D1127224

Diccionario Técnico Inglés
Spanish Technical Dictionary

Routledge
Diccionario Técnico Inglés
Spanish Technical Dictionary

Tomo/Volume
2

INGLÉS–ESPAÑOL
ENGLISH–SPANISH

London and New York

First published 1997
by Routledge
11 New Fetter Lane, London EC4P 4EE

Simultaneously published in the USA and Canada
by Routledge
29 West 35th Street, New York, NY 10001

Conversion tables adapted from *Dictionary of Scientific Units*, H. G. Jerrard and
D. B. McNeill, London: Chapman & Hall, 1992.

Typeset in Monotype Times, Helvetica 55 and Bauer Bodoni
by Routledge

Printed in England by TJ Press (Padstow) Ltd., Cornwall

Printed on acid-free paper

British Library Cataloguing-in-Publication Data
A catalogue record for this book is available from the British Library

Library of Congress Cataloging-in-Publication Data
Applied for

Vol 1 Spanish–English 0–415–11272–9
Vol 2 English–Spanish 0–415–11273–7
2-volume set 0–415–11274–5

Marcas registradas ®

Hemos hecho el máximo esfuerzo para señalar
los términos que estimamos protegidos por un
registro de marca. Sin embargo, la ausencia o
presencia de esta mención no surte efecto sobre su
estado legal.

Registered trademarks ®

Every effort has been made to label terms which
we believe constitute trademarks. The legal status
of these, however, remains unchanged by the
presence or absence of any such label.

Índice de contenidos/Contents

Introducción   xiii–xiv

Prólogo   xv–xvi

Estructura del diccionario   xvii–xix

Consejos para la utilización de este diccionario   xxi–xxiii

Abreviaturas utilizadas en este diccionario   xxix–xxx

DICCIONARIO INGLÉS–ESPAÑOL   1–836

     Tablas de conversión   837–846
     Longitud
     Superficie
     Volumen
     Ángulo
     Tiempo
     Masa
     Fuerza
     Potencia
     Energía, trabajo, calor
     Presión
     Flujo de inducción magnética
     Inducción magnética
     Fuerza magnetomotriz
     Intensidad de campo magnético
     Iluminación
     Luminancia

Elementos químicos   847–848

Introduction   xiii–xiv

Preface   xv–xvi

Features of the dictionary   xvii–xix

Using this dictionary   xxv–xxvii

Abbreviations used in this dictionary   xxix–xxx

ENGLISH–SPANISH DICTIONARY   1–836

     Conversion tables   837–846
     Length
     Area
     Volume
     Angle
     Time
     Mass
     Force
     Power
     Energy, work, heat
     Pressure
     Magnetic flux
     Magnetic flux density
     Magnetomotive force
     Magnetic field strength
     Illumination
     Luminance

Chemical elements   847–848

Diccionario Técnico Inglés
Spanish Technical Dictionary

Dirección del Proyecto/Project Manager
Gemma Belmonte Talero

Dirección Editorial/Managing Editor
Sinda López

Dirección del Programa/Programme Manager
Elizabeth White

Redacción/Editorial
Martin Barr   Justine Bird
Lisa Carden   Janice McNeillie
Jessica Ramage   Robert Timms

Marketing
Vanessa Markey   Rachel Miller

Sistemas Informáticos/Systems
Omar Raman   Simon Thompson

Administración/Administration
Amanda Brindley

Producción/Production
Maureen James   Nigel Marsh   Joanne Tinson

Asesores Técnicos Especialistas/
Specialist Consultants

Augustín Catalán
Agencia COVER

Antonio Castillo González
Agencia Industrial del Estado (INI)

John Camm
British Ceramic Research Limited

Dr Juan Domínguez
Centro de Investigación y Desarrollo Agrario,
Córdoba

Manuel Estany Segalás
Consejo Intertextil Español

Enrique Cuñetti
Facultad de Ingeniería, Universidad de la
República, Uruguay

Philip Maylor
Brian Patterson
IDPM, Institute for the Management of
Information Systems

Juan Carlos Miguez
IEEE, Uruguay

Dr A. Lopez-Soler
Dr X. Querol
Institute of Earth Sciences "Jaume Almera"
(CSIC), Barcelona

J.E.H. Leach
Institute of Energy

Christopher Wolfe
Institute of Physics

Celia Kirby
D.B. Smith
Institute of Hydrology

Malcolm Horlick
Institute of Refrigeration

Don Goodsell
Institution of Mechanical Engineers and Society
of Automotive Engineers

J. Salvador Santiago Páez
Instituto de Acústica (CSIC), Madrid

Dra Menchu Comas
Instituto Andaluz de Ciencias de la Tierra
(CSIC and Universidad de Granada)

María Ofelia Cirone
Dr Adan Edgardo Pucci
Instituto Argentino de Oceanografía
(CONICET)

Jesús Espinosa
Instituto del Frío (CSIC), Madrid

José Manuel Olías Jiménez
Instituto de la Grasa (CSIC), Sevilla

Dr Jaime Tornos Cubillo
Alejandro Mira Monerris
Dr Pedro Osuna Rey
Dr Fernando Hevia
(*coordinador de equipo/team co-ordinator*)
Marinela García Fernández
(*coordinadora de equipo/team co-ordinator*)
Ismael Arinas
M. Paloma M. Fradejas
Victoria Machuca
Carmen Sancho
Instituto de la Ingeniería de España

Nora Susana Fígoli
José Miguel Parera
Instituto de Investigaciones en Catálisis y
Petroquímica (FIQ-UNL-CONICET),
Argentina

Dr Manuel de León
Instituto de Matemáticas y Física Fundamental
(CSIC), Madrid

Dr Jesús A. Pajares
Instituto Nacional del Carbón (CSIC), Oviedo

José Torres Riera
Instituto Nacional de Técnica Aeroespacial

Miguel A. Gaspar Paricio
Instituto Papelero Español

Guillermo González Gómez
Katholieke Universiteit Leuven

Beni Ortiz
LA REVISTA de EL MUNDO

J.E. Lunn
Locomotive and Carriage Institution, Surrey

Pablo A. Fossati Fischer
Ministerio de Defensa Nacional de Uruguay

Julio Riet
Ministerio de Industria, Energía y Minería de
Uruguay

Gill Wilkinson
National Radiological Protection Board

Dr Guillermo H. Crapiste
Roberto Echarte
Luis A. Herrera
PLAPIQUI (U.N.S.-CONICET)

Dr Graham Moore
Diana Deavin
Pira International

Dr Jim Smith
Prince Edward Island Food Technology Centre

Dr A. Ballester
Dr N. Gómez
Dr C. Otero
Dr C. Pando
Dr J. A. Rodríguez Renuncio
Real Sociedad Española de Química

David Rojo
Revista CINEMANÍA

Ronald Ridout
Ridout Associates and Chartered Institute of
Building

Col. R.G. Lee
Royal Military College of Science

Miriam Andrioli
Servicio Meteorológico Nacional, Argentina

Paul Dinsdale
Society of Dyers and Colorists

Gillian Strachan-Gray
Specsavers Optical Superstores

Miguel A. Alonso del Pino
Mª Concepción Avilero Nieto
Jesús M. Frades Payo
Dr José M. Iraizoz Fernández
Luis Mansilla Plaza
Juan Antonio Martínez Martínez
Fernando Pedrazuela González
Manuel Sánchez Martínez
Fernando J. Terán Sierra
Universidad de Castilla-La Mancha

J. L. Escudero Soto
Universidad Complutense de Madrid

Alfredo Álvarez García
Antonio Díaz Parralejo
Juan Félix González González
Alejandro Martín Sánchez
Manuel Reino Flores
Pilar Suárez Marcelo
José Valverde Sánchez
Nuria Esther Vaquerizo Martín
Blas M. Vinagre Jara
Fernando Zayas Hinojosa
Universidad de Extremadura

Mark Hempsell
University of Bristol

Aurora Gutiérrez Sosa
University of Manchester

Dr John A. Elliot
University of Manchester Institute of Science
and Technology

Colaboradores/Contributors

Lucía Alvarez de Toledo
Rodolfo Antonelli
Emilio Aparicio Fernández
Beatriz A. Bonnet
Carolina Bovino de Morgan
Mª Luisa Casado López
María Fernanda Cid
Julio Alejandro Cid
Alfonso Cuevas y Fajardo
Laura Viviana Demoy
Dr Marco A. Díaz
Enric S. Dolz-Ferrer
Carmen Fernández-Marsden
Amelia Garcia-Leigh
Margarita García de Cortázar Nebreda
Lourdes García de Reece
M. Antonio Gavilanez
Jorge Hernández Osuna
John E. Kennedy
Edmund Knox

Patricia S. Luna
Eduardo Maleubre Nogales
Montserrat Maleubre Pablos
Dr Juan M. Nieves Pamplona
Carlos Novi
Carlos de Osma Calvo
María Cristina Plencovich
Eugene Polisky
Michael Rawson
Estefanía Rodríguez de Santos
Juan Rojo
Dr Sonia Roquet de Savage
Amparo Ruiz-Vera
Joaquín M. Sallarés
Norma Sánchez Meana
Oscar L. Spraggon
Mónica Liliana Suárez
Marina Tei
Daniel Ricardo Yagolkowski
Beatriz R. Zylberfisz de Yagolkowski

La lista de términos ingleses está extraída de nuestra base de datos terminológicos que fue publicada por primera vez en el *Diccionario Técnico Francés Routledge*, en 1994. Agradecemos la contribución original de las siguientes personas:

The English term list is based on our database of terminology first published in the *Routledge French Technical Dictionary*, 1994. We gratefully acknowledge the original contribution of the following:

Yves Arden, Réjane Amery, Josephine Bacon, John P. Bryon, Michael Carpenter, Anna Cordon, Maguy Couette, Elisabeth Coyne, P.J. Doyle, J.V. Drazil, Bill Duffin, James Dunster, Christopher Freeland, Crispin Geoghegan, Susan Green, Freda Klipstein, C.A. Lagall, David Larcher, Virginia Lester, Pamela Mayorcas, James Millard, Charles Polley, Michael Rawson, Louis Rioual, Tom Williams, Stephen Wilson, Stewart Wittering

Lexicógrafos y Correctores de pruebas/Lexicographers & Proofreaders

Tom Barlett
Soraya Bermejo
Michael Britton
Ximena Castillo
Harry Campbell
Yolanda Cerdá
Anna Cooke
Alison Crann
Mel Fraser
Fiona Greenall
Zoë Hambling
Kenneth Hillman
Margaret Jull Costa
Fiona Mackintosh
Isabel Mancebo-Portela
Philip Maxwell

Suzanne McCloskey
Héloïse McGuinness
Karen Miller
Julie Muleba
Jeremy Munday
Stephanie Parker
Zoë Petersen
Kathryn Phillips-Miles
Anna Reid
Mary Rigby
Jonathan Roper
Alisa Salamon
Malihe Sanatian
Martin Stark
Carmen Suárez
Gillian Wolfe

Mecanógrafos/Keyboarders

Debbie Thomas
Carmen Alpin, Emmanuelle Bels, Kristoffer Blegvad, Pedro Contreiras,
Antonio Fernández Entrena, Beatriz Fernández Martínez, Rosa Gálvez López,
Christiane Grosskopf, Michael Jopling, Ute Krebs, Ilona Lehmann, Géraldine Monnereau,
Geir Moulson, Roger Pena Muiño, Fabienne Rangeard, Beate Schmitt, Robert Timms, Jeremy Vine

Agradecimientos/Acknowledgements

Queremos agradecer la valiosa contribución de Gonzalo Álvarez Pineda, Esteban Gozalo Crespo, John Thristan y Enrique Cama Gómez, quienes revisaron las materias de Defensa y Armamento, Tecnología del Petróleo, Sistemas de Seguridad y Cinematografía respectivamente.

También expresamos nuestro agradecimiento a Jaime Tornos Cubillo, del Instituto de la Ingeniería de España; Ruperto Belmonte Monforte, de las Fuerzas Armadas Españolas; a la Universidad de Castilla-La Mancha; a Carlos Márquez Linares y a la Universidad de Extremadura por su grata colaboración en la compilación de este diccionario.

We wish to acknowledge the valuable contribution of Gonzalo Álvarez Pineda, Esteban Gozalo Crespo, John Thristan and Enrique Cama Gómez, who checked the subject areas of Military Technology, Petroleum Technology, Safety Engineering and Cinematography respectively.

We are also particularly grateful to Jaime Tornos Cubillo of the Instituto de la Ingeniería de España; Ruperto Belmonte Monforte from the Spanish Armed Forces; the Universidad de Castilla-La Mancha; Carlos Márquez Linares and the Universidad de Extremadura for their kind assistance during the compilation of this dictionary.

Introducción/Introduction

El *Diccionario Técnico Inglés Routledge* responde a una necesidad concreta en un área digna de reseñarse en vista del avance y la rápida evolución de la tecnología y de la ciencia en el mundo de hoy. Bien es cierto que avances tecnológicos los hubo siempre en la historia de la Humanidad; sin embargo, ha sido en los últimos decenios cuando tales avances han invadido todos los ámbitos del saber y del conocimiento humano y se han adueñado, valga la expresión, de casi todas las esferas o sectores de la vida humana. Estos avances se hacen patentes en la industria, cada vez más tecnificada así como en los negocios y la ciencia. Por esta razón, el conocimiento tecnológico se hace totalmente necesario en la transmisión de los saberes y en el aprendizaje de nuevos métodos.

Se podría argumentar que una lengua adquiere su madurez cuando es capaz de responder a las nuevas realidades que surgen en el entorno de sus hablantes. Es decir, cuando se forma una terminología adecuada a las realidades, que sea producto de la invención humana, del avance tecnológico y científico o de los cambios de mentalidades. Una lengua ha de ser capaz de demostrar día a día su capacidad de adaptación y adecuación a los cambios que requieran nuevas formas de expresión o definición.

El español está ganando auge y sirve, como se puede demostrar, para definir y determinar nuevas realidades científicas, experimentaciones técnicas e invenciones propias ya de un nuevo milenio. La realidad iberoamericana se torna cada vez más influyente en las esferas del comercio y de la comunicación. Cuando todas estas realidades se conjugan, surge la necesidad de elaborar un nuevo diccionario técnico que responda con su realización a los requerimientos que desde ámbitos distintos se están llevando a cabo.

Para la realización de este diccionario se ha contado con la colaboración de más de cien especialistas, pertenecientes a la industria, al mundo académico universitario y al de los negocios. La calidad y la precisión de las

The *Routledge Spanish Technical Dictionary* meets a specific need in an important field in view of the rapid developments currently taking place across the world in the spheres of technology and science. While it is true that there have been technological advances throughout the history of humanity, those which have come about in the last decade have impacted on every facet of human knowledge and understanding and hold sway over virtually every sphere of human life. They do so especially in industry, which has become increasingly mechanized, as well as in business and science. Technological know-how has become central to the acquisition of skills and the adoption of new working methods.

It could be argued that a language only comes of age when it is capable of responding to any new realities which arise in the living environment inhabited by its users; in other words, when the terminology of a language accounts for any changes in contingent reality which may result from factors, such as human inventions, technological or scientific advances or changing attitudes. A language must be able to demonstrate its adaptability to any changes which may occur, which might require corresponding shifts in expression or definition.

Spanish is gaining widespread usage and is demonstrably well-equipped to express and define existing scientific fact, future technological advances and inventions worthy of the new millennium. The Latin-American subcontinent is also becoming increasingly influential in the areas of trade and communication. If we take all these factors as a whole, the need for a new technical dictionary, designed to meet a variety of needs, becomes apparent.

The creation of this dictionary has involved the participation of over one hundred specialists from industry, the academic world and the corporate sector. The quality and accuracy of translations between the two languages has been tightly controlled by a team of professional translators from Spain, Latin America, the United States and the United Kingdom.

traducciones han sido revisadas por traductores profesionales procedentes de España, América Latina, Estados Unidos y Reino Unido.

El *Diccionario Técnico Inglés Routledge*, que es el resultado de una cuidadosa planificación inicial y especializada realización por parte de los traductores, académicos, expertos e investigadores que en él aparecen, viene a llenar un vacío existente: el de no poseer un instrumento eficaz y útil en la traducción de términos técnicos entre el español y el inglés.

The *Routledge Spanish Technical Dictionary*, which is the result of careful initial planning and skilled execution on the part of translators, academics and experts, meets the demand for an efficient and easy-to-use aid to the translation of technical terms between Spanish and English.

César Chaparro Gómez
Rector de la Universidad de Extremadura/
Vice Chancellor of the University of Extremadura

Prólogo/Preface

El diccionario técnico bilingüe español–inglés que presenta la editorial Routledge es el tercero de una serie especializada que se inició en 1994 con el Diccionario Técnico Francés y se continuó al año siguiente con el Diccionario Técnico Alemán.

Dos son los factores que han intervenido para hacer posible la creación de esta serie de diccionarios: la red de la base de datos y el método de compilación del repertorio léxico.

Podemos afirmar que no habría sido posible realizar una obra de estas características en un tiempo razonable si no hubiera sido por el uso de una base de datos que se creó específicamente para esta obra.

El rasgo que distingue a esta base de datos es su estructura relacional, mediante la cual el léxico de cada lengua se almacena en un fichero y las relaciones entre los términos en otros diferentes. Las conexiones entre los términos que se encuentran en los ficheros de cada lengua funcionan como traducciones gracias a las cuáles podemos tratar de manera compleja diversos tipos de equivalencias traducibles de una a muchas acepciones y de muchas a una. Las relaciones entre los vocablos dentro de una misma lengua actúan como remisiones, que cubren a su vez una gran variedad de categorías: variantes ortográficas o geográficas y abreviaturas.

El contenido de la base de datos se gestó en tres fases. Una proporción muy considerable del vocabulario inglés ya se había elaborado para editar el Diccionario Técnico Francés y el Diccionario Técnico Alemán. Un equipo de traductores con experiencia demostrada en las distintas especialidades y con un interés particular en la lexicografía cientificotécnica se ocupó de la terminología española. Los traductores se encargaron de delimitar los centros de interés para el público español. El léxico de cada lengua se sometió posteriormente a la consideración de diversos especialistas nativos en contacto directo con los últimos avances en cada ámbito tecnológico para asegurarse de su pertinencia, la exactitud de la información contextualizada y la

This is the third dictionary to be published from Routledge's programme of bilingual specialist and technical dictionaries, following on from the Routledge French Technical Dictionary in 1994 and the Routledge German Technical Dictionary in 1995.

The two main factors that have enabled us to create this generation of new bilingual technical dictionaries are the database system and the method of compilation.

It would not have been possible to compile this dictionary within a realistic timescale, and to the standard achieved, without the use of a custom-designed database.

The database's most significant feature is that it is designed as a relational database: term records for each language are held in separate files, with further files consisting only of link records. Links between terms in different language files represent translations which enable us to handle, in a complex way, various types of one-to-many and many-to-one translation equivalences. Links between terms within a single language file represent cross-references of various types: spelling variants, geographical variants and abbreviations.

The content of the database for this dictionary was created in three principal phases. A considerable proportion of the English term list was already available following the publication of our French and German Technical Dictionaries. The Spanish terminology was then solicited from specialist translators with current practical experience of a narrowly-defined specialist subject area and an interest in the collection and dissemination of technology. The specialist translators targeted the coverage to the Spanish market. The terms in each language were then vetted by native-speaker subject specialists working at the leading edge of the respective technology in order to ensure their currency, the accuracy of contextual information, and the adequacy of coverage. Finally, each language file was reviewed by editors to ensure coverage of American English and Latin American terms and

extensión del vocabulario. Por último, los editores revisaron los ficheros de cada lengua para cerciorarse de la inclusión del vocabulario específico y las variantes léxicas y fonéticas, tanto del español latino-americano como del inglés norteamericano, que aparecen claramente especificados.

Con todo, la creación y edición de una base de datos léxicos fue sólo el primer peldaño en la elaboración del diccionario. En una base de datos no es pertinente la distinción entre lengua de origen y de destino, así que a la hora de imprimir el diccionario fue necesario organizar los datos para elaborar de manera separada los volúmenes español–inglés e inglés–español. Los datos se elaboraron en otro módulo de software para obtener las listas alfabéticas del español al inglés y viceversa, sin olvidar los cuadros de variantes de palabras compuestas, los diferentes tipos de remisiones y demás características, siguiendo un algoritmo complejo.

Llegados a este punto un experimentado equipo de lexicógrafos españoles y británicos, cuya tarea consistía en eliminar redundancias e incoherencias, revisó el texto. Dicho equipo se encargó asimismo de redactar las explicaciones e informaciones contextuales y de suprimir aquellos términos cuyo carácter pecaba de demasiado general o demasiado especializado para ser incluído en un diccionario general técnico. Este método de trabajo por etapas nos ha permitido establecer altísimas cotas de control de calidad.

El equipo editorial

spelling variants; these are clearly labelled and distinguished.

The creation and editing of the database of terms was, however, only the first stage in the making of the dictionary. Within the database the distinction between source and target languages is not meaningful, but for this printed dictionary it has been necessary to format the data to produce separate Spanish–English and English–Spanish volumes. The data was processed by a further software module to produce two alphabetic sequences, of Spanish headwords with English translations and vice versa, each displaying the nesting of compounds, ordering of translations, style for cross-references of different types, and other features according to a complex algorithm.

At this stage the formatted text was edited by a team of experienced Spanish and English lexicographers whose task it was to eliminate duplication or inconsistency; edit the contextual information and explanations; and remove terms that were on the one hand too general, or on the other, too specialized for inclusion in a general technical dictionary. This phased method of working has enabled us to set extremely high standards of quality control.

The editorial team

Estructura del diccionario/Features of the dictionary

Los principales rasgos del diccionario están señalados en el extracto que aparece en la página siguiente. Para obtener una explicación más detallada de cada uno de estos rasgos así como información sobre la óptima utilización del diccionario, consúltense las páginas xxi-xxiii.

The main features of the dictionary are highlighted in the text extract on the opposite page. For a more detailed explanation of each of these features and information on how to get the most out of the dictionary, see pages xxv-xxvii.

Se indican los géneros para los nombres españoles —— **sphene** *n* MINERAL esfena *f*

sphere *n* GEOM, PHYS esfera *f*; ~ **gap** *n* ELEC ENG explosor de esferas *m*; ~ **of reflection** *n* CRYSTALL esfera de reflexión *f*

spherical[1] *adj* GEN esférico

spherical[2]: ~ **aberration** *n* CINEMAT, PHOTO, PHYS, TELECOM aberración de esfericidad *f*, aberración esférica *f*; ~ **aerial** *n* BrE (*cf spherical antenna AmE*) TELECOM antena esférica *f*; ~ **antenna** *n*

Las variantes del inglés británico y americano se dan de forma completa y aparecen indicadas pertinentemente —— AmE (*cf spherical aerial BrE*) TELECOM antena esférica *f*; ~ **container** *n* TRANSP contenedor esférico *m*; ~ **coordinates** *n pl* PHYS coordenadas esféricas *f pl*; ~ **distortion** *n* CINEMAT distorsión esférica *f*; ~ **geometry** *n* GEOM geometría esférica *f*; ~ **harmonic** *n* SPACE armonía esférica *f*; ~ **joint** *n* VEH *steering* junta de rótula *f*; ~ **lens** *n* CINEMAT, INSTR, OPT, PHOTO objetivo esférico *m*, PHYS lentes esféricas *f pl*; ~ **mirror** *n* INSTR, LAB, OPT,

Los compuestos siguen el orden alfabético a partir de su primer elemento —— PHYS, TELECOM espejo esférico *m*; ~ **sector** *n* GEOM sector esférico *m*; ~ **tank** *n* SPACE depósito esférico *m*; ~ **triangle** *n* GEOM triángulo esférico *m*; ~ **wave** *n* ACOUST, ELEC ENG, PHYS, WAVE PHYS onda esférica *f*

sphericity *n* GEOM esfericidad *f*

spherics *n pl* METEO atmosféricos *m pl*, esferas *f pl*, esféricos *m pl*, parásitos atmosféricos *m pl*

Los indicadores de materia ordenados alfabéticamente muestran la traducción apropiada —— **spheroid** *n* GEOM elipsoide atachado *m*, elipsoide de revolución *m*, esferoide *m*, PHYS esferoide *m*

spherometer *n* PHYS esferómetro *m*

spherosiderite *n* MINERAL esferosiderita *f*

spherulite *n* GEOL, MINERAL, PETR TECH esferulita *f*

spherulitic: ~ **texture** *n* GEOL textura esferolítica *f*

sphingosine *n* CHEM esfingosina *f*

sphragidite *n* MINERAL esfragidita *f*

Las remisiones entre las abreviaturas y sus formas plenas aparecen tanto para los términos españoles como para los ingleses —— **SPI** *abbr* (*secondary porosity index*) PETR TECH IPS (*índice de porosidad secundaria*)

spider *n* C&G araña *f*, CINEMAT cangrejo *m*, PETR TECH araña *f*, grapa a cuñas *f*, PROD *for mould or core* armadura *f*, *of amalgamating pan* cursor *m*, VEH cruceta *f*; ~ **and slips** *n pl* MINE anillo de maniobra *m*; **type armature** *n* ELEC cepo de armadura *m*; ~ **unit** *n* AIR TRANSP araña *f*, cruceta *f*

Los contextos ofrecen información suplementaria para ayudar a encontrar la traducción correcta —— **spigot** *n* CONST *cock or faucet* llave *f*, *plug of cock* canilla *f*, tubo *m*, *vent peg* espiga *f*; **and-faucet joint** *n* CONST empalme de enchufeo y cordón *m*; **and-faucet joint pipes** *n pl* CONST tuberías con uniones de cordón y grifo *f pl* (*Esp*), tuberías con uniones de enchufe y cordón *f pl* (*AmL*); ~ **joint** *n* CONST empalme de cordón *m*

Las variantes lingüísticas de España y América Latina se dan de forma completa y aparecen indicadas pertinentemente —— **spike** *n* AGRIC espiga *f*, marlo *m* (*AmL*), mazorca *f* (*Esp*), C&G pico *m*, CINEMAT impulso *m*, CONST perno *m*, ELEC ENG corriente de fuga *f*, MINE *quarrying* escarpiador *m* (*AmL*), perno *m* (*Esp*), NUCL semilla *f*, TRANSP punta *f*, TV pico *m*, impulso de hiperamplitud *m*; ~ **driver** *n* RAIL martillo neumático para clavar *m*; ~ **nail** *n* CONST clavo *m*; ~ **puller** *n* AmE (*cf sleeper-screw extractor BrE*) RAIL extractor de tirafondos *m*; **tooth harrow** *n* AGRIC grada de dientes rígidos *f*

spikelet *n* AGRIC espiguilla *f*

Right column annotations:

— Genders indicated at Spanish nouns

— British English and American English variants given in full and labelled accordingly

— Compound terms nested alphabetically at the first element

— Subject area labels given in alphabetical order to show appropriate translation

— Cross-references from abbreviations to full forms are shown for both Spanish and English

— Contexts give supplementary information to help locate the right translation

— Spanish and Latin American variants given in full and labelled accordingly

Consejos para la utilización de este diccionario

Delimitación de los contenidos

Éste es el volumen inglés–español del diccionario técnico general que presentamos. En él se da cuenta de todos los ámbitos de la tecnología moderna y del conocimiento científico en que se basa. Su acervo terminológico abarca desde los dominios tradicionales de la tecnología como la ingeniería mecánica, la industria de la construcción, la ingeniería eléctrica y electrónica a las especialidades de vanguardia como las fuentes de energía renovables, la ingeniería de seguridad y el control de calidad.

Selección del vocabulario

Hemos tratado de incluir el vocabulario esencial de cada materia. Un equipo de prominentes especialistas se ha ocupado de revisar los resultados, para asegurarnos de que tanto los términos españoles como los ingleses son precisos y actuales, de que las traducciones tienen equivalentes válidos y de que no quedaban lagunas en los campos léxicos seleccionados.

Hemos tomado la precaución de incluir únicamente aquellos términos cuyo carácter técnico resultaba incuestionable y de excluir los que carecían de significado específico en este campo y, si bien el vocabulario técnico esencial se encuentra a menudo adecuadamente representado en los diccionarios generales, no por eso hemos dejado de incluirlo en toda su extensión. En aquellos casos en los que una palabra permitía varias traducciones, hemos optado por la que los especialistas han considerado más plausible.

La extensión concedida a cada materia es proporcional a su importancia, de modo que a una especialidad del peso específico de la ingeniería mecánica se le dedican 12.000 términos, en tanto que a un campo nuevo como el de las fuentes de energía renovables que sólo ahora empieza a desarrollar un léxico propio, le corresponde un ámbito terminológico mucho más reducido.

Exclusiones y supresiones

A la hora de buscar una palabra en inglés no se tomarán en cuenta los siguientes morfemas:

a, all, an, any, anybody, anyone, anything, anywhere, are, be, by, during, each, every, everybody, everyone, everything, everywhere, for, from, here, if, in, is, it, no, nobody, no one, nor, not, nothing, nowhere, of, off, on, or, out, over, so, some, somebody, someone, something, somewhere, the, that, then, there, they, thing, this, to, too, under, very, where, while, who, with

Las palabras compuestas siguen el orden alfabético a partir de su primer elemento. Cuando varios compuestos participan de un lexema inicial común, éste se reemplaza por una virgulilla (~), por ejemplo:

adjacent[2]: **~ angle** *n* GEOM ángulo adyacente *m*; **~ bed effect** *n* PETROL efecto de lecho adyacente *m*; **~ channel** *n* TV canal adyacente *m*; **~ channel rejection ratio** *n* TELECOM relación de rechazo de canal adyacente *f*

Cuando el primer elemento es una entrada dotada de uno o varios significados técnicos, las acepciones correspondientes aparecen al principio, seguidas de los compuestos en orden alfabético. Por ejemplo:

adhesive[2] *n* MECH adhesivo *m*, P&R adhesivo *m*, pegamento *m*, PACK, PROD, SAFE adhesivo *m*; **~ applicator** *n* PACK aplicador de adhesivos *m*; **~ coat** *n* COATINGS capa adherente *f*, capa adhesiva *f*

Cuando el primer elemento no se traduce, los compuestos aparecen precedidos de dos puntos (:). Por ejemplo:

bainitic: **~ ferrite** *n* METALL ferrita bainítica *f*

Orden de las entradas

Las entradas se ordenan alfabéticamente e idéntico criterio se aplica a las locuciones y a las palabras compuestas. A este respecto debe considerarse irrelevante la carga semántica de los diferentes lexemas.

Los compuestos sólidos y aquellos unidos por guión se ordenan alfabéticamente, siguiendo así la secuencia de compuestos abiertos que contienen idéntico comienzo. Por ejemplo:

bridged *adj* PROD con puentes, de puente
bridged-H: ~ **network** *n* ELEC ENG *quadripole* red con puente en H *f*
bridged-T: ~ **network** *n* ELEC ENG *quadripole* red con puente en T *f*

Los artículos *a, an, the* y la preposición *of* no se toman en cuenta a la hora de determinar el orden de las palabras compuestas en un artículo. Por ejemplo:

beginning: ~ **of call demand** *n* TELECOM comienzo de llamada *m*; ~ **of life** *n* NUCL comienzos de vida *m pl*

En las entradas que registran gran cantidad de acepciones se utilizan marcadores para facilitar la localización de los términos. Por ejemplo:

double^2:
[**a**] ~~**acting pump** *n* PROD bomba de doble efecto *f*; ~~**armature relay** *n* ELEC relé de doble armadura *m*;
[**b**] ~~**balanced mixer** *n* ELECTRON mezclador doble compensado *m*; ~~**band projector** *n* AmE (*cf double-headed projector BrE*) CINEMAT proyector de banda doble *m*, proyector de cabezal doble *m*; ~~**base diode** *n* ELECTRON diodo de base doble *m*; ~~**battened case** *n* PACK caja doblemente reforzada *f*; ~~**beat valve** *n* HYDRAUL válvula de doble asiento *f*; ~ **bevel** *n* C&G doble bisel *m*

Se distingue entre las abreviaturas y acrónimos, escritos en mayúsculas y las palabras plenas correspondientes que se escriben en minúsculas. Por ejemplo:

age^1 *n* AGRIC, GEOL época *f*, PETROL época *f*, era *f*; ~ **dating** *n* GEOL antigüedad *f*, datación de la época *f*; ~ **of groundwater** *n* GEOL antigüedad del agua freática *f*, HYDROL, WATER antigüedad del agua freática, *f*, edad del agua freática *f*; ~ **hardening** *n* CRYSTALL endurecimiento estructural *m*, envejecimiento *m*, METALL, P&R endurecimiento por envejecimiento *m*
age^2 *vt* METALL endurecerse por envejecimiento, THERMO estabilizar por reposo
AGE *abbr (allyl glycidyl ether)* CHEM, P&R alilglicidiléter *m*

Los términos que incluyen cifras y símbolos se ordenan alfabéticamente, como si estuvieran escritos en letra. Por ejemplo:

3-D: ~ **log** *n* PETROL perfil tridimensional *m*
threose *n* CHEM treosa *f*

Homógrafos

Tras cada término se indica su categoría gramatical mediante abreviatura. Puede consultarse una lista completa de las abreviaturas en la página xxix. En el caso de términos cuyo elemento inicial es idéntico pero pertenecen a diferentes categorías gramaticales, las acepciones se distinguen por la inclusión de un supraíndice tras la entrada, ya sea dicha entrada semánticamente plena o tenga mero valor significante. El orden seguido es el de abreviatura, adjetivo, adverbio, sustantivo y verbo, seguidos por otras categorías gramaticales de uso más restringido, por ejemplo:

exponential^1 *adj* COMP&DP, ELEC, ELECTRON, MATH exponencial
exponential^2 *n* ELEC, MATH exponencial *m*; ~ **amplifier** *n* ELEC, MATH amplificador exponencial *m*; ~ **curve** *n* ELEC, MATH curva exponencial *f*; ~ **decay** *n* ELECTRON amortiguación exponencial *f*; ~ **distribution** *n* COMP&DP distribución exponencial *f*

Orden de las traducciones

Cada término se acompaña de uno o más indicadores que remiten al ámbito tecnológico en que se utiliza. En las páginas xxxi–xxxii se encuentra una lista completa de tales indicadores así como de sus formas léxicas plenas.

Cuando una acepción se utiliza en varios ámbitos tecnológicos, se consignan alfabéticamente los indicadores pertinentes.

Cuando la traducción de un término es la misma en varios ámbitos tecnológicos, dicha traducción va precedida de los indicadores pertinentes. Por ejemplo:

face^2 *vt* PROD *lathe work* tornear al aire, TEXTIL encarar

Cuando un vocablo acepta diferentes traducciones, dependiendo del campo en que se use, la traducción pertinente se consigna tras cada indicador o conjunto de indicadores. Por ejemplo:

facility *n* AIR TRANSP, PROD instalación *f*, TELECOM capacidad *f*; ~ **accepted message** *n (FAA)* TELECOM capacidad de aceptación de mensajes *f*

Información complementaria

Se da el género para cada término español que posea la categoría de nombre. Con respecto a los compuestos, éstos no llevan el género del último elemento, sino el de la unidad completa (es decir, el de su radical). Por ejemplo:

setter: ~ **sight** n MILIT *artillery* alza reguladora *f*

En muchos casos se ofrecen datos adicionales para precisar el uso de un término. Dicha información puede consistir en:

(a) El sujeto u objeto típicos de un verbo, por ejemplo:

set[3] *vt* CINEMAT ajustar, COMP&DP montar, *variable* poner a uno, fijar, *counter* ajustar, CONST *rivet* fijar, asentar

(b) Nombres usados habitualmente con un adjetivo, por ejemplo:

air[1]: ~ **-cooled** *adj* ELEC *equipment* de enfriamiento por aire, enfriado por aire, refrigerado por aire

(c) Palabras que indican la referencia de un nombre, por ejemplo:

cab n CONST *of crane* cabina *f*, TRANSP taxi *m*, coche de alquiler *m*, *of locomotive* garita *f*, *of motor, van* cabina *f*

(d) Información complementaria de la abreviatura, por ejemplo:

agreed: ~ **spillover** n TV *networks* desbordamiento acordado *m*

(e) una paráfrasis o equivalente funcional, por ejemplo:

bench n CONST *work table* banco *m*

En los casos en que una palabra puede traducirse de varias maneras en un mismo ámbito, se utiliza la información contextual para mostrar cuál es la traducción más apropiada en cada caso. Por ejemplo:

carcass n AGRIC res muerta *f*, CONST *carpentry* armazón *m*, ELEC ENG *of motor* entramado eléctrico *m*, carcasa *f*, TEXTIL armazón *m*

Remisiones

Dado que este diccionario incluye tanto los términos ingleses como los americanismos, se indica siempre su procedencia geográfica mediante indicador. La cobertura de este diccionario también incluye términos de América Latina y España. Para una lista completa de estos indicadores y de sus correspondencias, por favor consúltense la página xxix.

En el caso de variantes léxicas se ofrece una información completa y detallada en cada entrada, incluyendo las traducciones y referencias a la forma alternativa. Por ejemplo:

braked: ~ **car** n AmE (*cf braked wagon* BrE) RAIL vagón frenado *m*; ~ **wagon** n BrE (*cf braked car* AmE) RAIL vagón frenado *m*; ~ **weight percentage** n RAIL porcentaje del peso de frenado *m*

Las abreviaturas y sus formas plenas correspondientes se consignan alfabéticamente. La información completa, incluyendo las traducciones y las remisiones a las palabras completas o a las abreviaturas, según corresponda, aparece en cada entrada. Por ejemplo:

CNC[1] *abbr* (*computerized numerical control*) COMP&DP, MECH ENG CNC (*control numérico computerizado*)

Using the dictionary

Range of coverage

This is one volume (the English–Spanish volume) of a general technical dictionary that covers the whole range of modern technology and the scientific knowledge that underlies it. It contains a broad base of terminology drawn from traditional areas of technology such as mechanical engineering, the construction industry, electrical engineering and electronics, but also includes the vocabulary of newly prominent subject areas such as fuelless energy sources, safety engineering and quality assurance.

Selection of terms

We have aimed to include the essential vocabulary of each subject area, and the material has been checked by leading subject experts to ensure that both the Spanish and the English terms are accurate and current, that the translations are valid equivalents, and that there are no gaps in coverage.

We have been careful about including only genuine technical terms and not allowing general vocabulary with no technical value. At the same time, we have entered the core vocabulary of technical discourse in its totality, although some of these items may also be found in general dictionaries. Although other variant translations would often be permissible in a particular subject area, we have given the term most widely preferred by specialists in the area.

Coverage of the subject areas is given proportionally so that an established and wide-ranging area such as mechanical engineering has a count of around 12,000 terms whereas a new area in which terminology is still developing, such as fuelless energy sources, will have considerably fewer terms.

Stoplists

Terms in English are not entered under the following elements:

a, all, an, any, anybody, anyone, anything, anywhere, are, be, by, during, each, every, everybody, everyone, everything, everywhere, for, from, here, if, in, is, it, no, nobody, no one, nor, not, nothing, nowhere, of, off, on, or, out, over, so, some, somebody, someone, something, somewhere, the, that, then, there, they, thing, this, to, too, under, very, where, while, who, with

Compounds are listed at their first element. In these nested listings, the simple form is replaced by a swung dash (~). For example:

adjacent[2]: ~ **angle** *n* GEOM ángulo adyacente *m*; ~ **bed effect** *n* PETROL efecto de lecho adyacente *m*; ~ **channel** *n* TV canal adyacente *m*; ~ **channel rejection ratio** *n* TELECOM relación de rechazo de canal adyacente *f*

When the first element is itself a headword with one or more technical senses, compounds follow the simple form in alphabetical order. For example:

adhesive[2] *n* MECH adhesivo *m*, P&R adhesivo *m*, pegamento *m*, PACK, PROD, SAFE adhesivo *m*; ~ **applicator** *n* PACK aplicador de adhesivos *m*; ~ **coat** *n* COATINGS capa adherente *f*, capa adhesiva *f*

If the first element is not itself translated, a colon (:) precedes the compounds. For example:

bainitic: ~ **ferrite** *n* METALL ferrita bainítica *f*

Ordering of terms

All terms are ordered alphabetically at their first element. This is also the policy for hyphenated compounds. Compound terms are never entered under their second or third element, regardless of the semantic structure of the unit.

Hyphenated and solid compounds are entered in alphabetical sequence, and will thus follow a nest of open compounds with the same first element. For example:

bridged *adj* PROD con puentes, de puente

bridged-H: ~ **network** *n* ELEC ENG *quadripole* red con puente en H *f*
bridged-T: ~ **network** *n* ELEC ENG *quadripole* red con puente en T *f*

Articles (*a, an, the*) and the preposition *of* are ignored in determining the sequence of nested open compounds. For example:

beginning: ~ **of call demand** *n* TELECOM comienzo de llamada *m*; ~ **of life** *n* NUCL comienzos de vida *m pl*

In the case of very long compound nests, marginal markers have been used to make it easy to find a term more quickly. For example:

double[2]:

■ **a** ~~**acting pump** *n* PROD bomba de doble efecto *f*; ~~**armature relay** *n* ELEC relé de doble armadura *m*;

■ **b** ~~**balanced mixer** *n* ELECTRON mezclador doble compensado *m*; ~~**band projector** *n AmE* (*cf double-headed projector BrE*) CINEMAT proyector de banda doble *m*, proyector de cabezal doble *m*; ~~**base diode** *n* ELECTRON diodo de base doble *m*; ~~**battened case** *n* PACK caja doblemente reforzada *f*; ~~**beat valve** *n* HYDRAUL válvula de doble asiento *f*; ~ **bevel** *n* C&G doble bisel *m*

Abbreviations and acronyms written in upper case appear separately from vocabulary words of the same form written in lower case:

age[1] *n* AGRIC, GEOL época *f*, PETROL época *f*, era *f*; ~ **dating** *n* GEOL antigüedad *f*, datación de la época *f*, HYDROL, WATER antigüedad del agua freática, *f*, edad del agua freática *f*; ~ **hardening** *n* CRYSTALL endurecimiento estructural *m*, envejecimiento *m*, METALL, P&R endurecimiento por envejecimiento *m*
age[2] *vt* METALL endurecerse por envejecimiento, THERMO estabilizar por reposo
AGE *abbr* (*allyl glycidyl ether*) CHEM, P&R alilglicidiléter *m*

Terms containing figures and symbols are alphabetized according to the usual expansion when written out in full:

3-D: ~ **log** *n* PETROL perfil tridimensional *m*
threose *n* CHEM treosa *f*

Homographs

Every term is accompanied by a label indicating its part of speech. For a complete list of these labels and their expansions, please see page x.

When terms beginning with the same element fall into two or more part-of-speech categories,

the different nests will be distinguished by a raised number immediately following the head of the nest, whether the head has technical senses of its own or is a dummy. The sequence is abbreviation, adjective, adverb, noun and verb followed by less frequent parts of speech. For example:

exponential[1] *adj* COMP&DP, ELEC, ELECTRON, MATH exponencial
exponential[2] *n* ELEC, MATH exponencial *m*; ~ **amplifier** *n* ELEC, MATH amplificador exponencial *m*; ~ **curve** *n* ELEC, MATH curva exponencial *f*; ~ **decay** *n* ELECTRON amortiguación exponencial *f*; ~ **distribution** *n* COMP&DP distribución exponencial *f*

Ordering of translations

Every term is accompanied by one or more labels indicating the technological area in which it is used. For a complete list of these labels and their expansions, please see pages xxix-xxx.

Where the same term is used in more than one technological area, multiple labels are given as appropriate. These labels appear in alphabetical order.

Where a term has the same translation in more than one technological area, this translation is given after the sequence of the labels. For example:

face[2] *vt* PROD *lathe work* tornear al aire, TEXTIL encarar

Where a term has different translations according to the technological area in which it is used, the appropriate translation is given after each label or set of labels. For example:

facility *n* AIR TRANSP, PROD instalación *f*, TELECOM capacidad *f*; ~ **accepted message** *n* (*FAA*) TELECOM capacidad de aceptación de mensajes *f*

Supplementary information

The gender is given for every Spanish noun term. In the case of compound terms this is the gender of the term as a whole (that is, its noun head) rather than the final element. For example:

setter: ~ **sight** *n* MILIT *artillery* alza reguladora *f*

In many cases additional data is given about a term in order to show how it is used. Such contextual information can be:

(a) the typical subject or object of a verb, for example:

set[3] *vt* CINEMAT ajustar, COMP&DP montar, *variable* poner a uno, fijar, *counter* ajustar, CONST *rivet* fijar, asentar

(b) typical nouns used with an adjective, for example:

air[1]: ~ **-cooled** *adj* ELEC *equipment* de enfriamiento por aire, enfriado por aire, refrigerado por aire

(c) words indicating the reference of a noun, for example:

cab *n* CONST *of crane* cabina *f*, TRANSP taxi *m*, coche de alquiler *m*, *of locomotive* garita *f*, *of motor, van* cabina *f*

(d) information which supplements the subject area label, for example:

agreed: ~ **spillover** *n* TV *networks* desbordamiento acordado *m*

(e) a paraphrase or broad equivalent, for example:

bench *n* CONST *work table* banco *m*

When various different translations apply in the same subject area, contextual information is also used to show which translation is appropriate in different circumstances. For example:

carcass *n* AGRIC res muerta *f*, CONST *carpentry* armazón *m*, ELEC ENG *of motor* entramado eléctrico *m*, carcasa *f*, TEXTIL armazón *m*

Cross-references

Both British and North American terms are covered, and these are differentiated by regional labels. Coverage also includes terms from Latin America and Spain. For a complete list of these labels and their expansions, please see page xxix.

In the case of lexical variants, full information – including translations and cross-references to the other form – is given at each entry. For example:

braked: ~ **car** *n AmE (cf braked wagon BrE)* RAIL vagón frenado *m*; ~ **wagon** *n BrE (cf braked car AmE)* RAIL vagón frenado *m*; ~ **weight percentage** *n* RAIL porcentaje del peso de frenado *m*

Both abbreviations and their full forms are entered in the main body of the dictionary in alphabetical sequence. Full information – including translations and cross-references to the full form or abbreviations as appropriate – is given at each entry. For example:

CNC[1] *abbr (computerized numerical control)* COMP&DP, MECH ENG CNC *(control numérico computerizado)*

Abreviaturas utilizadas en este diccionario/ Abbreviations used in this dictionary

Categorías gramaticales/Parts of speech

abbr	abbreviation	abreviatura
adj	adjective	adjetivo
adv	adverb	adverbio
f	feminine	femenino
f pl	feminine plural	femenino plural
m	masculine	masculino
m pl	masculine plural	masculino plural
n	noun	sustantivo
n pl	noun plural	sustantivo plural
phr	phrase	frase
pref	prefix	prefijo
prep	preposition	preposición
vi	intransitive verb	verbo intransitivo
vt	transitive verb	verbo transitivo
vti	transitive and intransitive verb	verbo transitivo e intransitivo

Indicadores geográficos/Geographic codes

Esp	Spain	España
AmL	Latin America	América Latina
BrE	British English	Inglés británico
AmE	American English	Inglés americano

Indicadores de materia/Subject area labels

ACOUST	Acoustics	Acústica
AGRIC	Agriculture	Agricultura
AIR TRANSP	Air Transport	Transporte Aéreo
AUTO	Automotive Engineering	Ingeniería de Automoción
C&G	Ceramics and Glass	Cerámica y Vidrio
CHEM	Chemistry	Química
CHEM TECH	Chemical Technology Processes	Procesos de Tecnología Química
CINEMAT	Cinematography	Cinematografía
COAL	Coal Technology	Tecnología del Carbón
COATINGS	Coatings Technology	Revestimientos
COLOUR	Colours Technology	Tecnología del Color
COMP&DP	Computing and Data Processing	Informática y Procesamiento de Datos
CONST	Construction	Construcción
CRYSTALL	Crystallography	Cristalografía
DETERG	Detergents	Detergentes
ELEC	Electricity	Electricidad
ELEC ENG	Electrical Engineering	Ingeniería Eléctrica
ELECTRON	Electronic Engineering	Ingeniería Electrónica
FLUID	Fluid Physics	Física de los Fluidos
FOOD	Food Technology	Tecnología de la Alimentación
FUELLESS	Fuelless Energy Sources	Fuentes de Energías Renovables
GAS	Gas Technology	Tecnología de Gas

GEN	General Technology	Tecnología General
GEOL	Geology	Geología
GEOM	Geometry	Geometry
GEOPHYS	Geophysics	Geofísica
HEAT	Heat Equipment	Equipos Térmicos
HEAT ENG	Heating Engineering Components	Componentes de la Ingeniería Térmica
HYDRAUL	Hydraulic Equipment	Instalaciones Hidráulicas
HYDROL	Hydrology	Hidrología
INSTR	Instrumentation	Instrumentación
LAB	Laboratory Equipment	Equipamiento de Laboratorio
MAR POLL	Marine Pollution	Contaminación Marina
MATH	Mathematics	Matemáticas
MECH	Mechanics	Mecánica
MECH ENG	Mechanical Engineering	Ingeniería Mecánica
METALL	Metallurgy	Metalurgia
METEO	Meteorology	Meteorología
METR	Metrology	Metrología
MILIT	Military Technology	Defensa y Armamento
MINE	Mining	Minería
MINERAL	Mineralogy	Mineralogía
NUCL	Nuclear Technology	Tecnología Nuclear
OCEAN	Oceanography	Oceanografía
OPT	Optics	Óptica
PACK	Packaging	Envasado/Embalaje
P&R	Plastics and Rubber	Plásticos y Cauchos
PAPER	Paper Technology	Tecnología del Papel
PART PHYS	Particle Physics	Física de las Partículas
PETROL	Petrology	Petrología
PETR TECH	Petroleum Technology	Tecnología del Petróleo
PHOTO	Photography	Fotografía
PHYS	Physics	Física
POLL	Pollution	Contaminación
PRINT	Printing	Imprenta
PROD	Production Engineering	Gestión de la Producción
QUALITY	Quality Assurance	Control de la Calidad
RAD PHYS	Radiation Physics	Física de las Radiaciones
RAIL	Railway Engineering	Sistemas Ferroviarios
RECYCL	Recycling	Reciclaje
REFRIG	Refrigeration	Refrigeración
SAFE	Safety Engineering	Sistemas de Seguridad
SPACE	Space Technology	Tecnología Espacial
TELECOM	Telecommunications	Telecomunicaciones
TEXTIL	Textiles	Textiles
THERMO	Thermodynamics	Termodinámica
TRANSP	Transport	Transportes
TV	Television	Televisión
VEH	Vehicle Components	Piezas de Vehículos
WATER	Water Supply Engineering	Abastecimiento de Agua
WATER TRANSP	Water Transport Engineering	Transporte Marítimo
WAVE PHYS	Wave Physics	Física de las Ondas

DICCIONARIO INGLÉS–ESPAÑOL
ENGLISH–SPANISH DICTIONARY

A

a- *abbr* (*atto-*) METR a- (*ato*)

A[1] *abbr* CHEM, ELEC, ELEC ENG, ELECTRON, METR (*ampere*) A (*ampere, amperio*), PART PHYS (*atomic mass, atomic weight, mass number*) A (*masa atómica, peso atómico, ampere, amperio*), PHYS (*ampere*) A (*ampere, amperio*)

A[2]: **~ and B printing** *n* CINEMAT copiado A y B *m*; **~ and B roll cutting** *n* CINEMAT corte de rollos A y B *m*; **~ and B windings** *n pl* CINEMAT bobinados A y B *m pl*; **~ frame** *n* CONST estructura en A *f*; **~ level** *n* CONST nivel A *m*

AA *abbr* (*aggregate abrasion value*) CONST nivel de abrasión agregado *m*

AADT *abbr* (*average annual daily traffic*) TRANSP TMAD (*tráfico medio anual por día*), capacidad absoluta *f*, promedio anual de tráfico diario *m*

AAL[1] *abbr* (*ATM adaptative layer*) TELECOM AAL (*capa adaptable de ATM*)

AAL[2]: **~ protocol control information** *n* (*AAL-PCI*) TELECOM información de control de protocolos AAL *f*; **~ service data unit** *n* (*AAL-SDU*) TELECOM unidad datos de servicio AAL *f*

Aalenian *adj* GEOL Aaleniense

AAL-PCI *abbr* (*AAL protocol control information*) TELECOM información de control de protocolos AAL *f*

AAL-SDU *abbr* (*AAL service data unit*) TELECOM unidad datos de servicio AAL *f*

AAM *abbr* (*air-to-air missile*) MILIT misil aire-aire *m*

AARE *abbr* (*A-associate response*) TELECOM respuesta asociada A *f*

A-associate: **~ response** *n* (*AARE*) TELECOM respuesta asociada A *f*

aback *adv* WATER TRANSP *sails* en facha

abacus: **~ major** *n* MINE ábaco *m*

abaft *adv* WATER TRANSP *aft of* hacia popa, *in the stern half of ship* a popa

abandon: **~ ship** *vi* WATER TRANSP *emergency situation* abandonar el buque

abandoned: **~ workings** *n pl* MINE labores mineras abandonadas *f pl*

abandonment: **~ of ship** *n* WATER TRANSP abandono del buque *m*

abatement *n* PRINT disminución *f*

abattoir *n* FOOD, REFRIG matadero *m*

Abb: **~ number** *n* PHYS *constringence* número de Abbe *m*; **~ value** *n* C&G medida de dispersión de un cristal *f*

Abbé: **~ refractometer** *n* PHYS refractómetro de Abbé *m*; **~ theory** *n* PHYS *mechanism* teoría de Abbé *f*

abbreviated: **~ dialing** *AmE*, **~ dialling** *BrE n* TELECOM llamada abreviada *f*, llamada simplificada *f*; **~ number** *n* TELECOM número abreviado *m*

ABC *abbr* (*automatic brightness control*) TV CAB (*control automático de brillo*)

abeam *adv* SPACE en ángulo recto a la quilla, por el través, WATER TRANSP por el través

abelian *adj* MATH abeliano

aberration *n* GEN aberración *f*

abietate *n* CHEM abietato *m*

abietic: **~ acid** *n* CHEM, PAPER ácido abiético *m*

ablated: **~ ion** *n* NUCL ión extirpado *m*

ablating: **~ cone** *n* SPACE *missile warheads* cono de carga *m*; **~ momentum** *n* NUCL impulso de extirpación *m*

ablation *n* GEOL ablación *f*, HYDROL ablación *f*, desgaste *m*, fusión *f*, METEO ablación *f*, enfriamiento por ablación *m*, NUCL extirpación *f*, PHYS, SPACE ablación *f*; **~ shield** *n* SPACE escudo ablativo *m*, protector de ablación *m*

ablative[1] *adj* SPACE *material* ablativo

ablative[2]: **~ cooling** *n* SPACE enfriamiento ablacionante *m*; **~-method recording** *n* (*cf PIT-forming mode*) OPT grabación por el método ablativo *f*

ablaze *adj* THERMO encendido, llameante

abnormal: **~ pressure** *n* GEOL, PETR TECH presión anormal *f*; **~ structure** *n* METALL estructura anormal *f*; **~ termination** *n* COMP&DP finalización anormal *f*, terminación anormal *f*

aboard *adv* WATER TRANSP *ship* a bordo

abort[1] *n* COMP&DP aborto *m*, cancelación *f*, SPACE aborto *m*

abort[2] *vt* COMP&DP abortar, interrumpir, SPACE abortar

aborted: **~ landing** *n* AIR TRANSP aterrizaje abortado *m*; **~ takeoff** *n* AIR TRANSP despegue abortado *m*, despegue interrumpido *m*

above[1]: **~-ground** *adj* MINE en el exterior (*AmL*), sobre tierra (*Esp*)

above[2]: **~-ground** *adv* MINE al descubierto, en el exterior (*AmL*), sobre tierra (*Esp*)

above[3]: **~-ground worker** *n* MINE obrero que trabaja en el exterior *m*

abradant *n* COAL abradante *m*, abrasivo *m*

abrade *vt* MECH desgastar por rozamiento

abraded: **~ yarn** *n* TEXTIL hilado desgastado *m*

abrading: **~ wheel** *n* PROD rueda abrasiva *f*

abraser *n* PAPER abrasímetro *m*

abrasion[1]: **~-proof** *adj* MECH *communications* anti-abrasivo; **~-resistant** *adj* PRINT resistente a la abrasión

abrasion[2] *n* COAL, GEOL, HYDROL abrasión *f*, MECH, P&R abrasión *f*, desgaste por rozamiento *m*, PAPER abrasión *f*; **~ factor** *n* MECH *communications* factor de abrasión *m*; **~ fretting corrosion** *n* MECH desgaste por frotamiento de ajuste *m*; **~ resistance** *n* P&R, PAPER resistencia a la abrasión *f*; **~ resistance index** *n* P&R, PAPER índice de resistencia a la abrasión *m*; **~ resistant coating** *n* COATINGS revestimiento resistente a la abrasión *m*; **~ test** *n* MECH ENG prueba de desgaste por abrasión *f*, PRINT ensayo de desgaste por abrasión *m*; **~ tester** *n* COAL, HYDROL, INSTR, MECH, P&R abrasímetro *m*, PAPER medidor de resistencia a la abrasión *m*

abrasive[1] *adj* GEN abrasivo

abrasive[2] *n* COATINGS, MECH, MECH ENG, SAFE abrasivo *m*; **~ agent** *n* CHEM agente abrasivo *m*; **~ belt** *n* C&G *for grinding glass*, MECH ENG cinta abrasiva *f*; **~ cloth** *n* MECH ENG tela de esmeril *f*; **~ coating** *n* COATINGS revestimiento abrasivo *m*; **~ cut-off machine** *n* MECH

ENG máquina de cortar de disco abrasivo *f*; ~ **disc** *BrE,* ~ **disk** *n AmE* MECH ENG disco abrasivo *m*; ~ **dust** *n* SAFE polvo abrasivo *m*; ~ **flap wheel** *n* MECH ENG rueda abrasiva de aletas *f*; ~ **paper** *n* ELEC *cleaning* papel abrasivo *n*, papel de lija *m*, MECH *pipelines* papel abrasivo *m*; ~ **sheet** *n* MECH ENG papel abrasivo *m*; ~ **shot** *n* MECH *for protection against particles* abrasivo metálico *m*; ~ **tester** *n* GEOL abrasímetro *m*; ~ **wear** *n* CONST desgaste por abrasión *m*, P&R desgaste abrasivo *m*, desgaste por abrasión *m*; ~ **wheel** *n* MECH, MECH ENG, SAFE rueda abrasiva *f*; ~ **wheel combination** *n* INSTR combinación de muelas abrasivas *f*; ~ **wheels regulations** *n pl* SAFE *fixed equipment* normas sobre esmeriles *f pl*
abrasiveness *n* GEN abrasividad *f*
abreast *adv* WATER TRANSP por el través, tanto avante
abridged: ~ **edition** *n* PRINT edición abreviada *f*
abrupt: ~ **junction** *n* ELECTRON unión abrupta *f*
ABS *abbr* AUTO *(anti blocking system)* ABS *(sistema antibloqueo)*, P&R *(acrylonitrile-butadiene-styrene)* ABS *(acrilonitrilo-butadieno-estireno)*
abscissa *n* COMP&DP, MATH abscisa *f*
absence *n* ACOUST *of harmonic waves* ausencia *f*, carencia *f*, falta *f*, SPACE *of convection* ausencia *f*, carencia *f*
absent: ~ **reflection** *n* CRYSTALL *from diffraction patterns* reflexión ausente *f*; ~ **subscriber** *n* TELECOM abonado ausente *m*; ~ **subscriber service** *n* TELECOM servicio de abonados ausentes *m*
absinthe *n* CHEM licor de ajenjo *m*
absinthole *n* CHEM aceite de absenta *m*
absolute: ~ **activity** *n* PHYS actividad absoluta *f*; ~ **address** *n* COMP&DP dirección absoluta *f*; ~ **code** *n* COMP&DP código absoluto *m*; ~ **error** *n* COMP&DP error absoluto *m*; ~ **gain** *n* SPACE incremento isotrópico *m*, *communications* ganancia absoluta *f*, incremento absoluto *m*, aumento absoluto *m*; ~ **humidity** *n* HEAT ENG, HYDROL humedad absoluta *f*, METEO *device* concentración del vapor *f*, humedad absoluta *f*, PHYS humedad absoluta *f*; ~ **loader** *n* COMP&DP cargador absoluto *m*; ~ **measuring system** *n* ELECTRON sistema de medición absoluta *m*; ~ **motion** *n* PHYS movimiento absoluto *m*; ~ **movement** *n* CHEM movimiento absoluto *m*; ~ **permeability** *n* ELEC *magnetism*, ELEC ENG, PETROL permeabilidad absoluta *f*; ~ **permittivity** *n* ELEC *electrical field* constante dieléctrica absoluta *f*, permitividad absoluta *f*, ELEC ENG, PHYS permitividad absoluta *f*; ~ **potential** *n* ELEC potencial absoluto *m*; ~ **pressure** *n* REFRIG presión absoluta *f*; ~ **refractive index** *n* RAD PHYS índice de refracción absoluto *m*; ~ **speed variation** *n* ELEC *electrical machine* variación absoluta de velocidad *f*; ~ **stability** *n* TELECOM estabilidad absoluta *f*; ~ **stop signal** *n* RAIL *fixed equipment* señal de parada absoluta *f*; ~ **temperature** *n* PHYS, REFRIG, THERMO temperatura absoluta *f*; ~ **threshold** *n* TV *programming* umbral absoluto *m*; ~ **vacuum** *n* REFRIG vacío absoluto *m*; ~ **value** *n* CHEM, COMP&DP, MATH valor absoluto *m*; ~ **velocity** *n* MECH velocidad absoluta *f*; ~ **water velocity** *n* FUELLESS velocidad absoluta de agua *f*; ~ **zero** *n* CHEM, FOOD, PHYS, REFRIG, THERMO cero absoluto *m*
absorb *vt* GEN absorber, MECH ENG amortiguar
absorbable *adj* CHEM absorbible
absorbance *n* GEN absorbencia *f*
absorbed: ~ **dose** *n* PHYS, RAD PHYS dosis absorbida *f*;

~ **dose rate** *n* PHYS, RAD PHYS tasa de dosis absorbida *f*; ~ **energy** *n* METALL, RAD PHYS energía absorbida *f*
absorbency *n* GEN absorbencia *f*
absorbent¹ *adj* GEN absorbente
absorbent² *n* GEN absorbente *m*; ~ **belt skimmer** *n* POLL desescoriador de cinta absorbente *m*, desnatador de cinta absorbente *m*, espumador de cinta absorbente *m*
absorber¹ *adj* GEN absorbedor, absorbente
absorber² *n* GEN absorbedor *m*, absorbente *m*; ~ **column** *n* CHEM TECH columna absorbente *f*; ~ **member** *n* NUCL elemento absorbente *m*; ~ **plate** *n* FUELLESS, NUCL placa absorbente *f*; ~ **rod** *n* NUCL barra absorbente *f*; ~ **trap** *n* CHEM TECH colector absorbente *m*; ~ **tubing** *n* CHEM TECH tubería absorbente *f*
absorbing: ~ **capacity** *n* MECH *diaphragm* capacidad de absorción *f*; ~ **well** *n* WATER pozo absorbente *m*, pozo de drenaje *m*, pozo de fondo arenoso *m*, pozo drenante *m*
absorptiometer *n* PAPER absorciómetro *m*
absorptiometry *n* NUCL absorciometría *f*
absorption *n* GEN absorción *f*; ~ **band** *n* PHYS, RAD PHYS banda de absorción *f*; ~ **cell** *n* CHEM TECH celda de absorción *f*; ~ **circuit** *n* ELEC circuito de absorción *m*; ~ **coefficient** *n* ACOUST, PHYS, RAD PHYS coeficiente de absorción *m*; ~ **column** *n* COAL columna de absorción *f*, PETR TECH torre de absorción *f*; ~ **cooling** *n* FUELLESS refrigeración absorbente *f*; ~ **correction** *n* CRYSTALL corrección de absorción *f*; ~ **cross-section** *n* RAD PHYS sección eficaz de absorción *f*; ~ **current** *n* ELEC corriente de absorción *f*; ~ **edge** *n* CRYSTALL *X-ray spectra* borde de absorción *m*, margen de absorción *m*, NUCL borde de absorción *m*; ~ **factor** *n* ACOUST, TELECOM factor de absorción *m*; ~ **filter** *n* CINEMAT, INSTR filtro de absorción *m*; ~ **fringes** *n pl* PHYS, RAD PHYS franja de absorción *f*; ~ **in the soil** *n* WATER absorción del suelo *f*; ~ **ink test** *n* PRINT ensayo de absorción de tinta *m*; ~ **of ionizing radiation** *n* RAD PHYS, WAVE PHYS absorción de radiación ionizante *f*; ~ **of light** *n* RAD PHYS absorción de luz *f*; ~ **line** *n* PHYS raya de absorción *f*, raya oscura *f*; ~ **loss** *n* ELEC ENG, TV pérdida por absorción *f*; ~ **peak** *n* ELEC ENG absorción máxima *f*; ~ **plant** *n* PETR TECH, SAFE instalación de absorción *f*; ~ **of radiation** *n* RAD PHYS, WAVE PHYS absorción de radiación *f*; ~ **reactor** *n* CHEM TECH reactor de absorción *m*; ~ **refrigerating cycle** *n* REFRIG ciclo frigorífico de absorción *m*; ~ **refrigerating installation** *n* MECH ENG, REFRIG instalación de refrigeración por absorción *f*; ~ **refrigerating machine** *n* REFRIG máquina frigorífica de absorción *f*; ~ **refrigeration system** *n* REFRIG sistema frigorífico de absorción *m*; ~ **refrigerator** *n* REFRIG frigorífico de absorción *m*, refrigerador de absorción *m*, THERMO frigorífico de absorción *m*; ~ **silencer** *n* SAFE *cross-piece to which rail is attached* silenciador de absorción *m*; ~ **spectroanalysis** *n* RAD PHYS espectroanálisis de absorción *m*; ~ **spectrometer** *n* INSTR, LAB espectrómetro de absorción *m*; ~ **spectrometry** *n* TELECOM espectrometría de absorción *f*; ~ **spectrophotometer** *n* RAD PHYS espectrofotómetro de absorción *m*; ~ **spectroscopy** *n* PHYS, RAD PHYS espectroscopía de absorción *f*; ~ **spectrum** *n* PHYS, RAD PHYS, SPACE espectro de absorción *m*;

~ tower *n* CHEM TECH, COAL, FOOD torre de absorción *f*, PETR TECH torre de absorción *f*, torre de extracción *f*; **~ tube** *n* LAB *navigation* tubo de absorción *m*; **~-type refrigerator** *n* THERMO refrigerador de absorción *m*; **~ vessel** *n* CHEM TECH matraz de absorción *m*

absorptive: **~ attenuator** *n* ELECTRON, TELECOM atenuador absorbente *m*; **~ capacity** *n* HYDROL *for injection moulding*, PACK capacidad de absorción *f*; **~ dielectric** *n* ELEC dieléctrico absorbente *m*, dieléctrico de absorción *m*; **~ modulator** *n* ELECTRON modulador absorbente *m*; **~-type ink** *n* PRINT cubierta de botes *f*, tinta que seca por absorción *f*

abstract[1] *adj* COMP&DP abstracto

abstract[2]: **~ data type** *n* COMP&DP tipo de datos resumidos *m*; **~ symbol** *n* COMP&DP símbolo abstracto *m*; **~ topological principle** *n* GEOM *of screw* principio topológico abstracto *m*

abstract[3] *vt* COMP&DP abstraer, extractar, resumir

abstracting: **~ of heat** *n* HYDRAUL pérdida de calor *f*

abstraction *n* COMP&DP abstracción *f*, extracción *f*

abundance *n* NUCL, PHYS abundancia *f*; **~ pattern** *n* GEOL concentración media de un elemento *f*; **~ ratio** *n* NUCL razón de abundancias *f*, relación de abundancias *f*, PART PHYS *of isotopes* relación de abundancia *f*

aburton: **~ stowage** *n* WATER TRANSP estiba atravesada *f*

abut[1] *vt* CONST *carpentry* empotrar, encastrar

abut[2] *vi* CONST *carpentry* adosar

abutment *n* CONST *architecture* estribo *m*, tope *m*, *carpentry* rebaje *m*, empotramiento *m*, muesca *f*

abutting: **~ joint** *n* CONST junta a tope *f*, PETR TECH junta plana de empalme *f*, junta vertical *f*

abyssal[1] *adj* GEOL, OCEAN abisal

abyssal[2]: **~ cone** *n* OCEAN cono abisal *m*; **~ hill** *n* OCEAN colina abisal *f*; **~ knoll** *n* OCEAN colina abisal *f*; **~ pass** *n* OCEAN brecha abisal *f*, desfiladero abisal *m* (*Esp*); **~ plain** *n* GEOL llanura abisal *f*, GEOPHYS llano abisal *m*, llanura abisal *f*, planicie abisal *f*, OCEAN llanura abisal *f*, PETROL planicie abisal *f*; **~ spit** *n* OCEAN flecha abisal *f*, lengua abisal *f*

Ac *abbr* (*actinium*) CHEM, METALL, RAD PHYS Ac (*actinio*)

AC[1] *abbr* GEN (*alternating current*) CA (*corriente alterna, corriente alternativa*)

AC[2]: **~ operated** *adj* PROD accionado por CA

AC[3]: **~ ammeter** *n* ELEC, ELEC ENG amperímetro CA *m*; **~ amplifier** *n* ELECTRON amplificador de CA *m*; **~ armature relay** *n* ELEC ENG relé de dínamo de CA *m*, relé de inducido de CA *m*; **~ capacitor** *n* ELEC ENG capacitor de CA *m* (*AmL*), condensador de capacidad fija de CA *m* (*AmL*), relé de dínamo de CA *m*; **~ circuit** *n* ELEC ENG circuito de CA *m*; **~ contactor** *n* PROD contactor de CA *m*; **~ discharge** *n* ELEC ENG descarga de CA *f*; **~ electromotive force** *n* ELEC, ELEC ENG, PHYS fuerza electromotriz de CA *f*; **~ excitation** *n* ELEC ENG excitación de CA *f*; **~ generation** *n* ELEC ENG generación de CA *f*; **~ generator** *n* ELEC ENG generador de CA *m*; **~ input** *n* ELEC ENG alimentación de CA *f*, entrada de CA *f*; **~ Josephson effect** *n* ELECTRON efecto Josephson de CA *m*; **~ line** *n* ELEC ENG línea de CA *f*; **~ load** *n* ELEC ENG línea de carga de CA *f*; **~ machine** *n* ELEC ENG máquina de CA *f*; **~ magnetic biasing** *n* TV polarización magnética por CA *f*; **~ marker** *n*

WATER TRANSP *radar* indicador CA *m*; **~ meter** *n* ELEC *instrument* medidor de CA *m*; **~ motor** *n* ELEC alternomotor *m*, motor de CA *m*, ELEC ENG, PHYS motor de CA *m*; **~ operation** *n* ELEC ENG operación de CA *f*; **~ output** *n* ELEC ENG potencia de salida de CA *f*, potencia útil de CA *f*; **~ potentiometer** *n* ELEC component potenciómetro de CA *m*; **~ power failure** *n* ELEC ENG falta de tensión de CA *f*; **~ power line** *n* ELEC, ELEC ENG línea de alto voltaje de CA *f*, línea de energía de CA *f*; **~ power system** *n* SPACE *spacecraft* sistema de alimentación por CA *m*, sistema de corriente CA *m*; **~ resistance** *n* ELEC ENG resistencia de CA *f*; **~ source** *n* ELEC fuente de CA *f*, ELEC ENG fuente de CA *f*, generador de CA *m*; **~ voltmeter** *n* ELEC ENG voltímetro de CA *m*

academy: **~ aperture** *n* CINEMAT abertura académica *f*; **~ leader** *n* CINEMAT guía académica *f*; **~ mask** *n* CINEMAT máscara académica *f*

acanticone *n* MINERAL acanticona *f*

acanthite *n* MINERAL acantita *f*

accelerate[1]: **~-stop distance** *n* AIR TRANSP distancia aceleración-parada *f*; **~-stop distance available** *n* AIR TRANSP distancia aceleración-parada disponible *f*; **~-stop distance required** *n* AIR TRANSP distancia aceleración-parada requerida *f*

accelerate[2] *vt* GEN acelerar

accelerate[3] *vi* PHYS acelerar

accelerated[1] *adj* AUTO, PHYS acelerado

accelerated[2]: **~ ageing test** *n* P&R prueba de envejecimiento acelerado *f*; **~ commutation** *n* ELEC *electrical machine* conmutación acelerada *f*; **~ creep** *n* METALL deformación acelerada *f*, estiramiento acelerado por termofluencia *m*; **~ filtration** *n* CHEM TECH, FOOD filtración acelerada *f*; **~ freeze drying** *n* (*AFD*) AGRIC criodeshidratación *f*, liofilización acelerada *f*, secado por congelación *m*, FOOD, PACK, REFRIG, THERMO liofilización acelerada *f*; **~ motion** *n* MECH movimiento acelerado *m*; **~ storage test** *n* PACK ensayo de almacenado acelerado *m*; **~ weathering** *n* P&R alteración por exposición a la intemperie artificial *f*, deterioro por exposición a la intemperie artificial *m*

accelerating: **~ anode** *n* ELEC ENG, RAD PHYS ánodo acelerador *m*; **~ chamber** *n* CHEM TECH cámara de aceleración *f*; **~ electrode** *n* NUCL electrodo acelerador *m*; **~ force** *n* PHYS, SPACE fuerza aceleradora *f*, fuerza de aceleración *f*; **~ period** *n* CHEM TECH período de aceleración *m*; **~ power** *n* AUTO poder de aceleración *m*, VEH poder de aceleración *m*, potencia de aceleración *f*; **~ tube** *n* CHEM TECH, PART PHYS, PHYS tubo de aceleración *m*; **~ voltage** *n* ELEC *charged particles* tensión aceleradora *f*, tensión acelerante *f*, tensión aceleratriz *f*, ELEC ENG tensión de aceleración *f*, voltaje acelerador *m*

acceleration *n* GEN aceleración *f*; **~ control unit** *n* AIR TRANSP unidad de control de aceleración *f*; **~ detector** *n* AIR TRANSP detector de aceleración *m*; **~ device** *n* TRANSP mecanismo de aceleración *m*; **~ due to gravity** *n* GEOL, GEOPHYS, PHYS, SPACE aceleración por la gravedad *f*, aceleración debida a la gravedad *f*; **~ jet** *n* AUTO chicle de aceleración *m*, surtidor de aceleración *m*; **~ lane** *n* CONST, TRANSP carril de aceleración *m* (*Esp*); **~ relay** *n* ELEC relé de aceleración *m*; **~ time** *n* COMP&DP tiempo de aceleración *m*

accelerator *n* GEN *engine, boat building* acelerador *m*;

~ **breeder** n NUCL acelerador reproductor m; ~ **cavity** n PART PHYS cavidad del acelerador f; ~ **driven light water reactor** n NUCL reactor de agua ligera activado por acelerador m (*Esp*), reactor de agua liviana activado por acelerador m (*AmL*); ~ **jet** n VEH surtidor de alimentación m; ~ **linkage** n AUTO varillaje del acelerador m, RAIL acoplamiento del acelerador m, articulación del acelerador f, junta del acelerador f, VEH sistema de mando del acelerador m, varillaje del acelerador m; ~ **pedal** n (*cf gas pedal AmE*) AUTO acelerador m, pedal del acelerador m, VEH pedal del acelerador m, acelerador m; ~ **pump** n AUTO, VEH bomba de aceleración f

accelerometer n GEN acelerómetro m

accent n PRINT acento m; ~ **light** n CINEMAT luz para destacar f

accented: ~ **letter** n PRINT letra acentuada f

accentuate vt PRINT acentuar

acceptable: ~ **quality level** n (*AQL*) QUALITY nivel de calidad aceptable m

acceptance n MECH, QUALITY aceptación f, SPACE recepción f; ~ **angle** n CINEMAT ángulo de aceptación m, ELEC ENG ángulo de admisión m, OPT ángulo de aceptación m, ELECTRON ángulo de recepción m, PRINT, TELECOM ángulo de recepción m; ~ **of a beam** n ELECTRON, NUCL aceptación de un haz f; ~ **certificate** n QUALITY certificado de aceptación m; ~ **criterion** n SPACE criterio aceptación m, criterio de recepción m; ~ **firing test** n SPACE prueba de tiro de recepción f; ~ **flight** n AIR TRANSP vuelo de recepción m; ~ **inspection** n MECH ENG inspección de recepción f, QUALITY control de aceptación m; ~ **report** n MECH informe de aceptación m; ~ **specification** n QUALITY especificación de aceptación f; ~ **test** n COAL ensayo de aceptación m, prueba de aceptación f, COMP&DP, SPACE prueba de aceptación f, prueba de recepción f, TELECOM, WATER TRANSP prueba de recepción f; ~ **test sheet** n PROD hoja para pruebas de recepción f; ~ **testing** n MECH ensayos de recepción m pl; ~ **trial** n AIR TRANSP, WATER TRANSP *ships* prueba de recepción f

accepted: ~ **stock** n PACK mercancía recibida f, PAPER pasta aceptada f (*Esp*), pasta depurada f (*AmL*)

acceptor n CHEM *atom, molecule* aceptor m, COMP&DP *semiconductor* aceptador m, aceptor m, ELEC *induction, circuit*, ELECTRON, PART PHYS, PHYS aceptor m; ~ **atom** n ELECTRON átomo aceptor m, PART PHYS, PHYS átomo aceptor m, átomo receptor m; ~ **circuit** n ELEC *induction* circuito aceptor m, circuito de admisión m, circuito resonante m; ~ **concentration** n ELECTRON concentración de aceptores f; ~ **impurity** n ELECTRON aceptor de impurezas m; ~ **level** n ELECTRON nivel de aceptor m; ~ **resonance** n ELEC *AC circuit* resonancia aceptora f

access[1] n COAL, COMP&DP, ELECTRON, RAIL acceso m, SPACE acceso m, aumento m, TELECOM acceso m; ~ **arm** n COMP&DP brazo de acceso m; ~ **burst signal** n TELECOM señal de estallido de acceso f; ~ **channel** n TELECOM canal de acceso m; ~ **charge rate** n TELECOM tarifa inicial f; ~ **circuit** n TELECOM circuito de acceso m; ~ **concentrator** n TELECOM concentrador de acceso m; ~ **connection element** n TELECOM elemento de conexión de acceso m; ~ **control** n TELECOM control de acceso m; ~ **control list** n TELECOM relación de controles de acceso f; ~ **door** n AIR TRANSP puerta de acceso f; ~ **line** n COMP&DP línea de

acceso f; ~ **link** n TELECOM enlace de acceso m; ~ **list** n COMP&DP lista de acceso f; ~ **matrix** n TELECOM matriz de acceso f; ~ **method** n COMP&DP método de acceso m; ~ **mode** n COMP&DP modalidad de acceso f, modo de acceso m; ~ **network** n TELECOM red de acceso f; ~ **node** n TELECOM nodo de acceso m; ~ **number** n TELECOM número de acceso m; ~ **panel** n AIR TRANSP panel de acceso m, SPACE panel de acceso m, tablero de acceso m; ~ **path** n COMP&DP camino de acceso m, ruta de acceso f; ~ **port** n NUCL *for plastics* orificio de acceso m, TELECOM puerto de acceso m; ~ **ramp** n CONST, TRANSP rampa de acceso f; ~ **road** n AmE (*cf slip road BrE*) CONST calle de acceso f, camino de acceso m, vía de acceso f, TRANSP calle de acceso f, camino de acceso m, carretera de acceso f; ~ **road census** n AmE (*cf slip road census BrE*) TRANSP carretera de entrada censada f, censo de carreteras de acceso m, censo de vías de acceso m; ~ **road control** n AmE (*cf slip road control BrE*) TRANSP control de carretera de acceso m, control del camino de acceso m; ~ **road count** n AmE (*cf slip road count BrE*) TRANSP recuento de carreteras de acceso m, recuento de vías de acceso m; ~ **road metering** n AmE (*cf slip road metering BrE*) TRANSP medición de carretera de acceso f, medición de la vía de acceso f; ~ **speed** n ELEC ENG velocidad de acceso f; ~ **subsystem** n TELECOM subsistema de acceso m; ~ **time** n COMP&DP, ELEC ENG, OPT, PRINT tiempo de acceso m; ~ **to platforms** n RAIL acceso a los andenes m; ~ **unit** n (*AU*) TELECOM unidad de acceso f

access[2] vt COMP&DP acceder, ingresar, obtener acceso

accessibility n MECH, QUALITY accesibilidad f

accessible: ~ **coast** n WATER TRANSP costa abordable f; ~ **resource base** n FUELLESS base de recursos accesibles f

accessory n MECH ENG accesorio m; ~ **drive** n AIR TRANSP arrastre de accesorios m, conductor de accesorios m, transmisión accesoria f; ~ **gearbox** n AIR TRANSP engranaje accesorio m; ~ **shoe** n CINEMAT terminal para accesorios m, PHOTO *for cable* pie para accesorios m, respaldo para accesorios m

accident[1]: --**prone** adj SAFE propenso a sufrir accidentes

accident[2] n SAFE *rail* accidente m; ~ **advisory sign** n TRANSP señal de advertencia de incidente f, señalización de accidente f; ~ **analysis** n NUCL análisis de accidentes m; ~ **at work** n CONST, SAFE accidente laboral m; ~ **conditions** n pl NUCL condiciones de accidente f pl; ~ **data reporting** n AIR TRANSP informe de datos de accidente m; ~ **detector** n SAFE, TRANSP detector de accidentes m; ~ **prevention** n SAFE prevención de accidentes f; ~ **prevention advertising sign** n SAFE letrero para prevenir accidentes m, señal para prevenir accidentes f

accidental: ~ **alteration** n ACOUST alteración accidental f; ~ **braking** n RAIL, VEH frenado accidental m; ~ **discharge** n MAR POLL, POLL descarga accidental f

acclimatization n HEAT ENG climatización f, METEO aclimatación f

accommodation n MECH alojamiento m, MECH ENG alojamiento m, adaptación f, WATER TRANSP *boat building* alojamiento m; ~ **deck** n WATER TRANSP cubierta de alojamientos f; ~ **ladder** n WATER TRANSP escala real f; ~ **plan** n WATER TRANSP plano de alojamientos m; ~ **platform** n PETR TECH plata-

forma-hotel *f*; **~ rig** *n* PETR TECH plataforma-hotel *f*, torre de perforación fuera de la costa *f*
accordance *n* MECH ENG armonía *f*
accordion: **~ fold** *n* PAPER plegado en acordeón *m*, PRINT plegado en acordeón *m*, plegado en zigzag *m*
accountability *n* TELECOM responsabilidad *f*
accounting: **~ file** *n* COMP&DP archivo contable *m*, archivo de contabilidad *m*; **~ machine** *n* COMP&DP máquina contable *f*, máquina de contabilidad *f*; **~ ratio** *n* CONST ratio contable *m*, relación contable *f*
accretion *n* GEOL, METEO, WATER *of node* acreción *f*
accretionary: **~ prism** *n* GEOL prisma accrecional *m*
accumulating: **~ counter** *n* ELECTRON contador acumulador *m*
accumulation *n* GEOL acumulación *f*, yacimiento *m*, METEO *process* acumulación *f*
accumulator *n* AUTO acumulador *m*, batería de acumuladores *f*, CHEM, COMP&DP acumulador *m*, ELEC *collection of cells* batería de acumuladores *f*, acumulador *m*, ELECTRON acumulador *m*, ELEC ENG acumulador *m*, batería de acumuladores *f*, HEAT ENG, HYDRAUL, NUCL acumulador *m*, PHYS acumulador *m*, batería de acumuladores *f*, REFRIG acumulador *m*, SPACE, TELECOM batería de acumuladores *f*, THERMO acumulador *m*, TRANSP batería de acumuladores *f*, VEH elemento de batería *m*, batería de acumuladores *f*, acumulador *m*, WATER TRANSP batería de acumuladores *f*, *electrics* acumulador *m*; **~ cell** *n* AUTO vaso acumulador *m*, ELEC celda de acumulador *f*; **~ charge** *n* ELEC carga de acumulador *f*; **~ discharge** *n* ELEC descarga de acumulador *f*; **~ plate** *n* ELEC placa de acumulador *f*; **~ railcar** *n* RAIL automotor por acumuladores *m*; **~ register** *n* COMP&DP registro acumulador *m*, registro totalizador *m*; **~ tank** *n* PETR TECH tanque acumulador *m*
accuracy *n* COMP&DP precisión *f*, MECH, MECH ENG, METR, PHYS exactitud *f*, precisión *f*; **~ of measurement** *n* METR exactitud de medida *f*; **~ of parallel gears** *n* MECH ENG precisión de engranajes paralelos *f*; **~ of ship's position** *n* WATER TRANSP *navigation* exactitud de la situación del buque *f*, precisión de la situación del buque *f*; **~ test** *n* MECH ENG prueba de precisión *f*
accurate: **~ print registration** *n* PACK impresión con registro exacto *f*; **~ reproduction** *n* PHOTO reproducción fiel *f*
ACD *abbr* (*automatic call distributor*) TELECOM distribuidor automático de llamadas *m*
AC/DC: **~ converter** *n* ELECTRON inversor de CC/CA *m*; **~ motor converter set** *n* RAIL, VEH grupo convertidor de corriente alterna a continua *m*
acetal[1] *adj* FOOD acetal
acetal[2] *n* CHEM, P&R acetal *m*
acetaldehyde *n* CHEM, FOOD *coil* acetaldehído *m*
acetanilide *n* CHEM acetanilida *f*
acetate *n* CHEM, FOOD, P&R, TEXTIL acetato *m*; **~ adhesive** *n* PACK adhesivo de acetato *m*; **~ base** *n* PRINT soporte de acetato *m*; **~ color** *AmE*, **~ colour** *BrE n* COLOUR pintura para plásticos *f* (*AmL*), pintura plástica *f* (*Esp*); **~ film** *n* PACK película de acetato *f*; **~ glue** *n* PACK goma de acetato *f*; **~ laminate** *n* PACK película de acetato laminada *f*; **~ proof** *n* PRINT *surveying* prueba sobre hoja de acetato *f*
acetic[1] *adj* CHEM acético
acetic[2]: **~ acid** *n* CHEM, FOOD, P&R ácido acético *m*;

~ acid bacteria *n pl* FOOD, HYDROL, RECYCL, WATER bacteria del ácido acético *f*; **~ anhydride** *n* FOOD ácido acético *m*; **~ fermentation** *n* FOOD fermentación acética *f*
acetification *n* CHEM acetificación *f*
acetify *vt* CHEM acetificar
acetin *n* CHEM acetina *f*
acetobacterium *n* FOOD acetobacteria *f*
acetolysis *n* CHEM, FOOD acetólisis *f*
acetone *n* CHEM, COATINGS, FOOD acetona *f*, P&R acetona *f*, propanona *f*; **~ extract** *n* P&R extracto de acetona *m*; **~ lacquer** *n* COATINGS, COLOUR laca de acetona *f*; **~ resin** *n* P&R, PACK resina acetónica *f*
acetonitrile *n* CHEM acetonitrilo *m*
acetonuria *n* CHEM acetonuria *f*
acetophenone *n* CHEM fenilmetilcetona *f*
acetoxy- *pref* CHEM acetoxi-
acetoxyl *n* CHEM, FOOD acetosil *m*, peróxido de benzoílo *m*, P&R peróxido de benzoilo *m*
acetyl *n* CHEM acetilo *m*; **~ cellulose lacquer** *n* COATINGS, COLOUR laca de acetilcelulosa *f*; **~ iodide** *n* CHEM yoduro de acetilo *m*; **~ value** *n* P&R índice de acetato *m*
acetylene *n* CHEM, CONST, GAS, MECH, SAFE, THERMO acetileno *m*; **~ blowpipe** *n* CONST soplete para soldadura de acetileno *m*, soplete para acetileno *m*; **~ cutting** *n* MECH corte de acetileno *m*; **~ cylinder** *n* MECH *aviation* cilindro para acetileno *m*; **~ generator** *n* CHEM TECH gasógeno de acetileno *m*, generador de acetileno *m* (*AmL*), CONST, GAS generador de acetileno *m*; **~ lamp** *n* CONST lámpara de acetileno *f*; **~-oxygen torch** *n* MECH soplete oxiacetilénico *m*
acetylenic *adj* CHEM, CONST, GAS, MECH, SAFE, THERMO acetilénico
acetylide *n* CHEM colorante ácido *m*
acetylsalicylic *adj* CHEM acetilsalicílico
ACF *abbr* (*advanced communications function*) COMP&DP ACF (*función avanzada de comunicaciones*)
achievable: **~ availability** *n* PROD disponibilidad factible *f*; **~ burn-up** *n* NUCL grado de quemado potencial *m*
achrematite *n* MINERAL acrematita *f*
achroite *n* MINERAL acroíta *f*
achromat *n* OPT objetivo acromático *m*, PHYS lente acromática *f*
achromatic[1] *adj* GEN acromático
achromatic[2]: **~ aerial** *n* BrE (*cf achromatic antenna AmE*) TV antena acromática *f*; **~ antenna** *n* AmE (*cf achromatic aerial BrE*) TV antena acromática *f*; **~ color** *AmE see achromatic colour BrE*; **~ color removal** *AmE*, **~ colour** *BrE n* PRINT color acromático *m*; **~ colour removal** *n* BrE PRINT decoloración acromática *f*; **~ doublet** *n* PHYS doblete acromático *m*; **~ fringes** *n pl* PHYS franjas acromáticas *f pl*; **~ lens** *n* CINEMAT, PHOTO objetivo acromático *m*, PHYS lente acromática *f*, PRINT objetivo acromático *m*; **~ quartz fluoride lens** *n* INSTR lente de fluoruro de cuarzo acromática *f*
ACI *abbr* (*automatic car identification AmE, automatic wagon identification BrE*) TRANSP IAC (*identificación automática de coches*)
acicular *adj* GEOL, METALL acicular
aciculite *n* MINERAL aciculita *f*
acid[1]: **~-free** *adj* PAPER libre de ácidos; **~-proof** *adj* PAPER a prueba de ácidos, PRINT resistente a los ácidos; **~-resistant** *adj* PACK resistente a los ácidos,

POLL resistente al ataque de los ácidos, PRINT resistente al ácido; **~-stressed** *adj* POLL fatigado con ácido

acid² *n* CHEM, FOOD, POLL, TEXTIL, WATER ácido *m*; **~ acceptor** *n* P&R aceptor de ácidos *m*; **~ aerosol** *n* POLL aerosol ácido *m*; **~ badging** *n* C&G grabado al ácido *m*; **~ bath** *n* CHEM TECH baño ácido *m*; **~ chloride** *n* CHEM, FOOD cloruro de ácido *m*; **~ color** *AmE*, **~ colour** *BrE n* COLOUR, PRINT colorante ácido *m*; **~ concentration** *n* POLL concentración ácida *f*; **~ content** *n* PACK contenido en ácido *m*; **~ deposit** *n* MINE yacimiento ácido *m*, POLL depósito ácido *m*, precipitado ácido *m*, sedimento ácido *m*, yacimiento ácido *m*; **~ dye** *n* TEXTIL colorante ácido *m*, tinte ácido *m*; **~ earth** *n* POLL suelo ácido *m*, tierra ácida *f*; **~ elevator** *n* CHEM TECH elevador ácido *m*; **~ embossing** *n* C&G grabado en relieve al ácido *m*; **~-etched frosted glass** *n* C&G cristal matizado mordentado al ácido *m*; **~ etching** *n* C&G grabado al ácido *m*; **~ fallout** *n* POLL lluvia radiactiva ácida *f*, precipitación radiactiva ácida *f*; **~ fixing bath** *n* CHEM TECH, CINEMAT, PHOTO baño fijador ácido *m*; **~ fog** *n* POLL neblina ácida *f*; **~-free glue** *n* PHOTO cola neutra *f*, pegamento neutro *m*, pegamento sin ácido *m*; **~-free paper** *n* PACK, PAPER papel libre de ácido *m*; **~ hardening bath** *n* CINEMAT, PHOTO *fuel* baño endurecedor ácido *m*; **~ hydrometer** *n* AUTO densímetro *m*, densímetro de ácidos *m*, hidrodensímetro *m*; **~ injecting tank** *n* CHEM TECH tanque inyector de ácido *m*; **~ lake** *n* POLL lago ácido *m*; **~ level** *n* AUTO, CONST nivel de ácido *m*; **~ loading** *n* POLL alimentación ácida *f*, carga ácida *f*; **~ mark** *n* C&G marcado al ácido *m*; **~ neutralizing** *n* POLL neutralizador de ácidos *m*, neutralizante de ácidos *m*; **~-neutralizing capacity** *n* POLL capacidad neutralizadora de ácidos *f*; **~ number** *n* PETR TECH índice de acidez *m*; **~ particle** *n* POLL partícula acídica *f*; **~ pickling technology** *n* NUCL tecnología de decapado con ácidos *f*; **~ polishing** *n* C&G pulido al ácido *m*; **~ pollution** *n* POLL contaminación ácida *f*; **~ precipitation** *n* POLL lluvia ácida *f*, precipitación ácida *f*; **~ prepickling** *n* NUCL decapado preliminar con ácido *m* (*Esp*), decapado previo con ácido *m* (*AmL*); **~ process** *n* PAPER proceso ácido *m*; **~-proof coat** *n* COLOUR revestimiento a prueba de ácidos *m*, revestimiento antiácido *m*; **~-proof enamel** *n* COATINGS esmalte antiácido *m*, esmalte resistente al ácido *m*, COLOUR esmalte a prueba de ácidos *m*; **~-proof lining** *n* COATINGS revestimiento interior antiácido *m*; **~-proof protective gloves** *n pl* SAFE guantes protectores a prueba de ácidos *m pl*; **~-proof varnish** *n* COATINGS barniz a prueba de ácidos *m*, barniz resistente a los ácidos *m*, COLOUR barniz resistente a los ácidos *m*, PACK barniz a prueba de ácidos *m*, barniz resistente a los ácidos *m*; **~ radical** *n* CHEM radical ácido *m*; **~ rain** *n* GAS lluvia ácida *f*, precipitación ácida *f* (*AmL*), POLL lluvia ácida *f*, precipitación ácida *f*; **~ recovery plant** *n* PETR TECH, RECYCL planta de recuperación de ácidos *f*; **~ resistance** *n* P&R resistencia al ácido *f*; **~-resisting covering** *n* SAFE cubierta resistente al ácido *f*; **~-resisting paint** *n* CONST pintura antiácida *f*; **~ rock** *n* GEOL roca ácida *f*; **~ runoff** *n* POLL derrame ácido *m*; **~ salt** *n* FOOD sal ácida *f*; **~ shock** *n* POLL cambio brusco de la acidez *m*,

cambio brusco del PH *m*; **~ snow** *n* POLL nieve ácida *f*; **~ solution** *n* FOOD solución ácida *f*; **~ stop bath** *n* CINEMAT, PHOTO baño de paro ácido *m* (*Esp*), baño detenedor ácido *m* (*AmL*); **~ strength** *n* CHEM fuerza ácida *f*; **~ stress** *n* POLL esfuerzo ácido *m*; **~ tolerance** *n* POLL tolerancia al ácido *f*; **~ value** *n* FOOD *of substance* contenido de ácido libre *m*, valor ácido *m*, P&R índice de acidez *m*; **~ water** *n* HYDROL, POLL, WATER agua ácida *f*; **~ well treatment** *n* (*AWT*) PETR TECH, PETROL acidificación del pozo *f*

acidic¹ *adj* CHEM, HYDROL, POLL acídico

acidic²: **~ area** *n* CHEM intervalo de acidez *m*, POLL intervalo de acidez *m*, zona de acidez *f*, área ácida *f*; **~ chloride** *n* CHEM cloruro ácido *m*; **~ particle** *n* POLL partícula acídica *f*; **~ precursor** *n* POLL precursor ácido *m*; **~ rock** *n* CHEM, GEOL roca ácida *f*

acidiferous *adj* CHEM acidífero

acidifiable *adj* CHEM acidificable

acidification *n* GEN acidificación *f*

acidified: **~ lake** *n* POLL lago acidificado *m*, lago acidulado *m*

acidifier *n* CHEM, MAR POLL, PETR TECH, POLL, TEXTIL acidificador *m*

acidify *vt* CHEM acidificar, FOOD acidificar, acidular, HYDROL, MAR POLL acidificar, POLL acidificar, acidular, TEXTIL, WATER acidificar

acidifying¹ *adj* PETR TECH acidificador, POLL acidificador, acidificante

acidifying²: **~ agent** *n* CHEM, TEXTIL agente acidificante *m*; **~ beck** *n* TEXTIL barca acidificante *f*

acidimeter *n* CHEM, CHEM TECH acidímetro *m*, acidómetro *m*, FOOD, INSTR acidómetro *m*, PAPER acidímetro *m*

acidimetric *adj* CHEM, CHEM TECH, PAPER acidimétrico

acidimetry *n* CHEM, CHEM TECH, PAPER acidimetría *f*

acidity *n* GEN acidez *f*; **~ level** *n* POLL grado de acidez *m*, nivel de acidez *m*

acidless *adj* PACK libre de ácido

acidolysis *n* CHEM, CHEM TECH, FOOD *communications* acidólisis *m*

acidulate *vt* CHEM, CHEM TECH acidular

acidulated *adj* CHEM acidificado

aciform *adj* CHEM acicular

ACK *abbr* (*acknowledgement*) COMP&DP REC (*reconocimiento*)

acknowledge¹ *n* COMP&DP confirmación de recepción *f*; **~ character** *n* COMP&DP carácter de reconocimiento *m*

acknowledge² *vt* COMP&DP reconocer, acusar recibo de, confirmar recepción de

acknowledged: **~ information transfer service** *n* TELECOM servicio de traslado de información reconocida *m*

acknowledgement *n* (*ACK*) COMP&DP acuse de recibo *m*, confirmación de recepción *f*, reconocimiento *m* (*REC*), PRINT lanzamiento del codaste *m*, TELECOM acuse de recibo *m*, aviso de recepción *m*, reconocimiento de recibo *m*; **~ flag** *n* TELECOM bandera de confirmación *f*, señalizador *m*; **~ request** *n* TELECOM petición de confirmación *f*; **~ signal** *n* TELECOM señal de confirmación *f*

aclinic: **~ line** *n* GEOPHYS línea aclínica *f*

Acme: **~ thread** *n* MECH ENG *trapezoidal thread* rosca Acme *f*, rosca de 29 grados *f*; **~ thread tap** *n* MECH ENG macho de rosca de 29 grados *m*

acmite *n* MINERAL acmita *f*

aconitase *n* CHEM aconitasa *f*
aconitate *n* CHEM aconitato *m*
aconitic[1] *adj* CHEM aconítico
aconitic[2]: ~ **acid** *n* CHEM ácido aconítico *m*
aconitine *n* FOOD aconitina *f*
acorn: ~ **nut** *n* AIR TRANSP tuerca ciega *f*; ~ **tube** *n* ELECTRON tubo de capuchón *m*
acouphene *n* ACOUST acuófeno *m*
acoustic: ~ **absorption coefficient** *n* PHYS coeficiente de absorción acústica *m*; ~ **admittance** *n* ACOUST, ELEC admitancia acústica *f*, ELEC ENG admitancia acústica *f*, entrada acústica *f*, PHYS admitancia acústica *f*; ~ **aerial** *n BrE* TELECOM antena acústica *f*; ~ **antenna** *n AmE* TELECOM antena acústica *f*; ~ **attenuation** *n* ELECTRON atenuación acústica *f*; ~ **attenuation constant** *n* ELECTRON constante de atenuación acústica *f*; ~ **barrier** *n* ACOUST barrera acústica *f*, pantalla acústica *f*; ~ **blanket** *n* SPACE cobertor acústico *m*, neutralizador acústico *m*; ~ **board** *n* SAFE tablero acústico *m*; ~ **branch** *n* PHYS *communications* rama acústica *f*; ~ **calibrator** *n* ACOUST calibrador acústico *m*; ~ **capacitance** *n* ACOUST capacitancia acústica *f*; ~ **carrier** *n* ELECTRON transportador acústico *m*; ~ **cell** *n* ACOUST célula ciliada *f*; ~ **channel** *n* OCEAN canal sonoro *m*, canal de transmisión acústica *m*; ~ **compliance** *n* ACOUST elasticidad acústica *f*; ~ **coupler** *n* ACOUST, COMP&DP, ELECTRON acoplador acústico *m*; ~ **coupling** *n* ACOUST, ELECTRON, TELECOM acoplamiento acústico *m*; ~ **current meter** *n* OCEAN correntómetro acústico *m*; ~ **delay line** *n* ACOUST, COMP&DP, ELECTRON línea de retardo acústico *m*; ~ **diffraction** *n* ACOUST difracción acústica *f*; ~ **dispersion** *n* ACOUST dispersión acústica *f*; ~ **elasticity** *n* ACOUST elasticidad acústica *f*; ~ **emission** *n* NUCL emisión acústica *f*; ~ **enclosure** *n* ACOUST recinto acústico *m*, encapsulado acústico *m*; ~ **energy** *n* ACOUST energía acústica *f*, ELEC ENG energía acústica *f*, potencia acústica *f*; ~ **engineering** *n* ACOUST, MECH ENG ingeniería acústica *f*; ~ **fencing** *n* ACOUST, CONST barrera de protección acústica *f*, protección acústica *f*; ~ **field** *n* ACOUST campo acústico *m*; ~ **filter** *n* ACOUST, ELECTRON, MECH ENG filtro acústico *m*; ~ **frequency** *n* (*VF*) ELECTRON frecuencia acústica *f*; ~ **generator** *n* MECH ENG generador acústico *m*, generador de ondas acústicas *m*; ~ **impedance** *n* ACOUST, ELEC ENG, PHYS impedancia acústica *f*; ~ **inertance** *n* PHYS inertancia acústica *f*; ~ **insulating material** *n* POLL material aislante acústico *m*; ~ **interferometer** *n* ACOUST interferómetro acústico *m*; ~ **isolation** *n* ACOUST acustiaislamiento *m*, aislamiento acústico *m*, WATER TRANSP aislamiento acústico *m*; ~ **log** *n* GEOPHYS registro acústico *m*, sondeo acústico *m*, PETR TECH diagrafía acústica *f*, perfil acústico *m*, registro acústico *m*; ~ **mass** *n* ACOUST masa acústica *f*; ~ **modem** *n* COMP&DP módem acústico *m*; ~ **noise** *n* TELECOM perturbaciones acústicas *f pl*, ruido acústico *m*; ~ **oscillation** *n* ACOUST oscilación acústica *f*; ~ **plaster** *n* COATINGS enlucido acústico *m*, enlucido antisonoro *m*, mortero antisonoro *m*; ~ **pressure** *n* SPACE *spacecraft* presión acústica *f* (*Esp*), presión sonora *f* (*AmL*); ~ **propagation constant** *n* ACOUST constante de propagación acústica *f*; ~ **pulse** *n* ACOUST, ELECTRON impulso acústico *m*; ~ **radiometer** *n* ACOUST radiómetro acústico *m*;

~ **reactance** *n* ACOUST, ELEC ENG, PHYS reactancia acústica *f*; ~ **resistance** *n* ACOUST resistencia acústica *f*; ~ **resonator** *n* ACOUST, ELECTRON resonador acústico *m*; ~ **screen** *n* ACOUST barrera acústica *f*, pantalla acústica *f*; ~ **sensor** *n* ELECTRON sensor acústico *m*; ~ **signal** *n* ELECTRON, MECH ENG señal acústica *f*; ~ **signal generator** *n* MECH ENG generador de señales acústicas *m*; ~ **stiffness** *n* ACOUST, PHYS rigidez acústica *f*; ~ **system** *n* ACOUST sistema acústico *m*; ~ **testing room** *n* MECH ENG sala de pruebas acústicas *f*; ~ **transmission line** *n* ELEC, ELEC ENG línea de transmisión acústica *f*; ~ **trauma** *n* ACOUST trauma acústico *m*; ~ **velocity level** *n* ACOUST nivel de velocidad acústica *m*; ~ **velocity log** *n* FUELLESS registro de la velocidad de sonido *m*; ~ **vibration** *n* ACOUST vibración acústica *f*; ~ **wave** *n* ELEC ENG onda superficial acústica *f*; ~ **wave filter** *n* ACOUST, ELECTRON filtro de onda acústica *m*; ~ **wave propagation** *n* ELEC ENG propagación de la onda acústica *f*; ~ **waveband** *n* ACOUST, OCEAN banda de frecuencias sonoras *f*, banda de ondas sonoras *f*, WAVE PHYS banda de ondas sonoras *f*; ~ **well logging** *n* PETR TECH diagrafiado acústico de pozos *m*, perfilaje acústico de pozos *m*, registro acústico de pozos *m*
acoustical: ~ **field** *n* ACOUST campo acústico *m*; ~ **spectrum** *n* ACOUST espectro acústico *m*
acoustically: ~-**coupled modem** *n* COMP&DP módem con acoplamiento acústico *m*
acoustics *n* ACOUST, PHYS, SAFE acústica *f*
acousto: ~-**electric effect** *n* TELECOM efecto electroacústico *m*; ~-**optic effect** *n* OPT efecto acustoóptico *m*; ~-**optic modulation** *n* ELECTRON modulación acústico-óptica *f*; ~-**optic modulator** *n* ELECTRON modulador acústico-óptico *m*, OPT modulador acustoóptico *m*; ~-**optic processor** *n* ELECTRON procesador acústico-óptico *m*; ~-**optical modulator** *n* ELECTRON modulador acústico-óptico *m*, OPT modulador acustoóptico *m*
acquisition *n* SPACE captación del objetivo *f*, localización del objetivo *f*; ~ **of attitude** *n* SPACE captación de posición de vuelo *f*, localización de posición de vuelo *f*; ~ **of normal mode** *n* SPACE captación de modo normal *f*, localización de modalidad normal *f*; ~ **of orbit** *n* SPACE captación de órbita *f*, localización de órbita *f*
acre *n* METR acre *m*
acridine: ~ **dye** *n* COLOUR colorante de acridina *m*
acrolein *n* AIR TRANSP acroleína *f*
acrometer *n* METR acrómetro *m*
across[1]: ~ **flats** *adj* MECH ENG a traves de las caras, entre caras
across[2]: ~ **the bow** *adv* WATER TRANSP a través de proa
across[3]: ~-**the-line motor** *n* ELEC motor en la línea *m*, motor entre los lados de la línea *m*; ~-**the-line starter** *n* ELEC arrancador en la línea *m*, arrancador entre los lados de la línea *m*; ~-**track error** *n* SPACE error de seguimiento oblicuo *m*, error de seguimiento transversal *m*
acrylate *n* CHEM, P&R acrilato *m*
acrylated: ~ **epoxy resin** *n* P&R resina epoxi acrílica *f*, resina epóxica acrílica *f*
acrylic[1] *adj* CHEM acrílico, CONST de material acrílico, acrílico, MECH *metal, cell*, TEXTIL acrílico
acrylic[2] *n* CONST, MECH, TEXTIL acrílico *m*; ~ **paint** *n* CONST pintura acrílica *f*; ~ **plastic** *n* PACK plástico

acrílico *m*; ~ **resin** *n* MECH *metal, cell,* P&R, PACK resina acrílica *f*; ~ **resin coating** *n* COATINGS revestimiento de resina acrílica *m*; ~ **rubber** *n* PACK caucho acrílico *m*, goma acrílica *f*; ~ **size** *n* TEXTIL apresto acrílico *m*
acrylonitrile *n* CHEM acrilonitrilo *m*, cianuro de vinilo *m*; ~-**butadiene-styrene** *n* (*ABS*) P&R acrilonitrilo-butadieno-estireno *m* (*ABS*); ~ **rubber** *n* MECH *spacecraft,* P&R caucho de acrilonitrilo *m*, goma de acrilonitrilo *f*
ACSE *abbr* (*association control service element*) TELECOM elemento para el control de asociación *m*
act[1] *n* BrE SAFE ley *f*
act[2] *vi* PHYS actuar
acted: ~ **upon by a force** *phr* PHYS sometido a una fuerza
actin *n* FOOD, PHOTO, PHYS actina *f*
acting: ~ **area** *n* CINEMAT área de actuación *f*
actinic[1] *adj* FOOD, PHOTO, PHYS actínico
actinic[2]: ~ **light** *n* CINEMAT, RAD PHYS luz actínica *f*; ~ **radiation** *n* RAD PHYS radiación actínica *f*
actinide *n* CHEM, NUCL, PHYS, RAD PHYS actínido *m*; ~ **element** *n* CHEM, NUCL, PHYS, RAD PHYS actínido *m*; ~ **series** *n* RAD PHYS serie de los actínidos *f*
actinism *n* PHOTO, PHYS, RAD PHYS actinismo *m*
actinium *n* (*Ac*) CHEM, METALL, RAD PHYS actinio *m* (*Ac*); ~ **series** *n* RAD PHYS serie del actinio *f*
actinolite *n* MINERAL actinolita *f*
actinometer *n* INSTR, METEO, PHYS, RAD PHYS actinómetro *m*
actinometry *n* METEO, PHYS, RAD PHYS actinometría *f*
actinon *n* (*An*) CHEM, RAD PHYS actinón *m* (*An*)
actinote *n* MINERAL actinota *f*
action[1]: **out of** ~ *adj* ELEC, MECH ENG inutilizado
action[2] *n* MECH *spacecraft* accionamiento *m*, acción *f*, funcionamiento *m*, marcha *f*, MECH ENG acción *f*, funcionamiento *m*, movimiento *m*, PHYS acción *f*; ~ **entry** *n* COMP&DP *decision table* entrada de acción *f*; ~ **outline** *n* CINEMAT descripción general de la acción *f*; ~ **still** *n* CINEMAT foto fija de acción *f*, fotografía de acción *f*; ~ **turbine** *n* HYDRAUL turbina de acción *f*; ~ **of viscosity between wall and fluid** *n* FLUID acción de la viscosidad entre la pared y el fluido *f*
activate *vt* COAL activar
activated: ~ **alumina** *n* CHEM, FOOD alúmina activada *f*; ~ **carbon** *n* CHEM carbón activado *m*, CHEM TECH carbón activado *m*, carbón activo *m*, GAS, HYDROL, P&R, WATER carbón activado *m*; ~ **carbon black** *n* P&R negro de humo activado *m*; ~ **carbon filter** *n* HYDROL, NUCL filtro de carbón activado *m*; ~ **charcoal** *n* CHEM, FOOD, P&R *filler* carbón activado *m*; ~ **charcoal bed** *n* NUCL lecho de carbón activado *m*; ~ **complex** *n* METALL compuesto activado *m*; ~ **molecule** *n* RAD PHYS molécula activada *f*; ~ **recycled sludge** *n* HYDROL *geophysics* cieno reciclado activado *m*, lodo reciclado activado *m*; ~ **return sludge** *n* HYDROL cieno de retorno activado *m*, fango de retorno activado *m*, lodo de retorno activado *m*; ~ **sludge** *n* HYDROL *orbitography* cieno activado *m*, cieno activo *m*, fango activado *m*, fango activo *m*, lodo activado *m*, lodo activo *m*, POLL lodo activado *m*, lodo activo *m*, cieno activo *m*, fango activo *m*, cieno activado *m*, fango activado *m*, RECYCL cieno activado *m*, cieno activo *m*, fango activado *m*, fango activo *m*, lodo activado *m*, lodo activo *m*, sedimento activado *m*; ~ **sludge process** *n*

WATER método de cienos activos *m*, método de fangos activados *m*; ~ **sludge tank** *n* HYDROL *diodes* tanque de fango activado *m*; ~ **sludge treatment plant** *n* HYDROL *spacecraft* planta de tratamiento de fangos activados *f*; ~ **state** *n* METALL estado activado *m*, marcha activada *f*; ~ **zinc oxide** *n* CHEM, P&R óxido de zinc activado *m*
activating: ~ **agent** *n* COAL agente activador *m*
activation *n* GEN activación *f*; ~ **analysis** *n* PHYS análisis de activación *m*; ~ **area** *n* METALL superficie de activación *f*, área de activación *f*; ~ **comprising three successive levels of decision** *n* RAD PHYS activación con tres niveles sucesivos de decisión *f*; ~ **energy** *n* CRYSTALL, METALL, NUCL, RAD PHYS energía de activación *f*; ~ **entropy** *n* METALL entropía de activación *f*; ~ **log** *n* PETR TECH perfil de activación *m*, perfilaje de activación *m*, registro de activación *m*; ~ **parameter** *n* METALL parámetro de activación *m*
activator *n* CHEM, COAL, ELEC ENG, P&R activador *m*
active[1] *adj* COMP&DP activo, ELEC ENG impulsor; **in** ~ **service** *adj* PROD en servicio
active[2]: ~ **aerial** *n* BrE TELECOM antena activa *f*; ~ **antenna** *n* AmE TELECOM antena activa *f*; ~ **band-pass filter** *n* ELECTRON filtro de paso de banda activo *m*; ~ **band-stop filter** *n* ELECTRON filtro eliminador de banda activo *m*; ~ **beacon collision avoidance system** *n* AIR TRANSP sistema de prevención de colisión de radiofaro activo *m*, sistema preventivo anticolisión de radiofaro activo *m*; ~ **carbon absorption** *n* POLL absorción por carbón activado *f*; ~ **chlorine** *n* DETERG cloro activo *m*; ~ **circuit** *n* PHYS circuito activo *m*; ~ **component** *n* ELEC *electronics* componente activo *m*, ELEC ENG componente activo *m*, *of a current* componente impulsor *m*, PHYS, TELECOM componente activo *m*; ~ **control** *n* SPACE control activo *m*; ~ **current** *n* ELEC, PHYS corriente activa *f*; ~ **development** *n* PROD desarrollo activo *m*; ~ **dipole** *n* ELEC ENG, PHYS, TELECOM dipolo activo *m*; ~ **earth pressure** *n* COAL presión terrestre activa *f*; ~ **effluent holdup tank** *n* NUCL depósito de retención de efluentes activos *m*; ~ **effluent system** *n* NUCL sistema de efluentes activos *m*; ~ **element** *n* ELEC ENG elemento activo *m*, generatriz activa *f*; ~ **emanation** *n* NUCL emanación activa *f*; ~ **energy** *n* ELEC *of system* energía activa *f*; ~ **energy meter** *n* ELEC contador de energía activa *m*; ~ **field period** *n* TV período de campo activo *m*; ~ **filler** *n* P&R carga activa *f*; ~ **filter** *n* ELECTRON, TELECOM filtro activo *m*; ~ **filtering** *n* ELECTRON filtrado activo *m*; ~ **guidance** *n* SPACE guiado *m*, guía activa *f*; ~ **impedor** *n* ELEC *component* impedancia activa *f*, impedor activo *m*; ~ **infrared detector** *n* ELECTRON, PHYS, TRANSP detector de infrarroja activo *m*, detector de infrarrojos activos *m*; ~ **integrator** *n* ELECTRON integrador activo *m*; ~ **laser medium** *n* OPT medio laser activo *m*, TELECOM medio activo de laser *m*; ~ **layer** *n* ELECTRON estratificador activo *m*; ~ **length** *n* NUCL zona activa *f*; ~ **line** *n* ELECTRON, TV línea activa *f*; ~ **load** *n* ELEC *ohmic, resistive* carga activa *f*, ELEC ENG carga activa *f*, carga impulsora *f*; ~ **margin** *n* GEOL margen activo *m*; ~ **material** *n* ELEC ENG material fisionable *m*; ~ **microwave integrated circuit** *n* ELECTRON circuito integrado de microondas activo *m*; ~ **mine** *n* MINE mina en actividad *f*, mina en explotación *f*; ~ **mixer** *n* MECH ENG mezclador activo *m*; ~ **motor vehicle**

safety n TRANSP seguridad activa de vehículos de motor f; ~ **network** n ELEC ENG red activa f, red impulsora f; ~ **notch filter** n ELECTRON filtro entallado activo m; ~ **plate margin** n GEOL margen convergente activo m; ~ **potential** n ELEC potencial activo m; ~ **power** n ELEC alternating current potencia activa f, ELEC ENG consumed by semiconductor memory fuerza activa f, fuerza impulsora f, energía activa f, PHYS potencia activa f; ~ **power meter** n ELEC instrument contador de potencia activa m, medidor de potencia activa m; ~ **power relay** n ELEC contactor-disyuntor de potencia activa m, relé de potencia activa m; ~ **pressure** n MECH, MECH ENG presión efectiva f; ~ **processor** n TELECOM procesador activo m; ~ **pullup device** n ELECTRON dispositivo de actuación activo m; ~ **quadripole** n ELEC ENG cuadrípolo activo m; ~ **region** n ELECTRON mass zona activa f; ~ **runway** n AmE (cf runway in use BrE) AIR TRANSP pista en activo f, pista en servicio f; ~ **satellite** n SPACE estación repetidora orbital f, satélite activo m, satélite transmisor de señales m; ~ **sensor** n SPACE captador activo m, detector activo m, sistema registrador activo m, sonda activa f; ~ **solar system** n FUELLESS sistema solar activo m; ~ **solvent** n PACK disolvente activo m; ~ **star** n COMP&DP network estrella activa f; ~ **supervisor** n TELECOM supervisor activo m; ~ **suspension** n TRANSP suspensión activa f; ~ **system** n ACOUST sistema activo m; ~ **test loop** n NUCL lazo de prueba activo m; ~ **threat** n TELECOM amenaza activa f; ~ **transducer** n ELEC, ELEC ENG transductor activo m; ~ **volcano** n GEOL volcán en actividad m; ~ **voltage** n ELEC alternating current tensión activa f, voltaje activo m, ELEC ENG voltaje activo m, voltaje en fase de corriente m, tensión activa f, PHYS voltaje activo m; ~ **water** n HYDROL, WATER agua activa f

activity n COMP&DP, PHYS actividad f; ~ **coefficient** n PHYS coeficiente de actividad m; ~ **factor** n SPACE communications factor de actividad m, factor de energía m; ~ **inventory** n NUCL inventario de actividad m; ~ **overvoltage** n SPACE sobretensión de energía f, sobrevoltaje de energía m

actomyosin n FOOD actomiosina f

actual: ~ **aperture** n CINEMAT, PHOTO, TV abertura real f; ~ **evapotranspiration** n HYDROL, WATER evapotranspiración real f; ~ **flight path** n AIR TRANSP trayectoria de vuelo actual f; ~ **horsepower** n MECH potencia al freno f, potencia efectiva f; ~ **horsepower hour** n MECH caballo-hora efectivo m; ~ **key** n COMP&DP COBOL clave actual f, clave real f; ~ **parameter** n COMP&DP parámetro real m; ~ **power** n MECH materials potencia efectiva f; ~ **pressure** n HYDRAUL presión efectiva f; ~ **running speed** n MECH velocidad de funcionamiento real f; ~ **size** n MECH ENG medida real f; ~ **state** n NUCL estado real m; ~ **value** n PRINT valor real m; ~ **weight** n PRINT gramaje real m

actuate vt ELEC, ELEC ENG actuar, MECH accionar, poner en acción, MECH ENG accionar, actuar, impulsar, PRINT machine activar

actuating: ~ **plate** n AIR TRANSP plato accionador m; ~ **rod** n AIR TRANSP barra accionadora f; ~ **signal** n NUCL señal de actuación f

actuation n AIR TRANSP accionamiento m, SPACE impulsión f, operación f

actuator n AIR TRANSP, COMP&DP accionador m, actuador m, ELEC transducer accionador m, actuador m, actuante m, ELEC ENG impulsor m, accionador m, MECH accionador m, servomotor m, actuador m, impulsor m, MECH ENG accionador m, PROD accionador m, actuador m, SPACE accionador m, actuador m; ~ **attachment** n MECH ENG accesorio de actuador m; ~-**control valve** n AIR TRANSP válvula de control del accionador f; ~ **disc** BrE, ~ **disk** n AmE AIR TRANSP disco accionador m

ACU abbr (automatic calling unit) COMP&DP ULA (unidad de llamada automática)

acuity: ~ **projector** n INSTR projector de acuidad m, proyector de agudeza m

acutance n PHOTO acutancia f

acute[1]: ~-**angular** adj GEOM acutangular

acute[2]: ~ **angle** n GEOM ángulo agudo m, acutángulo m; ~ **effect** n POLL efecto agudo m; ~ **triangle** n GEOM triángulo agudo m

acuteness n GEOM of screw agudeza f

ACV abbr (air cushion vehicle) TRANSP vehículo con amortiguación por aire m

acyclic[1] adj CHEM acíclico

acyclic[2]: ~ **dynamo** n ELEC, ELEC ENG dinamo acílica f; ~ **generator** n ELEC generador acíclico m

acyl n CHEM acilo m

acylate vt CHEM acilar

acylation n CHEM, CHEM TECH acilación f

ad: ~ **face** n PRINT tipo para publicidad m

adamantine: ~ **luster** AmE, ~ **lustre** BrE n MINERAL brillo adamantino m; ~ **spar** n MINERAL corindón m

adamine n MINERAL adamina f

adamite n MINERAL adamita f

adamsite n MINERAL adamsita f

adapt: ~ **to space conditions** vt SPACE adaptar a las condiciones del espacio

adaptation n PRINT jack plane and trying plane adaptación f

adaptive[1] adj COMP&DP adaptable, adaptativo, MECH machines, workers adaptable

adaptive[2]: ~ **aerial** n BrE TELECOM antena adaptativa f; ~ **antenna** n AmE TELECOM antena adaptativa f; ~-**channel allocation** n COMP&DP asignación de canal adaptivo f; ~ **coding** n TELECOM codificación adaptiva f; ~ **control** n ELEC ENG control por adaptación m; ~ **control system** n COMP&DP sistema de control autoadaptable m, ELEC ENG sistema de control adaptable m, MECH protection sistema de control autoadaptable m; ~ **differential pulse coded modulation** n (ADPCM) TELECOM modulación adaptable diferencial de impulsos en código f (ADCPM); ~ **equalization** n ELEC ENG ecualización de adaptamiento f; ~ **filter** n ELECTRON filtro adaptivo m; ~ **filtering** n COMP&DP filtrado adaptivo m, TELECOM filtración por adaptiva f; ~ **process** n COMP&DP proceso adaptivo m; ~ **routing** n COMP&DP asignación de ruta adaptable f, direccionamiento adaptable m, encaminamiento adaptable m; ~ **signal processing** n ELECTRON procesamiento de señales autoadaptivos m; ~ **system** n COMP&DP sistema adaptivo m; ~ **tuning** n ELECTRON sintonización adaptable f

adaptor n COMP&DP adaptador m, ELEC connector adaptador m, alargadera f, enchufe múltiple m, ladrón m, ELEC ENG reductor de voltaje m, ladrón m, reductor de tensión m, adaptador m, ELECTRON adaptador m, LAB safety-dog or backstay of mine-car,

MECH, MECH ENG, TELECOM, TEXTIL adaptador *m*; **~ plate** *n* MECH ENG *to fit a chuck* plato adaptador *m*; **~ ring** *n* CINEMAT anillo adaptador *m*, aro adaptador *m*, PHOTO anillo adaptador *m*

ADC *abbr* COMP&DP, ELEC, ELECTRON, PART PHYS, PHYS, TELECOM (*analog-to-digital conversion*) conversión analógico-digital *f*, (*analog-to-digital converter*) conversor analógico-digital *m*, convertidor A/D *m*, convertidor analógico-digital *m*

add *vt* COMP&DP sumar, añadir, MATH sumar; **~ and delete** *vt* PRINT agregar y eliminar; **~ thin space** *vt* PRINT *text justification* agregar espacio fino

ADD *abbr* (*address prompt*) TELECOM indicador visual de una dirección del ordenador *m*

add-and-divide: **~ principle** *n* ELECTRON principio de acumulación y distribución *m*

add-drop: **~ multiplexer** *n* TELECOM multiplexor sumar-restar *m*

added[1]: **~-on component** *n* SPACE *spacecraft* componente de tipo aditivo *m*, elemento de tipo aditivo *m*

added[2]: **no ~ sugar** *phr* FOOD sin azúcar

addend *n* COMP&DP sumando *m*

addendum *n* MECH altura *f*, MECH ENG *gear* cabeza *f*, *height of a gear tooth, above the pitch-line* altura *f*, PRINT adición *f*, apéndice *m*, suplemento *m*; **~ circle** *n* MECH ENG addendum *m*, circunferencia de cabeza *f*

adder *n* COMP&DP sumador *m*, TV circuito aditivo *m*

add-in: **~ board** *n* ELECTRON cuadro aditivo *m*

adding: **~ counter** *n* ELECTRON contador de acumulación *m*; **~ network** *n* ELEC *circuit* red de adición *f*, red sumadora *f*

addition *n* COMP&DP adición *f*, MATH, MECH ENG adición *f*, suma *f*; **~ polymer** *n* P&R polímero de adición *m*; **~ polymerization** *n* P&R polimerización de adición *f*

additional[1] *adj* MECH ENG suplementario

additional[2]: **~ keyboard** *n* PRINT teclado adicional *m*; **~ tank** *n* SPACE depósito adicional *m*, tanque adicional *m*

additive[1]: **~-free** *adj* FOOD sin aditivo

additive[2] *n* GEN aditivo *m*; **~ color** *AmE see additive colour BrE*; **~ color printer** *AmE see additive colour printer BrE*; **~ color process** *AmE see additive colour process BrE*; **~ color system** *AmE see additive colour system BrE*; **~ color theory** *AmE*, **~ colour** *BrE* COLOUR color aditivo *m*; **~ colour printer** *n BrE* CINEMAT positivadora aditiva de color *f*; **~ colour process** *n BrE* CINEMAT proceso aditivo de color *m*, PHOTO procedimiento aditivo de color *m*; **~ colour system** *n BrE* CINEMAT sistema aditivo de color *m*; **~ colour theory** *n BrE* PRINT teoría de adición de colores *f*; **~ lamphouse** *n* CINEMAT portalámparas aditivo *m*; **~ method** *n* CINEMAT, ELECTRON método aditivo *m*; **~ mixing** *n* ELECTRON mezcla aditiva *f*; **~ noise** *n* TELECOM ruido aditivo *m*; **~ primaries** *n pl* CINEMAT, COLOUR, PRINT colores primarios aditivos *m pl*; **~ primary colors** *AmE*, **~ primary colours** *BrE* *n pl* CINEMAT, COLOUR, PRINT colores primarios aditivos *m pl*; **~ printer** *n* CINEMAT positivadora aditiva *f*; **~ process** *n* ELECTRON proceso aditivo *m*; **~ synthesis** *n* PHOTO, PRINT síntesis aditiva *f*

add-on: **~ edit** *n* TV edición de tipo aditivo *f*; **~ memory** *n* COMP&DP memoria adicional *f*, memoria de añadidura; **~ to the packaging** *n* PACK acompaña al embalaje *f*

address[1] *n* COMP&DP dirección *f*; **~ bus** *n* COMP&DP bus de direcciones *m*; **~ code** *n* CINEMAT código de dirección *m*; **~ format** *n* COMP&DP formato de dirección *m*; **~ generation** *n* COMP&DP generación de dirección *f*; **~ label** *n* PACK etiqueta del destinatario *f*, identificación del destinatario *f*; **~ mapping** *n* COMP&DP mapa de direcciones *m*, mapeado de dirección *m*; **~ presentation restricted indicator** *n* TELECOM indicador restringido de presentación de dirección *m*; **~ prompt** *n* (*ADD*) TELECOM indicador visual de una dirección del ordenador *m*; **~ register** *n* COMP&DP registro de dirección *m*; **~ space** *n* COMP&DP espacio de direcciones *m*; **~ stencil** *n* PACK cliché de destinatario *m*, clisé de destinatario *m*

address[2] *vt* COMP&DP direccionar, especificar

addressable[1] *adj* COMP&DP direccionable

addressable[2]: **~ location** *n* COMP&DP ubicación direccionable *f*

addressee *n* COMP&DP destinatario *m*

addressing *n* COMP&DP, TELECOM direccionamiento *m*; **~ system** *n* COMP&DP sistema de direccionamiento *m*

add-subtract: **~ time** *n* COMP&DP tiempo de suma-resta *m*

adduct *n* CHEM aducto *m*, complejo de inclusión *m*, HYDROL aducto *m*

adduction *n* CHEM, HYDROL aducción *f*

adelpholite *n* MINERAL adelfolita *f*

adenine *n* CHEM, FOOD adenina *f*

adenosine *n* CHEM adenosina *f*; **~ triphosphate** *n* (*ATP*) CHEM, FOOD, PETROL trifosfato de adenosina *m*, adenosina trifosfato *f* (*ATP*)

ADF[1] *abbr* (*automatic direction finding*) AIR TRANSP, TELECOM ADF (*goniometría automática*)

ADF[2]: **~ letdown** *n* AIR TRANSP aterrizaje por radiogoniómetro automático *m*

adhere *vi* P&R adherirse, PACK adherirse, pegarse

adherence *n* PACK adherencia *f*

adherend *n* P&R superficie de adhesión *f*

adhering: **~ nappe** *n* HYDROL capa adherente *f*

adherometer *n* INSTR, P&R adherómetro *m*

adhesion *n* COAL, CONST adhesión *f*, P&R adherencia *f*, adhesión *f*, PACK adhesión *f*; **~ coefficient** *n* AUTO coeficiente de adhesión *m*; **~ promoter** *n* P&R promotor de adhesión *m*; **~ strength test** *n* MECH ENG prueba de resistencia de adhesión *f*; **~ system** *n* TRANSP sistema de adherencia *m*; **~ test** *n* P&R prueba de adherencia *f*, prueba de adhesión *f*

adhesive[1] *adj* P&R, PACK, PAPER, PROD adhesivo

adhesive[2] *n* MECH adhesivo *m*, P&R adhesivo *m*, pegamento *m*, PACK, PROD, SAFE adhesivo *m*; **~ applicator** *n* PACK aplicador de adhesivos *m*; **~ coat** *n* COATINGS capa adherente *f*, capa adhesiva *f*; **~ film** *n* COATINGS película adherente *f*, PACK película adhesiva *f*; **~ fumes** *n pl* SAFE humos adhesivos *m pl*; **~ glue** *n* PACK pegamento *m*; **~ insulating tape** *n* ELEC ENG cinta aisladora *f*, cinta aislante *f*, cinta aislante adhesiva *f*; **~ machine** *n* PACK máquina aplicadora de adhesivos *m*; **~ shear strength** *n* P&R resistencia del adhesivo al corte *f*; **~ side** *n* PACK lateral adhesivo *m*, lateral encolado *m*; **~ strength** *n* P&R fuerza adhesiva *f*; **~ tape** *n* CINEMAT, ELEC ENG cinta adhesiva *f*, MECH *safety* cinta adhesiva *f*, cinta aislante *f*, P&R *article* cinta adhesiva *f*, PACK cinta adhesiva *f*, precinto adhesivo *m*; **~ varnish** *n* COLOUR barniz adhesivo *m*

adiabatic[1] *adj* FLUID, MECH, PHYS, THERMO adiabático

adiabatic[2]: **~ calorimeter** *n* THERMO calorímetro

adiabático *m*; ~ **change** *n* THERMO cambio adiabático *m*, transformación adiabática *f*, variación adiabática *f*; ~ **coefficient** *n* THERMO coeficiente adiabático *m*; ~ **compression** *n* FLUID, THERMO compresión adiabática *f*; ~ **curve** *n* PHYS, THERMO curva adiabática *f*; ~ **demagnetization** *n* PHYS desmagnetización adiabática *f*; ~ **efficiency** *n* PHYS eficiencia adiabática *f*, THERMO eficiencia adiabática *f*, rendimiento adiabático *m*; ~ **expansion** *n* PHYS, THERMO expansión adiabática *f*; ~ **invariant** *n* PHYS invariante adiabática *f*; ~ **lapse rate** *n* AIR TRANSP ritmo del lapso adiabático *m*, THERMO decrecimiento adiabático *m*, gradiente adiabático *m*, velocidad de caída adiabática *f*; ~ **pressure drop** *n* AIR TRANSP bajada de presión adiabática *f*, FLUID caída adiabática de presión *f*; ~ **process** *n* THERMO proceso adiabático *m*; ~ **shock wave** *n* SPACE onda de choque adiabática *f*; ~ **sound wave** *n* WAVE PHYS onda de sonido adiabático *f*; ~ **system** *n* THERMO sistema adiabático *m*; ~ **temperature gradient** *n* FLUID gradiente adiabático de temperatura *m*; ~ **transformation** *n* METALL transformación adiabática *f*; ~ **wall** *n* PHYS pared adiabática *f*
adiabatically *adv* FLUID, MECH, PHYS, THERMO adiabáticamente
adiabatism *n* FLUID, MECH, PHYS, THERMO adiabatismo *m*
adinole *n* GEOL adinola *f*
adipic[1] *adj* CHEM adípico
adipic[2]: ~ **ester** *n* CHEM hexanoato de dialquilo *m*, P&R hexanoato de dialquilo *m*, éster adípico *m*
adipocerite *n* PHYS adipocerito *m*
adit *n* COAL *entry* acceso *m*, galería de acceso *f*, socavón *m*, MINE *sewage* galería de desagüe *f*
adjacence *n* GEOM adyacencia *f*
adjacency *n* GEOM adyacencia *f*
adjacent[1] *adj* GEOM adyacente
adjacent[2]: ~ **angle** *n* GEOM ángulo adyacente *m*; ~ **bed effect** *n* PETROL efecto de lecho adyacente *m*; ~ **channel** *n* TV canal adyacente *m*; ~ **channel rejection ratio** *n* TELECOM relación de rechazo de canal adyacente *f*; ~ **channel selectivity** *n* TELECOM selectividad contra canales adyacentes *f*; ~ **coil** *n* ELEC bobina adyacente *f*; ~ **sides** *n pl* GEOM lados adyacentes *m pl*; ~ **waters** *n pl* OCEAN aguas adyacentes *f pl* (*Esp*), aguas colindantes *f pl* (*AmL*)
adjust *vt* CONST *levelling instrument* ajustar, MECH regular, graduar, ajustar, METR *microscope* ajustar, PRINT graduar, PROD regular, rectificar, verificar, SAFE ajustar, WATER TRANSP *compass* compensar; ~ **focus** *vt* CINEMAT enfocar, hacer foco
adjustable[1] *adj* ELECTRON ajustable, MECH ajustable, regulable, MECH ENG ajustable, regulable, variable; ~ **at will** *adj* MECH ENG ajustable a voluntad
adjustable[2]: ~ **adaptor** *n* MECH ENG *for multispindle heads* adaptador ajustable *m*; ~ **aperture** *n* PHYS diafragma ajustable *m*; ~ **axle** *n* RAIL eje graduable *m*; ~ **bandwidth filter** *n* ACOUST filtro de ancho de banda ajustable *m*; ~ **blade reamer** *n* MECH ENG escariador de cuchillas ajustables *m*; ~ **capacitor** *n* ELEC capacitor ajustable *m*, condensador ajustable *m*, ELEC ENG condensador ajustable *m*, condensador graduable *m*, condensador regulable *m*; ~ **ceramic capacitor** *n* ELEC ENG condensador cerámico graduable *m*; ~ **core** *n* ELEC ENG núcleo compensable *m*; ~ **curtain wall** *n* C&G muro de cortina ajustable *m*;

~-**discharge pump** *n* MECH ENG bomba de agotamiento ajustable *f*, bomba de descarga variable *f*; ~-**edge doctor blade** *n* PRINT cuchilla tangente de borde regulable *f*; ~ **eyepiece** *n* CINEMAT ocular ajustable *m*, ocular regulable *m*, OPT ocular ajustable *m*, PHOTO ocular ajustable *m*, ocular regulable *m*; ~ **gib** *n* MECH ENG chaveta ajustable *f*; ~ **hacksaw frame** *n* MECH ENG portasierra de mano regulable *m*; ~ **inductance** *n* ELEC inductancia ajustable *f*; ~ **inductance coil** *n* ELEC bobina de inductancia ajustable *f*, inductor ajustable *m*, ELEC ENG bobina de inductancia ajustable *f*; ~ **lens holder** *n* CINEMAT portaobjetivo ajustable *m*; ~ **lens hood barrel** *n* CINEMAT tubo ajustable para montaje del parasol *m*; ~ **nozzle** *n* MECH ENG boquilla ajustable *f*, tobera ajustable *f*; ~-**pitch propeller** *n* AIR TRANSP, MAR POLL hélice de paso regulable *f*; ~ **reamer** *n* MECH ENG escariador ajustable *m*; ~ **rear-view mirror** *n* AUTO, TRANSP, VEH espejo retrovisor regulable *m*; ~ **resistor** *n* ELEC resistor ajustable *m*, resistor variable *m*, ELEC ENG resistor graduable *m*; ~ **short circuit** *n* ELEC ENG, PHYS cortocircuito ajustable *m*; ~ **shutter** *n* CINEMAT obturador ajustable *m*, obturador con ajuste B *m*, PHOTO obturador ajustable *m*; ~ **spanner** *n* (*cf adjustable wrench*) MECH llave ajustable *f*, llave de tuercas ajustable *f*, MECH ENG llave de gusano *f*, llave inglesa *f*, llave de moleta *f*, VEH llave de gancho ajustable *f*, llave inglesa *f*, llave regulable *f*; ~-**speed motor** *n* ELEC motor de velocidad ajustable *m*, motor de velocidad regulable *m*, MECH motor de velocidad regulable *m*; ~ **stilt** *n* MINE trípode ajustable *m*; ~ **stop** *n* CINEMAT diafragma ajustable *m*, MECH, MECH ENG tope graduable *m*; ~ **stroke shaper** *n* MECH ENG cepilladora de carrera ajustable *f*; ~ **submersion weir** *n* POLL aliviadero de inmersión regulable *m*, vertedor ajustable sumergible *m*; ~ **transformer** *n* ELEC transformador ajustable *m*; ~ **trip setting** *n* PROD límite de desconexión regulable *m*; ~ **tripod** *n* METR trípode ajustable *m*; ~ **varying speed motor** *n* ELEC motor de velocidad regulable *m*, motor de velocidad variable *m*; ~ **voltage divider** *n* ELEC divisor de tensión ajustable *m*, divisor de voltaje ajustable *m*; ~ **wrench** *n* (*cf adjustable spanner*) MECH llave ajustable *f*, llave de moleta *f*, llave de tuercas ajustable *f*, MECH ENG llave de gusano *f*, llave inglesa *f*, VEH llave de gancho ajustable *f*, llave inglesa *f*, llave regulable *f*
adjusting[1] *adj* ELECTRON, MECH ajustable, MECH ENG ajustable, graduable, regulable
adjusting[2]: ~ **arm** *n* MECH ENG brazo regulador *m*; ~ **circuit** *n* ELEC ENG circuito corrector *m*, circuito de ajuste *m*; ~ **gib** *n* MECH ENG chaveta de reglaje *f*; ~ **knob** *n* CINEMAT, GEOPHYS botón de ajuste *m*, MECH botón corrector *m*, botón de ajuste *m*, PHOTO botón de ajuste *m*; ~ **potentiometer** *n* AIR TRANSP potenciómetro de ajuste *m*; ~ **screw** *n* MECH tornillo de ajuste *m*, tornillo de regulación *m*, MECH ENG tornillo de ajuste *m*, tornillo de corrección *m*, PRINT tornillo de ajuste *m*; ~ **sleeve** *n* AUTO manguito de ajuste *m*; ~ **telescope** *n* INSTR telescopio de ajuste *m*; ~ **valve** *n* GAS válvula de ajuste *f*; ~ **voltage** *n* ELEC tensión de ajuste *f*, voltaje de ajuste *m*
adjustment *n* C&G, CRYSTALL, ELECTRON, MECH ajuste *m*, MECH ENG ajuste *m*, reglaje *m*, regulación *f*, METR ajuste *m*, *of a balance* equilibrado *m*, PRINT ajuste *m*; ~ **knob** *n* CINEMAT botón de ajuste *m*, botón de

reglaje *m*, GEOPHYS botón de ajuste *m*, botón de regulación *m*, INSTR botón de reglaje *m*, MECH botón de ajuste *m*, PHOTO botón de ajuste *m*, botón de reglaje *m*; ~ **of the stroke without stopping the machine** *n* MECH ENG ajuste de la carrera sin parar la máquina *m*

adjuvant *n* COAL adjuvante *m*

administration: ~ **building** *n* MINE edificio administrativo *m*

administrative: ~ **area** *n* CONST campo administrativo *m*, materia administrativa *f*, zona administrativa *f*; ~ **processor** *n* TELECOM procesador administrativo *m*; ~ **unit** *n* (*AU*) TELECOM unidad administrativa *f*; ~ **unit group** *n* TELECOM grupo de unidad administrativa *m*

admiral *n* WATER TRANSP *navy* almirante *m*

Admiralty: ~ **chart** *n* BrE WATER TRANSP carta del Almirantazgo *f*, carta náutica del Almirantazgo *f*

admissible: ~ **interrupting current** *n* ELEC *circuit breaker* corriente interruptora admisible *f*

admission: ~ **pipe** *n* HYDRAUL tubo de admisión *m*; ~ **port** *n* HYDRAUL lumbrera de admisión *f*, orificio de admisión *m*; ~ **valve** *n* HYDRAUL válvula de admisión *f*, MECH ENG válvula de admisión *f*, válvula de toma *f*

admittance[1] *n* ACOUST, ELEC, ELEC ENG, PHYS, TELECOM admitancia *f*

admittance[2]: **no** ~ *phr* SAFE prohibida la entrada, prohibido el paso, se prohíbe la entrada

admix *n* C&G mezcla *f*

admixture *n* CONST aditivo *m*, P&R aditivo *m*, agregado *m*, ingrediente *m*, TEXTIL mezcla *f*

adobe *n* C&G, CONST adobe *m*

adornment *n* PRINT adorno *m*

ADPCM[1] *abbr* (*adaptive differential pulse coded modulation*) TELECOM ADPCM (*modulación adaptable diferencial de impulsos en código*)

ADPCM[2]: ~ **decoder** *n* TELECOM decodificador ADPCM *m*; ~ **encoder** *n* TELECOM codificador de señales ADPCM *m*

adrift *adv* WATER TRANSP *navigation* a la deriva

adsorb *vt* CHEM, COAL, FOOD, GAS, P&R, WATER adsorber

adsorbable[1] *adj* CHEM, COAL, FOOD, GAS, P&R, WATER adsorbible

adsorbable[2]: ~ **organic halogens** *n pl* (*AOX*) PAPER compuestos organohalogenados adsorbibles *m pl*

adsorbent[1] *adj* CHEM, COAL, GAS, P&R, WATER adsorbente

adsorbent[2] *n* CHEM, COAL, FOOD, GAS, P&R, WATER adsorbente *m*; ~ **pads** *n pl* PAPER productos adsorbentes *m pl*

adsorber *n* CHEM, COAL, FOOD, GAS, P&R, WATER adsorbedor *m*

adsorption *n* CHEM, COAL, FOOD, GAS, P&R, WATER adsorción *f*; ~ **heat** *n* NUCL calor de adsorción *m*; ~ **isotherm** *n* NUCL isoterma de adsorción *f*; ~ **trap** *n* NUCL trampa de adsorción *f*

ADT *abbr* (*average daily traffic*) TRANSP promedio de tráfico diario *m*

adularia *n* MINERAL adularia *f*

adulterant *n* FOOD adulterante *m*

adulterate *vt* FOOD adulterar

adulterated *adj* FOOD adulterado

adulteration *n* FOOD adulteración *f*

advance[1] *n* CINEMAT adelanto *m*, COAL mejora *f*, progreso *m*, ELEC *phase* avance *m*, progresión *f*, MECH ENG avance *m*, PHYS *fixed equipment* adelanto *m*, VEH avance *m*; ~ **angle** *n* ELEC ángulo de adelanto *m*; ~ **ball** *n* ACOUST regulador de fuerza centrífuga *m*, regulador de velocidad *m*; ~ **booking charter** *n* AIR TRANSP chárter de reserva anticipada *m*, chárter de reserva por adelantado *m*; ~ **classification track** *n* RAIL vía de clasificación cubierta por una señal *f*; ~ **copy** *n* PRINT copia preliminar *f*; ~ **diameter ratio** *n* AIR TRANSP *propeller* proporción del diámetro de avance *f*; ~ **information** *n* TRANSP adelanto de información *m*, avance informativo *m*; ~ **mechanism** *n* VEH sistema de avance del encendido *m*; ~ **mining** *n* MINE minería de vanguardia *f*; ~ **purchase excursion fare** *n* (*APEX fare*) AIR TRANSP precio de la excursión de reserva por adelantado *m* (*precio APEX*); ~ **sheet** *n* PRINT capilla *f*, hoja de prueba *f*, primera prueba *f*, prueba de prensa *f*; ~ **termination** *n* PROD terminación avanzada *f*

advance[2]: ~ **the throttle** *vi* AIR TRANSP adelantar el regulador de gases, adelantar la palanca de gases

advanced: ~ **airborne fire support system** *n* AIR TRANSP sistema avanzado de apoyo de fuego aéreo *m*; ~ **communications function** *n* (*ACF*) COMP&DP función avanzada de comunicaciones *f* (*ACF*); ~ **fuel cycle** *n* NUCL ciclo de combustible avanzado *m*; ~ **ignition** *n* AUTO, VEH avance al encendido *m*, ignición de avance *f*; ~ **light source** *n* (*ALS*) PART PHYS *third generation synchrotron* fuente luminosa avanzada *f* (*ALS*); ~ **passenger train** *n* (*APT*) RAIL tren moderno de viajeros *m*; ~ **signal processing** *n* ELECTRON proceso de señal avanzada *m*; ~ **trainer** *n* AIR TRANSP entrenador avanzado *m*

advancing: ~ **blade** *n* AIR TRANSP pala en estado de avance *f*; ~ **blade concept** *n* AIR TRANSP *rotary winged aircraft* concepto de avance de la pala *m*; ~ **face** *n* COAL frente de ataque *m*

advantage: ~ **factor** *n* NUCL factor de irradiación óptima *m*, factor de ventaja *m*

advection *n* METEO, PHYS advección *f*

advertisement *n* PRINT anuncio *m*; ~ **layout** *n* PRINT boceto del anuncio *m*; ~ **page** *n* PRINT página de anuncios *f*

advertising *n* PRINT propaganda *f*, publicidad *f* (*Esp*); ~ **copy** *n* PRINT original de anuncio *m*, tiras *f pl*; ~ **department** *n* PRINT departamento de publicidad *m*; ~ **photography** *n* PHOTO fotografía publicitaria *f*; ~ **slot** *n* TV espacio publicitario *m*, hueco publicitario *m*, tanda publicitaria *f*

advise: ~ **duration and charge** *vi* TELECOM consultar duración e importe, notificar duración e importe

advisory: ~ **diversion** *n* TRANSP desviación señalizada *f*; ~ **message** *n* TRANSP mensaje de recomendación *m*, recomendación *f*

adze *n* CONST azuela *f*

AE *abbr* (*application entry*) TELECOM entrada de aplicaciones *f*

aegirine *n* MINERAL egirina *f*

aegirite *n* MINERAL egirita *f*

aegyrite *n* MINERAL egirita *f*

aenigmatite *n* MINERAL animagtita *f*

aeolian *adj* GEOL, PETROL eólico

aerate *vt* COAL, CONST airear, FOOD gasificar, PRINT airear, RECYCL airear, ventilar, SAFE, THERMO, WATER TRANSP airear

aerated: ~ **mud** n PETR TECH lodo aireado m, lodo con aire m; ~ **sludge** n PETR TECH lodo aireado m, lodo con aire m

aeration n COAL, CONST aireación f, HYDROL steam engine aireación f, ventilación f, MECH ENG, PACK aireación f, RECYCL aireación f, ventilación f; ~ **basin** n WATER depósito de aireación m; ~ **tank** n RECYCL cisterna de aireación f, cisterna de ventilación f, tanque de aireación m; ~ **time** n HYDROL T T tiempo de aireación m

aerator n AIR TRANSP, AUTO, HYDROL aireador m, RECYCL aparato de aireación m, VEH aireador m; ~ **silencer** n AIR TRANSP silenciador del aireador m

aeraulics n GAS aeráulica f

aerial n BrE (cf antenna AmE) AIR TRANSP antena f, PHYS antena aérea f, spacecraft antena f, SPACE, TELECOM, TV, VEH, WATER TRANSP radio, radar antena f; ~ **array** n BrE SPACE red de antenas f; ~ **cable** n ELEC ENG, TELECOM cable aéreo m; ~ **camera** n CINEMAT cámara para aerofotografía f; ~ **collision** n AIR TRANSP colisión aérea f; ~ **conveyor** n PACK transportador aéreo m, transportador elevado m; ~ **directivity** n BrE TELECOM, TV directividad de la antena f; ~ **efficiency** n BrE TV eficacia de la antena f; ~ **fog** n CINEMAT neblina f, niebla f; ~ **gain** n BrE PHYS, SPACE, TV ganancia de antena f; ~ **image** n CINEMAT, PHOTO, TV imagen aérea f; ~ **image animation** n CINEMAT animación de imagen aérea f; ~ **insulated cable** n ELEC cable aéreo aislado m; ~ **lead** n BrE TV bajada de antena f; ~ **mapping camera** n PHOTO cámara de aerofotogrametría f; ~ **mast** n BrE TV, WATER TRANSP mástil de antena m; ~ **matching** n TELECOM adaptación de antenas f; ~ **photographic survey** n GEOL prospección fotográfica aérea f, reconocimiento topográfico por fotografía aérea m; ~ **photography** n PHOTO aerofotografía f (AmL), fotografía aérea f (Esp); ~-**pointing loss** n BrE TELECOM pérdida por apuntamiento de la antena f; ~ **reconnaissance** n MAR POLL reconocimiento aéreo m; ~ **resistance** n PHYS resistencia de la antena f; ~ **shot** n CINEMAT toma aérea f; ~ **surveillance** n MAR POLL vigilancia aérea f; ~ **survey** n AIR TRANSP reconocimiento aéreo m; ~ **system** n BrE SPACE sistema de antenas m; ~ **terminal** n BrE TV borne de antena m

aerification n CHEM aerificación f

aeroacustics n ACOUST aeroacústica f

aerobic[1] adj FOOD, HYDROL, RECYCL aeróbico

aerobic[2]: ~ **digester** n RECYCL digestor aeróbico m; ~ **digestion** n RECYCL digestión aeróbica f, putrefacción aeróbica f; ~ **fermentation** n FOOD fermentación aeróbica f; ~ **sludge digestion** n WATER digestión aeróbica de fangos f

aerobiology n METEO aerobiología f

aerobiosis n RECYCL aerobiosis f

aerobrake[1] n BrE (cf air brake AmE) AIR TRANSP, MECH ENG, SPACE craft aerofreno m

aerobrake[2] vi BrE (cf air brake AmE) AIR TRANSP, MECH ENG, SPACE craft aerofrenar

aerodrome n BrE AIR TRANSP aeródromo m

aerodynamic[1] adj GEN aerodinámico

aerodynamic[2]: ~ **axis** n WATER TRANSP ship design eje aerodinámico m; ~ **balance** n AIR TRANSP equilibrio aerodinámico m; ~ **braking** n SPACE spacecraft frenado aerodinámico m; ~ **center** AmE, ~ **centre** BrE n AIR TRANSP, WATER TRANSP centro aerodiná-

mico m; ~ **coefficient** n SPACE coeficiente aerodinámico m; ~ **control surface** n SPACE superficie aerodinámica de control f; ~ **drag** n AIR TRANSP, PHYS, SPACE resistencia aerodinámica f, TRANSP arrastre aerodinámico m; ~ **efficiency** n AIR TRANSP eficiencia aerodinámica f; ~ **factor** n AIR TRANSP factor aerodinámico m; ~ **form** n VEH forma aerodinámica f, perfil aerodinámico m; ~ **heating** n SPACE craft calentamiento aerodinámico m, calentamiento por aerodinámica m; ~ **lift** n TRANSP elevador aerodinámico m; ~ **load** n AIR TRANSP carga aerodinámica f; ~ **mast** n WATER TRANSP palo aerodinámico m; ~ **missile** n MILIT misil aerodinámico m, proyectil aerodinámico m; ~ **noise** n ACOUST, AIR TRANSP ruido aerodinámico m; ~ **power** n FUELLESS energía aerodinámica f; ~ **pressure** n AIR TRANSP presión aerodinámica f; ~ **shape** n VEH estructura aerodinámica f; ~ **sound** n ACOUST sonido aerodinámico m; ~ **twist** n AIR TRANSP torsión aerodinámica f; ~-**type air-cushion vehicle** n AIR TRANSP, TRANSP aerodeslizador de tipo aerodinámico m

aerodynamical: ~ **levitation** n TRANSP elevación aerodinámica f, levitación aerodinámica f

aerodynamics n GEN ship, boat design aerodinámica f

aeroelasticity n FUELLESS wind power, NUCL aeroelasticidad f

aeroembolism n OCEAN embolia gaseosa f

aerofoil n BrE AIR TRANSP plano aerodinámico m, superficie aerodinámica f, superficie sustentadora f, FUELLESS perfil de ala m, superficie sustentadora f, WATER TRANSP ship, boat design superficie sustentadora f, superficie sustentadora aerodinámica f; ~ **chord** n BrE AIR TRANSP cuerda alar f, cuerda de la superficie aerodinámica f; ~ **de-icing** n BrE AIR TRANSP deshielo de la superficie aerodinámica f; ~ **de-icing valve** n BrE AIR TRANSP válvula de deshielo de la superficie aerodinámica f; ~ **fan** n BrE REFRIG ventilador de paletas aerodinámicas m; ~ **hull** n BrE WATER TRANSP casco aerodinámico m

aeroglide n TRANSP aerodeslizamiento m

aerograph n C&G, PACK, PHOTO, PRINT aerógrafo m

aerography n C&G, PACK, PHOTO, PRINT aerografía f

aerogyro n AIR TRANSP aerogiroscopio m

aerolite n SPACE aerolito m

aerology n METEO aerología f

aeromagnetic[1] adj GEOL, PETROL aeromagnético

aeromagnetic[2]: ~ **survey** n GEOL, PETROL estudio aeromagnético m, prospección aeromagnética f; ~ **train** n TRANSP tren aeromagnético m

aerometer n ELEC accumulator aerómetro m, densímetro m (AmL), densímetro de flotación m, hidrómetro m, HYDROL, INSTR, PETR TECH, PHYS aerómetro m

aerometry n ELEC, HYDROL, PETR TECH, PHYS aerometría f

aeronautical: ~ **chart** n AIR TRANSP carta de navegación aeronáutica f; ~ **fixed circuit** n AIR TRANSP circuito fijo aeronáutico m; ~ **fixed service** n BrE (cf aeronautical fixed system AmE) AIR TRANSP red fija aeronáutica f, servicio fijo aeronáutico m, sistema fijo aeronáutico m; ~ **fixed station** n AIR TRANSP estación fija aeronáutica f; ~ **fixed system** n AmE (cf aeronautical fixed service BrE) AIR TRANSP sistema fijo aeronáutico m, network of ground radio stations red fija aeronáutica f, servicio fijo aeronáutico m; ~ **fixed telecommunication network** n AIR TRANSP red fija de telecomunicaciones aeronáuticas *f*; ~ **information circular** *n* AIR TRANSP circular de información aeronáutica *f*; ~ **information service** *n* AIR TRANSP servicio de información aeronáutico *m*; ~ **meteorological station** *n* AIR TRANSP estación meteorológica aeronáutica *f*; ~ **mobile satellite service** *n* SPACE *communications* servicio aeronáutico móvil por satélite *m*, servicio aeronáutico satelital móvil *m*; ~ **radio navigation service** *n* AIR TRANSP servicio de radionavegación aeronáutica *m*; ~ **register** *n* AIR TRANSP registro aeronáutico *m*; ~ **route chart** *n* AIR TRANSP carta de ruta aeronáutica *f*

aeronautics *n* AIR TRANSP aeronáutica *f*

aeronomy *n* AIR TRANSP, METEO, SPACE aeronomía *f*

aeroplane *n BrE* AIR TRANSP avión *m*; ~ **mass ratio** *n BrE* AIR TRANSP proporción de la masa del aeroplano *f*; ~ **tow launch** *n BrE* AIR TRANSP despegue de avión remolcado *m*

aeropulse *n* TRANSP pulsorreactor *m*

aerosite *n* MINERAL aerosita *f*

aeroslides *n pl* MECH ENG *handling equipment* guías aéreas *f pl*

aerosol *n* FLUID, METEO aerosol *m*, PACK aerosol *m*, pulverizador *m*, PHYS, POLL, PROD aerosol *m*; ~ **can** *n* PACK bote aerosol *m*; ~ **cap** *n* PACK cápsula aerosol *f*, tapón aerosol *m*; ~ **container** *n* MECH ENG recipiente aerosol *m*, envase de aerosol *m*, PACK recipiente aerosol *m*; ~ **and dust measuring and analysis apparatus** *n* INSTR, SAFE aparato para medir y analizar aerosoles y polvos *m*; ~ **packing** *n* PACK embalaje del aerosol *m*; ~ **propellant** *n* PETR TECH propulsor por aerosol *m*; ~ **spray container** *n* MECH ENG atomizador de aerosoles *m*; ~ **valve** *n* PACK válvula aerosol *f*

aerospace *n* SPACE aeroespacio *m*, espacio aéreo *m*; ~ **medicine** *n* SPACE medicina aeroespacial *f*

aerospatial *adj* SPACE aeroespacial

aerostatic: ~-**type air cushion vehicle** *n* TRANSP vehículo con colchón de aire tipo aerostático *m*

aerostatics *n* METEO aerostática *f*

aerothermodynamic: ~ **duct** *n* TRANSP conducto aerotermodinámico *m*

aerotow: ~ **flight** *n BrE* AIR TRANSP vuelo de aeroremolque *m*

aerotrain *n* RAIL aerotren *m*, TRANSP aerotren *m*, tren aéreo *m*

AES *abbr* (*Auger electron spectroscopy*) CHEM, PHYS EEA (*espectroscopía de electrones Auger*)

aeschynite *n* MINERAL aschynita *f*

AF *abbr* (*audio frequency*) ACOUST, ELECTRON, TELECOM frecuencia acústica *f*, frecuencia audible *f*

AFC *abbr* (*automatic frequency control*) ELEC, ELECTRON, PROD, TELECOM, TV CAF (*control automático de frecuencia*)

AFD *abbr* (*accelerated freeze drying*) AGRIC, FOOD, PACK, REFRIG, THERMO liofilización acelerada *f*

affiliate *n* COMP&DP, ELEC, TELECOM, TV abonado *m* (*Esp*), afiliado *m* (*AmL*)

affine: ~ **geometry** *n* GEOM geometría afín *f*; ~ **transformation** *n* METALL transformación afín *f*

affinity *n* CHEM, ELECTRON, NUCL, PART PHYS, TEXTIL afinidad *f*

affusion *n* CHEM afusión *f*

AFI *abbr* (*authority and format identifier*) TELECOM identificador de autorización y formato *m*

aflatoxin *n* FOOD aflatoxina *f*

AFNOR *abbr* (*Association Française de Normalisation*) PROD AFNOR (*Asociación Francesa para la Normalización*)

A4: ~ **size** *n* PAPER, PRINT tamaño A4 *m*

A-frame *n* MECH *equipment* cercha *f*

aft[1] *adv* SPACE a popa, atrás, WATER TRANSP *of ship* hacia popa

aft[2]: ~ **gate** *n* WATER *of canal-lock* compuerta de aguas abajo *f*; ~ **perpendicular** *n* WATER TRANSP *ship design* perpendicular de popa *f*; ~ **rake** *n* WATER TRANSP lanzamiento del codaste *m*; ~ **section** *n* WATER TRANSP *of ship* sección de popa *f*; ~ **stay** *n* WATER TRANSP *standing rigging* estay de mesana *m*

after[1]: ~-**shrinkage** *adj* PACK tras la contracción, tras la retractilación

after[2] *adv* WATER TRANSP hacia popa

after[3]: ~-**effect** *n* RAD PHYS efecto posterior *m*, efecto secundario *m*; ~ **sales service** *n* CONST, QUALITY servicio postventa *m*; ~ **sales servicing** *n* QUALITY apoyo postventa *m*

afterbay *n* WATER cámara de salida *f*

afterblow *n* PROD *steel manufacture* sobresoplado *m*

afterbody *n* SPACE cola *f*, cuerpo de popa *m*

afterburner *n* AIR TRANSP postquemador *m*, MECH ENG inyector de combustible en los gases calientes de exhaustación *m*, postquemador *m*, quemador trasero *m*, NUCL *blast furnace* posquemador *m*, THERMO postquemador *m*, VEH quemador auxiliar *m*

afterburning *n* THERMO combustión retardada *f*, persistencia de la combustión durante el periodo de expansión *f*

aftercooler *n* HEAT ENG posenfriador *m*, radiador de salida *m*

afterdamp *n* GAS, MINE *blasting tunnel* gases tóxicos *m pl*

afterdeck *n* WATER TRANSP cubierta de popa *f*

afterdryer *n* PAPER postsecador *m*

afterglow *n* ELECTRON incandescencia residual *f*, PAPER persistencia lumínica *f*, RAD PHYS luminiscencia residual *f*, posluminiscencia *f*, SPACE incandescencia residual *f*, posluminiscencia *f*, THERMO fosforescencia *f*, luminiscencia remanente *f*, luminiscencia residual *f*, persistencia luminosa *f*, persistencia lumínica *f*, TV luminiscencia residual *f*, WATER TRANSP *radar* persistencia lumínica *f*

afterimage *n* CINEMAT imagen secundaria *f*, TV imagen posterior *f*

AFV *abbr* (*tracked armoured fighting vehicle BrE*) MILIT vehículo blindado de combate sobre orugas *m*

afwillite *n* MINERAL afwilita *f*

AFWS *abbr* (*auxiliary feedwater system*) NUCL AFWS (*sistema de agua de alimentación auxiliar*)

Ag *abbr* (*silver*) C&G, CHEM, ELEC ENG, METALL, PHOTO Ag (*plata*)

against[1]: ~ **the grain** *adv* PRINT *under a load* en sentido transversal; ~ **the light** *adv* CINEMAT a contraluz

against[2]: ~ **text** *n* PRINT texto superpuesto *m*

agalite *n* MINERAL agalita *f*

agalmatolite *n* MINERAL agalmatolita *f*

agaphite *n* MINERAL agafita *f*

agar: ~-**agar** *n* FOOD agar-agar *m*; ~ **slant** *n* FOOD agar inclinado *m*, tubo inclinado de agar *m*

agaric: ~ **mineral** *n* MINERAL mineral agárico *m*

agate *n* C&G, MINERAL ágata *f*; ~ **line** *n* PRINT línea

ágata *f*; ~ **mortar** *n* CHEM mortero de ágata *m*;
~ **ware** *n* C&G productos de ágata *m pl*
agaty *n* MINERAL agatino *m*
AGC *abbr* (*automatic gain control*) ELECTRON, TELECOM
CGA (*control automático de ganancia*)
age[1] *n* AGRIC, GEOL época *f*, PETROL era *f*, época *f*;
~ **dating** *n* GEOL antigüedad *f*, datación de la época *f*;
~ **of groundwater** *n* GEOL antigüedad del agua
freática *f*, HYDROL, WATER antigüedad del agua
freática *f*, edad del agua freática *f*; ~ **hardening** *n*
CRYSTALL endurecimiento estructural *m*, envejecimiento *m*, METALL, P&R endurecimiento por
envejecimiento *m*
age[2] *vt* METALL endurecerse por envejecimiento,
THERMO estabilizar por reposo
AGE *abbr* (*allyl glycidyl ether*) CHEM, P&R alilglicidiléter *m*
aged *adj* THERMO endurecido por envejecimiento,
estabilizado
ageing[1]: ~**-resistant** *adj* PACK resistente al envejecimiento
ageing[2] *n* C&G *of glass, thermometer* relajación térmica
f, cura por reposo *f*, CHEM TECH vaporizado húmedo
m, CINEMAT *of film stock*, CONST, CRYSTALL, ELEC
envejecimiento *m*, FOOD *bakery, milling* añejamiento
m, curado *m*, envejecimiento *m*, P&R *of coatings*,
PACK, PAPER, PRINT envejecimiento *m*, REFRIG *of meat*
maduración *f*, curado *m*, TELECOM envejecimiento *m*;
~ **room** *n* REFRIG cámara de maduración de carnes *f*,
sala de curado *f*; ~ **study** *n* SPACE estudio del
envejecimiento *m*; ~ **test** *n* PACK ensayo de envejecimiento *m*
agency *n* AIR TRANSP, SPACE, TELECOM, TEXTIL agencia
f
agent *n* GEN agente *m*
agglomerate[1] *n* CHEM TECH aglomerado *m*, GEOL
aglomeración *f*, aglomerado *m*, PETROL aglomerado
m
agglomerate[2] *vt* CHEM TECH aglomerar
agglomerate[3] *vi* COAL aglomerarse
agglomeration *n* CHEM TECH, P&R aglomeración *f*
agglutinant *adj* GEN aglutinante
agglutinate *vti* CHEM, CHEM TECH, FOOD aglutinar
agglutination *n* CHEM, CHEM TECH, FOOD, P&R aglutinación *f*
agglutinin *n* CHEM, CHEM TECH, FOOD aglutinina *f*
aggradation *n* WATER acreación *f*, agradación *f*
aggradational: ~ **deposit** *n* WATER depósito aluvial *m*
aggrade *vt* GEOL depositar sedimentos en (*AmL*),
rellenar (*Esp*)
aggregate[1] *n* C&G aglomerado *m*, COAL aglomerado *m*,
agregado *m*, CONST árido *m*, METALL aglomerado *m*,
conjunto *m*, PETROL árido *m*; ~ **abrasion value** *n*
(*AA*) CONST nivel de abrasión agregado *m*, valor de
abrasión de los áridos *m*; ~ **cooling** *n* REFRIG
enfriamiento de agregados *m*, refrigeración centralizada *f*; ~ **crushing value** *n* CONST tensión de rotura
del árido *f*; ~ **output** *n* PROD producción global *f*,
rendimiento global *m*, rendimiento total *m*;
~ **scraper** *n* TRANSP escariadora de áridos *f*, rascadora de áridos *f*; ~ **signal** *n* TELECOM señal total *f*;
~ **stripping** *n* CONST arranque de los áridos *m*;
~ **stripping test** *n* CONST prueba de separación del
árido *f*
aggregate[2] *vi* GEOL agregar

aggressive: ~ **water** *n* HYDROL, WATER agua agresiva *f*,
agua con materia corrosiva *f*
agitate *vt* CHEM TECH agitar, PHOTO agitar, mover,
revolver, PRINT batir
agitator *n* AGRIC, COAL, FOOD agitador *m*, MECH ENG
agitador *m*, mezclador *m*, PETR TECH agitador *m*
agonic: ~ **line** *n* GEOPHYS línea ágona *f*
agreed: ~ **spillover** *n* TV *networks* desbordamiento
acordado *m*
agribusiness *n* AGRIC, FOOD agroindustria *f*
agricolite *n* MINERAL agricolita *f*
agricultural: ~ **machine** *n* AGRIC, MECH maquinaria
agrícola *f*
agropiron: ~ **repens** *n* AGRIC grama *f*
aground[1] *adj* OCEAN *of ship* embarrancado, encallado,
WATER TRANSP *of ship* embarrancado, encallado,
varado
aground[2] *adv* WATER TRANSP en seco
ahead[1] *adj* SPACE anterior, delantero
ahead[2] *adv* SPACE a la cabeza, adelante, avante, con
anticipación, más allá, por la proa, WATER TRANSP
por la proa, avante
ahull *adv* WATER TRANSP *sailing* a palo seco, con las
velas cargadas
AI *abbr* ACOUST (*articulation index*) AI (*índice de
articulación*), AGRIC (*artificial insemination*) IA (*inseminación artificial*), COMP&DP, TELECOM (*artificial
intelligence*) IA (*inteligencia artificial*)
AIA *abbr* (*audio indicator active*) TELECOM indicador de
audio activo *m*
aigrette *n* GEOPHYS corona *f*
aiguille *n* MINE espigueta *f*
aikinite *n* MINERAL aikinita *f*
aileron *n* AIR TRANSP alerón *m*; ~ **control** *n* AIR TRANSP
control del alerón *m*; ~ **control wheel** *n* AIR TRANSP
volante de control del alerón *m*; ~ **deflection** *n* AIR
TRANSP deflexión del alerón *f*; ~ **follow-up** *n* AIR
TRANSP timón de cola *m*; ~**-position indicator** *n* AIR
TRANSP indicador de posición del alerón *m*
AIM *abbr* (*audio indicator muted*) TELECOM indicador
de audio silencioso *m*
ainalite *n* MINERAL ainalita *f*
air[1]: ~**-and-sea** *adj* WATER TRANSP *forces* aeronaval;
~**-conditioned** *adj* AUTO, CONST con aire acondicionado, HEAT, REFRIG, THERMO acondicionado, con
aire acondicionado, VEH con aire acondicionado;
~**-cooled** *adj* ELEC *equipment* de enfriamiento por
aire, enfriado por aire, refrigerado por aire, MECH
ENG refrigerado por aire, con enfriamiento por aire,
enfriado por chorro de aire, enfriado por aire, PAPER
enfriado por aire, REFRIG aerorrefrigerado, THERMO
aerorrefrigerado, enfriado al aire, refrigerado por
aire; ~**-dried** *adj* FOOD, PACK secado al aire, PAPER
seco al aire
air[2] *n* GAS gas de aire *m*, TV aire *m*;
▬ **b** ~ **bag** *n* AUTO bolsa de aire *f*; ~ **bag restraint
system** *n* TRANSP sistema de contención por bolsa de
aire *m*; ~ **base** *n* AIR TRANSP base aérea *f*; ~ **bearing** *n*
CINEMAT cojinete neumático *m*; ~ **bell** *n* C&G, CINE-
MAT burbuja *f*; ~ **blade** *n* PAPER cuchilla de aire *f*;
~ **blast** *n* COAL chorro de aire *m*, inyección de aire *f*,
MINE caja de aire *f*, caja de viento *f*, corriente de aire
f; ~ **blast breaker** *n* ELEC *circuit breaker* disyuntor a
chorro de aire *m*, interruptor a chorro de aire *m*,
ruptor a chorro de aire *m*; ~**-blast burner** *n* MECH
ENG quemador de chorro de aire *m*; ~ **blast circuit**

breaker *n* ELEC ENG disyuntor de chorro de aire *m*; **~-blast cooling** *n* REFRIG enfriamiento por corriente de aire *m*; **~-blast freezer** *n* REFRIG congelador por aire forzado *m*; **~ blast freezing** *n* REFRIG congelación por corriente de aire *f*; **~ blast labeling** *AmE*, **~ blast labelling** *BrE n* PACK etiquetado por aire a presión *m*; **~-blast refining** *n* METALL afino por chorro de aire *m*, afino por corriente de aire *m*; **~ blast switch** *n* ELEC *circuit breaker* conmutador a chorro de aire *m*; **~ blast transformer** *n* ELEC transformador a chorro de aire *m*; **~-bleed valve** *n* AIR TRANSP válvula de purga de aire *f*, FOOD válvula de extracción de aire *f*, válvula de sangrado de aire *f*; **~ blowing** *n* MECH ENG soplado de aire *m*; **~ box** *n* MECH ENG arca de viento *f*, caja de viento *f*, cajón de ventilación *m*, colector de barrido *m*, MINE caja de aire *f*, caja de viento *f*, PETR TECH cámara de aire *f*, cámara de ventilación *f*; **~ brake** *n* (*cf aerobrake BrE*) AIR TRANSP freno aerodinámico *m*, aerofreno *m*, MECH *engine* freno aerodinámico *m*, freno de aire comprimido *m*, MECH ENG aerofreno *m*, freno de aire *m*, freno neumático *m*, servofreno *m*, freno de aire comprimido *m*, freno aerodinámico *m*, SPACE aerofreno *m*, TRANSP freno aerodinámico *m*, VEH freno de aire *m*; **~-brake hose** *n* MECH ENG manga flexible de freno de aire comprimido *f* (*AmL*), tubo flexible de freno de aire comprimido *m* (*Esp*), P&R manga para freno neumático *f* (*AmL*), tubo para freno neumático *m* (*Esp*); **~ brattice** *n* MINE compartimiento de ventilación *m* (*Esp*), tabique de ventilación *m* (*AmL*); **~-break switch** *n* ELEC, ELEC ENG interruptor de aire *m*; **~ breaker** *n* ELEC *switch* disyuntor al aire *m*; **~ breather** *n* PROD consumidor de aire *m*; **~-breathing engine** *n* AIR TRANSP motor aerobio *m*; **~ brick** *n* CONST ladrillo ventilador *m*; **~ bridge** *n* MINE cruzamiento de vías de ventilación *m*; **~ brush** *n* P&R pistola de pintar *f*; **~ bubble** *n* PHYS burbuja de aire *f*; **~-bubble bag** *n* PACK bolsa con acolchado burbujas de aire *f*; **~-bubble cushioning** *n* PACK material de acolchado de burbujas de aire *m*; **~ bubble wrap** *n* PACK embalado con un material con acolchamiento de burbujas;

~ c **~ capacitor** *n* ELEC capacitor de aire *m*, condensador con dieléctrico de aire *m*, PHYS capacitor de aire *m*; **~ cargo** *n* PACK carga aérea *f*; **~ cell** *n* ELEC ENG pila de aire *f*, pila de despolarización por aire *f*; **~-cell diesel engine** *n* AUTO motor diesel con cámara de precombustión *m*; **~-charging valve** *n* AIR TRANSP válvula de carga de aire *f*; **~ chuck** *n* MECH ENG, PRINT plato neumático *m*; **~ circuit breaker** *n* ELEC *switch* disyuntor al aire *m*; **~ classification** *n* FOOD clasificación por aire *f*; **~ cleaner** *n* COAL, MECH ENG depurador de aire *m*, filtro de aire *m*, purificador de aire *m*, VEH filtro de aire *m*, purificador de aire *m*; **~ cleaning** *n* COAL depuración del aire *f*; **~ clutch** *n* MECH ENG embrague neumático *m*; **~ combat simulator** *n* AIR TRANSP, MILIT simulador de combate aéreo *m*; **~ compressor** *n* AUTO, HYDRAUL, LAB, MECH, MECH ENG compresor de aire *m*; **~ compressor set** *n* MECH ENG unidad compresora de aire *f*; **~ conditioner** *n* AUTO climatizador *m*, MECH ENG aparato climatizador *m*, climatizador del aire *m*, VEH aire acondicionado *m*; **~ conditioning** *n* AUTO acondicionamiento de aire *m*, COAL acondicionamiento *m*, climatización *f*, eliminación de defectos superficiales *f*, humidificación *f*, tratamiento *m*, CONST

acondicionamiento de aire *m*, HEAT aire acondicionado *m*, climatización *f*, acondicionamiento de aire *m*, MECH ENG acondicionamiento de aire *m*, acondicionamiento de ambientes *m*, aire acondicionado *m*, climatización *f*, METEO acondicionamiento de aire *m*, climatización *f*, PRINT acondicionamiento de aire *m*, REFRIG acondicionamiento de aire *m*, aire acondicionado *m*, THERMO acondicionamiento de aire *m*; **~-conditioning installations** *n pl* SAFE instalaciones para acondicionamiento de aire *f pl*; **~-conditioning master valve** *n* MECH ENG válvula maestra de climatización *f*; **~-conditioning plant** *n* HEAT, REFRIG planta de aire acondicionado *f*; **~-conditioning unit** *n* AUTO, CONST, HEAT, MECH ENG acondicionador de aire *m*, REFRIG acondicionador de aire *m*, climatizador *m*, THERMO acondicionador de aire *m*; **~ conduction** *n* ACOUST conducción aerotimpánica *f*, conducción aérea *f*; **~ conduit** *n* MECH ENG conducto aerífero *m* (*Esp*), conducto de aire *m*, célula aerífera *f* (*AmL*), MINE conducto aerífero *m* (*Esp*), célula aerífera *f* (*AmL*); **~ connection** *n* MECH ENG racor para tubería de aire *m*; **~-cooled air conditioning unit** *n* HEAT, REFRIG, THERMO acondicionador por aire enfriado *m*; **~-cooled compressor** *n* REFRIG compresor enfriado por aire *m*; **~-cooled condenser** *n* HEAT ENG condensador refrigerado por aire *m*, REFRIG condensador enfriado por aire *m*; **~-cooled engine** *n* VEH motor refrigerado por aire *m*; **~-cooled motor** *n* MECH ENG motor enfriado por aire *m*; **~-cooled surface condenser** *n* MECH ENG condensador de superficie enfriado por aire *m*; **~-cooled system** *n* MECH ENG sistema de enfriado por aire *m*; **~-cooled transformer** *n* ELEC transformador con refrigerante de aire *m*, transformador enfriado por aire *m*, transformador refrigerado por aire *m*, ELEC ENG transformador con refrigerante de aire *m*, transformador de enfriamiento por agua *m*, transformador refrigerado por aire *m*; **~-cooled tube** *n* ELECTRON tubo de refrigeración por aire *m*; **~ cooler** *n* NUCL, REFRIG enfriador de aire *m*; **~ cooling** *n* AUTO refrigeración por aire *f*, ELEC ENG enfriamiento por aire *m*, ventilación *f*, MECH ENG enfriamiento por aire *m*, refrigeración por aire *f*; **~-cooling installation** *n* MECH ENG, REFRIG instalación de refrigeración por aire *f*; **~ core inductance** *n* ELEC inducción con núcleo de aire *f*; **~ core transformer** *n* ELEC, ELEC ENG transformador de núcleo de aire *m*, transformador sin núcleo *m*, transformador sin núcleo magnético *m*; **~ core winding** *n* SPACE tortuosidad de núcleo de aire *f*; **~ correction jet** *n* AUTO boquilla de corrección de aire *f*, chicle de corrección de aire *m*; **~ corridor** *n* AIR TRANSP corredor aéreo *m*, pasillo aéreo *m*; **~ course** *n* WATER TRANSP *ship building* conducto de ventilación *m*; **~ coursing** *n* MINE instalación para distribuir el aire de ventilación *f*; **~-cross bleed valve** *n* AIR TRANSP válvula de purga cruzada de aire *f*; **~ cure** *n* P&R curado al aire *m*, curado en frío *m*, polimerización a temperatura ambiente *f*; **~ curtain** *n* HEAT, REFRIG, TRANSP cortina de aire *f*; **~ curtain installation** *n* SAFE *vehicles* cortina de aire *f*; **~ cushion** *n* AIR TRANSP amortiguador de aire *m*, colchón de aire *m*, MECH ENG *handling equipment*, TRANSP amortiguador de aire *m*, WATER TRANSP *hovercraft* colchón de aire *m*; **~ cushion levitation** *n* TRANSP elevación con amortiguación por aire *f*, elevación mediante colchón de aire *f*; ~ **cushion restraint system** *n* TRANSP sistema de contención con amortiguación por aire *m*; ~ **cushion vehicle** *n* AIR TRANSP, TRANSP, WATER TRANSP aerodeslizador *m*, vehículo con amortiguación por aire *m*; ~**-cycle refrigeration machine** *n* REFRIG máquina frigorífica de aire *f*; ~ **cylinder** *n* MECH *fuel* cilindro de aire *m*;

~ d ~ **dashpot** *n* AIR TRANSP amortiguador de aire *m*, retardador de aire *m*, MECH ENG, TRANSP amortiguador de aire *m*; ~ **data computer** *n* AIR TRANSP computador de datos de aire *m* (*AmL*), computadora de datos de aire *f* (*AmL*), ordenador de datos de aire *m* (*Esp*); ~ **date** *n* TV fecha de salida al aire *f*; ~ **defence** *n* BrE MILIT defensa aérea *f*; ~ **defence gun** *n* BrE MILIT ametralladora antiaérea *f*; ~ **defense** *AmE see air defence BrE*; ~ **defense gun** *AmE see air defence gun BrE*; ~ **dehumidifier** *n* SAFE deshumidificador de aire *m*; ~**-depolarized battery** *n* ELEC ENG batería despolarizada por aire *f*; ~ **dielectric** *n* ELEC dieléctrico de aire *m*; ~ **diffuser** *n* REFRIG difusor de aire *m*; ~**-disaster investigation** *n* AIR TRANSP investigación de accidente aéreo *f*; ~ **discharge** *n* MECH *knot* salida de aire *f*; ~ **discharge nozzle** *n* MECH *type of fixing of rail to rail* tobera de salida del aire *f*; ~ **doctor** *n* PAPER, PRINT cepillo de aire *m*; ~ **doctor dampening system** *n* PAPER, PRINT sistema de mojado por cortina de aire *m*; ~ **door** *n* MINE compuerta de ventilación *f*; ~ **draft** *AmE see air draught BrE*; ~ **drain** *n* NUCL purga de aire *f*; ~**-drain valve** *n* NUCL válvula de purga de aire *f*; ~ **draught** *n* BrE WATER TRANSP *ship design* guinda *f*; ~ **drill** *n* MECH *device*, MECH ENG perforadora de aire comprimido *f*; ~ **drilling** *n* PETR TECH perforación por aire comprimido *f*, sondeo por aire *m*, PETROL perforación neumática *f*; ~**-dry mass** *n* PAPER *of pulp* peso de la pasta seca al aire *m*; ~**-dry pulp** *n* PAPER pasta seca al aire *f*; ~ **dryer** *n* PRINT secador por chorro de aire *m*; ~ **drying** *n* PRINT secado por chorro de aire *m*; ~ **duct** *n* COAL aeroducto *m*, HEAT conducto de aire *m*, MECH ENG conducto de aire *m*, conducto de ventilación *m*, ducto de aire *m*, manguerote de ventilación *m*, tubo de ventilación *m*, REFRIG conducto de aire *m*; ~ **ducting** *n* MECH ENG canalización del aire *f*;

~ e ~ **embolism** *n* OCEAN embolia gaseosa *f*; ~ **engine** *n* MECH ENG motor neumático *m*; ~**-entrained concrete** *n* CONST concreto ligero *m* (*AmL*), hormigón ligero *m* (*Esp*); ~ **entraining admixture** *n* CONST mezcla de arrastre de aire *f*; ~ **eraser** *n* PRINT corrector por chorro de aire *m*; ~ **exhaust** *n* PETR TECH salida de aire *f*; ~ **exhauster** *n* OCEAN arrastrador de partículas *m*, aspirador de partículas *m*, exhaustor *m*;

~ f ~ **ferry** *n* AIR TRANSP transbordador aéreo *m*; ~**-filed flight plan** *n* AIR TRANSP plan de vuelo archivado en vuelo *m*; ~ **film system** *n* TRANSP sistema de película de aire *m*; ~ **filter** *n* AUTO, CHEM TECH, COAL, HEAT ENG, MECH, VEH filtro de aire *m*; ~ **fit to breathe** *n* SAFE aire limpio respirable *m*; ~**-float drier** *n* PAPER secador por flotación en corriente de aire *m*; ~ **flooding** *n* PETR TECH inyección de aire *f*; ~ **flotation** *n* HYDRAUL, HYDROL flotación por aire *f*, POLL flotación por aire *f*, separación por contracorriente de aire *f*; ~ **flotation dryer** *n* PRINT secador por flotación de aire *m*; ~ **flow** *n* SPACE

circulación del aire *f*; ~ **flue** *n* PROD conducto de aire *m*, *of furnace* canal de aire *m*; ~ **fog** *n* CINEMAT neblina *f*, niebla *f*; ~ **freight** *n* AIR TRANSP carga aérea *f*, cargo aéreo *m*, PACK envío de la carga por avión *m*, flete aéreo *m*; ~ **friction** *n* SPACE fricción aérea *f*; ~ **friction heating** *n* SPACE calentamiento por fricción con el aire *m*; ~**-fuel ratio** *n* TRANSP relación del aire al combustible *f*; ~ **furnace** *n* HEAT horno de aire *m*;

~ g ~ **gage** *AmE see air gauge BrE*; ~ **gap** *n* COMP&DP entrehierro *m*, ELEC *capacitor, transformer* entrehierro *m*, intervalo de aire *m*, espacio entre los electrodos *m*, ELEC ENG *magnetic or electric circuit* entrehierro *m*, PETR TECH capa de aire *f*, PHYS *materials* entrehierro *m*, TRANSP intersticio de aire *m*, intervalo de aire *m*; ~**-gap coil** *n* ELEC bobina con entrehierro *f*, bobina con espacio de aire *f*; ~**-gap induction** *n* ELEC *coil* inducción con entrehierro *f*, inducción con espacio de aire *f*; ~ **gap protector** *n* ELEC *safety* dispositivo de protección con espacio de aire *m*, dispositivo protector con espacio de aire *m*, protector con espacio de aire *m*, SAFE dispositivo de protección con espacio de aire *m*, dispositivo protector con espacio de aire *m*; ~ **gas** *n* GAS aire *m*; ~ **gauge** *n* BrE MECH ENG manómetro de aire *m*, METR calibrador neumático *m*, manómetro de aire *m*; ~ **gun exploration method** *n* GEOPHYS método de exploración por pistola de aire comprimido *m*;

~ h ~ **hammer** *n* MECH *process* martillo neumático *m*; ~ **heater** *n* HEAT, MECH ENG calentador de aire *m*; ~ **hoist** *n* MECH ENG grúa neumática *f*, malacate neumático *m* (*Esp*), torno de aire comprimido *m*, torno neumático *m*, winchy *m* (*AmL*), PETR TECH malacate neumático *m* (*Esp*), torno neumático *m* (*Esp*), winchy *m* (*AmL*), PROD grúa neumática *f*; ~ **hole** *n* PROD *flaw in casting* toma de aire *f*, *vent* respiradero *m*; ~ **hose** *n* CONST manguera de aire *f*, MECH manguera de aire *f*, manguera de aire comprimido *f*, MECH ENG conducto de aire *m*, manguera de aire comprimido *f*, MINE conducto de aire *m* (*AmL*), manguera de aire *f*; ~ **humidifier** *n* SAFE humedificador de aire *m*;

~ i ~**-impermeable clothing materials** *n pl* SAFE materiales textiles impermeables al aire *m pl*; ~**-infiltration loss** *n* HEAT pérdida por infiltración de aire *f*; ~ **injection compressor** *n* HYDRAUL compresor de inyección de aire *m*; ~ **injection reactor** *n* (*AIR*) TRANSP reactor de inyección de aire *m*; ~ **injector** *n* MECH ENG inyector de aire *m*; ~ **inlet** *n* C&G entrada de aire *f*, MECH ENG admisión de aire *f*, llegada del viento *f*, toma de aire *f*, *of blower* entrada de aire *f*; ~ **inlet cock** *n* MECH ENG llave de admisión del aire *f*; ~ **inlet nozzle** *n* MECH ENG tobera de entrada de aire *f*; ~ **inlet pipe** *n* MECH ENG tubo de entrada de aire *m*; ~ **inlet purifier** *n* PROD depurador de entrada de aire *m*; ~ **inlet valve** *n* MECH ENG válvula de admisión de aire *f*, válvula de entrada de aire *f*, válvula de toma de aire *f*; ~ **input well** *n* PETR TECH pozo de inyección de aire *m*; ~ **insulation** *n* ELEC, ELEC ENG aislación de aire *f*, aislamiento de aire *m*; ~ **intake** *n* MECH ENG entrada de aire *f*, toma de aire *f*, WATER TRANSP toma de aire *f*, tubo portaviento *m*; ~ **intake pressure** *n* AIR TRANSP presión de la toma de aire *f*; ~ **intake valve** *n* AIR TRANSP válvula de toma de aire *f*;

~ j ~ **jet coater** *n* PAPER estucadora con tobera de aire *f*; ~ **jig** *n* COAL caja de depuración neumática *f*;

~ k ~ **knife** n P&R cuchilla a chorro de aire f, PAPER labio soplante m; ~ **knife coater** n PAPER estucadora de labio soplante f; ~ **knife coating** n PAPER estucado con labio soplante m; ~-**knife-coated paper** n PAPER papel estucado con labio soplante m;

~ l ~ **leak** n AUTO fuga de aire f, pérdida de aire f; ~ **leg** n MINE soporte neumático m; ~ **level** n CONST instrument nivel de aire m; ~ **lift** n AIR TRANSP puente aéreo m; ~ **lock** n HEAT ENG hot water heating systems bolsa de aire f, WATER of caisson esclusa neumática f;

~ m ~ **main** n MECH ENG canalización de aire comprimido f, canalización neumática f, principal canalización neumática f, tubería principal del viento f; ~ **mass classification** n METEO clasificación de las masas de aire f; ~ **meter** n MECH ENG contador de aire m, medidor de aire m; ~ **moisture** n COAL humedad del aire f; ~ **monitor** n TV monitor aéreo m, monitor de aire m (AmL), monitor de ambiente m; **off ~ monitor** n TV monitor que no transmite m; ~ **motor** n AIR TRANSP motor de aire m, MECH ENG rotary pneumatic engine motor de aire comprimido m, motor neumático m;

~ n ~~-**no-fuel vent valve** n AIR TRANSP válvula de combustible sin paso de aire f; ~ **nozzle** n COAL boquilla de ventilación f, tobera de aire f, tobera de ventilación f, MECH ENG boquilla de ventilación f, tobera de aire f;

~ o ~~-**oil actuator** n PROD accionador oleoneumático m; ~~-**operated chuck** n MECH ENG manguito porta-herramienta neumático m, plato neumático m, portabrocas neumático m; ~~-**operated gage** AmE, ~~-**operated gauge** BrE n METR calibrador accionado por aire m; ~~-**operated position switch** n PROD interruptor neumático de posición m; ~~-**operated valve grinder** n AUTO esmerilador de válvulas por aire m, esmerilador neumático de válvulas m; ~~-**or-oil cooling** n THERMO programming enfriamiento por aire o aceite m, refrigeración por aire o aceite f; ~ **outlet** n MECH ENG salida de aire f, of blower salida del viento f, venteo m; ~ **oven** n P&R horno de tiro natural m;

~ p ~ **passage** n MECH ENG conducto de aire m, conducto de aireación m, célula aerífera f (AmL), paso de aire m, MINE conducto aerífero m (Esp), conducto de aireación m, célula aerífera f (AmL), paso de aire m, vía aerífera f; ~ **passageway** n MINE galería aerífera f; ~ **permeability** n HEAT ENG, PRINT permeabilidad al aire f; ~~-**photo interpretation** n COAL interpretación de fotografía aérea f; ~ **pin block** n PRINT under a load bloque de pistones m; ~ **pipe** n MECH ENG cañería de aire f, conducto del viento m, conductor de aire m, tubo de aire m, MINE canal m, conducto del viento m; ~ **pipeline** n MECH ENG tubería de aire f; ~ **piston** n MECH ENG pistón neumático m, émbolo del cilindro de aire m; ~ **pocket** n AIR TRANSP, HEAT ENG bolsa de aire f; ~ **pollutant** n POLL contaminante atmosférico m, substancia contaminante atmosférica f, substancia contaminante del aire f; ~ **pollutants** n pl POLL contaminantes del aire m pl; ~~-**polluting substance** n POLL contaminante atmosférico m, substancia contaminante atmosférica f, substancia contaminante del aire f; ~ **pollution** n POLL contaminación atmosférica f, SAFE contaminación del aire f; ~ **pollution control** n POLL control de la contaminación atmosférica m; ~ **pollution emission** n POLL emisión

de contaminante atmosférico f; ~ **pollution incident** n POLL episodio de contaminación atmosférica m, incidente de contaminación atmosférica m; ~ **pollution problem** n POLL episodio de contaminación atmosférica m, incidente de contaminación atmosférica m, problema de contaminación atmosférica m; ~ **preheater** n MECH ENG precalentador de aire m; ~ **pressure** n COAL presión de aire f, MECH ENG presión atmosférica f, presión del aire f; ~ **pressure brake** n AUTO freno de aire comprimido m, freno neumático m; ~ **pressure gage** AmE, ~ **pressure gauge** BrE n PETR TECH manómetro de aire comprimido m, manómetro de presión del aire m; ~ **pressure relief duct** n RAIL conducto para aliviar la presión del aire m; ~ **propeller** n TRANSP ventilador rotatorio m; ~ **pulse** n PETROL pulso de aire m; ~ **pump** n MECH ENG for compression, drawing, PHYS bomba de aire f, bomba de vacío f, bomba de ventilación f, bomba neumática f; ~ **pump exhaust pipe** n MECH ENG tubo de escape de bomba de aire m; ~ **pump lubricator** n MECH ENG lubricador de bomba de aire m; ~ **pump throttle** n MECH ENG regulador de bomba de aire m; ~ **purger** n PACK purgador de aire m; ~ **purification and deodorization equipment** n SAFE equipo para purificar y desodorizar aire m; ~ **purity** n POLL pureza del aire f;

~ q ~ **quality** n TV calidad del aire f;

~ r ~ **rate change** n HEAT cambio en la velocidad del aire m; ~ **ratio** n AUTO proporción de aire f; ~ **reactor** n ELEC motor de reacción neumático m, reactor de aire comprimido m, reactor neumático m; ~ **receiver** n MECH ENG cámara de aire f, depósito de aire m, cámara de aire comprimido f, depósito de aire comprimido m; **off ~ recording** n TV grabación no transmitida f; ~ **refractive index** n WAVE PHYS índice de refracción del aire m; ~ **refrigeration cycle** n REFRIG ciclo frigorífico de aire m; ~ **regulator** n MECH ENG of gas burner regulador de aire m; ~ **reheater** n MECH ENG recalentador de aire m; ~ **renewal** n AIR TRANSP renovación de aire f; ~ **repressuring** n PETR TECH represurización de aire f; ~ **reservoir** n MINE caldecín m (Esp), depósito de aire m (AmL); ~ **roll** n PAPER rodillo soplador m, rodillo soplante m; ~~-**route facilities** n pl AIR TRANSP instalaciones de la ruta aérea f pl, servicios de la ruta aérea m pl;

~ s ~ **safety regulations** n pl AIR TRANSP normativas de seguridad aérea f pl; ~ **sample** n SAFE muestra de aire f; ~~-**sampling technique** n SAFE técnica de muestreo de aire f; ~ **scoop** n AIR TRANSP recogedor de aire m, MECH ENG tolva de aire f, toma de aire dinámica f; ~ **screen blow gun** n PROD soplete de pantalla de aire m; ~ **scrubber** n MINE depurador de aire m, filtro de aire m; ~~-**sea rescue** n MILIT rescate aeromarítimo m, salvamento aeromarítimo m, WATER TRANSP salvamento con medios marítimos y aéreos m; ~~-**sea rescue equipment** n MILIT, SAFE, TRANSP equipo de rescate aeromarítimo m; ~ **search radar** n WATER TRANSP navy radar de exploración aérea m; ~ **separation** n CHEM TECH separación de aire f, FOOD separación por aire f; ~ **separator** n MECH ENG separador de aire m; ~ **shaft** n MINE pozo de aireación m, respiradero m (AmL); ~ **shed** n POLL separación de aire f; ~ **shower** n PAPER pulverizador de aire m; ~~-**snifting valve** n MECH ENG válvula de alivio f, válvula de desahogo *f*, válvula de entrada de aire *f*; ~ **squeegee** *n* CINEMAT escobilla neumática *f*; ~ **stack** *n* MINE chimenea de ventilación *f*; ~ **stairs** *n* AIR TRANSP escaleras del avión *f pl*; ~ **starter** *n* MECH ENG motor de arranque por aire comprimido *m*; ~ **supply** *n* AIR TRANSP suministro de aire *m*;

■ **t** ~ **tank** *n* PETR TECH depósito de aire *m*, tanque de aire *m*, WATER TRANSP *ship* depósito de aire de arranque *m*; ~ **tap** *n* MECH ENG grifo de aire *m*; ~ **taxi** *n* AIR TRANSP taxi aéreo *m*; ~ **terminal** *n* AIR TRANSP terminal aérea *f*; ~ **terminal device** *n* REFRIG terminal de aire *f*; ~ **time** *n* TELECOM tiempo de permanencia en el aire *m*; **~-to-air heat exchanger** *n* MECH ENG intercambiador de calor de aire a aire *m*; **~-to-air missile** *n* (*AAM*) MILIT misil aire-aire *m*; **~-to-air refueling** *AmE*, **~-to-air refuelling** *BrE n* MILIT aprovisionamiento en vuelo *m*, repostaje en vuelo *m*; ~ **traffic** *n* AIR TRANSP tráfico aéreo *m*; ~ **traffic control** *n* AIR TRANSP control de tráfico aéreo *m*; ~ **traffic control center** *AmE*, ~ **traffic control centre** *BrE n* AIR TRANSP centro de control de tráfico aéreo *m*; ~ **traffic control clearance** *n* AIR TRANSP autorización del control de tráfico aéreo *f*; ~ **traffic control service** *n* AIR TRANSP servicio de control de tráfico aéreo *m*; ~ **traffic controller** *n* AIR TRANSP controlador de tráfico aéreo *m*; ~ **traffic pattern** *n* AIR TRANSP pauta del tráfico aéreo *f*; ~ **transformer** *n* ELEC transformador de aire *m*; ~ **treatment** *n* REFRIG tratamiento del aire *m*; ~ **trimmer capacitor** *n* ELEC ENG condensador de ajuste de aire *m*; ~ **turbine** *n* MECH ENG turbina atmosférica *f*, turbina de aire *f*, turbina de aire comprimido *f*;

■ **u** ~ **unfit for respiration** *n* SAFE aire no respirable *m*;

■ **v** ~ **valve** *n* HYDRAUL válvula de descarga *f*, MECH ENG purga de aire *f*, purgador de aire *m*, *tyre* válvula de aire *f*; ~ **variable capacitor** *n* ELEC ENG condensador variable de aire *m*; ~ **velocity** *n* HEAT velocidad del aire *f*; ~ **vent** *n* MECH ENG agujero de ventilación *m*, venteo *m*, venteo de aire *m*, ventosa de aire *f*, NUCL respiradero *m*, tubo de venteo de aire *m*, PETR TECH orificio de ventilación *m*, ventiladero *m*, PRINT, WATER TRANSP respiradero *m*; **~-vent pin** *n* MECH ENG pasador de ventosa de aire *m*; **~-vent valve** *n* AIR TRANSP válvula de escape de aire *f*, válvula de purgado de aire *f*, MECH ENG válvula de purga de aire *f*

air³ *vt* COAL, CONST, PRINT, RECYCL, SAFE, THERMO airear, WATER TRANSP *hold, bilges* airear, ventilar; **~-condition** *vt* CONST, HEAT, REFRIG, THERMO acondicionar; **~-cool** *vt* REFRIG aerorrefrigerar, THERMO aerorrefrigerar, enfriar al aire, refrigerar con aire

air⁴: ~ **brake** *vi AmE* (*cf aerobrake BrE*) AIR TRANSP, MECH ENG, SPACE *craft* aerofrenar

air⁵: **on** ~ *phr* TV en el aire

AIR *abbr* (*air injection reactor*) TRANSP reactor de inyección de aire *m*

airborne¹ *adj* AIR TRANSP aerotransportado

airborne² *adv* AIR TRANSP en el aire

airborne³: ~ **acoustical noise** *n* SAFE ruido transmitido a través del aire *m*; ~ **collision avoidance system** *n* AIR TRANSP sistema de prevención de colisión de a bordo *m*, sistema preventivo anticolisión de a bordo *m*; ~ **dust** *n* SAFE polvo en suspensión *m*; ~ **dust concentrations** *n pl* SAFE

concentraciones de polvo suspendido en el aire *f pl*; ~ **earth station** *n* SPACE *communications* estación terrestre aerotransportada *f*, estación terrestre para aeronaves *f*; ~ **laser** *n* ELECTRON láser de a bordo *m*; ~ **marker balloon** *n* MILIT radiobaliza aerotransportada *f*; ~ **noise** *n* ACOUST ruido aéreo *m*, MECH ENG *emitted by earthmoving machinery, chain saws* ruido llevado por el viento *m*, SAFE *emitted by machine tools* ruido transmitido a través del aire *m*; ~ **particle** *n* METEO partícula en suspensión en el aire *f*; ~ **pollutants** *n pl* POLL contaminantes atmosféricos *m pl*; ~ **proximity-warning indicator** *n* AIR TRANSP indicador de aviso de proximidad de a bordo *m*; ~ **radar** *n* TELECOM radar aerotransportado *m*; ~ **remote sensing** *n* MAR POLL teledetección aérea *f*, teledetección desde el aire *f*; ~ **sound** *n* ACOUST sonido aéreo *m*; ~ **survey** *n* GEOL prospección aerotransportada *f*, prospección efectuada desde un avión *f*; ~ **television** *n* TV televisión de la aeronave *f*

airbridge *n* AIR TRANSP aeropuente *m*

airbrush *n* C&G aerógrafo *m*, PACK aerógrafo *m*, pistola de pintar *f*, pulverizador de aire comprimido *m*, PHOTO, PRINT aerógrafo *m*

airbrushing *n* C&G, PACK, PHOTO, PRINT aerografía *f*

airbus *n* AIR TRANSP airbus *m*

aircheck *n* TV respiradero *m*; ~ **tape** *n* TV cinta de respiradero *f*

aircraft *n* AIR TRANSP *type* aeronave *f*, avión *m*; ~ **axis** *n* AIR TRANSP eje del avión *m*; ~ **balance** *n* AIR TRANSP equilibrio del avión *m*; ~ **call sign** *n* AIR TRANSP indicativo de llamada del avión *m*; ~ **carrier** *n* MILIT, WATER TRANSP buque portaviones *m*, portaviones *m*; ~ **category** *n* AIR TRANSP categoría del aeroplano *f*, categoría del avión *f*; ~ **classification** *n* AIR TRANSP clasificación del avión *f*; ~ **effectivity** *n* AIR TRANSP efectividad del avión *f*; ~ **engine emissions** *n pl* AIR TRANSP emisiones del motor del avión *f pl*; ~ **equipment** *n* AIR TRANSP equipo de a bordo del avión *m*; ~ **icing indicator** *n* AIR TRANSP indicador de formación de hielo del avión *m*, indicador de hielo del avión *m*; ~ **identification** *n* AIR TRANSP identificación del avión *f*; ~ **kilometer performed** *AmE*, ~ **kilometre performed** *BrE n* AIR TRANSP kilometraje efectuado por el avión *m*; ~ **lift** *n* AIR TRANSP sustentación del avión *f*; ~ **light** *n* AIR TRANSP luz del avión *f*; ~ **mains** *n* AIR TRANSP red eléctrica del avión *f*; ~ **maintenance engineer** *n* AIR TRANSP ingeniero de mantenimiento de aviones *m*; ~ **maintenance mechanic** *n* AIR TRANSP mecánico de mantenimiento de aviones *m*; ~ **maintenance rating** *n* AIR TRANSP clasificación del mantenimiento del avión *f*; ~ **movement** *n* AIR TRANSP movimiento del avión *m*; ~ **noise** *n* ACOUST ruido de aeronaves *m*; ~ **overhaul rating** *n* AIR TRANSP clasificación del mantenimiento del avión *f*, clasificación del servicio del avión *f*; ~ **tail unit** *n* AIR TRANSP empenaje *m*

airdraulic: ~ **gun** *n* AUTO pistola de aire *f*, pistola neumática *f*

airdrome *AmE see aerodrome BrE*

airdrop *vt* AIR TRANSP lanzar en paracaídas

airflow *n* AIR TRANSP, CONST flujo de aire *m*, FLUID caudal de aire *m*; ~ **rate** *n* HEAT caudal de aire *m*, grado del flujo de aire *m*, relación del flujo de aire *f*, velocidad del flujo de aire *f*; ~ **sensor** *n* AUTO sensor del flujo de aire *m*

airfoil *AmE see aerofoil BrE*

airframe: ~ **bonding lead** n AIR TRANSP cable conductor de conexión con la célula m, cable de masa con la célula m; ~ **noise** n ACOUST ruido del fuselaje m; ~ **reference plane** n AIR TRANSP plano de referencia de la célula del aparato m

airgun n GEOPHYS pistola de aire comprimido f, PETROL martillo neumático m

airhead n COAL galería de ventilación f, MINE galería de avance f (Esp), galería de ventilación f, galería del frente de ataque f (AmL)

airheading n COAL galería de ventilación f, MINE galería de avance f (Esp), galería de ventilación f, galería del frente de ataque f (AmL)

airlift n TRANSP elevador neumático m, transportador neumático m; ~ **pump** n CHEM TECH bomba de elevación por aire comprimido f

airline n AIR TRANSP aerolínea f, línea aérea f, C&G burbuja alargada en tubos de vidrio f, MECH ENG línea neumática f, tubería neumática f, TRANSP compañía aérea f (Esp), compañía de aeronavegación f (AmL), línea aérea f; ~ **pressure regulator** n MECH ENG regulador de presión en tuberías neumáticas m

airliner n AIR TRANSP avión de pasajeros m

airlock n AIR TRANSP blocaje de aire m, cierre de aire m, esclusa neumática f, FLUID embolsamiento de aire m, MINE bolsa de aire f, esclusa neumática f, PRINT recipiente de descarga de sólidos pulverizados m, REFRIG antecámara pequeña f, SAFE pipes compuerta f, SPACE compuerta de aire f, esclusa de aire f; ~ **feeder** n PAPER alimentador de esclusa neumática m; ~ **system** n NUCL sistema de esclusas m

airmail n AIR TRANSP correo aéreo m; ~ **paper** n PAPER papel de avión m (Esp), papel para correo aéreo m (AmL)

airplane AmE see aeroplane BrE; ~ **mass ratio** n AmE AIR TRANSP proporción de la masa del aeroplano f; ~ **noise** n ACOUST ruido de aviones m; ~ **tow launch** n AmE AIR TRANSP despegue de avión remolcado m

airport n AIR TRANSP aeropuerto m; ~ **charge** n AIR TRANSP impuesto del aeropuerto m; ~ **manager** n AIR TRANSP director de aeropuerto m; ~ **noise** n ACOUST ruido de aeropuertos m; ~ **security committee** n AIR TRANSP comité de seguridad del aeropuerto m; ~ **tax** n AIR TRANSP impuesto del aeropuerto m; ~ **terminal** n AIR TRANSP terminal de aeropuerto f; ~ **traffic** n AIR TRANSP tráfico aéreo del aeropuerto m

airscrew n AIR TRANSP hélice f

airspace n AIR TRANSP espacio aéreo m, MINE cámara de aire f, espacio vacío m, hueco m; ~ **insulation** n HEAT ENG aislación por capa de aire f; ~ **restriction** n AIR TRANSP restricción del espacio aéreo f

airspeed n AIR TRANSP velocidad con respecto al aire f, velocidad relativa f; ~ **indicator** n AIR TRANSP indicador de la velocidad con respecto al aire m, indicador de la velocidad del aire m, indicador de la velocidad relativa m, SPACE indicador de la velocidad del aire m

airstream: ~ **separation** n AIR TRANSP separación de la corriente de aire f

airtight adj FOOD, PETR TECH estanco, hermetizado

airtime n TV tiempo en el aire m

airtow: ~ **flight** AmE see aerotow flight BrE

airwave n PETROL onda de aire f, WAVE PHYS onda aérea f

airway n AIR TRANSP ruta aérea f, MINE conducto de ventilación m (AmL), galería de ventilación f (Esp), pozo de ventilación m (AmL); ~ **bill** n AIR TRANSP billete de avión m, billete de pasaje aéreo m, PRINT carta de porte aéreo f

airworthiness n AIR TRANSP aeronavegabilidad f

airworthy adj AIR TRANSP aeronavegable

Airy: ~ **disc** BrE, ~ **disk** n AmE PHYS disco de Airy m

AKD abbr (alkyl ketone dimers) PAPER dímeros alquilceténicos m pl

akerite n PETROL aquerita f

Al abbr (aluminium BrE, aluminum AmE) CHEM, METALL Al (aluminio)

alabaster n MINERAL alabastro m; ~ **glass** n C&G cristal de alabastro m

alalite n MINERAL alalita f

alanine n CHEM alanina f

alarm n GEN of ribbed bulkheads alarma f; ~ **bell** n ELEC campanilla de alarma f, SAFE campana de alarma f; ~ **call** n TELECOM llamada de alarma f; ~ **card** n TELECOM tarjeta de alarma f; ~ **circuit** n TELECOM circuito de alarma m; ~ **flashing light** n SAFE alarma luminosa intermitente f; ~ **function** n TELECOM función de alarma f; ~ **fuse** n ELEC fusible con alarma m, fusible con indicador m, MECH ENG fusible con alarma m, fusible con indicador de alarma m; ~ **gage** AmE, ~ **gauge** BrE n MECH ENG indicador del nivel bajo del agua m, manómetro de alarma m; ~ **indication lamp** n TELECOM lámpara de alarma f, piloto de indicación de alarma m; ~ **indication signal** n TELECOM señal de indicación de alarma f; ~ **and logging system** n SAFE of ribbed bulkheads sistema de alarma y registro m; ~ **printout facility** n TELECOM medios para impresión de alarma m; ~ **relay** n ELEC relé con alarma m, relé con indicador m; ~ **setting** n TELECOM ajuste de alarma m, calibración de alarma f; ~ **signal** n WATER TRANSP emergency radio call señal de alarma f; ~ **system** n SAFE sistema de alarma m; ~ **thermometer** n MECH ENG termostato con alarma m, termómetro avisador m; ~ **whistle** n MECH ENG pito de alarma m, silbato de alarma m; ~ **whistle signal** n HYDRAUL señal sonora de alarma por silbido f, silbato de alarma m

alaskaite n MINERAL, PETROL alascaíta f

alban n CHEM albana f, albán m

albedo n GEOPHYS, METEO albedo m, SPACE albedo m, albedo neutrónico m, coeficiente de reflexión del mar m, potencia reflectora f

albertite n MINERAL albertita f

albian n GEOL albiense m

albite n C&G albita f, MINERAL albita f, alvita f

albumen n CHEM, FOOD albúmina f; ~ **process** n PHOTO procedimiento a la albúmina m

albumenized: ~ **paper** n PAPER, PHOTO papel fotográfico con capa fotosensible a la albúmina m

albumin n CHEM, FOOD albúmina f

albuminate n CHEM, FOOD albuminato m

albuminoid[1] adj CHEM albuminoide

albuminoid[2] n CHEM albuminoide m, escleroproteína f

albumose n CHEM, FOOD albumosa f

alcaptone n CHEM alcaptona f

alcohol n GEN alcohol m; ~ **addition** n CHEM adición de alcohol f; ~ **ink** n PRINT tinta al alcohol f; ~ **-proof printing** n PRINT impresión a prueba de alcohol f; ~ **thermometer** n REFRIG termómetro de alcohol m

alcoholate n CHEM alcoholato m

alcoholic[1] adj FOOD alcohólico

alcoholic[2]: ~ **fermentation** *n* FOOD fermentación alcohólica *f*
alcoholysis *n* CHEM *of ester* alcohólisis *f*
aldehyde *n* CHEM, FOOD, P&R aldehído *m*; ~ **acid** *n* CHEM aldehído ácido *m*, ácido de aldehído *m*, FOOD ácido de aldehído *m*
aldehydic *adj* CHEM, FOOD, P&R aldehídico
alder *n* PAPER aliso *m*
aldohexose *n* CHEM, FOOD aldohexosa *f*
aldol *n* CHEM acetaldol *m*, aldol *m*
aldose *n* CHEM, FOOD aldosa *f*
aldosterone *n* CHEM, FOOD aldosterona *f*
alee *adj* WATER TRANSP *rudder* metido en orza
A-leg *n* TELECOM cadena regional en A *f*
alerting *n* TELECOM alerta *f*, vigilancia *f*
alexandrite *n* MINERAL alexandrita *f*
alfalfa *n* AmE (*cf lucerne BrE*) AGRIC alfalfa *f*
alga *n* HYDROL, MAR POLL, PETROL alga *f*
algal: ~ **bloom** *n* OCEAN floración algácea *f*, florecimiento algáceo *m* (*AmL*), florescencia algológica *f*; ~ **destruction** *n* HYDROL *diodes* destrucción algácea *f*; ~ **growth potential** *n* HYDROL potencial de crecimiento algáceo *m*; ~ **limestone** *n* PETROL caliza biomicrítica *f*; ~ **mat** *n* OCEAN algazos *m pl*, argazos *m pl*; ~ **reef** *n* GEOL, OCEAN arrecife de algas *m*
algebra *n* COMP&DP, MATH álgebra *f*
algebraic[1] *adj* COMP&DP, MATH algebraico
algebraic[2]: ~ **geometry** *n* GEOM geometría algebraica *f*
Algerian: ~ **onyx** *n* MINERAL ónix argelino *m*, ónix calcáreo *m*, ónix de Argelia *m*
algicide[1] *adj* HYDROL alguicida
algicide[2] *n* HYDROL alguicida *m*
alginate *n* P&R alginato *m*
alginic: ~ **acid** *n* CHEM, FOOD ácido algínico *m*
algoculture *n* OCEAN algocultura *f*, alguicultura *f*
algodonite *n* MINERAL algodonita *f*
algology *n* OCEAN algología *f*
algorithm *n* COMP&DP, MATH, SPACE *communications* algoritmo *m*
algorithmic[1] *adj* COMP&DP, MATH, SPACE algorítmico
algorithmic[2]: ~ **language** *n* COMP&DP lenguaje algorítmico *m*
algorithmics *n* COMP&DP, MATH, SPACE algoritmia *f*
ALI *abbr* (*annual limit on intake*) NUCL LAI (*límite anual de incorporación*)
alias *n* COMP&DP alias *m*
aliased: ~ **frequency** *n* ELECTRON frecuencia ajena *f*; ~ **signal** *n* ELECTRON señal ajena *f*; ~ **spectrum** *n* ELECTRON espectro ajeno *m*
aliasing[1] *adj* COMP&DP *graphics* espúreo
aliasing[2] *n* ELECTRON ajeno *m*; ~ **error** *n* PETROL error de equivalencia de designación *m*
alidade *n* CONST, INSTR alidada *f*
align[1]: ~-**reaming box** *n* AIR TRANSP caja alineadora-ensanchadora *f*, caja plantilla de alineación *f*
align[2] *vt* CINEMAT alinear, CONST alinear, alinearse, MECH alinear, MECH ENG alinear, encuadrar, PHOTO, PRINT, TELECOM, TV alinear
aligned *adj* GEN alineado
aligning: ~ **plug** *n* ELEC ENG clavija de alineación *f*; ~ **tool** *n* PRINT alineador *m*, bracear
alignment *n* CONST *ground plan* trazado *m*, alineación *f*, MECH alineación *f*, PRINT alineación *f*, alineamiento *m*, TELECOM alineación *f*, alineamiento *m*, sincronización *f*, TV *networks* alineación *f*, alineamiento *m*, WATER TRANSP *coastal navigation* enfilación *f*; ~ **fault** *n* TELECOM error de alineación *m*; ~ **frame** *n* PETROL cuadro de alineación *m*; ~ **mark** *n* PRINT marca de alineación *f*; ~ **pin** *n* MECH clavija de alineamiento *f*; ~ **tape** *n* TV cinta de alineación *f*, cinta de alineamiento *f*; ~ **telescope** *n* INSTR telescopio de alineación *m*
aliphatic[1] *adj* PETR TECH alifático
aliphatic[2]: ~ **hydrocarbon** *n* CHEM, P&R hidrocarburo alifático *m*; ~ **polyamine** *n* CHEM, P&R poliamina alifática *f*; ~ **solvent** *n* CHEM, PETR TECH disolvente alifático *m*
alive[1] *adj* ELEC *circuit* activo, bajo tensión, con corriente, ELEC ENG con corriente
alive[2]: ~ **matter** *n* PRINT composición para reutilizar *f*
alkadiene *n* CHEM alcadieno *m*
alkali[1]: ~-**fast** *adj* CHEM, DETERG alcalirresistente; ~-**proof** *adj* CHEM, DETERG alcalirresistente; ~-**soluble** *adj* CHEM, DETERG alcalisoluble
alkali[2] *n* GEN álcali *m*; ~ **cellulose** *n* PAPER álcali-celulosa *m*; ~ **content** *n* DETERG contenido alcalino *m*; ~ **feldspar** *n* PETR TECH feldespato alcalino *m*; ~ **halide** *n* CRYSTALL haluro alcalino *m*; ~ **metal** *n* METALL metal alcalino *m*; ~-**proof paper** *n* PACK papel resistente a los álcalis *m*; ~ **resistance** *n* P&R resistencia a las bases *f*, resistencia a los álcalis *f*; ~ **treatment** *n* DETERG tratamiento alcalino *m*
alkalic *adj* GEN alcalino
alkalimeter *n* CHEM, DETERG, FOOD alcalímetro *m*
alkalimetry *n* CHEM, DETERG, FOOD alcalimetría *f*
alkaline[1] *adj* GEN alcalino
alkaline[2]: ~ **battery** *n* ELEC batería alcalina *f*, ELEC ENG batería alcalina *f*, pila alcalina *f*; ~ **cell** *n* ELEC ENG elemento alcalino *m*; ~ **cleaning** *n* DETERG desengrase alcalino *m*, limpieza alcalina *f*; ~-**earth metal** *n* METALL metal alcalinotérreo *m*; ~ **medium-level radioactive waste** *n* NUCL residuo radiactivo alcalino de media actividad *m*; ~ **papermaking** *n* PAPER fabricación en medio alcalino *f*; ~ **photocell** *n* PHOTO célula fotoeléctrica alcalina *f*, fotocélula alcalina *f*; ~-**resistant lining** *n* SAFE *in fuel pellet* revestimiento resistente a los álcalis *m*; ~ **solution** *n* DETERG disolución alcalina *f*; ~ **storage battery** *n* ELEC acumulador alcalino *m*, batería alcalina *f*, ELEC ENG batería de acumuladores alcalinos *f*, acumulador alcalino *m*, batería alcalina *f*, TRANSP batería de acumuladores alcalinos *f*; ~ **storage cell** *n* ELEC ENG, ELECTRON elemento de acumuladores alcalinos *m*
alkalinity *n* GEN alcalinidad *f*
alkalization *n* CHEM, HYDROL alcalización *f*
alkalize[1] *vt* CHEM alcalizar
alkalize[2] *vti* CHEM alcalinizar, HYDROL alcalinizar, alcalizar
alkaloid *n* CHEM alcaloide *m*
alkane *n* CHEM, DETERG, PETR TECH, PETROL alcano *m*; ~ **sulfonate** *AmE*, ~ **sulphonate** *BrE n* CHEM, DETERG sulfonato de alcano *m*
alkene *n* CHEM, DETERG, PETR TECH alqueno *m*
alkenyl[1] *adj* CHEM alquenilo
alkenyl[2]: ~ **succinic anhydride** *n* (*ASA*) CHEM, PAPER anhídrido alquenil succínico *m*
alkoxide *n* CHEM alcóxido *m*
alkoxy- *pref* CHEM alcoxi-
alkyd *n* CHEM alquid *m*; ~ **resin** *n* P&R resina alquílica *f*
alkyde: ~-**resin varnish** *n* COATINGS, COLOUR barniz de resina alkídica *m*, barniz de resina alquídica *m*

alkyl *n* CHEM, DETERG, PETR TECH alquilo *m*; **~ benzene** *n* CHEM, DETERG alquil benceno *m* (*Esp*), alquilobenceno *m* (*AmL*); **~ ketone dimers** *n pl* (*AKD*) PAPER dímeros alquil-ceténicos *m pl*; **~ sulphonic acid** *n* CHEM, DETERG ácido alquilsulfónico *m*

alkylamine *n* CHEM, DETERG alquilamina *f*

alkylaromatics *n* PETR TECH alquiloaromáticos *m*

alkylation *n* CHEM *process*, DETERG, PETR TECH alquilación *f*; **~ plant** *n* DETERG planta de alquilación *f*; **~ unit** *n* CHEM TECH, DETERG unidad de alquilación *f*

alkylene *n* CHEM alquileno *m*, DETERG alquileno *m*, alquiloaromáticos *m*

alkyne *n* CHEM *compound*, PETR TECH alquino *m*

allactite *n* MINERAL alactita *f*

allagite *n* MINERAL alagita *f*

allanite *n* MINERAL alanita *f*

Allan: **~'s link motion** *n* MECH ENG distribución por sector Allan *f*

allantoin *n* CHEM alantoína *f*

all-around: **~ swing crane** *n* AmE CONST grúa giratoria de 360 grados *f*

all-capacitor: **~ filtering** *n* ELECTRON filtrado de capacidad total *m*

all-cargo: **~ charter flight** *n* AIR TRANSP vuelo charter de carga *m*; **~ load factor** *n* AIR TRANSP coeficiente de carga de avión de carga *m*; **~ service** *n* AIR TRANSP servicio de transporte de carga *m*

all-current: **~ motor** *n* AmE (*cf all-mains motor BrE*) ELEC motor de alimentación universal *m*, motor para toda corriente *m*, motor universal *m*

allelotropic *adj* CHEM alelótropo

allemontite *n* MINERAL alemontita *f*

Allen: **~ key** *n* BrE (*cf Allen wrench AmE*) AUTO, MECH ENG, VEH llave Allen *f*; **~ screw** *n* MECH ENG prisionero con cavidad hexagonal *m*; **~ valve** *n* MECH ENG válvula Allen *f*; **~ wrench** *n* AmE (*cf Allen key BrE*) AUTO, MECH ENG, VEH *tool* llave Allen *f*

allene *n* CHEM *compound* aleno *m*

Allen: **~'s loop test** *n* ELEC prueba de lazo de Allen *f*, prueba en bucle de Allen *f*, prueba por el método del anillo de Allen *f*

alleviation: **~ factor** *n* AIR TRANSP factor de mitigación *m*

alley: **~ cropping** *n* AGRIC cultivo en franjas *m*

alleyway *n* WATER TRANSP *boat building* pasillo *m*

all-freight: **~ service** *n* AIR TRANSP servicio de carga *m*, servicio de mercancías *m*

all-gear: **~ head** *n* MECH ENG cabezal de monopolea *m*; **~ single-pulley drive** *n* MECH ENG accionamiento por monopolea y caja de velocidades *m*

all-geared: **~ headstock** *n* MECH ENG cabezal de monopolea *m*

all-glass: **~ cockpit** *n* AIR TRANSP cabina con indicadores a base de pantallas electrónicas *f*; **~ optical fiber** *AmE*, **~ optical fibre** *BrE* *n* OPT, TELECOM fibra óptica de vidrio *f*, fibra óptica totalmente de vidrio *f*

alligator *n* MINE machacadora de mandíbulas *f*; **~ clamp** *n* CINEMAT pinza cocodrilo *f*, pinza de conexión *f*, pinza de mandíbulas *f*; **~ clip** *n* ELEC *connection* pinza cocodrilo *f*, presilla boca de caimán *f*, presilla cocodrilo *f*, ELEC ENG pinza cocodrilo *f*, pinza de conexión *f*, MECH ENG cocodrilo *m*, pinza de conexión *f*; **~ wrench** *n* MECH ENG llave de caños *f*, llave de mandíbulas *f*, llave para tubos *f*

alligatoring *n* AIR TRANSP cuarteado *m*, COATINGS cuarteado *m*, cuarteamiento *m*, P&R cuarteado *m*, cuarteamiento *m*, formación de grietas irregulares *f*, resquebrajamiento *m*

all-in: **~ tariff** *n* ELEC *supply* tarifa con todo incluído *f*

all-insulated: **~ switch** *n* ELEC conmutador totalmente aislado *m*, interruptor totalmente aislado *m*

all-mail: **~ service** *n* AIR TRANSP servicio sólo para correos *m*

all-mains: **~ motor** *n* BrE (*cf all-current motor AmE*) ELEC motor de alimentación universal *m*, motor para toda corriente *m*, motor universal *m*

allocate *vt* COMP&DP, PROD asignar

allocated: **~ frequency** *n* TV frecuencia distribuida *f*, frecuencia localizada *f*; **~ stock** *n* PROD existencias asignadas *f pl*

allocation *n* COMP&DP repartición *f*, asignación *f*, PROD asignación *f*

allochem *n* GEOL aloquímico *m*, granos aloquímicos *m pl*, PETROL aloquema *m*

allochroite *n* MINERAL allocroíta *f*

allochthon *n* GEOL material transportado *m*

allochthonous[1] *adj* PETROL, POLL alóctono

allochthonous[2]: **~ matter** *n* POLL materia alóctona *f*

allomorphite *n* MINERAL alomorfita *f*

allopalladium *n* MINERAL alopaladio *m*

allophane *n* MINERAL alófana *f*

all-or-nothing: **~ control** *n* SPACE control de todo o nada *m*; **~ relay** *n* ELEC relé de cierre-apertura *m*, relé de todo-nada *m*, ELEC ENG relé de todo-nada *m*

allotment *n* COMP&DP, PROD asignación *f*

allotriomorphic *adj* GEOL, PETROL alotriomórfico

allotrope *n* CHEM *of element*, CRYSTALL, METALL alótropo *m*

allotropic *adj* CHEM, CRYSTALL, METALL alotrópico

allotropy *n* CHEM, CRYSTALL, METALL alotropía *f*, polimorfismo *m*

allow: **~ to breed** *vt* PROD *fire of a blast furnace* dejar reproducir

allowable: **~ landing mass** *n* AIR TRANSP masa de aterrizaje permisible *f*; **~ load** *n* AIR TRANSP carga permisible *f*, ELEC *equipment* carga admisible *f*, carga nominal *f*, carga permisible *f*, carga tolerable *f*; **~ takeoff mass** *n* AIR TRANSP masa de despegue permisible *f*

allowance *n* MECH holgura *f*, margen *m*, tolerancia *f*, MECH ENG *machining*, PROD tolerancia *f*; **~ for machining** *n* PROD *founding* margen de acabado *m*; **~ for shrinkage** *n* MECH ENG tolerancia por contracción *f*

allowed: **~ electron dipole transition** *n* RAD PHYS transición electrónica dipolar permitida *f*; **~ energy band** *n* NUCL, PHYS, RAD PHYS banda energética permitida *f*; **~ spectrum** *n* NUCL espectro permitido *m*; **~ transition** *n* NUCL, PHYS, RAD PHYS transición permitida *f*

alloy[1] *n* CHEM *metals*, COAL, ELECTRON, MECH, MECH ENG, METALL, PROD aleación *f*; **~ carbide** *n* METALL carburo metálico de aleación *m*; **~ diode** *n* ELECTRON diodo de aleación *m*; **~ junction** *n* ELECTRON empalme de aleación *m*; **~ junction transistor** *n* ELECTRON transistor de unión de aleación *m*

alloy[2] *vt* CHEM alear, ligar, COAL alear, ELECTRON alear, ligar, MECH, MECH ENG alear, METALL, PROD alear, ligar

alloyed: **~ steel** *n* COAL, METALL, MINE acero aleado *m*

alloying: ~ **method** n ELECTRON método de aleación m

all-pass: ~ **filter** n ELECTRON, TELECOM filtro de todo paso m

all-plastic: ~ **fiber** AmE, ~ **fibre** BrE n OPT, TELECOM fibra de plástico f; ~ **optical fiber** AmE, ~ **optical fibre** BrE n OPT, TELECOM fibra óptica de plástico f, fibra óptica totalmente de plástico f

all-purpose: ~ **adhesive** n PACK adhesivo multiuso m; ~ **trailer** n TRANSP remolque de uso múltiple m, trailer de uso múltiple m, trailer multiuso m

all-round: ~ **light** n WATER TRANSP luz todo horizonte f; ~ **swing crane** n BrE (cf all-around swing crane AmE) CONST grúa giratoria de 360 grados f

all-silica: ~ **fiber** AmE, ~ **fibre** BrE n OPT, TELECOM fibra de sílice f

all-solid: ~ **state** n ELECTRON grupo compacto m

all-speed: ~ **aileron** n TRANSP alerón de varias velocidades m, alerón multi-velocidad m

all-tantalum: ~ **capacitor** n ELEC ENG condensador totalmente de tantalio m

all-terrain: ~ **tire** AmE, ~ **tyre** BrE n VEH neumático para todo terreno m; ~ **vehicle** n (AT vehicle) AUTO vehículo todo terreno m

alluaudite n MINERAL aluaudita f

all-up: ~ **weight** n (AUW) TRANSP peso en orden de vuelo m (PMA), peso total de despegue m (PMA)

alluvial: ~ **area** n CONST zona aluvial f; ~ **bed** n WATER lecho aluvial m; ~ **cone** n HYDROL, WATER cono aluvial m; ~ **deposit** n HYDROL aluvión m, MINE aluvión m, yacimiento aluvial m, OCEAN aluvión m, terrero aluvial m, PETROL aluvión m, depósito aluvial m, WATER aluvión m, depósito aluvial m, terreno de aluvión m, yacimiento aluvial m; ~ **fan** n GEOL abanico aluvial m; ~ **mining** n MINE explotación de aluviones f; ~ **nappe** n HYDROL capa aluvial f, manto aluvial m; ~ **plain** n GEOL llanura aluvial f, WATER planicie aluvial f

alluviation n OCEAN sedimentación aluvial f

alluvium n HYDROL, MINE, OCEAN, PETROL, WATER aluvión m

all-volatile: ~ **chemistry** n (AVT) NUCL química de los volátiles f; ~ **chemistry regime** n NUCL secondary side control régimen de control químico por volátiles m

all-watt: ~ **motor** n ELEC motor para toda potencia m, motor para todo vatio m, motor para todo watt m

all-weather: ~ **helicopter** n AIR TRANSP helicóptero todo tiempo m; ~ **operations** n pl AIR TRANSP operaciones todo tiempo f pl; ~ **search aircraft** n AIR TRANSP aeronave de búsqueda para todo tiempo f, MILIT aeronave de búsqueda para todo tiempo f, avión de búsqueda para todo tiempo m

allyl n CHEM alilo m; ~ **alcohol** n CHEM alcohol alílico m, alcohol propenílico m; ~ **glycidyl ether** n (AGE) CHEM, P&R alilglicidiléter m

almandine n MINERAL almandino m

almandite n MINERAL almandita f

alnoeite n MINERAL alnoeita f, alnoíta f

alnoite n MINERAL alnoeita f, alnoíta f

aloin n CHEM aloína f

along[1]: ~ **the line of strike** adv MINE a lo largo de la línea de filones

along[2]: ~**track error** n SPACE error de seguimiento lateral m

along[3]: ~ **the strike** prep MINE en dirección

alongshore adv WATER TRANSP navigation a lo largo de la costa

alongside adv WATER TRANSP ship, quay abarloado, al costado, atracado

alpha: ~ **cellulose** n PAPER alfa celulosa f; ~ **decay** n PART PHYS, PHYS, RAD PHYS desintegración alfa f; ~ **disintegration energy** n PART PHYS, PHYS, RAD PHYS energía de desintegración alfa f; ~**-elimination mechanism** n RAD PHYS mecanismo de eliminación alfa m; ~ **emitter** n PART PHYS, PHYS, RAD PHYS emisor alfa m; ~ **ionization gas analyser** n BrE NUCL analizador de gases por ionización alfa m; ~ **ionization gas analyzer** AmE see alpha ionization gas analyser BrE; ~ **particle** n ELEC helión m, partícula alfa f, NUCL, PART PHYS, PHYS, RAD PHYS partícula alfa f; ~ **profile** n OPT perfil alfa m; ~ **radiation** n ELEC, RAD PHYS radiación alfa f; ~ **ray** n PHYS radiación alfa f, rayo alfa m; ~ **ray spectrometry** n RAD PHYS espectrometría alfa f; ~ **wrap** n TV memory recubrimiento de alfas m

alphabetic: ~ **code** n COMP&DP código alfabético m

alphageometric: ~ **display** n TELECOM dispositivo visualizador m, visualizador alfageométrico m

alphameric adj COMP&DP, TELECOM alfanumérico

alphamosaic adj COMP&DP alfamosaico

alphanumeric[1] adj COMP&DP, TELECOM alfanumérico

alphanumeric[2]: ~ **character** n COMP&DP, TELECOM carácter alfanumérico m; ~ **code** n COMP&DP, TELECOM código alfanumérico m; ~ **display** n COMP&DP, TELECOM visualizador alfanumérico m; ~ **pager** n TELECOM avisador alfanumérico m; ~ **sort** n COMP&DP clasificación alfanumérica f

alquifou n MINERAL alquifol m

alquifoux n MINERAL alquifol m

ALS abbr (advanced light source) PART PHYS ALS (fuente luminosa avanzada)

alstonite n MINERAL alstonita f

altaite n MINERAL altaíta f

altazimuth: ~ **mounting** n INSTR montaje altazimutal m

alterable: ~ **optical memory** n OPT memoria óptica reprogramable f

alteration n ACOUST alteración f; ~ **of course** n SPACE alteración de la trayectoria f, WATER TRANSP navigation cambio de rumbo m

alternaria n AGRIC disease alternaria f

alternate: ~**-action switch** n ELEC, ELEC ENG interruptor de acción alternada m; ~ **exterior angle** n GEOM ángulo exterior alterno m; ~ **interior angle** n GEOM ángulo interior alterno m; ~ **landing site** n SPACE lugar alternativo de descenso m; ~ **mark inversion** n TELECOM inversión alternativa de señales f; ~ **mode** n ELECTRON modo alterno m; ~ **routing** n PROD asignación de ruta alternativa f; ~ **speech service** n TELECOM servicio alternativo de palabras m

alternating[1] adj MECH alternante, alternativo, alterno, MECH ENG alternado, alternante, alternativo, alterno

alternating[2]: ~ **burst** n TV burst alternante m (AmL), estallido alternante m (Esp); ~ **colored lights** AmE, ~ **coloured lights** BrE n pl WATER TRANSP luces de color de destellos f pl; ~ **component** n ELEC componente alternado m, componente alternativo m, componente alterno m; ~ **current** n (AC) CHEM, ELEC, ELEC ENG, ELECTRON, METALL, PHYS, PROD, SPACE, TELECOM, TV corriente alterna f (CA), corriente alternativa f (CA); ~**-current arc** n ELEC arco de corriente alterna *m*; **~-current balancer** *n* ELEC compensador de corriente alterna *m*, equilibrador de corriente alterna *m*, igualador de corriente alterna *m*; **~-current bridge** *n* ELEC *measurement* puente de corriente alterna *m*, puente de medidas con corriente alterna *m*, PHYS puente de corriente alterna *m*; **~-current circuit** *n* ELEC circuito de corriente alterna *m*; **~-current component** *n* ELEC componente de corriente alterna *f*; **~-current coupler** *n* TELECOM acoplador de corriente alterna *m*; **~-current field** *n* ELEC *electromagnetism* campo de corriente alterna *m*, inductor de corriente alterna *m*; **~-current generator** *n* ELEC, ELEC ENG, FUELLESS, PHYS, VEH alternador *m*; **~-current hum** *n* ELEC *amplifier* zumbido de corriente alterna *m*; **~-current machine** *n* ELEC máquina de corriente alterna *f*, ELEC ENG dispositivo de corriente alterna *m*; **~-current meter** *n* ELEC medidor de corriente alterna *m*; **~-current motor** *n* ELEC ENG, PHYS, TRANSP alternomotor,motor de corriente alterna *m*; **~-current network** *n* ELEC red de corriente alterna *f*; **~-current output** *n* ELEC ENG potencia de salida de CA *f*, salida de corriente alterna *f*; **~-current power system** *n* SPACE sistema de alimentación por CA *m*; **~-current relay** *n* ELEC relevador para corriente alterna *m*, relé de corriente alterna *m*; **~-current servomotor** *n* ELEC ENG servomotor de corriente alterna *m*; **~-current source** *n* ELEC ENG generador de corriente alterna *m*; **~-current supply** *n* ELEC, ELEC ENG, ELECTRON fuente de alimentación de corriente alterna *f*; **~-current transmission line** *n* ELEC, ELEC ENG *supply network* línea de transmisión de corriente alterna *f*; **~-current voltmeter** *n* ELEC *instrument* voltímetro de corriente alterna *m*; **~ electric field** *n* ELEC ENG campo eléctrico alternativo *m*; **~ electromotive force** *n* ELEC, ELEC ENG, PHYS fuerza electromotriz alterna *f*; **~ field** *n* ELEC ENG campo alternativo *m*; **~ flux** *n* ELEC *electromagnetism*, PHYS flujo alterno *m*; **~ magnetic field** *n* ELEC ENG campo magnético alternativo *m*; **~ motion** *n* MECH ENG movimiento alternativo *m*, movimiento de vaivén *m*, tren alternativo *m*; **~ saw** *n* MECH ENG sierra alternativa *f*; **~ voltage** *n* ELEC tensión alterna *f*, voltaje alterno *m*, ELEC ENG tensión alternativa *f*, voltaje alternativo *m*

alternation *n* MECH alternante *m*, MECH ENG alternación *f*, alternante *m*; **~ of movement** *n* MECH ENG alternación del movimiento *f*

alternative: **~ current generator** *n* ELEC, PHYS generador de corriente alterna *m*; **~ route** *n* TELECOM ruta alternativa *f*; **~ routing** *n* TELECOM enrutamiento alternativo *m*; **~ test method** *n* (*ATM*) OPT método de ensayo alternativo *m*, TELECOM método alternativo de pruebas *m* (*ATM*)

alternator *n* ELEC *generator* alternador *m*, ELEC ENG alternador *m*, generador de corriente alterna *m*, FUELLESS *hydroelectricity, windpower*, PHYS alternador *m*, VEH *electrical system* alternador *m*, generador *m*; **~ field voltage** *n* ELEC tensión de excitación *f*, tensión del inductor del alternador *f*, voltaje del inductor del alternador *m*

altimeter *n* AIR TRANSP, GEOPHYS, METR, PHYS, SPACE altímetro *m*; **~ setting** *n* AIR TRANSP, GEOPHYS, PHYS, SPACE ajuste del altímetro *m*, fijación del altímetro *f*, graduación del altímetro *f*

altimetry *n* AIR TRANSP, GEOPHYS, METR, PHYS, SPACE, TRANSP altimetría *f*

altitude *n* AIR TRANSP altitud *f*, altura *f*, COMP&DP, FUELLESS, GEOM, GEOPHYS altura *f*, MECH ENG altitud *f*, altura *f*, METR altura *f*, PHYS altitud *f*, altura *f*, altura sobre el nivel del mar *f*, SPACE altitud *f*, altura *f*, elevación *f*, TRANSP, WATER TRANSP altura *f*, WAVE PHYS altitud *f*, altura *f*; **~ controller** *n* AIR TRANSP controlador de altitud *m*; **~ corrector** *n* AUTO corrector de altitud *m*; **~ of optimum rainfall** *n* METEO precipitación idónea *f*; **~ and orbit control system** *n* (*AOCS*) SPACE sistema para control de posición y órbita *m* (*SCPO*)

altocumulus *n* (*AC*) AIR TRANSP, METEO altocúmulo *m* (*AC*)

altostrati *n* WATER TRANSP altostrato *m*

altostratus *n* (*AS*) AIR TRANSP, METEO altoestrato *m*, altostratus *m* (*AS*)

ALU *abbr* (*arithmetic and logic unit*) COMP&DP UAL (*unidad aritmetica y lógica*)

alum *n* CHEM, MINERAL alumbre *m*, PAPER alumbre *m*, alúmina *f*

alumina *n* CHEM, COAL, FOOD, MINERAL alúmina *f*; **~ content** *n* COAL contenido en aluminio *m*

aluminate[1] *n* CHEM aluminato *m*

aluminate[2] *vt* CHEM aluminar

alumination *n* CHEM aluminación *f*

aluminic *adj* CHEM alumínico

aluminiferous *adj* CHEM aluminífero

aluminite *n* MINERAL aluminita *f*

aluminium[1]: **~-coated** *adj* BrE COATINGS, METALL aluminizado

aluminium[2] *n* BrE (*Al*) CHEM, METALL aluminio *m* (*Al*); **~ alloy** *n* BrE MECH ENG, METALL *for solid bearings* aleación de aluminio *f*; **~ anode** *n* BrE ELEC ENG ánodo alumínico *m*, ánodo de aluminio *m*; **~ bottle** *n* BrE PACK botella de aluminio *f*; **~ bronze** *n* BrE MECH *materials* bronce de aluminio *m*; **~ can** *n* BrE PACK bote de aluminio *m*; **~ can bank** *n* BrE RECYCL cámara de combustión de aluminio *f*, depósito de latas de aluminio *m*; **~ capsule** *n* BrE PACK cápsula de aluminio *f*; **~ chlorohydrate** *n* BrE CHEM, HYDROL clorohidrato de aluminio *m*; **~ coating** *n* BrE COATINGS revestimiento de aluminio *m*; **~ conductor** *n* BrE ELEC conductor de aluminio *m*; **~ content** *n* BrE COAL contenido en aluminio *m*, contenido en alúmina *m*; **~ electrolytic capacitor** *n* BrE ELEC ENG condensador electrolítico de aluminio *m*; **~ foil** *n* BrE FOOD hoja de aluminio *f*, HEAT ENG hoja de aluminio *f*, papel de aluminio *m*, PACK hoja de aluminio *f*; **~ foil printing ink** *n* BrE PRINT tinta para imprimir sobre hojas de aluminio *f*; **~ garnet** *n* BrE MINERAL granate alumínico *m*; **~ gate** *n* BrE ELECTRON puerta de aluminio *f*; **~ hydroxide** *n* BrE CHEM, HYDROL, P&R hidróxido de aluminio *m*; **~-killed steel** *n* BrE MECH *materials*, METALL acero calmado con aluminio *m*; **~ oxide** *n* BrE CHEM óxido de aluminio *m*; **~ sheet** *n* BrE PACK lámina de aluminio *f*; **~ silicate** *n* BrE CHEM, DETERG silicato de aluminio *m*; **~ silicate fibre** *n* BrE HEAT ENG fibra de silicato de aluminio *f*; **~ sulphate** *n* BrE CHEM, HYDROL sulfato de aluminio *m*; **~ tape** *n* BrE PACK banda de aluminio *f*

aluminized: **~ screen** *n* ELECTRON pantalla de aluminio *f*; **~ teflon**® *n* SPACE teflón aluminizado® *m*

alumino- *pref* CHEM alumino-

aluminosilicate n CHEM, MINERAL aluminosilicato m;
~ **brick** n HEAT *disk drive actuator* ladrillo de silicato
de aluminio m

aluminothermic: ~ **welding** n MECH soldadura aluminotérmica f

aluminous adj CHEM aluminoso

aluminum AmE see aluminium BrE

alunite n MINERAL alunita f

alunogen n MINERAL alunógeno m

alurgite n MINERAL alurgita f

alveolar: ~ **dolomite** n GEOL *fixed equipment* dolomita
alveolar f

AM[1] abbr (*amplitude modulation*) GEN AM (*modulación
de amplitud*)

AM[2]: ~ **transfer coefficient** n SPACE *communications*
coeficiente de transferencia de modulación de amplitud m

Am abbr (*americium*) CHEM, NUCL, RAD PHYS Am
(*americio*)

amalgam n CHEM *of metal and mercury,* COAL, GEOL,
MECH ENG, MINERAL, NUCL, PROD *of metal and
mercury* amalgama f; ~ **barrel** n COAL barril de
amalgamación m, cilindro de amalgamación m

amalgamate vt GEN amalgamar

amalgamating: ~ **table** n COAL mesa de amalgamación f

amalgamation n GEN amalgamación f; ~ **plate** n COAL
placa de amalgamación f

amalgamator n CHEM amalgamador m, COAL amalgamador m, máquina amalgamadora f, substancia
amalgamadora f, GEOL amalgamador m, MECH ENG
amalgamador m, máquina de amalgamación f,
MINERAL, NUCL, PROD amalgamador m

amarine n CHEM amarina f

amateur: ~ **radio service** n TELECOM servicio de
radioaficionados m

amausite n MINERAL amausita f

Amazon: ~ **stone** n MINERAL amazonita f, microclina
f, piedra de las Amazonas f

amazonite n MINERAL amazonita f

amber n MINERAL ámbar m; ~ **varnish** n COATINGS,
COLOUR barniz color ámbar m

amberoid n MINERAL amberoide m, ambroide m,
ámbar prensado m

ambience: ~ **track** n CINEMAT banda de sonido
ambiental f

ambient[1] adj GEN ambiente

ambient[2]: ~ **air** n POLL, REFRIG aire ambiente m;
~ **emission standard** n POLL *quality factor* norma
de emisiones ambientales f; ~ **fluid** n FLUID fluido
ambiente m; ~ **light** n CINEMAT luz ambiental f;
~ **noise** n ACOUST ruido ambiental m, ruido ambiente
m, TELECOM ruido ambiente m; ~ **pollutant
concentration** n POLL concentración de contaminante ambiental f; ~ **quality standard** n POLL *of
compound* grado de calidad ambiental m, norma de
calidad ambiental f; ~ **radioactivity** n RAD PHYS
radiactividad ambiental f, radiactividad de fondo f;
~ **temperature** n GAS, HEAT, METALL, METR, PHYS,
THERMO temperatura ambiente f

ambiguity: ~ **resolution** n SPACE *communications* definición de ambigüedad f, resolución de una
ambigüedad f

amblygonite n MINERAL ambligonita f

ambrain n CHEM ambreína f

ambrite n MINERAL ambrita f

ambroid n MINERAL amberoide m, ambroide m

ambulance n AUTO, VEH ambulancia f; ~ **installation** n
AIR TRANSP equipo de a bordo de ambulancia m;
~ **station** n SAFE estación de ambulancias f

amend vt AGRIC enmendar, MECH ENG corregir,
enmendar, modificar, reformar

amendment n AGRIC *soils* enmienda f, MECH ENG
enmienda f, modificación f; ~ **file** n COMP&DP archivo
para enmiendas m; ~ **record** n COMP&DP registro de
enmiendas m

American: ~ **National Standards Institute** n (*ANSI*)
TELECOM Instituto Americano de Normalización
Nacional m (*ANSI*); ~ **National Taper Pipe thread**
n (*American NPT*) MECH ENG rosca cónica de tubos
American National f (*rosca NPT, rosca cónica NPT*);
~ **NPT** n (*American National Taper Pipe thread*)
MECH ENG rosca NPT f (*rosca cónica de tubos
American National*), rosca cónica NPT f (*rosca cónica
de tubos American National*); ~ **Society of Mechan-
ical Engineers** n (*ASME*) MECH ASME (*Sociedad
Norteamericana de Ingenieros Mecánicos*); ~ **Standard Code for Information Interchange** n (*ASCII*)
PRINT ASCII; ~ **standard pipe thread** n MECH ENG
rosca de tubo Brigg f; ~ **wire gage** n AmE, ~ **wire
gauge** BrE n PROD sistema norteamericano de
calibres de alambres y de chapas m

americium n (*Am*) CHEM, NUCL, RAD PHYS americio m
(*Am*)

amesite n MINERAL amesita f

amethyst n MINERAL amatista f

amiant n MINERAL amianto m

amianthinite n MINERAL amiantinita f

amianthus n MINERAL amianto m

amic: ~ **acid** n CHEM ácido amíctico m

Amici: ~ **prism** n PHYS *communications* prisma de
Amici m

amide n CHEM *compound, group,* DETERG, P&R amida f;
~ **hardener** n P&R endurecedor de amidas m

amidine n CHEM amidina f

amidogen n CHEM amidógeno m

amidships adv WATER TRANSP en el centro del buque

amination n CHEM aminación f

amine n CHEM, DETERG, P&R amina f; ~~**cured epoxy** n
P&R epoxi endurecida con amina f, resina epoxi
curada con amina f; ~ **curing agent** n COATINGS, P&R
agente endurecedor de amina m

amino[1]: ~ **acid** n CHEM *plant and animal tissues,* FOOD
aminoácido m; ~ **resin** n P&R resina amínica f

amino-[2] pref CHEM amino-

aminoazo adj CHEM aminoazo

ammeter n ELEC *instrument,* ELEC ENG, INSTR, LAB,
PHYS, TV, VEH amperímetro m

ammiolite n MINERAL amiolita f

ammonia n (*NH₃*) CHEM amoníaco m (*NH₃*); ~ **carboy**
n DETERG botellón de amoníaco m; ~ **dynamite** n
MINE dinamita amoniacal f; ~ **gas** n DETERG, GAS,
HYDROL gas amoníaco m; ~ **maser** n ELECTRON
maser de amoníaco m

ammoniacal adj CHEM amoniacal

ammonite n GEOL *final safety analysis report* amonite
m

ammonium n CHEM amonio m; ~ **chloride** n CHEM
cloruro de amonio m, *expectorant for bronchitis*
cloruro amónico m; ~ **hydroxide** n CHEM, PETR
TECH hidróxido amónico m; ~ **nitrate fuel oil** n
(*ANFO*) MINE explosivo compuesto de nitrato amó-

nico y fueloil *m* (*NAFO*); ~ **perchlorate** *n* CHEM, SPACE perclorato de amonio *m*

ammunition *n* MILIT munición *f*; ~ **box** *n* MILIT caja de armón *f*, caja de municiones *f*; ~ **depot** *n* MILIT depósito de municiones *m*; ~ **dump** *n* MILIT depósito de municiones *m*; ~ **paper** *n* PAPER papel para cartuchos *m*

amorphism *n* CHEM amorfismo *m*

amorphous[1] *adj* CHEM, COAL, CRYSTALL, ELECTRON, GEOL, P&R amorfo

amorphous[2]: ~ **layer** *n* ELECTRON estratificador amorfo *m*; ~ **semiconductor** *n* ELECTRON semiconductor amorfo *m*; ~ **silicon** *n* ELECTRON silicio amorfo *m*; ~ **structure** *n* P&R estructura amorfa *f*; ~ **substrate** *n* ELECTRON substrato amorfo *m*

amount: ~ **of substance** *n* PHYS cantidad de sustancia *f*

amp: ~ **rating** *n* PROD valor nominal del amperaje *m*

ampelite *n* PETROL ampelita *f*

amperage *n* ELEC *current* amperaje *m*, intensidad en amperios *f*, ELEC ENG amperaje *m*

ampere *n* (*A*) CHEM, ELEC, ELEC ENG, ELECTRON, METR, PHYS amperio *m* (*A*), ampere *m* (*A*); ~ **balance** *n* ELEC *instrument* balance de intensidad *m*, equilibrio de amperios *m*, simetría de amperios *f*, INSTR equilibrio de amperios *m*; ~ **conductor** *n* ELEC amperio-conductor *m*; ~ **density** *n* ELEC densidad de un amperio *f*; ~**-hour** *n* ELEC *quantity*, PHYS amperio-hora *m*; ~**-hour capacity** *n* PHOTO capacidad en amperios-hora *f*; ~**-second** *n* ELEC, PHYS *quantity* amperio-segundo *m*; ~ **turn** *n* ELEC *winding* ampere-vuelta *m*, amperio-vuelta *m*, ampervuelta *m*, PHYS amperio-vuelta *m*, ampervuelta *m*

Ampère: ~**-Laplace theorem** *n* ELEC *electromagnetism* teorema de Ampère-Laplace *m*; ~**'s law** *n* ELEC, PHYS ley de Ampère *f*; ~**'s rule** *n* ELEC *electromagnetism* regla de Ampère *f*; ~**'s theorem** *n* ELEC *electromagnetism* teorema de Ampère *m*

Amperian: ~ **currents** *n pl* PHYS corrientes amperianas *f pl*, corrientes de Ampère *f pl*

ampersand *n* PRINT signo & *m*

amphibian[1] *adj* WATER TRANSP anfibio

amphibian[2] *n* WATER TRANSP avión anfibio *m*, vehículo anfibio *m*

amphibious: ~ **armored car** *AmE*, ~ **armoured car** *BrE* *n* MILIT coche blindado anfibio *m*; ~ **tank** *n* MILIT tanque anfibio *m*; ~ **vehicle** *n* MILIT vehículo anfibio *m*

amphibole *n* CHEM *crystal structures*, MINERAL anfíbol *m*

amphibolite *n* PETROL anfibolita *f*

amphiboloid *adj* MINERAL anfiboloide

amphimixis *n* AGRIC anfimixis *f*

amphiphilic[1] *qdj* DETERG anfifílico

amphiphilic[2]: ~ **compound** *n* DETERG compuesto anfifílico *m*

amphitalite *n* MINERAL anfitalita *f*

amphodelite *n* MINERAL anfodelita *f*

ampholyte *n* CHEM anfólito *m*

amphoteric[1] *adj* CHEM, DETERG anfotérico

amphoteric[2]: ~ **compound** *n* CHEM, DETERG compuesto anfótero *m*

amplidyne *n* ELEC ENG amplidina amplificador magnético rotativo *f*

amplification *n* ELEC *signal*, ELECTRON amplificación *f*;

~ **factor** *n* CINEMAT, ELECTRON, INSTR factor de amplificación *m*

amplified: ~ **circuit** *n* TELECOM circuito con amplificador *m*; ~ **handset** *n* TELECOM micrófono con amplificador *m*

amplifier *n* GEN amplificador *m*; ~ **chip** *n* ELECTRON chip amplificador *m*; ~ **circuit** *n* ELECTRON circuito amplificador *m*; ~ **class** *n* ELECTRON clase de amplificador *f*, tipo de amplificador *m*; ~ **gain** *n* ELECTRON, PHYS ganancia de amplificación *f*; ~ **noise** *n* ELECTRON ruido de señal de amplificación *m*; ~ **stage** *n* ELECTRON fase de amplificación *f*; ~ **tube** *n* ELECTRON tubo amplificador *m*

amplify *vt* ELECTRON amplificar, PHYS, TELECOM, WATER TRANSP, WAVE PHYS ampliar

amplifying[1] *adj* COMP&DP de amplificación, ELEC *intensity* amplificador, de amplificación, ELECTRON, PHYS, TELECOM, WATER TRANSP de amplificación, WAVE PHYS amplificado, de amplificación

amplifying[2]: ~ **circuit** *n* ELECTRON circuito amplificador *m*; ~ **transistor** *n* ELECTRON transistor de amplificación *m*

amplitron *n* ELECTRON, PHYS amplitrón *m*

amplitude[1]: ~**-modulated** *adj* ELECTRON modulado en amplitud

amplitude[2] *n* GEN amplitud *f*; ~ **adjustment** *n* ELECTRON ajuste de amplitud *m*; ~**-amplitude distortion** *n* ELECTRON, PHYS, TELECOM, WAVE PHYS distorsión de amplitud *f*; ~**-amplitude response** *n* ELECTRON respuesta de amplitud *f*; ~**-amplitude response curve** *n* ELECTRON curva de respuesta de amplitud *f*; ~ **calibration** *n* ELECTRON calibración de la amplitud *f*, comprobación de amplitud *f*; ~ **calibrator** *n* ELECTRON calibrador de amplitud *m*; ~ **control** *n* WAVE PHYS control de amplitud *m*; ~ **corrector** *n* TV corrector de amplitud *m*; ~ **demodulation** *n* COMP&DP, ELECTRON, TELECOM, TV demodulación de la amplitud *f*; ~ **distortion** *n* ACOUST, ELECTRON, PHYS, TELECOM, WAVE PHYS distorsión de amplitud *f*; ~ **division** *n* PHYS división de la amplitud *f*; ~ **equalizer** *n* TELECOM ecualizador de amplitud *m*; ~**-frequency distortion** *n* ELECTRON, PHYS, TELECOM, WAVE PHYS distorsión de amplitud de frecuencia *f*; ~**-frequency response** *n* ELECTRON respuesta de amplitud de frecuencia *f*; ~**-frequency response curve** *n* ELECTRON curva de respuesta de amplitud de frecuencia *f*; ~ **gate** *n* ELECTRON puerta de control de amplitud *f*; ~ **information** *n* ELECTRON información de amplitud *f*; ~ **limiter** *n* ELECTRON, TELECOM limitador de amplitud *m*; ~ **limiter circuit** *n* TV circuito de limitación de amplitud *m*; ~**-modulated carrier** *n* ELECTRON portadora modulada en amplitud *f*; ~ **modulation** *n* (*AM*) GEN modulación de amplitud *f* (*AM*); ~ **probability distribution** *n* TELECOM distribución de probabilidad de amplitud *f*; ~ **resonance** *n* PHYS resonancia de amplitud *f*; ~ **response** *n* ELECTRON respuesta de amplitud *f*; ~ **spectrum** *n* PETROL, WAVE PHYS espectro de amplitud *m*; ~ **threshold** *n* ELECTRON umbral de amplitud *m*

AM-PM: ~ **conversion coefficient** *n* SPACE *communications* coeficiente de conversión antemeridiano AM-PM *m*; ~ **transfer coefficient** *n* SPACE coeficiente de transferencia antemeridiano AM-PM *m*

ampoule *n* BrE C&G, LAB, PACK ampolla *f*; ~ **box** *n* BrE PACK caja de ampollas *f*, estuche de ampollas *f*

ampule *AmE see* **ampoule** *BrE*

AMU *abbr* (*atomic mass unit*) PHYS UMA (*unidad de masa atómica*)

amyl *n* CHEM amilo *m*; **~ acetate** *n* CHEM, P&R acetato de amilo *m*

amylaceous *adj* FOOD amiláceo

amylase *n* AGRIC *enzyme* amilasa *f*

amylopectin *n* TEXTIL amilopectina *f*

An *abbr* (*actinon*) CHEM, RAD PHYS An (*actinón*)

anabatic: **~ front** *n* METEO frente anabático *m*

anabiosis *n* AGRIC anabiosis *f*

anachromatic: **~ lens** *n* CINEMAT, INSTR, OPT, PHOTO, PHYS objetivo anacromático *m*

anaerobe *n BrE* (*cf* **anaerobium** *AmE*) FOOD, HYDROL, OCEAN, P&R, RECYCL anaerobio *m*, anoxibiótico *m*

anaerobic[1] *adj* FOOD, HYDROL, OCEAN, P&R, RECYCL anaeróbico

anaerobic[2]**:** **~ adhesive** *n* P&R, PACK adhesivo anaeróbico *m*; **~ decomposition** *n* HYDROL, RECYCL descomposición anaeróbica *f*; **~ digestion** *n* RECYCL digestión anaeróbica *f*, putrefacción anaeróbica *f*; **~ treatment** *n* RECYCL tratamiento anaeróbico *m*

anaerobiosis *n* RECYCL anaerobiosis *f*

anaerobium *n AmE* (*cf* **aenerobe** *BrE*) FOOD, HYDROL, OCEAN, P&R, RECYCL anaerobio *m*, anoxibiótico *m*

anafront *n* METEO anafrente *m*

anaglyph: **~ process** *n* CINEMAT proceso anaglífico *m*

anaglypta *n* COATINGS anaglifo *m*

anaglyptic: **~ wall-paper** *n* COATINGS papel pintado en relieve *m*

analog[1] *adj* COMP&DP, ELEC ENG, ELECTRON, PETROL, PHYS, TELECOM analógico; **~-to-digital** *adj* TV analógico a digital (*A-a-D*)

analog[2]**:** **~ actuator** *n* ELEC ENG accionador analógico *m*, impulsor analógico *m*; **~ ammeter** ELEC, ELEC ENG, INSTR amperímetro analógico *m*; **~ bipolar integrated circuit** *n* ELECTRON circuito integrado bipolar analógico *m*; **~ board** *n* ELECTRON cuadro analógico *m*; **~ calculation** *n* COMP&DP cálculo analógico *m*; **~ call processor** *n* TELECOM procesador analógico de llamadas *m*; **~ carrier system** *n* COMP&DP sistema de portadora analógico *m*; **~ channel** *n* COMP&DP canal analógico *m*; **~ chip** *n* ELECTRON chip analógico *m*; **~ circuit** *n* ELEC ENG, ELECTRON, TELECOM circuito analógico *m*; **~ circuit design** *n* ELEC ENG, ELECTRON, TELECOM diseño de circuito analógico *m*; **~ comparator** *n* ELECTRON comparador analógico *m*; **~ data** *n* ELECTRON datos analógicos *m pl*; **~ delay line** *n* TV línea de retardo analógico *m*; **~ device** *n* TELECOM dispositivo analógico *m*; **~-to-digital conversion** *n* (*ADC*) COMP&DP, ELEC, ELECTRON, PART PHYS, PHYS, TELECOM conversión analógico-digital *f*; **~-to-digital converter** *n* (*ADC*) COMP&DP, ELEC, ELECTRON, PART PHYS, PHYS, TELECOM conversor analógico-digital *m*, convertidor A/D *m*, convertidor analógico-digital *m*; **~ filter** *n* ELECTRON filtro analógico *m*; **~ filtering** *n* ELECTRON filtrado analógico *m*; **~ gate** *n* ELECTRON puerta analógica *f*; **~-incremental system** *n* COMP&DP sistema incremental-analógico *m*; **~ information** *n* ELECTRON información analógica *f*, información análoga *f*; **~ integrated circuit** *n* ELECTRON circuito integrado analógico *m*; **~ interface** *n* TELECOM interfaz analógico *m*; **~ line driver** *n* COMP&DP controlador de línea analógica *m*; **~ measuring instrument** *n* ELEC instrumento de medición analó-

gico *m*, instrumento de medición análogo *m*, INSTR instrumento de medición analógico *m*, instrumento de medición análogo *m*, instrumento de medidas analógicas *m*, METR instrumento de medidas analógicas *m*; **~ measuring system** *n* COMP&DP sistema de medición analógica *m*; **~ meter** *n* ELEC ENG contador analógico *m*, medidor analógico *m*; **~ modulation** *n* ELECTRON, PHYS modulación analógica *f*; **~ output** *n* INSTR salida analógica *f*; **~ private wire** *n* TELECOM circuito analógico de uso privado *m*; **~ quantity** *n* COMP&DP cantidad analógica *f*; **~ recording** *n* TELECOM registro analógico *m*; **~ signal** *n* COMP&DP, ELECTRON, PHYS, TELECOM señal analógica *f*; **~ signal generator** *n* ELECTRON generador de señal analógica *m*; **~ signal processing** *n* ELECTRON proceso de señal analógica *m*; **~ switching system** *n* TELECOM sistema de conmutación analógica *m*; **~ system** *n* TELECOM sistema analógico *m*; **~ transmission** *n* TELECOM transmisión analógica *f*; **~ videodisc** *n* OPT videodisco analógico *m*; **~ voltmeter** *n* ELEC ENG voltímetro analógico *m*

analyse *vt BrE* GEN analizar

analyser *n BrE* GEN analizador *m*

analysing: **~ projector** *n BrE* CINEMAT proyector analizador *m*

analysis *n* GEN análisis *m*, ensayo *m*; **~ error** *n* COAL error analítico *m*, tolerancia *f*; **~ laboratory** *n* COAL laboratorio analítico *m*; **~ sample** *n* COAL muestra para análisis *f*; **~ of variance** *n* (*ANOVA*) COMP&DP análisis de varianza *m* (*ANOVA*)

analyst *n* GEN analista *m*

analytic[1] *adj* GEN analítico

analytic[2]**:** **~ geometry** *n* GEOM geometría analítica *f*; **~ projector** *n* CINEMAT proyector analítico *m*

analytical[1] *adj* GEN analítico

analytical[2]**:** **~ balance** *n* LAB balanza analítica *f*, balanza de laboratorio *f*, PHYS balanza de laboratorio *f*; **~ engine** *n* COMP&DP máquina analítica *f*; **~ geometry** *n* GEOM geometría analítica *f* (*AmL*); **~ mechanics** *n* PHYS mecánica analítica *f*; **~ sample** *n* COAL muestra para análisis *f*

analyze *AmE see* **analyse** *BrE*

analyzer *AmE see* **analyser** *BrE*

analyzing: **~ protector** *AmE see* **analysing projector** *BrE*

anamesite *n* PETROL anamesita *f*

anamorphic[1] *adj* CINEMAT, INSTR, PHOTO, TELECOM anamórfico

anamorphic[2]**:** **~ lens** *n* CINEMAT objetivo anamórfico *m*, INSTR lente anamórfica *f*, PHOTO, PHYS objetivo anamórfico *m*; **~ print** *n* CINEMAT copia anamórfica *f*; **~ squeeze** *n* CINEMAT compresión anamórfica *f*; **~ system** *n* CINEMAT sistema anamórfico *m*

anamorphoser *n* CINEMAT equipo anamorfizador *m*

anamorphosing: **~ printing** *n* CINEMAT copiado anamorfósico *m*

anamorphosis *n* CINEMAT, PHOTO, TELECOM anamorfosis *m*

anastigmat *n* OPT, PHOTO objetivo anastigmático *m*; **~ lens** *n* OPT, PHOTO lente anastigmática *f*

anastigmatic: **~ lens** *n* CINEMAT, OPT, PHOTO, PHYS objetivo anastigmático *m*

anatexis *n* GEOL anatexia *f*

anatto *n* FOOD achiote *m*

ancestor *n* COMP&DP *of node* antepasado *m*

anchor[1] *n* CONST *building* ancla *f*, anclaje *m*, MECH armadura *f*, tirante *m*, anclaje *m*, WATER TRANSP ancla *f*; ~ **arm** *n* WATER TRANSP brazo de ancla *m*; ~ **bearing** *n* WATER TRANSP demora del fondeadero *f*; ~ **bill** *n* WATER TRANSP pico de loro *m*; ~ **bolt** *n* CONST perno de anclaje *m*, MECH bulón de anclaje *m*, MECH ENG perno de anclaje *m*; ~ **boss** *n* WATER TRANSP núcleo del ancla *m*; ~ **buoy rope** *n* WATER TRANSP orinque *m*; ~ **cable attachment** *n* WATER TRANSP arraigada de la cadena del ancla *f*; ~ **chain** *n* WATER TRANSP cadena del ancla *f*; ~ **deck** *n* WATER TRANSP cubierta del castillo *f*; ~ **fluke** *n* WATER TRANSP uña *f*; ~ **ice** *n* OCEAN hielo de fondo *m*; ~ **in the form of an S** *n* CONST anclaje en forma de S *m*; ~ **in the form of an X** *n* CONST anclaje en forma de X *m*; ~ **light** *n* WATER TRANSP luz de fondeo *f*; ~ **nut** *n* MECH ENG tuerca de anclaje *f*; ~ **plate** *n* COAL placa de anclaje *f*; ~ **post** *n* CONST poste de anclaje *m*; ~ **ring** *n* WATER TRANSP arganeo *m*; ~ **rod** *n* COAL piquete de anclaje *m*; ~ **shackle** *n* WATER TRANSP grillete de ancla *m*; ~ **stock** *n* WATER TRANSP cepo del ancla *m*; ~ **watch** *n* MILIT guardia de puerto *f*; ~ **well** *n* WATER TRANSP varadero del ancla *m*

anchor[2]: ~ **in the roads** *phr* WATER TRANSP estar al ancla en la rada, fondear en la rada

anchor[3] *vt* CONST *floor joist* amarrar, anclar, sujetar, WATER TRANSP *ship* fondear

anchor[4] *vti* SPACE *craft* afianzar, anclar, WATER TRANSP anclar

anchor[5] *vi* WATER TRANSP surgir

anchorage *n* WATER TRANSP fondeo *m*, surgidero *m*; ~ **block** *n* CONST bloque de anclaje *m*; ~ **system** *n* NUCL sistema de anclaje *m*

anchoring *n* SPACE amarre *m*, anclaje *m*; ~ **bolt** *n* CONST perno para anclajes *m*; ~ **ground** *n* WATER TRANSP tenedero *m*; ~ **plate** *n* CONST placa de anclaje *f*; ~ **tower** *n* ELEC *supply network* torre de amarre *f*

ancillary[1] *adj* MECH, MECH ENG, SPACE auxiliar

ancillary[2]: ~ **equipment** *n* MECH equipo accesorio *m*, equipo auxiliar *m*

AND: ~ **gate** *n* COMP&DP puerta AND *f*, puerta Y *f*, PHYS compuerta Y *f*; ~ **operation** *n* COMP&DP operación AND *f*, operación Y *f*

Anderson: ~ **bridge** *n* ELEC *circuit* puente Anderson *m*, puente de medida Anderson *m*

andesite *n* PETROL andesita *f*

andesitic *adj* PETROL andesítico

andradite *n* MINERAL andradita *f*, topazolita *f*

anechoic: ~ **chamber** *n* TELECOM cámara anecoica *f*; ~ **room** *n* ACOUST cámara anecoica *f*, PHYS sala anecoica *f*; ~ **termination** *n* ACOUST terminación anecoica *f*

anelasticity *n* METALL, PHYS inelasticidad *f*

anemograph *n* FUELLESS, HYDROL, METEO, PHYS, WATER TRANSP anemógrafo *m*

anemometer *n* FUELLESS *tidal power*, HYDROL, LAB, METEO, PHYS, WATER TRANSP anemómetro *m*

anemometry *n* FUELLESS *tidal power*, HYDROL, LAB, METEO, PHYS, WATER TRANSP anemometría *f*

aneroid: ~ **altimeter** *n* AIR TRANSP altímetro aneroide *m*; ~ **barometer** *n* AIR TRANSP, CONST, LAB, METEO, PHYS barómetro aneroide *m*

anethole *n* CHEM anetol *m*

aneurin *n* CHEM aneurina *f*

ANFO *abbr* (*ammonium nitrate fuel oil*) MINE NAFO (*explosivo compuesto de nitrato amónico y fueloil*)

angiographic: ~ **examination table** *n* INSTR mesa de examen angiográfico *f*

angiography *n* INSTR angiografía *f*

angle *n* CINEMAT ángulo *m*, CONST angular *m*, ángulo de muro *m*, GEOM ángulo *m*, MECH ENG esquina *f*, ángulo *m*, PHYS, WATER TRANSP ángulo *m*; ~ **of acceptance** *n* NUCL *navigation* ángulo de aceptación *m*; ~ **of advance** *n* AUTO, ELEC, ELEC ENG ángulo de avance *m*, MECH ENG avance angular *m*, ángulo de avance *m*; ~ **of arrival** *n* TELECOM ángulo de llegada *m*; ~ **of attack** *n* AIR TRANSP, PHYS ángulo de ataque *m*; ~ **of attack indicator** *n* AIR TRANSP indicador del ángulo de ataque *m*; ~ **bar** *n* PRINT barra desviadora *f*; ~ **box** *n* PRINT casilla angular *f*; ~ **box wrench** *n* MECH ENG llave de muletilla angular *f*, llave de tubo angular *f*; ~ **brace** *n* CONST riostra diagonal *f*; ~ **bracket** *n* CONST ménsula en escuadra *f*, *shafting* escuadra *f*, palomilla *f*, MECH consola en escuadra *f*, escuadra *f*, ménsula *f*, MECH ENG consola en escuadra *f*, soporte de ángulo *m*; ~ **of brush lag** *n* ELEC *motor* ángulo de atraso de escobilla *m*, ángulo de retardo de escobilla *m*, ángulo de retraso de escobilla *m*; ~ **of clearance** *n* MECH ENG, PROD *machine tool* ángulo de despojo *m*; ~ **of contact** *n* PROD ángulo de contacto *m*; ~ **of coverage** *n* CINEMAT ángulo de cobertura *m*, ángulo de vista *m*; ~ **of cut-off** *n* CINEMAT ángulo de corte *m*; ~ **cutter** *n* MECH *process* fresa cónica de ángulo *f*, MECH ENG *of a milling machine* cortadora diagonal *f*, fresa cónica de ángulo *f*; ~ **of departure** *n* HYDRAUL ángulo de salida *m*, velocidad de salida *f*, OPT, PROD, TELECOM ángulo de salida *m*; ~ **of dip** *n* GEOPHYS ángulo de inclinación de la aguja magnética *m*, PHYS ángulo de inclinación *m*; ~ **drive** *n* MECH transmisión de ángulo *f*; ~ **of elevation** *n* AIR TRANSP, CONST, GEOM, SPACE, TELECOM ángulo de elevación *m*; ~ **error** *n* METR error de ángulo *m*; ~ **fishplate** *n* RAIL brida de angular *f*; ~ **fishplating** *n* RAIL aplicación de bridas de angular *f*; ~ **of friction** *n* COAL ángulo de fricción *m*, CONST ángulo de rozamiento *m*, PHYS ángulo de fricción *m*, PROD ángulo de rozamiento *m*; ~ **of hade** *n* GEOL complemento de buzamiento *m*; ~ **of heel** *n* WATER TRANSP *ship design* ángulo de escora *m*; ~ **in radians** *n* GEOM ángulo en radianes *m*, ángulo en radio *m*; ~ **of incidence** *n* AIR TRANSP, CINEMAT, FUELLESS, OPT, PHYS, PROD, TELECOM, WAVE PHYS ángulo de incidencia *m*; ~ **of inclination** *n* PROD ángulo de inclinación *m*; ~ **iron** *n* CONST angular de hierro *m*; ~ **iron joint** *n* CONST junta con angular de hierro *f*; ~ **joint** *n* CONST junta en ángulo *f*; ~ **of keying** *n* MECH ENG ángulo de calaje *m*; ~ **of lag** *n* ELEC *motor brush* ángulo de atraso *m*, ángulo de retraso *m*; ~ **of lap** *n* MECH ENG *of slide-valve* ángulo de recubrimiento *m*; ~ **of lead** *n* ELEC *motor brush* ángulo de adelanto *m*, ángulo de adelanto de fase *m*, ángulo de avance *m*, ELEC ENG ángulo de avance *m*, MECH ENG *of slide-valve* avance angular a la admisión *m*, ángulo de avance *m*, ángulo de avance a la admisión *m*; ~ **of lead of brushes** *n* ELEC *motor* ángulo de adelanto de escobillas *m*, ángulo de avance de escobillas *m*; ~ **of loll** *n* WATER TRANSP *ship design* ángulo de escora de transición *m*; ~ **of magnetic declination** *n* PHYS ángulo de declinación magnética *m*; ~ **of magnetic inclination** *n* PHYS ángulo de inclinación magnética *m*; ~ **mark** *n* PRINT marca angular *f*; ~ **measurement** *n* METR medida angular *f*;

~ meter *n* METR goniómetro *m*; **~ modulation** *n* ELECTRON modulación angular *f*; **~ of obliquity** *n* MECH ENG *gearing* ángulo de oblicuidad *m*; **~ of overlap** *n* ELEC *rectifier* ángulo de recubrimiento *m*, ángulo de solapamiento *m*, ángulo de superposición *m*; **~ peeling test** *n* P&R prueba de adherencia de ángulos *f*; **~ of phase difference** *n* ELEC *alternating current* ángulo de desfasaje *m*, ángulo de desfase *m*, ELEC ENG diferencia del ángulo de fase *f*, PHYS, WAVE PHYS ángulo de desfasaje *m*, ángulo de desfase *m*; **~ pin** *n* MECH ENG *diecasting die* pasador angular *m*; **~ of pitch** *n* AIR TRANSP ángulo de cabeceo *m*, C&G ángulo de inclinación *m*, WATER TRANSP ángulo de cabeceo *m*; **~ plate** *n* MECH ENG escuadra de apoyo *f*, escuadra para trazar *f*, soporte de escuadra *m*, METR *deck fittings* ángulo de enderezamiento *m*, *shipbuilding* escuadra de apoyo *f*, escuadra de ángulo *f*; **~ of precession** *n* FUELLESS ángulo de precesión *m*; **~ of prerelease** *n* MECH ENG avance angular al escape *m*, ángulo de avance al escape *m*; **~ of pressure** *n* MECH *switch*, MECH ENG ángulo de presión *m*; **~ of pull** *n* MECH ángulo de tracción *m*, WATER TRANSP *rope* ángulo de arrastre *m*, ángulo de tracción *m*; **~ rafter** *n* CONST alfarda *f*, lima tesa *f*; **~ of rake** *n* CINEMAT, MECH ENG *of cutting tool* ángulo de inclinación *m*; **~ of reflection** *n* PHYS, WAVE PHYS ángulo de reflexión *m*; **~ of refraction** *n* PHYS, WAVE PHYS ángulo de refracción *m*; **~ of relief** *n* MECH ENG *of cutting tool* ángulo de incidencia *m*, ángulo de rebajo *m*; **~ of repose** *n* CONST, PACK ángulo de talud natural *m*; **~ section** *n* MECH sector angular *m*; **~ sensor** *n* MECH sensor angular *m*; **~ shot** *n* CINEMAT toma angular *f*, toma en ángulo *f*; **~ sieve** *n* AGRIC zaranda *f*; **~ of sight** *n* MILIT ángulo de situación *m*, TELECOM ángulo de mira *m*, ángulo de visión *m*; **~ of stall** *n* AIR TRANSP ángulo de pérdida *m*; **~ steel** *n* MECH *eliquated metals* angular de acero *m*; **~ of taper** *n* MECH *switch* ángulo de ahusamiento *m*; **~ of 30 degrees** *n* GEOM ángulo de 30 grados *m*; **~ tie** *n* CONST escuadra en ángulo *f*, esquina *f*; **~ of tilt** *n* CINEMAT ángulo de inclinación *m*, ángulo de picado *m*, PHOTO, TV ángulo de picado *m*; **~ of traction** *n* MECH, WATER TRANSP ángulo de tracción *m*; **~ of twist** *n* MECH *eliquated metals* ángulo de torsión *m*; **~ of view** *n* CINEMAT ángulo de campo *m*, ángulo de vista *m*; **~ of wing setting** *n* AIR TRANSP ajuste del ángulo del ala *m*

angled: **~ column** *n* PHOTO *for protection against particles* columna angulada *f*, columna inclinada *f*; **~ core slide** *n* MECH ENG *injection moulds* corredera de macho angular *f*; **~ drill** *n* MINE perforación inclinada *f*; **~ key** *n* MECH ENG chaveta angular *f*; **~ open socket wrench** *n* MECH ENG llave de casquillo abierto angular *f*, llave de tuerca de boca tubular *f*; **~ socket wrench** *n* MECH ENG bocallave *f*, llave de cubo angulado *f*

angledozer *n* CONST explanadora de hoja oblicua *f*

angling *n* PRINT angulación *f*; **~ error** *n* PRINT error de angulación *m*

angstrom *n* METR angstrom *m*

angular[1] *adj* CONST, GEOM angular, MECH angular, anguloso

angular[2] *n* WATER TRANSP *shipbuilding* angular *m*; **~ ball bearing** *n* MECH cojinete de bolas angular *m*; **~ deviation** *n* ELEC ENG desviación angular *f*; **~ diameter** *n* SPACE diámetro angular *m*;

~ disconformity *n* GEOL disconformidad angular *f*; **~ displacement** *n* ELEC *alternating current* desplazamiento angular *m*; **~ displacement sensitivity** *n* AIR TRANSP *between two directions or axes* sensitividad de desplazamiento angular *f*; **~ distortion** *n* CINEMAT distorsión angular *f*; **~ frequency** *n* (*W*) ACOUST frecuencia angular *f* (*W*), ELEC *AC supply* frecuencia angular *f* (*W*), pulsación *f*, velocidad angular *f*, ELEC ENG, PHYS, RAD PHYS, WAVE PHYS frecuencia angular *f* (*W*); **~ grooved-and-tongued joint** *n* CONST junta angular machihembrada *f*; **~ kinetic energy** *n* MECH ENG energía cinética angular *f*, energía cinética de rotación *f*; **~ lead** *n* MECH ENG avance angular a la admisión *m*, ángulo de avance a la admisión *m*; **~ magnification** *n* PHYS magnificación angular *f*; **~ meshing** *n* MECH *colours in clothes* engrane angular *m*; **~ milling cutter** *n* MECH *colours in clothes* fresa angular *f*; **~ misalignment loss** *n* OPT, TELECOM pérdida por desalineación angular *f*; **~ momentum** *n* AIR TRANSP, MECH, PART PHYS, PHYS momento angular *m*; **~ pitch rate** *n* AIR TRANSP frecuencia del cabeceo angular *f*; **~ pre-release** *n* MECH ENG avance angular al escape *m*; **~ pulsing** *n* ACOUST pulsación angular *f*; **~ roll rate** *n* AIR TRANSP frecuencia del alabeo angular *f*; **~ roller bearing** *n* MECH cojinete de rodillos angular *m*; **~ rotor speed** *n* AIR TRANSP velocidad del rotor angular *f*; **~ separation** *n* TELECOM separación angular *m*; **~-thread screw** *n* MECH tornillo de paso angular *m*; **~ three-axis rate sensor** *n* AIR TRANSP sensor de la frecuencia triaxial angular *m*; **~ unconformity** *n* GEOL discordancia angular *f*; **~ velocity** *n* ELEC ENG, FUELLESS velocidad angular *f*, MECH ENG cambio de ángulo por unidad de tiempo *m*, velocidad angular *f*, PHYS, SPACE velocidad angular *f*; **~ velocity of precession** *n* FUELLESS velocidad angular de precesión *f*; **~ velocity rate sensor** *n* AIR TRANSP sensor de la proporción de la velocidad angular *m*; **~ viewfinder** *n* CINEMAT visor angular *m*; **~ yaw rate** *n* AIR TRANSP frecuencia de la guiñada angular *f*

angulometer *n* METR goniómetro *m*, OCEAN goniómetro *m*, radiogoniómetro *m*

anhedral *adj* GEOL anhédrico

anhidrosis *n* AGRIC *animal husbandry* anhidrosis *f*

anhydration *n* CHEM, FOOD anhidración *f*

anhydride *n* CHEM, DETERG, P&R, PAPER anhídrido *m*; **~ hardener** *n* P&R endurecedor de anhídrido *m*

anhydrite *n* GAS, PETR TECH, PETROL *conservation* anhidrita *f*

anhydrous[1] *adj* CHEM, FOOD anhidro, anhídrico, HYDROL, PETR TECH, POLL, WATER anhidro

anhydrous[2]: **~ ammonia** *n* CHEM, PETR TECH amoníaco anhidro *m*

anilide *n* CHEM anilida *f*

aniline: **~ dye** *n* CHEM, COLOUR, PHOTO colorante de anilina *m*; **~ formaldehyde resin** *n* PACK resina de anilina-formaldehído *f*; **~ ink** *n* COLOUR tinta de anilina *f*; **~ printing** *n* PACK impresión a la anilina *f*, PRINT flexografía *f*; **~ rubber-plate printing** *n* PRINT flexografía *f*, impresión en flexografía *f*; **~ value** *n* P&R índice de anilina *m*

anilox: **~ roll** *n* PRINT rodillo anilox *m*

animal[1]: **~-drawn** *adj* AGRIC por tracción animal

animal[2]: **~ building** *n* AGRIC edificio para el ganado *m*; **~ dealer** *n* AGRIC tratante de ganado *m*; **~ fat** *n* FOOD grasa animal *f*; **~ feed** *n* AGRIC pienso para animales *m*; ~ **glue** *n* PAPER cola animal *f*; ~ **health** *n* AGRIC sanidad animal *f*; ~ **husbandry** *n* AGRIC ganadería *f*; ~ **industry** *n* AGRIC producción pecuaria *f*; ~ **production** *n* AGRIC zootecnia *f*; ~ **protein factor** *n* (*APF*) AGRIC, FOOD factor de proteína animal *m* (*FPA*); ~ **research** *n* AGRIC investigación animal *f*, investigación pecuaria *f*; ~ **size** *n* COLOUR cola *f*, gelatina *f*; ~ **starch** *n* FOOD almidón animal *m*; ~ **unit** *n* (*AU*) AGRIC unidad animal *f* (*UA*)

animate *vt* CINEMAT animar

animated: ~ **cartoon** *n* CINEMAT dibujo animado *m*; ~ **film** *n* CINEMAT película animada *f*

animation: ~ **backlight** *n* CINEMAT iluminación posterior para animación *f*; ~ **bench** *n* CINEMAT mesa de animación *f*; ~ **camera** *n* CINEMAT cámara para animación *f*; ~ **cell** *n* CINEMAT celda de animación *f*; ~ **director** *n* CINEMAT director de animación *m*

animator *n* CINEMAT animador *m*

anime: ~ **varnish** *n* COATINGS, COLOUR barniz anímico *m*

anion *n* CHEM, COAL anión *m*, ELEC, ELEC ENG, ELECTRON anión *m*, ión negativo *m*, FOOD anión *m*, PART PHYS anión *m*, ión negativo *m*, átomo ionizado negativamente *m*, PHYS, RAD PHYS anión *m*, ión negativo *m*; ~ **exchanger** *n* COAL intercambiador de aniones *m*

anionic[1] *adj* GEN aniónico

anionic[2]: ~ **detergent** *n* DETERG detergente aniónico *m*; ~ **exchanger** *n* DETERG intercambiador aniónico *m*; ~ **surface-active agent** *n* CHEM surfactante aniónico *m*, DETERG agente tensoactivo aniónico *m*, surfactante aniónico *m*

anionotropy *n* CHEM anionotropía *f*

anisaldehyde *n* CHEM *perfumes* anisaldehído *f*

anisian *n* GEOL *metal, cell* anisiense *m*

anisidine *n* CHEM anisidina *f*

anisochronous: ~ **transmission** *n* COMP&DP transmisión anisócrona *f*

anisoelastic[1] *adj* SPACE *gyroscopes* anisoelástico

anisoelastic[2]: ~ **drift** *n* SPACE *gyroscopes* variación anisoelástica *f*

anisoelasticity *n* SPACE *gyroscopes* anisoelasticidad *f*; ~ **factor** *n* SPACE *gyroscopes* factor de anisoelasticidad *m*

anisole *n* CHEM *perfumes*, FOOD anisol *m*

anisotropic *adj* GEN anisotrópico, anisótropo

anisotropy *n* GEN anisotropía *f*; ~ **of turbulence** *n* FLUID anisotropía de turbulencia *f*

ankaramite *n* PETROL ankaramita *f*

ankerite *n* MINERAL ankerita *f*

annatto *n* FOOD bija *f*

anneal[1] *n* C&G, CRYSTALL, HEAT, MECH, NUCL, THERMO *metallurgy* recocido *m*

anneal[2] *vt* C&G fijar por calor, recocer, HEAT recocer, MECH *process* destemplar, fijar por calor, recocer, revenir (*Esp*), METALL destemplar, NUCL, THERMO recocer

annealed *adj* C&G, CRYSTALL, HEAT, MECH, NUCL, THERMO recocido; ~ **under gas** *adj* THERMO recocido con gas

annealing *n* C&G, CRYSTALL, HEAT, MECH, NUCL, THERMO recocido *m*; ~ **bath** *n* THERMO baño de recocido *m*; ~ **furnace** *n* C&G horno de recocer *m*, MECH *process*, NUCL, THERMO horno de recocido *m*; ~ **kiln** *n* C&G horno de recocido *m*; ~ **lehr** *n* C&G *for plate glass* horno de recocido *m*; ~ **lehr with rollers** *n*

C&G *for flat glass* horno de recocido con rodillos *m*; ~ **range** *n* C&G temperatura de recocido *f*; ~ **schedule** *n* C&G programa de recocido *m*

annex *AmE see* **annexe** *BrE*

annexe *n* *BrE* CONST anejo *m*, anexo *m*; ~ **block** *n* *BrE* MECH ENG edificio anexo *m*

annihilation *n* NUCL, PART PHYS, PHYS aniquilación *f*; ~ **photon** *n* RAD PHYS fotón de aniquiliación *m*; ~ **radiation** *n* RAD PHYS radiación de aniquilación *f*

annotation *n* COMP&DP, PROD, TELECOM anotación *f*

announcement: ~ **machine** *n* TELECOM máquina de avisos *f*

annual *n* AGRIC *plant* planta anual *f*; ~ **bluegrass** *n* AGRIC pastillo de invierno *m*; ~ **capacity factor** *n* FUELLESS factor de capacidad anual *m*; ~ **dose equivalent limit** *n* NUCL límite de dosis equivalente anual *m*; ~ **evaporation** *n* WATER evaporación anual *f*; ~ **flood** *n* WATER crecida anual *f*; ~ **flow** *n* WATER caudal anual *m*; ~ **limit on intake** *n* (*ALI*) NUCL límite anual de incorporación *m* (*LAI*); ~ **load** *n* WATER carga anual *f*; ~ **mean water level** *n* WATER nivel medio anual del agua *m*; ~ **natural background radiation** *n* RAD PHYS tasa anual de radiación de fondo *f*; ~ **ring** *n* AGRIC anillo de crecimiento *m*; ~ **runoff** *n* WATER aportación *f*, escorrentía anual *f*

annular[1] *adj* AIR TRANSP, C&G, ELECTRON, GAS anular, GEOM, MECH anular, en forma de anillo, MECH ENG en forma de anillo, PHYS, SPACE, TV, WATER anular

annular[2]: ~ **air gap** *n* NUCL huelgo anular *m*; ~ **borer** *n* MINE sondeadora de corona *f*; ~ **bushing** *n* C&G casquillo anular *m*; ~ **channel** *n* NUCL canal anular *m*; ~ **core** *n* NUCL *fixed equipment* núcleo anular *m*; ~ **crack** *n* C&G *in bottle finish* hendidura anular *f*; ~ **drainage** *n* WATER drenaje anular *m*; ~ **film boiling** *n* NUCL ebullición pelicular anular *f*; ~ **fuel element** *n* NUCL elemento de combustible anular *m*; ~ **gear** *n* MECH ENG engranaje de dientes interiores *m*; ~ **kiln** *n* C&G horno anular *m*; ~ **magnet** *n* PHYS imán anular *m* (*Esp*), imán con forma de anillo *m* (*AmL*), TV imán anular *m*, imán con forma de anillo *m* (*AmL*); ~ **momentum** *n* AIR TRANSP momento anular *m*; ~ **resonator** *n* ELECTRON resonador anular *m*; ~ **saw** *n* MECH ENG sierra circular *f*; ~ **space** *n* GAS, PETR TECH espacio anular *m*

annulus *n* AIR TRANSP anillo *m*, corona *f*, GEOM anillo *m*, ánulo *m*, PETR TECH anillo *m*, anular *m*, corona circular *f*, PETROL espacio anular *m*, SPACE anillo *m*, corona circular *f*, toro *m*

annunciator *n* ELEC ENG cuadro indicador *m*, panel de señalización eléctrica *m*, SPACE avisador *m*; ~ **panel** *n* PROD cuadro indicador *m*

anode *n* GEN ánodo *m*; ~ **characteristic** *n* ELEC ENG característica del ánodo *f*, ánodo característico *m*; ~ **circuit** *n* ELEC, ELEC ENG circuito del ánodo *m*; ~ **circuit breaker** *n* ELEC, ELEC ENG cortacircuito anódico *m*, cortacircuito de ánodo *m*; ~ **current** *n* ELEC ENG corriente del ánodo *f*; ~ **drop** *n* GAS caída anódica de voltaje *f*, caída de tensión anódica *f*; ~ **modulation** *n* ELECTRON modulación del ánodo *f*; ~ **ray** *n* ELEC ENG rayo del ánodo *m*, RAD PHYS rayo anódico *m*; ~ **saturation** *n* ELEC ENG saturación del ánodo *f*; ~ **voltage** *n* ELEC ENG voltaje del ánodo *m*

anodic[1] *adj* GEN anódico

anodic[2]:~ **coat** *n* COATINGS capa anódica *f*; ~ **coating** *n* COATINGS revestimiento anódico *m*

anodize *vt* CHEM, COATINGS, PRINT, WATER TRANSP anodizar

anodized: ~ **aluminium plate** *n* BrE PRINT plancha de aluminio anodizada *f*; ~ **aluminum plate** *AmE see anodized aluminium plate BrE*

anomalous: ~ **dispersion** *n* PHYS dispersión anómala *f*; ~ **scattering** *n* CRYSTALL dispersión anómala *f*; ~ **Zeeman effect** *n* PHYS efecto Zeeman anómalo *m*

anomaly *n* GEN anomalía *f*, irregularidad *f*

anomer *n* CHEM anómero *m*

anorogenic *adj* GEOL anorogénico

anorthite *n* C&G anortita *f*

anorthosite *n* PETROL anortosita *f*

ANOVA *abbr* (*analysis of variance*) COMP&DP ANOVA (*análisis de varianza*)

ANSI *abbr* (*American National Standards Institute*) PROD ANSI (*Instituto Americano de Normalización Nacional*)

answer: ~ **print** *n* CINEMAT primera copia *f*; ~ **signal** *n* TELECOM señal de respuesta *f*

answerback *n* TELECOM respuesta automática *f*

answering: ~ **pennant** *n* WATER TRANSP *international code of signals* gallardete característico *m*, gallardete de inteligencia *m*; ~ **service** *n* TELECOM servicio de contestador *m*

antacid *n* CHEM antiácido *m*

antagonistic: ~ **torque** *n* AIR TRANSP par antagonista *m*

antechamber *n* AUTO antecámara *f*

antenna *n* AmE (*cf aerial BrE*) GEN antena *f*; ~ **array** *n* AmE SPACE red de antenas *f*; ~ **directivity** *n* AmE TELECOM, TV directividad de la antena *f*; ~ **efficiency** *n* AmE TV eficacia de la antena *f*; ~ **gain** *n* AmE PHYS, SPACE, TV ganancia de antena *f*; ~ **lead** *n* AmE TV bajada de antena *f*; ~ **mast** *n* AmE TV, WATER TRANSP mástil de antena *m*; ~-**pointing loss** *n* AmE TELECOM pérdida por apuntamiento de la antena *f*; ~ **system** *n* AmE SPACE sistema de antenas *m*; ~ **terminal** *n* AmE TV borne de antena *m*

antennafier *n* TV antena amplificadora *f*

anthracene *n* CHEM antraceno *m*; ~ **dye** *n* CHEM colorante de antraceno *m*; ~ **oil** *n* CHEM aceite de antraceno *m*

anthracite *n* COAL hulla brillante *f*; ~ **coal** *n* COAL carbón de antracita *m*

anthracnose *n* AGRIC *plant pathology* antracnosis *f*

anthragallol *n* CHEM antragalol *m*

anthropic: ~ **soil** *n* AGRIC suelo antrópico *m*

anthropogenic: ~ **acidification** *n* POLL acidificación antropogénica *f*

anthryl *n* CHEM antril *m*, antrilo *m*

anti-abrasion: ~ **coating** *n* CINEMAT revestimiento antiabrasivo *m*; ~ **layer** *n* COATINGS capa antiabrasiva *f*, capa resistente a la abrasión *f*

anti-acid: ~ **film** *n* COATINGS película antiácida *f*

anti-adhesive: ~ **paper** *n* PACK papel anti-adhesivo *m*

anti-air: ~ **camouflage equipment** *n* MILIT equipo de camuflaje antiaéreo *m*

anti-aliasing *n* COMP&DP antisolapamiento *m*; ~ **filter** *n* ELECTRON filtro anti-ajeno *m*; ~ **filtering** *n* ELECTRON filtrado anti-ajeno *m*

anti-armor: ~ **warhead** *AmE see anti-armour warhead BrE*

anti-armour: ~ **warhead** *n* BrE MILIT cabeza de combate contra blindaje *f*

antibaryon *n* PART PHYS antibarión *m*

antiblocking: ~ **agent** *n* CHEM agente antibloqueante *m*, P&R agente antibloqueante *m*, antibloqueante *m*; ~ **system** *n* (*ABS*) AUTO sistema antibloqueo *m* (*ABS*)

antibonding: ~ **atomic orbital** *n* RAD PHYS orbital atómico antienlazante *m*; ~ **electron** *n* RAD PHYS electrón antienlazante *m*; ~ **molecular orbital** *n* RAD PHYS orbital molecular antienlazante *m*

anticaking: ~ **agent** *n* CHEM agente antipelmazante *m*, FOOD agente antiapelmazante *m*

anticapillary: ~ **course** *n* CONST capa anticapilar *f*

anticatalyst *n* FOOD anticatalizador *m*, inhibidor de catálisis *m*

anticathode *n* ELEC *X-ray tube*, PART PHYS, PHYS anticátodo *m*

antication *n* RAD PHYS anticatión *m*

anticipated: ~ **operating conditions** *n pl* AIR TRANSP condiciones de operación previstas *f pl*; ~ **transient without scream** *n* (*ATWS*) NUCL transitorio previsto sin parada de emergencia *m* (*ATWS*)

anticlinal[1] *adj* GAS anticlinal

anticlinal[2]: ~ **trap** *n* PETR TECH trampa anticlinal *f*

anticline *n* GEOL anticlinal *m*, MINE anticlinal *m*, bóveda *f*, portada *f*, PETR TECH anticlinal *m*

anticlinical *adj* MINE anticlinical

anticlinorium *n* GEOL anticlinorio *m*

anticlockwise: ~ **rotation** *n* MECH rotación a izquierdas *f*, rotación en dirección contraria a las agujas del reloj *f*, rotación siniestrosa *f*, rotación sinistrorsa *f*

anticlutter: ~ **control** *n* WATER TRANSP *radar* mando del supresor de parásitos *m*

anticoincidence *n* ELECTRON *heat unit*, NUCL, PHYS anticoincidencia *f*; ~ **circuit** *n* PHYS circuito de anticoincidencia *m*

anticollision: ~ **light** *n* AIR TRANSP luz anticolisión *f*; ~ **marker** *n* WATER TRANSP indicador para evitar abordajes *m*

anticorrosion: ~ **additive** *n* PETR TECH aditivo anticorrosión *m*; ~ **agent** *n* CHEM, PETR TECH agente anticorrosivo *m*; ~ **coating** *n* NUCL revestimiento anticorrosión *m*; ~ **oil** *n* PROD aceite anticorrosivo *m*; ~ **paint** *n* COATINGS pintura anticorrosiva *f*; ~ **paper** *n* PACK papel anti-corrosivo *m*

anticorrosive[1] *adj* COLOUR, MECH, P&R, PACK anticorrosivo

anticorrosive[2]: ~ **coating** *n* COATINGS baño anticorrosivo *m*, P&R baño anticorrosivo *m*, pintura anticorrosiva *f*; ~ **film** *n* PACK película anti-corrosiva *f*; ~ **paint** *n* COLOUR pintura anticorrosiva *f*; ~ **primer** *n* COATINGS imprimación anticorrosiva *f*

anticyclogenesis *n* METEO anticiclogénesis *f*

anticyclone *n* METEO alta *f*, anticlón *m*, zona de alta presión *f*

anticyclonic: ~ **circulation** *n* METEO circulación anticiclónica *f*, rotación anticiclónica *f*; ~ **growth** *n* METEO incremento de situación anticiclónica *m*, intensificación del anticiclón *f*; ~ **rotation** *n* METEO rotación anticiclónica *f*

antidazzle[1] *adj* C&G, CINEMAT, INSTR, SAFE, VEH antideslumbrante

antidazzle[2]: ~ **glass** *n* C&G, SAFE cristal antideslumbrante *m*; ~ **glasses** *n pl* INSTR gafas antideslumbrantes *f pl*; ~ **visor** *n* BrE (*cf antiglare vizor AmE*) VEH visera antideslumbrante *f*

antideflection: ~ **roll** *n* PAPER rodillo para evitar el combado *m*

antidive: ~ **fork** *n* VEH horquilla estabilizadora *f*; ~ **suspension** *n* VEH *motorcycle* suspensión *f*

antidote *n* CHEM, SAFE antídoto *m*

anti-drift: ~ **units** *n pl* MECH, MECH ENG antideslizantes *m pl*, antidesplazantes *m pl*

antidust: ~ **filter** *n* GAS filtro antipolvo *m*

anti-enzyme *n* FOOD inhibidor enzimático *m*

antiferromagnetic *adj* ELEC, PHYS antiferromagnético

antiferromagnetism *n* ELEC, PHYS antiferromagnetismo *m*

antiflash: ~ **varnish** *n* COATINGS, COLOUR barniz antiveteado *m*

anti-flicker: ~ **blade** *n* CINEMAT paleta antivibratoria *f*

antifoamer *n* CHEM, COAL, P&R, PACK, PAPER, PETR TECH antiespumante *m*

antifoaming: ~ **agent** *n* CHEM, COAL, P&R agente antiespumante *m*, antiespumante *m*, PACK, PAPER antiespumante *m*, PETR TECH agente antiespumante *m*, antiespumante *m*

antifog: ~ **film** *n* PACK película antivaho *f*

antifoggant *n* CINEMAT, PHOTO antivelo *m*

antifogging: ~ **agent** *n* CHEM, CINEMAT, PHOTO agente antivelo *m*

antifouling: ~ **composition** *n* COATINGS composición antiincrustante *f*; ~ **paint** *n* COATINGS pintura antiincrustante *f* (*AmL*), pintura antiséptica *f* (*Esp*), P&R pintura antiincrustante *f*, pintura antipútrida *f*, WATER TRANSP *ship maintenance* pintura antiincrustante *f*

antifreeze *n* GEN anticongelante *m*; ~ **agent** *n* PACK, REFRIG agente anticongelante *m*; ~ **paper** *n* PAPER papel anticongelante *m*

antifreezing *adj* GEN anticongelante

antifret: ~ **plate** *n* SPACE placa antirozamiento *f*

antifriction[1] *adj* MECH, MECH ENG, PROD antifricción

antifriction[2]: ~ **bearing** *n* MECH ENG *roller bearing* cojinete de metal antifricción *m*, PROD cojinete antifricción *m*; ~ **lining** *n* MECH ENG recubrimiento antifricción *m*

antifroth *n* CHEM, COAL, P&R, PACK, PAPER, PETR TECH antiespumante *m*

anti-G *abbr* (*antigravity*) SPACE antigravitatorio

anti-g: ~ **suit** *n* SPACE *spacecraft* traje para contrarrestar de la aceleración *m*

anti-gas: ~ **shelter** *n* MILIT refugio contra gases *m*

antigen *n* CHEM antígeno *m*

antiglare *n* C&G, CINEMAT, SAFE, VEH antideslumbrante *m*; ~ **coating** *n* TELECOM revestimiento antideslumbrante *m*; ~ **glasses** *n pl* INSTR gafas antideslumbrantes *f pl*; ~ **vizor** *n* AmE (*cf antidazzle visor BrE*) VEH *accessory* visera antideslumbrante *f*

antigravity[1] *adj* (*anti-G*) SPACE antigravitatorio

antigravity[2] *n* SPACE antiaceleración de la gravedad *f*, compensación de la gravedad *f*

antihalation: ~ **backing** *n* PHOTO respaldo antihalo *m*, PRINT capa protectora antihalo *f*; ~ **layer** *n* CINEMAT capa antihalo *f* (*AmL*)

antihalo: ~ **layer** *n* PHOTO capa antihalo *f* (*AmL*), revestimiento antihalo *m* (*Esp*)

anti-icing *n* SPACE anticongelamiento *m*, antihielo *m*; ~ **system** *n* SPACE sistema anticongelamiento *m*, sistema antihielo *m*

anti-interference[1] *adj* ELEC *protection* contra las interferencias

anti-interference[2] *n* ELEC *protection* antiinterferencia *f*

antiknock: ~ **additive** *n* AUTO, POLL, VEH aditivo antidetonante *m*; ~ **agent** *n* AUTO, POLL, VEH aditivo antidetonante *m*

antilock: ~ **brake system** *n* VEH sistema antibloqueo de frenos *m*; ~ **system** *n* VEH sistema antibloqueo *m*

antilocking: ~ **system** *n* MECH *position of spacecraft* dispositivo antienclavamiento *m*

antilogarithm *n* MATH antilogaritmo *m*

antilogous: ~ **pole** *n* CRYSTALL *pyroelectricity* polo antílogo *m*

antimatter *n* NUCL, PART PHYS, PHYS antimateria *f*

antimonial *adj* CHEM antimoniado

antimoniate *n* CHEM antimoniato *m*

antimonic *adj* CHEM antimónico

antimonide *n* CHEM antimoniuro *m*

antimonite *n* CHEM, MINERAL antimonita *f*

antimony *n* (*Sb*) C&G, CHEM, METALL antimonio *m* (*Sb*)

antineutrino *n* NUCL, PART PHYS antineutrino *m*

antineutron *n* PHYS antineutrón *m*

antinodal: ~ **line** *n* ACOUST línea antinodal *f*

antinode *n* ACOUST, ELEC antinodo *m*, vientre *m*, ELEC ENG, PHYS antinodo *m*, WAVE PHYS antinodo *m*, sección ventral *f*

antinoise[1] *adj* ACOUST, SAFE antiparasitario

antinoise[2] *n* ACOUST antiparásito *m*, antirruido *m*, SAFE antiparásito *m*

anti-offset: ~ **spray** *n* PRINT rociador antimaculante *m*

antioxidant[1] *adj* AUTO, COATINGS, FOOD, MECH, P&R, PACK antioxidante

antioxidant[2] *n* AUTO, COATINGS, FOOD, MECH, P&R, PACK antioxidante *m*

antiparallel[1] *adj* ELEC anticipado, ELECTRON, GEOM antiparalelo

antiparallel[2] *n* GEOM antiparalelo *m*; ~ **arrangement** *n* ELEC ENG disposición antiparalelo *f*; ~ **connection** *n* ELEC acoplamiento antiparalelo *m*, conexión antiparalela *f*

antiparticle *n* PART PHYS, PHYS antipartícula *f*

antipersonnel[1] *adj* (*AP*) MILIT antipersonal

antipersonnel[2]: ~ **mine** *n* MILIT mina contra tropas *f*

antiperthite *n* MINERAL antipertita *f*

antiphase[1] *adv* TV antifase, contrafase

antiphase[2]: ~ **boundary** *n* CRYSTALL límite de antifase *m*

antipodes *n pl* GEOM antípodas *m pl*

antipollution *adj* AUTO, MAR POLL, MECH, POLL, VEH contra la contaminación

antiproton *n* PART PHYS, PHYS antiprotón *m*

antiquark *n* PART PHYS, PHYS antiquark *m*

antique: ~ **drawn glass** *n* C&G vidrio estirado *m*; ~ **face** *n* PRINT tipo antiguo *m*; ~ **glass** *n* C&G cristalería soplada *f*

anti-radiation: ~ **missile** *n* (*ARM*) MILIT misil antirradiación *m*

antiredepositing *n* DETERG antirredeposición *f*

antiredeposition: ~ **agent** *n* CHEM, DETERG agente de antirredeposición *m*

antireflecting: ~ **treatment** *n* C&G tratamiento antirreflector *m*

antireflection: ~ **coating** *n* C&G, CINEMAT revestimiento antirreflector *m*, OPT revestimiento antirreflector *m*, revestimiento antirreflejante *m*, PHOTO revestimiento antirreflector *m*, SPACE recubrimiento antirreflexión *m*, TELECOM revestimiento antirreflector *m*

antireflective: ~ **coating** *n* COATINGS revestimiento antirreflectante *m*, TELECOM revestimiento antirreflector *m*

antireset: ~ **wind-up** *n* PROD mecanismo de contrarreajuste *m*

antiresonance *n* ACOUST, ELECTRON antirresonancia *f*

antiresonant: ~ **circuit** *n* AIR TRANSP, ELECTRON, PHYS circuito antirresonante *m*

antiroll: ~ **bar** *n* AIR TRANSP barra antialabeo *f*, AUTO barra estabilizadora *f*, MECH, SPACE barra antibalanceo *f*, VEH barra estabilizadora *f*

antirolling: ~ **device** *n* WATER TRANSP dispositivo antibalance *m*

antirust[1] *adj* AUTO antioxidante, COATINGS antiherrumbroso, antioxidante, FOOD antioxidante, MECH, P&R, PACK antiherrumbroso, antioxidante

antirust[2]: ~ **paint** *n* COATINGS pintura anticorrosiva *f*, P&R pintura antioxidante *f*; ~ **paper** *n* PACK, PAPER papel antioxidante *m*

antirusting: ~ **primer** *n* COATINGS imprimación antioxidante *f*

antisatellite: ~ **laser** *n* ELECTRON láser antisatélite *m*

antiscorching: ~ **agent** *n* CHEM, P&R agente antichamuscante *m*

antiscratch: ~ **solution** *n* CHEM agente antimancha *m*, CINEMAT agente antimancha *m*, solución antirrayas *f*

antiseasickness: ~ **pill** *n* WATER TRANSP píldora contra el mareo *f*

antisettling *adj* P&R antisedimentante

antishrink: ~ **treatment** *n* TEXTIL tratamiento inencogible *m*

antishrinkage: ~ **admixture** *n* CONST aditivo anticontracción *m*

antisidetone *adj* TELECOM eliminador de efectos locales *m*

antiskating *n* ACOUST regulación de fuerza centrípeta *f*

antiskid: ~ **braking system** *n* AUTO sistema de frenado antideslizante *m*; ~ **device** *n* AUTO, VEH dispositivo contra el derrapaje *m*, dispositivo contra el deslizamiento *m*; ~ **unit** *n* AIR TRANSP unidad antideslizante *f*

antiskinning: ~ **agent** *n* CHEM, P&R agente antidespellejante *m*, PRINT producto que evita que la tinta forme una película durante su almacenado *m*

antislide: ~ **pad** *n* PROD almohadilla antirresbaladiza *f*

antislip: ~ **material floor covering** *n* SAFE recubrimiento anti-deslizante para suelos *m*; ~ **operating lever clamp** *n* PROD abrazadera de palanca de funcionamiento antirresbaladizo *f*

antispattering: ~ **agent** *n* CHEM, FOOD agente antisalpicaduras *m*, SPACE *craft* agente salpicaduras *m*

antispill: ~ **bottle** *n* PACK botella inderramable *f*

antisplash: ~ **head** *n* LAB cabeza antisalpicadura *f*

antistain: ~ **agent** *n* CINEMAT antióxido *m*

antistaling: ~ **agent** *n* CHEM, FOOD agente antienvejecimiento *m*

antistatic[1] *adj* CINEMAT, COMP&DP, DETERG antiestático, ELEC *materials* antiestático, contra la estática, ELECTRON contra la estática, MECH, P&R, PHOTO, PRINT, SAFE, TEXTIL antiestático

antistatic[2]: ~ **agent** *n* CHEM, DETERG, P&R, TEXTIL agente antiestático *m*; ~ **backing** *n* PHOTO respaldo antiestático *m*; ~ **brush** *n* PRINT cepillo antiestático *m*; ~ **footwear** *n* SAFE calzado antiestático *m*; ~ **mat** *n* COMP&DP esterilla antiestática *f*; ~ **material** *n* SAFE material antiestático *m*; ~ **protection** *n* MECH ENG protección antiestática *f*; ~ **protective clothing** *n*

SAFE prendas protectoras antiestáticas *f pl*; ~ **rubber** *n* P&R caucho antiestático *m*; ~ **spray** *n* COMP&DP rociador antiestático *m*, PRINT aerosol antiestático *m*, porta de carga *f*

antistiction: ~ **oscillator** *n* ELECTRON oscilador compensador de rozamientos *m*

antistorm: ~ **glazing** *n* C&G esmaltado a prueba de intemperie *m*

antisubmarine[1] *adj* (*A/S*) MILIT antisubmarino

antisubmarine[2]: ~ **defence** *n* BrE MILIT, WATER TRANSP defensa antisubmarina *f*; ~ **defense** AmE *see antisubmarine defence BrE*; ~ **helicopter** *n* AIR TRANSP helicóptero antisubmarino *m*

antisurge: ~ **baffle** *n* AIR TRANSP deflector contra la agitación del aceite *m*, pantalla amortiguadora de oscilación eléctrica *f*, pantalla antisobretensión eléctrica *f*, pantalla antisobrevoltaje *f*; ~ **valve** *n* AIR TRANSP válvula antiagitación *f*, válvula antisobretensión *f*, válvula antisobrevoltaje *f*

antisymmetric: ~ **wave function** *n* PHYS, WAVE PHYS función de onda antisimétrica *f*

antitamper: ~ **cover** *n* PROD protección contra intrusos *f*

antitank: ~ **grenade** *n* MILIT granada anticarro *f*; ~ **guided missile** *n* (*ATGM*) MILIT misil guiado anticarro *m*; ~ **gun** *n* MILIT cañón anticarro *m*; ~ **helicopter** *n* AIR TRANSP helicóptero antitanque *m*; ~ **mine** *n* MILIT mina anticarro *f*

antitarnish: ~ **paper** *n* PAPER papel antivaho *m*

antitheft[1] *adj* AUTO antirrobo, PACK a prueba, QUALITY antirrobo, SAFE antirrobo, contra robos

antitheft[2]: ~ **ignition lock** *n* AUTO cerrojo de ignición antirrobo *m*, llave de contacto antirrobo *f*

antithetic: ~ **fault** *n* GEOL falla antitética *f*

antitorque: ~ **device** *n* AIR TRANSP dispositivo antipar *m*, dispositivo antitorsión *m*; ~ **propeller** *n* AIR TRANSP hélice antitorsión de cola *f*, rotor antitorsión de cola *m*; ~ **rotor** *n* TRANSP rotor antipar *m*

antitrades *n pl* WATER TRANSP *wind* contralísios *m pl*

antivacuum: ~ **valve** *n* FUELLESS *hydroelectricity* válvula contra vacío *f*

antivibration: ~ **table** *n* LAB mesa antivibratoria *f*

antozonite *n* MINERAL antozonita *f*

anular *adj* NUCL nuclear

anvil *n* ACOUST, MECH yunque *m*, MECH ENG *of micrometer* boca *f*, yunque *m*, MINE boca *f* (*AmL*), yunque *m*, PRINT yunque *m*; ~ **block** *n* MECH ENG pilón de forja *m*, *of power hammer* chabota *f*; ~ **die** *n* MECH ENG yunque *m*; ~ **vice** *n* BrE MECH ENG yunque de tornillo de banco *m*; ~ **vise** *AmE see anvil vice BrE*

AOCS *abbr* (*altitude and orbit control system*) SPACE SCPO (*sistema para control de posición y órbita*)

AOQL *abbr* (*average outgoing quality limit*) QUALITY límite de calidad media después de control *m*

AOX *abbr* (*adsorbable organic halogens*) PAPER compuestos organohalogenados adsorbibles *m pl*

AP[1] *abbr* (*antipersonnel*) MILIT antipersonal

AP[2]: ~ **horizon** *n* AGRIC horizonte AP *m*

apastron *n* SPACE apastro *m*, estrella binaria *f*

apatelite *n* MINERAL apatelita *f*

apatite *n* MINERAL apatito *m*

APC *abbr* ELECTRON (*automatic phase control*) control automático de fase *m*, MILIT (*armored personnel carrier AmE, armoured personnel carrier BrE*) transporte de tropas acorazado *m*, TV (*automatic phase control*) control automático de fase *m*

APD *abbr* (*avalanche photodiode*) ELECTRON fotodiodo de avalancha *m*, fotodiodo de descarga *m*, OPT fotodiodo de avalancha *m*

aperiodic[1] *adj* ELEC *galvanometer*, ELECTRON, PHYS, TV aperiódico

aperiodic[2]: ~ **aerial** *n* BrE (*cf aperiodic antenna* AmE) TV antena aperiódica *f*; ~ **antenna** *n* AmE (*cf aperiodic aerial* BrE) TV antena aperiódica *f*; ~ **circuit** *n* ELECTRON circuito aperiódico *m*

aperture *n* AIR TRANSP apertura *f*, C&G agujero *m*, CINEMAT, COMP&DP abertura *f*, CONST apertura *f*, ELEC ENG agujero *m*, apertura *f*, ELECTRON apertura *f*, INSTR apertura *f*, MAR POLL abertura *f*, MECH abertura *f*, agujero *m*, orificio *m*, paso *m*, portillo *m*, rendija *f*, MECH ENG abertura *f*, agujero *m*, METALL abertura *f*, orificio *m*, paso *m*, PHOTO, PHYS abertura *f*, PROD agujero *m*, SPACE *communications* abertura *f*, apertura *f*, TELECOM, TV apertura *f*; ~ **aerial** *n* BrE TELECOM antena de apertura *f*; ~ **angle** *n* CINEMAT, OPT, PHOTO, TV ángulo de abertura *m*; ~ **antenna** *n* AmE TELECOM antena de apertura *f*; ~ **card** *n* COMP&DP tarjeta de apertura *f*; ~ **diaphragm** *n* METALL diafragma de abertura *m*; ~ **distortion** *n* ELECTRON distorsión de abertura *f*; ~ **grill** AmE, ~ **grille** BrE *n* ELECTRON rejilla de abertura *f*, ventana de abertura *f*; ~ **guide** *n* CINEMAT guía de abertura *f*; ~ **mask** *n* ELECTRON máscara de abertura *f*, TV máscara de apertura *f*; ~ **plate** *n* CINEMAT diafragma *m*; ~ **preselector** *n* PHOTO preselector de la abertura *m*; ~ **ratio** *n* CINEMAT abertura relativa *f*; ~ **ring** *n* CINEMAT anillo de abertura *m*, aro de abertura *m*, aro de diafragma *m*, PHOTO, TV anillo de abertura *m*; ~ **scale** *n* PHOTO escala de la abertura *f*; ~**setting lever** *n* PHOTO control para fijar la abertura *m*; ~**setting ring** *n* CINEMAT, PHOTO, TV anillo para fijar la abertura *m*; ~ **stop** *n* CINEMAT, PHOTO, PHYS, TV abertura de diafragma *f*; ~ **top slide** *n* INSTR apertura superior del cursor *f*

apex *n* AGRIC, COAL ápice *m*, GEOM vértice *m*, ápice *m*, MINE enganche superior *m*, cúspide *f* (*Esp*), parte superior *f* (*AmL*), SPACE vértice *m*, ápice *m*

APEX: ~ **fare** *n* (*advance purchase excursion fare*) AIR TRANSP precio APEX *m* (*precio de la excursión de reserva por adelantado*)

APF *abbr* (*animal protein factor*) AGRIC, FOOD FPA (*factor de proteína animal*)

aphanesite *n* MINERAL afanesita *f*

aphanite *n* GEOL, PETROL afanita *f*

aphanitic *adj* GEOL, PETROL afanítico

aphelion *n* PHYS, SPACE afelio *m*

aphid *n* AGRIC *plant pathology* pulgón *m*, áfido *m*

aphrite *n* MINERAL afrita *f*, caliza espumosa *f*

aphrizite *n* MINERAL afrizita *f*

aphrodite *n* MINERAL afrodita *f*

aphrosiderite *n* MINERAL afrosiderita *f*

aphthalmometer *n* OPT oftalmómetro *m*

aphthalose *n* MINERAL aftalosa *f*

aphthitalite *n* MINERAL aftitalita *f*

aphthonite *n* MINERAL aftonita *f*

aphthous: ~ **fever** *n* AGRIC fiebre aftosa *f*, glosopeda *f*

aphyric *adj* GEOL *equipment* afírico

API: ~ **gravity** *n* PETR TECH densidad API *f*, PETROL gravedad API *f*

apiculture *n* AGRIC apicultura *f*

apiin *n* CHEM apiína *f*

apionol *n* CHEM apionol *m*

apjohnite *n* MINERAL apjohnita *f*

aplanatic: ~ **lens** *n* CINEMAT, PHOTO objetivo aplanático *m*

aplite *n* GEOL, PETROL aplita *f*

aplitic *adj* GEOL, PETROL aplítico

aplome *n* MINERAL andradita *f*, aplomo *m*

apnea AmE *see* apnoea BrE

apnoea *n* BrE OCEAN apnea *f*, suspensión de la respiración *f*

apochromat *n* CINEMAT, OPT, PHOTO, PHYS objetivo apocromático *m*

apochromatic[1] *adj* PRINT apocromático

apochromatic[2]: ~ **correction** *n* PHOTO corrección apocromática *f*; ~ **lens** *n* CINEMAT, OPT, PHOTO, PHYS objetivo apocromático *m*

apogee *n* PHYS apogeo *m*, SPACE apogeo *m*, auge *m*; ~ **maneuver** AmE, ~ **manoeuvre** BrE *n* SPACE maniobra de apogeo *f*; ~ **motor** *n* SPACE motor de apogeo *m*

apophyllite *n* MINERAL apofilita *f*

apostrophe *n* PRINT *bed* apóstrofo *m*

apothem *n* GEOM apotema *f*

apotome *n* ACOUST apótome *m*

apparatus *n* ELEC, ELECTRON, LAB, MECH, MECH ENG aparato *m*, PHOTO *of liquids* aparato *m*, equipo *m*, WATER TRANSP aparato *m*; ~ **charge rate** *n* TELECOM régimen de carga de aparatos *m*; ~ **dew point** *n* REFRIG punto de rocío equivalente *m*

apparent: ~ **altitude** *n* WATER TRANSP *sextant* altura aparente *f*; ~ **density** *n* COAL, P&R, PAPER *of board* densidad aparente *f*; ~ **energy** *n* ELEC energía aparente *f*; ~ **energy meter** *n* ELEC contador de energía aparente *m*; ~ **modulus of elasticity** *n* P&R límite aparente de elasticidad *m*, módulo aparente de elasticidad *m*; ~ **pitch** *n* MECH ENG *screws* paso aparente *m*; ~ **porosity** *n* C&G porosidad aparente *f*; ~ **powder density** *n* P&R densidad aparente *f*, densidad aparente de los polvos de moldeo *f*; ~ **power** *n* ELEC potencia aparente *f*, ELEC ENG energía aparente *f*, PHYS energía aparente *f*, potencia aparente *f*; ~ **power meter** *n* ELEC contador de energía aparente *m*, medidor de potencia aparente *m*; ~ **resistivity** *n* PETROL resistividad aparente *f*; ~ **sedimentation density** *n* CHEM TECH densidad aparente de sedimentación *f*; ~ **specific gravity** *n* PAPER peso específico aparente *m*; ~ **utilization of oxygen** *n* OCEAN utilización aparente de oxígeno *f*; ~ **velocity** *n* GEOPHYS velocidad aparente *f*; ~ **water table** *n* WATER nivel aparente del agua *m*, nivel freático aparente *m*; ~ **wind** *n* WATER TRANSP *navigation* viento aparente *m*

appearance *n* PAPER aspecto *m*; ~ **cover** *n* COATINGS capa final *f*

appendix *n* PRINT apéndice *m*

Applegate: ~ **diagram** *n* ELECTRON *coil* diagrama de posición electrónica *m*

Appleton: ~ **layer** *n* PHYS *at canal-lock* capa de Appleton *f*

appliance *n* AIR TRANSP instrumento *m*, MECH ENG dispositivo *m*, instrumento *m*, mecanismo *m*, máquina *f*, PETR TECH instrumento *m*, PROD artefacto *m*, instrumento *m*, SPACE, TELECOM, TRANSP, VEH, WATER TRANSP instrumento *m*

application *n* COMP&DP aplicación *f*, MECH aplicación

f, empleo *m*, utilización *f*; ~ **appliance label** *n* TELE-COM etiqueta para la utilización de aplicaciones *f*; ~ **association** *n* TELECOM asociación de aplicaciones *f*; ~ **consideration** *n* PROD consideración de aplicación *f*; ~ **context** *n* TELECOM contexto de aplicaciones *m*; ~ **entry** *n* (*AE*) TELECOM entrada de aplicaciones *f*; ~ **layer** *n* COMP&DP, TELECOM *open systems interconnection* capa de aplicación *f*, nivel de aplicación *m*; ~ **layer structure** *n* TELECOM estructura de capas de aplicación *f*; ~ **level gateway** *n* TELECOM acceso a nivel de aplicaciones *m*; ~ **of microprocessors to gaging systems** *AmE*, ~ **of microprocessors to gauging systems** *BrE n* MECH ENG aplicación de microprocesores a sistemas de calibración *f*; ~**-oriented language** *n* COMP&DP lenguaje orientado a aplicaciones *m*; ~ **package** *n* COMP&DP paquete de aplicación *m*; ~ **program** *n* COMP&DP programa de aplicación *m*; ~ **rate** *n* CONST porcentaje de aplicación *m*, MAR POLL tasa de aplicación *f*; ~ **reference** *n* TELECOM referencia de aplicación *f*; ~ **roller** *n* PACK rodillo aplicador *m*; ~ **service element** *n* (*ASE*) TELECOM elemento del servicio de aplicación *m*; ~**-specific integrated circuit** *n* (*ASIC*) COMP&DP circuito integrado de aplicación específica *m* (*CIAE*)

applications: ~ **processor** *n* TELECOM procesador de aplicaciones *m*; ~ **software** *n* COMP&DP software de aplicación *m*

applicative: ~ **language** *n* COMP&DP lenguaje aplicativo *m*

applicator: ~ **head** *n* PACK cabeza aplicadora *f*; ~ **roll** *n* PAPER rodillo aplicador *m*

applied: ~ **chemistry** *n* CHEM química aplicada *f*; ~ **electromagnetic force** *n* PART PHYS, PHYS fuerza electromagnética aplicada *f*; ~ **electromotive force** *n* ELEC *voltage*, ELEC ENG, PHYS fuerza electromotriz aplicada *f*; ~ **research** *n* POLL investigación aplicada *f*; ~ **stress** *n* METALL esfuerzo aplicado *m*, esfuerzo real *m*; ~ **thermodynamics** *n* MECH ENG termodinámica aplicada *f*; ~ **thread** *n* C&G filete del husillo aplicado *m*

apply *vt* CINEMAT, COATINGS, ELEC ENG aplicar, MECH aplicar, fijar, poner; ~ **for** *vt* MECH, PROD, TEXTIL *patents, permissions* solicitar; ~ **power to** *vt* ELEC ENG aplicar energía a

applying: ~ **joint bar** *n* *AmE* RAIL eclisa *f*

apportion *vt* PROD aplicar, prorratear, repartir

apportioned *adj* COMP&DP, PROD repartido

apportionment *n* METR dosificación *f*

appraisal: ~ **cost** *n* QUALITY costo de valoración *m*; ~ **drilling** *n* PETR TECH perforación de evaluación *f*, sondeo de apreciación *m*; ~ **well** *n* PETR TECH pozo de evaluación *m*, sondeo de evaluación *m*, PETROL pozo de evaluación *m* (*Esp*)

approach[1] *n* AIR TRANSP *flight* aproximación *f*, CONST *means of access* vía de acceso *f*, OCEAN aterrada *f*, acceso *m*, SPACE aproximación *f*, acercamiento *m*, WATER TRANSP *to land* aproximación *f*; ~ **channel** *n* WATER TRANSP canal de acceso *m*; ~ **chart** *n* AIR TRANSP carta de aproximación *f*; ~ **clearance** *n* AIR TRANSP permiso de aproximación *m*; ~ **control** *n* AIR TRANSP control de aproximación *m*; ~ **control office** *n* AIR TRANSP oficina de control de aproximación *f*; ~ **control rating** *n* AIR TRANSP clasificación de control de aproximación *f*; ~ **control service** *n* AIR TRANSP servicio de control de aproximación *m*;

~ **elevation guidance** *n* AIR TRANSP guía de elevación de aproximación *f*; ~ **fix** *n* AIR TRANSP fijación de aproximación *f*, posición de aproximación *f*; ~ **flow** *n* PAPER candal de pasta que llega a la máquina de papel *m*; ~ **funnel** *n* AIR TRANSP cono de aproximación *m*, embudo de aproximación *m*; ~ **guidance** *n* SPACE guía de acercamiento *f*, guía de aproximación *f*; ~ **idling conditions** *n pl* AIR TRANSP condiciones de aproximación en ralentí *f pl*, condiciones de espera de aproximación *f pl*; ~ **light beacon** *n* AIR TRANSP baliza luminosa de aproximación *f*; ~ **lighting system** *n* AIR TRANSP sistema de alumbrado de aproximación *m*, sistema de balizado luminoso de aproximación *m*; ~**-locked route** *n* RAIL itinerario con enclavamiento de aproximación *m*; ~ **noise measurement point** *n* AIR TRANSP punto de medida del ruido de aproximación *m*; ~ **path** *n* AIR TRANSP trayectoria de aproximación *f*; ~ **phase** *n* AIR TRANSP fase de aproximación *f*; ~ **point** *n* AIR TRANSP punto de aproximación *m*; ~ **procedure** *n* SPACE procedimiento de acercamiento *m*; ~ **reference noise measurement point** *n* AIR TRANSP punto de medida del ruido de referencia de aproximación *m*; ~ **sequence** *n* AIR TRANSP orden de aproximación *m*; ~ **speed** *n* AIR TRANSP velocidad de aproximación *f*, SPACE velocidad de acercamiento *f*; ~ **time** *n* AIR TRANSP tiempo de aproximación *m*

approach[2] *vt* AIR TRANSP aproximar, MINE acercar, aproximar, WATER TRANSP aproximar

appropriate: ~ **airworthiness requirements** *n pl* AIR TRANSP requerimientos de aeronavegabilidad apropiados *m pl*

approval *n* AIR TRANSP aceptación *f*, aprobación *f*, QUALITY aprobación *f*, VEH aprobación *f*, visto bueno *m*; ~ **certificate** *n* AIR TRANSP certificado de aceptación *m*, certificado de aprobación *m*; ~ **cost** *n* QUALITY costo de aprobación *m*; ~ **period** *n* QUALITY período de aprobación *m*; ~ **print** *n* CINEMAT copia de aprobación *f*; ~ **sign** *n* METR *communications* visto bueno *m*; ~ **standard** *n* QUALITY norma de aprobación *f*; ~ **system** *n* QUALITY sistema de aprobación *m*; ~ **test** *n* QUALITY prueba de aprobación *f*, SPACE ensayo de aprobación *m*, prueba de aprobación *f*; ~ **testing** *n* QUALITY ensayo de aprobación *m*

approve *vt* AIR TRANSP, QUALITY, SAFE aprobar

approved[1] *adj* AIR TRANSP, QUALITY, SAFE, TELECOM aprobado

approved[2]: ~ **first aid certificate** *n* SAFE certificado aprobado de primeros auxilios *m*; ~ **footwear** *n* SAFE calzado aprobado *m*; ~ **organization** *n* QUALITY organización autorizada *f*; ~ **safety area** *n* SAFE zona de seguridad autorizada *f*; ~ **safety lamp** *n* COAL lámpara protectora aprobada *f*

approximate[1] *adj* MATH aproximado

approximate[2]: ~ **execution time** *n* PROD tiempo aproximado de ejecución *m*; ~ **weight** *n* PACK peso aproximado *m*

approximate[3] *vt* MATH aproximar

approximation *n* MATH aproximación *f*; ~ **error** *n* TELECOM error de aproximación *m*; ~ **to the nearest millimeter** *AmE*, ~ **to the nearest millimetre** *BrE n* MATH aproximación al milímetro más cercano *f*

apron *n* AGRIC *grading machines* correa sinfín para transportar frutas o vegetales *f*, CONST plataforma *f*, HYDROL *nuclear power plant* muro de defensa *m*, PAPER delantal *m*, PRINT margen suplementario *m*,

PROD *conveyor belt* tablero *m*, SAFE *in fuel pellet delantal m*, WATER TRANSP *boat building* contrarroda *f*; **~ applicator** *n* C&G aplicador de cubierta de protección *m*; **~ board** *n* PAPER placa del delantal *f*; **~ conveyor** *n* CONST transportador de plataforma *m*, MECH ENG *continuous handling equipment* transportador de banda articulada *m*, transportador de estera *m*, transportador de mandil *m*, PACK transportador de banda articulada *m*, transportador de cadena *m*, TRANSP cinta transportadora de mandil *f*, transportador de banda articulada *m*, transportador de mandil *m*; **~ floodlight** *n* ELEC *lighting* lámpara de alta intensidad del proscenio *f*, lámpara de gran amperaje del proscenio *f*, proyector del proscenio *m*; **~ of a lathe** *n* MECH ENG escudo *m*, placa frontal *f*; **~ lip** *n* PAPER labio del delantal *m*; **~ management service** *n* AIR TRANSP servicio de dirección de pistas *m*; **~ taxiway** *n* AIR TRANSP pista de rodaje *f*

aprotic: **~ solvent** *n* CHEM disolvente aprótico *m*

APS *abbr* (*automatic protection switching*) TELECOM conmutación automática de protección *f*

APT *abbr* (*automatic programming tool*) COMP&DP APT (*herramienta de programación automática*)

apterous *adj* AGRIC áptero

Aptian *n* GEOL *metal, cell* Aptiense *m*

APU *abbr* (*auxiliary power unit*) MILIT unidad de energía auxiliar *f*

apyrous *adj* CHEM apiro

AQL *abbr* (*acceptable quality level*) QUALITY nivel de calidad aceptable *m*

aqua: **~ ammonia** *n* AGRIC hidróxido de amonio *m*; **~ regia** *n* CHEM agua regia *f*

aquaculture *n* AGRIC, OCEAN, WATER acuacultura *f*, acuicultivo *m*, acuicultura *f*

aquaculturist *n* AGRIC, OCEAN, WATER acuicultor *m*

aqualung *n* OCEAN equipo respiratorio autónomo *m*, escafandra autónoma *f*

aquamarine *n* MINERAL aguamarina *f*

aquanaut *n* OCEAN acuanauta *m*, oceanauta *m*

aquaplane *n* OCEAN, WATER TRANSP acuaplano *m*

aquaplaning *n* AIR TRANSP hidrodeslizamiento *m*, aquaplaning *m*, AUTO aquaplaning *m*, hidrodeslizamiento *m*

aquatic[1] *adj* HYDROL, OCEAN acuático

aquatic[2]: **~ acidification** *n* HYDROL, MAR POLL, POLL, WATER acidificación acuática *f*, acidificación del agua *f*; **~ pollutant** *n* WATER contaminante acuático *m*, polutante acuático *m*; **~ system** *n* WATER sistema acuático *m*

aqueduct *n* CONST, FUELLESS, HYDROL acueducto *m*, WATER acueducto *m*, conducto de abastecimiento *m*

aqueous[1] *adj* CHEM, FLUID, GEOL, HYDROL, PETR TECH, WATER acuoso

aqueous[2]: **~ effluent** *n* POLL efluente acuoso *m*, efluente acuífero *m*; **~ ink** *n* PRINT tinta de base acuosa *f*; **~ phase** *n* COAL fase acuosa *f*

aquiclude *n* WATER acuicludo *m*, acuiclusa *f*

aquiculture *n* AGRIC, OCEAN, WATER acuacultura *f*, acuicultivo *m*, acuicultura *f*

aquifer *n* GAS, GEOL, HYDROL, PETR TECH acuífero *m*, WATER capa acuífera *f*, acuífero *m*; **~ recharge** *n* HYDROL recarga acuífera *f*

aquiferous *adj* GAS, GEOL, HYDROL, MINE, PETR TECH, WATER acuífero

aquifuge *n* GEOL, WATER acuifugo *m*

aquitard *n* WATER acuitardo *m*

Ar *abbr* (*argon*) CHEM, ELECTRON, METALL Ar (*argón*)

arabinose *n* CHEM arabinosa *f*

arabitol *n* CHEM arabitol *m*

arachic *adj* CHEM aráquico

arachidonic: **~ acid** *n* CHEM, FOOD ácido araquidónico *m*

arachis: **~ oil** *n* AGRIC, CHEM, FOOD aceite de cacahuete *m* (*Esp*), aceite de maní *m* (*AmL*)

araeometer *n* COAL, HYDROL, PHYS areómetro *m*

araeometry *n* COAL, HYDROL, PHYS areometría *f*

aragonite *n* MINERAL, PETROL aragonito *m*

aramid *n* P&R arámida *f*

Ar-Ar: **~ step heating method** *n* GEOL método de calentamiento escalonado Ar-Ar *m*, método de calentamiento gradual Ar-Ar *m*

arbitrary: **~ constant** *n* PHYS constante arbitraria *f*; **~ signs** *n pl* PRINT signos convencionales *m pl*

arbor *n* CHEM arborización *f*, MECH ENG eje portaherramienta *m*, mandril *m*; **~ press** *n* MECH ENG, PROD prensa de husillo *f*; **~ support** *n* MECH ENG *of a milling machine* soporte de árbol *m*

arboriculture *n* AGRIC arboricultura *f*

arc[1] *n* ELEC *discharge*, GEOM arco *m*; **~ back** *n* ELEC ENG arco inverso *m*; **~ brazing** *n* PROD soldadura fuerte por arco *f*; **~ breaker** *n* ELEC apagador del arco *m*, cortacircuito del arco *m*, ELEC ENG ruptor del arco *m*; **~ carbon** *n* CINEMAT carbono del arco *m*; **~ of contact** *n* MECH ENG *of the belt* arco de contacto *m*; **~ current** *n* ELEC corriente del arco *f*; **~ cutter** *n* MECH ENG cortadora por arco eléctrico *f*; **~ cutting** *n* CONST corte por arco *m*, PROD corte por arco eléctrico *m*; **~ discharge** *n* ELEC, ELEC ENG descarga del arco *f*, descarga en arco *f*, GAS captación en abanico *f*, descarga de arco *f*; **~ discharge with transfer** *n* GAS captación en abanico con transferencia *f*; **~ discharge tube** *n* ELEC ENG tubo de descarga del arco *m*; **~ extinction** *n* ELEC apagado del arco *m*, apagamiento del arco *m*, extinción del arco *f*; **~ feed** *n* CINEMAT suministro del arco *m*; **~ feed control** *n* CINEMAT control de alimentación del arco *m*; **~ furnace** *n* HEAT horno de arco *m*; **~ heater** *n* MECH ENG calentador al arco eléctrico *m*, calentador por arco eléctrico *m*; **~ heating** *n* ELEC ENG calentamiento por arco *m*; **~ ignition** *n* CINEMAT encendido del arco *m*, ELEC encendido de arco *m*, ignición de arco *f*, inflamación de arco *f*, ELEC ENG encendido del arco *m*; **~ jet engine** *n* MECH ENG motor de chorro al arco *m*; **~ lamp** *n* ELEC lámpara de arco *f*; **~ lamp carbon** *n* MECH ENG carbono para arco voltaico *m*; **~ light** *n* CINEMAT luz de arco voltaico *f*, ELEC luz de arco *f*; **~ minute** *n* PHYS minuto del arco *m*; **~~over** *n* ELEC arco *m*, descarga exterior *f*, salto de arco *m*; **~ pitch** *n* MECH ENG *of gear wheel* paso circular *m*, paso circunferencial *m*; **~ projector** *n* CINEMAT proyector del arco *m*; **~ quench chamber** *n* ELEC ENG cámara de apagado de arco *f*; **~ quenching** *n* ELEC ENG soplado de arco *m*; **~ rectifier** *n* CINEMAT, ELEC ENG rectificador del arco *m*; **~ regulator** *n* ELEC regulador del arco *m*; **~ rheostat** *n* ELEC resistencia variable del arco *f*, reóstato del arco *m*; **~ second** *n* PHYS segundo del arco *m*; **~ spectrum** *n* PHYS espectro del arco *m*; **~ striking** *n* ELEC cebado de arco *m*, encendido de arco *m*, inicio de arco *m*; **~ suppression** *n* ELEC ENG supresión del arco *f*; **~ suppression coil** *n* ELEC *relay*, ELEC ENG bobina apagadora del arco *f*, bobina de apagado de arco *f*, bobina de apagado por rejillas *f*; ~ **welder** *n* MECH soldador del arco eléctrico *m*, soldadora por arco *f*; ~ **welding** *n* CONST, ELEC soldadura por arco *f*, MECH arcosoldadura *f*, PROD arcosoldadura *f*, soldadura con arco eléctrico *f*, soldadura por arco *f*, THERMO soldeo con arco eléctrico *m*, arcosoldadura *f*; ~ **welding electrode** *n* ELEC *application* electrodo de soldadura por arco *m*; ~ **welding machine** *n* MECH máquina para arcosoldadura *f*; ~ **width** *n* CINEMAT ancho del arco *m*

arc² *vt* CINEMAT iluminar con luz de arco voltaico, ELEC ENG cebar el arco

arcade *n* ĊONST arcada *f*

arcanite *n* MINERAL arcanita *f*

arch¹ *n* C&G *of glass-making pot* horno para el precaldeo de crisoles *m*, CONST *dome-shaped part of furnace* bóveda *f*, *structure* arco *m*, MINE arco *m*, bóveda *f*, portada *f*; ~ **brick** *n* CONST ladrillo abovedado *m*; ~ **dam** *n* CONST presa arco *f*, presa de arco simple *f*, presa-bóveda *f*, WATER presa arco *f*, presa bóveda *f*, presa de arco simple *f*; ~ **of discharge** *n* CONST *architecture* arco de descarga *m*; ~ **panel** *n* CONST panel en arco *m*; ~ **pillar** *n* MINE pilar de bóveda *m*; ~ **stone** *n* CONST dovela *f*

arch² *vt* CONST arquear, MINE arquear, curvar

arch³ *vi* MINE abovedarse

Archaean *n* GEOL *communications* Arcaica *f*, *stratigraphy* arqueozoica *f*

Archean *AmE see* **Archaean** *BrE*

arched¹ *adj* CONST arqueado, en forma de arco, MINE arqueado

arched²: ~**-beam bridge** *n* CONST puente con vigas en arco *m*; ~ **tile** *n* CONST teja convexa *f*

Archie: ~**'s formula** *n* PETROL fórmula de Archie *f*

Archimedean: ~ **screw** *n* HYDRAUL tornillo de Arquímedes *m*, tornillo hidráulico *m*

Archimedes': ~ **principle** *n* PHYS principio de Arquímedes *m*

Archimedes: ~ **screw** *n* HYDRAUL tornillo hidráulico *m*

arching *n* CONST *of roof*, MINE arqueado *m*

archipelagic: ~ **passage** *n* OCEAN pasaje archipelágico *m*

archipelago *n* GEOL, OCEAN, WATER TRANSP archipiélago *m*

architectural: ~ **acoustics** *n* ACOUST acústica arquitectónica *f*

archival: ~ **film** *n* CINEMAT película de archivo *f*; ~ **paper** *n* PAPER papel para documentos *m*

archive¹ *n* CINEMAT, COMP&DP archivo *m*

archive² *vt* COMP&DP archivar

archived: ~ **file** *n* COMP&DP archivo guardado en memoria *m*

arcing *n* ELEC ENG formación del arco eléctrico *f*, proyección de chispas del arco *f*, PROD formación del arco eléctrico *f*; ~ **contacts** *n* ELEC *circuit breaker* parachispas *m pl*; ~ **time** *n* ELEC *pole, fuse, switch* duración del arco *f*

ardennite *n* MINERAL ardenita *f*

area *n* GEN zona *f*; ~ **broadcasting** *n* TRANSP emisión local *f*, radiodifusión local *f*; ~ **broadcasting station** *n* TRANSP emisora de difusión local *f*, emisora de radiodifusión local *f*; ~ **code** *n* TELECOM código de zona *m*; ~ **control** *n* TRANSP control de área *m*; ~ **of deep weathering** *n* CONST zona de inclemencias meteorológicas *f*; ~ **defence** *n* BrE, ~ **defense** *n* AmE MILIT defensa aérea *f*; ~ **emission source** *n* POLL campo de acción de la fuente de emisión *m*, campo de influencia de la fuente de emisión *m*; ~ **of influence** *n* WATER área de influencia *f*; ~ **program** *AmE*, ~ **programme** *BrE n* TRANSP programa de zona *m*, programa de área *m*, programa local *m*; ~ **rule** *n* AIR TRANSP regla de las áreas *f*; ~ **traffic information** *n* TRANSP información del tráfico de la zona *f*

arecaine *n* CHEM arecaína *f*

arenaceous *adj* FUELLESS *rocks* arenoso

arendalite *n* MINERAL arendalita *f*

arenite *n* OCEAN arenita *f*, roca de playa *f*

arfvedsonite *n* MINERAL arfvedsonita *f*

argentic *adj* CHEM argéntico

argentiferous *adj* MINERAL argentífero

argentine *n* COLOUR, MINERAL argentina *f*

argentite *n* CHEM, MINERAL argentita *f*

argentopyrite *n* MINERAL argentopirita *f*

argil *n* C&G, CONST arcilla cerámica *f*

argillaceous *adj* FUELLESS *rocks*, GEOL arcilloso

argillite *n* PETROL argilita *f*

arginase *n* CHEM arginasa *f*

arginine *n* CHEM arginina *f*

argol *n* CHEM tártaro bruto *m*

argon *n* (*Ar*) CHEM, ELECTRON, METALL argón *m* (*Ar*); ~ **arc welding** *n* PROD soldadura por arco en atmósfera de argón *f*; ~ **gas blanket** *n* NUCL recubrimiento de gas argón *m*; ~ **gas laser** *n* GAS, RAD PHYS láser de gas argón *m*; ~ **laser** *n* ELECTRON láser de argón *m*

Argos: ~ **transmitter** *n* WATER TRANSP *oceanographic and environmental research* transmisor Argos *m*

argument *n* COMP&DP, MATH argumento *m*, PRINT longitud de línea *f*

argyric *adj* CHEM argírico

argyrodite *n* MINERAL argirodita *f*

argyropyrite *n* MINERAL argiropirita *f*

argyrose *n* MINERAL argirita *f*, argirosa *f*

argyrythrose *n* MINERAL argiritrosa *f*

arheic *adj* HYDROL, WATER arreico

aril *n* AGRIC *seed* arilo *m*

Aristoxene: ~ **comma** *n* ACOUST coma de Aristoxene *f*

Aristoxene-Zarlin: ~ **scale** *n* ACOUST escala Aristoxene-Zarlin *f*

arithmetic: ~ **capability** *n* PROD capacidad para cálculos aritméticos *f*; ~ **circuit** *n* ELECTRON circuito aritmético *m*; ~ **function** *n* MATH, PROD función aritmética *f*; ~ **instruction** *n* COMP&DP instrucción aritmética *f*; ~ **and logic unit** *n* (*ALU*) COMP&DP unidad aritmética y lógica *f* (*UAL*); ~ **mean** *n* COMP&DP media aritmética *f*, MATH media aritmética *f*, promedio aritmético *m*; ~ **operation** *n* COMP&DP operación aritmética *f*; ~ **operator** *n* COMP&DP operador aritmético *m*; ~ **shift** *n* COMP&DP desplazamiento aritmético *m*; ~ **unit** *n* (*AU*) COMP&DP unidad aritmética *f* (*UA*)

arizonite *n* MINERAL arizonita *f*

arkansite *n* MINERAL arkansita *f*

arkose *n* C&G, GEOL, PETROL arcosa *f*

arksutite *n* MINERAL arksutita *f*

arm¹ *n* INSTR *of plough* esteva *f*, *of gears* palanca de arrastre *f*, *of mill* aspa *f*, *of capstan* barra *f*, *of spindles* pezón *m*, *of angular iron* lado *m*, *of tools* pierna *f*, *of wheels* radio *m*, MECH ENG *of epicyclic train* brazo *m*, PETROL ramal *m*, brazo *m*, afluente *m*, PROD aspa *f*,

WATER TRANSP *of anchor* brazo *m*; ~ **rocker** *n* MECH ENG balancín *m*; ~ **swinger** *n* CINEMAT operador de pluma de grúa *m*; ~**-type brush holder** *n* ELEC *machine* portaescobillas tipo brazo *m*, portaescobillas tipo palanca *m*

arm² *vt* COMP&DP disponer, preparar

ARM *abbr (anti-radiation missile)* MILIT misil antirradiación *m*

ARMA *abbr (autoregressive moving average)* COMP&DP ARMA *(media móvil autorregresiva)*

armament *n* WATER TRANSP *ship building* armamento *m*

armature *n* ELEC *circuit* inducido *m*, ELEC ENG *circuit* inducido *m*, rotor *m*, PHYS armadura *f*, inducido *m*; ~ **bar** *n* ELEC *machine* barra del inducido *f*, ELEC segmento del inducido *m*; ~ **casing** *n* ELEC ENG cobertura del inducido *f*; ~ **circuit** *n* ELEC *machine* circuito del inducido *m*; ~ **coil** *n* ELEC *machine*, ELEC ENG bobina del inducido *f*; ~ **conductor** *n* ELEC *machine* conductor del inducido *m*; ~ **control** *n* ELEC *machine* control del inducido *m*; ~**-controlled motor** *n* ELEC motor controlado por el inducido *m*; ~ **core** *n* ELEC *generator*, ELEC ENG núcleo del inducido *m*; ~ **current** *n* ELEC *machine*, ELEC ENG corriente del inducido *f*; ~ **end connection** *n* ELEC *machine* borne del inducido *m*, conexión final del inducido *f*, conexión frontal del inducido *f*, enlaces extremos del inducido *m pl*; ~ **end plate** *n* ELEC *machine* borne del inducido *m*, placa de fondo del inducido *f*, placa extrema del inducido *f*, placa terminal del inducido *f*; ~ **field** *n* ELEC *machine* campo del inducido *m*; ~ **induction** *n* ELEC *machine* inducción del inducido *f*; ~ **iron** *n* ELEC ENG hierro del inducido *m*; ~ **reactance** *n* ELEC *machine* reactancia del inducido *f*; ~ **reaction** *n* ELEC *machine* reacción de inducción *f*, reacción del inducido *f*, ELEC ENG reacción del inducido *f*; ~ **reaction compensation** *n* ELEC ENG compensación de la reacción del inducido *f*; ~ **relay** *n* ELEC ENG relé del inducido *m*; ~ **resistance** *n* ELEC *machine* resistencia del inducido *f*, resistencia interna del inducido *f*, ELEC ENG resistencia del inducido *f*; ~ **shaft** *n* ELEC *machine* eje del inducido *m*; ~ **spider** *n* ELEC *machine* estrella del inducido *f*, soporte del inducido *m*, ELEC ENG cuerpo del inducido *m*, soporte del inducido *m*; ~ **tester** *n* ELEC *instrument* comprobador de inducidos *m*, probador de inducidos *m*; ~ **tooth** *n* ELEC *machine* diente del inducido *m*; ~ **winding** *n* ELEC *machine* arrollamiento del inducido *m*, devanado del inducido *m*, ELEC ENG devanado del inducido *m*

armor¹: ~**-clad** *AmE see armour-clad BrE*

armor² *AmE see armour BrE*

armored *AmE see armoured BrE*

armory *AmE see armoury BrE*

armour¹: ~**-clad** *adj BrE* ELEC, ELEC ENG blindado

armour² *n BrE* ELEC *cable conductor* armadura *f*, blindaje *m*, armadura exterior *f*, ELEC ENG *of cable* armadura exterior *f*, blindaje *m*, revestimiento *m*, MILIT fuerzas acorazadas *f pl*, coraza *f*; ~ **clamp** *n BrE* ELEC *cable* aprietacable para armaduras *m*, grampa para armaduras *f* (*AmL*), grapa para armaduras *f* (*Esp*), mordaza de cable para armaduras *f* (*AmL*); ~**-piercing bullet** *n BrE* MILIT bala perforante *f*; ~ **plate** *n BrE* CONST chapa de blindaje *f*, MECH placa de blindaje *f*, plancha de blindaje *f*; ~ **plate mill** *n BrE* PROD muela de acero de blindaje *f*,

muela de plancha de blindaje *f*; ~ **wire** *n BrE* OPT hilo de blindaje *m*

armour³ *vt BrE* MILIT, WATER TRANSP acorazar

armoured¹ *adj BrE* ELEC *cable* armado, blindado, ELEC ENG blindado, MILIT acorazado, TELECOM armado, WATER TRANSP acorazado

armoured²: ~ **battery** *n BrE* TRANSP batería blindada *f*; ~ **cable** *n BrE* ELEC ENG cable armado *m*, MECH ENG cable armado *m*, cable blindado *m*, TELECOM cable armado *m*; ~ **capillary** *n BrE* PROD tubo capilar blindado *m*; ~ **car** *n BrE* MILIT coche blindado *m*; ~ **face conveyor** *n BrE* MINE panzer *m* (*Esp*), transportador para el frente de arranque blindado *m* (*AmL*); ~ **glass** *n* C&G cristal blindado *m*, vidrio blindado *m*, CONST, SAFE cristal blindado *m*; ~ **hose** *n BrE* CONST manguera blindada *f*; ~ **personnel carrier** *n BrE* MILIT transporte de tropas acorazado *m*; ~ **reconnaissance car** *n BrE* MILIT coche blindado de reconocimiento *m*; ~ **recovery vehicle** *n BrE* (*ARV*) MILIT vehículo acorazado de recuperación *m*; ~ **train** *n BrE* MILIT tren blindado *m*

armoury *n BrE* MILIT armería *f*

armrest *n* AUTO apoyabrazo *m*, VEH apoyabrazo *m*, reposabrazo *m*

arms: ~ **rack** *n* MILIT bastidor para armas *m*

army: ~ **cutworm** *n* AGRIC gusano cortador *m*; ~ **worm** *n* AGRIC gusano del ejército *m*, gusano militar *m*

aromatic¹ *adj* FOOD, PETR TECH aromático

aromatic²: ~ **compound** *n* FOOD, PETR TECH compuesto aromático *m*; ~ **hydrocarbon** *n* CHEM, P&R hidrocarburo aromático *m*; ~ **series** *n* CHEM serie aromática *f*

aromaticity *n* CHEM, FOOD aromaticidad *f*

aromatization *n* CHEM, FOOD, PETR TECH aromatización *f*

aromatize *vt* CHEM, CHEM TECH aromatizar

ARPA *abbr (automatic radar plotting aid)* WATER TRANSP APRA *(ayuda de punteo radar automático)*

arrangement *n* ELEC ENG disposición *f*, MECH ENG arreglo *m*, *of workshop* disposición *f*

array *n* COMP&DP matriz *f*, arreglo *m*, MATH arreglo *m*, fila *f*, ordenamiento *m*, serie *f*, PETROL hilera transversal de perforaciones *f*, SPACE arreglo *m*, fila *f*, ordenamiento *m*, serie *f*, TELECOM array *m*, arreglo *m*, matriz *f*, reticulado *m* (*AmL*); ~ **aerial** *n BrE* (*cf array antenna AmE*) SPACE red de antenas *f*, antena en serie *f*, serie de elementos radiantes *f*, TELECOM antena en array *f*, antena matricial *f*; ~ **antenna** *n AmE* (*cf array aerial BrE*) SPACE antena en serie *f*, red de antenas *f*, serie de elementos radiantes *f*, TELECOM antena en array *f*, antena matricial *f*; ~ **interconnection** *n* COMP&DP interconexión de matrices *f*; ~ **processor** *n* COMP&DP procesador de matrices *m*

arrest *n* WATER TRANSP *of boat* embargo preventivo *m*

arrester *n* ELEC ENG chispero *m*, supresor *m*

arresting: ~ **hook** *n* AIR TRANSP *landing* gancho de frenado *m*

arrhenite *n* MINERAL arrhenita *f*

Arrhenius: ~ **equation** *n* CHEM ecuación de Arrhenius *f*

arris *n* C&G filo *m*

arrissed: ~ **edge** *n* C&G borde afilado *m*

arrow *n* AGRIC *sugar cane* inflorescencia *f*, CONST *surveying peg* aguja de cadeneo *f*

arrowhead *n* CONST punta de flecha *f*, PACK punta de flecha *f*, punta de lanza *f*; ~ **drill** *n* MECH ENG taladradora en punta de flecha *f*; ~ **wing** *n* AIR TRANSP, TRANSP ala punta-flecha *f*

arrowroot *n* AGRIC, FOOD arruzuz *m*

arsenate *n* CHEM arseniato *m*

arsenic *n* (*As*) C&G, CHEM, METALL arsénico *m* (*As*); ~ **implantation** *n* ELECTRON implantación de arsénico *f*; ~ **trioxide** *n* CHEM trióxido de arsénico *m*

arsenide *n* CHEM arsenido *m*

arseniferous *adj* MINERAL arsenífero

arseniopleite *n* MINERAL arseniopleíta *f*

arseniosiderite *n* MINERAL arseniosiderita *f*

arsenite *n* CHEM arsenita *f*

arsenolite *n* MINERAL arsenolita *f*

arsenopyrite *n* MINERAL arsenopirita *f*

arsine *n* CHEM arsina *f*

arson *n* THERMO incendio doloso *m*, incendio intencionado *m*

arsonist *n* THERMO incendiario *m*

Arsonval: d'~ galvanometer *n* ELEC ENG galvanómetro de Arsonval *m*

art *n* PRINT ilustraciones *f pl*, originales *m pl*; ~ **canvas** *n* PRINT bucarán *m*; ~ **color preparation** *AmE*, ~ **colour preparation** *n* PRINT preparación del original en color *f*; ~ **insert** *n* PRINT encarte publicitario *m*, inserción gráfica *f*; ~ **metal work** *n* CONST *railings, gates* trabajo de forja artística *m*; ~ **paper** *n* PAPER papel arte *m*; ~ **of printing** *n* PRINT arte de imprimir *m*

arterial: ~ **drainage** *n* WATER drenaje arterial *m*; ~ **highway** *n* TRANSP autopista principal *f*, arteria principal *f*, carretera de acceso limitado *f*, carretera troncal *f*; ~ **railway** *n* BrE (*cf articulated railroad AmE*) RAIL vía férrea principal *f*; ~ **road** *n* AUTO carretera principal *f*; ~ **system** *n* WATER sistema arterial *m*

artesian[1] *adj* PETR TECH artesiano, WATER artesiano, surgente

artesian[2] *n* HYDROL artesiano *m*; ~ **water** *n* COAL, HYDROL agua artesiana *f*; ~ **well** *n* HYDROL, WATER pozo artesiano *m*

arthropod *n* AGRIC artrópodo *m*

articulated[1] *adj* MECH, MECH ENG, TRANSP articulado

articulated[2]: ~ **blade** *n* AIR TRANSP *helicopter* pala articulada *f*; ~ **bus** *n* AUTO autobús articulado *m* (*Esp*); ~ **coupling** *n* TRANSP enganche articulado *m*; ~ **diving suit** *n* OCEAN escafandra articulada *f* (*Esp*), traje de inmersión articulado *m* (*AmL*); ~ **joint** *n* MECH ENG junta articulada *f*; ~ **lorry** *n* BrE (*cf articulated truck AmE*) VEH camión articulado *m*; ~ **railroad** *n* AmE TRANSP vía férrea principal *f*; ~ **railway** BrE *n* (*cf articulated railroad AmE*) TRANSP vía férrea principal *f*; ~ **rotor** *n* AIR TRANSP *helicopter* rotor articulado *m*; ~ **stinger** *n* PETROL espolón articulado *m*; ~ **trolleybus** *n* AUTO trolebús articulado *m*; ~ **truck** *n* AmE (*cf articulated lorry BrE*) VEH camión articulado *m*; ~**-type moving pavement** *n* BrE (*cf articulated-type moving sidewalk AmE*) TRANSP pavimento móvil articulado *m*, pavimento rodante articulado *m*; ~**-type moving sidewalk** *n* AmE (*cf articulated-type moving pavement BrE*) TRANSP pavimento móvil articulado *m*, pavimento rodante articulado *m*

articulation: ~ **index** *n* (*AI*) ACOUST índice de articulación *m* (*AI*), TELECOM índice de nitidez *m*

artificer *n* MECH ENG mecánico ajustador *m*, MILIT artificiero *m*

artificial: ~ **acidification** *n* POLL acidificación artificial *f*; ~ **aerial** *n* BrE TV antena artificial *f*; ~ **ageing** *n* METALL, THERMO curado artificial *m*, envejecimiento artificial *m*, revenido *m*, temple artificial *m*, tratamiento por precipitación *m*; envejecimiento artificial *m*, tratamiento por precipitación *m*; ~ **antenna** *n* AmE TV antena artificial *f*; ~ **ear** *n* ACOUST oído artificial *m*; ~ **feel failure detector** *n* AIR TRANSP detector de fallos por sensación artificial *m*; ~ **horizon** *n* AIR TRANSP, SPACE horizonte artificial *m*; ~ **insemination** *n* (*AI*) AGRIC inseminación artificial *f* (*IA*); ~ **intelligence** *n* (*AI*) COMP&DP, TELECOM inteligencia artificial *f* (*IA*); ~ **lake** *n* WATER lago artificial *m*; ~ **leather** *n* PAPER cuero artificial *m*; ~**-light color film** *AmE*, ~**-light colour film** *BrE n* CINEMAT película color para luz artificial *f*, película en color para luz artificial *f*, PHOTO película en color para luz artificial *f*; ~**-light photography** *n* PHOTO fotografía con luz artificial *f*; ~ **manure** *n* AGRIC, POLL, RECYCL abono artificial *m*; ~ **mastoid** *n* ACOUST mastoide artificial *f*; ~ **mouth** *n* ACOUST boca artificial *f*; ~ **noise** *n* SPACE, TELECOM ruido artificial *m*; ~ **nuclear reaction** *n* NUCL reacción nuclear artificial *f*; ~ **port** *n* WATER TRANSP puerto artificial *m*; ~ **radioactivity** *n* PHYS, RAD PHYS radiactividad artificial *f*; ~ **recharge** *n* HYDROL *person* recarga artificial *f*; ~ **reef** *n* GEOL, OCEAN arrecife artificial *m*; ~ **satellite** *n* TELECOM satélite artificial *m*; ~ **ventilation** *n* SAFE ventilación artificial *f*; ~ **voice** *n* ACOUST voz artificial *f*; ~ **weathering** *n* P&R alteración por exposición a la intemperie artificial *f*, deterioro por exposición a la intemperie artificial *m*

artificially[1]: ~ **aged** *adj* THERMO curado artificialmente, envejecido artificialmente, templado artificialmente

artificially[2]: ~ **age** *vt* THERMO curar artificialmente, envejecer artificialmente, templar artificialmente

artillery *n* MILIT artillería *f*; ~ **fire** *n* MILIT tiro de artillería *m*; ~ **park** *n* MILIT parque de artillería *m*; ~ **spotter** *n* MILIT observador de artillería *m*

Artinskian *adj* GEOL Artinskiense

artistic: ~ **porcelain** *n* C&G porcelana artística *f*; ~ **pottery** *n* C&G, PROD alfarería artística *f*

artist's: ~ **proof** *n* PRINT primera prueba *f*

artwork *n* PRINT ilustraciones *f pl*, labor artística *f*

ARV *abbr* (*armoured recovery vehicle BrE*) MILIT vehículo acorazado de recuperación *m*

aryl *n* CHEM arilo *m*

arylamine *n* CHEM arilamina *f*

A/S *abbr* (*antisubmarine*) MILIT antisubmarino

AS *abbr* (*altostratus*) AIR TRANSP, METEO altostrato *m*

As *abbr* (*arsenic*) C&G, CHEM, METALL As (*arsénico*)

ASA: ~ **standard** *n* CINEMAT *heat unit* norma ASA *f*

asbestos *n* C&G amianto *m*, CHEM, CONST asbesto *m*, MECH amianto *m*, asbesto *m*, MINERAL asbesto *m*, P&R amianto *m*, asbesto *m*, SAFE asbesto *m*, TEXTIL amianto *m*, asbesto *m*; ~ **board** *n* PAPER cartón de amianto *m*; ~ **cement** *n* CONST amianto-cemento *m*, asbesto-cemento *m*, fibrocemento *m*, PAPER cemento de amianto *m*; ~ **control in the workplace** *n* SAFE control de asbesto en áreas de trabajo *m*; ~**-free insulating plates** *n pl* SAFE placas aislantes sin amianto *f pl*; ~**-free protective clothing** *n* SAFE prendas protectoras sin amianto *f pl*; ~ **mat** *n* TEXTIL esterilla de asbesto *f*; ~ **millboard** *n* CONST cartón de amianto *m* (*AmL*), cartón de asbesto *m*; ~**-plaited packing** *n* CONST envoltorio de amianto *m* (*AmL*), envoltorio de asbesto *m* (*Esp*); ~ **roll disc** *BrE*, ~ **roll disk** *n AmE* C&G disco cilíndrico de amianto *m*; ~ **sheeting** *n* CONST revestimiento de amianto *m* (*AmL*), revestimiento de asbesto *m* (*Esp*); ~ **string** *n* CONST fibra de amianto *f* (*AmL*), fibra de asbesto *f* (*Esp*); ~ **thread** *n* CONST filamento de amianto *m* (*AmL*), filamento de asbesto *m* (*Esp*); ~ **twine** *n* CONST hilo de amianto *m* (*AmL*), hilo de asbesto *m* (*Esp*); ~ **washer** *n* MECH ENG arandela de amianto *f*; ~ **wool** *n* NUCL hilaza de amianto *f* (*Esp*), lana de amianto *f* (*AmL*)

asbestosis *n* CONST asbestosis *f*
asbolane *n* MINERAL asbolana *f*
asbolite *n* MINERAL asbolita *f*
ascaricide *n* CHEM ascaricida *m*
ascenders *n pl* PRINT rasgos ascendentes *m pl*
ascending: ~ **letter** *n* PRINT letra alta con trazo alto *f*; ~ **node** *n* SPACE nodo ascendente *m*
ascension *n* OCEAN ascensión *f*
ascent *n* OCEAN regreso a la superficie *m*, subida *f*; ~ **stage** *n* SPACE etapa de ascenso *f*
aschistic *adj* PETROL esquistoso
ASCII[1] *abbr* (*American Standard Code for Information Interchange*) PRINT *cabin* ASCII
ASCII[2]: ~ **code** *n* COMP&DP código ASCII *m*
ascorbic *adj* CHEM ascórbico
ASE *abbr* (*automatic stabilization equipment*) TRANSP equipo de estabilización automática *m*
aseptic[1] *adj* CHEM, FOOD, PACK aséptico
aseptic[2]: ~ **engineering** *n* SAFE ingeniería aséptica *f*; ~ **filling** *n* FOOD *of sea* rellenado aséptico *m*, relleno aséptico *m*, PACK llenado en condiciones asépticas *m*; ~ **packaging** *n* PACK embalaje aséptico *m*; ~ **room clothing** *n* SAFE prendas asépticas *f pl*, prendas estirilizadas *f pl*
ash[1]: ~**-free** *adj* POLL exento de ceniza, libre de ceniza, sin ceniza
ash[2] *n* COAL cenizas *f pl*, P&R ceniza *f*, cenizas *f pl*, PETROL, POLL ceniza *f*, THERMO ceniza *f*, escoria *f*; ~ **bin** *n* PROD cenicero *m*; ~ **box** *n* HEAT cenicero *m*, recipiente para ceniza *m*; ~ **and combustion residue** *n* POLL ceniza y residuo de combustión *f*; ~ **content** *n* FOOD, PAPER contenido de ceniza *m*, PROD contenido de ceniza *m*, proporción de ceniza *f*; ~ **dump** *n* PROD depósito de cenizas *m*; ~ **pit** *n* PROD cenicero *m*
ashless: ~ **filter paper** *n* FOOD filtro de papel sin ceniza *m*, LAB papel de filtro sin cenizas *m*; ~ **paper** *n* PAPER papel sin cenizas *m*
ashore *adv* WATER TRANSP a tierra, en tierra
ASIC *abbr* (*application-specific integrated circuit*) COMP&DP CIAE (*circuito integrado de aplicación específica*)
askarel *n* ELEC ENG askarel *m*
asmanite *n* MINERAL asmanita *f*
ASME[1] *abbr* (*American Society of Mechanical Engineers*) MECH ASME (*Sociedad Norteamericana de Ingenieros Mecánicos*)
ASME[2]: ~ **code** *n* MECH código ASME *m*
aspartame *n* FOOD aspartamo *m*
aspartic[1] *adj* CHEM, FOOD aspártico
aspartic[2]: ~ **acid** *n* CHEM ácido aspártico *m*
aspatron *n* NUCL aspatrón *m*

aspect: off ~ *n* RAIL *of mechanical signal* desconexión de señal mecánica *f*; ~ **ratio** *n* AIR TRANSP *of wing* alargamiento *m*, proporción del aspecto *f*, CINEMAT relación del ancho a la altura de la imagen *f*, COMP&DP relación de aspecto *f*, cociente dimensional *m*, ELEC ENG relación entre dimensiones *f*, MECH proporción dimensional *f*, PHYS alargamiento geométrico *m*, relación entre dimensiones *f*; ~**-ratio adjustment** *n* TV corrección de alargamiento *f*
asperolite *n* MINERAL asperolita *f*
asphalt[1] *n* GEN asfalto *m*; ~ **boiler** *n* CONST caldera para asfalto *f*; ~ **concrete** *n* CONST concreto asfáltico *m* (*AmL*), hormigón asfáltico *m* (*Esp*); ~ **paper** *n* PAPER papel asfaltado *m*; ~ **plant** *n* CONST planta asfáltica *f*; ~**-spreading machine** *n AmE* (*cf road-metal-spreading machine BrE*) CONST, TRANSP asfaltadora *f*, máquina asfaltadora *f*; ~ **surfacing** *n* CONST revestimiento asfáltico *m*; ~ **tanking** *n* CONST impermeabilización asfáltica *f*; ~ **varnish** *n* COATINGS, COLOUR barniz de asfalto *m*
asphalt[2] *vt* CONST, TRANSP asfaltar
asphaltene *n* MINERAL asfalteno *m*
asphalting *n* CONST asfaltado *m*, TRANSP asfaltado *m*, asfalto *m*
asphaltite *n* MINERAL asfaltita *f*
aspheric: ~ **corrector plate** *n* TV placa correctora asférica *f*
aspherical: ~ **lens** *n* CINEMAT objetivo asférico *m*
aspidolite *n* MINERAL aspidolita *f*
aspirated: ~ **psychrometer** *n* REFRIG psicrómetro aspirado *m*, sicrómetro aspirado *m*
aspiration: ~ **psychrometer** *n* REFRIG psicrómetro de aspiración *m*, sicrómetro de aspiración *m*; ~ **pump** *n* FOOD bomba aspirante *f*, HYDRAUL bomba aspirante *f*, bomba de aspiración *f*, MECH ENG bomba aspirante *f*, WATER bomba aspirante *f*, bomba de aspiración *f*
aspirator *n* LAB, PROD aspirador *m*
aspiring: ~ **pump** *n* FOOD bomba aspirante *f*, HYDRAUL bomba aspirante *f*, bomba de aspiración *f*, MECH ENG bomba aspirante *f*, máquina neumática *f*, WATER bomba aspirante *f*, bomba de aspiración *f*; ~ **tube** *n* HYDRAUL tubería de descarga *f*, tubo de aspiración *m*, tubo de exhaustación *m*
ASR *abbr* (*automatic send-receive*) COMP&DP ASR (*envío-recepción automáticos, terminal emisor-receptor automático*)
assault: ~ **rifle** *n* MILIT fusil de asalto *m*
assay[1] *n* CHEM ensayo *m*, prueba *f*, COAL comprobación *f*, ensayo *m*; ~ **balance** *n* CHEM balanza de ensayos *f*; ~ **furnace** *n* CHEM mufla de ensayos *f*, HEAT horno de ensayos *m*; ~ **grade** *n* COAL grado de contraste *m*; ~ **office** *n* CHEM laboratorio de análisis *m*, COAL contraste *m*; ~ **sample** *n* CHEM muestra de ensayo *f*; ~ **value** *n* COAL *of mineral* riqueza *f*
assay[2] *vi* CHEM ensayar, probar
assayer *n* CHEM verificador *m*
assemble[1]: ~ **edit** *n* TV montaje *m*, montaje de película *m*
assemble[2] *vt* COMP&DP ensamblar, CONST empalmar, montar, PRINT componer; ~ **to order** *vt* PROD montar según pedido
assemble[3]: ~ **edit** *vi* CINEMAT, TV montar inicialmente
assembler *n* COMP&DP ensamblador *m*, programa de ensamblaje *m*; ~ **directive** *n* COMP&DP mandato ensamblador *m*

assembling *n* MECH ENG armado *m*, ensamblaje *m*, montaje *m*; ~ **bolt** *n* MECH ENG perno de unión *m*

assembly *n* CINEMAT conjunto *m*, COMP&DP ensamblador *m*, CONST construcción *f*, montaje *m*, ELEC armado *m*, montaje *m*, GAS conjunto de equipos *m*, instalación *f*, montaje *m*, MECH montaje *m*, MECH ENG conjunto *m*, ensamblado *m*, montaje *m*, PRINT montaje *m*, VEH conjunto *m*, montaje *m*; ~ **area** *n* WATER TRANSP *for on board emergency* puesto de reunión *m*, zona de reunión *f*; ~ **building** *n* SPACE ensamblaje *m*, montaje *m*; ~ **coefficient** *n* PROD coeficiente de montaje *m*; ~ **drawing** *n* MECH, MECH ENG dibujo de montaje *m*; ~ **hall** *n* WATER TRANSP *ship building* taller de montaje *m*; ~ **jig** *n* MECH ENG bastidor de montaje *m*, plantilla de montaje *f*, útil de montaje *m*; ~ **language** *n* COMP&DP lenguaje ensamblador *m*; ~ **line** *n* MECH, MECH ENG, PACK, PROD cadena de montaje *f*, cadena de producción *f*, línea de montaje *f*, línea de producción *f*, WATER TRANSP *of shipyard* cadena de producción *f*, línea de montaje *f*, línea de producción *f*, *shipbuilding* cadena de montaje *f*; ~ **list** *n* MECH, MECH ENG, PACK cadena de montaje *f*, PROD cadena de montaje *f*, lista de montaje *f*, WATER TRANSP cadena de montaje *f*; ~ **pitch** *n* NUCL paso de elementos *m*, paso del conjunto *m*; ~ **plan** *n* MECH ENG plano de ensamblaje *m*; ~ **point** *n* TRANSP punto de reunión *m*; ~ **robot** *n* MECH robot de montaje *m*; ~ **sheet** *n* PROD hoja de montaje *f*; ~ **shop** *n* MECH taller de montaje *m*; ~ **tools** *n pl* MECH ENG herramientas de montaje *f pl*

assess *vt* QUALITY apreciar, TEXTIL evaluar; ~ **the distribution of** *vt* MECH ENG evaluar la distribución de

assessed: ~ **quality** *n* QUALITY calidad apreciada *f*

assessment *n* GEN evaluación *f*, apreciación *f*

asset *n* PETR TECH caudal existente *m*

assign *vt* COMP&DP asignar, designar, destinar, PROD asignar

assignable: ~ **cause** *n* QUALITY causa asignable *f*

assigned: ~ **flight path** *n* AIR TRANSP trayectoria asignada de vuelo *f*

assignment: ~ **map** *n* TELECOM mapa de asignaciones *m*; ~ **message** *n* TELECOM aviso de asignaciones *m*; ~ **statement** *n* COMP&DP sentencia de asignación *f*, instrucción de asignación *f*

assistant: ~ **driller** *n* PETROL perforador asistente *m*, perforador ayudante *m*

assisted: ~ **resonance** *n* ACOUST resonancia asistida *f*

associated: ~ **gain** *n* ELECTRON ganancia asociada *f*; ~ **gas** *n* GAS, PETR TECH gas asociado *m*; ~ **liquid** *n* PETR TECH líquido asociado *m*

association *n* CHEM, GEOL, TELECOM asociación *f*; ~ **control service element** *n* (*ACSE*) TELECOM elemento para el control de asociación *m*; ~ **initiator** *n* TELECOM iniciador de asociaciones *m*

associative: ~ **addressing** *n* COMP&DP direccionamiento asociativo *m*; ~ **memory** *n* COMP&DP memoria asociativa *f*; ~ **processor** *n* TELECOM procesador asociativo *m*; ~ **store** *AmE*, ~ **store** *BrE* *n* COMP&DP almacenamiento asociativo *m*, memoria asociativa *f*

assortment *n* PROD clasificación *f*

assumption: ~ **analysis** *n* PROD análisis de hipótesis *m*

assured: ~ **water supply** *n* HYDROL abastecimiento de agua asegurado *m*, WATER abastecimiento de agua asegurado *m*, suministro de agua asegurado *m*

astable: ~ **circuit** *n* ELECTRON circuito astable *m*; ~ **multivibrator** *n* ELECTRON multivibrador astable *m*

A-stage: ~ **resin** *n* P&R resina en estado A *f*, resina termoendurecible en estado inicial *f*

astatic[1] *adj* PHYS astático

astatic[2]: ~ **ammeter** *n* ELEC, ELEC ENG, INSTR amperímetro astático *m*; ~ **galvanometer** *n* ELEC ENG, PHYS *instrument* galvanómetro astático *m*; ~ **voltmeter** *n* ELEC *instrument* voltímetro astático *m*

astatine *n* (*At*) CHEM, RAD PHYS astato *m* (*At*)

astatki *n* PETROL residuo de petróleo *m*

astern *adv* WATER TRANSP a popa, hacia popa, por la popa

asteroid *n* SPACE asteroide *m*

asthenosphere *n* GEOL, PETROL astenosfera *f*

asthma: ~ **paper** *n* PAPER papel para el asma *m*

astigmatic: ~ **lens** *n* CINEMAT, OPT, PHOTO objetivo astigmático *m*, PHYS lente astigmática *f*, objetivo astigmático *m*

astigmatism *n* OPT, PHYS, TV astigmatismo *m*

astragal *n* CONST *moulding* astrágalo *m*

astrakanite *n* MINERAL astrakanita *f*

astro: ~ **fix** *n* SPACE punto de intersección con la órbita de un astro *m*, situación relativa de un astro *f*

astrocompass *n* SPACE astrobrújula *f*

astrodome *n* SPACE astropuerto *m*

astrodrome *n* SPACE astrodomo *m*, cúpula *f*

astrodynamics *n* SPACE astrodinámica *f*

astrometry *n* SPACE astrometría *f*

astronaut *n* SPACE astronauta *m*

astronavigation *n* WATER TRANSP astronavegación *f*

astronomer *n* SPACE astrónomo *m*

astronomic: ~ **longitude** *n* SPACE longitud astronómica *f*

astronomical: ~ **camera** *n* PHOTO cámara astronómica *f* (*AmL*), cámara de astrofotográfica *f* (*Esp*); ~ **navigation** *n* WATER TRANSP navegación astronómica *f*; ~ **position** *n* WATER TRANSP *astronavigation* situación astronómica *f*; ~ **telescope** *n* INSTR, PHYS telescopio astronómico *m*; ~ **tide** *n* OCEAN marea astronómica *f*

astrophyllite *n* MINERAL astrofilita *f*

astrophysics *n* PHYS, SPACE astrofísica *f*

asymmetric[1] *adj* COMP&DP, GEOM, MATH asimétrico

asymmetric[2]: ~ **circuit** *n* ELEC circuito asimétrico *m*, circuito disimétrico *m*, circuito no simétrico *m*; ~ **suspension** *n* TRANSP suspensión asimétrica *f*

asymmetrical[1] *adj* COMP&DP, GEOM, MATH asimétrico

asymmetrical[2]: ~ **circuit** *n* ELEC circuito asimétrico *m*, circuito disimétrico *m*, circuito no simétrico *m*; ~ **deflection** *n* TV deflexión asimétrica *f*; ~ **trapezoidal-screw thread** *n* MECH ENG hilo de rosca trapezoidal asimétrico *m*

asymmetry *n* CHEM, COMP&DP, GEOM, MATH asimetría *f*

asymptomatic: ~ **approximation** *n* TELECOM aproximación asintomática *f*

asymptomatical: ~ **approximation** *n* TELECOM aproximación asintomática *f*

asymptote *n* GEOM, MATH asíntota *f*

asymptotic *adj* GEOM, MATH asintótico

asynchronism *n* CINEMAT, COMP&DP, ELEC, PHYS, TV asincronismo *m*

asynchronous[1] *adj* CINEMAT, COMP&DP, ELEC, PHYS, TV asincrónico, asíncrono

asynchronous[2]: ~ **alternator** *n* ELEC, ELEC ENG alternador asíncrono *m*; ~ **channel adaptor** *n* COMP&DP adaptador de canal asíncrono *m*; ~ **circuit** *n* COMP&DP, TELECOM circuito asíncrono *m*; ~ **generator** *n* ELEC generador asíncrono *m*; ~ **linear induction motor** *n* ELEC, TRANSP motor de inducción lineal asíncrono *m*; ~ **link** *n* ELEC *of two AC systems* conectador acoplador asincrónico *m*, pieza corta de conexión asincrónica *f*, puente de conexión asincrónico *m*; ~ **machine** *n* ELEC ENG máquina asíncrona *f*; ~ **modem** *n* ELECTRON módem asincrono *m*; ~ **motor** *n* ELEC motor asincrónico *m*, motor asíncrono *m*, ELEC ENG motor asincrónico *m*, RAIL motor asincrónico *m*, motor asíncrono *m*; ~ **operation** *n* ELEC *motor* accionamiento asincrónico *m*, accionamiento asíncrono *m*, funcionamiento asíncrono *m*, operación asincrónica *f*, operación asíncrona *f*; ~ **port** *n* TELECOM puerto asíncrono *m*; ~ **running** *n* ELEC circulación asincrónica *f*, funcionamiento asíncrono *m*, marcha asincrónica *f*; ~ **sound** *n* CINEMAT sonido asincrónico *m*; ~ **time division multiplexing** *n* (*ATDM*) TELECOM multiplexión por división en tiempo asíncrono *f* (*ATDM*); ~ **transfer mode** *n* (*ATM*) TELECOM modo de transferencia asíncrona *m*; ~ **transmission** *n* COMP&DP, TELECOM transmisión asíncrona *f*

At *abbr* (*astatine*) CHEM, RAD PHYS At (*astato*)

atacamite *n* MINERAL atacamita *f*

atactic *adj* CHEM *polymers* atáctico

ATDM *abbr* (*asynchronous time division multiplexing*) TELECOM ATDM (*multiplexión por división en tiempo asíncrono*)

ATE *abbr* (*automatic test equipment*) COMP&DP EPA (*equipo de pruebas automático*)

atelestite *n* MINERAL atelesita *f*

atelite *n* MINERAL atelita *f*

ATGM *abbr* (*antitank guided missile*) MILIT misil guiado anticarro *m*

athermal *adj* CHEM atérmico

athermancy *n* PHYS atermancia *f*

athodyd *n* AIR TRANSP *ramjet* estatorreactor *m*

athwartships *adv* WATER TRANSP de babor a estribor, de banda a banda

ATK *abbr* (*aviation turbine kerosene*) PETR TECH keroseno de turbina de aviación *m*

atlasite *n* MINERAL atlasita *f*

ATM¹ *abbr* COMP&DP (*automatic teller machine*) ATM (*cajero automático Esp, máquina medidora automática AmL*), OPT (*alternative test method*) ATM (*método de ensayo alternativo*), TELECOM (*asynchronous transfer mode*) ATM (*modo de transferencia asíncrona*)

ATM²: ~ **adaptative layer** *n* (*AAL*) TELECOM capa adaptable de ATM (*AAL*)

atmolysis *n* CHEM atmólisis *f*

atmosphere *n* MECH ENG, METEO, METR, PHYS, PROD, RAD PHYS atmósfera *f*

atmospheric¹ *adj* METEO, PHYS atmosférico

atmospheric²: ~ **absorption** *n* METEO, RAD PHYS absorción atmosférica *f*; ~ **acidity** *n* METEO, POLL acidez atmosférica *f*; ~ **agent** *n* CHEM, PETR TECH agente atmosférico *m*; ~ **brake** *n* MECH, MECH ENG freno de aire comprimido *m*; ~ **burner** *n* THERMO quemador atmosférico *m*; ~ **chemical process** *n* POLL proceso químico atmosférico *m*; ~ **chemistry** *n* POLL meteorología química *f*, química atmosférica *f*; ~ **circulation** *n* METEO circulación atmosférica *f*;

~ **concentration** *n* POLL concentración atmosférica *f*; ~ **conditions** *n pl* WATER TRANSP condiciones atmosféricas *f pl*; ~ **degassing** *n* HYDROL desgasificación atmosférica *f*; ~ **disturbance** *n* METEO perturbación atmosférica *f*; ~ **electric field** *n* GEOPHYS campo eléctrico atmosférico *m*; ~ **electricity** *n* GEOPHYS, METEO electricidad atmosférica *f*; ~ **fallout** *n* POLL lluvia radiactiva atmosférica *f*, polvo radiactivo atmosférico *m*, precipitación radiactiva atmosférica *f*; ~ **haze** *n* PHOTO bruma atmosférica *f*; ~ **interference** *n* GEOPHYS interferencia atmosférica *f*; ~ **inversion** *n* METEO, POLL inversión atmosférica *f*; ~ **lifetime** *n* POLL longevidad atmosférica *f*, vida atmosférica *f*; ~ **line** *n* PHYS línea atmosférica *f*; ~ **load** *n* POLL carga a presión atmosférica *f*; ~ **loading** *n* POLL carga atmosférica *f*; ~ **noise** *n* ELECTRON, SPACE ruido atmosférico *m*; ~ **obscurity** *n* POLL obscuridad atmosférica *f*, oscuridad atmosférica *f*; ~ **phenomenon** *n* POLL fenómeno atmosférico *m*, fenómeno metereológico *m*; ~ **pollution** *n* POLL contaminación atmosférica *f*; ~ **pressure** *n* AIR TRANSP, GAS, METEO, PHYS presión atmosférica *f*; ~ **radiation** *n* METEO radiación atmosférica *f*; ~ **reentry** *n* SPACE reentrada a través de la atmósfera *f*; ~ **refiner** *n* PAPER refino a presión atmosférica *m*; ~ **scrubbing** *n* POLL depuración atmosférica *f*, lavado atmosférico *m*, limpieza atmosférica *f*; ~ **sulfur** *AmE*, ~ **sulphur** *BrE n* POLL azufre atmosférico *m*; ~ **tide** *n* GEOPHYS marea atmosférica *f*; ~ **window** *n* PHYS, RAD PHYS región de transmisiones atmosféricas *f*

atmospherics *n pl* ELEC ENG, ELECTRON atmosféricos *m pl*, GEOPHYS parásitos atmosféricos *m pl*, perturbaciones atmosféricas *f pl*

A-to-D *abbr* (*analog-to-digital*) TV conversión de sistema analógico a sistema digital *f*

atoll *n* OCEAN, WATER TRANSP atolón *m*

atom *n* GEN átomo *m*; ~**-atom collision** *n* NUCL colisión entre átomos *f*

atomic¹ *adj* CHEM, NUCL, PART PHYS, PHYS atómico

atomic²: ~ **absorption** *n* INSTR espectrómetro de absorción atómica *m*; ~ **absorption analysis** *n* RAD PHYS análisis de absorción atómica *m*; ~ **absorption spectrometer** *n* LAB espectrómetro de absorción atómica *m*; ~ **absorption spectrophotometer** *n* RAD PHYS espectrofotómetro de absorción atómica *m*; ~ **absorption spectroscopy** *n* CHEM *analysis*, PHYS espectroscopía de absorción atómica *f*; ~ **air-to-air rocket** *n* MILIT cohete atómico de aire a aire *m*; ~ **beam** *n* ELECTRON, NUCL haz atómico *m*; ~ **beam diffraction** *n* NUCL difracción del haz atómico *f*; ~ **beam frequency standard** *n* NUCL patrón de frecuencia del haz atómico *m*; ~ **bomb** *n* NUCL bomba atómica *f*; ~ **clock** *n* PHYS, TELECOM reloj atómico *m*; ~ **coordinates** *n pl* CRYSTALL coordenadas atómicas *f pl*; ~ **core** *n* NUCL núcleo atómico *m*; ~ **cross-section** *n* NUCL sección eficaz atómica *f*; ~ **density** *n* RAD PHYS densidad atómica *f*; ~ **displacement** *n* METALL desplazamiento atómico *m*; ~ **energy level** *n* NUCL nivel de energía atómica *m*; ~ **fluorescence analysis** *n* PHYS, RAD PHYS análisis por fluorescencia atómica *m*; ~ **gas laser** *n* ELECTRON láser de gas atómico *m*; ~ **heat capacity** *n* RAD PHYS capacidad calorífica atómica *f*; ~ **hydrogen maser** *n* ELECTRON maser de hidrógeno atómico *m*; ~ **hydrogen welding** *n* NUCL soldadura por hidrógeno atómico *f*; ~ **interspace** *n* NUCL espacio interno del átomo *m*; ~ **mass** *n* (*A*) CHEM, PART PHYS *of element* masa atómica *f* (*A*), peso atómico *m* (*A*); ~ **mass unit** *n* (*AMU*) PHYS unidad de masa atómica *f* (*UMA*); ~ **nucleus** *n* NUCL, PART PHYS núcleo atómico *m*; ~ **number** *n* (*Z*) CHEM, PART PHYS, PHYS número atómico *m* (*Z*); ~ **orbit width** *n* CHEM, PART PHYS, PHYS amplitud de la órbita atómica *f*; ~ **orbital** *n* CHEM, PART PHYS, PHYS, RAD PHYS orbital atómico *m*; ~ **physics** *n* PART PHYS, PHYS física atómica *f*; ~ **pile** *n* NUCL, PHYS pila atómica *f*; ~ **polarization** *n* RAD PHYS polarización atómica *f*; ~ **radiation** *n* NUCL radiación atómica *f*; ~ **radius** *n* CHEM, NUCL radio atómico *m*; ~ **ratio** *n* NUCL razón atómica *f*; ~ **research** *n* NUCL investigación atómica *f*; ~ **rocket** *n* MILIT cohete atómico *m*; ~ **scattering** *n* NUCL dispersión atómica *f*; ~ **scattering factor** *n* CRYSTALL factor de dispersión atómica *m*; ~ **shuffling** *n* METALL mezcla atómica *f*; ~ **spectroscopy** *n* RAD PHYS espectroscopía atómica *f*; ~ **spectrum** *n* NUCL, PHYS espectro atómico *m*; ~ **state** *n* NUCL estado atómico *m*; ~ **structure** *n* PART PHYS estructura atómica *f*; ~ **test** *n* MILIT ensayo atómico *m*, prueba atómica *f*; ~ **volume** *n* NUCL volumen atómico *m*; ~ **weapon** *n* MILIT, NUCL arma atómica *f*, arma nuclear *f*; ~ **weight** *n* (*A*) CHEM, PART PHYS, PHYS peso atómico *m* (*A*); ~ **weight unit** *n* (*AWU*) PHYS unidad de masa atómica *f* (*UMA*)

atomicity *n* CHEM, COMP&DP, PART PHYS, PHYS atomicidad *f*

atomistic: ~ **structure** *n* NUCL, SPACE *craft* estructura atómica *f*

atomization *n* CHEM *of liquid* atomización *f*, pulverización *f*, CHEM TECH atomización *f*, NUCL pulverización *f*, atomización *f*, PART PHYS, PETR TECH atomización *f*

atomize *vt* CHEM, NUCL, PART PHYS, PETR TECH, PHYS atomizar

atomizer *n* CHEM atomizador *m*, CHEM TECH atomizador *m*, pulverizador *m*, LAB atomizador *m*, PACK atomizador *m*, pulverizador *m*, PETR TECH, TRANSP atomizador *m*; ~ **injection nozzle** *n* CHEM TECH tobera de inyección del atomizador *f*; ~ **nozzle** *n* CHEM TECH tobera de atomización *f*

atomizing: ~ **burner** *n* THERMO quemador atomizante *m*, quemador de pulverización *m*, quemador pulverizante *m*; ~ **cone** *n* CHEM TECH tobera de atomización *f*; ~ **nozzle** *n* FOOD boquilla para pulverizar *f*, boquilla pulverizadora *f*; ~ **oil burner** *n* HEAT ENG quemador pulverizador de aceite *m*; ~ **process** *n* CHEM TECH proceso de atomización *m*

atonal: ~ **space** *n* ACOUST espacio atonal *m*, zona atonal *f*

atopite *n* MINERAL atopita *f*

ATP *abbr* CHEM, FOOD, PETROL (*adenosine triphosphate*) ATP (*adenosina trifosfato*), RAIL (*automatic train protection*) protección automática del tren *f*

atropic *adj* CHEM atrópico

attach *vt* COMP&DP conectar, interconectar, MECH acoplar, MECH ENG acoplar, enganchar, junta *f*, unir, SPACE acoplar, unir

attached[1] *adj* COMP&DP interconectado

attached[2]: ~ **eddies** *n pl* FLUID torbellinos readheridos *m pl*

attaching: ~ **gun** *n* PACK pistola para aplicar grapas *f*; ~ **part** *n* MECH ENG elemento de fijación *m*

attachment *n* COAL dispositivo de sujeción *m*, COMP&DP aditamento *m*, conexión *f*, interconexión *f*, INSTR accesorio *m*, dispositivo de sujeción *m*, enlace *m*, MECH ENG acoplamiento *m*, SPACE acoplamiento *m*, unión *f*, TEXTIL accesorio *m*; ~ **fitting** *n* MECH ENG elemento de enganche *m*; ~ **link** *n* MECH ENG manija de enganche *f*

attack *n* ACOUST, COAL ataque *m*; ~ **angle** *n* AIR TRANSP ángulo de ataque *m*, MINE ángulo de acometida *m*, PHYS ángulo de ataque *m*; ~ **helicopter** *n* MILIT helicóptero de ataque *m*

attacked: ~ **by acids** *adj* CHEM, CHEM TECH, POLL atacado por ácidos

attacolite *n* MINERAL atacolita *f*

attapulgite *n* PETROL atapulgita *f*

attended: ~ **operation** *n* COMP&DP funcionamiento con operador *m*, operación vigilada *f*, CONST, TELECOM funcionamiento con operador *m*

attenuating: ~ **element** *n* ELECTRON elemento atenuador *m*

attenuation *n* GEN atenuación *f*; ~ **band** *n* ELECTRON *ring winding* banda de atenuación *f*; ~ **coefficient** *n* ACOUST, ELECTRON, OPT, PHYS, TELECOM coeficiente de atenuación *m*; ~ **constant** *n* ELECTRON, PHYS *communications, antennae, aircraft* constante de atenuación *f*; ~ **contour** *n* ELECTRON contorno de atenuación *m*; ~ **distortion** *n* ELECTRON, PHYS *communications, antennae, aircraft* distorsión de atenuación *f*; ~~**limited operation** *n* OPT procedimiento limitado por atenuación *m*, TELECOM operación de atenuación limitada *f*

attenuator *n* GEN atenuador *m*; ~ **diode** *n* ELECTRON diodo atenuador *m*

attitude *n* SPACE posición de vuelo *f*; ~ **acquisition** *n* SPACE adquisición de posición de vuelo *f*; ~ **control** *n* AIR TRANSP control de actitud *m*; ~ **control unit** *n* SPACE unidad para control de posición de vuelo *f*; ~ **reference unit** *n* SPACE unidad de referencia para posición de vuelo *f*; ~ **sensor** *n* SPACE detector de posición *m*, sensor de posición *m*

attle *n* MINE blancarte *m* (*AmL*), desechos *m pl* (*AmL*), ganga *f* (*AmL*), labores abandonadas *f pl*, materias estériles *f pl*, ripios *m pl* (*Esp*), tepetate *m* (*AmL*)

atto- *pref* (*a-*) METR ato (*a-*)

attract *vi* ELEC, ELEC ENG, PHYS, SPACE atraerse

attraction *n* ELEC, ELEC ENG, SPACE atracción *f*

attractive[1] *adj* ELEC, ELEC ENG, PHYS, SPACE atractivo

attractive[2]: ~ **effect** *n* TRANSP efecto de atracción *m*; ~ **force** *n* ELEC *electromagnetism*, PHYS fuerza atractiva *f*, fuerza de atracción *f*; ~ **forces of very short range** *n pl* PART PHYS fuerzas de atracción de muy corto alcance *f pl*

attribute *n* COMP&DP, TELECOM atributo *m*

attrition *n* C&G desgaste por rozamiento *m*, COAL desgaste *m*, rozamiento *m*, CONST desgaste *m*, roce *m*, rozamiento *m*, MECH ENG desgaste *m*, frote *m*, roce *m*, rozadura *f*; ~ **test** *n* MECH ENG prueba de desgaste por frotamiento *f*

Atwater: ~ **factor** *n* FOOD actividad del agua *f*

Atwood's: ~ **machine** *n* PHYS máquina de Atwood *f*

ATWS *abbr* (*anticipated transient without scream*) NUCL ATWS (*transitorios previstos sin parada de emergencia*)

A-type: ~ **color film** *AmE*, ~ **colour film** *BrE n* CINEMAT película en color de tipo A *f*; ~ **facsimile** *n* PRINT facsímil tipo A *m*

AU *abbr* AGRIC (*animal unit*) UA (*unidad animal*), COMP&DP (*arithmetic unit*) UA (*unidad aritmética*), TELECOM (*access unit*) unidad de acceso *f*, (*administrative unit*) unidad administrativa *f*

Au *abbr* (*gold*) CHEM, METALL Au (*oro*)

audible: ~ **alarm** *n* SAFE, TELECOM alarma audible *f*; ~ **emergency evacuation signal** *n* SAFE señal acústica de evacuación de urgencia *f*; ~ **frequency range** *n* ACOUST margen de frecuencias audibles *m*; ~ **machmeter** *n* AIR TRANSP medidor audible de número de Mach *m*; ~ **runout indicator** *n* CINEMAT indicador audible de fin de cinta *m*; ~ **signal** *n* TELECOM señal audible *f*; ~ **warning system** *n* PACK sistema de alarma acústica *m*

audio¹ *adj* ACOUST, ELECTRON, TELECOM audio

audio² *n* COMP&DP audio *m*; ~ **amplifier** *n* ACOUST amplificador de audio *m*, ELECTRON amplificador de audio *m*, audio amplificador *m*; ~ **attenuator** *n* ELECTRON atenuador de audio *m*, atenuador de audiofrecuencia *m*, audio atenuador *m*; ~ **bearer service** *n* TELECOM servicio de portador *m*; ~ **CD player** *n* OPT reproductor de CD de audio *m*; ~ **compact disc** *n BrE* OPT disco compacto de audio *m*; ~ **compact disc player** *n BrE* OPT reproductor de discos compactos de audio *m*; ~ **compact disk** *AmE see audio compact disc BrE*; ~ **compact disk player** *AmE see audio compact disc player BrE*; ~ **feedback circuit** *n* TV circuito de realimentación de audio *m*; ~ **filter** *n* ELECTRON filtro de sonido *m*; ~ **frequency** *n* (*AF*) ACOUST audiofrecuencia *f*, ELECTRON audiofrecuencia *f*, frecuencia de sonido *f*, frecuencia acústica *f*, frecuencia audible *f*, TELECOM audiofrecuencia *f*, frecuencia audible *f*, WAVE PHYS audiofrecuencia *f*; ~~**frequency amplifier** *n* ACOUST amplificador de audio frecuencia *m*, ELECTRON amplificador de audio frecuencia *m*, amplificador de frecuencia de sonido *m*; ~~**frequency oscillator** *n* ELECTRON oscilador de audio frecuencia *m*, oscilador de frecuencia de sonido *m*; ~~**frequency signal generator** *n* ELECTRON generador de audiofrecuencia *m*, generador de señal de frecuencia audio *m*; ~ **indicator active** *n* (*AIA*) TELECOM indicador de audio activo *m*; ~ **indicator muted** *n* (*AIM*) TELECOM indicador de audio silencioso *m*; ~ **loop** *n* TELECOM bucle de audio *m*; ~ **modulation** *n* ELECTRON modulador de audio *m*, modulador de sonido *m*; ~ **oscillator** *n* RAD PHYS audiooscilador *m*, oscilador de frecuencia acústica *m*; ~ **playback** *n* TV reproducción de audio *f*; ~ **power amplifier** *n* ACOUST amplificador de audio *m*, ELECTRON amplificador de audio *m*, amplificador de potencia de sonido *m*; ~ **range** *n* ACOUST, RAD PHYS gama de frecuencias acústicas *f*; ~ **record** *n* TV grabación de audio *f*; ~ **response** *n* ELECTRON respuesta acústica *f*; ~ **response unit** *n* COMP&DP, ELECTRON unidad de respuesta de audio *f*, unidad de respuesta oral *f*; ~ **signal** *n* ELECTRON señal acústica *f*; ~ **splitter** *n* TELECOM separador de audio *m*; ~ **tape machine** *n* TV grabadora de audio *f*, grabadora de audio a cinta *f*; ~ **track** *n* TV pista de audio *f*; ~~**videotext** *n* TELECOM audio videotexto *m*

audiogram *n* ACOUST audiograma *m*

audiometer *n* ACOUST, INSTR, SAFE, WAVE PHYS audiómetro *m*

audiometric: ~ **room** *n* ACOUST, WAVE PHYS cámara audiométrica *f*

audiometry *n* ACOUST, METR, WAVE PHYS audiometría *f*

audit *n* QUALITY investigación de la calidad *f*, TELECOM comprobación *f*; ~ **of inspection procedure** *n* METR transformer, machine auditoría en proceso de inspección *f*; ~ **trail** *n* COMP&DP pista de auditoría *f*, pista de comprobación *f*, seguimiento de auditoría *m*, PROD, TELECOM pista de auditoría *f*

auditee *n* QUALITY examinado sobre la investigación de la calidad *m*

auditory: ~ **acuity** *n* ACOUST agudeza auditiva *f*; ~ **sensation area** *n* ACOUST área de sensación auditiva *f*; ~ **signals** *n pl* SAFE señales audibles *f pl*

augelite *n* MINERAL augelita *f*

augen: ~ **structure** *n* GEOL textura lenticular en fláser *f*

augend *n* COMP&DP co-sumando *m*

auger *n* AGRIC transportador a tornillo sinfín *m*, COAL barrena *f*, berbiquí *m*, cuchara *f*, hélice *f*, sonda *f*, taladro *m*, CONST *for wood* barrena *f*, perforador *m*, taladro *m*, GEOL broca *f*, MECH, MECH ENG barrena *f*, MINE barrena *f* (*AmL*), sonda *f*, barrena helicoidal *f* (*Esp*), barrena para tirafondos *f* (*AmL*), PETROL barrena *f*; ~ **bank** *n* AGRIC comedero de animales con distribución a través de sinfín *m*; ~ **bit** *n* MECH ENG *drilling device* broca de berbiquí *f*, gusanillo de rosca *m*; ~ **table** *n* AGRIC plataforma de corte de cosechadoras *f*

Auger: ~ **effect** *n* PHYS efecto Auger *m*, RAD PHYS efecto Auger *m*, transición Auger *f*; ~ **electron** *n* PHYS, RAD PHYS electrón Auger *m*; ~ **electron spectroscopy** *n* (*AES*) CHEM, PHYS espectroscopía de electrones Auger *f* (*EEA*); ~ **yield** *n* PHYS rendimiento Auger *m*

augite *n* MINERAL augita *f*

augmented: ~ **interval** *n* ACOUST intervalo aumentado *m*

aulacogen *n* GEOL aulacógeno *m*

aural: ~ **flutter** *n* ACOUST vibración aural *f*; ~ **harmonic** *n* ACOUST, SPACE, TELECOM armónico aural *m*; ~ **null loop** *n* TRANSP conexión de recepción nula *f*

auralite *n* MINERAL aurolita *f*

aurichalcite *n* MINERAL auricalcita *f*

auriferous¹ *adj* METALL, MINE, MINERAL aurífero

auriferous²: ~ **pyrite** *n* MINERAL pirita aurífera *f*

aurocyanide *n* CHEM aurocianuro *m*

aurora *n* GEOPHYS, METEO, SPACE aurora *f*; ~ **australis** *n* GEOPHYS aurora austral *f*, METEO aurora austral *f*, resplandor del sur *m*, SPACE, WATER TRANSP aurora austral *f*; ~ **borealis** *n* GEOPHYS aurora boreal *f*, METEO aurora boreal *f*, resplandor del norte *m*, SPACE, WATER TRANSP aurora boreal *f*; ~ **polaris** *n* GEOPHYS, METEO, SPACE, WATER TRANSP aurora polaris *f*

auroral: ~ **belt** *n* GEOPHYS zona auroral *f*; ~ **zone** *n* SPACE zona auroral *f*

aurous *adj* CHEM áureo

austenitic¹ *adj* MECH *safety* austenítico

austenitic²: ~ **stainless steel** *n* MECH ENG, METALL, PROD acero inoxidable austenítico *m*; ~ **steel** *n* MECH *pipelines*, METALL acero austenítico *m*

authenticate *vt* COMP&DP, QUALITY, TELECOM autenticar

authentication *n* COMP&DP autentificación *f*, autenticación *f*, QUALITY autenticación *f*, autentificación *f*, TELECOM autentificación *f*, autenticación *f*; ~ **code** *n* COMP&DP código de autentificación *m*; ~ **exchange** *n*

TELECOM intercambio de autentificación *m*; ~ **information** *n* TELECOM información de autentificación *f*; ~ **procedure** *n* TELECOM procedimiento de autentificación *m*

authigenesis *n* GEOL, PETROL autigénesis *f*

authigenic *adj* GEOL, PETROL autígeno

authority *n* PROD autoridad *f*; ~ **and format identifier** *n* (*AFI*) TELECOM identificador de autorización y formato *m*

authorization *n* COMP&DP, TELECOM autorización *f*; ~ **information** *n* TELECOM información de autorización *f*; ~ **information qualifier** *n* TELECOM calificador de información de autorización *m*

auto: ~ **winding** *n* CINEMAT, PHOTO bobinado automático *m* (*AmL*), rebobinado automático *m* (*Esp*)

autocatalysis *n* CHEM *process*, CHEM TECH autocatálisis *f*

autocatalytic: ~ **effect** *n* METALL efecto autocatalítico *m*

autochart *n* COMP&DP tabla automática *f*

autochthon *n* GEOL, PETROL, POLL autóctono *m*

autochthonal *adj* GEOL, PETROL, POLL autóctono

autochthonous[1] *adj* GEOL, PETROL, POLL autóctono

autochthonous[2]: ~ **matter** *n* POLL materia autóctona *f*

autoclastic *adj* GEOL autoclástico

autoclave *n* GEN autoclave *f*

autocollimator *n* INSTR, METR *equipment* autocolimador *m*

autocorrelation *n* ELECTRON, TELECOM autocorrelación *f*; ~ **function** *n* PETROL función de autocorrelación *f*

autocue *n* TV indicador automático visual *m*

autodefrost *n* REFRIG desescarche automático *m*

autodyne *n* ELECTRON autodino *m*

auto-editing *n* TV edición automática *f*

auto-equalization *n* TV ecualización automática *f*

autofeathering *n* AIR TRANSP *propeller* puesta en bandera automática *f*

autofocus *n* CINEMAT, PHOTO enfoque automático *m*; ~ **window** *n* PHOTO ventana de enfoque automático *f*

autogenous[1] *adj* COAL, MECH ENG *welding* autógeno

autogenous[2]: ~ **mill** *n* COAL molino autógeno *m*; ~ **milling** *n* COAL molienda autógena *f*, molturación autógena *f*

autogiro *n* AIR TRANSP autogiro *m*

autographic: ~ **ink** *n* COLOUR tinta autográfica *f*

autogyro *n* AIR TRANSP autogiro *m*

autoignition *n* AIR TRANSP autoencendido *m*, encendido automático *m*, VEH autoencendido *m*

autoionization *n* ELECTRON, PHYS autoionización *f*

autoiris *n* CINEMAT, PHYS, TV iris automático *m*

autoland *n* AIR TRANSP aterrizaje automático *m*

autoload *n* COMP&DP carga automática *f*

autolysis *n* FOOD autólisis *m*

automanual: ~ **switchboard** *n* TELECOM panel conmutador automático-manual *m*

automate *vt* COMP&DP, CONST, MECH ENG, PROD, SPACE automatizar

automated[1] *adj* COMP&DP, MECH ENG, PROD automatizado

automated[2]: ~ **personal rapid transit** *n* TRANSP tránsito privado rápido automatizado *m*

automatic:

~**a** ~ **ADC** *n* TELECOM ADC automático *m*; ~ **adjustment to light intensity** *n* SAFE ajuste automático a la intensidad de la luz *m*; ~ **approach**

control *n* AIR TRANSP control de aproximación automático *m*; ~ **arc welding** *n* MECH ENG soldadura al arco automática *f*; ~ **assembly machine** *n* MECH ENG máquina de ensamblar automática *f*; ~ **assembly work** *n* PACK montaje automático *m*; ~ **attempt** *n* TELECOM prueba automática *f*;

~**b** ~ **blade-folding system** *n* AIR TRANSP *helicopter* sistema de plegado de pala automático *m*; ~ **blowout preventer** *n* PETR TECH impiderreventones automático *m*; ~ **brake** *n* VEH freno automático *m*; ~ **brightness control** *n* (*ABC*) TV control automático de brillo *m* (*CAB*); ~ **burette** *n* LAB bureta automática *f*;

~**c** ~ **call distributor** *n* (*ACD*) TELECOM distribuidor automático de llamadas *m*; ~ **call recording** *n* PRINT registro de llamada automática *m*, timón compensado *m*; ~ **call transfer** *n* TELECOM transferencia automática de llamadas *f*; ~ **calling unit** *n* (*ACU*) COMP&DP unidad de llamada automática *f* (*ULA*); ~ **capper** *n* PACK cerrador automático *m*, encapsulador automático *m*; ~ **car identification** *n* AmE (*cf automatic wagon identification BrE*) TRANSP identificación automática de coches *f* (*IAC*), identificación automática de vagones *f*; ~ **changeover** *n* ELEC *switch* conmutación automática *f*, transferencia automática *f*, TELECOM cambio automático *m*, relevo automático *m*; ~ **check** *n* COMP&DP comprobación automática *f*; ~ **choke** *n* AUTO estrangulador automático *m*, mariposa automática *f*, VEH estrangulador automático *m*; ~ **chrominance control** *n* TV control automático de crominancia *m*; ~ **chucking lathe** *n* MECH ENG torno de plato automático *m*; ~ **circuit-recloser** *n* ELEC *switch* recierre automático de circuito *m*, reconexión automática de circuito *f*; ~ **clutch** *n* VEH cambio automático *m*, embrague automático *m*; ~ **collation** *n* PACK intercalado automático *m*; ~ **control** *n* CONST control automático *m*, ELEC autorregulación *f*, control automático *m*, mando automático *m*, PACK control automático *m*; ~ **control assembly** *n* NUCL conjunto de control automático *m*; ~ **control equipment** *n* PETR TECH equipo de control automático *m*; ~ **control of headway** *n* TRANSP control automático de avance *m*; ~ **control switch** *n* ELEC *relay* conmutador automático de control *m*, conmutador de control automático *m*, conmutador de mando automático *m*, conmutador de regulación automática *m*; ~ **control system** *n* PROD sistema de control automático *m*; ~ **copying lathe** *n* MECH ENG torno de copiar automático *m*; ~ **coupling** *n* RAIL enganche automático *m*; ~ **credit card service** *n* TELECOM servicio automático de tarjetas de crédito *m*; ~ **crossfeed range** *n* PROD gama de avances automáticos *f*, gama de avances transversales *f*; ~ **current controller** *n* ELEC *relay* control automático de corriente *m*, regulador automático de corriente *m*; ~ **cut-out switch** *n* ELEC *safety* cortacircuito automático *m*, dispositivo de desconexión automática *m*, SAFE cortacircuito automático *m*, disyuntor automático *m*; ~ **cutter** *n* C&G cortadora automática *f*;

~**d** ~ **data conversion** *n* COMP&DP conversión automática de datos *f*; ~ **data processing** *n* COMP&DP procesamiento automático de datos *m*; ~ **decurling** *n* PACK sistema automático para eliminar el abarquillado *m*; ~ **device** *n* TELECOM dispositivo automático *m*; ~ **dialing** *AmE*, ~ **dialling** *BrE* *n* TELECOM marcación automática *f*; ~ **direction finder** *n* AIR TRANSP radiogoniómetro automático *m*; ~ **direction finding** *n* (*ADF*) AIR TRANSP, TELECOM goniometría automática *f* (*ADF*); ~ **down feed** *n* MECH ENG *machine-tools* avance automático vertical hacia abajo *m*;

~ e ~ **editing** *n* TV edición automática *f*; ~ **enlarger** *n* PHOTO, PRINT ampliadora automática *f*; ~ **error correction** *n* AIR TRANSP, TELECOM corrección automática de errores *f*; ~ **expansion gear** *n* MECH ENG mecanismo del distribuidor de expansión automático *m*; ~ **exposure** *n* PHOTO exposición automática *f*;

~ f ~ **feed** *n* CHEM TECH suministro automático *m*, MECH ENG *cutting tool* avance automático *m*, PETR TECH alimentación automática *f*, suministro automático *m*, reposición automática *f*; ~ **feeder** *n* PROD alimentador automático *m*; ~ **feeding** *n* C&G alimentación automática *f*; ~ **feeding system** *n* PACK, PROD sistema automático de alimentación *m*; ~ **film-threading** *n* CINEMAT enhebrado automático de la película *m*; ~ **fire alarm** *n* CONST alarma automática contraincendios *f*, alarma de incendios automática *f*, SAFE alarma automática contra incendios *f*, alarma de incendios automática *f*, THERMO alarma automática contraincendios *f*; ~ **fire detection system** *n* SAFE sistema automático de detección de incendios *m*; ~ **fire sprinkler** *n* WATER TRANSP rociador automático contraincendios *m*; ~ **fire-fighting system** *n* SAFE sistema automático contra incendios *m*; ~ **firing unit** *n* MILIT mecanismo automático de fuego *m*; ~ **flexible bag-filling machine** *n* PACK máquina para llenar automáticamente bolsas flexibles *f*; ~ **flight control system** *n* AIR TRANSP sistema de control de vuelo automático *m*; ~ **focusing** *n* PHOTO enfoque automático *m*; ~ **forming** *n* C&G formado automático *m*; ~ **frequency control** *n* (*AFC*) ELEC, ELECTRON, PHYS, PROD, TELECOM, TV control automático de frecuencia *m* (*CAF*);

~ g ~ **gain control** *n* (*AGC*) ELECTRON, GEOPHYS, TELECOM control automático de ganancia *m* (*CAG*); ~ **gear change** *n* VEH cambio de velocidades automático *m*; ~ **gear shift** *n* VEH cambio de velocidades automático *m*; ~ **governor** *n* FUELLESS regulador automático *m*; ~ **guidance system** *n* ELEC ENG sistema de guía automático *m*; ~ **gun** *n* MILIT cañón automático *m*;

~ h ~ **helm** *n* WATER TRANSP automatimonel *m*;

~ i ~ **ignition** *n* GAS encendido automático *m*, ignición automática *f*; ~ **infringement recorder** *n* TRANSP registrador automático de infracciones *m*; ~ **intercept system** *n* TELECOM sistema automático de interceptación *m*; ~ **isolating valve** *n* PETR TECH válvula de aislamiento automático *f*;

~ l ~ **laser shutdown** *n* TELECOM desconexión láser automática *f*; ~ **lathe** *n* MECH ENG torno automático *m*; ~ **level control** *n* AUTO control de nivel automático *m*; ~ **light signals** *n pl* RAIL señales luminosas automáticas *f pl*; ~ **load transfer** *n* ELEC *supply* transferencia automática de la carga *f*; ~ **loading system** *n* PHOTO sistema automático de carga *m*; ~ **location registration of ships** *n* TELECOM localización automática de matrículas de buques *f*; ~ **lock** *n* CINEMAT, TV bloqueo automático *m*;

~ m ~ **message switching center** *AmE*, ~ **message switching centre** *BrE n* TELECOM centro automático

conmutador de mensajes *m*; ~ **microscope camera** *n* INSTR cámara microscópica automática *f*;

~ n ~ **numbering equipment** *n* TELECOM equipo de numeración automática *m*;

~ o ~ **oil burner** *n* HEAT ENG quemador automático de aceite *m*; ~ **operation** *n* CONST funcionamiento automático *m*;

~ p ~ **page numbering** *n* COMP&DP numeración automática de páginas *f*, numerado automático de páginas *m*; ~ **peak limiter** *n* TV limitador automático de valor máximo *m*; ~ **phase control** *n* (*APC*) ELECTRON, TV control automático de fase *m*; ~ **pirn change** *n* TEXTIL cambio automático de canilla *m*; ~ **pressing** *n* C&G prensado automático *m*; ~ **printer** *n* PHOTO positivadora automática *f*; ~ **programming tool** *n* (*APT*) COMP&DP herramienta de programación automática *f* (*APT*); ~ **protection switching** *n* (*APS*) TELECOM conmutación automática de protección *f*; ~ **punch** *n* COMP&DP *tape* perforación automática *f*;

~ r ~ **radar plotting aid** *n* (*ARPA*) WATER TRANSP ayuda de punteo radar automático *f* (*APRA*); ~ **rammer** *n* MILIT atacador automático *m*; ~ **ramp down** *n* PROD rampa descendente automática *f*; ~ **recall** *n* TELECOM llamada automática *f*; ~ **regulation** *n* MECH ENG autorregulación *f*; ~ **regulator** *n* MECH ENG autorregulador *m*; ~ **release** *n* MECH ENG desembrague automático *m*; ~ **repair** *n* TEXTIL reparación automática *f*; ~ **report generation** *n* PROD producción automática de informes *f*; ~ **reset** *n* ELEC *control* puesta a cero automática *f*, reposición automática *f*; ~ **rewinder** *n* PHOTO rebobinadora automática *f*; ~ **roaming** *n* TELECOM recorrido automático *m*; ~ **running and braking control** *n* TRANSP funcionamiento automático y control de frenado *m*;

~ s ~ **sampler** *n* COAL tomamuestra automático *m*; ~ **sampling** *n* PROD, QUALITY muestreo automático *m*; ~ **screen printing** *n* TEXTIL estampación automática en pantalla *f*; ~ **screw machine** *n* MECH roscadora automática *f*, torno de roscar automático *m*; ~ **send-receive** *n* (*ASR*) COMP&DP envío-recepción automáticos *m* (*ASR*), terminal emisor-receptor automático *m* (*ASR*); ~ **sewage flow regulator** *n* HYDROL regulador automático del flujo de aguas residuales *m*; ~ **side and bottom loading machine** *n* PACK máquina de carga automática por el fondo y el lateral *f*; ~ **sidelay control** *n* PRINT armazón *m*, control automático de registro lateral *m*; ~ **slide changer** *n* PHOTO proyector automático de diapositivas *m*; ~ **speed checker** *n* MECH ENG verificador automático de velocidad *m*; ~ **speed control** *n* AUTO control de velocidad automático *m*; ~ **spur gear cutting machine** *n* MECH ENG máquina automática para tallar engranajes de dentadura recta *f*; ~ **stabilization equipment** *n* (*ASE*) TRANSP equipo de estabilización automática *m*; ~ **starting unit** *n* AIR TRANSP unidad de arranque automático *f*, unidad de encendido automático *f*; ~ **switch** *n* ELEC conmutador automático *m*; ~ **switchboard** *n* TELECOM central telefónica automática *f*; ~ **switching** *n* ELEC ENG, TRANSP conmutación automática *f*; ~ **system** *n* SPACE sistema automático *m*;

~ t ~ **telephone exchange** *n* TELECOM central telefónica automática *f*; ~ **telephone switching** *n* ELEC ENG conmutación telefónica automática *f*; ~ **teller**

machine n (*ATM*) COMP&DP cajero automático m (*Esp*) (*ATM*), máquina medidora automática f (*AmL*) (*ATM*); ~ **test equipment** n (*ATE*) COMP&DP equipo de pruebas automático m (*EPA*); ~ **timer** n PHOTO disparador automático m; ~ **titration** n LAB titulación automática f (*AmL*), valoración automática f (*Esp*); ~ **tracking** n WATER TRANSP *radar* seguimiento automático m; ~ **traffic light signals** n pl RAIL señales automáticas de tráfico f pl; ~ **train control** n (*ATC*) RAIL mando automático del tren m; ~ **train protection** n (*ATP*) RAIL protección automática del tren f; ~ **transmission** n AUTO, MECH, TELECOM, VEH transmisión automática f; ~ **transportation system** n TRANSP sistema de transporte automático m; ~ **trunk working** n TELECOM circuito automático de enlaces m;

~v ~ **vacuum brake** n MECH ENG, RAIL, VEH freno de vacío automático m; ~ **valve** n PETR TECH, REFRIG válvula automática f; ~ **vehicle identification** n (*AVI*) TRANSP identificación automática de vehículos f; ~ **vehicle location** n (*AVL*) TELECOM localización automática de vehículos f; ~ **verification** n QUALITY comprobación automática f, verificación automática f; ~ **voltage control** n ELEC autorregulador de tensión m, autorregulador de voltaje m, control automático de voltaje m; ~ **volume control** n (*AVC*) ELEC ENG *radio*, OPT, PHYS control automático de volumen m;

~w ~ **wagon identification** n BrE (*cf automatic car identification AmE*) TRANSP identificación automática de coches f (*IAC*), identificación automática de vagones f; ~ **weather station** n METEO estación meteorológica automática f; ~ **white balance** n TV compensación automática de blancos f

automation n COMP&DP, CONST, MECH ENG, PROD automatización f, SPACE automatismo m, automatización f, WATER TRANSP automatimonel m, automatización f, piloto automático m

automatize vt COMP&DP, CONST, MECH ENG, PROD, SPACE automatizar

automaton n COMP&DP autómata m

autometamorphism n FUELLESS autometamorfismo m

automodulation n TELECOM automodulación f

automorphic adj GEOL automórfico, enhédrico, idiomórfico, PETROL automórfico

automorphous adj GEOL, PETROL automorfo

automotive[1] adj TRANSP automotor, automotriz, automóvil

automotive[2]: ~ **heating** n AUTO, HEAT calefacción de automóvil f; ~ **industry** n AUTO, PROD industria de automoción f, industria del automóvil f

autonomous[1] adj SPACE autónomo

autonomous[2]: ~ **submersible** n OCEAN sumergible autónomo m

autonomy n SPACE autonomía f

autopaster n PRINT empalmadora f

autopilot n AIR TRANSP autopiloto m, piloto automático m, SPACE piloto automático m, autopiloto m, WATER TRANSP autotimonel m; ~ **control unit** n AIR TRANSP unidad de control del piloto automático f; ~ **disengage push button** n AIR TRANSP botón de desconexión del piloto automático m; ~ **disengagement** n AIR TRANSP desenganche del piloto automático m; ~ **gyro unit** n AIR TRANSP equipo giroscópico del piloto automático m, unidad

del giróscopo del piloto automático f; ~ **pitch sensitivity system** n AIR TRANSP sistema de sensitividad de cabeceo del piloto automático m; ~ **turn knob** n AIR TRANSP manilla de conexión del piloto automático f, manilla de enganche del piloto automático f

autopositioning: ~ **unit** n AIR TRANSP unidad autosituadora f, unidad de autoposición f

autoradiography n PHYS, RAD PHYS autorradiografía f

autoradiolysis n (*cf radiolysis*) PHYS, RAD PHYS autorradiólisis f

autoreclosing: ~ **system** n PRINT sistema de autorreposición m

autoregression n COMP&DP autorregresión f

autoregressive: ~ **moving average** n (*ARMA*) COMP&DP media móvil autorregresiva f (*ARMA*)

autoreverse n CINEMAT inversión automática f

autorotation: ~ **flight** n AIR TRANSP vuelo de autorotación m; ~ **transition time** n AIR TRANSP tiempo de transición de autorotación m

autorotative: ~ **flight** n AIR TRANSP *helicopter* vuelo autorotativo m

autosampler n LAB muestrador automático m

autoservo: ~ **mode** n TV modo autoservo m

auto-stop: ~ **and rewind** n PHOTO bloqueo y rebobinado automático m

autosynchronization n TELECOM autosincronización f

autotension n TV autotensión f

autothermic: ~ **piston** n AUTO pistón autotérmico m

autothrottle n AIR TRANSP autorregulador de gases m

autotracking n SPACE rastreo automático m, seguimiento automático m, TV seguimiento automático m

autotransformer n ELEC ENG, PHYS autotransformador m; ~ **starter** n ELEC *motor*, ELEC ENG autotransformador de arranque m

autotroph n FOOD autótrofo m

autotype: ~ **paper** n PAPER papel para formularios m

autoxidation n CHEM, FOOD autooxidación f

autunite n MINERAL autunita f

AUW abbr (*all-up weight*) TRANSP PMA (*peso en orden de vuelo, peso total de despegue*)

auxiliary[1] adj MECH, MECH ENG, SPACE auxiliar

auxiliary[2]: ~ **boiler** n HEAT caldera auxiliar f; ~ **boiler feeder** n HEAT ENG, HYDRAUL, THERMO alimentador de caldera auxiliar m; ~ **close-up lens** n CINEMAT, PHOTO, TV lente auxiliar para primeros planos f; ~ **contact** n ELEC ENG, PROD contacto auxiliar m; ~ **contact accessory** n ELEC, PROD accesorio de contacto auxiliar m; ~ **contact deck** n PROD tablero de contacto auxiliar m; ~ **cut** n C&G corte auxiliar m; ~ **electrode** n C&G electrodo auxiliar m; ~ **engine** n MECH ENG máquina auxiliar f, WATER TRANSP motor auxiliar m, máquina auxiliar f; ~ **engine sailing ship** n WATER TRANSP buque de vela con motor auxiliar m, velero con motor auxiliar m; ~ **feedwater system** n (*AFWS*) NUCL sistema de agua de alimentación auxiliar m (*AFWS*); ~ **jet** n VEH surtidor auxiliar m; ~ **machinery** n WATER TRANSP máquina auxiliar f; ~ **memory** n COMP&DP memoria auxiliar f; ~ **mirror** n PHOTO espejo auxiliar m; ~ **motor** n ELEC, MECH ENG motor auxiliar m; ~ **parachute** n MILIT paracaídas auxiliar m; ~ **power unit** n (*APU*) AIR TRANSP equipo de potencia auxiliar m, equipo generador de fuerza eléctrica auxiliar m, MILIT unidad de energía auxiliar f; ~ **rotor** n AIR TRANSP *helicopter* rotor auxiliar m; ~ **service position** n TELECOM posición auxiliar de marcha f; ~ **servo control** n MECH ENG servocontrol auxiliar m; ~ **shoe** n PHOTO pie auxiliar m; ~ **storage** n AmE COMP&DP almacenamiento auxiliar m, almacén auxiliar m, memoria auxiliar f; ~ **store** BrE n COMP&DP almacenamiento auxiliar m, almacén auxiliar m, memoria auxiliar f; ~ **switch** n ELEC conmutador auxiliar m, PROD interruptor auxiliar m, TELECOM conmutador auxiliar m; ~ **switching point** n TELECOM punto auxiliar de conmutación m; ~ **switching unit** n TELECOM unidad auxiliar de conmutación f; ~ **track** n RAIL vía auxiliar f; ~ **transformer** n ELEC transformador auxiliar m; ~ **valve** n MECH ENG válvula auxiliar f; ~ **vessel** n WATER TRANSP embarcación auxiliar f

auxin n AGRIC *hormones*, CHEM auxina f

auxochrome n CHEM auxocromo m

available[1] *adj* AGRIC *nutrients* asimilable

available[2]: ~ **chlorine** n PAPER cloro disponible m; ~ **heat** n THERMO calor disponible m; ~ **inventory** n PROD inventario disponible m; ~ **light** n CINEMAT, PHOTO, TV iluminación disponible f; ~ **list** n COMP&DP lista disponible f; ~ **power** n FUELLESS energía disponible f, MECH ENG energía máxima disponible f, potencia disponible f, potencia útil f, TELECOM potencia disponible f; ~ **stock** n PROD existencias disponibles $f pl$; ~ **time** n COMP&DP tiempo disponible m; ~ **train path** n RAIL itinerario disponible para el tren m; ~ **water-holding capacity** n AGRIC capacidad de retención de agua aprovechable f

avalanche n ELEC ENG avalancha f, ionización acumulativa f, METEO alud m, avalancha f; ~ **breakdown** n ELEC *semi-conductor diode* disrupción en avalancha f, ruptura por avalancha f, ELECTRON descarga en avalancha f, descarga por ionización acumulativa f; ~ **diode** n ELECTRON diodo de avalancha m, diodo de descarga m, PHYS, TELECOM diodo de avalancha m; ~ **gain** n ELECTRON ganancia en proceso de avalancha f; ~ **photodiode** n (APD) ELECTRON, OPT fotodiodo de avalancha m, fotodiodo de descarga m; ~ **transit-time diode** n PHYS diodo de tiempo de tránsito por avalancha m; ~ **voltage** n ELEC tensión en avalancha f, voltaje en avalancha m

avalent *adj* CHEM sin valencia

avalite n MINERAL avalita f, fucsita f

AVC *abbr* (*automatic volume control*) ELEC ENG, OPT, PHYS CVA (*control automático de volumen*)

avenine n CHEM avenina f

aventurine n C&G venturina f; ~ **feldspar** n MINERAL feldespato aventurina m; ~ **orientale** n MINERAL aventurina oriental f; ~ **quartz** n MINERAL cuarzo aventurina m

average n MATH promedio m, PHYS media aritmética f, promedio m; ~ **adjuster** n WATER TRANSP *insurance* tasador de averías m; ~ **annual daily traffic** n ($AADT$) TRANSP promedio anual de tráfico diario m; ~ **annual flow** n HYDROL promedio de caudal anual m; ~ **bits per sample** n TELECOM media de bits por muestra f; ~ **casting** n PROD pieza media f; ~ **characteristic flow** n HYDROL promedio de caudal característico m; ~ **cladding diameter** n OPT diámetro promedio de revestimiento m, TELECOM diámetro medio de chapeado m; ~ **core diameter** n OPT diámetro promedio del núcleo m, TELECOM diámetro medio del alma m; ~ **crossing rate** n TELECOM velocidad media de cruce f; ~ **daily flow** n HYDROL promedio de caudal diario m; ~ **daily output** n

FUELLESS rendimiento diario promedio m, PROD producción media diaria f; ~ **daily traffic** n (ADT) TRANSP promedio de tráfico diario m; ~ **delay per vehicle** n TRANSP promedio de demora por vehículo m, promedio de retraso por vehículo m; ~ **density** n TRANSP densidad-promedio f; ~ **deviation** n ELEC desviación media f, desviación promedio f, MATH desviación media f; ~ **distribution diagram** n HYDROL diagrama del promedio de distribución m; ~ **in turbulent flow** n FLUID valor medio de un flujo turbulento m; ~ **journey time** n TRANSP promedio tiempo por jornada m, promedio tiempo por viaje m; ~ **life** n PHYS vida media f; ~ **load** n ELEC carga media f, carga promedio f; ~ **logarithmic energy decrement** n NUCL decremento logarítmico medio m; ~ **mean temperature** n REFRIG temperatura media normal f; ~ **monthly flow** n HYDROL promedio del caudal mensual m; ~ **outgoing quality** n (AOQ) QUALITY calidad media después de control f; ~ **outgoing quality limit** n ($AOQL$) QUALITY límite de calidad media después de control m; ~ **output** n THERMO rendimiento promedio m; ~ **overall travel speed** n TRANSP promedio global de la velocidad del viaje m; ~ **power** n TELECOM potencia media f; ~ **running speed** n PRINT velocidad media de funcionamiento f, TRANSP velocidad media de marcha f; ~ **sound power per unit area** n ACOUST potencia sonora media por unidad de área f; ~ **sound pressure level difference** n ACOUST aislamiento acústico bruto m; ~ **speech power** n ACOUST potencia media de la palabra f; ~ **speed including stoppages** n PROD velocidad media incluyendo paradas f; ~ **spot speed** n TRANSP velocidad media en un punto f; ~ **steady state pressure** n MECH ENG *in closed circuit* presión media en estacionamiento f, presión promedio en estado de régimen f; ~ **stopped time** n TRANSP promedio de tiempo parado m, tiempo medio de parada m; ~ **time interval** n TRANSP promedio de intervalo de tiempo m; ~ **value** n ELEC promedio m, valor medio m, valor promedio m, PHYS valor medio m; ~ **vehicle length** n TRANSP longitud media de vehículos f; ~ **wind speed** n FUELLESS, METEO velocidad media del viento f; ~ **yearly flow** n HYDROL promedio de control anual m

AVI *abbr* (*automatic vehicle identification*) TRANSP IAV (*identificación automática de vehículos*)

aviation: ~ **fuel** n AIR TRANSP combustible de aviación m; ~ **gasoline** n AmE PETR TECH gasolina de aviación f; ~ **petrol** BrE n PETR TECH gasolina de aviación f; ~ **turbine kerosene** n (ATK) PETR TECH keroseno de turbina de aviación m

avionics n AIR TRANSP aviónica f, electrónica aeronáutica f, equipo electrónico aeronáutico de a bordo m, SPACE aviónica f

AVL *abbr* (*automatic vehicle location*) TELECOM localización automática de vehículos f

avoiding: ~ **line** n RAIL línea de desviación f

avoirdupois: ~ **ounce** n METR onza avoirdupois f; ~ **weight** n METR peso de las unidades m

AVT *abbr* (*all-volatile chemistry*) NUCL química de los volátiles f

awaruite n MINERAL awaruíta f

awash *adj* WATER TRANSP a flor de agua

A-weighting: ~ **curve** n ACOUST curva de ponderación A f

AWG *abbr* (*American wire gage AmE, American wire*

gauge BrE) PROD sistema norteamericano de calibres de alambres y de chapas *m*

awl *n* CONST lezna *f*

awn *n* AGRIC arista *f*, barba de espiga de los cereales *f*

awner *n* AGRIC desbarbador *m*

AWT *abbr* (*acid well treatment*) PETR TECH, PETROL acidificación del pozo *f*

AWU *abbr* (*atomic weight unit*) PHYS UMA (*unidad de masa atómica*)

axial[1] *adj* GEOM, MATH axial

axial[2]: ~ **actuator** *n* SPACE accionador axial *m*, actuador axial *m*; ~ **armature** *n* ELEC, ELEC ENG inducido axial *m*, inducido provisto de eje *m*; ~ **backlash** *n* MECH, MECH ENG juego axial *m*; ~ **blower** *n* SAFE abanico axial *m*, fuelle axial *m*; ~ **clearance** *n* MECH huelgo axial *m*, juego axial *m*, MECH ENG juego axial *m*; ~ **compressor** *n* AIR TRANSP, MECH compresor axial *m*; ~ **culmination** *n* GEOL culminación axial *f*; ~ **cylindrical roller bearing** *n* MECH ENG cojinete de rodillos cilíndricos axial *m*; ~ **deposition** *n* C&G deposición axial *f*; ~ **depression** *n* GEOL depresión axial *f*; ~ **displacement** *n* TV desplazamiento axial *m*; ~ **efficiency** *n* ACOUST eficacia axial *f*; ~ **flow** *n* AIR TRANSP, VEH flujo axial *m*; ~ **flow fan** *n* HEAT ENG ventilador de flujo axial *m*; ~ **flow lift fan** *n* TRANSP ventilador axial de elevación *m*, ventilador impulsor de flujo axial *m*; ~ **flow pump** *n* MECH ENG, MINE bomba de flujo axial *f*; ~-**flow turbine** *n* HYDRAUL turbina de caudal paralelo *f*, turbina de flujo axial *f*; ~ **interference** *n* OPT interferencia axial *f*; ~ **interference microscopy** *n* OPT, TELECOM microscopía por interferencia axial *f*; ~ **interferometry** *n* OPT interferometría axial *f*; ~ **line** *n* GEOM eje *m*, línea axial *f*; ~ **load fatigue testing** *n* MECH ENG prueba de fatiga con carga axial *f*; ~ **loading** *n* METALL carga axial *f*; ~ **magnification** *n* PHYS aumento axial *m*; ~ **period** *n* SPACE período axial *m*; ~ **piston pump** *n* MECH bomba de pistón axial *f*; ~ **plane** *n* GEOL plano axial *m*; ~ **plane cleavage** *n* GEOL exfoliación del plano axial *f*; ~ **plane foliation** *n* GEOL exfoliación del plano axial *f*; ~ **plasma deposition** *n* TELECOM deposición axial de plasma *f*; ~ **propagation coefficient** *n* OPT, TELECOM coeficiente de propagación axial *m*; ~ **pump** *n* MECH ENG bomba axial *f*; ~-**radial bearing** *n* INSTR conexión axial radial *f*; ~ **radius** *n* OPT radio axial *m*; ~ **ratio** *n* CRYSTALL elipticidad *f*, relación axial *f*, SPACE razón axial *f*, relación axial *f*; ~ **ray** *n* OPT, TELECOM rayo axial *m*; ~ **rift zone** *n* GEOL zona de rift axial *f*; ~ **scanning** *n* OPT barrido axial *m*; ~ **shield** *n* NUCL blindaje axial *m*; ~ **slab interferometry** *n* TELECOM interferometría axial *f*; ~ **symmetry** *n* GEOM, MATH simetría axial *f*; ~ **thrust bearing** *n* MECH ENG cojinete de empuje axial *m*, rodamiento de empuje axial *m*; ~ **trace** *n* GEOL traza axial *f*; ~ **velocity** *n* FUELLESS velocidad axial *f*; ~ **velocity sensor** *n* SPACE detector de velocidad axial *m*; ~ **ventilator** *n* SAFE ventilador axial *m*

axially[1]: ~ **symmetric** *adj* CRYSTALL, GEOL axialmente simétrico

axially[2]: ~-**collapsing steering column** *n* TRANSP columna de dirección de derrumbe axial *f*, eje de dirección de derrumbe axial *m*

axillary: ~ **branching** *n* AGRIC ramificación axilar *f*; ~ **bud** *n* AGRIC yema axilar *f*

axinite *n* MINERAL axinita *f*

axiom *n* GEOM, MATH axioma *m*

axiomatic *adj* GEOM, MATH axiomático

axis *n* CRYSTALL, GEOM, MECH eje *m*, METEO *switch* eje de la depresión *m*, eje *m*, PHYS eje *m*; ~ **of an anticyclone** *n* METEO eje del anticiclón *m*; ~ **of commutation** *n* ELEC *machine* eje de conmutación *m*, línea de conmutación *f*; ~ **of inertia** *n* MECH eje de inercia *m*; ~ **of oscillation** *n* PHYS eje de oscilación *m*; ~ **of projection** *n* CINEMAT eje de proyección *m*; ~ **of revolution** *n* MECH eje de revolución *m*; ~ **of rotation** *n* MECH eje de rotación *m*; ~ **of symmetry** *n* CRYSTALL, GEOM, MECH ENG eje de simetría *m*

axle *n* CONST eje *m*, VEH eje *m*, árbol *m*; ~ **box** *n BrE* (*cf journal box AmE*) MECH ENG caja de engranajes *f*, caja de grasas *f*, *bearing block* chumacera *f*, cojinete *m*, RAIL caja de grasas *f*, cojinete *m*; ~ **bush** *n* VEH casquillo *m*; ~ **bushing** *n* VEH casquillo antifricción *m*, mangueta *f*; ~ **cap** *n* AUTO casquillo del eje *m*, sombrerete del eje *m*; ~ **casing** *n* AUTO, MECH alojamiento del eje *m*, VEH alojamiento del eje *m*, cárter del eje *m*; ~ **crank** *n* MECH ENG codo del eje *m*; ~ **fit** *n* MECH ENG ajuste de eje *m*; ~ **flange** *n* AUTO, VEH brida del eje *f*; ~ **guide** *n* RAIL placa de guarda *f*; ~ **guide stay** *n* RAIL tirante de placa de guarda *m*; ~ **housing** *n* AUTO, MECH alojamiento del eje *m*, VEH alojamiento del eje *m*, cárter del eje *m*; ~ **lathe** *n* MECH ENG torno para ejes *m*; ~ **load** *n* CONST carga axial *f*, carga del eje *f*, carga por eje *f*; ~ **pulley** *n* CONST *hardware* cabrestante *m*, polea *f*, roldana de eje *f*; ~ **ratio** *n* VEH relación de desmultiplicación *f*; ~ **seat** *n* MECH ENG asiento de eje *m*; ~ **shaft** *n* VEH palier *m*, semieje *m*

Az-El: ~ **mount** *n* SPACE montaje azimut-elevación *m*, soporte azimut-elevación *m*

azelaic *adj* CHEM acelaico, azelaico

azeotrope *n* CHEM, REFRIG, THERMO aceótropo *m*, azeótropo *m*

azeotropic[1] *adj* CHEM, REFRIG, THERMO azeotrópico

azeotropic[2]: ~ **distillation** *n* FOOD destilación azeotrópica *f*; ~ **mixture** *n* FOOD, REFRIG mezcla azeotrópica *f*; ~ **point** *n* REFRIG punto azeotrópico *m*

azeotropy *n* CHEM, REFRIG azeotropía *f*

AZERTY: ~ **keyboard** *n* COMP&DP *French keyboard* tablero AZERTY *m*

azide *n* CHEM azida *f*

azimino[1] *adj* CHEM azimino

azimino[2]: ~ **compound** *n* CHEM compuesto azimídico *m*

azimuth *n* CONST acimut *m*, azimut *m*, GEOL, PETROL, PHYS, SPACE, TV, WATER TRANSP *navigation* azimut *m*; ~ **adjustment** *n* TV ajuste de acimut *m*, ajuste azimutal *m*, ajuste de azimut *m*; ~ **angle** *n* FUELLESS ángulo acimutal *m*; ~ **bearing** *n* OCEAN marcación azimutal *f*, marcación relativa *f*; ~ **coarse motion clamp** *n* INSTR prensador de movimiento rápido acimutal *m*; ~ **compass** *n* WATER TRANSP compás azimutal *m*; ~ **distortion** *n* TV distorsión azimutal *f*; ~ **gyro** *n* SPACE giróscopo azimutal *m*; ~ **loss** *n* TV pérdida azimutal *f* (*Esp*), pérdida de azimut *f* (*AmL*); ~ **stabilization** *n* WATER TRANSP *radar* estabilización en azimut *f*; ~ **thrust** *n* SPACE impulso de azimut *m*

azimuthal: ~ **control** *n* AIR TRANSP control acimutal *m*; ~ **quantum number** *n* PHYS, RAD PHYS número cuántico azimutal *m*

azo: ~ **compounds** *n pl* CHEM compuestos azoicos *m pl*; ~ **dye** *n* CHEM colorante azoico *m*
azobenzene *n* CHEM azobenceno *m*
azobenzoic *adj* CHEM azobenzoico
azoic: ~ **dye** *n* TEXTIL colorante azoico *m*

azorite *n* MINERAL azorita *f*
azulene *n* CHEM azuleno *m*
azulin *n* CHEM azulina *f*
azulmin *n* CHEM azulmín *m*
azurite *n* CHEM, MINERAL azurita *f*

B

b *abbr* ACOUST, COMP&DP, ELEC ENG (*belio*), NUCL, PART PHYS, PHYS, RAD PHYS (*bel, barn*) b (*belio, barn, barnio*)
B *abbr* (*boron*) CHEM B (*boro*)
B: ~ **sizes** *n pl* PRINT tamaños B *m pl*
Ba *abbr* (*barium*) CHEM Ba (*bario*)
BA: ~ **screw thread** *n* (*British Association screw thread*) MECH ENG hilo de rosca de British Association *m*
babbited: ~ **cast-iron bearing** *n* MECH ENG cojinete de hierro fundido antifriccionado *m*
Babbitt's: ~ **metal** *n* MECH ENG metal Babbit *m*, metal antifricción *m*, metal blanco *m*
Babcock: ~ **plan** *n* TELECOM plan de Babcock *m*
Babinet: ~ **compensator** *n* PHYS compensador de Babinet *m*; ~**'s principle** *n* PHYS principio de Babinet *m*
babingtonite *n* MINERAL babingtonita *f*
baby *n* CINEMAT bombilla incandescente pequeña *f*; ~ **beef** *n* AGRIC carne de ternera blanca *f*; ~ **dryer** *n* PAPER cilindro secador embarcador *m*; ~ **legs** *n pl* CINEMAT trípode de patas cortas *m*, trípode bajo *m*; ~ **press** *n* PAPER rodillo tomador en la forma redonda *m*; ~ **tripod** *n* CINEMAT trípode bajo *m*
bacca: ~**-box smoother** *n* MECH ENG alisador de seta *m*
bacillus *n* FOOD bacilo *m*
back[1]: ~**-connected** *adj* ELEC *switch* conectado por detrás, de conexión posterior; ~**-to-back** *adj* CONST dorso contra dorso, PROD adosado, espalda con espalda
back[2] *n* COAL diaclasa longitudinal *f*, CONST *of arch* parte trasera *f*, reverso *m*, trasdós *m*, GEOL diaclasa longitudinal *f*, MECH ENG lomo *m*, MINE diaclasa longitudinal *f*, crucero principal *m*, techo *m*, cruce de galerías *m* (*Esp*), PHOTO parte posterior *f*, respaldo *m*, PRINT retiración *f*; ~ **adjustment** *n* PHOTO *spacecraft* ajuste posterior *m*; ~**-and-forth motion** *n* MECH ENG movimiento de avance y retroceso *m*, movimiento de vaivén *m*; ~**-and-forth printing** *n* CINEMAT copiado de vaivén *m*; ~**-arc basin** *n* GEOL cuenca de arco volcánico *f*, OCEAN cuenca marginal interna *f*; ~ **axle** *n* VEH puente trasero *m*; ~ **azimuth guidance** *n* AIR TRANSP *navigation* guía acimutal inversa *f*; ~ **balance** *n* MECH ENG contrapeso *m*; ~ **beam** *n* TEXTIL plegador posterior *m*; ~ **boiler** *n* MECH ENG *for hot water* bullidor *m*; ~ **center** *AmE*, ~ **centre** *BrE* *n* MECH ENG *of lathe* contrapunto *m*, punto de atrás *m*, punto posterior *m*; ~ **contact** *n* ELEC *relay* contacto de reposo *m*; ~ **cover** *n* PHOTO tapa posterior *f*; ~**-cover release** *n* PHOTO desenganche de la tapa posterior *m*; ~**-cross** *n* AGRIC retrocruza *f*, retrocruzamiento *m*; ~ **current** *n* HYDRAUL sobreflujo *m*; ~**-cylinder cover** *n* HYDRAUL culata del cilindro posterior *f*, tapa del cilindro posterior *f*, MECH ENG *of horizontal stationary engine* fondo de cilindro *m*, fondo de cilindro posterior *m*; ~ **diffusion** *n* NUCL retrodifusión *f*; ~ **diffusion loss** *n* NUCL pérdida por retrodifusión *f*; ~**-discharge car** *n* *AmE* (*cf back-*

discharge wagon BrE) RAIL vagón basculante con descarga hacia atrás *m*, vagón basculante hacia atrás *m*; ~**-discharge wagon** *BrE* *n* (*cf back-discharge car AmE*) RAIL vagón basculante con descarga hacia atrás *m*, vagón basculante hacia atrás *m*; ~ **eddy** *n* HYDROL corriente turbulenta de retorno *f*, remolino de retorno *m*; ~**-edge margin** *n* PRINT margen del borde posterior *m*; ~ **electromotive force** *n* (*back emf*) ELEC, ELEC ENG, PHYS, RAIL, VEH fuerza contraelectromotriz *f*; ~ **emf** *n* (*back electromotive force*) ELEC, ELEC ENG, PHYS, RAIL, VEH fuerza contraelectromotriz *f*; ~ **end of nuclear fuel cycle** *n* NUCL *from reactor onwards* segunda parte del ciclo de combustible nuclear *f*; ~**-end plate** *n* MECH ENG placa lado posterior *f*; ~ **filler** *n* CONST material para rellenar *m*, TRANSP máquina rellenadora *f* (*Esp*), rellenador de calas *m* (*AmL*), rellenazanjas *m* (*Esp*); ~ **finish** *n* COATINGS acabado del reverso *m*, acabado interior *m*; ~**-fire aerial** *n* *BrE* (*cf back-fire antenna AmE*) SPACE antena de radiación regresiva *f*; ~**-fire antenna** *n* *AmE* (*cf back-fire aerial BrE*) SPACE antena de radiación regresiva *f*; ~ **flow** *n* HYDRAUL flujo de retorno *m*; ~ **focus** *n* CINEMAT foco del fondo *m*; ~ **freight** *n* WATER TRANSP flete de vuelta *m*; ~ **gap** *n* TV intervalo *m*; ~ **gear** *n* MECH ENG contramarcha *f*; ~ **gutter** *n* PRINT medianil posterior *m*; ~**-hoe** *n* AGRIC pala mecánica trasera de tractor *f*; ~ **iron** *n* CONST *of plane* hierro de relleno *m*; ~ **label** *n* PACK etiqueta posterior *f*; ~ **lens** *n* INSTR lente posterior *f*; ~ **lining** *n* PRINT contralomo *m*, *of book* forro del lomo *m*; ~ **loader** *n* CONST cargador trasero *m*; ~ **margin** *n* PRINT margen posterior *m*; ~ **marks** *n pl* PRINT señales para el alzado *f pl*; ~ **matter** *n* PRINT apéndice *m*, suplemento *m*; ~ **observation** *n* CONST *levelling* observación posterior *f*; ~ **panel layout** *n* PROD distribución del cuadro posterior *f*; ~ **plate** *n* COMP&DP placa base *f*, placa matriz *f*, ELECTRON *coil* placa posterior *f*, MECH ENG *lathe-spindle* contraplato *m*; ~ **porch** *n* TV umbral posterior *m*; ~**-porch clamping** *n* TV fijación del umbral posterior *f*; ~ **pressure** *n* C&G contrapresión *f*, HYDRAUL presión de retroceso *f*; ~**-pressure valve** *n* HYDRAUL válvula de impulsión de retroceso *f*; ~ **printing** *n* PRINT impresión del dorso *f*, impresión invertida *f*; ~ **projection** *n* CINEMAT transparencia *f*; ~**-projection screen** *n* CINEMAT pantalla para transparencias *f*, pantalla translúcida *f*; ~ **puppet** *n* MECH ENG contrapunto *m*; ~ **reef** *n* GEOL zona detrás de una barrera de arrecifes *f*; ~**-reflection method** *n* CRYSTALL método de reflexión de retroceso *m*, retrodifracción *f*; ~ **rounding** *n* PRINT redondeo del lomo *m*; ~ **run** *n* CINEMAT rodaje marcha atrás *m*; ~ **saw** *n* CONST serrucho de costilla *f*; ~ **sheet of fire box** *n* MECH ENG chapa posterior de la caja de fuegos *f*; ~ **signal** *n* ELECTRON señal posterior *f*; ~ **speed** *n* MECH ENG reducción de engranajes *f*; ~ **splice** *n* WATER TRANSP *ropework* pata de conejo *f*, pata de ganso *f*; ~ **spotfacing** *n* MECH ENG refrentado posterior *m*; ~ **stope** *n* CONST testero *m*; ~ **stroke** *n*

HYDRAUL carrera de retorno f, carrera de vuelta f, recorrido de retorno m; **~ surface** n C&G *of drawn glass sheet* superficie posterior f; **~ thrust** n GEOL retrocabalgamiento m; **~ title** n PRINT *of book* título del lomo m; **~ titration** n CHEM retrotitulación f, retrovaloración f, titulación por retorno f; **~-to-back** n TEXTIL envés contra envés m, espalda contra espalda f; **~-to-back arrangement** n ELEC ENG *capacitors* ajuste de dos máquinas eléctricas acopladas m, *diodes etc* ajuste adosado añadido m, disposición en oposición f; **~-to-back commercials** n pl TV anuncios contiguos m pl; **~-tube sheet** n MECH ENG placa tubular de caja de fuegos f; **~ tweel** n C&G puerta de guillotina trasera f; **~ valve** n HYDRAUL válvula de contrapresión f; **~-wall photovoltaic cell** n ELEC ENG célula fotovoltaica de carrera posterior f; **~ water** n PAPER agua de retorno f; **~ weld** n PROD soldadura espaldar f

back[3] *vt* MECH ENG *tap* respaldar, *drill* retirar, PRINT imprimir el dorso, retirar, WATER TRANSP *sail* fachear, *anchor* engalgar; **~ off** *vt* MECH ENG *give clearance, relieve* desbloquear, *milling cutter* aflojar; **~ titrate** *vt* CHEM retrotitular, retrovalorar; **~ up** *vt* COMP&DP hacer una copia de reserva de, PRINT calzar la matriz de, imprimir el reverso del pliego de

back[4]: **~ off** *vi* PROD desbloquear; **~ up** *vi* RAIL dar marcha atrás

backbone: **~ bus** n COMP&DP bus principal m

backcoating n TEXTIL revestimiento de envés m

backed: **~-off cutter** n MECH ENG fresa de dientes destalonados f, fresa de perfil constante f, fresa de perfil invariable f; **~-off teeth** n pl MECH ENG *of gear or rack* dientes destalonados m pl

backfill[1] n COAL relleno de zanjas m, CONST relleno m, NUCL *phase of LOCA* rellenado m, POLL relleno m; **~ material** n NUCL material de relleno m

backfill[2] *vt* CONST rellenar

backfire n AUTO explosiones al carburador f pl, CONST explosión prematura f, retroceso transitorio de la llama en el soplete m, VEH encendido prematuro m, explosiones al carburador f pl

backflow n WATER contracorriente f

backfolding n GEOL retroplegamiento m

backfurrow n AGRIC contrasurco m

backgap n ACOUST retroespacio m

background n PHOTO campo m, fondo m, segundo plano m, PRINT fondo m; **~ absorption** n RAD PHYS absorción de fondo f; **~ art** n PRINT ilustración que forma el fondo f; **~ blur** n PHOTO fondo borroso m; **~ concentration** n POLL concentración de fondo f, nivel de fondo m; **~ film** n CINEMAT película de fondo f; **~ gas** n (*BG*) GAS, PETR TECH gas de background m; **~ intensity** n CRYSTALL *X-rays* intensidad de fondo f; **~ level** n POLL concentración de fondo f, nivel de fondo m; **~ lighting** n CINEMAT iluminación del fondo f, luz de fondo f, PHOTO, TV iluminación del fondo f; **~ monitor** n TV monitor de fondo m; **~ negative** n CINEMAT negativo de fondo m; **~ noise** n ACOUST, ELECTRON, GEOPHYS, PHYS, SPACE, TELECOM ruido de fondo m; **~ pattern** n PRINT dibujo tramado de fondo m, patente de navegación f; **~ planting** n AGRIC siembra de respaldo f; **~ pollution** n POLL contaminación de fondo f; **~ processing** n COMP&DP procesamiento de fondo m, procesamiento de prioridad subordinada m, procesamiento subordinado m; **~ program** n COMP&DP programa de base m,

programa de fondo m; **~ radiation** n NUCL, PHYS, RAD PHYS radiación de fondo f; **~ vorticity** n FLUID régimen turbulillonario de fondo m

backhand: **~ welding** n MECH, PROD soldadura de revés f

backhead n MECH ENG *tailstock of lathe* cabeza trasera f, contrapunto m

backhoe n MAR POLL retroexcavadora f; **~ loader** n TRANSP excavadora f, pala retroexcavadora f

backhole n MINE barreno de techo m

backing n AIR TRANSP *of seat* retroceso m, soporte m, apoyo m, COATINGS relleno m, MECH ENG forro m, marcha atrás f, PAPER hoja de respaldo f, PRINT *of book, plate, blanket* retiración f, RAIL *vehicles* marcha atrás f, TEXTIL tela de sostén f, *of book* refuerzo m, WATER TRANSP *of wind* rolada f; **~ bar** n AIR TRANSP barra de apoyo f, barra de soporte f; **~ bricks** n pl PROD ladrillos de respaldo m pl; **~ fabric** n TEXTIL tela de refuerzo de envés f; **~ movement** n RAIL movimiento de retroceso m, movimiento marcha atrás m; **~ off** n MECH ENG *machining* rebajado m, *relief or clearance* destalonado m; **~-off lathe** n MECH ENG torno de despojar m, torno de destalonar m; **~ paper** n PHOTO papel posterior protector m, respaldo m; **~ pass** n PROD *welding* doble pase f; **~ plate** n MECH ENG chapa de respaldo f, chapa soporte f, contraplaca f, VEH placa de apoyo f; **~ removal** n CINEMAT retirada del respaldo f; **~ roll** n PAPER rodillo de soporte m; **~ roller** n PRINT rodillo de apoyo m; **~ signal** n RAIL señal de marcha atrás f, señal de retroceso f; **~ storage** n AmE COMP&DP almacenamiento de respaldo m, memoria auxiliar f, memoria secundaria f; **~ store** BrE n COMP&DP almacenamiento de respaldo m, memoria auxiliar f, memoria secundaria f; **~ tape** n COMP&DP cinta auxiliar f; **~-up** n HYDRAUL retención f, PRINT impresión del dorso f, retiración f; **~ wire** n PAPER tela de soporte f

backlash n CINEMAT contragolpe m, HYDRAUL contrapresión f, MECH desajuste m, huelgo m, juego m, movimiento inútil m, MECH ENG *of gear* huelgo m, repercusión f, MINE zona muerta f, efecto reactivo m, repercusión f, PRINT holgura f, SPACE *communications* juego m, holgura f, VEH reenvío m, WATER TRANSP *radar* inversión de fase f; **~ error** n AIR TRANSP *in altimeter* error de contrapresión m, error del juego de los engranajes m

backlight[1] n CINEMAT luz posterior f, proyector de fondo m, iluminación posterior f

backlight[2] *vt* PHOTO iluminar con luz posterior

backlighting n CINEMAT, ELEC ENG, PHOTO, TV iluminación a contraluz f

backlining n PRINT *of book* forro del lomo m

backlit[1] *adj* PHOTO iluminado con luz posterior

backlit[2]: **~ push button** n PROD botón de iluminación a contraluz m

backlog n MECH acumulación de materiales f, material pendiente de clasificar m, PROD acumulación de trabajo f; **~ of orders** n PROD pedidos pendientes m pl

backpack: **~ radio** n MILIT radio de mochila f

backplane n COMP&DP, ELECTRON, PROD panel de fondo m, plano posterior m

backplate n TV placa posterior f

backrest n AUTO respaldo m, MECH ENG *lathe* luneta f, VEH respaldo m

backrush n OCEAN resaca f

backscatter[1] *n* SPACE retrodifusión *f*; ~ **effect** *n* NUCL efecto de retrodispersión *m*; ~ **gage** *AmE*, ~ **gauge** *BrE n* NUCL *of tyre* indicador de retrodispersión *m*; ~ **peak** *n* RAD PHYS pico de retrodispersión *m*
backscatter[2] *vt* OPT retrodifundir, retrodispersar, retrorreflejar
backscatter[3] *vi* OPT retrodifundirse
backscattered: ~ **light beam method** *n* ACOUST método del haz luminoso retrodispersado *m*
backscattering *n* ELECTRON dispersión *f*, OPT retrodifusión *f*, retroesparcimiento *m*, RAD PHYS retrodispersión *f*, SPACE dispersión inversa *f*, retrodispersión *f*, TELECOM retrodispersión *f*; ~ **factor** *n* PART PHYS factor de retrodifusión *m*, SPACE factor de retrodifusión *m*, factor de retrodispersión *m*, TELECOM factor de retrodispersión *m*; ~ **technique** *n* OPT técnica por retroesparcimiento *f*, TELECOM técnica de retrodispersión *f*
backset *n* HYDRAUL contracorriente *f*
backshore *n* OCEAN ribera posterior *f*, trasplaya *f*
backside *n* PAPER lado del accionamiento *m*, reverso *m*, PRINT reverso *m*; ~ **batt** *n* TEXTIL batán posterior *m*; ~ **coating** *n* CINEMAT revestimiento posterior protector *m*
backsight *n* CONST *levelling* visual inversa *f*
backspace[1] *n* (*BS*) COMP&DP, PRINT espacio de retroceso *m*, retroceso *m*, retroseguimiento *m*, tecla de retroceso *f*; ~ **character** *n* COMP&DP carácter de retroceso *m*
backspace[2] *vi* COMP&DP retroceder
backstay *n* WATER TRANSP *standing rigging* burda *f*
backstep: ~ **sequence** *n* PROD *welding* secuencia de retroceso *f*
backstop *n* PRINT tope de retención *m*
backtrack *vi* AIR TRANSP retroceder
backtracking *n* COMP&DP retroseguimiento *m*
backup[1] *adj* COMP&DP de apoyo, de reserva, de seguridad
backup[2] *n* COMP&DP copia de reserva *f*, ELEC ENG elemento de reserva *m*, PETR TECH equipo de reserva *m*, PROD apoyo *m*; ~ **battery** *n* ELEC, ELEC ENG, PROD batería de emergencia *f*; ~ **bearing** *n* SPACE marcación de reserva *f*, soporte de reserva *m*; ~ **circuit** *n* PROD circuito de reserva *m*; ~ **communication** *n* PROD comunicación de emergencia *f*; ~ **configuration** *n* PROD configuración de reserva *f*, configuración de respaldo *f*; ~ **line** *n* PETR TECH cable de soporte *m* (*Esp*), cable de sujeción *m* (*Esp*), línea de aguante *f* (*AmL*), línea de soporte *f* (*AmL*); ~ **mode** *n* PROD modo de emergencia *m*; ~ **post** *n* PETR TECH poste de retención *m*; ~ **power** *n* PROD abastecimiento de reserva *m*; ~ **power supply** *n* ELEC ENG suministro de energía de reserva *m*, TELECOM reserva de fuente de energía *f*; ~ **processor** *n* PROD procesador de respaldo *m*; ~ **roll** *n* C&G cilindro de respaldo *m*; ~ **service** *n* TRANSP servicio de reserva *m*; ~ **signal** *n* RAIL señal de marcha atrás *f*; ~ **supervisor** *n* TELECOM supervisor de reserva *m*; ~ **switch** *n* PROD interruptor de reserva *m*, interruptor de retorno de potencia *m*, interruptor subsidiario *m*
Backus: ~ **normal form** *n* COMP&DP forma normal de Backus *f*
backward[1] *adv* PROD mirando hacia atrás
backward[2]: ~**-and-forward motion** *n* MECH ENG movimiento de avance y retroceso *m*; ~ **channel** *n* COMP&DP canal de retroceso *m*, clasificación de retroceso *f*; ~ **diode** *n* ELECTRON diodo inverso *m*; ~ **explicit congestion notification** *n* (*BECN*) TELECOM notificación explícita de bloqueo regresivo *f*; ~ **flight** *n* AIR TRANSP vuelo hacia atrás *m*; ~**-input signal** *n* TELECOM señal de entrada regresiva *f*; ~**-interworking telephony event** *n* TELECOM acontecimiento de telefonía entrelazada hacia atrás *m*; ~ **motion** *n* MECH ENG movimiento de retroceso *m*, PRINT retroceso *m*; ~ **movement** *n* MECH ENG movimiento retrógrado *m*; ~ **scheduling** *n* PROD retroprogramación *f*; ~ **sort** *n* COMP&DP clasificación inversa *f*, clasificación regresiva *f*; ~ **stroke** *n* MECH ENG carrera retrógrada *f*; ~ **takeoff** *n* AIR TRANSP *helicopter* despegue hacia atrás *m*; ~ **wave** *n* ELEC ENG onda regresiva *f*, *transmission lines* onda de retorno *f*; ~**-wave guide** *n* TELECOM guía de onda regresiva *f*; ~**-wave oscillator** *n* (*BWO*) ELECTRON oscilador de onda regresiva *m*, PHYS oscilador de onda de retorno *m*, TELECOM oscilador de onda regresiva *m*; ~**-wave tube** *n* ELECTRON, PHYS tubo de onda regresiva *m*; ~ **welding** *n* PROD soldadura con la llama dirigida hacia la parte ya soldada *f*
backwash *n* HYDROL contracorriente *f*, *of sea* resaca *f*, OCEAN contracorriente submarina *f*, resaca *f*; ~ **tank** *n* NUCL depósito de reextracción *m*, tanque de reextracción *m*; ~ **water** *n* HYDROL agua estancada *f*, remanso *m*, WATER agua estancada *f*, agua lanzada hacia atrás *f*
backwashing *n* HYDROL *paper, board*, WATER lavado a contracorriente *m*
backwater *n* HYDROL remolino *m*, WATER contracorriente *f*; ~ **effect** *n* FUELLESS efecto de remanso *m*
backwind[1]: ~ **handle** *n* CINEMAT manivela de rebobinado *f*
backwind[2] *vt* CINEMAT, PHOTO rebobinar
backwind[3] *vi* CINEMAT, PHOTO rebobinar
baconer *n* AGRIC cerdo pancetero *m*
bacteria: ~ **bed** *n* WATER cama bacteriana *f*; ~ **beds** *n pl* RECYCL cultivos de bacterias *m pl*; ~ **propagation tank** *n* FOOD depósito para la propagación de bacterias *m*
bacterial: ~ **bed** *n* HYDROL lecho bacterial *m*, lecho bacteriano *m*; ~ **blight** *n* AGRIC muerte bacteriana *f*; ~ **count** *n* WATER conteo bacteriano *m*; ~ **leaf-blight of corn** *n* AGRIC muerte bacteriana de la hoja del maíz *f*; ~ **leaf-spot** *n* AGRIC mancha foliar bacteriana *f*; ~ **pustule** *n* AGRIC pústula bacteriana *f*; ~ **spot** *n* AGRIC mancha bacteriana *f*; ~ **stem-blight** *n* AGRIC muerte bacteriana del tallo *f*; ~ **streak** *n* AGRIC xantomoniasis *f*; ~ **stripe** *n* AGRIC estría bacteriana *f*
bactericidal *adj* HYDROL, RECYCL, WATER bactericida
bactericide *n* CHEM, FOOD, HYDROL, RECYCL, WATER bactericida *m*
bacteriological: ~ **oven** *n* LAB estufa bacteriológica *f*, horno bacteriológico *m*; ~ **warfare** *n* MILIT guerra bacteriológica *f*
bacteriolysis *n* CHEM, FOOD bacteriolisis *f*
bacteriophage *n* CHEM, FOOD bacteriófago *m*
bacteriostat *n* AGRIC producto que retarda el crecimiento de bacterias *m*, CHEM, FOOD bacteriostato *m*
bacteriotoxin *n* CHEM, FOOD bacteriotoxina *f*
bacterium *n* CHEM, FOOD, HYDROL, RECYCL bacteria *f*
bad: ~ **air** *n* MINE aire viciado *m*; ~ **annealing** *n* C&G mal recocido *m*; ~ **break** *n* PRINT separación incorrecta *f*; ~ **contact** *n* ELEC ENG falso contacto *m*;

~ **copy** *n* PRINT cero de la carta *m*, original ilegible *m*; ~ **ground** *n* CONST terreno inadecuado *m*; ~-**weather zone** *n* OCEAN zona de mal tiempo *f*; ~ **work** *n* PROD trabajo mal hecho *m*; ~ **workmanship** *n* PROD mano de obra mala *f*

badge¹ *n* C&G timbrado *m*, COMP&DP tarjeta de identificación *f*; ~ **plate** *n* PROD *boiler test plate* timbre *m*; ~ **reader** *n* COMP&DP lector de identificadores *m*

badge² *vt* PROD *boiler* timbrar

badging *n* C&G acción de timbrar una caldera *f*

baffle¹ *n* ACOUST caja acústica *f*, pantalla acústica *f*, C&G canal de colada *m*, CHEM TECH compuerta *f*, deflector *m*, CONST *plate or wall for deflecting gases or liquids* desviación *f*, MECH ENG deflector *m*, placa de desviación *f*, MINE compuerta *f*, deflector *m*, manga *f*, reductor de tiro *m*, NUCL barrilete *m*, pantalla deflectora *f*, PAPER placa deflectora *f*, VEH deflector *m*; ~ **board** *n* CONST pantalla aislante *f*; ~ **brick** *n* CONST *between crucible and fire* ladrillo aislante *m*; ~ **hole** *n* C&G orificio de llenado del molde *m*; ~ **mark** *n* C&G punto de llenado del molde *m*; ~ **plate** *n* C&G parallamas *m*, CONST, REFRIG placa deflectora *f*; ~ **ring** *n* PETR TECH anillo deflector *m*; ~ **silencer** *n* AUTO silenciador de pantallas *m*, silenciador de placas *m*; ~-**type separator** *n* CHEM TECH separador de choque *m*, separador de tabiques *m*; ~ **wall** *n* PAPER pared desviadora *f*

baffle² *vt* MINE escapar

baffler *n* CONST *for deflecting gases or liquids* placa deflectora *f*

baffling: ~ **wind** *n* METEO viento a ráfagas *m*, viento rafagoso *m*

bag¹ *n* GEN bolsa *f*; ~ **chute** *n* AGRIC rampa para sacos o bolsas *f*; ~ **conveyor** *n* TRANSP transportador de sacos *m*; ~ **filling** *n* PACK llenado de bolsas *m*; ~-**filling machine** *n* AGRIC embolsadora *f* (*AmL*), ensacadora *f* (*Esp*), PACK llenadora de bolsas *f*, máquina para llenar bolsas *f*; ~ **filter** *n* COAL filtro de sacos *m*; ~ **holder** *n* PACK soporte de la bolsa *m*; ~-**in-a-box packaging** *n* PACK envase "bolsa en caja" *m*; ~-**in-a-can packaging** *n* PACK envase "bolsa en lata" *m*; ~-**loading machine** *n* PACK máquina de cargar bolsas *f*; ~-**making machine** *n* PACK máquina para fabricar bolsas *f*; ~ **opener** *n* PACK abridor de la bolsa *m*; ~ **packaging** *n* PACK embolsado *m* (*Esp*), ensacado *m* (*AmL*), envasado en bolsa *m*; ~ **paper** *n* PACK papel para bolsas *m*; ~-**placing system** *n* PACK método para colocar las bolsas *m*, sistema de colocación de las bolsas *m*; ~ **reel** *n* PACK bolsa separable unida formando una bobina *f*; ~ **rolling** *n* PROD enrollado de sacos *m*; ~-**sealing equipment** *n* PACK maquinaria para cerrar bolsas *f*; ~-**sealing machine** *n* AGRIC, PACK máquina selladora de sacos o bolsas *f*; ~ **staple** *n* PACK grapa para cerrar bolsas *f*; ~-**stitching machine** *n* PACK cosedora de bolsas *f*, máquina de coser bolsas *f*

bag² *vt* FOOD embolsar

bagasse *n* PAPER bagazo de la caña de azúcar *m*; ~ **roller** *n* FOOD rodillo de bagazo *m*, rodillo de residuo *m*

baggage: ~ **car** *n* AmE (*cf luggage van BrE*) RAIL, VEH furgón de equipajes *m*; ~ **compartment** *n* AmE (*cf luggage compartment BrE*) TRANSP compartimiento de equipaje *m* (*AmL*), departamento de equipaje *m*; ~ **loader** *n* TRANSP cargador de equipaje *m*;

~ **retrieval** *n* TRANSP recuperación de equipaje *f*; ~ **room** *n* AmE (*cf luggage compartment BrE*) TRANSP compartimiento de equipaje *m*, departamento de equipaje *m*, pañol de equipajes *m*, sala de equipaje *f*; ~ **terminal** *n* TRANSP terminal de equipaje *f*

bagging *n* AGRIC tela para sacos o bolsas *f*, PACK embolsado *m*; ~ **machine** *n* PACK embolsadora *f*, máquina embolsadora *f*; ~ **platform** *n* AGRIC plataforma de embolsado *f*, plataforma de ensacado *f*

baghouse *n* COAL cámara de filtros de sacos *f*, cámara de sacos para filtrar gases *f*, precipitador de polvos *m*, POLL cámara de filtros de bolsas o mangas *f*

bagmaker *n* PACK fabricante de bolsas *m*

Bahia: ~ **grass** *n* AGRIC hierba bahía *f*

baikalite *n* MINERAL baikalita *f*

bail¹ *n* PROD *bow handle of foundry ladle* enrollado de sacos *m*, gancho *m*

bail² *vt* FLUID achicar; ~ **out** *vt* AIR TRANSP lanzar en paracaídas, FLUID, WATER TRANSP *boat* achicar

bail³: ~ **out** *vi* AIR TRANSP lanzarse en paracaídas, SPACE lanzarse, saltar

bailer *n* FLUID achicador *m*, PETROL *solids from liquids*, WATER TRANSP achicador *m*, cuchara *f*

Bailey: ~ **bridge** *n* CONST puente militar portátil *m*, MILIT puente Bailey *m*

bailing *n* PETROL achique *m*; ~ **tank** *n* WATER tanque de achique *m*

bainite *n* METALL bainita *f*

bainitic: ~ **ferrite** *n* METALL ferrita bainítica *f*

bait *n* C&G refuerzo de una pieza *m*, OCEAN cebadura *f* (*AmL*), cebo *m*

baiting *n* OCEAN cazarete *m*, colocación de la carnada *f*, colocación del cebo *f*

Bajocian *adj* GEOL Bajociense

bake¹ *n* C&G *of clay* cocido *m*; ~ **and UV-irradiation test** *n* C&G prueba de cocido e irradiación UV *f*

bake² *vt* C&G *clay* cocer, PRINT termoendurecer, PROD *cores, moulds* hornear, TEXTIL calentar en seco, secar, THERMO cocer

baked: ~ **enamel** *n* COATINGS esmalte secado al horno *m*, COLOUR esmalte recocido *m*; ~-**glass painting** *n* COLOUR pintura para cristal recocido *f*; ~ **sand** *n* PROD *founding* arena estufada *f*

Bakelite® *n* COATINGS, ELEC, P&R *plastics* bakelita *f*

bakery: ~ **concentrate** *n* FOOD concentrado para panadería *m*

baking *n* C&G, P&R cocción *f*, TEXTIL secado *m*; ~ **core** *n* PROD macho de fundería *m*; ~ **enamel** *n* COLOUR esmalte para horno *m*, PROD esmalte de hornear *m*; ~ **fault** *n* PROD defecto de horneado *m*; ~ **loss** *n* FOOD pérdida de horneado *f*; ~ **mold** *AmE*, ~ **mould** *BrE n* PROD molde para hornear *m*; ~ **process** *n* PRINT proceso de termoendurecimiento *m*; ~ **quality** *n* FOOD calidad de horneado *f*; ~ **sheet** *n* FOOD placa de hornear *f*; ~ **soda** *n* FOOD levadura química *f*; ~ **varnish** *n* COATINGS, COLOUR barniz secado al horno *m*

balance¹: **out of** ~ *adj* METR desequilibrado

balance² *n* GEN equilibrio *m*; ~ **arm** *n* AIR TRANSP brazo de balanza *m*; ~ **bar** *n* WATER *of lock-gate* barra compensadora *f*; ~ **beam** *n* MECH ENG, METR astil de balanza *m*, balancín compensador *m*, brazo de balanza *m*; ~ **bob** *n* MINE balancín de contrapeso *m*; ~ **bridge** *n* CONST puente basculante *m*, puente levadizo *m*; ~ **brush** *n* LAB *tools* cepillo de balanza *m*; ~ **chain** *n* MECH ENG cadena de contrapeso *f*; ~ **coil** *n*

ELEC bobina de equilibrio *f*, bobina de simetría *f*; ~ **crank** *n* MECH ENG manivela de contrapeso *f*; ~ **gear** *n* MECH ENG compensador diferencial *m*, engranaje diferencial *m*; ~ **horn** *n* AIR TRANSP palomilla de equilibrio *f*; ~ **lever** *n* MECH ENG balancín *m*, palanca de contrapeso *f*; ~ **piston** *n* HYDRAUL pistón compensador *m*; ~ **of plant** *n* (*BOP*) NUCL *non-nuclear part of plant* instalaciones complementarias de la central *f pl*; ~ **plough** *BrE*, ~ **plow** *AmE n* AGRIC arado báscula *m*; ~ **point** *n* AIR TRANSP punto de equilibrio *m*; ~ **pressure** *n* REFRIG presión de equilibrio *f*; ~ **relay** *n* ELEC relé de equilibrio *m*, relé de simetría *m*; ~ **step** *n* CONST *stair building* escalón compensado *m*; ~ **stripe** *n* CINEMAT banda de equilibrio *f*; ~ **tab** *n* AIR TRANSP aleta compensadora *f*; ~ **tank** *n* REFRIG recipiente de equilibrio *m*; ~ **washer** *n* AIR TRANSP arandela de compensador *f*; ~ **weight** *n* AIR TRANSP peso de compensación *m*, MECH, MECH ENG contrapeso *m*, peso equilibrador *m*; ~ **wheel** *n* CINEMAT volante regulador *m*

balance[3] *vt* HYDRAUL descargar

balanced[1] *adj* AIR TRANSP equilibrado; ~ **to earth** *adj* ELEC ENG equilibrado con respecto tierra

balanced[2]: ~ **aileron** *n* AIR TRANSP alerón equilibrado *m*; ~ **amplifier** *n* ELECTRON amplificador compensado *m*; ~ **-armature unit** *n* ELEC *motor* grupo de inducido equilibrado *m*, unidad de armadura balanceada *f*, unidad de armadura equilibrada *f*; ~ **-bridge interferometer switch** *n* TELECOM conmutador interferométrico de puente equilibrado *m*; ~ **control surface** *n* AIR TRANSP superficie de control equilibrada *f*; ~ **currents** *n pl* ELEC ENG corrientes balanceadas *f pl*; ~ **disc valve** *n BrE*, ~ **disk valve** *n AmE* FUELLESS válvula de mariposa *f*; ~ **error** *n* COMP&DP error compensado *m*; ~ **field length** *n* AIR TRANSP longitud de campo equilibrada *f*; ~ **flow** *n* REFRIG corriente equilibrada *f*, flujo equilibrado *m*; ~ **-frame cultivator** *n* AGRIC cultivador con armazón balanceado *m*; ~ **grading group** *n* TELECOM grupo de líneas equilibradas *m*; ~ **input** *n* ELEC ENG entrada equilibrada *f*; ~ **line** *n* ELEC *supply*, ELEC ENG línea compensada *f*, línea equilibrada *f*; ~ **load** *n* ELEC, ELEC ENG carga equilibrada *f*; ~ **mixer** *n* ELEC ENG mezclador equilibrado *m*, ELECTRON mezclador compensado *m*; ~ **modulator** *n* ELECTRON modulador compensado *m*; ~ **network** *n* ELEC *supply* red de equilibrio *f*, red equilibrada *f*, ELEC ENG red de equilibro *f*, red equilibrada *f*; ~ **process inks** *n* PRINT gama equilibrada de tintas *f*, quijada *f*; ~ **ration** *n* AGRIC ración balanceada *f*; ~ **rudder** *n* WATER TRANSP timón compensado *m*; ~ **slide valve** *n* MECH ENG válvula de corredera compensada *f*, válvula deslizante balanceada *f*; ~ **tension block** *n* MECH ENG contrapeso tensor *m*; ~ **valve** *n* HYDRAUL válvula equilibrada *f*

balancer *n* ELEC ENG compensador *m*, dinamo de compensación *m*

balancing *n* AIR TRANSP compensación *f*, equilibrado *m*, AUTO equilibrado *m*, nivelado *m*, NUCL equilibrado *m*, PHYS *architecture* compensador *m*, TELECOM equilibrado *m*; ~ **machine** *n* MECH ENG máquina compensadora *f*; ~ **magnetic strip** *n* TV pista magnética compensadora *f*; ~ **motion** *n* MECH ENG movimiento bascular *m*; ~ **network** *n* ELEC ENG red de compensación *f*; ~ **piston** *n* HYDRAUL pistón compensador *m*; ~ **relay** *n* ELEC relé equilibrador *m*;

~ **resistor** *n* ELEC resistencia compensadora *f*, resistencia de compensación *f*, resistor compensador *m*, resistor de compensación *m*; .~ **weight** *n* MECH contrapeso *m*, peso equilibrador *m*

balas: ~ **ruby** *n* MINERAL espinela rosa *f*, rubí balas *m*

balata *n* P&R balata *f*; ~ **belt** *n* MECH ENG correa de balata *f*

balcony *n* C&G balcón *m*

bald: ~ **tire** *AmE*, ~ **tyre** *BrE n* VEH neumático desgastado *m*, neumático sin talón *m*

bale *n* AGRIC, PACK, PAPER, TEXTIL bala *f*, fardo *m*; ~ **chamber** *n* AGRIC cámara de balas *f*, cámara de fardos *f*; ~ **ejector** *n* AGRIC expulsador de balas *m*, expulsador de fardos *m*; ~ **hoop** *n* PACK fleje de fardo *m*; ~ **loader** *n* AGRIC cargador de balas *m*, cargador de fardos *m*, TRANSP cargadora de fardos *f*, cargadora de pacas *f*; ~ **pulper** *n* PAPER desintegrador de balas *m*

baler *n* AGRIC embaladora *f*, empacadora *f*, enfardadora *f*

baling: ~ **press** *n* PACK enfardadora *f*, enfardonadora *f*, prensa para hacer balas *f*, prensa para hacer fardos *f*, PAPER prensa de embalar *f*, prensa de enfardar *f* (*AmL*)

balk *AmE see* **baulk** *BrE*

ball *n* AGRIC cepellón *m*, CONST *float* bola *f*, flotador *m*, MECH ENG *machine governor, bearing* bola *f*, *of pendulum* lenteja *f*; ~ **-and-socket** *n* PHOTO rótula esférica *f*; ~ **-and-socket head** *n* CINEMAT, PHOTO rótula *f* (*Esp*); ~ **-and-socket joint** *n* MECH, MECH ENG articulación de rótula *f*, articulación esférica *f*, junta de rótula esférica *f*, junta esférica *f*; ~ **bearing** *n* MECH cojinete de bolas *m*, MECH ENG cojinete de bolas *m*, rodamiento de bolas *m*, VEH rodamiento de bolas *m*; ~ **-bearing cage** *n* MECH ENG jaula de bolas del rodamiento *f*, marco portabolas del cojinete *m*; ~ **-bearing guideway** *n* MECH ENG guía de cojinete de bolas *f*, resbaladera de cojinete de bolas *f*; ~ **-bearing plummet block** *n* MECH ENG pedestal de cojinete de bolas *m*; ~ **-bearing race** *n* VEH anillo de rodadura *m*, pista del rodamiento de bolas *f*; ~ **-bearing reactor** *n* MECH ENG reactor de cojinete de bolas *m*; ~ **-bearing roller** *n* PROD rodillo de cojinetes de bolas *m*; ~ **bushing** *n* MECH ENG cojinete cilíndrico *m*, cojinete de bolas *m*; ~ **cage** *n* MECH ENG jaula *f*, marco portabolas *m*; ~ **check valve** *n* NUCL válvula esférica de retención *f*; ~ **circulating lead screw** *n* MECH ENG husillo circulante esférico *m*, tornillo de avance esférico *m*, tornillo de guía esférico *m*, tornillo regulador esférico *m*; ~ **circulating nut** *n* MECH ENG tuerca esférica circulante *f*; ~ **clay** *n* GEOL canto arcilloso *m*, PETR TECH arcilla plástica *f*, canto arcilloso *m*; ~ **cock** *n* CONST llave de flotador *f*, HYDRAUL válvula esférica *f*, MECH ENG grifo de flotador *m*, llave de flotador *f*; ~ **cup** *n* MECH ENG copa esférica *f*; ~ **end** *n* MECH ENG lado esférico *m*; ~ **-ended linkage** *n* MECH, MECH ENG articulación de extremidades esféricas *f*; ~ **gage** *AmE*, ~ **gauge** *BrE n* METR indicador esférico *m*, indicador flotador *m*; ~ **governor** *n* MECH ENG regulador de Watt *m*, regulador de bolas *m*; ~ **inner race** *n* MECH, MECH ENG, PROD anillo de rodadura interno *m*; ~ **joint** *n* MECH ENG junta esférica *f*, VEH junta de rótula *f*; ~ **-joint cage** *n* MECH ENG jaula de articulación esférica *f*; ~ **knob** *n* MECH ENG botón esférico *m*; ~ **lock** *n* MECH ENG *tools* cierre esférico *m*; ~ **lock**

retainer *n* MECH ENG *for punches* retén de cierre esférico *m*; **~-lock round-punch** *n* MECH ENG punzón redondo de cierre esférico *m*; **~ mill** *n* C&G, CHEM TECH, COAL, FOOD molino de bolas *m* (*Esp*), triturador de bolas *m* (*AmL*), LAB desintegrador de bolas *m* (*AmL*), molino de bolas *m* (*Esp*), pulverizador de bolas *m* (*AmL*), MINE, P&R molino de bolas *m* (*Esp*), triturador de bolas *m* (*AmL*); **~ milling** *n* COAL molienda de bolas *f*, molturación de bolas *f*; **~ pad** *n* MECH ENG amortiguador esférico *m*; **~ pane** *n* MECH ENG martillo con bolita *m*, peña bombeada *f*; **~ peen** *n* MECH ENG *of hammer* boca bombeada *f*, peña bombeada *f*; **~ race** *n* MECH ENG camino de rodadura *m*, canal de bolas *m*, anillo guía *m*, PRINT anillo guía *m*; **~ register** *n* MECH ENG registro de bolas *m*; **~ screw** *n* MECH ENG tornillo esférico *m*; **~-socket seat** *n* MECH ENG asiento de rótula *m*; **~-stage microscope** *n* INSTR microscopio con portaobjetos esférico *m*; **~ stop** *n* MECH ENG tope esférico *m*; **~-thrust bearing** *n* MECH, MECH ENG cojinete de empuje de bolas *m*; **~ valve** *n* HYDRAUL, MECH válvula de bola *f*, válvula de flotador *f*, válvula esférica *f*, MECH ENG válvula de bola *f*, *float type* válvula de flotador *f*; **~ vein** *n* MINE estrato con concreciones de siderita *m*

ballast[1]: **in ~** *adj* WATER TRANSP *ship* en lastre

ballast[2] *n* AIR TRANSP lastre *m*, CONST balasto *m*, lastre *m*, reactancia *f*, *for making concrete* capa de grava *f*, ELEC ENG reactancia auxiliar *f*, RAIL balasto *m*, WATER TRANSP *boat building* lastre *m*; **~ keel** *n* WATER TRANSP *boat building* quilla de lastre *f*; **~ resistor** *n* ELEC resistencia autorreguladora *f*, resistencia autorreguladora de corriente *f*, resistencia compensadora *f*, resistencia reguladora *f*, ELEC ENG resistencia de carga *f*; **~ retainer** *n* RAIL guardabalasto *m*; **~ screening** *n* RAIL cribado del balasto *m*; **~ tank** *n* WATER TRANSP tanque de lastre *m*; **~ valve** *n* HYDRAUL válvula de estrangulación *f* (*AmL*), válvula reguladora *f* (*Esp*)

ballasting *n* CONST *material* balasto *m*, grava *f*; **~ circuit** *n* ELEC ENG circuito de carga *m*

ballastless: **~ track** *n* TRANSP vía sin balasto *f*

balling *n* COAL aglomeración *f*; **~ drum** *n* COAL tambor de molturación *m*

ballistic[1] *adj* SPACE balístico

ballistic[2]: **~ galvanometer** *n* ELEC, PHYS galvanómetro balístico *m*; **~ missile** *n* ELECTRON, MILIT, SPACE misil balístico *m*, proyectil balístico *m*; **~ path** *n* SPACE recorrido balístico *m*; **~ trajectory** *n* MILIT, SPACE trayectoria balística *f*

ballistics *n* SPACE *mechanics* balística *f*

balloon *n* CHEM *flask* matraz *m* (*Esp*), redoma *f* (*AmL*), PRINT círculo bordeando un texto *m*; **~-release station** *n* SPACE estación de lanzamiento de globos *f*; **~ surfacing** *n* OCEAN regreso a la superficie con ayuda del globo de ascensión *m*; **~ system** *n* MILIT sistema de globo aerostático *m*; **~ tire** *AmE*, **~ tyre** *BrE n* AUTO neumático con cámara *m*

ballooning *n* OCEAN subida en globo *f*; **~ mass** *n* SPACE masa aerostática *f*

Balmer: **~'s formula** *n* PHYS fórmula de Balmer *f*; **~ series** *n* PHYS serie de Balmer *f*; **~ series lines** *n pl* PART PHYS líneas de Balmer *f pl*

baltimorite *n* MINERAL baltimorita *f*

baluster *n* CONST balaústre *m*

balustrade *n* CONST balaustrada *f*

bamboo *n* C&G bizcocho de porcelana de color de caña *m*; **~ pulp** *n* PAPER pasta de bambú *f*

ban *n* RAD PHYS banda *f*

banal: **~ slip** *n* METALL error trivial *m*

banana: **~-handling terminal** *n* TRANSP terminal de carga y descarga platanera *f*; **~ jack** *n* ELEC ENG clavija con punta cónica *f*; **~ orbit** *n* NUCL órbita arriñonada *f*; **~ plug** *n* CINEMAT, ELEC ENG, PHOTO clavija banana *f*, clavija con punta cónica *f*

Banbury: **~ mixer** *n* P&R mezclador Banbury *m*, mezcladora Banbury *f*

band[1] *n* COMP&DP banda *f*, faja *f*, CONST *round chimney-shaft, kiln* abrazadera *f*, correa *f*, fleje *m*, zuncho *m*, MECH ENG *machine belt* banda *f*, fleje *m*, zuncho *m*, PACK fleje *m*, PHYS banda *f*, banda de espectro *f*, PRINT banda *f*, PROD fleje *m*, RAD PHYS banda *f*, WAVE PHYS banda *f*, banda de espectro *f*; **~ application** *n* AGRIC *of fertilizers* aplicación en banda *f*; **~ brake** *n* MECH, MECH ENG freno de banda *m*, freno de cinta *m*; **~ chain** *n* CONST *surveying* cadena de unión *f*; **~ clutch** *n* MECH ENG embrague de cinta *m*; **~ conveyor** *n* AGRIC transportador de banda sinfín *m*, PACK, PROD cinta transportadora *f*, transportador de correa sinfín *m*; **~ coupling** *n* MECH ENG acoplamiento de cinta *m*; **~ heater** *n* MECH ENG *injection moulds* calentador de cinta *m*; **~ label** *n* PACK etiqueta autoadhesiva *f*, etiqueta separable formando una banda *f*; **~-limited channel** *n* COMP&DP canal de banda limitada *m*; **~-limited signal** *n* ELECTRON señal de ajuste de banda limitada *f*; **~ model** *n* METALL modelo de banda *m*, modelo de fleje *m*; **~ pass** *n* PETROL paso banda *m*; **~-pass amplifier** *n* ELECTRON amplificador de paso de banda *m*, amplificador pasabanda *m*; **~-pass filter** *n* (*BPF*) ACOUST, COMP&DP filtro de frecuencia *m*, ELECTRON filtro banda-paso *m*, filtro de banda pasante, filtro de frecuencia *m*, ENG ELEC, PHYS filtro de frecuencia *m*, RAD PHYS filtro de paso de banda *m* (*Esp*), SPACE *communications* filtro de frecuencia *m* (*Esp*), TELECOM filtro paso-banda *m* (*AmL*), filtro de paso de banda *m* (*Esp*), filtro de banda pasante *m*, filtro de frecuencia *m*; **~-pass filtering** *n* ACOUST, COMP&DP, ELEC filtración de paso de banda *f*, ELECTRON, PETROL, PHYS, TELECOM filtración de paso de banda *f*, filtrado de pasobanda *m* (*AmL*), filtrado de paso de banda *m*; **~ printer** *n* COMP&DP, PRINT impresora de banda *f*; **~ pulley** *n* MECH ENG polea para correa *f*; **~-rejection filter** *n* RAD PHYS filtro de supresión de banda *m*; **~ saw** *n* MECH ENG sierra de banda *f*, sierra sin fin *f*; **~-saw brazing apparatus** *n* MECH ENG máquina para soldar cuchillas de sierras de banda *f*; **~-saw brazing, sharpening and setting machine** *n* MECH ENG máquina para soldar, afilar y ajustar sierras de banda *f*; **~-saw pulley** *n* MECH ENG polea portacuchillas *f*, polea portasierra *f*; **~ sawing machine** *n* MECH ENG serrería de banda *f*; **~ sealer** *n* PACK aplicador de bandas *m*, aplicador de precintos *m*; **~ sealing** *n* PACK cierre mediante precinto *m*, sellado mediante precinto *m*; **~ seeding** *n* AGRIC siembra en banda *f*; **~ separation** *n* ELECTRON separación de banda *f*; **~ spectrum** *n* PHYS, RAD PHYS espectro de banda *m*; **~-stop filter** *n* COMP&DP filtro eliminador de banda *m*, filtro de eliminación de banda *m*, ELECTRON, TELECOM filtro de detención de banda *m* (*AmL*), filtro de eliminación de banda *m*, filtro eliminador de banda *m*; **~-stop filtering** *n* ELECTRON filtrado de eliminación de banda *m*; **~ tape** *n* CONST cinta *f*; **~ theory** *n* PHYS teoría de bandas *f*; **~ wheel** *n* MECH ENG polea para correa *f*, polea portasierra *f*

band^2: **~ limit** *vi* ELECTRON restringir banda

banded^1 *adj* GEOL bandeado, rayado

banded^2: **~ structure** *n* METALL estructura acanalada *f*, estructura zunchada *f*

banderole *n* PACK insignia *f*

banding *n* C&G bandeo *m*, MECH ENG cordaje *m*, estratificación *f*, PACK enfajillado *m*, TV sintonización de paso de banda *f*; **~ machine** *n* PACK enfajilladora *f*, máquina de cantonear *f*; **~ on hue** *n* TV control de tonalidad de banda *m*; **~ on noise** *n* TV control de ruido de banda *m*; **~ on saturation** *n* TV control de saturación de banda *m*

bandoleered: **~ component** *n* ELEC ENG componente en canana *m*

bandspread *n* RAD PHYS ensanche de banda *m*

B&W *abbr* (*black and white*) CINEMAT, PHOTO, PRINT, TV B y N (*blanco y negro*)

bandwidth *n* GEN ancho de banda *m* (*AmL*), anchura de banda *f* (*Esp*); **~ compression** *n* ELECTRON, TV compresión del ancho de banda *f*; **~ expansion** *n* ELECTRON expansión de ancho de banda *f*; **~-limited operation** *n* OPT procedimiento limitado por el ancho de banda *m*, TELECOM funcionamiento en banda limitada *m*

banger *n* PAPER golpeadora *f*

Bang: **~'s disease** *n* AGRIC brucelosis *f*, fiebre de Malta *f*

banjo: **~ bolt** *n* MECH ENG perno banjo *m*, *hollow bolt* perno hueco *m*; **~-type housing** *n* VEH cárter tipo partido *m*; **~ union** *n* MECH ENG conectador orientable *m*

bank^1 *n* AIR TRANSP inclinación *f*, COAL banqueta *f*, boca de pozo *f*, CONST *of sand, rock* banco *m*, *of cut* talud *m*, *of canal, road, railway, cut* orilla *f*, margen *m*, ribera *f*, *of earth* terraplén *m*, terreno *m*, ELEC ENG *buttons, contacts* situación en paralelo *f*, *group of capacitors* paralelo *m*, ELECTRON *ring winding* banco *m*, bloque *m*, conjunto *m*, HYDROL *boat building* ribera *f*, orilla *f*, MINE frente de trabajo *m*, barra *f*, inclinación lateral *f*, bocamina *f*, enganche de la calle *m*, OCEAN *radioactivity* banca *f*, banco *m*, ribera *f*, PHOTO banca *f*, PRINT subtítulo *m*, mesa *f*, RAIL rampa *f*, RECYCL contenedor *m*, receptáculo *m*, recipiente *m*, WATER TRANSP *of river* ribera *f*, orilla *f*, banco *m*; **~-and-pitch indicator** *n* BrE (*cf turn-and-bank indicator AmE*) AIR TRANSP indicador de inclinación y cabeceo *m*, indicador de viraje e inclinación *m*; **~ of capacitors** *n* ELEC ENG grupo de condensadores *m*; **~ of cells** *n* COAL batería *f*; **~ clearance angle** *n* MECH ENG ángulo de incidencia *m*; **~ contact** *n* TELECOM contacto de banco *m*; **~ of dryers** *n* PAPER mesa de secadoras *f*; **~ of lights** *n* CINEMAT batería de lámparas *f*; **~ of oscillators** *n* ELECTRON bloque de osciladores *m*; **~ of RAMs** *n* ELEC ENG conjunto de RAMs *m*; **~ of relays** *n* PROD batería de relés *f*; **~ switching** *n* COMP&DP conmutación de bancos *f*; **~ winding** *n* ELEC *coil* arrollamiento en capas superpuestas *m*, arrollamiento superpuesto *m*, devanado de capas múltiples *m*, enrollamiento yuxtapuesto *m*

bank^2 *vt* CONST apilar, crear un talud, crear un terraplén, MINE apilar; **~ up** *vt* COAL terraplenar, CONST amontonar, terraplenar, *to heap or pile up* rellenar, apilar, embalsar, MAR POLL terraplenar, MINE apilar, taluzar (*Esp*), terraplenar, amontonar (*AmL*), RAIL, RECYCL, TRANSP terraplenar; **~ up with earth** *vt* CONST *wall* rellenar para formar un talud

bank^3 *vi* SPACE inclinar; **~ up** *vi* METEO *clouds* amontonarse

banked^1: **~ up** *adj* THERMO amontonado, apilado, cubierto, respaldado

banked^2: **~ configuration** *n* NUCL configuración por bancos *f*; **~ winding** *n* ELEC *coil* devanado de capas múltiples *m*, arrollamiento anular *m*, arrollamiento en capas superpuestas *m*, enrollamiento yuxtapuesto *m*, arrollamiento superpuesto *m*, ELEC ENG enrollamiento yuxtapuesto *m*

banker: **~ shape** *n* PAPER sobre postal *m*

banket *n* MINE conglomerado aurífero *m*

bankhead *n* MINE boca del socavón *f*

banking *n* MINE enganche superior *m*, RAIL doble tracción con unidad tractora en cola *f*, subida de rampas con tracción en cola *f*; **~ locomotive** *n* BrE (*cf pusher locomotive AmE*) RAIL locomotora de refuerzo para subida de rampas *f*, locomotora empujadora *f*, locomotora trasera *f*

banknote: **~ paper** *n* PAPER papel moneda *m* (*AmL*), papel para billetes de banco *m* (*Esp*)

banquette *n* CONST *berm* banqueta *f*

BAPTA *abbr* (*bearing and power-transfer assembly*) SPACE CTCP (*conjunto de giro y transferencia de potencia*)

bar^1 *n* ACOUST *unit of pressure* baria *f*, COAL barra *f*, baria *f*, CONST barra *f*, GEOL, HYDROL *at mouth of river* banco de arena *m*, barra *f*, MECH ENG *of foundry flask* barra transversal *f*, MINE afuste *m*, barra *f*, lingote *m*, OCEAN *pressure unit* baria *f*, *at mouth of river* banco de arena *m*, *rivers* alfaque *m*, *sand banks* barra *f*, PAPER barra *f*, PETR TECH barra *m*, varilla *f*, PHYS baria *f*, TEXTIL varilla *f*, WATER TRANSP *geography* barra *f*, alfaque *m*, *at mouth of the river* banco de arena *m*; **~ armature** *n* ELEC *of machine* inducido de barras *m*; **~ bolt** *n* CONST perno arponado *m*; **~ chamfering tool** *n* MECH ENG herramienta biseladora para barras *f*; **~ channeler** *AmE*, **~ channeller** *BrE n* MINE rafadora de afuste *f*; **~ chart** *n* COMP&DP diagrama de barras *f* (*Esp*), gráfico de barras *m*, histograma *m*, tabla de barras *f* (*AmL*), MATH, PHYS, TELECOM gráfico de barras *m*, histograma *m*; **~ chuck** *n* MECH ENG *machine tools* portabarras *m*; **~ coach** *n* RAIL vagón del bar *m*; **~ coal-cutting machine** *n* MINE máquina rafadora de barra *f*, rozadora *f*; **~ coater** *n* P&R máquina revestidora para perfiles laminados *f*; **~ code** *n* COMP&DP, PACK, PRINT, TELECOM código de barras *m*; **~-code label printer** *n* PACK impresora de etiquetas con el código de barras *f*; **~-code labeling system** *AmE*, **~-code labelling system** *BrE n* PACK sistema de etiquetado mediante código de barras *m*; **~-code pen** *n* COMP&DP lápiz lector de código de barras *m*; **~-code reader** *n* PACK lector de código de barras *m*; **~-code scanner** *n* COMP&DP escáner para código de barras *m*, lector de código de barras *m*, PROD escáner para código de barras *m*; **~-code scanner and decoder logic** *n* COMP&DP, PACK lógica de lectura y desciframiento de códigos de barras *f*; **~ facing-tool** *n* MECH ENG herramienta de refrentar barras *f*; ~ **frame** *n* TEXTIL bastidor de varillas *m*; ~ **generator** *n* TV generador de barras *m*; ~ **hanger** *n* MECH ENG aparato de suspensión de barra *m*; ~ **hole** *n* MECH ENG *of capstan* alojamiento para barra *m*; ~ **magnet** *n* PHYS imán recto *m*; ~ **mill** *n* MECH ENG laminador para perfiles *m*; ~ **pattern** *n* TV carta de ajuste de barras *f* (*Esp*), patrón de ajuste de barras *m* (*AmL*); ~ **screen** *n* HYDROL *tool-, cutter-, drill-sharpening* emparrillado de barrotes *m*, MECH ENG parrilla de barrotes *f*, reja de barrotes *f*; ~**-shearing machine** *n* MECH ENG cizalladora de barras *f*; ~ **shears** *n pl* MECH ENG cizallas de barras *f pl*; ~ **turning-tool** *n* MECH ENG torno para redondos *m*; ~**-type transformer** *n* ELEC transformador de barras *m*; ~ **weir** *n* WATER esclusa de barras *f*; ~ **winding** *n* ELEC *armature* devanado de barras *m*

bar² *vt* HYDRAUL bloquear

barbed: ~ **bolt** *n* CONST tornillo dentado *m*; ~ **wire** *n* AGRIC, CONST, MILIT alambre de espino *m*, alambre de púas *m*; ~**-wire entanglement** *n* MILIT alambrada *f*; ~**-wire nail** *n* CONST punta para alambre de espino *f*

barbiturate *n* CHEM barbiturato *m*

barbituric: ~ **acid** *n* CHEM ácido barbitúrico *m*

Bardeen-Cooper-Schrieffer: ~ **theory** *n* (*BCS theory*) ELECTRON, PHYS teoría de Bardeen-Cooper-Schrieffer *f* (*teoría de BCS*)

bare¹ *adj* ELEC ENG al descubierto, gastado, pelado, raído, sin revestir, PROD sencillo

bare² *n* CONST parte descubierta *f*; ~**-boat charter** *n* PETR TECH flete de embarcación descubierta *m*, flete por embarcación *m*, WATER TRANSP arrendamiento a casco desnudo *m*, flete de embarcación descubierta *m*; ~ **conductor** *n* ELEC conductor desnudo *m*, conductor sin aislación *m*, conductor sin aislamiento *m*; ~ **drain wire** *n* ELEC hilo de drenaje desnudo *m*, hilo de retorno por tierra desnudo *m*, ELEC ENG hilo de retorno por tierra desnudo *m*, PROD alambre desnudo de drenaje *m*; ~ **fallow** *n* AGRIC barbecho negro *m*; ~ **hull** *n* AIR TRANSP casco desnudo *m*; ~ **light** *n* CINEMAT lámpara desnuda *f*; ~ **metal** *n* METALL metal desnudo *m*, metal puro *m*; ~ **particle** *n* NUCL partícula desnuda *f*; ~ **reactor** *n* NUCL reactor desnudo *m*; ~**-root method** *n* AGRIC plantación a raíz desnuda *f*; ~ **wire** *n* ELEC ENG, PROD alambre desnudo *m*, TELECOM hilo desnudo *m*

barefaced: ~ **tenon** *n* CONST espiga de cara visible *f*

barefoot: ~ **completion** *n* PETROL terminación a pozo abierto *f*

barge *n* PETROL barcaza *f*, chalana *f*, chalán *m* (*AmL*), gabarra *f*, pontón *m*, TRANSP barcaza *f*, gabarra *f*, WATER TRANSP chata *f*, chata velera *f*, gabarra *f*, barcaza *f*; ~ **carrier** *n* WATER TRANSP buque portabarcazas *m*, buque portagabarras *m*; ~ **container** *n* TRANSP contenedor de gabarras *m*

bargee *n* BrE (*cf bargeman AmE*) WATER TRANSP gabarrero *m*

bargeman *n* AmE (*cf bargee BrE*) WATER TRANSP gabarrero *m*

baric *adj* CHEM bárico

baring *n* MINE destape *m*

barite *n* C&G, CHEM, MINERAL, P&R barita *f*, baritina *f*, PETR TECH baritina *f*, barita *f*, PETROL barita *f*, baritina *f*

BARITT: ~ **diode** *n* (*barrier injection transit-time diode*) PHYS diodo de tiempo de tránsito por inyección en barrera *m*

barium *n* (*Ba*) CHEM bario *m* (*Ba*); ~ **chromate pigment** *n* COLOUR pigmento de cromato de bario *m*

bark *n* PAPER corteza *f*; ~ **boiler** *n* PAPER caldera que quema cortezas *f*; ~ **burner** *n* PAPER quemador de cortezas *m*; ~ **power boiler** *n* PAPER caldera de vapor que quema cortezas *f*; ~ **press** *n* PAPER prensa de cortezas *f*; ~ **specks** *n pl* PAPER motas de corteza *f pl* (*Esp*), puntos negros *m pl* (*AmL*), suciedad *f* (*Esp*)

barked: ~ **timber** *n* CONST *bark removed* madera de revestimiento *f*

barkevikite *n* MINERAL barkevikita *f*

Barkhausen: ~ **effect** *n* PHYS efecto Barkhausen *m*

barley: ~ **anthracnose** *n* AGRIC antracnosis de la cebada *f*; ~**-leaf rust** *n* AGRIC roya de hoja de cebada *f*; ~ **stripe** *n* AGRIC mancha listada de cebada *f*; ~ **yellow-dwarf** *n* AGRIC enanismo amarillo de la cebada *m*

Barlow's: ~ **wheel** *n* PHYS rueda de Barlow *f*

barn *n* (*b*) NUCL, PART PHYS, PHYS barn *m* (*b*), barnio *m* (*b*)

barndoor *n* CINEMAT visera *f*

Barnett: ~ **effect** *n* PHYS efecto Barnett *m*

barney *n* CINEMAT funda *f*

barnhardite *n* MINERAL barnhardtita *f*

barnyard: ~ **grass** *n* AGRIC pasto colorado *m*, pata de gallo *f*; ~ **manure** *n* AGRIC abono de corral *m*

barograph *n* AIR TRANSP barógrafo *m*, LAB, METEO, PHYS, WATER TRANSP barógrafo *m*, barómetro registrador *m*

barometer *n* GEN barómetro *m*; ~ **reading** *n* WATER TRANSP lectura barométrica *f*

barometric¹ *adj* GEN barométrico

barometric²: ~ **altitude controller** *n* AIR TRANSP controlador de altitud barométrico *m*; ~ **controller** *n* AIR TRANSP controlador barométrico *m*; ~ **height of pressure** *n* METEO altura barométrica de la presión atmosférica *f*; ~ **maximum** *n* METEO máxima barométrica *f*; ~ **pressure** *n* METEO presión barométrica *f*; ~ **switch** *n* AIR TRANSP interruptor barométrico *m*; ~ **trough** *n* METEO vaguada barométrica *f*

barometrical: ~ **variation** *n* METEO variación barométrica *f*

baroscope *n* PHYS baroscopio *m*

barostat *n* AIR TRANSP barostato *m*

barothermograph *n* PHYS barotermógrafo *m*

barotrauma *n* ACOUST barotrauma *m*

barracks *n pl* CONST barracas *f pl*, barracones *m pl*

barrage *n* CONST barrera *f*, cierre *m*, HYDROL *windows of building* presa *f*, MILIT *artillery* tiro de barrera *m*, OCEAN barrera *f*, presa de contención *f*, WATER azud *m*, presa *f*, presa de derivación *f*

barrandite *n* MINERAL barrandita *f*

barrel *n* CONST *of lock* cañón *m*, tubo *m*, *of screw* cilindro *m*, FOOD *cabin*, GEOL, HYDRAUL, LAB barril *m*, cuerpo *m*, MECH cuerpo *m*, tambor *m*, cilindro *m*, barril *m*, MECH ENG *of pump* cilindro *m*, *of headstock, lathe or tailstock* cañón *m*, *of capstan* tambor *m*, *of boiler* cuerpo cilíndrico *m*, *of rolling mill* tabla *f*, MINE tambor *m*, PETROL barril *m*, TRANSP barrica *f*, tambor *m*, tonel *m*, barril *m*; ~ **amalgamation** *n* PROD amalgamación en barriles *f*; ~ **boiler** *n* HYDRAUL caldera cilíndrica *f*; ~ **bolt** *n* CONST *locksmithing* cerrojo pasador *m*; ~ **buoy** *n* WATER TRANSP boya cilíndrica *f*; ~ **cam** *n* MECH ENG leva de cilindro *f*, leva de tambor *f*, PROD leva de cilindro *f*;

~ distortion n CINEMAT, PHOTO, PHYS distorsión esferoide f, distorsión negativa f; **~ finishing** n PROD acabado en tambor giratorio m; **~ key** n AmE (cf pipe key BrE) CONST llave principal f, pasador m; **~ mixer** n FOOD barril mezclador m; **~ nipple** n MECH ENG pipe fitting niple tubular m, tetón tubular m; **~ oil equivalent** n (BOE) PETR TECH equivalente a un barril de crudo m; **~ plating** n PROD recubrimiento electrolítico en tambor m, retrogalvanostegia f; **~ plotter** n BrE (cf drum plotter AmE) COMP&DP impresora de tambor f, plotter de tambor m, tambor de traza m, trazador de rodillo m, trazador de tambor m, PRINT impresora de tambor f; **~ printer** n BrE (cf drum printer AmE) COMP&DP, PRINT impresora de rodillo f, impresora de tambor f; **~ roller bearing** n MECH ENG cojinete de rodillos cilíndricos m; **~-shaped roller bearing** n MECH ENG cojinete de rodillos abarrilados m; **~ vault** n CONST bóveda de cañón f

Barremian adj GEOL materials Barremiense

barren[1] adj AGRIC erial, COAL estéril, improductivo, sin fósiles, árido, GEOL azoico, sin fósiles, MINE improductivo, sin fósiles

barren[2]: **~ brome** n AGRIC pasto valcheta m; **~ gangue** n COAL ganga improductiva f; **~ solution** n COAL disolución de ganga f

barrette: **~ file** n MECH ENG lima triangular achatada f

barretter n ELEC voltage stabilizer resistencia autorreguladora f, resistencia compensadora f, resistencia reguladora f, ELEC ENG lámpara estabilizadora de tensión f, lámpara de resistencia f, detector m, resistencia compensada f, PHYS resistencia autorreguladora f, resistencia de compensación f

barricade[1] n CONST barrera f, barricada f, empalizada f, valla f, SAFE, SPACE barricada f

barricade[2] vt CONST hacer barricadas

barrier n CONST barrera f, MINE barrera f (Esp), muro m (AmL), muro de protección m, pilar de seguridad m; **~ beach** n GEOL cordón litoral m; **~-coated paper** n PAPER papel con revestido barrera m; **~ film** n PACK película barrera f, película protectora f; **~ grid** n ELECTRON rejilla aislante f; **~-grid storage tube** n ELECTRON tubo de almacenamiento de material aislante m; **~ injection transit-time diode** n (BARITT diode) PHYS diodo de tiempo de tránsito por inyección en barrera m; **~ layer** n ELEC ENG barrera de potencial f, ELECTRON capa de detención f, OPT capa de detención f, PHYS, POLL, TELECOM barrera de potencial f, capa barrera f, capa de detención f; **~-layer cell** n ELEC ENG elemento de la capa de detención m; **~ material** n PACK material barrera m, material de protección m; **~ packaging** n PACK embalaje barrera m, embalaje de protección m; **~ reef** n GEOL, OCEAN arrecife barrera m

barriness n TEXTIL barrado m; **~ in the weft** n TEXTIL barrado por trama m

barring n PAPER barras f pl

barrow n AGRIC cerdo joven castrado m, CONST carretilla f, montículo m, MECH carretilla f, MINE pila de estériles f, vagoneta f, TRANSP carretilla f, remolque portaequipajes m

barrowful n CONST capacidad de una carretilla f, contenido de una carretilla m

barrowing n CONST transporte en carretilla m

Bartlett: **~ force** n NUCL fuerza de Bartlett f

barycenter AmE see barycentre BrE

barycentre n BrE MATH, SPACE baricentro m

barylite n MINERAL barilita f

baryon n PART PHYS, PHYS barión m; **~ number** n PART PHYS número de barión m, PHYS número bariónico m

barysphere n GEOPHYS barisfera f

baryta: **~ paper** n TRANSP papel couché m, papel revestido de sulfato de bario m

barytocalcite n MINERAL baritocalcita f

barytocelestine n MINERAL baritocelestina f

barytocelestite n MINERAL baritocelestina f

basal: **~ crystal** n METALL cristal basal m, cristal columnar m; **~ plane** n METALL plano basal m; **~ slip** n METALL deslizamiento basal m

basalt n CONST, FUELLESS, GEOL, PETROL basalto m; **~ glass** n PETROL traquita f

basaltic: **~ column** n GEOL columna basáltica f

basaltine n MINERAL basaltina f

basanite n PETROL basanita f

bascule n MECH ENG báscula f; **~ bridge** n CONST puente levadizo m

base[1]: **~ down** adj CINEMAT con el soporte hacia abajo

base[2] n C&G of neck fondo m, CHEM base f, CINEMAT for injection moulding soporte m, COMP&DP base f, CONST block to receive fitting base f, surveying línea de base f, ELEC ENG electrode casquillo m, base f, ELECTRON mass base f, GEOM pie m, base f, INSTR soporte m, MATH base f, MECH ENG of machine bancada f, of plummer-block pedestal m, PHYS vibration test base f, PRINT soporte de película m, pie del tipo de imprenta m, plate base f, TELECOM base f; **~ address** n COMP&DP direccionamiento de base m; **~ address register** n COMP&DP registro de direccionamiento de base m; **~ board** n AmE (cf skirting board BrE) CONST rodapié m, zócalo m; **~ cation** n POLL catión base m; **~-centered lattice** AmE, **~-centred lattice** BrE n METALL red centrada en la base f; **~ check** n AIR TRANSP comprobación de base f, verificación de base f; **~ circle** n MECH ENG of involute gear círculo de base m, círculo primitivo m; **~ coat** n P&R, PROD capa de base f; **~ contact** n ELEC ENG contacto de base m, contacto del casquillo m; **~ course** n CONST capa de asiento f; **~ cup** n PACK parte inferior de una botella f; **~ density** n CINEMAT densidad del soporte f; **~ design** n NUCL diseño base m; **~ diffusion** n ELECTRON heat unit difusión de base f; **~ displacement** n COMP&DP desplazamiento base m; **~ doping** n ELECTRON heat unit alteración de base f, dopado de base m; **~ drive** n ELECTRON excitación de base f; **~ drive signal** n ELECTRON señal de excitación de base f; **~ electrode** n ELEC ENG electrodo base m, electrodo del casquillo m; **~ failure** n COAL insuficiencia de pasta f, CONST fallo de base m, GEOL insuficiencia de pasta f; **~ film** n TV película base f; **~ flow** n HYDROL caudal intrínseco m; **~ flow effect** n SPACE efecto de caudal intrínseco m; **~ fog** n PHOTO velo de la base m; **~ glass** n C&G vidrio base m; **~ impurities** n pl ELECTRON impurezas de base f pl; **~ modulation** n ELECTRON modulación de base f; **~ of operations** n PROD base de operaciones f; **~ paper** n PAPER papel soporte m; **~ paper for diazotype** n PAPER papel soporte para diazotipo m; **~ plate** n CONST placa de apoyo f, placa de asiento f, MECH ENG placa de asiento f, placa de fundación f; **~ power** n NUCL potencia base f; **~ region** n ELECTRON zona de base f; **~ resistance** n ELEC ENG resistencia de base f, resistencia del casquillo f;

~ scratch n PHOTO rayadura de la base f; **~ of a sluice gate** n WATER busco m; **~ station** n MILIT, TELECOM estación base f; **~ station controller** n TELECOM controlador de la estación base m; **~ stock** n PAPER soporte m; **~ tint** n PRINT tintura de base f; **~-to-mobile relay** n TELECOM relé base-móvil m; **~ unit** n (BU) TELECOM unidad base f; **~ of verification** n CONST triangulation base de comprobación f; **~ volume** n TRANSP volumen base m; **~ wall** n CONST muro base m; **~ washer** n MECH ENG arandela de la base f; **~ web** n PAPER soporte m; **~ widening** n ELECTRON ensanche de base m; **~ width** n ELECTRON anchura de base f

baseband n COMP&DP, ELECTRON, TELECOM, TV banda base f; **~ modem** n COMP&DP, TELECOM módem de banda base m; **~ response function** n OPT, TELECOM función de respuesta de la banda base f; **~ signal** n ELECTRON señal de banda base f; **~ transfer function** n OPT, TELECOM función de transferencia de banda base f

baseboard n PHOTO tablero para ampliaciones m

baseline n CONST surveying línea de tierra f, INSTR, PRINT, WATER TRANSP ship design, navigation línea de base f; **~ inspection** n MECH inspección de línea base f; **~ shift** n PETROL desviación de la línea base f

basement n GEOL anteposo m, basamento m, sótano m, zócalo m, PETR TECH, PETROL antepozo m, basamento m, sótano m, zócalo m; **~ complex** n GEOL basamiento m; **~ wall** n CONST muro del sótano m, pared del sótano f

baseness n MINE pobreza f

baseplate n CINEMAT placa de base de cámara f, INSTR placa para el montaje f, MECH placa base f, placa de asiento f, placa de fondo f, plancha soporte f; **~ for fine blanking** n MECH ENG die set placa de base para troquelados finos f

basher n CINEMAT luz de relleno sobre la cámara f

basic: **~ access** n TELECOM acceso básico m; **~ amplifier** n ELECTRON amplificador básico m; **~ bit rate** n TELECOM tasa básica de bits f; **~ call charge** n TELECOM precio base de llamada m; **~ capacity** n TRANSP capacidad básica f; **~ coding** n COMP&DP codificación básica f, enlace básico m; **~ crops** n pl AGRIC cosechas principales f pl, cultivos básicos m pl; **~ dye** n CHEM, PAPER, TEXTIL colorante básico m; **~ failure** n AIR TRANSP fallo básico m; **~ fiber** AmE, **~ fibre** BrE n C&G fibra básica f; **~ frame alignment** n (BFA) TELECOM, TV alineación básica de imagen f; **~ frequency** n ELECTRON, TV frecuencia básica f, frecuencia de base f; **~ group** n ELEC ENG conjunto básico m, TELECOM grupo básico m; **~ instrument flight trainer** n AIR TRANSP entrenador básico de vuelo de instrumentos m; **~ legislation** n SAFE legislación básica f; **~ lining** n METALL revestimiento básico m; **~ linkage** n COMP&DP enlace básico m; **~ noise** n ELECTRON ruido básico m; **~ open-hearth furnace** n C&G horno de solera básico m; **~ petrochemical** n PETR TECH petroquímico básico m, producto petroquímico básico m, PETROL petroquímico básico m, producto petroquímico básico m; **~ rack** n MECH ENG gears cremallera base f, cremallera de referencia f, cremallera tipo f; **~ rate access** n (BRA) TELECOM precio base de acceso m; **~ rate service** n TELECOM precio base de servicio m; **~ safety rules** n pl SAFE machine operations normas básicas de seguridad f pl; **~ salt** n

CHEM sal básica f; **~ trainer** n AIR TRANSP entrenador básico m; **~ triangle** n METALL triángulo básico m; **~ weight** n PRINT gramaje m

BASIC abbr (Beginner's All-purpose Symbolic Instruction Code) COMP&DP, PRINT BASIC (código de instrucciones simbólicas de carácter general para principiantes)

basicity n CHEM basicidad f

basification n CHEM, GEOL basificación f

basify vt CHEM, GEOL basificar

basilar: **~ membrane** n ACOUST membrana basilar f

basin n COAL, GEOL braquisinclinal f, cubeta f, cuenca f, cuenca sedimentaria f, HYDROL cuenca f, telephone lines depósito m, LAB cápsula de porcelana f, MINE braquisinclinal f, PETR TECH cuenca geológica f, PROD of table tablero m, WATER pileta f, estanque m, cuenca f, hoya f; **~-and-range structure** n GEOL estructura de falla inclinada f; **~ irrigation** n AGRIC riego por compartimiento m

basis: **~ vector** n PHYS vector base m; **~ weight** n PAPER gramaje m

basket n SPACE barquilla f; **~ centrifuge** n COAL centrifugadora de cesta f; **~ coil** n ELEC ENG bobina de fondo de cesta f; **~ handle arch** n CONST arco realzado m; **~ trap** n OCEAN cesta f, nasa f

basketweave: **~ packing** n C&G embalaje reticulado m

bass n ACOUST bajo m, OCEAN perca f, **~ boost** n ELECTRON amplificador de bajas frecuencias m

bastard: **~ cut** n MECH ENG of file, rasp picadura bastarda f; **~ file** n MECH appliance, mechanism lima bastarda f; **~ pitch** n MECH ENG of screw paso bastardo m; **~ title** n PRINT título de contraportada m

bastite n MINERAL bastita f

bastnaesite n MINERAL bastnasita f

bat n CONST trozo de ladrillo m; **~ bolt** n CONST perno arponado m

batardeau n CONST ataguía f, dique m, presa f, HYDRAUL, HYDROL, WATER, WATER TRANSP dams, locks ataguía f, buque puerta m

batch[1]: **~-free** adj C&G exento de carga

batch[2] n C&G of glass-making raw materials pasta f, of bricks hornada f, CINEMAT tanda f, COMP&DP batch m, lote m, grupo de documentos m, grupo de programas m, FOOD lote m, MECH motorcycles partida de material f, lote m, partida f, remesa f, serie f, P&R hornada f, PAPER lote m, PETR TECH cantidad fija f, PROD lote m, SPACE grupo de documentos m, grupo de programas m, lote m, tanda f, TELECOM lote m, TEXTIL lote de material m, tanda f, partida f, lote m, partida de material f, TRANSP tanda f, lote de material m, partida f, lote m, partida de material f; **~ card** n PROD tarjeta de lote f, tarjeta de remesa f; **~ charger** n C&G cargador de pasta m; **~ code** n PACK código de la partida m, código de la remesa m; **~ composition** n C&G composición de la carga f; **~ crust** n C&G costra de carga f; **~ digester** n PAPER lejiadora discontinua f; **~ distillation** n NUCL destilación por etapas f, destilación por lotes f; **~ dust** n C&G polvo de carga m; **~ extraction** n NUCL extracción por etapas f, extracción por lotes f; **~ formula** n C&G fórmula de carga f; **~ freezer** n FOOD congelador de lotes m; **~ fuel-loading** n NUCL carga de combustible por lotes f; **~ furnace** n CHEM TECH, THERMO horno de carga por paquetes m, horno discontinuo m, horno intermitente m; **~ house** n C&G emplazamiento de carga m; **~ melting line** n C&G

eflorescencia de cuarzo *f*, línea de fusión de carga *f*; ~ **meltout line** *n* C&G línea de fundición *f*; ~ **mix** *n* CONST mezcla de amasado *f*; ~ **mixer** *n* C&G mezcladora del tipo Eirich *f*, CHEM TECH mezclador por cargas *m*, FOOD mezclador discontinuo *m*; ~ **mixing** *n* C&G mezcla de la carga *f*; ~ **mode** *n* PROD modo de lotes *m*; ~ **number** *n* CONST número de amasado *m*, PACK número de la remesa *m*; ~ **plant** *n* CONST planta de amasado *f*; ~ **process** *n* PROD muestreo discontinuo *m*, tratamiento por cargas *m*, tratamiento por lotes *m*; ~ **processing** *n* CHEM TECH, COMP&DP procesamiento por batch *m*, procesamiento por lotes *m*, total de batch *m* (*AmL*), total de lotes *m*, PAPER procesamiento en discontinuo *m*, PRINT procesado en discontinuo *m*; ~ **pulper** *n* PAPER desintegrador discontinuo *m*; ~ **roll** *n* PAPER bobina de final de máquina *f*; ~ **sampling** *n* PROD muestreo discontinuo *m*; ~ **stone** *n* C&G piedra de carga *f*; ~ **tabbing** *n* PACK comprobación de la remesa *f*; ~ **test** *n* PROD prueba por lote *f*; ~ **total** *n* COMP&DP total de lotes *m*; ~ **tower** *n* C&G torre de carga *f*; ~**-type freezer** *n* REFRIG congelador discontinuo *m*; ~ **wetting** *n* C&G mojado de carga *m*
batching *n* METR dosificación *f*
batchwise: ~ **operation** *n* CHEM TECH operación en forma discontinua *f*, operación intermitente *f*, operación discontinua *f*, FOOD operación discontinua *f*, operación intermitente *f*
bath *n* C&G, CINEMAT, PRINT, TEXTIL baño *m*; ~ **atmosphere** *n* C&G medio ambiente del baño *m*
batholith *n* PETROL batolito *m*
bathometer *n* FUELLESS, OCEAN, PHYS, WATER TRANSP batometro *m*
Bathonian *adj* GEOL Batoniense
bathymeter *n* FUELLESS, OCEAN, PHYS, WATER TRANSP batímetro *m*
bathymetric: ~ **chart** *n* WATER TRANSP *navigation* carta barimétrica *f*
bathymetry *n* FUELLESS, OCEAN, PHYS, WATER TRANSP batimetría *f*
bathyscaph *n* OCEAN batiscafo *m*
bathysphere *n* OCEAN batisfera *f*
bathytachymetry *n* OCEAN batitaquimetría *f*
bathythermograph *n* OCEAN batitermógrafo *m*
bathythermography *n* OCEAN batitermografía *f*
bathythermy *n* OCEAN batitermia *f*
batt *n* TEXTIL guata *f*; ~ **anchorage** *n* TEXTIL anclaje del batán *m*; ~**-anchorage testing device** *n* TEXTIL dispositivo de prueba para el anclaje del batán *m*
batten[1] *n* CINEMAT entarimado *m*, CONST tabla para piso de madera *f*, refuerzo *m*, *slate-lath* larguero *m*, listón *m*, MECH ENG listón *m*, WATER TRANSP sable *m*, serreta *f*; ~ **pocket** *n* ELEC ENG vaina *f*
batten[2] *vt* CONST clavar, entablillar; ~ **down** *vt* WATER TRANSP *hatches* cerrar
battening *n* CONST colocación de listones de madera *f*
batter[1] *n* C&G *of wall* pilote inclinado *m*, CONST *engineering, architecture* desplome *m*, *of wall* derrumbe *m*, inclinación *f*
batter[2] *vt* CONST derrumbar, golpear, *ditch* destruir, MECH ENG ataludar, *head of bolt* forzar
battering *n* CONST *of ditch* inclinación *f*, talud *m*, PAPER aplastamiento *m*
battery[1]: ~**-charged** *adj* SPACE cargado de baterías, cargado de pilas; ~**-powered** *adj* CINEMAT alimentado por baterías, ELEC ENG accionado por batería,

equipado con batería, PHOTO, PROD, TV alimentado por baterías
battery[2] *n* AUTO, CHEM batería *f*, COMP&DP batería *f*, pila *f*, ELEC acumulador eléctrico *m*, acumulador simple *m*, batería *f*, pila eléctrica *f*, ELEC ENG batería *f*, pila eléctrica *f*, acumulador eléctrico *m*, *single cell* acumulador simple *m*, HYDRAUL batería *f*, MECH ENG batería *f*, *of rolls, cylinders* tren *m*, MINE batería *f*, nivel *m*, piso *m* (*AmL*), PAPER, PHOTO, PHYS, REFRIG batería *f*, SPACE *spacecraft* batería *f*, grupo de pilas *m*, grupo de acumuladores *m*, grupo de condensadores *m*, TELECOM batería *f*, pila eléctrica *f*, VEH, WATER TRANSP *electrics* batería *f*; ~ **assembly** *n* PROD conjunto de baterías *m*, montaje en batería *m*; ~ **backup** *n* ELEC ENG batería de repuesto *f*, batería de reserva *f*, PROD reserva de baterías *f*; ~ **belt** *n* CINEMAT batería de cinturón *f*; ~ **box** *n* AUTO, PAPER caja de batería *f*; ~ **bus** *n* TRANSP autobús eléctrico de batería *m* (*Esp*), bus eléctrico *m* (*AmL*), ómnibus *m* (*AmL*); ~ **cable** *n* CINEMAT cable de las baterías *m*; ~ **cell** *n* AUTO elemento de la batería *m*, vaso de batería *m*, ELEC, ELEC ENG elemento de batería *m*, elemento de pila *m*, SPACE *spacecraft* acumulador *m*, célula energética *f*, elemento de una batería *m*, pila *f*; ~ **chamber** *n* PHOTO compartimiento para pilas *m*; ~ **chamber cover** *n* PHOTO tapa de la cámara para pilas *f*; ~ **changeover relay** *n* AUTO relé conmutador de batería *m*; ~ **charge** *n* ELEC, ELEC ENG carga de acumulador *f*, carga de batería *f*; ~ **charger** *n* ELEC ENG cargador de baterías *m*, dinamo para carga de baterías *m*, PHOTO cargador de las pilas *m*, TRANSP cargador de baterías *m*; ~ **check** *n* CINEMAT comprobación de las baterías *f*; ~ **clip** *n* ELEC ENG abrazadera de batería *f*; ~**-compartment cover** *n* PHOTO tapa del compartimiento para pilas *f*; ~ **condition** *n* TELECOM estado del acumulador *m*; ~ **cradle** *n* AUTO soporte de batería *m*, soporte de la batería *m*; ~ **discharge** *n* ELEC, SPACE descarga de batería *f*; ~ **drain** *n* SPACE purga de batería *f*; ~ **drive** *n* CINEMAT accionamiento por baterías *m*; ~ **exchange point** *n* TRANSP punto de cambio *m*; ~ **fuse** *n* MINE cebo eléctrico de cantidad *m*; ~ **grip** *n* PHOTO empuñadura para pilas *f*; ~ **holder** *n* PROD soporte de batería *m*; ~ **house** *n* MINE taller de bocartes *m*; ~ **housing** *n* ELEC caseta de acumuladores *f*, PROD local para baterías *m*; ~ **ignition** *n* AUTO encendido por acumuladores *m*; ~ **jar** *n* C&G vaso de pila *m*; ~ **loading point** *n* TRANSP punto de carga de baterías *m*, sitio de carga de baterías *m*; ~ **lorry** *n* BrE (*cf battery truck AmE*) TRANSP camión eléctrico *m*, camión eléctrico de acumuladores *m*; ~ **low LED** *n* PROD LED indicador de bajo nivel de carga de acumulador *m*; ~ **master switch** *n* AUTO, VEH interruptor maestro de batería *m*; ~ **operation** *n* ELEC ENG, TELECOM funcionamiento con batería *m*; ~ **pack** *n* CINEMAT conjunto de baterías *m*, PHOTO conjunto de pilas *m*, PROD paquete de baterías *m*; ~ **plate** *n* AUTO placa de batería *f*, ELEC electrodo de batería *m*, electrodo de una pila *m*, placa de batería *f*, ánodo de batería *m*, ELEC ENG placa de la batería *f*; ~**-powered electric vehicle** *n* TRANSP vehículo eléctrico accionado por acumuladores *m*; ~**-powered flash unit** *n* PHOTO unidad de flash alimentada por pilas *f*; ~**-powered viewer** *n* PHOTO visor alimentado por pilas *m*; ~ **of rolls** *n* MECH ENG *mill* serie de laminadores *f*, tren de laminadores *m*;

~ switch *n* PHOTO interruptor para las pilas *m*; **~ terminal** *n* AUTO, ELEC ENG borne de batería *m*, terminal de batería *m*, PHOTO terminal para las pilas *m*, VEH borne de batería *m*; **~ terminal pliers** *n pl* MECH ENG alicates terminales *m pl*; **~ transfer bus** *n* SPACE conductor colectivo de transferencia para batería *m*; **~ truck** *n* AmE (*cf* battery lorry BrE) TRANSP camión eléctrico *m*, camión eléctrico de acumuladores *m*; **~ vehicle** *n* ELEC ENG vehículo accionado por acumuladores *m*, vehículo impulsado por baterías *m*

battle: **~ cruiser** *n* WATER TRANSP crucero de combate *m*; **~ sight** *n* MILIT alza abatida *f*

battledore *n* C&G pala de enhornar *f*

battlefield *n* MILIT campo de batalla *m*

baud *n* COMP&DP baudio *m*; **~ rate** *n* COMP&DP tasa en baudios *f* (*AmL*), velocidad de línea en baudios *f* (*Esp*), velocidad de transmisión *f*, PROD velocidad de línea en baudios *f*

baulite *n* PETROL baulita *f*

baulk *n* BrE CONST *timber* listón *m*, viga de madera *f*

Baum: **~ box** *n* COAL vagoneta Baum *f*; **~ jig** *n* COAL caja Baum *f*, enganche de vagoneta Baum *m*; **~ washbox** *n* COAL cuba de lavado de Baum *f*

Baumé: **~ scale** *n* FOOD, PHYS escala de Baumé *f*, escala hidrométrica de Baumé *f*

bauxite *n* C&G, CHEM, GEOL, MINERAL, PETROL bauxita *f*

BAW *abbr* (*bulk acoustic-wave*) ELEC ENG onda acústica volumétrica *f*

bay *n* CONST *recess* entrante de pared *m*, mirador *m*, *civil engineering* compartimiento de un edificio *m*, ojo de puente *m*, FUELLESS bahía *f*, HYDROL compuerta de dique *f*, HYDROL compuerta de dique *f*, bahía *f*, MECH nave *f*, SPACE compartimiento *m*, elemento de una red de antena *m*, estante *m*, bodega *f*, TELECOM módulo *m*, WATER TRANSP ancón *m*, bahía *f*; **~ bolt** *n* CONST perno arponado *m*

Bayes': **~ theorem** *n* MATH teorema de Bayes *m*

baymouth: **~ bar** *n* GEOL, OCEAN, WATER TRANSP barra de bahía *f*, barra en la entrada de una bahía *f*

bayonet *n* ELEC ENG bayoneta *f*; **~ base** *n* ELEC ENG, PHOTO casquillo de bayoneta *m* (*AmL*), montura de bayoneta *f* (*Esp*); **~ cap** *n* ELEC casquillo de bayoneta *m* (*AmL*), montura de bayoneta *f* (*Esp*); **~ cap finish** *n* C&G acabado a casquillo de bayoneta *m*; **~ catch** *n* PACK asidero de bayoneta *m*; **~ coupling** *n* ELEC ENG acoplamiento de bayoneta *m*; **~ fitting** *n* CONST accesorio de bayoneta *m*; **~ joint** *n* ELEC conexión de bayoneta *f*, unión de bayoneta *f*; **~ lamp holder** *n* ELEC portalámparas de bayoneta *m*; **~ locking** *n* MECH cierre de bayoneta *m*; **~ mount** *n* CINEMAT montura de bayoneta *f*, PHOTO montaje de bayoneta *m*; **~ socket** *n* CINEMAT zócalo de bayoneta *m*, ELEC enchufe de bayoneta *m*, portalámparas de bayoneta *m*, zócalo de bayoneta *m*, zócalo para casquillo de bayoneta *m*, PHOTO casquillo de bayoneta *m* (*AmL*), montura de bayoneta *f* (*Esp*)

Bazin: **~'s formula** *n* HYDRAUL fórmula de Bazin *f*

BBD *abbr* (*bucket-brigade device*) ELEC ENG dispositivo de compresor axial *m*, TELECOM dispositivo de actuación rápida *m*

BC *abbr* PETR TECH (*bit change*) cambio de barrena *m*, cambio de trépano *m*, TELECOM (*bearer channel*) canal de corriente portadora *m*, radiodifusión *f*, TV (*broadcast*) emisión *f*

BCC: **~ lattice** *n* (*cf* body-centred cubic lattice BrE) CRYSTALL red CC *f* (*red cúbica centrada*)

BCD *abbr* (*binary-coded decimal*) COMP&DP, ELECTRON, PRINT DCB (*decimal codificado en binario, decimal codificado binario*)

B-channel: **~ virtual circuit service** *n* TELECOM canal B del servicio del circuito virtual *m*

BCS: **~ theory** *n* (*Bardeen-Cooper-Schrieffer theory*) ELECTRON, PHYS teoría de BCS *f* (*teoría de Bardeen-Cooper-Schrieffer*)

BCU *abbr* (*big close up*) CINEMAT primerísimo plano *m*

BDC *abbr* (*bottom dead center AmE, bottom dead centre BrE*) AUTO, MECH, VEH PMI (*punto muerto inferior*)

BE *abbr* (*binding energy*) CHEM, CRYSTALL, PART PHYS, RAD PHYS energía de enlace *f*, energía de unión *f*

Be *abbr* (*beryllium*) CHEM Be (*berilio*)

beach[1] *n* GEOL, OCEAN playa *f*; **~ berm** *n* COAL, GEOL, OCEAN berma *f*; **~ cusp** *n* OCEAN orla de playa *f* (*AmL*), punta de arena *f*; **~ fishing** *n* OCEAN pesca desde la playa *f*; **~ growth** *n* OCEAN evolución de la playa *f*, vegetación de playa *f*; **~ ridge** *n* OCEAN cresta de playa *f*, restinga *f*; **~ rock** *n* GEOL, OCEAN arenita *f*, roca de playa *f*; **~ seine** *n* OCEAN arte de playa *m*, jábega *f*, red de cerco *f*

beach[2] *vt* WATER TRANSP *vessel* varar

beaching: **~ leg** *n* WATER TRANSP escora *f*

beacon[1] *n* CONST *surveying* baliza *f*, faro *m*, radiofaro *m*, MILIT baliza *f*, OPT *of lighthouse* luz *f*, RAIL radiobaliza *f*, baliza *f*, radiofaro *m*, SPACE baliza *f*, radiofaro *m*, radiobaliza *f*, VEH *of lighthouse* luz *f*, WATER TRANSP boyarín *m*, boyarín del ancla *m*, *navigation marks* baliza *f*, *of lighthouse* luz *f*; **~ generator** *n* SPACE dinamo de baliza *f*, generador de baliza *m*

beacon[2] *vt* CONST balizar, iluminar

beaconing *n* CONST balizamiento *m*

bead[1] *n* C&G *of glass* reborde *m*, *in fiberizing glass* perla *f*, *on bottle* gollete de boca rebordeada *m*, COMP&DP cuenta *f*, sección de un programa *f*, CONST *joinery* moldura *f*, cuenta *f*, MECH *spacecraft* perla *f*, MECH ENG gubia *f*, PROD *moulder's tool* anillo de centrar *m*, VEH talón *m*; **~ core** *n* AUTO alambre de talón *m*, armadura metálica del neumático *f*, núcleo del aislador *m*; **~ tool** *n* PROD gubia para molduras convexas *f*

bead[2]: **~ down** *vt* C&G rebordear; **~ over** *vt* CONST rebordear

beaded[1] *adj* PROD rebordeado

beaded[2]: **~ bevel** *n* C&G canteador en bisel *m*; **~ chain** *n* MECH ENG cadena de rosario *f*; **~ esker** *n* GEOL montículo alargado de grava y arena estratificado *m*; **~ extrusion** *n* MECH ENG extrusión en rosario *f*; **~ screen** *n* CINEMAT, PHOTO pantalla alveolar *f*

beak: **~ iron** *n* MECH ENG pico de bigornia *m*

beaker *n* C&G vaso de boca ancha *m*, FOOD vaso de boca ancha *m*, vaso de laboratorio *m*, LAB vaso de precipitados *m*, PAPER cubilete *m*; **~ holder** *n* LAB portavaso *m*; **~ with spout** *n* LAB *wire* vaso de precipitados con pico *m*

beam[1] *n* CINEMAT haz *m*, CONST larguero *m*, *small* haz de luz *m*, viga *f*, dintel *m*, CRYSTALL, ELECTRON haz *m*, GAS rayo *m*, balancín *m*, MECH ENG viga *f*, *of machine* vigueta *f*, PART PHYS rayo *m*, haz *m*, PHYS *number* haz *m*, *communications* viga *f*, PRINT puente *m*, RAD PHYS rayo *m*, haz *m*, SPACE *communications* alcance efectivo *m*, onda dirigida *f*, haz *m*, TELECOM haz de rayos *m*, TEXTIL plegador *m*, TV haz *m*, WATER TRANSP *of lighthouse* bao *m*, manga *f*, haz *m*; ~ **aerial** *n BrE* (*cf beam antenna AmE*) TV antena de haz *f*, antena de haz dirigido *f*; ~ **alignment** *n* ELECTRON, TV alineación del haz *f*; ~ **angle** *n* ELECTRON, OPT, RAD PHYS, TELECOM ángulo de radiación *m*; ~ **antenna** *n AmE* (*cf beam aerial BrE*) TV antena de haz *f*, antena de haz dirigido *f*; ~ **attenuation** *n* ELECTRON atenuación de radiación *f*; ~ **blanking** *n* ELECTRON, TV supresión del haz *f*; ~ **bracket** *n* WATER TRANSP *shipbuilding* cartabón de bao *m*; ~ **caliper** *AmE see beam calliper BrE*; ~ **caliper gage** *AmE see beam calliper gauge BrE*; ~ **calliper** *BrE n* METR calibrador del balancín *m*; ~ **calliper gauge** *n BrE* METR tablero de calibración del balancín *m*; ~ **capture** *n* AIR TRANSP captura de haz *f*, sujeción de viga *f*; ~ **compasses** *n pl* METR brazo de compás *m*; ~ **cut-off** *n* TV corte del haz *m*; ~ **diameter** *n* OPT diámetro del haz *m*; ~ **divergence** *n* OPT, TELECOM divergencia del haz *f*; ~ **dividers** *n pl* MECH ENG divisores *m pl*; ~ **drive** *n* MECH ENG transmisión por balancín *f*; ~ **dyeing** *n* TEXTIL tintura en plegador *f*; ~ **-dyeing machine** *n* TEXTIL máquina de teñir en plegador *f*; ~ **engine** *n* MECH ENG motor de balancín *m*, máquina de balancín *f*; ~ **fixed at one end** *n* MECH ENG viga encastrada por una extremidad *f*; ~ **focusing** *n* ELECTRON enfoque del haz *m*; ~ **forming** *n* ELECTRON modelación del haz *f*; ~ **gate** *n* TV circuito discriminador del haz *m*; ~ **hook** *n* PROD *foundry* gancho del plegador *m*; ~ **impact point** *n* TV punto de impacto del haz *m*; ~ **injection** *n* NUCL inyección del haz *f*; ~ **intercept** *n* AIR TRANSP intercepción de haz *f*; ~ **jitter** *n* ELECTRON, TV inestabilidad del haz *f*; ~ **knee** *n* WATER TRANSP consola de bao *f*; ~ **lead** *n* ELECTRON *mass* hilo conductor del haz *m*; ~ **lead chip** *n* ELECTRON *mass* chip soporte del haz *m*; ~ **lead device** *n* ELECTRON dispositivo de conducción del haz *m*; ~ **loading** *n* TV carga del haz *f*; ~ **pattern** *n* TV diagrama direccional de radiación *m*; ~ **-plasma interaction** *n* NUCL interacción haz-plasma *f*; ~ **-positioning magnet** *n* TV imán posicionador haz *m*; ~ **-positioning system** *n* TV sistema posicionador del haz *m*; ~ **power** *n* ELECTRON potencia del haz *f*; ~ **-power density** *n* ELECTRON densidad de potencia del haz *f*; ~ **pulser** *n* NUCL pulsador del haz *m*; ~ **reach** *n* WATER TRANSP *sailing* ceñida a la cuadra *f*; ~ **reactor** *n* NUCL reactor de haz *m*; ~ **return** *n* TV retorno del haz *m*; ~ **-reversing lens** *n* TV lente de inversión del haz *f*; ~ **and scales** *n pl* METR balanzas y básculas *f f pl*; ~ **scales** *n* METR escala del fiel *f*; ~ **scanning** *n* ELECTRON exploración del haz *f*; ~ **sea** *n* WATER TRANSP mar de través *m*; ~ **shaft** *n* TEXTIL eje del plegador *m*; ~ **shaping** *n* ELECTRON formación del haz *f*; ~ **signal** *n* ELECTRON señal del haz *f*; ~ **splitter** *n* CINEMAT divisor de la luz *m*, divisor del haz *m*, OPT divisor del haz *m*, PRINT separador de haces *m*, TV divisor del haz *m*; ~ **splitting** *n* ELECTRON descomposición del haz *f*; ~ **-splitting prism** *n* CINEMAT prisma divisor del haz *m*, INSTR escisión de haces prismática *f*; ~ **-splitting system** *n* CINEMAT sistema divisor del haz *m*; ~ **support** *n* METR *of delicate balance* protección del fiel *f*; ~ **switching** *n* SPACE *communications* conmutación de haz *f*, orientación del haz *f*; ~ **tilt** *n* TV *pipes* inclinación del haz *f*; ~ **-to-beam sizing** *n* TEXTIL encolado de plegador a

plegador *m*; ~ **well** *n* PETR TECH pozo de bombeo mecánico *m*; ~ **width** *n* ELECTRON amplitud del haz *f*
beam² *vt* ELECTRON *compound* emitir
beamed: ~ **yarn** *n* C&G haz de urdimbre *m*
beamer *n* TEXTIL arrollador *m*
beaming *n* TEXTIL arrollado *m*
beamwidth *n* OPT abertura del haz *f*, amplitud angular del haz *f*, ángulo de abertura del haz *m*
bean *n* PETROL *solids from liquids* estrangulador *m*
bear¹ *n* C&G, PROD cuesco *m*, lobo *m*
bear² *vt* CONST soportar, MECH ENG apoyar, soportar, sostener
bear³: ~ **away** *vi* WATER TRANSP *sailing* desatracarse, arribar; ~ **stock-holding costs** *vi* TEXTIL correr con los costes del accionariado
bearded: ~ **needle frame** *n* TEXTIL bastidor de agujas de ganchillo *m*
bearding *n* TV línea del chaflán *f*
bearer *n* MECH ENG *of rolling mill* caja *f*, PRINT banda lateral de apoyo *f*, PROD *furnace* montante *m*; ~ **bracket** *n* PROD consola del montante *f*; ~ **capacity** *n* TELECOM capacidad del portador *f*; ~ **channel** *n* (*BC*) TELECOM canal de corriente portadora *m*, radiodifusión *f*; ~ **cradle** *n* PROD *grate* cuna del montante *f*; ~ **height** *n* PRINT altura de la banda lateral de apoyo *f*; ~ **service** *n* TELECOM servicio de corriente portadora *m*; ~ **set** *n* MINE marco portador *m* (*AmL*), marco soporte *m* (*Esp*)
bearing *n* CONST *points of compass* cojinete *m*, punto de apoyo *m*, apoyo *m*, *of several faces of building* soporte *m*, ELEC *machine* punto de apoyo *m*, rangua *f*, chumacera *f*, cojinete *m*, GEOL orientación *f*, MECH cojinete *m*, punto de apoyo *m*, soporte *m*, MECH ENG *component* cojinete *m*, *shaft, axle* soporte *m*, chumacera *f*, MINE aguante *m*, *ore* dirección *f*, PROD *of core print* portamacho *m*, RAIL tope de aguja *m*, VEH rodamiento *m*, cojinete *m*, WATER TRANSP *navigation* marcación *f*, demora *f*; ~ **axle box** *n* RAIL caja del eje portador *f*; ~ **block** *n* MECH ENG pedestal *m*; ~ **bracket** *n* PROD ménsula del porta-macho *f*; ~ **bush** *n* MECH ENG cojinete cilíndrico *m*; ~ **cage** *n* MECH ENG alojamiento del cojinete *m*; ~ **cap** *n* AUTO, MECH ENG casquete del cojinete *m*, casquillo del cojinete *m*, tapa del cojinete *f*; ~ **capacity** *n* COAL capacidad de carga *f*, carga admisible *f*, CONST capacidad portante *f*; ~ **compass** *n* WATER TRANSP aguja de marcar *f*; ~ **end** *n* MECH ENG *of shaft, axle* extremo del cojinete *m*, lado del cojinete *m*; ~ **lined with antifriction metal** *n* MECH ENG cojinete guarnecido con metal antifricción *m*, cojinete revestido con metal antifricción *m*; ~ **lining** *n* MECH revestimiento del cojinete *m*; ~ **lubrication system** *n* PROD sistema de lubricación de cojinetes *m*; ~ **-marker** *n* WATER TRANSP *radar* indicador de marcaciones *m*; ~ **materials** *n pl* MECH ENG materiales para cojinetes *m pl*; ~ **plate** *n* MECH ENG *disk-shaped* disco de presión *m*; ~ **point** *n* MECH ENG punto de apoyo *m*; ~ **and power-transfer assembly** *n* (*BAPTA*) SPACE conjunto de giro y transferencia de potencia *m* (*CTCP*); ~ **race** *n* MECH ENG anillo guía del cojinete *m*; ~ **rail** *n* TRANSP carril de apoyo *m*, rail de soporte *m*, riel de sustentación *m*; ~ **RTD** *n* PROD cojinete PTC *m*; ~ **surface** *n* MECH ENG superficie de apoyo *f*, superficie de rozamiento *f*, superficie portante *f*
beat¹ *n* ACOUST batido *m*, AIR TRANSP *of engine* batido *m*, pulsación *f*, ELECTRON pulsación *f*, PHYS batido *m*,

oscilación f, vibración f; ~ **frequency** n ACOUST, ELEC, PHYS frecuencia acústica f, frecuencia de pulsación f; **~-frequency oscillator** n (BFO) AIR TRANSP, ELECTRON, PHYS, TELECOM, TV oscilador de frecuencia de batido m, oscilador de frecuencia de impulsos m, oscilador de frecuencia de pulsación m; **~-frequency wavemeter** n WAVE PHYS cimómetro de frecuencia de pulsación m, medidor de onda de frecuencia acústica m, ondámetro de frecuencia acústica m; ~ **note** n WAVE PHYS nota de batido f; **~-note detector** n ELECTRON detector de tonalidad del impulso m; **~-note pitch** n WAVE PHYS tono de frecuencia audible m, tono de nota de batido m; ~ **signal** n ELECTRON señal de impulso f

beat² vt ELECTRON generar, PAPER batir, TEXTIL golpear con el batán

beat³ vi WATER TRANSP sailing voltejear

beatability n PAPER aptitud al refino f

beaten adj PAPER refinado

beater n CONST platelayer's batidor m, plumber's mallet martillo m, mezclador m, maza f, PAPER pila holandesa f, pila refinadora f; ~ **bar** n PAPER barra de la holandesa f; **~-breaker** n PAPER desintegrador de la pila m; ~ **plate** n PAPER platina f; ~ **roll** n PAPER cilindro de la pila holandesa m, molón m; ~ **sizing** n PAPER encolado en masa m, encolado interno m

beating n ELECTRON pulsación f, PAPER refinado m, PROD batido m; ~ **hammer** n MECH ENG martillo batidor m, martillo pulsante m; ~ **mill** n PAPER batán m; ~ **pick** n CONST platelayer's espadilla f

Beaufort: ~ **scale** n METEO, WATER TRANSP escala de Beaufort f

beaumontage n PROD mástique para tapar m

beaumontite n PETROL beaumontita f

beauty: ~ **quark** n (b-quark) PART PHYS beauty quark m, quark belleza m (b-quark)

becket n WATER TRANSP ropes vinatera f; ~ **bend** n WATER TRANSP knot vuelta de vinatera f

Beckmann: ~ **rearrangement** n CHEM of ketoxime reagrupamiento de Beckmann m, transposición de Beckmann f; ~ **thermometer** n PHYS termómetro de Beckmann m

BECN abbr (backward explicit congestion notification) TELECOM notificación explícita de bloqueo regresivo f

becquerel n (Bq) METR, NUCL, PHYS, RAD PHYS bequerelio m (Bq)

Becquerel: ~ **effect** n ELEC electrolytic cell efecto Becquerel m

bed¹ n COAL álveo m, filón m, lecho m, madre f, yacimiento m, CONST base f, lecho m, plataforma f, soporte m, capa f, estrato m, of clay asiento m, GAS estrato m, capa f, camada f, lecho m, GEOL camada f, estrato m, lecho m, capa f, HYDROL machine lecho m, MECH ENG machine-tool bancal m, OCEAN cama f, fondo del mar m, fondos marinos m pl, PETR TECH lecho m, PRINT platina f; ~ **bars** n pl MECH ENG of lathe mordazas de bancada f pl; ~ **deposit** n HYDROL sedimentos del lecho m pl; ~ **gage** AmE, ~ **gauge** BrE n METEO medidor de profundidad m; ~ **knife** n PAPER cuchilla de platina f; ~ **lathe** n MECH ENG torno de bancada m; ~ **level** n HYDROL nivel del lecho m; ~ **load** n GEOL carga de tracción f, carga de fondo f; **~-load transport** n HYDROL transporte de sólidos del fondo m; ~ **plate** n PAPER platina f, PETR TECH placasoporte f, platina de la perforadora f, WATER TRANSP

engine bancada f; ~ **rock** n WATER lecho de roca m; ~ **roll** n PAPER rodillo soportante m; ~ **sequence** n COAL serie alveal f; ~ **sizes** n pl TEXTIL tamaños de cama m pl; ~ **strata** n HYDROL estratos del lecho m pl; **~-type surfacing-and-boring lathe** n MECH ENG torno de taladrar y desbastar tipo bancada m

bed² vt CONST foundations apoyar; ~ **in** vt MILIT artillery asentar; ~ **out** vt CONST masonry asentar

bedding n ELEC cable almohadilla f, lecho m, relleno m, GEOL estratificación f, MILIT artillery acomodamiento m, PETR TECH estratificación f; **~-in** n PROD cimentación f; ~ **mortar** n CONST mortero de asiento m; ~ **surface** n CONST superficie de asiento f

bedplate n CONST placa de asiento f, MECH ENG of engine placa de fundación f, solera f, zócalo m, PROD of loam mould placa de fondo f; ~ **box** n PAPER asiento de la platina m

bedrock n GEOPHYS, OCEAN, PETR TECH fondo rocoso m

beef n AGRIC carne de vacuno f, GEOL capa de calcita fibrosa f, lentejones de calcita fibrosa m pl; ~ **cattle** n AGRIC ganado de abasto m, ganado vacuno m; ~ **herd** n AGRIC ganado de engorde m; ~ **and veal** n AGRIC carne bovina f; ~ **yield** n AGRIC rendimiento en carne de vaca m

beehive: ~ **kiln** n C&G horno circular intermitente m; ~ **oven** n PROD coking horno circular intermitente m

beekeeping n AGRIC apicultura f

beep: ~ **switch** n AIR TRANSP on cycle stick interruptor de tono m; ~ **tone** n CINEMAT tono audible m

beeper: ~ **trim** n AIR TRANSP of helicopter ajuste de tono m, regulador de tono m

beer: ~ **cooler** n REFRIG enfriador de cerveza m; ~ **crate** n PACK caja de cervezas f

beetle n AGRIC escarabajo m, CONST paviour's rammer mazo m; ~ **head** n CONST cabeza de mazo f

Beginner: **~'s All-purpose Symbolic Instruction Code** n (BASIC) COMP&DP, PRINT código de instrucciones simbólicas de carácter general para principiantes m

beginning: ~ **of call demand** n TELECOM comienzo de llamada m; ~ **of life** n NUCL comienzos de vida m pl; ~ **of life of the core** n NUCL comienzos de vida del núcleo m pl; ~ **of message** n (BOM) TELECOM comienzo de mensaje m; ~ **of tape** n (BOT) COMP&DP inicio de la cinta m (BOT); ~ **of tape marker** n COMP&DP marcador de principio de cinta m

behavior AmE see behaviour BrE

behaviour n BrE CONST comportamiento m, conducta f, MAR POLL comportamiento m

beheaded: ~ **river** n WATER río decapitado m

behenic¹ adj CHEM behénico, docosanoico

behenic²: ~ **acid** n CHEM ácido behénico m

beidellite n MINERAL beidelita f

bel n (b) ACOUST, COMP&DP, ELEC ENG, PART PHYS, PHYS, RAD PHYS belio m (b)

belay vt WATER TRANSP rope dar vuelta a

belaying: ~ **cleat** n WATER TRANSP cornamusa f; ~ **pin** n WATER TRANSP cabilla de maniobra f

bell n COAL martinete m, timbre m, PROD of blast furnace cono de cierre m; **~-and-hopper** n PROD blast furnace dispositivo de tolva y cono m; ~ **buoy** n WATER TRANSP navigation marks boya de campana f; **~-centering punch** AmE, **~-centring punch** BrE n MECH ENG punzón autocentrador m; ~ **character** n COMP&DP carácter de atención m, carácter de aviso m;

~ **chuck** n MECH ENG *of lathe* mandril de tornillos m, plato de tornillos m; **~-code signaling** AmE, **~-code signalling** BrE n RAIL señales mediante código por campana f pl; ~ **cone** n C&G cono de cierre m; ~ **furnace** n PROD horno de campana m; ~ **gear** n MECH ENG engranaje acampanado m; ~ **housing** n AUTO, VEH campana del embrague f, cárter del embrague m; ~ **jar** n C&G *for clock* recinto campana m, CHEM campana f, LAB campana de vidrio f; ~ **mouth** n MECH ENG, SPACE abocinamiento m, boca acampanada f, ensanchamiento m, ensanche m; **~-shaped curve** n GEOM curva de forma de campana f; **~-shaped insulator** n ELEC, ELEC ENG aislador acampanado m, aislante acampanado m, aislante bajo carpa m; ~ **transformer** n ELEC, ELEC ENG transformador de timbre m; **~-type armature** n ELEC *generator* inducido de timbre m; ~ **valve** n HYDRAUL válvula de campana f; ~ **wire** n ELEC ENG cable de timbre m

Bell: ~ **operating company** n (*BOC*) TELECOM empresa operativa de Bell f

bellcrank n AIR TRANSP *helicopter* palanca acodada f, MECH ENG leva acodada f; ~ **block** n MECH ENG bloque de palancas acodadas m; ~ **system** n MECH sistema de manivela m, sistema de palanca acodada m

bellhousing n PROD nicho m

bellied: ~ **core** n PROD *founding* macho ensanchado m

bellows n AUTO, C&G fuelle m, CINEMAT fuelle m, tubo flexible ondulado m, FOOD fuelle m, MECH, MECH ENG, PHOTO, PROD, SPACE fuelle m, tubo flexible ondulado m; ~ **attachment** n PHOTO accesorio de fuelle m; ~ **covering** n PHOTO cubierta del fuelle f; ~ **expansion joint** n MECH ENG junta de expansión de fuelle f; ~ **extension** n PHOTO extensión de fuelle f; ~ **frame** n PHOTO estructura del fuelle f; ~ **pump** n LAB *wire* bomba de fuelle f; ~ **seal** n SPACE cierre hermético del fuelle m; ~ **shutter** n CINEMAT, PHOTO obturador de fuelle m; **~-type folding camera** n PHOTO cámara plegable tipo fuelle f; **~-type pressure switch** n PROD interruptor automático de tipo fuelle m; ~ **valve** n MECH ENG válvula obturada por fuelle f, REFRIG válvula de fuelle f

belly[1] n C&G *of shaft furnace* vientre m, CONST *of wall* parte redondeada f, panza f, PROD panza f, *of flask* vientre m; ~ **landing** n AIR TRANSP aterrizaje sobre el vientre del avión m; ~ **pipe** n PROD *blast furnace* toma de aire f

belly[2] vi CONST pandear; ~ **out** vi CONST hincharse

belonite n MINERAL belonita f

below[1]: ~ **deck** adv WATER TRANSP *on ship* bajo cubierta

below[2]: **~-cloud scavenging** n POLL basurero a cielo abierto m (*Esp*), pepena a cielo abierto f (*AmL*)

belshazzar n C&G peligro de belios m

belt[1]: **~-driven** adj PROD accionado por correa; **~-fed** adj CHEM TECH alimentado por correa

belt[2] n AIR TRANSP, GEOL, HEAT ENG cinturón m, MECH, MECH ENG cinta f, correa f, correa de transmisión f, PETR TECH cinturón m, PROD *of machine* correa de transmisión f, RAD PHYS, TRANSP, VEH cinturón m; ~ **bolt** n PROD perno de la correa m; ~ **cleaner** n MINE cuchara de correa f; ~ **conveyor** n AGRIC, MECH ENG cinta transportadora f, correa transportadora f, transportador de cinta m, transportador de correa m, MINE cinta transportadora f (*Esp*), correa trans-

portadora f, transportador de cinta m, transportador de correa m, PACK, PROD cinta transportadora f, correa transportadora f, transportador de cinta m, transportador de correa m; ~ **conveyor with carrying idlers** n MECH ENG transportador de correa con polea guía m; ~ **drive** n MECH, MECH ENG, PROD transmisión por correa f; **~-driven pump** n PROD bomba accionada por correa f; ~ **dryer** n CHEM TECH secador de correa m; ~ **elevator** n AGRIC elevador de cinta m, elevador de correa m; ~ **fastener** n PROD sujetador de correa m; ~ **feed** n CHEM TECH alimentación de correa f; ~ **fork** n PROD horquilla de desembrague f; ~ **freezing** n REFRIG congelación sobre cinta transportadora f; ~ **friction** n MECH ENG fricción de correa f; ~ **guard** n MECH ENG defensa de correa f, guardacorrea m, SAFE defensa de correa f, *mechanism* guardabanda m; ~ **idler** n AUTO polea tensacorreas f, tensor de correa m, PROD anillo tensor m; ~ **lace** n PROD tireta para coser correas f; ~ **lacing** n PROD *steel* costura de correa f; ~ **marks** n pl C&G puntos de referencia en la cinta transportadora m pl; ~ **mounter** n PROD montador de correa m; **~-outgoing conveyor** n PROD cinta transportadora de salida f; ~ **press** n PRINT prensa de correa f; ~ **printer** n COMP&DP, PRINT impresora de banda f, impresora de cinta f; ~ **pulley** n PROD polea para correa f; ~ **pump** n PROD correa hidráulica f; ~ **rivet** n PROD remache para correa m; ~ **shifter** n PROD cambiacorreas m; ~ **shipper** n PROD cargador por correa m; ~ **skimmer** n MAR POLL rasera f, rasera de cinta f, POLL desescoriador de cinta m, desnatador de banda m, espumador de cinta m; ~ **stress** n MECH ENG esfuerzo de correa m; ~ **tension** n MECH ENG tensión de correa f; **~-type moving pavement** n BrE (*cf belt-type moving sidewalk AmE*) TRANSP adoquinado rodante tipo cinta m (*Esp*), andén móvil tipo cinta m, pavimento rodante tipo cinta m (*AmL*); **~-type moving sidewalk** n AmE (*cf belt-type moving pavement BrE*) TRANSP adoquinado rodante tipo cinta m (*Esp*), andén móvil tipo cinta m, pavimento rodante tipo cinta m (*AmL*); **~-type sling** n SAFE eslinga de tipo cinto f

belting n P&R conjunto de correas m, PROD correaje m; **~-in** n AIR TRANSP, SAFE acción de ponerse los cinturones de seguridad f

benzine n CHEM bencina f

bench n CONST *work-table* banco m, LAB mesa de laboratorio f, OCEAN, WATER TRANSP banco m, bancada de popa f; ~ **blasting** n MINE pega de banco f (*Esp*), pega de la grada recta f (*AmL*), pega del antepecho f, pega del piso f; ~ **cloth** n C&G cubierta de banco f; ~ **drill** n MECH, MECH ENG taladradora de banco f; **~-drilling machine** n MECH ENG taladradora de banco f; ~ **grinder** n MECH ENG rectificadora de banco f; ~ **height** n MINE altura del piso f; ~ **hole** n MINE abertura del piso f; ~ **lathe** n MECH torno para banco m, MECH ENG torno de banco m; ~ **molding machine** AmE, ~ **moulding machine** BrE n PROD máquina de moldear para banco f; **~-pillar drilling machine** n MECH ENG perforadora de columna de banco f, taladradora de columna de banco f; ~ **plane** n CONST cepillo de banco m; ~ **rammer** n PROD *moulder's* atacador para banco m; ~ **screw** n CONST tornillo de banco m, tornillo de carpintero m; ~ **seat** n VEH asiento corrido m, asiento posterior m; ~ **shears** n pl CONST cizallas f pl; ~ **stake** n CONST

bigorneta de banco *f*; ~ **stop** *n* CONST tope del banco *m*; ~ **time** *n* FOOD tiempo de espera *m*; ~**-type shaping machine** *n* MECH ENG conformadora tipo banco *f*, limadora tipo banco *f*, prensa de embutir tipo banco *f*; ~**-vice with clamp** *n BrE*, ~**-vise with clamp** *AmE* CONST tornillo de carpintero con mordaza *m*; ~ **work** *n* CINEMAT trabajo en el banco *m*
benchmark[1] *n* COMP&DP programa de evaluación de prestaciones *m*, prueba de rendimiento *f*, CONST *surveying* hito *m*, referencia *f*, MECH marca fija *f*
benchmark[2] *vt* COMP&DP evaluar el rendimiento de, evaluar prestaciones
benchmarking *n* COMP&DP evaluación de prestaciones *f*, evaluación del rendimiento *f*
bend[1] *n* C&G curva *f*, CONST *pipe-elbow* acodamiento *m*, codo *m*, ELEC ENG *waveguides* desviación *f*, *of fibre optics* plegado *m*, HYDROL *civil engineering* meandro *m*, MECH pliegue *m*, recodo *m*, curvatura *f*, acodamiento *m*, codo *m*, tubo curvado *m*, WATER TRANSP *of river, channel, pipe* codo *m*, recodo *m*; ~ **angle** *n* PROD ángulo de plegado *m*; ~ **coupling** *n* MECH ENG *pipe fitting* acoplamiento acodado *m*; ~ **radius** *n* PROD radio de plegado *m*; ~**-up lock washer** *n* MECH ENG arandela de taza *f*
bend[2] *vt* CONST *piece of wood* curvar, *pipe* acodar, *osier* cimbrear, MECH acodar, MINE arquear, PROD curvar, WATER TRANSP *anchor chain* entalingar, *rope* ajustar, *sail* envergar
bend[3] *vi* CONST arquearse, *branch* ramificar, combarse, *under a load* deformarse, MINE arquearse, PROD retorcerse
benday *n* PRINT sombreado mecánico *m*
bender *n* PRINT dobladora *f*
bending *n* C&G *of flat glass* curvatura *f*, CONST *of wood* cimbra *f*, MECH pliegue *m*, doblado *m*, doblez *m*, OPT curvatura *f*, PROD plegado *m*, SPACE codo *m*, curvatura *f*, doblez *m*, empalme *m*, pliegue *m*; ~ **circumferential stress** *n* WATER TRANSP *shipbuilding* esfuerzo de inflexión circunferencial *m*; ~ **die** *n* MECH ENG *press tools* estampa de doblar *f*, matriz de curvar *f*, matriz de doblar *f*; ~ **loss** *n* ELEC ENG *fibre optics* pérdida por codo *f*; ~ **machine** *n* MECH, PACK máquina curvadora *f*, máquina dobladora *f*; ~ **mold** *AmE see bending mould BrE*; ~ **moment** *n* CONST momento flector *m*, PHYS momento de flexión *m*, PROD, WATER TRANSP *ship design* momento flector *m*; ~ **mould** *n BrE* C&G molde para curvar *m*; ~ **movement** *n* CONST movimiento de flexión *m*, movimiento de giro *m*; ~ **press** *n* MECH ENG plegadora *f*, prensa para curvar *f*; ~ **radius** *n* MECH, PROD radio de curvatura *m*; ~ **roll** *n* MECH ENG cilindro de curvar *m*, rodillo de curvar *m*; ~ **roller** *n* C&G rodillo de curvar *m*; ~ **stiffness tester** *n* PAPER aparato para medir la resistencia a la flexión *m*; ~ **strength** *n* NUCL, PAPER resistencia a la flexión *f*; ~ **stress** *n* MECH, P&R esfuerzo de flexión *m*; ~ **test** *n* PRINT ensayo de resistencia al doblado *m*; ~ **tester** *n* P&R medidor de flexión *m*; ~ **vibrations** *n pl* RAD PHYS vibraciones de curvatura *f pl*, vibraciones de flexión *f pl*
Bendix: ~ **starter**® *n* AUTO Béndix® *m*, arranque Béndix® *m*, piñón del motor de arranque *m*, VEH Béndix® *m*, arranque Béndix® *m*, piñón del motor de arranque *m*; ~**-type starter** *n* AUTO arrancador tipo Béndix® *m*
bends *n pl* OCEAN ataque de presión *m*, enfermedad del

buzo *f*, PETR TECH curvas *f pl*, WATER TRANSP *diving illness* aeroembolsismo *m*, enfermedad del buzo *f*
beneficiation *n* C&G beneficiación *f*
Benioff: ~ **plane** *n* GEOL plano de Benioff *m*; ~ **zone** *n* FUELLESS *geothermal resources* zona de Benioff *f*
bent[1] *adj* C&G encorvado
bent[2]: ~ **finish** *n* C&G acabado encorvado *m*; ~ **glass** *n* C&G vidrio encorvado *m*; ~ **neck** *n* C&G gollete encorvado *m*; ~**-nose pliers** *n pl* MECH ENG alicates de mordazas curvadas *m pl*; ~ **spanner** *n* MECH ENG llave acodada *f*; ~ **tool** *n* MECH ENG *lathe* herramienta *f*, útil acodado *m*
benthonic *adj* GEOL bentónico
bentonite *n* COAL, DETERG, MINERAL, PETR TECH, PETROL bentonita *f*
benzaldehyde *n* CHEM benzaldehído *m*
benzaldoxime *n* CHEM benzaldoxima *f*
benzamide *n* CHEM benzamida *f*
benzanilide *n* CHEM benzanilida *f*
benzene *n* CHEM benceno *m*, benzol *m*, PETR TECH benzina *f*; ~ **hexachloride** *n* CHEM, FOOD hexacloruro de benceno *m*; ~ **ring** *n* CHEM anillo bencénico *m*
benzenoid *adj* CHEM bencenoide
benzidine *n* CHEM bencidina *f*
benzil *n* CHEM bencilo *m*
benzoate *n* CHEM benzoato *m*
benzohydrol *n* CHEM benzohidrol *m*
benzoic[1] *adj* CHEM benzoico
benzoic[2]: ~ **acid** *n* CHEM, FOOD ácido benzoico *m*
benzoin *n* CHEM benzoína *f*
benzol *n* CHEM benzol *m*; ~ **dyestuff** *n* COLOUR pigmento benzol *m*
benzole *n* CHEM benceno *m*, benzol *m*
benzonaphthol *n* CHEM benzonaftol *m*
benzonitrile *n* CHEM benzonitrilo *m*
benzophenone *n* CHEM benzofenona *f*
benzopyrene *n* CHEM benzopireno *m*
benzoquinone *n* CHEM benzoquinona *f*
benzoyl: ~ **chloride** *n* CHEM cloruro de benzoílo *m*; ~ **peroxide** *n* CHEM, FOOD acetosil *m*, peróxido de benzoílo *m*, P&R peróxido de benzoilo *m*
benzyl: ~ **alcohol** *n* CHEM alcohol bencílico *m*; ~ **cinnamate** *n* FOOD cinamato de bencilo *m*
BER *abbr* (*bit error rate*) COMP&DP, ELECTRON, TELECOM BER (*porcentaje de error de bit*), tasa de bits erróneos *f*
bergmannite *n* MINERAL bergamaskita *f*
berkelium *n* (*Bk*) CHEM, RAD PHYS berquelio *m* (*Bk*)
berm *n* COAL andén *m*, berma *f*, escalón *m*, zanja *f*, CONST *civil engineering* zanja de saneamiento *f*, GEOL berma *f*, OCEAN bancal *m*, berma *f*; ~ **ditch** *n* WATER cuneta de guardia *f*
Berne: ~ **key** *n* RAIL llave Berne *f*; ~ **rectangle** *n* RAIL rectángulo Berne *m*
Bernoulli: ~'s **equation** *n* FLUID ecuación de Bernoulli *f*; ~'s **theorem** *n* PHYS teorema de Bernoulli *m*
Berriasian *adj* GEOL Berriasiense
berth[1] *n* WATER TRANSP *bed* litera *f*, *cabin* cámara *f*, *mooring* puesto de atraque *m*, atraque *m*
berth[2] *vt* WATER TRANSP *shiphandling* atracar
berth[3] *vi* WATER TRANSP *mooring* atracar
berthierite *n* MINERAL berthierita *f*
berthing *n* SPACE atracamiento *m*, atraque *m*, fondeadero *m*, WATER TRANSP *of passengers* alojamiento *m*, atraque *m*
bertrandite *n* MINERAL bertrandita *f*

beryl *n* C&G, MINERAL berilo *m*
beryllia *n* C&G berilea *f*
beryllium *n* (*Be*) CHEM berilio *m* (*Be*); ~ **content meter** *n* NUCL medidor del contenido de berilio *m*; ~ **copper casting** *n* MECH ENG fundición de cobre de berilio *f*; ~ **copper die** *n* MECH ENG matriz de cobre de berilio *f*; ~-**moderated reactor** *n* NUCL reactor moderado por berilio *m*; ~-**prospecting meter** *n* NUCL berilómetro *m*
beryllonite *n* MINERAL berilonita *f*
berzelianite *n* MINERAL berzelianita *f*
Bessemer: ~ **converter** *n* HEAT, MECH ENG, PROD convertidor Bessemer *m*; ~ **iron** *n* PROD fundición Bessemer *f*; ~ **pig** *n* PROD fundición Bessemer *f*; ~ **process** *n* PROD proceso Bessemer *m*; ~ **steel** *n* METALL, PROD acero Bessemer *m*
best[1]: ~ **before date** *n* FOOD, NUCL, PACK, PART PHYS, RAD PHYS fecha de caducidad *f*; ~-**climb angle** *n* AIR TRANSP ángulo de ascenso óptimo *m*, ángulo óptimo de ascenso *m*; ~ **coal** *n* COAL carbón de roca *m*
best[2]: ~ **before** *phr* PACK consumir preferentemente antes de
beta: ~-**amylase** *n* FOOD beta amilasa *f*; ~-**backscatter gage** *AmE*, ~-**backscatter gauge** *BrE n* NUCL medidor de retrodispersión beta *m*; ~-**cellulose** *n* PAPER beta-celulosa *f*; ~ **decay** *n* PART PHYS, PHYS, RAD PHYS desintegración beta *f*; ~-**density gage** *AmE*, ~-**density gauge** *BrE n* NUCL medidor de la densidad beta *m*; ~ **disintegration energy** *n* PART PHYS, PHYS, RAD PHYS energía de desintegración beta *f*; ~ **emission** *n* RAD PHYS emisión beta *f*; ~ **emitter** *n* PART PHYS, PHYS, RAD PHYS emisor beta *m*; ~ **particle** *n* ELEC, NUCL, PART PHYS, PHYS, RAD PHYS partícula beta *f*; ~-**particle absorption analysis** *n* RAD PHYS análisis de absorción de partículas beta *m*; ~-**particle backscattering analysis** *n* RAD PHYS análisis de retrodispersión de partículas beta *m*; ~ **radiation** *n* ELEC, NUCL radiación beta *f*; ~ **ray** *n* ELEC, NUCL flujo de partículas beta *m*, rayo beta *m*, PART PHYS, PHYS flujo de partículas beta *m*, radiación beta *f*, rayo beta *m*; ~-**ray spectrum** *n* PHYS, RAD PHYS espectro beta *m*; ~ **test** *n* COMP&DP ensayo piloto *m*, prueba beta *f*
betatron *n* NUCL, PHYS, RAD PHYS betatrón *m*
Bethe-Goldstone: ~ **equation** *n* NUCL ecuación Bethe-Goldstone *f*
between: ~ **decks** *n* WATER TRANSP entrepuente *m*; ~-**the-lens filter** *n* CINEMAT filtro dentro del objetivo *m*, filtro entre lentes *m*; ~-**the-lens shutter** *n* PHOTO obturador de sector *m*
beudantine *n* MINERAL beudantina *f*
beudantite *n* MINERAL beudantita *f*
bevel[1] *n* INSTR baivel *m*, bisel *m*, cartabón *m*, rueda dentada cónica *f*, MECH bisel *m*, MECH ENG chaflán *m*, METR cartabón *m*, PROD bisel *m*; ~ **cutter** *n* MECH ENG fresa de ángulo *f*; ~ **edge** *n* MECH ENG bisel *m*, chaflán *m*; ~-**edged flat** *n* MECH ENG pletina biselada *f*; ~ **gear** *n* MECH, MECH ENG engranaje cónico *m*, engranaje de ángulo *m*; ~-**gear drive** *n* MECH ENG accionamiento de engranajes cónicos *m*; ~-**gear housing** *n* AIR TRANSP *helicopter* caja de engranajes cónicos *f*; ~-**gear set** *n* VEH engranaje cónico *m*; ~ **gearing** *n* AUTO, MECH ENG engranado angular *m*, engranaje cónico *m*; ~ **gears with straight and spiral tooth system** *n pl* MECH ENG engranajes cónicos con sistema de dientes rectos y helicoidales

m pl; ~-**headed bolt** *n* CONST *of lock* tornillo de cabeza biselada *m*; ~ **joint** *n* CONST unión biselada *f*, MECH ENG junta con chaflán *f*, junta en bisel *f*; ~ **protractor** *n* METR escuadra-transportador *f*; ~ **ring** *n* MECH ENG anillo en bisel *m*; ~ **ring flared stub shaft** *n* AIR TRANSP *helicopter* eje corto acampanado de anilla achaflanada *m*, eje corto acampanado de anilla cónica *m*; ~ **square** *n* METR baivel *m*, falsa escuadra *f*; ~ **wheel** *n* MECH ENG rueda cónica *f*
bevel[2] *vt* GEN achaflanar, biselar, ingletar
beveled *AmE see* bevelled *BrE*
beveling *AmE see* bevelling *BrE*
bevelled: ~ **chisel** *n BrE* MECH ENG formón de achaflanado *m*, formón en bisel *m*; ~ **washer** *n BrE* MECH ENG arandela achaflanada *f*, arandela de caras no paralelas *f*
bevelling *n BrE* C&G biselación *f*, corte biselado *m*, CONST biselación *f*, biselado *m*, ingletado *m*, INSTR biselación *f*, biselado *m*, escantillón *m*, sesgadura *f*, MECH, MECH ENG, PETR TECH biselación *f*, PETROL biselación *f*, truncamiento *m*, PRINT, PROD biselación *f*; ~ **machine** *n BrE* MECH ENG escantilladora *f*, máquina de achaflanar *f*; ~ **tool** *n BrE* INSTR herramienta escantilladora *f*
beverage: ~ **dispenser** *n* REFRIG distribuidor de bebidas *m*
Bewoid: ~ **size** *n* PAPER cola Bewoid *f*
beyond: ~ **repair** *adj* GEN irreparable, sin reparación posible
bezel *n* INSTR, MECH, PROD bisel *m*
BFA *abbr* (*basic frame alignment*) TELECOM, TV alineación básica de imagen *f*
BFO *abbr* (*beat-frequency oscillator*) AIR TRANSP, ELECTRON, PHYS, TELECOM oscilador de frecuencia de batido *m*, oscilador de frecuencia de impulsos *m*, oscilador de frecuencia de pulsación *m*, TV oscilador de frecuencia de batido *m*, oscilador de frecuencia de impulsos *m*
B-format: ~ **video recorder** *n* TV grabador de video en formato B *m* (*AmL*), grabador de vídeo en formato B *m* (*Esp*)
BG *abbr* (*background gas*) GAS, PETR TECH gas de background *m*
B/H: ~ **loop** *n* ELEC *magnetism* ciclo de histéresis *m*, curva de histéresis *f*
BHA *abbr* FOOD (*butylated hydroxyanisole*) BHA (*butilhidroxianisol*), PETR TECH (*bottom-hole assembly*) sarta de fondo *f*
BHP *abbr* (*brake horsepower*) MECH ENG, PROD, TRANSP BHP (*potencia al freno en caballos de fuerza*)
BHT *abbr* (*butylated hydroxytoluene*) FOOD BHT (*butilhidroxitolueno*)
Bi *abbr* (*bismuth*) CHEM, METALL Bi (*bismuto*)
bias[1] *n* COAL bies *m*, diagonal *f*, oblicuidad *f*, pendiente *f*, sesgo *m*, COMP&DP desviación *f*, polarización *f*, sesgo *m*, ELEC ENG derivación *f*, polarización *f*, voltaje medio *m*, MATH sesgo *m*, TV polarización *f*; ~ **battery** *n* ELEC ENG batería de polarización *f*; ~ **chase** *n* PRINT clasificación del buque *f*, rama sesgada *f*; ~ **circuit** *n* ELEC ENG circuito de derivación *m*; ~ **generator** *n* ELEC ENG generador de voltaje de polarización *m*; ~ **oscillator** *n* ELECTRON oscilador de polarización *m*; ~ **ply** *n* TEXTIL capa al bies *f*; ~-**ply tire** *n AmE* (*cf cross-ply tyre BrE*) VEH neumático con capas de tejido cruzadas *m*, neumático con capas de tejido sesgadas *m*, neumático con tejido en diagonal

m; ~ **resistor** *n* ELEC ENG resistencia de cátodo *f*, resistencia de polarización de rejilla *f*, resistencia de derivación *f*, PHYS resistencia de polarización *f*; ~ **source** *n* ELEC ENG fuente de polarización *f*, generador de polarización *m*; ~ **voltage** *n* PHYS voltaje de polarización *m*; ~ **winding** *n* ELEC, ELEC ENG bobinado de derivación *m*, devanado de derivación *m*, inducido de derivación *m*
bias[2] *vt* ELEC ENG, PHYS derivar, polarizar
biased[1] *adj* PHYS polarizado
biased[2]: ~ **exponent** *n* COMP&DP *floating point notation* exponente polarizado *m*; ~ **relay** *n* ELEC, ELEC ENG relé de retención *m*, relé polarizado *m*
biasing *n* TV polarización *f*; ~ **current** *n* TV corriente de polarización *f*, corriente polarizante *f*
biatomic: ~ **gas** *n* GAS gas biatómico *m*
biaxial: ~ **cable** *n* ELEC cable biaxial *m*; ~ **loading** *n* METALL carga biaxial *f*; ~ **orientation** *n* P&R orientación biaxial *f*
biaxially: ~~**oriented film** *n* P&R película orientada biaxialmente *f*
bib *n* CONST canilla *f* (*AmL*), espita *f*, grifo de boca roscada *m*; ~~**cock** *n* CONST grifo de manguera *m*, llave de paso *f*, MECH ENG grifo de boca curva *m*; ~ **nozzle** *n* CONST *of bib-cock* canilla curva *f* (*AmL*), grifo curvo *m*; ~ **tap** *n* MECH ENG grifo de desagüe *m*
bible: ~ **paper** *n* PAPER papel biblia *m*
bicarbonate: ~ **of soda** *n* CHEM, DETERG, FOOD bicarbonato de sodio *m*, bicarbonato sódico *m*
Bickford: ~ **fuse** *n* MINE mecha de Bickford *f* (*AmL*), mecha lenta *f* (*Esp*)
BICMOS: ~ **transistor** *n* COMP&DP transistor BICMOS *m*
bicolored *AmE see* **bicoloured** *BrE*
bicoloured *adj BrE* COLOUR bicolor
biconcave: ~ **lens** *n* INSTR, PHYS lente bicóncava *f*
biconical: ~ **aerial** *n BrE* (*cf biconical antenna AmE*) TELECOM antena bicónica *f*; ~ **antenna** *n AmE* (*cf biconical aerial BrE*) TELECOM antena bicónica *f*
biconvex: ~ **lens** *n* INSTR, PHYS lente biconvexa *f*
bicrystal *n* METALL bicristal *m*
bicycle *n* TRANSP bicicleta *f*; ~ **nipple adjuster** *n* TRANSP ajustador de tetilla para bicicleta *m*; ~ **pump** *n* TRANSP bomba de bicicleta *f*; ~ **tools** *n pl* TRANSP herramientas de bicicleta *f pl*
bicyclic *adj* CHEM bicíclico
bicycling[1] *adj* PRINT de tingladillo
bicycling[2] *n* PRINT uso de originales en varias obras *m*
bid *n* COMP&DP propuesta *f*, MECH *spacecraft* licitación *f*, oferta *f*, TELECOM intento de ocupación *m*, propuesta *f*
bidirectional[1] *adj* ACOUST, COMP&DP, PROD, TELECOM bidireccional
bidirectional[2]: ~ **block transfer** *n* PROD transferencia bidireccional de bloques *f*; ~ **counter** *n* ELECTRON contador bidireccional *m*, contador reversible *m*; ~ **coupler** *n* ELEC ENG detector bidireccional *m*; ~ **flow** *n* COMP&DP flujo bidireccional *m*; ~ **I/O module group** *n* PROD grupo bidireccional de módulos de E/S *m*; ~ **microphone** *n* ACOUST micrófono bidireccional *m*; ~ **network** *n* ELEC ENG red bidireccional *f*; ~ **switch** *n* ELEC, ELEC ENG interruptor bidireccional *m*; ~ **transducer** *n* ELEC ENG transductor bidireccional *m*, transformador bidireccional *m*; ~ **wind vane** *n* METEO biveleta *f*, veleta bidireccional *f*

bi-drum: ~ **boiler** *n* HEAT caldera de tambor doble *f*
bieberite *n* MINERAL bieberita *f*
bi-ergol: ~ **technology** *n* TRANSP tecnología biergológica *f*
bifilar[1] *adj* ELEC *winding*, PHYS bifilar, de dos hilos
bifilar[2]: ~ **electrometer** *n* ELEC electrómetro bifilar *m*, electrómetro de dos hilos *m*; ~ **suspension** *n* ELEC, PHYS suspensión bifilar *f*; ~ **winding** *n* ELEC *of inductor* arrollamiento bifilar *m*, devanado bifilar *m*
bifocal: ~ **glasses** *n pl* INSTR, OPT lentes bifocales *f pl*; ~ **lens** *n* C&G, INSTR lente bifocal *f*
bifurcated: ~ **mating-contact** *n* ELEC, PROD contacto bifurcado de acoplamiento *m*, contacto complementario bifurcado *m*, contacto de acoplamiento bifurcado *m*; ~ **movable-contact** *n* PROD contacto movible bifurcado *m*; ~ **rivet** *n* MECH ENG, PROD remache bifurcado *m*, remache de caña hendida *m*
bifurcation *n* TRANSP bifurcación *f*
big: ~ **bang** *n* PHYS, SPACE big Bang *m*, gran explosión *f*; ~ **bang radiation** *n* PHYS, SPACE *astronomy* radiación de fondo *f*, radiación del big bang *f*; ~ **bang theory** *n* PHYS, SPACE teoría de la gran explosión *f*; ~ **close up** *n* (*BCU*) CINEMAT primerísimo plano *m*; ~ **end** *n* AUTO, VEH cabeza de biela *f*; ~~**end bearing** *n* AUTO cojinete de cabeza de biela *m*, VEH cojinete de la cabeza *m*; ~ **hole** *n* PETR TECH hueco de gran diámetro *m*
bight *n* WATER TRANSP *ropes* seno *m*
biguanide *n* CHEM biguanida *f*
bilateral: ~ **aerial** *n BrE* TV antena bilateral *f*; ~ **amplifier** *n* ELECTRON amplificador bilateral *m*; ~ **antenna** *n AmE* (*cf bilateral aerial BrE*) TV antena bilateral *f*; ~ **transducer** *n* ELEC ENG transductor bidireccional *m*
bile: ~ **acid** *n* CHEM ácido biliar *m*
bilevel: ~ **operation** *n* ELEC ENG funcionamiento a dos niveles *m*
bilge *n* WATER TRANSP sentina *f*; ~ **blower** *n* WATER TRANSP ventilador de sentinas *m*; ~ **keel** *n* WATER TRANSP quilla de balance *f*; ~ **plate** *n* WATER TRANSP plancha de pantoque *f*; ~ **plating** *n* WATER TRANSP forro del pantoque *m*; ~ **pump** *n* WATER TRANSP bomba de sentina *f*; ~ **shore** *n* WATER TRANSP puntal de pantoque *m*; ~ **strake** *n* WATER TRANSP traca del pantoque *f*; ~ **stringer** *n* WATER TRANSP vagra del pantoque *f*; ~ **water** *n* WATER TRANSP agua de sentina *f*
bilirubin *n* CHEM bilirrubina *f*
bill: ~ **of health** *n* WATER TRANSP patente de sanidad *f*; ~ **of lading** *n* PETR TECH, WATER TRANSP conocimiento de embarque *m*, manifiesto de carga *m*; ~ **of material** *n* PROD lista de materiales *f*
billet: ~ **shears** *n pl* MECH ENG cizallas para tochos *f pl*
Billet: ~ **split lens** *n* PHYS lente dividida de Billet *f*
billeting: ~ **roll** *n* MECH ENG cilindro desbastador *m*, tren desbastador *m*
billiard: ~~**ball collision** *n* NUCL colisión elástica *f*
billing *n* TELECOM facturación *f*; ~ **center** *AmE*, ~ **centre** *BrE n* TELECOM centro de facturación *m*
billow *n* OCEAN oleada *f*, WATER TRANSP *of sea* ola grande *f*, oleada *f*
billyboy: ~ **dolly** *n* CINEMAT, TV dolly *f*
bimetal: ~ **piston** *n* AUTO pistón bimetálico *m*; ~ **plate** *n* PRINT plancha bimetálica *f*
bimetallic: ~ **contact** *n* ELEC ENG contacto bimetálico *m*; ~ **electrode** *n* ELEC electrodo bimetálico *m*;

~ element *n* REFRIG elemento bimetálico *m*; **~ strip** *n* ELEC bimetal *m*, elemento bimetálico *m*, lámina bimetálica *f*, par bimetálico *m*, PHYS tira bimetálica *f*; **~ switch** *n* ELEC conmutador bimetálico *m*; **~ wire** *n* ELEC, ELEC ENG alambre bimetálico *m*

bimodal: **~ bus** *n* AUTO, TRANSP autobús articulado *m* (*Esp*), autobús bimodal *m* (*Esp*), autobús oruga *m* (*Esp*), bus articulado *m* (*AmL*), bus bimodal *m* (*AmL*), bus oruga *m* (*AmL*), ómnibus articulado *m* (*AmL*), ómnibus bimodal *m* (*AmL*), ómnibus oruga *m* (*AmL*)

bimolecular *adj* CHEM bimolecular

bin *n* CINEMAT *screen* recipiente *m*, MECH tolva *f*, depósito *m*, PACK silo *m*, PROD depósito *m*; **~ liner** *n* PACK recubrimiento interior del silo *m*

binary[1] *adj* CHEM, COMP&DP, MATH, METALL binario

binary[2]: **~ adder** *n* ELECTRON sumador binario *m*; **~ addition** *n* ELECTRON suma binaria *f*; **~ arithmetic** *n* COMP&DP, ELECTRON, MATH aritmética binaria *f*; **~ chop** *n* COMP&DP troceador binario *m*, búsqueda binaria *f*, búsqueda dicotómica *f*; **~ circuit** *n* ELECTRON circuito binario *m*; **~ code** *n* COMP&DP, ELECTRON código binario *m*; **~-coded decimal** *n* (*BCD*) COMP&DP decimal codificado en binario *m* (*DCB*), decimal codificado binario *m* (*DCB*), ELECTRON decimal codificado en binario *m* (*DCB*), PRINT decimal codificado binario *m* (*DCB*); **~-coded octal** *n* COMP&DP, PROD octal codificado en binario *m*; **~-coded signal** *n* ELECTRON señal de código binario *f*; **~ coding** *n* TELECOM codificación binaria *f*; **~ column** *n* COMP&DP columna binaria *f*; **~ command language** *n* PROD lenguaje de mandatos codificado en binario *m*; **~ counter** *n* COMP&DP, ELECTRON contador binario *m*; **~ delay line** *n* TV línea de retardo binario *f*; **~ digit** *n* (*bit*) COMP&DP, ELECTRON, PETROL, PRINT, TELECOM cifra binaria *f* (*bit*), dígito binario *m* (*bit*); **~ digital** *n* COMP&DP digital binario *m*; **~ divider** *n* ELECTRON distribuidor binario *m*; **~ division** *n* ELECTRON división binaria *f*; **~ dump** *n* COMP&DP vuelco binario *m*; **~ engine** *n* MECH ENG máquina de vapores combinados *f*; **~ error-rate** *n* TELECOM tasa de errores binarios *f*; **~-heat engine** *n* MECH ENG máquina de vapores combinados *f*; **~ image** *n* SPACE, TELECOM imagen binaria *f*; **~ logic** *n* COMP&DP lógica binaria *f*; **~ modulation** *n* TELECOM modulación binaria *f*; **~ multiplication** *n* ELECTRON multiplicación binaria *f*; **~ multiplier** *n* ELECTRON, TELECOM multiplicador binario *m*; **~ notation** *n* COMP&DP notación binaria *f*; **~ number** *n* COMP&DP número binario *m*; **~ operation** *n* COMP&DP operación binaria *f*; **~ pair** *n* ELECTRON par binario *m*; **~ phase-shift keying** *n* (*BPSK*) TELECOM manipulación por desviación de fase binaria *f*; **~ representation** *n* COMP&DP representación binaria *f*; **~ scaler** *n* ELECTRON contador binario *m*; **~ search** *n* COMP&DP búsqueda binaria *f*, búsqueda dicotómica *f*; **~-search procedure** *n* TELECOM procedimiento de búsqueda binaria *m*; **~ sequence** *n* COMP&DP, TELECOM secuencia binaria *f*; **~ signal** *n* COMP&DP, ELECTRON, TELECOM señal binaria *f*; **~ sort** *n* COMP&DP clasificación binaria *f*; **~ subtraction** *n* COMP&DP subtracción binaria *f*, ELECTRON sustracción binaria *f*; **~ subtractor** *n* ELECTRON dispositivo de limitación binaria *m*; **~ synchronous transmission** *n* (*BSC*) COMP&DP transmisión sincrónica binaria *f*; **~ system** *n*

COMP&DP, ELECTRON sistema binario *m*; **~ tree** *n* COMP&DP árbol binario *m*

binaural *adj* ACOUST binaural, estereofónico

bind[1] *vt* COMP&DP atar, ligar, vincular, CONST *two wires* enlazar, conectar, ligar, atar, empalmar, PACK, PRINT encuadernar

bind[2] *vi* CONST *become wedged* ligarse, sujetarse

binder *n* AGRIC agavilladora *f*, C&G aglutinante *m*, CONST *of double floor* adhesivo *m*, *civil engineering* aglomerante *m*, *masonry* cementador *m*, *tie, fastening* unión *f*, *to effect cohesion* ligante *m*, GEOL consolidante *m*, P&R aglutinante *m*, PACK ligante *m*, encuadernador *m*, SPACE aglutinante *m*, amarre *m*, aglomerante *m*, TV ligador *m*; **~ course** *n* CONST capa de aglomerante *f*; **~ heater** *n* CONST calentador del aglomerante *m*

bindery *n* PRINT taller de encuadernación *m*

binding *n* AIR TRANSP *of engine* agarrotamiento *m*, COAL ligazón *m*, METALL fijación *f*, unión *f*; **~ agent** *n* CHEM, FOOD agente aglutinante *m*, MAR POLL aglutinante *m*; **~ beam** *n* CONST viga de sujeción *f*; **~ closure** *n* PACK cierre por pegado *m*; **~ edge** *n* PRINT margen del lomo *m*; **~ energy** *n* (*BE*) CHEM, CRYSTALL, PART PHYS, RAD PHYS energía de enlace *f*, energía de unión *f*; **~-energy curve** *n* NUCL curva de energía de enlace *f*; **~-head screw** *n* PROD tornillo de fijación *m*; **~ machine** *n* PACK encoladora *f*, encuadernadora *f*; **~ post** *n* ELEC ENG borne de conexión *m*; **~ pulley** *n* MECH ENG polea de tensión *f*, rodillo de tensión *m*; **~ stone** *n* CONST *masonry* piedra de unión *f*; **~ thread** *n* PRINT hilo de encuadernar *m*

bindweed *n* AGRIC correvuela *f*, enredadera europea *f*

binnacle *n* WATER TRANSP bitácora *f*; **~ compass** *n* WATER TRANSP *sailing* aguja de la bitácora *f*

binocular[1] *adj* INSTR, LAB, PHYS binocular

binocular[2]: **~ head** *n* INSTR cabezal binocular *m*; **~ microscope** *n* INSTR, LAB microscopio binocular *m*; **~ refractometer** *n* INSTR refractómetro binocular *m*

binomial *n* MATH binomio *m*; **~ coefficient** *n* MATH coeficiente binómico *m*, número combinatorio *m*; **~ distribution** *n* MATH, PHYS distribución binomial *f*; **~ theorem** *n* MATH teorema binomial *m*

bio: **~-indicator** *n* HYDROL, POLL indicador biológico *m*; **~-oxidation ditch** *n* HYDROL *steel rods*, WATER foso de bio-oxidación *m*

biobleaching *n* PAPER bioblanqueo *m*

biochemical: **~ oxygen demand** *n* (*BOD*) HYDROL, PETR TECH, POLL demanda bioquímica de oxígeno *f* (*DBO*); **~ tracer** *n* POLL trazador bioquímico *m*

bioclast *n* GEOL, PETROL bioclasto *m*

bioclastic *adj* GEOL, PETROL bioclástico

biodegradability *n* DETERG, HYDROL, MAR POLL, PACK, POLL, RECYCL biodegradabilidad *f*

biodegradable[1] *adj* DETERG, HYDROL, MAR POLL, PACK, POLL, RECYCL biodegradable

biodegradable[2]: **~ packaging** *n* PACK, RECYCL envase biodegradable *m*; **~ plastic** *n* RECYCL plástico biodegradable *m*; **~ substance** *n* POLL sustancia biodegradable *f*

biodegradation *n* DETERG, HYDROL biodegradación *f*, degradación biológica *f*, MAR POLL degradación biológica *f*, biodegradación *f*, PACK biodegradación *f*, degradación biológica *f*, POLL, RECYCL degradación biológica *f*, biodegradación *f*

biodiversity *n* AGRIC diversidad biológica *f*

biofilter *n* CHEM TECH, HYDROL filtro biológico *m*, POLL biofiltro *m*

biogas *n* GAS biogás *m*

biogenic[1] *adj* PETR TECH biogénico

biogenic[2]: ~ **rock** *n* PETROL roca biogénica *f*; ~ **sedimentation** *n* GEOL sedimentación biogénica *f*

biogeochemical: ~ **cycle** *n* GEOL ciclo biogeoquímico *m*

bioglass *n* C&G biovidrio *m*

biological: ~ **agent** *n* POLL agente biológico *m*; ~ **clearance rate** *n* NUCL tasa de eliminación biológica *f*; ~ **effects** *n pl* RAD PHYS efectos biológicos *m pl*; ~ **filter** *n* CHEM TECH, HYDROL, POLL filtro biológico *m*; ~ **hazard** *n* SAFE peligro biológico *m*, riesgo biológico *m*; ~ **indicator** *n* HYDROL, POLL indicador biológico *m*; ~ **oxidation** *n* HYDROL *craft* oxidación biológica *f*; ~-**protection cooling system** *n* NUCL sistema de refrigeración del blindaje biológico *m*; ~ **purification** *n* HYDROL *circuit* purificación biológica *f*; ~ **shield** *n* NUCL blindaje biológico *m*; ~ **sludge** *n* HYDROL *circuit* sedimento biológico *m*; ~ **treatment** *n* POLL tratamiento biológico *m*; ~ **water treatment** *n* WATER tratamiento biológico de agua *m*

biomass *n* FUELLESS, GAS, HYDROL, WATER biomasa *f*; ~ **from trees** *n* AGRIC biomasa arbórea *f*

biomicrite *n* PETROL biomicrita *f*

biophysics *n* PHYS biofísica *f*

biorotor *n* HYDROL *with grinding disc* biorrotor *m*

biose *n* CHEM biosa *f*, glúcido *m*

biosparite *n* PETROL bioesparita *f*

biosphere *n* METEO, POLL biosfera *f*

biostratigraphy *n* GEOL bioestratigrafía *f*

biostrome *n* GEOL biostroma *m*

biosynthesis *n* CHEM biosíntesis *f*

biotech *n* AGRIC, FOOD biotecnología *f*

biotechnology *n* AGRIC, FOOD biotecnología *f*

biotin *n* AGRIC, FOOD biotina *f*

biotite *n* C&G, MINERAL, PETROL biotita *f*

Biot-Savart: ~'**s law** *n* PHYS ley de Biot-Savart *f*

bioturbation *n* GEOL bioturbación *f*

biozone *n* GEOL biozona *f*, unidad bioestratigráfica *f*

BIP *abbr* (*bit-interleaved parity*) TELECOM paridad por bit intercalado *f*

bipack *n* CINEMAT película de dos capas *f*

biphase[1] *adj* ELEC, ELEC ENG bifásico

biphase[2]: ~ **current** *n* ELEC, ELEC ENG corriente bifásica *f*

biphasic: ~ **flow** *n* GAS flujo bifásico *m*

biphenyl *n* CHEM bifenilo *m*, difenilo *m*

bipolar[1] *adj* COMP&DP, ELEC, ELECTRON, PHYS bipolar

bipolar[2]: ~ **amplifier** *n* ELECTRON amplificador bipolar *m*; ~ **code** *n* TELECOM código bipolar *m*; ~ **code with three-zero substitution** *n* (*B3ZS*) TELECOM código bipolar con sustitución de tres ceros *m* (*B3ZS*); ~ **diode** *n* ELECTRON diodo bipolar *m*; ~ **electrode** *n* ELEC electrodo bipolar *m*; ~-**integrated circuit** *n* COMP&DP, ELECTRON circuito integrado bipolar *m*; ~ **line** *n* ELEC, ELEC ENG *supply* línea bipolar *f*; ~ **logic** *n* ELECTRON circuito lógico bipolar *m*; ~ **machine** *n* ELEC máquina bipolar *f*; ~ **power supply** *n* ELEC ENG suministro de energía bipolar *m*; ~ **power transistor** *n* ELECTRON transistor de potencia bipolar *m*; ~ **signal** *n* TELECOM señal bipolar *f*; ~ **technology** *n* ELECTRON tecnología bipolar *f*; ~ **transistor** *n* COMP&DP, ELECTRON, PHYS, TELECOM transistor bipo-

lar *m*; ~ **winding** *n* ELEC *machine* arrollamiento bipolar *m*, devanado bipolar *m*

bipropellant *n* SPACE biimpelente *m*, bipropelante *m*

biquinary[1] *adj* COMP&DP, MATH biquinario

biquinary[2]: ~ **code** *n* COMP&DP, MATH código biquinario *m*

bird: ~ **cage** *n* C&G efecto jaula *m*; ~ **'s nest** *n* C&G efecto nido de pájaro *m*; ~ **strike hazard** *n* AIR TRANSP peligro de choque con aves *m*

birdsfoot: ~ **trefoil** *n* AGRIC cuernecillo *m*

birefringence *n* CRYSTALL, OPT, PHYS, RAD PHYS birrefringencia *f*

birefringent[1] *adj* CRYSTALL, OPT, PHYS, RAD PHYS birrefringente

birefringent[2]: ~ **medium** *n* CRYSTALL, OPT, PHYS, RAD PHYS medio birrefringente *m*

bis: ~-**azo dye** *n* CHEM colorante bis-azoico *m*

biscuit: ~-**baked porcelain** *n* C&G loza cocida al bizcocho *f*; ~ **dipper** *n* C&G máquina de aspersión *f*; ~-**fired porcelain** *n* C&G loza cocida al bizcocho *f*; ~ **ware** *n* C&G loza bizcochada no vidriada *f*

B-ISDN[1] *abbr* (*broadband-integrated services digital network*) TELECOM RDSI-BA (*red digital de servicios integrados de banda ancha*)

B-ISDN[2]: ~ **network termination 1** *n* (*NT1-LB*) TELECOM terminación 1 de red digital de servicios integrados *f* (*terminación 1 de RDSI-BA*); ~ **network termination 2** *n* (*NT2-LB*) TELECOM terminación 2 de red digital de servicios integrados *f* (*terminación 2 de RDSI-BA*); ~ **terminal adaptor** *n* TELECOM adaptador terminal B de la red de transmisión digital de RDSI-BA *m*; ~ **terminal equipment** *n* (*TE-LB*) TELECOM equipo terminal B de la RDSI-BA *m*

bisect *vt* GEOM bisecar, bisectar

bisecting *adj* GEOM bisecado, bisectado

bisection *n* GEOM bisección *f*

bisector *n* GEOM bisector *m*

bisilicate *n* CHEM bisilicato *m*

bismite *n* MINERAL bismita *f*

bismuth *n* (*Bi*) CHEM, METALL bismuto *m* (*Bi*)

bismuthate *n* CHEM bismutato *m*

bismuthine *n* MINERAL bismutina *f*

bismuthinite *n* MINERAL bismutinita *f*

bismutite *n* MINERAL bismutita *f*

bisphenol: ~ **A** *n* P&R bisfenol A *m*

bistability *n* COMP&DP, ELEC ENG, ELECTRON, PHYS, TELECOM biestabilidad *f*

bistable[1] *adj* COMP&DP, ELEC ENG, ELECTRON, PHYS, TELECOM biestable

bistable[2]: ~ **circuit** *n* ELECTRON circuito biestable *m*; ~ **multivibrator** *n* ELECTRON multivibrador biestable *m*; ~ **relay** *n* ELEC ENG relé biestable *m*

bisulfate *AmE see bisulphate BrE*

bisulfide *AmE see bisulphide BrE*

bisulfite *AmE see bisulphite BrE*

bisulphate *n BrE* CHEM bisulfato *m*

bisulphide *n BrE* CHEM bisulfuro *m*

bisulphite *n BrE* CHEM bisulfito *m*

BISYNC *abbr* (*binary synchronous transmission*) COMP&DP transmisión sincrónica binaria *f*

bit[1] *abbr* (*binary digit*) COMP&DP, ELECTRON, PETROL, PRINT, TELECOM bit (*cifra binaria, dígito binario*)

bit[2] *n* COAL barrena *f*, COMP&DP bit *m*, CONST *of key* mecha *f*, barrena *f*, filo *m*, cabeza cortadora *f*, broca *f*, ELECTRON *mass* bit *m*, unidad binaria *f*, MECH barrena *f*, mecha *f*, broca *f*, MECH ENG *of brace, drill* mecha *f*, broca *f*, barrena *f*, MINE barrena *f*, PETR TECH barrena de arrastre *f*, bit *m*, mecha *f* (*AmL*), taladro *m*, broca *f*, trépano *m*, PETROL barrena de arrastre *f* (*AmL*), bit *m*, broca de arrastre *f* (*Esp*), mecha *f*, taladro *m*, trepano *m* (*Esp*), PRINT, TELECOM bit *m*; ~ **bearing** *n* PETROL cojinete para trépano *m*; ~ **brace** *n* MECH ENG berbiquí *m*; ~ **breaker** *n* PETR TECH bit breaker *m*, liberador de barrenas *m*, plato para conectar las barrenas *m*, plato para conectar las brocas *m*; ~**-by-bit encoding** *n* TELECOM codificación bit a bit *f*; ~ **change** *n* (*BC*) PETR TECH cambio de barrena *m*, cambio de trépano *m*; ~**-controlling instruction** *n* PROD instrucción controladora de bit *f*; ~ **density** *n* COMP&DP densidad de bits *f*, PETR TECH, PETROL densidad del trépano *f*; ~ **error rate** *n* (*BER*) COMP&DP, ELECTRON, TELECOM porcentaje de error de bit *m* (*BER*), tasa de bits erróneos *f*; ~ **examining** *n* PROD examen de bit *m*, revisión de bits *f*, revisión de las herramientas *f*; ~**-examining instruction** *n* PROD instrucción examinadora de bit *f*; ~ **holder** *n* MECH ENG portabarrenas *m*, portabrocas *m*; ~**-interleaved parity** *n* (*BIP*) TELECOM paridad por bit intercalado *f*; ~ **load** *n* PETROL carga del trépano *f*; ~ **location** *n* PROD celda de bit *f*; ~ **map** *n* COMP&DP, PRINT mapa de bits *m*; ~ **mapping** *n* ELECTRON configuración de la unidad binaria *f*; ~ **parallel transfer** *n* COMP&DP transferencia de bits en paralelo *f*, transferencia paralela de bit *f*; ~ **pattern** *n* COMP&DP configuración binaria *f*; ~ **position** *n* COMP&DP fila de ficha *f*, posición de bit *f*; ~ **rate** *n* COMP&DP, SPACE, TELECOM tasa de bits *f*, velocidad de transmisión de bits *f*; ~ **serial transfer** *n* COMP&DP transferencia en serie de bit *f*; ~**-shift register** *n* PROD registro de decalaje de bit *m*; ~ **slice** *n* ELECTRON sector de unidad binaria *m*; ~ **stock** *n* MECH ENG berbiquí *m*; ~**-stock drill** *n* MECH ENG barrena para berbiquí *f*; ~ **stream** *n* COMP&DP flujo de bit *m*; ~ **string** *n* COMP&DP cadena de bits *f*, serie de bits *f*, ELECTRON cadena binaria *f*; ~ **stuffing** *n* COMP&DP relleno de bits *m*; ~ **switch** *n* TELECOM conmutador de bit *m*; ~ **wear** *n* PETR TECH desgaste de la barrena *m*, desgaste del trépano *m*; ~ **weight** *n* PETROL peso del trépano *m*

bite¹ *n* CONST poder cortante *m*, *file or sand* filo *m*, MECH ENG mordedura *f*

bite² *vt* CONST *to cut, pierce, take hold of* agarrar, *of screw* ajustar, aferrar, *to enter, bury in, cling to* taladrar, perforar, MECH ENG morder; ~ **into** *vt* MECH ENG morder

bite³ *vi* WATER TRANSP *of anchor* agarrar

biting *n* MECH ENG mordiente *m*, *of rolling mill* mordedura *f*

bitone: ~ **ink** *n* COLOUR tinta de dos tonos *f*

bits: ~ **per inch** *n pl* (*BPI*) COMP&DP bits por pulgada *m pl* (*BPP*); ~ **per second** *n pl* (*BPS*) COMP&DP bits por segundo *m pl* (*BPS*)

bitt *n* WATER TRANSP bita *f*

bitter: ~ **dock** *n* AGRIC *weeds* lengua de vaca amarga *f*; ~ **end** *n* WATER TRANSP *of cable, of rope* chicote de a bordo *m* (*AmL*), final de a bordo *m*

Bitter: ~ **magnet** *n* PHYS imán de Bitter *m*; ~ **pattern** *n* PHYS figuras de Bitter *f pl*

bitterweed *n* AGRIC rama negra *f*

bitumen *n* CHEM alquitrán *m*, CHEM TECH alquitrán *m*, asfalto *m*, betún *m*, bitumen *m*, COAL alquitrán *m*, CONST, ELEC alquitrán *m*, asfalto *m*, betún *m*, bitumen *m*, GEOL bitumen *m*, asfalto *m*, betún *m*,

alquitrán *m*, MECH ENG bitumen *m*, betún *m*, asfalto *m*, alquitrán *m*, MINERAL asfalto *m*, P&R alquitrán *m*, betún *m*, bitumen *m*, asfalto *m*, PETR TECH, PETROL alquitrán *m*, betún *m*, asfalto *m*, bitumen *m*, TRANSP asfalto *m*, WATER TRANSP alquitrán *m*; ~**-coated paper** *n* PACK, PAPER papel bituminado *m*, papel embreado *m*; ~ **coating** *n* COATINGS revestimiento bituminoso *m*, revestimiento de betún *m*; ~ **emulsion** *n* CONST emulsión de asfáltica *f*, MECH ENG emulsión de bitumen *f*; ~ **pipe-coating** *n* MECH ENG revestimiento asfáltico para tuberías *m*

bituminization *n* CONST asfaltado *m*, TRANSP asfaltado *m*, asfalto *m*

bituminize *vt* CONST, TRANSP asfaltar

bituminized¹ *adj* CONST asfaltado, TRANSP asfaltado, asfalto

bituminized²: ~ **paper** *n* CONST papel asfáltico *m*

bituminous¹ *adj* GEN bituminoso

bituminous²: ~ **coal** *n* COAL carbón de piedra *m*, carbón mineral *m*, hulla *f*, hulla bituminosa *f*, carbón bituminoso *m*; ~ **membrane** *n* CONST membrana bituminosa *f*; ~ **paint** *n* COLOUR, CONST, P&R pintura bituminosa *f*; ~ **sand** *n* PETROL arena bituminosa *f*; ~ **shale** *n* GEOL pizarra bituminosa *f* (*Esp*)

bivalence *n* CHEM, COMP&DP bivalencia *f*

bivalent *adj* CHEM, COMP&DP bivalente

bixin *n* FOOD bixina *f*

Bk *abbr* (*berkelium*) CHEM, RAD PHYS Bk (*berquelio*)

black¹: ~ **and white** *adj* (*B&W*) CINEMAT, PHOTO, PRINT, TV blanco y negro (*B y N*)

black²: ~ **absorber-rod** *n* NUCL varilla absorbente negra *f*; ~ **art** *n* PRINT componente negro *m*; ~ **bindweed** *n* AGRIC enredadera anual *f*; ~ **body** *n* CINEMAT, PHYS, PRINT, RAD PHYS, SPACE, TV cuerpo absorbente de neutrones incidentes *m*, cuerpo negro *m*, radiador de Planck *m*; ~**-body radiation** *n* PHYS, RAD PHYS radiación de cuerpo negro *f*; ~**-body radiator** *n* PHYS, RAD PHYS radiador de cuerpo negro *m*; ~**-body temperature** *n* PHYS temperatura de cuerpo negro *f*; ~ **box** *n* AIR TRANSP, COMP&DP, INSTR caja negra *f*, registrador electrónico de las incidencias de vuelo *m*; ~ **chert** *n* GEOL sílex negro *m*; ~ **clipper** *n* TV separador del negro *m*; ~ **cobalt ocher** *AmE*, ~ **cobalt ochre** *BrE* *n* MINERAL ocre de cobalto negro *m*; ~ **compression** *n* TV compresión del negro *f*; ~ **crush** *n* TV compresión del negro *f*; ~ **diamond** *n* MINERAL diamante negro *m*; ~ **finishing** *n* PROD acabado en negro *m*; ~ **hole** *n* PHYS, SPACE agujero negro *m*; ~ **ice** *n* METEO, REFRIG, TRANSP hielo oscuro *m*; ~ **iron oxide** *n* CHEM, COLOUR óxido de hierro negro *m*; ~ **iron sand** *n* PROD arena negra ferruginosa *f*; ~ **japan** *n* COATINGS, COLOUR barniz japonés *m*; ~ **lead** *n* COLOUR grafito *m*; ~**-lead crucible** *n* PROD crisol de plomo negro *m*; ~ **leader** *n* CINEMAT, TV guía negra *f*; ~ **letter** *n* PRINT letra negrita *f*; ~ **level** *n* TV nivel del negro *m*; ~**-level frequency** *n* TV frecuencia de nivel del negro *f*; ~ **lift** *n* TV elevación del negro *f*; ~ **liquor** *n* HYDROL *of light* líquido residual *m*, PAPER lejía negra *f*; ~ **mold** *AmE*, ~ **mould** *BrE* *n* AGRIC moho negro *m*, negrón *m*; ~ **mustard** *n* AGRIC *weeds* mostaza negra *f*; ~ **nightshade** *n* AGRIC duraznillo negro *m*, hierba mora *f*; ~ **peak** *n* TV cresta del negro *f* (*Esp*), pico del negro *m* (*AmL*); ~ **porch** *n* TV umbral negro *m*; ~ **printer** *n* PRINT plancha del negro *f*; ~ **rot** *n* AGRIC podredumbre negra *f*; ~ **sand** *n* PROD *founding* arena usada *f*; ~ **shading** *n* TV sombreado negro *m*; ~ **shale** *n* GEOL pizarra negra *f*; ~ **spacing** *n* CINEMAT espaciado en negro *m*; ~ **speck** *n* C&G punto negro *m*; ~ **squall** *n* OCEAN turbonada negra *f*; ~ **stain** *n* C&G mancha negra *f*; ~ **staining** *n* C&G manchas negras *f pl*; ~ **stretch** *n* TV intervalo negro *m*; ~ **tellurium** *n* MINERAL teluro negro *m*; ~ **tide** *n* MAR POLL, POLL derrame de petróleo en el mar *m*, marea negra *f*; ~ **varnish** *n* COATINGS, COLOUR barniz negro *m*; ~ **water** *n* COAL, CONST, HYDROL aguas de desecho *f pl*, aguas negras *f pl*, POLL aguas de albañal *f pl*, aguas de desecho *f pl*, aguas negras *f pl*, aguas residuales *f pl*, RECYCL, WATER aguas de desecho *f pl*, aguas negras *f pl*, aguas residuales *f pl*; ~ **and white film** *n* CINEMAT, PHOTO película en blanco y negro *f*; ~**-white monitoring** *n* TV comprobación de blanco-negro *f*, monitoreo de blanco-negro *m*; ~ **and white television** *n* TV *broadcasting* televisión en blanco y negro *f*

black³: ~ **out** *vt* CINEMAT apagar

blacken *vt* THERMO ennegrecer

blackened *adj* C&G, COAL, PAPER, THERMO ennegrecido

blackening *n* C&G, PAPER ennegrecimiento *m*, PROD *foundry facing* negro de fundición *m*

blacking *n* PROD *foundry facing* negro de fundición *m*; ~ **bag** *n* PROD *founding* saquete para ennegrecer *m*

blackleg *n* AGRIC pie negro *m*

blackout *n* ELEC, ELEC ENG, NUCL apagón *m*, TELECOM apagón *m*, bloqueo de transmisión *m*, supresión *f*; ~ **curtain** *n* TEXTIL cortina opaca *f*

blacksmith¹ *adj* MECH forjador

blacksmith² *n* CONST, MECH ENG, PROD forjador *m*, herrero *m*; ~**'s bellows** *n* MECH ENG fuelle de herrero *m*; ~**'s forge** *n* MECH ENG, PROD forja de herrero *f*; ~**'s hammer** *n* MECH ENG martillo de mano *m*; ~**'s shop** *n* CONST herrería *f*, MECH ENG taller de forja *m*, herrería *f*, PROD herrería *f*; ~**'s tongs** *n pl* MECH ENG tenazas de herrero *f pl*

blackwall: ~ **hitch** *n* WATER TRANSP vuelta de gancho *f*

blackwash *n* COATINGS lavado en negro *m*, negro de fundición *m*, PROD *founding* negro líquido *m*

bladder: ~ **tank** *n* AIR TRANSP *flexible* depósito flexible *m*

blade *n* AIR TRANSP *of helicopter* pala *f*, álabe *m*, CONST pala *f*, cuchilla *f*, ELEC álabe *m*, FUELLESS paleta *f*, HYDRAUL álabe *m*, paleta *f*, pala *f*, MECH cuchilla *f*, álabe *m*, paleta *f*, aleta *f*, pala *f*, MECH ENG paleta *f*, aleta *f*, cuchilla *f*, álabe *m*, NUCL álabe *m*, PAPER cuchilla *f*, PROD, REFRIG álabe *m*, SPACE lámina *f*, álabe *m*, pala *f*, hoja *f*, WATER TRANSP *of propeller* pala *f*; ~ **aerodynamic center** *AmE*, ~ **aerodynamic centre** *BrE n* AIR TRANSP centro aerodinámico de la pala *m*; ~**-and-slot drive** *n* AIR TRANSP impulsor de pala y ranura *m*; ~ **angle** *n* AIR TRANSP ángulo de pala *m*; ~ **angle of attack** *n* AIR TRANSP, PHYS ángulo de ataque de la pala *m*; ~**-angle check-gage** *AmE*, ~**-angle check-gauge** *BrE n* AIR TRANSP galga de comprobación del ángulo de la pala *f*; ~**-aspect ratio** *n* AIR TRANSP proporción del aspecto de la pala *f*; ~**-attachment fitting** *n* AIR TRANSP adaptador de fijación de la pala *m*; ~ **balance** *n* AIR TRANSP equilibrado de la pala *m*; ~ **balance-weight** *n* AIR TRANSP peso de equilibrado de la pala *m*; ~ **bit** *n* PETR TECH trépano de aletas *m*; ~ **center of pressure** *AmE*, ~ **centre of pressure** *BrE n* AIR TRANSP centro

de presión de la pala *m*; ~ **chord** *n* AIR TRANSP cuerda de la pala *f*; ~ **coater** *n* PAPER estucadora de cuchilla *f*; ~ **coating** *n* PAPER estucado a cuchilla *m*; ~ **control system** *n* AIR TRANSP sistema de control de la pala *m*; ~ **cross-section** *n* AIR TRANSP corte transversal de la pala *m*, sección transversal de la pala *f*; ~ **cuff** *n* AIR TRANSP puño de la pala *m*; ~ **depth** *n* AIR TRANSP profundidad de la pala *f*; ~ **distortion** *n* AIR TRANSP deformación de la pala *f*; ~ **duct** *n* AIR TRANSP conducto de la pala *m*; ~ **efficiency factor** *n* AIR TRANSP factor de eficacia de la pala *m*; ~ **flapping angle** *n* AIR TRANSP ángulo de batimiento de la pala *m*; ~ **folder** *n* PRINT plegadora de cuchilla *f*; ~ **folding** *n* AIR TRANSP pliegue de la pala *m*; ~ **folding-hinge** *n* AIR TRANSP charnela de plegado de la pala *f*; ~ **holder** *n* MECH ENG portacuchillas *m*; ~ **leading edge** *n* AIR TRANSP borde de ataque de la pala *m*; ~ **life** *n* AIR TRANSP vida de la pala *f*; ~ **lift** *n* AIR TRANSP sustentación de la pala *f*; ~**-lift coefficient** *n* AIR TRANSP coeficiente de sustentación de la pala *m*; ~ **loading** *n* AIR TRANSP carga de la pala *f*; ~ **lower surface** *n* AIR TRANSP superficie inferior de la pala *f*; ~ **materials** *n pl* FUELLESS materias de paleta *f pl*; ~ **moment of inertia** *n* AIR TRANSP momento de inercia de la pala *m*; ~ **pitch** *n* AIR TRANSP, FUELLESS *turbines* paso de paleta *m*, paso de álabe *m*; ~**-pitch angle** *n* AIR TRANSP ángulo de paso de la pala *m*; ~**-pitch change-hinge** *n* AIR TRANSP charnela de cambio de paso de la pala *f*; ~**-pitch control compensator** *n* AIR TRANSP compensador del control de paso de la pala *m*; ~**-pitch indicator** *n* AIR TRANSP indicador de paso de la pala *m*; ~**-pitch reversal** *n* AIR TRANSP, TRANSP inversión del paso de las palas *f*; ~**-pitch setting** *n* AIR TRANSP posición del paso de la pala *f*, reglaje del paso de la pala *m*; ~**-pitch transmitter** *n* AIR TRANSP transmisor de paso de la pala *m*; ~**-pitch variation** *n* AIR TRANSP variación de paso de la pala *f*; ~ **pitch-change rod** *n* AIR TRANSP barra de cambio de paso de la pala *f*; ~ **pocket** *n* AIR TRANSP bolsillo de la pala *m*; ~ **profile** *n* AIR TRANSP perfil de la pala *m*; ~ **quantity** *n* FUELLESS número de paletas *m*; ~ **radius** *n* AIR TRANSP radio de la pala *m*; ~ **retention-strap** *n* AIR TRANSP abrazadera de retención de la pala *f*; ~ **root** *n* AIR TRANSP raíz de la pala *f*; ~ **setting** *n* AIR TRANSP reglaje de la pala *m*; ~**-setting angle** *n* AIR TRANSP ángulo de colocación de la pala *m*; ~ **shank** *n* AIR TRANSP espiga de la pala *f*, mango de la pala *m*; ~ **shutter** *n* CINEMAT obturador de laminilla *m*; ~ **slap** *n* AIR TRANSP bofetada de la pala *f*, golpeo de la pala *m*; ~ **sleeve** *n* AIR TRANSP manga de la pala *f*; ~**-spacing system** *n* AIR TRANSP sistema de separación de las palas *m*; ~**-span axis** *n* AIR TRANSP eje de longitud de la pala *m*; ~ **speed** *n* FUELLESS velocidad de las paletas *f*; ~ **spindle** *n* AIR TRANSP husillo de la pala *f*; ~ **spring** *n* MECH ENG resorte de flexión *m*, resorte de hojas *m*; ~ **stall** *n* AIR TRANSP pérdida de la pala *f*; ~ **stop** *n* AIR TRANSP paro de la pala *m*; ~ **sweep** *n* AIR TRANSP desvío tangencial de la pala *m*; ~**-taper ratio** *n* AIR TRANSP proporción de estrechamiento de la pala *f*, proporción de la conicidad de la pala *f*; ~ **tilt** *n* AIR TRANSP inclinación de la pala *f*; ~ **tip** *n* AIR TRANSP extremo de la pala *m*, punta de la pala *f*; ~**-tip cap** *n* AIR TRANSP casquillo del extremo de la pala *m*; ~**-tip fairing** *n* AIR TRANSP carenado del extremo de la pala *m*; ~**-tip loss factor** *n* AIR TRANSP factor de pérdida del extremo de la pala *m*; **~-tip nozzle** *n* AIR TRANSP tobera del extremo de la pala *f*; **~-tip stall** *n* AIR TRANSP pérdida en la punta de la pala *f*; **~-tip vortex** *n* AIR TRANSP torbellino de la punta de la pala *m*, turbulencia del extremo de la pala *f*, vórtice de la punta de la pala *m*; **~ tracking** *n* AIR TRANSP derrota de la pala *f*; **~ trailing edge** *n* AIR TRANSP borde de fuga de una pala *m*; **~-trim tab** *n* AIR TRANSP lengüeta de calibración de la pala *f*; **~-twisting moment** *n* AIR TRANSP momento de torsión de la pala *m*; **~ upper surface** *n* AIR TRANSP superficie superior de la pala *f*; **~-width ratio** *n* AIR TRANSP proporción del ancho de la pala *f*

blading *n* MECH empaletado *m*, paletaje *m*

blanch *vt* FOOD blanquear, escaldar

bland: **~ formula** *n* PROD fórmula suave *f*

blank[1] *n* COMP&DP blanco *m*, espacio en blanco *m*, MECH alambre para hacer tornillos *m*, espacio *m*, hueco *m*, llave ciega *f*, material en bruto *m*, obturador *m*, pieza bruta *f*, pieza sin terminar *f*, PRINT espacio en blanco *m*, PROD lingote de acero fundido *m*, pieza tosca de forja *f*; **~-and-burst message** *n* TELECOM mensaje de borrado y error *m*; **~ cartridge** *n* MILIT cartucho de fogueo *m*, cartucho sin bala *m*, MINE cartucho de fogueo *m*; **~ circle** *n* MECH ENG *gearing* círculo exterior *m*; **~ cracking** *n* C&G rajado de pieza tosca *m*; **~ door** *n* CONST puerta sin modular *f*; **~ flange** *n* MECH ENG brida ciega *f*, brida de obturación *f*; **~ frame** *n* CINEMAT cuadro en blanco *m*, fotograma en blanco *m*, TV fotograma en blanco *m*; **~ glass** *n* C&G vidrio tosco *m*; **~ groove** *n* ACOUST surco en blanco *m*; **~ liner** *n* PETR TECH camisa lisa *f*, liner liso *m*, liner sin perforaciones *m*, revestidor sin perforaciones *m*; **~-magnetic tape** *n* TV cinta magnética en blanco *f*; **~ mold** *AmE see blank mould BrE*; **~ mold seam** *AmE see blank mould seam BrE*; **~ mold turnover** *AmE see blank mould turnover BrE*; **~ mould** *n BrE* C&G estampa formadora *f*; **~ mould seam** *n BrE* C&G junta de la estampa formadora *f*; **~ mould turnover** *n BrE* C&G rendimiento de la estampa formadora *m*; **~ nut** *n* PROD tuerca sin roscar *f*; **~ seam** *n* C&G junta de la pieza en tosco *f*; **~ table** *n* C&G mesa de piezas en tosco *f*; **~ tear** *n* C&G rasgadura de la pieza en tosco *f*; **~ ticket** *n* PACK etiqueta en blanco *f*; **~ transfer** *n* C&G transferencia en blanco *f*; **~ wall** *n* CONST pared sin carga *f*; **~ washer** *n* MECH ENG arandela obturadora *f*; **~ window** *n* CONST falsa ventana *f*

blank[2] *vt* PROD cortar; **~ off** *vt* PROD obturar

blanked: **~ beam** *n* ELECTRON haz eliminado *m*; **~-off channel** *n* TELECOM canal aislado *m*

blanket[1]: **~-to-blanket** *adj* PRINT mantilla contra mantilla

blanket[2] *n* C&G compuesto para proteger la superficie de un metal *m*, NUCL manto *m*, zona fértil *f*, PRINT mantilla *f*, SPACE *spacecraft* medio fértil *m*, suspensión de bióxido de sodio en aguas pesadas *f*, cobertura *f*, manta *f*, materia fértil *f*, capa fértil *f*, TEXTIL manta *f*; **~ charger** *n* C&G cargador general *m*; **~ contamination** *n* PRINT contaminación de la mantilla *f*; **~ cylinder** *n* PRINT cilindro de la mantilla *m*; **~ feed** *n* C&G carga general *f*; **~ gas** *n* GAS, NUCL gas protector *m*; **~ low spot** *n* PRINT área hundida en la mantilla *f*; **~ make-ready** *n* PRINT puesta a punto de la mantilla *f*, tráfico de cabotaje *m*; **~-type**

insulant *n* REFRIG aislante en mantas flexible *m*; **~ washer** *n* PRINT lavamantillas *m*; **~ wrap** *n* PRINT buque de cabotaje *m*, protección de la mantilla *f*

blanketing *n* NUCL inertización *f*, PETR TECH inertización *f*, SAFE inertización *f*

blanking *n* ELECTRON borrado *m*, eliminación *f*, PROD obturación *f*, TV borrado *m*; **~ circuit** *n* TV circuito de borrado *m* (*AmL*); **~ cover** *n* AIR TRANSP tapa de obturación *f*; **~ cover for air-cooling unit outlet** *n* AIR TRANSP cubierta de la salida de la unidad de enfriamiento de aire *f*; **~ die** *n* MECH ENG *for small intricate processes* matriz de punzonar *f*, *press tools* cortador *m*; **~ effect** *n* AIR TRANSP efecto de obturación *m*; **~ generator** *n* ELECTRON generador de impulsos de supresión *m*; **~ interval** *n* TELECOM, TV intervalo de borrado *m*; **~ level** *n* TV nivel de borrado *m*; **~ operation** *n* MECH ENG *blanks* fabricación de piezas en tosco *f*, fabricación de primordios *f*; **~ plate** *n* AIR TRANSP placa de obturación *f*; **~ plug** *n* PROD tapón obturador *m*; **~ press** *n* MECH ENG prensa de troquelar *f*, prensa punzonadora *f*; **~ pulse** *n* TV pulso de borrado *m*; **~ signal** *n* ELECTRON señal de supresión *f*, TV señal de borrado *f*; **~ and sync signal** *n* TV señal de borrado y sincronismo *f*; **~ and sync signal mixer** *n* TV mezclador de la señal de borrado y sincronismo *m*; **~ voltage** *n* TV voltaje de borrado *m*

blast[1] *n* AIR TRANSP chorro *m*, PROD chorro de viento *m*, SPACE chorro *m*, explosión *f*, inyección *f*, TELECOM explosión *f*, voladura *f*; **~ fence** *n* AIR TRANSP barrera contra el chorro *f*; **~ forming** *n* P&R formación por inyección de aire *f*, moldeado por inyección de aire *m*; **~ freezing** *n* FOOD congelación por chorro de aire *f*; **~ furnace** *n* C&G, COAL, HEAT, MECH ENG alto horno *m*, PROD horno alto *m*, THERMO alto horno *m*; **~-furnace campaign** *n* PROD campaña de horno alto *f*; **~-furnace cement** *n* CONST cemento siderúrgico *m*; **~-furnace coke** *n* COAL coque de alto horno *m*, coque metalúrgico *m*; **~-furnace for coke** *n* PROD horno alto para coque *m*; **~-furnace gas** *n* PROD gas de alto horno *m*; **~-furnace slag** *n* PROD escoria de horno alto *f*; **~ gage** *AmE see blast gauge BrE*; **~ gate** *n* PROD *furnace* registro de la tubería del viento *m*; **~ gauge** *n BrE* PROD manómetro del viento *m*; **~-hole** *n* MINE barreno *m*, abertura de ventilación *f*; **~ main** *n* PROD *of furnace, cupola* tubería principal del viento *f*; **~ nozzle** *n* PROD tobera soplante *f*, *tuyere* bocín de tobera *m*; **~-off** *n* SPACE *spacecraft* despegue *m*, lanzamiento *m*; **~ pipe** *n* PROD *of blower* tubería del viento *f*; **~ preheater** *n* THERMO precalentador de alto horno *m*; **~ pressure** *n* PROD *furnace* presión del viento *f*; **~ pump** *n* HYDRAUL bomba impelente *f*; **~ shelter** *n* COAL protección contra explosiones *f*; **~ of steam** *n* HYDRAUL chorro de vapor de agua *m*

blast[2] *vt* COAL abrir, derribar, explotar, perforar, volar, CONST chorrear con arena; **~ by heating** *vt* COAL derribar con calor

blasted: **~ stone** *n* COAL roca volada *f*

blaster *n* COAL, CONST dinamitero *m*, explosor *m*, polvorero *m*, MINE dinamitero *m*, disparador de barrenos *m* (*Esp*), explosor *m*, polvorero *m* (*AmL*)

blasting *n* COAL explosión *f*, voladura *f*, CONST voladura *f*, MINE pega *f* (*AmL*), voladura *f*; **~-cap** *n* MINE cebo *m* (*AmL*), detonador *m* (*Esp*), fulminante *m* (*Esp*); **~-charge** *n* MINE carga de voladura *f*, carga explosiva *f* (*AmL*); **~ foreman** *n* CONST capataz encargado de las voladuras *m*; ~ **forewoman** *n* CONST capataz encargada de las voladuras *f*; **~-fuse** *n* MINE mecha de Bickford *f*, mecha lenta *f*; ~ **gelatine** *n* MINE dinamita goma *f*, gelatina detonante *f*, gelatina explosiva *f*; ~ **machine** *n* MINE explosor *m*; **~-pattern** *n* MINE disposición de los explosivos *f*

blastomylonite *n* GEOL blastomilonita *f*

blaze[1] *n* CHEM, HEAT ENG, SAFE llama *f*, THERMO hoguera *f*, llama *f*, *flame* llamarada *f*

blaze[2]: ~ **up** *vi* CHEM inflamarse, THERMO destellar, inflamarse, llamear

blazed: ~ **grating** *n* PHYS red de difracción glaseada *f*

blazing: ~ **fire** *n* CONST llamarada de fuego *f*

bleach[1]: ~ **bath** *n* CINEMAT, PHOTO baño de blanqueo *m*; ~ **liquor** *n* PROD solución de cloruro cálcico *f*

bleach[2] *vt* CHEM blanquear, decolorar, desoxidar, purificar, CINEMAT, FOOD, PAPER, PRINT, TEXTIL blanquear; ~ **out** *vt* PHOTO blanquear

bleached: ~ **flour** *n* FOOD harina blanqueada *f*; ~ **lined** *n* PAPER *folding boxboard* cartoncillo con la cara superior blanca *m*, cartulina con la cara superior blanca *f*; ~ **pulp** *n* PAPER pasta blanqueada *f*, pulpa blanqueada *f*

bleacher *n* DETERG blanqueador *m*, PAPER blanqueador *m*, pila blanqueadora *f*

bleaching[1]: **~-resistant** *adj* COLOUR resistente al blanqueo

bleaching[2] *n* CHEM blanqueado *m*, decoloración *f*, DETERG blanqueo *m*, decoloración *f*, FOOD blanqueado *m*, PAPER blanqueo *m*; ~ **agent** *n* CHEM agente blanqueador *m*, agente de blanqueo *m*, DETERG agente blanqueador *m*, agente de blanqueo *m*, blanqueador *m*, FOOD agente blanqueador *m*, PAPER blanqueador *m*, TEXTIL agente blanqueador *m*, agente de blanqueo *m*; ~ **bath** *n* CINEMAT, PHOTO baño de blanqueo *m*; ~ **chest** *n* PAPER tina de blanqueo *f*; ~ **clay** *n* C&G arcilla decoloradora *f*; ~ **earth** *n* DETERG tierra de blanqueo *f*; ~ **lime** *n* DETERG cal viva de blanqueo *f*; ~ **liquor** *n* PAPER lejía de blanqueo *f*, licor de blanqueo *m*; ~ **powder** *n* DETERG polvo de blanqueo *m*, FOOD polvo blanqueador *m*, PAPER cloruro de cal *m*; ~ **tower** *n* PAPER torre de blanqueo *f*; ~ **washer** *n* PAPER lavador del sistema del blanqueo *m*

bleed[1]: ~ **elbow** *n* MECH ENG codo purgador *m*; ~ **flow** *n* PROD flujo de purga *m*; **~-off** *n* REFRIG trasiego *m*; ~ **plug** *n* MECH ENG purgador *m*; ~ **printing** *n* PRINT impresión a sangre *f*; ~ **screw** *n* MECH ENG tornillo de purga *m*; ~ **valve** *n* AUTO válvula de sangrado *f*, MECH ENG, PETR TECH grifo de purga *m*, válvula de purga *f*, válvula de sangrado *f*

bleed[2] *vt* CINEMAT sangrar, MECH perder, purgar, sangrar, MECH ENG purgar, PRINT imprimir a sangre; ~ **down** *vt* PETROL purgar; ~ **off** *vt* PETROL purgar

bleed[3] *vi* P&R exudar, sangrar, PRINT correrse; ~ **off** *vi* COLOUR desteñir

bleeder *n* ELEC ENG divisor de tensión *m*, divisor de voltaje *m*; ~ **resistor** *n* ELEC ENG resistencia de compensación *f*, resistencia derivadora *f*; ~ **screw** *n* AUTO tornillo de sangrado *m*; **~-type condenser** *n* REFRIG condensador de extracción *m*; ~ **winding** *n* ELEC *regulation* arrollamiento de drenaje *m*, devanado de drenaje *m*

bleeding *n* MECH extracción de vapor *f*, sangradura *f*, sangría *f*, sangría de vapor *f*, MECH ENG, NUCL, PETR TECH purga *f*, PRINT corrimiento de la tinta *m*, VEH *brake system* purga *f*; **~-cock** *n* WATER grifo de purga *m*; **~-valve** *n* HYDRAUL, WATER válvula de desahogo *f*, válvula de purga *f*, válvula equilibrada *f*; ~ **whites** *n pl* TV blancos sangrientes *m pl*

bleep *vi* WATER TRANSP blip

B-leg *n* TELECOM rama B *f*

blemish: ~ **on copy** *n* PRINT defecto en el original *m*

blend[1] *n* P&R combinación *f*, mezcla *f*, TEXTIL mezcla *f*; ~ **ratio** *n* TEXTIL porcentaje de mezcla *m*, proporción de mezcla *f*

blend[2] *vt* MECH ENG, TEXTIL combinar, mezclar

blende *n* CHEM blenda *f*, MINERAL blenda *f*, esfalerita *f*

blender *n* C&G mezcladora *f*, P&R máquina mezcladora *f*

blending *n* PROD *founding* mezcla de fundiciones *f*, RAIL fusión *f*; **~-chest** *n* PAPER tina de mezcla *f*; ~ **plant** *n* PETR TECH instalación de matizado *f*, planta de mezclado *f*; ~ **radius** *n* MECH ENG radio de mezcla *m*, relación de mezcla *f*

blendous *adj* PROD blendoso

blendy *adj* PROD blendoso

blight *n* AGRIC añublo *m*, muerte generalizada *f*, tizón *m*

blimp[1] *n* CINEMAT blindaje insonoro para la cámara *m*

blimp[2] *vt* CINEMAT blindar

blimped: ~ **camera** *n* CINEMAT cámara contenida en blindaje insonoro *f*, cámara insonora *f*

blind *n* MECH persiana *f*, SPACE ceguera de los hielos *f*, proyectil que no ha estallado *m*, VEH cortina *f*; ~ **alley** *n* CONST callejón sin salida *m*; ~ **angle** *n* AIR TRANSP ángulo ciego *m*; ~ **arch** *n* CONST *architecture* arco simulado *m*; ~ **auction** *n* PETR TECH remate ciego *m*; ~ **blocking** *n* PRINT grabado ilegible *m*, impresión en seco *f*; ~ **door** *n* CONST puerta falsa *f*; ~ **drainage area** *n* WATER área de drenaje ciega *f*; ~ **drill roll** *n* PAPER rodillo con agujeros ciegos *m*; ~ **embossing** *n* PRINT en seco estampado, gofrado *m*; ~ **flange** *n* MECH ENG brida ciega *f*, brida de obturación *f*; ~ **flight** *n* AIR TRANSP vuelo a ciegas *m*; ~ **hole** *n* CONST orificio ciego *m*; ~ **image** *n* PRINT imagen cegada *f*; ~ **keyboard** *n* PRINT teclado ciego *m*; ~ **landing** *n* AIR TRANSP aterrizaje a ciegas *m*; ~ **level** *n* MINE fondo de saco *m*, galería ciega *f* (*AmL*), galería de sifón *f* (*AmL*), galería falsa *f* (*Esp*), piso intermedio *m* (*AmL*); ~ **navigation** *n* SPACE navegación por instrumentos *f*, vuelo sin visibilidad *m*; ~ **pit** *n* CONST pozo ciego *m*; ~ **printing** *n* PRINT impresión en seco *f*, litoral *m*; ~ **rivet** *n* MECH ENG remache ciego *m*; ~ **roaster** *n* PROD horno de mufla *m*; ~ **sector** *n* AIR TRANSP *without traffic rights* sector ciego *m*; ~ **sector without traffic rights** *n* TRANSP calle peatonal sin salida *f*, sarna *f*, zona sin tráfico rodado *f*; ~ **shaft** *n* CONST conducto ciego *m*; ~ **stamp** *n* PRINT gobernador *m*, imagen incolora en bajo relieve *f*; ~ **stud bolt** *n* MECH ENG prisionero ciego *m*; ~ **thrust** *n* GEOL cabalgamiento ciego *m*; ~ **wall** *n* CONST muro ciego *m*; ~ **washer** *n* MECH ENG arandela ciega *f*, arandela de obturación *f*; ~ **window** *n* CONST ventana ciega *f*; ~ **workings** *n pl* CONST obras de blindaje *f pl*; ~ **zone** *n* PETROL zona oculta *f*

blinding *n* PROD *of screen, sieve*, WATER obturación *f*; ~ **concrete** *n* CONST concreto de blindaje *m* (*AmL*), hormigón de blindaje *m* (*Esp*)

blink *vi* COMP&DP *graphic display* parpadear

blinker *n* AUTO, VEH intermitente *m*, luz intermitente *f*, lámpara de señalización por destellos *f*
blinking[1] *adj* COMP&DP parpadeante
blinking[2] *n* COMP&DP parpadeo *m*; ~ **light** *n* SPACE luz centelleante *f*, lámpara de destellos *f*
blip *n* TELECOM señal detectible *f*, señal luminosa en la pantalla *f*; ~ **tone** *n* CINEMAT tono audible *m*
blister *n* AIR TRANSP *of helicopter* vejiga *f*, C&G ampolla *f*, burbuja *f*, P&R burbuja *f*, ampolla *f*, PROD *air-bubble in casting* poro *m*, WATER TRANSP *paint* ampolla *f*, burbuja *f*; ~ **card** *n* PACK envase en lámina al vacío *m*; ~ **cut** *n* PAPER corte de pliegue *m*; ~**-edge-and-foil machine** *n* PACK máquina para envasar en láminas al vacío *f*; ~ **pack** *n* PACK envase en lámina al vacío *m*; ~**-pack tooling** *n* MECH ENG utillaje para emblistado *m*; ~**-packaging machine** *n* PACK máquina para envasar en láminas al vacío *f*; ~**-packing line** *n* PACK cadena de envasado en láminas al vacío *f*; ~ **rust** *n* AGRIC roya vesicular *f*; ~ **sealer** *n* PACK sistema para el sellado de envases en láminas al vacío *m*
blistering *n* PAPER, PRINT formación de ampollas *f*, formación de burbujas *f*
blizzard *n* METEO blizzard *f*, ventisca *f*
bloach *n* C&G ondulación *f*
bloat *n* AGRIC empaste *m*, timpanismo *m*
bloating *n* OCEAN curado *m*, PAPER hinchazón *f*
block[1] *n* C&G conjunto de lentes en bruto *m*, COAL calza *f*, COMP&DP bloque *m*, CONST bloque *m*, cuadra *f* (*AmL*), macizo *m*, manzana *f* (*Esp*), MECH ENG *of anvil* cepo *m*, *wedge* cuña *f*, PETR TECH bloque *m*, concesión *f*, permiso *m*, PRINT clisé *m*, grabado *m*, PROD bloque *m*, WATER TRANSP cuadernal *m*, motón *m*, polea *f*; ~**-and-tackle** *n* MECH ENG aparejo de poleas *m*, polipasto *m*; ~ **capitals** *n pl* PRINT mayúsculas de imprenta *f pl*; ~ **carriage** *n* MECH ENG *of overhead travelling crane* carro de rodadura *m*; ~ **chain** *n* MECH ENG cadena articulada *f*, cadena de eslabones macizos *f*, cadena de rodillos *f*; ~ **coding** *n* TELECOM codificación de bloque *f*; ~ **compaction** *n* COMP&DP compactación de bloques *f*, comprensión de bloques *f*; ~ **compression** *n* COMP&DP compactación de bloques *f*; ~ **copolymer** *n* P&R copolímero de bloque *m*; ~ **diagram** *n* COMP&DP diagrama de bloques *m*, ELEC ENG diagrama de bloques *m*, diagrama funcional *m*, MECH ENG diagrama de ensamblaje *m*, TELECOM diagrama de conjuntos *m*; ~**-dropping indicator** *n* TELECOM indicador de deposición de bloques *m*; ~ **error rate** *n* COMP&DP tasa de errores en bloques *f*; ~ **faulting** *n* GEOL fracturación en bloques *f*; ~ **grease** *n* MECH ENG grasa en bloque *f*; ~ **headway** *n* RAIL, SAFE distancia de seguridad entre convoyes *f*; ~ **lava** *n* GEOL lava en bloques *f*; ~ **length** *n* COMP&DP longitud de bloque *f*; ~ **letter** *n* PRINT tipo de madera de gran tamaño *m*; ~ **making** *n* PRINT fabricación de clisés *f*; ~ **number** *n* PETR TECH número de bloque *m*; ~ **polymer** *n* DETERG polímero en bloque *m*; ~ **polymerization** *n* DETERG polimerización en bloque *f*; ~ **print** *n* PRINT impresión mediante grabados de madera *f*; ~ **printing** *n* PRINT impresión mediante grabados de madera *f*, TEXTIL estampación con molde *f*; ~ **quantization** *n* TELECOM cuantificación de bloques *f*; ~ **salt cake** *n* FOOD sal en bloque *f*; ~ **section** *n* RAIL sección de tramo *f*; ~ **sensor** *n* PROD sensor de bloque *m*; ~**-shear test** *n* MECH ENG ensayo de corte en bloque *m*, prueba de cizallamiento en bloque *f*; ~ **signal**

locked *n* RAIL señal de tramo cerrada *f*; ~ **size** *n* COMP&DP tamaño del bloque *m*; ~ **sort** *n* COMP&DP clasificación de bloques *f*; ~ **speed** *n* AIR TRANSP velocidad de bloque *f*; ~ **structure** *n* COMP&DP estructura de bloques *f*; ~**-structured language** *n* COMP&DP lenguaje estructurado por bloques *m*; ~ **system** *n* RAIL sistema de señales por tramos de vía *m*; ~ **terminal** *n* TELECOM terminal de bloque *m*; ~ **time** *n* AIR TRANSP tiempo de bloque *m*, tiempo total del vuelo *m*; ~ **tin** *n* PROD estaño en lingotes *m*; ~**-to-block time** *n* AIR TRANSP tiempo de bloque a bloque *m*; ~ **transfer** *n* COMP&DP transferencia de bloques *f*; ~**-transfer read** *n* PROD lectura de transferencia en bloques *f*; ~**-transfer write** *n* PROD escritura de transferencia en bloques *f*; ~ **transmission** *n* TELECOM transmisión de bloques *f*; ~**-type insulant** *n* REFRIG aislante en paneles *m*, aislante en planchas *m*
block[2] *vt* MECH ENG bloquear, interceptar, WATER TRANSP *port* bloquear, obstruir; ~ **out** *vt* PRINT sobreimprimir tapando
blockade[1] *n* WATER TRANSP bloqueo *m*
blockade[2] *vt* WATER TRANSP bloquear
blockage: ~ **effects** *n pl* TELECOM efectos de blocaje *m pl*
blocked: ~ **impedance** *n* ELEC ENG impedancia bloqueada *f*, impedancia sin carga *f*; ~**-out halftone** *n* PRINT semitono sobreimpreso tapando *m*; ~ **reactance** *n* ELEC ENG reactancia bloqueada *f*, reactancia controlada *f*
blockhouse *n* MILIT fortín *m*
blocking *n* COAL bloqueo *m*, COMP&DP bloqueado *m*, ELEC ENG *of conduction* bloqueo *m*, P&R adherencia entre capas *f*, PRINT estampado *m*, PROD conformación aproximada a la definitiva *f*, TELECOM, TV, WATER bloqueo *m*; ~ **anticyclone** *n* METEO anticiclón de bloqueo *m*; ~ **board** *n* MINE entibado de la galería transversal *m*; ~ **capacitor** *n* ELEC, ELEC ENG, PHYS capacitor de bloqueo *m*, condensador de bloqueo *m*; ~ **device** *n* ELEC ENG dispositivo de bloqueo *m*; ~ **loss** *n* SPACE *communications* pérdida por bloqueo *f*; ~ **network** *n* ELEC ENG, TELECOM red de bloqueo *f*; ~ **oscillator** *n* ELECTRON oscilador de bloqueo *m*, PHYS oscilador de relajación *m*; ~ **period** *n* ELEC ENG período de bloqueo *m*; ~ **state** *n* ELECTRON bloqueo *m*; ~ **temperature** *n* GEOL temperatura de reforzamiento *f*
blockout *n* PRINT sobreimpresión que tapa la anterior *f*
blocks *n pl* PETR TECH aparejo de bloques *m*, polipasto *m*
blödite *n* MINERAL blödita *f*
bloedite *n* MINERAL bloedita *f*
blood: ~ **albumen** *n* FOOD albúmina sanguínea *f*; ~ **albumin** *n* FOOD albúmina sanguínea *f*; ~ **bank** *n* REFRIG banco de sangre *m*; ~ **meal** *n* AGRIC *animal rations* harina de sangre *f*; ~ **transfusion equipment** *n* SAFE equipo para transfusión de sangre *m*
blooded: ~ **stock** *n* AGRIC ganado de pura sangre *m*
bloodstone *n* MINERAL heliotropo *m*, piedra sangre *f*
bloom *n* C&G empañamiento *m*, FOOD eflorescencia *f*, pelusa *f*; ~ **shears** *n pl* MECH ENG cizallas para tochos *f pl*, tijeras para lupias *f pl*
bloomed[1] *adj* C&G tratado con película antirreflectora
bloomed[2]: ~ **lens** *n* CINEMAT, PHOTO objetivo antirreflector *m*, PHYS lente con película antirreflectora *f*
blooming *n* AGRIC floración *f*, foliación *f*, C&G

luminosidad excesiva *f*, CINEMAT tratamiento con material antirreflector *m*, COATINGS florecido *m*, PHOTO blooming *m*; ~ **mill** *n* MECH ENG laminador de desbaste *m*, laminador preliminar *m*; ~ **roll** *n* MECH ENG cilindro del tren desbastador *m*

bloop[1] *n* CINEMAT ruido de empalme *m*

bloop[2] *vt* CINEMAT marcar con tinta opaca

blooping: ~ **ink** *n* CINEMAT tinta opaca *f*; ~ **notch** *n* CINEMAT empalme defectuoso *m*; ~ **patch** *n* CINEMAT registro sonoro defectuoso *m*

blotch *n* TEXTIL mota *f*

blotter: ~ **material** *n* CONST material secante *m*

blotting: ~ **paper** *n* PAPER papel absorbente *m*, papel secante *m*

blow[1] *n* PROD corriente de aire *f*, *casing* carga fundida *f*; ~**-and-blow process** *n* C&G procedimiento soplado y resoplado *m*; ~ **back** *n* C&G resoplado *m*; ~ **ball** *n* LAB perilla neumática *f*; ~**-bending test** *n* MECH ENG prueba de flexión al choque *f*; ~ **coil** *n* ELEC ENG bobina de extinción *f*, electroimán de soplado *m*; ~**-fill-seal system** *n* PACK sistema de llenado y cierre *m*; ~ **fuse** *n* ELEC ENG fusible apagachispas *m*; ~**-head** *n* C&G cabeza de soplado *f*; ~**-mold** *AmE see blow-mould BrE*; ~**-molding** *AmE* ~**-mould** *n BrE* MECH ENG *for plastics* molde por insuflación de aire comprimido *m*; ~**-moulding** *n BrE* P&R moldeo por insuflación de aire comprimido *m* (*AmL*), moldeo por soplado *m* (*Esp*); ~**- off** *n* COAL purga *f*; ~**-off cock** *n* WATER grifo de purga *m*; ~**-off valve** *n* REFRIG válvula de escape *f*; ~ **roll** *n* PAPER rodillo soplador *m*; ~ **table** *n* C&G mesa de soplado *f*; ~**-up** *n* CINEMAT, PHOTO, PRINT ampliación *f*; ~**-up ascent** *n* OCEAN descompresión explosiva *f*; ~**-up printing** *n* CINEMAT copiado para obtener ampliaciones *m*; ~**-valve** *n* HYDRAUL válvula de seguridad *f*

blow[2]: ~ **up** *vi* SPACE estallar

blow[3] *vt* PROD *cupola* soplar, *fire* inyectar aire a, SPACE fundir, inyectar aire a, inyectar, escapar; ~ **down** *vt* HEAT ENG *cursor*, WATER purgar; ~ **in** *vt* PROD *blast furnace* encender; ~ **off** *vt* WATER evacuar, purgar; ~ **out** *vt* PROD *blast furnace* apagar ~ **up** *vt* CINEMAT ampliar, PHOTO ampliar, aumentar, PRINT ampliar, SPACE aumentar

blowdown *n* HEAT ENG purga, *f* NUCL *loss of coolant accident* fase de purga *f*, WATER purga *f*; ~ **accident** *n* NUCL, SAFE accidente de purga *m*; ~ **pressurization** *n* SPACE presionización de caída *f* (*AmL*), presurización de caída *f*; ~ **valve** *n* HEAT ENG *tools* válvula de purga *f*

blower *n* AUTO, C&G fuelle *m*, soplador *m*, ventilador *m*, ventilador impelente *m*, CINEMAT fuelle *m*, FOOD, MECH fuelle *m*, soplador *m*, ventilador *m*, ventilador impelente *m*, MECH ENG fuelle *m*, PAPER soplante *m*, PHOTO fuelle *m*, PROD *force fan* soplante *m*, fuelle *m*, ventilador *m*, *engine, as for blast furnace* máquina de soplar *f*, *collective* turbosoplante *m*, REFRIG ventilador de impulsión *m*, SPACE fuelle *m*, VEH ventilador *m*; ~**-brush** *n* CINEMAT, PHOTO pincel soplador *m*; ~**-cock** *n* PROD grifo del fuelle *m*, grifo del ventilador impelente *m*; ~**-fan** *n* PROD ventilador del soplante *m*; ~**-wheel** *n* MECH ENG rueda de soplador *f*

blowhole *n* OCEAN bufadero *m*, PROD *in casing* sopladura *f*

blowing *n* C&G *glass* soplado *m*, FOOD abombamiento *m*; ~**-agent** *n* P&R neumatógeno *m*, sustancia productora de gas *f*; ~**-crown** *n* C&G cabeza de soplar *f*;

~**-engine** *n* PROD máquina soplante *f*; ~ **ring** *n* C&G anillo refractorio flotante *m*; ~ **snow** *n* METEO arrastre eólico alto de nieve *m*, ventisca de nieve *f*

blowlamp *n* CONST *brazing lamp* soplete de soldar *m*, HEAT ENG soplete de soldar *m*, lamparilla de soldar *f*, MECH ENG lámpara de soldar *f*, lámpara para quemar pintura *f*

blown[1]: **not** ~ **up** *adj* C&G no soplado

blown[2]: ~ **bottle** *n* C&G, PACK botella fabricada por soplado *f*; ~ **fiber** *AmE*, ~ **fibre** *BrE n* TELECOM fibra soplada *f*; ~ **film** *n* P&R película soplada *f*; ~ **fire** *n* PROD fuego apagado *m*; ~ **flap** *n* AIR TRANSP *boundary layer control*, TRANSP flap soplado *m*; ~**-flap system** *n* AIR TRANSP sistema de flap soplado *m*; ~ **fuse** *n* ELEC, ELEC ENG fusible fundido *m*, fusible quemado *m*; ~**-fuse indicator** *n* PROD indicador de fusible fundido *m*, indicador de fusible quemado *m*; ~ **glass** *n* PROD cristal soplado *m*; ~**-glass tube** *n* LAB tubo de vidrio para soplado *m*; ~ **sheet** *n AmE* (*cf cylinder glass BrE*) C&G lámina soplada *f*, vidrio en cilindros *m*, vidrio plano soplado *m*

blowout *n* COAL explosión *f*, PETR TECH, PETROL erupción *f*, reventón *m*, POLL erosión eólica *f*, escape de aire *m*, fuga de aire *f*, SPACE *communications* estallido *m*, suspensión súbita *f*; ~ **preventer** *n* (*BOP*) PETR TECH impide-erupciones *m*, impide-reventones *m*, protector de erupción *m*, válvula de control de explosión *f*, válvula impide-reventones *f* (*AmL*), PETROL antirreventón *m*

blowpipe *n* C&G caña de vidriero *f*, CONST soplete *m*, MECH ENG caña de soplar *f*, soplete *m*, tubo de escape *m*, tubo portaviento *m*, PROD *of tyre* soplete *m*, tubo de escape *m*

blowpiping *n* CONST sopleteado *m*

blowtorch *n* CONST lámpara de soldar *f*, MECH ENG lámpara de soldar *f*, lámpara para quemar pintura *f*

blub *n* P&R *paint defect* ampolla *f*

blue[1]: ~ **adder** *n* TV circuito aditivo azul *m*; ~ **beam** *n* ELECTRON, TV haz azul *m*; ~**-beam magnet** *n* TV imán de haz azul *m*; ~**-black level** *n* TV nivel azul negro *m*; ~ **brittleness** *n* MECH falta de plasticidad *f*, METALL falta de plasticidad *f*, fragilidad azul *f*; ~ **clay** *n* C&G arcilla azul *f*; ~ **devil** *n* AGRIC *weeds* flor morada *f*; ~**-glaze pigment** *n* COLOUR pigmento azul satinado *m*; ~**-green laser** *n* ELECTRON láser verde-azul *m*; ~ **gun** *n* TV cañón azul *m*, disparador de azul *m*; ~ **key** *n* PRINT montaje azul *m*; ~ **litmus paper** *n* CHEM papel tornasol azul *m*; ~ **peak level** *n* TV nivel máximo de azul *m*; ~ **pot** *n* PROD crisol de grafito *m*; ~ **primary** *n* TV azul primario *m*; ~ **printer** *n* PRINT plancha del azul *f*; ~ **quark** *n* PHYS quark azul *m*; ~ **quartz** *n* MINERAL cuarzo azul *m*; ~ **reflectance factor** *n* PAPER factor de reflectancia en el azul *m*; ~ **sapphire** *n* MINERAL zafiro azul *m*; ~ **screen grid** *n* TV pantalla rejilla azul *f*; ~**-screen process** *n* CINEMAT proceso con pantalla azul *m*; ~ **signal** *n* ELECTRON señal azul *m*; ~ **silica-gel** *n* CHEM, PACK gel de sílice azul *m*; ~**-spar** *n* MINERAL espato azul *m*; ~ **tourmaline** *n* MINERAL turmalina azul *f*; ~ **vitriol** *n* CHEM vitriolo azul *m*

blue[2] *vt* PRINT azular

bluegrass *n* AGRIC pasto azul de Kentucky *m*

blueground *n* GEOL aglomerado descompuesto *m*

blueing *n* COLOUR, PAPER azulado *m*

blueprint *n* CONST copia en borrada *f*, copia en forroprusiato *f*, copia heliográfica *f*, MECH ENG calco azul de dibujo *m*, copia heliográfica *f*, PRINT, PROD cianocopia *f*, copia heliográfica *f*, TEXTIL cianotipo *m*

blueschist *n* GEOL esquisto azul *m*

bluestone *n* CHEM piedra azul *f*

bluff[1]: **~-bowed** *adj* WATER TRANSP *ship* de roda limpia

bluff[2] *n* CONST, GEOL acantilado *m*, OCEAN farallón *m* (*AmL*), morro *m*, acantilado *m*, WATER TRANSP acantilado *m*, promontorio *m*

blunt[1] *adj* MECH ENG embotado, obtuso, romo, PRINT desgatado

blunt[2] *n* PRINT tipo desgatado *m*; **~ body** *n* AIR TRANSP cuerpo romo *m*

blunt[3] *vt* MECH embotar, MECH ENG embotar, enromar

blur: **~ pan** *n* CINEMAT panorámica rápida de transición *f*

blurred[1] *adj* C&G, PHYS borroso

blurred[2]: **~ image** *n* PHYS imagen borrosa *f*, imagen no nítida *f*

blurring *n* CINEMAT *geophysics* emborronamiento *m*

blushing *n* P&R aspecto blancuzco y turbio *m*, PRINT rubor *m*

blustery *adj* METEO *switch* violento

board[1]: **on ~** *adv* MILIT, WATER TRANSP a bordo

board[2] *n* COMP&DP *circuits* placa *f*, módulo electrónico *m*, tarjeta *f*, CONST *notice-board* tablón de anuncios *m*, *timber* tabla *f*, pizarra *f*, tablero *m*, ELECTRON cuadro *m*, placa *f*, PAPER cartón *m*, PRINT tablero *m*, PROD *of bellows* tablilla *f*, TELECOM trama *f*, WATER TRANSP *of ship* bordo *m*; **~ felt** *n* PAPER fieltro de cartón *m*; **~ for pressing** *n* PAPER cartón para embutir *m*; **~-level modem** *n* ELECTRON módem sobre placa *m*; **~ liner** *n* PAPER tripa del cartón *f*; **~ locking tab** *n* PROD orejeta de cierre *f*; **~ machine** *n* PAPER máquina de cartón *f*; **~ sheathing** *n* COATINGS recubrimiento de madera *m*; **~-type insulant** *n* REFRIG aislante en paneles *m*, aislante en planchas *m*

board[3] *vt* CONST *cover with boards* entarimar, revestir de madera, WATER TRANSP *ship, goods* abordar, embarcar, visitar

board[4] *vi* WATER TRANSP embarcar, embarcarse

board[5]: **on ~** *prep* WATER TRANSP a bordo de

boarding *n* CONST entablado *m*, entarimado *m*, TEXTIL hormado *m*, WATER TRANSP *ship* abordaje *m*, embarque *m*, visita *f*; **~ bridge** *n* AIR TRANSP puente aéreo *m*; **~ party** *n* WATER TRANSP abordaje *m*, visita de cortesía *f*, visita de inspección *f*; **~ platform** *n* TRANSP andén de abordaje *m* (*AmL*), andén de embarque *m* (*Esp*), muelle de embarque *m* (*Esp*), plataforma de embarque *f* (*Esp*)

boat[1] *n* CONST *travelling cradle* barco *m*, bote *m*, embarcación *f*, LAB *measuring* cápsula *f* (*Esp*), navecilla *f* (*AmL*), MAR POLL embarcación *f*, bote *m*, OCEAN bote *m*, embarcación *f*, PROD *founding* tapón *m*, WATER TRANSP bote *m*, embarcación *f*; **~ carriage** *n* TRANSP transporte en barca *m*, transporte en barco, transporte en buque *m*; **~ chock** *n* WATER TRANSP *shipbuilding* calzo de bote *m*; **~ deck** *n* WATER TRANSP *in a ship* cubierta de botes *f*; **~ drill** *n* WATER TRANSP ejercicio de botes *m*; **~ elevator** *n* TRANSP, WATER TRANSP elevador de barcas *m*, elevador de barcos *m*; **~ falls** *n pl* WATER TRANSP *of lifeboat* tiras *f pl*; **~ heading** *n* WATER TRANSP rumbo del bote *m*; **~-hook** *n* WATER TRANSP bichero *m*; **~ launching crane** *n* TRANSP grúa para la botadura de embarcaciones *f*; **~ lift** *n* TRANSP amantillo de verga para botes *m*, elevador de barcos *m*, montabarcos *m*, WATER

TRANSP elevador de barcos *m*; **~ sling** *n* WATER TRANSP cable de suspensión *m*, cadena de suspensión *f*; **~ station** *n* WATER TRANSP *in lifeboats* puesto de embarque *m*; **~ tackle** *n* WATER TRANSP aparejo *m*; **~ tank** *n* TRANSP cámara de aire del bote *f*; **~ trailer** *n* TRANSP remolque de barca *m*

boat[2]: **~ up the furnace** *vi* PROD *founding* tapar el agujero de colada

boatbuilder *n* WATER TRANSP constructor de botes *m*

boathouse *n* TRANSP embarcadero *m*

boatload *n* WATER TRANSP *of passengers* barcada *f*, lanchada *f*

boatman *n* WATER TRANSP amarrador *m*, lanchero *m*

boatswain *n* WATER TRANSP contramaestre *m*; **~'s chair** *n* WATER TRANSP guindola *f*

bob *n* CONST *of plumb-line* plomada *f*, METR *of steelyard* peso cursor *m*, PROD *of leaver-driven pump* volante del balancín *m*

bobbin *n* C&G, CINEMAT bobina *f*, carrete *m*, ELEC ENG carrete *m*, devanadera *f*, devanadora *f*, PROD devanadera *f*, devanadora *f*, TEXTIL, TV bobina *f*, carrete *m*

bobierrite *n* MINERAL bobierrita *f*

bobstay *n* WATER TRANSP barbiquejo *m*

BOC *abbr* (*Bell operating company*) TELECOM empresa operativa de Bell *f*

BOD *abbr* (*biochemical oxygen demand*) HYDROL, PETR TECH, POLL DBO (*demanda bioquímica de oxígeno*)

body *n* C&G pasta *f*, HYDROL *of ore* consistencia *f*, densidad *f*, INSTR carrocería *f*, caja *f*, PRINT *of ink, of types* densidad *f*, cuerpo *m*, PROD *of rolling-mill roll* mesa *f*, *water, petroleum* capa *f*, RAIL caja *f*, TELECOM cuerpo *m*, TEXTIL carta *f*, cuerpo *m*, VEH carrocería *f*, WATER *of carriage, wagon* caja *f*, WATER TRANSP *of ship* cuerpo *m*; **~ at rest** *n* MECH cuerpo en reposo *m*; **~ brace** *n* CINEMAT soporte de cuerpo *m*; **~-centered cubic** *AmE see body-centred cubic BrE*; **~-centered cubic lattice** *AmE see body-centred cubic lattice BrE*; **~-centered lattice** *AmE see body-centred lattice BrE*; **~-centred cubic** *n BrE* CHEM cúbico de cuerpo centrado *m*; **~-centred cubic lattice** *n BrE* (*BCC lattice*) CRYSTALL red cúbica centrada *f* (*red CC*); **~-centred lattice** *n BrE* METALL red de cuerpo centrado *f*, red de malla centrada *f*; **~ filler** *n* VEH masilla para carrocerías *f*, tapaporos *m*; **~ force** *n* METALL presión de endurecimiento *f*; **~ gasket** *n* PROD empaquetadura de la mesa *f*; **~-icing** *n* REFRIG aplicación directa del hielo en seno de carga *f*; **~ in motion** *n* MECH cuerpo en movimiento *m*; **~ in white** *n* VEH carrocería tratada con parafina *f*; **~ matter** *n* PRINT composición de texto *f*; **~ mold** *AmE*, **~ mould** *BrE n* C&G molde de la pasta *m*; **~ paper** *n* PAPER papel base *m* (*AmL*), papel soporte *m*; **~ plan** *n* WATER TRANSP *ship design* plano de formas *m*; **~ of the print** *n* TEXTIL motivo del estampado *m*; **~ section** *n* WATER TRANSP *ship design* sección transversal *f*; **~ shell** *n* VEH carrocería *f*; **~ size** *n* PRINT tamaño de letra *m*; **~ stock** *n* PAPER papel soporte *m*; **~-transmitted vibration hazard** *n* SAFE riesgo originado por vibraciones transmitidas corporalmente *m*; **~ tube** *n* INSTR barrilete *m*; **~ type** *n* PRINT tipo común *m*; **~ waves** *n pl* GEOL ondas de volumen sin ser influidas por discontinuidades *f pl*

bodying *n* PRINT *of ink* viscosidad *f*; **~ agent** *n* PRINT espesante *m*

BOE *abbr* (*barrel oil equivalent*) PETR TECH equivalente a un barril de crudo *m*

boehmite *n* MINERAL boehmita *f*

bog: ~ **butter** *n* COAL turba fósil *f*; ~ **peat** *n* COAL turba de pantanos *f*

bogey *n* MECH ENG carretón *m*

boggy *adj* COAL pantanoso

boghead *n* COAL carbón de algas *m*

bogie *n* BrE (*cf truck AmE*) CONST, MECH, MECH ENG, RAIL, VEH bogie *m* (*Esp*), boje *m* (*AmL*), carretilla *f*, carretón *m*, remolque *m*, remolque articulado *m* (*AmL*), trailer *m* (*Esp*), vagón de mercancías *m*; ~ **bolster** *n* BrE (*cf truck bolster AmE*) RAIL traviesa del pivote del bogie *f*, traviesa del pivote del carretón *f*; ~ **frame** *n* BrE RAIL bastidor del bogie *m*, bastidor del carretón *m*; ~ **kiln** *n* HEAT horno de secado giratorio *m*; ~ **open self-discharge wagon** *n* BrE (*cf truck open self-discharge car AmE*) TRANSP carretón de descarga auto-basculante *m*, vagón de auto-descarga con caja abierta *m*; ~ **pin** *n* BrE (*cf truck pin AmE*) VEH *trailer* pivote de remolque *m*, pivote del bogie *m*, pivote del enganche *m*; ~ **pivot** *n* BrE (*cf truck pivot AmE*) VEH *trailer* pivote de arrastre *m*, pivote de remolque *m*, pivote del bogie *m*; ~ **wagon with swivelling roof** *n* BrE TRANSP carretón con techo giratorio *m*, furgón con techo corredizo *m*

bogus *n* PAPER imitación *f*

Bohemian: ~ **crystal** *n* C&G cristal de Bohemia *m*

Bohr: ~ **magneton** *n* PHYS, RAD PHYS magnetón de Bohr *m*; ~ **radius** *n* PHYS radio de Bohr *m*

Bohr-Sommerfeld: ~ **model** *n* PHYS modelo de Bohr-Sommerfeld *m*

boil[1] *n* COAL remolino vertical *m*; ~ **period** *n* PROD *Bessemer process* período de descarburación *m*

boil[2] *vt* PHYS hervir, THERMO bullir, cocer, hervir; ~ **down** *vt* FOOD, THERMO reducir; ~ **in bag** *vt* FOOD, PACK hervir sin sacar de la bolsa

boil[3] *vti* FOOD hervir

boil[4]: ~ **away** *vi* FOOD, THERMO consumirse, evaporarse; ~ **fast** *vi* THERMO hervir a borbotones; ~ **over** *vi* THERMO irse, rebosarse; ~ **slowly** *vi* THERMO cocer a fuego lento

boilable: ~ **pouch** *n* PACK bolsa que se puede hervir *f*

boiled: ~ **linseed oil** *n* CHEM, COATINGS, CONST, WATER TRANSP aceite de linaza cocido *m*; ~ **starch** *n* FOOD almidón reducido *m*

boiler *n* FOOD *of screw* hervidor *m*, HYDRAUL, MECH caldera *f*, cámara de combustión *f*, MECH ENG caldera *f*, generador de vapor *m*, PAPER, PHYS, RAIL caldera *f*, REFRIG hervidor *m*, THERMO hervidor *m*, caldera *f*, WATER TRANSP *engine* caldera *f*; ~ **alarm** *n* HYDRAUL indicador de alarma en la caldera *m*, indicador de silbato de alarma *m*; ~ **capacity** *n* HEAT capacidad de la caldera *f*; ~~**cleaning compound** *n* HEAT producto de limpieza para calderas *m*; ~ **coal** *n* COAL carbón de caldera *m*; ~ **economizer** *n* HYDRAUL economizador *m*; ~ **efficiency** *n* HEAT eficiencia de la caldera *f*; ~ **emergency float** *n* HYDRAUL flotador de alarma en la caldera *m*; ~ **explosion** *n* HYDRAUL, SAFE explosión de caldera *f*; ~ **feed pump** *n* HEAT bomba de alimentación de caldera *f*; ~ **feeding** *n* HYDRAUL alimentación de la caldera *f*; ~ **fitting** *n* HYDRAUL, PROD, THERMO accesorio de caldera *m*; ~ **float** *n* HYDRAUL boya de alarma en la caldera *f*, flotador de alarma en la caldera *m*; ~ **flue** *n* HYDRAUL hogar de caldera *m*, horno de caldera *m*; ~ **front** *n* HYDRAUL frente de caldera *m*; ~ **furnace** *n* HYDRAUL hogar de caldera *m*, horno de caldera *m*; ~ **grate** *n* HEAT rejilla de la caldera *f*; ~ **house** *n* HEAT local de calderas *m*, HYDRAUL hogar de caldera *m*; ~ **inspection** *n* HEAT, SAFE, THERMO inspección de calderas *f*; ~ **jacket** *n* HYDRAUL guarnición de caldera *f*; ~ **jacketing** *n* HYDRAUL envuelta de chapa aislando la caldera *f*, guarnición de aislamiento de la caldera *f*, revestimiento de caldera *m*; ~ **lagging** *n* HYDRAUL camisa aislante de la caldera *f*; ~ **pipe shaping-mandrel** *n* HYDRAUL mandril para dar forma a la canalización de la caldera *m*; ~ **plate** *n* HYDRAUL chapa para caldera *f*; ~ **rivet** *n* HYDRAUL remache de caldera *m*; ~~**room** *n* HEAT, HYDRAUL cámara de calderas *f*, sala de calderas *f*; ~ **scale** *n* DETERG escama de caldera *f*, FOOD acumulación calcárea *f*; ~~**scaling appliance** *n* RAIL máquina de desincrustar calderas *f*; ~~**scaling hammer** *n* HYDRAUL martillo para desincrustar calderas *m*; ~ **shell** *n* HYDRAUL cuerpo de caldera *m*; ~ **shop** *n* HYDRAUL taller de calderería *m*; ~ **stay** *n* MECH ENG estay de caldera *m*, tirante de caldera *m*; ~~**stay screwing-tap** *n* MECH ENG macho de roscar estays de caldera *m*; ~ **test-plate** *n* HYDRAUL chapa de caldera *f*, timbre de la caldera *m*; ~ **tube** *n* MECH ENG tubo de caldera *m*; ~~**tube expander** *n* HYDRAUL mandril para tubos de caldera *m*; ~~**water treatment** *n* HEAT tratamiento del agua de calderas *m*; ~ **works** *n pl* HYDRAUL taller de calderería *m*

boilermaker *n* HYDRAUL caldedera *f*, calderero *m*, fabricante de calderas *m*, MECH fabricante de calderas *m*

boilermaking *n* HEAT calderería *f*, HYDRAUL construcción de calderas *f*

boilersmith *n* HYDRAUL forjador de calderas *m*

boiling[1] *adj* PHYS, THERMO de ebullición, en ebullición, hirviendo, hirviente

boiling[2] *n* CHEM, CHEM TECH ebullición *f*, FOOD hervido *m*, PAPER digestión *f*, lejiado *m*, PHYS ebullición *f*, REFRIG ebullición *f*, hervido *m*, THERMO hervido *m*; ~ **fermentation** *n* CHEM TECH fermentación por ebullición *f*; ~ **flask** *n* CHEM TECH matraz de ebullición *m*; ~~**heavy-water moderated reactor** *n* NUCL reactor moderado por agua pesada en ebullición *m*; ~ **plate** *n* CHEM TECH placa de ebullición *f*; ~~**point** *n* FOOD, P&R, PHYS, THERMO punto de ebullición *m*; ~ **range** *n* PETR TECH gama de destilación *f*, gama de ebullición *f*; ~~**water reactor** *n* (*BWR*) NUCL, PHYS reactor de agua en ebullición *m*

bold *n* PRINT negrita *f*; ~ **face** *n* PRINT negrita *f*; ~ **shore** *n* OCEAN costa brava *f*; ~ **type** *n* PRINT *equipment* tipo de letra negrita *m*, PROD tipo negrilla *m*

boleite *n* MINERAL boleíta *f*

boll *n* AGRIC cápsula de algodón *f*

bollard *n* WATER TRANSP bolardo *m*, noray *m*

bolometer *n* ELEC ENG *microwaves*, PHYS, REFRIG, SPACE bolómetro *m*

bolster *n* CONST *of a knife* cabezal *m*, *of knife, chisel* larguero *m*, mango *m*, travesaño *m*, MECH ENG matriz *f*, plano de apoyo *m*; ~ **plate** *n* MECH ENG *injection moulds* placa portaestampa *f*

bolt[1] *n* AIR TRANSP perno *m*, AUTO abrazadera *f*, CONST *of door* pasador *m*, cerrojo *m*, perno *m*, MECH bulón *m*, tarugo *m*, perno *m*, MECH ENG *of door* tornillo *m*, pestillo *m*, cerrojo *m*, perno *m*, falleba *f*, MILIT perno *m*, PRINT *of book* canto doblado *m*, RAIL, TRANSP,

VEH perno *m*; ~ **circle** *n* PROD círculo de los agujeros de los pernos *m*; ~ **cropper** *n* MECH ENG, WATER TRANSP *ship repair* cortapernos *m*; ~ **cutter** *n* MECH cortador de pernos *m*, MECH ENG fabricante de pernos *mf*, máquina de hacer pernos *f*, tijera cortapernos *f*; **~-forging machine** *n* PROD *for making bolts, rivets, spikes etc* máquina para forjar pernos *f*; ~ **head** *n* LAB, MECH cabeza de perno *f*, MECH ENG cabeza de perno *f*, cabeza de tornillo *f*; **~-head flask** *n BrE* (*cf matrass AmE*) LAB *of measuring instrument* matraz *m*; ~ **header** *n* PROD máquina de encabezar pernos *f*; ~ **hole** *n* MECH ENG agujero de perno *m*; ~ **mounting** *n* PROD montaje empernado *m*; ~ **rope** *n* WATER TRANSP *sails* relinga *f*; **~-screwing and nut-tapping machine** *n* PROD roscadora de pernos y tuercas *f*; ~ **tongs** *n pl* PROD tenazas para pernos *f pl*

bolt² *vt* CONST *to fasten* atornillar, *to secure* echar el cerrojo, *to sift* unir con pernos

bolted: ~ **connection** *n* SPACE conexión con perno *f*, unión con pernos *f*; ~ **joint** *n* MECH ENG junta empernada *f*

bolting *n* CONST *sifting* empernado *m*, unión con pernos *f*, MECH ENG empernado *m*, SAFE *equipment* atornillamiento *m*; ~ **cloth** *n* C&G paño de ampliar *m*; ~ **fabric** *n* TEXTIL etamín *m*

Boltzmann: **~'s constant** *n* PHYS, SPACE *communications* constante de Boltzmann *f*; **~'s equation** *n* RAD PHYS ecuación de Boltzmann *f*

BOM *abbr* (*beginning of message*) TELECOM comienzo de mensaje *m*

bomb: ~ **bay** *n* MILIT almacén de bombas *m*, compartimiento para las bombas *m*; ~ **calorimeter** *n* PHYS calorímetro a volumen constante *m*, calorímetro de bomba *m*; **~-disposal team** *n* MILIT equipo de desactivación de explosivos *m*; ~ **rack** *n* MILIT bastidor para bombas *m*; ~ **sight** *n* MILIT mira de bombardeo *f*, mira de bombardeo aéreo *f*

bombardment *n* ELECTRON, GAS, METALL, MILIT, RAD PHYS bombardeo *m*

bombing *n* MILIT *general* bombardeo *m*, *with grenades* ataque con granadas de mano *m*; ~ **area** *n* MILIT área de bombardeo *f*

bond¹ *n* C&G ligazón *m*, CHEM enlace *m*, ligadura *f*, unión *f*, CONST adherencia *f*, *fastening* enlace *m*, unión *f*, ligante *m*, *brickwork* aparejo *m*, CRYSTALL enlace *m*, NUCL *motor vehicles* unión *f*, ligadura *f*, P&R unión *f*, enlace *m*, PACK *chemical* enlace *m*, unión *f*, PRINT sustancia adhesiva *f*, PROD *of emery wheel* adhesión *f*; ~ **angle** *n* CRYSTALL ángulo de enlace *m*; **~-breaker** *n BrE* COATINGS antiadherente *m*; ~ **energy** *n* METALL capacidad de adherencia *f*, energía de adherencia *f*, energía de enlace *f*, energía de unión *f*; ~ **length** *n* CRYSTALL longitud de enlace *f*; ~ **paper** *n* PAPER papel para títulos *m*; ~ **separation** *n* P&R separación del adhesivo *f*; ~ **stone** *n* CONST perpiaño *m*; ~ **strength** *n* CRYSTALL fuerza de enlace *f*, P&R fuerza de adherencia *f*, solidez de unión *f*

bond² *vt* CHEM unir, CONST adherir, *masonry* aglomerar, *masonry joint* ligar, MECH aglomerar

bond³ *vi* REFRIG conectar eléctricamente

bonded¹ *adj* C&G ligado

bonded²: ~ **abrasive products** *n pl* MECH ENG productos abrasivos aglomerados *m pl*; ~ **area** *n* WATER TRANSP *port* zona franca *f*; ~ **finish** *n* COATINGS acabado ligado *m*; ~ **goods** *n pl* PETR TECH mercancías en depósito *f pl*; ~ **masonry** *n* CONST

mampostería de aglomerado *f*; ~ **mat** *n* C&G ligado mate *m*; ~ **seal** *n* PACK sello pegado *m*; ~ **steel plate** *n* CONST placa de acero soldada *f*; ~ **thread** *n* TEXTIL hilo termoadherido *m*; ~ **value** *n* WATER TRANSP valor en aduana *m*; ~ **warehouse** *n* WATER TRANSP depósito franco *m*

bonder *n* CONST tizón *m*

bonding *n* CONST *building* aparejo *m*, *masonry* ligamento *m*, MECH enlace *m*, empalme *m*, conexión *f*, unión *f*, P&R adherencia *f*, unión *f*, PETR TECH enlace *m*, PROD ligante *m*, REFRIG aglutinación *f*, SPACE unión eléctrica *f*, enlace *m*, interconexionado a masa *m*, ligamiento *m*, conexión a tierra *f*, WATER TRANSP *construction* unión *f*; ~ **agent** *n* MECH adhesivo *m*, P&R adhesivo *m*, sustancia adhesiva *f*, PACK, PROD, SAFE adhesivo *m*, SPACE material adhesivo *m*; ~ **angle** *n* PROD ángulo de unión *m*; ~ **gun** *n* MECH ENG pistola de unión *f*; ~ **jumper** *n* ELEC ENG puente de conexión a tierra *m*, PROD puente de unión *m*; ~ **layer** *n* COATINGS capa adherente *f*; ~ **material** *n* NUCL material de ligadura *m*, material ligador *m*; ~ **pad** *n* ELECTRON *workmen* pieza de unión *f*; ~ **strap** *n* SPACE brazo *m*; ~ **strip** *n* PROD placa de unión *f*; ~ **strut** *n* PROD contrete de unión *m*; ~ **tab** *n* PROD tira de unión *f*; ~ **test** *n* PACK ensayo de adhesión *m*, PROD ensayo de unión *m*

bone¹: **~-dry** *adj* PAPER al seco absoluto, TEXTIL completamente seco

bone²: ~ **ash** *n* C&G, CHEM ceniza de huesos *f*; ~ **audiometry** *n* ACOUST audiometría por vía ósea *f*; ~ **bank** *n* REFRIG banco de huesos *m*; ~ **china** *n* C&G china de hueso *f*; ~ **coal** *n* COAL carbón terroso *m*, esquisto carbonoso *m*, hulla pizarrosa *f*, MINE carbón terroso *m*, esquistoso carbonoso *m*, hulla pizarrosa *f*; ~ **conduction** *n* ACOUST conducción ósea *f*; ~ **glue** *n* TEXTIL oseína *f*; **~-seeker** *n* NUCL osteófilo *m*; ~ **taint** *n* REFRIG alteración en profundidad *f*; ~ **vibrator** *n* ACOUST vibrador óseo *m*

bone³ *vt* CONST *surveying* alinear, nivelar

boning *n* CONST *of road* alineación *f*, nivelación *f*; **~-rod** *n* CONST *surveying* mira *f*; **~-stick** *n* CONST *surveying* estaca *f*

bonnet *n* (*cf hood AmE*) MINE cumbrera *f*, VEH capó *m*, WATER TRANSP *funnel* tapa *f*; ~ **catch** *n BrE* (*cf hood catch AmE*) AUTO, VEH enganche del capó *m*, pestillo del capó *m*; ~ **lock** *n BrE* (*cf hood lock AmE*) AUTO cierre del capó *m*, pestillo del capó *m*

bonneted: ~ **lamp** *n* CONST lámpara protegida con metal *f*

book¹: ~ **capacitor** *n* ELEC condensador de placas articuladas *m*, condensador variable de armaduras articuladas *m*, condensador variable tipo libro *m*; ~ **case** *n* PRINT tapas con lomo *f pl*; ~ **ink** *n* COLOUR tinta de libro *f*; ~ **makeup** *n* PRINT arreglo y compaginación de libros *m*, biela *f*; ~ **paper** *n* PAPER papel para edición *m*

book² *vi* TELECOM *a call* retener

bookbinder *n* PRINT encuadernador *m*; **~'s needle** *n* PRINT aguja de encuadernar *f*; **~'s shavings** *n* PAPER blanco 3ª con alcance *m*

bookbinding *n* PRINT encuadernación *f*; ~ **board** *n* PAPER cartón para encuadernación *m*

booked: ~ **call** *n* TELECOM llamada retenida *f*

bookface *n* PRINT estilo de tipo para libros *m*

bookfont *n* PRINT tipo de letra para libros *m*

bookplate *n* PRINT plancha para libros *f*

Boolean: ~ **algebra** n COMP&DP, MATH álgebra booleana f, álgebra de Boole f; ~ **operator** n COMP&DP operador booleano m; ~ **search** n COMP&DP búsqueda de Boole f; ~ **type** n COMP&DP tipo booleano m; ~ **value** n COMP&DP valor booleano m; ~ **variable** n COMP&DP variable booleana f

boom[1] n CINEMAT boom m, pértiga f, CONST cordón m, of crane brazo m, pluma f, aguilón m, MAR POLL barrera flotante f, MECH coated with abrasive brazo m, botalón m, pluma f, aguilón m, PETR TECH brazo de grúa m, SPACE estallido m, larguero m, TV pértiga f, WATER TRANSP at harbour entrance obstrucción de la bocana f; ~ **arm** n CINEMAT brazo del boom m; ~ **dolly** n CINEMAT, TV dolly para el boom f; ~ **dollyman** n CINEMAT, TV operador del dolly para el boom m; ~ **guy** n WATER TRANSP yachts osta f, retenida de botavara f; ~**-laying configuration** n MAR POLL configuración del fondeo de la barrera flotante f; ~ **mike** n CINEMAT, TV micrófono de la pértiga m, micrófono del boom m; ~ **operator** n CINEMAT, TV operador del boom m; ~ **pack** n MAR POLL barrera enfardada f; ~ **plate** n CONST of built-up girder placa metálica de viga f, pluma metálica f; ~ **retrieval** n MAR POLL recuperación de la barrera f; ~ **shot** n CINEMAT toma con boom f; ~**-towing** n MAR POLL remolque m; ~ **vang** n WATER TRANSP of yacht trapa de la botavara f

boom[2]: ~ **out** vi WATER TRANSP navegar a orejas de mulo

boomerang n FLUID bumerán m

boost[1] n ELEC ENG larguero m (Esp), reforzador m (AmL); ~ **charge** n TRANSP carga de refuerzo f; ~ **pressure** n AIR TRANSP presión de empuje f, presión de soberempuje f, presión de sobrealimentación f, SPACE presión de empuje f; ~ **pump** n SPACE bomba de impulsión f

boost[2] vt ELECTRON aumentar, MECH alzar, empujar, levantar, SPACE amplificar, elevar la potencia de, intensificar

booster n MINE propulsor m, SPACE acelerador intermedio m, motor principal del cohete m, catapulta de lanzamiento f, cohete auxiliar m, VEH servo de mando m, sobrealimentador m; ~ **battery** n TRANSP batería de urgencia f, batería elevadora de voltaje f; ~ **coil** n AIR TRANSP, AUTO, TRANSP, VEH adujada de refuerzo f (AmL), bobina de inducción cebada con acumulador para el arranque f (Esp); ~ **compressor** n REFRIG booster m, precompresor m; ~ **control** n TRANSP control de refuerzo m; ~ **dynamo** n ELEC dinamo elevadora de tensión f, dinamo elevadora de voltaje f, ELEC ENG dinamo elevadora de tensión f, dinamo elvadora de voltaje f; ~ **element** n NUCL elemento de sobrerreactividad m; ~ **generator** n ELEC generador autorregulador m; ~ **heating system** n FUELLESS sistema de calefacción aumentador m; ~ **light** n CINEMAT luz de refuerzo f, lámpara de refuerzo f; ~ **mill** n FUELLESS planta aumentadora f; ~ **platform** n PETR TECH plataforma de apoyo f, plataforma de refuerzo f; ~ **pump** n AIR TRANSP, MECH, MECH ENG, PETR TECH, TRANSP bomba cebadora f, bomba de carga f, bomba reforzadora f; ~ **rod** n NUCL barra de sobrerreactividad f; ~ **station** n PETROL estación auxiliar f, estación de refuerzo f, estación elevadora de presión f, TV emisora auxiliar de televisión f, emisora de TV de refuerzo f; ~ **transformer** n ELEC transformador elevador m,

transformador elevador de voltaje m, ELEC ENG negative transformador elevador de tensión m, positive transformador regulador m, ELECTRON transformador elevador m, transformador elevador de tensión m, transformador elevador de voltaje m; ~ **ventilation fan** n MINE ventilador secundario m

boosting: ~ **main** n HYDRAUL canalización f; ~ **regulator** n SPACE spacecraft regulador de impulsión m; ~ **station** n HYDROL estación de refuerzo f

boot[1] n AIR TRANSP funda antihielo f, guardapolvo de protección m, AUTO maletero m, portaequipajes m, funda f, portamaletas m, C&G tolva f, CONST bottom of rainwater downpipe manguito m; ~ **area** n PROD área de la tolva f; ~ **handle** n BrE (cf trunk handle AmE) VEH asa del portaequipajes f, manilla de apertura del maletero f; ~ **lid** n BrE (cf trunk lid AmE) VEH tapa del maletero f; ~ **topping** n WATER TRANSP boatbuilding pintura de flotación f

boot[2] vt COMP&DP arrancar

bootable: ~ **disk** n COMP&DP, PROD disco con secuencia de arranque m

booth n CINEMAT, PRINT cabina f

bootleg n TV ilegalidad f

bootstrap n COMP&DP autocarga f, autocargador m, cebado m (AmL), PRINT autocarga f, autocargador m, TV autoelevación f; ~ **system** n REFRIG sistema de bootstrap m

bootstrapping n COMP&DP, PRINT autocarga f, autocargado m

BOP[1] abbr OCEAN (blowout preventer) RDP (rompevientos de playa), PETR TECH (blowout preventer) impide-erupciones m, impide-reventones m, protector de erupción m, válvula de control de explosión f, válvula impide reventones f (AmL)

BOP[2]: ~ **stack** n OCEAN torre del RDP f

boracite n MINERAL boracita f

borane n CHEM borano m

borate n CHEM borato m

borax n AGRIC, C&G, CHEM, CONST, DETERG, MINERAL bórax m; ~ **bead** n CONST perla de bórax f; ~ **lake** n DETERG boratera f

borazon n CHEM borazón m, nitruro de boro sintetizado m

Borda: ~ **mouthpiece** n HYDRAUL boquilla de borda f

border n AGRIC faja sin arar f, C&G orla ornamental f, PRINT orla f; ~ **irrigation** n AGRIC riego por tablares m, WATER riego por amelgas m, riego por bordes m

bore[1] n AUTO calibre m, diámetro interior m, C&G entaponado m, perforado m, diámetro interior de cilindros m, FUELLESS water power aguaje m, GAS perforación f, HYDROL sondeo m, MECH ENG diámetro interior m, ánima f, MINE barreno m, OCEAN pororoca f, barreno m, VEH diámetro interior m, calibre m, WATER TRANSP of river macareo m; ~ **bit** n CONST earth-boring barreno m, broca f, PETR TECH drilling barreno m (Esp); ~ **core** n MINE testigo m; ~ **gage** AmE, ~ **gauge** BrE n METR calibrador del ánima m; ~ **rod** n CONST vara de calibrado f

bore[2] vt COAL barrenar, horadar (AmL), perforar, sondar, taladrar, trepar, CONST horadar (AmL), perforar, sondar, taladrar, trepar, barrenar, MECH agujerear, barrenar, penetrar, taladrar, MECH ENG abrir, barrenar, horadar (AmL), perforar, sondear, taladrar, MINE abrir, barrenar, horadar (AmL), perforar (Esp), sondear, taladrar, PETR TECH barrenar, PROD *hole* mandrilar, perforar; ~ **out** *vt* PROD *a hole* mandrilar

bore³ *vi* MINE barrenar (*Esp*), hacer excavaciones, hacer maniobras (*AmL*), taladrar; ~ **against water** *vi* MINE perforar en medio acuífero; ~ **for water** *vi* CONST hacer sondeos, WATER hacer sondeos para encontrar agua

bored: **~-and-plain plates** *n pl* MECH ENG chapas perforadas y sin perforar *f pl*; ~ **well** *n* HYDROL, WATER pozo barrenado *m*, pozo de sondeo *m*

borehole *n* COAL barreno *m*, pozo de sondeo *m*, CONST taladro *m*, GAS, GEOL, GEOPHYS, HYDROL agujero de perforación *m*, perforación *f*, pozo de sondeo *m*, MINE, PETROL barreno *m*, perforación *f*, pozo de sondeo *m*; ~ **effect** *n* PETROL efecto de perforación *m*; ~ **logging** *n* GEOPHYS calibrado en sondeos *m*, registro en sondeos *m*; ~ **logging-equipment** *n* GEOPHYS equipo de calibrado en pozos de perforación *m*; ~ **pump** *n* CONST bomba de la sonda *f*, WATER bomba de sondeos *f*

boreholing *n* CONST sondeo *m*; ~ **plant** *n* CONST planta de sondeo *f*, sonda *f*

borer *n* AGRIC *insect* barrenador *m*, MINE pistolete de mina *m* (*AmL*), barrenero *m*, barreno *m* (*Esp*), *rock drilling, earth boring* máquina de mandrinar *f*

boric: ~ **acid** *n* C&G, CHEM, COATINGS ácido bórico *m*; ~ **acid blender** *n* NUCL mezclador de ácido bórico *m*; ~ **oxide** *n* C&G, CHEM óxido de boro *m*

boride *n* CHEM boruro *m*

boring *n* COAL, CONST, MECH ENG, MINE, PROD barrenación *f*, mandrinado *m*, perforación *f*, sondeo *m*, taladrado *m*, taladro *m*; ~ **against water** *n* WATER barrenado por agua *m*; **~-and-turning mill** *n* MECH ENG taladradora *f*, torneadora *f*, torno de plato horizontal *m*; ~ **bar** *n* MECH ENG barra de mandrinar *f*, barra taladradora *f*, varilla de sondeo *f*; ~ **bit** *n* CONST *mortising* barrenado *m*, perforación *f*; ~ **with the bit** *n* CONST perforación con barrena *f*; ~ **by percussion** *n* CONST perforación por percusión *f*; ~ **by percussion with rods** *n* CONST perforación por percusión con varillas *f*; ~ **by rotation** *n* CONST perforación por rotación *f*; ~ **by shot drills** *n* CONST perforación por granalla *f*; ~ **chisel** *n* MINE trépano de sondeo *m*; ~ **contractor** *n* CONST contratista de sondeos *m*; ~ **cutter** *n* MECH ENG mandrinadora *f*, perforadora *f*; ~ **head** *n* MECH ENG, MINE cabezal barrenador *m*, corona *f*, corona cortante *f*, trépano compuesto *m* (*AmL*), trépano de cabeza *m* (*Esp*); ~ **machine** *n* MECH, MECH ENG, MINE mandrinadora *f*, máquina de barrenar *f*, máquina de taladrar *f*, perforadora *f*, taladradora *f*; ~ **mill** *n* MECH torno de plato horizontal *m*; ~ **plant** *n* MINE instalación de sondeos *f* (*AmL*), plataforma de sondeos *f* (*Esp*); ~ **rod** *n* CONST varilla para perforación *f*; ~ **site** *n* CONST lugar de sondeo *m*; ~ **spindle** *n* MECH, MECH ENG *of machine* eje portabrocas *m*, eje portaherramientas *m*; ~ **tool** *n* COAL barrena *f*, CONST barrena *f*, perforadora *f*, sondeo *m*, taladro *m*, MECH barrena *f*, broca *f*, herramienta de sondeo *f*, taladradora *f*, *for roughing* herramienta de taladrar en desbaste *f*, *for finishing* herramienta de taladrar en acabado *f*, MECH ENG broca *f*, *for roughing* herramienta de taladrar en desbaste *f*, herramienta de sondeo *f*, taladradora *f*, barrena *f*, *for finishing* herramienta de taladrar en acabado *f*, MINE barrena *f*, broca *f*, herramienta de taladrar en acabado *f*, taladradora *f*, herramienta de

taladrar en desbaste *f*, herramienta de sondeo *f*, PETROL barrena *f*

borneol *n* CHEM borneol *m*

bornite *n* MINERAL bornita *f*

bornyl *n* CHEM bornilo *m*; ~ **acetate** *n* CHEM acetato de bornilo *m*; ~ **alcohol** *n* CHEM alcohol bornílico *m*

borofluoride *n* CHEM borofluoruro *m*

boron *n* (*B*) CHEM boro *m* (*B*)

boronated: **~-steel absorber** *n* NUCL *motor vehicles* elemento absorbente de acero borado *m*

borosilicate *n* CHEM borosilicato *m*; ~ **glass** *n* C&G, HEAT ENG, LAB vidrio de borosilicato *m*, vidrio resistente al calor *m*

borrow *n* CONST material de préstamo *m*, PROD *excavations* zanja de préstamo *f*; ~ **pit** *n* COAL cantera de préstamo *f*, zanja de préstamo *f*, CONST zanja de préstamo *f*

bort *n* MINE bort *m*, PROD *for polishing* polvo de diamante *m*

Bose-Einstein: ~ **condensation** *n* PHYS condensación de Bose-Einstein *f*; ~ **distribution** *n* PHYS distribución de Bose-Einstein *f*; ~ **statistics** *n pl* PHYS estadística de Bose-Einstein *f*

bosh *n* C&G cuba para enfriar *f*

boson *n* PART PHYS, PHYS bosón *m*

boss *n* MECH ENG saliente *m*, refuerzo *m*, *of crank* realce *m*, MINE perno *m* (*AmL*), bulón *m*, PROD *on casting* saliente superficial *m*, VEH saliente *m*; ~ **grip** *n* CINEMAT jefe maquinista *m*, jefe tramoyista *m*; ~ **head** *n* LAB adaptador en cruz *m*

bossing: ~ **mallet** *n* CONST *plumber's* mazo para estampar *m*

BOT¹ *abbr* (*beginning of tape*) COMP&DP BOT (*inicio de la cinta*)

BOT²: ~ **marker** *n* COMP&DP marcador BOT *m*

both¹: ~ **justified** *adj* PRINT ambos justificados

both²: **~-way circuit** *n* TELECOM circuito bidireccional *m*; **~-way group** *n* TELECOM grupo bidireccional *m*; **~-way line** *n* TELECOM línea bidireccional *f*

botryogen *n* MINERAL botriógeno *m*

botryoidal *adj* MINERAL arracimado, botroidal

bott *n* PROD *founding* taponamiento de la piquera *m*, tapón cónico para la piquera de escoria *m*; ~ **stick** *n* PROD *founding* barra de cierre para la piquera *f*

bottle¹: ~ **bank** *n* RECYCL contenedor de botellas *m*; ~ **cap** *n* PACK tapón roscado *m*; **~-capping machine** *n* PACK máquina para colocar los tapones roscados *f*; ~ **carrier** *n* PACK transportador de botellas *m*; **~-casing machine** *n* C&G máquina de entubación de vidrio verde *f*; **~-closing machine** *n* PACK cerradora de botellas *f*; ~ **closure** *n* PACK cierre de la botella *m*; ~ **cooler** *n* REFRIG enfriador de botellas *m*; **~-corking machine** *n* PACK encorchadora de botellas *f*; ~ **deposit** *n* PACK depósito de botellas *m*; ~ **filler** *n* AGRIC, FOOD, PACK embotellador *m*; ~ **glass** *n* C&G vidrio verde *m*; ~ **industry** *n* C&G industria botellera *f*; ~ **jack** *n* MECH ENG gato en forma de botella *m*; ~ **jacket** *n* PACK funda de botella *f*; **~-leak detector** *n* PACK detector de fugas de las botellas *m*; ~ **with molded neck** *AmE*, ~ **with moulded neck** *BrE n* C&G, LAB *glassware* botella con cuello moldeado *f*; **~-packing machine** *n* PACK empaquetadora de botellas *f*; **~-rinsing machine** *n* PACK enjuagadora de botellas *f*; ~ **screw** *n* WATER TRANSP *rigging* tensor de cuerpo cerrado *m*; **~-sealing machine** *n* PACK precintadora de botellas *f*; ~ **sleeve** *n* PACK manguito de malla para la botella *m*; ~ **stopper** *n* PACK corcho de la botella *m*, tapón de la botella *m*; ~**-type liquid cooler** *n* REFRIG enfriador de botella *m*; ~ **unscrambler** *n* PACK clasificador de botellas *m*; ~**-washing machine** *n* FOOD, PACK lavadora de botellas *f*

bottle[2] *vt* AGRIC, FOOD, PACK embotellar

bottled[1] *adj* AGRIC, FOOD, PACK embotellado

bottled[2]: ~ **gas** *n* GAS gas en botellones *m*, gas envasado *m*, THERMO gas embotellado *m*, gas en botellones *m*; ~ **liquefied petroleum gas** *n* GAS gas de petróleo licuado envasado *m*

bottleneck *n* FOOD embotellamiento *m*, MECH *antennas, waveguides*, PROD atasco *m*, obstrucción *f*, TRANSP atasco *m*, embotellamiento *m*, estrechamiento de la calzada *m*

bottling: ~ **line** *n* PACK cadena de embotellado *f*, tren de embotellado *m*; ~ **machine** *n* FOOD, PACK embotelladora *f*, máquina embotelladora *f*; ~ **tank** *n* FOOD depósito para embotellado *m*

bottom[1] *n* COAL *of coal seam* residuo de destilación *m*, muro *m*, piso *m*, fondo *m*, suelo *m*, CONST *of valley* planicie *f*, pie *m*, fondo del valle *m*, HYDROL *of basin, reservoir* fondo *m*, lecho *m*, MINE labor de fondo *f*, trabajo en el interior *m*, fondo *m*, muro *m* (*AmL*), piso *m*, residuo de destilación *m*, suelo *m*, OCEAN extremo *m* (*AmL*), sedimento *m* (*Esp*), PRINT pie de página *m*; ~ **block** *n* C&G macizo de fondo *m*; ~ **brass** *n* MECH ENG cojinete inferior *m*; ~**-cementing plug** *n* PETR TECH tapón inferior de cementación *m*; ~ **charge** *n* MINE carga de fondo *f* (*Esp*), carga inferior *f* (*AmL*); ~ **coder** *n* PACK codificador del fondo *m*; ~ **culvert** *n* HYDROL, WATER alcantarilla de fondo *f*; ~ **current** *n* OCEAN, WATER corriente de fondo *f*; ~ **dead center** *n* AmE, ~ **dead centre** *n* BrE (*BDC*) AUTO, MECH, VEH punto muerto inferior *m* (*PMI*); ~ **deposit** *n* WATER depósito de fondo *m*; ~ **die** *n* PROD *of power hammer* estampa hembra *f*, estampa inferior *f*; ~ **dressing** *n* AGRIC abono de base *m*; ~ **dyeing** *n* COLOUR teñido de fondo *m*; ~ **filling** *n* PACK llenado del fondo *m*; ~ **flange** *n* CONST brida de base *f*; ~ **flap** *n* PACK aleta fondo *f*; ~ **flow** *n* WATER corriente de fondo *f*; ~ **flue** *n* HEAT ENG conducto inferior de humos *m*; ~ **fold** *n* PACK doblez del fondo *m*; ~**-folding-and-seaming machine** *n* PACK máquina dobladora y cosedora del fondo *f*; ~ **glass** *n* C&G vidrio de fondo *m*; ~ **heat** *n* C&G calor del fondo *m*; ~ **hole** *n* MINE agujero de fondo *m*, barreno tendido *m* (*AmL*), barreno de suelo *m* (*Esp*), PETR TECH agujero de fondo *m*, fondo del hueco *m*, fondo del pozo *m*; ~**-hole assembly** *n* (*BHA*) PETR TECH sarta de fondo *f*; ~**-hole conditions** *n pl* PETR TECH estado del fondo del pozo *m*; ~**-hole pressure** *n* PETROL presión de fondo *f*; ~ **ice** *n* OCEAN hielo de fondo *m*; ~ **level** *n* MINE galería de fondo *f*, nivel de fondo *m*; ~ **lighting** *n* CINEMAT, TV iluminación inferior *f*; ~ **outlet** *n* HYDROL *of water above crest of weir* boca de salida *f*, WATER salida por el fondo *f*; ~ **pallet** *n* PROD *of power hammer* estampa inferior *f*; ~ **paving** *n* C&G revestimiento del fondo *m*; ~ **pillar** *n* MINE macizo de protección del pozo *m*; ~ **plate** *n* CONST placa inferior *f*, PROD *of loam mould* placa del fondo *f*; ~ **plating** *n* WATER TRANSP *boat building* planchas del fondo *f pl*; ~ **pouring** *n* PROD *founding* colada en fuente *f*; ~ **press** *n* PAPER prensa inferior *f*; ~ **profile** *n* OCEAN perfil batimétrico *m*, perfil del fondo *m*; ~ **rail** *n* CONST *of door-frame, sash-frame* cabio bajo *m*; ~ **ripples** *n pl* HYDROL ondulaciones residuales del cauce *f pl*; ~ **road** *n* MINE galería de base *f* (*Esp*), galería de fondo *f*, galería inferior *f* (*AmL*); ~**-road bridge** *n* CONST puente de tablero inferior *m*; ~ **roll** *n* PROD *rolling mill* cilindro inferior *m*; ~ **shot** *n* MINE barreno de suelo *m* (*Esp*), barreno tendido *m* (*AmL*); ~ **spool box** *n* CINEMAT caja del carrete inferior *f*; ~ **sprocket** *n* CINEMAT engranaje inferior *m*; ~ **station** *n* COAL, MINE estación inferior del pozo *f*; ~ **structure** *n* AIR TRANSP estructura inferior *f*; ~ **surge** *n* OCEAN onda irruptiva del fondo *f*; ~ **swage** *n* PROD estampa inferior *f*; ~ **tear** *n* C&G rasgado del fondo *m*; ~ **topography** *n* OCEAN topografía submarina *f*; ~ **transport** *n* HYDROL transporte de sedimentos *m*; ~**-up methodology** *n* COMP&DP metodología del fondo hacia arriba *f*; ~ **water** *n* HYDROL, OCEAN agua de fondo *f*; ~ **workings** *n pl* MINE laboreo de fondo *m*; ~ **yeast** *n* FOOD levadura baja *f*, levadura de depósito *f*, levadura de fondo *f*, levadura de solera *f*

bottom[2] *vi* OCEAN *programme* tocar fondo

bottomer: ~ **slab** *n* REFRIG placa de endurecimiento de fondos *f*

bottoming: ~ **indicator** *n* AIR TRANSP *aviation* indicador de fondo *m*; ~ **tap** *n* MECH ENG macho cilíndrico *m*, macho de ahondar *m*, macho de roscar final *m*

bottoms *n pl* FOOD residuos *m pl*, PETR TECH fondos *m pl*, residuos *m pl*

bottomset: ~ **beds** *n pl* GEOL sedimentos del fondo *m pl*

botulinum: ~ **cook** *n* FOOD cocción botulina *f*

botulism *n* FOOD botulismo *m*

boudinage *n* GEOL estructura de deformación *f*

Bouguer: ~ **anomaly** *n* GEOL, GEOPHYS anomalía de Bouguer *f*; ~ **correction** *n* GEOPHYS corrección de Bouguer *f*

boulangerite *n* MINERAL boulangerita *f*

boulder *n* COAL bloque de mineral *m*, bloque errático *m*, piedra *f*, CONST, PETROL canto rodado *m*; ~ **clay** *n* COAL, GEOL acarreo glaciar *m*, arcilla glaciar *f*; ~ **soil** *n* COAL tierra en bloques *f*

boulet *n* COAL briqueta *f*, ovoide pequeño *m*

bounce: ~ **board** *n* CINEMAT plancha para hacer rebotar la luz *f*; ~ **light** *n* TV iluminación por rebote *f*; ~ **lighting** *n* CINEMAT, PHOTO iluminación por rebote *f*

bounced: ~ **landing** *n* AIR TRANSP aterrizaje de rebote *m*, aterrizaje rebotado *m*

bound: ~ **book** *n* PRINT libro encuadernado *m*; ~ **electron** *n* PART PHYS electrón enlazado *m*, electrón ligado *m*; ~ **mode** *n* OPT, TELECOM modo ligado *m*; ~ **water** *n* CHEM agua combinada químicamente *f*, FOOD agua retenida *f*, GEOL, HYDROL, PETR TECH, PETROL, WATER agua combinada químicamente *f*, agua de formación *f*, agua ligada *f*

boundary *n* CONST hito *m*, lindero *m*, límite *m*, mojón *m*, GEOL contorno *m*, límite *m*, METALL contorno *m*; ~ **conditions** *n pl* ELEC condiciones frontera *f pl*; ~ **dimensions** *n pl* MECH ENG *overall size* cotas límite *f pl*; ~ **fence** *n* CONST valla limítrofe *f*; ~ **film** *n* COATINGS capa límite *f*; ~ **layer** *n* ACOUST, AIR TRANSP, COATINGS, FLUID, FUELLESS, MECH capa límite *f*, superficie limitante *f*, METALL superficie limitante *f*, OCEAN, PHYS, REFRIG capa límite *f*, superficie limitante *f*; **~-layer control** *n* TRANSP control de la capa límite *m*; **~-layer formation** *n* FLUID formación de la capa límite *f*; **~-layer separation** *n* FLUID separación de la capa límite *f*; **~-layer stability** *n* FLUID estabilidad de la capa límite *f*; **~ light** *n* AIR TRANSP luz de demarcación *f*; **~ line** *n* CONST línea divisoria *f*; **~ lubrication** *n* AIR TRANSP lubricación periférica *f*; **~ mark** *n* CONST mojón *m*; **~ pillar** *n* MINE macizo de protección *m*; **~ post** *n* CONST marca de límite *f*; **~ stone** *n* CONST hito *m*

boundstone *n* GEOL roca de boundstone *f*, PETROL hito *m*, mojón *m*

bour: **~ foxtail** *n* AGRIC cola de zorro *f*

Bourdon: **~ gage** *AmE*, **~ gauge** *BrE* *n* PETR TECH, PHYS instrumento Bourdon *m*, manómetro de Bourdon *m*, medidor Bourdon *m*, tubo Bourdon *m*

bournonite *n* MINERAL bournonita *f*

bovine: **~ rabies** *n* AGRIC rabia bovina *f*; **~ spongiform encephalopathy** *n* (*BSE*) AGRIC encefalopatía espongiforme bovina *f* (*BSE*)

bow[1] *n* CONST curvatura *f*, jabalcón *m*, arco *m*, *of padlock* asa *f*, comba *f*, *of key* anilla *f*, MECH ENG marco *m*, asa *f*, arco *m*, PROD *of foundry ladle* asa *f*, RAIL arco *m*, WATER TRANSP amura *f*, proa *f*; **~ anchor** *n* WATER TRANSP ancla de leva *f*; **~ and bias** *n* TEXTIL inclinación y bies *f*; **~ calipers** *AmE*, **~ callipers** *BrE* *n pl* CONST compás de espesores *m*, compás de gruesos *m*; **~ chock** *n* WATER TRANSP *shipbuilding* guía de amura *f*; **~ compass** *n* CONST bigotera *f* (*Esp*), compás *m*, compás de puntas *m*, MECH ENG compás de espesores *m*, compás de muelle de precisión *m*; **~ dividers** *n pl* CONST bigotera *f*; **~ drill** *n* MECH ENG berbiquí de violín *m*; **~ entrance** *n* WATER TRANSP *boat design* finos de proa *m pl*; **~ fender** *n* WATER TRANSP *deck equipment* defensa de proa *f*; **~ handle** *n* PROD *of foundry ladle* asa *f*; **~ hanger** *n* PROD arco de suspensión *m*; **~ lathe** *n* MECH ENG torno de arco *m*; **~ shock** *n* GEOPHYS *magnetic storm* frente de choque *m*, SPACE arco choque *m*; **~ spring** *n* WATER TRANSP *mooring* esprín de proa *m*; **~-spring compass** *n* CONST compás de muelle *m*; **~ stopper** *n* WATER TRANSP *deck fittings* estopor *m*; **~ and warp** *n AmE* (*cf warped sheet BrE*) C&G hoja pandeada *f*; **~ wave** *n* AIR TRANSP onda del morro *f*, WATER TRANSP ola de proa *f*

bow[2] *vt* PROD curvar

bow[3] *vi* PROD retorcerse

Bowden: **~ cable** *n* MECH, VEH cable Bowden *m*

bowed: **~ roll** *n* PAPER rodillo curvado *m*

bowenite *n* MINERAL bowenita *f*

bowl *n* COAL embudo *m*, METR *of balance or scales* platillo *m*, PROD cuba *f*; **~ centrifuge** *n* COAL centrifugadora de taza *f*; **~ classifier** *n* COAL clasificador de taza *m*, clasificador de vasija *m*; **~ mill crusher** *n* COAL trituradora de rodillos *f*

bowline *n* WATER TRANSP *knot* as de guía *m*

bowlingite *n* MINERAL bowlingita *f*, piedra jabón *f*, saponita *f*

bowser *n* AIR TRANSP camión cisterna *m*, SPACE camión para repostar *m*

bowsprit *n* WATER TRANSP bauprés *m*

bowstring: **~ bridge** *n* CONST puente de cuerdas *m*; **~ girder** *n* CONST viga elástica *f*

box[1] *n* CONST *keeper of lock-bolt* cerrojo *m*, PRINT cajetín *m*, recuadro *m*, PROD *moulding flask* molde de fundición *m*, TRANSP caja control *f* (*AmL*), jaula *f*

(*Esp*), espacio de ocupación *m*, contenedor *m*; **~ camera** *n* PHOTO cámara de cajón *f*, cámara rectangular *f*, cámara rígida *f*; **~ casting** *n* MECH ENG fundición en cajas *f*; **~-connecting rod end** *n* MECH ENG cabeza de biela de caja cerradas *f*; **~ coupling** *n* MECH ENG acoplamiento de manguito *m*; **~ culvert** *n* CONST, HYDROL, WATER alcantarilla rectangular *f*; **~-erecting machine** *n* PACK máquina normadora de cajas *f*; **~-filling machine** *n* PACK llenadora de cajas *f*; **~ fold** *n* GEOL pliegue en caja *m*; **~ frame** *n* MECH ENG *machine tools* bastidor de cajón *m*; **~ furnace** *n* HEAT horno de caja *m*; **~ girder** *n* CONST viga cajón *f*, viga tubular *f*; **~-girder bridge** *n* CONST puente de viga cajón *m*; **~ gutter** *n* CONST *building* canalón rectangular *m*; **~ kiln** *n* HEAT horno de secar de caja *m*; **~ lock** *n* CONST cerradura a nivel *f*; **~ lug** *n* PROD *gearing* terminal del cárter *m*; **~-making machine** *n* PACK máquina para fabricar cajas de cartón *f*; **~ molding** *AmE*, **~ moulding** *BrE* *n* PROD moldeo en cajas *m*; **~ nut** *n* MECH ENG tuerca ciega *f*, tuerca de sombrerete *f*; **~ pallet** *n* PACK paleta de carga para cajas *f*; **~ pallet with mesh** *n* PACK paleta con caja alambrada *f*; **~ pass** *n* PROD *rolling mill* canal hembra *m*; **~ and pin** *n* MINE macho y hembra *m*; **~ pin** *n* MECH ENG pasador de caja *m*; **~ relay** *n* ELEC conmutador de caja *m*, relé de caja *m*; **~ screw** *n* CONST tornillo *m*; **~-section track-girder** *n* TRANSP traviesa de sección rectangular hueca *f*, traviesa hueca de sección rectangular *f*; **~ spanner** *n* (*cf box wrench*) MECH, MECH ENG llave de cazoleta *f*, llave de muletilla *f*, llave de tubo *f*, llave de vaso *f*; **~ staple** *n* CONST *lock-staple* caja del cerrojo *f*, hembra del cerrojo *f*; **~ switch** *n* ELEC interruptor de caja *m*; **~-type stiffener** *n* AIR TRANSP refuerzo tipo caja *m*; **~-type structure** *n* AIR TRANSP estructura tipo caja *f*; **~ wagon** *n BrE* (*cf boxcar AmE*) RAIL *vehicles* vagón cerrado *m*, vagón de bordes altos *m*; **~ wrench** *n* (*cf box spanner*) MECH llave de cazoleta *f*, llave de cubo *f*, llave de muletilla *f*, llave de vaso *f*, MECH ENG llave de cazoleta *f*, llave de muletilla *f*, llave de tubo *f*, llave de vaso *f*; **~ yard** *n* PROD *foundry* patio de cajas *m*

box[2] *vt* CONST *tenon in mortise* encajonar

box[3]: **~ the compass** *vi* WATER TRANSP cuartear la aguja

boxcar *n AmE* (*cf box wagon BrE*) RAIL vagón cerrado *m*, vagón de bordes altos *m*; **~ pulse** *n* ELECTRON pulsos largos separados por pausas cortas *m pl*

boxed: **~ head** *n* PRINT título recuadrado *m*

boxing *n* CONST enmaderado *m*; **~ machine** *n* PACK máquina para hacer cajas *f*

boxspun: **~ yarn** *n* TEXTIL hilado por centrifugación *m*

Boyle: **~'s law** *n* PHYS ley de Boyle *f*; **~ temperature** *n* PHYS temperatura de Boyle *f*

BPF *abbr* (*band-pass filter*) GEN filtro de frecuencia *m* (*Esp*), filtro paso-banda *m* (*AmL*), filtro banda-paso *m*, filtro de pasa de banda *m* (*Esp*), filtro de banda pasante *m*

BPI *abbr* (*bits per inch*) COMP&DP BPP (*bits por pulgada*)

BPS *abbr* (*bits per second*) COMP&DP BPS (*bits por segundo*)

BPSK *abbr* (*binary phase-shift keying*) TELECOM manipulación por desviación de fase binaria *f*

Bq *abbr* (*becquerel*) METR, NUCL, PHYS, RAD PHYS Bq (*bequerelio*)

b-quark n (*beauty quark*) PART PHYS b-quark m (*quark belleza*)

Br abbr (*bromine*) CHEM Br (*bromo*)

BRA abbr (*basic rate access*) TELECOM precio base de acceso m

brace[1] n AIR TRANSP abrazadera f, atadura f, refuerzo m, COAL piso de maniobra m, tirante m, CONST in *lattice truss* tirante m, riostra f, *trussed frame or partition* anclaje m, *wooden roof truss* puntal m, abrazadera f, *face of timbers* jabalcón m, *carpenter's bitstock* berbiquí m, *engineer's racketbrace* taladro m, HYDRAUL abrazadera f, anclaje m, MECH berbiquí m, taladro m, MINE piso de maniobra m, SPACE riostra f, tirante m; ~ **bit** n MECH ENG broca de berbiquí f; ~ **head** n MINE cabeza de maniobra f, herramienta de giro (*Esp*) f, llave de maniobra f, mango de maniobra m (*AmL*); ~ **key** n MINE herramienta de giro f, llave de maniobra f, mango de maniobra m (*AmL*); ~ **roots** n pl AGRIC raíces adventicias f pl; ~ **strut** n MECH ENG tirante m

brace[2] vt CONST *framing* amarrar, ensamblar, *beam* atirantar, armar, cercar, rodear, *banks of cut* apuntalar, MECH, MECH ENG abrazar, apuntalar, armar, reforzar, WATER TRANSP *yard* bracear, brazar; ~ **against wind pressure** vt CONST *roof, truss* contraventear; ~ **together** vt CONST *shores* entibar

braces n pl CONST *of system of shoring* soportes m pl

brachistochrone n GEOM braquistócrono m

bracing n C&G *of tank blocks* armadura f, CONST *strengthening* apuntalamiento m, *trussing* arriostramiento m; ~ **against wind pressure** n CONST contraviento m; ~ **truss** n MECH ENG riostra f

bracket[1] n CONST *support* ménsula f, ELEC ENG *for electric light* palomilla f, HYDRAUL abrazadera f, MECH ménsula f, repisa f, pedestal m, MECH ENG pedestal m, ménsula f, repisa f, MINE plataforma en la boca del pozo f, puntal m, WATER TRANSP consola f; ~ **crab** n MINE varillaje m; ~ **hanger** n MINE silleta f, soporte m (*Esp*)

bracket[2] vt PRINT encerrar entre corchetes·

brackets n pl PRINT paréntesis rectangulares m pl

Brackett: ~ **series** n PHYS serie de Brackett f

brackish[1] adj CONST salado, FOOD, GEOL, HYDROL, OCEAN, WATER salobre

brackish[2]: ~ **marl and limestone** n GEOL marga y caliza de aguas salobres f; ~ **water** n AGRIC, GEOL, HYDROL, WATER agua salada f, agua salobre f

bract n AGRIC *cluster* bráctea f

brad n CONST *slender nail* clavo m, punta f

bradawl n CONST lezna f

bradenhead: ~ **cap for the casing** n PETR TECH tapadera del cabezal de pozo f

Bradford: ~ **breaker** n MECH ENG machacadora de Bradford f, trituradora de Bradford f

Bragg: ~ **angle** n CRYSTALL ángulo de Bragg m; ~ **cell** n CRYSTALL celda de Bragg f, ELEC ENG elemento de Bragg m; ~ **indices** n pl CRYSTALL índices de Bragg m pl; ~**'s law** n CRYSTALL ley de Bragg f; ~ **reflection** n CRYSTALL reflexión de Bragg f

braid[1] n C&G cordoncillo m, ELEC *cable* malla f, tejido m, trenzado m, ELEC ENG *copper-wire shielding* trencilla f, *insulation of electric wire* trenza f, ELECTRON trenza f, PROD trenza f, TEXTIL galón m, trenza f, pasamanería f

braid[2] vt ELEC, ELEC ENG, TEXTIL trenzar

braided: ~ **hose** n P&R manguera trenzada f; ~ **river** n GEOL río anastomosado m; ~ **stream** n PETROL curso de agua anastomizante m, río de cauces interconectados m; ~ **wire** n ELEC ENG alambre trenzado m

braiding n ELEC ENG revestimiento de material trenzado m, TEXTIL trenzado m; ~ **of river** n HYDROL separación y cruzamiento de los ríos f; ~ **technique** n TEXTIL técnica del trenzado f

brailer: ~ **boom** n WATER TRANSP *fishing* pluma auxiliar del salabardo f, pluma del salabardo f

brain: ~ **train** n TRANSP tren inteligente m

braise vt FOOD cocer en poca agua, estofar

brake n AUTO freno m, MECH dobladora de chapas f, espeque m, plegadora de palastro f, MECH ENG, VEH freno m; ~ **anchor-plate** n AUTO, VEH plato fijo del freno m; ~ **application** n AUTO, RAIL, VEH acción de frenado f; ~ **band** n AUTO, MECH, MECH ENG, VEH cinta del freno f, freno de mano m; ~ **bleeder unit** n AUTO equipo de drenaje del freno m, equipo de purga del freno m, equipo de sangrado del freno m; ~ **block** n MECH ENG portazapata de freno m, zapata de freno f (*Esp*), RAIL, VEH zapata de freno f; ~ **cable** n AUTO, VEH cable de freno m; ~ **caliper** AmE, ~ **calliper** BrE n MECH zapata de freno f; ~ **cam** n AUTO excéntrica del freno f, leva de freno f, MECH, VEH leva de freno f; ~ **chute** n SPACE deslizadera para frenado f, rampa de freno f; ~ **clearance** n AUTO, VEH holgura del freno f; ~ **compensator** n VEH compensador de frenada m, regulador de frenado m; ~ **connecting-rod** n VEH varilla de apriete del freno f; ~ **crank** n MECH ENG manivela del freno f; ~ **cylinder** n AUTO, MECH ENG, VEH bombín de freno m, cilindro de mando m, cilindro del freno m; ~ **disc** n BrE, ~ **disk** AmE n MECH, VEH disco de freno m; ~ **drum** n AUTO, MECH, MECH ENG, VEH plato portafreno m, tambor del freno m; ~ **dynamo** n ELEC *generator*, ELEC ENG dinamofreno f; ~ **effort** n TRANSP esfuerzo de frenado m; ~ **fade** n VEH pérdida de eficacia de los frenos f; ~ **failure** n TRANSP fallo de frenos m; ~ **flange** n RAIL disco de freno m; ~ **fluid** n AUTO líquido de frenos m, MECH ENG fluido para frenos hidráulicos m, VEH líquido de frenos m; ~**-fluid reservoir** n AUTO depósito del líquido de frenos m; ~**-fluid tank** n MECH ENG depósito del líquido de frenos m; ~ **force** n MECH ENG fuerza de frenado f; ~ **forks** n pl AUTO, VEH horquillas del freno f pl; ~ **horsepower** n (*BHP*) MECH ENG, PROD potencia al eje f, potencia al freno en caballos de fuerza f (*BHP*), potencia de freno f, potencia efectiva en caballos de fuerza f, TRANSP potencia al eje f, potencia al freno en caballos de fuerza f (*BHP*); ~ **horsepower hour** n MECH ENG caballo-hora efectivo m, PROD potencia al freno en caballos hora f; ~ **hose** n VEH manguito de acoplamiento de la canalización de frenos m; ~**-hose coupling-head** n AmE RAIL manguera de acoplamiento de la tubería del freno f; ~ **housing** n AUTO, VEH alojamiento del freno m; ~ **jaw** n MECH ENG mordaza de freno f; ~ **lever** n MECH ENG, RAIL palanca de freno f; ~ **light switch** n AUTO, VEH interruptor de luz de frenado m; ~ **line** n AUTO tuberías del sistema de frenado f pl, tubos del sistema de frenado m pl, VEH latiguillo m, tubería de freno f; ~ **lining** n AUTO forro de freno m, guarnición de freno f, C&G forro de freno m, guarnición de freno f (*AmL*), zapata de freno f (*Esp*), MECH forro de freno m, guarnición de freno f, zapata de freno f, MECH ENG forro de freno m, guarnición de freno f

(*AmL*), zapata de freno *f* (*Esp*), VEH forro de freno *m*, guarnición de freno *f*, zapata de freno *f*; **~-lining wear-indicator** *n* AUTO, VEH indicador de desgaste del forro del freno *m*; **~ linkage** *n* AUTO, MECH ENG, VEH varillaje del freno *m*; **~ master cylinder** *n* AUTO cilindro maestro del freno *m*, cilindro principal *m*, cilindro principal de freno *m*; **~ mean-effective pressure** *n* AIR TRANSP presión media efectiva del freno *f*; **~ motor** *n* ELEC motor de freno *m*; **~ noise** *n* ACOUST ruido de frenos *m*; **~ pad** *n* AUTO forro de la zapata del freno *m*, MECH patín de freno *m*, VEH pastilla de freno *f*, forro de la zapata del freno *m*; **~ parachute** *n* TRANSP paracaídas de frenado *m*; **~ pedal** *n* AUTO, VEH pedal del freno *m*; **~-pipe coupling-head** *n* BrE (*cf brake-hose coupling-head AmE*) RAIL manguera de acoplamiento de la tubería del freno *f*; **~ pitch** *n* TRANSP recorrido del freno *m*; **~ plate** *n* VEH disco del freno *m*; **~ power** *n* MECH ENG fuerza de frenado *f*, potencia al freno *f*, potencia efectiva *f*; **~-power distributor** *n* AUTO distribuidor de fuerza del freno *m*, distribuidor de potencia del freno *m*; **~ pressure** *n* AUTO presión del freno *f*; **~-pressure regulator** *n* MECH ENG regulador de la fuerza de frenado *m*; **~ reaction** *n* TRANSP reacción del freno *f*; **~ release** *n* AUTO, RAIL, VEH acción de soltar los frenos *f*; **~-release spring** *n* AUTO muelle de recuperación del freno *m*, resorte de recuperación del freno *m*; **~ rigging** *n* RAIL mecanismo de accionamiento de frenos *m*; **~ ring** *n* MECH ENG anillo de freno *m*, aro de freno *m*; **~ rod** *n* VEH varilla de freno *f*; **~-screw handle** *n* RAIL manivela del husillo de freno *f*, manivela del tornillo de freno *f*; **~ servo** *n* VEH servofreno *m*; **~ shaft** *n* AUTO, VEH eje de freno *m*; **~ shield** *n* AUTO, VEH placa protectora del freno *f*; **~ shoe** *n* AUTO, MECH calzo *m*, patín de freno *m*, zapata de freno *f*, MECH calzo *m*, patín de freno *m*, zapata de freno *f* (*Esp*), VEH calzo *m*, patín de freno *m*, zapata de freno *f*; **~ squeal** *n* ACOUST chirrido de frenos *m*; **~ strap** *n* MECH ENG tirante de freno *m*; **~ system** *n* MECH ENG, VEH sistema de frenos *m*; **~ test** *n* MECH ENG ensayo al freno *m*, prueba del freno *f*; **~ testing** *n* CONST prueba de frenado *f*; **~ torque** *n* AIR TRANSP par del freno *m*; **~-turbine air-cycle** *n* REFRIG ciclo de aire con turbina de expansión *m*; **~ valve** *n* RAIL válvula de frenado *f*, válvula de freno *f*; **~ warning-light** *n* VEH luz de aviso del funcionamiento de los frenos *f*; **~-wheel cylinder** *n* AUTO cilindro del freno de la rueda *m*

braked: **~ car** *n* AmE (*cf braked wagon BrE*) RAIL vagón frenado *m*; **~ wagon** BrE *n* (*cf braked car AmE*) RAIL vagón frenado *m*; **~-weight percentage** *n* RAIL porcentaje del peso de frenado *m*

brakeman *n* RAIL guardafrenos *m*; **~'s cabin** *n* RAIL garita del guardafrenos *f*

brakes: **~ off** *n* AUTO acción de soltar los frenos *f*, RAIL acción de soltar los frenos *f*, desapriete de frenos *m*, saltar del freno *m*, VEH acción de soltar los frenos *f*

braking *n* MECH agramado *m*, curvatura *f*, deflexión *f*, frenado *m*, RAIL frenado *m*; **~ airscrew** *n* TRANSP tornillo neumático de frenado *m*; **~ deceleration** *n* TRANSP desaceleración de frenado *f*; **~ distance** *n* AUTO, VEH distancia de frenado *f*; **~ governor** *n* TRANSP regulador de frenado *m*; **~ pitch** *n* AIR TRANSP *helicopter* cabeceo de frenado *m*; **~ power** *n* TRANSP potencia de frenado *f*; **~ resistance** *n* TRANSP

resistencia de frenado *f*; **~ shield** *n* SPACE escudo para frenado *m*; **~ system** *n* MECH ENG sistema de frenado *m*; **~ time** *n* TRANSP tiempo de frenado *m*

bran *n* AGRIC afrecho *m*, salvado *m*; **~ finisher** *n* FOOD eliminador de salvado *m*

branch[1] *n* COMP&DP *circuit* bifurcación *f*, CONST *metal piece at end of hose* derivación *f*, bifurcación *f*, ELEC *of supply network* rama *f*, derivación *f*, brazo *m*, ELEC ENG *of network* derivación *f*, ELECTRON bifurcación *f*, *workmen* ramificación *f*, PHYS ramal *m*; **~ box** *n* ELEC *connection* caja de derivación *f*; **~ circuit** *n* PHYS, PROD circuito derivado *m*; **~-circuit protective-device** *n* PROD mecanismo protector de circuito derivado *m*; **~ close** *n* PROD terminación de bifurcación *f*; **~-close instruction** *n* PROD instrucción para terminar bifurcación *f*; **~ end** *n* PROD fin de bifurcación *m*; **~ group** *n* PROD grupo de bifurcación *m*; **~ instruction** *n* COMP&DP instrucción de bifurcación *f*; **~ line** *n* ELEC *supply network* línea derivada *f*, RAIL línea secundaria *f*, ramal *m*, vía lateral *f*, vía secundaria *f*; **~-open instruction** *n* PROD instrucción para abrir bifurcación *f*; **~ pipe** *n* CONST *metal piece at end of hose* tubería secundaria *f*, tubo bifurcado *m*, *plumbing* ramal de tubería *m*, MECH *of colloid* tubo bifurcado *m*, WATER *for extinguishing fire* ramal de tubería *m*, tubo bifurcado *m*, bifurcación *f*; **~ point** *n* COMP&DP, ELECTRON *mass* punto de bifurcación *m*; **~ sewer** *n* WATER cloaca derivada *f*, ramal cloacal *m*; **~ start** *n* PROD comienzo de bifurcación *m*; **~ terminal** *n* ELEC *connection* terminal de derivación *m*; **~ warehouse** *n* PROD depósito secundario *m*

branch[2] *vt* COMP&DP *program, circuit* bifurcar, CONST derivar, *one pipe on another* empalmar, conectar, bifurcar

branch[3] *vi* CONST bifurcarse, ramificar; **~ off** *vi* CONST bifurcarse, dividirse, esparcirse, separarse

branch[4]: **~ open** *phr* PROD bifurcación abierta *f*

branched[1] *adj* CHEM ramificado

branched[2]: **~ chain** *n* CHEM cadena ramificada *f*; **~ polymer** *n* P&R polímero ramificado *m*

branching *n* PHYS bifurcación *f*, derivación *f*, ramificación *f*, WATER ramificación *f*; **~ condition** *n* PROD condición de ramificación *f*; **~ device** *n* PROD dispositivo de bifurcación *m*, dispositivo de ramificación *m*; **~ filter** *n* ELECTRON *measuring* filtro de bifurcación *m*; **~ instruction** *n* PROD instrucción de bifurcación *f*, instrucción de ramificación *f*; **~ ratio** *n* PHYS relación de ramificación *f*

branding: **~ iron** *n* PACK hierro de marcar en caliente *m*

brandisite *n* MINERAL brandisita *f*

brasilin *n* CHEM brasilina *f*

brass *n* CHEM, COLOUR bronce *m*, ELEC casquillo de cojinete *m*, cojinete *m*, collar *m*, rangua *f*, MECH bronce *m*, latón *m*, MECH ENG latón *m*, PROD bronce *m*; **~-finisher's lathe** *n* CONST torno para el acabado de bronce *m*; **~ foundry** *n* CONST fundición de bronce *f*; **~ insert-ring** *n* PROD anillo de inserción de bronce *m*; **~ rod** *n* FUELLESS *in windmill pump* árbol de latón *m*; **~ round-head woodscrew** *n* CONST tornillo de madera con cabeza redonda de bronce *m*; **~ screw** *n* MECH ENG tornillo de bronce *m*, tornillo de latón *m*; **~ smith** *n* CONST artesano en bronce *m*; **~ solder** *n* CONST soldador de bronce *m*, soldadura de bronce *f*; **~ type** *n* PRINT tipo de latón *m*; **~ wire** *n* CONST cable de bronce *m*; **~-wire gauze** *n* CONST tela metálica de alambre de bronce *f*

brassing *n* CONST trabajo del bronce *m*

brassworking: ~ **tools** *n pl* PROD *lathe* herramientas de latón *f pl*

brassworks *n* CONST trabajos en bronce *m pl*

brattice *n* MINE caño de aire *m*, compartimiento de ventilación *m* (*Esp*), tabique de ventilación *m* (*AmL*); ~ **cloth** *n* MINE lona para tabiques de ventilación *f*

braunite *n* MINERAL braunita *f*

Bravais: ~ **lattice** *n* CRYSTALL red cristalina de Bravais *f*

brayer *n* PRINT rodillo para entintar a mano *m*, torreta de control *f*

braze[1]: ~ **welding** *n* CONST soldadura de cobre *f*, soldadura de latón *f*

braze[2] *vt* CONST, MECH ENG, PROD, THERMO broncesoldar, cobresoldar, soldar con latón, soldar con suelda fuerte

brazeability *n* CONST, MECH ENG, PROD, THERMO cobresoldabilidad *f*

brazed[1] *adj* CONST, MECH ENG, PROD, THERMO broncesoldado, cobresoldado

brazed[2]: ~~**on tips** *n pl* MECH ENG cuchillas cobresoldadas *f pl*

brazier: ~ **head rivet** *n* PROD remache superior de caldera de cobre *m*

Brazilian: ~ **ruby** *n* MINERAL rubí de Brasil *m*, topacio rosa *m*

brazing *n* CONST broncesoldadura *f*, cobresoldadura *f*, cobresoldeo *m*, HEAT soldadura con metal no ferroso *f*, soldadura fuerte *f*, MECH ENG broncesoldadura *f*, cobresoldadura *f*, cobresoldeo *m*, PROD cobresoldeo *m*, soldadura de latón *f* (*AmL*), soldadura fuerte *f*, latonado *m*, cobresoldadura *f*, broncesoldadura *f*, SAFE, SPACE soldadura fuerte *f*, THERMO broncesoldadura *f*, cobresoldadura *f*, cobresoldeo *m*, latonado *m*, soldadura con aleación de cinc y cobre *f*, soldadura con latón *f*, soldadura fuerte *f*, suelda fuerte *f*; ~ **blowpipe** *n* CONST soplete de cobresoldadura *m*; ~ **flux** *n* CONST fundente de soldadura *m*; ~ **hazard** *n* SAFE peligro originado por soldadura fuerte *m*; ~ **lamp** *n* PROD lámpara para cobresoldadura *f*; ~ **metal** *n* PROD aleación de cobre para cobresoldar *f*; ~ **solder** *n* PROD aleación para soldar *f*

breach *n* WATER brecha *f*; ~ **of the safety rules** *n* SAFE desobediencia de las reglas de seguridad *f*, incumplimiento de las normas de seguridad *m*

breached: ~ **anticline** *n* GEOL anticlinal brechificado *m*

bread: ~ **grain** *n* AGRIC cereal panificador *m*, FOOD grano panadero *m*; ~ **improver** *n* FOOD mejorador de pan *m*; ~ **texture** *n* FOOD textura de pan *f*

breadboard *n* COMP&DP placa experimental para componentes electrónicos *f*, tablero experimental para componentes electrónicos *m* (*Esp*), tablero inicial para componentes electrónicos *m* (*AmL*); ~ **model** *n* ELEC ENG panel experimental *m*

breadmaking *n* FOOD industria panadera *f*

breadstuff *n* AGRIC cereal *m*, granos *m pl*

breadth *n* COMP&DP, PAPER, PRINT anchura *f*, WATER TRANSP *ship design* manga *f*

break[1]: ~~**free** *adj* TELECOM desencadenado

break[2] *n* COAL avance *m*, falla *f*, intercalación *f*, quiebra *f*, COMP&DP interrupción *f*, ruptura *f*, CONST *of curb roof* abertura *f*, hueco *m*, *of hinge* ángulo *m*, MINE avance *m*, falla *f*, intercalación *f*, quiebra *f*, PAPER rotura *f*, PROD derrame *m*, interrupción *f*,

ruptura *f*, TEXTIL rotura *f*; ~~**before-make switch** *n* TV conmutador previo de ruptura *m*; ~~**break contact** *n* ELEC contacto de reposo-reposo *m*; ~ **bulk** *n* TRANSP descarga *f*; ~ **character** *n* PROD carácter de enlace *m*; ~ **contact** *n* ELEC *relay* contacto abierto *m*, contacto de reposo *m*, ELEC ENG contacto de ruptura *m*, contacto de desconexión *m*, contacto de apertura *m*, PROD conmutador de interrupción *m*, conmutador de ruptura *m*; ~ **distance** *n* ELEC ENG distancia de interrupción *f*, distancia disruptiva *f*; ~~**even point** *n* TEXTIL punto de quiebre *m*; ~~**induced current** *n* ELEC ENG, ELECTRON corriente inducida de desconexión *f*; ~ **joint** *n* CONST junta partida *f*; ~ **line** *n* PRINT línea incompleta *f*; ~~**of-slope** *n* GEOL cambio de pendiente *m*, cambio de rasante *m*; ~ **roller** *n* FOOD rodillo molturador *m*, rodillo triturador *m*; ~ **stone** *n* WATER grava *f*; ~ **tailings** *n pl* FOOD *essayer's mark* residuos *m pl*; ~ **thrust** *n* GEOL deslizamiento de la grieta *m*, pliegue-falla *m*; ~ **time** *n* ELEC *relay* tiempo de apertura *m*, tiempo de ruptura *m*, ELEC ENG sincronización de apertura del circuito *f*, tiempo de apertura *m*

break[3] *vt* COMP&DP interrumpir, CONST fracturar, romper, *a lock* desmontar, ELEC ENG *circuit* abrir, PROD interrumpir, SAFE romper, WATER TRANSP *flag* romper la canasta, soltar; ~ **down** *vt* CINEMAT *diodes* dividir, CONST *timber* desmontar, desarmar, MINE desbastar en caliente (*AmL*), desgastar en caliente; ~ **an emulsion** *vt* CHEM, POLL, WATER desemulsionar; ~ **for colors** *AmE*, ~ **for colours** *BrE vt* PRINT separar para impresión en colores; ~ **off** *vt BrE* C&G desmoldar; ~ **open** *vt* SAFE abrir; ~ **with a pick** *vt* CONST *ground* escarvar con pico; ~ **up** *vt* CONST *separate into fragments or parts* desarmar

break[4] *vi* CONST desprenderse, separarse, quebrarse, romper, WATER TRANSP *wave* romper, romperse; ~ **coal** *vi* COAL extraer carbón; ~ **down** *vi* CONST averiarse, SAFE *communications* descomponerse, TEXTIL averiarse; ~ **edges** *vi* MECH cortar los bordes; ~ **open** *vi* CONST *door* abrirse, romperse; ~ **out** *vi* PROD *run from mould* rebosar, reventar, SAFE *fire* iniciarse; ~ **up** *vi* CONST *become separated into fragments or parts* desarmarse

breakage *n* MINE arranque *m* (*AmL*), recorte *m* (*Esp*); ~ **rate** *n* PAPER velocidad de trituración *f*, TEXTIL coeficiente de rotura *m*

breakaway: ~ **prop** *n* CINEMAT utillería que puede destruirse rápidamente *f*; ~ **starting current** *n* ELEC corriente de arranque *f*

breakdown *n* CHEM *pressure, stress* ruptura *f*, COMP&DP avería *f*, CONST descarga eléctrica *f*, descomposición *f*, desglose *m*, fallo *m*, ruptura *f*, ELEC avería *f*, *of dielectric* descarga disruptiva *f*, disrupción *f*, perforación *f*, ruptura *f*, ELEC ENG avería *f*, *of insulator, p-n junction* descarga a través de un aislante *f*, interrupción del servicio *f*, ELECTRON avería *f*, *communications*, perturbación *f*, GAS avería *f*, GEOL disgregación *f*, MECH, MECH ENG avería *f*, fallo *m*, MINE descomposición *f*, NUCL avería *f*, descarga *f*, P&R avería *f*, descarga disruptiva *f*, descomposición *f*, desintegración *f* PHYS, fallo *m*, *for cable* descarga a través de un aislante *f*, interrupción del servicio *f*, interrupción del suministro eléctrico *f*, PROD avería *f*, discontinuidad *f*, QUALITY, SAFE, SPACE avería *f*, TELECOM avería *f*, interrupción del servicio *f*, TEXTIL desglose *m*, WATER TRANSP avería *f*; ~ **car** *n AmE* (*cf breakdown wagon BrE*) RAIL vagón de socorro *m*; ~ **gang** *n* CONST equipo de reparación de averías *m*; ~ **manual** *n* RAIL manual de averías *m*; ~ **operator** *n* CINEMAT *orbitography* separador de negativos *m*; ~ **voltage** *n* ELEC, ELEC ENG *of dielectric* tensión de disparo *f*, tensión de perforación *f*, tensión de ruptura *f*, voltaje de perturbación del suministro *m*, voltaje de ruptura *m* MECH ENG tensión de disparo *f*, tensión de perforación *f*, tensión de ruptura *f*, voltaje de ruptura *m*, PHYS voltaje de perturbación del suministro *m*, voltaje de ruptura *m*, TELECOM voltaje de ruptura *m*; ~ **wagon** *n BrE* (*cf breakdown car AmE*) RAIL vagón de socorro *m*

breaker *n* AUTO interruptor *m*, ruptor *m*, CHEM TECH quebradora *f*, trituradora *f*, MECH ENG *crushing or grinding machine* machacadora *f*, quebrantadora *f*, trituradora *f*, OCEAN golpe de mar *m*, rompiente *m*, PAPER filocho *m*, pila desintegradora de trapos *f*, WATER TRANSP *in sea* rompiente *m*; ~ **board** *n* MAR POLL *brazing-lamp* paleta batidora *f*; ~ **contact** *n* VEH contactos del ruptor *m pl*; ~ **plough** *n BrE* AGRIC arado de desfonde *m*, subsolador *m*; ~ **plow** *AmE see breaker plough BrE*; ~ **point** *n* CONST punto de rotura *m*; ~ **spring** *n* AUTO muelle del ruptor *m*, resorte del ruptor *m*; ~ **stack** *n* PACK, PAPER lisa *f*; ~ **steel** *n* CONST, METALL acero duro *m*; ~ **strip** *n* REFRIG varilla de fijación aislante *f*; ~ **triggering** *n* AUTO disparador de interruptor *m*

breakerless: ~ **triggering** *n* AUTO disparador sin interruptor *m*

breaking *n* CHEM TECH fractura *f*, ruptura *f*, CONST *of lock* rotura *f*, fractura *f*, colapso *m*, MINE arranque *m* (*AmL*), recorte *m* (*Esp*), OCEAN *programme* reventazón *f*, rompimiento *m*; ~ **arc** *n* ELEC, ELEC ENG arco de ruptura *m*; ~ **capacity** *n* ELEC *of switch, fuse* capacidad de desconexión *f*, capacidad de ruptura *f*, capacidad interruptora *f*, poder de ruptura *m*, ELEC ENG *of switch, fuse* capacidad de desconexión *f*, capacidad de ruptura *f*, capacidad interruptora *f*, poder de ruptura *m*, ELECTRON *of switch, fuse* capacidad de ruptura *f*, capacidad de desconexión *f*, poder de ruptura *m*; ~ **of a circuit** *n* ELEC ENG desconexión de un circuito *f*; ~ **current** *n* ELEC *of relay* corriente de ruptura *f*; ~ **down** *n* C&G *pot* descomposición *f*, COAL *of coal* arranque *m*, CONST *of logs* serrado *m*, disgregación *f*, rotura *f*, MECH ENG *roll* rodillo desbrozador *m*, MINE derrumbe *m*; ~ **ground** *n* MINE derrumbe de tierra *m*; ~ **-in** *n* MECH derribo *m*, desfondamiento *m*, MECH ENG rodaje *m*; ~ **-in hole** *n* MINE taladrado de pozos *m*; ~ **-in shot** *n* MINE barrenado de alcance *m*, *blasting* barrenado de franqueo *m*; ~ **length** *n* PAPER longitud de rotura *f*, TEXTIL longitud de la rotura *f*; ~ **load** *n* COAL, MECH, MECH ENG, PACK, PAPER, WATER TRANSP *of rope, chain* carga de fractura *f*, carga de rotura *f*, carga de ruptura *f*; ~ **-off** *n* C&G ruptura *f*; ~ **pattern** *n* MECH *of electrode* modelo de rotura *m*; ~ **point** *n* MECH límite de rotura *m*; ~ **shot** *n* MINE barreno de alcance *m*, barreno de calado *m* (*Esp*), barreno de franqueo *m* (*AmL*); ~ **strain** *n* WATER TRANSP *of rope* esfuerzo de rotura *m*; ~ **strength** *n* MECH, P&R, TEXTIL resistencia a la rotura *f*, resistencia a la rotura por tensión *f*; ~ **-strength tester** *n* PAPER caja de entrada de pasta *f*; ~ **stress** *n* MECH, MECH ENG carga de rotura *f*, esfuerzo de rotura *m*; ~ **test** *n* MECH *of oil*

prueba de resistencia *f*, prueba de rotura *f*; ~ **up** *n* CONST desmembramiento *m*, HYDROL *of ice in rivers* deshielo *m*, MECH desintegración *f*, fragmentación *f*, punto de inicio *m*; ~ **wave** *n* OCEAN ola rompiente *f*

breakout *n* MECH ENG rebaba *f*, PETR TECH desenroscado *m*, PROD *blast furnace* escape de escoria *m*, *from mould* escape de metal líquido *m*, *of molten iron* rebaba *f*

breakpoint *n* COMP&DP, PROD punto de interrupción *m*; ~ **chlorination** *n* HYDROL cloración hasta el punto de aumento rápido del cloro residual *f*

breakthrough *n* CONST perforación *f*, GEOL afloramiento *m*, calada *f*, canal de comunicación entre galerías adyacentes *m*, interrupción *f*, MINE afloramiento *m*, calada *f* (*AmL*), canal de comunicación entre galerías adyacentes *m*, interrupción *f*, PRINT, TELECOM ruptura *f*; ~ **point** *n* COAL punto de ruptura *m*

breakwater *n* CONST dique *m*, escollera *f*, malecón *m*, rompeolas *m*, tajamar *m*, terraplén *m* (*Esp*), OCEAN, WATER dique *m*, escollera *f*, malecón *m*, rompeolas *m*, tajamar *m*, terraplén *m*, WATER TRANSP dique *m*, escollera *f*, malecón *m* (*AmL*), rompeolas *m*, tajamar *m*, terraplén *m*

breast *n* COAL cámara *f*, frente *m*, *face of mine* testero *m*, *furnace* pared *f*, *high furnace* vientre *m*; ~ **box** *n* PAPER cajetín de alimentación *m*; ~ **drill** *n* MECH ENG berbiquí de pecho *m*, taladro de pecho *m*; ~ **face** *n* MINE barreno de cara *m*, frente de ataque *m*; ~ **hole** *n* MINE, PROD agujero de evacuación de escorias *m*, barreno de cara *m*, barreno de costado *m*; ~ **line** *n* WATER TRANSP *mooring* amarra de través *f*; ~ **roll** *n* PAPER rodillo cabecero *m*; ~ **wall** *n* C&G muro de sostenimiento *m*, muro lateral *m*, CONST *breast-high wall* pared frontal *f*, *retaining wall* muro de retención *m*; ~ **wheel** *n* HYDRAUL rueda de costado *f*

breasting: ~ **parapet** *n* HYDRAUL defensa *f*, escudo *m*

breastplate *n* MECH ENG pectoral *m*

breastsummer *n* CONST viga muestra *f*

breath: ~ **-holding** *n* OCEAN apnea voluntaria *f*, retención de la respiración *f*

breathable: ~ **air** *n* SAFE aire respirable *m*

breather *n* AUTO respiradero *m*, HYDRAUL válvula de descarga *f*, MECH ENG, PROD, VEH respiradero *m*, tubo de aireación *m*, válvula de aire *f*; ~ **pipe** *n* AUTO respiradero *m*, tubo de respiración *m*

breathing: ~ **apparatus** *n* COAL, MINE, OCEAN, PETR TECH, SAFE aparato de respirar *m*, aparato respiratorio *m*; ~ **mixture** *n* OCEAN mezcla respiratoria *f*

breccia *n* PETROL brecha *f*

bred: ~ **cow** *n* AGRIC vaca grávida *f*, vaca preñada *f*

breech *n* MILIT cierre *m*, culata *f*, recámara *f*; ~ **block** *n* MILIT bloque del cierre *m*; ~ **cover** *n* MILIT cubreculata *m*; ~ **screw** *n* MILIT tornillo del cierre *m*

breeches: ~ **buoy** *n* WATER TRANSP *for rescue* canasta salvavidas *f*, través de popa *m*, través de proa *m*; ~ **joint** *n BrE* ELEC *cable connection* unión posterior *f*; ~ **pipe** *n* MECH, MECH ENG, PROD tubo ahorquillado *m*, tubo bifurcado *m*, tubo en Y *m*

breeching *n* PROD *of boiler* cajas de humo *f pl*; ~ **piece** *n* PROD *Y-pipe connection* pieza de cierre *f*

breed¹ *vt* AGRIC criar, reproducir

breed² *vi* AGRIC, PROD reproducirse

breeder *n* AGRIC genetista *m*, reproductor *m*; ~ **reactor** *n* NUCL, PHYS reactor reproductor *m*; ~ **seed** *n* AGRIC semilla del mejorador *f*

breeding *n* AGRIC mejoramiento genético *m*, cría *f*;
~ **cycle** *n* NUCL ciclo de reproducción *m*; ~ **process**
n NUCL proceso de reproducción *m*; ~-**process**
efficiency *n* NUCL eficacia del proceso de reproducción *f*, reproductividad neta *f*; ~ **station** *n* AGRIC
centro de reproducción *m*; ~ **stock** *n* AGRIC material
de reproducción *m*, parentales *m pl*, reproductores *m*
pl; ~ **unit** *n* AGRIC centro de genética ganadera *m*
breeze *n* COAL cenizas de horno *f pl*, cisco de coque *m*,
menudo de cok *m*, polvo de coque *m*, rescoldo *m*,
METEO brisa *f*
breezing *n* C&G cenizas de horno *f pl*
breithauptite *n* MINERAL breithauptita *f*, níquel antimonial *m*
bremsstrahlung *n* PHYS, RAD PHYS radiación de
bremsstrahlung *f*, radiación fotónica de frenado
electromagnético *f*; ~ **source** *n* NUCL, RAD PHYS
fuente de radiación de frenado *f*
bressummer *n* BrE CONST dintel de madera *m*
brestsummer *AmE see bressummer BrE*
breunnerite *n* MINERAL breunnerita *f*
brewer's: ~ **grain** *n* FOOD *airworthiness* grano para
elaboración cervecera *m*
brewing *n* FOOD elaboración cervecera *f*; ~ **industry** *n*
FOOD industria cervecera *f*; ~ **liquor** *n* FOOD licor
cervecero *m*
Brewster: ~ **incidence** *n* PHYS incidencia de Brewster *f*
brewsterite *n* MINERAL brewsterita *f*
Brewster's: ~ **angle** *n* OPT ángulo de Brewster *m*
brick[1] *n* C&G, CONST ladrillo *m*; ~-**and-tile machine** *n*
C&G máquina cortadora de ladrillos y azulejos *f*,
máquina para cortar ladrillos y azulejos *f*; ~ **arch** *n*
CONST *of furnace firebox* arco de ladrillo *m*, horno de
ladrillo *m*; ~-**arch bearer** *n* CONST soporte del arco de
ladrillo *m*, soporte del horno de ladrillo *m*; ~ **clay** *n*
C&G, CONST arcilla para ladrillo *f*; ~ **earth** *n* CONST
tierra de ladrillos *f*; ~ **field** *n* CONST ladrillal *m*; ~ **kiln**
n CONST horno para cocer ladrillos *m*; ~-**molding**
machine *AmE*, ~-**moulding machine** *BrE n* C&G
máquina de moldear ladrillos *f*, máquina ladrillera *f*;
~ **pavement** *n* CONST enladrillado *m*; ~ **paving** *n*
CONST pavimento de ladrillo *m*; ~ **trowel** *n* CONST
llana *f*, trulla *f*; ~ **wall** *n* CONST muro de ladrillos *m*,
pared de ladrillos *f*
brick[2] *vt* CONST revestir de ladrillo; ~ **up** *vt* CONST
tapiar con ladrillos
bricked: ~-**up core** *n* CONST centro de ladrillos *m*
bricklayer *n* C&G, CONST albañil *m*; ~'s **trowel** *n* CONST,
MECH ENG cuchara de albañil *f* (*AmL*), llana de
albañil *f* (*Esp*), llana para enlucir *f* (*Esp*), trulla de
albañil *f*
brickwork *n* C&G, CONST albañilería *f*
brickworks *n* CONST fábrica de ladrillo *f*
bridge[1] *n* C&G, COMP&DP puente *m*, CONST puente-grúa
m, ELEC *instrument* puente *m*, puente de medida *m*,
INSTR, MECH ENG brida *f*, puente *m*, PROD *furnaces*,
TELECOM, WATER TRANSP *of control* puente *m*;
~ **amplifier** *n* ELECTRON amplificador de puente *m*;
~ **arm** *n* INSTR brazo del puente *m*; ~ **balancing** *n*
ELEC ENG compensación de puente de medida *f*;
~ **castle** *n* WATER TRANSP ciudadela *f*; ~ **circuit** *n*
ELEC circuito en puente *m*, circuito puente *m*, ELEC
ENG circuito en derivación *m*, circuito en puente *m*;
~ **connection** *n* ELEC conexión en puente *f*, montaje
en puente *m*; ~ **crane** *n* CONST puente-grúa *m*;
~ **deck** *n* WATER TRANSP cubierta puente *f*;

~-**deflective recorder** *n* CONST registrador de deformación del puente *m*, registrador de desviación del
puente *m*; ~ **with diminished arches** *n* CONST puente
con arcos disminuidos *m*; ~ **with equal bays** *n* CONST
puente de tramos iguales *m*; ~-**house** *n* WATER
TRANSP *of ship* ciudadela *f*; ~-**keeper** *n* WATER
TRANSP operador de puente móvil *m*; ~-**layer tank**
n MILIT carro tiendepuentes *m*; ~ **plate** *n* CONST *back*
support of grate-bars placa puente *f*, MECH ENG
injection moulds placa de sujeción *f*; ~ **rail** *n* CONST
baranda del puente *f* (*AmL*), barandilla del puente *f*
(*Esp*); ~ **reamer** *n* MECH ENG escariador estructural
m; ~ **rectifier** *n* ELEC, ELEC ENG rectificador de
puente *m*; ~ **resistance** *n* ELEC resistencia en paralelo
f; ~ **shown in cross-section** *n* CONST sección
transversal de un puente *f*; ~ **truss** *n* CONST estructura del puente *f*; ~ **under railroad** *n* AmE TRANSP
puente bajo la línea férrea *m*; ~ **under railway** *BrE n*
(*cf bridge under railroad AmE*) RAIL puente bajo la
línea férrea *m*
bridge[2] *vt* CONST *span* salvar mediante un puente, unir
mediante puentes, *valley* conectar, cruzar; ~ **over** *vt*
CONST *valley* atravesar mediante un puente, cruzar
mediante un puente
bridged *adj* PROD con puentes, de puente
bridged-H: ~ **network** *n* ELEC ENG *quadripole* red con
puente en H *f*
bridged-T: ~ **network** *n* ELEC ENG *quadripole* red con
puente en T *f*
bridging *n* CONST *strutting between floor joists* arriostramiento *m*; ~ **contacts** *n pl* ELEC ENG *on-off switch*
contactos de láminas *m pl*, contactos en paralelo *m*
pl; ~ **piece** *n* CONST riostra *f*, travesaño *m*; ~ **shot** *n*
CINEMAT toma de transición *f*; ~ **tank** *n* MILIT carro
tiendepuentes *m*
bridle *n* PETROL brida *f*, WATER TRANSP *towing,*
anchoring pie de gallo *m*; ~ **chain** *n* MINE cadena de
retención *f*; ~ **joint** *n* CONST machihembrado *m*
brief *n* PROD informe *m*
Briet-Wigner: ~ **resonance** *n* NUCL resonancia Briet-
Wigner *f*
Brigg's: ~ **pipe thread** *n* MECH ENG rosca de tubo
Brigg *f*
bright[1] *adj* CINEMAT luminoso, OPT brillante, luminoso,
TEXTIL vivo, TV luminoso; ~ **all over** *adj* MECH ENG
tool todo pulido
bright[2]: ~-**annealed wire** *n* MECH ENG alambre
recocido brillante *m*; ~ **annealing** *n* HEAT esmaltado
por calor *m*, recocido brillante *m*; ~ **bolt** *n* MECH ENG
perno pulido *m*; ~ **coal** *n* COAL carbón brillante *m*;
~ **etching** *n* C&G grabado al ácido brillante *m*; ~ **field**
n METALL soldadura pulida *f*; ~-**field illumination** *n*
PHYS iluminación en campo claro *f*; ~-**field image** *n*
CRYSTALL imagen de campo claro *f*; ~ **fringe** *n* PHYS
franja brillante *f*; ~ **gold** *n* C&G oro brillante *m*;
~ **hard-drawn wire** *n* MECH ENG alambre brillante
estirado en frío *m*; ~ **level** *n* TV nivel del blanco *m*;
~ **line spectrum** *n* SPACE espectro de líneas luminosas
m; ~-**line viewfinder** *n* PHOTO visor luminoso *m*;
~ **silver** *n* C&G plata brillante *f*
brightening *n* PROD abrillantamiento *m*
brightness *n* ELECTRON, OPT brillo *m*, PAPER blancura
f, *metal* claridad *f*, PHYS *spacecraft* brillo *m*, PRINT
blancura *f*, TV brillo *m* (*AmL*), luminosidad *f* (*Esp*);
~ **control** *n* TV regulación de la luminosidad *f* (*Esp*),
regulación del brillo *f* (*AmL*); ~ **curve** *n* TV curva de

brillo *f* (*AmL*), curva de luminosidad *f* (*Esp*);
~ **modulation** *n* ELECTRON modulación de brillo *f*;
~ **range** *n* PHOTO gama de intensidad luminosa *f*;
~ **ratio** *n* CINEMAT proporción de brillos *f*, TV
contraste de brillos *m*, rango del brillo *m* (*AmL*);
~ **theorem** *n* OPT teorema del brillo *m*; ~ **value** *n* TV
valor de la luminosidad *m* (*Esp*), valor del brillo *m*
(*AmL*)
brilliance *n* ELECTRON luminosidad *f*
brilliant: ~ **cutting** *n* C&G tallado en brillante *m*;
~ **polish** *n* PROD pulimiento brillante *m*; ~ **varnish** *n*
COLOUR barniz brillante *m*
Brillouin: ~ **zone** *n* METALL, PHYS zona de Brillouin *f*
brim: ~ **capacity** *n* C&G capacidad máxima *f*
brine *n* CHEM, GAS, HYDROL, NUCL, OCEAN, REFRIG
salmuera *f*; ~ **cooler** *n* REFRIG enfriador de salmuera
m; ~ **cooling** *n* FOOD refrescadura en salmuera *f*,
refrescamiento en salmuera *m*; ~ **drum** *n* REFRIG
acumulador de salmuera *m*; ~ **fermentation** *n*
OCEAN fermentación en salmuera *f*; ~ **header** *n*
REFRIG colector de salmuera *m*; ~ **line** *n* REFRIG
conducto de salmuera *m*, línea de salmuera *f*;
~ **pickling** *n* OCEAN *graphic display* conservación en
salmuera *f*, salmuerado *m*; ~ **pump** *n* REFRIG bomba
de salmuera *f*; ~ **return-tank** *n* REFRIG depósito de
retorno de salmuera *m*; ~ **sparge** *n* REFRIG agitador
de salmuera por inyección de aire comprimido *m*;
~ **spray** *n* REFRIG pulverización de salmuera *f*;
~ **tank** *n* REFRIG depósito de salmuera *m*
Brinell: ~ **ball test** *n* MECH, MECH ENG ensayo de
dureza Brinell *m*, prueba a la bola Brinell *f*;
~ **hardness** *n* MECH *vehicles*, MECH ENG dureza
Brinell *f*; ~~**hardness number** *n* MECH, MECH ENG
número de dureza de Brinell *m*; ~~**hardness testing-
machine** *n* MECH, MECH ENG máquina para determinar la dureza por el método Brinell *f*; ~ **test** *n* MECH,
MECH ENG prueba de Brinell *f*
brinelling *n* MECH ENG brinelación *f*
bring[1]: ~ **into position for use** *vt* PROD *drill* colocar
para uso; ~ **to the boil** *vt* THERMO llevar a hervor;
~ **to the surface** *vt* MINE subir al exterior; ~ **up** *vt*
PRINT poner a la altura; ~ **up to date** *vt* MECH ENG
poner al día
bring[2]: ~ **the air bubble to the center of its run** *AmE*,
~ **the air bubble to the centre of its run** *BrE vi*
CONST nivelar con nivel de burbuja; ~ **down the face**
vi MINE descender el fondo; ~ **up** *vi* WATER TRANSP
moor dar fondo
briny *adj* HYDROL, OCEAN salado, salobre
briquette *n* C&G briqueta *f*, COAL aglomerado de
carbón *m*, briqueta *f*
brisance *n* MINE potencia explosiva *f* (*AmL*), potencial
enérgico *m* (*Esp*)
bristly: ~ **lady's thumb** *n* AGRIC *weeds* polígono
cerdoso *m*
British: ~ **Association screw thread** *n* (*BA screw
thread*) MECH ENG hilo de rosca de British Association *m*; ~ **Standard fine screw thread** *n* (*BSF screw
thread*) MECH ENG hilo de rosca de paso pequeño de
British Standards *m*; ~ **Standard parallel pipe
thread** *n* (*BSP*) MECH ENG hilo de rosca en paralelo
de British Standards *m*; ~ **Standard taper pipe
thread** *n* (*BSPT*) MECH ENG hilo de rosca cónico de
British Standards *m*; ~ **Standard Whitworth thread**
n (*BSW thread*) MECH ENG hilo de rosca Whitworth
de British Standards *m*; ~ **Standards Institution** *n*

(*BSI*) PROD Instituto Británico de Normalización *m*
(*BSI*); ~ **Standards Specification** *n* (*BSS*) MECH
ENG especificación de British Standards *f*; ~ **thermal
unit** *n* (*BTU*) GAS, HEAT ENG, MECH ENG, PETROL
unidad térmica británica *f* (*BTU*)
brittle[1] *adj* C&G, CRYSTALL, GEOL frágil, quebradizo,
MECH *vehicles* frágil, agrio, quebradizo, METALL
quebradizo, agrio, frágil, P&R frágil, quebradizo
brittle[2]: ~ **crack** *n* NUCL grieta por fragilización *f*;
~ **ductile transition** *n* METALL, NUCL transición
frágil-dúctil *f*; ~ **failure** *n* NUCL fractura por fragilización *f*, rotura frágil *f*; ~ **fracture** *n* CRYSTALL,
MECH, METALL fractura por fragilidad *f*; ~~**fracture
resistance** *n* METALL resistencia de fractura frágil *f*;
~~**fracture transition-temperature** *n* MECH *vehicles*
temperatura de transición a la rotura frágil *f*
brittleness *n* C&G, CRYSTALL, GEOL fragilidad *f*, MECH,
METALL agrura *f*, falta de plasticidad *f*, fragilidad *f*,
P&R fragilidad *f*
Brix: ~ **scale** *n* FOOD escala de Brix *f*
broach[1] *n* CONST *pin of lock* agujas chapitel *f pl*, lezna *f*,
punzón *m*, MECH brocha *f*, brochar, MECH ENG
escariador de tracción *m*, fresa rectilínea de cremallera *f*, mandril *m*, brocha *f*, MINE brocha *f*, brochar
broach[2] *vt* MECH ENG brochar, mandrilar .
broach[3] *vi* WATER TRANSP *parcel, barrel* encentar,
espitar
broaching *n* MECH, MECH ENG, MINE brochado *m*,
mandrinado *m*; ~ **bit** *n* MINE broca abierta *f* (*Esp*),
brochadora *f* (*AmL*); ~ **machine** *n* MECH brochadora
f, MECH ENG brochadora *f*, fresadora con cremallera
f, mandriladora *f*; ~ **tool** *n* MECH, MECH ENG
herramienta para brochar *f*
broad[1]: **on a** ~ **reach** *adv* WATER TRANSP *sailing* con
viento libre a popa del través
broad[2]: ~~**crested weir** *n* HYDRAUL, WATER vertedero
de pared gruesa *m*; ~~**flange girder** *n* CONST viga de
ala ancha *m*; ~~**gage railroad** *n* *AmE* RAIL ferrocarril
de vía ancha *m*; ~~**gauge railway** *BrE n* RAIL
ferrocarril de vía ancha *m*; ~ **irrigation** *n* AGRIC,
HYDROL irrigación extensa *f*, WATER irrigación
extensa *f*, riego con aguas cloacales *m*, riego con
aguas negras *m*; ~~**side aerial** *n* *BrE* (*cf broad-side
antenna AmE*) SPACE antena de radiación lateral *f*,
antena de radiación transversal *f*; ~~**side antenna** *n*
AmE (*cf broad-side aerial BrE*) SPACE antena de
radiación lateral *f*, antena de radiación transversal *f*
broadband *n* COMP&DP, TV banda ancha *f*; ~ **aerial** *n*
BrE (*cf broadband antenna AmE*) SPACE, TV antena de
banda ancha *f*; ~ **amplifier** *n* ELECTRON amplificador
de banda ancha *m*; ~ **antenna** *n* *AmE* (*cf broadband
aerial BrE*) SPACE, TV antena de banda ancha *f*;
~ **crosspoint** *n* TELECOM contacto de cruce de banda
ancha *m*; ~~**integrated services digital network** *n*
(*B-ISDN*) TELECOM red digital de servicios integrados de banda ancha *f* (*RDSI-BA*); ~ **sound** *n* ACOUST
sonido de banda ancha *m*; ~ **switch** *n* TELECOM
conmutador de banda ancha *m*; ~ **switching
network** *n* TELECOM red de conmutación de banda
ancha *f*
broadcast[1] *n* (*BC*) AGRIC aplicación a voleo *f*, TELE-
COM radiodifusión *f*, TV emisión *f*; ~ **quality** *n* TV
calidad de la emisión *f*; ~ **seeding** *n* AGRIC siembra al
voleo *f*; ~~**signaling virtual channel** *AmE*,
~~**signalling virtual channel** *BrE n* (*BSVC*) TELE-
COM canal virtual de señalización de radiodifusión *m*;

~ **standard** *n* TV emisión estándar *f*; ~ **transmitter** *n* TELECOM transmisor de radiodifusión *m*; ~ **video Umatic** *n* (*BVU*) TV emisión por video Umatic *f* (*AmL*), emisión por vídeo Umatic *f* (*Esp*); ~ **videographics** *n* TV emisión de videográficos *f*

broadcast[2] *vt* TELECOM emitir, radiar, TV emitir, WAVE PHYS emitir, radiar, transmitir

broadcasting *n* SPACE radiodifusión *f*, radiodifusor *m*, TELECOM radiodifusión *f*, TV emisión *f*; ~ **network** *n* TV red de radiodifusión *f*; ~ **rights** *n* TV derechos de radiodifusión *m pl*; ~ **satellite** *n* SPACE *communications*, TV satélite de radiodifusión *m*; ~ **satellite service** *n* SPACE servicio de satélites de radiodifusión *m*; ~ **station** *n* TV radioemisora *f*; ~ **times** *n pl* TV horas de radiodifusión *f pl*

broadleaf: ~ **weed** *n* AGRIC maleza de hojas anchas *f*

broadloom: ~ **carpet** *n* TEXTIL alfombra en rollo *f*

broadsheet *n* PRINT hoja grande *f*

broadside *n* PRINT pliego anuncio de gran tamaño *m*; ~ **array aerial** *n* BrE (*cf broadside array antenna AmE*) TELECOM antena en array de radiación transversal *f*; ~ **array antenna** *n* AmE (*cf broadside array aerial BrE*) TELECOM antena en array de radiación transversal *f*; ~ **page** *n* PRINT página apaisada *f*

brocade *n* TEXTIL brocado *m*

brochantite *n* MINERAL brochantita *f*

broke *n* PAPER papel averiado *m*

broken[1] *adj* GEN averiado, WATER TRANSP falto; ~-**backed** *adj* WATER TRANSP *ship* quebrantado

broken[2]: ~ **circuit** *n* ELEC ENG circuito abierto *m*; ~ **country** *n* CONST contorno de líneas de puntos *m*; ~-**down timber** *n* CONST madera partida *f*; ~ **end** *n* TEXTIL cabo roto *m*; ~ **ice** *n* REFRIG hielo troceado *m*; ~ **line** *n* GEOM línea cortada *f*; ~ **ore** *n* MINE pilar de mineral *m*, mineral machacado *m*, mineral quebrantado *m*, mineral triturado *m*; ~ **rice** *n* AGRIC, FOOD arroz machacado *m*, arroz partido *m*; ~ **rock** *n* COAL pilar de carbón *m*; ~ **seed** *n* C&G burbuja ampollada *f*, fragmentación de burbujas *f*; ~ **stone** *n* CONST piedra irregular *f*; ~ **white line** *n* CONST línea blanca discontinua *f*; ~ **working** *n* COAL arranque *m*

broker *n* PETR TECH intermediario *m*

bromal *n* CHEM bromal *m*

bromargyrite *n* MINERAL bromargirita *f*

bromate *n* CHEM bromato *m*

brome: ~ **grass** *n* AGRIC bromo *m*, cebadilla *f*

bromelain *n* FOOD bromelina *f*

bromhidric *adj* CHEM bromhídrico

bromic *adj* CHEM brómico

bromide *n* CHEM, DETERG, PHOTO bromuro *m*; ~ **paper** *n* PHOTO papel bromuro *m*, papel de gelatinobromuro *m*; ~ **print** *n* PHOTO copia de bromuro *m*, PRINT copia en papel bromuro *f*

bromine *n* (*Br*) CHEM bromo *m* (*Br*)

bromite *n* MINERAL bromita *f*

bromoacetic *adj* CHEM bromoacético

bromoacetone *n* CHEM bromoacetona *f*

bromobenzene *n* CHEM bromobenceno *m*

bromoform *n* CHEM bromoformo *m*

bromoil: ~ **print** *n* PHOTO copia de bromoleotipia *f*

bromomethane *n* CHEM bromometano *m*

bromophenol *n* CHEM bromofenol *m*

bromyrite *n* MINERAL bromargirita *f*, bromuro de plata *m*

bronze[1]: ~-**chromate finished** *adj* PROD acabado de cromado de bronce

bronze[2] *n* CHEM *alloy* bronce *m*, aleación de cobre y estaño *f*, COLOUR, MECH bronce *m*, METALL *alloy* aleación de cobre y estaño *f*, PROD bronce *m*; ~ **guide bush** *n* MECH ENG casquillo de guía de bronce *m*, manguito de guía de bronce *m*; ~ **ink** *n* COLOUR tinta de bronce *f*; ~ **pigment** *n* COLOUR pigmento de bronce *m*; ~ **powder** *n* COLOUR polvo de bronce *m*; ~-**powder ink** *n* PRINT tinta metálica de bronce *f*; ~ **varnish** *n* COATINGS barniz metálico *m*, COLOUR barniz bronceado *m*, barniz metálico *m*; ~ **welding** *n* CONST soldadura de bronce *f*

bronzeworking: ~ **tools** *n pl* PROD herramientas de bronce *f pl*

bronzing *n* PRINT impresión en bronce *f*; ~ **tincture** *n* COLOUR tintura bronceadora *f*

bronzite *n* MINERAL broncita *f*

brook *n* GEOL, HYDROL arroyo *m*, arroyuelo *m*

Brookfield: ~ **viscosity** *n* P&R viscosidad de Brookfield *f*

brookite *n* MINERAL brookita *f*

broom *n* CONST escoba *f*; ~ **millet** *n* AGRIC sorgo forrajero *m*

brow *n* CONST *of hill* cima *f*, cumbre *f*, MINE cumbre *f* (*Esp*), cresta *f* (*AmL*), frente de pliegue *m* (*AmL*), borde *m* (*Esp*), pozo inclinado *m*

brown: ~ **coal** *n* THERMO carbón bituminoso *m*; ~-**coal gas** *n* GAS gas de lignito *m*; ~ **haematite** *n* BrE CHEM hematites parda *f*; ~ **hematite** *AmE see brown haematite BrE*; ~ **iron ore** *n* CHEM mineral de hierro pardo *m*; ~ **mechanical pulp** *n* PAPER pulpa mecánica parda *f*; ~ **mechanical pulp board** *n* PAPER cartón de pulpa mecánica parda *m*, pasta mecánica parda *f*; ~ **millboard** *n* PAPER cartón pardo *m*; ~ **mixed-pulp board** *n* PAPER cartón gris *m* (*AmL*), cartón pardo *m*; ~ **print** *n* PRINT copia cianográfica en papel sepia *f*; ~ **spar** *n* MINERAL espato bruno *m*; ~ **stock** *n* PAPER pasta de descarga *f*; ~ **tourmaline** *n* MINERAL turmalina parda *f*

Brownian: ~ **motion** *n* PHYS, RAD PHYS movimiento browniano *m*, movimiento de Brown *m*; ~ **movement** *n* PHYS, RAD PHYS movimiento browniano *m*, movimiento de Brown *m*

browning *n* COLOUR oscurecimiento *m*

brownout *n* ELEC ENG, ELECTRON, PROD oscurecimiento parcial *m*

browse *vt* COMP&DP curiosear, examinar, hacer un browse, hojear

brucellosis *n* AGRIC brucelosis *f*, fiebre de Malta *f*

brucine *n* CHEM, FOOD brucina *f*

brucite *n* MINERAL brucita *f*

Bruckner: ~ **cycle** *n* METEO ciclo de Brückner *m*

bruise *n* C&G grieta *f*, raspadura *f*, FOOD golpe *m*, machacadura *f*

brush *n* AUTO escobilla *f*, COLOUR brocha *f*, CONST brocha *f*, cepillo *m*, escobilla *f*, *wood* matorral *m*, ELEC *in machine* escobilla *f*, ELEC ENG descarga azulada *f*, LAB *act* escobillón *m*, MECH *for injection moulding* cepillo *m*, escobilla *f*, PAPER cepillo *m*, PROD escobilla *f*; ~ **angle** *n* ELEC *for machine* ángulo de escobilla *m*; ~-**coated paper** *n* PAPER papel estucado con cepillo *m*; ~ **coater** *n* PAPER estucadora de cepillos *f*; ~ **coating** *n* COATINGS pincelada *f*, revestimiento aplicado con brocha *m*, PAPER estucado con cepillo *m*; ~-**contact resistance** *n* ELEC *in machine*

resistencia de contacto de escobillas f; ~ **discharge** n ELEC *in machine* chispa de colector f, efluvio eléctrico m, descarga en abanico f, chispa de escobilla f, descarga radiante f, ELEC ENG descarga radiante f, efluvio eléctrico m, descarga en abanico f, chispa de colector f, chispa de escobilla f, PHYS descarga en abanico f, chispa de escobilla f, descarga radiante f, chispa de colector f, efluvio eléctrico m; ~ **dyeing** n COLOUR teñido a pincel m; ~ **finish** n PAPER cepillado m; ~ **glazing** n PAPER satinado por cepillado m; ~-**holder** n ELEC *in machine*, ELEC ENG portaescobillas m; ~-**lifting device** n ELEC *in machine* dispositivo elevador de escobillas m; ~ **plating** n COATINGS electrodeposición f; ~ **polishing** n PAPER abrillantado a cepillo m; ~-**polishing machine** n PAPER cepilladora f; ~ **position** n ELEC ENG colocación de las escobillas f; ~ **proof** n PRINT prueba a pincel f; ~-**rocker** n ELEC ENG portaescobillas regulable m, puente de las escobillas m; ~ **rod** n ELEC ENG electrodo de escobilla m; ~-**roller** n PAPER rodillo cepillador m; ~-**selector** n ELEC *in machine* selector de escobilla m; ~ **sparking** n ELEC *in machine* chispa de escobilla f, chispa eléctrica de escobilla f, descarga disruptiva de escobilla f; ~ **spring** n ELEC ENG muelle de la escobilla m, resorte de la escobilla m; ~-**type DC motor** n ELEC ENG motor de CC por escobillas m; ~ **washer** n TEXTIL lavacepillos m; ~ **yoke** n ELEC *generator* yugo de escobilla m
brushed *adj* MECH cepillado
brushing n TEXTIL cepillado m
brushite n MINERAL brushita f
brushless: ~ **DC motor** n ELEC, ELEC ENG motor CC sin escobillas m; ~ **generator** n ELEC, ELEC ENG generador sin escobillas m; ~ **motor** n ELEC, ELEC ENG motor sin escobillas m
brushlines n pl C&G marcas del cepillo f pl, rayas agrietadas verticales f pl
brushmarks n pl C&G rayas agrietadas verticales f pl
brute n CINEMAT *diodes* bruto m, lámpara de arco eléctrico f, ELEC lámpara de arco eléctrico f
BS *abbr* (*backspace*) COMP&DP, PRINT espacio de retroceso m, retroceso m, retroseguimiento m, tecla de retroceso f
BSC *abbr* (*binary synchronous transmission*) COMP&DP transmisión sincrónica binaria f
BSE *abbr* (*bovine spongiform encephalopathy*) AGRIC BSE (*encefalopatía espongiforme bovina*)
BSF: ~ **screw thread** n (*British Standard fine screw thread*) MECH ENG hilo de rosca de paso pequeño de British Standards m
BSI *abbr* (*British Standards Institution*) PROD BSI (*Instituto Británico de Normalización*)
BSP *abbr* (*British Standard parallel pipe thread*) MECH ENG hilo de rosca en paralelo de British Standards m
BSPT *abbr* (*British Standard taper pipe thread*) MECH ENG hilo de rosca cónico de British Standards m
BSS *abbr* (*British Standards Specification*) MECH ENG especificación de British Standards f
B-stage: ~ **resin** n P&R resina termoplástica en estado blando f, resitol m
BSVC *abbr* (*broadcast-signaling virtual channel AmE, broadcast-signalling virtual channel BrE*) TELECOM canal virtual de señalización de radiodifusión m
BSW: ~ **thread** n (*British Standard Whitworth thread*) MECH ENG hilo de rosca Whitworth de British Standards m

B3ZS *abbr* (*bipolar code with three-zero substitution*) TELECOM B3ZS (*código bipolar con sustitución de tres ceros*)
BU *abbr* (*base unit*) TELECOM unidad base f
bubble[1] n C&G, CHEM TECH burbuja f, COAL nivel m, sopladura f, P&R, PHYS burbuja f; ~ **barrier** n MAR POLL barrera de burbujas f; ~ **cap** n FOOD casquete de burbujeo m, PETR TECH campana burbujeadora f, casquete de burbujeo m; ~ **chamber** n PART PHYS, PHYS cámara de burbujas f; ~-**coated paper** n PAPER papel con estucado esponjoso m; ~ **detector** n OCEAN detector de burbujas m; ~ **film** n PACK película con acolchado de burbujas f; ~ **flowmeter** n LAB caudalímetro de burbuja m, fluxímetro de burbuja m; ~ **gage** *AmE*, ~ **gauge** *BrE* n CHEM TECH calibrador de burbuja m, caudalímetro de burbuja m; ~-**jet printer** n COMP&DP, PRINT impresora a chicler de tinta f (*AmL*), impresora de chorro de tinta f (*Esp*), impresora de inyección de tinta f (*Esp*); ~ **level** n MECH *screen* nivel de burbuja de aire m; ~ **memory** n COMP&DP memoria de burbuja f, ELEC ENG memoria de tránsito f; ~ **model** n METALL modelo de burbujas m; ~ **nut** n CONST tornillo de nivelación m; ~ **pack** n PACK empaquetado con un material con acolchado de burbujas m; ~-**point pressure** n PETROL presión de punto de burbujeo f; ~ **sort** n COMP&DP clasificación en onda f, clasificación por el método de burbuja f; ~ **tray** n CHEM TECH plato de burbujeo m; ~-**tray column** n CHEM TECH columna de platos de burbujeo f; ~ **tube** n CONST tubo de burbuja m; ~ **type** n TEXTIL tipo burbuja m
bubble[2]: ~ **through** *vi* PHYS burbujear a través
bubbler n C&G burbujeador f, cuentaburbujas m, PHYS borboteador m
bubbling[1] *adj* PHYS burbujeante, efervescente
bubbling[2] n C&G burbujeado m, burbujeado del esmalte m, CHEM, OCEAN, PHYS burbujeo m
Buchmann: ~ **and Meyer pattern** n ACOUST modelo de Buchmann y Meyer m
Buchner: ~ **flask** n LAB matraz de Buchner m; ~ **funnel** n LAB cubeta f, cubo m, embudo de Buchner m
buck n CONST banco de madera m, marco m; ~-**boost regulator** n SPACE regulador reductor-elevador m
bucket n AGRIC *elevator* cangilón m, COMP&DP *memory* cubo m (*AmL*), balde de acero m, balde m, cubeta f, CONST álabe m, balde de acero m, cubo m, *crane* draga f, *of elevator, dredge* cangilón m, balde m, *for aerial ropeway* vagoneta f, paleta f, cuchara f, FUELLESS *turbine* cangilón m, HYDRAUL paleta f, MAR POLL *brazing-lamp* balde de acero m, balde m, MECH *geophysics* paleta f, MINE jaula de extracción f, WATER *of water-wheel*, WATER TRANSP *dredge* cangilón m; ~ **angle** n FUELLESS ángulo de cangilón m; ~-**brigade device** n (*BBD*) ELEC ENG dispositivo de compresor axial m, TELECOM dispositivo de actuación rápida m; ~ **chain** n CONST *dredger or elevator* cadena de cangilón f; ~-**chain excavator** n MINE excavadora de cucharón f (*Esp*), excavadora de rosario f (*Esp*), rotopala f (*Esp*); ~ **conveyor** n CONST transportador de cangilones m; ~ **dredger** n CONST, WATER, WATER TRANSP draga de cangilones f; ~ **drogue** n WATER TRANSP ancla flotante f; ~ **with drop-bottom** n CONST cubo con fondo móvil m; ~ **elevator** n AGRIC elevador a cangilones m, CONST elevador de cangilones m; ~ **excavator** n CONST

excavadora de cangilones *f* (*AmL*), rotopala *f*; ~ **ladder** *n* CONST *of dredge* escalera de cangilones *f*; ~ **pump** *n* HYDRAUL, MECH ENG, WATER bomba aspirante-impelente *f*, bomba aspirante-impelente con válvulas en el pistón *f*; ~ **seat** *n* AUTO, VEH asiento bajo *m*, asiento de cubeta *m*; ~ **velocity** *n* FUELLESS velocidad de cangilón *f*; ~ **wheel** *n* CONST rueda de cangilones *f*; ~~**wheel excavator** *n* MINE excavadora con rueda de rosario *f* (*AmL*), excavadora de cangilones *f* (*AmL*), rotopala *f* (*Esp*)

bucketful *n* CONST cuchara *f*

bucketless: ~ **system** *n* PROD sistema sin cubo *m*

bucking: ~ **circuit** *n* ELEC circuito compensador *m*, circuito de compensación *m*; ~ **coil** *n* ELEC bobina en oposición *f*, ELEC ENG bobina compensadora *f*, bobina en oposición *f*; ~ **regulator** *n* SPACE estabilizador compensador *m*

buckle[1] *n* C&G deformación *f*, CINEMAT combeo *m*, MECH ENG *of leaf spring* brida *f*, *of strap* hebilla *f*, PETROL hebilla *f*, argolla *f*, combadura *f*, pandeo *m*, lazo *m*, abrazadera *f*; ~~**folder machine** *n* PRINT plegado a bolsillo *m*; ~ **folding** *n* GEOL plegamiento en bucles *m*; ~ **trip** *n* CINEMAT dispositivo de seguridad antienganche de la película *m*

buckle[2] *vt* MECH, MECH ENG alabear, deformar, pandear

buckle[3] *vi* MECH curvarse, deformarse, pandear, torcerse

buckling *n* CINEMAT combado *m*, GEOL pliegue en bucle *m*, MECH *diodes* pandeo *m*, deformación *f*, ondulación superficial *f*, MECH ENG *distorting* flexión lateral *f*, pandeo *m*, alabeo *m*, NUCL deformación *f*, pandeo *m*, PHOTO deformación *f*, alabeo *m* (*AmL*), combeo *m*, combado *m* (*Esp*), PROD *of boiler plate* pandeo *m*; ~ **load** *n* MECH *diodes* carga de pandeo *f*

buckram *n* PRINT bucarán *m*

buckstay *n* C&G varilla del horno *f*, viga de anclaje *f*

buckwheat *n* AGRIC alforfón *m*, trigo sarraceno *m*, FOOD trigo sarraceno *m*

bud[1]: ~ **worm** *n* AGRIC gusano de las yemas *m*

bud[2] *vti* AGRIC brotar, injertar

buddle *n* COAL, MINE artesa *f*, gamella *f*

buff[1]: ~ **wheel** *n* PROD disco de pulir *m*

buff[2] *vt* PROD pulimentar, pulir

buffalo: ~ **grass** *n* AGRIC niveladora *f*

buffer[1] *n* CHEM amortiguador *m*, buffer *m*, tampón *m*, COMP&DP memoria intermedia *f*, registro intermedio *m*, ELEC ENG acumulador intermedio *m*, circuito intermedio *m*, MECH amortiguador *m*, regulador *m*, MECH ENG amortiguador *m*, pulidora *f*, tope *m*, P&R regulador *m*, solución reguladora *f*, tampón *m*, PRINT memoria intermedia *f*, RAIL tope *m*, TV *ring network* separador *m*; ~ **action** *n* CHEM, DETERG acción amortiguadora *f*, acción de un buffer *f*, acción tamponadora *f*, acción tampón *f*; ~ **amplifier** *n* ELECTRON amplificador compensador *m*; ~ **battery** *n* ELEC ENG batería de compensación *f*, batería compensadora *f*, TRANSP batería compensadora *f*, batería de compensación *f*; ~ **beam** *n* RAIL travesaño de tope *m*; ~ **circuit** *n* ELECTRON circuito de compensación *m*; ~ **dynamo** *n* ELEC *generator* dinamo de compensación *f*; ~ **memory** *n* ELEC ENG memoria intermedia *f*, TELECOM memoria dinámica *f*; ~ **register** *n* COMP&DP registrador intermedio *m*; ~ **salt** *n* FOOD sal reguladora *f*; ~ **solution** *n* FOOD solución reguladora *f*, PROD *chroming* solución

amortiguadora *f*, solución retardadora *f*, solución tope *f*; ~ **stage** *n* PROD paso amortiguador *m*; ~ **stop** *n* RAIL tope de parada *m*; ~~**stop block** *n* RAIL parachoques *m*, tope de choque *m*; ~ **storage** *n* NUCL almacenamiento de reserva *m*; ~ **tank** *n* GAS tanque compensador *m*

buffer[2] *vt* CHEM regular, COMP&DP almacenar en la memoria intermedia, efectuar en registro intermedio (*AmL*)

buffered: ~ **fiber** *AmE*, ~ **fibre** *BrE* *n* OPT, TELECOM fibra protegida *f*; ~ **input-output** *n* COMP&DP entrada-salida mediante registro intermedio *f*, memoria intermedia de entrada-salida *f*

buffering *n* COMP&DP almacenamiento en memoria intermedia *m*, almacenamiento en registro intermedio *m*, OPT protección *f*; ~ **agent** *n* CINEMAT agente de tamponación *m*

buffet *n* SPACE embate *m*; ~ **car** *n* RAIL coche restaurante *m*, vagón restaurante *m*

buffeting *n* AIR TRANSP vibración *f*, SPACE bataneo *m*, conmoción estructural *f*, meneo *m*, sacudida *f*, vibración estructural *f*, WATER TRANSP meneo *m*

buffing *n* PROD pulimento *m*; ~ **gear** *n* RAIL aparato de choque *m*; ~ **wheel** *n* PROD rueda bruñidora *f*, rueda pulidora *f*

bufotoxin *n* CHEM bufotoxina *f*

bug *n* AGRIC chinche *f*, insecto *m*, COMP&DP, PRINT defecto *m*

buggy *n* COAL, MINE carretilla *f*, trole *m*

build[1]: ~ **up factor** *n* NUCL factor de acumulación *m*

build[2] *vt* CONST construir, *house* edificar, PRINT *page* rellenar; ~~**up** *vt* CONST *girder* edificar

builder *n* CONST *building contractor* constructor *m*; ~'s **certificate** *n* WATER TRANSP *of ship* certificado de construcción *m*; ~'s **hardware** *n* CONST herramientas de construcción *f pl*; ~ **hardware merchant** *n* CONST vendedor de herramientas de construcción *m*; ~ **timber** *n* CONST madera para construcción *f*

building *n* MINE relleno *m*, PROD *mantle of blast furnace* construcción *f*; ~ **acoustics** *n pl* ACOUST acústica de edificios *f*; ~ **berth** *n* WATER TRANSP *shipbuilding* cama de construcción *f*; ~ **construction** *n* CONST edificación *f*, edificio *m*; ~ **line** *n* CONST límite de la construcción *m*; ~ **materials** *n pl* CONST materiales de construcción *m pl*; ~~**penetration loss** *n* TELECOM pérdidas por penetración *f pl*; ~ **ring** *n* CONST *loam-moulding* anillo para ensayos *m*; ~ **slip** *n* WATER TRANSP *shipbuilding* cama de varada *f*; ~ **stone** *n* CONST piedra para construcción *f*; ~ **trade** *n* CONST sector de la construcción *m*

built[1]: ~~**in** *adj* ELEC ENG incorporado, MECH, MECH ENG empotrado, incorporado

built[2]: ~~**in beam** *n* MECH ENG viga empotrada *f*, viga empotrada en los dos extremos *f*; ~~**in charger** *n* TRANSP cargador incorporado *m*; ~~**in exposure meter** *n* PHOTO exposímetro incorporado *m*; ~~**in filter** *n* CINEMAT filtro incorporado *m*; ~~**in function** *n* COMP&DP función incorporada *f*; ~~**in light meter** *n* CINEMAT, PHOTO fotómetro incorporado *m*; ~~**in motor** *n* ELEC ENG motor incorporado *m*; ~~**in tank** *n* MECH ENG tanque incorporado *m*; ~~**up crank** *n* MECH ENG cigüeñal ensamblado *m*, cigüeñal no enterizo *m*; ~~**up edge** *n* MECH ENG *tools* cuña de metal que queda adherida al filo de la cuchilla *f*, viruta con sobrecorte *f*; ~~**up girder** *n* CONST viga armada *f*

bulb *n* AUTO bombilla *f*, C&G bulbo *m*, CINEMAT bombilla *f*, ELEC *light* ampolleta *f*, bombilla *f*, ELEC ENG *lamp* lámpara *f*, bombilla *f*, MECH ENG *light* bola *f*, bombilla *f*, cubeta *f*; ~ **alternator** *n* ELEC alternador de ampollas *m*, alternador de bombillas *m*; ~ **edge** *n* C&G orilla del bulbo *f*; ~ **generator** *n* ELEC generador de ampollas *m*, generador de bombillas *m*; ~ **plate** *n* MECH chapa con bulbo *f*; ~~**type temperature switch** *n* PROD termistor de tipo bulbo *m*

bulbous: ~ **bow** *n* WATER TRANSP *boat building* proa de bulbo *f*

bulge¹ *n* CONST comba *f*, curva *f*, pandeo *m*, *of wall* engrosamiento *m*, MECH ENG bombeo *m*, comba *f*, pandeo *m*

bulge² *vt* CONST pandear

bulge³ *vi* CONST combarse, abombarse, MECH ENG combar, hacer comba, pandear

bulged: ~ **finish** *n* C&G angina *f*; ~ **wall** *n* CONST muro con comba *m*, pared con comba *f*

bulging *n* CONST combadura *f*; ~ **wall** *n* CONST muro con comba *m*, pared con comba *f*

bulk¹: **in** ~ *adv* COAL al por mayor, en masa, globalmente

bulk² *n* COMP&DP, CONST, MECH volumen *m*, tamaño *m*, PACK tamaño *m*, PAPER índice de volumen *m*, volumen específico *m*, *binding* grueso del libro sin tapas *m*, *of ink, paper* cuerpo *m*, *of paper* volumen de hoja *m*, PHOTO tamaño *m*, PHYS grosor *m*, volumen *m*, masa *f*, PRINT índice de volumen *m*, TEXTIL masa *f*, WATER TRANSP *cargo* cargamento a granel *m*; ~ **acoustic-wave** *n* (*BAW*) ELEC ENG onda acústica volumétrica *f*; ~ **carrier** *n* CONST transportador de graneles *m*, WATER TRANSP granelero *m*; ~ **cement** *n* CONST cemento a granel *m*; ~ **channel** *n* ELECTRON *cosmology* canal colectivo *m*; ~ **container with gravity discharge** *n* TRANSP contenedor de descarga por gravedad *m*; ~ **container with pressure discharge** *n* TRANSP contenedor con descarga por presión *m*; ~ **density** *n* C&G, COAL, P&R, PETR TECH densidad aparente *f*, densidad en masa *f*, densidad por unidad de volumen *f*, densidad total *f*, densidad volumétrica aparente *f*; ~ **deposition** *n* POLL almacenaje a granel *m*; ~ **diffusion** *n* METALL difusión conjunta *f*, difusión de volumen *f*; ~ **eraser** *n* TV borrador volumétrico *m*; ~ **fiber** *AmE*, ~ **fibre** *BrE* *n* PAPER materia fibrosa *f*, pasta *f*; ~ **film** *n* PHOTO película a granel *f* (*AmL*), película en lata *f*, película en rollo *f* (*Esp*); ~ **film loader** *n* PHOTO cargador de película a granel *m* (*AmL*), cargador de película en rollo *m* (*Esp*); ~ **flotation** *n* COAL flotación colectiva *f*, flotación simultánea *f*; ~ **freezing** *n* REFRIG congelación a granel *f*; ~ **goods** *n pl* PACK mercancía a granel *f*; ~ **index** *n* PAPER, PRINT índice de volumen *m*; ~ **lifetime** *n* ELECTRON *communications* duración de memoria *f*; ~ **material** *n* COAL material bruto *m*; ~ **memory** *n* COMP&DP memoria de gran capacidad *f*; ~ **modulus** *n* PETROL módulo de volumen *m*, PHYS módulo de elasticidad cúbica *m*, módulo volumétrico *m*; ~ **modulus of elasticity** *n* MECH ENG módulo de elasticidad volumétrico *m*; ~~**oil circuit-breaker** *n* ELEC disyuntor de baño de aceite *m*; ~ **properties** *n pl* ELECTRON características del volumen de información *f pl*; ~ **property** *n* METALL capacidad *f*; ~ **resistivity** *n* ELEC ENG resistencia volumétrica *f*; ~ **semiconductor** *n* ELECTRON semiconductor de

memoria *m*; ~~**ship train** *n* TRANSP convoy de buques graneleros *m*; ~~**solids handling technology** *n* MECH ENG tecnología de manipulación de sólidos voluminosos *f*; ~ **of steam** *n* HYDRAUL volumen de vapor *m*; ~ **transport** *n* PACK, TRANSP transporte de mercancías a granel *m*; ~ **volume** *n* PETROL volumen de capacidad *m*; ~ **wafer** *n* ELECTRON pastilla de memoria *f*; ~~**wave oscillator** *n* ELECTRON oscilador de onda de medición de volumen *m*; ~~**wave resonator** *n* ELECTRON resonador de onda de medición de volumen *m*

bulk³ *vt* WATER agrupar, reunir

bulkhead *n* MECH pieza de obturación *f*, tabique divisorio *m*, MECH ENG caída bruta *f*, mampara *f*, muro de contención *m*, SPACE *spacecraft* mampara *f*, muro de muelle *m*, tabique divisorio *m*, WATER TRANSP *ship, boat building* mamparo *m*; ~ **coupling** *n* MECH ENG *pipe fitting* acoplamiento de mamparo *m*; ~ **plan** *n* WATER TRANSP *ship design* plano constructivo de mamparas *m*; ~ **plate** *n* WATER TRANSP *shipbuilding* plancha para mamparas *f*; ~ **stiffener** *n* WATER TRANSP *shipbuilding* refuerzo de mampara *m*

bulking *n* CONST abultamiento *m*, *expansion of earth when excavated* esponjamiento *m*, RECYCL *of sludge* amontonamiento *m*, acumulación *f*, WATER abultamiento *m*; ~ **index** *n* PAPER, PRINT cuerpo del papel, índice de volumen *m*; ~ **paper** *n* PAPER papel pluma *m*; ~ **thickness** *n* PAPER espesor medio de una hoja *m*

bulky: ~ **group** *n* CHEM grupo voluminoso *m*; ~ **waste** *n* POLL desperdicio voluminoso *m*, RECYCL basura voluminosa *f*, desperdicio voluminoso *m*

bull *n* PROD *of foundry ladle* brazo largo *m*; ~ **block** *n* MECH ENG cabezal estirador *m*, pasteca grande *f*; ~ **for service** *n* AGRIC toro reproductor *m*; ~ **handle** *n* PROD *foundry* asa de cazo mayor *f*; ~ **ladle** *n* MECH ENG cazo con dos brazos largos *m*, cazo mayor *m*, PROD *founding* cazo mayor con brazos *m*; ~ **pump** *n* MINE bomba de vapor de acción simple *f*

bullbar *n* AUTO parachoques delantero *m*

bulldog: ~~**casing spear** *n* MINE arpón pescatubos *m*

bulldozer *n* AUTO, CONST bulldozer *m*, explanadora *f*, MINE empujadora niveladora *f* (*AmL*), locomotora para movimientos de vagones *f*, motoniveladora *f* (*Esp*)

bulldozing *n* CONST movimiento de tierras con bulldozer *m*

bullet *n* PRINT línea de puntos *f*, punto negro de adorno *m*

bulletin: ~ **board** *n* COMP&DP boletín electrónico *m*, tablero de anuncios *m*

bulletproof: ~ **jacket** *n* MILIT chaleco a prueba de balas *m*, chaleco antibalas *m*; ~ **vest** *n* MILIT chaleco antibalas *m*

bullhead: ~ **rivet** *n* CONST remache de cabeza redonda *m*

bullheaded: ~ **rail** *n* RAIL carril de doble seta *m*; ~ **rivet** *n* CONST remache de cabeza redonda *m*

bullion *n* C&G *gold* oro bruto *m*, *silver* plata bruta *f*, METALL metales preciosos *m pl*, metálico *m*, oro bruto *m*

bulwark *n* WATER TRANSP amurada *f*; ~ **rail** *n* WATER TRANSP *shipbuilding* pasamanos *m*

bump¹: ~ **exposure** *n* PRINT exposición suplementaria *f*

bump²: ~ **up** *vt* CINEMAT entrar en cuadro por arriba

bumper n AUTO, VEH parachoques m; ~ **rod** n MECH ENG diecasting die vástago impulsor m

bumping: ~ **hammer** n MECH ENG martillo de chapista m, martillo desabollador m; ~ **screen** n PROD criba de sacudidas f; ~ **table** n PROD mesa de sacudidas f, mesa de vaivén f; ~ **tray** n PROD mesa de sacudidas f

bumpkin n WATER TRANSP pequeña botavara f, percha f

bumpless: ~ **transfer** n PROD transferencia sin sacudidas f

bunched: ~ **cable** n BrE (cf bundled cable AmE) ELEC, ELEC ENG, ELECTRON cable de conductores múltiples m, haz de cables m; ~ **conductor** n BrE (cf bundled conductor AmE) ELEC, ELEC ENG, ELECTRON haz de conductores m

buncher: ~ **resonator** n ELECTRON resonador de entrada m; ~ **space** n ELECTRON espacio de modulación m

bunching n AIR TRANSP air traffic control agrupamiento m, ELECTRON agrupación f; ~ **space** n ELECTRON espacio para cables agrupados m

bunchy n MINE yacimiento irregular m

bundle[1] n C&G atado m, haz m, OPT mazo m, PACK bulto m, empaquetado m, fardo m, paquete m, TELECOM manojo m; ~ **tier** n PRINT empaquetador m; ~**-tying machine** n PACK atadora de paquetes f; ~**-type machine** n PRINT máquina embaladora f

bundle[2] vt PAPER empaquetar

bundled: ~ **cable** n AmE (cf bunched cable BrE) ELEC, ELEC ENG, ELECTRON cable de conductores múltiples m, haz de cables m; ~ **conductor** n AmE (cf bunched conductor BrE) ELEC, ELEC ENG, ELECTRON haz de conductores m

bundling: ~ **machine** n PACK empaquetadora f; ~ **press** n PAPER prensa de empaquetar f

bung n FOOD tapón m, bitoque m, LAB tapón m, PROD techo móvil m; ~ **of saggars** n C&G pila de gacetas f

bunghole n FOOD tools agujero del bitoque m, agujero del tapón m

bunging: ~**-up** n PROD high furnace atascamiento m

bunk n WATER TRANSP litera f

bunker[1] n COAL carbonera f, pañol del carbón m, CONST depósito m, MAR POLL combustible líquido m, MINE banco m, carbonera f, combustible m, WATER TRANSP tanque de combustible m; ~ **C** n AIR TRANSP, MAR POLL búnker C m; ~ **car** n MINE vagoneta para combustible f; ~ **coal** n COAL carbón de carboneras m; ~ **conveyor** n MINE transportador de combustible m; ~ **fuel** n MAR POLL combustible líquido m; ~ **oil** n TRANSP combustible para buques m; ~ **system** n MINE instalación para el suministro de combustible f; ~ **tank** n POLL depósito de carbones m, depósito de petróleo m, tanque petrolero m; ~ **vibrator** n MINE vibrador de combustible m

bunker[2] vi WATER TRANSP tomar

bunkering n WATER TRANSP toma de combustible f

Bunsen: ~ **burner** n LAB mechero Bunsen m; ~ **cell** n ELEC pila de Bunsen f

bunsenine n MINERAL bunsenina f

bunsenite n MINERAL bunsenita f

buoy[1] n PETROL boya f, WATER TRANSP navigation marks baliza f, boya f; ~ **rope** n WATER TRANSP for anchor orinque m; ~ **tender** n WATER TRANSP balizador m, buque balizador m

buoy[2] vt WATER TRANSP navigation marks balizar

buoyancy n AIR TRANSP, FLUID, HYDRAUL, HYDROL, PHYS, WATER TRANSP flotabilidad f; ~ **adjustment** n OCEAN ajuste de lastre m; ~ **compensator** n OCEAN chaleco ascensional m; ~ **curve** n WATER TRANSP ship design curva de empujes f; ~ **force** n FLUID fuerza de empuje f; ~ **tank** n WATER TRANSP ship, floating booms tanque de flotabilidad m

buoyant adj WATER TRANSP boyante

buoyline n WATER TRANSP orinque m

buratite n MINERAL buratita f

burette n CHEM, LAB bureta f, pipeta f; ~ **stand** n LAB soporte de bureta m, soporte de pipeta m

burgee n C&G gallardete m

Burgers: ~ **circuit** n METALL circuito Burgers m; ~ **vector** n CRYSTALL vector de Burgers m

burglar[1]: ~**-proof** adj SAFE a prueba de robos

burglar[2]: ~ **alarm** n SAFE alarma antirrobo f, alarma contra ladrones f

burglary n SAFE robo m

burgundy: ~ **bottle** n C&G botella de Borgoña f

burial n GEOL, PETR TECH enterramiento m; ~ **metamorphism** n GEOL metamorfismo estático m

buried[1] adj ELECTRON subterráneo

buried[2]: ~ **channel CCD** n (buried channel charge-coupled device) ELECTRON aparato de acoplamiento cargado m, canal subterráneo AAC m; ~ **channel charge-coupled device** n (buried channel CCD) ELECTRON aparato acoplado de carga m, canal subterráneo AAC m; ~ **loop** n TRANSP circuito enterrado m, derivación subterránea f, nudo de comunicaciones bajo tierra m, raqueta subterránea f; ~ **pipeline** n GAS tubería enterrada f; ~ **topography** n GEOL topografía subterránea f

burk: ~**-oil circuit breaker** n ELEC interruptor en baño de aceite m

burlap: ~ **finish** n PAPER acabado arpillera m

burn[1] n CINEMAT quemado m, SAFE injury quemadura f, TV persistencia de la imagen f (AmL), remanencia de la imagen f (Esp); ~ **cut** n MINE cuele canadiense m; ~**-in** n PROD, SPACE testing envejecimiento m; ~ **mark** n C&G mancha rojiza por pulido f; ~ **pit** n PETROL pozo de quemado m; ~ **time** n MILIT tiempo de combustión m; ~**-up** n NUCL quemado m; ~**-up fraction** n NUCL grado de quemado m

burn[2] vt AGRIC artigar, PROD encender, THERMO abrasar, calcinar, encender, incendiar, quemar; ~ **in** vt CINEMAT encender, TV bruñir; ~ **off** vt C&G despintar con soplete, THERMO despintar con soplete, eliminar quemando

burn[3] vi THERMO arder, quemarse

burnable: ~ **poison** n NUCL veneno consumible m

burned[1] adj THERMO slates que se adhiere fuertemente al carbón

burned[2]: ~ **brick** n CONST ladrillo quemado m; ~ **sand** n PROD founding arena gris f

burner n GAS, HEAT ENG, LAB, TELECOM, THERMO quemador m; ~ **block** n C&G bloque refractario del quemador m; ~ **brick** n HEAT ladrillo del quemador m; ~ **can** n SPACE cámara de combustión f

burning n C&G cocción f, PROD soldadura con soplete f, soldadura por fusión líquida f, baking calcinación f, THERMO ardor m, quemadura f; ~ **agent** n MAR POLL comburente m; ~**-coal** n COAL brasa f; ~**-heat** n THERMO calor de combustión m; ~**-house** n PROD kiln horno de calcinar m; ~**-in** n PRINT termoendurecido m; ~**-mirror** n INSTR espejo ustorio m; ~**-off and edge-melting machine** n C&G cortadora de oxígeno f, máquina de oxicorte y refundición f; ~ **reflector** n

INSTR espejo ustorio *m*; ~ **surface-to-throat area ratio** *n* SPACE cociente zona de combustión superficie-garganta *m*

burnish[1] *n* C&G pulido *m*

burnish[2] *vt* C&G, PRINT bruñir

burnisher *n* C&G bruñidora *f*, pulidora *f*

burnishing *n* C&G, MECH, PRINT bruñido *m*, pulido *m*, satinado *m*; ~ **gold** *n* C&G oro para bruñir *m*; ~ **silver** *n* C&G plata para bruñir *f*

burnout *n* NUCL abrasamiento *m*, SPACE fundido de cojinetes *m*, sobrecarga destructiva *f*, *craft* abrasamiento *m*, avería por calor excesivo *f*, fallo *m*, *jet engine* extinción *f*, *electric appliances* quemado *m*, THERMO *jet engine* extinción de la llama *f*; ~ **velocity** *n* SPACE velocidad al extinguirse el motor *f*

burnt[1] *adj* THERMO calcinado

burnt[2]: ~ **clay** *n* C&G barro cocido *m*; ~ **contact** *n* VEH contacto quemado *m*; ~ **earthenware** *n* C&G loza cocida *f*; ~ **mold** *AmE*, ~ **mould** *BrE n* C&G molde quemado *m*; ~**-sugar coloring** *AmE*, ~**-sugar colouring** *BrE n* COLOUR colorante de azúcar quemada *m*; ~ **valve** *n* VEH válvula quemada *f*

burr *n* MECH *casting* rebaba *f*, virola *f*, *tool* buril *m*, MECH ENG *casting* virola *f*, buril *m*, rebaba *f*, PAPER moleta de repicar *f*, PROD *on piece of metal* rebaba *f*, protuberancia *f*

burring: ~ **reamer** *n* MECH ENG *burr remover* escariador desbarbador *m*, escariador quitarrebabas *m*

Burrus: ~ **diode** *n* OPT, TELECOM diodo de Burrus *m*

burst[1] *n* COMP&DP *of errors* ráfaga *f*, MILIT *of firing* descarga *f*, ráfaga *f*, andanada *f*, RAD PHYS ionización instantánea *f*, SPACE ráfaga *f*, irrupción *f*, incremento súbito *m*, aumento instantáneo *m*, ionización instantánea *f*, impulso de sincronización *m*, TELECOM, TEXTIL estallido *m*, TV ráfaga *f*, señal de sincronismo de color *f*; ~ **amplifier** *n* ELECTRON amplificador de la señal de sincronismo de color *m*, amplificador de ráfagas *m*, amplificador estellante *m*, TV amplificador de la señal de sincronismo de color *m*, amplificador estellante *m*; ~ **can** *n* NUCL vaina reventada *f*; ~**-error correcting-capability** *n* TELECOM capacidad para corregir errores impulsivos *f*; ~ **factor** *n* PAPER factor de estallido *m*; ~ **gate** *n* TV compuerta de sincronización cromática *f*; ~ **index** *n* PAPER índice de estallido *m*; ~**-locked oscillator** *n* ELECTRON, TV oscilador de sincronización cromática *m*; ~ **mode** *n* COMP&DP modo de ráfaga *m*, separador de páginas *m*; ~ **phase** *n* TV fase de sincronización cromática *f*; ~ **separator** *n* TV separador de sincronización cromática *m*; ~ **tester** *n* PAPER medidor de estallido *m*; ~ **word** *n* SPACE *communications* aumento brusco del nivel de voz *m*

burst[2] *vt* CONST estallar, romper, *pipes* reventar

burst[3] *vi* COMP&DP reventar, MECH estallar, explotar, hacer explosión, MECH ENG reventar; ~ **its banks** *vi* HYDROL *of river* desbordarse bruscamente, salir de madre, salirse del cauce

bursting *n* CONST explosión *f*, rotura *f*; ~ **disc** *BrE*, ~ **disk** *n* *AmE* MECH cápsula de seguridad *f*, diafragma protector *m*; ~**-off** *n* C&G rotura por presión *f*; ~ **pressure** *n* C&G, PACK, PAPER presión de estallido *f*, presión de rotura por estallido *f*, presión de ruptura *f*; ~ **shot** *n* MINE barreno de franqueo *m* (*AmL*), barreno de calado *m* (*Esp*); ~ **strength** *n* P&R resistencia a compresión a la rotura *f*, PACK, PAPER, TEXTIL resistencia al estallido *f*

bury: ~ **barge** *n* PETR TECH barcaza de tendido submarino *f*, gabarra para conducción submarina *f*, PETROL barcaza de tendido submarino *f*

bus *n* COMP&DP barra distribuidora *f*, bus *m*, carretera *f*, conductor común *m*, enlace de comunicaciones *m*, ELEC, ELEC ENG, MECH ENG, SPACE, TELECOM, TV barra colectora *f*; ~ **arbitrator** *n* TELECOM controlador del bus *m*; ~ **bay** *n* AUTO plataforma de autobús *f*; ~ **choke** *n* PROD bobina colectora *f*; ~ **configuration** *n* TELECOM configuración del sistema bus *f*; ~**-discharge board** *n* PROD tablero de descarga de la barra colectora *m*; ~ **duct plug-in unit** *n* ELEC *connection* sistema de conexión de conductos eléctricos *m*, unidad enchufable del conducto portacable de la barra colectora *f*; ~ **interface** *n* COMP&DP interfase de base común *f* (*AmL*), interfase de conductor común *f*, interfaz de bus *m*; ~**-lane equipped with guiding device** *n* TRANSP carril bus equipado con dispositivo-guía *m*, carril de autobús equipado con dispositivo de guiado *m*; ~ **line** *n* ELEC línea colectiva *f*; ~**-mouse adaptor** *n* COMP&DP adaptador bus-ratón *m*, adaptador de bus del ratón *m*, adaptador de conductor común *m*, barra de conductor común *f*; ~ **network** *n* COMP&DP red de conductores comunes *f*, red en bus *f*, terminación de conductores comunes *f* (*AmL*), terminador de bus *m*; ~ **on railroad car** *n* *AmE* (*cf bus on railway wagon BrE*) TRANSP autobús montado sobre vagón de ferrocarril *m* (*Esp*), bus montado en vagón de ferrocarril *m* (*AmL*), ómnibus *m* (*AmL*); ~ **on railroad tracks** *n* *AmE* TRANSP autobús sobre la vía de ferrocarril *m* (*Esp*), bus sobre la vía de ferrocarril *m* (*AmL*), ómnibus *m* (*AmL*); ~ **on railway tracks** *BrE n* (*cf bus on railroad tracks AmE*) TRANSP autobús sobre la vía de ferrocarril *m* (*Esp*), bus sobre la vía de ferrocarril *m* (*AmL*), ómnibus *m* (*AmL*); ~ **on railway wagon** *n* *BrE* (*cf bus on railroad car AmE*) TRANSP autobús montado sobre vagón de ferrocarril *m* (*Esp*), bus montado en vagón de ferrocarril *m* (*AmL*), ómnibus *m* (*AmL*); ~ **shelter** *n* TRANSP cochera *f*; ~ **topology** *n* COMP&DP topología de bus *f*, topología de conductores comunes *f* (*AmL*)

busbar *n* ELEC *connection* barra colectora *f*, barra conductora *f*, barra de distribución *f*, barra ómnibus *f*, ELEC ENG barra colectora *f*, barra conductora *f*, barra ómnibus *f*, barra de distribución *f*, MECH ENG barra ómnibus *f*, barra colectora *f*, barra conductora *f*, barra de distribución *f*, SPACE barra colectora *f*, TELECOM barra colectora *f*, barra conductora *f*, barra de distribución *f*, barra ómnibus *f*, TV barra colectora *f*; ~ **coupler** *n* ELEC *switch* acoplador de barra colectora *m*, unión de barra colectora *f*; ~**-sectionalizing switch** *n* ELEC seccionador de barra colectora *m*; ~ **system** *n* ELEC *connection* sistema de barra colectora *m*

bush *n* MECH ENG, VEH casquillo *m*, cojinete *m*, manguito *m*; ~ **fallow** *n* AGRIC barbecho en maleza *m*

bushel *n* METR bushel *m*

bushing *n* C&G casquillo *m*, orificio refractario *m*, MECH, MECH ENG boquilla *f*, casquillo *m*, codo doble *m*, cojinete de polea *m*, manguito *m*, reductor roscado *m*; ~ **assembly** *n* C&G portaorificio *m*

business: ~ **communication system** *n* TELECOM sistema de comunicaciones comerciales *m*; ~ **form** *n* PRINT *highway* impreso comercial *m*; ~ **forms** *n pl* PAPER formularios continuos comerciales *m pl*;

~-forms printing n PRINT impresión de formularios f;
~ graphics n COMP&DP, PRINT gráficos comerciales m
pl; **~ system** n TELECOM sistema comercial m;
~ traffic n TRANSP tráfico comercial m
bustamite n MINERAL bustamita f
buster: ~ shot n MINE barreno de alcance m
busting: ~ shot n MINE barreno de franqueo m (AmL),
barreno de calado m (Esp)
bustle: ~ pipe n PROD of blast furnace busa f
bustline n TEXTIL contorno de busto m; **~ ruffle** n
TEXTIL volante en el contorno de busto m
busway: ~ for rapid transit n TRANSP carril bus de
tránsito rápido m, carril de tránsito rápido para
autobús m, vía rápida de autobús f, vía rápida de bus
f
busy: ~ hour n TELECOM hora de carga f; **~ number** n
TELECOM número ocupado m; **~ period** n TELECOM
período cargado m; **~ signal** n COMP&DP señal de
ocupado f; **~ state** n TELECOM estado de ocupación
m; **~ status** n TELECOM estado de ocupación m
butadiene n CHEM, PETR TECH butadieno m; **~ acrylonitrile rubber** n P&R caucho de butadieno-
acrilonitrilo m; **~ rubber** n P&R caucho de butadieno
m; **~ styrene copolymer** n PETR TECH copolímero
butadieso-estireno m
butane n CHEM, PETR TECH butano m; **~ carrier** n PETR
TECH buque para transporte de butano líquido m,
ship barco butanero m, buque butanero m, butanero
m, vehicle camión butanero m, vagón butanero m,
TRANSP ship butanero m, barco butanero m, buque
butanero m, vehicle vagón butanero m, camión
butanero m, WATER TRANSP buque para transporte
de butano líquido m; **~ tanker** n PETR TECH vehicle
camión cisterna de butano m, ship buque para
transporte de butano líquido m, buque petrolero de
butano m, buque butanero m, buque cisterna de
butano m, TRANSP ship buque petrolero de butano m,
buque butanero m, camión cisterna de butano m,
buque cisterna de butano m, WATER TRANSP buque
cisterna de butano m, buque petrolero de butano m,
buque para transporte de butano líquido m, buque
cisterna m
butanol n CHEM alcohol butílico m, butanol m, DETERG
alcohol butílico m
butanone n P&R butanona f
butenal n CHEM butenal m, crotonaldehído m
butene n CHEM, DETERG buteno m
butt[1] n CONST tope m, carpentry bisagra f, MECH ENG of
connecting rod cabeza f, MILIT culata f, WATER TRANSP
shipbuilding junta a tope f; **~-and-strap hinge** n
CONST bisagra cubrejuntas f; **~ cock** n CONST canilla
de base f (AmL), grifo de base m; **~ contact** n ELEC of
relay contacto a tope m; **~ coupling** n MECH ENG
acoplamiento de manguito m; **~ end** n CONST
carpentry tope m; **~-end splicer** n CINEMAT empalmadora a tope f; **~ hinge** n CONST bisagra de tope f;
~ joint n CONST square-joint junta a tope f, plumbing
cubrejunta f, MECH ENG nudo de unión m, junta a
tope f, junta a tope con cubrejunta f, junta plana f,
PROD riveting junta a tope con cubrejunta f, welding
junta a tope f, junta plana f; **~ plate** n MECH
cubrejunta f; **~ riveting** n PROD remachado de juntas
transversales m; **~ seal** n PROD costura transversal f;
~-seam welding n PROD soldadura de costuras
transversales f; **~ strap** n PROD cubrejunta f;
~-strap joint n PROD unión del cubrejunta f; **~ strip**

n PROD cubrejunta f, eclisa f; **~ weld** n CONST, MECH,
MECH ENG, PROD soldadura a tope f; **~ welding** n
CONST, MECH, MECH ENG, PROD soldadura a tope f,
soldadura por aproximación f; **~-welding machine** n
PROD máquina para soldadura a tope f
butt[2]: **~-joint** vt CONST unir a tope
butter: ~ coloring AmE, **~ colouring** BrE n COLOUR
colorante de cloruro m; **~ oil** n FOOD aceite de
mantequilla m
butterfly n AUTO estrangulador m, mariposa f;
~ damper n HEAT ENG amortiguador de mariposa
m; **~-damper** n REFRIG registro de mariposa m; **~ nut**
n CONST tuerca de mariposa f; **~ screw** n CONST,
MECH ENG tornillo de mariposa m, tornillo de
orejetas m; **~ throttle valve** n HYDRAUL válvula de
mariposa f; **~ valve** n FUELLESS dams, HYDRAUL,
MECH ENG fast closing válvula de mariposa f
Butterworth: ~ filter n ELECTRON, PHYS filtro Butterworth m
butting n CONST carpentry colocación a tope f
buttock: ~ lines n pl WATER TRANSP ship design perfil
longitudinal f pl, sección longitudinal f
buttocks n pl WATER TRANSP shipbuilding anca f,
cucharros de popa m pl
button[1] n GEN botón m; **~-fastener** n PROD for
machine-belts fijador de botones m; **~-head bolt** n
CONST, MECH ENG perno de cabeza semiesférica m;
~-head rivet n CONST, PROD remache de cabeza
esférica m
button[2] vt TEXTIL abrochar
buttress n CONST of wall or bridge contrafuerte m;
~ dam n CONST, HYDROL presa de contrafuertes f;
~ screw thread n MECH ENG asymmetrical thread
rosca de perfil trapezoidal f; **~ thread** n CONST screws
rosca en forma de trapecio f
buttressing n CONST apuntalamiento m, colocación de
un contrafuerte f, sostenimiento m
butyl: ~ acetate n CHEM, P&R acetato de butilo m;
~ alcohol n DETERG alcohol butílico m; **~ ether** n
FOOD éter butílico m; **~ phthalate** n P&R ftalato de
butilo m; **~ rubber** n P&R caucho butílico m
butylated: ~ hydroxyanisole n (BHA) FOOD butilhidroxianisol m (BHA); **~ hydroxytoluene** n (BHT)
FOOD butilhidroxitolueno m (BHT)
butylene n DETERG butileno m
butyraldehyde n CHEM butiraldehído m
butyrate n CHEM butirato m
butyric: ~ acid n AGRIC, CHEM, FOOD ácido butírico m
butyrin n CHEM butirina f
butyrite n COAL butirita f
buy: ~-back price n PETR TECH precio de readquisición
m, precio de recompra m
buzzer n ELEC ENG, TELECOM zumbador m
BVU abbr (broadcast video Umatic) TV emisión por
video Umatic f (AmL), emisión por vídeo Umatic f
(Esp)
B-weighting: ~ curve n ACOUST curva de ponderación
B f
B-wind n CINEMAT, TV bobinado B m (AmL), rebobinado B m (Esp)
BWO abbr (backward-wave oscillator) TELECOM oscilador de onda regresiva m
BWR abbr (boiling-water reactor) NUCL, PHYS reactor
de agua en ebullición m
B-Y: ~ axis n TV vehicles eje B-Y m; **~ signal** n TV
vehicles señal B-Y f

bypass[1] *adj* PHYS derivado, desviado

bypass[2] *n* COAL, CONST derivación *f*, desviación *f*, desvío *m*, ELEC *circuit* derivación *f*, desviación *f*, desvío *m* (*Esp*), interruptor *m*, GAS desviación *f*, desvío *m*, derivación *f*, HYDRAUL desvío *m*, desviación *f*, derivación *f*, MECH ENG desviación *f*, derivación *f*, desvío *m*, PETR TECH desvío *m*, desviación *f*, derivación *f*, PROD desviación *f*, derivación *f*, desvío *m*, TRANSP derivación *f*, desviación *f*, desvío *m*; ~ **anode** *n* ELEC ENG ánodo de derivación *m*; ~ **bore** *n* AUTO agujero de desviación *m*, taladro de desvío *m*; ~ **capacitor** *n* PHYS capacitor de paso *m*; ~ **engine** *n* AIR TRANSP, TRANSP motor de derivación *m*, motor de desviación *m*; ~ **line** *n* TRANSP línea de desvío *f*, vía de desviación *f*, vía de desvío *f*; ~-**oil cleaner** *n* AUTO filtro de aceite en derivación *m*; ~ **ratio** *n* AIR TRANSP proporción de desvío *f*; ~ **road** *n* TRANSP carretera de desvío *f*, desvío provisional *m*; ~ **switch** *n* ELEC interruptor de sobrepaso *m*, interruptor derivante *m*; ~ **valve** *n* LAB válvula de derivación *f*

bypassable: ~ **traffic** *n* TRANSP tráfico desviable *m*

bypassing *n* PETROL derivación *f*, desvío *m*

by-product *n* CHEM *of reaction* derivado *m*, producto secundario *m*, subproducto *m*, CHEM TECH subproducto *m*, COAL subproducto *m*, derivado *m*, producto secundario *m*, MECH ENG, PETR TECH derivado *m*, producto secundario *m*, subproducto *m*, POLL subproducto *m*, derivado *m*, producto secundario *m*, PROD producto secundario *m*, derivado *m*, subproducto *m*; ~ **gas** *n* GAS subproducto gaseoso *m*

byroad *n* CONST, TRANSP atajo *m*, camino secundario *m*

byssolite *n* MINERAL bisolita *f*

byte *n* COMP&DP, PROD, TELECOM byte *m*, octeto *m*; ~ **designation** *n* COMP&DP, PROD, TELECOM designación de byte *f*; ~ **machine** *n* COMP&DP, PROD, TELECOM máquina de byte *f*; ~ **switch** *n* TELECOM conmutador de bytes *m*, conmutador de octetos *m*

bytownite *n* MINERAL bitownita *f*

byway *n* CONST camino secundario *m*, sendero *m*, TRANSP camino secundario *m*

C

c *abbr* (*centi-*) METR c (*centi-*)

C *abbr* CHEM (*carbon, Celsius*) C (*carbono, Celsio*), ELEC, ELEC ENG, ELECTRON (*coulomb*) C (*culombio*), MECH, METEO (*Celsius*) C (*Celsius*), METR (*Celsius, coulomb*) C (*Celsio, culombio*), PHYS (*Celsius, coulomb*) C (*Celsio, culombio*), PETR TECH (*carbon*) C (*carbono*)

C: ~ **operation** *n* PART PHYS operación de la carga *f*; ~ **wrench** *n* MECH ENG llave de maquinista *f*

Ca *abbr* (*calcium*) CHEM, FOOD, METALL Ca (*calcio*)

CA: ~ **packaging** *n* PACK embalaje caducado *m*

cab *n* CONST *of crane* cabina *f*, TRANSP coche de alquiler *m*, taxi *m*, *of locomotive* garita *f*, *of locomotive, motor van* cabina *f*, VEH *of locomotive, motor van* cabina *f*; **~-and-pillar distribution service** *n* TELECOM servicio de distribución principal *m*; **~-over-engine** *n* VEH cabina sobre el motor *f*; ~ **signal** *n* RAIL señal de la cabina *f*; ~ **signaling** *AmE*, ~ **signalling** *BrE* *n* TRANSP señalización de cabina *f*, señalización de garita guarda-vías *f*, señalización de guardabarrera *f*, señalización para taxis *f*

cabal: ~ **glass** *n* C&G vidrio cabal *m*

cabin *n* AIR TRANSP cabina *f*, CONST *of crane* cabina *f*, casa *f*, caseta *f* (*Esp*), cabina cósmica *f*, cámara *f* (*AmL*), RAIL, SPACE cabina *f*, WATER TRANSP *accommodation* camarote *m*, cámara *f*; ~ **altimeter** *n* AIR TRANSP altímetro de cabina *m*; ~ **altitude** *n* AIR TRANSP altitud de cabina *f*; ~ **attendant** *n* AIR TRANSP, TRANSP asistente de cabina *m*, ayudante de cabina *m*; ~ **baggage** *n* AIR TRANSP, TRANSP equipaje de cabina *m*; ~ **class** *n* TRANSP clase preferente *f*; ~ **conveyor** *n* TRANSP portacabinas *m*; ~ **crew** *n* AIR TRANSP, TRANSP tripulación de cabina *f*; ~ **cruiser** *n* WATER TRANSP motocrucero con cámara *m*; ~ **differential pressure** *n* AIR TRANSP presión diferencial de cabina *f*; ~ **differential pressure gage** *AmE*, ~ **differential pressure gauge** *BrE* *n* AIR TRANSP indicador de presión diferencial de cabina *m*, manómetro diferencial de cabina *m*; ~ **floor** *n* AIR TRANSP suelo de la cabina *m*; ~ **headroom** *n* WATER TRANSP *yacht* altura de paso *f*; ~ **layout** *n* AIR TRANSP distribución interior de la cabina *f*, esquema de distribución de la cabina *m*; ~ **pressure** *n* AIR TRANSP, SPACE presión de la cabina *f*; ~ **pressurization** *n* AIR TRANSP presionización de la cabina *f*, presurización de la cabina *f*, SPACE presionización de la cabina *f*; ~ **pulley cradle** *n* TRANSP base de la polea de la cabina *f*; ~ **services** *n pl* AIR TRANSP, TRANSP servicios de cabina *m pl*; ~ **sole** *n* WATER TRANSP *ship building* plan de la cámara *m*; ~ **sole reinforcement** *n* WATER TRANSP *ship building* refuerzo del plan de la cámara *m*; ~ **system on rail** *n* TRANSP sistema de cabina sobre rieles *m*; ~ **telephone** *n* AIR TRANSP teléfono de cabina *m*; ~ **temperature** *n* AIR TRANSP temperatura de la cabina *f*; ~ **temperature indicator** *n* AIR TRANSP indicador de la temperatura de la cabina *m*, termómetro de cabina *m*; **~-type moving pavement** *n* *BrE*

(*cf cabin-type moving sidewalk AmE*) TRANSP acera móvil capotada *f* (*Esp*), adoquinado móvil cubierto *m* (*Esp*), adoquinado rodante cubierto *m* (*Esp*), pavimento móvil cubierto *m* (*AmL*), pavimento rodante cubierto *m* (*AmL*), vereda móvil capotada *f* (*AmL*); **~-type moving sidewalk** *n* *AmE* (*cf cabin-type moving pavement BrE*) TRANSP acera móvil capotada *f* (*Esp*), adoquinado móvil cubierto *m* (*Esp*), adoquinado rodante cubierto *m* (*Esp*), pavimento móvil cubierto *m* (*AmL*), pavimento rodante cubierto *m* (*AmL*), vereda móvil capotada *f* (*AmL*)

cabinet *n* MECH armario *m* (*Esp*), caja *f*, gabinete *m* (*AmL*), P&R armario *m* (*Esp*), cabina *f*, gabinete *m* (*AmL*), sala *f*, vitrina *f*, TELECOM armario *m*; ~ **shell** *n* REFRIG cuba exterior *f*

cabinetmaker *n* CONST ebanista *m*

cabinetmaking *n* CONST ebanistería *f*

cabinetwork *n* CONST marquetería *f*

cable[1]: **~-laid** *adj* WATER TRANSP *of rope, hawser* acalabrotado

cable[2] *n* COMP&DP cable *m*, cordón *m*, ELEC cable *m*, acción de agrupar por pares *f*, acción de casar por pares *f*, acción de formar pares *f*, ELEC ENG cable *m*, MECH acanaladura *f*, cable *m*, estría *f*, MECH ENG, P&R, PETROL cable *m*, TELECOM amarra *f*, cable *m*, VEH, WATER TRANSP *communications* cable *m*; ~ **angle indicator** *n* WATER TRANSP indicador de ángulo del cable *m*; ~ **assembly** *n* OPT, TELECOM conjunto de cables *m*, montaje de cables *m*; ~ **box** *n* ELEC *connection*, ELEC ENG caja de empalme de cables *f*, registro de conexiones *m*; ~ **bundle** *n* ELEC, ELEC ENG, ELECTRON haz de cables *m*; ~ **chain** *n* MINE cable de alambres *m*, cadena de ancla *f*, WATER TRANSP cadena *f*; ~ **clamp** *n* ELEC, ELEC ENG abrazadera de cables *f*, MECH grampa para cable *f* (*AmL*), grapa para cable *f* (*Esp*), mordaza de cable *f*; ~ **clinch** *n* WATER TRANSP entalingadura *f*, malla *f*; ~ **clip** *n* ELEC, ELEC ENG collar para cable *m*, grapa de cable *f*, sujetacable *m*, VEH grapa de cable *f*; ~ **communications** *n pl* TELECOM comunicaciones por cable *f f pl*; ~ **compensation circuit** *n* TV circuito compensador de cable *m*; ~ **conduit** *n* ELEC, ELEC ENG manguito de cable *m*; ~ **connector** *n* ELEC conexión de cable *f*, ELEC ENG empalmador de cable *m*; ~ **conveyor** *n* PAPER transportador de cable *m*; ~ **core** *n* ELEC, ELEC ENG alma del cable *f*, P&R alma del cable *f*, eje del cable *m*, núcleo del cable *m*; ~ **coupling** *n* ELEC, ELEC ENG acoplamiento de cables *m*, unión de cables *f*, TELECOM unión de cables *f*; ~ **covering** *n* *AmE* ELEC, ELEC ENG, P&R cubierta del cable *f*, forro del cable *m*, revestimiento del cable *m*; ~ **defects** *n pl* ELEC, ELEC ENG defectos en el cable *m pl*, falla en el cable *f*; ~ **detector** *n* ELEC, ELEC ENG, INSTR detector de cable *m*; ~ **distribution point** *n* ELEC, ELEC ENG punto de distribución de cables *m*, sitio de distribución de cables *m*; ~ **distributor** *n* ELEC, ELEC ENG distribuidor de cables *m*; ~ **drilling** *n* PETR TECH, PETROL perforación por cable *f*; **~-drilling bit** *n* PETR TECH, PETROL barrena de perforación con cadena *f*; ~ **drum** *n* CONST carrete para enrollar cables *m*, ELEC bobina para arrollar cable eléctrico *f*, tambor de cable *m*, tambor para cables *m*, ELEC ENG bobina de cable *f*, OCEAN tambor *m*, PACK bobina para enrollar cables *f*; ~ **duct** *n* ELEC, ELEC ENG conducto de cable *m*; ~ **end** *n* ELEC, ELEC ENG extremidad del cable *f*, extremo del cable *m*, punta del cable *f*, MINE chicote del cable *m* (*AmL*), extremo del cable *m*, final del cable *m* (*Esp*), punta del cable *f*; ~ **fitting** *n* ELEC, ELEC ENG adaptación de cables *f*, ajuste de cable *m*, empalme de cables *m*; ~ **form** *n* ELEC, ELEC ENG forma de cables *f*; ~ **gage** *AmE*, ~ **gauge** *BrE* *n* ELEC, ELEC ENG, INSTR instrumento medidor de cable *m*, medidor de cable *m*; ~ **grease** *n* ELEC, ELEC ENG grasa de cable *f*; ~ **guide** *n* VEH guía de cable *f*; ~**-handling system** *n* ELEC, ELEC ENG sistema de manejo de cables *m*; ~ **harness** *n* ELEC ENG dispositivo del cable de elevación *m*; ~ **head** *n* ELEC, ELEC ENG cabeza del cable *f*, inicio del cable *m*; ~ **insulation** *n* ELEC, ELEC ENG aislación del cable *f*, aislamiento del cable *m*, aislante de cable *m*; ~ **insulator** *n* ELEC, ELEC ENG aislador del cable *m*; ~ **isolator** *n* ELEC, ELEC ENG aislante de cable *m*; ~ **joint** *n* ELEC *connection*, ELEC ENG, TELECOM empalme de cables *m*, junta de cables *f*, unión de cables *f*; ~ **jointer** *n* TELECOM empalmador de cables *m*; ~ **junction** *n* ELEC, ELEC ENG empalme de cableado *m*; ~ **junction box** *n* ELEC *connection*, ELEC ENG caja de empalmes para cables *f*; ~ **laying** *n* ELEC, ELEC ENG colocación de cables *f*, tendido de cables *m*; ~**-laying ship** *n* WATER TRANSP buque dedicado al tendido de cables *m*, cablero *m*; ~ **link** *n* TV conexión de cables *f*; ~ **locator** *n* ELEC, ELEC ENG, INSTR localizador de cables *m*; ~ **locker** *n* WATER TRANSP caja de cables *f*, caja de cadenas *f*; ~ **loss** *n* ELEC, ELEC ENG pérdida en el cable *f*; ~ **lug** *n* ELEC, ELEC ENG talón de cable *m*; ~ **manhole** *n* ELEC *supply*, ELEC ENG galería de cables *f*, registro de cables *m*; ~ **network** *n* ELEC, ELEC ENG cableado *m*, red de cables *f*; ~ **pair** *n* COMP&DP cable de un par *m*, ELEC, ELEC ENG par de cables *m*; ~ **rack** *n* ELEC, ELEC ENG bandeja para cables *f*, palomillas de cables *f pl*, portacables *m*; ~ **railway** *n* MECH ENG, RAIL, TRANSP funicular *m*, teleférico *m*, transportador por cable *m*; ~ **reel** *n* PACK bobina de cable *f*, rollo de cable *m*, PETROL carrete para cable *m*, carretel para cable *m*, devanador de cable *m*; ~ **release** *n* PHOTO disparador de cable *m*; ~ **release socket** *n* PHOTO clavija del disparador de cable *f*; ~ **repeater** *n* ELEC, ELEC ENG repetidor de cable *m*, restablecedor de cable *m*; ~ **run** *n* ELEC *supply*, ELEC ENG recorrido del cable *m*, ruta del cable *f*, tendido del cable *m*; ~ **screen** *n* ELEC *conductor*, ELEC ENG blindaje del cable *m*, pantalla eléctrica del cable *f*; ~ **section** *n* ELEC, ELEC ENG sección de cable *f*; ~ **shaft** *n* ELEC, ELEC ENG cuerpo del cable *m*; ~ **sheath** *n* ELEC, ELEC ENG, MECH ENG camisa del cable *f*, funda de cable *f*, vaina del cable *f*; ~**-sheath stripper** *n* ELEC, ELEC ENG, MECH ENG desforradora de cables *f*, máquina para desnudar cables *f*; ~ **sheathing** *n* *BrE* ELEC, ELEC ENG, P&R cubierta del cable *f*, forro del cable *m*, revestimiento del cable *m*; ~ **ship** *n* TELECOM, WATER TRANSP buque cablero *m*, cablero *m*; ~ **splicing** *n* ELEC, ELEC ENG ajuste de cable *m*, empalme de cables *m*, junta de cables *f*, TELECOM junta de cables *f*; ~**-stayed bridge** *n* CONST puente colgante *m*; ~ **storage hold** *n* TELECOM

bodega almacenamiento cables *f*; ~ **support** *n* TRANSP soporte del cable *m*, torreta *f*; ~ **suspension wire** *n* ELEC, ELEC ENG alambre de sujeción del cable *m*, alambre de suspensión del cable *m*, alambre de sustentación del cable *m*; ~ **television network** *n* TELECOM, TV red de televisión por cable *f*; ~ **television system** *n* TELECOM, TV sistema de televisión por cable *m*; ~ **tensioner** *n* ELEC, ELEC ENG tensor del cable *m*; ~ **terminal box** *n* CINEMAT caja terminal para cables *f*; ~ **termination** *n* ELEC, ELEC ENG *connection* cabeza de cable *f*, caja de corte *f*, caja terminal *f*; ~ **transmission** *n* TV transmisión por cable *f*; ~ **trench** *n* ELEC *supply*, ELEC ENG canal de cables *m*, lecho de cables *m*, surco de cables *m*; ~ **trough** *n* ELEC, ELEC ENG canalón del cable *m*, macarrón del cable *m*; ~ **weight** *n* AIR TRANSP peso del cable *m*; ~ **winch** *n* ELEC, ELEC ENG cabrestante del cable *m*, TRANSP torno de cable *m*

cablecast *n* TV transmisión por cable *f*

cabled: ~ **network** *n* TV red por cable *f*

cablegram *n* ELEC, ELEC ENG cablegrama *m*

cable's: ~ **length** *n* WATER TRANSP cumplido de cable *m*

cableway *n* MECH ENG, RAIL funicular *m*, TRANSP cable aéreo *m*, funicular *m*, funivía *f*, teleférico *m*

cabling *n* ELEC *supply* cableado *m*, cableaje *m*, tendido *m*, ELEC ENG cableado *m*, tendido *m*, cableaje *m*, TELECOM cableaje *m*, cableado *m*, tendido *m*, TV cableado *m*, cableaje *m*, tendido *m*

caboose *n* *AmE* (*cf guard's van BrE*) RAIL furgón de cola *m*, vagón freno *m*, VEH furgón de cola *m*

cabotage *n* TRANSP cabotaje *m*

cabrerite *n* MINERAL cabrerita *f*

cabriolet *n* TRANSP, VEH cabriolet *m*, cabriolé *m*

cache *n* COMP&DP *memory* caché *m*, escondrijo *m*; ~ **memory** *n* COMP&DP memoria caché *f*, memoria intermedia *f*

cacoxenite *n* MINERAL cacoxenita *f*, cacoxeno *m*

CAD *abbr* (*computer-aided design*) COMP&DP, ELEC, MECH, PRINT, PROD, TELECOM CAD (*diseño asistido por computadora AmL, diseño asistido por ordenador Esp*)

cadastral: ~ **survey** *n* CONST levantamiento catastral *m*

cadaverine *n* CHEM cadaverina *f*, pentametilendiamina *f*

cadmium[1]: ~**-plated** *adj* CHEM, MECH, METALL *unit* cadmiado

cadmium[2] *n* (*Cd*) CHEM, ELEC, ELEC ENG, METALL, MINERAL cadmio *m* (*Cd*); ~ **blende** *n* MINERAL blenda cadmífera *f*; ~ **cell** *n* ELEC pila Weston *f*; ~**-nickel cell** *n* ELEC ENG célula fotoeléctrica de cadmio-níquel *f*; ~ **ocher** *AmE*, ~ **ochre** *BrE* *n* MINERAL ocre cadmífero *m*; ~ **sulfide cell** *AmE*, ~ **sulphide cell** *BrE* *n* ELEC, ELEC ENG célula de sulfuro de cadmio *f*, fotocélula de sulfuro de cadmio *f*, pila de sulfuro de cadmio *f*

caesium *n* *BrE* (*Cs*) CHEM, ELEC ENG, ELECTRON, SPACE cesio *m* (*Cs*); ~ **beam resonator** *n* *BrE* ELECTRON resonador de haz de cesio *m*; ~ **cathode** *n* *BrE* ELEC ENG cátodo de cesio *m*; ~ **clock** *n* *BrE* SPACE *communications* reloj de cesio *m*; ~**-doped glass** *n* *BrE* SPACE cristal dopado con cesio *m*, cristal impurificado con cesio *m*; ~ **phototube** *n* *BrE* ELECTRON, INSTR fototubo de cesio *m*, tubo fotoeléctrico de cesio *m*

caffeic[1] *adj* CHEM, FOOD cafeico

caffeic^2: ~ **acid** n CHEM, FOOD ácido cafeico m
caffeine n CHEM, FOOD cafeína f
caffetannic adj CHEM, FOOD cafetánico
cage^1 n MINE cuba f (AmL), jaula f (Esp); ~ **armature** n ELEC generator, ELEC ENG inducido de jaula m; ~ **guides** n pl MINE guiaderas de la jaula de extracción f pl; ~ **relay** n ELEC ENG relé de camarín m, relé de jaula m; ~ **rotor** n ELEC ENG rotor enjaulado m; ~ **sheets** n pl MINE intercalación de vagones f; ~ **shuts** n pl MINE tacos de jaula de extracción m pl, taquetes de la jaula de minas m pl; ~ **slides** n pl MINE guías de la jaula f pl; ~ **winding system** n MINE sistema de extracción por jaulas m
cage^2 vt MINE introducir en la jaula de extracción, trucks enjaular
CAI abbr (computer-assisted instruction) COMP&DP CAI (enseñanza asistida por computadora AmL, enseñanza asistida por ordenador Esp)
caisson n CONST, HYDRAUL, HYDROL ataguía f, cajón m, camello m, WATER ataguía f, cajón m, camello m, compuerta flotante f, WATER TRANSP ataguía f, cajón m, camello m; ~ **disease** n OCEAN, WATER TRANSP enfermedad de las cámaras de sumersión f, enfermedad de los cajones f, parálisis de los buzos f; ~ **master** n OCEAN jefe de la cámara hiperbárica m; ~ **worker** n OCEAN trabajador en cajón de hinca m (AmL), trabajador en cámara hiperbárica m (Esp)
cake^1: ~-**dyed** adj TEXTIL teñido en corona
cake^2 n PROD loam moulding masa coalescida de polvo sin prensar f
cake^3 vt CHEM aglutinarse, CHEM TECH, FOOD aglutinarse, apelmazar
cake^4 vi CHEM, CHEM TECH aglutinarse
caking n CHEM, CHEM TECH aglutinación f, FOOD apelmazamiento m, P&R aglutinación f, PRINT acumulación de partículas de tinta f; ~ **coal** n COAL carbón aglutinante m
CAL abbr (computer-assisted learning) COMP&DP CAL (enseñanza auxiliada por computadora AmL, enseñanza auxiliada por ordenador Esp)
calamine n AmE (cf smithsonite BrE) COAL, MINE, MINERAL calamina f
calamite n MINERAL calamita f, tremolita f
calaverite n MINERAL calaverita f
calc^1: ~-**alkaline** adj GEOL alcalinocalcífera
calc^2: ~-**schist** n GEOL calco-esquisto m, esquisto calcáreo m; ~-**silicate hornfels** n GEOL corneana calco-lilicatada f
calcarenite n GEOL calcarenita f
calcareous^1 adj CHEM, GEOL calcáreo, calizo
calcareous^2: ~ **alga** n GEOL alga calcárea f; ~ **dolomite** n GEOL dolomita calcárea f, dolomita caliza f; ~ **ooze** n GEOL barro calcáreo m; ~ **sandstone** n GEOL arenisca calcárea f, arenisca caliza f; ~ **tufa** n GEOL toba calcárea f, toba caliza f
calcic adj CHEM, GEOL cálcico
calciferol n CHEM, GEOL calciferol m
calciferous adj CHEM, GEOL calcífero
calcify vt CHEM, GEOL calcificar
calcimine n COLOUR calcimina f
calcin n HYDRAUL tueste m
calcination n CHEM, COAL, HEAT calcinación f
calcine vt CHEM, COAL, HEAT calcinar
calcined: ~ **magnesia** n P&R magnesia calcinada f
calcining n CHEM, COAL, HEAT calcinación f, calcinado m; ~ **kiln** n C&G horno de calcinación m, COAL horno

de calcinación m, horno de tostación m, HEAT horno de calcinación m, PROD, THERMO estufa f, horno m, horno de calcinación m, horno de cuba m
calciocelestine n MINERAL calciocelestina f
calcioferrite n MINERAL calcioferrita f
calciothorite n MINERAL calciotorita f
calcite n MINERAL calcita f
calcitic: ~ **dolomite** n GEOL dolomita calcítica f
calcium n (Ca) CHEM, FOOD, METALL calcio m (Ca); ~ **carbide** n CHEM carburo cálcico m, carburo de calcio m; ~ **carbonate** n FOOD carbonato cálcico m; ~ **chloride** n CHEM, FOOD cloruro cálcico m, cloruro de calcio m; ~ **naphthenate** n P&R naftenato de calcio m; ~ **pantothenate** n CHEM, FOOD pantotenato cálcico m; ~ **petroleum sulfanates** AmE, ~ **petroleum sulphanates** BrE n pl PETR TECH sulfanatos de petróleo y calcio m pl; ~ **phosphate** n CHEM, FOOD fosfato cálcico m; ~ **silicate** n DETERG silicato de calcio m; ~ **sulfate** AmE, ~ **sulphate** BrE n CHEM, FOOD sulfato cálcico m
calcrete n GEOL calcreta f, tosca f, travertino m
calculable: ~ **capacitor** n PHYS capacitor calculable m
calculate vt COMP&DP, MATH, PHYS calcular
calculating: ~ **machine** n COMP&DP, ELECTRON, MATH, PHYS máquina de calcular f
calculation n COMP&DP, MATH, PHYS cálculo m
calculator n COMP&DP, ELECTRON, MATH, PHYS calculador m, calculadora f
calculus n MATH cálculo diferencial m; ~ **of variations** n MATH cálculo de variaciones m
caldera n GEOL caldera f
caledonite n MINERAL caledonita f
calender^1 n P&R calandria f, PACK alisadora f, lisa f, PAPER calandra f, lisa f, TEXTIL calandria f; ~ **bowl** n PAPER rodillo de la calandra m; ~ **bowl paper** n PAPER papel para rodillos de la calandra m; ~ **roll** n PAPER rodillo de la calandra m; ~ **smash** n PAPER aplastamiento de la calandra m; ~ **unit** n PACK alisadora f, laminadora f; ~ **water box** n PAPER caja de agua de la calandra f
calender^2 vt P&R, PAPER calandrar
calendered: ~ **film** n P&R película calandrada f; ~ **paper board** n PAPER cartón calandrado m, papel calandrado m
calendering n P&R, PAPER calandrado m; ~ **felt** n PAPER fieltro abrillantador m
calf: ~ **binding** n PRINT encuadernación en piel de becerro f
calibrate vt GEN calibrar
calibrated: ~ **air speed** n AIR TRANSP velocidad relativa calibrada f; ~ **dial** n PROD cuadrante calibrado m; ~ **valve** n MECH ENG válvula calibrada f, válvula tarada f; ~ **watershed** n POLL cuenca hidrográfica calibrada f, vertiente calibrada f, vierteaguas calibrado m; ~ **weir** n HYDROL esclusa calibrada f
calibration n GEN calibración f, calibrado m, tarado m; ~ **chart** n COMP&DP cuadro de calibración m; ~ **flight** n AIR TRANSP vuelo de calibración m; ~ **flume** n WATER canalón de calibración m; ~ **instrument** n INSTR instrumento de calibración m; ~ **module** n AIR TRANSP módulo de calibración m; ~ **pressure** n AIR TRANSP presión de calibración f; ~ **ring** n WATER TRANSP radar anillo de distancia m; ~ **service** n METR servicio de calibrado m; ~ **signal** n ELECTRON señal de comprobación f; ~ **test** n AIR TRANSP prueba

de calibración *f*; ~ **weight** *n* LAB peso de calibración *m*

calibrator *n* ELECTRON comprobador *m*

calico *n* PRINT, TEXTIL calicó *m*; ~ **mop** *n* PROD rueda de trapo de calicó *f*, disco de trapo para pulir *m*

California: ~ **Bearing Ratio** *n* (*CBR*) CONST índice de resistencia del terreno *m* (*CBR*)

californium *n* (*Cf*) CHEM, RAD PHYS californio *m* (*Cf*)

caliper *AmE see* **calliper** *BrE*

calipers *AmE see* **callipers** *BrE*

call[1] *n* TELECOM llamada *f*; ~ **acceptance signal** *n* TELECOM señal de aceptación de llamada *f*; ~ **accounting system** *n* TELECOM sistema de contabilizar llamadas *m*; ~ **attempt** *n* TELECOM intento de llamada *m*; ~ **barring** *n* TELECOM interdicción de llamadas *f*; ~**-barring equipment** *n* TELECOM equipo de interdicción de llamadas *m*; ~ **bell** *n* ELEC ENG campanilla *f*, timbre de llamada *m*; ~ **button** *n* ELEC ENG *bell* botón de llamada *m*; ~ **by name** *n* COMP&DP llamada por el nombre *f*; ~ **by reference** *n* COMP&DP llamada por referencia *f*; ~**-by value** *n* COMP&DP instrucción de llamada *f*, llamada por valor *f*; ~ **charge** *n* TELECOM precio de llamada *m*; ~ **charge rate** *n* TELECOM tarifa de llamada *f*; ~**-charging equipment** *n* TELECOM equipos de tarificación de llamadas *m pl*; ~ **control** *n* TELECOM control de llamadas *m*; ~ **control agent** *n* (*CCA*) TELECOM agente de control de llamadas *m*; ~ **distributor** *n* TELECOM distribuidor de llamadas *m*; ~ **diversion** *n* TELECOM desvío de llamadas *m*; ~ **diverter** *n* TELECOM desviador de llamadas *m*; ~ **duration** *n* TELECOM duración de llamada *f*; ~ **flow** *n* TELECOM flujo de llamadas *m*, volumen de llamadas *m*; ~**-forwarding installation** *n* TELECOM instalación de envío de llamadas *f*; ~**-forwarding-may-occur indicator** *n* TELECOM indicador de posible traslado de llamada *m*; ~ **handling** *n* TELECOM tratamiento de llamadas *m*; ~ **held** *n* TELECOM llamada retenida *f*; ~ **hold** *n* TELECOM llamada en espera *f*; ~ **holding** *n* TELECOM retención de llamadas *f*; ~ **identification** *n* TELECOM identificación de llamada *f*; ~ **identity** *n* TELECOM identidad de llamada *f*; ~**-indicating device** *n* TELECOM dispositivo indicador de llamada *m*; ~**-in-progress cost information** *n* TELECOM información del precio de la llamada en curso *f*; ~ **interception** *n* TELECOM intercepción de llamada *f*; ~ **logging** *n* TELECOM registro de llamadas *m*, registro del mensaje *m*; ~ **loss priority** *n* (*CLP*) TELECOM prioridad de pérdida de llamada *f*; ~ **message supervisory** *n* (*CMS*) TELECOM supervisión de mensaje de llamada *f*; ~ **metering** *n* TELECOM cómputo de llamadas *m*; ~ **modification completed message** *n* (*CMC*) TELECOM modificación de llamada mensaje concluído *f*; ~ **modification reject message** *n* (*CMRJ*) TELECOM modificación de llamada rechazar mensaje *f*; ~ **modification request message** *n* (*CMR*) TELECOM modificación de llamada solicitar mensaje *f*; ~ **origin** *n* TELECOM origen de llamada *m*; ~ **portability** *n* TELECOM movilidad de llamada *f*; ~ **processor** *n* TELECOM procesador de llamadas *m*; ~ **queued** *n* TELECOM llamada en espera *f*; ~**-queueing facility** *n* TELECOM sistema de puesta en fila de espera de llamadas *m*; ~ **reference** *n* TELECOM referencia de llamada *f*; ~ **retrieval** *n* TELECOM recuperación de llamada *f*; ~ **sender** *n* TELECOM emisor de llamada *m*; ~ **sequence** *n* TELECOM

secuencia de llamada *f*; ~ **set-up** *n* TELECOM establecimiento de llamadas *m*; ~**-set-up delay** *n* TELECOM demora para establecer la comunicación *f*; ~**-set-up packet** *n* TELECOM paquete para establecer la comunicación *m*; ~**-set-up phase** *n* TELECOM fase para establecer una comunicación *f*; ~ **sheet** *n* CINEMAT nómina *f*; ~ **sign** *n* TELECOM, WATER TRANSP *radio* distintivo de llamada *m*; ~ **store** *n* TELECOM memoria de llamadas *f*; ~ **success rate** *n* TELECOM índice de éxito de llamadas *m*; ~ **trace** *n* TELECOM localizador de llamada *m*; ~ **transfer** *n* TELECOM transferencia de llamada *f*; ~**-tufa** *n* PETROL toba caliza *f*; ~ **waiting** *n* TELECOM llamada en espera *f*; ~**-waiting indication** *n* TELECOM indicación de llamada en espera *f*; ~**-waiting signal** *n* TELECOM señal de llamada en espera *f*

call[2]: ~ **collect** *vi AmE* (*cf make a reverse charge call BrE*) TELECOM hacer una llamada a cobro revertido; ~ **for help** *vi* SAFE pedir socorro

callainite *n* MINERAL callainita *f*

called: ~**-line identification** *n* (*CLI*) TELECOM identificación de la línea de llamada *f*; ~**-line identity** *n* (*CDLI*) TELECOM identidad de la línea de llamada *f*, identidad del abonado llamado *f*; ~ **number display** *n* TELECOM dispositivo visualizador del número llamado *m*; ~ **party** *n* TELECOM abonado llamado *m*; ~**-station identity** *n* (*CSI*) TELECOM identidad de la estación llamada *f*; ~ **telephone** *n* TELECOM teléfono llamado *m*

caller *n* TELECOM abonado que llama *m*

calling: ~ **channel** *n* TELECOM canal de llamadas *m*; ~ **indicator** *n* TELECOM indicador de llamadas *m*; ~ **lamp** *n* TELECOM lámpara de llamada *f*; ~ **line** *n* TELECOM línea de llamada *f*; ~ **line identification display** *n* (*CLID*) TELECOM visualizador de identificación de línea de llamada *m*; ~ **line identification presentation** *n* TELECOM presentación de identificación de línea de llamada *f*; ~**-line identification restriction** *n* (*CLIR*) TELECOM restricción de identificación de línea de llamada *f*; ~**-party address request indicator** *n* TELECOM indicador solicitando dirección del abonado que llama *m*; ~**-party address response indicator** *n* TELECOM indicador contestando dirección del abonado que llama *m*; ~**-party category request indicator** *n* TELECOM indicador solicitando dirección del abonado que llama *m*; ~**-party category response indicator** *n* TELECOM indicador contestando categoría del abonado que llama *m*; ~**-party number incomplete indicator** *n* TELECOM indicador de número incompleto del abonado que llama *m*; ~ **sequence** *n* COMP&DP secuencia de llamada *f*; ~ **signal** *n* TELECOM señal de llamada *f*; ~ **telephone** *n* TELECOM teléfono que llama *m*

calliper[1] *n BrE* AUTO calibre *m*, portapinza *m*, MECH calibrador *m*, calibre *m*, diámetro interior *m*, MECH ENG calibre *m*, PAPER calibre *m*, espesor *m*, PETROL calibre *m*, PRINT caja de cables *f*, espesor *m*, VEH *of a brake* calibrador *m*, portapinza *m*; ~ **calender** *n BrE* PAPER calandra calibradora *f*; ~ **compasses** *n pl BrE* METR compás de calibración *m*; ~ **gauge** *n BrE* MECH ENG calibre plano *m*; ~ **log** *n BrE* PETR TECH calibre *m*, perfil de calibración *m*, registro de calibración *m*, PETROL perfil de calibración *m*; ~ **square** *n BrE* MECH ENG escuadra calibradora *f*, pie de rey *m*

calliper² *vt BrE* MECH ENG calibrar

callipers *n pl BrE* C&G calibradores *m pl*, LAB calibrador *m*, METR *beam, digital, vernier* compás de brazos curvos *m*, compás de calibres *m*, compás de gruesos *m*

callout *n* PRINT rótulo *m*

Callovian *adj* GEOL Calloviense

calm¹ *adj* HYDROL, METEO, OCEAN en calma

calm² *n* HYDROL, METEO, OCEAN calma *f*; ~ **sea** *n* HYDROL, METEO, OCEAN, WATER TRANSP mar calmo *m*

calm³ *vt* WATER TRANSP *ship* calmar

calomel *n* CHEM, MINERAL calomel *m*, calomelano *m*; ~ **electrode** *n* ELEC electrodo de calomelanos *m*

caloric¹ *adj* THERMO calorífico, calórico, térmico

caloric²: ~ **conductibility** *n* THERMO conductibilidad calórica *f*; ~ **content** *n* THERMO contenido calórico *m*; ~ **power** *n* THERMO potencia calorífica *f*, potencia calórica *f*, potencia térmica *f*

calorie *n* FOOD, HEAT ENG, PHYS, THERMO caloría *f*

calorific¹ *adj* FOOD, HEAT ENG, PHYS, REFRIG, THERMO calorífico

calorific²: ~ **balance** *n* REFRIG, THERMO balance calorífico *m*, balance térmico *m*; ~ **output** *n* REFRIG, THERMO rendimiento calorífico *m*, rendimiento térmico *m*; ~ **power** *n* THERMO poder calorífico *m*, potencia calorífica *f*; ~ **value** *n* GEOL, HEAT ENG, PETR TECH, PHYS, THERMO poder calorífico *m*, potencia calorífica *f*, valor calorífico *m*

calorifier *n* MECH ENG calorífero *m*

calorimeter *n* GEN calorímetro *m*; ~ **assembly** *n* RAD PHYS conjunto calorímetro *m*

calorimetric¹ *adj* GEN calorimétrico

calorimetric²: ~ **bomb** *n* LAB *memories*, PHYS bomba calorimétrica *f*; ~ **thermometer** *n* THERMO termómetro calorimétrico *m*

calorimetry *n* GEN calorimetría *f*

calving *n* AGRIC parición *f*, paridera *f*; ~ **rate** *n* AGRIC tasa de parición *f*; ~ **season** *n* AGRIC paridera *f*, época de parición *f*

calyx: ~ **drill** *n* MINE barrena de cáliz *f* (*Esp*), barrena tubular *f* (*AmL*)

cam¹: ~ **action** *adj* MECH ENG accionado por leva

cam² *n* AIR TRANSP, AUTO, CINEMAT, MECH, MECH ENG, VEH excéntrica *f*, leva *f*; ~ **angle** *n* AUTO, VEH ángulo de leva *m*; ~ **cleat** *n* WATER TRANSP *equipment* mordaza *f*; ~ **contour** *n* AIR TRANSP contorno de excéntrica *m*, contorno de leva *m*; ~ **follower** *n* AIR TRANSP, MECH, MECH ENG biela de excéntrica *f*, empujador de leva *m*, seguidor de leva *m*; ~ **following** *n* VEH accionamiento sobre la leva *m*, empuje de leva *m*; ~ **lobe** *n* AIR TRANSP, AUTO, VEH lóbulo de leva *m*, resalto de leva *m*, saliente de leva *m*; ~ **measuring equipment** *n* METR equipo de medición excéntrica *m*; ~ **profile** *n* VEH perfil de la leva *m*; ~ **shape** *n* MECH forma de leva *f*; ~ **switch** *n* ELEC conmutador de levas *m*

CAM *abbr* COMP&DP (*content-addressable memory*), memoria de contenido direccionable *f*, COMP&DP, ELEC, PROD, TELECOM (*computer-aided manufacturing*) CAM (*fabricación asistida por computadora AmL, fabricación asistida por ordenador Esp*)

camber¹ *n* ACOUST curvatura *f*, AIR TRANSP *runway* comba *f*, curbadura *f*, COATINGS curvado *m*, CONST abombamiento *m*, *of road* bombeo *m*, *of piece of wood* combadura *f*, peralte *m*, rampa *f*, OCEAN cimbra de la ola *f*, varadero carenero *f*, VEH caída *f*, ángulo de caída *m*, WATER TRANSP *ship building* brusca reglamentaria *f*; ~ **bar** *n* PAPER barra desarrugadora *f*

camber² *vt* CONST dar peralte

camber³ *vi* CONST curvarse

cambered: ~ **deck** *n* WATER TRANSP *boat construction* cubierta con brusca *f*, cubierta con curvatura transversal *f*; ~ **suction box** *n* PAPER caja aspirante desplegadora *f*

cambering *n* CONST *of road* bombeo *m*, peralte *m*, rampa *f*

Cambrian *adj* GEOL Cámbrico

cambric *n* TEXTIL cambray *m*

CAMC *abbr* (*customer access maintenance centre BrE*) TELECOM centro de mantenimiento acceso para abonados *m*, centro de mantenimiento atención al cliente *m*

camcorder *n* TV cámara de video de mano *f* (*AmL*), cámara de vídeo de mano *f* (*Esp*), cámara portátil *f*

camel *n* WATER TRANSP camello *m*, defensa flotante de muelle *f*

cameo *n* C&G camafeo *m*

camera¹: ~-**ready** *adj* PRINT listo para reproducir

camera² *n* GEN cámara *f*, cámara fotográfica *f*; ~ **angle** *n* CINEMAT, PHOTO, TV ángulo de cámara *m*; ~ **body** *n* CINEMAT, PHOTO, TV cuerpo de la cámara *m*; ~ **boom** *n* CINEMAT, TV boom de la cámara *m*; ~ **bracket** *n* CINEMAT, TV soporte de la cámara *m*; ~ **with built-in exposure meter** *n* PHOTO cámara fotográfica con exposímetro incorporado *f*; ~ **car** *n* CINEMAT, TV cámara-car *f*; ~ **channel** *n* CINEMAT, TV canal de cámara *m*; ~ **with collapsible mount** *n* PHOTO cámara con montura plegable *f*; ~ **control unit** *n* (*CCU*) CINEMAT, TV unidad de control de la cámara *f*; ~ **with coupled exposure meter** *n* PHOTO cámara fotográfica con exposímetro incorporado *f*; ~ **with coupled rangefinder** *n* PHOTO cámara con telémetro acoplado *f*; ~ **crew** *n* TV equipo de cámara *m*; ~ **with detachable reflex viewfinder** *n* PHOTO cámara fotográfica con visor reflex desmontable *f*; ~ **with diaphragm shutter** *n* PHOTO cámara fotográfica con obturador de entre lentes *f*; ~ **drive** *n* CINEMAT, TV transmisión de la cámara *f*; ~ **equipment** *n* CINEMAT, TV equipo de cámara *m*; ~ **extension** *n* PHOTO distancia del objetivo a la placa *f*; ~ **front** *n* PHOTO parte delantera de la cámara *f*, parte frontal de la cámara *f*; ~ **gate** *n* CINEMAT, TV ventanilla de cámara *f*; ~ **housing** *n* CINEMAT, PHOTO, TV caja de la cámara *f*; ~ **with interchangeable lens** *n* PHOTO cámara fotográfica con objetivo intercambiable *f*; ~ **with large bellows extension** *n* PHOTO cámara fotográfica con extensión de fuelle grande *f*; ~ **line-up** *n* CINEMAT, TV puesta a punto de cámara *f*; ~ **log** *n* CINEMAT, TV registro de cámara *m*; ~ **lucida** *n* CINEMAT, PHOTO, TV cámara lúcida *f*; ~ **matching** *n* CINEMAT, TV adaptación de cámaras *f*; ~ **with mirror-reflex focusing** *n* PHOTO cámara fotográfica con enfoque reflex por espejos *f*; ~ **monitor** *n* CINEMAT, TV monitor de cámara *m*; ~ **mount** *n* CINEMAT, PHOTO, TV montura de la cámara *f*; ~ **movement** *n* CINEMAT, PHOTO, TV movimiento de cámara *m*; ~ **opticals** *n pl* CINEMAT, TV efectos ópticos efectuados con la cámara *m pl*; ~ **original** *n* CINEMAT, TV original de cámara *m*; ~-**prompting system** *n* CINEMAT, TV sistema de indicación de cámara *m*; ~-**ready copy** *n* (*CRC*) PRINT original listo para reproducir m (*CRC*); ~ **report** n CINEMAT informe de cámara m, parte de cámara f, PHOTO informe de cámara m, TV informe de cámara m, parte de cámara f; ~ **with rising and swinging front** n PHOTO cámara fotográfica con objetivo descentrable f; ~ **with short bellows extension** n PHOTO cámara fotográfica con extensión de fuelle corto f; ~ **signal** n CINEMAT, TV señal de vídeo f; ~ **slate** n CINEMAT, TV claqueta de cámara f; ~ **speed** n CINEMAT, TV velocidad de la cámara f; ~**speed checker** n CINEMAT, TV verificador de la velocidad de la cámara m; ~ **stand** n PHOTO trípode m; ~ **switching** n CINEMAT, TV conmutador de cámara m; ~ **tape** n CINEMAT, TV cinta de cámara f; ~ **test** n CINEMAT, TV prueba de cámara f; ~ **tube** n CINEMAT, ELECTRON, TV tubo de cámara m; ~ **viewpoint** n CINEMAT, TV punto de vista de cámara m

cameraman n CINEMAT filmador m, operador de cámara m, TV camarógrafo m (*AmL*), cámara m (*Esp*), filmador m

camouflage: ~ **paint** n COLOUR pintura de camuflaje f; ~ **supports** n pl MILIT protección de camuflaje f; ~ **system** n MILIT sistema de camuflaje m

campaign n C&G of glass furnace campaña f, COAL período de trabajo sin interrupción m, campaña f, MILIT, PROD of furnace campaña f

Campanian adj GEOL Campaniense

Campbell-Stokes: ~ **recorder** n FUELLESS contador tipo Campbell-Stokes m

camper n VEH caravana f

camphane n CHEM canfano m

camphene n CHEM canfeno m

camphol n CHEM borneol m, canfol m

camphor n CHEM alcanfor m; ~ **oil** n CHEM aceite alcanforado m, aceite de alcanfor m

camphorate n CHEM canforato m

camphorated adj CHEM alcanforado

camphoric adj CHEM canfórico

camping: ~ **gas** n GAS, PETR TECH gas de campamento m

campylite n MINERAL campilita f

camshaft n AUTO, ELEC, MECH, MECH ENG, VEH, WATER TRANSP eje de distribución m, eje de levas m, árbol de distribución m, árbol de levas m; ~ **bushing** n AUTO, VEH casquillo del árbol de levas m, cojinete del árbol de levas m, manguito del árbol de levas m; ~ **clearance** n AUTO, VEH holgura del árbol de levas f, juego del árbol de levas m, tolerancia del árbol de levas f; ~ **controller** n ELEC switch controlador del árbol de distribución m, regulador del eje de levas m, regulador del árbol de levas m; ~ **drive** n AUTO, VEH volante del árbol de levas m; ~ **drive chain** n VEH cadena de mando de la distribución f; ~ **gear** n MECH ENG engranaje del eje de levas m; ~ **grinding machine** n MECH ENG rectificadora de eje de levas f

can[1] n CINEMAT lata de película f, recipiente de hojalata m, HYDRAUL bidón m, tambor m, PROD for holding lubricating oil lata f; ~ **bank** n RECYCL cámara de combustión f, depósito de latas m; ~ **buoy** n WATER TRANSP navigation mark boya cilíndrica f; ~**closing machine** n AmE (*cf tin-closing machine BrE*) PACK cerradora de botes f, máquina cerradora de latas f; ~ **delabeling** n AmE (*cf tin delabelling BrE*) PACK desetiquetado de la lata m; ~**filling line** n AmE (*cf tin-filling line BrE*) PACK cadena de llenado de latas f; ~**filling machine** n AmE (*cf tin-filling*

machine *BrE*) PACK llenadora de latas f, máquina llenadora de latas f; ~**packing machine** n AmE (*cf tin-packing machine BrE*) PACK empaquetadora de latas f, máquina enlatadora f; ~ **relabeling** n AmE (*cf tin relabelling BrE*) PACK reetiquetado de latas m; ~**sealing compound** n AmE (*cf tin-sealing compound BrE*) PACK material usado para el sellado de la lata m

can[2] vt FOOD, PACK enlatar

CAN abbr (*cancel*) COMP&DP carácter de instrucción que indica dejar sin efecto m

Canadian: ~ **switched network** n (*CSN*) TELECOM red conmutada canadiense f

canal n C&G of sheet glass tank furnace chorreado-alimentador m, WATER caz m, WATER TRANSP waterway canal m; ~ **boat** n WATER TRANSP embarcación para navegación en canales f; ~ **lock** n WATER esclusa f; ~ **lock gate** n WATER compuerta de esclusa f, puerta de esclusa f; ~ **ray** n NUCL rayo canal m, PHYS rayo canal m, rayo positivo m; ~**ray analysis** n NUCL, PHYS análisis de rayos canales m; ~**ray discharge** n NUCL, PHYS descarga de rayos canales f; ~ **transport** n TRANSP transporte por canal m

canalization n WATER canalización f

canalize vt WATER canalizar, encauzar

canard: ~ **wing aircraft** n AIR TRANSP avión con alas de canard m

cancel n (*CAN*) COMP&DP character carácter de instrucción que indica dejar sin efecto m

cancrinite n MINERAL cancrinita f

candel: ~ **coal** n COAL carbón de llama larga m

candela n (*cd*) ELEC, ELEC ENG, METR, OPT, PHYS candela f (*cd*)

candite n MINERAL candita f

candle: ~ **power** n PHOTO poder luminoso m

cane: ~ **crop** n AGRIC zafra f; ~ **juice** n AGRIC, FOOD jugo de caña m; ~ **plantation** n AGRIC cañaveral m; ~ **sugar** n AGRIC, FOOD azúcar de caña m

canister n PACK caja de hojalata f

canless: ~ **fuel assembly** n NUCL conjunto combustible sin vaina m, elemento de combustible sin vaina m

cannage n TEXTIL rejilla f

canned[1] adj FOOD, PACK enlatado

canned[2]: ~ **food** n AmE (*cf tinned food BrE*) FOOD, PACK alimento en conserva m, alimento enlatado m, comida enlatada f; ~ **motor** n MECH CGS unit motor eléctrico provisto de diafragma m

cannel: ~ **coal** n COAL, MINE carbón de bujía m, carbón de gas m, hulla de llama larga f, hulla seca f

canning n AmE (*cf tinning BrE*) FOOD, PACK enlatado m; ~ **crop** n AGRIC cosecha destinada a ser enlatada f; ~ **industry** n (*cf tinning industry BrE*) AGRIC, FOOD, PACK industria conservera f; ~ **jar** n AmE (*cf preserving jar BrE*) C&G, FOOD, PACK botella para conserva f, jarro para conservas m; ~ **tooling** n MECH ENG utillaje para envasado m

Cannizzaro: ~ **reaction** n CHEM reacción de Cannizzaro f

cannon n MILIT cañón m; ~ **plug** n CINEMAT conector cannon m

canoe n TV concavidad f, WATER TRANSP craft canoa f; ~ **fold** n GEOL sinclinal elongado m; ~ **stern** n WATER TRANSP sailing boats, yachts popa de canoa f

canola: ~ **oil** n AGRIC, FOOD aceite de colza m

canonical: ~ **distribution** n PHYS distribución canó-

nica *f*; ~ **ensemble** *n* PHYS conjunto canónico *m*;
~ **equations** *n pl* PHYS ecuaciones canónicas *f pl*

canopy *n* AGRIC dosel vegetal *m*, AIR TRANSP cubierta *f*,
cúpula *f*, WATER TRANSP *of long boats* capota abatible
f, carroza *f*

cant[1] *n* CONST *inclination, slope* esquina *f*, inclinación *f*,
pendiente *f*, MECH ENG inclinación *f*, oblicuidad *f*,
peralte *m*, sobreelevación *f*, RAIL peralte *m*; ~ **file** *n*
MECH ENG lima espada *f*, lima para colas de milano *f*,
lima triangular isósceles *f*

cant[2] *vt* WATER TRANSP enmendar el rumbo, escorar

cant[3]: ~ **over** *vi* WATER TRANSP *navigation* escorar a
una banda

cantharidine *n* CHEM cantaridina *f*

cantilever *n* CONST construcción de puentes de vigas en
voladizo *f*, ménsula *f*, viga en voladizo *f*, MECH ENG
ménsula *f*, soporte-pescante *m*, viga voladiza *f*,
PAPER, RAIL ménsula *f*; ~ **beam** *n* CONST ménsula *f*,
viga en voladizo *f*, PHYS viga en voladizo *f*; ~ **bridge** *n*
CONST puente de vigas en voladizo *m*; ~ **loaded at
free end** *n* CONST viga en voladizo con carga en la
punta *f*; ~ **retaining wall** *n* CONST muro de contención en voladizo *m*; ~ **wing** *n* AIR TRANSP, TRANSP ala
de cantilever *f*

cantilevered[1] *adj* MECH, PHYS en voladizo

cantilevered[2]: ~ **Fourdrinier** *n* PAPER mesa plana con
viga voladiza *f*

cantilevering *n* CONST *of bridges*, MECH ENG, PHYS
voladizo *m*

cantonite *n* MINERAL cantonita *f*

canvas *n* PRINT lona *f*, TEXTIL cañamazo *m* (*AmL*),
entretela *f*, lona *f*, WATER TRANSP *sails* lona *f*, trapo *m*;
~ **brattice** *n* CONST cañamazo *m* (*AmL*), tabique de
lona *m* (*Esp*); ~ **filter** *n* MINE filtro de cañamazo *m*
(*AmL*), filtro de lona *m* (*Esp*); ~ **table** *n* MINE
entablamiento de lona *m*

cap[1] *n* C&G, CINEMAT tapa *f*, CONST *of pile* capitel *m*, *of
sheer-legs* travesaño *m*, tapón ciego *m*, *well-boring*
tapa *f*, *blasting* casquillo aislante *m*, *connecting
uprights* techo *m*, moldura de plinto *f*, ELEC ENG *of
electric lamp* casquillo *m*, GEOL capuchón *m*, HY-
DRAUL válvula *f*, INSTR casquete *m*, sombrerete *m*,
válvula *f*, MECH válvula *f*, sombrerete *m*, casquete *m*,
MECH ENG casquete *m*, sombrerete *m*, válvula *f*, MINE
cumbrera *f*, detonador *m* (*Esp*), montera *f*, PETROL
tapa *f*, casquete *m*, sombrerete *m*, cúpula *f*, detonador *m*, fulminante *m*, PHOTO tapa del objetivo *f*,
TEXTIL capa *f*; ~ **nut** *n* MECH, MECH ENG capuchón
roscado *m*, tapón roscado *m*, tuerca ciega *f*, tuerca de
sombrerete *f*; ~ **piece** *n* MINE cabeza *f*, cabezal *m*,
cojinete *m* (*AmL*), cumbrera *f*, dintel *m*, travesaño *m*
(*Esp*); ~ **and pin insulator** *n* ELEC ENG casquillo y
clavija aislantes *m*; ~ **rock** *n* FUELLESS, GEOL, MINE,
PETR TECH capa impermeable *f*, roca de cubierta *f*,
roca improductiva *f*; ~ **and rod insulator** *n* ELEC ENG
casquillo y barra aislantes *m*; ~ **sealing** *n* PACK
cerrado de la tapa *m*; ~~**sealing compound** *n* PACK
material usado para el cerrado de la tapa *m*;
~~**sealing equipment** *n* PACK equipo para cerrar la
tapa *m*; ~~**spinning frame** *n* TEXTIL continua de hilar
de campana *f*; ~ **of steam chest** *n* HYDRAUL válvula
del depósito de vapor *f*; ~ **still** *n* WATER *of a sluice
gate* cumbrera *f*

cap[2] *vt* C&G capar, CONST *ridge of roof* rematar,
coronar, cubrir, *well* tapar; ~ **up** *vt* CINEMAT tapar

capability *n* QUALITY aptitud *f*, capacidad *f*, TELECOM

capacidad *f*; ~ **approval** *n* QUALITY aprobación de
aptitud *f*, aprobación de capacidad *f*

capable: ~ **of detonation** *adj* MINE susceptible de
detonación

capacitance *n* ELEC, ELEC ENG, OPT, PHYS, TELECOM
capacidad *f*, capacitancia *f*; ~ **box** *n* ELEC, ELEC ENG,
INSTR cajetín de capacitancia *m*; ~ **bridge** *n* ELEC,
ELEC ENG, INSTR puente capacímetro *m*, puente de
capacidades *m*, puente de capacitancias *m*;
~ **coupling** *n* ELEC, ELEC ENG acoplamiento de
capacidad *m*; ~ **disc** *BrE*, ~ **disk** *n* *AmE* OPT disco
de capacitancia *m*; ~ **electronic disc** *BrE*, ~ **electronic disk** *n* *AmE* OPT disco electrónico de
capacitancia *m*; ~ **relay** *n* ELEC relé capacitivo *m*;
~ **sensing** *n* OPT detección de capacitancia *f*;
~ **tolerance** *n* PROD margen de capacitancia *m*

capacitive: ~ **component** *n* ELEC, ELEC ENG compo-
nente capacitivo *m*; ~ **coupling** *n* ELEC, ELEC ENG,
TELECOM acoplamiento capacitivo *m*; ~ **feedback** *n*
ELEC, ELEC ENG reacción capacitiva *f*; ~ **load** *n* ELEC,
ELEC ENG, TELECOM carga capacitiva *f*; ~ **reactance**
n ELEC, ELEC ENG, PHYS reactancia capacitiva *f*,
reactancia de capacidad *f*; ~ **resistance** *n* ELEC,
ELEC ENG resistencia capacitiva *f*; ~ **tuning** *n* ELEC
ENG sintonía por condensadores *f*; ~ **voltage divider**
n ELEC ENG divisor de voltaje capacitivo *m*

capacitor *n* GEN capacitor *m*, condensador *m*; ~ **bank**
n ELEC ENG batería de condensadores *f*; ~ **discharge**
n ELEC ENG descarga de condensador *f*; ~ **film** *n* ELEC
película de condensador *f*; ~ **ignition** *n* AUTO, VEH
arranque con condensador *m*, ignición por condensador *f*; ~ **leakage current** *n* ELEC ENG fuga de
corriente del condensador *f*; ~ **motor** *n* ELEC ENG
motor de inducción monofásico *m*, motor monofásico con condensador *m*; ~ **plate** *n* ELEC, ELEC ENG,
PHYS armadura de condensador *f*, placa de condensador *f*; ~ **reactance** *n* ELEC ENG reactancia del
condensador *f*; ~ **start motor** *n* ELEC, ELEC ENG
motor de arranque con capacitor *m*, motor de
arranque por condensador *m*; ~ **start-and-run
motor** *n* ELEC, ELEC ENG motor de arranque y
arrastre con capacitor *m*, motor de arranque y
funcionamiento con condensador *m*; ~ **storage** *n*
AmE COMP&DP almacenamiento por capacitor *m*,
memoria capacitiva *f*; ~ **store** *BrE* *n* COMP&DP
almacenamiento por capacitor *m*, memoria capacitiva *f*; ~ **tissue paper** *n* PAPER papel para
condensadores *m*

capacity *n* CONST, ELEC ENG, MECH ENG capacidad *f*,
potencia *f*, METR *of a micrometer* capacidad *f*, NUCL
tools capacidad *f*, potencia *f*, PROD *productive power*
capacidad *f*, potencia *f*, REFRIG capacidad *f*, TRANSP
capacidad *f*, VEH capacidad *f*, WATER *of a
pump* capacidad *f*; ~ **bridge** *n* ELEC *circuit* puente de
capacidad *m*, puente para medidas de capacidad *m*;
~ **clause** *n* AIR TRANSP cláusula capacitoria *f*,
cláusula de capacidad *f*; ~ **control** *n* AIR TRANSP
control de capacidad *m*, REFRIG regulación de
potencia frigorífica *f*, variación de potencia *f*;
~ **controller** *n* REFRIG dispositivo de variación de
potencia *m*, regulador de potencia *m*; ~ **factor** *n* (*cf
load factor BrE*) PETR TECH factor de capacidad *m*,
factor de carga *m*; ~ **of output** *n* PROD *of a fan*
capacidad *f*, caudal *m*; ~ **plan** *n* WATER TRANSP *cargo
ship* plano de capacidades *m*; ~ **reducer** *n* REFRIG
reductor de potencia *m*; ~ **requirement planning** *n*

PROD planeamiento de las necesidades de producción *m*; ~ **under prevailing conditions** *n* TRANSP capacidad en condiciones predominantes *f*

cape *n* OCEAN, WATER TRANSP cabo *m*

capillarimeter *n* COAL capilarímetro *m*

capillarity *n* CHEM, COAL, CONST, PHYS capilaridad *f*; ~-**breaking layer** *n* COAL capa de rotura de capilaridad *f*

capillary[1] *adj* MECH ENG capilar

capillary[2]: ~ **action** *n* FLUID, PETR TECH acción capilar *f*, acción de la capilaridad *f*; ~ **conductivity** *n* HYDROL conductividad capilar *f*; ~ **crack** *n* NUCL grieta capilar *f*; ~ **diffusion** *n* HYDROL difusión capilar *f*; ~ **filling** *n* MECH ENG llenado capilar *m*; ~ **flowmeter** *n* LAB *recording* fluxímetro capilar *m*; ~ **fringe** *n* HYDROL franja capilar *f*; ~ **instability** *n* FLUID inestabilidad capilar *f*; ~ **molding** *AmE*, ~ **moulding** *BrE* *n* PROD moldeo por capilaridad *m*; ~ **rise** *n* COAL ascensión capilar *f*, subida capilar *f*; ~ **soil water** *n* HYDROL, WATER agua absorbida por capilaridad *f*; ~ **solder fitting** *n* MECH ENG *for copper tubes* accesorio de suelda capilar *m*; ~ **tube** *n* LAB, PETR TECH, PHYS tubo capilar *m*; ~-**type temperature switch** *n* PROD termistor *m*; ~ **viscometer** *n* CHEM TECH, LAB viscosímetro capilar *m*; ~ **viscosimeter** *n* CHEM TECH, LAB viscosímetro capilar *m*; ~ **water** *n* AGRIC, COAL, HYDROL agua capilar *f*; ~ **wave** *n* OCEAN, PHYS ola capilar *f*, onda capilar *f*

capital *n* PRINT mayúscula *f*; ~ **cost** *n* QUALITY costo de inversión *m*; ~ **letter** *n* PRINT ataguía *f*, mayúscula *f*

capper *n* (*cf cutoff man BrE*) C&G cortador de vidrio estirado verticalmente *m*, PACK encapsuladora *f*

capping *n* MINE control de la producción *m*, control para limitar el flujo *m*, terreno de recubrimiento *m*, PACK colocación del tapón roscado *f*, encapsulado *m*, WATER cumbrera *f*; ~ **shutter** *n* CINEMAT obturador protector *m*

capric[1] *adj* CHEM cáprico

capric[2]: ~ **acid** *n* CHEM ácido cáprico *m*

caproic *adj* CHEM caproico

caproin *n* CHEM caproína *f*

caprolactam *n* CHEM caprolactama *f*

caproyl *n* CHEM caproilo *m*

capryl *n* CHEM caprilo *m*

caprylic *adj* CHEM caprílico

capsaicin *n* CHEM capsaicina *f*

capsicin *n* CHEM capsicina *f*

capsize *vt* WATER TRANSP *vessel* hacer volcar, volcar, zozobrar

capsizing *n* WATER TRANSP zozobra *f*

capstan *n* ACOUST cabezal móvil *m*, CINEMAT, ELEC ENG, MECH, MECH ENG, TV, WATER TRANSP cabezal móvil *m*, cabrestante *m*; ~ **drive** *n* TV servo cabrestante *m*; ~ **drum** *n* WATER TRANSP madre *f*, tambor *m*; ~-**headed screw** *n* CONST tornillo con cabeza redonda *m*; ~ **lathe** *n* MECH, MECH ENG torno revólver *m*; ~ **motor control** *n* CINEMAT control del motor del cabezal móvil *m*; ~ **pit** *n* CONST pozo para cabrestante *m*; ~ **screw** *n* CONST cuerpo del cabrestante *m*; ~ **servo** *n* CINEMAT servomecanismo del cabezal móvil *m*; ~ **servolock** *n* CINEMAT mecanismo de servobloqueo del cabezal móvil *m*; ~ **tach lamp** *n* CINEMAT lámpara giratoria de cabezal móvil *f*

capsule *n* MINE *blasting*, SPACE cápsula *f*

captain *n* AIR TRANSP, MILIT, WATER TRANSP *navy* capitán *m*; ~ **call** *n* AIR TRANSP llamada del capitán *f*

captaincy *n* AIR TRANSP, MILIT, WATER TRANSP capitanía *f*

captation: ~ **drag** *n* TRANSP rastreo de captación *m*

caption *n* CINEMAT subtítulo *m*, PRINT pie *m*; ~ **roller** *n* CINEMAT operador de máquina tituladora *m*; ~ **scanner** *n* TV explorador de títulos *m*; ~ **stand** *n* TV posición de titulares *f*

captive[1] *adj* MECH cautivo, imperdible, prisionero

captive[2] *n* MILIT cautivo *m*; ~ **cross-head terminal screw** *n* PROD tornillo cautivo de cabeza de cruceta *m*; ~ **flight** *n* SPACE vuelo cautivo *m*; ~ **head terminal** *n* ELEC *connection* terminal del cabezal imperdible *m*; ~ **screw** *n* MECH ENG tornillo imperdible *m*

capture[1] *n* AIR TRANSP *beam*, PHYS *communications*, SPACE *of satellite* captura *f*, WATER *programme* captación *f*; ~ **cross-section** *n* PETROL corte transversal de captación *m*, corte transversal de captura *m*; ~ **effect** *n* ELECTRON, TELECOM efecto de captura *m*; ~ **range** *n* ELECTRON margen de captura *m*; ~ **unit** *n* PETROL unidad de captación *f*, unidad de captura *f*

capture[2] *vt* SPACE recobrar

car *n* (*cf wagon BrE*) MINE vagón *m*, RAIL vagón de mercancías *m*, TRANSP coche *m* (*Esp*), vagón *m*, carro *m* (*AmL*), vagón de mercancías *m*; ~ **accessory** *n* AUTO, VEH accesorio del automóvil *m*; ~ **body tooling** *n* MECH ENG utillaje de chapistería *m*; ~ **distributor office** *n* AmE (*cf wagon distributor office BrE*) RAIL despacho del distribuidor de vagones *m*; ~ **elevator** *n* AmE (*cf wagon lift BrE*) RAIL montacargas para vagones *m*, montavagones *m*; ~ **ferry** *n* TRANSP, WATER TRANSP canguro *m*, transbordador de automóviles *m*; ~ **for internal yard use** *n* AmE (*cf wagon for internal yard use BrE*) RAIL, VEH vagón para uso interno en la estación *m*; ~ **ladle** *n* PROD *founding* cucharón sobre vagoneta *m*; ~ **polish** *n* COATINGS pulido para carros *m* (*AmL*), pulido para coches *m* (*Esp*); ~ **pool** *n* TRANSP aparcamiento *m*, depósito de coches *m*; ~ **pooling** *n* TRANSP aparcamiento de coches *m* (*Esp*), utilización en común de automóviles *f* (*AmL*); ~ **repair shop** *n* AmE (*cf workshop BrE*) RAIL taller *m*, taller para la reparación de vagones *m*; ~ **sleeper train** *n* AmE (*cf wagon sleeper train BrE*) RAIL tren de coches-cama *m*; ~ **telephone** *n* TELECOM, TRANSP teléfono de automóvil *m* (*AmL*), teléfono de carro *m* (*AmL*), teléfono de coche *m* (*Esp*)

carrageenan *n* MAR POLL carraguín *m*

caramel *n* COLOUR, FOOD caramelo *m*; ~ **sugar** *n* FOOD caramelo *m*

caramelized: ~ **sugar** *n* BrE FOOD azúcar caramelizado *m*

carat *n* METR *of diamond* carate *m* (*AmL*), quilate *m* (*Esp*); ~ **fine** *n* METR carate *m* (*AmL*), quilate *m* (*Esp*)

caravan *n* BrE (*cf trailer*) TRANSP, VEH caravana *f*, remolque *m*, trailer *m*

carbamate *n* CHEM carbamato *m*

carbamic: ~ **acid** *n* CHEM ácido carbámico *m*

carbamyl *n* CHEM carbamilo *m*

carbamyle *n* CHEM carbamila *f*

carbanil *n* CHEM carbanilo *m*

carbanilide *n* CHEM carbanilida *f*

carbanion *n* CHEM carbanión *m*

carbazide *n* CHEM carbazida *f*

carbazole *n* CHEM carbazol *m*

carbene *n* CHEM carbeno *m*

carbide *n* CHEM, MECH, MECH ENG, METALL carburo *m*; ~ **cracking** *n* METALL craqueado carbúrico *m*, pirólisis de carburo metálico *f*; ~ **formation** *n* METALL formación de carburos metálicos *f*; ~ **tip** *n* MECH ENG punta de carburo *f*; ~**-tipped hole saw** *n* MECH, MECH ENG sierra de perforación con puntas de carburo *f*; ~**-tipped tool** *n* MECH, MECH ENG herramienta con puntas de carburo *f*; ~ **tools** *n pl* MECH ENG herramientas con cuchillas de carburo *f*

carbinol *n* CHEM carbinol *m*

carbocyclic *adj* CHEM carbocíclico

carbohydrase *n* CHEM, FOOD carbohidrasa *f*

carbohydrate *n* CHEM, FOOD carbohidrato *m*; ~ **size** *n* TEXTIL apresto de carbohidrato *m*

carbolic *adj* CHEM carbólico, fénico

carbon[1]: ~**-free** *adj* METALL exento de carbono, libre de carbono

carbon[2] *n* (*C*) CHEM carbono *m* (*C*), CINEMAT lámpara de carbón *f*, ELEC, ELEC ENG carbón *m*, PETR TECH carbono *m* (*C*), VEH *engine* hollín *m*; ~ **advancing** *n* CINEMAT adelanto de la lámpara de carbón *m*; ~ **arc** *n* ELEC, ELEC ENG arco con electrodos de carbón *m*, arco eléctrico con electrodos de carbón *m*; ~ **arc lamp** *n* ELEC, ELEC ENG lámpara de arco con electrodos de carbón *f*; ~ **arc welding** *n* PROD soldadura con arco con electrodo de carbón *f*; ~ **bisulfide** *AmE*, ~ **bisulphide** *BrE n* CHEM bisulfuro de carbono *m*, disulfuro de carbono *m*; ~ **black** *n* COAL negro de carbón *m*, negro de humo *m*, P&R negro de humo *m*, PETR TECH negro de humo de gas natural *m*; ~ **brick** *n* HEAT ladrillo carbónico *m*; ~ **brush** *n* ELEC *generator*, ELEC ENG, MECH ENG escobilla de carbón *f*; ~ **composition resistor** *n* ELEC, ELEC ENG, PHYS resistencia de carbón *f*; ~ **contact** *n* ELEC, ELEC ENG, MECH contacto de carbón *m*; ~ **copy paper** *n* PAPER papel para copias *m*; ~ **cycle** *n* FOOD ciclo del carbono *m*; ~ **dating** *n* RAD PHYS datación por carbono *f*; ~ **dioxide** *n* CHEM anhídrido carbónico *m*, dióxido de carbono *m*, COAL anhídrido carbónico *m*, dióxido de carbono *m*, nieve carbónica *f*, ELECTRON (*CO₂*) carbón dióxido *m* (*CO₂*), MECH ENG dióxido de carbono *m*; ~ **dioxide fire-extinguisher** *n* SAFE extinguidor de bióxido de carbono *m*, extintor de bióxido de carbono *m*; ~ **dioxide greenhouse effect** *n* POLL, efecto invernadero por dióxido de carbono *m*; ~ **dioxide laser** *n* ELECTRON láser de dióxido de carbono *m*; ~ **dioxide snow** *n* REFRIG nieve carbónica *f*; ~ **disulfide** *AmE*, ~ **disulphide** *BrE n* FOOD disulfuro de carbono *m*; ~ **electrode** *n* ELEC *cell*, ELEC ENG electrodo de carbón *m*; ~ **fiber** *AmE see carbon fibre BrE*; ~ **fiber felt** *AmE see carbon fibre felt BrE*; ~ **fiber reinforced plastic** *AmE see carbon fibre reinforced plastic BrE*; ~ **fiber tool** *AmE see carbon fibre tool BrE*; ~ **fibre** *n BrE* P&R, SPACE, VEH fibra de carbono *f*; ~ **fibre felt** *n BrE* SPACE fieltro de fibra de carbono *m*; ~ **fibre reinforced plastic** *n BrE* P&R plástico reforzado con fibra de carbono *m*; ~ **fibre tool** *n BrE* MECH ENG herramienta de fibra de carbono *f*, herramienta de fibra de carbón *f*; ~ **filament lamp** *n* ELEC ENG lámpara de filamento de carbón *f*; ~ **film** *n* ELEC ENG película de carbón *f*; ~ **film resistor** *n* ELEC ENG resistencia-película de carbón *f*; ~ **holder** *n* CINEMAT sujetador de lámparas de carbón *m*; ~**-holder lamp** *n* ELEC ENG lámpara de portafilamento de carbón *f*; ~ **ink** *n* COLOUR tinta al

carbón *f*; ~ **microphone** *n* ACOUST micrófono de carbón *m*; ~ **monoxide** *n* CHEM monóxido de carbono *m*, oxido de carbono *m*, COAL monóxido de carbono *m*, óxido de carbono *m*, gas de alumbrado *m*, MECH ENG, POLL, VEH monóxido de carbono *m*, óxido de carbono *m*; ~ **monoxide filter** *n* SAFE filtro para monóxido de carbono *m*; ~ **monoxide laser** *n* ELECTRON láser de monóxido de carbono *m*; ~ **paper** *n* PAPER papel carbón *m*; **no ~ required** *n* (*NCR*) PAPER autocopiativo no carbonado *m* (*NCR*); ~ **resistor** *n* ELEC, ELEC ENG, PHYS resistencia de carbón *f*; ~ **steel** *n* COAL, MECH, MECH ENG, METALL, NUCL acero al carbono *m*; ~ **steel dust** *n* COAL granalla de acero al carbono *f*; ~ **steel tool** *n* MECH ENG herramienta de acero al carbono *f*; ~ **tet** *n* (*carbon tetrachloride*) CHEM, CINEMAT tetracloruro de carbono *m*; ~ **tetrachloride** *n* (*carbon tet*) CHEM, CINEMAT tetracloruro de carbono *m*

carbonaceous *adj* CHEM, GEOL carbonoso, carbonáceo

carbonado *n* MINERAL carbonado *m*

carbonatation *n* CHEM, PAPER carbonatación *f*

carbonate[1] *n* CHEM, DETERG, PAPER carbonato *m*; ~ **alkalinity** *n* HYDROL alcalinidad carbonatada *f*; ~ **hardness** *n* HYDROL dureza de carbonatos *f*; ~ **platform** *n* GEOL plataforma de carbonatos *f*

carbonate[2] *vt* CHEM, FOOD carbonatar

carbonated *adj* CHEM, FOOD, GEOL carbonatado

carbonation *n* DETERG, HYDROL carbonación *f*

carbonatite *n* PETROL carbonatita *f*

carbonatization *n* GEOL carbonatización *f*

carbon-14: ~ **analysis** *n* GEOL, RAD PHYS análisis por carbono 14 *m*; ~ **dating** *n* GEOL, RAD PHYS datación por carbono-14 *f*

carbonic[1] *adj* CHEM carbónico

carbonic[2]: ~ **acid equilibrium** *n* HYDROL equilibrio del anhídrido carbónico *m*

carboniferous *adj* COAL, MINERAL, PETR TECH carbonífero

carbonization *n* COAL, THERMO carbonización *f*

carbonize[1] *vt* COAL, THERMO carbonizar

carbonize[2] *vi* COAL, MINE cementar, hullificarse

carbonized[1] *adj* COAL, THERMO carbonizado

carbonized[2]: ~ **forms** *n pl* PAPER formularios con papeles carbonados *m pl*

carbonizing: ~ **base paper** *n* PAPER papel soporte carbón *m*

carbonless: ~ **copy paper** *n* PAPER papel autocopiativo *m*; ~ **copy paper forms** *n pl* PAPER formularios de papel autocopiativo *m pl*

carbonyl *n* CHEM carbonilo *m*; ~ **chloride** *n* CHEM cloruro de carbonilo *m*; ~ **sulfide** *AmE*, ~ **sulphide** *BrE n* POLL sulfuro de carbonilo *m*

carborundum® *n* CHEM carborundum® *m*, carburo de silicio *m*, MECH ENG carborundo *m*; ~ **wheel**® *n* PROD rueda de carborundo *f*

carbostyril *n* CHEM carboestirilo *m*

carboxyl *n* CHEM carboxilo *m*

carboxylate *n* CHEM carboxilato *m*

carboxylated *adj* P&R carboxílico

carboxylic *adj* CHEM carboxílico

carboxymethyl: ~ **cellulose** *n* (*CMC*) DETERG, FOOD, P&R carboximetilcelulosa *f*, celulosa de carboximetilo *f*

carboy *n* C&G damajuana *f*, garrafón *m*, FOOD bombona *f*, LAB bombona *f*, *data* garrafón *m*

carbro: ~ **color print** *AmE*, ~ **colour print** *BrE* *n* PHOTO copia a color en papel carbro *f*, copia coloreada en papel carbro *f*; ~ **printing** *n* PHOTO, PRINT impresión en papel carbro *f*

carburation *n* HEAT carburación *f*

carburet *vt* CHEM carburar

carburetor *AmE see carburettor BrE*; ~ **barrel** *AmE see carburettor barrel BrE*; ~ **control cable** *AmE see carburettor control cable BrE*; ~ **engine** *AmE see carburettor engine BrE*; ~ **float** *AmE see carburettor float BrE*; ~ **float chamber** *AmE see carburettor float chamber BrE*; ~ **jacket** *AmE see carburettor jacket BrE*; ~ **linkage** *AmE see carburettor linkage BrE*; ~ **needle** *AmE see carburettor needle BrE*

carburettor *n BrE* AUTO, C&G, MECH, MECH ENG, VEH, WATER TRANSP *engine* carburador *m*; ~ **barrel** *n BrE* AUTO, VEH barril del carburador *m*, cuba del carburador *f*; ~ **control cable** *n BrE* AUTO, VEH cable de control del carburador *m*; ~ **engine** *n BrE* AUTO, VEH motor con carburador *m*; ~ **float** *n BrE* AUTO, VEH boya del carburador *f*, flotador del carburador *m*; ~ **float chamber** *n BrE* AUTO, VEH cuba del carburador *f*; ~ **jacket** *n BrE* AUTO, VEH camisa del carburador *f* (*AmL*), camisa del cilindro *f*, chaqueta del carburador *f* (*AmL*), chaqueta del cilindro *f*; ~ **linkage** *n BrE* AUTO, VEH conexión del carburador *f*, varillaje de carburador *m*; ~ **needle** *n BrE* AUTO, VEH válvula de aguja del carburador *f*

carburizing *n* MECH ENG carbocementación *f*, carburación *f*, cementación *f*; ~ **furnace** *n* MECH ENG horno de cementación *m*

carbylamine *n* CHEM carbilamina *f*

carcass *n* AGRIC res muerta *f*, CONST *carpentry* armazón *m*, ELEC ENG *of motor* entramado eléctrico *m*, carcasa *f*, TEXTIL armazón *m*; ~ **chilling** *n* FOOD, REFRIG oreo refrigerado *m*, preenfriamiento de canales *m*; ~ **dressing percentage** *n* AGRIC, FOOD porcentaje de carne en canal *m*; ~ **meat** *n* AGRIC, FOOD carne en canal *f*; ~ **weight** *n* AGRIC peso en canal *m*; ~ **yield** *n* FOOD cantidad de carne *f*, rendimiento en canal *m*

carcinogen *n* CHEM, FOOD, SAFE cancerígeno *m*

carcinogenic[1] *adj* CHEM, FOOD, SAFE cancerígeno

carcinogenic[2]: ~ **substance** *n* SAFE substancia cancerígena *f*

carcinotron *n* ELECTRON, PHYS, TELECOM carcinotrón *m*, oscilador *m*

card[1] *n* ELECTRON tarjeta *f*, TEXTIL carda *f*; ~ **clothing** *n* TEXTIL guarnición de carda *f*; ~ **cutting** *n* TEXTIL picado de los cartones *m*; ~ **module** *n* ELECTRON módulo de tarjeta *m*; ~ **molding** *AmE*, ~ **moulding** *BrE* *n* PROD *founding* moldeo sobre placa-modelo *m*; ~-**operated payphone** *n* TELECOM teléfono de pago con tarjeta *m*; ~ **reader** *n* TELECOM lector de tarjetas *m*; ~ **system** *n* COMP&DP sistema de fichas *m*, sistema de tarjetas *m*; ~ **wire** *n* HYDRAUL envuelta *f*

card[2] *vt* TEXTIL cardar

cardamom: ~ **oil** *n* FOOD aceite de cardamomo *m*

cardan *n* AIR TRANSP, AUTO, MECH ENG cardan *m*; ~ **coupling** *n* MECH ENG acoplamiento cardan *m*; ~ **joint** *n* AUTO, MECH, MECH ENG, VEH junta cardan *f*, junta cardánica *f*; ~ **shaft** *n* AUTO eje cardan *m*, MECH eje cardánico *m*, eje con juntas universales *m*

Cardan: ~ **'s suspension** *n* MECH ENG suspensión cardán *f*

cardboard *n* PACK, PAPER cartulina *f*; ~ **backing** *n* PACK, PAPER refuerzo de cartón *m*; ~ **packaging** *n* PACK, PAPER envase de cartulina *m*; ~ **tray** *n* PACK, PAPER bandeja de cartulina *f*; ~ **tube** *n* PACK, PAPER tubo de cartulina *m*

carded: ~ **packaging** *n* PACK embalaje programado *m*; ~ **pattern** *n* PROD *founding* placa portamodelo *f*

Cardew: ~ **voltmeter** *n* ELEC voltímetro Cardew *m*

cardinal: ~ **number** *n* MATH número cardinal *m*; ~ **points** *n pl* PHYS *pipelines*, WATER TRANSP *compass* puntos cardinales *m pl*; ~ **system** *n* WATER TRANSP *navigation marks* sistema cardinal *m*

carding *n* TEXTIL cardado *m*, cardadura *f*

cardioid *n* MECH ENG cardiode; ~ **microphone** *n* ACOUST micrófono cardioide *m*

cardphone *n* TELECOM teléfono de pago con tarjeta *m*

cardroom *n* TEXTIL sala de cardado *f*

care *n* SAFE *materials* cuidado *m*, TEXTIL conservación *f*, cuidado *m*, mantenimiento *m*; ~ **labeling** *AmE*, ~ **labelling** *BrE* *n* TEXTIL etiquetado de conservación *m*, etiquetado de cuidado *m*, etiquetado de mantenimiento *m*

careen *vi* WATER TRANSP carenar, poner la quilla a carenar

careening *n* WATER TRANSP carenadura *f*; ~ **grid** *n* WATER TRANSP carenero *m*

carene *n* CHEM careno *m*

caret *n* PRINT signo de intercalación *m*

cargo *n* AIR TRANSP cargo *m*, PETR TECH flete *m*, SPACE avión de carga *m*, carga *f*, cargamento *m*, flete *m*, WATER TRANSP carga *f*, cargamento *m*, flete *m*; ~ **aircraft** *n* AIR TRANSP avión de transporte de carga *m*; ~ **bay** *n* SPACE compartimiento para la carga *m*, nave de cargamento *f*; ~ **boom** *n* WATER TRANSP puntal de carga *m*; ~ **capacity** *n* WATER TRANSP *ship design* capacidad de carga *f*; ~-**carrier support** *n* AIR TRANSP *helicopter* apoyo del transporte de carga *m*, soporte del transporte de carga *m*; ~ **compartment** *n* AIR TRANSP compartimiento de cargo *m*; ~ **compartment door** *n* AIR TRANSP puerta del compartimiento de cargo *f*; ~ **compartment equipment** *n* AIR TRANSP equipo del compartimiento de carga *m*; ~ **crane** *n* WATER TRANSP *shipbuilding* grúa de carga *f*; ~ **derrick** *n* WATER TRANSP *shipbuilding* pluma de carga *f*; ~ **gear** *n* WATER TRANSP *shipbuilding* medios de carga y descarga *m pl*; ~ **handling** *n* AIR TRANSP manejo de la carga *m*, WATER TRANSP manipulación de la carga *f*; ~ **hatch** *n* SPACE, TRANSP, WATER TRANSP escotilla de carga *f*; ~ **hatchway** *n* TRANSP compuerta de carga *f*, escotilla de carga *f*; ~ **helicopter** *n* AIR TRANSP helicóptero de carga *m*; ~ **hold** *n* SPACE bodega de carga *f*, TRANSP, WATER TRANSP bodega de carga *f*, bodega de estibado de la carga *f*, bodega para estibar la carga *f*; ~ **hook** *n* WATER TRANSP gancho de carga *m*; ~ **manifest** *n* AIR TRANSP, TRANSP, WATER TRANSP declaración de carga *f*, manifiesto de carga *m*; ~ **officer** *n* WATER TRANSP oficial responsable de la carga *m*; ~ **and passenger ship** *n* WATER TRANSP buque de carga y pasaje *m*; ~ **plan** *n* WATER TRANSP plano de carga *m*, plano de estiba *m*; ~ **port** *n* WATER TRANSP *shipbuilding* porta de carga *f*; ~ **pump** *n* MAR POLL, WATER TRANSP *tanker* bomba de carga *f*; ~ **release hook** *n* AIR TRANSP *of a helicopter* gancho de suelta de la carga *m*; ~ **satellite** *n* SPACE satélite de carga *m*; ~ **ship** *n* WATER TRANSP buque de carga *m*, carguero *m*; ~ **sling** *n* AIR TRANSP *of a helicopter* eslinga de carga *f*; ~ **space** *n* AIR TRANSP, TRANSP,

VEH, WATER TRANSP cabida de caja f, espacio de carga m; ~ **swing** n AIR TRANSP *of a helicopter* oscilación de la carga f; ~ **tank** n POLL cisterna de carga f, depósito de carga m, tanque de carga m, tolva de carga f; ~ **terminal** n AIR TRANSP terminal de carga f; ~ **warehouse** n TRANSP almacén de carga m; ~ **winch** n WATER TRANSP chigre de carga m

carinated: ~ **propeller** n TRANSP hélice carenada f

carload n AmE (*cf wagonload BrE*) TRANSP carga de vagón f, vagón m

CARM abbr (*chemical-agent-resisting material*) MILIT material resistente a los agentes químicos m

carmine n CHEM, FOOD carmesí m, carmín m; ~ **lacquer** n COATINGS, COLOUR laca de carmín f

carminic adj CHEM carmínico

carnallite n MINERAL carnalita f

carnauba: ~ **wax** n FOOD cera de carnauba f

Carnian adj GEOL Karniense

carnitine n CHEM carnitina f

Carnot: ~ **cycle** n HEAT, PHYS, THERMO ciclo de Carnot m; ~ **engine** n PHYS motor de Carnot m; ~ **theorem** n PHYS teorema de Carnot m

carnotite n MINERAL carnotita f

carob n FOOD algarroba m

carone n CHEM carona f

carotene n CHEM, FOOD caroteno m

carousel: ~ **structure** n SPACE *communications* estructura en carrusel f

carpel n AGRIC *pistil* carpelo m

carpenter n CONST carpintero m; ~'**s bench** n CONST banco de carpintero m; ~'**s gage** AmE, ~'**s gauge** BrE n CONST calibre de carpintero m, galga de carpintero f; ~'**s joint** n CONST junta de carpintero f

carpentry n CONST carpintería f

carpet n CONST *road* capa de rodadura f; ~ **cleaner** n DETERG limpiador de alfombras m; ~ **shampoo** n DETERG lavador de alfombras m; ~ **underlay** n TEXTIL basamento de alfombra m; ~ **yarn** n TEXTIL hilado para alfombra m

carpholite n MINERAL carfolita f

carrageen n FOOD carragenato m, carragenina f, MAR POLL carraguín m

carrageenan n FOOD carragenato m, carragenina f

carriage n COMP&DP carro m, MECH carro m, carro corredizo m, soporte móvil m, tren de rodadura m, MECH ENG carro m, gastos de acarreo m pl, gastos de transporte m pl, vagón m, vehículo m, MILIT cureña f, PACK acarreo m, transporte m, PROD vagón m, RAIL vagón de mercancías m, TRANSP vagón de pasajeros m, acarreo m, capacidad de carga f, vagón m, vehículo m; ~ **A** n TRANSP transporte A m; ~ **by sea** n PACK, WATER TRANSP transporte por mar m, transporte por vía marítima m; ~ **key** n RAIL llave de vagón f; ~ **planing machine** n MECH ENG cepilladora de carro f; ~ **return** n (*CR*) COMP&DP carácter de retorno del carro m, PRINT retorno del carro m; ~ **spring** n MECH ENG ballesta de coche f, ballesta de hojas f, resorte de coche m, resorte de hojas m

carrick: ~ **bend** n WATER TRANSP *knot* grupo doble de calabrote m

carrier n COMP&DP portador m, ELECTRON transportador m, PHYS corriente portadora f, *for protection against particles* portador m, PRINT *of data* conductor m, PROD carro m, SPACE *communications* transportista m, transportador m, TELECOM onda portadora f,

TEXTIL transportador m, TV portadora f; ~ **acquisition** n ELECTRON adquisición de la portadora f; ~ **amplifier** n ELECTRON amplificador de la portadora m; ~ **analysis** n NUCL análisis de portadores m; ~ **balance** n TV balance de la onda portadora m, equilibrio de la onda portadora m; ~ **bandwidth** n ELECTRON ancho de banda de la portadora m; ~ **bed** n PETROL capa productora f; ~-**borne aircraft** n AIR TRANSP, MILIT aviación embarcada f, avión transportado en portaviones m; ~ **box** n PACK caja de transporte f; ~ **detection** n ELECTRON, TELECOM detección de la onda portadora f, detección de portadora f; ~ **difference system** n TV sistema de diferencias de la onda portadora m; ~ **frequency** n COMP&DP frecuencia de la portadora f, ELECTRON, TELECOM, TV frecuencia de la onda portadora f, frecuencia de la portadora f; ~-**frequency offset** n TELECOM desplazamiento de frecuencia de la onda portadora m; ~-**frequency oscillator** n ELECTRON oscilador de frecuencia portadora m; ~ **gas** n GAS, NUCL, POLL gas portador m; ~ **generation** n ELECTRON generador de portadora m; ~ **level** n ELECTRON nivel de conducción m; ~ **mobility** n PHYS movilidad del portador f; ~ **modulation** n ELECTRON modulación de portadora f; ~ **noise** n ELECTRON ruido de la portadora m; ~ **reinsertion operator** n ELECTRON operador de reinserción de la portadora m; ~ **repeater** n ELECTRON repetidor de la portadora m; ~ **sense multiple access** n (*CSMA*) TELECOM acceso múltiple por detención de portadora m; ~ **sense multiple access with collision detection** n (*CSMA/CD*) COMP&DP, ELECTRON acceso múltiple en dirección a la onda portadora con detección de colisiones m; ~ **sense signal** n TELECOM señal de dirección de la onda portadora f; ~ **sense system** n TELECOM sistema de dirección de la onda portadora m; ~-**ship-borne helicopter** n AIR TRANSP helicóptero con base en portaviones m, helicóptero con base en portahelicópteros m; ~ **signal** n COMP&DP señal de portadora f, señal portadora f; ~ **suppression** n ELECTRON, TELECOM supresión de la onda portadora f, supresión de la portadora f; ~-**to-intermodulation noise density ratio** n TELECOM relación densidad onda portadora-ruido intermodulación f; ~-**to-noise density ratio** n TELECOM relación de densidad onda portadora-ruido f; ~ **wagon** n CONST vagón de carga m; ~ **wave** n PHYS, TV, WATER TRANSP, WAVE PHYS onda portadora f, onda transmisora f; ~-**wave generator** n WAVE PHYS generador de onda portadora m, generador de onda transmisora m; ~-**wave modulation** n WAVE PHYS modulación de onda portadora f, modulación de onda transmisora f

carry[1] n COMP&DP *arithmetic* acarreo m, arrastre m, arrastre de unidades m, ELECTRON transporte m; ~ **digit** n COMP&DP dígito de acarreo m, dígito de arrastre m; ~ **level** n PROD nivel de transporte m; ~ **lookahead** n COMP&DP acarreo anticipado m, previsión de acarreo f; ~-**off** n NUCL arrastre m; ~-**over** n C&G arrastre de polvos en la mezcla m

carry[2] vt COMP&DP *arithmetic* acarrear, arrastrar, CONST *road* transportar, *support* soportar, MECH ENG transportar, acarrear, soportar, TELECOM, TEXTIL transportar; ~ **out to sea** vt HYDROL acarrear hacia el mar

carry[3]: ~ **the load safely** *vi* SAFE transportar cargas con seguridad

carry[4]: ~ **a canal as far as the sea** *phr* WATER conducir un canal hasta el mar

carrying *n* TEXTIL transporte *m*; ~ **axle** *n* AUTO, MECH ENG, RAIL, VEH eje portador *m*; ~ **bogie** *n* BrE (*cf carrying truck AmE*) RAIL carretón portador *m*; ~ **capacity** *n* FUELLESS *of a pipe* capacidad *f*, MECH *fail* capacidad de potencia *f*, carga útil *f*, MECH ENG cabida *f*, capacidad de carga *f*, carga útil *f*, PACK capacidad de carga *f*, carga útil *f*; ~ **handle** *n* INSTR, MECH, PACK asa de transporte *f*, asa para facilitar el transporte *f*; ~ **idler** *n* MECH ENG rodillo de apoyo *m*; ~-**in fork** *n* C&G tenedor de carga *m*; ~ **medium** *n* PRINT soporte conductor *m*; ~ **roller** *n* C&G rodillo de acarreo *m*; ~ **truck** *n* AmE (*cf carrying bogie BrE*) RAIL carretón portador *m*; ~ **wheel** *n* TRANSP rueda portadora *f*

CARS *abbr* (*coherent anti-Stokes Raman scattering*) PHYS dispersión Raman coherente anti-Stokes *f*

Carson's: ~ **rule bandwidth** *n* SPACE *communications* ancho de banda según la regla de Carson *m*

cart *n* CONST carretón *m*, carro *m*

Cartesian: ~ **coordinate** *n* CONST, ELECTRON, GEOM, MATH, PHYS coordenada Cartesiana *f*; ~ **coordinate system** *n* CONST, ELECTRON, GEOM, MATH, PHYS sistema coordinado Cartesiano *m*; ~ **geometry** *n* GEOM geometría Cartesiana *f*; ~ **product** *n* COMP&DP producto Cartesiano *m*

carton *n* PACK cartón *m*; ~ **compact** *n* PAPER cartón compacto *m*, cartón contracolado *m*; ~-**dosing machine** *n* PACK máquina suministradora de cajas *f*; ~ **erector and closer** *n* PACK máquina de montaje y cierre de cajas *f*; ~ **filler** *n* PACK máquina de llenado de cajas *f*

cartoner *n* PACK encartonadora *f*

cartoning: ~ **machine** *n* PACK máquina de hacer envases de cartón *f*

cartoon *n* CINEMAT, TV dibujo animado *m*

cartridge *n* COMP&DP, MILIT, MINE cartucho *m*, PHOTO carrete *m*, rollo *m*; ~ **belt** *n* MILIT cinta de ametralladora *f*, cinta de cartuchos *f*; ~ **brass** *n* MECH, MECH ENG latón para cartuchería *m*; ~ **case** *n* MILIT vaina metálica del cartucho *f*; ~ **depot** *n* MILIT depósito de cartuchos *m*; ~ **drive** *n* COMP&DP unidad de cartucho *f*; ~ **factory** *n* MILIT fábrica de cartuchos *f*; ~ **filter** *n* MECH ENG, VEH cartucho filtrante *m*, filtro de cartucho *m*; ~ **for indexable inserts** *n* MECH ENG *cutting tools* cartucho para inserto rotatorio *m*; ~ **fuse** *n* ELEC, ELEC ENG fusible de cartucho *m*, fusible encapsulado *m*; ~ **heater** *n* MECH ENG *injection moulds* calentador de cartuchos *m*; ~ **loading** *n* COMP&DP carga de cartucho *f*; ~ **pen** *n* PRINT pluma estilográfica de cartuchos *f*; ~ **recorder** *n* INSTR unidad de grabación *f*; ~-**relief valve** *n* PROD válvula de seguridad de cartucho *f*

carve *vt* CONST labrar

carved *adj* CONST labrado

carvel: ~-**built** *adj* WATER TRANSP *boatbuilding* de construcción a tope, de forro liso

carving: ~ **machine** *n* PROD máquina de desbastar *f*; ~ **tool** *n* PROD herramienta para entallar *f*

CAS *abbr* MILIT (*close air support*) apoyo aéreo cercano *m*, TELECOM (*channel associated signaling AmE*, *channel associated signalling BrE*) señalización asociada a las vías de transmisión *f*

cascadable: ~ **counter** *n* COMP&DP contador conectable en cascada *m*

cascade[1] *n* GEN cascada *f*; ~ **aerator** *n* HYDROL aireador de cascada *m*; ~ **amplifier** *n* ELECTRON amplificador de cascada *m*; ~ **arrangement** *n* ELEC, ELEC ENG acoplamiento en serie *m*; ~ **blades** *n pl* AIR TRANSP palas en cascada *f pl*; ~ **connection** *n* ELEC *wire*, ELEC ENG, NUCL *wire* conexión en cascada *f*; ~ **furnace** *n* HEAT, THERMO horno en cascada *m*; ~ **milk cooler** *n* AGRIC, REFRIG enfriador de leche por aspersión *m*; ~ **mill** *n* COAL molino de cascada *m*; ~ **printer** *n* CINEMAT positivadora en cascada *f*; ~ **process** *n* RAD PHYS proceso en cascada *m*; ~ **set** *n* ELEC ENG calaje en cascada *m*; ~ **vane** *n* AIR TRANSP paleta en cascada *f*, álabe de cascada *m*; ~ **washing** *n* PHOTO lavado en serie *m*

cascade[2] *vt* ELEC, ELEC ENG acoplar en serie

cascaded: ~ **carry** *n* ELECTRON *of sonic boom* arrastre en serie *m*

cascading *n* COAL caída en cascada *f*; ~ **counters** *n pl* PROD contadores en cascada *m pl*; ~ **timer** *n* PROD temporizador en cascada *m*

case[1] *n* AIR TRANSP, CONST caja *f*, MECH caja *f*, camisa *f*, estuche *m*, cubierta *f*, MECH ENG carcasa *f*, bastidor *m*, caja *f*, marco *m*, METR *of balance of precision* urna *f*, SPACE funda *f*; ~ **of box spanners** *n* BrE (*cf case of box wrenches AmE*) AUTO, VEH estuche de llaves *m*, estuche de llaves de tubo *m*, estuche de llaves de vaso *m*; ~ **of box wrenches** *n* AmE (*cf case of box spanners BrE*) AUTO, VEH estuche de llaves *m*, estuche de llaves de tubo *m*, estuche de llaves de vaso *m*; ~ **depth** *n* MECH ENG profundidad de cementación *f*; ~-**erecting, filling and closing machine** *n* PACK máquina para montar, llenar y cerrar *f*; ~-**hardened steel** *n* MECH, MECH ENG, METALL acero de cementación *m*; ~ **hardening** *n* MECH, MECH ENG carbocementación *f*, cementación en caja *f*; ~-**lining paper** *n* PACK papel para forrar cajas *m*; ~ **loader** *n* PACK cargador de cajas *m*; ~-**making machine** *n* PRINT máquina para hacer las tapas *f*; ~ **packing** *n* PACK caja de embalaje *f*, estuche de llaves *m*, estuche de llaves de tubo *m*, estuche de llaves de vaso *m*; ~-**packing and unpacking of ampoules machine** *n* PACK máquina para colocar y extraer objetos envasados en láminas al vacío *f*; ~-**sealing machine** *n* PACK precintadora de cajas *f*

case[2] *vt* CONST *well, borehole* embalar, entubar, PRINT poner tapas a

case[3]: **in** ~ **of fire** *phr* SAFE en caso de incendio

CASE *abbr* (*computer-aided software engineering*) COMP&DP ingeniería de software asistida por ordenador *f* (*Esp*), ingeniería de soporte lógico auxiliada por computadora *f* (*AmL*)

cased: ~ **beam** *n* CONST viga cajón *f*; ~ **book** *n* PRINT libro en cartoné *m*; ~ **well** *n* HYDROL pozo cementado *m*, pozo enfundado *m*

casein *n* CHEM, FOOD, P&R caseína *f*; ~ **acid** *n* CHEM, FOOD ácido de caseína *m*; ~ **glue** *n* FOOD goma de caseína *f*; ~ **hydrolysate** *n* CHEM, FOOD hidrolisado de caseína *m*; ~ **paint** *n* COLOUR pintura de caseína *f*

caseinate: ~ **gum** *n* FOOD goma de caseinato *f*

casement *n* C&G bastidor *m*, CONST cerco *m*, marco *m*; ~ **cloth** *n* TEXTIL tejido para cortinas *m*; ~ **fastener** *n* CONST cerrojo de marco de ventana *m*; ~ **window** *n* CONST ventana practicable *f*

cash: ~ **crop** n AGRIC cultivo comercial m; ~ **farming economy** n AGRIC economía agrícola comercial f
cashew: ~-**nut oil** n FOOD, P&R aceite de anacardo m
casing n C&G carcasa f, cubierta f, CINEMAT funda f, CONST around door, window marco m, ELEC of motor caja f, carcaza f, FOOD cubierta f, envoltura f, GAS cañería de entubación f, cañería de revestimiento f, tubería de entubación f, tubería de revestimiento f, HYDRAUL revestimiento m, estator m, MECH caja f, revestimiento m, encofrado m, carcasa f, PETR TECH cañería f (AmL), tubería de revestimiento f, entubado m, equipo de reserva m, PETROL tubería de revestimiento f, REFRIG cuerpo de compresor centrífugo m, SPACE armazón m, carcasa f, cubierta f, envoltura f, revestimiento m, VEH alojamiento m, cárter m; ~ **clamp** n PETR TECH collarín de seguridad del revestimiento m, mordaza de varillaje f; ~ **clamps** n pl CONST grapas para marco f pl; ~ **cutter** n PETR TECH cortatubo de revestimiento tubular de pozo m; ~ **elevator** n AmE (cf casing lift BrE) CONST elevador para tubería de pozo m; ~ **expander** n CONST ensanchador de contramarcos m; ~ **grab** n CONST agarradero de marco de ventana m, agarradero de tubería de pozo m; ~ **hanger** n PETROL sujeción de tubería de revestimiento f; ~ **head** n CONST cabezal m, PETR TECH cabezal de tubería de revestimiento m, cabezal del revestimiento m; ~ **head gasoline** n AmE PETR TECH gasolina condensada de gas natural f, gasolina obtenida en el separador f; ~ **head petrol** BrE n (cf casing head gasoline AmE) PETR TECH gasolina condensada de gas natural f, gasolina obtenida en el separador f; ~-**in** n PRINT colocación de tapas f; ~-**in machine** n PRINT máquina de colocar tapas f; ~ **lift** n BrE (cf casing elevator AmE) CONST elevador para tubería de pozo m; ~ **line** n CONST línea de tubería f; ~ **packer** n CONST obturador m; ~ **perforation** n PETR TECH cañoneo m (Esp), cañoneo del revestimiento m (Esp), perforación por tubos f (Esp), punzado de la cañería m (AmL); ~ **pipe** n MINE boring tubería de entubación f, tubería de revestimiento f, WATER tubería de revestimiento f; ~ **set** n PETR TECH anclaje de la tubería de revestimiento m, colocación de la tubería f; ~ **shoe** n GAS zapato de entubación m; ~ **spear** n CONST arpón pescatubos f
Cassegrain: ~ **telescope** n PHYS, SPACE telescopio de Cassegrain m
cassette n CINEMAT, OPT casete f, PHOTO cinta f, TV casete f; ~ **loading** n CINEMAT carga de casettes f; ~ **recorder** n INSTR casete grabadora f
cassia: ~ **oil** n FOOD aceite de cassia m
cassiterite n MINERAL casiterita f
cast[1]: **as** ~ adj PROD en estado tosco de fundición; ~-**coated** adj PAPER estucado de alto brillo
cast[2] n C&G vaciado m (AmL), PROD colada f; ~ **bronze** n MECH, METALL bronce fundido m; ~ **coating** n PAPER estucado de alto brillo m; ~ **film** n P&R película fundida f, película moldeada por colada f; ~ **gate** n PROD founding agujero de colada m; ~ **glass** n C&G vidrio vaciado m; ~ **house** n PROD blast furnace nave de colada f; ~-**in-place pile** n COAL pila moldeada in situ f; ~ **iron** n CONST, MECH, MECH ENG, METALL fundición f, hierro colado m, hierro fundido m; ~-**iron elbow** n CONST, NUCL codo de fundición m; ~-**iron joint** n CONST unión de hierro fundido f; ~-**iron pipe** n CONST tubería de fundición

f; ~-**iron pipeline** n MECH ENG tubería de hierro fundido f; ~ **nail** n CONST clavo de fundición m; ~ **scrap** n PROD chatarra de fundición f; ~ **steel** n MECH, METALL acero colado m, acero fundido m, acero moldeado m
cast[3] vt C&G vaciar, MECH ENG derretir, fundir, moldear, PROD fundir, lathe bed moldear, iron colar, WATER TRANSP anular float soltar; ~ **in open sand** vt PROD fundir al descubierto; ~ **off** vt PRINT calcular el espacio tipográfico, WATER TRANSP mooring lines largar
cast[4] vi WATER TRANSP abatir; ~ **anchor** vi WATER TRANSP echar el ancla; ~ **off** vi WATER TRANSP sailing arribar, caer a sotavento, ship levar anclas
castable adj C&G vaciable
castellated: ~-**head fastener** n MECH ENG perno cabezal almenado m; ~ **nut** n CONST tuerca entallada f, MECH ENG tuerca almenada f (Esp), tuerca castilla f (AmL)
caster n PRINT máquina fundidora de tipos f, PROD person fundidor m, swivelling, roller roldana pivotante f
casting n C&G vaciada f, MECH boat building colada f, fundición f, moldeo m, MECH ENG pieza fundida f, fundición f, colada f, P&R fusión f, pieza fundida f, pieza colada f, PRINT fundición f, PROD colada f, ingot pieza fundida f, metals vaciado m (AmL), SPACE propulsion abatimiento m, tiro m; ~ **box** n PROD caja de moldeo f; ~ **crane** n C&G grúa para vaciar f; ~ **in molds** AmE, ~ **in moulds** BrE n PROD colada en molde f; ~ **ladle** n PROD foundry cucharón de fundir m; ~ **lip** n C&G boca de vaciado f; ~ **mold** AmE, ~ **mould** BrE n MECH ENG lingotera f, P&R molde de colada m; ~-**on** n PROD founding soldadura por fundición líquida f; ~ **pattern** n MECH plantilla de fundición f; ~ **pit** n PROD iron foundry, steel works foso de colada m; ~ **roller** n C&G rodillo de vaciado m; ~ **scar** n C&G cicatriz de vaciado f, falla de vaciado f; ~ **table** n C&G mesa de vaciado f; ~ **unit** n C&G unidad de vaciado f
castle: ~ **nut** n CONST, MECH ENG tuerca almenada f (Esp), tuerca castilla f (AmL), tuerca entallada f
castor n MECH ENG rueda pivotante f, rueda pequeña pivotante f; ~ **oil** n P&R aceite de ricino m
castorin n CHEM castorina f
casualty: ~ **at sea** n SAFE, WATER TRANSP siniestro m
cat: ~ **cracker** n PETR TECH desintegrador catalítico m; ~ **head** n MECH ENG carrete m, luneta f, manguito de refuerzo m; ~ **whisker** n PROD buscador m; ~-**whisker head** n PROD cabezal de buscador m
CAT abbr COMP&DP (computer-aided testing) CAT (prueba auxiliada por computadora AmL, prueba auxiliada por ordenador Esp), PRINT (computer-assisted typesetting) CAT (fotocomposición asistida por computadora AmL, fotocomposición asistida por ordenador Esp)
cataclasis n GEOL cataclasis f
cataclasite n GEOL cataclasita f
cataclasm n GEOL fragmentación f
cataclysm n GEOL cataclismo m
catadioptric adj PHYS catadióptrico
catalase n CHEM, FOOD catalasa f
catalog AmE see catalogue BrE
catalogue n BrE COMP&DP, PROD catálogo m; ~ **number** n BrE PROD número del catálogo m
catalysis n FOOD catálisis f

catalyst *n* GEN, catalizador *m*; ~ **bed** *n* NUCL capa catalizadora *f*; ~ **poison** *n* POLL veneno de catalizador *m*

catalytic¹ *adj* CHEM catalítico

catalytic²: ~ **converter** *n* AUTO, POLL, VEH convertidor catalítico *m*, reactor catalítico *m*; ~ **cracking** *n* CHEM *of heavy oil*, PETR TECH desintegración catalítica *f*, termodesintegración catalítica *f*; ~-**cracking plant** *n* PETR TECH instalación de desintegración catalítica *f*, planta de cracking catalítico *f*; ~ **muffler** *n* AmE (*cf catalytic silencer BrE*) POLL amortiguador de sonido catalítico *m* (*Esp*), mofle catalítico *m* (*AmL*), silenciador catalítico *m* (*AmL*); ~ **poison** *n* CHEM TECH veneno de un catalizador *m*; ~ **process** *n* POLL proceso catalítico *m*; ~ **pump** *n* CHEM TECH bomba catalítica *f*; ~ **reaction** *n* GAS reacción catalítica *f*; ~ **reactor** *n* CHEM TECH reactor catalítico *m*; ~ **reforming** *n* PETR TECH reformado catalítico *m*; ~ **silencer** *n* BrE (*cf catalytic muffler AmE*) POLL amortiguador de sonido catalítico *m* (*Esp*), mofle catalítico *m* (*AmL*), silenciador catalítico *m* (*AmL*)

catalyze *vt* CHEM, P&R catalizar

catalyzed: ~ **deuterium reaction** *n* NUCL reacción de deuterio catalizado *f*

catamaran *n* WATER TRANSP catamarán *m*; ~ **dredge** *n* WATER draga en catamarán *f*

cataphoresis *n* CHEM cataforesis *f*

catapleite *n* MINERAL catapleíta *f*

catapult *n* AIR TRANSP *aircraft carrier*, MILIT catapulta *f*

cataract *n* C&G *glassworker* catarata *f*, HYDRAUL, WATER regulador hidráulico *m*

cataracting *n* COAL caída en catarata *f*

catastrophic: ~ **failure** *n* ELEC ENG fallo catastrófico *m*, rotura catastrófica *f*

catch *n* CONST *fastener* pestillo *m*, MECH pasador *m*, fiador *m*, retén *m*, garra *f*, MECH ENG gancho *m*, fiador *m*, pestillo *m*, falleba *f*, MINE *landing dog* sujetador *m* (*Esp*), trinquete *m* (*AmL*), garfio *m* (*Esp*), tope *m* (*AmL*), OCEAN captura *f*, calada *f*; ~ **basin** *n* WATER cuenca de recepción *f*, depósito de fangos *m*, sumidero *m*; ~ **feeder** *n* WATER canal de irrigación *m*, canal de riego *m*; ~ **index** *n* OCEAN índice de capturas *m*; ~ **light** *n* CINEMAT luz de detalle *f*; ~ **line** *n* PRINT línea corta de texto *f*, línea corta *f*; ~ **pans** *n pl* C&G charolas *f pl*; ~ **per unit effort** *n* (*CUE*) OCEAN captura por unidad de esfuerzo *f*; ~ **pin** *n* MECH ENG clavija de embrague *f*, clavija de retención *f*, *of lathe catch-plate* dedo de arrastre *m*, uña de arrastre *f*, RAIL clavija de embrague *f*; ~ **pit** *n* CONST sumidero *m*; ~ **plate** *n* MECH ENG plato de retención *m*, *of lathe* plato portamandrín *m*; ~ **quota** *n* OCEAN cuota de pesca *f*

catchability: ~ **coefficient** *n* OCEAN coeficiente de capturabilidad *m*

catcher: ~ **cavity** *n* ELECTRON *communications* cavidad de captación *f*; ~ **space** *n* ELECTRON espacio de captación *m*

catching *n* WATER captación *f*

catchment *n* HYDROL desagüe *m*, WATER captación *f*; ~ **area** *n* CONST cuenca colectora *f*, FUELLESS zona de captación *f*, HYDROL *impluvium* cuenca hidrográfica *f*, cuenca imbrífera *f*; ~ **area response lag** *n* HYDROL retraso de respuesta de la cuenca colectora *m*; ~ **basin** *n* HYDROL depósito de desagüe *m*, WATER cuenca de captación *f*, cuenca hidrográfica *f*

catchpit *n* PETR TECH divisor *m*, sumidero *m*

catechol *n* CHEM catecol *m*, pirocatequina *f*

catecholamine *n* CHEM catecolamina *f*

catechutannic *adj* CHEM tanino catecútico

catenary *n* GEOM, MECH, PHYS, RAIL, WATER TRANSP catenaria *f*; ~ **support** *n* RAIL cable soportado por catenaria *m*, soporte por catenaria *m*

catenation *n* CHEM *chain formation* catenación *f*

catenoid *n* GEOM catenoide *f*

caterpillar *n* AGRIC, MILIT oruga *f*; ~ **grinder** *n* PAPER desfibrador de cadenas *m*; ~ **hauling scraper** *n* TRANSP excavadora-transportadora de origen *f*, pala transportadora de oruga *f*; ~ **tractor** *n* AGRIC, MILIT tractor oruga *m*

cathartic *adj* CHEM catártico

cathead *n* PETROL carretel de maniobras *m*, torno auxiliar *m*

cathedral: ~ **glass** *n* C&G vidrio emplomado *m*

cathepsin *n* CHEM catepsina *f*

cathetometer *n* INSTR, LAB, PHYS catetómetro *m*

cathode *n* GEN cátodo *m*; ~ **amplifier** *n* ELEC ENG, ELECTRON, PHYS amplificador catódico *m*; ~ **beam** *n* ELEC ENG, ELECTRON, TV haz de cátodos *m*; ~ **circuit** *n* ELEC ENG, ELECTRON circuito catódico *m*; ~ **dark space** *n* ELEC ENG, ELECTRON espacio negro del cátodo *m*; ~ **disintegration** *n* ELEC ENG, ELECTRON desintegración catódica *f*; ~ **drop** *n* ELECTRON, GAS caída catódica de voltaje *f*, caída de tensión de cátodo *f*; ~ **follower** *n* PHYS seguidor de cátodo *m*; ~ **glow** *n* PHYS brillo catódico *m*, luminosidad catódica *f*; ~ **modulation** *n* ELECTRON modulación de cátodo *f*; ~ **ray** *n* (*CRO*) ELEC ENG, ELECTRON, PHYS, RAD PHYS, TV rayo catódico *m*; ~-**ray beam** *n* ELEC ENG, ELECTRON, TV haz catódico *m*; ~-**ray direction finder** *n* ELECTRON, TELECOM goniómetro de rayos catódicos *m*; ~-**ray oscilloscope** *n* (*CRO*) ELECTRON, INSTR, PHYS, RAD PHYS, TV osciloscopio de rayos catódicos *m* (*ORC*); ~-**ray screen** *n* TELECOM pantalla de rayos catódicos *f*; ~-**ray tube** *n* (*CRT*) COMP&DP, ELEC, ELECTRON, PRINT, SAFE, TV tubo de rayos catódicos *m* (*TRC*); ~ **spot** *n* ELEC ENG, ELECTRON trazo luminoso catódico *m*; ~ **sputtering** *n* ELEC, ELEC ENG pulverización catódica *f*, METALL volatilización catódica en el vacío *f*

cathodic: ~ **etching** *n* METALL ataque catódico *m*; ~-**oxide coating** *n* COATINGS capa de óxido catódico *f*, revestimiento obtenido por oxidación catódica *m*; ~ **protection** *n* COAL, HYDROL protección catódica *f*

cathodoluminescence *n* ELEC ENG, PHYS catodoluminiscencia *f*

cation *n* CHEM, ELEC, ELECTRON, PART PHYS, PHYS, RAD PHYS catión *m*, ión positivo *m*; ~ **exchange** *n* HYDROL, PETR TECH canje catiónico *m*; ~ **exchange capacity** *n* (*CEC*) PETR TECH capacidad de canje catiónico *f*, POLL capacidad de intercambio catiónico *f*, capacidad de intercambio de cationes *f*; ~ **exchanger** *n* COAL permutador de cationes *m*

cationic *adj* CHEM, COAL, HYDROL, PART PHYS, PHYS catiónico

cat: ~'**s eye** *n* C&G ojo de gato *m*, CONST elemento reflectante *m*, MINERAL crisoberilo *m*, ojo de gato *m*; ~'**s eye quartz** *n* MINERAL cuarzo ojo de gato *m*; ~'**s whisker transistor** *n* ELECTRON transistor de filamento fibroso *m*

catspaw *n* METEO, WATER TRANSP boca de lobo *f*, mar rizado *m*, ventolina *f*

cattle *n* AGRIC ganado vacuno *m*; ~ **brand** *n* AGRIC marca del ganado *f*; ~ **breeding** *n* AGRIC mejoramiento del ganado *m*; ~ **car** *n* AmE (*cf cattle wagon BrE*) AGRIC jaula de ganado *f*, jaula de granate *f*, RAIL, TRANSP vagón para ganado *m*; ~ **dealer** *n* AGRIC ganadero *m*; ~ **dip** *n* AGRIC baño *m*; ~ **feed** *n* AGRIC alimento para ganado vacuno *m*; ~ **grid** *n* AGRIC, CONST enrejado para el ganado *m*; ~ **hide** *n* AGRIC cuero de res *m*; ~ **lorry** *n* BrE (*cf cattle truck AmE*) AGRIC, TRANSP camión de transporte de ganado *m*, camión para transportar ganado *m*, vagón para transporte de ganado *m*; ~ **management** *n* AGRIC manejo de animales *m*; ~ **on the hoof** *n* AGRIC ganado en pie *m*; ~ **performance** *n* AGRIC tasa de eficiencia bovina *f*; ~ **raiser** *n* AGRIC ganadero *m*; ~ **ranch** *n* AGRIC estancia *f* (*Esp*), hacienda *f*; ~ **sanitation** *n* AGRIC sanidad pecuaria *f*; ~ **tick** *n* AGRIC garrapata *f*; ~ **truck** *n* AmE (*cf cattle lorry BrE*) AGRIC, TRANSP camión de transporte de ganado *m*, camión para transportar ganado *m*, vagón para transporte de ganado *m*; ~ **unit** *n* AGRIC unidad ganadera *f*; ~ **wagon** *n* BrE (*cf cattle car AmE*) AGRIC jaula de ganado *f*, jaula de granate *f*, RAIL, TRANSP vagón para ganado *m*

catwalk *n* CONST acera *f*, corredor estrecho *m*, MECH pasarela de servicio *f*, pasillo de servicio *m*

Cauer: ~ **filter** *n* PHYS filtro de Cauer *m*

cauldron *n* MINE caldera *f*, caldero *m* (*AmL*), caldero grande *m* (*Esp*), PROD caldera *f*

caulk *vt* MECH, MECH ENG, PROD calafatear, taponar, WATER TRANSP *boat building* calafatear, retacar

caulked: ~ **joint** *n* WATER TRANSP junta calafateada *f*, junta retacada *f*

caulker *n* MECH, MECH ENG, PROD, WATER TRANSP calafate *m*, retacador *m*

caulking *n* MECH calafateado *m*, calafateo *m*, MECH ENG, PROD calafateo *m*, calafateado *m*, WATER TRANSP calafateado *m*, calafateo *m*, retacado *m*; ~ **chisel** *n* MECH, MECH ENG, PROD cincel para calafatear *m*; ~ **hammer** *n* MECH ENG martillo de calafate *m*, PROD mazo de calafate *m*; ~ **iron** *n* MECH, MECH ENG, PROD cincel de calafatear *m*, WATER TRANSP hierro de calafate *m*, retacador *m*, retacador neumático *m*; ~ **mallet** *n* MECH, MECH ENG, PROD mazo de calafatear *m*

cause[1]: ~ **value** *n* TELECOM valor de causa *m*

cause[2]: ~ **to subside** *vt* CONST causar un asiento de, causar un hundimiento de

causeway *n* CONST andén *m*, calzada *f*, piso *m*, vereda *f* (*AmL*), WATER TRANSP *to cross boggy areas* calzada *f*, calzada elevada *f*

caustic[1] *adj* CHEM, DETERG, PHYS cáustico

caustic[2]: ~ **alkali** *n* CHEM, DETERG álcali cáustico *m*; ~ **curve** *n* PHYS curva cáustica *f*; ~ **potash** *n* DETERG potasa cáustica *f*; ~ **soda** *n* CHEM, DETERG sosa cáustica *f*; ~ **stress corrosion cracking** *n* NUCL agrietamiento por tensocorrosión en medio cáustico *m*; ~ **surface** *n* CHEM, PHYS superficie cáustica *f*

causticity *n* CHEM, DETERG, PHYS causticidad *f*

causticize *vt* CHEM, DETERG, PHYS caustificar

caution: ~ **label** *n* PACK, SAFE etiqueta de advertencia *f*, rótulo de aviso *m*; ~ **signal** *n* RAIL, SAFE señal de precaución *f*

cautive *adj* MILIT cautivo

CAV[1] *abbr* (*constant angular velocity*) COMP&DP, OPT velocidad angular constante *f*

CAV[2]: ~ **disc** BrE, ~ **disk** *n* AmE OPT disco de velocidad angular constante *m*

caved[1] *adj* GEOL, MINE cavernoso, desplomado

caved[2]: ~ **area** *n* GEOL, MINE zona desplomada *f*

Cavendish: ~ **experiment** *n* PHYS experimento de Cavendish *m*

cavern *n* MINE socavón *m*

cavernous *adj* GEOL cavernoso

caving *n* CONST desmoronamiento *m*, MINE laboreo por derrumbe *m*, PETR TECH, PETROL derrumbamiento *m*, derrumbe *m*, desmoronamiento *m*; ~**-in** *n* MINE derrumbamiento *m*

cavitate *vi* GEN cavitar

cavitating *adj* GEN cavitante

cavitation *n* GEN cavitación *f*; ~ **failure** *n* METALL avería por cavitación *f*

cavity *n* COAL cavidad *f*, rechupe *m*, ELECTRON, GAS cavidad *f*, METALL cavidad *f*, oquedad *f*, MINE rechupe *m*, *containing gas or water* caverna *f*, cavidad *f*, hueco *m*, oquedad *f*, NUCL, PETR TECH, PETROL, PHYS, SPACE *communications* cavidad *f*; ~ **absorber** *n* ACOUST absorbedor de cavidad *m*; ~ **filler** *n* ELECTRON material de relleno de cavidad *m*; ~ **insert** *n* MECH ENG *injection moulds* inserto para cavidades *m*; ~ **magnetron** *n* ELECTRON, PHYS magnetrón de cavidad *m*; ~ **mirror** *n* INSTR espejo de cavidad *m*; ~ **oscillator** *n* ELECTRON oscilador de cavidad *m*; ~ **plate** *n* MECH ENG placa portaestampa *f*; ~ **resonance** *n* ELECTRON, PHYS, TELECOM, TV resonancia de cavidad *f*; ~ **resonator** *n* ELECTRON, PHYS, TELECOM, TV resonador de cavidad *m*

CAW *abbr* (*channel address word*) COMP&DP palabra de dirección en canal *f*, palabra del canal de cambio *f*, palabra direccional del canal *f*

cay *n* OCEAN cayo *m*

CB[1] *abbr* PHYS, RAD PHYS (*conduction band*) BC (*banda de conducción*), TELECOM (*citizen band*) banda ciudadana *f*

CB[2]: ~ **switchboard** *n* TELECOM panel de conmutación *m*

Cb *abbr* (*cumulonimbus*) METEO Cb (*cumulonimbo, cumulonimbus*)

CBDS *abbr* (*connectionless broadband data service*) TELECOM servicio de datos de banda ancha sin conexiones *m*

CBL *abbr* (*cement bond log*) PETR TECH CBL (*perfil de adherencia del cemento, registro de adherencia del cemento*)

CBO *abbr* (*continuous bit stream oriented*) TELECOM orientado a la transmisión contínua de bits

CBR *abbr* (*California Bearing Ratio*) CONST CBR (*índice de resistencia del terreno*)

CC *abbr* TELECOM (*connect confirm*) confirmación de conexión *f*, TELECOM (*control channel*) canal de control *m*, TELECOM (*country code*) código del país *m*

Cc *abbr* (*cirrocumulus*) METEO Cc (*cirrocúmulo*)

CCA *abbr* (*call control agent*) TELECOM agente de control de llamadas *m*

CCD[1] *abbr* (*charge-coupled device*) COMP&DP, ELEC ENG, ELECTRON, PHYS, TELECOM, TV DAC (*dispositivo acoplado por carga*)

CCD[2]: ~ **filter** *n* ELECTRON filtro DAC *m*; ~ **signal processing** *n* ELECTRON proceso de señal DAC *m*

CCF *abbr* (*channel-centre frequency BrE*) TELECOM frecuencia central del canal *f*

CCIR *abbr* (*International Radio Consultative*

Committee) SPACE *communications* Comité Consultivo Internacional de Radiocomunicaciones *m*

CCITT *abbr* (*International Telegraph and Telephone Consultative Committee*) TELECOM CCITT (*Comité Consultivo Internacional de Telefonía y Telegrafía*)

CCM *abbr* (*communication countermeasures*) TELECOM contramedidas en las comunicaciones *f pl*

CCO *abbr* (*crystal-controlled oscillator*) ELECTRON, TELECOM oscilador controlado por cristal de cuarzo *m*

CCS *abbr* (*common channel signaling AmE, common channel signalling BrE*) TELECOM señalización por canal común *f*

CCTV *abbr* (*closed-circuit television*) TELECOM, TV circuito cerrado de televisión *m*, televisión en circuito cerrado *f*

CCU *abbr* (*camera control unit*) CINEMAT, TV unidad de control de la cámara *f*

ccw: **~ rotation** *n* PROD rotación a izquierdas *f*, rotación en dirección contraria a las agujas del reloj *f*, rotación siniestrosa *f*, rotación sinistrorsa *f*

CCWS *abbr* (*component-cooling water system*) NUCL CCWS (*sistema de agua de refrigeración de componentes*)

cd *abbr* (*candela*) ELEC, ELEC ENG, METR, OPT, PHYS cd (*candela*)

Cd *abbr* (*cadmium*) CHEM, ELEC, ELEC ENG, METALL, MINERAL Cd (*cadmio*)

CD[1] *abbr* COMP&DP (*compact disc*), OPT (*compact disc*) CD (*disco compacto*), TELECOM (*collision detection*) detección de colisiones *f*

CD[2]: **~ audio disc** *BrE*, **~ audio disk** *n AmE* OPT disco compacto de audio *m*; **~ audio player** *n* OPT reproductor de discos compactos de audio *m*; **~ drive** *n* COMP&DP unidad de disco compacto *f*

CDF *abbr* MATH (*cumulative distribution function*) DFA (*distribución de frecuencias acumulativas*), TELECOM (*combined distribution frame*) distribución combinada *f*

CD-I *abbr* (*compact disc-interactive*) OPT disco compacto interactivo *m*

CDLI *abbr* (*called-line identity*) TELECOM identidad de la línea de llamada *f*, identidad del abonado llamado *f*

CDM *abbr* TELECOM (*code-division multiplexing*) multiplexión por división de códigos *f*, TELECOM (*companded delta modulation*) modulación delta compandida *f*

CDMA *abbr* (*code-division multiple access*) SPACE *communications* acceso múltiple por división de código *m*

CDO *abbr* TELECOM (*connect data overflow*) conexión de sobrecarga de datos *f*, TELECOM (*community dial office*) central telefónica comunitaria *f*

CD-PROM *abbr* (*compact disc programmable read-only memory*) OPT disco compacto de memoria de sólo lectura programable *m*

CDR *abbr* (*critical design review*) SPACE RCD (*revisión crítica de diseño*)

CD-ROM[1] *abbr* (*compact disc read-only memory*) COMP&DP, OPT CD-ROM (*disco compacto de memoria de sólo lectura*)

CD-ROM[2]: **~ disc drive** *n* COMP&DP, OPT unidad de disco de CD-ROM *f*; **~ drive** *n* COMP&DP, OPT unidad de CD-ROM *f*; **~ player** *n* COMP&DP, OPT reproductor de CD-ROM *m*

CDU *abbr* (*crude distillation unit*) PETR TECH unidad de refinado de crudo *f*

CE *abbr* (*connection element*) TELECOM elemento de conexiones *m*

Ce *abbr* (*cerium*) CHEM Ce (*cerio*)

cease[1] *n* TELECOM suspensión *f*

cease[2]: **~ work** *vt* MINE cesar el trabajo, suspender el trabajo

ceased: **~ subscriber** *n* TELECOM abonado dado de baja *m*

CEB *abbr* (*consecutive error block*) TELECOM bloque de errores consecutivos *m*

CEC *abbr* (*cation exchange capacity*) PETR TECH capacidad de canje catiónico *f*

CED *abbr* (*capacitance electronic disc BrE*) OPT disco electrónico de capacitancia *m*

cedrene® *n* CHEM cedrene® *m*

cedrol *n* CHEM cedrol *m*

ceiling *n* AIR TRANSP, SPACE techo *m*, techo operativo *m*, visibilidad *f*; **~ altitude** *n* AIR TRANSP, SPACE altitud de techo *f*, altitud de visibilidad *f*; **~ coil** *n* REFRIG serpentín de techo *m*; **~ diffuser** *n* REFRIG difusor de techo *m*; **~ fitting** *n* ELEC *lighting* accesorio para cielo raso *m*, accesorio para montaje en el techo *m*, ajuste para techo *m*; **~ joist** *n* CONST vigueta de techo *f*; **~ rose** *n* ELEC roseta para cielo raso *f*, ELEC ENG rosetón de techo *m*; **~ tile** *n* CONST losa del techo *f*

ceilometer *n* AIR TRANSP nefoscópico *m*, telémetro de nubes *m*

celadonite *n* MINERAL celadonita *f*

celestial[1] *adj* AIR TRANSP, SPACE, WATER TRANSP celeste

celestial[2]: **~ body** *n* SPACE cuerpo celeste *m*; **~ guidance** *n* SPACE guiado astronómico *m*, guiado por referencia celeste *m*; **~ longitude** *n* SPACE longitud celeste *f*, longitud eclíptica *f*; **~ mechanics** *n* SPACE mecánica celeste *f*; **~ navigation** *n* AIR TRANSP, SPACE, WATER TRANSP navegación astronómica *f*, navegación celestial *f*

celestine *n* MINERAL celestina *f*

celestite *n* MINERAL celestita *f*

cell *n* CINEMAT celda *f*, elemento *m*, COMP&DP celda *f*, célula *f*, ELEC *supply* elemento de batería *m*, pila *f*, vaso *m*, ELEC ENG célula *f*, *of battery* elemento *m*, FUELLESS célula *f*, INSTR celda *f*, pila *f*, LAB celda *f*, cubeta *f*, PHOTO, PHYS célula *f*, PRINT celda *f*, SPACE elemento *m*, célula *f*, TELECOM célula *f*; **~ boundary** *n* TELECOM límite de la célula *m*; **~ definition** *n* PRINT definición de la celda *f*; **~ flare** *n* CINEMAT resplandor de la celda *m*; **~ parameter** *n* CRYSTALL parámetro de la celda unidad *m*; **~ polarization** *n* ELEC ENG polarización celular *f*; **~ shape** *n* PRINT forma de la celda *f*; **~ side** *n* CINEMAT lado de la celda *m*

cellar *n* PETR TECH, PETROL antepozo *m*, sótano *m*; **~ deck** *n* PETR TECH, PETROL piso del sótano *m*

cellophane: **~ film** *n* PACK película de celofán *f*

cellular[1] *adj* AIR TRANSP, CONST, HYDRAUL, WATER, WATER TRANSP celular

cellular[2]: **~ array** *n* ELECTRON agrupación celular *f*; **~ bottom** *n* WATER TRANSP *shipbuilding* doble fondo celular *m*, doble fondo de construcción celular *m*; **~ cofferdam** *n* CONST, HYDROL, WATER, WATER TRANSP ataguía celular *f*; **~ dolomite** *n* GEOL dolomita celular *f*; **~ glass** *n* HEAT ENG vidrio celular *m*; **~ logic** *n* ELECTRON lógica celular *f*; **~ network** *n* TELECOM red celular *f*; **~ plastic** *n* P&R, REFRIG

plástico celular *m*; ~ **radio** *n* COMP&DP radio celular *f*;
~ **rubber** *n* HEAT ENG, P&R, REFRIG caucho celular *m*,
goma celular *f*; ~ **structure** *n* TELECOM estructura
celular *f*; ~ **system** *n* TELECOM sistema celular *m*;
~ **technique** *n* TELECOM técnica celular *f*
celluloid *n* CHEM, CINEMAT, PACK celuloide *m*
cellulose *n* CHEM, CINEMAT, P&R, PACK celulosa *f*;
~ **acetate** *n* CHEM, CINEMAT, P&R, PACK acetato de
celulosa *m*; ~~**acetate base** *n* CINEMAT soporte de
acetato de celulosa *m*; ~~**acetate film** *n* PACK película
de acetato de celulosa *f*; ~ **acetobutyrate** *n* CHEM,
P&R acetato-butirato de celulosa *m*; ~ **lacquer** *n*
COATINGS, COLOUR laca de celulosa *f*; ~ **nitrate** *n*
CINEMAT, P&R nitrato de celulosa *m*; ~~**nitrate base** *n*
CINEMAT soporte de nitrato de celulosa *m*, P&R
soporte de acetato de celulosa *m*; ~ **paint** *n* P&R
pintura celulósica *f*; ~ **triacetate** *n* CINEMAT, P&R
triacetato de celulosa *m* (*CTA*); ~~**triacetate base** *n*
CINEMAT soporte de triacetato de celulosa *m*;
~ **wadding** *n* PAPER guata de celulosa *f*
cellulosic *adj* CHEM, TEXTIL celulósico
Celsius *n* (*C*) CHEM, MECH, METEO, METR, PHYS, PROD
Celsio *m* (*C*); ~ **temperature** *n* CHEM, MECH, METEO,
METR, PHYS, PROD temperatura Celsius *f*
cement[1] *n* C&G, CHEM, CINEMAT cemento *m*, CONST
mortar cemento *m*, pegamento *m*, GEOL cemento *m*,
SPACE cemento *m*, pegamento *m*, vínculo *m*; ~ **bond
log** *n* (*CBL*) PETR TECH perfil de adherencia del
cemento *m* (*CBL*), registro de adherencia del
cemento *m* (*CBL*); ~ **dust** *n* CONST polvo de cemento
m; ~~**injection process** *n* CONST proceso de inyección
de cemento *m*; ~ **kiln** *n* C&G horno de cemento *m*;
~ **maker** *n* CONST cementera *f*, molino de cemento *m*;
~ **manufacturer** *n* CONST fabricante de cemento *m*;
~ **marl** *n* CONST marga para cemento *f*; ~ **mill** *n*
CONST molino de cemento *m*; ~ **paint** *n* COLOUR
pintura de cemento *f*; ~ **plug** *n* PETR TECH tapón de
cemento *m*; ~ **slurry** *n* CONST pasta de cemento *f*;
~ **splice** *n* CINEMAT empalme por cemento *m*;
~ **splicer** *n* CINEMAT empalmadora por cemento *f*;
~ **stabilization** *n* CONST estabilización con cemento *f*;
~ **stone** *n* CONST piedra de cemento *f*; ~ **works** *n* C&G
fábrica de cemento *f*, CONST trabajos con cemento *m*
pl
cement[2] *vt* C&G, CONST, GAS, NUCL, PETR TECH,
THERMO cementar
cementation *n* C&G *with mortar*, CONST, GAS, NUCL,
PETR TECH, THERMO cementación *f*; ~ **factor** *n* PE-
TROL factor de cementación *m*; ~ **furnace** *n* HEAT,
THERMO horno de cementación *m*; ~ **process** *n*
CONST proceso de cementación *m*
cemented: ~ **glass** *n* C&G vidrio cementado *m*;
~ **lenses** *n pl* C&G lentes cementadas *f pl*
cementing *n* CONST *mortar*, PETR TECH cementación *f*;
~ **material** *n* CONST adhesivo *m*, aglutinante *m*;
~ **plug** *n* PETR TECH tapón de cemento *m*; ~ **string** *n*
PETR TECH sarta de cementación *f*, tubería de
cementación *f*
CEN *abbr* (*Comité Européen de Normalisation*) PROD
CEN (*Comité Europeo de Normalización*)
CENELEC *abbr* (*Comité Européen de Normalisation
Électronique*) ELEC, ELEC ENG CENELEC (*Comité
Europeo de Normalización Electrónica*)
Cenomanian *adj* GEOL Cenomaniense
Cenozoic *adj* GEOL Cenozoico
censured: ~ **test** *n* SPACE ensayo censurado *m*

center *AmE see* centre *BrE*
centerboard *AmE see* centreboard *BrE*
centered: ~ **system** *AmE see* centred system *BrE*
centerfold *AmE see* centrefold *BrE*
centering *AmE see* centring *BrE*
centerless: ~ **grinder** *AmE see* centreless grinder *BrE*;
~ **grinding** *AmE see* centreless grinding *BrE*; ~ **precision grinding** *AmE see* centreless precision grinding
BrE
centerline: ~ **bulkhead** *AmE see* centreline bulkhead
BrE
centerplate *AmE see* centreplate *BrE*
centi- *pref* (*c*) METR centi- (*c*)
centiare *n* METR centiárea *f*
centigrade *adj* CHEM, MECH, METEO, METR, PHYS,
THERMO centígrado
centigram *n* METR centigramo *m*
centigramme *n see* centigram
centiliter *AmE see* centilitre *BrE*
centilitre *n BrE* METR centilitro *m*
centimeter *AmE see* centimetre *BrE*
centimetre *n BrE* METR centímetro *m*; ~~**gram-
second** *n BrE* (*CGS*) METR cegesimal *m* (*CGS*);
~~**gram-second system** *n BrE* (*CGS system*) METR
sistema cegesimal *m* (*sistema cgs*); ~ **wave** *BrE* PHYS
onda centimétrica *f*
centinormal *adj* CHEM centinormal
centipoise *n* P&R centipoise *m*
centner *n* METR *weight of metal* quintal *m*
central: ~ **battery switchboard** *n* TELECOM cuadro
central de distribución de acumuladores *m*; ~ **charging equipment** *n* TELECOM equipos centrales de
carga *m pl*; ~ **claw** *n* CINEMAT, MECH ENG garfio
central *m*; ~ **column of a tripod** *n* PHOTO columna
central de un trípode *f*; ~ **control** *n* TELECOM control
central *m*; ~ **control room** *n* TV sala central de
control *f*; ~ **exchange** *n* TELECOM central telefónica
f; ~ **focusing wheel** *n* INSTR rueda de enfoque central
f; ~ **force** *n* PHYS fuerza central *f*; ~ **gangway** *n*
TRANSP pasarela central *f*; ~ **heating** *n* CONST, HEAT,
THERMO calefacción central *f*; ~~**heating boiler** *n*
HEAT, THERMO caldera para calefacción central *f*;
~ **limit theorem** *n* MATH teorema central del límite *m*,
teorema del límite central *m*; ~ **load-bearing
element** *n* OPT elemento central de soporte de carga
m; ~ **locking** *n* AUTO, MECH ENG, VEH cierre centralizado *m*; ~ **nuclear force** *n* NUCL, PART PHYS fuerza
nuclear central *f*; ~ **nuclear potential** *n* NUCL
potencial nuclear central *m*; ~~**office switch** *n* TELE-
COM conmutador oficina central *m*; ~ **office trunk** *n*
TELECOM enlace oficina central *m*; ~ **power plant** *n*
ELEC ENG planta central de energía *f*; ~ **processing
unit** *n* (*CPU*) COMP&DP, TELECOM unidad central de
proceso *f* (*UCP*); ~ **processor** *n* COMP&DP, TELECOM
procesador central *m* (*UCP*); ~ **pulse distributor** *n*
TELECOM distribuidor central de impulsos *m*;
~ **refrigerating plant** *n* MECH ENG, REFRIG, THERMO
instalación frigorífica central *f*; ~ **splitter edge** *n*
FUELLESS *turbines* partidor central *m*; ~ **station** *n*
GAS estación central *f*; ~ **strength member** *n* OPT
miembro central de resistencia *m*; ~ **switching unit** *n*
TELECOM unidad central de conmutación *f*;
~ **vacuum cleaning system** *n* SAFE sistema de
aspiración central *m*
centralized[1] *adj* COMP&DP, MECH ENG, TELECOM centralizado

centralized^2: ~ **control** *n* TELECOM control centralizado *m*; ~ **control system** *n* TELECOM sistema de control centralizado *m*; ~ **lubricating system** *n* MECH ENG sistema de lubricación centralizado *m*; ~ **operation** *n* COMP&DP operación centralizada *f*; ~ **routing** *n* COMP&DP direccionamiento centralizado *m*, encaminamiento centralizado *m*, enrutamiento centralizado *m*; ~ **system** *n* TELECOM sistema centralizado *m*; ~ **traffic division system** *n* TELECOM sistema centralizado para la separación de tráfico *m*

centralizer *n* PETR TECH centralizador *m*

centre *n BrE* CONST centro *m*, cimbra *f*, GEOM centro *m*, MECH ENG *of a lathe* punto *m*, PACK centro *m*, eje vertical *m*, PROD, SAFE, TELECOM centro *m*; ~ **bearing** *n BrE* AUTO cojinete central *m*; ~**-bearing plate** *n BrE* MECH ENG placa soporte central *f*, plato central de soporte *m*; ~ **bit** *n BrE* MECH ENG broca de centrar *f*, broca de guía *f*, mecha centradora *f*; ~ **bit for bit stock** *n BrE* MECH ENG broca de centrar *f*, broca de tres puntas *f*, mecha centradora *f*; ~ **brace bit** *n BrE* MECH ENG broca de centro *f*, broca de guía *f*; ~ **of buoyancy** *n BrE* HYDROL centro de empuje *m*, WATER TRANSP *boatbuilding* centro de carena *m*; ~ **core** *n BrE* MINE núcleo central *m*; ~ **of curvature** *n BrE* GEOM, PHYS, RAD PHYS centro de curvatura *m*; ~ **cut** *n BrE* MINE corte central *m* (*Esp*), corte en Y *m* (*AmL*); ~ **cut hole** *n BrE* MINE barreno de cuele *m*, barreno de cuña *m*, barreno de franqueo *m*; ~ **of displacement** *n BrE* HYDROL centro de desplazamiento *m*; ~ **distance** *n BrE* MECH ENG distancia entre centros *f*; ~ **drill** *n BrE* MECH ENG broca para centrar *f*, mecha para centrar *f*; ~ **engine** *n BrE* AUTO, VEH motor central *m*; ~ **finder** *n BrE* METEO buscador de núcleo *m*; ~ **of flotation** *n BrE* WATER TRANSP *ship design* centro de flotación *m*; ~ **folding tubing** *n BrE* PACK tubo plegable según el eje vertical *m*; ~ **frequency** *n BrE* ELECTRON frecuencia nominal *f*; ~ **girder** *n BrE* WATER TRANSP *shipbuilding* quilla vertical *f*; ~ **of gravity** *n BrE* AIR TRANSP, CONST, MECH, PHYS, SPACE, WATER TRANSP centro de gravedad *m*; ~ **hole** *n BrE* MECH ENG agujero de centrado *m*; ~**-hole with protecting chamfer** *n BrE* MECH ENG agujero de centrado con chaflán protector *m*; ~**-hung window** *n BrE* CONST ventana de balancín *f*, ventana-basculante *f*; ~ **of impact** *n BrE* MECH centro de impacto *m*; ~ **of inertia** *n BrE* MECH centro de inercia *m*, centro de masa *m*; ~ **key** *n BrE* MECH ENG broca de botar *f*, sacamecha *f*; ~ **knife edge** *n BrE* METR *balance* soporte de cuchilla central *m*; ~ **of lateral resistance** *n BrE* WATER TRANSP *ship design* centro de deriva *m*; ~ **lathe** *n BrE* MECH ENG torno de puntos *m*; ~ **line** *n BrE* MECH, MECH ENG, PROD, SPACE eje longitudinal *m*, línea central *f*, línea de centros *f*, WATER TRANSP *ship design* eje de crujía *m*, eje longitudinal del buque *m*; ~ **line of rudderstock** *n BrE* WATER TRANSP *ship design* eje de la mecha del timón *m*; ~ **of low pressure** *n BrE* METEO centro de baja presión *m*; ~ **of mass** *n BrE* MECH, PHYS, SPACE centro de masa *m*; ~ **of mass coordinates** *n pl BrE* MECH, PHYS, SPACE coordenadas de centro de masa *f pl*; ~ **of mass system** *n BrE* MECH, NUCL sistema de centro de masas *m*; ~ **of motion** *n BrE* MECH centro de movimiento *m*; ~ **of oscillation** *n BrE* PHYS centro de oscilación *m*; ~ **panel** *n BrE* AIR TRANSP panel central *m*; ~ **of percussion** *n BrE* PHYS centro de percusión *m*; ~ **pin** *n BrE* MECH ENG *of turntable*

pivote central *m*; ~ **plate** *n BrE* RAIL *fixed equipment* placa de centrado *f*; ~ **point** *n BrE* MECH ENG pivote *m*, *of centre bit* punto central *m*; ~ **pop** *n BrE* MECH, MECH ENG, PROD granetazo *m*; ~ **of pressure** *n BrE* AIR TRANSP *aerodynamics*, PHYS centro de presión *m*; ~ **punch** *n BrE* MECH, MECH ENG granete *m*, punzón de marcar *m*, punzón de perforar *m*; ~ **punch mark** *n BrE* MECH, MECH ENG granetazo *m*, PROD granetazo *m*, granete punzón de marca *m*; ~ **rest** *n BrE* MECH ENG *of lathe* luneta *f*, luneta fija *f*, soporte central *m*; ~ **spread** *n BrE* PRINT cabullería *f*, plana doble *f*; ~**-stable relay** *n BrE* ELEC relevador estable en la posición central *m*, relé estable en la posición central *m*; ~ **of symmetry** *n BrE* CRYSTALL centro de simetría *m*; ~ **tap** *n BrE* ELEC *transformer* derivación central *f*, toma central *m*; ~ **of thrust** *n BrE* SPACE centro de empuje *m*, centro de impulsión *m*; ~ **to centre** *n BrE* MECH ENG entreejes *m*; ~ **of waterplane area** *n BrE* WATER TRANSP *ship design* centro del área de flotación *m*; ~ **of wind pressure** *n BrE* WATER TRANSP *ship design* centro vélico *m*; ~**-wind reel** *n BrE* PAPER bobina con mandril *f*; ~ **winding** *n BrE* PAPER bobinado sobre mandril *m*; ~ **wing section** *n BrE* AIR TRANSP sección central del ala *f*

centreboard *n BrE* WATER TRANSP *boatbuilding* orza *f*, orza de deriva *f*, orza de eje *f*

centred: ~ **system** *n BrE* PHYS *solids from solids* sistema centrado *m*

centrefold *n BrE* PRINT pliegue central *m*

centreless: ~ **grinder** *n BrE* MECH, MECH ENG rectificadora sin puntos *f*; ~ **grinding** *n BrE* MECH, MECH ENG rectificado sin puntos *m*; ~ **precision grinding** *n BrE* MECH, MECH ENG rectificado de precisión sin puntos *m*

centreline: ~ **bulkhead** *n BrE* WATER TRANSP *ship design* mamparo de crujía *m*

centreplate *n BrE* WATER TRANSP *boatbuilding* orza de deriva metálica *f*, orza metálica *f*

Centrex: ~ **system**® *n* TELECOM sistema Centrex® *m*

centrifugal^1 *adj* AIR TRANSP, AUTO, CHEM TECH, MECH, PHYS, VEH centrífugo

centrifugal^2 *n* CHEM TECH, MECH, PHYS centrifugadora *f*, centrífuga *f*; ~ **acceleration** *n* AIR TRANSP aceleración centrífuga *f*; ~ **advance mechanism** *n* AUTO, VEH mecanismo de avance centrífugo *m*; ~ **casting** *n* C&G vaciado centrifugado *m*, PROD fundición centrífuga *f*; ~ **cleaner** *n* CHEM TECH limpiador centrífugo *m*; ~ **clutch** *n* AUTO, VEH embrague centrífugo *m*; ~ **compressor** *n* MECH ENG compresor centrífugo *m*; ~ **drawing** *n* C&G secado por centrífuga *m*; ~ **dryer** *n* CHEM TECH, COAL secadora centrífuga *f*; ~ **evaporator** *n* INSTR, LAB *glassware* evaporador centrífugo *m*; ~ **exhauster** *n* CHEM TECH extractor centrífugo *m*; ~ **extractor** *n* CHEM TECH, NUCL extractor centrífugo *m*; ~ **fan** *n* HEAT ENG, REFRIG, THERMO ventilador centrífugo *m*; ~ **filter** *n* CHEM TECH, COAL, MECH ENG filtro centrífugo *m*; ~ **filtration** *n* CHEM TECH, COAL, MECH ENG filtración centrífuga *f*; ~ **flow fan** *n* TRANSP ventilador centrífugo *m*; ~ **force** *n* AIR TRANSP, CHEM TECH, FLUID, PHYS, POLL, SPACE fuerza centrífuga *f*; ~**-force calibrator** *n* CHEM TECH, PHYS calibrador de fuerza centrífuga *m*; ~ **hydroextractor** *n* CHEM TECH hidroextractor centrífugo *m*; ~ **machine** *n* CHEM TECH centrífuga *f*; ~ **mass** *n* NUCL masa centrífuga *f*; ~ **mill** *n* CHEM TECH molino centrífugo *m*; ~ **pump** *n* CHEM

TECH, MAR POLL, MECH ENG, REFRIG bomba centrífuga *f*; ~ **relay** *n* ELEC relé accionado por fuerza centrífuga *m*, relé centrífugo *m*; ~ **separator** *n* CHEM TECH separador centrífugo *m*; ~ **skimmer** *n* MAR POLL rasera centrífuga *f*; ~ **supercharger** *n* AUTO sobrealimentador centrífugo *m*, VEH sobrealimentador centrifugo *m*; ~ **switch** *n* ELEC, ELEC ENG, MECH ENG interruptor centrífugo *m*; ~ **and vacuum governor** *n* AIR TRANSP gobernador de centrifugación y vacío *m*

centrifugally: ~ **operated** *adj* FUELLESS de maniobra centrífuga

centrifugation *n* CHEM, CHEM TECH, WATER centrifugación *f*

centrifuge[1] *n* CHEM, CHEM TECH centrifugadora *f*, centrífuga *f*, máquina centrífuga *f*, COAL centrífuga *f*, HYDROL, LAB, MECH, P&R, PHYS centrifugadora *f*, centrífuga *f*, máquina centrífuga *f*; ~ **bucket** *n* LAB cubeta de centrífuga *f*; ~ **drive** *n* MECH ENG accionamiento centrífugo *m*, accionamiento de centrífuga *m*; ~ **mill** *n* CHEM TECH molino centrífugo *m*; ~ **rotor** *n* LAB rotor centrífugo *m*; ~ **screen** *n* CHEM TECH criba centrífuga *f*; ~ **tube** *n* LAB tubo de centrífuga *m*

centrifuge[2] *vt* GEN centrifugar

centrifuged: ~ **latex** *n* P&R látex centrifugado *m*

centrifuging *n* COAL centrifugación *f*

centring *n* BrE CONST centrado *m*, cimbra *f*, cimbra de arco *f*, MECH, MECH ENG centrado *m*, centraje *m*, centramiento *m*; ~ **bridge** *n* BrE PROD puente de centrar *m*; ~ **bush** *n* BrE MECH, MECH ENG manguito de centrado *m*; ~ **control** *n* BrE TV control de centrado *m*; ~ **lathe** *n* BrE MECH ENG torno de centrar *m*, torno de puntos *m*; ~ **lens with ruled cross** *n* BrE C&G ocular con cruz y escala *m*; ~ **machine** *n* BrE MECH, MECH ENG máquina de centrar *f*; ~ **nut** *n* BrE MECH ENG tuerca de centrado *f*, tuerca de centrar *f*; ~ **pin** *n* BrE MECH ENG pasador de centrar *m*; ~ **ring** *n* BrE TV anillo de centrado *m*; ~ **rod** *n* BrE MECH ENG varilla de centrar *f*; ~ **screw** *n* BrE MECH ENG tornillo de centrar *m*; ~ **sleeve** *n* BrE MECH ENG manguito de centrar *m*; ~ **suction holder** *n* BrE INSTR recipiente de aspiración centrado *m*; ~ **wedge** *n* BrE PRINT calce de centrado *m*, carburador *m*

centripetal[1] *adj* AIR TRANSP, MECH ENG, PHYS centrípeto

centripetal[2]: ~ **acceleration** *n* AIR TRANSP aceleración centrípeta *f*; ~ **filter** *n* MECH ENG filtro centrípeto *m*; ~ **force** *n* PHYS fuerza centrípeta *f*

centroid[1] *adj* GEOM, PHYS centroide

centroid[2] *n* GEOM, PHYS centroide *m*

Centronics: ~ **interface** *n* PRINT interfaz Centronics *m*

centrosphere *n* GEOPHYS barisfera *f*, centrosfera *f*

centrosymmetric *adj* CRYSTALL centrosimétrico

cephalopod *n* GEOL cefalópodo *m*

cephalosporin *n* CHEM cefalosporina *f*

cepstrum *n* ELECTRON cepstrum *m*

CEQ *abbr* (*customer equipment*) TELECOM equipo del abonado *m*, equipo del cliente *m*

ceramic *n* C&G, CHEM *substance* cerámica *f*; ~ **art** *n* C&G arte cerámico *m*; ~ **capacitor** *n* C&G ELEC, ELEC ENG, PHYS, TELECOM capacitor cerámico *m*, capacitor de dieléctrico cerámico *m*, condensador cerámico *m*; ~~**chip capacitor** *n* C&G, ELEC ENG condensador de chip cerámico *m*, condensador de microplaqueta cerámica *m*; ~ **coating** *n* C&G, COATINGS revesti-

miento cerámico *m*; ~ **color** *AmE*, ~ **colour** *BrE* *n* COLOUR colorante cerámico *m*; ~ **fiber** *AmE*, ~ **fibre** *BrE* *n* C&G, HEAT fibra cerámica *f*; ~ **glaze** *n* C&G vidriado cerámico *m*; ~ **industry** *n* C&G industria de la cerámica *f*; ~ **insulating material** *n* ELEC, ELEC ENG material aislante cerámico *m*; ~ **insulator** *n* ELEC, ELEC ENG aislador cerámico *m*, aislante cerámico *m*; ~ **kiln** *n* C&G horno para cerámica *m*, mufa para cerámica *f*; ~ **machine** *n* C&G máquina para hacer cerámica *f*; ~ **pavement slab** *n* C&G mosaico cerámico para pavimentar *m*; ~ **slip gage** *AmE*, ~ **slip gauge** *BrE* *n* MECH ENG calibrador cerámico de espesores *m*, calibrador de espesores de cerámica *m*, galga de bloques de cerámica *f*; ~ **tile** *n* C&G, GAS baldosa de cerámica *f*; ~ **transfer** *n* C&G transferencia cerámica *f*; ~ **wall tile** *n* C&G azulejo cerámico *m*

ceramist *n* C&G ceramista *m*

cerargyrite *n* MINERAL cerargirita *f*

cerealin *n* CHEM cerealina *f*

cerealose *n* CHEM cerealosa *f*

Cerenkov: ~ **counter** *n* PART PHYS, RAD PHYS contador Cerenkov *m*; ~ **detector** *n* PART PHYS, RAD PHYS detector Cerenkov *m*; ~ **radiation** *n* PART PHYS, RAD PHYS radiación de Cerenkov *f*

cerite *n* MINERAL cererita *f*

ceresin *n* CHEM ceresina *f*

ceresine *n* CHEM ceresina *f*

ceric *adj* CHEM cérico

cerine *n* CHEM, MINERAL cerina *f*, ortita *f*

cerite *n* MINERAL cerita *f*

cerium *n* (*Ce*) CHEM cerio *m* (*Ce*)

cermet *n* MECH cerametal *m*, cermet *m*

CERN *abbr* (*Conseil Européen pour la Recherche Nucléaire*) PART PHYS CERN (*Laboratorio Europeo de Física de Partículas*)

cerolite *n* MINERAL cerolita *f*

cerotic *adj* CHEM cerótico

cerous[1] *adj* CHEM ceroso

cerous[2]: ~ **oxide** *n* CHEM óxido ceroso *m*

certificate: ~ **of airworthiness** *n* AIR TRANSP certificado de aeronavegabilidad *m*; ~ **of compliance** *n* QUALITY certificado de conformidad *m*; ~ **of conformity** *n* MECH ENG certificado de conformidad *m*, certificado de homologación *m*, QUALITY certificado de conformidad *m*; ~ **of registration** *n* AIR TRANSP certificado de registro *m*, WATER TRANSP *logbook* certificado de inscripción en el Registro Mercantil *m*; ~ **of registry** *n* WATER TRANSP certificado del Registro Marítimo *m*, patente de navegación *f*; ~ **of seaworthiness** *n* WATER TRANSP certificado de navegabilidad *m*

certification *n* COMP&DP homologación *f*, VEH certificación *f*; ~ **body** *n* QUALITY organismo de aprobación *m*; ~ **noise** *n* ACOUST ruido de certificación *m*; ~ **organization** *n* QUALITY organización de aprobación *f*; ~ **system** *n* QUALITY sistema de certificación *m*; ~ **test** *n* AIR TRANSP, GAS prueba de certificación *f*; ~ **weight** *n* AIR TRANSP peso de certificación *m*

certified: ~ **company** *n* QUALITY empresa certificada *f*, sociedad certificada *f*; ~ **seed** *n* AGRIC semilla certificada *f*

certify *vt* AIR TRANSP *as airworthy*, QUALITY, WATER TRANSP *as seaworthy* certificar

ceruleum *n* CHEM cerúleo *m*

ceruse *n* CHEM blanco de plomo *m*, cerusa *f*

cerusite *n* MINERAL cerusita *f*, plomo blanco *m*
cervantite *n* MINERAL cervantita *f*
cerylic *adj* CHEM cerílico
cesium *n* AmE *see* caesium *BrE*
cesspit *n* WATER letrina *f*, pozo negro *m*
cesspool *n* WATER buzón *m*, pileta de patio *f*
cetane *n* CHEM cetano *m*
cetyl *n* CHEM cetilo *m*
cevadine *n* CHEM cevadina *f*
ceylonite *n* MINERAL ceilanita *f*
ceylonite *n* MINERAL ceilonita *f*
Cf *abbr* (*californium*) CHEM, RAD PHYS Cf (*californio*)
CFC *abbr* (*chlorofluorocarbon*) PACK, POLL CFC (*clorofluorocarbono*)
CFD *abbr* (*computational fluid dynamics*) AIR TRANSP CFD (*dinámica de fluidos computacional*), FLUID dinámica de fluidos computacional *f*
C-format: ~ **videotape recorder** *n* TV grabador de video en formato C *m* (*AmL*), grabador de vídeo en formato C *m* (*Esp*)
CG *abbr* GAS (*connexion gas*), PETR TECH (*connection gas*) gas de conexión *m*
CGA *abbr* (*color graphics adaptor* AmE, *colour graphics adaptor* BrE) COMP&DP CGA (*adaptador gráfico de colores*)
CGS *abbr* (*centimeter-gram-second* AmE, *centimetre-gram-second* BrE) METR CGS (*cegesimal*)
chabasite *n* MINERAL chabasita *f*
chad *n* COMP&DP recorte *m* (*Esp*)
chafer *n* AGRIC escarabajo escoriador *m*, TEXTIL desfibradora *f*
chaff *n* AGRIC cáscara *f*, granza *f*, FOOD paja *f*, MILIT virutas metálicas *f pl*; ~ **cutter** *n* AGRIC cortadora de forraje *f*
chafing *n* NUCL fatiga acelerada por rozamiento *f*, vibrocorrosión *f*, WATER TRANSP *of sails* desgaste *m*, rozamiento *m*; ~ **plate** *n* MECH ENG chapa de fricción *f*, chapa de rozamiento *f*; ~ **strip** *n* AIR TRANSP banda de rozamiento *f*, guarnición *f*
chain[1]: **~-driven** *adj* MECH ENG accionado por cadena
chain[2] *n* GEN cadena *f*; ~ **block** *n* MECH *aircraft, spacecraft* cadena de eslabones *m*, MECH ENG aparejo diferencial de cadena *m*, garrucha diferencial de cadena *f*, montacarga de cadena *f*, *sheave* polea diferencial *f*; ~ **bolt** *n* MECH ENG pasador de cadena *m*, perno de cadena *m*; ~ **bridge** *n* CONST puente de cadena *m*; ~ **cable** *n* MECH ENG cable de cadena *m*, WATER TRANSP *mooring* cadena *f*; ~ **case** *n* SAFE cárter de la cadena *m*, guardacadena *f*; ~ **coal cutting machine** *n* MINE rafadora de cadena para carbón *f*; ~ **code** *n* COMP&DP código de la cadena puntera *m*, código en cadena *m*; ~ **conveyor** *n* MECH ENG cadena transportadora *f*, transportador de cadena *m*; ~ **coupling** *n* MECH ENG acoplamiento de cadena *m*, enganche de cadena *m*; ~ **drive** *n* MECH, MECH ENG, VEH accionamiento por cadena *m*, transmisión por cadena *f*; ~ **elevator** *n* AmE (*cf chain lift* BrE) MECH ENG elevador de cadena *m*; ~ **formation** *n* CHEM *compounds* formación en cadena *f*; ~ **gear** *n* MECH ENG engranaje de cadena *m*, rueda dentada para cadena *f*; ~ **grate** *n* MECH ENG parrilla articulada *f*; ~ **grinder** *n* PAPER desfibrador de cadena *m*; ~ **guard** *n* MECH ENG cubrecadena *f*, guardacadena *f*, VEH protector de cadena *m*, protector del catello *m*; ~ **guide** *n* MECH ENG, VEH guía de cadena *f*; ~ **haulage** *n* COAL arrastre de vagonetas en

cadena *m*; ~ **hoist** *n* MECH ENG grúa de cadena *f*, montacargas de cadena *m*; ~ **ladder** *n* CONST escalera de cadena *f*; ~ **length** *n* P&R longitud de cadena *f*; ~ **lever** *n* MECH ENG palanca de cadena *f*; ~ **lift** *n* BrE (*cf chain elevator* AmE) MECH ENG elevador de cadena *m*; ~ **lifter** *n* WATER TRANSP *on windlass* barbotén *m*, barbotún *m*; ~ **link** *n* AUTO, VEH eslabón de cadena *m*; ~ **locker** *n* WATER TRANSP caja de anclas *f*; ~ **maker** *n* PROD *person* cadenero *m*; **~-oiled bearing** *n* MECH ENG cojinete de lubricación automática por cadena *m*; ~ **pillar** *n* MINE pilar de protección de galerías *m*; ~ **pin** *n* MINE aguja de cadeneo *f*, pasador de cadena *m*; ~ **pipe wrench** *n* MECH ENG llave de cadena para tubos *f*; ~ **plate** *n* WATER TRANSP *rigging* cadenote *m*; ~ **printer** *n* AmE (*cf train printer* BrE) COMP&DP, PRINT impresora de cadena *f*, impresora de tren *f*; ~ **pulley** *n* MECH ENG polea de cadena *f*, rueda de cadena *f*; ~ **pulley block** *n* MECH ENG aparejo de cadena *m*, polipasto de cadena *m*; ~ **pump** *n* MECH ENG, WATER bomba de cadena *f*, bomba de rosario *f*; ~ **reaction** *n* MECH ENG, METALL, PHYS, RAD PHYS reacción en cadena *f*; ~ **saw** *n* MECH ENG sierra de cadena *f*, *for wood* sierra de dientes articulados *f*; ~ **scraper** *n* HYDROL excavadora de arrastre concatenada *f*; ~ **shearing machine** *n* MINE rozadora de cadena para entalladuras verticales *f*; ~ **sheave** *n* MECH ENG polea de cadena *f*, *cupped* rueda de cadena *f*; ~ **sling** *n* SAFE estrobo de cadena *m*; ~ **sprocket** *n* MECH ENG rueda dentada de cadena *f*; ~ **and sprocket drive** *n* AUTO transmisión de cadena y rueda dentada *f*; ~ **and sprocket wheels** *n pl* MECH ENG cadena y ruedas dentadas *f*; ~ **tensioner** *n* VEH tensor de cadena *m*; ~ **vice** *n* BrE MECH ENG grampa a cadena *f*, prensa a cadena *f*, prensa de cadena *f*, tornillo de cadena *m*; ~ **vise** *n* AmE *see* chain vice BrE; ~ **wheel** *n* MECH ENG piñón de cadena *m*, polea de cadena *f*, rueda dentada para cadena *f*; ~ **winding** *n* ELEC ENG devanado en cadena *m*
chain[3] *vt* CONST *surveying* medir con cadena
chainage *n* CONST cadeneo *m*
chaincase *n* VEH cárter de la cadena *m*
chained: ~ **file** *n* COMP&DP archivo encadenado *m*; ~ **list** *n* COMP&DP lista encadenada *f*
chaining *n* CONST cadeneo *m*; ~ **search** *n* COMP&DP búsqueda encadenada *f*
chainmail: ~ **garments** *n pl* SAFE prendas de malla de acero *f pl*
chainman *n* CONST *surveying* portacadenas *m*
chainsmith *n* PROD *person* herrero *m*
chair *n* C&G silla *f*, MECH ENG *at universities* cátedra *f*; ~ **arm** *n* C&G brazo de la silla *m*; ~ **lift** *n* TRANSP telesilla *f*
chalcanthite *n* MINERAL calcantita *f*
chalcedony *n* MINERAL calcedonia *f*
chalcedonyx *n* MINERAL calcedonix *m*
chalcocite *n* MINERAL calcosita *f*
chalcogenide: ~ **glass** *n* C&G vidrio con elementos en forma metálica *m*
chalcolite *n* MINERAL calcolita *f*
chalcomenite *n* MINERAL calcomenita *f*
chalcone *n* CHEM calcona *f*
chalcophanite *n* MINERAL calcofanita *f*
chalcophyllite *n* MINERAL calcofilita *f*
chalcopyrite *n* MINERAL calcopirita *f*
chalcopyrrhotine *n* MINERAL calcopirrotina *f*

chalcosiderite *n* MINERAL calcosiderita *f*
chalcosine *n* MINERAL calcosina *f*
chalcostibite *n* MINERAL calcoestibina *f*, güejarita *f*, wolfsbergita *f*
chalcotrichite *n* MINERAL calcotriquita *f*
chalk *n* C&G clarión *m*, gis *m*, tiza *f*, GEOL carbonato cálcico *m*, creta *f*, PETR TECH creta *f*; ~ **formation** *n* WATER yacimiento de caliza *m*; ~ **marl** *n* CONST marga *f*, GEOL marga de creta *f*; ~ **stratum** *n* CONST capa de yeso *f*, capa yesífera *f*, estrato de yeso *m*, estrato yesífero *m*
chalking *n* PRINT desprendimiento de partículas de tinta ya impresa *m*
chalkomorphite *n* MINERAL calcomorfita *f*
chalky[1] *adj* GEOL carbonatado, cretáceo, PETR TECH, PETROL cretáceo
chalky[2]: ~ **clay** *n* WATER arcilla gredosa *f*
chalybite *n* MINERAL calibita *f*, espato ferrífero *m*, siderita *f*
chamber *n* CHEM cámara *f*, MECH caja *f*, cuerpo *m*, cámara *f*, mezclador *m*, MECH ENG *of injector* cámara *f*, MILIT recámara *f*, MINE anchurón *m* (*AmL*), hornillo *m* (*AmL*), cámara subterránea *f*, sala *f*, cámara *f*, WATER *of canal lock* cuenco *m*; ~ **acid** *n* CHEM, CHEM TECH ácido de cámaras *m*; ~ **process** *n* CHEM TECH proceso de las cámaras de plomo *m*; ~-**type vacuum sealing** *n* PACK precintado al vacío *m*
chambered: ~ **core** *n* PROD *founding* macho bombeado *m*; ~ **eccentric** *n* MECH ENG excéntrica lobulada *f*; ~ **hole** *n* MINE barreno con el fondo ensanchado *m*
chambering *n* MINE ensanchamiento del fondo *m*
chambre: ~ **blanche** *n* PACK cámara de aclarado *f*
chamfer[1] *n* CONST bisel *m*, chaflán *m*, inglete *m*; ~ **stop** *n* CONST *joinery* punto de terminación del biselado *m*
chamfer[2] *vt* C&G biselar, CONST achaflanar, biselar, ingletar, INSTR, MECH biselar, MECH ENG achaflanar, biselar, espatillar, sesgar, PETR TECH, PETROL, PRINT, PROD biselar
chamfered: ~ **joint** *n* CONST junta de inglète *f*, MECH ENG junta en bisel *f*
chamfering *n* CONST biselado *m*, ingletado *m*
chamois *n* PROD gamuza *f*
chamosite *n* MINERAL chamosita *f*
champagne: ~ **bottle** *n* C&G botella para champaña *f*; ~ **finish** *n* C&G acabado champaña *m*
chandelier *n* C&G, ELEC *lighting* araña de luces *f*, candelabro *m*, candelero *m*
change[1] *n* FLUID variación *f*, PART PHYS *in shape of nucleus* cambio *m*; ~ **dump** *n* COMP&DP vuelco de cambios *m*; ~ **feed box** *n* MECH ENG *machine tools* caja de alimentación *f*; ~ **file** *n* COMP&DP archivo de cambios *m*; ~ **gear** *n* MECH ENG engranaje de cambio de velocidad *m*, engranaje de cambio *m*, mecanismo de inversión de marcha *m*; ~ **hook** *n* MECH ENG garfio doble *m*; ~-**of-gage station** *AmE*, ~-**of-gauge station** *BrE n* RAIL estación de cambio de ancho de vía *f*; ~ **order** *n* MECH orden de cambio *f*; ~ **record** *n* COMP&DP registro de cambios *m*; ~ **speed gear** *n* MECH ENG cambio de velocidad *m*; ~ **of state** *n* PHYS, THERMO cambio de estado *m*; ~ **tape** *n* COMP&DP cinta de cambios *f*; ~ **wheel** *n* MECH ENG *for screw-cutting lathe* rueda de filetear *f*, rueda de recambio *f*
change[2] *vt* WATER TRANSP *course* enmendar; ~ **over** *vt* CINEMAT cambiar
change[3]: ~ **over from gear-drive to belt-drive** *vi*

MECH ENG pasar de la marcha por engranajes a la marcha por correa
changeover *n* CINEMAT, TV cambio *m*; ~ **cue** *n* CINEMAT, TV aviso de cambio *m*, señal de cambio *f*; ~ **procedure** *n* PACK procedimiento de cambio *m*, procedimiento de permuta *m*; ~ **relay** *n* ELEC, ELEC ENG relé de conmutación *m*, relé inversor *m*; ~ **switch** *n* ELEC conmutador *m*, inversor de corriente *m*, ELEC ENG conmutador *m*, conmutador inversor *m*, inversor de corriente *m*, WATER TRANSP *electrical* conmutador de dos posiciones *m*; ~ **to stand-by** *n* TELECOM permutación a estado de espera *f*; ~ **valve** *n* PROD válvula inversora *f*
changing: ~ **bag** *n* CINEMAT saco de carga *m*, saco negro *m*, PHOTO bolsa oscura de carga *f* (*Esp*), cambiaplacas a plena luz *m* (*AmL*)
channel[1] *n* ACOUST, COMP&DP canal *m*, CONST aspirador *m* (*Esp*), canaleta *f* (*AmL*), *long gutter, groove* aliviadero *m*, conducto *m*, lecho de río *m*, ELEC, ELEC ENG, ELECTRON circuito eléctrico *m*, canal *m*, FUELLESS, GEOL canal *m*, HYDRAUL aliviadero *m*, aspirador *m* (*Esp*), canaleta *f* (*AmL*), HYDROL aspirador *m* (*Esp*), canal *m*, canaleta *f* (*AmL*) MECH conducto *m*, ranura *f*, canal *m*, MECH ENG conducto *m*, SPACE canal *m*, TELECOM vía de transmisión *f*, TV canal *m*, WATER aspirador *m* (*Esp*), canaleta *f* (*AmL*) WATER TRANSP aliviadero *m*, aspirador *m* (*Esp*), canal *m*, canaleta *f* (*AmL*); ~ **address word** *n* (*CAW*) COMP&DP palabra de dirección en canal *f*, palabra del canal de cambio *f*, palabra direccional del canal *f*; ~ **allocation** *n* TV distribución de canales *f*; ~ **allocation time** *n* TELECOM tiempo de asignación de canal *m*; ~ **amplifier** *n* TV amplificador de canales *m*; ~ **associated signaling** *n* *AmE*, ~ **associated signalling** *BrE n* TELECOM señalización asociada a las vías de transmisión *f*, señalización asociada al canal *f*; ~ **bandwidth** *n* TV ancho de banda del canal *m*; ~ **bed** *n* WATER cauce *m*; ~ **capacity** *n* COMP&DP, TELECOM capacidad del canal *f*; ~ **center frequency** *n* *AmE*, ~-**centre frequency** *BrE n* TELECOM frecuencia central del canal *f*; ~ **command word** *n* COMP&DP palabra de comando en canal *f*, palabra de mandato en canal *f*, palabra de orden del canal *f*; ~ **control** *n* TELECOM control del canal *m*; ~ **doping** *n* ELECTRON alteración de canal *f*; ~ **efficiency** *n* TELECOM eficiencia del canal *f*; ~ **equipment** *n* TELECOM equipo de canales *m*; ~ **fill** *n* GEOL relleno de canal *m*; ~ **filter** *n* ELECTRON filtro de canal *m*; ~ **induction furnace** *n* HEAT horno de canal de inducción *m*; ~ **iron** *n* CONST *square section* hierro en U *m*, viga en U *f*, *U section* tubo en U *m*; ~ **lag** *n* GEOL depósitos basales de un canal *m pl*; ~ **loading** *n* TELECOM carga del canal *f*; ~ **marking** *n* TRANSP baliza de canal *f*; ~ **marks** *n pl* TRANSP señalizaciones de canal *f pl*; ~ **modulation** *n* ELECTRON modulación de canal *f*; ~ **noise** *n* ELECTRON ruido de canal *m*; ~ **occupancy** *n* TELECOM ocupancia del canal *f*; ~ **sample** *n* COAL muestra de roza *f*; ~ **selector** *n* TELECOM, TV selector de canales *m*; ~-**selector switch** *n* TELECOM, TV conmutador de selección de canales *m*, llave selectora de canales *f*; ~ **spacing** *n* COMP&DP, TV espaciado de canales *m*; ~ **status table** *n* COMP&DP tabla de categoría de canales *f*, tabla de estado de canal *f* (*Esp*); ~ **status word** *n* COMP&DP palabra de categoría de canales *f*, palabra de estado de canal *f*; ~ **stopper** *n* ELEC ENG supresor del circuito *m*;

~ track n TRANSP canalización f; **~ using lower sideband** n TV canal utilizando banda lateral inferior m; **~ using upper sideband** n TV canal utilizando banda lateral superior m; **~ vocoder** n TELECOM vocoder de canales m

channel^2 vt CONST canalizar, FUELLESS canalizar, encauzar, GEOL acanalar, encauzar, PROD encauzar

channel^3: **~ out** vi PROD encauzar hacia la salida

channeler AmE see channeller BrE

channeling AmE see channelling m; **~ machine** AmE see channelling machine BrE

channelization n TRANSP canalización f

channeller n BrE MINE acanaladora f (Esp), rafadora f (AmL), rozadora f

channelling n BrE FUELLESS dams, geothermal power canalización f, encauzamiento m, GEOL dams, geothermal power encauzamiento m, PROD grooving, blast furnace chimeneas f pl, dams, geothermal power encauzamiento m, TELECOM canalización f, WATER dams, geothermal power encauzamiento m; **~ machine** n BrE MINE acanaladora f (Esp), rafadora f (AmL), rozadora f

channels: **in ~** phr FLUID en canales

channelway n WATER cauce de una corriente de agua m

chaos: **~ theory** n MATH teoría del caos f

chapelet n WATER bomba de cadena sin fin f, bomba de rosario f

chaplet n PROD founding soporte para machos m

chaps n pl MECH ENG of vice mordazas f

char^1 n TELECOM carbonizado m

char^2 vt COAL carbonizar, chamuscar

character n COMP&DP, ELECTRON, PRINT, TELECOM, TV carácter m; **~ code** n COMP&DP código de carácter m; **~-coupling switch** n TELECOM conmutador de acoplamiento de caracteres m; **~ generator** n COMP&DP, ELECTRON, TELECOM, TV generador de caracteres m; **~-oriented machine** n COMP&DP computador orientado a los caracteres m (AmL), computadora orientada a los caracteres f (AmL), ordenador orientado a los caracteres m (Esp); **~ outline** n COMP&DP contorno de un carácter m, perfil de caracteres m; **~ pitch** n PRINT número de caracteres por unidad de longitud m; **~ printer** n COMP&DP, PRINT impresora de caracteres f; **~ reader** n COMP&DP lectura de caracteres f; **~-reading vision system** n COMP&DP, PACK sistema visual de lectura de caracteres m; **~ recognition** n COMP&DP reconocimiento de caracteres m; **~ set** n COMP&DP conjunto de caracteres m, juego de caracteres m; **~ string** n COMP&DP cadena de caracteres f, PRINT línea de caracteres f; **~ subset** n COMP&DP juego parcial de caracteres m, subconjunto de caracteres m; **~ switch** n TELECOM conmutador de caracteres m; **~ tracer** n INSTR rastreador decodificador m; **~ type** n COMP&DP, PRINT tipo de carácter m; **~ width** n PRINT anchura del carácter f

characteristic^1 adj COMP&DP característico

characteristic^2 n GEN característica f; **~ admittance** n ACOUST, ELEC, ELEC ENG, PHYS admitancia característica f; **~ curve** n ACOUST, CINEMAT, ELEC, ELECTRON, PHOTO, PHYS, SPACE curva característica f; **~ efficiency** n ACOUST eficacia característica f; **~ equation** n SPACE ecuación característica f; **~ floodwater flow rate** n HYDROL porcentaje característico de evacuación de aguas m; **~ flow** n HYDROL flujo característico m; **~ frequency** n RAD PHYS frecuencia característica f; **~ impedance** n ACOUST, ELEC ENG, PHYS impedancia característica f; **~ low-water flow rate** n HYDROL porcentaje característico del nivel de estiaje m; **~ shape** n MECH ENG of roughness profile forma característica f; **~ X-ray spectrum** n RAD PHYS espectro característico de rayos X m

characters: **~ per inch** n (CPI) PRINT caracteres por pulgada m pl (CPP); **~ per second** n (CPS) COMP&DP, PRINT caracteres por segundo m pl (CPS)

charcoal n CHEM carbón m, COAL carbón de leña m, carbón vegetal m; **~ duff** n COAL desperdicios de carbón de leña m pl, desperdicios de carbón vegetal m pl; **~ filter** n LAB filtro de carbón m; **~ root** n AGRIC carbón de raíz m

charge^1 n C&G, ELEC, ELEC ENG, ELECTRON carga f, MINE cartucho m, carga f, PART PHYS carga f, PHYS carga f, carga eléctrica f, TELECOM carga f; **~ amplifier** n ELECTRON amplificador de carga m; **~ area** n NUCL zona de carga f; **~ build-up** n ELEC ENG recarga f; **~ carrier** n ELEC ENG onda portadora electrizada f, SPACE portador de carga m; **~ chamber** n PROD of reverbatory furnace laboratorio m; **~ cloud** n RAD PHYS distribución espacial de la carga eléctrica f, nube de carga f; **~ conjugation operation** n PART PHYS operación de la carga f; **~ couple device camera** n PACK cámara con dispositivo de acoplamiento de carga f; **~-coupled device** n (CCD) COMP&DP, ELEC ENG, ELECTRON, PHYS, TELECOM, TV dispositivo acoplado por carga m (DAC); **~ density** n ELEC of a capacitor, PHYS, RAD PHYS densidad de carga f; **~ discharge cycle** n TRANSP ciclo de carga y descarga m; **~ face** n NUCL paramento de carga m; **~ hand** n PROD capataz m, encargado m; **~ indicator** n WATER TRANSP of batteries indicador de carga m; **~ leakage** n ELEC of a capacitor dispersión de carga f, escape de carga m, fuga de carga f; **~ mass ratio** n PHYS carga específica f; **~-metering converter** n TELECOM convertidor del contador de carga m; **~ multiplets** n pl RAD PHYS multipletes de carga m pl; **~ neutralization** n ELEC neutralización de carga f; **~ parity symmetry** n PART PHYS, RAD PHYS simetría paritaria de carga f; **~ pump** n ELEC ENG carga inestable f, inestabilidad de la carga f; **~ rate** n TELECOM tasa de carga f; **~ storage** n ELEC ENG acumulación de carga f; **~-storage diode** n ELECTRON diodo de almacenamiento de carga m; **~-storage tube** n ELECTRON tubo de almacenamiento de carga m; **~ stratification** n TRANSP estratificación de la carga f; **~ transfer** n NUCL, RAD PHYS transferencia de carga f; **~-transfer band** n NUCL, RAD PHYS banda de transferencia de carga f; **~-transfer device** n (CTD) ELEC ENG, PHYS, SPACE, TELECOM dispositivo de transferencia de carga m (DTC)

charge^2 vt PROD, TELECOM cargar, THERMO alimentar, cargar; **~ by friction** vt PHYS cargar por fricción; **~ the call to** vt TELECOM cargar la llamada a

chargecard n TELECOM tarjeta de pago f

charged: **~ particle** n ELEC ENG, ELECTRON, NUCL, PART PHYS, POLL, RAD PHYS partícula cargada f; **~-particle activation analysis** n PART PHYS, RAD PHYS análisis de activación por partículas cargadas m; **~-particle beam** n ELECTRON, PART PHYS haz de partículas cargado m; **~-particle radiography** n

NUCL, PART PHYS, RAD PHYS radiografía por partículas cargadas *f*

charger *n* PROD *furnace* cargador *m*

charging *n* C&G carga *f*, ELEC ENG carga *f*, cargador *m*, MINE, PROD *furnace* carga *f*; ~ **circuit** *n* ELEC *of a battery, accumulator* circuito de carga *m*; ~ **connection** *n* REFRIG conexión de carga *f*, racor de carga *m*; ~ **cullet only** *n* C&G carga de vidrio de desecho solo *f*; ~ **current** *n* ELEC *of a battery, accumulator* corriente de carga *f*; ~ **door** *n* PROD *of a furnace* compuerta de carga *f*; ~ **end** *n* C&G lado de carga *m*; ~ **equipment** *n* TELECOM equipo de carga *m*; ~ **hole** *n* PROD *of cupola* abertura de carga *f*; ~ **information** *n* TELECOM información de carga *f*; ~ **machine** *n* PROD *of a furnace* máquina cargadora *f*; ~ **platform** *n* PROD *of a furnace* plataforma de carga *f*; ~ **point** *n* TRANSP punto de carga *m*; ~ **pump** *n* NUCL bomba de carga *f*; ~ **rectifier** *n* ELEC *of a battery, accumulator* rectificador de carga *m*; ~ **regulator** *n* SPACE regulador de carga *m*; ~ **scaffold** *n* PROD andamio de carga *m*; ~ **station** *n* ELEC *of an accumulator, battery*, ELEC ENG *of accumulator, a battery* central eléctrica de carga *f*, punto de carga *m*; ~ **voltage** *n* ELEC, ELEC ENG *of an accumulator, battery* tensión de carga *f*, voltaje de carga *m*

Charles: ~ **'s law** *n* PHYS ley de Charles *f*

charm *n* NUCL, PART PHYS encanto *m*; ~ **quark** *n* PART PHYS, PHYS charm quark *m*, quark encanto *m*

Charpy: ~ **impact test** *n* MECH prueba de impacto Charpy *f*, prueba de resilencia Charpy *f*, METALL prueba de impacto Charpy *f*, prueba de resilencia Charpy *f*, P&R prueba de impacto Charpy *f*, prueba de resilencia Charpy *f*; ~ **impact tester** *n* P&R medidor Charpy de resistencia a la rotura bajo impacto *m*; ~ **test** *n* PHYS prueba de Charpy *f*; ~ **V-notch impact specimen** *n* NUCL probeta con entalla en V para prueba de impacto Charpy *f*; ~ **V-notch test** *n* MECH *craft* prueba con entalla Charpy en V *f*

charred *adj* CHEM carbonizado

charring *n* CHEM carbonización *f*, CONST *preservation of timber* limpieza de fachada *f*

chart[1] *n* ACOUST ábaco *m*, PHYS cuadro *m*, PRINT gráfico *m*, WATER TRANSP *map* carta de marear *f*, carta náutica *f*; ~ **correction** *n* WATER TRANSP *navigation* corrección de la carta *f*; ~ **datum** *n* WATER TRANSP *navigation* cero de la carta *m*, datum de la carta *m*; ~ **paper** *n* PAPER papel para diagramas *m*, papel para ábacos *f*; ~ **recorder** *n* INSTR, LAB *device to check shades* grabador gráfico *m*, registro gráfico *m*; ~ **strip** *n* ELEC banda de papel para registro gráfico *f*, carta de rollo *f*, gráfica de rollo *f*, gráfica en banda de papel *f*, rollo de papel gráfico *m*; ~ **table** *n* WATER TRANSP mesa de marear *f*, mesa de marear las cartas *f*

chart[2] *vt* HYDROL, WATER TRANSP *navigation, hydrography* cartografiar

charted: ~ **depth** *n* WATER TRANSP *navigation* profundidad cartografiada *f*

charter *n* AIR TRANSP, PETR TECH, WATER TRANSP fletamento *m*; ~ **company** *n* AIR TRANSP compañía chárter *f*, WATER TRANSP sociedad flotadora *f*; ~ **party** *n* PETR TECH, WATER TRANSP contrato de fletamento *m*, póliza de fletamento *f*

charterage *n* AIR TRANSP, PETR TECH, WATER TRANSP fletamento *m*

charterer *n* AIR TRANSP, PETR TECH, WATER TRANSP fletador *m*

chartering *n* AIR TRANSP, PETR TECH, WATER TRANSP fletamentos *m pl*; ~ **broker** *n* WATER TRANSP corredor fletador *m*

chartroom *n* WATER TRANSP *boat building* caseta de derrota *f*, cuarto de derrota *m*

chase[1] *n* MINE *seam* guía *f*, PRINT rama *f*, forma *f*

chase[2] *vt* MECH ENG *screw-cutting* filetear, repasar, MINE trazar, PROD *rivets* roscar

chaser *n* MECH ENG *screw-cutting* peine para roscar *m*; ~ **die screwing stock** *n* MECH ENG terraja de peines *f*

chasing *n* MECH ENG *screw-cutting* peinado *m*, roscado *m*; ~ **lathe** *n* MECH ENG torno de embutir *m*, torno para roscar *m*; ~ **machine** *n* MECH ENG máquina de filetear *f*

chassis *n* VEH bastidor *m*, chasis *m*; ~ **cab** *n* VEH armazón de la cabina *m*, bastidor de cabina *m*, chasis de cabina *m*; ~ **member** *n* VEH larguero del bastidor *m*

chat: ~ **roller** *n* COAL apisonadora de sílex *f*

chatoyant *adj* MINERAL efecto ojo de gato *m*, efecto tornasolado *m*

chatter[1]: ~ **mark** *n* GEOL marca falciforme *f*

chatter[2] *vi* PROD vibrar

chattering *n* PROD vibración *f*

chauffer *n* PROD *kettle for skin-drying* recalentador *m*

chavibetol *n* CHEM chavibetol *m*

chavicol *n* CHEM chavicol *m*

cheap: ~ **call** *n* TELECOM llamada económica *f*; ~ **call rate** *n* TELECOM tarifa reducida de llamadas *f*

Chebyshev: ~ **filter** *n* ELECTRON, PHYS filtro de Chebyshev *m*

check[1] *n* C&G trampa de retroceso *f*, COMP&DP comprobación *f*, control *m*, verificación *f*, MECH ENG comprobación *f*, control *m*, revisión *f*, verificación *f*, PACK, SPACE comprobación *f*, WATER TRANSP *shipbuilding* gualdera de litera *f*; ~ **analysis** *n* CHEM análisis de prueba *m*; ~ **assay** *n* CHEM contraprueba *f*, ensayo de verificación *m*; ~ **bit** *n* ELECTRON bit de verificación *m*, clave de control *f*; ~ **character** *n* COMP&DP carácter de control *m*; ~ **code** *n* COMP&DP código de comprobación *m*; ~ **digit** *n* COMP&DP dígito de control *m*; ~ **point** *n* SPACE punto de verificación *m*; ~ **print** *n* CINEMAT prueba *f*; ~ **rail** *n* RAIL contracarril *m*; ~ **row planting** *n* AGRIC siembra en cuadros *f*; ~ **sample** *n* CHEM, COAL muestra de contraste *f*, muestra de control *f*, muestra testigo *f*; ~ **sequence** *n* TELECOM secuencia de comprobación *f*; ~ **switch** *n* ELEC, ELEC ENG conmutador de comprobación *m*, conmutador de control *m*, conmutador de prueba *m*; ~ **valve** *n* AUTO, FUELLESS, HYDRAUL válvula de contención *f*, válvula de retención *f*, MECH válvula de frenado *f*, válvula de retención *f*, MECH ENG válvula de retención *f*, válvula de frenado *f*, SPACE, VEH, WATER válvula de retención *f*; ~ **weighing** *n* PACK comprobación del peso *f*; ~ **weighing machine** *n* PACK balanza *f*, báscula *f*

check[2] *vt* CINEMAT, CONST comprobar, verificar, METR *measurements* verificar, SAFE revisar, WATER TRANSP *rope* aguantar, filar poco a poco, lascar, quitar andar; ~ **out** *vt* SPACE verificar

checked: ~ **finish** *n* C&G acabado cuadriculado *m*

checker *n* (*cf chequer*) METALL termorrecuperador *m*, recuperador de calor *m*, PROD recuperador de calor *m*, termorrecuperador *m*, *tallyman* controlador *m*, verificador *m*; ~ **brick** *n* C&G ladrillo refractario para cámara de precalentamiento *m*; ~ **chamber** *n* C&G cámara de precalentamiento de gases *f*; ~ **pattern** *n* C&G fondo ajedrezado *m*; ~ **plate** *AmE see chequer plate BrE*

checkerboarding *AmE see chequerboarding BrE*

checkered: ~ **plate** *AmE see chequered plate BrE*

checkering *AmE see chequering BrE*

checkers *AmE see chequers BrE*

checking *n* PACK, QUALITY comprobación *f*, verificación *f*; ~ **apparatus** *n* PACK, QUALITY aparato de comprobación *m*, instrumento de verificación *m*; ~ **fixture** *n* MECH ENG *machine tools* montaje de verificación *m*

checklist *n* MECH ENG lista de control *f*

checknut *n* MECH ENG contratuerca *f*, tuerca de seguridad *f*, tuerca de sujeción *f*

checkout *n* *AmE* SPACE verificación *f*; ~ **system** *n* SPACE sistema de verificación *m*

checkpoint *n* COMP&DP punto de control *m*; ~ **recovery** *n* COMP&DP recuperación del punto de control *f*

checkrail *n* CONST carretera inferior *f*, travesaño de encuentro *m*

checks *n pl* TEXTIL cuadros *m pl*, tejido a cuadros *m*

checkshot *n* PETR TECH disparo de verificación *m*

checksum *n* COMP&DP, ELECTRON suma de control *f*, total de control *m*

checkweigher *n* PACK balanza comprobadora de pesos *f*

cheek *n* CONST *of mortise* cara *f*, MECH ENG quijada *f*, cara firme *f*, montante *m*, parte central *f*, jamba *f*, PROD *of flask* parte central *f*, WATER TRANSP *of block* quijada *f*; ~ **block** *n* WATER TRANSP *deck fittings* motón de quijada *m*

cheeks *n pl* MECH ENG *of lathe* mordazas *f pl*, MINE costero *m* (*Esp*), hastial *m* (*AmL*), pared *f*

cheese *n* TEXTIL queso *m*; ~ **adaptor** *n* TEXTIL adaptador de la bobina plana *m*; ~-**drying room** *n* FOOD, REFRIG secadero para quesos *m*; ~-**head fastener** *n* MECH ENG elemento de sujeción de cabeza chata ranurada *m*; ~-**head rivet** *n* CONST remache de cabeza plana *m*; ~-**head screw** *n* CONST tornillo con cabeza plana *m*; ~ **tube** *n* TEXTIL tubo de la bobina plana *m*

chelate[1] *n* CHEM, DETERG, HYDROL, NUCL quelato *m*; ~ **formation** *n* NUCL formación de quelatos *f*

chelate[2] *vt* CHEM, DETERG, HYDROL, NUCL quelatar

chelating *n* CHEM, DETERG, HYDROL, NUCL quelación *f*; ~ **agent** *n* CHEM, DETERG, HYDROL agente quelatante *m*, quelatador *m*

chelation *n* CHEM, DETERG, HYDROL, NUCL quelación *f*

chemi: ~-**groundwood** *n* PAPER pasta químico-mecánica *f*

chemical: ~ **agent** *n* CHEM, MILIT, POLL, TEXTIL agente químico *m*; ~-**agent-resisting material** *n* (*CARM*) MILIT material resistente a los agentes químicos *m*; ~ **altering** *n* CHEM, PETROL alteración química *f*; ~ **analysis** *n* COAL análisis químico *m*, análisis por vía húmeda *m*, ensayo por vía húmeda *m*; ~ **balance** *n* CHEM, LAB, PHYS balanza de laboratorio *f*, balanza química *f*; ~ **bond** *n* CHEM, CRYSTALL, PETR TECH enlace químico *m*; ~ **burn** *n* CHEM, SAFE quemadura química *f*; ~ **coal cleaning** *n* CHEM, COAL, POLL depuración química del carbón *f*, limpieza química del carbón *f*; ~ **coating** *n* CHEM, COATINGS, NUCL

revestimiento químico *m*; ~ **component** *n* CHEM, GEOL componente químico *m*; ~ **decanning** *n* CHEM, CHEM TECH, NUCL desenvainado por medios químicos *m*; ~ **decladding** *n* CHEM, CHEM TECH, NUCL desenvainado por medios químicos *m*; ~ **development** *n* CHEM, PHOTO revelado químico *m*; ~ **dosimetry** *n* CHEM, RAD PHYS dosimetría química *f*; ~ **drains** *n pl* NUCL drenajes químicos *m pl*; ~ **durability** *n* C&G, CHEM durabilidad química *f*; ~ **fogging** *n* CINEMAT velo químico *m*; ~ **grouting and freezing** *n* MINE consolidación y solidificación química *f*; ~ **hardening** *n* CHEM, METALL endurecimiento químico *m*, temple químico *m*; ~ **hazard** *n* CHEM, SAFE peligro químico *m*, riesgo químico *m*; ~ **intensification** *n* CHEM, PHOTO intensificación química *f*; ~ **laser** *n* CHEM, ELECTRON láser químico *m*; ~ **leavening** *n* FOOD levadura química *f*; ~ **machining** *n* MECH maquinado químico *m*; ~ **milling** *n* PROD fresado químico *m*; ~ **oxygen demand** *n* (*COD*) CHEM, HYDROL, POLL demanda química de oxígeno *f* (*DQO*); ~ **plant** *n* CHEM TECH fábrica de productos químicos *f*; ~ **polishing** *n* CHEM, METALL pulido químico *m*; ~ **potential** *n* CHEM, PHYS potencial químico *m*; ~ **precipitation** *n* CHEM, HYDROL precipitación química *f*; ~ **pulp** *n* PAPER pulpa química *f*; ~ **pulping** *n* PAPER cocción química *f*; ~ **purification** *n* HYDROL purificación química *f*; ~ **reprocessing plant** *n* CHEM TECH, NUCL planta de reprocesamiento químico *f*; ~ **resistance** *n* C&G, P&R resistencia química *f*; ~-**resistant coating** *n* CHEM, COATINGS revestimiento resistente a los productos químicos *m*; ~-**rocket engine** *n* MECH ENG motor de cohete químico *m*; ~ **sedimentation** *n* CHEM, GEOL sedimentación química *f*; ~ **stability** *n* COAL estabilidad química *f*; ~ **stabilization** *n* HYDROL *quality factor* estabilización química *f*; ~ **tanker** *n* WATER TRANSP buque tanque quimiquero *m*; ~ **treatment** *n* CHEM, COAL tratamiento químico *m*; ~ **vapor deposition** *n* *AmE*, ~ **vapour deposition** *n* *BrE* (*CVD*) ELECTRON, OPT, TELECOM deposición de vapor químico *f* (*DVQ*); ~ **and volume control system** *n* (*CVCS*) NUCL sistema de control químico y de volumen *m*; ~ **water treatment** *n* CHEM, HYDROL, WATER tratamiento químico de agua *m*; ~ **weathering** *n* GEOL alteración química *f*, PETROL desgaste por acción química *m*

chemically[1]: ~-**resistant** *adj* PACK resistente a la acción de productos químicos

chemically[2]: ~-**neutral oil** *n* PETR TECH aceite neutralizado químicamente *m*; ~-**resistant glass** *n* C&G vidrio resistente a substancias químicas *m*

chemicoanalytical *adj* CHEM quimicoanalítico

chemicometallurgical *adj* CHEM, METALL quimicometalúrgico

chemicometallurgy *n* CHEM, METALL quimicometalurgia *f*

chemicomineralogical *adj* CHEM, MINERAL quimicomineralógico

chemicophysical *adj* CHEM, PHYS quimicofísico

chemicothermo: ~ **mechanical pulp** *n* (*CTMP*) PAPER pasta químico-termomecánica *f*

chemiluminescence *n* PHYS, RAD PHYS quimioluminiscencia *f*

chemistry *n* CHEM química *f*

chemonuclear: ~ **fuel reactor** *n* CHEM, NUCL reactor quimiconuclear *m*

chemotherapy *n* CHEM quimioterapia *f*

chenille: ~ **fabric** *n* TEXTIL tejido de chenilla *m*, tejido de felpilla *m*; ~ **yarn** *n* TEXTIL hilo de chenilla *m*

chenopodium: ~ **album** *n* AGRIC quinoa *f*

chequer *n* BrE METALL, PROD recuperador de calor *m*, termorrecuperador *m*; ~ **plate** *n* BrE PROD chapa estriada *f*

chequerboarding *n* BrE CINEMAT edición en tablero de ajedrez *f*

chequered: ~ **plate** *n* BrE PROD chapa estriada *f*

chequering *n* BrE PROD cuadriculado *m*

chequers *n pl* BrE C&G ajedrezados *m pl*

cherry: ~ **coal** *n* COAL, MINE hulla grasa de llama larga *f*, hulla semigrasa *f*

cherrying *n* MECH ENG *machine tools* accesorio de fresado *m*

chert *n* GEOL chert *m*, sílex *m*; ~ **nodule** *n* GEOL nódulo de silex *m*

cherty[1] *adj* GEOL silíceo

cherty[2]: ~ **bed** *n* GEOL capa silícea *f*; ~ **limestone** *n* GEOL caliza silícea *f*; ~ **marl** *n* GEOL marga silícea *f*

chessylite *n* CHEM, MINERAL azurita *f*, chessylita *f*

chest *n* C&G arca *f*, PAPER tina *f*; ~ **freezer** *n* FOOD, REFRIG, THERMO arcón congelador *m*

chestpod *n* CINEMAT estativo *m*

chevron *n* MECH ENG cheurón *m*; ~ **cut gears** *n pl* MECH ENG engranajes a cheurones *m pl*; ~ **fold** *n* GEOL pliegue en zig-zag *m*; ~ **runner bar** *n* C&G barra engalonada *f*

chewing: ~ **insect** *n* AGRIC insecto masticador *m*

Chezy: ~ **'s formula** *n* HYDROL fórmula de Chezy *f*

chiaroscuro *n* CINEMAT claroscuro *m*

chiastolite *n* MINERAL quiastolita *f*

chickencorn *n* AGRIC guinea de gallina *f*

chief: ~ **building authority** *n* CONST organismo con competencias en urbanismos *m*; ~ **cameraman** *n* CINEMAT, TV primer operador *m*; ~ **designer** *n* CONST proyectista principal *m*; ~ **engineer** *n* CONST ingeniero jefe *m*, WATER TRANSP *aboard ship* maquinista naval jefe *m*; ~ **erecting engineer** *n* CONST ingeniero jefe de montaje *m*; ~ **factor** *n* PROD factor principal *m*; ~ **guard** *n* BrE RAIL jefe de tren *m*; ~ **petty officer** *n* WATER TRANSP *navy* contramaestre mayor *m*; ~ **superintendent engineer** *n* CONST ingeniero jefe de obra *m*

child: ~-**resistant closure** *n* PACK, SAFE cierre a prueba de niños *m*; ~-**resistant packaging** *n* PACK, SAFE embalaje a prueba de niños *m*

childproof: ~ **finish** *n* C&G, COATINGS, SAFE acabado a prueba de niños *m*

childrenite *n* MINERAL quildrenita *f*

chileite *n* MINERAL chileíta *f*

chill[1]: ~ **casting** *n* PROD *action* fundición en concha *f*, *object cast* fundición de coquilla *f*; ~ **hardening** *n* PROD *founding* endurecimiento superficial *m*, temple al aire *m*; ~ **mark** *n* BrE (*cf chill wrinkle AmE*) C&G marca de enfriamiento *f*, marca fría *f*; ~ **mold** *AmE*, ~ **mould** *BrE n* PROD *founding* coquilla de colada *f*, moldeo en coquilla *m*; ~-**permanent adhesive** *n* PACK adhesivo que sigue actuando a baja temperatura *m*; ~-**proofing** *n* REFRIG estabilización por frío *f*; ~ **roll** *n* P&R rodillo de enfriamiento *m*, PRINT rodillo enfriador *m*; ~ **room** *n* REFRIG, THERMO sala de congelación *f*, sala de enfriamiento *f*, sala de refrigeración *f*; ~ **wrinkle** *n* AmE (*cf chill mark BrE*) C&G marca de enfriamiento *f*, marca fría *f*

chill[2] *vt* PROD *founding* colocar; ~ **harden** *vt* PROD endurecer superficialmente, templar al aire

chill[3] *vti* FOOD, MECH, REFRIG, THERMO congelar, enfriar

chilled[1] *adj* FOOD, REFRIG, THERMO enfriado, refrigerado

chilled[2]: ~ **cast iron** *n* PROD fundición de concha *f*; ~ **goods** *n pl* FOOD, PACK, REFRIG mercancías en frío *f pl*, mercancías refrigeradas *f pl*; ~ **iron** *n* PROD hierro en moldes *m*; ~-**iron casting** *n* PROD fundición en coquilla *f*; ~-**iron roll** *n* PROD cilindro de función de templada *m*; ~ **shot** *n* PROD granalla de acero templado *f*; ~ **water** *n* HYDROL, REFRIG agua refrigerada *f*

chilling[1] *adj* CHEM, MECH ENG, REFRIG, THERMO refrigerante

chilling[2] *n* PROD *founding* fundición en concha *f*, temple en coquilla *m*, REFRIG, THERMO enfriamiento *m*; ~ **injury** *n* REFRIG daño por frío *m*; ~ **process** *n* REFRIG, THERMO proceso de refrigeración *m*; ~ **tower** *n* PRINT torre de enfriamiento *f*

chimney *n* CONST chimenea *f* (*AmL*), HEAT ENG chimenea *f*, MINE chimenea *f* (*AmL*), clavo *m* (*AmL*), clavo de chimenea *m*, columna rica *f*, PROD bóveda *f*; ~ **cooler** *n* CONST sistema de refrigeración de chimenea *m*; ~ **effect** *n* HEAT ENG efecto chimenea *m*; ~ **flue** *n* CONST cañón de chimenea *m*, conducto de humos de chimenea *m*, tragante de chimenea *m*; ~ **stack** *n* CONST tubo de chimenea *m*; ~ **valve** *n* PROD *of a hot-blast stove, blast furnace* válvula de bóveda *f*

china *n* C&G porcelana tipo china *f*; ~ **clay** *n* C&G, COATINGS, GEOL, MINERAL, P&R arcilla blanca muy pura *f*, caolín *m*; ~-**clay quarry** *n* C&G mina de caolín *f*; ~-**clay washing** *n* C&G lavado de caolín *m*; ~ **grass** *n* PAPER ramio *m*; ~ **insulator** *n* C&G, ELEC, ELEC ENG aislante de porcelana *m*; ~ **ornamentation** *n* C&G ornamento de porcelana *m*; ~ **painter** *n* C&G pintor de porcelana *m*; ~ **painting** *n* C&G pintura en porcelana *f*; ~ **water** *n* COATINGS tinta de China *f*

chinch: ~ **bug** *n* AGRIC chinche *f*

chine *n* AIR TRANSP arista *f*, borde *m*; ~ **tyre** *n* AIR TRANSP *motor* neumático de borde *m*, neumático de faldilla *m*

Chinese: ~ **blue** *n* C&G, COLOUR azul chino *m*; ~ **ink** *n* COLOUR tinta china *f*; ~ **lacquer** *n* COATINGS, COLOUR laca china *f*; ~ **paper** *n* PAPER papel de china *m*

chiolite *n* MINERAL quiolita *f*

chip[1]: **off** ~ *adj* ELECTRON fuera del chip; **on** ~ *adj* ELECTRON dentro del chip

chip[2] *n* C&G despostillada *f*, COMP&DP chip *m*, plaqueta *f*, circuito integrado *m*, CONST ripio *m*, *of stone* bloque pequeño *m*, ELEC lasca *f*, chip *m*, ELECTRON chip *m*, MECH viruta *f*, brizna *f*, rebaba *f*, astilla *f*, MECH ENG cuña cilíndrica *f*, lasca *f*, viruta *f*, ripio *m*, PAPER troceado *m*, PROD *of wood, metal* rebaba *f*, SPACE chip *m*, cubo *m*, microprocesador *m*, circuito integrado *m*, TELECOM chip *m*; ~-**and-wire hybrid circuit** *n* ELECTRON chip de tecnología híbrida *m*; ~ **area** *n* ELECTRON área del chip *f*; ~ **breaker** *n* MECH ENG rompevirutas *m*; ~ **card** *n* COMP&DP circuito estampado para plaquetas *m*, tarjeta con chip *f*; ~ **complexity** *n* ELECTRON complejidad de microplaca *f*, complejidad del chip *f*; ~ **design** *n* ELECTRON diseño del chip *m*; ~ **layout** *n* ELECTRON esquema del chip *m*; ~ **rate** *n* TELECOM velocidad del chip *f*; ~ **refining** *n* PAPER refino de troceados *m*; ~ **removal**

n MECH ENG desprendimiento de virutas *m*; ~ **set** *n* ELECTRON conjunto de chips *m*

chip³ *vt* CONST *with cold-chisel* cincelar, picar, PROD *whittle* trocear

chipboard *n* PACK, PAPER cartón gris *m*

chipped: ~ **corner** *n* C&G esquina despostillada *f*; ~ **edge** *n* C&G orilla despostillada *f*; ~ **ice** *n* REFRIG hielo en laminillas *m*

chipper *n* CONST cincelador *m*, PAPER troceadora *f*; ~ **knife** *n* PAPER cuchillas de la troceadora *f pl*

chipping *n* CONST *of stone* lasca *f*, piedra de árida para carretera *f*, raspado *m*, PROD *of wood, metal* desbarbado *m*, *with cold-chisel* desbastación *f*; ~ **chisel** *n* PROD cincel de desbarbar redondo *m*, *diamond point* cincel de desbarbar *m*, cincel de desbastar *m*, desbarbador de punta de diamante *m*, *flat* cincel de desbarbar plano *m*; ~ **hammer** *n* PROD martillo de cincelar *m*; ~ **to the weight** *n* C&G rebaje hasta su peso *m*; ~ **tool** *n* C&G herramienta para rebajar *f*

chippings *n pl* COAL gravilla *f*, virutas *f pl*

chips *n pl* PAPER silo de troceados *m*

chiral *adj* CHEM quiral

chirp *n* COMP&DP chirrido *m* (*Esp*), gorjeo *m* (*AmL*); ~ **modulation** *n* SPACE *communications* modulación por impulsos de frecuencia variable *f*

chirping *n* TELECOM chirrido *m* (*Esp*), gorgojeo *m* (*AmL*)

chisel *n* CONST *for wood, stone* buril *m*, cincel *m*, formón *m*, MECH *circuit* cincel *m*, trincha *f*, escoplo *m*, cortafríos *m*, MECH ENG escoplo *m*, formón *m*, gubia *f*, cincel *m*, MINE cortafríos *m*, cincel *m* (*AmL*), escoplo *m*, trépano *m*, PROD *for metal* cincel *m*; ~**-and-point pick** *n* CONST, MECH ENG formón *m*; ~ **bit** *n* MINE trépano cortante *m*, barrena de cincel *f*, PETR TECH barrena de percusión *f*, trépano cortante *m*; ~ **marking** *n* MECH ENG marcado a cincel *m*; ~ **plough** *n* BrE AGRIC arado cincel *m*, subsolador *m*; ~ **plow** *AmE see* chisel plough *BrE*; ~ **subsoiler** *n* AGRIC arado de subsuelo *m*

chiseler *AmE see* chiseller *BrE*

chiseling *AmE see* chiselling *BrE*

chiseller *n* BrE PROD *person* burilador *m*

chiselling *n* BrE PROD burilado *m*

chitin *n* CHEM quitina *f*

chitosamine *n* CHEM quitosamina *f*

chiviatite *n* MINERAL chiviatita *f*

chloanthite *n* MINERAL chloantita *f*

chloracetate *n* CHEM cloracetato *m*

chloracetic *adj* CHEM cloracético

chloral *n* CHEM cloral *m*

chloralamide *n* CHEM cloralamida *f*

chloralbenzene *n* CHEM cloralbenceno *m*

chloralbutol *n* CHEM cloralbutol *m*

chloralformate *n* CHEM cloralformatio *m*

chloralhydrate *n* CHEM cloral hidratado *m*, hidrato de cloral *m*

chloralose *n* CHEM cloralosa *f*

chloranil *n* CHEM cloranil *m*

chlorastrolite *n* MINERAL clorastrolita *f*

chlorate *n* CHEM clorato *m*; ~ **explosive** *n* MINE explosivo cloratado *m*

chloric¹ *adj* CHEM clórico

chloric²: ~ **acid** *n* CHEM, FOOD ácido clórico *m*

chloride *n* CHEM, COAL cloruro *m*; ~ **of lime bleaching** *n* DETERG blanqueo con polvos de blanqueo *m*; ~ **paper** *n* PHOTO papel cloruro *m*

chlorinate *vt* CHEM, DETERG, HYDROL clorar, tratar con cloro

chlorinated¹ *adj* CHEM, DETERG, HYDROL clorado

chlorinated²: ~ **lime** *n* DETERG hipoclorito cálcico *m*, polvo de blanqueo *m*, FOOD cal clorada *f*; ~ **polyethylene** *n* P&R polietileno clorado *m*; ~ **polyvinyl chloride** *n* (*CPVC*) P&R cloruro de polivinilo clorado *m* (*CPVC*); ~ **rubber** *n* P&R caucho clorado *m*; ~ **water** *n* HYDROL, PROD, WATER agua clorada *f*

chlorination *n* CHEM, DETERG, HYDROL cloración *f*; ~ **tank** *n* HYDROL contenedor de cloración *m*, depósito de cloración *m*; ~ **vessel** *n* HYDROL contenedor de cloración *m*, depósito de cloración *m*

chlorine¹: ~**-fast** *adj* CHEM, DETERG clororresistente

chlorine² *n* (*Cl*) CHEM, DETERG, HYDROL, POLL, SAFE cloro *m* (*Cl*); ~**-ammonia process** *n* HYDROL proceso de cloro-amoníaco *m*; ~ **bleaching agent** *n* DETERG blanqueador clorado *m*; ~ **contact chamber** *n* HYDROL cámara de contacto de cloro *f*; ~ **demand** *n* HYDROL demanda de cloro *f*; ~**-free pulp** *n* PAPER papel libre de cloro *m*, pasta libre de cloro *f*

chlorite *n* CHEM clorito *m*, COAL clorita *m*, MINERAL, PETR TECH clorita *f*; ~ **spar** *n* MINERAL espato clorítico *m*

chloritization *n* GEOL cloritización *f*

chloritoid *n* MINERAL cloritoide *m*

chlorocalcite *n* MINERAL clorocalcita *f*

chlorofiber *AmE see* chlorofibre *BrE*

chlorofibre *n* BrE TEXTIL clorofibra *f*

chlorofluorocarbon *n* (*CFC*) PACK, POLL clorofluorocarbono *m* (*CFC*)

chlorohydrin *n* CHEM clorhidrina *f*

chloromelanite *n* MINERAL cloromelanita *f*

chloropal *n* MINERAL clorópalo *m*

chlorophane *n* MINERAL fluorita *f*

chlorophenol *n* CHEM clorofenol *m*

chlorophyl *AmE see* chlorophyll *BrE*

chlorophyll *n* BrE CHEM clorofila *f*

chloropicrin *n* CHEM cloropicrina *f*

chloroplatinate *n* CHEM cloroplatinato *m*

chloroprene *n* CHEM cloropreno *m*; ~ **rubber** *n* P&R caucho de cloropreno *m*

chlororubber *n* CHEM, P&R clorocaucho *m*

chlorosis *n* AGRIC clorosis *f*

chlorospinel *n* MINERAL cloroespinela *f*

chlorosulfonated *AmE see* chlorosulphonated *BrE*

chlorosulfonation *AmE see* chlorosulphonation *BrE*

chlorosulphonated *adj* BrE CHEM, DETERG clorosulfonado

chlorosulphonation *n* BrE CHEM, DETERG clorosulfonación *f*

chlorous *adj* CHEM cloroso

chock¹: ~ **block** *adj* PROD *mining* estemple

chock² *n* MECH *stranded ship* calzo *m*, PROD *scotch, stopping-block* taco *m*, *of rolling-mill* caldero *m*, WATER TRANSP *shipbuilding* alavante *m*, calzo *m*, galápago *m*, guía *f*

chock³ *vt* PROD *scotch* calzar

chocolate: ~ **coating** *n* FOOD cobertura de chocolate *f*, revestimiento de chocolate *m*; ~**-coating machine** *n* FOOD máquina para cubrir chocolate *f*; ~ **mousse** *n* MAR POLL, POLL crema de chocolate *f*, derrame de petróleo en el mar *m*, marea negra *f*

choke¹ *n* AUTO ahogador *m* (*Esp*), estrangulador *m*, estrangulador de aire *m*, obturador *m*, C&G estrangulador *m*, ELEC *inductor*, ELEC ENG bobina de

choque *f*, choque *m*, transformador reductor *m*,
MECH *steel rods* cebador del carburador *m* (*AmL*),
ahogador *m* (*Esp*), OCEAN obturador *m*, cebador *m*
(*AmL*), estrangulador *m*, PETR TECH estrangulador
m, regulador *m*, TELECOM bobina de autoinducción *f*,
bobina de choque *f*, VEH estrangulador *m*, ahogador
m (*Esp*); ~ **circuit** *n* ELEC circuito de choque *m*; ~ **coil**
n AUTO bobina de reacción *f*, ELEC *inductor*, ELEC ENG
bobina de choque *f*, bobina de impedancia *f*, bobina
de reactancia *f*, PHYS bobina de reactancia *f*, VEH
bobina de reacción *f*; ~ **damp** *n* MINE mofeta *f*;
~ **feed** *n* ELEC *supply* alimentación por choque *f*,
corriente de alimentación por choque *f*; ~ **flange** *n*
ELEC, ELEC ENG brida de choque *f*; ~ **input filter** *n*
ELEC, ELEC ENG, ELECTRON filtro de entrada inductiva
m; ~ **plunger** *n* ELEC ENG succionador de choque *m*
choke² *vt* PROD obstruir
choke³ *vi* PROD atascarse
choked: ~ **nozzle** *n* AIR TRANSP boquilla bloqueada *f*
choker: ~ **plate** *n* AUTO, VEH mariposa *f*, obturador *m*,
palomilla del estrangulador *f*, placa estrangulador *f*,
placa obturadora *f*; ~ **valve** *n* COAL válvula de
estrangulación *f*, válvula reguladora *f* (*Esp*)
choking *n* AIR TRANSP, AUTO bloqueo *m*, estrangulamiento *m*, obstrucción *f*, PROD obstrucción *f*
cholate *n* CHEM colato *m*
cholecystography *n* INSTR colescitografía *f*
cholesteric *adj* CHEM colestérico
cholesterol *n* CHEM, FOOD colesterol *m*
cholic *adj* CHEM cólico
choline *n* FOOD colina *f*
cholinergic *adj* CHEM colinérgico
cholinesterase *n* CHEM colinesterasa *f*
chondrarsenite *n* MINERAL condroarsenita *f*
chondrin *n* CHEM condrina *f*
chondrite *n* GEOL, PETR TECH condrita *f*
chondritic *adj* GEOL, PETR TECH condrítico
chondrodite *n* MINERAL condrodita *f*
chop¹ *n* MECH ENG *of joiner's vice* mordaza *f*
chop² *vt* AGRIC picar, ELECTRON interrumpir
chopped: ~ **mode** *n* ELECTRON modo interrumpido *m*;
~ **signal** *n* ELECTRON señal interrumpida *f*; ~ **strand**
n C&G fibra cortada *f*; ~ **strand mat** *n* C&G colchoneta de fibra de vidrio *f*, P&R fieltro de fibra
recortada *m*, malla de filamentos discontinua *f*, WA-
TER TRANSP esterilla de fibra troceada *f*
chopper *n* AGRIC desmenuzadora *f*, AIR TRANSP
cortador *m*, ELECTRON interruptor *m*, PAPER cortadora *f*; ~ **amplifier** *n* ELECTRON amplificador de
interrupción *m*, amplificador de muestreo *m*;
~ **circuitry** *n* SPACE circuito cortador *m*; ~ **fold** *n*
PRINT plegado en ángulo recto *m*; ~-**fold blade** *n*
PRINT cuchilla de plegado en ángulo recto *f*;
~-**stabilized amplifier** *n* ELECTRON amplificador
estabilizado de interrupción *m*, amplificador estabilizado de muestreo *m*
choppiness *n* AIR TRANSP, METEO, OCEAN, WATER
TRANSP agitación *f*
chopping: ~ **bit** *n* MINE trépano cortante *m*
choppy: ~ **sea** *n* METEO, OCEAN, WATER TRANSP mar
picado *m*
chord *n* ACOUST acorde *m*, cuerda *f*, AIR TRANSP,
FUELLESS, GEOM, WATER TRANSP cuerda *f*; ~ **line** *n*
FUELLESS línea de cuerda *f*; ~ **member** *n* AIR TRANSP
of truss miembro de la cuerda *m*

chordal: ~ **thickness** *n* AIR TRANSP *of gears* grosor de
la cuerda *m*
christianite *n* MINERAL cristianita *f*
Christmas: ~ **tree** *n* PETR TECH arbolito de producción
m, cruz de producción *f*, árbol de Navidad *m*, PETROL
armadura de surgencia *f*, árbol de conexiones *m*
chroma *n* PRINT intensidad del color *f*, TV crominancia
f; ~ **control** *n* TV control de crominancia *m*; ~ **delay** *n*
TV línea de retardo cromático *f* (*AmL*), retardo
cromático *m* (*Esp*); ~ **flutter** *n* TV parpadeo cromático *m*; ~ **pilot** *n* TV piloto cromático *m*
chromakey *n* TV separador de crominancia *m*
chromate *n* CHEM cromato *m*
chromatic¹ *adj* CHEM, COLOUR, OPT, PHOTO, PHYS, TV
cromático
chromatic²: ~ **aberration** *n* GEN aberración cromática
f; ~ **balance** *n* TV balance cromático *m*, equilibrio
cromático *m*; ~ **color** *AmE*, ~ **colour** *BrE* *n* COLOUR
color cromático *m*; ~ **component** *n* TV componente
cromático *m*; ~ **coordinates** *n pl* PHYS coordenadas
cromáticas *f pl*; ~ **dispersion** *n* OPT dispersión
cromática *f*; ~ **distortion** *n* OPT distorsión cromática
f; ~ **flicker** *n* TV parpadeo cromático *m*; ~ **resolving
power** *n* PHYS poder de resolución cromático *m*;
~ **scale** *n* ACOUST escala cromática *f*; ~ **semitone** *n*
ACOUST semitono cromático *m*; ~ **spectrum** *n* PHOTO
espectro cromático *m*; ~ **splitting** *n* TV repartición
cromática *f* (*AmL*), separación cromática *f* (*Esp*)
chromaticity *n* GEN cromaticidad *f*; ~ **aberration** *n*
OPT, PHYS, RAD PHYS, TELECOM, TV aberración de
cromaticidad *f*; ~ **coordinates** *n pl* PHYS coordenadas de cromaticidad *f pl*; ~ **diagram** *n* TV diagrama
de cromaticidad *m*
chromatography *n* CHEM, LAB cromatografía *f*;
~ **column** *n* CHEM, LAB columna de cromatografía
f; ~ **papers** *n pl* CHEM, LAB papeles de cromatografía
m pl; ~ **tank** *n* CHEM, LAB celda cromatográfica *f*,
cuba de cromatografía *f*, tanque de cromatografía *m*
chrome¹ *adj*: ~-**plated** MECH ENG, VEH, VS cromado
chrome²: ~ **alum** *n* CHEM alumbre crómico *m*; ~ **color**
AmE, ~ **colour** *BrE* *n* COLOUR color cromático *m*,
color de cromo *m*, colorante al cromo *m*; ~-**dioxide
tape** *n* TV cinta de dióxido de cromo *f*; ~ **green** *n*
C&G, COLOUR verde de cromo *m*, verde de cromo *m*;
~-**green lead pigment** *n* COLOUR pigmento de cromo
verde de plomo *m*; ~ **intensifier** *n* PHOTO intensificador de cromo *m*; ~ **ocher** *AmE*, ~ **ochre** *BrE* *n*
MINERAL ocre de cromo *m*; ~ **ore** *n* C&G, MINERAL
mineral de cromo *m*; ~-**phthalocyanine blue lead
pigment** *n* COLOUR pigmento de cromo-ftalocianino
azul de plomo *m*; ~ **strip** *n* VEH moldura de cromo *f*
chromic¹ *adj* C&G, CHEM, COLOUR crómico
chromic²: ~ **oxide** *n* C&G, CHEM, COLOUR óxido de
cromo *m*; ~ **oxide pigment** *n* COLOUR pigmento de
óxido crómico *m*
chrominance *n* ELECTRON cromeado *m*, SPACE, TV
crominancia *f*; ~ **amplifier** *n* ELECTRON amplificador
cromeado *m*; ~ **bandwidth** *n* TV ancho de banda de
crominancia *m*; ~-**carrier output** *n* TV salida de la
portadora de crominancia *f* (*Esp*), salida de la
subportadora de color *f* (*AmL*); ~ **component** *n* TV
componente cromático *m*, componente de crominancia *m*; ~ **demodulator** *n* TV demodulador de
crominancia *m*; ~ **phase** *n* TV fase de crominancia
f; ~ **signal** *n* ELECTRON señal de cromeado *f*, SPACE
communications, TV señal de crominancia *f*;

~ **subcarrier** n ELECTRON subportadora de cromeado f, TV subportadora de crominancia f; ~ **subcarrier demodulation** n ELECTRON demodulación de subportador de cromeado f; ~ **subcarrier demodulator** n ELECTRON demodulador de subportador de cromeado m; ~ **subcarrier modulator** n ELECTRON modulador de subportador de cromeado m; ~ **subcarrier oscillator** n ELECTRON oscilador de subportador de cromeado m; ~ **subcarrier reference** n TV referencia de subportadora de crominancia f; ~ **subcarrier signal** n TV señal de subportadora de crominancia f

chromite n C&G, MINERAL cromita f

chromium[1]: ~-**plated** adj COATINGS, MECH ENG, VEH cromado

chromium[2] n (Cr) CHEM, COATINGS, METALL cromo m (Cr); ~ **deposit** n COATINGS depósito de cromo m; ~ **plating** n COATINGS, MECH ENG, VEH cromado m

chromogen n CHEM cromóforo m, cromógeno m

chromophoric adj CHEM cromofórico

chromosphere n SPACE cromosfera f

chromotropic adj CHEM cromotrópico

chromous adj CHEM cromoso

chronic: ~ **effect** n POLL efecto crónico m, efecto desagradable m, efecto insoportable m

chronograph n INSTR cronógrafo m

chronology n SPACE cronología f

chronometer n LAB, PHYS, WATER TRANSP cronómetro m; ~ **rate** n WATER TRANSP precisión f

chronostratigraphic: ~ **division** n GEOL división cronostratigráfica f; ~ **unit** n GEOL unidad cronostratigráfica f

chrysene n CHEM criseno m

chrysoberyl n MINERAL crisoberilo m

chrysocolla n MINERAL crisócola f

chrysoidine n CHEM crisoidina f

chrysolite n MINERAL crisolita f

chrysophanic adj CHEM crisofánico

chrysoprase n MINERAL crisoprasa f

chrysotile n MINERAL crisotilo m

chuck n MECH with grinding disc portabrocas m, portaherramientas m, MECH ENG manguito portaherramienta m, portabrocas m, of lathe plato m, part mandril m, MINE calzo m, cuña f; ~ **adaptor** n MECH ENG adaptador portaherramienta m; ~ **back** n MECH ENG of lathe contraplato m; ~ **bushing** n MECH ENG casquillo de plato m; ~ **face** n MECH ENG plato de agujeros m; ~ **faceplate dogs** n pl MECH ENG plato de agujeros con cuatro garras m; ~ **guard** n MECH ENG protector del plato m; ~ **plate** n MECH ENG portaplato m

chucking n MECH of light montaje de una pieza sobre el plato m, MECH ENG independent of support from back centre montaje al aire m; ~ **between centers** AmE, ~ **between centres** BrE n MECH ENG lathe montaje entre puntos m; ~ **reamer** n MECH ENG escariador para máquina m, escariador de mandril m

chuffing n SPACE resoplaido m, combustión irregular f

chugging n NUCL borbolleo resonante m, SPACE escape m, golpeteo m, expulsión periódica f

churn[1] n FOOD batido m, mantequera f; ~ **drill** n MINE barrena de cable f, sonda de percusión f, taladro giratorio m, trépano para sondeo a la cuerda m (AmL), trépano para sondeo al cable m (Esp), PETR TECH perforación por cable f; ~ **drill bit** n COAL, MINE trépano m; ~ **drilling** n COAL, MINE apertura de

galerías con perforadoras neumáticas f; ~ **milk cooler** n AGRIC, REFRIG enfriador de leche en cántaros m

churn[2] vt FOOD batir, PROD founding agitar

churning n FOOD batido m

chute n AGRIC canal de descarga m, manga f (AmL), C&G canal m, chimenea f (AmL), descarga f, COAL alcancía f (AmL), canaleta f (Esp), chimenea f (AmL), coladero f (Esp), deslizadera f, paso m, tolua f (Esp), vertedera f, CONST canal m chimenea f (AmL), MECH canal m, canaleta f, conducto m, deslizadera f, MECH ENG conducto m, MINE alcancía f (AmL), aspirador m (Esp), canaleta f (AmL), chimenea f (AmL), coladero m (Esp), conducto m, deslizadera f, paso m (AmL), pozo de comunicación m (AmL), tolua f (Esp), SPACE caída f, conducto m, descenso m, paracaídas m, rampa f; ~ **door** n MINE buzón de alcancía m, buzón de chimenea m (AmL), puerta de coladero f (Esp); ~ **gate** n CONST compuerta de rápido f, MINE buzón de alcancía m, buzón de chimenea m (AmL), puerta de coladero f (Esp); ~ **hang-up** n MINE bloqueo de chimenea m; ~ **spillway** n FUELLESS dams saetín m, vertedero m, vertedor m (AmL)

CI abbr TELECOM (concatenation indication) indicación de concatenación f, TELECOM (conversation impossible) conversación imposible f

Ci abbr METEO (cirrus) Ci (cirrus), PHYS (curie), RAD PHYS (curie) Ci (curie)

CIC abbr (combat information center AmE, combat information centre BrE) MILIT centro de información de combate m

cicero n PRINT cabuyería f, cícero m

CID abbr (consecutive identical digits) TELECOM dígitos idénticos consecutivos m pl

CIF abbr (cost insurance freight) PROD coste y seguro y flete m

cigar: ~ **aerial** n BrE (cf cigar antenna AmE) SPACE communications antena fusiforme f; ~ **antenna** n AmE (cf cigar aerial BrE) SPACE communications antena fusiforme f; ~ **box** n PACK caja de puros f; ~ **lighter** n VEH encendedor m

cigarette: ~ **pack** n AmE (cf cigarette packet BrE) PACK cajetilla f, cajetilla de cigarrillos f, paquete de cigarrillos m; ~ **packet** BrE n (cf cigarette pack AmE) PACK cajetilla f, cajetilla de cigarrillos f, paquete de cigarrillos m

CIM abbr (computer-integrated manufacturing) COMP&DP CIM (fabricación informatizada, fabricación integrada por computador AmL, fabricación integrada por computadora AmL, fabricación integrada por ordenador Esp)

CIME abbr (customer installation maintenance entities) TELECOM entidades de mantenimiento instalaciones de abonados f pl

Cimmerian: ~ **orogeny** n GEOL, PETR TECH orogenia cimeriana f, orogenia cimerianense f; ~ **unconformity** n GEOL, PETR TECH discordancia del kimeridgiense f

cimolite n MINERAL cimolita f

cinch n TV cincha f

cinching n TV cincha f

cinchona n CHEM quina f

cinchonidine n CHEM cinconidina f

cinchonin n CHEM cinconina f

cinder: ~ **bank** n PROD escorial m; ~ **bed** n PROD capa de escorias *f*, lecho de cenizas *m*; ~ **chute** *n* PROD tubo de descarga de cenizas *m*; ~ **cone** *n* GEOL cono de escorias *m*; ~ **notch** *n* PROD piquera para la escoria *f*; ~ **pit** *n* PROD picadura *f*; ~ **pocket** *n* PROD colector de cenizas *m*; ~ **wool** *n* PROD lana de escoria *f*

cinders *n pl* PROD *forge scale* cenizas *f pl*, escorias *f pl*

cinema: ~ **projector** *n* BrE (*cf movie projector* AmE) CINEMAT, ELEC *lighting* proyector cinematográfico *m*, proyector de cine *m*

Cinemascope *n* CINEMAT Cinemascope *m*

cinematographer *n* CINEMAT cineasta *m*

cinemicrography *n* CINEMAT cinemicrografía *f*

cineol *n* CHEM cineol *m*, eucaliptol *m*

cineolic *adj* CHEM cineólico

cineradiography *n* CINEMAT cinerradiografía *f*

cinerama *n* CINEMAT cinerama *m*

cinerite *n* GEOL cinerita *f*

cinnabar *n* CHEM, MINE, MINERAL cinabrio *m*

cinnamate *n* CHEM, FOOD cinamato *m*

cinnamic *adj* CHEM cinámico

cinnamyle *n* CHEM cinamilo *m*

cinnoline *n* CHEM cinolina *f*

CIP *abbr* (*cleaning in place*) FOOD *brazing lamp* CIP (*limpieza en el lugar*)

ciphertext *n* TELECOM texto cifrado *m*

CIR *abbr* (*committed information rate*) TELECOM velocidad de información obligada *f*

circle *n* CINEMAT círculo *m*, GEOM circunferencia *f*, círculo *m*, *sailing* ruedo *m*, MECH ENG, PHOTO, PHYS círculo *m*; ~ **of confusion** *n* CINEMAT, PHOTO círculo de confusión *m*; ~ **of least confusion** *n* CINEMAT, PHOTO círculo de mínima confusión *m*; ~ **wipe** *n* CINEMAT, TV agrandamiento gradual circular de la imagen *m*

circling: ~ **approach** *n* AIR TRANSP aproximación circular *f*; ~ **guidance light** *n* AIR TRANSP baliza luminosa de guía para vuelos de circunvalación *f*, luces de guía para vuelos de circunvalación *f pl*

circlip *n* AUTO anillo de pistón *m*, anillo de seguridad *m*, anillo elástico de retención *m*, MECH, MECH ENG anillo de pistón *m*, fiador de perno de pistón *m*, grapa circular *f*, resorte circular *m*, resorte circular de obturación *m*, VEH anillo de pistón *m*, anillo de seguridad *m*, anillo elástico de retención *m*; ~ **pliers** *n pl* MECH ENG alicates para resortes circulares *m*

circuit *n* COMP&DP, ELEC, ELECTRON, PHYS, TELECOM circuito *m*, circuito eléctrico *m*; ~ **analysis** *n* ELEC ENG análisis del circuito *m*; ~ **availability** *n* TELECOM disponibilidad de circuitos *f*; ~ **board** *n* ELEC, ELECTRON cuadro del circuito *m*, placa del circuito *f*; ~ **breaker** *n* CINEMAT disyuntor *m*, CONST disyuntor *m*, interruptor automático *m*, ELEC *switch*, ELEC ENG cortacircuito *m*, disyuntor *m*, interruptor *m*; ~ **closer** *n* ELEC, ELEC ENG cierracircuito *m*, conmutador conjuntor *m*; ~ **delay** *n* ELECTRON circuito de retardo *m*, temporizador de circuito *m*; ~ **design** *n* ELEC ENG, ELECTRON diseño del circuito *m*; ~ **diagram** *n* ELEC, ELEC ENG, ELECTRON diagrama de circuito *m*, esquema de conexiones *m*, esquema eléctrico *m*, TV diagrama de circuito *m*, diagrama del circuito *m*; ~ **element** *n* ELEC ENG, ELECTRON elemento circuital *m*, elemento de circuito *m*; ~ **group** *n* TELECOM grupo de circuitos *m*; ~ **group query message** *n* (*CQM*) TELECOM mensaje de consulta destinado a grupo de circuitos *m*; ~ **group query response message** *n* (*CQR*) TELECOM mensaje de respuesta de consulta

destinado a grupo de circuitos *m*; ~ **integration** *n* ELECTRON integración del circuito *f*; ~ **mode bearer service** *n* TELECOM modo circuito para servicio portador *m*; ~ **noise** *n* ELECTRON ruido del circuito *m*; ~ **power requirement** *n* ELEC consumo del circuito *m*, demanda de energía de alimentación del circuito *f*, demanda de energía del circuito *f*, demanda de energía eléctrica del circuito *f*, energía necesaria del circuito *f*, PROD demanda de energía del circuito *f*; ~ **state indicator** *n* TELECOM indicador del estado del circuito *m*; ~ **switch** *n* TELECOM conmutador de circuito *m*; ~**-switched exchange** *n* TELECOM central de circuitos conmutados *f*; ~**-switched network** *n* COMP&DP red con conmutación de circuitos *f*, red de circuitos conmutados *f*; ~ **switching** *n* COMP&DP, TELECOM conmutación de circuitos *f*; ~**-switching center** AmE, ~**-switching centre** BrE *n* COMP&DP, TELECOM centro de conmutación de circuitos *m*; ~**-switching network** *n* TELECOM red de conmutación de circuitos *f*; ~ **switching system** *n* TELECOM sistema de conmutación de circuitos *m*; ~ **switching unit** *n* TELECOM unidad de conmutación de circuitos *f*; ~ **theory** *n* ELEC ENG teoría de circuitos *f*

circular: ~ **aerial** *n* BrE (*cf circular antenna* AmE) TV antena circular *f*; ~ **antenna** *n* AmE (*cf circular aerial* BrE) TV antena circular *f*; ~ **aperture** *n* PHYS abertura circular *f*; ~ **arc** *n* GEOM arco circular *m*; ~ **blast aim** *n* PROD *of a furnace* conducto circular del viento *m*; ~ **combing machine** *n* TEXTIL peinadora circular *f*; ~ **cut file** *n* MECH ENG lima fresadora de mano *f*; ~ **diamond-cutting apparatus** *n* MECH ENG aparato de cortar diamante circular *m*; ~ **die set** *n* MECH ENG juego de matrices circulares *m*; ~ **die stock** *n* MECH ENG portadados circular *m*; ~ **gear** *n* MECH ENG engranaje cilíndrico *m*; ~ **gearing** *n* MECH ENG engranaje cilíndrico *m*; ~**-knitted fabric** *n* TEXTIL tejido de punto circular *m*; ~ **level** *n* INSTR nivel esférico *m*; ~ **measure** *n* GEOM medida circular *f*; ~ **milling attachment** *n* MECH ENG accesorio para fresar circularmente *m*; ~ **motion** *n* PHYS movimiento circular *m*; ~ **orbit** *n* SPACE órbita circular *f*; ~ **pitch** *n* MECH, MECH ENG paso circular *m*, paso circunferencial *m*; ~ **points at infinity** *n pl* GEOM puntos circulares en infinito *m pl*; ~ **polarization** *n* PHYS, RAD PHYS, TELECOM polarización circular *f*; ~ **polarization of light** *n* PHYS, RAD PHYS polarización circular de la luz *f*; ~ **protractor** *n* GEOM graduador circular *m*, transportador circular *m*; ~ **reflector** *n* INSTR espejo esférico *m*; ~ **saw** *n* CONST, MECH, MECH ENG sierra circular *f*; ~ **scan** *n* ELECTRON exploración circular *f*; ~ **screwing die** *n* MECH ENG matriz circular de filetear *f*; ~ **screwing die for parallel pipe threads** *n* MECH ENG matriz circular de filetear para roscas paralelas de tubería *f*; ~ **shafts** *n pl* MECH ENG ejes circulares *m pl*; ~ **shift** *n* COMP&DP decalaje circular *m*, desplazamiento circular *m*, rotación *f*, ELECTRON rotación *f*; ~ **slide valve** *n* HYDRAUL válvula de disco *f*, válvula distribuidora cilíndrica *f*; ~ **thickness** *n* MECH ENG *of gears* espesor circular *m*, espesor curvilíneo *m*, espesor de arco *m*; ~ **vibrating screen** *n* COAL pantalla vibratoria *f*; ~ **wave** *n* NUCL, WAVE PHYS onda circular *f*; ~ **waveguide** *n* ELEC ENG, PHYS, WAVE PHYS guía de ondas circular *f*

circularization *n* SPACE *of orbit* circularización *f*

circularize *vt* SPACE *orbit* poner en órbita circular

circularly: **~-polarized wave** *n* ACOUST, PHYS onda polarizada circularmente *f*
circulate: **~ in opposite directions** *vi* PART PHYS beams circular en direcciones opuestas
circulating: **~ ball lead screw** *n* MECH ENG tornillo de avance esférico circulante *m*, tornillo regulador esférico circulante *m*; **~ ball spindle** *n* MECH ENG husillo circulante *m*; **~ boiler** *n* HYDRAUL caldera de circulación *f*; **~ fan** *n* REFRIG, THERMO ventilador de recirculación *m*; **~ load** *n* COAL carga circulante *f*; **~ pump** *n* FOOD, HEAT ENG, HYDRAUL, REFRIG bomba de circulación *f*; **~ shift register** *n* PROD memoria de línea de retardo *f*; **~ system** *n* MECH ENG *lubrication* sistema de circulación *m*; **~ water system** *n* NUCL sistema de agua de circulación *m*
circulation *n* PETR TECH, PHYS *solids from liquids*, WATER circulación *f*; **~ pump** *n* FOOD, HEAT ENG, HYDRAUL, REFRIG bomba de circulación *f*
circulator *n* COMP&DP distribuidor *m*, SPACE *communications* circulador *m*, distribuidor *m*, propagador de noticias *m*, TELECOM circulador *m*
circumaural: **~ earphone** *n* ACOUST auricular circumaural *m*
circumcenter *AmE see* circumcentre *BrE*
circumcentre *n BrE* GEOM circuncentro *m*
circumcircle *n* GEOM circuncírculo *m*
circumference *n* GEOM circunferencia *f*
circumferential: **~ register** *n* PRINT registro periférico *m*; **~ speed** *n* AIR TRANSP velocidad circunferencial *f*; **~ stress** *n* METALL tensión circunferencial *f*, tensión periférica *f*
circumnavigation *n* WATER TRANSP circunnavegación *f*
circumpolar *adj* WATER TRANSP circumpolar
circumscribe *vt* GEOM circunscribir
circumscribed: **~ circle** *n* GEOM círculo circunscrito *m*
cirque *n* GEOL circo glaciar *m*
cirrocumulus *n* (*Cc*) METEO cirrocúmulo *m* (*Cc*)
cirrolite *n* MINERAL cirrolita *f*
cirrostratus *n* (*Cs*) METEO cirrostrato *m* (*Cs*)
cirrus *n* (*Ci*) METEO cirrus *m* (*Ci*)
cis *adj* CHEM cis; **~-trans** *adj* CHEM cis-trans
CISC *abbr* (*complex instruction set computer*) COMP&DP CISC (*computador de conjuntos de instrucciones complejas AmL, computadora de conjunto de instrucciones complejas AmL, ordenador de conjunto de instrucciones complejas Esp*)
cissing *n* COATINGS incisiones *f pl*, P&R cisuras *f pl*, incisiones *f pl*
cistern *n* WATER aljibe *m*, cisterna *f*
citizen: **~ band** *n* (*CB*) TELECOM banda ciudadana *f*
citral *n* CHEM citral *m*, geranial *m*
citrate *n* CHEM citrato *m*
citric[1] *adj* CHEM, DETERG, FOOD cítrico
citric[2]: **~ acid** *n* CHEM, DETERG, FOOD ácido cítrico *m*
citrine *n* MINERAL citrino *m*, cuarzo amarillo *m*; **~ color** *AmE*, **~ colour** *BrE n* COLOUR color cetrino *m*; **~ quartz** *n* MINERAL cuarzo citrino *m*
citronella *n* FOOD citronela *f*
citronellal *n* CHEM citronelal *m*
citronyl *n* CHEM citronilo *m*
citrulline *n* CHEM citrulina *f*
city: **~ gas** *n* GAS gas para consumo urbano *m*; **~ terminal** *n* AIR TRANSP terminal de la ciudad *f*; **~ water** *n AmE* (*cf mains water BrE*) HYDROL, WATER agua industrial *f*, canalización principal de aguas *f*
civetone *n* CHEM civetona *f*

civil: **~ defence** *n BrE* MILIT defensa civil *f*; **~ defense** *AmE see* civil defence *BrE*; **~ engineer** *n* CONST ingeniero civil *m*, ingeniero de caminos, canales y puentes *m*, ingeniero técnico de obras públicas *m*; **~ engineering** *n* CONST ingeniería civil *f*, obra civil *f*
Cl *abbr* (*chlorine*) CHEM, DETERG, HYDROL, POLL, SAFE Cl (*cloro*)
clack *n* MECH ENG chapaleta *f*, charnela *f*; **~ box** *n* MECH ENG caja de válvulas *f*; **~ valve** *n* HYDRAUL válvula de charnela *f*, MECH ENG válvula de charnela *f*, válvula de retención *f*
clad: **~ fuel clearance** *n* NUCL huelgo vaina-pastilla *m*; **~ pressure vessel** *n* MECH ENG recipiente de presión chapado *m*, recipiente de presión revestido *m*
cladding *n* MECH plaqueado *m*, chapeado *m*, NUCL encamisado *m*, OPT, PHYS revestimiento *m*, SPACE encamisado *m*, envainado *m*, revestimiento exterior *m*, TELECOM revestimiento *m*; **~ center** *AmE*, **~ centre** *BrE n* OPT centro del revestimiento *m*, TELECOM centro de chapado *m*; **~ diameter** *n* OPT diámetro del revestimiento *m*; **~-diameter tolerance** *n* OPT tolerancia del diámetro del revestimiento *f*; **~ material** *n* NUCL material de la vaina *m*; **~ mode** *n* OPT modo que se propaga por el revestimiento *m*; **~ mode stripper** *n* OPT supresor de modos en el revestimiento *m*; **~ temperature limit** *n* NUCL límite de temperatura de la vaina *m*; **~ tolerance field** *n* OPT, TELECOM campo de tolerancia del chapado *m*, campo de tolerancia del revestimiento *m*
claim *n* MINE concesión *f* (*Esp*), pertenencia *f* (*AmL*)
claire *n* OCEAN ostrera *f*
Claisen: **~ condensation** *n* CHEM, CHEM TECH condensación de Claisen *f*; **~ flask** *n* CHEM, CHEM TECH matraz de Claisen *m*
clam: **~ shell bucket** *n* CONST cuchara bivalva *f*; **~ shell bucket dredger** *n* CONST draga de cuchara bivalva *f*
clamp[1] *n* ELEC *cable* abrazadera *f*, grapa *f*, sujetador *m*, LAB *paint, pigments* abrazadera *f*, pinza *f*, MECH grapa *f*, zuncho *m*, tornillo de banco *m*, mordaza *f*, abrazadera *f*, grampa *f*, MECH ENG *for rubber tubes* pinza para tubos de goma *f*, motón *m*, abrazadera *f*, prensa de sujeción *f*, tornillo de presión *m*, *of levelling instrument* pinza *f*, zuncho *m*, grapa *f*, MINE, OCEAN abrazadera *f*, PHOTO pinza *f*, PROD abrazadera *f*, TRANSP, VEH mordaza *f*, abrazadera *f*, grampa *f*; **~ course** *n* CONST recorrido de tornillos de carpintero *m*; **~ with jaws** *n* LAB pinza con mordazas *f*; **~-on type amp probe** *n* PROD amperímetro de tipo empotrable *m*; **~ pin** *n* PROD pasador de fijación *m*; **~ pulse generator** *n* CINEMAT, TV generador de impulsos de bloqueo *m*; **~ screw** *n* PROD tornillo de fijación *m*; **~ slot** *n* MECH ENG ranura de mordaza *f*; **~ washer** *n* PROD arandela de abrazadera *f*
clamp[2] *vt* CONST grapar, sujetar con mordazas, ELEC grapar, MECH embridar, fijar, sujetar, grapar, MECH ENG grapar, PROD empotrar, fijar; **~ together** *vt* PROD *pipes* empotrar
clamped[1] *adj* CONST, ELEC, MECH, MECH ENG, PACK, PROD empotrado, grapado, sujeto
clamped[2]: **~ pipe connection** *n* MECH ENG conexión embridada de tubería *f*
clamping *n* ELECTRON, MECH, MECH ENG, PROD apriete *m*, fijación *f*, junta *f*, TV fijación *f*; **~ band** *n* MECH ENG banda de sujeción *f*; **~ circuit** *n* ELECTRON circuito de fijación *m*, circuito de fijación de

amplitud *m*, TV circuito de fijación *f*, circuito de fijación de amplitud *m*; ~ **diode** *n* ELECTRON, PHYS diodo de bloqueo *m*, diodo de fijación *m*; ~ **dog** *n* PROD *of timber-clip, of log-carriage, of log-sawing machine* pata de sujeción *f*; ~ **fixture** *n* MECH ENG *machine tools* plato de fijación *m*; ~ **force** *n* PACK fuerza de apriete *f*, fuerza de sujeción *f*; ~ **handle** *n* MECH ENG *of lathe* empuñadura de sujeción *f*, mango de apriete *m*; ~ **lever** *n* MECH ENG palanca de inmovilización *f*; ~ **mechanism** *n* MECH ENG mecanismo de bloqueo *m*; ~ **pin** *n* PROD pasador de fijación *m*; ~ **pulses** *n pl* TV impulsos de fijación *m pl*; ~ **reflector** *n* PHOTO reflector de sujeción *m*; ~ **ring** *n* PACK anillo de fijación *m*, arandela de sujeción *f*; ~ **screw** *n* PROD tornillo de apriete *m*

clamshell: ~ **blister** *n* PACK cápsula termoformada en forma concha *f*

clap: ~ **sill** *n* WATER umbral de asiento *m*

Clapeyron: ~'**s equation** *n* PHYS ecuación de Clapeyron *f*

clapper *n* HYDRAUL, MECH ENG válvula de charnela *f*; ~ **board** *n* CINEMAT claqueta *f*; ~ **person** *n* CINEMAT claquetista *m*; ~ **seat** *n* MECH ENG asiento de charnela *m*; ~ **valve** *n* HYDRAUL obturador de pulsómetro *m*, sangrador *m*

clarification *n* CHEM, COAL, QUALITY, WATER clarificación *f*; ~ **plant** *n* WATER planta de clarificación *f*

clarified: ~ **butter** *n* FOOD mantequilla clarificada *f*

clarifier *n* FOOD clarificador *m*, HYDROL clarificadora *f*, depósito de decantación *m*

clarify *vt* GEN clarificar

clarifying *n* GEN clarificación *f*; ~ **basin** *n* PETR TECH balsa de clarificación *f*, estanque de clarificación *m*

clarite *n* MINERAL clarita *f*

clarity *n* TELECOM claridad *f*

Clarke: ~ **number** *n* GEOL número de Clarke *m*

clarkeite *n* MINERAL clarkeíta *f*

clashing *n* TELECOM colisión *f*

clasp[1] *n* MECH ENG corchete *m*, presilla *f*; ~ **brake** *n* TRANSP freno de dos zapatas opuestas entre sí *m*; ~ **nut** *n* MECH ENG tuerca del husillo *f*

clasp[2] *vt* MECH abrazar, MECH ENG encorchetar, TEXTIL abrochar

clasp[3] *vi* MECH ENG abrazar, enganchar

class *n* COMP&DP, CRYSTALL clase *f*, MECH ENG categoría *f*, clase *f*, rango *m*; ~ **A amplifier** *n* ELECTRON, PHYS amplificador de clase A *m*; ~ **A evaporating pan** *n* HYDROL depósito de evaporación de clase A *m*; ~ **of accuracy** *n* METR tipo de exactitud *m*

CLASS *abbr* (*containerized lighter aboard ship system*) TRANSP sistema de buques remolcadores para transporte de gabarras cargadas con contenedores *m*

classic: ~ **thermodynamics** *n* THERMO termodinámica clásica *f*

classical: ~ **radius** *n* GEOM, PHYS radio clásico *m*

classification *n* COAL, QUALITY, RAIL, TRANSP, WATER clasificación *f*; ~ **detector** *n* TRANSP detector de clasificación *m*; ~ **of ship** *n* WATER TRANSP *insurance* clasificación del buque *f*; ~ **siding** *n* TRANSP playa de clasificación *f*; ~ **society** *n* WATER TRANSP *insurance* sociedad de clasificación *f*; ~ **system** *n* QUALITY sistema de clasificación *m*; ~ **track** *n* TRANSP vía de clasificación *f*; ~ **of type design** *n* PRINT clasificación de estilo de tipo *f*; ~ **yard** *n* AmE (*cf marshalling yard BrE, shunting yard*

BrE) RAIL estación de clasificación *f*, TRANSP estación de clasificación *f*, zona de clasificación *f*; ~ **yard tower** *n* TRANSP torre de la estación de clasificación *f*; ~ **yardline** *n* RAIL línea de estación de clasificación *f*

classifier *n* C&G, CHEM TECH clasificador *m*, COAL lavador *m*

classify *vt* C&G, CHEM TECH, COAL, QUALITY clasificar

classifying: ~ **drum** *n* CHEM TECH tambor de clasificación *m*

clast *n* GEOL, PETROL, RECYCL clasto *m*, detritos *m pl*, detritus *m*

clastic[1] *adj* GEOL, PETROL, RECYCL clástico, detrítico

clastic[2]: ~ **rocks** *n* GEOL rocas clásticas *f pl*, rocas detríticas *f pl*; ~ **terrigenous rock** *n* GEOL roca terrígena clástica *f*

clathrate: ~ **compound** *n* CHEM compuesto clatrático *m*

clatter *vi* MECH ENG tintinear, traquetear

claudetite *n* MINERAL claudetita *f*

claused: ~ **bill of lading** *n* WATER TRANSP conocimiento de embarque sucio *m*

Clausius: ~ **statement** *n* PHYS enunciado de Clausius *m*

Clausius-Mosotti: ~ **formula** *n* PHYS fórmula de Clausius-Mosotti *f*

clausthalite *n* MINERAL clausthalita *f*

claw[1] *n* CINEMAT garfio *m*, CONST gancho *m*, garra *f*; ~ **bar** *n* CONST sacaclavos de horquilla *m*; ~ **carriage** *n* CINEMAT mecanismo de avance del garfio *m*; ~ **clutch** *n* MECH ENG embrague de garras *m*; ~-**feed system** *n* CINEMAT sistema de alimentación del garfio *m*; ~ **hammer** *n* CONST martillo de orejas *m*; ~ **movement** *n* CINEMAT movimiento del garfio *m*

claw[2]: ~ **off** *vi* WATER TRANSP zafarse

clay *n* GEN arcilla *f*, barro *m*; ~-**based mud** *n* PETR TECH lodo a base de arcilla *m*; ~-**based sludge** *n* PETR TECH lodo a base de arcilla *m*; ~ **brick** *n* C&G ladrillo de barro *m*; ~ **composition** *n* C&G composición del barro *f*; ~ **content** *n* COAL contenido en arcilla *m*; ~ **crucible** *n* C&G crisol de barro *m*; ~ **cutter** *n* C&G cortador de barro *m*; ~ **dust** *n* C&G polvo de barro *m*; ~ **with flints** *n* GEOL arcilla con sílex *f*; ~ **flowage** *n* GEOL flujo de arcilla *m*; ~ **gouge** *n* GEOL pulverización por falla *f*; ~ **industry** *n* C&G industria del barro *f*; ~ **kneader** *n* C&G amasador de barro *m*; ~-**kneading machine** *n* C&G máquina amasadora de barro *f*; ~ **loam** *n* C&G, CONST arcilla para moldear *f*; ~ **marl** *n* WATER marga arcillosa *f*; ~ **mass** *n* C&G masa de barro *f*; ~ **mill** *n* C&G molino de barro *m*, molino de bolas *m*; ~ **mineral** *n* COAL, GEOL mineral arcilloso *m*, mineral de arcilla *m*; ~ **mining** *n* MINE explotación de canteras de arcilla *f*; ~ **mixer** *n* C&G mezclador de barro *m*; ~-**mixing machine** *n* C&G máquina mezcladora de barro *f*; ~ **mortar** *n* C&G mortero de barro *m*; ~ **parting** *n* MINE intercalación de arcilla *f*; ~ **pipe** *n* C&G tubo de barro *m*; ~ **pit** *n* MINE barrera *f* (*AmL*), barrero *m*, barrizal *m*, cantera de arcilla *f*, fosa de barro *f*, mina de arcilla *f*; ~-**plate press** *n* C&G prensa para loseta de barro *f*; ~ **powder** *n* C&G barro molido *m*, polvo de barro *m*; ~ **press** *n* C&G prensa para barro *f*; ~ **roller** *n* C&G rodillo de barro *m*; ~ **silt** *n* WATER sedimento arcilloso *m*; ~ **slip** *n* PAPER lechada de caolín *f*; ~ **soil** *n* AGRIC, COAL suelo arcilloso *m*, tierra arcillosa *f*; ~ **suspension** *n* WATER suspensión en arcilla *f*; ~ **tamping** *n* CONST consolidación de arcillas *f*; ~ **wetting** *n* C&G humedecedor de barro *m*; ~ **worker** *n* C&G alfarero *m*; ~-**working machine** *n* C&G máquina para trabajar el barro *f*

claypan *n* AGRIC capa de arcilla *f*

claystone *n* GEOL argilita *f*

CLCP *abbr* (*connectionless convergence protocol*) TELECOM protocolo de convergencia sin conexiones *m*

cleading *n* HYDRAUL funda *f*, revestimiento *m*

clean[1] *adj* COAL puro

clean[2]: ~-**air car** *n* TRANSP coche ecológico *m*; ~-**air device** *n* SAFE aditamento de aire limpio *m*; ~ **bill of lading** *n* WATER TRANSP conocimiento de embarque limpio *m*; ~ **coal** *n* COAL carbón lavado *m*, carbón limpio *m*; ~ **configuration** *n* AIR TRANSP configuración limpia *f*; ~ **cut** *n* C&G corte limpio *m*; ~ **printing** *n* PRINT impresión limpia *f*; ~ **proof** *n* PRINT prueba limpia *f*, prueba nítida *f*; ~ **rain** *n* POLL lluvia limpia *f*; ~ **room** *n* ELECTRON unidad limpia *f*, LAB cuarto limpio *m*, sala limpia *f*, PACK nave vacía *f*, REFRIG cámara aséptica *f*, SAFE cuarto limpio *m*, SPACE sala aséptica *f*, sala blanca *f*, sala limpia *f*; ~ **snow** *n* POLL nieve limpia *f*; ~ **space** *n* REFRIG espacio aséptico *m*; ~-**up** *n* MAR POLL limpieza *f*; ~-**up technique** *n* MAR POLL, POLL procedimiento de limpieza *m*; ~ **water** *n* HYDROL, MAR POLL, WATER agua limpia *f*; ~-**work station** *n* REFRIG puesto de trabajo aséptico *m*

clean[3] *vt* COAL lavar, purificar, PAPER depurar, PROD limpiar, *by removing sand* desarenar, *file* desbastar; ~ **off** *vt* CONST *carpentry* cepillar, lijar; ~ **out** *vt* PROD limpiar; ~ **up** *vt* CONST *wood* limpiar totalmente, MINE limpiar, PROD *casting on emery wheel* rectificar, RECYCL recoger, limpiar

Clean: ~ **Air Act** *n* POLL Acta del Aire Limpio *f*

cleanable: ~ **air filter** *n* HEAT ENG, POLL filtro de aire limpiable *m*

cleaned: ~ **coal** *n* COAL carbón lavado *m*; ~ **gas** *n* GAS gas limpio *m*

cleaner *n* CHEM, CHEM TECH limpiador *m*, MINE cuchara *f* (*AmL*), cuchara limpiadora *f* (*Esp*), PAPER depurador *m*, PROD *moulding tool* limpiadora *f*, desarenador *m*, aparato de limpieza *m*, SAFE, WATER *programme* limpiador *m*; ~ **cell** *n* COAL celda de acabado *f*; ~ **jig** *n* COAL caja de lavado *f*

cleaning *n* PAPER depuración *f*, PROD *of boiler tubes* limpieza *f*, *of castings* desarenado *m*; ~ **agent** *n* CHEM, DETERG, MAR POLL limpiador *m*; ~ **barrel** *n* PROD *founding* tonel para desarenar *m*; ~ **brush** *n* PRINT cepillo limpiador *m*; ~ **door** *n* PROD puerta de limpieza *f*; ~ **equipment** *n* SAFE equipo limpiador de gases *m*; ~ **fluid** *n* INSTR líquido limpiador *m*; ~ **hole** *n* PROD abertura de limpieza *f*; ~ **machine** *n* PROD máquina para limpiar *f*; ~ **material** *n* DETERG material limpiador *m*; ~-**off** *n* CONST *carpentry* eliminación de obstrucciones *f*; ~ **pit** *n* PROD foso de limpieza *m*; ~ **shop** *n* PROD *founding* taller de desarenar *m*; ~ **tools** *n pl* MINE herramientas de desarenado *f pl*; ~-**up** *n* PROD *of piece of work* repaso *m*, RECYCL, WATER *of sluices* limpieza *f*

cleanse *vt* WATER depurar, purificar, *river* sanear

cleansing *n* WATER depuración *f*, purificación *f*, *of a river* saneamiento *m*

clear[1] *adj* METEO claro, transparente

clear[2] *n* COMP&DP borrado *m*; ~-**air turbulence** *n* AIR TRANSP turbulencia de aire claro *f*, turbulencia de aire limpio *f*; ~ **base** *n* CINEMAT soporte transparente *m*;

~ **binder** *n* TV ligador transparente *m*; ~ **channel** *n* TELECOM canal despejado *m*; ~-**channel capability** *n* TELECOM capacidad de canales despejados *f*; ~ **copy** *n* PRINT original limpio *m*; ~ **etching** *n* C&G grabado con ácido *m*; ~-**etching bath** *n* C&G baño para grabado con ácido *m*; ~ **frit** *n* C&G frita clara *f*; ~ **ice** *n* REFRIG hielo transparente *m*; ~ **leader** *n* CINEMAT, TV guía transparente *f*; ~ **light** *n* RAIL *fixed equipment* luz libre *f*; ~ **pond** *n* COAL balsa de decantación *f*, estanque de decantación *m*, MINE balsa de decantación *f*; ~ **request** *n* COMP&DP petición de despeje *f*, petición de liberación *f*; ~-**request packet** *n* TELECOM paquete de solicitud de desconexión *m*; ~ **sixty-four service** *n* TELECOM locución despejada *f*, servicio sesenta y cuatro de desconexión *m*; ~ **spot** *n* C&G mancha clara *f*; ~ **text** *n* TELECOM texto despejado *m*; ~ **to zero** *n* COMP&DP puesta a cero *f*; ~ **transmission** *n* TELECOM transmisión despejada *f*; ~ **varnish** *n* COATINGS, COLOUR barniz transparente *m*; ~ **water** *n* HYDROL, WATER agua clarificada *f*; ~ **weather** *n* AIR TRANSP, METEO, WATER TRANSP tiempo bonancible *m*; ~ **zone** *n* COMP&DP zona de seguridad *f*, zona despejada *f*

clear[3] *vt* COMP&DP borrar, despejar, eliminar, MINE desenredar, despejar, PROD *drill* borrar, separar, WATER TRANSP *anchor* desencepar, escapular, montar, despachar, abrirse de, izar arriba y claro; ~ **away** *vt* CONST *sand bank* dragar, eliminar obstáculos; ~ **out** *vt* CONST *earth, rubbish* despejar, limpiar

clearance *n* AIR TRANSP *of propeller, wing, etc* distancia *f*, margen *m*, margen de seguridad *m*, COMP&DP *security* acreditación *f*, autorización *f*, ELEC ENG separación *f*, tolerancia *f*, HYDRAUL espacio perjudicial *m*, holgura *f*, tolerancia de ajuste positiva *f*, MECH luz *f*, despeje *m*, huelgo *m*, juego *m*, resguardo *m*, margen *m*, espacio libre *m*, MECH ENG huelgo *m*, holgura *f*, espacio muerto *m*, juego *m*, despeje *m*, resguardo *m*, destalonado *m*, intersticio *m*, distancia entre la cabeza de un diente y la raíz del diente conjugado *f*, paso libre *m*, MINE separación vertical *f* (*Esp*), franqueo vertical *m* (*AmL*), holgura *f* (*Esp*), margen de altura *m* (*AmL*), NUCL huelgo *m*, PROD huelgo *m*, holgura *f*, *negative lap of slide-valve* límite *m*, WATER TRANSP *customs* despacho *m*; ~ **angle** *n* MECH ENG *machine tools* ángulo de despojo anterior *m*; ~ **circle** *n* MECH ENG *gearing* círculo límite *m*; ~ **hole** *n* MECH ENG *for threaded bolt for shaft* agujero de paso *m*; ~ **level** *n* COMP&DP nivel de acreditación *m*, nivel de autorización *m*; ~ **line** *n* MECH ENG *straight gearing* línea límite *f*; ~ **period** *n* TRANSP tiempo de despacho *m*; ~ **space** *n* HYDRAUL cámara *f*, espacio perjudicial *m*, holgura *f*, huelgo *m*, interisticio *m*, tolerancia de ajuste positiva *f*

cleared: ~ **for take-off** *adj* AIR TRANSP autorizado para despegar, permitido

clearer *n* MECH ENG *tools* purgador *m*

clearing *n* AGRIC claro *m*, desmonte *m*, MINE alzado *m* (*AmL*), desenredado *m*, espaciado *m* (*Esp*); ~-**away** *n* PROD *of rubbish* limpieza *f*; ~ **bath** *n* CINEMAT, PHOTO baño clarificador *m*; ~ **of the cage** *n* MINE alzado de la jaula *m*; ~ **and grubbing** *n* CONST limpieza y desbroce *f*; ~ **operations** *n pl* CONST operaciones de limpieza *f pl*; ~ **procedure** *n* TELECOM procedimiento de despeje *m*; ~ **time** *n* PRINT tiempo de recuperación *m*

clearness *n* HYDROL, WATER claridad *f*, limpidez *f*

clearscan *n* WATER TRANSP *radar* circuito clearscan *m*
clearview: ~ **screen** *n* WATER TRANSP vistaclara *m*
clearway *n* MECH ENG zona libre de obstáculos *f*
cleat *n* CONST *wood* listón *m*, tablita *f*, GEOL fisura *f*, grieta *f*, MECH ENG bita *f*, listón *m*, travesero *m*, *for rope* abrazadera *f*, WATER TRANSP *deck equipment* cornamusa *f*
cleavage *n* CRYSTALL exfoliación *f*, fisura *f*, GEOL exfoliación *f*, METALL exfoliación *f*, hendidura *f*, partición *f*; ~ **crack** *n* METALL fisuración por fragmentación *f*; ~ **facet** *n* METALL faceta de despegue *f*, faceta de exfoliación *f*; ~ **plane** *n* CHEM, CRYSTALL plano de clivaje *m*
cleaver *n* CONST *for wood* hacha *f*, instrumento para resquebrajar *m*
cleaving *n* CONST corte de madera y leña *m*, resquebrajamiento *m*; ~ **saw** *n* CONST sierra para leña *f*, sierra para resquebrajar *f*
cleft *n* OCEAN cortada *f*; ~ **water** *n* COAL agua de grieta *f*; ~ **weld** *n* PROD soldadura de muesca *f*; ~ **welding** *n* PROD soldadura de muesca *f*
cleveite *n* MINERAL cleveíta *f*
clevis *n* MECH *safety hook, spring hook, clip hook* ojete *m*, abrazadera *f*, horquilla *f*, MECH ENG horquilla *f*, *safety hook, spring hook, clip hook* ojete *m*, abrazadera *f*, *shackle, U bolt with pin or screw* grillete *m*; ~ **bolt** *n* MECH, MECH ENG abrazadera roscada *f*, horquilla roscada *f*; ~ **link** *n* MECH, MECH ENG acoplamiento de conexión en U *m*, unión en U *f*, varilla de conexión en U *f*; ~ **pin** *n* MECH chaveta de horquilla *f*, espiga de horquilla *f*, pasador de horquilla *m*, *without head* pivote de horquilla *m*, MECH ENG pasador de horquilla *m*, chaveta de horquilla *f*, *without head* pivote de horquilla *m*, espiga de horquilla *f*
clew *n* WATER TRANSP *on sails* puño *m*, puño de escota *m*
CLI *abbr* (*called-line identification*) TELECOM identificación de la línea de llamada *f*
click *n* ACOUST chasquido *m*, MECH ENG *horology* fiador *m*, lingüete *m*, trinquete *m*; ~ **footage counter** *n* CINEMAT indicador sonoro del metraje *m*; ~ **stop** *n* CINEMAT, PHOTO parada *f*; ~ **wheel** *n* MECH ENG rueda de trinquete *f*, rueda dentada de trinquete *f*
CLID *abbr* (*calling line identification display*) TELECOM visualizador de identificación de línea de llamada *m*
cliff *n* CONST, GEOL, OCEAN, WATER TRANSP acantilado *m*, cantil *m*
climagram *n* METEO climagrama *m*, climograma *m*, diagrama climático *m*
climate *n* METEO clima *m*; ~ **environment** *n* METEO medio climático *m*
climatic: ~ **anomaly** *n* METEO anomalía climática *f*; ~ **chamber** *n* PACK, REFRIG, THERMO cámara climática *f*, cámara climatizada *f*; ~ **conditions** *n pl* PACK condiciones climáticas *f pl*; ~ **detector** *n* TRANSP detector climático *m*; ~ **graph** *n* METEO diagrama climático *m*; ~ **hazard** *n* METEO, SAFE peligro climatológico *m*, riesgo climatológico *m*; ~ **protection** *n* SAFE protección climática *f*; ~ **test** *n* PACK, SPACE ensayo climático *m*, prueba climática *f*
climatogram *n* METEO climatograma *m*
climatology *n* METEO climatología *f*
climb[1] *n* AIR TRANSP ascenso *m*, subida *f*, toma de altura *f*, CRYSTALL *of dislocation* ascensión *f*, SPACE ascenso *m*, subida *f*, toma de altura *f*; ~ **corridor** *n*

AIR TRANSP, SPACE corredor de ascenso *m*, corredor de subida *m*, pasillo de ascensión *m*, pasillo de trepada *m*; ~ **cruise** *n* AIR TRANSP crucero ascendente *m*, crucero de subida *m*; ~ **gradient** *n* AIR TRANSP gradiente del ascenso *m*, inclinación de subida *f*, ángulo de ascenso *m*, SPACE gradiante del ascenso *m*, inclinación de subida *f*, ángulo de ascenso *m*; ~-**out** *n* AIR TRANSP ascenso *m*, subida *f*, toma de altura *f*; ~ **performance** *n* AIR TRANSP prestaciones en ascenso *f pl*, resultado de la subida *m*; ~ **phase** *n* AIR TRANSP fase de ascenso *f*, fase de subida *f*; ~ **rate** *n* SPACE rapidez de ascenso *f*, velocidad de ascenso *f*; ~ **setting** *n* AIR TRANSP reglaje de subida *m*; ~ **speed** *n* AIR TRANSP, SPACE velocidad de ascenso *f*, velocidad de subida *f*; ~ **turn** *n* AIR TRANSP viraje en subida *m*
climb[2] *vi* AIR TRANSP, SPACE ascender
climbing: ~ **lane** *n* CONST camino en pendiente *m*, vía en pendiente *f*; ~ **speed** *n* AIR TRANSP, SPACE velocidad escalar de ascenso *f*
clinch[1]: ~ **rivet** *n* MECH ENG remache de redoblar *m*
clinch[2] *vt* PROD remachar, WATER TRANSP *chain* entalingar
clinched *adj* PROD cerrado
cling: ~ **film** *n* PACK película adherente *f*, revestimiento adhesivo *m*
clinker[1]: ~-**built** *adj* WATER TRANSP *boatbuilding* de tingladillo
clinker[2] *n* CHEM TECH escoria *f*, CONST clinker *m*, escoria *f*, PROD grasa de fundición *f*, cenizas voltantes *f pl*, clinquer *m*, *iron slag* escorias *f pl*; ~ **brick** *n* C&G ladrillo clinker *m*, ladrillo refractario *m*; ~ **cement** *n* C&G clinker *m*
clinkstone *n* GEOL fonolita *f*, PETROL, PROD fonolita *f*, piedra de campana *f*
clinochlore *n* MINERAL clinocloro *m*
clinoclase *n* MINERAL clinoclasa *f*
clinoclasite *n* MINERAL clinoclasita *f*
clinohedrite *n* MINERAL clinoedrita *f*
clinohumite *n* MINERAL clinohumita *f*
clinometer *n* COAL, CONST, GEOL, GEOPHYS, INSTR, METR clinómetro *m*, eclímetro *m*, indicador de pendiente *m*, MINE clinómetro *m*, eclínometro *m*, indicador de pendiente *m*, SPACE clinómetro *m*, eclímetro *m*, indicador de pendiente *m*; ~ **alidade** *n* CONST, INSTR alidada de eclímetro *f*
clinometry *n* GEN clinometría *f*
clinozoisite *n* MINERAL clinozoisita *f*
clintonite *n* MINERAL clintonita *f*
clip[1] *n* CINEMAT corto *m*, ELEC ENG *signal* abrazadera *f*, presilla *f*, LAB pinza *f* (*Esp*), presilla *f* (*AmL*), MECH sujetador *m*, collar *m*, mordaza *f*, abrazadera *f*, brida *f*, pinza *f*, grapa *f*, grampa *f*, MECH ENG abrazadera *f*, pinza *f*, mordaza *f*, grapa *f*, collar *m*, sujetador *m*, brida *f*, TEXTIL presilla *f*; ~ **frame** *n* TEXTIL bastidor de pinzas *m*; ~ **gage** *AmE*, ~ **gauge** *BrE n* METALL calibre de mordaza *m*; ~ **hook** *n* MECH ENG *sister hook* gancho en ancla *m*, gancho de enlace *m*, gancho de seguridad doble *m*, *spring hook, safety hook* gancho de seguridad *m*; ~-**on carrier** *n* PACK corte en marcha *m*; ~-**on instrument** *n* ELEC, INSTR instrumento de mordazas *m*, instrumento que se fija con presilla *m*; ~-**on refrigerating unit** *n* REFRIG grupo frigorífico amovible *m*; ~ **stenter** *n* TEXTIL rame de pinzas *m*
clip[2] *vt* AGRIC esquilar, PROD *shear* rebabar

clipped: ~ **wing** n AIR TRANSP, TRANSP ala de punta recortada f

clipper n AIR TRANSP circuito limitador m, ELECTRON limitador de amplitud m, TELECOM limitador de amplitud m, recortador m, separador de amplitud m, separador de sincronización m, TV nivelador m, recortador m; ~ **amplifier** n ELECTRON amplificador de limitación m; ~ **circuit** n ELECTRON circuito limitador m; ~ **diode** n ELECTRON, TV diodo limitador m; ~ **dryerfelt** n TEXTIL munidora f

clipping n COMP&DP recorte m; ~ **circuit** n ELECTRON circuito recortador m; ~ **level** n ELECTRON nivel de limitación m, TV nivel de recorte m

clique n TELECOM grupo de personas con intereses comunes m

CLIR abbr (calling-line identification restriction) TELECOM restricción de identificación de línea de llamada f

CLLM abbr (consolidated link-layer management message) TELECOM mensaje de gestión consolidada de enlace entre capas m

CLNP abbr (connectionless network layer protocol) TELECOM protocolo a nivel de red sin conexiones m

CLNS abbr (connectionless network layer service) TELECOM servicio a nivel de red sin conexiones m

clock[1] n ELECTRON, METR reloj m; ~ **circuit** n ELECTRON circuito de reloj m, circuito de sincronización m; ~ **cycle** n COMP&DP, ELECTRON ciclo cronometrado m, ciclo de reloj m; ~ **-face reference** n AIR TRANSP referencia de la cara del reloj f; ~ **frequency** n COMP&DP, ELECTRON frecuencia de base f, frecuencia de reloj f; ~ **period** n ELECTRON período de reloj m, período empleado m; ~ **pulse** n COMP&DP, ELECTRON impulso de reloj m, impulso de sincronización m, impulso de tiempo m; ~ **rate** n COMP&DP frecuencia de base f, frecuencia de reloj f, registro de reloj m, PROD ritmo del patrón m; ~ **recovery** n SPACE communications recuperación del reloj f; ~ **register** n COMP&DP registro cronométrico m; ~ **relay** n ELEC relé de reloj m; ~ **screw plate** n PROD hilera para relojería f; ~ **signal** n ELECTRON señal de reloj f, señal sincronizada f; ~ **track** n COMP&DP pista cronométrica f, pista de reloj f

clock[2] vt CINEMAT, COMP&DP, ELECTRON cronometrar, registrar

clocked: ~ **circuit** n ELECTRON circuito sincronizado m; ~ **flip-flop** n ELECTRON basculador cronometrado m

clocking n COMP&DP sincronización f, transmisión sincrónica f, ELECTRON cronometrado m; ~ **sequence** n ELECTRON secuencia cronometrada f

clockwise[1]: ~ **rotation** n FOOD of measuring equipment, MECH rotación de izquierda a derecha f, rotación según las agujas del reloj f

clockwise[2]: ~ **-rotating** phr FOOD of measuring instrument, MECH que gira en el sentido de las agujas del reloj

clockwork n MECH mecanismo de relojería m, mecanismo de resorte m; ~ **camera** n CINEMAT cámara de cuerda f

clod n CONST terrón m

clog vt MECH ENG atascar, obstruir, trabar, PAPER, PROD obstruir, WATER programme atascar

clogged[1] adj MECH, MECH ENG atascado, atorado, obstruido, trabado

clogged[2]: ~ **felt** n C&G felpa obturada f; ~ **head** n TV cabeza obstruida f

clogging n COAL, MECH ENG, MINE atascamiento m, obstrucción f, PAPER acolmatado, PROD obstrucción f, WATER atascamiento m

clone n COMP&DP, PHYS clon m

cloning n COMP&DP, PHYS clonación f

clopanar: ~ **waveguide** n ELEC ENG guía de ondas coplanar f

close[1]: ~ **-hauled** adj WATER TRANSP sailing ciñendo, de bolina

close[2]: ~ **air support** n (CAS) MILIT apoyo aéreo cercano m; ~ **-burning coal** n COAL carbón aglomerante m, carbón aglutinante m; ~ **buttress** n CONST contrafuerte m; ~ **-cell foam** n PACK espuma para cerrar compartimientos f; ~ **-coil spring** n MECH ENG muelle en espiral m, muelle helicoidal cerrado m, resorte helicoidal cerrado m; ~ **collision** n NUCL colisión próxima f; ~ **couple** n CONST building cercha de dos pares f; ~ **-couple truss** n CONST armadura de cercha de dos pares f; ~ **coupling** n COMP&DP acoplamiento compacto m, acoplamiento estrecho m, ELEC, ELEC ENG inductance acoplamiento cerrado m, acoplamiento estrecho m, acoplamiento fuerte m, acoplamiento rígido m; ~ **-fit thread** n MECH ENG rosca de paso de precisión f, rosca de paso fino f; ~ **frequency signals** n pl ELECTRON señales de frecuencia de cierre f pl; ~ **joint** n PROD junta estanca f; ~ **lathing** n PROD torno cerrado m; ~ **medium shot** n CINEMAT primer plano medio m; ~ **-packed lattice** n METALL red de malla compacta f, red de malla pequeña f; ~ **-packed structure** n CRYSTALL estructura de empaquetamiento compacto f; ~ **packing** n CRYSTALL empaquetamiento compacto m; ~ **piling** n CONST apilamiento estrecho m; ~ **set** n MINE instalación de extracción f (AmL), instalación fija f (Esp), marco de ajuste m pl (Esp), marco de entibación m (AmL), marco de mina m; ~ **-sliding fit** n MECH, MECH ENG ajuste corredizo cerrado m, ajuste deslizante cerrado m; ~ **-spiral spring** n MECH ENG muelle helicoidal cerrado m, resorte helicoidal cerrado m; ~ **string** n CONST stair building zanca cerrada f; ~ **supervision** n SAFE supervisión rigurosa f; ~ **-talking efficiency** n ACOUST eficacia parafónica f; ~ **-timbered level** n MINE galería entibada adosada f (AmL), galería entibada ajustada f (Esp); ~ **timbering** n MINE entibado adosado m (AmL), entibado ajustado m (Esp); ~ **tolerance spacer** n MECH ENG espaciador de precisión m, galgas de precisión f pl, plantilla de precisión f; ~ **-up** n CINEMAT primer plano m, SPACE examen minucioso m, primer plano m, vista cercana f; **very ~-up** n CINEMAT examen minucioso m, plano de detalles m, vista cercana f; ~ **-up attachment** n CINEMAT lente de aproximación f, lente de aproximación para primeros planos f, lente para retraso f, lente para retratos f, OPT lente para retratos f, PHOTO lente de aproximación f, lente de aproximación para primeros planos f, lente para retratos f, TV lente de aproximación f, lente de aproximación para primeros planos f, lente para retraso f; ~ **-up lens** n INSTR, PHOTO lente de ampliación f

close[3] vt CONST road bloquear, cerrar, ELEC ENG cerrar, PROD rivet tapar, mould, plate cerrar, tube taponar; ~ **down** vt CINEMAT, PHOTO cerrar, reducir; ~ **up** vt

CINEMAT, PHOTO hacer una vista detallada, tomar un primer plano, PRINT juntar

close[4]: **on a ~ reach** *phr* WATER TRANSP con viento a proa del través sin ceñir todo

closed[1] *adj* MATH *curves, intervals, topological spaces* cerrado

closed[2]: **~-and-sealed cooling system** *n* AUTO sistema de refrigeración autónomo *m*, sistema de refrigeración hermético *m*; **~ bolts** *n pl* PRINT signaturas plegadas sin perforar *f pl*; **~ box girder** *n* TRANSP viga tubular cerrada *f*; **~ butt joint** *n* PROD *welding* junta a tope sin huelgo *f*; **~ cell** *n* P&R célula cerrada *f*; **~-cell cellular plastic** *n* P&R plástico celular de célula cerrada *m*; **~-cell foamed plastic** *n* P&R, REFRIG plástico celular de celdillas cerradas *m*; **~ chain** *n* CHEM cadena cerrada *f*, compuesto cíclico *m*; **~ circuit** *n* COAL, ELEC, ELEC ENG, MECH ENG, PHYS, TELECOM circuito cerrado *m*; **~-circuit grinding** *n* COAL molienda en circuito cerrado *f*, molturación en circuito cerrado *f*; **~-circuit television** *n* (*CCTV*) TELECOM, TV circuito cerrado de televisión *m*, televisión en circuito cerrado *f*; **~-circuit voltage** *n* ELEC, ELEC ENG voltaje de servicio *m*; **~-coil armature** *n* ELEC *generator*, ELEC ENG inducido de devanado cerrado *m*; **~ container** *n* TRANSP contenedor cerrado *m*; **~-cup flash point** *n* P&R punto de inflamabilidad en cubeta cerrada *m*; **~ curve** *n* GEOM curva cerrada *f*; **~-cycle cooling system** *n* NUCL, THERMO sistema de refrigeración de ciclo cerrado *m*; **~-cycle gas turbine** *n* TRANSP turbina de gas de ciclo cerrado *f*; **~-cycle hot-air turbine** *n* TRANSP turbina de aire caliente de ciclo cerrado *f*; **~-cyle cooling system** *n* ELEC sistema de refrigeración de ciclo cerrado *m*; **~ demand** *n* PROD demanda cerrada *f*; **~ diaphragm** *n* ACOUST diafragma cerrado *m*; **~-face calender** *n* PAPER calandra de construcción cerrada *f*; **~ folds** *n pl* PRINT cantos doblados *m pl*; **~ fuel cycle** *n* NUCL ciclo de combustible cerrado *m*; **~ interval** *n* MATH intervalo cerrado *m*; **~ locker** *n* WATER TRANSP *accommodation* pañol cerrado *m*; **~ loop** *n* AIR TRANSP círculo cerrado *m*, ELEC, ELEC ENG, ELECTRON *circuit* lazo cerrado *m*, circuito cerrado *m*, bucle cerrado *m*; **~-loop control** *n* ELEC, ELECTRON control en bucle cerrado *m*, funcionamiento en bucle cerrado *m*; **~-loop control system** *n* ELEC, ELEC ENG, ELECTRON sistema de control en bucle cerrado *m*; **~-loop feedback** *n* ELEC, ELEC ENG, ELECTRON, PROD realimentación en circuito cerrado *f*; **~-loop gain** *n* ELEC, ELEC ENG, ELECTRON ganancia en bucle cerrado *f*; **~-loop traffic control system** *n* ELEC sistema de control de tráfico en circuito cerrado *m*, ELEC ENG sistema de control de tráfico en circuito cerrado *m*, ELECTRON sistema de control de tráfico en circuito cerrado *m*, TRANSP sistema de control de tráfico en circuito cerrado *m*; **~ pass** *n* PROD *rolling mill* canal embutido *m*; **~ position** *n* ELEC *relay* posición cerrada *f*; **~ pot** *n* C&G crisol cerrado *m*; **~ ring** *n* CHEM *structure* anillo cerrado *m*; **~ sea** *n* OCEAN mar cerrado *m*; **~ shell** *n* PHYS capa cerrada *f*; **~-slot armature** *n* ELEC *generator* inducido dentado cerrado *m*; **~ system** *n* THERMO sistema cerrado *m*; **~-throat wind tunnel** *n* PHYS túnel aerodinámico de garganta cerrada *m*; **~-turbine chamber** *n* PROD cámara de turbina cerrada *f*; **~ user group** *n* (*CUG*) COMP&DP, TELECOM grupo cerrado de usuarios *m*; **~ vessel** *n* LAB

recipiente cerrado *m*; **~ work** *n* MINE explotación subterránea *f*

closedown *n* COMP&DP *of a program* cierre definitivo *m*, cierre *m*

closest: **~ approach distance** *n* WATER TRANSP *radar navigation* distancia de aproximación máxima *f*; **~ point of approach** *n* WATER TRANSP *radar navigation* punto de aproximación máxima *m*

closet *n* C&G closet *m*, guardarropa *m*

closing *n* CONST *of a street* bloqueo *m*, cierre *m*, corte *m*, PROD cierre *m*; **~ contact** *n* ELEC *relay* contacto de cierre *m*; **~ credits** *n pl* CINEMAT, TV títulos finales *m pl*; **~ machine** *n* PACK máquina cerradora *f*; **~ operation** *n* ELEC *relay* funcionamiento cerrado *m*; **~ panel** *n* MECH ENG panel de cierre *m*, tablero de cierre *m*; **~ speed** *n* ELEC *relay* velocidad de cierre *f*, WATER TRANSP *navigation* velocidad de aproximación *f*; **~ time** *n* ELEC *relay* hora de cierre *f*, tiempo de cierre *m*

closure *n* C&G *of bottles* tapa *f*, CHEM *of ring* ciclización *f*, cierre *m*, ELEC ENG *of a circuit*, GEOL, PACK cierre *m*; **~ production line** *n* PACK cadena de producción de cierres *f*; **~ rail** *n* RAIL carril de unión *m*

cloth *n* SPACE tela *f*, trapo *m*, velamen *m*, TEXTIL tela *f*; **~-centered board** *AmE*, **~-centred board** *BrE* *n* PAPER cartón entretelado de dos caras *m*; **~ lap** *n* OCEAN pliegue de velamen *m*; **~-lined paper** *n* PAPER papel entretelado en una cara *m*; **~ polisher** *n* C&G pulidor de tela *m*; **~ turnout** *n* TEXTIL atuendo de tela *m*

clothing *n* HYDRAUL envuelta *f*, guarnición de carda *f*, revestimiento *m*, PAPER vestiduras *f pl*, SAFE prendas *f pl*, vestimenta *f*, TEXTIL vestiduras *f pl*; **~ plate** *n* HYDRAUL chapa de envuelta del revestimiento calorífugo *f*, chapa del revestimiento *f*

clotting *n* CHEM, FOOD coagulación *f*, engrumación *f*

cloud[1]: **~ amount** *n* METEO nubosidad *f*; **~ ceiling** *n* AIR TRANSP, METEO techo de nubes *m*; **~ chamber** *n* PART PHYS cámara de niebla *f*, WAVE PHYS cámara de ionización *f*, cámara de niebla *f*; **~ collision warning system** *n* AIR TRANSP, SAFE sistema de aviso de colisión en nubes *m*; **~ cover** *n* METEO, WATER TRANSP nubosidad *f*; **~ formation** *n* METEO formación de las nubes *f*; **~ layer** *n* METEO, SPACE capa de nubes *f*; **~ point** *n* DETERG punto de turbidez *m*, temperatura de enturbiamiento *f*, REFRIG punto de enturbamiento *m*; **~ pulse** *n* ELEC ENG *charge-storage tubes* impulso de nube *m*; **~ system** *n* METEO sistema nuboso *m*

cloud[2]: **~ over** *vi* METEO anublarse

cloudbase *n* AIR TRANSP, METEO base de nubes *f*; **~ measuring instrument** *n* AIR TRANSP, INSTR, METEO instrumento de medición de la base de las nubes *m*

cloudburst *n* METEO chaparrón *m*, chaparrón fuerte *m*

cloudiness *n* GAS nebulosidad *f*, opacidad *f*, turbidez *f*

clouding *adj* TV anubarrado, nublado

cloudy *adj* METEO nuboso

clout: **~ nail** *n* MECH ENG clavo de cabeza ancha *m*, tacha *f*

clove: **~ hitch** *n* WATER TRANSP *knot* ballestrinque *m*

clover: **~-leaf aerial** *n* *BrE* (*cf clover-leaf antenna AmE*) TV antena dipolo magnético de trébol *f*; **~-leaf antenna** *n* *AmE* (*cf clover-leaf aerial BrE*) TV antena dipolo magnético de trébol *f*

CLP *abbr* (*call loss priority*) TELECOM prioridad de pérdida de llamada *f*

CLS *abbr* (*connectionless server*) TELECOM servidor sin conexiones *m*

CLSF *abbr* (*connectionless service function*) TELECOM función de servicio sin conexiones *f*

club[1]: ~ **car** *n* *AmE* RAIL coche salón *m*

club[2] *vi* WATER TRANSP *mooring* ir a la deriva arrastrando el ancla

clump *n* PRINT lingote *m*

clupeine *n* CHEM clupeína *f*

cluster[1] *n* AGRIC racimo *m*, COMP&DP agrupamiento *m*, MECH ENG aglomeración *f*, agrupación *f*, batería *f*, grupo *m*, juego *m*, *of gear wheels* tren *m*, PROD batería *f*, SPACE *of galaxies* enjambre *m*, conglomerado *m*, TEXTIL hato *m*, TRANSP aglomeración *f*, conjunto *m*, conjunto de engranajes *m*, grupo de hombres para un lanzamiento *m*; ~ **controller** *n* COMP&DP controlador de agrupamientos *m*; ~ **formation** *n* METALL formación en grupo *f*; ~ **indicator light** *n* PROD luz indicadora de grupo *f*; ~ **spring** *n* MECH ENG resorte múltiple *m*

cluster[2]: ~ **together** *vi* GEOL agrupar

clustered *adj* TRANSP aglomerado, agrupado, recogido

clustering *n* METALL agrupación *f*

clutch *n* AUTO embrague *m*, CINEMAT llave de cambio *f*, MECH embrague *m*, garra *f*, manguito de embrague *m*, MECH ENG, VEH, WATER TRANSP *of an engine* embrague *m*; ~ **cable** *n* AUTO, VEH cable de embrague *m*; ~ **casing** *n* AUTO, VEH cárter de embrague *m*; ~ **clearance** *n* AUTO, VEH juego del embrague *m*; ~ **collar** *n* MECH ENG collar de embrague *m*; ~ **coupling** *n* MECH ENG acoplamiento del embrague *m*; ~ **disc** *BrE*, ~ **disk** *n* AUTO, VEH disco de embrague *m*; ~ **drive plate** *n* AUTO, VEH plato de accionamiento del embrague *m*; ~ **drum** *n* AUTO, MECH ENG tambor del embrague *m*, VEH tambor del embrage *m*; ~ **fork** *n* AUTO, MECH ENG, VEH embragador *m*, horquilla del embrague *f*; ~ **gear** *n* AUTO engranaje del embrague *m*, MECH ENG, VEH engranaje del embrage *m*; ~ **housing** *n* AUTO, VEH campana del embrague *f*; ~ **lining** *n* AUTO, MECH forro del embrague *m*, revestimiento del embrage *m*, MECH ENG forro del embrague *m*, revestimiento del embrague *m*, VEH forro del embrague *m*, revestimiento del embrague *m*; ~ **linkage** *n* AUTO, VEH varillaje de mando del embrague *m*; ~ **master cylinder** *n* AUTO, VEH cilindro maestro del embrague *m*; ~ **output cylinder** *n* AUTO cilindro de salida del embrague *m*, cilindro impulsor del embrague *m*, cilindro motor del embrague *m*, VEH cilindro de salida de embrague *m*, cilindro impulsor del embrague *m*, cilindro motor del embrague *m*; ~ **pedal** *n* AUTO, VEH pedal de embrague *m*; ~~**pedal clearance** *n* AUTO, VEH juego del pedal del embrague *m*; ~~**pedal push rod** *n* AUTO, VEH empujador del pedal de embrague *m*; ~~**pedal release** *n* VEH palanca de desenganche del pedal del embrague *f*; ~~**pedal release lever** *n* AUTO palanca de desenganche del pedal del embrague *f*; ~ **pick-off** *n* AIR TRANSP derivador del embrague *m*, transductor del embrague *m*; ~ **plate** *n* AUTO, VEH disco de embrague *m*; ~ **pressure plate** *n* MECH ENG placa de presión del embrague *f*, plato de presión del embrague *m*; ~ **release bearing** *n* AUTO, VEH manguito del cojinete de empuje *m*; ~ **release fork** *n* AUTO varilla de embrague *f*, VEH horquilla de desembrague *f*; ~ **rod** *n* AUTO, VEH varilla de embrague *f*; ~ **shaft** *n* AUTO, VEH eje del embrague

m; ~ **slave cylinder** *n* AUTO, VEH cilindro auxiliar del embrague *m*; ~ **sleeve** *n* AUTO, VEH manguito del embrague *m*; ~ **slip** *n* AUTO deslizamiento del embrague *m*, patinamiento del embrague *m*, resbalamiento del embrague *m*, VEH patinamiento del embrague *m*, resbalamiento del embrague *m*, deslizamiento del embrague *m*; ~ **spring** *n* MECH ENG, VEH muelle del embrague *m*, resorte del embrague *m*; ~ **throwout** *n* AUTO, VEH carrera del embrague *f*, desembrague *m*

clutter *n* ELECTRON *communications* ecos parásitos de pantalla *m pl*, ecos perturbadores de radar *m pl*, emborronamiento de pantalla *m*, perturbación *f*, señales parásitas en pantalla *f pl*, SPACE señales parásitas en pantalla *f pl*, ecos perturbadores de radar *m pl*, emborronamiento de pantalla *m*, perturbación *f*, ecos parásitos de pantalla *m pl*, TELECOM ecos parásitos de pantalla *m pl*, ecos perturbadores de radar *m pl*, emborronamiento de pantalla *m*, perturbación *f pl*, señales parásitas en pantalla *f pl*, WATER TRANSP *radar screen* ecos parásitos de pantalla *m pl*, ecos perturbadores de radar *m pl*, emborronamiento de pantalla *m*, perturbación *f*, señales parásitas en pantalla *f pl*; ~ **filter** *n* ELECTRON *communications* filtro de señales parásitas *m*

CLV[1] *abbr* (*constant linear velocity*) OPT velocidad lineal constante *f*

CLV[2]: ~ **disc** *BrE*, ~ **disk** *n* *AmE* OPT disco de velocidad lineal constante *m*

Clyburn: ~ **wrench** *n* MECH ENG llave ajustable de rolleta *f*

CM *abbr* COMP&DP (*configuration management*) administración de configuración *f*, gestión de configuración *f*, TELECOM (*connection matrix*) matriz de conexión *f*, condicionalmente obligatorio

Cm *abbr* (*curium*) CHEM, RAD PHYS Cm (*curio*)

CMC *abbr* DETERG, FOOD, P&R (*carboxymethyl cellulose*) CMC (*carboximetilcelulosa*), TELECOM (*call modification completed message*) modificación de llamada mensaje concluido *f*

CMI *abbr* (*coded mark inversion*) TELECOM inversión de la señal codificada *f*

CMIP *abbr* (*common management information protocol*) TELECOM protocolo de información de gestión común *m*

CMIPM *abbr* (*common management information protocol machine*) TELECOM máquina de protocolos de información de gestión común *f*

CMIS *abbr* (*common management information service*) TELECOM servicio de información de gestión común *m*

CMISE[1] *abbr* (*common management information service element*) TELECOM elemento de servicio de información de gestión común *m*

CMISE[2]: ~ **service provider** *n* TELECOM suministrador de servicios CMISE *m*

CMO *abbr* (*common master oscillator*) TELECOM oscilador maestro general *m*

CMOS[1] *abbr* (*complementary metal oxide semiconductor*) ELECTRON, PROD SCOM (*semiconductor complementario de óxido de metal*)

CMOS[2]: ~ **crosspoint** *n* TELECOM contacto de cruce CMOS *m*; ~ **logic** *n* ELECTRON circuito lógico de SCOM *m*; ~ **RAM memory module** *n* PROD módulo de memoria RAM de CMOS *m*; ~ **transistor** *n* ELECTRON transistor de SCOM *m*

C-mount *n* CINEMAT montura C *f*; ~ **adaptor** *n* CINEMAT adaptador para montaje C *m*

CMR *abbr* (*call modification request message*) TELECOM modificación de llamada solicitar mensaje *f*

CMRJ *abbr* (*call modification reject message*) TELECOM modificación de llamada rechazar mensaje *f*

CMS *abbr* (*call message supervisory*) TELECOM supervisión de mensaje de llamada *f*

CN *abbr* (*customer network*) TELECOM red de abonados *f*

C-n *abbr* (*container-n*) TELECOM contenedor-n *m*

CNC[1] *abbr* (*computerized numerical control*) COMP&DP, MECH ENG CNC (*control numérico computerizado*)

CNC[2]: ~ **controlled** *adj* MECH ENG *machine tools* controlado por CNC

CNC[3]: ~ **cylindrical grinder** *n* MECH ENG pulidora cilíndrica de control numérico computarizado *f*, rectificadora cilíndrica de control numérico computarizado *f*; ~ **production internal grinding machine** *n* MECH ENG pulidora interna de producción de control numérico computarizado *f*; ~ **surface grinder** *n* MECH ENG pulidora de superficies exteriores de control numérico computarizado *f*

Co *abbr* (*cobalt*) C&G, CHEM, COLOUR, METALL, NUCL Co (*cobalto*)

coacervate *n* CHEM coacervato *m*

coacervation *n* CHEM coacervación *f*

coach *n* RAIL coche *m*, TRANSP carruaje *m*, vagón de viajeros *m*, autobús de línea *m*, autocar *m*, carroza *f*, omnibús *m*; ~ **bolt** *n* MECH ENG fijador roscado para madera *m*, pasador para madera *m*, perno para madera *m*; ~ **class** *n* TRANSP vagón de clase turista *m*; ~ **screw** *n* MECH ENG perno para madera *m*, tirafondo *m*

coachroof *n* WATER TRANSP *yachts* tambucho *m*

coagulant *n* CHEM, CHEM TECH, FOOD, HEAT ENG, HYDROL, P&R coagulante *m*

coagulate *vt* CHEM, CHEM TECH, FOOD, HEAT ENG, HYDROL, P&R coagular

coagulated *adj* CHEM, CHEM TECH, FOOD, HEAT ENG, HYDROL, P&R coagulado

coagulating *n* CHEM, CHEM TECH, FOOD, HEAT ENG, HYDROL, P&R coagulante *m*; ~ **agent** *n* P&R coagulante *m*; ~ **tank** *n* CHEM TECH tanque de coagulación *m*

coagulation *n* CHEM, CHEM TECH, HEAT ENG, HYDROL, P&R coagulación *f*; ~ **liquid** *n* CHEM TECH líquido de coagulación *m*

coagulator *n* CHEM TECH coagulador *m*

coagulum *n* P&R coágulo *m*

coal[1]: ~-**bearing** *adj* COAL carbonífero; ~-**fired** *adj* COAL calentado por carbón

coal[2] *n* COAL, GEOL, MINE, PETROL, THERMO carbón *m*, carbón de piedra *m*; ~ **ash** *n* COAL ceniza de carbón *f*; ~ **basin** *n* COAL, GEOL cuenca carbonífera *f*; ~ **basket** *n* COAL cesto de carbón *m*, quintal *m*; ~ **bean** *n* COAL granulado de carbón *m*; ~-**bearing rock** *n* COAL, GEOL, MINE lecho carbonífero *m*, roca carbonífera *f*; ~ **bed** *n* COAL, GEOL, MINE yacimiento de carbón *m*; ~ **belt** *n* COAL, GEOL, MINE cinta transportadora de carbón *f*; ~ **breaker** *n* COAL, MINE trituradora de carbón *f*; ~ **bunker** *n* COAL, MINE carbonera *f*, pañol de carbón *m*, RAIL carbonera *f*; ~ **chute** *n* COAL, MINE boca de carbonera *f*, chimenea para carbón *f*; ~ **cracker** *n* COAL quebrantadora *f*; ~ **crusher** *n* COAL, MINE quebrantadora de

carbón *f*, trituradora de carbón *f*; ~ **cutter** *n* COAL, MINE máquina rafadora para carbón *f*, picador de carbón *m*, rozadora para carbón *f*, socavadora *f*; ~-**cutting machine** *n* COAL, MINE máquina rafadora para carbón *f*; ~ **deposit** *n* COAL, GEOL, MINE yacimiento hullero *m*; ~ **dressing** *n* COAL, MINE preparación mecánica de carbones *f*; ~ **drift** *n* COAL, MINE galería de carbón *f*; ~ **drill** *n* COAL, MINE perforadora rotativa para carbón *f*; ~ **dust** *n* COAL cisco *m*, polvo de carbón *m*, POLL polvo de carbón *m*; ~ **dust feeder** *n* COAL *furnance*, HEAT *furnace* alimentación con carbón pulverizado *f*; ~ **extraction** *n* COAL, MINE extracción del carbón *f*; ~ **field** *n* COAL, GEOL, MINE cuenca carbonífera *f*; ~-**fired boiler** *n* HEAT caldera a carbón *f*; ~ **formation** *n* COAL, GEOL, MINE formación carbonífera *f*; ~ **gas** *n* COAL gas de carbón *m*, GAS gas de carbón *m*, gas de hulla *m*; ~ **gasification** *n* COAL, GAS, PETR TECH gasificación del carbón *f*; ~ **getting** *n* COAL, MINE arranque de carbón *m*; ~-**handling plant** *n* COAL, MINE planta de manejo del carbón *f*; ~ **liquefaction** *n* CHEM, COAL, GAS, MINE, PETR TECH, PHYS, REFRIG, THERMO licuefacción del carbón *f*; ~ **measure** *n* COAL, GEOL, MINE capa de carbón *f*, filón de carbón *m*, yacimiento de carbón *m*; ~ **mine** *n* COAL, MINE hullera *f*, mina de carbón *f*; ~ **mining** *n* COAL, MINE explotación de minas de carbón *f*, minería del carbón *f*; ~ **mining explosive** *n* MINE explosivo para la explotación de minas de carbón *m*; ~-**mining explosive** *n* COAL explosivo para la explotación de minas de carbón *m*; ~-**mining machine** *n* COAL, MINE deshulladora *f*, rafadora para carbón *f*, rozadora para carbón *f*; ~ **naphtha** *n* COAL benzol *m*; ~ **oil** *n* COAL petróleo bruto obtenido por pirólisis *m*; ~ **pick** *n* COAL, MINE pico para carbón *m*; ~ **pillar** *n* COAL, MINE pilar de carbón *m*; ~ **pit** *n* COAL, MINE mina de carbón *f*; ~ **powder** *n* COAL, MINE cisco *m*, granalla de carbón *f*, polvo de carbón *m*; ~ **preparation** *n* COAL, MINE preparación del carbón *f*; ~ **prepared and blended** *n* COATINGS pasta de carbón *f*; ~ **road** *n* COAL, MINE galería de carbón *f*; ~ **seam** *n* COAL, MINE capa de carbón *f*, filón *m*; ~ **ship** *n* COAL, MINE, WATER TRANSP buque carbonero *m*, carbonero *m*; ~ **sizer** *n* COAL, MINE calibrador de carbón *m*; ~ **slack** *n* COAL, MINE menudo de carbón *m*; ~ **slake** *n* COAL, MINE finos de carbón *m pl*, menudos de carbón *m pl*; ~ **sludge** *n* COAL, MINE fangos de carbón *m pl*; ~ **stockyard** *n* COAL almacenamiento de carbón *m*, MINE almecenamiento de carbón *m*; ~ **and stone breaker** *n* MINE trituradora de carbón y roca *f*; ~ **tar** *n* COAL alquitrán de hulla *m*; ~-**tar dye** *n* COAL, COLOUR colorante de alquitrán *m*; ~-**tar naphtha** *n* COAL benzol *m*; ~-**tar pitch** *n* COAL brea *f*, brea de alquitrán *f*; ~ **wall** *n* COAL, MINE frente de arranque del carbón *m*; ~ **washer** *n* COAL lavadero de carbón *m*; ~ **washery** *n* COAL lavadero de carbón *m*; ~-**washing plant** *n* COAL lavadero de carbón *m*; ~ **wharf** *n* COAL, TRANSP muelle para carbón *m*; ~ **winning** *n* COAL, MINE arranque de carbón *m*; ~ **yard** *n* COAL, MINE almacenamiento de carbón *m*, parque de carbón *m*

coal[3] *vt* COAL, MINE, THERMO alimentar con carbón

coalesce *vi* CHEM combinarse (*AmL*), fundirse (*Esp*)

coalescence *n* METEO coalescencia *f*

coalface *n* COAL, MINE frente de arranque del carbón

m; ~ **system** *n* MINE formación del frente de arranque del carbón *f*

coalification *n* COAL carbonificación *f*, carbonización *f*, GEOL carbonificación *f*, carbonificación *f*, MINE carbonificación *f*, carbonización *f*

coaltitude *n* SPACE coaltitud *f*

coalworks *n* COAL, MINE hullera *f*

coaming *n* AIR TRANSP armazón *m*, brazola *f*, reborde de protección *m*, visera *f*, WATER TRANSP *shipbuilding, boat building* brazola *f*

Coanda: ~ **effect** *n* FLUID efecto Coanda *m*

coarse[1] *adj* AGRIC *grain*, GEOL grueso, MECH áspero, MECH ENG grueso, basto, áspero, recio, tosco, aproximado; ~**-grained** *adj* CINEMAT, GEOL, METALL, PAPER, PHOTO, PRINT de grano grueso

coarse[2]: ~ **adjustment** *n* ELEC ajuste aproximativo *m*, ajuste grueso *m*, INSTR ajuste aproximado *m*, ajuste grueso *m*; ~ **aggregate** *n* CONST gravilla *f*; ~ **batt** *n* TEXTIL batán grueso *m*; ~ **concentration mill** *n* MINE chimenea de mineral *f* (*AmL*), coladero *m* (*Esp*), pozo vertedero *m* (*AmL*), tolua *f* (*AmL*); ~ **count** *n* TEXTIL título grueso *m*; ~ **crops** *n pl* AGRIC cosechas de grano grueso *f pl*; ~ **crusher** *n* COAL trituradora de grueso *f*, triturador de grueso *m*, MINE triturador de grueso *m*, trituradora de gruesos *f*, PROD triturador de grueso *m*, trituradora de grueso *f*; ~ **crushing** *n* COAL, MINE, PROD trituración de grueso *f*; ~ **crushing mill** *n* CHEM TECH trituradora gruesa de rodillos *f*; ~ **feed** *n* MECH ENG *machine tools* avance rápido *m*; ~ **filter** *n* WATER filtro de malla ancha *m*; ~ **filtration** *n* COAL filtración primaria *f*, lixiviación primaria *f*; ~ **grain** *n* CINEMAT, GEOL, METALL, MINE, PAPER, PHOTO, PRINT grano grueso *m*; ~**-grain image** *n* CINEMAT, PHOTO, TV imagen de grano grueso *f*; ~ **grinding** *n* COAL, MINE desbaste a la muela *m*, trituración basta *f*, trituración gruesa *f*; ~ **groove** *n* ACOUST surco grueso *m*; ~ **meal** *n* AGRIC harina de grano grueso *f*; ~ **mesh screen** *n* COAL criba de malla ancha *f*; ~ **ore** *n* MINE mineral en trozos *m*; ~ **pitch** *n* AIR TRANSP *of propeller* paso ancho *m*, MECH ENG paso largo *m*; ~**-pitch screw** *n* CONST tornillo de paso ancho *m*; ~**-pitch thread** *n* AIR TRANSP *of propeller* hilo de paso largo *m*; ~ **pottery** *n* C&G cacharro *m*; ~ **sand** *n* CONST, GEOL arena gruesa *f*, MINE arena basta *f* (*Esp*), arena granugienta *f* (*AmL*), arena gruesa *f*; ~ **sand middlings** *n pl* MINE mixtos de arena gruesa *m pl*; ~ **sands** *n pl* MINE gruesos *m pl*; ~ **scanning** *n* TV exploración aproximada *f*; ~ **screen** *n* COAL criba de granos *f*, tamiz de malla ancha *m*, PRINT trama gruesa *f*; ~ **silt** *n* GEOL limo grueso *m*; ~ **soil** *n* COAL suelo grueso *m*; ~ **solder** *n* PROD suelda de plomo *f*; ~ **texture** *n* GEOL textura gruesa *f*; ~ **thread** *n* MECH ENG *of nuts, bolts* paso grande *m*; ~ **trommel** *n* MINE criba para gruesos *f*; ~ **yarn** *n* TEXTIL hilo de título grueso *m*

coarsening *n* METALL aumento de tamaño de grano *m*, engrosamiento *m*; ~**-up sequence** *n* GEOL secuencia granocreciente *f*, secuencia negativa *f*

coarser: ~ **woven fabric** *n* TEXTIL tejido de calada más grueso *m*

coast[1] *n* GEOL costa *f*, litoral *m*, HYDROL *communications* costa *f*, orilla *f*, WATER TRANSP *geography* costa *f*; ~ **battery** *n* MILIT batería de costa *f*; ~ **earth station** *n* WATER TRANSP *navigation by satellite* estación terrestre costera *f*

coast[2] *vi* VEH descender con motor desembragado,

marchar por inercia, WATER TRANSP costear; ~**-to-stop** *vi* PROD desplazar por inercia hasta parar

coastal[1] *adj* GEOL, HYDROL, WATER TRANSP *geography* con litoral, costero

coastal[2]: ~ **artillery** *n* MILIT artillería de costa *f*; ~ **chart** *n* WATER TRANSP carta costera *f*; ~ **defence** *n BrE* HYDROL, MILIT, WATER TRANSP defensa costera *f*, defensa de costa *f*; ~ **defense** *AmE see coastal defence BrE*; ~ **deposit** *n* WATER sedimento costero *m*; ~ **erosion** *n* HYDROL erosión costera *f*; ~ **fisherman-farmer** *n* OCEAN pescador agricultor *m*, pescador campesino *m*; ~ **fishery** *n* OCEAN pesca costera *f*, pesca de bajura *f*; ~ **navigation** *n* HYDROL, OCEAN, WATER TRANSP navegación costera *f*, navegación de cabotaje *f*; ~ **plain** *n* GEOL llanura costera *f*; ~ **platform** *n* GEOL, GEOPHYS, OCEAN plataforma litoral *f*; ~ **ridge** *n* GEOL, GEOPHYS, OCEAN ribazo *m*; ~ **ring road** *n* CONST carretera costera de circulación *f*, costanera *f* (*AmL*); ~ **river** *n* WATER río costero *m*; ~ **shipping** *n* HYDROL, WATER TRANSP navegación costera *f*; ~ **station** *n* TELECOM estación costera *f*; ~**-station identity** *n* TELECOM identidad de estación costera *f*; ~ **trade** *n* WATER TRANSP tráfico de cabotaje *m*; ~ **waters** *n pl* HYDROL, OCEAN, WATER, WATER TRANSP aguas costeras *f pl*, aguas litorales *f pl*; ~ **zone** *n* GEOL, HYDROL, OCEAN, WATER TRANSP zona costera *f*

Coastal: ~ **Studies Institute** *n* (*CSI*) MAR POLL, POLL Instituto de Estudios Costeros *m*

coaster *n* WATER TRANSP buque de cabotaje *m*, cabotero *m*

coastguard *n* WATER TRANSP servicio de vigilancia costera *m*; ~ **cutter** *n* WATER TRANSP guardacostas *m*

coasting: ~ **lugger** *n* WATER TRANSP *fishing* lugre cabotero *m*; ~ **trade** *n* WATER TRANSP *merchant navy* cabotaje *m*

coastline *n* GEOL, HYDROL, OCEAN, WATER TRANSP litoral *m*, línea de costa *f*

coastwise: ~ **trade** *n* WATER TRANSP *merchant navy* tráfico de cabotaje *m*

coat[1] *n* CONST *roads* capa *f*, mano *f*, PAPER estucado *m*, SPACE capa *f*, recubrimiento *m*, forro *m*; ~ **of paint** *n* COATINGS, PAINT mano de pintura *f*; ~ **trough** *n* COATINGS cuba empleada para aplicación de revestimientos *f*; ~ **of varnish** *n* COATINGS capa de barniz *f*

coat[2] *vt* CINEMAT emulsionar, revestir, COATINGS estucar, forrar, *with gum* engomar, *with lead* emplomar, bañar, recubrir, revestir, *with whitewash, distemper* pintar, *with slip* empastar, FOOD cubrir, P&R dar una mano de pintura, dar una capa de pintura, revestir, PAPER revestir, estucar; ~ **lenses** *vt* COATINGS revestir lentes

coated[1] *adj* COATINGS revestido, FOOD *in breadcrumbs* cubierto

coated[2]: ~ **abrasive** *n* COATINGS, MECH ENG abrasivo de recubrimiento *m*, cinta de lija *f*, papel abrasivo *m*, papel de lija *m*, tela de lija *f*; ~ **back** *n* COATINGS, PRINT lomo estucado *m*; ~ **board** *n* COATINGS madera revestida *f*; ~ **electrode** *n* MECH *civil engineering* electrodo recubierto *m*, electrodo revestido *m*; ~ **fabric** *n* COATINGS, P&R, TEXTIL tela forrada *f*, tela revestida *f*; ~ **folding board** *n* PAPER cartón estucado para cajas plegables *m*; ~ **glass** *n* C&G vidrio recubierto *m*; ~ **lens** *n* CINEMAT lente con revestimiento antirreflejante *f*, objetivo con revestimiento antirreflejante *m*, recubrimiento con propiedades ópticas *m*, COATINGS, INSTR lente con recubrimiento *f*, objetivo con revestimiento antirreflejante *m*, recubrimiento con propiedades ópticas *m*, OPT, PHOTO lente con revestimiento antirreflejante *f*, objetivo con revestimiento antirreflejante *m*, recubrimiento con propiedades ópticas *m*, PHYS lente con revestimiento antirreflejante *f*, objetivo con revestimiento antirreflejante *m*, recubrimiento con propiedades ópicas *m*; ~ **paper** *n* COATINGS papel revestido *m*, PACK, PAPER papel estucado *m*, papel revestido *m*; ~ **thickness measurement** *n* MECH ENG medición del grosor del revestimiento *f*; ~ **wire** *n* COATINGS alambre forrado *m*, cable forrado *m*

coater *n* COATINGS revoque *m*, PAPER estucadora *f*; ~ **pan** *n* COATINGS recipiente para recubrir *m*; ~ **trough** *n* COATINGS cuba de sedimentación *f*

coating *n* AGRIC *of seed* cobertura *f*, CINEMAT revestimiento *m*, COATINGS capa *f*, baño *m*, recubierto *m*, revestimiento *m*, recubrimiento *m*, CONST revestimiento *m*, ELEC ENG recubierto *m*, P&R mano *f*, revestimiento *m*, capa *f*, PACK capa protectora *f*, revestimiento *m*, PAPER estucado *m*, PETR TECH mano de pintura *f*, revestimiento *m*, recubrimiento *m*, baño *m*, PETROL mano de pintura *f*, recubrimiento *m*, revestimiento *m*, baño *m*, PHYS *of an optical fibre* revestimiento *m*, PROD capa *f*, TEXTIL tejido para abrigos *m*; ~ **base paper** *n* COATINGS, PAPER papel soporte para estucar *m* (*AmL*); ~ **binder** *n* COATINGS, PAPER adhesivo para estucado *m*, ligante para estucados *m*; ~ **color** *AmE*, ~ **colour** *BrE n* COATINGS color del revestimiento *m*, PAPER baño de estucado *m*, formulación de estucado *f*, salsa de estucado *f*; ~ **compound** *n* COATINGS, PACK agente de revestido *m*; ~ **drum** *n* COATINGS tambor para revestimientos *m*; ~ **film** *n* COATINGS capa de revestimiento *f*; ~ **finish** *n* COATINGS acabado de revestimiento *m*; ~ **head** *n* CINEMAT, PHOTO cabezal de emulsionado *m*; ~ **kitchen** *n* COATINGS, PAPER cocina de estucado *f*, sala para preparar las formulaciones de estucado *f*; ~ **machine** *n* COATINGS máquina de revestir *f*, estucadora *f*, P&R máquina de revestir *f*, PAPER estucadora *f*; ~ **material** *n* COATINGS material de revestimiento *m*; ~ **powder** *n* COATINGS recubrimiento pulvimetalúrgico *m*; ~ **property** *n* COATINGS propiedad del revestimiento *f*; ~ **roller system** *n* COATINGS sistema de rodillos para revestimiento *m*; ~ **sheet** *n* COATINGS chapa para revestimiento *f*; ~ **slip** *n* COATINGS deslizamiento de la capa de revestimiento *m*; ~ **thickness** *n* COATINGS, P&R espesor de la capa de revestimiento *m*, espesor de la mano *m*; ~ **thickness measurement apparatus** *n* COATINGS, INSTR, METR aparato de medida para calcular el grosor de una capa *m*; ~ **trough** *n* COATINGS cuba de sedimentación *f*, cuba empleada para aplicación de revestimientos *f*; ~ **varnish** *n* COATINGS barniz de revestimiento *m*, barniz de cobertura *m* (*AmL*), barniz de recubrimiento *m* (*Esp*), COLOUR barniz de cobertura *m* (*AmL*), barniz de recubrimiento *m* (*Esp*), barniz de revestimiento *m*; ~ **wax** *n* COATINGS cera para revestimiento *f*; ~ **weight** *n* COATINGS, PRINT gramaje de la capa del estucado *m*

coax *n* COMP&DP, ELEC cable coaxial *m*, ELEC ENG cable coaxial *m*, cable concéntrico *m*, PHYS cable coaxial *m*, TELECOM, TV cable coaxial *m*, coaxial *m*

coaxial[1] *adj* GEN coaxial, coaxil

coaxial[2]: ~ **aerial** *n* BrE (*cf coaxial antenna AmE*) TELECOM, TV antena de alimentador coaxial *f*; ~ **antenna** *n* AmE TELECOM, TV antena de alimentador coaxial *f*; ~ **attenuator** *n* ELECTRON atenuador coaxial *m*; ~ **cable** *n* COMP&DP, ELEC, ELEC ENG, PHYS, TELECOM, TV cable coaxial *m*, cable concéntrico *m*; ~ **cavity** *n* ELECTRON cavidad coaxial *f*; ~ **connector** *n* ELEC ENG conector coaxial *m*; ~ **diode** *n* ELECTRON diodo coaxial *m*; ~ **filter** *n* ELECTRON filtro coaxial *m*; ~ **fixed load** *n* ELEC ENG carga fija coaxial *f*; ~ **helicopter** *n* AIR TRANSP helicóptero coaxial *m*; ~ **line** *n* ELEC ENG, TELECOM línea coaxial *f*; ~ **line** *n* PHYS línea coaxial *f*; ~ **line system** *n* ELEC ENG, PHYS, TELECOM sistema de línea coaxial *m*; ~ **load** *n* ELEC ENG carga concéntrica *f*; ~ **loudspeaker** *n* ACOUST altavoz coaxial *m*; ~ **magazine** *n* CINEMAT chasis coaxial *m*; ~ **magnetron** *n* ELECTRON magnetrón coaxial *m*; ~ **pair** *n* ELEC ENG par coaxial *m*; ~ **pair cable** *n* ELEC ENG cable de par coaxial *m*; ~ **phase shifter** *n* ELEC ENG conmutador de fase coaxial *m*; ~ **propeller** *n* AIR TRANSP hélice coaxial *f*; ~ **resonator** *n* ELECTRON resonador coaxial *m*

cob[1] *n* AGRIC marlo *m* (*AmL*), mazorca *f* (*Esp*), zuro *m*, CONST ladrillo crudo *m*; ~ **coal** *n* COAL carbón seleccionado a mano *m*

cob[2] *vt* BrE COAL, MINE clasificar a mano, escoger a mano

cobalamin *n* CHEM cobalamina *f*

cobalt *n* (*Co*) C&G, CHEM, COLOUR, METALL, NUCL cobalto *m* (*Co*); ~ **bloom** *n* MINERAL eritrina *f*, flores de cobalto *f pl*; ~ **bottle** *n* C&G botella color cobalto *f*; ~ **chloride** *n* C&G, CHEM cloruro de cobalto *m*; ~ **color** *AmE*, ~ **colour** *BrE n* COLOUR colorante de cobalto *m*; ~ **glance** *n* MINERAL cobaltina *f*; ~ **naphthenate** *n* P&R naftenato cobáltico *m*, naftenato de cobalto *m*; ~ **60 gamma irradiation** *n* NUCL irradiación gamma por cobalto 60 *f*; ~ **60 irradiation plant** *n* NUCL equipo de irradiación por cobalto 60 *m*

cobaltammines *n pl* CHEM cobaltaminas *f pl*

cobaltic *adj* CHEM cobáltico

cobaltine *n* MINERAL cobaltina *f*

cobaltite *n* MINERAL cobaltita *f*

cobb *AmE see cob BrE*

cobble *n* GEOL canto rodado *m*, guijarro *m*

cobbles *n pl* COAL carbón en galleta *m*, carbón en pedazos pequeños *m*, exudación *f*, galleta *f*, guijarros *m pl*

cocaine *n* CHEM cocaína *f*

coccolite *n* MINERAL cocolita *f*

coccolith *n* GEOL cocolito *m*

co-channel: ~ **interference** *n* TV interferencia del canal propio *f*

cochineal *n* COLOUR, FOOD cochinilla *f*; ~ **dye** *n* COLOUR carmín *m*

cochlea *n* ACOUST cóclea *f*

cochlear: ~ **duct** *n* ACOUST rampa coclear *f*; ~ **microphonic effect** *n* ACOUST efecto microfónico coclear *m*; ~ **microphonics** *n* ACOUST microfónico coclear *m*; ~ **potentials** *n pl* ACOUST potenciales cocleares *m pl*

cock[1] *n* CONST *tap* canilla *f*, grifo *m*, HYDRAUL grifo de purga *m*, distribuidor rotativo *m*, LAB *screen* llave *f*, MECH *vehicles* grifo *m*, distribuidor rotativo *m*, WATER TRANSP *sea* llave de paso *f*, grifo *m*; ~ **brass** *n* CONST canilla de bronce *f*, grifo de bronce *m*; ~ **key** *n* CONST llave de paso *f*; ~ **metal** *n* CONST canilla de metal *f*, grifo de metal *m*

cock² *vt* CINEMAT *person*, PHOTO montar

cocking: ~ **lever** *n* CINEMAT, PHOTO control de montaje *m*; ~ **ring** *n* CINEMAT, PHOTO anillo de montaje *m*

cockle *n* PRINT torcedura de hojas *f*; ~ **finish** *n* PAPER crispado *m*; **--finished paper** *n* PAPER papel crispado *m*

cocklebur *n* AGRIC *weed* bardana menor *f*

cockpit *n* AIR TRANSP cabina de mando *f*, SPACE *of a spacecraft* cabina del piloto *f*, carlinga *f*, VEH puesto de pilotaje *m*, WATER TRANSP bañera *f*; ~ **drainage** *n* WATER TRANSP desagüe de la bañera *m*, imbornales de la bañera *m pl*; ~ **light** *n* AIR TRANSP luz de la cabina de mando *f*; ~ **temperature indicator** *n* AIR TRANSP indicador de la temperatura de la cabina de mando *m*; ~ **voice recorder** *n* AIR TRANSP grabadora de sonidos y voces de la cabina de mando *f*, registrador de voces de la cabina de mando *m*

cocks: ~ **and fittings** *n pl* CONST grifería con accesorios *f*

cocoa: ~ **mass** *n* FOOD masa de cacao *f*; ~ **solids** *n pl* FOOD sólidos de cacao *m pl*

cocoon *n* AGRIC capullo *m*

co-current: ~ **line** *n* OCEAN línea cocorriente *f*

cod: **--liver oil** *n* FOOD aceite de hígado de bacalao *m*

COD *abbr* (*chemical oxygen demand*) CHEM, HYDROL, POLL DQO (*demanda química de oxígeno*)

code¹ *n* COMP&DP, ELECTRON código *m*, TELECOM código *m*, clave *f*; ~ **checking** *n* WATER TRANSP prueba de recepción *f*; ~ **conversion** *n* COMP&DP, ELEC ENG conversión de código *f*; ~ **converter** *n* COMP&DP, ELEC ENG convertidor de código *m*; **--decode system** *n* TRANSP sistema de codificación y descodificación *m*; **--decoder** *n* COMP&DP, ELECTRON, TELECOM codificador *m*, códec *m*; **--division multiple access** *n* (*CDMA*) SPACE acceso múltiple por división de código *m*; **--division multiplexing** *n* (*CDM*) TELECOM multiplexión asíncrona por división en el tiempo *f*; ~ **extension** *n* COMP&DP extensión de código *f*; **--extension character** *n* COMP&DP carácter de extensión de código *m*; ~ **flag** *n* WATER TRANSP bandera de señales *f*; ~ **number** *n* CINEMAT *of paper, board* número de código *m*; ~ **violation** *n* (*CV*) TELECOM violación de código *f*

code² *vt* COMP&DP, TV codificar

codec *n* COMP&DP, ELECTRON, TELECOM codificador-decodificador *m*, códec *m*

coded: ~ **mark inversion** *n* (*CMI*) TELECOM inversión de la señal codificada *f*; ~ **transmission** *n* TELECOM transmisión codificada *f*

codeine *n* CHEM codeína *f*, metilmorfina *f*

coder *n* COMP&DP, ELECTRON, TELECOM, TV cifrador *m*, codificador *m*; **--decoder** *n* COMP&DP, ELECTRON, TELECOM codificador-decodificador *m*, códec *m*

coding *n* COMP&DP, ELECTRON, TELECOM codificación *f*; ~ **device** *n* TRANSP dispositivo de codificación *m*, mecanismo de codificación *m*, mecanismo de codificación *m*; ~ **error** *n* COMP&DP, ELECTRON error de codificación *m*; ~ **scheme** *n* ELECTRON modelo de codificación *m*; ~ **standard** *n* TELECOM norma de codificación *f*; ~ **theory** *n* COMP&DP teoría de codificación *f*; ~ **type** *n* TELECOM tipo de codificación *m*

coefficient *n* ELEC, HYDRAUL, MATH, PHYS, PROD coeficiente *m*; ~ **of abundance** *n* WATER coeficiente de abundancia *m*; ~ **of capture** *n* OCEAN coeficiente de captura *m*; ~ **of consolidation** *n* COAL coeficiente de consolidación *m*; ~ **of contraction** *n* HYDRAUL coeficiente de contracción *m*; ~ **of coupling** *n* ELEC *inductor* coeficiente de acoplamiento *m*; ~ **of discharge** *n* HYDRAUL coeficiente de caudal *m*, coeficiente de descarga *m*, coeficiente de gasto *m*; ~ **of drag** *n* FUELLESS coeficiente de resistencia al avance *m*; ~ **of drainage** *n* HYDROL coeficiente de drenaje *m*; ~ **of efficiency** *n* MECH coeficiente de eficiencia *m*; ~ **of efflux** *n* HYDRAUL coeficiente de descarga *m*; ~ **of elasticity** *n* P&R coeficiente de elasticidad *m*; ~ **of expansion** *n* CONST coeficiente de expansión *m*, P&R coeficiente de dilatación *m*, coeficiente de expansión *m*; ~ **of fineness** *n* WATER TRANSP *ship design* coeficiente de afinamiento *m*; ~ **of friction** *n* CONST, MECH, METR, P&R, PHYS coeficiente de fricción *m*, coeficiente de rozamiento *m*; ~ **of groundwater flow** *n* HYDROL coeficiente del flujo de agua subterránea *m*; ~ **of haze** *n* POLL coeficiente de bruma *m*, coeficiente de enturbiamiento atmosférico *m*; ~ **of infiltration** *n* HYDROL coeficiente de infiltración *m*; ~ **of magnetic dispersion** *n* ELEC coeficiente de dispersión magnética *m*; ~ **of mutual induction** *n* ELEC coeficiente de inducción mutua *m*, coeficiente de inducción múltiple *m*; ~ **of permeability** *n* HYDROL coeficiente de permeabilidad *m*; ~ **of reduction** *n* WATER TRANSP *scantlings* coeficiente de reducción *m*; ~ **of roughness** *n* HYDROL coeficiente de agitación del mar *m*; ~ **of runoff** *n* HYDROL coeficiente de escurrimiento *m*; ~ **of safety** *n* PROD, SAFE coeficiente de seguridad *m*; ~ **of thermal conduction** *n* MECH, P&R, THERMO coeficiente de termoconducción *m*; ~ **of thermal conductivity** *n* MECH, P&R, THERMO coeficiente de conductividad térmica *m*; ~ **of thermal expansion** *n* MECH, PHYS, THERMO *physical geography* coeficiente de expansión térmica *m*; ~ **of thermal insulance** *n* MECH, P&R, PHYS, THERMO coeficiente de aislamiento térmico *m*; ~ **of torque** *n* FUELLESS coeficiente de torsión *m*; ~ **of usable groundwater** *n* HYDROL coeficiente de aguas subterráneas utilizables *m*

coenzyme *n* FOOD coenzima *f*

coercitivity *n* ELEC ENG coercitividad *f*

coercive: ~ **field strength** *n* ELEC *magnetism* intensidad de campo coercitivo *f*; ~ **force** *n* ELEC *magnetism*, ELEC ENG, METALL, PHYS fuerza coerciva *f*; ~ **intensity** *n* ELEC *magnetism* intensidad coerciva *f*

coercivity *n* ELEC, ELECTRON, METALL, PHYS, TV coercitividad *f*

coeval *adj* GEOL coetáneo, contemporáneo

co-extruded: ~ **film** *n* PACK película coextrusionada *f*

coffer *n* WATER *on canal* cámara *f*

cofferdam *n* CONST ataguía *f*, compartimiento estanco *m*, dique de presa *m*, HYDRAUL ataguía *f*, HYDROL compartimiento estanco *m*, dique de presa *m*, ataguía *f*, WATER, WATER TRANSP ataguía *f*, comportamiento estanco *m*, dique de presa *m*

coffering *n* CONST, HYDROL, WATER construcción de ataguías *f*

cog¹ *n* CONST diente *m*, MECH diente *m*, lengüeta *f*, leva *f*, MECH ENG *tooth* diente *m*; ~ **belt** *n* MECH ENG cinta de resaltos *f*, cinta dentada *f*, cinta transportadora corrugada *f*, polea dentada *f*, VEH correa dentada *f*;

~ **rail** *n* MECH ENG cremallera *f*, rail dentado *m*; ~ **and round** *n* MECH ENG engranaje de linterna *m*

cog² *vt* AUTO, MECH, MECH ENG *scotch, chock* acuñar

cogged¹ *adj* AUTO, MECH, MECH ENG, VEH dentado

cogged²: ~ **belt** *n* AUTO, VEH correa dentada *f*; ~ **belt timing** *n* AUTO sincronización por correa dentada *f*, sincronizado por polea dentada *m*, VEH sincronización por correa dentada *f*, sincronizado por polea centrada *m*

cogging: ~ **mill** *n* PROD tren desbastador *m*

cogwheel *n* MECH ENG engranaje *m*, piñón *m*, rueda dentada *f*; ~ **ore** *n* MINERAL bournonita *f*

cohere *vi* GEOL adherirse

coherence *n* ELECTRON, OPT, PHYS, TELECOM, WAVE PHYS coherencia *f*; ~ **area** *n* OPT, PHYS, TELECOM área de coherencia *f*; ~ **bandwidth** *n* TELECOM ancho de banda de coherencia *m*; ~ **length** *n* OPT, PHYS, TELECOM longitud de coherencia *f*; ~ **time** *n* OPT, PHYS, TELECOM tiempo de coherencia *m*

coherent¹ *adj* ELECTRON, METALL, OPT, PHYS, TELECOM, WAVE PHYS coherente

coherent²: ~ **anti-Stokes Raman scattering** *n* (*CARS*) PHYS dispersión Raman coherente anti-Stokes *f*; ~ **area** *n* OPT, TELECOM área coherente *f*; ~ **boundary** *n* METALL contorno coherente *m*; ~ **detection** *n* ELECTRON detección coherente *f*; ~ **interface** *n* METALL zona interfacial coherente *f*; ~ **light** *n* ELECTRON, OPT, TELECOM, WAVE PHYS luz coherente *f*; ~ **monochromatic beam** *n* RAD PHYS haz monocromático coherente *m*; ~ **noise** *n* GEOPHYS interferencia coherente *f*, ruido coherente *m*; ~ **oscillator** *n* ELECTRON oscilador coherente *m*; ~ **particle** *n* METALL partícula coherente *f*; ~ **phase-shift keying** *n* (*CPSK*) TELECOM transmisión por desplazamiento coherente de fase *f*; ~-**pulse radar** *n* RAD PHYS radar de impulsos sincronizados *m*; ~ **radiation** *n* OPT, TELECOM radiación coherente *f*; ~ **signal processing** *n* ELECTRON proceso de señal coherente *m*; ~ **transmission** *n* OPT, TELECOM transmisión coherente *f*; ~ **wave** *n* PHYS, WAVE PHYS onda coherente *f*

cohesion *n* COAL, CONST, METALL, PHYS cohesión *f*; ~ **pile** *n* COAL tablestaca de cohesión *f*

cohesive¹ *adj* COAL, CONST, METALL, PHYS coherente, cohesivo

cohesive²: ~ **energy** *n* METALL energía de cohesión *f*; ~ **force** *n* PHYS fuerza de cohesión *f*; ~ **soil** *n* COAL suelo cohesivo *m*

cohobate *vt* CHEM cohobar, destilar repetidas veces

cohobation *n* CHEM cohobación *f*

coil¹ *n* CONST *piping* bobina *f*, serpentín *m*, ELEC *inductance*, ELEC ENG carrete *m*, bobina *f*, HEAT ENG *wire* serpentín *m*, MECH bobina *f*, rollo *m*, MECH ENG rollo *m*, bobina *f*, serpentín *m*, espira *f*, aduja *f*, PACK rollo *m*, PAPER bobina muy estrecha *f*, PHYS bobina *f*, arrollamiento *m*, PROD *of wire*, VEH bobina *f*, WATER TRANSP *of rope* aduja *f*; ~ **clutch** *n* MECH ENG embrague de espiral *m*; ~ **core** *n* ELEC, ELEC ENG núcleo de la bobina *m*; ~ **form** *n* ELEC, ELEC ENG forma para bobina *f*; ~ **header** *n* REFRIG cabezal del serpentín *m*; ~-**loaded cable** *n* ELEC ENG cable de carga por bobinas *m*; ~ **loading** *n* ELEC ENG carga de bobinas *f*, pupinización *f*; ~ **pitch** *n* ELEC paso en la bobina *m*; ~ **Q-factor** *n* ELEC, PHYS factor-Q de la bobina *m*; ~ **section** *n* ELEC sección de bobina *f*; ~ **spring** *n* AUTO, MECH, MECH ENG, VEH muelle

espiral *m*, muelle helicoidal *m*, resorte espiral *m*, resorte helicoidal *m*; ~-**spring clutch** *n* AUTO, MECH, MECH ENG, VEH embrague de resorte helicoidal *m*; ~-**to-coil insulation** *n* ELEC *transformer* aislamiento entre bobinas *m*; ~ **voltage code** *n* PROD código de tensión de la bobina *m*; ~ **winding** *n* ELEC devanado de bobina *m*

coil² *vt* ELEC, PROD *wires* enrollar

coiled: ~ **coil filament** *n* ELEC *light bulb* filamento doblemente arrollado *m*, filamento en doble espiral *m*; ~ **coil lamp** *n* ELEC *light bulb* lámpara de filamento doblemente arrollado *f*; ~ **spring** *n* AUTO, MECH, MECH ENG, VEH muelle espiral *m*, muelle helicoidal *m*, resorte espiral *m*, resorte helicoidal *m*

coiler *n* PROD bobinador *m*

coiling *n* PROD enrollamiento *m*

coin: ~-**box relay** *n* ELEC relé de alcancía de pago previo *m*, relé de caja de monedas *m*; ~-**operated payphone** *n* TELECOM teléfono monedero *m*, teléfono operado con monedas *m*, teléfono público *m*; ~-**slot operator** *n* PROD accionador de ranura de monedas *m*; ~-**slot selector switch** *n* PROD interruptor selector de ranura de monedas *m*

coincidence: ~ **circuit** *n* ELECTRON, PHYS circuito de coincidencia *m*; ~ **dip** *n* ACOUST bache de coincidencia *m*; ~ **effect** *n* ACOUST efecto de coincidencia *m*; ~ **frequency** *n* ACOUST frecuencia de coincidencia *f*

coining: ~ **die** *n* MECH ENG troquel de acuñar *m*

coir *n* TEXTIL, WATER TRANSP *ropes* fibra de coco *f*

coke¹: ~-**fired** *adj* PROD caldeado con coque

coke² *n* CHEM, COAL, MINE, PROD, THERMO coque *m*; ~ **basket** *n* COAL cesto de coque *m*; ~ **bed** *n* COAL capa de coque *f*, lecho de coque *m*; ~ **blast furnace** *n* COAL, PROD, THERMO horno alto de coque *m*; ~ **breaker** *n* COAL, MINE trituradora de coque *f*; ~-**cooling tower** *n* COAL, MINE instalación para enfriar coque *f*; ~ **dust** *n* COAL, MINE coque pulverizado *m*; ~ **fork** *n* COAL orquilla para escoger el coque *f*, MINE orquilla para coger el coque *f*; ~ **mill** *n* COAL molino de coque *m*; ~ **oven** *n* C&G, COAL, HEAT, MINE, PROD, THERMO horno de coque *m*; ~-**quenching tower** *n* COAL, MINE instalación para apagar el coque *f*

coke³ *vt* COAL, MINE convertir en coque, coquificar, coquizar

coked: ~ **coal dust** *n* MINE costra de coque *f*

coking¹ *adj* COAL, MINE coquificante, coquizable

coking² *n* COAL carbonización *f*, coquificación *f*, coquización *f*, MINE coquización *f*; ~ **coal** *n* COAL carbón de coque *m*; ~ **cracking** *n* COAL craqueo de coque *m*; ~ **duff** *n* COAL finos de coque *m pl*, menudos de coque *m pl*; ~ **plant** *n* MINE planta de carbonización *f*; ~ **plate** *n* PROD *of furnace* mesa para descargar el coke *f*

colchiceine *n* CHEM colchiceína *f*, colquiceína *f*

colchicine *n* CHEM colchicina *f*, colquicina *f*

colcothar *n* CHEM, PROD colcótar *m*, óxido férrico *m*

cold¹: ~-**cured** *adj* PROD, THERMO vulcanizado en frío; ~-**drawn** *adj* PROD, THERMO estirado en frío; ~-**forged** *adj* MECH ENG, THERMO forjado en frío; ~-**rolled** *adj* MECH, PROD, THERMO laminado en frío; ~-**smoked** *adj* FOOD ahumado en frío

cold²: ~ **appearance** *n* C&G apariencia fría *f*; ~ **bending** *n* MECH doblado en frío *m*; ~-**blast valve** *n* PROD *stove, furnace* válvula de viento *f*; ~ **bond** *n* THERMO enlace en frío *m*; ~ **bonding** *n*

THERMO enlace en frío *m*, proceso de enlace en frío *m*; ~ **brittleness** *n* MECH, REFRIG, THERMO fragilidad en frío *f*; ~ **casting** *n* THERMO electroformación *f*; ~ **cathode** *n* ELEC ENG, ELECTRON cátodo frío *m*; ~**-cathode counter tube** *n* ELEC ENG, ELECTRON tubo contador de cátodo frío *m*; ~**-cathode tube** *n* ELECTRON tubo de cátodo frío *m*; ~ **chain** *n* REFRIG cadena del frío *f*; ~ **chamber** *n* REFRIG cámara frigorífica *f*; ~ **chisel** *n* AGRIC cincel *m*, MECH ENG, PROD buril *m*, cincel de acero templado *m*, cortafríos *m*, cortahierros *m*; ~ **creep** *n* THERMO fluencia en frío *f*, termodeformación en frío *f*; ~ **curing** *n* PROD, THERMO vulcanización en frío *f*; ~**-cut varnish** *n* COATINGS, COLOUR barniz en frío *m*; ~ **dimpling process** *n* MECH ENG proceso de abollado en frío *m*; ~ **drawing** *n* MECH estiramiento en frío *m*; ~ **dyeing** *n* COLOUR teñido en frío *m*; ~ **emission** *n* ELEC ENG emisión fría *f*; ~ **end coating** *n* C&G recubrimiento en frío *m*; ~ **flow** *n* MECH *heat unit* flujo en frío *m*, P&R plasticidad en frío *f*; ~ **forging** *n* MECH ENG, PROD, THERMO forja en frío *f*, forjadura en frío *f*; ~**-forging die** *n* MECH ENG, PROD estampa de forjado en frío *f*, matriz de forjado en frío *f*, molde de forjado en frío *m*, troquel de forjado en frío *m*, THERMO estampa ede forjado en frío *f*, matriz de forjado en frío *f*, molde de forjado en frío *m*, troquel de forjado en frío *m*; ~ **frame** *n* AGRIC cama fría *f*, *to cover young plants* caja de paredes de cristal *f*, cajonera *f*; ~ **front** *n* METEO frente frío *m*; ~ **gas system** *n* SPACE sistema de gas frío *m*; ~**-gluing system** *n* PACK método de engomado en frío *m*, sistema de engomado en frío *m*; ~ **hobbing** *n* MECH ENG estampado en frío *m*, fresado en frío *m*, moldeado en frío *m*, troquelado en frío *m*; ~ **injury** *n* REFRIG daño por frío *m*; ~ **junction** *n* ELEC *thermocouple* extremos fríos *m pl*, extremos libres *m pl*, soldadura fría *f*, ELEC ENG *thermocouple* extremos fríos *m pl*, extremos libres *m pl*, juntura fría *f*, soldadura fría *f*; ~ **leg** *n* NUCL rama fría *f*; ~ **leg LOCA** *n* NUCL LOCA de rotura de la rama fría *m*; ~ **light** *n* CINEMAT luz fría *f*; ~, **low-density nebula** *n* SPACE *type* HI nebulosa fría de baja densidad *f*; ~**-mirror reflector** *n* CINEMAT reflector de espejo frío *m*; ~ **mix** *n* CONST mezcla en frío *f*; ~ **mold** *AmE see cold mould BrE*; ~**-molded wood** *AmE see cold-moulded wood BrE*; ~ **molding** *AmE see cold moulding BrE*; ~ **mould** *BrE* *n* C&G molde frío *m*; ~**-moulded wood** *n* *BrE* WATER TRANSP *boat construction* madera moldeada en frío *f*; ~ **moulding** *n* *BrE* C&G, P&R moldeado en frío *m*; ~ **pressure welding** *n* CONST, MECH soldadura a presión en frío *f*; ~ **resistance** *n* ELEC ENG criorresistencia *f*, resistencia en frío *f*; ~ **riveting** *n* CONST remachado en frío *m*; ~**-rolled joist** *n* THERMO perfil laminado en frío *m*; ~ **rolling** *n* THERMO laminación en frío *f*; ~ **saw** *n* MECH ENG sierra para cortar metales *f*; ~ **seal** *n* PRINT sellado en frío *m*; ~ **section** *n* AIR TRANSP *of jet engine* sección fría *f*; ~**-set ink** *n* COLOUR tinta de secado en frío *f*; ~ **setting** *n* P&R endurecimiento en frío *m*, solidificación en frío *f*; ~**-setting adhesive** *n* P&R, PACK adhesivo de endurecimiento en frío *m*; ~ **shortening** *n* REFRIG contracción por frío *f*; ~ **shot** *n* PROD *founding* cierre por enfriamiento *m*, granalla en frío *f*; ~ **shrink-fitting** *n* REFRIG machiembrado por frío *m*; ~ **shut** *n* PROD *founding* discontinuidad en un metal fundido *f*; ~ **shutdown** *n*

NUCL parada fría *f*; ~ **stabilization** *n* REFRIG estabilización por frío *f*; ~ **start** *n* COMP&DP arranque en frío *m*, arranque inicial *m*, THERMO *disk drive actuator*, VEH arranque en frío *m*; ~**-start device** *n* AUTO, VEH dispositivo de arranque en frío *m*; *n* ELEC *lighting* lámpara de cebado en frío *f*; ~ **static base** *n* REFRIG soporte fijo para sistema de frío *m*; ~ **storage** *n* FOOD, REFRIG, SAFE, THERMO almacenamiento en frío *m*, almacén frío *m*, conservación en frío *f*; ~ **storage injury** *n* FOOD lesión producida por conservación en frío *f*; ~ **storage room** *n* FOOD, REFRIG, THERMO cámara de almacenamiento frigorífico *f*; ~ **storage ship** *n* WATER TRANSP buque frigorífico *m*; ~ **store** *n* FOOD, MECH ENG, REFRIG, THERMO almacén frigorífico *m*, armario frigorífico *m*; ~ **store complex** *n* REFRIG complejo frigorífico *m*; ~ **strength** *n* THERMO resistencia al frío *f*; ~ **surface** *n* C&G superficie fría *f*; ~ **test** *n* AGRIC prueba de frío *f*; ~ **trap** *n* REFRIG condensador de frío *m*; ~ **type** *n* PRINT composición sin plomo *f*; ~ **water down-welling zone** *n* OCEAN zona generadora de aguas frías *f*; ~ **working** *n* PROD *blast furnace* marcha fría *f*

cold[3]: ~**-bond** *vt* PROD, THERMO unir en frío *m*; ~**-cure** *vt* PROD, THERMO vulcanizar en frío; ~**-draw** *vt* PROD estampar en frío, THERMO estampar en frío, estirar en frío; ~**-forge** *vt* MECH ENG, PROD, THERMO forjar en frío; ~**-harden** *vt* PROD, THERMO endurecer en frío; ~**-roll** *vt* THERMO laminar en frío; ~**-shear** *vt* MECH ENG, THERMO cizallar en frío

coldroom *n* MECH ENG, REFRIG, THERMO cuarto frío *m*, cámara frigorífica *f*, sala fría *f*

colemanite *n* MINERAL colemanita *f*

coleoptile *n* AGRIC coleóptilo *m*

COLI *abbr* (*connected-line identity*) TELECOM identidad de línea conectada *f*

colics *n* OCEAN cólicos *m*

coliform: ~ **bacterium** *n* FOOD bacilo coliforme *m*

collagen *n* CHEM, FOOD colágeno *m*

collapse[1] *n* CONST colapso *m*, derrumbe *m*, GEOL desplome *m*, hundimiento *m*, MINE *of ground* colapso *m*; ~ **depth** *n* OCEAN profundidad destructiva *f*

collapse[2] *vi* GEOL derrumbarse, desplomarse

collapsible[1] *adj* MECH ENG *dismantlement* desarmable, abatible, plegable, desmontable, PROD abatible, desarmable, desmontable, plegable

collapsible[2]: ~ **aerial** *n* *BrE* (*cf collapsible antenna AmE*) SPACE antena plegable *f*; ~ **antenna** *n* *AmE* SPACE *communications* antena plegable *f*; ~ **boat** *n* WATER TRANSP bote plegable *m*; ~ **bottle** *n* PHOTO botella semirrígida *f*; ~ **case** *n* PACK caja desmontable *f*; ~ **core** *n* MECH ENG *injection moulding* macho desmontable *m*, nocho perecedero *m*; ~ **finder** *n* PHOTO visor plegable *m*; ~ **freight container** *n* TRANSP contenedor de carga plegable *m*; ~ **gate** *n* CONST puerta abatible *f*; ~ **and reusable packaging system** *n* PACK sistema de embalaje desmontable y reutilizable *m*; ~ **section** *n* TRANSP sección desmontable *f*, sección plegable *f*; ~ **stand** *n* CINEMAT soporte plegable *m*, PHOTO soporte logable *m*; ~ **steering column** *n* AUTO, VEH columna de dirección desarmable *f*; ~ **take-up core** *n* CINEMAT núcleo receptor plegable *m*; ~ **tube** *n* PACK tubo desmontable *m*; ~ **water hose** *n* MECH ENG manguera plegable *f*

collapsing *n* MECH ENG colapso *m*, derrumbe *m*

collar[1] *n* C&G *Danner tube drawing process* collarín *m*,

CONST *headpiece or cap of set* collar *m*, MECH collarín *m*, anillo *m*, cuello *m*, manguito *m*, aro *m*, collar *m*, espiga *f*, casquillo *m*, MECH ENG collarín *m*, collar *m*, *on shaft* cuello *m*, *on coupling* aro *m*, anillo *m*, *tools* espiga *f*, manguito *m*, casquillo *m*, PETR TECH, PETROL aro *m*, collar *m*, cuello *m*, cupla *f*, unión *f*; ~ **beam** *n* MECH ENG *building* falso tirante *m*, jabalcón *m*, viga de trabazón *f*; ~~**beam truss** *n* CONST armadura de falso tirante *f*; ~ **grab** *n* MINE excavadora desplazable *f*; ~ **joint** *n* MECH ENG ajuste de anillo *m*, ajuste de aro *m*, ajuste de collar *m*; ~ **plate** *n* MECH ENG *lathe steady rest* luneta *f*; ~ **roof** *n* CONST cubierta con falso tirante *f*; ~ **tie** *n* MECH ENG *building* falso tirante *m*; ~ **truss** *n* CONST viga de falso tirante *f*

collar² *vt* MECH ENG poner aro, poner manguito

collared: ~ **coupling** *n* MECH ENG acoplamiento de collar *m*

collargol *n* CHEM colargol *m*

collate *vt* COMP&DP comparar, cotejar, PRINT alzar, intercalar

collating: ~ **machine** *n* PRINT alzadora de papel *f*, alzadora *f*; ~ **marks** *n pl* PRINT señales para el alzado *f pl*; ~ **sequence** *n* COMP&DP orden de clasificación de caracteres *m*, secuencia de colación *f*, secuencia de intercalación *f*; ~ **system** *n* PACK sistema de intercalación *m*; ~ **table** *n* PRINT mesa para el alzado *f*; ~ **transit tray** *n* PACK intercalado de bandejas en movimiento *m*

collation *n* COMP&DP colacionado *m*, intercalación clasificada *f*

collator *n* COMP&DP comparador *m*, cotejador *m*, dispositivo de colación *m*, programa de intercalación *m*

collect¹: ~ **call** *n* AmE (*cf reverse-charge call BrE*) TELECOM llamada a cobro revertido *f* (*Esp*), llamada pagadera en destino *f* (*AmL*); ~ **cylinder** *n* PRINT cilindro recolector *m*; ~ **run** *n* PRINT tiro combinado *m*

collect² *vt* WATER captar

collecting: ~ **agent** *n* COAL colector *m*, reactivo *m*; ~ **ditch** *n* WATER pozo colector *m*; ~ **electrode** *n* POLL *gas treatment* electrofiltro *m*, precipitador electrostático *m*; ~ **pit** *n* CONST fosa colectora *f*, pozo colector *m*; ~ **reagent** *n* COAL colector *m*, reactivo captante *m*; ~ **vat** *n* MINE artesa colectora *f* (*Esp*), cuba colectora *f* (*Esp*)

collection *n* ELEC ENG *of current* toma *f*, MAR POLL *paint-burning lamp* recogida *f*, PROD cobro *m*, cobranza *f*, WATER toma *f*, captación *f*; ~ **basin** *n* MAR POLL *of oil* cuba de recogida *f*; ~ **and delivery** *n* RAIL recogida y entrega *f*; ~ **device** *n* MAR POLL, POLL dispositivo de recogida *m*; ~ **tray** *n* PAPER bandeja recogedora *f*

collective: ~ **aerial** *n* BrE (*cf collective antenna AmE*) TELECOM, TV antena colectiva *f*; ~ **antenna** *n* AmE (*cf collective aerial BrE*) TELECOM, TV antena colectiva *f*; ~ **bellcrank** *n* AIR TRANSP *helicopters* palanca acodada del colectivo *f*; ~ **effective dose equivalent** *n* NUCL dosis equivalente efectiva colectiva *f*; ~ **effective dose equivalent commitment** *n* NUCL compromiso de dosis equivalente efectiva colectiva *m*; ~ **effective dose equivalent rate** *n* NUCL tasa de dosis equivalente efectiva colectiva *f*; ~ **excitation** *n* RAD PHYS excitación colectiva *f*; ~ **model** *n* PHYS modelo colectivo *m*; ~ **pitch** *n* AIR TRANSP *helicopters* paso del colectivo *m*; ~~**pitch angle** *n* AIR TRANSP

helicopters ángulo de paso del colectivo *m*; ~~**pitch anticipator** *n* AIR TRANSP *helicopters* anticipador del paso del colectivo *m*; ~~**pitch control** *n* AIR TRANSP *helicopters* control del paso del colectivo *m*; ~~**pitch follow-up** *n* AIR TRANSP *helicopters* regulador del paso del colectivo *m*, timón del paso del colectivo *m*; ~~**pitch indicator** *n* AIR TRANSP *helicopters* indicador del paso del colectivo *m*; ~~**pitch lever** *n* AIR TRANSP *helicopters* palanca del paso del colectivo *f*; ~~**pitch switch** *n* AIR TRANSP *helicopters* interruptor del paso del colectivo *m*; ~~**pitch synchronizer** *n* AIR TRANSP *helicopters* sincronizador del paso del colectivo *m*; ~ **protection shelter** *n* MILIT *chemical warfare* refugio de protección colectiva *m*; ~ **protective system** *n* MILIT *chemical warfare* sistema de protección colectiva *m*

collector *n* CHEM TECH colector *m*, ELEC ENG *of dynamo-electric machine* toma de corriente *f*, HYDRAUL, PHYS, TELECOM, TRANSP colector *m*; ~ **contact** *n* ELEC ENG contacto de la toma *m*; ~ **doping** *n* ELECTRON alteración del captador *f*; ~ **efficiency** *n* FUELLESS rendimiento de colector solar *m*; ~ **electrode** *n* ELEC ENG electrodo captador *m*, electrodo de la toma de corriente *m*; ~ **motor** *n* ELEC ENG motor del colector de corriente *m*; ~ **region** *n* ELEC ENG zona del colector de corriente *f*; ~ **ring** *n* ELEC *of commutator* anillo colector *m*, anillo rozante *m*, ELEC ENG, MECH ENG anillo rozante *m*, anillo colector *m*; ~ **shoe** *n* ELEC *of commutator* patín *m*, zapata *f*, ELEC ENG, RAIL zapata de la toma colectora *f*; ~ **tilt angle** *n* FUELLESS ángulo de inclinación de colector solar *m*; ~ **well** *n* HYDROL pozo de captación *m*

collet *n* MECH ENG boquilla *f*, pinza portapiezas *f*, portaherramientas *m*, VEH anillo metálico *m*, collar *m*, collarín *m*; ~ **chuck** *n* MECH ENG *machine tools* boquilla de mordazas *f*, plato de pinzas *m*; ~~**type spindle** *n* MECH ENG *machine tools* eje de mordazas *m*, eje de pinzas *m*, husillo de mordazas *m*, husillo de pinzas *m*

collidine *n* CHEM colidina *f*

colliding: ~~**beam accelerator** *n* ELECTRON, NUCL acelerador de choque frontal *m*

collier *n* COAL, MINE buque carbonero *m*, mina de carbón *f*, minero *m*, vapor *m*, WATER TRANSP buque carbonero *m*, carbonero *m*

colliery *n* COAL, MINE comercio de carbón *m*, hullera *f*, mina de carbón *f*, parque de carbones *m*

colligative *adj* CHEM coligativo

collimate *vt* CINEMAT colimar, ELECTRON, INSTR alinear, colimar, OPT, PHOTO, PHYS, TELECOM colimar

collimated: ~ **beam** *n* ELECTRON haz de luz colimado *m*; ~ **lens** *n* CINEMAT, OPT, PHOTO lente colimada *f*; ~ **light** *n* FUELLESS luz colimada *f* (*Esp*), luz paralelada *f* (*AmL*); ~ **point source** *n* NUCL fuente puntual colimada *f*

collimating: ~ **fault** *n* CINEMAT, PHOTO defecto de colimación *m*

collimation *n* GEN colimación *f*

collimator *n* GEN colimador *m*

collinear¹ *adj* GEOM colineal

collinear²: ~ **aerial** *n* BrE (*cf collinear antenna AmE*) TELECOM antena colineal *f*; ~ **antenna** *n* AmE (*cf collinear aerial BrE*) TELECOM antena colineal *f*

collision *n* COAL choque *m*, colisión *f*, COMP&DP colisión *f*, PHYS, SAFE, TRANSP choque *m*, colisión *f*,

WATER TRANSP *accident* abordaje *m*, colisión *f*; ~ **avoidance aid** *n* SAFE, WATER TRANSP ayuda para prevenir los abordajes *f*; ~ **course** *n* SPACE trayectoria de colisión *f*, trayectoria de impacto *f*, WATER TRANSP *navigation* rumbo con riesgo de abordaje *m*; ~ **density** *n* RAD PHYS densidad de colisión *f*; ~ **detection** *n* (*CD*) COMP&DP detección de colisiones *f*, percepción de colisión *f*, TELECOM detección de colisiones *f*; ~ **energy** *n* PART PHYS energía de colisión *f*; ~ **experiment** *n* PART PHYS experimento de colisión *m*; ~ **of the first kind** *n* NUCL colisión de primera especia *f*; ~ **integral** *n* PHYS, RAD PHYS integral de colisión *f*; ~ **ionization** *n* PHYS, RAD PHYS ionización por choque *f*, ionización por colisión *f*; ~ **rate** *n* TELECOM tasa de colisiones *f*; ~ **test** *n* TRANSP ensayo de colisión *m*, prueba de colisión *f*; ~ **warning system** *n* AIR TRANSP, SPACE sistema de alerta anticolisiones *m*; ~ **wave** *n* MINE onda de choque *f* (*Esp*), onda prolongada *f* (*AmL*)

collocated: ~ **concentrator** *n* TELECOM concentrador colocado *m*

collodion *n* CHEM colodión *m*, nitrocelulosa *f*; ~ **plate** *n* PHOTO placa de colodión *f*; ~ **process** *n* PRINT procedimiento al colodión *m*

colloid *n* GEN coloide *m*; ~ **disperse system** *n* POLL sistema de dispersión coloidal *m*; ~ **mill** *n* FOOD molino coloidal *m*; ~ **propulsion** *n* SPACE propulsión coloidal *f*

colloidal¹ *adj* GEN coloidal

colloidal²: ~ **mud** *n* PETR TECH lodo coloidal *m*; ~ **silica** *n* DETERG sílice coloidal *f*; ~ **sludge** *n* PETR TECH lodo coloidal *m*

colloxylin *n* CHEM coloxilina *f*

collyrite *n* MINERAL colirita *f*

colon: ~ **bacillus** *n* HYDROL bacilo del colon *m*

colophene *n* CHEM colofeno *m*

colophon *n* CHEM colofón *m*

colophonite *n* MINERAL colofonita *f*

colophony *n* CHEM, P&R colofonia *f*

color *AmE see* **colour** *BrE*

coloradoite *n* MINERAL coloradoíta *f*

colored *AmE see* **coloured** *BrE*

colorfast *AmE see* **colourfast** *BrE*

colorful *AmE see* **colourful** *BrE*

colorimeter *n* GEN colorímetro *m*

colorimetric: ~ **pyrometer** *n* THERMO pirómetro colorimétrico *m*

colorimetry *n* GEN colorimetría *f*

coloring *AmE see* **colouring** *BrE*

colorless *AmE see* **colourless** *BrE*

colors *AmE see* **colours** *BrE*

colorwork *AmE see* **colourwork** *BrE*

colour¹ *n* *BrE* CHEM color *m*, colorante *m*, COMP&DP color *m*, FOOD color *m*, colorante *m*, MINE mineral de valor *m*, PAPER color *m*, teñido *m*, PHOTO color *m*, PRINT colorante *m*, TELECOM color *m*, TEXTIL color *m*, colorante *m*; ~ **adaptor** *n* *BrE* COMP&DP adaptador de color *m*; ~ **analyser** *n* *BrE* CINEMAT analizador de color *m*, cromoanalizador *m*, PHOTO analizador de color *m*, TV analizador de color *m*, cromoanalizador *m*; ~ **analysis** *n* *BrE* CINEMAT, PHOTO análisis de color *m*, TV análisis de colores *m*; ~ **automatic time base corrector** *n* *BrE* TV corrector automático de la aberración cromática *m*; ~**background generator** *n* *BrE* CINEMAT, TV generador de colores de fondo *m*; ~ **balance** *n* *BrE*

CINEMAT, PHOTO equilibrio de colores *m*, TV colores de fondo *m pl*; ~ **bar** *n* *BrE* TV barra de color *f*; ~**bar generator** *n* *BrE* TV generador de barras de color *m*; ~ **bar test pattern** *n* *BrE* TV carta de prueba de barras de color *f* (*EsP*), patrón de prueba de barras de color *m* (*AmL*); ~ **break-up** *n* *BrE* TV separación de colores *f*; ~ **burst** *n* *BrE* TV pulso de sincronización de la subportadora de color *m*; ~ **cap** *n* *BrE* PROD *for push-button* tapa de color *f*; ~ **cast** *n* *BrE* CINEMAT, PHOTO emisión en color *f*; ~ **change** *n* *BrE* C&G cambio de color *m*; ~ **chart** *n* *BrE* CINEMAT, PRINT, TV carta cromática *f*; ~ **chart and grey scale** *n* *BrE* CINEMAT, PRINT carta cromática y escala de grises *f*, TV carta crómatica y escala de grises *f*; ~ **code letter** *n* *BrE* PROD etiqueta de código de colores *f*, letra de código de colores *f*; ~ **compensating filter** *n* *BrE* CINEMAT, TV filtro compensador de color *m*, filtro de compensación de colores *m*; ~**conversion filter** *n* *BrE* CINEMAT, TV filtro de conversión de color *m*; ~ **coordinates** *n pl* *BrE* RAD PHYS coordenadas de color *f pl*; ~**corrected lens** *n* *BrE* CINEMAT objetivo con corrección de colores *m*, OPT, PHOTO lente con corrección de colores *f*, objetivo con corrección de colores *m*; ~ **correction** *n* *BrE* CINEMAT corrección de la abrerración cromática *f*, TV corrección de la aberración cromática *f*; ~**correction filter** *n* *BrE* CINEMAT, ELECTRON, TV filtro corrector de color *m*, filtro de corrección del color *m*; ~ **decoder** *n* *BrE* CINEMAT, TV decodificador de color *m*; ~ **densimeter** *n* *BrE* PAPER densitómetro de color *m*; ~ **developer** *n* *BrE* PHOTO revelador para color *m*; ~ **development** *n* *BrE* PHOTO revelado en color *m*; ~ **difference** *n* *BrE* TV diferencia de color *f*; ~**difference signal** *n* *BrE* TV control de diferencia de color *m*, señal de diferencia de color *f*; ~ **display** *n* *BrE* AIR TRANSP pantalla de color *f*, pantalla en color *f*, COMP&DP pantalla en color *f*, visualización en colores *f* (*AmL*), LAB imagen cromática *f*, PHOTO pantalla en color *f*, SPACE imagen cromática *f*, monitor de color *m*, pantalla de color *f*, representación visual cromática *f*, pantalla en color *f*; ~ **dupe neg** *n* *BrE* CINEMAT negativo dupe a color *m*; ~ **dupe print** *n* *BrE* CINEMAT copia dupe a color *f*; ~ **error** *n* *BrE* TV error de color *m*; ~ **fastness** *n* *BrE* COLOUR permanencia del color *f*, color permanente *m*, P&R color permanente *m*, permanencia del color *f*; ~ **field** *n* *BrE* TV cuadro cromático *m*; ~**field corrector** *n* *BrE* TV corrector del cuadro cromático *m*; ~ **film analyser** *n* *BrE* CINEMAT, PHOTO, TV analizador de película a color *m*; ~ **finish** *n* *BrE* COLOUR acabado de color *m*; ~ **form** *n* *BrE* PRINT forma de color subsiguiente en impresiones a varios colores *f*; ~ **formulation** *n* *BrE* COLOUR formulación del color *f*; ~ **framing** *n* *BrE* TV ajuste del color de la imagen *m*; ~ **fringing** *n* *BrE* TV bordeamiento de color *m*; ~ **gate** *n* *BrE* TV circuito de desconexión de color *m*, gatillo de desconexión de color *m*; ~ **gradation** *n* *BrE* COLOUR clasificación cromática *f*; ~ **graphic** *n* *BrE* COMP&DP dibujo de color *m* (*AmL*), gráfico en color *m* (*Esp*); ~ **graphics adaptor** *n* *BrE* (*CGA*) COMP&DP adaptador gráfico de colores *m* (*CGA*); ~ **guides** *n pl* *BrE* COLOUR, PRINT guías de colores *f pl*; ~ **head** *n* *BrE* CINEMAT, PHOTO cabezal de color *m*; ~ **hue** *n* *BrE* COLOUR tono cromático *m*; ~ **indicators of dose** *n pl* *BrE* RAD PHYS indicadores cromáticos de dosis *m pl*; ~ **key** *n* *BrE* PRINT clave de colores *f*; ~ **kill** *n BrE* TV supresión del color *f*, supresor de color *m*; ~ **limit** *n BrE* COLOUR límite de colorante *m*; ~ **line plate** *n BrE* PRINT clisé de trama de colores *m*; ~ **lock** *n BrE* TV fijación del color *f*; ~ **map** *n BrE* COMP&DP mapa de colores *m*; ~ **match** *n BrE* COLOUR ajuste cromático *m*, equilibrio cromático *m*; ~ **matching** *n BrE* CINEMAT compensación de colores *f*, igualación de colores *f*, COLOUR ajuste cromático *m*, equilibrio cromático *m*, ajuste de color *m*, PRINT ajuste de color *m*; ~ **metallography** *n BrE* METALL cromometalografía *f*; ~ **mix** *n BrE* C&G, COLOUR mezcla de colores *f*; ~ **modulator** *n BrE* TV modulación del color *f*, modulador de color *m*; ~ **noise** *n BrE* TV ruido cromático *m*; ~ **palette** *n BrE* COMP&DP paleta de colores *f*; ~ **phase** *n BrE* TV fase del color *f*; ~**-phase diagram** *n BrE* TV diagrama de la fase de color *m*; ~ **photography** *n BrE* PHOTO cromofotografía *f*, fotografía coloreada *f*, fotografía en color *f*; ~ **picture** *n BrE* PHOTO fotografía en color *f*, imagen a color *f*; ~ **print** *n BrE* PHOTO copia a color *f*, copia coloreada *f*, PRINT ajuste cromático *m*, policromía *f*; ~**-printing machine** *n BrE* PHOTO impresora en color *f*, PRINT impresora en color *f*, proceso de impresión en color *m*; ~**-printing process** *n BrE* PHOTO, IMPR cromotipia *f*, proceso de impresión en color *m*; ~ **processing** *n BrE* CINEMAT, PHOTO revelado en color *m*; ~**-processing chemicals** *n pl BrE* CHEM productos para el revelado en color *m pl*, químicos para el revelado en color *m pl*, CINEMAT productos para el revelado en color *m pl*, químicos para el revelado en color *m pl*, PHOTO productos para el revelado en color *m pl*, químicos para el revelado en color *m pl*; ~ **pyrometer** *n BrE* RAD PHYS cromopirómetro *m*; ~ **reference signal** *n BrE* TV señal de referencia del color *f*; ~ **removal** *n BrE* P&R alteración del color *f*, coloración anormal *f*, decoloración *f*; ~ **removing** *n BrE* PRINT descoloración *f*; ~ **rendition** *n BrE* CINEMAT reproducción de los colores *f*; ~ **response** *n BrE* CINEMAT respuesta de color *f*; ~ **reversal film** *n BrE* CINEMAT, PHOTO película reversible a color *f*; ~ **reversal intermediate** *n BrE* CINEMAT, PHOTO copia intermedia reversible a color *f*; ~ **reversal process** *n BrE* CINEMAT, PHOTO proceso reversible a color *m*; ~**-sampling frequency** *BrE* RAD PHYS frecuencia de muestreo cromático *f*; ~**-sampling rate** *n BrE* TV frecuencia de conmutación de colores *f*, promedio de conmutación de colores *m*; ~**-sampling sequence** *n BrE* TV secuencia de conmutación de colores *f*; ~ **saturation** *n BrE* ELECTRON saturación de color *f*; ~ **screen** *n BrE* PHOTO pantalla de color *f*, pantalla ortocromática *f*, trama de color *f*; ~ **separation** *n BrE* CINEMAT, PHOTO separación de colores *f*, PRINT selección de colores *f*, TV separación de colores *f*; ~**-separation filter** *n BrE* CINEMAT, PHOTO, TV filtro de separación de colores *m*; ~**-separation negative** *n BrE* CINEMAT negativo para la separación de colores *m*, PHOTO, TV negativo para la selección de colores *m*; ~**-separation overlay** *n BrE* CINEMAT, PHOTO, TV separación de colores *f*, separador de colores *m*; ~ **shift** *n BrE* PRINT cambio de color *m*; ~ **signal** *n BrE* TV señal de color *f*; ~ **splitter** *n BrE* CINEMAT, TV separador de colores *m*; ~ **streaks** *n pl BrE* C&G vetas de color *f pl*; ~ **strength** *n BrE* COLOUR, P&R *paint, pigments* poder de tinción *m*, poder tintoreo *m*; ~ **striking** *n BrE* C&G vetas de color *f pl*; ~ **subcarrier** *n BrE* TV subportadora cromática *f*; ~ **sync signal** *n*

BrE TV señal de sincronismo de colores *f*; ~ **synthesizer** *n BrE* TV sintetizador de colores *m*; ~ **television** *n BrE* TV televisión en color *f*; ~ **temperature** *n BrE* CINEMAT, PHOTO temperatura de color *f*; ~ **temperature meter** *n BrE* CINEMAT, PHOTO termocolorímetro *m*; ~ **threshold** *n BrE* TV umbral del color *m*; ~ **timer** *n BrE* CINEMAT cronómetro para color *m*; ~ **tone** *n BrE* COLOUR, P&R *paint* tono de color *m*; ~ **triangle** *n BrE* PHYS triángulo de colores *m*; ~ **wheel** *n BrE* COLOUR, TEXTIL rueda de colores *f*

colour[2] *vt BrE* PAPER teñir
coloured *BrE adj* GEN coloreado; ~ **clay** *n BrE* C&G barro de colores *m*; ~ **edges** *n pl BrE* PRINT bordes coloreados *m pl*; ~ **glass** *n BrE* C&G vidrio coloreado *m*; ~ **lake** *n BrE* COATINGS, COLOUR laca coloreada *f*; ~ **light signal** *n BrE* RAIL señal luminosa de color *f*; ~ **pigment** *n BrE* COLOUR pigmento colorante *m*, pigmento coloreado *m*; ~ **strapping** *n BrE* PACK sujeción con correas de color *f*, zunchado con bandas de color *m*
colourfast *adj BrE* COLOUR de color permanente, PACK de color resistente, TEXTIL de color sólido
colourful *adj BrE* COLOUR colorido
colouring *n BrE* CHEM color *m*, COLOUR color *m*, colorante *m*, FOOD color *m*, coloración *f*, colorante *m*, teñido *m*, PAPER, PHOTO, PRINT, TEXTIL color *m*, colorante *m*; ~ **agent** *n BrE* C&G, CHEM, COLOUR agente colorante *m*; ~ **body** *n BrE* COLOUR consistencia del colorante *f*; ~ **matter** *n BrE* CHEM, COLOUR, FOOD, PAPER, PRINT, TEXTIL colorante *m*; ~ **pigment** *n BrE* COLOUR pigmento colorante *m*; ~ **power** *n BrE* COLOUR poder colorante *m*; ~ **substance** *n BrE* COLOUR sustancia colorante *f*; ~ **value** *n BrE* COLOUR poder colorante *m*
colourless[1] *adj BrE* CHEM, COLOUR, FOOD incoloro
colourless[2]: ~ **flux** *n BrE* C&G fundente incoloro *m*; ~ **glass** *n BrE* C&G vidrio incoloro *m*, vidrio transparente *m*
colours *n pl BrE* WATER TRANSP *national flag* bandera nacional *f*, colores nacionales *m pl*; ~ **of the spectrum** *n pl BrE* RAD PHYS colores del espectro *m pl*
colourwork *n BrE* PRINT impresión en color *f*
COLP *abbr* (*connected-line identification presentation*) TELECOM presentación de identificación de línea conectada *f*
Colpitts: ~ **oscillator** *n* ELECTRON oscilador Colpitts *m*
COLR *abbr* (*connected-line identification restriction*) TELECOM restricción de identificación de línea conectada *f*
colter *AmE see* **coulter** *BrE*
columbite *n* CHEM, MINERAL columbita *f*, niobita *f*
columbium *n* CHEM columbio *m*
columbus: ~ **grass** *n* AGRIC sorgo negro *m*
column *n* GAS, MATH columna *f*, MINE perforadora de columna *f*, PRINT columna *f*; ~ **box** *n* PROD *founding* chasis de columnas *m*; ~ **charge** *n* MINE carga de columna *f*; ~ **matter** *n* PRINT composición en columnas *f*; ~**-type drilling machine** *n* MECH ENG taladradora de columna *f*
columnar: ~ **basalt** *n* GEOL basalto columnar *m*; ~ **charge** *n* MINE carga columnar *f*; ~ **composition** *n* PRINT composición en columnas *f*; ~ **crystal** *n* CRYSTALL, METALL cristal basal *m*, cristal columnar *m*; ~ **jointing** *n* GEOL diaclasado columnar *m*

COM *abbr* COMP&DP (*computer output on microfilm*) salida de computadora en microfilm *f* (*AmL*), salida de ordenador en microfilm *f* (*Esp*), TELECOM (*continuation of message*) continuación de mensaje *f*

coma *n* ELECTRON, PHOTO, PHYS coma *f*

comagmatic *adj* GEOL comagmático

comb[1] *n* TEXTIL peine *m*; ~ **filter** *n* ELECTRON, TELECOM filtro de peine *m*; ~ **filtering** *n* ELECTRON, TELECOM filtrado de peine *m*; ~-**shaped electrode** *n* SPACE electrodo en forma de peine *m*

comb[2] *vt* TEXTIL peinar

combat: ~ **aircraft** *n* AIR TRANSP, MILIT avión de combate *m*; ~ **helicopter** *n* AIR TRANSP, MILIT helicóptero de combate *m*; ~ **information center** *n* AmE, ~ **information centre** BrE *n* MILIT centro de información de combate *m*; ~ **intelligence** *n* MILIT información de combate *f*

combed[1] *adj* TEXTIL peinado

combed[2]: ~ **top** *n* TEXTIL cinta peinada *f*; ~-**wool fabric** *n* TEXTIL tejido de lana peinada *m*; ~ **yarn** *n* TEXTIL hilo peinado *m*

combination *n* AIR TRANSP, CHEM, COMP&DP, MATH combinación *f*; ~ **board** *n* PAPER cartón multicapa *m*; ~ **bulk carrier** *n* TRANSP transporte mixto a granel *m*, transporte combinado *m*; ~ **chuck** *n* MECH ENG plato combinado *m*, plato de garras independientes *m*, plato de mordazas independientes *m*, plato universal *m*; ~ **lathe** *n* MECH ENG torno de plato combinado *m*; ~ **lock** *n* CONST cerradura de combinación *f*; ~ **pliers** *n pl* MECH ENG *press tools* alicates ajustables *m pl*, pinzas ajustables *f pl*; ~ **run** *n* PRINT tirada de combinación *f*; ~ **sound** *n* ACOUST sonido combinado *m*; ~ **surface gage** AmE, ~ **surface gauge** BrE *n* MECH ENG gramil de ajustador *m*, gramil de prisma combinado *m*, gramil de trazador *m*, gramil de trazar combinado *m*, verificador combinado de planos *m*; ~ **tap assembly** *n* MECH, MECH ENG juego de machos de roscar *m*; ~ **tone** *n* ACOUST acorde combinado *m*, tono combinado *m*, tono de combinación *m*; ~ **tools** *n pl* MECH ENG *press tools* herramientas de combinación *f pl*, herramientas de corte y embutido *f pl*, herramientas múltiples *f pl*

combinational: ~ **circuit** *n* AmE (*cf combinatorial circuit* BrE) COMP&DP, ELECTRON circuito combinacional *m*, circuito combinatorio *m*; ~ **setting** *n* COMP&DP ajuste combinatorio *m*, parámetro combinatorio *m*

combinatorial[1] *adj* COMP&DP, ELECTRON, MATH combinational, combinatorio

combinatorial[2]: ~ **analysis** *n* MATH análisis combinatorio *m*; ~ **circuit** *n* BrE (*cf combinational circuit* AmE) COMP&DP, ELECTRON circuito combinacional *m*, circuito combinatorio *m*; ~ **logic** *n* ELECTRON circuito lógico combinacional *m*, circuito lógico combinatorio *m*

combinatorics *n* GEOM, MATH *probability theory* combinatoria *f*

combine[1] *n* AGRIC cosechadora autopropulsada *f*, cosechadora trilladora *f*

combine[2] *vt* COMP&DP, MECH ENG *diagrams* combinar

combined: ~ **bending, shrinking, and welding machine** *n* MECH ENG máquina combinada de soldadura, contracción y doblado *f*; ~ **braking** *n* RAIL, VEH frenado combinado *m*; ~ **diagram** *n* MECH ENG *engine output* diagrama general *m*, diagrama totalizado *m*, plano general *m*, plano total *m*; ~ **distribution frame** *n* (*CDF*) TELECOM distribución combinada *f*, trama de distribución combinada *f*; ~ **drill and countersink** *n* MECH ENG, PROD broca y avellanadora combinadas *f*; ~-**flow turbine** *n* HYDRAUL turbina mixta *f*; ~ **grinder and sieve** *n* MECH ENG, PROD trituradora y criba combinadas *f*; ~ **heat and power station** *n* THERMO estación térmica y eléctrica combinada *f*; ~ **local-toll system** *n* TELECOM sistema combinado local-interurbano *m*; ~ **packaging** *n* PACK embalaje combinado *m*; ~ **parallel vice** *n* BrE MECH ENG *for drilling machines* tornillo paralelo combinado *m*, tornillo paralelo de combinación *m*; ~ **parallel vise** AmE *see combined parallel vice* BrE; ~ **print** *n* CINEMAT, PRINT copia combinada *f*; ~ **sewer** *n* HYDROL, WATER alcantarilla para aguas negras y de lluvia *f*; ~ **sewer system** *n* HYDROL, WATER alcantarilla para aguas negras y de lluvia *f*; ~ **side-deliver rake and swath turner** *n* AGRIC rastrillo henificador combinado *m*; ~ **sight** *n* MILIT alza conjugada *f*; ~ **stamping, forging, shearing, and punching machine** *n* MECH ENG máquina combinada de punzonar, cortar, forjar y estampar *f*; ~ **stoping** *n* MINE explotación por bancos *f*, explotación por escalones *f*, explotación por gradas *f*; ~ **sulfur** AmE, ~ **sulphur** BrE *n* P&R azufre combinado *m*; ~ **surfacing, planing, moulding, and slot-mortising machine** *n* MECH ENG máquina combinada de mortajar, moldear, cepillar y acabado *f*; ~ **vessel** *n* TRANSP barco de cabotaje mixto *m*; ~ **water** *n* HYDROL, WATER agua combinada *f*, agua de constitución *f*

combiner *n* TELECOM combinador *m*; ~ **circuit** *n* ELECTRON, TV circuito combinador *m*, circuito de combinación *m*

combing: ~ **machine** *n* TEXTIL peinadora *f*

combining: ~ **circuit** *n* TELECOM circuito combinador *m*; ~ **cone** *n* MECH ENG *of injector* tobera convergente *f*, tobera de mezcla *f*, tobera inyectora *f*; ~ **nozzle** *n* MECH ENG *of injector* boquilla convergente *f*, boquilla inyectora *f*; ~ **tube** *n* MECH ENG *of injector* tobera convergente *f*

combust *vi* MINE *explosively* quemar

combustibility *n* GEN combustibilidad *f*

combustible[1] *adj* GEN combustible

combustible[2] *n* COAL, PACK, THERMO combustible *m*; ~ **fossil fuel** *n* POLL combustible fósil *m*; ~ **gas** *n* GAS gas combustible *m*; ~ **material** *n* POLL, SAFE material combustible *m*; ~ **waste** *n* POLL desperdicio combustible *m*, residuo combustible *m*

combustion *n* CHEM, COAL, P&R, PACK, SAFE, THERMO combustión *f*; ~ **air** *n* THERMO aire de combustión *m*; ~ **analysis** *n* THERMO análisis de combustión *m*; ~ **axial-gas fan** *n* HEAT ENG, MECH ENG ventilador de gas axial de combustión *m*; ~ **boat** *n* LAB, THERMO recipiente para incineración *m*; ~ **chamber** *n* AIR TRANSP, AUTO, HEAT, HYDRAUL, MECH ENG, SPACE, THERMO, WATER TRANSP *of engine* cámara de combustión *f*, cámara de explosión *f*; ~-**chamber annular case** *n* AIR TRANSP caja anular de la cámara de combustión *f*; ~ **control** *n* WATER TRANSP *engines* regulación de la combustión *f*; ~ **deposits** *n pl* THERMO depósitos de combustión *m pl*; ~ **efficiency** *n* SPACE eficacia de combustión *f*, THERMO eficiencia de combustión *f*, rendimiento de combustión *m*; ~ **energy** *n* THERMO energía de combustión *f*; ~ **engine** *n* THERMO, TRANSP motor de combustión *m*; ~ **engineering** *n* THERMO ingeniería de combustión *f*; ~ **gas** *n* GAS, HEAT ENG, PROD, SPACE, THERMO gas de combustión *m*; ~**-gas turbine** *n* GAS, PROD, SPACE, THERMO turbina de combustión *f*; ~ **index** *n* THERMO relación de combustión *f*, índice de combustión *m*; ~ **instability** *n* THERMO inestabilidad de la combustión *f*; ~ **prechamber** *n* THERMO, TRANSP antecámara de combustión *f*; ~ **starter** *n* AIR TRANSP, THERMO iniciador de combustión *m*

combustor *n* SPACE, THERMO cámara de combustión *f*

come: ~ **apart** *vi* MECH ENG desarmar, desmontar, separar; ~ **away** *vi* MECH ENG desprenderse, partirse, romperse, zafarse; ~ **back to the center of its run** *AmE*, ~ **back to the centre of its run** *BrE* *vi* CONST *air bubble* centrar; ~ **into gear** *vi* MECH ENG entrar en marcha, ponerse en marcha; ~ **off** *vi* MECH ENG desprenderse, partirse, romperse, zafarse; ~ **to** *vi* WATER TRANSP *shiphandling* orzar; ~ **to a standstill** *vi* MECH ENG pararse

comeback *n* THERMO retroceso *m*

comenic *adj* CHEM coménico

comet *n* SPACE cometa *m*; ~ **core** *n* SPACE núcleo del cometa *m*; ~ **in coating** *n* PRINT ráfaga en la capa sensible *f*

cometary: ~ **nebula** *n* SPACE nebulosa cometaria *f*

comfort: ~ **cooling** *n* REFRIG, THERMO refrigeración confortable *f*

comforter *n* TEXTIL bufanda *f*

coming: ~ **into gear** *n* MECH ENG puesta en marcha *f*; ~ **out of hole** *n* PETR TECH salida del agujero *f*, subida del pozo *f*

comingled: ~ **yarn** *n* TEXTIL madeja enredada *f*

comma *n* ACOUST, PRINT coma *f*

command *n* COMP&DP, MILIT, SPACE señal de control *f*, telemando *m*; ~ **buffer** *n* PROD memoria tampón de mandatos *f*; ~ **channel** *n* MILIT canal de mando *m*, SPACE canal de mando *m*, canal para señales de control *m*; ~ **and control center** *AmE*, ~ **and control centre** *BrE* *n* WATER TRANSP *of ship* centro de gobierno y mando *m*; ~ **and control system** *n* (*CSM*) COMP&DP sistema de orden y control *m*; ~**-driven interface** *n* COMP&DP interfase accionada por órdenes *f*, interfaz controlado por órdenes *m*, TELECOM interfaz controlado por órdenes *m*; ~ **earth station** *n* SPACE estación terrena de mando *f*, estación terrena emisora de la señal de control *f*; ~ **language** *n* COMP&DP guía de orden *f*, lenguaje de comandos *m*, lenguaje de órdenes *m*, petición de orden *f*; ~ **link** *n* SPACE enlace de señal de control *m*; ~ **module** *n* SPACE módulo de mando *m*; ~ **receiver** *n* SPACE receptor de la señal de control *m*; ~ **and service module** *n* SPACE módulo de mando y servicio *m* (*MMS*); ~ **ship** *n* MILIT, WATER TRANSP *navy* buque en que se halla el mando naval *m*; ~ **system** *n* COMP&DP sistema de órdenes *m*

commander *n* MILIT capitán de fragata *m*, SPACE comandante *m*, WATER TRANSP *navy* capitán de fragata *m*, comandante *m*

commensurable *adj* MATH conmensurable

comment: ~ **line** *n* PROD línea de comentarios *f*

commentary: ~ **track** *n* CINEMAT banda de comentarios *f*

commercial *n* TV anuncio publicitario *m* (*Esp*), propaganda *f* (*AmL*), tanda comercial *f*; ~ **amplifier** *n* ELECTRON amplificador comercial *m*,

amplificador industrial *m*; ~ **coal** *n* COAL carbón comercial *m*; ~ **coefficiency** *n* PROD coeficiencia comercial *f*; ~ **computing** *n* COMP&DP informática comercial *f*; ~ **condensing unit** *n* REFRIG grupo compresor-condensador comercial *m*; ~ **electric vehicle** *n* TRANSP vehículo eléctrico comercial *m*; ~ **field** *n* PETR TECH campo comercial *m*; ~ **language** *n* COMP&DP lenguaje comercial *m*; ~ **life** *n* SPACE vida útil comercial *f*; ~ **photography** *n* PHOTO fotografía corporativa *f*; ~ **port** *n* WATER TRANSP puerto comercial *m*; ~ **power frequency** *n* ELEC, ELEC ENG frecuencia de energía comercial *f*; ~ **press** *n* PRINT prensa industrial *f*; ~ **printing** *n* PRINT impresos comerciales *m pl*; ~ **sector** *n* GAS sector comercial *m*; ~ **standard** *n* PROD patrón industrial *m*; ~ **traffic** *n* TRANSP tráfico comercial *m*; ~ **type** *n* PRINT tipo comercial *m*; ~ **value** *n* MINE valor venal *m*; ~ **vehicle** *n* VEH vehículo comercial *m*; ~ **water** *n* HYDROL, WATER agua industrial *f*

comminution *n* CHEM TECH, HYDROL, NUCL trituración *f*

comminutor *n* CHEM TECH, HYDROL, NUCL triturador *m*

commission[1]: **in** ~ *adj* PROD, WATER TRANSP *ship* en servicio

commission[2] *vt* CONST encomendar, poner en marcha

commissioned: ~ **work** *n* PROD trabajo encargado *m*, *rendering of services* trabajo realizado por encargo *m*

commissioning *n* CONST puesta a punto *f*, puesta en marcha *f*, MECH *heat unit* puesta en servicio *f*; ~ **test** *n* TELECOM prueba de puesta en servicio *f*

commit: ~ **to silicon** *vt* ELECTRON tratar con silicio

commitment *n* PROD compromiso *m*

committed: ~ **effective dose equivalent** *n* NUCL dosis equivalente efectiva integrada *f*; ~ **information rate** *n* (*CIR*) TELECOM velocidad de información obligada *f*

commodities *n pl* AGRIC productos básicos *m pl*

commodity: ~ **group** *n* PACK grupo de mercancías *m*

commodore *n* WATER TRANSP *navy* comodoro *m*

common: ~ **aerial** *n* *BrE* (*cf common antenna AmE*) TELECOM, TV antena común *f*; ~**-anode connection** *n* ELEC ENG conexión de ánodo común *f*; ~ **antenna** *n* *AmE* (*cf common aerial BrE*) TELECOM, TV antena común *f*; ~ **area** *n* COMP&DP zona común *f*, área común *f*; ~**-base amplifier** *n* ELECTRON amplificador en base común *m*; ~**-base connection** *n* ELEC ENG conexión de base común *f*; ~**-base transistor** *n* ELECTRON transistor en base común *m*; ~ **battery switchboard** *n* TELECOM cuadro conmutador central *m*; ~ **branch** *n* ELEC *supply*, ELEC ENG brazo central *m*, derivación central *f*, derivación común *f*, rama central *f*, rama común *f*; ~ **carrier** *n* PRINT conductor común *m*, TV portadora común *f*, WATER TRANSP *satellite communications* portador común *m*; ~ **cathode** *n* ELEC ENG cátodo común *m*; ~ **cause of accidents** *n* SAFE causa común de accidentes *f*; ~ **channel signaling** *n* *AmE* TELECOM señalización por canal común *f*; ~ **channel signalling** *BrE* *n* (*CCS*) TELECOM señalización por canal común *f*; ~ **clay** *n* C&G barro *m*; ~**-collector amplifier** *n* ELECTRON amplificador de colector común *m*; ~**-collector connection** *n* ELEC ENG conexión de colector común *f*; ~ **control equipment** *n* TELECOM equipo de control común *m*; ~ **control switching system** *n* TELECOM sistema de conmutación de control común *m*; ~ **control system** *n* TELECOM sistema de control común *m*;

~ crossing n RAIL cruzamiento agudo m; **~ depth point** n GEOL, PETR TECH, PETROL punto de profundidad común m; **~ difference** n MATH diferencia común f; **~-drain amplifier** n ELECTRON amplificador en drenaje común m; **~-drain connection** n ELEC ENG conexión de consumo de energía f, conexión de pérdida de energía f; **~-drain transistor** n ELECTRON transistor de consumo común m, transistor en drenaje común m; **~-emitter amplifier** n ELECTRON amplificador de emisor común m; **~-emitter connection** n ELEC ENG conexión de emisor común f; **~-emitter transistor** n ELECTRON transistor de emisión común m; **~ equipment** n TELECOM equipo común m; **~ fuse** n MINE mecha común f (Esp), mecha de Bickford f (AmL), mecha ordinaria f; **~-gate amplifier** n ELECTRON amplificador en puerta común m; **~-gate connection** n ELEC ENG conexión de puerta común f; **~-gate transistor** n ELECTRON transistor en puerta común m; **~ highway** n TELECOM conductor común m; **~ injury in the workplace** n SAFE lesión común en el área de trabajo f; **~ logarithm** n MATH logaritmo de Briggs m, logaritmo decimal m; **~ management information protocol** n (CMIP) TELECOM protocolo de información de gestión común m; **~ management information protocol machine** n (CMIPM) TELECOM máquina de protocolos de información de gestión común f; **~ management information service** n (CMIS) TELECOM servicio de información de gestión común m; **~ management information service element** n (CMISE) TELECOM elemento de servicio de información de gestión común m; **~ master oscillator** n (CMO) TELECOM oscilador maestro general m; **~ mode** n ELECTRON, TELECOM modo común m; **~-mode gain** n ELECTRON, TELECOM ganancia en modo común f; **~-mode rejection** n ELECTRON supresión del modo común f, TELECOM rechazo del modo común m; **~-mode rejection ratio** n ELECTRON, TELECOM porcentaje de rechazo de modo común m, razón de rechazo del modo común f; **~-mode signal** n ELECTRON, TELECOM señal en modo común f; **~-mode voltage** n ELEC ENG tensión unimodal común f; **~ properties of electromagnetic waves** n pl RAD PHYS propiedades comunes de las ondas electromagnéticas f pl; **~ quality** n PROD calidad corriente f; **~ rafter** n CONST cabio común m; **~ ratio** n MATH razón común f, relación común f; **~ reactance** n ELEC inductors reactancia común f; **~-repair tools** n pl MECH ENG herramientas de reparación común f pl; **~ return** n TELECOM retorno combinado m; **~ scaffold** n CONST andamiaje común m, andamio común m; **~-source amplifier** n ELECTRON amplificador en fuente común m; **~-source transistor** n ELECTRON transistor en fuente común m; **~ store** n TELECOM memoria común f; **~ wire** n PROD alambre común m

communal: **~ farm** n AGRIC explotación agrícola colectiva f

communicating: **~ vessels** n pl LAB vasos comunicantes m pl

communication: **~ channel** n COMP&DP canal de comunicaciones m; **~ countermeasures** n (CCM) TELECOM contramedidas en las comunicaciones f pl; **~ link** n COMP&DP enlace de comunicación m; **~ medium** n COMP&DP medio de comunicaciones m, soporte de comunicaciones m; **~ network** n COMP&DP red de comunicación f; **~ satellite** n SPACE satélite de comunicaciones m; **~ server** n COMP&DP procesador de comunicación m, servidor de comunicaciones m; **~ system** n COMP&DP sistema de comunicación m; **~ theory** n COMP&DP teoría de comunicación f

communications: **~ agreement** n TELECOM acuerdo de comunicaciones m; **~ cable** n ELEC ENG, TELECOM cable de comunicaciones m; **~ circuit** n ELEC ENG, TELECOM circuito de comunicaciones m, vía de comunicaciones f; **~ filter** n ELECTRON filtro de comunicaciones m; **~ line** n ELEC ENG línea de comunicaciones f; **~ processor** n TELECOM procesador de comunicaciones m; **~ satellite** n (COMSAT) WATER TRANSP satélite de telecomunicaciones m; **~ signal** n ELECTRON señal de comunicaciones f; **~ software** n COMP&DP software de comunicaciones m, soporte lógico de comunicación m (AmL); **~ system monitoring** n (CSM) SPACE control del sistema de comunicaciones m (CSS)

community: **~ aerial** n BrE (cf community antenna AmE) TELECOM, TV antena colectiva f; **~ antenna** n AmE (cf community aerial BrE) TELECOM, TV antena colectiva f; **~ broadcasting** n TV emisión comunitaria f; **~ dial office** n TELECOM central telefónica comunitaria f; **~ noise** n ACOUST ruido comunitario m; **~ sewage works** n HYDROL, RECYCL, WATER planta de depuración de aguas residuales comunitarias f

commutating: **~ pole** n ELEC polo auxiliar m, polo de conmutación m; **~ winding** n ELEC devanado de conmutación m

commutation n ELEC, ELEC ENG, MATH conmutación f

commutative adj ELEC, ELECTRON, MATH conmutativo

commutator n ELEC colector m, colector de delgas m, conmutador m, interruptor m, ELEC ENG colector m, conmutador m, remote measurement recopilador de delgas m, TRANSP colector de delgas m, conmutador m; **~ bar** n ELEC, ELEC ENG delga f, delga de colector f; **~ brush** n ELEC, ELECTRON escobilla de colector f; **~ DC motor** n (commutator direct current motor) ELEC ENG motor de colector de CC m (motor de colector de corriente continua); **~ direct current motor** n (commutator DC motor) ELEC ENG motor de colector de corriente continua m (motor de colector de CC); **~ motor** n ELEC, ELEC ENG, TRANSP motor de colector m; **~ segment** n ELEC, ELEC ENG delga de colector f; **~ sparking** n ELEC, ELECTRON chispas del colector f pl; **~ switch** n ELEC, ELECTRON conmutador de dirección m, interruptor del colector m; **~-type frequency** n ELEC converter, ELECTRON convertidor de frecuencia con colector m

commuter: **~ traffic** n TRANSP tráfico de cercanías m

comp n PRINT tipógrafo m

compact[1]: **~ CNC universal cylindrical grinding machine** n MECH ENG máquina rectificadora cilíndrica universal de control numérico f; **~ disc** n (CD) COMP&DP, OPT disco compacto m (CD); **~ disc read only memory** n (CD-ROM) OPT disco compacto de memoria de sólo lectura m (CD-ROM); **~ disc-interactive** n (CD-I) OPT disco compacto interactivo m; **~ music disc** n OPT disco compacto de música m; **~ music disc drive** n COMP&DP unidad de disco compacto de música f

compact[2] vt GEOL, PROD compactar

compaction n COMP&DP compactación f, compresión f, GEOL compactación f

compacted: **~ apparent density** n CHEM TECH densidad aparente de compactación *f*; ~ **conductor** *n* ELEC *cable* conductor compactado *m*; ~ **thickness** *n* CONST espesor compactado *m*

compaction *n* COAL, CONST, GEOL, PETR TECH compactación *f*, consolidación *f*; ~ **disequilibrium** *n* GEOL, PETR TECH desequilibrio de la compactación *m*; ~ **piling** *n* COAL apilamiento por compactación *m*; ~ **trend** *n* GEOL, PETR TECH dirección de compactación *f*

companded: ~ **delta modulation** *n* (*CDM*) TELECOM modulación delta compandida *f*; ~ **signal** *n* ELECTRON señal limitada *f*

compander *n* COMP&DP, ELECTRON, SPACE *communications* compresor-expansor *m*

companding *n* ELECTRON, SPACE compresión-expansión *f*, TELECOM compansión *f*

companion: ~ **chip** *n* ELECTRON chip de acoplamiento *m*, microplaca de acoplamiento *f*; ~ **crop** *n* AGRIC cultivo asociado *m*; ~ **source** *n* ELECTRON fuente de acoplamiento *f*

companionway *n* WATER TRANSP bajada *f*, bajada a la cámara *f*; ~ **hatch** *n* WATER TRANSP escotilla de bajada *f*, escotilla de tambucho *f*; ~ **ladder** *n* WATER TRANSP escala de bajada a la cámara *f*, escala de cámara *f*; ~ **posts** *n pl* WATER TRANSP puntales de la escotilla de bajada *m pl*

company: ~-**wide quality control** *n* (*CWQC*) QUALITY control de calidad en toda la empresa *m*, control de calidad en toda la sociedad *m*

comparative: ~ **dyeing** *n* COLOUR teñido comparado *m*; ~ **test** *n* PHYS prueba comparativa *f*

comparator *n* COMP&DP, ELECTRON comparador *m*, INSTR, METR ampliador óptico *m*, comparador *m*, PHYS, TELECOM comparador *m*; ~ **circuit** *n* ELECTRON circuito comparador *m*; ~ **densitometer** *n* CINEMAT densitómetro comparador *m*

compare *vt* COMP&DP comparar

comparison: ~ **circuit** *n* TELECOM circuito de comprobación *m*

compartment *n* COAL compartimiento *m*, cuartel *m*, COMP&DP compartimiento *m*, MECH ENG compartimiento *m*, departamento *m*, división *f*, sección *f*, REFRIG, TRANSP compartimiento *m*; ~ **case** *n* PACK caja-compartimiento *f*, estantería *f*; ~ **mill** *n* COAL molinos de compartimientos *m pl*

compartmental: ~ **model** *n* TELECOM modelo compartimentado *m*

compartmentalization *n* COMP&DP compartimentación *f*, compartimentalización *f*

compartmentation *n* WATER TRANSP *naval architecture* compartimentado *m*

compartmented: ~ **insert** *n* PACK intercalado en compartimientos *m*; ~ **tray** *n* PACK bandeja de compartimientos *f*

compass *n* CONST, GEOPHYS, MILIT, PHYS, SPACE brújula *f*, compás *m*, WATER TRANSP *navigation* aguja *f*, aguja de marear *f*, aguja náutica *f*, compás *m*; ~ **bearing** *n* AIR TRANSP marcación de la brújula *f*, GEOL rumbo marcado por la brújula *m*, WATER TRANSP demora de aguja *f*, marcación de la brújula *f*; ~ **bowl** *n* PHYS cubeta de bitácora *f*; ~ **card** *n* INSTR rosa de la brújula *f*, WATER TRANSP rosa de la aguja *f*, rosa de los vientos *f*; ~ **compensating** *n* AIR TRANSP compensador de brújula *m*; ~ **compensation base** *n* AIR TRANSP base de compensación de la brújula *f*; ~ **dial** *n* WATER TRANSP limbo *m*, limbo graduado de

la rosa *m*; ~ **error** *n* WATER TRANSP desvío *m*, error de ajuste *m*; ~ **heading** *n* AIR TRANSP rumbo de la brújula *m*, WATER TRANSP *navigation* rumbo de aguja *m*; ~ **input** *n* WATER TRANSP *radar* entrada de información de la giroscópica *f*; ~ **lens** *n* C&G lente de brújula *f*; ~ **locator** *n* AIR TRANSP localizador de brújula *m*; ~ **meridian line** *n* INSTR línea meridiana magnética *f*; ~ **needle** *n* WATER TRANSP imán director *m*; ~ **plane** *n* CONST cepillo redondo *m*; ~ **repeater** *n* WATER TRANSP aguja repetidora *f*; ~ **saw** *n* CONST serrucho de marquetería *m*, serrucho de punta *m*, sierra de contornear *f*; ~ **survey** *n* MINE levantamiento de planos con brújula *m*; ~ **variation** *n* WATER TRANSP variación de la aguja *f*

compasses *n pl* GEOM, MECH ENG compases *m pl*, compás *m*; ~ **with pen point** *n pl* MECH ENG compases con punta de bolígrafo *m pl*; ~ **with pencil point** *n pl* MECH ENG compases con punta de lápiz *m pl*

compatibility *n* ACOUST compatibilidad *f*, COAL coherencia *f*, compacidad *f*, compatibilidad *f*, consistencia *f*, COMP&DP, ELECTRON, MECH ENG, P&R, QUALITY, TV compatibilidad *f*; ~ **between elastometric materials and fluids** *n* MECH ENG compatibilidad entre fluidos y materiales elastométricos *f*

compatible[1] *adj* GEN compatible

compatible[2]: ~ **groove modulation** *n* ACOUST modulación de surco compatible *f*; ~ **logic** *n* ELECTRON circuito lógico compatible *m*; ~ **plug** *n* ELEC ENG enchufe compatible *m*

compensate[1] *vt* ELECTRON, MECH ENG, RAIL compensar, SAFE *for industrial injuries* indemnizar, WATER TRANSP *compass* compensar

compensate[2] *vi* PHYS compensar; ~ **for wear** *vi* MECH compensar por desgaste

compensated: ~ **amplifier** *n* ELECTRON amplificador compensado *m*; ~ **brake rigging** *n* RAIL mecanismo de accionamiento de frenos compensado *m*; ~ **foundation** *n* COAL cimentación compensada *f*; ~ **induction motor** *n* ELEC motor asincrónico compensado *m*, motor de inducción compensado *m*; ~ **motor** *n* ELEC motor compensado *m*; ~ **pendulum** *n* PHYS péndulo compensado *m*; ~ **semiconductor** *n* ELEC ENG semiconductor intrínseco por compensación *m*

compensating: ~ **beam** *n* MECH ENG balancín compensador *m*; ~ **buffer** *n* RAIL freno compensador *m*, tope compensador *m*; ~ **circuit** *n* ELEC circuito de compensación *m*; ~ **coupling** *n* MECH ENG acoplamiento elástico *m*; ~ **current** *n* ELEC corriente compensadora *f*; ~ **developer** *n* PHOTO revelador compensador *m*; ~ **filter** *n* PHOTO filtro compensador *m*; ~ **gear** *n* MECH ENG engranaje diferencial *m*; ~ **jet** *n* VEH surtidor compensador *m*; ~ **reservoir** *n* HYDROL, WATER contraembalse *m*, embalse secundario *m*; ~ **spool** *n* PROD carrete compensador *m*; ~ **voltage** *n* ELEC tensión compensadora *f*, voltaje compensador *m*

compensation *n* ELEC ENG, ELECTRON, HYDROL, OCEAN, PHYS compensación *f*, SAFE *for industrial injuries*, indemnización *f*; ~ **basin** *n* HYDROL depósito de compensación *m*; ~ **circuit** *n* TELECOM circuito de comparación *m*; ~ **current** *n* OCEAN corriente de compensación *f*; ~ **depth** *n* OCEAN profundidad de compensación *f*; ~ **for wear** *n* MECH compensación por desgaste *f*; ~ **reservoir** *n* HYDROL depósito de compensación *m*; ~ **theorem** *n* PHYS teorema de

compensación *m*; ~ **winding** *n* ELEC ENG devanado compensador *m*
compensator *n* ELEC *alternating current circuits*, ELEC ENG, ELECTRON, PETR TECH, PHYS autotransformador *m*, compensador *m*
competent *adj* GEOL competente
competing: ~ **demands** *n pl* PROD demandas competidoras *f pl*
competition: ~ **growth** *n* METALL aumento de la competencia *m*, desarrollo de prueba *m*
competitive: ~ **edge** *n* PROD ventaja competitiva *f*
compilation *n* COMP&DP, PRINT, TELECOM compilación *f*; ~ **time** *n* COMP&DP tiempo de compilación *m*
compiler *n* COMP&DP, PRINT, TELECOM compilador *m*; ~-**compiler** *n* COMP&DP compilador-compilador *m*; ~ **diagnostic** *n* COMP&DP diagnóstico de compilador *m*; ~ **directive** *n* COMP&DP directiva de compilador *f*, directriz de compilación *f*
complement *n* COMP&DP, ELECTRON complemento *m*
complementarity *n* COMP&DP, PART PHYS complementariedad *f*
complementary: ~ **angle** *n* GEOM ángulo complementario *m*; ~ **code** *n* TELECOM código complementario *m*; ~ **colors** *AmE*, ~ **colours** *BrE n pl* COLOUR, PHOTO, PHYS colores complementarios *m pl*; ~ **input rack** *n* PROD planchero complementario de entrada *m*; ~ **I/O addressing** *n* PROD direccionamiento complementario de E/S *m*; ~ **matte** *n* CINEMAT trama complementaria *f*; ~ **metal oxide semiconductor** *n* (*CMOS*) ELECTRON, PROD semiconductor complementario de metal (*SCOM*); ~ **outputs** *n pl* ELECTRON salidas complementarias *f pl*; ~ **pair** *n* ELECTRON par complementario *m*; ~ **set** *n* MATH conjunto complementario *m*; ~ **transistors** *n pl* ELECTRON transistores complementarios *m pl*
complete[1]: ~-**assembly** *adj* MECH ENG, PROD de conjunto completo, de juego completo, de montaje completo, de unidad completa
complete[2]: ~ **combustion** *n* GAS, THERMO combustión completa *f*; ~ **diversion** *n* TRANSP desviación total *f*; ~ **fertilizer** *n* AGRIC, POLL, RECYCL abono completo *m*; ~ **purification** *n* NUCL purificación completa *f*
completely: ~ **stable layer** *n* METEO capa totalmente estable *f*
completion *n* PETR TECH completación *f*; ~ **time** *n* CONST plazo de ejecución *m*
complex *n* GEOL complejo *m*; ~ **admittance** *n* ELEC *alternating current circuits*, ELEC ENG, PHYS admitancia compleja *f*; ~ **fraction** *n* MATH fracción compleja *f*, fracción compuesta *f*, quebrado complejo *m*, quebrado compuesto *m*; ~ **impedance** *n* ELEC *alternating current circuits*, ELEC ENG, PHYS impedancia compleja *f*; ~ **instruction set computer** *n* (*CISC*) COMP&DP computador de conjuntos de instrucciones complejas *m* (*AmL*) (*CISC*), computadora de conjunto de instrucciones complejas *f* (*AmL*) (*CISC*), ordenador de conjunto de instrucciones complejas *m* (*Esp*) (*CISC*); ~ **number** *n* COMP&DP, MATH número complejo *m*; ~ **ore** *n* COAL mineral complejo *m*; ~ **permeability** *n* ELEC *alternating current circuits* permeabilidad compleja *f*; ~ **power** *n* ELEC energía compleja *f*, potencia compleja *f*; ~ **refractive index** *n* PHYS índice de refracción complejo *m*; ~ **signal** *n* ELECTRON señal compleja *f*; ~ **tone** *n* ACOUST tono complejo *m*; ~ **type** *n* COMP&DP tipo complejo *m*; ~ **wave** *n* ELECTRON, TELECOM onda compleja *f*;

~ **waveform** *n* ACOUST, COMP&DP, ELEC, ELEC ENG, ELECTRON, PHYS, WAVE PHYS forma de onda compleja *f*
complexing: ~ **agent** *n* NUCL complexante *m*
complexity *n* COMP&DP complejidad *f*
complexometric: ~ **titration** *n* CHEM titulación complejométrica *f*, valoración complejométrica *f*
compliance *n* ACOUST compilancia *f*, elasticidad *f*, QUALITY conformidad *f*; ~ **test** *n* QUALITY prueba de conformidad *f*
component[1] *adj* MECH ENG componente
component[2] *n* COAL elemento *m*, pieza *f*, ELEC *of force, current* componente *m*, *part* elemento *m*, pieza *f*, ELECTRON *of car* componente *m*, MECH elemento *m*, pieza *f*, componente *m*, elemento componente *m*, MECH ENG, NUCL, PHYS, PROD, TELECOM componente *m*; ~-**cooling water system** *n* (*CCWS*) NUCL sistema de agua de refrigeración de componentes *m* (*CCWS*); ~ **data element separator** *n* TELECOM separador por elementos de los datos de componentes *m*; ~ **density** *n* ELECTRON densidad del componente *f*; ~ **failure** *n* PROD fallo de los componentes *m*; ~ **identification marker** *n* PROD marca de identificación del componente *f*; ~ **layout** *n* ELECTRON instalación del componente *f*; ~ **level** *n* ELECTRON nivel del componente *m*; ~ **manufacturer** *n* PROD fabricante de los componentes *m*; ~ **procurement** *n* SPACE compra de componentes *f*, obtención de componentes *f*; ~ **selection** *n* SPACE selección de componentes *f*; ~ **side** *n* TELECOM lado de componentes *m*; ~ **spacing** *n* PROD separación de los componentes *f*
compose *vt* PRINT componer
composing: ~ **machine** *n* PRINT componedora *f*; ~ **stick** *n* PRINT regleta de componer *f*
composite *n* METALL material compuesto *m*, metal compuesto *m*, P&R compuesto *m*, mezclado *m*, mixtura *f*; ~ **absorber** *n* NUCL absorbente compuesto *m*; ~ **aircraft** *n* AIR TRANSP avión compuesto *m*; ~ **cable** *n* ELEC ENG cable mixto *m*; ~ **check print** *n* CINEMAT prueba combinada *f*; ~ **color signal** *AmE*, ~ **colour signal** *BrE n* TV señal de color compuesta *f*; ~ **container** *n* PACK contenedor mixto *m*; ~ **dike** *n* GEOL dique mixto *m*; ~ **girder** *n* CONST viga compuesta *f*; ~ **log** *n* GEOL perfil mixto *m*; ~ **material** *n* SPACE material compuesto *m*; ~ **number** *n* MATH número compuesto *m*, número no primo *m*; ~ **pass band** *n* ELECTRON banda de paso compuesta *f*; ~ **pile** *n* COAL aguja compuesta *f*; ~ **print** *n* CINEMAT copia combinada *f*; ~ **sample** *n* COAL, QUALITY muestra compuesta *f*; ~ **shot** *n* CINEMAT toma combinada *f*; ~ **signal** *n* ELECTRON, TELECOM, TV señal compuesta *f*; ~ **signal coding** *n* ELECTRON, TELECOM, TV codificación de señal compuesta *f*; ~ **sill** *n* GEOL manto compuesto *m*, sill mixto *m*; ~ **synchronization signal** *n* TV señal de sincronismo compuesta *f*; ~ **video signal** *n* TV señal de video compuesta *f* (*AmL*), señal de vídeo compuesta *f* (*Esp*); ~ **volcano** *n* GEOL volcán compuesto *m*; ~ **wave** *n* TELECOM onda compuesta *f*
composition *n* CHEM, MECH, NUCL, PAPER, PRINT composición *f*; ~ **board** *n* PRINT mesa de composición *f*; ~ **caster** *n* PRINT fundidora de la composición *f*; ~ **sizes** *n pl* PRINT tamaños de composición *m pl*
compositor *n* PRINT cajista *m*
compost: ~ **heap** *n* AGRIC, RECYCL montón de abono vegetal *m*

composting n AGRIC, POLL, RECYCL abono compuesto m

compound n CHEM compuesto m, mezcla f, P&R combinación f, compuesto m, mezcla f, PROD compuesto m; **~ blowpipe** n PROD soplete oxídrico m; **~ clarification** n HYDROL clarificación compuesta f; **~ compression** n MECH ENG of air compresión escalonada f, compresión por fases f; **~ compressor** n MECH ENG of air compresor de fases escalonadas m; **~ die** n MECH ENG press tools troquel combinado m, troquel compuesto m; **~ engine** n MECH ENG motor alternativo con turbina de gases de escape m, motor de pluriexpansión m; **~ expansion engine** n MECH ENG motor de pluriexpansión m; **~ fertilizer** n AGRIC compuesto químico m; **~ gage** AmE, **~ gauge** BrE n REFRIG manovacuómetro m, manómetro compuesto m; **~ girder** n CONST viga compuesta f; **~ glass fiber** AmE, **~ glass fibre** BrE n OPT fibra de vidrio compuesta f, fibra de vidrio compuesto f; **~ helicopter** n AIR TRANSP helicóptero compuesto m; **~ interest** n PETR TECH interés compuesto m; **~ lens** n OPT, PHOTO lente compuesta f, objetivo compuesto m; **~ lever** n MECH ENG palanca compuesta f; **~ magnet** n PHYS imán laminado m; **~ microscope** n INSTR, PHYS microscopio compuesto m; **~ modulation** n ELECTRON modulación compuesta f; **~ motion** n MECH movimiento compuesto m, movimiento mixto m; **~ motor** n ELEC, ELEC ENG motor de excitación compuesta m, motor de excitación mixta m, motor en compound m; **~ nucleus** n NUCL, PHYS, RAD PHYS núcleo compuesto m; **~ oil** n PROD mezcla de aceites minerales y vegetales f; **~ pendulum** n PHYS péndulo compuesto m, péndulo de compensación m; **~ screw** n MECH ENG differential tornillo de pasos contrarios m, tornillo diferencial m; **~ slide rest** n MECH ENG soporte de carro transversal y longitudinal m, soporte de desplazamiento transversal y longitudinal m; **~ slotted worktable** n MECH ENG portapiezas ranurado compuesto m; **~ statement** n COMP&DP program declaración compuesta f, instrucción compuesta f, sentencia compuesta f; **~ table** n MECH ENG for drilling machines mesa ortogonal f; **~ tide** n OCEAN marea compuesta f; **~ tool holder** n MECH ENG portaherramientas compuesto m, portaherramientas múltiple m; **~ twinning** n METALL germinación compuesta f, maclaje compuesto m; **~ wedge** n MINE cuña múltiple f; **~ winding** n ELEC direct current devanado compound m, devanado doble m, devanado en serie y derivación m, devenado mixto m, ELEC ENG devanado compound m, devanado doble m, devanado en serie y derivación m, devanado mixto m; **~-winding motor** n ELEC, ELEC ENG motor de devanado mixto m; **~-wound motor** n ELEC, ELEC ENG motor de excitación compound m, motor de excitación compuesta m, motor de excitación mixta m

compounding n ELEC, ELEC ENG devanado mixto m

comprehensive n PRINT boceto definitivo m; **~ treatment plant** n WATER planta de tratamiento completa f

compress vt COMP&DP comprimir, condensar, CONST, ELECTRON, MECH ENG, MINE, NUCL, TELECOM comprimir

compressed: **~ air** n CONST, MECH ENG, MINE aire a presión m, aire comprimido m; **~-air cylinder** n MECH ENG cilindro de aire comprimido m; **~-air drill** n CONST, MECH ENG perforadora de aire comprimido f, perforadora neumática f; **~-air engine** n CONST, MECH ENG motor de aire caliente comprimido m; **~-air equipment** n CONST, MECH ENG equipo de aire comprimido m; **~-air line** n CONST, MECH ENG canalización de aire comprimido f, línea de aire comprimido f, manguera de aire comprimido f, tubo de aire comprimido m; **~-air lubricator** n CONST, MECH ENG engrasador de aire a presión m, engrasador de aire comprimido m, lubrificador de aire comprimido m; **~-air motor** n MINE motor de aire comprimido m; **~-air socket** n MECH ENG encastre de aire a presión m, enchufe de aire a presión m, toma de aire a presión f; **~-air sprayer** n AGRIC pulverizador de aire comprimido m; **~-air system** n MECH ENG sistema de aire a presión m, sistema de aire comprimido m, sistema neumático m; **~ air-conditioning unit** n CONST equipo de aire acondicionado con compresor m; **~ digital transmission** n TELECOM transmisión digital comprimida f; **~ fitting** n MECH ENG of pipes accesorio a presión m, ajuste a presión m; **~ nuclear matter** n NUCL materia nuclear comprimida f; **~-pulse width** n ELECTRON amplitud de impulso comprimido f; **~ signal** n ELECTRON señal comprimida f; **~ speech** n ELECTRON, TELECOM diálogo comprimido m; **~ steel shafting** n MECH ENG transmisión con ejes de acero en compresión f; **~ video level** n TV nivel de video comprimido m (AmL), nivel de vídeo comprimido m (Esp)

compressibility n GEN compresibilidad f; **~ coefficient** n COAL, PHYS coeficiente de compresibilidad m; **~ curve** n THERMO curva de compresibilidad f; **~ drag** n AIR TRANSP resistencia aerodinámica de la compresibilidad f; **~ effects** n pl AIR TRANSP efectos de compresibilidad m pl; **~ factor** n PETR TECH, PETROL, THERMO factor de compresibilidad m; **~ of gases** n THERMO compresibilidad de los gases f; **~ modulus** n COAL coeficiente de compresibilidad m

compressible[1] adj GEN compresible

compressible[2]: **~ flow** n FLUID flujo compresible m

compressing: **~ fan** n MECH ENG ventilador impelente m

compression n GEN compresión f; **~ chamber** n AUTO, COAL cámara de compresión f, HYDRAUL cámara de compresión f, PETR TECH, VEH cámara de compresión f; **~ cock** n HYDRAUL grifo de descompresión m; **~ curve** n COAL curva de compresión f; **~ damage** n PACK deterioro debido a la compresión m; **~ filter** n ELECTRON filtro de compresión m; **~ ignition engine** n MECH ENG motor de ignición por compresión m, motor diesel m, motor por autoencendido m; **~ index** n COAL índice de compresión m; **~ installation** n GAS instalación de compresión f; **~ load** n PACK carga de compresión f; **~ modulus** n P&R coeficiente de compresión m, módulo de compresión m; **~ mold** AmE see compression mould BrE; **~ molding** AmE see compression moulding BrE; **~-molding machine** AmE see compression-moulding machine BrE; **~ mould** n BrE MECH ENG, P&R molde de compresión m, moldeo por compresión m; **~ moulding** n BrE C&G, P&R, PACK moldeo por compresión m, moldeo por prensado m; **~-moulding machine** n BrE MECH ENG, P&R, PACK máquina de moldeo por compresión f; **~ period** n HYDRAUL período de compresión m;

~ **plant** *n* THERMO planta de compresión *f*; ~ **point** *n* HYDRAUL principio de compresión *m*; ~ **pump** *n* HYDRAUL bomba de compresión *f*, bomba de presión *f*; ~ **ratio** *n* ELECTRON relación de compresión *f*, MECH ENG grado de compresión *m*, relación de compresión *f*, relación volumétrica *f*, índice de compresión *m*, REFRIG, THERMO, VEH relación de compresión *f*; ~ **refrigerating cycle** *n* REFRIG, THERMO ciclo frigorífico de compresión *m*; ~ **refrigerator** *n* MECH ENG, REFRIG, THERMO refrigerador de compresión *m*; ~ **ring** *n* AUTO, VEH anillo de compresión *m*, segmento de compresión *m*; ~ **set** *n* P&R endurecimiento por compresión *m*, solidificación por compresión *f*; ~ **spring** *n* HYDRAUL muelle de compresión *m*, resorte de compresión *m*; ~ **stage** *n* MECH ENG escalón de compresión *m*, etapa de compresión *f*, fase de compresión *f*; ~ **strength** *n* MECH *quality factor*, P&R, PACK resistencia a la compresión *f*; ~ **stress** *n* MECH *communications* resistencia a la compresión *f*, METALL tensión de compresión *f*; ~ **stroke** *n* AUTO carrera de compresión *f*, THERMO carrera de compresión *f*, tiempo de compresión *m*, VEH carrera de compresión *f*; ~ **system** *n* REFRIG sistema de compresión *m*; ~ **test** *n* COAL, MECH, METALL, PACK ensayo de compresión *m*, prueba de compresión *f*; ~ **test machine** *n* PACK aparato para realizar el ensayo de resistencia a la compresión *m*; ~ **tester** *n* PAPER aparato para medir la compresión *m*
compressional: ~ **wave** *n* ACOUST, GEOL, WAVE PHYS onda compresional *f*, onda de compresión *f*
compressive: ~ **force** *n* MECH ENG fuerza compresiva *f*; ~ **strain** *n* GEOL deformación compresiva *f*, MECH *ring winding* deformación por compresión *f*; ~ **stress** *n* GEOL esfuerzo de compresión *m*
compressometer *n* COAL compresómetro *m*
compressor *n* GEN compresor *m*; ~ **air bleed** *n* MECH ENG purga de aire del compresor *f*; ~ **blade** *n* AIR TRANSP pala del compresor *f*; ~ **-expander** *n* TELECOM compresor-expansor *m*; ~ **rotor** *n* AIR TRANSP *helicopters* rotor del compresor *m*; ~ **stall** *n* AIR TRANSP *turbine engines* pérdida del compresor *f*; ~ **stator** *n* AIR TRANSP estator del compresor *m*; ~ **surge** *n* AIR TRANSP sobrecarga del compresor *f*; ~ **terminal box** *n* REFRIG caja de terminales del compresor *f*
Compton: ~ **continuum** *n* PHYS, RAD PHYS continuo de Compton *m*; ~ **effect** *n* PHYS, RAD PHYS efecto de Compton *m*; ~ **scattering** *n* PHYS, RAD PHYS dispersión de Compton *f*; ~ **wavelength** *n* NUCL, PHYS, RAD PHYS longitud de onda de Compton *f*
Compur: ~ **shutter** *n* PHOTO obturador de Compur *m*
computation *n* COMP&DP, TELECOM *data processing* computación, cálculo *m*, cómputo *m*, *theory* computación *f* (*AmL*), informática *f* (*Esp*); ~ **of center of gravity** *AmE*, ~ **of centre of gravity** *BrE n* AIR TRANSP cálculo del centro de gravedad *m*
computational: ~ **fluid dynamics** *n* (*CFD*) AIR TRANSP, FLUID dinámica de fluidos computacional *f* (*CFD*)
computer[1]: ~ **-aided** *adj* COMP&DP auxiliado por computador (*AmL*), auxiliado por computadora (*AmL*), auxiliado por ordenador (*Esp*); ~ **-assisted** *adj* COMP&DP asistido por computador (*AmL*), asistido por computadora (*AmL*), asistido por ordenador (*Esp*), auxiliado por computador (*AmL*), auxiliado por computadora (*AmL*), auxiliado por

ordenador (*Esp*); ~ **-based** *adj* COMP&DP informatizado (*Esp*), PROD computadorizado (*AmL*), informatizado (*Esp*); ~ **-controlled** *adj* PROD, TELECOM controlado por computadora (*AmL*), controlado por ordenador (*Esp*)
computer[2] *n* COMP&DP computador *m* (*AmL*), computadora *f* (*AmL*), ordenador *m* (*Esp*), ELEC aparato computador de distancias *m*, calculadora electrónica *f*, computador *f* (*AmL*), computadora *f* (*AmL*), ordenador *m* (*Esp*); ~ **-aided design** *n* (*CAD*) COMP&DP, ELEC, MECH, PRINT, PROD, TELECOM diseño asistido por computador *m* (*AmL*) (*CAD*), diseño asistido por computadora *m* (*AmL*) (*CAD*), diseño asistido por ordenador *m* (*Esp*) (*CAD*); ~ **-aided design and manufacture** *n* COMP&DP, PROD diseño y fabricación asistidos por computador *m* (*AmL*), diseño y fabricación asistidos por computadora *m* (*AmL*), diseño y fabricación asistidos por ordenador *m* (*Esp*); ~ **-aided manufacturing** *n* (*CAM*) COMP&DP, ELEC, PROD, TELECOM fabricación asistida por computador *f* (*AmL*) (*CAM*), fabricación asistida por computadora *f* (*AmL*) (*CAM*), fabricación asistida por ordenador *f* (*Esp*) (*CAM*); ~ **-aided software engineering** *n* (*CASE*) COMP&DP ingeniería de software asistida por ordenador *f* (*Esp*), ingeniería de soporte lógico auxiliada por computadora *f* (*AmL*); ~ **-aided testing** *n* (*CAT*) COMP&DP prueba asistida por ordenador *f* (*Esp*) (*CAT*), prueba auxiliada por computador *f* (*AmL*) (*CAT*), prueba auxiliada por computadora *f* (*AmL*) (*CAT*); ~ **animation** *n* CINEMAT, COMP&DP animación por computadora *f* (*AmL*), animación por ordenador *f* (*Esp*), TV animación por computadora *f* (*Esp*), animación por ordenador *f*; ~ **art** *n* COMP&DP arte por computador *m* (*AmL*), arte por computadora *m* (*AmL*), arte por ordenador *m* (*Esp*); ~ **-assisted instruction** *n* (*CAI*) COMP&DP enseñanza asistida por computador *f* (*AmL*) (*CAI*), enseñanza asistida por computadora *f* (*AmL*) (*CAI*), enseñanza asistida por ordenador *f* (*Esp*) (*CAI*); ~ **-assisted learning** *n* (*CAL*) COMP&DP enseñanza auxiliada por computador *f* (*AmL*) (*CAL*), enseñanza auxiliada por computadora *f* (*AmL*) (*CAL*), enseñanza auxiliada por ordenador *f* (*Esp*) (*CAL*); ~ **-assisted setting** *n* COMP&DP composición por computador *f* (*AmL*), composición por computadora *f* (*AmL*), composición por ordenador *f* (*Esp*), PRINT composición asistida por computador *f* (*AmL*), composición asistida por computadora *f* (*AmL*), composición asistida por ordenador *f* (*Esp*); ~ **-assisted translation** *n* COMP&DP traducción por ordenador *f* (*Esp*), traducción auxiliada por computadora *f* (*AmL*); ~ **-assisted typesetting** *n* (*CAT*) COMP&DP, PRINT fotocomposición asistida por computador *f* (*AmL*), fotocomposición asistida por computadora *f* (*AmL*), fotocomposición asistida por ordenador *f* (*Esp*); ~ **bank** *n* COMP&DP, TELECOM banco de memoria *m*; ~ **-based training** *n* COMP&DP, TELECOM formación basada en computadores *f* (*AmL*), formación basada en ordenadores *f* (*Esp*); ~ **-controlled all-relay interlocking** *n* COMP&DP, RAIL enclavamiento mediante relés controlados por computadora *m* (*AmL*), enclavamiento mediante relés controlados por ordenador *m* (*Esp*); ~ **family** *n* COMP&DP familia de computadoras *f* (*AmL*), familia de computadores *f* (*AmL*), familia de orde-

nadores *f* (*Esp*); ~ **graphics** *n* COMP&DP, TV gráficos de computador *m pl* (*AmL*), gráficos de computadora *m pl* (*AmL*), gráficos de ordenador *m pl* (*Esp*); ~-**integrated manufacturing** *n* (*CIM*) COMP&DP fabricación informatizada *f* (*Esp*) (*CIM*), fabricación integrada por computadora *f* (*AmL*) (*CIM*); ~ **interface** *n* COMP&DP, TELECOM interfaz de computador *m* (*AmL*), interfaz de computadora *m* (*AmL*), interfaz de ordenador *m* (*Esp*); ~ **literacy** *n* COMP&DP alfabetismo en computadoras *m* (*AmL*), alfabetismo en ordenadores *m* (*Esp*), fundamentos informáticos *m pl*; ~ **logic** *n* COMP&DP lógica de computadoras *f* (*AmL*), lógica de ordenadores *f* (*Esp*), lógica informática *f*; ~ **network** *n* COMP&DP red de computadoras *f* (*AmL*), red de ordenadores *f* (*Esp*), red informática *f*, TELECOM red de computadores *f* (*AmL*), red de ordenadores *f* (*Esp*), red informática *f*; ~-**network architecture** *n* COMP&DP arquitectura de red de computadoras *f* (*AmL*), arquitectura de red de computadores *f* (*AmL*), arquitectura de red de ordenadores *f* (*Esp*); ~ **output on microfilm** *n* (*COM*) COMP&DP salida de computadora en microfilm *f* (*AmL*), salida de ordenador en microfilm *f* (*Esp*); ~ **science** *n* COMP&DP ciencia de computadoras *f* (*AmL*), informática *f* (*Esp*); ~ **security** *n* COMP&DP seguridad de computadora *f* (*AmL*), seguridad de ordenadores *f* (*Esp*), seguridad informática *f*; ~ **system** *n* COMP&DP sistema informático *m*, ELEC sistema informatico *m*, TELECOM sistema informático *m*; ~ **technology** *n* COMP&DP tecnología de computadoras *f* (*AmL*), tecnología de ordenadores *f* (*Esp*)

computerized[1] *adj* COMP&DP informatizado (*Esp*), PROD computadorizado (*AmL*), informatizado (*Esp*)

computerized[2]: ~ **interlocking system** *n* RAIL sistema de enclavamiento controlado por computador *m* (*AmL*), sistema de enclavamiento controlado por computadora *m* (*AmL*), sistema de enclavamiento controlado por ordenador *m* (*Esp*); ~ **numerical control** *n* (*CNC*) COMP&DP, MECH ENG control numérico computerizado *m* (*CNC*); ~ **signal box** *n* RAIL cabina de cambio de agujas controlada por computadora *f* (*AmL*), cabina de cambio de agujas controlada por ordenador *f* (*Esp*); ~ **signaling equipment** *AmE*, ~ **signalling equipment** *BrE n* RAIL equipo de señalización por computadora *m* (*AmL*), equipo de señalización por ordenador *m* (*Esp*)

computer-PBX: ~ **interface** *n* (*CPI*) COMP&DP, TELECOM interfaz computador-PBX *m* (*AmL*), interfaz computadora-PBX *m* (*AmL*), interfaz ordenador-PBX *m* (*Esp*)

computing *n* COMP&DP, TELECOM computación *f* (*AmL*), informática *f* (*Esp*); ~ **device** *n* COMP&DP dispositivo de cálculo *m*, dispositivo de cómputo *m*, dispositivo informático *m*; ~ **facility** *n* COMP&DP instalación de cálculo *f*, instalación informática *f*, servicio de cómputo *m*; ~ **sciences** *n pl* COMP&DP, TELECOM informática *f*

CON *abbr* (*concentrator*) COMP&DP, ELECTRON, HEAT, TELECOM concentrador *m*

concatenate *vt* COMP&DP, ELEC ENG, ELECTRON, PRINT, TELECOM concatenar

concatenation *n* COMP&DP, ELEC ENG, ELECTRON, PRINT, TELECOM concatenación *f*; ~ **indication** *n* (*CI*) TELECOM indicación de concatenación *f*

concave *n* COAL cóncavo *m*, excavado *m*, hueco *m*; ~ **bow** *n* C&G arco cóncavo *m*; ~-**convex lens** *n* CINEMAT, INSTR, OPT, PHOTO, TV lente cóncava-convexa *f*; ~ **grating** *n* PHYS, SPACE rejilla cóncava *f*; ~ **lens** *n* CINEMAT, INSTR, MECH ENG, OPT, PHOTO lente cóncava *f*; ~ **mirror** *n* INSTR, PHYS espejo cóncavo *m*; ~ **optical tool** *n* C&G, OPT herramienta óptica cóncava *f*; ~ **surface** *n* GEOM superficie cóncava *f*; ~ **weld** *n* NUCL soldadura cóncava *f*

concealed[1] *adj* GEOL enterrado, oculto

concealed[2]: ~ **signal** *n* RAIL señal oculta *f*

concentrate[1] *n* AGRIC pienso concentrado *m*, COAL, FOOD concentrado *m*

concentrate[2] *vt* CHEM, CHEM TECH, COAL, FOOD concentrar

concentrated[1] *adj* CHEM, CHEM TECH, COAL, FOOD concentrado

concentrated[2]: ~ **sludge** *n* COAL cieno concentrado *m*, fango concentrado *m*, lodo concentrado *m*, sedimento concentrado *m*; ~ **solution** *n* CHEM solución concentrada *f*

concentrates: ~ **box** *n* METALL, MINE caja de concentrados *f*

concentrating: ~ **mirror** *n* INSTR espejo de concentración *m*; ~ **reflector** *n* INSTR reflector de concentración *m*; ~ **table** *n* COAL mesa concentradora *f*, mesa de concentración *f*

concentration *n* GEN concentración *f*; ~ **basin** *n* OCEAN cuenca de concentración *f*; ~ **cell** *n* ELEC pila de dos líquidos *f*; ~ **column** *n* CHEM TECH columna de concentración *f*; ~ **mortar** *n* MINE mortero concentrado *m* (*Esp*), mortero sin amalgamación interior *m* (*AmL*); ~ **network** *n* TELECOM red de concentración *f*; ~ **overvoltage** *n* SPACE sobretensión de concentración *f*; ~ **ratio** *n* COAL coeficiente de concentración *m*, FUELLESS relación de concentración *f*; ~ **stage** *n* TELECOM etapa de concentración *f*

concentrator *n* (*CON*) COMP&DP, ELECTRON concentrador *m*, FUELLESS dispositivo concentrador *m*, HEAT concentrador *m*, MINE transformador concentrador *m*, instalación para concentrar minerales *f*, TELECOM concentrador *m*

concentric[1] *adj* CONST, ELEC, GEOL, GEOM, MATH, MECH concéntrico

concentric[2]: ~ **circle** *n* GEOM círculo concéntrico *m*; ~ **conductor** *n* ELEC *cable* conductor concéntrico *m*; ~ **dike** *n* GEOL falla concéntrica *f*; ~ **folds** *n pl* GEOL pliegues concéntricos *m pl*; ~ **Fresnel lens** *n* INSTR, OPT lente concéntrica de Fresnel *f*; ~ **loading** *n* CONST carga concéntrica *f*; ~ **magazine** *n* CINEMAT chasis concéntrico *m*; ~ **optical cable** *n* OPT, TELECOM, TV cable óptico concéntrico *m*; ~ **pipe** *n* GAS tubería concéntrica *f*; ~ **track** *n* OPT pista concéntrica *f*; ~ **winding** *n* ELEC *of a machine, transformer* devanado de bobinas concéntricas *m*

concentrically: ~-**stranded circular conductor** *n* ELEC *cable* conductor circular trenzado concéntricamente *m*

concentricity *n* MECH concentricidad *f*; ~ **tolerance** *n* MECH tolerancia de concentricidad *f*

conceptual *adj* COMP&DP conceptual

concertina: ~ **fold** *n* PRINT plegado en acordeón *m*, plegado en zigzag *m*

concession *n* PETR TECH concesión *f*

conche *vt* FOOD conchar

conchoidal: ~ **fracture** *n* C&G fractura concoidal *f*, fractura concoide f, CRYSTALL fractura concoide f, fractura concoidal f

concordance n COMP&DP conformidad f, OCEAN screen concordancia f

concourse n HYDROL afluencia f, TRANSP marquesina f, sala de espera f, confluencia f, convergencia f, WATER afluencia f

concrete[1] n C&G, CONST concreto m (AmL), hormigón m (Esp); ~ **apron** n HYDROL batiente de concrete m (AmL), batiente de hormigón m (Esp), plataforma de concreto f (AmL), plataforma de hormigón f (Esp); ~ **base** n GEOPHYS base concreta f; ~ **batching and mixing plant** n CONST planta de concreto f (AmL), planta de hormigón f (Esp); ~ **block** n C&G, CONST bloque de concreto m (AmL), bloque de hormigón m (Esp); ~ **breaker** n CONST rompedor de concreto m (AmL), rompedor de hormigón m (Esp); ~ **coating** n COATINGS, COLOUR, PETROL recubrimiento de concreto m (AmL), recubrimiento de hormigón m (Esp), revestimiento de concreto m (AmL), revestimiento de hormigón m (Esp); ~ **durability** n CONST durabilidad del concreto f (AmL), durabilidad del hormigón f (Esp); ~ **enamel** n COLOUR esmalte de concreto m (AmL), esmalte de hormigón m (Esp); ~ **lining** n COATINGS, CONST revestimiento de concreto m (AmL), revestimiento de hormigón m (Esp); ~ **masonry** n CONST obra de fábrica de concreto f (AmL), obra de fábrica de hormigón f (Esp); ~ **mixer** n COAL, CONST, MECH ENG hormigonera f; ~ **pile** n COAL pilote de hormigón armado m; ~ **pipe** n CONST tubería de concreto f (AmL), tubería de hormigón f (Esp); ~ **platform** n PETR TECH plataforma de cemento f, plataforma de concreto f (AmL), plataforma de hormigón f (Esp); ~ **ring** n CONST anillo de concreto m (AmL), anillo de hormigón m (Esp); ~ **roofing tile** n CONST placa de cubierta de concreto f (AmL), placa de cubierta de hormigón f (Esp), techo de concreto m (AmL), techo de hormigón m (Esp); ~ **saw** n CONST sierra para concreto f (AmL), sierra para hormigón f (Esp); ~ **scraper** n TRANSP escariador de concreto m (AmL), escariador de hormigón m (Esp), excavadora de hormigón f, rascadora de concreto f (AmL), rascadora de hormigón f (Esp); ~ **sleeper** n BrE (cf concrete tie AmE) CONST, RAIL durmiente de concreto m (AmL), durmiente de hormigón m (Esp), traviesa de concreto f (AmL), traviesa de hormigón f (Esp); ~ **structure** n CONST estructura de concreto f (AmL), estructura de hormigón f (Esp); ~ **tie** n AmE (cf concrete sleeper BrE) CONST, RAIL durmiente de concreto m (AmL), durmiente de hormigón m (Esp), traviesa de concreto f (AmL), traviesa de hormigón f (Esp); ~ **work** n CONST hormigonado m (Esp), obra de hormigón f (Esp), obra de concreto f (AmL)

concrete[2] vt CONST hormigonar (Esp), concretar (AmL), to form into a mass verter hormigón

concreting n CONST hormigonado m; ~ **train** n RAIL tren de hormigonado m

concretion n GEOL, PETR TECH, PETROL concreción f

concurrent[1] adj COMP&DP simultáneo

concurrent[2]: ~ **execution** n COMP&DP ejecución concurrente f, ejecución simultánea f; ~ **lines** n pl GEOM líneas concordantes f pl, rectas concordantes f pl; ~ **processing** n COMP&DP, ELECTRON procesamiento simultáneo m, proceso concurrente m

concussion: ~ **table** n MECH ENG mesa de sacudidas f

condensable[1] adj CHEM, GAS, PHYS condensable

condensable[2]: ~ **gas** n GAS gas condensable m

condensate n GEN condensado; ~ **gas** n GAS gas de condensado m; ~ **gas reservoir** n GAS yacimiento de gas condensado m; ~ **line** n REFRIG conducto del condensado m; ~ **polishing system** n NUCL sistema de purificación del condensado m; ~ **system** n NUCL sistema del condensado m; ~ **well** n GAS pozo de condensado m

condensating: ~ **pump** n CHEM TECH bomba de condensación f

condensation n GEN condensación f; ~ **by injection** n CHEM TECH condensación por inyección f; ~ **by surface cooling** n CHEM TECH condensación por enfriamiento superficial f; ~ **calorimeter** n CHEM TECH calorímetro por condensación m; ~ **column** n CHEM TECH columna de condensación f; ~ **hygrometer** n CHEM TECH higrómetro de condensación m, higrómetro de punto de rocío m; ~ **nucleus** n METEO, POLL núcleo de condensación m; ~ **nucleus counter** n METEO, POLL contador de núcleos de condensación m; ~ **polymer** n P&R polímero por condensación m; ~ **polymerization** n P&R polimerización por condensación f; ~ **trail** n AIR TRANSP estela de condensación f; ~ **trap** n CHEM TECH colector de condensación m

condense vt GEN condensar

condensed[1] adj GEN condensado

condensed[2]: ~ **face** n PRINT tipo estrecho m; ~ **ring** n CHEM anillo condensado m; ~ **sequence** n GEOL secuencia condensada f; ~ **system** n CHEM TECH sistema condensado m

condenser n GEN condensador m, refrigerante m; ~ **adjustment knob** n INSTR, PHOTO botón de reglaje de la lente condensadora m; ~ **discharge exploder** n MINE detonador por descarga del condensador m; ~ **heat** n REFRIG calor cedido en el condensador m, potencia del condensador f; ~ **hotwell** n NUCL cámara caliente del condensador f; ~ **lamp** n CINEMAT, PHOTO, TV lámpara condensadora f; ~ **lens** n CINEMAT, INSTR, OPT, PHOTO lente condensadora de luz f; ~ **microphone** n ACOUST micrófono de condensador m; ~ **system** n PHOTO sistema condensador m

condensing n TELECOM condensación f; ~ **lens** n CINEMAT, INSTR, OPT, PHOTO lente condensadora f, objetivo condensador m; ~ **plant** n CHEM TECH planta de condensación f; ~ **pressure** n REFRIG presión de condensación f; ~ **trap** n LAB sequence trampa de condensación f; ~ **turbine** n HEAT turbina de condensación f; ~ **unit** n REFRIG grupo compresor-condensador m

condition[1] n COMP&DP condición f; ~ **-based maintenance** n QUALITY mantenimiento basado en condiciones m; ~ **instruction** n PROD instrucción de condición f, instrucción de situación f

condition[2] vt COAL tratar

conditional[1] adj COMP&DP condicional m

conditional[2]: ~ **expression** n COMP&DP expresión condicional f; ~ **instability** n METEO inestabilidad condicional f; ~ **instruction** n COMP&DP instrucción condicional f; ~ **jump** n COMP&DP salto condicional m

conditionally[1]: ~ **mandatory** adj (CM) TELECOM condicionalmente obligatorio

conditionally[2]: ~ **unstable unsaturated layer** *n* METEO capa condicionalmente inestable sin saturar *f*

conditioned *adj* TEXTIL acondicionado

conditioning *n* C&G acondicionamiento *m*, DETERG tratamiento *m*, ELECTRON acontecimiento *m*, HYDROL tratamiento *m*, P&R acondicionamiento *m*, POLL *communications* tratamiento *m*, PRINT acondicionamiento *m*; ~ **instruction** *n* PROD instrucción de acondicionamiento *f*; ~ **tank** *n* COAL tanque de humidificación *m*; ~ **zone** *n* C&G zona de acondicionamiento *f*

conditions: ~ **for dynamic similarity of two flows** *n pl* FLUID condiciones para la semejanza dinámica de dos flujos *f pl*; ~ **of testing** *n pl* PACK condiciones *f pl*

conductance *n* ELEC, ELEC ENG, ELECTRON, PHYS, TELECOM conductancia *f*; ~ **bridge** *n* ELEC, ELEC ENG, PHYS puente de conductancia *m*; ~ **cell** *n* ELECTRON, LAB celda conductimétrica *f*, cuba conductimétrica *f*

conducted: ~ **spurious emission** *n* TELECOM emisión espuria conducida *f*, emisión parásita conducida *f*

conductimetric: ~ **titration** *n* CHEM titulación conductimétrica *f*, valoración conductimétrica *f*

conducting[1] *adj* ELEC *property* en estado de conducción

conducting[2]: ~ **state** *n* ELECTRON volumen conductor *m*; ~ **zone** *n* ELEC ENG zona de conducción *f*

conduction *n* GEN conducción *f*; ~ **angle** *n* ELEC ENG ángulo conductivo *m*; ~ **band** *n* (*CB*) PHYS, RAD PHYS banda de conducción *f* (*BC*); ~ **charge** *n* ELEC, PHYS carga de conducción *f*; ~ **current** *n* ELEC, PHYS corriente conductiva *f*, corriente de conducción *f*; ~ **heater** *n* MECH ENG, THERMO calentador por conducción *m*; ~ **pump** *n* ELEC ENG accionador conductivo *m*

conductive: ~ **grease** *n* SPACE lubricante conductor *m*; ~ **lacquer** *n* COATINGS laca conductora *f*; ~ **varnish** *n* COATINGS barniz con propiedades conductoras *m*

conductivity *n* GEN conductividad *f*; ~ **meter** *n* LAB conductibilímetro *m* (*AmL*), conductímetro *m* (*Esp*); ~ **modulation** *n* ELECTRON modulación de conductividad *f*

conductor *n* ELEC conductor *m*, conductor electrónico *m*, hilo conductor *m*, ELEC ENG canalón *m*, conducto *m*, hilo conductor *m*, macarrón *m*, PETR TECH conductor *m*, tubería de revestimiento *f*, PHYS conductor *m*, RAIL conductor *m*, jefe de tren *m*, TELECOM conductor *m*; ~ **pipe** *n* MINE tubo conductor *m*, tubo guía *m*; ~ **rail** *n* ELEC, ELEC ENG, RAIL carril conductor *m*, rail conductor *m*; ~ **screen** *n* ELEC, ELEC ENG pantalla conductora *f*; ~ **wire** *n* ELEC, ELEC ENG hilo conductor *m*

conduit *n* CONST acueducto *m*, conducto *m*, ELEC *supply* canaleta por la que pasa el cableado *f*, conducto *m*, conducto para cables *m*, tubería para conductores *f*, ELEC ENG tubo de protección de cables *m*, conducto portacables *m*, tubo aislante *m*, FUELLESS, HYDROL conducto *m*, acueducto *m*, PROD conducto portacables *m*, WATER cañería *f*, acueducto *m*, conducto *m*, tubería *f*; ~ **box** *n* ELEC ENG caja de derivaciones *f*, caja de distribución *f*, caja de empalmes *f pl*; ~ **capacity** *n* FUELLESS capacidad de conducto *f*; ~ **entry** *n* PROD entrada del conducto *f*; ~ **hub** *n* PROD eje del conducto *m*; ~ **pipe** *n* CONST tubería *f*

condurrite *n* MINERAL condurrita *f*

cone *n* C&G cono *m*, embudo *m*, ELECTRON, GEOM, GEOPHYS, MATH cono *m*, MECH ENG cono *m*, polea de cono *f*, tobera de inyector *f*, PROD *of a blast furnace* tolva *f*, SPACE, TEXTIL, TV cono *m*; ~ **bit** *n* MECH ENG escariador cónico *m*, PETR TECH barrena cónica *f* (*Esp*), mecha cónica *f* (*AmL*), trépano cónico *m* (*AmL*); ~ **classifier** *n* COAL, PROD *for ore* clasificador cónico *m*; ~ **clutch** *n* AUTO, MECH ENG, VEH embrague cónico *m*, embrague de cono *m*; ~ **countersink** *n* MECH, MECH ENG, PROD avellanador cónico *m*; ~ **crusher** *n* COAL quebrantadora de conos *f*, trituradora de conos *f*; ~ **cut** *n* MINE corte en cono *m*; ~ **delta** *n* GEOL cono aluvial *m*; ~ **drive** *n* MECH ENG impulsor de conos de fricción *m*, mando por conos de fricción *m*, motor de conos de fricción *m*; ~ **drum** *n* MECH ENG tambor cónico *m*; ~ **for overhead motion** *n* MECH ENG cono de sobre cabeza *m*, cono para transmisión alta *m*; ~ **gear** *n* MECH ENG mecanismo de conos de fricción *m*, polea cónica *f*, transmisión por conos de fricción *f*; ~**-head rivet** *n* CONST remache de cabeza cónica *m*, remache de cabeza de cono truncado *m*; ~ **light** *n* ELEC proyector intensificador *m*; ~ **pliers** *n pl* MECH ENG alicates cónicos *m pl*, tenazas cónicas *f pl*; ~ **pulley** *n* MECH ENG polea de cono *f*, polea escalonada *f*; ~**-pulley drive** *n* MECH ENG impulsor de polea cónica *m*, transmisor de polea escalonada *m*; ~ **of revolution** *n* GEOM cono de revolución *m*; ~ **sampler** *n* COAL muestra cónica *f*; ~ **separator** *n* COAL embudo de decantación *m*; ~ **sheave** *n* MECH ENG garrucha *f*, polea acanalada cónica *f*, polea acanalada escalonada *f*, roldana *f*; ~ **of silence** *n* MECH ENG cono de silencio *m*; ~ **and socket joint** *n* LAB *circuits* junta cónica, macho y hembra *f* (*Esp*), junta de cono y socket *f* (*AmL*), junta tipo Quickfit *f* (*AmL*); ~ **tube** *n* TEXTIL tubo cónico *m*; ~ **union body** *n* MECH ENG cuerpo de acoplamiento *m*, cuerpo de unión del cono *m*, unión cónica *f*; ~ **valve** *n* HYDRAUL válvula cónica *f*; ~ **wheel** *n* MECH ENG rueda cónica *f*

confectionery: ~ **mold** *AmE*, ~ **mould** *BrE* *n* MECH ENG molde de panadero *m*

conference: ~ **bridge** *n* TELECOM puente de conferencia *m*; ~ **call** *n* TELECOM comunicación colectiva *f*; ~**-call chairman** *n* TELECOM coordinador de comunicación colectiva *m*; ~**-call chairperson** *n* TELECOM coordinador de comunicación colectiva *m*; ~ **network** *n* TV red de comunicación colectiva *f*

confidence: ~ **interval** *n* COMP&DP, MATH *statistics* intervalo de confianza *m*

confidentiality *n* TELECOM confidencialidad *f*

configuration *n* COMP&DP, ELECTRON, SPACE, TELECOM configuración *f*; ~ **control** *n* PROD control de configuración *m*; ~ **management** *n* (*CM*) COMP&DP administración de configuración *f*, gestión de configuración *f*; ~ **plug** *n* PROD tapón de configuración *m*; ~ **space** *n* GEOM, PHYS espacio de configuración *m*

configurational: ~ **entropy** *n* METALL entropía configuracional *f*

configure *vt* COMP&DP configurar

confined: ~ **aquifer** *n* GEOL, HYDROL, WATER acuífero cerrado *m*; ~ **ground water** *n* COAL, HYDROL, WATER agua artesiana *f*, agua de profundidad limitada *f*; ~ **space** *n* SAFE espacio cerrado *m*

confinement *n* AGRIC *of livestock* encierro *m*, MINE confinamiento *m*, limitación *f*, PETR TECH limitación *f*, restricción *f*, PHYS confinamiento *m*

confirm[1] *n* TELECOM confirmación *f*
confirm[2] *vt* TELECOM confirmar
confirmation *n* TELECOM confirmación *f*
confirmed: ~ **service** *n* TELECOM servicio confirmado *m*
conflicting: ~ **traffic flow** *n* TRANSP afluencia de tráfico encontrada *f*, afluencia de tráficos opuestos *f*
confluence *n* HYDROL, WATER afluencia *f*, confluencia *f*
confluent[1] *adj* HYDROL, WATER confluente
confluent[2] *n* HYDROL, WATER afluente *m*
conform *vt* CINEMAT conformar; ~ **in shape to** *vt* PROD ajustarse a la forma de
conformal: ~ **aerial** *n* BrE (*cf conformal antenna AmE*) SPACE *communications* antena conformada *f*, antena conforme *f*; ~ **antenna** *n* AmE (*cf conformal aerial BrE*) SPACE *communications* antena conformada *f*, antena conforme *f*
conformance *n* COMP&DP conformidad *f*; ~ **statement** *n* PROD declaración de conformidad *f*
conformer *n* CINEMAT conformador *m*
conformity *n* GEOL conformidad *f*, PETR TECH concordancia *f*, QUALITY conformidad *f*; ~ **test** *n* QUALITY prueba de conformidad *f*
confused: ~ **sea** *n* WATER TRANSP *weather* mar confuso *m*
confusion: ~ **cone** *n* AIR TRANSP cono de confusión *m*; ~ **message** *n* TELECOM mensaje de confusión *m*
congealing: ~ **point** *n* FLUID punto de congelación *m*
congestion *n* COAL aglomeración *f*, congestión *f*, TELECOM congestión *f*
conglomerate *n* CONST, FUELLESS, GEOL aglomerado *m*, conglomerado *m*, PETR TECH, PETROL conglomerado *m*, pudinga *f*
congruence: ~ **arithmetic** *n* MATH aritmética congruente *f*
congruent[1] *adj* MATH, GEOM congruente
congruent[2]: ~ **triangle** *n* GEOM triángulo congruente *m*
Coniacian *adj* GEOL Coniaciense
conic[1] *adj* GEOM, TEXTIL cónico
conic[2] *n* GEOM cónica *f*
conical: ~ **beaker** *n* LAB vaso cónico *m*; ~ **buoy** *n* WATER TRANSP *navigation marks* boya cónica *f*; ~ **clamping connection** *n* MECH ENG *pipe fitting* conexión cónica *f*, unión de asiento cónico *f*; ~ **flask** *n* LAB matraz Erlenmeyer *m*, matraz cónico *m*; ~ **gear** *n* MECH ENG engranaje cónico *m*; ~ **ground glass point** *n* LAB junta cónica de vidrio esmerilado *f*; ~ **horn** *n* ACOUST bocina cónica *f*; ~ **mill** *n* COAL chimenea cónica *f*; ~ **projection** *n* GEOM proyección cónica *f*; ~ **refiner** *n* PAPER refino cónico *m*; ~ **reinforced rim** *n* C&G orilla cónica reforzada *f*; ~ **-seat valve** *n* HYDRAUL válvula de asiento cónico *f*; ~ **shaft end** *n* MECH ENG extremo cónico del eje *m*; ~ **shell** *n* SPACE chapa cónica *f*, célula cónica *f*; ~ **sieve** *n* FOOD chino *m*, colador cónico *m*; ~ **snoot** *n* CINEMAT aditamento cónico *m*; ~ **spacer** *n* MECH ENG aro cónico *m*, espaciador cónico *m*, separador cónico *m*; ~ **surface** *n* GEOM superficie cónica *f*; ~ **tubing** *n* CONST *tube made in sections or lengths* tubo en virolas *m*
conics *n* GEOM *sheet of paper* cónica *f*
coniferin *n* CHEM coniferina *f*
coniine *n* CHEM conicina *f*, coniína *f*
conine *n* CHEM conina *f*

coning: ~ **angle** *n* AIR TRANSP *helicopter* ángulo de conicidad *m*
conjoined: ~ **pitches** *n pl* ACOUST alturas tonales conjuntas *f pl*, tonos conjuntos *m pl*
conjugacy *n* GEOM, MATH, PHYS conjugación *f*, conjugancia *f*
conjugate[1] *adj* GEOM, MATH, PHYS conjugada
conjugate[2] *n* GEOM, MATH, PHYS conjugado *m*; ~ **branch** *n* ELEC ENG rama conjugada *f*; ~ **impedances** *n pl* ACOUST impedancias conjugadas *f pl*; ~ **jointing** *n* GEOL fisuración conjugada *f*; ~ **plane** *n* METALL, MATH plano conjugado *m*; ~ **points** *n pl* PHYS puntos conjugados *m pl*; ~ **slip** *n* METALL deslizamiento conjugado *m*
conjugated *adj* CHEM *compound, bond*, MATH conjugado
conjugation *n* CHEM *of a compound, bond*, MATH conjugación *f*
conjunction *n* COMP&DP conjunción *f*, ELECTRON unión *f*
conn *n* WATER TRANSP *piloting* gobernador *m*
connate: ~ **water** *n* GEN agua de formación *f*, agua fósil *f*, agua intersticial *f*, agua nativa *f*, agua singenética *f*,
connect[1]: ~ **confirm** *n* (*CC*) TELECOM confirmación de conexión *f*; ~ **data overflow** *n* (*CDO*) TELECOM conexión de sobrecarga de datos *f*; ~ **and disconnect signaling** AmE, ~ **and disconnect signalling** BrE *n* TELECOM señalización de conexión y desconexión *f*; ~ **time** *n* COMP&DP tiempo de conexión *m*
connect[2] *vt* CINEMAT conectar, COMP&DP conectar, enlazar, ELEC, ELEC ENG enlazar, *communications* enlazar, *device* acoplar, *in series, parallel etc* conectar, *several components* empalmar, PHYS, PROD conectar; ~ **in parallel** *vt* ELEC, ELEC ENG acoplar en paralelo; ~ **in series** *vt* ELEC, ELEC ENG acoplar en serie; ~ **up** *vt* ELEC, ELEC ENG conectar
connected[1] *adj* COMP&DP, ELEC, ELEC ENG conectado, MECH ENG conectado, unido, acoplado, PHYS conectado; ~ **in parallel** *adj* ELEC, ELEC ENG, PHYS conectado en paralelo; ~ **in series** *adj* ELEC, ELEC ENG, PHYS conectado en serie; ~ **to the current** *adj* AmE (*cf connected to the mains BrE*) ELEC *installation*, ELEC ENG conectado a la corriente, conectado a la línea de alimentación, conectado a la red eléctrica, conectado a la red principal; ~ **to earth** *adj* BrE (*cf connected to ground AmE*) ELEC ENG conectado a toma de tierra; ~ **to ground** *adj* AmE (*cf connected to earth BrE*) ELEC ENG conectado a toma de tierra, situado a tierra; ~ **to the mains** *adj* BrE (*cf connected to the current AmE*) ELEC *installation*, ELEC ENG conectado a la corriente, conectado a la línea de alimentación, conectado a la red eléctrica, conectado a la red principal
connected[2]: ~ **data set to line** *n* TELECOM datos conectados preparados para línea *m pl*; ~ **-line identification presentation** *n* (*COLP*) TELECOM presentación de identificación de línea conectada *f*; ~ **-line identification restriction** *n* (*COLR*) TELECOM restricción de identificación de línea conectada *f*; ~ **-line identity** *n* (*COLI*) TELECOM identidad de línea conectada *f*; ~ **-line identity request indicator** *n* TELECOM indicador de solicitud de identidad de línea conectada *m*; ~ **network** *n* ELEC *supply*, ELEC ENG red conexa *f*
connecting: ~ **-brake lever rods** *n pl* MECH ENG

palanca de freno de conexión *f*; ~ **cable** *n* CINEMAT, ELEC ENG, PHOTO, TV cable de conexión *m*; ~ **cord** *n* CINEMAT, ELEC ENG, PHOTO cable de conexión *m*; ~ **dimensions** *n pl* MECH ENG dimensiones de conexión *f pl*; ~ **dimensions of chucks** *n pl* MECH ENG dimensiones de conexión del manguito portaherramientas *f pl*, dimensiones de conexión del plato *f pl*, dimensiones de conexión del portabrocas *f pl*; ~ **flange** *n* SPACE brida conectora *f*, reborde conector *m*; ~ **lead** *n* ELEC ENG cable de conexión *m*; ~ **link** *n* MECH ENG *shackle of clevis* grillete de unión *m*, *split mending-link* eslabón de unión *m*; ~ **rod** *n* AIR TRANSP barra de conexión *f*, AUTO biela *f*, MECH, MECH ENG barra de conexión *f*, barra de unión *f*, biela *f*, varilla de conexión *f*, varilla de maniobra *f*, varilla de unión *f*, RAIL varilla de maniobra *f*, VEH, WATER TRANSP *alternative engine* biela *f*; ~-**rod bearing** *n* AUTO, MECH ENG cojinete de biela *m*; ~-**rod big end** *n* AUTO, MECH ENG, VEH cabeza de biela *f*; ~-**rod with box end** *n* AUTO, MECH ENG, VEH biela con cabeza de caja cerrada *f*; ~-**rod cap** *n* AUTO, MECH ENG, VEH sombrerete de biela *m*; ~-**rod end** *n* AUTO, MECH ENG, VEH cabeza de biela *f*; ~-**rod with fork end** *n* AUTO, MECH ENG, VEH biela con cabeza en horquilla *f*; ~-**rod of infinite length** *n* MECH ENG barra de conexión de longitud infinita *f*, varilla de conexión de longitud infinita *f*; ~-**rod shank** *n* AUTO, MECH ENG, VEH cuerpo de biela *m*; ~-**rod small end** *n* AUTO, MECH ENG, VEH pie de biela *m*; ~-**rod with strap end** *n* AUTO, MECH ENG, VEH biela con cabeza de caja *f*; ~ **scene** *n* CINEMAT escena de transición *f*; ~ **screw** *n* MECH ENG tornillo de conexión *m*, tornillo de unión *m*; ~ **shaft** *n* AIR TRANSP eje de conexión *m*; ~ **skirt** *n* SPACE faldón conector *m*; ~ **terminal** *n* ELEC *of cable, connection*, ELEC ENG terminal de conexión *m*; ~ **train** *n* RAIL tren de conexión *m*; ~ **tunnel** *n* SPACE túnel de conexión *m*; ~ **twin-yoke** *n* AIR TRANSP brida doble de conexión *f*, horquilla doble de conexión *f*, yugo doble de conexión *m*; ~ **wire** *n* ELEC, ELEC ENG cable de conexión *m*, hilo de conexión *m*

connection *n* COMP&DP conexión *f*, CONST conexión *f*, *pipes* acoplamiento *m*, *union of wires, tubes* empalme *m*, unión *f*, ELEC *circuit* conexión *f*, acometida *f*, contacto *m*, ELEC ENG *of conductors* contacto *m*, conexión *f*, acometida *f*, montaje *m*, GAS conexión *f*, MECH ENG acoplamiento *m*, acople *m*, conexión *f*, unión *f*, PHYS, TELECOM conexión *f*; ~ **between two shafts** *n* MECH ENG conexión entre dos ejes *f*; ~ **box** *n* ELEC ENG caja de conexiones *f*; ~ **diagram** *n* ELEC ENG diagrama de conexiones *m*, esquema de montaje *m*; ~ **element** *n* (*CE*) TELECOM elemento de conexiones *m*; ~ **gas** *n* (*CG*) PETR TECH gas de conexión *m*; ~ **matrix** *n* (*CM*) TELECOM matriz de conexión *f*; ~ **port** *n* MECH ENG abertura de conexión *f*, lumbrera de conexión *f*, orificio de conexión *m*; ~-**related function** *n* (*CRF*) TELECOM función relacionada con la conexión *f*; ~ **request** *n* (*CR*) TELECOM petición de comunicación *f*, solicitud de conexión *f*; ~ **strip** *n* TELECOM regleta de conexión *f*; ~ **to earth** *n* BrE (*cf connection to ground AmE*) ELEC ENG toma a tierra *f*, unión a tierra *f*; ~ **to ground** *n* AmE (*cf connection to earth BrE*) ELEC ENG unión a tierra *f*, toma a tierra *f*

connectionless[1] *adj* TELECOM sin conexiones

connectionless[2]: ~ **bearer service** *n* TELECOM servicio portador sin conexiones *m*; ~ **broadband data service** *n* (*CBDS*) TELECOM servicio de datos de banda ancha sin conexiones *m*; ~ **convergence protocol** *n* (*CLCP*) TELECOM protocolo de convergencia sin conexiones *m*; ~ **mode network service** *n* TELECOM servicio de red sin conexiones *m*; ~ **mode transmission** *n* TELECOM transmisión sin conexiones *f*; ~ **network layer protocol** *n* (*CLNP*) TELECOM protocolo a nivel de red sin conexiones *m*; ~ **network layer service** *n* (*CLNS*) TELECOM servicio a nivel de red sin conexiones *m*; ~ **server** *n* (*CLS*) TELECOM servidor sin conexiones *m*; ~ **service function** *n* (*CLSF*) TELECOM función de servicio sin conexiones *f*

connective *n* COMP&DP conectivo *m*, conjuntivo *m*

connectivity *n* COMP&DP conectividad *f*

connector *n* CHEM, CINEMAT, COMP&DP conector *m*, ELEC ENG empalme *m*, LAB, TELECOM conector *m*, VEH conector *m*, racor *m*; **out-~** *n* COMP&DP conector de salida *m*, TELECOM conector fuera de circuito *m*, conector fuera de servicio *m*; ~ **socket** *n* ELEC ENG hembra del enchufe *f*; ~ **socket for trailer** *n* AUTO, ELEC alvéolo conector para remolques *m*, enchufe conector para remolques *m*

connexion: ~ **gas** *n* (*CG*) GAS gas de conexión *m*

conning: ~ **tower** *n* WATER TRANSP *submarine* torreta de control *f*

conscience *n* PROD *breastplate* placa de pecho *f*

consecutive[1] *adj* COMP&DP, TELECOM consecutivo

consecutive[2]: ~ **error block** *n* (*CEB*) TELECOM bloque de errores consecutivos *m*; ~ **identical digits** *n pl* (*CID*) TELECOM dígitos idénticos consecutivos *m pl*

conservation *n* OPT conservación *f*, PETR TECH conservación *f*, preservación *f*, PETROL, THERMO conservación *f*; ~ **of brightness** *n* OPT, PHYS, TELECOM conservación del brillo *f*; ~ **of charge** *n* PHYS conservación de la carga *f*; ~ **of energy** *n* PHYS conservación de la energía *f*; ~ **of mass** *n* PHYS conservación de la masa *f*; ~ **of momentum** *n* PHYS conservación de la cantidad de movimiento lineal *f*; ~ **of parity** *n* PHYS conservación de la paridad *f*; ~ **of radiance** *n* OPT, PHYS, TELECOM conservación de la radiancia *f*; ~ **tillage** *n* AGRIC labranza conservacionista *f*

conservationist *adj* AGRIC conservacionista

conservative: ~ **estimate** *n* PROD evaluación prudente *f*; ~ **force** *n* PHYS fuerza conservativa *f*; ~ **plate margin** *n* GEOL margen de placa no-destructivo *m*

consigned: ~ **component** *n* PROD componente consignado *m*

consignment *n* PROD remesa *f*

consignor *n* PROD consignador *m*, consignatario *m*

consistency *n* COAL compatibilidad *f*, consecuencia *f*, consistencia *f*, COMP&DP coherencia *f*, consistencia *f*, uniformidad *f*, FOOD consistencia *f*, PAPER consistencia *f*, densidad *f*; ~ **index** *n* COAL índice de consistencia *m*; ~ **limit** *n* COAL límite de consistencia *m*; ~ **regulator** *n* PAPER regulador de consistencia *m*

console *n* AIR TRANSP consola *f*, panel de mandos *m*, puesto de control *m*, tablero de mandos *m*, COMP&DP consola *f*, ELEC *control* consola *f*, pupitre de control *m*, pupitre de mando *m*, WATER TRANSP *electronic equipment* consola de control *f*; ~ **air conditioning unit** *n* REFRIG acondicionador mural *m*

consolidated: ~ **link-layer management message** *n* (*CLLM*) TELECOM mensaje de gestión consolidada de enlace entre capas *m*

consolidation *n* COAL, PETR TECH, PETROL, TRANSP consolidación *f*, reducción del volumen y aumento de densidad *f*; ~ **test** *n* COAL, PETR TECH, PETROL ensayo de consolidación *m*, prueba de consolidación *f*

consonance *n* ACOUST consonancia *f*

constant[1] *adj* COMP&DP, ELECTRON, MATH, MECH, PHYS constante

constant[2] *n* COMP&DP, ELECTRON, MATH, MECH, PHYS constante *f*, invariante *f*; **~-amplitude mechanical reading** *n* ACOUST lectura mecánica de amplitud constante *f*; **~-amplitude modulation** *n* ELECTRON modulación de amplitud constante *f*; ~ **angular velocity** *n* (*CAV*) COMP&DP, OPT velocidad angular constante *f*; ~ **angular velocity disc** *BrE*,~ **angular velocity disk** *n* *AmE* OPT disco de velocidad angular constante *m*; ~ **bit rate** *n* TELECOM tasa de bits constante *f*; ~ **boiling mixture** *n* CHEM mezcla azeotrópica *f*; ~ **current** *n* ELEC, ELEC ENG intensidad constante *f*; **~-current dynamo** *n* ELEC, ELEC ENG *generator* dinamo de corriente constante *f*, dinamo de voltaje constante *f*; **~-current modulation** *n* ELEC, ELECTRON modulación de corriente constante *f*; **~-current oscillator** *n* ELECTRON oscilador de corriente constante *m*; **~-current transformer** *n* ELEC ENG transformador de amperaje constante *m*; ~ **delay line** *n* ELECTRON línea de temporización constante *f*; ~ **differential pressure** *n* AIR TRANSP presión diferencial constante *f*; ~ **duty** *n* ELEC *equipment* rendimiento constante *m*; ~ **failure rate period** *n* QUALITY período de falla a ritmo constante *m*; ~ **field** *n* ELEC campo constante *m*, campo inductor constante *m*; ~ **flow pump** *n* MECH ENG bomba de caudal constante *f*, bomba de desplazamiento positivo *f*, bomba de flujo constante *f*; ~ **line number operation** *n* TV operación por número de línea constante *f*; ~ **linear velocity** *n* (*CLV*) OPT velocidad lineal constante *f*; ~ **linear velocity disc** *BrE*, ~ **linear velocity disk** *n* *AmE* OPT disco de velocidad lineal constante *m*; ~ **load** *n* ELEC *of a machine* carga constante *f*; ~ **mesh** *n* VEH piñón de engranaje constante *m*; **~-mesh gears** *n* *pl* AUTO engranajes a conexión continua *m pl*; ~ **motor torque** *n* PROD momento torsional constante del motor *m*; ~ **percentage band width filter** *n* ELECTRON amplitud de filtro de banda de porcentaje constante *f*; **~-pressure operation** *n* SPACE funcionamiento a presión constante *m*, operación a presión constante *f*; ~ **rate** *n* TELECOM velocidad constante *f*; ~ **speed** *n* MECH, MECH ENG, PHYS, TRANSP velocidad constante *f*; **~-speed belt head** *n* PROD *lathe* cabezal de monopolea *m*; **~-speed drive** *n* MECH ENG impulsión de velocidad constante *f*, motor de velocidad constante *m*; **~-speed propeller** *n* AIR TRANSP hélice de velocidad constante *f*; **~-speed pulley** *n* PROD polea de velocidad constante *f*; ~ **temperature oven** *n* LAB, THERMO estufa de temperatura constante *f*, horno de temperatura constante *m*; **~-velocity mechanical reading** *n* ACOUST lectura mecánica de velocidad constante *f*; **~-velocity universal joint** *n* VEH junta homocinética *f*; ~ **voltage** *n* ELEC, ELEC ENG tensión constante *f*; **~-voltage dynamo** *n* ELEC *generator*, ELEC ENG dinamo de voltaje constante *f*; **~-voltage source** *n* ELEC fuente de tensión constante *f*, generador de voltaje constante *m*, ELEC ENG generador de voltaje constante *m*; **~-voltage transformer** *n* ELEC, PROD transformador de voltaje constante *m*; ~ **volume**

sampling *n* (*CVS*) POLL muestreo de volumen constante *m*

constantan *n* ELEC *thermocouple* constantan *m*

constitutive: ~ **alteration** *n* ACOUST alteración estructural *f*

constraint *n* COMP&DP limitación *f*

constricted: ~ **node** *n* METALL nodo estrechado *m*

constriction *n* METALL contracción *f*, encogimiento *m*; ~ **energy** *n* METALL energía de contracción *f*, potencia de contracción *f*; ~ **power** *n* METALL energía de contracción *f*

constringence *n* PHYS *materials* constringencia *f*

constructed: ~ **limestone** *n* GEOL caliza bioconstruida *f*

construction: ~ **joint** *n* CONST junta de construcción *f*; ~ **nozzle** *n* SPACE tobera de suspensión *f*; ~ **plan** *n* CONST plano constructivo *m*, plano de construcción *m*; ~ **program** *AmE*, ~ **programme** *BrE* *n* CONST plan de trabajos *m*, programa de construcción *m*, programa de obra *m*; ~ **schedule** *n* CONST plan de construcción *m*, programa de construcción *m*; ~ **sheet** *n* WATER TRANSP *ship or boat building* hoja de construcción *f*; ~ **site** *n* CONST lugar de construcción *m*, ubicación de la obra *f*; ~ **time** *n* CONST plazo de construcción *m*; ~ **water line** *n* CONST *boat building*, TRANSP, WATER TRANSP *boat building* línea de flotación de construcción *f*; ~ **work** *n* CONST trabajo de construcción *m*; ~ **yard** *n* WATER TRANSP *boat building* astillero *m*

constructional: ~ **defect** *n* CONST defecto de construcción *m*; ~ **features** *n* *pl* WATER TRANSP *shipbuilding* características constructivas *f pl*

constructive: ~ **interference** *n* PHYS, WAVE PHYS interferencia constructiva *f*; ~ **plate margin** *n* GEOL margen de placa constructivo *m*

consulting: ~ **engineer** *n* PROD ingeniero asesor *m*, ingeniero consultor *m*

consumable: ~ **electrode** *n* CONST electrodo consumible *m*, electrodo fungible *m*

consumer *n* ELEC, GAS, PACK, QUALITY, TEXTIL consumidor *m*; ~ **awareness** *n* TEXTIL conciencia de consumidor *f*; ~ **electronic equipment** *n* ELEC ENG equipo electrónico del usuario *m*; ~ **electronics** *n* ELECTRON electrónica para el consumidor *f*; ~ **goods** *n pl* PACK artículos de consumo *m pl*, bienes de consumo *m pl*; **~-goods sector** *n* PACK sector de bienes de consumo *m*

consumption *n* AUTO consumo *m*, gasto *m*, HYDROL consumo *m*, MECH, VEH consumo *m*, gasto *m*, WATER consumo *m*; ~ **deviation** *n* PROD desviación del consumo *f*; ~ **of smoke** *n* CHEM, COAL fumividad *f*; ~ **water** *n* HYDROL, WATER agua de consumo *f*

contact *n* AIR TRANSP, AUTO, COMP&DP, ELEC, ELEC ENG contacto *m*, GEOL contacto *m*, plano de separación *m*, P&R, PROD contacto *m*; ~ **adhesive** *n* P&R, PACK adhesivo de contacto *m*, autoadhesivo *m*; ~ **aerator** *n* HYDROL aireador por contacto *m*; ~ **angle** *n* COAL ángulo de abrazamiento *m*; ~ **arrangement** *n* ELEC ENG disposición de los contactos *f*; ~ **aureole** *n* GEOL aureola por contacto *f*; ~ **blade** *n* ELEC *relay* hoja de contacto *f*, lengüeta de contacto *f*, álabe de contacto *m*; ~ **block** *n* ELEC ENG bloque de contacto *m*; ~ **bounce** *n* ELEC *relay* capacidad de contacto *f*, contacto incierto *m*, rebote de contacto *m*, PROD rebote de contacto *m*; ~ **breaker** *n* AUTO, VEH ruptor *m*, WATER TRANSP *electrics* disyuntor *m*; ~ **breaker-**

point n (cf points AmE) AUTO, VEH platino del ruptor m, punto de interrupción de contacto m, ruptor m; ~ **button** n ELEC ENG pulsador de contacto m; ~ **chatter** n AUTO vibración de los contactos f, vibración de los platinos f, ELEC relay vibración del contacto f; ~ **column** n HYDROL tubo de purificación por contacto m; ~ **continuity** n ELEC, PROD continuidad de contacto f; ~ **detector** n TRANSP detector de contacto m; ~ **EMF** n ELEC between two metals, PHYS FEM de contacto f, potencial de contacto m; ~ **fault** n ELEC ENG defecto de contacto m; ~ **flight** n AIR TRANSP vuelo de contacto m; ~ **freezer** n REFRIG, THERMO congelador por contacto m; ~ **freezing** n REFRIG, THERMO congelación por contacto f; ~ **gap** n ELEC relay separación de contacto f; ~ **hardening** n REFRIG, THERMO endurecimiento por contacto m; ~ **heater** n MECH ENG, THERMO calentador de contacto m; ~ **histogram** n ELEC, PROD histograma de contactos m; ~ **icing** n REFRIG aplicación directa del hielo f; ~ **lens** n C&G lente de contacto f, INSTR lentilla de contacto f, OPT lente de contacto f; ~ **lithography** n ELECTRON, PRINT litografía de contacto f; ~ **log** n PETR TECH perfil de contacto m, registro de contacto m; ~ **mask** n ELECTRON capa de contacto f; ~ **masking** n ELECTRON tapado por contacto m; ~ **material** n PROD material de contacto m; ~ **metamorphism** n GEOL metamorfismo de contacto m; ~ **metasomatism** n GEOL metasomatismo de contacto m; ~ **microphone** n ACOUST micrófono de contacto m; ~ **molding** AmE, ~ **moulding** BrE n C&G moldeo por contacto m; ~ **negative** n PHOTO negativo de contacto m; ~ **noise suppression** n PROD eliminación de ruido de fritura f; ~ **pin** n ELEC ENG clavija de contacto f; ~ **point** n AIR TRANSP, MECH ENG punto de contacto m; ~ **point file** n MECH ENG lima de punto de contacto f; ~ **points gap** n AUTO, VEH separación de los contactos f, separación de los platinos f; ~ **poison** n AGRIC tóxico de contacto m; ~ **potential** n ELEC thermocouple potencial de contacto m; ~ **print** n CINEMAT, PHOTO, PRINT copia por contacto f; ~ **printer** n CINEMAT, PHOTO, PRINT impresora por contacto f, positivadora por contacto f; ~ **printing** n CINEMAT, PHOTO, PRINT impresión por contacto f; ~ **printing frame** n CINEMAT, PHOTO, PRINT bastidor para la impresión por contacto m, prensa de contactos f; ~ **profile meter** n MECH ENG medidor de perfil de contacto m; ~ **ramp** n RAIL fixed equipment rampa de acceso f; ~ **rating** n ELEC ENG clase de contacto f; ~ **resistance** n ELEC between two metals, ELEC ENG resistencia de contacto f; ~ **scanning** n COMP&DP exploración por contacto f; ~ **set** n AUTO, VEH juego de contactos del ruptor m, juego de platinos m; ~ **spring** n ELEC relay manantial resurgente m, muelle de contacto m, WATER manantial de desbordamiento m, manantial de ladera m, manantial resurgente m; ~ **twin** n CRYSTALL macla de contacto f, macla de yuxtaposición f; ~ **window** n ELEC ENG circuito periódico de contacto m

contactless: ~ **ignition** n BrE (cf pointless ignition AmE) AUTO encendido sin platinos m, ignición sin contactos f, ignición sin platinos f, VEH emendido sin platinos m, ignición sin contactos f, ignición sin platinos f; ~ **pickup** n BrE (cf pointless pickup AmE) ELEC transductor sin contactos m; ~ **support vehicle** n TRANSP vehículo aislado de apoyo m; ~ **transistor-**

ized ignition n BrE (cf pointless transistorized ignition AmE) AUTO arranque transistorizado sin platinos m, ignición transistorizada sin platinos f

contactor n ELEC relay, ELEC ENG conjuntor m, contactor m, interruptor automático m; ~ **with overload relay** n ELEC, ELEC ENG, PROD contactor con relé de máxima m, contactor con relé de sobrecarga m; ~ **starter** n AUTO, ELEC, ELEC ENG, VEH arrancador contactor m, dispositivo de arranque contactor m

container n (CT) AGRIC for fertilizers, pesticides recipiente m, COAL envase m, depósito m, cubeta f, PACK recipiente m, contenedor m, TELECOM contenedor m, TRANSP contenedor m, cisterna f, depósito m; ~ **of the beaker type** n PROD cuba de tipo de vaso de análisis f; ~ **berth** n TRANSP muelle para carga y descarga de contenedores m; ~ **board box** n PACK contenedor de cartón m; ~ **capsule** n TRANSP cápsula recipiente f; ~ **car** n AmE (cf container wagon BrE) RAIL, TRANSP vagón contenedor m; ~**-carrier lorry** n BrE (cf container-carrier truck AmE) TRANSP camión portacontenedores m; ~**-carrier truck** n AmE (cf container-carrier lorry BrE) TRANSP camión portacontenedores m; ~ **destuffing** n TRANSP vaciado de contenedores m; ~ **with fixed wheels** n TRANSP contenedor de ruedas fijas m; ~ **glass** n C&G vidrio para envases m; ~ **lighter** n TRANSP barcaza portacontenedores f, barcaza-contenedor f; ~**-n** n (C-n) TELECOM contenedor-n m; ~ **with opening top** n TRANSP contenedor con abertura superior m; ~**-rinsing equipment** n PACK equipo para enjuagar contenedores m; ~ **ship** n WATER TRANSP buque portacontenedores m; ~ **station** n TRANSP estación de contenedores f, terminal de contenedores f; ~ **stripping** n TRANSP descarga de los contenedores f, desmontaje de los contenedores m; ~ **terminal** n TRANSP terminal de contenedores f; ~ **unpacking** n TRANSP descarga de contenedores f; ~ **unstuffing** n TRANSP vaciado de contenedores m; ~ **wagon** n BrE (cf container car AmE) RAIL, TRANSP vagón contenedor m; ~ **wharf** n TRANSP muelle de contenedores m

containerization n PACK, TRANSP contenedorización f

containerize vt PACK poner en contenedores, TRANSP poner en contenedores, transportar en recipientes cerrados

containerized: ~ **lighter aboard ship system** n (CLASS) TRANSP sistema de buques remolcadores para transporte de gabarras cargadas con contenedores m

containment n NUCL contención f, recinto de contención m, PHYS confinamiento m; ~ **boom** n PETR TECH barrera de contención f; ~ **integrity** n NUCL integridad del recinto de contención f; ~ **spray system** n NUCL sistema de rociado de contención f; ~ **sump** n NUCL sumidero de contención m

contaminant: ~ **determination** n FOOD, QUALITY determinación de contaminación f

contaminate vt GEN contaminar

contaminated: ~ **mud** n PETR TECH lodo contaminado m; ~ **sludge** n PETR TECH lodo contaminado m

contamination n GEN contaminación f; ~ **fallout** n POLL contaminación por lluvia radiactiva f, contaminación por polvo radiactivo f, precipitación radiactiva f (Esp); ~ **meter** n MILIT, NUCL, POLL, SAFE medidor de contaminación m

contemporaneous[1] adj GEOL contemporáneo

contemporaneous[2]: ~ **fault** *n* GEOL falla contemporánea *f*, falla sincrónica *f*

content *n* COAL capacidad *f*, contenido *m*, volumen *m*, CONST *of field* contenido *m*, METALL contenido *m*, ley *f*, MINE ley *f*, superficie *f*, P&R, TELECOM, TEXTIL contenido *m*; **~-addressable memory** *n* (*CAM*) COMP&DP memoria de contenido direccionable *f*; **~-addressable storage** *n AmE* COMP&DP almacenamiento de contenido direccionable *m*, guarde de contenido direccionable *m* (*AmL*), memoria de contenido direccionable *f*; **~-addressable store** *BrE n* COMP&DP almacenamiento de contenido direccionable *m*, guarde de contenido direccionable *m* (*AmL*), memoria de contenido direccionable *f*

contention *n* COMP&DP contención *f*, contienda *f*, ELECTRON capacidad *f*, contenido *m*, TELECOM contención *f*; ~ **control** *n* TELECOM control de contención *m*

contents *n pl* MINE tabla de materias *f*; ~ **declaration** *n* PACK declaración del contenido *f*, manifiesto del contenido *m*; ~ **directory** *n* COMP&DP directorio de contenido *m*

contest *n* COAL contienda *f*, controversia *f*, debate *m*, lucha *f*, oposición *f*, pugna *f*, torneo *m*

context[1]: **~-free** *adj* COMP&DP independiente del contexto, libre de contexto; **~-sensitive** *adj* COMP&DP contextual, sensible a contexto

context[2]: ~ **switching** *n* COMP&DP cambio de contexto *m*, conmutación contextual *f*

contiguous[1] *adj* COMP&DP, GEOM, OCEAN contiguo

contiguous[2]: ~ **angle** *n* GEOM ángulo contiguo *m*; ~ **waters** *n pl* OCEAN aguas contiguas *f pl*; ~ **zone** *n* OCEAN zona contigua *f*

continental: ~ **accretion** *n* GEOL aglomeración continental *f*; ~ **air** *n* METEO aire continental *m*; ~ **anticyclone** *n* METEO anticiclón continental *m*; ~ **borderland** *n* OCEAN borde continental *m*; ~ **climate** *n* METEO clima continental *m*; ~ **drift** *n* GEOL, OCEAN deriva continental *f*; ~ **fringe** *n* OCEAN franja continental *f*; ~ **margin** *n* OCEAN margen continental *m*; ~ **mass** *n* GEOL, GEOPHYS masa continental *f*; ~ **plate** *n* GEOL, GEOPHYS altiplano continental *m*, meseta continental *f*, placa continental *f* (*Esp*); ~ **platform** *n* GEOL plataforma continental *f*; ~ **rise** *n* GEOL elevación continental *f*, OCEAN glacis continental *m*; ~ **shelf** *n* GEOL, GEOPHYS, OCEAN, PETR TECH plataforma continental *f*; **~-shelf waters** *n* OCEAN aguas de la plataforma continental *f pl*, aguas epicontinentales *f pl*; ~ **shield** *n* GEOL, GEOPHYS cratón *m*, escudo continental *m*; ~ **slope** *n* GEOL, GEOPHYS, OCEAN, PETR TECH declive continental *m*, talud continental *m*; ~ **terrace** *n* OCEAN terraza continental *f*

contingency: ~ **plan** *n* MAR POLL, NUCL, SAFE plan para contingencias *m*; ~ **table** *n* MATH tabla de contingencia *f*

continual: ~ **mechanical twinning** *n* METALL germinación mecánica continua *f*, maclaje mecánico continuo *m*

continuation: ~ **of message** *n* (*COM*) TELECOM continuación de mensaje *f*; ~ **sheets** *n pl* PRINT hojas de continuación *f pl*

continuity: ~ **control** *n* CINEMAT, TV control de continuidad *m*; ~ **editing** *n* CINEMAT, TV montaje de continuidad *m*; ~ **fault** *n* TELECOM fallo en la continuidad *m*; ~ **log** *n* CINEMAT, TV registro de continuidad *m*; ~ **sheet** *n* CINEMAT, TV hoja de continuidad *f*; ~ **switch** *n* ELEC interruptor de continuidad *m*; ~ **test** *n* ELEC *of a circuit* prueba de continuidad *f*; ~ **tester** *n* ELEC *instrument* probador de continuidad *m*

continuous[1] *adj* GEN continuo; ~ **bit stream oriented** *adj* (*CBO*) TELECOM orientado a la transmisión contínua de bits

continuous[2]: **~-access public transport system** *n* TRANSP sistema de acceso continuo de transporte público *m*; ~ **adjustment** *n* ELECTRON ajuste continuo *m*; ~ **automatic train control** *n* RAIL, TRANSP control automático de tren *m*; ~ **beam** *n* CONST viga continua *f*, ELECTRON haz continuo *m*; ~ **beam modulation** *n* TV modulación continua de intensidad *f*; ~ **belt** *n* PROD correa sin fin *f*; ~ **casting** *n* C&G vaciado continuo *m*, MECH *of a batch* proceso de fundición con solidificación continua *m*; **~-casting process** *n* C&G proceso de vaciado continuo *m*; ~ **chart recorder** *n* INSTR, LAB grabador de gráficos continuo *m*; ~ **control** *n* COMP&DP control continuo *m*; ~ **controlled squelch system** *n* (*CTCSS*) TELECOM sistema silenciador de control continuo *m*; ~ **cooker** *n* FOOD cocina continua *f*, placa continua *f*; ~ **counting station** *n* TRANSP estación de recuento continuo *f*; ~ **cross-bonding** *n* ELEC conexión cruzada continua *f*, empalme cruzado continuo *m*; ~ **current** *n* (*CC*) ELEC ENG, RAIL corriente continua *f* (*CC*); ~ **digester** *n* PAPER lejiadora continua *f*; **~-drawing process** *n* C&G proceso de estirado continuo *m*; ~ **duty** *n* ELEC *equipment* servicio continuo *m*; ~ **dyeing** *n* COLOUR teñido continuo *m*; ~ **feed head** *n* MECH ENG *machine tools* cabeza de avance continuo *f*; ~ **feed paper** *n* *AmE* (*cf continuous stationery BrE*) COMP&DP, PAPER, PRINT formulario continuo *m*, papel de alimentación continua *m*; ~ **fiber** *AmE*, ~ **fibre** *BrE n* METALL fibra continua *f*; ~ **filament** *n* C&G filamento continuo *m*; ~ **flood** *n* HYDROL, WATER flujo continuo *m*, flujo elevado continuo *m*; **~-flow dryer** *n* AGRIC secadora de flujo continuo *f*; ~ **form** *n* *AmE* (*cf continuous stationery BrE*) COMP&DP, PAPER, PRINT formulario continuo *m*, papel de alimentación continua *m*; ~ **freeze drying** *n* AGRIC, FOOD, PACK, REFRIG, THERMO liofilización continua *f*; ~ **freezer** *n* REFRIG congelador continuo *m*; ~ **grinder** *n* PAPER desfibrador continuo *m*; ~ **grinder and polisher** *n* C&G pulidor-esmerilador continuo *m*; ~ **high flow** *n* HYDROL, WATER flujo continuo *m*, flujo elevado continuo *m*; ~ **kiln** *n* HEAT horno de secado continuo *m*; ~ **laser** *n* ELECTRON láser continuo *m*; **~-laser action** *n* ELECTRON accionamiento con láser continuo *m*; **~-laser beam** *n* ELECTRON haz de láser continuo *m*; ~ **load** *n* ELEC, ELEC ENG carga continua *f*; ~ **loading** *n* ELEC, ELEC ENG carga continua *f*; ~ **loop** *n* CINEMAT bucle continuo *m*; **~-loop projector** *n* CINEMAT proyector de bucle continuo *m*; ~ **mechanical handling equipment** *n* MECH ENG equipo de manejo mecánico continuo *m*, equipo manipulador mecánico continuo *m*; ~ **mechanical handling equipment for loose bulk materials** *n* MECH ENG equipo manipulador mecánico continuo para materiales a granel *m*; ~ **motion weight filling** *n* PACK proceso de llenado en continuo *m*; ~ **oscillation** *n* ELECTRON oscilación contínua *f*; ~ **output** *n* ELEC *generator* potencia de salida continua *f*, potencia generada continua *f*, potencia suministrada continua *f*, ELEC ENG potencia útil *f*; ~ **polisher** *n* C&G pulidor continuo *m*; ~ **precipitation** *n* METALL, METEO precipitación continua *f*; ~~**presence detector** *n* TRANSP detector de presencia constante *m*; ~ **processing machine** *n* PHOTO equipo para el revelado continuo *m*; ~ **production** *n* PACK, PROD producción continua *f*; ~ **production line** *n* PACK, PROD cadena de producción continua *f*; ~ **rating** *n* ELEC *of a generator* régimen continuo *m*, régimen permanente *m*; ~ **recirculation lehr** *n* C&G horno de revenido de recirculación continua *m*, templador continuo *m*; ~ **ringing bell** *n* ELEC ENG timbre de sonido continuo *m*; ~ **sampling** *n* QUALITY muestreo continuo *m*; ~ **saw** *n* MECH ENG sierra continua *f*, sierra de cinta *f*; ~ **shield-bonding** *n* ELEC conexión cruzada continua *f*, empalme cruzado continuo *m*; ~ **signal** *n* ELECTRON señal continua *f*; ~ **slab** *n* CONST losa continua *f*; ~ **spectrum** *n* ACOUST, ELECTRON, PHYS, RAD PHYS, SPACE espectro continuo *m*; ~~**spun yarn** *n* TEXTIL hilo de hilatura continua *m*; ~ **stationery** *n* BrE (*cf continuous feed paper AmE, cf continuous form AmE*) COMP&DP, PAPER, PRINT formulario continuo *m*, papel de alimentación continua *m*; ~ **strand mat** *n* C&G colchoneta de filamento continuo *f*, P&R fieltro de fibra continua *m*, malla de filamentos continua *f*; ~ **surface** *n* RAIL superficie continua *f*; ~ **thread** *n* PACK rosca sin fin *f*; ~~**thread cap** *n* PACK tapa de rosca sin fin *f*; ~~**thread closure** *n* PACK cierre de rosca sin fin *m*; ~ **tone** *n* PRINT tono continuo *m*; ~ **transport** *n* TRANSP transporte continuo *m*; ~ **transportation system** *n* TRANSP sistema de transporte continuo *m*; ~ **tuning** *n* ELECTRON sintonización continua *f*; ~ **vulcanization** *n* P&R vulcanización continua *f*; ~ **wave** *n* (*CW*) ELEC ENG, PHYS, TV, WAVE PHYS onda continua *f* (*OC*); ~~**wave laser** *n* ELECTRON, PHYS, WAVE PHYS láser de onda continua *m*; ~~**wave radar** *n* WATER TRANSP radar de onda continua *m*; ~~**wave radar detector** *n* TRANSP, WATER TRANSP, WAVE PHYS detector constante de ondas de radar *m*; ~~**wave ultrasonic detector** *n* TRANSP, WAVE PHYS detector ultrasónico de ondas continuas *m*; ~ **web products** *n pl* PRINT productos de banda continua *m pl*; ~ **welded rail** *n* (*CWR*) RAIL carril continuo soldado *m*, riel continuo soldado *m*; ~ **white line** *n* CONST línea continua *f*; ~ **yarn** *n* TEXTIL hilo continuo *m*

continuously[1]: ~ **adjustable** *adj* ELECTRON ajustable continuamente

continuously[2]: ~~**loaded cable** *n* ELEC ENG, TELECOM cable cargado continuamente *m*, cable cargado de continuo *m*; ~~**tunable oscillator** *n* ELECTRON oscilador sintonizable continuamente *m*; ~~**variable attenuator** *n* ELECTRON atenuador variable continuamente *m*

contorted: ~ **bedding** *n* GEOL estratificación contorsionada *f*

contour *n* AGRIC curva de nivel *f*, CONST *of pillar* contorno *m*, *of dome* perímetro *m*, GEOL contorno *m*, perfil *m*; ~ **effect** *n* ACOUST efecto de contorno *m*; ~ **farming** *n* AGRIC cultivo por curvas de nivel *m*; ~ **follower** *n* MECH ENG perfilómetro *m*; ~ **fringes** *n pl* PHYS franjas de contorno *f pl*; ~ **generation** *n* PROD producción de contornos *f*; ~ **grinding** *n* PROD rectificado por muela de superficies curvas *m*; ~ **interval** *n* GEOL distancia entre los contornos de

nivel *f*; ~ **line** *n* CONST, GEOL curva de nivel *f*; ~ **map** *n* CONST plano topográfico *m*, PRINT plano fotográfico *m*; ~~**measuring equipment** *n* METR equipo de medida del contorno *m*; ~ **planting** *n* AGRIC siembra a nivel *f*; ~ **ploughing** *n* BrE AGRIC arada en curva de nivel *f*; ~ **plowing** *AmE see contour ploughing BrE*

contoured: ~ **beam aerial** *n* BrE (*cf contoured beam antenna AmE*) SPACE *communications* antena de haz conformado *f*, antena de haz contorneado *f*; ~ **beam antenna** *n* AmE (*cf contoured beam aerial BrE*) SPACE *communications* antena de haz conformado *f*, antena de haz contorneado *f*

contract[1]: **on** ~ *adv* PROD a destajo

contract[2]: ~ **blister packaging service** *n* PACK cápsula termoformada a medida del objeto a envasar *f*; ~ **boring** *n* MINE sondeo a tanto alzado *m* (*AmL*), sondeo por contracta *m* (*Esp*); ~ **drilling** *n* MINE sondeo a tanto alzado *m* (*AmL*), sondeo por contracta *m* (*Esp*); ~ **packaging** *n* PACK embalaje a medida *m*; ~ **pegging** *n* PROD estabilización de tipos de cambio en contratos *f*; ~ **price** *n* PROD precio según contrato *m*; ~ **work** *n* PROD obra por contrata *f*

contract[3] *vti* GEN contraer

contractant: ~ **soil** *n* COAL suelo contraíble *m*

contracted: ~ **section** *n* HYDRAUL sección contraída *f*; ~ **weir** *n* WATER vertedero con contracción *m*

contractibility *n* COAL contractibilidad *f*

contractible: ~ **soil** *n* COAL suelo contraíble *m*

contractile *adj* TEXTIL contráctil

contraction *n* HYDROL *of river bed*, MECH ENG contracción *f*, estrechamiento *m*, MINE estrechamiento *m*, contracción *f*, PHYS, TEXTIL contracción *f*, estrechamiento *m*; ~ **coefficient** *n* FUELLESS, HYDRAUL coeficiente de acortamiento *m*, coeficiente de contracción *m*; ~ **crack** *n* PROD *founding* grieta de contracción *f*, grieta de refracción *f*; ~ **due to cold** *n* THERMO contracción por frío *f*; ~ **joint** *n* CONST junta de contracción *f*; ~ **rule** *n* PROD *founding* regla que considera la contracción de los metales *f*

contractor *n* CONST *person* constructor *m*, empresa constructora *f*, contratista *m*, QUALITY *company* empresa constructora *f*, *person* constructor *m*, contratista *m*

contralode *n* MINE filón crucero *m*

contrast *n* CINEMAT, PHOTO, PHYS, TV contraste *m*; ~ **control** *n* CINEMAT, PHOTO, PHYS, TV control de contraste *m*; ~ **effect** *n* CINEMAT, PHOTO, PHYS, TV efecto de contraste *m*; ~ **medium injector** *n* INSTR inyector medio de contraste *m*; ~ **photometer** *n* PHOTO fotómetro de contraste *m*; ~ **ratio** *n* CINEMAT relación de contraste *f*, PAPER opacidad de contraste *f*, TV relación de contraste *f*; ~ **reduction** *n* CINEMAT, PHOTO, PHYS, TV reducción de contraste *f*

contrasted: ~ **negative** *n* CINEMAT, PHOTO negativo contrastado *m*

contrasting: ~ **phase microscope** *n* INSTR microscopio de fase de contraste *m*

contrasty *adj* CINEMAT con gran contraste

contravene *vt* SAFE *regulations* contravenir

contrivance *n* MECH ENG artefacto *m*, dispositivo *m*, invención *f*, máquina *f*

control[1] *n* COMP&DP control *m*, ELEC control *m*, mando *m*, regulación *f*, ELECTRON control *m*, SPACE control *m*, gobierno *m*, manejo *m*, TELECOM, TEXTIL control *m*, TRANSP gobierno *m*, VEH control *m*, mando *m*, WATER TRANSP *ship* gobierno *m*; ~ **arm** *n* CINEMAT, TV brazo de control *m*, VEH brazo oscilante *m*; ~ **assay** *n* CHEM ensayo de control *m*, prueba de control *f*, COAL ensayo de control *m*; ~ **band** *n* CINEMAT, TV banda de control *f*; ~ **barrier** *n* CONST barrera de control *f*; ~ **bit** *n* COMP&DP bit de control *m*; ~ **board** *n* ELEC panel de control *m*, tablero de control *m*; ~ **box** *n* MECH ENG caja de control *f*; ~ **burst** *n* SPACE *communications* señal de sincronización de control *f*; ~ **bus** *n* COMP&DP bus de control *m*, conductor común de control *m*; ~ **cable** *n* MECH ENG cable de control *m*; ~ **center** *AmE*, ~ **centre** *BrE n* PROD centro de mando *m*, RAIL centro de control *m*, SPACE centro de control *m*, control de misión *m*, TV centro de control *m*; ~ **channel** *n* (*CC*) TELECOM canal de control *m*; ~ **character** *n* COMP&DP carácter de control *m*; ~ **characteristic** *n* ELEC ENG característica de control *f*, característica de orden *f*; ~ **chart** *n* QUALITY cuadro de control *m*; ~ **circuit** *n* CINEMAT, COMP&DP circuito de control *m*, ELEC circuito de control *m*, circuito de regulación *m*, REFRIG, TELE- COM circuito de control *m*; ~ **column** *n* AIR TRANSP columna de control *f*; ~ **column boss** *n* AIR TRANSP buje de la palanca de control *m*; ~ **column whip** *n* AIR TRANSP sacudida de la columna de control *f*; ~ **console** *n* ELEC consola de control *f*, pupitre de mando *m*, TV consola de control *f*; ~ **damper** *n* AIR TRANSP amortiguador de control *m*; ~ **data** *n pl* COMP&DP datos de control *m pl*; ~ **deck** *n* TV pista de control *f*; ~ **desk** *n* INSTR mesa de control *f*, pupitre de mando *m*; ~ **discrepancy switch** *n* ELEC conmu- tador de control de discrepancias *m*; ~ **and display unit** *n* SPACE unidad de control y representación visual *f*; ~ **driving** *n* COAL mecanismo de control *m*; ~ **dynamo** *n* ELEC *generator*, ELEC ENG dinamo de control *f*; ~ **early warning radar rating** *n* AIR TRANSP clasificación del radar de aproximación de vigilancia *f*; ~ **electrode** *n* ELEC ENG electrodo de mando *m*, electrodo regulador *m*; ~ **equipment** *n* PROD equipo de maniobra *m*, TELECOM equipo de control *m*; ~ **of exposure to fumes from welding and brazing** *n* SAFE control de exposición a humos de soldadura *m*; ~ **field** *n* COMP&DP campo de control *m*; ~ **film band** *n* CINEMAT, TV banda de película de control *f*; ~ **flow** *n* COMP&DP flujo de control *m*; ~ **frequency** *n* TV frecuencia piloto *f*; ~ **function** *n* TELECOM función de control *f*; ~ **fuse** *n* MECH ENG, PROD fusible de control *m*; ~ **gear** *n* ELEC equipo de combinador *m*, equipo de control *m*, ELEC ENG maquinaria de mando *f*, mecanismo de gobierno *m*; ~ **gearing ratio** *n* AIR TRANSP proporción de los engranajes de control *f*; ~ **grid** *n* ELEC ENG *of a vacuum tube* rejilla de control *f*, *of an electron gun* enrejado de control *m*; ~ **gyro** *n* AIR TRANSP *of a helicopter*, SPACE giróscopo de control *m*; ~ **gyro and amplifier** *n* SPACE giróscopo y amplificador de control *m*; ~ **key** *n* COMP&DP clave de control *f*, tecla de control *f*; ~ **knob** *n* CINEMAT mando de control *m*, ELEC botón de mando *m*, perilla de mando *f*; ~ **lever** *n* AIR TRANSP palanca de control *f*, palanca de juego *f*, MINE palanca de mando *f*, palanca de maniobra *f*; ~ **lever quadrant** *n* AIR TRANSP cuadrante de la palanca de control *m*; ~ **light** *n* CINEMAT luz de control *f*; ~ **limit** *n* QUALITY límite de control *m*; ~ **malfunction** *n* PROD malfun- cionamiento de control *m*; ~ **memory** *n* TELECOM memoria de control *f*; ~ **of minimum headway** *n* TRANSP control de avance mínimo *m*; ~ **panel** *n* AIR

TRANSP, COMP&DP, CONST, MECH, SPACE panel de control *m*, tablero de control *m*, TEXTIL cuadro de mandos *m*, WATER TRANSP *of instruments* cuadro de control *m*; ~ **pedestal** *n* AIR TRANSP pedestal de control *m*; ~ **piston** *n* MECH ENG pistón de control *m*; ~ **plane** *n* AIR TRANSP plano de control *m*; ~ **potentiometer** *n* ELEC ENG potenciómetro de con- trol *m*; ~ **program** *AmE*, ~ **programme** *BrE n* TRANSP programa de control *m*; ~ **register** *n* COMP&DP registro de control *m*; ~ **relay** *n* ELEC relé de control *m*; ~ **register** *n* COMP&DP registro de control *m*; ~ **reversal** *n* AIR TRANSP inversión de control *f*; ~ **rocket** *n* SPACE cohete de control *m*; ~ **rod** *n* AIR TRANSP barra de control *f*, AUTO barra de control *f*, varilla de mando *f*, varilla de reglaje *f*, PHYS barra de control *f*; ~ **rod drive housing** *n* (*CRDH*) NUCL alojamiento del mecanismo de accionamiento de las barras de control *m* (*CRDH*); ~ **rod drive mechanism** *n* (*CRDM*) NUCL mecanismo de accio- namiento de las barras de control *m* (*CRDM*); ~**rod ejection accident** *n* NUCL, SAFE accidente de eyec- ción de barras *m*; ~**rod resonance** *n* AIR TRANSP *helicopter* resonancia de la barra de control *f*; ~ **rod worth** *n* NUCL valor de una barra de control *m*; ~ **room** *n* ELEC sala de control *f*, sala de mando *f*, NUCL, TV sala de control *f*, WATER TRANSP *of ship* cámara de mando *f*; ~**room window** *n* TV ventana de la sala de control *f*; ~ **rotor** *n* AIR TRANSP rotor de control *m*; ~ **routine** *n* COMP&DP rutina de control *f*; ~ **and safety device** *n* HEAT, SAFE dispositivo de seguridad y control *m*; ~ **sample** *n* AGRIC muestra testigo *f*; ~ **screen** *n* INSTR pantalla de control *f*; ~ **sector** *n* AIR TRANSP sector de control *m*; ~ **sequence** *n* COMP&DP secuencia de control *f*; ~ **signal** *n* ELECTRON, TV señal de control *f*; ~ **size** *n* COAL tamaño de control *m*; ~ **stage** *n* AIR TRANSP nivel de control *m*; ~ **strip** *n* CINEMAT franja de control *f*; ~ **of substances hazardous to health** *n* (*COSHH*) SAFE control de substancias peligrosas para la salud *m*; ~ **surface** *n* AIR TRANSP, PHYS superficie de control *f*; ~**surface angle** *n* AIR TRANSP ángulo de la superficie de control *m*; ~**surface locking** *n* AIR TRANSP blocaje de la superficie de control *m*; ~ **switch** *n* ELEC conmutador de control *m*, conmutador de mando *m*, llave de mando *f*, ELEC ENG interruptor de mando *m*; ~ **system** *n* AIR TRANSP sistema de control *m*, ELEC sistema de mando automático *m*, sistema de regula- ción *m*, TELECOM, TEXTIL sistema de control *m*; ~ **tag** *n* PACK etiqueta de control *f*, tarjeta de control *f*; ~ **tape** *n* COMP&DP cinta de control *f*; ~ **total** *n* COMP&DP suma de control *f*, total de control *m*; ~ **tower** *n* AIR TRANSP torre de control *f*; ~ **of toxicity at work** *n* SAFE control de toxicidad en el trabajo *m*; ~ **of toxicity in the workplace** *n* SAFE control de toxicidad en el lugar de trabajo *m*; ~ **track** *n* ACOUST, TV pista de control *f*; ~**track signal** *n* ACOUST, TV señal de la pista de control *f*; ~**track time code** *n* ACOUST, TV sincronización de la pista de control *f*; ~ **transformer** *n* ELEC, ELEC ENG transformador de mando *m*; ~ **unit** *n* CINEMAT, COMP&DP unidad de control *f*, ELEC, ELEC ENG caja de control *f*, dispositivo de control *m*, unidad de control *f*, MECH ENG, TELECOM unidad de control *f*; ~ **valve** *n* HY- DRAUL válvula de control *f*, válvula de estrangulación *f* (*AmL*), válvula de maniobra *f*, válvula reguladora *f*

(*Esp*), MECH válvula de control *f*, válvula de estrangulación *f*, válvula de maniobra *f*, válvula reguladora *f* (*Esp*); ~ **voltage** *n* ELEC, PROD voltaje de control *m*; ~ **wedge** *n* CINEMAT cuña de control *f*; ~ **weir** *n* WATER vertedero de control *m*; ~ **wheel** *n* C&G rueda de control *f*; ~ **word** *n* COMP&DP palabra de control *f*
control² *vt* COMP&DP controlar, SPACE, TELECOM controlar, gobernar
controllability *n* AIR TRANSP controlabilidad *f*
controllable: ~ **pitch propeller** *n* WATER TRANSP hélice de palas orientables *f*, hélice de paso controlable *f*
controlled¹: ~**-atmosphere packed** *adj* FOOD envasado bajo atmósfera controlada
controlled²: ~ **airspace** *n* AIR TRANSP espacio aéreo controlado *m*; ~ **atmosphere** *n* HEAT atmósfera controlada *f*; ~ **carrier modulation** *n* ELECTRON modulación controlada de la portadora *f*; ~ **combustion system** *n* AUTO, THERMO, VEH sistema de combustión controlada *m*; ~ **delay lock** *n* TV demora de sincronizado controlada *f*; ~ **dumping** *n* POLL, RECYCL descarga controlada *f*, vertido controlado *m*; ~ **emission toilet** *n* RAIL retrete de expulsión controlada *m*; ~**-environment storage system** *n* PACK sistema de almacenaje ambientalmente controlado *m*; ~**-environment storage system** *n* PROD sistema de almacenaje ambientalmente controlado *m*; ~ **flight** *n* AIR TRANSP vuelo controlado *m*; ~ **frequency** *n* ELECTRON frecuencia controlada *f*; ~ **oscillator** *n* ELECTRON oscilador controlado *m*; ~ **outlet** *n* MECH ENG salida controlada *f*; ~ **pressure** *n* MECH ENG presión controlada *f*; ~ **slip differential** *n* MECH, VEH diferencial de deslizamiento controlado *m*; ~ **spillway** *n* HYDRAUL, WATER aliviadero controlado *m*; ~ **spin** *n* AIR TRANSP barrena controlada *f*, espín controlado *m*; ~ **temperature** *n* HEAT ENG, THERMO temperatura controlada *f*; ~ **tipping** *n* POLL, RECYCL vertido controlado *m*; ~ **variable** *n* ELEC ENG variable controlada *f*; ~ **zone** *n* NUCL zona controlada *f*
controller *n* COMP&DP controlador *m*, ELEC ENG, MECH ENG regulador *m*, OPT, PROD controlador *m*, SPACE comandante de zona de defensa antiaérea *m*, controlador *m*, regulador *m*; ~ **layout** *n* PROD diagrama del controlador *m*
controlling: ~ **valve** *n* HYDRAUL válvula de control *f*, válvula de estrangulación *f* (*AmL*), válvula de maniobra *f*, válvula reguladora *f* (*Esp*)
controls: ~ **and indicators** *n pl* AIR TRANSP controles e indicaciones *m pl*
convected: ~ **heat** *n* HEAT, THERMO calor de convección *m*
convection *n* GEN convección *f*; ~ **cooler** *n* REFRIG enfriador de convección *m*, refrigerador por convección *m*, THERMO enfriador de convección *m*, refrigerador, de convección *m*; ~ **cooling** *n* REFRIG, THERMO enfriamiento por convección *m*, refrigeración por convección *f*; ~ **current** *n* C&G corriente de convección *f*, ELEC ENG corriente conveccional *f*, corriente normal *f*, PHYS, THERMO corriente de convección *f*; ~ **dryer** *n* REFRIG corriente de convección *f*, THERMO secador de convección *m*; ~ **drying** *n* THERMO secado por convección *m*; ~ **heat** *n* THERMO calor de convección *m*; ~ **oven** *n* CHEM, HEAT, THERMO horno por convección *m*; ~ **superheater** *n* HEAT, THERMO sobrecalentador por convección *m*
convective¹ *adj* GEN convectivo

convective²: ~ **exchange** *n* GAS intercambio convectivo *m*; ~ **flow** *n* FLUID flujo convectivo *m*; ~ **heat transfer coefficient** *n* HEAT ENG coeficiente de transferencia de calor por convección *m*; ~ **superheater** *n* HEAT sobrecalentador por convección *m*; ~ **turbulence** *n* AIR TRANSP turbulencia convectiva *f*
convector *n* HEAT, HEAT ENG, THERMO convector *m*; ~ **heater** *n* HEAT, HEAT ENG, THERMO calentador convector *m*
conventional: ~ **cable** *n* OPT cable convencional *m*; ~ **gas** *n* GAS gas común *m*; ~ **milling** *n* MECH ENG fresado convencional *m*, fresado en dirección contraria al avance *m*, fresado en sentido contrario al avance *m*, fresado paralelo *m*; ~ **takeoff and landing** *n* (*CTOL*) AIR TRANSP, MILIT despegue y aterrizaje convencional *m*; ~ **takeoff and landing aircraft** *n* AIR TRANSP, MILIT avión de despegue y aterrizaje convencional *m*; ~ **transportable pallet** *n* PACK paleta transportable de forma convencional *f*
convergence: ~ **assembly** *n* TV conjunto de convergencia *m*; ~ **circuit** *n* TV circuito de convergencia *m*; ~ **error** *n* TV error de convergencia *m*; ~ **sublayer** *n* (*CS*) TELECOM subcapa de convergencia *f*; ~**-sublayer protocol data unit** *n* (*CSPDU*) TELECOM unidad de datos protocolarios de la subcapa de convergencia *f*
convergent¹ *adj* GEN convergente
convergent²: ~ **beam** *n* OPT haz convergente *m*; ~ **lines** *n pl* GEOM líneas convergentes *f pl*, rectas convergentes *f pl*; ~ **margin** *n* GEOL margen convergente activo *m*; ~ **reaction** *n* NUCL reacción convergente *f*; ~ **sequence** *n* MATH secesión convergente *f*, secuencia convergente *f*
converging: ~ **energy** *n* WAVE PHYS energía convergente *f*, potencia convergente *f*; ~ **lens** *n* C&G, CINEMAT, INSTR, OPT, PHOTO, PHYS lente convergente *f*; ~ **power** *n* WAVE PHYS potencia convergente *f*
conversation: ~ **impossible** *n* (*CI*) TELECOM conversación imposible *f*
conversational¹ *adj* COMP&DP conversacional, interactivo
conversational²: ~ **frequencies** *n pl* ACOUST frecuencias conversacionales *f pl*; ~ **mode** *n* COMP&DP modo conversacional *m*, modo interactivo *m*
conversion *n* COMP&DP conversión *f*, ELEC, ELEC ENG, ELECTRON conversión *f*, transformación *f*; ~ **coating** *n* COATINGS recubrimiento de conversión *m*; ~ **coefficient** *n* NUCL coeficiente de conversión *m*; ~ **conductance** *n* ELEC ENG conductancia de conversión *f*; ~ **degree** *n* TRANSP grado de conversión *m*; ~ **electron** *n* ELECTRON, RAD PHYS electrón de conversión *m*; ~ **filter** *n* CINEMAT filtro de conversión *m*; ~ **frequency** *n* ELECTRON frecuencia de conversión *f*; ~ **gain** *n* ELECTRON ganancia de conversión *f*; ~ **layer** *n* COLOUR capa de conversión *f*; ~ **machinery** *n* PACK maquinaria de conversión *f*; ~ **oil** *n* PETR TECH aceite de conversión *m*; ~ **oscillator** *n* ELECTRON oscilador de conversión *m*; ~ **pig** *n* PROD lingote de afino *m*; ~ **quantum efficiency** *n* NUCL rendimiento cuántico de conversión *m*; ~ **rate** *n* ELECTRON porcentaje de conversión *m*; ~ **voltage gain** *n* ELEC ENG ganancia de tensión de conversión *f*
convert *vt* COMP&DP convertir, ELEC, ELEC ENG, ELECTRON convertir, transformar, PAPER manipular; ~ **to diesel** *vt* TRANSP transformar en diesel

converted: ~ **top** n TEXTIL pieza superior transformada f
converter n CINEMAT convertidor m, ELEC, ELEC ENG, ELECTRON convertidor m, transformador m, HEAT convertidor m, PAPER manipulador m, TELECOM conversor m, convertidor m, VEH convertidor m; ~ **cabinet** n TELECOM armario del convertidor m, armario del conversor m; ~ **chip** n ELEC, ELECTRON chip convertidor m, chip transformador m; ~ **gas** n DETERG, GAS gas convertidor m; ~ **pig** n PROD fundición de afino f; ~ **set** n ELEC ENG grupo transformador m, conjunto convertidor m; ~ **tube** n INSTR tubo mezclador m, tubo convertidor m
convertible n VEH descapotable m; ~ **top** n VEH techo convertible m, techo descapotable m
converting n PAPER manipulación f; ~ **pot** n PROD cementation furnace caja de cementación f; ~ **station** n ELEC transformer, ELEC ENG central de conversión f, central eléctrica de conversión f, estación de conversión f, planta de conversión f
convex: ~ **bow** n C&G arco convexo m; ~ **immersions of closed surfaces** n pl GEOM inmersiones convexas de superficies cerradas f pl; ~ **lens** n INSTR, OPT, PHOTO, PHYS lente convexa f; ~ **mirror** n INSTR, PHYS espejo convexo m; ~ **optical tool** n C&G, OPT herramienta óptica convexa f; ~ **programming** n COMP&DP programación convexa f; ~ **surface** n C&G of plano-convex lens, GEOM, OPT superficie convexa f
convey: ~ **power** vt MECH ENG transferir fuerza motriz, transportar fuerza motriz, trasladar fuerza motriz
conveyor n AGRIC, C&G transportador m, CONST cinta transportadora f, transportador m, conductor m, INSTR, MECH ENG transportador m, MINE cinta transportadora f (Esp), máquina transportadora f (AmL), PACK, PROD transportador m; ~ **belt** n AGRIC, CONST, MECH, MECH ENG cinta transportadora f, correa transportadora f, MINE cinta transportadora f (Esp), correa transportadora f, PROD, TRANSP cinta transportadora f, correa transportadora f; ~~**belt lehr** n C&G horno de revenido con banda transportadora m, templador con banda transportadora m; ~~**belt skimmer** n POLL desescoriador de cinta transportadora m, desnatador de banda transportadora m, espumador de cinta transportadora m; ~~**belt with a textile carcass** n MECH ENG correa transportadora con armazón textil f; ~ **belting** n TEXTIL cinta transportadora f; ~ **chain** n MECH ENG cadena transportadora f; ~ **drive** n MINE correa transportadora f; ~ **for silvering** n C&G transportador para plateado m; ~ **handling system** n PACK forma de manejar el transportador f, sistema de manutención mediante transportador m; ~ **road** n COAL galería conductora f; ~ **system** n CONST sistema de transporte m
convolute: ~ **lamination** n GEOL laminación convulta f
convolution n ELECTRON espira f, MECH ENG circunvolución f, convolución f, enrollamiento m, enroscadura f, paso m, pliegue m, PETROL circunvolución f, sinuosidad f; ~ **code** n TELECOM código convolucional m; ~ **product** n ELECTRON material en espiras m
convolutional: ~ **code** n TELECOM código convolucional m; ~ **coding** n TELECOM codificación convolucional f; ~ **filter** n ELECTRON filtro en espira m; ~ **filtering** n ELECTRON filtrado en espira m

convolutive: ~ **code** n TELECOM código convolutivo m
convolver n ELECTRON arrollamiento m
convolvulin n CHEM convolvulina f
convoy[1] n MILIT, WATER TRANSP navy convoy m
convoy[2] vt MILIT, WATER TRANSP navy convoyar, escoltar
convulvulus: ~ **sepium** n AGRIC campanilla f
cook: ~-**chill meal** n FOOD, PACK comida cocinada y refrigerada f
cooker n PAPER lejiadora f, THERMO cocedor m
cooking n PAPER lejiación f (Esp), digestión f (AmL), THERMO cocción f
cool[1]: ~ **water inlet** n INSTR entrada de agua fría f
cool[2]: ~ **down** vti C&G enfriar
coolant n AUTO líquido refrigerante m, CONST refrigerante m, MECH ENG in refrigerators enfriador m, refrigerante m, in machine tools líquido refrigerante m, PHYS refrigerante m, REFRIG, THERMO fluido frigorífico m, VEH líquido refrigerante m
cooled[1] adj REFRIG, THERMO enfriado, refrigerado
cooled[2]: ~ **incubator** n LAB, REFRIG incubador refrigerado m
cooler n HEAT ENG enfriador m, radiador m, MECH ENG enfriador m, refrigerador m, NUCL, PETR TECH, PROD enfriador m, REFRIG cámara de refrigeración f, enfriador m, refrigerador m, THERMO enfriador m, refrigerador m, cámara de refrigeración f; ~ **cock** n PROD grifo del enfriador m
cooling[1] adj CHEM, HEAT ENG, MECH ENG, REFRIG, THERMO refrigerante
cooling[2] n C&G, GAS, MECH ENG, REFRIG, TEXTIL, THERMO enfriamiento m, refrigeración f; ~ **age** n GEOL período de enfriamiento m; ~ **air** n MECH ENG, REFRIG, THERMO aire de enfriamiento m, aire refrigerante m; ~ **banks and roller conveyors** n pl MECH ENG, REFRIG, THERMO bancos de enfriamiento y transportadores de rodillos m pl, bancos de refrigeración y transportadores de rodillos m pl, baterías de enfriamiento y transportadores de rodillos f pl, baterías de refrigeración y transportadores de rodillos f pl; ~ **basin** n PROD, REFRIG, THERMO cuba de enfriamiento f; ~ **bath** n REFRIG baño de enfriamiento m; ~ **battery** n REFRIG batería refrigerante f; ~ **cavity** n NUCL cavidad de enfriamiento f, piscina de enfriamiento f, REFRIG cavidad de enfriamiento f; ~ **coil** n GAS, NUCL, REFRIG serpentín de enfriamiento m, serpentín refrigerador m; ~ **and conveying unit** n MECH ENG, REFRIG, TRANSP unidad de transporte y refrigeración f; ~ **cylinder** n PAPER, REFRIG cilindro refrigerador m; ~ **down** n REFRIG puesta en temperatura f; ~~**down period** n C&G, NUCL, REFRIG período de enfriamiento m; ~ **duct** n MECH ENG, REFRIG conducto de enfriamiento m, conducto de refrigeración m, conducto refrigerante m; ~ **equipment** n MECH ENG, REFRIG, TEXTIL equipo de refrigeración m, equipo refrigerante m; ~ **fan** n AUTO, CINEMAT, REFRIG ventilador de enfriamiento m, ventilador de refrigeración m, VEH ventilador de refrigeración m; ~ **fin** n AIR TRANSP, MECH ENG aleta de refrigeración f, aleta refrigeradora f, NUCL aleta disipadora de calor f, REFRIG, THERMO aleta de refrigeración f, aleta refrigeradora f; ~ **flap** n AIR TRANSP, TRANSP flap de refrigeración m; ~ **load** n REFRIG, THERMO carga térmica f; ~ **medium** n REFRIG, THERMO fluido frigorífico m, refrigerante secundario m; ~ **mixture** n REFRIG, THERMO mezcla

refrigerante *f*; ~ **oil** *n* MECH ENG, REFRIG, THERMO aceite de refrigeración *m*, aceite refrigerante *m*; ~ **period** *n* NUCL *of waste* período de enfriamiento *m*; ~ **pond** *n* WATER estanque de enfriamiento *m*, piscina de desactivación *f*; ~ **range** *n* REFRIG amplitud de enfriamiento *f*; ~ **rate** *n* REFRIG grado de refrigeración *m*; ~ **rib** *n* CINEMAT aleta de enfriamiento *f*; ~ **section** *n* FOOD, REFRIG sección de enfriamiento *f*; ~ **spiral** *n* MECH ENG *injection moulds*, REFRIG serpentín refrigerante *m*; ~ **system** *n* AUTO, CONST, ELEC, POLL, TEXTIL, THERMO sistema de enfriamiento *m*, sistema de refrigeración *m*, sistema refrigerante *m*; ~ **tank** *n* CINEMAT tanque de enfriamiento *m*; ~ **to low temperature** *n* REFRIG, THERMO enfriamiento a una temperatura baja *m*, refrigeración a baja temperatura *f*; ~ **tower** *n* CHEM TECH, CONST, HEAT ENG, MECH ENG torre de enfriamiento *f*, torre de refrigeración *f*, MINE enfriador de chimenea *m* (*AmL*), torre de enfriado *f* (*Esp*), torre de refrigeración *f*, NUCL, PROD, REFRIG, THERMO torre de enfriamiento *f*, torre de refrigeración *f*; ~ **tube** *n* MECH ENG, REFRIG tubo de refrigeración *m*; ~ **tunnel** *n* FOOD, REFRIG túnel de enfriamiento *m*, túnel de refrigeración *m*; ~ **turbine** *n* MECH ENG turbina de enfriamiento *f*; ~ **water pipe** *n* MECH ENG, REFRIG, WATER tubería de agua de refrigeración *f*; ~ **zone** *n* C&G, REFRIG zona de enfriamiento *f*

coop *n* AGRIC gallinero *m*

Cooper: ~ **pairs** *n pl* PHYS pares de Cooper *m pl*

cooperative: ~ **emission** *n* METALL emisión cooperativa *f*; ~ **phenomenon** *n* PHYS fenómeno cooperativo *m*

coordinate[1] *n* COMP&DP, CONST, GEOM, MATH, MECH ENG, PHYS coordenada *f*; ~ **axes** *n pl* GEOM ejes de coordenadas *m pl*; ~ **boring-and-milling machine** *n* MECH ENG máquina coordinada de fresar y mandrinas *f*, máquina mandrinadora coordinada *f*, máquina taladradora y fresadora coordinada *f*; ~ **geometry** *n* GEOM geometría analítica *f*; ~ **linkage** *n* METALL acoplamiento coordinado *m*, enlace coordinado *m*; ~ **measuring machine** *n* METR aparato de medida coordinado *m*; ~ **system** *n* MATH, PHYS sistema de coordenadas *m*; ~ **transformation** *n* ELECTRON transformación coordinada *f*

coordinate[2] *vt* CONST, TELECOM coordinar

coordinated: ~ **universal time** *n* (*UTC*) TELECOM hora universal coordinada *f*

coordinating: ~ **gap** *n* ELEC *spark* distancia de salto *f*, distancia interelectródica *f*

coordination: ~ **area** *n* SPACE zona de coordinación *f*; ~ **bond** *n* CHEM enlace de coordinación *m*; ~ **number** *n* CHEM, CRYSTALL, METALL número de coordinación *m*

co-owner *n* WATER TRANSP *of ship* copropietario *m*, socio *m*; ~ **of private siding** *n* RAIL copropietario de apartadero particular *m*

cop: ~-**dyed** *adj* COLOUR teñido en canillas

copal: ~ **varnish** *n* COLOUR barniz de copal *m*

copaline *n* MINERAL copalina *f*

copalite *n* MINERAL copalita *f*

cope[1] *n* PROD *moulding-flask, loam mould* semicaja superior *f*; ~ **ring** *n* PROD *founding* anillo de la semicaja superior *m*

cope[2] *vt* CONST *architecture* recortar, *stones* rebajar

copiapite *n* MINERAL copiapoíta *f*

copilot *n* AIR TRANSP copiloto *m*

coping *n* CONST *architecture* albardilla *f*, WATER *of side walls of lock* coronamiento *m*

coplanar[1] *adj* ACOUST, GEOM, PHYS coplanar

coplanar[2]: ~ **cartridge** *n* ACOUST cartucho coplanar *m*, cápsula fonocaptora coplanar *f*; ~ **forces** *n pl* PHYS fuerzas coplanares *f pl*; ~ **waveguide** *n* PHYS, WAVE PHYS guía de ondas coplanar *f*

copolar: ~ **attenuation** *n* SPACE *communications* atenuación copolar *f*; ~ **pattern** *n* SPACE *communications* diagrama de copolarización *m*

copolymer *n* CHEM, P&R, PETR TECH, TEXTIL copolímero *m*

copolymerization *n* CHEM, P&R, PETR TECH, TEXTIL copolimerización *f*

copper[1]: ~-**bearing** *adj* MINE cuprífero; ~-**clad** *adj* COATINGS, ELEC *cable* blindado con hoja de cobre, con recubrimiento de cobre, cubierto con hoja de cobre; ~-**colored** *AmE*, ~-**coloured** *BrE adj* COLOUR de color cobre

copper[2] *n* (*Cu*) CHEM, ELEC, METALL cobre *m* (*Cu*); ~ **alloy bush** *n* MECH ENG buje de aleación de cobre *m*, casquillo de aleación de cobre *m*, cojinete de aleación de cobre *m*, manguito de aleación de cobre *m*; ~ **asbestos gasket** *n* AUTO junta de cobre y amianto *f*, MECH ENG junta de asbestos al cobre *f*, VEH junta de cobre y amianto *f*; ~ **bit** *n* PROD *of soldering iron* soldador *m*; ~ **braid** *n* ELEC, ELECTRON, PROD trenza de cobre *f*; ~-**braid shielding** *n* ELEC *cable* blindaje de trenza de cobre *m*, pantalla de trenza de cobre *f*, ELECTRON, PROD pantalla de trenza de cobre *f*, blindaje de trenza de cobre *m*; ~ **cable** *n* ELEC, ELECTRON, TELECOM cable de cobre *m*; ~ **conductor** *n* ELEC *cable*, ELECTRON conductor de cobre *m*; ~ **lap** *n* PROD taco abrasivo de cobre *m*; ~ **light** *n* C&G luz de cobre *f*; ~ **loss** *n* ELEC *transformer* pérdida en el cobre *f*, pérdida por efecto Joule *f*, pérdida óhmica *f*, ELEC ENG, PHYS pérdida en el cobre *f*; ~ **mine** *n* MINE mina de cobre *f*; ~ **nickel** *n* MINERAL niquelina *f*, níquel arsenical *m*; ~-**oxide rectifier** *n* ELEC ENG rectificador de óxido de cobre *m*; ~ **pyrite** *n* MINERAL pirita cuprífera *f*, pirita de cobre *f*; ~ **rivet** *n* CONST remache de cobre *m*; ~ **sheet** *n* CONST lámina de cobre *f*, plancha de cobre *f*; ~ **staining** *n* C&G cobreado *m*; ~ **sulfate** *AmE*, ~ **sulphate** *BrE n* CHEM, PHOTO sulfato de cobre *m*; ~ **test cell** *n* RAD PHYS celda de ensayo de cobre *f*; ~ **uranite** *n* NUCL torbernita *f*; ~ **wire** *n* COATINGS, CONST, ELEC, ELEC ENG *conductor* alambre de cobre *m*, cable de cobre *m*, hilo de cobre *m*; ~ **works** *n* PROD *for treatment of ores* fundición de cobre *f*, *foundry* fundería de cobre *f*

copperas *n* CHEM caparrosa *f*

copperasine *n* MINERAL sulfato de hierro y cobre *m*

copperplate *n* COLOUR, PRINT plancha de cobre *f*; ~ **engraving ink** *n* COLOUR, PRINT tinta para grabado en plancha de cobre *f*; ~ **printing press** *n* PRINT prensa para impresión en plancha de cobre *f*

copperplated: ~ **cylinder** *n* PRINT cilindro cobreado *m*

copperworking: ~ **tools** *n pl* PROD herramientas de cobre *f pl*

coprecipitation *n* NUCL coprecipitación *f*

coprocessor *n* COMP&DP coprocesador *m*

coprolite *n* GEOL coprolito *m*

coprostanol *n* CHEM coprostanol *m*

copy[1] *n* COMP&DP copia *f*, PRINT copia *f*, ejemplar *m*; ~ **camera** *n* PHOTO cámara de reproducción *f*, cámara para copiado *f*; ~ **fitting** *n* PRINT cálculo de originales *m*; ~ **frame** *n* PRINT marco portaoriginales *m*; **~-in** *n* COMP&DP importación *f*; ~ **milling** *n* MECH ENG fresado de copia *m*, fresado de reproducción *m*; **~-milling lathe** *n* MECH ENG *machine tool* torno fresador copiador *m*; **~-milling machine** *n* MECH ENG fresadora copiadora *f*, fresadora de reproducción *f*; **~-out** *n* COMP&DP exportación *f*; ~ **punch press** *n* MECH ENG prensa punzonadora copiadora *f*, prensa recortadora copiadora *f*, prensa troqueladora copiadora *f*, punzonadora copiadora *f*; ~ **stand** *n* PHOTO portaoriginales *m*, tablero para copias y reproducciones *m*

copy^2 *vt* PRINT reproducir

copying: ~ **attachment** *n* MECH ENG *machine tools* acoplamiento copiador *m*, aparato copiador *m*, dispositivo copiador *m*; ~ **ink** *n* COLOUR tinta de copiar *f*; ~ **lathe** *n* MECH ENG torno copiador *m*; ~ **lathe tool** *n* MECH ENG herramienta de torno copiador *f*; ~ **stand** *n* PHOTO tablero para copias y reproducciones *m*; ~ **unit** *n* MECH ENG dispositivo copiador *m*, unidad copiadora *f*

coquina: ~ **limestone** *n* GEOL caliza lumaquélica *f*

coracite *n* MINERAL, NUCL coracita *f*

coral^1 *adj* GEOL, OCEAN coralífero

coral^2 *n* GEOL, OCEAN coral *m*; ~ **reef** *n* GEOL arrecife coralígeno *m*, arrecife de coral *m*, OCEAN arrecife de coral *m*, arrecife coralígeno *m*; ~ **ridge** *n* GEOL, OCEAN cresta de coral *f*

coralline *adj* GEOL, OCEAN coralino

corbel *n* CONST *architecture* can *m*, saliente *m*, voladizo *m*

cord *n* C&G cuerda *f*, ELEC *cable* cable *m*, cordón *m*, cuerda *f*, MECH ENG cordón *m*, cuerda *f*, cable *m*, PAPER cuerda *f*, TELECOM conductor flexible *m*, cordón *m*, dicordio *m*, TEXTIL cordón *m*; ~ **carpet** *n* TEXTIL alfombra de cuerda *f*; ~ **circuit** *n* TELECOM circuito de conductos flexibles *m*, dicordios *m pl*; ~ **switch** *n* ELEC conmutador con cordones *m*, conmutador de cables *m*; ~ **switchboard** *n* TELECOM panel de conmutación por conductos flexibles *m*, panel de conmutación por dicordios *m*; **~-to-coating bond test** *n* MECH ENG prueba de adhesión del recubrimiento del cable *f*; ~ **of wood** *n* METR cuerda de leña *f*

cordage *n* WATER TRANSP *rigging* cabuyería *f*

cordierite *n* C&G cordierita *f*, MINERAL cordierita *f*, dicroíta *f*, iolita *f*

cordless: ~ **power drill** *n* MECH ENG taladradora a pilas *f*, taladradora eléctrica a pilas *f*; ~ **power screwdriver** *n* MECH ENG destornillador eléctrico a pilas *m*; ~ **switchboard** *n* TELECOM cuadro conmutador sin dicordios *m*, cuadro de distribución sin hilos conductores *m*, panel de conmutación sin dicordios *m*; ~ **sync** *n* CINEMAT sincronizador sin cable *m*; ~ **synchronization** *n* CINEMAT sincronizador sin cable *m*; ~ **telephone** *n* TELECOM teléfono inalámbrico *m*

cordon: ~ **line** *n* TRANSP acordonado *m*; **~-line survey** *n* TRANSP reconocimiento del acordonado *m*

corduroy *n* TEXTIL pana *f*

cordwood *n* CONST cuerda de leña *f*, leña *f*

core^1 *n* AGRIC hueso *m*, pepita *f*, CINEMAT *of carbon arc*, COMP&DP núcleo *m*, CONST núcleo *m*, alma *f*, *of building* interior *m*, ELEC *machine transformer* núcleo de hierro *m*, núcleo *m*, *safety* alma *f*, ELEC ENG *of a*

wire rope, cable conductor de cable eléctrico multifilar *m*, conductor de cable eléctrico monofilar *m*, alma *f*, *of fibre-optic cable* conductor interno aislado *m*, *magnetic memory* núcleo de memoria *m*, *magnetic, relay* soporte de cátodo *m*, GEOL, GEOPHYS testigo *m*, núcleo *m*, HYDROL muro de impermeabilización *m*, MINE testigo *m* (*Esp*), muestra *f* (*AmL*), NUCL *measuring* núcleo *m*, OPT núcleo *m*, alma *f*, PACK núcleo *m*, PAPER mandril *m*, PART PHYS núcleo *m*, núcleo atómico *m*, PETR TECH núcleo *m* (*AmL*), testigo *m* (*Esp*) *equipment, aircraft* núcleo magnético *m*, *safety* alma *f*, región activa *f*, núcleo central *m*, PROD *founding* macho de fundición *m*, *of crushing roll* macho *m*, SPACE centro *m*, núcleo *m*, TELECOM alma *f*, núcleo *m*, TEXTIL núcleo *m*, TV, WATER TRANSP *of rope* alma *f*; ~ **analysis** *n* PETR TECH análisis de núcleos *m* (*AmL*), análisis de testigos *m* (*Esp*); ~ **arbor** *n* PROD *founding* eje del macho *m*; ~ **area** *n* OPT área del núcleo *f*, REFRIG sección total de rejilla *f*, TELECOM región del alma *f*; ~ **average burn-up** *n* NUCL quemado medio del núcleo *m*; ~ **barrel** *n* MINE sacamuestras *m* (*AmL*), sacatestigos *m* (*Esp*), tubo sacatestigos *m*, PETR TECH barril cortanúcleos *m*, barril de testigos *m* (*Esp*), testiguero *m* (*AmL*), PROD *founding* macho *m*; ~ **bit** *n* MINE corona de sondeo *f*, sacamuestras *m* (*AmL*), sacatestigos *m* (*Esp*), PETR TECH barrena cortanúcleos *f* (*AmL*), barrena cortatestigos *f*, barrena sacatestigos *f* (*Esp*), broca *f*, mecha sacatestigos *f* (*Esp*), trépano sacatestigos *m* (*Esp*); **~-blowing machine** *n* MECH ENG soplador para machos *m*; ~ **board** *n* PROD *founding* tabla de machos *f*; ~ **borer** *n* MINE *for soft rock and large diameter holes* sonda para muestras *f* (*AmL*), sonda para testigos *f* (*Esp*); ~ **box** *n* PROD *founding* caja de machos *f*; ~ **box-boring machine** *n* PROD taladradora de machos *f*; ~ **breaker** *n* MINE extractor de testigos *m* (*Esp*), sacamuestras *m* (*AmL*), sacatestigos *m* (*Esp*); ~ **carriage** *n* PROD *founding* carro de estufa de machos *m*; ~ **casting** *n* PROD *founding* fundición con macho *f*; ~ **catcher** *n* MINE extractor de testigos *m* (*Esp*), sacamuestras *m* (*AmL*), sacatestigos *m* (*Esp*), NUCL recipiente del núcleo *m*; ~ **center** *AmE*, ~ **centre** *BrE n* OPT centro del núcleo *m*, TELECOM centro del alma *m*, centro del núcleo *m*; **~-cladding concentricity error** *n* OPT, TELECOM error de concentricidad en el revestimiento del alma *m*, error de concentricidad núcleo-revestimiento *m*; **~-cladding interface** *n* OPT, TELECOM superficie de contacto de chapado del núcleo *f*, superficie de separación entre el núcleo y el revestimiento *f*; **~-cladding ratio** *n* OPT, TELECOM relación entre el diámetro del alma y el espesor del aislamiento *f*; ~ **coolant flow rate** *n* NUCL tasa de caudal del refrigerante del núcleo *f*; ~ **cutter** *n* MINE corona testiguera *f* (*Esp*), trépano para testigos *m* (*AmL*); ~ **diameter** *n* OPT, TELECOM diámetro del núcleo *m*; **~-diameter tolerance** *n* OPT, TELECOM tolerancia del diámetro del alma *f*, tolerancia del diámetro del núcleo *f*; ~ **drill** *n* MECH ENG barrena sacamuestras *f*, broca hueca *f*, PETR TECH sondeo estratigráfico *m*; ~ **drill carbide-tipped for concrete** *n* MECH ENG broca hueca de plaquitas de carburo para hormigón *f*; ~ **drilling** *n* MINE barrena sacamuestras *f*, broca hueca *f*, corona de sondeo *f*, sonda para testigos *f* (*Esp*), sondeo estratigráfico *m* (*AmL*), sondeo testiguero *m* (*Esp*), tren de sondeos *m*, PETROL perforación con sacatestigos *f*; ~ **driver** *n* MECH ENG *mortising machine* conductor de tubo *m*; ~ **dump** *n* COMP&DP vuelco de la memoria central *m*; ~ **extractor** *n* MINE sacatestigos *m*; ~-**flooding train** *n* NUCL tren de inundación del núcleo *m*, tren de inyección de seguridad *m*; ~ **grid** *n* PROD *founding* armadura del macho *f*; ~ **grid structure** *n* NUCL estructura reticular del núcleo *f*; ~ **head plug unit** *n* NUCL tapón superior del núcleo *m*; ~ **iron** *n* PROD *founding* armadura del macho *f*; ~ **laminations** *n pl* ELEC ENG discos del núcleo *m pl*; ~ **lathe** *n* PROD *founding* torno para machos *m*; ~ **lifter** *n* MINE sacatestigos *m*; ~ **loss** *n* ELEC *transformer*, PHYS pérdida en el hierro *f*, pérdida en el núcleo *f*; ~ **making** *n* PROD *founding* fabricación de machos *f*; ~ **nail** *n* CONST clavo central *m*; ~ **outlet thermocouple** *n* NUCL termopar de salida del núcleo *m*; ~ **oven** *n* PROD estufa de machos *f*; ~ **pin** *n* PROD pasador de machos *m*; ~ **plane** *n* ELEC ENG plano del núcleo *m*; ~ **plate** *n* MECH ENG *injection mould* disco del núcleo *m*, placa de machos *f*, placa de refuerzos de noyos *f*, PROD *founding* placa de machos *f*; ~ **plunger** *n* MINE núcleo móvil *m*; ~ **print** *n* PROD *founding* alojamiento para machos *m*, portada para machos *f*, saliente del macho *m*; ~ **pusher** *n* MINE expulsatestigos *m*; ~ **rack** *n* PROD *founding* planchero de machos *m*; ~ **reference surface concentricity error** *n* OPT, TELECOM error de concentricidad de la superficie de referencia del núcleo *m*; ~ **sample** *n* COAL, GAS, MINE, PETR TECH muestra del sondeo *f*, testigo *m*; ~ **sampling** *n* CONST testigo de sondeo *m*; ~ **sand** *n* PROD *founding* arena para machos *f*; ~ **screen** *n* ELEC *cable conductor* blindaje del núcleo *m*, pantalla del alma *f*; ~ **shuffling** *n* NUCL redistribución de los elementos de combustible en el núcleo *f*; ~ **slicer** *n* PETROL rebanadora de testigos *f*; ~ **slide retaining plate** *n* MECH ENG placa de fijación del carro *f*, placa de retención de la maza *f*, placa de retención del carro *f*, placa de retención del porta-estampas *f*; ~ **stock** *n* PROD *founding* caja de machos *f*; ~ **storage** *n* AmE COMP&DP almacenamiento por núcleos *m*, almacén por núcleos *m*, memoria de núcleos *f*; ~ **store** BrE *n* COMP&DP almacenamiento por núcleos *m*, almacén por núcleos *m*, memoria de núcleos *f*; ~ **stove** *n* PROD *founding* estufa de machos *f*; ~ **test** *n* ELEC *machine* prueba del núcleo *f*; ~ **tolerance field** *n* OPT campo de tolerancia del núcleo *m*, TELECOM campo de tolerancia del alma *m*; ~ **transformer** *n* ELEC, ELEC ENG transformador de núcleo *m*; ~ **trestle** *n* PROD *founding* armazón para machos *m*; ~ **tube** *n* MINE tubo testigos *m*, PROD *founding* tubo de machos *m*; ~-**type transformer** *n* ELEC, ELEC ENG transformador de columnas *m*, transformador de núcleo de hierro *m*; ~ **uncovery** *n* NUCL descubrimiento del núcleo *m*

core² *vt* GEOL, PETR TECH testificar, PROD ahuecar con macho, *in castings* ahuecar, formar con un macho; ~ **out** *vt* PROD *in castings* ahuecar, formar con un macho; ~ **up** *vt* PROD formar con un macho

cored: ~ **casting** *n* PROD fundición con macho *f*; ~ **passage** *n* MECH ENG agujero de desarenar *m*, agujero moldeado *m*; ~ **solder** *n* ELEC *connections* soldadura de almas *f*, soldante de almas *m*

coreless: ~ **armature** *n* ELEC, ELEC ENG inducido sin núcleo *m*; ~ **induction furnace** *n* HEAT, THERMO horno de inducción sin núcleo *m*

corer *n* PETR TECH extractor de testigos *m*

coring *n* MECH ENG colocación de machos *f*, cristalización *f*, heterogeneidad *f*, moldeo con machos *m*, solución sólida nucleada *f*, METALL cristalización *f*, heterogeneidad *f*, solución sólida nucleada *f*, PETR TECH, PETROL corte núcleos *m* (*AmL*), extracción de testigos *f* (*Esp*), PROD *in castings* colocación de machos *f*; ~ **machine** *n* PROD *founding* máquina para colocar machos *f*; ~-**out** *n* PROD ahuecamiento *m*; ~ **tool** *n* PETR TECH cortanúcleos *m* (*AmL*), herramienta sacatestigos *f* (*Esp*), utillaje del sacatestigos *m* (*Esp*); ~-**up** *n* PROD colocación de machos *f*

Coriolis: ~ **acceleration** *n* MECH, SPACE aceleración de Coriolis *f*; ~ **effect** *n* FLUID efecto de Coriolis *m*; ~ **force** *n* FLUID, METEO, PHYS fuerza de Coriolis *f*

cork *n* CONST corcho *m*, LAB corcho *m*, tapón *m*, REFRIG corcho *m*; ~ **borer** *n* LAB taladracorchos *m*; ~ **finish** *n* C&G, COATINGS acabado al corcho *m*; ~ **polishing** *n* C&G pulido con corcho *m*; ~ **washer** *n* MECH ENG arandela de corcho *f*

corkage *n* AmE (*cf bore BrE*) C&G diámetro interior de cilindros *m*, entaponado *m*, perforado *m*

corking: ~ **machine** *n* PACK máquina de colocar tapones *f*; ~ **plug** *n* PACK tapón de cierre *m*

corkscrew: ~ **aerial** *n* BrE (*cf corkscrew antenna AmE*) TELECOM antena helicoidal *f*; ~ **antenna** *n* AmE (*cf corkscrew aerial BrE*) TELECOM antena helicoidal *f*; ~ **rule** *n* ELEC *electromagnetism* norma de poner conductores eléctricos en espiral *f*, regla del sacacorchos *f*, regla del tirabuzón *f*, ELEC ENG regla del tirabuzón *f*, regla del sacacorchos *f*, norma de poner conductores eléctricos en espiral *f*, PHYS norma de poner conductores eléctricos en espiral *f*, regla del sacacorchos *f*, regla del tirabuzón *f*; ~ **stairs** *n pl* CONST escalera helicoidal *f*

corn *n* AmE (*cf maize BrE*) AGRIC maíz *m*; ~ **belt** *n* AmE (*cf maize belt BrE*) AGRIC zona maicera *f*, zona núcleo *f* (*AmL*); ~ **binder** *n* AmE (*cf maize binder BrE*) AGRIC cortadora-empacadora de maíz *f*; ~-**borer** *n* AmE (*cf maize-borer BrE*) AGRIC barrenador del maíz *m*; ~ **breeding** *n* AmE (*cf maize breeding BrE*) AGRIC mejoramiento genético de maíz *m*; ~-**cob** *n* AGRIC mazorca de maíz *f*, zuro del maíz *m*; ~ **cob with grains** *n* AGRIC mazorca de maíz con grano *f*; ~ **crib** *n* AmE (*cf maize drying shed BrE*) AGRIC criba de maíz *f*; ~ **drill** *n* AmE (*cf maize drill BrE*) AGRIC sembradora de maíz *f*; ~ **flake** *n* AGRIC copo de maíz *m*; ~ **gluten feed** *n* AmE (*cf maize gluten feed BrE*) AGRIC alimento de gluten de maíz *m*; ~ **grower** *n* AmE (*cf maize grower BrE*) AGRIC agricultor de maíz *m*, productor de maíz *m*; ~ **growing area** *n* AmE (*cf maize growing area BrE*) AGRIC región productora de maíz *f*; ~ **husk** *n* AmE (*cf maize husk BrE*) AGRIC chala de maíz *f* (*AmL*), espata de maíz *f* (*Esp*); ~ **husker** *n* AmE (*cf maize husker BrE*) AGRIC deschaladora de maíz *f* (*AmL*), deshojadora de maíz *f* (*Esp*); ~ **leaf aphid** *n* AmE (*cf maize leaf aphid BrE*) AGRIC pulgón de la hoja del maíz *m*; ~-**meal** *n* (*cf Indian meal BrE*) AGRIC harina de maíz *f* (*Esp*), polenta *f* (*AmL*); ~ **picker** *n* AmE (*cf maize picker BrE*) AGRIC cosechadora de maíz *f*; ~ **picker-husker** *n* AmE (*cf maize picker-husker BrE*) AGRIC cosechadora-deshojadora de maíz *f* (*Esp*), espigadora-deschaladora de maíz *f* (*AmL*); ~ **picker-sheller** *n* AmE (*cf maize picker-sheller BrE*) AGRIC cosechadora-desgranadora de maíz *f*, espigadora-desgranadora de maíz *f* (*AmL*); **~ sap beetle** *n* AGRIC escarabajo de savia del maíz *m*; **~ sheller** *n* AmE (*cf maize sheller BrE*) AGRIC desgranadora de maíz *f*; **~ silage** *n* AmE (*cf maize silage BrE*) AGRIC ensilado de maíz *m*; **~ snapper** *n* AmE (*cf maize snapper BrE*) AGRIC espigadora de maíz *f*; **~ stalk** *n* AmE (*cf maize stalk BrE*) AGRIC tallo del maíz *m*; **~ stunt** *n* AmE (*cf maize stunt BrE*) AGRIC enanismo del maíz *m*; **~ syrup** *n* AmE (*cf maize syrup BrE*) AGRIC jarabe de maíz *m*; **~ thresher** *n* AmE (*cf maize thresher BrE*) AGRIC trilladora de maíz *f*

corner: **~ band** *n* CONST guardavivos *m*; **~ block** *n* C&G piedra angular *f*; **~ cut** *n* PRINT redondeo de esquina *m*; **~ detail** *n* TV detalle del ángulo *m*; **~ loss** *n* TELECOM pérdida angular *f*; **~ mount** *n* PHOTO esquina *f*, ángulo *m*; **~ pillar** *n* CONST pilar de esquina *m*; **~ post** *n* CONST cornijal *m*, esquinal *m*; **~ reflector aerial** *n* BrE TV antena con reflector angular *f*; **~ reflector antenna** *n* AmE (*cf corner-reflector aerial BrE*) TV antena con reflector angular *f*; **~-rounding cutters** *n pl* MECH ENG *right-hand, left-hand, double* cortadora redondeadora de esquinas *f*, tijeras curvadas para planchas *f pl*; **~ slick** *n* PROD *founding* alisado de escuadra *m*; **~ smoother** *n* PROD *founding* alisador de escuadra *m*; **~ stapling** *n* PACK, PRINT grapado del ángulo *m*; **~-stapling machine** *n* PACK, PRINT máquina grapadora de ángulos *f*; **~ tile** *n* CONST teja de esquina *f*

cornice *n* CONST *architecture* cornisa *f*
corolla *n* AGRIC corola *f*
corollary *n* MATH corolario *m*
corona *n* ELEC ENG, ELECTRON, GAS, P&R, PHYS, SPACE corona *f*; **~ discharge** *n* ELEC, ELEC ENG, GAS, P&R, PHYS, SPACE descarga en corona *f*, descarga por efecto corona *f*, efecto corona *m*; **~ effect** *n* ELEC *discharge*, ELEC ENG, GAS, P&R, SPACE efecto corona *m*; **~ resistance** *n* P&R resistencia a la corona *f*
coronal: **~ emission line** *n* RAD PHYS línea coronal de emisión *f*
coronene *n* CHEM coroneno *m*
corral *vt* MAR POLL cerrar
corrected: **~ data** *n pl* COMP&DP datos corregidos *m pl*; **~ result** *n* METR resultado corregido *m*
correcting: **~ lens** *n* CINEMAT, OPT, PHOTO lente correctora *f*; **~ optics** *n* OPT, PHOTO óptica correctora *f*; **~ plate** *n* INSTR placa correctora *f*
correction *n* MECH ENG corrección *f*; **~ factor** *n* AIR TRANSP, METR factor de corrección *m*; **~ factor for induced drag** *n* AIR TRANSP factor de corrección para la resistencia aerodinámica *m*, factor de corrección para retardo inducido *m*; **~ filter** *n* PHOTO filtro de corrección *m*; **~ lens** *n* CINEMAT, OPT, PHOTO lente correctora *f*; **~ maneuver** *AmE*, **~ manoeuvre** *BrE* *n* SPACE maniobra de corrección *f*
corrective: **~ action** *n* QUALITY acción correctiva *f*; **~ maintenance** *n* COMP&DP mantenimiento correctivo *m*; **~ measure** *n* TELECOM medida correctiva *f*
correctness *n* METR *of balance* exactitud *f*
corrector: **~ circuit** *n* TV circuito corrector *m*
correlated *adj* GEN correlacionado
correlation *n* GEN correlación *f*; **~ coefficient** *n* COMP&DP, FLUID coeficiente de correlación *m*; **~ function** *n* ELECTRON función de correlación *f*
correlative: **~ phase-shift keying** *n* TELECOM manipulación por desviación de fase correlativa *f*
correlator *n* ELECTRON, TELECOM correlador *m*

correspondence *n* ACOUST correspondencia *f*; **~ analysis** *n* MATH análisis de correspondencia *m*; **~ envelope** *n* PACK, PAPER bolsa postal *f*; **~ pocket** *n* PACK, PAPER sobre postal *m*; **~ principle** *n* PHYS principio de correspondencia *m*
corresponding: **~ angle** *n* GEOM ángulo correspondiente *m*
corridor: **~ control** *n* TRANSP control del corredor *m*, control del pasillo *m*, control mediante pasillo *m*
corrodent *n* CHEM, SAFE corrosivo *m*
corrodibility *n* GEN corrosividad *f*
corrodible *adj* GEN corrosible
corrosion *n* GEN corrosión *f*; **~ fatigue** *n* METALL fatiga por corrosión *f*; **~-fatigue crack** *n* METALL, NUCL grieta por fatiga bajo corrosión *f*; **~ inhibitor** *n* AUTO, COATINGS, FOOD, MECH, P&R, PACK, SPACE, VEH antioxidante *m*, inhibidor anticorrosivo *m*, inhibidor de corrosión *m*; **~ nodule** *n* NUCL *measuring* nódulo de corrosión *m*; **~ pickling** *n* NUCL decapado por baño ácido *m* (*AmL*), desoxidación por baño ácido *f* (*Esp*); **~ prevention** *n* PACK prevención de la corrosión *f*; **~ preventive** *n* PACK agente para evitar la corrosión *m*; **~-preventive paper** *n* PACK papel a prueba de corrosión *m*; **~ resistance** *n* CONST, P&R resistencia a la corrosión *f*; **~-resistant stainless steel fastener** *n* MECH ENG abrazadera de acero inoxidable anti-corrosivo *f*, fiador de acero inoxidable anti-corrosivo *m*, sujetador de acero inoxidable anti-corrosivo *m*
corrosive[1] *adj* CHEM, SAFE corrosivo
corrosive[2]: **~ atmosphere** *n* PROD atmósfera corrosiva *f*; **~ substance** *n* SAFE substancia corrosiva *f*; **~ water** *n* HYDROL, WATER agua corrosiva *f*
corrugated[1] *adj* MECH ENG acanalado, arrugado, corrugado, estriado, ondulado, PAPER corrugado, ondulado
corrugated[2]: **~ board** *n* PACK, PAPER cartón corrugado *m*, cartón ondulado *m*; **~-board box** *n* PACK, PAPER caja de cartón ondulado *f*; **~-board with broadly spaced flutes** *n* PACK, PAPER cartón ondulado de onda ancha *m*; **~-board with narrowly spaced flutes** *n* PACK, PAPER cartón microondulado *m*; **~ cardboard** *n* FOOD cartón corrugado *m*, PACK, PAPER cartulina ondulada *f*; **~ expansion joint** *n* NUCL junta de expansión ondulada *f*; **~ fiberboard** *AmE*, **~ fibreboard** *BrE* *n* PACK cartón ondulado *m*; **~ glass** *n* C&G vidrio corrugado *m*, vidrio rolado *m*; **~ iron** *n* CONST chapa ondulada *f*, placa ondulada *f*; **~ jaws** *n pl* MINE mordazas acanaladas *f pl*; **~ paper** *n* PACK, PAPER papel ondulado *m*; **~ products** *n pl* PACK materiales ondulados *m pl*; **~ roll** *n* PROD lámina ondulada *f*; **~ sheet iron** *n* CONST placa ondulada *f*; **~ wired glass** *n* C&G vidrio rolado alambrado *m*
corrugating: **~ medium** *n* PAPER papel para corrugar *m* (*AmL*), papel para ondular *m* (*Esp*)
corrugation *n* C&G corrugado *m*, PAPER corrugación *f*, ondulación *f*
corrugator *n* PAPER onduladora *f*, tren ondulador *m*
corrupt[1]: **~ file** *n* COMP&DP archivo corrupto *m*
corrupt[2] *vt* COMP&DP corromper
corsite *n* PETROL corsita *f*
corticoid *n* CHEM corticoide *m*
corticosteroid *n* CHEM corticoesteroide *m*
corticosterone *n* CHEM corticosterona *f*
corticotrophic *adj* CHEM corticotrófico
corticotrophin *n* CHEM corticotrofina *f*

corticotropic *adj* CHEM corticotrópico

corticotropin *n* CHEM corticotropina *f*

cortisone *n* CHEM cortisona *f*

corundellite *n* MINERAL corundelita *f*

corundophilite *n* MINERAL corundofilita *f*

corundum *n* C&G, MINERAL corindón *m*; ~ **wheel** *n* PROD disco de corindón *m*

corynite *n* MINERAL corinita *f*

cos *abbr* (*cosine*) COMP&DP, CONST, GEOM, MATH *trigonometry* cos (*coseno*)

cosalite *n* MINERAL cosalita *f*

cosec *abbr* (*cosecant*) COMP&DP, CONST, GEOM, MATH *trigonometry* cosec (*cosecante*)

cosecant *n* (*cosec*) COMP&DP, CONST, GEOM, MATH *trigonometry* cosecante *f* (*cosec*)

coset: ~ **deposits** *n pl* GEOL depósitos clasificados por grupos *m pl*

COSHH *abbr* (*control of substances hazardous to health*) SAFE control de substancias peligrosas para la salud *m*

cosine *n* (*cos*) COMP&DP, CONST, GEOM, MATH *trigonometry* coseno *m* (*cos*); ~ **emission law** *n* OPT ley de emisión del coseno *f*; ~ **equalizer** *n* TV igualador de coseno *m*; ~ **rule** *n* GEOM ley de los cosenos *f*, regla del coseno *f*; ~ **tables** *n* GEOM tablas de cosenos *f pl*; ~ **wave** *n* GEOM cusinusoide *f*, onda de coseno *f*

cosmic: ~ **background radiation** *n* PART PHYS, PHYS, RAD PHYS, SPACE radiación cósmica de fondo *f*; ~ **noise** *n* SPACE ruido cósmico *m*; ~ **radiation** *n* PART PHYS, PHYS, RAD PHYS, SPACE radiación cósmica *f*; ~ **ray** *n* PHYS, RAD PHYS, SPACE rayo cósmico *m*; ~ **ray background** *n* PHYS, RAD PHYS, SPACE radiación cósmica de fondo *f*; ~ **shower** *n* SPACE lluvia cósmica *f*; ~ **space** *n* SPACE espacio cósmico *m*; ~ **velocity** *n* SPACE velocidad cósmica *f*

cosmodrome *n* SPACE cosmódromo *m*

cosmogony *n* SPACE cosmogonía *f*

cosmography *n* SPACE cosmografía *f*

cosmology *n* SPACE cosmología *f*

cosmonaut *n* SPACE cosmonauta *m*

cossyrite *n* MINERAL cosirita *f*

cost[1]: ~-**effective** *adj* MECH ENG económico

cost[2] *n* PROD coste *m*; ~ **center** *AmE*, ~ **centre** *BrE n* PROD centro de coste *m*, centro de cálculo de costes *m*; ~-**effective maintenance** *n* MECH ENG mantenimiento económico *m*, mantenimiento rentable *m*; ~ **insurance freight** *n* (*CIF*) PROD coste y seguro y flete *m*; ~ **overrun** *n* SPACE rebasamiento de costos *m*; ~ **price** *n* PROD precio de coste *m*, precio de factura *m*, precio de venta *m*; ~ **reduction in mechanical assembly** *n* MECH ENG reducción de coste en el montaje mecánico *f*; ~ **of space** *n* PACK costo de espacio *m*; ~ **variance** *n* PROD variación del coste *f*

Costas: ~ **loop** *n* TELECOM bucle de Costas *m*

costean[1]: ~ **pit** *n* MINE pocillo de investigación *m* (*Esp*), pozo de cateo *m* (*AmL*), pozo de exploración *m*, pozo de prospección *m* (*Esp*); ~ **trench** *n* MINE zanja de exploración *f*

costean[2] *vi* MINE catear, explorar, hacer sondeos

cot *abbr* (*cotangent*) COMP&DP, CONST, GEOM, MATH *trigonometry* cotg (*cotangente*)

cotangent *n* (*cot*) COMP&DP, CONST, GEOM, MATH *trigonometry* cotangente *f* (*cotg*)

cotidal[1] *adj* GEOPHYS coetáneo con la amplitud de marea

cotidal[2]: ~ **line** *n* GEOPHYS mareograma *m*

cotter: ~ **bolt** *n* MECH ENG perno con chaveta *m*; ~ **file** *n* MECH ENG carleta plana *f*, lima ranuradora *f*; ~ **pin** *n* MECH chaveta de retén *f*, chaveta guía *f*, clavija hendida *f*, pasador abierto *m*, pasador de aletas *m*, pasador de chaveta *m*, MECH ENG chaveta de retén *f*, chaveta guía *f*, pasador abierto *m*, clavija hendida *f*, pasador de aletas *m*, pasador de chaveta *m*, WATER TRANSP pasador de chaveta *m*; ~ **slot** *n* MECH ENG ranura de chaveta *f*, ranura de pasador *f*; ~ **stud bolt** *n* MECH ENG prisionero de chaveta *m*

cottered: ~ **joint** *n* CONST unión con pasador *f*

cottering *n* MECH ENG chavetaje *m*

cotton[1]: ~-**covered** *adj* COATINGS, ELEC, ELEC ENG *wire* forrado de algodón, revestido de algodón

cotton[2] *n* AGRIC, TEXTIL algodón *m*; ~ **belt** *n* AGRIC zona algodonera *f*; ~ **braid** *n* ELEC ENG trenza de algodón *f*, TEXTIL galón de algodón *m*, pasamanería de algodón *f*; ~ **condenser spinning** *n* TEXTIL hilatura del algodón por condensador *f*; ~ **field** *n* AGRIC, TEXTIL algodonal *m*; ~ **insulation** *n* ELEC, ELEC ENG aislación de algodón *f*, aislamiento de algodón *m*; ~ **linter** *n* P&R borra de algodón *f*; ~ **picker** *n* AGRIC, TEXTIL cosechadora de algodón *f*; ~-**seed oil** *n* FOOD aceite de semilla de algodón *m*; ~ **spinning** *n* TEXTIL hilatura del algodón *f*; ~ **stainer** *n* AGRIC, TEXTIL chinche tintórea *f*; ~ **stripper** *n* AGRIC recolectora de algodón *f*; ~ **waste** *n* PROD, TEXTIL borra de algodón *f*, desperdicios de algodón *m pl*; ~ **yarn** *n* TEXTIL hilo de algodón *m*

Cotton: ~ **balance** *n* PHYS balanza de Cotton *f*

Cotton-Mouton: ~ **effect** *n* PHYS efecto Cotton-Mouton *m*

cottonseed *n* AGRIC semilla de algodón *f*

cotunnite *n* MINERAL cotunnita *f*

CO₂ *n* (*carbon dioxide*) ELECTRON CO_2 *m* (*dióxido de carbono, carbón dióxido*)

cotyledon *n* AGRIC cotiledón *m*

couch: ~ **press** *n* PAPER prensa húmeda *f*, prensa manchón *f*; ~ **roll jacket** *n* PAPER camisa del rodillo manchón *f*

Couette: ~ **flow** *n* FLUID flujo de Couette *m*

coulomb *n* (*C*) ELEC, ELEC ENG, ELECTRON, METR, PHYS culombio *m* (*C*); ~ **energy** *n* RAD PHYS energía culombiana *f*; ~ **gage** *AmE*, ~ **gauge** *BrE n* METEO, PHYS culombímetro *m*; ~ **repulsion** *n* PHYS repulsión culombiana *f*

coulombmeter *n* ELEC, ELEC ENG, INSTR, METR, PHYS coulómetro *m*, voltámetro *m*

Coulomb: ~'**s law** *n* ELEC *electrostatics*, PHYS ley de Coulomb *f*; ~ **theorem** *n* ELEC, PHYS teorema de Coulomb *m*; ~ **torsion balance** *n* PHYS balanza de torsión de Coulomb *f*

coulometer *n* ELEC, ELEC ENG, INSTR, METR, PHYS coulómetro *m*, voltámetro *m*

coulter *n* *BrE* AGRIC reja de arado *f*

coumalic *adj* CHEM cumálico

coumalin *n* CHEM cumalina *f*

coumaline *n* CHEM cumalina *f*

coumaran *n* CHEM cumarana *f*

coumarane *n* CHEM cumarana *f*

coumaric *adj* CHEM cumárico

coumarin *n* CHEM cumarina *f*

coumarine *n* CHEM cumarina *f*

coumarone: ~ **resin** *n* P&R resina de cumarona *f*

count *n* COMP&DP número *m*, TEXTIL número *m*, título

m; **~-up counter** *n* ELECTRON contador de impulsos *m*; **~-up done bit** *n* PROD bit de terminación del recuento *m*

countdown *n* ELECTRON, SPACE cuenta atrás *f*, cuenta regresiva *f*; **~ counter** *n* ELECTRON, SPACE contador de cuenta atrás *m*

counter *n* COMP&DP, ELECTRON, MECH ENG contador *m*, MINE subnivel *m*, filón crucero *m*, filón transversal *m*, veta transversal *f*, galería intermedia *f*, nivel *m*, contrafilón *m*, TELECOM contador *m*, WATER TRANSP *stun structure* bovedilla *f*; **~ address** *n* PROD dirección del contador *f*; **~ circuit** *n* ELECTRON circuito contador *m*; **~ EMF** *n* ELEC medidor de FEM *m*; **~ gangway** *n* MINE contragalería *f*, galería intermedia *f*; **~ key light** *n* CINEMAT contraluz principal *f*; **~ lathe** *n* CONST tabla de la bovedilla *f*; **~-revolving axial fan** *n* TRANSP ventilador axial contrarrotativo *m*, ventilador axial de hélices contrarrotativas *m*; **~-rotating propeller** *n* TRANSP hélice contrarrotatoria *f*; **~ tube** *n* ELECTRON, NUCL tubo contador *m*; **~-tube probe** *n* NUCL sonda con tubo contador *f*

counteracting: **~ force** *n* MECH ENG fuerza neutralizadora *f*, fuerza opuesta *f*

counterbalance[1] *n* AIR TRANSP contrabalance *m*; **~ carriage** *n* MINE carro del contrapeso *m*

counterbalance[2] *vt* MECH, MECH ENG compensar, equilibrar

counterbalanced: **~ drilling spindle** *n* MECH ENG eje perforador equilibrado *m*; **~ lever** *n* MECH ENG palanca equilibrada *f*

counterbalancing: **~ rope** *n* MINE contracable de equilibrio *m* (*AmL*), contrapeso de equilibrio *m* (*Esp*)

counterbore[1] *n* MECH ENG agujero escariado *m*, contrataladro *m*, ensanchador *m*, escariador *m*; **~ with detachable pilot** *n* MECH ENG escariador con piloto desmontable *m*; **~ with solid pilot** *n* MECH ENG escariador con piloto sólido *m*

counterbore[2] *vt* MECH ENG, PROD ensanchar, escariar

counterboring *n* MECH ENG, PROD ensanchamiento *m*, escariado *m*

counterclockwise: **~ rotation** *n* MECH, PROD rotación a izquierdas *f*, rotación en dirección contraria a las agujas del reloj *f*, rotación siniestrosa *f*

countercurrent *n* CHEM, ELEC ENG, HYDROL, NUCL, OCEAN, WATER contracorriente *f*; **~ classifier** *n* COAL lavador a contracorriente *m*; **~-diffusion plant** *n* NUCL planta de difusión en contracorriente *f*

counterdie *n* PRINT contramatriz *f*

counterdriving: **~ motion** *n* MECH ENG transmisión intermedia *f*

counterelectromotive: **~ force** *n* ELEC, ELEC ENG, PHYS, RAIL, VEH fuerza contraelectromotriz *f*

counterflooding *n* WATER TRANSP equilibrado *m*

counterflow *n* COAL contracorriente *f*, contraflujo *m*; **~ classifier** *n* COAL lavador a contracorriente *m*; **~ heat exchanger** *n* FOOD intercambiador de calor a contracorriente *m*, REFRIG cambiador de calor de corrientes cruzadas *m*, THERMO intercambiador de calor a contracorriente *m*

countergear *n* MECH ENG transmisión intermedia *f*

counterlevel *n* MINE galería intermedia *f*

counterlode *n* MINE contrafilón *m*, filón crucero *m*, filón transversal *m*, veta transversal *f*

countermatte *n* CINEMAT contratrama *f*

countermotion *n* MECH ENG movimiento contrario *m*, movimiento opuesto *m*

counterplate *n* MECH ENG contraplato *m*

counterpoise: **~ bridge** *n* CONST puente de contrapeso *m*, puente levadizo *m*

counterpressure *n* HYDRAUL contrapresión *f*

counterpunch[1] *n* MECH ENG contrapunzón *m*

counterpunch[2] *vt* MECH ENG contrapunzar

countershaft *n* AUTO eje intermedio *m*, eje secundario *m*, árbol contraeje *m*, MECH ENG contramarcha *f*, eje intermedio *m*, eje secundario *m*, transmisión intermedia *f*, árbol auxiliar con engranajes *m*; **~ cone** *n* MECH ENG cono del eje conducido *m*; **~ gear** *n* AUTO engranaje de eje secundario *m*, VEH piñón del eje intermediario *m*

countershafting *n* MECH ENG transmisión intermedia *f*, contramarcha *f*

countershot *n* CINEMAT contratoma *f*

countersink[1] *n* GEN avellanado *m*; **~ bit** *n* MECH, MECH ENG, PROD avellanador *m*, broca de avellanar *f*

countersink[2] *vt* MECH, MECH ENG, PROD abocardar, avellanar

countersinking *n* GEN avellanado *m*

counterstern *n* WATER TRANSP *boat building* popa con bovedilla *f*

counterstream: **~ line** *n* HYDRAUL línea de retroceso del flujo *f*

countersunk: **~ buttonhead rivet** *n* CONST remache de cabeza redonda embutida *m*; **~ fastener** *n* MECH ENG sujetador avellanado *m*, sujetador embutido *m*; **~-head bolt** *n* CONST, MECH, MECH ENG perno de cabeza avellanada *m*; **~-head rivet** *n* CONST, MECH, MECH ENG remache de cabeza embutida *m*; **~-head screw** *n* CONST, MECH, MECH ENG tornillo de cabeza avellanada *m*, tornillo de cabeza embutida *m*, tornillo de cabeza perdida *m*; **~ hole** *n* MECH ENG agujero avellanado *m*, PROD orificio hundido *m*; **~ mount** *n* PHOTO *for a camera lens* montaje embutido *m*; **~ riveting** *n* CONST, MECH, MECH ENG remache avellanado *m*; **~ screw** *n* CONST, MECH, MECH ENG tornillo embutido *m*; **~ setting** *n* PHOTO montaje embutido *m*; **~ woodscrew** *n* CONST tornillo embutido para madera *m*

countertest *n* MECH ENG contraprueba *f*

countertop: **~ machine** *n* PACK máquina contadora de tapas *f*

counterweight *n* CONST, INSTR, MECH, MECH ENG contrapeso *m*

counting *n* ELECTRON contador *m*; **~ device** *n* PACK contador *m*; **~ rate** *n* ELECTRON porcentaje de recuento *m*; **~ station** *n* TRANSP estación de recuento *f*

country: **~ code** *n* (*CC*) TELECOM código del país *m*; **~ rock** *n* GEOL roca encajante *f*, MINE roca de los respaldos *f* (*AmL*), roca esteril *f* (*Esp*), filón *m* (*AmL*), roca madre *f* (*Esp*)

county: **~ agent** *n* AGRIC agente de extensión *m*

couplability *n* RAIL posibilidad de enganche *f*

couple[1] *n* ELEC, ELEC ENG elemento *m*, par *m*, MECH ENG conexión *f*, empalme *m*, enganche *m*, ensample *m*, junta *f*, pareja *f*, unión *f*, PHYS par *m*; **~ roof** *n* CONST par con tirantes *m*

couple[2] *vt* ELEC, ELEC ENG acoplar, conectar, MECH, MECH ENG acoplar, MINE acoplar, empalmar, RAIL enganchar; **~ in parallel** *vt* ELEC, ELEC ENG acoplar en derivación, conectar en paralelo

coupled: **~ circuit** *n* ELEC, ELEC ENG circuito acoplado *m*; **~ engines** *n pl* MECH ENG motores acoplados *m pl*;

~ **exposure meter** n PHOTO exposímetro acoplado m; ~ **lid-base bottle tray** n PACK bandeja para botellas con tapa movible incorporada f; ~ **modes** n pl ACOUST, OPT, SPACE, TELECOM modos acoplados m pl; ~ **oscillators** n pl ELECTRON, PHYS osciladores acoplados m pl; ~ **rangefinder** n PHOTO telémetro acoplado m; ~ **speed and F-stop setting** n CINEMAT, PHOTO, TV ajuste acoplado de abertura y velocidad del diafragma m; ~ **systems** n pl PHYS sistemas acoplados m pl

coupler n GEN acoplador m; ~ **connector** n ELEC conector acoplador m; ~ **development** n CINEMAT revelado de acoplador m; ~ **loss** n OPT pérdida por acoplamiento f, TELECOM pérdida de acoplador f; ~ **plug and socket connection** n ELEC enchufe acoplador y zócalo conector m; ~ **socket-connector** n ELEC zócalo conector acoplador m

coupling n ACOUST acoplador m, AIR TRANSP acoplamiento m, conexión f, unión f, CHEM acoplamiento m, aparejamiento m, CINEMAT acoplador m, COMP&DP acoplador m, acoplamiento m, ELEC connection, induction acoplamiento m, acoplador m, ELEC ENG waveguides acoplador m, enganche m, acoplamiento m, conexión f, empalme m, ELECTRON acoplador m, MECH acoplamiento m, conexión f, acoplador m, empalme m, unión f, junta f, MECH ENG device acoplamiento m, conexión f, empalme m, two shafts unión f, acoplador m, junta f, PHYS empalme m, acoplamiento m, acoplador m, RAIL acoplamiento m, enganche m, TELECOM acoplador m, acoplamiento m, TRANSP conexión f, enganche m, acoplamiento m, VEH conexión f, acoplamiento m, enganche m, WATER TRANSP of engine acoplamiento m; ~ **agent** n P&R agente de acoplamiento m; ~ **between stages** n ELECTRON fases entre acoplamiento f pl; ~ **blanking plug** n PROD tapón obturador de empalme m; ~ **box** n MECH ENG collar de acoplamiento m, manguito de acoplamiento m; ~ **buffer** n AIR TRANSP amortiguador de acoplamiento m; ~ **capacitor** n ELEC capacitor de acoplamiento m, condensador de acoplamiento m, PHYS capacitor de acoplamiento m; ~ **coefficient** n PHYS coeficiente de acoplamiento m; ~ **coil** n ELEC bobina de acoplamiento f; ~ **constant** n NUCL, PHYS constante de acoplamiento f; ~ **cover** n AIR TRANSP helicopter cubierta de unión f; ~ **efficiency** n OPT, TELECOM eficacia del acoplamiento f, eficiencia de acoplamiento f; ~ **flange** n MECH brida de acoplamiento f, brida de empalme f, brida de unión f; ~ **hook** n MECH ENG gancho de acoplamiento m, RAIL dispositivo de enganche m; ~ **hose** n RAIL manguera de acoplamiento f; ~ **impedance** n ELEC impedancia de acoplamiento f; ~ **link** n MECH ENG enganche m, unión f; ~ **loop** n ELEC ENG nudo de empalme m; ~ **loss** n OPT, TELECOM pérdida en el acoplamiento f, pérdida por acoplamiento f; ~ **nut** n MECH ENG tensor de acoplamiento m, tensor de empalme m, tuerca de acoplamiento f, tuerca de unión f; ~ **pin** n MECH ENG for trailer pasador de enganche m, pasador de unión m; ~ **resistance** n ELEC resistencia de acoplamiento f; ~ **ring** n MECH ENG anillo de acoplamiento m; ~ **rod** n RAIL biela de acoplamiento f; ~ **sleeve** n MECH manguito de acoplamiento m, MECH ENG manguito de acoplamiento m, pipe fitting manguito de unión m; ~**spigot with thread** n MECH ENG die set espiga de acoplamiento con rosca f; ~ **spindle** n MECH ENG eje de acoplamiento de plato m; ~ **transformer** n ELEC, ELEC ENG transformador de acoplamiento m; ~ **tube** n MECH ENG tubo de acoplamiento m

course[1]: ~-**up** adv WATER TRANSP radar proa arriba

course[2] n AIR TRANSP rumbo m, C&G of bricks or blocks carrera f, CONST masonry hilada f, of road recorrido m, contorno m, HYDROL of river curso m, MINE dirección f, PHYS desarrollo m, SPACE curso m, dirección f, ruta f, trayectoria f, recorrido m, TEXTIL recorrido m, pasada f, WATER TRANSP navigation rumbo m; ~ **alignment** n AIR TRANSP alineación de rumbo f, corrección de rumbo f; ~ **angle** n AIR TRANSP ángulo de rumbo m; ~ **blip pulse** n TELECOM pulso de la señal en curso m; ~-**data generator** n AIR TRANSP generador de datos de rumbo m; ~ **indicator** n AIR TRANSP, WATER TRANSP navigation indicador de rumbo m; ~ **indicator selector** n AIR TRANSP, WATER TRANSP selector de indicador de rumbo m; ~ **line** n AIR TRANSP, WATER TRANSP línea de rumbo f; ~ **made good** n WATER TRANSP navigation rumbo corregido m, rumbo efectivo m; ~-**of-face stitches** n TEXTIL pasada de puntadas del derecho f; ~-**of-reverse stitches** n TEXTIL pasada de puntadas del revés f; ~ **of ore** n MINE filón alargado horizontalmente m; ~ **selector** n AIR TRANSP selector de rumbo m; ~ **through the water** n WATER TRANSP navigation rumbo real por el agua m; ~ **to steer** n WATER TRANSP navigation derrota f; ~ **tracer** n AIR TRANSP trazador de rumbo m

course[3]: **be on** ~ vi WATER TRANSP estar a rumbo

courses: ~ **per minute** n pl TEXTIL pasadas por minuto f pl

courseware n COMP&DP software didáctico m (Esp), soporte lógico de un curso de enseñanza m (AmL)

coursing n MINE instalación para distribuir el aire de ventilación f; ~ **bubble** n COAL nivel de ventilación m

courtesy: ~ **ensign** n WATER TRANSP of visited country bandera de cortesía f; ~ **flag** n WATER TRANSP of visited country bandera de cortesía f

couverture n FOOD cobertura f

Couvinian adj GEOL Couviniense

covalence n CHEM, NUCL covalencia f

covalency n CHEM, NUCL covalencia f

covalent[1] adj CHEM, NUCL covalente

covalent[2]: ~ **bond** n CHEM enlace covalente m, enlace sigma m, unión covalente f, CRYSTALL enlace covalente m, METALL adherencia covalente f, enlace covalente m, unión covalente f

covariance n COMP&DP covarianza f

covariant n COMP&DP covariante f; ~ **electrodynamics** n ELEC electrodinámica covariante f

cove n OCEAN cala f, caleta f, ensenada f, WATER TRANSP geography ancón m, cala f

covelline n MINERAL covellina f

covellite n MINERAL covellita f

cover n CINEMAT funda f, CONST welt tablero m, GEOL, HYDRAUL recubrimiento m, INSTR sombrerete m, cubierta f, MECH cubierta f, tapa f, MECH ENG cubierta f, sombrerete m, placa de recubrimiento f, tapa f, PRINT, SAFE cubierta f, SPACE tapa f, cubierta f, TEXTIL funda f, tapa f, VEH tapa f; ~ **crop** n AGRIC cultivo de cobertura m; ~ **gas** n GAS, NUCL gas protector m; ~-**gas discharge line** n GAS, NUCL línea de descarga del gas protector f; ~ **glass** n C&G, LAB microscopy cubreobjeto m; ~-**glass gage** AmE,

~-glass gauge *BrE n* C&G, LAB cubreobjeto con escala *m*; **~ plate** *n* FUELLESS *of collector* placa de cubierta *f*, MECH ENG cubierta protectora de tubos catódicos *f*, placa de recubrimiento *f*, NUCL cubierta protectora *f*; **~ slab** *n* NUCL losa superior del reactor *f*; **~ slip** *n* C&G, INSTR, LAB cubreobjeto *m*; **~ strip** *n* MECH ENG listón tapajuntas *m*, platabanda *f*; **~ strip of root rib** *n* AIR TRANSP *helicopter* tira de cubierta de la nervadura de la raíz *f*; **~ tile** *n* BrE (*cf spout cover AmE*) C&G cubierta de la noria *f*, tapón *m*, CONST tapón *m*; **~ to prevent accidents** *n* SAFE cubierta para prevenir accidentes *f*

coverage *n* AGRIC *pesticide*, SPACE, TELECOM cobertura *f*; **~ area** *n* SPACE zona de cobertura *f*

coveralls *n pl* AmE (*cf overalls BrE*) SAFE bata de trabajo *f* (*Esp*), mono de trabajo *m* (*Esp*), overoles *m pl* (*AmL*)

covercoat *n* C&G capa de sellado *f*

covered[1] *adj* COATINGS forrado, ELEC *conductor*, ELEC ENG forrado, recubierto, revestido

covered[2]: **~ car** *n* AmE (*cf covered wagon BrE*) RAIL vagón cerrado *m*; **~ container** *n* TRANSP contenedor cubierto *m*; **~ electrode** *n* CONST electrodo revestido *m*; **~ pot** *n* C&G crisol cubierto *m*; **~ wagon** *n* BrE (*cf covered car AmE*) RAIL vagón cerrado *m*; **~ yarn** *n* TEXTIL hilo recubierto *m*

covering *n* COATINGS recubierto *m*, CONST *over pit-top* cubierta *f*, ELEC ENG, PACK recubrimiento *m*, PHOTO funda *f*; **~ board** *n* WATER TRANSP *shipbuilding* regala *f*; **~ fire** *n* MILIT tiro de protección *m*; **~ joint** *n* CONST junta de recubrimiento *f*; **~ paint** *n* COATINGS, P&R pintura de cobertura *f*, pintura de recubrimiento *f*; **~ plate** *n* PROD cubierta protectora *f*, placa protectora *f*; **~ power** *n* COATINGS, COLOUR, P&R poder de cobertura *m*, poder de cubrimiento *m*; **~ varnish** *n* COATINGS, COLOUR barniz protector *m*

cow: **~ catcher** *n* RAIL máquina exploradora *f*, quitapiedras *m*

COW *abbr* (*crude-oil washing*) PETR TECH lavado de crudo *m*

cowl *n* AIR TRANSP *motor* capó *m*, CONST *of chimney*, HEAT ENG *wire* sombrerete *m*, MECH capó *m*; **~ flap** *n* AIR TRANSP *of engine, gill* portezuela del capó *f*

cowling *n* AIR TRANSP capó *m*; **~ flaps** *n pl* VEH *cooling* aleta de enfriamiento *f*

Cowper: **~ stove** *n* C&G estufa de Cowper *f*

CPI *abbr* COMP&DP (*computer-PBX interface*) interfaz computador-PBX *m* (*AmL*), interfaz computadora-PBX *m* (*AmL*), interfaz ordenador-PBX *m* (*Esp*), PRINT (*characters per inch*) CPP (*caracteres por pulgada*), TELECOM (*computer-PBX interface*) interfaz computador-PBX *m* (*AmL*), interfaz computadora-PBX *m* (*AmL*), interfaz ordenador-PBX *m* (*Esp*)

CPM *abbr* (*critical-path method*) COMP&DP CPM (*método del camino crítico*)

CPS *abbr* (*characters per second*) COMP&DP, PRINT CPS (*caracteres por segundo*)

CPSK *abbr* (*coherent phase-shift keying*) TELECOM transmisión por desplazamiento coherente de fase *f*

CPT: **~ theorem** *n* PART PHYS, PHYS teorema CPT *m*

CPU *abbr* (*central processing unit*) COMP&DP, TELECOM UCP (*unidad central de proceso*)

CPVC *abbr* (*chlorinated polyvinyl chloride*) P&R CPVC (*cloruro de polivinilo clorado*)

CQM *abbr* (*circuit group query message*) TELECOM mensaje de consulta destinado a grupo de circuitos *m*

CQR[1] *abbr* (*circuit group query response message*) TELECOM mensaje de respuesta de consulta destinado a grupo de circuitos *m*

CQR[2]: **~ anchor** *n* SAFE, WATER TRANSP *mooring* ancla CQR de seguridad *f*

c-quark *n* PART PHYS quark encanto *m*

CR[1] *abbr* COMP&DP (*carriage return*) carácter de retorno del carro *m*, TELECOM (*connection request*) petición de comunicación *f*

CR[2]: **~ rubber** *n* CHEM caucho CR *m*

Cr *abbr* (*chromium*) CHEM, COATINGS, METALL Cr (*cromo*)

crab[1] *n* MECH *machine* malacate *m*, pala mecánica *f*, torno para elevar pesos *m*, PROD *hoisting* carro *m*; **~ angle** *n* AIR TRANSP ángulo de deriva *m*; **~ winch** *n* PROD torno de izar *m*

crab[2] *vi* WATER TRANSP *ship* irse a la ronza

Crab: **~ nebula** *n* SPACE nebulosa del Cangrejo *f*

crack[1] *n* COAL cascada *f*, chasquido *m*, estallido *m*, estampido *m*, fisura *f*, grieta *f*, hendidura *f*, raja *f*, CONST diaclasa *f*, fisura *f*, grieta *f*, CRYSTALL grieta *f*, MECH fisura *f*, grieta *f*, hendidura *f*, rajadura *f*, METALL estallido *m*, grieta *f*, hendidura *f*, TEXTIL rasgadura *f*; **~ arrest temperature** *n* METALL temperatura de contención de grietas *f*, temperatura de interrupción de grietas *f*; **~ branching** *n* METALL desintegración por estallido *f*; **~ detector** *n* MECH ENG, NUCL detector de grietas *m*; **~ extension force** *n* METALL capacidad de extensión de la grieta *f*; **~ formation** *n* METALL formación de grietas *f*, formación de hendiduras *f*; **~ initiation** *n* METALL inicio de la entalla *m*, inicio de la grieta *m*, inicio de la hendidura *m*; **~ nucleation** *n* METALL nucleación de la grieta *f*, nucleación de la hendidura *f*; **~ opening displacement** *n* NUCL desplazamiento de la punta de la grieta *m*; **~ propagation rate** *n* NUCL velocidad de propagación de una grieta *f*; **~ resistance** *n* P&R resistencia a la rotura *f*, resistencia al resquebrajamiento *f*; **~ test** *n* MECH ENG prueba de grietas *f*; **~ tip** *n* METALL extremo de la grieta *m*; **~ velocity** *n* METALL velocidad de propagación de una grieta *f*

crack[2] *vi* CRYSTALL, MECH ENG, P&R agrietarse

cracked *adj* MECH, MECH ENG agrietado, rajado

cracker *n* COAL alambique pirolizador *m*, cilindro pulverizador *m*

cracking *n* CONST fisura *f*, grieta *f*, MECH *colours, ink* pirólisis catalítica a presión *f*, agrietamiento *m*, grieta *f*, crujido *m*, MECH ENG formación de grietas pequeñas *f*, agrietamiento *m*, NUCL, P&R agrietamiento *m*, PETR TECH desintegración catalítica *f*, cracking *m*, QUALITY resquebrajamiento *m*, THERMO agrietamiento *m*; **~ coal** *n* C&G carbón para craqueo *m*; **~ equipment with fluidized catalyst** *n* CHEM TECH equipo de craqueo con catalizador fluidizado *m*; **~ open** *n* MECH ENG *of a valve* ligera apertura *f*, pequeña apertura *f*; **~ plant** *n* PETR TECH planta de cracking *f*

crackle[1] *n* ACOUST, CHEM crepitación *f*

crackle[2] *vi* ACOUST, CHEM crepitar

crackled: **~ finish** *n* PROD acabado craquelado *m*; **~ glass** *n* C&G vidrio agrietado *m*

cradle *n* CINEMAT mecanismo basculante *m*, CONST *hanging scaffold* cama *f*, cuna *f*, INSTR apoyo *m*, soporte *m*, bastidor *m*, cojinete *m*, MECH bastidor *m*,

apoyo *m*, soporte *m*, cojinete *m*, MECH ENG *tooling*
escala suspendida *f*, escala volante *f*, MINE artesa *f*,
criba lavadora *f*, gamella *f*, WATER TRANSP *for storage
or transport of boat* calzo *m*; ~ **dynamo** *n* ELEC
generator, ELEC ENG dinamo de cuna *f*; ~ **gear head**
n CINEMAT cabeza de engranaje basculante *f*; ~ **head**
n CINEMAT cabeza basculante *f*; ~ **iron** *n* CONST cuna
de hierro *f*; ~ **mounting** *n* MILIT montaje de la cuna
m; ~ **rocker** *n* MINE cuna *f*; ~ **stirrup** *n* CONST estribo
de apoyo *m*

craft *n* SPACE artefacto *m*, avión *m*, embarcación *f*, nave
f, WATER TRANSP *boat* artefacto *m*, embarcación *f*;
~ **porcelain** *n* C&G porcelana artesanal *f*; ~ **pottery** *n*
C&G, PROD alfarería artesanal *f*

cramp[1] *n* CONST *carpenter's* grapa *f*, *for stonework*
corchete *m*, laña *f*, MECH ENG gatillo *m*, grapa *f*,
grapón *m*, sujeción *f*, traba *f*; ~ **iron** *n* CONST
carpenter's grapa de hierro *f*, *for stonework* corchete
de hierro *m*; ~ **iron with stone hook** *n* CONST
corchete de hierro con ganchos *m*; ~ **with turned-
down ends** *n* CONST corchete con extremos invertidos *m*

cramp[2] *vt* MECH ENG sujetar, trabar

cramping *n* TV sujeción *f*

cranage *n* MECH ENG *in workshop* engruado *m*, gastos
de grúa *m pl*, gruaje *m*, sistema de grúas *m*; ~ **of 20
tonnes capacity** *n* MECH ENG sistema de grúa de 20
toneladas de capacidad *m*; ~ **up to 20 tonnes
capacity** *n* MECH ENG sistema de grúa de hasta 20
toneladas *m*

cranch *n* MINE pilar de mineral *m*

crane *n* CINEMAT, CONST, MECH, WATER TRANSP *dockyard, cargo vessel* grúa *f*; ~ **barge** *n* PETR TECH
gabarra grúa *f*; ~ **helicopter** *n* AIR TRANSP helicóptero grúa *m*; ~ **hook** *n* CONST gancho de grúa *m*; ~ **jib**
n MECH, MECH ENG brazo de grúa *m*, pluma de grúa *f*;
~ **ladle** *n* PROD *founding* cucharón de grúa *m*;
~ **operator** *n* CINEMAT operador de grúa *m*, WATER
TRANSP conductor de grúa *m*; ~ **rail** *n* CONST carril de
grúa *m*, riel de grúa *m*

craneman *n* CONST maquinista de grúa *m*

crank *n* AIR TRANSP *reactor* manivela *f*, manubrio *m*,
AUTO manivela *f*, cigüeña *f*, codo *m*, brazo de
manivela *m*, MECH manivela *f*, manubrio *m*, MECH
ENG brazo de manivela *m*, eje acodado *m*, cigüeña *f*,
codo de manubrio *m*, cigüeñal *m*, codo de palanca *m*,
VEH manivela *f*, brazo de manivela *m*, cigüeñal *m*;
~ **arm** *n* AUTO, MECH ENG, VEH brazo de manivela *m*;
~ **bearing** *n* MECH ENG cojinete de bancada *m*,
cojinete de cigüeñal *m*; ~ **blasting machine** *n* MINE
máquina con funcionamiento defectuoso *f*; ~ **cheek**
n AUTO, MECH ENG, VEH brazo de manivela *m*; ~ **and
connecting rod system** *n* MECH ENG cigüeña y
sistema de varilla de conexión *f*, codo y sistema de
varilla de conexión *m*; ~ **drive slotting machine** *n*
MECH ENG limadora vertical de manivela *f*, mortajadora de manivela *f*, ranuradora de manivela *f*; ~ **end**
n MECH ENG extremo delantero *m*, extremo posterior
m; ~ **end dead center** *AmE*, ~ **end dead centre** *BrE*
n MECH ENG centro muerto delantero *m*, centro
muerto trasero *m*, punto muerto delantero *m*, punto
muerto trasero *m*; ~ **end release** *n* MECH ENG escape
delantero *m*; ~ **handle** *n* RAIL manivela *f*; ~ **link** *n*
PROD articulación de la placa de apoyo *f*; ~ **pin** *n*
AUTO muñequilla del cigüeñal *f*, muñón del cigüeñal
m, pasador del cigüeñal *m*, MECH pasador de

manivela *m*, VEH muñequilla de biela del cigüeñal *f*,
muñón del cigüeñal *m*; ~ **shaping machine** *n* MECH,
MECH ENG limadora accionada por biela *f*; ~ **switch**
n AIR TRANSP, AUTO, VEH interruptor de arranque del
motor *m*

crankcase *n* AUTO, MECH, VEH caja del cigüeñal *f*,
cárter del motor *m*, cárter inferior del cigüeñal *m*;
~ **breather** *n* AUTO, VEH respiradero del cárter motor
m; ~ **heater** *n* REFRIG calentador del cárter *m*; ~ **top
half** *n* AUTO, MECH, VEH cárter superior del cigüeñal
m; ~ **ventilation** *n* AUTO, MECH, VEH ventilación del
cárter motor *f*

cranked: ~ **facing tool** *n* MECH ENG herramienta de
refrentar acodada *f*; ~ **finishing tool** *n* MECH ENG
herramienta de acabado acodada *f*; ~ **knife tool** *n*
MECH ENG herramienta de corte acodada *f*; ~ **knife
tool for copy turning** *n* MECH ENG herramienta de
corte acodada para torneado de reproducción *f*;
~ **link** *n* MECH ENG *chain* junta acodada *f*, unión
acodada *f*; ~ **link transmission chain** *n* MECH ENG
cadena de transmisión de enlace acodada *f*, cadena
de transmisión de unión acodada *f*; ~ **spanner** *n*
MECH ENG llave acodada *f*; ~ **tool** *n* MECH ENG *metal
turning* herramienta acodada *f*; ~ **turning and facing
tool** *n* MECH ENG herramienta de tornear y refrentar
acodada *f*

cranking *n* AIR TRANSP *of a piston engine* arranque del
motor por medio de manivela *m*, rotación del motor
por medio de manivela *f*

crankpath *n* MECH ENG paso acodado *m*

crankpin *n* MECH ENG *of engine crank* muñequilla *f*,
muñón *m*

crankshaft *n* AUTO, MECH, MECH ENG, VEH, WATER
TRANSP *engine* cigüeñal *m*, eje del cigüeñal *m*, árbol
del cigüeñal *m*; ~ **alignment gage** *AmE*, ~ **alignment gauge** *BrE* *n* MECH ENG galga para la
alineación de cojinetes del cigüeñal *f*, galga para
medir la caída del cigüeñal *f*; ~ **bearing** *n* AUTO, VEH
cojinete del cigüeñal *m*; ~ **bearing cap** *n* AUTO, VEH
casquillo del cojinete del cigüeñal *m*, sombrerete del
soporte del cigüeñal *m*; ~ **front end** *n* AUTO, VEH
extremo delantero del cigüeñal *m*; ~ **gear** *n* AUTO,
VEH engranaje del cigüeñal *m*

crankweb *n* AUTO, MECH, VEH brazo de cigüeñal
m, brazo de manivela *m*, guitarra del cigüeñal *f*

crash[1] *n* COMP&DP caída del sistema *f*, choque *m*,
PRINT gasa para encuadernar *f*, SPACE impacto *m*;
~ **barrier** *n* SAFE barrera de impacto *f*, TRANSP muro
de protección *m*; ~ **landing** *n* AIR TRANSP aterrizaje de
emergencia *m*, aterrizaje forzoso *m*, SPACE *aircraft*
aterrizaje de emergencia *m*; ~ **numbering** *n* PRINT
numeración continua *f*; ~ **perforation** *n* PRINT perforación continua *f*; ~ **printing** *n* PRINT impresión
consecutiva *f*; ~ **switch** *n* AIR TRANSP interruptor de
impacto *m*

crash[2]: ~ **into** *vt* SAFE chocar contra, impactar contra

crash[3] *vi* COMP&DP fallar

crate *n* AGRIC jaula *f*, PACK cajón *m*, jaula *f*; ~ **pallet** *n*
TRANSP bandeja-jaula *f*, paleta-jaula *f*, pálet-jaula *m*
(*AmL*)

crater *n* GEOL cráter *m*, MINE cráter *m*, embudo *m*, P&R
cráter *m*, poro *m*, SPACE cráter *m*; ~ **cut** *n* MINE
socavación *f*

craton *n* GEOL cratón *m*

crawfish *n* WATER cangrejo de río *m*, ástaco *m*

crawler *n* MECH tractor oruga *m*; ~ **base** *n* MINE planta rastrera *f*; ~ **dragline excavator** *n* CONST *civil engineering* draga excavadora sobre orugas *f*, dragalina sobre orugas *f*; ~ **track** *n* MECH ENG banda de rodamiento *f*, carrilera de rodamiento *f*, oruga de rodamiento *f*

crawling *n* ELEC ENG enganche *m*, enlace *m*, P&R formación de arrugas *f*, TV enganche *m*

crayfish *n* WATER cangrejo de río *m*, ástaco *m*

craze[1] *n* TEXTIL último grito *m*

craze[2] *vt* CONST agrietar

craze[3] *vi* C&G agrietar

crazing *n* C&G, CONST agrietamiento *m*, formación de grietas pequeñas *f*, CRISTALL, MECH ENG, NUCL, P&R formación de grietas pequeñas *f*

crazy: ~ **top** *n* AGRIC deformación de la inflorescencia *f*, panoja loca *f*

CRC[1] *abbr* COMP&DP, ELECTRON, TELECOM (*cyclic redundancy check*) CRC (*verificación de redundancia cíclica*), PRINT (*camera-ready copy*) CRC (*original listo para reproducir*), TELECOM (*cyclic redundancy code*) CRC (*código de redundancia cíclica*)

CRC[2]: ~ **message bloc** *n* (*CMB*) TELECOM bloque de mensajes CRC *m*

CRDH *abbr* (*control rod drive housing*) NUCL CRDH (*alojamiento del mecanismo de accionamiento de las barras de control*)

CRDM *abbr* (*control rod drive mechanism*) NUCL CRDM (*mecanismo de accionamiento de las barras de control*)

cream: ~ **separator** *n* FOOD separador de nata *m*; ~ **of tartar** *n* CHEM bitartrato potásico *m*, crémor tártaro *m*, FOOD crémor tártaro *m*, tartrato ácido de potasio *m*

creamed: ~ **latex** *n* P&R látex desnatado *m*

creamery: ~ **butter** *n* FOOD mantequilla cremosa *f*

creaming *n* C&G, FOOD, P&R desnatado *m* (*Esp*), desnate *m* (*AmL*); ~ **agent** *n* CHEM, P&R agente cremante *m*

crease[1] *n* PRINT arruga *f*, estría *f*, TEXTIL arruga *f*, doblez *m*, pliegue *m*; ~ **recovery** *n* TEXTIL recuperación de las arrugas *f*, recuperación del pliegue *f*; ~**-resistant finish** *n* COATINGS, TEXTIL acabado resistente a las arrugas *m*; ~ **resistance** *n* TEXTIL resistencia a las arrugas *f*, resistencia al pliegue *f*; ~**-resistant finish** *n* COATINGS, TEXTIL acabado a prueba de arrugas *m*

crease[2] *vt* PACK plegar, PRINT, TEXTIL arrugar

crease[3] *vi* TEXTIL arrugarse

creaseability *n* PAPER aptitud al plegado *f*

creaser *n* PRINT hendedor *m*

creasing: ~**-and-gluing machine** *n* PACK máquina plegadora y encoladora *f*; ~**-and-scoring machine** *n* PACK máquina plegadora y ranuradora *f*

create[1] *vt* COMP&DP crear

create[2]: ~ **a draft** *AmE*, ~ **a draught** *BrE* *vi* MECH ENG crear aspiración, crear succión, crear una corriente de aire, *drawing* crear un dibujo, crear un diseño, crear un esquema a borrador, crear un plano

credential *n* TELECOM credencial *m*

credit *n* CINEMAT título *m*; ~**-card call** *n* TELECOM, TV llamada con tarjeta de crédito *f*; ~ **indicator** *n* TELECOM indicador de crédito *m*

credits *n pl* CINEMAT, TV títulos *m pl*, títulos de crédito *m pl*

creek *n* WATER TRANSP caleta *f*, caño *m*

creel *n* TEXTIL cántara *f*, fileta *f*; ~ **fishing** *n* OCEAN pesca con nasa *f*

creep[1] *n* COAL arrastre *m*, cadencia elástica *f*, corrimiento *m*, fluencia *f*, formación de cristales en la superficie *f*, levantamiento gradual del piso por subpresiones *m*, percolación *f*, resbalamiento *m*, termodeformación plástica *f*, CONST corrimiento *m*, CRYSTALL fluencia a alta temperatura *f*, GAS deslizamiento *m*, HEAT ENG termodeformación lenta *f*, MECH deformación progresiva *f*, estiramiento continuo y lento *m*, fluencia *f*, termodeformación plástica *f*, MINE estiramiento *m*, levantamiento gradual del piso por subpresiones *m*, P&R termodeformación plástica *f*, PETR TECH arrastre *m*, deslizamiento *m*, movimiento paulatino de terreno *m*, PROD *of belt* resbalamiento *m*; ~ **feeding** *n* AGRIC alimentación suplementaria de terneros *f*; ~ **limit** *n* METALL límite de fluencia *m*; ~ **properties** *n pl* MECH propiedades de fluencia *f pl*; ~ **resistance** *n* P&R resistencia a la fluencia *f*; ~ **rupture elongation** *n* METALL alargamiento de la rotura por fluencia *m*; ~ **strain** *n* METALL deformación dependiente del tiempo *f*, termodeformación plástica *f*; ~ **strength** *n* COAL carga máxima de tracción sin deformación apreciable *f*, resistencia a la fluencia *f*, resistencia a la termofluencia *f*, METALL carga máxima de tracción sin deformación *f*; ~ **test** *n* C&G prueba de escurrimiento *f*

creep[2] *vi* GEOL deformarse

creeper: ~ **chain** *n* MINE cadena transportadora *f*

creeping[1] *adj* AGRIC reptante, GEOL deformándose continuamente, móvil

creeping[2]: ~ **motion** *n* FLUID deformación plástica *f*; ~ **wheatgrass** *n* AGRIC grama *f*

cremator *n* HEAT, THERMO horno crematorio *m*

crenulation *n* GEOL crenulación *f*

creosote *n* CHEM creosota *f*

crepe *n* CHEM, P&R crepé *m*, TEXTIL crespón *m*; ~ **paper** *n* PACK, PAPER papel crespado *m*; ~ **rubber** *n* P&R crepé de caucho *m*

creped *adj* PAPER crespado

creping *n* PAPER crespado *m*

crescent: ~**-shaped** *adj* GEOM luniforme

cresol: ~ **resin** *n* P&R resina de cresol *f*

crest *n* CONST cresta *f*, *of roof* cima *f*, FUELLESS *of dams* coronamiento *m*, GEOL cresta *f*, cima *f*, HYDROL *spacecraft* cresta *f*, *unit of measurement of absorbed dose* coronamiento *m*, WATER *of dam, weir* coronamiento *m*, coronación *f*; ~ **factor** *n* ELEC ENG *alternating current* factor de amplitud *m*, factor de cresta *m*; ~ **height** *n* FUELLESS altura de coronamiento *f*; ~ **line** *n* OCEAN línea de cresta *f*; ~ **province** *n* OCEAN zona de crestas *f*; ~ **tile** *n* CONST teja *f*

crested: ~ **wheatgrass** *n* AGRIC agropiro *m*

cretaceous *adj* GEOL, PETR TECH, PETROL cretáceo

Cretaceous: ~ **Period** *n* GEOL, PETR TECH período Cretáceo *m*

crevice *n* COAL bolsa *f*, fisura *f*, grieta *f*, hendidura *f*

crew[1] *n* AGRIC cuadrilla *f*, AIR TRANSP tripulación *f*, CINEMAT equipo *m*, PETR TECH cuadrilla *f*, turno *m*, PROD equipo *m*, SPACE tripulación *f*, WATER TRANSP *of a boat, ship* dotación *f*, tripulación *f*; ~ **compartment** *n* AIR TRANSP compartimiento de la tripulación *m*; ~ **door** *n* AIR TRANSP puerta de la tripulación *f*; ~ **escape module** *n* SPACE módulo para escape de la tripulación *m*; ~ **list** *n* WATER TRANSP *ship's papers* lista de tripulación *f*; ~ **operating manual** *n* AIR TRANSP manual de operación de la tripulación *m*; ~'s **quarters** *n pl* WATER TRANSP cámaras de la tripulación *f pl*; ~ **rescue vehicle** *n* SPACE vehículo de rescate de la tripulación *m*; ~ **service module** *n* (*CSM*) SPACE módulo de servicio de la tripulación *m*; ~ **station** *n* AIR TRANSP estación de la tripulación *f*

crew[2] *vti* WATER TRANSP *vessel* tripular

crewmate *n* SPACE miembro de la tripulación *m*

CRF *abbr* TELECOM (*connection-related function*), TELECOM (*virtual channel connection*) función relacionada con la conexión *f*, conexión de canal virtual *f*

CRI: ~ **print** *n* CINEMAT copia CRI *f*

crib *n* MINE cuadro portátil *m* (*Esp*), pilar de madera *m* (*AmL*), entibado *m*, PROD *mines* encofrado de madera *m*, entibado *m*, llave de madera *f*

cribble *n* COAL cedazo *m*, criba *f*, harnero *m*, tamiz *m*, PROD criba *f*

cribwork *n* PROD encribado *m*

crichtonite *n* MINERAL crictonita *f*

crime: ~ **prevention device** *n* SAFE aditamento para prevenir crímenes *m*

crimp[1] *n* C&G corrugado *m*, estrechez *f*, obstrucción *f*, TEXTIL rizado *m*; ~ **lock** *n* PRINT cierre fruncido *m*; ~**-on closure** *n* PACK cierre mediante rizado *m*; ~ **paper cup** *n* PACK naso de papel rizado *m*; ~ **terminal lug** *n* ELEC ENG lengüeta de conexión a presión *f*, lengüeta de conexión terminal fruncida *f*

crimp[2] *vt* MECH fijar por presión, plegar, rebordear, MINE doblar, ondular (*AmL*), plegar, rizar (*Esp*), PRINT marcar con rayas, PROD aboquillar, TEXTIL fruncir

crimped: ~ **connection** *n* ELEC ENG conexión en rizo *f*; ~ **fiber** *AmE*, ~ **fibre** *BrE* *n* TEXTIL fibra rizada *f*; ~ **yarn** *n* TEXTIL hilo ondulado *m*

crimper *n* C&G plegador *m*

crimping *n* MINE ondulación *f*, pliegue *m* (*AmL*), rizo *m* (*Esp*), PROD rebordeado *m*; ~ **bush** *n* MECH ENG casquillo de ondulación *m*, casquillo de pliegue *m*, engarce *m*, manguito de ondulación *m*, manguito de pliegue *m*; ~ **pliers** *n pl* MECH ENG alicates de engarzar *m pl*; ~ **tool** *n* ELEC, MECH tenaza dobladora *f*, tenaza engarzadora *f*, MECH ENG engarzador de cartuchos *m*, herramienta engarzadora *f*; ~ **washer** *n* MECH ENG arandela engarzadora *f*

crimson[1]: ~ **lake** *n* COATINGS, COLOUR laca de carmesí *f*

crimson[2] *vt* COLOUR teñir de carmesí

cringle *n* WATER TRANSP *sail* garrucho de cabo *m*

crinkle: ~ **washer** *n* MECH ENG arandela rizada *f*

crinkled: ~ **finish** *n* PROD ondulado *m*

crinoidal: ~ **limestone** *n* GEOL caliza encrinítica *f*

crisp[1] *adj* TEXTIL rizado

crisp[2]: ~ **handle** *n* TEXTIL tacto crujiente *m*; ~ **linen** *n* TEXTIL ropa blanca crujiente *f*; ~ **paper-like finish** *n* TEXTIL acabado con aspecto de papel rizado *m*

cristobalite *n* MINERAL cristobalita *f*

criterion: ~ **of failure** *n* MECH, QUALITY criterio de falla *m*

critical[1] *adj* AIR TRANSP, CHEM, MECH ENG, NUCL, QUALITY crítico

critical[2]: ~ **altitude** *n* AIR TRANSP altitud crítica *f*; ~ **amount** *n* NUCL cantidad crítica *f*, masa crítica *f*; ~ **angle** *n* CHEM ángulo crítico *m*, OPT ángulo crítico *m*, ángulo de incidencia límite *m*, PETROL, PHYS, TELECOM ángulo crítico *m*; ~ **backing pressure** *n*

MECH ENG *of vacuum pump* contrapresión crítica *f*; ~ **band** *n* ACOUST banda crítica *f*; ~ **constants** *n pl* CHEM constantes críticas *f pl*; ~ **crack-length** *n* METALL extensión crítica de la grieta *f*; ~ **damping** *n* ACOUST amortiguamiento crítico *m*, ELEC ENG amortiguación crítica *f*, PETR TECH, PETROL amortiguamiento crítico *m*, PHYS amortiguación crítica *f*; ~ **defect** *n* QUALITY defecto crítico *m*; ~ **density** *n* TRANSP densidad crítica *f*; ~ **design review** *n* (*CDR*) SPACE *project management* revisión crítica de diseño *f* (*RCD*); ~ **diameter** *n* MINE calibre crítico *m*; ~ **distance** *n* PETR TECH, PETROL distancia crítica *f*; ~ **energy** *n* METALL energía crítica *f*; ~ **engine** *n* AIR TRANSP motor crítico *m*; ~ **engine inoperative** *n* AIR TRANSP motor crítico inoperativo *m*; ~ **event** *n* PROD evento crítico *m*; ~ **field** *n* ELEC, ELEC ENG campo inductor crítico *m*, *of magnetron* campo magnético crítico *m*; ~ **flicker frequency** *n* CINEMAT frecuencia de centelleo crítica *f*, TV frecuencia de centelleo crítica *f*; ~ **flux ratio** *n* NUCL razón de flujo crítico *f*; ~ **fracture stress** *n* METALL esfuerzo crítico de la fractura *m*; ~ **frequency** *n* SPACE *communications* frecuencia crítica *f*; ~ **heat flow** *n* NUCL flujo crítico de calor *m*, límite de la ebullición nucleada *m*; ~ **heat flux** *n* HEAT ENG, PROD flujo calorífico crítico *m*; ~ **isotherm** *n* CHEM isoterma crítica *f*; ~ **mass** *n* PHYS masa crítica *f*; ~ **path** *n* COMP&DP camino crítico *m*, senda crítica *f*, CONST camino crítico *m*; ~**-path analysis** *n* TEXTIL análisis de trayectoria crítica *m*; ~**-path method** *n* (*CPM*) COMP&DP método del camino crítico *m* (*CPM*), programa de control para microprocesadores *m*; ~ **pathway** *n* NUCL camino crítico *m* (*AmL*), vía crítica *f* (*Esp*); ~ **pigment volume concentration** *n* (*CVPC*) P&R concentración de volumen crítico de pigmentos *f*; ~ **point** *n* PHYS punto crítico *m*; ~ **power unit** *n* AIR TRANSP *airworthiness* grupo de potencia crítico *m*, grupo motor crítico *m*; ~ **pressure** *n* HEAT ENG, PHYS presión crítica *f*; ~ **reaction** *n* RAD PHYS reacción crítica *f*; ~ **resistance** *n* ELEC resistencia crítica *f*; ~ **resource** *n* COMP&DP recurso crítico *m*; ~ **safety function** *n* NUCL, SAFE función crítica de seguridad *f*; ~ **section** *n* COMP&DP sección crítica *f*; ~ **shear strain** *n* METALL esfuerzo cortante crítico *m*; ~ **speed** *n* AIR TRANSP, MECH, TRANSP velocidad crítica *f*; ~ **stress** *n* METALL carga crítica *f*, esfuerzo crítico *m*; ~ **temperature** *n* HEAT ENG, PETR TECH, PHYS, REFRIG, THERMO temperatura crítica *f*; ~**-temperature curve** *n* THERMO curva de temperatura crítica *f*; ~**-temperature range** *n* THERMO gama de temperatura crítica *f*, intervalo de temperatura crítica *m*, rango de temperatura crítica *m*; ~ **velocity** *n* PHYS velocidad crítica *f*; ~ **voltage** *n* ELEC, ELEC ENG tensión crítica *f*; ~ **volume** *n* HEAT ENG volumen crítico *m*; ~ **water level** *n* WATER nivel de agua crítico *m*; ~ **wing** *n* AIR TRANSP, TRANSP *airworthiness* ala crítica *f*

criticality *n* QUALITY criticidad *f*; ~ **analysis** *n* QUALITY análisis de criticidad *m*

crizzle *n* C&G arruga *f*

crizzled: ~ **finish** *n* C&G labio estrellado *m*

CRO *abbr* (*cathode-ray oscilloscope*) ELECTRON, INSTR, PHYS, RAD PHYS, TV ORC (*osciloscopio de rayos catódicos*)

crocein *n* CHEM croceína *f*

crocidolite n MINERAL crocidolita f

crocin n CHEM crocina f

crockery: ~ **maker** n C&G alfarero m; ~ **ware** n C&G, PROD alfarería f

crocodile: ~ **clip** n ELEC connection brida de cocodrilo f, pinza cocodrilo f, presilla cocodrilo f, ELEC ENG pinza cocodrilo f, mordaza de cocodrilo f, brida de cocodrilo f, MECH ENG brida de cocodrilo f, mordaza de cocodrilo f, pinza cocodrilo f; ~ **squeezer** n PROD for puddled iron cinglador de quijadas m

crocoisite n MINERAL crocoíta f

crocoite n MINERAL crocoíta f

croconic adj CHEM crocónico

crocus: ~ **cloth** n MECH ENG arpillera f, tela de esmeril de óxido de hierro f

cronstedtite n MINERAL cronstedtita f

crook[1] vt PROD curvar

crook[2] vi PROD retorcerse

crooked: ~ **hole** n PETR TECH, PETROL pozo torcido m

Crookes: ~ **dark space** n ELECTRON, PHYS espacio oscuro de Crookes m; ~ **glass** n C&G vidrio de Crookes m; ~ **tube** n ELECTRON tubo de Crookes m

crop[1] n AGRIC cosecha f, cultivo m; ~ **dusting** n AGRIC, AIR TRANSP aerofumigación de cosechas f; ~ **end** n PROD of iron or steel bar punta f; ~ **ratio** n AGRIC distribución de superficies cultivadas f; ~ **residue** n AGRIC residuo de cosecha m; ~ **rotation** n AGRIC rotación de cultivos f; ~ **year** n AGRIC campaña f

crop[2] vt CINEMAT, PRINT recortar, TEXTIL tundir, TV recortar

cropped adj TEXTIL tundido

cropping n CINEMAT, PRINT, TV recorte m (Esp); ~ **delay** n AGRIC retraso de cosecha m; ~ **plan** n AGRIC plan de cultivo m; ~ **system** n AGRIC sistema de cultivos m

cross[1] n CONST pipe connection cruce m, surveying escuadra f; ~ **assembler** n COMP&DP ensamblador cruzado m; ~ **assembly** n COMP&DP ensamblaje cruzado m; ~ **bearer** n PROD of furnace grate cruciferario m, travesaño m; ~ **bedding** n GEOL estratificación cruzada f; ~ **bombardment** n RAD PHYS bombardeo cruzado m, bombardeo múltiple m; ~ **bonding** n ELEC conexión blindada f, conexión cruzada f, ligadura blindada f; ~**border system** n TELECOM sistema de límites cruzados m; ~ **brace** n WATER TRANSP shipbuilding arriostramiento en cruz m, riostra transversal f; ~**color noise** AmE, ~**colour noise** BrE n TV ruido por diacromía m, ruido por diacronía m; ~ **compilation** n COMP&DP compilación cruzada f; ~ **compiler** n COMP&DP compilador cruzado m; ~**connect cabinet** n TELECOM armario interconectado m; ~**connect unit** n TELECOM unidad interconectada f; ~ **correlation** n ELECTRON correlación cruzada f; ~**correlation function** n ELECTRON, PETROL función de correlación cruzada f; ~ **correlator** n ELECTRON correlador cruzado m; ~**country lorry** n BrE (cf cross-country truck AmE) TRANSP camión todo-terreno m; ~**country truck** n AmE (cf cross-country lorry BrE) TRANSP camión todo-terreno m; ~ **coupling** n ELEC ENG acoplamiento cruzado m, in symmetric assemblies conexión cruzada f, of waves acoplamiento en cruce m; ~ **direction** n PAPER dirección transversal f, PRINT sentido transversal m; ~ **drift** n MINE socavón m; ~ **driving** n MINE apertura f, avance m, perforación f; ~ **entry** n COAL, MINE galería de arrastre f

(AmL), galería de transporte f (Esp), galería de ventilación f, galería principal f, PROD galería de arrastre f (AmL), galería de transporte f (Esp); ~**esterification** n CHEM transesterificación f; ~ **fade** n ACOUST atenuación cruzada f, CINEMAT desvanecimiento cruzado m, fundido cruzado m, ELECTRON atenuación cruzada f, TV fundido cruzado m; ~ **file** n PROD lima doble f; ~**fired furnace** n C&G horno de fuego cruzado m; ~ **fold** n GEOL pliegue cruzado m; ~**garnet hinge** n CONST bisagra con granata transversal f; ~ **girth** n MECH ENG of bed of lathe bancada transversal f, nervadura cruzada f, nervadura transversal f; ~ **grain** n PRINT contra fibra f; ~ **grinding** n PAPER desfibrador transversal m; ~ **hair** n CINEMAT cruz f, COMP&DP cursor cruz f, mirilla f, PRINT hilo del retículo m; ~**hatch pattern** n CINEMAT, MECH ENG diseño de rayado cruzado m; ~ **hatching** n MECH ENG rayado cruzado m, sombreado a rayas m; ~ **link** n CHEM enlace cruzado m, ligadura transversal f, P&R entrecruzamiento m, ligadura transversal f; ~ **linking** n CHEM, P&R entrecruzamiento m; ~**linking agent** n P&R agente de reticulación m; ~ **lode** n MINE filón crucero m, veta atravesada f; ~**magnetizing effect** n ELEC efecto de magnetización cruzada m; ~ **member** n RAIL traviesa f, VEH travesaño m, traviesa f; ~ **modulation** n ELECTRON, TV modulación cruzada f; ~**modulation** n TELECOM modulación cruzada f; ~**pane hammer** n CONST martillo de peña m; ~**peen hammer** n CONST martillo de boca cruzada m; ~**peen sledgehammer** n CONST martillo de dos manos de peña transversal m; ~ **perforation** n PRINT taladrado transversal m; ~**ply tyre** n BrE VEH neumático con capas de tejido cruzadas m, neumático con capas de tejido sesgadas m, neumático con tejido en diagonal m; ~**polar pattern** n SPACE, TELECOM communications diagrama de polarización cruzada m; ~ **polarization** n SPACE, TELECOM polarización cruzada f; ~ **pollination** n AGRIC polinización cruzada f; ~ **products** n pl ELECTRON productos cruzados m pl; ~**ratio** n GEOM cociente cruzado m, razón armónica f; ~**recess for screw** n MECH ENG cruz hendida para tornillos f, rebaje cruzado para tornillos m; ~**recessed pan head screw** n MECH ENG tornillo de cabeza troncocónica de cruz hendida m; ~ **ripple** n OCEAN escarceo m; ~ **riveting** n PROD remachado al tresbolillo m; ~ **section** n CONST of road, GEOL sección transversal f, MECH ENG perfil transversal m, corte transversal m, sección transversal f, METALL corte transversal m, PAPER sección transversal f, PHYS sección eficaz f, PROD of girder, rail, TEXTIL, WATER, WATER TRANSP shipbuilding sección transversal f; ~**section density** n NUCL densidad de la sección eficaz f; ~**section iron** n PROD rolled section hierro de sección cruciforme m, hierro en corte transversal m; ~**sectional cut** n PAPER corte en dirección transversal m; ~**sectional cutting** n PAPER corte en dirección transversal m; ~**sectional drawing** n WATER TRANSP ship design plano de la sección transversal m; ~ **slide** n MECH ENG machine-tools carro transversal m, of tail-stock carro superior m; ~ **slip** n CRYSTALL deslizamiento cruzado m, deslizamiento transversal m, METALL deslizamiento transversal m; ~ **springs** n pl WATER TRANSP mooring esprines de proa y de popa m pl; ~ **staff** n CONST jalón m, mira f; ~**staff head** n CONST surveying punta de jalón f; ~ **stone** n GEOL mineral en forma de cruz *m*; **~ tie** *n* WATER TRANSP *shipbuilding* riostra transversal *f*; **~-track error** *n* WATER TRANSP *navigation by satellite or radar* error en la intersección de trayectorias *m*; **~ traverse** *n* PROD *lathe-work* carro transversal *m*; **~-tube boiler** *n* HEAT, THERMO caldera de tubos cruzados *f*; **~ union** *n* MECH ENG unión cruzada *f*, unión transversal *f*; **~ valve** *n* HYDRAUL válvula de desvío *f*, válvula de tres vías *f*; **~ vein** *n* GEOL filón transversal *m*, MINE filón atravesado *m*, filón crucero *m* (*AmL*), filón transversal *m*; **~ wall** *n* CONST muro transversal *m*, pared transversal *f*; **~ web** *n* PRINT reticulado *m* (*AmL*), retículo *m* (*Esp*)

cross² *vt* CONST *from one side to other* atravesar, cruzar, GEOL cruzar, franquear, PROD *screw-thread* dar concavidad a; **~ the bows** *vt* WATER TRANSP *of ship* cortar; **~-cut** *vt* PROD *with saw* picar cruzado; **~-fertilize** *vt* AGRIC fecundar por fertilización; **~-hatch** *vt* PROD rayar en cruz, sombear; **~ link** *vt* P&R reticular; **~ over** *vt* RAIL cruzar

crossbar *n* AIR TRANSP travesaño *m*, barra cruzada *f*, cruceta *f*, CONST barra transversal *f*, travesaño *m*, PROD *of foundry flask* travesaño *m*, barra cruzada *f*, RAIL varilla transversal *f*; **~ exchange** *n* TELECOM central de barras cruzadas *f*; **~ selector** *n* ELEC ENG selector de barras cruzadas *m*; **~ system** *n* TELECOM sistema de barras cruzadas *m*

crossbeam *n* CONST, WATER TRANSP *shipbuilding* travesaño *m*, viga transversal *f*

crossbit *n* PETR TECH barrena de percusión *f*

crossbond *n* RAIL conexión entre el alimentador y el carril *f*

crosscurves *n pl* WATER TRANSP *ship design* curvas cruzadas de estabilidad *f pl*

crosscut¹ *n* MECH ENG corte transversal *m*, PROD picadura doble *f*; **~ chisel** *n* PROD buril *m*; **~ file** *n* PROD lima muza *f*; **~ saw** *n* PROD sierra de tumba *f*, sierra tronzadera *f*; **~-saw hazard** *n* PROD, SAFE peligro de corte con sierra tronzadera *m*; **~ tooth** *n* PROD *of saw* diente contorneado *m*

crosscut² *vi* GEOL cortar transversalmente

crosscutting¹ *adj* GEOL cortado transversalmente

crosscutting² *n* CINEMAT montaje intercalado *m*, GEOL, MINE perforación de galerías transversales *f*, TV montaje intercalado *m*

crossdrive *vt* MINE abrir, avanzar, horadar (*AmL*), perforar

crossed: **~ ends** *n pl* TEXTIL cabos cruzados *m pl*; **~ field** *n* ELECTRON, PHYS, TELECOM campo cruzado *m*; **~-field amplifier** *n* ELECTRON, PHYS, TELECOM amplificador de campo cruzado *m*; **~-field tube** *n* ELECTRON, PHYS, TELECOM tubo de campo cruzado *m*; **~ Nicols** *n pl* PHYS nicoles cruzados *m pl*

crossfall *n* CONST bombeo *m*, pendiente transversal *f*

crossfeed *n* MECH ENG *machine tools* avance transversal *m*; **~ line** *n* AIR TRANSP línea de alimentación cruzada *f*, línea de suministro cruzado *f*

crossfire *n* MILIT fuego cruzado *m*

crossflow *n* TRANSP afluencia transversal *f*, VEH flujo transversal *m*; **~ fan** *n* HEAT ENG ventilador de flujo cruzado *m*; **~ heat exchanger** *n* REFRIG, THERMO intercambiador de calor por cruce de corrientes *m*; **~ radiator** *n* AUTO, VEH radiador de flujo cruzado *m*

crosshatching *n* PRINT contrarrayado *m*

crosshead *n* MECH pie de biela *m*, MECH ENG, PHYS *knot*, PROD *of piston* cruceta *f*; **~ block** *n* MECH ENG corredera de la cruceta *f*; **~ body** *n* MECH ENG cuerpo de la cruceta *m*; **~ displacement rate** *n* PHYS velocidad de desplazamiento de la cruceta *f*; **~ engine** *n* WATER TRANSP máquina con biela conectada a una cruceta *f*; **~ gib** *n* MECH ENG patín de cruceta *m*; **~ guide** *n* MECH ENG guía de la cruceta *f*, guía rectilínea *f*; **~ pin** *n* MECH ENG muñequilla de la cruceta *f*, pasador de la cruceta *m*, perno de la cruceta *m*; **~ shoe** *n* MECH ENG patín de la cruceta *m*; **~ slipper** *n* MECH ENG patín de la cruceta *m*, zapata de la cruceta *f*; **~-terminal screw** *n* PROD tornillo de cabeza avellanada *m*; **~ with 4-bar guide** *n* MECH ENG cruceta con guía de 4 barras *f*

crossheading *n* MINE conducto de ventilación *m* (*AmL*), frente de extracción *m*, galería de ventilación *f* (*Esp*), pozo de ventilación *m* (*AmL*)

crossing *n* WATER TRANSP *sea* travesía *f*; **~ the line** *n* WATER TRANSP *ceremony* Paso de la Línea *m*, Paso del Ecuador *m*; **~ timber** *n* RAIL viga de cruce *f*; **~ time** *n* WATER TRANSP duración de la travesía *f*

crossite *n* MINERAL crossita *f*

crossover *n* CONST paso de enlace *m*, vía de enlace *f*, RAIL cruce *m*, cruzamiento *m*, vía de cruzamiento *f*, vía diagonal de enlace *f*, TELECOM cruce *m*, transición *f*, TV punto de cruce *m*; **~ area** *n* ELECTRON área de cruce *f*; **~ between curved track** *n* RAIL cruce entre vías curvas *m*; **~ distortion** *n* TELECOM distorsión cruzada *f*; **~ frequency** *n* ELECTRON, TELECOM frecuencia de cruce *f*, frecuencia de transición *f*

crosspiece *n* CONST travesaño *m*, WATER *of lock gate* cruceta *f*, WATER TRANSP *shipbuilding* cruz de las bitas *f*, maimonete *m*

crossplot *n* PETROL trazado transversal *m*

crossply: **~ tire** *AmE*, **~ tyre** *BrE n* P&R neumático cubierto con pliegues transversales *m*

crosspoint *n* TELECOM contacto de cruce *m*

crossroads *n pl* CONST, TRANSP cruce de caminos *m*, cruce de carreteras *m*

crosstail: **~ hinge** *n* CONST bisagra de guía transversal *f*

crosstailed: **~ hinge** *n* CONST bisagra de guía cruzada *f*

crosstalk *n* ACOUST diafonía *f*, COMP&DP conversación cruzada *f*, diafonía *f*, PHYS diafonía *f*, TELECOM cruce *m*, TV interferencia cruzada *f*, interferencia entre los canales *f*

crosstree *n* WATER TRANSP *rigging* cruceta *f*, cruceta de palo *f*

crosswind *n* AIR TRANSP viento cruzado *m*; **~ landing** *n* AIR TRANSP aterrizaje con vientos cruzados *m*

crosswise¹ *adv* PRINT transversalmente

crosswise²: **~ ribs** *n pl* TEXTIL canal transversal *m*; **~ veneer-splicing machine** *n* MECH ENG máquina empalmadora transversal de chapas de madera *f*

crotonaldehyde *n* CHEM crotonaldehído *m*, aldehído crotónico *m*

crotonic *adj* CHEM crotónico

crotylic *adj* CHEM crotílico

crow *n* CONST gancho *m*

crowbar *n* CONST palanca *f*, ELEC ENG circuito para cortocircuitar carga *m*, MECH barra de punta *f*, barreta *f*

crowd: **~ safety** *n* SAFE seguridad en caso de aglomeración *f*

crowdion *n* METALL agrupación local de iones *f*

crowfoot *n* CINEMAT soporte de cámara de tres patas *m*

crown *n* AGRIC corona *f*, C&G bóveda *f*, CONST *of arch* coronación *f*, vértice *m*, MECH cabeza de pistón *f*, rueda de levas *f*, MECH ENG *engines* circunferencia externa *f*, corona *f*, MINE pliegue *m*, corona *f* (*Esp*), cumbrera *f* (*AmL*), cabezal *m*, PETR TECH corona *f*, PROD *of anvil* mesa de yunque *f*, *of furnace* bóveda *f*, *of crown-faced pulley* bombeo *m*, WATER TRANSP *of anchor* cruz *f*; ~ **bearer** *n* MINE cercha *f* (*Esp*), marco *m* (*AmL*); ~ **bit** *n* PETR TECH barrena de arrastre *f*, broca *f*, mecha de corona *f*, trépano de corona *m*; ~ **block** *n* PETR TECH bloque de corona *m*, corona de torre *f*, portapoleas de corona *m*, travesaño portapolea *m*, PROD *of derrick* caballete portapoleas *m*; ~ **closure** *n* PACK chapa *f*, tapón corona *m*; ~ **cork** *n* PACK tapón corona con opérculo de corcho *m*; ~ **cup** *n* PACK embutición del tapón corona *f*; ~ **face pulley** *n* PROD polea de cara combada *f*; ~ **gall** *n* AGRIC agalla de la corona *f*; ~ **gate** *n* WATER *of canal lock* compuerta de aguas arriba *f*; ~ **glass** *n* C&G vidrio crown *m*, vidrio soda *m*; ~**-glass lens** *n* C&G, CINEMAT, INSTR, OPT, PHOTO, PHYS lente convergente *f*; ~ **impregnated with diamonds** *n* MINE corona de diamantes *f*; ~ **piece** *n* MINE cabezal *m*, cumbrera *f*; ~ **and pinion** *n* VEH conjunto de piñón y corona *m*, par de reducción *m*; ~ **post** *n* CONST *of roof truss* montaje vertical *m*; ~ **process** *n* C&G proceso crown *m*; ~ **pulley** *n* PROD *derrick* polea maestra *f*; ~ **tile** *n* CONST *arched* losa del empino *f*, teja cimera *f*; ~ **tree** *n* MINE cabezal *m*; ~ **wheel** *n* AUTO corona del diferencial *f*, corona dentada cónica *f*, rueda corona *f*, MECH ENG rueda dentada cónica *f*, rueda dentada mayor *f*, VEH corona dentada *f*; ~ **wheel and pinion** *n* VEH conjunto de corona y piñón *m*, par cónico *m*

crowned: ~ **pulley** *n* PROD polea abombada *f*

crowning *n* CONST *architecture* coronación *f*, remate *m*, PROD abombamiento *m*; ~ **pulley** *n* PROD polea abombada *f*

CRT[1] *abbr* (*cathode-ray tube*) COMP&DP, ELEC, ELECTRON, PRINT, SAFE, TV TRC (*tubo de rayos catódicos*)

CRT[2]: ~ **cathode-ray pencil** *n* ELEC pincel de rayos catódicos TRC *m*; ~ **controller** *n* ELECTRON controlador de TRC *m*

crucible *n* CHEM, HEAT, LAB, PROD, THERMO crisol *m*; ~ **furnace** *n* CHEM, HEAT, LAB, PROD, THERMO horno de crisol *m*, mufla *f*; ~ **tongs** *n pl* LAB pinzas de mufla *f pl*, tenazas de mufla *f pl*

cruciform: ~ **head fastener** *n* MECH ENG sujetador de cabeza cruciforme *m*

crud *n* NUCL lodos de corrosión *m pl*

crude[1] *adj* CHEM crudo, COAL crudo, no refinado, PETR TECH crudo

crude[2] *n* PETR TECH, PETROL crudo *m*; ~ **assay** *n* PETR TECH, PETROL análisis de crudo *m*, prueba de crudo *f*; ~ **carrier** *n* MAR POLL, PETR TECH, PETROL, POLL, WATER TRANSP buque para el transporte de crudos *m*, petrolero para crudos *m*, petrolero para el transporte de crudos *m*; ~ **distillation unit** *n* (*CDU*) PETR TECH unidad de destilación de crudo *f*; ~ **fiber** *AmE*, ~ **fibre** *BrE n* AGRIC fibra cruda *f*, FOOD fibra bruta *f*; ~ **oil** *n* MAR POLL, PETR TECH, PETROL, POLL crudo *m*, petróleo crudo *m*; ~**-oil analysis** *n* PETR TECH análisis de crudo *m*; ~**-oil tanker** *n* PETR TECH, PETROL, WATER TRANSP buque cisterna de crudo *m*, buque petrolero de crudo *m*; ~**-oil washing** *n* (*COW*) PETR TECH lavado de crudo *m*; ~ **ore** *n* COAL mineral

no refinado *m*; ~ **protein** *n* FOOD proteína bruta *f*; ~ **rubber** *n* P&R caucho bruto *m*, caucho crudo *m*

crude[3]: **in a ~ state** *phr* PROD en estado bruto

cruise[1] *n* AIR TRANSP, WATER TRANSP crucero *m*; ~ **climb** *n* AIR TRANSP subida de crucero *f*; ~**-climb drift up** *n* AIR TRANSP deriva ascendente de subida de crucero *f*; ~ **control** *n* VEH marcha a velocidad de crucero *f*; ~ **control device** *n* TRANSP dispositivo de control de navegación *m*, mecanismo de control de crucero *m*; ~ **descent** *n* AIR TRANSP *drift down* descenso de crucero *m*; ~ **missile** *n* MILIT misil de crucero *m*, misil de gran alcance *m*, WATER TRANSP *navy* misil de crucero *m*, misil de gran alcanze *m*; ~ **ship** *n* WATER TRANSP buque para cruceros *m*

cruise[2] *vi* WATER TRANSP cruzar, hacer un crucero

cruiser *n* AUTO automóvil policial con radioteléfono *m*, MILIT crucero *m*, TRANSP *boat* crucero *m*, lancha de motor *f*, yate de recreo *m*, *car* automóvil policial con radioteléfono *m*, coche policía con radioteléfono *m*, WATER TRANSP *warship* crucero *m*, yate para cruceros *m*; ~ **stern** *n* WATER TRANSP *boat building* popa de crucero *f*

cruising: ~ **altitude** *n* AIR TRANSP altitud de crucero *f*; ~ **cutter** *n* WATER TRANSP cúter de crucero *m*; ~ **power** *n* AIR TRANSP potencia de crucero *f*; ~ **range** *n* SPACE alcance de crucero *m*, VEH recorrido efectuado a velocidad de crucero *m*; ~ **speed** *n* AIR TRANSP, WATER TRANSP velocidad de crucero *f*

crumb: ~ **elasticity** *n* FOOD elasticidad de miga *f*; ~ **firmness** *n* FOOD dureza de miga *f*; ~ **formation** *n* FOOD formación de miga *f*; ~ **structure** *n* MECH ENG estructura grumosa *f*; ~ **texture** *n* FOOD textura de la miga de pan *f*

crumble *vi* CONST *walls* colapsar, derrumbarse, desmoronarse

crumple: ~ **zone** *n* MINE zona de contracción *f*, zona de derrumbamiento *f*

crush[1]: ~**-resistant** *adj* TEXTIL resistente al estrujamiento

crush[2]: ~ **barrier** *n* SAFE barrena de colisión *f*, barrera de choque *f*; ~ **belt** *n* GEOL zona de fractura *f*; ~ **breccia** *n* GEOL brecha de trituración *f*, brecha por fractura *f*, HYDRAUL brecha de fricción *f*; ~ **resistance** *n* TEXTIL resistencia al estrujamiento *f*; ~ **rock** *n* GEOL brecha *f*

crush[3] *vt* AGRIC triturar, COAL aplastar, machacar, triturar, CONST machacar, triturar, aplastar, FOOD machacar, PAPER aplastar, PROD triturar, TEXTIL estrujar

crushed: ~ **aggregate** *n* COAL agregado triturado *m*; ~ **grain** *n* AGRIC grano triturado *m*; ~ **ice** *n* REFRIG hielo triturado *m*; ~ **material** *n* COAL, CONST material de machaqueo *m*, material triturado *m*; ~ **ore** *n* MINE mineral machacado *m*, mineral quebrantado *m*, mineral triturado *m*; ~ **stone** *n* CONST roca machacada *f*

crusher *n* AGRIC *for grapes* estrujadora *f*, COAL trituradora *f*, rodillo perfilador *m*, quebrantadora *f*, medidor de presiones *m*, CONST machacadora *f*, MECH ENG triturador *m*, quebrantadora *f*, perfilador *m*, PROD triturador *m*; ~ **gage** *AmE*, ~ **gauge** *BrE n* MECH medidor de presiones *m*; ~ **jaw** *n* CHEM TECH mandíbula trituradora *f*; ~ **roll** *n* CHEM TECH, PROD cilindro triturador *m*

crushing *n* COAL machaqueo *m*, molienda *f*, trituración *f*, CONST aplastamiento *m*, machaqueo *m*, rotura por comprensión *f*, trituración *f*, MINE bocarteo *m* (*AmL*), fresado *m* (*Esp*), machaqueo *m*, trituración *f*, P&R aplastamiento *m*, molienda *f*, trituración *f*, PAPER aplastamiento *m*, PROD trituración *f*, SAFE *communications, antennas, aircraft* aplastamiento *m*, TEXTIL rotura *f*; ~ **cylinder** *n* CHEM TECH trituradora de cilindros *f*; ~ **efficiency** *n* COAL rendimiento de la trituradora *m*; ~ **machine** *n* CHEM TECH trituradora *f*; ~ **machine for ice** *n* MECH ENG machacadora de hielo *f*, quebrantadora de hielo *f*, trituradora de hielo *f*; ~ **plant** *n* CHEM TECH, COAL planta trituradora *f*; ~ **power** *n* SAFE potencia de aplastamiento *f*; ~ **resistance** *n* PAPER resistencia al aplastamiento *f*; ~ **roll** *n* CHEM TECH cilindro triturador *m*, rodillo de trituración *m*, MECH ENG *for screw threads*, PROD rodillo triturador *m*

crushproof: ~ **safety bonnet** *n* BrE (*cf crushproof safety hood AmE*) TRANSP capó anti-choque *m*, capó anti-golpes *m*; ~ **safety hood** *n* AmE (*cf crushproof safety bonnet BrE*) TRANSP capó anti-choque *m*, capó anti-golpes *m*

crust *n* GEOL, PETROL capa *f*, corteza *f*, costra *f*; ~ **freezing** *n* REFRIG congelación superficial *f*

crutch *n* WATER TRANSP *support for boom* horquilla *f*; ~ **handle** *n* PROD mango de muletilla *m*; ~ **key** *n* CONST llave de horquilla *f*, PROD *of cock* muletilla *f*

cryobiology *n* REFRIG criobiología *f*

cryobranding *n* REFRIG croiomarcado *m*

cryocooling *n* REFRIG enfriamiento criogénico *m*

cryoetching *n* REFRIG criodecapado *m*

cryogenic[1] *adj* PHYS, REFRIG, SPACE, THERMO criogénico

cryogenic[2]: ~ **fluid** *n* REFRIG fluido criogénico *m*; ~ **fuel** *n* SPACE combustible criogénico *m*; ~ **liquid** *n* MECH ENG líquido criogénico *m*; ~ **memory** *n* COMP&DP memoria criogénica *f*; ~ **pressure vessel** *n* MECH ENG contenedor criogénico de presión *m*, recipiente criogénico de presión *m*, vasija de presión criogénica *f*; ~ **propellant** *n* SPACE propulsante criogénico *m*; ~ **refrigerator** *n* REFRIG refrigerador criogénico *m*; ~ **stage** *n* SPACE etapa criogénica *f*; ~ **tank** *n* SPACE cuba criogenica *f*, depósito criogénico *m*, tanque criogénico *m*

cryogenically: ~ **treated** *adj* MECH ENG tratado criogénicamente

cryogenics *n* HEAT ENG, MECH ENG, PHYS, REFRIG, SPACE, THERMO criogenia *f*, criogénica *f*

cryolite *n* C&G criolita *f*, CHEM criolita *f*, espato de Groenlandia *m*, MINERAL criolita *f*

cryology *n* REFRIG criología *f*

cryomagnetism *n* REFRIG criomagnetismo *m*

cryomedicine *n* REFRIG criomedicina *f*

cryophysics *n* REFRIG criofísica *f*

cryopump *n* SPACE bomba criogénica *f*, criostato *m*

cryoscopy *n* REFRIG crioscopia *f*

cryostat *n* LAB, PHYS, SPACE criostato *m*

cryosurgery *n* REFRIG criocirugía *f*

cryotechnic: ~ **arm** *n* SPACE brazo criotécnico *m*

cryotron *n* ELEC ENG criotón *m*

cryptanalysis *n* COMP&DP, TELECOM análisis críptico *m*, criptoanálisis *m*

cryptocrystalline *adj* CRYSTALL, GEOL criptocristalina

cryptographic[1] *adj* COMP&DP, SPACE, TELECOM criptográfico

cryptographic[2]: ~ **check valve** *n* TELECOM válvula de retención criptográfica *f*

cryptography *n* COMP&DP, SPACE, TELECOM criptografía *f*

cryptosteady: ~ **pressure exchanger** *n* TRANSP intercambiador de presión criptofija *m*

crystal *n* C&G, CHEM, CRYSTALL, ELECTRON, OPT, TELECOM cristal *m*; ~ **axes** *n pl* CRYSTALL ejes cristalinos *m pl*; ~ **control** *n* AIR TRANSP control por cristal *m*; ~**-controlled oscillator** *n* (*CCO*) ELECTRON, TELECOM oscilador controlado por cristal de cuarzo *m*; ~ **defect** *n* CRYSTALL, OPT, QUALITY imperfección cristalina *f*; ~ **diode** *n* ELECTRON diodo de cristal *m*; ~ **face** *n* CRYSTALL capa cristalina *f*, cara de un cristal *f*; ~ **field** *n* CRYSTALL, RAD PHYS campo cristalino *m*; ~**-field splitting energy** *n* CRYSTALL, RAD PHYS energía de escisión del campo cristalino *f*; ~ **filter** *n* CRYSTALL, ELECTRON, TELECOM filtro de cristal *m*; ~ **frequency** *n* CRYSTALL, ELECTRON frecuencia por cristal *f*; ~ **frequency drift** *n* CRYSTALL, ELECTRON variación de la frecuencia por cristal *f*; ~ **glass** *n* C&G cristal *m*; ~ **growth** *n* CRYSTALL crecimiento cristalino *m*, crecimiento de cristales *m*, METALL dilatación del cristal *f*, expansión del cristal *f*; ~ **holder** *n* CRYSTALL, ELECTRON soporte de cristal *m*; ~ **ice** *n* REFRIG hielo cristalino *m*; ~ **ladder filter** *n* CRYSTALL, ELECTRON filtro celular de cristal *m*; ~ **laser** *n* CRYSTALL, ELECTRON láser de cristal *m*; ~ **lattice** *n* CRYSTALL, ELECTRON red cristalina *f*; ~**-lattice filter** *n* CRYSTALL, ELECTRON filtro de malla de cristal *m*; ~**-lattice parameter** *n* METALL constante de red *f*, constante de retículo *f*, parámetro de red *m*; ~ **oscillator** *n* CRYSTALL, ELEC, ELECTRON, RAD PHYS oscilador cristalino *m*, oscilador de cristal *m*, oscilador estabilizado por cristal *m*, oscilador regulado por cristal *m*; ~ **plasticity** *n* CRYSTALL, METALL plasticidad del cristal *f*; ~ **resonator** *n* CRYSTALL, ELECTRON resonador de cristal *m*; ~ **sheet glass** *n* AmE (*cf thick sheet glass BrE*) C&G luna de cristal *f*; ~ **spectrometer** *n* CRYSTALL, RAD PHYS espectrómetro de cristal *m*; ~ **structure** *n* COAL, CRYSTALL, METALL estructura cristalina *f*; ~ **symmetry** *n* CRYSTALL simetría cristalina *f*; ~ **system** *n* CRYSTALL sistema cristalino *m*; ~ **time base** *n* CRYSTALL, ELECTRON base de tiempo de cristal *f*; ~ **tuff** *n* CRYSTALL, GEOL toba cristalina *f*

crystalline[1] *adj* CHEM, CRYSTALL cristalino

crystalline[2]: ~ **basement** *n* CRYSTALL, GEOL basamento cristalino *m*; ~ **fracture** *n* CRYSTALL, METALL fractura cristalina *f*; ~ **limestone** *n* CRYSTALL, GEOL caliza cristalina *f*; ~ **silica dust** *n* CRYSTALL, SAFE polvo de sílice cristalino *m*

crystallization *n* CHEM TECH, CRYSTALL, P&R cristalización *f*; ~ **basin** *n* CHEM TECH, CRYSTALL cuenco de cristalización *m*; ~ **point** *n* CHEM TECH, CRYSTALL punto de cristalización *m*

crystallize: ~ **out** *vi* CHEM TECH, CRYSTALL separar por cristalización

crystallizer *n* CHEM, CHEM TECH, CRYSTALL cristalizador *m*

crystallizing: ~ **dish** *n* CRYSTALL, LAB cristalizador *m* (*Esp*), vidrio de reloj *m* (*AmL*); ~ **pond** *n* CHEM TECH, COAL, CRYSTALL alberca de cristalización *f*

crystallographic: ~ **plane** *n* CRYSTALL, INSTR plano cristalográfico *m*; ~ **slip** *n* CRYSTALL, METALL desprendimiento cristalográfico *m*

cumulus

crystallography *n* CRYSTALL, METALL, RAD PHYS
cristalografía *f*

CS *abbr* (*convergence sublayer*) TELECOM subcapa de
convergencia *f*

Cs *abbr* CHEM, ELEC ENG, ELECTRON (*caesium BrE*,
cesium AmE) Cs (*cesio*), METEO (*cirrostratus*) Cs
(*cirrostrato*), SPACE (*caesium BrE*, *cesium AmE*) Cs
(*cesio*)

C-shaped: ~ **frame** *n* INSTR molde en forma de C *m*

CSI *abbr* MAR POLL, POLL (*Coastal Studies Institute*)
Instituto de Estudios Costeros *m*, TELECOM (*called-
station identity*) identidad de la estación llamada *f*

CSM *abbr* COMP&DP (*command and control system*)
sistema de orden y control *m*, SPACE (*crew service
module, communications system monitoring*) módulo
de servicio de la tripulación *m*, CSS (*control del
sistema de comunicaciones*)

CSMA *abbr* (*carrier sense multiple access*) TELECOM
acceso múltiple por detención de portadora *m*

CSMA/CD *abbr* (*carrier sense multiple access with
collision detection*) COMP&DP, ELECTRON AMDOP/
DC (*acceso múltiple en dirección a la onda portadora
con detección de colisiones*)

CSN *abbr* (*Canadian switched network*) TELECOM red
conmutada canadiense *f*

CSPDU *abbr* (*convergence-sublayer protocol data unit*)
TELECOM unidad de datos protocolarios de la
subcapa de convergencia *f*

C-stage: ~ **resin** *n* P&R resina termoendurecible en su
fase final *f*, resita *f*

CT *abbr* (*container*) TELECOM contenedor *m*

CTD *abbr* (*charge-transfer device*) ELEC ENG, PHYS,
SPACE, TELECOM DTC (*dispositivo de transferencia de
carga*)

CTMP *abbr* (*chemicothermo mechanical pulp*) PAPER
pasta químico-termomecánica *f*

CTOL[1] *abbr* (*conventional takeoff and landing*) AIR
TRANSP, MILIT despegue y aterrizaje convencional *m*

CTOL[2]: ~ **aircraft** *n* AIR TRANSP, MILIT avión de
despegue y aterrizaje convencional *m*

Cu *abbr* CHEM, ELEC, METALL (*copper*) Cu (*cobre*),
METEO (*cumulus*) CU (*cúmulo*)

cubage *n* COAL, METR cubicación *f*

cubanite *n* MINERAL cubanita *f*

cubature *n* METR cubicación *f*

cube[1] *n* GEOM cubo *m*; ~ **problem** *n* GEOM problema
cúbico *m*, problema de la duplicación del cubo *m*

cube[2] *vt* MATH elevar al cubo

cubebin *n* CHEM cubebina *f*

cubic[1] *adj* CONST, CRYSTALL, GEOM, MATH, METR
cúbico

cubic[2]: ~ **boron nitride** *n* MECH ENG nitruro de boro
cúbico *m*; ~ **boron nitride grinding wheel** *n* MECH
ENG rueda trituradora de nitruro de boro cúbico *f*;
~ **boron nitride saw** *n* MECH ENG sierra de nitruro de
boro cúbico *f*; ~ **capacity** *n* MECH *measuring*, METR,
WATER TRANSP *of stowage area* capacidad cúbica *f*,
volumen *m*; ~ **centimeter** *AmE*, ~ **centimetre** *BrE n*
METR centímetro cúbico *m*; ~ **decimeter** *AmE*,
~ **decimetre** *BrE n* METR decímetro cúbico *m*;
~ **expansion coefficient** *n* PHYS coeficiente de
expansión cúbica *m*; ~ **expansivity** *n* PHYS expansi-
vidad cúbica *f*; ~ **foot** *n* METR pie cúbico *m*; ~ **inch** *n*
METR pulgada cúbica *f*; ~ **measure** *n* METR medida
cúbica *f*; ~ **measurement** *n* METR cubicación *f*;
~ **meter** *AmE*, ~ **metre** *BrE n* MATH, METR metro

cúbico *m*; ~ **octahedron** *n* GEOM octaedro cúbico *m*,
octahedro cúbico *m*; ~ **system** *n* METR sistema
cúbico *m*; ~ **yard** *n* METR yarda cúbica *f*

cubical: ~ **distortion** *n* METALL distorsión cúbica *f*;
~ **expansion** *n* METALL expansión cúbica *f*

cubicite *n* MINERAL cubicita *f*

cubing *n* METR cubicación *f*

cuboid *n* GEOM cuboide *m*

cud *n* AGRIC bolo alimenticio *m*

cue[1] *n* CINEMAT indicación *f*, pie *m*, TV punto de
referencia *m*; ~ **light** *n* CINEMAT, TV luz de aviso *f*;
~ **mark** *n* CINEMAT, TV marca indicadora *f*; ~ **print** *n*
CINEMAT, TV copión *m*; ~ **screen** *n* CINEMAT, TV
pantalla de aviso *f*; ~ **sheet** *n* CINEMAT, TV programa
escrito del trabajo de cada parte *m*; ~ **track** *n*
CINEMAT, TV pista avisadora *f*, pista de aviso *f*;
~~**track address code** *n* CINEMAT, TV código de
dirección de la pista de aviso *m*

cue[2] *vt* CINEMAT, TV indicar

CUE *abbr* (*catch per unit effort*) OCEAN captura por
unidad de esfuerzo *f*

cueing *n* ACOUST, CINEMAT, TV guía *f*, indicación *f*,
referencia *f*, señal *f*

cuer *n* CINEMAT, TV avisador *m*

CUG *abbr* (*closed user group*) COMP&DP, TELECOM
grupo cerrado de usuarios *m*

cull *vt* AGRIC desviejar; ~ **by hand** *vt* COAL escoger a
mano

cullet *n* C&G vidrio de deshecho *m*; ~ **catcher** *n* C&G
recogedor de vidrio sobrante *m*; ~ **chute** *n* C&G canal
para vidrio de deshecho *m*; ~ **crush** *n* C&G vidrio
molido *m*; ~ **crusher** *n* C&G molino de vidrio *m*

culling *n* COAL elección *f*

culm *n* AGRIC tallo de los cereales *m*, C&G antracita *f*,
COAL cisco *m*, culm *m*, polvo de antracita *m*, polvo de
carbón *m*

cultipacker *n* AGRIC rodillo compactador *m*

cultivator *n* CONST cultivadora *f*

culture *n* AGRIC cultivo *m*; ~ **plate** *n* AGRIC, LAB caja
Petri *f*, placa de cultivo *f*; ~ **starter** *n* AGRIC cultivo
inicial *m*

culvert *n* COAL alcantarilla *f*, CONST, HYDROL alcantarilla *f*, conducto subterráneo *m*, MECH ENG, RECYCL,
WATER alcantarilla *f*

cumaldehyde *n* CHEM aldehído cumínico *m*, cumal-
dehído *m*

cumarin *n* CHEM cumarina *f*

cumene *n* CHEM cumeno *m*, isopropilbenceno *m*

cumengeite *n* MINERAL cumengeíta *f*

cumic *adj* CHEM cúmico

cummingtonite *n* MINERAL cummingtonita *f*

cumulative: ~ **discharge** *n* FUELLESS gasto acumulativo *m*; ~ **distribution diagram** *n* HYDROL diagrama
de distribución acumulativa *m*; ~ **distribution
function** *n* (*CDF*) MATH distribución de frecuencias
acumulativas *f* (*DFA*); ~ **fission yield** *n* NUCL
rendimiento acumulado de fisión *m*; ~ **ionization** *n*
NUCL ionización en cascada *f*; ~ **toxic effect** *n* POLL
efecto tóxico acumulativo *m*; ~ **working time** *n* PROD
tiempo de funcionamiento acumulativo *m*

cumulo: ~ **dome** *n* GEOL cresta de cúmulo volcánico *f*,
domo volcánico *m*; ~ **volcano** *n* GEOL cúmulo
volcánico *m*, domo volcánico *m*

cumulonimbus *n* (*Cb*) METEO banda de conducción *f*
(*Cb*), cumulonimbo *m*, cumulonimbus *m* (*Cb*)

cumulus *n* (*Cu*) METEO cumulus *m* (*Cu*); ~ **congestus**

n METEO cumulus congestus *m*; ~ **humilis** *n* METEO cumulus humilis *m*

cumyl *n* CHEM cumil *m*

cup *n* LAB, P&R cubeta *f*, PACK vaso *m*; **~-and-ball joint** *n* PROD junta de cono y esfera *f*; ~ **chuck** *n* MECH ENG plato de copa *m*; ~ **and cone** *n* PROD *blast-furnace* cono y embudo *m*; ~ **and cone fracture** *n* METALL fractura de cono y copa *f*, fractura de cono y embudo *f*; **~-head bolt** *n* MECH ENG perno de cabeza redonda *m*, perno de cabeza semiesférica *m*, tornillo de cabeza redonda *m*, tornillo de cabeza semiesférica *m*; **~-head rivet** *n* CONST remache de cabeza redonda *m*; ~ **joint** *n* PROD *lead pipe* unión de taza *f*; ~ **leather** *n* PROD cuero embutido en forma de U *m*; ~ **valve** *n* HYDRAUL válvula de doble asiento *f*; ~ **washer** *n* MECH ENG arandela acopada *f*, arandela cóncava *f*; ~ **wheel** *n* PROD *emery wheel* muela de cubeta *f*

cupboard *n* LAB armario *m* (*Esp*), gabinete *m* (*AmL*)

cupel *n* CHEM copela *f*

cupola *n* C&G cubilote *m*, COAL bóveda *f*, cúpula *f*, garita *f*, horno de ladrillos *m*, GEOL bóveda *f*, HEAT cubilote *m*, PROD bóveda *f*, cubilote *m*, RAIL garita *f*; ~ **furnace** *n* C&G horno de cubilote *m*, PROD cubilote *m*; ~ **with receiver** *n* PROD cubilote con antecristol *m*

cupped: ~ **chain sheave** *n* PROD polea cónica de cadena con cono *f*

cuprammonium *n* CHEM, TEXTIL cuproamonio *m*

cuprate *n* CHEM cuprato *m*

cupreous *adj* CHEM cuproso

cupric *adj* CHEM cúprico

cupride *n* CHEM cúprido *m*

cuprite *n* CHEM, MINERAL cuprita *f*

cuproapatite *n* CHEM, MINERAL cuproapatito *m*

cuprodescloizite *n* CHEM, MINERAL cuprodescloizita *f*

cupromagnesite *n* CHEM, MINERAL cupromagnesita *f*

cupromanganese *n* CHEM, MINERAL cupromanganeso *m*

cuproplumbite *n* CHEM, MINERAL cuproplumbito *m*

cuproscheelite *n* CHEM, MINERAL cuproscheelita *f*

cuprotungstite *n* CHEM, MINERAL cuprotungstita *f*

cuprous *adj* CHEM cuproso

curb *n* CONST *AmE* (*cf kerb BrE*) declive lateral de la carretera *m*, bordillo *m*, bordillo de la acera *m*, *building* solera *f*, MINE cuadro portador *m*, aro de fundición para hinca de pozos *m*, poceta para recoger el agua de un pozo *f*; ~ **plate** *n* CONST *building* viga carrera *f*; ~ **ring** *n* MINE *in mine-shaft* anillo portador *m*, fortificación *f*; ~ **roof** *n* CONST tejado tipo masandra *m*

curbed: ~ **chain** *n* PROD cadena de barbada *f*

curbstone *n* *AmE* (*cf kerbstone BrE*) CONST loseta del bordillo *f*, piedra para bordillo *f*

curcumine *n* CHEM curcumina *f*

cure[1] *n* CHEM, ELEC, MECH, P&R vulcanización *f*; ~ **period** *n* CONST curado *m*, período de curado *m*

cure[2] *vt* CHEM, ELEC vulcanizar, FOOD curar, madurar, MECH, P&R vulcanizar, TEXTIL curar

cured: ~ **malt** *n* FOOD malta tostada *f*; ~ **seed** *n* AGRIC semilla curada *f*

curfew *n* ACOUST toque de queda *m*

curie *n* (*Ci*) PHYS, RAD PHYS curie *m* (*Ci*)

Curie: ~ **constant** *n* PHYS, RAD PHYS constante de Curie *f*; **~'s law** *n* PETR TECH, PETROL, PHYS, RAD PHYS ley de Curie; ~ **point** *n* ELEC *paramagnetism*, PETR TECH, PETROL, PHYS, REFRIG punto de Curie *m*; ~ **temperature** *n* RAD PHYS temperatura de Curie *f*; *f*

Curie-Weiss: ~ **law** *n* PHYS, RAD PHYS ley de Curie-Weiss *f*

curing *n* CHEM vulcanización *f*, CONST curado *m*, ELEC vulcanización *f*, MECH *communications, equipment* curación *f*, curado *m*, endurecimiento *m*, vulcanización *f*, OCEAN curado *m*, P&R vulcanización *f*, TEXTIL curado *m*, THERMO vulcanización *f*, WATER TRANSP *material* endurecimiento *m*; ~ **agent** *n* COATINGS, P&R agente endurecedor *m*; ~ **cellar** *n* REFRIG cámara de curado *f*, cámara de salazón *f*; ~ **compound** *n* CONST aditivo para curado *m*; ~ **membrane** *n* CONST membrana de curado *f*; ~ **oven** *n* TEXTIL horno de polimerización *m*; ~ **time** *n* P&R tiempo de vulcanización *m*; ~ **tunnel** *n* CONST túnel de curado *m*

curium *n* (*Cm*) CHEM, RAD PHYS curio *m* (*Cm*); ~ **series** *n* RAD PHYS serie del curio *f*

curl[1] *n* ELECTRON rizo *m*, FLUID rotacional *m*, PACK, PAPER abarquillado *m*, PHYS *device* rotacional *m*, PRINT abarquillado *m*, TEXTIL rizo *m*; ~ **corresponding to vorticity** *n* FLUID ondulación correspondiente a la vorticidad *f*; ~ **field** *n* ELEC ENG campo rotacional *m*

curl[2] *vt* C&G, TEXTIL rizar

curled: ~ **edge** *n* C&G orilla rizada *f*

curling[1] *adj* PACK, PAPER, PRINT abarquillado

curling[2] *n* PACK, PAPER, PRINT abarquillado *m*, TEXTIL rizado *m*

current[1]: **~-operated** *adj* *AmE* (*cf mains-operated BrE*) ELEC *appliance*, ELEC ENG accionado por la corriente, alimentado por la red, enchufado a la red

current[2] *n* (*cf mains BrE*) ELEC, ELEC ENG corriente *f*, corriente eléctrica *f*, red de distribución eléctrica *f*, HYDROL, OCEAN corriente *f*, corriente marina *f*, PHYS corriente *f*, corriente eléctrica *f*, RAD PHYS, TELECOM corriente eléctrica *f*, TV suministro principal *m* (*AmL*), corriente *f*, red eléctrica *f*, WATER red de distribución *f*, tubería principal *f*, WATER TRANSP *navigation tides* corriente *f*, corriente marina *f*; ~ **amplification** *n* ELEC, ELECTRON amplificación de corriente *f*; ~ **amplifier** *n* ELEC, ELECTRON amplificador de corriente *m*; ~ **antinode** *n* ELEC ENG punto de máxima corriente *m*; ~ **balance** *n* ELEC equilibrador de corriente *m*, balanza electrodinámica *f*, INSTR, PHYS balanza electrodinámica *f*, equilibrador de corriente *m*; ~ **balance relay** *n* ELEC relé de equilibrado de corriente *m*; ~ **bedding** *n* GEOL estratificación entrecruzada *f*; ~ **cable** *n* *AmE* (*cf mains cable BrE*) ELEC cable de la corriente *m*, ELEC ENG cable de la corriente *m*, cable de la red eléctrica *m*; **~-carrying capacity** *n* ELEC *line* capacidad de conducción de corriente *f*, capacidad de corriente *f*, ELEC ENG, ELECTRON, PHYS capacidad de corriente *f*, capacidad de conducción de corriente *f*; **~-carrying coil** *n* ELECTRON, PHYS arrollamiento recorrido por la corriente *m*; ~ **chart** *n* WATER TRANSP *navigation* atlas de corrientes de marea *m*; ~ **coater** *n* COATINGS estucadora de cortina *f*; **~-collecting brush** *n* ELEC ENG escobilla para la toma de corriente *f*; ~ **collector** *n* ELEC ENG, RAIL toma de corriente *f*; **~-conducting pin** *n* PROD pasador conductor de corriente *m*; ~ **control** *n* ELEC ENG control de la corriente *m*; **~-controlled device** *n* ELEC ENG dispositivo controlado por corriente *m*; **~-controlled oscillator** *n* ELECTRON oscilador de corriente controlada *m*; ~ **core** *n* OCEAN núcleo de la corriente *m*; ~ **density** *n* ELEC, ELEC ENG, GEOPHYS, METALL, PHYS densidad de corriente *f*; ~ **differential protection** *n* ELEC protección diferencial de corriente *f*; ~ **direction** *n* ELEC, ELEC ENG dirección de la corriente *f*; ~ **distribution** *n* ELEC distribución de corriente *f*; ~ **divider** *n* ELEC *circuit* divisor de corriente *m*; ~ **drift** *n* ELEC, ELECTRON, TELECOM deriva de la corriente *f*; ~ **element** *n* PHYS elemento de corriente *m*; ~ **feedback** *n* ELEC, ELEC ENG, ELECTRON realimentación en corriente *f*; ~ **fluctuation** *n* ELEC fluctuación de corriente *f*, variación de corriente *f*; ~ **frequency** *n* AmE (*cf mains frequency BrE*) ELEC *supply*, ELEC ENG frecuencia de alimentación eléctrica *f*, frecuencia de la corriente *f*, frecuencia de la red eléctrica *f*, frecuencia de red *f*; ~ **gain** *n* ELEC, ELECTRON, PHYS ganancia de corriente *f*; ~ **generator** *n* ELEC, ELEC ENG, PHYS generador de corriente *m*; ~ **hum** *n* AmE (*cf mains hum BrE*) ELEC *supply*, ELEC ENG murmullo de la corriente *m*, zumbido de corriente *m*, zumbido de la red *m*; ~ **input** *n* ELEC ENG entrada de corriente *f*; ~ **intensity** *n* ELEC, ELEC ENG intensidad de la corriente *f*; ~ **lead** *n* AmE (*cf mains lead BrE*) ELEC, ELEC ENG cable conductor de corriente *m*, cable conductor de la red *m*, cable de corriente *m*; ~ **lead cleat** *n* AmE (*cf mains lead cleat BrE*) ELEC, ELEC ENG mordaza del cable de toma de corriente *f*; ~ **limiter** *n* ELEC, ELEC ENG limitador de corriente *m*, limitador de sobreintensidad *m*; ~ **limiting** *n* ELEC, ELEC ENG limitación de sobreintensidad *f*; ~~-**limiting circuit breaker** *n* ELEC, ELEC ENG cortacircuito limitador de corriente *m*; ~~-**limiting fuse link** *n* ELEC conexión de fusible limitador de corriente *f*; ~~-**limiting inductor** *n* ELEC, ELEC ENG inductor limitador de corriente *m*; ~~-**limiting reactor** *n* ELEC, ELEC ENG bobina de reactancia limitadora de corriente *f*, reactor limitador de corriente *m*; ~ **loop** *n* PHYS antinodo de la corriente *m*, cresta de la corriente *f*; ~ **meter** *n* FUELLESS contador de corrientes *m*, HYDRAUL contador de corrientes *m*, corrientímetro *m*, medidor de corrientes *m*, HYDROL correntómetro *m*, molinete hidráulico *m*, OCEAN currentímetro *m*, WATER correntómetro *m*, fluviómetro *m*, medidor de corrientes *m*, molinete hidrométrico *m*, WATER TRANSP correntímetro *m*; ~~-**mode logic** *n* ELEC ENG lógica del modo de corriente *f*; ~ **modulation** *n* ELECTRON modulación de corriente *f*; ~ **output** *n* ELEC ENG salida de corriente *f*; ~ **path** *n* ELEC ENG trayecto de la corriente *m*; ~ **peak** *n* ELEC máximo de corriente *m*, pico de corriente *m*; ~ **plug** *n* AmE (*cf mains plug BrE*) ELEC clavija de conexión a la red *f*, enchufe de conexión a la red *m*, enchufe de la corriente *m*, enchufe tomacorriente *m*, ELEC ENG clavija de conexión a la red *f*, enchufe a la red *m*, enchufe de conexión a la red *m*, enchufe de la corriente *m*, enchufe tomacorriente *m*; ~ **pulse** *n* ELEC ENG impulso de corriente *m*; ~ **ramp** *n* PROD curva de la corriente *f*; ~ **rate** *n* WATER TRANSP *sea* velocidad de corrientes *f*; ~ **rating** *n* PROD gama actual *f*, gama de corriente *f*; ~ **rectifier** *n* AmE (*cf mains rectifier BrE*) ELEC, ELEC ENG rectificador de corriente *m*, rectificador de red *m*, rectificador de voltaje de la red *m*; ~ **regulation** *n* ELEC, ELEC ENG regulación de corriente *f*; ~ **regulator** *n* ELEC, ELEC ENG regulador de corriente *m*; ~ **relay** *n* ELEC, ELEC ENG relevador de intensidad *m*, relé de corriente *m*, relé de intensidad *m*; ~ **requirement** *n* ELEC requerimiento de corriente

m, PROD demanda de corriente *f*; ~ **reverser** *n* ELEC, ELEC ENG inversor de corriente *m*; ~ **ripple** *n* ELEC ENG ondulación de la corriente *f*, GEOL riple de corriente *f*, OCEAN rosa de las corrientes *f*; ~ **sensing** *n* ELEC ENG detección de corriente *f*; ~~-**sensing resistor** *n* ELEC ENG resistencia para medida de la corriente *f*; ~ **set** *n* WATER TRANSP *sea* dirección de la corriente *f*; ~ **sink** *n* ELEC ENG inmersión de corriente *f*; ~ **socket** *n* AmE (*cf mains socket BrE*) ELEC, ELEC ENG clavija de corriente *f*, clavija hembra de corriente *f*, enchufe de corriente *m*; ~ **source** *n* ELEC, ELEC ENG generador de corriente *m*, PHYS fuente de la corriente *f*, generador de corriente *m*; ~ **state of the art** *n* TELECOM estado actual de la tecnología *m*; ~ **stream** *n* OCEAN flujo de la corriente *m*; ~ **strength** *n* ELEC, ELEC ENG intensidad de la corriente *f*; ~ **supply** *n* AmE (*cf mains supply BrE*) ELEC *network* alimentación eléctrica *f*, alimentación por la red *f*, corriente *f*, red *f*, red eléctrica *f*, ELEC ENG alimentación eléctrica *f*, suministro de la red *m*, PHYS suministro de corriente *m*; ~ **surge** *n* ELEC ENG sobrecorriente *f*; ~ **switch** *n* AmE (*cf mains switch BrE*) ELEC, ELEC ENG interruptor de corriente *m*, interruptor de red *m*, interruptor de voltaje de la red *m*, llave de la corriente *f*; ~~-**testing meter** *n* ELEC ENG medidor para pruebas de intensidad *m*; ~~-**transformation ratio** *n* ELEC relación de transformación de corriente *f*; ~ **transformer** *n* AmE (*cf mains transformer BrE*) ELEC, ELEC ENG transformador de alimentación *m*, transformador de corriente *m*, transformador de intensidad *m*, transformador de la red de corriente eléctrica *m*, transformador de la red principal *m*, ELECTRON transformador de alimentación *m*, transformador de corriente *m*, transformador de intensidad *m*, transformador de la red de corriente *m*, transformador de la red principal *m*; ~ **voltage** *n* AmE (*cf mains voltage BrE*) ELEC *of supply* voltaje de la red *m*, tensión de la corriente *f*, voltaje de la corriente *m*, voltaje de alimentación *m*, ELEC ENG, TV voltaje de la red *m*, voltaje de alimentación *m*, voltaje de la corriente *m*, tensión de la corriente *f*; ~~-**voltage characteristic** *n* ELEC ENG curva característica voltaje-corriente *f*, SPACE característica corriente de voltaje *f*
cursor *n* COMP&DP, PRINT cursor *m*; ~ **hit** *n* PROD por cursor; ~ **key** *n* COMP&DP tecla del cursor *f*
curtain *n* C&G *Foucault process*, TEXTIL cortina *f*; ~ **boom** *n* MAR POLL barrera flotante con faldilla *f*; ~~-**coated paper** *n* COATINGS, PAPER papel revestido por cortina *m*; ~ **coater** *n* COATINGS, PAPER estucadora de cortina *f*; ~~-**coating machine** *n* COATINGS, MECH ENG máquina de revestimiento de cortinas *f*, máquina recubridora de cortinas *f*, PAPER máquina de revestimiento de cortinas *f*, máquina recubridora de cortinas *f*; ~ **of fire** *n* MILIT barrera de fuego *f*; ~ **loop** *n* TEXTIL lazo de cortina *m*; ~ **wall** *n* CONST muro cortina *m*
curtaining *n* P&R arrugamiento *m*
curvature *n* GEOM curvatura *f*, inflexión *f*, MATH, PHYS curvatura *f*; ~ **of field** *n* CINEMAT, PHYS curvatura de campo *f*; ~ **of surfaces** *n* GEOM curvatura de superficies *f*
curve[1] *n* CONST *of arch*, GEOM, MATH curva *f*; ~ **of contact** *n* MECH ENG *gearing* circunferencia primitiva *f*, curva de contacto *f*; ~ **factor** *n* FUELLESS factor de

curva *m*; ~ **widening** *n* CONST ensanchamiento de curva *m*

curve^2 *vt* MATH curvar, PROD encorvar, curvar

curve^3 *vi* PROD retorcerse

curved^1 *adj* GEOM, MATH curvado

curved^2: ~ **approach** *n* AIR TRANSP aproximación curvada *f*; ~ **azimuth approach path** *n* AIR TRANSP *microwave landing system* trayectoria curvada de aproximación por acimuz *f*; ~ **common crossing** *n* RAIL cruzamiento agudo en curva *m*; ~ **line** *n* GEOM línea curva *f*; ~ **spanner** *n* MECH ENG llave curvada *f*; ~ **step** *n* CONST *stair* escalón curvo *m*; ~ **vane** *n* HYDRAUL paleta curvada *f*; ~ **worm gear** *n* MECH ENG engranaje helicoidal *m*, tornillo sinfín curvado *m*

curvilinear^1 *adj* GEOM, PHYS curvilíneo

curvilinear^2: ~ **coordinate** *n* GEOM, PHYS coordenada curvilínea *f*

cushion^1 *n* HYDRAUL compresión *f*, MECH ENG amortiguador *m*, chumacera *f*, cojinete *m*; ~ **borne** *n* TRANSP soporte de amortiguador *m*; ~ **car** *n* *AmE* (*cf cushion wagon BrE*) RAIL vagón escudo *m*; ~ **distortion** *n* CINEMAT distorsión amortiguada *f*; ~ **gas** *n* GAS gas de amortiguación *m*; ~ **spring** *n* VEH muelle de retorno *m*; ~ **wagon** *n* *BrE* (*cf cushion car AmE*) RAIL vagón escudo *m*

cushion^2 *vt* HYDRAUL amortiguar

cushioning *n* HYDRAUL compresión *f*, PROD amortiguamiento *m*; ~ **product** *n* PACK material almohadillado *m*, material para protección contra golpes *m*

cusp *n* METALL arista *f*

custom^1: ~-**designed** *adj* PACK hecho de encargo; ~-**made** *adj* PACK hecho de encargo; ~-**ordered** *adj* TEXTIL encargado a medida

custom^2: ~ **calling service** *n* TELECOM servicio de llamadas por especificación *m*; ~ **chip** *n* COMP&DP chip personalizado *m*, plaqueta de encargo *f*; ~-**designed chip** *n* ELECTRON chip diseñado sobre pedido *m*, microplaca sobre pedido *f*,. microplaca diseñada sobre pedido *f*; ~ **LSI** *n* ELECTRON integración a gran escala sobre pedido *f*; ~ **production** *n* PROD fabricación sobre pedido *f*, producción por encargo *f*

customer: ~ **access maintenance center** *n* *AmE* TELECOM centro de mantenimiento acceso para abonados *m*, centro de mantenimiento atención al cliente *m*; ~ **access maintenance centre** *BrE* *n* (*CAMC*) TELECOM centro de mantenimiento acceso para abonados *m*, centro de mantenimiento atención al cliente *m*; ~ **equipment** *n* (*CEQ*) TELECOM equipo del abonado *m*, equipo del cliente *m*; ~ **installation maintenance entities** *n* (*CIME*) TELECOM entidades de mantenimiento instalaciones de abonados *f pl*; ~**'s model** *n* MECH ENG modelo del cliente *m*; ~ **network** *n* (*CN*) TELECOM red de abonados *f*; ~ **order servicing** *n* PROD cumplimentación de pedidos de clientes *f*; ~ **premises equipment** *n* TELECOM equipo en locales del abonado *m*

customerization *n* PROD personalización *f*

customization *n* ELECTRON adaptación *f*, PROD fabricación de encargo *f*

customize *vt* ELECTRON adaptar, PRINT personalizar, TEXTIL hacer a medida

customized^1 *adj* ELECTRON adaptado, PRINT personalizado

customized^2: ~ **form** *n* PRINT impreso personalizado *m*

customs: ~ **clearance** *n* WATER TRANSP despacho de aduanas *m*; ~ **patrol boat** *n* WATER TRANSP embarcación patrullera del servicio de aduanas *f*

cusum: ~ **chart** *n* QUALITY *statistics* cuadro de suma acumulada *m*

cut^1: ~ **from bar** *adj* PROD *bolts, nuts and screws* tallado en la barra; ~ **from the solid** *adj* PROD *gears* tallado en el primordio *m*; ~ **from the solid banks** *adj* PROD *gears* tallado en el primordio *m*; ~-**off** *adj* ELEC ENG incomunicado; ~ **on the bias** *adj* TEXTIL cortado al biés; ~-**staple spun** *adj* TEXTIL hilado de fibra cortada; ~-**to-length** *adj* PROD cortado a medida

cut^2 *n* C&G, CINEMAT corte *m*, COAL corte *m*, roza *f*, socavación *f*, talla *f*, CONST *open excavation, trench* corte *m*, tajo *m*, MECH *sheet of paper* corte *m*, pasada *f*, picadura *f*, recorte *m* (*Esp*), MECH ENG *of machine tool* corte *m*, pasada *f*, picadura *f*, MINE arranque *m* (*AmL*), roza para estemple *f*, cuele *m* (*Esp*), descalce *m* (*AmL*), desmonte *m* (*Esp*), huida *f* (*AmL*), perforación *f*, corte mineral *m*, PROD *of rasp* pasada *f*; ~ **chain incline** *n* MINE corte al sesgo *m*; ~ **and cover** *n* CONST excavación y revestimiento *f*; ~ **and cover method** *n* CONST método de excavación y revestimiento *m*; ~ **end** *n* CONST *of timber* borde sin rematar *m*; ~ **film** *n* PHOTO película rígida *f*; ~ **gears** *n pl* MECH ENG engranajes fresados *m pl*; ~ **glass** *n* C&G cristal cortado *m*; ~ **hole** *n* MINE perforación *f*; ~-**in wind speed** *n* FUELLESS velocidad de viento de intercalar *f*; ~ **locus** *n* GEOM *topology* lugar de corte *m*; ~ **negative** *n* CINEMAT, PHOTO negativo cortado *m*; ~ **oil** *n* PETR TECH, PETROL corte de petróleo *m*, petróleo emulsionado *m*; ~ **and paste** *n* COMP&DP, PRINT cortado y pegado *m*; ~ **piece** *n* SAFE pieza cortada *f*; ~ **point** *n* GEOM *topology* punto de corte *m*; ~ **sizes** *n pl* C&G tamaños de corte estándar *m pl*; ~ **slide** *n* TV película rígida *f*; ~ **stone** *n* CONST piedra labrada *f*; ~-**stone quarry** *n* CONST cantera de piedra *f*; ~ **string** *n* CONST *stair building* zanca cerrada *f*; ~-**to-length line** *n* PROD instalación para cortar a la longitud deseada *f*; ~ **wall string** *n* CONST *stair building* zanca cerrada *f*

cut^3 *vt* CINEMAT cortar, *craft* apagar, CONST *veneers*, GEOM cortar, MECH cortar, tallar, desbastar, MINE *coal* picar, socavar, P&R disolver, diluir, PRINT *astronomy* cortar, PROD *rack, teeth of file* desbastar; ~ **down** *vt* MINE abrir; ~ **with a jig** *vt* SAFE cortar con plantilla; ~ **off** *vt* C&G *edges of glass* cortar, HYDRAUL cerrar, cortar, PROD *sever connections* cortar, *sever with tool* trocear; ~ **out** *vt* MECH ENG *machine tools* cortar, desconectar, PROD separar; ~ **plat** *vt* MINE cargar, enganchar; ~ **to** *vt* CINEMAT cortar; ~ **to the required length** *vt* PROD *tube* cortar a medidas especificadas; ~ **up** *vt* CONST cortar

cut^4: ~ **a landing** *vi* MINE extraer la jaula, sacar la jaula; ~ **a lode** *vi* MINE explotar un filón, extraer un filón; ~ **a shaft** *vi* MINE excavar; ~ **a station** *vi* MINE enganchar

cutaway: ~ **view** *n* MECH ENG vista de corte *f*, vista recortada *f*

cutback *n* TEXTIL reducción *f*; ~ **fiber technique** *AmE*, ~ **fibre technique** *BrE* *n* OPT técnica de medida cortando la fibra *f*; ~ **technique** *n* TELECOM método de alteración *m*

cutoff *n* CINEMAT, ELEC ENG corte *m*, HYDRAUL cierre

m, fin de inyección *m*, fin de la emisión *m*, PRINT límite de cada impresión *m*, PROD desconexión *f*, corte *m*, TV corte *m*, WATER *cut by river across bend* meandro recortado *m*, corta *f*, *crescent-shaped body of water* brazo muerto *m*; ~ **cock** *n* CONST llave de cierre *f*; ~ **current** *n* ELEC *circuit breaker* corriente de corte *f*, corriente residual *f*; ~ **device** *n* HYDRAUL dispositivo de cierre *m*; ~ **ditch** *n* CONST zanja perimetral *f*; ~ **frequency** *n* ACOUST, ELEC, ELECTRON, PHYS, TELECOM frecuencia de cierre *f*, frecuencia de corte *f*; ~ **grade** *n* COAL dureza de corte *f*; ~ **man** *n* BrE (*cf capper AmE*) C&G cortador de vidrio estirado verticalmente *m*; ~ **plate** *n* HYDRAUL teja de expansión *f*; ~ **point** *n* HYDRAUL punto de corte del flujo *m*; ~ **relay** *n* ELEC relé de corte *m*; ~ **switch** *n* CINEMAT conmutador de corte *m*; ~ **trench** *n* OCEAN, WATER *dam* zanja antisocavación *f*, zanja interceptora *f*; ~ **valve** *n* CONST válvula de cierre *f*, HYDRAUL válvula de contención *f*, válvula de retención *f*; ~ **wall** *n* WATER *dam* diente de aguas arriba *m*, muro de guardia *m*, muro interceptor *m*; ~ **wavelength** *n* OPT, PHYS longitud de onda crítica *f*, TELECOM longitud de onda de corte *f*; ~ **wheel** *n* MECH ENG rueda de recortar *f*

cutout *n* C&G corte *f*, ELEC ENG disyuntor *m*, MECH ENG abertura *f*, corte *m*, muesca *f*, PRINT recortado *m*, RAIL vía de desmonte *f*, vía en trinchera *f*; ~ **device** *n* SAFE aditamento de corte *m*, aditamento de paro *m*; ~ **dial** *n* MECH ENG reloj desconectador *m*; ~ **photograph** *n* PHOTO fotografía silueteada *f*; ~ **switch** *n* ELEC ELEC ENG interruptor *m*, conmutador de corte *m*; ~ **wind speed** *n* FUELLESS velocidad de viento de cortar *f*

cutter *n* CONST *of stone, wood* cortadora *f*, MECH broca *f*, cortador *m*, tronchador *m*, MECH ENG cuchilla *f*, portaherramientas *m*, barra de corte *f*, broca *f*, fresa *f*, máquina de cortar *f*, herramienta de corte *f*, cortadora *f*, MINE cantero *m* (*AmL*), cortador *m*, cortador de piedra *m*, PRINT guillotina *f*, WATER TRANSP *vessel* cúter *m*; ~ **adaptor** *n* MECH ENG *machine tools* adaptador de cuchilla *m*, adaptador de fresa *m*; ~ **arbor** *n* MECH ENG *milling-machine* eje portafresas *m*; ~ **arm** *n* COAL acanaladora *f* (*Esp*), barra portacuchillas *f*, eje portaherramienta *m*, rafadora *f* (*AmL*); ~ **bar** *n* MECH ENG *for boring machine* herramienta para interiores *f*, *machine-tool work* cuchilla *f*, portaherramientas *m*, barra de corte *f*; ~'s **bay** *n* C&G departamento de corte *m*; ~ **blade** *n* C&G hoja cortadora *f*; ~ **chain** *n* COAL cadena portacuchillas *f*; ~ **dredger** *n* WATER TRANSP draga disgregadora *f*; ~ **head** *n* CONST cabeza cortante *f*, MECH ENG cabezal portacuchillas *m*, cabezal portafresas *m*, MINE cabezal cortador *m*; ~ **with hub** *n* MECH ENG fresa con buje *f*; ~'s **lathe** *n* C&G torno de cortador *m*; ~ **loader** *n* COAL cargador de cuchillas *m*; ~ **mandrel** *n* MECH ENG barrón portaherramientas *m* ; ~'s **pliers** *n* C&G pinzas del cortador *f pl*; ~ **with shank** *n* MECH ENG fresa con eje *f*, portaherramientas con espiga *m*, portaherramientas con mango *m*, portaherramientas con vástago *m*; ~ **spindle** *n* MECH ENG eje portacuchillas *m*, eje portaherramientas *m*; ~'s **straight edge** *n* C&G regla del cortador *f*; ~'s **table** *n* C&G mesa del cortador *f*; ~'s **table ruler** *n* C&G regla de la mesa para cortar *f*; ~ **with tapped hole** *n* MECH ENG fresa con agujero roscado *f*, portaherramientas con agujero roscado *m*; ~ **wheel**

n MECH ENG moleta *f*; ~ **wound** *n* SAFE herida por cortadora *f*

cutting¹ *adj* GEOL cortante

cutting² *n* C&G corte *m*, CINEMAT corte del negativo *m*, COAL corte *m*, erosión *f*, esqueje *m*, excavación *f*, talla *f*, CONST *trench* excavación *f*, MINE cateo *m* (*AmL*), corte *m* (*Esp*), talla *f* (*AmL*), busca de minerales *f* (*AmL*), excavación *f*, cata *f* (*Esp*), sondeo *m*, exploración *f*, prospección *f* (*Esp*), calicata *f*, PROD *of a gearwheel* corte *m*, *of a chip* troceo *m*, *of metal by oxygen jet* erosión *f*, RAIL vía en trinchera *f*, SAFE cortado *m*, corte *m*, TEXTIL corte *m*, muestra *f*; ~ **angle** *n* FOOD, MECH *machine tool* ángulo de corte *m*; ~ **bit** *n* COAL trépano cortante *m*; ~ **blowpipe** *n* CONST soplete de corte *m*; ~ **copy** *n* CINEMAT copia de trabajo *f*; ~ **diamond** *n* C&G cortador de vidrio *m*; ~ **die** *n* PAPER troqueladora *f*; ~ **drift** *n* MECH ENG mandril cortador *m*; ~ **driftpin** *n* MECH ENG broca de corte *f*, mandril de ensanchar *m*, pasador cónico de ensanchar *m*; ~ **edge** *n* C&G *of diamond* orilla de corte *f*, CONST *of tool* borde afilado *m*, borde cortante *m*, borde penetrante *m*, filo cortante *m*, MECH, MECH ENG arista cortante *f*, filo cortante *m*, labio cortante *m*, TEXTIL borde del corte *m*; ~ **fluid** *n* PROD lubricante para cuchillas *m*; ~ **frame** *n* C&G marco de corte *m*; ~ **gage** *AmE see cutting gauge BrE*; ~ **gas** *n* GAS gas de cortes *m*; ~ **gauge** *n* BrE CONST gramil de cuchilla *m*; ~ **head** *n* MINE cabezal cortante *m*; ~**-in** *n* MECH ENG inserto *m*, intercalación *f*, intervención *f*; ~ **machine** *n* MINE cortador mecánico *m*; ~ **nippers** *n pl* CONST tenazas de corte *f pl*; ~**-off** *n* CONST *of heads of piles* corte *m*, HYDRAUL corte *m*, cierre *m*, PROD *of gates* cierre *m*, *of pieces of iron* traceo *m*; ~ **off the edges** *n* C&G desbastado de orillas *m*; ~**-off and forming lathe** *n* MECH ENG torno troceador y de perfiles *m*, torno troceador y de repetición *m*; ~**-off lathe** *n* MECH ENG torno troceador *m*; ~**-off piece** *n* PROD *from tube* pieza de separación *f*; ~**-off slide** *n* MECH ENG carro de corte *m*, guía de corte *f*; ~**-off tool** *n* MECH ENG *lathe* herramienta de corte *f*, herramienta de trocear *f*; ~**-off wheel** *n* MECH ENG muela de corte *f*, rueda de corte *f*; ~ **oil** *n* MECH ENG lubricante para cuchillas *m*; ~ **pliers** *n pl* CONST alicates de corte *m pl*, pinzas de corte *f pl*, MECH ENG alicates de corte *m pl*, PROD pinzas de corte *f pl*, alicates de corte *m pl*; ~ **point** *n* CINEMAT punto de corte *m*; ~ **ring** *n* MINE *of ore stamp* abrazadera *f*, anillo cortante *m*, caja *f*; ~ **shop** *n* C&G taller de corte *m*; ~ **speed** *n* MECH ENG velocidad de corte *f*; ~ **stroke** *n* MECH ENG *machine tool work* carrera de corte *f*, carrera útil *f*, distancia de corte *f*, distancia útil *f*; ~ **stylus** *n* ACOUST estilete arrancamaterial *m*, punzón para grabar en disco virgen *m*; ~ **teeth** *n pl* CONST dientes cortantes *m pl*; ~ **tool** *n* MECH, MECH ENG escoplo *m*, herramienta de corte *f*, MINE escoplo *m*; ~ **torch** *n* MECH ENG soplete cortador *m*, soplete de corte *m*; ~ **veneer** *n* CONST chapa cortante *f*; ~ **wheel** *n* C&G rueda abrasiva *f*, MECH ENG moleta cortante *f*

cuttings *n pl* COAL muestras de formaciones *f pl*, retales *m pl*, sedimentos *m pl*, PETR TECH cortes *m pl*, muestras de formaciones *f pl*, recortes *m pl*, ripios *m pl*, muestra de formaciones *f*; ~ **gas** *n* GAS gas de ripios *m*, PETR TECH gas de cortes *m*, gas de ripios *m*; ~ **removal** *n* PETR TECH retirada de ripios *f*

cutwater *n* CONST *of bridge-pier* espolón *m*

cutworm *n* AGRIC gusano cortador *m*

CV *abbr* (*code violation*) TELECOM violación de código *f*

CVCS *abbr* (*chemical and volume control system*) NUCL sistema de control químico y de volúmen *m*

CVD *abbr* (*chemical vapor deposition AmE, chemical vapour deposition BrE*) ELECTRON, OPT, TELECOM DVQ (*deposición de vapor químico*)

CVPC *abbr* (*critical pigment volume concentration*) P&R concentración de volumen crítico de pigmentos *f*

CVS *abbr* (*constant volume sampling*) POLL muestreo de volumen constante *m*

CW¹ *abbr* (*continuous wave*) ELEC ENG, PHYS, TV, WAVE PHYS OC (*onda continua*)

CW²: ~ **gas laser** *n* ELECTRON láser de gas y funcionamiento continuo *m*; ~ **laser** *n* ELECTRON láser de funcionamiento continuo *m*; ~ **laser beam** *n* ELECTRON haz de láser de funcionamiento continuo *m*; ~ **laser diode** *n* ELECTRON diodo de láser de funcionamiento continuo *m*; ~ **signal** *n* ELEC ENG señal OC *f*

C-weighting: ~ **curve** *n* ACOUST curva de ponderación C *f*

CWQC *abbr* (*company-wide quality control*) QUALITY control de calidad en toda la empresa *m*, control de calidad en toda la sociedad *m*

CWR *abbr* (*continuous welded rail*) RAIL carril continuo soldado *m*, riel continuo soldado *m*

cyamelid *n* CHEM ciamélida *f*

cyamelide *n* CHEM ciamélida *f*

cyan *n* PRINT cian *m*

cyanacetic *adj* CHEM cianoacético

cyanamide *n* CHEM cianamida *f*

cyanate *n* CHEM cianato *m*

cyanic *adj* CHEM ciánico

cyanidation *n* CHEM, CHEM TECH, COAL cianuración *f*

cyanide *n* CHEM cianuro *m*; ~ **process** *n* CHEM, CHEM TECH, COAL cianuración *f*

cyanite *n* MINERAL cianita *f*, distena *f*

cyanization *n* CHEM cianización *f*

cyanogen *n* CHEM cianógeno *m*

cyanose *n* MINERAL cianosa *f*

cyanosite *n* MINERAL cianosita *f*

cyanotrichite *n* MINERAL cianotriquita *f*

cybernetics *n* COMP&DP, SPACE cibernética *f*

cyberspace *n* COMP&DP ciberespacio *m*

cyc *n* CINEMAT ciclorama *m*

cyclamate *n* CHEM ciclamato *m*

cycle *n* GEN ciclo *m*; ~ **counting** *n* PROD contaje de ciclos *m*, recuento de ciclos *m*; ~ **of intervals** *n* ACOUST ciclo de intervalos *m*; ~ **path** *n* TRANSP calzada para ciclistas *f* (*AmL*), carril para bicicletas *m* (*Esp*); ~ **of sedimentation** *n* GEOL ciclo de sedimentación *m*; ~ **split adjustment** *n* TRANSP ajuste fraccionado del ciclo *m*; ~ **stealing** *n* COMP&DP parada del ciclo *f*, robo de ciclo informático *m*; ~ **time** *n* COMP&DP tiempo del ciclo *m*; ~ **track** *n* CONST, TRANSP vía para bicicletas *f*

cyclic¹ *adj* GEN cíclico, periódico

cyclic²: ~ **block code** *n* TELECOM código cíclico de bloque *m*; ~ **code** *n* TELECOM código cíclico *m*; **~-control step** *n* AIR TRANSP *of a helicopter* etapa de control cíclico *f*; **~-flapping angle** *n* AIR TRANSP *of a helicopter* ángulo de batimiento cíclico *m*; ~ **inventory** *n* PROD inventario periódico *m*; ~ **noise** *n* ACOUST ruido cíclico *m*; ~ **pitch** *n* AIR TRANSP *of a helicopter* paso cíclico *m*; **~-pitch control** *n* AIR

TRANSP *of a helicopter* control de paso cíclico *m*; **~-pitch control stick** *n* AIR TRANSP *of a helicopter* palanca de control de paso cíclico *f*; **~-pitch servo trim** *n* AIR TRANSP *of a helicopter* servo regulador de paso cíclico *m*; **~-pitch stick** *n* AIR TRANSP *of a helicopter* palanca de paso cíclico *f*; ~ **redundancy check** *n* (*CRC*) COMP&DP, ELECTRON, MATH, TELECOM comprobación de la redundancia cíclica *f* (*CRC*), verificación de redundancia cíclica *f* (*CRC*); ~ **redundancy code** *n* (*CRC*) TELECOM código de redundancia cíclica *m* (*CRC*); ~ **sedimentation** *n* GEOL sedimentación cíclica *f*; ~ **shift** *n* COMP&DP desplazamiento cíclico *m*; ~ **stick** *n* AIR TRANSP *of a helicopter* palanca cíclica *f*

cyclical: ~ **stress** *n* METALL esfuerzo alternativo *m*, esfuerzo cíclico *m*

cycling *n* AIR TRANSP *of a helicopter* cíclico *m*

cyclization *n* CHEM, CHEM TECH ciclación *f*, ciclización *f*

cycloaliphatic: ~ **amine** *n* CHEM, P&R amina cicloalifática *f*

cycloalkene *n* CHEM, PETR TECH ciclo alqueno *m*

cyclogyro *n* AIR TRANSP ciclogiróscopo *m*

cyclohexane *n* CHEM, PETR TECH ciclohexano *m*

cyclohexanol *n* CHEM ciclohexanol *m*

cyclohexene *n* CHEM ciclohexeno *m*

cycloid *n* GEOM cicloide *f*

cycloidal: ~ **gear** *n* MECH engranaje cicloidal *m*

cyclomethylene *n* CHEM ciclometileno *m*

cyclone *n* CHEM TECH ciclón *m*, COAL ciclón *m*, clasificador de aire seco *m*, extractor de polvo *m*, FOOD ciclón *m*, METEO ciclón *m*, depresión *f*, PETR TECH ciclón *m*, clasificador *m*, POLL ciclón *m*, extractor de polvo *m*; ~ **furnace** *n* C&G horno de ciclón *m*, HEAT horno de turbulencia *m*; ~ **recovery skimmer** *n* POLL desescoriador por ciclón *m*, desnatadora por ciclón *f*, espumador por ciclón *m*

cyclonic: ~ **circulation** *n* METEO circulación ciclónica *f*; ~ **rotation** *n* METEO rotación ciclónica *f*

cycloolefin *n* CHEM, PETR TECH cicloolefina *f*

cycloparaffin *n* CHEM, PETR TECH cicloparafina *f*

cyclopean: ~ **concrete** *n* CONST concreto ciclópeo *m* (*AmL*), hormigón ciclópeo *m* (*Esp*); ~ **concrete gravity dam** *n* HYDROL presa de gravedad de concreto ciclópeo *f* (*AmL*), presa de gravedad de hormigón ciclópeo *f* (*Esp*)

cyclopic: ~ **barrage** *n* WATER presa ciclópea *f*

cyclothem *n* GEOL ciclotema *m*

cyclotron *n* ELECTRON, NUCL, PART PHYS, PHYS, acelerador cíclico *m*, acelerador contínuo *m*, acelerador de electrones *m*, acelerador de iones *m*, ciclotrón *m*; ~ **frequency** *n* ELECTRON, NUCL, PART PHYS, PHYS frecuencia ciclotrónica *f*; ~ **radiation** *n* PHYS, RAD PHYS radiación ciclotrónica *f*; ~ **safety** *n* PHYS, RAD PHYS, SAFE seguridad del ciclotrón *f*

cyclotronic: ~ **resonance** *n* TELECOM resonancia ciclotrónica *f*

cylinder *n* AUTO cilindro *m*, perno de la culata *m*, C&G, COMP&DP, GEOM cilindro *m*, HEAT ENG turbina *f*, HYDRAUL cuerpo *m*, MECH cilindro *m*, cuerpo *m*, tambor *m*, MINE cilindro *m*, tambor *m*, turbina *f*, P&R cilindro *m*, PAPER cilindro *m*, rodillo *m*, PROD cilindro *m*, *of pump* cuerpo *m*, REFRIG, THERMO turbina *f*, VEH, WATER TRANSP *of engine* cilindro *m*; ~ **bank angling** *n* AUTO, VEH ángulo de inclinación del cilindro *m*; ~ **barrel** *n* HYDRAUL, MECH ENG, PROD,

VEH barril del cilindro *m*, cuerpo del cilindro *m*;
~ **block** *n* AUTO bloque *m*, bloque de cilindros *m*,
bloque del motor *m*, MECH, MECH ENG bloque del
motor *m*, VEH bloque de cilindros *m*, bloque del
motor *m*; ~ **boiler** *n* HYDRAUL caldera cilíndrica *f*;
~ **bore** *n* MECH ENG calibre del cilindro *m*, diámetro
interior del cilindro *m*; ~ **cam** *n* MECH ENG, PROD leva
de cilindro *f*; ~ **capacity** *n* AUTO, VEH capacidad del
cilindro *f*; ~ **casing** *n* PROD chaqueta del cilindro *f*;
~ **cock** *n* CONST canilla cilíndrica *f* (*AmL*), grifo
cilíndrico *m*, llave de desagüe *f*; ~ **cover** *n* HYDRAUL
culata *f*, tapa del cilindro *f*, PROD tapa del cilindro *f*;
~ **drawing process** *n* C&G proceso de cilindro de
vidrio plano *m*; ~ **drying machine** *n* TEXTIL secadora
cilíndrica *f*; ~ **flange** *n* VEH pestaña de asiento del
cilindro *f*; ~ **gasket** *n* REFRIG junta cilíndrica *f*;
~ **glass** *n* BrE (*cf blown sheet AmE*) C&G lámina
soplada *f*, vidrio en cilindros *m*, vidrio plano soplado
m; ~ **head** *n* AUTO culata *f*, HYDRAUL, MECH ENG
culata *f*, tapa del cilindro *f*, PROD culata del cilindro *f*,
REFRIG cabeza de cilindro *f*, VEH culata *f*, WATER
TRANSP *of engine* cabeza del cilindro *f*, tapa del
cilindro *f*; ~**-head gasket** *n* AUTO, VEH junta de
culata *f*; ~**-head stud** *n* MECH ENG espárrago de la
culata del cilindro *m*, pasador de culata del cilindro
m, perno sin cabeza de la culata del cilindro *m*;
~ **jacket** *n* PROD camisa exterior del cilindro *f*,
chaqueta del cilindro *f*; ~ **lagging** *n* HEAT ENG,
PROD, THERMO forro calorífugo del cilindro *m*;
~ **liner** *n* AUTO, MECH, VEH camisa de cilindro *f*,
camisa interior del cilindro *f*; ~ **lock** *n* PROD cerradura del cilindro *f*; ~**-lock operator** *n* PROD
accionador de la cerradura del cilindro *m*;
~ **machine** *n* PAPER máquina de rodillos *f*; ~ **mold**
AmE, ~ **mould** *BrE n* PAPER forma redonda *f*;
~ **piston rod** *n* MECH ENG barra del pistón del
cilindro *f*, vástago del pistón del cilindro *m*, RAIL
barra del pistón del cilindro *f*; ~ **poppet head** *n* PROD
of lathe contrapunto de manguito *m*; ~ **printing
machine** *n* PRINT prensa cilíndrica *f*; ~ **process** *n*
C&G proceso por cilindro *m*; ~ **rheostat** *n* ELEC
reóstato de cilindro *m*; ~ **rod** *n* MECH ENG barra del
cilindro *f*; ~**-sizing machine** *n* TEXTIL máquina de

aprestar cilíndrica *f*; ~ **sleeve** *n* AUTO, VEH manguito
del cilindro *m*; ~ **tailstock** *n* PROD *of lathe* contrapunto del cilindro *m*; ~ **wall** *n* AUTO, VEH pared del
cilindro *f*; ~ **wrench** *n* PROD llave para tubos *f*
cylindrical[1] *adj* GEOL, GEOM, MECH ENG cilíndrico
cylindrical[2]: ~ **abrasive sheet** *n* MECH ENG hoja
abrasiva cilíndrica *f*; ~ **balanced valve** *n* FUELLESS
válvula equilibrada *f*; ~ **boiler** *n* HYDRAUL caldera
cilíndrica *f*; ~ **capacitor** *n* PHYS capacitor cilíndrico
m; ~ **coordinates** *n pl* PHYS coordenadas cilíndricas *f*
pl; ~ **flue boiler** *n* HYDRAUL caldera de hogar interior
cilíndrico *f*; ~ **gage** *AmE*, ~ **gauge** *BrE n* PROD
calibrador cilíndrico *m*, calibre de anillos *m*, calibre
de topes *m*; ~ **gear pair** *n* AUTO pareja de engranajes
cilíndricos *f*; ~ **gears** *n pl* MECH ENG engranajes
cilíndricos *m pl*; ~ **gears for heavy engineering** *n pl*
MECH ENG engranajes cilíndricos para ingeniería
pesada *m pl*; ~ **grinder** *n* MECH, MECH ENG rectificadora cilíndrica *f*; ~ **grinding** *n* MECH, MECH ENG
rectificado cilíndrico *m*; ~ **irradiator** *n* NUCL irradiador cilíndrico *m*; ~ **lens** *n* INSTR lente cilíndrica *f*;
~ **mouthpiece** *n* HYDRAUL boquilla cilíndrica *f*,
tobera cilíndrica *f*; ~ **pin** *n* MECH ENG pasador
cilíndrico *m*; ~ **reflecting aerial** *n* BrE (*cf cylindrical
reflecting antenna AmE*) TELECOM antena reflectora
cilíndrica *f*; ~ **reflecting antenna** *n* AmE (*cf cylindrical reflecting aerial BrE*) TELECOM antena reflectora
cilíndrica *f*; ~ **roller bearing** *n* MECH ENG cojinete
axial de rodillos cilíndricos *m*; ~ **rotor machine** *n*
ELEC máquina de rotor cilíndrico *f*; ~ **shell** *n* SPACE
capa cilíndrica *f*; ~ **solid of revolution** *n* GEOM
cilindro de revolución *m*, sólido cilíndrico de una
revolución *m*; ~ **spring** *n* PROD resorte cilíndrico *m*;
~ **wave** *n* ACOUST onda cilíndrica *f*; ~ **winding** *n* ELEC
coil bobinado cilíndrico *m*
cylindroconic *adj* PROD cilindrocónico
cymene *n* CHEM cimeno *m*
cymogene *adj* PETROL cimógeno
cymophane *n* MINERAL cimófana *f*
cyprine *n* MINERAL ciprina *f*, vesubiana azul *f*
cyst *n* AGRIC agalla *f*, quiste *m*; ~ **nematode** *n* AGRIC
nemátodo cecidio *m*
cytogenetics *n* AGRIC citogenética *f*

D

D *abbr* (*deuterium*) CHEM, NUCL, PHYS D (*deuterio*)

dab *vt* PRINT entintar con tampón

dabber *n* PRINT tampón *m*, PROD *of loamplate, loam mould* varilla de refuerzo *f*

DAC *abbr* COMP&DP, ELECTRON, TELECOM, TV (*digital-analog conversion*) DAC (*conversión digital-analógica f*), (*digital-analog converter*) DAC (*conversor digital-analógico m, convertidor digital-analógico m*), NUCL (*derived air concentration*) CDA (*concentración derivada en aire*)

dacite *n* MINERAL, PETROL dacita *f*

Dacron® *n* TEXTIL, WATER TRANSP *sailcloth* Dacrón® *m*

daggerboard *n* WATER TRANSP dique de presa *m*

dailies *n pl* CINEMAT rodaje diario *m*

daily: ~ **consumption** *n* WATER consumo diario *m*; ~ **specific consumption** *n* HYDROL consumo específico diario *m*; ~ **use** *n* PROD uso diario *m*; ~ **water flow** *n* WATER caudal de agua diario *m*

dairy: ~ **belt** *n* AGRIC cuenca lechera *f*; ~ **cattle** *n* AGRIC ganado lechero *m*, ganado vacuno de leche *m*; ~ **cow** *n* AGRIC vaca lechera *f*; ~ **farm** *n* AGRIC granja lechera *f*, tambo *m* (*AmL*); ~ **farming** *n* AGRIC explotación lechera *f*; ~ **industry** *n* AGRIC, FOOD industria lechera *f*; ~ **plant** *n* REFRIG central lechera *f*; ~ **produce** *n pl* AGRIC, FOOD productos lácteos *m pl*; ~ **product** *n* FOOD producto lácteo *m*

dairyman *n* AGRIC lechero *m*

daisychain *n* ELECTRON, PROD cadena *f*; ~ **bus** *n* COMP&DP bus de encadenamiento *m*, bus de encadenamiento mariposa *m*, conductores comunes de forma encadenada *m pl*

daisywheel *n* COMP&DP margarita *f*, rueda de mariposa *f*, PRINT cabezal de margarita *m*; ~ **printer** *n* COMP&DP, PRINT impresora a rueda de mariposa *f* (*AmL*), impresora de margarita *f* (*Esp*), impresora de tipo margarita *f* (*Esp*)

dalton *n* RAD PHYS daltón *m*

Dalton's: ~ **law** *n* PHYS ley de Dalton *f*

dam¹ *n* FUELLESS presa *f*, HYDROL pantano *m*, presa *f*, MINE cerramiento *m*, presa *f*, PROD dama *f*, WATER dique *m*, presa *f*; ~ **plate** *n* PROD placa de damas *f*

dam² *vt* MINE, WATER embalsar, represar

damage *n* GEN avería *f*; ~ **assessment** *n* WATER TRANSP evaluación de los daños *f*, tasación de los daños *f*

damaged¹ *adj* TELECOM deteriorado

damaged²: ~ **car** *n* AmE (*cf damaged wagon BrE*) RAIL vagón averiado *m*; ~ **fuel assembly** *n* NUCL elemento de combustible dañado *m*; ~ **wagon** *n* BrE (*cf damaged car AmE*) RAIL vagón averiado *m*; ~ **yarn** *n* C&G fibra dañada *f*

damming *n* MINE represamiento *m*, WATER remanso *m*, represamiento *m*

damourite *n* MINERAL damourita *f*

damp¹ *n* MINE apajado *m*; ~ **fog** *n* METEO niebla que moja *f*; ~**-proof course** *n* CONST tratamiento de hidrofugación *m*, tratamiento de impermeabilización

m; ~ **sheet** *n* MINE lona de ventilación *f*; ~ **streak** *n* PAPER banda húmeda *f*

damp² *vt* ELEC *oscillation*, ELEC ENG, PHYS amortiguar

damped: ~ **oscillation** *n* ELECTRON oscilación amortiguada *f*; ~ **sinusoidal quantity** *n* ELEC ENG cantidad sinusoidal amortiguada *f*; ~ **vibrations** *n pl* WAVE PHYS vibraciones amortiguadas *f pl*

dampener *n* PAPER rodillo humectador *m*

dampening *n* METALL humedecimiento *m*; ~ **etch** *n* PRINT mordido húmedo *f*; ~ **solution** *n* PRINT solución humectadora *f*

damper *n* ACOUST, AUTO amortiguador *m*, CONST *of furnace, chimney* regulador de tiro *m*, ELEC ENG amortiguador *m*, HEAT ENG humedecedor *m*, amortiguador *m*, MECH ENG amortiguador *m*, PROD *of superheater* registro *m*, RAIL amortiguador *m*, REFRIG registro *m*, compuerta *f*, SPACE *mechanical acoustics* amortiguador *m*, VEH amortiguador *m*, taco elástico *m*

damping *n* GEN amortiguación *f*, amortiguamiento *m*, atenuación *f*, humedecimiento *m*; ~ **capacitor** *n* ELEC ENG condensador de atenuación *m*; ~ **coefficient** *n* PHYS coeficiente de amortiguación *m*; ~ **coil** *n* ELEC, ELEC ENG bobina de amortiguamiento *f*; ~ **device** *n* MECH ENG aparato amortiguador *m*; ~ **down** *n* PROD *of blast furnace* parada temporal *f*; ~ **factor** *n* ELEC, PHYS factor de amortiguación *m*; ~ **moment** *n* AIR TRANSP momento de amortiguación *m*; ~ **off** *n* AGRIC podredumbre de plántula *f*; ~ **resistance** *n* PHYS resistencia de amortiguación *f*; ~ **resistor** *n* ELEC resistor de amortiguación *m*; ~ **roll** *n* PACK cilindro humidificador *m*; ~ **stretch** *n* PAPER alargamiento debido a la humedad *m*

danaide *n* HYDRAUL rueda hidráulica de pera *f*

danaite *n* MINERAL danaíta *f*

danalite *n* MINERAL danalita *f*

danburite *n* MINERAL danburita *f*

dance *vt* CONST *step* oscilar

dancing: ~ **seat** *n* HYDRAUL ajuste oscilante *m*; ~ **sleeper** *n* BrE (*cf dancing tie AmE*) RAIL traviesa oscilante *f*; ~ **step** *n* CONST *stair building* escalón oscilante *m*; ~ **tie** *n* AmE (*cf dancing sleeper BrE*) RAIL traviesa oscilante *f*

dandy: ~ **roll** *n* PAPER rodillo desgotador *m*, rodillo afiligranador *m*, rodillo para marcas de agua *m*

Danforth: ~ **anchor** *n* WATER TRANSP ancla Danforth *f*

danger *n* SAFE peligro *m*, riesgo *m*; ~ **area** *n* SAFE área peligrosa *f*; ~ **point** *n* SAFE punto peligroso *m*; ~ **signal** *n* SAFE señal de peligro *f*; ~ **zone** *n* SAFE zona de peligro *f*

dangerous: ~ **environment** *n* RAD PHYS, SAFE ambiente peligroso *m*, entorno peligroso *m*; ~ **goods** *n pl* PACK, SAFE, TRANSP mercancías peligrosas *f pl*; ~ **materials** *n pl* CHEM, SAFE, TRANSP materiales peligrosos *m pl*; ~ **substance** *n* CHEM, SAFE, TRANSP substancia peligrosa *f*

Danian *adj* GEOL Daniense

Danish: ~ **seine** *n* OCEAN cerco danés *m*, red de cerco danesa *f*

dannemorite *n* MINERAL dannemorita *f*

DAO *abbr* (*deasphalted oil*) PETR TECH crudo desasfaltado *m*

daphnetin *n* CHEM dafnetina *f*

daphnin *n* CHEM dafnina *f*

daphnite *n* MINERAL dafnita *f*

darcy *n* HYDROL darcy *m*, unidad de permeabilidad *f*

dark[1]: **~-colored** *AmE*, **~-coloured** *BrE adj* GEOL color oscuro

dark[2]: **~ conduction** *n* ELEC ENG conducción residual *f*; **~ current** *n* ELEC ENG corriente en la oscuridad *f*, OPT corriente de oscuridad *f*, PHYS, TELECOM corriente residual *f*; **~-field illumination** *n* PHYS iluminación en campo oscuro *f*; **~-field image** *n* CRYSTALL imagen de campo oscuro *f*; **~ filter** *n* INSTR filtro oscuro *m*; **~ fringe** *n* PHYS franja oscura *f*; **~ glass** *n* C&G vidrio oscuro *m*; **~-ground illumination** *n* PHYS iluminación sobre fondo oscuro *f*; **~ line spectrum** *n* SPACE espectro de líneas oscuras *m*; **~ nebula** *n* SPACE nebulosa oscura *f*; **~ resistance** *n* ELEC ENG *photocell* resistencia de reposo *f*, NUCL resistencia de reposo *f*, resistencia oscura *f*; **~ shade** *n* TEXTIL tonalidad oscura *f*; **~ slide** *n* PHOTO chasis *m*, placa negra *f*; **~ tone** *n* COLOUR tono oscuro *m*; **~-trace screen** *n* ELECTRON pantalla de trazo oscuro *f*

darkening *n* C&G opacado *m*; **~ index** *n* C&G índice de opacidad *m*

darkroom *n* CINEMAT, PHOTO cuarto oscuro *m*; **~ lighting** *n* CINEMAT, PHOTO iluminación de seguridad *f*, iluminación inactínica *f*; **~ timer** *n* CINEMAT, PHOTO reloj para cuarto oscuro *m*

dart *n* TEXTIL pinza *f*; **~ impact test** *n* C&G prueba de impacto con dardo *f*

darting: **~ flame** *n* THERMO *burner* dardo de llama *m*

dash *n* PRINT guión *m*

dashboard *n* AUTO, VEH cuadro de instrumentos *m*, tablero de instrumentos *m*

dashpot *n* MECH, MECH ENG amortiguador *m*, retardador *m*, NUCL zona de amortiguación *f*, TRANSP, VEH amortiguador *m*; **~ valve** *n* MECH ENG válvula de amortiguación *f*, válvula del amortiguador *f*, válvula del retardador *f*

DAT *abbr* (*digital audio tape*) COMP&DP cinta digital de audio *f*

data *n pl* GEN datos *m pl*, información *f*; **~ abstraction** *n* COMP&DP abstracción de datos *f*, extracción de datos *f*; **~ acquisition** *n* COMP&DP, ELECTRON adquisición de datos *f*; **~ aggregate** *n* COMP&DP agregación de datos *f*, conjunto de datos *m*; **~ amplifier** *n* ELECTRON amplificador de datos *m*; **~ array** *n* COMP&DP arreglo de datos *m*, matriz de datos *f*; **~ burst** *n* SPACE ráfaga de datos *f*; **~ bus** *n* COMP&DP bus de datos *m*, conductor común de datos *m*, SPACE canal de datos *m*; **~ capture** *n* COMP&DP captura de datos *f*; **~ carrier** *n* COMP&DP portador de datos *m*, TELECOM portadora de datos *f*; **~ carrier detector** *n* (*DCD*) TELECOM detector de portadora de datos *m*; **~ carrier failure detector** *n* TELECOM detector de fallo en la portadora de datos *m*; **~ cartridge** *n* COMP&DP cartucho de datos *m*; **~ chaining** *n* COMP&DP encadenamiento de datos *m*; **~ channel** *n* COMP&DP canal de datos *m*; **~ channel multiplexer** *n* COMP&DP multiplexor de canales de datos *m*; **~ circuit terminal equipment** *n* TELECOM equipo terminal del circuito de datos *m*; **~ circuit-**

terminating equipment *n* TELECOM equipo del circuito de terminación de datos *m*; **~ collection** *n* COMP&DP, TELECOM recogida de datos *f*, recolección de datos *f*; **~ collection center** *AmE*, **~ collection centre** *BrE n* (*DCC*) TELECOM centro de recogida de datos *m*, centro de recolección de datos *m*; **~ collection equipment** *n* TELECOM equipo de recogida de datos *m*; **~ collection platform** *n* (*DCP*) METEO plataforma para recogida de datos *f*, SPACE equipo para recolección de datos *m*, plataforma para la recolección de datos *f*; **~-collection satellite** *n* SPACE satélite para recolección de datos *m*; **~ collection system** *n* (*DCS*) TELECOM sistema de recogida de datos *m*; **~ communication** *n* COMP&DP comunicación de datos *f*, telemática *f*, transmisión de datos *f*; **~ communication channel** *n* (*DCC*) TELECOM canal de comunicación de datos *m*, canal de transmisión de datos *m*; **~ communication network** *n* COMP&DP red de comunicación de datos *f*, red telemática *f*; **~ communication terminal** *n* COMP&DP terminal de comunicación de datos *m*, terminal de transmisión de datos *m*, terminal telemático *m*; **~ compaction** *n* COMP&DP, ELECTRON, TELECOM compactación de datos *f*, compresión de datos *f*; **~ compression** *n* COMP&DP, ELECTRON, TELECOM compactación de datos *f*, compresión de datos *f*; **~ compression technique** *n* (*DCT*) COMP&DP, ELECTRON, TELECOM técnica de compresión de datos *f*; **~ concentrator** *n* COMP&DP concentrador de datos *m*; **~ convention** *n* AIR TRANSP convención de datos *f*; **~ conversion** *n* COMP&DP, ELECTRON conversión de datos *f*; **~ converter** *n* COMP&DP, ELECTRON convertidor de datos *m*; **~ declaration** *n* COMP&DP declaración de datos *f*; **~ definition** *n* COMP&DP definición de datos *f*; **~ description** *n* COMP&DP descripción de datos *f*; **~ description language** *n* (*DDL*) COMP&DP lenguaje de descripción de datos *m*; **~ dictionary** *n* COMP&DP diccionario de datos *m*; **~ display terminal** *n* TV terminal de visualización de datos *m*; **~ division** *n* COMP&DP *COBOL* división de datos *f*; **~ domain** *n* ELECTRON campo de datos *m*; **~ element** *n* COMP&DP elemento de datos *m*, ELECTRON elemento de información *m*, TELECOM elemento de datos *m*; **~ element separator** *n* TELECOM separador de elementos de datos *m*; **~ encryption** *n* COMP&DP cifrado de datos *m*, encriptación de datos *f*; **~ entry** *n* COMP&DP, ELECTRON entrada de datos *f*, ingreso de datos *m*, introducción de datos *f*; **~ extraction** *n* COMP&DP, ELECTRON extracción de datos *f*; **~ field** *n* COMP&DP campo de datos *m*; **~ file** *n* COMP&DP archivo de datos *m*, fichero de datos *m*; **~ flowchart** *n* COMP&DP organigrama de datos *m*; **~ format** *n* COMP&DP formato de datos *m*; **~ gathering** *n* COMP&DP acumulación de datos *f*, recolección de datos *f*; **~ hierarchy** *n* COMP&DP jerarquía de datos *f*; **~ independence** *n* COMP&DP independencia de datos *f*; **~ integrity** *n* TELECOM integridad de datos *f*; **~ interchange message store** *n* ELECTRON almacenamiento de mensajes por intercambio de datos electrónicos *m*; **~ item** *n* COMP&DP unidad de información *f*, ítem de datos *m*; **~ link** *n* COMP&DP, ELECTRON enlace de datos *m*, SPACE *communications* canal de datos *m*, enlace de datos *m*, TELECOM transmisión de datos *f*; **~ link connection** *n* (*DLC*) TELECOM conexión para la transmisión de datos *f*, enlace para la transmisión de datos *m*; **~ link**

connection identifier n (*DLCI*) TELECOM identificador de conexión para la transmisión de datos m, identificador del enlace para la transmisión de datos m; ~ **link control** n AIR TRANSP control intercambio de datos m, COMP&DP control de enlace de datos m; ~ **link control protocol** n COMP&DP protocolo de control de enlace de datos m; ~ **link escape** n (*DLE*) COMP&DP escape de enlace de datos m (*DLE*), transmisión transparente f; ~ **link layer** n COMP&DP capa de enlace de datos f, nivel de enlace de datos m, TELECOM nivel de transmisión de datos m; ~ **link service** n (*DLS*) TELECOM servicio de transmisión de datos m; ~ **logger** n COMP&DP registrador de datos m, INSTR tabulador electrónico de datos m; ~ **logging** n COMP&DP, NUCL, TELECOM registro de datos m; ~ **management** n (*DM*) COMP&DP, TELECOM administración de datos f (*DM*), gestión de datos f; ~ **manipulation language** n (*DML*) COMP&DP lenguaje de manipulación de datos m (*DML*); ~ **medium** n COMP&DP medio de almacenamiento de datos m, medio de datos m, soporte de datos m; ~ **model** n COMP&DP modelo de datos m; ~ **modulation** n TELECOM modulación de datos f; ~ **multiplexer** n TELECOM multiplex de datos m, TRANSP multiplexor de datos m; ~ **multiplexing** n ELECTRON, TELECOM transmisión simultánea de datos f; ~ **name** n COMP&DP nombre de datos m; ~ **network** n COMP&DP, TELECOM red de datos f; ~ **network identification code** n (*DNIC*) TELECOM código de identificación de la red de datos m; ~ **origin authentication** n COMP&DP, TELECOM autenticación del origen de datos f; ~ **origination** n COMP&DP creación de datos f; ~ **output** n COMP&DP, INSTR salida de datos f; ~ **packet** n TELECOM paquete de datos m; ~ **path** n COMP&DP senda de datos f, vía de acceso a los datos f, ELECTRON canalización de datos f; ~ **phase** n TELECOM fase de datos f; ~ **port** n TELECOM puerto de datos m; ~ **preparation** n COMP&DP preparación de datos f; ~ **privacy** n COMP&DP confidencialidad de los datos f, secreto de datos m; ~ **private wire** n TELECOM circuito de uso privado de datos m; ~ **processing** n (*DP*) COMP&DP, TELECOM sistema de explotación de datos m, proceso de datos m (*PD*), tratamiento de la información m (*PD*); ~ **processing center** AmE, ~ **processing centre** BrE n (*DPC*) COMP&DP, TELECOM centro de procesamiento de datos m (*DPC*), centro de proceso de datos m (*DPC*), centro informático m; ~ **processing system** n COMP&DP sistema de proceso de datos m, sistema de procesamiento de datos m, sistema informático m; ~-**processing terminal equipment** n TELECOM equipo terminal para el proceso de datos m; ~ **protection** n COMP&DP protección de datos f; ~ **query** n COMP&DP consulta de los datos f, interrogación de datos f; ~ **rate** n COMP&DP velocidad de transmisión de datos f; ~ **record** n COMP&DP registro de datos m; ~ **recorder** n COMP&DP grabadora de datos f, registrador de datos m; ~ **recording** n COMP&DP grabación de datos f, registro de datos m, ELEC apunte de datos m, registro de datos m, TELECOM grabación de datos f; ~ **recording back** n PHOTO soporte para la grabación de información m; ~ **recovery system** n RAD PHYS sistema de recuperación de datos m; ~ **reduction** n COMP&DP reducción de datos f; ~-**relay satellite** n (*DRS*) SPACE satélite de recogida de datos m, satélite para transmisión de

datos m, satélite retransmisor de datos m; ~ **representation** n COMP&DP representación de datos f; ~ **retrieval** n COMP&DP recuperación de datos f; ~ **security** n COMP&DP protección de datos f, seguridad de datos f; ~ **set** n COMP&DP conjunto de datos m; ~ **set definition** n COMP&DP definición del conjunto de datos f; ~ **set ready** n (*DSR*) COMP&DP módem listo para comunicar m, módem listo para funcionar m, TELECOM conjunto de datos listo m, conjunto de datos preparados m; ~ **sheet** n VEH documentación f, ficha técnica f; ~ **signaling rate** AmE, ~ **signalling rate** BrE n TELECOM régimen de señalización de datos m; ~ **sink** n ELEC ENG equipo que recibe los datos m, TELECOM colector de datos m; ~ **source** n COMP&DP generador de datos m, ELEC ENG fuente de datos f, generador de datos m; ~ **station** n COMP&DP estación de datos f; ~ **storage** AmE, ~ **store** BrE n (*DS*) COMP&DP, NUCL, TELECOM almacenamiento de datos m, memoria de datos f; ~ **stream** n COMP&DP, ELEC ENG, TELECOM corriente de datos f, flujo de datos m; ~ **structure** n COMP&DP estructura de datos f; ~ **switch** n TELECOM conmutador de datos m; ~ **switching** n TELECOM conmutación de datos f; ~-**switching exchange** n (*DSE*) COMP&DP, TELECOM central de comunicación de datos f (*CCD*), central de conmutación de datos f (*CCD*), TELECOM panel de conmutación de datos m; ~ **table** n PROD tabla de datos f; ~ **table failure** n PROD fallo de la tabla de datos m; ~ **table section specifier** n PROD especificador de la sección de tabla de datos m; ~ **table word address** n PROD dirección con palabra de la tabla de datos f; ~ **tablet** n COMP&DP bloque de datos m, tabla de datos f, tableta de datos f; ~ **terminal** n COMP&DP, TELECOM terminal de datos m; ~ **terminal equipment** n (*DTE*) AIR TRANSP, COMP&DP, TELECOM conjunto terminal de datos m (*DTE*), equipo terminal de datos m (*DTE*); ~ **terminal ready** n TELECOM terminal de datos preparado m; ~ **transfer** n COMP&DP transferencia de datos f; ~ **transfer rate** n COMP&DP, TELECOM velocidad de transferencia de datos f, velocidad de transmisión de datos f; ~ **transfer requested** n TELECOM transferencia de datos solicitada f; ~ **transfer system** n TELECOM sistema de transferencia de datos m; ~ **transmission** n COMP&DP transmisión de datos f; ~-**transmission balloon** n MILIT globo aerostático de transmisión de datos m; ~ **transmission channel** n COMP&DP canal de transmisión de datos m; ~ **transmission rate switch** n COMP&DP, PROD interruptor de la velocidad de transmisión de datos m; ~-**transport network** n COMP&DP, TELECOM red de transporte de datos f; ~ **type** n COMP&DP tipo de datos m; ~ **validation** n COMP&DP validación de datos f; ~ **vet** n COMP&DP revisión de datos f, verificación de datos f; ~ **word** n COMP&DP palabra de datos f

databank n COMP&DP, ELECTRON, TELECOM banco de datos m

database n COMP&DP, ELECTRON, TELECOM base de datos f; ~ **administrator** n (*DBA*) COMP&DP, TELECOM administrador de la base de datos m; ~ **management** n (*DBM*) COMP&DP, TELECOM administración de la base de datos f, gestión de la base de datos f; ~ **management system** n (*DBMS*) COMP&DP, TELECOM sistema de administración de base de datos m (*SABD*), sistema de gestión de base de datos *m*; ~ **query** *n* COMP&DP consulta de la base de datos *f*, interrogación de la base de datos *f*

datagram *n* COMP&DP, TELECOM datagrama *m*

dataphone® *n* COMP&DP, ELECTRON, SAFE, TELECOM datáfono® *m*

datarom® *n* OPT datarom® *f*

date *n* AGRIC época *f*, GEOL era *f*, época *f*, PETROL época *f*; ~ **code** *n* PACK código de fecha *m*; ~ **freight inward** *n* PROD fecha de llegada del flete *f*; ~ **line** *n* WATER TRANSP línea de cambio de fecha *f*; ~ **of manufacture** *n* PACK fecha de fabricación *f*; ~ **and time of transmission** *n* TELECOM fecha y hora de transmisión *f*

dater *n* COMP&DP fechador *m*

dating *n* GEOL, PHYS datación *f*; ~ **program** *n* COMP&DP programa de fechado *m*

datiscin *n* CHEM datiscina *f*

datolite *n* MINERAL datolita *f*

datum *n* CONST dato *m*, información *f*, referencia *f*, SPACE dato *m*; ~ **horizon** *n* GEOL horizonte de referencia *m*; ~ **level** *n* CONST nivel de referencia *m*, punto de referencia *m*; ~ **line** *n* CONST línea de referencia *f*, MECH, MECH ENG línea de comparación *f*, línea de referencia *f*, plano de nivel *m*, SPACE línea de comparación *f*, línea de datos *f*, línea de referencia *f*, línea de tierra *f*; ~ **plane** *n* (*DP*) CONST, GEOL plano de referencia *m* (*PR*); ~ **point** *n* CONST punto de referencia *m*

daub *vt* PROD embadurnar

daubing *n* PROD guarnecimiento *m*

daughter *n* NUCL hija *f*; ~ **board** *n* ELECTRON cuadro de filiación *m*, placa subordinada *f*; ~ **isotope** *n* GEOL isótopo descendiente *m*; ~ **nuclide** *n* RAD PHYS nucleido hijo *m*; ~ **product** *n* PHYS, RAD PHYS descendiente radiactivo *m*, nucleido hijo *m*

davit *n* MECH grúa de botes *f*, pescante *m*, WATER TRANSP pescante *m*; ~ **fall** *n* WATER TRANSP tira *f*

Davy: ~ **lamp** *n* COAL, MINE, SAFE lámpara de seguridad *f*

davyne *n* MINERAL davyna *f*

day: ~ **boat** *n* WATER TRANSP bote velero de recreo sin cámara *m*; ~ **drift** *n* MINE socavón *m*; ~ **exterior** *n* CINEMAT toma exterior de día *f*; ~ **for night** *n* CINEMAT noche americana *f*; ~ **fuel tank** *n* NUCL tanque diario de combustible *m*; ~ **hole** *n* MINE socavón *m*; ~ **level** *n* MINE socavón *m*; ~ **night mirror** *n* VEH espejo interior día-noche *m*; ~ **range** *n* AIR TRANSP radio de acción diario *m*; ~ **tank** *n* C&G crisol *m*, NUCL tanque diario *m*; ~ **to-busy-hour ratio** *n* TELECOM relación día-hora cargada *f*; ~ **traffic** *n* TELECOM tráfico diario *m*

Day-Glo: ~ **paint**® *n* COLOUR, P&R pintura Day-Glo® *f*

daylight *n* MECH ENG, P&R abertura *f*; ~ **colliery** *n* COAL, MINE mina de carbón a cielo abierto *f*; ~ **color film** *AmE*, ~ **colour film** *BrE* *n* CINEMAT, PHOTO película en color para la luz del día *f*; ~ **exposure** *n* PHOTO exposición para la luz del día *f*; ~ **film** *n* CINEMAT, PHOTO película para la luz del día *f*; ~ **lamp** *n* CINEMAT lámpara de luz del día *f*; ~ **loading** *n* CINEMAT carga a la luz del día *f*; ~ **loading tank** *n* PHOTO tanque de carga para la luz diurna *m*; ~ **magazine** *n* CINEMAT chasis para la luz del día *m*; ~ **mine** *n* MINE mina a cielo abierto *f*; ~ **photography** *n* PHOTO fotografía a la luz del día *f*; ~ **screen** *n* CINEMAT pantalla para la luz del día *f*

dayworks *n pl* CONST jornadas *f pl*

dazzle *n* SAFE deslumbramiento *m*

dB *abbr* (*decibel*) GEN dB (*decibelio*)

dBA *abbr* (*decibel A*) GEN dBA (*decibelio A*)

DBA *abbr* (*database administrator*) COMP&DP, TELECOM administrador de la base de datos *m*

dBB *abbr* (*decibel B*) GEN dBB (*decibelio B*)

dBC *abbr* (*decibel C*) GEN dBC (*decibelio C*)

dBD *abbr* (*decibel D*) GEN dBD (*decibelio D*)

DBM *abbr* (*database management*) COMP&DP, TELECOM administración de la base de datos *f*, gestión de la base de datos *f*

DBMS *abbr* (*database management system*) COMP&DP, TELECOM SABD (*sistema de administración de base de datos*)

DBS *abbr* TELECOM (*direct broadcasting by satellite*) difusión en directo por satélite *f*, radiodifusión directa vía satélite *f*, TV (*direct broadcast satellite*) satélite de difusión en directo *m*

DBST *abbr* (*double bituminous surface treatment*) CONST tratamiento superficial doble bituminoso *m*

DC[1] *abbr* COMP&DP (*device control*) control de la unidad *m*, control del dispositivo *m*, ELEC (*direct current*) CC (*corriente continua*)

DC[2]: ~ **ammeter** *n* ELEC, ELEC ENG amperímetro de CC *m*; ~ **amplifier** *n* ELECTRON amplificador de corriente continua *m*; ~ **balancer** *n* ELEC equilibrador de CC *m*; ~ **biasing** *n* TV polarización por corriente continua *f*; ~ **boost** *n* PROD refuerzo de corriente continua *m*; ~ **bridge** *n* ELEC ENG puente de CC *m*; ~ **centering** *AmE*, ~ **centring** *BrE* *n* TV centrado por corriente continua *m*; ~ **circuit** *n* ELEC ENG circuito de CC *m*; ~ **clamp diode** *n* ELECTRON diodo de enclavamiento por corriente continua *m*, diodo de fijación por corriente continua *m*, TV diodo de fijación por corriente continua *m*; ~ **component** *n* TELECOM componente CC *m*; ~ **converter** *n* ELEC convertidor de CC *m*, transformador de CC *m*; ~ **coupled amplifier** *n* ELECTRON amplificador de corriente continua acoplada *m*; ~ **generation** *n* ELEC ENG generación de CC *f*; ~ **generator** *n* ELEC, ELEC ENG, PHYS generador de CC *m*; ~ **high-tension power transmission** *n* ELEC ENG transmisión de energía de alta tensión en CC *f*; ~ **input** *n* ELEC ENG entrada de CC *f*; ~ **insertion** *n* TV inserción por corriente continua *f*; ~ **isolation** *n* ELEC, ELEC ENG aislamiento de CC *m*; ~ **Josephson effect** *n* ELEC ENG, PHYS efecto Josephson de CC *m*; ~ **level** *n* TV nivel de corriente continua *m*; ~ **machine** *n* ELEC ENG máquina de CC *f*; ~ **meter** *n* ELEC, INSTR medidor de CC *m*; ~ **motor** *n* ELEC, ELEC ENG, PHYS motor de CC *m*; ~ **network** *n* ELEC ENG red de CC *f*; ~ **output** *n* ELEC ENG salida de CC *f*; ~ **potentiometer** *n* ELEC *relay* potenciómetro de CC *m*; ~ **relay** *n* ELEC ENG relé de CC *m*; ~ **resistance** *n* ELEC ENG resistencia de CC *f*; ~ **servomotor** *n* ELEC ENG servomotor de CC *m*; ~ **signaling** *AmE*, ~ **signalling** *BrE* *n* ELECTRON señalización de CC *f*; ~ **supply** *n* ELEC fuente de alimentación de CC *f*, ELEC ENG suministro de CC *m*, fuente de alimentación de CC *f*; ~ **switching** *n* ELEC ENG conmutación de CC *f*; ~ **to-AC conversion** *n* ELEC ENG conversión de CC en CA *f*; ~ **to-AC converter** *n* ELEC ENG convertidor de CC en CA *m*; ~ **to-DC conversion** *n* ELEC ENG conversión de CC en CC *f*; ~ **to-DC converter** *n* ELEC ENG convertidor de CC en CC *m*; ~ **transducer** *n* ELEC ENG transductor de CC *m*, transformador de CC *m*; ~ **transformer**

n ELEC ENG transformador de CC *m*; ~ **voltage** *n* ELEC ENG tensión de CC *f*; ~ **voltage source** *n* ELEC ENG generador de voltaje de CC *m*; ~ **voltmeter** *n* ELEC ENG voltímetro de CC *m*

DCC *abbr* ELEC (*double cotton-covered*) con cubierta de dos capas de algodón, TELECOM (*data collection center AmE, data collection centre BrE*) centro de recogida de datos *m*, centro de recolección de datos *m*, (*data communication channel*) canal de transmisión de datos *m*

DCD *abbr* (*data carrier detector*) TELECOM detector de portadora de datos *m*

DC/DC: ~ **converter** *n* SPACE conversor CC/CC *m*

DCE¹ *abbr* (*despun control electronics*) TELECOM conjunto electrónico de rotación *m*

DCE²: ~ **source** *n* TELECOM fuente DCE *f*

D-channel *n* TELECOM canal D *m*; ~ **virtual circuit** *n* TELECOM circuito virtual canal D *m*

DCL *abbr* (*direct-coupled logic*) TELECOM lógica de acoplamiento directo *f*

DCME¹ *abbr* (*digital circuit multiplication equipment*) TELECOM DCME (*equipo de multiplicación del circuito digital*)

DCME²: ~ **frame** *n* TELECOM cuadro DCME *m*; ~ **function** *n* TELECOM función DCME *f*; ~ **gain** *n* TELECOM amplificador DCME *m*; ~ **overload** *n* TELECOM sobrecarga DCME *f*

DCMG *abbr* (*digital circuit multiplication gain*) TELECOM sistema de multiplicación del circuito digital *m*

DCMS *abbr* (*digital circuit multiplication system*) TELECOM sistema de amplificación del circuito digital *m*

DCP *abbr* (*data collection platform*) SPACE plataforma para la recolección de datos *f*

DCS *abbr* TELECOM (*defined context set*) conjunto de contextos definidos *m*, (*digital command signal*) señal de mando digital *f*, (*defence communication system BrE, defense communication system AmE*) sistema de comunicación de defensa *m*, (*data collection system*) sistema de recogida de datos *m*

DCT *abbr* (*data compression technique*) COMP&DP, ELECTRON, TELECOM técnica de compresión de datos *f*

DDC *abbr* (*direct digital control*) COMP&DP, TELECOM control digital directo *m*

DDD *abbr* (*direct distance dialling BrE, direct distance dialing AmE*) TELECOM llamada directa a distancia *f*, marcación directa a distancia *f*

DDE *abbr* (*direct data entry*) COMP&DP, ELECTRON DDE (*entrada directa de datos*)

DDES *abbr* (*digital data exchange standard*) PRINT norma para el intercambio de datos digitales *f*, norma para el intercambio de datos numéricos *f*

DDI *abbr* (*direct digital interface*) TELECOM comunicación interurbana automática en directo *f*, interfaz digital directa *m*

DDL *abbr* (*data description language*) COMP&DP lenguaje de descripción de datos *m*

DDP *abbr* (*distributed data processing*) COMP&DP informática distribuida *f*, procesamiento de datos distribuidos *m*

de Broglie: ~ **wave** *n* ELEC ENG, PHYS, RAD PHYS onda de de Broglie *f*

de luxe: ~ **edition** *n* PRINT edición de lujo *f*

DEA *abbr* (*diethanolamine*) CHEM DEA (*dietanolamina*)

deacidification *n* HYDROL desacidificación *f*

deactivate *vt* CHEM desactivar, COAL desactivar, desoxigenar, MECH ENG desactivar

deactivation *n* CHEM, COAL, MECH ENG desactivación *f*

dead¹ *adj* COAL inerte, no ventilado; ~**-burned** *adj* THERMO calcinado

dead²: ~ **ahead** *adv* WATER TRANSP a fil de roda; ~ **astern** *adv* WATER TRANSP a fil de popa; ~ **slow ahead** *adv* WATER TRANSP avante poco a poco; ~ **slow astern** *adv* WATER TRANSP atrás poco a poco

dead³: ~ **air** *n* TV aire viciado *m*; ~ **anneal** *n* THERMO recocido a fondo *m*; ~ **axle** *n* AUTO, MECH ENG eje fijo *m*, eje muerto *m*; ~ **band** *n* ELEC ENG banda inactiva *f*; ~ **bolt** *n* CONST cerrojo muerto *m*; ~ **calm** *n* HYDROL calma chicha *f*, calma profunda *f*, WATER TRANSP calma chicha *f*, calmazo *m*; ~ **center** *AmE* *see dead centre BrE*; ~**-center notch** *AmE see dead-centre notch BrE*; ~ **centre** *n* BrE MECH contrapunto *m*, punto fijo *m*, punto muerto *m*, MECH ENG contrapunto *m*, torno de puntos fijos *m*, VEH punto muerto *m*; ~**-centre notch** *n* BrE MECH ENG muesca de punto muerto *f*, ranura de punto muerto *f*; ~ **dike** *n* FUELLESS dique sin central *m*; ~ **dyeing** *n* COLOUR teñido pesado *m*; ~ **end** *n* MECH ENG espira inactiva *f*; ~ **end feeder** *n* ELEC ENG alimentador extremo *m*; ~ **end station** *n* TRANSP estación terminal *f*; ~ **end switch** *n* MINE vía muerta *f*; ~ **end tower** *n* ELEC torre extrema *f*; ~ **end trap** *n* REFRIG trampa en la aspiración *f*; ~**-ended feeder** *n* ELEC alimentador extremo *m*; ~ **freight** *n* PETR TECH falso flete *m*; ~ **front connector** *n* ELEC ENG conector frente muerto *m*, conector frente protegido *m*; ~ **furrow** *n* AGRIC surco muerto *m*; ~ **ground** *n* MINE ganga *f*, roca estéril *f*, terreno estéril *m*; ~ **halt** *n* COMP&DP parada terminal *f*, tiempo muerto *m*; ~**-length-type chuck** *n* MECH ENG portabrocas de longitud exacta *m*, portaherramientas de longitud exacta *m*; ~ **line anchor** *n* PETR TECH anclaje de línea muerta *m*; ~ **load** *n* CONST carga muerta *f*, carga permanente *f*; ~ **lock** *n* CONST cerradura muerta *f*; ~ **loss system** *n* PROD sistema de pura pérdida *m*; ~ **man's control** *n* SAFE, TRANSP control de macizo de anclaje *m*, control de seguridad *m*; ~ **oil** *n* PETR TECH petróleo muerto *m*, petróleo sin movilidad *m*; ~ **plate** *n* PROD *of grate-bars* mesa del horno *f*; ~ **pulley** *n* MECH ENG polea fija *f*; ~ **reckoning** *n* AIR TRANSP estimación *f*, OCEAN, WATER TRANSP estima *f*, navegación a ciegas *f*, navegación a la estima *f*; ~ **reckoning position** *n* AIR TRANSP, OCEAN, WATER TRANSP situación estimada *f*; ~ **room** *n* ACOUST cámara anecoica *f*, cámara sorda *f*, habitación insonorizada *f*, sala sorda *f*, PHYS cámara anecoica *f*; ~ **sand** *n* PROD arena gris *f*; ~ **sector** *n* RAIL sector muerto *m*; ~ **short circuit** *n* ELEC ENG cortocircuito perfecto *m*; ~ **smooth cut** *n* PROD *of file* picadura totalmente dulce *f*; ~ **soft anneal** *n* THERMO recocido blando a fondo *m*, recocido suave a fondo *m*; ~ **spindle** *n* MECH ENG eje muerto *m*, husillo fijo *m*, punto fijo *m*; ~ **spot** *n* CINEMAT zona muerta *f*; ~ **steam** *n* HYDRAUL, THERMO vapor de escape *m*; ~**-stick landing** *n* AIR TRANSP aterrizaje sin motor *m*; ~ **time** *n* COMP&DP, ELECTRON tiempo muerto *m*; ~ **wall** *n* CONST pared ciega *f*; ~ **water** *n* OCEAN aguaje producido por la resistencia de apéndices *m*, revesas de la estela *f pl*, agua remansada *f*, aguas muertas *f pl*; ~ **weight** *n* MECH, PETR TECH, WATER TRANSP peso muerto *m*; ~ **weight pressure gage** *AmE*, ~ **weight pressure**

gauge *BrE n* PHYS manómetro de contrapeso *m*; **~ weight scale** *n* WATER TRANSP escala de peso muerto *f*; **~ weight tonnage** *n* MECH peso muerto *m*, PETR TECH lastre *m*, peso muerto *m*, tonelaje de carga *m*, tonelaje de peso muerto *m*, WATER TRANSP peso muerto *m*; **~ weight tons** *n pl* PETR TECH toneladas de peso muerto *f pl*; **~ work** *n* MINE labores preparatorias *f pl* (*Esp*), trabajo preparatorio *m* (*AmL*); **~ workings** *n pl* MINE explotación preparatoria *f* (*AmL*), labores preparatorias *f pl* (*Esp*); **~ zone** *n* COMP&DP zona muerta *f*

deadbeat: ~ galvanometer *n* ELEC, INSTR galvanómetro aperiódico *m*

deaden *vt* MECH ENG amortiguar, apagar

deadening *n* CONST insonorización *f*

deadhead *n* MECH ENG *of a lathe* contrapunto *m*, PROD *shrinkage head* canal de colada *m*

deading *n* PROD *lagging* envuelta *f*

deadlight *n* WATER TRANSP tapa ciega *f*

deadline *n* CINEMAT plazo *m*, TV fin de plazo *m*, vencimiento *m*; **~ conformity** *n* PROD conformidad con el plazo *f*

deadlock *n* COMP&DP bloqueo *m*, punto muerto *m*

deadly: ~ embrace *n* COMP&DP bloqueo fatal *m*

deadman *n* PETR TECH anclaje *m*, macizo de anclaje *m*, WATER TRANSP *deck fittings* contrapeso de pluma de carga giratoria *m*

deadrise *n* WATER TRANSP astilla muerta *f*

deads *n pl* MINE desechos *m pl*, escombros *m pl*, estériles *m pl*

deadwood *n* WATER TRANSP durmiente *m*

deadworks *n pl* WATER TRANSP obra muerta *f*

deaerator *n* AIR TRANSP, PETR TECH desaireador *m*

deal *n* CONST *thick board, plank* tablón *m*, tablón americano y canadiense *m*

dealer: ~ room technology *n* TELECOM tecnología para salas de operaciones de bolsa *f*

dealkalization *n* C&G, CHEM desalcalinización *f*

deaminase *n* CHEM desaminasa *f*

Dean and Stark: ~ apparatus *n* LAB aparato de Dean y Stark *m*

deanamorphoser *n* CINEMAT equipo desanamorfizador *m*

deasphalted: ~ oil *n* (*DAO*) PETR TECH crudo desasfaltado *m*

debacle *n* OCEAN gran deshielo *m*

deballasting: ~ water *n* MAR POLL, POLL, WATER TRANSP deslastraje del agua de lastre *m*

debarker *n* PAPER descortezadora *f*

debarking *n* PAPER descortezado *m*; **~ drum** *n* PAPER tambor descortezador *m*

debiteuse *n* C&G debituse *m*; **~ bubble** *n* C&G burbuja de debituse *f*

debituminization *n* COAL desbituminación *f*

deblock *vt* COMP&DP desbloquear

deblocking *n* COMP&DP desbloqueado (*AmL*), desbloqueo *m*

debottlenecking *n* PETR TECH limpieza de restricciones *f*

debriefing *n* AIR TRANSP, SPACE informe de vuelo *m*

debris *n* COAL acarreos *m pl*, derribos *m pl*, desechos *m pl*, despojos *m pl*, detritos *m pl*, detritus *m*, fragmentos *m pl*, GEOL derribos *m pl*, detritos *m pl*, detritus *m*, METALL deshechos *m pl*, residuos *m pl*, POLL detritos *m pl*; **~ flow** *n* GEOL corriente de barro con cantos

gruesos *f*; **~ removal** *n* PETR TECH retirada de escombros *f*

debug *vt* COMP&DP depurar, eliminar errores

debugger *n* COMP&DP depurador *m*

debugging *n* COMP&DP depuración *f*

debunching *n* ELECTRON dispersión *f*

debur *vt* MECH, MECH ENG desbarbar

deburring *n* C&G rebabeo *m*, MECH desbarbado *m*, MECH ENG desbarbado *m*, desbastado *m*; **~ machine** *n* MECH ENG máquina de desbarbar *f*; **~ tool** *n* MECH ENG herramienta de desbarbar *f*

Debye: ~ frequency *n* PHYS frecuencia de Debye *f*; **~ model** *n* PHYS modelo de Debye *m*; **~ temperature** *n* PHYS temperatura de Debye *f*

Debye-Waller: ~ factor *n* CRYSTALL factor de Debye-Waller *m*

decade *n* AIR TRANSP, ELECTRON, NUCL década *f*; **~ attenuator** *n* ELECTRON atenuador de décadas *m*; **~ box** *n* AIR TRANSP, ELEC ENG caja de décadas *f*; **~ capacitance box** *n* AIR TRANSP, ELEC ENG caja de décadas de condensadores *f*; **~ inductance box** *n* AIR TRANSP, ELEC ENG caja de décadas de inductancias *f*; **~ oscillator** *n* ELECTRON oscilador de décadas *m*; **~ resistance box** *n* AIR TRANSP, ELEC ENG caja de décadas de resistencias *f*; **~ scaler** *n* ELECTRON contador de décadas *m*, contador electrónico de décadas *m*

decaffeinated *adj* FOOD descafeinado

decagon *n* GEOM decágono *m*

decagram *n* METR decagramo *m*

decahedral *adj* GEOM decaedral, decaédrico

decahedron *n* GEOM decaedro *m*, decahedro *m*

decahydronaphthalene *n* CHEM decahidronaftaleno *m*

decal *n* AmE (*cf transfer BrE*) C&G calcomanía *f*

decalcification *n* CHEM, HYDROL descalcificación *f*

decalcify *vt* CHEM, HYDROL descalcificar

decalin *n* CHEM decahidronaftaleno *m*, decalina® *f*

decaliter *AmE see* **decalitre** *BrE*

decalitre *n BrE* METR decalitro *m*

decameter *AmE see* **decametre** *BrE*

decametre *n BrE* METR decámetro *m*

decametric: ~ wave *n* TELECOM onda decamétrica *f*

decane *n* CHEM decano *m*

decanning *n* NUCL *arithmetic* desenvainado *m*, eliminación de la vaina *f*

decanoic: ~ acid *n* CHEM ácido decanoico *m*

decanol *n* CHEM decanol *m*

decant *vt* CHEM, CHEM TECH, FOOD, PETR TECH, POLL decantar

decantation *n* CHEM, CHEM TECH, FOOD, PETR TECH, POLL decantación *f*; **~ glass** *n* CHEM TECH vaso de decantación *m*; **~ rate** *n* CHEM TECH tasa de decantación *f*, velocidad de decantación *f*; **~ reactor** *n* CHEM TECH reactor de decantación *m*; **~ tank** *n* CHEM TECH tanque de decantación *m*; **~ vessel** *n* CHEM TECH matraz de decantación *m*

decanter *n* CHEM, CHEM TECH, FOOD, PETR TECH, POLL decantador *m*

decanting *n* CHEM, CHEM TECH, FOOD, PETR TECH, POLL decantación *f*; **~ glass** *n* CHEM, CHEM TECH, FOOD, PETR TECH, POLL vaso de decantación *m*

decarbonate *vt* COAL descarbonatar, descarbonizar, eliminar el anhídrido carbónico, GEOL descarbonatar

decarbonation *n* COAL, GEOL descarbonatación *f*

decarbonization *n* CHEM descarbonización *f*, COAL

descarbonización *f*, descarburación *f*, THERMO descarbonización *f*

decarbonize *vt* CHEM descarbonizar, COAL descarbonizar, descarburar, THERMO descarbonizar

decarbonizing *n* CHEM descarbonización *f*, COAL descarbonización *f*, descarburación *f*, THERMO descarbonización *f*

decarboxylase *n* CHEM descarboxilasa *f*

decarboxylation *n* CHEM descarboxilación *f*

decatize *vt* TEXTIL decatizar

decatizing *n* TEXTIL decatizado *m*; ~ **machine** *n* TEXTIL decatizadora *f*

decay[1] *n* ELECTRON desintegración *f*, extinción *f*, NUCL decaimiento *m*, desactivación *f*, RAD PHYS desintegración *f*, TV amortiguamiento *m*; ~ **cavity** *n* NUCL cavidad de desactivación *f*, piscina de desactivación *f*; ~ **chain** *n* PART PHYS, PHYS cadena de desintegración *f*; ~ **characteristic** *n* ELEC ENG característica de disminución de intensidad lumínica *f*; ~ **constant** *n* GEOL, NUCL, PHYS, RAD PHYS constante de desintegración *f*; ~ **curve** *n* RAD PHYS curva de desintegración *f*; ~ **date** *n* SPACE fecha de caída *f*; ~ **factor** *n* ELEC ENG factor de disminución *m*; ~ **law** *n* NUCL, PHYS, RAD PHYS ley de desintegración radiactiva *f*; ~ **modes** *n pl* RAD PHYS modos de desintegración *m pl*; ~ **particle** *n* PART PHYS partícula de desintegración *f*; ~ **product** *n* NUCL descendiente *m*; ~ **rate** *n* ACOUST velocidad de caída *f*, ELECTRON índice de desintegración *m*, RAD PHYS tasa de desintegración *f*, TV velocidad de amortiguamiento *f*; ~ **time** *n* COMP&DP tiempo de caída *m*, tiempo de decaimiento *m*, ELEC ENG *of device dial* tiempo de extinción *m*, ELECTRON tiempo de desintegración *m*, PETROL tiempo de persistencia *m*, tiempo de extinción *m*, tiempo de declinación *m*, PHYS *eliquated metals* tiempo de desintegración *m*

decay[2] *vi* ELECTRON, PHYS, RAD PHYS desintegrarse

decelerate *vt* MECH, PHYS decelerar, retardar

deceleration *n* MECH aceleración negativa *f*, desaceleración *f*, retardo *m*, MECH ENG aceleración negativa *f*, PHYS desaceleración *f*, SPACE desaceleración *f*, frenada *f*; ~ **lane** *n* TRANSP carril de desaceleración *m*; ~ **parachute** *n* TRANSP paracaídas de frenado *m*; ~ **time** *n* COMP&DP tiempo de deceleración *m*

decelerometer *n* INSTR, METR desacelerómetro *m*, medidor de frenada *m*, SPACE medidor de frenada *m*, desacelerómetro *m*

decentralized[1] *adj* COMP&DP, TELECOM descentralizado

decentralized[2]: ~ **system** *n* TELECOM sistema descentralizado *m*

deception: ~ **signal** *n* ELECTRON señal confusa *f*

dechenite *n* MINERAL dechenita *f*

dechlorination *n* HYDROL descloración *f*

decibel *n* (*dB*) GEN decibelio *m* (*dB*); ~ **A** *n* (*dBA*) GEN decibelio A *m* (*dBA*); ~ **B** *n* (*dBB*) GEN, decibelio B *m* (*dBB*); ~ **C** *n* (*dBC*) GEN, decibelio C *m* (*dBC*); ~ **D** *n* (*dBD*) GEN, decibelio D *m* (*dBD*)

deciduous: ~ **wood** *n* PAPER madera de frondosas *f*

decigram *n* (*dg*) METR decígramo *m* (*dg*)

decimal: ~ **candle** *n* METR candela decimal *f*; ~ **notation** *n* COMP&DP, MATH, TELECOM notación decimal *f*; ~ **point** *n* COMP&DP, MATH coma decimal *f*, punto decimal *m*; ~**-to-binary conversion** *n* ELECTRON conversión de sistema decimal a binario *f*; ~**-to-**

binary converter *n* ELECTRON convertidor de sistema decimal a binario *m*

decimeter *AmE see decimetre BrE*

decimetre *n* *BrE* METR decímetro *m*

decineper *n* (*dN*) ACOUST, ELECTRON, METR, TELECOM, TV decineperio *m* (*dN*)

decinormal *adj* CHEM decinormal

decipher *vt* ELECTRON, TELECOM descifrar, descodificar

deciphering *n* ELECTRON, TELECOM descodificación *f*

decision *n* AIR TRANSP, COMP&DP, MATH decisión *f*; ~ **content** *n* COMP&DP contenido de decisión *m*; ~ **height** *n* AIR TRANSP altura de decisión *f*; ~ **speed** *n* (*V1*) AIR TRANSP velocidad de decisión *f*; ~ **table** *n* COMP&DP tabla de decisión *f*; ~ **theory** *n* MATH teoría de decisiones *f*; ~ **tree** *n* COMP&DP árbol de decisión *m*

deck *n* COMP&DP *for magnetic tapes* unidad *f*, CONST plataforma *f*, *of bridge* cubierta *f*, MINE cubierta *f* (*Esp*), plataforma *f* (*Esp*), suelo *m* (*AmL*), piso *m* (*AmL*), PRINT plataforma de las rotativas *f*, WATER TRANSP cubierta *f*; ~ **beam** *n* WATER TRANSP bao de cubierta *m*; ~ **bridge** *n* CONST puente de tablero superior *m*; ~ **cargo** *n* WATER TRANSP cubertada *f*, mercancías en cubierta *f pl*; ~ **crane** *n* WATER TRANSP grúa de cubierta *f*; ~ **fittings** *n pl* WATER TRANSP equipo de cubierta *m*; ~ **gear** *n* WATER TRANSP accesorio de cubierta *m*, equipo de cubierta *m*; ~ **girder** *n* WATER TRANSP eslora *f*; ~**-hull bonding** *n* WATER TRANSP unión de la cubierta al casco *f*; ~ **light** *n* WATER TRANSP claraboya *f*, lumbrera *f*; ~ **line** *n* WATER TRANSP línea de cubierta *f*; ~ **load** *n* WATER TRANSP cargamento en cubierta *m*, cubertada *f*; ~ **longitudinal** *n* WATER TRANSP longitudinal de cubierta *m*; ~ **officer** *n* WATER TRANSP oficial de puente *m*; ~ **pillar** *n* WATER TRANSP puntal de entrepuente *m*; ~ **plan** *n* WATER TRANSP plano de la cubierta superior resistente *m*, plano de tracas de la cubierta superior resistente *m*; ~ **plate** *n* WATER TRANSP chapa de cubierta *f*, plancha para cubiertas *f*; ~ **plating** *n* WATER TRANSP tracas de cubierta *f pl*; ~ **sprinkler system** *n* WATER TRANSP instalación de rociadores de cubierta *f*; ~ **stringer** *n* WATER TRANSP trancanil *m*; ~ **structure** *n* WATER TRANSP estructura de cubierta *f*; ~ **switch** *n* ELEC, ELEC ENG interruptor de pantalla *m*; ~ **transverse** *n* WATER TRANSP bao reforzado *m*; ~ **valve** *n* HYDRAUL válvula de disco *f*, válvula distribuidora cilíndrica *f*

decked *adj* WATER TRANSP con cubierta

decker *n* PAPER espesador *m*

deckhead *n* WATER TRANSP forro de cubierta *m*, techo *m*; ~ **light** *n* WATER TRANSP claraboya *f*, lumbrera *f*

decking *n* CONST tablero *m*, WATER TRANSP revestimiento de cubierta *m*

deckle *n* PAPER barba *f*, borde irregular *m*; ~ **board** *n* PAPER regleta *f*

decladding *n* NUCL eliminación de la vaina *f*

declarative[1] *adj* COMP&DP declarativo

declarative[2]: ~ **statement** *n* COMP&DP sentencia declarativa *f*

declination *n* AIR TRANSP, PETROL, PHYS, WATER TRANSP declinación *f*; ~ **angle** *n* AIR TRANSP, PHYS ángulo de declinación *m*; ~ **axis** *n* INSTR eje de declinación *m*; ~ **bearing** *n* INSTR cojinete en declive *m*; ~ **circle** *n* INSTR, PHYS círculo de declinación *m*; ~ **gear** *n* INSTR mecanismo de declinación *m*

decline *n* HYDROL disminución *f*

declinometer *n* PHYS declinómetro *m*

declutch *vi* AUTO, MECH, MECH ENG, VEH desembragar

decoction *n* FOOD decocción *f*

decode *vt* COMP&DP decodificar, ELECTRON decodificar, descifrar, SAFE descifrar, SPACE decodificar, TELECOM, TV decodificar, descifrar; **~-encode** *vt* TV decodificar-codificar

decoder *n* COMP&DP, ELECTRON decodificador *m*, descifrador *m*, SAFE descifrador *m*, SPACE, TELECOM decodificador *m*, descifrador *m*, TV descifrador *m*

decoding *n* COMP&DP, ELECTRON, SPACE, TELECOM, TV decodificación *f*, descifrado *m*; **~ device** *n* COMP&DP, ELECTRON, SPACE, TELECOM, TV dispositivo descodificador *m*, mecanismo de desciframiento *m*; **~ matrix** *n* TV matriz descifradora *f*

decohesion *n* METALL descohesión *f*

decoiler *n* PROD desbobinador *m*

decollate *vt* COMP&DP desglosar, separar, PRINT separar

decollator *n* COMP&DP desglosador *m*, separador *m*, PRINT separador *m*

decolorizer *AmE see decolourizer BrE*

decolourizer *n BrE* C&G decolorante *m*

decommutation *n* ELECTRON desconmutación *f*

decommutator *n* ELECTRON desconmutador *m*

decompiler *n* COMP&DP decompilador *m*

decompose *vt* GEN descomponer

decomposing: **~ agent** *n* CHEM agente de descomposición *m*

decomposition *n* GEN descomposición *f*; **~ temperature** *n* PACK temperatura de descomposición *f*

decompression *n* OCEAN, PETROL descompresión *f*; **~ chamber** *n* PETR TECH, PETROL, WATER TRANSP cámara de descompresión *f*; **~ chart** *n* OCEAN plano de descompresión *m*; **~ sickness** *n* OCEAN embolia de nitrógeno *f*; **~ tables** *n pl* PETROL tablas de descompresión *f pl*; **~ time** *n* PETROL tiempo de descompresión *m*

decontaminated *adj* GEN descontaminado

decontamination *n* CHEM, CHEM TECH, NUCL, POLL, RAD PHYS descontaminación *f*; **~ factor** *n* RAD PHYS factor de descontaminación *m*; **~ system** *n* NUCL sistema de descontaminación *m*

deconvolution *n* ELECTRON, GEOL, TELECOM desconvolución *f*, eliminación de espiras *f*

deconvolved *adj* GEOL desenvolvente

decorating: **~ kiln** *n* C&G horno de decorado *m*

decoration: **~ firing** *n* C&G horneado del decorado *m*

decorative: **~ cutting** *n* C&G corte decorativo *m*; **~ varnish** *n* P&R barniz decorativo *m*

decorticator *n* FOOD descascarador *m*, descortezador *m*

decoupled *adj* COMP&DP, ELEC, TELECOM desacoplado

decoupling *n* CHEM desacoplamiento *m*, desacoplo *m*, desapareamiento *m*, ELEC *in AC circuit*, ELEC ENG desacoplamiento *m*, desacoplo *m*, SPACE desacoplamiento de señales *m*, desacoplo *m*, TELECOM desacoplamiento *m*; **~ capacitor** *n* ELEC ENG condensador de desconexión *m*; **~ filter** *n* ELECTRON filtro de desacoplamiento *m*

decoy: **~ tank** *n* MILIT tanque de señuelo *m*

decrab *vt* AIR TRANSP corregir la deriva *f*

decrease: **~ in definition** *n* PHOTO disminución de la definición *f*

decrement[1] *n* COMP&DP disminución *f*, ELECTRON atenuación *f*, disminución *f*, PHYS decremento *m*; **~ in reactivity** *n* NUCL decremento de reactividad *m*

decrement[2] *vt* COMP&DP decrementar

decrementer *n* COMP&DP decrementador *m*

decrepitation: **~ test** *n* C&G prueba de decrepitación *f*

decrypt *vt* ELECTRON descifrar

decryption *n* COMP&DP descifre *m*, descriptación *f*, TELECOM descriptación *f*

decyl *n* CHEM decilo *m*; **~ alcohol** *n* CHEM alcohol decílico *m*; **~ bromide** *n* CHEM bromuro decílico *m*

dedendum *n* MECH, MECH ENG altura del pie del diente *f*; **~ circle** *n* MECH ENG circunferencia de base *f*, circunferencia de raíz *f*, círculo del pie *m*; **~ line** *n* MECH ENG *in straightgearing* círculo del pie *m*

dedicated[1] *adj* COMP&DP, TELECOM dedicado, especializado

dedicated[2]: **~ channel** *n* TELECOM, TV canal dedicado *m*; **~ chip** *n* ELECTRON chip especializado *m*, microplaca especial *f*; **~ computer** *n* COMP&DP computador especializado *m* (*AmL*), computadora especializada *f* (*AmL*), ordenador especializado *m* (*Esp*); **~ frequency** *n* TELECOM frecuencia dedicada *f*; **~ line** *n* COMP&DP línea dedicada *f*, línea especializada *f*, TELECOM línea dedicada *f*; **~ mode** *n* COMP&DP modo dedicado *m*; **~ port** *n* TELECOM puerto dedicado *m*; **~ signaling channel** *AmE*, **~ signalling channel** *BrE n* TELECOM canal de señalización dedicado *m*

dedust *vt* COAL aspirar

deduster *n* COAL aspirador de polvo *m*

dedusting: **~ unit** *n* CONST equipo para captación de polvo *m*

dee *n* PHYS electrodo hueco semicilíndrico *m*

deed: **~ paper** *n* PAPER papel para documentos *m*

de-emphasis *n* ACOUST, ELECTRON desacentuación *f*, SPACE debilitamiento *m*, desacentuación *f*, suavizamiento de contrastes *m*

de-emulsifier *n* CHEM, FOOD desmulsificante *m*, MAR POLL desemulsionador *m*

de-emulsifying: **~ agent** *n* CHEM, FOOD, MAR POLL agente desmulsificante *m*

de-energization *n* ELEC, ELEC ENG, PHYS desexcitación *f*

de-energize[1] *vt* ELEC ENG, PROD desexcitar

de-energize[2] *vi* PHYS desenergizarse

de-energized: **~ position** *n* PROD posición de desexcitación *f*

deep[1] *adj* COLOUR, TEXTIL *shade* subido; **~-frozen** *adj* FOOD congelado rápidamente, THERMO criotratado; **~-rooted** *adj* AGRIC profundamente arraigado

deep[2]: **~ adit** *n* WATER galería inferior de desagüe *f*; **~ borehole** *n* MINE sondeo a gran profundidad *m*; **~ boring** *n* MINE sondeo a gran profundidad *m*; **~ color** *AmE see deep colour BrE*; **~ color tone** *AmE see deep colour tone BrE*; **~ colour** *BrE n* COLOUR color intenso *m*; **~ colour tone** *n BrE* COLOUR, P&R tono intenso de color *m*; **~ cut** *n* C&G corte profundo *m*; **~ depletion** *n* ELEC ENG vaciado a fondo *m*; **~ depression** *n* METEO depresión profunda *f*; **~ drawing** *n* MECH embutición profunda *f*; **~ drawing die** *n* MECH ENG estampa honda de embutir *f*, matriz honda de embutir *f*; **~ drawing film** *n* PACK película para embutir *f*; **~ drawing foil** *n* PACK hoja para embutir *f*; **~-drawing machine** *n* PACK máquina embutidora *f*; **~-drawn packaging** *n* PACK embalaje embutido *m*; ~ **drillhole** *n* MINE agujero de sondeo profundo *m*; ~ **drilling** *n* MINE sondeo profundo *m*; ~ **etching** *n* C&G grabado profundo *m*; ~~**etching bath** *n* C&G baño para grabado profundo *m*; ~ **etching paste** *n* C&G pasta para grabado profundo *f*; ~ **fading** *n* ELECTRON desvanecimiento intenso *m*; ~ **foundation** *n* COAL cimentación reforzada *f*; ~~**freeze** *n* FOOD, REFRIG congelado *m*, THERMO criotratamiento *m*; ~~**freeze packaging** *n* PACK, REFRIG embalaje para productos ultracongelados *m*; ~~**freeze ship** *n* OCEAN buque frigorífico *m*; ~~**freezing** *n* PACK ultracongelación *f*, REFRIG congelación rápida *f*, THERMO criotratamiento *m*; ~~**fryer** *n* FOOD freidora *f*; ~~**furrow drill** *n* AGRIC abresurcos *m*, sembradora en líneas *f*; ~ **geological waste disposal** *n* NUCL almacenamiento geológico de residuos a gran profundidad *m*; ~ **groove ball bearing** *n* MECH ENG cojinete de bolas de guías hondas *m*, cojinete de bolas de ranuras profundas *m*; ~ **groundwater** *n* WATER agua freática profunda *f*; ~~**hole boring** *n* MECH ENG perforado de profundidad *m*, sondeado de profundidad *m*; ~ **inelastic collision** *n* NUCL colisión inelástica profunda *f*; ~ **mine** *n* MINE explotación minera profunda *f*; ~~**mined coal** *n* COAL carbón explotado en profundidad *m*; ~ **nut** *n* CONST tuerca profunda *f*; ~ **page** *n* PRINT página vertical *f*; ~ **pattern G cramp** *n* CONST corchete grande en forma de G *m*; ~ **ploughing** *n* BrE AGRIC labranza profunda *f*; ~ **plowing** *AmE see* deep ploughing *BrE*; ~ **rejection trap** *n* ELECTRON circuito obturador de gran potencia *m*; ~ **scattering layer** *n* (*DSL*) OCEAN capa profunda de dispersión *f*; ~ **sea** *n* GEOL, OCEAN, WATER TRANSP alta mar *f*; ~~**sea cable** *n* WATER TRANSP cable submarino *m*; ~~**sea diver** *n* PETROL, WATER TRANSP buceador en aguas profundas *m*, buceadora en aguas profundas *f*; ~~**sea fan** *n* GEOL, OCEAN abanico abisal *m*, abanico oceánico *m*, abanico submarino *m*; ~~**sea fishery** *n* OCEAN pesquería de aguas profundas *f*, pesquería de altura *f*; ~~**sea fishing** *n* OCEAN pesca de aguas profundas *f*, WATER TRANSP pesca de altura *f*; ~~**sea floor** *n* GEOPHYS, OCEAN fondo profundo marino *m*; ~~**sea navigation** *n* WATER TRANSP navegación oceánica *f*; ~~**sea oasis** *n* OCEAN oasis abisal *m*; ~~**sea pilot** *n* WATER TRANSP práctico de altura *m*; ~~**sea trench** *n* GEOL, GEOPHYS, OCEAN fosa profunda del fondo marino *f*, fosa profunda del mar *f*; ~~**sea trough** *n* OCEAN cubeta abisal *f*; ~ **shade** *n* COLOUR, TEXTIL tono subido *m*; ~ **sleek** *n* C&G bruñido profundo *m*; ~ **space** *n* SPACE espacio profundo *m*; ~ **space mission** *n* SPACE misión al espacio profundo *f*, sonda para el espacio profundo *f*; ~ **space probe** *n* SPACE sonda para el espacio profundo *f*; ~~**space transponder** *n* SPACE baliza para espacio profundo *f*, respondedor para espacio profundo *m*, transpondedor para espacio profundo *m*; ~ **stabilization** *n* COAL estabilización a gran profundidad *f*; ~ **tank** *n* TRANSP tanque de lastre *m*, tanque profundo *m*, tanque vertical *m*; ~ **ultraviolet radiation** *n* ELEC ENG, RAD PHYS radiación ultravioleta profunda *f*; ~~**water diving** *n* PETR TECH, WATER TRANSP buceo en aguas profundas *m*; ~~**water dock** *n* CONST dique de aguas profundas *m*; ~~**water harbor** *AmE*, ~~**water harbour** *BrE n* WATER TRANSP puerto de gran calado *m*, puerto en aguas profundas *m*; ~~**water line** *n* WATER TRANSP flotación de máxima carga *f*; ~~**water**

wave *n* OCEAN, PHYS, WATER TRANSP ola de aguas profundas *f*; ~ **well** *n* HYDROL, WATER pozo profundo *m*; ~ **well thermometer** *n* (*DWT*) PETROL termómetro para pozos profundos *m*

deep³: ~~**freeze** *vt* FOOD, REFRIG congelar rápidamente, THERMO congelar a baja temperatura, criotratar

deepest: ~ **ballast condition** *n* WATER TRANSP condición de máximo lastre *f*; ~ **seagoing draft** *AmE*, ~ **seagoing draught** *BrE n* WATER TRANSP calado máximo en agua salada *m*

de-excitation *n* GEOPHYS desexcitación *f*

default *n* COMP&DP valor por defecto *m*, valor por omisión *m*; ~ **value** *n* COMP & DP, TELECOM valor por omisión *m*

defect *n* GEN defecto *m*; ~ **analysis** *n* RAD PHYS análisis de defectos *m*; ~ **annealing** *n* ELECTRON esmaltación defectuosa *f*; ~ **conduction** *n* ELEC ENG conducción defectuosa *f*; ~ **counting** *n* QUALITY cuenta de defectos *f*; ~ **density** *n* ELECTRON densidad defectuosa *f*; ~ **in distribution** *n* C&G defecto de distribución *m*; ~ **structure** *n* METALL estructura de defectos *f*

defective¹ *adj* GEN defectuoso

defective²: ~ **fuel rod** *n* NUCL varilla de combustible defectuosa *f*; ~ **packaging** *n* PACK embalaje defectuoso *m*; ~ **scale** *n* ACOUST escala defectuosa *f*

defence: ~ **communication system** *n* BrE TELECOM sistema de comunicación de defensa *m*; ~ **in depth criterion** *n* NUCL criterio de defensa a ultranza *m*

defense: ~ **communication system** *n* AmE see defence communication system *BrE*

deferred: ~ **addressing** *n* COMP&DP direccionamiento diferido *m*; ~ **charges** *n pl* PROD cobro directo *m*, gastos diferidos *m pl*

defiberer: ~ **pit** *AmE see* defibrer pit *BrE*

defibering *AmE see* defibring *BrE*

defibrer: ~ **pit** *n* BrE PAPER fosa de la desfibradora *f*

defibring *n* BrE PAPER desfibrado *m*

deficit: ~ **reactivity** *n* NUCL déficit de reactividad *m*

defile *n* CONST, GEOL desfiladero *m*

defined: ~ **context set** *n* (*DCS*) TELECOM conjunto de contextos definidos *m*

definite: ~ **integral** *n* MATH integral definida *f*

definition *n* CINEMAT, COMP&DP, ELECTRON, PHOTO definición *f*, nitidez *f*; ~ **chart** *n* CINEMAT carta de nitidez *f*; ~ **test pattern** *n* TV cuadro-patrón de imágenes *m*

definitive: ~ **time relay** *n* ELEC relé de retardo independiente *m*

deflagrate *vi* CHEM deflagrar, incendiar, MINE, SAFE architecture deflagrar

deflagrating: ~ **explosive** *n* MINE explosivo deflagrante *m*

deflagration *n* CHEM, MINE, SAFE deflagración *f*

deflaker *n* PAPER despatillador *m*

deflash *vt* P&R rebabarse

deflation *n* MECH ENG, VEH pérdida de presión *f*

deflect *vt* CHEM TECH, MECH ENG, RAD PHYS, TV apartar, curvar, desviar, ladear, WATER desviar

deflected: ~ **beam** *n* TV haz divergente *m*

deflecting: ~ **coil** *n* NUCL, PHYS bobina deflectora *f*; ~ **electrode** *n* NUCL electrodo deflector *m*; ~ **plate** *n* CHEM TECH placa de desviación *f*; ~ **tubing** *n* CHEM TECH tubería de desviación *f*; ~ **valve** *n* HYDRAUL válvula desviadora *f*

deflection n GEN curvatura f, deflexión f, deformación f, desviación f; ~ **amplifier** n ELECTRON amplificador de desviación m; ~ **angle** n TV ángulo de desviación m; ~ **by electric fields** n RAD PHYS deflexión por campos eléctricos f; ~ **by magnetic fields** n RAD PHYS deflexión por campos magnéticos f; ~ **coil** n ELEC ENG bobina de desviación electromagnética f; ~ **electrode** n ELEC ENG electrodo de deflexión electromagnética m; ~ **factor** n ELECTRON factor de desviación m; ~ **magnet** n TV imán de desviación m; ~ **magnetometer** n RAD PHYS magnetómetro de deflexión m; ~ **plate** n ELECTRON placa de desviación f, placa desviadora f, RAD PHYS, SPACE placa deflectora f, TV placa de desviación f, placa desviadora f; ~ **sensitivity** n ELECTRON sensibilidad de desviación f; ~ **system** n TV sistema de desviación m; ~ **tube** n RAD PHYS tubo de deflexión m; ~ **yoke** n ELECTRON bobina de desviación f; ~ **yoke pullback** n TV efecto retrógrado del yugo de deflexión m
deflector n AIR TRANSP, CHEM TECH deflector m, desviador m, FUELLESS dispositivo desviador m, PAPER, TELECOM deflector m; ~ **chute** n C&G canal deflector m; ~ **plate** n AIR TRANSP placa deflectora f, plancha deflector f, CHEM TECH placa deflectora f
deflocculant n CHEM, HYDROL, P&R desfloculante m
deflocculating: ~ **agent** n CHEM, HYDROL, P&R desfloculador m
deflocculation n CHEM, HYDROL, P&R desfloculación f
defoamer n GEN desespumante m
defoaming: ~ **agent** n CHEM agente desespumante m, agente eliminador de espuma m, antiespumante m, COAL antiespumante m, FOOD agente desespumante m, P&R, PACK, PAPER antiespumante m, PETR TECH agente desespumante m, antiespumante m
defocus[1]: ~ **effect** n CINEMAT efecto de desenfoque m; ~ **transition** n CINEMAT transición por desenfoque f
defocus[2] vt CINEMAT, ELECTRON desenfocar
defogging: ~ **fan** n AIR TRANSP fan anticondensación m
defoliant n AGRIC, CHEM defoliante m
deforestation n AGRIC deforestación f
deform vt GEN deformar
deformable: ~ **rear section** n TRANSP parte trasera deformable f
deformation n GEN alteración f, deformación f, desfiguración f; ~ **ellipsoid** n GEOL elipsoide por deformación m; ~ **modulus** n COAL módulo de deformación m; ~ **point** n C&G punto de deformación m
deformational: ~ **phase** n GEOL fase de deformación f
defrost[1]: ~ **cycle** n REFRIG ciclo de desescarche m
defrost[2] vt FOOD descongelar, REFRIG descongelar, desescarchar
defroster n AUTO, VEH calentador de parabrisas m
defrosting n FOOD descongelación f, MECH ENG descongelación f, REFRIG descongelación f, desescarche m; ~ **test** n MECH ENG of refrigerated cabinet prueba de descongelación f, prueba de deshielo f
degas[1] vt CHEM TECH, ELECTRON desgasar, desgasificar, MINE extraer gas de
degas[2] vti HYDROL desgasificar
degasification n CHEM TECH, ELECTRON, HYDROL, MINE desgasificación f
degasifying n CHEM TECH desgasificación f, destilación seca f

degasser n CHEM TECH desgasificador m, GEOL bomba de extracción de agua f, HEAT ENG desgasificador m
degassing n CHEM TECH desgasado m, destilación seca f, ELECTRON desgasificación f
degauss vt GEN degaussar, desimantar, desmagnetizar
degausser n COMP&DP, PHYS, TV desmagnetizador m, desmagnetizante m
degaussing n COMP&DP, PHYS degaussado m, desimantado m, desmagnetización f, desmagnetizado m, TV desmagnetización f, desmagnetizado m; ~ **coil** n TV bobina desmagnetizante f
degeneracy n CHEM, CRYSTALL, ELECTRON, METALL, PHYS, RAD PHYS degeneración f
degenerate[1] adj CHEM, ELECTRON, METALL, PHYS degenerado
degenerate[2]: ~ **electron gas** n ELECTRON, GAS, PHYS gas de electrones degenerados m; ~ **matter** n CHEM materia degenerada f; ~ **semiconductor** n ELECTRON semiconductor degenerado m
degradation n GEN degeneración f, degradación f
degraded: ~ **minute** n (DM) TELECOM minuto degradado m; ~ **operating conditions** n pl SPACE condiciones degradadas de funcionamiento f pl, regímenes degradados m pl; ~ **signal** n TV señal degradada f; ~ **sync** n TV sincronización degradada f; ~ **synchronization** n TV sincronización degradada f
degrease vt GEN desengrasar, desgrasar
degreaser n GEN desengrasador m, desgrasador m
degreasing n GEN desengrasado m, desengrasante m, desengrase m; ~ **agent** n GEN agente desengrasante m; ~ **compound** n GEN composición desengrasante f, compuesto desengrasante m; ~ **tank** n FOOD depósito de desengrasado m
degree n GEN, grado m; ~ **Celsius** n METR grado Celsius m; ~ **of coherence** n OPT, TELECOM grado de coherencia m; ~ **of compaction** n COAL grado de compactación m, CONST grado de consolidación m; ~ **of compliance** n TRANSP grado de conformidad m; ~ **of consolidation** n COAL grado de consolidación m; ~ **of crimp** n TEXTIL grado de rizado m; ~ **of drying** n CONST grado de secado m; ~ **of freedom** n ACOUST grado de libertad m; ~ **of heat** n THERMO grado de calor m; ~ **of incombustibility** n PAPER grado de incombustibilidad m; ~ **Kelvin** n METR grado Kelvin m; ~ **of non-flammability** n PAPER grado de ininflamabilidad m; ~ **of pollution** n MAR POLL grado de contaminación m, POLL grado de contaminación m, nivel de contaminación m; ~ **of polymerization** n P&R grado de polimerización m; ~ **of protection** n PROD grado de protección m, nivel de protección m; ~ **of purification** n HYDROL, WATER grado de depuración m; ~ **of saturation** n COAL, TRANSP grado de saturación m; ~ **of temperature** n THERMO grado de temperatura m; ~ **of utilization** n TRANSP grado de utilización m
degum vt FOOD, TEXTIL desgomar
degumming n FOOD, TEXTIL desgomado m
dehorn vti AGRIC desmochar
dehumidification n HEAT, NUCL, REFRIG, SAFE deshumidificación f
dehumidifier n HEAT, NUCL, REFRIG, SAFE deshumidificador m
dehumidify vt HEAT, NUCL, REFRIG, SAFE deshumidificar
dehydrate vti GEN deshidratar
dehydrated adj GEN deshidratado

dehydrating: ~ **agent** n GEN agente deshidratante m
dehydration n GEN deshidratación f
dehydrator n CHEM TECH, REFRIG deshidratador m
dehydrofreezing n REFRIG deshidratación-congelación f
dehydrogenase n CHEM, DETERG, FOOD deshidrogenasa f
dehydrogenate vt CHEM, FOOD deshidrogenar
dehydrogenated adj CHEM, FOOD deshidrogenado
dehydrogenation n CHEM, FOOD deshidrogenación f
dehydroluminosterol n CHEM deshidroluminosterol m
de-ice vti AIR TRANSP, AUTO, HEAT, REFRIG deshelar
de-icer n AIR TRANSP deshelador m, desincrustador de hielo m, AUTO deshelador m, HEAT descongelador m, deshelador m, REFRIG deshelador m, SPACE descongelador m, desincrustador de hielo m, VEH descongelador m; ~ **boot** n AIR TRANSP neumático antihielo m, SPACE protección antihielo f
de-icing n AIR TRANSP descongelación f, deshielo m, HEAT descongelación f, REFRIG fusión de pista de hielo f; ~ **air** n AIR TRANSP aire deshelador m; ~ **air outlet** n AIR TRANSP salida de aire deshelador f; ~ **air temperature indicator** n AIR TRANSP indicador de la temperatura del aire deshelador m; ~ **duct** n AIR TRANSP conducto deshelador m; ~ **pump** n AIR TRANSP bomba deshealdora f
de-inked: ~ **paper stock** n PAPER pasta destintada f
de-inking n PAPER destintado m
de-interleave vt ELECTRON desintercalar
de-interleaving n ELECTRON desintercalado m
de-ionized: ~ **water** n ELEC, WATER agua desionizada f
de-ionizer n LAB desionizador m
de-ionizing: ~ **grid** n ELECTRON rejilla de desionización f
de-iron vt C&G eliminar hierro
DEL abbr (delete character) COMP&DP carácter de supresión m
delaminate vt P&R exfoliar
delamination n C&G delaminación f, P&R delaminación f, exfoliación f
delay[1]: **on** ~ adv PROD con retardo, retardado
delay[2] n GEN aplazamiento m, demora f, retardo m, retraso m; **off** ~ n PROD retardo en desconexión m; ~ **cable** n TV cable de retardo m; ~ **cap** n MINE detonador de retardo m; ~ **circuit** n ELEC, ELECTRON, TELECOM, TV circuito de retardo m; ~ **component** n NUCL componente de retardo m; **off** ~ PROD retardo en desconexión m; ~ **detonator** n MINE detonador de retardo m; ~ **distortion** n TV distorsión debida al retardo f; ~ **firing** n MINE pega de varios barrenos en secuencia f; ~ **generator** n ELECTRON generador de retardo m; ~ **line** n COMP&DP, ELECTRON, PHYS, TV línea de demora f, línea de retardo f; ~**-line storage** n NUCL almacenamiento en línea de retardo m; ~**-mode relay** n TELECOM relé de retardo m; ~ **multivibrator** n ELECTRON multivibrador de retardo m; ~ **relay** n ELEC relé de retardo m, ELEC ENG relé temporizado m; ~ **switch** n ELEC conmutador de retardo m; ~ **time** n ELEC of switch, TELECOM, TV tiempo de retardo m
delay[3] vt ELEC, ELEC ENG, ELECTRON demorar, retrasar
delay[4] vi ELEC, ELECTRON retardar, tardar
delayed: ~ **action circuit-breaking** n ELEC ENG desconexión circuital de acción retardada f; ~**-action detonator** n MINE detonador de acción retardada m; ~**-action fuse** n ELEC ENG fusible de acción

diferida m; ~ **action release** n PHOTO disparador de acción retardada m; ~ **AGC** n (delayed automatic gain control) ELECTRON CGA retardada f (control de ganancia automática retardada); ~ **automatic gain control** n (delayed AGC) ELECTRON control de ganancia automática retardada m (CGA retardada); ~ **blanking signal** n TV señal de supresión retardada f; ~ **broadcast** n TV emisión en diferido f, emisión retardada f; ~ **coincidence** n RAD PHYS coincidencia retardada f; ~ **coking** n THERMO coquificación retardada f; ~ **critical reactor** n NUCL reactor crítico con neutrones retardados m; ~ **explosion** n MINE explosión retardada f; ~ **fracture** n METALL fractura retardada f; ~ **hardening** n THERMO endurecimiento retardado m; ~ **modified phase-shift keying** n (delayed MPSK) ELECTRON variación de fase por efecto de retardo f (VFE de retardo); ~ **MPSK** n (delayed modified phase-shift keying) ELECTRON VFE de retardo f (variación de fase por efecto de retardo); ~ **neutron** n PHYS, RAD PHYS neutrón retardado m; ~ **scanning** n TV exploración retardada f; ~ **sweep** n ELECTRON exploración retardada f
delaying: ~ **sweep** n ELECTRON exploración retardada f; ~ **time base** n ELECTRON base de tiempo retardada f
deleatur n PRINT borrado m
delessite n MINERAL delessita f
delete[1]: ~ **character** n (DEL) COMP&DP carácter de borrado m, carácter de supresión m
delete[2] vt COMP&DP, PRINT borrar, suprimir
deletion n COMP&DP, PRINT borrado m, supresión f, TELECOM anulación f; ~ **record** n COMP&DP registro de borrado m, registro de supresión m
Delezenne: ~ **scale** n ACOUST escala Delezenne f
Delf: ~ **flask** n HYDROL matraz de Delf m
Delft n C&G cerámica de Holanda f
delftware n C&G cerámica f
delimiter n COMP&DP delimitador m, separador m, PRINT delimitador m
deliquesce vi CHEM hacerse líquido
deliquescence n CHEM, FOOD delicuescencia f
deliquescent adj CHEM, FOOD delicuescente
delivered: ~ **site** n CONST terreno entregado al constructor para ejecutar la obra m
deliverer n PACK abastecedor m, abastecedora f, expedidor m, suministrador m
delivery n C&G entrega f, FOOD entrega f, producción f, MECH ENG abastecimiento m, capacidad f, suministro m, NUCL descarga f, PRINT entrega f, salida f, PROD entrega f, of a drawtaper abastecimiento m, desagüe m, extremo de salida m, WATER pump caudal m, rendimiento m; ~ **box** n PROD of pump caja de descarga f; ~ **channel** n WATER canal de descarga m; ~ **cone** n PROD of injector tobera divergente f; ~ **cycle** n PROD ciclo de suministro m; ~ **date** n PACK, PROD fecha de entrega f; ~ **delay** n PACK demora en la entrega f, retraso en la entrega m; ~ **head** n NUCL, WATER altura de impulsión f; ~ **hose** n WATER manguera de descarga f; ~ **into the mains** n BrE (cf delivery into the utility network AmE) ELEC, NUCL suministro a la red m; ~ **into the utility network** n AmE (cf delivery into the mains BrE) ELEC, NUCL suministro a la red m; ~ **jogger** n PRINT igualador de la pila de salida m; ~ **lead time** n PROD plazo de entrega m, tiempo de espera m; ~ **lift** n WATER altura de descarga f, altura de impulsión f; ~ **main** n WATER

ducto de descarga *m*; ~ **nozzle** *n* PROD boquilla de descarga *f*; ~ **of pattern from mold** *AmE*, ~ **of pattern from mould** *BrE n* PROD extracción del modelo *f*; ~ **pipe** *n* AUTO tubería de suministros *f*, WATER tubo de descarga *m*; ~ **pressure** *n* WATER presión de descarga *f*, presión de impulsión *f*; ~ **race** *n* WATER canal distribuidor *m*; ~ **schedule** *n* PROD plan de entregas *m*; ~ **sheet** *n* PROD hoja de entregas *f*; ~ **side** *n* NUCL lado de descarga *m*; ~ **tanker** *n* PROD, WATER TRANSP buque cisterna de entregas *m*; ~ **ticket** *n* PROD albarán *m*, hoja de entregas *f*; ~ **time** *n* PROD hora de entrega *f*; ~ **tube** *n* PROD tubo de alimentación *m*, *of injector* tobera divergente *f*; ~ **valve** *n* HYDRAUL válvula de descarga *f*, válvula de escape *f*, válvula de impulsión *f*, válvula de suministro *f*

delocalized: ~ **electron** *n* ELECTRON, PHYS electrón deslocalizado *m*

delorenzite *n* METALL, MINERAL, NUCL delorencita *f*

DELPHI: ~ **detector** *n* PART PHYS detector DELPHI *m*

delphinin *n* CHEM, MINERAL *anthocyanin* delfinidina *f*

delphinine *n* CHEM, MINERAL delfinina *f*

delphinite *n* CHEM, MINERAL delfinita *f*, epídota *f*

delta *n* ELEC ENG triángulo *m*, GEOL, HYDROL, OCEAN, PETR TECH delta *m*; ~ **bonding** *n* CHEM enlace delta *m*; ~ **connection** *n* ELEC conexión en delta *f*, conexión en triángulo *f*, ELEC ENG montaje en triángulo *m*, conexión en triángulo *f*, PHYS conexión en triángulo *f*; ~ **fitting** *n* MECH ENG ajuste en delta *m*, montaje en delta *m*; ~ **fold** *n* PRINT pliegue triangular *m*; ~ **function** *n* PETROL función delta *f*; ~**-matched aerial** *n BrE* (*cf delta-matched antenna AmE*) TV antena adaptada en delta *f*; ~**-matched antenna** *n AmE* (*cf delta-matched aerial BrE*) TV antena adaptada en delta *f*; ~ **modulation** *n* COMP&DP modulación delta *f*, ELECTRON modulación triangular *f*, SPACE, TELECOM modulación delta *f*; ~ **network** *n* ELEC ENG red en delta *f*, red en triángulo *f*; ~ **plain** *n* GEOL llanura deltaica *f*; ~ **ray** *n* NUCL, RAD PHYS rayo delta *m*; ~**-star connection** *n* ELEC conexión triángulo-estrella *f*; ~**-to-star conversion** *n* ELEC conversión triángulo-estrella *f*; ~ **wing** *n* AIR TRANSP, TRANSP ala en delta *f*

deltaic[1] *adj* GEOL, HYDROL, OCEAN, PETR TECH deltaico

deltaic[2]: ~ **platform** *n* GEOL, GEOPHYS, OCEAN plataforma deltaica *f*

deluge *n* METEO diluvio *m*

deluster *AmE see delustre BrE*

delustre *vt BrE* TEXTIL deslustrar

demagnetization *n* COAL, ELEC, MECH, MECH ENG, PHYS, TV desimanación *f*, desimantación *f*, desmagnetización *f*

demagnetize[1] *vt* COAL, ELEC, MECH, MECH ENG, PHYS, TV desimanar, desimantar, desmagnetizar

demagnetize[2] *vi* COAL, ELEC, MECH, MECH ENG, PHYS, TV desimanarse, desimantarse, desmagnetizarse

demagnetizer *n* COAL, COMP&DP desmagnetizante *m*, MECH ENG desimanador *m*, desmagnetizador *m*, desmagnetizante *m*, PHYS, TV desmagnetizante *m*

demagnetizing: ~ **equipment** *n* PROD equipo de desimanación *m*; ~ **field** *n* ELEC, PHYS campo desimanante *m*, campo desmagnetizante *m*

demand: ~ **assignment** *n* SPACE asignación de función *f*; ~ **management** *n* PROD gestión de la demanda *f*; ~ **meter** *n* ELEC ENG contador de demanda máxima *m*; ~ **on plant busses** *n* NUCL demanda en barras de

central *f*; ~ **paging** *n* COMP&DP localización inmediata de personal *f*, paginación discrecional *f*; ~**-responsive system** *n* TRANSP sistema de demanda flexible *m*, sistema sensible a la demanda *m*; ~**-scheduled bus service** *n* TRANSP servicio de autobuses con horario según demanda *m*

demantoid *n* MINERAL demantoide *f*

demethylate *vt* CHEM desmetilar

demethylation *n* CHEM desmetilación *f*

demijohn *n* C&G damajuana *f*

demineralization *n* CHEM TECH, HEAT ENG, HYDROL desmineralización *f*

demineralize *vti* CHEM TECH, HEAT ENG, HYDROL desmineralizar

demineralized: ~ **water** *n* CONST, HYDROL, WATER agua desmineralizada *f*

demineralizing: ~ **plant** *n* NUCL planta desmineralizadora *f*

demister *n* AIR TRANSP, AUTO, HYDROL, VEH aireador *m*; ~ **system** *n* VEH sistema de desempañamiento *m*

demo: ~ **reel** *n* CINEMAT carrete de demostración *m*

demodulate *vt* COMP&DP, ELECTRON, PHYS, SPACE, TELECOM, TV demodular, desmodular

demodulated *adj* COMP&DP, ELECTRON, PHYS, SPACE, TELECOM, TV demodulado

demodulation *n* COMP&DP, ELECTRON, PHYS, SPACE, TELECOM, TV demodulación *f*, desmodulación *f*

demodulator *n* COMP&DP demodulador *m*, desmodulador *m*, ELEC demodulador *m*, ELECTRON, PHYS, SPACE, TELECOM, TV demodulador *m*, desmodulador *m*

demold *AmE see demould BrE*

demolding *see demoulding BrE*

demonstrated: ~ **capacity** *n* PROD capacidad comprobada *f*

demonstration: ~ **plot** *n* AGRIC parcela demostrativa *f*

demould *n BrE* C&G, P&R desmoldeo *m*

demoulding *n BrE* C&G, P&R desmoldeado *m*, desmoldeo *m*

demulsifying: ~ **product** *n* POLL producto desemulsificante *m*, producto desemulsionante *m*

demultiplex *vt* ELECTRON, TELECOM desmultiplexar

demultiplexer *n* COMP&DP, ELECTRON, PHYS, TELECOM, TV demultiplexador *m*, demultiplexor *m*

demultiplexing *n* COMP&DP, ELECTRON demultiplexación *f*, demultiplexado *m*, desmultiplexado *m*, PHYS demultiplexación *f*, demultiplexado *m*, TELECOM demultiplexación *f*, demultiplexado *m*, TV demultiplexado *m*

demurrage *n* PETR TECH gastos de demora *m pl*, penalización por demora *f*

denatured: ~ **alcohol** *n* CHEM, COLOUR, FOOD alcohol desnaturalizado *m*

dendrite *n* CHEM, CRYSTALL, GEOL, METALL, MINERAL dendrita *f*

dendritic[1] *adj* CHEM, CRYSTALL, GEOL, METALL, MINERAL dendrítico

dendritic[2]: ~ **drainage pattern** *n* HYDROL característica de drenaje dendrítico *f*, estructura de drenaje dendrítico *f*; ~ **form** *n* CHEM, CRYSTALL, GEOL, METALL, MINERAL forma dendrítica *f*

denesting: ~ **magazine** *n* PACK almacén de desestibado *m*

denial *n* TELECOM negación *f*

denier *n* TEXTIL denier *m*

denitrification n HYDROL, POLL denitrificación f, desnitrificación f

denominator n MATH denominador m

dense: ~ **crown** n C&G corona densa f; ~ **flint** n C&G cristal de roca denso m; ~ **liquid** n COAL líquido denso m; ~ **medium** n COAL medio denso m

densimeter n FOOD, PETR TECH densímetro m

densimetric: ~ **curve** n COAL curva densimétrica f

densimetry n FOOD, PETR TECH densimetría f

densitometer n ACOUST, CINEMAT, OPT, PHOTO, PHYS densitómetro m

densitometry n ACOUST, CINEMAT, OPT, PHOTO, PHYS densitometría f

density n GEN densidad f; ~ **bottle** n LAB picnómetro m; ~ **current** n HYDROL corriente variable en función de la densidad f; ~ **curve** n PRINT curva de densidad f; ~ **filling machine** n PACK máquina rellenadora por densidad f; ~ **log** n GEOPHYS registro de la densidad m, PETR TECH perfil de densidad m, registro de la densidad m; ~ **modifier** n FOOD modificador de densidad m; ~ **modulation** n ELECTRON modulación de densidad f; ~ **of pile** n TEXTIL densidad de pelo f; ~ **range** n PRINT gama de densidad f; ~ **test** n CONST ensayo de densidad m, prueba de densidad f

dent vt MECH abollar, mellar, MECH ENG, METALL, NUCL abollar

dental: ~ **ceramic** n C&G cerámica dental f

dented: ~ **knob** n MECH ENG cabeza dentada f, manilla dentada f

denting n NUCL abolladura f

denudation n GEOL, METALL denudación f

denuded: ~ **zone** n METALL zona desnuda f

deodorizing n HYDROL desodorización f

deoxidation n MINE desoxigenación f

deoxidization n CHEM desoxidación f

deoxidizer n CHEM desoxidante m

deoxyribonucleic: ~ **acid** n (DNA) CHEM ácido desoxirribonucleico m (ADN)

depacketizer n TELECOM despaquetificador m

depalletization n PACK despaletizado

departure: ~ **curves** n pl PETROL curvas de desviación f pl; ~ **from nuclear boiling** n (DNB) NUCL apartamiento de la ebullición nucleada m; ~ **terminal** n TRANSP terminal de salidas f

dependability n MECH ENG fiabilidad f, seguridad de funcionamiento f, seguridad de servicio f, QUALITY confiabilidad f, fiabilidad f, seguridad f

dependent[1] adj PROD dependiente

dependent[2]: ~ **exchange** n TELECOM central telefónica dependiente f, central telefónica subordinada f; ~ **navigation** n SPACE navegación dependiente f; ~ **variable** n MATH variable dependiente f

dephased adj ACOUST, ELEC desfasado

dephasing: ~ **coefficient** n ACOUST coeficiente de desfasador m

dephlegmate vt CHEM, NUCL deflegmar

dephlegmator n CHEM, NUCL deflegmador m

deplete vt CHEM, ELECTRON, NUCL, WATER agotar, empobrecer

depletion n CHEM agotamiento m, enrarecimiento m, rebaja de concentración f, ELECTRON empobrecimiento m, agotamiento m, GEOL depleción f, NUCL empobrecimiento m, agotamiento m, WATER agotamiento m, recesión f; ~ **layer** n ELECTRON capa agotada f, capa de transición f, PHYS capa de transición f; ~ **layer photodiode** n ELECTRON fotodiodo de empobreci-

miento m; ~ **mode** n ELECTRON modo de mínima m; ~-**mode FET** n ELECTRON TEC mínimo m; ~ **rate** n PETR TECH, PETROL rata de agotamiento f (AmL), ritmo de agotamiento m, tasa de agotamiento f (Esp); ~ **of subsoil resources** n AGRIC agotamiento de los recursos del subsuelo m

deployable: ~ **aerial** n BrE (cf deployable antenna AmE) SPACE antena desplegable f; ~ **antenna** n AmE (cf deployable aerial BrE) SPACE antena desplegable f

depocenter AmE see depocentre BrE

depocentre n BrE GEOL depocentro m (AmL), depósito central m (Esp)

depoisoning n NUCL desenvenenamiento m

depolarization n CHEM, ELEC ENG, PHYS despolarización f, SPACE communications depolarización f

depolarize vt CHEM, ELEC ENG, PHYS despolarizar

depolarizer n CHEM, ELEC ENG, PHYS despolarizador m

depolarizing: ~ **agent** n ELEC, PHYS agente despolarizador m, agente despolarizante m; ~ **field** n ELEC, PHYS campo despolarizante m

depolluted adj POLL descontaminado, da

depolluting: ~ **ship** n MAR POLL, POLL barco descontaminador m, buque descontaminador m

depolymerization n CHEM, P&R despolimerización f

deposit n CHEM depósito m, COAL metal depositado m, incrustación f, depósito m, sedimento m, precipitado electrolítico m, CONST yacimiento m, depósito m, GEOL sedimento m, depósito m, PACK, WATER depósito m; ~ **bottle** n PACK botella de depósito f; ~ **copy** n pl PRINT copia para el depósito legal del libro f; ~ **of ore** n MINE depósito de mineral m

deposited: ~ **layer** n ELECTRON estratificador depositado m; ~ **matter** n POLL material depositado m, material sedimentado m

deposition n ELECTRON deposición f, METALL deposición f, electrodeposición f, POLL deposición f, depósito m, electrodeposición f, precipitación f, sedimentación f; ~ **rate** n POLL velocidad de deposición f, velocidad de sedimentación f; ~ **speed** n POLL velocidad de deposición f, velocidad de sedimentación f; ~ **value** n POLL valor de depósito m; ~ **velocity** n POLL velocidad de deposición f, velocidad de sedimentación f

depositional: ~ **fabric** n PETR TECH textura deposicional f; ~ **fault** n GEOL falla deposicional f; ~ **sequence** n GEOL secuencia de depósito f

depot n MINE depósito almacén m, estación de distribución f, RAIL almacén de estación m, estación de ferrocarril principal f, almacén m, depósito m

depreciation n PROD depreciación f

depress vt COAL rebajar

depressed: ~ **cladding** n OPT chapado sin recubrimiento, TELECOM chapado deprimido m; ~ **deck car** n AmE (cf depressed deck wagon BrE) RAIL vagón batea de plataforma rebajada m; ~ **deck wagon** BrE n (cf depressed deck car AmE) RAIL vagón batea de plataforma rebajada m; ~ **thread** n C&G rosca hundida f

depression n MECH ENG depresión f, reducción f, METEO depresión f, zona de baja presión f; ~ **bar** n C&G barra depresora f; ~ **cone** n WATER cono de depresión m; ~ **spring** n WATER manantial de depresión m, manantial descendente m

depressurization n AIR TRANSP, NUCL, OCEAN, PROD, SPACE, WATER TRANSP descompresión f, despresurización f; ~ **accident** n NUCL, SAFE accidente de despresurización *m*; ~ **valve** *n* MECH ENG válvula de despresurización *f*

depressurize *vt* AIR TRANSP, NUCL, OCEAN, PROD, SPACE descomprimir, despresionizar, despresurizar,

depressurized: ~ **condition** *n* PROD estado despresionizado *m*

depth *n* MINE, OCEAN, PHYS, WATER profundidad *f*, WATER TRANSP puntal *m*; ~ **below pitch line** *n* MECH ENG *gearing* profundidad bajo la circunferencia primitiva *f*, profundidad bajo la curva primitiva *f*; ~ **charge** *n* MILIT carga antisubmarinos *f*, carga de profundidad *f*; ~ **controller** *n* PETR TECH controlador de profundidad *m*; ~ **curve** *n* OCEAN curva de profundidad *f*; ~ **of cut** *n* MECH, MECH ENG, PROD profundidad de corte *f*; ~ **dose** *n* RAD PHYS dosis en profundidad *f*; ~ **of field** *n* CINEMAT, METALL, OPT, PHOTO, TV profundidad de campo *f*; ~ **of field scale** *n* CINEMAT, PHOTO escala de profundidad de campo *f*; ~ **finder** *n* WATER TRANSP ecosondador *m*; ~ **of focus** *n* CINEMAT profundidad de campo *f*, GEOPHYS, PHOTO, PHYS profundidad de foco *f*, TV profundidad de enfoque *f*; ~ **of focus scale** *n* CINEMAT, PHOTO escala de profundidad de foco *f*; ~ **for freeboard** *n* WATER TRANSP puntal de francobordo *m*; ~ **of frictional influence** *n* OCEAN friccional *f*, profundidad de la influencia *f*; ~ **gage** *AmE*, ~ **gauge** *BrE* *n* MECH calibre de profundidad *m*, hidrobarómetro *m*, manómetro de profundidad *m*, METR manómetro de profundidad *m*, regulador de profundidad *m*, testigo de profundidad *m*, limnímetro *m*, calibre de profundidad *m*, galga para medir profundidades *f*, hidrobarómetro *m*, OCEAN escala hidrométrica *f*, limnímetro *m*, PROD testigo de profundidad *m*; ~ **of immersion** *n* TRANSP profundidad de inmersión *f*; ~ **of investigation** *n* GEOPHYS, PETROL profundidad de investigación *f*; ~ **meter** *n* OCEAN medidor de profundidad *m*, sonda de profundidad *f*; ~ **of penetration** *n* NUCL profundidad de penetración *f*; ~ **point** *n* PETROL punto de profundidad *m*; ~ **recorder** *n* OCEAN registrador de profundidad *m*; ~ **rudder** *n* OCEAN timón de profundidad *m*; ~ **of shade** *n* TEXTIL profundidad de matiz *f*; ~ **sounder** *n* OCEAN sonda ecoica *f*, WATER TRANSP ecosondador *m*; ~ **of sowing** *n* AGRIC profundidad de siembra *f*; ~ **of thread** *n* CONST profundidad de la rosca *f*; ~**-to-draft ratio** *AmE*, ~**-to-draught ratio** *BrE* *n* WATER TRANSP relación puntal-calado *f*; ~ **of water** *n* FUELLESS, HYDROL, WATER TRANSP profundidad de agua *f*

depulping: ~ **screen** *n* COAL filtro de depulpación *m*

depurator *n* CHEM TECH depurador *m*

depuration *n* CHEM despurinación *f*

deputy *n* MINE maderista *m*, representante local del propietario de una mina *m*, supervisor *m*

derail *vt* RAIL descarrilar

derailing: ~ **points** *n pl* *BrE* (*cf derailing switch AmE*) RAIL aguja de descarrilamiento *f*, aguja descarriladora *f*; ~ **switch** *n* *AmE* (*cf derailing points BrE*) RAIL aguja de descarrilamiento *f*, aguja descarriladora *f*

derailment *n* RAIL descarrilamiento *m*

derating *n* ELEC ENG disminución de potencia por causas ajenas al mecanismo *f*

derivative *n* CHEM, ELECTRON, MATH derivado *m*; ~ **control** *n* ELEC regulación derivada *f*

derive *vt* GEN derivar

derived: ~ **air concentration** *n* (*DAC*) NUCL concen-

tración derivada en aire *f* (*CDA*); ~ **circuit** *n* ELEC circuito bifurcado *m*, ELEC ENG circuito derivado *m*; ~ **current** *n* ELEC *branch* corriente bifurcada *f*; ~ **energy** *n* PETR TECH energía derivada *f*; ~ **fossil** *n* GEOL fósil derivado *m*; ~ **fuel** *n* PETR TECH combustible derivado *m*, fuel derivado *m*; ~ **gust velocity** *n* AIR TRANSP velocidad de ráfaga derivada *f*; ~ **product** *n* CHEM producto derivado *m*; ~ **unit** *n* MECH ENG, PHYS unidad derivada *f*

dernbachite *n* MINERAL dernbachita *f*

deroofing *n* GEOL descubrimiento *m*, desmantelamiento *m*

derrick *n* AIR TRANSP grúa de brazo móvil *f*, CONST grúa *f*, pluma *f*, FUELLESS, MECH grúa *f*, PETR TECH torre de sondeo *f*, torre de perforación *f*, cabria *f*, PETROL castillete *m*, torre *f*, WATER TRANSP abanico *m*, pluma de carga *f*; ~ **boom** *n* WATER TRANSP pluma *f*; ~ **cellar** *n* PETR TECH, PETROL antepozo *m*; ~ **crane** *n* CONST grúa fija *f*; ~ **crown** *n* PETR TECH cornisa de la cabria *f* (*AmL*), corona de la torre *f* (*AmL*), cúpula de la torre *f* (*Esp*); ~ **floor** *n* PETR TECH piso de trabajo *m*, piso del equipo *m*, piso del taladro *m*, planchada *f*, planchada de perforación *f*, suelo de la torre *m*; ~ **girt** *n* CONST pluma de grúa *f*; ~ **man** *n* PETR TECH encuellador *m*, torrero *m*; ~ **monkey board** *n* PETR TECH encuelladero *m*, plataforma del encuellador *f*; ~ **post** *n* CONST poste de grúa *m*

derricking: ~ **crane** *n* CONST manejo de grúa *m*

derusting *n* MECH ENG desoxidación *f*, extracción de la herrumbre *f*, extracción del óxido *f*

desalinate *vt* CHEM TECH, HYDROL desalar, desalinizar, PETR TECH desalinizar, WATER, WATER TRANSP desalar, desalinizar

desalination *n* CHEM TECH, HYDROL, OCEAN, WATER desalación *f*, desalinización *f*; ~ **plant** *n* CHEM TECH, CONST, HYDRAUL, WATER instalación de desalinización de agua de mar *f*, planta desalinizadora *f*; ~ **reactor** *n* NUCL reactor de desalación *m*

desalt *vt* CHEM TECH, PETR TECH desalar, desalinizar

desalting *n* CHEM TECH, PETR TECH desalación *f*, desalinización *f*

desander *n* PETR TECH, PETROL desarenador *m*

desaturate *vt* TV desaturar

desaturated: ~ **color** *AmE*, ~ **colour** *BrE* *n* COLOUR color desvanecido *m*, TV color desaturado *m*

desaturation *n* OCEAN desaturación *f*

descale *vt* DETERG desescamar, desincrustar, MECH decapar, descascarillar, desescamar, remover la capa de óxido de, PROD desincrustar

descaling *n* DETERG desescamado *m*, desincrustación *f*, MECH desescamado *m*, PROD desincrustación *f*

descendant *n* COMP&DP descendiente *m*

descender *n* PRINT trazo descendente *m*

descending: ~ **node** *n* SPACE nodo descendente *m*

descent *n* SPACE descenso *m*; ~ **engine** *n* SPACE motor de descenso *m*; ~ **orbit** *n* SPACE trayectoria de descenso *f*, órbita de descenso *f*; ~ **path** *n* SPACE trayectoria descendente *f*; ~ **stage** *n* SPACE etapa de descenso *f*

descloizite *n* MINERAL descloizita *f*

descramble *vt* SAFE desencriptar, descifrar, SPACE descifrar, TELECOM desencriptar

descrambler *n* SAFE desencriptador *m*, descifrador *m*, SPACE descifrador *m*, TELECOM descifrador *m*, desencriptador *m*, TV descifrador *m*

descrambling *n* SAFE desencriptado *m*, SPACE descifrado *m*, TELECOM descifrado *m*, desencriptado *m*, TV descifrado *m*

descriptor *n* COMP&DP descriptor *m*

deseasonalize *vt* PROD usar fuera de temporada

desensitization *n* MINE insensibilización *f*, PHOTO, TELECOM desensibilización *f*

desensitize *vt* MINE insensibilizar, PHOTO, TELECOM desensibilizar

desensitizer *n* MINE insensibilizador *m*, PHOTO, TELE-COM desensibilizador *m*

desensitizing: ~ **bath** *n* CINEMAT, PHOTO baño desensibilizador *m*

desert: ~ **pediment** *n* GEOL pedimiento desértico *m*

deshrinking: ~ **process** *n* CINEMAT proceso de desencogimiento *m*

desiccant[1] *adj* CHEM, HEAT, PACK, REFRIG, THERMO desecante

desiccant[2] *n* CHEM, CHEM TECH desecante *m*, FOOD secante *f*, PACK desecante *m*, REFRIG deshidratante *m*, THERMO desecante *m*; ~ **bag** *n* PACK bolsa que contiene un desecante *f*

desiccate *vt* CHEM, CHEM TECH desecar, FOOD desecar, secar, HEAT, PACK, PETR TECH, REFRIG, THERMO desecar

desiccated *adj* GEN desecado

desiccation *n* GEN desecación *f*; ~ **crack** *n* GEOL grieta de desecación *f*; ~ **ratio** *n* REFRIG relación de desecación *f*

desiccative: ~ **agent** *n* CHEM, CHEM TECH agente desecante *m*

desiccator *n* CHEM, CHEM TECH, FOOD, HEAT, LAB desecador *m*; ~ **screen** *n* CHEM TECH pantalla desecadora *f*

design[1] *n* COMP&DP, CONST proyecto *m*, PRINT boceto *m*, WATER TRANSP plan *m*, plano *m*, proyecto *m*; ~ **aid** *n* COMP&DP asistencia al diseño *f*, auxilio de diseño *m*, auxilio de proyecto *m*; ~ **airspeed** *n* AIR TRANSP velocidad relativa de diseño *f*; ~ **automation** *n* COMP&DP automatización del diseño *f*, automatización del proyecto *f*, informatización del diseño *f*; ~ **base earthquake** *n* NUCL seísmo de base de diseño *m*; ~ **basis case** *n* SPACE marco de diseño básico *m*; ~ **basis event** *n* NUCL incidente de base de diseño *m*; ~ **to buckling strength** *n* SPACE diseño para esfuerzo de pandeo *m*; ~ **burn-up** *n* NUCL grado de quemado de diseño *m*; ~ **criterion** *n* NUCL criterio de diseño *m*, PROD criterio de proyección *m*; ~ **cruising speed** *n* AIR TRANSP velocidad de crucero de diseño *f*; ~ **department** *n* PROD departamento de diseño *m*, WATER TRANSP departamento de proyectos *m*, oficina de proyectos *f*; ~ **diving speed** *n* AIR TRANSP velocidad de picado de diseño *f*; ~ **draftsman** *AmE*, ~ **draughtsman** *BrE n* MECH dibujante-proyectista *m*, MECH ENG delineante proyectista *m*, dibujante-proyectista *m*; ~ **flaps-extended speed** *n* AIR TRANSP velocidad de diseño con flaps extendidos *f*; ~ **flight weight** *n* AIR TRANSP peso de vuelo de diseño *m*; ~ **flood** *n* HYDROL flujo previsto *m*; ~ **flow** *n* HYDROL flujo previsto *m*; ~ **irradiation level** *n* NUCL nivel de irradiación de diseño *m*; ~ **landing speed** *n* AIR TRANSP velocidad de aterrizaje de diseño *f*; ~ **landing weight** *n* AIR TRANSP peso de aterrizaje de diseño *m*; ~ **language** *n* COMP&DP lenguaje del diseño *m*, lenguaje del proyecto *m*; ~ **load** *n* AIR TRANSP carga de diseño *f*; ~ **maneuvering speed** *AmE*, ~ **manoeuvring speed** *BrE n* AIR TRANSP

velocidad de maniobra de diseño *f*; ~ **office** *n* CONST oficina de diseño *f*, oficina de proyectos *f*; ~ **outside temperature** *n* HEAT temperatura exterior de diseño *f*, temperatura exterior proyectada *f*; ~ **pressure** *n* REFRIG presión de cálcula *f*, presión máxima de servicio *f*; ~**-related defect** *n* NUCL defecto de diseño *m*; ~ **rough air speed** *n* AIR TRANSP velocidad de diseño de turbulencia de aire *f*; ~ **rules for drive power** *n pl* MECH ENG normas de construcción para unidad motriz *f pl*, reglas de construcción para potencia de conducción *f pl*, reglas de diseño para potencia motriz *f pl*; ~ **specification and requirements** *n pl* PROD, QUALITY especificaciones y requisitos del diseño *f pl*; ~ **speed** *n* TRANSP velocidad de régimen *f*; ~ **speed for maximum gust intensity** *n* AIR TRANSP velocidad de diseño para ráfagas de máxima intensidad *f*; ~ **storm** *n* HYDROL precipitación prevista *f*; ~ **takeoff mass** *n* AIR TRANSP masa de despegue de diseño *f*; ~ **taxi weight** *n* AIR TRANSP peso de rodaje de diseño *m*; ~ **to ultimate strength** *n* SPACE diseño para esfuerzos máximos *m*, diseño para obtener resistencia máxima *m*; ~ **to yield point** *n* SPACE diseño a punto de rotura *m*, diseño para punto de deformación *m*; ~ **volume** *n* TRANSP volumen de diseño *m*; ~ **waterline** *n* WATER TRANSP flotación de proyecto *f*; ~ **waterplane** *n* WATER TRANSP plano de flotación de proyecto *m*; ~ **weight** *n* AIR TRANSP peso de diseño *m*; ~ **wheel load** *n* AIR TRANSP carga de diseño por rueda *f*; ~ **wing area** *n* AIR TRANSP área del ala de diseño *f*

design[2] *vt* CONST proyectar, MECH calcular, proyectar, trazar

designate *vt* TELECOM designar

designated: ~ **frequency** *n* TELECOM frecuencia designada *f*

designed: ~ **power required output** *n* NUCL potencia de salida de diseño *f*

designer *n* PROD *person* proyectista *m*; ~ **draftsman** *AmE*, ~ **draughtsman** *BrE n* MECH dibujante-proyectista *m*; ~ **handbook** *n* TELECOM manual del diseñador *m*

desilter *n* PETR TECH desiltor *m* (*AmL*), separador de granos finos *m* (*Esp*), separador de limolita *m* (*Esp*)

desilting: ~ **basin** *n* HYDROL estanque de desenlodamiento *m*

disintegrate *vt* CHEM desintegrar

desire: ~ **line** *n* TRANS línea adecuada *f*, línea conveniente *f*

desired: ~ **value** *n* NUCL valor deseado *m*

desize *vt* TEXTIL desencolar

desizing *n* TEXTIL desencolado *m*

desktop: ~ **computer** *n* COMP&DP computador de sobremesa *m* (*AmL*), computadora de sobremesa *f* (*AmL*), ordenador de sobremesa *m* (*Esp*), microcomputadora *f* (*AmL*), microordenador *m* (*Esp*), microcomputadora de mesa *f* (*AmL*), microordenador de mesa *m* (*Esp*); ~ **publishing** *n* (*DTP*) COMP&DP autoedición *f*, autoedición de textos *f*, programa de edición publicitario *m*, publicación de mesa *f* (*AmL*), tratamiento de textos con opciones gráficas *m*, PRINT autoedición *f*

deslag *vt* COAL desescoriar, sangrar la escoria

deslime *vt* COAL desenlodar, eliminar lodos, quitar los fangos, METALL, MINE desenlodar

desliming *n* COAL desenlodadura *f*; ~ **screen** *n* COAL filtro desenlodador *m*, criba para eliminar lodos *f*, desenlodador *m*

deslurry *vt* COAL extraer finos por métodos húmedos

deslurrying *n* COAL extracción de finos por métodos húmedos *f*

desmine *n* MINERAL desmina *f*

desmotropy *n* CHEM desmotropía *f*

desorb *vt* CHEM, COAL desorber

desorption *n* CHEM, COAL desorción *f*

despiking: ~ **circuit** *n* ELEC ENG circuito despuntador *m*

despun[1] *adj* SPACE estabilizado

despun[2]: ~ **control electronics** *n* (*DCE*) TELECOM conjunto electrónico de rotación *m*

destack *vt* PACK, PROD desapilar

destination: ~ **bin** *n* PROD tolva de destino *f*; ~ **network** *n* (*DN*) TELECOM red de destino *f*

destroyer *n* MILIT, WATER TRANSP destructor *m*

destruction *n* RAD PHYS destrucción *f*

destructive: ~ **breakdown** *n* ELEC ENG descarga destructiva *f*, ELECTRON interrupción destructiva *f*; ~ **element** *n* SAFE elemento destructivo *m*; ~ **interference** *n* ELEC ENG, PHYS, WAVE PHYS interferencia destructiva *f*; ~ **plate margin** *n* GEOL margen de placa destructivo *m*; ~ **read** *n* COMP&DP lectura destructiva *f*; ~ **test** *n* MECH ENG prueba destructiva *f*

destructor *n* THERMO destructor *m*, horno para incineración de basuras *m*

destuffing *n* TRANSP vaciado *m*

desulfonation *AmE see* desulphonation *BrE*

desulfurization *AmE see* desulphurization *BrE*

desulfurize *AmE see* desulphurize *BrE*

desulfurizing: ~ **furnace** *AmE see* desulphurizing furnace *BrE*

desulphonation *n* *BrE* CHEM desulfonación *f*

desulphurization *n* *BrE* CHEM desulfuración *f*, desulfuramiento *m*, COAL, PETR TECH, POLL, PROD desulfuración *f*, desulfuramiento *m*, desulfurización *f*

desulphurize *vt* *BrE* CHEM, COAL, PETR TECH, POLL, PROD desulfurar

desulphurizing: ~ **furnace** *n* *BrE* PROD horno para piritas *m*

desuperheat *vt* HEAT ENG desobrecalentar

desuperheater *n* HEAT ENG desobrecalentador *m*

detachable[1] *adj* MECH ENG desconectable, desmontable, móvil, postizo, separable, PHOTO desmontable

detachable[2]: ~ **handle** *n* MECH ENG manecilla desmontable *f*; ~ **jaws** *n pl* MECH ENG *of vice* mordazas desmontables *f pl*, mordazas postizas *f pl*; ~ **keyboard** *n* COMP&DP teclado desconectable *m*, teclado desplazable *m*, PROD teclado desmontable *m*, teclado desplazable *m*; ~ **nose cone** *n* AIR TRANSP cono de morro desmontable *m*; ~ **pod** *n* AIR TRANSP *helicopter* contenedor de equipo desmontable *m*; ~ **pressure plate** *n* PHOTO placa de presión desmontable *f*; ~ **union** *n* MECH ENG *pipe fitting* junta desmontable *f*

detaching: ~ **hook** *n* MINE gancho de desprendimiento *m*

detachment *n* MECH ENG desprendimiento *m*, separación *f*; ~ **device** *n* MECH ENG aparato de desprendimiento *m*, aparato de separación *m*

detail: ~ **gage** *AmE*, ~ **gauge** *BrE* *n* MECH ENG calibrador de pieza *m*, indicador de pieza *m*, medidor de pieza *m*, verificador de pieza *m*; ~ **log** *n* PETROL

perfil de detalle *m*; ~ **rendition** *n* TV plano de detalles *m*

detailed: ~ **survey** *n* CONST investigación detallada *f*, levantamiento de detalle *m*

detassel *vt* AGRIC despanojar

detasseling *AmE see* detasselling *BrE*; ~ **machine** *AmE see* detasselling machine *BrE*

detasselling *n* *BrE* AGRIC despanojado *m*, remoción de la inflorescencia masculina del maíz *f*; ~ **machine** *n* *BrE* AGRIC máquina despanojadora *f*, máquina que corta inflorescencias masculinas *f*

detection *n* ACOUST, ELECTRON, RAD PHYS, SPACE detección *f*; ~ **loop** *n* TRANSP circuito de detección *m*; ~ **system inside the vehicle** *n* TRANSP sistema de detección en el interior del vehículo *m*; ~ **system outside the vehicle** *n* TRANSP sistema de detección en el exterior del vehículo *m*; ~ **threshold** *n* OPT, TELECOM umbral de detección *m*

detectivity *n* OPT, TELECOM detectividad *f*

detector *n* GEN detector *m*; ~ **circuit** *n* ELECTRON circuito detector *m*; ~ **diode** *n* ELECTRON diodo detector *m*; ~ **signal** *n* ELECTRON señal detectora *f*; ~ **tubes for short-term sampling** *n pl* SAFE *vibration test* tubos detectores para muestreo a corto plazo *m pl*

detent *n* MECH ENG bloqueador *m*, fiador *m*, retén *m*, seguro *m*

detention: ~ **basin** *n* WATER depósito de retención *m*, embalse de detención *m*; ~ **reservoir** *n* HYDROL, WATER depósito de retención *m*, embalse de retención *m*

detergency *n* CHEM, DETERG detergencia *f*

detergent *n* CHEM, DETERG, PETR TECH, TEXTIL detergente *m*; ~ **additive** *n* CHEM, DETERG aditivo detergente *m*; ~ **effect** *n* DETERG efecto detergente *m*; ~ **oil** *n* DETERG, VEH aceite detergente *m*; ~ **paste** *n* DETERG pasta detergente *f*; ~ **power** *n* DETERG poder detergente *m*

deterioration *n* GAS desgaste *m*, deterioro *m*, P&R deterioro *m*

determinant *n* COMP&DP, MATH determinante *m*

detonable *adj* MINE detonable

detonatable *adj* THERMO detonable

detonate *vt* MILIT, MINE, THERMO detonar

detonating: ~ **card** *n* MILIT, SPACE plaqueta iniciadora *f*, tarjeta explosiva *f*; ~ **cord** *n* MINE cordón detonante *m*, cuerda detonante *f*, mecha detonante *f*; ~ **explosive** *n* MINE explosivo detonante *m*; ~ **fuse** *n* MINE cuerda detonante *f*, mecha detonante *f*; ~ **point** *n* MINE temperatura de detonación *f*; ~ **relay** *n* MINE relé detonante *m*

detonation *n* MINE, THERMO detonación *f*; ~ **pressure** *n* MINE presión de detonación *f*; ~ **temperature** *n* MINE temperatura de detonación *f*; ~ **wave** *n* MINE onda de detonación *f*, onda explosiva *f*

detonator *n* MILIT cápsula fulminante *f*, detonador *m*, MINE detonador *m*, RAIL petardo *m*, señal detonante *f*, SPACE detonador *m*, THERMO fulminante *m*, detonador *m*; ~ **cap** *n* MINE cápsula detonadora *f*

detrain *vi* RAIL desembarcar

detrital[1] *adj* PETROL detrítico

detrital[2]: ~ **sediment** *n* OCEAN sedimento detrítico *m*

detune *vt* ELECTRON, TELECOM, TV desintonizar

detuning *n* ELECTRON, TELECOM, TV desintonización *f*

deuteric: ~ **alteration** *n* GEOL alteración deutérica *f*

deuteride *n* CHEM hidruro pesado *m*

deuterium *n* (*D*) CHEM, NUCL, PHYS deuterio *m* (*D*);
~ **oxide** *n* (*D₂O*) CHEM, NUCL, PHYS óxido de deuterio
m (*D₂O*)
deuteron *n* CHEM, PART PHYS, PHYS deuterón *m*
deuteroproteose *n* CHEM deuteroproteosa *f*
deuton *n* CHEM, PART PHYS, PHYS deutón *m*
Deutsche: ~ **Industrienorm** *n* (*DIN*) MECH ENG,
PHOTO, PRINT, PROD, QUALITY Deutsche Industrienorm *m* (*DIN*)
develop *vt* CINEMAT revelar, CONST, GEOM desarrollar,
MECH ENG desarrollar, producir, progresar, MINE
reconocer, explotar, extraer, examinar, sacar, trazar,
PHOTO revelar
developed: ~ **image** *n* CINEMAT, PHOTO imagen revelada *f*; ~ **luminosity** *n* RAD PHYS luminosidad
desarrollada *f*
developer *n* CINEMAT, PHOTO revelador *m*; ~ **for soft
contrast** *n* CINEMAT, PHOTO revelador para contraste
tenue *m*; ~ **formula** *n* CINEMAT, PHOTO fórmula de
revelado *f*; ~ **streaks** *n pl* CINEMAT, PHOTO rayas del
revelador *f pl*
developing: ~ **bath** *n* CINEMAT, PHOTO baño revelador
m; ~ **clip** *n* PHOTO pinza para colgar el material
revelado *f*; ~ **drum** *n* CINEMAT tambor de revelado *m*;
~ **reel** *n* PHOTO bobina de revelado *f* (*AmL*), guía de
revelado *f* (*Esp*); ~ **spiral** *BrE n* (*cf developing spool
AmE*) PHOTO bobina de revelado *f* (*AmL*), carrete de
revelado *m* (*AmL*), espiral de relevado *f* (*Esp*), guía
de revelado *f*; ~ **spool** *n AmE* (*cf developing spiral
BrE*) PHOTO bobina de revelado *f* (*AmL*), carrete de
revelado *m*; ~ **tank** *n* CINEMAT, PHOTO tanque de
revelado *m*; ~ **tank thermometer** *n* CINEMAT, PHOTO
termómetro para el tanque de revelado *m*; ~ **time** *n*
CINEMAT tiempo de revelado *m*; ~ **tongs** *n pl*
CINEMAT, PHOTO pinzas para revelado *f pl*
development *n* CONST desarrollo *m*, MECH ENG
ampliación *f*, desarrollo *m*, producción *f*, MINE
reconocimiento *m*, trazado *m*, PETR TECH desarrollo
m, THERMO desarrollo *m*, evolución *f*; ~ **by rock
chutes** *n* MINE reconocimiento por chimeneas de
relleno *m*; ~ **fog** *n* CINEMAT velo por revelado *m*;
~ **heading** *n* MINE galería de trazado *f*; ~ **phase** *n*
PETR TECH fase de desarrollo *f*; ~ **project** *n* PETR TECH
proyecto de desarrollo *m*, proyecto de producción *m*;
~ **and subsequent manufacture** *n* MECH ENG desarrollo y producción subsiguiente *m*, proyecto y
fabricación subsiguiente *m*; ~ **tank** *n* PHOTO tanque
de revelado *m*; ~ **test** *n* SPACE ensayo de desarrollo *m*,
prueba de desarrollo *f*; ~ **time** *n* CINEMAT tiempo de
revelado *m*; ~ **well** *n* PETR TECH pozo de desarrollo *m*;
~ **work** *n* MINE trabajos de trazado y de acceso *m pl*
deviated: ~ **drilling** *n* PETR TECH perforación desviada
f; ~ **well** *n* PETR TECH pozo desviado *m*
deviation *n* GEN desvío *m*; ~ **detector** *n* AIR TRANSP
detector de desviación *m*; ~ **from criticality** *n* NUCL
desviación de condiciones de criticidad *f*; ~ **indicator**
n AIR TRANSP indicador de desviación *m*;
~ **measurement** *n* TELECOM medida de la desviación
f; ~ **mirror** *n* INSTR espejo de desviación *m*; ~ **prism** *n*
INSTR, TELECOM prisma de desviación *m*; ~ **ratio** *n*
ELECTRON porcentaje de desviación *m*; ~ **signal** *n* AIR
TRANSP señal de desviación *f*; ~ **well** *n* PETR TECH
pozo desviado *m*
device *n* COMP&DP dispositivo *m*, unidad *f*, ELEC,
ELECTRON, LAB aparato *m*, MAR POLL dispositivo *m*,
MECH aparato *m*, MECH ENG aparato *m*, artefacto *m*,

dispositivo *m*, mecanismo *m*, PHOTO aparato *m*, PROD
mecanismo *m*, TELECOM dispositivo *m*, WATER
TRANSP aparato *m*; ~ **control** *n* (*DC*) COMP&DP
control de la unidad *m*, control del dispositivo *m*;
~ **controller** *n* TELECOM controlador de dispositivo
m; ~ **driver** *n* COMP&DP controlador de dispositivo *m*,
impulsor de dispositivo *m*; ~ **queue** *n* COMP&DP cola
de dispositivo *f*, fila de espera del dispositivo *f*;
~ **reserve** *n* COMP&DP reserva de dispositivo *f*
devil *n* PROD caldera de asfalto *f*
devitrification *n* C&G, GEOL desvitrificación *f*, devitrificación *f*; ~ **stone** *n* C&G piedra de devitrificación *f*
devitrify[1] *vt* C&G, GEOL desvitrificar
devitrify[2] *vi* C&G, GEOL desvitrificar
Devonian *adj* GEOL Devónico
dew *n* METEO rocío *m*, REFRIG condensación *f*, rocío *m*;
~ **cap** *n* INSTR detonador a distancia *m*; ~ **indicator** *n*
TV indicador del punto de rocío *m*; ~ **point** *n* AIR
TRANSP punto de rocío *m*, FOOD punto de goteo *m*,
HEAT ENG punto de condensación *m*, punto de rocío
m, *wire* punto de saturación *m*, METEO, NUCL punto
de rocío *m*, PETROL punto de condensación *m*, punto
de niebla *m*, punto de rocío *m*, PHYS, REFRIG,
THERMO punto de rocío *m*; ~ **point depression** *n*
REFRIG separación del punto de rocío *f*; ~~**point
hygrometer** *n* REFRIG higrómetro de punto de rocío
m; ~ **point measurement** *n* C&G medición del punto
de rocío *f*; ~ **point temperature** *n* NUCL temperatura
de punto de rocío *f*, THERMO temperatura de punto
de rocío *f*, temperatura de saturación *f*; ~ **retting** *n*
TEXTIL enriado por rociado *m*
Dewar: ~ **flask** *n* CHEM TECH, LAB, PHYS frasco Dewar
m, matraz Dewar *m*, termo *m*, vaso Dewar *m*
dewater *vt* HYDRAUL achicar, descebar, desecar, deshidratar, MINE *mine* achicar, agotar, desaguar, TEXTIL
extraer el agua de
dewatered: ~ **waste** *n* NUCL residuos deshidratados *m*
pl
dewaterer *n* MINE desaguador *m*, deshidratador *m*,
tanque decantador *m*
dewatering *n* CHEM deshidratación *f*, CONST desagüe
m, deshidratación *f*, secado *m*, MINE agotamiento *m*,
desagüe *m*, PETR TECH, PETROL deshidratación *f*,
TEXTIL extracción del agua *f*; ~ **point** *n* TEXTIL punto
de extracción del agua *m*; ~ **press** *n* PAPER prensa
desgotadora *f*; ~ **pump** *n* MINE, WATER bomba de
achique *f*; ~ **roll** *n* PAPER rodillo desgotadora *m*;
~ **under load** *n* TEXTIL extracción del agua bajo carga
f
deweylite *n* MINERAL deweylita *f*
dextral[1] *adj* GEOL dextral
dextral[2]: ~ **fault** *n* GEOL falla en dirección dextral *f*
dextran *n* CHEM dextrano *m*
dextrin *n* CHEM, FOOD, P&R dextrina *f*, goma de
almidón *f*
dextrorotatory *adj* CHEM, FOOD, PHYS dextrógiro
dextrose *n* AGRIC, CHEM, FOOD dextrosa *f*
Deybe-Hückel: ~ **theory** *n* CHEM teoría de Deybe-
Hückel *f*
DF[1] *abbr* (*direction finding*) AIR TRANSP, TELECOM
goniometría *f*
DF[2]: ~ **receiver** *n* WATER TRANSP receptor del goniómetro *m*
DFA *abbr* (*diphenylamine*) CHEM DFA (*difenilamina*)
dg *abbr* (*decigram*) METR dg (*decígramo*)

DHA *abbr (dihydroxyacetone)* CHEM DHA *(dihidroxia-cetona)*
D-handle *n* CONST *of a shovel* mango *m*
diabase *n* AmE *(cf dolerite BrE)* GEOL, PETROL diabasa *f*
diacetic: ~ **acid** *n* CHEM ácido diacético *m*
diacetyl *n* CHEM diacetilo *m*
diacetylacetone *n* CHEM diacetilacetona *f*
diacetylene *n* CHEM diacetileno *m*
diacetylmorphine *n* CHEM diacetilmorfina *f*
diachronous *adj* GEOL diácrono
diacid *n* CHEM diácido *m*
diaclasite *n* MINERAL bastita *f*, diaklasita *f*
diacritical *adj* COMP&DP diacrítico
diadochite *n* MINERAL diadoquita *f*
diadochy *n* GEOL diadoquia *f*
diaeresis *n* BrE PRINT diéresis *f*
diagenesis *n* FUELLESS transformación sedimentaria *f*, GEOL, PETR TECH, PETROL diagénesis *f*
diagenetic *adj* GEOL, PETR TECH, PETROL diagenético
diagnostic[1] *adj* COMP&DP diagnóstico
diagnostic[2]: ~ **aid** *n* TELECOM ayuda al diagnóstico *f*; ~ **error message** *n* COMP&DP mensaje de error de diagnóstico *m*; ~ **program** *n* COMP&DP programa de diagnóstico *m*; ~ **report** *n* COMP&DP informe de diagnóstico *m*; ~ **test** *n* COMP&DP prueba de diagnóstico *f*
diagonal[1] *adj* GEOM diagonal
diagonal[2] *n* NUCL diagonal *f (AmL)*, jabalcón *m (Esp)*; ~ **brace** *n* WATER *of lock-gate* riostra *f*; ~ **cutters** *n pl* MECH ENG cortadores diagonales *m pl*, fresas diagonales *f pl*; ~ **cutting nippers** *n pl* MECH ENG, PROD alicates de corte diagonal *m pl*; ~ **joiner** *n* CINEMAT empalme diagonal *m*; ~ **lines** *n pl* WATER TRANSP líneas diagonales *f pl*; ~ **ply tire** *AmE*, ~ **ply tyre** *BrE* *n* P&R cubierta con pliegues diagonales *f*, neumático con pliegues diagonales *m*; ~ **ram longwall face** *n* MINE frente de tajo largo diagonal *m*; ~ **register** *n* PRINT registro diagonal *m*; ~ **scale** *n* MECH ENG escala de proporciones *f*; ~ **splice** *n* CINEMAT empalme diagonal *m*; ~ **stay** *n* HYDRAUL soporte en diagonal *m*; ~ **strength** *n* CONST resistencia diagonal *f*; ~ **weir** *n* HYDROL, WATER aliviadero inclinado *m*
diagram *n* COMP&DP, ELEC, ELECTRON, MATH, PHYS diagrama *m*, PROD diagrama *m*, *for calculation of spiral springs* esquema *m*, gráfico *m*, TELECOM, TV diagrama *m*; ~ **of Corliss valve gear** *n* PROD diagrama de válvulas de Corliss; ~ **of output** *n* PROD gráfico de producción *m*
dial[1] *n* ELEC *of instrument* cuadrante *m*, esfera *f*, MECH ENG *face-plate of instrument or clock* cara del reloj *f*, círculo indicador *m*, esfera del reloj *f*, MINE brújula de trípode *f*, TELECOM disco *m*, VEH esfera *f*, *on instrument panel* indicador en el cuadro de instrumentos *m*; ~**-a-bus** *n* TRANSP autobús con tacógrafo *m (Esp)*, bus con tacógrafo *m (AmL)*, ómnibus *m (AmL)*; ~ **gage** *AmE*, ~ **gauge** *BrE* *n* MECH ENG comparador de cuadrante *m*, galga de cuadrante *f*, METEO sensor analógico *m*; ~**-indicating calipers** *AmE*, ~**-indicating callipers** *BrE n pl* METR compás de calibres indicador de cuadrante *m*; ~**-indicating gage** *AmE*, ~**-indicating gauge** *BrE n* METR galga indicadora de cuadrante *f*; ~**-indicating micrometer** *n* METR micrómetro indicador de cuadrante *m*; ~ **plate** *n* MECH ENG *faceplate* cuadrante graduado *m*; ~ **sight** *n* MILIT alza circular *f*, alza panorámica *f*,

goniómetro *m*; ~ **telephone** *n* TELECOM teléfono de disco *m*; ~ **thermometer** *n* REFRIG termómetro de cuadrante *m*; ~**-tone delay** *n* TELECOM retardo en la señal de línea *m*; ~**-type metallic pressure gage** *AmE*, ~**-type metallic pressure gauge** *BrE n* MECH ENG manómetro de presión metálico tipo cuadrante *m*, manómetro metálico de esfera *m*, manómetro metálico de presión tipo cuadrante *m*; ~**-up port** *n* TELECOM puesto de marcación *m*
dial[2] *vt* TELECOM marcar
dialing *AmE see dialling BrE*
dialkene *n* CHEM, MINERAL, PETR TECH dialqueno *m*
diallage *n* MINERAL diálaga *f*
dialling *n* BrE MINE levantamiento con la brújula *m*, TELECOM marcación *f*; ~ **code** *n* TELECOM código de marcación *m*; ~ **error** *n* TELECOM error de marcación *m*; ~ **period** *n* TELECOM período de marcación *m*
dialog *AmE see dialogue BrE*
dialogite *n* MINERAL dialogita *f*, espato manganoso *m*
dialogue *n* BrE COMP&DP diálogo *m*; ~ **replacement** *n* CINEMAT cambio de diálogo *m*, sustitución de diálogo *f*; ~ **track** *n* CINEMAT banda de diálogos *f*, TV banda de diálogos *f*, pista de sonido *f*
dialuric: ~ **acid** *n* CHEM ácido dialúrico *m*
dialysate *n* CHEM dialisado *m*
dialytic *adj* CHEM dialítico
diamagnetic[1] *adj* CHEM, ELEC, PETROL, PHYS, RAD PHYS diamagnético
diamagnetic[2]: ~ **anisotropy** *n* PHYS, RAD PHYS anisotropía diamagnética *f*; ~ **material** *n* ELEC, PHYS material diamagnético *m*; ~ **shielding** *n* PHYS, RAD PHYS *of the nucleus* apantallamiento diamagnético *m*; ~ **susceptibility** *n* PHYS, RAD PHYS susceptibilidad diamagnética *f*
diamagnetics *n* PHYS, RAD PHYS diamagnética *f*
diamagnetism *n* CHEM, ELEC, ELEC ENG, PETROL, PHYS, RAD PHYS diamagnetismo *m*
diameter *n* GEOM diámetro *m*; ~ **across flats** *n* MECH ENG diámetro através de planos *m*; ~ **equalization** *n* ACOUST diámetro de ecualización *m*
diametral: ~ **groove pitch** *n* ACOUST paso diametral del surco *m*
diametric *adj* ELEC, GEOM diametral, diamétrico
diametrical[1] *adj* ELEC, GEOM diametral, diamétrico
diametrical[2]: ~ **winding** *n* ELEC, ELEC ENG bobinado diametral *m*
diametrically: ~ **opposed** *adv* GEOM diametralmente opuesto
diamide *n* CHEM diamida *f*
diamine *n* CHEM diamina *f*
diaminodiphenylmethane *n* CHEM, P&R diaminodifenilmetano *m*
diamond[1]: ~**-bearing** *adj* MINE diamantífero
diamond[2] *n* GEN diamante *m*; ~ **bit** *n* PETR TECH barrena de diamantes *f*, broca de diamante *f*, corona de diamante *f*; ~ **boring crown** *n* PROD corona de puntas de diamante *f*; ~ **cleaving** *n* PROD rajadura del diamante *f*; ~ **cold chisel** *n* MECH ENG cincel con punta rómbica *m*, cortafríos con punta rómbica *m*; ~ **core drill** *n* PETR TECH barrena sacatestigos de diamantes *f*, corona de diamante *f (Esp)*, cortanúcleos de diamante *m (AmL)*, cortatestigos de diamante *m (Esp)*, sondadora a base de diamantes *m*, PROD taladrador con núcleo de diamante *m*; ~ **crossing** *n* RAIL cruzamiento oblicuo *m*; ~ **crown set** *n* MINE trépano de corona adiamantada *m*; ~ **cut**

n MINE talla del diamante *f*; ~ **cut pattern** *n* C&G corte en diamante *m*; ~ **cutter** *n* PROD *person* tallador de diamante *m*; ~ **cutting** *n* PROD talla del diamante *f*; ~ **drill** *n* GAS barrena con punta de diamante *f*, perforadora a diamante *f*, PROD sonda de barrera de diamantes *f*, trépano adiamantado *m*; ~ **drilling** *n* MINE perforación al diamante *f*, sondeo con corona de diamantes *m*, sondeo con trépano de diamantes *m*, PETR TECH perforación con barrena de diamantes *f*, perforación con broca de diamantes *f*, sondeo con corona de diamantes *m*; ~ **dust** *n* MINE brujido *m*, polvo de diamante *m*; ~ **field** *n* MINE campo diamantífero *m*; ~ **glass cutting** *n* C&G corte de vidrios con diamante *m*; ~ **grinding-wheel** *n* MECH ENG muela adiamantada *f*; ~ **ink** *n* COLOUR tinta de diamante *f*; ~ **lattice** *n* METALL malla adiamantada *f*, red adiamantada *f*; ~ **matrix** *n* MINE roca madre del diamante *f*; ~ **mine** *n* MINE mina de diamantes *f*; ~ **mining** *n* MINE extracción del diamante *f*; ~ **nose chisel** *n* MECH ENG cincel con punta rómbica *m*, cortafríos con punta rómbica *m*; ~ **paper** *n* PRINT papel de tamaño 8,8 x 13,3 cm *m*; ~ **paste** *n* METALL pasta adiamantada *f*; ~ **pencil** *n* C&G, CONST lápiz de diamante *m*; ~ **point** *n* CONST, MECH ENG *lathe* punta de diamante *f*, punta rómbica *f*; ~ **point chisel** *n* MECH ENG cincel de punta de diamante *m*; ~ **point cold chisel** *n* MECH ENG cincel de punta de diamante *m*, cortafríos de punta de diamante *m*; ~**-point engraving** *n* C&G grabado con punta de diamante *m*; ~ **powder** *n* MINE brujido *m*, polvo de diamante *m*; ~ **riffle** *n* WATER *sluices* rejilla de diamante *f*; ~ **saw** *n* MECH ENG sierra de diamante *f*, sierra de dientes adiamantados *f*; ~**-slitting wheel** *n* C&G rueda de corte de diamante *f*; ~**-tipped pen** *n* LAB marcador de punta de diamante *m* (*Esp*), pluma de punta de diamante *f* (*AmL*); ~ **tool** *n* CONST, MECH, MECH ENG herramienta con punta adiamantada *f*, herramienta con punta de diamante *f*; ~ **winding** *n* ELEC devanado en rombo *m*, ELEC ENG devanado uniforme *m*; ~ **wire lattice** *n* CONST enrejado con cable con forma de diamante *m*

diamondiferous *adj* MINE diamantífero
diaphasic *adj* TRANSP difásico
diaphone *n* WATER TRANSP diáfono *m*
diaphorite *n* MINERAL diaforita *f*
diaphragm *n* ACOUST, CINEMAT, MECH, MECH ENG, PHOTO diafragma *m*; ~ **cellular cofferdam** *n* HYDROL compartimiento estanco celular de diafragma *m*; ~ **clutch** *n* AUTO embrague de diafragma *m*; ~ **compressor** *n* MECH ENG compresor de diafragma *m*; ~ **fuel pump** *n* AUTO, VEH bomba de combustible de diafragma *f*; ~ **jig** *n* MINE caja diafragma *f*; ~ **meter** *n* GAS medidor de diafragma *m*; ~ **presetting** *n* CINEMAT preajuste del diafragma *m*; ~ **pressure vessel** *n* MECH ENG contenedor de presión de diafragma *m*; ~ **pump** *n* MAR POLL, WATER bomba de diafragma *f*, bomba de membrana *f*; ~**-type washbox** *n* COAL cuba de lavado de diafragma *f*; ~ **valve** *n* MECH ENG válvula de diafragma *f*, válvula de membrana *f*

diapir *n* GEOL, PETR TECH diapiro *m*
diapositive *n* PHOTO diapositiva *f*
diaryls *n pl* CHEM diarilos *m pl*
diaschistic *adj* GEOL, PETR TECH, PETROL diaesquístico
diaspore *n* MINERAL diáporo *m*
diastase *n* CHEM, FOOD diastasa *f*

diastem *n* GEOL, PETROL diastema *m*
diastereo: ~ **isomer** *n* CHEM diastereoisómero *m*
diastereomer *n* CHEM diastereómero *m*
diathermal *adj* PHYS, THERMO diatérmico
diathermanous *adj* THERMO diatérmano
diathermic *adj* THERMO diatérmico
diatom *n* GEOL, PETROL diatomea *f*
diatomaceous: ~ **brick** *n* HEAT ENG ladrillo de diatomeas *m*; ~ **earth** *n* FOOD kieselguhr *m*, GEOL tierra de diatomeas *f*, HYDROL harina fósil *f*, REFRIG tierra de diatomeas *f*
diatomic[1] *adj* CHEM, GAS, PHYS, PHYS RAD diatómico
diatomic[2]: ~ **gas** *n* GAS, PHYS gas diatómico *m*; ~ **molecule** *n* CHEM, PHYS, RAD PHYS molécula diatómica *f*
diatomite *n* GEOL, HEAT ENG diatomita *f*, MINERAL diatomita *f*, trípoli *m*, PETROL diatomita *f*
diatonic[1] *adj* ACOUST diatónica
diatonic[2]: ~ **semitone** *n* ACOUST semitono diatónico *m*; ~ **tetrachord** *n* ACOUST tetracordo *m*
diatreme *n* GEOL diatrema *f*
diazo *n* CHEM, PRINT diazo *m*
diazoacetic *adj* CHEM diazoacético
diazobenzene *n* CHEM diazobenceno *m*
diazoimide *n* CHEM diazoimida *f*
diazole *n* CHEM diazol *m*
diazomine *n* CHEM diazomina *f*
diazonium *n* CHEM diazonio *m*
diazotize *vt* CHEM diazotar, diazotizar
dibasic *adj* CHEM dibásico
dibenzanthracene *n* CHEM dibenzoantraceno *m*
dibenzopyrrole *n* CHEM dibenzopirrol *m*
dibenzoyl *adj* CHEM dibenzoil
dibenzylamine *n* CHEM dibencilamina *f*
dibromobenzene *n* CHEM dibromobenceno *m*
dibromohydrin *n* CHEM dibromohidrina *f*
dibromosuccinic: ~ **acid** *n* CHEM ácido dibromosuccínico *m*
dibutyl: ~ **phthalate** *n* P&R ftalato de dibutilo *m*
dibutyrin *n* CHEM dibutirina *f*
dice *vt* FOOD cortar en cubitos, cortar en dados pequeños
dichloracetic: ~ **acid** *n* CHEM ácido dicloroacético *m*
dichloride *n* CHEM dicloruro *m*
dichloroacetone *n* CHEM dicloroacetona *f*
dichlorobenzene *n* CHEM diclorobenceno *m*
dichlorodifluoromethane *n* CHEM, REFRIG diclorodifluorometano *m*
dichloroethane *n* CHEM dicloroetano *m*
dichlorohydrin *n* CHEM diclorohidrina *f*
dichotomizing: ~ **search** *n* COMP&DP búsqueda dicotómica *f*
dichroic[1] *adj* CINEMAT, ELECTRON, OPT, PHOTO, PHYS, TELECOM dicroico
dichroic[2]: ~ **filter** *n* CINEMAT, ELECTRON, OPT, TELECOM filtro dicroico *m*; ~ **fog** *n* CINEMAT, PHOTO velo dicroico *m*; ~ **LCD** *n* ELECTRON VCL dicroico *m*; ~ **liquid crystals** *n pl* ELECTRON cristales líquidos dicroicos *m pl*; ~ **liquid visual display** *n* ELECTRON panel de visualización de cristal líquido dicroico *m*; ~ **mirror** *n* CINEMAT, OPT, TELECOM espejo dicroico *m*
dichroism *n* CHEM, CRYSTALL, PHYS dicroísmo *m*
dichromate *n* CHEM dicromato *m*
dichrote *n* MINERAL cordierita *f*, dicroíta *f*, iolita *f*
dickinsonite *n* MINERAL dickinsonita *f*
dicotyledon *n* AGRIC dicotiledón *m*

DID *abbr* (*direct inward dialing AmE, direct inward dialling BrE*) TELECOM marcación directa entrante *f*

Didyme: ~ **comma** *n* ACOUST coma Didyme *f*

didymium *n* CHEM didimio *m*

die[1]: **~-cast** *adj* MECH *founding* fundido a presión, fundido a troquel, troquelado

die[2] *n* C&G dado *m*, CINEMAT troquel *m*, MECH *of clay* forjado *m*, matriz *f*, caja de terraja *f*, cojinete de roscar *m*, cojinete de terraja *m*, estampa *f*, troquel *m*, matriz de trefilar *f*, MECH ENG boquilla *f*, *in conjunction with punches* punzón de mano *m*, estampa *f*, *for threading* terraja de roscar *f*, *press tools* troquel *m*, cojinete de roscar *m*, hilera de trefilar *f*, molde *m*, terraja *f*, *for wire, bar, tube drawing* hilera de estirar *f*, *engine link-block* corredera del sector Stephenson *f*, matriz de trefilar *f*, *forming* forjado *m*, *for cold heading* matrices *f pl*, MINE troquel *m* (*Esp*), triturador de mineral *m* (*AmL*), bocarte *m* (*AmL*), PRINT troquel *m*, PROD *for wiredrawing* hilera de estirar *f*, *for power-hammer* agarradero *m*, *of amalgamating pan* matriz *f*, *for anvil of power-hammer* troquel *m*, dado *m*, forjado *m*; ~ **bar** *n* MECH ENG barra de trefilar *f*; **~-cast** *n* PROD fundido a presión *m*, fundido en coquilla *m*; **~-cast body** *n* PROD cuerpo fundido a presión *m*; ~ **casting** *n* PROD fundido de matrices *m*; **~-casting die** *n* MECH ENG estampa *f*, matriz *f*, molde *m*, troquel *m*; **~-casting machine** *n* MECH ENG máquina estampadora *f*, máquina moldeadora *f*, máquina troqueladora *f*; ~ **chuck** *n* PROD *in lathe* plato de roscar *m*, plato portacojinete *m*; ~ **cut** *n* PRINT troquelado *m*; ~ **cutting** *n* PRINT troquelado *m*; ~ **for metallic powders** *n* MECH ENG estampa para polvos metálicos *f*, matriz para polvos metálicos *f*; ~ **for motor body panels** *n pl* MECH ENG *press tools* estampa para paneles de automóviles *f*, estampa para paneles de coches *f*, matriz para paneles de automóviles *f*, matriz para paneles de coches *f*; ~ **for pressing** *n* MECH ENG estampa para embutir *f*, estampa para estampar *f*, matriz para estampar *f*, matriz para estampar *f*; ~ **for punching** *n* MECH ENG matriz para perforar *f*, matriz para punzonar *f*, troquel para perforar *m*; ~ **for stamping** *n* MECH ENG matriz para estampar *f*; ~ **forging** *n* MECH ENG, PROD forja con estampa *f*, forja en matriz *f*, forja en troquel *f*; ~ **guide** *n* PROD *screw stock* guiacojinetes de roscar *m*; ~ **head** *n* PROD *screw cutting* hilera *f*; ~ **holder** *n* MECH ENG *in a press*, PROD *for punching machine* portaestampa *m*, portamatriz *m*, portatroquel *m*; ~ **in one piece** *n* PROD *screw-stock* estampado en una sola pieza *m*; ~ **in two halves** *n* PROD *screw-stock* estampado en dos piezas *m*; ~ **nut** *n* PROD tuerca para repasar roscas *f*; ~ **plate** *n* PROD *screw cutting* estampa *f*, *wiredrawing* hilera *f*; ~ **set** *n* MECH ENG *fine blanking* juego de matriz y troquel *m*, *for stamping, punching* juego de moldes *m*, juego de punzones *m*, juego de estampas *m*, portaestampa *m*, portamatriz *m*, juego de troqueles *m*; ~ **sinking** *n* MECH ENG grabado de matrices en hueco *m*; **~-sinking machine** *n* MECH ENG fresadora de estampas *f*, máquina de grabar matrices en hueco *f*; **~-stamper** *n* MECH *founding* pieza estampada en frío *f*, troquel estampador *m*; **~-stamping** *n* PRINT estampado en relieve *m*; **~-stamping press** *n* PAPER prensa troqueladora por estampación *f*; ~ **stock** *n* PROD portadados *m*; **~-threading machine** *n* MECH ENG roscadora de terrajas *f*

die[3]: **~-cast** *vt* MECH ENG colar en matriz, fundir a presión, presofundir, troquelar; **~-cut** *vt* PRINT troquelar; ~ **out** *vt* GEOL terminar, PRINT matrizar

dieback *n* AGRIC acronecrosis *f*

diehead *n* PROD *for screwing bolts or tubes* portaluneta *m*

dieldrin *n* CHEM, FOOD dieldrina *f*

dielectric[1] *adj* CHEM, ELEC,ENG ELEC, PHYS, TELECOM dieléctrico

dielectric[2]: ~ **absorption** *n* ELEC, ELEC ENG absorción dieléctrica *f*; ~ **aerial** *n* BrE (*cf dielectric antenna AmE*) SPACE, TELECOM antena dieléctrica *f*; ~ **antenna** *n* AmE (*cf dielectric aerial BrE*) SPACE, TELECOM antena dieléctrica *f*; ~ **breakdown** *n* ELEC perforación dieléctrica *f*, ruptura del dieléctrico *f*, ruptura dieléctrica *f*; ~ **charge** *n* TELECOM carga dieléctrica *f*; ~ **condenser** *n* ELEC condensador dieléctrico *m*; ~ **constant** *n* ELEC ENG constante dieléctrica *f*, permitividad específica *f*, P&R capacidad inductiva específica *f*, constante dieléctrica *f*, PHYS constante dieléctrica *f*; ~ **current** *n* ELEC ENG corriente de fuga *f*; ~ **heater** *n* MECH ENG calentador dieléctrico *m*; ~ **heating** *n* ELEC, ELEC ENG caldeo dieléctrico *m*, calentamiento dieléctrico *m*, HEAT calefacción dieléctrica *f*, P&R calentamiento con microondas *m*, calentamiento dieléctrico *m*; ~ **hysteresis** *n* ELEC, ELEC ENG histéresis dieléctrica *f*; ~ **insulation** *n* ELEC, ELEC ENG aislación dieléctrica *f*; ~ **loss** *n* ELEC, ELEC ENG, PHYS pérdida dieléctrica *f*, pérdida en el dieléctrico *f*; ~ **loss angle** *n* ELEC ángulo de pérdida del dieléctrico *m*; ~ **material** *n* ELEC ENG, PHYS material dieléctrico *m*; ~ **medium** *n* ELEC ENG, PHYS medio dieléctrico *m*; ~ **polarization** *n* ELEC ENG, PHYS polarización dieléctrica *f*; ~ **property** *n* ELEC, PHYS propriedad dieléctrica *f*; ~ **resistance** *n* ELEC resistencia dieléctrica *f*; ~ **resonator** *n* SPACE, TELECOM resonador dieléctrico *m*; ~ **resonator filter** *n* ELECTRON, SPACE filtro resonador dieléctico *m*; ~ **rigidity test** *n* ELEC ENG prueba de rigidez dieléctrica *f*; ~ **strength** *n* ELEC rigidez dieléctrica *f*, ELEC ENG, PHYS resistencia dieléctrica *f*; ~ **susceptibility** *n* ELEC susceptibilidad dieléctrica *f*; ~ **swelling** *n* NUCL hinchamiento dieléctrico *m*; ~ **thawing** *n* REFRIG descongelación dieléctrica *f*

Diels-Alder: ~ **reaction** *n* CHEM reacción de Diels-Alder *f*

diene *n* CHEM dieno *m*

dieresis *n* PRINT diéresis *f*

diergol: ~ **head** *n* PROD *for screwing bolts or tube* portaluneta *m*; ~ **technology** *n* SPACE tecnología diergólica *f*

diesel: ~ **compression tester** *n* AUTO comprobador de compresión de diesel *m*; **~-driven generating set** *n* ELEC ENG grupo electrógeno accionado por motor diesel *m*; **~-electric drive** *n* TRANSP propulsión diesel-eléctrica *f*, tracción diesel-eléctrica *f*; **~-electric engine** *n* RAIL locomotora diesel-eléctrica *f*; **~-electric power station** *n* ELEC ENG central de energía diesel-eléctrica *f*; **~-electric railcar** *n* RAIL automotor diesel-eléctrico *m*; **~-electric shunting motor tractor** *n* RAIL locomotora diesel-eléctrica de maniobras *f*; ~ **engine** *n* AUTO, PROD, VEH, WATER TRANSP motor diesel *m*; ~ **fuel** *n* AUTO, PETR TECH combustible diesel *m*, gas-oil *m*, gasóleo *m*, THERMO gas-oil *m*, VEH combustible diesel *m*, gas-oil *m*, gasóleo *m*; ~ **gas** *n* GAS gas diesel *m*; ~ **generator**

standby power plant n NUCL generador diesel de reserva m; ~ **generator unit service wagon** n RAIL vagón de servicio con generador diesel m; ~ **hammer** n COAL martillo diesel m; ~~**hydraulic engine** n MECH ENG motor diesel-hidráulico m; ~~**hydraulic locomotive** n RAIL locomotora diesel con transmisión hidráulica f; ~ **oil** n TRANSP gas-oil m, gasóleo m; ~~**powered compressor** n MECH ENG compresor a diesel m

dieseling n AUTO autoencendido m

dietary: ~ **fiber** AmE, ~ **fibre** BrE n FOOD fibra dietética f; ~ **sugar** n FOOD azúcar dietético m

diethanolamine n (*DEA*) CHEM, DETERG dietanolamina f (*DEA*)

diethyl: ~ **ether** n DETERG éter dietílico m

diethylene n DETERG dietileno m

diethylenic: ~ **acid** n CHEM ácido dietilénico m

difference: ~ **frequency** n ELECTRON frecuencia diferencial f; ~ **limen** n ACOUST umbral diferencial m; ~ **signal** n ELECTRON señal diferencial f

differential[1] adj MATH diferencial

differential[2] n AUTO, C&G, MATH, MECH, MECH ENG, VEH diferencial m; ~ **ammeter** n ELEC, ELEC ENG, INSTR amperímetro diferencial m; ~ **amplifier** n ELECTRON, PHYS, TELECOM amplificador diferencial m; ~ **bevel gear** n VEH engranaje cónico del diferencial m, piñón cónico del diferencial m; ~ **braking** n AIR TRANSP frenado diferencial m; ~ **calculus** n MATH cálculo diferencial m; ~ **capacitance** n ELEC ENG capacidad incremental f; ~ **carrier** n AUTO portador del diferencial m; ~ **case** n AUTO caja del diferencial f, cárter del diferencial m; ~ **Cerenkov counter** n PART PHYS contador de Cerenkov diferencial m; ~ **chain block** n MECH cadena diferencial f, NUCL aparejo diferencial de cadena m; ~ **coefficient** n MATH coeficiente diferencial m; ~ **coil** n ELEC bobina diferencial f; ~ **comparator** n ELECTRON comparador diferencial m; ~ **control rod worth** n NUCL valor diferencial de una barra de control m; ~ **corrections** n pl WATER TRANSP correcciones diferenciales f pl; ~ **delay** n ELECTRON temporizador diferencial m; ~ **effect** n AIR TRANSP efecto diferencial m; ~ **equation** n MATH ecuación diferencial f; ~ **focusing** n CINEMAT enfoque diferencial m; ~ **gain** n ELECTRON, TV diferencia de ganancia f, ganancia diferencial f; ~ **galvanometer** n ELEC, ELEC ENG, INSTR galvanómetro diferencial m; ~ **geometry** n GEOM geometría diferencial f; ~ **head** n FUELLESS salto de agua diferencial m; ~ **input** n ELECTRON corriente de entrada diferencial f, entrada diferencial f; ~ **lock** n AUTO, VEH bloqueo del diferencial m; ~ **magnetometer** n ELEC, INSTR magnetómetro diferencial m; ~ **measuring instrument** n INSTR instrumento de medida diferencial m; ~ **microphone** n ACOUST micrófono diferencial m; ~~**mode** n ELECTRON modo diferencial m; ~ **mode attenuation** n ELECTRON atenuación diferencial de modos f, OPT, TELECOM atenuación diferencial de modos f, atenuación en modo diferencial f; ~ **mode delay** n OPT, TELECOM retardo del modo diferencial m; ~ **mode signal** n ELECTRON señal de modo diferencial f; ~ **modulation** n ELECTRON modulación diferencial f; ~ **phase** n ELECTRON, TV diferencia de fase f, fase diferencial f; ~ **phase shift keying** n (*DPSK*) ELECTRON manipulación de variación de fase diferencial f (*MVFD*); ~ **pinion** n AUTO piñón del

diferencial m; ~ **pressure** n HYDRAUL, PETR TECH diferencia de presión f, presión diferencial f; ~ **pressure gage** AmE, ~ **pressure gauge** BrE n MECH calibre de diferencia de presión m; ~ **protection relay** n ELEC relé de protección diferencial m; ~ **pulley** n PHYS polea diferencial f; ~ **pulse code modulation** n (*DPCM*) ELECTRON modulación diferencial de código pulsado f (*MDCP*); ~ **quantum efficiency** n OPT eficiencia cuántica diferencial f, TELECOM rendimiento cuántico diferencial m; ~ **ratio** n AUTO relación del diferencial f; ~ **relay** n ELEC, ELEC ENG relevador diferencial m, relé diferencial m; ~ **scanning calorimetry** n P&R, RAD PHYS, THERMO calorimetría de exploración diferencial f; ~ **settlement** n CONST, GEOL asentamiento diferencial m; ~ **shaft** n AUTO eje del diferencial m; ~ **shrinkage** n TEXTIL encogimiento diferencial m; ~ **side gear** n AUTO engranaje planetario del diferencial m; ~ **signal** n ELECTRON señal diferencial f; ~ **signal source** n ELECTRON fuente de señal diferencial f; ~ **spider** n VEH cruceta del diferencial f; ~ **spider pinion** n VEH piñón planetario del diferencial m, piñón satélite del diferencial m; ~ **temperature** n PETR TECH temperatura diferencial f; ~ **thermal analysis** n (*DTA*) CHEM, P&R, POLL, THERMO análisis térmico diferencial m; ~ **thermocouple** n THERMO termopar diferencial m; ~ **thermometer** n THERMO termómetro diferencial m; ~ **threshold** n ACOUST umbral diferencial m; ~ **threshold of frequency** n ACOUST umbral diferencial de frecuencia m; ~ **threshold of sound pressure level** n ACOUST umbral diferencial de nivel de presión del sonora m; ~ **time** n ELECTRON tiempo diferencial m; ~ **topology** n GEOM topología diferencial f; ~ **transducer** n ELEC ENG transductor diferencial m; ~ **transformer** n ELEC, ELEC ENG transformador diferencial m; ~ **voltage** n ELEC ENG tensión diferencial f, voltaje diferencial m; ~ **voltmeter** n ELEC, INSTR voltímetro diferencial m; ~ **winding** n ELEC ENG devanado diferencial m

differentially: ~~**excited compound generator** n ELEC, ELEC ENG generador de excitación mixta diferencial m

differentiated adj ELECTRON, GEOL, MATH diferenciado

differentiating: ~ **circuit** n ELECTRON circuito diferenciado m

differentiation n GEOL, MATH diferenciación f

diffracted: ~ **beam** n CRYSTALL haz difractado m; ~ **wave** n PHYS, WAVE PHYS onda difractada f

diffraction n GEN difracción f; ~ **grating** n OPT red de difracción f, PHYS red de difracción f, rejilla de difracción f, TELECOM rejilla de difracción f, WAVE PHYS crática de difracción f, red difractora f, rejilla de difracción f, retículo de difracción m; ~ **pattern** n CRYSTALL diagrama de difracción m, figura de difracción f, METALL figura de difracción f, modelo de difracción m, patrón de difracción m, OPT figura de difracción f; ~ **spectrograph** n NUCL, OPT, PHYS, RAD PHYS espectrógrafo de difracción m, espectrógrafo difractivo m; ~ **spectrum** n NUCL, OPT, PHYS, RAD PHYS espectro de difracción m; ~ **spot** n CRYSTALL mancha de difracción f

diffractometer n CRYSTALL, GEOL, INSTR, PETR TECH, RAD PHYS difractómetro m

diffractometry n CRYSTALL, GEOL, INSTR, PETR TECH, RAD PHYS difractometría f

diffuse[1]: ~ **blue reflectance factor** n PAPER factor de reflectancia difusa en el azul m; ~ **field** n ACOUST campo difuso m; ~ **light density** n OPT densidad luminosa difusa f; ~**-light recorder** n INSTR grabador de luz difusa m; ~ **metal oxide semiconductor** n (*DMOS*) ELECTRON semiconductor de óxido de metal difuso m (*SOMD*); ~ **nebula** n SPACE nebulosa difusa f; ~ **radiation** n FUELLESS, SPACE radiación difusa f; ~ **reflection** n ELEC ENG, RAD PHYS reflexión difusa f; ~ **scattering method** n NUCL método de dispersión difusa m

diffuse[2] vt GEN difundir

diffused: ~ **alloy transistor** n ELECTRON transistor de aleación por difusión m; ~ **emitter-collector transistor** n ELECTRON transistor emisor-captador por difusión m; ~ **junction** n ELECTRON unión por difusión f; ~ **layer** n ELECTRON estratificado por difusión m; ~ **light** n CINEMAT, PHOTO, TV iluminación difusa f; ~ **photodiode** n ELECTRON fotodiodo de difusión m

diffuser n GEN difusor m; ~ **blade** n CHEM TECH navaja difusora f; ~ **lens** n INSTR lente difusora f; ~ **scrim** n CINEMAT gasa difusora f

diffusing adj C&G *glass* difusor

diffusiometer n OCEAN difusómetro m

diffusion n ACOUST, CHEM CHEM difusión f, COAL difusión f, dispersión f, CONST, ELECTRON, PHYS difusión f, POLL difusión f, dispersión f, TV difusión f; ~ **annealing** n CHEM TECH recocido por difusión m; ~ **apparatus** n CHEM TECH, INSTR difusómetro m; ~ **area** n REFRIG área de difusión f; ~ **cell** n CHEM TECH celda de difusión f; ~ **coefficient** n ELECTRON, PHYS coeficiente de difusión m; ~ **current** n ELEC *electrolysis* corriente de difusión f; ~ **defect** n ELECTRON defecto de difusión m; ~ **doping** n ELECTRON dopado por difusión m; ~ **effect filter** n CINEMAT filtro de efecto de difusión m; ~ **kernel** n NUCL núcleo de difusión m; ~ **length** n ELECTRON extensión de difusión f; ~ **mean free path** n NUCL, PHYS recorrido libre medio m; ~ **oven** n CHEM TECH, ELECTRON horno de difusión m; ~ **pump** n INSTR, MECH ENG, PHYS bomba de difusión f; ~ **tower** n CHEM TECH columna de difusión f, torre de difusión f

diffusionless: ~ **reaction** n METALL reacción sin difusión f

diffusivity n FLUID coeficiente de difusión m, PHYS difusividad f

dig: ~ **in manure** vt AGRIC estercolar

digest vt RECYCL resumir

digested: ~ **sludge** n HYDROL fango digerido m

digester n C&G, CHEM, COAL, FOOD autoclave f, HYDROL *mass* digestor m, LAB autoclave f, PAPER lejiadora f, digestor m, PROD autoclave f, RECYCL digestor m, autoclave f, THERMO autoclave f, digestor m; ~ **gas** n GAS, HYDROL gas de tanque digestor m, RECYCL autoclave a gas f, THERMO gas de tanque digestor m

digestibility n AGRIC digestibilidad f

digestible: ~ **fiber** n AmE, ~ **fibre** n BrE AGRIC fibra digestible f; ~ **organic matter** n (*DOM*) RECYCL materia orgánica digestible f

digestion n CHEM digestión f, PAPER lejiado m, RECYCL digestión f, putrefacción f; ~ **apparatus** n LAB aparato de digestión m; ~ **tank** n HYDROL, THERMO tanque digestor m; ~ **time** n HYDROL, THERMO tiempo de digestión m

digestive: ~ **enzyme** n RECYCL enzima digestiva f; ~ **system** n RECYCL sistema digestivo m

digger n AGRIC arrancadora f, COAL arrancadora f, excavadora f, picador m, MINE arrancadora f, picador m, pocero m

digging n COAL arranque m, excavación f, CONST excavación f; ~ **bucket** n TRANSP cuchara excavadora f; ~ **face** n MINE frente de excavación m; ~ **ladder** n MINE cadena de arrastre f (*Esp*), escala f (*AmL*); ~ **machine** n CONST excavadora f; ~ **technique** n CONST técnica de excavación f

diggings n pl MINE excavaciones f pl, labores mineras f pl, minas f pl, yacimientos m pl

digital[1] adj COMP&DP digital, ELECTRON digital, numérico; ~**-to-analog** adj COMP&DP, TV digital a analógico (*D-a-A*)

digital[2]: ~ **actuator** n ELEC ENG accionador digital m, accionador numérico m; ~ **adder** n ELECTRON sumador digital m; ~ **ammeter** n ELEC, ELEC ENG, INSTR amperímetro digital m; ~ **analog conversion** n TELECOM conversión analógica-digital f; ~ **analog converter** n TELECOM conversor analógico-digital m; ~ **attenuator** n ELECTRON atenuador digital m; ~ **audio tape** n (*DAT*) COMP&DP cinta digital de audio f; ~ **camera** n TV cámara digital f; ~ **carrier module** n TELECOM módulo de portadora digital m; ~ **cassette** n COMP&DP casete digital f; ~ **chip** n ELECTRON chip digital m; ~ **circuit** n COMP&DP, ELECTRON, TELECOM circuito digital m; ~ **circuit design** n ELEC ENG, ELECTRON, TELECOM diseño de circuito digital m; ~ **circuit multiplication equipment** n (*DCME*) TELECOM equipo de multiplicación del circuito digital m (*DCME*); ~ **circuit multiplication gain** n (*DCMG*) TELECOM ganancia de multiplicación del circuito digital f, sistema de multiplicación del circuito digital m; ~ **circuit multiplication system** n (*DCMS*) TELECOM sistema de amplificación del circuito digital m; ~ **code** n ELECTRON código digital m; ~ **coding** n ELECTRON, TELECOM codificación digital f; ~ **command signal** n (*DCS*) TELECOM señal de comando digital f; ~ **communications** n COMP&DP comunicaciones digitales f pl; ~ **computer** n COMP&DP, ELECTRON computador dedicado m (*AmL*), computador digital m (*AmL*), computadora dedicada f (*AmL*), computadora digital f (*AmL*), ordenador dedicado m (*Esp*), ordenador digital m (*Esp*); ~ **connection** n TELECOM conexión digital f; ~ **control** n TELECOM, TV control digital m; ~ **control box** n AUTO caja de control digital f; ~ **converter** n ELECTRON convertidor digital m; ~ **cross-connect** n TELECOM interfaz digital m; ~ **cross-connect equipment** n (*DXC*) TELECOM equipo de interconexión digital m; ~ **data** n pl ELECTRON datos digitales m pl, información digital f; ~ **data exchange standard** n (*DDES*) PRINT norma para el intercambio de datos digitales f, norma para el intercambio de datos numéricos f; ~ **device** n ELECTRON aparato digital m, dispositivo digital m; ~ **display** n ELECTRON elemento de visualización digital m, INSTR pantalla digital f; ~ **distribution frame** n TELECOM repartidor digital m; ~ **domain** n ELECTRON campo digital m; ~ **error** n TELECOM error digital m; ~ **exchange** n TELECOM central telefónica digital f; ~ **feedback** n ELEC ENG, ELECTRON, TELECOM realimentación digital f; ~ **filling** n TELECOM relleno digital m; ~ **filter** n ELECTRON, TELECOM filtro digital *m*; ~ **filtering** *n* COMP&DP, ELECTRON, TELE-COM filtrado digital *m*; ~ **flight-data recorder** *n* AIR TRANSP grabadora digital de datos de vuelo *f*, registrador digital de datos de vuelo *m*; ~ **frame** *n* CINEMAT ajustador de imagen digital *m*; ~ **frame structure** *n* TELECOM estructura de tramas digitales *f*; ~ **framer** *n* TV ajustador de imagen digital *m*; ~ **hierarchy** *n* TELECOM jerarquía digital *f*; ~ **identification frame** *n* TELECOM trama de identificación digital *f*; ~ **image** *n* ELECTRON imagen digital *f*; ~ **image processing** *n* ELECTRON procesado de imagen digital *m*; ~ **input** *n* ELECTRON entrada digital *f*; ~ **input signal** *n* ELECTRON señal de entrada digital *f*; ~ **instantaneous frequency measurement** *n* ELECTRON medición de frecuencia instantánea digital *f*; ~ **instrument** *n* ELEC, INSTR instrumento digital *m*; ~ **integrated circuit** *n* ELECTRON circuito integrado digital *m*; ~ **integration** *n* ELECTRON integración digital *f*; ~ **integrator** *n* ELECTRON integrador digital *m*; ~ **interface** *n* TELECOM interconexión digital *f*; ~ **interference** *n* TELECOM interferencia digital *f*; ~ **logic** *n* ELECTRON circuito lógico digital *m*; ~ **loop** *n* TELECOM bucle digital *m*; ~ **main network switching center** *n* AmE, ~ **main network switching centre** *n* BrE TELECOM centro de conmutación digital de la red principal *m*; ~ **matched filter** *n* ELECTRON filtro adaptable digital *m*; ~ **modulation** *n* ELECTRON, PHYS, TELECOM modulación digital *f*; ~ **modulation link** *n* TELECOM enlace de modulación digital *m*; ~ **modulation system** *n* TELECOM sistema de modulación digital *m*; ~ **multimeter** *n* ELEC ENG multímetro digital *m*; ~ **multiplex** *n* ELECTRON multiplexado digital *m*, transmisión múltiple digital *f*; ~ **multiplexing** *n* ELECTRON transmisión múltiple digital *f*; ~ **multiplication** *n* ELECTRON multiplicación digital *f*; ~ **multiplier** *n* ELECTRON multiplicador digital *m*; ~ **optical disc** BrE, ~ **optical disk** *n* AmE OPT disco óptico digital *m*; ~ **output** *n* ELECTRON salida de corriente digital *f*; ~ **output signal** *n* ELECTRON señal de salida digital *f*; ~ **pad** *n* TELECOM relleno digital *m*; ~ **phase modulation** *n* TELECOM modulación de fase digital *f*; ~ **phase shifting** *n* ELECTRON variación de fase digital *f*; ~ **plotter** *n* COMP&DP plotter digital *m*, trazador de gráficos digital *m*, trazador digital *m*; ~ **process computer system** *n* NUCL computador digital de proceso *m* (*AmL*), computadora digital de proceso *f* (*AmL*), ordenador digital de proceso *m* (*Esp*); ~ **processing** *n* ELECTRON tratamiento digital *m*, TELECOM proceso digital *m*; ~ **pseudonoise sequence** *n* TELECOM secuencia de pseudorruidos digitales *f*; ~~**pulse stream** *n* TELECOM tren de impulsos digitales *m*; ~ **read-out** *n* COMP&DP lectura de salida digital *f*, lectura digital *f*, ELEC dispositivo de indicación digital *m*, dispositivo de indicación numérica *m*, indicación digital *f*, indicación numérica *f*, INSTR lectura digital *f*, TELECOM presentador visual digital *m*; ~ **read-out measuring instrument** *n* METR instrumento de lectura digital de medidas *m*; ~ **read-out micrometer** *n* METR micrómetro de lectura digital *m*; ~ **recorder** *n* NUCL, TELECOM, TV registrador digital *m*; ~ **recording** *n* TELECOM, TV registro digital *m*; ~ **regeneration** *n* ELECTRON regeneración digital *f*; ~ **regenerator** *n* ELECTRON regenerador digital *m*; ~ **representation** *n* COMP&DP, ELECTRON representación digital *f*; ~ **satellite concentrator** *n*

TELECOM concentrador satélite digital *m*; ~ **section** *n* (*DS*) TELECOM sección digital *f*; ~ **selective calling** *n* (*DSC*) TELECOM llamada selectiva digital *f*; ~ **signal** *n* COMP&DP, ELECTRON, PHYS, TELECOM señal digital *f*; ~ **signal analyser** *n* BrE ELECTRON analizador de señal digital *m*; ~ **signal analysis** *n* ELECTRON análisis de señal digital *m*; ~ **signal analyzer** *AmE see digital signal analyser BrE*; ~ **signal processing** *n* (*DSP*) COMP&DP procesamiento de señal digital *m*, ELECTRON proceso de señal digital *m* (*PSD*), tratamiento de señal digital *m* (*TSD*); ~ **signature** *n* TELECOM firma digital *f*; ~ **simulation model** *n* GAS modelo digital de simulación *m*; ~ **speech** *n* ELECTRON audición digital *f*; ~ **speech compression** *n* TELECOM compresión vocal digital *f*; ~ **speech interpolation** *n* (*DSI*) TELECOM interpolación vocal digital *f*; ~ **speech synthesis** *n* ELECTRON síntesis de audición digital *f*; ~ **subscriber access unit** *n* TELECOM unidad digital de acceso al abonado *f*; ~ **subtractor** *n* ELECTRON restador digital *m*, subtractor digital *m*; ~ **switch** *n* TELECOM conmutador digital *m*; ~ **switching** *n* TELECOM conmutación digital *f*; ~ **switching center** *n* AmE, ~ **switching centre** *n* BrE TELECOM centro de conmutación digital *m*; ~ **switching element** *n* (*DSE*) TELECOM elemento de conmutación digital *m*; ~ **switching equipment** *n* ELEC ENG equipo conmutador digital *m*; ~ **switching matrix** *n* TELECOM matriz de conmutación digital *f*; ~ **switching network** *n* TELECOM red de conmutación digital *f*; ~ **switching system** *n* TELECOM sistema de conmutación digital *m*; ~ **television** *n* TV televisión digital *f*; ~~**to-analog conversion** *n* (*DAC*) COMP&DP, ELECTRON, TELECOM, TV conversión digital-analógica *f*; ~~**to-analog converter** *n* (*DAC*) COMP&DP, ELECTRON, TELECOM, TV conversor digital-analógico *m*, convertidor digital-analógico *m*; ~ **transit command** *n* TELECOM comando de tránsito digital *m*; ~ **transmission** *n* TELECOM transmisión digital *f*; ~ **trunk interface** *n* (*DTI*) TELECOM interfaz de enlace digital *m*; ~ **tuning** *n* ELECTRON sintonización digital *f*; ~ **TV receiver** *n* TV receptor de televisión digital *m*; ~ **video effects** *n pl* (*DVE*) TV efectos digitales de vídeo *m pl* (*AmL*) , efectos digitales de video *m pl* (*Esp*); ~ **videodisc** *n* BrE OPT videodisco digital *m*; ~ **videodisk** *AmE see digital videodisc BrE*; ~ **videotape recorder** *n* (*DVTR*) TV grabador de cinta de video digital *m* (*AmL*), grabador de cinta de vídeo digital *m* (*Esp*), grabador de video digital *m* (*AmL*), grabador de vídeo digital *m* (*Esp*); ~ **voltmeter** *n* ELEC ENG voltímetro digital *m*

digitalin *n* CHEM digitalina *f*

digitalis *n* FOOD digital *m*

digitalization *n* MECH ENG digitalización *f*

digitalized[1] *adj* SPACE digitalizado

digitalized[2]: ~ **speech** *n* ELECTRON, TELECOM voz digitalizada *f*

digitally: ~~**encoded videodisc** *n* BrE OPT videodisco codificado digitalmente *m*; ~~**encoded videodisk** *AmE* OPT videodisco codificado digitalmente *m*

digitization *n* COMP&DP, ELECTRON, NUCL, PHYS, TELECOM, TV digitalización *f*

digitize *vt* COMP&DP digitalizar, ELEC traducir a la forma digital, traducir en valor digital, traducir en valor numérico, cifrar, ELECTRON digitalizar, MECH ENG cifrar, codificar en dígito, convertir en valor numérico, digitalizar,numerizar, NUCL, PHYS digitalizar, PRINT convertir en digitales, TELECOM, TV digitalizar

digitized[1] *adj* GEN digitalizado

digitized[2]: **~ data** *n* COMP&DP, ELECTRON, TELECOM datos digitalizados *m pl*, información digitalizada *f*; **~ image** *n* COMP&DP, ELECTRON imagen digitalizada *f*, imagen numérica *f*; **~ signal** *n* ELECTRON señal digitalizada *f*; **~ speech** *n* ELECTRON, TELECOM voz digitalizada *f*

digitizer *n* COMP&DP, ELECTRON, TELECOM digitalizador *m*

digitizing: **~ rate** *n* COMP&DP, ELECTRON, TELECOM cadencia de digitalización *f*, ritmo de digitalización *m*; **~ tablet** *n* COMP&DP tableta de digitalización *f*

diglycidyl: **~ ether** *n* CHEM éter diglicidílico *m*, P&R diglicidiléter *m*, éter diglicidílico *m*

diguanide *n* CHEM diguanida *f*

dihedral[1] *adj* GEOM diedro, diédrico

dihedral[2] *n* AIR TRANSP diedro *m*; **~ aerial** *n* BrE (*cf dihedral antenna AmE*) TELECOM antena de diedro *f*; **~ angle** *n* GEOM, METALL ángulo diedro *m*; **~ antenna** *n* AmE (*cf dihedral aerial BrE*) TELECOM antena de diedro *f*

dihydroacridine *n* CHEM dihidroacridina *f*

dihydrobenzene *n* CHEM dihidrobenceno *m*

dihydrocarveol *n* CHEM dihidrocarveol *m*

dihydrocarvone *n* CHEM dihidrocarvona *f*

dihydroergotamine *n* CHEM dihidroergotamina *f*

dihydronaphthalene *n* CHEM dihidronaftaleno *m*

dihydrostreptomycin *n* CHEM dihidroestreptomicina *f*

dihydrotachysterol *n* CHEM dihidrotaquisterol *m*

dihydroxyacetone *n* (*DHA*) CHEM dihidroxiacetona *f* (*DHA*)

diiodomethane *n* CHEM diyodometano *m*

dike *n* CONST dique *m*, presa *f*

dilatable *adj* COAL dilatable

dilatancy *n* COAL, P&R dilatancia *f*

dilatant *adj* COAL *soil* dilatador, dilatante

dilatation *n* GAS dilatación *f*, HYDRAUL dilatación *f*, expansión *f*

dilatational: **~ wave** *n* GEOL onda de dilatación *f*

dilation *n* GEOM dilatación *f*

dilatometer *n* PHYS dilatómetro *m*

dilator *n* GEOM dilatador *m*

diluent *n* CHEM diluyente *m*, P&R diluente *m*, diluyente *m*, disolvente *m*

dilute[1] *adj* METALL atenuado, diluido, disuelto

dilute[2] *vt* CHEM, CHEM TECH diluir, COAL clarificar, diluir, lavar a la cuba, METALL, P&R diluir

diluting: **~ agent** *n* CHEM, CHEM TECH agente de dilución *m*

dilution *n* CHEM, CHEM TECH, PETR TECH dilución *f*; **~ refrigerator** *n* PHYS, REFRIG refrigerador de dilución *m*

dim *vt* CINEMAT, PHOTO atenuar

dimension[1]: **~ line** *n* MECH ENG línea de cota *f*

dimension[2] *vt* MECH ENG, PROD acotar

dimensional: **~ compatibility** *n* TELECOM compatibilidad dimensional *f*; **~ control** *n* PROD control dimensional *m*; **~ equation** *n* PHYS ecuación dimensional *f*; **~ measuring instruments** *n pl* INSTR, METR instrumentos de medidas dimensionales *m pl*; **~ requirements** *n pl* SAFE normas dimensionales *f pl*; **~ stability** *n* CINEMAT, NUCL, PACK, PAPER, PRINT estabilidad dimensional *f*

dimensioned: **~ sketch** *n* PROD croquis acotado *m*, dibujo acotado *m*

dimensioning *n* COMP&DP ajuste de dimensión *m*, dimensionamiento *m*, MECH ENG acotación *f*, dimensionamiento *m*, medición *f*, PROD acotación *f*, dimensionamiento *m*

dimer *n* CHEM dímero *m*

dimeric *adj* CHEM dimérico

dimethoxymethane *n* CHEM dimetoximetano *m*

dimethyl *n* CHEM dimetilo *m*; **~ sulfate** *AmE see dimethyl sulphate BrE*; **~ sulfone** *AmE see dimethyl sulphone BrE*; **~ sulphate** *n* BrE CHEM sulfato de dimetilo *m*; **~ sulphone** *n* BrE CHEM dimetilsulfona *f*

dimethylacetic *adj* CHEM dimetilacético

dimethylamine *n* (*DMA*) CHEM dimetilamina *f* (*DMA*)

dimethylaniline *n* CHEM dimetilanilina *f*

dimethylarsine *n* CHEM dimetilarsina *f*

dimethylbenzene *n* CHEM dimetilbenceno *m*

dimethylformamide *n* (*DMF*) CHEM dimetilformamida *f* (*DMF*)

dimethylglyoxime *n* CHEM dimetilglioxima *f*

diminished: **~ arch** *n* CONST *architectural structure, bridge* arco rebajado *m*, *curve described* bóveda rebajada *f*; **~ interval** *n* ACOUST intervalo decreciente *m*

dimmed: **~ beams** *n pl* AmE (*cf dipped headlights BrE*) AUTO faros basculantes *m pl*, VEH faros basculantes *m pl*, luces cortas *f pl*, luz de cruce *f*

dimmer *n* CINEMAT atenuador *m*, ELEC amortiguador de luz *m*, reductor de alumbrado *m*, reductor de iluminación *m*, reductor de luz *m*; **~ quadrant** *n* CINEMAT cuadrante atenuador *m*; **~ switch** *n* ELEC, ELEC ENG conmutador reductor *m*, interruptor de graduación de la luz *m*; **~ system** *n* AIR TRANSP sistema regulador de voltaje *m*

dimorphism *n* CHEM, CRYSTALL dimorfismo *m*

dimple *n* C&G hoyuelo *m*, METALL embutido superficial *m*, muesca efectuada con punzón *f*

dimpled: **~ hole** *n* MECH ENG embutido superficial *m*, hoyuelo superficial *m*

dimpling *n* MECH ENG aboyado con punzón especial *m*

DIN[1] *abbr* (*Deutsches Institut für Normung*) PROD DIN (*Instituto Alemán para la Normalización*)

DIN[2]: **~ rail** *n* PROD riel DIN *m*; **~ size** *n* PRINT tamaño DIN *m*; **~ speed** *n* PHOTO sensibilidad DIN *f*

dinaphthyl *n* CHEM dinaftilo *m*

dinghy *n* MILIT, P&R, WATER TRANSP chinchorro *m*

dinging: **~ hammer** *n* MECH ENG martillo de chapista *m*, martillo desaboyador *m*

dinitrobenzene *n* CHEM dinitrobenceno *m*

dinitrocresol *n* CHEM dinitrocresol *m* (*DNC*)

dinitronaphthalene *n* CHEM dinitronaftaleno *m*

dinitrophenol *n* CHEM dinitrofenol *m*

dinitrotoluene *n* (*DNT*) CHEM dinitrotolueno *m* (*DNT*)

dinky *n* CINEMAT dinky *m*; **~ reel** *n* PAPER, PRINT bobina de papel de mitad de anchura *f*

dintheader *n* MINE excavadora *f*, picador de carbón *m*

dinucleotide *n* CHEM dinucleótido *m*

dioctyl: **~ phthalate** *n* P&R ftalato de dioctilo *m*

diode *n* GEN diodo *m*; **~ amplifier** *n* ELECTRON amplificador de diodo *m*; **~ anode** *n* ELECTRON ánodo del diodo *m*; **~ array** *n* TELECOM array de diodos *m*; **~ characteristic** *n* ELECTRON característica del diodo *f*; **~-connected transistor** *n* ELECTRON transistor de diodo conectado *m*; **~-connected tube**

n ELECTRON tubo de diodo conectado *m*; ~ **crosspoint** *n* TELECOM contacto de cruce de diodos *m*; ~ **forward impedance** *n* ELECTRON impedancia directa del diodo *f*; ~ **frequency multiplier** *n* ELECTRON multiplicador de diodo de frecuencia *m*; ~ **gate** *n* ELECTRON puerta de diodo *f*; ~ **impedance** *n* ELECTRON impedancia del diodo *f*; ~ **laser** *n* ELECTRON, OPT láser de diodo *m*; ~ **limiter** *n* ELECTRON diodo limitador *m*, limitador de diodo *m*, TV diodo limitador *m*; ~ **logic** *n* ELECTRON circuito lógico de diodo *f*; ~ **mixer** *n* ELECTRON diodo mezclador *m*; ~ **modulation** *n* ELECTRON modulación de diodo *f*; ~ **oscillator** *n* ELECTRON oscilador de diodo *m*; ~ **peak detector** *n* ELECTRON detector de picos a diodos *m*; ~ **phase shifter** *n* ELECTRON variador de fase de diodo *m*; ~ **photodetector** *n* ELECTRON diodo fotodetector *m*, fotodetector de diodos *m*, TELECOM diodo fotodetector *m*; ~ **rectifier** *n* ELECTRON rectificador a diodo *m*; ~ **series resistance** *n* ELECTRON resistencia serie del diodo *f*; ~ **string** *n* ELECTRON cadena de diodos *f*; ~ **suppression** *n* ELECTRON eliminación de diodo *f*; ~ **suppressor** *n* ELECTRON eliminador de diodos *m*; ~ **switch** *n* ELECTRON diodo de conmutación *m*, TELECOM diodo conmutador *m*, diodo de conmutación *m*, TV diodo de conmutación *m*; ~ **transducer** *n* ELECTRON transductor a diodo *m*; ~**transistor logic** *n* (*DTL*) COMP&DP, ELECTRON circuito a base de diodos y transistores *m* (*DTL*); ~ **tube** *n* AmE (*cf diode valve BrE*) ELECTRON tubo de diodo *m*; ~**type dual input** *n* PROD, TV ingreso dual de tipo diodo *m*; ~ **valve** *n* BrE (*cf diode tube AmE*) ELECTRON tubo de diodo *m*; ~ **voltage** *n* ELECTRON voltaje de diodo *m*

dioecious *adj* AGRIC dioico

diol *n* CHEM diol *m*

diolefin *n* PETR TECH diolefina *f*

Dion: ~ **axle** *n* AUTO eje de Dion *m*

diopside *n* MINERAL diópsido *m*

dioptase *n* MINERAL dioptasa *f*

diopter *AmE see* **dioptre** *BrE*

dioptre *n* BrE OPT, PHOTO, PHYS, SPACE dioptría *f*; ~ **lens** *n* CINEMAT lente de aproximación *f*, lente dióptrica *f*, PHOTO, TV lente de aproximación *f*

dioptric: ~ **adjuster** *n* CINEMAT, TV ajustador dióptrico *m*

diorite *n* PETROL diorita *f*

dioxide *n* CHEM bióxido *m*, dióxido *m*

dioxin *n* CHEM dioxina *f*

dioxytartaric *adj* CHEM dioxitartárico

dip¹ *n* AGRIC *for animals* baño *m*, C&G *of bait in making sheet glass* inmersión *f*, COAL *of overhead line* flecha *f*, inclinación *f*, inflexión *f*, pendiente *f*, FUELLESS buzamiento *m*, GEOL buzamiento *m*, inclinación *f*, MINE pendiente *f*, lugar en declive *m* (*Esp*), chiflón *m* (*AmL*), declive *m*, inclinación *f*, inmersión *f*, buzamiento *m*, galería inclinada *f* (*AmL*), recuesto *m* (*AmL*), PETROL baño *m*, inmersión *f*, buzamiento *m*, inclinación *f*, TEXTIL baño *m*, WATER TRANSP *of sextant* depresión aparente *f*; ~ **angle** *n* GEOL inclinación magnética *f*, GEOPHYS inclinación magnética *f*, ángulo magnético *m*, PETR TECH, PETROL inclinación magnética *f*; ~ **brazing** *n* CONST soldadura por inmersión *f*; ~ **circle** *n* GEOPHYS círculo magnético *m*, inclinómetro *m*; ~ **circle needle** *n* GEOPHYS aguja de inclinómetro *f*; ~ **coat**

n COATINGS revestimiento por inmersión *m*; ~-**coated paper** *n* PAPER papel revestido por inmersión *m*; ~ **coating** *n* COATINGS aplicación de revestimiento por inmersión *f*, recubrimiento por inmersión *m*, P&R aplicación de revestimiento por inmersión *f*, PAPER revestido por inmersión *m*, PROD recubrimiento por inmersión *m*; ~ **compass** *n* GEOPHYS brújula de inclinación *f*, brújula de minero *f* (*dated*), clinómetro para inclinación marina *m*; ~ **dyeing** *n* COLOUR teñido de inmersión *m*; ~ **equator** *n* GEOPHYS ecuador magnético *m*; ~ **fault** *n* GEOL falla ortogonal *f*, PETROL falla transversal *f*; ~ **freezing** *n* PACK congelación por inmersión *f*; ~ **net** *n* OCEAN ábaco de inclinación *m*; ~ **pickup** *n* TEXTIL absorción del baño *f*; ~ **roller** *n* PRINT rodillo humectador *m*; ~ **selector switch** *n* ELEC *automotive* conmutador para bascular *m*, conmutador selector para bascular *m*; ~ **slip** *n* GEOL desplazamiento de inclinación *m*; ~ **slope** *n* GEOL pendiente de buzamiento *f*, pendiente inclinada *f*; ~ **switch** *n* ELEC *automotive* conmutador para bascular *m*, conmutador selector para bascular *m*, PROD interruptor de inmersión *m*

dip² *vt* PROD *into liquids*, TEXTIL hundir, sumergir; ~ **varnish** *vt* COATINGS, COLOUR barnizar por inmersión

dip³ *vi* GEOL buzar

DIP¹ *abbr* (*dual-in-line package*) COMP&DP, ELEC ENG DIP (*empaque doble en línea, paquete en línea doble*)

DIP²: ~ **battery** *n* ELEC ENG batería PLD *f*; ~ **relay** *n* ELEC ENG relé PLD *m*; ~ **switch** *n* ELEC ENG interruptor PLD *m*

dipalmitin *n* CHEM dipalmitina *f*

diparachlorobenzyl *n* CHEM diparaclorobencilo *m*

diphase *adj* ELEC, ELEC ENG bifásico

diphead *n* MINE chiflón *m*

diphenyl *n* CHEM difenilo *m*

diphenylamine *n* (*DFA*) CHEM difenilamina *f* (*DFA*)

diphenylcarbinol *n* CHEM difenilcarbinol *m*

diphenylmethane: ~ **diisocyanate** *n* (*MDI*) P&R diisocianato de difenilmetano *m* (*MDI*)

diplacusis *n* ACOUST diploacusia *f*, diplacusia *f*

diplexer *n* TELECOM diplexor *m*

diploid *adj* AGRIC diploide

dipolar¹ *adj* CHEM dipolar

dipolar²: ~ **ion** *n* CHEM ión dipolar *m*; ~ **moment** *n* CHEM momento dipolar *m*

dipole *n* ACOUST, ELEC, ELEC ENG, METALL, PHYS, TELECOM dipolo *m*; ~ **aerial** *n* BrE (*cf dipole antenna AmE*) TV antena de doblete *f*, antena dipolo *f*, WATER TRANSP antena dipolo *f*; ~ **antenna** *n* AmE (*cf dipole aerial BrE*) TV antena de doblete *f*, antena dipolo *f*, WATER TRANSP antena dipolo *f*; ~-**dipole interaction** *n* PHYS interacción dipolo-dipolo *f*; ~ **moment** *n* ELEC ENG momento dipolar *m*

dipped: ~ **headlights** *n pl* BrE (*cf dimmed beams AmE*) AUTO faros basculantes *m pl*, VEH faros basculantes *m pl*, luces cortas *f pl*, luz de cruce *f*

dipper *n* WATER TRANSP achicador *m*; ~ **dredger** *n* WATER TRANSP pala excavadora flotante *f*, draga de almeja *f*, draga de cuchara *f*

dipping *n* PRINT inmersión *f*; ~ **refractometer** *n* INSTR refractómetro de inmersión *m*; ~ **roller** *n* PRINT rodillo mojador *m*; ~ **varnish** *n* COATINGS, COLOUR barniz de inmersión *m*

dipstick *n* AUTO, VEH varilla del nivel del aceite *f*, varilla para medición del nivel *f*

dipyre *n* MINERAL dipiro *m*

Dirac: ~ **constant** *n* PHYS constante de Dirac *f*; ~ **function** *n* PETROL función de Dirac *f*

direct[1] *adj* GEN directo; ~-**coupled** *adj* COMP&DP acoplado directamente

direct[2]: ~ **AC converter** *n* ELEC convertidor de CA directa *m*, transformador de CA directa *m*; ~ **access** *n* COMP&DP, ELEC ENG, ELECTRON acceso directo *m*; ~ **access memory** *n* ELEC ENG memoria de acceso directo *f*; ~ **access storage** *n* AmE, ~ **access store** BrE *n* COMP&DP almacenamiento de acceso directo *m*, memoria de acceso directo *f*; ~-**acting overhead camshaft** *n* AUTO, MECH, VEH árbol de levas en culata de acción directa *m*; ~-**acting pump** *n* HYDRAUL, WATER bomba de acción directa *f*; ~ **action pump** *n* HYDRAUL, WATER bomba de acción directa *f*; ~ **address** *n* COMP&DP direccional directo *m*, dirección directa *f*; ~ **addressing** *n* COMP&DP direccionamiento directo *m*; ~ **arc furnace** *n* HEAT horno de arco directo *m*; ~ **axis subtransient electromotive force** *n* ELEC fuerza electromotriz subtransitoria longitudinal *f*, ELEC ENG fuerza electromotriz subtransitoria longtitudinal *f*, PHYS fuerza electromotriz subtransitoria longitudinal *f*; ~ **axis transient electromotive force** *n* ELEC, ELEC ENG, PHYS fuerza electromotriz transitoria longitudinal *f*; ~ **broadcasting by satellite** *n* (*DBS*) TELECOM difusión en directo por satélite *f*, radiodifusión directa via satélite *f*; ~ **broadcast satellite** *n* (*DBS*) TV satélite de difusión en directo *m*; ~ **casting** *n* PROD fundición de primera fusión *f*; ~ **cell** *n* TRANSP célula directa *f*; ~ **cold hydrogen cell** *n* TRANSP pila de hidrógeno con refrigeración directa *f*; ~ **component** *n* ELEC componente continuo *m*; ~ **contact condenser** *n* PROD condensador de contacto directo *m*; ~ **control** *n* MECH ENG control directo *m*; ~ **conversion** *n* FUELLESS conversión directa *f*; ~-**coupled amplifier** *n* ELECTRON amplificador de acoplo directo *m*, amplificador directamente acoplado *m*; ~-**coupled logic** *n* (*DCL*) TELECOM lógica de acoplamiento directo *f*; ~ **coupling** *n* ELEC *AC circuits*, ELEC ENG, ELECTRON, FUELLESS acoplamiento directo *m*; ~ **current** *n* (*DC*) C&G *of flow of glass in furnace* corriente directa *f*, ELEC corriente continua *f* (*CC*), RAIL corriente directa *f* (*CC*); ~ **current component** *n* ELEC componente de corriente continua *f*; ~ **current converter** *n* TELECOM convertidor de corriente continua *m*; ~-**current coupler** *n* TELECOM acoplador de corriente continua *m*; ~ **current distortion** *n* NUCL distorsión por corriente continua *f*; ~-**current generator** *n* ELEC generador de corriente continua *m*; ~ **current traction motor** *n* TRANSP motor de tracción de corriente continua *m*; ~ **current transformer** *n* ELEC transformador de corriente continua *m*; ~ **current voltage source** *n* ELEC fuente de corriente continua *f*, ELEC ENG fuente de corriente continua *f*, generador de tensión de corriente continua *m*; ~ **cycle boiling reactor** *n* NUCL reactor de agua en ebullición de ciclo directo *m*; ~ **data entry** *n* (*DDE*) COMP&DP, ELECTRON entrada directa de datos *f* (*DDE*); ~ **DC converter** *n* ELEC convertidor de CC *m*, transformador de CC *m*; ~ **debit payment** *n* TELECOM pago de cargo directo *m*; ~ **delivery** *n* PROD entrega directa *f*;

~ **dialing in** *AmE*, ~ **dialling in** *BrE* *n* TELECOM marcación directa entrante *f*; ~ **digital control** *n* (*DDC*) COMP&DP, TELECOM control digital directo *m*; ~ **digital interface** *n* (*DDI*) TELECOM comunicación interurbana automática en directo *f*, interfaz digital directa *m*; ~ **disc** *BrE*, ~ **disk** *n* *AmE* OPT disco directo *m*; ~ **distance dialing** *n* *AmE*, ~ **distance dialling** *BrE* *n* TELECOM llamada directa a distancia *f*, marcación directa a distancia *f*; ~ **draught boiler** *n* PROD caldera de llama directa *f*; ~ **drive** *n* MECH ENG accionamiento directo *m*, acoplamiento directo *m*, toma directa *f*, transmisión directa *f*; ~ **drive propeller** *n* AIR TRANSP hélice de propulsión directa *f*; ~ **duplicating film** *n* PHOTO película para duplicación directa *f*; ~ **dye** *n* TEXTIL colorante directo *m*; ~ **electron beam writing** *n* ELECTRON introducción de información directa por haz de electrones *f*; ~ **emulsion** *n* PRINT emulsión directa *f*; ~ **energy conversion** *n* ELEC ENG conversión de energía directa *f*; ~ **expansion** *n* REFRIG expansión directa *f*; ~ **expansion refrigeration system** *n* REFRIG sistema de enfriamiento por expansión directa *m*; ~ **file** *n* COMP&DP archivo directo *m*; ~-**fitting shank** *n* MECH ENG espiga de acoplamiento directo *f*; ~ **flight** *n* AIR TRANSP vuelo directo *m*; ~ **force** *n* MECH ENG fuerza directa *f*; ~ **frequency modulation** *n* ELECTRON modulación de frecuencia directa *f*; ~ **frequency synthesis** *n* ELECTRON síntesis de frecuencia directa *f*; ~ **frequency synthesizer** *n* ELECTRON sintetizador de frecuencia directa *m*; ~ **gravure** *n* PRINT fotograbado directo *m*; ~ **hydrogen-oxygen cell** *n* TRANSP célula directa de oxígeno-hidrógeno *f*; ~ **injection** *n* AUTO, TRANSP inyección directa *f*; ~ **injection engine** *n* AUTO, TRANSP motor de inyección directa *m*; ~ **input** *n* ELECTRON entrada directa *f*; ~ **interception** *n* POLL intercepción directa *f*; ~ **inward dialing** *n* *AmE*, ~ **inward dialling** *BrE* *n* (*DID*) TELECOM marcación directa entrante *f*; ~ **irrigation** *n* HYDROL riego directo *m*; ~ **leaching** *n* GAS lixiviación directa *f*; ~ **light** *n* PHOTO luz directa *f*; ~ **line** *n* TELECOM línea directa *f*; ~ **link wiring** *n* TEXTIL instalación eléctrica por enlace directo *f*; ~ **loss** *n* HYDROL pérdida directa *f*; ~ **loudspeaker** *n* ACOUST altavoz directo *m*; ~ **maintenance** *n* NUCL *software* mantenimiento directo *m*; ~ **memory access** *n* (*DMA*) COMP&DP, ELECTRON acceso directo a la memoria *m* (*DMA*); ~ **metal mastering** *n* (*DMM*) PROD matrización de discos *f*; ~ **methanol-air cell** *n* TRANSP célula directa metanol-aire *f*; ~ **modulation** *n* ELECTRON modulación directa *f*; ~ **orbit** *n* SPACE órbita directa *f*; ~ **output** *n* ELECTRON salida directa *f*; ~ **outward dialing** *n* *AmE*, ~ **outward dialling** *BrE* *n* TELECOM marcación directa saliente *f*; ~ **overcurrent release** *n* ELEC *tripping device* aparato de máximo de corriente continua *m*; ~ **pattern generation** *n* ELECTRON generación de estructuras directa *f*; ~ **photonuclear effect** *n* NUCL efecto fotonuclear directo *m*; ~ **piezoelectric effect** *n* ELEC ENG, PHYS efecto piezoeléctrico directo *m*; ~ **poisoning** *n* POLL envenenamiento directo *m*; ~ **positive process** *n* CINEMAT proceso positivo directo *m*; ~-**pouring gate** *n* PROD *in mould* canal de colada en caída directa *m*; ~ **power component** *n* ELEC ENG componente de potencia directa *f*; ~ **print** *n* CINEMAT copia directa *f*; ~ **radiation** *n* FUELLESS radiación directa *f*; ~ **rail fastening** *n* RAIL conexión directa de carriles *f*; ~ **read after write** *n* (*DRAW*) OPT lectura directa después de escritura *f*; ~ **reading** *n* ELEC, MECH ENG lectura directa *f*; ~ **reading instrument** *n* ELEC, INSTR aparato de lectura directa *m*, instrumento de lectura directa *m*; ~ **read-out instrument** *n* ELEC dispositivo de lectura de continua *m*, dispositivo indicador de continua *m*; ~ **runoff** *n* HYDROL escurrimiento directo *m*, inclinación directa *f*; ~ **satellite broadcasting** *n* TELECOM radiodifusión por satélite directa *f*; ~ **screen** *n* PRINT trama directa *f*; ~ **starting** *n* ELEC arranque directo *m*, puesta en marcha directa *f*, ELEC ENG, MECH ENG arranque directo *m*; ~ **strand cable** *n* OPT cable trenzado directo *m*; ~ **stress** *n* MECH ENG esfuerzo longitudinal *m*; ~-**suction skimmer** *n* MAR POLL rasera de succión directa *f*; ~-**to-plate imaging system** *n* PRINT sistema de imagen directa en una plancha *m*; ~-**view storage tube** *n* ELECTRON tubo para la reproducción directa de la imagen *m*; ~ **viewfinder** *n* CINEMAT visor directo *m*; ~ **vision prism** *n* PHYS prisma de visión directa *m*; ~ **voltage regulation** *n* ELEC regulación de tensión continua *f*; ~ **wave** *n* GEOL onda directa *f*; ~ **writing** *n* ELECTRON introducción directa de la información *f*

direct[3] *vt* CINEMAT, TELECOM dirigir

directed: ~ **beam display** *n* ELECTRON visualizador de haz dirigido *m*; ~ **bond** *n* CRYSTALL enlace dirigido *m*

directing *n* ELECTRON dirección *f*; ~ **line** *n* MECH ENG línea direccional *f*

direction: ~ **commutator** *n* ELEC conmutador inversor de marcha *m*; ~-**control valve** *n* MECH ENG válvula de control de dirección *f*; ~ **finder** *n* AIR TRANSP, OCEAN radiogonómetro *m*; ~ **finder aerial** *n* BrE (*cf direction finder antenna AmE*) TRANSP antena de radiogoniómetro *f*; ~ **finder antenna** *n* AmE (*cf direction finder aerial BrE*) TRANSP antena de radiogoniómetro *f*; ~ **finding** *n* (*DF*) AIR TRANSP goniometría *f*, TELECOM goniometría *f*, radiogoniometría *f*; ~-**finding receiver** *n* WATER TRANSP receptor del goniómetro *m*; ~ **of flow** *n* HYDROL dirección de la corriente *f*, dirección del curso *f*; ~ **indicator** *n* AUTO, VEH indicador de dirección *m*, intermitente *m*; ~ **of lay** *n* ELEC *of cable component* dirección del paso del cableado *f*, sentido del paso del cableado *m*; ~ **sign** *n* CONST señal de dirección *f*; ~ **switch** *n* ELEC conmutador inversor de marcha *m*; ~ **of traffic** *n* RAIL sentido del tráfico *m*; ~ **of twist** *n* TEXTIL sentido de la torsión *m*

directional: ~ **aerial** *n* BrE (*cf directional antenna AmE*) SPACE, TELECOM antena direccional *f*, antena directiva *f*, antena dirigida *f*, TV antena bidireccional *f* (*AmL*), antena direccional *f*, antena directiva *f*, antena dirigida *f*; ~ **aid** *n* TRANSP panel informativo de dirección *m*; ~ **antenna** *n* AmE (*cf directional aerial BrE*) SPACE, TELECOM antena direccional *f*, antena directiva *f*, antena dirigida *f*, TV antena bidireccional *f* (*AmL*), antena direccional *f*, antena directiva *f*, antena dirigida *f*; ~ **beam** *n* ELECTRON, TELECOM, TV haz direccional *m*; ~ **beam transmitter** *n* ELECTRON, TELECOM, TV transmisor direccional de un haz *m*; ~ **blue reflectance factor** *n* PAPER factor de reflectancia direccional en el azul *m*; ~ **census** *n* TRANSP censo direccional *m*; ~ **control valve** *n* PROD válvula de maniobra direccional *f*; ~ **coupler** *n* ELEC ENG, PHYS, TELECOM acoplador direccional *m*; ~ **coupler switch** *n* ELEC ENG, PHYS, TELECOM

conmutador del acoplador direccional *m*; ~ **coupling** *n* ELEC ENG, ELECTRON, TELECOM acoplamiento direccional *m*; ~ **detector** *n* TRANSP detector direccional *m*; ~ **drilling** *n* PETR TECH perforación direccional controlada *f*, perforación dirigida *f*; ~ **fabric** *n* GEOL textura direccional *f*; ~ **filter** *n* ELECTRON filtro direccional *m*; ~ **gyro** *n* AIR TRANSP giróscopo direccional *m*, TRANSP brújula giroscópica *f*, giroscopio direccional *m*; ~ **lighting** *n* CINEMAT, PHOTO, TV iluminación direccional *f*; ~ **microphone** *n* ACOUST micrófono direccional *m*; ~ **optical coupler** *n* ELEC ENG, OPT acoplador óptico direccional *m*, acoplamiento óptico direccional *m*, TELECOM acoplador óptico direccional *m*; ~ **pattern** *n* ACOUST modelo direccional *m*; ~ **relay** *n* ELEC, ELEC ENG relé direccional *m*; ~ **response** *n* ELECTRON respuesta direccional *f*; ~ **selectivity** *n* TV selectividad direccional *f*; ~ **stability** *n* AIR TRANSP estabilidad de ruta *f*, SPACE, TRANSP estabilidad contra la guiñada *f*, estabilidad de ruta *f*; ~ **structure** *n* GEOL estructura direccional *f*; ~ **well** *n* PETR TECH pozo direccional *m*, pozo direccional controlado *m*

directionality: ~ **factor** *n* FUELLESS factor direccionador *m* (*Esp*), factor directivo *m* (*AmL*)

directionally: ~-**structured raschel goods** *n pl* TEXTIL géneros raschel estructurados direccionalmente *m pl*

directions *n pl* TEXTIL instrucciones *f pl*, instrucciones de empleo *f pl*; ~ **for use** *n* PACK instrucciones de uso *f pl*, instrucciones de empleo *f pl*

directive *n* COMP&DP directriz *f*

directivity *n* SPACE, TELECOM, TV directividad *f*; ~ **factor** *n* ACOUST factor de directividad *m*; ~ **index** *n* ACOUST índice de directividad *m*

directly[1]: ~-**earthed** *adj* BrE (*cf directly-grounded AmE*) ELEC ENG conectado directo a tierra; ~-**grounded** *adj* AmE (*cf directly-earthed BrE*) ELEC ENG conectado directo a tierra

directly[2]: ~-**heated cathode** *n* ELEC ENG cátodo caldeado directamente *m*

director *n* CINEMAT, SPACE director *m*; ~**'s finder** *n* CINEMAT visor para el director *m*; ~ **of photography** *n* (*DP*) CINEMAT director de fotografía *m*; ~ **valve** *n* PROD válvula directriz *f*

directory *n* COMP&DP, TELECOM directorio *m*; ~ **assistance** *n* AmE (*cf directory enquiries BrE*) TELECOM información del directorio *f*, servicio de información *m*; ~ **control system** *n* TELECOM sistema de control del directorio *m*; ~ **enquiries** *n* BrE (*cf enquiries assistance AmE*) ELECTRON información *f*, servicio de información *m*, TELECOM (*cf directory assistance AmE, cf enquiries service AmE*) información *f*, información del directorio *f*, servicio de información *m*; ~ **information tree** *n* (*DIT*) TELECOM árbol de información del directorio *m*; ~ **number** *n* TELECOM número del directorio *m*; ~ **store** *n* TELECOM almacenamiento en directorio *m*; ~ **user** *n* TELECOM usuario del directorio *m*

dirt *n* C&G polvo *m*, COAL barro *m*, fango *m*, roca estéril *f*, sedimentos *m pl*, tierra de aluvión *f*, tierra excavada *f*; ~ **band** *n* COAL capa de estériles *f*; ~-**packing machine** *n* MINE bateadora de aluviones *f*; ~ **trap** *n* MECH ENG *for pipeline, valve, fitting* colector de impurezas *m*, colector de sedimentos *m*

dirty: ~ **shoulder** *n* C&G hombro sucio *m*; ~-**water pump** *n* NUCL bomba de aguas residuales *f*

DIS *abbr* (*draft international standard*) COMP&DP, TELECOM borrador de norma internacional *m*
disable *vt* COMP&DP desactivar, neutralizar, ELEC ENG desactivar, deshabilitar
disabled: ~ **equipment** *n* TELECOM equipo inhabilitado *m*
disabling *n* ELEC ENG, COMP&DP desactivación *f*
disaccharide *n* CHEM disacárido *m*
disappearing: ~~**filament pyrometer** *n* PHYS pirómetro de filamento desvanecedor *m*
disarm¹ *vt* MILIT desactivar, desarmar
disarm² *vti* COMP&DP desarmar
disassemble *vt* COMP&DP abatir, desensamblar, MECH ENG abatir, desarmar, desmontar
disassembler *n* COMP&DP desensamblador *m*
disassembly *n* COMP&DP, MECH ENG abatimiento *m*, desarme *m*, desmontaje *m*
disbudding *n* AGRIC desbrote *m*
disc *n* BrE AIR TRANSP disco *m*, MECH ENG disco *m*, platillo *m*, PACK, TV disco *m*; ~ **aerial** *n* BrE (*cf disk antenna AmE*) TELECOM, TV antena de disco *f*; ~ **area** *n* BrE AIR TRANSP área del disco *f*; ~ **armature** *n* BrE ELEC, ELEC ENG inducido de anillo plano *m*, inducido de disco *m*; ~ **brake** *n* BrE AUTO, MECH, MECH ENG, VEH freno de disco *m*; ~ **brake calliper** *n* BrE RAIL calibrado del freno de disco *m*, frenos de zapatas *m pl*, VEH frenos de zapatas *m pl*; ~ **brake pad** *n* BrE AUTO forro del freno de disco *m*, pastilla del freno de disco *f*, MECH, VEH forro del freno de disco *m*; ~ **brake tools** *n pl* BrE AUTO, VEH herramientas del freno de disco *f*; ~ **braking system** *n* BrE AUTO, CONST sistema de frenado de disco *m*, sistema de freno de disco *m*; ~ **capacitor** *n* BrE ELEC ENG condensador de disco *m*; ~ **centre wheel** *n* BrE VEH rueda de disco *f*, rueda de plato compacto *f*; ~ **clutch** *n* BrE MECH, VEH embrague de discos *m*, embrague monodisco *m*; ~ **coulter** *n* BrE AGRIC reja circular *f*; ~ **crank** *n* BrE PROD manivela de platillo *f*, manivela de plato *f*; ~ **filter** *n* BrE COAL filtro distribuidor *m*; ~ **grinder** *n* BrE C&G esmeril de disco *m*, PROD rectificador de disco *m*; ~ **grinding** *n* BrE C&G, PROD esmerilado con disco *m*; ~ **harrow** *n* BrE AGRIC grada de discos *f*; ~ **head** *n* BrE OPT cabeza del disco *f*; ~ **key** *n* BrE MECH ENG chaveta circular *f*, chaveta de disco *f*; ~ **loading** *n* BrE AIR TRANSP carga de disco *f*; ~ **mastering** *n* BrE OPT negativización del disco *f*; ~ **mill** *n* BrE COAL, FOOD molino de discos *m*; ~ **piston** *n* BrE HYDRAUL pistón de plato *m*; ~ **platter** *n* BrE OPT bandeja del disco *f*; ~ **player** *n* BrE OPT reproductor de discos *m*; ~ **plough** *n* BrE AGRIC arado de discos *m*; ~ **polishing** *n* BrE C&G pulido con disco *m*; ~ **recorder** *n* BrE ACOUST grabador de discos *m*, ELEC grabador de discos *m*, registrador de disco *m*; ~ **refiner** *n* BrE PAPER refino de discos *m*; ~ **resonator filter** *n* BrE ELECTRON filtro resonador de disco *m*; ~ **sander** *n* BrE CONST, MECH ENG lijadora rotatoria a discos *f*, pulidora a discos *f*, pulidora circular *f*, pulidora de disco *f*; ~ **sanding machine** *n* BrE CONST, MECH ENG máquina lijadora a discos *f*, máquina pulidora circular *f*, máquina pulidora de discos *f*; ~ **sandpapering machine** *n* BrE CONST, PROD lijadora de disco *f*, máquina lijadora de disco *f*; ~ **seal tube** *n* BrE ELECTRON tubo de hermeticidad de disco *m*; ~ **sector** *n* BrE COMP&DP sector de disco *m*; ~ **shutter** *n* BrE CINEMAT, PHOTO obturador de disco *m*; ~ **signal** *n*

BrE RAIL señal de disco *f*; ~ **skimmer** *n BrE* MAR POLL rasera de disco *f*, POLL desescoriador de disco *m*, desnatador de disco *m*, espumador de disco *m*; ~ **tiller** *n BrE* AGRIC grada de discos *f*; ~ **valve** *n BrE* HYDRAUL válvula de disco *f*, válvula distribuidora cilíndrica *f*; ~ **winding** *n BrE* ELEC, ELEC ENG devanado en disco *m*
discard¹ *n* MECH pieza rechazada por defectuosa *f*
discard² *vt* MECH ENG abandonar, desechar, rechazar, PROD, QUALITY rechazar, TEXTIL desechar, rechazar
discharge¹ *n* COAL caudal *m*, desprendimiento *m*, ELEC *of condenser, arc*, ELEC ENG descarga *f*, GEOL caudal *m*, HYDROL descarga *f*, *of a river* canal *m*, MAR POLL descarga *f*, MECH ENG *of pump* impulsión *f*, desagüe *m*, caudal *m*, salida *f*, descarga *f*, NUCL, PHYS descarga *f*, POLL caudal *m*, descarga *f*, RECYCL descarga *f*, vertido *m*, REFRIG impulsión *f*, descarga *f*, TELECOM descarga *f*, WATER descarga *f*, caudal *m*; ~ **at sea** *n* MAR POLL descarga al mar *f*, descarga en la mar *f*, POLL descarga al mar *f*, descarga en el mar *f*; ~ **button** *n* MECH ENG botón de descarga *m*, interruptor de descarga *m*; ~ **canal** *n* WATER canal de descarga *m*; ~ **capacitor** *n* ELEC ENG condensador de descarga *m*; ~ **channel** *n* HYDROL canal de descarga *m*, canal de evacuación *m*; ~ **circuit** *n* ELEC ENG circuito de descarga *m*; ~ **coefficient** *n* FUELLESS coeficiente de descarga *m*; ~ **current** *n* ELEC, ELEC ENG corriente de descarga *f*; ~ **flume** *n* WATER presa de descarga *f*; ~ **head** *n* HYDROL, NUCL altura de descarga *f*, altura de impulsión *f*; ~ **lamp** *n* ELEC lámpara de descarga *f*, ELEC ENG lámpara de descarga luminosa *f*, lámpara de tubo fluorescente *f*; ~ **lift** *n* WATER altura de impulsión *f*; ~ **mass curve** *n* HYDROL curva de volúmenes acumulados en el desagüe *f*; ~ **nozzle** *n* NUCL tobera de descarga *f*; ~ **pipe** *n* RECYCL conducto de descarga *m*, tubería de descarga *f*, tubo de descarga *m*, WATER tubo de descarga *m*, tubo de impulsión *m*; ~ **pond** *n* NUCL piscina de combustible gastado *f* (*Esp*), piscina de combustible quemado *f* (*AmL*); ~ **pressure** *n* MECH ENG, REFRIG presión de descarga *f*; ~ **printing** *n* TEXTIL estampado por corrosión *m*; ~ **rate** *n* RECYCL régimen de descarga *m*, velocidad de descarga *f*; ~ **regulator** *n* FUELLESS, SPACE regulador de descarga *m*; ~ **resistor** *n* ELEC resistencia de descarga *f*; ~ **sluice** *n* WATER esclusa de descarga *f*; ~ **temperature** *n* REFRIG, THERMO temperatura de descarga *f*; ~ **tube** *n* ELECTRON, PHYS tubo de descarga *m*; ~ **valve** *n* HYDRAUL válvula de descarga *f*, válvula de escape *f*, válvula de impulsión *f*, válvula de suministro *f*, MECH ENG, REFRIG válvula de descarga *f*; ~ **velocity** *n* HYDROL velocidad de descarga *f*; ~ **welding** *n* PROD soldadura de descarga *f*
discharge² *vt* MAR POLL descargar, MILIT desembarcar, disparar, POLL descargar, deslastrar, desprender, RECYCL verter, descargar, WATER TRANSP *cargo, ballast* descargar, deslastrar, *slops* efectuar descargas de
discharge³: ~ **into the sea** *vi* HYDROL desembocar en el mar, *rivers* salir al mar
discharged *adj* ELEC, WATER descargado ·
discharging: ~ **arch** *n* CONST arco de descarga *m*
disclination *n* METALL desclinación *f*
discoloration *AmE see* **discolouration** *BrE*
discolouration *n BrE* C&G decoloración *f*

disconformity n GEOL discordancia f, disconformidad f

disconnect[1]: ~ **relay** n ELEC ENG relé de desconexión m; ~ **rod** n NUCL barra de desconexión f; ~ **switch** n ELEC ENG, PROD desconectador m

disconnect[2] vt CHEM, COMP&DP, ELEC ENG, MECH ENG, NUCL, TELECOM desconectar

disconnecting: ~ **switch** n ELEC interruptor de seccionamiento m, seccionador m

disconnection n CHEM, COMP&DP, ELEC ENG, MECH ENG, NUCL, TELECOM desconexión f

disconnector n RAIL disyuntor m

discontinued: ~ **approach** n AIR TRANSP aproximación interrumpida f; ~ **manufacturing** n PROD fabricación discontinua f

discontinuity: ~ **layer** n OCEAN capa de discontinuidad f

discontinuous: ~ **amplifier** n ELECTRON amplificador discontinuo m; ~ **glide** n METALL deslizamiento discontinuo m; ~ **spectrum** n RAD PHYS espectro discontinuo m

discordance n ACOUST, GEOL discordancia f

discovery n PETR TECH descubrimiento m; ~ **shaft** n MINE pozo de exploración m, pozo descubridor m; ~ **well** n PETR TECH pozo descubridor m; ~ **work** n MINE labor de descubrimiento f

discrepancy n MATH, MECH ENG, PHYS discrepancia f

discrete[1] adj COMP&DP, ELECTRON, TELECOM discontinuo, discreto

discrete[2]: ~ **amplifier** n ELECTRON amplificador discreto m; ~ **bipolar transistor** n ELECTRON transistor bipolar discreto m; ~ **capacitor** n ELEC ENG condensador discontinuo m, condensador discreto m; ~ **channel** n TELECOM canal discreto m; ~ **component** n ELEC ENG, TELECOM componente discreto m; ~ **electronic circuit** n ELECTRON circuito electrónico discreto m; ~ **filter** n ELECTRON filtro discreto m; ~ **Fourier transform** n ELECTRON transformación discreta Fourier f, transformada discreta de Fourier f; ~ **frequency** n ELECTRON frecuencia discreta f; ~ **input-output** n PROD entrada y salida discontínuas f pl, entrada y salida discretas f pl; ~ **manufacturing** n PROD fabricación discreta f; ~ **resistor** n ELEC ENG resistencia discreta f; ~ **sampling** n QUALITY muestreo sencillo m; ~ **semiconductor device** n ELECTRON dispositivo semiconductor discreto m; ~ **signal** n ELECTRON señal discreta f

discretionary: ~ **wiring** n ELECTRON instalación discrecional f

discriminant n MECH ENG discriminante m; ~ **function** n MATH función discriminante f

discriminating: ~ **circuit breaker** n ELEC cortocircuito discriminante m; ~ **protective system** n ELEC sistema de protección discriminante m; ~ **relay** n ELEC relé diferenciador m, relé discriminador m, relé selector m; ~ **satellite exchange** n TELECOM central telefónica discriminante de satélite f

discrimination n ELECTRON, MECH ENG, OPT, TELECOM, TV discriminación f

discriminator n ELECTRON, MECH ENG, OPT, TELECOM, TV discriminador m

discussion: ~ **tube arrangement** n INSTR dispositivo del conducto de debate m

disease: ~ **control method** n AGRIC método de control sanitario m; ~ **resistance** n AGRIC resistencia a enfermedades f

disengage vt AUTO desembragar MECH, MECH ENG desembragar, desenganchar, desprender, desunir

disengaging: ~ **gear in front** n MECH ENG engranaje de desembrague delantero m, mecanismo de desembrague delantero m; ~ **lever** n MECH ENG palanca de desembrague f

dish[1] n C&G for roller in manufacture of rolled plate cuchara f, CHEM plato m, vidrio de reloj m, LAB vidrio de reloj m, cápsula f, PHOTO cubeta f; ~ **aerial** n BrE (cf dish antenna AmE) SPACE communications, TELECOM antena de plato f, antena parabólica f; ~ **antenna** n AmE (cf dish aerial BrE) SPACE communications, TELECOM antena de plato f, antena parabólica f; ~~**ended boiler** n HYDRAUL caldera de fondo abombado f; ~ **heater** n PHOTO calentador de cubeta m; ~ **rocker** n PHOTO mecedora de cubetas f; ~ **thermometer** n PHOTO termómetro para cubetas m

dish[2] vt PROD embutir

disharmonic adj GEOL disarmónico

dished[1] adj MECH abombado, ahuecado, cóncavo, embutido

dished[2]: ~ **bottom** n NUCL casquete inferior m; ~ **head** n MECH cabeza embutida f; ~ **washer** n MECH ENG arandela acopada f; ~ **wheel** n PROD muela abrasiva de cubeta f

dishing: ~ **shallow depression** n NUCL extremo embutido m

dishpan n TV deflector parabólico m; ~ **spacer** n MECH ENG espaciador acopado m, separador de plato m

disilane n CHEM disilano m

disincrustant n PROD for boiler desincrustante m

disinfect vt HYDROL, SAFE, WATER desinfectar

disinfectant n HYDROL, SAFE, WATER desinfectante m

disinfection n HYDROL, SAFE, WATER desinfección f

disinfest vt SAFE desinfestar

disintegrate vi PART PHYS, PHYS, RAD PHYS desintegrarse

disintegration: ~ **energy** n PART PHYS, PHYS, RAD PHYS energía de desintegración f

disintegrator n FOOD desintegrador m, PROD disgregador m, molino desintegrador m

disjoint[1] adj MATH disjunto, inconexo

disjoint[2] vt MECH ENG desarticular, desconectar

disjointing n MECH ENG desarticulación f, desarticulado m

disjunction n COMP&DP disyunción f, ELECTRON disgregación f

disk[1] n AmE see disc BrE

disk[2]: ~~**resident** adj COMP&DP residente en disco

disk[3] n COMP&DP disco m; ~ **cartridge** n COMP&DP cartucho de disco m; ~ **controller** n COMP&DP controlador de disco m; ~ **drive** n COMP&DP unidad de disco f; ~ **file** n COMP&DP archivo de disco m; ~ **operating system** n (DOS) COMP&DP sistema operativo de discos m (DOS); ~ **pack** n COMP&DP pila de discos f; ~ **unit** n COMP&DP, PRINT, TELECOM unidad de disco f

diskette n COMP&DP, PRINT, TELECOM disquete m; ~ **drive** n COMP&DP, PRINT, TELECOM unidad de disquete f

dislevelment n CONST desnivel m

dislocation n CRYSTALL, GEOPHYS, METALL dislocación f; ~ **annihilation** n METALL aniquilación de la dislocación f; ~ **core** n METALL núcleo de dislocación

m; ~ **debris** *n* METALL residuos de dislocación *m pl*;
~ **density** *n* METALL densidad de dislocación *f*;
~ **junction** *n* METALL unión de la dislocación *f*;
~ **kink** *n* METALL alabeamiento por dislocación *m*,
pliegue de dislocación *m*; ~ **line** *n* CRYSTALL línea de
dislocación *f*, zona de dislocación *f*; ~ **loop** *n*
CRYSTALL bucle de dislocación *m*; ~ **velocity** *n* ME-
TALL velocidad de dislocación *f*; ~ **wall** *n* CRYSTALL
pared de dislocación *f*

dismantle *vt* MECH ENG, MILIT desarmar, desmontar

dismantlement *n* MECH ENG, MILIT desmontaje *m*

dismantling *n* MECH ENG desarmado *m*, desmontado
m, desmontaje *m*, NUCL desmantelamiento *m*, *screen*
desmontaje *m*; ~ **chamber** *n* CONST taller de desmontaje *m*

dismast *vti* WATER TRANSP desarbolar

dismasting *n* WATER TRANSP desarbole *m*

dismount[1] *n* MECH ENG desmontaje *m*

dismount[2] *vt* MECH ENG desmontar

dismutation *n* CHEM dismutación *f*

disorder *n* METALL irregularidad *f*

disordered: ~ **chain** *n* CHEM *of polymer* cadena
desordenada *f*, cadena irregular *f*

disorientation *n* METALL desorientación *f*

dispatch *vt* PROD, TRANSP despachar

dispatcher *n* COMP&DP despachador *m*, distribuidor
m, TRANSP expedidor *m*, repartidor *m*

dispatching *n* PROD, TRANSP distribución *f*; ~ **cold
store** *n* REFRIG acumulación de frío para su
distribución *f*

dispenser *n* FOOD dosificador *m*, vertedero *m*, vertedor *m*, LAB surtidor *m*, PACK distribuidor *m*;
~ **cathode** *n* ELEC ENG cátodo emisor *m*, cátodo
suministrador *m*

dispensing *n* PACK, TEXTIL distribución *f*; ~ **machine** *n*
PACK dispensadora *f*, máquina distribuidora *f*

dispersant *n* CHEM agente dispersante *m*, CHEM TECH
agente dispersante *m*, disolvente *m*, dispersante *m*,
FOOD, HYDROL agente dispersante *m*, PETR TECH,
POLL agente dispersante *m*, disolvente *m*, dispersante
m; ~ **spraying** *n* MAR POLL aspersión del dispersante *f*

disperse: ~ **dye** *n* TEXTIL colorante disperso *m*

dispersed *adj* CHEM, TELECOM disperso

dispersing: ~ **agent** *n* CHEM, CHEM TECH agente
dispersante *m*, COAL medio dispersante *m*, FOOD,
HYDROL agente dispersante *m*, P&R dispersante *m*,
PETR TECH, POLL agente dispersante *m*

dispersion *n* GEN dispersión *f*; ~ **coefficient** *n* CHEM
TECH coeficiente de dispersión *m*; ~ **cone** *n* CHEM
TECH cono de dispersión *m*; ~-**cooled reactor** *n*
NUCL reactor refrigerado por dispersión *m*;
~ **equation** *n* PHYS ecuación de dispersión *f*; ~ **fuel**
n NUCL combustible disperso *m*; ~ **grating** *n* CHEM
TECH rejilla de dispersión *f*; ~ **hardening** *n* METALL
endurecimiento por dispersión *m*; ~ **kneader** *n* CHEM
TECH amasador dispersador *m*; ~ **paint** *n* COLOUR
pintura de dispersión *f*; ~ **relation** *n* PHYS relación de
dispersión *f*; ~ **strengthening** *n* CHEM TECH reforzamiento por dispersión *m*; ~ **test** *n* GAS prueba de
dispersión *f*; ~ **train** *n* NUCL tren de dispersión *m*

dispersive: ~ **delay line** *n* ELECTRON línea de retardo
dispersora *f*; ~ **medium** *n* CHEM TECH, PHYS medio
dispersivo *m*; ~ **power** *n* PHYS poder dispersor *m*

dispersivity *n* CHEM TECH dispersividad *f*

dispersoid *n* CHEM TECH dispersoide *m*

displace *vt* ELEC ENG decalar, desplazar

displaced[1] *adj* MECH ENG desajustado, descentrado,
desplazado, NUCL, SPACE desplazado

displaced[2]: ~ **threshold** *n* AIR TRANSP *of runway*
humbral desplazado *m*

displacement *n* ACOUST desplazamiento *m*, elongación *f*, AUTO desplazamiento *m*, COMP&DP *of
addresses* desplazamiento *m*, reemplazo *m*, ELEC
ENG decalaje *m*, GEOL, GEOPHYS, MECH ENG, PHYS,
WATER, WATER TRANSP desplazamiento *m*; ~ **current**
n ELEC *Maxwell's equations, dielectric*, ELEC ENG,
PHYS corriente de desplazamiento *f*; ~ **error** *n* AIR
TRANSP error de desplazamiento *m*; ~ **fan** *n* PROD
ventilador estático *m*; ~ **phase** *n* ELEC fase de
desplazamiento *f*; ~ **spike** *n* NUCL zona de desplazamientos *f*; ~ **thickness** *n* MECH ENG espesor de
desplazamiento *m*; ~ **variable** *n* SPACE variable de
desplazamiento *f*, variable de desviación *f*; ~ **vector** *n*
ELEC vector desplazamiento *m*

display[1] *n* COMP&DP pantalla *f*, presentación *f*, visualización *f*, ELEC presentación *f*, presentación visual *f*,
representación *f*, visualización *f*, PACK expositor *m*,
PRINT composición *f*, presentación *f*, SPACE pantalla *f*,
representación visual *f*, TELECOM visualizador *m*,
TEXTIL escaparate *m*, exhibición *f*, TRANSP expositor
m, WATER TRANSP presentación *f*; ~ **adaptor** *n*
COMP&DP adaptador de pantalla *m*, PACK
caja expositora *f*; ~ **brilliance** *n* AIR TRANSP, WATER
TRANSP *radar* brillo *m*, brillo de la imagen *m*; ~ **case**
n REFRIG mostrador *m*, vitrina *f*; ~ **console** *n*
COMP&DP consola de visualización *f*; ~ **controller** *n*
COMP&DP controlador de pantalla *m*, controlador de
visualización *m*; ~ **device** *n* COMP&DP dispositivo de
visualización *m*; ~ **driver** *n* COMP&DP controlador de
visualización *m*, impulsor de visualización *m*; ~ **face**
n PRINT tipo para titulares *m*; ~ **format** *n* NUCL
formato de presentación visual *m*, PROD formato de
visualización *m*; ~ **menu** *n* COMP&DP menú de
pantalla *m*, menú de visualización *m*; ~ **packaging**
n PACK embalaje expositor *m*; ~ **processor** *n*
COMP&DP procesador de pantalla *m*, procesador de
visualización *m*; ~ **retention** *n* ELECTRON retención
de visualización *f*; ~ **screen** *n* ELECTRON pantalla de
visualización *f*, TELECOM pantalla luminosa *f*;
~ **setting** *n* COMP&DP ajuste de visualización *m*,
parámetro de visualización *m*; ~ **storage tube** *n*
ELECTRON tubo de retención de imagen *m*; ~ **terminal**
n SPACE terminal de representación visual *f*; ~ **tube** *n*
ELECTRON tubo de visualización *m*; ~ **type** *n* PRINT *in
WYSIWYG system* tipo en pantalla *m*; ~ **window** *n*
C&G vitrina *f*

display[2] *vt* COMP&DP mostrar, visualizar, ELECTRON
visualizar, SPACE presentar en pantalla, representar,
TELECOM visualizar, TEXTIL exhibir

displayed: ~ **speed system** *n* TRANSP sistema de
velocidad visualizada *m*; ~ **waveform** *n* ELECTRON
forma de onda visualizada *f*

disposable: ~ **protective clothing** *n* SAFE prendas
protectoras desechables *f pl*; ~ **syringe** *n* LAB jeringa
desechable *f*

disposal *n* MAR POLL eliminación *f*; ~ **site** *n* CONST
escombrera *f*, vertedero *m*; ~ **tank** *n* SPACE *spacecraft*
cubo de desechos *m*, tanque de desechos *m*

disruption *n* NUCL disrupción *f*

disruptive[1] *adj* ELEC ENG disruptivo, MINE rompedor

disruptive[2]: ~ **discharge** *n* ELEC ENG descarga disruptiva *f*; ~ **strength** *n* ELEC ENG, PHYS resistencia

dieléctrica *f*; ~ **voltage** *n* ELEC tensión disruptiva *f*, ELEC ENG voltaje de la descarga disruptiva *m*

dissecting: ~ **microscope** *n* INSTR microscopio de disección *m*; ~ **scissors** *n pl* LAB pinzas de disección *f pl*; ~ **tray** *n* LAB bandeja de disección *f*

dissection *n* GEOM, LAB disección *f*; ~ **needle** *n* LAB aguja de disección *f*

dissector: ~ **tube** *n* TV tubo disector *m*

dissipated: ~ **power** *n* ELEC energía disipada *f*, potencia disipada *f*

dissipation *n* ELEC, ELEC ENG degradación de la energía *f*, derroche *m*, RAD PHYS disipación *f*; ~ **coefficient** *n* PHYS coeficiente de disipación *m*; ~ **factor** *n* ELEC, PHYS factor de disipación *m*

dissipative: ~ **loss** *n* ELEC ENG, ELECTRON, PHYS pérdida por disipación *f*; ~ **medium** *n* PHYS medio disipativo *m*

dissociable *adj* CHEM, COAL, CRYSTALL, GAS disociable

dissociate *vi* CHEM, COAL, CRYSTALL, GAS disociar

dissociated *adj* CHEM, COAL, CRYSTALL, GAS disociado

dissociation *n* CHEM, COAL, CRYSTALL, GAS *of defect* disociación *f*; ~ **constant** *n* CHEM constante de disociación *f*, constante de ionización *m*; ~ **energy** *n* GAS energía de disociación *f*

dissolubility *n* CHEM, CHEM TECH disolubilidad *f*, solubilidad *f*

dissolution *n* CHEM, CHEM TECH disolución *f*

dissolve[1] *n* CINEMAT disolvencia *f*

dissolve[2] *vt* CHEM, CINEMAT, GAS disolver

dissolve[3]: ~ **away** *vi* CHEM TECH disolver; ~ **out** *vi* CHEM TECH desvanecer

dissolved[1] *adj* CHEM, POLL disuelto

dissolved[2]: ~ **gas** *n* GAS gas disuelto *m*; ~ **inorganic carbon** *n* POLL carbono inorgánico disuelto *m*; ~ **organic carbon** *n* POLL carbono orgánico disuelto *m*; ~ **organic matter** *n* POLL materia orgánica disuelta *f*; ~ **oxygen** *n* (*DO*) POLL oxígeno disuelto *m* (*OD*)

dissolvent *n* CHEM, CHEM TECH disolvente *m*

dissolver *n* CHEM, CHEM TECH disolvente *m*

dissolving *n* CHEM disolución *f*; ~ **pulp** *n* PAPER pasta noble *f*, pulpa para disolver *f*; ~ **shutter** *n* CINEMAT, PHOTO obturador para fundidos *m*; ~ **tank** *n* PAPER disolvedor *m*

dissonance *n* ACOUST, WAVE PHYS disonancia *f*

dissymmetric *adj* CHEM, GEOM, MATH disimétrico

dissymmetrical *adj* CHEM, GEOM, MATH disimétrico

dissymmetry *n* CHEM, GEOM, MATH disimetría *f*

distance *n* MATH, MECH ENG, METR, PHYS distancia *f*; ~ **apart** *n* MECH ENG distancia de separación *f*; ~ **bar** *n* MECH ENG barra de distancia *f*, barra separadora *f*; ~ **between centers** *AmE see* distance between centres *BrE*; ~ **between centers of journals** *AmE see* between centres of journals *BrE*, ~ **between centres** *BrE n* MECH ENG distancia entre centros *f*, distancia entre puntos *f*; ~ **between centres of journals** *n BrE* MECH ENG distancia entre centros de chumacera *f*, distancia entre centros de cojinete *f*, distancia entre centros de muñones *f*; ~ **of drill from column** *n* MECH ENG distancia de la broca a la columna *f*; ~ **finder** *n* WATER TRANSP *sonar, asdic* indicador de distancias *m*; ~-**measuring equipment** *n* (*DME*) AIR TRANSP, METR equipo de medición de distancias *m*; ~ **meter** *n* CINEMAT indicador de distancias *m*; ~ **piece** *n* CONST *between bars of grate* distancia *f*, vano *m*, MECH ENG espaciador *m*, pieza de separación *f*;

~ **piece spacer** *n* MECH ENG espaciador *m*, pieza de separación *f*; ~ **relay** *n* ELEC relé de distancia *m*, relé de protección de distancia *m*; ~ **scale** *n* CINEMAT, PHOTO escala de distancias *f*; ~ **switch** *n* ELEC conmutador de distancia *m*

distant: ~ **caution signal** *n* RAIL señal avanzada de precaución *f*; ~ **collision** *n* NUCL colisión lejana *f*; ~ **field** *n* TELECOM campo distante *m*; ~ **source** *n* POLL fuente distante *f*; ~ **water fishing** *n* OCEAN pesca de altura *f*; ~ **water supply** *n* HYDROL, WATER abastecimiento de agua de altura *m*

distemper[1] *n* COLOUR diluyente *m*, P&R templa *f*, PROD pintura al temple *f*, temple *m*

distemper[2] *vt* COLOUR diluir

distensional: ~ **fault** *n* GEOL falla distensiva *f*

disthene *n* MINERAL cianita *f*, distena *f*

distil *vt BrE* CHEM, CHEM TECH, HYDROL, THERMO, VEH destilar; ~ **off** *vt BrE* CHEM extraer por destilación, CHEM TECH, HYDROL destilar, THERMO extraer por destilación, separar por destilación

distill *AmE see* distil *BrE*

distillate *n* CHEM, CHEM TECH, PETR TECH, THERMO destilado *m*

distillation *n* CHEM *product* destilación *f*, CHEM TECH destilado *m*, PETR TECH, THERMO *product* destilación *f*; ~ **by ascent** *n* CHEM TECH destilación por ascensión *f*, THERMO destilación por elevación de temperatura *f*, destilación por subida de temperatura *f*; ~ **by descent** *n* CHEM TECH destilación por caída *f*, THERMO destilación por bajada de temperatura *f*, destilación por caída de temperatura *f*; ~ **chamber** *n* CHEM TECH cámara de destilación *f*; ~ **flask** *n* CHEM, CHEM TECH, LAB, THERMO matraz de destilación *m*; ~ **gas** *n* CHEM, CHEM TECH, GAS, THERMO gas de destilación *m*; ~ **range** *n* CHEM, THERMO producto de destilación *m*; ~ **retort** *n* CHEM, LAB, THERMO retorta de destilación *f*; ~ **tail** *n* CHEM, CHEM TECH, THERMO cola de destilación *f*; ~ **test** *n* CHEM, CHEM TECH prueba por destilación *f*; ~ **tower** *n* CHEM TECH, PETR TECH, THERMO torre de destilación *f*

distilled *adj* CHEM, CHEM TECH, HYDROL, THERMO, VEH destilado

distiller *n* CHEM, CHEM TECH aparato de destilación *m*, destilador *m*, LAB aparato de destilación *m*

distillery: ~ **residue** *n* FOOD residuo de destilería *m*

distilling: ~ **apparatus** *n* CHEM, CHEM TECH, LAB aparato de destilación *m*; ~ **column** *n* CHEM, CHEM TECH columna de destilación *f*; ~ **flask** *n* CHEM, CHEM TECH matraz de destilación *m*; ~ **tower** *n* CHEM TECH torre de destilación *f*; ~ **tube** *n* CHEM, CHEM TECH tubo de destilación *m*

distorted[1] *adj* ELECTRON deformado

distorted[2]: ~ **wave method** *n* NUCL método de ondas distorsionadas *m*

distorting[1] *adj* C&G *mirror* distorsionante

distorting[2]: ~ **lens** *n* INSTR, OPT lente deformante *m*

distortion *n* ACOUST, ELEC, ELECTRON distorsión *f*, MECH ENG, P&R deformación *f*, PHYS, TELECOM, TV distorsión *f*; ~ **lens** *n* CINEMAT, OPT, PHOTO, TV lente de distorsión *f*; ~-**limited operation** *n* TELECOM operación de distorsión limitada *f*

distress[1]: **in** ~ *adj* WATER TRANSP en peligro, siniestro

distress[2]: ~ **alert** *n* WATER TRANSP alerta de una situación de peligro *f*; ~ **alerting** *n* TELECOM señal de socorro *f*; ~ **beacon** *n* SPACE baliza de llamada de atención *f*, baliza de señalización *f*, WATER TRANSP radiobaliza de localización de siniestros *f*; ~ **call** *n* AIR TRANSP llamada de socorro *f*; ~ **flare** *n* WATER TRANSP bengala para señales de socorro *f*; ~ **radio call system** *n* TELECOM sistema de llamadas de socorro radiotelefónicas *m*; ~ **signal** *n* AIR TRANSP, WATER TRANSP señal de socorro *f*

distributary: ~ **channel** *n* GEOL canal distributario *m*

distribute *vt* COMP&DP, PROD repartir

distributed[1] *adj* COMP&DP, PROD repartido

distributed[2]: ~ **architecture** *n* COMP&DP arquitectura distribuida *f*; ~ **array processor** *n* COMP&DP procesador de matriz distribuida *m*, procesador matricial distribuido *m*; ~ **capacitance** *n* ELEC ENG capacitancia distribuida *f*; ~ **control system** *n* PROD, TELECOM sistema de control distribuido *m*; ~ **data processing** *n* (*DDP*) COMP&DP informática distribuida *f*, procesamiento de datos distribuidos *m*; ~ **database** *n* COMP&DP, ELECTRON, TELECOM base de datos distribuida *f*; ~ **digital processing** *n* NUCL procesamiento digital distribuido *m*; ~ **element circuit** *n* ELEC ENG circuito elemental distribuido *m*; ~ **inductance** *n* ELEC ENG autoinducción distribuida *f*; ~ **multiantenna system** *n* TELECOM sistema distribuido multi-antena *m*; ~ **network** *n* COMP&DP red distribuida *f*, red repartida *f*; ~ **operating system** *n* COMP&DP sistema operativo distribuido *m*; ~ **PBX** *n* TELECOM central telefónica privada distribuida *f*; ~ **processing** *n* COMP&DP procesamiento distribuido *m*, PROD proceso distribuido *m*

distributing *n* HYDRAUL distribución *f*; ~ **board** *n* ELEC, VEH cuadro de distribución *m*, tablero de distribución *m*; ~ **canal** *n* WATER canal de distribución *m*; ~ **pipe** *n* NUCL línea de distribución *f*, WATER cañería de distribución *f*, tubería de distribución *f*

distribution *n* GEN distribución *f*; ~ **amplifier** *n* ELECTRON, TELECOM, TV amplificador de distribución *m*; ~ **board** *n* ELEC ENG cuadro de distribución *m*, panel de distribución *m*, TELECOM cuadro de distribución *m*; ~ **box** *n* ELEC caja de derivación *f*, caja de distribución *f*, ELEC ENG caja de distribución *f*; ~ **bus** *n* ELEC barra de distribución *f*; ~ **cabinet** *n* ELEC ENG armario de distribución *m*; ~ **cable** *n* ELEC, ELEC ENG cable de distribución *m*; ~ **center** *AmE*, ~ **centre** *BrE* *n* ELEC centro de distribución *m*; ~ **chain** *n* TRANSP cadena de distribución *f*; ~ **chamber** *n* MECH ENG cámara de distribución *f*; ~ **diagram** *n* HYDROL, MECH ENG diagrama de distribución *m*; ~ **of electricity** *n* ELEC distribución de electricidad *f*; ~ **frame** *n* TELECOM marco repartidor *m*; ~ **function** *n* MATH función de distribución *f*; ~ **fuse board** *n* ELEC cuadro de fusibles de distribución *m*; ~ **list** *n* (*DL*) TELECOM lista de distribución *f*; ~ **network** *n* CONST, ELEC, ELEC ENG, TELECOM red de distribución *f*; ~ **primary link** *n* (*DPL*) TELECOM enlace principal de distribución *m*; ~ **ring** *n* NUCL anillo de distribución *m*; ~ **stage** *n* TELECOM etapa de distribución *f*; ~ **station** *n* ELEC ENG central de distribución *f*; ~ **steel** *n* CONST armadura de distribución *f*; ~ **substation** *n* ELEC,ELEC ENG subestación de distribución *f*; ~ **system** *n* ELEC, ELEC ENG, GAS, WATER red de distribución *f*, sistema de distribución *m*; ~ **technique** *n* PACK técnica de distribución *f*; ~ **valve** *n* MECH ENG válvula de distribución *f*

distributive: ~ **fault** *n* GEOL falla distributiva *f*

distributor *n* AUTO, ELEC, MECH, MECH ENG distribuidor *m*, PACK distribuidor *m*, repartidor *m*, VEH distribuidor *m*; ~ **arm** *n* AUTO, VEH pipa del distribuidor *f*; ~ **cam** *n* VEH leva del distribuidor *f*; ~ **cap** *n* AUTO tapa del distribuidor *f*, VEH tapa del ruptor *f*; ~**clamp bolt** *n* AUTO abrazadera del distribuidor *f*, tornillo de fijación del distribuidor *m*; ~ **drive** *n* VEH mecanismo de accionamiento del distribuidor *m*; ~ **finger** *n* AUTO dedo del distribuidor *m*; ~ **housing** *n* AUTO, VEH alojamiento del distribuidor *m*; ~ **injection pump** *n* AUTO bomba de inyección con distribuidor *f*; ~ **roll** *n* PAPER rodillo distribuidor *m*; ~ **rotor** *n* AUTO, VEH rotor del distribuidor *m*; ~ **shaft** *n* AUTO, VEH eje del distribuidor *m*; ~ **suppressor** *n* VEH resistencia antiparasitaria del distribuidor *f*, supresor del distribuidor *m*

district: ~ **heating** *n* HEAT calefacción por distritos *f*, THERMO calefacción centralizada *f*; ~ **heating station** *n* THERMO estación de calefacción centralizada *f*

disturb *vt* CONST, METEO, PETROL perturbar

disturbance *n* METEO, PETROL perturbación *f*

disturbed: ~ **compass** *n* WATER TRANSP aguja loca *f*; ~ **field** *n* METEO campo inestable *m*, campo perturbado *m*

disulfide *AmE see* disulphide *BrE*

disulphide *n* *BrE* CHEM bisulfuro *m*, disulfuro *m*

disused: ~ **quarry** *n* MINE cantera abandonada *f*

DIT *abbr* (*directory information tree*) TELECOM árbol de información del directorio *m*

ditch *n* AIR TRANSP aterrizaje forzoso *m*, COAL acequia *f*, aspirador *m* (*Esp*), canal *m*, canaleta *f* (*AmL*), cuneta *f*, foso *m*, trinchera *f*, zanja *f*, CONST aspirador *m* (*Esp*), canaleta *f* (*AmL*), HYDROL aspirador *m* (*Esp*), canaleta *f* (*AmL*), foso *m*, zanja *f*, PETROL aspirador *m* (*Esp*), calicata *f*, canaleta *f* (*AmL*) cuneta *f*, WATER acequia *f*, aspirador *m* (*Esp*), canaleta *f* (*AmL*), foso *m*, trinchera *f*, zanja *f*; ~ **canal** *n* WATER canal a nivel *m*; ~ **drainage** *n* HYDROL drenaje mediante zanjas *m*; ~ **irrigation** *n* AGRIC, HYDROL, WATER irrigación por acequias *f*; ~ **line** *n* WATER línea de fosos *f*

ditcher *n* CONST zanjadora *f*

ditching *n* AIR TRANSP aterrizaje forzoso *m*

dither *n* ELECTRON oscilación de pequeña amplitud *f*; ~ **oscillator** *n* ELECTRON oscilador de pequeña amplitud *m*

dithering *n* COMP&DP *graphics* motivo de tramado *m*

dithiobenzoic: ~ **acid** *n* CHEM ácido ditiobenzoico *m*

dithionate *n* CHEM ditionato *m*

dithionic: ~ **acid** *n* CHEM ácido ditiónico *m*

diurnal[1] *adj* GEOPHYS, METEO diurno

diurnal[2]: ~ **tide** *n* OCEAN onda diurna *f*, WATER TRANSP marea diurna *f*; ~ **variation** *n* WATER TRANSP marea barométrica *f*, variación diaria *f*; ~ **wave** *n* OCEAN onda diurna *f*

divalence *n* CHEM divalencia *f*

divalent *adj* CHEM divalente

dive[1] *n* AIR TRANSP picado *m*, SPACE buceo *m*, inmersión *f*, picado *m*, sumersión *f*

dive[2] *vi* AIR TRANSP, SPACE picar

diver *n* OCEAN, PETR TECH buzo *m*

divergence *n* AIR TRANSP, MATH, NUCL, OPT, PHYS, SPACE divergencia *f*

divergent[1] *adj* AIR TRANSP, MATH, NUCL, OPT, PHYS, SPACE divergente

divergent[2]: ~ **lens** *n* CINEMAT, INSTR, OPT, PHOTO, PHYS lente divergente *f*; ~ **meniscus** *n* PHOTO menisco divergente *m*; ~ **nozzle** *n* PHYS tobera divergente *f*; ~ **plate boundary** *n* GEOL límite de placas divergentes *m*

diverging *n* TRANSP divergente *m*; ~ **lens** *n* CINEMAT, INSTR, OPT, PHOTO, PHYS lente divergente *f*; ~ **volume** *n* TRANSP volumen divergente *m*

diver: ~'**s cramp** *n* OCEAN calambres *m pl*

diversion *n* TRANSP desviación *f*, WATER derivación *f*, desviación *f*; ~ **canal** *n* HYDROL canal de derivación *m*, WATER canal de derivación *m*, canal de desviación *m*, canal desviador *m*; ~ **channel** *n* HYDROL canal de derivación *m*; ~ **cut** *n* HYDROL paso de derivación *m*; ~ **dam** *n* HYDROL presa de derivación *f*, WATER dique de desvío *m*; ~ **sluice** *n* WATER esclusa de desviación *f*; ~ **tunnel** *n* HYDROL túnel de derivación *m*

divert *vt* CONST desviar, derivar

diverter *n* PETR TECH desviador *m*, desviador de flujo *m*

diverting *n* WATER *of river, stream* desviación *f*, desvío *m*

divide[1]: ~ **circle** *n* INSTR círculo divisorio *m*

divide[2] *vt* COMP&DP, MATH dividir

divided: ~ **beam** *n* METR balancín graduado *m*; ~ **circle** *n* GEOM círculo dividido *m*; ~ **dial** *n* MECH ENG cuadrante graduado *m*; ~ **highway** *n* AmE (*cf dual carriageway BrE*) CONST autopista de doble calzada *f*, autopista de dos carriles por sentido *f*, carretera de doble sentido *f*, carretera troncal *f*, TRANSP autopista de doble calzada *f*, autopista de dos carriles por sentido *f*; ~ **pitch** *n* MECH ENG *of screw* paso aparente *m*

dividend *n* COMP&DP, MATH dividendo *m*

divider *n* COMP&DP, ELECTRON divisor *m*, MECH ENG bifurcador *m*, divisor *m*, reductor *m*, separador *m*, PROD separador *m*, TELECOM divisor *m*

dividers *n pl* GEOM divisores *m pl*, METR compás de dividir *m*, compás de medir *m*, compás de puntas secas *m*, MINE travesaños diagonales *m pl*, PROD separadores *m pl*, WATER TRANSP compás de proporción *m*, compás de puntas *m*

dividing: ~ **apparatus** *n* PROD aparato separador *m*; ~ **attachment** *n* MECH ENG dispositivo de separación *m*, dispositivo distribuidor *m*, dispositivo divisor *m*; ~ **box** *n* ELEC caja de derivación *f*; ~ **circle** *n* MECH ENG círculo de contacto *m*, círculo primitivo *m*; ~ **circuit** *n* ELECTRON circuito divisor *m*; ~ **heads** *n pl* MECH ENG cabezales divisores *m pl*; ~ **into compartments** *n* MINE división en compartimientos *f*; ~ **multivibrator** *n* ELECTRON multivibrador de división *m*; ~ **wheel** *n* MECH ENG rueda divisora *f*

diving *n* OCEAN, PETROL buceo *m*; ~ **bell** *n* OCEAN campana de buceo *f*, PETR TECH, PETROL campana de buzo *f*, WATER TRANSP campana de buceo *f*, cámara de salvamento *f*; ~ **brake** *n* AIR TRANSP freno aerodinámico de picado *m*, freno de picado *m*; ~ **cylinder** *n* OCEAN cilindro de buceo *m*; ~ **depth** *n* OCEAN profundidad de buceo *f*; ~ **equipment** *n* PETROL equipo de buceo *m*; ~ **gear** *n* OCEAN equipo de buceo *m*; ~ **helmet** *n* OCEAN casco rígido de buceo *m*; ~ **hood** *n* OCEAN capucha de neopreno *f*; ~ **mask** *n* OCEAN máscara de buceo *f*; ~ **operation** *n* OCEAN operación de buceo *f*; ~ **plate** *n* OCEAN plancha de arrastre de buceo *f*; ~ **rudder** *n* WATER TRANSP timón horizontal *m*; ~ **saucer** *n* OCEAN mini-submarino *m*; ~ **suit** *n* OCEAN traje de buceo *m*, WATER TRANSP ropa aceitada *f*, traje de buzo *m*, traje estanco *m*; ~ **sup-**

port barge *n* OCEAN barco de apoyo al buceo *m*; ~ **tank** *n* OCEAN tanque de buceo *m*

divinyl *n* CHEM divinilo *m*

divisible *adj* MATH divisible

division *n* CONST *partition*, GEOL, MATH división *f*, PHYS *safety* separación *f*; ~**-inserting equipment** *n* PACK equipo para insertar una señal de división *m*; ~ **plate** *n* MECH ENG disco divisor *m*, plato divisor *m*; ~ **point** *n* MECH ENG punto de división *m*, punto de separación *m*; ~ **wheel** *n* MECH ENG rueda de división *f*

divisor *n* COMP&DP, MATH divisor *m*

divorced: ~ **perlite** *n* METALL perlita con cementita esferoidizada *f*, perlita globular *f*, perlita granular *f*

DL *abbr* (*distribution list*) TELECOM lista de distribución *f*

D-layer *n* GEOPHYS, PHYS capa D *f*

DLC *abbr* (*data link connection*) TELECOM conexión para la transmisión de datos *f*

DLCI *abbr* (*data link connection identifier*) TELECOM identificador de conexión para la transmisión de datos *m*, identificador del enlace para la transmisión de datos *m*

DLE *abbr* (*data link escape*) COMP&DP DLE (*escape de enlace de datos*)

D-link *n* RAIL enganche D *m*

DLS *abbr* (*data link service*) TELECOM servicio de transmisión de datos *m*

DM *abbr* AGRIC (*dry matter*) MS (*materia seca*), COMP&DP (*data management*) gestión de datos *f*, TELECOM (*data management*) administración de datos *f*, gestión de datos *f*, (*degraded minute*) minuto degradado *m*

DMA *abbr* CHEM (*dimethylamine*) DMA (*dimetilamina*), COMP&DP, ELECTRON (*direct memory access*) DMA (*acceso directo a la memoria*)

DME *abbr* (*distance-measuring equipment*) AIR TRANSP, METR equipo de medición de distancias *m*

DMF *abbr* (*dimethylformamide*) CHEM DMF (*dimetilformamida*)

DML *abbr* (*data manipulation language*) COMP&DP DML (*lenguaje de manipulación de datos*)

DMM *abbr* (*direct metal mastering*) PROD matrización de discos *f*

DMNSC *abbr* (*digital main network switching center AmE, digital main network switching centre BrE*) TELECOM centro de conmutación digital de la red principal *m*

DMOS[1] *abbr* (*diffuse metal oxide semiconductor*) ELECTRON SOMD (*semiconductor de óxido de metal difuso*)

DMOS[2]: ~ **technology** *n* ELECTRON tecnología de SOMD *f*; ~ **transistor** *n* ELECTRON transistor de SOMD *m*

dN *abbr* (*decineper*) ACOUST, ELECTRON, METR, PHYS, TELECOM, TV dN (*decineperio*)

DN *abbr* (*destination network*) TELECOM red de destino *f*

DNA *abbr* (*deoxyribonucleic acid*) CHEM ADN (*ácido desoxirribonucleico*)

DNB *abbr* (*departure from nuclear boiling*) NUCL apartamiento de la ebullición nucleada *m*

DNC *abbr* (*dinitrocresol*) CHEM DNC (*dinitrocresol*)

DNIC *abbr* (*data network identification code*) TELECOM código identificador de la red de datos *m*

DNT *abbr* (*dinitrotoluene*) CHEM DNT (*dinitrotolueno*)

do: ~ **not drop** *phr* PACK no volcar; ~ **not throw** *phr* PACK no tirar

DO *abbr* (*dissolved oxygen*) CHEM, POLL OD (*oxígeno disuelto*)

dobby *n* TEXTIL maquineta *f*, maquinilla *f*; ~ **weave fabric** *n* TEXTIL tejido de ligamento por maquinita *m*

dock[1] *n* WATER TRANSP dique *m*, dársena *f*; ~ **wall** *n* CONST muro del muelle *m*, WATER TRANSP pared del dique *f*, pared lateral del dique *f*, muro del muelle *m*; ~ **warehouse** *n* WATER TRANSP almacén en los muelles *m*, tinglado *m*; ~ **work** *n* PROD trabajo de muelles *m*

dock[2] *vt* SPACE acortar, atracar, WATER TRANSP atracar, meter en dársena

dock[3] *vi* SPACE acoplarse, WATER TRANSP abordar, entrar en dársena

dockage *n* FOOD abaleo *m*, extracción *f*, WATER TRANSP muellaje *m*

docker *n* BrE (*cf longshoreman AmE*) WATER TRANSP cargador de muelle *m*, estibador *m*, obrero portuario *m*

docket *n* PROD rótulo *m*

docking *n* SPACE acoplamiento *m*, atraque *m*, WATER TRANSP atracada *f*; ~ **adaptor** *n* SPACE adaptador para acoplamiento *m*; ~ **guidance system** *n* AIR TRANSP sistema de guía de aparcamiento *m*; ~ **maneuver** *AmE*, ~ **manoeuvre** *BrE n* WATER TRANSP maniobra de amarre *f*, maniobra de atraque *f*; ~ **piece** *n* SPACE pieza para acoplamiento *f*; ~ **port** *n* SPACE puerta para acoplamiento *f*; ~ **probe** *n* SPACE sonda para acoplamiento *f*; ~ **procedure** *n* AIR TRANSP procedimiento de aparcamiento *m*; ~ **tunnel** *n* SPACE túnel para acoplamiento *m*; ~ **unit** *n* SPACE unidad para acoplamiento *f*

dockyard *n* WATER TRANSP arsenal *m*, arsenal de marina *m*, *shipbuilding* astillero *m*, atarazana *f*

doctor: ~ **blade** *n* PACK rasqueta *f*, PAPER cuchilla *f*, rasqueta *f*, PRINT cuchilla tangente *f*, rasqueta *f*; ~ **roll** *n* PAPER rodillo de rasqueta *m*

docudrama *n* CINEMAT, TV drama documental *m*

document *n* COMP&DP documento *m*; ~ **film** *n* PHOTO película para documentos *f*; ~ **reader** *n* COMP&DP lector de documentos *m*; ~ **reading** *n* COMP&DP lectura de documentos *f*; ~ **retrieval** *n* COMP&DP recuperación de documentos *f*; ~ **sorter** *n* COMP&DP clasificador de documentos *m*

documentary *n* CINEMAT, TV documental *m*; ~ **film-maker** *n* CINEMAT, TV cineasta documental *m*, realizador de documentales *m*; ~ **proof** *n* MAR POLL justificantes *m pl*

DOD *abbr* (*direct outward dialing AmE, direct outward dialling BrE*) TELECOM marcación directa saliente *f*

dodder *n* AGRIC cuscuta *f*

dodecagon *n* GEOM dodecágono *m*

dodecahedral *adj* GEOM dodecaédrico

dodecahedron *n* GEOM dodecaedro *m*

dodecane *n* CHEM, DETERG dodecano *m*

dodecyl: ~ **benzene** *n* CHEM, DETERG dodecilbenceno *m*

dodge *vt* PHOTO puntear

dodgers *n pl* PRINT hojas sueltas *f pl*

doeglic *adj* CHEM doéglico

doffer: ~ **comb** *n* TEXTIL peine desprendedor *m*

doffing *n* TEXTIL mudada *f*; ~ **devices** *n pl* TEXTIL dispositivos de la mudada *m pl*

dog *n* MECH fiador *m*, gancho *m*, grapa *f*, retén *m*,

seguro *m*, trinquete *m*, MECH ENG *lathe-carrier* corazón de arrastre *m*, *pawl* garra *f*, retén *m*, perro *m*, fiador *m*, perro de arrastre *m*, *for lathe faceplate* perro de plato de torno *m*, trinquete *m*, MINE *casing* retén *m* (*Esp*), enganchador *m*, perno *m* (*Esp*), arrancatubos *m* (*AmL*), topes de fin de carrera *m pl*, PROD *for box-lugs* garra *f* (*Esp*), perro *m* (*AmL*); ~ **chuck** *n* MECH ENG *of lathe* plato de garras *m*; ~ **clutch** *n* AUTO embrague de garras *m*, embrague de uñas *m*, MECH ENG acoplamiento de garras *m*, embrague de garras *m*, embrague de uñas *m*, VEH embrague de garras *m*, embrague por dientes *m*; ~ **hook** *n* MECH ENG gancho de apriete *m*, gancho de arrastre *m*, uña de apriete *f*; ~ **hook sling** *n* MECH ENG eslinga de gancho de arrastre *f*; ~ **iron** *n* PROD gancho de unión *m*; ~ **spike** *n* RAIL clavo de uña *m*; ~ **wheel** *n* MECH ENG *on ratchet* rueda de trinquete *f*

doghouse *n* BrE (*cf filling end AmE*) C&G cargador del horno *m*, PETR TECH casa del perforador *f*, caseta *f*, casa de perro *f*

dogleg *n* PETR TECH pata de perro *f*, PETROL codo *m*, doblez *m*; ~ **stairs** *n pl* CONST escalera cerrada *f*

DOHC: ~ **engine** *n* AUTO motor de doble árbol de levas en cabeza *m*

doldrums *n pl* METEO, OCEAN, WATER TRANSP calmas ecuatoriales *f pl*, zona de calmas ecuatoriales *f*

dolerite *n* (*cf diabase AmE*) GEOL diabasa *f*, dolerita *f*, MINERAL dolerita *f*, PETROL diabasa *f*, dolerita *f*

doleritic: ~ **texture** *n* PETROL textura dolerítica *f*

dolerophane *n* MINERAL dolerofana *f*

dolerophanite *n* MINERAL dolerofanita *f*

doline *n* WATER dolina *f*

dolly[1] *n* C&G carretilla de rodillos *f*, CINEMAT dolly *f*, MECH carretilla *f*, cepillo pulidor *m*, estampa *f*, PROD carretilla *f*, plataforma móvil *f*, *riveting* sufridor *m*, TV dolly *f*; ~ **shot** *n* CINEMAT toma con dolly *f*; ~ **track** *n* CINEMAT vía de la dolly *f*

dolly[2] *vi* CINEMAT efectuar una toma con dolly; ~ **back** *vi* CINEMAT efectuar una toma con dolly, ampliando la imagen; ~ **in** *vi* CINEMAT efectuar una toma con dolly, reduciendo la imagen

dolomite *n* C&G, CHEM, GEOL, MINERAL, PETR TECH, PETROL dolomita *f*; ~ **brick** *n* CONST ladrillo de dolomita *m*

dolomitic: ~ **limestone** *n* GEOL caliza dolomítica *f*

dolostone *n* GEOL dolomía *f*

dolphin *n* WATER TRANSP *mooring post, beacon* duque de alba *m*, muerto de amarre *m*

DOM *abbr* (*digestible organic matter*) RECYCL materia orgánica digestible *f*

domain *n* ELECTRON campo *m*, MATH *of a function*, PHYS dominio *m*; ~ **of integrity** *n* MATH dominio de integridad *m*, dominio entero *m*; ~~**specific part** *n* (*DSP*) TELECOM parte específica del dominio *f*; ~ **structure** *n* METALL, PHYS estructura de dominios *f*

dome *n* C&G cúpula *f*, CONST *of a cock, tap* tapa *f*, *architecture* cúpula *f*, GAS diapiro *m*, domo *m*, bóveda *f*, cúpula *f*, GEOL domo *m*, HYDRAUL bóveda *f*, PETR TECH domo *m*, *of a furnace* bóveda *f*; ~ **cap** *n* PROD sombrerete *m*; ~ **casing** *n* PROD revestimiento cerámico *m*, revestimiento del tambor *m*; ~ **cover** *n* PROD revestimiento cerámico *m*, revestimiento del tambor *m*; ~ **gas** *n* GAS gas de diapiro *m*, gas de domo *m*; ~ **head** *n* PROD culata abovedada *f*; ~ **nut** *n* MECH ENG tuerca abovedada *f*, tuerca en bóveda *f*, tuerca en cúpula *f*, tuerca en domo *f*; ~ **pad** *n* MECH

ENG amortiguador abovedado *m*, disco de taladrar abovedado *m*, portabrocas abovedado *m*; ~ **riveter** *n* HYDRAUL remachadora hidráulica de bóvedas *f*; ~ **roof** *n* CONST techo de la cúpula *m*

domeless: ~ **telescope** *n* INSTR telescopio sin cúpula *m*

domestic: ~ **appliance** *n* ELEC aparato casero *m*, aparato de uso doméstico *m*, aparato doméstico *m*, utensilio para el hogar *m*; ~ **boiler** *n* MECH ENG caldera doméstica *f*; ~ **coal** *n* COAL carbón doméstico *m*; ~ **consumer** *n* ELEC consumidor casero *m*, consumidor doméstico *m*; ~ **electric installation** *n* ELEC, ELEC ENG instalación eléctrica doméstica *f*; ~ **electronic equipment** *n* ELEC ENG equipo electrónico doméstico *m*; ~ **emission** *n* POLL emisión doméstica *f*; ~ **flight** *n* AIR TRANSP vuelo doméstico *m*, vuelo interno *m*; ~ **freezer** *n* REFRIG congelador doméstico *m*; ~ **fuel oil** *n* PETR TECH combustible doméstico *m*, fuel-oil *m*; ~ **gas** *n* GAS gas nacional *m*, gas para el mercado interno *m*, gas para uso doméstico *m*; ~ **gas appliance** *n* GAS, HEAT aparato doméstico a gas *m*; ~ **refrigerator** *n* MECH ENG refrigerador doméstico *m*, REFRIG, THERMO frigorífico doméstico *m*; ~ **service** *n* AIR TRANSP servicio doméstico *m*; ~ **sewage** *n* POLL basura doméstica *f*, RECYCL basura doméstica *f*, residuos domésticos *m pl*, WATER basura doméstica *f*; ~ **sewage system** *n* COAL, HYDROL, POLL, RECYCL, WATER alcantarillado *m*; ~ **waste water** *n* HYDROL aguas residuales de servicios propios *f pl*, POLL aguas negras *f pl*, RECYCL, WATER aguas negras *f pl*, aguas residuales de servicios propios *f pl*; ~ **waste water sewage** *n* HYDROL aguas negras *f pl*; ~ **water** *n* HYDROL agua para servicio propio *f*, aguas cloacales sanitarias *f pl*, RECYCL, WATER aguas cloacales sanitarias *f pl*; ~-**water supply** *n* HYDROL, WATER abastecimiento de agua doméstica *m*

domeykite *n* MINERAL cobre blanco *m*, domeykita *f*
dominant[1] *adj* ACOUST dominante
dominant[2]: ~ **anion** *n* POLL anión predominante *m*, ion negativo predominante *m*; ~ **cation** *n* POLL catión predominante *m*, ion positivo predominante *m*; ~ **mode** *n* ELEC ENG *waveguides*, PHYS *for a funnel* modo dominante *m*

donor *n* CHEM *atom* dador *m*, donante *m*, COMP&DP *chip manufacturing* donador *m*, donante *m*, ELECTRON donador *m*, PART PHYS, PHYS dador *m*; ~ **atom** *n* ELECTRON, PART PHYS, PHYS átomo donador *m*; ~ **impurity** *n* ELECTRON impureza donadora *f*; ~ **level** *n* ELECTRON nivel donador *m*

do-nothing: ~ **instruction** *n* COMP&DP instrucción nula *f*

door *n* PROD VEH puerta *f*; ~ **bar** *n* CONST barra de la puerta *f*; ~ **blocking** *n* RAIL bloqueo de puertas *m*; ~ **bolt** *n* CONST cerrojo de la puerta *m*, tirador de la puerta *m*; ~ **brand** *n* CONST tipo de puerta *m*; ~ **case** *n* CONST marco *m*; ~ **casing** *n* CONST marco *m*, VEH marco de puerta *m*; ~ **catch** *n* VEH pestillo de puerta *m*; ~ **framing** *n* CONST jambaje *m*; ~ **glass** *n* VEH cristal de puerta *m*; ~ **handle** *n* CONST tirador de la puerta *m*, VEH manecilla de la puerta *f*; ~ **hinge** *n* CONST, VEH bisagra de la puerta *f*; ~ **lock** *n* VEH cerradura de puerta *f*; ~ **locking** *n* RAIL, VEH cierre de puertas *m*; ~-**locking mechanism** *n* VEH mecanismo de bloqueo de puerta *m*; ~ **opening** *n* CONST hueco de la puerta *m*, vano de la puerta *m*; ~ **panel** *n* CONST

panel de la puerta *m*; ~ **pillar** *n* VEH montante de puerta *m*; ~ **rack** *n* REFRIG estanterías de compuerta *m*; ~ **sill** *n* CONST *off the ground* solera de la puerta *f*, *resting on ground* umbral de la puerta *m*; ~-**to-door delivery** *n* RAIL entrega a domicilio *f*, transporte puerta a puerta *m*

doorframe *n* CONST marco de la puerta *m*
doorknob *n* CONST tirador de la puerta *m*
doorpost *n* CONST jamba de la puerta *f*
doorway *n* CONST *opening* portal *m*, vano de la puerta *m*

dopamine *n* CHEM dopamina *f*, hidroxitiramina *f*
dopant *n* COMP&DP dopante *m*, ELECTRON adulterante *m*, dopante *m*, átomo dopante *m*, OPT dopante *m*, PHYS adulterante *m*, impurificador *m*
dope[1] *n* COLOUR aditivo *m*, PETROL grasa para rosca *f*, aditivo *m*; ~ **mark** *n* C&G marca de lubricante *f*; ~ **sheet** *n* CINEMAT información de última hora *f*; ~ **station** *n* PETROL estación para recubrir tubería *f*
dope[2] *vt* COLOUR modificar por adición, COMP&DP dopar, ELECTRON adulterar, dopar, OPT dopar, PHYS adulterar, añadir un aditivo a, impurificar, TELECOM dopar
doped[1] *adj* COMP&DP *chip manufacturing* dopado, ELECTRON dopado, adulterado, PHYS impurificado, adulterado
doped[2]: ~ **fiber** *AmE*, ~ **fibre** *BrE n* OPT fibra dopada *f*; ~ **semiconductor** *n* ELECTRON semiconductor dopado *m*; ~ **silica fiber** *AmE*, ~ **silica fibre** *BrE n* OPT, TELECOM fibra de sílice dopada *f*
doping *n* ELECTRON, FOOD, PHYS adulteración *f*, PRINT modificación de las características de la tinta mediante aditivos *f*, TELECOM dopaje *m*; ~ **agent** *n* ELECTRON agente adulterador *m*, agente dopante *m*; ~ **compensation** *n* ELECTRON compensación por dopado *f*, compensación por impurezas *f*; ~ **level** *n* ELECTRON nivel de dopado *m*

Doppler: ~ **bandwidth** *n* ELECTRON ancho de banda Doppler *m*; ~ **broadening** *n* CRYSTALL *of a line* PHYS, RAD PHYS ensanchamiento de una línea espectral *m*, ensanchamiento Doppler *m*; ~ **effect** *n* ELECTRON, NUCL, PETROL, PHYS, RAD PHYS, WAVE PHYS corrimiento Doppler *m*, efecto Doppler *m*; ~ **filter** *n* ELECTRON filtro Doppler *m*; ~ **filtering** *n* ELECTRON filtrado Doppler *m*; ~ **frequency** *n* ELECTRON frecuencia Doppler *f*; ~-**inertial loop** *n* SPACE lazo Doppler-inercial *m*; ~ **modulation** *n* ELECTRON modulación Doppler *f*; ~ **navigation** *n* PETROL, SPACE navegación por efecto Doppler *f*; ~ **shift** *n* PETROL deslizamiento Doppler *m*, variación de la frecuencia por efecto Doppler *f*, SPACE corrimiento Doppler *m*, desplazamiento Doppler *m*; ~ **width** *n* RAD PHYS amplitud Doppler *f*

Doppler-Fizeau: ~ **displacement shift** *n* ACOUST desplazamiento de frecuencia por efecto Doppler-Fizeau *m*; ~ **effect** *n* ACOUST efecto Doppler-Fizeau *m*

dopplerite *n* MINERAL doplerita *f*
dormancy *n* AGRIC latencia *f*
dormant: ~ **lock** *n* CONST pestillo incrustado *m*; ~ **period** *n* AGRIC reposo vegetal *m*; ~ **terminal** *n* COMP&DP terminal inactivo *m*
dormer *n* CONST ventana de buharda *f*
DOS *abbr* (*disk operating system*) COMP&DP DOS (*sistema operativo de discos*)
dosage *n* COAL, METR dosaje *m*, dosificación *f*

dose *n* CHEM, METR, RAD PHYS dosis *f*; ~ **accumulated by workers** *n* RAD PHYS dosis acumulada del personal *f*; ~ **constant** *n* RAD PHYS constante de dosis *f*; ~ **equivalent** *n* PHYS, RAD PHYS dosis equivalente *f*; ~**-meter** *n* ACOUST dosímetro *m*; ~ **rate** *n* PHYS tasa de dosis *f*, RAD PHYS razón de dosis *f*, tasa de dosis *f*, velocidad de acumulación de dosis *f*; ~ **rate effect** *n* RAD PHYS efecto de la tasa de dosis *m*; ~ **response** *n* POLL dosis de respuesta *f*; ~**-response relationship** *n* POLL relación de la dosis de respuesta *f*
dosimeter *n* PHYS, RAD PHYS dosímetro *m*; ~ **glass** *n* C&G vidrio de dosímetro *m*
dosimetry *n* PHYS, RAD PHYS dosimetría *f*
dosing *n* CHEM, PACK dosificación *f*; ~ **apparatus** *n* PACK dosificador *m*; ~ **feeder** *n* PACK alimentador-dosificador *m*; ~ **machine** *n* PACK dosificadora *f*; ~ **packing** *n* PACK embalaje dosificador *m*; ~ **pump** *n* PACK bomba dosificadora *f*
dot[1]: ~**-to-dot** *adv* PRINT punto por punto
dot[2] *n* COMP&DP, ELECTRON, PRINT, TEXTIL, TV punto *m*; ~ **etching** *n* PRINT reducción del punto *f*; ~ **generator** *n* ELECTRON generador de puntos *m*; ~ **grating** *n* TV diagrama de puntos *m*; ~ **interlace scanning** *n* TV exploración por puntos sucesivos *f*; ~ **leaders** *n pl* PRINT puntos conductores *m pl*; ~ **matrix** *n* COMP&DP, ELECTRON matriz de puntos *f*; ~ **matrix printer** *n* COMP&DP, PRINT impresora de matriz de puntos *f*, impresora de puntos *f*, impresora matricial *f*; ~ **printer** *n* COMP&DP, PRINT impresora de puntos *f*
dotted: ~ **frame** *n* PRINT marco punteado *m*
double[1]: ~**-acting** *adj* AUTO de doble acción, FUELLESS de doble efecto, MECH de doble acción, de doble efecto, MECH ENG de acción doble, de efecto doble, REFRIG de doble efecto; ~**-battened** *adj* PACK con refuerzo de madera doble; ~ **cotton-covered** *(DCC)* ELEC con cubierta de dos capas de algodón; ~**-cut** *adj* PROD de picadura cruzada; ~**-cutting** *adj* MECH ENG de corte bifacial, de corte doble; ~**-decked** *adj* PACK de dos pisos; ~**-fed** *adj* ELEC de doble alimentación; ~**-headed** *adj* CINEMAT de cabezal doble; ~ **layer** *adj* COATINGS doble capa *f*; ~**-pure-rubber-covered** *adj* *(DPRC)* ELEC con cubierta de goma pura doble; ~**-skinned** *adj* MECH ENG de revestimiento doble; ~**-threaded** *adj* CONST de doble torsión, *screw* con doble rosca *f*; ~ **twist** *adj* GEOM doble torsión
double[2]:
~ **a** ~**-acting pump** *n* PROD bomba de doble efecto *f*; ~**-armature relay** *n* ELEC relé de doble armadura *m*;
~ **b** ~**-balanced mixer** *n* ELECTRON mezclador doble compensado *m*; ~**-band projector** *n* AmE *(cf double-headed projector BrE)* CINEMAT proyector de banda doble *m*, proyector de cabezal doble *m*; ~ **base diode** *n* ELECTRON diodo de base doble *m*; ~**-battened case** *n* PACK caja doblemente reforzada *f*; ~ **beat valve** *n* HYDRAUL válvula de doble asiento *f*; ~ **bevel** *n* C&G doble bisel *m*; ~**-beveled chisel** *AmE see double-bevelled chisel BrE*; ~**-beveled turning chisel** *AmE see double-bevelled turning chisel BrE*; ~**-bevelled chisel** *n BrE* CONST formón de doble biselado *m*; ~**-bevelled turning chisel** *n BrE* CONST formón de doble biselado *m*, formón de tornero con doble biselado *m*; ~ **bituminous surface treatment** *(DBST)* CONST tratamiento superficial doble bituminoso *m*; ~ **blackwall hitch** *n* WATER TRANSP vuelta de

gancho doble *f*; ~ **blade cutter** *n* PAPER cortadora de doble cuchilla *f*; ~ **bond** *n* CHEM doble enlace *m*, doble ligadura *f*; ~ **bottom** *n* WATER TRANSP doble fondo *m*; ~**-bottom plan** *n* WATER TRANSP plano del doble fondo *m*; ~**-break switch** *n* ELEC, PROD interruptor bipolar *m*, interruptor de doble ruptura *m*; ~ **bridge** *n* INSTR puente doble *m*; ~ **bucket collector** *n* POLL electrodofiltros de doble etapa *m pl*, electrodos colectores de doble etapa *m pl*, electrodos colectores de dos cámaras *m pl*; ~ **buffering** *n* COMP&DP almacenamiento en doble búfer *m*, almacenamiento en memoria intermedia doble *m*, registramiento doble *m*;
~ **c** ~ **cable release** *n* PHOTO disparador de dos cables *m*; ~ **calipers** *AmE*, ~ **callipers** *BrE n pl* CONST calibrador doble *m*, calibre doble *m*; ~**-camera extension** *n* PHOTO extensión para dos cámaras *f*; ~ **casing** *n* MECH ENG revestimiento doble *m*; ~ **cavity mold** *AmE*, ~ **cavity mould** *BrE n* C&G molde de doble cavidad *m*; ~**-circuit brake** *n* TRANSP freno de doble circuito *m*; ~ **claw** *n* CINEMAT garfio doble *m*; ~**-condenser pole piece** *n* INSTR masa polar del condensador doble *f*; ~ **conversion** *n* ELECTRON conversión doble *f*; ~**-cord switchboard** *n* TELECOM panel de conmutación dicordio *m*; ~ **core cable** *n* ELEC cable de doble par *m*, cable de dos almas *m*; ~ **crew operation** *n* AIR TRANSP operación de tripulación doble *f*; ~ **cropping** *n* AGRIC cultivos dobles *m pl*; ~ **crossover** *n* CONST cruce doble *m*, vía de enlace doble *f*, RAIL cruce doble *m*; ~ **crossover road** *n* CONST carretera de cruce de doble sentido *f*; ~ **crucible method** *n* OPT método de crisol doble *m*; ~ **crucible technique** *n* OPT técnica de crisol doble *f*; ~**-cylinder engine** *n* MECH ENG motor bicilíndrico *m*;
~ **d** ~ **deck crown furnace** *n* C&G horno de doble corona *m*; ~ **delta connection** *n* ELEC sistema de conexiones en delta dobles *m*, sistema de conexiones en triángulo dobles *m*; ~ **delta wing** *n* AIR TRANSP, TRANSP ala de doble delta *f*; ~ **density** *n* COMP&DP doble densidad *f*; ~**-density recording** *n* COMP&DP grabación de doble densidad *f*, registro de doble densidad *m*; ~ **diamond crossing with slips** *n* RAIL doble cruzamiento oblicuo con deslizamientos *m*; ~**-diffused transistor** *n* ELECTRON transistor difuso doble *m*; ~ **diffusion** *n* ELECTRON difusión doble *f*, doble difusión *f*; ~ **disc sandpapering machine** *n* BrE PROD máquina lijadora de doble disco *f*; ~ **disc winding** *n* BrE ELEC *of transformer* devanado en disco doble *m*; ~ **disk sandpapering machine** *AmE see double disc sandpapering machine BrE*; ~ **disk winding** *AmE see double disc winding BrE*; ~ **drum dryer** *n* FOOD secador de doble cilindro *m*; ~ **dyeing** *n* TEXTIL doble teñido *m*;
~ **e** ~ **earth fault** *n* BrE *(cf double ground fault AmE)* ELEC tierra accidental doble *f*, tierra doble *f*; ~**-edge grinder** *n* C&G esmeril de dos filos *m*; ~ **8 film** *n* AmE *(cf double 8 stock BrE)* CINEMAT película de 8 mm doble *f*; ~ **8 stock** *BrE n* *(cf double 8 film AmE)* CINEMAT película de 8 mm doble *f*; ~**-ended** *n* PROD de dos bocas; ~**-ended break** *n* NUCL *of pipe* seccionamiento total *m*; ~**-ended handsaw file** *n* PROD lima de tres bordes y extremos iguales *f*; ~**-ended match plane** *n* CONST cepillo machihembrado con dos extremos *m*; ~**-ended piston rod cylinder** *n* MECH ENG vástago del pistón de extremo doble *m*, vástago del émbolo de extremo doble *m*;

~ **engine** n MECH ENG motor doble m; ~ **entries** n pl MINE galerías gemelas f pl; ~ **equal angle cutter** n MECH fresa cónica de ángulo doble f, MECH ENG fresa cónica de ángulo doble f, fresa diagonal de corte doble f; ~ **exposure** n CINEMAT, PHOTO doble exposición f, exposición doble f;

■ **f** ~ **face corrugated board** n PACK cartón ondulado de doble cara m; ~ **face crepe paper** n PACK, PAPER papel crespado doble cara m; ~~**face wax paper** n PACK papel encerado por ambas caras m; ~~**faced sledgehammer** n CONST martillo de doble cara m; ~~**flanged traveling wheel** AmE, ~~**flanged travelling wheel** BrE n PROD rodillo de dos pestañas m; ~ **flat** n ACOUST doble bemol f; ~ **floor** n CONST with more than one binder doble piso m, with one binder entramado doble m;

■ **g** ~ **glazing** n CONST, HEAT ENG cristal doble m, doble vidrio m; ~ **glazing unit** n C&G unidad de glaseado doble f; ~ **gobbing** n C&G vela doble f; ~ **ground fault** n AmE (cf double earth fault BrE) ELEC tierra accidental doble f, tierra doble f; ~ **gun tube** n TV tubo de doble cañón m;

■ **h** ~ **hairline** n PRINT filete extrafino doble m; ~ **half round file** n PROD lima de media caña de doble picadura f; ~~**headed projector** n BrE (cf double-band projector AmE) CINEMAT proyector de banda doble m, proyector de cabezal doble m; ~~**headed rail** n RAIL carril de doble cabeza m, riel de doble seta m; ~~**headed shaping machine** n MECH ENG limadora de cabezal doble f; ~ **helical gear** n MECH ENG engranaje helicoidal doble m; ~ **housing planing machine** n MECH ENG cepilladora de puente f; ~ **hull** n WATER TRANSP doble casco m;

■ **i** ~ **image** n CINEMAT imagen doble f; ~ **inlet fan** n MECH ENG, REFRIG ventilador de doble entrada m, ventilador de dos oídos m; ~ **insulation** n ELEC ENG doble aislación f; ~ **insulator** n ELEC, ELEC ENG aislante doble m;

■ **j** ~ **joint** n PETROL unión doble f;

■ **k** ~ **Kelvin bridge** n INSTR puente Kelvin doble m, puente Thomson doble m;

■ **l** ~ **layer** n COATINGS bicapa f; ~~**layer coating** n TELECOM revestimiento de doble capa m; ~~**layer winding** n ELEC of coil arrollamiento bifilar m, arrollamiento en doble capa m, devanado bifilar m, doble arrollamiento m; ~ **legend** n PROD leyenda doble f; ~ **letter** n PRINT letra doble f;

■ **m** ~ **moding** n ELECTRON selector doble m; ~ **modulation** n ELECTRON doble modulación f, modulación doble f; ~ **mortise-and-tenon joint** n CONST unión de espiga y mortaja doble f;

■ **o** ~ **offset gravure** n PRINT grabado de doble composición m; ~ **overhead camshaft** n VEH doble árbol de levas en cabeza m;

■ **p** ~ **pass boiler** n HEAT caldera de doble paso f; ~~**perf stock** n CINEMAT película de perforación doble f; ~ **perforation** n CINEMAT perforación doble f; ~ **pitch roof** n CONST tejado a dos aguas m; ~ **plate dry clutch** n AUTO embrague de disco doble en seco m; ~ **platform pallet** n PACK paleta de doble plataforma f; ~~**pole double-throw knife switch** n ELEC conmutador bipolar bidireccional m, conmutador de dos polos y dos vías m, conmutador bipolar de dos vías m, ELEC ENG conmutador bipolar bidireccional m; ~~**pole double-throw switch** n (DPDTS) ELEC conmutador bipolar bidireccional m

(CBB), conmutador bipolar bidireccional m, ELEC ENG conmutador bipolar bidireccional m (CBB); ~~**pole single-throw relay** n ELEC ENG relé unipolar bidireccional m; ~~**pole single-throw switch** n (DPSTS) ELEC ENG conmutador unipolar bidireccional m (CUB); ~~**pole snap switch** n (DPSS) ELEC conmutador de acción rápida de dos polos m, conmutador instantáneo de dos polos m; ~~**pole switch** n (DPS) CINEMAT, ELEC, ELEC ENG conmutador bipolar m, conmutador de doble polo m, conmutador de dos polos m; ~ **precision** n COMP&DP doble precisión f; ~ **precision arithmetic** n COMP&DP, MATH aritmética de doble precisión f; ~ **pump** n PROD bomba doble f;

■ **r** ~ **rail** n ELECTRON to form scale in carril doble m, doble carril m, doble vía f; ~~**reduction rear axle** n AUTO puente trasero de doble reducción m; ~~**reflector aerial** n BrE (cf double-reflector antenna AmE) TELECOM antena de doble reflector f; ~~**reflector antenna** n AmE (cf double-reflector aerial BrE) TELECOM antena de doble reflector f; ~ **refraction** n CRYSTALL, OPT, PHYS, RAD PHYS birrefringencia f; ~ **ridge waveguide** n ELEC ENG guiaondas de cresta doble m; ~ **roller chain** n AUTO cadena de rodillos doble f; ~ **row ball bearing** n MECH ENG cojinete de bolas de doble fila m; ~ **rule** n PRINT mediacaña f; ~ **ruling** n PRINT mediacaña f;

■ **s** ~ **sharp** n ACOUST doble sostenido m; ~ **sheet detector** n PRINT detector de doble hoja m; ~ **sideband modulation** n ELECTRON modulación de banda lateral doble f; ~ **sideband modulator** n ELECTRON modulador de banda lateral doble m; ~~**sideband transmission** n TELECOM transmisión en banda lateral doble f, TV transmisión con dos bandas laterales f, transmisión en banda lateral doble f; ~~**sided disc** BrE, ~~**sided disk** AmE n COMP&DP disco de doble cara m; ~~**sided distribution frame** n TELECOM marco repartidor de dos caras m; ~~**sided floppy diskette** n COMP&DP disco de doble cara m, disco flexible de doble lado m, disquete de doble cara m; ~~**sided insert** n PRINT inserción a dos caras f; ~~**sided printed circuit** n ELECTRON circuito impreso a doble cara m; ~~**sided printed-circuit board** n ELECTRON placa de circuito impreso a doble cara f; ~~**sided substrate** n ELECTRON substrato de doble capa m; ~~**sided tape** n PACK cinta adhesiva por ambos lados f; ~ **16 film** n AmE (cf double 16 stock BrE) CINEMAT película de 16 mm doble f; ~ **16 stock** n BrE (cf double 16 film AmE) CINEMAT película de 16 mm doble f; ~ **skin** n WATER TRANSP doble forro m; ~ **speed motor** n ELEC motor de doble velocidad m; ~ **spread** n PRINT composición que abarca una página doble f, texto que abarca una página doble m; ~~**squirrel cage motor** n ELEC motor de doble jaula de ardilla m, motor de jaula de ardilla Boucherot m; ~~**squirrel cage winding** n ELEC ENG devanado en doble jaula de ardilla m; ~ **strap butt joint** n MECH ENG junta a tope doble f, junta de abrazadera doble f, junta de estriba doble f, junta plana doble f; ~ **stub** n PRINT talonario doble m; ~ **suction riser** n REFRIG conducto ascendente doble m; ~ **supereffect** n TV superefecto doble m;

■ **t** ~ **tackle** n WATER TRANSP aparejo doble m; ~ **take** n CINEMAT reacción tardía f; ~ **tenon joint** n CONST unión de espiga doble f; ~ **Thomson bridge** n INSTR puente Thomson doble m; ~~**throw contact** n ELEC ENG contacto bidireccional m; ~~**throw knife**

switch *n* ELEC conmutador de cuchilla de dos direcciones *m*, conmutador de cuchilla de dos vías *m*, interruptor de palanca de dos posiciones de contacto *m*; **~-throw switch** *n* ELEC conmutador de dos direcciones *m*, conmutador de dos posiciones de contacto *m*, conmutador de dos vías *m*, interruptor bidireccional *m*, ELEC ENG conmutador bidireccional *m*, interruptor bidireccional *m*; **~ timbering** *n* MINE marco ordinario *m*; **~ tone ink** *n* COLOUR tinta de dos tonos *f*; **~ triode** *n* ELECTRON triodo doble *m*; **~-tuned amplifier** *n* ELECTRON amplificador de doble sintonización *m*; **~-tuned cavity** *n* ELECTRON cavidad de doble sintonización *f*; **~-tuned circuit** *n* ELECTRON circuito de doble sintonización *m*; **~-tuned filter** *n* ELECTRON filtro de doble sintonización *m*;

~ v **~ velocity correlation** *n* FLUID correlación doble de velocidad *f*;

~ w **~ weight paper** *n* PHOTO papel de soporte grueso *m*; **~-wheel lathe** *n* MECH ENG torno de rueda doble *m*; **~-winding armature** *n* ELEC, ELEC ENG inducido de arrollamiento bifilar *m*, inducido de devanado bifilar *m*, inducido de doble arrollamiento *m*, inducido de doble devanado *m*, inducido de dos arrollamientos *m*; **~ window fiber** *AmE*, **~ window fibre** *BrE* *n* OPT, TELECOM fibra de ventana doble *f*; **~ wire system** *n* ELEC sistema de conexión bifilar *m*; **~ wishbone suspension** *n* AUTO suspensión de horquilla doble *f*; **~-wound armature** *n* ELEC, ELEC ENG inducido de arrollamiento bifilar *m*, inducido de devanado bifilar *m*, inducido de doble arrollamiento *m*, inducido de doble devanado *m*, inducido de dos arrollamientos *m*; **~-wound generator** *n* ELEC generador de dos arrollamientos *m*; **~-wound transformer** *n* ELEC transformador de dos devanados *m*, ELEC ENG transformador bifilar *m*

double[3] *vt* WATER TRANSP *cape, mooring lines* doblar; **~-print** *vt* CINEMAT copiar dos veces, PRINT sobreimprimir, sobreimprimir tapando

doubled: **~ lens** *n* CINEMAT, INSTR, OPT, PHOTO, PHYS objetivo doble *m*

doubler *n* MECH ENG duplicador *m*, TELECOM doblador de voltaje *m*

doublet *n* CHEM *spectroscopy* doblete *m*, CINEMAT objetivo doble *m*, FUELLESS *geothermal power* sistema de dos pozos *m*, INSTR, OPT, PHOTO objetivo doble *m*, PHYS *spectroscopy* doblete *m*, objetivo doble *m*, PRINT doblete *m*, THERMO sistema de dos pozos *m*; **~ aerial** *n* *BrE* (*cf doublet antenna AmE*) TV antena de doblete *f*, antena dipolo *f*, WATER TRANSP antena dipolo *f*; **~ antenna** *n* *AmE* (*cf doublet aerial BrE*) TV antena de doblete *f*, antena dipolo *f*, WATER TRANSP antena dipolo *f*; **~ lens** *n* CINEMAT, INSTR, OPT objetivo doble *m*, PHOTO lente doble *f*, objetivo doble *m*, PHYS *spectroscopy* objetivo doble *m*

dough *n* FOOD, P&R masa *f*, pasta *f*; **~ mixer** *n* P&R mezclador de pasta *m*

doughnut *n* GEOM donut *m*, toro *m*

Dove: **~ prism** *n* OPT prisma de Dove *m*

dovetail[1] *n* CONST, INSTR, MECH, PROD cola de milano *f*; **~ cutter** *n* MECH ENG fresa de colas de milano *f*, fresadora de colas de milano *f*, PROD lima de cola de milano *f*; **~-form tool** *n* MECH ENG herramienta para formar colas de milano *f*; **~ halved joint** *n* CONST empalme a media madera con cola de milano *m*; **~ joint** *n* CONST empalme de cola de milano *m*, junta de cola de milano *f*, MECH ensambladura en cola de

milano *f*; **~ lap joint** *n* CONST junta de cola de milano a solape *f*

dovetail[2] *vt* CONST ensamblar con cola de milano

dovetailed: **~ joint** *n* CONST junta de cola de milano *f*

dowel[1] *n* CONST clavija *f*, espiga *f*, pitón *m*, PROD *of core box* clavija *f*; **~ hole** *n* CONST *of draw-pinned slot mortice and tenon joint* orificio para clavija *m*; **~ pin** *n* CONST clavija *f*, pasador *m*, espiga *f*, PROD espiga de madera *f*; **~ pin with extracting thread** *n* MECH ENG clavija con rosca extractora *f*, clavija con rosca para extracción *f*, espiga con rosca extractora *f*, espiga con rosca para extracción *f*, pasador con rosca extractora *m*; **~-pin parallel** *n* MECH ENG paralela enclavijada *f*

dowel[2] *vt* CONST empernar, enclavijar, ensamblar con espigas, PROD enclavijar

down[1]: **~ by the head** *adj* WATER TRANSP hundido de proa, metido de proa; **~ by the stern** *adj* WATER TRANSP hundido de popa, metido de popa

down[2]: **~ converter** *n* TELECOM convertidor de RF a IF *m*; **~ counter** *n* ELECTRON contador descendente *m*, PROD contador decreciente *m*; **~ counter rung** *n* PROD peldaño de contador decreciente *m*; **~ cut milling** *n* MECH ENG fresadora de corte descendente *f*; **~ dip** *n* PETR TECH buceo hacia abajo *m*, buzamiento descendente *m*, buzamiento hacia abajo *m*; **~-enable bit** *n* COMP&DP, PROD bit habilitador de decrecimiento *m*; **~ gust** *n* AIR TRANSP ráfaga descendente *f*; **~ line** *n* RAIL línea descendente *f*; **~ link** *n* SPACE, TELECOM enlace descendente *m*; **~ lock** *n* AIR TRANSP bloqueo inferior *m*; **~ pulse** *n* ELECTRON impulso descendente *m*; **~ quark** *n* PART PHYS, PHYS quark abajo *m*; **~ runner** *n* PROD *in mould* agujero de colada *m*

downbending *n* GEOL inclinación descendente *f*

downbuckle *n* GEOL tectógeno *m*

downcast *n* MINE corriente de aire descendente *f*, pozo de entrada de aire *m*, pozo de ventilación *m*; **~ shaft** *n* MINE pozo de entrada de aire *m*, pozo de ventilación *m*

downcomer *n* NUCL espacio anular de bajada *m*, PETR TECH tubo vertical de bajada *m*, tubo vertical de bajada en una torre de destilación *m*, PROD *of blast furnace* toma de gas lateral *f*, tubo vertical de bajada *m*

downdip *adv* GEOL en el sentido de la inclinación

downdraft *AmE see downdraught BrE*; **~ carburetor** *AmE see downdraught carburettor BrE*

downdraught *n* *BrE* AIR TRANSP, MECH ENG corriente de aire descendente *f*; **~ carburettor** *n* *BrE* AUTO, VEH carburador de tiro descendente *m*, carburador de tiro invertido *m*

downfaulted[1] *adj* GEOL hundido por una falla

downfaulted[2]: **~ block** *n* GEOL bloque de dislocación descendente *m*; **~ side** *n* GEOL bloque hundido *m*

downfeed *n* MECH ENG *of machine tools* avance vertical descendente *m*, avance vertical hacia abajo *m*

downgrading *n* MECH ENG reclasificación en un nivel inferior *f*, METALL *of alloys* empobrecimiento *m*, PROD *of alloys* empobrecimiento *m*, reclasificación en un nivel inferior *f*

downhaul *n* WATER TRANSP cargadera *f*

downhill: **~ slope** *n* CONST pendiente *f*

downhole[1] *adj* PETR TECH fondo del pozo *m*

downhole[2]: **~ conditions** *n pl* PETR TECH condiciones en el fondo del pozo *f pl*; **~ measurements** *n pl* PETR TECH medidas del fondo del pozo *f pl*; **~ safety valve**

n PETR TECH válvula de seguridad de agujero de perforación *f*, válvula de seguridad para el fondo del pozo *f*

download: ~ **operation** *n* PROD operación de descarga *f*

downloading *n* COMP&DP, TELECOM transferencia de un ordenador a otro *f*

downpipe *n* BrE (*cf downspout*) CONST bajante *m*, tubo de bajada de aguas *m*

downrange: ~ **station** *n* SPACE estación situada en la trayectoria *f*

downspout *n* AmE (*cf downpipe BrE*) CONST bajante *m*, tubo de bajada de aguas *m*

downstream[1] *adj* FLUID, HYDROL descendente, TEXTIL del final

downstream[2] *adv* CONST aguas abajo, río abajo, FLUID, GAS aguas abajo, corriente abajo, río abajo, HYDROL aguas abajo, MECH, PHYS aguas abajo, corriente abajo, río abajo, WATER aguas abajo, WATER TRANSP *river* aguas abajo, corriente abajo, río abajo

downstream[3]: ~ **cutwater** *n* WATER *of bridge pier* tajamar de salida *m*; ~ **face** *n* HYDROL *founding* adoruos de aguas abajo *m pl*, sobrecubierta *f*; ~ **fairing** *n* REFRIG carenado corriente abajo *m*; ~ **level** *n* HYDROL nivel de aguas abajo *m*; ~ **process** *n* CHEM TECH, PROD, TEXTIL proceso que sigue *m*; ~ **wake** *n* FLUID estela formada aguas abajo *f*

downstroke *n* AUTO, MECH, MECH ENG, P&R, VEH carrera descendente *f*; ~ **press** *n* P&R prensa de carrera descendente *f*

downtake *n* PROD *of blast furnace* toma de gas lateral *f*

downtime *n* AIR TRANSP tiempo fuera de funcionamiento *m*, COMP&DP tiempo de inactividad *m*, tiempo de parada *m*, MECH período de interrupción del servicio *m*, tiempo de parada *m*, tiempo improductivo *m*, tiempo muerto *m*, NUCL, PACK tiempo muerto *m*, PETR TECH período de paralización por avería *m*, PROD tiempo de inactividad *m*, tiempo de parada *m*, tiempo improductivo *m*, TELECOM tiempo improductivo *m*, TV tiempo inactivo *m*; ~ **cost** *n* PACK coste debido al retraso *m*, coste debido al tiempo de parada *m*

downward[1]: ~ **compatible** *adj* COMP&DP compatible con revisión anterior, compatible hacia abajo

downward[2]: ~ **compatibility** *n* COMP&DP compatibilidad con revisión anterior *f*, compatibilidad descendente *f*, compatibilidad hacia abajo *f*; ~ **gradient** *n* CONST pendiente descendente *f*; ~ **modulation** *n* ELECTRON modulación descendente *f*; ~ **motion** *n* PROD movimiento descendente *m*; ~ **stroke** *n* MECH ENG carrera descendente *f*

downwarp *n* GEOL subsidencia regional *f*

downwash *n* AIR TRANSP torbellino descendiente *m*, torbellino hacia abajo *m*

downwind[1] *adv* AIR TRANSP a favor del viento, de viento de cola, FUELLESS de viento en popa, POLL a favor del viento, WATER TRANSP con el viento

downwind[2] *n* AIR TRANSP viento de cola *m*, FUELLESS viento en popa *m*, METEO viento descendente *m*, WATER TRANSP viento en popa *m*; ~ **leg** *n* AIR TRANSP tramo a favor del viento *m*, tramo con viento de cola *m*

downy: ~ **mildew** *n* AGRIC mildiú enanizante *m*, FOOD moho velloso *m*

dowser *n* CINEMAT obturador de proyector *m*, HYDROL varita de zahorí *f*

DP[1] *abbr* CINEMAT (*director of photography*) director de fotografía *m*, COMP&DP (*data processing*) PD (*procesamiento de datos, proceso de datos*), sistema de explotación de datos *m*, CONST, GEOL (*datum plane*) PR (*plano de referencia*), TELECOM (*data processing*) PD (*procesamiento de datos, proceso de datos*)

DP[2]: ~ **end of data** *n* COMP&DP fin de datos *m*

DPC *abbr* (*data processing center AmE, data processing centre BrE*) COMP&DP, TELECOM centro de procesamiento de datos *m* (*DPC*)

DPCM *abbr* (*differential pulse code modulation*) ELECTRON MDCP (*modulación diferencial de código pulsado*)

DPDT: ~ **relay** *n* ELEC ENG relé de CBB *m*; ~ **switch** *n* ELEC ENG conmutador CBB *m*

DPDTS *abbr* (*double-pole double-throw switch*) ELEC, ELEC ENG CBB (*conmutador bipolar bidireccional*), conmutador bipolar de dos vías *m*

DPL *abbr* (*distribution primary link*) TELECOM enlace principal de distribución *m*

DPRC *abbr* (*double-pure-rubber-covered*) ELEC con cubierta de goma pura doble *adj*

DPS *abbr* (*double-pole switch*) CINEMAT, ELEC, ELEC ENG conmutador bipolar *m*, conmutador de doble polo *m*, conmutador de dos polos *m*

DPSK *abbr* (*differential phase shift keying*) ELECTRON MVFD (*manipulación de variación de fase diferencial*)

DPSS *abbr* (*double-pole snap switch*) ELEC conmutador de acción rápida de dos polos *m*, conmutador instantáneo de dos polos *m*

DPST: ~ **relay** *n* ELEC ENG relé UB *m*; ~ **switch** *n* ELEC ENG conmutador UB *m*

DPSTS *abbr* (*double-pole single-throw switch*) ELEC, ELEC ENG CUB (*conmutador unipolar bidireccional*)

d-quark *n* PART PHYS quark abajo *m*

dracone *n* BrE MAR POLL dracone *m*, dragón *m*

draft[1] *AmE see draught BrE*

draft[2] *n* CONST, MECH ENG *sketch, outline* borrador *m*, plano *m*, proyecto *m*

drafting *n* TEXTIL remetido *m*; ~ **system** *n* TEXTIL sistema de remetido *m*

draftsman *AmE see draughtsman BrE*

drag[1] *n* AIR TRANSP resistencia aerodinámica *f*, resistencia al avance *f*, retardo *m*, FLUID resistencia hidrodinámica *f*, *on a sphere* resistencia al avance *f*, FUELLESS *wind power* resistencia al avance *f*, MECH draga *f*, freno *m*, galga *f*, retardo *m*, zapata *f*, METALL arrastre *m*, MINE retardo *m*, zapata *f*, resistencia *f*, draga *f*, galga *f*, PHYS resistencia aerodinámica *f*, frenado *m*, arrastre *m*, PRINT mancha *f*, PROD *founding* estiraje *m*, draga *f*, resistencia a ventilación en minas *f*, SPACE arrastre *m*, frenado *m*, resistencia aerodinámica *f*, WATER TRANSP resistencia al avance *f*; ~ **angle** *n* AIR TRANSP ángulo de la resistencia *m*, ángulo de la resistencia aerodinámica *m*; ~ **axis** *n* AIR TRANSP eje de arrastre *m*, eje de resistencia aerodinámica *m*; ~ **bit** *n* PETR TECH barrena de arrastre *f*, broca *f*, mecha de arrastre *f*; ~ **brace** *n* AIR TRANSP tirante de arrastre *m*; ~ **brake** *n* AIR TRANSP, TRANSP flap de resistencia al arrastre *m*; ~ **chute** *n* AIR TRANSP, SPACE *spacecraft* paracaídas de frenado *m*; ~ **chute cover** *n* AIR TRANSP cubierta del paracaídas de frenado *f*; ~ **coefficient** *n* AIR TRANSP, AUTO coeficiente de resistencia aerodinámica *m*, FLUID

coeficiente de resistencia al avance *m*, PHYS coeficiente de retardo *m*, VEH coeficiente de resistencia al aire *m*, WATER TRANSP coeficiente de resistencia al avance *m*; ~ **cup** *n* AIR TRANSP casco de frenado *m*; ~ **cup skirt** *n* AIR TRANSP falda del casco de frenado *f*; ~ **damper** *n* AIR TRANSP amortiguador de arrastre *m*, amortiguador de frenado *m*; ~ **fold** *n* GEOL pliegue de arrastre *m*; ~ **hinge** *n* AIR TRANSP *of helicopter* charnela de arrastre *f*, charnela de resistencia *f*; ~ **lift** *n* TRANSP elevador de arrastre *m*; ~ **link** *n* AIR TRANSP eslabón de arrastre *m*, AUTO, VEH barra de acoplamiento *f*; ~ **moment** *n* AIR TRANSP momento de resistencia aerodinámica *m*; ~ **parachute** *n* AIR TRANSP paracaídas de frenado *m*; ~ **rake** *n* AGRIC rastrillo de arrastre *m*; ~ **roller** *n* CINEMAT rodillo de arrastre *m*; ~ **rudder** *n* AIR TRANSP timón de dirección de arrastre *m*; ~ **screw** *n* MECH ENG tornillo de arrastre *m*; ~ **stop** *n* AIR TRANSP parada de arrastre *f*
drag²: ~ **anchor** *phr* WATER TRANSP garrear el ancla
drag³ *vt* WATER TRANSP *sea bottom* rastrear
dragging *n* WATER TRANSP *of the sea bottom* rastreo *m*, *on anchor, moored buoy, etc* garreo *m*
dragline: ~ **excavator** *n* CONST draga excavadora *f*, dragalina *f*
dragnet *n* OCEAN red de arrastre *f*; ~ **fishing** *n* OCEAN pesca de arrastre *f*
dragrope *n* OCEAN sonda *f*
drain¹ *n* AGRIC desaguadero *m*, drenaje *m*, COAL acequia *f*, alcantarilla *f*, avenamiento *m*, cloaca *f*, orificio de rebosadero *m*, pozo *m*, pozo absorbente *m*, sumidero *m*, zanja *f*, CONST alcantarilla *f*, desagüe *m*, dren *m*, *sewer* zanja *f*, ELEC ENG consumo de energía *m*, pérdida de energía *f*, HYDROL drenaje *m*, avenamiento *m*, alcantarilla *f*, MECH ENG alcantarilla *f*, PETR TECH desagüe *m*, drenaje *m*, PHYS drenaje *m*, POLL boca de alcantarilla *f*, PROD desagüe *m*, drenaje *m*, purga *f*, RECYCL boca de alcantarilla *f*, alcantarilla *f*, canal de drenaje *m*, desagüe *m*, WATER acequia *f*, alcantarilla *f*, avenamiento *m*, boca de alcantarilla *f*, WATER TRANSP desagüe *m*, purga *f*; ~ **bias** *n* ELEC ENG derivación de fuga de energía *f*; ~ **cock** *n* CONST llave de desagüe *f*, MECH ENG, PROD grifo de desagüe *m*, grifo de drenaje *m*, grifo de purga *m*, llave de purga *f*, VEH grifo de purga *m*, grifo de vaciado *m*, WATER grifo de purga *m*; ~ **connector** *n* MECH ENG conector de desagüe *m*, conector de drenaje *m*; ~ **contact** *n* ELEC ENG contacto de pérdida de energía *m*; ~ **cup** *n* PROD embudo de desagüe *m*; ~ **current** *n* ELEC ENG corriente de drenaje *f*; ~ **nipple** *n* MECH ENG niple de desagüe *m*, niple de drenaje *m*, niple de purga *m*; ~ **pan** *n* MECH ENG, REFRIG depósito de desagüe *m*, depósito de drenaje *m*; ~ **plug** *n* AUTO, VEH tapón de drenaje *m*, tapón de vaciado *m*; ~ **shaft** *n* MINE pozo de evacuación *m*; ~ **solenoid** *n* MECH ENG solenoide de drenaje *m*; ~ **tap** *n* PETR TECH agujero de drenaje *m*; ~ **terminal** *n* ELEC ENG terminal de drenaje *m*; ~ **testing and cleaning equipment** *n* CONST equipo de limpieza y de comprobación de desagües *m*; ~ **trap** *n* CONST sifón de drenaje *m*; ~ **valve** *n* MECH ENG válvula de desagüe *f*, válvula de drenaje *f*, válvula de purga *f*, RAIL purgador *m*, WATER TRANSP válvula de purga *f*; ~ **well** *n* MINE pozo de evacuación *m*; ~ **wire** *n* ELEC hilo de drenaje *m*, hilo de retorno por tierra *m*, PROD alambre de drenaje *m*
drain² *vt* CHEM drenar, COAL purgar, CONST *land* sanear, *ditch* drenar, HYDRAUL descebar, achicar, desecar,

deshidratar, HYDROL evacuar, drenar, desaguar, avenar, MECH drenar, purgar, evacuar, descebar, vaciar, MECH ENG vaciar, MINE desaguar, agotar, evacuar, PAPER desgotar, PROD vaciar, purgar, RECYCL desaguar, filtrar, vaciar, drenar, evacuar, WATER desaguar, avenar, drenar, descebar, agotar, achicar; ~ **off** *vt* WATER agotar
drainability *n* PAPER aptitud al desgote *f*
drainable: ~ **fuel** *n* AIR TRANSP combustible desechable *m*
drainage *n* AGRIC, CONST, HYDROL drenaje *m*, MECH ENG desagüe *m*, drenaje *m*, purga *f*, MINE achique *m*, agotamiento *m*, desagüe *m*, desecación *f*, drenaje *m*, sistema de alcantarillado *m*, PAPER desgote *m*, drenaje *m*, PETR TECH, PROD drenaje *m*, RECYCL desagüe *m*, WATER drenaje *m*, agotamiento *m*; ~ **aid** *n* PAPER agente favorecedor del drenado *m*; ~ **area** *n* CONST cuenca de drenaje *f*, zona de desagüe *f*, HYDROL cuenca de captación *f*, PETROL área de drenaje *f*, WATER área de drenaje *f*, cuenca *f*, área colectora *f*, área de escurrimiento *f*, hoya *f*; ~ **basin** *n* HYDROL cuenca fluvial *f*, cuenca hidrográfica *f*, WATER cuenca hidrográfica *f*, cuenca vertiente *f*, cuenca de captación *f*, hoya hidrológica *f*; ~ **channel** *n* AGRIC canal de drenaje *m*, zanja de drenaje *f*, OCEAN canal de agotamiento *m*, canal de desagüe *m*, WATER canal de drenaje *m*, zanja de desagüe *f*; ~ **chest** *n* PAPER tina de desgote *f*; ~ **density** *n* HYDROL densidad de drenaje *f*, densidad de la red de avenamiento *f*; ~ **ditch** *n* HYDROL canal de desagüe *m*, zanja para avenamiento *f*, WATER zanja de drenaje *f*, zanja para avenamiento *f*, zanja de agotamiento *f*; ~ **foil** *n* PAPER cuchilla desgotadora *f*; ~ **gallery** *n* HYDROL *traffic* galería de drenaje *f*; ~ **level** *n* MINE galería de desagüe *f*, socavón *m*; ~ **pattern** *n* GEOL estructura de drenaje *f*; ~ **pump** *n* WATER bomba de agotamiento *f*, bomba de desagüe *f*; ~ **structure** *n* CONST sistema de drenaje *m*, sistema de saneamiento *m*; ~ **system** *n* COAL, HYDROL, POLL alcantarillado *m*, RECYCL alcantarillado *m*, sistema de desagüe *m*, WATER alcantarillado *m*, WATER TRANSP instalación de purga *f*; ~ **terrace** *n* AIR TRANSP plataforma de drenaje *f*, terraza de desagüe *f*; ~ **well** *n* MINE pozo de desagüe *m*
drainer *n* PAPER desgotador *m*
draining *n* COAL avenamiento *m*, purga *f*, HYDROL avenamiento *m*, MINE achique *m*, agotamiento *m*, desagüe *m*, desecación *f*, drenaje *m*, WATER avenamiento *m*, drenaje *m*, escurrimiento *m*; ~ **engine** *n* WATER bomba de agotamiento *f*, bomba de desagüe *f*; ~ **pump** *n* WATER bomba de agotamiento *f*, bomba de desagüe *f*; ~ **rack** *n* FOOD escurridor *m*, LAB escurridera *f*, gradilla *f*; ~ **screen** *n* COAL tamiz de desagüe *m*
drainpipe *n* CONST caño del desagüe *m*, tubo de desagüe *m*, tubo de drenaje *m*
DRAM *abbr* (*dynamic random access memory*) COMP&DP DRAM (*memoria dinámica de acceso aleatorio*)
dram *n* METR dracma *m*
drape¹ *n* TEXTIL drapeado *m*; ~ **folds** *n pl* GEOL pliegues con capas más potentes en flancos que en el eje *m pl*
drape² *vt* GEOL cubrir
draping: ~ **properties** *n pl* TEXTIL características de la caída *f pl*

draught *n* *BrE* CONST *ventilation* aspiración *f*, *in chimney* tiro *m*, succión *f*, HEAT corriente *f*, MECH ángulo de retiro *m*, MECH ENG ángulo de retiro *m*, corriente de aire *f*, desmoldeo *m*, PROD desmoldeo *m*, corriente de aire *f*, tiro *m*, reducción en tamaño *f*, conicidad *f*, ángulo de retiro *m*, TEXTIL estiraje *m*, WATER TRANSP calado *m*; ~ **bar** *n* *BrE* RAIL barra de tracción *f*; ~ **box** *n* *BrE* HYDRAUL distribuidor de descarga *m*, tubo de succión *m*; ~ **engine** *n* *BrE* MINE turbina de succión *f*, locomotora *f*; ~ **gauge** *n* *BrE* HEAT, PROD indicador del tiro *m*; ~ **hole** *n* *BrE* PROD *of furnace* agujero de colada *m*, ventosa *f*; ~ **machine** *n* *BrE* PROD *pattern-drawing* máquina de desmoldear *f*; ~ **marks** *n pl* *BrE* WATER TRANSP *ship design* escala de calados *f*; ~ **quality** *n* *BrE* PROD calidad de prueba *f*; ~ **regulator** *n* *BrE* HEAT regulador de corriente de aire *m* PROD registro regulador del tiro *m*, regulador del tiro *m*; ~ **tube** *n* *BrE* FUELLESS tubo de aspiración *m*, HYDRAUL tubería de descarga *f*, tubo de aspiración *m*, tubo de exhaustación *m*, tubo de succión *m*; ~ **zone** *n* *BrE* TEXTIL zona de estiraje *f*

draughtsman *n* *BrE* MECH dibujante *m*, MECH ENG delineante *m*, PROD delineante *m*, dibujante *m*, WATER TRANSP delineante *m*

draw[1] *n* MECH, MECH ENG ángulo de retiro *m*, PAPER tracción *f*, tiro *m*, PROD ángulo de retiro *m*, *casting* rechupe *m*; ~ **bench** *n* PROD banco de trefilar *m*; ~ **bore** *n* CONST *of tenon* agujero de llamada *m*; ~ **bore pin** *n* CONST pasador de llamada *m*; ~ **casting** *n* CONST *well boring* estirado *m*; ~**-down** *n* PETR TECH período de flujo *m*, PROD estirado, estiraje *m*, WATER aspiración adicional *f*, descenso del nivel de extracción *f*; ~**-down of water in aquifer** *n* FUELLESS descenso del nivel de agua acuífera *m*; ~ **gate** *n* WATER compuerta *f*; ~ **gear spring plate** *n* RAIL soporte del muelle del mecanismo de tracción *m*; ~ **hook** *n* PROD *moulder's tool*, RAIL gancho de tracción *m*; ~ **hook bar** *n* RAIL gancho de tracción *m*; ~**-in chuck** *n* MECH ENG plato de mordazas convergentes *m*, plato de quijadas convergentes *m*; ~**-in spring chuck** *n* MECH ENG plato de resortes de mordazas convergentes *m*, plato de resortes de quijadas convergentes *m*; ~**-off** *n* WATER extracción *f*; ~**-off tap** *n* MECH ENG grifo de extracción *m*; ~**-out switchgear** *n* ELEC conmutador de elementos amovibles *m*, dispositivo de distribución extraíble *m*; ~**-out unit** *n* ELEC unidad de elementos amovibles *f*, unidad extraíble *f*; ~ **ring** *n* MECH ENG anillo de tracción *m*; ~ **rod** *n* C&G caña *f*; ~ **roll** *n* PAPER rodillo de tiro *m*; ~ **screw** *n* MECH ENG tornillo de extracción *m*, tornillo sinfín tractor *m*; ~ **spike** *n* PROD *moulder's tool* aguja de desmoldear *f*; ~ **stick** *n* PROD *moulder's tool* aguja de desmoldear *f*; ~ **taper** *n* PROD *founding* inclinación de las caras laterales del molde *f*; ~ **water** *n* OCEAN, WATER TRANSP agua de calado *f*; ~ **works** *n* PETR TECH malacate *m*, PETROL cuadro de maniobras *m*, malacate *m*

draw[2] *vt* MECH ENG trefilar, PROD *metal into tubes, bars, etc* revenir, *metal into wire* desmoldear, TEXTIL estirar, WATER TRANSP arriar, calar; ~ **down** *vt* WATER descender, extraer; ~ **out** *vt* MECH ENG trefilar; ~ **out of a kiln** *vt* PROD trefilar

draw[3] *vi* CONST *chimney* tirar; ~ **the charge** *vi* PROD deshornar; ~ **the plug** *vi* PROD quitar el tapón

DRAW *abbr* (*direct read after write*) OPT lectura directa después de escritura *f*

drawback *n* PROD *founding* revenido *m*; ~ **spring** *n* MECH ENG muelle de llamada *m*, resorte de retracción *m*

drawbar *n* MECH ENG barra de tiro *f*, barra de tracción *f*, barra tractora *f*, varilla de llamada *f*, RAIL barra de enganche *f*, barra de tracción *f*, tensor *m*, travesaño posterior *m*, VEH barra de enganche *f*; ~ **bolt** *n* VEH perno de barra de enganche *m*; ~ **guide** *n* RAIL guía de la barra de tracción *f*

drawbridge *n* CONST *bascule bridge* puente móvil *m*, *rolling* puente giratorio *m*, *turning* puente levadizo *m*

drawframe *n* TEXTIL manuar *m*

drawhole *n* PROD agujero de colada *m*

drawing *n* CHEM TECH, CONST *plans* trazado *m*, GEOM trazado *m*, plano *m*, MECH ENG *plans* trazado *m*, METALL *wire* estiraje trefilado *m*, MINE recuperación *f*, rechupado *m*, revenido *m* (*Esp*), recorte *m* (*Esp*), extracción *f*, arranque *m* (*AmL*), P&R moldeado por estiramiento *m*, moldeo por estirado *m*, PROD *founding, of pattern* embutición *f*, *wire* estiraje *m*, TEXTIL estiraje *m*, WATER *of water from well* extracción *f*, aspiración *f*, WATER TRANSP trazado *m*, plano *m*; ~ **alongside** *n* WATER TRANSP atracada *f*; ~ **bench** *n* PROD *wiredrawing* banco de estiraje *m*; ~ **block** *n* PROD *wiredrawing* cabezal de estirar *m*; ~ **board** *n* CONST, MECH, WATER TRANSP tablero de dibujo *m*; ~ **engine** *n* MINE maquinaria de arranque *f*, motor de estiraje *m*; ~ **file** *n* PROD lima de embutición *f*; ~ **height** *n* MINE altura de extracción *f* (*AmL*), altura fija *f* (*Esp*); ~ **ink** *n* COLOUR, PRINT tinta de dibujo *f*; ~ **list** *n* PROD lista de dibujos *f*, lista de planos *f*; ~ **machine** *n* C&G máquina de estirado *f*; ~ **off** *n* HYDRAUL admisión *f*, aspiración *f*, toma *f*, toma de vapor *f*; ~ **office** *n* WATER TRANSP oficina de proyectos *f*, sala de trazado *f*; ~ **paper** *n* GEOM papel de trazado *m*; ~ **press** *n* MECH ENG prensa de embutir *f*, prensa de estirar *f*, prensa estiradora *f*; ~ **print** *n* CONST copia de un plano *f*, impresión de un plano *f*; ~ **process** *n* TELECOM proceso de extracción *m*; ~ **punch** *n* MECH ENG punzón embutidor *m*; ~ **tower** *n* C&G torre de estirado *f*

drawknife *n* CONST cuchilla de dos mangos *f*, cuchilla desbastadora *f*

drawn *adj* C&G *glass*, COATINGS *galvanized coating* estirado, MECH ENG *wire* estirado, revenido, trefilado, PROD *tube* estirado; ~ **from the wood** *adj* FOOD sacado del barril

drawplate *n* PROD calibre de estirar *m*

drawtube *n* INSTR tubo portaocular *m*

dredge[1] *n* AGRIC, CONST draga *f*, MINE draga *f*, mineral de calidad inferior *m*, rastra *f*, WATER TRANSP draga *f*; ~ **boat** *n* MINE dragalina *f* (*Esp*), gánguil *m* (*AmL*); ~ **bucket** *n* MINE rosario de la draga *m*; ~ **bucket ladder** *n* MINE escala de draga *f*, escala del rosario de la draga *f*; ~ **chain** *n* MINE, WATER TRANSP rosario de draga *m*; ~ **elevator** *n* MINE transportador vertical de cangilones *m*; ~ **ladder** *n* MINE escala *f*; ~ **mining** *n* MINE dragado de aluviones *m*; ~ **net** *n* WATER TRANSP *fishing* rastra *f*; ~ **plant** *n* MINE planta de dragados *f*; ~ **pump** *n* WATER TRANSP bomba de dragado *f*

dredge[2] *vt* MAR POLL, WATER TRANSP dragar

dredger *n* MAR POLL draga *f*, MINE draga *f*, excavadora de rosario *f*, obrero dragador *m*, pescador de rastra *m*, WATER TRANSP gánguil *m*, *person* obrero dragador *m*, pescador de rastra *m*; ~ **bucket** *n* TRANSP cangilón de draga *m*

dredging *n* HYDROL, MAR POLL, MINE, WATER TRANSP dragado *m*; ~ **face** *n* MINE frente de dragado *m*; ~ **field** *n* MINE zona de dragado *f*; ~ **ground** *n* MINE terreno de dragado *m*; ~ **operations** *n pl* WATER TRANSP operaciones de dragado *f pl*; ~ **sand** *n* CONST dragado de arena *m*, succión *f*, succión de arena *f*
dreg *n* PAPER lodos de decantación *m pl*
Dreschel: ~ **bottle** *n* LAB botella de Dreschel *f*
dress[1]: ~ **material** *n* TEXTIL género para vestidos *m*
dress[2] *vt* CONST *stone* labrar, PROD *casting* desbarbar
dress[3]: ~ **ship overall** *phr* WATER TRANSP engalanar
dressed[1] *adj* FOOD aderezado, CONST *stone* labrado
dressed[2]: ~ **beef** *n* AGRIC carne limpia de res *f*; ~ **carcass weight** *n* AGRIC peso en canal limpio *m*; ~ **poultry** *n* AGRIC aves limpias *f pl*; ~ **stone** *n* CONST piedra labrada *f*; ~ **width of warp** *n* TEXTIL ancho de la urdimbre encolado *m*; ~ **wool** *n* AGRIC lana cardada *f*
dresser *n* COAL aplanadora *f*, preparador *m*, PROD dispositivo reavivador *m*, *founding* desbastador *m*; ~ **cutter** *n* MECH ENG diamante reavivador *m*, reacondicionadora *f*, reavivador de muelas *m*, reavivamuelas *m*
dressing *n* C&G terminado *m*, COAL preparación mecánica *f*, CONST *of stone* acabado *m*, labrado *m*, PAPER repicado *m*, PROD *of emery wheel* reavivado *m*, reafilado *m*, restauración de la superficie de corte *f*, *of castings* desarenado *m*; ~ **equipment** *n* MECH ENG equipo de desarenado *m*, equipo de reavivado *m*, equipo de rebarbado *m*; ~ **shop** *n* PROD taller de desarenado *m*; ~ **works** *n* MINE taller de concentraciones *m*, taller de preparación mecánica *m*
dribble: ~ **irrigation** *n* AGRIC riego por goteo *m*
dried *adj* CONST *brick*, FOOD, THERMO seco
drift[1] *n* ACOUST deriva *f*, AIR TRANSP desplazamiento *m*, deriva *f*, desviación *f*, CONST *of bore hole* túnel de comunicación *m*, galería *f*, GEOL desplazamiento *m*, HYDROL desplazamiento *m*, *direction of current* dirección *f*, sentido *m*, INSTR variación del cero *f*, dispersión *f*, MAR POLL deriva *f*, MECH *coil* botador de pernos *m*, mandril cuadrado *m*, ensanchador *m*, punzón cuadrado *m*, MECH ENG *for taper shank drills* punzón expulsador *m*, holgura *f*, desplazamiento *m*, distancia entre centro de agujeros que deben coincidir *f*, desalineación *f*, *key* sacapernos *m*, huelgo *m*, desviación lateral *f*, sacachavetas *m*, sacabrocas *m*, botador de chavetas *m*, diferencia de diámetro entre el perno y el agujero correspondiente *f*, punzón cilíndrico *m*, botador de pernos *m*, MINE dirección en que se perfora un tunel *f*, túnel de exploración *m*, empuje horizontal *m*, intersección *f*, morrena *f*, desviación de la vertical *f*, socavón *m*, OCEAN desplazamiento *m*, PETROL desviación *f*, desplazamiento *m*, deriva *f*, PROD *casing swedge* estampa *f*, deriva *f*, SPACE abatimiento *m*, deriva *f*, desviación *f*, deslizamiento *m*, desplazamiento *m*, TELECOM deriva *f*, WATER TRANSP *of current* abatimiento *m*, deriva *f*, intensidad *f*; ~ **angle** *n* AIR TRANSP ángulo de deriva *m*, ángulo de desplazamiento *m*; ~ **azimuth** *n* PETROL azimut de deriva *m*; ~ **bolt** *n* PROD cabilla *f*; ~ **current** *n* OCEAN, WATER TRANSP corriente de deriva *f*; ~ **error** *n* AIR TRANSP error de deriva *m*, error de desplazamiento *m*; ~ **ice** *n* WATER TRANSP hielo a la deriva *m*; ~ **indicator** *n* AIR TRANSP indicador de deriva *m*; ~ **lock** *n* TV estabilización de la deriva *f*; ~ **mining** *n* MINE explotación por galerías *f*, explotación por

socavones *f*, explotación subterránea de yacimientos auríferos *f*; ~ **net** *n* WATER TRANSP red de enmalle de deriva *f*; ~ **orbit** *n* SPACE órbita de deriva *f*; ~ **pin** *n* MECH ENG *rivet* pasador cónico *m*; ~ **plate** *n* MECH ENG placa de deriva *f*, placa de deslizamiento *f*; ~ **punch** *n* MECH ENG pasador cónico *m*; ~ **region** *n* ELECTRON región de movilidad de la corriente *f*; ~ **soil** *n* AGRIC suelo de arrastre *m*; ~ **space** *n* ELECTRON distancia de agrupación *f*; ~ **stope** *n* MINE taje de avance *m* (*AmL*), tajo de avance *m* (*Esp*); ~ **tube** *n* ELECTRON tubo de deslizamiento *m*, tubo de variación *m*, MECH ENG tubo de deslizamiento *m*; ~ **tunnel** *n* ELECTRON tunel de variación *m*, túnel de control *m*; ~ **velocity** *n* METALL velocidad de derivación *f*, velocidad de ensanchamiento *f*
drift[2] *vt* HYDROL arrastrar
drift[3] *vi* METR derivar, WATER TRANSP abatir, derivar, ir a la deriva
drifting *n* CONST *piling into heaps* apilado, MECH ENG *a hole* ensanchamiento de taladros con mandril *m*, mandrilado *m*, MINE acarreo *m*, perforación de galerías en dirección al filón *f*; ~ **buoy** *n* METR boya largada a la deriva *f*; ~ **flight** *n* AIR TRANSP vuelo a la deriva *m*; ~ **float** *n* OCEAN flotador de deriva *m*; ~ **level** *n* MINE galería de dirección *f*, galería horizontal de avance *f*; ~ **snow** *n* METEO ventisca de nieve *f*
driftmeter *n* AIR TRANSP derivómetro *m*
driftpin *n* MECH ENG mandril de ensanchar *m*, pasador para casar agujeros *m*, pasador cónico *m*, pasador igualador de agujeros *m*, pasador de unión *m*
drill[1] *n* AGRIC hilera *f*, surco *m*, COAL perforadora *f*, perforar, taladro *m*, MECH agujereadora *f*, broca *f*, taladradora *f*, taladro *m*, MECH ENG *holder, stock* broca *f*, perforador *m*, portabarrenas *m*, portabrocas *m*, MINE broca *f*, perforadora *f*, portabrocas *m*, taladro mecánico *m*, pistolete de mina *m* (*AmL*), agujereadora *f*, barreno *m* (*Esp*), PROD agujereadora *f*; ~ **barge** *n* PETR TECH gabarra de perforación *f*, perforadora montada sobre embarcación *f*, torre de perforación sobre barcaza *f*; ~ **bit** *n* MINE barrena para martillo perforador *f* (*AmL*), boca de barrena *f* (*Esp*), trépano para roca *m*, PETR TECH barrena de arrastre *f*, broca *f*, mecha *f* (*AmL*), trépano de perforación *m*; ~ **bushing** *n* MECH, MECH ENG casquillo guía para taladrar con plantilla *m*; ~ **casing** *n* MINE tubería de entubación *f*, tubería de revestimiento *f*; ~ **chain** *n* MINE cadena de perforación *f*; ~ **chuck** *n* MECH ENG portabrocas *m*, portamechas *m* (*AmL*); ~ **collar** *n* PETR TECH barrena de carga *f* (*AmL*), collar de perforación *m* (*Esp*), lastrabarrena *f* (*Esp*), portamechas *m* (*AmL*), PETROL portamechas *m*; ~ **column** *n* PETROL columna de perforación *f*; ~ **core** *n* MINE testigo de la perforación *m*, testigo de sondeo *m*; ~ **cuttings** *n pl* COAL detritos de sondeos *m pl*, detritus de sondeos *m*, GAS detritos de perforación *m pl*, detritos de sondeos *m pl*, detritus de perforación *m*, detritos de sondeos *m pl*, ripios *m pl*, virutas de perforación *f pl*, PETR TECH cortes *m pl*, detritos de perforación *m pl*, detritos de sondeos *m pl*, detritus de perforación *m*, detritos de sondeos *m*, ripios *m pl*; ~ **floor** *n* PETROL piso de perforación *m*; ~ **gage** *AmE*, ~ **gauge** *BrE n* MECH ENG calibrador de brocas *m*, galga de brocas *f*, *for measuring angle of twistdrill bevel* galga de ángulos de corte de brocas *f*; ~ **grinder** *n* MECH ENG afiladora de brocas *f*; ~ **head**

n MECH ENG cabezal portabrocas *m*; ~ **holder** *n* MECH ENG *metalwork*, MINE portabrocas *m*; ~ **hole** *n* MINE agujero de sondeo *m*, barreno *m* (*Esp*), orificio de mina *m* (*AmL*); ~ **jar** *n* MINE sonda de percusión *f*, trépano *m*; ~ **joint** *n* MINE conexión para brocas *f*, junta de unión para brocas *f*; ~ **locater** *n* MECH ENG *of drilling machine* localizador de taladro *m*; ~ **pin** *n* CONST *of lock* barreno *m*; ~ **pipe** *n* MINE, PETR TECH, PETROL tubería de perforación *f*, tubería vástago *f*, tubo de perforación *m*, varilla de sondeo *f*, varillaje *m*; ~ **pipe coupling** *n* MINE empalme de las varillas de perforación *m*; ~ **planting** *n* AGRIC siembra en hilera *f*; ~ **pole joint** *n* MINE conexión de las varillas de perforación *f*; ~ **press** *n* MECH, MECH ENG prensa taladradora *f*, taladradora de columna *f*; ~ **rig** *n* MINE *boring* carro perforador *m* (*Esp*), perforadora montada sobre carrillo *f* (*AmL*); ~ **rod** *n* MINE barra para fabricar barrenas *f*, varilla de perforación *f*, varilla de sonda *f*, vástago para broca postiza *m*, PETROL varilla de perforación *f*; ~ **rod grab** *n* MINE arrancasonda *m*; ~ **rope** *n* MINE cable de sondeo *m*; ~ **sharpener** *n* MECH ENG afiladora de brocas *f*; ~ **ship** *n* PETR TECH barco de perforación *m*, buque de perforación *m*, buque de prospección de hidrocarburos *m*, PETROL buque de perforación *m*, buque de prospección de hidrocarburos *m*, WATER TRANSP buque de prospección de hidrocarburos *m*, buque para perforaciones *m*; ~ **site** *n* MINE emplazamiento de perforación *m*; ~ **socket** *n* MECH ENG boquilla para taladro *f*, taladro *m*; ~ **spout** *n* AGRIC distribuidor de semilla *m*; ~ **steel** *n* MECH ENG acero para brocas *m*, METALL, MINE acero para barrenas *m*, acero para brocas *m*, acero para picos *m*; ~ **stem** *n* PETROL columna perforadora *f*, vástago de perforación *m*; ~ **stem test** *n* (*DST*) FUELLESS prueba del árbol *f*, PETR TECH prueba de producción con tubería de perforación *f* (*DST*); ~ **string** *n* PETR TECH sarta de perforación *f*, PETROL columna perforadora *f*; ~ **string drag** *n* PETR TECH arrastre *m*

drill² *vt* COAL barrenar, CONST taladrar, *borehole* barrenar, perforar, MECH barrenar, taladrar, agujerear, perforar, MECH ENG taladrar, barrenar, MINE barrenar, taladrar, PETR TECH barrenar

drill³ *vi* MINE hacer maniobras (*AmL*), perforar (*Esp*); ~ **offshore** *vi* WATER TRANSP perforar mar adentro

drillability *n* PETR TECH perforabilidad *f*, propiedad de las rocas al ser perforadas *f*

drillable *adj* PETR TECH perforable, taladrable

drilled: ~ **fillister head screw** *n* MECH ENG cabeza cilíndrica taladrada *f*, cabeza redonda taladrada *f*; ~ **well** *n* HYDROL pozo perforado *m*

driller *n* PETR TECH barrenadora *f*, perforador *m*, perforista *m*, sondista *m*, taladradora *f*, PETROL perforador *m*; ~ **box** *n* MINE caja de sonda *f*

drilling *n* COAL maniobras *f pl*, perforación *f*, sondeo *m*, taladrado *m*, taladradura *f*, *of blast hole* barrenado *m*, GAS perforación *f*, MECH ENG *in metal* taladrado *m*, MINE barrenado *m*, perforación *f*, PROD, WATER perforación *f*; ~ **attachment** *n* MECH ENG accesorio de taladradora *m*; ~ **barge** *n* PETROL barcaza de perforación *f*; ~ **bit** *n* COAL, CONST, MECH, MECH ENG barrena *f*, MINE barrena *f*, trépano *m*, tricono *m* (*Esp*), trépano de sondeo *m* (*AmL*), PETROL broca *f*, trépano *m*, barrena *f*; ~ **break** *n* PETROL avance de penetración *m*, cambio de velocidad de avance de la perforación *m*; ~ **cable** *n* MINE

cable de perforación *m*; ~ **conditions** *n pl* PETR TECH condiciones de perforación *f pl*, condiciones de sondeo *f pl*; ~ **contractor** *n* PETROL contratista de perforaciones *m*; ~ **crew** *n* PETR TECH cuadrilla de perforación *f*, cuadrilla de sondeo *f*, personal de perforación *m*; ~ **debris** *n* COAL detritos de la perforación *m pl*, detritus de la perforación *m*; ~ **engineer** *n* PETR TECH, PETROL ingeniero de perforación *m*; ~ **equipment** *n* MINE equipo de sondeo *m*, equipo para perforar *m*; ~ **floor** *n* PETR TECH planchada *f*, plataforma *f*; ~ **jar** *n* MINE corredera *f*; ~ **jig** *n* MECH ENG plantilla para taladrar *f*, taladradora portátil *f*; ~ **line** *n* PETR TECH, PETROL cable de perforación *m* (*Esp*), guaya *f* (*AmL*), línea de perforación *f* (*Esp*); ~ **machine** *n* MECH máquina de barrenar *f*, máquina de perforar *f*, perforadora *f*, taladradora *f*, MECH ENG *metal-drilling* máquina de perforar *f*, máquina de taladrar *f*, taladradora para ángulos *f*, perforadora *f*, taladradora *f*, MINE martillo perforador *m*, máquina de perforar *f*; ~ **machine table** *n* COAL mesa de taladrar *f*; ~ **mast** *n* PETROL mástil de perforación *m*; ~ **mud** *n* PETR TECH, PETROL lodo de perforación *m*; ~ **operations** *n pl* PETR TECH operaciones de la perforación *f pl*, operaciones de sondeo *f pl*; ~ **pillar** *n* MECH ENG columna de taladradora *f*; ~ **plant** *n* MINE instalación de sondeos *f* (*AmL*), plataforma de sondeos *f* (*Esp*); ~ **platform** *n* PETR TECH, PETROL equipo de perforación *m*, plataforma de perforación *f*, taladro *m*, WATER TRANSP plataforma de perforación *f*; ~ **program** *AmE*, ~ **programme** *BrE* *n* PETR TECH programa de perforación *m*, programación de perforación *f*; ~ **rate** *n* CONST rendimiento de perforación *m*, PETR TECH tasa de penetración *f* (*ROP*), velocidad de avance *f*; ~ **rig** *n* MINE equipo de perforación *m*, máquina perforadora *f*, tren de sondeo *m*, PETR TECH equipo de perforación *m*, taladro *m*; ~ **site** *n* MINE zona de sondeos *f*, PETROL emplazamiento de perforación *m*; ~ **sludge** *n* PETR TECH lodo de perforación *m*; ~ **spindle** *n* MECH ENG eje de la taladradora *m*; ~ **superintendent** *n* PETROL superintendente de perforación *m*; ~ **template** *n* MECH ENG plantilla para taladrar *f*; ~ **tool** *n* CONST *earth boring* taladradora *f*; ~ **winch** *n* MINE cabrestante de sondeo *m*, torno de sondeo *m*

drillings *n pl* COAL fango de sondeo *m*, virutas de taladrar *f pl*, MINE fangos de sondeo *m pl*, polvo de barreno *m*

drinkable *adj* FOOD potable

drinking: ~ **trough** *n* AGRIC abrevadero *m*; ~ **water** *n* CONST, FOOD, HYDROL, WATER agua potable *f*; ~-**water cooler** *n* REFRIG enfriador de agua potable *m*; ~-**water quality** *n* WATER calidad de agua potable *f*; ~-**water supply** *n* HYDROL, WATER abastecimiento de agua potable *m*, fuente de agua potable *f*

drip¹: ~-**dry** *adj* TEXTIL secado por goteo; ~-**proof** *adj* MECH ENG protegido contra goteo, protegido contra goteras, protegido contra salpicaduras; ~-**proof screen-protected** *adj* MECH ENG protegido contra goteo, protegido contra goteras, protegido contra salpicaduras

drip² *n* FOOD goteo *m*, REFRIG exudado *m*; ~ **cock** *n* CONST llave de desagüe *f*; ~ **cup** *n* CONST colector de goteo *m*; ~ **feed lubrication** *n* MECH ENG lubricación de goteo *f*; ~ **feed lubricator** *n* MECH ENG lubricador a gotas *m*; ~ **irrigation** *n* AGRIC riego por goteo *m*;

~ **pump** n WATER bomba para purgar agua f; ~ **tray** n PROD bandeja para recoger el goteo f, REFRIG cubeta de desescarcha f

drive[1] adj MECH ENG motriz

drive[2] n COMP&DP dispositivo m, mecanismo m, unidad f, MECH accionamiento m, impulsión f, impulso m, propulsión f, MECH ENG impulsor m, motor m, propulsor m, transmisor m, MINE galería f, galería en dirección f, piso de galería m, TEXTIL impulso m, VEH eje rotativo m, árbol m; ~ **battery** n TRANSP batería de accionamiento f; ~ **block** n MINE calza f, carrucha f (Esp), chabota f (AmL), polea f; ~ **bolt** n PROD perno de transmisión m; ~ **chain** n AUTO, VEH cadena de transmisión f; ~ **coil** n ELEC ENG relay bobina de excitación f, impulsora f; ~ **end** n ELEC ENG terminal extremo de excitación m; ~ **fit** n MECH ENG montaje a frotamiento duro m, montaje forzado m; ~ **head** n MINE cabeza golpeadora de hinca f; ~ **knob** n INSTR botón de mando m; ~ **line** n AUTO, VEH línea de conducción f; ~ **mechanism** n CINEMAT mecanismo de accionamiento m; ~ **motor** n CINEMAT motor de accionamiento m, ELEC ENG motor de arrastre m, motor de impulsión m, PHOTO motor de accionamiento m; ~ **pin** n CINEMAT garfio de arrastre m, MECH ENG dedo de arrastre m, uña de arrastre f; ~ **pinion** n AUTO, VEH piñón conductor m, piñón de ataque m, piñón de mando m, piñón motriz m; ~ **pinion shaft** n AUTO, VEH eje del piñón de ataque m; ~ **pipe** n MINE tubo de perforación m, tubo de revestimiento m, tubo de sondeo m, tubo hincado m; ~ **power** n MECH ENG fuerza de propulsión f, fuerza de transmisión f, fuerza motriz f; ~ **pulley** n VEH polea conductora f, polea de mando f; ~ **sampler** n MINE muestreo por tubo hincado m; ~ **shaft** n AmE (cf propeller shaft BrE) AUTO eje de la transmisión m, eje impulsor m, eje motriz m, árbol de mando m, árbol de transmisión m, árbol impulsor m, MECH ENG eje conductor m, eje motor m, árbol de transmisión m, VEH eje de la transmisión m, eje propulsor m, árbol de transmisión m, árbol impulsor m, árbol de mando m; ~**-shaft tunnel** n AmE (cf propeller-shaft tunnel BrE) AUTO, VEH alojamiento del árbol de mando m, túnel del árbol de transmisión m; ~ **shoe** n MINE zapata cortante f, zapata encajadora f, zapata propulsora f; ~ **side** n PAPER lado de la transmisión m, lado del accionamiento m; ~ **sprocket** n CINEMAT rueda dentada motriz f, TV rueda de transmisión f, VEH rueda dentada motriz para cadena f; ~ **system** n MECH ENG sistema conductor m, sistema motor m, TEXTIL sistema de impulsión m; ~ **train** n VEH grupo de engranajes conductores m; ~ **tube** n MINE canal de arrastre m (AmL), canal de transmisión m (Esp); ~ **voltage** n TV voltaje de excitación m; ~ **wheel** n AUTO, VEH rueda de tracción f, rueda motriz f, rueda propulsora f

drive[3] vt CONST screw clavar, atornillar, MECH activar, mover, impulsar, hacer funcionar, accionar, MECH ENG propulsar, impulsar, transmitir, SPACE accionar, TEXTIL conducir; ~ **in** vt CONST clavar, MECH ENG introducir, meter; ~ **into** vt MECH ENG empujar, introducir, meter

drive[4] vi WATER conducir

driven: ~ **disc** n BrE, ~ **disk** AmE MECH ENG disco conducido m; ~ **element** n MECH ENG elemento conducido m; ~ **plate** n AUTO, VEH disco conducido m; ~ **plate assembly** n AUTO montaje del disco conducido m; ~ **tool holder** n MECH ENG portaherramientas conducido m; ~ **wheel** n MECH ENG engranaje conducido m, rueda conducida f

driver n ACOUST explorador m, paso excitador m, COMP&DP controlador m, impulsor m, MECH ENG conductor de arrastre m, fuerza motriz de arrastre f, motor de arrastre m, rivet drift remache de arrastre m, key drift chaveta de arrastre f, clavija de arrastre f, pasador de arrastre m, lathe dog, carrier perro de arrastre m, PROD troquel m, RAIL maquinista m; ~'s **cab** n RAIL, VEH cabina del maquinista f; ~'s **cabin** n VEH cabina del maquinista f; ~ **card** n PROD tarjeta de gestión f; ~ **chuck** n MECH ENG of lathe plato de arrastre m; ~ **plate** n MECH ENG of lathe plato de arrastre m; ~ **stage** n AUTO etapa conductora f, SPACE etapa excitadora f, paso excitador m; ~'s **windscreen** n BrE (cf driver's windshield AmE), ~'s **windshield** n AmE VEH parabrisas m

driverless adj TRANSP sin conductor

driving[1] adj MECH ENG motriz

driving[2] n COAL hinca f, CONST of a screw apriete m, well-sinking hincado m, MECH ENG impulsor m, transmisor m, conductor m, motor m, MINE cuele m, avance m, perforación f, apertura f, hinca f, RAIL, VEH conducción f; ~ **axle** n AUTO eje motriz m, VEH eje de mando m; ~ **belt** n MECH ENG correa conductora f, correa motriz f, correa transmisora f, for conveying motion cinta conductora f, cinta motriz f; ~ **block** n CONST well casing cabeza de percursión f; ~ **crew** n RAIL equipo del maquinista m; ~ **desk** n RAIL pupitre del maquinista m; ~ **disc** n BrE, ~ **disk** AmE MECH ENG disco conductor m; ~ **dog** n MECH ENG perro de arrastre m; ~ **drum** n TRANSP tambor de impulsos m, tambor motor m; ~ **element** n MECH ENG elemento conductor m; ~ **end** n MECH lado de la transmisión m; ~ **fit** n MECH ENG ajuste a presión m; ~ **force** n METALL fuerza motriz f, TEXTIL fuerza de transmisión f; ~ **gear** n MECH ENG aparato conductor m, aparato motor m, aparato motriz m, engranaje conductor m, engranaje motor m, engranaje motriz m, piñón conductor m, piñón motor m, piñón motriz m, engranaje de transmisión m, engranaje principal m; ~ **head** n MECH ENG cabezal conductor m; ~**-in** n CONST of nail remachado m, of screw apriete m; ~ **level** n MINE galería de avance f (Esp), galería del frente de ataque f (AmL); ~ **mirror** n INSTR espejo retrovisor m; ~ **pinion** n MECH ENG piñón conductor m, piñón de arrastre m, piñón de ataque m, piñón motor m; ~ **potential** n ELEC ENG tensión de trabajo f; ~ **pressure** n MECH ENG presión de ataque f, presión motriz f; ~ **propeller** n TRANSP hélice impulsora f; ~ **pulley** n MECH ENG, PROD polea conductora f, polea impulsora f, polea motriz f; ~ **pulse** n TV pulso de excitación m; ~ **shaft** n MECH ENG eje conductor m, eje impulsor m, eje motor m, eje motor principal m, WATER TRANSP eje de accionamiento m; ~ **side** n PROD of belt ramal tenso m; ~ **signals** n pl TV señales de arrastre f pl (Esp), señales de excitación f pl (AmL); ~ **tenon** n MECH ENG for parallel shank tools espiga conductora f; ~ **test** n VEH prueba de aptitud para conducir f; ~ **trailer car** n TRANSP cabeza tractora del remolque f, cabeza tractora del trailer f; ~ **unit** n PROD, TRANSP unidad motora f; ~ **wheel** n CINEMAT rueda motriz f, MECH ENG rueda de arrastre f, rueda transmisora f, rueda de impulsión f, flywheel rueda motora f, rueda conductora *f*, rueda motriz *f*, volante *m*, TRANSP volante *m*

drizzle[1] *n* METEO llovizna *f*

drizzle[2] *vi* METEO garuar, lloviznar

drogue *n* AIR TRANSP cesta *f*, SPACE embudo *m*, WATER TRANSP *emergency* ancla flotante *f*; ~ **chute** *n* SPACE paracaídas troncoidal *m*

drone *n* AIR TRANSP, SPACE avión teledirigido *m*; ~ **helicopter** *n* AIR TRANSP helicóptero radiodirigido *m*, helicóptero teledirigido *m*

droop *n* ELECTRON disminución *f*; ~ **flap** *n* AIR TRANSP flap de inclinación *m*, TRANSP aleta hipersustentadora de inclinación *f*, flap de inclinación *m*; ~ **nose** *n* AIR TRANSP morro Krueger *m*; ~~**nose aircraft** *n* AIR TRANSP avión de morro caído *m*; ~ **rate** *n* ELECTRON porcentaje de disminución *m*; ~ **restrainer** *n* MECH ENG soporte *m*; ~~**restraining ring** *n* MECH ENG anilla de soporte *f*, aro de soporte *m*; ~~**restraining shaft** *n* MECH ENG eje rígido *m*

drop[1]: ~~**forged** *adj* PROD estampado en caliente

drop[2] *n* C&G gota *f*, COAL gota *f*, pajuela *f*, partícula *f*, caída *f*, descenso *m*, desnivel *m*, CONST caída *f*, gota *f*, pendiente *f*, FOOD gota *f*, GEOL caída *f*, descenso *m*, desnivel *m*, PROD *of pattern-withdrawing machine* indicador de disco abatible *m*, REFRIG caída *f*, WATER TRANSP *of sail* baluma de popa *f*, caída *f*, caída de popa *f*; ~ **arm** *n* AIR TRANSP brazo de caída *m*, AUTO brazo de mando *m*, VEH brazo de mando *m*, palanca de mando *f*; ~ **arrow** *n* CONST *surveying* jalón *m*; ~ **bed frame** *n* VEH chasis con piso descendente *m*; ~ **box** *n* WATER caja inferior de descarga *f*; ~ **cable** *n* TV cable de caída de voltaje *m*; ~ **center rim** *AmE*, ~ **centre rim** *BrE* *n* AUTO reborde central de caída de la llanta *m*, VEH llanta de centrado de la rueda *f*; ~ **counter** *n* PACK cuentagotas *m*; ~~**down menu** *n* COMP&DP menú desplegable *m*, menú drop down *m*; ~ **folio** *n* PRINT numeración a pie de página *f*; ~~**forged rivetless chain** *n* MECH ENG cadena sin remaches estampada en caliente *f*; ~~**forged steel dog** *n* PROD *of lathe* garra de acero forjada en caliente *f*; ~~**forged steel spanner** *n* PROD llave de acero forjada en caliente *f*; ~ **forging** *n* MECH estampado por caída *m*, MECH ENG forja a martinete *f*, forja con troquel *f*, forja de estampado en caliente *f*, PROD forja con troquel *f*, pieza matrizada *f*, estampación en caliente *f*, forja de estampado en caliente *f*, forja a martinete *f*; ~ **formation** *n* FLUID formación de gotas *f*; ~~**frame indicator** *n* TV indicador de caída de imagen *m*; ~ **frame mode** *n* TV modo de caída de imagen *m*; ~ **grate** *n* PROD *of furnace* emparrillado basculante *m*; ~ **hammer** *n* COAL martillo pilón *m*, martinete de caída libre *m*, martinete de forja *m*, CONST maza *f*, MECH ENG, PROD martillo de fragua *m*, martillo pilón *m*, martinete de caída libre *m*; ~ **height** *n* COAL, PACK altura de caída *f*; ~ **hole** *n* COAL pozo de sondeo por tierra *m*; ~~**in** *n* COMP&DP información parásita *f*, ELEC ENG error por exceso *m*, información parásita *f*; ~~**in package** *n* ELEC ENG paquete de añadidura por goteo *m*; ~ **initial** *n* PRINT inicial que ocupa más de una línea de altura *f*; ~ **keel** *n* WATER TRANSP quilla retráctil *f*; ~ **line wiring** *n* PROD línea de caída de tensión *f*; ~~**out** *n* COMP&DP desaparición *f*, pérdida de información *f*, ELEC *insufficient amplitude* intensidad de desexcitación *f*, ELEC ENG *relay* disparo *m*, *of mains* desenganche *m*, *insufficient amplitude* intensidad de desexcitación *f*, PRINT *computing* fallo

de la señal *m*, TV caída *f*; ~~**out compensator** *n* TV compensador de caída *m*; ~~**out current** *n* ELEC *of relay* corriente de desaccionamiento *f*, corriente de paso al reposo *f*, corriente de vuelta al reposo *f*, ELEC ENG corriente de desenganche *f*; ~~**out switch signal** *n* TV señal de caída *f*; ~~**out time** *n* ELEC *of relay* tiempo de desaccionamiento *m*, tiempo de desactivación *m*, PROD tiempo de desexcitación *m*, tiempo de paso a la posición de reposo *m*, PROD tiempo de desexcitación *m*; ~~**out voltage** *n* ELEC ENG tensión de desprendimiento *f*; ~ **pan** *n* PROD bandeja para recoger el goteo *f*; ~ **pile hammer** *n* MECH martillo pilón *m*; ~ **point** *n* FLUID punto de condensación *m*, REFRIG punto de fusión *m*; ~ **point apparatus** *n* LAB aparato de punto de goteo *m*; ~ **of pressure** *n* HYDRAUL caída de presión *f*, pérdida de carga *f*; ~ **runner** *n* PROD canal de colada en caída directa *m*; ~ **shadow** *n* PRINT sombreado bajo letras *m*; ~ **shipment** *n* PROD envío directo *m*; ~ **test** *n* PACK ensayo de caída *m*; ~ **valve** *n* HYDRAUL válvula invertida *f*; ~ **valve gear** *n* HYDRAUL mecanismo de válvula invertida *m*; ~ **wire** *n* TEXTIL caballero *m*; ~ **zone** *n* MILIT zona de lanzamiento *f*, SPACE zona de descenso *f*

drop[3] *vt* ELEC ENG *voltage* bajar, PRINT descender; ~~**forge** *vt* PROD estampar en caliente

drop[4] *vi* WATER TRANSP *of wind* amainar; ~ **anchor** *vi* WATER TRANSP fondear, largar el ancla

droplet *n* METEO gota de nube *f*, gotita *f*, POLL gotita *f*, gotícula *f*

dropmaster *n* MILIT jefe de salto *m*

dropped[1]: ~ **axle** *n* VEH eje inferior *m*; ~ **side** *n* GEOL labio inferior *m*

dropped[2]: **not to be ~** *phr* PACK no volcar

dropper *n* LAB cuentagotas *m*, gotero *m*

dropping: ~ **bottle** *n* C&G botella cuentagotas *f*, LAB botella cuentagotas *f*, gotero *m*; ~ **resistor** *n* ELEC ENG resistor reductor de tensión *m*; ~ **tube** *n* LAB tubo cuentagotas *m*, tubo de goteo *m*; ~ **zone** *n* MILIT zona de lanzamiento *f*

dross *n* COAL carbón de calidad inferior *m*, escoria *f*, espuma *f*; ~ **filter** *n* GAS filtro de impurezas *m*

drought: ~ **resistance** *n* AGRIC resistencia a sequía *f*; ~ **stress** *n* AGRIC período crítico de sequía *m*

drowned: ~ **flow** *n* FLUID flujo ahogado *m*; ~ **nappe** *n* HYDROL capa anegada *f*; ~ **river valley** *n* OCEAN valle de un río inundado *m*; ~ **turbine** *n* HYDRAUL turbina anegada *f*, turbina hidráulica *f*; ~ **valley** *n* HYDROL valle anegado *m*; ~ **weir** *n* HYDRAUL, HYDROL, WATER azud sumergido *m*, vertedero sumergido *m*

DRS *abbr* (*data-relay satellite*) SPACE satélite de recogida de datos *m*, satélite retransmisor de datos *m*

drum *n* GEN tambor *m*; ~ **altimeter** *n* AIR TRANSP altímetro de tambor *m*; ~ **armature** *n* ELEC, ELEC ENG inducido de tambor *m*; ~ **brake** *n* AUTO freno de tambor *m*; ~ **brake tools** *n pl* AUTO herramientas del freno de tambor *f pl*; ~ **cam** *n* PROD leva de tambor *f*; ~ **cobber** *n* COAL clasificador de tambor *m*, separador de tambor *m*; ~ **controller** *n* ELEC combinador cilíndrico *m*, combinador de tambor *m*; ~ **cooler** *n* REFRIG enfriador de tambor *m*; ~ **debarker** *n* PAPER descortezadora de tambor *f*; ~ **development** *n* CINEMAT revelado en tambor *m*; ~ **drive** *n* MECH ENG conductor de cilindro *m*, conductor de tambor *m*, motor de cilindro *m*, motor de tambor *m*; ~ **dryer** *n* COAL secador de tambor *m*, FOOD secador de rodillos *m*, TEXTIL secadora de tambor *f*, THERMO secador de tambor *m*; ~ **dyeing** *n* COLOUR teñido en tambor *m*; ~ **feeder** *n* MECH ENG, TEXTIL alimentador de tambor *m*; ~ **filter** *n* COAL, HYDROL filtro giratorio *m*, tambor filtrante *m*; ~ **freeze dryer** *n* REFRIG liofilizador de tambor *m*; ~ **furnace** *n* THERMO horno de tambor *m*; ~ **gate** *n* FUELLESS *dams* compuerta de tambor *f*; ~ **kiln** *n* THERMO horno de tambor *m*; ~ **lens** *n* INSTR tambor de lentes *m*; ~ **membrane** *n* ACOUST membrana timpánica *f*; ~ **mix** *n* CONST mezcla de bidón *f*; ~ **plotter** *n* *AmE* (*cf* barrel plotter *BrE*) COMP&DP impresora de tambor *f*, plotter de tambor *m*, tambor de traza *m*, trazador de rodillo *m*, trazador de tambor *m*, PRINT impresora de tambor *f*; ~ **printer** *n* *AmE* (*cf barrel printer BrE*) COMP&DP, PRINT impresora de rodillo *f*, impresora de tambor *f*; ~ **scanner** *n* PRINT escáner de tambor *m*, TV tambor de exploración *m*; ~ **screen** *n* HYDROL criba cilíndrica *f*, criba de tambor *f*; ~ **separator** *n* COAL separador cilíndrico *m*; ~ **shaft** *n* MECH ENG eje de tambor *m*; ~ **skimmer** *n* MAR POLL rasera de tambor *f*; ~ **starter** *n* ELEC *switch*, ELEC ENG arrancador de tambor *m*; ~ **store** *n* TELECOM almacenamiento de tambor *m*; ~ **switch** *n* ELEC conmutador de tambor *m*, interruptor de tambor *m*; ~ **titler** *n* CINEMAT tituladora de tambor *f*; ~ **washer** *n* CONST arandela *f*, roldana del tambor *f*; ~ **winding** *n* ELEC ENG devanado de tambor *m*

drumhead *n* PROD *of capstan* corona *f*

druse *n* GEOL drusa *f*

drusy *adj* GEOL drúsico

dry¹ *adj* GEN seco

dry²: ~ **acid deposit** *n* POLL depósito ácido seco *m*; ~ **acidic fallout** *n* POLL polvo radiactivo ácido y seco *m*, precipitación acídica seca *f*, precipitación radiactiva ácida-seca *f*; ~ **adiabatic lapse rate** *n* POLL gradiente adiabático seco *m*, razón adiabática de secado *f*, THERMO gradiente adiabático seco *m*; ~ **air** *n* METEO aire seco *m*; ~ **air filter** *n* HEAT ENG filtro de aire seco *m*; ~ **back** *n* PRINT alteración de la tinta durante su secado *f*; ~ **battery** *n* ELEC ENG batería seca *f*; ~ **broke** *n* PAPER desechos secos *m pl*; ~ **bulb temperature** *n* HEAT ENG temperatura de bulbo seco *f*; ~ **bulb thermometer** *n* HEAT ENG, REFRIG, THERMO termómetro de bola seca *m*, termómetro de bulbo seco *m*, termómetro seco *m*; ~ **bulk carrier** *n* WATER TRANSP buque de carga seca a granel *m*; ~ **bulk container** *n* TRANSP contenedor de volúmenes secos *m*; ~ **cargo ship** *n* WATER TRANSP buque de carga seca *m*; ~ **cell** *n* ELEC, ELEC ENG, PHYS pila seca *f*; ~ **circuit** *n* ELEC ENG circuito con bajo nivel de señal *m*, circuito de mínima potencia *m*; ~ **cleaning** *n* DETERG limpieza en seco *f*; ~ **cleaning agent** *n* CHEM, DETERG agente de limpieza en seco *m*; ~ **clutch** *n* VEH embrague con funcionamiento en seco *m*; ~ **color** *AmE*, ~ **colour** *BrE* *n* COLOUR colorante en polvo *m*; ~ **compression** *n* REFRIG compresión seca *f*, funcionamiento en régimen seco *m*; ~ **connection** *n* ELEC ENG conexión en seco *f*; ~ **connector** *n* ELEC ENG conector seco *m*; ~ **content** *n* PAPER contenido en sólidos *m*; ~ **cooling tower** *n* REFRIG torre de enfriamiento seco *f*; ~ **creping** *n* PAPER crespado en seco *m*; ~ **crops** *n pl* AGRIC cosechas de secano *f pl*; ~ **crushing** *n* COAL molienda en seco *f*; ~ **crust** *n* COAL corteza seca *f*; ~ **density** *n* COAL, CONST densidad en estado seco *f*, densidad seca *f*; ~ **deposition** *n* POLL depósito seco *m*, electrodeposición seca *f*, precipitación seca *f*, sedimentación

seca *f*; ~ **desulfurization process** *AmE*, ~ **desulphurization process** *BrE* *n* POLL proceso de desulfuración por vía seca *m*; ~ **distillation** *n* CHEM destilación seca *f*; ~ **dock** *n* CONST, WATER TRANSP dique de carenas *m*, dique seco *m*; ~ **dust removal** *n* SAFE eliminación de polvo seco *f*; ~ **electrolyte** *n* ELEC ENG electrólito seco *m*; ~ **end** *n* PAPER parte seca *f*; ~ **engine** *n* AIR TRANSP motor seco *m*; ~ **expansion evaporator** *n* REFRIG evaporador en régimen seco *m*; ~ **farming** *n* AGRIC cultivo de secano *m*; ~ **flashover voltage** *n* ELEC *of arc* tensión de contorneamiento en seco *f*, tensión de salto arco con aislador seco *f*, tensión disruptiva en seco *f*, voltaje de contorneamiento en seco *m*, voltaje de salto arco con aislador seco *m*; ~ **fraction** *n* HEAT ENG *of steam* fracción seca *f*; ~ **freeze** *n* PACK congelación a seco *f*; ~ **gas** *n* GAS, PETROL gas seco *m*; ~ **heat** *n* TEXTIL calor seco *m*; ~ **hole** *n* MINE agujero de sondeo hecho en seco *m*, barreno seco *m* (*Esp*), barreno sin utilizar agua para mitigar el polvo *m* (*AmL*), perforación hacia arriba *f*, pozo donde no se encuentra ni gas ni petróleo *m*, pozo estéril *m* (*AmL*), pozo improductivo *m*, pozo seco *m* (*Esp*), PETR TECH, PETROL pozo estéril *m* (*AmL*), pozo improductivo *m*, pozo seco *m* (*Esp*); ~ **ice** *n* CHEM dióxido de carbono sólido *m*, hielo seco *m*, FOOD, REFRIG hielo seco *m*; ~ **ice bunker** *n* REFRIG compartimiento de nieve carbónica *m*; ~ **ink** *n* COLOUR tinta en polvo *f*, tóner *m*; ~ **joint** *n* ELEC, HYDRAUL junta de dilatación *f*; ~ **lens** *n* LAB lente seca *f*; ~ **line** *n* PAPER línea seca *f*; ~ **mass** *n* SPACE masa seca *f*; ~ **matter** *n* (*DM*) AGRIC materia seca *f* (*MS*), HYDROL material impuro *m*; ~ **measure** *n* AGRIC medida para áridos *f*; ~ **mounting press** *n* PHOTO prensa para montaje en seco *f*; ~ **mounting tissue** *n* PHOTO papel de seda para montaje en seco *m*; ~ **mud** *n* PETR TECH lodo seco *m*; ~ **natural gas** *n* GAS, PETR TECH gas natural seco *m*; ~ **offset** *n* PRINT offset seco *m*; ~ **offset ink** *n* PRINT tóner para offset *m*; ~ **out** *n* NUCL secado *m*; ~ **powder fire extinguisher** *n* SAFE extintor de incendios de polvo *m*, extintor de incendios de polvo químico seco *m*; ~ **power** *n* AIR TRANSP potencia seca *f*; ~ **precipitation** *n* POLL precipitación seca *f*; ~ **precision grinding** *n* MECH ENG rectificado de precisión en seco *m*; ~ **pulp** *n* PAPER pasta seca *f*, pulpa seca *f*; ~ **rot** *n* AGRIC, CONST podredumbre seca *f*, WATER TRANSP *in wood* caries seca *f*, pudrición seca *f*; ~ **run** *n* PROD ensayo *m*; ~ **running compressor** *n* MECH ENG compresor de funcionamiento en seco *m*, compresor de funcionamiento sin lubricante *m*; ~ **season** *n* AGRIC, METEO estación seca *f*; ~ **sludge** *n* PETR TECH lodo seco *m*; ~ **solids content** *n* PAPER contenido en sólidos *m*, materia seca *f*; ~ **splicer** *n* CINEMAT empalmadora en seco *f*; ~ **spray** *n* C&G aspersión seca *f*; ~ **standpipe** *n* CONST depósito en seco *m*; ~ **steam** *n* FUELLESS, HEAT vapor seco *m*; ~ **stone wall** *n* CONST mampostería en seco *f*; ~ **storage** *n* NUCL almacenamiento en seco *m*; ~ **storage battery** *n* ELEC, ELEC ENG acumulador seco *m*, batería de acumuladores secos *f*; ~ **sump** *n* AUTO, VEH cárter en seco *m*; ~ **sump lubrication** *n* AUTO, VEH lubricación por cárter seco *f*; ~ **transfer lettering** *n* PRINT rotulación con letras autoadhesivas *f*; ~ **tree** *n* PETR TECH árbol seco *m*; ~ **type cooler** *n* REFRIG enfriador de tipo seco *m*; ~ **type power transformer** *n* ELEC

ENG transformador en seco *m*; **~-type transformer** *n* ELEC, ELEC ENG transformador de tipo seco *m*; ~ **valley** *n* HYDROL valle árido *m*; ~ **weight** *n* AIR TRANSP, PACK peso en seco *m*, SPACE masa seca *f*, masa seca sin combustible *f*, peso en seco *m*, peso sin combustible *m*; ~ **well** *n* NUCL pozo estéril *m* (*AmL*), pozo seco *m* (*Esp*), PETR TECH pozo seco, WATER cámara seca *f*, pozo estéril *m* (*AmL*), pozo seco *m* (*Esp*)

dry³ *vt* COAL agotar, secar, HEAT desecar, THERMO desecar, secar; ~ **by cold air** *vt* THERMO secar con aire frío; ~ **by heat** *vt* THERMO secar por calor; **~-clean** *vt* TEXTIL limpiar en seco; **~-dock** *vt* WATER TRANSP meter en dique seco; **~-heat-set** *vt* TEXTIL fijar con calor en seco; **~-mount** *vt* PHOTO montar en seco, pegar en seco; ~ **up** *vt* HYDRAUL achicar, descebar, desecar, deshidratar

dry⁴: ~ **up** *vti* HYDROL desecar completamente

dry⁵ *vi* COAL agotarse, secarse; **~-dock** *vi* WATER TRANSP entrar en dique seco

dryer *n* AGRIC secadora *f*, CHEM desecador *m*, secador *m*, COAL desecador *m*, secadora *f*, MECH ENG secadora *f*, P&R máquina secadora *f*, secador *m*, PRINT *ink* secador *m*, secante *m*, TEXTIL secadora *f*, THERMO desecador *m*, secador *m*, secadero *m*; ~ **fabric** *n* TEXTIL género para secadora *m*; ~ **felt** *n* PAPER fieltro secador *m*, filtro secador *m*; ~ **filter** *n* CHEM TECH filtro desecador *m*; ~ **for grinding wheel** *n* MECH ENG secadora para muela rectificadora *f*; ~ **glazer** *n* PHOTO secadora esmaltadora *f*; ~ **mill** *n* COAL molino en seco *m*; ~ **pocket** *n* PAPER bolsa secadora *f*; ~ **pocket ventilation duct** *n* PAPER conducción para ventilar las bolsas secadoras *f*; ~ **section** *n* PAPER sección de secado *f*, tren de secado *m*

drying *n* CHEM secado *m*, seco, COAL desecación *f*, secado *m*, agotamiento *m*, P&R, PAPER, PETR TECH, TEXTIL, THERMO secado *m*; ~ **agent** *n* PACK secante *f*, THERMO desecante *m*; ~ **air** *n* COAL aire desecante *m*, aire secante *m*; ~ **area** *n* FOOD zona de secado *f*; ~ **cabinet** *n* CINEMAT, FOOD armario de secado *m*, MECH ENG armario secadero *m*, armario secador *m*, P&R cabina de secado *f*, gabinete de secado *m*; ~ **chamber** *n* PROD cámara de desecación *f*, cámara de desecar *f*, THERMO cámara de secado *f*; ~ **column** *n* LAB columna de secado *f*; ~ **cupboard** *n* CINEMAT, FOOD armario de secado *m*; ~ **cylinder** *n* DETERG cilindro de secado *m*, cilindro secador *m*, PAPER cilindro secador *m*, TEXTIL cilindro de secado *m*, cilindro secador *m*; ~ **drum** *n* CONST, DETERG tambor de secado *m*; ~ **floor** *n* PROD secadero *m*; ~ **frame** *n* PHOTO bastidor de secado *m*; ~ **furnace** *n* MECH ENG horno de secado *m*, horno secador *m*, PROD horno de desecar *m*; ~ **house** *n* PROD cámara de secado *f*; ~ **kiln** *n* COAL, FOOD, PROD horno de secado *m*; ~ **machine** *n* PACK secadora *f*; ~ **mark** *n* CINEMAT marca de secado *f*; ~ **oil** *n* FOOD aceite de secado *m*, P&R, PROD *paints* aceite secante *m*; **~-out** *n* THERMO desecado *m*; ~ **oven** *n* COAL estufa de desecación *f*, FOOD, PACK, PAPER, TEXTIL horno de secado *m*; ~ **room** *n* PROD secadero *m*; ~ **section** *n* FOOD sección de secado *f*; ~ **shrinkage** *n* CONST contracción por desecación *f*, contracción por fraguado *f*; ~ **stove** *n* PROD estufa de secado *f*, horno para secar moldes *m*, TEXTIL estufa de secado *f*; ~ **system** *n* GAS sistema de secado *m*; ~ **tower** *n* FOOD torre de secado *f*; ~ **tunnel** *n* FOOD, PACK túnel de secado *m*; **~-up** *n*

HYDROL agotamiento *m*; ~ **varnish** *n* COATINGS barniz de secado *m*

dryness *n* COAL aridez *f*, sequedad *f*, sequía *f*, GEOL, MINERAL aridez *f*, PAPER, TEXTIL sequedad *f*; ~ **fraction** *n* HYDRAUL porcentaje de vapor seco *m*, porcentaje relativo de vapor seco *m*; ~ **ratio** *n* REFRIG relación de sequedad *f*; ~ **test** *n* REFRIG prueba de sequedad *f*

DS *abbr* COMP&DP, NUCL (*data storage AmE, data store BrE*) almacenamiento de datos *m*, TELECOM (*data storage AmE, data store BrE*) almacenamiento de datos *m*, memoria de datos *f*, (*digital section*) sección digital *f*

DSC *abbr* (*digital selective calling*) TELECOM llamada selectiva digital *f*

DSE *abbr* COMP&DP, TELECOM (*data-switching exchange*) CCD (*central de comunicación de datos, central de conmutación de datos*), TELECOM (*digital switching element*) elemento de conmutación digital *m*

D-shackle *n* WATER TRANSP grillete en forma de D *m*

DSI *abbr* (*digital speech interpolation*) TELECOM interpolación vocal digital *f*

DSL *abbr* (*deep scattering layer*) OCEAN capa profunda de dispersión *f*

DSP *abbr* ELECTRON (*digital signal processing*) PSD (*proceso de señal digital*), TSD (*tratamiento de señal digital*), TELECOM (*domain-specific part*) sección específica del dominio *f*

DSR *abbr* (*data set ready*) COMP&DP módem listo para comunicar *m*, módem listo para funcionar *m*, TELECOM conjunto de datos listo *m*

DST *abbr* (*drill stem test*) FUELLESS prueba del árbol *f*, PETR TECH DST (*prueba de producción con tubería de perforación*)

D-star *n* OPT, TELECOM *normalized detectivity* estrella D *f*

DTA *abbr* (*differential thermal analysis*) CHEM, P&R, POLL, THERMO análisis térmico diferencial *m*

DTE *abbr* (*data terminal equipment*) AIR TRANSP, COMP&DP, TELECOM DTE (*conjunto terminal de datos, equipo terminal de datos*)

DTI *abbr* (*digital trunk interface*) TELECOM interfaz de enlace digital *m*

DTL *abbr* (*diode-transistor logic*) COMP&DP, ELECTRON DTL (*circuito a base de diodos y transistores*)

D-to-A *abbr* (*digital-to-analog*) COMP&DP, TV D-a-A (*digital a analógico*)

DTP *abbr* (*desktop publishing*) COMP&DP autoedición *f*, autoedición de textos *f*, programa de edición publicitario *m*, publicación de mesa *f* (*AmL*), tratamiento de textos con opciones gráficas *m*, PRINT autoedición *f*

D₂O *abbr* (*deuterium oxide*) CHEM, NUCL, PHYS D_2O (*óxido de deuterio*)

D-type: ~ **flip-flop** *n* ELECTRON basculador tipo D *m*, biestable D *m*

dual¹ *adj* GEOM doble, dual; **~-ganged** *adj* ELEC doble mando, doblemente acoplado

dual²: **~-beam cathode ray tube** *n* ELECTRON tubo de rayos catódicos de doble haz *m*; **~-capacitor motor** *n* ELEC motor de doble capacitor *m*, motor de doble condensador *m*; ~ **carburetor** *AmE*, ~ **carburettor** *BrE* *n* AUTO, MECH, VEH carburador doble *m*; ~ **carriageway** *n* BrE (*cf divided highway AmE*) CONST autopista de doble calzada *f*, autopista de dos carriles por sentido *f*, carretera de doble sentido *f*, TRANSP autopista de doble calzada *f*, autopista de dos carriles por sentido *f*, carretera de acceso limitado *f*, carretera troncal *f*; **~-carrier transmission** *n* TELECOM transmisión de doble portadora *f*; **~-circuit brake** *n* TRANSP freno de doble circuito *m*; **~ clevis** *n* MECH ENG abrazadera doble *f*, horquilla doble *f*; **~-coil latching relay** *n* ELEC ENG relé de enganche a bobina doble *m*; **~ compressor** *n* MECH ENG compresor de doble efecto *m*, compresor doble *m*; **~ control** *n* AIR TRANSP control doble *m*; **~-control switch** *n* RAIL conmutador de mando doble *m*; **~-current locomotive** *n* ELEC, RAIL locomotora para dos voltajes *f*; **~-cycle reactor** *n* NUCL reactor de ciclo doble *m*; **~ discharge head** *n* MECH ENG cabeza doble de descarga *f*; **~ flight-control system** *n* AIR TRANSP sistema de control de vuelo doble *m*; **~-flow jet engine** *n* AIR TRANSP motores a reacción de flujo doble *m pl*, motor de flujo doble *m*; **~-format camera** *n* PHOTO cámara de dos formatos *f*; **~ fuel** *n* SPACE combustible dual *m*; **~-fuel engine** *n* TRANSP motor de doble combustible *m*; **~-fuel pressure gage** *AmE*, **~-fuel pressure gauge** *BrE n* AIR TRANSP manómetro de presión de doble combustible *m*; **~-fuel system** *n* TRANSP sistema de doble combustible *m*, sistema dual de combustible *m*; **~ indicator** *n* MECH ENG indicador doble *m*, indicador dual *m*; **~-induction log** *n* PETROL perfil de inducción doble *m*; **~-in-line package** *n* (*DIP*) COMP&DP caja de doble hilera de conexiones *f*, empaque doble en línea *m* (*DIP*), paquete en línea doble *m* (*DIP*), ELEC ENG empaque doble en línea *m* (*DIP*), paquete en línea doble *m* (*DIP*); **~-in-line package relay** *n* ELEC ENG relé de paquete en línea doble *m*; **~ input** *n* PROD, TV ingreso dual *m*; **~-input conversion kit** *n* PROD equipo de conversión de doble ingreso *m*; **~ instruction** *n* AIR TRANSP instrucciones dobles *f pl*; **~ instruction time** *n* AIR TRANSP tiempo de instrucción doble *m*; **~-knife cutter** *n* PAPER guillotina de dos cuchillas *f*; **~-level plan** *n* TELECOM plan de doble nivel *m*; **~-mode bus** *n* TRANSP autobús bimodal *m* (*Esp*), bus bimodular *m*, omnibús bimodal *m* (*AmL*); **~ network** *n* PHYS, TV circuito recíproco *m*; **~ platform** *n* AIR TRANSP plataforma doble *f*; **~-point breaker** *n* AUTO, VEH interruptor de platinos dobles *m*, interruptor de puntos dobles *m*; **~-port memory** *n* COMP&DP memoria de doble acceso *f*; **~ power supply** *n* ELEC ENG doble alimentación *f*; **~-pressure controller** *n* REFRIG presostato combinado de alta y baja presión *m*; **~-pressure valve** *n* PROD válvula de dos presiones *f*; **~-processor load-sharing system** *n* TELECOM sistema de reparto de la carga de doble procesador *m*; **~-processor system** *n* TELECOM sistema de doble procesador *m*; **~-purpose cattle** *n* AGRIC ganado de doble finalidad *m*; **~-purpose dredger** *n* WATER TRANSP draga mixta *f*; **~-purpose vehicle** *n* VEH vehículo de doble uso *m*; **~ rod** *n* AIR TRANSP barra doble *f*; **~-rotor helicopter** *n* AIR TRANSP helicóptero de doble rotor *m*; **~-signaling telephone** *AmE*, **~-signalling telephone** *BrE n* TELECOM teléfono de doble señalización *m*; **~ slot** *n* PROD doble ranuración *f*; **~-spin satellite** *n* SPACE satélite de doble giro *m*, satélite de doble rotación *m*; **~-spin stabilization** *n* SPACE estabilización por doble rotación *f*; **~-standard monitor** *n* TV monitor de doble columna *m*;

~-supply voltage *n* ELEC ENG voltaje de suministro doble *m*; **~ tandem wheel undercarriage** *n* AIR TRANSP tren de aterrizaje de ruedas dobles en tándem *m*; **~-temperature refrigerator** *n* REFRIG refrigerador de doble temperatura *m*; **~ track** *n* ACOUST pista doble *f*; **~ wheels** *n pl* AIR TRANSP ruedas dobles *f pl*; **~-window fiber** *AmE*, **~-window fibre** *BrE n* OPT fibra de ventana doble *f*

dub *vt* CINEMAT, TV doblar

dubbed: **~ version** *n* CINEMAT versión doblada *f*

dubbing *n* ACOUST combinación de dos o más registros sonoros *f*, mezcla de sonidos *f*, montaje *m*, reunión *f*, CINEMAT doblaje *m*, COATINGS igualado de la madera *m*, TV doblaje *m*; **~ chart** *n* CINEMAT carta de doblaje *f*; **~ studio** *n BrE* (*cf dubbing theater AmE*) CINEMAT estudio de doblaje *m*; **~ theater** *n AmE* (*cf dubbing studio BrE*) CINEMAT estudio de doblaje *m*

duckbill: **~ pliers** *n pl* MECH alicates de boca plana *m pl*, MECH ENG alicates de boca plana *m pl*, pinzas de punta de aguja *f pl*, tenazas de boca plana *f pl*, PROD alicates de boca plana *m pl*

duckboard *n* CONST loneta *f*

duct *n* ACOUST conducto *m*, MECH, MECH ENG canal *m*, conducto *m*, ducto *m*, tubo *m*, PROD conducto *m*, REFRIG conducto *m*, TELECOM conducto *m*, WATER canal *m*; **~ distribution** *n* REFRIG distribución por conductos *f*; **~ layout** *n* PROD plano de los conductos *m*; **~ work** *n* PROD canalización *f*, REFRIG conducciones *f pl*, red de conductos *f*

ducted: **~ fan** *n* MECH ENG, TRANSP ventilador entubado *m*; **~-fan engine** *n* AIR TRANSP motor de fan canalizado *m*, MECH ENG motor de hélice entubada *m*, motor de ventilador entubado *m*; **~-fan turbo engine** *n* TRANSP turbomotor con ventilador entubado *m*; **~ propeller** *n* TRANSP hélice canalizada *f*, hélice en tobera fija *f*

ductile[1] *adj* CRYSTALL, METALL dúctil

ductile[2]: **~-brittle transition** *n* METALL transición de la rotura dúctil a la rotura frágil *f*; **~ crack** *n* METALL grieta dúctil *f*; **~ fracture** *n* CRYSTALL fractura astillosa *f*, fractura dúctil *f*, METALL fractura dúctil *f*; **~ iron pipe** *n* MECH ENG caño de hierro dúctil *m*, tubo de hierro dúctil *m*

ductility *n* CRYSTALL, MECH ENG, METALL ductilidad *f*

ducting *n* MECH ENG canalización *f*; **~ gas** *n* GAS gas transportado mediante conductos *m*

ductor: **~-type ink fountain** *n* COLOUR tintero tipo conducto *m*

due: **~ date** *n* PROD día del vencimiento *m*, fecha de vencimiento *f*, plazo de vencimiento *m*

duff *n* COAL capa de humus *f*, finos de antracita *m pl*, mantillo *m*, menudos de carbón *m pl*

dufrenite *n* MINERAL dufrenita *f*

dufrenoysite *n* MINERAL dufrenoysita *f*

dugout *n* MILIT, TELECOM abrigo *m*, abrigo subterráneo *m*

dulcin *n* CHEM dulcina *f*, parafenetolcarbamida *f*, FOOD dulcina *f*

dulcine *n* CHEM dulcita *f*

dull[1] *adj* COLOUR apagado, MECH *coil* desafilado, embotado, sin filo, sin punta, PETR TECH *bit* desgastado, sin punta, TEXTIL apagado

dull[2]: **~ coal** *n* COAL, MINE carbón mate *m*, hulla muerta *f*; **~ finish** *n* COLOUR, TEXTIL acabado mate *m*

dulling: **~ spray** *n* CINEMAT aerosol opacificante *m*

dullness *n* P&R deslustre *m*

Dulong: ~ **and Petit's law** *n* PHYS ley de Dulong y Petit *f*

dumb: ~ **barge** *n* WATER TRANSP aljibe sin propulsión *m*, gabarra sin propulsión propia *f*; ~ **drift** *n* MINE galería de aireación *f*; ~ **furnace** *n* MINE hogar de aireación *m*; ~ **plate** *n* PROD placa de antehogar *f*; ~ **terminal** *n* COMP&DP terminal simple *m*, terminal sin procesador *m*

dumbbell: ~ **test strip** *n* METALL elemento de prueba con los extremos de mayor sección que la parte central bajo prueba *m*

dummy *n* PRINT boceto *m*; ~ **aerial** *n* BrE TV antena artificial *f*; ~ **antenna** *AmE see dummy aerial BrE*; ~ **bearing race** *n* MECH ENG anillo de cojinete falso *m*, guía de cojinete falso *f*; ~ **cartridge** *n* MINE cartucho de fogueo *m*, cartucho de instrucción *m* (*AmL*), cartucho de prueba *m* (*Esp*), cartucho falso *m* (*Esp*), cartucho sin carga *m* (*AmL*); ~ **fiber** *AmE*, ~ **fibre** *BrE* *n* OPT, TELECOM fibra ficticia *f*; ~ **grenade** *n* MILIT granada de instrucción *f*, granada sin carga *f*; ~ **instruction** *n* COMP&DP instrucción ficticia *f*; ~ **pack** *n* PACK falso embalaje *m*; ~ **part** *n* MECH ENG parte falsa *f*; ~ **piston** *n* HYDRAUL pistón compensador *m*; ~ **stage** *n* SPACE etapa ficticia *f*, etapa simulada *f*; ~ **target** *n* MILIT blanco de prueba *m*

dumortierite *n* MINERAL dumortierita *f*

dump[1] *n* *AmE* (*cf tip BrE*) AGRIC descarga *f*, COAL escombrera *f*, escorial *m*, COMP&DP vaciado *m*, vuelco *m*, CONST vertedero *m*, GEOL desmonte *m*, MINE escombrera *f*, vertedero *m*, RECYCL escombrera *f*, vertedero *m*; ~ **area** *n* PROD área de descarga *f*; ~ **bucket** *AmE* (*cf tipping bucket BrE*) CONST balde basculante *m*, cubo basculante *m*; ~ **car** *n* *AmE* (*cf dump wagon BrE*) TRANSP vagón basculante *m*; ~ **cart** *n* COAL volquete *m*; ~ **check** *n* COMP&DP verificación de vuelco *f*; ~ **cooling** *n* SPACE enfriamiento por descarga *m*; ~ **grate** *n* PROD emparrillado basculante *m*; ~ **heap** *n* MINE mecanismo basculante *m*; ~ **site** *n* CONST vertedero *m*, MINE zona de descarga *f*, RECYCL escombrera *f*, vertedero *m*; ~ **skip** *n* CONST escombrera *f*; ~ **trap liquid return** *n* REFRIG purgador del retorno del líquido *m*; ~ **truck** *n* *AmE* (*cf tipper BrE*) AGRIC camión volquete *m*, COAL basculante *m*, camión volquete *m*, vagoneta basculante *f*, volcador de vagones *m*, volcador de vagonetas *m*, CONST basculante *m*, camión basculante *m*, TRANSP camión basculante *m*; ~ **wagon** *n* BrE (*cf dump car AmE*) TRANSP vagón basculante *m*

dump[2] *vt* COAL descargar, tirar, verter, MAR POLL descargar, verter, MINE bascular, RECYCL descargar, tirar, verter, SPACE vaciar

dumper *n* *AmE* (*cf tipper BrE*) CONST volquete *m*, camión basculante *m*, dumper *m*, basculante *m*, TRANSP dumper *m*, volquete *m*; ~ **truck** *n* *AmE* (*cf tipper BrE*) CONST basculante *m*, camión basculante *m*

dumping *n* AIR TRANSP vaciado *m*, frenado aerodinámico *m*, CONST vuelco *m*, MINE descarga *f* (*Esp*), basculamiento *m* (*AmL*), PAPER, POLL descarga *f*, PROD basculamiento *m*, vuelco *m*, RECYCL descarga *f*, vertido *m*; ~ **bucket** *n* CONST cubo de descarga *m*, TRANSP cubo de descarga *m*, cucharón de descarga *m*; ~ **circuit** *n* TV circuito de descarga *m*; ~ **ground** *n* MINE terreno de abono *m*, vaciadero de productos de dragado *m*, vertedero de productos de dragado *m*,

RECYCL escombrera *f*, terreno para escombros *m*, vertedero *m*; ~ **mechanism** *n* PACK mecanismo de descarga *m*; ~ **station** *n* CONST centro de vaciado *m*

dumpy: ~ **level** *n* CONST nivel de Troughton *m*, nivel de anteojo corto *m*, nivel rígido *m*

dune *n* GEOL duna *f*

dunite *n* GEOL, MINERAL, PETROL dunita *f*

duodecimo *n* PRINT doceavo *m*

duotone *n* PRINT reproducción bicolor *f*; ~ **ink** *n* COLOUR tinta de dos tonos *f*

duotype *n* PRINT impresión con dos fotograbados superpuestos *f*

dupe[1] *n* CINEMAT dupe *m*, PRINT copia *f*; ~ **negative** *n* CINEMAT negativo dupe *m*, negativo duplicado *m*; ~ **positive** *n* CINEMAT positivo dupe *m*, positivo duplicado *m*

dupe[2] *vt* CINEMAT generar un dupe

duplex[1] *adj* COMP&DP dúplex, ELEC ENG bidireccional simultáneo, duplo, TELECOM dúplex

duplex[2] *n* COMP&DP, TELECOM dúplex *m*; ~ **automatic vacuum brake** *n* MECH ENG freno de vacío automático doble *m*, vacuofreno automático dúplex *m*, RAIL, VEH freno de vacío automático doble *m*; ~ **board** *n* PACK cartón dúplex *m*; ~ **boring machine** *n* MECH ENG mandrinadora dúplex *f*, perforadora dúplex *f*, taladradora dúplex *f*; ~ **burner** *n* TRANSP quemador con varias entradas y una salida *m*; ~ **cable** *n* ELEC, ELEC ENG cable de dos conductores trenzados *m*, cable dúplex *m*; ~ **chain** *n* AUTO, VEH doble cadena *f*; ~ **compound winding engine** *n* MECH ENG motor de bobinado compuesto dúplex *m*; ~ **compressor** *n* HYDRAUL compresor bicilíndrico *m*, compresor con dos cilindros de vapor *m*; ~ **crank** *n* MECH ENG acodado doble *m*, manubrio doble *m*; ~**-cylinder engine** *n* MECH ENG motor bicilíndrico *m*; ~ **engine** *n* MECH ENG motor bicilíndrico *m*; ~ **filter** *n* PROD filtro doble *m*; ~ **halftone** *n* PRINT semitono en dos colores *m*; ~ **ink** *n* COLOUR tinta dúplex *f*, tinta en dos colores *f*; ~ **lap winding** *n* ELEC arrollamiento dúplex *m*, devanado de dos circuitos *m*, devanado doble *m*, devanado dúplex *m*; ~ **lever punch** *n* MECH ENG punzón de palanca doble *m*; ~ **operation** *n* COMP&DP funcionamiento dúplex *m*; ~ **pump** *n* HYDRAUL bomba bicilíndrica *f*, bomba impelente de doble asiento *f*; ~ **punching bear** *n* MECH ENG punzonadora doble *f*, punzón doble *m*, sacabocados dúplex *m*; ~ **waterproof board** *n* PACK cartón dúplex resistente al agua *m*

duplexer *n* COMP&DP, TELECOM duplexor *m*

duplicate[1] *n* PHOTO reproducción *f*; ~ **feeder** *n* ELEC alimentador doble *m*; ~ **I/O addressing** *n* PROD direccionamiento duplicado de entrada y salida *m*; ~ **supply** *n* ELEC, ELEC ENG fuente de alimentación doble *f*

duplicate[2] *vt* COMP&DP duplicar, PHOTO copiar, duplicar, reproducir, TV duplicar

duplicating: ~ **film** *n* PHOTO película para copias duplicadas *f*; ~ **recorder** *n* INSTR grabador duplicador *m*; ~ **stencil-base paper** *n* PAPER papel base para esténcil *m*, papel soporte para ciclostilo *m*

duplication *n* GEN duplicación *f*

durability *n* MECH ENG durabilidad *f*, METR durabilidad *f*, duración *f*, longevidad *f*, resistencia *f*, P&R, PACK, QUALITY durabilidad *f*, TEXTIL duración *f*; ~ **test** *n* PACK ensayo de duración *m*

durable *adj* QUALITY duradero

duralumin *n* MECH, METALL duraluminio *m*

durangite *n* GEOL, MINERAL durangita *f*

duration *n* HYDRAUL, MECH ENG, PROD duración *f*; **~ of expansion of steam** *n* HYDRAUL duración de la expansión del vapor *f*

durene *n* CHEM dureno *m*

durn *n* MINE marco *m*

durometer *n* LAB, P&R, PAPER, PRINT durómetro *m*

durra *n* AGRIC *sorghum* durra *f*, zahine *f*

durum: **~ wheat** *n* AGRIC, FOOD trigo duro *m*

dust¹: **~-laden** *adj* COAL, SAFE cargado de polvo; **~-tight** *adj* ELEC, MECH ENG, PACK, PROD hermético al polvo

dust² *n* COAL basura *f*, cenizas *f pl*, ennegrecimiento de moldes *m*, escombros *m pl*, partículas de tamaño menor de 76 milímetros *f pl*, polvareda *f*, polvo *m*, serrín *m*, CONST polvo *m*, P&R, PAPER cenizas *f pl*, POLL, SAFE polvo *m*; **~ aspirator** *n* PACK aspirador de polvo *m*; **~ bag** *n* SAFE bolsa para polvos *f*; **~ blouse** *n* SAFE blusa para polvo *f*; **~ boot** *n* VEH guardapolvo *m*; **~ cap** *n* MECH ENG casquillo guardapolvos *m*, tapa guardapolvos *f*; **~ catcher** *n* CHEM TECH caja colectora del polvo *f*, colector de polvo *m*, COAL separador de polvo *m*; **~ chamber** *n* COAL colector de polvos *m*, cámara para polvos *f*; **~ coal** *n* COAL carbón en polvo *m*; **~ collector** *n* COAL, P&R captador de polvo *m*, colector de polvo *m*, PROD instalación de desempolvamiento *f*; **~ content** *n* POLL contenido de polvos *m*, volumen de polvos *m*; **~ control** *n* CHEM TECH control de polvos *m*; **~ counter** *n* INSTR contador de polvos *m*; **~ cover** *n* MECH ENG cubierta guardapolvos *f*, SAFE cubierta para polvos *f*; **~ exhaust fan** *n* COAL, PROD sistema de aspiración de polvos *m*, SAFE abanico extractor de polvos *m*; **~-exhausting device** *n* PACK aparato aspirador de polvo *m*; **~ explosion** *n* COAL explosión de polvos *f*; **~ filter** *n* COAL filtro de polvo *m*; **~ guard** *n* COAL guardapolvo *m*, guardapolvos *m*, PACK protección contra el polvo *f*; **~ hood** *n* SAFE capucha para polvos *f*; **~ mask** *n* SAFE careta contra polvos *f*, mascarilla antipolvo *f*; **~ mill** *n* FOOD molino de polvo *m*; **~ monitor** *n* NUCL monitor de polvo *m*; **~ particle** *n* POLL partícula de polvo *f*; **~ removal** *n* PROD despolvoreo *m*; **~ removal plant** *n* POLL, SAFE unidad extractora de polvo *f*; **~ removal system** *n* PACK, POLL, PROD sistema para quitar el polvo *m*; **~ seal** *n* AUTO guardapolvos *m*; **~ separator** *n* SAFE colector de polvos *m*; **~ and spray protective hood** *n* SAFE capucha protectora contra polvo y aspersión *f*; **~ suppression system** *n* CONST sistema de eliminación de polvo *m*

dust³ *vt* AGRIC espolvorear, pulverizar, FOOD, PRINT espolvorear

duster *n* AGRIC espolvoreador *m*, pulverizador *m*, PETROL pozo improductivo *m*, PHOTO cepillo para quitar el polvo *m*, quitapolvo *m*

dusting *n* PAPER fragmentos de fibras *m pl*, pelusa *f*, *action* desprendimiento de polvillo *m*, *fibre fragments* celulosa en copos *f*; **~ bag** *n* PROD saquete de espolvorear *m*; **~ brush** *n* PHOTO cepillo para quitar el polvo *m*; **~ unit** *n* PRINT espolvoreadora *f*

dustproof¹ *adj* ELEC resguardado del polvo, a prueba de polvo, impenetrable al polvo, hermético al polvo, MECH ENG hermético al polvo, PACK, PROD protegido contra el polvo, hermético al polvo, SAFE a prueba de polvo

dustproof²: **~ motor** *n* ELEC motor protegido contra el polvo *m*

dusty *adj* COAL polvoriento

Dutch: **~ roll** *n* AIR TRANSP inestabilidad lateral oscilatoria *f*

duty *n* PROD *of machine* servicio *m*, trabajo *m*; **~ cycle** *n* MECH coeficiente de utilización *m*, factor de trabajo *m*, régimen de trabajo *m*, PROD ciclo de servicio *m*, factor de trabajo *m*; **~ pump** *n* PROD bomba de régimen *f*

D-valve *n* HYDRAUL distribuidor de concha *m*, válvula D *f*

DVE *abbr* (*digital video effects*) TV efectos digitales de video *m pl* (*AmL*), efectos digitales de vídeo *m pl* (*Esp*)

DVTR *abbr* (*digital videotape recorder*) TV grabador de cinta de video digital *m* (*AmL*), grabador de cinta de vídeo digital *m* (*Esp*), grabador de video digital *m* (*AmL*), grabador de vídeo digital *m* (*Esp*)

dwarf: **~ star** *n* SPACE estrella enana *f*

dwarfism *n* AGRIC enanismo *m*

D-weighting: **~ curve** *n* ACOUST curva de ponderación D *f*

dwell: **~ angle** *n* AUTO, VEH ángulo de apertura de los contactos del ruptor *m*, ángulo del dwell *m*; **~ setting** *n* PROD parada para escape de gases *f*

dwelling: **~ time** *n* TEXTIL tiempo de permanencia *m*

DWT *abbr* (*deep well thermometer*) PETROL termómetro para pozos profundos *m*

DX: **~-stuffing signal** *n* TELECOM señal de relleno DX *f*

DXC *abbr* (*digital cross-connect equipment*) TELECOM equipo de interconexión digital *m*

Dy *abbr* (*dysprosium*) CHEM, COAL, METALL Dy (*disprosio*)

dyadic *adj* COMP&DP diádico

dye¹ *n* CHEM pigmento *m*, tinte *m*, tintura *f*, COLOUR, PAPER, PRINT, TEXTIL colorante *m*; **~ laser** *n* ELECTRON, PHYS láser de color *m*; **~ liquor** *n* TEXTIL líquido colorante *m*; **~ penetrant test** *n* MECH ensayo con líquidos penetrantes *m*; **~ room** *n* COLOUR sala de teñido *f*; **~ shop** *n* COLOUR tienda de teñido *f*; **~ toning** *n* CINEMAT viraje *m*; **~ transfer process** *n* CINEMAT, PHOTO proceso de transferencia de colorante *m*, proceso de transferencia de tintes *m*

dye² *vt* COLOUR teñir, PAPER, PHOTO colorear, teñir, TEXTIL teñir; **~ in the piece** *vt* TEXTIL teñir en pieza; **~ under pressure** *vt* TEXTIL teñir a presión

dyed¹ *adj* COLOUR, TEXTIL teñido

dyed²: **~ yarn** *n* TEXTIL hilo teñido *m*

dyehouse *n* COLOUR, TEXTIL taller de teñido *m*

dyeing *n* COLOUR, TEXTIL teñido *m*, tintura *f*; **~ affinity** *n* TEXTIL afinidad a la tintura *f*

dyer *n* COLOUR tinte *m*

dyestuff *n* COLOUR, PAPER, PRINT, TEXTIL colorante *m*

dying *n* MECH ENG decreciente, troquelado *m*

dynamic: **~ address translation** *n* COMP&DP conversión dinámica de direcciones *f*, traducción dinámica de direcciones *f*; **~ allocation** *n* COMP&DP asignación dinámica *f*, vuelco dinámico *m*; **~ balance** *n* MECH ENG equilibrio dinámico *m*; **~ balancing** *n* AIR TRANSP equilibrio dinámico *m*; **~ braking** *n* RAIL frenado dinámico *m*, TRANSP frenado dinámico *m*, frenado reostático *m*, VEH frenado dinámico *m*; **~ component** *n* AIR TRANSP componente dinámico *m*; **~ conditions** *n pl* ELEC ENG condiciones dinámicas *f pl*; **~ convergence** *n* TV conversión dinámica *f*;

~ **correction** *n* PETROL corrección dinámica *f*; ~ **distortion** *n* ACOUST distorsión dinámica *f*; ~ **dump** *n* COMP&DP vuelco dinámico *m*; ~ **focusing** *n* TV focalización dinámica *f*; ~ **force calibration** *n* MECH ENG calibración por fuerza dinámica *f*, calibración por fuerza viva *f*; ~ **friction** *n* PHYS fricción dinámica *f*; ~ **heating** *n* HEAT ENG, THERMO calentamiento dinámico *m*; ~ **interaction** *n* METALL interacción dinámica *f*; ~ **load control** *n* TELECOM control de carga dinámica *m*; ~ **loading** *n* CONST, METALL carga dinámica *f*; ~ **loudspeaker** *n* ACOUST altavoz dinámico *m*; ~ **memory** *n* COMP&DP memoria dinámica *f*; ~ **metamorphism** *n* FUELLESS metamorfismo dinámico *m*, GEOL metamorfismo dinámico *m*, metamorfismo mecánico *m*; ~ **model** *n* SPACE modelo dinámico *m*; ~ **movement detector** *n* TRANSP detector de movimiento dinámico *m*; ~ **overvoltage** *n* ELEC ENG sobretensión dinámica *f*; ~ **parameter** *n* COMP&DP parámetro dinámico *m*; ~ **positioning** *n* PETR TECH, PETROL posicionamiento dinámico *m*; ~ **power consumption** *n* ELEC ENG consumo de energía dinámica *m*; ~ **presence detector** *n* TRANSP detector de presencia dinámica *m*; ~ **pressure** *n* AIR TRANSP, METEO presión dinámica *f*; ~ **programming** *n* COMP&DP programación dinámica *f*; ~ **property** *n* P&R propiedad dinámica *f*; ~ **RAM** *n* COMP&DP RAM dinámica *f*; ~ **range** *n* ACOUST gama dinámica *f*, margen dinámico *m*, ELECTRON gama dinámica *f*, PETROL, RAD PHYS, TV gama dinámica *f*, margen dinámico *m*; ~ **resistance** *n* ELEC resistencia dinámica *f*; ~ **response** *n* TELECOM respuesta dinámica *f*; ~ **similarity** *n* FLUID semejanza dinámica *f*; ~ **sounding** *n* COAL acción de probar el techo golpeándolo *f*, sondeo dinámico *m*; ~ **stability** *n* AIR TRANSP, TELECOM estabilidad dinámica *f*; ~ **test** *n* METALL prueba dinámica *f*; ~ **tide** *n* OCEAN dinamó-metro *m*; ~ **toe angle** *n* VEH ángulo de convergencia dinámica *m*; ~ **trimming** *n* ELEC ENG compensación dinámica *f*; ~ **viscosity** *n* FLUID, FUELLESS, P&R, PHYS viscosidad dinámica *f*

dynamical *adj* FLUID, METALL dinámico

dynamics *n* GEN dinámica *f*

dynamite *n* MINE dinamita *f*; ~ **cartridge** *n* MINE cartucho de dinamita *m*; ~ **store** *n* MINE depósito de dinamita *m* (*AmL*), polvorín *m* (*Esp*)

dynamo[1]: ~~**electric** *adj* ELEC ENG dinamoeléctrico

dynamo[2] *n* ELEC dinamo *f*, ELEC ENG dinamo *f*, dínamo *f*, VEH dinamo *f*, generador *m*, WATER TRANSP dinamo *f*; ~ **blaster** *n* MINE explosor de dinamo *m*; ~ **effect** *n* SPACE efecto dinamo *m*; ~ **exploder** *n* MINE explosor de dinamo *m*

dynamograph *n* MECH dinamógrafo *m*

dynamometer *n* INSTR, LAB, MECH dinamómetro *m*; ~ **wattmeter** *n* INSTR vatímetro dinamométrico *m*

dynamometric: ~ **dynamo** *n* ELEC dinamo dinamométrico *f*

dynamotor *n* ELEC, ELEC ENG dinamotor *m*, transformador giratorio *m*

dyne *n* METR dina *f*

dynode *n* PHYS dínodo *m*

dysanalyte *n* MINERAL disanalita *f*

dysclasite *n* MINERAL disclasita *f*

dyscrasite *n* MINERAL discrasita *f*

dysluite *n* MINERAL disluíta *f*

dysodile *n* MINERAL disodilo *m*

dyspnea *n AmE see* dyspnoea *BrE*

dyspnoea *n* OCEAN disnea *f*

dysprosium *n* (*Dy*) CHEM, COAL, METALL disprosio *m* (*Dy*)

Dzus: ~ **fastener** *n* SPACE brida Dzus *f*, remache hueco *m*

E

e *abbr* (*electron*) GEN e (*electrón*)

E[1] *abbr* (*exa-*) METR E (*exa-*)

E[2]: **~ bend** *n* ELEC ENG, WAVE PHYS desviación E *f*; **~ and M signaling** *AmE*, **~ and M signalling** *BrE n* TELECOM señalización E y M *f*; **~ mode** *n* OPT, TELECOM modo E *m*; **~ plane** *n* ELEC ENG, WAVE PHYS plano E *m*; **~ wave** *n* ELEC ENG, WAVE PHYS onda E *f*

E&OE *abbr* (*errors and omissions excepted*) PRINT s.e.u.o. (*salvo error u omisión*)

EA *abbr* (*external access equipment*) TELECOM equipo de acceso externo *m*

EAF[1] *abbr* (*electric-arc furnace*) COAL, ELEC, ELEC ENG, HEAT, MECH ENG, THERMO horno de arco eléctrico *m*, horno de arco voltaico *m*

EAF[2]: **~ dust** *n* COAL, THERMO brasa del horno de arco eléctrico *f*

ear *n* AGRIC espiga *f*, marlo *m* (*AmL*), mazorca *f* (*Esp*), MECH ENG abertura *f*, entrada *f*, *of fan, centrifugal pump* oído *m*; **~-drier** *n* AGRIC secadora de mazorcas *f*; **~-dryer** *n* AGRIC secadora de espigas *f*, secadora de mazorcas *f*; **~-drying** *n* AGRIC secado en espiga *m*, secado en mazorca *m*; **~ protection** *n* ACOUST, CONST, SAFE protección auditiva *f*; **~-protector** *n* ACOUST, CONST, LAB, SAFE protector auditivo *m*, protector de oídos *m*; **~ protectors** *n pl* ACOUST, CONST, LAB, SAFE orejeras *f pl*; **~-setting** *n* AGRIC formación de las espigas *f*; **~ tag** *n* AGRIC *cattle* arete *m*, etiqueta de oreja *f*

eardrum *n* ACOUST membrana timpánica *f*, tímpano *m*

early[1] *adj* GEOL inicial, primario, temprano

early[2]: **~ admission** *n* PROD *slide valve* admisión anticipada *f*, avance a la admisión *m*; **~ blight** *n* AGRIC añublo precoz *m*, muerte generalizada temprana *f*; **~ failure** *n* ELEC ENG fallo prematuro *m*; **~-failure period** *n* QUALITY período de defectos rápido *m*, período de fallas rápido *m*; **~ finish** *n* TV fin anticipado *m*; **~-finish audio** *n* TV fin anticipado de audio *m*; **~-finish video** *n* TV fin anticipado de video *m*; **~ release** *n* PROD *slide valve* avance al escape *m*, escape anticipado *m*; **~ start** *n* TV comienzo anticipado *m*; **~-start audio** *n* TV comienzo anticipado de audio *m*; **~-start video** *n* TV comienzo anticipado de video *m*; **~ variety** *n* AGRIC variedad temprana *f*; **~-warning radar** *n* WATER TRANSP radar de alerta previa *m*; **~ white milo** *n* AGRIC milo blanco precoz *m*

Early: **~ effect** *n* ELECTRON efecto Early *m*

earmuffs *n pl* ACOUST, CONST, LAB, SAFE orejeras *f pl*, protectores auditivas *m pl*, protectores de oídos *m pl*

Earnshaw's: **~ theorem** *n* PHYS teorema de Earnshaw *m*

earphone *n* ACOUST audífono *m*

earpiece *n* ACOUST, TELECOM auricular *m*

earplug *n* ACOUST, CONST, LAB, SAFE protector auditivo *m*, protector auricular *m*, tapón para el oído *m*

earth[1]: **~-free** *adj BrE* (*cf ground-free AmE*) ELEC libre de tierra; **~-orbiting** *adj* SPACE en órbita terrestre

earth[2] *n BrE* (*cf ground AmE*) COAL suelo *m*, tierra *f*, ELEC, ELEC ENG, PHYS, PROD, TELECOM, VEH masa *f*, masa eléctrica *f*, puesta a tierra *f*, tierra *f*, toma de tierra *f*; **~ arrester** *n BrE* (*cf ground arrester AmE*) ELEC, ELEC ENG cortacircuito de puesta a tierra *m*, interruptor de voltaje a tierra *m*; **~'s atmosphere** *n* METEO, SPACE atmósfera terrestre *f*; **~-auger** *n* MINE barrena para abrir agujeros para postes *f*; **~'s axis** *n* SPACE eje terrestre *m*; **~ bar** *n BrE* (*cf ground bar AmE*) ELEC *connection*, ELEC ENG, PROD barra de tierra *f*; **~-borer** *n* MINE barrena de cateo *f*, trépano de sondar *m*; **~ bus** *n BrE* (*cf ground bus AmE*) ELEC, ELEC ENG, PROD barra colectora de tierra *f*, barra de puesta a tierra *f*, conductor ómnibus de tierra *m*; **~-bus mounting** *n BrE* (*cf ground-bus mounting AmE*) ELEC, ELEC ENG, PROD montaje de barra de puesta a tierra *m*; **~ cable** *n BrE* (*cf ground cable AmE*) ELEC, ELEC ENG, VEH cable de masa *m*, cable de toma de tierra *m*; **~-capture vehicle** *n* SPACE vehículo terrestre de captura *m*; **~ clamp** *n BrE* (*cf ground clamp AmE*) ELEC, ELEC ENG abrazadera de conexión a tierra *f*, abrazadera de tierra *f*; **~ clip** *n BrE* (*cf ground clip AmE*) ELEC, ELEC ENG presilla de conexión a masa *f*, presilla de conexión a tierra *f*; **~ conductor** *n BrE* (*cf ground conductor AmE*) ELEC, ELEC ENG conductor de masa *m*, conductor de tierra *m*; **~ connection** *n BrE* (*cf ground connection AmE*) AUTO, ELEC, ELEC ENG, PROD, VEH conexión a tierra *f*, masa *f*, tierra *f*, toma a masa *f*, toma de tierra *f*, unión a tierra *f*; **~ connector** *n BrE* (*cf ground connector AmE*) ELEC toma de tierra *f*, ELEC ENG unión a tierra *f*, PROD toma de tierra *f*; **~ core** *n* GEOPHYS núcleo terrestre *m*; **~'s core** *n* FUELLESS, GEOL, GEOPHYS núcleo terrestre *m*; **~ current** *n BrE* (*cf ground current AmE*) ELEC, ELEC ENG corriente de retorno por tierra *f*, corriente de vuelta por tierra *f*, GEOPHYS corriente de fuga *f*, corriente de tierra *f*, corriente telúrica *f*, corriente terrestre *f*, PROD corriente telúrica *f*; **~'s crust** *n* FUELLESS, GEOL, GEOPHYS corteza terrestre *f*; **~ curvature** *n* SPACE curvatura terrestre *f*; **~ dam** *n* HYDROL, WATER dique de tierra *m*, presa de terraplén *f*, presa de tierra *f*; **~ detector** *n BrE* (*cf ground detector AmE*) ELEC, ELEC ENG defectoscopio de aislamiento *m*, detector de defectos de puesta a masa *m*, indicador de tierra *m*; **~ detector light** *n BrE* (*cf ground detector light AmE*) ELEC, ELEC ENG, PROD lámpara indicadora del detector de tierra *f*; **~ electrode** *n BrE* (*cf ground electrode AmE*) AUTO, ELEC, ELEC ENG, PHYS, VEH electrodo de conexión a tierra *m*, electrodo de masa *m*, electrodo de tierra *m*; **~ escape stage** *n* SPACE etapa de escape de la tierra *f*; **~-escape velocity** *n* SPACE velocidad para escapar de la Tierra *f*; **~ fall** *n* CONST derrumbamiento *m*, desprendimiento *m*; **~ fault** *n BrE* (*cf ground fault AmE*) ELEC, ELEC ENG, PROD fuga a tierra *f*, pérdida a tierra *f*, tierra accidental *f*; **~-fault protection** *n BrE* (*cf ground-fault protection AmE*) ELEC, ELEC ENG, PROD protección contra fuga a tierra *f*, protección contra pérdida a tierra *f*, protección contra tierra accidental *f*; **~-fault tray** *n BrE* (*cf ground-fault tray*

AmE) ELEC, ELEC ENG, PROD banda de conexión a tierra *f*, bandeja de pérdida a tierra *f*; ~ **grab** *n* COAL cuchara excavadora *f*; ~ **indicator** *n BrE* (*cf ground indicator AmE*) ELEC, ELEC ENG indicador de defectos de aislamiento *m*, indicador de tierra *m*; ~ **inductor** *n* GEOPHYS inductor de tierra *m*, inductor terrestre *m*; ~ **lead** *n BrE* (*cf ground lead AmE*) ELEC, ELEC ENG, PHYS, PROD, TELECOM cable a tierra *m*, hilo de puesta a masa *m*, TV cable de tierra *m*, hilo de puesta a masa *m*; ~ **leakage** *n BrE* (*cf ground leakage AmE*) ELEC, ELEC ENG derivación a tierra *f*, dispersión a tierra *f*, fuga a tierra *f*, pérdida a tierra *f*, PROD fuga a tierra *f*; ~~**leakage circuit breaker** *n BrE* (*cf ground-leakage circuit breaker AmE*) ELEC, ELEC ENG cortocircuito de fuga a tierra *m*, cortocircuito de pérdida a tierra *m*; ~~**leakage current** *n BrE* (*cf ground-leakage current AmE*) ELEC, ELEC ENG corriente de fuga a tierra *f*; ~~**leakage detector** *n BrE* (*cf ground-leakage detector AmE*) ELEC, ELEC ENG detector de fuga a tierra *m*; ~~**leakage meter** *n BrE* (*cf ground-leakage meter AmE*) ELEC, ELEC ENG medidor de fuga a tierra *m*, medidor de tierra accidental *m*; ~ **line** *n BrE* (*cf ground line AmE*) ELEC, ELEC ENG línea a tierra *f*; ~ **lug** *n BrE* (*cf ground lug AmE*) ELEC, ELEC ENG, PROD lengüeta de puesta a tierra *f*, terminal de masa *f*, terminal de tierra *m*; ~**'s magnetic field** *n* ELEC, GEOPHYS, PHYS, SPACE campo magnético terrestre *m*; ~ **oil** *n* PETROL petróleo *m*; ~ **orbit** *n* SPACE órbita terrestre *f*; ~~**orbit rendezvous** *n* SPACE encuentro en órbita terrestre *m*; ~~**orbiting mission** *n* SPACE misión terrestre en órbita *f*; ~~**parking orbit** *n* SPACE órbita de aparcamiento terrestre *f*; ~ **pin** *n BrE* (*cf ground pin AmE*) ELEC, ELECTRON, PROD patilla de conexión a tierra *f*, terminal de tierra *m*; ~ **plane** *n* GEOM, PHYS plano de tierra *m*; ~ **plate** *n* ELEC, ELEC ENG placa de conexión a tierra *f*, toma de tierra *f*, GEOPHYS meseta terrestre *f*; ~ **potential** *n BrE* (*cf ground potential AmE*) ELEC, ELEC ENG, SPACE potencial de tierra *m*, potencial terrestre *m*; ~ **pressure** *n* COAL empuje de tierras *m*, presión terrestre *f*; ~~**pressure at rest** *n* COAL presión terrestre en calma *f*; ~~**pressure coefficient** *n* COAL coeficiente de presión terrestre *m*; ~ **radiation** *n* GEOPHYS radiación terrestre *f*; ~~**rammer** *n* CONST apisonadora *f*; ~ **receiver** *n* SPACE receptor en tierra *m*; ~~**reentry altitude** *n* SPACE altitud para reingreso en la tierra *f*; ~ **remote-sensing satellite** *n* SPACE satélite de observación de la tierra *m*, satélite de percepción remota *m*, satélite terrestre con recepción a distancia *m*; ~ **reservoir** *n* WATER embalse de tierra *m*; ~ **resistance** *n BrE* (*cf ground resistance AmE*) ELEC, ELEC ENG resistencia de tierra *f*; ~~**resistance meter** *n BrE* (*cf ground-resistance meter AmE*) ELEC, ELEC ENG medidor de resistencia de tierra *m*; ~~**resources research satellite** *n* SPACE satélite de observación de recursos terrestres *m*, satélite investigación de recursos terrestres *m*; ~ **return** *n BrE* (*cf ground return AmE*) ELEC ENG, GEOPHYS, PROD, TELECOM retorno por tierra *m*; ~ **rod** *n BrE* (*cf ground rod AmE*) ELEC varilla de toma de tierra *f*, barra de tierra *f*, varilla de tierra *f*, ELEC ENG varilla de toma de tierra *f*, varilla de tierra *f*, GEOPHYS barra de tierra *f*, vástago de tierra *m*, PROD barra de tierra *f*; ~ **satellite** *n* SPACE satélite terrestre *m*; ~ **sensor** *n* GEOPHYS detector terrestre *m*, sensor terrestre *m*; ~ **spike** *n* GEOPHYS punta de descarga terrestre *f*; ~ **station** *n* PHYS estación terrena

f, estación terrestre *f*, SPACE, TELECOM, TV estación terrestre *f*, estación terrena *f*; ~ **switch** *n BrE* (*cf ground switch AmE*) ELEC, ELEC ENG conmutador de puesta a tierra *m*; ~~**synchronous orbit** *n* SPACE sincrónica ecuatorial *f*, órbita geoestacionaria *f*, órbita sincrónica con la Tierra *f*; ~~**synchronous satellite** *n* SPACE satélite en órbita sincrónica con la Tierra *m*; ~ **terminal** *n BrE* (*cf ground terminal AmE*) ELEC, ELEC ENG borne de puesta a tierra *m*, borne de tierra *m*, terminal de tierra *m*, WATER TRANSP borne de puesta a tierra *m*; ~~**terminal arrester** *n BrE* (*cf ground-terminal arrester AmE*) ELEC, ELEC ENG protector de terminal de tierra *m*; ~ **tide** *n* OCEAN marea terrestre *f*; ~~**to-orbit shuttle** *n* SPACE, TELECOM transbordador Tierra-órbita *m*; ~ **tremor** *n* GEOPHYS temblor de tierra *m*; ~ **wire** *n BrE* (*cf ground wire AmE*) ELEC, ELEC ENG, PHYS, PROD, TELECOM, TV conductor de tierra *m*, hilo de masa *m*, hilo de puesta a tierra *m*

earth³ *vt BrE* (*cf ground AmE*) GEN conectar a masa, conectar a tierra, poner a masa, poner a tierra, unir a masa

Earth: ~ **exploration satellite service** *n* SPACE servicio de exploración de la tierra por satélite *m*

earthdrill *n* COAL barrena para tierra *f*

earthed¹ *adj BrE* (*cf grounded AmE*) ELEC, ELEC ENG, TELECOM puesto a tierra, unido a tierra

earthed²: ~ **base connection** *n BrE* ELEC, ELEC ENG conexión base a tierra *f*; ~ **collector connection** *n BrE* ELEC, ELEC ENG conexión colector a masa *f*, conexión de electrodo captador a masa *f*; ~ **earth terminal** *n BrE* ELEC, ELEC ENG, PROD borne de tierra aterrado *m*; ~ **emitter connection** *n BrE* ELEC ENG conexión del cuerpo emisor a tierra *f*; ~ **neutral system** *n BrE* ELEC, ELEC ENG sistema con neutro a tierra *m*; ~ **switch** *n BrE* ELEC, ELEC ENG conmutador con conexión a tierra *m*, conmutador de puesta a tierra *m*; ~ **system** *n BrE* ELEC, ELEC ENG, PROD sistema de puesta a tierra *m*

earthenware *n* C&G, PROD alfarería *f*; ~ **decorator** *n* C&G decorador *m*; ~ **glazing** *n* C&G, PROD alfarería vidriada *f*; ~ **jar** *n* C&G jarra de barro *f*; ~ **pipe** *n* C&G tubo de barro *m*, CONST tubería de barro *f*; ~ **sieve** *n* C&G criba de alfarero *f*; ~ **slab** *n* C&G loseta de barro *f*; ~ **tank** *n* C&G tanque de barro *m*

earthing *n BrE* (*cf grounding AmE*) CONST, ELEC, ELEC ENG, ELECTRON, RAIL conexión a masa *f*, conexión a tierra *f*, puesta a tierra *f*, unión a tierra *f*, SPACE conexión a masa *f*, conexión a tierra *f*, descenso en tierra *m*, puesta a masa *f*, puesta a tierra *f*; ~ **bus** *n BrE* ELEC barra colectora de puesta a tierra *f*, conductor ómnibus de puesta a tierra *m*, ELEC ENG conductor ómnibus de puesta a tierra *m*, barra colectora de puesta a tierra *f*, PROD barra colectora de puesta a tierra *f*; ~ **clip** *n BrE* ELEC, ELEC ENG presilla de conexión a masa *f*, presilla de puesta a tierra *f*; ~ **electrode conductor** *n BrE* ELEC, ELEC ENG, PROD conductor de electrodo de puesta a tierra *m*; ~ **electrode system** *n BrE* ELEC, ELEC ENG, PROD sistema de electrodos de conexión a tierra *m*, sistema de electrodos de puesta a tierra *m*; ~ **paddle** *n BrE* RAIL varilla de tierra *f*; ~ **pole** *n BrE* RAIL piquete de toma de tierra *m*; ~ **position** *n BrE* ELEC posición de conexión a masa *f*, posición de conexión a tierra *f*; ~ **reactor** *n BrE* ELEC, ELEC ENG reactancia de puesta a tierra *f*, reactor a tierra *m*; ~ **regulation** *n BrE* PROD regulación de puesta a tierra *f*; ~ **rod** *n BrE* ELEC varilla de tierra *f*, RAIL piquete de toma de tierra *m*; ~ **strip** *n BrE* ELEC, ELEC ENG tira de toma de tierra *f*; ~ **switch** *n BrE* ELEC, ELEC ENG conmutador de puesta a tierra *m*, interruptor de puesta a tierra *m*; ~**-up** *n* AGRIC aporcamiento *m*

earthmover *n* AGRIC, MECH ENG excavadora *f*

earthmoving: ~ **machinery** *n* MECH ENG equipo de excavaciones *m*, equipo de movimiento de tierra *m*, excavadora *f*, maquinaria de excavaciones *f*, maquinaria de movimiento de tierra *f*

earthquake *n* CONST, GEOPHYS temblor de tierra *m*, terremoto *m*; ~ **focus** *n* GEOL, GEOPHYS centro sísmico *m*, hipocentro *m*; ~ **intensity** *n* GEOL, GEOPHYS intensidad del terremoto *f*, intensidad sísmica *f*; ~**-proof construction** *n* CONST edificación antisísmica *f*

earthshine *n* SPACE claro de Tierra *m*, luz cenicienta *f*

earthwork *n* CONST *operation* movimiento de tierras *m*; ~ **cubature** *n* CONST volumen del movimiento de tierras *m*; ~ **cubing** *n* CONST volumen del movimiento de tierras *m*; ~ **embankment** *n* CONST talud *m*, terraplén *m*

ease[1]: ~ **of access** *n* MECH facilidad de acceso *f*; ~ **of machining** *n* MECH facilidad de maquinado *f*; ~ **of operation** *n* MECH facilidad de manejo *f*

ease[2]: ~ **forward** *vt* AIR TRANSP adelantar con cuidado, mover hacia adelante con cuidado

easer *n* COLOUR aditivo *m*, MINE barreno de ayuda *m*; ~ **hole** *n* MINE agujero de alivio *m* (*Esp*), agujero de desahogo *m* (*AmL*), orificio de alivio *m* (*Esp*), orificio de desahogo *m* (*AmL*)

easterly: ~ **wind** *n* METEO, WATER TRANSP viento del este *m*

eastward *adj* WATER TRANSP que mira al este *phr*

easy: ~ **connection** *n* TELECOM conexión fácil *f*; ~ **fire** *n* C&G quemado fácil *m*; ~ **glide** *n* CRYSTALL deslizamiento fácil *m*; ~ **glide region** *n* METALL región de deslizamiento suave *f*; ~**-opening tag** *n* PACK etiqueta fácil de quitar *f*; ~ **payment** *n* TELECOM pago fácil *m*; ~**-peel-off self-adhesive label** *n* PACK etiqueta autoadhesiva fácil de quitar *f*

eave *n* CONST alero *m*

eaves: ~ **board** *n* CONST tabla del canalón del alero *f*; ~ **gutter** *n* CONST canalón del alero *m*; ~ **trough** *n* CONST canal *m*, canalón *m*, puente-canal *m*

ebb[1] *n* OCEAN menguante *m*, reflujo *m*, WATER TRANSP reflujo *m*; ~ **current** *n* FUELLESS, HYDROL, OCEAN, WATER TRANSP corriente menguante *f*; ~ **generation** *n* FUELLESS, HYDROL, WATER TRANSP generación menguante *f*; ~ **stream** *n* FUELLESS, HYDROL, OCEAN, WATER TRANSP corriente de la marea menguante *f*, corriente menguante *f*; ~ **tide** *n* FUELLESS, HYDROL, OCEAN, WATER, WATER TRANSP bajamar *m*, marea alta *f*, marea descendente *f*, marea menguante *f*, marea vaciante *f*

ebb[2] *vi* FUELLESS, HYDROL, WATER, WATER TRANSP bajar, menguar

EBC *abbr* (*electron-beam curing*) NUCL, PRINT curado por haz electrónico *m*, endurecimiento por haz de electrones *m*, endurecimiento por haz electrónico *m*

EBCDIC[1] *abbr* (*extended binary-coded decimal-interchange code*) COMP&DP EBCDIC (*código ampliado de caracteres decimales codificados en binario*)

EBCDIC[2]: ~ **code** *n* ELECTRON código de EBCDIC *m*

EBS[1] *abbr* (*European barge-carrier system*) TRANSP sistema EBCS (*Sistema Europeo de Transporte de Barcazas*)

EBCS[2]: ~ **lighter** *n* TRANSP gabarra EBCS *f*

ebonite *n* ELEC, P&R ebonita *f*

EBS *abbr* (*electron-bombarded semiconductor*) ELECTRON, NUCL, PART PHYS SBE (*semiconductor de bombardeo electrónico*)

ECC *abbr* (*embedded control channel*) TELECOM canal de control embebido *m*

eccentric *n* MECH, MECH ENG, TEXTIL excéntrica *f*; ~ **anomaly** *n* SPACE anomalía excéntrica *f*, excentricidad *f*; ~ **bit** *n* MINE, PETR TECH barrena excéntrica *f*, trépano excéntrico *m*; ~ **bush** *n* MECH ENG casquillo excéntrico *m*; ~ **cam** *n* MECH ENG leva excéntrica *f*; ~ **chisel** *n* MINE trépano excéntrico *m*; ~ **chuck** *n* MECH ENG *lathe* mandril excéntrico *m*, plato excéntrico *m*, portabrocas excéntrico *m*; ~ **collar** *n* MECH ENG collar excéntrico *m*; ~ **disc** *BrE*, ~ **disk** *AmE* *n* MECH ENG disco de excéntrica *m*, disco excéntrico *m*; ~ **drive slotting machine** *n* MECH ENG limadora de excéntrica *f*, mortajadora de excéntrica *f*, ranuradora de excéntrica *f*; ~ **gear** *n* MECH ENG mecanismo de excéntrica *m*, sector Stephenson *m*; ~ **hook** *n* MECH ENG gancho excéntrico *m*; ~ **hoop** *n* MECH ENG anillo excéntrico *m*, aro excéntrico *m*, collar excéntrico *m*; ~ **loading** *n* CONST carga excéntrica *f*; ~ **rod** *n* AIR TRANSP biela de excéntrica *f*, MECH, MECH ENG biela de excéntrica *f*, varilla excéntrica *f*; ~ **shaft** *n* MECH ENG eje descentrado *m*, eje excéntrico *m*; ~ **sheave** *n* MECH ENG disco de excéntrica *m*; ~ **strap** *n* MECH ENG collar de excéntrica *m*, collarín de excéntrica *m*

eccentricity *n* ACOUST excentricidad *f*, MECH descentramiento *m*, excentricidad *f*

ECD *abbr* COMP&DP (*error-control device*) dispositivo de control de errores *m*, PETR TECH (*equivalent circulating density*) ECD (*densidad de circulación equivalente*), TELECOM (*error-control device*) dispositivo de control de errores *m*

ecdysone *n* CHEM ecdisona *f*

ecgonine *n* CHEM ecgonina *f*

echelette: ~ **grating** *n* PHYS rejilla en escalones *f*

echelon: ~ **grating** *n* PHYS rejilla en escalones *f*; ~ **lens** *n* INSTR, OPT lente de escalones *f*

echinochromes *n pl* CHEM equinocromos *m pl*

echinoderms *n pl* GEOL, OCEAN equinodermos *m pl*

echo *n* GEN eco *m*; ~**-canceling chip** *AmE see echo-cancelling chip BrE*; ~ **cancellation** *n* ELECTRON eliminación de ecos *f*; ~ **canceller** *n* ELECTRON eliminador de ecos *m*; ~**-cancelling chip** *n BrE* ELECTRON chip para la cancelación de ecos *m*; ~ **chamber** *n* ACOUST, MECH ENG, TELECOM cámara de resonancia *f*, cámara de reverberación *f*; ~ **check** *n* COMP&DP control por eco *m*, verificación por eco *f*; ~ **detection** *n* OCEAN detección por eco *f*; ~ **distortion** *n* ELECTRON distorsión del eco *f*, distorsión ecoica *f*; ~ **image** *n* PRINT imagen fantasma *f*; ~ **location** *n* OCEAN ubicación por eco *f*; ~ **ranging** *n* OCEAN posicionador acústico *m*; ~ **signal** *n* ELECTRON señal de eco *f*; ~ **sounder** *n* OCEAN, WATER TRANSP, WAVE PHYS ecosonda *f*, sonda por eco *f*, sondador acústico *m*; ~ **sounding** *n* OCEAN, WATER TRANSP, WAVE PHYS sonda acústica *f*, sonda por eco *f*, sondador acústico *m*; ~ **suppression** *n* COMP&DP, ELECTRON, SPACE, TELECOM supresión del eco *f*; ~**-suppressor** *n* COMP&DP, ELECTRON, SPACE, TELECOM supresor de ecos *m*

echograph *n* PHYS ecógrafo *m*
echoless: ~ **chamber** *n* ACOUST, MECH ENG, TELECOM cámara anecoica *f*, cámara sin reverberaciones *f*
echolocation *n* ACOUST, WATER TRANSP ecolocación *f*
echometry *n* GAS ecometría *f*
echoplex *n* COMP&DP ecoplex *m*
ECL[1] *abbr* (*emitter-coupled logic*) COMP&DP LEA (*lógica de emisor acoplado*), ELECTRON CLEA (*circuito lógico de emisor acoplado*)
ECL[2]: ~ **gate array** *n* ELECTRON circuito lógico predifundido de EA *m*
eclipse *n* SPACE eclipse *m*
eclogite *n* PETROL eclogita *f*
ECM *abbr* (*electronic countermeasures*) MILIT, SPACE contramedidas electrónicas *f pl*
ECN *abbr* (*explicit congestion notification*) TELECOM notificación explícita de congestión *f*
ecological: ~ **factor** *n* POLL factor ecológico *m*; ~ **niche** *n* AGRIC nicho ecológico *m*; ~ **pyramid** *n* POLL pirámide ecológica *f*
ecology *n* POLL ecología *f*; ~ **cullet** *n* C&G cullet ecológico *m*, fundente ecológico *m*, RECYCL eliminación ecológica *f*
economic: ~ **order quantity** *n* PROD cantidad de orden económico *f*; ~ **project** *n* PETR TECH proyecto económico *m*; ~ **quality** *n* QUALITY calidad económica *f*; ~ **risk** *n* QUALITY riesgo económico *m*
economical: ~ **speed** *n* WATER TRANSP velocidad económica *f*
economizer *n* HEAT, HYDRAUL economizador *m*; ~ **jet** *n* VEH surtidor economizador *m*
economy: ~~**size pack** *n* PACK paquete de tamaño económico *m*; ~ **of space** *n* PACK ahorro de espacio *m*
ecosystem *n* POLL ecosistema *m*
ecru *n* COLOUR color crudo *m*; ~ **finish** *n* COLOUR acabado semimate *m*
edaphic *adj* AGRIC edáfico
edaphology *n* AGRIC edafología *f*, COAL edafología *f*, pedología *f*
EDAX *abbr* (*energy dispersive analysis by X-rays*) CHEM análisis dispersivo de energía por rayos X *m*
eddy[1] *n* ACOUST remolino *m*, FLUID torbellino *m*, HYDROL corriente turbulenta *f*, remolino *m*, OCEAN, PHYS remolino *m*, WATER TRANSP remolino *m*, revesa *f*; ~ **brake** *n* BrE (*cf eddy-current brake AmE*) ELEC ENG, MECH, RAIL freno de corrientes parásitas *m*, freno magnético *m*, VEH freno de corrientes parásitas *m*; ~ **current** *n* ELEC, ELEC ENG, MECH, NUCL, PHYS, RAIL, TV corriente de Foucault *f*, corriente en remolino *f*, corriente parásita *f*; ~~**current brake** *n* AmE (*cf eddy brake BrE*) ELEC ENG, MECH, RAIL freno de corrientes parásitas *m*, freno magnético *m*, VEH freno de corrientes parásitas *m*; ~~**current braking** *n* ELEC *motor* acción frenante de la corriente de Foucault *f*, frenado de corrientes parásitas *m*, frenado de la corriente de Foucault *m*, ELEC ENG detención por corrientes de Foucault *f*, frenado de corrientes parásitas *m*, frenado de la corriente de Foucault *m*; ~~**current circuit** *n* ELEC, ELEC ENG circuito de corriente de Foucault *m*; ~~**current flow meter** *n* ELEC, NUCL medidor del flujo de corrientes de Foucault *m*, medidor del flujo de corrientes inducidas *m*; ~~**current inspection** *n* ELEC ENG, MECH, RAIL inspección por corrientes magnéticas *f*, inspección por corrientes parásitas *f*; ~~**current loss**

n ELEC, PHYS, TV pérdida por corrientes parásitas *f*; ~ **diffusion** *n* NUCL difusión turbulenta *f*; ~ **flow** *n* COAL, REFRIG corriente turbulenta *f*, flujo turbulento *m*; ~ **wind** *n* METEO remolino *m*, OCEAN viento arremolinado *m*, WATER TRANSP *against a sail* contraste *m*, remolino *m*
eddy[2] *vi* WATER TRANSP arremolinarse, saltar
eddying: ~ **current** *n* OCEAN corriente de Foucault *f*
edenite *n* MINERAL edenita *f*
edestin *n* CHEM edestina *f*
EDG *abbr* (*electronic dot generator*) PRINT generador electrónico de puntos *m*
edge[1] *n* COMP&DP *of card* borde *m*, CRYSTALL arista *f*, borde *m*, ELECTRON flanco *m*, GEOM arista *f*, canto *m*, INSTR borde *m*, arista *f*, lado *m*, limbo *m*, reborde *m*, MECH canto *m*, borde *m*, MECH ENG *of blade* corte *m*, *of slide-valve, of cylinder port* arista *f*, bisel *m*, filo *m*, PACK reborde *m*, borde *m*, canto *m*, PETROL canto *m*, PHYS, TEXTIL borde *m*; ~ **as cut** *n* C&G orillas burdas *f pl*; ~~**box member** *n* AIR TRANSP miembro de la caja lateral *m*; ~ **coals** *n pl* COAL capas empinadas de carbón *f pl*; ~ **coding** *n* CINEMAT codificación marginal *f*; ~ **connector** *n* ELEC ENG conector de borde *m*; ~~**control assembly** *n* NUCL conjunto de control periférico *m*; ~~**control element** *n* NUCL elemento de control periférico *m*; ~ **correction** *n* TV corrección del contorno *f*; ~ **crack** *n* C&G grieta de orilla *f*; ~ **creep** *n* C&G encogimiento de la orilla *m*; ~ **cushion** *n* PACK almohadillado del borde *m*; ~~**cutter** *n* PAPER cortabordes *m*; ~ **dislocation** *n* CRYSTALL dislocación de Taylor-Orowan *f*, dislocación tipo cuña *f*, METALL dislocación en cuña *f*; ~ **distance** *n* MECH ENG distancia del borde al centro del remache *f*; ~ **doctor** *n* PRINT cuchilla lateral *f*; ~ **effect** *n* ELEC ENG, PHYS efecto de borde *m*; ~~**emitting diode** *n* ELECTRON, OPT diodo de emisión de borde *m*; ~~**emitting light-emitting diode** *n* (*ELED*) TELECOM diodo fotoemisor de emisión marginal *m*; ~ **enhancement** *n* TV nitidez del contorno *f*; ~ **fine-grinding** *n* C&G esmerilado fino de bordes *m*; ~ **flare** *n* CINEMAT resplandor marginal *m*; ~ **fogging** *n* CINEMAT velo marginal *m*; ~ **fracture** *n* C&G fractura de borde *f*; ~ **fusion** *n* C&G fusión de borde *f*; ~ **guide** *n* C&G guía *f*, CINEMAT guía marginal *f*; ~~**gumming machine** *n* PACK engomadora de bordes *f*, máquina encoladora de bordes *f*; ~ **holder** *n* C&G sujetador de borde *m*; ~ **latching** *n* ELECTRON unión de bordes *f*; ~ **lighting** *n* ELEC ENG iluminación de borde *f*; ~ **melting** *n* C&G fundido de bordes *m*; ~ **mill** *n* P&R laminador de canto *m*, PROD fresa estrecha *f*, fresa sierra *f*; ~ **notch** *n* CINEMAT muesca marginal *f*; ~ **nozzle** *n* PAPER chorro cortador de bordes *m*; ~ **number** *n* CINEMAT número marginal *m*; ~ **numbering** *n* CINEMAT numeración marginal *f*; ~~**numbering machine** *n* CINEMAT máquina de numeración marginal *f*; ~ **peeling** *n* C&G descascarillado del borde *m*; ~ **plate** *n* CONST placa de borde *f*; ~ **preparation** *n* MECH *heat unit* preparación de los cantos *f*; ~ **protection** *n* PACK protección de los bordes *f*; ~ **rate** *n* ELECTRON porcentaje de bordes *m*; ~ **roll** *n* C&G rodillo de borde *m*; ~ **runner** *n* PAPER molino de muelas *m*, PROD muela vertical *f*; ~ **seam** *n* COAL, MINE estrato empinado *m*; ~ **of the sheet** *n* C&G borde de la hoja *m*; ~~**socket connector** *n* ELEC ENG, PROD conector de enchufe de borde *m*; ~ **spray** *n* PAPER chorro cortador de bordes *m*; ~ **steepness** *n*

ELECTRON cualidad del borde *f*; ~ **stripe** *n* CINEMAT banda marginal *f*; ~ **tools** *n* *pl* PROD herramientas cortantes *f pl*; ~ **track** *n* CINEMAT banda marginal *f*; ~ **of track banding** *n* TV margen de la banda de pista *m*; ~**-triggered flip-flop** *n* ELECTRON biestable sincrono activado por cambios de nivel *m*; ~ **trim** *n* TEXTIL cenefa *f*; ~**-trimmer** *n* MECH ENG repasadora de aristas *f*; ~ **water** *n* HYDROL acuífero lateral *m*, PETR TECH acuífero lateral *m*, agua subyacente *f*; ~**-wheel** *n* PROD muela vertical *f*; ~ **wheel grinding machine** *n* PROD máquina de rectificar muelas verticales *f*; ~ **winding** *n* ELEC devanado inclinado *m*

edge[2]: ~ **with a groove** *vt* C&G bordear con ranura

edge[3]: ~**-to-edge** *phr* MECH ENG de arista a arista, de lado a lado

edgestone *n* PROD guardacantón *m*

edgewise: ~ **bend** *n* ELEC ENG flexión periférica *f*; ~ **growth** *n* METALL crecimiento de lado a lado *m*, germinación de costado *f*

edging *n* C&G borde *m*, MECH ENG borde *m*, bordeado *m*, corte *m*, guarnición del borde *f*; ~ **iron** *n* CONST reborde de hierro *m*; ~ **machine** *n* INSTR máquina de preparar cantos de chapa *f* (*AmL*), máquina rebordeadora *f* (*Esp*); ~ **panel** *n* AIR TRANSP lámina de pestaña *f*; ~ **paper** *n* PAPER papel para bordear *m*

EDI[1] *abbr* (*electronic data interchange*) TELECOM intercambio de datos electrónicos *m*

EDI[2]: ~ **forwarding** *n* TELECOM envío de intercambio de datos electrónicos *m*; ~ **message** *n* (*EDIM*) TELECOM mensaje por intercambio de datos electrónicos *m*; ~**-message store** *n* (*EDI-MS*) TELECOM almacenamiento de mensajes por intercambio de datos electrónicos *m*; ~ **messaging** *n* (*EDIMG*) TELECOM mensajería por intercambio de datos electrónicos *f*; ~**-messaging environment** *n* (*EDIME*) TELECOM entorno de mensajería por intercambio de datos electrónicos *m*; ~**-messaging system** *n* (*EDIMS*) TELECOM sistema de mensajería por intercambio de datos electrónicos *m*; ~**-messaging user** *n* TELECOM usuario de mensajería por intercambio de datos electrónicos *m*; ~ **notification** *n* (*EDIN*) TELECOM notificación de intercambio de datos electrónicos *f*; ~ **user** *n* TELECOM usuario de intercambio de datos electrónicos *m*; ~**-user agent** *n* (*EDI-UA*) TELECOM agente usuario de intercambio de datos electrónicos *m*

edible: ~ **acid** *n* FOOD ácido comestible *m*; ~ **crops** *n pl* AGRIC cultivos comestibles *m pl*

EDIFACT *abbr* (*electronic data interchange for administration, commerce and transport*) TELECOM intercambio de datos electrónicos para la administración, el comercio y el transporte *m*

EDIM[1] *abbr* (*EDI message*) TELECOM mensaje por intercambio de datos electrónicos *m*

EDIM[2]: ~ **responsibility** *n* TELECOM responsabilidad del mensaje por intercambio de datos electrónicos *f*

EDIME *abbr* (*EDI-messaging environment*) TELECOM entorno de mensajería por intercambio de datos electrónicos *m*

EDIMG[1] *abbr* (*EDI messaging*) TELECOM mensajería por intercambio de datos electrónicos *f*

EDIMG[2]: ~ **user** *n* TELECOM usuario de mensajería por intercambio de datos electrónicos *m*

EDIMS *abbr* (*EDI-messaging system*) TELECOM sistema de mensajería por intercambio de datos electrónicos *m*

EDI-MS *abbr* (*EDI-message store*) TELECOM almacenamiento de mensajes por intercambio de datos electrónicos *m*

EDIN *abbr* (*EDI notification*) TELECOM notificación de intercambio de datos electrónicos *f*

edingtonite *n* MINERAL edingtonita *f*

Edison: ~ **cell** *n* ELEC elemento Edison *m*, elemento de acumulador Edison *m*

edit[1]: ~**-in** *n* CINEMAT, TV añadido en montaje *m*; ~ **master** *n* CINEMAT, TV copia maestra de montaje *f*; ~ **mode** *n* CINEMAT, TV modo edición *m*; ~**-out** *n* CINEMAT, TV eliminado en montaje *m*; ~ **pulse** *n* CINEMAT, TV pulso de montaje *m*; ~ **sync** *n* CINEMAT, TV sincronización de montaje *f*; ~ **synchronization** *n* CINEMAT, TV sincronización de montaje *f*

edit[2] *vt* CINEMAT montar, COMP&DP editar, TV montar

edited: ~ **print** *n* CINEMAT, TV copia montada *f*

editing[1] *adj* CINEMAT, TV de montaje

editing[2] *n* CINEMAT modificación *f*, montaje *m*, COMP&DP edición *f*, programa de edición *m*, PRINT, TV modificación *f*, montaje *m*; ~ **machine** *n* CINEMAT, TV máquina montadora *f*; ~ **on original** *n* CINEMAT, TV montaje sobre original *m*; ~ **rack** *n* CINEMAT, TV bastidor de montaje *m*; ~ **room** *n* CINEMAT, TV sala de montaje *f*; ~ **shot list** *n* CINEMAT, TV lista de tomas para montaje *f*

editor *n* CINEMAT montador *m*, COMP&DP editor *m*, TV montador *m*, técnico de montaje *m*

editorial: ~ **newsroom** *n* TV sala de redacción *f*

EDI-UA *abbr* (*electronic data interchange user agent*) COMP&DP agente usuario de intercambio de datos electrónicos *m*, TELECOM agente usuario de intercambio de datos electrónicos *m*, unidad de acceso al intercambio de datos electrónicos *f*

EDM *abbr* (*electro-discharge machining*) MECH ENG, PROD elaboración por electroerosión *m*, fabricación por descarga eléctrica *m*, fabricación por electroerosión *m*, maquinación por electrodescarga *m*, maquinado por electrodescarga *m*

EDP *abbr* (*electronic data processing*) COMP&DP EDP (*procesamiento electrónico de datos*), ELECTRON TDE (*tratamiento de datos electrónico*)

EDTA *abbr* (*ethylenediamin tetra-acetic acid*) CHEM, DETERG EDTA (*ácido etilendiamino tetra-acético*)

EDTV *abbr* (*extended definition television*) TV televisión de alta definición *f* (*Esp*), televisión por definición extendida *f* (*AmL*)

educational: ~ **broadcasting** *n* TV programación educativa *f*

eduction *n* HEAT, HYDRAUL escape *m*; ~ **port** *n* HYDRAUL orificio de escape *m*, orificio de evacuación *m*; ~ **valve** *n* HYDRAUL válvula de escape *f*, válvula de evacuación *f*

eductor *n* MECH ENG eductor *m*, eyector *m*

EE *abbr* (*electronic editing*) CINEMAT, TV edición electrónica *f*

E-E *abbr* (*electronic-to-electronic*) ELECTRON, TV electrónico a electrónico

EEROM *abbr* (*electrically-erasable ROM*) COMP&DP EEROM (*ROM borrable eléctricamente*), ROMBE (*ROM borrable eléctricamente*)

EFA *abbr* (*essential fatty acid*) CHEM, FOOD EFA (*ácido graso esencial*)

effect: ~ **filter** *n* CINEMAT filtro de efectos *m*; ~ **lighting** *n* CINEMAT, PHOTO, TV iluminación para efectos *f*

effective: ~ **address** *n* COMP&DP direccional efectivo *m*

(*AmL*), dirección efectiva *f* (*Esp*); ~ **aperture** *n* CINEMAT, PHOTO, TV abertura eficaz *f*, abertura útil *f*; ~ **area** *n* SPACE área efectiva *f*; ~ **boron cut-off** *n* NUCL umbral efectivo del boro *m*; ~ **candle-power** *n* PHOTO poder luminoso eficaz *m*; ~ **center of acoustic source** *AmE*, ~ **centre of acoustic source** *BrE n* ACOUST centro efectivo de fuente acústica *m*; ~ **cross-sectional area** *n* MECH área de sección eficaz *f*; ~ **current** *n* ELEC ENG corriente eficaz *f*; ~ **data-transfer rate** *n* COMP&DP tasa efectiva de transferencia de datos *f*, velocidad efectiva de transmisión de datos *f*; ~ **delayed-neutron fraction** *n* NUCL fracción efectiva de neutrones diferidos *f*; ~ **drop height** *n* COAL altura de caída efectiva *f*; ~ **electromotive force** *n* ELEC, ELEC ENG, PHYS fuerza electromotriz eficaz *f*; ~ **evaporation** *n* WATER evaporación efectiva *f*; ~ **freezing-time** *n* REFRIG tiempo efectivo de congelación *m*; ~ **gap length** *n* ACOUST anchura efectiva de entrehierro *f*, TV longitud de intervalos efectiva *f*; ~ **grain size** *n* COAL tamaño de grano útil *m*; ~ **head** *n* FUELLESS salto de agua efectivo *m*, HYDRAUL caída efectiva *f*, caída útil *f*, desnivel efectivo *m*; ~ **heating-surface** *n* HEAT ENG, THERMO *paint, pigments* superficie de caldeo real *f*; ~ **horsepower** *n* MECH ENG caballos efectivos *m pl*, potencia al freno en caballos *f*, potencia efectiva *f*; ~ **horsepower hour** *n* MECH ENG caballos efectivos hora *m pl*; ~ **image-field** *n* PHOTO campo de imagen eficaz *m* (*AmL*), profundidad de cambio *f* (*Esp*); ~ **latent heat of fusion** *n* THERMO calor latente de fusión efectivo *m*; ~ **load** *n* PACK carga efectiva *f*; ~ **mass** *n* ACOUST masa efectiva *f*; ~ **mode volume** *n* OPT volumen de modal efectivo *m*, TELECOM volumen de modo efectivo *m*; ~ **neutron number** *n* NUCL factor eta *m*; ~ **particle density** *n* NUCL densidad efectiva de partículas *f*; ~ **perceived-noise level** *n* (*EPNL*) ACOUST nivel efectivo de ruido percibido *m* (*EPNL*); ~ **permeability** *n* PETROL permeabilidad efectiva *f*; ~ **picture signal** *n* TV señal de imagen efectiva *f*; ~ **pile length** *n* COAL longitud de aguja útil *f*; ~ **pitch** *n* AIR TRANSP *propeller* paso efectivo *m*; ~ **porosity** *n* PETROL porosidad efectiva *f*; ~ **power** *n* ELEC energía eficaz *f*, MECH ENG potencia al freno *f*, potencia efectiva *f*, trabajo útil *m*; ~ **precipitation** *n* METEO precipitación efectiva *f*; ~ **pressure** *n* HYDRAUL presión efectiva *f*; ~ **radiated-power** *n* (*ERP*) TELECOM potencia radiada efectiva *f* (*PRE*); ~ **range** *n* MILIT alcance efectivo *m*; ~ **resistance** *n* ELEC ENG, PHYS resistencia efectiva *f*; ~ **slit-width** *n* TV ancho efectivo de la línea de sonido *m*; ~ **sound pressure** *n* ACOUST, POLL presión acústica efectiva *f*, presión acústica eficaz *f*, presión sonora efectiva *f*, presión sonora eficaz *f*; ~ **steam pressure** *n* HYDRAUL, NUCL presión de vapor efectiva *f*; ~ **stress** *n* COAL, PETR TECH carga efectiva *f*, esfuerzo efectivo *m*, tensión efectiva *f*; ~ **temperature** *n* THERMO temperatura efectiva *f*; ~ **-temperature range** *n* THERMO gama de temperatura efectiva *f*, intervalo de temperatura efectiva *m*, rango de temperatura efectiva *m*; ~ **tension** *n* MECH ENG esfuerzo útil de tensión *m*, esfuerzo útil de tracción *m*; ~ **traffic** *n* TELECOM tráfico efectivo *m*; ~ **value** *n* ELEC ENG valor eficaz *m*; ~ **voltage** *n* ELEC ENG tensión efectiva *f*

effectiveness *n* MAR POLL eficacia *f*

effectivity: ~ **terms** *n pl* PROD términos de puesta en aplicación *m pl*

effects *n pl* (*FX*) CINEMAT, TV efectos *m pl*, efectos especiales *m pl*, efectos sonoros *m pl*; ~ **bank** *n* CINEMAT, TV banco de efectos *m*; ~ **box** *n* CINEMAT, TV caja de efectos sonoros *f*; ~ **bus** *n* CINEMAT, TV bus de efectos *m*; ~ **generator** *n* CINEMAT, TV generador de efectos *m*

effervescence *n* CHEM, FOOD efervescencia *f*

effervescent *adj* CHEM, FOOD efervescente

efficiency *n* GEN eficacia *f*, eficiencia *f*, rendimiento *m*; ~ **diode** *n* ELECTRON diodo de ganancia *m*, diodo de recuperación *m*

efficient: ~ **packaging** *n* PACK embalaje eficaz *m*

effloresce *vi* C&G, CHEM, COATINGS, FOOD eflorescer

efflorescence *n* C&G, CHEM, COATINGS, FOOD eflorescencia *f*

efflorescent *adj* C&G, CHEM, COATINGS, FOOD eflorescente

effluent *n* GAS, HYDROL, NUCL, PETR TECH, RECYCL, WATER efluente *m*, emanación *f*, emisión *f*; ~ **channel** *n* WATER canal de efluente *m*; ~ **discharge** *n* RECYCL vertido de efluyentes *m*, vertido de emanaciones *m*; ~ **monitor** *n* RECYCL, WATER monitor de efluentes *m*, monitor de emisiones *m*; ~~**purification process** *n* RECYCL proceso de depuración de las emanaciones *m*, proceso de depuración de los efluentes *m*, tratamiento de depuración de las emanaciones *m*, tratamiento de depuración de los efluentes *m*; ~ **standard** *n* RECYCL efluente standard *m*, emisión estándar *f*, emisión standard *f*; ~ **stream** *n* HYDROL corriente de agua efluente *m*; ~ **treatment plant** *n* MAR POLL, POLL instalación para el tratamiento del efluente *f*, WATER instalación para el tratamiento del efluente *f*, planta de tratamiento de efluentes *f*; ~ **weir** *n* NUCL vertedero del efluente *m*

effluvium *n* CHEM efluvio *m*

efflux *n* HYDRAUL, WATER caudal *m*, circulación *f*, corriente *f*

effusion *n* ELECTRON, NUCL, PHYS efusión *f*; ~ **oven** *n* ELECTRON, NUCL, PHYS horno de efusión *m*

EFT *abbr* (*electronic funds transfer*) TELECOM transferencia electrónica de fondos *f*

EFTPOS *abbr* (*electronic funds transfer at point of sale*) TELECOM transferencia electrónica de fondos en punto de venta *f*

EFTS *abbr* (*electronic funds transfer system*) COMP&DP EFTS (*sistema de transferencia electrónica de fondos*)

EGA *abbr* (*extended graphic arrangement*) COMP&DP EGA (*arreglo gráfico extendido*)

egg[1]: ~ **laying** *adj* AGRIC ovíparo; ~~**shaped** *adj* GEOM ovalado

egg[2]: ~ **batch** *n* AGRIC puesta de huevos *f*; ~ **calipers** *AmE*, ~ **callipers** *BrE n pl* MECH ENG compases de exteriores *m pl*, compases de puntas para diámetros exteriores *m pl*; ~ **candler** *n* AGRIC oviscopio *m*; ~ **hatch** *n* AGRIC eclosión de huevos *f*; ~ **producer** *n* AGRIC productor de huevos *m*; ~~**shaped thimble** *n* PROD *for rope* dedal oviforme *m*, guardacabo oviforme *m*; ~~**yolk index** *n* FOOD índice de yema de huevo *m*

Egyptian *n* PRINT egipcio *m*

Ehrenfest: ~'s **equations** *n pl* PHYS ecuaciones de Ehrenfest *f pl*

EHT[1] *abbr* (*extra-high tension*) TV MAT (*muy alta tensión*)

EHT^2: ~ **rectifier** n TV válvula rectificadora de MAT f; ~ **supply** n TV suministro de tensión muy elevada m

eicosane n CHEM eicosano m

eicosyl: ~ **alcohol** n CHEM alcohol icosílico m

eiderdown n TEXTIL edredón m

eigenfrequency n GEN eigenfrecuencia f, frecuencia propia f

eigenfunction n ACOUST, PHYS autofunción f, función propia f

eigenshadow n SPACE sombra propia f

eigenvalue n COMP&DP valor eigen m, ELECTRON, PHYS autovalor m, valor propio m

eigenvector n COMP&DP vector eigen m, ELECTRON, PHYS autovector m, vector propio m

eight: ~-**bit accuracy** n COMP&DP, ELECTRON precisión de octeto f; ~-**bit byte** n COMP&DP, ELECTRON octeto m; ~-**bit conversion** n COMP&DP, ELECTRON conversión de octeto f; ~-**bit converter** n COMP&DP, ELECTRON convertidor de octeto m; ~-**bit output** n COMP&DP, ELECTRON byte de salida m, salida de octeto f; ~-**channel recorder** n INSTR grabador de ocho pistas m; ~-**column card** n COMP&DP ficha de ocho columnas f, tarjeta de ocho columnas f; ~-**level code** n ELECTRON código de ocho niveles m; ~-**phase shift keying** n ELECTRON variación en la octava fase f; ~-**ply belting** n PROD correas de ocho capas f pl; ~-**point recorder** n INSTR grabador de ocho puntos m

eighth: ~-**order Chebyshev filter** n ELECTRON, PHYS filtro Chebyshev en octava posición m

eightvo n (*8vo*) PRINT octavo m

8vo n (*eightvo*) PRINT octavo m

Einstein: ~ **coefficients** n pl RAD PHYS coeficientes de Einstein m pl; ~-**de-Haas effect** n PHYS efecto Einstein-de-Haas m; ~ **photoelectric equation** n ELEC PHYS ecuación fotoeléctrica de Einstein f; ~ **temperature** n PHYS temperatura de Einstein f

einsteinium n (*Es*) CHEM, PHYS, RAD PHYS einstenio m (*Es*)

Einthoven: ~ **galvanometer** n ELEC, ELEC ENG galvanómetro de Einthoven m

EIRP *abbr* (*equivalent isotropically-radiated power*) SPACE *communications* EEII (*potencia equivalente radiada isotrópica*)

EIT *abbr* (*encoded information type*) TELECOM tipo de información codificada m

ejecta n pl GEOL eyecciones volcánicas f pl, materias proyectadas f pl, eyecciones f pl

ejectable: ~ **capsule** n SPACE cápsula eyectable f; ~ **nose cone** n SPACE cono eyectable de la ojiva m

ejectamenta n pl GEOL deyecciones volcánicas f pl, materias proyectadas f pl

ejected: ~ **beam** n NUCL haz extraído m (*Esp*), haz eyectado m (*AmL*)

ejection n MECH evacuación f, expulsión f, eyección f, SAFE expulsado; ~ **force** n SPACE fuerza de expulsión f; ~-**guide bush** n MECH ENG manguito de guía de eyección m; ~-**guide pillar** n MECH ENG pilar de guía de eyección m; ~ **pin** n MECH ENG pasador eyector m, pivote eyector m; ~ **seat** n AIR TRANSP, MILIT, SPACE asiento eyectable m

ejector n MECH, MECH ENG, P&R expulsor m, eyector m; ~ **condenser** n HYDRAUL condensador de chorro m, condensador de eyector m, condensador por eyección m; ~-**cycle refrigeration system** n REFRIG sistema frigorífico de eyección de vapor m; ~ **pin** n

MECH pasador del expulsor m, MECH ENG pivote eyector m; ~ **plate** n MECH ENG *injection mould* plato eyector m, P&R placa del eyector f; ~ **pump** n MECH ENG bomba expulsora f, bomba eyectora f; ~ **retaining-plate** n MECH ENG *diecasting* placa de retención del expulsor f, placa de retención del eyector f, plato de retención del expulsor m, plato de retención del eyector m; ~ **seat** n AIR TRANSP, MILIT, SPACE asiento eyectable m; ~ **sleeve** n MECH ENG manguito del eyector m, manguito expulsor m; ~ **stop-piece** n MECH ENG pieza de paro del eyector f, tope del expulsor m, tope del eyector m; ~-**type trim exhaust system** n PACK sistema de extracción del recorte tipo eyector m; ~ **valve** n MECH ENG válvula del eyector f, válvula expulsora f

ekebergite n MINERAL ekebergita f

Ekman: ~ **flow** n HYDROL flujo de Ekman m, OCEAN caudal de Ekman m; ~ **forcing** n OCEAN fuerza de Ekman f; ~ **layer** n HYDROL capas estratificadas Ekman f pl, OCEAN sustrato de Ekman m; ~ **spiral** n OCEAN espiral de Ekman m

elaeolite n MINERAL eleolita f, nefelina f

elaidic *adj* CHEM elaídico

elaidin n CHEM elaidina f

elapsed: ~ **time** n COMP&DP, MECH tiempo transcurrido m; ~-**time counter** n MECH contador de intervalos m

elasmosine n MINERAL elasmosina f

elastic: ~ **after-effects** n pl FLUID efectos elásticos m pl; ~ **bitumen** n MINERAL betumen elástico m (*AmL*), betún elástico m (*Esp*); ~ **coefficient** n METALL coeficiente elástico m; ~ **collision** n NUCL colisión elástica f, PHYS choque elástico m, colisión elástica f; ~ **constant** n FLUID constante de elasticidad f, METALL constante elástica f; ~ **deformation** n PACK deformación elástica f; ~ **elongation** n PACK alargamiento elástico m; ~ **impact** n NUCL impacto elástico m; ~ **impedance** n PETROL impedancia elástica f; ~ **instability** n AIR TRANSP inestabilidad elástica f; ~ **limit** n CONST, MECH, P&R, PACK, PHYS límite elástico m, límite de elasticidad m; ~ **mode** n SPACE modo elástico m; ~ **nut** n MECH ENG, PROD tuerca elástica f; ~ **properties** n pl FLUID propiedades de elasticidad f pl; ~ **range** n MECH *mass* zona de deformaciones elásticas f; ~ **scattering** n PART PHYS, PHYS, RAD PHYS dispersión elástica f; ~ **scattering of high-energy electrons** n PART PHYS, PHYS, RAD PHYS dispersión elástica de electrones de alta energía f; ~ **stop-nut** n MECH ENG, PROD tuerca de paro elástica f, tuerca de tope elástica f; ~ **stretch** n PACK alargamiento elástico m; ~ **wave** n ELEC ENG, PHYS, WAVE PHYS onda elástica f; ~ **wheel** n TRANSP rueda elástica f

elasticity n GEN elasticidad f

elastomer n CHEM, P&R, PETR TECH, PROD, REFRIG, SPACE elastómero m; ~ **seal** n PROD junta elastomérica f

elastomeric: ~ **membrane tank** n SPACE tanque con membrana elastómerica m

elaterite n MINERAL elaterita f

E-layer n GEOPHYS capa E f, capa de Kennelly-Heaviside f, ionosfera f, PHYS capa E f, ionosfera f, WAVE PHYS ionosfera f

elbow^1: ~-**high** *adj* CONST hasta el codo m

elbow^2 n LAB, MECH, NUCL codo m, tubo acodado m; ~-**height handrail** n CONST pasamanos a la altura del codo *m*; ~ **joint** *n* MECH articulación de codo *f*, MECH ENG articulación de codo *f*, junta articulada *f*, unión en T *f*; ~ **pad** *n* SAFE codera *f*; ~ **tongs** *n pl* PROD tenazas de boca curva *f pl*, tenazas de bujes *f pl*; ~ **union** *n* CONST junta acodada *f*

Elcometer: ~ **thickness gage** *AmE*, ~ **thickness gauge** *BrE n* INSTR, P&R indicador de espesor Elcometer *m*

elderflower *n* FOOD flor de saúco *f*

electret *n* PHYS electreto *m*; ~-**foil microphone** *n* ACOUST micrófono de electrete *m*

electric[1] *adj* GEN eléctrico

electric[2]: ~ **actuator** *n* ELEC, SPACE actuador eléctrico *m*; ~ **arc** *n* COAL, ELEC, ELEC ENG, GAS, PHYS arco eléctrico *m*, arco voltaico *m*; ~-**arc cutting** *n* THERMO corte por arco eléctrico *m*; ~-**arc furnace** *n* (*EAF*) COAL, ELEC, ELEC ENG, HEAT, MECH ENG, THERMO horno de arco eléctrico *m*, horno de arco voltaico *m*; ~-**arc heater** *n* ELEC, MECH ENG calentador de arco eléctrico *m*; ~-**arc welding** *n* ELEC, PROD, THERMO soldeo por arco eléctrico *m*; ~ **bell** *n* COAL timbre *m*, ELEC campana eléctrica *f*; ~ **blanket** *n* ELEC, HEAT ENG manta eléctrica *f*; ~-**blanket heating** *n* ELEC, HEAT ENG calentamiento por manta eléctrica *m*; ~ **blasting** *n* MINE pega eléctrica *f*; ~ **blasting machine** *n* MINE explosor eléctrico *m*; ~ **blasting cap** *n* MINE cebo eléctrico *m*, explosor *m*; ~ **braking** *n* ELEC frenado eléctrico *m*; ~-**cable joint** *n* RAIL empalme de cable eléctrico *m*; ~ **calamine** *n* MINERAL calamina *f*; ~ **cell** *n* ELEC, ELEC ENG pila eléctrica *f*; ~ **charge** *n* ELEC, ELEC ENG, PART PHYS, PHYS, TELECOM carga eléctrica *f*; ~ **circuit** *n* ELEC, ELEC ENG, ELECTRON circuito eléctrico *m*; ~ **coil** *n* ELEC, ELEC ENG bobina eléctrica *f*; ~ **conduction** *n* ELEC, ELEC ENG conducción eléctrica *f*; ~ **conductor** *n* ELEC, ELEC ENG, PHYS conductor eléctrico *m*; ~ **conduit** *n* ELEC, ELEC ENG conducto portacables eléctricos *m*; ~ **constant** *n* ELEC ENG *permittivity* permisividad eléctrica del vacío *f*, *resistance, capacitance, inductance of circuit element* constante eléctrica *f*, PHYS constante eléctrica *f*; ~ **contact** *n* ELEC, ELEC ENG contacto eléctrico *m*; ~ **control** *n* ELEC, ELEC ENG control eléctrico *m*, mando eléctrico *m*; ~ **convector** *n* ELEC, THERMO convector eléctrico *m*, estufa eléctrica *f*; ~ **current** *n* ELEC, ELEC ENG, PHYS, RAD PHYS, TELECOM corriente eléctrica *f*; ~-**current carrier** *n* ELEC, ELEC ENG, PHYS, RAD PHYS portador de carga eléctrica *m*, portador de corriente eléctrica *m*; ~ **defrosting** *n* ELEC, REFRIG desescarche eléctrico *m*; ~ **delay detonator cap** *n* ELEC, MINE cebo eléctrico de retardo *m*; ~ **delay line** *n* ELEC, ELECTRON línea eléctrica de retardo *f*; ~ **delivery lorry** *n BrE* (*cf electric delivery truck AmE*) AUTO camión de distribución eléctrica *m*; ~ **delivery truck** *n AmE* (*cf electric delivery lorry BrE*) AUTO camión de distribución eléctrica *m*; ~ **detonator** *n* MINE detonador eléctrico *m*; ~ **dipole** *n* ELEC, ELEC ENG, PHYS dipolo eléctrico *m*; ~ **dipole moment** *n* ELEC, ELEC ENG, PHYS momento del dipolo eléctrico *m*, momento dipolar eléctrico *m*; ~ **discharge** *n* ELEC, ELEC ENG, ELECTRON descarga eléctrica *f*; ~-**discharge laser** *n* ELECTRON láser de descarga eléctrica *m*; ~ **displacement** *n* ELEC, ELEC ENG, PHYS desplazamiento eléctrico *m*; ~ **drill** *n* CONST, ELEC, MECH sonda eléctrica *f*, taladro eléctrico *m*, taladro mecánico eléctrico *m*; ~ **dryer** *n* ELEC, HEAT secador

eléctrico *m*; ~ **efficiency** *n* ELEC ENG rendimiento eléctrico *m*; ~ **energy** *n* ELEC, ELEC ENG, PHYS energía eléctrica *f*; ~ **eye** *n* ELEC, ELEC ENG célula fotoeléctrica *f*, ojo eléctrico *m*; ~ **fence** *n* AGRIC, ELEC cerca eléctrica *f*; ~ **field** *n* ELEC, ELEC ENG, PETROL, PHYS, RAD PHYS, TELECOM, TV campo eléctrico *m*; ~-**field gradient** *n* ELEC, ELEC ENG, PHYS gradiente de campo eléctrico *m*; ~-**field intensity** *n* ELEC, ELEC ENG, PETROL, PHYS, RAD PHYS intensidad del campo eléctrico *f*; ~-**field strength** *n* ELEC, ELEC ENG, PETROL, PHYS, RAD PHYS intensidad del campo eléctrico *f*; ~ **fire** *n* ELEC, HEAT fuego eléctrico *m*; ~ **firing** *n* MINE disparo por medios eléctricos *m* (*AmL*), explosión por medios eléctricos *f*, explosor *m* (*Esp*); ~ **flux** *n* ELEC, ELEC ENG, PHYS flujo de desplazamiento *m*, flujo eléctrico *m*; ~ **force** *n* ELEC, ELEC ENG fuerza eléctrica *f*; ~ **fuel-pump** *n* AUTO, ELEC, VEH bomba de combustible eléctrica *f*; ~ **furnace** *n* COAL, ELEC electrohorno *m*, horno eléctrico *m*, HEAT, THERMO horno eléctrico *m*; ~ **generator** *n* ELEC, ELEC ENG, NUCL, TV electrogenerador *m*, generador eléctrico *m*; ~ **heater** *n* ELEC, HEAT electrocalefactor *m*, estufa eléctrica *f*, radiador eléctrico *m*, MECH ENG, THERMO calentador eléctrico *m*; ~ **heating** *n* ELEC, HEAT ENG calefacción eléctrica *f*; ~ **heating-pad** *n* THERMO manta eléctrica *f*; ~ **hoist** *n* ELEC, MECH elevador eléctrico *m*, montacargas eléctrico *m*, torno eléctrico *m*; ~ **hot-plate** *n* ELEC, THERMO calentador eléctrico *m*, electrocalentador *m*, parilla eléctrica *f*, placa calentadora eléctrica *f*; ~ **image** *n* ELEC imagen eléctrica *f*, ELEC ENG característica eléctrica *f*, imagen eléctrica *f*; ~-**induction furnace** *n* ELEC ENG horno de electroinducción *m*; ~ **interlock** *n* ELEC, PROD enclavamiento eléctrico *m*; ~ **interlocking system** *n* ELEC, PROD, SAFE sistema de enclavamiento eléctrico *m*; ~ **lighter** *n* ELEC alumbrador eléctrico *m*, encendedor eléctrico *m*, mecha eléctrica *f*; ~ **lighting** *n* ELEC iluminación eléctrica *f*; ~ **linkage** *n AmE* (*cf electric transmission BrE*) ELEC transmisión eléctrica *f*; ~ **locomotive** *n* ELEC, RAIL locomotora eléctrica *f*; ~ **log** *n* PETR TECH perfil eléctrico *m*, registro eléctrico *m*; ~ **loss** *n* ELEC pérdida eléctrica *f*; ~ **machine** *n* ELEC, ELEC ENG máquina eléctrica *f*; ~ **magnet** *n* CHEM, ELEC, ELEC ENG, PART PHYS, PHYS, TELECOM, TV electroimán *m*; ~ **meter** *n* ELEC contador de electricidad *m*, contador eléctrico *m*; ~ **mixer** *n* ELEC, FOOD batidora eléctrica *f*; ~ **moped** *n* AUTO, ELEC ciclomotor eléctrico *m*; ~ **motor** *n* AUTO, ELEC, ELEC ENG, TRANSP electromotor *m*, motor eléctrico *m*; ~ **noise** *n* ELECTRON ruido eléctrico *m*; ~ **oscillation** *n* ELECTRON oscilación eléctrica *f*; ~ **oven** *n* COAL horno eléctrico *m*, ELEC electrohorno *m*, horno eléctrico *m*, HEAT horno eléctrico *m*, THERMO electrohorno *m*, horno eléctrico *m*; ~ **pickup** *n* TRANSP camioneta eléctrica de reparto *f* (*Esp*), chatita *f* (*AmL*); ~ **plug** *n* ELEC, ELEC ENG, LAB clavija eléctrica *f*, enchufe macho *m*; ~ **polarization** *n* ELEC, PHYS polarización eléctrica *f*; ~ **pole** *n* ELEC, ELEC ENG polo eléctrico *m*; ~ **potential** *n* ELEC, ELEC ENG, PHYS potencial eléctrico *m*; ~ **power** *n* ELEC, ELEC ENG, THERMO energía eléctrica *f*, potencia eléctrica *f*; ~ **power line** *n* ELEC, ELEC ENG, THERMO línea de energía eléctrica *f*; ~-**power station** *n* ELEC estación eléctrica *f*, ELEC ENG central de electricidad *f*, central eléctrica *f*; ~-**power substation** *n* ELEC, ELEC ENG subestación eléctrica *f*; ~-**power system** *n* ELEC, ELEC ENG, THERMO red eléctrica *f*; ~-**power transmission** *n* ELEC, ELEC ENG, THERMO transmisión de energía eléctrica *f*; ~ **propulsion lorry** *n BrE* (*cf electric propulsion truck AmE*) AUTO, ELEC camión de propulsión eléctrica *m*; ~ **propulsion truck** *n AmE* (*cf electric propulsion lorry BrE*) AUTO, ELEC camión de propulsión eléctrica *m*; ~ **pulse** *n* ELEC, ELEC ENG impulso eléctrico *m*; ~ **quadrupole** *n* ELEC, ELEC ENG, RAD PHYS choque eléctrico *m*, cuadrípolo eléctrico *m*; ~ **quadrupole transition** *n* ELEC, ELEC ENG, RAD PHYS transición del cuadrípolo eléctrico *f*; ~ **railcar** *n* ELEC, VEH autovía eléctrica *f*; ~ **relay** *n* ELEC, ELEC ENG relé eléctrico *m*; ~ **resistance** *n* ELEC, ELEC ENG, PHYS resistencia eléctrica *f*; ~-**resistance furnace** *n* ELEC horno de resistencia eléctrico *m*, ELEC ENG, PHYS electrohorno de resistencia *m*, horno de resistencia eléctrico *m*, THERMO horno de resistencia eléctrico *m*; ~ **road vehicle** *n* AUTO, VEH automóvil eléctrico *m*; ~-**rocket engine** *n* MECH ENG motor de cohete eléctrico *m*; ~ **saw** *n* CONST, ELEC serrucho eléctrico *m*, sierra eléctrica *f*; ~ **shock** *n* ELEC electrochoque *m*, electroshock *m*, sacudida eléctrica *f*, ELEC ENG electrochoque *m*, electroshock *m*, SAFE choque eléctrico *m*, electrochoque *m*; ~ **shot-firer** *n* MINE pega de barrenos eléctrica *f*; ~ **shot-firing** *n* MINE pega de barrenos eléctrica *f*; ~ **signal** *n* ELEC, ELEC ENG señal eléctrica *f*; ~ **smelting** *n* ELEC, ELEC ENG electrofusión *f*; ~ **socket** *n* CINEMAT enchufe hembra *m*, ELEC enchufe hembra *m*, zócalo *m*, ELEC ENG enchufe hembra *m*, LAB enchufe hembra *m*, zócalo *m*, PROD, TELECOM enchufe hembra *m*; ~ **spark** *n* ELEC chispa eléctrica *f*; ~ **stapling-machine** *n* ELEC, PROD engrapadora eléctrica automática *f*; ~ **starter** *n* AUTO, ELEC aparato de arranque eléctrico *m*; ~ **steam-boiler** *n* ELEC, MECH ENG caldera eléctrica *f*, electrocaldera *f*; ~ **surface-heater** *n* ELEC, MECH ENG calentador eléctrico de superficies *m*, calentador superficial eléctrico *m*; ~ **susceptibility** *n* ELEC, PHYS susceptibilidad eléctrica *f*; ~ **transducer** *n* ELEC, ELEC ENG transductor eléctrico *m*; ~ **transmission** *n* *BrE* (*cf electric linkage AmE*) ELEC *supply network* transmisión eléctrica *f*; ~ **transport vehicle** *n* ELEC, TRANSP vehículo eléctrico de transporte *m*; ~ **trolley** *n* ELEC, TRANSP carrito eléctrico *m*, trole eléctrico *m*; ~ **tuning** *n* ELECTRON sintonización eléctrica *f*; ~ **utility** *n* ELEC, ELEC ENG empresa electrocomercial *f*, empresa eléctrica *f*; ~ **variable** *n* ELEC variable eléctrica *f*; ~ **vehicle** *n* ELEC, TRANSP, VEH vehículo eléctrico *m*; ~ **wave** *n* ELEC, ELEC ENG, WAVE PHYS onda eléctrica *f*, onda hertziana *f*; ~ **welding** *n* ELEC, ELEC ENG soldadura eléctrica *f*; ~ **wire-break alarm** *n* ELEC, SAFE alarma de cortocircuito eléctrico *f*, alarma de interrupción de cable eléctrico *f*; ~ **wiring** *n* ELEC, ELEC ENG cableado *m*, conjunto de conexiones eléctricas *m*, VEH cableado de la instalación eléctrica *m*

electrical: ~ **accident** *n* ELEC, ELEC ENG, SAFE accidente eléctrico *m*; ~ **admittance** *n* ACOUST, ELEC, ELEC ENG, PHYS, TELECOM admitancia eléctrica *f*; ~ **appliance** *n* ELEC, TEXTIL aparato eléctrico *m*; ~ **blasting** *n* ELEC, MINE pega eléctrica *f*; ~ **breakdown** *n* ELEC ENG descarga disruptiva *f*; ~ **capacitance** *n* ELEC, TELECOM capacitancia eléctrica *f*; ~ **characteristic** *n* ELEC, ELEC ENG, ELECTRON característica eléctrica *f*; ~ **charge** *n* ELEC, ELEC ENG,

PHYS, TELECOM carga eléctrica *f*; ~ **circuit** *n* ELEC, TELECOM circuito eléctrico *m*; ~ **component** *n* ELEC, ELEC ENG componente eléctrico *m*; ~ **conductance** *n* ELEC, TELECOM conductancia eléctrica *f*; ~ **conduction** *n* ELEC, ELEC ENG conducción eléctrica *f*; ~ **conductivity** *n* ELEC, ELEC ENG conductividad eléctrica *f*; ~ **conductor** *n* ELEC, ELEC ENG canalón eléctrico *m*, conductor eléctrico *m*, PHYS conductor eléctrico *m*; ~ **connection** *n* ELEC, ELEC ENG conexión eléctrica *f*; ~ **connector** *n* ELEC, ELEC ENG conector eléctrico *m*; ~ **contact** *n* ELEC, ELEC ENG contacto eléctrico *m*; ~ **continuity** *n* ELEC, ELEC ENG continuidad eléctrica *f*; ~ **control board** *n* ELEC, NUCL cuadro de control eléctrico *m*; ~ **double-layer** *n* CHEM *surface* capa eléctrica doble *f*; ~ **drive** *n* ELEC, ELEC ENG, NUCL, PHOTO accionamiento eléctrico *m*; ~ **earth connector** *n BrE* (*cf electrical ground connector AmE*) ELEC, ELEC ENG, WATER TRANSP borne de puesta a masa *m*, borne de puesta a tierra *m*; ~ **efficiency** *n* ELEC eficacia eléctrica *f*, eficiencia eléctrica *f*, rendimiento eléctrico *m*; ~ **energy** *n* ELEC, ELEC ENG, PHYS energía eléctrica *f*; ~ **engineering** *n* ELEC, ELEC ENG electrotecnia *f*, ingeniería eléctrica *f*; ~ **equipment** *n* ELEC, ELEC ENG equipo eléctrico *m*; ~ **fault** *n* QUALITY falla eléctrica *f*; ~ **filter** *n* ELEC, ELEC ENG, ELECTRON filtro eléctrico *m*; ~ **fire risk** *n* ELEC, SAFE peligro de incendio eléctrico *m*; ~ **firing** *n* ELEC, MINE disparo eléctrico *m*; ~ **ground connector** *n AmE* (*cf electrical earth connector BrE*) ELEC, ELEC ENG, WATER TRANSP borne de puesta a masa *m*, borne de puesta a tierra *m*; ~ **hazard** *n* ELEC, SAFE peligro eléctrico *m*, riesgo eléctrico *m*; ~ **household appliance** *n* ELEC electrodoméstico *m*, enser doméstico eléctrico *m*; ~ **hygrometer** *n* ELEC, REFRIG higrómetro eléctrico *m*; ~ **images** *n pl* ELEC imágenes eléctricas *f pl*; ~ **input** *n* ELEC, ELEC ENG, ELECTRON entrada de corriente *f*, entrada de energía eléctrica *f*; ~ **installation** *n* ELEC, ELEC ENG, WATER TRANSP instalación eléctrica *f*; ~-**installation work** *n* ELEC, ELECTRON, WATER TRANSP trabajo de instalación eléctrica *m*; ~ **insulating board** *n* PAPER cartón dieléctrico *m*; ~ **insulating paper** *n* PAPER papel dieléctrico *m*; ~ **insulation** *n* ELEC, ELEC ENG aislamiento eléctrico *m*; ~-**kinetic impedance** *n* ACOUST, ELEC impedancia electrocinética *f*; ~ **log** *n* PETROL perfil eléctrico *m*, registro eléctrico *m*; ~ **machine** *n* ELEC, ELEC ENG máquina eléctrica *f*; ~ **measuring-apparatus** *n* ELEC, SAFE aparato eléctrico para mediciones *m*, medidor eléctrico *m*; ~ **network** *n* ELEC, ELECTRON, PHYS red eléctrica *f*; ~ **noise** *n* ELECTRON perturbación eléctrica *f*; ~-**optical** *n* (*E-O*) ELEC, OPT, PROD, TELECOM electroóptico *m*, eléctrico-óptico *m*; ~-**optical isolation** *n* ELEC, ELEC ENG, OPT, PROD aislamiento eléctrico y óptico *m*; ~ **oscillation** *n* ELEC, WAVE PHYS oscilación eléctrica *f*; ~ **oscillator** *n* ELEC, WAVE PHYS oscilador eléctrico *m*; ~ **output** *n* ELEC ENG, ELECTRON salida de corriente *f*, salida de energía eléctrica *f*, NUCL rendimiento eléctrico *m*; ~ **panel** *n* WATER TRANSP cuadro de control *m*; ~ **path** *n* ELEC, PROD circuito eléctrico *m*; ~ **power** *n* ELEC, ELEC ENG, ELECTRON, NUCL, TELECOM energía eléctrica *f*, potencia eléctrica *f*; ~-**power supply** *n* ELEC, ELEC ENG, ELECTRON, NUCL, TELECOM suministro de energía eléctrica *m*; ~ **properties** *n pl* CONST, ELEC, ELEC ENG propiedades eléctricas *f pl*; ~ **protection equipment** *n* ELEC, SAFE equipo eléctrico de protección *m*, equipo protector eléctrico *m*; ~ **ratings** *n pl* PROD valores eléctricos nominales *m pl*; ~ **resistivity** *n* ELEC, P&R resistividad eléctrica *f*; ~ **resonator** *n* ELEC, ELECTRON resonador eléctrico *m*; ~ **safety requirements** *n pl* ELEC, SAFE normas de seguridad eléctrica *f pl*; ~ **shot-firing** *n* MINE disparo eléctrico *m*; ~ **signal** *n* ELEC, ELEC ENG, ELECTRON señal eléctrica *f*; ~ **soil-heating** *n* AGRIC, ELEC, HEAT calentamiento eléctrico del suelo *m*; ~ **solenoid** *n* PROD solenoide eléctrico *m*; ~ **storm** *n* METEO tormenta eléctrica *f*; ~ **survey** *n* PETROL levantamiento con método eléctrico *m*, perfilado eléctrico *m*; ~ **tape** *n* PROD cinta aislante *f*; ~ **test** *n* ELEC, ELEC ENG prueba eléctrica *f*, test eléctrico *m*; ~ **transmission line** *n* ELEC, ELEC ENG electroducto *m*, línea de transmisión eléctrica *f*; ~ **wiring** *n* ELEC, ELEC ENG cableado *m*; ~ **wiring diagram** *n* ELEC ENG, WATER TRANSP diagrama del circuito eléctrico *m*; ~ **zero** *n* ELEC, INSTR cero eléctrico *m*; ~ **zero adjuster** *n* ELEC, INSTR ajustador del cero eléctrico *m*

electrically[1]: ~**-driven** *adj* ELEC, ELEC ENG, MECH, PHOTO accionado eléctricamente, electroaccionado, electroimpulsado

electrically[2]: ~**-erasable ROM** *n* (*EEROM*) COMP&DP ROM borrable eléctricamente *f* (*EEROM, ROMBE*); ~**-held crosspoint** *n* TELECOM punto de contacto eléctrico *m*; ~**-operated valve** *n* ELEC, PROD electroválvula *f*; ~**-pumped laser** *n* ELECTRON láser bombeado eléctricamente *m*; ~**-tuned oscillator** *n* ELEC, ELECTRON, WAVE PHYS oscilador sintonizado eléctricamente *m*

electricity *n* GEN electricidad *f*; ~ **generated** *n* ELEC, ELEC ENG, NUCL electricidad generada *f*; ~ **generating station** *n* CONST, ELEC, ELEC ENG, NUCL central de generación eléctrica *f*; ~ **generation** *n* ELEC generación de electricidad *f*, producción de electricidad *f*, ELEC ENG producción de electricidad *f*, FUELLESS, NUCL generación de electricidad *f*; ~ **meter** *n* ELEC, ELEC ENG contador de electricidad *m*, contador eléctrico *m*; ~ **pylon** *n* CONST, ELEC' mástil de electricidad *m*, torre metálica de electricidad *f*; ~ **supply** *n* CONST, ELEC, ELEC ENG, MECH ENG suministro de electricidad *m*, suministro eléctrico *m*; ~ **supply system** *n* CONST, ELEC, ELEC ENG, MECH ENG sistema de suministro de electricidad *m*; ~ **transmission** *n* ELEC, ELECTRON, THERMO transmisión de electricidad *f*

electrification *n* ELEC, ELEC ENG, PHYS electrificación *f*

electrify *vt* ELEC, ELEC ENG, PHYS electrificar, electrizar

electro[1]: ~**-optic** *adj* OPT, TELECOM electroóptico; ~**-optical** *adj* ELECTRON, OPT electroóptico; ~**-osmotic** *adj* CHEM electroosmótico

electro[2] *n* PRINT electrotipo *m*; ~**-discharge machining** *n* (*EDM*) MECH ENG, PROD elaboración por electroerosión *f*, fabricación por descarga eléctrica *f*, fabricación por electroerosión *f*, maquinación por electrodescarga *f*; ~**-extraction** *n* CHEM electroextracción *f*; ~**-optic effect** *n* ELEC, OPT, TELECOM efecto electroóptico *m*; ~**-optic switch** *n* ELEC, OPT, TELECOM conmutador electroóptico *m*; ~**-optical distance-measuring equipment** *n* ELEC, INSTR, OPT, TELECOM instrumento de medida de distancia electroóptica *m*; ~**-optical distance-measuring instrument** *n* ELEC, INSTR, OPT, TELECOM instrumento de medida de distancia electroóptica *m*; ~**-optical modulator** *n* ELECTRON, OPT modulador

electroóptico *m*; ~**-optical signal processing** *n* ELECTRON, OPT tratamiento de señal electroóptico *m*; ~**-osmosis** *n* CHEM electroósmosis *f*; ~**-spark machining** *n* MECH ENG maquinación electroerosivo *f*, maquinación por chispa eléctrica *f*, maquinación por fulguración *f*

electroacoustic: ~ **chain** *n* ACOUST, ELEC ENG cadena electroacústica *f*; ~ **transducer** *n* ACOUST, ELEC ENG transductor electroacústico *m*

electroacoustical: ~ **reciprocity coefficient** *n* ACOUST, ELEC ENG coeficiente de reciprocidad electroacústica *n*

electroacoustics *n* ACOUST, ELEC ENG electroacústica *f*

electroanalysis *n* CHEM electroanálisis *m*

electrobus *n* ELEC, TRANSP autobús eléctrico *m*, electrobús *m*

electrocapillarity *n* CHEM electrocapilaridad *f*

electrocapillary *adj* CHEM electrocapilar

electrochemical[1] *adj* CHEM, ELEC, ELEC ENG electroquímico

electrochemical[2]: ~ **capacitor** *n* CHEM, ELEC, ELEC ENG, TELECOM condensador electroquímico *m*; ~ **energy** *n* CHEM, ELEC, ELEC ENG energía electroquímica *f*; ~ **series** *n* CHEM, ELEC, ELEC ENG serie electroquímica *f*

electrochemistry *n* CHEM, ELEC, ELEC ENG electroquímica *f*

electrocochleography *n* ACOUST electrococleografía *f*

electrode *n* GEN electrodo *m*; ~ **admittance** *n* ELEC, ELEC ENG, PHYS admitancia de electrodo *f*; ~ **bias** *n* ELEC derivación electródica *f*, ELEC ENG derivación electródica *f*, polarización del electrodo *f*; ~**-bias voltage** *n* ELEC ENG voltaje medio del electrodo *m*; ~ **boiler** *n* ELEC, HEAT ENG caldera de electrodos *f*; ~ **carbon** *n* ELEC ENG carbón de electrodos *m*; ~ **characteristic** *n* ELEC, ELEC ENG, PHYS característica electródica *f*; ~ **configuration** *n* ELEC, TELECOM configuración del electrodo *f*; ~ **gap** *n* ELEC, ELEC ENG separación del electrodo *f*; ~ **holder** *n* CONST, ELEC, ELEC ENG portaelectrodos *m*; ~ **potential** *n* CHEM, ELEC, ELEC ENG, PHYS potencial del electrodo *m*; ~ **tip** *n* ELEC hilo de punta de electrodo *m*

electrodeposit *n* COATINGS, CONST, ELEC, ELEC ENG depósito electrolítico *m*, electrodepósito *m*

electrodeposition *n* COATINGS, CONST, ELEC ENG, ELEC, PROD deposición electrolítica *f*, electroplastia *f*, galvanoplastia *f*

electrodermal: ~ **effect** *n* ACOUST efecto electrodérmico *m*

electrodialysis *n* CHEM, ELEC electrodiálisis *f*

electrodrilling *n* COAL taladro eléctrico *m*

electrodynamic: ~ **instrument** *n* ELEC, INSTR aparato electrodinámico *m*; ~ **levitation** *n* ELEC, TRANSP elevación electrodinámica *f*, levitación electrodinámica *f*; ~ **loudspeaker** *n* ACOUST, ELEC altavoz electrodinámico *m*; ~ **microphone** *n* ACOUST, ELEC micrófono electrodinámico *m*; ~ **relay** *n* ELEC relé electrodinámico *m*

electrodynamics *n* ACOUST, ELEC, PHYS electrodinámica *f*

electrodynamometer *n* ELEC, INSTR, PHYS electrodinamómetro *m*

electrofluorescence *n* ELEC, NUCL electrofluorescencia *f*

electroforming *n* CONST, COATINGS, ELEC, ELEC ENG, PROD galvanoplastia *f*

electrofusion *n* ELEC, GAS electrofusión *f*
electroglow *n* COMP&DP electroluminiscencia *f*, ELEC electroluminiscencia *f*, halo eléctrico *m*, ELECTRON, NUCL, OPT, PHYS electroluminiscencia *f*, SPACE electroluminiscencia *f*, halo eléctrico *m*, TELECOM electroluminiscencia *f*
electrographic: ~ **analysis** *n* ELEC, RAD PHYS análisis electrográfico *m*; ~ **ink** *n* COLOUR, ELEC tinta electrográfica *f*; ~ **printer** *n* COMP&DP, ELEC, PRINT impresora electrográfica *f*
electrokinetic[1] *adj* CHEM, ELEC, ELEC ENG, PHYS electrocinético
electrokinetic[2]: ~ **energy** *n* CHEM, ELEC, ELEC ENG, PHYS energía electrocinética *f*, potencia electrocinética *f*
electrokinetics *n* CHEM, ELEC, ELEC ENG, PHYS electrocinética *f*
electroluminescence *n* GEN electroluminiscencia *f*
electroluminescent: ~ **display** *n* COMP&DP, ELEC, ELECTRON display electroluminiscente *m* (*AmL*), pantalla electroluminiscente *f* (*Esp*), visualización electroluminiscente *f*
electrolysis *n* GEN electrólisis *f*
electrolyte *n* GEN electrólito *m*; ~ **battery** *n* TRANSP batería con electrolito *f*
electrolytic[1] *adj* GEN electrolítico
electrolytic[2]: ~ **bath** *n* ELEC, ELEC ENG, PHYS baño electrolítico *m*, inmersión electrolítica *f*; ~ **capacitor** *n* ELEC, ELEC ENG, PHYS capacitor electrolítico *m*, condensador electrolítico *m*; ~ **cell** *n* ELEC, ELEC ENG, PHYS cuba electrolítica *f*, célula electrolítica *f*; ~ **conductivity** *n* ELEC, ELEC ENG, PHYS conductividad electrolítica *f*; ~ **display** *n* ELECTRON visualización electrolítica *f*; ~ **etching** *n* ELEC, NUCL ataque electrolítico *m*; ~ **hydrometer** *n* ELEC hidrómetro electrolítico *m*; ~ **hygrometer** *n* REFRIG higrómetro electrolítico *m*; ~ **marking** *n* MECH ENG *on metal conductors* marcado electrolítico *m*; ~ **rectifier** *n* ELEC, ELEC ENG, PHYS rectificador electrolítico *m*; ~ **unit** *n* ELEC, ELEC ENG, PHYS módulo electrolítico *m*, unidad electrolítica *f*
electrolyze *vt* CHEM, ELEC, PHYS electrolizar
electrolyzer *n* CHEM, ELEC, PHYS electrolizador *m*
electromagnet *n* GEN electroimán *m*
electromagnetic[1] *adj* GEN electromagnético
electromagnetic[2]: ~ **brake** *n* AUTO, RAIL, TRANSP, VEH freno electromagnético *m*; ~ **calorimeter** *n* ELEC, PART PHYS, RAD PHYS calorímetro electromagnético *m*; ~ **chuck** *n* MECH ENG plato electromagnético *m*, portabrocas electromagnético *m*, portaherramientas electromagnético *m*; ~ **clutch** *n* ELEC, MECH, TRANSP embrague electromagnético *m*; ~ **compatibility** *n* (*EMC*) SPACE compatibilidad electromagnética *f*; ~ **coupling** *n* ELEC, ELEC ENG, TRANSP acoplamiento electromagnético *m*; ~ **current meter** *n* OCEAN correntómetro electromagnético *m*; ~ **damper** *n* ELEC, GEOPHYS amortiguador electromagnético *m*; ~ **damping** *n* ELEC, GEOPHYS amortiguación electromagnética *f*, amortiguamiento electromagnético *m*; ~ **deflection** *n* ELEC ENG desviación electromagnética *f*, ~ **disturbance** *n* SPACE, TELECOM perturbación electromagnética *f*; ~ **energy** *n* ELEC, ELEC ENG, PHYS energía electromagnética *f*; ~~**energy pulse** *n* ELEC, ELEC ENG impulso de energía electromagnética *m*; ~ **environment** *n* SPACE ambiente electromagnético *m*; ~ **field** *n* ELEC, ELEC ENG, PHYS, TELECOM, WAVE

PHYS campo electromagnético *m*; ~ **fixing-device** *n* MECH ENG dispositivo de fijación electromagnética *m*, dispositivo de sujeción electromagnética *m*; ~ **flowmeter** *n* ELEC, ELEC ENG medidor electromagnético de caudal *m*; ~ **focusing** *n* ELEC ENG enfoque electromagnético *m*; ~ **force** *n* ELEC, ELEC ENG, PART PHYS, PHYS fuerza electromagnética *f*; ~ **ignition** *n* AUTO, ELEC arranque electromagnético *m*, ignición electromagnética *f*, ELEC ENG arranque electromagnético *m*, VEH ignición electromagnética *f*, arranque electromagnético *m*; ~ **induction** *n* (*EMI*) PHYS, PROD inducción electromagnética *f* (*IEM*); ~ **interaction** *n* PART PHYS, RAD PHYS interacción electromagnética *f*; ~ **interference** *n* (*EMI*) COMP&DP, TELECOM interferencia electromagnética *f* (*IEM*); ~ **interference filter** *n* ELEC, ELEC ENG, ELECTRON filtro de interferencia electromagnético *m*; ~ **interference filtering** *n* ELEC, ELEC ENG, ELECTRON filtración de interferencia electromagnética *f*; ~ **isolation** *n* ELEC, ELEC ENG aislamiento electromagnético *m*; ~ **lateral-guidance system** *n* TRANSP sistema lateral de guiado electromagnético *m*; ~ **lens** *n* CINEMAT, ELEC, ELEC ENG, OPT, TV lente electromagnética *f*; ~ **levitation** *n* ELEC, PHYS, TRANSP levitación electromagnética *f*; ~ **loudspeaker** *n* ACOUST, ELEC altavoz electromagnético *m*; ~ **microphone** *n* ACOUST, ELEC micrófono electromagnético *m*; ~ **mode** *n* OPT modo electromagnético *m*; ~ **moment** *n* ELEC momento electromagnético *m*; ~ **momentum** *n* ELEC, PHYS momento electromagnético *m*; ~ **overload relay** *n* ELEC, ELEC ENG relevador electromagnético de sobrecarga *m*, relé electromagnético de sobrecarga *m*; ~ **pulse** *n* ELEC, ELEC ENG, TELECOM impulso electromagnético *m*; ~ **pump** *n* ELEC, ELECTRON, NUCL bomba electromagnética *f*; ~ **radiation** *n* ELEC, ELEC ENG, ELECTRON, METEO, OPT, PHYS, PROD, RAD PHYS, TELECOM, WAVE PHYS radiación electromagnética *f*; ~ **relay** *n* ELEC, ELEC ENG relé electromagnético *m*; ~ **resonator** *n* ELEC, ELECTRON resonador electromagnético *m*; ~ **screen** *n* ELEC, PHYS pantalla electromagnética *f*; ~ **shielding** *n* ELEC blindaje electromagnético *m*; ~ **shutter-release** *n* ELEC, PHOTO disparador electromagnético *m*; ~ **spectrum** *n* ELEC, ELEC ENG, ELECTRON, RAD PHYS espectro electromagnético *m*; ~ **tuning** *n* ELECTRON sintonización electromagnética *f*; ~ **unit** *n* ELEC unidad electromagnética *f*; ~ **vulnerability** *n* ELEC ENG vulnerabilidad electromagnética *f*; ~ **wave** *n* ELEC, ELEC ENG, ELECTRON, PHYS, RAD PHYS, TELECOM, WAVE PHYS onda electromagnética *f*; ~~**wave equations** *n pl* ELEC, PHYS, RAD PHYS, WAVE PHYS ecuaciones de las ondas electromagnéticas *f pl*; ~~**wave polarization** *n* ELEC, ELEC ENG, WAVE PHYS polarización de la onda electromagnética *f*
electromagnetically: ~~**operated** *adj* ELEC, ELEC ENG accionado electromagnéticamente
electromagnetism *n* GEN electromagnetismo *m*
electromechanical: ~~**coupling factor** *n* ACOUST, ELEC factor de acoplamiento electromecánico *m*; ~ **device** *n* ELEC, ELEC ENG mecanismo electromecánico *m*; ~ **exchange** *n* ELEC, ELEC ENG, TELECOM central electromecánica *f*; ~ **filter** *n* ELEC, ELEC ENG, ELECTRON filtro electromecánico *m*; ~ **relay** *n* ELEC, ELEC ENG relé electromecánico *m*; ~ **switching** *n* ELEC, TELECOM conmutación electromecánica *f*; ~~**switching system** *n* ELEC, TELECOM sistema de

conmutación electromecánica *m*; ~~**switching unit** *n* ELEC, TELECOM unidad de conmutación electromecánica *f*; ~ **transducer** *n* ACOUST, ELEC, ELEC ENG transductor electromecánico *m*

electromechanics *n* ACOUST, ELEC, ELEC ENG, TELECOM electromecánica *f*

electromeric: ~ **effect** *n* CHEM, ELEC efecto electromérico *m*

electrometeor *n* ELEC, GEOPHYS electrometeoro *m*

electrometer *n* GEN electrómetro *m*; ~ **amplifier** *n* ELEC, ELEC ENG, ELECTRON amplificador electrométrico *m*; ~ **tube** *n* ELEC, ELEC ENG, ELECTRON tubo electrométrico *m*

electrometric: ~ **titration** *n* CHEM titulación electrométrica *f*, titulación potenciométrica *f*, valoración potenciométrica *f*

electrometry *n* ELEC, ELEC ENG, ELECTRON electrometría *f*

electromobile *n* TRANSP electromóvil *m*

electromotive: ~ **force** *n* (*EMF*) ELEC, ELEC ENG, PHYS fuerza electromotriz *f* (*FEM*)

electromotor *n* ELEC, ELEC ENG, MECH ENG, TRANSP electromotor *m*

electron *n* (*e*) GEN electrón *m* (*é*); ~ **accelerator** *n* ELECTRON, NUCL, PART PHYS acelerador de electrones *m*, ciclotrón *m*, sincrotrón *m*; ~ **affinity** *n* ELECTRON, NUCL, PART PHYS afinidad electrónica *f*; ~ **attachment** *n* ELECTRON, NUCL, PART PHYS adhesión del electrón *f*; ~ **beam** *n* CHEM, COMP&DP, ELEC, ELECTRON, METALL, NUCL, PART PHYS, TELECOM, TV haz de electrones *m*, haz electrónico *m*, WAVE PHYS haz de electrones *m*, rayo de electrones *m*, haz electrónico *m*; ~~**beam acceleration** *n* ELEC, ELECTRON, NUCL aceleración de haz de electrones *f*; ~~**beam alignment method** *n* ELECTRON método de alineación de haz de electrones *m*; ~~**beam annealing** *n* ELECTRON fortalecimiento del haz de electrones *m*; ~~**beam bombardment furnace** *n* ELECTRON, NUCL, PART PHYS horno de bombardeo por haz electrónico *m*; ~~**beam column** *n* ELECTRON columna de haz de electrones *f*; ~~**beam curing** *n* (*EBC*) NUCL, PRINT curado por haz electrónico *m*, endurecimiento por haz de electrones *m*, endurecimiento por haz electrónico *m*; ~~**beam cutting** *n* ELECTRON interrupción por haz de electrones *f*; ~~**beam direct writing** *n* ELECTRON escritura directa de haz de electrones *f*; ~~**beam focusing** *n* ELECTRON enfoque de haz de electrones *m*; ~~**beam laser** *n* ELECTRON láser de haz de electrones *m*; ~~**beam lithography** *n* ELECTRON litografía de haz de electrones *f*; ~~**beam lithography machine** *n* ELECTRON máquina de litografía de haz de electrones *f*; ~~**beam machining** *n* ELECTRON mecanizado por haz de electrones *m*; ~~**beam mask** *n* ELECTRON ocultación del haz de electrones *f*; ~~**beam melting** *n* ELECTRON, NUCL fusión por haz electrónico *f*; ~~**beam parametric amplifier** *n* ELECTRON amplificador paramétrico del haz de electrones *m*; ~~**beam processing** *n* ELECTRON tratamiento del haz de electrones *m*; ~~**beam projection lithography** *n* ELECTRON litografía por proyección de haz de electrones *f*; ~~**beam projection printing** *n* ELECTRON, PRINT impresión por proyección de haz de electrones *f*; ~~**beam pumping** *n* ELECTRON bombeo de haz de electrones *m*; ~~**beam resist** *n* ELECTRON protección del haz de electrones *f*; ~~**beam**

scanning *n* ELECTRON exploración por haz de electrones *f*; ~~**beam test** *n* ELECTRON, RAD PHYS prueba del haz electrónico *f*; ~~**beam tube** *n* ELECTRON tubo de haz de electrones *m*; ~~**beam voltage** *n* ELECTRON, TV voltaje del haz electrónico *m*; ~~**beam welding** *n* CONST, ELECTRON, NUCL soldadura de haz de electrones *f*; ~~**bombarded semiconductor** *n* (*EBS*) ELECTRON, NUCL, PART PHYS semiconductor de bombardeo electrónico *m* (*SBE*); ~ **bombardment** *n* ELECTRON, NUCL, PART PHYS bombardeo de electrones *m*; ~~**bombardment thruster** *n* SPACE impulsor de bombardeo electrónico *m*; ~ **capture** *n* ELECTRON, NUCL, PHYS, RAD PHYS captura electrónica *f*; ~~**capture detector** *n* POLL detector de captura electrónica *m*; ~ **cascade** *n* ELECTRON, NUCL, PART PHYS cascada electrónica *f*; ~ **cloud** *n* CHEM, ELECTRON, NUCL, RAD PHYS, TV nube de electrones *f*, nube electrónica *f*; ~ **collision** *n* ELECTRON, TELECOM colisión electrónica *f*; ~ **conductivity** *n* ELECTRON, RAD PHYS conductividad electrónica *f*; ~ **continuum** *n* ELECTRON, NUCL, PART PHYS espectro continuo electrónico *m*; ~ **cooling** *n* ELECTRON, PART PHYS enfriamiento de electrones *m*; ~ **coupling** *n* ELEC ENG, ELECTRON, PART PHYS acoplamiento de electrones *m*, acoplamiento electrónico *m*; ~~**coupling oscillator** *n* ELECTRON oscilador de acoplamiento electrónico *m*; ~ **current** *n* ELEC ENG, ELECTRON corriente electrónica *f*; ~ **cyclotron** *n* ELECTRON, NUCL, PART PHYS ciclotrón de electrones *m*; ~~**cyclotron frequency** *n* ELECTRON, NUCL, PART PHYS, PHYS frecuencia del ciclotrón de electrones *f*; ~ **density** *n* CHEM, CRYSTALL, ELECTRON, PART PHYS, PHYS densidad de los electrones *f*, densidad electrónica *f*; ~~**density distribution** *n* CHEM, CRYSTALL, ELECTRON, PART PHYS, PHYS distribución de la densidad electrónica *f*; ~ **detection** *n* ELECTRON, PART PHYS detección de electrones *f*; ~ **device** *n* ELEC ENG, ELECTRON dispositivo electrónico *m*, mecanismo electrónico *m*; ~ **diffraction** *n* CRYSTALL, ELECTRON, RAD PHYS difracción de electrones *f*; ~~**diffraction pattern** *n* CRYSTALL diagrama de difracción de electrones *m*; ~ **drift** *n* ELECTRON, NUCL arrastre electrónico *m*, desplazamiento de los electrones *m*; ~ **emission** *n* ELECTRON, PART PHYS emisión de electrones *f*; ~ **emitter** *n* ELECTRON, PART PHYS emisor de electrones *m*; ~~**energy filter** *n* ELECTRON, PART PHYS, RAD PHYS filtro de energía electrónica *m*; ~~**energy loss** *n* RAD PHYS pérdida de energía electrónica *f*; ~~**energy-loss spectroscopy** *n* RAD PHYS espectroscopía por pérdida electroenergética *f*; ~~**flood lithography** *n* ELECTRON litografía por flujo de electrones *f*; ~ **gas** *n* ELECTRON, GAS, PHYS gas de electrones *m*; ~ **gun** *n* ELECTRON, INSTR, PHYS, RAD PHYS, TV cañón de electrones *m*, cañón electrónico *m*; ~ **gun current** *n* ELECTRON, PHYS, TV corriente del cañón de electrones *f*; ~ **image** *n* ELECTRON imagen electrónica *f*; ~ **imaging** *n* ELECTRON proyección de imágenes electrónicas *f*; ~~**impact ion engine** *n* SPACE motor de impacto de iones electrónicos *m*; ~~**induced activation** *n* ELECTRON, RAD PHYS activación electrónica *f*, activación inducida por electrones *f*; ~ **irradiation** *n* SPACE radiación de electrones *f*; ~ **lens** *n* CINEMAT, ELECTRON, INSTR, OPT, PHYS, TV lente electrónica *f*; ~ **magnetic moment** *n* ELECTRON, NUCL, PHYS momento magnético del electrón *m*; ~ **mass** *n* CHEM, ELECTRON, PART

PHYS masa del electrón *f*, masa electrónica *f*; **~ micrograph** *n* RAD PHYS micrografía electrónica *f*; **~ microscope** *n* ELECTRON, INSTR, LAB, METALL, PART PHYS, PHYS, TELECOM microscopio electrónico *m*; **~ microscope tube** *n* INSTR tubo electrónico del microscopio *m*; **~ microscopy** *n* ELECTRON, PHYS microscopía electrónica *f*; **~ mirror** *n* ELECTRON, INSTR cátodo secundario *m*, dínodo *m*, espejo electrónico *m*; **~ multiplier** *n* ELECTRON, RAD PHYS multiplicador de electrones *m*, multiplicador electrónico *m*; **~-multiplier phototube** *n* ELECTRON, INSTR, RAD PHYS fototubo multiplicador electrónico *m*; **~-multiplier tube** *n* ELECTRON, INSTR, RAD PHYS tubo multiplicador electrónico *m*; **~ neutrino** *n* ELECTRON, PHYS neutrino electrónico *m*; **~ optics** *n* ELECTRON, OPT, PHYS óptica electrónica *f*; **~ pair** *n* ELECTRON, PART PHYS, RAD PHYS par de electrones *m*; **~ paramagnetic resonance** *n* ELECTRON, NUCL, PHYS resonancia paramagnética electrónica *f*; **~ path** *n* ELECTRON, NUCL, PART PHYS, TV recorrido del electrón *m*; **~ population** *n* SPACE población de electrones *f*; **~-positron annihilation** *n* ELECTRON, NUCL, PART PHYS aniquilación electrón positrón *f*; **~-positron collider** *n* PART PHYS cámara de reacción electrón-positrón *f*; **~-positron interaction** *n* PART PHYS colisión del electrón-positrón *f*, encuentro del electrón-positrón *m*, interacción del electrón-positrón *f*; **~ probe** *n* NUCL sonda electrónica *f*; **~ radiography** *n* ELECTRON, NUCL radiografía electrónica *f*; **~ ray** *n* ELECTRON radiación electrónica *f*; **~ scanning** *n* ELECTRON, NUCL barrido electrónico *m*; **~ scanning beam** *n* TV haz explorador de electrones *m*; **~ shell** *n* CHEM, ELECTRON, NUCL, PART PHYS, PHYS capa del electrón *f*, capa electrónica *f*; **~ shower** *n* ELECTRON, NUCL, PART PHYS chaparrón electrónico *m*; **~ source** *n* ELECTRON, RAD PHYS fuente de electrones *f*; **~ specific charge** *n* NUCL carga específica del electrón *f*; **~-spectroscopic diffraction** *n* PHYS, RAD PHYS difracción de espectroscopia electrónica *f*; **~-spectroscopic imaging** *n* PHYS, RAD PHYS formación de imágenes por espectroscopia electrónica *f*, reproducción de imágenes por espectroscopía electrónica *f*; **~ spectroscopy** *n* PHYS, RAD PHYS espectroscopía electrónica *f*; **~ spin** *n* CHEM, ELECTRON, NUCL, PART PHYS, PHYS espín del electrón *m*; **~-spin resonance** *n* NUCL, PART PHYS, PHYS resonancia del espín del electrón *f*; **~-spin resonance magnetometer** *n* NUCL, PART PHYS, PHYS magnetómetro de resonancia del espín del electrón *m*; **~-storage ring** *n* ELECTRON, PART PHYS anillo de almacenamiento de electrones *m*; **~ stream** *n* PART PHYS, TV flujo de electrones *m*; **~ synchrotron** *n* ELECTRON, NUCL, PART PHYS sincrotrón de electrones *m*; **~ theory of metals** *n* RAD PHYS teoría electrónica de los metales *f*; **~-to-atom ratio** *n* NUCL, PART PHYS razón electrónica-atómica *f*, relación de electrón a átomo *f*; **~ trajectory** *n* ELECTRON, NUCL trayectoria electrónica *f*; **~-transfer diode** *n* PHYS diodo de transferencia electrónica *m*; **~ tube** *n* ELECTRON tubo electrónico *m*; **~-tube base** *n* ELECTRON base de tubo electrónico *f*; **~-tube envelope** *n* ELECTRON funda de tubo electrónico *f*; **~-tube grid** *n* ELECTRON rejilla de tubo electrónico *f*; **~-tube heater** *n* ELECTRON filamento de tubo electrónico *m*; **~-tube holder** *n* ELECTRON anclaje de tubo electrónico *m*; **~-tube neck** *n* ELECTRON collarín de tubo electrónico

m; **~ tube oscillator** *n* ELECTRON oscilador de tubo electrónico *m*; **~-volt** *n* (*eV*) ELEC ENG, ELECTRON, NUCL, PART PHYS, PHYS electronvoltio *m* (*eV*); **~-wave magnetron** *n* ELECTRON, WAVE PHYS magnetrón de ondas electrónicas *m*; **~-wave tube** *n* ELECTRON, WAVE PHYS tubo de ondas electrónicas *m*

Electron: ~ Spectroscopy for Chemical Analysis *n* (*ESCA*) CHEM Espectroscopía Electrónica para Análisis Químico *f* (*ESCA*)

electronegative *adj* CHEM, RAD PHYS electronegativo

electronic[1] *adj* ELEC, ELECTRON electrónico; **~-to-electronic** *adj* (*E-E, E-to-E*) ELECTRON, TV electrónico a electrónico

electronic[2]: **~ anti-locking device** *n* TRANSP mecanismo electrónico antibloqueo *m*; **~ anti-skid system** *n* TRANSP sistema electrónico antideslizante *m*; **~ balance** *n* LAB balanza electrónica *f*; **~-beam forming** *n* ELECTRON formación de haz electrónico *f*; **~-beam steering** *n* ELECTRON dirección del haz electrónico *f*; **~ bearing line** *n* WATER TRANSP línea de rumbos electrónica *f*; **~ bearing-cursor** *n* WATER TRANSP cursor de rumbos electrónico *m*; **~ bearing-marker** *n* WATER TRANSP indicador de marcaciones electrónico *m*; **~ braking-control** *n* TRANSP control electrónico de frenado *m*; **~ car** *n* AUTO, ELECTRON coche electrónico *m*; **~ carburetor** *AmE*, **~ carburettor** *BrE* *n* ELECTRON, TRANSP carburador electrónico *m*; **~ chart** *n* WATER TRANSP carta electrónica *f*; **~ chart display** *n* WATER TRANSP presentación de la carta electrónica *f*, presentación en pantalla de la carta electrónica *f*; **~ chopper** *n* ELECTRON interruptor electrónico *m*; **~ circuit** *n* ELECTRON, TELECOM circuito electrónico *m*; **~ circuit integration** *n* ELECTRON, TELECOM integración de circuito electrónico *f*; **~ clock** *n* ELECTRON, TELECOM reloj electrónico *m*; **~ commutation** *n* TRANSP conmutación electrónica *f*; **~ comparator** *n* MECH ENG comparador electrónico *m*; **~ component** *n* COMP&DP, ELECTRON, TELECOM componente electrónico *m*; **~ compound** *n* METALL compuesto electrónico *m*; **~ configuration** *n* PHYS configuración electrónica *f*; **~ control system** *n* ELECTRON sistema de control electrónico *m*; **~ control unit** *n* AUTO unidad de control electrónico *f*; **~ counter** *n* ELECTRON contador electrónico *m*; **~ countermeasures** *n pl* (*ECM*) MILIT, SPACE contramedidas electrónicas *f pl*; **~ counting** *n* ELECTRON contador electrónico *m*; **~ crosspoint** *n* TELECOM punto de contacto electrónico *m*; **~ data interchange** *n* (*EDI*) TELECOM intercambio de datos electrónicos *m*; **~ data interchange for administration, commerce and transport** *n* (*EDIFACT*) TELECOM intercambio de datos electrónicos para la administración, el comercio y el transporte *m*; **~ data interchange forwarding** *n* TELECOM envío de intercambio de datos electrónicos *m*; **~ data interchange message stores** *n* TELECOM almacenamiento de mensajes por intercambio de datos electrónicos; **~ data interchange user agent** *n* (*EDI-UA*) COMP&DP, TELECOM agente usuario de intercambio de datos electrónicos *m*; **~ data processing** *n* (*EDP*) COMP&DP procesamiento electrónico de datos *m* (*EDP*), ELECTRON tratamiento de datos electrónico *m* (*TDE*); **~ device** *n* ELEC ENG, ELECTRON dispositivo electrónico *m*, mecanismo electrónico *m*; **~ digital theodolite** *n* CONST teodolito digital electrónico *m*; ~ **direction-reverser** *n* TRANSP recuperador de dirección electrónico *m*; ~ **directory** *n* TELECOM directorio electrónico *m*; ~-**display micrometric head** *n* METR cabezal micrométrico del indicador electrónico *m*; ~ **dot generator** *n* (*EDG*) PRINT generador electrónico de puntos *m*; ~ **editing** *n* (*EE*) CINEMAT, TV edición electrónica *f*; ~ **engineering** *n* ELECTRON ingeniería electrónica *f*; ~ **engraving** *n* PRINT grabado electrónico *m*; ~ **equipment** *n* ELECTRON equipo electrónico *m*; ~ **exchange** *n* TELECOM central electrónica *f*; ~-**field production** *n* TV producción del campo electrónico *f*; ~ **filing** *n* COMP&DP archivo electrónico *m*; ~ **frequency-control** *n* ELECTRON control de frecuencia electrónico *m*; ~ **funds transfer** *n* (*EFT*) TELECOM transferencia electrónica de fondos *f*; ~ **funds transfer at point of sale** *n* (*EFTPOS*) TELECOM transferencia electrónica de fondos en punto de venta *f*; ~ **funds transfer system** *n* (*EFTS*) COMP&DP sistema de transferencia electrónica de fondos *m* (*EFTS*); ~ **gage** *AmE*, ~ **gauge** *n* *BrE* METR dispositivo electrónico *m*; ~ **gauging probe** *n* *BrE* MECH ENG probeta medidora electrónica *f*, sonda medidora electrónica *f*; ~ **heat capacity** *n* ELECTRON, PHYS capacidad térmica electrónica *f*; ~ **heat conductivity** *n* ELECTRON, NUCL, PHYS conductividad térmica electrónica *f*; ~ **heating** *n* ELEC ENG, ELECTRON caldeo por histéresis dieléctrica *m*, calentamiento electrónico *m*; ~ **ignition** *n* AUTO, ELEC, ELECTRON, VEH arranque electrónico *m*, encendido electrónico *m*, ignición electrónica *f*; ~ **imaging** *n* ELECTRON proyección electrónica de imágenes *f*; ~ **injection** *n* AUTO, ELECTRON, VEH inyección electrónica *f*; ~ **integrated circuit** *n* ELECTRON circuito integrado electrónico *m*; ~ **intelligence** *n* ELECTRON inteligencia electrónica *f*; ~-**key system** *n* TELECOM sistema de manipulación electrónica *m*; ~ **mail** *n* (*e-mail*) COMP&DP, ELECTRON, TELECOM correo electrónico *m*; ~ **mail service** *n* (*e-mail service*) COMP&DP, ELECTRON, TELECOM servicio de correo electrónico *m*; ~ **mailbox** *n* (*e-mail box*) COMP&DP, ELECTRON, TELECOM buzón de correo electrónico *m*, buzón electrónico *m*; ~ **matting** *n* TV aglutinamiento electrónico *m*; ~ **memory** *n* ELEC ENG, ELECTRON memoria electrónica *f*; ~ **message switch** *n* TELECOM conmutador electrónico de mensajes *m*; ~ **message system** *n* TELECOM sistema electrónico de mensajes *m*; ~ **messaging** *n* COMP&DP, ELECTRON, TELECOM mensajería electrónica *f*; ~ **metering of fuel injection** *n* TRANSP medición electrónica de inyección de combustible *f*; ~ **module** *n* ELECTRON módulo electrónico *m*; ~ **music** *n* ELECTRON música electrónica *f*; ~ **news gathering** *n* (*ENG*) TV recolección electrónica de noticias *f*; ~ **office** *n* COMP&DP oficina electrónica *f*; ~**plate** *n* ELEC, ELECTRON placa electrónica *f*, plancha electrónica *f*; ~ **point of sale** *n* (*EPOS*) COMP&DP punto de ventas electrónico *m*, terminal punto de venta *m* (*TPV*); ~ **polarization** *n* PHYS, RAD PHYS polarización electrónica *f*; ~ **power supply** *n* ELEC fuente de suministro electrónica *f*, ELEC ENG, ELECTRON fuente de suministro electrónica *f*, suministro de energía electrónica *m*; ~ **publishing** *n* COMP&DP, ELECTRON edición electrónica *f*, publicación electrónica *f*; ~ **relay** *n* ELEC, ELECTRON relevador electrónico *m*, relé electrónico *m*; ~ **rocket-engine** *n* SPACE motor de propulsión para cohete electrónico

m; ~ **scanning** *n* PRINT exploración electrónica *f*; ~ **semiconductor** *n* NUCL semiconductor electrónico *m*; ~-**signal processing** *n* ELECTRON tratamiento de señal electrónica *m*; ~ **signature** *n* COMP&DP firma electrónica *f*; ~-**speech synthesis** *n* ELECTRON síntesis de audiofrecuencia electrónica *f*; ~ **speed controller** *n* TRANSP controlador electrónico de velocidad *m*; ~ **speed-control** *n* TRANSP control electrónico de velocidad *m*; ~ **structure** *n* NUCL estructura electrónica *f*; ~ **subshell** *n* RAD PHYS subcapa electrónica *f*; ~ **surveillance** *n* TELECOM vigilancia electrónica *f*; ~ **switch** *n* COMP&DP, TELECOM conmutador electrónico *m*; ~ **switching** *n* COMP&DP, TELECOM conmutación electrónica *f*; ~ **switching system** *n* (*ESS*) TELECOM sistema de conmutación electrónico *m*; ~ **test-pattern** *n* ELECTRON patrón de prueba electrónico *m*; ~ **timer** *n* ELECTRON temporizador electrónico *m*, PHOTO reloj electrónico *m*; ~ **traffic aid** *n* TRANSP ayuda electrónica para el tráfico *f*; ~ **tube** *n* ELECTRON tubo electrónico *m*; ~ **tuning** *n* ELECTRON, TELECOM sintonización electrónica *f*; ~-**tuning range** *n* ELECTRON, TELECOM gama de sintonización electrónica *f*; ~-**tuning sensitivity** *n* ELECTRON, TELECOM sensibilidad de sintonización electrónica *f*; ~ **valve** *n* ELECTRON válvula electrónica *f*; ~ **warfare** *n* (*EW*) ELECTRON, MILIT guerra electrónica *f* (*GE*); ~ **weighing scales** *n* ELEC, PACK balanza electrónica *f*
electronically[1]: ~ **controlled** *adj* ELECTRON electrónicamente controlado
electronically[2]: ~-**controlled surface grinder** *n* CONST, ELECTRON, MECH ENG pulidora de superficies de control electrónico *f*, rectificadora de superficies de control electrónico *f*; ~-**controlled valve** *n* CONST, ELECTRON, MECH ENG válvula de control electrónico *f*; ~-**tuned filter** *n* ELECTRON, TELECOM filtro de sintonización electrónica *m*; ~-**tuned oscillator** *n* ELECTRON, TELECOM oscilador sintonizado electrónicamente *m*
electronographic: ~ **camera** *n* PART PHYS cámara electronográfica *f*
electrophilic *adj* CHEM electrofílico
electrophoresis *n* CHEM, ELEC, LAB electroforesis *f*; ~ **cell** *n* CHEM, ELEC, LAB celda de electroforesis *f*, cuba electroforética *f*
electrophoretic: ~ **enameling** *AmE*, ~ **enamelling** *BrE* *n* COLOUR esmaltado electroforético *m*; ~ **migration** *n* NUCL migración electroforética *f*
electrophorus *n* ELEC ENG electróforo *m*
electrophotographic: ~ **printer** *n* COMP&DP, ELEC, PRINT impresora electrofotográfica *f*
electrophotography *n* COMP&DP, PRINT electrofotografía *f*
electroplatable *adj* COATINGS con revestimiento electrolítico
electroplate[1] *n* COATINGS galvanoplastia *f*, recubrimiento electrolítico *m*, CONST galvanoplastia *f*, ELEC, ELEC ENG galvanoplastia *f*, recubrimiento electrolítico *m*, PROD galvanoplastia *f*
electroplate[2] *vt* COATINGS electrochapar, electrodepositar, galvanoplastiar, CONST galvanoplastiar, ELEC, ELEC ENG electrochapar, electrodepositar, galvanoplastiar, PROD galvanoplastiar
electroplated[1] *adj* COATINGS electrochapado, electrodepositado, electrorrevestido, galvanoplastiado, CONST galvanoplastiado, ELEC, ELEC ENG electro-

chapado, electrodepositado, electrorrevestido, galvanoplastiado, PROD galvanoplastiado; ~ **with tin** adj COATINGS revestido electrolíticamente con estaño

electroplated[2]: ~ **coating** n COATINGS, ELEC, ELEC ENG revestimiento electrolítico m; ~ **terne** n COATINGS, ELEC, ELEC ENG recubrimiento electrolítico de plomo m

electroplating n COATINGS electrochapado m, electroplastia f, galvanoplastia f, CONST galvanoplastia f, ELEC, ELEC ENG electrochapado m, electroplastia f, galvanoplastia f, PROD electroplastia f, galvanoplastia f; ~ **bath** n COATINGS, ELEC, ELEC ENG baño de galvanoplastia m; ~ **vat** n COATINGS, ELEC, ELEC ENG cuba de electrochapado f, cuba de electrolítica f

electropneumatic: ~ **brake** n RAIL, TRANSP, VEH freno electroneumático m

electropolishing n METALL electropulido m

electropositive[1] adj CHEM, RAD PHYS electropositivo

electropositive[2]: ~ **elements** n pl CHEM, RAD PHYS elementos electropositivos m pl

electroscope n ELEC, INSTR, PHYS electroscopio m

electrosensitive: ~ **paper** n COMP&DP, PRINT papel electrosensible m; ~ **printer** n COMP&DP, ELEC, PRINT impresora electrosensible f; ~ **safety system** n SAFE, SPACE sistema electrosensible de seguridad m

electrosilver vt COATINGS, ELEC, ELEC ENG platear por electrólisis

electrosilvering n COATINGS, ELEC, ELEC ENG plateado galvanoplástico m

electroslag: ~ **welding** n CONST soldadura por inclusión eléctrica f, soldadura eléctrica con escorias f, soldadura con escoria eléctricamente conductora f, MECH soldadura con escoria eléctricamente conductora f, soldadura eléctrica con escorias f, NUCL soldadura por deslizamiento eléctrico f

electrostatic[1] adj ELEC, ELEC ENG, ELECTRON, PHYS, TELECOM electrostático

electrostatic[2]: ~ **air filter** n ELEC, HEAT ENG, SAFE filtro de aire electrostático m; ~ **attraction** n ELEC, ELEC ENG, PHYS, SPACE atracción electrostática f; ~ **cathode ray tube** n (electrostatic CRT) ELECTRON tubo de rayos catódicos electrostático m (TRC electrostático); ~ **charge** n ELEC carga electrostática f; ~ **collector** n NUCL colector electrostático m, dispositivo de captura electrostática m; ~ **CRT** n (electrostatic cathode ray tube) ELECTRON TRC electrostático m (tubo de rayos catódicos electrostático); ~ **enameling** AmE, ~ **enamelling** BrE n COLOUR, ELEC esmaltado electrostático m; ~ **exciter** n ACOUST excitador electrostático m; ~ **field** n ELEC, PHYS campo electrostático m; ~ **filter** n ELEC, ELECTRON filtro electrostático m; ~ **flux** n ELEC flujo electrostático m; ~ **flux density** n ELEC densidad del flujo electrostático f; ~ **focusing** n ELEC ENG enfoque electrostático m; ~ **force** n ELEC, ELEC ENG fuerza electrostática f; ~ **generator** n ELEC, ELEC ENG generador electrostático m, máquina de influencia f, máquina electrostática de influencia f; ~ **induction** n ELEC, ELEC ENG, PHYS inducción electrostática f; ~ **ink transfer** n ELEC, PRINT transferencia electrostática de la tinta f; ~ **ion-oscillation** n NUCL oscilación iónica electrostática f; ~ **lens** n ELEC ENG, OPT, PHYS, RAD PHYS lente electrostática f; ~ **loudspeaker** n ACOUST, ELEC altavoz electrostático m; ~ **microphone** n ACOUST micrófono electrostático m; ~ **plotter** n COMP&DP, ELEC plotter electrostático

m, trazador electrostático m; ~ **potential energy** n GEOPHYS energía potencial electrostática f; ~ **powder coating** n COATINGS, COLOUR, P&R recubrimiento electrostático con pintura en polvo m, revestimiento de polvo electrostático m; ~ **precipitator** n (ESP) GAS, POLL precipitador electrostático m; ~ **printer** n COMP&DP, ELEC, PRINT impresora electrostática f; ~ **relay** n ELEC relevador electrostático m, relé electrostático m; ~ **screen** n ELECTRON, PHYS, VEH pantalla electrostática f; ~ **spray-painting** n COLOUR, CONST pintura de pulverización electrostática f

electrostatics n ELEC, ELEC ENG, ELECTRON, PHYS electrostática f

electrostriction n PHYS electroestricción f

electrosynthesis n CHEM electrosíntesis f

electrotechnical: ~ **porcelain** n C&G, ELEC ENG porcelana electrotécnica f

electrotechnics n ELEC electrotecnia f

electrotechnology n ELEC electrotecnología f

electrothermal[1] adj ELEC electrotérmico

electrothermal[2]: ~ **booster** n ELEC, SPACE propulsión electrotérmica f; ~ **printer** n COMP&DP, ELEC, PRINT impresora electrotérmica f

electrotype n PRINT electrotipo m, galvanotipia f

electrovan n TRANSP carretilla eléctrica de equipaje f, furgoneta eléctrica f, VEH furgoneta eléctrica f

electroweak: ~ **theory** n PART PHYS, PHYS teoría de la interacción electrodébil f, teoría electrodébil f; ~ **unification energy** n PART PHYS, PHYS energía de unificación electrodébil f

ELED abbr (edge-emitting light-emitting diode) TELECOM diodo fotoemisor de emisión marginal m

element n GEN elemento m; ~ **specific activity** n NUCL, PHYS actividad específica del elemento f

elemental: ~ **particle** n PART PHYS, PHYS partícula elemental f

elementary: ~ **charge** n PHYS carga elemental f; ~ **enrichment factor** n NUCL factor de enriquecimiento elemental m; ~ **loudspeaker** n ACOUST altavoz elemental m; ~ **particle** n PART PHYS, PHYS partícula elemental f; ~ **separation effect** n NUCL efecto de separación elemental m; ~ **separative power** n NUCL poder de separación elemental m; ~ **servicing sheet** n PROD hoja de mantenimiento básico f

elephant: ~ **boiler** n HYDRAUL caldera de hervidores f

elevated: ~ **line** n TRANSP línea elevada f; ~ **platform** n RAIL plataforma elevada f; ~ **rapid-transit system** n TRANSP sistema de carreteras elevadas para tránsito rápido m, sistema de tránsito rápido elevado m; ~ **runway** n CONST vía elevada f; ~ **stress level** n PROD nivel elevado de esfuerzo m; ~ **track** n RAIL vía elevada f

elevating: ~ **machinery** n MECH ENG maquinaria elevadora f; ~ **screw** n MECH ENG tornillo elevador m; ~ **table** n MECH mesa elevadora f; ~ **wheel** n MECH ENG rueda elevadora f, volante elevador m, MILIT volante de puntería en elevación m

elevation n CONST alzado m, elevación f, altitud f, cota f, front view of building fachada f, MECH cota f, elevación f, WATER TRANSP altura f, elevación f; ~ **above sea level** n METEO elevación sobre el nivel del mar f; ~ **adjusting screw** n INSTR tornillo de ajuste elevador m; ~ **angle** n AIR TRANSP, CONST, GEOM, SPACE, TELECOM ángulo de elevación m; ~ **guidance** n AIR TRANSP guía de elevación f;

~ **head** *n* HYDRAUL desnivel *m*, NUCL carga hidráulica *f*

elevator *n* (*cf lift BrE*) AGRIC silo *m*, AIR TRANSP izador *m*, CONST *for goods* ascensor *m*, elevador *m*, montacargas *m*, transportador vertical *m*, MECH *for goods* elevador *m*, montacargas *m*, escalera mecánica *f*, ascensor *m*, transportador vertical *m*, PETR TECH, PROD elevador *m*; ~ **bucket** *n* PROD cangilón del elevador *m*; ~ **control** *n* AIR TRANSP control del izador *m*; ~ **cup** *n* PROD cangilón del elevador *m*; ~ **deflection** *n* AIR TRANSP deflexión del izador *f*, desviación del izador *f*; ~ **follow-up** *n* AIR TRANSP mando de maniobra del izador *m*, timón del izador *m*; ~ **hoist** *n* AIR TRANSP elevador del izador *m*; ~ **trim** *n* AIR TRANSP reglaje del timón de profundidad *m*

elevon *n* TRANSP elevón *m*

ELF *abbr* (*extremely low frequency*) ELEC, ELECTRON, TELECOM FEB (*frecuencia extremadamente baja*)

ellagic *adj* CHEM elágico

ellagitannin *n* CHEM elagitanina *f*

ellipse *n* GEOM elipse *f*; ~ **of inertia** *n* MECH elipse de inercia *f*

ellipsis *n* PRINT puntos suspensivos *m pl*

ellipsoid[1] *adj* GEOL, GEOM, MECH ENG, PHYS elipsoide

ellipsoid[2] *n* GEOL, GEOM, MECH ENG, PHYS elipsoide *m*

ellipsometer *n* PHYS elipsómetro *m*

elliptic[1] *adj* ELECTRON, GEOM elíptico

elliptic[2]: ~ **filter** *n* ELECTRON filtro elíptico *m*; ~ **response curve** *n* ELECTRON curva de respuesta elíptica *f*; ~ **spring** *n* MECH ENG muelle elíptico *m*, resorte elíptico *m*

elliptical[1] *adj* ELECTRON, GEOM elíptico

elliptical[2]: ~ **arch** *n* CONST *of bridge* arco circular *m*, arco elíptico *m*; ~ **gear** *n* MECH ENG engranaje elíptico *m*; ~ **geometry** *n* GEOM geometría elíptica *f*; ~ **mirror** *n* INSTR, PHYS espejo elíptico *m*; ~ **orbit** *n* PHYS, SPACE órbita elíptica *f*; ~ **polarization** *n* PHYS, RAD PHYS polarización elíptica *f*, SPACE elipticidad *f*; ~ **space** *n* GEOM espacio elíptico *m*; ~ **stern** *n* WATER TRANSP popa elíptica *f*

elliptically: ~-**polarized wave** *n* ACOUST, PHYS, WAVE PHYS onda polarizada elípticamente *f*

elliptone *n* CHEM eliptona *f*

elongated[1] *adj* MECH alargado, PRINT apaisado

elongated[2]: ~ **grain** *n* METALL grano alargado *m*; ~ **hole** *n* MECH, MECH ENG agujero alargado *m*, agujero extendido *m*

elongation *n* C&G, MECH ENG, METALL, P&R, PHYS alargamiento *m*, elongación *f*, prolongación *f*; ~ **at break** *n* P&R alargamiento al romperse *m*; ~ **at rupture** *n* PHYS alargamiento de ruptura *m*; ~ **of the cylinder** *n* C&G elongación del cilindro *f*

ELT *abbr* (*emergency locator transmitter*) TELECOM transmisor localizador de emergencia *m*, WATER TRANSP transmisor de localización de siniestros *m*

eluate *n* CHEM, CHEM TECH, FOOD, NUCL eluido *m*

eluent *n* CHEM, CHEM TECH, FOOD, NUCL eluyente *m*

elute *vt* CHEM, CHEM TECH, FOOD, NUCL eluir

eluting: ~ **agent** *n* CHEM, NUCL agente eluyente *m*

elution *n* CHEM, CHEM TECH, FOOD, NUCL elución *f*

elutriate *vt* C&G, CHEM, CHEM TECH elutriar, levigar

elutriating: ~ **funnel** *n* CHEM, CHEM TECH embudo de levigación *m*; ~ **machine** *n* CHEM, CHEM TECH equipo de levigación *m*

elutriation *n* C&G arrastre *m*, elutriación *f*, levigación *f*, CHEM, CHEM TECH elutriación *f*, levigación *f*;

~ **chamber** *n* CHEM, CHEM TECH cámara de elutriación *f*; ~ **test** *n* CONST ensayo de levigación *m*

elvan *n* GEOL elvan *m*

elvanite *n* PETROL elvanita *f*

em *n* PRINT cuadratín *m*; ~ **quad** *n* PRINT cuadratín *m*

EM *abbr* (*end of medium*) COMP&DP EM (*fin del medio, fin del soporte*)

e-mail *n* (*electronic mail*) COMP&DP, ELECTRON, TELECOM correo electrónico *m*; ~ **address** *n* COMP&DP, ELECTRON, TELECOM casilla electrónica *f*, dirección electrónica *f*; ~ **box** *n* (*electronic mailbox*) COMP&DP, ELECTRON, TELECOM buzón de correo electrónico *m*, buzón electrónico *m*; ~ **service** *n* (*electronic mail service*) COMP&DP, ELECTRON, TELECOM servicio de correo electrónico *m*

emanating: ~ **power** *n* RAD PHYS potencia de emanación *f*

emanation *n* CHEM, NUCL, PHYS, RAD PHYS emanación *f*

emasculation *n* AGRIC castración *f*, emasculación *f*

embankment *n* COAL, CONST, MINE, RAIL dique *m* (*AmL*), malecón *m* (*AmL*), terraplén *m* (*Esp*); ~ **pile** *n* COAL aguja de terraplén *f*, pilar terraplenado *m*, aguja terraplén *f*, MINE aguja terraplén *f*; ~ **piling** *n* COAL amontonamiento en terraplén *m*, avance con agujas de terraplén *m*, MINE avance con agujas de terraplén *m*

embattlement *n* P&R fragilización *f*

embed *vt* COMP&DP incrustar, CONST, MECH ENG embutir, empotrar, incrustar

embedded[1] *adj* COMP&DP incrustado, intercalado, CONST, MECH ENG embutido, empotrado, incrustado; ~ **in the wall** *adj* CONST empotrado

embedded[2]: ~ **control channel** *n* (*ECC*) TELECOM canal de control embebido *m*; ~ **loop** *n* TRANSP bucle integrado *m*, circuito integrado *m*; ~ **operations channel** *n* (*EOC*) TELECOM canal operativo embebido *m*

embedment *n* CONST empotramiento *m*

embelin *n* CHEM ácido embélico *m*

embodied *adj* MECH incorporado, MECH ENG compilado, incluido, incorporado

embolden *vt* COMP&DP, PRINT poner en negritas

embolite *n* MINERAL embolita *f*

emboss *vt* MECH ENG, PACK, PAPER, PRINT gofrar

embossed[1] *adj* MECH ENG, PACK, PAPER, PRINT en relieve, estampado, gofrado

embossed[2]: ~ **label** *n* PACK etiqueta gofrada *f*; ~ **paper** *n* PACK, PAPER, PRINT papel gofrado *m*

embossing *n* P&R estampado en relieve *m*, grabado en relieve *m*, PACK, PAPER, PRINT estampado *m*, gofrado *m*; ~ **calender** *n* PACK, PAPER calandra gofradora *f*; ~ **closure** *n* PACK cierre mediante gofrado *m*; ~ **machine** *n* PACK, PAPER, PRINT máquina para estampar en relieve *f*; ~ **press** *n* PACK, PAPER, PRINT prensa gofradora *f*, prensa para estampar en seco *f*; ~ **roll** *n* PACK, PAPER, PRINT rodillo gofrador *m*

embossment *n* MECH ENG realce *m*, relieve *m*

embrittlement *n* C&G, CRYSTALL, GEOL, MECH, METALL, NUCL fragilización *f*

embroider *vt* TEXTIL labrar

embroidered *adj* TEXTIL labrado

embryo *n* AGRIC embrión *m*

EMC *abbr* (*electromagnetic compatibility*) SPACE compatibilidad electromagnética *f*

emerald *n* MINERAL esmeralda *f*; ~ **copper** *n* MINERAL dioptasa *f*
emerged *adj* AGRIC, GEOL emergido
emergence *n* AGRIC, GEOL emergencia *f*
emergency: ~ **aid** *n* TRANSP ayuda de emergencia *f*, servicio de socorro *m*, servicio de urgencia *m*; ~ **airlock** *n* NUCL esclusa de emergencia *f*; ~ **attention** *n* TELECOM servicio de emergencia *m*; ~ **battery** *n* ELEC, ELEC ENG batería de emergencia *f*, batería de socorro *f*, batería de urgencia *f*, PROD batería de emergencia *f*, SAFE batería de socorro *f*; ~ **beacon** *n* AIR TRANSP, SPACE radiobaliza de emergencia *f*; ~ **brake** *n* AIR TRANSP, VEH freno de emergencia *m*; ~-**brake system** *n* AIR TRANSP, VEH sistema de frenado de emergencia *m*; ~ **button** *n* ELEC, SAFE botón de emergencia *m*; ~ **cable** *n* TRANSP cable de emergencia *m*; ~ **call** *n* TELECOM, TRANSP llamada de emergencia *f*; ~-**call system** *n* TELECOM, TRANSP sistema de llamada de emergencia *m*; ~ **capsule** *n* SPACE cápsula de emergencia *f*; ~ **case** *n* SAFE caso de emergencia *m*; ~ **center** *AmE*, ~ **centre** *BrE* *n* SAFE centro de emergencias *m*; ~ **condition** *n* NUCL condición de emergencia *f*; ~ **control** *n* AIR TRANSP, SAFE control de emergencia *m*; ~ **core coolant** *n* NUCL refrigerante de emergencia del núcleo *m*; ~ **crash barrier** *n* SAFE, TRANSP barrera de emergencia anti-choque *f*; ~ **crop** *n* AGRIC cultivo de emergencia *m*; ~ **descent** *n* AIR TRANSP descenso de emergencia *m*; ~ **diesel-generator** *n* NUCL generador diesel de emergencia *m*; ~ **door** *n* CONST puerta de emergencia *f*; ~ **drill** *n* SAFE, WATER TRANSP ejercicio de emergencia *m*, ejercicio de evacuación para casos de emergencia *m*; ~ **equipment** *n* AIR TRANSP, SAFE equipo de emergencia *m*; ~ **escape** *n* SPACE salida de emergencia *f*; ~-**escape tower** *n* SPACE torre para escape de emergencia *f*; ~ **evacuation of buildings** *n* SAFE evacuación de emergencia de edificios *f*; ~ **exit** *n* AIR TRANSP, CONST, SAFE salida de emergencia *f*; ~ **exposure to external radiations** *n* NUCL exposición a radiaciones externos por emergencia *f*, irradiación excepcional concertada *f*; ~ **exposure to radioactive materials** *n* NUCL contaminación excepcional concertada *f*, exposición a materiales radiactivos por emergencia *f*; ~ **first-aid procedure** *n* SAFE técnica de primeros auxilios en casos de emergencia *f*; ~ **fishplating** *n* RAIL eclisaje de emergencia *m*; ~ **flotation gear** *n* AIR TRANSP equipo de flotación de emergencia *m*; ~ **installation** *n* TELECOM instalación de emergencia *f*; ~ **landing** *n* AIR TRANSP aterrizaje de emergencia *m*, aterrizaje forzoso *m*, SPACE aterrizaje de emergencia *m*; ~ **lighting** *n* ELEC alumbrado de emergencia *m*, alumbrado de socorro *m*, iluminación de emergencia *f*; ~-**location beacon** *n* AIR TRANSP radiobaliza de localización de emergencia *f*; ~ **locator transmitter** *n* (*ELT*) TELECOM transmisor localizador de emergencia *m*, WATER TRANSP transmisor de localización de siniestros *m*; ~ **maintenance** *n* COMP&DP mantenimiento de emergencia *m*, mantenimiento de urgencia *m*; ~ **measures** *n pl* SAFE medidas de emergencia *f pl*; ~ **mode** *n* SPACE modo de emergencia *m*; ~ **operating procedure** *n* NUCL procedimiento de operación de emergencia *m*; ~ **plan** *n* MAR POLL, SAFE plan de emergencia *m*; ~ **position-indicating radio beacon** *n* (*EPIRB*) TELECOM radiofaro indicador de posición para emergencias *m*, WATER TRANSP radiobaliza de

localización de siniestros *f* (*RLS*); ~ **power supply** *n* ELEC alimentación de emergencia *f*, sistema de alimentación de emergencia *m*; ~ **power-generator** *n* MECH grupo electrógeno de emergencia *m*; ~ **preparedness** *n* NUCL estado de preparación para emergencias *m*; ~ **procedure** *n* AIR TRANSP procedimiento de emergencia *m*; ~ **radio-call** *n* WATER TRANSP señal de alarma *f*; ~ **response** *n* NUCL respuesta de emergencia *f*; ~ **rocket** *n* WATER TRANSP bengala de emergencia *f*, bengala para casos de emergencia *f*; ~ **service** *n* SAFE, SPACE servicio médico de urgencia *m*; ~ **services** *n pl* TELECOM servicios de emergencia *m pl*; ~ **shutdown** *n* COMP&DP cierre de emergencia *m*, parada de emergencia *f*, NUCL parada de emergencia *f*; ~ **shutdown of the reactor** *n* NUCL parada de emergencia del reactor *f*; ~-**shutdown rod** *n* NUCL barra de parada de emergencia *f*; ~ **sign** *n* SAFE, SPACE letrero de emergencia *m*; ~ **slide** *n* AIR TRANSP, SAFE deslizador de escape de emergencia *m*, tobogán de emergencia *m*; ~ **spillway** *n* HYDRAUL, HYDROL, SAFE, WATER aliviadero de seguridad *m*; ~ **stop** *n* SAFE parada de emergencia *f*; ~-**stopping device** *n* SAFE aditamento para el paro de emergencia *m*; ~ **supply tank** *n* AIR TRANSP depósito de suministro de emergencia *m*; ~ **system** *n* AIR TRANSP sistema de emergencia *m*; ~ **telephone** *n* TELECOM, TRANSP teléfono de emergencia *m*; ~ **treatment** *n* SAFE tratamiento de urgencia *m*; ~ **turn** *n* WATER TRANSP evolución de emergencia *f*, viraje de emergencia *m*
emergent[1] *adj* AGRIC, GEOL emergente
emergent[2]: ~ **velocity** *n* HYDRAUL velocidad de salida *f*
emerging: ~-**foil craft** *n* TRANSP, WATER TRANSP balsa auto-emergente *f*
emerizing *n* TEXTIL esmerilación *f*
emery *n* C&G lija *f*, MECH, MECH ENG, METALL, PROD esmeril *m*; ~-**belt polishing machine** *n* PROD pulidora de correa de esmeril *f*; ~ **cloth** *n* MECH, MECH ENG, PROD tela de esmeril *f*; ~ **grinder** *n* PROD esmeriladora *f*; ~-**grinding machine** *n* PROD máquina esmeriladora *f*; ~ **machine** *n* PROD máquina esmeriladora *f*; ~ **paper** *n* MECH, PAPER, PROD papel de esmeril *m*; ~ **powder** *n* MECH ENG, PROD polvo de esmeril *m*; ~ **washing** *n* C&G lavado con lija *m*; ~ **wheel** *n* MECH, PROD muela de esmeril *f*, rueda de esmeril *f*; ~-**wheel attachment** *n* MECH, PROD accesorio para muela de esmeril *m*; ~-**wheel dresser** *n* PROD aparato para reavivar muelas de esmeril *m*; ~-**wheel spindle** *n* PROD huso de la muela de esmeril *m*
emerylite *n* MINERAL emerylita *f*
emetin *n* CHEM emetina *f*
EMF *abbr* (*electromotive force*) ELEC, ELEC ENG, PHYS FEM (*fuerza electromotriz*)
EMI *abbr* COMP&DP, (*electromagnetic interference*) IEM (*interferencia electromagnética*), ELEC, ELEC ENG (*electromagnetic induction*) IEM (*inducción electromagnética*), (*electromagnetic interference*) IEM (*interferencia electromagnética*), ELECTRON (*electromagnetic interference*) IEM (*interferencia electromagnética*), PHYS (*electromagnetic induction*) IEM (*inducción electromagnética*), PROD (*electromagnetic induction*) IEM (*inducción electromagnética*), (*electromagnetic interference*) IEM (*interferencia

electromagnética), SPACE, TELECOM (*electromagnetic interference*) IEM (*interferencia electromagnética*)

emission *n* AIR TRANSP, PART PHYS, POLL, RAD PHYS, VEH emisión *f*; ~ **band** *n* PHYS banda de emisión *f*; ~ **chamber** *n* INSTR cámara de emisión *f*; ~ **data** *n pl* POLL datos de emisión *m pl*; ~ **electron microscope** *n* ELECTRON, INSTR microscopio electrónico de emisión *m*; ~ **inventory** *n* POLL inventario de emisiones *m*; ~ **line** *n* PHYS línea de emisión *f*; ~ **microscope** *n* INSTR microscopio de emisión *m*; ~ **microscopy** *n* METALL microscopía de emisión *f*; ~ **nebula** *n* SPACE nebulosa emisión *f*; ~ **point** *n* POLL foco de emisión puntal *m*, punto de emisión *m*; ~ **source** *n* POLL fuente de emisión *f*, fuente emisora *f*; ~ **spectral analysis** *n* RAD PHYS espectrometría de emisiones *f*; ~ **spectrum** *n* PHYS, RAD PHYS, SPACE espectro de emisión *m*; ~ **standard** *n* POLL estándar de emisión *m*, norma de emisión *f*, valor de emisión fijado por la ley *m*

emissive: ~ **diode** *n* ELECTRON diodo emisivo *m*

emissivity *n* HEAT ENG, OPT, PHYS, RAD PHYS, TELECOM emisividad *f*

emit *vt* COMP&DP emitir, THERMO desprender, emitir

emittance *n* FUELLESS emisión *f*

emitted: ~ **radiation** *n* RAD PHYS radiación emitida *f*

emitter *n* COMP&DP emisor *m*, ELEC, ELEC ENG, ELECTRON cuerpo emisor *m*, cátodo emisor *m*, emisor *m*, PHYS, RAD PHYS, TELECOM emisor *m*; **~-base breakdown** *n* ELECTRON avería de la base del emisor *f*; **~-base junction** *n* ELECTRON unión emisor base *f*; ~ **bias circuit** *n* ELECTRON circuito de polarización de emisor *m*; ~ **contact** *n* ELEC ENG contacto emisor *m*; **~-coupled logic** *n* (*ECL*) COMP&DP lógica de emisor acoplado *f* (*LEA*), ELECTRON circuito lógico de emisor acoplado *m* (*CLEA*); **~-coupled logic gate array** *n* ELECTRON circuito lógico predifundido de emisor acoplado *m*; ~ **diode** *n* ELEC ENG, ELECTRON diodo emisor *m*; ~ **electrode** *n* ELEC ENG, ELECTRON electrodo emisor *m*; ~ **follower** *n* ELEC ENG, PHYS seguidor de emisor *m*; **~-receiver** *n* COMP&DP emisor-receptor *m*; ~ **region** *n* ELEC, ELEC ENG área del emisor *f*

emodic *adj* CHEM emódico

emodin *n* CHEM emodina *f*

empennage *n* AIR TRANSP empenaje *m*

empirical: ~ **formula** *n* CHEM fórmula empírica *f*; ~ **operation factor** *n* MECH ENG factor de operación empírico *m*, porcentaje empírico de utilización *m*; ~ **temperature** *n* THERMO temperatura empírica *f*

emplacement: ~ **age** *n* GEOL edad de emplazamiento *f*, época de emplazamiento *f*

emplectite *n* MINERAL emplectita *f*

empties *n* PACK envases vacíos *m pl*; ~ **siding** *n* RAIL, TRANSP apartadero para vagones vacíos *m*

empty[1] *adj* COMP&DP vacío, PROD en vacío, sin carga

empty[2]: ~ **band** *n* PHYS banda vacía *f*; ~ **hole** *n* PETROL pozo vacío *m*; ~ **machine** *n* PROD máquina marchando en vacío *f*; ~ **medium** *n* COMP&DP medio vacío *m*, soporte vacío *m*; ~ **string** *n* COMP&DP cadena vacía *f* (*Esp*), serie vacía *f* (*AmL*); ~ **weight** *n* AIR TRANSP peso en vacío *m*

emptying: ~ **plug** *n* PROD tapón de vaciado *m*

EMS *abbr* (*expanded-memory specification*) COMP&DP EMS (*especificación de memoria expandida*)

Emsian *adj* GEOL Emsiense

emulate *vt* COMP&DP, ELECTRON, TELECOM emular

emulation *n* COMP&DP, ELECTRON, TELECOM emulación *f*

emulator *n* COMP&DP, ELECTRON, TELECOM emulador *m*

emulsifiability *n* CHEM, CHEM TECH, FOOD, P&R, PAPER emulsionabilidad *f*

emulsifiable *adj* CHEM, CHEM TECH, FOOD, NUCL, P&R, PAPER emulsificable

emulsification *n* CHEM, CHEM TECH, FOOD, NUCL, P&R, PAPER emulsificación *f*

emulsified[1] *adj* CHEM, CHEM TECH, FOOD emulsificado, emulsionado, NUCL emulsificado, P&R emulsionado, PAPER emulsificado

emulsified[2]: ~ **fuel** *n* AIR TRANSP combustible emulsificado *m*

emulsifier *n* CHEM, CHEM TECH, FOOD, NUCL, P&R, PAPER emulgente *m*, emulsificador *m*, emulsionante *m*, emulsor *m*, emulsificante *m*

emulsify *vt* GEN emulsificar (*AmL*), emulsionar (*Esp*)

emulsifying[1] *adj* CHEM, CHEM TECH, FOOD emulgente, emulsionante, NUCL emulgente, P&R emulgente, emulsionante, PAPER emulgente

emulsifying[2]: ~ **agent** *n* GEN agente emulgente *m*, agente emulsionante *m*; ~ **liquid** *n* CHEM TECH, SAFE líquido emulgente *m*, líquido emulsionante *m*; ~ **machine** *n* CHEM TECH equipo emulsionante *m*

emulsion[1]: **~-coated** *adj* COATINGS, PACK revestido por emulsión

emulsion[2] *n* GEN emulsión *f*; ~ **adhesive** *n* P&R, PACK adhesivo en emulsión *m*; ~ **batch** *n* CINEMAT, PHOTO lote de emulsión *m*; ~ **batch-number** *n* CINEMAT, PHOTO número de lote de la emulsión *m*; ~ **binder** *n* CHEM, CHEM TECH, FOOD, P&R emulgente *m*, emulsionante *m*; **~-breaker** *n* CHEM, MAR POLL, POLL, WATER desemulsificante *m*, producto desemulsificante *m*, producto desemulsionante *m*; **~-coated paper** *n* PAPER papel revestido por emulsión *m*; ~ **layer** *n* COATINGS capa de emulsión *f*; ~ **mud** PETROL lodo de emulsión *m*; ~ **paint** *n* COLOUR, CONST, P&R, PROD pintura de emulsión *f*; ~ **persistence** *n* CHEM TECH persistencia de la emulsión *f*; ~ **pile-up** *n* CINEMAT acumulación de emulsión *f*; ~ **polymerization** *n* P&R polimerización por emulsión *f*; ~ **position** *n* CINEMAT posición de la emulsión *f*; ~ **side** *n* CINEMAT, TV lado de la emulsión *m*; ~ **speed** *n* CINEMAT velocidad de la emulsión *f*; ~ **stripping** *n* PRINT emulsión despegable *f*; ~ **test** *n* CHEM TECH prueba de emulsión *f*

emulsion[3]: ~ **in** *phr* CINEMAT con la emulsión hacia adentro; ~ **out** *phr* CINEMAT con la emulsión hacia afuera

EMW *abbr* (*equivalent mud weight*) PETR TECH EMW (*densidad de lodo equivalente, peso de lodo equivalente*)

en: ~ **echelon folds** *n pl* GEOL pliegues en relevo *m pl*; ~ **space** *n* PRINT espacio de medio cuadratín *m*, semicuadratín *m*

enable[1]: ~ **pulse** *n* COMP&DP impulso de activación *m*, ELECTRON impulso autorizado *m*, pulso de habilitación *m*; ~ **signal** *n* ELECTRON señal autorizada *f*, señal de habilitación *f*

enable[2] *vt* COMP&DP activar, habilitar, ELECTRON autorizar, habilitar, PROD habilitar

enabled: ~ **gate** *n* ELECTRON puerta electrónica habilitada *f*

enabling *n* ELECTRON autorización *f*, habilitación *f*; ~ **signal** *n* COMP&DP señal de activación *f*

enamel[1]: **~-covered** *adj* COATINGS cubierto de esmalte
enamel[2] *n* C&G, COATINGS, COLOUR, CONST, P&R, PROD
esmalte *m*; **~ colors** *AmE*, **~ colours** *BrE n pl* C&G,
COLOUR colores de esmalte *m pl*; **~-firing** *n* C&G
horneado de esmalte *m*; **~ paint** *n* COATINGS, COLOUR
pintura al esmalte *f*, pintura vidriada *f*, pintura vítrea
f; **~ varnish** *n* COATINGS, COLOUR barniz al esmalte
m, barniz esmaltado *m*
enamel[3] *vt* COATINGS, COLOUR esmaltar; **~-bake** *vt*
COLOUR hornear al esmalte
enameled *AmE see* enamelled *BrE*
enameling *AmE see* enamelling *BrE*
enamelled[1] *adj BrE* COATINGS, COLOUR esmaltado,
vitrificado, HEAT, PROD esmaltado
enamelled[2]: **~ copper wire** *n BrE* COATINGS, CONST,
ELEC, ELEC ENG alambre de cobre esmaltado *m*;
~ iron *n BrE* METALL, PROD hierro esmaltado *m*;
~ paper *n BrE* COATINGS papel esmaltado *m*; **~ wire**
n BrE COATINGS, ELEC, ELEC ENG alambre esmaltado
m, hilo esmaltado *m*
enameller *n* COATINGS esmaltador *m*
enamelling *n BrE* COATINGS, COLOUR, HEAT, PROD
esmaltado *m*; **~ furnace** *n BrE* COATINGS horno de
esmaltado *m*; **~ kiln** *n BrE* COATINGS horno de
esmaltado *m*; **~ line** *n BrE* COATINGS línea de
esmaltado *f*; **~ sheet** *n BrE* COATINGS chapa de acero
para esmaltar *f*; **~ stove** *n BrE* COATINGS estufa de
esmaltado *f*
enanthal *n* CHEM enantal *m*
enanthic *adj* CHEM enántico
enanthin *n* CHEM enantina *f*
enanthol *n* CHEM enantol *m*
enanthylate *n* CHEM enantilato *m*
enanthylic *adj* CHEM enantílico
enantiomer *n* CHEM, CRYSTALL enantiomorfo *m*,
enantiómero *m*
enantiomorph *n* CHEM, CRYSTALL enantiomorfo *m*
enantiomorphic *adj* CHEM, CRYSTALL enantiomórfico
enantiomorphism *n* CHEM, CRYSTALL enantiomor-
fismo *m*
enantiomorphous *adj* CHEM, CRYSTALL enantiomórfico
enantiotropic *adj* CHEM, CRYSTALL enantiotrópico
enargite *n* MINERAL enargita *f*
encapsulated: **~ dye** *n* COLOUR colorante encapsulado
m, tinte encapsulado *m*; **~ source** *n* NUCL fuente
encapsulada *f*; **~ type** *n* COMP&DP tipo encapsulado
m
encapsulating: **~ glass** *n* C&G vidrio para encapsular
m
encapsulation *n* NUCL, P&R encapsulación *f*; **~ mould**
n MECH ENG molde encapsulador *m*
encase *vt* CONST empotrar, encajar
encased[1] *adj* CONST embutido, empotrado, encajado,
oculto
encased[2]: **~ beam** *n* CONST viga oculta *f*
encasing *n* HYDRAUL recubrimiento *m*
encipher *vt* ELECTRON, TELECOM cifrar
encipherment *n* ELECTRON, TELECOM cifrado *m*
enclave *n* PETROL enclave *m*
enclosed[1] *adj* MECH ENG blindado, encartado, encerrado, enclaustrado, PACK se adjunta
enclosed[2]: **~ casing** *n* HYDRAUL envuelta *f*, revestimiento *m*; **~ fuse** *n* ELEC, ELEC ENG fusible dentro *m*,
fusible encerrado *m*, MECH ENG fusible encerrado *m*;
~ gears *n pl* MECH ENG engranajes enclaustrados *m*

pl; **~ motor** *n* ELEC motor cerrado *m*, ELEC ENG
motor blindado *m*; **~ sea** *n* OCEAN mar encerrado *m*
enclosing: **~ wall** *n* CONST muro de cerramiento *m*
enclosure *n* ACOUST caja *f*, recinto *m*, CONST cerca *f*,
cerramiento *m*, valla *f*, *of palisades* empalizada *f*,
NUCL, PHYS recinto *m*, PROD armario *m*
encode *vt* COMP&DP, ELECTRON, TELECOM, TV codificar
encoded: **~ information type** *n* (*EIT*) TELECOM tipo
de información codificada *m*; **~ pulses** *n pl* TV pulsos
codificados *m pl*; **~ signal** *n* ELECTRON señal codificada *f*
encoder *n* COMP&DP, ELECTRON, PROD, TELECOM, TV
cifrador *m*, codificador *m*; **~ module** *n* PROD módulo
codificador *m*; **~ shaft** *n* PROD eje codificador *m*
encoding *n* AIR TRANSP, COMP&DP, ELECTRON, PACK,
SPACE, TELECOM cifrado *m*, codificación *f*;
~ altimeter *n* AIR TRANSP altímetro cifrado *m*,
altímetro codificado *m*; **~ potentiometer** *n* SPACE
potenciómetro cifrado *m*
encompass *vt* MECH ENG encerrar, rodear
encounter: **~ rate** *n* MAR POLL tasa de hallazgo *f*
encrinite *n* GEOL encrinita *f*
encrinitic: **~ limestone** *n* GEOL caliza encrinítica *f*
encrypt *vt* COMP&DP, ELECTRON, TELECOM, TV cifrar,
codificar, encriptar
encrypted: **~ speech** *n* TELECOM palabra criptogra-
fiada *f*
encryption *n* COMP&DP, ELECTRON, TELECOM, TV
cifrado *m*, codificación *f*, criptografía *f*, encriptación
f; **~ chip** *n* ELECTRON chip codificador *m*
end[1]: **~-to-end** *adj* COMP&DP de extremo a extremo
end[2]: **~ of address** *n* COMP&DP fin de dirección *m*, fin
direccional *m*; **~ address field** *n* PROD zona de
dirección final *f*; **~-and-end lease** *n* TEXTIL cruz
hilo a hilo *f*; **~-around carry** *n* COMP&DP acarreo
circular *m*, arrastre circular *m*; **~-around shift** *n*
COMP&DP desplazamiento lógico *m*; **~ of block** *n*
(*EOB*) COMP&DP fin de bloque *m* (*EOB*); **~ box** *n*
WATER *sluices* caja de cola *f*; **~ bracket** *n* MINE
abrazadera de extremo *f*, escuadra *f*; **~-bunker
refrigerated truck** *n* REFRIG vagón refrigerante con
depósito de hielo en los testeros *m*; **~ cap** *n* ELEC ENG
wire capacete *m*, cápsula extrema *f*; **~ cleat** *n* COAL
plano secundario de crucero *m*; **~ of connecting-rod**
n MECH ENG extremo de biela *m*, extremo de varilla de
conexión *m*; **~ contraction** *n* HYDROL contracción
lateral *f*; **~ credits** *n pl* CINEMAT, TV títulos finales *m*
pl; **~-cutting nippers** *n pl* PROD tenazas de corte de
extremos *f pl*; **~ of data** *n* (*EOD*) COMP&DP fin de
datos *m* (*EOD*); **~ deckle** *n* PAPER carro final *m*;
~ distortion *n* ELECTRON distorsión final *f*; **~ door** *n*
C&G puerta trasera *f*; **~ dump** *n* CONST descarga por
el extremo *f*, volquete al extremo *m*; **~ fence** *n* PROD
límite final *m*; **~ of file** *n* (*EOF*) COMP&DP fin de
archivo *m* (*EOF*), fin de fichero *m* (*EOF*); **~-fire
aerial** *n BrE* (*cf* end-fire antenna *AmE*) SPACE antena
de fase progresiva *f*, TELECOM antena de radiación
longitudinal *f*; **~-fire antenna** *n AmE* (*cf* end-fire
aerial *BrE*) SPACE antena de fase progresiva *f*, TELE-
COM antena de radiación longitudinal *f*, **~ fire array
aerial** *n BrE* (*cf* end fire array antenna *AmE*) TELE-
COM antena de array con radiación máxima en la
dirección del eje *f*; **~ fire array antenna** *n AmE* (*cf*
end fire array aerial *BrE*) TELECOM antena de array
con radiación máxima en la dirección del eje *f*; **~ of
flight** *n* AIR TRANSP, SPACE fin del vuelo *m*; **~-frame**

member n PACK miembro del extremo de la montura m; ~ **group** n CHEM grupo terminal m; ~ **of job** n (EOJ) COMP&DP fin de tarea m (EOJ), fin de trabajo m (EOJ); ~ **leader** n CINEMAT, TV guía final f; **--leaf paper** n PAPER papel de guardas m; ~ **of lehr** n C&G final del templador m; ~ **mark** n COMP&DP marca final f; ~ **measure** n METR medida final f; ~ **of medium** n (EM) COMP&DP fin del medio m (EM), fin del soporte m (EM); ~ **member** n GEOL miembro final m; ~ **of message** n (EOM) COMP&DP, TELECOM fin de mensaje m (EOM); ~ **mill** n MECH ENG fresa universal de espiga f, fresa universal frontal f, fresa universal radial f; ~ **mill with indexable inserts** n MECH ENG fresa radial con insertos graduables f, fresa universal con adaptador graduable f; ~ **nippers** n pl MECH ENG tenazas planas f pl; **--of-communication signal** n TELECOM señal de fin de comunicación f; **--of-life cladding rupture** n NUCL rotura de la vaina a finales de vida f; ~ **panel** n MECH ENG, PACK panel del extremo m, panel extremo m, placa terminal f; ~ **piece** n SPACE pieza de cierre f; ~ **plate** n PROD boiler placa tubular f; ~ **play** n MECH, MECH ENG holgura longitudinal f, juego axial m, juego longitudinal m; ~ **point** n CHEM of a reaction punto de equivalencia m; ~ **pointer** n PROD indicador de finalización m, indicador de punta m; ~ **of query** n (ENQ) COMP&DP fin de consulta m (ENQ); ~ **of reel** n COMP&DP fin del carrete m; ~ **rib** n AIR TRANSP costilla final f; ~ **rung** n PROD peldaño extremo m; ~ **of runway approach** n AIR TRANSP aproximación al límite de la pista f; ~ **screen** n ELECTRON pantalla final f; ~ **section** n NUCL sección final f, tobera f; ~ **sheet** n PRINT hoja final f; ~ **slate** n CINEMAT claqueta final f; **--statement address** n PROD dirección de fin de instrucción f; ~ **stop** n MECH ENG tope final m; ~ **of stroke** n MECH ENG final de carrera m; ~ **suction centrifugal pump** n MECH ENG bomba centrífuga de aspiración final f, bomba centrífuga de succión final f; ~ **system** n TELECOM sistema de end m, sistema de fin m; ~ **of tape marker** n (EOT marker) COMP&DP marcador de fin de cinta m; ~ **of text** n (ETX) COMP&DP fin de texto m (FDT); ~ **thrust bearing** n MECH ENG cojinete final de empuje m; **--to-end control** n COMP&DP control de extremo a extremo m; **--to-end digital connectivity** n TELECOM conectividad digital de extremo a extremo f; **--to-end encipherment** n TELECOM cifrado de extremo a extremo m; **--to-end information indicator** n TELECOM indicador de datos de extremo a extremo m; **--to-end method indicator** n TELECOM indicador de método de extremo a extremo m; **--to-end protocol** n COMP&DP protocolo de extremo a extremo m, protocolo entre extremos m; ~ **of transaction** n (EOT) TELECOM fin de movimiento m (EOT); ~ **of transmission** m (EOT) COMP&DP, TELECOM fin de transmisión m (EOT); ~ **of transmission block** n (ETB) COMP&DP fin del bloque de transmisión m (FBT); ~ **of travel** n MECH ENG of tool, piston etc final de carrera m, final de pasada m; ~ **use** n MECH ENG, PROD, QUALITY, SAFE uso final m, TEXTIL artículo final m, uso final m; ~ **user** n COMP&DP, CONST, ELEC ENG, TELECOM, TRANSP, WATER usuario final m; **--wall bracket** n MINE apoyo empotrado de la galería m, brazo de pared de la galería m, consola mural de la galería f

endless: ~ **belt** n VEH correa sin fin f; ~ **cable** n TRANSP, VEH cable sinfín m; ~ **chain** n VEH cadena sin fin f; ~ **hexagonal belt** n MECH ENG correa hexagonal sin fin f; ~ **magnetic-loop cartridge** n ACOUST cartucho de bucle magnético sin fin m; ~ **pin-chain** n TEXTIL cadena de grapas sin fin f; ~ **printing** n PRINT impresión continua f; ~ **screw** n MECH ENG tornillo sin fin m; ~ **variable speed of V-belt** n MECH ENG velocidad variable continua de correa trapezoidal f; ~ **V-belt** n MECH ENG correa trapezoidal sin fin f; ~ **wide V-belt** n MECH ENG correa trapezoidal ancha sin fin f

endlink n CHEM of polymer enlace terminal m
endoatmospheric adj SPACE endoatmosférico
endoenzyme n CHEM endoenzima f
endogenetic adj PETROL endogenético
endogenic adj PETROL endógeno
endolymph n ACOUST endolinfa f
endomorph n MINERAL endomorfo m
endoscope n INSTR, NUCL, PHYS, SPACE endoscopio m
endoscopy n INSTR, NUCL, PHYS, SPACE endoscopia f
endosperm n AGRIC, FOOD endosperma f
endothermic[1] adj C&G, CHEM, PETR TECH, SPACE endotérmico
endothermic[2]: ~ **process** n PETR TECH proceso endotérmico m; ~ **reaction** n FUELLESS solar power, GAS reacción endotérmica f
endurance n AIR TRANSP autonomía f, resistencia f, PROD resistencia a la fatiga f, SPACE autonomía f, resistencia a la fatiga f; ~ **limit** n CRYSTALL, METALL límite de fatiga m; ~ **ratio** n NUCL relación del límite de fatiga a la resistencia de rotura por tracción f; ~ **tensile strength** n MECH ENG resistencia a la tensión f, resistencia a las fuerzas de tensión f; ~ **test** n MECH ENG, METR prueba de resistencia f, PROD prueba de duración f, prueba de resistencia a esfuerzos alternos cíclicos f, QUALITY ensayo de aguante m, SPACE prueba de resistencia f
energization n ELEC energización f, ELEC ENG cebado magnético m, energización f, PROD, RAD PHYS energización f
energize vt ELEC, ELEC ENG, PROD activar, dar energía, excitar
energized[1] adj ELEC, ELEC ENG, PROD activado, excitado
energized[2]: ~ **relay** n PROD relé excitado m
energizing: ~ **circuit** n ELEC ENG circuito activador m; ~ **current** n ELEC ENG corriente de excitación f
energy[1]: **--intensive** adj THERMO de gran consumo de energía
energy[2] n GEN energía f, potencia f; ~ **absorption** n TELECOM absorción de carga f; **--availability factor** n ELEC ENG factor de disponibilidad de energía m; ~ **balance** n THERMO, WATER balance energético m; ~ **balance in turbulence** n FLUID equilibrio de energía en turbulencia m; ~ **balance of the soil** n AGRIC, HYDROL equilibrio energético del suelo m; **--band gap** n NUCL salto de la banda de energía m; ~ **budget** n POLL balance de energía m, balance energético m, presupuesto de energía m; ~ **cascade** n FLUID cascada de energía f; ~ **conservation** n THERMO conservación de energía f; ~ **consumption** n PHYS, THERMO consumo de energía m; ~ **content** n THERMO contenido de energía m; ~ **conversion** n ELEC ENG, TELECOM, THERMO conversión de energía f; **--conversion factor** n RAD PHYS factor energético de conversión m; ~ **converter** n ELEC ENG, TELECOM,

THERMO conversor de energía *m*; ~ **crisis** *n* THERMO crisis energética *f*; ~ **degradation** *n* NUCL degradación energética *f*; ~ **demand** *n* THERMO demanda de energía *f*; ~ **densities of radiation** *n pl* RAD PHYS densidades energéticas de la radiación *f pl*; ~ **density** *n* SPACE densidad de energía *f*; ~ **dispersal** *n* SPACE dispersión de energía *f*; ~ **dispersive analysis by X-rays** *n* (*EDAX*) CHEM análisis dispersivo de energía por rayos X *m*; ~ **and dissipation spectra in turbulence** *n pl* FLUID espectros de energía y disipación en turbulencia *m pl*; ~ **dissipator** *n* HYDROL disipador de energía *m*; ~ **efficiency** *n* THERMO rendimiento energético *m*; ~ **equilibrium** *n* GAS equilibrio energético *m*; ~**exchange reaction** *n* NUCL reacción de intercambio energético *f*; ~ **exitance** *n* OPT exitación energética *f*; ~ **extraction** *n* FUELLESS rendimiento de energía *m*; ~**flow chart** *n* THERMO diagrama de circulación de energía *m*, diagrama de flujo energético *m*; ~ **fluence** *n* PHYS fluencia energética *f*; ~**fluence rate** *n* PHYS tasa de fluencia energética *f*; ~ **flux** *n* OPT, RAD PHYS, TELECOM, THERMO flujo energético *m*; ~ **form** *n* GAS forma de energía *f*; ~ **gap** *n* PHYS *solar power* separación energética *f*; ~ **irradiance** *n* OPT irradiancia energética *f*; ~ **level** *n* GEOPHYS, PART PHYS, PHYS, RAD PHYS nivel de energía *m*, nivel energético *m*; ~ **loss** *n* ELEC, GAS, PHYS pérdida de energía *f*, pérdida energética *f*; ~ **meter** *n* ELEC ENG ergómetro *m*, medidor de energía *m*; ~**pattern factor** *n* FUELLESS factor de modelo de energía *m*; ~ **range** *n* RAD PHYS gama de energía *f*, intervalo de energía *m*, rango de energía *m*; ~ **recovery** *n* FUELLESS, RECYCL, THERMO recuperación de energía *f*; ~**recovery factor** *n* FUELLESS, RECYCL, THERMO factor de recuperación de energía *m*; ~ **recuperation** *n* FUELLESS, RECYCL, THERMO recuperación de energía *f*; ~ **regeneration** *n* THERMO regeneración de energía *f*; ~ **saving** *n* PROD, THERMO ahorro de energía *m*; ~**selecting electron microscope** *n* INSTR microscopio electrónico selector de energía *m*; ~ **source** *n* SPACE fuente de energía *f*; ~ **spectrum** *n* SPACE espectro de energía *m*; ~ **storage** *n* ELEC almacenamiento de energía *m*, ELEC ENG acumulación de energía *f*, almacenamiento de energía *m*, NUCL almacenamiento de energía *m*, SPACE, THERMO acumulación de energía *f*, almacenamiento de energía *m*; ~**storage capacitor** *n* ELEC ENG, SPACE, THERMO condensador de almacenaje de energía *m*; ~**storage device** *n* ELEC ENG, SPACE, THERMO dispositivo para almacenamiento de energía *m*; ~ **supply** *n* ELEC, ELEC ENG, FUELLESS, MECH ENG, NUCL, SPACE, THERMO abastecimiento de energía *m*, suministro de energía *m*; ~ **technology** *n* POLL tecnología energética *f*; ~ **transfer** *n* GEOPHYS traspaso de energía *m*, PHYS, THERMO transferencia de energía *f*; ~**transfer coefficient** *n* PHYS coeficiente de transferencia de energía *m*; ~ **transference by vibration** *n* WAVE PHYS transferencia de energía por vibraciones *f*; ~ **transformation** *n* ELEC, ELEC ENG, THERMO conversión de energía *f*, transformación de energía *f*; ~ **transmission** *n* THERMO transmisión de energía *f*; ~ **valley** *n* NUCL valle energético *m*; ~ **waste** *n* GAS derroche de energía *m*

ENG *abbr* (*electronic news gathering*) TV recolección electrónica de noticias *f*

engage[1] *vt* MECH, MECH ENG acoplar, embragar, endentar, enganchar, engranar

engage[2] *vi* MECH, MECH ENG embragar, engranar

engagement *n* MECH, MECH ENG engranaje *m*, *of clutch* embrague *m*

engaging *n* MECH engranaje *m*, *of clutch* embrague *m*, MECH ENG embragado *m*, engranado *m*

engine[1]: ~**driven** *adj* PROD accionado por máquina

engine[2] *n* AIR TRANSP, AUTO, MECH, MECH ENG, VEH motor *m*, WATER TRANSP motor *m*, máquina *f*; ~ **air-intake** *n* AIR TRANSP entrada de aire del motor *f*, toma de aire del motor *f*; ~ **air-intake extension** *n* AIR TRANSP extensión de la entrada de aire del motor *f*, extensión de la toma de aire del motor *f*; ~ **angle command** *n* SPACE comando del ángulo del motor *m*; ~ **anti-icing gate valve** *n* AIR TRANSP válvula de corredera antihielo del motor *f*; ~ **bearing** *n* MECH ENG cojinete de motor *m*, WATER TRANSP cojinete *m*, rodamiento *m*; ~ **block** *n* AUTO, MECH, MECH ENG, VEH bloque del motor *m*; ~ **body** *n* SPACE cuerpo de motor *m*; ~ **brake** *n* AUTO, VEH freno del motor *m*; ~ **breakdown** *n* AUTO fallo del motor *m*, VEH avería del motor *f*, fallo del motor *m*, WATER TRANSP avería del motor *f*; ~ **builder** *n* MECH ENG constructor de motores *m*, fabricante de motores *mf*, fabricante de máquinas *mf*; ~ **bypass air** *n* AIR TRANSP aire de desvío del motor *m*, aire de derivación del motor *m*; ~ **capacity** *n* VEH rendimiento del motor *m*; ~ **coasting-down time** *n* AIR TRANSP tiempo de funcionamiento por inercia del motor *m*; ~ **combustion-chamber** *n* MECH ENG cámara de combustión del motor *f*; ~ **compartment** *n* VEH compartimiento del motor *m*; ~**cooling system** *n* WATER TRANSP sistema de refrigeración de las máquinas *m*; ~ **cradle** *n* AIR TRANSP, AUTO, VEH bancada del motor *f*; ~ **crank** *n* MECH ENG manubrio del motor *m*; ~ **de-icing** *n* AIR TRANSP deshielo del motor *m*; ~**driven pump** *n* AIR TRANSP bomba accionada por motor *f*; ~**emission control** *n* MECH ENG control de emisiones del motor *m*; ~ **exhaust system** *n* MECH ENG, WATER TRANSP sistema de escape de la máquina *m*, sistema de escape del motor *m*; ~ **failure** *n* VEH avería del motor *f*, WATER TRANSP avería de la máquina *f*, avería del motor *f*; ~ **fan** *n* AUTO ventilador del motor *m*; ~ **fitting** *n* MECH ENG accesorio del motor *m*; ~ **flameout** *n* AIR TRANSP, SPACE apagado del motor *m*, apague el motor *m*, extinción del motor *f*, VEH extinción del motor *f*; ~ **flywheel** *n* MECH ENG volante del motor *m*; ~ **frame** *n* MECH ENG batiente de la máquina *m*, batiente del motor *m*, WATER TRANSP polín de la máquina principal *m*; ~ **fuel supply** *n* MECH ENG, WATER TRANSP abastecimiento de combustible para la máquina *m*; ~ **fuel system** *n* MECH ENG sistema de combustible del motor *m*; ~ **hoist** *n* AIR TRANSP elevador del motor *m*; ~**hours indicator** *n* MECH ENG, WATER TRANSP registrador de horas de funcionamiento de la máquina *m*, registrador de horas de funcionamiento del motor *m*; ~ **house** *n* PROD casa de máquinas *f*; ~ **instruments** *n pl* AIR TRANSP instrumentos del motor *m pl*; ~**jet wash** *n* AIR TRANSP chorro del motor a reacción *m*, chorro del reactor *m*; ~ **maintenance** *n* WATER TRANSP mantenimiento de las máquinas *m*; ~ **maker** *n* MECH ENG, PROD *person* constructor de máquinas *m*; ~ **manufacturer** *n* MECH ENG, SPACE fabricante de motor *m*; ~ **mounting** *n* AUTO soporte del motor *m*; ~ **mountings** *n* SPACE bancada de motores *f*; ~ **muffler** *n* AmE (*cf engine silencer BrE*) AUTO, MECH, MECH ENG silenciador del escape del motor *m*; ~ **nacelle** *n* AIR TRANSP compartimiento del motor *m*, cápsula del motor *f*, góndola del motor *f*; ~**nacelle stub** *n* AIR TRANSP muñón de la góndola del motor *m*; ~**nozzle cluster** *n* AIR TRANSP agrupación de la tobera del motor *f*; ~ **oil** *n* AUTO, MECH, MECH ENG, VEH aceite del motor *m*; ~ **operation** *n* WATER TRANSP funcionamiento de la máquina *m*; ~ **overhaul** *n* WATER TRANSP recorrida de la máquina *f*, recorrida del motor *f*, revisión de la máquina *f*, revisión del motor *f*; ~ **pedestal** *n* MECH soporte de la máquina *m*; ~ **pick-up** *n* VEH capacidad de aceleración *f*; ~ **pit** *n* PROD foso *m*; ~ **pod** *n* AIR TRANSP compartimiento del motor *m*, cápsula del motor *f*, góndola del motor *f*; ~**pressure ratio** *n* AIR TRANSP proporción de presión del motor *f*; ~ **rating** *n* AIR TRANSP categoría del motor *f*; ~**relight push-button** *n* AIR TRANSP botón de reencendido del motor *m*; ~ **room** *n* PROD sala de máquinas *f*, WATER TRANSP compartimiento de máquinas *m*, espacio de máquinas *m*, cámara de máquinas *f*; ~**room log** *n* WATER TRANSP cuaderno de máquinas *m*, cuaderno diario de máquinas *m*; ~**room telegraph** *n* WATER TRANSP telégrafo de máquinas *m*; ~ **run-up** *n* AIR TRANSP calentamiento del motor *m*; ~ **seating** *n* WATER TRANSP asiento de máquinas *m*, polín *m*; ~**shaft bearing** *n* AIR TRANSP cojinete del eje del motor *m*; ~ **shed** *n* BrE (*cf locomotive depot AmE*) RAIL depósito de locomotoras *m*, depósito de máquinas *m*; ~ **shop** *n* AUTO taller de motores *m*; ~ **shutdown in flight** *n* AIR TRANSP apagado del motor en vuelo *m*, cierre del motor en vuelo *m*; ~ **shut-off stop** *n* AIR TRANSP tope del cierre del motor *m*; ~ **silencer** *n* BrE (*cf engine muffler AmE*) AUTO, MECH, MECH ENG silenciador del escape del motor *m*; ~ **speed** *n* AIR TRANSP, VEH velocidad del motor *f*; ~ **stand** *n* AIR TRANSP banco del motor *m*; ~ **starter** *n* AIR TRANSP, AUTO, VEH interruptor de arranque del motor *m*; ~**starting control box** *n* AIR TRANSP caja de control de arranque del motor *f*, caja de control de encendido del motor *f*; ~ **support** *n* AIR TRANSP, AUTO, VEH bancada del motor *f*, soporte del motor *m*; ~ **support arch** *n* AIR TRANSP, AUTO, VEH arco de soporte del motor *m*; ~ **support lug** *n* AUTO, VEH taco de suspensión del motor *m*; ~ **support plug** *n* AUTO, VEH tapón del cárter *m*; ~ **test stand** *n* AIR TRANSP banco de pruebas del motor *m*, SPACE banco de pruebas del motor *m*, plataforma de pruebas del motor *f*; ~ **torque** *n* AIR TRANSP, AUTO fuerza de par del motor *f*, par del motor *m*, VEH fuerza de par del motor *f*; ~ **trolley** *n* AIR TRANSP carretilla del motor *f*; ~ **valve** *n* MECH ENG válvula del motor *f*; ~ **ventilation system** *n* WATER TRANSP sistema de ventilación de la máquina *m*, sistema de ventilación del motor *m*; ~ **vibration** *n* AIR TRANSP vibración del motor *f*; ~ **winding-house** *n* MINE grúa de extracción *f*; ~ **windmilling** *n* AIR TRANSP *helicopter* autorrotación de la hélice del motor *f*

engineer *n* MECH ingeniero *m*, RAIL ingeniero *m*, maquinista *m*, WATER TRANSP maquinista naval *m*; ~**'s cab** *n* RAIL, VEH cabina del maquinista *f*; ~ **officer** *n* WATER TRANSP oficial de máquinas *m*; ~**'s surface plate** *n* PROD mármol de ajustador *m*

engineered: ~ **barrier** *n* NUCL barrera tecnológica *f*

engineering: ~ **calculations record** *n* MECH ENG registro de cálculos de ingeniería *m*; ~ **change** *n* PROD modificación de la concepción *f*; ~ **data** *n* PROD datos técnicos *m pl*; ~ **department** *n* MECH, MECH ENG departamento de ingeniería *m*, PROD oficina técnica *f*; ~ **and design department** *n* MECH ENG departamento de diseño e ingeniería *m*; ~ **drawing** *n* MECH ENG dibujo técnico *m*, plano de construcción mecánica *m*, WATER TRANSP plano de construcción *m*; ~ **drawing block** *n* MECH ENG cabezal de estirado *m*; ~ **facilities** *n pl* MECH instalaciones técnicas *f pl*; ~ **issue level** *n* PROD nivel de distribución de datos técnicos *m*; ~ **and methods** *n pl* PROD concepción tecnológica y métodos de fabricación *f*; ~ **model** *n* SPACE modelo de ingeniería *m*; ~ **office** *n* MECH, MECH ENG departamento técnico *m*; ~ **order wire** *n* (*EOW*) TELECOM línea de órdenes de ingeniería *f*; ~ **standards** *n pl* MECH ENG estándares de ingeniería *m pl*; ~ **unit** *n* PROD unidad técnica *f*; ~ **work-station** *n* COMP&DP puesto de trabajo de ingeniería *m*

engineer: ~**s' stores** *n pl* PROD fornituras para mecánicos *f pl*

engines: **all** ~ **operating** *phr* AIR TRANSP todos los motores en funcionamiento, todos los motores en operación

English: ~ **china** *n* C&G porcelana inglesa *f*; ~ **finish paper** *n* PAPER papel fuertemente alisado *m*; ~**type axis mounting** *n* INSTR montaje axial de tipo inglés *m*

engrave *vt* C&G, ELECTRON, PRINT grabar

engraved: ~ **blanket** *n* PRINT mantilla con depresiones *f*

engraver *n* C&G, PRINT grabador *m*

engraving *n* ACOUST, C&G, ELECTRON, PRINT grabado *m*; ~ **depth** *n* PRINT profundidad de grabado *f*; ~ **head** *n* PRINT cabeza grabadora *f*; ~ **in relief** *n* C&G grabado en relieve *m*; ~ **lathe** *n* C&G torno para grabar *m*; ~ **rubber** *n* PRINT caucho para grabar *m*

enhance *vt* FOOD mejorar, TEXTIL realzar

enhanced: ~ **oil recovery** *n* (*Eof*) PETR TECH recuperación mejorada de petróleo *f*; ~ **service** *n* TELECOM servicio reforzado *m*

enhancement *n* TELECOM refuerzo *m*; ~ **mode** *n* ELECTRON modo de activación *m*; ~ **mode FET** *n* ELECTRON transistor de efecto campo de empobrecimiento *m*; ~ **mode field-effect transistor** *n* ELECTRON transistor de efecto campo de empobrecimiento *m*

enharmonic: ~ **note** *n* ACOUST nota enarmónica *f*

enhydrite *n* MINERAL enhidrita *f*

enlarge *vt* CINEMAT ampliar, INSTR ensanchar, PHOTO, PRINT ampliar

enlarged: ~ **image** *n* CINEMAT, PHOTO, PHYS, PRINT imagen ampliada *f*

enlargement *n* CINEMAT ampliación *f*, INSTR ampliación *f*, dilatación *f*, expansión *f*, PHOTO, PRINT ampliación *f*; ~ **print** *n* CINEMAT, PHOTO copia ampliada *f*

enlarger *n* CINEMAT, INSTR, PHOTO, PRINT ampliadora *f*; ~ **baseboard** *n* PHOTO tablero para ampliaciones *m*; ~ **camera** *n* CINEMAT ampliadora *f*, INSTR, PHOTO, PRINT ampliadora *f*, cámara ampliadora *f*; ~ **column** *n* PHOTO, PRINT columna para ampliaciones *f*; ~ **support** *n* PHOTO, PRINT respaldo para ampliaciones *m*

enlarging *n* CINEMAT ampliación *f*, INSTR ampliación *f*, ensanchamiento *m*, PHOTO, PRINT ampliación *f*;

~ **camera** *n* CINEMAT, INSTR ampliadora *f*, PHOTO, PRINT ampliadora *f*, ampliadora fotográfica *f*, cámara ampliadora *f*; **~-hole** *n* MINE orificio de ensanchamiento *m*; **~-meter** *n* PHOTO, PRINT exposímetro para ampliaciones *m*; **~-paper** *n* PHOTO, PRINT papel para ampliaciones *m*

enol *n* CHEM enol *m*

enolase *n* CHEM enolasa *f*

enolic *adj* CHEM enólico

enolization *n* CHEM enolización *f*

ENQ *abbr* (*end of query*) COMP&DP ENQ (*fin de consulta*)

enquiries: ~ **service** *n* AmE (*cf directory enquiries BrE*) ELECTRON, TELECOM información *f*, servicio de información *m*

enquiry *n* COMP&DP consulta *f*

enrich *vt* COAL lavar, FOOD, NUCL, RAD PHYS enriquecer

enriched: ~ **fuel** *n* NUCL combustible enriquecido *m*; ~ **material** *n* RAD PHYS material enriquecido *m*; ~ **nuclear fuel** *n* NUCL combustible nuclear enriquecido *m*; ~ **ration** *n* AGRIC ración reforzada *f*; ~ **reactor** *n* NUCL reactor enriquecido *m*; ~ **uranium** *n* NUCL, PHYS uranio enriquecido *m*

enrichment *n* COAL lavado *m*, FOOD enriquecimiento *m*, mejora *f*, NUCL, PHYS enriquecimiento *m*; ~ **tails** *n* NUCL colas de enriquecimiento *f pl*

ensemble: ~ **activity** *n* TELECOM actividad colectiva *f*

enstatite *n* MINERAL enstatita *f*

ensure: ~ **the health, safety and welfare of** *phr* SAFE asegurar la salud, la seguridad y el bienestar de

entablature *n* PROD *of power hammer, forging press etc* entablamiento *m*

entangle *vt* SAFE, TEXTIL enredar

entangled *adj* SAFE, TEXTIL enredado

entanglement *n* SAFE embrollo *m*, enredo *m*

enter *vt* COMP&DP introducir, registrar, ELECTRON introducir, MECH ENG morder, WATER TRANSP asentar

enteramine *n* CHEM enteramina *f*

entering: ~ **air temperature** *n* REFRIG temperatura del aire de entrada *f*; ~ **file** *n* PROD lima cuadrada puntiaguda *f*, lima de lengua de pájaro *f*; ~ **tap** *n* PROD macho cónico *m*, macho de aterrajado preliminar *m*; ~ **traffic** *n* TRANSP tráfico de entrada *m*

enthalpy *n* GEN entalpia *f*; ~ **of formation** *n* THERMO calor latente de formación *m*, entalpia de formación *f*; ~ **of vaporization** *n* CHEM TECH, THERMO calor latente de vaporización *m*, entalpia de vaporización *f*

entrainment *n* FLUID arrastre *m*; ~ **current** *n* OCEAN corriente de arrastre *f*

entrance *n* HYDRAUL admisión *f*; ~ **pupil** *n* PHYS pupila de entrada *f*

entrap *vt* MAR POLL *tools* encerrar

entrapped: ~ **air** *n* P&R burbuja de aire *f*, PACK aire ocluido *m*; ~ **gas** *n* GAS gas atrapado *m*

entropic: ~ **flux** *n* THERMO flujo entrópico *m*

entropy *n* GEN entropía *f*; ~ **of fusion** *n* THERMO entropía de fusión *f*; ~ **of vaporization** *n* THERMO entropía de vaporización *f*

entry *n* COAL boca *f*, galería de transporte *f*, galería principal *f*, COMP&DP entrada *f*, ingreso *m*, introducción *f*, ELECTRON ingreso *m*; ~ **in stock** *n* PROD entrada de existencias *f*; ~ **instruction** *n* COMP&DP instrucción de entrada *f*; ~ **into orbit** *n* SPACE entrada en órbita *f*; ~ **pillar** *n* COAL pilar de carbón *m*, pilar de galería *m*; ~ **point** *n* COMP&DP punto de entrada *m*, punto de introducción *m*; ~ **queue** *n* COMP&DP cola

de entrada *f*, fila de entrada *f*; ~ **stump** *n* COAL pilar de carbón *m*, pilar de galería *m*; ~ **timbering** *n* COAL entibación de la galería principal *f*

enumeration *n* MATH enumeración *f*; ~ **type** *n* COMP&DP tipo de enumeración *m*

envelope *n* ELEC ENG envolvente *m*, ELECTRON funda *f*, TELECOM, TV envoltura *f*; ~ **curve** *n* MECH curva envolvente *f*; ~ **delay** *n* SPACE retardo de propagación de grupo *m*, retardo envolvente *m*; ~ **delay distortion** *n* SPACE distorsión de retardo de la envolvente *f*; ~ **paper** *n* PAPER papel para sobres postales *m*; ~ **switch** *n* TELECOM conmutador de grupo *m*; ~ **velocity** *n* TELECOM velocidad de grupo *f*

enveloping: ~ **machine** *n* PACK máquina de envolver *f*; **~-tooth wheel** *n* MECH ENG *worm-gearing* engranaje de dientes helicoidales *m*

envelopment *n* ELEC ENG envolvente *m*, ELECTRON funda *f*, PACK funda *f*, sobre *m*

environment[1]: **~-friendly** *adj* DETERG, PACK, POLL, PROD, QUALITY medioambientalmente inocuo

environment[2] *n* GEN ambiente *m*; ~ **cooling** *n* REFRIG enfriamiento de ambientes *m*; ~ **division** *n* COMP&DP división de ambiente *f*; **~-survey satellite** *n* SPACE satélite para exploración del ambiente *m*

environmental[1] *adj* GEN ambiental, del medio ambiente

environmental[2]: **~-and-safety engineering** *n* SAFE ingeniería de seguridad y medio ambiente *f*; ~ **cleanliness** *n* SAFE limpieza ambiental *f*; ~ **cleanliness in enclosed spaces** *n* SAFE limpieza ambiental en espacios cerrados *f*; ~ **compatibility** *n* POLL compatibilidad ambiental *f*; ~ **conditions** *n pl* METR, PROD condiciones ambientales *f pl*; **~-control system** *n* SPACE sistema para control de las condiciones ambientales *m*; ~ **engineering** *n* AGRIC ingeniería ambiental *f*; ~ **hazard** *n* QUALITY peligro del ambiente *m*; ~ **health** *n* AGRIC, SAFE higiene ambiental *f*; ~ **impact** *n* MAR POLL, NUCL, POLL impacto ambiental *m*, impacto ecológico *m*; **~-impact assessment** *n* NUCL, POLL evaluación del impacto medioambiental *f*; **~-impact statement** *n* NUCL, POLL declaración de impacto ambiental *f*; ~ **law** *n* POLL legislación ambiental *f*, leyes sobre el medio ambiente *f pl*; ~ **noise** *n* ACOUST, SAFE ruido ambiental *m*; ~ **noise pollution** *n* ACOUST, POLL contaminación ambiental por ruido *f*; ~ **planning** *n* POLL planeación ambiental *f* (*AmL*), planificación ambiental *f* (*Esp*); ~ **protection** *n* POLL, PROD protección ambiental *f*; ~ **protection agency** *n* (*EPA*) POLL Agencia para la Protección del Medio Ambiente *f*; ~ **radioactivity** *n* RAD PHYS radiactividad ambiental *f*, radiactividad de fondo *f*; ~ **risk** *n* QUALITY riesgo del ambiente *m*; ~ **stress** *n* SPACE ensayo de adaptación ambiental *m*, fatiga ambiental *f*; ~ **test** *n* SPACE ensayo ambiental *m*; ~ **test chamber** *n* SPACE cámara de ensayo en condiciones ambientales *f*, cámara de simulación espacial *f*; ~ **testing** *n* MECH ensayo en condiciones ambientales controladas *m*, ensayos de resistencia al ambiente *m pl*, QUALITY prueba del ambiente *f*; **~-testing procedure** *n* SAFE técnica de ensayo ambiental *f*; ~ **torque** *n* SPACE momento torsional en condiciones ambientales *m*

enzyme *n* CHEM, DETERG, FOOD, RECYCL enzima *f*

E-O *abbr* (*electrical-optical*) ELEC, OPT, PROD, TELECOM electroóptico[1] *m*, eléctrico-óptico *m*

EOB *abbr* (*end of block*) COMP&DP EOB (*fin de bloque*)

EOC *abbr* (*embedded operations channel*) TELECOM canal operativo embebido *m*

Eocene *adj* GEOL Eoceno

EOD *abbr* (*end of data*) COMP&DP EOD (*fin de datos*)

EOF *abbr* (*end of file*) COMP&DP EOF (*fin de archivo, fin de fichero*)

Eof *n* (*enhanced oil recovery*) PETR TECH recuperación mejorada de petróleo *f*

EOJ *abbr* (*end of job*) COMP&DP EOJ (*fin de tarea, fin de trabajo*)

EOM *abbr* (*end of message*) COMP&DP, TELECOM EOM (*fin de mensaje*)

eosin *n* CHEM eosina *f*

EOT[1] *abbr* COMP&DP (*end of transmission*), TELECOM (*end of transaction, end of transmission*) EOT (*fin de transmisión, fin de movimiento*)

EOT[2]: **~ marker** *n* (*end of tape marker*) COMP&DP marcador de fin de cinta

Eötvös: **~ balance** *n* PHYS balanza de Eötvös *f*

EOW *abbr* (*engineering order wire*) TELECOM línea de órdenes de ingeniería *f*

EP *abbr* GEOPHYS (*equilibrium potential*) EP (*equilibrio potencial*), TELECOM (*erroneous period*) período erróneo *m*

EPA *abbr* (*Environmental Protection Agency*) POLL Agencia para la Protección del Medio Ambiente *f*

epeiric: **~ sea** *n* GEOL mar epírico *m*

epeirogenesis *n* GEOL epirogénesis *f*

ephedrine *n* CHEM efedrina *f*

ephemerides *n pl* SPACE efemérides *f*

epicadmium: **~ neutron** *n* NUCL neutrón epicádmico *m*

epicenter *AmE see* **epicentre** *BrE*

epicentral: **~ area** *n* GEOL, GEOPHYS, PHYS zona epicéntrica *f*

epicentre *n BrE* GEOL, GEOPHYS, PHYS epicentro *m*

epichlorhydrin *n* CHEM epiclorhidrina *f*

epicinchonine *n* CHEM epicinconina *f*

epiclastic *adj* PETROL epiclástico

epicontinental[1] *adj* GEOL, PETROL epicontinental

epicontinental[2]: **~ sea** *n* GEOL, PETROL mar epicontinental *m*

epicoprostanol *n* CHEM epicoprostanol *m*

epicyclic[1] *adj* MECH, MECH ENG, WATER TRANSP epicíclico

epicyclic[2]: **~ gear** *n* MECH, WATER TRANSP engranaje epicíclico *m*; **~-gear train** *n* MECH, MECH ENG tren de engranaje epicíclico *m*; **~ train** *n* MECH, MECH ENG tren epicíclico *m*

epicycloid *n* GEOM epicicloide *f*

epicycloidal[1] *adj* MECH, MECH ENG, WATER TRANSP epicicloidal

epicycloidal[2]: **~ gear** *n* MECH, MECH ENG engranaje epicicloidal *m*

epidehydroandrosterone *n* CHEM epidehidroandrosterona *f*

epidemic: **~ disease** *n* AGRIC livestock epizootia *f*

epidiascope *n* INSTR, OPT, PHOTO epidiascopio *m*

epidiorite *n* PETROL epidiorita *f*

epidote *n* CHEM, MINERAL delfinita *f*, epídota *f*

epigenetic *adj* GEOL epigenético

epigenic *adj* GEOL epigénico

epimer *n* CHEM epímero *m*

epimerization *n* CHEM epimerización *f*

EPIRB *abbr* (*emergency position-indicating radio beacon*) TELECOM radiofaro indicador de posición para emergencias *m*, WATER TRANSP RLS (*radiobaliza de localización de siniestros*)

epirogenic: **~ movement** *n* GEOL movimiento epirogénico *m*

epistilbite *n* MINERAL epistilbita *f*

epitaxial[1] *adj* CHEM TECH, CRYSTALL, ELECTRON, METALL, RAD PHYS, TELECOM epitaxial

epitaxial[2]: **~ deposition** *n* CRYSTALL, ELECTRON deposición epitaxial *f*; **~ dislocation** *n* METALL dislocación epitaxial *f*; **~ growth** *n* CRYSTALL, ELECTRON crecimiento epitaxial *m*; **~ layer** *n* CRYSTALL, ELECTRON, TELECOM capa epitaxial *f*; **~ wafer** *n* ELECTRON pastilla epitaxial *f*

epitaxy *n* CHEM TECH, CRYSTALL, ELECTRON, METALL, RAD PHYS, TELECOM epitaxia *f*; **~ reactor** *n* CHEM TECH, CRYSTALL, ELECTRON, METALL reactor de epitaxia *m*

epithermal *adj* GEOL epitermal

epizone *n* GEOL epizona *f*

E-plane: **~ bend** *n* ELEC ENG desviación en el plano E *f*

EPNL *abbr* (*effective perceived-noise level*) ACOUST EPNL (*nivel efectivo de ruido percibido*)

EPOS *abbr* (*electronic point of sale*) COMP&DP TPV (*terminal punto de venta*)

epoxide *n* CHEM, P&R epóxido *m*

epoxidized: **~ oil** *n* P&R aceite epoxi *m*, aceite epoxídico *m*, aceite epóxido *m*

epoxy *n* CHEM epoxi *m*; **~ buffer** *n* TELECOM buffer de epoxi *m*; **~ matrix** *n* SPACE matriz epóxica *f*; **~ resin** *n* CHEM, CONST, ELEC, P&R, PACK resina epoxi *f*, resina epóxica *f*

EPROM *abbr* (*erasable PROM*) COMP&DP EPROM (*PROM borrable*)

epsomite *n* MINERAL epsomita *f*

equal: **~-area projection** *n* GEOL proyección sobre superficie uniforme *f*; **~-arm bridge** *n* ELEC brazo idéntico del puente *m*, lado idéntico del puente *m*, rama idéntica del puente *f*; **~-loudness contour** *n* ACOUST curva de igual sonoridad *f*; **~ pressure** *n* OCEAN línea isobárica *f*; **~-sided angle** *n* CONST angular de lados iguales *m*; **~ temperament** *n* ACOUST temperamento uniforme *m*; **~-time point** *n* AIR TRANSP punto de tiempos iguales *m*

equality *n* COMP&DP igualdad *f*

equalization *n* GEN compensación *f*, ecualización *f*, equilibrio *m*, igualación *f*; **~ curve** *n* ELECTRON curva de compensación *f*

equalizer *n* GEN compensador *m*, ecualizador *m*, equilibrador *m*, igualador *m*; **~ bar** *n* AUTO, VEH barra estabilizadora *f*; **~ circuit** *n* TELECOM circuito de igualador *m*; **~ spring** *n* MECH ENG muelle compensador *m*; **~ tank** *n* REFRIG recipiente equilibrador *m*

equalizing: **~ amplifier** *n* ELECTRON, TV amplificador de ecualización *m*; **~ damper** *n* REFRIG registro de equilibrio *m*; **~ feeder** *n* ELEC alimentador de compensación *m*; **~ file** *n* PROD lima de igualar *f*; **~ gear** *n* MECH ENG engranaje compensador *m*; **~ pulses** *n pl* TV pulsos de ecualización *m pl*; **~ reservoir** *n* HYDROL, WATER contraembalse *m*; **~ tank** *n* WATER tanque compensador *m*; **~ temperature** *n* THERMO temperatura de compensación *f*; **~ valve** *n* HYDRAUL válvula de equilibrio *f*, válvula de manguito *f*

equally: ~-**spaced** *adj* CONST, GEOM, MECH ENG equidistante

equant *adj* GEOL equidimensional

equation *n* CHEM, ELEC, MATH, MECH, PHYS, THERMO ecuación *f*; ~ **of continuity** *n* ELEC, PHYS ecuación de continuidad *f*; ~ **of equilibrium** *n* MECH ecuación de equilibrio *f*; ~ **of nth degree** *n* MATH ecuación de enésimo grado *f*; ~ **of radiative transfer** *n* RAD PHYS ecuación de la transferencia radiativa *f*; ~ **of state** *n* MECH ecuación de estado *f*; ~ **of thermal state** *n* THERMO ecuación de estado térmico *f*

equations: ~ **of creeping motion** *n pl* FLUID ecuaciones para deformación plástica de fluencia *f pl*

equator *n* GEOPHYS, METEO, OCEAN, SPACE, WATER TRANSP ecuador *m*

equatorial: ~ **calms** *n* METEO, OCEAN calmas ecuatoriales *f pl*; ~ **climate** *n* METEO zona climática ecuatorial *f*; ~ **crossing** *n* SPACE cruce del ecuador *m*; ~ **orbit** *n* SPACE órbita ecuatorial *f*; ~-**orbiting satellite** *n* SPACE satélite en órbita ecuatorial *m*; ~ **zone** *n* METEO zona ecuatorial *f*, zona tórrida *f*

equiangular[1] *adj* GEOM equiangular

equiangular[2]: ~ **triangle** *n* GEOM triángulo equiangular *m*, triángulo equilátero *m*

equiaxed: ~ **grain** *n* METALL grano equiaxial *m*, grano equidimensional *m*

equidistant *adj* CONST, GEOM, MECH ENG equidistante

equigranular *adj* GEOL equigranular

equilateral *adj* GEOM equilateral, equilátero

equilenin *n* CHEM equilenina *f*

equilibrated: ~ **valve** *n* HYDRAUL válvula de equilibrio *f*

equilibrium[1] *n* GEN equilibrio *m*; ~ **constant** *n* CHEM constante de equilibrio *f*; ~ **density** *n* PETR TECH densidad de equilibrio *f*; ~ **length** *n* OPT, TELECOM longitud de equilibrio *f*; ~-**mode distribution** *n* OPT, TELECOM distribución en modo equilibrio *f*; ~-**mode distribution length** *n* OPT, TELECOM longitud de distribución en modo equilibrado *f*; ~ **potential** *n* (*EP*) GEOPHYS equilibrio potencial *m* (*EP*); ~ **radiation pattern** *n* OPT, TELECOM diagrama de radiación de equilibrio *m*; ~ **saturation** *n* PETROL saturación de equilibrio *f*; ~ **system** *n* GEOPHYS sistema de equilibrio *m*; ~ **tide** *n* FUELLESS marea ideal *f*, OCEAN marea de equilibrio *f*

equilibrium[2]: **not in** ~ *phr* PHYS no en equilibrio

equimolecular *adj* CHEM equimolecular

equinoctial: ~ **tide** *n* FUELLESS marea equinoccial *f*, WATER TRANSP aguas de mareas *f pl*, marea equinoccial *f*, mareas mayores *f pl*

equip *vt* MINE, PROD, TELECOM equipar, WATER TRANSP aparejar, equipar, armar

equipartition *n* PHYS equipartición *f*

equiphase: ~ **surface** *n* ELEC ENG superficie equifásica *f*

equipment *n* CONST, MECH ENG, PROD equipamiento *m*, equipo *m*; ~ **layer** *n* TELECOM capa de equipos *f*; ~ **manufacturer** *n* WATER TRANSP fabricante de aparejos y pertrechos *m*; ~ **services** *n pl* AIR TRANSP servicios de equipo *m pl*; ~ **specification** *n* QUALITY especificación del equipo *f*

equipotential[1] *adj* ELEC, ELEC ENG, GEOPHYS, PHYS, SPACE equipotencial

equipotential[2] *n* ELEC, ELEC ENG, PHYS, SPACE equipotencial *m*; ~ **line** *n* ELEC, ELEC ENG, PHYS, SPACE línea equipotencial *f*; ~ **surface** *n* ELEC, ELEC ENG, GEOPHYS, PHYS, SPACE plano equipotencial *m*, superficie equipotencial *f*

equipressure *n* OCEAN presión de equilibrio *f*

equity: ~ **capital** *n* PETR TECH capital en acciones ordinarias *m*

equivalence *n* COMP&DP, MATH, NUCL, TRANSP equivalencia *f*; ~ **gate** *n* COMP&DP puerta de equivalencia *f*; ~ **operation** *n* COMP&DP operación de equivalencia *f*

equivalent: ~ **absorption area** *n* ACOUST área de absorción equivalente *f*; ~ **airspeed** *n* AIR TRANSP velocidad con respecto al aire equivalente *f*; ~ **area** *n* SPACE *mathematical integration* superficie equivalente *f*; ~ **circuit** *n* ELEC, ELEC ENG, ELECTRON, PHYS circuito equivalente *m*; ~ **circulating density** *n* (*ECD*) PETR TECH densidad de circulación equivalente *f* (*ECD*); ~ **conductance** *n* THERMO conductancia equivalente *f*; ~ **continuous-sound level** *n* ACOUST nivel sonoro continuo equivalente *m*; ~ **density** *n* PETR TECH densidad equivalente *f*; ~ **depth** *n* PETR TECH profundidad equivalente *f*; ~ **isotropically-radiated power** *n* (*EIRP*) SPACE potencia equivalente radiada isotrópica *f* (*EEII*); ~ **mud weight** *n* (*EMW*) PETR TECH densidad de lodo equivalente *f* (*EMW*), peso de lodo equivalente *m*; ~ **neutral density** *n* PRINT densidad neutral equivalente *f*; ~ **noise temperature** *n* SPACE temperatura de ruido equivalente *f*; ~ **per million** *n* POLL equivalente por millón *m*; ~ **proportions** *n* CHEM proporciones equivalentes *f pl*; ~ **random-traffic intensity** *n* TELECOM intensidad de tráfico aleatorio equivalente *f*; ~ **resistance** *n* ELEC resistencia equivalente *f*; ~ **shaft-horsepower** *n* MECH ENG potencia de eje equivalente *f*; ~ **step index** *n* (*ESI*) OPT, TELECOM índice escalonado equivalente *m*; ~ **step-index profile** *n* (*ESI profile*) OPT, TELECOM perfil de índice escalonado equivalente *m* (*perfil ESI*); ~ **thermal conductivity** *n* HEAT ENG, THERMO conductividad térmica equivalente *f*; ~ **thermal network** *n* HEAT ENG, THERMO red térmica equivalente *f*; ~ **vertical gust speed** *n* AIR TRANSP velocidad de ráfaga vertical equivalente *f*

Er *abbr* (*erbium*) CHEM Er (*erbio*)

era *n* AGRIC época *f*, GEOL, PETROL era *f*, época *f*

erasable: ~ **data disk** *n* COMP&DP disco de datos borrable *m*; ~ **disk drive** *n* COMP&DP unidad de disco borrable *f*; ~ **optical disc** *BrE*, ~ **optical disk** *AmE n* OPT disco óptico borrable *m*; ~ **optical drive** *n* COMP&DP, OPT unidad óptica borrable *f*; ~ **optical memory** *n* OPT memoria óptica borrable *f*; ~ **optical storage** *n* OPT almacenamiento óptico borrable *m*; ~ **PROM** *n* (*EPROM*) COMP&DP PROM borrable *f* (*EPROM*); ~ **storage** *n* *AmE* COMP&DP almacenamiento borrable *m*, memoria borrable *f*; ~ **store** *BrE n* COMP&DP almacenamiento borrable *m*, memoria borrable *f*

erase[1]: ~ **head** *n* COMP&DP, TV cabezal de borrado *m*

erase[2] *vt* COMP&DP, OPT, TV borrar

eraser *n* COMP&DP, TV borrador *m*

erasing: ~ **current** *n* TV corriente de borrado *f*; ~ **head** *n* COMP&DP, TV cabezal de borrado *m*; ~ **magnetic head** *n* ACOUST cabeza magnética borradora *f*

erasure *n* ACOUST, COMP&DP, TV borrado *m*

erathem *n* GEOL eratema *m*

erbium *n* (*Er*) CHEM erbio *m* (*Er*)

erect: ~ **burner** *n* PROD quemador recto *m*; ~-**image**

viewfinder *n* PHOTO proyector de opaco *m*, visor de imágenes directas *m*

erecting: ~ **lens** *n* INSTR, OPT ocular erector *m*; ~-**prism telescope** *n* INSTR telescopio de prisma erector *m*; ~ **shop** *n* MECH taller de construcción *m*, PROD taller de montaje *m*, WATER TRANSP taller de montaje *m*, taller de prefabricación *m*

erection *n* CONST *of buildings*, PROD *of machinery* montaje *m*; ~ **jig** *n* WATER TRANSP posicionador para montajes *m*; ~ **plan** *n* PROD *for machinery* plano de montaje *m*

erector *n* MECH constructor *m*, instalador *m*, MECH ENG instalador *m*, RAIL montador *m*

eremeyevite *n* MINERAL eremeyevita *f*

erg *n* METR ergio *m*

ergmeter *n* INSTR, METR ergómetro *m*

ergol *n* SPACE, THERMO ergol *m*

ergonomic[1] *adj* COMP&DP, MECH ENG, PACK, PROD, SAFE, SPACE ergonómico

ergonomic[2]: ~ **design principle** *n* SAFE principio de diseño ergonómico *m*

ergonomics *n* COMP&DP, MECH ENG, PACK, PROD, SAFE, SPACE ergonomía *f*

ergonomist *n* COMP&DP, MECH ENG, PACK, PROD, SAFE, SPACE ergonomista *m*

ergot *n* AGRIC, FOOD cornezuelo *m*; ~ **alkaloids** *n pl* CHEM alcaloides del ergot *m pl*

ergotinine *n* CHEM ergotinina *f*

erinite *n* MINERAL erinita *f*

eritrosine *n* CHEM eritrosina *f*

Erlenmeyer: ~ **flask** *n* LAB matraz Erlenmeyer *m*

erode *vt* CONST, GEOL, HYDROL, METEO desgastar, erosionar

erosion *n* GEN erosión *f*; ~ **by water** *n* HYDROL erosión por el agua *f*; ~ **control** *n* AGRIC lucha contra erosión *f*; ~ **rate** *n* SPACE índice de erosión *m*

erosional: ~ **unconformity** *n* GEOL discordancia erosional *f*

erosive: ~ **burning** *n* SPACE combustión erosiva *f*

ERP *abbr* (*effective radiated-power*) TELECOM PRE (*potencia radiada efectiva*)

ERRA *abbr* (*European Recycling and Recovery Association*) PACK, RECYCL AERR (*Asociación Europea de Reciclado y Recuperación*)

erratic: ~ **block** *n* GEOL bloque errático *m*, canto errático *m*

erroneous: ~ **block** *n* TELECOM bloque erróneo *m*; ~ **period** *n* (*EP*) TELECOM período erróneo *m*

error *n* COMP&DP, ELECTRON, PHYS error *m*; ~ **analysis** *n* COMP&DP análisis de errores *m*; ~ **check** *n* TELECOM verificación de errores *f*; ~-**check character** *n* TELECOM carácter de control de errores *m*; ~-**check signal** *n* TELECOM señal de control de errores *f*; ~ **code** *n* COMP&DP código de error *m*; ~ **control** *n* COMP&DP, TELECOM control de errores *m*; ~-**control device** *n* (*ECD*) COMP&DP, TELECOM dispositivo de control de errores *m*; ~-**correcting code** *n* COMP&DP, ELECTRON, SPACE, TELECOM código corrector de errores *m*, código de corrección de errores *m*; ~ **correction** *n* COMP&DP, ELECTRON, TELECOM corrección de errores *f*; ~-**correction code** *n* COMP&DP, ELECTRON código corrector de errores *m*, TELECOM código corrector de errores *m*, código de corrección de errores *m*; ~-**correction coding** *n* COMP&DP, ELECTRON código con corrección de errores *m*, TELECOM codificación con corrección de errores *f*; ~ **density** *n* TELECOM densidad de errores *f*; ~-**detecting code** *n* COMP&DP, ELECTRON, TELECOM código de detección de errores *m*; ~ **detection** *n* COMP&DP detección de errores *f*, detección de fallas *f*, ELECTRON, TELECOM, TV detección de errores *f*; ~-**detection code** *n* COMP&DP, ELECTRON, TELECOM código de detección de errores *m*; ~-**detection coding** *n* COMP&DP, ELECTRON, TELECOM codificación para la detección de errores *f*; ~ **detector** *n* COMP&DP, ELECTRON, TELECOM detector de errores *m*; ~ **detector code** *n* COMP&DP, ELECTRON, TELECOM código detector de errores *m*; ~ **diagnosis** *n* COMP&DP, TELECOM diagnóstico de error *m*; ~ **diagnostics** *n* COMP&DP, TELECOM diagnóstico de errores *m*; ~ **distribution** *n* MATH distribución de error *f*; ~ **estimation** *n* MATH valoración del error *f*; ~ **list** *n* COMP&DP lista de errores *f*; ~ **management** *n* COMP&DP administración de errores *f*, gestión de errores *f*, TELECOM administración de errores *f*; ~ **message** *n* COMP&DP, TELECOM mensaje de error *m*; ~ **of omission** *n* QUALITY error por omisión *m*; ~ **pattern** *n* TELECOM curva de error *f*; ~ **probability** *n* TELECOM probabilidad de error *f*; ~ **program** *n* COMP&DP programa de errores *m*; ~ **protection** *n* ELECTRON protección de errores *f*, TELECOM protección de error *f*; ~ **protection code** *n* TELECOM código de protección de error *m*; ~ **rate** *n* COMP&DP, ELECTRON, TELECOM frecuencia de error *f*, porcentaje de error *m*, tasa de error *f*; ~-**rate measurement** *n* COMP&DP, ELECTRON, TELECOM medición de la tasa de error *f*; ~ **recovery** *n* COMP&DP, TELECOM recuperación de errores *f*; ~ **report** *n* COMP&DP captura de errores *f*, detección y corrección de errores *f*, informe de errores *m*; ~ **retrieval** *n* QUALITY investigación de errores *f*; ~ **signal** *n* AIR TRANSP, ELECTRON señal de error *f*; ~ **susceptibility** *n* TELECOM susceptibilidad de errores *f*

errored: ~ **second** *n* (*ES*) TELECOM segundo erróneo *m*

errors: ~ **and omissions excepted** *phr* (*E&OE*) PRINT salvo error u omisión (*s.e.u.o.*)

erubescite *n* MINERAL bornita *f*

erucic *adj* CHEM erúcico

eruption *n* FLUID erupción *f*, irrupción *f*, GAS erupción *f*; ~ **point** *n* GEOL centro de erupción *m*

eruptive: ~ **rock** *n* GEOL roca eruptiva *f*

erythrin *n* CHEM eritrina *f*

erythrite *n* MINERAL eritrita *f*

erythritol *n* CHEM eritritol *m*

erythropsin *n* CHEM eritropsina *f*

erythrose *n* CHEM eritrosa *f*

erythrosine *n* CHEM eritrosina *f*

erythrulose *n* CHEM eritrulosa *f*

ES *abbr* (*errored second*) TELECOM segundo erróneo *m*

Es *abbr* (*einsteinium*) CHEM, PHYS, RAD PHYS Es (*einstenio*)

ESA *abbr* (*European Space Agency*) SPACE ESA (*Agencia Espacial Europea*)

Esaki: ~ **diode** *n* ELECTRON, PHYS diodo Esaki *m*

ESC *abbr* (*escape key*) COMP&DP ESC (*tecla de escape, tecla de salida*)

ESCA *abbr* (*Electron Spectroscopy for Chemical Analysis*) CHEM ESCA (*Espectroscopía Electrónica para Análisis Químico*)

escalator *n* CONST, TRANSP escalera mecánica *f*, escalera móvil *f*

escape: ~ **capsule** *n* PETR TECH cápsula de escape *f*; ~ **chute** *n* AIR TRANSP rampa de escape *f*, SPACE tobogán de escape *m*; ~ **device** *n* SAFE aditamento de escape *m*; ~ **hatch** *n* SPACE escotilla de salvamiento *f*; ~ **key** *n* (*ESC*) COMP&DP tecla de escape *f* (*ESC*), tecla de salida *f* (*ESC*); ~ **lane** *n* TRANSP carril de escape *m*, carril de salida *m*; ~ **peak** *n* RAD PHYS pico de fugas *m*; ~ **rope** *n* AIR TRANSP cuerda de escape *f*; ~ **sequence** *n* COMP&DP secuencia de escape *f*; ~ **valve** *n* HYDRAUL válvula de descarga *f*, válvula de escape *f*, válvula de evacuación *f*; ~ **velocity** *n* PHYS velocidad de escape *f*, velocidad de fuga *f*

escapement: ~ **mechanism** *n* MECH ENG mecanismo de escape *m*

escarpment *n* OCEAN escarpe *m*, escarpia *f*

eschinite *n* MINERAL eschinita *f*

escort: ~ **ship** *n* WATER TRANSP buque escolta *m*

esculin *n* CHEM esculina *f*

escutcheon *AmE see scutcheon BrE*

eserine *n* CHEM eserina *f*

ESI[1] *abbr* (*equivalent step index*) OPT, TELECOM índice escalonado equivalente *m*

ESI[2]: ~ **profile** *n* (*equivalent step-index profile*) OPT, TELECOM perfil ESI *m* (*perfil de índice escalonado equivalente*); ~ **refractive-index difference** *n* OPT diferencia del índice de refracción *f*, TELECOM diferencia de índice refractivo del perfil de índice escalonado *f*

ESP *abbr* (*electrostatic precipitator*) POLL precipitador electrostático *m*

espacement *n* MECH separación *f*

esparite *n* PETROL esparita *f*

esparto: ~ **pulp** *n* PAPER pasta de esparto *f*, pulpa de esparto *f*

ESS *abbr* (*electronic switching system*) TELECOM sistema de conmutación electrónico *m*

essential: ~ **fatty acid** *n* (*EFA*) CHEM, FOOD ácido graso esencial *m* (*EFA*); ~ **oil** *n* FOOD aceite esencial *m*; ~**services water** *n* NUCL agua de servicios esenciales *f*

essonite *n* MINERAL esonita *f*

establishing: ~ **shot** *n* CINEMAT, TV plano de situación *m*, plano general *m*

estar: ~ **base** *n* CINEMAT soporte de estar *m*

estate: ~ **car** *n* BrE (*cf station wagon AmE*) AUTO, VEH furgoneta *f*

ester *n* CHEM, DETERG, P&R éster *m*; ~ **gum** *n* P&R goma éster *f*; ~ **interchange** *n* DETERG intercambio estérico *m*; ~ **number** *n* DETERG número estérico *m*; ~ **resin** *n* DETERG resina estérica *f*; ~ **value** *n* DETERG valor estérico *m*

esterification *n* CHEM, FOOD esterificación *f*

esterify *vt* CHEM, FOOD esterificar

estimate *vt* METR estimar

estimated: ~ **elapsed time** *n* AIR TRANSP tiempo transcurrido aproximado *m*; ~ **flight time** *n* AIR TRANSP tiempo de vuelo previsto *m*; ~ **normal payload** *n* AIR TRANSP carga normal prevista *f*; ~ **off-block time** *n* AIR TRANSP tiempo fuera de servicio previsto *m*; ~ **position** *n* WATER TRANSP situación estimada *f*; ~ **reckoning** *n* OCEAN rumbo estimado *m*; ~ **time of arrival** *n* (*ETA*) AIR TRANSP, TRANSP, WATER TRANSP hora de llegada prevista *f*, hora estimada de llegada *f*; ~ **time of departure** *n* (*ETD*) AIR TRANSP, TRANSP, WATER TRANSP hora de salida prevista *f*, hora estimada de salida *f*

estimation *n* MATH estimación *f*, valoración *f*

estimator *n* MATH estimador *m*, inclinómetro *m*

estradiol *n* CHEM estradiol *m*

estriol *n* CHEM estriol *m*

estrone *n* CHEM estrona *f*

estuarine *adj* GEOL, OCEAN, WATER TRANSP estuarino

estuary *n* FUELLESS, GEOL, HYDROL, OCEAN, WATER TRANSP estuario *m*

ESV *abbr* (*experimental safety vehicle*) SAFE, TRANSP vehículo experimental de seguridad *m*

ET *abbr* (*exchange termination*) TELECOM terminal de central telefónica *m*

eta: ~ **factor** *n* PHYS factor eta *m*; ~~**meson** *n* PART PHYS, PHYS mesón eta *m*; ~ **neutral meson** *n* PART PHYS, PHYS mesón neutro eta *m*, neutreto eta *m*

ETA *abbr* (*estimated time of arrival*) AIR TRANSP, TRANSP, WATER TRANSP hora de llegada prevista *f*, hora estimada de llegada *f*

etalon *n* PHYS etalón *m*

ETB *abbr* (*end of transmission block*) COMP&DP FBT (*fin del bloque de transmisión*)

etch[1]: ~ **pit** *n* CRYSTALL figura de corrosión *f*, hoyo de ataque químico *m*, picadura *f*, METALL figura de corrosión *f*

etch[2] *vt* CHEM, CRYSTALL, ELECTRON, METALL, PRINT atacar con un ácido, grabar

etched: ~~**surface printing** *n* PRINT impresión sobre superficie grabada *f*

etching *n* CHEM ataque químico *m*, decapante *m*, ELECTRON grabación *f*, METALL, PRINT grabado *m*; ~ **ink** *n* COLOUR tinta de grabar *f*; ~ **machine** *n* PRINT máquina para grabar *f*; ~ **solution** *n* METALL solución de grabado químico *f*

ETD *abbr* (*estimated time of departure*) AIR TRANSP, TRANSP, WATER TRANSP hora de salida prevista *f*, hora estimada de salida *f*

ethal *n* CHEM etal *m*

ethanal *n* CHEM acetaldehído *m*, etanal *m*, FOOD acetaldehído *m*

ethane *n* CHEM, PETR TECH etano *m*

ethanethiol *n* CHEM etanotiol *m*, etil mercaptano *m*

ethanoic: ~ **acid** *n* CHEM, FOOD ácido etanoico *m*

ethanol *n* CHEM, FOOD, PETR TECH, PHOTO alcohol etílico *m*, etanol *m*

ethanolamine *n* CHEM, DETERG etanolamina *f*

ethanolysis *n* CHEM etanólisis *f*

ethene *n* CHEM, DETERG, FOOD, GAS, P&R, PETR TECH eteno *m*, etileno *m*

ether *n* CHEM, DETERG éter *m*; ~ **linkage** *n* DETERG enlace etérico *m*; ~ **oxide** *n* CHEM, DETERG éter óxido *m*

ethereal *adj* CHEM etéreo

etherlene: ~ **linkage** *n* DETERG enlace eterlénico *m*

ethionic *adj* CHEM etiónico

ethoxylation *n* DETERG etoxilación *f*

ethyl *n* CHEM, PETR TECH etilo *m*; ~ **acetate** *n* CHEM, FOOD, P&R acetato de etilo *m*; ~ **alcohol** *n* CHEM, FOOD, PETR TECH, PHOTO alcohol etílico *m*; ~ **cellulose** *n* P&R celulosa de etilo *f*; ~ **cinnamate** *n* FOOD cinamato de etilo *m*; ~ **vanillin** *n* FOOD vainillina de etilo *f*

ethylamine *n* CHEM aminoetano *m*, etilamina *f*

ethylaniline *n* CHEM etilanilina *f*

ethylate[1] *n* CHEM etilato *m*

ethylate[2] *vt* CHEM etilar

ethylation *n* CHEM etilación *f*

ethylene *n* CHEM, DETERG, FOOD, GAS, P&R, PETR TECH eteno *m*, etileno *m*; ~ **glycol** *n* CHEM, DETERG etilenglicol *m*; ~ **oxide** *n* CHEM, DETERG óxido de etileno *m*; ~**-propylene rubber** *n* P&R caucho de etilenopropileno *m*; ~**-vinyl acetate** *n* (*EVA*) P&R etileno-acetato de vinilo *m* (*EVA*), copolímero etileno *m* (*EVA*)

ethylenediamin: ~**tetra-acetic acid** *n* (*EDTA*) CHEM, DETERG ácido etilendiamino tetra-acético *m* (*EDTA*)

ethylenic *adj* CHEM etilénico

ethylic *adj* CHEM etílico

ethylidene *n* CHEM etilideno *m*

ethylmorphine *n* CHEM etilmorfina *f*

ethylsulfuric *AmE see* ethylsulphuric *BrE*

ethylsulphuric *adj BrE* CHEM etilsulfúrico

ethylthioethanol *n* PETR TECH tiotetanol etílico *m*

ethyne *n* CHEM acetileno *m*, etino *m*, CONST, GAS, MECH, SAFE, THERMO acetileno *m*

E-to-E *abbr* (*electronic-to-electronic*) ELECTRON, TV electrónico a electrónico

ETS *abbr* (*European Telecommunication Standard*) TELECOM Norma Europea de Telecomunicaciones *f*

ETSI *abbr* (*European Telecommunication Standardization Institute*) TELECOM Instituto Europeo de Normas de Telecomunicaciones *m*

ETX *abbr* (*end of text*) COMP&DP FDT (*fin de texto*)

Eu *abbr* (*europium*) CHEM Eu (*europio*)

eucairite *n* MINERAL eucairita *f*

eucalyptol *n* CHEM eucaliptol *m*

euchroite *n* MINERAL eucroíta *f*

euclase *n* MINERAL euclasa *f*

Euclidean[1] *adj* GEOM euclídeo, euclídico

Euclidean[2]: ~ **geometry** *n* GEOM geometría euclídica *f*; ~ **space** *n* GEOM, PHYS espacio euclídeo *m*, espacio euclídico *m*

Euclid: ~**'s parallel postulate** *n* GEOM axioma paralelo de Euclides *m*, postulado del paralelo de Euclides *m*, MATH axioma paralelo de Euclides *m*

eucolite *n* MINERAL eucolita *f*, titanita *f*

eudialite *n* MINERAL eudialita *f*

eudialyte *n* MINERAL eudialita *f*

eudiometer *n* CHEM, INSTR eudiómetro *m*

eudiometry *n* CHEM, INSTR eudiometría *f*

eudnophite *n* MINERAL eudnofita *f*

eugenol *n* CHEM eugenol *m*

eugeosyncline *n* GEOL eugeosinclinal *f*

euhedral *adj* GEOL euhédrico

eukairite *n* MINERAL eucairita *f*

Euler: ~ **angle** *n* PHYS ángulo de Euler *m*; ~**'s formula** *n* GEOM fórmula de Euler *f*

eulytine *n* MINERAL eulitina *f*

euosmite *n* MINERAL euosmita *f*

Eurobeer: ~ **bottle** *n* C&G botella para cerveza europea *f*

European: ~ **Alcohol Brandy and Spirit Union** *n* FOOD Unión Europea de Brandis y Licores *f*; ~ **barge-carrier system** *n* (*EBCS*) TRANSP Sistema Europeo de Transporte de Barcazas *m* (*sistema EBCS*); ~ **corn-borer** *n* AmE AGRIC barrenador europeo de maíz *m*; ~ **laboratory for particle physics** *n* (*CERN*) PART PHYS laboratorio de física de partículas *m* (*CERN*); ~ **maize-borer** *n* BrE (*cf European corn-borer AmE*) AGRIC barrenador europeo de maíz *m*; ~ **Recycling and Recovery Association** *n* (*ERRA*) PACK, RECYCL Asociación Europea de Reciclado y Recuperación *f* (*AERR*); ~ **Space Agency** *n* (*ESA*) SPACE Agencia Espacial Europea *f* (*ESA*); ~ **Telecommunication Standard** *n* (*ETS*) TELECOM Norma Europea de Telecomunicaciones *f*; ~ **Telecommunication Standardization Institute** *n* (*ETSI*) TELECOM Instituto Europeo de Normas de Telecomunicaciones *m*

europic *adj* CHEM európico

europium *n* (*Eu*) CHEM europio *m* (*Eu*)

europous *adj* CHEM europoso

Eustachian: ~ **tube** *n* ACOUST trompa de Eustaquio *f*

eustatic[1] *adj* FUELLESS, GEOL, GEOPHYS eustático

eustatic[2]: ~ **movement** *n* OCEAN movimiento eustático *m*

eusynchite *n* MINERAL eusinquita *f*

eutectic[1] *adj* C&G, CHEM, METALL eutéctico

eutectic[2] *n* C&G, CHEM, METALL eutéctico *m*; ~**-alloy overload relay** *n* PROD relé de sobrecarga de aleación eutéctica *m*; ~ **point** *n* CHEM, METALL punto eutéctico *m*; ~ **reaction** *n* CHEM, METALL reacción eutéctica *f*; ~ **transformation** *n* CHEM, METALL transformación eutéctica *f*

eutectoid *n* METALL eutectoide *m*

eutexia *n* CHEM eutexia *f*

eutrophic[1] *adj* DETERG, RECYCL eutrófico

eutrophic[2]: ~ **lake** *n* RECYCL embalse eutrófico *m*, lago eutrófico *m*

eutrophication *n* DETERG, RECYCL eutrofización *f*

eutrophy[1] *n* DETERG, RECYCL eutrofia *f*

eutrophy[2] *vt* DETERG, RECYCL eutrofiar

euxenite *n* MINERAL euxenita *f*

euxinic *adj* GEOL euxínico

eV *abbr* (*electron-volt*) ELEC ENG, ELECTRON, NUCL, PART PHYS, PHYS eV (*electronvoltio*)

EVA *abbr* (*ethylene-vinyl acetate*) P&R EVA (*etileno-acetato de vinilo, copolímero etileno*)

evacuate *vt* ELECTRON evacuar, MECH desocupar, evacuar, vaciar, MECH ENG vaciar, PHYS evacuar, PROD vaciar, SAFE desocupar

evacuated: ~**-tube collector** *n* FUELLESS colector de tubos vaciados *m*

evanescent: ~ **field** *n* OPT, TELECOM campo evanescente *m*; ~ **wave** *n* PHYS onda evanescente *f*

evaporable *adj* HEAT evaporable

evaporate[1] *vt* CHEM, CHEM TECH, HEAT, PHOTO evaporar; ~ **dry** *vt* CHEM, CHEM TECH evaporar a sequedad

evaporate[2] *vi* CHEM, CHEM TECH, HEAT, PHOTO evaporarse

evaporated: ~ **latex** *n* P&R látex evaporado *m*; ~ **layer** *n* ELECTRON estratificador evaporado *m*; ~ **whole-milk** *n* FOOD leche entera evaporada *f*

evaporating: ~ **basin** *n* LAB vasija de evaporación *f*, cápsula de evaporación *f*; ~ **boiler** *n* CHEM TECH calentador del evaporador *m*; ~ **dish** *n* LAB cápsula de evaporación *f*; ~ **pan** *n* CHEM TECH evaporímetro *m*; ~ **point** *n* CHEM, CHEM TECH, HEAT punto de evaporación *m*; ~ **pump** *n* CHEM TECH bomba de evaporación *f*; ~ **temperature** *n* REFRIG temperatura de evaporación *f*; ~ **vessel** *n* CHEM TECH matraz de evaporación *m*

evaporation *n* GEN evaporación *f*, vaporización *f*; ~ **cooling** *n* CHEM TECH enfriamiento evaporativo *m*; ~ **enthalpy** *n* CHEM TECH, THERMO entalpia de vaporización *f*; ~ **loss** *n* CHEM TECH, WATER pérdida por evaporación *f*; ~ **meter** *n* CHEM TECH evaporímetro *m*; ~ **pan** *n* WATER tanque de evaporación *m*; ~ **product** *n* CHEM TECH producto de evaporación *m*;

~ **rate** *n* CHEM TECH, COATINGS velocidad de evaporación *f*; ~ **tank** *n* HYDROL depósito de evaporación *m*

evaporative: ~ **capacity** *n* CHEM TECH poder de vaporización *m*; ~ **condenser** *n* REFRIG condensador evaporativo *m*; ~ **cooling** *n* REFRIG, THERMO enfriamiento por evaporación *m*, refrigeración por evaporación *f*; ~ **ice** *n* CHEM TECH, REFRIG hielo evaporativo *m*

evaporator *n* GEN evaporador *m*, vaporizador *m*

evaporimeter *n* CHEM TECH, HYDROL, INSTR evaporímetro *m*

evaporite *n* FUELLESS, GEOL, PETR TECH, PETROL evaporita *f*

evapotranspiration *n* HYDROL, WATER evapotranspiración *f*

even¹ *adj* GEOL regular, uniforme, PROD *surface* liso, llano

even²: ~-**and-odd courses** *n* TEXTIL pasadas pares e impares *f pl*; ~-**even nucleus** *n* PHYS, RAD PHYS núcleo par-par *m*; ~-**grained soil** *n* COAL suelo liso *m*, terreno liso *m*; ~ **ground** *n* CONST terreno llano *m*; ~ **harmonic** *n* ELECTRON, PHYS par armónico *m*; ~-**odd nucleus** *n* PHYS, RAD PHYS núcleo par-impar *m*; ~-**order filter** *n* ELECTRON filtro en orden par *m*; ~ **parity** *n* COMP&DP, PHYS paridad par *f*; ~ **pitch** *n* MECH ENG *screws* paso constante *m*; ~-**sided angle** *n* GEOM, PROD ángulo equilátero *m*; ~-**thickness paper** *n* PAPER papel calibrado *m*

even³: ~ **with the ground** *phr* CONST a la altura del terreno; **on** ~ **keel** *phr* WATER TRANSP sin diferencias de calados

evener: ~ **roll** *n* PAPER rodillo igualador *m*

event¹: ~-**driven** *adj* PROD iniciado por un acontecimiento

event² *n* GEN acontecimiento *m*, evento *m*, suceso *m*; ~ **handling** *n* COMP&DP manipulación de sucesos *f*, tratamiento de acontecimientos *m*; ~-**presentation restriction error** *n* TELECOM error de restricción de presentación de acontecimientos *m*; ~ **recorder** *n* ELEC registrador de eventos *m*, registrador de fenómenos *m*, INSTR grabador de acontecimientos *m*

event³: **in the** ~ **of breakdown** *phr* SAFE en caso de descompostura

evolute *n* GEOM, MATH evoluta *f*

evolution *n* CHEM evolución *f*, MATH extracción de una raíz *f*, PHYS desarrollo *m*, evolución *f*

evolve *vi* CHEM desprender

EW *abbr* (*electronic warfare*) ELECTRON, MILIT GE (*guerra electrónica*)

ex: ~-**store** *phr* PROD en almacén; ~-**works** *phr* PROD en fábrica

EX *abbr* (*extinction ratio*) TELECOM coeficiente de extinción *m*

exa- *pref* (*E*) METR exa- (*E*)

exactitude *n* PROD exactitud *f*

exactness *n* PROD rigor *m*

examine: ~-**off** *n* PROD desconexión de interrogación *f*; ~-**off instruction** *n* PROD orden de desconexión de interrogación *f*; ~-**off key** *n* PROD tecla para desconectar interrogación *f*; ~-**on** *n* PROD conexión de interrogación *f*; ~-**on instruction** *n* PROD orden de conexión de interrogación *f*; ~-**on key** *n* PROD tecla para conectar interrogación *f*

excavatability *n* COAL, MINE excavabilidad *f*

excavated: ~ **material** *n* MINE material extraído por

extracción *m*, RAIL material extraído por excavación *m*

excavating *n* COAL, CONST, MINE excavación *f*

excavation *n* COAL, CONST, MINE excavación *f*

excavator *n* COAL, CONST, MINE, TRANSP excavadora *f*

excelsion *n* PACK virutas para embalar *f pl*

excelsior: ~ **tissue** *n* PAPER lana de papel *f*

exception: ~ **handler** *n* COMP&DP gestor de excepciones *m*, manipulador de excepciones *m*

excess: ~ **attenuation** *n* TELECOM exceso de atenuación *m*; ~ **baggage** *n* AIR TRANSP exceso de equipaje *m*; ~ **current** *n* ELEC sobrecarga de corriente *f*, sobrecorriente *f*; ~-**current switch** *n* ELEC conmutador de sobrecorriente *m*; ~ **energy** *n* THERMO exceso de energía *m*; ~ **energy meter** *n* ELEC contador de exceso de energía *m*, contador totalizador de exceso *m*; ~-**fare office** *n* RAIL oficina para pago de sobreprecio en billetes *f*; ~ **function** *n* METALL función excedente *f*; ~ **of operating overload** *n* PROD exceso de sobrecarga operativa *m*; ~ **pressure** *n* REFRIG exceso de presión *m*; ~ **temperature** *n* THERMO temperatura excesiva *f*; ~ **voltage** *n* ELEC sobretensión *f*, sobrevoltaje *m*; ~-**voltage protection** *n* ELEC, SAFE protección contra el sobrevoltaje *f*, protección contra la sobretensión *f*; ~ **weight** *n* PACK exceso de peso *m*

excessive: ~ **heat** *n* PROD calor excesivo *m*; ~ **production** *n* PETROL producción excesiva *f*

exchange *n* COMP&DP centralita *f*, intercambio *m*, MECH ENG, PROD cambio *m*, intercambio *m*, TELECOM central *f*, centralita *f*; ~ **clip** *n* PROD grapa de intercambio *f*; ~ **energy** *n* METALL energía de cambio *f*; ~ **jump** *n* COMP&DP salto de intercambio *m*; ~ **line** *n* TELECOM línea de la central *f*; ~ **switchboard** *n* TELECOM central telefónica *f*; ~ **termination** *n* (*ET*) TELECOM terminal de central telefónica *m*

exchangeable: ~ **disk** *n* COMP&DP disco cambiable *m*, disco intercambiable *m*

exchanger *n* MECH ENG intercambiador *m*

excitance *n* RAD PHYS excitancia *f*

excitation *n* GEN excitación *f*; ~ **anode** *n* ELEC ENG ánodo de excitación *m*; ~ **circuit** *n* ELEC ENG circuito de excitación *m*; ~ **current** *n* ELEC *electromagnetism* corriente de excitación *f*; ~ **energy** *n* RAD PHYS energía de excitación *f*; ~ **field** *n* ELEC ENG campo de excitación *m*; ~ **function** *n* RAD PHYS función de excitación *f*; ~ **source** *n* RAD PHYS fuente de excitación *f*; ~ **winding** *n* ELEC devanado de excitación *m*, devanado inductor *m*

excited¹ *adj* CHEM, GAS, PART PHYS, PHYS, RAD PHYS excitado

excited²: ~ **atom** *n* CHEM, ELEC, ELECTRON, GAS ión *m*, PART PHYS ión *m*, átomo excitado *m*, átomo ionizado *m*, PETR TECH ión *m*, PHYS ión *m*, átomo excitado *m*; ~ **component** *n* GAS componente excitado *m*; ~ **state** *n* CHEM *of atom*, METALL, PART PHYS, PHYS, RAD PHYS estado de excitación *m*, estado excitado *m*; ~-**state deactivation** *n* RAD PHYS desactivación del estado excitado *f*

exciter *n* ELEC *generator* excitador *m*, inductor *m*, ELEC ENG *exciting dynamo* dinamo excitadora *f*, *static dynamo* inductor *m*, FUELLESS *turbines* excitador *m*; ~ **lamp** *n* CINEMAT lámpara excitadora *f*, lámpara fónica *f*

exciting: ~ **dynamo** *n* ELEC dinamo excitatriz *f*, excitatriz *f*, ELEC ENG dinamo excitatriz *f*

exciton n PHYS excitón m
excitron n ELEC ENG excitrón m
exclusion: ~ **principle** n CHEM principio de exclusión m; ~ **zone** n NUCL zona de exclusión f
exclusive: ~ **fishing zone** n OCEAN zona exclusiva de pesca f; ~ **NOR circuit** n ELECTRON circuito NO-O exclusivo m, circuito exclusivo NO-O m; ~ **NOR gate** n COMP&DP puerta NI exclusiva f, puerta NOR exclusiva f, ELECTRON rejilla NO-O exclusiva f; ~ **OR circuit** n ELECTRON circuito O exclusivo m; ~ **OR gate** n COMP&DP puerta O exclusiva f, puerta OR exclusiva f, ELECTRON rejilla O exclusiva f; ~ **OR operation** n COMP&DP operación O exclusiva f, operación OR exclusiva f; ~ **site** n TRANSP emplazamiento exclusivo m, sitio exclusivo m
excursion: ~ **steamer** n TRANSP vapor turístico m
exducer n AIR TRANSP exductor m
executable: ~ **instruction** n COMP&DP instrucción ejecutable f; ~ **statement** n COMP&DP declaración ejecutable f, sentencia ejecutable f
execute[1]: ~ **phase** n COMP&DP fase de ejecución f
execute[2] vt COMP&DP ejecutar
execution n COMP&DP ejecución f; ~ **time** n COMP&DP tiempo de ejecución m
executive n COMP&DP ejecutivo m, ejecutor m; ~ **aircraft** n AIR TRANSP avión de ejecutivo m; ~ **helicopter** n AIR TRANSP helicóptero de ejecutivo m
exercise: ~ **area** n OCEAN área de ejercitación f
exert vt PHYS ejercer
exfoliation n GEOL, PHYS exfoliación f
exhalation: ~ **valve** n AIR TRANSP válvula de exhalación f
exhaust[1] n AIR TRANSP, AUTO, HEAT escape m, HEAT ENG tubo de escape m, tubo de expulsión m, PAPER salida de vahos f, VEH escape m; ~ **back-pressure** n AIR TRANSP presión del escape f; ~ **brake** n AUTO, VEH freno por compresión de aire en el motor m; ~ **case** n AIR TRANSP caja del escape f; ~ **cavity** n HYDRAUL hueco de la concha m; ~**cleaning installation** n SAFE instalación limpiadora de escape f; ~ **cone** n AIR TRANSP cono de escape m; ~ **cover** n HYDRAUL recubrimiento de escape m; ~ **draft** AmE, ~ **draught** BrE n MECH ENG corriente de escape f, corriente de extracción f, ventilación por aspiración f, ventilación por extracción f; ~ **edge** n HYDRAUL arista interior f; ~ **fan** n HEAT ENG, MECH, MECH ENG, PAPER extractor m, extractor de aire m, extractor de vahos m, ventilador de extracción m; ~ **fumes** n pl AIR TRANSP descarga del motor f, humos de escape m pl, AUTO, MECH, THERMO, TRANSP, VEH humos de escape m pl; ~ **gas cleaning** n GAS, THERMO limpieza de los gases de escape f; ~**gas combustion** n AUTO, MECH, TRANSP combustión de gases de escape f; ~**gas emission** n AUTO, MECH, TRANSP emisión de gases de escape f; ~**gas indicator** n AUTO, TRANSP, VEH indicador de gas del escape m; ~**gas recirculation** n AUTO, MECH, TRANSP recirculación de gases de escape f; ~**gas recirculation with air injection** n AUTO, TRANSP recirculación de gases de escape con inyección de aire f; ~**gas temperature** n AIR TRANSP, AUTO, TRANSP temperatura del gas de escape f; ~**gas turbine** n AUTO turbina de gases de escape f; ~ **gases** n pl AIR TRANSP, AUTO gases de escape m pl, humos de escape m pl, GAS gases de escape m pl, MECH gases de escape m pl, humos de escape m pl, THERMO chorro de gases m, gases de

escape m pl, humos de escape m pl, TRANSP, VEH gases de escape m pl, humos de escape m pl; ~ **lag** n HYDRAUL retardo de escape m; ~ **lap** n HYDRAUL recubrimiento de escape m; ~ **lead** n HYDRAUL avance de escape m; ~ **manifold** n AIR TRANSP colector de escape m, múltiple de escape m, AUTO, MECH, THERMO, VEH colector de escape m; ~ **nozzle** n AIR TRANSP tobera de escape f; ~**nozzle breeches** n pl AIR TRANSP bragas de la tobera de escape f pl; ~ **passage** n AUTO conducto del escape m; ~ **pipe** n AIR TRANSP, THERMO, WATER TRANSP tubería de escape f, tubo de escape m; ~ **port** n AUTO, HYDRAUL, VEH lumbrera de escape f, orificio de escape m; ~ **pump** n HYDRAUL, WATER bomba de aspiración f; ~ **recycling** n TRANSP reciclaje del escape m; ~ **steam** n FOOD vapor expulsado m, vapor perdido m, HEAT ENG, HYDRAUL vapor de escape m; ~ **steam turbine** n HEAT ENG turbina a vapor de escape f; ~ **stroke** n AUTO, VEH carrera de escape f, fase de escape f; ~ **system** n AUTO, VEH sistema de escape m; ~ **trail** n AIR TRANSP estela del escape del motor f; ~ **turbine** n HEAT ENG turbina de escape f; ~ **turbocharger** n AUTO turboalimentador de escape m; ~ **valve** n AUTO, HYDRAUL, LAB, VEH válvula de escape f; ~ **vent installations** n pl SAFE instalaciones ventiladoras de escape f pl
exhaust[2] vt METALL, NUCL agotar
exhausted: ~ **developer** n PHOTO revelador agotado m; ~ **vein** n MINE filón agotado m
exhauster n FOOD aspirador m, extractor m, MECH ENG aspirador m, extractor de aire m, ventilador aspirante m
exhausting n MINE aspiración f, escape m (Esp), vaciado m (AmL)
exhaustion n METALL, NUCL agotamiento m; ~ **box** n FOOD caja de expulsión f; ~ **creep** n METALL deformación por agotamiento f
exhumed: ~ **anticlinal fold** n GEOL anticlinal exhumado m
existing: ~ **light** n CINEMAT, PHOTO, TV iluminación existente f
exit n COMP&DP salida f; ~ **cone** n PHYS cono de salida m; ~ **point** n COMP&DP punto de salida m; ~ **pupil** n PHYS pupila de salida f; ~ **taxiway** n AIR TRANSP salida de rodaje f; ~ **velocity** n HYDRAUL velocidad de salida f
exjunction n COMP&DP disyunción exclusiva f, exyunción f
exoatmospheric adj SPACE exoatmosférico
exobase n SPACE base espacial f
EXOR: ~ **operation** n COMP&DP operación EXOR f
exosphere n SPACE exosfera f
exothermal adj CHEM, PETR TECH, SPACE, THERMO exotérmico
exothermic[1] adj CHEM, PETR TECH, SPACE, THERMO exotérmico
exothermic[2]: ~ **process** n PETR TECH proceso exotérmico m
exotic: ~ **chip** n ELECTRON microplaca artificial f; ~ **signal** n ELECTRON señal artificial f
expand vi GEOM expandirse, extenderse, HYDRAUL dilatarse, expandirse
expandable: ~ **pallet** n PACK paleta de carga extensible f
expanded: ~ **cellular plastic** n P&R, REFRIG plástico celular expandido m; ~ **cork** n REFRIG corcho

expandido *m*; ~-**data table** *n* PROD tabla de datos inflados *f*; ~-**memory manager** *n* COMP&DP gestor de memoria expandida *m*; ~-**memory specification** *n* (*EMS*) COMP&DP especificación de memoria expandida *f* (*EMS*); ~ **metal** *n* MECH metal poroso *m*; ~ **perlite** *n* HEAT ENG perlita expandida *f*; ~ **plastic** *n* P&R, REFRIG plástico expandido *m*; ~ **polystyrene** *n* PACK poliestireno expandido *m*; ~-**polythene packaging** *n* PACK embalaje de poliestireno expandido *m*; ~ **rubber** *n* P&R caucho expandido *m*; ~ **scale** *n* METR escala expandida *f*; ~ **sweep** *n* ELECTRON exploración ampliada *f*

expander *n* PROD extensor *m*; ~ **module** *n* PROD módulo extensor *m*

expanding: ~ **mandrel** *n* MECH ENG mandril de diámetro regulable *m*, mandril de expansión *m*

expansibility *n* THERMO expansibilidad *f*

expansion *n* GEN dilatación *f*, expansión *f*, extensión *f*; ~ **bellows** *n* MECH expansión de fuelle *f*; ~ **bend** *n* REFRIG lira de dilatación *f*; ~ **board** *n* COMP&DP circuito impreso de extensión *m*, tarjeta de ampliación *f*; ~ **bolt** *n* MECH ENG perno regulable *m*; ~ **box** *n* HYDRAUL caja de dilatación *f*; ~ **cable** *n* PROD cable de expansión *m*; ~ **cam** *n* HYDRAUL leva de dilatación *f*; ~ **card** *n* COMP&DP módulo de extensión *m*, tarjeta de ampliación *f*, ELECTRON tarjeta de expansión *f*; ~ **chamber** *n* MECH ENG cámara de expansión *f*, cámara de ionización *f*; ~ **coefficient** *n* MECH coeficiente de dilatación *m*; ~ **coupling** *n* HYDRAUL manguito de dilatación *m*; ~ **due to heat** *n* THERMO expansión por calor *f*; ~ **duration** *n* HYDRAUL duración de la expansión *f*; ~ **engine** *n* MECH ENG motor de expansión *m*; ~ **filter** *n* ELECTRON filtro de expansión *m*; ~ **gap** *n* HYDRAUL junta de dilatación *f*; ~ **gear** *n* MECH ENG mecanismo del distribuidor de expansión *m*; ~ **joint** *n* CONST junta de dilatación *f*, junta de expansión *f*, HYDRAUL junta de dilatación *f*; ~ **loop** *n* REFRIG codo de dilatación *m*; ~ **network** *n* TELECOM red de expansión *f*; ~ **notch** *n* HYDRAUL muesca de expansión *f*; ~ **nozzle** *n* AIR TRANSP *jet engine* tobera de expansión *f*; ~ **period** *n* HYDRAUL período de expansión *m*; ~ **plate** *n* HYDRAUL corredera de expansión *f*, teja de expansión *f*; ~ **point** *n* HYDRAUL principio de la expansión *m*; ~ **reamer** *n* PROD escariador de diámetro regulable *m*; ~ **ring** *n* PETR TECH anillo de expansión *m*; ~ **slide** *n* HYDRAUL corredera de expansión *f*, teja de expansión *f*; ~ **slot** *n* COMP&DP, ELECTRON conector de expansión *m*, ranura de extensión *f*; ~ **space** *n* C&G junta de expansión *f*; ~ **stage** *n* TELECOM etapa de expansión *f*; ~ **storage tube** *n* ELECTRON tubo memorizador de expansión *m*; ~ **stress** *n* HYDRAUL esfuerzo de dilatación *m*; ~ **stroke** *n* MECH ENG carrera de expansión *f*, THERMO carrera de expansión *f*, tiempo de expansión *m*, VEH *engine* carrera de expansión *f*, carrera de trabajo *f*; ~ **tank** *n* AUTO, HEAT ENG, HYDRAUL, MECH caja de dilatación *f*, depósito de expansión *m*, tanque de expansión *m*; ~ **trap** *n* HYDRAUL purgador de expansión *m*, trampilla de descarga *f*; ~ **tube** *n* LAB tubo de dilatación *m*, tubo de expansión *m*; ~ **turbine** *n* AIR TRANSP, REFRIG turbina de expansión *f*; ~ **valve** *n* HYDRAUL, MECH ENG, REFRIG válvula de expansión *f*; ~ **vessel** *n* MECH ENG recipiente de expansión *m*; ~ **wave** *n* AIR TRANSP *sonic boom* onda de expansión *f*

expected: ~ **approach time** *n* AIR TRANSP tiempo de aproximación previsto *m*

expedite *vt* PROD activar la entrega

expediting *n* PROD seguimiento de fabricación *m*

expeditor *n* PROD expedidor *m*

expeller: ~ **cake** *n* FOOD pastilla de extracción *f*, torta de extracción *f*

expendable[1] *adj* MECH de duración limitada, perecedero, SPACE consumible, desechable

expendable[2]: ~ **item** *n* MECH ENG componente desechable *m*, producto desechable *m*; ~ **pallet** *n* TRANSP bandeja desechable *f*, paleta desechable *f*, pálet desechable *m* (*AmL*)

experience: ~ **curve** *n* TEXTIL curva de experiencia *f*

experiment *n* GEN experimento *m*, prueba *f*; ~ **module** *n* SPACE módulo para experimentación *m*; ~ **package** *n* SPACE conjunto de experimentos *m*; ~ **station** *n* AGRIC estación experimental *f*

experimental[1] *adj* GEN experimental

experimental[2]: ~ **basin** *n* WATER cuenca experimental *f*; ~ **field** *n* AGRIC campo experimental *m*; ~ **helicopter** *n* AIR TRANSP helicóptero experimental *m*; ~ **model** *n* MECH modelo experimental *m*; ~ **physics** *n* PART PHYS, PHYS física experimental *f*; ~ **plot** *n* AGRIC parcela experimental *f*; ~ **safety vehicle** *n* (*ESV*) SAFE, TRANSP vehículo experimental de seguridad *m*; ~ **section** *n* CONST corte experimental *m*; ~ **solid-disc flywheel** *BrE*, ~ **solid-disk flywheel** *AmE* *n* MECH ENG disco sólido experimental *m*, volante macizo experimental *m*; ~ **television** *n* TV televisión experimental *f*

expert: ~ **system** *n* COMP&DP sistema experto *m*

expiration: ~ **of timer** *n* *AmE* (*cf expiry of timer BrE*) TELECOM caducidad del temporizador *f*

expiry: ~ **date** *n* CINEMAT fecha de vencimiento *f*, FOOD fecha de caducidad *f*; ~ **of timer** *n* *BrE* (*cf expiration of timer AmE*) TELECOM caducidad del temporizador *f*

explicit: ~ **address** *n* COMP&DP direccional explícito *m* (*AmL*), dirección explícita *f* (*Esp*), exponente *m*; ~ **congestion notification** *n* (*ECN*) TELECOM notificación explícita de congestión *f*

explode[1] *vt* GEN volar

explode[2] *vi* GEN explosionar, explotar, hacer explosión

exploded: ~ **view** *n* MECH *of car* despiece *f*, vista desarrollada *f*, MECH ENG *of drawing* vista detallada *f*

exploder *n* MINE cebo *m*, detonador *m* (*Esp*), explosor *m*

exploration *n* GAS, PETR TECH exploración *f*, prospección *f*; ~ **drilling** *n* GAS, PETR TECH perforación exploratoria *f*; ~ **drive** *n* MINE galería de cateo *f* (*AmL*), galería de exploración *f* (*Esp*), galería de reconocimiento *f* (*AmL*); ~ **level** *n* MINE galería de cateo *f* (*AmL*), galería de exploración *f* (*Esp*), galería de reconocimiento *f* (*AmL*); ~ **licence** *n* *BrE* PETR TECH licencia de exploración *f*, licencia de prospección *f*; ~ **license** *AmE see exploration licence BrE*; ~ **phase** *n* PETR TECH fase de exploración *f*; ~ **pit** *n* MINE pocillo de investigación *m* (*Esp*), pozo de cateo *m* (*AmL*), pozo de prospección *m* (*Esp*); ~ **platform** *n* SPACE plataforma de exploración *f*; ~ **rig** *n* PETR TECH equipo de exploración *m*, torre de sondeo de exploración *f*; ~ **shaft** *n* MINE pozo de cateo *m* (*AmL*), pozo de prospección *m* (*Esp*); ~ **trench** *n* MINE foso de cateo *m* (*AmL*), foso de exploración *m* (*Esp*), trinchera de cateo *f* (*AmL*), trinchera de exploración *f* (*Esp*); ~ **well** *n* PETR TECH pozo de exploración *m*, pozo exploratorio *m*, PETROL pozo de exploración *m*, pozo excavado hacia arriba *m* (*AmL*), pozo exploratorio *m*; ~ **work** *n* MINE labores de exploración *f pl*, trabajos de exploración *m pl*

exploratory: ~ **drilling** *n* GAS, PETR TECH perforación exploratoria *f*; ~ **well** *n* PETR TECH, PETROL pozo exploratorio *m*

exploring: ~ **coil** *n* ELEC *magnetic field* bobina exploradora *f*

explosimeter *n* INSTR, LAB explosímetro *m*

explosion[1]: ~-**proof** *adj* AIR TRANSP a prueba de explosión, MECH antidetonante, antiexplosivo, PACK protegido contra las explosiones, a prueba de explosión

explosion[2] *n* MECH ENG, PETR TECH, PROD, SAFE explosión *f*; ~ **breccia** *n* GEOL brecha de explosión *f*; ~ **die** *n pl* MECH ENG matrices de explosión *f pl*, troquel de explosión *m*; ~-**proof glazing** *n* C&G vidrio a prueba de explosiones *m*; ~ **wave** *n* MINE onda de explosión *f*

explosive[1] *adj* GEN explosivo

explosive[2] *n* GEN explosivo *m*; ~ **atmosphere** *n* SAFE atmósfera explosiva *f*; ~ **bolt** *n* MECH, SPACE bulón explosivo *m*; ~ **combustion** *n* MINE combustión explosiva *f*; ~ **decompression** *n* OCEAN, THERMO descompresión explosiva *f*; ~ **forming** *n* MECH, THERMO conformación de piezas por cargas explosivas *f*, conformación por explosión *f*; ~ **mixture** *n* AUTO mezcla explosiva *f*; ~ **sensitivity** *n* MINE sensibilidad del explosivo *f*; ~-**type rivet** *n* MECH remache explosivo *m*

explosives: ~ **magazine** *n* MINE almacenado de explosivos *m*, polvorín *m*

exponent *n* COMP&DP, ELEC, ELECTRON, MATH exponente *m*

exponential[1] *adj* COMP&DP, ELEC, ELECTRON, MATH exponencial

exponential[2] *n* ELEC, MATH exponencial *m*; ~ **amplifier** *n* ELECTRON amplificador exponencial *m*; ~ **curve** *n* ELEC, MATH curva exponencial *f*; ~ **decay** *n* ELECTRON amortiguación exponencial *f*; ~ **distribution** *n* COMP&DP distribución exponencial *f*; ~ **horn** *n* ACOUST bocina exponencial *f*; ~ **tube** *n* ELECTRON tubo exponencial *m*

export: ~ **licence** *BrE*, ~ **license** *AmE n* TRANSP, WATER TRANSP licencia de exportación *f*, permiso de exportación *m*; ~ **packaging** *n* PACK embalaje de exportación *m*

expose *vt* CINEMAT, PHOTO, PRINT, TV exponer

exposed: ~-**location single-buoy mooring** *n* (*ELSBM*) PETR TECH anclaje de baliza simple de localización descubierta *m*, boya simple de amarre de localización descubierta *f*; ~ **part** *n* CONST *of roofing-slate* parte descubierta *f*

exposure *n* CINEMAT, PHOTO, PHYS, PRINT, TV exposición *f*; ~ **at the surface** *n* OCEAN exposición en superficie *f*; ~-**calculating chart** *n* PHOTO guía de exposiciones *f*, tabla de exposiciones *f*; ~ **calculator** *n* CINEMAT, PHOTO, TV calculadora de exposición *f*; ~ **control-tape** *n* CINEMAT, PHOTO cinta de control de la exposición *f*; ~ **counter** *n* CINEMAT, PHOTO contador de exposiciones *m*; ~ **dose** *n* RAD PHYS dosis de exposición *f*; ~ **duration** *n* CINEMAT, PHOTO duración de la exposición *f*; ~ **factor** *n* CINEMAT, PHOTO factor de exposición *m*; ~ **index** *n* CINEMAT, PHOTO, TV

índice de exposición *m*; ~ **latitude** *n* CINEMAT, PHOTO latitud de exposición *f*; ~ **limit** *n* SAFE límite de exposición *m*; ~ **meter** *n* CINEMAT, PHOTO, PHYS exposímetro *m*, fotómetro *m*; ~-**meter needle** *n* CINEMAT, PHOTO, PHYS aguja del exposímetro *f*; ~ **meter using needle-matching system** *n* CINEMAT, PHOTO exposímetro por coincidencia de agujas *m*; ~ **rate** *n* PHYS tasa de exposición *f*; ~ **risk** *n* NUCL, RAD PHYS, SAFE riesgo de exposición *m*; ~ **scale** *n* CINEMAT, PHOTO escala de exposiciones *f*; ~ **test** *n* CINEMAT, PHOTO prueba de exposición *f*; ~ **time** *n* CINEMAT, PHOTO tiempo de exposición *m*; ~ **timer** *n* CINEMAT, PHOTO exposímetro *m*; ~ **to fumes** *n* SAFE exposición a humos *f*; ~ **to radiation** *n* NUCL, P&R, SAFE exposición a la radiación *f*; ~ **to weather** *n* P&R exposición a la intemperie *f*; ~ **value** *n* CINEMAT, PHOTO valor de exposición *m*

express: ~ **parcel service** *n* RAIL servicio de paquetería urgente *m*; ~ **train** *n* RAIL tren expreso *m*

expression *n* COMP&DP expresión *f*

expulsion *n* ELEC, ELEC ENG, PETR TECH eliminación *f*, expulsión *f*; ~ **fuse** *n* ELEC cortacircuito de expulsión *m*, fusible de expulsión *m*, ELEC ENG fusible de expulsión *m*; ~ **rate** *n* PETR TECH grado de expulsión *m*; ~-**type lightning arrester** *n* ELEC ENG pararrayos con fusible de expulsión *m*

extended: ~ **addressing** *n* COMP&DP direccionamiento extendido *m*; ~ **application layer structure** *n* (*XALS*) TELECOM estructura en capas de aplicación extendida *f*; ~ **bandwidth system** *n* TELECOM sistema de ancho de banda ampliado *m*; ~ **binary-coded decimal-interchange code** *n* (*EBCDIC*) COMP&DP código ampliado de caracteres decimales codificados en binario *m* (*EBCDIC*); ~ **definition television** *n* (*EDTV*) TV televisión de alta definición *f* (*Esp*), televisión por definición extendida *f* (*AmL*); ~ **graphic arrangement** *n* (*EGA*) COMP&DP arreglo gráfico extendido *m* (*EGA*); ~ **interaction oscillator** *n* ELECTRON oscilador de interacción ampliado *m*; ~-**interaction tube** *n* ELECTRON tubo de interacción ampliado *m*; ~ **nip** *n* PAPER línea de contacto ampliada *f*, línea de tangencia ampliada *f*; ~ **nip press** *n* PAPER prensa de línea de contacto ampliada *f*; ~ **node** *n* METALL nudo estirado *m*, nudo prolongado *m*; ~ **piston-rod** *n* MECH ENG contravarilla del pistón *f*; ~ **runway centerline** *AmE*, ~ **runway centreline** *BrE n* AIR TRANSP eje de pista extendido *m*, línea central de pista extendida *f*; ~-**surface heat exchanger** *n* MECH ENG intercambiador de calor de superficie extendida *m*; ~ **type** *n* PRINT tipo extra ancha *m*

extender *n* COLOUR diluente *m*; ~ **oil** *n* PETR TECH aceite para extender el caucho *m*

extensibility *n* COMP&DP, MECH ENG, P&R alargabilidad *f*, extensibilidad *f*

extensible: ~ **addressing** *n* COMP&DP direccionamiento extensible *m*; ~ **language** *n* COMP&DP lenguaje ampliable *m*, lenguaje extensible *m*

extension *n* GEOL, MECH ENG, PHOTO dilatación *f*, extensión *f*, PHYS *unit* alargamiento *m*, TELECOM supletorio *m*; ~ **bell** *n* TELECOM timbre supletorio *m*; ~ **bellows** *n* CINEMAT, PHOTO fuelle de extensión *m*, fuelle extensible *m*; ~ **bellows unit** *n* CINEMAT, PHOTO unidad de fuelle de extensión *f*; ~ **bit** *n* MECH ENG broca ajustable *f*, broca extensible *f*; ~ **cable** *n* CINEMAT cable alargador *m*, ELEC, ELEC ENG cable de

prolongación *m*; ~ **connector-plug** *n* MECH ENG clavija conectora de extensión *f*; ~ **cord** *n* AIR TRANSP cuerda de extensión *f*; ~ **ladder** *n* CONST escalera extensible *f*, escalera plegable *f*; ~ **lead** *n* CINEMAT guía de extensión *f*, LAB cable de extensión *m*; ~ **line** *n* MECH ENG *of drawing* línea de extensión *f*; ~ **piece** *n* MECH ENG *for box-spanner* alargadera *f*; ~ **reel** *n* ELEC ENG bobina extensible *f*, carrete extensible *m*; ~ **ring** *n* PHOTO anillo de extensión *m*; ~ **service** *n* AGRIC servicio de extensión *m*; ~ **shaft** *n* MECH ENG eje de expansión *m*, eje de extensión *m*; ~ **socket** *n* MECH ENG enchufe de extensión *m*, enchufe portátil *m*, enchufe supletorio *m*; ~ **spring** *n* MECH ENG muelle de extensión *m*, resorte de extensión *m*; ~ **tripod** *n* CINEMAT, PHOTO trípode de patas extensibles *m*, trípode telescópico *m*; ~ **tube** *n* CINEMAT tubo telescópico *m*, LAB tubo de extensión *m*, PHOTO tubo telescópico *m*; ~ **well** *n* PETR TECH pozo de extensión *m*
extensive: ~ **crops** *n pl* AGRIC cultivos extensivos *m pl*; ~ **quantity** *n* PHYS cantidad extensiva *f*
extensometer *n* MECH extensímetro *m*, METR extensómetro *m*
extent *n* MINE amplitud *f*, estimación *f* (*AmL*), extensión *f*, grado *m*, importancia *f*
exterior *n* CINEMAT exterior *m*; ~ **angle** *n* GEOM ángulo exterior *m*; ~ **finish** *n* COLOUR acabado exterior *m*; ~-**packaging machine** *n* PACK máquina de embalaje exterior *f*; ~-**pole generator** *n* ELEC generador de polos exteriores *m*; ~ **surface** *n* PACK superficie externa *f*
external: ~ **access equipment** *n* (*EA*) TELECOM equipo de acceso externo *m*; ~ **blocking** *n* TELECOM bloqueo exterior *m*; ~ **caliper gage** *AmE*, ~ **calliper gauge** *BrE n* MECH ENG calibrador plano de exteriores *m*; ~ **circuit** *n* ELEC circuito exterior *m*, circuito externo *m*, conexiones externas *f pl*; ~ **combustion engine** *n* MECH ENG, TRANSP motor de combustión externa *m*; ~ **cylindrical gage** *AmE*, ~ **cylindrical gauge** *BrE n* MECH ENG calibrador cilíndrico de exteriores *m*; ~ **defrosting** *n* REFRIG desescarche desde el exterior *m*; ~ **device** *n* COMP&DP dispositivo externo *m*; ~ **disturbance** *n* ELEC perturbación externa *f*; ~ **electromagnetic wave** *n* RAD PHYS, WAVE PHYS onda electromagnética externa *f*; ~ **force** *n* METALL fuerza externa *f*; ~ **gas-pressure cable** *n* ELEC cable exterior con gas a presión *m*; ~ **geomagnetic field** *n* GEOPHYS, PHYS campo geomagnético externo *m*; ~ **graticule** *n* ELECTRON cuadrícula externa *f*; ~ **inductance** *n* ELEC inductancia externa *f*; ~ **injection** *n* AUTO, VEH inyección externa *f*; ~ **input** *n* ELEC, ELECTRON entrada de corriente externa *f*; ~ **insulation** *n* ELEC, ELEC ENG aislación externa *f*, aislamiento externo *m*; ~ **interface** *n* ELECTRON interconexión externa *f*, SPACE *equipment* interconexión externa *f*, superficie externa de contacto *f*, zona interfacial externa *f*, TELECOM interconexión externa *f*; ~ **interrupt** *n* COMP&DP interrupción externa *f*; ~-**load carrier** *n* AIR TRANSP *helicopter* transportador de carga externa *m*; ~ **magnetic field** *n* ELEC campo magnético externo *m*; ~ **magnetosphere** *n* SPACE magnetosfera externa *f*; ~ **memory** *n* COMP&DP, ELEC ENG memoria externa *f*; ~ **micrometer** *n* MECH ENG micrómetro de exteriores *m*; ~ **modulation** *n* ELECTRON modulación externa *f*; ~ **noise** *n* ELECTRON perturbación exterior

f; ~ **parasite** *n* AGRIC ectoparásito *m*; ~ **photoelectric effect** *n* ELEC, OPT, PHOTO, TELECOM efecto fotoeléctrico externo *m*, efecto fotoeléctrico extrerno *m*; ~ **plasticizer** *n* P&R plastificante externo *m*; ~-**pole generator** *n* ELEC generador de polos exteriores *m*; ~ **pre-stressing** *n* CONST pretensado externo *m*; ~ **reference** *n* COMP&DP referencia externa *f*; ~ **resistance** *n* ELEC, ELEC ENG resistencia externa *f*; ~ **resistor** *n* ELEC, ELEC ENG resistencia exterior *f*; ~ **screw** *n* PROD tornillo macho *m*; ~ **set-up** *n* PROD montaje externo *m*; ~ **signal** *n* ELECTRON, TELECOM señal externa *f*; ~ **signal source** *n* ELECTRON, TELECOM fuente de señal externa *f*; ~ **sort** *n* COMP&DP clasificación externa *f*; ~ **source** *n* ELECTRON fuente externa *f*; ~ **storage** *n* *AmE* (*cf external store BrE*) COMP&DP almacenamiento externo *m*, memoria externa *f*; ~ **store** *BrE n* (*cf external storage AmE*) COMP&DP almacenamiento externo *m*, memoria externa *f*; ~ **sync** *n* ELECTRON sincronización externa *f*; ~ **synchronization** *n* ELECTRON sincronización externa *f*; ~ **thread** *n* MECH ENG filete externo *m*, hilo exterior *m*, roscado externo *m*; ~-**threaded fastener** *n* MECH ENG *bolts, studs, screws* fijador de rosca externa *m*, pasador de rosca externa *m*, perno de rosca externa *m*, sujetador de rosca externa *m*; ~ **threads** *n pl* MECH ENG filetes exteriores *m pl*, hilos externos *m pl*; ~ **torque** *n* MECH ENG par de fuerzas exterior *m*; ~ **traffic** *n* TRANSP tráfico exterior *m*; ~ **voltage** *n* ELEC, ELEC ENG voltaje exterior *m*; ~-**voltage source** *n* ELEC, ELEC ENG generador de voltaje exterior *m*
externides *n pl* GEOL arco secundario *m*, orogenia secundaria *f*
extinct: ~ **volcano** *n* GEOL volcán apagado *m*, volcán extinto *m*
extinction *n* ELEC ENG, MECH ENG, RAD PHYS *of light* extinción *f*; ~ **potential** *n* ELEC ENG potencial de extinción *m*; ~ **ratio** *n* (*EX*) TELECOM coeficiente de extinción *m*; ~ **zone** *n* GAS zona de extinción *f*
extinguisher *n* AIR TRANSP, CONST, MECH ENG matafuegos *m*, SAFE extinguidor de incendios *m* (*AmL*), matafuegos *m*, THERMO matafuegos *m*; ~ **percussion** *n* AIR TRANSP percusión del extintor *f*; ~ **striker** *n* AIR TRANSP accionador de extintor *m*
extinguishing: ~ **foam** *n* AIR TRANSP, SAFE, THERMO espuma extintora *f*
extra: ~-**hard paper** *n* PAPER, PHOTO papel extrafuerte *m*; ~-**high tension** *n* (*EHT*) TV tensión muy elevada *f* (*MAT*); ~-**high-voltage cable** *n* ELEC, ELEC ENG cable de alta tensión *m*; ~ **labor** *AmE*, ~ **labour** *BrE n* PROD mano de obra complementaria *f*; ~-**smooth file** *n* PROD lima extradulce *f*; ~-**soft paper** *n* PAPER, PHOTO papel extrasuave *m*; ~-**thin sheet glass** *n* C&G vidrio plano extra delgado *m*; ~-**vehicular pressure garment** *n* SPACE presión para actividad extravehicular *f*
extract[1] *n* CHEM, COAL, CONST, GAS extracto *m*
extract[2] *vt* CHEM, COAL, CONST, GAS extraer, sacar
extractable: ~ **sulfur** *AmE*, ~ **sulphur** *BrE n* P&R azufre extraíble *m*
extraction *n* GEN extracción *f*; ~ **fan** *n* LAB extractor *m*, ventilador aspirante *m*; ~ **hood** *n* LAB campana de extracción *f*; ~ **liquid** *n* CHEM TECH líquido de extracción *m*; ~ **process** *n* PETR TECH proceso de separación *m*; ~ **rate** *n* FOOD velocidad de extracción *f*, HYDROL *heat unit* porcentaje de extracción *m*;

~ **thimble** *n* FOOD abrazadera de extracción *f*, LAB cartucho de extracción *m*

extractive: ~ **distillation** *n* FOOD destilación extractiva *f*

extractor *n* GEN extractor *m*; ~ **basket** *n* CHEM TECH canasta del extractor *f*; ~ **fan** *n* MECH ENG ventilador de extracción *m*; ~-**fan system** *n* SAFE sistema extractor *m*

extrados *n* CONST *of an arch* extradós *m*, trasdós *m*

extradynamite *n* MINE dinamita de base explosiva *f*

extragalactic *adj* SPACE extragaláctico

extraneous: ~ **noise** *n* TELECOM ruido parásito *m*

extraordinary: ~ **ray** *n* PHYS rayo extraordinario *m*

extrapolate *vt* QUALITY extrapolar

extrapolation *n* QUALITY extrapolación *f*

extreme: ~ **breadth** *n* WATER TRANSP *ship design* manga en el fuerte *f*; ~ **close-up** *n* CINEMAT, TV primerísimo plano *m*; ~ **depth** *n* WATER TRANSP *shipbuilding* puntal máximo *m*; ~ **draft** *AmE*, ~ **draught** *BrE n* WATER TRANSP *ship design* calado máximo *m*; ~-**overtravel limit switch** *n* PROD interruptor de fin de carrera de sobrecarrera máxima *m*; ~-**pressure additive** *n* PETR TECH aditivo de presión extrema *m*

extremely: ~ **low frequency** *n* (*ELF*) ELEC, ELECTRON, TELECOM frecuencia extremadamente baja *f* (*FEB*)

extrinsic: ~ **conductivity** *n* ELEC ENG conductividad extrínseca *f*; ~-**joint loss** *n* OPT pérdida en el empalme extrínseco *f*, TELECOM pérdida de uniones extrínsecas *f*; ~-**junction loss** *n* OPT, TELECOM pérdida en el empalme extrínseco *f*; ~ **photoconductivity** *n* ELEC fotoconductividad extrínseca *f*; ~ **semiconductor** *n* COMP&DP, ELECTRON, PHYS semiconductor extrínseco *m*

extrudability *n* GEN extrudibilidad *f*

extrude *vi* GEN extrudir

extruded: ~ **cellular plastic** *n* REFRIG plástico celular extruido *m*; ~ **film** *n* P&R película extruida *f*; ~ **insulation** *n* ELEC, ELEC ENG aislamiento extruido *m*; ~ **seal** *n* MECH ENG sello extruido *m*

extruder *n* P&R extrusora *f*, PAPER extrusionadora *f*

extruding: ~ **machine** *n* P&R extrusora *f*, máquina para extruir *f*

extrusion *n* GEN extrusión *f*; ~-**blow molding** *AmE*, ~-**blow moulding** *BrE n* PACK moldeado por soplado y extrusión *m*; ~-**coated paper** *n* PAPER papel revestido por extrusión *m*; ~ **coating** *n* PAPER revestido por extrusión *m*; ~ **die** *n* MECH ENG *for plastics or metal* troquel extrusor *m*, matriz de extrusión *f*, troquel de extrusión *m*, matriz extrusora *f*, P&R molde de extrusión *m*; ~ **die-casting** *n* MECH ENG moldeado por extrusión *m*; ~ **flange** *n* MECH ENG flanja de extrusión *f*, reborde de extrusión *m*; ~ **gun** *n* MECH ENG pistola de extrusión *f*; ~ **head** *n* MECH ENG cabeza de extrusión *f*, cabezal del extrusor

m; ~ **machine** *n* P&R, PACK, PAPER extrusionadora *f*, máquina extrusionadora *f*, máquina para extruir *f*

extrusive: ~ **rock** *n* FUELLESS, GEOL roca extrusiva *f*, roca extrusora *f*

exudation *n* CHEM, P&R exudación *f*

exude *vt* CHEM, P&R exudar

eye[1] *n* C&G ojo *m*, MECH argolla *f*, MECH ENG *of tool* ojo *m*, anilla *f*, bucle *m*, argolla *f*, ojal *m*, METEO *of wind* filo *m*, PROD ojo *m*, WATER TRANSP *for mooring-ring, for anchor* gaza *f*, ojo *m*; ~ **bolt** *n* VEH perno de anilla *m*; ~-**cup** *n* CINEMAT ocular *m*, PHOTO lavaojos *m*; ~ **diagram** *n* TELECOM diagrama del ojo *m*; ~-**drop bottle** *n* C&G botella con gotero *f*; ~ **end** *n* MECH ENG anilla final *f*; ~, **face and neck protection** *n* SAFE protección de ojos, cara y cuello *f*; ~ **filter** *n* SAFE filtro ocular *m*; ~-**headed bolt** *n* PROD perno de anilla *m*; ~ **injury** *n* SAFE lesión ocular *f*, lesión a los ojos *f*; ~-**lens** *n* CINEMAT, INSTR, LAB, OPT, PHOTO, PHYS, PROD, SPACE lente ocular *f*; ~-**protection filter** *n* SAFE filtro de protección ocular *m*; ~-**protection glasses** *n pl* C&G, LAB, INSTR, OPT, PROD, SAFE anteojos de seguridad *m pl* (*AmL*), gafas de seguridad *f pl* (*Esp*), lentes de seguridad *f pl* (*Esp*); ~-**protector** *n* SAFE protección ocular *f*, protector ocular *m*; ~-**rinse bottle** *n* SAFE botella lavaojos *f*; ~-**shade** *n* INSTR, SAFE visera *f*; ~-**shape pattern** *n* TELECOM patrón de la estructura del ojo *m*; ~-**shields** *n pl* INSTR, SAFE visera del ocular *f*; ~-**wash** *n* SAFE lavado de ojos *m*, lavaojos *m*

eye[2]: **at ~ level** *phr* CONST a la altura de los ojos

eyebolt *n* MECH cáncamo *m*, perno de anilla *m*, perno de ojo *m*, *for lifting* perno de argolla *m*, tornillo de ojo *m*, MECH ENG perno de anilla *m*, perno de ojo *m*, perno de argolla *m*, tornillo de ojo *m*, cáncamo *m*, PROD cáncamo de ojo *m*, WATER TRANSP *deck fittings* cáncamo *m*

eyed: ~ **punch** *n* PROD punzón de ojo *m*; ~ **rivet-snap** *n* PROD remache de ojal *m*; ~ **rod** *n* PROD varilla de ojal *f*

eyehandle *n* PROD mango de ojo *m*

eyehook *n* PROD gancho cerrado *m*; ~ **and thimble** *n* PROD gancho cerrado y dedal *m*

eyelet *n* PACK abertura *f*, ojal metálico *m*, resquicio *m*, PRINT ojete *m*, PROD ojal *m*; ~ **hole** *n* WATER TRANSP *ropes, engine* frisa *f*, ollao con guardacabos metálico *m*, roñada *f*

eyepiece *n* GEN lente ocular *f*, ocular *m*, pieza ocular *f*; ~ **focusing knob** *n* INSTR, PHOTO botón de ajuste ocular *m*; ~ **holder** *n* INSTR portaocular *m*; ~ **lens** *n* CINEMAT, INSTR, LAB, OPT, PHOTO, PHYS, PROD, SPACE lente ocular *f*; ~ **micrometer** *n* INSTR, MECH ENG micrómetro de lente ocular *m*

eyeplate *n* WATER TRANSP arraigada de metal *f*, chapa cáncamo *f*

eyesplice *n* WATER TRANSP *rope* ajuste de gaza *m*

F

f *abbr* (*femto*) METR f (*femto*)

F *abbr* GEN (*farad, faraday*) F (*farad, faradio*)

FAA *abbr* (*facility accepted message*) TELECOM capacidad de aceptación de mensajes *f*

fabric *n* GEOL estructura *f*, textura *f*, PAPER tela *f*, PETROL tela *f*, textura *f*, SPACE estructuras de partes soldadas *f pl*, tela *f*, TEXTIL género *m*, tejido *m*, tela *f*; ~ **care** *n* TEXTIL cuidado del tejido *m*; ~ **construction** *n* TEXTIL construcción del tejido *f*; ~ **dust collector** *n* SAFE colector de polvos por bolsas *m*; ~ **element** *n* GEOL elemento de textura *m*; ~ **in rope form** *n* TEXTIL tejido en cuerda *m*; ~**-pasted paper** *n* PAPER papel con tela en el interior *m*; ~ **sample** *n* TEXTIL muestra de tejido *f*, muestra de tela *f*; ~ **sleeve** *n* PAPER manchón de tela plástica encogible *m*; ~ **softener** *n* DETERG, TEXTIL suavizante de telas *m*; ~ **weight** *n* TEXTIL peso del tejido *m*; ~ **width** *n* TEXTIL ancho de la tela *m*

fabricated: ~ **structure** *n* SPACE estructura fabricada *f*

fabricating: ~ **shop** *n* MECH taller de fabricación *m*

fabrication: ~**-related fuel defect** *n* NUCL defecto de fabricación en el combustible *m*; ~ **technique** *n* ELECTRON técnica de fabricación *f*; ~ **yield** *n* ELECTRON rendimiento de fabricación *m*

fabricator *n* CONST ferrallista *m*

Fabry-Pérot: ~ **interferometer** *n* INSTR, PHYS, SPACE interferómetro de Fabry-Pérot *m*

facade *n* CONST fachada *f*

face[1] *n* COAL cara *f*, paramento *m*, CONST frente *m*, *of wall* cara *f*, *of dam* parámetro *m*, GEOM lado *m*, cara *f*, MINE frente de trabajo *m* (*Esp*), cara de trabajo *f* (*AmL*), PHYS *CGS unit* lado *m*, PRINT ojo *m*, estilo *m*, PROD *of anvil* mesa *f*, *of a needle, of furnace, of cupola* ojo *m*, boca *f*; ~**-centered cubic** *n* AmE *see face-centred cubic BrE*; ~**-centered cubic lattice** *n* AmE *see face-centred cubic lattice BrE*; ~**-centered lattice** *n* AmE *see face-centred lattice BrE*; ~**-centred cubic** *n* FCC *BrE* CHEM, CRYSTALL, METALL cúbico de caras centradas *m* (*CCC*); ~**-centred cubic lattice** *n* BrE CHEM, CRYSTALL, METALL red cúbica de caras centradas *f* (*red CCC*); ~**-centred lattice** *n* BrE METALL red cúbica de caras centradas *f*; ~ **chuck** *n* MECH ENG *of lathe* plato al aire *m*; ~ **cleat** *n* COAL plano principal de crucero *m*; ~ **cutter** *n* MECH ENG fresa de refrentar *f*; ~ **dust** *n* PROD *founding* negro de espolvorear *m*; ~ **flange** *n* PROD barreta *f*; ~ **gear** *n* MECH ENG engranaje de dentadura frontal *m*; ~ **grinder** *n* MECH ENG, PROD rectificadora de superficies frontales *f*; ~ **grinding** *n* MECH ENG rectificador de superficies frontales *m*, rectificadora de superficies frontales *f*, PROD rectificado de superficies frontales *m*, rectificadora de superficies frontales *f*; ~ **hole** *n* MINE orificio del frente de arranque *m*; ~ **lathe** *n* MECH ENG plato sin contrapuntos *m*, torno al aire *m*, torno de plato *m*; ~ **milling cutter** *n* MECH ENG fresa de refrentar *f*, fresa frontal *f*, fresa frontal plana *f*; ~**-milling grinder** *n* MECH ENG afiladora de fresas de refrentar *f*, rectificadora de fresas de refrentar *f*; ~ **roll** *n* PAPER ancho de tabla *m*,

ancho del rodillo *m*; ~ **shield** *n* MILIT careta *f*, PROD , SAFE careta *f*, careta de protección *f* , pantalla protectora *f*; ~ **spanner** *n* MECH ENG llave con espigas al frente *f*, llave de tuercas de media luna de tetones *f*; ~ **string** *n* CONST *stair-building* zanca exterior *f*; ~ **and support system** *n* MINE sistema de trabajo y soporte *m*; ~ **visor** *BrE*, ~ **vizor** *AmE n* SAFE visor facial *m*; ~ **wall** *n* CONST muro de revestimiento *m*; ~ **wheel** *n* PROD *emery wheel* muela lapidaria *f*

face[2] *vt* PROD *lathe work* tornear al aire, TEXTIL encarar

faced[1]: ~ **with silk** *adj* TEXTIL revestido de seda

faced[2]: ~ **flange** *n* PROD brida con cara revestida *f*

faceplate *n* ELECTRON, MECH ENG *of lathe* placa frontal *f*, plato universal *m*, TV chapa frontal *f*, panel frontal *m*, WATER TRANSP *of ribbed bulkheads* ala *f*, llanta rigidizadora frontal *f*; ~ **chuck** *n* MECH ENG *of lathe* plato universal al aire *m*; ~ **coupling** *n* MECH ENG acoplamiento de platos *m*; ~ **dog** *n* MECH ENG *of lathe* garra del plato *f*, mordaza del plato *f*; ~ **jaw** *n* MECH ENG *of lathe* mordaza del plato *f*; ~ **mounting** *n* MECH ENG *of lathe* montaje al aire *m*; ~ **starter** *n* ELEC *of motor* arrancador de placa frontal *m*

facer *n* HYDRAUL chapa de envuelta del revestimiento calorífugo *f*

faceted[1] *adj* C&G, METALL, NUCL facetado

faceted[2]: ~ **bubble** *n* NUCL *in fuel pellet* hueco facetado *m*; ~ **expansion** *n* C&G, METALL dilatación facetada *f*, expansión facetada *f*; ~ **growth** *n* METALL dilatación facetada *f*, expansión facetada *f*; ~ **ring** *n* NUCL anillo facetado *m*

facies *n* GEOL, PETROL facies *f pl*

facilities *n pl* AIR TRANSP, PROD instalaciones *f pl*, TV instalaciones *f pl*, recursos *m pl*

facility *n* AIR TRANSP, PROD instalación *f*, TELECOM capacidad *f*; ~ **accepted message** *n* (*FAA*) TELECOM capacidad de aceptación de mensajes *f*; ~ **availability** *n* AIR TRANSP instalaciones disponibles *f pl*; ~ **failure** *n* AIR TRANSP fallo de las instalaciones *m*; ~ **indicator** *n* TELECOM indicador de capacidad *m*; ~ **rejected message** *n* (*FRJ*) TELECOM capacidad de rechazo de mensajes *f*; ~ **reliability** *n* AIR TRANSP fiabilidad de las instalaciones *f*; ~ **request message** *n* (*FAR*) TELECOM capacidad de petición de mensajes *f*

facing *n* CONST revestimiento *m*, *of dam* parámetro *m*, *of slope* cara *f*, GEOL encarado *m*, MECH ENG *machine tools* torneado al aire *m*, TEXTIL vista *f*; ~ **attachment** *n* MECH ENG *machine tools* pieza de refrentar *f*; ~ **block** *n* C&G block para hacer caras *m*; ~ **brick** *n* CONST ladrillo visto *m*; ~ **direction** *n* GEOL dirección de vergencia *f*; ~ **fabric** *n* TEXTIL tela de tapeta *f*; ~ **head** *n* MECH ENG *machine tools* soporte para refrentar *m*; ~ **matter** *n* PRINT página de anuncio opuesta a la de lectura *f*; ~ **tool** *n* MECH ENG herramienta de refrentar *f*; ~ **tool for roughing** *n* MECH ENG herramienta de refrentar para desbastar *f*

FACR *abbr* (*first-article configuration review*) SPACE revisión de la configuración según la cláusula primera *f*

facsimile *n* COMP&DP, PRINT, TELECOM facsímil *m*, telecopia *f*; ~ **compression** *n* COMP&DP, TELECOM compresión facsímil *f*; ~ **interworking function** *n* (*FAXFIF*) TELECOM función entrelazada de facsímil *f*; ~ **machine** *n* COMP&DP, PRINT, TELECOM máquina de facsímil *f*, telecopiadora *f*; ~ **message** *n* COMP&DP, TELECOM mensaje de facsímil *m*, telecopia *f*; ~ **telegraphy** *n* TELECOM telegrafía en facsímil *f*

factor: ~ **analysis** *n* MATH análisis factorial *m*; ~ **of safety** *n* CONST coeficiente de seguridad *m*

factorial[1] *adj* COMP&DP, MATH factorial

factorial[2] *n* COMP&DP, MATH factorial *m*; ~ **design** *n* COMP&DP, MATH diseño factorial *m*; ~ **magnification** *n* INSTR amplificación factorial *f*, aumento factorial *m*, OPT aumento factorial *m*, amplificación factorial *f*

factorization *n* MATH factorización *f*

factorize *vt* MATH factorizar

factory[1]: ~ **-adjusted** *adj* MECH ajustado de fábrica; ~ **-assembled** *adj* PROD montado en la fábrica

factory[2] *n* MECH centro fabril *m*, fábrica *f*, MECH ENG, PROD, SAFE fábrica *f*; ~ **acceptance** *n* MECH *space* verificación de fábrica *f*; ~ **-assembled system** *n* REFRIG sistema frigorífico autónomo *m*; ~ **cullet** *n* C&G cullet propio *m*, fundente propio *m*; ~ **fumes** *n pl* POLL, PROD, SAFE humos de fábrica *m pl*; ~ **inspection** *n* PROD, SAFE inspección de fábrica *f*; ~ **inspector** *n* PROD, SAFE inspector de fábricas *m*; ~ **ship** *n* OCEAN buque factoría *m*, REFRIG barco factoría *m*, WATER TRANSP buque factoría *m*; ~ **siding** *n* RAIL, TRANSP apartadero industrial *m*; ~ **supplies** *n pl* PROD materiales auxiliares *m pl*

factotum: ~ **initial** *n* PRINT inicial recuadrada *f*

facultative: ~ **aerobe** *n* FOOD aerobio facultativo *m*

fade[1]: ~ **-proof** *adj* PRINT resistente a la descoloración; ~ **-resistant** *adj* PRINT resistente a la descoloración

fade[2] *n* CINEMAT, PHOTO, TV desvanecimiento *m*; ~ **-in** *n* CINEMAT, TV aparición gradual de la imagen *f*; ~ **-out** *n* CINEMAT, TV desaparición gradual de la imagen *f*; ~ **shutter** *n* CINEMAT, PHOTO, TV obturador de desvanecimiento *m*; ~ **-to-black** *n* CINEMAT, TV desvanecimiento a negro *m*, fundido a negro *m*; ~ **-to-white** *n* CINEMAT, TV desvanecimiento a blanco *m*, fundido a blanco *m*

fade[3] *vi* CINEMAT desvanecer, COLOUR decolorarse, PHOTO desvanecer a blanco *m*, TEXTIL, desteñir, TV desvanecer

fader *n* GEN atenuador *m*

fading *n* ACOUST atenuación *f*, AGRIC marchitamiento *m*, CINEMAT desvanecimiento *m*, COMP&DP, ELEC, ELECTRON, PETROL atenuación *f*, PHYS atenuación *f*, decoloración *f*, PRINT desvanecimiento *m*, SPACE amortiguamiento *m*, debilitamiento *m*, desvanecimiento de la señal *m*, TELECOM desvanecimiento de la señal *m*, TV atenuación *f*

faecal[1] *adj BrE* HYDROL *sewage*, RECYCL fecal

faecal[2]: ~ **matter** *n BrE* HYDRAUL materia fecal *f*, substancia fecal *f*, HYDROL materias fecales *f pl*, RECYCL materia fecal *f*, materias fecales *f pl*, substancia fecal *f*

faeces *n pl BrE* HYDROL, RECYCL excrementos *m pl*, heces *f pl*

fahl: ~ **ore** *n* MINERAL tetraedrita *f*

fahlunite *n* MINERAL fahlunita *f*

Fahrenheit: ~ **scale** *n* METEO, PHYS escala Fahrenheit *f*

fail[1]: ~ **-safe** *adj* COMP&DP *mechanism* a prueba de fallos, a prueba de fallos leves, sin riesgo de fallo,
ELEC a prueba de averías, a prueba de fallos, a prueba de seguridad, ELEC ENG a prueba de seguridad, a prueba de averías, a prueba de fallos, MECH a prueba de averías, a prueba de seguridad, a prueba de fallos, NUCL a prueba de averías, a prueba de fallos, a prueba de seguridad, PROD a prueba de fallos, a prueba de averías, a prueba de seguridad, SAFE a prueba de seguridad, a prueba de averías, de doble seguridad, a prueba de fallos, SPACE, TRANSP a prueba de averías, a prueba de fallos, a prueba de seguridad; ~ **-soft** *adj* SPACE fallo leve

fail[2]: ~ **-safe** *n* ELEC autoprotección *f*, protección en caso de falla *f*; ~ **-safe design** *n* NUCL diseño de fallo a prueba de fallo *m*, diseño de fallo sin riesgo de fallo *m*; ~ **-safe device** *n* SAFE aditamento de seguridad *m*; ~ **-safe operation** *n* COMP&DP funcionamiento a prueba de fallos *m*, operación sin riesgo de fallo *f*; ~ **-safe work methods** *n pl* PROD métodos de trabajo a prueba de averías *m pl*

fail[3] *vi* CONST colapsar, romper, MECH averiarse, romperse, *injector* descebarse, PROD *injector* descebarse, romperse, averiarse

failed: ~ **circuit** *n* NUCL circuito fallado *m*; ~ **element detection system** *n* NUCL sistema de detección de elementos defectuosos *m*; ~ **fuel-element monitor** *n* NUCL monitor de elementos de combustible defectuosos *m*; ~ **loop** *n* NUCL lazo en condiciones de fallo *m*

failure *n* COMP&DP avería *f*, fallo *m*, CONST fallo *m*, *of a bridge* rotura *f*, CRYSTALL *by breaking* fractura *f*, ELEC *of equipment* interrupción *f*, malfuncionamiento *m*, falla *f*, avería *f*, ELEC ENG *of test* fallo *m*, *of equipment* avería *f*, ELECTRON avería *f*, GAS avería *f*, rotura *f*, falla *f*, MECH malfuncionamiento *m*, fallo *m*, avería *f*, MECH ENG malfuncionamiento *m*, avería *f*, fallo *m*, METALL malfuncionamiento *m*, fallo *m*, rotura *f*, NUCL, PHYS avería *f*, PROD *of injector* descebo *m*, avería *f*, QUALITY falla *f*, fallo *m*, avería *f*, SAFE avería *f*, SPACE *of equipment* insuficiencia *f*, fallo *m*, avería *f*, TELECOM avería *f*, fallo *m*, WATER TRANSP avería *f*; ~ **data card** *n* AIR TRANSP tarjeta de datos de fallos *f*; ~ **indicator** *n* CINEMAT indicador de fallos *m*; ~ **load** *n* COAL carga de rotura *f*; ~ **logging** *n* COMP&DP registro de averías *m*, registro de fallos *m*; ~ **mechanism** *n* QUALITY mecanismo de falla *m*; ~ **moment** *n* MECH momento de rotura *m*; ~ **rate** *n* COMP&DP, ELEC ENG frecuencia de fallos *f*, tasa de fallos *f*, MECH ENG frecuencia de fallos *f*, porcentaje de averías *m*, QUALITY ritmo de defecto *m*, ritmo de falla *m*, SPACE frecuencia de fallos *f*, porcentaje de fallos *m*, tasa de fallos *f*, TELECOM tasa de fallos *f*; ~ **recovery** *n* COMP&DP recuperación de fallos *f*

fairing[1] *adj* VEH fuselado

fairing[2] *n* AIR TRANSP, REFRIG carenado *m*, SPACE carenaje *m*, fuselado *m*, TELECOM cofia *f*, VEH fuselado *m*

fairlead *n* AIR TRANSP guía de entrada *f*, WATER TRANSP *deck equipment* alavante *m*, guiacabos *m*, guía *f*

fairway *n* FUELLESS canal *m*, paso *m*, OCEAN canalizado *m*, paso *m*, WATER TRANSP canal *m*, paso *m*; ~ **navigation** *n* WATER TRANSP navegación por un paso *f*

fake *n* PROD *cast-iron cement* mástique de fundición *m*

fakes *n* COAL arenisca pizarrosa *f*

fall[1] *n* HYDRAUL caída *f*, desnivel *m*, HYDROL *river level* salto de agua *m*, PHYS *steam engine* caída *f*, PROD *of* *drilling spindle, tool holder* descenso *m*, WATER salto *m*; **~ cleanup** *n* MINE bombeo de extracción *m* (*AmL*), bombeo de limpieza *m* (*Esp*); **~ of earth** *n* CONST desnivel del terreno *m*, pendiente del terreno *f*; **~ of ground** *n* CONST desnivel del terreno *m*, pendiente del terreno *f*; **~ in hydraulic head** *n* HYDROL desnivel de la carga hidráulica *m*; **~-off** *n* ELECTRON amortiguación *f*; **~ of potential** *n* ELEC caída de potencial *f*; **~ of rock** *n* CONST caída de piedras *f*, derrumbamiento *m*; **~-safe light metal ladder** *n* SAFE escalera de seguridad de metal ligero *f*; **~ of the tide** *n* OCEAN, WATER TRANSP bajada de la marea *f*; **~ time** *n* ELECTRON intervalo de caída *m*, PHYS tiempo de caída *m*

fall²: **~ in** *vi* CONST derrumbarse; **~ overboard** *vi* WATER TRANSP caer al agua

fallback *n* COMP&DP procedimiento de funcionamiento parcial *m*

falling: **~ edge** *n* ELECTRON flanco de bajada *m*, ángulo de caída *m*; **~ film** *n* DETERG película descendente *f*; **~ gradient** *n* CONST declive *m*, pendiente *f*; **~ rising** *n* ELECTRON flanco de subida *m*; **~ sluice** *n* HYDROL compuerta de inmersión *f*; **~ sphere viscometer** *n* INSTR, LAB viscosímetro de bolas *m* (*Esp*), viscosímetro de esfera de caída *m* (*AmL*); **~ tide** *n* FUELLESS, HYDROL marea descendente *f*, marea menguante *f*, reflujo *m*, OCEAN marea bajante *f*, WATER TRANSP marea descendente *f*, marea menguante *f*, reflujo *m*; **~ water table** *n* GEOPHYS, HYDROL descenso del nivel hidrostático *m*, regresión de la capa freática *f*

fallout *n* AGRIC poso radiactivo *m*, NUCL, PHYS, POLL, RAD PHYS deposición radiactiva *f* (*AmL*), poso radiactivo *m*, precipitación radiactiva *f* (*Esp*); **~ shelter** *n* NUCL refugio nuclear *m*

fallow *n* AGRIC barbecho *m*

false¹ *adj* COMP&DP falso

false²: **~ alarm** *n* TELECOM falsa alarma *f*; **~ alarm probability** *n* TELECOM probabilidad de falsa alarma *f*; **~ back** *n* PRINT lomo falso *m*; **~ body** *n* C&G, PRINT cuerpo falso *m*; **~ call** *n* TELECOM llamada falsa *f*; **~-calling rate** *n* TELECOM proporción de llamadas falsas *f*; **~ ceiling** *n* REFRIG falso techo *m*; **~ cleavage** *n* GEOL exfoliación menor *f*; **~ closure** *n* ELEC ENG cierre en falso *m*; **~ color** *AmE*, **~ colour** *BrE* *n* COLOUR, COMP&DP color falso *m*; **~ core** *n* PROD pieza batida *f*; **~ core molding** *AmE*, **~ core moulding** *BrE* *n* PROD moldeo de piezas batidas *m*; **~ echo** *n* OCEAN eco falso *m*; **~ floor** *n* REFRIG falso suelo *m*; **~ frame** *n* AIR TRANSP marco falso *m*; **~ plain** *n* TEXTIL falso liso *m*; **~ rib** *n* AIR TRANSP costilla falsa *f*, nervadura falsa *f*; **~ signal** *n* ELECTRON, TELECOM señal errónea *f*; **~ spar** *n* AIR TRANSP larguero falso *m*; **~ switching** *n* ELEC conmutador falso *m*; **~ topaz** *n* MINERAL cuarzocitrino *m*, falso topacio *m*; **~-to-true transition** *n* PROD transición de falso a verdadero *f*; **~ tripping** *n* ELEC disparo falso *m*; **~ warning** *n* AIR TRANSP aviso falso *m*

falsework *n* CONST *of vault* encofrado *m*

famatinite *n* MINERAL famatinita *f*

Famennian *adj* GEOL Fameniese

family: **~ of elements** *n* RAD PHYS familia de elementos *f*; **~ of particles** *n* PART PHYS familia de partículas *f*

fan¹ *n* GEN abanico *m*, ventilador *m*; **~-assisted air heater** *n* HEAT ENG convector de aire caliente con ventilador *m*, convector de aire con abanico *m*, SAFE convector de aire caliente con abanico *m*, convector de aire con abanico *m*; **~ beam** *n* ELECTRON haz en abanico *m*; **~ belt** *n* AUTO, MECH, VEH correa del ventilador *f*; **~ blade** *n* AUTO aspa del ventilador *f*, pala del ventilador *f*, paleta del ventilador *f*, MECH, REFRIG aspa del ventilador *f*, paleta del ventilador *f*, THERMO aspa del ventilador *f*, TRANSP, VEH aspa del ventilador *f*, paleta del ventilador *f*; **~ blower** *n* MECH ENG ventilador centrífugo *m*; **~ brake** *n* MECH ENG freno del ventilador *m*; **~ coil unit** *n* REFRIG ventiloconvector *m*; **~ cooling** *n* REFRIG, THERMO enfriamiento por ventilador *m*, refrigeración por ventilación *f*; **~ cut** *n* MINE excavación de aireación *f*, socavación *f*; **~ drift** *n* COAL, MINE galería de ventilación *f*; **~ efficiency** *n* HEAT ENG rendimiento del ventilador *m*; **~ efficiency curve** *n* HEAT ENG curva de rendimiento del ventilador *f*; **~ engine** *n* TRANSP motor de ventilador *m*; **~ guard** *n* REFRIG protector del ventilador *m*; **~ heater** *n* HEAT calefactor de ventilador *m*, calentador de ventilador *m*, ventilocalefactor *m*, MECH ENG, THERMO calefactor de ventilador *m*, calentador de ventilador *m*; **~-in** *n* COMP&DP entrada máxima *f*, número de señales que entran *m*, ELEC ENG *circuits* conductores de entrada *m pl*; **~-in factor** *n* ELEC ENG factor de entrada de elementos *m*; **~ jet engine** *n* THERMO, TRANSP reactor de doble flujo *m*; **~ jet turbine** *n* AIR TRANSP, THERMO, TRANSP turbina de doble chorro *f*; **~ marker beacon** *n* AIR TRANSP, WATER TRANSP radiobaliza de abanico *f*, radiobaliza de haz de abanico *f*; **~ motor** *n* REFRIG motor del ventilador *m*, TRANSP ventilador del motor *m*; **~-out** *n* COMP&DP número de señales que salen *m*, salida máxima *f*, ELEC ENG conductores de salida *m pl*; **~-powered burner** *n* MECH ENG quemador de ventilador *m*; **~ pulley** *n* AUTO, VEH polea de arrastre del ventilador *f*, polea del ventilador *f*; **~ pump** *n* PAPER bomba de cabeza de máquina *f*; **~ shroud** *n* AUTO cubierta del ventilador *f*; **~ station** *n* CONST instalación de ventilación *f*; **~ wheel** *n* MECH ENG volante del ventilador *m*, SAFE rotor de ventilador *m*

fan²: **~ cool** *vt* REFRIG, THERMO enfriar por ventilador, refrigerar con ventilador

fancy: **~ box** *n* PACK caja de adorno *f*, caja de fantasía *f*, caja de lujo *f*; **~ frame** *n* PRINT marco adornado *m*; **~ type** *n* PRINT tipo adornado *m*; **~ woven fabric** *n* TEXTIL tejido de calada de fantasía *m*; **~-woven-fabrics market** *n* TEXTIL mercado para los tejidos de calada de fantasía *m*; **~ yarn** *n* TEXTIL hilado de fantasía *m*

faneritic *adj* GEOL, PETROL fanerítico

fanfold *n* PRINT pliegue en abanico *m*, PROD plegado en acordeón *m*; **~ paper** *n* COMP&DP papel continuo doblado *m* (*AmL*), papel membretado fanfold *m* (*AmL*), papel plegado en acordeón *m* (*Esp*); **~ stationery** *n* COMP&DP papel continuo doblado *m* (*AmL*), papel membretado fanfold *m* (*AmL*), papel plegado en acordeón *m* (*Esp*)

fang¹ *n* MECH ENG espiga *f*, MINE conducto de ventilación *m*; **~ bolt** *n* CONST perno arponado *m*

fang² *vt* HYDRAUL cebar

fanned: **~-beam aerial** *n* *BrE* TV antena de haz en abanico *f*; **~-beam antenna** *AmE* see *fanned-beam aerial BrE*; **~ cable** *n* ELEC ENG cable en abanico *m*; **~ circulation** *n* HEAT circulación ventilada *f*

fanning: ~ **mill** n AGRIC separador de semillas m; ~ **out** n PROD salidas en abanico f pl

fantail n CONST carpentry cola de milano f, WATER TRANSP boat building abanico m, bovedilla f; ~ **joint** n CONST empalme de cola de milano m

FAQ abbr (frequently asked questions) COMP&DP FAQ (preguntas más frecuentes)

far: ~~**end block error** n (FEBE) TELECOM error de bloqueo distante m; ~~**field analysis** n OPT, TELECOM análisis en campo lejano m; ~~**field diffraction pattern** n OPT, TELECOM diagrama de difracción de campo lejano m, figura de difracción de campo lejano f; ~~**field intensity** n SPACE, TELECOM intensidad de campo distante f, intensidad de campo lejano f; ~~**field pattern** n OPT, TELECOM diagrama de campo lejano m; ~~**field radiation pattern** n OPT, TELECOM diagrama de radiación de campo lejano m; ~~**field region** n OPT, TELECOM región de campo lejano f; ~ **infrared** n PHYS, RAD PHYS infrarrojo lejano m; ~ **range** n SPACE distancia lejana f, espacio distante m, espacio lejano m; ~ **ultraviolet** n PHYS, RAD PHYS ultravioleta lejano m

FAR abbr (facility request message) TELECOM capacidad de petición de mensajes f

farad n (F) ELEC, ELEC ENG, ELECTRON, METR, NUCL, PHYS farad m (F), faradio m (F)

faraday n (F) ELEC, ELEC ENG, ELECTRON, METR, NUCL, PHYS farad m, (F), faradio m (F)

Faraday: ~ **cage** n ELEC, ELEC ENG, PHYS jaula de Faraday f, pantalla electrostática f; ~ **circulator** n ELEC ENG, ELECTRON, PHYS circulante Faraday m; ~ **constant** n PHYS constante de Faraday f; ~ **cylinder** n PHYS cilindro de Faraday m; ~ **dark-space** n ELECTRON, PHYS espacio oscuro de Faraday m; ~**'s disc** BrE, ~**'s disk** n AmE PHYS disco de Faraday m; ~ **effect** n ELEC, ELEC ENG, ELECTRON, PHYS efecto Faraday m; ~ **ice pail** n ELEC cilindro de Faraday m; ~**'s laws** n pl ELEC, ELEC ENG, ELECTRON, NUCL, PHYS leyes de Faraday f pl; ~ **rotation** n SPACE abrazadera f; ~ **screen** n ELEC, ELEC ENG, NUCL, PHYS pantalla de Faraday f; ~ **shield** n ELEC, ELEC ENG, NUCL, PHYS pantalla electrostática f

faredice vt COAL cerner, cribar, faradizar, seleccionar, tamizar

farelite n MINERAL farelita f

farinaceous adj FOOD farináceo, harinoso

farinograph n FOOD farinógrafo m

farm¹ n AGRIC explotación agrícola f, granja f; ~ **animal** n AGRIC animal de trabajo m; ~ **of economic size** n AGRIC explotación agrícola económicamente viable f; ~ **gate price** n AGRIC precio a nivel de explotación agrícola m; ~~**hand** n AGRIC bracero m, peón m; ~ **implement** n AGRIC apero m; ~ **income** n AGRIC ingresos agrícolas m pl; ~ **machinery** n AGRIC, MECH maquinaria agrícola f; ~ **management** n AGRIC administración agrícola f; ~ **mechanization** n AGRIC, MECH mecanización agrícola f; ~ **operations** n pl AGRIC tareas agrícolas f pl; ~ **price** n AGRIC precio al productor m

farm²: ~ **out** vt AGRIC arrendar

farmer n AGRIC agricultor m, granjero m, productor agrícola m

Farmer: ~**'s reducer** n PHOTO rebajador de Farmer m

farming n AGRIC agricultura f, cultivo m; ~ **demonstration** n AGRIC demostración agrícola f; ~~**out** n PETR TECH cesión de intereses f; ~ **plan** n

AGRIC plan de explotación agrícola m; ~ **sector** n AGRIC agro m, sector agrícola m; ~ **system** n AGRIC sistema de explotación agrícola m; ~ **systems research** n AGRIC investigación sobre sistemas de producción agrícola f; ~ **technique** n AGRIC técnica de cultivos f; ~ **unit** n AGRIC unidad agrícola f

farmstead n AGRIC cortijo m

farnesol n CHEM farnesol m

farrow vt AGRIC parir cerdos

FAS abbr TELECOM (flexible access switch) conmutador de acceso flexible m (frame alignment signal), señal de alineación de trama f, WATER TRANSP (free alongside ship) FAS (franco al costado del buque)

fascia n CONST facia f, imposta f; ~ **board** n CONST tabla de frontis f

fashioning: ~ **mechanism** n TEXTIL mecanismo de menguado m

fassaite n MINERAL fassaita f

fast¹ adj CHEM colour, COLOUR no desteñible, TEXTIL no desteñible, sólido; ~~**acting** adj ELEC ENG relay rápido, fuse de acción rápida, MECH ENG, PROD de acción rápida; ~~**changing** adj ELECTRON engine instantáneo; ~~**to-light** adj OPT, PRINT fotoestable

fast²: ~~**acting trip** n MECH ENG desenganche de acción rápida m, disyuntor de acción rápida m, gatillo de acción rápida m; ~~**acting trip valve** n NUCL válvula de disparo de accionamiento rápido f; ~~**beam experiment** n RAD PHYS experimento con haz rápido m; ~ **breathing** n OCEAN respiración agitada f; ~~**breeder reactor** n AGRIC incubador rápido m, NUCL, PHYS reactor reproductor rápido m; ~~**breeder reactor technology** n NUCL, PHYS tecnología de reactores reproductores rápidos f; ~ **burst** n NUCL fallo súbito m; ~ **circuit switch** n TELECOM conmutador rápido de circuitos m; ~ **color** AmE, ~ **colour** BrE n PRINT color sólido m; ~ **curing** n P&R curado rápido m, endurecimiento rápido m, vulcanización rápida f; ~ **developer** n PHOTO revelador rápido m; ~ **feed** n MECH ENG avance rápido m; ~ **film** n AmE CINEMAT película rápida f; ~~**fission factor** n NUCL, PART PHYS, PHYS factor de fisión rápida m; ~ **forward** n CINEMAT, TV avance rápido m; ~ **Fourier transform** n (FFT) COMP&DP, ELECTRON transformada rápida de Fourier f (TRF); ~ **frequency hopping** n ELECTRON trayecto rápido de frecuencia m; ~ **frequency-shift keying** n TELECOM transmisión rápida por desplazamiento de frecuencia f; ~ **fusion-fission assembly at zero thermal power** n NUCL conjunto de fusión-fisión rápida a potencia térmica cero m; ~ **head** n PROD cabezal fijo m; ~ **headstock** n PROD punto fijo m; ~ **insertion** n NUCL inserción rápida f; ~ **logic** n ELECTRON circuito lógico de alta velocidad m, circuito lógico rápido m; ~ **and loose pulleys** n pl PROD poleas locas y fijas f pl; ~ **motion** n TV movimiento rápido m; ~ **neutron** n NUCL, PART PHYS, PHYS neutrón rápido m; ~ **packet switch** n (FPS) TELECOM conmutador rápido de paquetes m; ~ **particle** n NUCL, PART PHYS, PHYS partícula rápida f; ~ **playback** n TV lectura rápida f; ~ **pulley** n PROD polea fija f; ~ **pulp** n PAPER pasta poco refinada f, pulpa poco refinada f; ~ **reactor** n NUCL, PART PHYS, PHYS reactor rápido m; ~~**recovery diode** n ELECTRON diodo de recuperación rápida m; ~~**reservation protocol** n (FRP) TELECOM protocolo de reserva rápida m; ~ **reverse-recovery rectifier** n ELEC ENG rectificador de rápida recuperación m; ~~**rise pulse** n

ELECTRON impulso de elevación rápida *m*, pulso de subida *m*; **~-rise signal** *n* ELECTRON señal de subida rápida *f*; **~-slaving** *n* AIR TRANSP atrapado rápido *m*; **~-slaving relay** *n* AIR TRANSP relé esclavo rápido *m*; **~ stock** *n* CINEMAT película rápida *f*; **~ sweep** *n* ELECTRON exploración rápida *f*; **~-switching power rectifier** *n* ELEC ENG rectificador de potencia de conmutación rápida *m*; **~-switching power transistor** *n* ELECTRON transistor de potencia de conmutación *m*; **~ train** *n* RAIL tren rápido *m*; **~-tuned filter** *n* ELECTRON filtro de sintonización rápida *m*; **~-tuned oscillator** *n* ELECTRON oscilador de sintonización rápida *m*; **~ update** *n* COMP&DP, TELECOM actualización rápida *f*; **~-update request** *n* TELECOM petición de actualización rápida *f*; **~ wave** *n* ELEC ENG, ELECTRON, WAVE PHYS onda rápida *f*; **~-wave tube** *n* ELEC ENG, ELECTRON tubo de onda rápida *m*; **~ wheel** *n* PROD rueda fija *f*

fast[3]: **~ forward** *vt* CINEMAT, TV avanzar con rapidez

fasten *vt* MECH asegurar, atar, fijar, trabar, TEXTIL abrochar

fastener *n* MECH, MECH ENG, PROD sujetador *m*, *rivet* remache *m*, *press stud* fiador *m*, *of box, window* cierre *m*, *clasp* abrazadera *f*, *of door* pasador *m*, cerrojo *m*, perno *m*, SPACE brida *f*

fastening *n* CONST *strap, stirrup*, MECH, MECH ENG, PROD fijación *f*, sujeción *f*, unión *f*, TEXTIL cierre *m*, corchete *m*

fastness *n* TEXTIL solidez *f*; **~ to light** *n* TEXTIL solidez a la luz *f*; **~ to perspiration** *n* TEXTIL solidez a la transpiración *f*; **~ to rubbing** *n* TEXTIL solidez al roce *f*; **~ to washing** *n* TEXTIL solidez al lavado *f*

fat *n* FOOD grasa *f*; **~ cattle** *n* AGRIC ganado gordo *m*; **~ clay** *n* PETR TECH arcilla muy plástica *f*; **~ coal** *n* COAL, MINE carbón graso *m*, hulla grasa *f*; **~ concrete** *n* CONST concreto con alta dosificación de cemento *m* (*AmL*), hormigón con alta dosificación de cemento *m* (*Esp*); **~ edge** *n* P&R borde craso *m*, exceso de pintura en el borde *m*; **~ mortar** *n* CONST mortero de cal grasa *m*; **~ test** *n* AGRIC prueba para determinar contenido graso *f*

fatal: **~ accident** *n* SAFE accidente fatal *m*; **~ error** *n* COMP&DP error fatal *m*

fate: **~ of oil** *n* MAR POLL suerte corrida por el derrame *f*

father: **~ file** *n* COMP&DP archivo original *m*, archivo padre *m*

fathom *n* METR, OCEAN, WATER TRANSP braza *f*

fatigue *n* AIR TRANSP, CRYSTALL, MECH, METALL fatiga *f*, P&R fatiga *f*, resistencia a largo plazo *f*; **~ crack** *n* METALL grieta por fatiga *f*, resquebrajadura por fatiga *f*, SPACE fisura por fatiga *f*; **~ failure** *n* METALL fractura por fatiga *f*; **~ fracture** *n* CRYSTALL fractura por fatiga *f*; **~ hardening** *n* METALL endurecimiento por fatiga *m*; **~ inspection** *n* AIR TRANSP inspección de fatiga *f*; **~ precrack** *n* NUCL grieta incipiente por fatiga *f*; **~ properties** *n pl* MECH características de fatiga *f pl*; **~ softening** *n* METALL reblandecimiento por fatiga *m*; **~ strength** *n* AIR TRANSP, CRYSTALL, MECH, METALL, P&R resistencia a la fatiga *f*, SPACE *spacecraft* carga de fatiga *f*; **~ test** *n* AIR TRANSP, CRYSTALL, MECH, METALL, P&R prueba de fatiga *f*

fatten *vt* AGRIC engordar

fattening *n* AGRIC engorde *m*; **~ ground** *n* OCEAN territorio de engorde *m*

fatty: **~ acid** *n* AGRIC, CHEM, DETERG, FOOD ácido graso *m*; **~ acid glyceride** *n* CHEM, FOOD glicérido de ácido graso *m*;, **~ alcohol** *n* CHEM, DETERG alcohol graso *m*; **~ amine** *n* CHEM, DETERG amina grasa *f*; **~ clay** *n* C&G barro grasoso *m*

faucet *n* (*cf tap BrE*) CONST *cock* espita *f*, grifo *m*, LAB *measuring* llave de paso *f*, válvula de cierre *f*, llave *f*, MECH grifo *m* (*AmL*), extremo ensanchado *m* (*Esp*), boquilla *f* (*AmL*), canilla *f* (*AmL*); **~ joint** *n* CONST *in pipes* junta tipo enchufe *f*; **~ key** *n* CONST llave de la canilla *f*, llave de la espita *f*, llave del grifo *f*

faujasite *n* MINERAL faujasita *f*

fault[1]: **~-tolerant** *adj* COMP&DP insensible a fallos, tolerante a fallos (*AmL*), ELEC ENG tolerante de defecto

fault[2] *n* GEN avería *f*; **~ basin** *n* GEOL cuenca de hundimiento tectónico *f*, PETR TECH cuenca fallada *f*; **~ boundary** *n* GEOL límite de falla *m*; **~ breccia** *n* HYDRAUL brecha de fricción *f*; **~ clearance** *n* TELECOM reparación de avería *f*; **~ code chart** *n* PROD tabla de código de fallas *f*; **~ condition** *n* PROD condición de falla *f*; **~ conglomerate** *n* MINE conglomerado de fallas *m*; **~ detection** *n* COMP&DP detección de averías *f*, ELEC, GAS, TELECOM detección de averías *f*, detección de fallas *f* (*AmL*), detección de fallo *f* (*Esp*); **~ detector** *n* ELEC detector de fallas *m*; **~ diagnosis** *n* COMP&DP diagnosis de averías *f*, diagnosis de fallos *f*; **~ display** *n* TELECOM indicador de averías *m*; **~ drag** *n* GEOL arrastre de falla *m*; **~-finding** *n* ELEC ENG localización de averías *f*; **~-finding table** *n* MECH ENG tabla de localización de averías *f*, tabla de localización de fallos *f*; **~ gouge** *n* GEOL pulverización por falla *f*; **~-identification code chart** *n* PROD tabla de código de identificación de fallas *m*; **~ indicator** *n* PROD indicador de averías *m*; **~ light** *n* PROD lámpara de fallas *f*; **~ maintenance** *n* TELECOM reparación de avería *f*; **~ plane** *n* GEOL plano de falla *m*; **~-reception center** *n* AmE, **~-reception centre** *BrE n* (*FRC*) TELECOM centro de recepción de averías *m*; **~ recovery** *n* PROD recuperación de averías *f*; **~ reporting** *n* PROD aviso de averías *m*; **~ resistance** *n* ELEC ENG resistencia de aislamiento *f*; **~ spring** *n* WATER manantial de falla *m*; **~ time** *n* COMP&DP intervalo de inactividad por avería *m*, tiempo de inactividad por avería *m*, tiempo del fallo *m*; **~ tolerance** *n* ELEC ENG tolerancia de fallo *f*; **~-tolerant system** *n* COMP&DP sistema insensible a fallos *m* (*Esp*), sistema tolerante a fallos *m* (*AmL*); **~ trace** *n* GEOL línea de falla *f*; **~ trap** *n* GEOL dislocación de falla *f*, PETR TECH dislocación de falla *f*, trampa por falla *f*; **~ voltage circuit breaker** *n* ELEC cortocircuito de tensión de la falla *m*

fault[3] **~-free** *phr* CHEM, FOOD, HYDROL, PETR TECH anhidro, POLL anhidro, libre de humedad, sin humedad, TEXTIL sin agua, WATER anhidro

faultless *adj* TEXTIL sin defectos

faulty[1] *adj* CINEMAT averiado, ELEC averiado, defectuoso, imperfecto, ELEC ENG imperfecto, MECH, MECH ENG, PACK, PROD, QUALITY averiado, defectuoso, imperfecto, TELECOM averiado, TEXTIL defectuoso

faulty[2]: **~ call** *n* TELECOM llamada errónea *f*; **~ connection** *n* SAFE conexión mal hecha *f*, TELECOM conexión errónea *f*; **~ insulation** *n* ELEC, ELEC ENG aislación defectuosa *f*; **~ line** *n* ELEC, ELEC ENG línea defectuosa *f*; **~ operation** *n* MECH ENG operación defectuosa *f*, operación errónea *f*, operación incorrecta *f*; ~-**sheet ejection signal** *n* PACK señal para extraer la hoja defectuosa *f*

faunal: ~ **province** *n* GEOL ámbito faunal *m*

faunistic: ~ **province** *n* GEOL ámbito faunístico *m*

fauserite *n* MINERAL fauserita *f*

fax *vt* COMP&DP, PRINT, TELECOM enviar por fax, faxear

FAXFIF *abbr* (*facsimile interworking function*) TELECOM función entrelazada de facsímil *f*

fayalite *n* MINERAL fayalita *f*

FCC[1] *abbr* (*face-centered cubic AmE, face-centred cubic BrE*) CHEM, CRYSTALL, METALL CCC (*cúbico de caras centradas*)

FCC[2]: ~-**based structure** *n* CHEM, CRYSTALL estructura formada por redes cúbicas de caras centradas *f*; ~ **lattice** *n* (*face-centered cubic lattice AmE, face-centred cubic lattice BrE*) CHEM, CRYSTALL, METALL red CCC *f* (*red cúbica de caras centradas*)

FDDI *abbr* (*fiber-distributed data interface AmE, fibre-distributed data interface BrE*) TELECOM interfase de datos distribuidos por fibra *f*

FDHM *abbr* (*full-duration half maximum*) OPT duración completa a mitad de altura *f*, TELECOM duración total mitad del máximo *f*

FDM *abbr* (*frequency-division multiplexing*) COMP&DP, ELECTRON, PHYS, TELECOM MDF (*multiplexación por división de frecuencias, multiplexado por división de frecuencias*)

FDMA *abbr* (*frequency-division multiple access*) SPACE, TELECOM AMDF (*acceso múltiple por división de frecuencias*)

FDR *abbr* (*final design review*) SPACE revisión final del diseño *f*

FDS: ~ **system** *n* (*frequency-division switching system*) TELECOM sistema de conmutación por división de frecuencias *m*

FDX *abbr* (*full duplex*) COMP&DP FDX (*sistema de transmisión birideccional*)

FE *abbr* (*functional entity*) TELECOM entidad funcional *f*

Fe *abbr* (*iron*) CHEM, METALL Fe (*hierro*)

FEA *abbr* (*functional entity action*) TELECOM acción de entidad funcional *f*

feasibility *n* MINE posibilidad de realización *f*, viabilidad *f*; ~ **study** *n* COMP&DP estudio de factibilidad *m*, estudio de viabilidad *m*, CONST estudio de factibilidad *m*

feather[1] *n* C&G pluma *f*, CONST *slip of wood* cuña *f*, *shaft-key* chaveta coorediza *f*, *tongue on edge of board* lengüeta *f*, barbilla *f*, canto *m*, MECH ENG *tongue on edge of board* canto *m*, chaveta corrediza *f*, cuña *f*, lengüeta *f*, barbilla *f*, PROD *shaft-key* chaveta corrediza *f*, *tongue on edge of board* barbilla *f*, lengüeta *f*, *slip of wood* cuña *f*, canto *m*; ~ **edge** *n* CONST canto en bisel *m*; ~ **edge file** *n* PROD lima de corte *f*; ~-**edged brick** *n* CONST ladrillo de canto de bisel *m*, ladrillo de cuña *m*; ~-**edged file** *n* PROD lima de cantos biselados *f*; ~ **joint** *n* CONST junta de falsa espiga *f*; ~ **meal** *n* AGRIC harina de plumas *f*; ~-**necked bolt** *n* PROD perno con cabeza en forma de saliente cuadrado *m*; ~ **ore** *n* MINERAL jamesonita sin hierro *f*, plumosita *f*; ~ **tongue** *n* CONST lengüeta *f*

feather[2] *vi* PRINT expandirse

feathered[1] *adj* AIR TRANSP *propeller* abanderado

feathered[2]: ~ **joint** *n* MECH ENG junta en bisel *f*; ~ **pitch** *n* AIR TRANSP *of propeller* paso abanderado *m*

feathering *n* AIR TRANSP *of propeller* abanderamiento

m, puesta en bandera *f*; ~ **angle** *n* AIR TRANSP ángulo de abanderamiento *m*, ángulo de puesta en bandera *m*; ~ **effect** *n* AIR TRANSP efecto de abanderamiento *m*

feature *n* GEN característica *f*; ~ **extraction** *n* COMP&DP extracción de características *f*

FEBE *abbr* (*far-end block error*) TELECOM error de bloqueo distante *m*

FEC *abbr* (*forward error correction*) COMP&DP, TELECOM corrección anticipada de errores *f* (*AmL*), corrección de errores hacia adelante *f* (*Esp*)

fecal[1] *AmE see* **faecal** *BrE*

feces *AmE see* **faeces** *BrE*

fed: ~-**in winding** *n* ELEC devanado de alimentación *m*

Fedorov: ~ **stage** *n* CRYSTALL platina de Fedorov *f*, platina universal *f*

feed[1] *n* AGRIC alimento *m*, distribuidor *m*, AUTO alimentación *f*, COAL caudal *m*, penetración por revolución del trépano *f*, COMP&DP, ELEC alimentación *f*, ELEC ENG *power supply* alimentación *f*, corriente de alimentación *f*, corriente de suministro eléctrico *f*, HYDRAUL caudal de aire *m*, alimentación *f*, caudal de agua *m*, MECH alimentación *f*, avance *m*, P&R carga *f*, alimento *m*, PETR TECH alimentación *f*, PROD alimentación *f*, *motion carrying work towards a tool* presión *f*, avance *m*, TV alimentación *f*, WATER *at canal-lock* esclusada *f*; ~ **balance** *n* AGRIC balance forrajero *m*; ~ **and bleed** *n* NUCL modo de aporte y purga *m*; ~ **box** *n* MECH ENG, PAPER, PROD caja de alimentación *f*, caja de avances *f*; ~ **bunk** *n* AGRIC comedero *m*; ~ **bush** *n* MECH ENG *injection mould* anillo de fondo de alimentación *m*, buje de alimentación *m*, casquillo de alimentación *m*, manguito de alimentación *m*; ~ **cable** *n* ELEC, ELEC ENG cable alimentador *m*, cable de alimentación *m*, conductor alimentador *m*, MECH ENG cable de alimentación *m*; ~ **chart** *n* MECH ENG tabla de avances *f*; ~ **circuit** *n* ELEC, ELEC ENG circuito de alimentación *m*; ~ **claw** *n* CINEMAT garfio de alimentación *m*; ~ **cock** *n* PROD válvula de alimentación *f*; ~ **conversion ratio** *n* AGRIC índice de aprovechamiento del forraje *m*; ~ **conveyor** *n* AGRIC acarreador *m*; ~ **crop** *n* AGRIC cultivo que se destina a forraje *m*; ~-**forward** *n* PROD avance *m*; ~-**forward AGC** *n* TELECOM alimentación hacia delante AGC *f*; ~-**forward control** *n* COMP&DP control por alimentación anticipada *m*, control por alimentación hacia adelante *m* (*Esp*); ~ **gear** *n* PROD engranaje de avance *m*, mecanismo de alimentación *m*; ~ **grain** *n* AGRIC cereal forrajero *m*; ~ **guides** *n pl* PRINT guías de entrada *f pl*; ~ **head** *n* PROD *founding* bebedero de colada *m*; ~ **hole** *n* COMP&DP ranura de alimentación *f*; ~ **hopper** *n* CONST, MECH, PACK, PROD almacén de alimentación *m*, depósito de alimentación *m*, tolva de alimentación *f*; ~-**hose union** *n* PETR TECH unión de la manguera de alimentación *f*; ~ **limiter** *n* MECH ENG limitador de alimentación *m*, limitador de avance *m*; ~ **magazine** *n* CINEMAT chasis de alimentación *m*, MECH ENG depósito de alimentación *m*; ~ **mashes** *n pl* AGRIC mezclas alimentarias *f pl*; ~ **mill** *n* AGRIC molino para hacer pienso *m*; ~ **motion** *n* PROD movimiento de avance *m*; ~ **pipe** *n* HYDRAUL tubo abductor *m*, tubo alimentador *m*, PROD tubo de alimentación *m*, *for supplying water to boiler* tubería de alimentación *f*; ~ **plate** *n* MECH ENG *injection mould* placa alimentadora *f*, plato alimentador *m*; ~ **pump** *n* HEAT bomba de alimentación *f*;

~ **rack** *n* MECH ENG *machine tools* cremallera de alimentación *f*, PROD *lubricating rack* rampa de engrase *f*; ~ **range** *n* MECH ENG alcance de alimentación *m*, gama de alimentación *f*, rango de alimentación *m*; ~ **rate** *n* COAL velocidad de alimentación *f*, velocidad de avance *f*; ~ **reel** *n* CINEMAT bobina de alimentación *f*; ~~**reversing gear** *n* MECH ENG mecanismo inversor del avance *m*; ~ **roll** *n* FOOD, MECH ENG rodillo alimentador *m*, rodillo de avance *m*, PAPER rodillo de alimentación *m*; ~ **roller** *n* FOOD rodillo de alimentación *m*, MECH ENG cilindro alimentador *m*, rodillo alimentador *m*, rodillo de avance *m*; ~ **runner** *n* P&R canal de colada de la carga *m*; ~ **screw** *n* MECH ENG *of lathe* husillo *m*, husillo de avance *m*, tornillo de avance *m*; ~ **shaft** *n* MECH ENG *of lathe* husillo principal del carro *m*; ~ **sleeve** *n* MECH ENG manguito de alimentación *m*, manguito de avance *m*; ~ **spool** *n* CINEMAT bobina de alimentación *f*; ~ **sprocket** *n* CINEMAT rueda dentada de alimentación *f*; ~ **system** *n* SPACE sistema de alimentación *m*; ~ **table** *n* PRINT mesa de alimentación *f*; ~ **tank** *n* PETR TECH tanque de suministro *m*, PROD tanque de alimentación *m*; ~ **unit** *n* AGRIC unidad forrajera *f*; ~ **valve** *n* PETR TECH válvula de alimentación *f*; ~ **waveguide** *n* ELEC, ELEC ENG, WAVE PHYS guía de ondas de alimentación *f*

feed[2] *vt* CINEMAT, COMP&DP alimentar, MECH alimentar, avanzar, *founding* bombear, MECH ENG *founding* bombear, alimentar, avanzar, PROD alimentar, avanzar, *founding* bombear, TV alimentar

feedback *n* GEN regeneración *f*, retroalimentación *f*; ~ **AGC** *n* TELECOM realimentación AGC *f*; ~ **amplifier** *n* ELECTRON amplificador de retroacción *m*, amplificador realimentado *m*; ~ **circuit** *n* TV circuito de realimentación *m*, circuito de retroacción *m*; ~ **coil** *n* ELEC, ELEC ENG bobina de realimentación *f*; ~ **control** *n* ELEC ENG control por realimentación *m*, regulación por contrarreacción *f*, ELECTRON control en lazo cerrado *m*; ~ **control system** *n* ELEC ENG, ELECTRON sistema de regulación por contrarreacción *m*; ~ **current** *n* ELEC ENG, ELECTRON corriente de realimentación *f*; ~ **loop** *n* ELECTRON circuito cerrado de realimentación *m*, lazo cerrado *m*, lazo de realimentación *m*, MECH circuito de realimentación *m*, PROD bucle de realimentación *m*; ~ **oscillator** *n* ELECTRON oscilador de realimentación *m*; ~ **ratio** *n* ELECTRON porcentaje de realimentación *m*; ~ **resistor** *n* ELEC ENG resistencia de realimentación *f*, resistencia de retropulsión *f*; ~ **signal** *n* ELECTRON señal de realimentación *f*, PROD señal de retorno *f*; ~ **stabilization** *n* ELECTRON estabilización por realimentación *f*; ~ **voltage** *n* ELEC ENG tensión de realimentación *f*; ~ **winding** *n* ELEC ENG devanado de realimentación *m*

feedboard *n* PRINT tablero de alimentación *m*, tablero marcador *m*

feeder *n* AGRIC ganado de engorde *m*, C&G alimentador *m*, chorreador *m*, ELEC *supply network* alimentador *m*, cable de alimentación *m*, circuito de alimentación *m*, conductor de alimentación *m*, ELEC ENG línea de alimentación *f*, GEOL alimentador *m*, ramal *m*, vía de aporte *f*, ramificación *f*, HYDRAUL canal de carga *m*, canal de llegada *m*, canal de trabajo *m*, MECH ENG, PACK, PRINT alimentador *m*, PROD aparato alimentador *m*, *shrinkage head* mazarota *f*, SPACE cable alimentador *m*, alimentador *m*, línea de

alimentación *f*, TEXTIL alimentador *m*; ~ **airline** *n* AIR TRANSP línea aérea secundaria *f*; ~ **bar** *n* ELEC *supply* barra de alimentación *f*; ~ **cable** *n* COMP&DP, ELEC, ELEC ENG, TV *supply network* cable alimentador *m*, cable de alimentación *m*, conductor alimentador *m*; ~ **calf** *n* AGRIC ternero para engordar *m*; ~ **gate** *n* C&G compuerta del alimentador *f*; ~ **header** *n* NUCL colector de alimentación *m*; ~ **line** *n* RAIL ramal *m*, ramificación *f*, vía lateral *f*, vía secundaria *f*; ~ **link** *n* SPACE *communications* enlace alimentador *m*, eslabón alimentador *m*; ~ **nose** *n* C&G media luna *f*; ~ **opening** *n* C&G orificio *m*; ~ **pipe** *n* NUCL tubería de alimentación *f*; ~ **plunger** *n* C&G tapón *m*; ~ **ship** *n* WATER TRANSP transbordador de contenedores *m*; ~ **steer** *n* AGRIC novillo destetado de engorde *m*; ~ **tank** *n* AIR TRANSP tanque secundario *m*; ~ **train** *n* RAIL tren de ramificación *m*; ~ **yarn** *n* TEXTIL hilo alimentador *m*

feedgrinder *n* AGRIC trituradora *f*

feeding *n* AGRIC alimentación *f*, PROD alimentación *f*, avance *m*, TEXTIL alimentación *f*; ~ **area** *n* AGRIC zona de engorde *f*; ~ **device** *n* PACK mecanismo de alimentación *m*; ~ **ground** *n* OCEAN territorio de alimentación *m*; ~ **rack** *n* AGRIC comedero *m*; ~ **roll** *n* PAPER rodillo de alimentación *m*; ~ **system** *n* PAPER sistema de alimentación *m*; ~ **table** *n* PACK mesa de alimentación *f*; ~ **transformer** *n* ELEC transformador de alimentación *m*; ~ **trough** *n* AGRIC comedero *m*

feedline *n* NUCL línea de alimentación *f*

feedlot *n* AGRIC corral de engorde *m*

feedstock *n* ELEC, ELEC ENG disponibilidad de suministro *f*

feedthrough *n* ELEC ENG alimentación directa *f*, MECH paso *m*, PHYS, SPACE alimentador a través *m*; ~ **capacitor** *n* ELEC ENG condensador de alimentador *m*; ~ **insulator** *n* ELEC, ELEC ENG aislador de alimentación *m*

feedwater *n* GEN agua de alimentación *f*; ~ **heater** *n* HEAT ENG, PROD calentador de agua de alimentación *m*; ~~**inlet nozzle** *n* NUCL tobera de entrada de alimentación *f*; ~ **manifold** *n* NUCL colector de agua de alimentación *m*, múltiple de agua de alimentación *m*; ~ **pump** *n* HYDROL, MECH ENG bomba de agua de alimentación *f*; ~ **softening** *n* HEAT ENG, HYDROL, WATER ablandamiento del agua de alimentación *m*; ~ **treatment** *n* HYDROL tratamiento del agua de alimentación *m*

feel: ~ **mechanism** *n* SPACE mecanismo de servomando *m*; ~ **plate** *n* P&R placa de contacto *f*; ~ **simulator** *n* SPACE simulador de sondeo *m*; ~~**simulator valve** *n* AIR TRANSP válvula simuladora de percepción *f*

feeler *n* PRINT sensor *m*; ~ **gage** *AmE*, ~ **gauge** *BrE n* METEO testeador *m*, METR calibrador de separaciones *m*, calibrador de verificación de piezas *m*, galga de espesores *f*, NUCL, VEH galga de espesores *f*

feet: ~ **per second** *n pl* CINEMAT pies por segundo *m pl*

Fehling's: ~ **solution** *n* CHEM solución de Fehling *f*

feint: ~ **rules** *n pl* PRINT rayas continuas *f pl*

feldspar *n* C&G, CHEM, MINERAL feldespato *m*

fell *vt* AGRIC talar, CONST *timber* cortar

felling *n* AGRIC tala *f*

felsite *n* PETROL felsita *f*

felspar *n* C&G, CHEM, MINERAL feldespato *m*

felt *n* PAPER, TEXTIL fieltro *m*; ~ **board** *n* PAPER cartón fieltro *m*; ~~**carrying roll** *n* PAPER rodillo conductor del fieltro *m*; ~ **conditioner** *n* PAPER acondicionador del fieltro *m*; ~**-direction mark** *n* PAPER marca de la dirección del fieltro *f*; ~ **dryer** *n* PAPER secador del fieltro *m*; ~ **and foam joint** *n* CONST unión de fieltro y espuma *f*; ~ **mark** *n* PAPER marca del fieltro *f*; ~ **polisher** *n* C&G pulidor de felpa *m*; ~ **roll** *n* PAPER rodillo-guía del fieltro *m*; ~ **side** *n* PAPER cara fieltro *f*; ~ **stretcher** *n* PAPER tensor del fieltro *m*; ~ **washer** *n* MECH ENG arandela de fieltro *f*, PAPER lavador del fieltro *m*; ~ **whipper** *n* PAPER batán de fieltro *m*

female: ~ **connector** *n* CINEMAT conector hembra *m*, ELEC, ELEC ENG connector hembra *m*, enchufe hembra *m*, LAB enchufe hembra *m*, PROD connector hembra *m*, enchufe hembra *m*, TELECOM enchufe hembra *m*; ~ **contact** *n* ELEC, ELEC ENG contacto hembra *m*; ~ **die** *n* PRINT matriz en bajo relieve *f*; ~ **guide** *n* TV guía hembra *f*; ~ **thread** *n* MECH ENG rosca hembra *f*, rosca interior *f*

femto *pref* (*f*) METR femto (*f*)

fence[1] *n* AGRIC, CONST cerca *f*; ~ **boom** *n* MAR POLL cerca flotante *f*; ~ **code** *n* PROD código de delimitación *m*

fence[2]: ~ **in** *vt* AGRIC, CONST alambrar, cercar

fenchene *n* CHEM fenqueno *m*

fenchone *n* CHEM fencona *f*

fenchyl *n* CHEM fenquilo *m*

fend: ~ **off** *vt* WATER TRANSP abrir de costado, desatracar, *collosion* mantenerse franco

fender *n* AmE (*cf mudguard BrE*) AUTO aleta *f*, guardabarros *m*, MAR POLL defensa *f*, MECH tapa de protección *f*, TRANSP, VEH aleta *f*, guardabarros *m*, WATER TRANSP defensa *f*

Fenske: ~ **helices** *n pl* LAB serpentines Fenske *m pl*

FEP *abbr* (*front-end processor*) COMP&DP procesador delantero *m*, procesador frontal *m*, TELECOM procesador front-end *m*

Fermat's: ~ **principle** *n* PHYS principio de Fermat *m*

ferment *vi* CHEM, FOOD, HYDROL fermentar

fermentation *n* CHEM, FOOD, HYDROL fermentación *f*

fermenter *n* CHEM, FOOD, HYDROL fermentador *m*

Fermi: ~ **energy** *n* PHYS energía de Fermi *f*; ~ **level** *n* PHYS nivel de Fermi *m*; ~ **sphere** *n* PHYS esfera de Fermi *f*; ~ **surface** *n* PHYS superficie de Fermi *f*; ~**-wave vector** *n* PHYS vector de ondas de Fermi *m*

Fermi-Dirac: ~ **distribution** *n* PHYS distribución de Fermi-Dirac *f*; ~ **statistics** *n pl* PHYS estadística de Fermi-Dirac *f*

fermion *n* PART PHYS, PHYS fermión *m*

fermium *n* (*Fm*) CHEM, RAD PHYS fermio *m* (*Fm*)

ferrate *n* CHEM ferrato *m*

ferredoxin *n* CHEM ferredoxina *f*

ferric[1] *adj* CHEM, PROD férrico

ferric[2]: ~ **oxide** *n* CHEM, PROD óxido férrico *m*

ferricyanide *n* CHEM ferricianuro *m*

ferricyanogen *n* CHEM ferricianógeno *m*

ferrimagnetic *adj* PHYS ferrimagnético

ferrimagnetism *n* PHYS ferrimagnetismo *m*

ferrioxalic *adj* CHEM ferrioxálico

ferrite *n* CHEM, ELEC, ELEC ENG ferrita *f*, ELECTRON núcleo de ferrita *m*, PHYS ferrita *f*; ~ **core** *n* COMP&DP, ELEC núcleo de ferrita *m*, ELEC ENG *bead memory* memoria de núcleos de ferrita *f*, *of transformer* núcleo de ferrita *m*, TV núcleo de ferrita *m*; ~ **head** *n* TV núcleo de ferrita *m*; ~ **isolator** *n* ELEC ENG seccionador de ferrita *m*; ~ **limiter** *n* ELEC ENG limitador de ferrita *m*; ~ **phase-shifter** *n* ELEC ENG cambiador de fase de ferrita *m*; ~ **rod** *n* ELEC ENG centro de ferrita *m*, PHYS barra de ferrita *f*; ~ **rotator** *n* ELEC ENG rotatorio de ferrita *m*

ferritic[1] *adj* MECH, METALL, SPACE ferrítico

ferritic[2]: ~ **stainless steel** *n* MECH, MECH ENG, METALL, PROD, SPACE acero inoxidable ferrítico *m*

ferritin *n* CHEM ferritina *f*

ferritizing: ~ **annealing** *n* METALL recocido ferritizante *m*

ferroan: ~ **dolomite** *n* GEOL dolomita férrica *f*

ferroconcrete *n* WATER TRANSP *ship building* concreto armado *m* (*AmL*), hormigón armado *m* (*Esp*)

ferrocyanate *n* CHEM ferrocianato *m*

ferrocyanide *n* CHEM ferrocianuro *m*

ferrocyanogen *n* CHEM ferrocianógeno *m*

ferrodynamic: ~ **wattmeter** *n* ELEC vatímetro ferrodinámico *m*

ferroelectric[1] *adj* ELEC, ELEC ENG, PHYS ferroeléctrico

ferroelectric[2]: ~ **crystal** *n* CRYSTALL, ELEC, ELEC ENG cristal ferroeléctrico *m*

ferroelectricity *n* ELEC, ELEC ENG, PHYS ferroelectricidad *f*

ferrogallic: ~ **ink** *n* COLOUR tinta ferrogálica *f*

ferromagnetic[1] *adj* ELEC, ELEC ENG, ELECTRON, PHYS ferromagnético

ferromagnetic[2]: ~ **amplifier** *n* ELECTRON amplificador ferromagnético *m*; ~ **instrument** *n* INSTR instrumento ferromagnético *m*; ~ **material** *n* ELEC, ELEC ENG, PETROL material ferromagnético *m*

ferromagnetism *n* ELEC, ELEC ENG, ELECTRON, PHYS ferromagnetismo *m*

ferromolybdenum *n* METALL ferromolibdeno *m*

ferronickel *n* METALL ferroníquel *m*; ~ **cell** *n* ELEC ENG elemento de ferroníquel *m*

ferroprussiate *n* CHEM ferroprusiato *m*

ferroresonance *n* ELEC ENG ferrorresonancia *f*, resonancia de cables eléctricos armados *f*; ~ **circuit** *n* ELEC ENG circuito de ferrorresonancia *m*

ferrosoferric *adj* CHEM ferrosoférrico

ferrous: ~ **oxide** *n* C&G, CHEM óxido ferroso *m*; ~ **sulfate** *AmE*, ~ **sulphate** *BrE n* CHEM sulfato ferroso *m*

ferruginous *adj* GEOL ferruginoso

ferrule *n* MECH, MECH ENG, OPT, TELECOM casquillo *m*, férula *f*, guarnición metálica *f*, regatón *m*, virola *f*; ~ **resistor** *n* ELEC ENG resistencia de la tapa de contacto *f*

ferry *n* TRANSP canguro *m*, transbordador *m*, WATER TRANSP buque transbordador *m*, buque transportador *m*, canguro *m*, transbordador *m*; ~ **flight** *n* AIR TRANSP vuelo de autotraslado *m*; ~ **service** *n* TRANSP, WATER TRANSP servicio de ferry *m*, servicio de transbordador *m*

ferryboat *n* WATER TRANSP buque transbordador de trenes y pasaje *m*, transbordador de trenes y pasaje *m*

ferrying *n* WATER TRANSP transbordo *m*

fertile: ~ **isotope** *n* PHYS isótopo fértil *m*; ~ **material** *n* NUCL material fértil *m*

fertility: ~ **rate** *n* AGRIC tasa de fecundidad *f*

fertilize *vt* AGRIC abonar, añadir abonos, fecundar, POLL, RECYCL abonar

fertilizer *n* AGRIC, POLL, RECYCL abono *m*; ~ **distribution** *n* AGRIC distribución de fertilizantes *f*; ~ **mixture** *n* AGRIC mezcla de fertilizantes *f*; ~ **proportioner** *n* AGRIC dosímetro *m*; ~ **spreader** *n* AGRIC distribuidor de fertilizantes *m*

ferulic *adj* CHEM ferúlico

fescue *n* AGRIC cañuela *f*

fest: **~-sulfite cellulose** *AmE*, **~-sulphite cellulose** *BrE n* PAPER pasta al sulfito fest *f*

festoon *n* GEOL festón *m*; **~ cross-bedding** *n* GEOL estratificación cruzada en festón *f*, estratificación cruzada en surco *f*; **~ dryer** *n* PAPER secador de banda colgante *m*

FET[1] *abbr* (*field-effect transistor*) COMP&DP, ELECTRON, OPT, PHYS, SPACE TEC (*transistor de efecto de campo*)

FET[2]: **~ amplifier** *n* ELECTRON, SPACE amplificador de TEC *m*; **~ front end** *n* ELECTRON extremo frontal del TEC *m*; **~ input** *n* ELECTRON entrada de corriente en el TEC *f*

fetch[1] *n* COMP&DP extracción *f* (*Esp*), traída *f* (*AmL*); **~ instruction** *n* COMP&DP instrucción de búsqueda *f*, instrucción de extracción *f* (*Esp*), instrucción de traída *f* (*AmL*)

fetch[2] *vt* COMP&DP extraer (*Esp*), traer (*AmL*)

fetch[3] *vi* WATER TRANSP alcanzar, coger

Feynman: **~ diagram** *n* PHYS diagrama de Feynman *m*

FF[1] *abbr* (*form feed*) COMP&DP, PRINT alimentación de papel *f*, avance de hoja *m*, avance de papel *m*, avance de página *m*

FF[2]: **~ carbon black** *n* (*fine furnace carbon black*) P&R negro de humo de horno y partícula fina *m*

FFT *abbr* (*fast Fourier transform*) COMP&DP, ELECTRON TRF (*transformada rápida de Fourier*)

F-head: **~ engine** *n* AUTO motor de culata en F *m*

FHP: **~ motor** *n* (*fractional horsepower motor*) ELEC, ELEC ENG motor de <1 HP *m* (*motor de potencia menor de un caballo*)

FI *abbr* (*fidelity*) ELECTRON FI (*fidelidad*)

fiber *AmE see* fibre *BrE*

fiberglass *AmE see* fibreglass *BrE*

fiberizer *n* PAPER separador de fibras *m*

Fibonacci: **~ search** *n* COMP&DP búsqueda de Fibonacci *f*; **~ sequence** *n* MATH serie de Fibonacci *f*, sucesión de Fibonacci *f*

fibre *n* BrE C&G, OPT, PAPER, TELECOM, TEXTIL fibra *f*; **~ axis** *n* BrE OPT eje de fibra *m*, eje de la fibra *m*, TELECOM eje de fibra *m*; **~ buffer** *n* BrE OPT protección de la fibra *f*, TELECOM fibra buffer *f*; **~ bundle** *n* BrE OPT, TELECOM haz de fibras *m*; **~ cladding** *n* BrE OPT, TELECOM revestimiento de fibras *m*; **~ coating** *n* BrE, OPT, TELECOM revestimiento de fibras *m*; **~ composition** *n* BrE PAPER composición fibrosa *f*; **~ content** *n* BrE TEXTIL contenido en fibras *m*; **~ core** *n* BrE OPT núcleo de la fibra *f*, TV alma de fibra *f*; **~ crop** *n* BrE AGRIC planta textil *f*; **~-distributed data interface** *n* BrE (*FDDI*) TELECOM interfase de datos distribuidos por fibra *f*; **~ drum** *n* BrE NUCL *for radioactive wastes* bidón de fibra *m*, PACK tambor de fibras *m*; **~ excess length** *n* BrE OPT longitud excedente de fibra *f*; **~ feeder** *n* BrE C&G chorreador de fibras *m*; **~ furnish** *n* BrE PRINT composición fibrosa *f*; **~ gasket** *n* BrE MECH junta de fibra *f*; **~ helix** *n* BrE OPT fibra helicoidal *f*, hélice de la fibra *f*; **~ jacket** *n* BrE OPT chaqueta de la fibra *f*, vaina de la fibra *f*, TELECOM camisa de fibra *f*; **~ joint** *n* BrE MECH junta de fibra *f*; **~-like material** *n* BrE CONST símil fibra *m*; **~-optic** *n* BrE C&G, COMP&DP, ELEC ENG, OPT, PHYS, SPACE fibra óptica *f*; **~-optic cable** *n* BrE COMP&DP, ELEC ENG, TELECOM cable de fibra óptica *m*, cable fibroóptico *m*; **~-optic cladding** *n*

BrE OPT, TELECOM chapeado de fibra óptica *m*; **~-optic connection** *n* BrE ELEC ENG, OPT, TELECOM conexión de fibra óptica *f*, conexión fibroóptica *f*; **~-optic connector** *n* ELEC ENG, OPT, TELECOM conector de fibra óptica *m*, conector fibroóptico *m*; **~-optic modem** *n* BrE COMP&DP, ELECTRON, OPT módem de fibra óptica *m*; **~-optic network** *n* BrE ELEC ENG, OPT, TELECOM red de fibra óptica *f*; **~-optic receiver** *n* BrE ELEC ENG, OPT, TELECOM receptor de fibra óptica *m*; **~-optic splice** *n* BrE OPT, TELECOM empalme de fibra óptica *m*; **~-optic technology** *n* BrE ELEC ENG, OPT, TELECOM tecnología de fibra óptica *f*, tecnología fibroóptica *f*; **~-optic terminal device** *n* BrE OPT, TELECOM dispositivo terminal de fibra óptica *m*, dispositivo terminal de fibroóptica *m*; **~-optic transducer** *n* BrE ELEC ENG, OPT, TELECOM transductor fibroóptico *m*; **~-optic transmission** *n* BrE ELEC ENG, OPT, TELECOM transmisión de fibra óptica *f*; **~-optic transmission system** *n* BrE ELEC ENG, OPT, TELECOM sistema de transmisión de fibra óptica *m*; **~-optic transmitter** *n* BrE ELEC ENG, OPT, TELECOM transmisor fibroóptico *m*; **~-optics** *n* BrE C&G, CINEMAT, COMP&DP, ELEC ENG, OPT, PHYS, TELECOM fibroóptica *f*, óptica de fibras *f*; **~-optics equipment** *n* BrE LAB, OPT, TELECOM equipo de fibra óptica *m*, equipo fibroóptico *m*; **~ pigtail** *n* BrE OPT espiral de fibra *f*, fibra terminal *f*; **~-reinforced sand** *n* BrE CONST arena reforzada con fibra *f*; **~ rope** *n* BrE MECH ENG cuerda de fibra textil *f*; **~ scattering** *n* BrE OPT esparcimiento de la fibra *m*, TELECOM dispersión por fibra *f*; **~ texture** *n* BrE METALL textura fibrosa *f*; **~ to the building** *n* BrE (*FTTB*) TELECOM fibra hasta el edificio *f*; **~ to the home** *n* BrE (*FTTH*) TELECOM fibra hasta el domicilio *f*; **~ to the kerb** *n* BrE (*FTTC*) TELECOM fibra hasta la acera *f*; **~ to the office** *n* BrE (*FTTO*) TELECOM fibra hasta la oficina *f*; **~-type sling** *n* BrE SAFE eslinga tipo fibra *f*, estrobo tipo fibra *m*; **~ washer** *n* BrE MECH junta de fibra *f*

fibreglass *n* BrE GEN fibra de vidrio *f*, fibravidrio *f*

fibrillating *n* PAPER fibrilación *f*

fibroin *n* CHEM fibroína *f*

fibrous: **~ fracture** *n* CRYSTALL fractura astillosa *f*, fractura fibrosa *f*, METALL, NUCL fractura fibrosa *f*; **~ insulation** *n* HEAT ENG aislación por material fibroso *f*, aislamiento fibroso *m*; **~ layer** *n* PAPER capa fibrosa *f*; **~ microstructure** *n* METALL microestructura fibrosa *f*; **~ peat** *n* COAL turba fósil *f*; **~ texture** *n* CRYSTALL textura fibrosa *f*; **~ waste** *n* TEXTIL borra fibrosa *f*

ficin *n* CHEM ficina *f*

Fick's: **~ law** *n* PHYS ley de Fick *f*

fictitious: **~ binding energy** *n* NUCL energía de enlace ficticia *f*

fiddle *n* WATER TRANSP *retaining bar* balancera *f*, violín *m*; **~ block** *n* WATER TRANSP *deck fittings* motón de briol *m*; **~ drill** *n* MECH ENG barbiquí de pecho *m*, taladro de mano *m*

fidelity *n* (*FI*) ELECTRON fidelidad *f* (*FI*)

field[1]: **~-engraved** *adj* PROD grabado en obra; **~-expandable** *adj* PROD extendible por el usuario; **~-tested** *adj* MECH ensayado in situ, ensayado sobre el terreno

field[2] *n* ACOUST campo *m*, CINEMAT imagen *f*, ELEC *electric, magnetic* campo *m*, inductor *m*, ELEC ENG campo *m*, *in a conductor* campo conductivo *m*, PETR

TECH, PETROL campo *m*, yacimiento *m*, PHOTO, TV imagen *f*; ~ **of action** *n* CINEMAT campo de acción *m*; ~ **artillery** *n* MILIT artillería de campaña *f*; ~-**balancing equipment** *n* MECH ENG *vibration test* equipo compensador de campo *m*, equipo equilibrador de campo *m*; ~ **battery** *n* MILIT batería de artillería de campaña *f*, batería de campaña *f*; ~ **book** *n* CONST cuaderno de campo *m*, libreta de campo *f*; ~-**breaking switch** *n* NUCL disyuntor de campo *m*; ~ **camera** *n* PHOTO cámara de campaña *f*, cámara de campo *f*; ~ **capacity** *n* AGRIC capacidad de campo *f*; ~-**centering control** *AmE*, ~-**centring control** *BrE n* TV control del centrado de la imagen *m*; ~ **circuit** *n* ELEC *of machine* circuito inductor *m*; ~ **coil** *n* ELEC, ELEC ENG bobina de campo *f*; ~ **convergence** *n* TV convergencia de la imagen *f*; ~ **crop** *n* AGRIC cultivo extensivo *m*; ~ **cultivator** *n* AGRIC cultivador subsuperficial *m*; ~ **current** *n* ELEC *of machine* corriente del inductor *f*, ELEC ENG corriente del campo inductor *f*, corriente inductora *f*; ~ **delimiter** *n* COMP&DP delimitador de campo *m*; ~ **depth** *n* TELECOM profundidad de campo *f*; ~ **diaphragm** *n* METALL diafragma de campo *m*, diafragma de montaje *m*; ~ **direction** *n* ELEC, ELEC ENG dirección del campo inductor *f*; ~-**discharge switch** *n* NUCL interruptor de excitación *m*, interruptor de ruptura del campo inductor *m*; ~ **distributor** *n* AGRIC sembradora a voleo distribuidora de fertilizantes *f*; ~ **divider** *n* TV divisor de la frecuencia de la imagen *m*; ~ **effect** *n* COMP&DP, ELECTRON, OPT, PHYS, SPACE, TELECOM efecto de campo *m*; ~-**effect amplifier** *n* ELECTRON, TELECOM amplificador de efecto de campo *m*; ~-**effect transistor** *n* (*FET*) COMP&DP, ELECTRON, OPT, PHYS, SPACE transistor de efecto de campo *m* (*TEC*); ~-**effect transistor amplifier** *n* ELECTRON, OPT, PHYS, SPACE *communications* amplificador del transistor de efecto de campo *m*; ~ **electron microscope** *n* INSTR microscopio de campo electrónico *m*; ~ **emission** *n* ELECTRON, PHYS emisión de campo *f*, emisión por efecto de campo *f*; ~ **emission microscope** *n* ELECTRON, INSTR, PHYS microscopio de emisión por efecto de campo *m*; ~ **engineer** *n* MECH ingeniero de campo *m*, ingeniero de obra *m*; ~ **excitation** *n* ELEC *of machine* excitación del inductor *f*; ~ **flutter** *n* NUCL distorsión de campo *f*; ~ **flyback** *n* TV retorno del haz *m*; ~ **of force** *n* ELEC ENG campo de fuerza *m*; ~ **frame** *n* AUTO cuadro de campo *m*; ~-**free emission current** *n* NUCL corriente de emisión con campo nulo *f*; ~ **frequency** *n* TV frecuencia de imagen *f*; ~-**gating circuit** *n* TV circuito de desbloqueo de la imagen *m*; ~ **glass magnifier** *n* C&G lupa de campo *f*; ~ **glasses** *n pl* INSTR, OPT gemelos de campaña *m pl*; ~ **illumination** *n* INSTR iluminación por efecto de campo *f*; ~ **of image** *n* CINEMAT campo de la imagen *m*; ~ **intensity** *n* ELEC, ELEC ENG intensidad de campo *f*; ~-**ion microscope** *n* INSTR, PHYS microscopio de iones de campo *m*, microscopio iónico de campo *m*; ~ **joint station** *n* PETROL estación conjunta de campo *f*; ~ **lens** *n* CINEMAT lente de campo *f*, INSTR, OPT, PHOTO lente de campo *f*, lente interior *f*; ~ **line** *n* ELEC ENG línea inductora *f*, PHYS línea de campo *f*; ~ **magnet** *n* ELEC ENG electroimán del campo *m*, polo inductor *m*; ~-**neutralizing magnet** *n* TV inductor neutralizante *m*; ~ **of nuclear forces** *n* NUCL campo de fuerzas

nucleares *m*; ~ **oxide** *n* ELECTRON óxido de campo *m*; ~ **pick-up** *n* TV imágenes recogidas en la calle por cámaras móviles *f pl*; ~ **pole** *n* ELEC ENG polo inductor *m*; ~ **potential** *n* PETROL potencial de campo *m*; ~ **processing** *n* PETROL procesado de campo *m*; ~-**programmable device** *n* COMP&DP dispositivo programable de campo *m*; ~-**programmable logic array** *n* (*FPLA*) COMP&DP arreglo lógico programable de campo *m* (*FPLA*); ~ **rate flicker** *n* CINEMAT, TV frecuencia de parpadeo de imagen *f*; ~ **regulator** *n* ELEC, ELEC ENG regulador de excitación *m*, regulador del campo inductor *m*; ~ **resistance** *n* AGRIC resistencia en campo *f*; ~ **reversal** *n* GEOL campo inverso *m*; ~ **rheostat** *n* ELEC *of machine* reóstato de campo *m*, reóstato de excitación *m*, ELEC ENG reóstato de campo *m*, reóstato regulador de excitación *m*; ~ **of sharpness** *n* CINEMAT campo de nitidez *m*; ~-**shift switch** *n* TV control de desplazamiento de imagen *m*; ~ **spider** *n* ELEC ENG armazón polar *m*; ~ **stop** *n* PHYS limitador del campo *m*; ~ **strength** *n* ELEC, ELEC ENG equipotencia del campo *f*, intensidad del campo *f*; ~-**strength meter** *n* ELEC, ELEC ENG, INSTR medidor de intensidad de campo *m*; ~ **strip cropping** *n* AGRIC *conservation* cultivo en franjas paralelas *m*; ~ **study** *n* AGRIC estudio en campo *m*; ~ **suppressor** *n* ELEC, ELEC ENG supresor de campo *m*; ~ **sync** *n* TV sincronización de imagen *f*; ~-**sync alignment** *n* TV alineación de la sincronización de imagen *f*; ~ **synchronization** *n* TV sincronización de imagen *f*; ~ **tilt** *n* TV corrección de la distorsión de imagen *f*; ~ **trial** *n* AGRIC ensayo de campo *m*, MAR POLL prueba en el mar *f*, prueba sobre el terreno *f*, SPACE experimento sobre el terreno *m*, TELECOM ensayo de campo *m*; ~ **unit** *n* AGRIC unidad de extensión *f*; ~ **vector** *n* ELEC ENG vector de campo *m*; ~ **of view** *n* CINEMAT campo visual *m*; ~ **voltage** *n* ELEC *of machine* tensión del inductor *f*; ~ **weld** *n* NUCL soldadura de montaje *f*; ~ **winding** *n* ELEC, ELEC ENG *of machine* devanado de campo *m*, devanado de excitación *m*, devanado inductor *m*; ~ **wire** *n* ELEC, ELEC ENG cable flexible aislado *m*; ~ **wiring** *n* PROD cableado del inductor *m*; ~ **wiring arm** *n* PROD brazo de cableado del inductor *m*; ~ **work** *n* MILIT trabajo en campaña *m*

FIFO *abbr* (*first-in-first-out*) COMP&DP *memories* primero en entrar, primero en salir

fifth *n* ACOUST quinta *f*; ~ **generation** *n* COMP&DP quinta generación *f*; ~-**generation computer** *n* COMP&DP computador de quinta generación *m* (*AmL*), computadora de quinta generación *f* (*AmL*), ordenador de quinta generación *m* (*Esp*); ~ **wheel** *n* VEH quinta rueda *f*, rueda auxiliar *f*; ~-**wheel kingpin** *n* VEH pivote de quinta rueda *m*; ~-**wheel kingpin axis** *n* VEH eje de giro de la rueda auxiliar *m*, eje del pivote de la rueda auxiliar *m*, eje del pivote de quinta rueda *m*

figurative: ~ **constant** *n* COMP&DP constante figurada *f*

figure *n* MATH cifra *f*, PRINT ilustración *f*; ~ **of merit** *n* ELECTRON, SPACE coeficiente de calidad *m*; ~-**of-eight calipers** *AmE*, ~-**of-eight callipers** *BrE n pl* MECH ENG calibrador en ocho *m*, compás calibrador en ocho *m*, compás de puntas en ocho *m*; ~-**of-eight knot** *n* WATER TRANSP lasca *f*; ~-**of-eight stairs** *n pl*

CONST escalera de ochos *f*; ~ **shift** *n* TELECOM cambio a cifras *m*; ~ **space** *n* PRINT espacio de cifra *m*

figured: ~ **rolled glass** *n* BrE (*cf patterned glass* AmE) C&G vidrio rolado *m*

figures: ~ **shift** *n* COMP&DP inversión de cifras *f* (*Esp*), movimiento de figuras *m* (*AmL*)

figuring *n* C&G grabado *m*

filament *n* CONST, ELEC, ELEC ENG, INSTR filamento *m*, P&R hilo *m*, filamento *m*, PHYS filamento *m*, filete *m*, TEXTIL filamento *m*, hebra *f*; ~ **current** *n* ELEC *of valve, tube* corriente de caldeo *f*, corriente de encendido *f*, corriente de filamento *f*, ELEC ENG corriente de filamento *f*; ~ **denier** *n* TEXTIL denier del filamento *m*; ~ **resistance** *n* ELEC *of valve, tube* resistencia de filamento *f*; ~ **temperature** *n* ELEC *of valve, tube* temperatura de filamento *f*; ~ **transformer** *n* ELEC, ELEC ENG transformador para filamentos *m*

file[1] *n* COMP&DP archivo *m*, fichero *m*, MECH *spacecraft* escofina *f*, lima *f*, PRINT fila *f*, fichero *m*, PROD archivo *m*, expediente *m*, lima *f*, fichero *m*, TELECOM fichero *m*, VEH lima *f*; ~ **access** *n* COMP&DP acceso a archivos *m*, acceso a ficheros *m*, acceso al fichero *m*; ~**activity ratio** *n* COMP&DP relación de actividad de fichero *f*, tasa de actividad de archivos *f*, tasa de actividad de ficheros *f*; ~ **creation** *n* COMP&DP creación de archivos *f*, creación de ficheros *f*; ~ **description** *n* COMP&DP descripción de archivos *f*, descripción de ficheros *f*; ~ **directory** *n* COMP&DP directorio de archivos *m*, directorio de ficheros *m*; ~ **folder** *n* COMP&DP archivador de documentos *m* (*Esp*), clasificadora de documentos *f* (*AmL*); ~ **identifier** *n* COMP&DP identificador de archivos *m*; ~ **label** *n* COMP&DP etiqueta de archivo *f*, etiqueta de fichero *f*; ~ **maintenance** *n* COMP&DP mantenimiento de archivos *m*, mantenimiento de ficheros *m*; ~ **management** *n* COMP&DP administración de archivos *f*, administración de fichero *f*, gestión de archivos *f*; ~ **mark** *n* COMP&DP marca de archivo *f*, marca de archivos *f*, marca de ficheros *f*; ~ **name** *n* COMP&DP nombre de archivo *m*, nombre de fichero *m*; ~ **operation** *n* COMP&DP, PROD operación de ficheros *f*; ~ **organization** *n* COMP&DP organización de archivos *f*, organización de ficheros *f*; ~ **picture** *n* PHOTO fotografía de archivo *f*; ~ **preparation** *n* COMP&DP preparación de archivos *f*, preparación de ficheros *f*, preparación del archivo *f*; ~ **processing** *n* COMP&DP procesamiento de archivos *m*, procesamiento de ficheros *m*, proceso de archivos *m*; ~ **protection** *n* COMP&DP protección de archivos *f*, protección de ficheros *f*; ~ **recovery** *n* COMP&DP recuperación de archivos *f*, recuperación de ficheros *f*, recuperación del archivo *f*; ~ **restore** *n* COMP&DP restauración de archivos *f*, restauración de ficheros *f*; ~ **security** *n* COMP&DP protección de ficheros *f*, seguridad de archivos *f*, seguridad de ficheros *f*; ~ **separator** *n* COMP&DP separador de archivos *m*, separador de ficheros *m*; ~ **server** *n* COMP&DP procesador de ficheros *m*, servidor de archivos *m*, servidor de ficheros *m*, servidor del fichero *m*; ~ **sharing** *n* COMP&DP compartimiento de archivos *m*, utilización compartida de ficheros *f*; ~ **size** *n* COMP&DP tamaño de archivo *m*; ~ **storage** *n* AmE (*cf file store* BrE) COMP&DP almacenamiento de archivos *m*, almacenamiento de ficheros *m*, almacén de archivo *m*, almacén de fichero *m*; ~ **store** BrE *n* (*cf file storage* AmE)

COMP&DP almacén de archivo *m*, almacén de fichero *m*, almacenamiento de archivos *m*, almacenamiento de ficheros *m*; ~ **structure** *n* COMP&DP estructura de archivos *f*, estructura de ficheros *f*; ~ **transfer** *n* COMP&DP transferencia de archivos *f*, transferencia de ficheros *f*; ~ **transfer access and manipulation service element** *n* (*FTAMSE*) COMP&DP, TELECOM acceso de transferencia de ficheros y elemento del servicio de manipulación *m*; ~ **transfer protocol** *n* (*FTP*) COMP&DP protocolo de transferencia de archivos *m* (*FTP*); ~ **updating** *n* COMP&DP actualización de archivos *f*, actualización de ficheros *f*

file[2]: ~ **a patent application** *vi* PROD, TEXTIL archivar una solicitud de patente

filicic *adj* CHEM filícico

filing *n* COMP&DP, PROD archivo *m*, clasificación *f*

filings *n pl* PROD virutas *f pl*

fill[1] *n* C&G relleno *m*, COAL carga *f*, terraplén *m*; ~**-and-seal machine** *n* PACK máquina de llenado y precintado *f*; ~ **hole** *n* PACK orificio de llenado *m*; ~**-in flash** *n* CINEMAT, PHOTO flash de relleno *m*; ~**-in light** *n* CINEMAT, PHOTO luz de relleno *f*; ~**-in screen** *n* CINEMAT pantalla de relleno *f*; ~ **level** *n* PACK nivel de llenado *m*; ~ **raise** *n* MINE chimenea de mineral *f* (*AmL*), chimenea de mineral para llenado *f* (*Esp*)

fill[2] *vt* C&G llenar, MINE cargar, hinchar (*AmL*), llenar (*Esp*), rellenar (*Esp*), verter (*AmL*), PACK llenar, PRINT rellenar, PROD llenar; ~ **up** *vt* CONST colmar, llenar a tope

filled[1] *adj* CONST *civil engineering* de relleno, lleno, relleno

filled[2]: ~ **binder** *n* CONST ligante de relleno *m*

filler *n* C&G llenador *m*, COLOUR aparejo *m* (*AmL*), tapaporos *m* (*Esp*), COMP&DP relleno *m*, CONST material de relleno *m*, masilla *f*, ELEC *for cable* compuesto lubricante *m*, relleno *m*, ELEC ENG *between wires of cable* ánima *f*, relleno *m*, NUCL *networks* tapaporos *m*, P&R carga *f*, relleno *m*, PAPER carga *f*, PROD embudo *m*, máquina rellenadora *f*, tapón de carga *m*, tubo de alimentación *m*; ~ **alloy** *n* CONST aleación de relleno *f*, mezcla de relleno *f*, METALL aleación de relleno *f*; ~ **cap** *n* AUTO tapón de llenado *m*, MECH *spacecraft* tapa de relleno *f* (*AmL*), tapa del combustible *f* (*AmL*), VEH tapón de llenado *m*; ~ **character** *n* COMP&DP carácter de relleno *m*; ~ **coat** *n* COLOUR capa de aparejo *f* (*AmL*), tapagrietas *m* (*Esp*); ~ **compartment flap** *n* VEH tapa del depósito de llenado *f*; ~ **metal** *n* CONST metal auxiliar *m*, metal de aportación *m*, filler *m*, MECH metal de aportación *m*, metal auxiliar *m*, PROD metal auxiliar *m*, metal de aportación *m*; ~ **rod** *n* CONST, MECH, PROD *welding* varilla de metal de aportación *f*; ~ **wire** *n* MECH alambre de relleno *m*

fillet *n* AIR TRANSP banda *f*, *of airframe* curva de enlace *f*, carenado de unión *m*, CONST *hollow moulding* filete *m*, *feather tongue* chaflán *m*, MECH ENG *of gear* curva de acordamiento *f*, curva de acuerdo *f*, PROD *of screw* hilo *m*, rosca *f*; ~ **gutter** *n* CONST *building* canalón de arista *m*; ~ **slick** *n* PROD *founding* filete de alisar *m*; ~ **weld** *n* MECH *communications* soldadura de filete *f*, soldadura en ángulo *f*, soldadura ortogonal *f*

filleted: ~ **joint** *n* CONST *carpentry* junta de tablones *f*

filleting: ~ **machine** *n* OCEAN fileteadora *f*

filling *n* C&G carga *f*, COMP&DP, CONST relleno *m*, FOOD llenado *m*, GAS relleno *m*, MINE cargamento de vagonetas *m* (*AmL*), llenado de vagonetas *m* (*Esp*),

NUCL relleno *m*; ~ **and capping machine** *n* PACK máquina llenadora y encapsuladora *f*; ~ **coefficient** *n* TELECOM coeficiente de relleno *m*; ~ **device** *n* PACK dispositivo de llenado *m*; ~ **and dosing machine** *n* PACK máquina llenadora y dosificadora *f*; ~ **end** *n* AmE (*cf doghouse BrE*) C&G cargador del horno *m*; ~ **hole** *n* MECH abertura de carga *f*, agujero de carga *m*, SPACE agujero de llenado *m*; ~ **line** *n* PACK cadena de llenado *f*; ~ **machine** *n* PACK máquina llenadora *f*; ~ **material** *n* NUCL material de relleno *m*; ~ **metal** *n* PROD *for autogenous welding* metal de aportación *m*; ~ **nozzle** *n* PACK boquilla de llenado *f*; ~ **pipe** *n* WATER TRANSP tubería de llenado *f*; ~ **plate** *n* WATER TRANSP *in deck* chapa de relleno *f*; ~ **plug** *n* PROD tapón de relleno *m*; ~ **point** *n* C&G puerta de carga *f*; ~ **raise** *n* MINE chimenea de relleno *f*; ~**-up** *n* PROD relleno *m*; ~ **valve** *n* SPACE válvula de alimentación *f*, válvula de carga *f*, válvula de llenado *f*; ~ **vibrator** *n* PACK vibrador de llenado *m*

fillister *n* CONST garlopín *m*, guillame *m*, *of window sash* ranura de encaje *f*; ~**-head machine screw** *n* MECH ENG, PROD tornillo de máquina de cabeza cilíndrica ranurada *m*, tornillo de máquina de cabeza redonda *m*; ~**-head screw** *n* PROD tornillo de cabeza cilíndrica ranurada *m*; ~ **plane** *n* CONST cepillo ranurador *m*

fillistered: ~ **joint** *n* CONST unión con ranura de encaje *f*

film¹: ~**-forming** *adj* P&R peliculígeno

film² *n* CHEM *thin membrane*, CINEMAT película *f*, COATINGS película *f*, capa *f*, HYDRAUL lámina *f*, película *f*, MECH capa delgada *f*, membrana *f*, película *f*, revestimiento delgado *m*, P&R capa delgada *f*, película *f*, PACK, PHOTO, PROD película *f*, SPACE lámina *f*, película *f*, revestimiento galvánico delgado *m*, velo *m*; ~ **aperture assembly** *n* CINEMAT conjunto de la abertura *m*; ~**-applying lid and heat-sealing machine** *n* PACK máquina retractiladora *f*; ~ **backing** *n* PHOTO respaldo de la película *m*; ~ **blowing** *n* P&R fabricación de película por soplado *f*; ~ **boiling** *n* NUCL ebullición pelicular *f*, REFRIG ebullición en película *f*; ~ **camera** *n* CINEMAT cámara de cine *f*, INSTR guía de la película *f*; ~ **capacitor** *n* ELEC ENG condensador de película *m*; ~ **cartoning** *n* PACK cartonaje para películas *m*; ~ **cassette** *n* INSTR casette de película *f*; ~ **casting** *n* P&R moldeado de película por colada *m*; ~ **channel** *n* CINEMAT guía de la película *f*; ~ **checker** *n* CINEMAT comprobador de película *m*; ~ **clip** *n* PHOTO pinza para película *f*; ~ **coating** *n* PACK película protectora *f*; ~ **cooling** *n* SPACE enfriamiento de la lámina *m*, TRANSP enfriamiento de la cubierta *m*, temple del revestimiento *m*; ~ **cutting** *n* PROD corte de film *m*; ~ **director** *n* CINEMAT director cinematográfico *m*; ~ **dosimeter** *n* RAD PHYS película dosimétrica *f*; ~ **drive** *n* CINEMAT mecanismo de arrastre de la película *m*; ~ **drum** *n* CINEMAT tambor para película *m*; ~ **dryer** *n* CINEMAT, PHOTO secador de película *m*; ~**-drying drum** *n* CINEMAT, PHOTO tambor de secado de película *m*; ~**-drying machine** *n* CINEMAT máquina de secado de película *f*; ~ **extrusion** *n* P&R extrusión de película *f*; ~ **extrusion equipment** *n* PACK equipo para obtener películas por extrusión *m*; ~ **fading** *n* CINEMAT desvanecimiento de la película *m*; ~ **feeder pin** *n* CINEMAT garfio de alimentación de la película *m*; ~**-footage counter** *n* CINEMAT, TV contador de metraje *m*; ~ **gage** *AmE see film gauge BrE*; ~ **gate**

n CINEMAT ventanilla para la película *f*; ~ **gauge** *n* BrE CINEMAT paso *m*; ~ **holder** *n* CINEMAT, PHOTO tensador de película *m*; ~ **horse** *n* CINEMAT cuña de tierra *f*; ~ **lamination** *n* PACK laminado de películas *m*; ~ **leader** *n* CINEMAT, PHOTO guía de película *f*; ~ **length** *n* CINEMAT longitud de la película *f*; ~**-maker** *n* CINEMAT cineasta *m*; ~ **pick-up** *n* CINEMAT, TV película captadora *f*; ~ **plane** *n* CINEMAT plano de la película *m*; ~ **rack** *n* CINEMAT, PHOTO colgador de películas *m*; ~ **register punch** *n* PRINT perforación de registro de la película *f*; ~ **resistor** *n* ELEC ENG resistencia de película *f*; ~**-rewind handle** *n* CINEMAT, PHOTO palanca para rebobinar la película *f*; ~ **scanner** *n* TV máquina de telecine *f*; ~ **shoot** *n* CINEMAT rodaje de la película *m*; ~ **speed** *n* CINEMAT, PHOTO sensibilidad de la película *f*, velocidad de la película *f*; ~ **spool** *n* CINEMAT, PHOTO carrete de película *m*; ~ **thickness** *n* P&R espesor de la película *m*; ~ **threading** *n* CINEMAT enhebramiento de la película *m*; ~**-to-tape transfer** *n* CINEMAT, TV transferencia de película a cinta *f*; ~ **transducer** *n* SPACE transductor de película *m*; ~ **transfer** *n* CINEMAT, TV transferencia de película *f*; ~ **transmitter** *n* CINEMAT, TV transmisor de película *m*; ~ **transport** *n* CINEMAT, PHOTO, TV transporte de la película *m*; ~**-transport lever** *n* CINEMAT, PHOTO control de transporte de la película *m*; ~**-transport sprocket** *n* CINEMAT, PHOTO engranaje de transporte de la película *m*; ~ **tree** *n* CINEMAT árbol para película *m*; ~**-type indicator** *n* CINEMAT, PHOTO, TV indicador del tipo de película *m*; ~ **winder** *n* CINEMAT, PHOTO, TV enrollador de película *m*, rebobinadora de película *f*; ~ **wrap** *n* PACK envoltura con película *f*; ~**-wrapping machine** *n* PACK máquina de envolver con película *f*, máquina retractiladora *f*; ~ **wrinkling** *n* CINEMAT arrugamiento de la película *m*

filming: ~ **speed** *n* CINEMAT velocidad de filmación *f*

filmset *n* BrE (*cf photocomposer AmE*) PRINT fotocompositora *f*

filmsetter *n* CINEMAT, PHOTO, PRINT fotocomponedora *f*

filter¹ *n* GEN filtro *m*; ~ **aid** *n* CHEM TECH coayudante de la filtración *m*; ~ **amplifier** *n* ELECTRON amplificador de filtro *m*; ~**-amplitude response** *n* ELECTRON respuesta de amplitud de filtro *f*; ~**-and-sample detector** *n* TELECOM detector de filtrado y muestreo *m*; ~ **attenuation** *n* ELECTRON atenuación de filtro *f*; ~ **bag** *n* CHEM TECH, COAL manga para filtrar *f*, saco para filtrar *m*; ~ **bank** *n* ELECTRON batería de filtros *f*; ~ **basin** *n* RECYCL embalse de filtrado *m*; ~ **bed** *n* CHEM TECH, NUCL, RECYCL, WATER lecho de filtración *m*, lecho filtrante *m*, lecho percolador *m*; ~ **bowl** *n* VEH vaso del filtro *m*; ~ **bypass** *n* PROD derivación del filtro *f*; ~ **cake** *n* CHEM TECH torta de filtración *f*, COAL costra de lodo *f*, torta de cachaza *f*, torta de filtro *f*; ~ **capacitor** *n* ELEC ENG condensador de filtro *m*; ~ **cartridge** *n* CHEM TECH, MECH, VEH cartucho del filtro *m*, cartucho filtrante *m*; ~ **characteristic-function** *n* ELECTRON función característica del filtro *f*; ~ **choke** *n* ELEC, ELEC ENG choque de filtro *m*, inductor de filtro *m*, reactancia de filtro *f*, reactor de filtro *m*; ~ **cloth** *n* C&G tela de filtro *f*, CHEM TECH, WATER tela de filtrar *f*, tela filtrante *f*; ~ **crystal** *n* ELECTRON cristal de filtro *m*; ~ **discrimination** *n* ELECTRON discriminación del filtro *f*; ~ **drum** *n* CHEM TECH tambor de filtración

m; **~-dryer** *n* REFRIG deshidratador con filtro *m*; **~ element** *n* PROD elemento del filtro *m*; **~ factor** *n* CINEMAT, PHOTO, TV factor del filtro *m*; **~ feed trough** *n* COAL canaleta alimentadora del filtro *f*; **~ feeder** *n* RECYCL alimentador de filtrado *m*; **~ flask** *n* CHEM TECH frasco de filtración *m*; **~ frame** *n* CHEM TECH bastidor de filtro *m*, marco de filtro *m*; **~ frequency** *n* ELECTRON, RAD PHYS frecuencia de filtrado *f*; **~-frequency response** *n* ELECTRON, RAD PHYS respuesta de frecuencia de filtrado *f*; **~ funnel** *n* CHEM, LAB embudo de filtración *m*; **~ gallery** *n* WATER galería filtrante *f*; **~ gravel** *n* CHEM TECH, WATER grava de filtración *f*, grava filtradora *f*, grava filtrante *f*; **~ holder** *n* CINEMAT portafiltros *m*, soporte del filtro *m*, PHOTO soporte del filtro *m*, TV portafiltros *m*, soporte del filtro *m*; **~ house** *n* NUCL caseta de filtros *f*; **~ jig** *n* SPACE *equipment* criba del filtro *f*, filtro de plantilla *m*; **~ kit** *n* CINEMAT, TV conjunto de filtros *m*; **~ layer** *n* CINEMAT, TV capa de filtros *f*; **~ lens** *n* INSTR, OPT, PHOTO lente filtradora *f*; **~ mask** *n* SPACE pantalla de filtro *f*; **~ order** *n* ELECTRON orden de filtrado *m*, orden del filtro *m*; **~ paper** *n* CHEM, CHEM TECH, LAB, PAPER papel de filtro *m*; **~ phase response** *n* ELECTRON respuesta de fase del filtro *f*; **~ pick-up** *n* INSTR fonocaptor filtrador *m*; **~ plant** *n* WATER estación de filtración *f*, instalación filtradora *f*, planta filtradora *f*; **~ plugging value** *n* CHEM TECH valor de taponamiento del filtro *m*; **~ pole** *n* ELECTRON polo del filtro *m*; **~ press** *n* C&G, CHEM TECH, COAL, FOOD, LAB, PAPER filtro prensa *m*, prensa filtradora *f*; **~ press cloth** *n* CHEM TECH lona del filtro prensa *f*; **~ pump** *n* LAB bomba filtrante *f* (*AmL*), trompa de vacío *f* (*Esp*); **~ response** *n* ELECTRON respuesta de filtro *f*; **~ screen** *n* P&R filtro de malla *m*, filtro de seda metálica *m*, filtro de tela metálica *m*, PHOTO pantalla del filtro *f*, PROD criba filtrante *f*, filtro de tela metálica *m*; **~ section** *n* ELECTRON sección de filtro *f*; **~ set** *n* PHOTO conjunto de filtros *m*, set de filtros *m*; **~ shaping** *n* ELECTRON estructura del filtro *f*; **~ siphon** *AmE see filter syphon BrE*; **~ slot** *n* CINEMAT ranura para filtros *f*; **~ stuff** *n* CHEM TECH estopa de filtración *f*; **~ support** *n* LAB anillo *m*, soporte de filtro *m*; **~ synthesis** *n* ELECTRON síntesis del filtro *f*; **~ syphon** *n BrE* CHEM TECH sifón de filtración *m*; **~ tank** *n* LAB frasco de filtración *m*, WATER tanque de filtración *m*; **~ template** *n* SPACE curva del filtro *f*, filtro de plantilla *m*; **~ thickener** *n* COAL espesador de filtro *m*, tanque de sedimentación a filtro *m*; **~ transmittance** *n* CHEM TECH transmitancia del filtro *f*; **~ well** *n* WATER pozo filtrante *m*; **~ zero** *n* ELECTRON anulación de filtro *f*, cero de filtro *m*
filter² *vt* GEN filtrar, CONST percolar; **~ out** *vt* CHEM TECH filtrar
filterability *n* COAL filtrabilidad *f*
filtered: **~ pulp** *n* CHEM TECH pulpa filtrada *f*
filtering *n* GEN filtración *f*, filtrado *m*; **~ charcoal** *n* COAL carbón vegetal *m*; **~ cloth** *n* CHEM TECH tela de filtración *f*; **~ facepiece** *n* SAFE *for protection against particles* mascarilla con filtro contra partículas *f*; **~ flask** *n* CHEM TECH frasco de filtración *m*; **~ layer** *n* CHEM TECH capa de filtración *f*, capa del filtro *f*; **~ limit** *n* CHEM TECH límite de filtración *m*, punto de obstrucción del filtro frío *m*; **~ plant for dust and fibres** *n* SAFE colector de polvos y fibras *m*; **~ pulp** *n* CHEM TECH pulpa de filtración *f*; **~ screen** *n* CHEM

TECH criba filtradora *f*; **~ separation** *n* CHEM TECH separación por filtración *f*; **~ tank** *n* LAB frasco de filtración *m*; **~ well** *n* CHEM TECH pozo de filtración *m*
filtrate *n* CHEM, CHEM TECH, COAL, RECYCL filtrado *m*; **~ loss** *n* PETROL pérdida de filtrado *f*
filtrating: **~ strainer** *n* CHEM TECH colador filtrante *m*
filtration *n* CHEM *solids from liquids* filtración *f*, COAL *solids from liquids* infiltración *f*, lixiviación *f*, filtración *f*, extracción de sólidos *f*, lavado de morteros *m*, CONST percolación *f*, destilación *f*, *solids from liquids* filtración *f*, PETR TECH, PROD, RECYCL, WATER *solids from liquids* filtración *f*; **~ flask** *n* LAB matraz de filtración *m*; **~ plant** *n* COAL planta de filtrado *f*; **~ vat** *n* WATER cuba de filtración *f*
fin *n* C&G, MECH, NUCL aleta *f*, PROD *founding* rebarba *f*, REFRIG aleta *f*, WATER TRANSP *shipbuilding* aleta *f*, plano de deriva *m*, timón horizontal *m*; **~ cooling** *n* NUCL disipación de calor por aletas *f*; **~ efficiency** *n* REFRIG efectividad de aleta *f*; **~ keel** *n* WATER TRANSP *shipbuilding* orza *f*, plano antideriva *m*; **~ leading edge** *n* AIR TRANSP borde de ataque del plano de deriva *m*; **~ slot** *n* REFRIG ranura de la aleta *f*; **~ spar box** *n* AIR TRANSP caja del larguero del estabilizador *f*; **~ stub frame** *n* AIR TRANSP marco del muñón del estabilizador *m*; **~ stub top rib** *n* AIR TRANSP costilla superior del muñón del estabilizador *f*
final: **~ amplification** *n* ELECTRON amplificación final *f*; **~ amplifier** *n* ELECTRON amplificador final *m*, amplificador final de etapa *m*; **~ anode** *n* TV ánodo final *m*; **~ approach** *n* AIR TRANSP aproximación final *f*; **~-approach fix** *n* AIR TRANSP posición de aproximación final *f*; **~-approach path** *n* AIR TRANSP trayectoria de aproximación final *f*; **~ approach point** *n* AIR TRANSP punto de aproximación final *m*; **~ assembly** *n* NUCL, PROD montaje final *m*; **~ blanking** *n* TV borrado final *m*; **~ blow** *n* C&G soplo final *m*; **~ coat** *n* COLOUR capa final *f*; **~ cut** *n* CINEMAT, TV montaje definitivo *m*; **~ design review** *n* (*FDR*) SPACE revisión final del diseño *f*; **~ drive** *n* AUTO transmisión final *f*; **~ fuel burn-up** *n* NUCL grado de quemado final del combustible *m*; **~-image tube** *n* INSTR colector de imagen final *m*; **~ inspection** *n* QUALITY control definitivo *m*, inspección definitiva *f*; **~ mix** *n* CINEMAT, TV mezclado definitivo *m*; **~ modulator** *n* ELECTRON modulador final *m*; **~ position setting** *n* NUCL ajuste final de posición *m*; **~ proof** *n* PRINT prueba final *f*; **~ safety analysis report** *n* (*FSAR*) NUCL *for plant licensing*, SAFE informe final de análisis de seguridad *m*; **~-settling tank** *n* WATER depósito de decantación final *m*, tanque de decantación final *m*; **~-shooting script** *n* CINEMAT, TV guión definitivo de rodaje *m*; **~ treatment** *n* PACK tratamiento final *m*; **~ trial composite** *n* CINEMAT copia de prueba combinada definitiva *f*; **~ trial print** *n* CINEMAT copia definitiva de prueba *f*
finally: **~ galvanized coating** *n* COATINGS acabado final por galvanizado *m*
finder *n* CINEMAT visor *m*, INSTR anteojo buscador *m*, enfocador *m*, portaobjetos cuadriculado *m*, visor *m*, PHOTO enfocador *m*; **~ hood** *n* PHOTO tapa del visor *f*; **~ point punch** *n* PROD punzón de punto *m*
fine¹: **~-grained** *adj* GEN de grano fino; **~-textured** *adj* GEOL de textura fina
fine²: **~ on the bow** *adv* WATER TRANSP a fil de roda
fine³: **~ adjustment** *n* ELECTRON, INSTR, NUCL, PROD,

TV ajuste fino *m*, ajuste preciso *m*, reglaje de precisión *m*; ~ **aggregate** *n* CONST árido fino *m*; ~ **batt** *n* TEXTIL batán fino *m*; ~ **blanking-die** *n* MECH ENG *press tool* cortador de precisión *m*, matriz de punzonar de precisión *f*, punzón sacabocados de precisión *m*; ~ **blanking-press** *n* MECH ENG cortadora de precisión *f*, prensa de troquelar de precisión *f*, prensa punzonadora de precisión *f*; ~ **castings** *n pl* PROD pieza pequeña de fundición *f*; ~ **coal** *n* COAL carbón menudo *m*; ~ **concentration mill** *n* PROD instalación de concentración de finos *f*; ~ **control** *n* NUCL control fino *m*; ~-**control member** *n* NUCL elemento de control fino *m*; ~-**control rod** *n* MECH ENG varilla de control de precisión *f*; ~ **count** *n* TEXTIL título fino *m*; ~-**counts yarns** *n pl* TEXTIL hilos de títulos finos *m pl*; ~ **crack** *n* MECH ENG fisura fina *f*, grieta fina *f*, hendidura fina *f*; ~ **crusher** *n* COAL, PROD trituradora de finos *f*; ~ **crushing** *n* COAL, PROD trituración fina *f*, trituración de finos *f*; ~-**crushing mill** *n* CHEM TECH molino de molienda en fino *m*, trituradora de finos *f*; ~ **cut** *n* CINEMAT, TV montaje de detalle *m*; ~ **emery cloth** *n* MECH ENG lija fina *f*, tela de esmeril fina *f*; ~-**fluted reamer** *n* MECH ENG escariador de ranuras finas *m*; ~ **focus sleeve** *n* INSTR tubo de alta definición *m*; ~ **furnace carbon black** *n* (*FF carbon black*) P&R negro de humo de horno y partícula fina *m*; ~ **gage** *AmE*, ~ **gauge** *BrE* *n* TEXTIL galga fina *f*; ~ **grain** *n* CINEMAT, METALL, MINE, PHOTO, PROD grano fino *m*; ~-**grain developer** *n* CINEMAT, PHOTO revelador de grano fino *m*; ~-**grain image** *n* CINEMAT, PHOTO, TV imagen de grano fino *f*; ~-**grain master** *n* CINEMAT, PHOTO copia maestra de grano fino *f*; ~-**grained wheel** *n* PROD muela de grano fino *f*; ~ **gravel** *n* CONST grava fina *f*; ~ **grinding** *n* COAL, PROD molienda fina *f*, molturación fina *f*, trituración fina *f*; ~ **line** *n* ELECTRON línea de precisión *f*, PRINT línea delgada *f*; ~-**line printed circuit** *n* ELECTRON circuito impreso con línea de precisión *m*; ~-**offals** *n pl* AGRIC subproductos de molienda *m pl*; ~ **papers** *n* PAPER papeles delgados *m pl*; ~ **pitch** *n* AIR TRANSP *of propeller* paso fino *m*; ~-**pitch screw** *n* CONST tornillo de paso pequeño *m*; ~ **sand** *n* COAL, CONST, PETR TECH, PETROL arena fina *f*, arenilla *f*; ~ **screen** *n* PRINT trama fina *f*; ~-**screen halftone** *n* PRINT semitono de trama fina *m*; ~ **silt** *n* GEOL limo fino *m*; ~ **slip** *n* METALL grieta fina *f*; ~ **soil** *n* AGRIC, COAL terreno liso *m*; ~ **solder** *n* PROD suelda de estaño y plomo *f*; ~ **structure** *n* NUCL, PHYS, RAD PHYS estructura fina *f*; ~-**structure constant** *n* NUCL, PHYS constante de estructura fina *f*; ~-**time based instruction** *n* PROD orden basada en tiempo finito *f*; ~ **trommel** *n* PROD tromel para finos *m*; ~ **tuning** *n* ELECTRON ajuste fino de sintonización *m*, TELECOM sincronización precisa *f*; ~ **worm drive** *n* MECH ENG engranaje de tornillo sinfín de precisión *m*

finely: ~-**threaded micrometer screw** *n* MECH ENG tornillo de micrómetro de paso de precisión *m*, tornillo de micrómetro de paso fino *m*

fineness *n* CONST, WATER TRANSP *shipbuilding* finura *f*; ~ **ratio** *n* AIR TRANSP *streamlined body* proporción de esbeltez *f*, relación de la fineza *f*, MECH ENG alargamiento *m*, esbeltez *f*

fines *n pl* COAL, CONST, MINE finos *m pl*, límites *m pl*, menudos *m pl*, PAPER fibras muy cortas *f pl*

finesse *n* OPT fuerza *f*

Fingal: ~ **process** *n* NUCL proceso Fingal *m*

finger *n* MECH ENG dedo de retención *m*, garra *f*, linguete *m*, uña *f*; ~ **bar** *n* MECH ENG linguete de retención *m*; ~-**grip clip** *n* AIR TRANSP gancho de agarre de dedo *m*; ~-**guide plate** *n* MECH ENG placa guía de garra *f*; ~ **millet** *n* AGRIC mijo africano *m*; ~ **nut** *n* CONST tuerca de orejetas *f*; ~ **plate** *n* CONST chapa de guarda *f*; ~ **post** *n* CONST poste indicador *m*; ~ **release** *n* PHOTO disparador de botón *m*; ~ **stall** *n* SAFE dedal *m*

fingering *n* GEOL, PETROL digitación *f*

finial *n* CONST pináculo *m*, remate *m*

fining: ~ **lap** *n* INSTR herramienta de afino *f*; ~ **period** *n* PROD *Bessemer process* período de afino *m*; ~-**up sequence** *n* GEOL secuencia granodecreciente *f*, secuencia positiva *f*

finings *n pl* FOOD cola de pescado *f*, gelatinas *f pl*

finish[1] *n* C&G acabado *m*, terminado *m*, COATINGS, COLOUR acabado *m*, MECH acabado *m*, capa superficial protectora *f*, última mano *f*, P&R, PAPER, PRINT, PROD, REFRIG acabado *m*, TEXTIL apresto *m*, acabado *m*

finish[2] *vt* GEN acabar, COAL pulir

finished: ~ **appearance** *n* TEXTIL aspecto acabado *m*; ~ **fabric** *n* TEXTIL tejido acabado *m*; ~ **goods** *n* TEXTIL productos acabados *m pl*; ~-**goods store** *n* PACK almacén de productos acabados *m*; ~ **quartz** *n* ELECTRON acabado del cuarzo *m*; ~ **width of cloth** *n* TEXTIL ancho acabado de la tela *m*

finisher *n* CONST *public works* afinadora *f*, cementista *m*, perfiladora *f*, pulidor *m*; ~ **scutcher** *n* TEXTIL desplegador acabador *m*

finishing *n* GEN acabado *m*; ~ **agent** *n* TEXTIL agente de acabado *m*; ~ **belt** *n* C&G banda de acabado *f*; ~ **cattle** *n pl* AGRIC vacunos en periodo final de engorde *m pl*, vacunos en terminación de engorde *m pl*; ~ **coat** *n* CONST, P&R última mano *f*; ~ **groove** *n* ACOUST surco finalizador *m*; ~ **reamer** *n* MECH ENG escariador de acabado *m*; ~ **reamer for Morse tapers** *n* MECH ENG escariador de acabado para conos morse *m*; ~ **sander** *n* MECH ENG pulidora de acabado *f*; ~ **stage** *n* TEXTIL fase de acabado *f*; ~ **technique** *n* TEXTIL técnica de acabado *f*; ~ **varnish** *n* C&G, COATINGS, COLOUR barniz de acabado *m*, barniz de lustre *m*, MECH barniz de acabado *m*

finite: ~ **element** *n* MECH, MECH ENG elemento finito *m*, elemento limitado *m*; ~-**element calculation method** *n* MECH, MECH ENG método de cálculo de elementos finitos *m*; ~-**element structural model** *n* SPACE modelo estructural de elemento finito *m*; ~ **elements for mechanical engineering** *n pl* MECH ENG elementos finitos para ingeniería mecánica *m pl*, elementos limitados para ingeniería mecánica *m pl*; ~ **elements methods** *n pl* MECH ENG métodos de elementos finitos *m pl*, métodos de elementos limitados *m pl*; ~ **impulse response** *n* (*FIR*) ELECTRON respuesta de impulso finito *f* (*RIF*); ~-**impulse response filter** *n* (*FIR filter*) ELECTRON, TELECOM filtro de respuesta de impulso finito *m*; ~-**range interaction** *n* NUCL interacción de alcance finito *f*

finned: ~ **can** *n* NUCL vaina con aletas disipadoras de calor *f*; ~ **cooler** *n* REFRIG enfriador de tubos de aletas *m*, THERMO enfriador de tubos de aletas *m*, refrigerador de aletas *m*; ~ **heater** *n* THERMO calefactor de aletas *m*, calentador de tubos de aletas *m*; ~ **radiator** *n* AUTO radiador de aletas *m*; ~ **surface** *n*

HEAT ENG *of measuring instrument* superficie aleteada *f*; **~ tube** *n* MECH tubo de aletas *m*

fiorite: **~ terrace** *n* GEOPHYS terraza de fiorita *f*

FIR *abbr* (*finite impulse response*) ELECTRON RIF (*respuesta de impulso finito*)

fire[1]: **~-polished** *adj* C&G pulido con fuego; **~-resistant** *adj* GEN ignífugo, HEAT, HEAT ENG, PROD, SAFE, THERMO pirorresistente, no propagador de llama; **~-resisting** *adj* GEN ignífugo, HEAT, HEAT ENG, PROD, SAFE, THERMO pirorresistente, no propagador de llama; **~-retarding** *adj* GEN ignífugo

fire[2] *n* GAS, HEAT, SAFE *diaphragm*, THERMO incendio *m*, lumbre *f*; **~ alarm** *n* AIR TRANSP alarma contra-incendios *f*, ELEC, SAFE alarma contraincendios *f*, alarma de fuego *f*, alarma de incendios *f*, avisador de incendios *m*, THERMO, WATER TRANSP alarma contra-incendios *f*, alarma de incendios *f*, avisador de incendios *m*; **~ area** *n* NUCL zona de incendio *f*; **~ blanket** *n* SAFE cobija contra incendios *f* (*AmL*), manta contra incendios *f* (*Esp*); **~ bridge** *n* PROD *of furnace* puente *m*, tranco *m*; **~ bulkhead** *n* SAFE mamparo contraincendios *m*, SPACE cabeza de encendido *f*, WATER TRANSP *ship design* mamparo contraincendios *m*; **~ chamber** *n* HYDRAUL *of metallurgical furnace*, PROD, THERMO cámara de combustión *f*, hogar *m*; **~-control line** *n* AGRIC línea de control de fuego *f*; **~-control plan** *n* WATER TRANSP plano de lucha contra incendios *m*; **~ correction** *n* MILIT corrección del tiro *f*; **~ curtain** *n* SAFE, THERMO cortina de fuego *f*; **~ cutoff** *n* HEAT ENG *protection* cortafuegos *m*; **~ damage** *n* QUALITY, SAFE avería por el incendio *f*, daños por el incendio *m pl*, daños por fuego *m pl*; **~ damper** *n* HEAT ENG cortafuegos *m*; **~ danger station** *n* AGRIC *conservation* observatorio contra incendios *m*; **~-detecting wire** *n* AIR TRANSP, SAFE cable de detección de incendio *m*; **~ detection and alarm system** *n* SAFE sistema de detección y alarma de incendios *m*; **~-detection harness** *n* AIR TRANSP, SAFE arnés de detección de incendios *m*; **~-detection system** *n* AIR TRANSP, SAFE, WATER TRANSP sistema de detección de incendios *m*; **~ detector** *n* SAFE detector de incendios *m*; **~ door** *n* PROD puerta del hogar *f*, SAFE puerta contra incendios *f*, puerta del hogar *f*, puerta del horno *f*, THERMO puerta contra incendios *f*, puerta contrafuegos *f*, puerta del hogar *f*, puerta del horno *f*; **~ drill** *n* PROD, SAFE, THERMO ejercicios de contraincendios *m pl*, ejercicios de salvamento de incendios *m pl*, simulacro de incendio *m*; **~-engine** *n* SAFE carro bomba contra incendios *m* (*AmL*), coche bomba contra incendios *m*, THERMO bomba de contra-incendios *f*, bomba de incendios *f*, VEH bomba de contraincendios *f*; **~-escape** *n* CONST, SAFE, THERMO escala de salvamento *f*, escalera para caso de incendio *f*, salida de incendio *f*; **~ exit** *n* CONST, SAFE, THERMO salida de emergencia *f*; **~ extinguisher** *n* AIR TRANSP, CONST, MECH ENG, SAFE, THERMO extinguidor de incendios *m* (*AmL*), extintor de incendios *m* (*Esp*), matafuegos *m*; **~-extinguisher filling** *n* AIR TRANSP, CONST, SAFE, THERMO, WATER TRANSP carga de los extinguidores de incendios *f* (*AmL*), carga de los extintores de incendios *f* (*Esp*); **~-extinguishing agent** *n* SAFE agente extintor de incendios *m*; **~ finish** *n* C&G acabado a fuego *m*; **~ finisher** *n* C&G, COATINGS acabador *m*; **~ grate** *n* PROD emparrillado *m*, parrilla

f (*AmL*); **~ hazard** *n* AIR TRANSP, CONST, SAFE, THERMO, WATER TRANSP peligro de incendio *m*, riesgo de incendio *m*; **~ hole** *n* PROD *of furnace* boca del hogar *f*; **~ hose** *n* CONST, SAFE, THERMO manguera de incendios *f*; **~-hose coupling** *n* CONST, SAFE, THERMO conector de manguera contra incendios *m*; **~-hose nozzle** *n* CONST, SAFE, THERMO boquilla de manguera contra incendios *f*, lanza de manguera contra incendios *f*; **~-hose reel** *n* CONST, SAFE, THERMO carrete para manguera contra incendios *m*; **~ hydrant** *n* BrE (*cf fireplug AmE*) CONST, SAFE, THERMO, WATER, WATER TRANSP boca contraincendios *f*, boca de incendios *f*, hidrante para incendios *m*, toma de agua contraincendios *f*; **~ ladder** *n* CONST, SAFE escalera de incendios *f*; **~ lamp** *n* PROD *for skin-drying* lámpara de flamear *f*; **~ load** *n* THERMO carga de fuego *f*; **~ lobby** *n* THERMO mosquete de rueda *m*; **~ marks** *n pl* C&G marcas de fuego *f pl*; **~ monitor** *n* MAR POLL can lanzaespuma *m*; **~ point** *n* REFRIG punto de combustión *m*, SAFE temperatura de inflamabilidad espontánea *f*; **~-polished edge** *n* C&G borde pulido a fuego *m*; **~-polishing** *n* C&G pulido a fuego *m*; **~ precautions** *n pl* SAFE, THERMO precauciones contra incendios *f pl*; **~ prevention** *n* SAFE, THERMO prevención contra-incendios *f*, prevención de incendios *f*; **~ protection** *n* SAFE, THERMO protección contra incendios *f*; **~-protection door** *n* CONST, SAFE, THERMO puerta de protección contra incendios *f*; **~-protection gate** *n* CONST, SAFE, THERMO compuerta contra incendios *f*; **~-protection plan** *n* SAFE, THERMO plan de protección contra incendios *m*; **~ pump** *n* CONST, SAFE, THERMO bomba de incendios *f*; **~ regulations** *n pl* SAFE normativa sobre incendios *f*; **~ rescue appliance** *n* SAFE, THERMO aparato para rescate en incendios *m*; **~ resistance** *n* P&R, THERMO resistencia al fuego *f*; **~-resistant bulkhead** *n* THERMO mampara ignífuga *f*, mampara pirorresistente *f*, tabique corta-fuegos *m*; **~-resistant coating** *n* COATINGS, THERMO revestimiento antinflamable *m*, revestimiento ignífugo *m*, revestimiento refractario *m*; **~-resistant door** *n* CONST, SAFE, THERMO puerta ignífuga *f*, puerta pirorresistente *f*; **~-resistant layer** *n* COATINGS, THERMO capa ignífuga *f*; **~-resistant paint** *n* COLOUR, CONST, THERMO pintura ignífuga *f*, pintura resistente al fuego *f*; **~-resistant paper** *n* PAPER, THERMO papel ignífugo *m*; **~-resisting bulkhead** *n* THERMO mampara ignífuga *f*; **~-retardant coat** *n* COATINGS, NUCL, THERMO reves-timiento ignífugo *m*; **~ riser** *n* THERMO tubería de fuego *f*, tubería de humos *f*; **~-rising main** *n* THERMO conducto ascendente de humos *m*; **~ room** *n* PROD *of blast furnace* cuba *f*, safety *n* MILIT, SAFE seguridad contra incendios *f*; **~ safety sign** *n* SAFE letrero de peligro contra incendio *m*, señales de peligro contra incendio *f pl*; **~ screen** *n* PROD pantalla ignífuga *f*, parachispas *m*, SAFE cortina contra fuego *f*; **~ siren** *n* SAFE sirena de incendio *f*; **~ spot** *n* AGRIC fuego secundario *m*; **~-spread prevention** *n* SAFE, THERMO prevención de la propagación del fuego *f*; **~ sprinkler** *n* SAFE, THERMO aspersor contra incendios *m*, rociador contra incendios *m*; **~ station** *n* THERMO cuartel de bomberos *m*; **~ stop** *n* SAFE altar *m*, muro *m*, THERMO altar *m*, muro cortafuegos *m*; **~ test** *n* SAFE prueba de inflamabilidad *f*; **~ test for furniture** *n* SAFE prueba de inflamabilidad para muebles *f*;

~-tube boiler n HEAT caldera con tubos de humos f, caldera humotubular f; **~ valve** n MECH ENG, SAFE, THERMO válvula del sistema contraincendios f; **~ wire** n AIR TRANSP cable de incendios m

fire³ vt C&G, FOOD encender, hornear, MILIT disparar; **~ up** vt THERMO activar

fireboat n SAFE, WATER TRANSP embarcación contraincendios f

firebox n HEAT fogón m, HYDRAUL cámara de combustión f, RAIL caja de fuegos f, cajón de fuegos m, THERMO caja de fuegos f, cámara de combustión f; **~ tube plate** n RAIL chapa tubular de la caja de fuegos f

firebreak n THERMO sendero cortafuegos m

firebrick n C&G, CONST, HEAT, THERMO ladrillo refractario m

fireclay n C&G barro refractario m, GEOL, THERMO arcilla refractaria f; **~ brick** n LAB mechanism ladrillo de arcilla refractaria m; **~ crucible** n C&G crisol de barro refractario m; **~ mold** AmE, **~ mould** BrE n C&G molde de barro refractario m

fired¹: **~-on** adj C&G horneado

fired²: **~ clay** n C&G barro quemado m; **~ earthenware** n C&G, PROD alfarería cocida f; **~ pressure vessel** n MECH ENG caldera a presión f; **~ tube** n ELECTRON tubo activado m

firedamp n COAL, MINE, THERMO grisú m, metano m, mofeta f; **~-proof machine** n COAL máquina a prueba de grisú f

firedog n HEAT morillo m

firefighter n CONST, SAFE, THERMO apagafuegos m, bombero m

firefighting n CONST, SAFE, THERMO combate de incendios m, extinción de incendios f, lucha contraincendios f; **~ equipment** n SAFE, THERMO equipo para combate de incendios m; **~ personnel** n SAFE, THERMO brigada de incendios f; **~ and rescue equipment** n SAFE, THERMO equipo para combate de incendios y rescate m; **~ vehicle** n SAFE, THERMO vehículo contra incendios m

fireguard n THERMO guardafuegos m, parachispas m

firelight n THERMO lumbre f

firelighter n HEAT ENG encendedor m

firelock n THERMO mosquete de rueda m

fireman n CONST, SAFE, THERMO bombero m; **~'s helmet** n SAFE casco de bombero m

fireplug n AmE (cf fire hydrant BrE) CONST, SAFE, THERMO, WATER, WATER TRANSP boca contraincendios f, boca de incendios f, hidrante para incendios m, toma de agua contraincendios f

fireproof¹ adj GEN a prueba de fuego, a prueba de incendios, antideflagrante, antillama, ignífugo, incombustible, ininflamable, refractario

fireproof²: **~ bulkhead** n SPACE conector ignífugo m, tabique cortafuego m; **~ clothing** n SAFE prendas ignífugas f pl, prendas incombustibles f pl; **~ coat** n COATINGS capa ignífuga f, revestimiento ignífugo m, COLOUR, THERMO revestimiento ignífugo m; **~ coating** n COATINGS pintura a prueba de fuego f, pintura incombustible f, sustancia retardante a las llamas f, CONST pintura a prueba de fuego f, P&R, THERMO pintura a prueba de fuego f, pintura incombustible f, sustancia retardante a las llamas f; **~ color** AmE, **~ colour** BrE n COLOUR colorante ignífugo m; **~ drilling machine** n MINE, SAFE, THERMO máquina perforadora ignífuga f;

~ enclosure n SAFE receptáculo a prueba de incendios m; **~ floor** n SAFE suelo refractario m; **~ glass** n C&G vidrio a prueba de fuego m; **~ lighting installation** n ELEC, ELEC ENG, SAFE, THERMO instalación eléctrica antideflagrante f, instalación eléctrica incombustible f; **~ motor** n ELEC ENG motor antideflagrante m, motor incombustible m, SAFE motor incombustible m, THERMO motor antideflagrante m, motor incombustible m; **~ paint** n COLOUR pintura ignífuga f, pintura resistente al fuego f, CONST pintura ignífuga f; **~ pottery** n C&G loza a prueba de fuego f; **~ stirrer** n LAB agitador refractario m; **~ switch** n ELEC conmutador antideflagrante m, conmutador incombustible m, conmutador que no produce llama m, SAFE, THERMO interruptor ignífugo m; **~ telephone system** n CONST sistema telefónico a prueba de incendios m

fireproof³ vt GEN ignifugar, incombustibilizar

fireproofed adj GEN ignifugado, incombustibilizado, SAFE, THERMO protegido del fuego

fireproofing n C&G, COATINGS ignifugación f, incombustibilización f, COLOUR incombustibilización f, MECH, P&R, PACK, SAFE, THERMO ignifugación f, incombustibilización f; **~ paint** n COLOUR, CONST pintura ignífuga f

fireseal n AIR TRANSP, SAFE hermético contra fuegos m

fireship n THERMO brulote m

firetrap n SAFE lugar propenso a incendios m

firewall n AIR TRANSP, CONST, PETR TECH, SAFE, SPACE barrera contra fuegos f, mampara cortafuegos f, muro cortafuegos m, pantalla cortafuegos f

firing n C&G cocimiento m, ELEC ENG of reactor encendido m, of gas tube, thyristor, triac activación f, ELECTRON activación f, alimentación f, MINE cambio de color por exposición al fuego m, disparo m, SPACE encendido m; **~ circuit** n MINE circuito de activación m, circuito de encendido m; **~ on** n C&G horneado m; **~ order** n VEH orden de encendido m; **~ pin** n MILIT percutor m; **~ pulse** n ELEC ENG of gas tube, thyristor, triac impulso actuante m, pulso de disparo m; **~ range** n C&G intervalo de cocción m, MILIT campo de tiro m; **~ temperature** n C&G temperatura de cocido f; **~ test** n SPACE prueba de tiro f; **~ time** n ELEC ENG tiempo de activación m; **~ voltage** n ELEC ENG tensión de activación f, voltaje de cebado m; **~ window** n SPACE ventana de lanzamiento f, ventana de tiro f, ventana especial de lanzamiento f

firkin n FOOD barrilito m

firm¹: **~-planned** adj PROD de planeamiento en firme

firm² n PROD, TEXTIL empresa f; **~ allocation** n PROD asignación en firme f; **~ ground** n CONST terreno firme m; **~ handle** n TEXTIL tacto firme m

firmer: **~ gouge** n MECH ENG gubia de maceta f, gubia punzón f

firmly: **~-asset fabric** n TEXTIL tejido tupido m

firmware n COMP&DP micro-instrucción m, soporte lógico inalterable m, PRINT microprogramación f; **~ chip set** n PROD juego de circuitos integrados para micrologicales m

first¹: **~ aid** n SAFE primeros auxilios m pl; **~-aid box** n SAFE botiquín de primeros auxilios m; **~-aid cabinet** n AmE (cf first-aid cupboard BrE) SAFE gabinete de primeros auxilios m; **~-aid class** n SAFE clase de primeros auxilios f; **~-aid cupboard** n BrE (cf first-aid cabinet AmE) SAFE gabinete de primeros auxilios m; **~-aid kit** *n* SAFE botiquín de primeros auxilios *m*; **~-aid personnel** *n* SAFE personal de primeros auxilios *m*; **~-aid post** *n* SAFE, WATER TRANSP puesto de primeros auxilios *m*; **~-aid procedure** *n* SAFE técnica de primeros auxilios *f*; **~-aid treatment room** *n* SAFE enfermería de primeros auxilios *f*; **~-aid work** *n* SAFE prácticas de primeros auxilios *f pl*; **~-aid worker** *n* SAFE socorrista *m*; **~ aider** *n* SAFE socorrista *m*; **~ anode** *n* ELEC ENG ánodo primario *m*; **~ answer print** *n* CINEMAT primera copia *f*; **~ arrivals** *n pl* GEOL primeras llegadas *f pl*; **~-article configuration review** *n* (*FACR*) SPACE revisión de la configuración según la cláusula primera *f*; **~ assembly** *n* CINEMAT primer montaje *m*; **~ bottom** *n* AGRIC llanura aluvial *f*; **~-choice group** *n* TELECOM grupo preferente *m*; **~ coat** *n* COATINGS, COLOUR primera capa *f*, primera mano *f*; **~ condenser lamp** *n* PHOTO lente condensadora primaria *f*; **~ condenser lens** *n* CINEMAT, INSTR, OPT lente condensadora primaria *f*; **~ connection to grid** *n* NUCL acoplamiento inicial a la red *m*; **~ critical experiment** *n* NUCL experimento de criticidad inicial *m*; **~ criticality** *n* NUCL criticidad inicial *f*; **~-degree burn** *n* SAFE quemadura de primer grado *f*; **~ detector** *n* ELECTRON detector principal *m*; **~ dogwatch** *n* MILIT primer cuartillo *m*; **~ down** *n* PRINT primero *m*; **~-down ink** *n* PRINT primera tinta *f*; **~ dryer** *n* PAPER primer grupo de secadores *m*; **~ firing** *n* C&G primer cocido *m*; **~ generation** *n* COMP&DP primera generación *f*; **~-generation computer** *n* COMP&DP computador de primera generación *m* (*AmL*), computadora de primera generación *f* (*AmL*), ordenador de primera generación *m* (*Esp*); **~ harmonic** *n* ELECTRON armónico fundamental *m*, primer armónico *m*, PHYS armónico fundamental *m*; **~ IF amplifier** *n* ELECTRON amplificador de primera FI *m*; **~ injection** *n* ELECTRON inyección de entrada *f*; **~ intermediate frequency** *n* ELEC, ELECTRON primera frecuencia intermedia *f*; **~ ionization potential** *n* PHYS primer potencial de ionización *m*; **~ law** *n* PHYS primera ley *f*; **~ local oscillator** *n* ELECTRON oscilador local principal *m*; **~ mate** *n* WATER TRANSP *merchant navy* piloto de primera clase *m*; **~ mixer** *n* ELECTRON mezclador inicial *m*; **~-nearest neighbors** *AmE*, **~-nearest neighbours** *BrE* *n* METALL vecindad próxima al origen *f*; **~ officer** *n* WATER TRANSP primer oficial *m*; **~-order filter** *n* ELECTRON filtro de primer orden *m*; **~-order quantity** *n* GEOM cantidad de primer orden *f*; **~-order reaction** *n* CHEM, METALL reacción de primer orden *f*; **~-order transition** *n* PHYS transición de primer orden *f*; **~ oxidizing firing** *n* C&G primer cocido oxidante *m*; **~ pair of rollers** *n* C&G primer par de rodillos *m*; **~ runnings** *n pl* FOOD aguas de cabeza *f pl*, primer licor *m*; **~-stage planet gear** *n* AIR TRANSP *helicopter* engranaje planetario de primera etapa *m*; **~-stage sun gear** *n* AIR TRANSP engranaje solar de primera etapa *m*; **~-trial composite** *n* CINEMAT primera copia combinada de prueba *f*; **~ unit** *n* CINEMAT primera unidad *f*; **~-window fiber** *AmE*, **~-window fibre** *n* *BrE* (*FWF*) OPT, TELECOM fibra de primera ventana *f*, fibra que opera en la primera ventana de longitudes de ondas *f*

first² : **~-in-first-out** *phr* (*FIFO*) COMP&DP *memories* primero en entrar, primero en salir

firth *n* OCEAN, WATER TRANSP brazo de mar *m*, ría *f*

fisetin *n* CHEM fisetina *f*

fish: **~ basket** *n* OCEAN nasa *f*; **~-breeding** *n* FOOD cría piscícola *f*; **~ corral** *n* OCEAN corral de peces *m*; **~ detector** *n* OCEAN detector de peces *m*; **~ eye** *n* PAPER ojo de pescado *m*; **~-eye lens** *n* CINEMAT lente de distorsión *f*, ojo de pez *m*, OPT lente de distorsión *f*, PHOTO, TV lente de distorsión *f*, ojo de pez *m*; **~ farmer** *n* OCEAN acuicultor *m*; **~ farming** *n* OCEAN acuicultura *f*, cultivo de peces *m*; **~ finder** *n* OCEAN patrón de pesca *m*; **~ gig** *n* OCEAN bote de pesca *m*; **~ hold** *n* OCEAN bodega *f*; **~ meal** *n* OCEAN alimento para peces *m*; **~ oil** *n* CHEM aceite de pescado *m*; **~ paper** *n* ELEC ENG fibra aislante *f*; **~ pass** *n* FUELLESS escalera de peces *f*; **~ protein concentrate** *n* (*FPC*) OCEAN concentrado de proteínas de peces *m*; **~ room** *n* OCEAN cámara de almacenamiento *f*; **~ smoking** *n* OCEAN abrumadero de peces *m*; **~ stock** *n* OCEAN captura *f*, stock de peces *m*; **~ trade** *n* FOOD industria pesquera *f*, OCEAN industria pesquera *f*, palanqueo *m*, WATER TRANSP comercio del pescado *m*; **~ traps** *n pl* OCEAN artes de pesca *f pl*, redes *f pl*

Fisher: **~ boom** *n* CINEMAT, TV pértiga Fisher *f*

fisherman: **~'s bend** *n* WATER TRANSP vuelta de rezón *f*

fishery *n* FOOD, WATER TRANSP pesquería *f*; **~ protection vessel** *n* WATER TRANSP guardapescas *m*

fishing *n* PETR TECH, PETROL pesca *f*, recuperación de herramientas perdidas *f*; **~ basin** *n* OCEAN cuenca de lavado *f*; **~ drift** *n* OCEAN, WATER TRANSP *net* arte de deriva *m*, arte de enmalle *m*; **~ drift-net** *n* WATER TRANSP red de deriva *f*, red de enmalle *f*; **~ efficiency** *n* OCEAN eficiencia pesquera *f*; **~ effort** *n* OCEAN esfuerzo pesquero *m*; **~ expert** *n* OCEAN experto en pesca *m*; **~ fleet** *n* WATER TRANSP flota pesquera *f*; **~ gear** *n* OCEAN aparejo *m*; **~ ground** *n* WATER TRANSP caladero *m*; **~ net** *n* OCEAN red de pesca *f*; **~ rights** *n pl* WATER TRANSP derechos de pesca *m pl*; **~ smack** *n* WATER TRANSP zumaca pesquera *f*; **~ socket** *n* PETR TECH pescante *m*; **~ tool** *n* PETR TECH pescaherramientas *m*, pescante *m*; **~ trip** *n* OCEAN crucero de pesca *m*; **~ vessel** *n* OCEAN, WATER TRANSP buque pesquero *m*; **~ zone** *n* OCEAN zona de pesca *f*

fishplate *n* *BrE* (*cf joint bar AmE*) RAIL eclisa *f*; **~ block** *n* RAIL cubrejunta *f*

fishplating *n* *BrE* (*cf applying joint bar AmE*) RAIL eclisa *f*, eclisaje *m*

fishpole *n* CINEMAT caña *f*

fishtail: **~ bit** *n* PETR TECH trépano en cola de carpa *m*

fissile¹ *adj* NUCL, PART PHYS, PHYS fisionable, fisil

fissile² : **~ inventory ratio** *n* NUCL razón del inventario fisionable *f*; **~ isotope** *n* NUCL, PART PHYS, PHYS isótopo fisionable *m*; **~ material** *n* NUCL, PHYS, RAD PHYS material fisionable *m*

fission: **~ cross-section** *n* PHYS sección eficaz de fisión *f*; **~ fragments** *n pl* NUCL, PART PHYS, PHYS fragmentos de fisión *m pl*; **~-gas plenum** *n* NUCL espacio para gases de fisión *m*; **~ ionization chamber** *n* NUCL, PART PHYS, PHYS cámara de ionización de fisión *f*; **~ neutron** *n* PART PHYS, RAD PHYS neutrón de fisión *m*; **~ recoil** *n* NUCL partícula de retroceso de fisión *f*; **~ spike** *n* NUCL pico de fisión *m*, semilla *f*; **~ track dating** *n* GEOL datación por trazos *f*, PHYS datación mediante trazas de fisión *f*

fissionable *adj* NUCL, PART PHYS, PHYS escindible, fisionable

fissium *n* NUCL fisio *m*

fissure *n* CONST, GEOPHYS, OCEAN fisura *f*, grieta *f*; ~ **water** *n* COAL manantial de fisura *m*

fist *n* PRINT signo de llamada *m*

fit[1]: ~ **to drink** *adj* FOOD potable

fit[2] *n* MECH ENG montaje *m*

fit[3] *vt* C&G ajustar, MECH adaptar, ajustar, MECH ENG adaptar, ajustar, montar, WATER TRANSP fijar, instalar; ~ **with** *vt* MECH ENG armar con, equipar con, proveer con; ~ **in** *vt* MECH ENG colocar en, introducir en, meter en, montar en; ~ **into** *vt* MECH ENG ajustar dentro de, colocar dentro de, meter dentro de; ~ **on** *vt* MECH ENG colocar al extremo de, montar al extremo de; ~ **out** *vt* MECH ENG armar, equipar, proveer, suministrar, surtir, WATER TRANSP *ship* armar; ~ **to** *vt* MECH ENG ajustar, colocar, montar

fit[4] *vi* PRINT adecuarse; ~ **together** *vi* GEOM encajarse

FIT *abbr* (*formation interval test*) PETROL prueba de intervalos de formación *f*

FITE *abbr* (*forward-interworking telephony event*) TELECOM circuito de telefonía entrelazada hacia adelante *m*

fitment *n* CONST, MECH ENG accesorio *m*, montaje *m*, montura *f*, soporte *m*

fits: ~ **and clearances** *n pl* MECH ENG ajustes y tolerancias *m pl*, medidas y tolerancias *f pl*

fitted: ~ **with** *adj* TELECOM equipado con

fitter *n* MECH, MECH ENG instalador *m*, mecánico *m*, montador *m*; ~'**s hammer** *n* MECH ENG martillo de ajustador *m*, martillo de mecánico *m*

fitting *n* CONST accesorio *m*, MECH *process* colocación *f*, adaptador *m*, conector *m*, accesorio *m*, montaje *m*, ajuste *m*, MECH ENG *device* ajuste *m*, accesorio *m*, conector *m*, adaptador *m*, *process* colocación *f*, montaje *m*, PROD accesorio *m*, WATER TRANSP *of ship* accesorio *m*, *shipbuilding* armamento *m*; ~ **bolt** *n* MECH ENG perno de montaje *m*, perno de sujeción *m*; ~ **device** *n* MECH ENG dispositivo de montaje *m*, dispositivo de sujeción *m*; ~ **dimensions** *n pl* MECH ENG medidas de ajuste *f pl*, medidas de instalación *f pl*, medidas de montaje *f pl*; ~ **out** *n* CONST equipamiento *m*, habilitación *f*, WATER TRANSP *of ship* armamento *m*; ~-**out berth** *n* WATER TRANSP dique de construcción *m*, dársena de construcción *f*; ~ **shop** *n* MECH ENG taller de ajuste *m*

five: ~-**axis numerical control** *n* MECH ENG control numérico de cinco ejes *m*, control numérico penta axial *m*; ~-**layer barrier film laminate** *n* PACK laminado de cinco capas de película barrera *m*; ~-**legged transformer** *n* ELEC transformador de cinco circuitos derivados *m*; ~-**sided broach** *n* MECH ENG broche pentagonal *m*

fix[1] *n* SPACE *position* punto de intersección *m*, situación relativa *f*, WATER TRANSP *navigation* punto *m*

fix[2] *vt* CONST fijar, inmovilizar, *beam* arreglar, instalar, poner en orden, reparar, *floor joist to wall* colocar, MECH ENG *piston firmly on rod* fijar, posicionar

fixed[1] *adj* MECH, MECH ENG colocado, fijo, montado, no regulable

fixed[2]: ~ **amplitude** *n* ELECTRON amplitud definitiva *f*; ~ **angle sounding** *n* OCEAN sondeo en ángulo fijo *m*; ~ **armature** *n* ELEC *generator*, ELEC ENG inducido fijo *m*; ~ **attenuator** *n* ELECTRON atenuador permanente *m*; ~-**base notation** *n* COMP&DP notación de base fija *f*, MECH ENG broche pentagonal *m*; ~ **beacon** *n* WATER TRANSP baliza fija *f*; ~ **beam** *n* CONST viga empotrada *f*; ~ **capacitor** *n* ELEC, ELEC ENG, PHYS capacitor no regulable *m*, condensador fijo *m*, condensador no regulable *m*; ~ **carbon** *n* CHEM carbono combinado *m*, GEOL carbono fijo *m*; ~ **coil** *n* ELEC bobina fija *f*; ~ **contact** *n* ELEC, ELEC ENG contacto fijo *m*; ~-**data processing terminal equipment** *n* TELECOM terminal de procesado de datos fijos *m*; ~ **delay** *n* ELEC *of relay switch* retardo fijo *m*; ~-**delivery pump** *n* PROD bomba de descarga constante *f*; ~ **disk** *n* COMP&DP disco fijo *m*; ~-**displacement motor** *n* PROD motor de desplazamiento constante *m*; ~-**distance lights** *n pl* AIR TRANSP luces de distancia fija *f pl*; ~-**end moment** *n* CONST momento de empotramiento *m*; ~ **equipment** *n* CONST equipo fijo *m*; ~ **error on radio altimeter** *n* AIR TRANSP error fijo en el radioaltímetro *m*; ~ **field** *n* COMP&DP campo fijo *m*; ~ **fire extinguisher** *n* SAFE extintor de incendios fijo *m*, extintor de incendios interconstruido *m*; ~-**focus** *n* CINEMAT, PHOTO, TV foco fijo *m*; ~-**focus camera** *n* CINEMAT, PHOTO, TV cámara fotográfica de foco fijo *f*; ~-**focus lens** *n* CINEMAT, OPT, PHOTO, TV lente de foco fijo *f*; ~ **format** *n* COMP&DP formato fijo *m*; ~-**frequency magnetron** *n* ELECTRON magnetrón de frecuencia constante *m*; ~-**frequency oscillator** *n* ELECTRON oscilador de frecuencia constante *m*; ~-**frequency synthesizer** *n* ELECTRON sintetizador de frecuencia constante *m*; ~-**gain filter** *n* ELECTRON filtro de ganancia constante *m*, filtro de ganancia permanente *m*; ~-**gain filtering** *n* ELECTRON filtrado de ganancia permanente *m*; ~ **generator** *n* SPACE alternador fijo *m*, generador inamovible *m*; ~ **grate** *n* HEAT parrilla fija *f*; ~ **guard** *n* SAFE protección fija *f*; ~ **head** *n* COMP&DP cabeza fija *f*, cabezal fijo *m*; ~ **length** *n* COMP&DP longitud fija *f*; ~-**length block** *n* COMP&DP bloque de longitud fija *m*; ~-**length record** *n* COMP&DP registro de longitud fija *m*; ~ **lift** *n* MINE altura fija *f* (*Esp*), piso fijo *m* (*Esp*), *thickness of ore* altura de extracción *f* (*AmL*); ~ **light** *n* WATER TRANSP luz fija *f*; ~ **load** *n* ELEC ENG carga constante *f*; ~ **loss** *n* ELEC pérdida fija *f*; ~ **member** *n* MECH ENG pieza fija *f*; ~ **oil** *n* CHEM aceite fijo *m*; ~-**order quantity** *n* PROD cantidad fija de pedido *f*; ~-**pitch propeller** *n* AIR TRANSP hélice de paso fijo *f*; ~ **plant** *n* PROD equipo inamovible *m*; ~ **point** *n* PROD coma fija *f*, CONST, TELECOM punto fijo *m*; ~-**point arithmetic** *n* COMP&DP, MATH aritmética de coma fija *f*; ~-**point notation** *n* COMP&DP notación de coma fija *f*; ~-**point part** *n* COMP&DP parte de coma fija *f*; ~ **pole** *n* ELEC, ELEC ENG polo fijo *m*; ~-**radix notation** *n* COMP&DP notación de base fija *f*; ~ **resistor** *n* ELEC, ELEC ENG, PHYS resistencia fija *f*, resistor no regulable *m*; ~-**ring gear** *n* AIR TRANSP engranaje anular fijo *m*; ~-**roller sluice gate** *n* FUELLESS compuerta rodante *f*; ~-**satellite service** *n* (*FSS*) SPACE servicio fijo por satélite *m*; ~ **sequencer** *n* TELECOM secuenciador fijo *m*; ~ **set** *n* MINE instalación de extracción *f* (*AmL*), instalación fija *f* (*Esp*); ~-**sieve jig** *n* PROD criba de rejilla fija *f*; ~-**spindle circular-saw bench** *n* PROD sierra circular de eje fijo *f*; ~-**stator vane** *n* AIR TRANSP aleta de estátor fija *f*; ~ **steady rest** *n* MECH ENG *of lathe* luneta fija *f*; ~-**stick stability** *n* AIR TRANSP estabilidad con la palanca de mandos fijada *f*; ~ **stinger** *n* PETROL espolón fijo *m*; ~ **stop** *n* MECH ENG tope fijo *m*; ~ **table** *n* C&G *in mirror-making* mesa fija *f*; ~-**target experiment** *n* PART PHYS experimento del anticátodo fijo *m*; ~ **tongs** *n pl* AUTO pinza de freno fija *f*; ~-**tuned cavity resonator** *n* ELECTRON resonador con cavidad de sintonización constante *m*; ~-**tuning** *n* ELECTRON sintonización constante *f*; ~ **wheel** *n* MECH ENG *fast on axle* engranaje fijo *m*, piñón fijo *m*, rueda fija *f*; ~ **wing** *n* AIR TRANSP, TRANSP ala fija *f*; ~-**wing aircraft** *n* AIR TRANSP avión de ala fija *m*; ~ **word length** *n* COMP&DP longitud de palabra fija *f*; ~-**wordlength computer** *n* COMP&DP computador de longitud de palabra fija *m* (*AmL*), computadora de longitud de palabra fija *f* (*AmL*), ordenador de longitud de palabra fija *m* (*Esp*)

fixer *n* CHEM TECH, CINEMAT, PHOTO baño fijador *m*

fixing *n* CONST inmovilización *f*, GAS arreglo *m*, compostura *f*, MECH ENG anclado *m*, colocación *f*, empotramiento *m*, fijación *f*, montaje *m*; ~ **bath** *n* CHEM TECH, CINEMAT, PHOTO baño fijador *m*; ~ **screw** *n* CONST, MECH ENG tornillo de fijación *m*, tornillo de montaje *m*

fixture *n* MECH ENG *machine tools* portapiezas *m*, montaje de sujeción *m*, plantilla sujetadora *f*, *object firmly in place* accesorio *m*, aparato *m*, dispositivo *m*, pieza fija *f*

fixtures *n pl* MECH ENG dispositivos de unión *m pl*; ~ **and fittings** *n pl* CONST aparatos *m pl*, enseres y accesorios *m pl*

Fizeau: ~ **fringes** *n pl* PHYS franjas de Fizeau *f pl*

fizzle *n* COAL bocazo *m*

flag[1] *n* CINEMAT bandera *f*, COMP&DP etiqueta *f*, marca *f*, indicador *m*, señalador *m*, CONST *paving stone* baldosa *f*, losa *f*, GEOL placa arenisca *f*, asperón *m*, PRINT señalador *m*, WATER TRANSP *navy* bandera *f*, insignia *f*; ~ **bit** *n* COMP&DP bit indicador *m*, bit señalador *m*, PROD bit indicador *m*; ~ **captain** *n* WATER TRANSP *navy* comandante del buque insignia *m*; ~ **of convenience** *n* WATER TRANSP bandera de conveniencia *f*, pabellón de conveniencia *m*; ~ **leaf** *n* AGRIC hoja bandera *f*, hoja terminal *f*; ~ **officer** *n* WATER TRANSP *navy* almirante *m*; ~ **signal** *n* WATER TRANSP *communications* señal emitida por banderas *f*; ~ **window** *n* AIR TRANSP ventana metálica bloqueada *f*

flag[2] *vt* COMP&DP etiquetar, marcar

flagging *n* CONST embaldosado *m*, enlosado *m*, TV señalización *f*

flagship *n* WATER TRANSP *navy* buque almirante *m*, buque insignia *m*

flagstaff *n* WATER TRANSP asta de bandera *f*

flagstone *n* CONST baldosa *f*, losa de piedra *f*, suelo de lajas *m*, GEOL roca laminar *f*; ~ **pavement** *n* CONST suelo de lajas *m*

flake *n* AGRIC copo *m*, desmalezado por fuego *m*, GEOL escama *f*, lasca *f*

flaked: ~ **rail** *n* RAIL carril descamado *m*, riel descamado *m*

flakiness: ~ **index** *n* CONST índice de descascaramiento *m*

flaking *n* PRINT separación en forma de escamas *f*

flame[1]: ~-**resistant** *adj* GEN antiinflamable, ignífugo, incombustible, resistente al fuego

flame[2] *n* CHEM, HEAT ENG, SAFE, THERMO llama *f*; ~ **arc** *n* ELEC, ELEC ENG arco de encendido *m*; ~ **arrester** *n* CONST, PETR TECH, SAFE, SPACE, THERMO apagallamas *m*, parallamas *m*; ~ **attenuation** *n* C&G reducción de la llama *f*; ~ **bridge** *n* PROD puente *m*; ~ **cleaning** *n* CONST limpieza por llama *f*; ~ **control** *n* HEAT control de llama *m*; ~-**cutter** *n* CONST máquina

de oxicorte *f*, MECH, THERMO máquina de oxicorte *f*, soplete *m*; ~ **cutting** *n* CONST, MECH, THERMO cortadura por soplete *f*, corte por soplete *m*, oxicortadura *f*; ~-**cutting torch** *n* THERMO soplete para oxicorte *m*; ~ **detector** *n* HEAT detector de llamas *m*; ~-**emission spectroscopy** *n* PHYS, THERMO espectroscopía de emisión por llama *f*; ~ **failure** *n* THERMO interrupción de la llama *f*; ~-**gouging** *n* CONST escopladura por llama *f*; ~ **holder** *n* AIR TRANSP mantenedor de llamas *m*, retardador de llamas *m*; ~ **hydrolysis** *n* OPT hidrólisis de llama *f*; ~ **photometer** *n* INSTR, LAB flamómetro *m* (*AmL*), fotómetro de llama *m* (*Esp*); ~ **plate** *n* PROD chapa de fuego *f*; ~-**projector** *n* MILIT lanzallamas *m*; ~-**resistant paint** *n* COLOUR, CONST, THERMO pintura ignífuga *f*, pintura resistente al fuego *f*; ~-**retardant conveyor belt** *n* MECH ENG cinta transportadora resistente al fuego *f*, cinta transportadora retardadora de llamas *f*; ~ **spectroscopy** *n* PHYS, THERMO espectroscopía a la llama *f*; ~ **spectrum** *n* PHYS, THERMO espectro de llama *m*; ~-**spray coating** *n* COATINGS, MECH, THERMO revestimiento realizado con soplete *m*, revestimiento realizado utilizando llama *m*; ~-**spraying** *n* NUCL metalización por soplete *f*; ~-**thrower** *n* MILIT lanzallamas *m*; ~ **trap** *n* AIR TRANSP atrapador de llamas *m*, atrapallamas *m*, CONST, PETR TECH apagallamas *m*, SAFE apagallamas *m*, parallamas *m*, SPACE apagallamas *m*, THERMO apagallamas *m*, parallamas *m*, VEH dispositivo antillamarada *m*; ~ **tube** *n* PROD *of brazing lamp* tubo quemador *m*; ~-**welding** *n* P&R soldadura con llama *f*

flame[3]: ~-**harden** *vt* THERMO templar a la llama, templar superficialmente con la llama

flameout *n* THERMO extinción de la llama *f*

flameproof[1] *adj* GEN a prueba de fuego, a prueba de incendios, antideflagrante, antillama, ignífugo, incombustible, ininflamable, refractario

flameproof[2]: ~ **clothing** *n* SAFE prendas ignífugas *f pl*, prendas incombustibles *f pl*; ~ **coat** *n* COATINGS capa ignífuga *f*, revestimiento ignífugo *m*; ~ **color** *AmE*, ~ **colour** *BrE* *n* COLOUR colorante ignífugo *m*; ~ **drilling machine** *n* MINE, SAFE, THERMO máquina perforadora ignífuga *f*; ~ **enclosure** *n* SAFE *of electrical apparatus* receptáculo a prueba de incendios *m*; ~ **floor** *n* SAFE suelo refractario *m*; ~ **glass** *n* C&G vidrio a prueba de fuego *m*; ~ **lighting installation** *n* ELEC, ELEC ENG, SAFE, THERMO instalación eléctrica antideflagrante *f*, instalación eléctrica incombustible *f*; ~ **motor** *n* ELEC ENG motor antideflagrante *m*, motor incombustible *m*, SAFE motor incombustible *m*, THERMO motor antideflagrante *m*, motor incombustible *m*; ~ **paint** *n* COLOUR pintura ignífuga *f*, pintura resistente al fuego *f*, CONST pintura ignífuga *f*; ~ **pottery** *n* C&G loza a prueba de fuego *f*; ~ **stirrer** *n* LAB agitador refractario *m*; ~ **switch** *n* ELEC conmutador antideflagrante *m*, conmutador incombustible *m*, conmutador que no produce llama *m*, SAFE, THERMO interruptor ignífugo *m*; ~ **telephone system** *n* CONST sistema telefónico a prueba de incendios *m*

flameproofed *adj* C&G ignifugado, incombustibilizado, CHEM ignifugado, COATINGS, COLOUR, MECH, P&R, PACK ignifugado, incombustibilizado, SAFE, THERMO ignifugado, incombustibilizado, protegido del fuego

flameproofing *n* C&G, COATINGS ignifugación *f*, incombustibilización *f*, COLOUR incombustibilización *f*, MECH, P&R, PACK, SAFE, THERMO ignifugación *f*, incombustibilización *f*; **~ paint** *n* COLOUR, CONST pintura ignífuga *f*

flaming: **~ coal** *n* COAL carbón de llama *m*, hulla bituminosa *f*

flamm: **~ yarn** *n* TEXTIL tejido inflamable *m*

flammability *n* GEN combustibilidad *f*, inflamabilidad *f*

flammable¹ *adj* GEN inflamable

flammable²: **~ atmosphere** *n* SAFE, THERMO atmósfera inflamable *f*; **~ liquid** *n* SAFE líquido inflamable *m*; **~ material** *n* SAFE material inflamable *m*; **~ vapor** *AmE*, **~ vapour** *BrE n* SAFE vapor inflamable *m*

flange¹ *n* ACOUST, AUTO pestaña *f*, reborde *m*, CONST *of girder* ala *f*, ELEC *connection* brida *f*, pestaña *f*, ELEC ENG abrazadera *f*, LAB brida *f* (*Esp*), reborde *m* (*AmL*), collarín *m* (*Esp*), borde *m* (*AmL*), MAR POLL brida *f*, MECH reborde *m*, brida *f*, resalte *m*, pestaña *f*, MECH ENG flanja *f*, brida *f*, llanta *f*, pestaña *f*, aleta *f*, saliente *m*, PETR TECH brida *f*, PROD *of grooved pulley* pestaña *f*, *of tube* aleta *f*, *of cylinder* brida *f*, *sheet-metal working* faldilla *f*, SPACE *mechanics* reborde *m*, pestaña *f*, TEXTIL balona *f*; **~ coupling** *n* MECH ENG acoplamiento de bridas *m*, acoplamiento de discos *m*, acoplamiento de platos *m*; **~ cutout** *n* PROD recorte de bridas *m*; **~ face** *n* PROD refrentado de bridas *m*; **~ joint** *n* MECH ENG junta de bridas *f*, junta de collarín *f*, junta de platos *f*; **~ motor** *n* ELEC motor de brida *m*, MECH motor vertical embridado *m*; **~ mounting** *n* PROD montaje sobre bridas *m*, SPACE aleta de montaje *f*, aleta de sustentación *f*, timón *m*; **~ pipe** *n* CONST tubería con brida *f*; **~ plate** *n* CONST plancha de cubierta *f*, plancha de ala *f*, platabanda *f*, PROD chapa con faldilla *f*; **~ pulley** *n* MECH ENG polea con pestañas *f*, polea de rebordes *f*; **~ smoother** *n* PROD *moulder's tool* lima para refrenar bridas *f*; **~ tile** *n* CONST pletina *f*; **~-to-rail clearance** *n* RAIL holgura entre la pestaña y el carril *f*; **~ wheel** *n* MECH ENG rueda de pestañas *f*

flange² *vt* MECH ENG embridar, poner bridas, PROD *plate* enfaldillar, *tube* poner bridas; **~ up** *vt* PETR TECH conectar mediante bridas, embridar

flanged¹ *adj* GEN con aletas, con bridas, con rebordes, embridado, rebordeado

flanged²: **~ ball valve** *n* MECH ENG válvula de bola de bridas *f*; **~ bolt** *n* MECH ENG perno con bridas *m*, perno con pestañas *m*; **~ bottom** *n* C&G fondo con pestaña *m*; **~ cap** *n* PACK tapa con pestaña *f*; **~ cast-iron pipe** *n* CONST tubería de fundición con brida *f*; **~ edge** *n* MECH ENG extremo alado *m*, PACK tapa con pestaña *f*; **~ fitting** *n* MECH ENG adaptador de brida *m*, adaptador de plato *m*, conector de brida *m*, conector de plato *m*, junta de brida *f*, junta de plato *f*; **~ gear** *n* MECH ENG engranaje protegido *m*; **~ guide** *n* MECH ENG guía alada *f*, guía con patín *f*; **~ nut** *n* MECH ENG tuerca tapón *f*; **~ pipeline** *n* MECH ENG tubo con bridas *m*, tubo con collarín *m*, tubo embridado *m*; **~ pressure pipe** *n* MECH ENG tubo de presión con bridas *m*, tubo de presión con collarín *m*; **~ shaft** *n* MECH ENG eje con plato *m*; **~ traveling wheel** *AmE*, **~ travelling wheel** *BrE n* MECH ENG rueda de traslación embridada *f*, rueda portadora embridada *f*; **~ tube radiator** *n* AUTO radiador de tubos con pestañas *m*; **~ union** *n* MECH ENG acoplamiento de bridas *m*, junta de bridas *f*, montaje de bridas *m*, unión de bridas *f*

flangeless: **~ brake block** *n* RAIL zapata de freno sin pestaña *f*

flanger *n* PROD pestañadora *f*, rebordeadora *f*, enfaldilladora *f*, prensa de embutir *f*

flanging *n* PROD enfaldillado *m*; **~ machine** *n* PACK ribeteadora *f*, PROD pestañadora *f*, *working by revolving mechanism* rebordeadora *f*; **~ press** *n* PROD prensa de rebordear *f*, *working by pressure* prensa de embutir *f*; **~ test** *n* PROD *for tube* prueba de rebatimiento del collarín *f*

flank *n* CONST, MECH, MECH ENG, SPACE flanco *m*; **~ gear** *n* MECH ENG engranaje de dientes de flancos rectos *m*; **~ wall** *n* CONST muro lateral *m*

flap *n* AIR TRANSP aleta *f*, flap *m*, portezuela *f*, CONST aleta *f*, faldilla *f*, MECH aleta *f*, flanco *m*, MECH ENG aleta *f*, falda *f*, faldilla *f*, faldón *m*, PACK aleta *f*, SPACE flap *m*, TEXTIL cartera *f*, pestaña *f*, TRANSP flap *m*; **~ attenuator** *n* ELECTRON atenuador de aleta *m*; **~ door** *n* CONST escotilla *f*, puerta de ventilación *f*, trampilla *f*; **~ gate** *n* FUELLESS compuerta *f*, HYDROL *of compound* compuerta de cierre oscilante *f*; **~ hinge** *n* CONST bisagra embutida *f*; **~ jack** *n* AIR TRANSP actuador hidráulico de flaps *m*, gato del flap *m*; **~ roller carriage** *n* AIR TRANSP carro de guiado de flaps *m*, portador de rodillos del flap *m*; **~ snap** *n* PACK a golpe de aleta; **~ track rib** *n* AIR TRANSP nervión de las guías del flap *m*; **~ valve** *n* CONST, HYDRAUL, MECH ENG, PROD válvula de charnela *f*, válvula de mariposa *f*; **~ valve pump** *n* PROD bomba de válvula de charnela *f*; **~-wheel with shaft** *n* MECH ENG *coated with abrasive* rueda de aletas con eje *f*, rueda de tiras abrasivas con eje *f*

flapping *n* AIR TRANSP *of helicopter* aleteo *m*, batimiento *m*; **~ angle** *n* AIR TRANSP *of helicopter* ángulo de batimiento *m*; **~ hinge** *n* AIR TRANSP *of helicopter* charnela de aleteo *f*, charnela de batimiento *f*; **~-hinge pin** *n* AIR TRANSP *of helicopter* pasador de la charnela de aleteo *m*; **~ moment** *n* AIR TRANSP *of helicopter* momento de batimiento *m*; **~ stress peak** *n* AIR TRANSP *of helicopter* punto máximo de la curva de esfuerzo del batimiento *m*, punto máximo de la curva del esfuerzo del aleteo *m*

flare¹ *n* AIR TRANSP bengala *f*, destello *m*, llama *f*, llamarada *f*, señal luminosa *f*, CINEMAT resplandor *m*, CONST baliza *f*, MILIT baliza *f*, bengala *f*, cohete luminoso *m*, señal luminosa *f*, PETR TECH antorcha *f*, RAIL, SPACE baliza *f*, WATER TRANSP bengala *f*; **~-out** *n* AIR TRANSP enderezamiento *m*, salida *f*; **~ pistol** *n* MILIT pistola de bengalas *f*, pistola de señales *f*; **~ spot** *n* CINEMAT mancha de resplandor *f*; **~ stack** *n* PETR TECH antorcha *f*

flare² *vt* C&G abocinar, acampanar, HEAT ENG abocinar, aborcadar, MECH, PROD abocinar, aborcadar, acampanar, TEXTIL acampanar, abocinar, THERMO abocinar, aborcadar

flare³: **~ up** *vi* THERMO *network* destellar

flared¹ *adj* MECH, TEXTIL abocinado, acampanado, ensanchado, evasé

flared²: **~ end** *n* C&G punta acampanada *f*; **~ landing** *n* AIR TRANSP aterrizaje abocardado *m*; **~ neck** *n* C&G cuello acampanado *m*; **~ section** *n* SPACE *antennas, waveguides* sección abocinada *f*, sección de diámetro progresivamente mayor *f*; **~ tube** *n* PROD tubo abocardado *m*

flaring¹ *adj* C&G, PROD abocinado, acampanado

flaring² *n* C&G acampanado *m*, PETR TECH quemado

por antorcha *m*, PROD abocinamiento *m*, acampanado *m*, ensanchamiento *m*

flash[1] *n* CINEMAT centelleo *m*, MINE luces *f pl*, P&R rebaba lateral *f*, PHOTO, PRINT flash *m*; ~ **ageing** *n* COLOUR vaporización rápida *f*; ~ **analog-to-digital conversion** *n* ELECTRON conversión paralela analógica-digital *f*; ~ **analog-to-digital converter** *n* ELECTRON convertidor paralelo analógico-digital *m*; ~ **bar** *n* PHOTO soporte para lámparas de flash *m*; ~ **boiler** *n* HEAT ENG, HYDRAUL, THERMO caldera de vaporización instantánea *f*, caldera de vaporización muy rápida *f*; ~ **bulb** *n* PHOTO lámpara de flash *f*; ~ **contact** *n* PHOTO contacto para flash *m*; ~ **conversion** *n* ELECTRON conversión rápida *f*; ~ **converter** *n* ELECTRON convertidor rápido *m*; ~ **cutting** *n* CINEMAT, TV montaje rápido *m*; ~ **distillation** *n* CHEM, FOOD, THERMO, WATER destilación de equilibrio *f*, destilación en corriente de vapor *f*, destilación instantánea *f*, destilación por expansión brusca *f*; ~ **duration** *n* PHOTO duración del flash *f*; ~ **evaporation** *n* CHEM, FOOD, NUCL evaporación instantánea *f*, evaporación súbita *f*; ~ **exposure** *n* PRINT exposición auxiliar *f*; ~ **fire** *n* THERMO explosión instantánea *f*; ~ **flood** *n* HYDROL riada repentina *f*; ~ **frame** *n* CINEMAT, TV cuadro instantáneo *m*, fotograma instantáneo *m*; ~ **gas** *n* REFRIG vapor instantáneo *m*; ~ **heating** *n* FOOD, HEAT ENG calentamiento instantáneo *m*; ~ **mold** *AmE*, ~ **mould** *BrE n* P&R molde de operación rápida *m*, molde de rebaba *m*; ~ **-off** *n* PRINT vaporización instantánea *f*; ~ **-over** *n* ELEC, ELEC ENG, THERMO cortocircuito con desprendimiento de chispas *m*, cortocircuito con emisión de chispas *m*, descarga disruptiva *f*; ~ **pan** *n* CINEMAT, TV panorámica rápida *f*; ~ **photolysis** *n* CHEM fotólisis instantánea *f*; ~ **point** *n* GEN punto de inflamación *m*, punto de vaporización *m*, temperatura de inflamabilidad *f*, temperatura de inflamación *f*; ~ **point apparatus** *n* LAB aparato de punto de inflamación *m*; ~ **shoe** *n* PHOTO pie del flash *m*; ~ **socket for F and X contact** *n* PHOTO clavija de conexión de flash para contactos F y X *f*; ~ **subcooling** *n* NUCL subenfriamiento por evaporación súbita *m*; ~ **switch** *n* PHOTO botón del flash *m*; ~ **test** *n* ELEC ENG prueba de aislamiento *f*, prueba disruptiva *f*; ~ **tester** *n* MECH ENG probador de rebabas de corte *m*, probador de rebabas de forja *m*, probador de rebabas de recalcar *m*; ~ **tube** *n* ELECTRON tubo de destellos *m*; ~ **welding** *n* CONST soldadura con arco a presión *f*, soldadura a tope por chispa *f*, PROD soldadura por centelleo *f*; ~ **wheel** *n* HYDRAUL rueda de paletas *f*

flash[2]: ~ **harden** *vt* METALL, PROD, THERMO templar instantáneamente

flash[3]: ~ **over** *vi* ELEC, THERMO hacer saltar un arco

flashback *n* CINEMAT escena retrospectiva *f*, CONST, THERMO retorno de la llama *m*, retroceso de la llama *m*; ~ **preventer** *n* SAFE, THERMO válvula contra el retroceso de la llama *f*

flashboard *n* WATER alza removible *f*, tabla de quitapón *f*, *of dam or sluice gate* alza *f*

flashcube *n* PHOTO cuboflash *m*, flash de cubo *m*

flasher *n* AUTO, ELEC interruptor intermitente *m*, HYDRAUL caldera de vaporización rápida *f*, VEH interruptor intermitente *m*, lámpara intermitente *f*

flashing *n* CINEMAT, ELEC ENG, PHOTO centelleo *m* (*AmL*), disparo de flash *m* (*Esp*); ~ **light** *n* WATER

TRANSP *navigation marks* luz de destellos *f*; ~ **lights** *n pl* SAFE luces intermitentes *f pl*; ~ **signal** *n* WATER TRANSP señal de destellos *f*; ~ **warning lights** *n pl* AUTO, SAFE, VEH luces intermitentes de aviso *f pl*

flashlight *n* ELEC, ELEC ENG foco de mano *m*, linterna *f*, linterna de bolsillo *f*, linterna eléctrica *f*, lámpara de bolsillo *f*, lámpara portátil *f*, PHOTO luz de magnesio *f*, luz del flash *f*

flashover: ~ **voltage** *n* ELEC ENG voltaje disruptivo *m*

flashstage: ~ **cooler** *n* REFRIG enfriador intermedio de expansión *m*

flask *n* FOOD envase *m*, LAB *narrow-necked* matraz *m*, matraz volumétrico *m*; ~ **with molded neck** *AmE see flask with moulded neck BrE*; ~ **molding** *AmE see flask moulding BrE*; ~ **with moulded neck** *n BrE* LAB matraz con cuello moldeado *m*; ~ **moulding** *n BrE* PROD moldeo en caja *m*; ~ **pin** *n* MECH ENG pasador de caja de moldear *m*, perno de caja de moldear *m*

flat[1] *adj* CONST llano, plano; ~ **-bottomed** *adj* WATER TRANSP *boat* chato

flat[2] *n* ACOUST bemol *m*, AGRIC cajonera *f*, CINEMAT bastidor *m*, MECH cara plana *f*, filo normal al eje *m*, parte plana *f*, OCEAN bajío *m*, PRINT plantilla de montaje *f*, WATER TRANSP bajío *m*; ~ **aerial** *n BrE* (*cf flat antenna AmE*) TELECOM antena plana *f*; ~ **amplifier** *n* ELECTRON amplificador plano *m*; ~ **-and-fitted width** *n* TEXTIL ancho plano y ajustado *m*; ~ **angle** *n* GEOM ángulo llano *m*, ángulo plano *m*; ~ **antenna** *n AmE* (*cf flat aerial BrE*) TELECOM antena plana *f*; ~ **arch** *n* CONST arco de descarga *m*; ~ **back** *n* PRINT lomo plano *m*; ~ **-back stoping method** *n* MINE método de laboreo a lo largo de las minas *m*; ~ **-band pass filter** *n* ELECTRON filtro de paso de banda constante *m*; ~ **battery** *n* TELECOM batería plana *f*; ~ **-bed cylinder press** *n* PRINT prensa planocilíndrica *f*; ~ **-bed editing table** *n* CINEMAT, TV mesa horizontal de montaje *f*; ~ **-bed plotter** *n* COMP&DP plotter plano *m*, trazador de base plana *m*, trazador plano *m*; ~ **-bed press** *n* PRINT prensa plana *f*; ~ **-bed proofing press** *n* PRINT prensa plana sacapruebas *f*; ~ **-bed scanner** *n* COMP&DP escáner plano *m*, explorador de base plana *m*, explorador plano *m*; ~ **belt drive** *n* MECH ENG conductor de correa plana *m*, transmisor de correa plana *m*; ~ **-bottom tappet** *n* AUTO empujaválvulas plano *m*, levantaválvulas plano *m*, VEH levantaválvulas plano *m*; ~ **-bottomed etch pit** *n* METALL grabado de corrosión de fondo plano *m*; ~ **-bottomed flask** *n* LAB matraz de fondo plano *m*; ~ **box** *n* PAPER caja aspirante plana *f*; ~ **brush** *n* COLOUR brocha plana *f*, pincel para aplicar el diluente *m*; ~ **cable** *n* ELEC, ELEC ENG cable plano *m*; ~ **canvas hose** *n* SAFE manguera plana de lona *f*; ~ **car** *n AmE* (*cf flat wagon BrE*) RAIL vagón plataforma *m*; ~ **chisel** *n* MECH ENG *engineer's* cortafríos plano *m*, trépano plano *m*, MINE cortafríos plano *m*, trépano plano *m*, escoplo plano *m*, cincel de boca plana *m*; ~ **cold chisel** *n* MECH ENG cortafríos plano *m*; ~ **color** *AmE*, ~ **colour** *BrE n* C&G color mate *m*; ~ **countersunk rivet** *n* PROD remache de cabeza perdida *m*; ~ **-crested weir** *n* HYDRAUL vertedero de cresta ancha *m*, vertedero de pared gruesa *m*; ~ **curve** *n* GEOM curva plana *f*; ~ **drill** *n* MECH ENG *arrow-headed* broca de cabeza de flecha *f*, broca plana *f*; ~ **edge** *n* C&G borde plano *m*; ~ **edge and bevel** *n* C&G borde plano y bisel *m*; ~ **ejector-pin** *n* MECH ENG pasador expulsor plano *m*, pasador eyector plano *m*; **~-end sack** *n* PACK saco de fondo plano *m*; **~ engine** *n* AUTO, VEH motor plano *m*, motor rebajado *m*; **~ etching** *n* PRINT grabado sin contraste *m*; **~ facet** *n* C&G faceta plana *f*; **~-flame burner** *n* LAB mechero-mariposa *m*; **~ form** *n* PRINT forma plana *f*; **~ formation** *n* ELEC *cable configuration*, ELEC ENG formación plana *f*; **~-four engine** *n* TRANSP motor de cuatro cilindros *m*, motor de cuatro tiempos *m*; **~ gasket** *n* NUCL junta plana *f*; **~ glass** *n* C&G vidrio plano *m*; **~-grinding machine** *n* C&G máquina de esmerilado plano *f*; **~-head bolt** *n* MECH ENG, PROD perno de cabeza plana *m*; **~-head screwdriver** *n* MECH ENG, PROD destornillador para tornillos de cabeza perdida *m*; **~-knitting machine** *n* TEXTIL tricotosa rectilínea *f*; **~ lens** *n* INSTR lente plana *f*; **~ lighting** *n* CINEMAT, PHOTO, TV iluminación plana *f*, iluminación sin contraste *f*, iluminación uniforme *f*; **~ mirror** *n* INSTR espejo plano *m*; **~-nose pliers** *n pl* MECH alicates de boca plana *m pl*, alicates planos *m pl*, pinzas de puntas planas *f pl*, MECH ENG alicates de boca plana *m pl*, alicates planos *m pl*, PROD alicates de boca plana *m pl*, alicates planos *m pl*, pinzas de puntas planas *f pl*; **~-nosed pliers** *n pl* MECH pinzas de puntas planas *f pl*, alicates de boca plana *m pl*, alicates planos *m pl*, MECH ENG alicates planos *m pl*, alicates de boca plana *m pl*, PROD alicates de boca plana *m pl*, alicates planos *m pl*, pinzas de puntas planas *f pl*; **~ optical tool** *n* C&G, OPT herramienta óptica plana *f*; **~ pack** *n* ELECTRON caja plana *f*, PACK paquete plano *m*; **~-packing gasket** *n* NUCL junta plana de cierre *f*; **~ paint** *n* COLOUR, CONST pintura opaca *f*; **~ pallet** *n* PACK paleta plana *f*; **~-panel display** *n* ELECTRON pantalla plana *f*; **~ plate** *n* FLUID, FUELLESS placa plana *f*; **~-plate collector** *n* FUELLESS *solar power* colector con placas planas *m*; **~ pleat** *n* TEXTIL pliegue plano *m*; **~ radiator** *n* HEAT radiador plano *m*; **~ rammer** *n* PROD *founding* pisón chato *m*; **~-rate service** *n* TELECOM servicio de tarifa plana *m*; **~-rate tariff** *n* ELEC *consumption* tarifa a tanto alzado *f*, tarifa uniforme *f*, tarifa única *f*; **~ relay** *n* ELEC ENG relé plano *m*; **~ response** *n* ELECTRON respuesta plana *f*; **~-response motor** *n* ELEC motor de respuesta uniforme *m*; **~-ring dynamo** *n* ELEC *generator*, ELEC ENG dinamo de anillo plano *f*; **~ rod** *n* MECH ENG varilla plana *f*; **~-running wheel** *n* MECH ENG rueda de traslación plana *f*; **~ sack** *n* PACK saco plano *m*; **~ screen** *n* COMP&DP pantalla plana *f*, PRINT trama sin contraste *f*, TELECOM, TV pantalla plana *f*; **~-screening** *n* PRINT tramado sin contraste *m*; **~ and self-tapping screw** *n* MECH ENG tornillo autoroscante plano *m*, tornillo autosuficiente plano *m*; **~-sheet delivery** *n* PRINT salida plana *f*; **~ shelf** *n* OCEAN plataforma plana *f*; **~ spin** *n* AIR TRANSP barrena plana *f*; **~ stern** *n* WATER TRANSP *boatbuilding* popa cuadra *f*, popa cuadrada *f*; **~ surface** *n* INSTR superficie plana *f*; **~ tile** *n* C&G loseta *f*; **~ tint** *n* PRINT fondo uniforme *m*; **~ tire** *AmE see flat tyre BrE*; **~ top** *n* WATER TRANSP cubierta de despegue *f*, portaviones *m*; **~-top chain** *n* MECH ENG cadena de articulaciones *f*, cadena de los chapones *f*; **~-top culvert** *n* CONST alcantarilla aplanada *f*; **~ trajectory** *n* MILIT trayectoria rasante *f*; **~ transmission belt** *n* MECH ENG correa transmisora plana *f*; **~ turn** *n* AIR TRANSP viraje plano *m*; **~ twin** *n* TRANSP plano bifilar *m*; **~ twin engine** *n* AUTO motor plano de dos

pistones *m*; **~ tyre** *n BrE* VEH neumático desinflado *m*; **~ wagon** *n BrE* (*cf flat car AmE*) RAIL vagón plataforma *m*; **~ washer** *n* MECH ENG arandela plana *f*; **~ wire** *n* ELEC, ELEC ENG alambre plano *m*; **~ yarn** *n* TEXTIL hilo plano *m*

flatness *n* MECH ENG, PAPER planeidad *f*, PRINT falta de contraste *f*, PROD lisura *f*; **~ quality** *n* MECH ENG *of measuring faces* calidad de planeidad *f*; **~ tolerance** *n* MECH ENG tolerancia de planeidad *f*

flatted: **~ parallel shank tool** *n* MECH ENG espiga achatada *f*, espiga cuadrada *f*, espiga de dos caras *f*

flattening *n* GEOL allanamiento *m*, aplastamiento *m*, PROD achacamiento *m*, aplanamiento *m*, aplastamiento *m*, VEH pérdida de presión *f*; **~ test** *n* PHYS prueba de aplastamiento *f*

flatter *n* PROD martillo aplanador *m*

flatting: **~ mill** *n* PROD, RAIL laminador para alambres *m*, laminadora *f*; **~ pigment** *n* P&R pigmento mate *m*; **~ varnish** *n* COATINGS barniz mate *m*, COLOUR barniz de base *m*, barniz mate *m*; **~ works** *n pl* PROD taller de laminación *m*

flavan *n* CHEM flavana *f*

flavanone *n* CHEM flavanona *f*

flavin *n* CHEM flavina *f*

flavone *n* CHEM, FOOD flavona *f*

flavonoid *n* CHEM, FOOD flavonoide *m*

flavonol *n* CHEM flavonol *m*

flavoprotein *n* CHEM, FOOD flavoproteína *f*

flavopurpurin *n* CHEM flavopurpurina *f*

flavor *AmE see flavour BrE*

flavoring *AmE see flavouring BrE*

flavour[1] *n BrE* FOOD sabor *m*; **~ enhancer** *n BrE* FOOD reforzador de sabor *m*; **~ potentiator** *n BrE* FOOD potenciador de sabor *m*; **~ of quark** *n BrE* PART PHYS tipo de quark *m*

flavour[2] *vt BrE* FOOD aderezar, condimentar, saborizar, sazonar

flavouring *n BrE* FOOD aderezo *m*, condimento *m*, saborizante *m*

flaw *n* CRYSTALL defecto *m*, MECH defecto *m*, falla *f*, imperfección *f*, tacha *f*, NUCL, PAPER, QUALITY defecto *m*

flawless *adj* PAPER sin defectos

F-layer *n* GEOPHYS capa F *f*, capa de Appleton *f*, PHYS capa F *f*

flea: **~ beetle** *n* AGRIC pulgón *m*

fleam: **~ tooth** *n* MECH ENG *of saw* diente biselado *m*, diente con bisel *m*; **~-tooth saw** *n* MECH ENG sierra de dientes biselados *f*

fleece: **~ former** *n* TEXTIL formadora de vellón *f*

fleet[1] *adj* WATER TRANSP somero

fleet[2] *n* MILIT armada *f*, RAIL parque de vagones *m*, WATER TRANSP armada *f*, *painting* cubrimiento parcial *m*; **~ admiral** *n* MILIT, WATER TRANSP *navy* capitán general de la armada *m*; **~ weight** *n* AIR TRANSP peso del fletado *m*

fleet[3] *vt* WATER TRANSP *ropes* lascar

Fleet: **~ Air Arm** *n BrE* (*cf Naval Air Service AmE*) MILIT, WATER TRANSP Arma Aérea Naval *f*, Fuerza Aeronaval *f*, Fuerza Aérea Naval *f*

Fleming's: **~ rules** *n pl* ELEC reglas de Fleming *f pl*

flesh: **~ side** *n* PROD *of belt* lado de la carne *m*

fleuron *n* PRINT ornamento floral *m*, adorno floral *m*, florón *m*

flexi: **~-arm** *n* CINEMAT, TV brazo flexible *m*

flexibility: **~ factor** *n* MECH ENG factor de flexibilidad *m*; ~ **strength** *n* TELECOM resistencia de la flexibilidad *f*

flexible: ~ **access switch** *n* (*FAS*) TELECOM conmutador de acceso flexible *m*; ~ **cable** *n* ELEC, ELEC ENG cable flexible *m*; ~ **conductor** *n* ELEC, ELEC ENG canalización flexible *f*, conductor flexible *m*; ~ **connection** *n* RAIL conexión flexible *f*; ~ **construction** *n* CONST construcción flexible *f*; ~ **control** *n* MECH ENG control de flexibilidad *m*; ~ **coupling** *n* MECH ENG acoplamiento flexible *m*, junta flexible *f*; ~ **drive** *n* MECH accionamiento flexible *m*; ~ **drive shaft** *n* MECH ENG eje conductor flexible *m*, eje motriz flexible *m*, eje transmisor flexible *m*; ~ **ducting** *n* CONST conducto flexible *m*; ~ **gasket** *n* MECH junta obturadora elástica *f*, junta obturadora flexible *f*, MECH ENG junta de estanqueidad elástica *f*, junta de estanqueidad flexible *f*, junta obturadora elástica *f*, junta obturadora flexible *f*, PROD junta obturadora elástica *f*, junta obturadora flexible *f*; ~ **hose** *n* CONST manguera flexible *f*, MAR POLL conducto flexible *m*, MINE tubo flexible *m*; ~-**hose connection** *n* MINE conexión de tubo flexible *f*; ~-**hose coupling** *n* MINE empalme de tubos flexibles *m*; ~-**hose union** *n* MINE conectador de tubo flexible *m*, unión de manguera *f*, unión de tubo flexible *f*; ~ **joint** *n* MECH ENG acoplamiento flexible *m*, junta flexible *f*, transmisión flexible *f*; ~ **metal conduit** *n* MECH ENG cañería metálica flexible *f*, conducto metálico flexible *m*, tubería metálica flexible *f*, tubo metálico flexible *m*; ~ **metal piping** *n* MECH ENG canalización metálica flexible *f*, cañería metálica flexible *f*, tuberías metálicas flexibles *f pl*; ~ **metallic hose** *n* MECH ENG manguera metálica flexible *f*; ~ **mounting** *n* MECH ENG montaje flexible *m*; ~ **oil storage tank** *n* MILIT tanque flexible para almacenamiento de combustible *m*; ~ **package** *n* PACK paquete flexible *m*; ~ **packaging machine** *n* PACK máquina para fabricar envases flexibles *f*; ~ **pipe** *n* MECH ENG cañería flexible *f*, tubería flexible *f*, tubo flexible *m*; ~ **printed circuit** *n* ELECTRON circuito impreso flexible *m*; ~ **reflector** *n* SPACE reflector flexible *m*; ~ **resistor** *n* ELEC ENG resistencia dúctil *f*; ~-**rotor balance** *n* MECH ENG equilibrado del rotor flexible *m*; ~ **shaft** *n* MECH ENG eje flexible *m*; ~-**shaft adaptor** *n* MECH ENG adaptador de eje flexible *m*; ~-**shaft coupling** *n* MECH ENG acoplamiento de eje flexible *m*; ~ **stay bolt** *n* MECH ENG tirante articulado *m*, virotillo articulado *m*; ~ **steel piping** *n* MECH ENG tuberías flexibles de acero *f pl*; ~ **tool-changing system** *n* MECH ENG *for injection moulding* sistema de cambio de herramientas flexible *m*; ~ **tubing** *n* MECH ENG canalización flexible *f*, entubado flexible *m*; ~ **waveguide** *n* ELEC ENG guía de ondas elástica *f*, guía de ondas flexible *f*, PHYS guía de ondas elástica *f*, SPACE, WAVE PHYS guía de ondas elástica *f*, guía de ondas flexible *f*; ~ **wire** *n* ELEC, ELEC ENG hilo conductor flexible *m*; ~ **wire saw** *n* MECH ENG sierra de cable flexible *f*, sierra de pelo flexible *f*, sierra helizoidal flexible *f*

flexing: ~ **endurance** *n* P&R resistencia a la flexión *f*; ~ **resistance** *n* P&R resistencia a la flexión *f*

flexion: ~ **spring** *n* MECH ENG muelle de flexión *m*, resorte de flexión *m*

flexo: ~-**folder-gluer** *n* PACK máquina flexográfica-dobladora-encoladora *f*

flexographic: ~ **ink** *n* PRINT tinta flexográfica *f*; ~ **printing** *n* P&R, PRINT impresión flexográfica *f*

flexography *n* PRINT flexografía *f*

flexural: ~ **rigidity** *n* MECH, NUCL, PHYS, PRINT rigidez a la flexión *f*; ~ **slip folding** *n* GEOL plegamiento en bucles *m*; ~ **strength** *n* MECH, NUCL, P&R resistencia a la flexión *f*, resistencia flexural *f*, PAPER resistencia a la flexión *f*, PRINT resistencia a la flexión *f*, resistencia flexural *f*

flexure: ~-**mode resonator** *n* ELECTRON resonador con modo flexible *m*

flick: ~ **pan** *n* CINEMAT, TV panorámica rápida *f*

flicker[1]: ~-**free** *adj* CINEMAT sin centelleo, COMP&DP *screen* libre de vacilación, sin parpadeo

flicker[2] *n* CINEMAT *screen* centelleo *m* (*AmL*), disparo de flash *m* (*Esp*), parpadeo *m*, vacilación *f*, COMP&DP, TV *screen* centelleo *m*, parpadeo *m*, vacilación *f*; ~ **blade** *n* CINEMAT, TV laminilla de centelleo *f*; ~ **frequency** *n* CINEMAT, TV frecuencia de centelleo *f*, frecuencia de parpadeo *f*; ~ **noise** *n* ELECTRON ruido fluctuante *m*; ~ **photometer** *n* PHYS fotómetro de destellos *m*

flicker[3] *vi* CINEMAT centellear, ELECTRON fluctuar

flickering *n* CINEMAT, TELECOM, TV parpadeo *m*

flier *n* CONST *stair-building* escalón normal *m*, escalón recto *m*

fliers *n pl* CONST escalones *m pl*

flight *n* AIR TRANSP vuelo *m*, CONST aspa *f*, PROD *push-plate of conveyor* rastra *f*; ~ **attitude** *n* AIR TRANSP actitud de vuelo *f*; ~ **clearance** *n* AIR TRANSP permiso de vuelo *m*; ~ **compartment** *n* AIR TRANSP compartimiento de vuelo *m*; ~-**compartment access stairway** *n* AIR TRANSP escalera de acceso al compartimento de vuelo *f*; ~-**compartment lights** *n pl* AIR TRANSP luces del compartimiento de vuelo *f pl*; ~ **computer** *n* AIR TRANSP computador de vuelo *m* (*AmL*), computadora de vuelo *f* (*AmL*), ordenador de vuelo *m* (*Esp*); ~ **controller** *n* AIR TRANSP controlador de vuelo *m*; ~ **controls** *n pl* AIR TRANSP controles de vuelo *m pl*; ~ **conveyor** *n* PROD transportador con listones *m*, transportador de paletas *m*, transportador de rastras *m*; ~ **crew** *n* AIR TRANSP tripulación de vuelo *f*; ~ **data** *n* AIR TRANSP datos de vuelo *m pl*; ~-**data recorder** *n* AIR TRANSP grabadora de datos de vuelo *f*, SPACE registrador de datos de vuelo *m*; ~-**data system** *n* SPACE sistema de información de vuelo *m*; ~ **deck** *n* AIR TRANSP cabina de vuelo *f*, cubierta de vuelo *f*, puente de mando *m*, WATER TRANSP *of aircraft carrier* cubierta de vuelo *f*; ~ **director** *n* AIR TRANSP director de vuelo *m*; ~ **display** *n* AIR TRANSP demostración de vuelo *f*; ~ **documentation** *n* AIR TRANSP documentación de vuelo *f*; ~ **engineer** *n* AIR TRANSP ingeniero de a bordo *m*, ingeniero de vuelo *m*, mecánico de a bordo *m*, mecánico de vuelo *m*; ~-**engineer's panel** *n* AIR TRANSP tablero de control del mecánico de vuelo *m*, tablero de instrumentos del mecánico de vuelo *m*; ~-**engineer's seat** *n* AIR TRANSP asiento del ingeniero de vuelo *m*, asiento del mecánico de vuelo *m*; ~ **envelope** *n* AIR TRANSP envolvente de vuelo *m*; ~ **formation** *n* AIR TRANSP formación de vuelo *f*; ~ **information** *n* AIR TRANSP información de vuelo *f*; ~ **information center** *AmE*, ~ **information centre** *BrE* *n* AIR TRANSP centro de información de vuelo *m*; ~ **information service** *n* AIR TRANSP servicio de información de vuelo *m*; ~ **instructor** *n* AIR TRANSP

instructor de vuelo *m*; ~ **instruments** *n pl* AIR TRANSP instrumentos de vuelo *m pl*; ~ **level** *n* AIR TRANSP nivel de vuelo *m*; ~ **of locks** *n* HYDROL, WATER TRANSP esclusas escalonadas *f pl*, esclusas superpuestas *f pl*; ~ **log** *n* AIR TRANSP diario de a bordo *m*, diario de navegación *m*, libro de vuelo *m*; ~ **maneuver** *AmE*, ~ **manoeuvre** *BrE n* AIR TRANSP maniobra de vuelo *f*; ~ **manual** *n* AIR TRANSP manual de vuelo *m*; ~ **model** *n* AIR TRANSP, SPACE modelo de vuelo *m*; ~ **occurrence** *n* SPACE *spacecraft* ocurrencia de vuelo *f*; ~ **path** *n* AIR TRANSP trayectoria de vuelo *f*; ~**-path recorder** *n* AIR TRANSP, INSTR grabador de la trayectoria de vuelo *m*; ~ **plan** *n* AIR TRANSP plan de vuelo *m*; ~**-plan data** *n* AIR TRANSP datos del plan de vuelo *m pl*; ~**-progress board** *n* AIR TRANSP pizarra del itinerario real de vuelo *f*, tablero de progresión de vuelo *m*; ~ **readiness review** *n* (*FRR*) SPACE revisión de disponibilidad de vuelo *f*; ~ **recorder** *n* AIR TRANSP grabadora de vuelo *f*, registrador de vuelo *m*; ~ **refueling probe** *AmE*, ~ **refuelling probe** *BrE n* AIR TRANSP sonda de reaprovisionamiento en vuelo *f*; ~**-regularity message** *n* AIR TRANSP mensaje de regularidad de vuelo *m*; ~ **report** *n* AIR TRANSP, SPACE informe de vuelo *m*; ~ **sequence** *n* AIR TRANSP, SPACE secuencia de vuelo *f*; ~ **simulator** *n* AIR TRANSP, COMP&DP simulador de vuelo *m*; ~ **spectrum** *n* AIR TRANSP espectro de vuelo *m*; ~ **of stairs** *n* CONST tramo de escalera *m*; ~ **status** *n* AIR TRANSP categoría de vuelo *f*; ~ **technical error** *n* AIR TRANSP error técnico de vuelo *m*; ~ **test** *n* AIR TRANSP, SPACE prueba de vuelo *f*; ~ **test center** *AmE*, ~ **test centre** *BrE n* AIR TRANSP, SPACE centro de pruebas de vuelo *m*; ~**-test recorder** *n* AIR TRANSP, SPACE grabadora de pruebas de vuelo *f*; ~ **transition** *n* AIR TRANSP transición de vuelo *f*; ~ **visibility** *n* AIR TRANSP visibilidad en vuelo *f*
flighted: ~ **departure** *n* RAIL salidas escalonadas *f pl*
flint *n* C&G sílex *m*, GEOL pedernal *m*, sílex *m*; ~ **paper** *n* PAPER papel de lija *m*
flinty: ~ **ash** *n* GEOL cenizas silíceas *f pl*; ~ **crush rock** *n* GEOL milonita muy compacta *f*
flip: ~ **chip** *n* ELECTRON pastilla dispersora *f*; ~ **coil** *n* ELEC ENG *electrotechnics* bobina exploradora *f*; ~**-flop** *n* ELECTRON biestable *m*, báscula *f*, PHYS circuito basculante *m*; ~**-flop circuit** *n* COMP&DP anillo de relés eléctricos *m*, circuito basculante *m*, ELEC anillo de relés eléctricos *m*, ELECTRON, PHYS anillo de relés eléctricos *m*, circuito basculante *m*; ~ **spout closure** *n* PACK cerrojo de retroceso *m*
float[1] *n* AUTO boya *f*, flotador *m*, COAL bloque para pulir mármol *m*, minerales finos que flotan al lavarlos *m pl*, neumatóforo *m*, pajuelas de oro *f pl*, yacimiento desprendido del filón *m*, CONST boya *f*, flotador *m*, talocha *f*, MECH desgaste *m*, desplazamiento leve *m*, escofina de picadura sencilla *f*, escofina de talla simple *f*, huelgo axial *m*, MECH ENG desgaste de una herramienta *m*, desplazamiento pequeño *m*, huelgo axial *m*, MINE yacimiento desprendido del filón *m*, PETROL, VEH flotador *m*, WATER flotador *m*, paleta *f*, WATER TRANSP boya *f*, chata *f*, flotador *m*, jangada *f* (*AmL*); ~ **altitude** *n* AIR TRANSP, SPACE altura de rebote *f*; ~**-and-sink analysis** *n* COAL ensayo de separación por líquidos de densidad intermedia *m*; ~ **chamber** *n* AUTO, VEH cuba de nivel constante *f*, cuba del flotador *f*; ~**-controlled alarm whistle** *n* HYDRAUL silbato de

alarma regulado por flotador *m*; ~**-cut file** *n* MECH ENG lima de picadura simple *f*; ~ **glass** *n* C&G vidrio flotado *m*; ~ **gold** *n* MINE oro de espuma *m*, oro flotante *m*, oro que flota *m*, pajuelas de oro *f pl*; ~ **life** *n* ELEC ENG carga lenta *f*; ~ **mineral** *n* MINE pajuelas metálicas *f pl*; ~ **needle** *n* AUTO aguja del flotador *f*; ~**-on/float-off vessel** *n* WATER TRANSP buque con sistema de transflotación de gabarras *m*; ~ **switch** *n* ELEC, ELEC ENG, REFRIG interruptor de flotador *m*; ~ **trap** *n* HYDRAUL purgador de agua de flotador *m*; ~ **valve** *n* HYDRAUL, MECH ENG, REFRIG válvula de flotador *f*, válvula esférica *f*; ~ **water wheel** *n* HYDRAUL rueda de paletas *f*
float[2] *vt* PHYS hacer flotar; ~ **off** *vt* WATER TRANSP *stranded ship* desembarrancar, desvarar
float[3]: ~ **off** *vi* WATER TRANSP *stranded ship* boyar, ponerse a flote
floatboard *n* WATER paleta *f*
floater *n* C&G, PROD flotador *m*
floating[1] *adj* MECH desplazable, libre, oscilante, variable
floating[2]: ~ **accent** *n* PRINT acento flotante *m*; ~ **anchor nut** *n* MECH ENG tuerca de sujeción flotante *f*; ~ **axle** *n* VEH puente trasero flotante *m*; ~ **beacon** *n* WATER TRANSP baliza flotante *f*; ~ **bridge** *n* MILIT puente de barcas *m*, puente de pontones *m*, puente flotante *m*, TRANSP puente de barcas *m*, WATER TRANSP puente de barcas *m*, puente de pontones *m*, puente flotante *m*; ~ **bush** *n* MECH ENG buje flotante *m*, manguito flotante *m*; ~**-carrier modulation** *n* ELECTRON modulación por portadora flotante *f*; ~ **charge** *n* ELEC ENG carga continua *f*; ~ **crane** *n* WATER TRANSP grúa flotante *f*; ~ **derrick** *n* CONST grúa sobre pontona *f*; ~ **dock** *n* CONST, WATER TRANSP dique flotante *m*; ~ **dredge** *n* MINE limo en suspensión en el agua turbia *m*; ~ **engine** *n* AUTO motor flotante *m*; ~ **flexible tank** *n* MAR POLL tanque flotante de material flexible *m*, tanque flotante flexible *m*; ~ **floor** *n* ACOUST suelo flotante *m*; ~ **gate** *n* ELECTRON puerta flotante *f*; ~ **gears** *n* AIR TRANSP *of helicopter* engranajes flotantes *m pl*; ~ **gold** *n* MINE espuma de oro *f*, oro flotante *m*; ~ **grid** *n* ELEC ENG rejilla libre *f*; ~ **hydrographic dredge** *n* OCEAN draga hidrogéfica *f*; ~ **input** *n* ELEC ENG entrada sin referencia a tierra *f*; ~ **line** *n* WATER TRANSP *for rescue* cabo salvavidas flotante *m*; ~ **output** *n* ELEC ENG salida sin referencia a tierra *f*; ~ **pile** *n* COAL pila flotante *f*; ~ **platen** *n* MECH ENG plato de prensa flotante *m*; ~ **platform** *n* OCEAN plataforma flotante *f*; ~ **point** *n* COMP&DP, TELECOM coma flotante *f*; ~**-point arithmetic** *n* COMP&DP, MATH aritmética de coma flotante *f*, aritmética de punto flotante *f*; ~**-point notation** *n* COMP&DP, TELECOM notación en coma flotante *f*, notación en punto flotante *f*; ~**-point number** *n* COMP&DP, TELECOM número de coma flotante *m*; ~**-point operation** *n* COMP&DP, TELECOM operación de coma flotante *f*, operación de punto flotante *f*; ~**-point processor** *n* (*FPP*) COMP&DP, TELECOM procesador de coma flotante *m*, procesador de punto flotante *m*; ~ **potential** *n* ELEC ENG potencial flotante *m*; ~ **rig** *n* PETR TECH equipo de perforación flotante *m*, torre de perforación flotante *f*; ~ **shaft** *n* MECH ENG eje desplazable *m*, eje flotante *m*; ~ **spindle** *n* MECH ENG eje flotante *m*, huso flotante *m*; ~ **supply** *n* ELEC suministro aislado *m*, suministro flotante *m*, sumi-

nistro sin conexiones *m*; ~ **tongs** *n pl* AUTO pinza flotante *f*; ~ **tool-holder** *n* MECH ENG portaherramientas oscilante *m*; ~-**zone melting method** *n* NUCL método de fusión por zonas flotantes *m*

floatplane *n* AIR TRANSP, TRANSP hidroavión *m*

flocculant *n* CHEM, CHEM TECH, COAL coagulante *m*, floculador *m*, floculante *m*, FOOD floculador *m*, floculante *m*, P&R coagulante *m*, floculador *m*, floculante *m*

flocculate[1] *n* CHEM, CHEM TECH, COAL, FOOD, P&R flóculo *m*

flocculate[2] *vi* CHEM, CHEM TECH, COAL, FOOD, P&R flocular

flocculation *n* CHEM, CHEM TECH, COAL, FOOD, P&R floculación *f*, PETR TECH agrumación *f*, floculación *f*; ~ **point** *n* CHEM TECH punto de floculación *m*; ~ **test** *n* CHEM TECH prueba de floculación *f*

flocculator *n* CHEM, CHEM TECH, COAL, FOOD, P&R floculador *m*

flocculence *n* CHEM, CHEM TECH, COAL, FOOD, P&R floculencia *f*

flocculent[1] *adj* CHEM, CHEM TECH, COAL, FOOD, P&R floculante

flocculent[2]: ~ **gypsum** *n* HEAT ENG yeso floculento *m*

flock *n* P&R pelusa *f*; ~ **printing** *n* PRINT impresión aterciopelada *f*

flocking *n* GAS floculación *f*

floe *n* OCEAN *of floating ice* masa *f*, masa flotante *f*

flong: ~ **board** *n* PAPER cartón para flanes de esterotipia *m*

flood[1]: **in** ~ *adj* HYDROL *river* crecido

flood[2] *n* AUTO ahogado *m*, CINEMAT luz de inundación *f*, HYDROL crecida *f*, inundación *f*, torrente *m*, MECH ahogado *m*, PRINT exceso de tinta *m*, VEH ahogado *m*, WATER, WATER TRANSP inundación *f*, marea entrante *f*; ~ **abatement** *n* WATER reducción de crecidas *f*; ~ **arch** *n* WATER arco de descarga para las crecidas *m*; ~ **basalt** *n* GEOL basalto de colada *m*; ~ **bed** *n* HYDROL *of river* lecho mayor *m*; ~ **cock** *n* WATER grifo de aspersión *m*; ~ **control** *n* AGRIC defensa contra las inundaciones *f*, FUELLESS, WATER control de crecidas *m*, control de inundaciones *m*; ~-**control irrigation** *n* AGRIC, HYDROL, WATER riego por inundación controlada *m*; ~-**control measures** *n pl* AGRIC, HYDROL, WATER medidas para el control de crecidas *f pl*; ~-**control reservoir** *n* HYDROL, WATER embalse de retención *m*; ~-**control works** *n pl* HYDROL, WATER instalaciones para el control de crecidas *f pl*; ~ **deposits** *n pl* HYDROL depósitos de crecidas *m pl*; ~ **gate** *n* HYDROL, WATER compuerta de inundación *f*; ~ **irrigation** *n* AGRIC, HYDROL, WATER irrigación por inundación *f*, riego por inundación *m*; ~ **loss** *n* FUELLESS, WATER pérdida por inundación *f*; ~-**mitigation measures** *n pl* HYDROL, WATER medidas para mitigar las crecidas *f pl*; ~ **peak** *n* HYDROL, WATER caudal máximo de crecida *m*; ~ **plain** *n* AGRIC terreno de aluvión *m*, GEOL llanura de inundación *f*, HYDROL lecho de creciente *m*, llanura aluvial *f*, planicie aluvial *f*, planicie de inundación *f*, WATER llanura aluvial *f*, planicie aluvial *f*, planicie de inundación *f*; ~ **prevention** *n* AGRIC, HYDROL, WATER prevención de crecidas *f*; ~-**recession crop** *n* AGRIC cultivo de decrecida *m*; ~-**relief measures** *n pl* HYDROL, WATER medidas de protección contra las riadas *f pl*; ~ **spillway** *n*

HYDROL, WATER aliviadero de avenidas *m*, evacuador de crecidas *m*; ~ **stream** *n* OCEAN corriente de inundación *f*, WATER TRANSP *of tide* flujo de la marea *m*; ~ **tide** *n* HYDROL marea ascendente *f*, pleamar *f*, OCEAN pleamar *f*, WATER TRANSP *navigation* marea creciente *f*; ~-**type cooling** *n* REFRIG enfriamiento por inmersión *m*; ~ **of water** *n* HYDROL, WATER crecida de las aguas *f*; ~ **wave** *n* HYDROL onda de la crecida *f*

flood[3] *vt* AUTO ahogar, HYDROL anegar, VEH ahogar, WATER TRANSP *tanks* anegar, inundar

flood[4] *vi* HYDROL *river* desbordarse, inundar, WATER TRANSP *tide* entrar, subir

flooded[1] *adj* AUTO ahogado, HYDROL anegado, inundado, MECH ahogado, OCEAN inundado, VEH ahogado, WATER inundado, anegado, WATER TRANSP *ship* anegado, inundado

flooded[2]: ~ **beam** *n* CINEMAT haz de inundación *m*; ~ **evaporator** *n* REFRIG evaporador inundado *m*

flooding *n* ELECTRON, HYDROL desbordamiento *m*, inundación *f*, OCEAN inundación *f*, PRINT empaste de la plancha por exceso de tinta *m*, WATER desbordamiento *m*, inundación *f*; ~ **gun** *n* ELECTRON disparador de inundación *m*; ~ **pattern** *n* GEOPHYS modelo de inundación *m*

floodlight *n* ELEC ENG luz de resalte *f*

floodlighting *n* ELEC alumbrado por proyección *m*, iluminación mediante proyectores *f*, iluminación proyectada *f*

floodplain: ~ **agriculture** *n* AGRIC agricultura en tierras de aluvión *f*

floods *n pl* HYDROL, WATER raudales *m pl*

floor[1] *n* CINEMAT piso *m*, COAL piso *m*, *of coal seam* suelo *m*, muro *m*, CONST *top face, tongued and grooved or made of wood block* tablero *m*, *of building, house, general structure* solar *m*, *top face, square-joined* piso *m* (*AmL*), suelo *m* (*Esp*), *storey of building* planta *f*, *of basin, reservoir* solera *f*, *top face, made of tile or cement block* tarima *f*, MINE muro de la galería de minas *m*, piso de la galería de minas *m*, PROD *of foundry* piso *m*, WATER *of chamber of lock* zampeado *m*, losa de fundación *f*, platea *f*, WATER TRANSP *shipbuilding* varenga *f*; ~ **beam** *n* AIR TRANSP viga del piso *f*; ~ **bedding** *n* PROD *founding* colocación en obra *f*; ~ **contact switch** *n* ELEC interruptor de contacto montado en el piso *m*; ~ **hanger** *n* MINE silleta de piso *f*; ~ **hatch** *n* AIR TRANSP compuerta del suelo *f*, portezuela del piso *f*; ~ **heave** *n* MINE descomposición *f* (*Esp*), desplazamiento de una capa *m* (*AmL*), dislocación del piso *f* (*AmL*), falla *f* (*Esp*), hinchamiento del piso *m*, levantamiento del suelo *m* (*Esp*), rechazo vertical *m* (*AmL*), recubrimiento horizontal *m*, resalto horizontal *m*; ~ **joist** *n* CONST vigueta de piso *f*; ~-**mounting** *n* MECH ENG *machine tool* montaje de piso *m*; ~ **pan** *n* VEH cárter inferior *m*; ~ **panel** *n* AIR TRANSP panel del piso *m*; ~ **plate** *n* MECH chapa de varenga *f*, chapa del piso *f*, WATER TRANSP *shipbuilding* varenga *f*; ~ **polish** *n* DETERG cera para pisos *f* (*AmL*), cera para suelos *f* (*Esp*); ~ **sand** *n* PROD *founding* arena vieja *f*; ~ **shift** *n* VEH manguito inferior *m*; ~ **shots** *n* COAL barreno de suelo *m* (*Esp*), barreno tendido *m* (*AmL*); ~ **space** *n* PACK espacio que ocupa la máquina *m*, superficie del piso *f*; ~ **stock** *n* PROD existencias en obra *f pl*; ~ **switch** *n* ELEC *of lift, elevator* conmutador de piso *m*, conmutador montado en el piso *m*; ~ **tile** *n* C&G

CONST baldosa *f*; **~-type surfacing-and-boring lathe** *n* MECH ENG torno de barrenar y cilindrar de tipo carrusel *m*, torno de barrenar y cilindrar de tipo vertical *m*, torno de taladrar y cilindrar de tipo carrusel *m*, torno de taladrar y cilindrar de tipo vertical *m*; ~ **varnish** *n* COATINGS barniz para suelos *m*; ~ **and wall self-adhesive PVC tile** *n* P&R loseta de PVC autoadhesivo para pisos y paredes *f*; **~-warming cable** *n* MECH ENG cable de calefacción del pavimento *m*, cable de calefacción del suelo *m*

floor² *vt* CONST *square-joined* entarimar, *with tile or cement block* recubrir

flooring *n* CONST, SAFE entarimado *m*, material para pavimentos *m*, material para suelos *m*, revestimiento del piso *m*; ~ **material** *n* CONST, SAFE material para pavimentos *m*; ~ **nail** *n* CONST clavo para pisos *m*; ~ **tile** *n* C&G, CONST baldosa *f*

floorman *n* PETR TECH cuñero *m*

floorspace *n* CONST *of building* superficie *f*; ~ **occupied** *n* CONST superficie útil *f*

flop *n* P&R descolgado *m*

flopover *n* TV vibrado de imagen *m*

floppy: ~ **disk** *n* COMP&DP, PRINT, TELECOM disco flexible *m*, disquete *m*; ~ **disk drive** *n* COMP&DP, PRINT, TELECOM unidad de disco *f*, unidad de disco flexible *f*, unidad de disquete *f*; ~ **disk reader** *n* COMP&DP, PRINT, TELECOM lector de discos flexibles *m*

florestry *n* AGRIC arte floral *m*

floriculture *n* AGRIC floricultura *f*

flos: ~ **ferri** *n* MINERAL flos ferri *m*

flotation *n* CHEM *of mineral*, CHEM TECH flotación *f*, COAL flotación por espuma *f*, MINE, PETR TECH, WATER TRANSP flotación *f*; ~ **chamber** *n* MAR POLL cámara de flotabilidad *f*; ~ **collar** *n* PETR TECH collar de flotación *m*, SPACE collarín de flotación *m*; ~ **equipment** *n* CHEM TECH equipo de flotación *m*; ~ **froth** *n* CHEM TECH espuma de flotación *f*; ~ **liquid** *n* CHEM TECH líquido de flotación *m*; ~ **method** *n* PETROL *solids from liquids* método de flotación *m*; ~ **plant** *n* CHEM TECH planta de flotación *f*; ~ **process** *n* COAL proceso de flotación *m*, MINE procedimiento de flotación *m*; ~ **tailings** *n* COAL estériles de flotación *m pl*; ~ **tank** *n* WATER TRANSP tanque de flotación *m*

flotel *n* PETR TECH plataforma de alojamiento *f*

flotilla *n* WATER TRANSP escuadrilla *f*

flotsam *n* WATER TRANSP echazón flotante *f*, restos flotantes *m pl*

flour: ~ **beetle** *n* AGRIC escarabajo de harina *m*

flourmill *n* AGRIC, FOOD molino harinero *m*

flow¹ *n* COAL caudal *m*, fluencia *f*, FLUID, FUELLESS caudal *m*, movimiento *m*, GEOL caudal *m*, fluencia *f*, plegamiento fluidal *m*, HYDRAUL caudal *m*, movimiento *m*, *of water* corriente *f*, HYDROL, MECH *of water* corriente *f*, caudal *m*, movimiento *m*, METALL circulación *f*, movimiento *m*, PACK movimiento *m*, circulación *f*, PETR TECH corriente *f*, PHYS caudal *m*, PROD colada *f*, REFRIG corriente *f*, TEXTIL movimiento *m*, caudal *m*, THERMO, WATER caudal *m*, movimiento *m*; ~ **alarm** *n* PROD avisador de flotador *m*; ~ **banding** *n* GEOL bandeado fluidal *m*; ~ **box** *n* PAPER fluidificador *m*; ~ **cleavage** *n* GEOL exfoliación pizarrosa *f*, pizarrosidad *f*; ~ **coefficient** *n* FLUID, FUELLESS coeficiente de flujo *m*; ~ **control** *n* COMP&DP, HEAT control de flujo *m*, PROD regulación del caudal *f*, TELECOM control de flujo *m*, TRANSP *on*

roadway control de afluencia *m*, control de flujo *m*; **~-control indicator** *n* PROD indicador de regulación del caudal *m*; **~-control valve** *n* MECH ENG válvula controlada de caudal *f*, válvula de control de flujo *f*, PROD válvula de regulación del caudal *f*; **~-controller** *n* PROD controlador del caudal *m*; ~ **cup** *n* LAB copa de flujo *f*; ~ **direction** *n* COMP&DP dirección de flujo *f*; ~ **distributor** *n* PAPER distribuidor del caudal *m*; ~ **divisor** *n* PROD divisor de flujo *m*; ~ **fatigue** *n* MECH ENG fatiga de flujo *f*; ~ **foam wrap** *n* PACK recubrimiento con espuma solidificado *m*; ~ **fold** *n* GEOL pliegue de flujo *m*; ~ **of heat** *n* HEAT ENG, THERMO flujo térmico *m*; **~-in process** *n* TEXTIL proceso de entrada a raudales *m*; ~ **instability** *n* FLUID inestabilidad del flujo *f*; ~ **limit** *n* ELEC ENG límite de flujo *m*; ~ **line** *n* COMP&DP línea de flujo *f*, PETR TECH, PETROL colector de flujo *m*, línea de flujo *f*, tubería de flujo *f*, TELECOM línea de flujo *f*; **~-line temperature** *n* PETR TECH punto de fluencia *m*, temperatura de la tubería de salida *f*; ~ **lobe** *n* GEOL lóbulo de descarga *m*; ~ **nozzle** *n* MECH ENG boquilla de flujo *f*, boquilla medidora de flujo *f*, tobería de caudal *f*; ~ **path** *n* PROD ruta de tratamiento *f*; ~ **pattern** *n* FLUID patrón de flujo *m*, REFRIG clase de corriente *f*, WATER configuración de flujo *f*, espectro de corriente *m*; ~ **pipe** *n* HYDRAUL tubo alimentador *m*; ~ **point** *n* FLUID punto de flujo *m*, PETR TECH temperatura de licuación de soldadura *f*, PRINT *inks* punto de fluencia *m*; ~ **rate** *n* COAL gasto *m*, FLUID caudal *m*, medida del caudal *f*, GAS velocidad del flujo *f*, HYDROL medición del caudal *f*, medida del caudal *f*, MECH medida del caudal *f*, PETR TECH magnitud de flujo *f*, PHYS medida del caudal *f*, WATER magnitud de flujo *f*, medida del caudal *f*, medida del gasto *f*; **~-rate controller** *n* MECH ENG control de caudal *m*, controlador del caudal del flujo *m*; **~-regulating valve** *n* WATER regulador de gasto *m*, válvula reguladora de la corriente *f*; ~ **resistance** *n* ACOUST resistencia al flujo *f*; **~-resistance coefficient** *n* HYDROL coeficiente de resistencia del caudal *m*; ~ **resistivity** *n* ELEC resistividad al flujo *f*; ~ **schedule** *n* PETROL programa de flujo *m*; ~ **sheet** *n* COAL diagrama de flujos *m*, MINE escorrentía laminar *f* (*AmL*), flujo laminar *m* (*Esp*), PETR TECH gráfico del flujo *m*; ~ **shop** *n* PROD taller de lavado *m*; ~ **speed** *n* FLUID velocidad de flujo *f*; ~ **spinning** *n* MECH ENG repulsado de aumento de fluencia plástica *m*; ~ **switch** *n* ELEC conmutador de flujo *m*, PROD interruptor de caudal *m*; ~ **tank** *n* PETROL tanque receptor *m*, tanque colector *m*; ~ **of water** *n* CONST, HYDROL, WATER caudal de agua *m*; **~-wrapping machine** *n* PACK máquina continua para envolver *f*

flow² *vti* COMP&DP circular

flow³: ~ **along** *vi* HYDROL, WATER manar

flow⁴: ~ **into** *vt* HYDROL *of river* desembocar en

flowable: ~ **solids reactor** *n* (*FSR*) NUCL reactor de flujo de sólidos *m*

flowchart *n* COMP&DP, PHYS diagrama de flujo *m* (*Esp*), flujograma *m* (*AmL*), organigrama *m* (*Esp*); ~ **block** *n* COMP&DP bloque de organigrama *m*, casilla de organigrama *f*; ~ **connector** *n* COMP&DP conector de flujograma *m* (*AmL*), conector de organigrama *m* (*Esp*); ~ **symbol** *n* COMP&DP símbolo de organigrama *m*; ~ **text** *n* COMP&DP texto de organigrama *m*

flowcharting *n* COMP&DP trazado de organigrama *m*

flowgraph *n* COMP&DP gráfica de flujo *f*

flowing¹ *adj* HYDROL, WATER fluyente

flowing²: ~ **pressure** *n* PETROL presión de flujo *f*, presión de surgencia *f*; ~ **well** *n* PETROL pozo artesiano *m*

flowmeter *n* GEN aforador *m*, caudalímetro *m*, fluidímetro *m*, flujómetro *m*, indicador de caudal *m*, medidor de flujo *m*, rotámetro *m*

FLS *abbr* (*frame loss second*) TELECOM segundo de pérdida de trama *m*

fluate *n* CHEM fluato *m*

fluctuate *vi* ELEC cambiar, fluctuar, variar

fluctuating: ~ **error** *n* TV error de fluctuación *m*; ~ **noise** *n* ACOUST ruido fluctuante *m*; ~ **stress** *n* METALL esfuerzo alternativo *m*, esfuerzo cíclico *m*

fluctuation *n* ELEC cambio *m*, fluctuación *f*, variación *f*

flue *n* C&G chimenea *f* (*Esp*), HEAT humero *m*, HEAT ENG cañón *m*, conducto de humos *m*, PROD *of furnace* canal de humos *m*, *of boiler* tubo de humos *m*, *of chimney* humero *m*, THERMO tubo de humos *m*; ~ **boiler** *n* PROD caldera de horno *f*; ~ **dust** *n* COAL polvo del tragante *m*; ~ **gas** *n* GAS gas de chimenea *m*, gas de combustión *m*, HEAT ENG, PROD, SPACE, THERMO gas de combustión *m*; ~~**gas cleaning installation** *n* SAFE instalación para limpieza de gases de chimenea *f*; ~~**gas scrubber** *n* GAS, HEAT ENG, THERMO lavador de gas de combustión *m*, lavadora de gas de combustión *f*; ~~**gas scrubbing** *n* HEAT ENG, THERMO lavado de gas de combustión *m*; ~ **lining** *n* HEAT ENG, THERMO forrado de tubos *m*, forro de chimenea *m*; ~ **net** *n* OCEAN trasmallo *m*; ~ **plate** *n* PROD *of boiler* placa tubular *f*; ~ **sheet** *n* PROD *of boiler* placa tubular *f*; ~ **shop** *n* HYDRAUL taller de calderería *m*; ~ **tube** *n* NUCL tubería de descarga de gases de combustión *f*

flued: ~ **heater** *n* HEAT ENG, MECH ENG calentador entubado *m*

flueless: ~ **heater** *n* HEAT ENG calentador de combustión limpia *m*, MECH ENG calentador sin tubos *m*

fluellite *n* MINERAL fluellita *f*

fluence *n* PHYS fluencia *f*

fluff *n* PAPER celulosa en copos *f*, pelusa *f*, obtención de copos *f*, repelado *m*

fluffing *n* PAPER obtención de copos *f*, repelado *m*

fluid: ~~**bed furnace** *n* CHEM TECH, NUCL horno de lecho fluidizado *m*, horno de lecho fluido *m*; ~~**bed granulator** *n* CHEM TECH, NUCL granulador de lecho fluidizado *m*; ~ **breathing** *n* OCEAN respiración fluida *f*; ~~**catalyst process** *n* CHEM TECH proceso catalítico fluidizado *m*; ~ **cooler** *n* REFRIG enfriador del fluido *m*; ~ **coupling** *n* PROD acoplamiento hidráulico *m*, VEH acoplamiento hidráulico *m*, acoplamiento por líquido *m*; ~ **cracking** *n* CHEM TECH craqueo fluidizado *m*; ~ **drive** *n* MECH accionamiento hidráulico *m*, transmisión hidráulica *f*, transmisión por un fluido *f*; ~ **dynamics** *n* FLUID dinámica de los fluidos *f*; ~ **engineering** *n* FLUID ingeniería de los fluidos *f*; ~ **flow** *n* FLUID flujo de fluidos *m*, PETR TECH corriente de fluidos *f*, corriente fluida *f*; ~~**gate printing** *n* CINEMAT copiado con ventanilla fluida *m*; ~ **head** *n* CINEMAT cabeza fluida *f*; ~ **inclusion** *n* GEOL inclusión fluida *f*; ~ **inlet** *n* MECH ENG entrada de fluido *f*; ~~**level switch** *n* PROD interruptor por nivel fluido *m*; ~ **logic circuit** *n* MECH ENG circuito lógico de fluido *m*; ~ **mechanics** *n* FLUID mecánica de los fluidos *f*; ~ **particle** *n* FLUID partícula de fluido *f*; ~ **permeability** *n* FLUID, HEAT ENG permeabilidad a

los fluidos *f*; ~ **physics** *n* FLUID física de los fluidos *f*; ~ **pipeline** *n* MECH ENG acueducto de fluidos *m*, canalización de fluidos *f*, cañería de fluidos *f*, tubería de fluidos *f*; ~~**power cylinder** *n* MECH ENG cilindro accionado por fluido *m*, cilindro hidráulico *m*; ~ **power system** *n* MECH ENG sistema de fuerza de fluido *m*; ~ **pressure** *n* FLUID presión de fluidos *f*; ~ **receiver** *n* FLUID, MECH ENG recibidor de fluidos *m*; ~~**tight packing** *n* PROD empaquetamiento estanco a los fluidos *m*; ~ **wave** *n* FLUID onda en fluido *f*

fluidal: ~ **structure** *n* GEOL estructura fluidal *f*; ~ **texture** *n* GEOL textura fluidal *f*

fluidic: ~ **device** *n* MECH ENG dispositivo fluídico *m*

fluidics *n* FLUID fluídica *f*, tecnología de los fluidos *f*

fluidization *n* COAL, FLUID, PETR TECH, PETROL fluidificación *f*, fluidización *f*

fluidized: ~ **bed** *n* CHEM TECH, HEAT lecho fluidificado *m*, lecho fluidizado *m*; ~~**bed coating** *n* CHEM TECH, COATINGS recubrimiento de lecho fluidizado *m*, revestimiento aplicado por lecho fluidizado *m*; ~~**bed dryer** *n* CHEM TECH, FOOD, HEAT secador de lecho fluidificado *m*, secador de lecho fluidizado *m*, secador de lecho fluido *m*; ~~**bed freezing** *n* CHEM TECH, FOOD, REFRIG congelación en lecho fluidificado *f*; ~~**bed gasification** *n* CHEM TECH gasificación en lecho fluidizado *f*; ~~**bed kiln** *n* CHEM TECH, NUCL horno de lecho fluidizado *m*; ~~**bed reduction** *n* CHEM TECH reducción en lecho fluidizado *f*; ~~**bed sintering** *n* CHEM TECH aglomeración en lecho fluidizado *f*, sinterización en lecho fluidizado *f*; ~~**bed vibro-cooler** *n* CHEM TECH, REFRIG vibroenfriador de lecho fluidizado *m*

fluke *n* WATER TRANSP *of anchor* uña *f*

flume *n* COAL canal de arrastre *m*, canal de descarga *m*, canaleta de distribución del hormigón *f*, canalizo *m*, caz *m*, chimenea de ventilación *f*, saetín *m*, separador de gas *m*, CONST canalón *m*, FUELLESS saetín *m*, PROD *of mill* canal de descarga *m*, WATER canalón *m*, *artificial open channel* canal abierto para agua *m*, *turbine chamber* caz *m*

fluoanthene *n* CHEM fluoanteno *m*

fluoanthrene *n* CHEM fluoantreno *m*

fluocerine *n* MINERAL fluocerina *f*

fluocerite *n* MINERAL fluocerita *f*

fluorene *n* CHEM fluoreno *m*

fluorenone *n* CHEM fluorenona *f*

fluorescein *n* CHEM fluoresceína *f*

fluorescence *n* GEN fluorescencia *f*; ~ **analysis** *n* PHYS, RAD PHYS análisis por fluorescencia *m*; ~ **excitation spectrum** *n* RAD PHYS espectro de excitación de fluorescencia *m*; ~ **microscope** *n* CHEM, INSTR, PHYS, RAD PHYS, WAVE PHYS microscopio de fluorescencia *m*; ~ **yield spectrometer** *n* INSTR, PHYS, RAD PHYS espectrómetro de fluorescencia *m*

fluorescent: ~~**discharge tubes** *n pl* RAD PHYS tubos de descarga fluorescente *m pl*; ~ **lamp** *n* ELEC, ELEC ENG, GAS, PHYS, RAD PHYS lámpara fluorescente *f*; ~ **lighting** *n* ELEC, ELEC ENG, GAS, PHYS, RAD PHYS iluminación fluorescente *f*; ~ **penetration test** *n* MECH ensayo de penetración fluorescente *m*; ~ **screen** *n* ELEC, ELECTRON, INSTR, PHYS, RAD PHYS pantalla fluorescente *f*; ~ **substance** *n* ELEC sustancia fluorescente *f*, OPT suspensión fluorescente *f*, PHYS, RAD PHYS sustancia fluorescente *f*; ~ **tube** *n* ELEC, ELEC ENG, GAS, PHYS, RAD PHYS *lighting* lámpara fluorescente *f*, tubo fluorescente *m*;

~ **whitening** *n* PAPER blanqueante fluorescente *m*; ~ **X-ray spectrometer** *n* ELEC, INSTR, PHYS, RAD PHYS espectrómetro de rayos X fluorescente *m*

fluoridation *n* CHEM fluoración *f*

fluoride *n* CHEM fluoruro *m*; ~ **opal glass** *n* C&G vidrio opalino *m*

fluorine *n* (*F*) C&G, CHEM, COAL flúor *m* (*F*)

fluorite *n* MINERAL fluorita *f*; ~ **lens** *n* INSTR lente de fluorita *f*

fluoritic *adj* CHEM fluorítico

fluoroborate *n* CHEM fluoborato *m*

fluoroboric: ~ **acid** *n* CHEM ácido fluobórico *m*

fluorocarbon: ~ **refrigerant** *n* REFRIG refrigerante fluorocarbonado *m*; ~ **resin** *n* P&R resina fluorocarbonada *f*

fluoroform *n* CHEM fluoformo *m*

fluorography *n* RAD PHYS fluorografía *f*, radiofotografía *f*

fluorophosphate *n* CHEM fluofosfato *m*

fluoroscopy *n* ELEC ENG fluoroscopia *f*, radioscopia *f*

fluorosilicate *n* CHEM fluosilicato *m*

fluorosilicic *adj* CHEM fluosilícico

fluorspar *n* C&G, CHEM, MINERAL espato flúor *m*, fluorita *f*

fluosulfonic *AmE see fluosulphonic BrE*

fluosulphonic *adj BrE* CHEM fluosulfónico

fluroaluminate *n* CHEM fluroaluminato *m*

flush[1] *adj* CONST, PROD a nivel, a paño, a ras; ~ **left** *adj* COMP&DP, PRINT justificado a la izquierda; ~**-operated** *adj* PROD operado a chorro *m*; ~ **right** *adj* COMP&DP, PRINT justificado a la derecha

flush[2] *n* WATER tromba de agua *f*; ~ **aerial** *n BrE* (*cf flush antenna AmE*) AIR TRANSP antena de fosa *f*, antena empotrada *f*, antena rasa *f*; ~ **antenna** *n AmE* (*cf flush aerial BrE*) AIR TRANSP antena de fosa *f*, antena empotrada *f*, antena rasa *f*; ~ **bolt** *n* PROD perno de cabeza embutida *m*; ~ **box** *n* WATER depósito de agua para limpiar *m*; ~ **cut** *n* PROD corte a ras *m*; ~ **deck** *n* WATER TRANSP *boat building* cubierta corrida *f*; ~ **gate** *n* WATER compuerta de limpia *f*; ~ **head** *n* MECH ENG, PROD cabeza embutida *f*; ~**-head rivet** *n* MECH ENG, PROD remache de cabeza embutida *m*; ~ **joint** *n* MECH ENG, PROD junta al tope *f*, junta lisa *f*, junta machihembra *f*; ~ **lifting ring** *n* WATER TRANSP *deck fitting* argolla de izada a paño *f*; ~ **lock** *n* CONST cerradura a nivel *f*; ~ **mount** *n* PROD montaje a paño *m*, montaje embutido *m*; ~**-mounted aerial** *n BrE* (*cf flush-mounted antenna AmE*) SPACE antena encastrada *f*; ~**-mounted antenna** *n AmE* (*cf flush-mounted aerial BrE*) SPACE antena encastrada *f*; ~**-mounted lens** *n* OPT, PHOTO lente montada a paño *f*; ~ **mounting** *n* ELEC *of switch* montaje embutido *m*, montaje empotrado *m*; ~ **plating** *n* WATER TRANSP *boat building* forro enrasado *m*; ~ **pond** *n* WATER depósito de limpia *m*; ~ **riveting** *n* PROD remachado a paño *m*, remachado embutido *m*; ~ **switch** *n* ELEC, ELEC ENG conmutador embutido *m*, conmutador embutido en la pared *m*; ~ **tank** *n* WATER depósito de limpia *m*; ~ **weir** *n* HYDRAUL vertedero sumergido *m*; ~ **wiring** *n* ELEC, ELEC ENG *supply network* cableado embutido *m*

flush[3] ~ *vt* COMP&DP, PRINT justificar la composición, PROD enrasar, igualar, nivelar, WATER mover por chorro de agua; ~ **up** *vt* PROD aflorar; **be** ~ **with** *vt* PROD estar a ras de, estar nivelado con

flushed: ~ **zone** *n* PETROL zona lavada *f*

flushing *n* AGRIC sobrealimentación antes del acoplamiento sexual *f*, MAR POLL chorro de flujo rápido *m*, MECH limpieza por descarga de agua *f*, purga *f*, MINE desescoriado *m* (*AmL*), dispersión de un contaminante desde un puerto o estuario *f*, extinción del fuego por descarga de agua *f*, lavado del oro *m*, limpieza del grisú acumulado por corriente de agua *f*, limpieza por descarga de agua *f*, PRINT recorte de la plancha al ras *m*, PROD limpieza por descarga de agua *f*, WATER baldeo *m*; ~ **connector** *n* MECH ENG conector de descarga *m*; ~ **tools** *n pl* MINE herramientas de lavado *f pl*, utensilios de lavado *m pl* (*AmL*)

flute *n* C&G canal *m*, CONST *groove* estría *f*, MECH pliegue *m*, acanaladura *f*, estría *f*, ondulación *f*, ranura *f*, canal *m*, PAPER acanalado *m*, SPACE flauta *f*; ~ **mark** *n* GEOL marca de erosión *f*

fluted *adj* MECH, MECH ENG con ranuras, estriado, ranurado, PAPER ondulado

fluteless[1] *adj* MECH, MECH ENG sin canales, sin estrías, sin ranuras

fluteless[2]: ~ **screwing tap** *n* MECH ENG macho de roscar sin estrías *m*

fluter *n* PAPER tren ondulador *m*

fluting *n* C&G acanalado *m*, CONST estriado *m*; ~ **corrugating medium** *n* PAPER papel para ondular *m*, tripa para ondular *f*; ~ **corrugating paper** *n* PAPER papel para ondular *m*, tripa para ondular *f*; ~ **medium** *n* PAPER papel para ondular *m*, tripa para ondular *f*; ~ **paper** *n* PAPER papel para ondular *m*, tripa para ondular *f*

flutter *n* ACOUST diafonía *f*, fluctuación *f*, lloro *m*, titilación *f*, trepidación *f*, AIR TRANSP *aerodynamics* flameo *m*, trepidación *f*, vibración *f*, fluctuación *f*, vibración aeroelástica *f*, TELECOM diafonía *f*, TV lloro *m*, vibración *f*; ~ **echo** *n* ACOUST eco fluctuante *m*, eco pulsante *m*, TV eco múltiple *m*; ~ **effect** *n* TV efecto ondulatorio *m*; ~ **factor** *n* ACOUST factor vibratorio *m*; ~ **rate** *n* TV velocidad de la vibración *f*

fluttering: ~ **of brightness level** *n* TV parpadeo del nivel de blanco *m*; ~ **seat** *n* HYDRAUL *pipes* alojamiento para pulsaciones hidráulicas del líquido circulante *m*; ~ **video level** *n* TV oscilación del nivel de video *f* (*AmL*), oscilación del nivel de vídeo *f* (*Esp*)

fluvial: ~ **alluvium** *n* WATER aluvión fluvial *m*; ~ **hydraulics** *n* WATER hidráulica fluvial *f*

fluviatile *adj* GEOL fluviatil

fluvio: ~**-glacial** *adj* GEOL fluvioglaciar; ~**-marine** *adj* GEOL fluviomarino

flux[1] *n* C&G, CONST, ELEC, ELEC ENG fundente *m*, MECH *of horizontal stationary engine* decapante *m*, fundente *m*, NUCL, PHYS fundente *m*; ~**-cored arc welding** *n* CONST soldadura por arco eléctrico con fundente *f*; ~**-cored arc welding with active-gas shielding** *n* CONST soldadura con arco sumergido y fundente en gas activo *f*; ~**-cored wire** *n* CONST cable con núcleo de fundente *m*; ~ **density** *n* ELEC *magnetism*, PHYS densidad de flujo *f*; ~**-flattened region** *n* NUCL zona de aplanamiento del flujo *f*; ~ **gate** *n AmE* (*cf flux valve BrE*) AIR TRANSP válvula de flujo magnético *f*; ~**-gate magnetometer** *n* ELEC ENG magnetómetro de saturación *m*, PETROL magnetómetro de apertura de flujo *m*; ~ **leakage** *n* ELEC ENG dispersión de flujo *f*; ~ **line** *n* C&G línea de nivel *f*, ELEC ENG línea de fuerza de flujo *f*; ~**-line attack** *n* C&G ataque por corrosión en la línea de nivel de vidrio *m*; ~ **linkage** *n* ELEC ENG acoplo inductivo *m*; ~ **map** *n* NUCL mapa de flujo *m*; ~ **powder** *n* COAL polvo bituminoso *m*; ~ **quantum** *n* PHYS cantidad de flujo *f*; ~ **of radiation** *n* RAD PHYS flujo de radiación *m*; ~ **tilting** *n* NUCL escorado del núcleo *m*; ~ **valve** *n* BrE (*cf flux gate AmE*) AIR TRANSP válvula de flujo magnético *f*

flux^2 *vt* PROD rociar con bórax

fluxmeter *n* CONST, ELEC, ELEC ENG, PHYS flujómetro *m*, fluxímetro *m*, fluxómetro *m*

fly^1 *n* MECH ENG vane, as of radiometer aleta *f*, PROD *vaned speed-regulating device* molinete regulador de paletas *m*; ~ **ash** *n* COAL cenizas *f pl*, cenizas volantes *f pl*; ~~**ball governor** *n* PROD regulador centrífugo *m*, regulador de Watt *m*, regulador de bolas *m*; ~~**bar with two balls** *n* PROD balancín a bolas *m*; ~~**by** *n* SPACE paso cercano *m*; ~~**by effect** *n* SPACE efecto de paso cercano *m*; ~~**by point** *n* SPACE punto de sobrevuelo *m*; ~~**by-wire flight controls** *n pl* AIR TRANSP controles de vuelo digitales fly-by-wire *m pl*; ~ **crank** *n* PROD contramanivela *f*; ~ **governor** *n* PROD *vaned speed-regulating device* volante *m*; ~ **nut** *n* PROD tuerca de orejetas *f*; ~~**off** *n* HYDROL cantidad de lluvia que se evapora *f*; ~ **press** *n* MECH ENG prensa de husillo *f*, PROD prensa de balancín *f*, prensa de husillo *f*; ~ **pulley** *n* MECH ENG polea volante *f*; ~ **roll** *n* PAPER rodillo guía del fieltro *m*; ~~**shuttle loom** *n* TEXTIL telar de lanzadera de aletas *m*; ~ **tipping** *n* RECYCL vertido de envergadura *m*

fly^2 *vt* WATER TRANSP *semaphore flag* arbolar, enarbolar, largar

fly^3 *vi* PROD *riveting* saltar; ~ **off** *vi* PROD *riveting* saltar

flyback *n* ELECTRON, TV retorno *m*, retroceso *m*; ~ **blanking** *n* TV tiempo de retroceso del borrado *m*; ~ **transformer** *n* TV transformador de retracción *m* (*Esp*), transformador vertical de alta tensión *m* (*AmL*)

flyer *n* CONST *stair-building* escalón *m*, paso *m*; ~~**spinning frame** *n* TEXTIL continua de hilar de aletas *f*

flying: ~ **boat** *n* AIR TRANSP hidroavión *m*; ~ **bridge** *n* CONST, WATER TRANSP puente volante *m*; ~ **buttress** *n* CONST arbotante *m*, arco botarel *m*; ~ **erase head** *n* TV cabeza de borrado volante *f*; ~ **hours** *n pl* AIR TRANSP horas de vuelo *f pl*; ~ **insert** *n* PRINT inserción volante *f*; ~ **lead** *n* PROD aleta adelantada *f*; ~ **paster** *n* PRINT empalmador volante *m*; ~ **scaffold** *n* CONST andamio suspendido y oscilante *m*; ~ **shore** *n* CONST apeo *m*, apuntalamiento *m*; ~ **sparks** *n pl* MECH ENG, PROD, SAFE chispas *f pl*; ~ **spot** *n* TV punto deslizante *m*; ~~**spot scanner** *n* SPACE explorador indirecto móvil *m*, TV explorador de punto deslizante *m*; ~~**spot tube scanner** *n* TV explorador de punto deslizante de tubo *m*, tubo de exploración por punto deslizante *m*; ~ **squad** *n* CONST brigada en voladizo *f*, cuadrilla en voladizo *f*; ~ **test bench** *n* AIR TRANSP banco de pruebas de vuelo *m*; ~ **time** *n* AIR TRANSP duración de vuelo *f*, tiempo de vuelo *m*

flyover *n* AUTO, CONST, TRANSP, VEH paso superior *m*; ~ **noise measurement point** *n* AIR TRANSP punto de medida de ruido del paso de vuelo *m*

flysch *n* GEOL, PETROL flysch *m*

flyweight *n* MECH ENG bola *f*, contrapeso *m*, contrapeso volante *m*

flywheel *n* AUTO, MECH, MECH ENG, REFRIG, VEH volante *m*; ~ **housing** *n* VEH cárter del volante *m*; ~ **ring gear** *n* MECH ENG, VEH engranaje anular del volante *m*; ~ **starter ring gear** *n* MECH ENG, VEH corona dentada de puesta en movimiento del volante *f*

Fm *abbr* (*fermium*) CHEM, RAD PHYS Fm (*fermio*)

FM: ~ **carrier** *n* ELECTRON portador de MF *m*; ~ **modem** *n* (*frequency-modulation modem*) ELECTRON módem de MF *m*; ~ **signal** *n* ELECTRON señal de MF *f*

FMBS *abbr* (*frame-mode bearer service*) TELECOM servicio portador del modo trama *m*

F-number *n* PHOTO, PHYS abertura relativa *f*, luminosidad *f*

foam^1 *n* C&G, CHEM, CHEM TECH espuma *f*, COAL cachaza *f*, espuma *f*, DETERG, FOOD espuma *f*, P&R caucho celular *m*, caucho esponjoso *m*, caucho espumado *m*, espuma *f*, goma espuma *f*, PAPER, TEXTIL, THERMO espuma *f*; ~ **backing** *n* TEXTIL refuerzo de espuma *m*; ~ **blanket** *n* AIR TRANSP capa de espuma *f*; ~ **booster** *n* FOOD aumentador de espuma *m*; ~ **boosting** *n* DETERG intensificación de la espumación *f*; ~ **breaker** *n* CHEM TECH desespumante *m*; ~ **compound** *n* AIR TRANSP compuesto de espuma *m*; ~ **dilution** *n* CHEM TECH dilución de espuma *f*; ~ **drainage** *n* CHEM TECH drenaje de espuma *m*; ~ **extinguisher** *n* AIR TRANSP, CONST, SAFE extintor de espuma *m*; ~ **extinguisher test** *n* AIR TRANSP, SAFE prueba de extintor de espuma *f*; ~ **fire-extinguisher** *n* AIR TRANSP, CONST, SAFE extintor de incendios a base de espuma *m*; ~ **glass** *n* C&G espuma de vidrio *f*; ~ **inhibitor** *n* CHEM TECH inhibidor de espuma *m*; ~ **layer** *n* TEXTIL lámina de espuma *f*; ~ **layer-forming flame-proofing agent** *n* SAFE agente protector que forma capas de espuma contra incendios *m*; ~ **line** *n* C&G línea de espuma *f*; ~ **mat drying** *n* FOOD secado de espuma en lecho *m*; ~ **material** *n* CONST, PACK, PROD material de espuma *m*; ~ **packaging and cushioning** *n* PACK embalaje relleno de espuma solidificable y almohadillado *m*; ~ **persistence** *n* CHEM TECH persistencia de espuma *f*; ~ **rubber** *n* P&R caucho celular *m*, caucho esponjoso *m*, caucho espumado *m*, goma espuma *f*; ~ **separation** *n* CHEM TECH separación por espuma *f*; ~ **tank** *n* PAPER tanque de espuma *m*; ~ **vacuum drying** *n* FOOD secado de espuma al vacío *m*

foam^2 *vt* CHEM TECH, TEXTIL espumar

foamed: ~ **glass** *n* C&G vidrio espumado *m*; ~ **plastic** *n* P&R plástico celular *m*, plástico esponjoso *m*, plástico espumado *m*; ~ **polystyrene and polyethylene molder** *AmE*, ~ **polystyrene and polyethylene moulder** *BrE* *n* PACK moldeador con espuma de poliestireno y polietileno *m*; ~ **slag aggregate** *n* HEAT ENG añadido de escoria porosa *m*

foamer *n* C&G, CHEM, CHEM TECH, DETERG, PETR TECH, PROD agente espumante *m*, espumante *m*

foaming *n* C&G, CHEM TECH, DETERG, FOOD, PETR TECH, PROD espumación *f*, espumado *m*; ~ **agent** *n* C&G, CHEM, CHEM TECH, DETERG agente espumante *m*, agente espumoso *m*, FOOD agente espumoso *m*, PETR TECH agente espumante *m*, PROD agente espumante *m*, agente espumoso *m*; ~ **test** *n* AIR TRANSP prueba de espuma *f*

foamy *adj* C&G, CHEM TECH, DETERG, P&R, PROD, TEXTIL espumoso

FOB *abbr* (*free on board*) PETR TECH, WATER TRANSP FOB (*franco a bordo*)

focal: ~ **depth** *n* GEOL profundidad focal *f*; ~ **length** *n*

CINEMAT, ELECTRON, PHOTO, PHYS, RAD PHYS, TV distancia focal *f*; ~ **plane** *n* CINEMAT, ELECTRON, PHOTO, PHYS, RAD PHYS, TV plano focal *m*; ~ **plane shutter** *n* CINEMAT, PHOTO, TV obturador de cortinilla *m*; ~ **point** *n* CINEMAT, PHOTO, TV punto focal *m*; ~ **range** *n* CINEMAT, PHOTO, TV gama focal *f*; ~ **spot** *n* ELECTRON punto focal *m*, trazo focal *m*; ~ **time** *n* CINEMAT, PHOTO, TV tiempo focal *m*

focimeter *n* INSTR focómetro *m*

focus[1]: **in** ~ *adv* CINEMAT, OPT, PHOTO, TV enfocado

focus[2] *n* CINEMAT, ELECTRON, PHOTO, TV enfoque *m*; ~ **knob** *n* CINEMAT, INSTR, PHOTO, TV botón de enfoque *m*; ~ **modulation** *n* CINEMAT, PHOTO, TV modulación del foco *f*; ~ **on film** *n* CINEMAT, TV enfoque en película *m*; ~ **pulling** *n* CINEMAT, PHOTO, TV ajuste del foco *m*; ~ **setting** *n* CINEMAT, PHOTO, TV ajuste del enfoque *m*, ajuste del foco *m*

focus[3] *vt* CINEMAT, ELECTRON, OPT, PHOTO, PHYS, TV concentrar, enfocar, WAVE PHYS ajustar, concentrar, enfocar, fijar, hacer converger; ~ **for infinity** *vt* PHOTO enfocar al infinito

focused[1] *adj* CINEMAT, ELECTRON, PHOTO, PHYS, TV, WAVE PHYS enfocado

focused[2]: ~ **beam** *n* ELECTRON haz convergente *m*, WAVE PHYS haz convergente *m*, haz dirigido *m*, haz enfocado *m*; ~ **ion beams** *n pl* RAD PHYS haces iónicos convergentes *m pl*; ~ **log** *n* PETROL perfil convergente *m*

focusing *n* CINEMAT, ELECTRON enfoque *m*, PHOTO enfoque *m*, aro de enfoque *m*, TV enfoque *m*; ~ **aid** *n* CINEMAT, PHOTO, TV ayuda de enfoque *f*; ~ **anode** *n* ELEC ENG ánodo de enfoque *m*; ~ **coil** *n* CINEMAT bobina de enfoque *f*, ELEC ENG bobina de concentración *f*, TV bobina de enfoque *f*; ~ **control** *n* CINEMAT, PHOTO, TV control de enfoque *m*; ~ **diode** *n* ELEC ENG, INSTR, TV diodo de enfoque *m*; ~ **electrode** *n* ELEC ENG, INSTR, TV electrodo de enfoque *m*; ~ **knob** *n* CINEMAT, INSTR, PHOTO, TV botón de enfoque *m*, mando de enfoque *m*; ~ **lamp** *n* ELEC lámpara de enfoque *f*; ~ **lens** *n* CINEMAT, INSTR, OPT, PHOTO, TV lente de enfoque *f*; ~ **lever** *n* CINEMAT, TV varilla de enfoque *f*; ~ **magnet** *n* CINEMAT, ELEC ENG, PHOTO, SPACE, TV electroimán de concentración *m*, electroimán de foco *m*, imán de enfoque *m*; ~ **magnifier** *n* INSTR amplificador de enfoque *m*; ~ **magnifying glass** *n* INSTR cristal de aumento convergente *m*, lupa de enfoque *f*; ~ **mount** *n* CINEMAT, TV montaje de enfoque *m*; ~ **range** *n* CINEMAT, PHOTO, TV escala de enfoque *f*; ~ **ring** *n* CINEMAT anillo de enfoque *m*, aro de enfoque *m*, INSTR, PHOTO anillo de enfoque *m*, TV anillo de enfoque *m*, aro de enfoque *m*; ~ **screen** *n* CINEMAT, INSTR, PHOTO, TV pantalla de enfoque *f*; ~-**screen frame** *n* CINEMAT, PHOTO, TV soporte de la pantalla de enfoque *m*; ~ **sleeve** *n* INSTR tubo focalizador *m*; ~ **stage** *n* CINEMAT, PHOTO área de enfoque *f*

fodder *n* AGRIC forraje *m*

foehn *n* METEO foehn *m*; ~ **wind** *n* METEO foehn *m*

FOF *abbr* (*freeze-out fraction*) SPACE, TELECOM fracción de bloqueo de conexión *f*, fracción de bloqueo momentáneo *f*

fog[1] *n* ACOUST, CINEMAT velo *m*, METEO niebla *f*, *sea* niebla marina *f*, niebla por advección *f*, PHOTO, PRINT velo *m*, REFRIG niebla *f*; ~ **bank** *n* METEO banco de niebla *m*; ~ **dispersal** *n* AIR TRANSP disipador de niebla *m*, dispersador de bruma *m*; ~ **gun** *n* CINEMAT,

TV generador de niebla *m*; ~ **lamp** *n* AUTO, TRANSP, VEH lámpara antiniebla *f*; ~ **signal** *n* WATER TRANSP señal de niebla *f*; ~ **warning** *n* METEO, WATER TRANSP aviso de niebla *m*, radioaviso de niebla *m*

fog[2] *vt* AGRIC nebulizar, CINEMAT, PHOTO velar

fogged: ~ **film** *n* CINEMAT, PHOTO película velada *f*

föhn *n* METEO föhn *m*; ~ **wind** *n* METEO föhn *m*

foil *n* CRYSTALL *electron microscope specimen* lámina metálica *f*, PACK lámina metálica delgada *f*, PAPER lámina desgotadora *f*, PROD hoja delgada de metal *f*, oropel *m*, papel metalizado *m*; ~ **backing machine** *n* PACK dispositivo de soporte de la hoja *m*, máquina de retorno de la hoja *f*; ~-**forming plant** *n* PROD fábrica de láminas metálicas delgadas *f*; ~ **paper** *n* PAPER papel de aluminio *m*; ~ **sampler** *n* COAL muestreador de pan de oro *m*, muestreador de pan de plata *m*; ~ **sealing** *n* PACK sellado de lámina metálica *f*; ~ **tooling** *n* MECH ENG herramientas de embotar *f pl*

fold[1] *n* GEOL, PETROL plegamiento *m*, pliegue *m*; ~ **axis** *n* GEOL, PETROL eje del pliegue *m*; ~ **brush setting** *n* PROD calaje de las escobillas plegable *m*; ~ **carton** *n* PACK caja plegable *f*, caja plegable de cartón *f*; ~ **limb** *n* GEOL flanco del pliegue *m*; ~ **nappe** *n* GEOL manto de recubrimiento *m*

fold[2] *vt* PAPER plegar; ~ **back** *vt* PROD plegar; ~ **down** *vt* PROD plegar hacia abajo; ~ **over** *vt* PROD superponer

foldaway *adj* MECH ENG plegable, plegadizo

folded[1]: ~ **and collated** *adj* PRINT plegado y clasificado

folded[2]: ~-**bottom box** *n* PACK caja de fondo plegable *f*; ~-**dipole aerial** *n* BrE (*cf folded-dipole antenna AmE*) TV antena dipolo doblado *f*; ~-**dipole antenna** *n* AmE (*cf folded-dipole aerial BrE*) TV antena dipolo doblado *f*; ~ **network** *n* TELECOM red plegada *f*

folder *n* PACK, PRINT, PROD plegadora *f*; ~-**gluer** *n* PACK plegadora-engomadora *f*; ~ **unit** *n* PRINT plegadora *f*

folding[1] *adj* MECH ENG, PROD plegable, plegadizo, plegado, plegador

folding[2] *n* ELECTRON plegador *m*, GEOL plegamiento *m*, PAPER plegado *m*, PROD plegadizo, plegado *m*, plegador *m*; ~-**and-seaming machine** *n* PACK, PROD máquina plegadora y cosedora *f*; ~ **axes** *n* AIR TRANSP *of helicopter* ejes plegables *m pl*; ~ **bed** *n* SAFE camilla *f*; ~ **bicycle** *n* TRANSP bicicleta plegable *f*; ~ **blade** *n* AIR TRANSP *of helicopter* pala plegable *f*; ~ **box** *n* PACK, PAPER caja plegable *f*; ~-**box erecting machine** *n* PACK montaje de máquinas con envase plegadizo *m*; ~-**box setting machine** *n* PACK máquina para montar cajas plegables *f*; ~ **boxboard** *n* PAPER cartoncillo para cajas plegables *m*, cartón para cajas plegables *m*; ~ **camera** *n* PHOTO cámara de campaña *f*, cámara fotográfica plegable *f*; ~ **carton** *n* PACK caja plegable *f*; ~ **cylinder** *n* PRINT cilindro plegador *m*; ~ **doors** *n pl* CONST puertas plegables *f pl*; ~ **drum** *n* PRINT tambor de plegado *m*; ~ **endurance** *n* PAPER resistencia al plegado *f*; ~ **frequency** *n* GEOL, PETROL frecuencia de plegamiento *f*; ~ **joint** *n* CONST unión plegable *f*; ~-**knife cylinder** *n* PAPER cilindro con cuchilla plegadora *m*; ~ **lens** *n* INSTR, OPT lente de desdoblamiento *f*; ~ **machine** *n* MECH ENG, PAPER, PROD plegadora *f*, plegadora mecánica *f*; ~ **machine for cardboard** *n* MECH ENG, PAPER, PROD plegadora de cartón *f*; ~ **pocket-magnifier** *n* INSTR amplificador de bolsillo por desdoblamiento *m*; ~ **propeller** *n* WATER TRANSP *boat building* hélice plegable *f*; ~ **pylon** *n* AIR TRANSP *of helicopter* columna plegable *f*; ~ **roller** *n* PRINT rodillo plegador *m*; ~ **rule** *n* AmE (*cf jointed rule BrE*) CONST metro plegable *m*, regla plegable *f*, METEO metro plegable *m*; ~ **seat** *n* AmE (*cf tip-up seat BrE*) AUTO, VEH asiento abatible *m*, asiento plegable *m*; ~ **sides** *n pl* PACK laterales plegables *m pl*; ~ **sight** *n* CONST visualrecíproca *f*; ~ **station** *n* PRINT sección de plegado *f*; ~ **strength** *n* PACK ensayo de doblado *m*, resistencia al doblado *f*, resistencia al plegado *f*; ~ **test** *n* PACK ensayo de plegado *m*; ~-**wing aircraft** *n* AIR TRANSP avión de ala plegable *m*

foldover *n* PETROL deflexión *f*; ~ **edge** *n* PRINT borde superpuesto *m*; ~ **leg** *n* PHOTO pie articulado *m*

foliated[1] *adj* GEOL foliado, laminado

foliated[2]: ~ **coal** *n* COAL, MINE carbón esquistoso *m*, hulla pizarrosa *f*; ~ **crystalline rock** *n* GEOL roca cristalina laminada *f*; ~ **tellurium** *n* MINERAL telurio foliado *m*, telurio hojoso *m*

foliation *n* GEOL esquistosidad *f*, exfoliación *f*

folic: ~ **acid** *n* CHEM, FOOD ácido fólico *m*

folinic *adj* CHEM folínico

folio[1] *n* PRINT libro en folio *m*

folio[2] *vt* PRINT foliar, paginar

follicle *n* AGRIC folículo *m*

follow[1]: ~ **focus** *n* CINEMAT, PHOTO, TV mando de foco *m*; ~ **range** *n* ELECTRON desplazamiento continuo *m*; ~ **rest** *n* MECH ENG *of lathe* luneta móvil *f*, soporte *m*, soporte móvil *m*; ~ **spot** *n* CINEMAT luz dirigida para seguimiento *f*

follow[2]: ~ **focus** *vi* CINEMAT, PHOTO, TV enfocar en movimiento; ~ **F-stop** *vi* CINEMAT, PHOTO, TV ajustar la abertura

follower *n* COAL contraaguja de vía muerta *f*, elevador *m*, polea mandada *f*, transportador *m*, MECH rodillo de leva *m*, MECH ENG tapa de pistón *f*, *driven pulley* polea conducida *f*, polea mandada *f*, *gearing* rueda conducida *f*, engranaje impulsado *m*, engranaje secundario *m*, *of planing machine* seguidor *m*, PROD *of stuffing box* casquillo *m*; ~ **bush** *n* PROD *of stuffing box* casquillo *m*; ~ **roll** *n* PAPER rodillo accionado *m*

following: ~ **gear** *n* MECH ENG engranaje conducido *m*; ~ **wind** *n* WATER TRANSP viento en popa cerrado *m*

F1: ~ **generation** *n* AGRIC primera generación filial *f*

font *n* COMP&DP, PRINT fuente *f*, juego de tipos de caracteres *m*, juego de tipos de letras *m*, tipo de letras *m*; ~ **valve** *n* HYDRAUL válvula de contención *f*

food *n* FOOD alimento *m*; ~ **additive** *n* FOOD aditivo alimenticio *m*; ~ **chemistry** *n* FOOD química de los alimentos *f*; ~ **control** *n* FOOD, QUALITY control alimentario *m*; ~ **freezer** *n* FOOD, MECH ENG, REFRIG congelador de alimentos *m*, congelador de comestibles *m*; ~-**grade film** *n* FOOD, PACK película para estar en contacto con alimentos *f*; ~ **grains** *n pl* AGRIC, FOOD granos alimenticios *m pl*; ~ **inspection** *n* FOOD, QUALITY inspección de alimento *f*; ~ **irradiation** *n* FOOD, RAD PHYS irradiación de los alimentos *f*; ~ **packaging** *n* FOOD, PACK embalaje de alimentos *m*, envase para alimentos *m*; ~ **plain** *n* HYDROL zona de inundación *f*; ~ **poisoning** *n* FOOD intoxicación *f*; ~ **preservative** *n* AGRIC sustancia conservante *f*, FOOD conservador de alimento *m*; ~ **processing plant** *n* FOOD planta de proceso de alimentos *f*; ~ **requirements** *n pl* FOOD exigencias alimenticias *f pl*; ~ **science** *n* FOOD ciencia de los alimentos *f*; ~ **tray** *n* PACK bandeja de alimentos *f*; ~ **value** *n*

AGRIC, FOOD valor nutritivo *m*; ~-**wrapping machinery** *n* PACK maquinaria para envolver alimentos *f*

foodstuff *n* FOOD producto alimenticio *m*

foot *n* CONST base *f*, pie *m*, METR *measure* pie *m*, MINE residuo *m*, WATER TRANSP *of topmast, juggle* coz *f*, pie *m*, *support* pujamen *m*; ~-**and-mouth disease** *n* AGRIC fiebre aftosa *f*, glosopeda *f*; ~ **candle** *n* CINEMAT bujía-pie *f*; ~ **change** *n* VEH cambio de velocidades de pedal *m*, cambio por pedal *m*; ~-**change lever** *n* VEH palanca del pedal de cambio de velocidades *f*; ~ **dimmer** *n* AUTO interruptor de pie *m*, conmutador de pie *m*, interruptor de conmutador de pie *m*, VEH interruptor de pie *m*; ~ **dipswitch** *n* (*cf foot dimmer AmE*) AUTO interruptor de pie *m*, conmutador de pie *m*, interruptor de conmutador de pie *m*, VEH interruptor de pie *m*; ~ **lambert** *n* CINEMAT pie-lambert *m*; ~-**operated control** *n* MECH ENG control de pedal *m*; ~ **pump** *n* AUTO, MECH ENG bomba de pie *f*; ~ **switch** *n* INSTR conmutador de pedal *m*; ~ **valve** *n* HYDRAUL válvula de contención *f*, válvula de retención *f*, MECH ENG válvula de aspiración *f*; ~-**wall seam** *n* CONST grieta en la parte inferior de la pared *f*

footage *n* CINEMAT metraje *m*

footboard *n* AmE (*cf monkey board BrE*) PETR TECH *drilling* encuelladero *m*, plataforma del encuellador *f*, tabla de piso *f*, PETROL plataforma astillero *f*, plataforma de la torre *f*

footbrake *n* AUTO, VEH freno de pie *m*

footbridge *n* CONST, RAIL pasarela *f*, puente para peatones *m*

foothold *n* CONST base de apoyo *f*, soporte de base *m*

footing *n* COAL pie *m*, CONST apoyo de la cimentación *m*, *of building* cimiento *m*, zapata *f*, GEOL zapata *f*; ~ **block** *n* CONST zócalo *m*

footlight *n* CINEMAT, TV candileja *f*

footnote: ~ **call out** *n* PRINT llamada de la nota al pie *f*

footprint *n* CINEMAT zona de caída *f*, SPACE cobertura *f*, TV zona de caída *f*

footrest *n* VEH reposapiés *m*

footscrew *n* MECH ENG tornillo nivelador *m*

footstep *n* MECH ENG rangua *f*, tajuelo *m*; ~ **bearing** *n* MECH ENG rangua *f*, tajuelo *m*

footstock *n* MECH ENG *of lathe* contracabezal *m*, contrapunto *m*

footwall *n* GEOL muro *m*, suelo *m*, MINE muro *m* (*AmL*), muro de base *m*, muro yacente *m*, piso *m*, suelo *m*

footway *n* CONST andén *m*, calzada *f*, piso *m*

footwear *n* SAFE calzado *m*; ~ **for protection against burns** *n* SAFE calzado protector para evitar quemaduras *m*

FOQ *abbr* (*free on quay*) WATER TRANSP franco en muelle

forage *n* AGRIC forraje *m*; ~ **chopper** *n* AGRIC picadora de forrajes *f*; ~ **crop** *n* AGRIC cultivo para forraje *m*; ~ **sorghum** *n* AGRIC sorgo forrajero *m*

foraminifera *n* GEOL, PETROL foraminífero *m*

foraminiferal *adj* GEOL, PETROL foraminífero

forbidden: ~ **band** *n* NUCL, PHYS, RAD PHYS banda prohibida *f*; ~ **decay modes** *n pl* RAD PHYS modos de desintegración prohibidos *m pl*; ~ **energy band** *n* NUCL, PHYS, RAD PHYS banda energética prohibida *f*; ~ **transition** *n* NUCL, PHYS, RAD PHYS transición prohibida *f*

force¹ n HYDROL violencia f, PHYS fuerza f; **~-balance transducer** n ELEC ENG transductor de equilibrio de fuerzas m; **~-disable command** n PROD comando forzado de desactivación m; **~-enable command** n PROD comando forzado de activación m; ~ **fan** n PROD ventilador soplante m; **~-feed lubrication** n MECH ENG lubricación con alimentación a presión f, PROD lubrificación con alimentación a presión f; ~ **fit** n MECH, MECH ENG ajuste forzado m, montaje de fuerza m; ~ **of friction** n MECH ENG, PHYS fuerza de fricción f; ~ **line** n GEOPHYS, MECH ENG línea de fuerza f; ~ **link** n AIR TRANSP enlace de fuerza m; **~-off command** n MECH ENG, PROD comando de desconexión m; **~-on command** n MECH ENG, PROD comando de conexión m; ~ **pump** n HYDRAUL, PROD, WATER bomba impelente f; ~ **selection** n PROD selección por fuerza f; ~ **table** n PROD cuadro de fuerzas m; ~ **unit** n MECH ENG, PHYS unidad de fuerza f

force² vt MINE forzar; ~ **off** vt MECH ENG, PROD desenmangar por presión; ~ **on** vt MECH ENG, PROD enmangar por presión

force³: ~ **open the points** vi RAIL talonar la aguja

forced: **~-air cooling** n MECH ENG, PROD, REFRIG enfriado por aire a presión m, enfriado por aire forzado m, refrigerado por aire a presión m, refrigerado por aire forzado m; **~-air furnace** n GAS, MECH ENG horno de aire forzado m, quemador de tiraje forzado m (AmL), quemador de tiro por aspiración m; **~-circulation boiler** n HEAT caldera de circulación forzada f; ~ **convection** n C&G, FLUID, GAS, HEAT ENG, PHYS, PRINT convección forzada f; **~-convection edge** n PRINT borde de convección forzada m; **~-convection lehr** n C&G horno de revenido de convección forzada m, templador de convección forzada m; ~ **cooling** n MECH ENG enfriado a presión m, lubricado a presión m, PROD enfriado a presión m, REFRIG enfriado a presión m, lubricado a presión m; ~ **development** n CINEMAT revelado forzado m; ~ **draft** AmE see forced draught BrE; **~-draft air-cooled condenser** AmE see forced-draught air-cooled condenser BrE; **~-draft burner** AmE see forced-draught burner BrE; **~-draft cooling** AmE see forced-draught cooling BrE; **~-draft furnace** AmE see forced-draught furnace BrE; ~ **draught** n BrE CONST in chimney tiro forzado m, HEAT corriente de aire forzada f, MECH ENG corriente de aire a presión f, ventilation ventilación mecánica por insuflación f, aireado forzado m, tiro forzado m, ventilación forzada f; **~-draught air-cooled condenser** n BrE REFRIG condensador enfriado por convección forzada de aire m, condensador refrigerado por corriente forzada de aire m; **~-draught burner** n BrE GAS, MECH ENG horno de aire forzado m, quemador de tiraje forzado m (AmL), quemador de tiro forzado m (Esp); **~-draught cooling** n BrE REFRIG enfriamiento por circulación forzada m; **~-draught furnace** n BrE HEAT ENG, MECH ENG, PROD horno de tiraje forzado m (AmL), horno de tiro forzado m (Esp); **~-feed lubrication** n AUTO engrase por alimentación forzada m, lubricación por alimentación forzada f; **~-fit bush** n MECH ENG casquillo de ajuste forzado m, manguito de ajuste forzado m; ~ **hot air** n HEAT, THERMO aire caliente forzado m; **~-input bit** n COMP&DP, PROD bit de entrada forzada m; ~ **I/O indicator** n PROD indicador de E/S forzado m; ~ **landing** n AIR TRANSP, SPACE descenso de emergencia m, descenso forzoso m; ~ **lubrification** n REFRIG engrase a presión m, engrase forzado m; **~-oil cooling** n MECH ENG, REFRIG refrigeración por aceite a presión f; ~ **oscillation** n ELECTRON, PHYS oscilación forzada f; ~ **ventilation** n ELEC, ELEC ENG, MECH ENG, PROD ventilación a presión f, ventilación forzada f; **~-ventilation motor** n ELEC, ELEC ENG, MECH ENG motor con ventilación forzada m; ~ **vibration** n ACOUST, PHYS vibración forzada f; ~ **warm air** n HEAT, THERMO aire caliente forzado m; **~-water cooling** n MECH ENG, REFRIG enfriamiento por agua a presión m, refrigeración por agua a presión f

forcing n CONST of lock acto de forzar m, forzamiento m, MINE forzamiento m, forzador m, rompimiento m (Esp), apertura f (AmL), separador m; ~ **down** n MINE forzamiento descendente m; ~ **indicator** n PROD indicador de función forzada m

ford¹ n CONST, HYDROL vado m

ford² vt CONST, HYDROL vadear

fording n CONST, HYDROL vado m

fore¹ adj WATER TRANSP proel, de proa

fore² adv WATER TRANSP a proa; ~ **and aft** adv WATER TRANSP en sentido longitudinal

fore³: **~-and-aft cyclic control support** n AIR TRANSP of helicopter apoyo de control cíclico longitudinal m; **~-and-aft cyclic pitch** n AIR TRANSP of helicopter paso cíclico longitudinal m; **~-and-aft line** n WATER TRANSP ship design eje de crujía m, eje longitudinal m, línea proa-popa f; ~ **deep** n GEOL pre-fosa f; ~ **edge** n PRINT borde anterior m, borde frontal m; ~ **observation** n CONST levelling observación directa f; **~-runnings** n pl FOOD aguas de cabeza f pl, primer licor m; ~ **vacuum** n PHYS vacío preliminar m

forebay n HYDRAUL cámara de agua f

foreboiler n HYDRAUL frente de caldera m

forecast n METEO predicción f; ~ **horizon** n PROD horizonte de pronóstico m; ~ **interval** n PROD intervalo de pronóstico m; ~ **period** n PROD período de pronóstico m

forecasting n COMP&DP previsión f, pronóstico m, METEO predicción f, predicción del tiempo f, predicción meteorológica f, pronóstico del tiempo m, WATER predicción f, previsión f

forecastle n WATER TRANSP shipbuilding castillo de proa m

foredeck n WATER TRANSP shipbuilding cubierta del castillo f

forefoot n WATER TRANSP shipbuilding pie de roda m

foreground¹ adj COMP&DP preferencial, preferente, prioritario

foreground²: **in the** ~ adv CINEMAT, PHOTO, TV en primer plano, en primer término

foreground³ n CINEMAT primer término m, COMP&DP primer plano m, PHOTO, TV primer plano m, primer término m; ~ **job** n COMP&DP tarea en primer plano f, tarea prioritaria f, trabajo preferencial m; ~ **miniature** n CINEMAT miniatura en primer plano f; ~ **processing** n COMP&DP procesamiento en primer plano m, procesamiento prioritario m; ~ **program** n COMP&DP programa de primer plano m, programa preferencial m

forehearth n C&G alimentador m, canal de distribución m, chorreador m; ~ **entrance** n C&G entrada al alimentador f, entrada al chorreador f

foreign: ~ **cullet** *n* C&G cullet foráneo *m*, fundente foráneo *m*; ~ **matter** *n* PROD materia extraña *f*

foreland *n* GEOL antepaís *m*, OCEAN cabo *m*, promontorio *m*

forelock *n* MECH ENG chaveta *f* (*AmL*), contrachaveta *f*; ~ **bolt** *n* MECH ENG perno de chaveta *m*

forelocking *n* MECH ENG enchavetado *m*

foreman *n* C&G mayordomo *m*, CONST capataz *m*, encargado *m*, PROD capataz *m*; ~ **shunter** *n* RAIL capataz de maniobras *m*

foremast *n* WATER TRANSP palo trinquete *m*

forepeak *n* WATER TRANSP pique de proa *m*

forepoling *n* MINE avance con tablestacas *m*, entibación con agujas *f* (*AmL*), entibación hincada *f*, entibo provisional *m*, posteo *f* (*Esp*), *workmen* primer relevo *m*

foresail *n* WATER TRANSP vela trinquete *f*

foreset: ~ **bed** *n* GEOL capa frontal *f*

foreshore *n* GEOL, HYDROL playa baja *f*, OCEAN cercanías de costa *f pl*

foresight *n* CONST *surveying* vista de frente *f*, MILIT *of rifle* punto de mira *m*, MINE croquis de nivel *m*, nivelación *f*, punto de mira *m* (*AmL*)

forest: ~ **area** *n* AGRIC, CONST zona forestal *f*; ~ **fallow** *n* AGRIC barbecho forestal *m*; ~ **fire** *n* AGRIC, THERMO incendio forestal *m*; ~ **floor** *n* AGRIC suelo forestal *m*; ~ **gallery** *n* AGRIC galería forestal *f*; ~ **management** *n* AGRIC manejo de bosque *m*

forestay *n* WATER TRANSP estay del trinquete *m*; ~ **pin** *n* WATER TRANSP arraigado del estay del trinquete *m*; ~ **sail** *n* WATER TRANSP trinquetilla *f*

forewinning: ~ **heading** *n* MINE galería de trazado *f*

forge *n* CONST, MECH, MECH ENG, METALL forja *f*, MINE fragua *f*, PROD fragua *f*, taller de forja *m*, *large ironworks* forja *f*; ~ **back** *n* PROD respaldo de fragua *m*; ~ **bellows** *n* PROD fuelle de fragua *m*; ~ **hammer** *n* PROD martillo de fragua *m*; ~ **roll** *n* PROD rodillo para forjar redondo *m*; ~ **scale** *n* PROD batiduras de forja *f pl*; ~ **welding** *n* CONST, PROD soldadura de forja *f*

forged¹ *adj* CONST, MECH, MECH ENG, METALL, PROD forjado, fraguado

forged²: ~ **shackle** *n* MECH ENG gancho de acero forjado *m*, gancho de hierro forjado *m*, grillete de acero forjado *m*, grillete de hierro forjado *m*, horquilla de acero forjado *f*, horquilla de hierro forjado *f*; ~ **steel lifting hook** *n* MECH ENG gancho de grúa de acero forjado *m*; ~ **wing attachment** *n* AIR TRANSP accesorio forjado de unión del ala *m*

forged¹: **as** ~ *adj* PROD en estado tosco de forjado

forging *n* CONST forja *f*, MECH *lathe* forja *f*, pieza forjada *f*, pieza estampada *f*, forjadura *f*, MECH ENG, PROD forjadura *f*, *piece of forged work* pieza forjada *f*, *process* forja *f*; ~ **die** *n* MECH ENG troquel de forjar *m*; ~ **press** *n* PROD prensa de forjar *f*

fork¹ *n* AGRIC, C&G horquilla *f*, CONST *of road, river, railway* bifurcación *f*, cruce de carreteras *m*, cruce de ferrocarril *m*, MECH ENG *of clutch*, VEH horquilla *f*; ~ **arm** *n* AUTO, MECH ENG, VEH brazo de horquilla *m*; ~ **bar** *n* MECH ENG barra de horquilla *f*; ~ **center** *AmE*, ~ **centre** *BrE n* MECH ENG *lathe* punto de tres dientes *m*; ~ **chuck** *n* MECH ENG plato ahorquillado *m*, plato de tres puntos *m*, plato de tulipa *m*; ~-**end connecting rod** *n* MECH ENG biela de cabeza ahorquillada *f*; ~ **head** *n* MECH articulación de horquilla *f*, MECH ENG articulación de horquilla *f*, cabeza de horquilla *f*; ~-**lever roller** *n* PROD rodillo de

palanca de horquilla *m*; ~ **lift** *n* AGRIC elevador de horquilla *m*; ~ **mounting** *n* INSTR montaje en horquilla *m*; ~ **oscillator** *n* ELECTRON oscilador de bifurcación *m*; ~ **push rod** *n* AUTO, VEH barra de empuje de horquilla *f*; ~ **return spring** *n* VEH muelle de retorno de horquilla *m*; ~ **truck** *n* AUTO carretilla elevadora *f*; ~ **wrench** *n* MECH ENG llave inglesa de horquilla *f*

fork²: ~ **a belt off** *vt* MECH ENG desconectar correa, desembragar correa; ~ **a belt on** *vt* MECH ENG conectar correa, embragar corre

forked: ~ **connection** *n* ELEC conexión bifurcada *f*; ~ **pipe** *n* CONST tubería en Y *f*, tubería horquillada *f*

forklift: ~ **truck** *n* GEN carretilla de horquilla elevadora *f*, carretilla elevadora *f*, vehículo montacargas de horquilla *m*

form *n* COMP&DP forma *f*, impreso *m*, papel *m*, CONST matriz *f*, molde *m*, PRINT *see forme BrE*, PROD molde *m*; ~ **drag** *n* AIR TRANSP resistencia aerodinámica de forma *f*, retardo de forma *m*; ~ **error** *n* METR error de hechura *m*; ~ **feed** *n* (*FF*) COMP&DP, PRINT alimentación de papel *f*, avance de hoja *m*, avance de papel *m*, avance de página *m*; ~-**feed character** *n* COMP&DP carácter de alimentación de papel *m*, carácter de avance de página *m*; ~-**fill-and-seal machine** *n* PACK máquina para formar, llenar y cerrar envases *f*; ~ **grinding** *n* MECH ENG rectificado de perfiles *m*; ~ **milling** *n* MECH fresa perfilada *f*, MECH ENG, PROD fresa perfilada *f*, fresado de perfiles *m*; ~-**milling cutter** *n* MECH ENG, PROD fresa de perfilar *f*, fresa de perfiles *f*; ~-**milling cutter with constant profile** *n* MECH ENG, PROD fresa de perfilar con perfil fijo *f*; ~ **shim** *n* MECH ENG galga de perfil *f*, suplemento de perfil *m*; ~ **stop** *n* COMP&DP parada de papel *f*, parada por falta de papel *f*, PRINT parada por falta de papel *f*; ~-**wound coil** *n* ELEC bobina arrollada sobre mandril *f*, bobina conformada *f*, devanado conformado *m*

formal: ~ **language** *n* COMP&DP lenguaje formal *m*; ~ **logic** *n* COMP&DP lógica formal *f*; ~ **parameter** *n* COMP&DP parámetro formal *m*; ~ **wear** *n* TEXTIL ropa de vestir *f*

formaldehyde *n* CHEM, FOOD, P&R, TEXTIL aldehído fórmico *m*, formaldehído *m*, metanal *m*; ~ **sulfoxylate** *AmE*, ~ **sulphoxylate** *BrE n* CHEM, FOOD sulfoxilato de formaldehído *m*

formalin *n* CHEM formalina *f*

formamide *n* CHEM formamida *f*

formant *n* ACOUST formante *m*; ~ **vocoder** *n* TELECOM vocoder formante *m*

format¹ *n* GEN formato *m*, tamaño *m*

format² *vt* COMP&DP dar formato, formatear

formate *n* CHEM formato *m*

formation *n* PAPER estructura de la hoja *f*, estructura *f*; ~ **energy** *n* METALL energía de desarrollo *f*, energía de formación *f*; ~ **evaluation** *n* GEOL, PETR TECH, PETROL evaluación de formación *f*; ~ **factor** *n* PETR TECH, PETROL factor de formación *m*; ~ **flight** *n* AIR TRANSP vuelo en formación *m*; ~ **fluid** *n* GEOL, PETR TECH fluido de formación *m*; ~ **interval test** *n* (*FIT*) PETROL prueba de intervalos de formación *f*; ~ **pressure** *n* GEOL, PETR TECH presión de reservorio *f*; ~-**pressure gradient** *n* GEOL, PETR TECH gradiente de presión de formación *m*; ~ **resistivity** *n* PETROL resistividad de formación *f*; ~ **test** *n* PETR TECH, PETROL prueba de formación *f*; ~ **tester** *n* PAPER medidor de la estructura *m*, PETROL ensayador de capas *m*; ~ **volume factor** *n* PETR TECH, PETROL factor de volumen de la formación *m*; ~ **water** *n* GEOL, HYDROL, PETR TECH, PETROL agua de formación *f*

formatter *n* COMP&DP formatador *m* (*AmL*), formateador *m* (*Esp*)

formatting *n* COMP&DP formateado *m*

formazyl *n* CHEM formazilo *m*

forme *n* BrE PRINT forma *f*

formed: ~ **cutter** *n* MECH fresa perfilada *f*, MECH ENG fresa de forma *f*, fresa perfilada *f*, PROD fresa perfilada *f*; ~ **milling cutter** *n* MECH fresa perfilada *f*, MECH ENG fresa de forma *f*, fresa perfilada *f*, PROD fresa perfilada *f*

former *n* C&G sacador *m*, ELEC ENG horma *f*, INSTR matriz *f*, molde *m*, MECH ENG cordón *m*, gálibo *m*, matriz *f*, mecánico formador *m*, molde *m*, plantilla guía *f*, PAPER formador *m*, PRINT amoldadora-sacadora *f*, PROD *strickle* matriz *f*, molde *m*, *templet* plantilla de devanado *f*, calibre reproductor *m*, gálivo *m*; ~ **folder** *n* PRINT dobladora a embudo *f*; ~ **roller** *n* C&G placa de rolado del sacador *f*

formic *adj* CHEM fórmico

forming *n* COATINGS, MECH, P&R, PROD confirmación *f*, embutición *f*, modelado *m*, moldeado *m*; ~ **fabric** *n* PAPER tela de formación *f*; ~ **lathe** *n* MECH ENG torno de repetición *m*; ~ **roll** *n* PAPER rodillo formador *m*; ~ **shoe** *n* PAPER zapata de formación *f*; ~ **temperature** *n* PACK temperatura de formación *f*; ~ **tool** *n* MECH ENG herramienta de copiar *f*, herramienta de perfilar *f*; ~ **tool holder** *n* MECH ENG portaherramientas de copiar *m*; ~ **tools** *n pl* MECH ENG herramientas de copiar *f pl*, herramientas de perfilar *f pl*

formula *n* CHEM fórmula *f*

formwork *n* CONST encofrado *m*; ~ **hammer** *n* MECH ENG martillo *m*, martillo mecánico de forja *m*, martillo pilón *m*, martinete de forja *m*, mazo *m*

formyl *n* CHEM formilo *m*

forsterite *n* MINERAL forsterita *f*

fort: ~ **valve** *n* HYDRAUL válvula de retención *f*

fortification *n* FOOD enriquecimiento *m*

fortified *adj* FOOD enriquecido

Fortin: ~ **barometer** *n* PHYS barómetro de Fortin *m*

forward[1] *adj* AIR TRANSP delantero, WATER TRANSP de proa, proel

forward[2] *adv* WATER TRANSP a proa, hacia proa; ~ **of the beam** *adv* WATER TRANSP a proa del través

forward[3]: ~ **amplifier** *n* ELECTRON amplificador de acción directa *m*; ~ **-backward counter** *n* TV contador de avance y retroceso *m*; ~ **bias** *n* ELEC ENG, PHYS polarización directa *f*, polarización negativa frontal *f*; ~ **characteristic** *n* ELECTRON características directas *f pl*; ~ **conductance** *n* ELEC, ELEC ENG, ELECTRON *of semiconductor* conductancia directa *f*; ~ **contactor** *n* PROD contador directo *m*; ~ **current** *n* ELEC corriente directa *f*, corriente en sentido directo *f*, ELEC ENG corriente activada *f*; ~ **-drive roll** *n* PAPER rodillo de rotorno de la tela *m*; ~ **error correction** *n* (*FEC*) COMP&DP, TELECOM corrección anticipada de errores *f* (*AmL*), corrección de errores hacia adelante *f* (*Esp*); ~ **-input signal** *n* TELECOM señal de entrada hacia adelante *f*; ~ **-interworking telephony event** *n* (*FITE*) TELECOM circuito de telefonía entrelazada hacia adelante *m*; ~ **link** *n* SPACE *communications*

enlace directo *m*; ~ **path** *n* ELEC ENG trayectoria directa *f*; ~ **perpendicular** *n* WATER TRANSP *ship design* perpendicular de proa *f*; ~ **resistance** *n* ELEC *of semiconductor* resistencia directa *f*, resistencia en sentido directo *f*; ~ **scheduling** *n* PROD programación directa *f*; ~ **station** *n* PROD estación directa *f*; ~ **-stroke interval** *n* TV intervalo de la carrera de ida *m*; ~ **-swept wing** *n* AIR TRANSP, TRANSP ala de flecha negativa *f*; ~ **takeoff** *n* AIR TRANSP despegue hacia adelante *m*; ~ **-traveling wave** *AmE*, ~ **-travelling wave** *BrE* *n* ELEC, ELEC ENG, WAVE PHYS onda directa avanzada *f*; ~ **wave** *n* ELEC ENG onda hacia adelante *f*

forward[4] *vt* PRINT poner guardas, recortar

forwarded: ~ **notification** *n* TELECOM notificación reenviada *f*

forwarding: ~ **agent** *n* BrE (*cf freight agent AmE*) FOOD agente cargador *m*, RAIL, TRANSP, WATER TRANSP agente aduanero *m*, agente cargador *m*, agente de aduanas *m*, agente de transporte *m*, agente despachador *m*, agente expedidor *m*, expedidor aduanero *m*, transitario *m*; ~ **office** *n* BrE (*cf freight office AmE*) TRANSP oficina de expediciones *f*, oficina de fletes *f*, oficina expedidora *f*; ~ **roller** *n* PRINT rodillo de avance *m*; ~ **sucker** *n* PRINT chupón de avance *m*

fossil[1]: ~ **-bearing** *adj* COAL, GEOL, PETROL que contiene fósiles

fossil[2]: ~ **copal** *n* MINERAL copal fósil *m*; ~ **fuel** *n* PETR TECH, PETROL, THERMO combustible fósil *m*; ~ **-fuel power station** *n* ELEC, THERMO central de fuerza motriz de combustible fósil *f*, central energética impulsada por combustibles fósiles *f*; ~ **imprint** *n* GEOL imprenta fósil *f*, marca fósil *f*; ~ **radiation** *n* SPACE radiación primigenia *f*, radiación primitiva *f*, radiación residual *f*; ~ **water** *n* GEOL, HYDROL agua de origen antiguo *f*, agua fósil *f*, PETR TECH, PETROL agua fósil *f*, WATER agua de origen antiguo *f*

fossiliferous *adj* COAL, GEOL, PETROL fosilífero

Foucault: ~ **pendulum** *n* PHYS péndulo de Foucault *m*

foul[1]: ~ **anchor** *n* WATER TRANSP ancla encepada *f*; ~ **bottom** *n* WATER TRANSP fondo sucio *m*, mal tenedero *m*, fondo de mal tenedero *m*; ~ **gas** *n* GAS gas sucio *m*; ~ **ground** *n* WATER TRANSP mal fondeadero *m*; ~ **mine-gas** *n* MINE gas minero tóxico *m*; ~ **water** *n* HYDROL, POLL, RECYCL aguas contaminadas *f pl*, aguas estancadas *f pl*, aguas sucias *f pl*, WATER aguas contaminadas *f pl*, aguas estancadas *f pl*; ~ **-weather gear** *n* WATER TRANSP indumentaria de mal tiempo *f*; ~ **wind** *n* METEO, WATER TRANSP viento contrario *m*

foul[2] *vt* MAR POLL ensuciar, MECH ENG atascar, enredar, obstruir

foul[3] *vi* WATER TRANSP *ship* enceparse, enredarse, ensuciarse

fouled[1] *adj* MECH atorado, MECH ENG, PROD atorado, sucio

fouled[2]: ~ **anchor** *n* WATER TRANSP ancla encepada *f*

fouling: ~ **factor** *n* REFRIG factor de incrustaciones *m*

foundation *n* COAL cimentación *f*, CONST cimentación *f* (*Esp*), cimiento *m* (*Esp*), fundación *f* (*AmL*); ~ **block** *n* CONST bloque de cimentación *m*; ~ **bolt** *n* CONST perno de anclaje *m*; ~ **plate** *n* CONST placa de cimentación *f*; ~ **seed** *n* AGRIC *plant breeding* semilla base *f*; ~ **stock** *n* AGRIC *livestock* ganado original de la explotación *m*

founder[1] *n* PROD *person* fundidor *m*

founder[2] *vi* WATER TRANSP *of boat* irse a pique
founder's: ~ **black** *n* COATINGS negro para fundición *m*
founding *n* PROD colada *f*, *art* fundición *f*
foundry *n* COAL, HEAT fundería *f*, fundición *f*, MECH fundición *f*, MECH ENG, PROD fundería *f*, fundición *f*;
~ **abrasive cutoff-and-grinding machine** *n* MECH ENG máquina de amolar y cortar de disco abrasivo *f*, máquina de esmerilar y cortar de disco abrasivo *f*;
~ **blower** *n* PROD ventilador para funderías *m*;
~ **flask** *n* PROD caja de moldeo *f*; ~ **iron** *n* PROD arrabio para moldería *m*; ~ **ladle** *n* PROD cazo de colada *m*; ~ **riddle** *n* PROD tamiz de moldear *m*;
~ **sand** *n* CONST arena de fundición *f*; ~ **scrap** *n* PROD chatarra de la fundición *f*
fountain *n* PRINT tintero *m*; ~ **blade** *n* PRINT rasqueta del tintero *f*; ~ **keys** *n pl* PRINT tornillos reguladores del tintero *m pl*; ~ **runner** *n* PROD *in mould* canal de colada en fuente *m*; ~ **screw** *n* PRINT tornillo del tintero *m*
four[1]: ~**-phase** *adj* ELECTRON tetrafásico; ~**-ply** *adj* PROD *belting* de cuatro espesores; ~**-polar** *adj* ELEC *generator* tetrapolar; ~**-pole** *adj* ELEC *generator* de cuatro polos; ~**-sided** *adj* GEOM cuadrilátero
four[2]: ~**-barrel carburetor** *AmE*, ~**-barrel carburettor** *BrE n* AUTO, VEH carburador de cuatro cubas *m*; ~**-centered arch** *AmE*, ~**-centred arch** *BrE n* CONST arco de cuatro centros *m*; ~**-channel amplifier** *n* ELECTRON amplificador de cuatro canales *m*; ~**-circle diffractometer** *n* CRYSTALL, INSTR difractómetro de cuarto círculos *m*; ~**-color printing** *AmE see four-colour printing BrE*; ~**-color process** *AmE see four-colour process BrE*; ~**-color process ink** *AmE see four-colour process ink BrE*; ~**-color theorem** *AmE see four-colour theorem BrE*; ~**-colour printing** *n BrE* PRINT impresión a cuatro colores *f*; ~**-colour process** *n BrE* PRINT proceso de cuatricromía *m*; ~**-colour process ink** *n BrE* PRINT tinta para cuatricromía *f*; ~**-colour theorem** *n BrE* GEOM teorema cuadricolor *m*, teorema de los cuatro colores *m*, teorema tetracromo *m*; ~**-column forging press** *n* PROD prensa de forja de cuatro columnas *f*; ~**-concentric-circle near-field template** *n* OPT, TELECOM plantilla de cuatro círculos concéntricos de campo cercano *f*; ~**-concentric-circle refractive-index template** *n* OPT, TELECOM plantilla de índice de refracción de cuatro círculos concéntricos *f*; ~**-cylinder motorcycle** *n* AUTO análisis foliar *m*; ~**-engine jet aircraft** *n* AIR TRANSP avión a reacción cuatrimotor *m*, avión a reacción tetramotor *m*; ~**-flute twist hand reamer** *n* MECH ENG escariador de mano de cuatro ranuras *m*; ~**-high** *n* PROD doble dúo *m*; ~**-high rod mill** *n* PROD tren de laminador doble dúo *m*; ~**-jaw independent chuck** *n* MECH ENG plato de cuatro garras independiente *m*, plato de tetragarra independiente *m*; ~**-layer diode** *n* ELECTRON diodo de cuatro capas *m*; ~**-level maser** *n* ELECTRON emisor de radiación de cuatro niveles *m*; ~**-master** *n* WATER TRANSP buque de cuatro palos *m*; ~**-plate** *n* CINEMAT base niveladora de cámara *f*; ~**-pole filter** *n* ELEC, ELECTRON filtro tetrapolar *m*; ~**-pole generator** *n* ELEC, ELECTRON generador de cuatro polos *m*; ~**-port directional control valve** *n* MECH ENG válvula de control direccional de cuatro polos *f*; ~**-quadrant multiplier** *n* ELECTRON multiplicador de cuatro cuadrantes *m*; ~**-roll reverse pan feed** *n* PRINT alimentación inversa de cola de cuatro

rodillos *f*; ~**-screw bell chuck** *n* MECH ENG plato de campana de cuatro tornillos *m*; ~**-seat aircraft** *n* AIR TRANSP avión de cuatro plazas *m*; ~**-signature coding system** *n* TELECOM sistema de codificación de cuatro firmas *m*; ~**-spindle drilling machine** *n* PROD perforadora de cuatro husillos *f*; ~**-star petrol** *n* AUTO, PETR TECH, PETROL, VEH gasolina super *f*; ~**-stroke cycle** *n* AUTO, MECH, MECH ENG, VEH, WATER TRANSP ciclo de cuatro tiempos *m*; ~**-stroke engine** *n* AUTO, MECH, MECH ENG, VEH, WATER TRANSP motor de cuatro tiempos *m*; ~**-terminal network** *n* ELEC ENG circuito de cuatro terminales *m*, cuadrípolo *m*, red eléctrica de cuatro bornes *f*, red eléctrica de cuatro terminales *f*; ~**-throw geared pump** *n* PROD bomba de engranaje tetracilíndrica *f*; ~**-tool tool post** *n* MECH ENG *of lathe* portaherramientas revólver de cuatro caras *m*; ~**-tool turret** *n* MECH ENG *of lathe* torreta de cuatro herramientas *f*, torreta portaherramientas revolver de cuatro caras *f*; ~**-way** *n* CINEMAT base niveladora de cámara *f*; ~**-way bit** *n* PETR TECH trépano de cuatro aletas *m*, trépano de cuatro puntas *m*; ~**-way cock** *n* WATER grifo de cuatro vías *m*, válvula de cuatro pasos *f*; ~**-way dusting** *n* PRINT espolvoreado en cuatro direcciones *m*; ~**-way extension socket** *n* ELEC, ELEC ENG enchufe de cuatro direcciones *m*; ~**-way pallet** *n* PACK paleta de carga de cuatro accesos *f*; ~**-way powdering** *n* PRINT empolvado cuádruple *m*; ~**-wheel brake system** *n* AUTO, VEH sistema de freno a las cuatro ruedas *m*; ~**-wheel drive** *n* AUTO, VEH tracción a las cuatro ruedas *f*; ~**-wheel drive vehicle** *n* AUTO, VEH vehículo con tracción a las cuatro ruedas *m*; ~**-wing bit** *n* PETR TECH mecha de cuatro aletas *f* (*AmL*), trépano de cuatro aletas *m* (*Esp*); ~**-wire circuit** *n* COMP&DP circuito de cuatro hilos *m*, circuito de cuatro hilos conductores *m*; ~**-wire crosspoint** *n* TELECOM contacto de cruce bifilar doble *m*; ~**-wire repeater** *n* ELECTRON repetidor de cuatro hilos *m*; ~**-wire switch** *n* TELECOM conmutador bifilar doble *m*; ~**-wire switching system** *n* TELECOM sistema de conmutación bifilar doble *m*; ~**-wire system** *n* ELEC ENG sistema tetrafilar *m*
4-D: ~ **reinforcement** *n* SPACE armazón 4-D *m*
Fourdrinier *n* PAPER Fourdrinier *m*; ~ **paper machine** *n* PAPER máquina de mesa plana *f*; ~ **shake** *n* PAPER dispositivo de traqueo *m*; ~ **wire** *n* PAPER tela de formación *f*, tela de mesa plana *f*
fourfold: ~ **rotation axis** *n* CRYSTALL eje de rotación cuaternario *m*, eje de simetría cuaternario *m*; ~ **tripod stand** *n* PHOTO montaje cuádruple de trípode *m*
Fourier: ~ **analysis** *n* ELECTRON, MATH, PHYS análisis de Fourier *m*; ~ **integral** *n* ACOUST, ELECTRON, MATH, PHYS integral de Fourier *f*; ~ **series** *n* ACOUST, CRYSTALL, ELECTRON, MATH, PHYS serie de Fourier *f*; ~ **transform** *n* ACOUST, CRYSTALL, ELECTRON, PHYS transformada de Fourier *f*; ~ **transform spectroscopy** *n* ELECTRON, PHYS espectroscopía por transformada de Fourier *f*; ~ **transformation** *n* ACOUST, CRYSTALL, ELECTRON, PHYS transformación de Fourier *f*
4 PST: ~ **switch** *n* ELEC ENG interruptor PST cuadripolar *m*, interruptor simple cuadripolar *m*
fourth: ~ **generation** *n* COMP&DP cuarta generación *f*; ~**-generation computer** *n* COMP&DP computador de cuarta generación *m* (*AmL*), computadora de cuarta

generación *f* (*AmL*), ordenador de cuarta generación *m* (*Esp*)

fowl: ~ **cholera** *n* AGRIC cólera aviar *f*; ~ **pest** *n* AGRIC peste aviar *f*

fowlerite *n* MINERAL fowlerita *f*

fox: ~ **wedge** *n* CINEMAT cuña variable *f*

foxing *n* PAPER manchas del papel *f pl*

foxtail: ~ **grass** *n* AGRIC cola de zorro *f*; ~ **millet** *n* AGRIC panizo blanco *m*

FPC *abbr* (*fish protein concentrate*) OCEAN concentrado de proteínas de peces *m*

FPLA *abbr* (*field-programmable logic array*) COMP&DP FPLA (*arreglo lógico programable de campo*)

FPP *abbr* (*floating-point processor*) COMP&DP, TELECOM procesador de coma flotante *m*, procesador de punto flotante *m*

FPS *abbr* (*fast packet switch*) TELECOM conmutador rápido de paquetes *m*

Fr *abbr* (*francium*) CHEM, METALL, NUCL, RAD PHYS Fr (*francio*)

fractal *n* COMP&DP, MATH fractal *m*

fraction *n* MATH, PETR TECH fracción *f*; ~ **distillation column** *n* CHEM TECH columna para destilación fraccionada *f*

fractional[1] *adj* MATH fraccionario

fractional[2]: ~ **crystallization** *n* CRYSTALL, GEOL cristalización fraccionada *f*; ~ **distillation** *n* CHEM TECH destilación fraccionada *f*, PETR TECH destilación de muestras *f*, destilación fraccionada *f*; ~**-frequency deviation** *n* ELECTRON desviación de frecuencia fraccionaria *f*; ~ **horsepower motor** *n* (*FHP motor*) ELEC, ELEC ENG motor de potencia menor de un caballo *m* (*motor de <1 HP*); ~ **low-power condensing unit** *n* REFRIG grupo frigorífico de pequeña potencia *m*; ~ **part** *n* COMP&DP parte fraccionaria *f*; ~ **pitch** *n* MECH ENG *of screw* paso bastardo *m*; ~ **pitch winding** *n* ELEC, ELEC ENG devanado de paso fraccionario *m*, devanado de paso parcial *m*; ~ **slot winding** *n* ELEC, ELEC ENG devanado de ranura fraccional *m*

fractionating: ~ **apparatus** *n* CHEM TECH equipo de fraccionación *m*; ~ **column** *n* PETR TECH columna de destilación fraccionada *f*; ~ **tower** *n* CHEM TECH torre de fraccionamiento *f*

fractionation *n* CHEM *of oil, solvent* fraccionamiento *m*; ~ **column** *n* LAB columna de fraccionamiento *f*

fracture *n* C&G, CRYSTALL fractura *f*, FUELLESS rotura *f*, GEOL disyunción *f*, MECH, MECH ENG fractura *f*, rotura *f*, ruptura *f*, METALL, NUCL, PETR TECH, PETROL fractura *f*, QUALITY rompimiento *m*; ~ **behavior** *AmE*, ~ **behaviour** *BrE* *n* METALL comportamiento de la fractura *m*; ~ **cleavage** *n* GEOL esfoliación por fractura *f*; ~ **cone** *n* C&G cono de fractura *m*; ~ **criterion** *n* METALL criterio de fractura *m*; ~ **gradient** *n* GEOL, PETR TECH gradiente de fractura *m*; ~ **log** *n* PETROL perfil de fractura *m*; ~ **mechanics** *n* MECH mecánica de rotura *f*; ~ **pattern** *n* C&G patrón de fractura *m*; ~ **plane** *n* GEOL, GEOPHYS, PETR TECH fractura plana *f*; ~ **pressure** *n* GEOL, GEOPHYS, PETR TECH presión de fracturación *f*; ~ **test** *n* MECH ENG ensayo de fractura *m*, ensayo de rotura *m*, prueba de fractura *f*, prueba de rotura *f*, tenacidad a la rotura *f*; ~ **toughness** *n* P&R tenacidad a la fractura *f*, tenacidad a la rotura *f*; ~ **zone** *n* GEOPHYS cinturón milonítico *m*

fractured: ~**-and-faulted chalk** *n* CONST yeso defectuoso y quebrado *m*

fracturing *n* GEOL, PETR TECH fractura *f*, fracturación *f*, PETROL fracturación *f*

fragment *vt* COAL reducir a fragmentos

fragmental: ~ **rock** *n* GEOL roca fragmentaria *f*

fragmentation *n* METALL fragmentación *f*

fragmenting: ~ **shell** *n* MILIT proyectil de fragmentación *m*

framboid *n* GEOL, MATH framboide *m*

frame[1]: ~ **by frame** *adv* PHOTO fotograma a fotograma

frame[2] *n* CINEMAT cuadro *m*, fotograma *m*, imagen *f*, COMP&DP imagen *f*, recuadro *m*, CONST *set of shores* cuaderna *f*, armazón *m*, *of roof, bridge* estructura *f*, *of door or window* marco *m*, *for walls or partitions* entramado *m*, ELEC ENG *of device* armazón *m*, trama *f*, estator *m*, estructura *f*, ELECTRON imagen *f*, secuencia *f*, MECH estructura *f*, banco de tornero *m*, armazón *m*, molde *m*, sistema articulado *m*, MECH ENG *of engine, machine tool, etc* sistema articulado *m*, chasis *m*, batiente *m*, bastidor *m*, banco de tornero *m*, construcción *f*, caja *f*, armazón *m*, PACK, PAPER bastidor *m*, PHOTO cuadro *m*, bastidor *m*, fotograma *m*, imagen *f*, PHYS sistema de referencia *m*, PRINT bastidor *m*, marco *m*, RAIL bastidor *m*, SPACE *communications* unidad de información *f*, zona explorada *f*, imagen *f*, cuadro *m*, TELECOM cuadro *m*, TEXTIL bastidor *m*, TV fotograma *m*, imagen *f*, VEH bastidor *m*, chasis *m*, armazón *m*, WATER *of sluice gate* cerco-guía *m*, marco *m*, WATER TRANSP *shipbuilding* cuaderna *f*; ~ **adjuster** *n* CINEMAT regulador del cuadro *m*; ~ **alignment** *n* SPACE *communications* cuadro de alineamiento *m*, TELECOM alineación de trama *f*; ~ **alignment signal** *n* (*FAS*) TELECOM señal de alineación de trama *f*; ~ **angle** *n* WATER TRANSP *shipbuilding* angular de cuaderna *m*; ~ **bridge** *n* CONST puente de celosía *m*; ~ **cap** *n* MECH ENG cubierta del bastidor *f*; ~ **counter** *n* CINEMAT, PHOTO contador de fotogramas *m* (*Esp*), cuentafotogramas *m* (*AmL*); ~ **crossbeam** *n* MECH ENG balancín transversal del armazón *m*, travesaño del armazón *m*, traviesa del armazón *f*, viga transversal del armazón *f*; ~ **cross-member** *n* MECH ENG travesaño del armazón *m*, travesaño del bastidor *m*, traviesa del armazón *f*, traviesa del bastidor *f*; ~ **edging** *n* MECH ENG bordeado del armazón *m*, guarnición del armazón *f*, ribeteado del armazón *m*; ~ **efficiency** *n* SPACE *communications* eficiencia de cuadro *f*; ~ **fixing** *n* CONST fijación de estructura *f*; ~ **by frame** *n* CINEMAT, TV cuadro a cuadro *m*; ~ **frequency** *n* CINEMAT, TV frecuencia de imágenes *f*; ~ **generator** *n* TELECOM generador de tramas *m*; ~ **grid** *n* ELECTRON cuadrícula de imagen *f*; ~ **house** *n* CONST casa desmontable *f*; ~ **length** *n* SPACE longitud de imagen *f*, longitud del cuadro *f*; ~ **line** *n* CINEMAT, TV línea de separación de dos imágenes *f*, línea del cuadro *f*; ~**-line leader** *n* CINEMAT, TV guía de la línea del cuadro *f*; ~ **loss second** *n* (*FLS*) TELECOM segundo de pérdida de trama *m*; ~**-mode bearer service** *n* (*FMBS*) TELECOM servicio portador del modo trama *m*; ~ **plan** *n* WATER TRANSP *ship design* plano de cuadernas *m*; ~ **pulse** *n* CINEMAT, TV pulso de imagen *m*; ~ **rate** *n* CINEMAT, TV frecuencia de imagen *f*, velocidad de cuadro *f*; ~ **saw** *n* PROD *hand* sierra ordinaria *f*, *powered* sierra de bastidor *f*; ~**-saw file** *n* MECH ENG lima de acanalar *f*; ~ **slip** *n* CINEMAT, TV deslizamiento de la imagen *m*; **~-slotted system** *n* TELECOM sistema de tramas ranuradas *m*; **~ spacing** *n* WATER TRANSP *shipbuilding* clara de cuadernas *f*; **~ store** *n* CINEMAT, TV almacenamiento de imágenes *m*; **~ sync** *n* TELECOM sincronización de trama *f*; **~-sync pulse** *n* TELECOM impulso sincronizador de trama *m*, TV impulso sincronizador de imagen *m*; **~ synchronization** *n* SPACE *communications* cuadro de sincronización *m*, TELECOM sincronización de trama *f*; **~-synchronization control** *n* TELECOM sincronizador de trama *m*, TV control sincronizador de imagen *m*

frame[3] *vt* CINEMAT, PHOTO, TV encuadrar
frame[4] *vi* WATER TRANSP armar y escorar las cuadernas
framed: **~ floor** *n* CONST suelo ensamblado *m*; **~ set square** *n* MECH ENG escuadra de dibujo sin centro *f*
framework *n* CONST armazón *m*, *of crane* armadura *f*
framing *n* CINEMAT ajuste de imagen *m*, CONST composición de un edificio *f*, ensamblaje *m*, esqueleto *m*, TV ajuste de imagen *m*; **~ chisel** *n* CONST, MECH ENG formón *m*; **~ control** *n* TV regulación de ajuste de imagen *f*; **~ knob** *n* CINEMAT, TV mando de encuadre *m*; **~ mask** *n* CINEMAT, TV recuadro *m*
Francis: **~ turbine** *n* FUELLESS turbina tipo Francis *f*
francium *n* (*Fr*) CHEM, METALL, NUCL, RAD PHYS francio *m* (*Fr*)
Franck-Hertz: **~ experiment** *n* PHYS experimento de Franck-Hertz *m*
frangulin *n* CHEM frangulina *f*, ramnoxantina *f*
Frank-Condon: **~ principle** *n* PHYS principio de Frank-Condon *m*
franklinite *n* MINERAL franklinita *f*
Frank-Read: **~ source** *n* CRYSTALL manantial de Frank-Read *m*
Frasnian *adj* GEOL Frasniense
Fraunhofer: **~ diffraction** *n* OPT, PHYS, TELECOM difracción de Fraunhofer *f*; **~-diffraction pattern** *n* OPT, PHYS, TELECOM diagrama de difracción de Fraunhofer *m*; **~ line** *n* PHYS línea de Fraunhofer *f*; **~ region** *n* SPACE *communications* campo lejano de radiación *m*, región de Fraunhofer *f*, región de campo *f*
FRC *abbr* (*fault-reception center AmE, fault-reception centre BrE*) TELECOM centro de recepción de averías *m*

freak: **~ wave** *n* OCEAN onda anormal *f*
free[1] *adj* CHEM *uncombined* libre; **~ alongside ship** *adj* (*FAS*) WATER TRANSP franco al costado del buque (*FAS*); **~-blown** *adj* C&G soplado al aire; **~ of charge** *adj* TELECOM libre de gastos; **~ from gas** *adj* THERMO exento de gas; **~ from slag** *adj* THERMO exento de escorias; **~ on board** *adj* (*FOB*) PETR TECH, WATER TRANSP franco a bordo (*FOB*); **~ on quay** *adj* (*FOQ*) WATER TRANSP franco en muelle
free[2]: **~ acidity** *n* CHEM acidez libre *f*; **~-air anomaly** *n* GEOL, GEOPHYS anomalía de Bouguer *f*, anomalía de aire libre *f*, anomalía de atmósfera libre *f*; **~-air correction** *n* GEOL, GEOPHYS corrección de aire libre *f*; **~-air crystal oscillator** *n* ELEC, ELECTRON oscilador de cristal de aire libre *m*; **~-air peak overpressure** *n* AIR TRANSP *of sonic boom* sobrepresión máxima de aire ambiente *f*; **~-air reduction** *n* GEOL, GEOPHYS reducción de aire libre *f*; **~ area** *n* REFRIG sección libre de paso de aire *f*; **~ atmosphere** *n* METEO atmósfera libre *f*; **~ bar**

filter *n* ELECTRON filtro de barra libre *m*; **~ beam** *n* CONST ménsula *f*, viga libre *f*; **~ charge** *n* PHYS carga libre *f*; **~ convection flow** *n* FLUID flujo de convección libre *m*; **~ delivery pump** *n* PROD bomba sin impulsión *f*; **~-drop height** *n* AIR TRANSP altura de caída libre *f*; **~ electrical motional impedance** *n* ACOUST, ELEC, ELEC ENG impedancia eléctrica mocional libre *f*; **~ electrical vibration impedance** *n* ACOUST impedancia electrovibratoria libre *f*; **~ electron** *n* ELEC, ELECTRON, PART PHYS, PHYS, RAD PHYS electrón libre *m*; **~-electron density** *n* ELEC, ELECTRON, PART PHYS, PHYS, RAD PHYS densidad de electrones libres *f*; **~ end** *n* MINE chicote *m* (*AmL*), extremo libre *m*, final *m* (*Esp*), ramal libre *m*, PROD *of rope, pulley block chain* ramal libre *m*; **~ energy** *n* CHEM, METALL, PHYS, THERMO energía libre *f*; **~ face** *n* MINE superficie libre *f*; **~ fall** *n* MINE sondeo de caída libre *m*; **~-fall boring** *n* CONST perforación de caída libre *f*; **~-fall drilling** *n* CONST taladrado libre *m*; **~-fall jump** *n* MILIT salto de caída libre *m*; **~-fall pump** *n* PROD bomba de émbolo aspirante *f*; **~-falling stamp** *n* CONST mazo de caída libre *m*; **~ field** *n* ACOUST, COMP&DP campo libre *m*; **~-field tension efficiency** *n* ACOUST eficacia de tensión de campo libre *f*; **~ flight** *n* SPACE vuelo libre *m*; **~-flight test** *n* SPACE prueba de vuelo libre *f*; **~-flow air-conditioning unit** *n* HEAT, REFRIG, THERMO acondicionador de insuflación directa *m*; **~-flow product** *n* PACK producto que fluye fácilmente *m*; **~ format** *n* COMP&DP formato libre *m*; **~ grid** *n* ELECTRON rejilla móvil *f*; **~ groundwater** *n* HYDROL, WATER agua freática libre *f*; **~ gyro** *n* AIR TRANSP giróscopo libre *m*; **~ heat** *n* HEAT ENG, THERMO calor libre *m*; **~ length** *n* MECH ENG longitud libre *f*, longitud natural *f*; **~ linear oscillation** *n* MECH ENG, TELECOM oscilación lineal libre *f*; **~ list** *n* COMP&DP lista libre *f*; **~ longitudinal oscillation** *n* MECH ENG, TELECOM oscilación longitudinal libre *f*; **~ mechanical impedance** *n* ACOUST, ELEC, ELEC ENG impedancia mecánica libre *f*; **~-milling ore** *n* MINE mineral cuyo metal es completamente amalgamable *m*; **~ nappe** *n* HYDROL capa libre *f*; **~ oscillation** *n* ELEC, ELEC ENG, PHYS oscilación libre *f*; **~ oscillation period** *n* GEOPHYS período de oscilación libre *m*; **~ overall weir** *n* HYDROL vertedero totalmente libre *m*; **~-piston gas turbine** *n* MECH ENG turbina a gas de pistón libre *f*; **~ port** *n* WATER TRANSP puerto franco *m*; **~ pratique** *n* WATER TRANSP libre plática *f*; **~ radical** *n* CHEM, FOOD, P&R radical libre *m*; **~-radical reaction** *n* CHEM, FOOD, P&R reacción de radicales libres *f*; **~-roller sluice gate** *n* FUELLESS *of dam* compuerta rodante *f*; **~ rotor** *n* AIR TRANSP *of helicopter* rotor libre *m*; **~-running frequency** *n* ELECTRON frecuencia de marcha continua *f*; **~-running mode** *n* ELECTRON modo de marcha continua *m*; **~-running oscillator** *n* ELEC, ELECTRON multivibrador astable *m*, oscilador astable *m*; **~-running signal** *n* ELECTRON señal de marcha libre *f*; **~-running timer** *n* PROD temporizador continuo *m*; **~ shaft** *n* MECH ENG eje libre *m*; **~ source** *n* NUCL fuente libre *f*; **~-space basic loss** *n* SPACE, TELECOM pérdida básica del espacio libre *f*; **~-space loss** *n* SPACE, TELECOM pérdida de espacio libre *f*; **~-standing insert** *n* PRINT inserción independiente *f*; **~ stock** *n* PAPER pasta magra *f*; **~-stream** *n* FLUID corriente libre; **~-stream velocity** *n* FLUID, PHYS velocidad de corriente libre *f*; **~-stream velocity outside the boundary layer** *n* FLUID, PHYS velocidad de corriente libre fuera de la capa límite *f*; **~ sulfur** *AmE*, **~ sulphur** *BrE* *n* P&R azufre libre *m*; **~ surface** *n* PHYS superficie libre *f*, WATER TRANSP *ship design* carena líquida *f*, superficie libre *f*; **~-surface effect** *n* WATER TRANSP *ship design* efecto de carena líquida *m*, efecto de superficie libre *m*; **~ travel** *n* AUTO movimiento libre *m*; **~ turbine** *n* AIR TRANSP turbina libre *f*; **~ vibration** *n* ACOUST, PHYS vibración libre *f*

free³: **~ from gas** *vt* THERMO eliminar el gas de

free⁴ *vi* WATER TRANSP *of wind* angularse

freeboard *n* WATER TRANSP *ship design* francobordo *m*; **~ allowances** *n pl* WATER TRANSP *ship design* deducciones en el franco bordo *f pl*

freefall *n* AIR TRANSP, PACK caída libre *f*

freemartin *n* AGRIC frimartin *f*, frimartinismo *m*

freeness *n* PAPER refino *m*; **~ tester** *n* PAPER refinómetro *m*; **~ value** *n* PAPER grado de refino *m*, índice de desgote *m*

freephone: **~ call** *n* BrE (*cf toll-free call AmE*) TELECOM comunicación interurbana no tasada *f* (*AmL*), llamada gratuita *f* (*Esp*); **~ number** *n* BrE (*cf toll-free number AmE*) TELECOM número de llamada gratuita *m*, número de teléfono gratuito *m*

freesheet: **~ paper** *n* PAPER papel sin pasta mecánica *m*

freestanding *adj* PACK autoestable

freeway *n* AmE (*cf motorway BrE*) AUTO, CONST, TRANSP, VEH autopista *f*, calzada *f*, carretera *f*

freewheel *n* MECH ENG rueda libre *f*; **~ and clutch unit** *n* AIR TRANSP conjunto de embrague y marcha libre *m*, unidad de embrague y desembrague *f*; **~-driven head** *n* MECH ENG cabezal conducido por rueda libre *m*; **~ mechanism** *n* MECH, MECH ENG mecanismo de rueda libre *m*

freewheeling: **~ diode** *n* ELECTRON, PROD diodo de rueda libre *m*

freeze¹: **~-dried** *adj* AGRIC liofilizado, CHEM TECH, FOOD, PACK, REFRIG, THERMO deshidratado por congelación, liofilizado

freeze²: **~ concentration** *n* CHEM TECH, FOOD, REFRIG concentración por congelación *f*; **~-dried product** *n* FOOD, PACK, REFRIG producto liofilizado *m*; **~-dryer** *n* AGRIC liofilizador *m*, CHEM TECH, FOOD deshidratador por congelación *m*, liofilizador *m*, secador por congelación *m*, PACK liofilizador *m*, REFRIG deshidratador por congelación *m*, liofilizador *m*, secador por congelación *m*, THERMO liofilizador *m*; **~-drying** *n* AGRIC liofilización *f*, CHEM TECH, FOOD, PACK, REFRIG, THERMO deshidratación por congelación *f*, liofilización *f*, secado por congelación *m*; **~-frame** *n* CINEMAT, PHOTO, TV cuadro bloqueado *m*, cuadro congelado *m*, cuadro fijo *m*; **~-out** *n* TELECOM bloqueo momentáneo *m*; **~-out fraction** *n* (*FOF*) SPACE, TELECOM fracción de bloqueo de conexión *f*, fracción de bloqueo momentáneo *f*; **~-picture** *n* TELECOM imagen congelada *f*; **~-picture request** *n* TELECOM petición de congelación de la imagen *f*; **~-thaw resistance** *n* CHEM TECH, FOOD, REFRIG resistencia a la congelación-descongelación *f*; **~-up** *n* REFRIG, THERMO congelación *f*

freeze³ *vt* GEN congelar; **~-dry** *vt* AGRIC, CHEM TECH, FOOD, PACK, REFRIG, THERMO liofilizar; **~ out** *vt* REFRIG separar por congelación

freeze⁴ *vi* CHEM TECH, FOOD, PHYS, REFRIG, THERMO congelarse

freezer *n* CHEM TECH, MECH ENG, REFRIG, THERMO congelador *m*, máquina frigorífica *f*, refrigerador *m*; **~ burn** *n* REFRIG quemadura por congelación *f*; **~ capacity** *n* FOOD, REFRIG capacidad del congelador *f*; **~ compartment** *n* FOOD, REFRIG compartimiento congelador *m*; **~ trawler** *n* OCEAN, REFRIG barco rastreador frigorífico *m*; **~ vessel** *n* REFRIG, TRANSP, WATER TRANSP barco frigorífico *m*

freezing *n* FOOD congelación *f*, METALL solidificación *f*, PACK, PHYS, REFRIG, THERMO congelación *f*; **~ capacity** *n* FOOD, REFRIG capacidad de congelación *f*; **~ liquid** *n* CHEM líquido congelante *m*; **~ machine** *n* FOOD, PROD, REFRIG máquina frigorífica *f*; **~ medium** *n* REFRIG agente congelante *m*; **~ mixture** *n* PHYS, REFRIG mezcla congeladora *f*, mezcla refrigerante *f*; **~ plant** *n* FOOD, MECH ENG, REFRIG instalación de congelación *f*; **~ plateau** *n* REFRIG meseta de congelación *f*; **~ point** *n* C&G, CHEM TECH, FOOD, MECH ENG, METALL, P&R, PACK, PHYS, REFRIG, THERMO, WATER TRANSP punto de congelación *m*, temperatura de congelación *f*; **~ rate** *n* REFRIG, THERMO velocidad de congelación *f*; **~ room** *n* FOOD, REFRIG cámara de congelación *f*; **~ section** *n* REFRIG sección de congelación *f*; **~ trawler** *n* OCEAN, REFRIG, WATER TRANSP arrastrero congelador *m*; **~ tube** *n* PROD tubo congelador *m*; **~ tunnel** *n* REFRIG túnel de congelación *m*

freibergite *n* MINERAL freibergita *f*

freieslebenite *n* MINERAL freieslebenita *f*

freight *n* AmE (*cf goods BrE*) PACK mercancías *f pl*, PETR TECH, SPACE flete *m*, WATER TRANSP carga *f*, flete *m*; **~ agent** *n* AmE FOOD, RAIL (*cf forwarding agent AmE*, *cf goods agent BrE*) agente aduanero *m*, agente cargador *m*, agente de aduanas *m*, agente expedidor *m*, transitario *m*, WATER TRANSP (*cf forwarding agent AmE*, *cf goods agent BrE*) agente aduanero *m*, agente cargador *m*, agente de aduanas *m*, agente de transporte *m*, agente despachador *m*, agente expedidor *m*, transitario *m*; **~ car** *n* AmE (*cf freight wagon BrE*) TRANSP vagón de mercancías *m*; **~ chute** *n* AmE (*cf goods chute BrE*) TRANSP tobogán de carga *m*, tobogán de mercancías *m*; **~ depot** *n* AmE (*cf goods depot BrE*) TRANSP almacén de mercancías *m*, depósito de carga *m*, estación de mercancías *f*, muelle de mercancías *m*; **~ house** *n* AmE (*cf warehouse BrE*) TRANSP alojamiento de mercancías *m*; **~ inwards** *n pl* AmE (*cf goods inwards BrE*) PROD entrada de mercancías *f*, RAIL entrada de cargamento *f*, entrada de mercancías *f*; **~ locomotive** *n* AmE (*cf goods locomotive BrE*) RAIL locomotora de tren de mercancías *f*; **~ office** *n* AmE (*cf forwarding office BrE*) TRANSP oficina de expediciones *f*, oficina de fletes *f*, oficina expedidora *f*; **~ porter** *n* AmE (*cf goods porter BrE*) RAIL locomotora de tren de mercancías *f*, peón de carga *m*, peón de mercancías *m*; **~ rate** *n* AmE (*cf goods rate BrE*) PACK, PETR TECH tarifa de la carga *f*, tarifa del flete *f*, tipo del flete *m*; **~ shed** *n* AmE (*cf goods shed BrE*) TRANSP depósito de mercancías *m*; **~ station** *n* AmE (*cf goods station BrE*) TRANSP almacén de mercancías *m*, depósito de carga *m*, estación de mercancías *f*, muelle de mercancías *m*;

~ **terminal** n AmE (cf goods terminal BrE) PACK terminal de carga m; ~ **train** n AmE (cf goods train BrE) RAIL tren de carga m, tren de mercancías m; ~ **truck** n AmE (cf goods lorry BrE) AUTO camión de mercancías m; ~ **van** n AmE (cf goods van BrE) TRANSP furgoneta de mercancías f, furgón de mercancías m; ~ **wagon** n BrE (cf freight car AmE) TRANSP vagón de mercancías m; ~ **yard** n AmE (cf goods yard BrE) RAIL patio de carga m, patio de mercancías m; ~**-yard foreman** n AmE (cf goods yard foreman BrE) RAIL capataz del patio de carga m, capataz del patio de mercancías m

freighter n WATER TRANSP buque de carga m (Esp), fletero m (AmL)

freightliner: ~ **train** n RAIL tren portacontenedores m

French[1]: ~ **boiler** n HYDRAUL caldera de hervidores f; ~ **casement** n CONST marco de ventana de dos hojas m; ~ **chalk** n MINERAL, TEXTIL jaboncillo de sastre m; ~ **doors** n pl AmE (cf French windows BrE) CONST puerta cristalera f, puerta de balcón f, puerta de cristales f, ventana practicable f; ~ **embossing** n C&G grabado francés m; ~ **fold** n PRINT plegado en cuarto sin corte m; ~ **folder** n PRINT plegado en cuatro sin cortes m; ~ **polish** n COATINGS, COLOUR barniz de alcohol m, barniz de muñeca m; ~ **quotes** n pl PRINT comillas f pl; ~ **standard** n MECH ENG estándar francés m; ~ **window** n C&G ventana francesa f; ~ **windows** n pl BrE (cf French doors AmE) CONST puerta cristalera f, puerta de balcón f, puerta de cristales f, ventana practicable f

French[2]: ~ **polish** vt COATINGS, COLOUR barnizar con muñequilla

Frenkel: ~ **defect** n CRYSTALL defecto Frenkel m

freon n CHEM diclorodifluorometano m, freón m, PROD diclorofluorometano m, freón m, REFRIG diclorodifluorometano m, freón m

frequency[1]: ~**-modulated** adj ELECTRON modulado en frecuencia

frequency[2] n GEN frecuencia f; ~ **adjustment** n ELECTRON ajuste de frecuencia m; ~ **agility** n ELECTRON agilidad de frecuencia f; ~ **alignment** n TELECOM alineación de frecuencias f; ~ **allocation** n TELECOM, TV distribución de frecuencias f; ~ **band** n AIR TRANSP, COMP&DP, ELEC, ELECTRON, RAD PHYS, TELECOM, TV, WATER TRANSP, WAVE PHYS banda de frecuencias f; ~ **calibrator** n ELECTRON calibrador de frecuencia m; ~ **change** n ELECTRON cambio de frecuencia m; ~ **changer** n ELEC, ELECTRON converter cambiador de frecuencia m, convertidor de frecuencia m; ~ **channel** n TELECOM canal de frecuencias m; ~ **characteristic** n TELECOM característica de frecuencia f; ~ **compensation** n ELECTRON compensación de frecuencia f; ~ **component** n ELECTRON componente de frecuencia m; ~ **compressive feedback demodulator** n SPACE communications demodulador de realimentación por compresión de frecuencia m; ~ **control** n ELECTRON, TELECOM control de frecuencias m; ~ **conversion** n ELEC, ELECTRON, TELECOM conversión de frecuencia f; ~ **converter** n ELEC, ELECTRON, TELECOM convertidor de frecuencia m; ~ **counter** n ELECTRON, INSTR, TELECOM contador de frecuencia m; ~ **coverage** n ELECTRON, TELECOM cobertura de frecuencia f; ~**-current converter** n ELEC, TELECOM convertidor de la frecuencia de corriente m; ~ **curve** n MATH curva de frecuencia f; ~ **cut-off** n ELECTRON interrupción de frecuencia f; ~ **demodulation** n COMP&DP, ELECTRON, TELECOM, TV demodulación de frecuencia f; ~ **demodulator** n COMP&DP, ELECTRON, TELECOM, TV demodulador de frecuencia m; ~ **departure** n ELECTRON desviación de frecuencia f; ~ **detector** n ELECTRON detector de frecuencia m; ~ **deviation** n ELEC, ELECTRON of wave corrimiento de frecuencia m, desviación de frecuencia f, error de frecuencia m; ~ **displacement** n ELECTRON, TELECOM desplazamiento en frecuencia m; ~ **distortion** n ELECTRON, PHYS, TELECOM, WAVE PHYS distorsión de frecuencia f; ~ **distribution** n COMP&DP, MATH, METALL distribución de frecuencias f; ~ **distribution curve** n (cf frequency distribution) MATH curva de distribución de frecuencia f; ~ **diversity** n TELECOM diversidad de frecuencias f; ~ **divider** n ELEC, TELECOM divisor de frecuencias m; ~**-division multiple access** n (FDMA) SPACE, TELECOM acceso múltiple por división de frecuencias m (AMDF); ~**-division multiplexing** n (FDM) COMP&DP, ELECTRON , PHYS, TELECOM multiplexación por división de frecuencias f (MDF), multiplexado por división de frecuencias m (MDF); ~**-division switching system** n (FDS system) TELECOM sistema de conmutación por división de frecuencias m; ~ **domain** n ELECTRON dominio de frecuencia m, ámbito de frecuencia m; ~**-domain signal processing** n ELECTRON tratamiento de señal de ámbito de frecuencia m; ~ **doubler** n ELEC, ELECTRON, PHYS, TELECOM doblador de frecuencia m, duplicador de frecuencia m; ~ **drift** n ELEC, ELECTRON, TELECOM corrimiento de frecuencia m, deriva de corriente f, deriva de frecuencia f; ~ **encoding** n ELECTRON, TELECOM codificación de frecuencia f; ~ **fall-off** n ELEC caída de frecuencia f, disminución de frecuencia f; ~ **flutter** n ACOUST vibración de frecuencia f; ~ **hopping** n ELECTRON desplazamiento de frecuencia m, TELECOM variación por saltos en la frecuencia f; ~**-hopping oscillator** n ELECTRON oscilador de desplazamiento de frecuencia m; ~ **interlace** n TV entrelazado de frecuencias m; ~ **inversion** n TELECOM inversión de frecuencia f; ~ **loss** n TV pérdida de frecuencia f; ~ **meter** n ELEC ENG, ELECTRON, INSTR, TELECOM frecuencímetro m; ~ **modulation** n COMP&DP, ELEC, ELECTRON frecuencia modulada f, modulación de frecuencia f, PART PHYS, PHYS, TELECOM modulación de frecuencia f, frecuencia modulada f, TV, WAVE PHYS frecuencia modulada f, modulación de frecuencia f; ~**-modulation modem** n (FM modem) ELECTRON módem de modulación de frecuencia m; ~**-modulation noise** n TELECOM ruido de modulación de frecuencia m; ~**-modulation transmitting signal** n ELECTRON, RAD PHYS, TELECOM señal de transmisión FM f, señal de transmisión de frecuencia modulada f; ~ **modulator** n COMP&DP, ELEC, ELECTRON, PART PHYS, PHYS, TELECOM, TV, WAVE PHYS modulador de frecuencia m; ~ **monitor** n TV monitor de frecuencia m; ~ **multiplexer** n ELECTRON multiplexor de frecuencias m; ~ **multiplexing** n TELECOM multiplexado de frecuencia m; ~ **multiplication** n ELECTRON multiplicación de frecuencia f; ~ **multiplier** n ELECTRON multiplicador de frecuencia m, TELECOM generador de armarios m; ~**-multiplier klystron** n ELECTRON multiplicador klystron de frecuencia m; ~ **noise** n ELECTRON ruido de frecuencia m; ~ **offset** n ELECTRON dispersión de frecuencias f; ~ **overlap** n TV solapamiento de frecuencias m; ~ **pulling** n ELECTRON variación de frecuencia f; ~ **pushing** n ELECTRON impulso de frecuencia m; ~ **range** n AIR TRANSP, COMP&DP banda de frecuencias f, ELEC banda de frecuencias f, gama de frecuencias f, intervalo de frecuencias m, margen de frecuencias m, ELECTRON banda de frecuencias f, gama de frecuencias f, intervalo de frecuencias m, margen de frecuencia m, RAD PHYS, TELECOM banda de frecuencias f, TV banda de frecuencias f, gama de frecuencias f, intervalo de frecuencias m, margen de frecuencias m, WATER TRANSP, WAVE PHYS banda de frecuencias f; ~ **regulation** n TELECOM regulación de frecuencia f; ~ **rejection** n ELECTRON supresión de frecuencia f; ~ **relay** n ELEC ENG relé de frecuencia m; ~ **resolution** n ELECTRON resolución de frecuencia f; ~ **response** n CINEMAT, ELEC, ELECTRON, OPT, TELECOM, WAVE PHYS respuesta de frecuencia f; ~-**response curve** n ELECTRON curva de respuesta de frecuencia f, curva de respuesta en frecuencia f; ~ **retrace** n ELECTRON retroceso de frecuencia m; ~ **reuse** n ELECTRON, SPACE, TELECOM reutilización de frecuencia f; ~ **scale** n ELECTRON escala de frecuencia f; ~ **scanner** n TELECOM explorador de frecuencias m, scanner de frecuencias m; ~ **scanning** n TELECOM exploración de frecuencias f; ~-**selective amplifier** n ELECTRON amplificador selectivo de frecuencia m; ~-**selective filter** n ELECTRON filtro selectivo de frecuencia m; ~ **selector** n TELECOM selector de frecuencias m; ~ **separation** n ELECTRON separación de frecuencia f; ~ **shift** n COMP&DP, ELECTRON, TV desplazamiento de frecuencia m; ~-**shift keying** n (FSK) COMP&DP, ELECTRON, TELECOM, TV manipulación por desplazamiento de frecuencia f (MDF); ~-**shift keying modem** n ELECTRON módem de manipulación por desplazamiento de frecuencia m; ~ **source** n ELECTRON fuente de frecuencia f; ~ **spectrum** n ACOUST, COMP&DP, ELECTRON, WAVE PHYS espectro de frecuencias m; ~ **stabilizer** n ELEC estabilizador de frecuencia m; ~ **standard** n ELECTRON patrón de frecuencia m; ~ **sweep** n ELECTRON, TELECOM barrido de frecuencia m; ~ **synthesis** n ELECTRON síntesis de frecuencia f; ~ **synthesizer** n ELECTRON sintetizador de frecuencia m; ~ **test** n RAD PHYS prueba de frecuencia f; ~ **tracking** n SPACE communications enganche de frecuencia m, rastreo de frecuencia m; ~ **transducer** n ELEC, ELEC ENG transductor de frecuencia m; ~ **transformer** n ELEC, ELEC ENG transformador de frecuencia m; ~ **translation** n ELECTRON, TELECOM, TV conversión de frecuencia f; ~ **tuning** n ELECTRON, TELECOM sintonización de frecuencia f; ~-**uncertainty band** n TELECOM banda de incertidumbre de frecuencias f

frequently: ~ **asked questions** phr (FAQ) COMP&DP preguntas más frecuentes (FAQ)

fresh: ~ **cow** n AGRIC vaca que acaba de parir f; ~ **fish trade** n OCEAN comercialización de pescado fresco f, WATER TRANSP comercio del pescado fresco m; ~ **fuel** n NUCL combustible nuevo m

freshet n GEOL avalancha f, HYDROL corriente de agua dulce f, riada f

freshness: ~ **seal** n PACK precinto intacto m

freshwater[1] adj GEN de agua dulce

freshwater[2] n AGRIC, GAS, HYDROL, PETROL, WATER, WATER TRANSP agua dulce f; ~ **allowance** n WATER TRANSP free on board deducción por agua dulce f; ~ **condenser** n WATER TRANSP condensador del generador de agua dulce m; ~ **drilling mud** n PETR TECH, PETROL lodo de perforación de agua dulce m; ~ **drilling sludge** n PETR TECH, PETROL lodo de perforación de agua dulce m; ~ **interface** n HYDROL superficie de separación de agua dulce f; ~ **mud** n PETR TECH lodo de agua dulce m; ~ **sludge** n PETR TECH lodo de agua dulce m; ~ **stock** n WATER provisión de agua dulce f

Fresnel: ~ **biprism** n PHYS biprisma de Fresnel m; ~ **diffraction** n ACOUST, OPT, PHYS, TELECOM difracción de Fresnel f; ~ **diffraction pattern** n ACOUST, OPT, PHYS, TELECOM diagrama de difracción de Fresnel m; ~'s **equation** n ACOUST ecuación de Fresnel f; ~'s **formulae** n pl PHYS fórmulas de Fresnel f pl; ~ **lens** n CINEMAT, INSTR, PHOTO, PHYS lente de Fresnel f; ~ **mirrors** n pl PHYS espejos de Fresnel m pl; ~ **reflection** n OPT, TELECOM reflexión de Fresnel f; ~ **reflection method** n OPT, TELECOM método de reflexión de Fresnel m; ~ **region** n COMP&DP, TELECOM región de Fresnel f; ~ **zone** n TELECOM zona de Fresnel f; ~ **zone blockage** n TELECOM blocaje de zona de Fresnel m

fret: ~ **cutting** n PROD corte de marquetería m; ~ **fret saw** n PROD sierra de calar f, sierra de marquetería f; ~ **saw blade** n PROD sierra de marquetería f, sierra de punta f; ~ **saw frame** n PROD portasierra de calar m, portasierra de marquetería m; ~ **sawing** n PROD calado m

fretting n MECH corrosión f, corrosión por frotamiento f, desgaste por rozamiento m, roce m, NUCL desgaste por rozamiento m, PROD calado m, corrosión por frotamiento f, desgaste por rozamiento m, ornamentación f; ~ **fatigue** n METALL fatiga por contacto f, fatiga por rozamiento f

fretwork n PROD calado m

friable adj P&R desmenuzable

friction[1]: ~-**glazed** adj PAPER satinado por fricción

friction[2] n GEN fricción f, frotamiento m, rozamiento m; ~ **ball** n MECH ENG bola de fricción f; ~ **brake** n VEH freno de fricción m; ~-**brake hoist** n PROD montacargas de freno de fricción m; ~ **calender** n PAPER calandra friccionadora f; ~ **clutch** n MECH ENG embrague de fricción m; ~ **cone drive** n MECH ENG conductor de cono de fricción m; ~ **coupling** n MECH ENG acoplamiento por fricción m; ~ **course** n CONST recorrido de frenado m; ~ **damper** n AIR TRANSP, MECH amortiguador de fricción m; ~ **disc** BrE, ~ **disk** AmE n MECH ENG disco de fricción m; ~ **draft gear** AmE see friction draught gear BrE; ~ **drag** n AIR TRANSP resistencia aerodinámica por rozamiento f; ~ **draught gear** n BrE MECH ENG aparato de tracción por fricción m; ~ **drive** n CINEMAT, MECH ENG transmisión por fricción f; ~ **facing** n AUTO cara de fricción f; ~ **force** n ELEC ENG fuerza friccional f, METALL energía de rozamiento f, fuerza de rozamiento f, poder de rozamiento m, PHYS fuerza de rozamiento f, fuerza friccional f, poder de rozamiento m; ~ **fuse** n MINE estopín de fricción m; ~ **gear** n MECH ENG transmisión por fricción f; ~ **gearing** n MECH ENG transmisión por rueda de fricción f; ~ **glazing** n PAPER satinado por fricción m; ~ **hammer** n PROD martinete de fricción m; ~ **head** n CINEMAT cabeza de fricción f; ~ **headstock** n MECH ENG of lathe cabezal de fricción m, contrapunto de fricción *m*; ~ **loss** *n* FUELLESS pérdida por fricción *f*; ~ **pile** *n* COAL, CONST pilote de fricción *m*, pilote de rozamiento *m*; ~ **plate** *n* PROD placa de fricción *f*; ~ **point** *n* MECH ENG punto de fricción *m*; ~ **reel** *n* PAPER bobina de fricción *f*; ~ **ring** *n* MECH ENG anillo de fricción *m*, anillo de rozamiento *m*; ~ **roller** *n* PAPER, PROD rodillo de fricción *m*; ~ **screw** *n* MECH ENG tornillo de fricción *m*; ~ **snap-on cap** *n* PACK cápsula que se abre por fricción *f*; ~ **spring** *n* MECH ENG muelle de fricción *m*, resorte de fricción *m*; ~ **stress** *n* METALL coeficiente de rozamiento *m*; ~**-type bearing** *n* MECH ENG cojinete tipo fricción *m*; ~ **welding** *n* CONST soldadura de fricción *f*; ~ **wheel** *n* MECH ENG polea de fricción *f*, rueda de fricción *f*, volante de fricción *m*

frictional[1] *adj* CONST de rozamiento
frictional[2]: ~ **drag** *n* MECH resistencia de rozamiento *f*; ~ **electricity** *n* ELEC electricidad estática engendrada por frotamiento *f*, triboelectricidad *f*; ~ **flow** *n* NUCL flujo friccional *m*; ~ **force** *n* MECH ENG, PHYS fuerza de fricción *f*; ~ **ignition** *n* MINE ignición de fricción *f*, ignición por rozamiento *f*; ~ **resistance** *n* WATER TRANSP *ship design* resistencia de fricción *f*; ~ **torque** *n* SPACE par de razamiento *m*
frictioning *n* P&R impregnación *f*
frictionless *adj* MECH sin fricción, MECH ENG sin fricción, sin resistencia, sin rozamiento
fridge *n* ELEC, REFRIG, THERMO refrigerador *m*; ~**-freezer** *n* ELEC, REFRIG, THERMO congelador *m*
Friedel-Crafts: ~ **reaction** *n* CHEM reacción de Friedel-Crafts *f*; ~ **synthesis** *n* CHEM TECH, DETERG síntesis de Friedel-Crafts *f*
friedelite *n* MINERAL friedelita *f*
friesete *n* MINERAL friseíta *f*
frigate *n* MILIT, WATER TRANSP *navy* fragata *f*
fringe *n* PHYS banda *f*, banda de espectro *f*, RAD PHYS banda *f*, WAVE PHYS banda *f*, banda de espectro *f*; ~ **effect** *n* AIR TRANSP efecto marginal *m*, ELEC ENG efecto peculiar *m*, TV efecto ondulatorio *m*; ~ **separation** *n* OPT, PHYS, WAVE PHYS separación de franja *f*
fringing *n* TV alteración cromática de los extremos *f*; ~ **reef** *n* GEOL arrecife *m*, OCEAN arrecife *m*, costanera de orla *f*
frisket *n* PRINT frasqueta *f*
frit *n* C&G frita *f*
fritted: ~ **glaze** *n* C&G vidriado con fritas *m*
fritting: ~ **furnace** *n* C&G, HEAT *disc* horno de sinterización *m*
FRJ *abbr* (*facility rejected message*) TELECOM capacidad de rechazo de mensajes *f*
frogleg: ~ **winding** *n* ELEC ENG devanado en cruce *m*
fromage: ~ **frais** *n* BrE FOOD queso blanco *m*, queso fresco *m*
front[1]: ~**-end** *adj* AUTO, COMP&DP, ELECTRON, INSTR anterior, central, delantero, frontal, PHOTO avanzado, central, delantero, frontal, VEH anterior, central, delantero, frontal; ~**-wheel drive** *adj* TRANSP tracción delantera *f*
front[2] *n* CONST frente *m*, *of edifice* fachada *f*, METEO frente *m*, PROD *of boiler, furnace* fachada *f*; ~ **arch** *n* C&G arco frontal *m*; ~ **axle** *n* VEH eje delantero *m*; ~ **blade** *n* MAR POLL cara activa *f*; ~ **bumper** *n* AUTO parachoques delantero *m*; ~ **cylinder cover** *n* HYDRAUL tapa frontal de cilindro *f*; ~ **cylinder head** *n* HYDRAUL tapa frontal de cilindro *f*; ~ **delivery** *n*

PRINT salida frontal *f*; ~ **diaphragm** *n* PHOTO diafragma frontal *m*; ~ **door** *n* AUTO puerta delantera *f*; ~ **element** *n* PHOTO elemento anterior *m*; ~ **elevation** *n* MECH ENG alzado *m*, elevación frontal *f*, vista de frente *f*, vista frontal *f*; ~**-end equipment** *n* PRINT equipo central *m*; ~**-end loader** *n* MAR POLL cargadora de ataque frontal *f*, pala mecánica de ataque frontal *f*; ~ **end of nuclear fuel cycle** *n* NUCL primera parte del ciclo de combustible nuclear *f*; ~**-end processor** *n* (*FEP*) COMP&DP procesador delantero *m*, procesador frontal *m*, TELECOM procesador front-end *m*; ~ **engine** *n* AUTO motor delantero *m*; ~ **face** *n* MECH ENG cara frontal *f*; ~**-facing roller** *n* PROD rodillo delantero *m*; ~ **fender** *n* AmE (*cf front wing* BrE) AUTO *of car* aleta delantera *f*, guardabarros delantero *m*, TRANSP, VEH guardabarros delantero *m*; ~ **flasher** *n* AUTO, VEH intermitente delantero *m*; ~ **focal plane** *n* CINEMAT, PHOTO plano focal anterior *m*; ~ **frame** *n* PHOTO cuadro anterior *m*; ~ **gap** *n* ACOUST abertura delantera *f*; ~ **guide** *n* PRINT guía delantera *f*; ~ **lay** *n* PRINT guía frontal *f*; ~ **lens** *n* INSTR, OPT lente frontal *f*; ~**-lens filter** *n* INSTR, OPT filtro de lente frontal *m*; ~ **lighting** *n* CINEMAT, PHOTO, TV iluminación frontal *f*; ~ **matter** *n* PRINT parte inicial *f*; ~**-mounted engine** *n* VEH motor delantero *m*; ~ **of pack labeler** *n* AmE, ~ **of pack labeller** *n* BrE *n* PACK etiquetador de la parte delantera del paquete *m*; ~ **panel** *n* MECH ENG panel frontal *m*; ~ **piston** *n* AUTO pistón delantero *m*; ~**-porch switch** *n* TV conmutador del umbral anterior *m*; ~ **projection** *n* CINEMAT, TV proyección frontal *f*; ~ **rake angle** *n* MECH ENG ángulo de ataque frontal *m*, ángulo de rebaje frontal *m*; ~ **ring** *n* INSTR anillo frontal *m*; ~ **scanning** *n* CINEMAT anillo frontal *m*, TV exploración frontal *f*; ~ **seat** *n* AUTO, VEH asiento delantero *m*; ~ **shock-absorber** *n* AUTO amortiguador delantero *m*; ~ **side** *n* PAPER lado del conductor *m*; ~ **sight** *n* MILIT punto de mira *m*; ~ **standard adjustment** *n* PHOTO ajuste estándar frontal *m*; ~ **stop** *n* PRINT tope frontal *m*; ~ **suspension** *n* AUTO, VEH suspensión delantera *f*; ~ **suspension cross-member** *n* AUTO miembro cruzado de la suspensión delantera *m*; ~ **wall** *n* C&G pared delantera *f*, pared frontal *f*; ~**-wall photovoltaic cell** *n* ELEC célula fotovoltaica con barrera anterior *f*; ~ **wheel** *n* TRANSP rueda frontal *f*; ~**-wheel alignment** *n* AUTO, TRANSP, VEH alineación de las ruedas delanteras *f*; ~**-wheel drive** *n* AUTO tracción a las ruedas delanteras *f*, MECH impulsión por eje delantero *f*, propulsión sobre las ruedas delanteras *f*, tracción delantera *f*, VEH impulsión por eje delantero *f*; ~ **wing** *n* BrE (*cf front fender* AmE) AUTO aleta delantera *f*, guardabarros delantero *m*, TRANSP, VEH guardabarros delantero *m*
front[3]: ~**-light** *vt* PHOTO iluminar frontalmente
frontal: ~ **area** *n* MECH ENG área frontal *f*
frontispiece *n* PRINT contraportada *f*
frost[1]: ~**-hardy** *adj* AGRIC, COAL resistente a heladas; ~**-resistant** *adj* AGRIC, COAL *soil* a prueba de heladas, resistente a heladas
frost[2] *n* CINEMAT filtro difusor *m*, GEOL, METEO congelación *f*, helada *f*, REFRIG escarcha *f*; ~ **action** *n* GEOL efecto de las heladas *m*; ~ **back** *n* REFRIG formación de escarcha en la aspiración *f*; ~ **deposit** *n* REFRIG depósito de escarcha *m*; ~ **formation** *n* REFRIG formación de escarcha *f*; ~**-free level** *n*

COAL nivel libre de helada *m*, nivel sin helar *m*; ~ **heave** *n* COAL levantamiento por congelación *m*, METEO levantamiento por helada *m*, REFRIG levantamiento del suelo por congelación *m*; **--level indicator** *n* REFRIG indicador del nivel de escarcha *m*; ~ **limit** *n* COAL límite de congelación *m*; **--penetration depth** *n* COAL profundidad de penetración de la helada *f*; ~ **point** *n* REFRIG punto de escarcha *m*; **--preventive agent** *n* AIR TRANSP, AUTO anticongelante *m*, CHEM agente anticongelante *m*, CONST anticongelante *m*, PACK agente anticongelante *m*, anticongelante *m*, PAPER anticongelante *m*, REFRIG agente anticongelante *m*, anticongelante *m*, THERMO, VEH anticongelante *m*; ~ **susceptibility** *n* COAL susceptibilidad a la helada *f*; ~ **work** *n* GEOL meteorización por heladas *f*

frostbite *n* REFRIG deterioro por congelación *m*

frosted[1] *adj* C&G, FOOD, METR, REFRIG escarchado

frosted[2]: ~ **glass** *n* C&G vidrio escarchado *m*; ~ **lacquer** *n* COATINGS, COLOUR laca mate *f*

frosting *n* C&G, FOOD, METR, REFRIG escarchado *m*; ~ **bath** *n* C&G baño de ácido *m*

froth *n* COAL espuma *f*; ~ **flotation** *n* COAL flotación por espuma *f*; ~ **flotation plant** *n* MINE planta de flotación por espuma *f*

frothing *n* P&R producción de burbujas relativamente estables *f*

Froude: ~ **number** *n* PHYS número de Froude *m*

frozen[1] *adj* FOOD, REFRIG, THERMO congelado, gélido; ~ **solid** *adj* FOOD, REFRIG, THERMO solidificado por congelación

frozen[2]: ~ **food** *n* FOOD, REFRIG, THERMO alimento congelado *m*; **--food storage cabinet** *n* FOOD, MECH ENG, REFRIG, THERMO armario de almacenamiento de comestibles congelados *m*; **--food storage room** *n* FOOD, REFRIG, THERMO cámara de almacenamiento para productos congelados *f*, cámara para productos congelados *f*; ~ **frame** *n* CINEMAT, PHOTO, TV cuadro congelado *m*, cuadro fijo *m*, fotograma congelado *m*; ~ **ground** *n* COAL, GEOL suelo helado *m*, terreno helado *m*; ~ **liquid** *n* CHEM líquido congelado *m*; ~ **product** *n* FOOD, PACK, PROD, REFRIG producto congelado *m*

FRP *abbr* (*fast-reservation protocol*) TELECOM protocolo de reserva rápida *m*

FRR *abbr* (*flight readiness review*) SPACE revisión de disponibilidad de vuelo *f*

fructan *n* CHEM fructana *f*

fructosan *n* CHEM fructosana *f*

fructose *n* CHEM, FOOD fructosa *f*

fruit: ~ **carrier** *n* WATER TRANSP buque frutero *m*; ~ **flesh** *n* AGRIC mesocarpio *m*; ~ **grower** *n* AGRIC fruticultor *m*; ~ **sugar** *n* CHEM, FOOD azúcar de fruta *m*; ~ **wrapper** *n* FOOD envoltura de fruta *f*

frusemide *n* CHEM frusemida *f*

frustum *n* GEOM frusto *m*, tronco *m*

FSAR *abbr* (*final safety analysis report*) NUCL, SAFE *for plant licensing* informe final de análisis de seguridad *m*

FSK[1] *abbr* (*frequency-shift keying*) COMP&DP, ELECTRON, TELECOM, TV MDF (*manipulación por desplazamiento de frecuencia*)

FSK[2]: ~ **modem** *n* ELECTRON módem de MDF *m*

FSR *abbr* (*flowable solids reactor*) NUCL reactor de flujo de sólidos *m*

FSS *abbr* (*fixed-satellite service*) SPACE servicio fijo por satélite *m*

F-stop *n* CINEMAT, PHOTO, PHYS, TV abertura de diafragma *f*, ajuste de abertura *m*

FTAMSE *abbr* (*file transfer access and manipulation service element*) COMP&DP, TELECOM acceso de transferencia de ficheros y elemento del servicio de manipulación *m*

FTP *abbr* (*file transfer protocol*) COMP&DP FTP (*protocolo de transferencia de archivos*)

FTTB *abbr* (*fiber to the building AmE, fibre to the building BrE*) TELECOM fibra hasta el edificio *f*

FTTC *abbr* (*fiber to the curb AmE, fibre to the curb BrE*) TELECOM fibra hasta la acera *f*

FTTH *abbr* (*fiber to the home AmE, fibre to the home BrE*) TELECOM fibra hasta el domicilio *f*

FTTO *abbr* (*fiber to the office AmE, fibre to the office BrE*) TELECOM fibra hasta la oficina *f*

F2: ~ **generation** *n* AGRIC segunda generación filial *f*

FU *abbr* (*functional unit*) COMP&DP, TELECOM unidad funcional *f*

fuchsin *n* CHEM fucsina *f*

fuchsite *n* MINERAL avalita *f*, fucsita *f*

fuchsone *n* CHEM fucsona *f*

fucose *n* CHEM fucosa *f*

fucosterol *n* CHEM fucosterol *m*

fucoxanthin *n* CHEM fucoxantina *f*

fuel[1]: **--efficient** *adj* THERMO de buen rendimiento, de uso eficiente de combustible

fuel[2] *n* COAL combustible líquido *m*, SPACE agente oxidante *m*, THERMO, VEH combustible *m*, WATER TRANSP *for engine* combustible *m*, combustible líquido *m*; **--air mixture** *n* THERMO mezcla carburante *f*; ~ **assembly** *n* NUCL elemento de combustible *m*, PHYS conjunto de combustibles *m*; ~ **backup pump** *n* SPACE bomba alternativa de combustible *f*, bomba de repuesto de combustible *f*; ~ **bunker** *n* PROD tanque de combustible *m*; ~ **cell** *n* SPACE pila de combustible *f*, pila energética *f*, THERMO compartimiento de un tanque de combustible *m*, célula energética *f*; ~ **charge** *n* NUCL carga de combustible *f*; ~ **cladding** *n* NUCL vaina del combustible *f*; ~ **cock** *n* AIR TRANSP llave de combustible *f*; ~ **consumption** *n* AIR TRANSP, THERMO consumo de combustible *m*; ~ **consumption meter** *n* AIR TRANSP, THERMO indicador de consumo de combustible *m*; ~ **control** *n* AIR TRANSP control de combustible *m*; **--control unit** *n* AIR TRANSP unidad de control de combustible *f*; **--coolant heat exchanger** *n* AIR TRANSP intercambiador de calor refrigerante del combustible *m*, permutador térmico refrigerador del combustible *m*, termopermutador refrigerante del combustible *m*; ~ **cooling** *n* REFRIG, THERMO refrigeración de combustible *f*; ~ **cost** *n* AIR TRANSP, SPACE gasto del combustible *m*; ~ **cross-feed valve** *n* AIR TRANSP válvula de alimentación cruzada de combustible *f*; ~ **cycle** *n* SPACE ciclo de combustible *m*; ~ **dump** *n* MILIT depósito de combustible *m*; ~ **dump valve** *n* SPACE válvula del depósito de combustible *f*; ~ **dumping** *n* SPACE descarga de combustible *f*; ~ **dumping system** *n* SPACE sistema de descarga de combustible *m*; ~ **economy** *n* THERMO economía de combustible *f*; ~ **efficiency** *n* SPACE rendimiento del combustible *m*; ~ **expansion box** *n* AIR TRANSP caja de expansión del combustible *f*; ~ **filter** *n* AIR TRANSP, AUTO filtro del combustible *m*; **--freeze system** *n*

REFRIG sistema con frigorífico carburante *m*; ~ **funnel** *n* HEAT embudo para el combustible *m*; ~ **gage** *AmE see fuel gauge BrE*; ~ **gage indicator** *AmE see fuel gauge indicator BrE*; ~ **gage transmitter** *AmE see fuel gauge transmitter BrE*; ~ **gas** *n* GAS gas combustible *m*; ~ **gauge** *n BrE* AIR TRANSP, AUTO, VEH indicador de combustible *m*; ~ **gauge indicator** *n BrE* AIR TRANSP, AUTO, VEH indicador de combustible *m*, medidor del combustible *m*; ~ **gauge transmitter** *n BrE* AIR TRANSP transmisor del indicador del combustible *m*, transmisor del nivel de combustible *m*, AUTO, TRANSP, VEH transmisor del indicador del combustible *m*; ~ **grade** *n* AIR TRANSP grado del combustible *m*; ~**-handling plant** *n* HEAT, THERMO planta para la manipulación del combustible *f*; ~ **high-pressure pump** *n* AUTO, VEH bomba de combustible de alta presión *f*; ~ **indicator** *n* AIR TRANSP, AUTO, VEH indicador de combustible *m*; ~ **injection** *n* AUTO, HEAT ENG, THERMO, VEH inyección de combustible *f*; ~**-injection pump** *n* AUTO, HEAT ENG, THERMO, VEH bomba de inyección de combustible *f*; ~ **injector** *n* AUTO, HEAT ENG, MECH ENG, THERMO, VEH inyector de combustible *m*; ~**-inlet valve** *n* AUTO válvula de entrada de combustible *f*; ~ **jettison** *n* AIR TRANSP lanzamiento de combustible *m*; ~**-level presetting controls** *n pl* AIR TRANSP controles de predeterminación del nivel del combustible *m pl*; ~**-level selector** *n* AIR TRANSP selector del nivel de combustible *m*; ~**-level transmitter** *n* AIR TRANSP transmisor del nivel de combustible *m*; ~ **line** *n* AUTO, VEH circuito de combustible *m*, línea de combustible *f*, tubería de combustible *f*; ~ **load** *n* AIR TRANSP carga de combustible *f*; ~ **man** *n* SPACE provisión de combustible *f*; ~ **measuring unit** *n* SPACE unidad de mediación de combustible *f*; ~ **nozzle** *n* AUTO, MECH ENG, VEH boquilla de combustible *f*, tobera de combustible *f*; ~ **oil** *n* CHEM aceite fuel *m* (*Esp*), aceite combustible (*AmL*), fueloil *m* (*AmL*), fuelóleo *m* (*Esp*), COAL, CONST fueloil *m* (*AmL*), fuelóleo *m* (*Esp*), HEAT gasóleo *m*, PETR TECH aceite pesado *m*; ~**-oxidizer mixture ratio** *n* SPACE proporción de mezcla del combustible oxidante *f*; ~ **pipe** *n* AUTO, VEH tubo de combustible *m*; ~ **pump** *n* AIR TRANSP, AUTO, MECH, MECH ENG, SPACE, VEH, WATER TRANSP bomba de alimentación *f*, bomba de alimentación de combustible *f*, bomba de combustible *f*, bomba de gasolina *f* (*Esp*), bomba de nafta *f* (*AmL*); ~ **reserve** *n* AIR TRANSP reserva de combustible *f*; ~ **rod** *n* PHYS varilla de combustible *f*; ~ **selector** *n* HEAT selector de combustible *m*; ~ **shut-off cock** *n* AIR TRANSP llave de cierre del combustible *f*; ~ **shut-off cock control link** *n* AIR TRANSP enlace de control de la llave de cierre del combustible *m*; ~ **system** *n* AIR TRANSP sistema de combustible *m*; ~**-system diagram** *n* WATER TRANSP diagrama del circuito de combustible *m*; ~ **tank** *n* AIR TRANSP, AUTO, MECH depósito de combustible *m*, tanque de combustible *m*, SPACE cuba de combustible *f*, tanque de combustible *m*, VEH depósito de combustible *m*; ~**-tank selector switch** *n* AIR TRANSP interruptor selector del depósito de combustible *m*; ~ **tanker** *n* TRANSP camión cisterna *m*; ~ **temperature probe** *n* AIR TRANSP sonda de temperatura del combustible *f*; ~ **transfer** *n* AIR TRANSP transvase de combustible *m*; ~ **ullage box** *n*

AIR TRANSP caja de expansión del combustible de punta del ala *f*

fuel³ *vt* THERMO aprovisionar

fueler *n AmE see fueller BrE*

fueling *AmE see fuelling BrE*; ~ **vehicle** *AmE see fuelling vehicle BrE*

fueller *n BrE* PETR TECH abastecedor de combustible *m*, suministrador de combustible *m*

fuelling *n BrE* AIR TRANSP, PETR TECH abastecimiento *m*, repostado *m*; ~ **vehicle** *n BrE* SPACE vehículo para repostar *m*

fugacity *n* CHEM, GAS, THERMO fugacidad *f*

fulcrum *n* PHYS fulcro *m*, punto de apoyo *m*; ~ **pin** *n* MECH ENG eje de articulación *m*

fulgurite *n* GEOL fulgurita *f*, PROD *lightning tube* fulgurito *m*

full¹: ~**-bodied** *adj* PRINT *ink* con cuerpo; ~**-bound** *adj* PRINT encuadernado a toda piel, encuadernado piel; ~**-color** *AmE*, ~**-colour** *BrE adj* PRINT a todo color; ~ **and down** *adj* WATER TRANSP completamente cargado hasta los calados permitidos; ~ **glueing** *adj* PACK totalmente pegado; ~**-voltage AC/DC** *adj* PROD de CA/CC a pleno voltaje

full²: ~ **ahead** *adv* WATER TRANSP *engine* avante toda; ~ **astern** *adv* WATER TRANSP *engine* atrás toda; ~ **and by** *adv* WATER TRANSP *sailing* a vela llena, en buena vela

full³: ~ **adder** *n* COMP&DP sumador *m*, sumador completo *m*, totalizador *m*; ~ **aperture** *n* PHOTO plena abertura *f*; ~ **band** *n* PHYS *circuit* banda completa *f*; ~ **bridge** *n* ELEC *of instrument* puente completo *m*, puente lleno *m*; ~ **circuit** *n* ELEC circuito completo *m*; ~**-coverage beam** *n* SPACE *communications* configuración de carga máxima *f*; ~**-custom circuit** *n* ELECTRON circuito totalmente manual *m*; ~ **dredging depth** *n* WATER altura total de dragado *f*; ~ **duplex** *n* (*FDX*) COMP&DP sistema de transmisión bidireccional *m* (*FDX*); ~**-duration half maximum** *n* (*FDHM*) OPT duración completa a mitad de altura *f*, TELECOM duración total mitad del máximo *f*; ~**-face tunnel borer** *n* MINE perforador del túnel con frente entero *m*; ~**-face type** *n* PRINT tipo de ojo pleno *m*; ~ **face-mask** *n* SAFE máscara *f*; ~ **finish** *n* COATINGS acabado a fondo *m*, acabado total *m*; ~**-floating axle** *n* AUTO eje flotante total *m*; ~**-flow oil filter** *n* VEH filtro de aceite de capacidad total *m*; ~**-forward gear** *n* MECH ENG distribución toda en marcha adelante *f*; ~**-frame** *n* CINEMAT, PHOTO, TV fotograma completo *m*; ~**-frame print** *n* PHOTO copia de negativo completo *f*; ~ **gear forward** *n* MECH ENG distribución toda en marcha hacia adelante *f*; ~ **handle** *n* TEXTIL tacto lleno *m*; ~ **head of water** *n* HYDRAUL, WATER altura máxima de caída del agua *f*; ~**-injection turbine** *n* HYDRAUL turbina de inyección total *f*; ~**-lead crystal glass** *n* C&G cristal de plomo *m*; ~**-length cloth** *n* TEXTIL tejido en toda su longitud *m*; ~ **load** *n* AIR TRANSP carga máxima *f*, ELEC *of generator*, PROD carga plena *f*, plena carga *f*; ~**-load configuration** *n* SPACE *spacecraft* configuración de plena carga *f*; ~**-load current** *n* ELEC, PROD corriente a plena carga *f*; ~**-motion videoconferencing** *n* TELECOM videoconferencia de movimiento total *f*; ~**-open throttle** *n* AIR TRANSP regulador de gases totalmente abierto *m*; ~**-out** *n* PRINT composición continua *f*; ~**-page advertisement** *n* PRINT anuncio a toda página *m*; ~ **pipe** *n* HYDRAUL conducto forzado *m*, tubería forzada *f*; **~-pitch coil** *n* ELEC bobina de paso entero *f*; **~-pitch winding** *n* ELEC *coil* devanado de paso entero *m*, ELEC ENG devanado diametral *m*; **~ point** *n* PRINT punto final *m*; **~ power** *n* WATER TRANSP *machinery* plena potencia *f*; **~-pressure suit** *n* SPACE conjunto de presión máxima *m*; **~ scale** *n* MECH ENG *drawing* escala completa *f*, escala uno a uno *f*, tamaño natural *m*; **~-screen editor** *n* COMP&DP editor de pantalla llena *m*, editor en pantalla de página completa *m*; **~-slipper piston** *n* AUTO pistón de falda estrecha *m*, pistón de patín *m*, pistón de zapatilla *m*; **~ stop** *n* PRINT punto final *m*; **~ subtractor** *n* COMP&DP, ELECTRON sustractor todo completo *m*; **~ sunlight** *n* SPACE insolación completa *f*, plena luz solar *f*; **~ throttle** *n* AIR TRANSP máxima potencia *f*; **~ thrust** *n* SPACE pleno empuje *m*; **~-tide duration** *n* OCEAN duración de una marea completa *f*; **~ track** *n* ACOUST pista completa *f*; **~ voltage** *n* ELEC, ELEC ENG, PROD pleno voltaje *m*, tensión plena *f*, voltaje máximo *m*; **~-wave rectification** *n* ELEC, ELEC ENG, PHYS, PROD rectificación de onda completa *f*; **~-wave rectified AC voltage** *n* ELEC, ELEC ENG, PROD voltaje de CA rectificado de onda completa *m*; **~-wave rectifier** *n* ELEC, ELEC ENG, PHYS, PROD rectificador de onda completa *m*; **~-width half maximum** *n* (*FWHM*) OPT, TELECOM anchura a mitad de altura *f*; **~-width sample** *n* TEXTIL muestra a todo el ancho *f*

full[4]: **in ~ swing** *phr* MECH ENG a toda máquina, en plena acción, en plena actividad, en plena producción; **in ~ working order** *phr* MECH ENG en condiciones de servicio, en estado de servicio, en perfecto estado de funcionamiento

Fuller-Bonot: ~ mill *n* COAL molino de Fuller-Bonot *m*

fuller's: ~ earth *n* GEOL tierra de batanero *f*

fulling *n* TEXTIL batanado *m*; **~ mill** *n* PAPER batán *m*

fully[1]: **~ automatic** *adj* INSTR, MECH ENG, PROD completamente automático, totalmente automático; **~-compressed** *adj* MECH ENG, PROD a compresión total

fully[2]: **~-automatic diaphragm** *n* PHOTO diafragma totalmente automático *m*; **~-automatic self-adhesive labeling machine** *AmE*, **~-automatic self-adhesive labelling machine** *BrE n* PACK máquina automática para aplicar etiquetas autoadhesivas *f*; **~-automatic stretch wrapper** *n* PACK empaquetadora con un material estirable totalmente automática *f*; **~-bleached pulp** *n* PAPER pulpa extrablanqueada *f*; **~-distributed control system** *n* TELECOM sistema de control totalmente distribuido *m*; **~-drawn yarns** *n pl* TEXTIL hilos totalmente estirados *m pl*

fulminate[1] *n* CHEM fulminato *m*

fulminate[2] *vi* CHEM fulminar

fulmination *n* CHEM fulminación *f*

fulminic: ~ acid *n* CHEM ácido fulmínico *m*

fulvene *n* CHEM fulveno *m*

fumaric *adj* CHEM fumárico

fumarole *n* GEOL fumarola *f*

fume: ~ cupboard *n* CHEM TECH, LAB campana de extracción *f*, campana de laboratorio *f*; **~ extractor** *n* CHEM TECH extractor de humos *m*; **~ hood** *n* CHEM TECH, LAB campana de extracción *f*, campana de laboratorio *f*; **~ incinerator** *n* CHEM TECH incinerador de humos *m*

fumes *n pl* AUTO, CHEM, HEAT ENG, SAFE humos *m pl*

fuming: ~ sulfuric acid *AmE*, **~ sulphuric acid** *BrE n* CHEM, DETERG ácido sulfúrico fumante *m*

fumivorous *adj* CHEM, COAL fumívoro

function[1]: **~-orientated** *adj* PROD organizado por funciones

function[2]: **~ code** *n* COMP&DP código de funcionamiento *m*, código de función *m*; **~-division system** *n* TELECOM sistema de división de funciones *m*; **~-division system architecture** *n* TELECOM arquitectura del sistema de división de funciones *f*; **~ generator** *n* ELECTRON generador de función *m*; **~ key** *n* COMP&DP tecla de función *f*; **~ selector** *n* ELEC conmutador de aplicaciones *m*, selector de funciones *m*

functional: ~ analysis *n* MATH análisis funcional *m*; **~ character** *n* PRINT carácter funcional *m*; **~ decomposition** *n* COMP&DP descomposición funcional *f*; **~ design** *n* COMP&DP diseño funcional *m*; **~ diagram** *n* COMP&DP diagrama funcional *m*, MECH ENG diagrama de funcionamiento de circuito *m*, diagrama funcional *m*; **~ entity** *n* (*FE*) TELECOM entidad funcional *f*; **~ entity action** *n* (*FEA*) TELECOM acción de entidad funcional *f*; **~ group** *n* CHEM grupo funcional *m*; **~-group header** *n* TELECOM cabecera de grupo funcional *f*; **~ language** *n* COMP&DP lenguaje funcional *m*; **~ test** *n* COMP&DP, TELECOM prueba de funcionamiento *f*, prueba funcional *f*; **~ unit** *n* (*FU*) COMP&DP, TELECOM unidad funcional *f*

functionally: ~-divided system *n* TELECOM sistema dividido funcionalmente *m*

fundamental: ~ chord *n* ACOUST acorde fundamental *m*; **~ component** *n* PHYS componente fundamental *f*; **~ frequency** *n* ACOUST, ELECTRON, TELECOM frecuencia fundamental *f*; **~ mode** *n* ELEC ENG modo básico *m*, modo fundamental *m*, OPT, PHYS, SPACE modo fundamental *m*; **~ programming** *n* PROD programación de base *f*; **~ tone** *n* ACOUST, WAVE PHYS tono fundamental *m*; **~ unit** *n* ELEC unidad fundamental *f*, MECH ENG unidad básica *f*, unidad fundamental *f*, PHYS unidad fundamental *f*; **~ vibration mode** *n* ACOUST modo de vibración fundamental *m*, SPACE modo fundamental de vibración *m*

fungicidal: ~ varnish *n* COATINGS, COLOUR barniz fungicida *m*

fungicide *n* AGRIC, CHEM, P&R fungicida *m*; **~ paint** *n* CONST, PROD pintura fungicida *f*

fungistat *n* FOOD fungistático *m*

fungus[1]: **~-proof** *adj* PROD antifúngico

fungus[2] *n* AGRIC hongo *m*

funicular *n* MECH ENG, RAIL, TRANSP funicular *m*

funnel *n* C&G, CHEM, CHEM TECH embudo *m*, CONST chimenea metálica *f*, embudo *m*, ELECTRON conducto *m*, FOOD, LAB embudo *m*, MECH embudo *m*, tubo de aireación *m*, PROD *gate or pouring hole of mould* embudo *m*, embocadura *f*, tubo de aireación *m*, WATER TRANSP *ship* chimenea *f*; **~ heater** *n* LAB calentador de embudo *m*; **~ stand** *n* LAB portaembudo *m*, soporte de embudo *m*

fur[1] *n* HEAT, HYDRAUL incrustación *f*, PROD *boiler scale* desincrustación *f*, incrustación *f*, TEXTIL piel *f*

fur[2] *vt* PROD, TEXTIL incrustar

fur[3] *vi* HEAT, HYDRAUL, PROD incrustarse

furfural *n* P&R furfural *m*

furfuraldehyde *n* P&R furfuraldehído *m*

furfuryl *adj* CHEM furfuril

furile *n* CHEM furilo *m*
furilic *adj* CHEM furílico
furl *vt* WATER TRANSP *sail* aferrar
Furling: ~ **speed** *n* FUELLESS *wind power* velocidad de aferrar *f*
furlong *n* METR estadio *m*
furnace *n* HEAT horno *m*, HYDRAUL hogar *m*, LAB *vehicles* horno *m*, PROD *for heating steam boiler* hogar *m*, *for smelting, melting, baking* horno *m*, THERMO horno *m*; ~ **bridge** *n* PROD altar del horno *m*; ~ **charge** *n* C&G carga del horno *f*; ~-**fill** *n* C&G llenado de horno *m*; ~ **gas** *n* PROD gas de alto horno *m*; ~ **grate** *n* PROD parrilla *f* (*AmL*); ~ **oil** *n* THERMO *central heating* aceite de calefacción *m*; ~ **plate** *n* PROD chapa del hogar *f*
furnish *n* PAPER composición de fabricación *f*; ~ **layer** *n* PAPER capa fibrosa *f*
furnishing *n pl* CONST accesorio *m*, equipo *m*, mobiliario *m*; ~ **fabric** *n* TEXTIL tejido para tapicería *m*
furniture: ~ **and fittings** *n pl* CONST herrajes y accesorios *m pl*; ~, **fixtures and fittings** *n pl* CONST mobiliario, lámparas y accesorios *m pl*
furon *n* CHEM furona *f*
furred *adj* HEAT, HYDRAUL, PROD *in boilers* incrustado
furring *n* CONST *of roof* enrasado *m*; ~ **hammer** *n* HYDRAUL martillo para desincrustar calderas *m*; ~ **piece** *n* CONST pieza de enrasar *f*
furrow *n* AGRIC, GEOL, WATER surco *m*; ~ **irrigation** *n* AGRIC, WATER riego por surcos *m*; ~ **slice** *n* AGRIC banda de tierra *f*, gleba *f*
fusarium: ~ **wilt** *n* AGRIC fusariosis *f*
fuse[1]: ~-**protected** *adj* ELEC ENG protegido por fusibles
fuse[2] *n* ELEC *electric circuit*, ELEC ENG, ELECTRON fusible *m*, MILIT cebo *m*, espoleta *f*, estopín *m*, mecha *f*, MINE cebo *m* (*Esp*), detonador *m* (*Esp*), espoleta *f*, estopín *m* (*AmL*), mecha *f* (*Esp*), SPACE, TV fusible *m*; ~ **array** *n* ELEC ENG serie de fusibles *f*; ~ **base** *n* ELEC ENG bayoneta del fusible *f*, casquillo del fusible *m*; ~-**blown status indicator** *n* PROD indicador de estado de fusible fundido *m*; ~ **board** *n* ELEC, ELEC ENG panel de fusibles *m*; ~ **box** *n* AUTO, ELEC, ELEC ENG, VEH caja de fusibles *f*, caja de fusores *f*; ~ **cap** *n* MILIT cápsula detonante *f*; ~ **carrier** *n* ELEC, ELEC ENG portafusibles *m*; ~ **clip** *n* PROD sujetafusible *m*; ~ **cord** *n* SPACE *spacecraft* cordón de espoleta *m*; ~ **cover** *n* ELEC cubierta de fusible *f*, tapa de fusible *f*, PROD tapafusibles *m*; ~ **element** *n* ELEC ENG, ELECTRON elemento de fusible *m*; ~ **holder** *n* ELEC portafusibles *m*, ELEC ENG, ELECTRON, TV cuadro de fusibles *m*, portafusibles *m*; ~ **link** *n* ELEC cinta fusible *f*, fusible de cinta *m*, lámina fusible *f*, ELEC

ENG elemento fusible de cartucho *m*, fusible de cinta *m*, lámina fusible *f*; ~ **protection** *n* ELEC ENG protección por fusibles *f*; ~ **puller** *n* PROD quitafusibles *m*, sacafusibles *m pl*; ~ **safety-pin** *n* MILIT pasador de seguridad de la espoleta *m*; ~ **strip** *n* ELEC fusible de cinta *m*, lámina fusible *f*, regleta de fusibles *f*, ELEC ENG fusible de cinta *m*, lámina fusible *f*; ~ **wire** *n* ELEC, ELEC ENG alambre fusible *m*, hilo fusible *m*
fuse[3] *vt* C&G, P&R, THERMO fundir
fused: ~ **bifocals** *n pl* C&G bifocales fundidos *m pl*; ~ **bundle** *n* C&G haz de fibras fundido *m*; ~ **quartz** *n* OPT, TELECOM cuarzo fundido *m*; ~ **silica** *n* C&G, OPT, TELECOM sílice fundida *f*; ~-**silica window** *n* SPACE ventana de sílice fundida *f*
fusee: ~ **wheel** *n* PROD *extraction* tambor cónico *m*
fusel: ~ **oil** *n* FOOD aceite de fusel *m*
fuselage *n* AIR TRANSP, SPACE, TRANSP fuselaje *m*; ~ **box** *n* AIR TRANSP caja del fuselaje *f*; ~-**box beam wall** *n* AIR TRANSP pared de la viga de la caja del fuselaje *f*; ~ **center box** *AmE*, ~ **centre box** *BrE n* AIR TRANSP caja central del fuselaje *f*; ~ **datum line** *n* AIR TRANSP línea de referencia del fuselaje *f*; ~ **dorsal fin** *n* AIR TRANSP aleta dorsal del fuselaje *f*; ~ **ground connection** *n* AIR TRANSP conexión de tierra del fuselaje *f*
fusible[1] *adj* C&G, THERMO fundible
fusible[2]: ~ **clay** *n* C&G barro fundible *m*; ~ **plug for steam boiler** *n* HYDRAUL tapón fusible para caldera de vapor *m*
fusing *n* C&G, P&R, THERMO fusión *f*; ~ **oven** *n* C&G, P&R, THERMO horno de fusión *m*; ~ **point** *n* C&G, P&R, THERMO temperatura de fusión *f*
fusion *n* GEN fusión *f*; ~ **drilling** *n* COAL foración por fusión *f*, perforación por fusión *f*; ~ **splice** *n* OPT, TELECOM empalme por fusión *m*; ~-**welded butt joint** *n* MECH ENG junta a tope soldada por fusión *f*, junta plana soldada por fusión *f*; ~ **welding** *n* CONST, PROD, THERMO fusiosoldeo *m*, soldadura por arco *f*, soldadura por fusión *f*
futures: ~ **market** *n* AGRIC mercado a término *m*
fuzz *n* PAPER, PRINT pelusa *f*
fuzzy: ~ **image** *n* PHOTO imagen borrosa *f*; ~ **logic** *n* COMP&DP lógica borrosa *f*, lógica de duda *f*, lógica de nebulosa *f*; ~ **theory** *n* COMP&DP teoría de duda *f*, teoría de nebulosa *f*
FWF *abbr* (*first-window fiber AmE, first-window fibre BrE*) OPT fibra de primera ventana *f*, fibra que opera en la primera ventana de longitudes de ondas *f*
FX *abbr* (*effects*) CINEMAT, TV efectos *m pl*, efectos especiales *m pl*, efectos sonoros *m pl*

G

G *abbr* (*giga-*) METR G (*giga-*)
GA *abbr* (*go ahead*) TELECOM adelante *m*
Ga *abbr* (*gallium*) CHEM, ELECTRON, METALL, OPT, PHYS Ga (*galio*)
GaAs: ~ laser *n* (*gallium arsenide laser*) RAD PHYS láser de arseniuro de galio *m*
gab *n* HYDRAUL gancho *m*; ~ hook *n* HYDRAUL palanca *f*
gabbro *n* PETROL gabro *m*
gabion *n* CONST gavión *m*
gable *n* CONST hastial *m* (*AmL*); ~ roof *n* CONST tejado a dos aguas *m*
gad *n* MINE barra puntiaguda *f* (*AmL*), chaveta *f* (*AmL*), cuña *f* (*Esp*), punterola *f* (*Esp*)
gadget: ~ bag *n* PHOTO bolsa para accesorios *f*
gadolinite *n* MINERAL gadolinita *f*
gadolinium *n* CHEM gadolinio *m* (*Gd*)
gaff *n* WATER TRANSP pico cangrejo *m*
gaffer *n* C&G capataz *m*; ~ grip *n* CINEMAT jefe electricista *m*, jefe eléctrico *m*; ~ tape *n* CINEMAT cinta para electricistas *f*
gage *AmE see* gauge *BrE*
gaged *AmE see* gauged *BrE*
gagger *n* PROD *founding* clavo de fundidor *m*, clavo de moldeador *m*, gancho de molde *m*
gaging *AmE see* gauging *BrE*
gain *n* COMP&DP ganancia *f*, ELEC *signal* amplificación *f*, ganancia *f*, ELEC ENG, ELECTRON amplificación *f*, SPACE *communications* ganancia *f*, amplificación *f*, aumento *m*, rendimiento *m*, TELECOM, TV, WATER TRANSP ganancia *f*; ~ ability *n* AGRIC habilidad para aumentar de peso *f*; ~ adjustment *n* ELECTRON ajuste de ganancia *m*; ~ change *n* ELECTRON modificación de ganancia *f*; ~ compression *n* ELECTRON compresión de ganancia *f*; ~ control *n* ELECTRON control de ganancia *m*; ~ curve *n* ELECTRON curva de ganancia *f*; ~ drift *n* ELECTRON variación de ganancia *f*; ~ frequency characteristic *n* ELECTRON característica de frecuencia de ganancia *f*; ~ function *n* ELECTRON función de ganancia *f*; ~ in live weight *n* AGRIC aumento de peso en vivo *m*; ~ setting *n* ELECTRON regulación de ganancia *f*; ~-to-noise-temperature ratio *n* (*G-T*) SPACE relación ganancia temperatura de ruido *f* (*G-T*); ~ trace *n* PETROL rastro de ganancia *m*; ~ trimming *n* ELECTRON regulación de ganancia *f*; ~-weighting factor *n* ELECTRON factor de ponderación de ganancia *m*
gaining *n* AGRIC ganancia de peso *f*; ~ stream *n* WATER corriente de crecida *f*
galactic: ~ cloud *n* SPACE nube galáctica *f*; ~ noise *n* ELECTRON ruido galáctico *m*
galactonic *adj* CHEM galactónico
galactosamine *n* CHEM galactosamina *f*
galactose *n* CHEM, FOOD galactosa *f*
gale *n* METEO temporal *m*, ventarrón *m*, viento duro *m*; ~ warning *n* METEO, WATER TRANSP aviso de temporal *m*, aviso de viento duro *m*
galena *n* CHEM galena *f*, MINERAL galenita *f*
galenobismutite *n* MINERAL galenobismutita *f*

Galilean: ~ frame *n* PHYS sistema de referencia de Galileo *m*; ~ telescope *n* PHYS telescopio de Galileo *m*; ~ transformation *n* PHYS transformación de Galileo *f*
gall *n* AGRIC, C&G agalla *f*; ~ midge *n* AGRIC mosquita de agalla *f*
gallate *n* CHEM galato *m*
galled: ~ spot *n* AGRIC, GEOL zona erosionada *f*
gallein *n* CHEM galeína *f*
gallery *n* COAL, GEOL, NUCL galería *f*; ~ furnace *n* PROD horno de galera *m*, horno de galerías *m*; ~ in dead ground *n* MINE galería en roca *f*
galley *n* PRINT galerada *f*, WATER TRANSP *of ship* cocina *f*; ~ furnishings *n pl* AIR TRANSP, WATER TRANSP muebles de cocina *m pl*; ~ proof *n* PRINT prueba de galerada *f*
gallic *adj* CHEM gálico
galling *n* NUCL corrosión por frotamiento *f*
gallium *n* (*Ga*) CHEM, ELECTRON, METALL, OPT, PHYS galio *m* (*Ga*); ~ arsenide *n* ELECTRON, OPT, PHYS arseniuro de galio *m*; ~ arsenide chip *n* ELECTRON, OPT, PHYS chip de arseniuro de galio *m*; ~ arsenide component *n* ELECTRON, OPT, PHYS componente de arseniuro de galio *m*; ~ arsenide diode *n* ELECTRON, OPT, PHYS diodo de arseniuro de galio *m*; ~ arsenide laser *n* (*GaAs laser*) RAD PHYS láser de arseniuro de galio *m*; ~ arsenide logic *n* ELECTRON circuito lógico de arseniuro de galio *m*; ~ arsenide MOS transistor *n* ELECTRON transistor SOM de arseniuro de galio *m*; ~ arsenide parametric amplifier diode *n* ELECTRON diodo de amplificador paramétrico de arseniuro de galio *m*; ~ arsenide solar cell *n* ELECTRON pila solar de arseniuro de galio *f*; ~ arsenide substrate *n* ELECTRON substrato de arseniuro de galio *m*
gallon *n* METR *British imperial measure* galón *m*; ~ jug *n* C&G galón *m*
gallow: ~ plough *n* BrE AGRIC arado con antetrén *m*; ~ plow *AmE see* gallow plough *BrE*
gallows: ~ frame *n* MINE castillete de extracción *m*
galvanic[1] *adj* GEN galvánico
galvanic[2]: ~ cell *n* CHEM, COATINGS celda galvánica *f*, célula galvánica *f*, ELEC célula galvánica *f*, celda galvánica *f*, ELEC ENG celda galvánica *f*, célula galvánica *f*; ~ couple *n* ELEC ENG par galvánico *m*; ~ current *n* ELEC, ELEC ENG corriente galvánica *f*; ~ deposition *n* COATINGS depósito galvánico *m*; ~ isolation *n* ELEC, ELEC ENG aislamiento galvánico *m*; ~ plating *n* COATINGS galvonoplastia *f*, plaqueado galvánico *m*, recubrimiento galvánico *m*
galvanization *n* GEN galvanización *f*
galvanize *vt* GEN galvanizar
galvanized[1] *adj* CHEM, COATINGS cincado, galvanizado, ELEC, ELEC ENG galvanizado, MECH, P&R cincado, galvanizado
galvanized[2]: ~ protective coating *n* COATINGS revestimiento protector galvanizado *m*
galvanometer *n* GEN galvanómetro *m*; ~ shunt *n* ELEC, ELEC ENG derivación de galvanómetro *f*, resistencia

en paralelo para galvanómetro *f*, shunt de galvanómetro *m*

galvanoplastics *n pl* COATINGS, CONST, ELEC, ELEC ENG, PROD galvanoplastia *f*

galvanoplates *n pl* PHYS galvanoplacas *f pl*

gambier *n* CHEM gambir *m*

gambrel: ~ **roof** *n* AmE (*cf mansard roof BrE*) CONST cubierta de la mansarda *f*

game: ~ **theory** *n* GEOM *statistics* teoría de juegos *f*

gamete *n* AGRIC gameto *m*

gamma *n* CINEMAT, NUCL, PETROL, TV gamma *f*; ~ **backscatter method** *n* NUCL método de retrodispersión gamma *m*; ~ **characteristic** *n* ELECTRON característica de rayos gamma *f*; ~ **correction** *n* CINEMAT corrección gamma *f*; ~ **corrector** *n* TV corrector gamma *m*; ~ **decay** *n* PART PHYS, PHYS, RAD PHYS desintegración gamma *f*; ~ **emission** *n* RAD PHYS emisión gamma *f*; ~ **error** *n* TV error gamma *m*; ~ **film** *n* RAD PHYS película gamma *f*, película gammamétrica *f*; ~ **fuel scanning** *n* NUCL barrido gamma del combustible *m*; ~~**gamma log** *n* PETR TECH diagrafía gamma-gamma *f*, perfil gamma-gamma *m*, registro gamma-gamma *m*; ~ **log** *n* FUELLESS, GAS, PETR TECH, PETROL perfil gamma *m*; ~ **particle** *n* ELEC, NUCL, PART PHYS, PHYS, RAD PHYS partícula gamma *f*; ~~**photon activation** *n* RAD PHYS activación inducida por fotones gamma *f*, activación por fotones gamma *f*; ~ **quench** *n* NUCL temple gamma *m*; ~ **radiation** *n* ELEC, PART PHYS, PHYS, RAD PHYS, WAVE PHYS radiación gamma *f*; ~ **radiography** *n* RAD PHYS radiografía gamma *f*; ~ **ray** *n* ELECTRON, PART PHYS, PETROL, PHYS, RAD PHYS, WAVE PHYS rayo gamma *m*; ~~**ray absorption analysis** *n* RAD PHYS análisis de absorción de rayos gamma *m*, análisis de absorción gamma *m*; ~~**ray activation analysis** *n* PHYS, RAD PHYS análisis de activación gamma *m*; ~~**ray astronomy** *n* RAD PHYS, SPACE astronomía de rayos gamma *f*; ~~**ray beam** *n* PART PHYS, RAD PHYS haz de rayos gamma *m*; ~~**ray conversion** *n* RAD PHYS conversión gamma *f*; ~~**ray escape peak** *n* RAD PHYS pico de fugas de rayos gamma *m*; ~~**ray heating** *n* RAD PHYS calentamiento gamma *m*; ~~**ray log** *n* FUELLESS, GEOPHYS registro de rayos gamma *m*, PETR TECH gammagrafía *f*, perfil de rayos gamma *m*, registro de rayos gamma *m*; ~~**ray logging** *n* PETR TECH perfilaje de rayos gamma *m*; ~~**ray photon** *n* RAD PHYS fotón gamma *m*; ~~**ray quantum** *n* PART PHYS, RAD PHYS cuanto de rayos gamma *m*; ~~**ray spectrometer** *n* INSTR, RAD PHYS, WAVE PHYS espectrómetro de rayos gamma *m*; ~~**ray spectrum** *n* RAD PHYS espectro gamma *m*; ~~**ray survey** *n* NUCL, RAD PHYS medición de rayos gamma *f*; ~~**ray well logging** *n* PETR TECH gammagrafía de pozo *f*, registrado de rayos gamma *m*; ~ **strip** *n* CINEMAT franja gamma *f*

gammametric: ~ **ore assay** *n* NUCL ensayo gamamétrico de minerales *m*

gammexane *n* CHEM gamexano *m*

gamut *n* ACOUST escala musical *f*

gang[1]: ~ **capacitor** *n* ELEC, ELEC ENG condensador múltiple *m*, condensador tándem *m*; ~ **channel** *n* MECH ENG canal múltiple *m*; ~ **drill** *n* PROD perforadora múltiple *f*, taladradora múltiple *f*, taladro de cabezales múltiples *m*; ~ **machining** *n* PROD mecanización en serie *f*; ~ **piece** *n* MECH ENG *lathe* pieza múltiple *f*; ~ **press** *n* MECH ENG prensa de matrices múltiples *f*, prensa de punzones múltiples *f*; ~ **punch**

n PROD multiperforadora *f*; ~ **saw** *n* PROD sierra de hojas múltiples *f*; ~ **switch** *n* ELEC, ELEC ENG, PROD conmutador múltiple *m*, interruptor acoplado *m*; ~ **tool** *n* MECH ENG herramienta múltiple *f*; ~~**tuning capacitor** *n* ELEC ENG condensador de ajuste de grupo *m*; ~ **work** *n* PROD fabricación en serie *f*

gang[2] *vt* MECH ENG ensamblar herramientas, operar simultáneamente herramientas, PETR TECH operar simultáneamente herramientas, PRINT agrupar moldes para ser impresos a la vez

ganged: ~ **capacitors** *n pl* ELEC ENG condensadores acoplados *m pl*; ~ **circuit** *n* ELEC ENG circuito de sintonización simultánea *m*, circuito de mando único *m*, TV circuito de mando único *m*; ~ **separations** *n pl* PRINT separaciones múltiples *f pl*; ~ **tuning** *n* ELEC ENG sintonización con mando único *f*, sintonía en tándem *f*

ganging *n* ELEC, ELEC ENG acoplamiento mecánico *m*, agrupamiento en un solo control *m*

gangplank *n* WATER TRANSP plancha de paso entre buques *f*

gangue *n* GEOL ganga *f*; ~ **mineral** *n* COAL ganga *f*

gangway *n* COAL galería de extracción *f*, galería de transporte *f*, galería maestra *f*, socavón *m*, vía de circulación *f*, MINE galería maestra *f*, VEH fuelle de comunicación *m*, WATER TRANSP plancha de desembarco *f*, portalón *m*

gantry *n* CONST, RAIL, WATER, WATER TRANSP pórtico *m*; ~ **crane** *n* CONST, NUCL, RAIL, WATER TRANSP grúa pórtico *f*; ~ **with hoist** *n* NUCL grúa pórtico con mecanismo de izado *f*; ~ **lathe** *n* MECH ENG torno de bancada prismática *m*

Gantt: ~ **chart** *n* PROD gráfico de Gantt *m*

gap *n* AIR TRANSP espacio entre alas adyacentes *m*, COMP&DP intervalo *m*, separación *f*, CONST distancia entre raíces *f*, ELEC *magnetic circuits* abertura *f*, *relays* separación *f*, ELEC ENG *relays* separación *f*, *magnetic circuits* abertura *f*, GEOL hiato *m*, MECH separación *f*, distancia *f*, espacio intermedio *m*, huelgo *m*, hueco *m*, MECH ENG distancia *f*, espacio *m*, huelgo *m*, escotadura *f*, *magnetism* entrehierro *m*, NUCL hueco *m*, huelgo *m*, PHYS separación *f*, RAIL distancia entre raíces *f*, SPACE escotadura *f*, espacio entre alas adyacentes *m*, espacio interlobular *m*, interespacio *m*, intervalo *m*, separación *f*, TRANSP distancia *f*, intervalo *m*, TV intervalo *m*; ~ **bed** *n* MECH ENG *lathe* bancada de escote *f*, bancada escotada *f*, bancada partida *f*; ~ **bridge** *n* MECH ENG *lathe* puente *m*; ~ **depth** *n* ACOUST profundidad de entrehierro *f*, TV profundidad de intervalo *f*; ~ **detector** *n* TRANSP detector de separación *m*; ~ **effect** *n* TV efecto de intervalo *m*; ~ **gage** AmE, ~ **gauge** BrE *n* METR *diaphragm* calibrador de paso *m*, *of screw* galga para dimensiones exteriores *f*; ~ **lathe** *n* MECH ENG torno de puente *m*; ~ **length** *n* ACOUST anchura de entrehierro *f*, ELEC ENG longitud del intersticio *f*; ~ **loss** *n* ACOUST, OPT pérdida en el entrehierro *f*, TELECOM pérdida de separación *f*, TV pérdida de intervalo *f*; ~ **setting** *n* TV fijación de intervalo *f*; ~ **spanner** *n* MECH ENG llave inglesa de horquilla *f*; ~~**to-gap adjustment** *n* PRINT ajuste de espacio a espacio *m*; ~ **width** *n* TV ancho de intervalo *m*

gapped: ~ **core** *n* ELEC ENG centro del intersticio *m*

gapping: ~ **switch** *n* TV conmutador de intervalos *m*

garage: ~ **ventilating apparatus** *n* SAFE aparato ventilador de cochera *m*

garbage[1] *n* (*cf rubbish BrE*) COMP&DP acumulación de información parasítica *f*, información parásita *f*, NUCL basura *f*, PACK, PROD basura *f*, desechos *m pl*, desperdicios *m pl*, despojos *m pl*, residuos *m pl*, RECYCL basura *f*, desechos *m pl*, desperdicios *m pl*, despojos *m pl*, escombros *m pl*, residuos *m pl*, SAFE basura *f*; **~ bag** *n* AmE (*cf rubbish bag BrE*) PACK bolsa de basura *f*; **~ chute** *n* AmE (*cf rubbish chute BrE*) RECYCL colector de basura *m*, vertedero de basura *m*; **~ collection** *n* COMP&DP reagrupación de vacíos *f*, recuperación de datos *f*, recuperación de espacio *f*; **~ truck** *n* AmE (*cf dustbin lorry BrE*) RECYCL camión de la basura *m*, camión de recolección de basura *m*

garbage[2] **~-in/garbage-out** *phr* (*GIGO*) COMP&DP basura entra/basura sale

garboard *n* WATER TRANSP *shipbuilding* aparadura *f*; **~ strake** *n* WATER TRANSP *shipbuilding* traca de aparadura *f*

garden: **~ trowel** *n* AGRIC transplantador *m*

garments *n pl* TEXTIL vestiduras *f pl*

garnet *n* CONST, MINERAL granate *m*; **~ hinge** *n* CONST bisagra continua *f*

garnierite *n* MINERAL garnierita *f*

gas[1]: **~-cooled** *adj* GAS, REFRIG, THERMO enfriado con gas, refrigerado con gas; **~-filled** *adj* GAS, THERMO de atmósfera gaseosa, lleno de gas; **~-fired** *adj* GAS, HEAT ENG, PROD, THERMO alimentado por gas, calentado con gas; **~-flushed** *adj* PACK limpiado con una corriente de gas; **~-packed** *adj* FOOD envasado con gas; **~-proof** *adj* CHEM, CHEM TECH, GAS, MECH, MECH ENG, PROD, THERMO estanco a gases, hermético al gas, impermeable al gas, a prueba de gases, resistente a los gases

gas[2] *n* AmE AUTO nafta *f* (*AmL*), gasolina *f* (*Esp*), CHEM gas *m*, COAL grisú *m*, HEAT ENG gas *m*, MINE grisú *m*, P&R AmE gasolina *f* (*Esp*), nafta *f* (*AmL*), PETR TECH gas *m*, gasolina *f* (*Esp*), nafta *f* (*AmL*), PETROL nafta *f* (*AmL*), gas *m*, gasolina *f* (*Esp*), PHYS, REFRIG gas *m*, THERMO gas *m*, grisú *m*, gasolina *f* (*Esp*), nafta *f* (*AmL*), VEH AmE gasolina *f* (*Esp*), nafta *f* (*AmL*); **~ absorption** *n* GAS, PETR TECH absorción de gas *f*; **~-air mixture** *n* GAS, THERMO mezcla de aire y gas *f*; **~ alarm system** *n* MINE sistema avisador de desprendimiento de gases *m* (*AmL*), sistema de alarma contra gas *m* (*Esp*); **~ alert** *n* MILIT alerta de gases *f*; **~ analyser** *n* BrE GAS, PETR TECH analizador de gas *m*; **~ analysis** *n* GAS, PETR TECH análisis de gas *m*; **~ analyzer** *AmE see gas analyser BrE*; **~-and-oil-resistant hose** *n* AmE P&R manguera resistente a la gasolina y al aceite *f* (*Esp*), manguera resistente a la nafta y al aceite *f* (*AmL*); **~ balance** *n* GAS balance de gas *m*; **~ band** *n* GAS banda de gas *f*; **~ bearing** *n* MECH fuerza del gas *f*; **~ blowpipe** *n* PROD soplete a gas *m*; **~ boiler** *n* GAS, HEAT, THERMO caldera de gas *f*; **~ bottle** *n* GAS, NUCL, PROD, THERMO botella de gas a presión *f*, cilindro de gas a presión *m*, recipiente para gas a presión *m*; **~ burette** *n* LAB bureta de gas *f*; **~ burner** *n* GAS, HEAT ENG, PROD, THERMO mechero de gas *m*, quemador de gas *m*; **~ cap** *n* MINE aureola *f*, capa gasífera *f*, PETR TECH capa gasífera *f*, casquete de gas *m*, montera de gas *f*, PETROL cúpula gasífera *f*; **~ cap drive** *n* GAS, PETR TECH drenaje por expansión de gas *m*, empuje por montera de gas *m*; **~ carbon** *n* COAL carbón de retorta *m*; **~ carburizing** *n* GAS, THERMO carbocementación de gas *f*, cementación gaseosa *f*, cementación por gas *f*; **~ carrier** *n* WATER TRANSP buque tanque para el transporte de gas *m*, gasero *m*; **~ cavity** *n* NUCL hueco de gas *m*; **~ chromatograph** *n* CHEM, FOOD, GAS, LAB, THERMO cromatógrafo de gases *m*; **~ chromatography** *n* CHEM, FOOD, THERMO cromatografía de gases *f*, cromatografía gaseosa *f*; **~ circuit** *n* HEAT circuito de gas *m*; **~ circulation loop** *n* NUCL lazo de circulación de gas *m*; **~ cleaner** *n* GAS limpiador de gas *m*; **~ cleaning** *n* GAS limpieza de gas *f*; **~ cloud** *n* GAS nube de gas *f*; **~ coal** *n* COAL carbón de gas *m*; **~ cock** *n* GAS grifo de gas *m*, PROD grifo de gas *m*, válvula de gas *f*; **~ coke** *n* COAL cok de gas *m*; **~ completion unit** *n* GAS unidad de acabado de gas *f*; **~ compressor** *n* GAS, PROD compresor de gas *m*; **~ constant** *n* PHYS constante de los gases perfectos *f*; **~ consumption** *n* AmE (*cf petrol consumption BrE*) AUTO, VEH *engine* consumo de gasolina *m* (*Esp*), consumo de nafta *m* (*AmL*); **~ content** *n* CHEM, GAS, THERMO contenido gaseoso *m*; **~-cooled breeder reactor** *n* (*GCBR*) NUCL reactor reproductor refrigerado por gas *m*; **~-cooled nuclear power plant** *n* NUCL central nuclear con reactor refrigerado por gas *f*; **~ cooler** *n* GAS, REFRIG enfriador de gases *m*; **~ cutting** *n* PROD, THERMO corte por llama oxiacetilénica *m*, oxicorte *m*; **~ cylinder** *n* GAS, MECH, MECH ENG, NUCL, PROD, THERMO botella de gas comprimido *f*, cilindro de gas a presión *m*, depósito de gas a presión *m*; **~ detector** *n* CHEM, CHEM TECH grisuscopio *m*, grisuómetro *m*, GAS detector de gases *m*, detector de metano *m*, grisuscopio *m*, grisuómetro *m*, INSTR detector de gases *m*, grisuscopio *m*, grisuómetro *m*, LAB, MILIT detector de gases *m*, MINE detector de gases *m*, detector de metano *m*, gasoscopio *m*, grisuscopio *m* (*AmL*), grisuómetro *m* (*Esp*); **~ diode** *n* ELECTRON, GAS diodo de gas *m*, fanotrón *m*; **~ discharge** *n* ELECTRON, GAS, NUCL descarga de gas *f*; **~-discharge gap** *n* ELECTRON, GAS, NUCL intervalo de descarga gaseosa *m*; **~-discharge lamp** *n* ELEC lámpara de descarga luminosa *f*, lámpara fluorescente *f*, ELEC ENG lámpara fluorescente *f*, GAS lámpara de descarga luminosa *f*, lámpara fluorescente *f*, PHYS, RAD PHYS lámpara fluorescente *f*; **~ dissociation** *n* GAS disociación de gas *f*; **~ drive** *n* GAS desplazamiento de petróleo por gas *m*, empuje gasífero *m*, empuje por gas en solución *m*; **~-drying plant** *n* GAS instalación de secado de gas *f*, planta de secado de gas *f*; **~ dump** *n* AmE MILIT depósito provisional de gasolina *m* (*Esp*), depósito provisional de nafta *m* (*AmL*); **~ dynamic laser** *n* ELECTRON, OPT láser dinámico de gas *m*; **~ embolism** *n* OCEAN embolia *f*; **~ engine** *n* AUTO motor de gasolina *m* (*Esp*), motor de nafta *m* (*AmL*), GAS motor de gas *m*, MECH ENG motor de gas *m*, motor de combustión *m*, PROD máquina de gas *f*, *of blast-furnace* motor de gas *m*, THERMO motor de nafta *m* (*AmL*), máquina de gas *f*, motor de gasolina *m* (*Esp*), motor de gas *m*, VEH motor de nafta *m* (*AmL*), motor de gasolina *m* (*Esp*), WATER TRANSP motor de gasolina *m* (*Esp*), motor de nafta *m* (*AmL*); **~-engine vehicle** *n* AmE AUTO, POLL, VEH vehículo con motor de gasolina *m* (*Esp*), vehículo con motor de nafta *m* (*AmL*); **~-enriching value** *n* GAS, THERMO poder gasificante *m*; ~ **enrichment** *n* GAS, THERMO enriquecimiento gaseoso *m*; ~ **equation** *n* GAS, MECH *boat fitting* ecuación de gas *f*; ~ **exploder** *n* GAS, PETROL detonante de gas *m*; ~ **explosion** *n* COAL, PETR TECH explosión de gas *f*; ~ **expulsion** *n* OCEAN expulsión de gas *f*; ~ **extraction** *n* OCEAN extracción de gas *f*;

▪ **f** ~ **factor** *n* GAS factor de gas *m*; ~ **fading** *n* COLOUR desteñido por gases *m*; ~ **feeder** *n* MINE depósito de grisú *m*; ~ **field** *n* GAS campo de gas *m*, yacimiento de gas *m*, yacimiento gasífero *m*, PETR TECH campo de gas *m*, campo de petróleo con presión de gas *m*, THERMO campo de petróleo con presión de gas *m*; ~**-filled cable** *n* ELEC, ELEC ENG, GAS cable lleno de gas *m*; ~**-filled rectifier** *n* ELEC, ELEC ENG, GAS rectificador de gas *m*; ~**-filled rectifier diode** *n* ELEC, ELEC ENG diodo rectificador de gas *m*; ~**-filled relay** *n* ELEC, ELEC ENG, ELECTRON, GAS relé de gas *m*, relé lleno de gas *m*; ~**-filled switching tube** *n* ELEC, ELECTRON, GAS tubo de conmutación de gas *m*, tubo de conmutación lleno de gas *m*; ~**-filled tube** *n* ELEC, ELECTRON, GAS tubo lleno de gas *m*; ~**-filled workings** *n* MINE fábrica de gas *f*; ~ **filter** *n* AmE AUTO, VEH filtro de gasolina *m* (*Esp*), filtro de nafta *m* (*AmL*); ~ **fire** *n* GAS, HEAT, THERMO alimentación por gas *f*, caldeo con gas *m*, radiador de gas *m*; ~**-fired furnace** *n* GAS, HEAT, HEAT ENG horno caldeado con gas *m*, horno de gas *m*, PROD horno de gas *m*, THERMO horno caldeado con gas *m*, horno de gas *m*; ~**-fired heater** *n* GAS, HEAT, MECH ENG, THERMO calentador a gas *m*; ~**-fired water heater** *n* GAS, HEAT, HYDROL, MECH ENG, THERMO calentador de agua a gas *m*, termo de agua por gas *m*; ~ **fissure** *n* MINE grieta gasífera *f*; ~ **fitter** *n* GAS, PROD *person* gasista *m*, instalador de gas *m*; ~ **fitting** *n* GAS, PROD accesorio para gas *m*, aparato de distribución de gas *m*; ~ **flare** *n* GAS, THERMO antorcha para gases *f*; ~ **flow** *n* FLUID, GAS flujo de gas *m*, flujo gaseoso *m*; ~ **flue** *n* GAS, HEAT, PROD humero de gas *m*; ~ **focusing** *n* ELECTRON concentración gaseosa *f*; ~ **formation volume factor** *n* PETROL factor de volumen de la formación de gas *m*; ~**-fueled bus** *n* AmE (*cf petrol-fuelled bus BrE*) AUTO, VEH autobús de gasolina *m* (*Esp*), autobús de nafta *m* (*AmL*); ~**-fueled car** *n* AmE (*cf petrol-fuelled car BrE*) AUTO coche de gasolina *m* (*Esp*), coche de nafta *m* (*AmL*); ~ **furnace** *n* GAS, HEAT, HEAT ENG, PROD, THERMO horno de gas *m*;

▪ **g** ~ **generator** *n* GAS, PROD, SPACE, THERMO gasógeno *m*, generador de gas *m*, generador de gases de combustión *m*, turbina de combustión *f*, turbina de gases *f*; ~ **grid** *n* GAS, PETR TECH, THERMO red de canalización de gas *f*, red de distribución de gas *f*, red de gasoductos *f*;

▪ **h** ~ **heating** *n* GAS, HEAT, HEAT ENG, PROD, THERMO calefacción a gas *f*; ~**-heating system** *n* GAS, HEAT ENG, THERMO sistema de calefacción a gas *m*; ~ **holder** *n* CHEM, CHEM TECH gasómetro *m*, GAS depósito de gas *m*, gasómetro *m*, recipiente de gas *m*, INSTR gasómetro *m*, PROD, THERMO depósito de gas *m*, gasómetro *m*, recipiente de gas *m*; ~ **hose** *n* AmE (*cf petrol hose BrE*) AUTO, P&R, VEH manguera de gasolina *f* (*Esp*), manguera de nafta *f* (*AmL*), tubo flexible de gasolina *m* (*Esp*), tubo flexible de nafta *m* (*AmL*); ~ **hydrocarbon** *n* CHEM, GAS hidrocarburo gaseoso *m*;

▪ **i** ~ **in place** *n* GAS, PETROL gas in situ *m*; ~ **injection** *n* GAS, PETR TECH inyección de gas *f*; ~**-insulated line** *n* ELEC *supply network* línea con aislación de gas *f*;

▪ **j** ~ **jet** *n* GAS, PROD chorro de gases *m*;

▪ **k** ~ **kinetics** *n* GAS, THERMO cinética de gases *f*;

▪ **l** ~ **laser** *n* ELECTRON, GAS, OPT, RAD PHYS láser de gas *m*; ~ **leak** *n* GAS, THERMO escape de gas *m*, fuga de gas *f*; ~**-leak detector** *n* GAS, SAFE, THERMO detector de fuga de gas *m*; ~ **leaking** *n* CHEM, CHEM TECH, GAS desprendimiento de gas *m*; ~ **lift** *n* PETR TECH recuperación de crudo por inyección de gas *f*; ~ **lighter** *n* GAS, HEAT ENG, PROD encendedor de gas *m*; ~ **liquid chromatography** *n* CHEM, GAS, THERMO cromatografía de gases en fase líquida *f*; ~ **liquid partition chromatography** *n* CHEM, GAS, THERMO cromatografía de gases en fase líquida *f*; ~**-loaded accumulator** *n* GAS, MECH ENG acumulador a gas *m*; ~ **lock** *n* REFRIG cierre de vapor *m*; ~ **log** *n* PETROL perfil de gas *m*; ~**-lubricated bearing** *n* MECH ENG, NUCL cojinete lubricado por gas *m*;

▪ **m** ~ **machine** *n* PROD carburador *m*; ~ **main** *n* GAS, PROD, THERMO canalización de gas *f*, cañería principal de gas *f*; ~**-making apparatus** *n* GAS, PROD aparato gasífero *m*; ~ **mantle** *n* THERMO manguito incandescente para gas *m*; ~ **maser** *n* ELECTRON, GAS emisor de gas *m*; ~ **mask** *n* MILIT careta antigás *f*, máscara antigás *f*; ~ **meter** *n* GAS medidor de gas *m*, LAB contador de gas *m*, medidor de gas *m*, PROD contador de gas *m*, THERMO contador de gas *m*, medidor de gas *m*; ~ **mixture** *n* AmE AUTO mezcla de gasolina *f*, mezcla de nafta *f* (*AmL*), VEH mezcla de gasolina *f* (*Esp*), mezcla de nafta *f* (*AmL*); ~ **motor** *n* PROD motor de gas industrial *m*; ~ **multiplication factor** *n* ELECTRON factor de multiplicación de gas *m*;

▪ **n** ~ **nitriding** *n* GAS, THERMO nitruración gaseosa *f*; ~ **noise** *n* ELECTRON ruido de gas *m*;

▪ **o** ~ **oil** *n* AUTO gas-oil *m*, PETR TECH, PETROL gas-oil *m*, gasoil para motores marinos *m*, gasóleo *m*, THERMO gas-oil *m*, gasóleo *m*, gasoil para motores marinos *m*, TRANSP, VEH gas-oil *m*; ~**-oil contact** *n* AmE (*petrol-oil contact BrE*) PETR TECH, PETROL contacto gas-petróleo *m*; ~**-oil mixture** *n* AmE (*cf petrol-oil mixture BrE*) AUTO, VEH mezcla aceite-gasolina *f* (*Esp*), mezcla aceite-nafta *f* (*AmL*), mezcla de aceite y gasolina *f* (*Esp*), mezcla de aceite y nafta *f* (*AmL*); ~**-only phase** *n* THERMO fase de sólo gas *f*; ~ **originally in place** *n* PETROL gas originariamente in situ *m*; ~ **outlet** *n* TRANSP salida de gases *f*;

▪ **p** ~ **pedal** *n* AmE (*cf accelerator pedal BrE*) AUTO, VEH acelerador *m*; ~ **permeability** *n* GAS, P&R, THERMO permeabilidad del gas *f*; ~ **phototube** *n* ELECTRON, INSTR fototubo de gas *m*; ~ **pipe** *n* CONST, GAS gasoducto *m*, tubo de gas *m*, MECH ENG gasoducto *m*, PETR TECH, PETROL canalización de gas *f*, gasoducto *m*, THERMO, TRANSP gasoducto *m*, tubo de gas *m*; ~ **pipeline** *n* CONST, GAS canalización de gas *f*, gasoducto *m*, MECH ENG gasoducto *m*, PETR TECH, PETROL, THERMO canalización de gas *f*, gasoducto *m*, TRANSP gasoducto *m*; ~ **pliers** *n pl* CONST pinzas de gasista *f pl*; ~ **pocket** *n* GAS bolsón de gas *m*; ~ **poker** *n* MECH ENG vara de gas *f*; ~ **precipitate** *n* METALL precipitado de gas *m*; ~ **pressure** *n* GAS, HEAT, PHYS, THERMO presión de gas *f*; ~**-pressure reducing valve** *n* GAS, HEAT, THERMO decompresor de gas *m*, válvula reductora de presión de gas *f*; **~-pressure regulator** *n* GAS, HEAT, PHYS, THERMO regulador de la presión del gas *m*; **~ producer** *n* PROD gasógeno *m*; **~ pump** *n* AmE (*cf petrol pump BrE*) AIR TRANSP, AUTO, MECH, MECH ENG, SPACE, VEH, WATER TRANSP bomba de alimentación *f*, bomba de combustible *f*, bomba de gasolina *f* (*Esp*), bomba de nafta *f* (*AmL*); **~ purger** *n* REFRIG purgador de aire *m*, purgador de gases no condensables *m*; **~ purging** *n* REFRIG purga de gas *f*, purgado del gas *m*; **~ purifier** *n* GAS, PROD depurador de gas *m*, lavador de gas *m*;

~ q **~ quench** *n* GAS, HEAT apagado de gas *m*, corte del suministro de gas *m*;

~ r **~ ratio** *n* ELECTRON porcentaje de gas *m*; **~ refrigerator** *n* GAS, MECH ENG, REFRIG, THERMO frigorífico a gas *m*, refrigerador a gas *m*; **~ resistance** *n* AmE P&R resistencia a la gasolina *f* (*Esp*), resistencia a la nafta *f* (*AmL*); **~ retort** *n* GAS, PROD retorta de gas *f*; **~ return safety device** *n* SAFE aditamento para retorno seguro de gases *m*; **~ ring** *n* GAS quemador de corona *m*;

~ s **~ saturation** *n* PETROL saturación de gas *f*; **~ scrubber** *n* CHEM TECH, NUCL depurador de gases *m*; **~-scrubbing plant** *n* CHEM TECH, GAS lavador de gases *m*; **~-shielded metal arc welding** *n* CONST soldadura con arco metálico sumergido en gas inerte *f*; **~ show** *n* GAS indicio de gas *m*, PETR TECH indicio de gas *m*, muestra de gas *f*; **~ spring** *n* GAS fuente de gas *f*, MECH ENG fuente de gas *f*, mofeta *f*; **~ station** *n* AmE (*cf petrol station BrE*) AUTO estación de gasolina *f* (*Esp*), estación de nafta *f* (*AmL*), estación de servicio *f*, gasolinera *f*, TRANSP gasolinera *f*, VEH estación de gasolina *f* (*Esp*), estación de nafta *f* (*AmL*), estación de servicio *f*, gasolinera *f*; **~ stock** *n* GAS, PROD hilera de gas *f*; **~ storage** *n* FOOD, GAS, PROD almacenamiento de gas *m*; **~ stripper** *n* GAS, NUCL extractor de gas *m*;

~ t **~ tank** *n* AUTO depósito de gasolina *m* (*Esp*), depósito de nafta *m* (*AmL*), CHEM, CHEM TECH gasómetro *m*, GAS gasómetro *m*, depósito de gas *m*, INSTR gasómetro *m*, PROD depósito de gas *m*, gasómetro *m*, THERMO gasómetro *m*, VEH depósito de gasolina *m* (*Esp*), depósito de nafta *m* (*AmL*); **~ tank cap** *n* AmE AUTO, VEH tapón del depósito de gasolina *m* (*Esp*), tapón del depósito de nafta *m* (*AmL*); **~ tap** *n* GAS, PROD terraja para tubos de gas *f*, *cock* grifo de gas *m*; **~ tar** *n* COAL alquitrán de gas *m*, alquitrán de hulla *m*; **~ tetrode** *n* ELECTRON tetrodo de gas *m*; **~ thermometer** *n* GAS, INSTR termómetro de dilatación de gases *m*, termómetro de gas *m*, PHYS termómetro de gas *m*, REFRIG termómetro de dilatación de gases *m*; **~ thread** *n* GAS, MECH ENG, PROD rosca de gas *f*, rosca de tubería de gas *f*, rosca fina de gas *f*; **~-thread pipe stock** *n* GAS, MECH ENG, PROD hilera para tubos de rosca de gas *f*; **~-to-oil ratio** *n* (*GOR*) PETR TECH relación gas-petróleo *f* (*GOR*); **~ transmission line** *n* GAS línea de transmisión de gas *f*; **~ triode** *n* ELECTRON triodo de gas *m*; **~ tube** *n* ELECTRON, GAS tubo de gas *m*; **~ turbine** *n* AIR TRANSP, GAS, MECH, PROD, THERMO, WATER TRANSP *engine* turbina de combustión interna *f*, turbina de gas *f*; **~-turbine bus** *n* TRANSP autobús con turbina de combustión interna *m*; **~-turbine engine** *n* AIR TRANSP motor de turbina a gas *m*; **~-turbine power station** *n* ELEC *supply*, GAS central de energía de turbina de combustión *f*, central

eléctrica de turbina de gas *f*; **~-turbine ship** *n* WATER TRANSP buque propulsado por turbina de gas *m*;

~ v **~ valve** *n* PROD *blast furnace* válvula de gas *f*; **~ vent** *n* GAS línea de descarga de gases *f*, MINE respiradero *m* (*AmL*), válvula de gas *f* (*Esp*), NUCL línea de descarga de gases *f*;

~ w **~-water contact** *n* PETROL contacto gas-agua *m*; **~ water heater** *n* GAS, HEAT, THERMO calentador de agua por medio de gas *m*; **~-welded system** *n* MECH, MECH ENG sistema de soldadura oxiacetilénica *m*, sistema soldado a gas *m*; **~ welding** *n* GAS, MECH, MECH ENG, THERMO soldadura oxiacetilénica *f*, soldadura por llama de gas *f* (*AmL*), soldeo oxiacetilénico *m*, soldeo por llama de gas *m* (*Esp*); **~ well** *n* PETROL pozo gasífero *m*; **~ works** *n* GAS, HEAT ENG, PROD factoría de gas industrial *f* (*AmL*), fábrica de gas *f* (*Esp*)

gaseous[1] *adj* CHEM gaseoso, GAS gaseoso, grisuoso, MINE gaseoso (*Esp*), grisuoso, PHYS gaseoso, THERMO gaseoso (*Esp*), grisuoso

gaseous[2]: **~-acid air pollution index** *n* SAFE índice de contaminación del aire por ácidos en estado gaseoso *m*; **~ active medium** *n* ELECTRON medio activo gaseoso *m*; **~ core reactor** *n* NUCL reactor de núcleo gaseoso *m*; **~ effluent** *n* GAS efluente gaseoso *m*; **~ fuel** *n* PETR TECH combustible gaseoso *m*; **~ phase** *n* THERMO fase gaseosa *f*; **~ state** *n* GAS estado gaseoso *m*; **~ vein** *n* GAS filón gaseoso *m*, vena gaseosa *f*, veta gaseosa *f*

gases: **~ and fumes** *n pl* AIR TRANSP, GAS, SAFE gases y humos *m pl*

gash *n* MECH ENG acanaladura *f*, desgarro *m*, entalladura *f*, rotura *f*

gasification *n* GEN gasificación *f*

gasify *vt* GEN gasificar

gasket *n* AUTO empaquetadura *f*, junta *f*, MECH burlete *m*, empaquetadura metálica *f*, junta *f*, junta obturadora *f*, obturador *m*, MECH ENG junta de estanqueidad *f*, junta desbloqueadora *f*, junta elástica *f*, junta ensanchadora *f*, junta obturadora *f*, PROD junta de estanqueidad *f*, trenza de cáñamo *f*, junta obturadora *f*, VEH junta *f*, WATER TRANSP *for furling sails* empaquetadura *f*, frisa *f*, tomador *m*; **~ paper** *n* PAPER papel para juntas *m*

gasogene *n* PROD gasógeno *m*

gasoline *n* AmE (*cf petrol BrE*) AUTO, P&R, PETR TECH, PETROL, THERMO, VEH gasolina *f* (*Esp*), nafta *f* (*AmL*); **~-and-oil-resistant hose** *n* AmE (*cf petrol-and-oil-resistant hose BrE*) P&R manguera resistente a la gasolina y al aceite *f* (*Esp*), manguera resistente a la nafta y al aceite *f* (*AmL*); **~ consumption** *n* AmE (*cf petrol consumption BrE*) AUTO, VEH consumo de gasolina *m* (*Esp*), consumo de nafta *m* (*AmL*); **~ dump** *n* AmE (*cf petrol dump BrE*) MILIT depósito provisional de gasolina *m* (*Esp*), depósito provisional de nafta *m* (*AmL*); **~ engine** *n* AmE (*cf petrol engine BrE*) AUTO, THERMO, VEH, WATER TRANSP motor de gasolina *m* (*Esp*), motor de nafta *m* (*AmL*); **~-engine vehicle** *n* AmE (*cf petrol-engine vehicle BrE*) AUTO, POLL, VEH vehículo con motor de gasolina *m* (*Esp*), vehículo con motor de nafta *m* (*AmL*); **~ filter** *n* AmE (*cf petrol filter BrE*) AUTO, VEH filtro de gasolina *m* (*Esp*), filtro de nafta *m* (*AmL*); **~ hose** *n* AmE (*cf petrol hose BrE*) AUTO, P&R, VEH manguera de gasolina *f* (*Esp*), manguera de nafta *f* (*AmL*), tubo flexible de gasolina *m* (*Esp*), tubo flexible de nafta *m* (*AmL*); ~ **mixture** *n* *AmE* (*cf petrol mixture BrE*) AUTO mezcla de gasolina *f*, mezcla de nafta *f* (*AmL*), VEH mezcla de gasolina *f* (*Esp*), mezcla de nafta *f* (*AmL*); **~-oil contact** *n* *AmE* (*cf petrol-oil contact BrE*) PETR TECH, PETROL contacto gas-petróleo *m*; **~-oil mixture** *n* *AmE* (*cf petrol-oil mixture BrE*) AUTO, VEH mezcla aceite-gasolina *f* (*Esp*), mezcla aceite-nafta *f* (*AmL*), mezcla de aceite y gasolina *f* (*Esp*), mezcla de aceite y nafta *f* (*AmL*); ~ **pump** *n* *AmE* (*cf petrol pump* (*BrE*) AIR TRANSP, AUTO, MECH, MECH ENG, SPACE, VEH, WATER TRANSP bomba de alimentación *f*, bomba de combustible *f*, bomba de gasolina *f* (*Esp*), bomba de nafta *f* (*AmL*); ~ **resistance** *n* *AmE* (*cf petrol resistance* (*BrE*) P&R resistencia a la gasolina *f* (*Esp*), resistencia a la nafta *f* (*AmL*); ~ **station** *n* *AmE* (*cf petrol station* (*BrE*) AUTO estación de gasolina *f* (*Esp*), estación de nafta *f* (*AmL*), estación de servicio *f*, gasolinera *f*, TRANSP gasolinera *f*, VEH estación de gasolina *f* (*Esp*), estación de nafta *f* (*AmL*), estación de servicio *f*, gasolinera *f*; ~ **tank** *n* *AmE* (*cf petrol tank* (*BrE*) AUTO, VEH depósito de gasolina *m* (*Esp*), depósito de nafta *m* (*AmL*); ~ **tank cap** *n* *AmE* (*cf petrol tank cap BrE*) AUTO, VEH tapón del depósito de gasolina *m* (*Esp*), tapón del depósito de nafta *m* (*AmL*)

gasometer *n* CHEM, CHEM TECH, GAS, INSTR gasoscopio *m*, gasómetro *m*, grisuscopio *m*, grisuómetro *m*, MINE gasoscopio *m*, grisuscopio *m* (*AmL*), grisuómetro *m* (*Esp*), PROD, THERMO gasómetro *m*

gasometric *adj* CHEM, CHEM TECH, GAS, PROD, THERMO gasométrico

gasometry *n* CHEM, CHEM TECH, GAS, PROD, THERMO gasometría *f*

gassed: ~ **yarn** *n* TEXTIL hilo gaseado *m*

gassing *n* CHEM absorción de gas *f*, tratamiento con gas *m*

gassy *adj* CHEM gaseoso, GAS gaseoso, grisuoso, MINE gaseoso (*Esp*), grisuoso, PHYS gaseoso, THERMO espumoso, gaseoso (*Esp*), grisuoso, lleno de gases

gastight *adj* CHEM, CHEM TECH, GAS, MECH, MECH ENG, PROD, THERMO estanco a gases, hermético al gas, impermeable al gas, a prueba de gases, resistente a los gases

gastropod *n* AGRIC, GEOL gasterópodo *m*

gate[1] *n* AGRIC *irrigation* compuerta *f*, CINEMAT ventanilla *f*, COMP&DP puerta *f*, CONST compuerta *f*, entrada *f*, puerta *f*, ELEC ENG, ELECTRON puerta *f*, HYDRAUL álabe giratorio *m*, HYDROL *mass* compuerta *f*, MECH álabe giratorio *m*, P&R orificio para inyectar *m*, PHYS compuerta *f*, PROD entrada *f*, metal que queda en el bebedero *m*, puerta *f*, barrera *f*, compuerta *f*, válvula de compuerta *f*, alza *f*, VEH placa guía *f*, WATER compuerta *f*, puerta *f*; ~ **accentuator** *n* MECH ENG acentuador de bebedero *m*, desbloqueador de bebedero *m*, ensanchador de bebedero *m*; ~ **amplifier** *n* PROD amplificador de desconexión periódica *m*; ~ **array** *n* COMP&DP arreglo de puerta *m*, matriz de puertas *f*, ELECTRON conjunto de puertas *m*, TELECOM array puertas *m*, arreglo de puerta *m*; ~ **array chip** *n* ELECTRON conjunto de puertas en un chip *m*; ~ **bias** *n* ELEC ENG polarización de la puerta *f*; ~ **chamber** *n* HYDROL, WATER *of a lock* cámara de puertas *f*; ~ **contact** *n* ELEC ENG contacto de puerta *m*; ~ **cutter** *n* MECH ENG cortador de esclusa *m*, interruptor de esclusa *m*, interruptor de puerta *m*; ~ **delay** *n* ELECTRON retardo de la señal a

través de la puerta *m*, retardo de respuesta de la puerta *m*; ~ **density** *n* ELECTRON densidad de paso *f*; ~ **dielectric** *n* ELEC ENG dieléctrico de puerta *m*; **~-drive board** *n* PROD tablero de gobierno de puertas *m*; **~-drive signal** *n* ELECTRON señal de mando de puerta *f*; **~-driving board** *n* PROD tablero de gobierno de puertas *m*; ~ **end box** *n* MINE cuadro de tajo *m*; ~ **gear** *n* HYDRAUL mecanismo de compuerta *m*; ~ **hook** *n* CONST pasador *m*; ~ **latch** *n* CONST candado de la puerta *m*, pestillo de la puerta *m*; ~ **leakage current** *n* ELEC ENG corriente de pérdida en puerta *f*; ~ **pin** *n* PROD *founding* modelo del bebedero *m*; ~ **shutter** *n* PROD *founding* esclusa *f*; ~ **sill** *n* WATER umbral de compuerta *m*; ~ **spool** *n* PROD *founding* montabebedero *m*; ~ **stem** *n* HYDRAUL vástago de válvula de compuerta *m*; ~ **stick** *n* PROD *founding* canilla de bebedero *f*; ~ **switch** *n* ELEC interruptor controlado por compuerta *m*; **~-to-cathode resistor** *n* ELEC ENG resistencia puerta-cátodo *f*; **~-to-drain capacitance** *n* ELEC ENG capacitancia puerta a drenaje *f*; **~-to-source capacitance** *n* ELEC ENG capacitancia puerta a generador *f*; **~-to-source voltage** *n* ELEC ENG tensión puerta a generador *f*; **~-to-substrate capacitance** *n* ELEC ENG capacitancia puerta a substrato *f*; ~ **valve** *n* HYDRAUL, MECH ENG válvula de compuerta *f*, válvula de corredera *f*, válvula de esclusa *f*, válvula de paso directo *f*; ~ **voltage** *n* ELEC ENG tensión de puerta *f*

gate[2] *vt* HYDRAUL mover las compuertas

gated[1]: ~ **off** *adj* PROD desincronizado; ~ **on** *adj* PROD sincronizado

gated[2]: ~ **beam tube** *n* TV tubo de haz periódico *m*; ~ **diode** *n* ELECTRON diodo con desbloqueo *m*; ~ **flip-flop** *n* ELECTRON circuito basculador de bloqueo *m*, circuito biestable de bloqueo *m*; ~ **signal** *n* ELECTRON señal de interrupción *f*

gatepost *n* CONST poste de la entrada *m*

gateway *n* COMP&DP pasarela *f*, portilla *f*, sistema de comunicaciones entre redes *m*, PROD carretera de acceso *f*, centro de tránsito internacional *m*, galería de arrastre *f* (*AmL*), galería de transporte *f*, procesador de comunicaciones inter-redes *m*, TELECOM acceso *m*; ~ **computer** *n* COMP&DP computador de portilla *m* (*AmL*), computador pasarela *m* (*AmL*), computador puente entre redes *m* (*AmL*), computadora de portilla *f* (*AmL*), computadora pasarela *f* (*AmL*), computadora puente entre redes *f* (*AmL*), ordenador de portilla *m* (*Esp*), ordenador pasarela *m* (*Esp*), ordenador puente entre redes *m* (*Esp*); ~ **network element** *n* TELECOM elemento de acceso a la red *m*

gather[1]: ~ **write** *n* COMP&DP escritura agrupada *f*

gather[2] *vt* C&G recoger, TEXTIL fruncir

gather[3]: ~ **way** *vi* WATER TRANSP *ship* empezar a tomar salida, tomar salida

gathered *adj* TEXTIL fruncido

gatherer *n* PRINT alzadora *f*

gathering *n* C&G acumulación *f*, concentración *f*, PRINT alzado *m*, TEXTIL frunce *m*, fruncido *m*; ~ **bubble** *n* C&G vela *f*; ~ **cylinder** *n* PRINT cilindro alzador *m*; ~ **end** *n* C&G cabeza de la caña *f*; ~ **hole** *n* C&G boca del horno *m*; ~ **iron** *n* C&G caña *f*; ~ **line** *n* HYDRAUL conducto de llegada *m*; ~ **table** *n* PRINT mesa para el alzado *f*; ~ **temperature** *n* C&G temperatura del vidrio *f*

gating *n* COMP&DP agitación *f*, conmutación *f*, puerta *f*,

ELECTRON cierre *m*, interrupción *f*, HYDRAUL movimiento de las compuertas *m*, TV supresión del haz *f*; ~ **pulse** *n* ELECTRON impulso de desconexión *m*, TV pulso de desconexión *m*; ~ **signal** *n* ELECTRON señal de interrupción *f*; ~ **transistor** *n* ELECTRON transistor selector *m*

GATT *abbr* (*General Agreement on Tariffs and Trade*) AGRIC GATT (*Acuerdo General sobre Aranceles y Comercio Aduaneros*)

gauge[1] *n BrE* CINEMAT paso *m*, COAL calibrador *m*, condensador *m*, separador *m*, CONST ancho de vía *m* (*Esp*), trocha de vía *f* (*AmL*), ELEC *measurement, manufacture* calibre *m*, medida *f*, INSTR calibrador *m*, calibre *m*, dispositivo de medida *m*, galga *f*, indicador *m*, instrumento *m*, medidor *m*, plantilla *f*, LAB calibrador *m*, calibre *m*, dispositivo de medida *m*, indicador *m*, medidor *m*, plantilla *f*, galga *f*, MECH plantilla *f*, calibrador *m*, indicador *m*, medidor *m*, calibre *m*, MECH ENG medidor *m*, calibre *m*, dispositivo de medida *m*, calibrador *m*, galga *f*, plantilla *f*, verificador *m*, METR *instrument* calibrado *m*, calibrador *m*, PROD calibrador *m*, galga *f*, calibre *m*, QUALITY *tools* calibrador *m*, *wire* calibre *m*, RAIL *fixed equipment* gálibo de carga *m*, ancho de vía *m*, TEXTIL, VEH galga *f*, calibre *m*; ~ **bar** *n BrE* CONST gálibo *m*, *rail* barra de calibrado *f*; ~ **block** *n BrE* MECH, METR bloque calibrador *m*; ~ **brick** *n BrE* CONST ladrillo aplantillado *m*; ~ **clearance** *n BrE* RAIL holgura del gálibo *f*; ~ **cock** *n BrE* WATER grifo de prueba *m*, llave de prueba *f*; ~ **door** *n BrE* MINE puerta reguladora interior de la ventilación *f*; ~ **glass** *n BrE* C&G tubo medidor *m*, PETR TECH vidrio de calibrar *m*, PROD indicador del nivel de agua *m*, tubo de nivel *m*, tubo del nivel de agua *m*, REFRIG indicador de nivel visible *m*; ~ **invariance** *n BrE* PHYS invarianza del calibre *f*; ~ **isolating valve** *n BrE* PROD válvula de aislamiento del indicador *f*; ~ **number** *n BrE* PROD *wire* número de calibre *m*, título de calibre *m*; ~ **plane** *n BrE* MECH ENG *of assembly* plano de verificación *m*; ~ **pressure** *n BrE* REFRIG presión manométrica *f*; ~ **stand** *n BrE* METR equipo calibrador *m*; ~ **widening** *n BrE* RAIL ensanchamiento de la vía *m*

gauge[2] *vt BrE* GEN aforar, PROD graduar, cubicar, tarar, *metal plate, iron wire* calibrar, TEXTIL calibrar

gauged: ~ **orifice** *n BrE* PETR TECH orificio calibrado *m*; ~ **restriction** *n BrE* PETR TECH restricción calibrada *f*, restricción dosificada *f*

gauging *n BrE* HYDRAUL aforo *m*, MECH ENG calibración *f*, calibrado *m*, medición *f*, verificación *f*, METR calibrado *m*, calibración *f*, *of measuring instrument* medición *f*, PETR TECH control *m*, control de la producción *m*, comprobación *f*, medición *f*, verificación *f*, PROD aforo *m*, calibración *f*, QUALITY estimación de las reservas de petróleo *f*, TELECOM aforo *m*, WATER calibración *f*, aforo *m*; ~ **plate** *n BrE* PROD chapa de calibrar *f*, placa de galga *f*; ~ **station** *n BrE* WATER estación de aforo *f*, estación fluviométrica *f*; ~ **tank** *n BrE* PETR TECH tanque de medición *m*

gault *n* CONST, GEOL terreno arcilloso duro *m*

Gault: ~ **clay** *n* C&G, CONST, GEOM arcilla dura *f*

gauss *n* ELEC *unit* gausio *m*, gauss *m*, GEOL gausio *m*

Gaussian[1] *adj* ACOUST, COMP&DP, OPT, PHYS, TELECOM, TV de Gauss, gaussiano

Gaussian[2]: ~ **beam** *n* OPT, TELECOM haz gaussiano *m*; ~ **circuit** *n* TV circuito gaussiano *m*; ~ **curvature** *n* GEOM curvatura de Gauss *f*, curvatura total *f*; ~ **curve** *n* GEOM curva de Gauss *f*; ~ **distribution** *n* COMP&DP, MATH, PHYS distribución de Gauss *f*, distribución gaussiana *f*; ~**-filtered minimum shift keying** *n* (*GMSK*) TELECOM codificación por mínimo desplazamiento de fase por filtrado gaussiano *f*; ~ **noise** *n* ACOUST, COMP&DP, ELECTRON, TELECOM ruido gaussiano *m*; ~ **pulse** *n* COMP&DP, ELECTRON, TELECOM impulso gaussiano *m*; ~ **quadrature** *n* COMP&DP cuadratura gaussiana *f*

gaussmeter *n* ELEC, INSTR gausiómetro *m*

Gauss's: ~ **law** *n* PHYS ley de Gauss *f*; ~ **theorem** *n* ELEC, PHYS teorema de Gauss *m*

gauze *n* PROD tamiz *m*, tela metálica *f*; ~ **strainer** *n* PROD tamiz metálico *m*

Gay-Lussac's: ~ **law** *n* PHYS ley de Gay-Lussac *f*

gaylussite *n* MINERAL gaylussita *f*, natrocalcita *f*

gazogene *n* PROD gasógeno *m*

GCBR *abbr* (*gas-cooled breeder reactor*) NUCL reactor reproductor refrigerado por gas *m*

G-clamp *n* MECH ENG prensa de encolar *f*, prensa de tornillo *f*

GCR *abbr* (*group code recording*) COMP&DP registro de código agrupado *m*

G-cramp *n* MECH ENG prensa de mano *f*

Gd *abbr* (*gadolinium*) CHEM Gd (*gadolinio*)

Ge *abbr* (*germanium*) CHEM, ELEC ENG, METALL Ge (*germanio*)

gear[1]: **out of** ~ *adj* MECH ENG desembragado

gear[2] *n* MECH engranaje *m*, engrane *m*, mecanismo *m*, MECH ENG multiplicación *f*, piñón *m*, rueda dentada *f*, engranaje *m*, desmultiplicación *f*, *appliance, mechanism* velocidad *f*, mecanismo *m*, artefacto *m*, dispositivo *m*, equipo *m*, WATER TRANSP *engine* engranaje *m*; ~ **assembly** *n* MECH ENG equipo de engranajes *m*, mecanismo de engranajes *m*, tren de engranajes *m*; ~ **blank** *n* MECH ENG disco para engranaje *m*, primordio de engranaje *m*, primordio de rueda dentada *m*; ~ **case** *n* MECH ENG caja de cambios *f*, caja de engranajes *f*, caja de velocidades *f*, cárter de engranajes *m*; ~ **casing** *n* MECH ENG caja de engranajes *f*, cárter de engranajes *m*; ~ **change** *n BrE* (*cf gear shift AmE*) AUTO cambio de velocidad por pedal *m*, cambio de velocidades *m*, VEH cambio de velocidades *m*, *motorcycles* cambio de velocidad por pedal *m*; ~ **change lever** *n BrE* (*cf gear shift lever AmE*) AUTO, VEH palanca de cambio de marchas *f*, palanca de cambio de velocidades *f*; ~ **cone angle** *n* MECH ENG ángulo de cono del engranaje *m*; ~ **cover** *n* MECH ENG caja de engranajes *f*, cárter de engranajes *m*; ~ **cutter** *n* MECH *of vehicle*, MECH ENG fresa de módulo *f*, fresa para engranajes *f*, fresadora de engranajes *f*; ~ **cutting** *n* MECH *of vehicle*, MECH ENG fresadora de engranajes *f*, máquina de tallar engranajes *f*, talla de engranajes *f*; ~**-cutting machine** *n* MECH *of vehicle*, MECH ENG fresadora de engranajes *f*, máquina de tallar engranajes *f*; ~ **drive** *n* MECH impulsión por engranajes *f*, mando por engranajes *m*, transmisión por engranajes *f*, *power transmission* impulsor por engranajes *m*, MECH ENG transmisión por engranajes *f*, impulsión por engranajes *f*, mando por engranajes *m*, *power transmission* impulsor por engranajes *m*; ~ **head** *n* MECH ENG cabezal de engranajes *m*; ~ **hob** *n* MECH fresa matriz *f*, MECH ENG fresa generatriz para tallar engranajes *f*,

fresa matriz *f*; **~-hobbing machine** *n* MECH ENG fresadora para tallar engranajes por fresa matriz *f*, máquina de tallar engranajes por fresa matriz *f*; **~-measuring cylinder** *n* METR cilindro de medición del engranaje *m*; **~-milling machine** *n* MECH ENG fresadora de tallar engranajes por disco *f*, fresadora de tallar engranajes por fresa *f*, máquina de tallar engranajes por disco *f*, máquina de tallar engranajes por fresa *f*; **~ puller** *n* VEH extractor de engranajes *m*; **~ pump** *n* AUTO, P&R, REFRIG, VEH bomba de engranajes *f*; **~ ratio** *n* MECH relación de engranajes *f*, relación de multiplicación *f*, relación de reducción *f*, MECH ENG engranaje reductor *m*, multiplicación *f*, reducción *f*, relación de engranajes *f*, relación de multiplicación *f*, relación de reducción *f*, relación de transmisión *f*, VEH relación de engranajes *f*, relación de multiplicación *f*, relación de reducción *f*, relación de transmisión *f*; **~ shaft** *n* MECH, MECH ENG eje de engranajes *m*; **~-shaping machine** *n* MECH ENG cepilladora de engranajes *f*, limadora de engranajes *f*, máquina de tallar engranajes con cuchilla *f*; **~-shaving machine** *n* MECH ENG cepilladora de engranajes blandos *f*, cepilladora de engranajes sin templar *f*, limadora de engranajes blandos *f*, limadora de engranajes sin templar *f*; **~ shift** *n* AmE (*cf gear change* BrE) AUTO, VEH cambio de velocidad por pedal *m*, cambio de velocidades *m*; **~ shift lever** *n* AmE (*cf gear change lever* BrE) AUTO, VEH palanca de cambio de marchas *f*, palanca de cambio de velocidades *f*; **~ streaks** *n pl* PRINT franjas en el impreso debidas a los engranajes *f pl*; **~-testing machine** *n* METR aparato verificador de transmisiones *m*; **~ tooth** *n* MECH ENG diente de engranaje *m*; **~ train** *n* AUTO juego de engranajes *m*, MECH ENG tren de engranajes *m*, VEH juego de engranajes *m*, tren de engranajes *m*; **~-type oil pump** *n* AUTO, VEH bomba de aceite de engranajes *f*; **~ wheel** *n* MECH, MECH ENG engranaje *m*, piñón *m*, rueda de fricción *f*, rueda dentada *f*; **~ work** *n* MECH ENG tren de engranajes *m*
gear[3] *vt* MECH ENG engranar
gear[4] *vi* MECH ENG engranar
gearbox *n* AUTO *engine*, MECH, MECH ENG, PROD, VEH, WATER TRANSP *engine* caja de cambio de velocidades *f*, caja de cambios *f*, caja de engranajes *f*, caja de velocidades *f*; **~ guard** *n* MECH ENG cárter de la caja de cambio de velocidades *m*, protector de la caja de cambio de velocidades *m*; **~ housing** *n* AUTO, VEH cárter de la caja de cambios *m*; **~ input shaft** *n* MECH ENG eje conductor de la caja de cambio de velocidades *m*, eje motor de la caja de cambio de velocidades *m*, eje primario de la caja de cambio de velocidades *m*, eje principal de la caja de cambio de velocidades *m*; **~ selector fork** *n* VEH horquilla selectora de velocidades *f*
geared[1] *adj* MECH, MECH ENG accionado por engranaje, de engranaje, engranado
geared[2]: **~ center column** *AmE*, **~ centre column** *BrE n* CINEMAT, PHOTO columna central engranada *f*; **~ head** *n* CINEMAT cabeza de manivelas *f*; **~ motor** *n* MECH motor de engranaje *m*, motor engranado *m*; **~ turbine** *n* MECH turbina engranada *f*
gearing[1] *adj* MECH ENG engranado, *gearwheels* dentado
gearing[2] *n* MECH ENG engrane *m*, mando *m*, mecanismo *m*, tren de engranajes *m*
gearless *phr* MECH de acoplo directo, de ataque

directo, de transmisión directa, sin engranajes, MECH ENG de acoplo directo, de ataque directo, sin engranajes
gears *n pl* AUTO juego de engranajes *m*, PROD engranajes *m pl*, VEH juego de engranajes *m*
Gedinnian *adj* GEOL Gediniense
gedrite *n* MINERAL gedrita *f*
gehlenite *n* MINERAL gehlenita *f*
Geiger: **~ counter** *n* NUCL, PART PHYS, PHYS, RAD PHYS contador Geiger *m*; **~ tube** *n* NUCL, PART PHYS, PHYS, RAD PHYS detector de Geiger *m*
Geiger-Müller: **~ tube** *n* PHYS tubo Geiger-Müller *m*, RAD PHYS detector de Geiger-Müller *m*
Geissler: **~ tube** *n* ELECTRON, PHYS tubo Geissler *m*
gel[1] *n* GEN gel *m*; **~ cell** *n* ELEC ENG célula de gel *f*, elemento gelatinizado *m*; **~ coat** *n* COATINGS, WATER TRANSP *GRP construction* capa de gel *f*; **~ permeation chromatography** *n* CHEM cromatografía de permeación en gel *f*, cromatografía por filtración en gel *f*, LAB cromatografía de permeación de gel *f*, cromatografía por filtración en gel *f*; **~ time** *n* P&R tiempo de gelatinización *m*, PACK tiempo de gelificación *m*
gel[2] *vi* CHEM gelificar
gelatine *n* CHEM, FOOD, MINE, PACK *adhesives* gelatina *f*; **~ capsule** *n* PACK cápsula de gelatina *f*; **~ dynamite** *n* MINE dinamita de gelatina *f*; **~ filter** *n* CINEMAT filtro de gelatina *m*
gelatino: **~-bromide process** *n* PHOTO proceso de gelatino-bromuro *m*; **~-chloride** *n* CHEM cloruro gelatinado *m*
gelation *n* CHEM, CHEM TECH, P&R formación de un gel *f*, gelación *f*
gelding *n* AGRIC caballo castrado *m*
gelignite *n* CHEM, MINE gelignita *f*
gelling: **~ agent** *n* CHEM agente de gelatinización *m*, agente gelificante *m*, CHEM TECH gelificante *m*, FOOD, MAR POLL agente de gelatinización *m*, agente gelificante *m*, gelificante *m*, P&R agente de gelatinización *m*, agente de solidificación *m*, agente gelificante *m*
gelose *n* CHEM agar-agar *m*, gelosa *f*
gelsemine *n* CHEM gelsemina *f*
gem: **~ magnifier** *n* INSTR amplificador de gema *m*
gene *n* AGRIC gene *m*; **~ bank** *n* AGRIC banco de germoplasma *m*; **~ loci** *n pl* AGRIC locis *m*
general[1]: **~-purpose** *adj* DETERG, ELEC ENG, MECH, MECH ENG, PROD de uso general, de uso universal, para aplicaciones diversas, para todo uso
general[2]: **~ arrangement** *n* CONST, MECH, MECH ENG disposición general *f*; **~-arrangement drawing** *n* CONST, MECH, MECH ENG plano de disposición general *m*; **~-arrangement plan** *n* CONST, MECH, WATER TRANSP *shipbuilding* plano de disposición general *m*; **~ assembly** *n* MECH ENG disposición general *f*, plano de montaje general *m*; **~ atmospheric circulation** *n* METEO circulación atmosférica general *f*; **~ cargo** *n* PACK carga general *f*; **~ drawing** *n* NUCL plano general *m*; **~ equation of the circle** *n* GEOM ecuación general del círculo *f*; **~-layout drawing** *n* CONST, MECH ENG plano de montaje general *m*; **~ localization** *n* TELECOM localización general *f*; **~ maintenance** *n* NUCL mantenimiento general *m*; **~ plan** *n* CONST, MECH ENG *technical drawing* plano de conjunto *m*, plano general *m*; **~-purpose board** *n* ELECTRON tablero multiuso *m*; **~-purpose chip** *n* ELECTRON chip de uso general *m*; **~-purpose**

computer n (GP computer) COMP&DP computador de uso general m (AmL), computador universal m (AmL) (CU), computadora de uso general f (AmL), computadora universal f (AmL) (CU), ordenador de uso general m (Esp), ordenador universal m (Esp); **~-purpose electric vehicle** n TRANSP vehículo eléctrico polivalente m; **~-purpose laminate** n ELECTRON panel multiuso m; **~-purpose language** n COMP&DP lenguaje universal m; **~-purpose machine tool** n PROD máquina herramienta para usos generales f; **~-purpose relay** n ELEC ENG relé para todas las aplicaciones m; **~-purpose resistor** n ELEC ENG resistencia para aplicaciones diversas f; **~-purpose screw thread** n MECH ENG hilo de uso general m, rosca de uso general f; **~ theory of relativity** n PHYS teoría general de la relatividad f; **~ tolerance** n MECH ENG tolerancia general f; **~ warning panel** n AIR TRANSP cuadro de aviso general m, SAFE tablón de anuncios m; **~ yield load** n METALL carga elástica general f

General: ~ Agreement on Tariffs and Trade n (GATT) AGRIC Acuerdo General sobre Aranceles y Comercio Aduaneros m (GATT)

generalized: ~ coordinates n pl PHYS coordenadas generalizadas f pl; **~ Pauli principle** n PART PHYS principio de Pauli generalizado m

generate vt ELEC, GEOM, NUCL, RAD PHYS generar

generated[1]: **~ on chip** adj ELECTRON generado sobre el chip

generated[2]: **~ address** n COMP&DP direccional generado m (AmL), dirección calculada f, dirección generada f (AmL)

generating[1] adj ELEC, ELEC ENG, ELECTRON, PROD generadora, generatriz, productora

generating[2] n ELEC, ELEC ENG, ELECTRON, FUELLESS, NUCL, PROD generación f; **~ capacity** n ELEC, ELEC ENG, FUELLESS, NUCL supply capacidad generadora f; **~ cutter** n MECH ENG fresa generadora f; **~ grid** n FLUID rejilla generadora f; **~ plant** n ELEC supply instalación generatriz f, planta de producción de energía eléctrica f, ELEC ENG, FUELLESS, NUCL planta de producción de energía eléctrica f, instalación generatriz f; **~ program** n COMP&DP programa generador m; **~ set** n ELEC supply grupo electrogenerador m, planta eléctrica f, ELEC ENG grupo electrógeno m

generation n ELEC supply, ELEC ENG, ELECTRON, FUELLESS generación f, producción f, MECH ENG producción f, NUCL generación f, producción f, PROD generación f; **~ copy** n TV programme generación de copias f; **~ data set** n COMP&DP conjunto de datos de generación m, grupo de datos de generación m; **~ number** n COMP&DP número de generación m

generator n GEN electrics generador m; **~ brush** n VEH escobilla del generador f; **~ coal** n COAL carbón de gasógeno m; **~ gas** n GAS gas de gasógeno m, gas pobre m, gas pobre de gasógeno m, PETROL gas pobre m, PROD gas de gasógeno m, gas pobre m, gas pobre de gasógeno m; **~ output** n ELEC, ELEC ENG salida del generador f; **~ output power** n ELEC, ELEC ENG potencia de salida del generador f; **~ set** n ELEC ENG grupo electrógeno m; **~ signaling** AmE, **~ signalling** BrE n ELEC ENG señalización del generador f; **~ speed** n FUELLESS velocidad del generador f

generic: ~ cascade n NUCL cascada genérica f; **~ flow**

control n (GFC) TELECOM control genérico del flujo m; **~ name** n COMP&DP nombre genérico m

genetic[1] adj AGRIC, RAD PHYS genético

genetic[2]: **~ engineering** n AGRIC manipulación genética f; **~ markers** n pl AGRIC marcadores genéticos m pl; **~ reservoir** n AGRIC reserva genética f

Geneva: ~ wheel n MECH ENG engranaje de cruz de malta m

genistein n CHEM genisteína f

genny n CINEMAT generador electrógeno m

genthite n MINERAL gentita f

gentian: ~ violet n FLUID violeta de genciana f

gentianin n CHEM gencianina f

gentiobiose n CHEM gentiobiosa f

gentiopicrin n CHEM gentiopicrina f

gentisate n CHEM gentisato m

gentisic adj CHEM gentisínico, gentísico

gentisin n CHEM gentisina f

gentle: ~ breeze n METEO brisa débil f, brisa suave f; **~ heat** n HEAT, THERMO calentamiento moderado m, calentamiento suave m

genus n GEOM of a surface género m

geobarometer n GEOL, INSTR geobarómetro m

geochemical: ~ cycle n CHEM, GEOL, PETR TECH, PETROL ciclo geoquímico m

geochemistry n CHEM, GEOL, PETR TECH, PETROL geoquímica f

geochronology n GEOL, PETROL geocronología f

geode n GEOL geoda f

geodesic: ~ line n GEOM línea geodésica f; **~ navigation** n WATER TRANSP navegación geodésica f; **~ station** n WATER TRANSP estación geodésica f; **~ survey** n COAL red geodésica f, CONST investigación geodésica f

geodesy n GEOL geodesia f

geodimeter n CONST, INSTR geodímetro m

geodynamics n GEOL, SPACE geodinámica f

geographical: ~ range n WATER TRANSP navigation alcance geográfico m

geohydrology n COAL geohidrología f

geoid n GEOL, OCEAN geoide m

geological[1] adj GEOL geológico

geological[2]: **~ column** n GEOL columna geológica f, perfil geológico m; **~ environment** n GAS, GEOL ambiente geológico m; **~ layer** n GAS, GEOL capa geológica f; **~ section** n GEOL corte geológico m, sección geológica f; **~ survey** n COAL, GEOL, PETR TECH investigación geológica f, reconocimiento geológico m; **~ time scale** n GEOL cronología geológica f (AmL), escala de tiempos geológicos f (Esp)

geology n COAL, GEOL, PETR TECH geología f

geomagnetic[1] adj GEOL, GEOPHYS, PHYS, SPACE geomagnético

geomagnetic[2]: **~ cutoff energy** n SPACE umbral de energía geomagnética m; **~ equator** n GEOPHYS ecuador geomagnético m; **~ latitude** n GEOPHYS, PHYS latitud geomagnética f; **~ meridian** n GEOPHYS meridiano geomagnético m; **~ pole** n GEOPHYS polo geomagnético m; **~ reversal** n GEOPHYS inversión geomagnética f; **~ secular variation** n GEOPHYS variación secular geomagnética f; **~ tail** n GEOPHYS, SPACE apéndice geomagnético m, cola geomagnética f

geomagnetism n GEOL, GEOPHYS, PHYS, SPACE geomagnetismo m

geometer n GEOM profession geómetra m

geometric[1] adj GEOM, MATH geométrico

geometric[2]: ~ **albedo** *n* GEOM, SPACE albedo geométrico *m*; ~ **beam resolution** *n* NUCL resolución geométrica del haz *f*; ~ **buckling** *n* NUCL autovalor geométrico *m*, curvatura geométrica *f*; ~ **calibration** *n* TV calibración geométrica *f*; ~ **data** *n* CONST, GEOM datos geométricos *m pl*; ~ **displacements** *n pl* GEOM, MECH ENG desplazamientos geométricos *m pl*; ~ **distribution** *n* GEOM, MATH distribución geométrica *f*; ~ **error** *n* TV error geométrico *m*; ~ **factor** *n* PETROL factor de forma *m*; ~ **isomer** *n* CHEM isómero geométrico *m*; ~ **optics** *n* OPT, PHYS, TELECOM óptica geométrica *f*; ~ **pitch** *n* AIR TRANSP *propeller* paso geométrico *m*; ~ **properties** *n pl* GEOM propiedades geométricas *f pl*; ~ **representation** *n* GEOM representación geométrica *f*; ~ **resolution length** *n* GEOM, NUCL intervalo de resolución geométrica *m*; ~ **sequence** *n* GEOM, MATH sucesión geométrica *f*; ~ **series** *n pl* MATH serie geométrica *f*; ~ **surface** *n* GEOM superficie geométrica *f*; ~ **tolerancing** *n* MECH ENG tolerancias geométricas *f pl*
geometrical *adj* GEOM, MATH geométrico
geometrician *n* GEOM *profession* geómetra *m*
geometry *n* AUTO, GEOM, MATH, METALL, NUCL, RAD PHYS geometría *f*; ~ **of absorption** *n* GEOM, RAD PHYS geometría de la absorción *f*; ~ **of glide** *n* GEOM geometría de deslizamiento *f*, METALL configuración del deslizamiento *f*, geometría de deslizamiento *f*; ~ **of irradiation** *n* GEOM, NUCL geometría de la irradiación *f*
geomorphology *n* GEOL geomorfología *f*
geon *n* GEOPHYS geón *m*
geopetal *adj* PETROL geopetal
geophone *n* COAL, GAS, GEOL, GEOPHYS, PETR TECH, PHYS geófono *m*
geophysical: ~ **exploration** *n* GEOPHYS exploración geofísica *f*, prospección geofísica *f*; ~ **log** *n* GEOL, GEOPHYS, PETR TECH registro geofísico *m*; ~ **measurement** *n* GAS, GEOPHYS medición geofísica *f*; ~ **prospecting** *n* GEOPHYS prospección geofísica *f*, radiestesia *f*; ~ **survey** *n* CONST, GEOL, GEOPHYS, PETR TECH investigación geofísica *f*, prospección geofísica *f*
geophysics *n* ACOUST, COAL, GEOL, GEOPHYS, PETR TECH, PHYS geofísica *f*
geopotential *n* GEOM, GEOPHYS geopotencial *m*; ~ **height** *n* GEOPHYS altura geopotencial *f*; ~ **meter** *n* GEOPHYS medidor geopotencial *m*
geopressure *n* GEOPHYS, PETR TECH presión geológica *f*
geostatic: ~ **pressure** *n* GEOPHYS, PETR TECH presión geostática *f*
geostationary: ~ **orbit** *n* GEOPHYS, PHYS, SPACE órbita geoestacionaria *f*; ~ **satellite** *n* PHYS, SPACE, TELECOM, TV, WATER TRANSP *navigation* satélite geoestacionario *m*; ~ **satellite orbit** *n* SPACE órbita de satélite geoestacionario *f*
geostrophic: ~ **wind** *n* GEOPHYS, METEO viento geostrófico *m*; ~ **wind level** *n* GEOPHYS, METEO nivel de viento geostrófico *m*
geosynchronous: ~ **orbit** *n* SPACE órbita geosincrónica *f*
geosynclinal *adj* GEOL, GEOPHYS, PETR TECH geosinclinal
geosyncline *n* GEOL, GEOPHYS, PETR TECH geosinclinal *m*
geotechnical: ~ **properties** *n pl* COAL, GEOL propiedades geotécnicas *f pl*

geotechnics *n* COAL, GEOL, GEOPHYS geotécnica *f*
geotectocline *n* GEOPHYS geotectoclino *m*
geotectonic *adj* COAL, GEOL, GEOPHYS geotectónico
geothermal[1] *adj* FUELLESS, GEOL, GEOPHYS, PETR TECH, PHYS, THERMO geotérmico
geothermal[2]: ~ **circuit** *n* FUELLESS, GEOPHYS circuito geotérmico *m*; ~ **drilling equipment** *n* FUELLESS equipo de perforación geotérmico *m*; ~ **energy** *n* GEOPHYS, PHYS energía geotérmica *f*; ~ **field** *n* FUELLESS campo geotérmico *m*; ~ **gradient** *n* FUELLESS, GEOL, GEOPHYS, PETR TECH gradiente geotérmico *m*, pendiente geotérmica *f*, THERMO gradiente geotérmico *m*; ~ **log** *n* FUELLESS, PETR TECH perfil geotérmico *m*, registro geotérmico *m*; ~ **logging** *n* FUELLESS, PETR TECH perfilaje geotérmico *m*; ~ **plant** *n* ELEC, FUELLESS instalación geotérmica *f*, planta geotérmica *f*, THERMO instalación geotérmica *f*; ~ **power** *n* FUELLESS energía geotérmica *f*; ~ **power station** *n* ELEC, ELEC ENG, FUELLESS central eléctrica geotérmica *f*, central geotérmica *f*; ~ **resources** *n pl* FUELLESS recursos geotérmicos *m pl*
geothermics *n* GEN geotérmica *f*
geothermometer *n* GEN geotermómetro *m*
geotropic: ~ **filling** *n* GEOL relleno geotrópico *m*
geraniol *n* CHEM geraniol *m*
geranyl *n* CHEM geranilo *m*
germ: ~ **killer** *n* AGRIC germicida *m*
German: ~~**-type mounting** *n* INSTR montaje de tipo germánico *m*
germanium *n* (*Ge*) CHEM, ELEC ENG, METALL germanio *m* (*Ge*); ~ **avalanche photodiode** *n* ELEC, ELECTRON fotodiodo de germanio de avalancha *m*; ~ **diode** *n* ELEC, ELECTRON diodo de germanio *m*; ~ **rectifier** *n* ELEC, ELECTRON rectificador de germanio *m*; ~ **transistor** *n* ELECTRON transistor de germanio *m*
gersdorffite *n* MINERAL gersdorfita *f*
get[1] *n* COAL producción *f*
get[2]: ~ **under way** *vi* WATER TRANSP *sailing* largarse, ponerse a la vela; ~ **up steam** *vi* HYDRAUL, PROD levantar presión, producir vapor
getter *n* ELEC *valve, oscilloscope* getter *m*, rarefactor *m*, reductor de presión *m*, ELEC ENG, GEOL, MINE desgaseador *m*, TELECOM getter *m*
getting: ~ **up steam** *n* HYDRAUL, PROD generación de vapor *f*, producción de vapor *f*
geyser *n* FUELLESS, GEOPHYS, HEAT ENG, HYDROL, THERMO fuente termal *f*, géiser *m*
geyserite *n* MINERAL geiserita *f*
g-factor *n* PHYS factor g *m*
GFC *abbr* (*generic flow control*) TELECOM control genérico del flujo *m*
g-force *n* AIR TRANSP, PHYS, SPACE fuerza G *f*, fuerza de la gravedad *f*
ghost *n* CINEMAT, PHOTO, TV imagen fantasma *f*; ~ **echo** *n* SPACE eco falso *m*, eco fantasma *m*; ~ **image** *n* CINEMAT, PHOTO, TV imagen fantasma *f*
giant: ~ **pulse** *n* ELECTRON impulso gigante *m*
gib *n* MECH ENG chaveta de talón *f*, contrachaveta *f*, corredera de ajuste *f*, cuña *f*, patín *m*, retenedor *m*; ~ **and cotter** *n* MECH ENG chaveta *f*, chaveta doble *f*, contrachaveta *f*; ~ **head key** *n* MECH ENG chaveta con cabeza *f*, chaveta con talón *f*; ~ **and key** *n* MECH ENG chaveta y contrachaveta *f*
Gibbs': ~ **free energy** *n* PHYS energía libre de Gibbs *f*; ~ **phase rule** *n* CHEM, NUCL regla de fase de Gibbs *f*
gibbsite *n* MINERAL gibbsita *f*

gieseckite *n* MINERAL gieseckita *f*
gig *n* PROD *founding* terraja transportable *f*
giga- *pref* (*G*) METR giga- (*G*)
gigabyte *n* COMP&DP, OPT, TELECOM gigabyte *m*, gigaocteto *m*
gigadisk *n* OPT gigadisco *m*
gigantolite *n* MINERAL gigantolita *f*
GIGO *abbr* (*garbage-in/garbage-out*) COMP&DP basura entra/basura sale
gilbert *n* ELEC ENG gilbertio *m*
gilbertite *n* MINERAL gilbertita *f*
gild *vt* METALL, PROD dar brillo a, dorar
gilder *n* METALL, PROD *person* dorador *m*
gilding *n* METALL dorado *m*, doradura *f*, PRINT dorado *m*, PROD dorado *m*, doradura *f*
gill *n* METR *liquid measure* gill *m*
gilled: ~ **tube** *n* PROD tubo con nervios *m*
gilt[1]: ~ **edge** *adj* PRINT de borde dorado
gilt[2]: ~ **edge** *n* PRINT borde dorado *m*
gimbal *n* MECH cuna *f*, suspensión a la cardán *f*; ~ **head** *n* CINEMAT cabeza de tercereje *f*; ~ **joint** *n* MECH ENG junta cardónica *f*, rótula *f* (*Esp*); ~ **mounting** *n* WATER TRANSP suspensión cardán *f*, suspensión cardánica *f*; ~ **suspensión** *n* MECH ENG suspensión cardánica *f*; ~ **tripod** *n* CINEMAT trípode cardánico *m*
gimp *n* TEXTIL galón *m*
gin[1] *n* CONST husillo *m*, molinete *m*, cabria *f*, poste grúa *m*; ~ **block** *n* PROD cuadernal de cabina *m*, cuadernal de cabria *m*; ~ **pulley** *n* PROD cuadernal de cabina *m*, cuadernal de cabria *m*; ~ **tackle** *n* PROD aparejo de cabria *m*; ~ **trash** *n* AGRIC residuo del despepitado *m*; ~ **wheel** *n* CONST rueda de torno *f*, molinete *m*
gin[2] *vt* AGRIC despepitar
ginning *n* AGRIC despepitado *m*
giobertite *n* MINERAL giobertita *f*
Giorgi: ~ **system** *n* METR sistema Giorgi *m*
girasol *n* MINERAL ópalo de fuego *m*, ópalo girasol *m*
girasole *n* MINERAL ópalo de fuego *m*, ópalo girasol *m*
girder *n* CONST *large beam* larguero *m*, *small* viga principal *f*, jácena *f*, *trussed* viga maestra *f*, WATER TRANSP *shipbuilding* eslora *f*, vagra *f*, viga *f*; ~ **bridge** *n* CONST puente de vigas *m*; ~**type frame** *n* PROD *steam engine* estructura bayoneta *f*
girdling *n* AGRIC *forest* incisión cortical *f*
girt *n* CONST *cross-piece of derrick* traviesa de piso *f*, vigueta *f*
girth: ~ **weld** *n* MECH, NUCL soldadura circunferencial *f*
gismondine *n* MINERAL gismondina *f*
git: ~ **cutter** *n* PROD *founding* barrena para abrir el agujero de colada *f*
give[1]: ~**way vessel** *n* WATER TRANSP buque que cede el paso *m*
give[2]: ~ **clearance to** *vt* MECH ENG dar juego a, dar tolerancia a; ~ **off** *vt* PHYS, THERMO desprender; ~ **a wide berth to** *vt* WATER TRANSP *shiphandling* dar un buen resguardo a
give[3]: ~ **the alarm** *vi* SAFE dar la alarma; ~ **out** *vi* PROD *fail* pararse; ~ **way** *vi* CONST vencerse, derrumbarse
given: ~ **code** *n* TELECOM código especificado *m*
Givetian *adj* GEOL Givetiense
glabrous *adj* AGRIC glabro
glacial[1] *adj* GEOL glacial
glacial[2]: ~ **acetic acid** *n* CHEM, FOOD ácido acético glacial *m*; ~ **clay** *n* COAL, GEOL arcilla glaciárica *f*;

~ **outburst** *n* OCEAN irrupción glacial *f*; ~ **stage** *n* GEOL época glacial *f*
glacier: ~ **lake** *n* HYDROL lago de glaciar *m*; ~ **mud** *n* HYDROL lodo de glaciar *m*; ~ **silt** *n* HYDROL fango glaciárico *m*; ~ **snow** *n* HYDROL nieve de helero *f*
glairin *n* CHEM glairina *f*
glance: ~ **coal** *n* COAL antracita *f*
glancing: ~ **collision** *n* NUCL colisión tangencial *f*
gland *n* MECH casquillo *m*, collarín *m*, cuello *m*, MECH ENG caja estancadora *f*, casquillo *m*, collarín *m*, prensaestopas *m*, MINE cable guía *m*, cuerda freno *f*, NUCL prensaestopas *m*, PETR TECH casquillo *m*, empaquetamiento de prensaestopas *m*, PROD caja estancadora *f*, collarín *m*, empaquetadura *f*, *of stuffing box* casquillo *m*, SPACE casquillo *m*, collarín *m*; ~ **steam system** *n* NUCL sistema de cierres de vapor *m*
glanded: ~ **pump** *n* NUCL bomba con prensaestopas *f*
glare[1]: ~**free** *adj* SAFE sin brillo
glare[2] *n* CINEMAT resplandor *m*, PRINT deslumbramiento *m*, SAFE brillo *m*; ~ **shield** *n* AIR TRANSP pantalla antideslumbrante *f*, pantalla reflectora *f*
glaserite *n* MINERAL glaserita *f*
glass[1]: ~**fiber reinforced** *AmE*, ~**fibre reinforced** *BrE adj* PACK, PROD reforzado con fibra de vidrio, reforzado con vitrofibra; ~**reinforced** *adj* PACK, PROD reforzado con vitrofibra
glass[2] *n* C&G vaso *m*, vidrio *m*, CHEM, PETROL vidrio *m*; ~ **analysis** *n* C&G análisis del vidrio *m*; ~ **bar** *n* C&G, CONST barra de vidrio *f*; ~ **bead** *n* C&G cuenta de vidrio *f*, gota de vidrio *f*; ~**beaded screen** *n* CINEMAT pantalla alveolar *f*; ~ **bit** *n* MECH ENG broca para vidrio *f*; ~ **block** *n* C&G bloque de vidrio *m*; ~ **blower** *n* C&G soplador de vidrio *m*; ~**bonded mica** *n* ELEC ENG *insulator* mica ligada con vidrio aislante *f*; ~ **box** *n* COMP&DP caja de vidrio *f*; ~ **brick** *n* C&G, CONST ladrillo de vidrio *m*; ~ **cameo** *n* C&G medallón de vidrio *m*; ~ **capacitor** *n* C&G, ELEC ENG condensador de vidrio *m*; ~ **ceramic** *n* C&G, NUCL vidrio cerámico *m*; ~ **cladding** *n* ELEC ENG recubierto de vidrio *m*; ~ **cloth** *n* PROD tela de fibra de vidrio *f*, WATER TRANSP *material* tejido de vidrio *m*; ~**coated ceramic capacitor** *n* ELEC ENG condensador cerámico revestido de vidrio *m*; ~ **color** *AmE*, ~ **colour** *BrE n* C&G, COLOUR color vítreo *m*; ~**concrete panel** *n* C&G panel de vidrio macizo *m*; ~ **container** *n* PACK contenedor de cristal o de vidrio *m*; ~ **continuous filament yarn** *n* C&G filamento continuo de vidrio *m*; ~ **cutter** *n* C&G , CONST diamante cortavidrios *m*, *person* cortador de vidrios *m*, vidriero *m*; ~**cutting wheel** *n* C&G rueda de corte para vidrio *f*; ~ **depth** *n* C&G profundidad del vidrio *f*; ~ **dish** *n* C&G plato de vidrio *m*; ~ **door** *n* CONST puerta vidriada *f*; ~ **drill** *n* C&G, MECH ENG broca para vidrio *f*, mecha para vidrio *f*; ~ **dust** *n* C&G polvo de vidrio *m*; ~ **electrode** *n* LAB electrodo de vidrio *m*; ~ **epoxprinted circuit board** *n* ELECTRON cuadro eléctrico impreso en resina de epoxia *m*; ~ **epoxy laminate** *n* ELECTRON resina de epoxia *f*; ~ **fabric** *n* C&G, PACK tejido de fibra de vidrio *m*; ~**fiber** *AmE see glass-fibre BrE*; ~**fiber cable** *AmE see glass-fibre cable BrE*; ~**fiber laminate** *AmE see glass-fibre laminate BrE*; ~**fiber mat** *AmE see glass-fibre mat BrE*; ~**fiber reinforced plastic** *AmE see glass-fibre reinforced plastic BrE*; ~**fiber reinforcement** *AmE*, ~**fibre** *BrE n* C&G, COMP&DP, CONST, ELEC fibra de

vidrio *f*, fibravidrio *f*, ELEC ENG fibra de vidrio *f*, fibravidrio *f*, hilo de vidrio *m*, HEAT ENG, OPT, P&R, PACK, PROD, REFRIG, TELECOM, TEXTIL, VEH, WATER TRANSP *boat building material* fibra de vidrio *f*, fibravidrio *f*; **~-fibre cable** *n BrE* C&G, CONST, ELEC, ELEC ENG, TELECOM cable de vitrofibra *m*, cable vitrofibra *m*; **~-fibre laminate** *n BrE* C&G, PACK laminado de fibra de vidrio *m*; **~-fibre mat** *n BrE* C&G colchoneta de fibra de vidrio *f*; **~-fibre reinforced plastic** *n BrE* C&G, P&R, PACK, SAFE plástico armado con fibra de vidrio *m*, plástico reforzado con fibra de vidrio *m*; **~-fibre reinforcement** *n BrE* C&G refuerzo de fibra de vidrio *m*; **~ former** *n* C&G soplador *m*; **~ frit** *n* C&G frita *f*; **~ glazing** *n* C&G, COATINGS pulido del vidrio *m*, recubrimiento vítreo *m*; **~-heating panel** *n* C&G panel de vidrio para calentar *m*; **~ holder** *n* C&G, ELEC ENG portalámparas de vidrio *m*; **~ insulator** *n* C&G, ELEC, ELEC ENG aislador de vidrio *m*; **~ jar** *n* C&G, PACK jarra de vidrio *f*, tarro de vidrio *m*; **~ laser** *n* C&G, ELECTRON láser para vidrio *m*; **~-level controller** *n* C&G, PROD controlador del nivel del vidrio *m*; **~ marble** *n* C&G canica de vidrio *f*; **~ melted from batch only** *n* C&G vidrio producido con 100% materia prima *m*; **~ melted from cullet** *n* C&G vidrio producido con 100% de fundente *m*; **~ microsphere** *n* C&G microesfera de vidrio *f*; **~ mosaic** *n* C&G mosaico de vidrio *m*; **~ paper** *n* C&G, PAPER papel abrasivo *m*, papel abrasivo con fibra de vidrio *m*, papel de lija *m*; **~ passivation** *n* C&G papel abrasivo de vidrio *m*, pasivación de vidrio *f*, tratamiento de vidrio *m*, ELECTRON pasivación de vidrio *f*, tratamiento de vidrio *m*; **~ paving slab** *n* C&G loseta vítrea para pavimento *f*; **~ plate** *n* C&G, LAB placa de vidrio *f*; **~ pocket** *n* C&G bolsa de vidrio *f*; **~-polyester enclosure** *n* C&G, PROD recipiente de poliéster de fibra de vidrio *m*; **~ pressure plate** *n* PHOTO plancha de cristal *f*; **~-reinforced concrete** *n* C&G, CONST, PROD cemento reforzado con vidrio *m*; **~-reinforced laminate** *n* C&G, CONST, NUCL material laminar reforzado con vidrio *m*; **~-reinforced plastic** *n* (*GRP*) C&V,EMB,P&C, SAFE plástico reforzado con fibra de vidrio *m* (*GRP*); **~-reinforced polyester** *n* (*GRP*) C&G, CONST, MECH, MECH ENG, P&R, PROD, WATER TRANSP poliéster reforzado con fibra de vidrio *m* (*GRP*); **~-reinforced polyester mold** *AmE*, **~-reinforced polyester mould** *BrE n* C&G, MECH, MECH ENG molde de poliester reforzado con fibra de vidrio *m*; **~ rod** *n* C&G, LAB varilla de vidrio *f*; **~ roof** *n* C&G, CONST techo de vidrio *m*; **~ roof-tile** *n* C&G, CONST teja de vidrio para techos *f*; **~ shot** *n* CINEMAT toma a través de un cristal *f*; **~ slide** *n* INSTR portaobjetos *m*; **~ stirring-rod** *n* C&G, LAB agitador de vidrio *m*; **~ stopper** *n* Ç&G, LAB tapón de vidrio *m*; **~ substrate** *n* ELECTRON substrato de vidrio *m*; **~ tank** *n* C&G, LAB cuba *f*, tanque de vidrio *m*; **~ transition temperature** *n* C&G, P&R temperatura de transición del estado vítreo *f*, temperatura de transición vítrea *f*; **~ tube** *n* C&G, ELECTRON, LAB tubo de vidrio *m*; **~ tubing** *n* C&G, LAB, MECH tubo de vidrio *m*; **~ wadding** *n* PACK guata de fibra de vidrio *f*; **~ washer** *n* C&G, LAB limpiador de vidrio *m*; **~ wool** *n* C&G, HEAT ENG, P&R, PACK, REFRIG lana de vidrio *f*; **~-wool filter** *n* C&G filtro de lana de vidrio *m*
glassblowing *n* C&G soplado de vidrio *m*
glasses *n pl* INSTR anteojos *m pl*, gafas *f pl*, lentes *f pl*,

OPT anteojos *m pl* (*AmL*), gafas *f pl*, SAFE anteojos de protección *m pl* (*AmL*), gafas protectoras *f pl* (*Esp*), lentes *f pl*
glassine *n* PAPER papel cristal *m*; **~ paper** *n* PAPER papel satinado *m*
glassivation *n* ELECTRON aplicación de vidrio *f*
glassmaker's: **~ tools** *n pl* C&G herramientas de vidriero *f pl*
glassmaking: **~ sand** *n* C&G arena silícea *f*
glassware *n* C&G, LAB material de vidrio *m*
glassy: **~ feldspar** *n* C&G feldespato vidrioso *m*; **~ state** *n* C&G estado vítreo *m*; **~ texture** *n* C&G, PETROL textura vidriosa *f*
glauberite *n* MINERAL glauberita *f*
glaucodote *n* MINERAL arsenopirita cobaltífera *f*, glaucodot *m*
glaucolite *n* MINERAL glaucolita *f*
glauconite *n* GEOL, MINERAL, PETROL glauconita *f*; **~ marl** *n* CONST marga *f*
glauconitic *adj* GEOL, MINERAL, PETR TECH, PETROL glauconítico
glaucophane *n* MINERAL glaucofana *f*
glaze[1] *n* C&G lustre *m*, vidriado *m*, COLOUR, P&R lustre *m*, PAPER satinado *m*, PROD lustre *m*, REFRIG capa de hielo *f*, película de hielo *f*, TEXTIL lustre *m*; **~ grinder** *n* C&G molino para vidrio *m*; **~ kiln** *n* C&G horno de vidriado *m*
glaze[2] *vi* C&G, PROD ponerse vidrioso
glaze[3] *vt* C&G *substrate* vitrificar, vidriar, *building* poner vidrios, CONST poner vidrios, FOOD glasear, PHOTO esmaltar, PROD glasear, esmaltar, vidriar, poner cristales, satinar, encristalar, TEXTIL lustrar, satinar, glasear
glazed[1] *adj* C&G *pottery* vidriado
glazed[2]: **~ blanket** *n* PRINT mantilla satinada *f*; **~ brick** *n* CONST ladrillo vidriado *m*; **~ door** *n* CONST puerta de vidrio *f*; **~ earthenware** *n* C&G loza vidriada *f*; **~ frame** *n* CONST *window* marco vidriado *m*; **~ frost** *n* METEO hielo liso *m*; **~ millboard** *n* PAPER cartón duro *m*; **~ paper** *n* COATINGS, PAPER papel esmaltado *m*, papel satinado *m*; **~ pottery** *n* C&G cerámica vidriada *f*; **~ sash** *n* CONST *window* hoja vidriada *f*; **~ tile** *n* C&G azulejo *m*, CONST azulejo *m*, valdosa vitrificada *f*; **~ yarn** *n* TEXTIL hilo satinado *m*
glazier *n* C&G, CONST *person* vidriero *m*
glazier's: **~ diamond** *n* C&G, CONST diamante de vidriero *m*; **~ pliers** *n pl* C&G pinzas de vidriero *f pl*
glazing *n* C&G *installing windows* colocación de ventanas *f*, *windows of building* instalación de vidrios en las ventanas *f*, CONST *setting glass* vidriera *f* (*AmL*), escaparate *m* (*Esp*), FOOD glaseado *m*, FUELLESS *flat plate collector* vidriado *m*, PAPER alisado *m*, satinado *m*, PROD encristalado *m*, esmaltado *m*, glaseado *m*, satinado *m*, TEXTIL glaseado *m*, lustrado *m*; **~ bar** *n* C&G barra de vidriera *f*, CONST barra de escaparate *f*, barra de vidriera *f*; **~ industry** *n* C&G industria vidriera *f*; **~ machine** *n* C&G máquina para poner vidrios *f*, PHOTO máquina esmaltadora *f*; **~ mill** *n* COATINGS pulidora *f*; **~ quality** *n* C&G calidad de vidriado *f*; **~ roller** *n* PAPER rodillo abrillantador *m*; **~ sheet** *n* PHOTO hoja esmaltadora *f*; **~ varnish** *n* COATINGS, COLOUR barniz transparente *m*
glebe *n* MINE mineral terroso *m*
glide *n* CHEM, CRYSTALL, METALL deslizamiento *m*, dislocación *f*; **~ aerial** *n BrE* (*cf glide antenna AmE*) AIR TRANSP antena de planeo *f*; **~ antenna** *n AmE* (*cf*

glide aerial BrE) AIR TRANSP antena de planeo *f*; **~ band** *n* METALL banda de deslizamiento *f*; **~ path** *n* AIR TRANSP, TRANSP trayectoria de planeo *f*; **--path beacon** *n* AIR TRANSP, TRANSP baliza de trayectoria de planeo *f*; **--path beam** *n* AIR TRANSP, TRANSP haz de trayectoria de planeo *m*; **--path localizer** *n* TRANSP localizador de trayectoria de planeo *m*; **~ plane** *n* CRYSTALL *symmetry element*, NUCL *ring network* plano de deslizamiento *m*; **~ ratio** *n* AIR TRANSP proporción de planeo *f*; **~ slope** *n* AIR TRANSP trayectoria de planeo *f*; **--slope aerial** *n* *BrE* (*cf glide-slope antenna AmE*) AIR TRANSP, TRANSP antena de la trayectoria de planeo *f*; **--slope antenna** *AmE* (*cf glide-slope aerial BrE*) antena de planeo *f*

glider *n* AIR TRANSP, MILIT planeador *m*; **~ tug** *n* MILIT remolcador del planeador *m*

gliding *n* CRYSTALL deslizamiento *m*; **~ angle** *n* AIR TRANSP ángulo de planeo *m*; **~ boat** *n* TRANSP, WATER TRANSP hidrodeslizador *m*; **~ distance** *n* AIR TRANSP distancia de planeo *f*; **~ flight** *n* AIR TRANSP planeo *m*, vuelo de planeo *m*; **~ fracture** *n* NUCL fractura deslizante *f*

glissile: **~ dislocation** *n* METALL dislocación por desplazamiento *f*

glitch *n* TV perturbación de baja frecuencia *f*

global[1] *adj* COMP&DP general, global, mundial, SPACE global, mundial, relativo al globo terráqueo, TELECOM mundial

global[2]: **~ beam** *n* SPACE *communications* haz global *m*; **~ call** *n* TELECOM llamada global *f*; **~ coverage** *n* TELECOM, WATER TRANSP cobertura global *f*; **~ positioning system** *n* (*GPS*) AIR TRANSP, WATER TRANSP sistema de posicionamiento global *m* (*GPS*); **~ variable** *n* COMP&DP variable global *f*

Global: **~ Marine Distress and Safety System** *n* (*GMDSS*) WATER TRANSP *sea rescue* Sistema Mundial de Socorro y Seguridad Marítimos *m* (*SMSSM*)

globe: **~ joint** *n* MECH ENG junta de rótula *f*; **~ tap** *n* MECH ENG grifo recto *m*; **~ valve** *n* HYDRAUL válvula esférica *f*, REFRIG válvula de esfera *f*

Globigerina: **~ ooze** *n* GEOL barro de globigerinas *m*, lodo de globigerinas *m*, OCEAN barro de globigerinas *m*

globoid: **~ gear** *n* MECH ENG engranaje globoide *m*

globular[1] *adj* CHEM globular, METALL globular, nodular

globular[2]: **~ coke** *n* COAL perlas de coque *f pl*

globule *n* CHEM glóbulo *m*

glory: **~ hole** *n* C&G horno de recalentamiento *m*

gloss *n* C&G, COLOUR lustre *m*, FOOD glaseado *m*, P&R brillo *m*, lustre *m*, PAPER, PRINT brillo *m*, PROD brillo *m*, glaseado *m*, lustre *m*, satinado *m*, TEXTIL lustre *m*; **~ calender** *n* PAPER calandra abrillantadora *f*; **~ effect** *n* COLOUR efecto brillante *m*; **~ finish** *n* COATINGS, COLOUR acabado brillante *m*; **~ ink** *n* COLOUR tinta brillante *f*; **~ meter** *n* P&R satinómetro *m*, PAPER aparato para medir el brillo *m*; **~ paint** *n* COLOUR, CONST pintura al esmalte *f*, pintura brillante *f*

glossiness *n* C&G lustre *m*, COLOUR aspecto brillante *m*, brillo *m*, lustre *m*, P&R lustre *m*, PROD aspecto brillante *m*, brillo *m*, lustre *m*, TEXTIL lustre *m*

glossing *n* FOOD glaseado *m*, PROD aguas *f pl*, glaseado *m*, lustrado *m*, TEXTIL aguas *f pl*

glossy[1] *adj* CINEMAT, P&R, PHOTO, TEXTIL, TV brillante

glossy[2]: **~ print** *n* PHOTO copia fotográfica esmaltada *f*, PRINT impreso satinado *m*

glove: **~ box** *n* NUCL caja de guantes *f*, VEH guantera *f*; **~ port** *n* NUCL portillo de guantes *m*

glow[1] *n* CHEM combustión lenta *f*; **~ discharge** *n* ELEC, ELEC ENG, ELECTRON, PHYS, RAD PHYS descarga luminiscente *f*, efluvio *m*; **--discharge cathode** *n* ELEC, ELEC ENG, ELECTRON, PHYS cátodo de descarga luminiscente *m*; **--discharge lamp** *n* ELEC, ELECTRON, PHYS lámpara de descarga luminiscente *f*; **--discharge rectifier** *n* ELEC ENG rectificador de efluvio *m*; **--discharge sputtering** *n* NUCL sublimación catódica con descarga luminosa *f*; **--discharge tube** *n* ELEC, ELEC ENG, ELECTRON tubo de descarga luminiscente *m*; **~ lamp** *n* ELEC, ELEC ENG lámpara de incandescencia *f*; **~ plug** *n* AUTO bujía incandescente *f*, THERMO bujía incandescente *f*, tapón incandescente *m*; **~ switch** *n* ELEC, ELEC ENG interruptor de descarga *m*

glow[2] *vi* CHEM inflamarse, THERMO abrasarse, arder, encenderse, inflamarse, radiar; **~ red** *vi* CHEM quemarse al rojo

glowing[1] *adj* CHEM ardiente, encendido, incandescente, inflamado, luminiscente, radiante, resplandeciente, rutilante, SPACE incandescente, THERMO ardiente, encendido, incandescente, inflamado, luminiscente, radiante, resplandeciente, rutilante

glowing[2]: **~ cloud** *n* GEOL nube ardiente *f*; **~ heat** *n* HEAT ENG, THERMO calor luminiscente *m*, calor radiante *m*, calor rutilante *m*; **~ tungsten filament** *n* RAD PHYS filamento de wolframio incandescente *m*

glucagon *n* CHEM factor hiperglicémico-glicogenolítico *m*, glucagón *m*

glucamine *n* CHEM glucamina *f*

glucaronic *adj* CHEM glucarónico

glucide *n* CHEM carbohidrato *m*, glúcido *m*

gluconic[1] *adj* CHEM glucónico

gluconic[2]: **~ acid** *n* CHEM, DETERG ácido glucónico *m*

glucoprotein *n* CHEM glucoproteína *f*

glucopyranose *n* CHEM glucopiranosa *f*

glucosamine *n* CHEM glucosamina *f*

glucosan *n* CHEM glucosana *f*

glucose *n* CHEM glucosa *f*

glucoside *n* CHEM, FOOD glucósido *m*

glue[1] *n* CHEM, COLOUR cola *f*, P&R cola *f*, goma arábiga *f*, PACK, PAPER, TEXTIL cola *f*; **~ color** *AmE*, **~ colour** *BrE* *n* COLOUR colorante adhesivo *m*; **~ etching** *n* C&G grabado engomado *m*; **~ film** *n* PACK película de cola *f*; **--gumming machine** *n* PACK máquina engomadora *f*; **~ joint** *n* PACK junta encolada *f*; **~ layer** *n* COATINGS capa de cola *f*; **~ line** *n* P&R capa de adhesivo entre dos superficies *f*; **~ press** *n* PACK prensa de encolar *f*; **~ size** *n* COLOUR adhesivo de cola *m*; **--spreading machine** *n* PACK máquina esparcidora de la cola *f*

glue[2] *vt* CHEM, P&R, PACK, PAPER, TEXTIL encolar

glued: **~ box** *n* PACK caja pegada *f*; **~ seal** *n* PACK precinto engomado *m*; **~ tab** *n* PACK etiqueta engomada *f*

gluing *n* PACK, PAPER, PRINT, PROD encolado *m*, encoladura *f*; **~ device** *n* PACK dispositivo para encolar *m*; **~ machine** *n* PACK, PRINT encoladora *f*

glume *n* AGRIC gluma *f*

gluon *n* PART PHYS, PHYS glúon *m*; **~ color** *AmE*, **~ colour** *BrE* *n* PART PHYS color del glúon *m*

glut *n* HYDRAUL bóveda *f*

glutaconic *adj* CHEM glutacónico
glutamate *n* CHEM glutamato *m*
glutamic *adj* CHEM glutámico
glutamine *n* CHEM glutamina *f*
glutaraldehyde *n* CHEM glutaraldehído *m*
glutaric *adj* CHEM glutárico
glutathione *n* CHEM glutatión *m*
gluten[1]: ~-free *adj* AGRIC, FOOD sin gluten
gluten[2] *n* AGRIC, FOOD gluten *m*; ~ extensibility *n* FOOD amplitud del gluten *f*; ~ meal *n* AGRIC harina de gluten *f*
glyceraldehyde *n* CHEM gliceraldehído *m*
glyceric *adj* CHEM glicérico
glyceride *n* CHEM, FOOD glicérido *m*
glycerine *n* CHEM glicerina *f*
glycerol *n* CHEM glicerol *m*
glycerophosphate *n* CHEM glicerofosfato *m*
glycerophosphoric *adj* CHEM glicerofosfórico
glyceryl *n* CHEM glicerilo *m*; ~ monacoleate *n* CHEM, FOOD monacolato de glicerilo *m*; ~ tristearate *n* CHEM, FOOD estearina *f*, triestearato de glicerilo *m*
glycidic *adj* CHEM glicídico
glycine *n* CHEM, FOOD glicina *f*, ácido aminoacético *m*
glycocide *n* CHEM glicósido *m*
glycogen *n* CHEM, FOOD glicógeno *m*
glycol *n* CHEM, DETERG, REFRIG etilenglicol *m*, glicol *m*; ~ ether *n* CHEM, DETERG éter glicólico *m*; ~ solution *n* CHEM, DETERG, REFRIG solución de glicol *f*
glycolic *adj* CHEM, DETERG, REFRIG glicólico
glycoline *n* CHEM glicolina *f*
glycolipid *n* CHEM glicolípido *m*
glycolysis *n* CHEM, FOOD glicólisis *f*
glycoside *n* CHEM, FOOD glucósido *m*
glycuronic *adj* CHEM glicurónico
glycylglycine *n* CHEM glicilglicina *f*
glycyrrhizine *n* CHEM glicirricina *f*
glyoxal *n* CHEM glioxal *m*
glyoxalidine *n* CHEM glioxalidina *f*
glyoxaline *n* CHEM glioxalina *f*, imidazol *m*
glyoxime *n* CHEM glioxima *f*
glyoxylic *adj* CHEM glioxílico
glyptal: ~ resin *n* P&R resina gliptálica *f*; ~ resin lacquer *n* COLOUR laca de resina gliptal *f*
GMDSS *abbr* (*Global Marine Distress and Safety System*) WATER TRANSP *sea rescue* SMSSM (*Sistema Mundial de Socorro y Seguridad Marítimos*)
gmelinite *n* MINERAL gmelinita *f*
GMSK *abbr* (*Gaussian-filtered minimum shift keying*) TELECOM codificación por mínimo desplazamiento de fase por filtrado gaussiano *f*
GMT *abbr* (*Greenwich Mean Time*) AIR TRANSP, PHYS, SPACE GMT (*hora solar media, hora del meridiano de Greenwich, hora media de Greenwich*)
gnat *n* AGRIC mosquito *m*
gneiss *n* CONST, GEOL, PETROL gneis *m*
gneissic *adj* CONST, GEOL, PETROL gneísico
gnomonic: ~ projection *n* WATER TRANSP *navigation* proyección centrográfica *f*, proyección gnomónica *f*
go[1]: ~-no-go *adj* MECH ENG máximo y mínimo; ~-and-not-go *adj* MECH ENG *limit-gauges* máximo y mínimo
go[2]: ~ ahead *adv* (*GA*) TELECOM adelante
go[3]: ~ ahead *n* (*GA*) TELECOM adelante *m*; ~ devil *n* PETR TECH conejo *m*, muñeco *m*; ~ gage *AmE*, ~ gauge *BrE n* MECH ENG calibrador de tolerancia

mínima *m*, calibrador fijo de medida exacta *m*, calibrador que pasa *m*
go[4]: ~ alongside *vt* WATER TRANSP abarloar a
go[5]: ~ about *vi* WATER TRANSP *sailing* virar por avante; ~ aground *vi* OCEAN, WATER TRANSP encallar, varar; ~ astern *vi* WATER TRANSP ciar, ir marcha atrás; ~ critical *vi* NUCL hacerse crítico; ~ down *vi* WATER TRANSP *ship* irse al fondo; ~ down by the bows *vi* WATER TRANSP *ship* colarse por ojo, pasarse por ojo; ~ into circuit *vi* TELECOM entrar en circuito; ~ out *vi* ELEC ENG *of light* apagarse, extinguirse; ~ plug *n* MECH tapón de ida *m*; ~ upstream *vi* HYDROL ir aguas arriba; ~ via the circuit *vi* TELECOM entrar a través del circuito
goaf *n* MINE relleno con desechos *m*
gob *n* C&G vela *f*, MINE atierre *m*, hundimiento *m*, macizo de relleno *m*; ~ distributor *n* C&G distribuidor de velas *m*; ~ feeding *n* C&G alimentación de vela *f*; ~ tail *n* C&G cola de la gota o carga *f*; ~ temperature *n* C&G temperatura de la gota o carga *f*
goethite *n* MINERAL goetita *f*, lepidocroita *f*, mica rubí *f*
goggles *n pl* LAB, MECH ENG, OPT, PROD, SAFE anteojos de protección *m pl* (*AmL*), gafas protectoras *f pl* (*Esp*)
going *n* CONST *of a step* descenso *m*; ~ over *n* PROD *screw-cutting* pasada *f*
Golay: ~ cell *n* PHYS célula de Golay *f*
gold[1]: ~-bearing *adj* METALL, MINE, MINERAL aurífero; ~-plated *adj* CHEM dorado, enchapado en oro
gold[2] *n* (*Au*) CHEM, METALL oro *m* (*Au*); ~ blocking *n* PRINT impresión en oro *f*; ~ chloride *n* CHEM cloruro áurico *m*; ~ cleanup *n* MINE lavado de oro *m*; ~ conglomerate *n* MINE conglomerado aurífero *m*; ~ content *n* COAL contenido en oro *m*, MINE contenido de diodo *m*; ~ cyanide *n* CHEM cianuro de oro *m*; ~ diggings *n* COAL aluvión aurífero *m*, placer *m*, MINE aluvión aurífero *m*; ~-doped diode *n* ELECTRON diodo dopado con oro *m*; ~ doping *n* ELECTRON dopado con oro *m*; ~ epoxy *n* ELECTRON epoxia en oro *f*; ~ field *n* MINE yacimiento aurífero *m*; ~ flashing *n* SPACE centelleo aurífero *m*, centelleo dorado *m*; ~ foil *n* PRINT lámina de oro *f*; ~ grade *n* MINE contenido en oro *m*, ley aurífera *f*; ~ leaf electroscope *n* ELEC ENG, INSTR, PHYS electroscopio de láminas de oro *m*; ~ mine *n* MINE mina aurífera *f*; ~-mining industry *n* MINE industria minera del oro *f*; ~ ore *n* MINE mineral aurífero *m*; ~ plating *n* METALL, SPACE dorado *m*, recubrimiento electrolítico de oro *m*; ~ probe method *n* NUCL método de la sonda de oro *m*; ~ reef *n* MINE filón de cuarzo aurífero *m*, filón tubular *m*; ~ tenor *n* MINE contenido en oro *m*, ley aurífera *f*; ~ toning *n* PHOTO viraje en oro *m*
golden: ~ beryl *n* MINERAL berilo dorado *m*; ~ section *n* GEOM proporción aurea *f*, razón aurea *f*, sección de oro *f*
goldenrod *n* PRINT hoja de montaje *f*, plantilla *f*
goliath: ~ crane *n* CONST grúa goliath *f*
gondola *n* SPACE barquilla *f*; ~ cableway *n* TRANSP teleférico con cabinas *m*, teleférico góndola *m*; ~ car *n AmE* (*cf open wagon BrE*) RAIL vagón abierto *m*, vagón batea *m*, vagón de bordes bajos *m*
Gondwanan *adj* GEOL de Gondwana
gong *n* WATER TRANSP gong *m*
goniometer *n* CRYSTALL, GEOM goniómetro *m*, radio-

goniómetro *m*, INSTR goniómetro *m*, OCEAN goniómetro *m*, radiogoniómetro *m*, RAD PHYS goniómetro *m*

Gooch: ~ **crucible** *n* LAB crisol de Gooch *m*

good: ~ **inwards test** *n* PROD prueba de mercancías de entrada *f*

goods *n pl BrE* (*cf freight AmE*) PACK mercancías *f pl*, PETR TECH, SPACE flete *m*, WATER TRANSP carga *f*, flete *m*; ~ **agent** *n BrE* FOOD agente cargador *m*, RAIL , TRANSP, WATER TRANSP agente aduanero *m*, agente cargador *m*, agente de aduanas *m*, agente de transporte *m*, agente despachador *m*, agente expedidor *m*, transitario *m*; ~ **chute** *n BrE* (*cf freight chute AmE*) TRANSP tobogán de carga *m*, tobogán de mercancías *m*; ~ **depot** *n BrE* (*cf freight depot AmE*) TRANSP almacén de mercancías *m*, depósito de carga *m*, estación de mercancías *f*, muelle de mercancías *m*; ~ **inwards** *n pl BrE* (*cf freight inwards AmE*) PROD entrada de mercancías *f*, RAIL entrada de cargamento *f*, entrada de mercancías *f*; ~ **lift** *n* PROD montacargas *m*; ~ **locomotive** *n BrE* (*cf freight locomotive AmE*) RAIL locomotora de tren de mercancías *f*; ~ **lorry** *n BrE* (*cf freight truck AmE*) AUTO camión de mercancías *m*; ~ **porter** *n BrE* (*cf freight porter AmE*) RAIL locomotora de tren de mercancías *f*, peón de carga *m*, peón de mercancías *m*; ~ **rate** *n BrE* (*cf freight rate AmE*) PACK, PETR TECH tarifa de la carga *f*, tarifa del flete *f*, tipo del flete *m*; ~ **shed** *n BrE* (*cf freight shed AmE*) TRANSP depósito de mercancías *m*; ~ **station** *n BrE* (*cf freight station AmE*) TRANSP almacén de mercancías *m*, depósito de carga *m*, estación de mercancías *f*, muelle de mercancías *m*; ~ **terminal** *n BrE* (*cf freight terminal AmE*) PACK terminal de carga *m*; ~ **train** *n BrE* (*cf freight train AmE*) RAIL tren de carga *m*, tren de mercancías *m*; ~ **van** *n BrE* (*cf freight van AmE*) TRANSP furgoneta de mercancías *f*, furgón de mercancías *m*; ~ **wagon** *n BrE* (*cf freight car AmE*) TRANSP vagón de mercancías *m*; ~ **yard** *n BrE* (*cf freight yard AmE*) RAIL patio de carga *m*, patio de mercancías *m*; ~ **yard foreman** *n BrE* (*cf freight yard foreman AmE*) RAIL capataz del patio de carga *m*, capataz del patio de mercancías *m*

goose: ~-**necked pot carriage** *n* C&G carro cuello de ganso *m*

gooseneck *n* CINEMAT cuello de cisne *m*, MECH barra curva *f*, cuello de cisne *m*, sifón *m*, PROD *blast furnace* codo del portaviento *m*, WATER TRANSP gancho de botavara *m*, tubo de ventilación *m*; ~ **pipe** *n* MECH tubo en S *m*, MECH ENG tubo de cuello de cisne *m*, tubo en S *m*; ~ **wrench** *n* MECH ENG llave de cuello de cisne *f*

gopher *n* COMP&DP gopher *m*; ~ **hole** *n* MINE túnel para voladura *m*

GOR *abbr* (*gas-to-oil ratio*) PETR TECH GOR (*relación gas-petróleo*)

goslarite *n* MINERAL goslarita *f*

gossan *n* GEOL montera de oxidación *f*, quijo *m*

gothic: ~ **face** *n* PRINT tipo gótico *m*

gouge *n* CONST *wood-working tool* gubia *f*, MINE salbanda *f*

gouging *n* PROD *welding* trabajo con la gubia *m*; ~ **blowpipe** *n* CONST soplete de corte *m*

governing *n* MECH ENG reglaje *m*

governor *n* AUTO activador *m*, regulador *m*, CINEMAT activador *m*, ELEC ENG, FUELLESS, MECH, MECH ENG,

VEH, WATER TRANSP activador *m*, regulador *m*; ~-**control stop** *n* AIR TRANSP tope del control del regulador *m*; ~ **rod** *n* MECH ENG varilla reguladora *f*; ~ **valve** *n* HYDRAUL válvula de estrangulación *f* (*AmL*), válvula reguladora *f* (*Esp*)

GP[1] *abbr* (*Guinier-Preston zone*) CRYSTALL zona de Guinier-Preston *f*

GP[2]: ~ **computer** *n* (*general-purpose computer*) COMP&DP computador de uso general *m* (*AmL*), computador universal *m* (*AmL*) (*CU*), computadora de uso general *f* (*AmL*), computadora universal *f* (*AmL*) (*CU*), ordenador de uso general *m* (*Esp*), ordenador universal *m* (*Esp*)

GPS *abbr* (*global positioning system*) AIR TRANSP, WATER TRANSP GPS (*sistema de posicionamiento global*)

GPU *abbr* (*ground power unit*) AIR TRANSP GPU (*grupo electrógeno de pista, grupo motopropulsor de tierra, unidad de potencia de tierra*)

grab *n* CONST agarradera *f*, asa *f*, mango *m*, MINE cubeta draga *f*, enganchador de sondas *m*, sondeo *m*, NUCL *boat* gancho *m*, WATER TRANSP *of dredger* cuchara *f*; ~ **bucket** *n* CONST balde de mandíbulas *m*, cuchara bivalva *f*, cucharón de mandíbulas *m*; ~ **crane** *n* CONST excavadora bivalva *f*; ~ **dredge** *n* CONST draga bivalva *f*; ~ **dredger** *n* CONST dragadora bivalva *f*, WATER TRANSP draga de almeja *f*

grabbing: ~ **clutch** *n* AUTO embrague de agarre *m*, embrague de garras *m*; ~ **tap** *n* MINE terraja enganchadora *f*

graceful: ~ **degradation** *n* COMP&DP degradación con garbo *f*, degradación parcial *f*

grad *n* CINEMAT degradación *f*

gradation *n* COLOUR gradación *f*, METR dosificación *f*, PRINT gradación *f*

gradding *n* CINEMAT degradación *f*

grade[1] *n* GEN calidad *f*; ~ **cattle** *n* AGRIC ganado vacuno seleccionado *m*; ~ **crossing** *n AmE* (*cf level crossing BrE*) CONST, RAIL paso a nivel *m*; ~ **of service** *n* TELECOM grado de servicio *m*; ~ **stake** *n* RAIL estaca de rasante *f*

grade[2] *vt* GEN clasificar, gradar, CONST allanar, aplanar, nivelar

graded: ~ **bedding** *n* GEOL estratificación gradada *f*; ~ **channel terrace** *n* AGRIC terraza de desagüe *f*; ~ **coal** *n* COAL carbón calibrado *m*, carbón clasificado *m*; ~ **index** *n* ELEC ENG perfil de índice gradual *m*, OPT índice gradual *m*; ~-**index core** *n* ELEC ENG núcleo del perfil de índices gradual *m*; ~-**index fiber** *AmE*, ~-**index fibre** *BrE n* OPT fibra de índice gradual *f*, PHYS fibra de índice enjaretada *f*, TELECOM fibra de índice gradual *f*, WATER TRANSP fibra de índice enjaretada *f*; ~-**index profile** *n* OPT, PHYS, TELECOM perfil de índice gradual *m*; ~ **profile** *n* GEOL perfil gradado *m*; ~ **seal** *n* C&G sello graduado *m*; ~ **sluice** *n* WATER compuerta de abertura graduada *f*; ~ **soil** *n* COAL terreno inclinado *m*

grader *n* CINEMAT clasificador *m*, CONST niveladora *f*, explanadora *f*, MAR POLL, TRANSP explanadora *f*, máquina explanadora *f*; ~ **leveling blade** *AmE*, ~ **levelling blade** *BrE n* TRANSP cuchilla niveladora de aplanadora *f*

gradient *n* GEN pendiente *f*; ~ **current** *n* OCEAN corriente de nivelación *f*; ~ **microphone** *n* ACOUST micrófono de gradiente *m*; ~ **post** *n* RAIL poste de cambio de rasante *m*, poste indicador de la pendiente *m*; ~ **of Reynolds stress** *n* FLUID gradiente de esfuerzo de Reynolds *m*; ~ **speed** *n* CINEMAT velocidad de gradiente *f*; ~ **of x per cent** *n* CONST pendiente de x por ciento *f*; ~ **of x in 1000** *n* CONST pendiente de x por 1000 *f*

grading *n* AGRIC clasificación *f*, C&G selección *f*, CINEMAT gradación *f*, COAL cribado *m*, granulometría *f*, nivelación *f*, regularización *f*, CONST granulometría *f*, graduación *f*, *bringing to level, to regular inclination* nivelación *f*, *civil engineering* explanación *f*, PACK, PROD, QUALITY clasificación *f*, TELECOM mejora *f*; ~ **analysis** *n* CONST ensayo granulométrico *m*; ~ **band** *n* CINEMAT banda de gradación *f*; ~ **copy** *n* CINEMAT copia de gradación *f*; ~**-coupling loss cable** *n* ELEC, TELECOM cable de pérdidas de acoplamiento de mejora *m*; ~ **curve** *n* COAL curva de nivelado *f*; ~ **envelope** *n* CONST cubierta de nivelación *f*; ~ **plant** *n* AGRIC planta clasificadora *f*; ~ **sheet** *n* CINEMAT, TV hoja de gradación *f*

gradiomanometer *n* PETROL gradiomanómetro *m*

graduated: ~ **braking** *n* RAIL, VEH frenado graduado *m*; ~ **circle** *n* INSTR círculo graduado *m*; ~ **dial** *n* INSTR cuadrante graduado *m*, MECH ENG disco graduado *m*; ~ **filter** *n* CINEMAT, PHOTO, TV filtro graduado *m*; ~ **flask** *n* LAB matraz graduado *m*; ~ **pipette** *n* LAB pipeta graduada *f*

graduating: ~ **engine** *n* MECH ENG motor graduador *m*

graduation *n* LAB escala *f*, graduación *f*, PRINT *transformer, electrical machine* graduación *f*; ~ **mark** *n* LAB marca de graduación *f*

graft: ~ **hybrid** *n* AGRIC híbrido de injerto *m*; ~ **polymer** *n* P&R polímero injertado *m*; ~ **polymerization** *n* P&R polimerización por injerto de una cadena *f*; ~ **union** *n* AGRIC soldadura *f*

grafting: ~ **in the dormant bud** *n* AGRIC injerto a ojo dormido *m*

graham: ~ **flour** *n* AGRIC harina de trigo sin cerner *f*

Graham: ~**'s law** *n* PHYS ley de Graham *f*

grain[1] *n* GEN grano *m*; ~ **alcohol** *n* FOOD alcohol de cereales *m*, alcohol de grano *m*; ~ **auger** *n* AGRIC sinfín *m*; ~ **boundary** *n* CRYSTALL contorno de grano *m*, junta de grano *f*, límite de grano *m*, METALL junta de grano *f*, límite de grano *m*, contorno de grano *m*, NUCL borde de grano *m*; ~**-boundary diffusion** *n* METALL difusión del plano de exfoliación *f*; ~**-boundary migration** *n* METALL migración del plano de exfoliación *f*; ~ **clumping** *n* PHOTO aglutinación del grano *f*; ~ **crop** *n* AGRIC cosecha de cereales *f*; ~ **dealer** *n* AGRIC cerealista *m*; ~ **direction** *n* PRINT sentido longitudinal *m*; ~ **drill** *n* AGRIC sembradora en línea *f*; ~ **equivalent** *n* AGRIC valor cereal *m*; ~ **feeder** *n* AGRIC tolva *f*; ~ **fraction** *n* COAL fraccionado por tamaños *m*; ~ **grower** *n* AGRIC productor de granos *m*; ~ **hay** *n* AGRIC heno de cereales *m*; ~ **legume** *n* AGRIC leguminosa de grano seco *f*; ~ **mill** *n* AGRIC molino de granos *m*; ~ **moth** *n* AGRIC polilla del grano *f*; ~**-producing country** *n* AGRIC país productor de granos *m*; ~ **product** *n* AGRIC producto de cereales *m*; ~ **refinement** *n* METALL afino del grano *m*, refino de grano *m*; ~**-refining anneal** *n* THERMO recocido afinante del grano *m*; ~ **season** *n* AGRIC campaña cerealista *f*; ~ **shape** *n* COAL forma de las partículas *f*; ~ **side** *n* PROD *of belt* cara del grano *f*, cara del pelo *f*; ~ **size** *n* COAL, CRYSTALL, METALL tamaño de la partícula *m*, tamaño del grano *m*; ~**-size analysis** *n* MECH ENG análisis del

tamaño del grano *m*; ~**-size distribution** *n* GEOL distribución granulométrica *f*; ~ **sorghum** *n* AGRIC sorgo granífero *m*; ~ **structure** *n* COAL estructura de garno *f*, estructura de la partícula *f*; ~ **test** *n* C&G prueba del grano *f*; ~ **year** *n* AGRIC campaña cerealista *f*

grain[2] *vt* PROD granular, granularse

graininess *n* CINEMAT, PHOTO, PRINT granulación *f*

grainless *adj* PHOTO sin grano

grainstone *n* GEOL roca granular *f*

gram *n* CHEM, METR, PHYS gramo *m*; ~ **calorie** *n* METR, PHYS *heat unit* caloría-gramo *f*; ~ **centimeter** *n* AmE, ~ **centimetre** *n* BrE METR centímetro-gramo *m*; ~ **equivalent** *n* CHEM *of compound* gramo equivalente *m*; ~ **in mass** *n* METR gramo-masa *m*; ~ **ion** *n* METR ión-gramo *m*; ~ **molecule** *n* METR molécula-gramo *f*

grammage *n* PAPER, PRINT gramaje *m*

grammatite *n* MINERAL grammatita *f*

gramme *see* gram

Gramme: ~ **ring** *n* ELEC *coil* anillo Gramme *m*; ~ **winding** *n* ELEC devanado Gramme *m*

gramophone: ~ **record** *n* ACOUST disco de gramófono *m*

granary *n* FOOD granero *m*

grand: ~ **unification energy** *n* PART PHYS gran energía de unificación *f*; ~ **unified theory** *n* (*GUT*) PART PHYS, PHYS teoría de gran unificación *f*

granite *n* CONST, GEOL, PETROL granito *m*; ~**-gneiss** *n* GEOL gneis granítico *m*; ~ **surface plate** *n* MECH ENG superficie plan de granito *f*

granitell *n* PETROL granitela *f*

granitite *n* PETROL granitita *f*

granitization *n* GEOL granitización *f*

granitoid *adj* GEOL granitoide

granny: ~ **knot** *n* WATER TRANSP nudo lleno mal hecho *m*

granodiorite *n* PETROL granodiorita *f*

granophyre *n* PETROL granofiro *m*

granular[1] *adj* CONST granulado, granular, GEOL granular

granular[2]: ~ **fracture** *n* NUCL fractura granular *f*; ~ **material** *n* CONST material granular *m*; ~ **noise** *n* TELECOM ruido granular *m*

granularity *n* COMP&DP, PHOTO granularidad *f*

granulate *vt* CHEM TECH, GEOL, PACK granular

granulated[1] *adj* GEOL, PACK granulado

granulated[2]: ~ **cork** *n* REFRIG corcho granulado *m*; ~ **glass** *n* C&G vidrio granulado *m*

granulates *n pl* CHEM TECH granulados *m pl*

granulating: ~ **crusher** *n* CHEM TECH granuladora *f*; ~ **hammer** *n* CHEM TECH bujarda *f*; ~ **machine** *n* CHEM TECH granuladora *f*, máquina granuladora *f*, PACK granuladora *f*, maquinaria granuladora *f*; ~ **roller** *n* CHEM TECH rodillo de granulación *m*

granulation *n* AGRIC granazón *m*, C&G, CHEM TECH granulación *f*, COAL graneado *m*; ~ **pitch** *n* CHEM TECH bitumen de granulación *m*

granulator *n* C&G, CHEM TECH granulador *m*

granule *n* PACK gránulo *m*; ~ **size distribution** *n* C&G distribución del tamaño de los granos *f*

granuled: ~ **material** *n* CHEM TECH material granulado *m*

granulite *n* PETROL granulita *f*

granulometric[1] *adj* C&G, CHEM TECH, COAL, CONST, NUCL granulométrico

granulometric[2]: ~ **analysis** *n* BrE (*cf screen analysis*

AmE) C&G, CHEM TECH, COAL, GEOL, NUCL análisis granulométrico *m*; ~ **classification** *n* C&G, CHEM TECH, COAL clasificación granulométrica *f*
granulometry *n* C&G, CHEM TECH, COAL granulometría *f*
grape: ~ **colaspis** *n* AGRIC colaspis flavida *f*; ~ **grower** *n* AGRIC viticultor *m*; ~ **growing** *n* AGRIC viticultura *f*; ~ **harvest** *n* AGRIC vendimia *f*; ~ **sugar** *n* AGRIC fructosa *f*, FOOD glucosa *f*
grapeseed: ~ **oil** *n* FOOD aceite de orujo *m*
grapeshot *n* MILIT metralla *f*
grapestone *n* PETROL pepita *f*
graph[1] *n* COMP&DP gráfico *m*, MATH gráfica *f*, gráfico *m*; ~ **plotter** *n* COMP&DP plotter gráfico *m*, trazador gráfico *m*; ~ **theory** *n* MATH teoría de grafos *f*, teoría de gráficas *f*
graph[2] *vt* MATH dibujar (*Esp*), dibujar una gráfica (*Esp*), graficar (*AmL*)
graphic *n* PRINT gráfico *m*; ~ **arts** *n* PRINT artes gráficas *f pl*; ~ **character** *n* COMP&DP carácter gráfico *m*; ~ **display adaptor** *n* COMP&DP adaptador de representación gráfica *m*; ~ **geometry** *n* GEOM geometría gráfica *f*; ~ **software package** *n* COMP&DP edición gráfica *f*, editor gráfico *m*, paquete de edición gráfico *m*, paquete de software gráfico *m*, paquete de soporte lógico gráfico *m*; ~ **tablet** *n* TV tablero gráfico *m*; ~ **texture** *n* PETROL textura gráfica *f*
graphical: ~ **editing** *n* COMP&DP edición gráfica *f*; ~ **representation** *n* COMP&DP representación gráfica *f*; ~ **symbol** *n* SAFE símbolo gráfico *m*
graphics *n* COMP&DP gráfico *m*; ~ **coordinated with bottle labels** *n* PACK gráficos coordinados con etiquetas de botella *m pl*; ~ **plotter** *n* COMP&DP plotter gráfico *m*, trazador gráfico *m*; ~ **tablet** *n* COMP&DP tableta gráfica *f*; ~ **work station** *n* COMP&DP puesto de trabajo gráfico *m*
graphite *n* CHEM, MINERAL grafito *m*; ~ **block** *n* NUCL bloque de grafito *m*; ~ **brush** *n* ELEC escobilla de grafito *f*; ~**clad fuel element** *n* NUCL elemento de combustible revestido de grafito *m*; ~ **coating** *n* COATINGS, NUCL revestimiento de grafito *m*; ~ **grease** *n* MECH *of transformer* grasa grafitada *f*; ~ **guide tube** *n* NUCL tubo-guía de grafito *m*; ~ **paint** *n* COLOUR pintura de grafito *f*; ~ **shielding** *n* NUCL blindaje de grafito *m*; ~ **structure** *n* NUCL estructura de grafito *f*
graphitization *n* METALL grafitización *f*
grapnel *n* MECH ENG anclote *m*, rezón *m*, WATER TRANSP rezón *m*
grapple *n* TRANSP cucharón bivalvo *m*, residuo acuoso *m*, WATER TRANSP arpeo *m*
grappling: ~ **hook** *n* WATER TRANSP arpeo *m*, garfio de arpeo *m*
graptolitic: ~ **shale** *n* GEOL esquisto graptolítico *m*
grasping: ~ **margin** *n* PRINT margen de entrada *m*
grass *n* ELECTRON señales parásitas *f pl*, MINE exterior *m* (*AmL*), suelo *m* (*Esp*), NUCL deflexión por ruido de la base de tiempos *f*; ~ **improvement** *n* AGRIC mejora de pastizales *f*; ~ **management** *n* AGRIC pasticultura *f*; ~ **sorghum** *n* AGRIC sorgo forrajero *m*
grasshopper *n* AGRIC saltamontes *m*
grate *n* HEAT parrilla *f* (*AmL*), PROD *fire* armadura *f*, parrilla *f* (*AmL*), *of ore stamp* tamiz *m*; ~ **area** *n* CONST zona enrejada *f*; ~ **bar** *n* PROD barra de emparrillado *f*, barrote de parrilla *m*; ~**shaking rig** *n* PROD mecanismo sacudidor de parrilla *m*

graticule *n* CINEMAT, ELECTRON, INSTR, METR, OPT, TV cuadrícula *f*, ocular cuadriculado *m*, reticulado *m* (*AmL*), retículo *m* (*Esp*)
grating *n* ELEC ENG *waveguides* trama *f*, PHYS rejilla de difracción *f*, PROD reja *f*, emparrillado *m*, rejilla *f*, *for cores or moulds* armadura *f*, TELECOM rejilla de difracción *f*, TV reticulado *m* (*AmL*), retículo *m* (*Esp*), WATER TRANSP *cockpit* enjaretado *m*, WAVE PHYS red difractora *f*, rejilla de difracción *f*; ~ **converter** *n* ELEC transformador de guía de ondas *m*, ELEC ENG convertidor reticular *m*, transformador de guía de ondas *m*; ~ **spectrograph** *n* NUCL espectrógrafo de retículo *m*
grave *vt* WATER TRANSP *ship maintenance* carenar, limpiar fondos
gravel *n* COAL arena aurífera *f*, pedregoso *m*, CONST grava *f*, ripio *m*, GEOL, PETROL grava *f*; ~ **mine** *n* COAL aluvión aurífero *m*, placer *m*, MINE aluvión aurífero *m*; ~ **pit** *n* CONST cantera de grava *f*, gravera *f*, WATER cascajal *m*, gravera *f*
graveyard: ~ **orbit** *n* SPACE órbita para aparcar satélites fuera de servicio *f*
gravimeter *n* COAL, GEOPHYS, INSTR, PETR TECH, PHYS gravímetro *m*
gravimetric[1] *adj* COAL, GEOPHYS, INSTR, PETR TECH, PHYS gravimétrico
gravimetric[2]: ~ **analysis** *n* CHEM TECH, COAL, GEOPHYS, INSTR, PETR TECH análisis gravimétrico *m*; ~ **survey** *n* GEOL, GEOPHYS, PETR TECH prospección gravimétrica *f*
gravimetry *n* GEN gravimetría *f*
graving: ~ **dock** *n* WATER TRANSP dique seco *m*
gravitation *n* PHYS, SPACE gravitación *f*; ~ **collapse** *n* SPACE colapso gravitacional *m*, derrumbamiento gravitacional *m*; ~ **constant** *n* SPACE constante de gravitación *f*
gravitational: ~ **acceleration** *n* GEOL, GEOPHYS, PHYS aceleración gravitacional *f*; ~ **constant** *n* GEOL, GEOPHYS, PHYS constante de gravitación *f*, constante gravitacional *f*; ~ **field** *n* GEOL, GEOPHYS, PHYS campo gravitacional *m*, campo gravitacional terrestre *m*; ~ **mass** *n* GEOL, GEOPHYS, PHYS masa gravitacional *f*; ~ **potential** *n* GEOL, GEOPHYS, PHYS potencial gravitacional *m*; ~ **water** *n* COAL, HYDROL, WATER agua de gravedad *f*; ~ **wave** *n* PHYS onda gravitacional *f*, RAD PHYS, WAVE PHYS onda de gravedad *f*; ~**wave aerial** *n* BrE (*cf gravitational-wave antenna AmE*) PHYS, RAD PHYS antena de ondas gravitacionales *f*; ~**wave antenna** *n* AmE (*cf gravitational-wave aerial BrE*) PHYS, RAD PHYS antena de ondas gravitacionales *f*
graviton *n* PHYS gravitón *m*
gravity[1]: ~**free** *adj* GEOPHYS, PHYS sin gravedad
gravity[2] *n* GEOPHYS, MECH ENG, NUCL, PETR TECH, PHYS, SPACE gravedad *f*; ~ **acceleration** *n* PHYS, SPACE aceleración de la gravedad *f*; ~ **anomaly** *n* GEOL, GEOPHYS anomalía gravitacional *f*; ~ **casting** *n* MECH ENG fundición colada a presión por gravedad *f*, fundición inyectada por gravedad *f*; ~**check irrigation** *n* AGRIC riego por tablares *m*; ~**collapse structure** *n* GEOL estructura de hundimiento por gravedad *f*; ~ **dam** *n* HYDROL presa de gravedad *f*; ~ **die-casting die** *n* MECH ENG matriz de fundición colada por gravedad *f*, matriz para colada por gravedad *f*, molde de fundición inyectada por gravedad *m*; ~ **draining** *n* PETROL drenaje por gravedad *m*; ~**drop absorber rod** *n* NUCL barra

absorbente de caída libre *f*, barra absorbente de caída por la gravedad *f*; ~ **filler plug** *n* AIR TRANSP tapón del repostador por gravedad *m*; ~ **filling** *n* SPACE relleno por gravedad *m*; ~**filling machine** *n* PACK llenadora por gravedad *f*; ~ **flow** *n* NUCL flujo por gravedad *m*; ~ **gliding** *n* GEOL deslizamiento gravitacional *m*; ~~**gradient boom** *n* SPACE brazo de gradiente de gravedad *m*; ~~**gradient stabilization** *n* SPACE estabilización por gradiente de gravedad *f*, estabilización por gradiente de gravitación *f*; ~~**gradient torque** *n* SPACE par del gradiente de gravedad *m*; ~ **incline** *n* CONST inclinación por gravedad *f*; ~ **irrigation** *n* AGRIC riego por gravedad *m*; ~ **meter** *n* COAL gravímetro *m*, GEOPHYS, INSTR gravímetro *m*, medidor de gravedad *m*, PETR TECH gravímetro *m*, PHYS gravímetro *m*, medidor de gravedad *m*; ~ **mold for casting** *AmE*, ~ **mould for casting** *BrE n* MECH ENG molde de gravedad para fundición *m*; ~ **plane** *n* CONST plano inclinado *m*; ~ **platform** *n* PETR TECH plataforma de gravedad *f*; ~ **railroad** *n* CONST línea férrea de gravedad *f*; ~ **refueling** *AmE*, ~ **refuelling** *BrE n* AIR TRANSP repostado por gravedad *m*, SPACE reaprovisionamiento por gravitación *m*, repostaje por gravitación *m*; ~ **roller** *n* PACK rodillo giratorio por gravedad *m*; ~~**roller conveyor** *n* PACK transportador de rodillo por gravedad *m*; ~ **slide** *n* GEOL deslizamiento por gravedad *m*, desprendimiento por gravedad *m*; ~ **spillway dam** *n* AIR TRANSP estanque de derrame de gravedad *m*, presa de aliviadero *f*; ~ **stamp** *n* PROD bocarte de caída libre *m*, pilón de caída libre *m*; ~ **survey** *n* PETROL levantamiento gravimétrico *m*; ~ **switch** *n* ELEC ENG disyuntor de gravedad *m*; ~ **unit** *n* PETROL unidad gravimétrica *f*; ~~**vacuum transit train** *n* (*GVT train*) TRANSP, VEH tren con vacío de gravedad *m*; ~ **water** *n* COAL, HYDROL, WATER agua de gravedad *f*; ~ **wave** *n* PHYS, WAVE PHYS onda de gravedad *f*

gravure *n* PRINT huecograbado *m*; ~~**coated paper** *n* PAPER papel estucado con rodillo grabado *m*; ~ **coating** *n* PAPER estucado con rodillo grabado *m*; ~ **ink** *n* COLOUR tinta para huecograbado *f*; ~ **printing** *n* PRINT impresión en huecograbado *f*; ~ **printing ink** *n* COLOUR tinta para impresión de huecograbado *f*; ~ **roller** *n* PRINT rodillo de huecograbado *m*

gray *AmE see* **grey** *BrE*

Gray: ~ **code** *n* SPACE código de Gray *m*

graywacke *AmE see* **greywacke** *BrE*

grazing[1] *adj* ACOUST, PHYS rasante

grazing[2] *n* AGRIC pastoreo *m*; ~ **incidence** *n* OPT, PHYS incidencia rasante *f*; ~ **season** *n* AGRIC época de pastoreo *f*

grease[1] *n* AUTO, ELEC ENG, MECH, MECH ENG, PROD, VEH grasa *f*; ~ **box** *n* PROD caja de grasa *f*; ~ **cap** *n* VEH engrasador *m*; ~ **cock** *n* PROD grifo engrasador *m*; ~ **cup** *n* PROD engrasador de copa *m*; ~ **gun** *n* AUTO, CONST, MECH ENG pistola de engrase *f*, VEH jeringa de engrase *f*, pistola de engrase *f*; ~ **lubricator** *n* PROD lubricador de grasa *m*; ~ **mark** *n* C&G marca de lubricante *f*; ~~**packing gland** *n* MECH ENG prensaestopas de grasa *m*; ~ **pencil** *n* CINEMAT lápiz graso *m*; ~~**resistant board** *n* PACK, PAPER cartón resistente a las grasas *m*; ~~**resistant paper** *n* PACK, PAPER papel resistente *m*, papel resistente a las grasas *m*; ~ **retainer** *n* MECH ENG retenedor de grasa lubricante *m*

grease[2] *vt* AUTO, MECH, MECH ENG, PROD, VEH engrasar, lubricar

greaseproof[1] *adj* PACK, PAPER a prueba de grasa, resistente a las grasas

greaseproof[2]: ~ **paper** *n* FOOD papel encerado *m*, PACK papel resistente a las grasas *m*, papel similsulfurizado *m*, PAPER papel encerado *m*, papel resistente a las grasas *m*, papel similsulfurizado *m*

greaser *n* PROD engrasador *m*

greasing *n* PROD engrase *m*; ~ **agent** *n* CHEM, FOOD agente grasiento *m*

great: ~ **circle** *n* PHYS círculo mayor *m*, círculo máximo *m*, ortodromo *f*; ~ **circle chart** *n* WATER TRANSP carta gnomónica *f*, carta nomónica *f*; ~~**circle course** *n* WATER TRANSP derrota ortodrómica *f*, rumbo por círculo máximo *m*; ~~**circle path** *n* SPACE trayectoria ortodrómica *f*, trayectoria según un círculo máximo *f*; ~~**circle route** *n* AIR TRANSP ruta ortodrómica *f*

greatest: ~ **common divisor** *n* MATH máximo común divisor *m* (*mcd*)

green[1]: ~~**stained** *adj* GEOL de tono verdoso

green[2] *n* TRANSP *traffic-light* abierto *m*; ~ **adder** *n* TV circuito aditivo verde *m*; ~ **beam** *n* ELECTRON, TV haz verde *m*; ~~**beam laser** *n* ELECTRON, TV láser de haz verde *m*; ~ **belt** *n* GEOL cinturón verde *m*; ~ **black level** *n* TV nivel verde negro *m*; ~ **chop** *n* AGRIC pasto verde cortado fino *m*; ~ **compact** *n* NUCL comprimido crudo *m*; ~ **concrete** *n* CONST concreto fresco *m* (*AmL*), hormigón fresco *m* (*Esp*); ~ **corn** *n* AGRIC maíz tierno *m*; ~ **earth** *n* MINERAL tierra verde *f*; ~ **fallow** *n* AGRIC barbecho verde *m*; ~ **feeding crop** *n* AGRIC cosecha destinada al corte *f*; ~ **feldspar** *n* MINERAL feldespato verde *m*; ~ **gun** *n* ELECTRON indicador con luz verde *m*, TV cañón verde *m*; ~ **hide** *n* PROD cuero en bruto *m*, cuero verde *m*, piel sin curtir *f*; ~ **LED status indicator DC power ON** *n* PROD indicador verde de diodo emisor de luz del estado de potencia conectada *m*; ~ **maize** *n* AGRIC maíz tierno *m*; ~ **manure** *n* AGRIC, POLL, RECYCL abono verde *m*; ~ **manure crop** *n* AGRIC cultivo de abono en verde *m*; ~ **mineral** *n* CHEM verde malaquita *m*; ~ **patch distortion** *n* C&G distorsión de parche verde *f*; ~ **peak level** *n* TV nivel máximo de verde *m*; ~ **pellet** *n* NUCL pastilla cruda *f*; ~ **period** *n* TRANSP período verde *m*; ~ **phase** *n* TRANSP fase de luz verde *f*, luz en verde *f*; ~ **primary** *n* TV verde primario *m*; ~ **print** *n* CINEMAT copia verde *f*; ~ **quark** *n* PHYS quark verde *m*; ~ **revolution** *n* AGRIC revolución verde *f*; ~ **screen grid** *n* TV rejilla pantalla verde *f*; ~ **sea** *n* OCEAN mar verde *m*; ~ **time** *n* TRANSP intervalo de luz verde *m*; ~ **vitriol** *n* CHEM vitriolo verde *m*

green[3] *vt* COLOUR enverdecer

greenbug *n* AGRIC pulgón verde *m*

greenhouse *n* AGRIC invernadero *m*; ~ **crop** *n* AGRIC cultivo en invernadero *m*; ~ **effect** *n* FUELLESS, GEOPHYS, METEO, PHYS, REFRIG efecto invernadero *m*

greenockite *n* MINERAL greenockita *f*

greenovite *n* MINERAL greenovita *f*

greensand *n* GEOL arena glauconítica *f*, arena verde *f*, PROD *founding* arena húmeda *f*

greenschist *n* GEOL esquisto verde *m*

greenstone *n* CONST, GEOL roca recién extraída de la cantera *f*, roca verde *f*, roca verdosa *f*

Greenwich: ~ **Mean Time** *n* (*GMT*) AIR TRANSP, PHYS,

SPACE hora media de Greenwich *f* (*TMG*), hora media solar *f*, hora del meridiano de Greenwich *f* (*TMG*), tiempo universal *m*

Gregorian: ~ **reflector aerial** *n BrE* (*cf Gregorian reflector antenna AmE*) TELECOM antena de reflector Gregoriana *f*; ~ **reflector antenna** *n AmE* (*cf Gregorian reflector aerial BrE*) TELECOM antena de reflector Gregoriana *f*; ~ **telescope** *n* PHYS telescopio gregoriano *m*

greisening *n* GEOL greisenización *f*

greisenization *n* GEOL greisenización *f*

grenade *n* MILIT granada *f*; ~ **launcher** *n* MILIT lanzagranadas *m*

grey[1]: **in the** ~ *adj BrE* TEXTIL en crudo

grey[2]: ~ **balance** *n BrE* PRINT equilibrio de grises *m*; ~ **board** *n BrE* C&G, PAPER, PROD cartón gris *m*; ~ **body** *n BrE* TV cuerpo gris *m*; ~ **cast iron** *n BrE* MECH fundición gris *f*; ~-**component replacement** *n BrE* PRINT sustitución del componente gris *f*; ~ **contents** *n pl BrE* PRINT contenido gris *m*; ~ **copper ore** *n BrE* MINERAL cobre gris *m*; ~ **glass filter** *n BrE* INSTR filtro de cristal gris *m*; ~-**iron pipe** *n BrE* MECH ENG cañería de hierro gris *f*, tubería de hierro gris *f*; ~ **manganese ore** *n BrE* MINERAL manganeso gris *m*; ~ **mould** *n BrE* AGRIC moho gris *m*; ~ **scale** *n BrE* CINEMAT, COMP&DP, PHOTO, TV escala de grises *f*; ~-**scale value** *n BrE* CINEMAT, COMP&DP, PHOTO, TV valor en la escala de grises *m*

greywacke *n BrE* GEOL, PETROL grauwaka *f*

grid *n* COAL alcantarillado *m*, rejilla *f*, ELEC *supply network* red nacional de energía eléctrica *f*, rejilla *f*, red de distribución *f*, red de energía eléctrica *f*, ELEC ENG *supply network* red de energía eléctrica *f*, red nacional de energía eléctrica *f*, red de distribución *f*, HYDROL alcantarillado *m*, rejilla *f*, POLL alcantarillado *m*, PROD *grate, grating* parrilla *f* (*AmL*), emparrillado *m*, rejilla *f*, *for cores, moulds* armadura *f*, RECYCL alcantarillado *m*, TEXTIL cuadrícula *f*, WATER alcantarillado *m*; ~ **bar** *n* PROD *rolled sections* barrote de parrilla *m*; ~ **bias** *n* ELEC ENG voltaje de polarización de rejilla *m*; ~ **capacitor** *n* ELEC ENG condensador de rejilla *m*; ~ **cathode capacitance** *n* ELEC ENG capacitancia del cátodo de rejilla *f*; ~ **characteristic** *n* ELECTRON característica de la rejilla *f*; ~ **coil** *n* PROD serpentín de parrilla *m*, serpentín plano *m*; ~-**controlled mercury arc rectifier** *n* ELEC ENG rectificador de arco de mercurio regulado por rejilla *m*; ~-**controlled tube** *n* ELECTRON tubo regulado por rejilla *m*; ~ **current** *n* ELEC, ELEC ENG corriente de rejilla *f*; ~-**driving power** *n* ELEC ENG potencia de excitación de la rejilla *f*; ~-**following behavior** *AmE*, ~-**following behaviour** *BrE n* NUCL operación por seguimiento de carga *f*; ~ **leak resistor** *n* PHYS resistencia de escape de electrones de la rejilla *f*; ~ **modulation** *n* ELECTRON modulación de rejilla *f*, TV modulación de grilla *f* (*AmL*), modulación de rejilla *f* (*Esp*); ~ **parameter** *n* ELECTRON parámetro de la rejilla *m*; ~ **probe** *n* NUCL sonda de rejilla *f*; ~ **sheet** *n* PROD hoja cuadriculada *f*; ~-**support plate** *n* NUCL rejilla de soporte del núcleo *f*; ~ **turbulence** *n* FLUID turbulencia en rejilla *f*

griddle *n* COAL, PROD criba *f*

griddling *n* COAL, PROD cribado *m*

gridiron: ~ **valve** *n* PROD corredera de parrilla *f*, válvula de parrilla *f*

Griffith: ~ **flaw** *n* C&G falla de Griffith *f*; ~'s **fracture criterion** *n* NUCL criterio de fractura de Griffith *m*

Grignard: ~ **reagent** *n* CHEM reactivo de Grignard *m*

grillage *n* C&G enrejado *m*

grille *n* AUTO parrilla *f* (*AmL*)

grind[1]: ~-**and-leach process** *n* NUCL proceso de trituración y lixiviación *m*

grind[2] *vt* CHEM moler, pulverizar, triturar, CHEM TECH afilar, amolar, moler, pulverizar, triturar, COAL moler, pulverizar, triturar, FOOD triturar, MECH, MECH ENG afilar, aguzar, amolar, bruáir, esmerilar, moler, molturar, pulimentar, pulir, rectificar, triturar, PROD afilar, aguzar, amolar, bruáir, esmerilar, rectificar, triturar, moler, molturar, pulimentar, pulir

grindability *n* CHEM TECH triturabilidad *f*

grinder *n* C&G esmeril *m*, FOOD molinillo *m*, MECH afiladora *f*, esmeriladora *f*, rectificadora *f*, MECH ENG afiladora *f*, muela *f*, máquina de afilar *f*, máquina de rectificar *f*, rectificadora *f*, PAPER desfibrador de muela *m*, PROD *person* afilador *m*, afiladora *f*; ~ **pit** *n* PAPER fosa de la muela desfibradora *f*; ~ **spindle** *n* C&G husillo del esmeril *m*

grinding *n* C&G esmerilado *m*, CHEM molido *m*, molienda *f*, trituración *f*, COAL molienda *f*, molturación *f*, pulverización *f*, trituración *f*, CONST, FOOD trituración *f*, MECH afilado *m*, esmerilado *m*, rectificado *m*, MECH ENG afilado *m*, amolado *m*, METALL abrasivo *m*, rectificado *m*, MINE molienda *f*, molturación *f*, trituración *f*, P&R desintegración en polvo *f*, pulverización *f*, PAPER desfibrado *m*, PROD *crushing* pulverización *f*, trituración *f*, *finishing* rectificado *m*, *sharpening* afilado *m*, amolado *m*; ~ **agent** *n* C&G agente esmerilador *m*; ~ **center** *AmE see grinding centre BrE*; ~ **center with seven axes** *AmE*, ~ **centre** *BrE n* MECH ENG centro de rectificado *m*; ~ **centre with seven axes** *n BrE* MECH ENG centro de rectificado con siete ejes *m*; ~ **cylinder** *n* CHEM TECH rueda de amolar *f*; ~ **device** *n* CHEM TECH amoladora *f*, trituradora *f*, MECH, MECH ENG, PROD amoladora *f*; ~ **drum** *n* CHEM TECH tambor de trituración *m*; ~ **in of a stopper** *n* C&G esmerilado de un tapón *m*; ~ **line** *n* PROD *twist-drill* eje central de broca espiral *m*; ~ **machine** *n* CHEM TECH amoladora *f*, MECH afiladora *f*, máquina de afilar *f*, máquina de rectificar *f*, rectificadora *f*, trituradora *f*, *roughing* amoladora *f*, desbarbadora *f*, máqina de amolar *f*, MECH ENG máquina de rectificar *f*, rectificadora *f*, trituradora *f*, afiladora *f*, máquina de afilar *f*, *roughing* amoladora *f*, desbarbadora *f*, máquina de amolar *f*, PAPER desfibradora *f*, PROD afiladora *f*, amoladora *f*; ~ **media** *n* COAL medios de molturar *m pl*, molinos *m pl*; ~ **mill** *n* AGRIC molino de muelas *m*, CHEM TECH molino de amolar *m*; ~ **pan** *n* PROD cuba de amalgamación *f*, cuba de trituración *f*, molino de amalgamación *m*; ~ **paste** *n* MECH, MECH ENG, PROD pasta abrasiva *f*, pasta para pulir *f*, pasta pulverizada *f*; ~ **plant** *n* CHEM TECH planta de amolar *f*; ~ **and polishing** *n* C&G esmerilado y pulido *m*; ~ **ring** *n* CHEM TECH anillo de rectificar *m*, anillo esmerilador *m*; ~ **runner** *n* C&G corredera de esmerilado *f*; ~ **sand** *n* C&G arena de esmerilado *f*; ~ **spindle** *n* MECH ENG eje de afiladora *m*, eje de rectificadora *m*; ~-**spindle carrier** *n* MECH ENG soporte del eje de afiladora *m*, soporte del eje de rectificadora *m*; ~ **unit** *n* C&G

esmeril *m*; ~ **wheel** *n* C&G muela abrasiva *f*, rueda abrasiva *f*, MECH *of a transformer* rueda de afilar *f*, MECH ENG rueda abrasiva *f*, muela abrasiva *f*, PROD muela abrasiva *f*, rueda abrasiva *f*; **~-wheel dressing equipment** *n* MECH ENG, PROD equipo de reavivar muelas abrasivas *m*, equipo de rectificar ruedas abrasivas *m*

grindstone *n* PAPER muela desfibradora *f*, PETROL asperón *m*, PROD esmiriladora *f*, muela abrasiva *f*, piedra de afilar *f*

grip[1] *n* C&G agarre *m*, CINEMAT maquinista *m*, tramoyista *m*, COAL pieza de enganche *f*, zanja pequeña de desagüe *f*, CONST agarre *m*, MECH ENG distancia entre dos cabezas de remache *f*, brida *f*, empuñadura *f*, fiador *m*, garra *f*, mango *m*, mangueta *f*, mordaza *f*, puño *m*, retén *m*, PROD asa *f*, mango *m*, presa *f*, agarre *m*, *hold* mordaza *f*, *clutching device* retén *m*, fiador *m*, sujetador *m*, WATER TRANSP agarre *m*; ~ **nut** *n* PROD contratuerca *f*; ~ **pipe wrench** *n* MECH ENG llave para tubos *f*

grip[2] *vt* MECH ENG morder, PROD agarrar, apretar, asir, empuñar, fijar, sujetar, WATER TRANSP *anchor* agarrar, morder

gripper: ~ **pad** *n* PRINT base de apoyo de las pinzas *f*; ~ **tool** *n* NUCL herramienta de sujeción *f*

grippers: ~ **and yarn carrier** *n* TEXTIL transportador de pinzas e hilado *m*

gripping: ~ **dog** *n* PROD perro de sujeción *m*; ~ **jaws** *n pl* PROD mordaza de apriete *f*, mordaza de sujeción *f*; ~ **pad** *n* PROD almohadilla sujetadora *f*, mordaza de apriete *f*; ~ **yoke** *n* MECH ENG *machinery* yugo de apriete *m*, yugo de sujeción *m*

grit *n* CONST arena *f*, arenisca silícea *f*, *civil engineering* limaduras *f pl*, GEOL arenisca silícea *f*, MECH limaduras *f pl*, polvo de muelas abrasivas *m*, grano de muela abrasiva *m*, PETROL gravilla *f*, PROD limaduras *f pl*, polvos *m pl*; ~ **blasting** *n* CONST, MECH chorro de arena *m*; ~ **spreader** *n* TRANSP enarenadora *f*, esparcidora de arena o grava *f*; ~ **trap** *n* HYDROL colector de sólidos arrastrados en el agua de alcantarillas *m*

grits *n pl* AGRIC maíz a medio moler *m*

gritter *n* AUTO mezcla de grava *f*

gritting *n* CONST engravillado *m*, formación de una barra de arena *f*, pulimento *m*

grizzly *n* COAL, PROD criba de barrotes *f*, cribón *m*

groats *n pl* AGRIC avena a medio moler *f*

grocer *n*: ~**'s bag** *n* PACK cesta de la compra *f*

groin *AmE see* **groyne** *BrE*

groined: ~ **vault** *n* CONST arco de encuentro *m*, bóveda de arista *f*

grommet *n* ELEC ENG ojal *m*, MECH ENG *separating part* arandela aislante *f*, WATER TRANSP *ropes* frisa *f*, ollao con guardacabos metálico *m*, roñada *f*

groove *n* ACOUST surco *m*, CONST, MECH acanaladura *f*, muesca *f*, ranura *f*, surco *m*, MECH ENG ranura *f*, estría *f*, *in rolling mill roll* canal *m*, muesca *f*, garganta *f*, NUCL ranura *f*, OPT surco *m*, ranura *f*, PROD estría *f*, cajera *f*, hendidura *f*, ranura *f*, *in boiler-plate* fisura *f*, garganta *f*, muesca *f*, acanaladura *f*; **~-cutting chisel** *n* MECH *of a transformer* buril de acanalar *m*; ~ **drift** *n* PROD mandarín para ranuras *m*; ~ **guard** *n* ACOUST protector de surco *m*; ~ **punch** *n* PROD punzón de garganta *m*; ~ **shape** *n* ACOUST forma del surco *f*; ~ **speed** *n* ACOUST velocidad del surco *f*

grooved[1] *adj* PROD con garganta, con ranuras, estriado, ranurado

grooved[2]: ~ **ball bearing** *n* MECH ENG cojinete de bolas acanalado *m*; ~ **cable** *n* OPT, TELECOM alambre acanalado *m*, cable acanalado *m*; ~ **cone** *n* MECH ENG cono acanalado *m*; ~ **cylinder cam** *n* MECH ENG excéntrica de cilindro acanalada *f*, leva de cilindro acanalada *f*; ~ **and feathered joint** *n* CONST junta acanalada y embadurnada *f*; ~ **pin** *n* MECH ENG pasador acanalado *m*; ~ **press** *n* PAPER prensa ranurada *f*; ~ **pulley** *n* MECH ENG polea de garganta *f*; ~ **rail** *n* RAIL carril acanalado *m*, riel acanalado *m*; ~ **roll** *n* MECH ENG cilindro acanalado *m*, cilindro de garganta *m*, PAPER rodillo ranurado *m*, PROD cilindro acanalado *m*; ~ **roller** *n* MECH ENG cilindro acanalado *m*, rodillo acanalado *m*; ~ **wheel** *n* MECH ENG *pulley for gut, or round band* polea de garganta *f*

grooving *n* MECH ENG mortajado *m*, ranurado *m*, PROD estriado *m*, fisuración *f*, ranurado *m*; ~ **iron** *n* CONST hierro ranurado *m*; ~ **machine** *n* MECH ENG máquina de acanalar *f*, máquina de ranurar *f*, ranuradora *f*; ~ **plane** *n* CONST cepillo de ranurar *m*

groroilite *n* MINERAL groroilita *f*

gross *n* METR gruesa *f*; ~ **area** *n* FUELLESS *of collector* área bruta *f*; ~ **calorific value** *n* GAS poder calorífico superior *m*, HEAT ENG valor calorífico bruto *m*; ~ **flow** *n* NUCL caudal bruto *m*; ~ **heat loss** *n* HEAT ENG, THERMO pérdida de calor bruta *f*; ~ **horsepower** *n* MECH ENG potencia total de caballos *f*; ~ **installed capacity** *n* NUCL potencia bruta instalada *f*; ~ **margin** *n* PROD beneficio bruto *m*, margen bruto *m*; ~ **profit** *n* PROD beneficio bruto *m*, ganancia bruta *f*; ~ **register** *n* WATER TRANSP arqueo bruto *m*; ~ **requirements** *n pl* PROD necesidades totales *f pl*; ~ **thrust** *n* AIR TRANSP empuje bruto *m*; ~ **ton** *n* METR tonelada larga *f*, WATER TRANSP tonelada de arqueo bruto *f*; ~ **tonnage** *n* PETR TECH tonelaje de registro bruto *m*, WATER TRANSP arqueo bruto *m*; ~ **vehicle weight** *n* (*GVW*) VEH peso total del vehículo *m* (*PTV*); ~ **volume** *n* PACK volumen total *m*; ~ **weight** *n* AIR TRANSP, METR, PACK, TEXTIL peso bruto *m*, peso total *m*, TRANSP peso total *m*

grossular *n* MINERAL grosularia *f*

grossularite *n* MINERAL grossularita *f*

ground[1]: **~-controlled** *adj* SPACE controlado desde tierra; **~-free** *adj AmE* (*cf* **earth-free** *BrE*) ELEC *circuit* libre de tierra

ground[2] *n* GEN masa *f*, masa eléctrica *f*, puesta a tierra *f*, toma de tierra *f*; ~ **absorption** *n* ACOUST absorción del terreno *f*; ~ **address** *n* TELECOM dirección terrestre *f*; ~ **angle** *n* AIR TRANSP ángulo de aterrizaje *m*; ~ **angle shot** *n* CINEMAT, TV toma a ras de suelo *f*; ~ **arrester** *n AmE* (*cf* **earth arrester** *BrE*) ELEC, ELEC ENG cortacircuito de puesta a tierra *m*, interruptor de voltaje a tierra *m*; ~ **bar** *n AmE* (*cf* **earth bar** *BrE*) ELEC, ELEC ENG, PROD barra de tierra *f*; ~ **base** *n* C&G base esmerilada *f*; ~ **bus** *n AmE* (*cf* **earth bus** *BrE*) ELEC, ELEC ENG, PROD barra colectora de tierra *f*, barra de puesta a tierra *f*, conductor ómnibus de tierra *m*; **~-bus mounting** *n AmE* (*cf* **earth-bus mounting** *BrE*) ELEC, ELEC ENG, PROD montaje de barra de puesta a tierra *m*; ~ **cable** *n AmE* (*cf* **earth cable** *BrE*) ELEC, ELEC ENG, VEH cable de masa *m*, cable de toma a tierra *m*, cable de toma de tierra *m*; ~ **clamp** *n AmE* (*cf* **earth clamp** *BrE*) ELEC, ELEC ENG abrazadera de conexión a tierra *f*, abrazadera de tierra *f*; ~ **clearance** *n* VEH distancia al suelo *f*; ~ **clip** *n AmE* (*cf earth clip BrE*) ELEC, ELEC ENG presilla de conexión a masa *f*, presilla de conexión a tierra *f*; ~ **cloth** *n* TEXTIL tela de fondo *f*; ~ **coat** *n* COATINGS capa de base *f*; ~ **color** *AmE*, ~ **colour** *BrE n* C&G color en polvo *m*, COLOUR color de fondo *m*; ~ **conductor** *n AmE* (*cf earth conductor BrE*) ELEC, ELEC ENG conductor de masa *m*, conductor de tierra *m*; ~ **connection** *n AmE* (*cf earth connection BrE*) AUTO conexión a tierra *f*, masa *f*, tierra *f*, toma a masa *f*, toma a tierra *f*, unión a tierra *f*, ELEC, ELEC ENG, PROD, VEH conexión a tierra *f*, masa *f*, tierra *f*, toma a masa *f*, toma de tierra *f*, unión a tierra *f*; ~ **connector** *n AmE* (*cf earth connector BrE*) ELEC conexión a tierra *f*, toma de tierra *f*, ELEC ENG conexión a tierra *f*, unión a tierra *f*, PROD conexión a tierra *f*, toma de tierra *f*; ~~**controlled approach** *n* AIR TRANSP aproximación controlada desde tierra *f*; ~~**controlled approach system** *n* AIR TRANSP sistema de aproximación controlado desde tierra *m*; ~ **current** *n AmE* (*cf earth current BrE*) ELEC, ELEC ENG corriente de retorno por tierra *f*, corriente de vuelta por tierra *f*, GEOPHYS corriente de fuga *f*, corriente de tierra *f*, corriente telúrica *f*, corriente terrestre *f*, PROD corriente telúrica *f*; ~ **detector** *n AmE* (*cf earth detector BrE*) ELEC, ELEC ENG defectoscopio de aislamiento *m*, detector de defectos de puesta a masa *m*, indicador de tierra *m*; ~ **detector light** *n AmE* (*cf earth detector BrE*) ELEC, ELEC ENG, PROD lámpara indicadora del detector de tierra *f*; ~ **effect** *n* AIR TRANSP efecto de tierra *m*; ~ **effect machine** *n* (*GEM*) TRANSP, VEH vehículo terrestre levitante por la reacción de chorros de aire sobre el terreno *m*; ~ **electrode** *n AmE* (*cf earth electrode BrE*) AUTO, ELEC, ELEC ENG, PHYS, VEH electrodo de conexión a tierra *m*, electrodo de masa *m*, electrodo de tierra *m*; ~ **fabric** *n* TEXTIL tejido de fondo *m*; ~ **facilities** *n* SPACE equipos de tierra *m pl*, instalaciones en tierra *f pl*; ~ **fault** *n AmE* (*cf earth fault BrE*) ELEC, ELEC ENG, PROD fuga a tierra *f*, pérdida a tierra *f*, tierra accidental *f*; ~ **fault current** *n* PROD corriente de pérdida a tierra *f*; ~~**fault protection** *n AmE* (*cf earth-fault protection BrE*) ELEC, ELEC ENG, PROD protección contra fuga a tierra *f*, protección contra pérdida a tierra *f*, protección contra tierra accidental *f*; ~~**fault tray** *n AmE* (*cf earth-fault tray BrE*) ELEC, ELEC ENG, PROD banda de conexión a tierra *f*, bandeja de pérdida a tierra *f*; ~ **fault trip** *n* ELEC, PROD disparo por perdida a tierra *m*; ~ **glass** *n* CINEMAT, PHOTO cristal esmerilado *m*; ~~**glass circle** *n* CINEMAT, PHOTO círculo de cristal esmerilado *m*; ~~**glass with Fresnel lens** *n* CINEMAT, PHOTO cristal esmerilado con lente de Fresnel *m*; ~~**glass joint** *n* LAB junta de vidrio esmerilado *f*; ~~**glass joint clamp** *n* LAB abrazadera de junta de vidrio esmerilado *f*, clip de junta de vidrio esmerilado *m*; ~~**glass screen** *n* CINEMAT, INSTR, PHOTO pantalla de cristal esmerilado *f*; ~~**glass screen with microprism spot** *n* PHOTO cristal esmerilado con microprisma *m*; ~~**glass screen with reticule** *n* CINEMAT, PHOTO cristal esmerilado con retícula *m*; ~ **hay** *n* AGRIC heno picado *m*; ~~**in cutting rake** *n* MECH ENG ángulo de corte *m*; ~ **indicator** *n AmE* (*cf earth indicator BrE*) ELEC, ELEC ENG indicador de defectos de aislamiento *m*, indicador de tierra *m*; ~ **installation** *n* AIR TRANSP instalación de tierra *f*; ~ **layer** *n* METEO capa cerca del

suelo *f*, capa límite superficial *f*; ~ **lead** *n AmE* (*cf earth lead BrE*) ELEC, ELEC ENG, PHYS, PROD, TELECOM cable a tierra *m*, hilo de puesta a masa *m*, TV cable de tierra *m*, hilo de puesta a masa *m*; ~ **leakage** *n AmE* (*cf earth leakage BrE*) ELEC, ELEC ENG derivación a tierra *f*, dispersión a tierra *f*, fuga a tierra *f*, pérdida a tierra *f*, PROD fuga a tierra *f*; ~~**leakage circuit breaker** *n AmE* (*cf earth-leakage circuit breaker BrE*) ELEC, ELEC ENG cortocircuito de fuga a tierra *m*, cortocircuito de pérdida a tierra *m*; ~~**leakage current** *n AmE* (*cf earth-leakage current BrE*) ELEC, ELEC ENG corriente de fuga a tierra *f*; ~~**leakage detector** *n AmE* (*cf earth-leakage detector BrE*) ELEC, ELEC ENG detector de fuga a tierra *m*; ~~**leakage meter** *n AmE* (*cf earth-leakage meter BrE*) ELEC, ELEC ENG medidor de fuga a tierra *m*, medidor de tierra accidental *m*; ~ **level** *n* NUCL nivel del suelo *m*; ~ **lighting** *n* AIR TRANSP iluminación de tierra *f*; ~ **line** *n AmE* (*cf earth line BrE*) ELEC, ELEC ENG línea a tierra *f*; ~ **loop** *n* PROD bucle de tierra *m*; ~ **lug** *n AmE* (*cf earth lug BrE*) ELEC, ELEC ENG, PROD lengüeta de puesta a tierra *f*, terminal de masa *f*, terminal de tierra *m*; ~ **maneuver** *AmE*, ~ **manoeuvre** *BrE n* AIR TRANSP maniobra de tierra *f*; ~ **movement** *n* GAS movimiento de tierra *m*, movimiento del suelo *m*; ~ **network** *n* TELECOM red de tierra *f*; ~ **noise** *n* ELECTRON ruido de fondo *m*; ~ **operation** *n* AIR TRANSP operación de tierra *f*, SPACE operación terrena *f*, operación terrestre *f*; ~ **pin** *n AmE* (*cf earth pin BrE*) ELEC, ELECTRON, PROD patilla de conexión a tierra *f*, terminal de tierra *m*; ~ **plane** *n AmE* (*cf earth plane BrE*) GEOM, PHYS plano de tierra *m*; ~ **plate** *n AmE* (*cf earth plate BrE*) ELEC, ELEC ENG placa de conexión a tierra *f*, toma de tierra *f*; ~ **potential** *n AmE* (*cf earth potential BrE*) ELEC, ELEC ENG, SPACE potencial de tierra *m*, potencial terrestre *m*; ~ **power supply** *n* AIR TRANSP suministro de fuerza de tierra *m*, suministro eléctrico de tierra *m*; ~ **power system** *n* SPACE sistema de energía terrestre *m*, sistema de potencia en tierra *m*; ~ **power unit** *n* (*GPU*) AIR TRANSP grupo electrógeno de pista *m* (*GPU*), grupo motopropulsor de tierra *m* (*GPU*), unidad de potencia de tierra *f* (*GPU*); ~~**proximity warning** *n* AIR TRANSP aviso de proximidad a tierra *m*; ~ **radio station** *n* AIR TRANSP estación de radio de tierra *f*; ~ **resistance** *n AmE* (*cf earth resistance BrE*) ELEC, ELEC ENG resistencia de tierra *f*; ~~**resistance meter** *n AmE* (*cf earth-resistance meter BrE*) ELEC, ELEC ENG medidor de resistencia de tierra *m*; ~ **resonance** *n* AIR TRANSP resonancia de tierra *f*; ~ **return** *n* ELEC ENG vuelta por tierra *f*, retorno por tierra *m*, GEOPHYS retorno por tierra *m*, PROD vuelta por tierra *f*, retorno por tierra *m*, TELECOM retorno por tierra *m*; ~ **rod** *n* ELEC varilla de toma de tierra *f*, barra de tierra *f*, varilla de tierra *f*, ELEC ENG varilla de toma de tierra *f*, varilla de tierra *f*, GEOPHYS vástago de tierra *m*, barra de tierra *f*, PROD barra de tierra *f*; ~ **segment** *n* SPACE segmento terreno *m*, segmento terrestre *m*; ~ **sensing** *n* PROD detección de tierra *f*; ~ **service equipment** *n* AIR TRANSP equipo de servicio de tierra *m*; ~ **speed** *n* AIR TRANSP velocidad absoluta *f*, velocidad en suelo *f*; ~ **staff** *n* AIR TRANSP personal de tierra *m*; ~ **state** *n* CHEM *atom*, PART PHYS, PHYS, RAD PHYS estado fundamental *m*; ~~**state frequency** *n* CHEM, PART PHYS, PHYS, RAD PHYS frecuencia del estado fundamental *f*; **~-state transition** *n* CHEM, PART PHYS, PHYS, RAD PHYS transición desde el estado fundamental *f*; **~ station** *n* SPACE estación terrena *f*, estación terrestre *f*; **~ stopper** *n* LAB, PACK tapón esmerilado *m*; **~ swell** *n* OCEAN *in shallow waters* mar tendido *m*, marejada *f*, maremoto *m*, oleada *f*, oleaje de fondo *m*, WATER TRANSP *in shallow waters* mar tendido *m*, oleada *f*, oleaje de fondo *m*; **~ switch** *n* AmE (*cf earth switch BrE*) ELEC, ELEC ENG conmutador de puesta a tierra *m*; **~ tackle** *n* WATER TRANSP *mooring* equipo de fondeo *m*; **~ target** *n* MILIT blanco terrestre *m*; **~ terminal** *n* AmE (*cf earth terminal BrE*) ELEC, ELEC ENG borne de masa *m*, borne de puesta a tierra *m*, borne de tierra *m*, terminal de tierra *m*, WATER TRANSP borne de puesta a tierra *m*; **~-terminal arrester** *n* AmE (*cf earth-terminal arrester BrE*) ELEC *connection*, ELEC ENG protector de terminal de tierra *m*; **~ test** *n* AIR TRANSP, SPACE prueba en tierra *f*, verificación en tierra *f*; **~ thread tap** *n* MECH ENG macho de roscar con rosca rectificada *m*; **~-to-air communication** *n* AIR TRANSP comunicaciones tierra-aire *f pl*; **~-to-air missile** *n* (*SAM*) MILIT misil de tierra a aire *m*, misil tierra-aire *m*; **~-to-ground missile** *n* MILIT misil de tierra a tierra *m*; **~ visibility** *n* AIR TRANSP visibilidad en tierra *f*; **~ water** *n* AGRIC, COAL, HYDROL agua de pozo *f*, agua del subsuelo *f*, agua freática *f*, agua subterránea *f*, capa acuífera subterránea *f*, POLL agua subterránea *f*, WATER agua de pozo *f*, agua del subsuelo *f*, agua freática *f*, agua subterránea *f*, capa acuífera subterránea *f*; **~-water basin** *n* AGRIC, COAL, HYDROL, WATER cuenca de aguas freáticas *f*; **~-water contour** *n* AGRIC, COAL, HYDROL, WATER contorno de agua subterránea *m*; **~-water contour map** *n* AGRIC, COAL, HYDROL, WATER carta del contorno de aguas subterráneas *f*; **~-water depth** *n* AGRIC, COAL, HYDROL, WATER profundidad del agua freática *f*; **~-water inrush** *n* AGRIC, COAL, HYDROL, WATER irrupción de agua freática *f*; **~-water investigation** *n* AGRIC, COAL, HYDROL, WATER búsqueda de agua subterránea *f*; **~-water level** *n* AGRIC, COAL, CONST, HYDROL, WATER capa freática *f*, nivel de agua freática *m*, nivel de agua subterránea *m*, nivel freático *m*; **~-water resources** *n* AGRIC, COAL, HYDROL, WATER recursos de agua subterránea *m pl*; **~-water supply** *n* AGRIC, COAL, HYDROL, WATER abastecimiento de agua subterránea *m*, suministro de agua subterránea *m*; **~-water table** *n* AGRIC, COAL, HYDROL, WATER capa freática *f*, nivel freático *m*; **~ wave** *n* OCEAN onda de tierra *f*, onda fundamental *f*, onda subterránea *f*, RAD PHYS, WATER TRANSP onda de tierra *f*, TELECOM onda terrestre; **~ wire** *n* AmE (*cf earth wire BrE*) ELEC, ELEC ENG, PHYS, PROD, TELECOM, TV conductor de tierra *m*, hilo de masa *m*, hilo de puesta a tierra *m*

ground[3] *vt* AmE (*cf earth BrE*) GEN conectar a masa, conectar a tierra, poner a masa, poner a tierra, unir a masa

ground[4] *vi* AIR TRANSP obligar a permanecer en tierra, OCEAN, WATER TRANSP *ship* encallar, varar

grounded[1] *adj* AmE (*cf earthed BrE*) ELEC, ELEC ENG, TELECOM puesto a tierra, unido a tierra

grounded[2]: **~ base connection** *n* AmE ELEC, ELEC ENG conexión base a tierra *f*; **~ collector connection** *n* AmE ELEC, ELEC ENG conexión colector a masa *f*, conexión de electrodo captador a masa *f*; **~ earth**

terminal *n* AmE ELEC, ELEC ENG, PROD borne de tierra aterrado *m*; **~ emitter connection** *n* AmE ELEC ENG conexión del cuerpo emisor a tierra *f*; **~ neutral system** *n* AmE ELEC, ELEC ENG sistema con neutro a tierra *m*; **~ switch** *n* AmE ELEC, ELEC ENG conmutador con conexión a tierra *m*, conmutador de puesta a tierra *m*; **~ system** *n* AmE ELEC, ELEC ENG, PROD sistema de puesta a tierra *m*

grounding *n* (*cf earthing BrE*) AIR TRANSP *of aircraft* suspensión de vuelos *f*, obligación a permanecer en tierra *f*, CONST conexión a masa *f*, unión a tierra *f*, conexión a tierra *f*, puesta a tierra *f*, ELEC, ELEC ENG conexión a tierra *f*, conexión a masa *f*, unión a tierra *f*, puesta a tierra *f*, ELECTRON puesta a tierra *f*, unión a tierra *f*, conexión a tierra *f*, conexión a masa *f*, MAR POLL varadura *f*, RAIL puesta a tierra *f*, conexión a tierra *f*, unión a tierra *f*, conexión a masa *f*, SPACE conexión a masa *f*, conexión a tierra *f*, puesta a tierra *f*, puesta a tierra *f*; **~ bar** *n* AIR TRANSP barra de anclaje a tierra *f*; **~ bus** *n* AmE (*cf earthing bus BrE*) ELEC conductor ómnibus de puesta a tierra *m*, barra colectora de puesta a tierra *f*, ELEC ENG barra colectora de puesta a tierra *f*, conductor ómnibus de puesta a tierra *m*, PROD barra colectora de puesta a tierra *f*; **~ clip** *n* AmE (*cf earthing clip BrE*) ELEC, ELEC ENG *connection* presilla de conexión a masa *f*, presilla de puesta a tierra *f*; **~ electrode conductor** *n* AmE (*cf earthing electrode conductor BrE*) ELEC, ELEC ENG, PROD conductor de electrodo de puesta a tierra *m*; **~ electrode system** *n* AmE (*cf earthing electrode system BrE*) ELEC, ELEC ENG, PROD sistema de electrodos de conexión a tierra *m*, sistema de electrodos de puesta a tierra *m*; **~ paddle** *n* AmE (*cf earthing paddle BrE*) RAIL varilla de tierra *f*; **~ path** *n* MECH ENG, PROD trayecto de la puesta a tierra *m*; **~ pole** *n* AmE (*cf earthing pole BrE*) RAIL piquete de toma de tierra *m*; **~ position** *n* AmE (*cf earthing position BrE*) ELEC *switch* posición de conexión a masa *f*, posición de conexión a tierra *f*; **~ reactor** *n* AmE (*cf earthing reactor BrE*) ELEC, ELEC ENG reactancia de puesta a tierra *f*, reactor a tierra *m*; **~ regulation** *n* AmE (*cf earthing regulation BrE*) PROD regulación de puesta a tierra *f*; **~ rod** *n* AmE (*cf earthing rod BrE*) ELEC varilla de tierra *f*, RAIL piquete de toma de tierra *m*; **~ strip** *n* AmE (*cf earthing strip BrE*) ELEC tira de toma a tierra *f*, ELEC ENG tira de toma de tierra *f*; **~ switch** *n* AmE (*cf earthing switch BrE*) ELEC, ELEC ENG conmutador de puesta a tierra *m*, interruptor de puesta a tierra *m*

groundsill *n* CONST *of door-frame* umbral *m*, *of timber frame* carretera inferior *f*, durmiente *m* (*AmL*), MINE durmiente *m* (*AmL*), muro transversal sumergido *m* (*AmL*), solera *f* (*Esp*)

groundwater: **~ catchment** *n* WATER cuenca de aguas subterráneas *f*

groundwood *n* PAPER pasta mecánica *f*; **~ pulp** *n* PAPER pulpa mecánica *f*

group[1] *n* GEN grupo *m*; **~ call identity** *n* TELECOM identidad de grupo llamante *f*; **~ code recording** *n* (*GCR*) COMP&DP registro de código agrupado *m*; **~ of commodities** *n* PACK conjunto de artículos *m*, grupo de mercancías *m*; **~ delay** *n* ELEC ENG, SPACE retardo de grupo *m*; **~-delay linear distortion** *n* ELEC ENG, SPACE distorsión lineal de retardo de grupo *f*; **~ distribution frame** *n* TELECOM trama de distribución de grupo *f*; **~ index** *n* OPT, TELECOM índice de

grupo *m*; ~ **mark** *n* COMP&DP marca de grupo *f*;
~ **occulting light** *n* WATER TRANSP *navigation marks*
luz de grupos de ocultaciones *f*; ~ **separator** *n* (*GS*)
COMP&DP separador de grupo *m* (*SG*); ~ **of sidings** *n*
RAIL grupo de apartaderos *m*; ~~**switching center**
AmE, ~~**switching centre** *BrE* *n* TELECOM centro de
conmutación de grupos *m*; ~~**switching centre
catchment area** *n* TELECOM área de recogida del
centro de conmutación de grupos *f*; ~~**switching
centre exchange area** *n* TELECOM área de intercambio del centro de conmutación de grupo *f*; ~ **theory** *n*
MATH teoría de grupos *f*; ~ **transmission delay** *n*
TELECOM demora en la transmisión de grupo *f*;
~ **velocity** *n* ACOUST, GEOPHYS, OPT, PHYS, TELECOM
velocidad de grupo *f*
group² *vt* ELEC, ELEC ENG acoplar
groupage: ~ **car** *n* *AmE* (*cf groupage wagon BrE*) RAIL
vagón de agrupamiento *m*, vagón de grupaje *m*;
~ **traffic** *n* RAIL tráfico de agrupamiento *m*, tráfico de
grupaje *m*; ~ **traffic forwarder** *n* RAIL expedidor de
agrupamiento de mercancías *m*, transportista de
mercancías en grupaje *m*; ~ **wagon** *n* *BrE* (*cf groupage car AmE*) RAIL vagón de agrupamiento *m*, vagón
de grupaje *m*
grouping *n* ELEC ENG, TELECOM acoplamiento *m*;
~ **switch** *n* ELEC ENG, TELECOM conmutador de
acoplamiento *m*
grout¹ *n* CONST lechada de cemento *f*, lechada para
inyección *f*, mortero *m*; ~ **curtain** *n* CONST pantalla
de inyección *f*
grout² *vt* CONST inyectar lechada
grouting *n* COAL cementación de grietas acuíferas *f*,
inyecciones de enlechado *f pl*, profundización de
pozos por cimentación del terreno *f*, CONST enlechado *m*, inyecciones de mortero *f pl*, inyecciones de
lechada *f pl*, NUCL enlechado *m*, lechada de cemento
f; ~ **equipment** *n* CONST equipo para inyecciones *m*
growing: ~ **crops** *n pl* AGRIC cultivos en pie *m pl*;
~ **period** *n* AGRIC período vegetativo *m*; ~ **point** *n*
AGRIC punto de crecimiento *m*
growler *n* ELEC, INSTR probador de aislamientos *m*,
probador de inducidos *m*, verificador de cortocircuitos *m*
grown: ~~**in dislocation** *n* METALL dislocación en
desarrollo *f*; ~ **junction** *n* ELECTRON conexión a
tierra *f*
growth *n* AGRIC, CRYSTALL, ELECTRON, FLUID crecimiento *m*, METALL crecimiento *m*, dilatación *f*,
expansión *f*, hinchamiento *m*, NUCL crecimiento *m*;
~ **anticline** *n* GEOL anticlinal de crecimiento *m*;
~ **fault** *n* GEOL falla de crecimiento *f*; ~ **pattern** *n*
METALL estructura de crecimiento *f*, patrón de
crecimiento *m*; ~ **rate** *n* AGRIC tasa de crecimiento
f; ~ **ring** *n* AGRIC anillo anual de crecimiento *m*;
~ **spiral** *n* METALL espiral de crecimiento *f*; ~ **step** *n*
METALL fase de crecimiento *f*, fase de dilatación *f*;
~ **twin** *n* METALL macla de crecimiento *f*
groyne *n* *BrE* CONST aristón *m*, dique *m*, espigón *m*,
OCEAN dique *m*, espolón, WATER estacada *f*, WATER
TRANSP *coastal protection* espigón *m*, estacada *f*
GRP *abbr* GEN (*glass-reinforced plastic*) GRP (*plástico
reforzado con fibra de vidrio*); (*glass-reinforced polyester*) GRP (*poliéster reforzado con fibra de vidrio*)
grub *n* AGRIC gorgojo *m*; ~ **screw** *n* MECH ENG pasador
prisionero *m*, pasador roscado *m*, tornillo de cabeza

hendida *m*, tornillo de presión *m*, tornillo fiador *m*,
tornillo sin cabeza *m*
grunerite *n* MINERAL grunerita *f*
GS *abbr* (*group separator*) COMP&DP SG (*separador de
grupo*)
GSC *abbr* (*group-switching center AmE, group-switching centre BrE*) TELECOM centro de conmutación de
grupos *m*
G-suit *n* AIR TRANSP traje anti-G *m*
G-T *abbr* (*gain-to-noise-temperature ratio*) SPACE G-T
(*relación ganancia temperatura de ruido*)
guaiac: ~ **gum** *n* FOOD goma de guayaco *f*, resina de
guayaco *f*
guaiacol *n* CHEM guaiacol *m*
guaiaconic *adj* CHEM guaiacónico
guaiaretic *adj* CHEM guaiarético
guanidine *n* CHEM guanidina *f*
guanine *n* CHEM guanina *f*
guano *n* CHEM guano *m*
guanosine *n* CHEM guanosina *f*
guanyl *n* CHEM guanilo *m*
guarantee: ~ **cap** *n* PACK tapón de rosca de garantía
m; ~ **closure** *n* PACK cierre de garantía *m*; ~ **period** *n*
PROD, SPACE período de garantía *m*
guaranteed: ~ **draw off** *n* FUELLESS decantación
garantizada *f*; ~ **flight path** *n* AIR TRANSP trayectoria
de vuelo garantizada *f*; ~ **thrust** *n* AIR TRANSP empuje
garantizado *m*; ~ **weight** *n* AIR TRANSP peso garantizado *m*
guard¹ *n* COMP&DP guarda *f*, ELEC *safety* protector *m*,
dispositivo de protección *m*, rejilla de protección *f*,
MECH dispositivo protector *m*, protección *f*, barrera *f*,
protector *m*, MECH ENG *to prevent bars wrapping
round rolling-mill rolls* barrera *f*, protección *f*,
protector *m*, dispositivo protector *m*, PRINT guarda
f, PROD guarda *f*, protector *m*, defensa *f*, RAIL
conductor *m*, jefe de tren *m*, SAFE *fuel* guarda tipo
jaula *f*, protección *f*, dispositivo de protección *m*,
dispositivo protector *m*, defensa *f*; ~ **against debris**
n MECH ENG barrera contra escombros *f*, guarda
contra escombros *f*, protección contra escombros *f*;
~ **band** *n* COMP&DP banda de guardar *f*, banda de
protección *f*; ~ **circuit** *n* ELEC ENG circuito de
seguridad *m*; ~ **iron** *n* RAIL máquina exploradora *f*,
quitapiedras *m*; ~ **log** *n* PETROL registro de guardia
m; ~ **plate** *n* PROD chapa protectora *f*, placa de
guarda *f*, placa de sangría *f*; ~ **ring** *n* ELEC anillo de
guarda *m*, anillo de protección *m*, anillo de seguridad
m, anillo protector *m*, ELEC ENG anillo de guarda *m*,
anillo de seguridad *m*, anillo protector *m*, PHYS, PROD
anillo de guarda *m*, anillo de protección *m*, anillo de
seguridad *m*, anillo protector *m*; ~~**ring capacitor** *n*
ELEC ENG condensador del anillo de seguridad *m*;
~ **space** *n* TELECOM espacio de protección *m*; ~ **time**
n SPACE tiempo de seguridad *m*; ~'**s van** *n* *BrE* (*cf
caboose AmE*) RAIL, VEH furgón de cola *m*, vagón
freno *m*; ~ **vessel** *n* NUCL blindaje antimisiles *m*,
recinto de protección del reactor *m*; ~ **wire** *n* ELEC
overhead line alambre de protección *m*, ELEC ENG hilo
de guardia *m*
guard²: ~ **against** *vt* SAFE proteger contra, resguardar
de
guarded¹ *adj* SAFE protegido
guarded²: ~ **gears** *n pl* MECH ENG engranajes encar-
tados *m pl*, engranajes protegidos *m pl*, SAFE
engranes resguardados *m pl*; ~ **input** *n* ELEC ENG

entrada protegida *f*; ~ **output** *n* ELEC ENG producción protegida *f*

guarding *n* SAFE protección *f*; ~ **relay** *n* ELEC ENG relé de seguridad *m*

guardrail *n* CONST guardarraíl *m*, *hand-rail* quitamiedos *m*, SAFE barrera *f*, baranda *f* (*AmL*), barandilla *f* (*Esp*), pasamanos *m*, barandal *m*, WATER TRANSP *deck equipment* baranda *f* (*AmL*), barandilla *f* (*Esp*)

gudgeon *n* CONST cuello de eje *m*, gorrón *m*, muñón *m*, MECH ENG *of shaft, pin, pivot, journal* clavija *f*, pasador *m*, muñón *m*, pivote *m*, perno *m*, MINE gorrón del castillete *m* (*Esp*), polea del castillete de extracción *f* (*AmL*), PROD *of winch barrel* pivote *m*; ~ **pin** *n* BrE (*cf wrist pin AmE*) MECH muñequilla del pistón *f*, muñón del pistón *m*, perno de émbolo *m*, MECH ENG *crosshead-pin* perno de la cruceta *m*, VEH muñequilla del pistón *f*, pasador *m*

guidance: ~ **aerial** *n* BrE (*cf guidance antenna AmE*) SPACE antena de guiado *f*; ~ **antenna** *n* AmE (*cf guidance aerial BrE*) SPACE antena de guiado *f*; ~ **cushion** *n* TRANSP amortiguador-guía *m*; ~ **magnet** *n* TRANSP imán de dirección *m*, imánguía *m*; ~ **navigation system** *n* SPACE sistema de guiado de navegación *m*; ~ **receiver** *n* SPACE receptor de guiado *m*

guide *n* C&G guía *f*, HYDRAUL directriz *f*, saetín *m*, MECH ENG *for solid die-stock* guía para cojinetes *f*, *tool* guía *f*, guiador *m*, referencia *f*, MINE corredera *f*, guiador *m*, guía *f*, TEXTIL guía *f*; ~ **bar** *n* MECH ENG barra de guía *f*, barra directriz *f*, resbaladera *f*, TEXTIL barra de pasadores *f*, barra guía *f*; ~ **beam** *n* TRANSP haz guía *m*, rayo-guía *m*; ~ **bearer** *n* MECH ENG *of cross-head guides* soporte de resbaladeras *m*; ~ **bearing** *n* INSTR cojinete de guía *m*; ~ **blade** *n* HYDRAUL paleta directriz *f*; ~ **block** *n* MECH ENG *injection mould* bloque guía *m*, *of cross-head guides* patín de la cruceta *m*; ~ **bush** *n* MECH ENG casquillo guía *m*, manguito guía *m*; ~ **bushing** *n* NUCL manguito guía *m*; ~ **clamp** *n* MECH ENG abrazadera de guía *f*, mordaza de guía *f*, tornillo de guía *m*; ~ **cross tie** *n* MECH ENG riostra travesal guía *f*, travesaño guía *m*; ~ **error** *n* TV error de referencia *m*; ~ **funnel** *n* PETROL embudo de guía *m*; ~ **line** *n* PETROL línea guía *f*; ~**-line tensioner** *n* PETROL tensor de las líneas guía *m*; ~ **mill** *n* PROD *iron and steel manufacture* laminador de guías *m*; ~ **number** *n* PHOTO número guía *m*; ~ **nut** *n* MECH ENG tuerca guía *f*; ~ **pillar** *n* MECH ENG columna guía *f*; ~ **pin** *n* MECH, MECH ENG espiga de guía *f*, perno de guía *m*, punzón de guía *m*, PRINT guía de entrada *f*; ~ **plate** *n* MECH ENG, PROD placa directriz *f*, placa guía *f*; ~ **post** *n* CONST hito *m*, poste indicador *m*, PETROL poste de guía *m*; ~ **pulley** *n* MECH ENG polea de desviación *f*, polea directriz *f*, polea guía *f*; ~ **ramp** *n* MECH ENG plataforma de guía *f*, rampa guía *f*; ~ **ring** *n* HYDRAUL anillo de guía *m*, corona directriz *f*; ~ **roll** *n* PAPER rodillo conductor *m*, rodillo guía *m*; ~ **roller** *n* CINEMAT, PROD rodillo guía *m*, TEXTIL cilindro guía *m*; ~ **rope** *n* PROD cable guía *m*; ~ **screw** *n* MECH ENG *lathe* husillo *m*, tornillo guía *m*; ~ **shoe** *n* MINE zapata de guía *f*; ~ **stock** *n* PROD rosca guía *f*; ~ **tooth** *n* MECH ENG diente guía *m*; ~ **tube** *n* MECH ENG, MINE tubo guiador *m*, tubo guía *m*; ~ **vane** *n* FUELLESS *turbines* paleta guiadora *f*, HYDRAUL encauzador *m*, álabe guía *m*, álabe del distribuidor *m*, álabe director *m*, MECH encauzador *m*, álabe guía

m, álabe del distribuidor *m*, álabe director *m*, aleta guiadora *f*, REFRIG álabe del distribuidor *m*, álabe director *m*, álabe guía *m*; ~ **vane servomotor** *n* FUELLESS servomotor de paleta guiadora *m*; ~ **vane vibration** *n* FUELLESS vibración de paleta guiadora *f*; ~ **wavelength** *n* PHYS longitud de onda de guía *f*; ~ **wheel** *n* TRANSP rueda de guía *f*; ~ **yoke** *n* MECH ENG *of cross-head guides* soporte de resbaladeras *m*

guided: ~ **air-cushion vehicle** *n* TRANSP, WATER TRANSP aerodeslizador guiado *m*; ~ **beam diameter** *n* OPT diámetro del haz guiado *m*; ~ **long-range missile** *n* MILIT misil guiado de gran alcance *m*; ~ **missile** *n* MILIT misil dirigido *m*, misil guiado *m*, misil radioguiado *m*, misil teledirigido *m*, misil teleguiado *m*; ~ **public mass transportation system** *n* TRANSP sistema de transporte público controlado *m*; ~ **radiation system** *n* TELECOM sistema de radiación dirigida *m*; ~ **road** *n* TRANSP carretera controlada *f*; ~ **wave** *n* OPT, TELECOM onda dirigida *f*, onda guiada *f*; ~ **weapon** *n* MILIT misil guiado *m*

guideline *n* MECH ENG, PROD directriz *f*, línea de conducta *f*

guidelines *n pl* MECH ENG, PROD, SAFE normas *f pl*

guidepoles *n pl* CONST *of a pile-driver* guías del martinete *f pl*

guiderail *n* MECH ENG carril de guía *m*, carril guiador *m*, contra carril *m*, rail *m*, TRANSP carril de dirección *m*, carril guía *m*

guideway *n* TRANSP deslizadera *f*; ~ **at grade** *n* TRANSP deslizadera en curso *f*

guiding *n* MECH ENG dirección *f*, directriz *f*, guiador *m*, guiante *m*, guía *f*, referencia *f*; ~ **line** *n* PROD trazo de referencia *m*; ~ **mark** *n* PROD referencia *f*, WATER TRANSP *navigation* marca de enfilación *f*

guillotine *n* SAFE guillotina *f*; ~ **gate** *n* MINE compuerta de guillotina *f*; ~ **shearing machine** *n* PROD tijeras de guillotina *f pl*; ~ **shears** *n* MECH, PROD tijeras de guillotina *f pl*; ~ **shutter** *n* CINEMAT, PHOTO, TV obturador de guillotina *m*; ~ **splicer** *n* CINEMAT, PHOTO, TV empalmadora guillotina *f*

guillotining *n* PAPER guillotinado *m*; ~ **trimming** *n* PAPER igualado *m*

Guinier-Preston: ~ **zone** *n* (*GP*) CRYSTALL zona de Guinier-Preston *f*

gulf *n* WATER TRANSP golfo *m*

gulleting: ~ **saw file** *n* PROD lima de cola de rata *f*

gulley: ~ **sucker** *n* MAR POLL orificio variador *m*

gulonic *adj* CHEM gulónico

gulose *n* CHEM gulosa *f*

gum[1] *n* CHEM chicle *m*; ~ **arabic** *n* FOOD goma arábiga *f*; ~ **lac** *n* COATINGS laca adhesiva *f*; ~ **lake** *n* COATINGS laca adhesiva *f*, laca gomosa *f*; ~ **tragacanth** *n* FOOD goma tragacanto *f*

gum[2] *vt* PROD encolar, engomar, pegar con goma; ~ **up** *vt* PROD embotarse, ensuciarse

gumbo *n* PETR TECH, PETROL arcilla pegajosa *f*, arcilla plástica *f*, lutita pegagosa *f*

gummed: ~ **edge** *n* PACK borde encolado *m*; ~ **label** *n* PACK etiqueta encolada *f*, etiqueta engomada *f*; ~ **paper** *n* PACK papel engomado *m*; ~ **paper tape** *n* PACK cinta de papel engomado *f*, precinto de papel engomado *m*

gumming *n* PAPER engomado *m*, PROD embotamiento *m*, ensuciamiento *m*; ~ **machine** *n* PACK encoladora *f*, engomadora *f*; **~-up** *n* PROD embotamiento *m*, ensuciamiento *m*

gummite *n* MINERAL gummita *f*

gun *n* MILIT ametralladora *f*, arma de fuego *f*, cañón *m*, escopeta *f*, pistola *f*, revólver *m*; **~ barrel** *n* MILIT cañón de fusil *m*; **~ carriage** *n* MILIT cureña de cañón *f*; **~ efficiency** *n* CINEMAT, TV eficacia de la cámara *f*; **~ perforator** *n* PETR TECH cañón *m*; **~ pit** *n* MILIT asentamiento del cañón *m*, pozo del cañón *m*; **~ shield** *n* MILIT abrigo del cañón *m*; **~ swab brush** *n* MILIT escobillón para cañones *m*

guncotton *n* MINE algodón pólvora *m*, fulmicotón *m* (*AmL*), mecha *f* (*Esp*), nitroalgodón *m* (*Esp*), piroxilina *f* (*AmL*)

gunfire *n* MILIT cañoneo *m*, disparo de cañón *m*, fuego de cañón *m*

gunite *n* CONST gunita *f*

guniting *n* C&G esparcido *m*, espreado *m*, CONST gunitado *m*

gunmetal *n* MECH bronce de cañón *m*, bronce industrial *m*, bronce mecánico *m*, MILIT bronce de cañón *m*; **~ bearing** *n* MECH ENG cojinete de bronce de cañón *m*; **~ bush** *n* MECH ENG casquillo de bronce de cañón *m*; **~ bushing** *n* MECH ENG encasquillado con bronce de cañón *m*

Gunn: **~ amplifier** *n* ELECTRON, PHYS amplificador Gunn *m*; **~ diode** *n* ELECTRON, PHYS diodo de Gunn *m*; **~ effect** *n* ELECTRON, PHYS efecto Gunn *m*; **~-effect diode** *n* ELECTRON, PHYS diodo de efecto Gunn *m*

gunnel *n* WATER TRANSP regala *f*

gunning *n* C&G esparcido *m*, espreado *m*

gunpod *n* CINEMAT soporte de microtono direccional *m*

gunpowder *n* MILIT pólvora *f*

Gunter: **~'s chain** *n* CONST cadena de agrimensor *f*

gunwale *n* WATER TRANSP falca *f*, regala *f*

gusset *n* PRINT pliegue *m*, WATER TRANSP *shipbuilding* cartabón *m*, cartabón de unión *m*, consola *f*, consola de refuerzo *f*; **~ wrinkle** *n* PRINT arruga del pliegue *f*

gusseted: **~ layflat tubing** *n* PACK tubo plano con fuelle *m*; **~ sack** *n* PACK saco de fuelle *m*

gust *n* AIR TRANSP, METEO, SPACE, WATER TRANSP *of wind* racha *f*, ráfaga *f*; **~ alleviation factor** *n* AIR TRANSP, SPACE, WATER TRANSP factor de atenuación de ráfagas *m*; **~ envelope** *n* AIR TRANSP, SPACE, WATER TRANSP diagrama V-N de ráfagas *m*; **~ formation time** *n* AIR TRANSP, SPACE, WATER TRANSP tiempo de formación de ráfaga *m*; **~ gradient distance** *n* AIR TRANSP, SPACE, WATER TRANSP distancia de formación de ráfaga *f*; **~ intensity** *n* AIR TRANSP, SPACE, WATER TRANSP fuerza de ráfaga *f*, intensidad de ráfaga *f*, intensidad de turbulencia *f*, rafagosidad *f*; **~ load factor** *n* AIR TRANSP, SPACE, WATER TRANSP factor de carga de ráfaga *m*; **~ load limit** *n* AIR TRANSP, SPACE, WATER TRANSP límite de carga de ráfaga *m*; **~ lock** *n* AIR TRANSP, SPACE, WATER TRANSP blocaje antirráfaga *m*, enganche contra ráfagas *m*; **~ V-n diagram** *n* AIR TRANSP, SPACE, WATER TRANSP diagrama V-N de ráfagas *m*

gusting: **~ wind** *n* METEO viento a ráfagas *m*, viento rafagoso *m*

gut[1] *n* OCEAN estrecho *m*

gut[2] *vt* OCEAN desentrañar

GUT *abbr* (*grand unified theory*) PART PHYS, PHYS teoría de gran unificación *f*

Gutenberg: **~ discontinuity** *n* GEOL discontinuidad de Gutenberg *f*

gutta: **~-percha** *n* CHEM, P&R gutapercha *f*

gutter *n* AIR TRANSP canalón *m*, corrosión fisurante *f*, CONST aspirador *m* (*Esp*), canaleta *f* (*AmL*), canalón *m*, MECH cuneta *f*, PRINT medianil *m*; **~ bleed** *n* PRINT ilustración que abarca dos páginas *f*; **~ bracket** *n* CONST *for attaching to rafter* palomilla del canalón *f*, *to drive* soporte del canalón *m*, fiador *m*, *to screw on* escuadra para la canaleta *f*; **~ space** *n* PRINT margen del medianil *m*; **~ tile** *n* C&G tubo de drenaje *m*

guttering *n* AIR TRANSP corrosión fisurante *f*

guy *n* CONST tensor *m*, MECH tensor *m*, tirante *m*, WATER TRANSP *rope* cabo de retenida *m*, retenida *f*, viento *m*; **~ anchor** *n* PETR TECH anclaje de viento *m*; **~ insolator** *n* ELEC, ELEC ENG aislante para cable de retenida *m*; **~ ring** *n* PETR TECH anillo de retenidas *m*; **~ rope** *n* CONST tirante *m*, viento *m*; **~ wire** *n* ELEC ENG cable de retenida *m*

guying *n* CONST, ELEC ENG tensar con vientos

guyot *n* GEOL guyot *m*, meseta submarina *f*, OCEAN guyot *m*

GVT: **~ train** *n* (*gravity-vacuum transit train*) TRANSP, VEH tren con vacío de gravedad *m*

GVW *abbr* (*gross vehicle weight*) VEH PTV (*peso total del vehículo*)

Gy *abbr* (*gray*) METR, PHYS Gy (*gray*)

G-Y: **~ axis** *n* TV eje V-Y *m*; **~ signal** *n* TV señal G-Y *f*

gymnite *n* MINERAL gimnita *f*

gynocardic *adj* CHEM ginocárdico

gypseous *adj* CHEM yesoso

gypsiferous[1] *adj* GEOL yesífero

gypsiferous[2]: **~ shale** *n* GEOL pizarra yesífera *f*

gypsum[1]: **~-bearing** *adj* GEOL yesífero

gypsum[2] *n* AGRIC, CHEM, GEOL, MINERAL, PETR TECH, PETROL yeso *m*; **~ quarry** *n* MINE yesar *m*

gypsy *n* WATER TRANSP cabirón *m*; **~ winch** *n* PROD torno de mano *m*, torno elevador de pared *m*

gyrating: **~ mass** *n* NUCL masa giratoria *f*

gyrator *n* PHYS girador *m*

gyratory: **~ crusher** *n* FOOD triturador giratorio *m*

gyro: **~ amplifier** *n* AIR TRANSP amplificador giroscópico *m*; **~ caging** *n* AIR TRANSP caja giroscópica *f*; **~ data-switching control** *n* AIR TRANSP control del interruptor de datos del giróscopo *m*; **~ horizon** *n* AIR TRANSP, SPACE horizonte del giróscopo *m*, horizonte giroscópico *m*; **~ instruments** *n pl* AIR TRANSP, SPACE instrumentos del giróscopo *m pl*, instrumentos giroscópicos *m pl*; **~ laser** *n* AIR TRANSP, ELECTRON, SPACE láser giroscópico *m*; **~ resetting** *n* AIR TRANSP calibración del giróscopo *f*, reglaje del giróscopo *m*; **~-stabilized platform** *n* SPACE *vehicles* plataforma giro-estabilizada *f*; **~ stabilization** *n* AIR TRANSP, CINEMAT, TRANSP estabilización del giro *f*, estabilización giroscópica *f*; **~ stabilizer** *n* AIR TRANSP, CINEMAT, TRANSP estabilizador giroscópico *m*; **~ unbalance** *n* AIR TRANSP desequilibrio giroscópico *m*

gyrobus *n* TRANSP autobús giroscópico *m* (*Esp*), bus giroscópico *m* (*AmL*), girobús *m* (*Esp*), ómnibus *m* (*AmL*), VEH autobús giroscópico *m* (*Esp*), bus giroscópico *m* (*Esp*), girobús *m* (*Esp*), ómnibus *m* (*AmL*)

gyroclinometer *n* SPACE clinómetro giroscópico *m*, giroclinómetro *m*

gyrocompass *n* AIR TRANSP brújula giroscópica *f*, compás giroscópico *m*, WATER TRANSP girocompás *m*

gyrodyne *adj* AIR TRANSP girodino

gyromagnetic: ~ **effects** *n pl* PHYS efectos giromagnéticos *m pl*; ~ **ratio** *n* PHYS relación giromagnética *f*

gyrometer *n* SPACE girómetro *m*

gyropilot *n* WATER TRANSP *compass* giropiloto *m*

gyroplane *n* AIR TRANSP giroplano *m*, plano del giróscopo *m*

gyroscope *n* AIR TRANSP, CINEMAT, FUELLESS, MECH, PHYS, SPACE giroscopio *m*

gyroscopic[1] *adj* GEN giroscópico

gyroscopic[2]: ~ **compass** *n* AIR TRANSP brújula giroscópica *f*, compás giroscópico *m*, WATER TRANSP aguja giroscópica *f*, compás giroscópico *m*; ~ **force** *n* FUELLESS fuerza giroscópica *f*; ~ **head** *n* CINEMAT cabeza giroscópica *f*; ~ **platform** *n* AIR TRANSP plataforma giroscópica *f*; ~ **sight** *n* MILIT alza giroscópica *f*; ~ **torque** *n* AIR TRANSP par de fuerzas giroscópico *m*; ~ **tripod head** *n* CINEMAT cabeza de trípode giroscópico *f*

gyrostat *n* CHEM, PHYS giróstato *m*

gyrostatic *adj* CHEM, PHYS girostático

gyrosyn: ~ **compass** *n* AIR TRANSP *helicopter* brújula de giróscopo direccional sincronizado *f*; ~ **compass indicator** *n* AIR TRANSP indicador de brújula girosincronizada *m*

gyrotron *n* TELECOM girotrón *m*

gyttja *n* COAL tasmanita *f*

H

h *abbr* METR (*hecto*) h (*hecto*), PHYS (*Planck's constant*) h (*constante de Planck*)

H *abbr* GEN (*henry, hydrogen*) H (*henrio, hidrógeno*)

H: ~ **armature** *n* ELEC *machine* inducción H *f*; ~ **bomb** *n* NUCL bomba *f*; ~ **cell** *n* ELEC ENG célula H *f*, elemento H *m*; ~ **hinge** *n* CONST bisagra en forma de H *f*, gozne en forma de H *m*; ~ **mode** *n* TELECOM modo H *m*; ~ **plane** *n* ELEC ENG plano H *m*; ~ **plane bend** *n* ELEC ENG curvatura de plano H *f*; ~ **wave** *n* ELEC ENG onda H *f*

ha *abbr* (*hectare*) METR ha (*hectárea*)

Ha *abbr* (*hahnium*) CHEM, RAD PHYS Ha (*hahnio*)

Haber: ~ **process** *n* CHEM proceso de Haber *m*

habit *n* CRYSTALL hábito cristalino *m*, METALL constitución dominante *f*, forma dominante *f*; ~ **plane** *n* CRYSTALL plano del hábito cristalino *m*, METALL plano estructural *m*

habitat *n* PETROL hábitat *m*

habitation: ~ **module** *n* SPACE *spacecraft* módulo de habitación *m*

hacking: ~ **knife** *n* CONST *glazing* cuchillo de corte *m*; ~ **stitch** *n* TEXTIL puntada de corte *f*

hackle[1] *n* AmE (*cf hackle mark BrE*) C&G marca de pelo *f*, pelo *m*; ~ **mark** BrE *n* (*cf hackle AmE*) C&G marca de pelo *f*, pelo *m*

hackle[2] *vt* TEXTIL rastrillar

hackling *n* TEXTIL rastrillado *m*

hacksaw *n* MECH *to heap or pile up* sierra de mecánico *f*, sierra para metales *f*, MECH ENG sierra alternativa para metales *f*, sierra de mecánico *f*; ~ **blade** *n* MECH ENG hoja de segueta *f*, hoja de sierra para metales *f*, PROD hoja de sierra para metales *f*; ~ **frame** *n* MECH ENG arco de segueta *m*, arco de sierra para metales *m*

hade *n* GEOL inclinación *f*, complemento de buzamiento *m*

Ha-Dec: ~ **mount** *n* SPACE montaje Ha-Dec *m*, montaje declinación ángulo horario *m*

hadron *n* PART PHYS, PHYS, RAD PHYS hadrón *m*; ~ **detection** *n* PART PHYS detección de hadrones *f*

hadronic: ~ **calorimeter** *n* PART PHYS, RAD PHYS calorímetro hadrónico *m*

haematein *n* BrE CHEM hemateína *f*

haematic *adj* BrE CHEM hemático

haematin *n* BrE CHEM hematina *f*

haematite *n* BrE CHEM hematites *f*

haematolite *n* BrE MINERAL hematolita *f*, hematolito *m*

haematoporphyrin *n* BrE CHEM hematoporfirina *f*

haematoxylin *n* BrE CHEM hematoxilina *f*

haemoglobin *n* BrE CHEM hemoglobina *f*

haemolysin *n* BrE CHEM hemolisina *f*

haemolysis *n* BrE CHEM hemólisis *f*

haemolytic *adj* BrE CHEM hemolítico

haemopyrrole *n* BrE CHEM hemopirrol *m*

haemosiderin *n* BrE CHEM hemosiderina *f*

haemotoxin *n* BrE CHEM hemotoxina *f*

hafnium *n* (*Hf*) CHEM, METALL hafnio *m* (*Hf*)

Hager: ~ **disc** BrE, ~ **disk** *n* AmE C&G disco Hager *m*

hahnium *n* CHEM (*Ha, Hn*), RAD PHYS (*Ha, Hn*) hahnio *m* (*Ha, Hn*)

Haidinger: ~ **fringes** *n pl* PHYS franjas de Haidinger *f pl*

hail[1] *n* METEO, PHYS granizada *f*, granizo *m*, WATER TRANSP *another ship* llamada a la voz *f*

hail[2] *vt* WATER TRANSP *another ship* llamar a la voz

hail[3] *vi* METEO, PHYS granizar; ~ **from a port** *vi* WATER TRANSP venir de cierto puerto

hailing: ~ **distance** *n* WATER TRANSP alcance de la voz *m*

hailstone *n* METEO granizo *m*, pedrisco *m*, PHYS granizo *m*

hailstorm *n* METEO granizada *f*, pedrisco *m*, PHYS granizada *f*

hair *n* TEXTIL pelo *m*; ~ **cell** *n* ACOUST célula ciliada *f*; ~ **hygrometer** *n* LAB, PHYS, REFRIG higrómetro de cabello *m*; ~ **light** *n* CINEMAT iluminación para resaltar el cabello *f*; ~ **protector** *n* SAFE protector del cabello *m*; ~ **pyrites** *n* MINERAL sulfuro de níquel capilar *m*, tricopirita *f*

haircord: ~ **carpet** *n* TEXTIL alfombra de cuerda de pelo *f*

hairiness *n* TEXTIL vellosidad *f*

hairline *n* PRINT filete extrafino *m*, *deck fittings* trazo extrafino *m*; ~ **crack** *n* CONST grieta capilar *f*, MECH *planting* grieta capilar interna *f*; ~ **register** *n* PRINT registro exacto *m*; ~ **space** *n* PRINT filete extrafino *m*

hairpin: ~ **cooler** *n* C&G enfriador de horquilla *m*; ~ **spring** *n* MECH ENG resorte de horquilla *m*, resorte en V *m*; ~ **tube** *n* MECH ENG tubo en U *m*

hairspring *n* MECH ENG muelle en espiral *m*

hairstroke *n* PRINT trazo fino *m*

hairy: ~ **crab grass** *n* AGRIC pasto cuaresma *m*; ~ **roving** *n* C&G rovín peludo *m*; ~ **vetch** *n* AGRIC arvejilla *f*

halation *n* ELECTRON halo *m*, PHOTO formación de halo *f*

half[1] *adj* ACOUST, MECH ENG medio; ~**-bound** *adj* PRINT encuadernado a media piel, ecuadernado a media pasta; ~ **bridge piece** *adj* MECH ENG *lathe* medio puente; ~ **bushing** *adj* MECH ENG medio buje, medio casquillo, medio manguito; ~**-mast** *adj* WATER TRANSP *flag* a media asta

half[2]: ~ **ahead** *adv* WATER TRANSP *engine* avante media; ~ **astern** *adv* WATER TRANSP *engine* atrás media

half[3]: ~**-adder** *n* COMP&DP, ELECTRON semisumador *m*; ~ **beam** *n* WATER TRANSP *shipbuilding* medio bao *m*; ~ **bog soil** *n* AGRIC suelo semi turboso *m*; ~**-breadth plan** *n* WATER TRANSP *shipbuilding* plano horizontal *m*, proyección horizontal del plano de formas *f*; ~ **bridge** *n* ELEC ENG semipuente *m*; ~ **bridge arrangement** *n* ELEC ENG semi-montaje en derivación *m*; ~ **clamp** *n* MECH ENG media brida *f*, semibrida *f*; ~ **cleat** *n* MECH ENG media abrazadera *f*; ~ **cup** *n* MECH ENG media copa *f*, semicopa *f*; ~ **cycle** *n* ELEC ENG semiciclo *m*, NUCL *atomic physics* hemiciclo *m*, semiciclo *m*; ~**-duplex** *n* (*HDX*) COMP&DP semi-dúplex *m* (*HDX*); ~ **duplex operation** *n* COMP&DP, TELECOM operación en semi-dúplex *f*, operación semidúplex *f*; **~-elliptic spring** *n* MECH ENG muelle semielíptico *m*, resorte semielíptico *m*; **~ flange** *n* MECH ENG media flanja *f*, media pestaña *f*, medio collarín *m*, medio reborde *m*, semialeta *f*, semillanta *f*, semiplato *m*; **~-gap bed** *n* MECH ENG *lathe* bancada de medio escote *f*; **~-integral spin** *n* PHYS espín semientero *m*; **~-life** *n* CHEM, GEOL período de semidesintegración *m*, vida media *f*, NUCL período de semidesintegración *m*, vida media radiactiva *f*, PART PHYS *of particle*, PHYS período de semidesintegración *m*, vida media *f*, RAD PHYS vida media radiactiva *f*; **~ line** *n* GEOM medialínea *f*, rayo *m*; **~ mask** *n* SAFE mascarilla *f*; **~-moon ring wrench** *n* MECH ENG llave de anillo de media luna *f*; **~-octave band** *n* ACOUST banda de media octava *f*; **~-plate camera** *n* PHOTO cámara fotográfica de medio clisé *f*; **~-power bandwidth** *n* SPACE anchura de banda a mitad de potencia *f*; **~-power beamwidth** *n* SPACE *communications* anchura de haz a mitad de potencia *f*; **~-power width** *n* ELECTRON amplitud reducida a la mitad *f*, anchura reducida a la mitad *f*; **~ pulse** *n* ELECTRON semiimpulso *m*; **~ round edge** *n* C&G borde de media caña *m*; **~ section** *n* PROD *drawing* semicorte *m*; **~ sectional beam** *n* TEXTIL plegador medio seccional *m*; **~ set** *n* MINE marco con un solo pie derecho *m*; **~ sheetwork** *n* PRINT imposición e impresión a blanco y vuelta *f*; **~-size drawing** *n* PROD dibujo a escala mitad *m*, dibujo a mitad de tamaño natural *m*; **~-sized board** *n* ELECTRON cuadro de tamaño medio *m*; **~ space** *n* CONST *stair-building* rellano *m*; **~ subtractor** *n* COMP&DP semisustractor *m*; **~ thickness** *n* PHYS *heat unit* espesor medio *m*; **~-thrust washer** *n* MECH ENG arandela de medio empuje *f*; **~ tide** *n* WATER TRANSP media marea *f*; **~ tide level** *n* OCEAN nivel medio de marea *m*; **~-timbering** *n* CONST entramado de madera *m*; **~-track lorry** *n BrE* (*cf half-track truck AmE*) VEH camión semioruga *m*; **~-track truck** *n AmE* (*cf half-track lorry BrE*) VEH camión semioruga *m*; **~-track vehicle** *n* MILIT autooruga *m*; **~ truss** *n* CONST *building* semicercha *f*; **~ turn stairs** *n* CONST escaleras de ida y vuelta *f pl*; **~ twist** *n* PROD media vuelta *f*; **~ union** *n* MECH ENG semiunión *f*; **~ value layer** *n* (*HVL*) NUCL espesor de semirreducción *m*; **~-value thickness** *n* PHYS espesor de semirreducción *m*; **~ wave** *n* ELEC *alternating current* media onda *f*, semionda *f*; **~-wave dipole** *n* ELEC ENG, PHYS, TELECOM dipolo de semionda *m*; **~-wave dipole aerial** *n BrE* (*cf half-wave dipole antenna AmE*) RAD PHYS, TV antena dipolo de media onda *f*; **~-wave dipole antenna** *n AmE* (*cf half-wave dipole aerial BrE*) RAD PHYS, TV antena dipolo de media onda *f*; **~ wave line** *n* PHYS línea de onda media *f*; **~-wave plate** *n* PHYS placa de onda media *f*; **~-wave rectification** *n* ELEC rectificación de media onda *f*, ELEC ENG rectificación de media onda *f*, rectificación en semilongitud de onda *f*; **~-wave rectifier** *n* ELEC rectificador de media onda *m*, ELEC ENG rectificador de media onda *m*, rectificador de semilongitud de onda *m*, PHYS rectificador de semionda *m*; **~-wave transmission line** *n* ELEC *supply* línea de transmisión de media onda *f*; **~ width** *n* PHYS media anchura *f*, RAD PHYS anchura de un pico *f*; **~ width printing press** *n* PRINT prensa de impresión de media anchura *f*; **~ word** *n* COMP&DP media palabra *f*, semipalabra *f*

halfbinding *n* PRINT encuadernación a media piel *f*
halfkraft: **~ board** *n* PAPER cartón semikraft *m*
halfshaft *n* VEH palier *m*, semieje *m*
halftone[1] *adj* ACOUST medio tono
halftone[2] *n* PRINT autotipia *f*, semitono *m*; **~ block** *n* PHOTO bloque de media tinta *m*; **~ coated paper** *n* PAPER papel estucado para ilustraciones *m*; **~ dot** *n* PRINT punto de la trama *m*; **~ exposure** *n* PRINT exposición de medio tono *f*; **~ ink** *n* PRINT tinta para ilustraciones *f*; **~ process** *n* PRINT proceso de semitonos *m*; **~ reproduction** *n* PRINT reproducción en semitonos *f*; **~ selection** *n* PRINT selección de semitonos *f*
halide *n* CHEM haluro *m*, halogenuro *m*
halite *n* MINERAL halita *f*, sal gema *f*
hall *n* RAIL vestíbulo *m*
Hall: **~ coefficient** *n* PHYS coeficiente de Hall *m*; **~ effect** *n* ELEC *magnetism, electromagnetism*, PHYS, RAD PHYS, SPACE efecto Hall *m*; **~ field** *n* PHYS campo de Hall *m*; **~ generator** *n* AUTO generador de Hall *m*; **~ IC** *n* (*Hall integrated circuit*) AUTO circuito integrado de Hall *m*; **~ integrated circuit** *n* (*Hall IC*) AUTO circuito integrado de Hall *m*; **~ ion-thruster** *n* SPACE *spacecraft* propulsor iónico de Hall *m*; **~ magnetometer** *n* PHYS magnetómetro de Hall *m*; **~ mobility** *n* PHYS movilidad de Hall *f*; **~ probe** *n* PHYS, RAD PHYS sonda de Hall *f*; **~ resistance** *n* PHYS resistencia de Hall *f*; **~ voltage** *n* PHYS voltaje de Hall *m*
hallmark *n* PROD marca de contraste *f*, punzón de garantía *m*
halloysite *n* MINERAL halloysita *f*
halmyrolysis *n* GEOL halmirolisis *f*
halo *n* ELECTRON, PRINT halo *m*, SPACE aureola *f*, corona *f*, halo *m*; **~ of dispersion** *n* NUCL halo de dispersión *m*; **~ orbit** *n* SPACE órbita de corona *f*
HALO *abbr* (*high-altitude low-opening*) MILIT *parachute insertion technique* salto de paracaídas a gran altitud *m*
halocarbon: **~ refrigerant** *n* REFRIG refrigerante halocarbonado *m*
halogen *n* CHEM halógeno *m*, CINEMAT lámpara halógena *f*; **~ lamp** *n* ELEC *lighting* lámpara halógena *f*
halogenated: **~ hydrocarbon solvent** *n* PROD disolvente hidrocarbúrico halogenado *m*
halogenation *n* CHEM halogenación *f*
halogenous *adj* CHEM halógeno
halography *n* CHEM halografía *f*
haloid[1] *adj* CHEM haloideo
haloid[2] *n* CHEM haloide *m*
halokinesis *n* GEOL haloquinesis *f*, PETR TECH alocinesis *f*, haloquinesis *f*
halon *n* SPACE halón *m*; **~ fire extinguisher** *n* SAFE extintor de halón *m*; **~, foam and powder firefighting installation** *n* SAFE instalación de combate de incendios con halón, espuma y polvo químico *f*
halotechny *n* CHEM halotecnia *f*
halotrichite *n* MINERAL halotriquita *f*
halt[1] *n* COMP&DP detención *f*, parada *f*; **~ instruction** *n* COMP&DP instrucción de parada *f*; **~ sign** *n* CONST señal de stop *f*
halt[2] *vt* COMP&DP detener, interrumpir
halt[3] *vti* COMP&DP parar
halt[4] *vi* COMP&DP detenerse
halved: **~ belt** *n* PROD correa cruzada *f*; **~ joint** *n*

CONST *woodwork* junta a media madera *f*, PROD *cast iron work* junta a media fundición *f*, *wrought iron work* junta a medio hierro *f*

halving *n* CONST empalme a media madera *m*, PROD *cast iron work* junta a media fundición *f*, *wrought iron work* junta a medio hierro *f*

halyard *n* WATER TRANSP *running rigging* driza *f*

Hamiltonian *adj* PHYS hamiltoniano

Hamilton-Jacobi: ~ **equation** *n* PHYS ecuación de Hamilton-Jacobi *f*

Hamilton's: ~ **equations** *n pl* PHYS ecuaciones de Hamilton *f pl*

hammer *n* ACOUST, C&G martillo *m*, COAL martinete de forja *m*, percusor *m*, MECH *on working barge* martillo *m*, maza *f*; ~ **crusher** *n* COAL quebrantadora de martillos *f*, trituradora de martillos *f*; ~ **die** *n* MECH ENG *for forming* troquel de martillo *m*; ~ **drill** *n* CONST perforadora de martillo *f*, taladro de percusión *m*, MECH ENG martillo perforador *m*, perforador de martillo *m*, perforadora de percusión *f*, MINE martillo perforador *m*, perforadora de percusión *f*; ~ **drive screw** *n* MECH ENG tornillo de martillo *m*; ~ **enamel** *n* COLOUR esmalte con efecto martillado *m*; ~ **finish** *n* P&R acabado abollado *m*; ~ **grab** *n* CONST mango del martillo *m*; ~ **head** *n* PROD pico de martillo *m*; ~ **head screw** *n* MECH ENG tornillo de cabeza de martillo *m*; ~ **mill** *n* FOOD molino de martillo *m*; ~ **pick** *n* PROD remachado de martillo *m*; ~ **plug** *n* CONST enchufe del martillo *m*; ~ **riveting** *n* PROD remachado al martillo *m*; ~ **scale** *n* PROD batiduras de forja *f pl*, batiduras de martillado *f pl*; ~ **seismics** *n* GEOPHYS sísmica de martillo *f*; ~ **slag** *n* PROD escoria de fragua *f*, escoria del martillado *f*; ~ **tone finish** *n* COLOUR acabado martillado *m*

hammered: ~ **glass** *n* C&G vidrio martillado *m*

hammering *n* CONST martilleo *m*, NUCL *of ribbed bulkheads* golpe de ariete *m*, PROD martilleo *m*, martillazos *m pl*, golpeteo *m*, REFRIG golpe de ariete *m*

Hamming: ~ **code** *n* SPACE *communications* código de Hamming *m*; ~ **distance** *n* TELECOM distancia de Hamming *f*

hammock *n* WATER TRANSP coy *m*

hand[1]: ~-**assembled** *adj* PACK montado a mano; ~-**held** *adj* SAFE *machine* manual; ~-**operated** *adj* MECH accionado a mano, manual, MECH ENG accionado a mano

hand[2]: **by** ~ *adv* PROD a mano; **by** ~ **power** *adv* PROD accionado a mano

hand[3] *n* LAB *at canal-lock* aguja *f*; ~ **baggage** *n* AIR TRANSP equipaje de mano *m*; ~ **bellows** *n* C&G fuelle de mano *m*, soplador manual *m*; ~ **block printing** *n* TEXTIL estampado a mano con molde *m*; ~-**blown glass** *n* C&G vidrio soplado a mano *m*; ~ **brace** *n* MECH ENG barbiquí de mano *m*; ~ **centrifuge** *n* LAB centrifugadora manual *f*; ~ **chain** *n* CONST cadena de mano *f*, PROD *of pulley-block, hoist* cadena de maniobra *f*; ~ **composition** *n* PRINT composición a mano *f*; ~-**cranked camera** *n* CINEMAT cámara accionada manualmente *f*; ~ **dog** *n* MINE gancho de mano *m*; ~ **dosing** *n* PACK dosificación manual *f*; ~ **downfeed** *n* MECH ENG *machine tools* descenso manual *m*; ~ **drill** *n* MECH *of headstock, lathe or tailstock* aparato de sondeo a mano *m*, barrena de mano *f*, perforadora de mano *f*, taladro de mano *m* (*AmL*); ~ **drive** *n* CINEMAT accionamiento manual *m*;

~-**expansion valve** *n* REFRIG válvula de expansión manual *f*; ~ **feed** *n* MECH ENG *machine tools* alimentación a mano *f*, alimentación manual *f*, avance a mano *m*, avance manual *m*, PACK, PRINT alimentación a mano *f*, alimentación manual *f*; ~ **file** *n* PROD lima carrelera *f*, lima plana de mano *f*; ~-**finishing stick** *n* MECH ENG *abrasives* varilla de acabado a mano *f*; ~ **flare** *n* WATER TRANSP *signal* bengala de mano *f*; ~ **flywheel pump** *n* PROD bomba de volante *f*; ~ **glass** *n* INSTR campana de vidrio *f*, espejo de mano *m*, lupa de mano *f*; ~-**guided machine** *n* SAFE máquina de mano *f*; ~ **hammer** *n* PROD martillo de mano *m*; ~-**held camera** *n* CINEMAT cámara de mano *f*, cámara sin trípode *f*; ~-**held machine** *n* SAFE máquina manual *f*; ~-**held mobile radio** *n* CONST radio portátil *f*; ~-**held power tool** *n* ELEC, MECH ENG, SAFE herramienta eléctrica de mano *f*, herramienta eléctrica portátil *f*; ~-**held programmer** *n* PROD programador portátil *m*; ~-**held receiver** *n* TELECOM receptor portátil *m*; ~-**held terminal** *n* TELECOM terminal portátil *m*; ~ **hole** *n* PROD *boiler* agujero de inspección *m*, agujero de lavado *m*; ~ **labeler** *AmE*, ~ **labeller** *BrE* *n* PACK etiquetador manual *m*; ~ **lever** *n* MECH ENG palanca de mano *f*; ~-**lever feed** *n* MECH ENG alimentación por palanca de mano *f*, avance por palanca de mano *m*; ~ **mirror** *n* INSTR espejo de mano *m*; ~-**mixed concrete** *n* CONST concreto mezclado a mano *m* (*AmL*), hormigón mezclado a mano *m* (*Esp*); ~ **nut** *n* PROD tuerca de mariposa *f*, tuerca de orejetas *f*; ~-**operation** *n* SPACE utilización manual *f*; ~-**operated machine** *n* PACK máquina manual *f*; ~-**operated power shovel** *n* MECH ENG excavadora mecánica de operación manual *f*, pala mecánica de operación manual *f*; ~-**operated switch** *n* ELEC conmutador accionado a mano *m*, conmutador manual *m*; ~-**power hacksaw** *n* PROD sierra alternativa de mano *f*; ~-**power warehouse goods lift** *n* PROD montacargas mecánico de mano *m*; ~ **press** *n* PRINT prensa manual *f*; ~ **pump** *n* PROD, SAFE *process* bomba de mano *f*, bomba manual *f*; ~ **rammer** *n* PROD *moulding* pisón de mano *m*; ~ **rope** *n* PROD *of pulley-block, hoist, etc* cuerda de maniobra *f*; ~ **screen printing** *n* TEXTIL estampado a la lionesa *m*; ~ **selection** *n* COAL clasificación a mano *f*, escogido a mano *m*, escogido manual *m*, muestreo manual *m*; ~ **shears** *n pl* PROD *for metal* cizallas de mano *f pl*; ~ **sheet machine** *n* PRINT máquina manual de hojas *f*; ~ **shield** *n* SAFE escudo de mano *m*; ~ **signal** *n* SAFE *switch* señal manual *f*, TRANSP señal manual *f*, señalización manual *f*; ~ **spike** *n* MECH ENG tirafondos de mano *m*, tirafondos manual *m*; ~ **stamp** *n* PROD *metalworking* estampa de mano *f*; ~ **tachometer** *n* PACK tacómetro manual *m*; ~ **tap** *n* PROD *screwcutting* macho de roscar a mano *m*; ~ **throttle control** *n* AUTO mando manual de la mariposa *m*; ~ **tool** *n* MECH herramienta manual *f*, *of headstock, lathe or tailstock* herramienta de mano *f*, PROD *lathe* herramienta manual *f*, herramienta de mano *f*; ~-**transmitted vibration** *n* SAFE vibración transmitida a través de la mano *f*; ~-**transmitted vibration hazard** *n* SAFE *switch* peligro originado por vibraciones transmitidas manualmente *m*; ~ **truck** *n* PROD carretilla *f*, carretilla de mano *f*; ~-**up** *n* COMP&DP colgado *m*, interrupción de la comunicación *f*; ~ **vice** *n* *BrE* MECH *into a wall* entenalla *f*,

MECH ENG entenalla *f*, tornillo de mano *m*; ~ **vise** *AmE see* hand vice *BrE*; ~ **wheel** *n* MECH rueda a mano *f*, volante de mano *m*, MECH ENG *for driving* volante *m*, *without handle* volante de maniobra *m*, volante de mano *m*, rueda de mano *f*; ~ **winch** *n* PROD guinche de manivela *m*, guinche de mano *m*

handbagging *n* PACK embolsado manual *m*

handbarrow *n* CONST angarillas *f pl*

handbinding *n* PRINT encuadernación manual *f*

handbook *n* MECH ENG, PROD manual *m*

handbrake *n* AUTO, MECH, MECH ENG, VEH freno de mano *m*; ~ **cable** *n* AUTO, VEH cable del freno de mano *m*; ~ **lever** *n* AUTO palanca del freno de mano *f*

handed: ~ **assembly** *n* MECH ENG montaje a mano *m*, montaje manual *m*

handgrip *n* CINEMAT empuñadura *f*, mango *m*, MECH ENG agarrador *m*, asidero *m*, empuñadura *f*, MINE asidero *m*, PACK asidero *m*, asa *f*, PHOTO empuñadura *f*, PROD, SPACE, VEH asidero *m*; ~ **with shutter release** *n* CINEMAT empuñadura con interruptor *f*, mango con disparador *m*

handle[1] *n* CONST asa *f*, mango *m*, tirador *m*, MECH *locksmithing* mango *m*, asa *f*, empuñadura *f*, puño *m*, MECH ENG manivela *f*, agarrador *m*, asidero *m*, empuñadura *f*, mango *m*, puño *m*, MINE asidero *m*, empuñadura *f*, asa *f*, mango *m*, PACK asa *f*, asidero *m*, PROD *of basket or pail* asa *f*, asidero *m*, *of tool* mango *m*, *of trying plane or jack plane* semipuño *m*, puño *m*, SPACE *spacecraft* empuñadura *f*, palanca de mando *f*, agarradera *f*, asidero *m*, TEXTIL manivela *f*, VEH empuñadura *f*, manija *f*, asidero *m*; ~ **lever** *n* MECH ENG manigueta *f*; ~ **plate** *n* MECH ENG cacha *f*; ~ **switch** *n* MECH ENG interruptor de puño *m*, interruptor extensible *m*; ~-**welding machine** *n* PROD máquina de soldar de mano *f*

handle[2] *vt* MECH manipular, poner mango, PROD *manipulate* manejar, tratar, comerciar en, ejecutar, manipular, TEXTIL manipular, WATER TRANSP *vessels* bracear, manejar, marcar

handling *n* COMP&DP tratamiento *m*, MECH ENG manejo *m*, maniobra *f*, manipulación *f*, tratamiento *m*, PACK manutención *f*, manipulado *m*, PAPER manipulación *f*, PROD *manipulation* manipulación *f*, *proving with handle* enmangamiento *m*, SAFE *fuel* manejo *m*, SPACE embarque *m*, maniobra *f*, TELECOM, TEXTIL manipulación *f*; ~ **characteristic** *n* SPACE característica de la maniobra *f*, característica del embarque *f*; ~ **equipment** *n* PACK equipo de manipulado *m*; ~-**and filling equipment** *n* PACK equipo de manutención y llenado *m*; ~ **and installing instructions** *n pl* MECH ENG, PACK instrucciones de manutención e instalación *f pl*; ~ **lug** *n pl* MECH ENG agarradera *f*, anillo *m*, asa de sujeción *f*, orejeta para izar *f*; ~ **time** *n* TEXTIL tiempo de manipulación *m*

handover *n* NUCL *in fuel pellet* cambio de turno *m*, entrega *f*

handpacking *n* PACK empaquetado manual *m*

handpick *vt* COAL recoger a mano

handprinting *n* PRINT impresión manual *f*

handpunch *n* COMP&DP perforador manual *mf*, perforadora de mano *f*, PROD punzón de mano *m*

handrail *n* CONST pasamanos *m*, MECH baranda *f* (*AmL*), barandilla *f* (*Esp*), pasamanos *m*, WATER TRANSP pasamanos *m*

handrailing *n* CONST, NUCL pasamanos *m*

handrest *n* INSTR reposabrazos *m*, MECH ENG *lathe*

apoyo de mano *m*, soporte de mano *m*; ~ **socket** *n* MECH ENG *lathe* soporte del carro portaherramientas *m*

hands[1]: ~-**free** *adj* TELECOM manos libres

hands[2]: ~-**off operation** *n* COMP&DP funcionamiento automático *m*, operación sin manos *f*, TELECOM funcionamiento asíncrono *m*; ~-**on introduction** *n* PROD introducción práctica *f*; ~-**on operation** *n* COMP&DP operación para ganar experiencia práctica *f*

handsaw *n* CONST *large* serrucho *m*, *small* sierra *f*, PROD sierra de mano *f*

handscreening *n* COAL selección a mano *f*

handscrew *n* MECH ENG gato *m*

handset *n* PROD microteléfono *m*, micrófono *m*, programador portátil *m*, TELECOM aparato telefónico *m*, microteléfono *m*; ~ **cord** *n* TELECOM cordón del microteléfono *m*

handshake *n* COMP&DP entrada en comunicación *f*, saludo inicial *m*

handshaking *n* COMP&DP *communications* comunicación amiga *f*

handsheet *n* PAPER hoja de ensayo *f*, hoja de laboratorio *f*

handspike *n* MECH *portion of brick* espeque *m*, palanca de maniobra *f*, palanqueta *f*

handwashing *n* PROD lavado de mano *m*

handwork *n* PROD obra hecha a mano *f*, trabajo a mano *m*, trabajo manual *m*

handworking *n* PROD trabajo manual *m*

handy[1] *adj* MECH *sailing* manuable

handy[2]: ~ **billy** *n* WATER TRANSP *tackle* aparato de mano *m*, bomba de achique portátil *f*

hang[1] *n* PROD *blast furnace* obstrucción *f*

hang[2] *vt* PROD colgar, suspender; ~ **up** *vt* COMP&DP, PROD colgar

hang[3] *vi* PROD *blast furnace* obstruirse; ~ **up** *vi* TELECOM colgar

hangar *n* AIR TRANSP hangar *m*

hanger *n* CONST *to carry end of joist* barra de suspensión *f*, MECH ENG *shaft* soporte colgante *m*, soporte suspendido *m*, PROD gancho de suspensión *m*, silleta *f*, soporte *m*; ~ **with bearings** *n* MECH ENG soporte colgante con cojinetes *m*, soporte suspendido con cojinetes *m*; ~ **pipe** *n* MECH tubería de suspensión *f*

hanging[1] *adj* PROD pendiente

hanging[2] *n* PROD *action* colgante *m*, suspensión *f*; ~ **bucket** *n* PROD cangilón suspendido *m*; ~ **indentation** *n* PRINT párrafo francés *m*; ~ **lamp** *n* ELEC, ELEC ENG lámpara colgante *f*; ~ **post** *n* CONST *of door or gate* colgante *m*; ~ **rod** *n* MINE varilla de suspensión *f*; ~ **scaffold** *n* CONST andamio colgante *m*; ~ **stage** *n* CONST andamio colgante *m*; ~ **stairs** *n* CONST escalera voladiza *f*; ~ **steps** *n* CONST escalones en voladizo *m*; ~ **thread** *n* TEXTIL hilo colgante *m*; ~ **tool** *n* PROD *metal turning* herramienta de gancho *f*; ~-**up** *n* PROD colgado *m*, suspensión *f*; ~ **wall** *n* GEOL labio levantado *m*, pared superior *f*

hangover *n* NUCL resonancia parásita *f*; ~ **time** *n* SPACE *communications* período de atenuación del eco *m*, período de persistencia *m*, TELECOM tiempo de persistencia *m*

hangtag *n* PACK etiqueta colgante *f*

hank *n* TEXTIL madeja *f*, WATER TRANSP *rope* garrucho *m*

Hanle: ~ **effect** n (cf magnetic depolarization of resonance radiation) RAD PHYS efecto Hanle m
haplite n GEOL, PETROL aplita f
haploid adj AGRIC haploide
harbor AmE see harbour BrE
harbour n BrE WATER TRANSP puerto m; ~ **dues** n pl BrE WATER TRANSP derechos de puerto m pl; ~ **master** n BrE WATER TRANSP capitán del puerto m; ~ **master's office** n BrE WATER TRANSP capitanía de puerto f; ~ **station** n BrE WATER TRANSP trade estación marítima f
hard[1] adj CINEMAT rígido; ~**-bound** adj PRINT encuadernado de tapas duras; ~**-coated** adj AGRIC de cáscara dura; ~**-faced** adj MECH ENG cementado, endurecido, resistente al desgaste; ~ **on the helm** adj WATER TRANSP ship duro al timón; ~**-sectored** adj COMP&DP disk de sector duro; ~**-wired** adj COMP&DP cableado, físicamente conectado
hard[2]: ~ **bromide paper** n PHOTO papel duro de bromuro m; ~ **chrome finish** n MECH ENG acabado en cromo duro m; ~ **chrome plating** n COATINGS revestimiento de cromo duro m, MECH ENG for tools, gauges, etc cromado duro m; ~ **coal** n COAL antracita f, carbón bituminoso m, hulla f; ~ **contact** n ELEC contacto duro m, PROD contacto hidrófobo m; ~ **copy** n COMP&DP copia impresa f, salida impresa f, PRINT, SPACE copia impresa f; ~ **decision decoding** n TELECOM decodificación de decisión dura f; ~ **disk** n COMP&DP, TELECOM disco duro m; ~**-edged matte** n CINEMAT trama de borde rígido f; ~ **facing** n MECH cementación f, endurecimiento superficial m, revestimiento con material duro m; ~**-fired gate drive** n PROD unidad de puerta de tiro duro f; ~ **of formation bit** n PETR TECH barrena de arrastre f, broca f, mecha para formación dura f, trépano para formación dura m; ~ **glass** n C&G vidrio duro m; ~ **grade** n PROD emery wheels grado de dureza duro m; ~ **ground** n GEOL capa endurecida f, suelo endurecido m; ~ **handle** n TEXTIL tacto duro m; ~ **landing** n AIR TRANSP aterrizaje brusco m, aterrizaje duro m, SPACE aterrizaje difícil m; ~ **limited signal** n ELECTRON señal muy limitada f; ~ **limiter** n ELECTRON limitador potente m; ~ **limiting** n ELECTRON gran limitación f; ~ **magnetic material** n MECH material magnético de gran remanencia m, PHYS material de gran remanencia magnética m; ~ **metal** n MECH ENG boruros, carburos, nitruros y siliciluros cementados m pl, carburo al tungsteno m, metal duro m; ~ **metal burr** n MECH ENG rebaba de metal duro f; ~**-over signal** n ELECTRON señal de exceso f; ~ **plating** n COATINGS cromado duro m, cromado resistente m; ~ **porcelain** n C&G porcelana dura f; ~ **pulse** n ELECTRON impulso violento m; ~ **radiation** n RAD PHYS radiación dura f; ~ **sectoring** n COMP&DP formato permanente en sectores por hardware m, sectorización dura f; ~ **shoulder** n CONST respaldo duro m; ~ **snow** n METEO nieve dura f; ~ **soldering** n CONST, MECH ENG cobresoldeo m, PROD brazing soldadura de latón f (AmL), cobresoldeo m, soldadura fuerte f, SPACE spacecraft soldadura de latón f (AmL), THERMO cobresoldeo m; ~ **sphere model** n CRYSTALL modelo de esfera dura m; ~ **vacuum** n ELECTRON alto vacío m; ~ **water** n HYDROL agua calcárea f, agua dura f, agua gruesa f, WATER agua calcárea f, agua dura f, agua gorda f, agua gruesa f; ~ **water filter** n WATER filtro para agua calcárea m;

~ **wheel** n PROD muela abrasiva dura f; ~ **X-ray** n PHYS rayo X duro m, RAD PHYS rayo X duro m, rayo X hiperenergético m
hard[3]: ~**-face** vt MECH ENG cementar
hardboard n CONST, PACK tablero de aglomerado m
hardcore n CONST lecho de grava m, núcleo resistente m
harden vt PROD cementar, endurecer, endurecerse, hidrogenar, templarse, THERMO endurecer
hardenability n CRYSTALL templabilidad f, METALL facilidad para el temple f, templabilidad f
hardened: ~ **dowel pin** n MECH ENG clavija cementada f, pasador cementado m, pasador endurecido m; ~ **oil** n PROD aceite hidrogenado m; ~ **stainless steel** n MECH ENG, METALL, PROD acero inoxidable cementado m
hardener n CINEMAT, P&R, PHOTO endurecedor m
hardening n CONST endurecimiento m, CRYSTALL, METALL endurecimiento m, temple m, P&R, REFRIG endurecimiento m, SPACE hidrogenación f, temple m, torsión suplementaria f; ~ **bath** n PRINT baño endurecedor m; ~ **on the glazing** n C&G endurecimiento del esmalte m; ~ **tunnel** n REFRIG túnel de endurecimiento m
hardfacing n CONST revestimiento de superficie m
hardiness n AGRIC resistencia a inclemencias f
hardness n CHEM of water, substance, CONST, CRYSTALL dureza f, MECH, METALL dureza f, solidez f, P&R dureza f; ~ **reference standards** n pl MECH ENG estándar de referencia de dureza m; ~ **scale** n MECH on ship escala de dureza f; ~ **test** n PHYS ensayo de dureza m; ~ **tester** n INSTR esclerómetro m, LAB durómetro m, esclerómetro m, MECH steel esclerómetro m, ensayo de dureza m, medidor de durezas m, durómetro m, MECH ENG probador de dureza m, durómetro m, METR durómetro m, esclerómetro m, medidor de durezas m, P&R durómetro m, medidor de dureza m, PHYS durómetro m
hardpan n GEOL capa de roca debajo del terreno blando f, capa endurecida f
hardware n COMP&DP equipo físico m, hardware m, MECH pieza metálica f, quincallería f, PETROL, TELECOM hardware m; ~ **check** n COMP&DP comprobación mediante hardware f; ~ **configuration** n COMP&DP configuración del equipo físico f, configuración del hardware f; ~ **error** n COMP&DP error de hardware m; ~ **handshaking** n PROD saludo inicial entre equipos m, secuencia de señales electrónicas entre equipos f; ~ **maintenance** n COMP&DP mantenimiento del equipo físico m, mantenimiento del hardware m; ~ **reliability** n COMP&DP fiabilidad del hardware f, confiabilidad de equipo físico f; ~ **resources** n COMP&DP recursos de equipo físico m pl, recursos de hardware m pl; ~ **review** n PROD control de equipamiento m; ~ **stack** n COMP&DP pila de equipo físico f (AmL), pila de hardware f; ~ **upgrade** n COMP&DP ampliación del hardware f, mejora del hardware f, modernización del equipo físico f, modernización del hardware f
hardwired[1] adj ELEC ENG permanentemente conectado
hardwired[2]: ~ **logic** n COMP&DP lógica de cableado f, lógica físicamente conectada f (Esp); ~ **programmable switching system** n TELECOM sistema de conmutación programable cableado m
hardwood n CONST madera dura f, PAPER madera de

frondosas *f*; ~ **pulp** *n* PAPER pasta de frondosas *f*, pulpa de frondosas *f*

harmaline *n* CHEM harmalina *f*

harmful[1] *adj* PETR TECH *substance*, SAFE dañino, nocivo; ~ **to the eyes** *adj* SAFE dañino a los ojos, lesivo a los ojos

harmful[2]: ~ **substance** *n* SAFE substancia nociva *f*

harmine *n* CHEM harmina *f*

harmonic[1] *adj* GEN armónico

harmonic[2] *n* GEN armónico *m*; ~ **analyser** *n* BrE ELECTRON, PHYS analizador armónico *m*; ~ **analysis** *n* ELECTRON, MECH, PHYS, TELECOM análisis armónico *m*; ~ **analyzer** *n* AmE ELECTRON, PHYS analizador armónico *m*; ~ **attenuation** *n* ELECTRON atenuación armónica *f*; ~ **content** *n* ELECTRON residuo armónico *m*; ~ **distortion** *n* ACOUST, ELECTRON, TELECOM distorsión armónica *f*; ~ **filter** *n* ELECTRON, SPACE, TELECOM filtro de armónicos *m*; ~ **function** *n* ELECTRON función armónica *f*; ~ **generation** *n* ELECTRON generación armónica *f*; ~ **generator** *n* ELEC generador de armónicos *m*, ELECTRON generador armónico *m*, PHYS generador de armónicos *m*, TELECOM multiplicador de frecuencias *m*; ~ **generator varactor** *n* ELECTRON reactancia variable de generador armónico *f*; ~ **mean** *n* MATH media armónica *f*; ~ **minor scale** *n* ACOUST escala de armónicos menores *f*; ~ **mixer** *n* ELECTRON mezclador armónico *m*; ~ **mode** *n* ELECTRON modo armónico *m*; ~ **order** *n* ELECTRON orden armónico *m*; ~ **oscillation** *n* PHYS oscilación armónica *f*; ~ **oscillator** *n* ELECTRON, PHYS oscilador armónico *m*; ~ **point** *n* GEOM punto armónico *m*; ~ **ratio** *n* GEOM cociente de armónicas *m*, razón armónica *f*; ~ **rejection** *n* ELECTRON supresión armónica *f*; ~ **response characteristic** *n* WAVE PHYS característica de respuesta armónica *f*; ~ **series** *n* ACOUST serie armónica *f*; ~ **suppressor** *n* ELECTRON, RAD PHYS supresor de armónicos *m*; ~ **waves** *n pl* WAVE PHYS ondas armónicas *f pl*

harmony *n* ACOUST armonía *f*

harmotome *n* GEOL, MINERAL harmotoma *m*

harness *n* AIR TRANSP arnés *m*, MILIT arnés *m*, correaje *m*, SAFE arnés *m*, SPACE *spacecraft* arnés *m*, cableado *m*; ~ **cable** *n* ELEC cable preformado *m*, MECH cable de conexionado *m*

harnessing *n* WATER aprovechamiento industrial *m*, puesta en explotación *f*, utilización *f*

harper: ~ **machine** *n* PAPER máquina de papel de mesa invertida *f*

harpoon *n* OCEAN arpón *m*; ~ **gun** *n* OCEAN cañón para disparar el arpón *m*

harriscut *n* WATER TRANSP solape *m*

harrow *n* AGRIC grada *f*; ~ **tooth** *n* AGRIC diente de rastra *m*

harsh: ~ **handle** *n* TEXTIL tacto áspero *m*

hartite *n* MINERAL hartita *f*

Hartley: ~ **oscillator** *n* ELECTRON oscilador Hartley *m*

harvest *n* AGRIC cosecha *f*

harvester: ~-**thresher** *n* AGRIC cosechadora-trilladora *f*

HASAWA *abbr BrE* (*Health and Safety at Work Act BrE*) SAFE ley de salud y seguridad en el trabajo *f*

hash *n* COMP&DP código de comprobación *m*, estática en la pantalla *f*, PRINT copia *f*; ~ **function** *n* COMP&DP función de creación de códigos de comprobación *f*, función para verificación de errores *f*; ~ **table** *n* COMP&DP tabla con códigos de comprobación *f*

hashing *n* COMP&DP método de claves *m*

hasp *n* CONST *locksmithing* pestillo *m*, picaporte *m*

hat: ~ **roller** *n* MINE polea soporte *f*

hatch *n* AIR TRANSP *of plane* escotilla *f*, portezuela *f*, SPACE *of spacecraft* compuerta *f*, escotilla *f*, WATER TRANSP *of boat* escotilla *f*; ~ **coaming** *n* WATER TRANSP brazola de escotilla *f*; ~ **cover** *n* WATER TRANSP *of ship* tapa de escotilla *f*

hatchback *n* TRANSP compuerta trasera *f*, escotilla trasera *f*; ~ **automobile** *n* AmE, ~ **car** *n* BrE AUTO, VEH automóvil con portón trasero *m*, coche con portón trasero *m*, coche con tres o cinco puertas *m*

hatchet *n* PROD hacha de mano *f*

hatchetine *n* MINERAL cera mineral *f*, hatchetina *f*, sebo mineral *m*

hatching *n* MECH ENG rayado *m*, sombreado a rayas *m*

hatchway *n* WATER TRANSP hueco de escotilla *m*

hauerite *n* MINERAL hauerita *f*

haul[1] *n* OCEAN arrastre *m*, WATER TRANSP *fishing* redada *f*, tirón *m*

haul[2] *vt* WATER TRANSP *rope, boat, net* cobrar, halar, mantenerse a rumbo; ~ **down** *vt* WATER TRANSP *flag, sail* arriar, cargar, *sails* abatir, quitar, recoger; ~ **in** *vt* WATER TRANSP *bowlines* ronzar, virar; ~ **on board** *vt* OCEAN halar a bordo; ~ **taut** *vt* WATER TRANSP *rope* templar, tesar; ~ **up** *vt* WATER TRANSP *boat* izar

haul[3]: ~ **alongside** *vi* WATER TRANSP atracar

haulage: ~ **cable** *n* TRANSP cable de arrastre *m*, cable de tracción *m* (*Esp*); ~ **contractor** *n* TRANSP contratista de acarreos *m*; ~ **road** *n* COAL, MINE, PROD galería de arrastre *f* (*AmL*), galería de transporte *f* (*Esp*); ~ **way** *n* COAL, MINE, PROD galería de arrastre *f* (*AmL*), galería de transporte *f* (*Esp*)

haulier *n* AUTO, TRANSP distribuidor *m*

hauling: ~ **and winding engine** *n* MINE motor de tracción y extracción *m*

haunch *n* CONST *bevelled* banqueta *f*, *of arch* costado de una bóveda *m*, ménsula *f*, riñón *m*, espaldón *m*

haunched: ~ **mortise-and-tenon joint** *n* CONST junta de espiga y mortaja reforzada *f*

hausmannite *n* MINERAL hausmannita *f*

Hauterivian *adj* GEOPHYS Hauteriviense *m*

hauyne *n* MINERAL hauyna *f*

hauynite *n* MINERAL hauyna *f*

Hawaiian: ~-**type volcano** *n* GEOL volcán de tipo Hawaiano *m*

hawk *n* CONST esparavel *m*, llana *f*

hawse *n* WATER TRANSP *ship* escobén *m*, zona de escobenes *f*; ~ **pipe** *n* WATER TRANSP *shipbuilding* bocina del escobén *f*

hawser *n* MECH ENG cable de remolque *m*, calabrote *m*, guindaleza *f*, WATER TRANSP estacha *f*, estacha de amarre *f*, guindaleza *f*

hay: ~ **baler** *n* AGRIC empacadora de heno *f*, enfardadora de heno *f*; ~ **band** *n* PROD *founding* cinta de paja *f*; ~ **chopper** *n* AGRIC picadora de heno *f*; ~ **conditioner** *n* AGRIC acondicionadora de heno *f*; ~ **crop** *n* AGRIC cultivo destinado a producción de heno *m*; ~ **crop silage** *n* AGRIC ensilaje hecho con materiales no curados *m*; ~ **rope** *n* PROD *founding* cinta de paja *f*

hayesine *n* MINERAL hayesina *f*

haylage *n* AGRIC ensilaje con condiciones de baja humedad *m*

hayloft *n* AGRIC henil *m*

haymaker *n* AGRIC henificadora *m*

haymaking *n* AGRIC henificación *f*

hayrack *n* AGRIC comedero para heno *m*

hazard *n* AIR TRANSP, AUTO, QUALITY peligro *m*, SAFE riesgo *m*; ~ **analysis** *n* QUALITY, SAFE análisis de fenómenos peligrosos *m*, análisis de riesgo *m*; ~ **beacon** *n* AIR TRANSP radiobalizada de peligro *f*, radiofaro de peligro *m*; ~ **prevention** *n* SAFE prevención de riesgos *f*; ~ **warning lamp** *n* VEH luz de emergencia *f*; ~ **warning system** *n* AUTO sistema de aviso de peligro *m*

hazardous: ~ **substance** *n* SAFE substancia peligrosa *f*; ~ **zone** *n* SAFE zona peligrosa *f*

haze *n* METEO calima *f*, P&R opacidad *f*, WATER TRANSP calima *f*; ~ **filter** *n* CINEMAT filtro para neblina *m*

hazy *adj* METEO calinoso, TEXTIL confuso, THERMO calinoso, WATER TRANSP *weather* brumoso, calinoso

h-bar *n* PHYS constante reducida de Planck *f*

H-bar *n* CONST barra en H *f*

H-beam *n* CONST viga en H *f*

HC *abbr* (*high-cube container*) TRANSP contenedor alto *m*

HCF *abbr* (*highest common factor*) MATH mcd (*máximo común divisor*)

HCP *abbr* (*hexagonal close-packed structure*) CRYSTALL EHC (*empaquetado hexagonal compacto*)

HD *abbr* (*heavy-duty oil*) PETR TECH lubricante para motores de gran potencia *m*, petróleo pesado *m*

HDB3 *abbr* (*high-density bipolar of order 3 code*) TELECOM código bipolar de alta densidad del orden 3 *m*

HDLC *abbr* (*high-level data link control*) COMP&DP, TELECOM control de enlace de datos de alto nivel *m*

HDPE *abbr* (*high-density polyethylene*) PACK PAD (*polietileno de alta densidad*)

HDTV *abbr* (*high-definition television*) TELECOM, TV televisión de alta definición *f* (*Esp*), televisión por definición extendida *f* (*AmL*)

HDW: ~ **barge carrier** *n* TRANSP transbordador portabarcazas HDW *m*

HDX *abbr* (*half-duplex*) COMP&DP HDX (*semi-dúplex*)

He *abbr* (*helium*) CHEM, NUCL, PETR TECH, RAD PHYS, REFRIG He (*helio*)

head[1]: ~**on** *adj* SAFE de frente, SPACE, TRANSP frontal; ~**sealed** *adj* PACK termosellado; ~**up** *adj* WATER TRANSP proa arriba

head[2] *n* AGRIC cabeza de ganado *f*, capítulo *m*, CINEMAT *machine* cabeza *f*, *of a timber clip, a log carriage, log sawing* cabezal *m*, COMP&DP *recording* cabezal *m*, CONST *of pile* cabecero *m*, *of slate* fondo *m*, cabeza *f*, HYDRAUL carga hidrostática *f*, carga de agua *f*, altura piezométrica *f*, LAB montera *f*, MECH ENG fondo *m*, potencia por flujo en peso *f*, *of cylinder* culata del cilindro *f*, *of lathe* cabezal *m*, desnivel *m*, cara *f*, tapa *f*, altura *f*, culata *f*, cabeza *f*, carga *f*, tapa del cilindro *f*, MINE galería de avance *f* (*Esp*), capitel *m*, galería del frente de ataque *f* (*AmL*), dirección del crucero más resistente *f*, PETR TECH altura *f*, fuente *f*, PRINT encabezamiento *m*, cabeza *f*, cabezal *m*, PROD *of screw, bolt, nail, rivet* cabeza *f*, mazarota *f*, WATER TRANSP *of groyne, jetty* morro *m*, *rudder stock* cabeza *f*, *triangular sail* grátil alto *m*, grátil *m*; ~ **adjustment** *n* TV ajuste de la cabeza *m*; ~ **alignment** *n* TV alineación de la cabeza *f*; ~ **amplifier** *n* ELECTRON amplificador de imagen *m*, SPACE *communications* amplificador de imagen *m*, amplificador previo *m*, preamplificador *m*; ~ **assembly** *n* TV conjunto de cabezal *m*; ~ **banding** *n* TV cabeceado *m*; ~ **bay** *n*

WATER canal anterior *m*, depósito de carga *m*, saetín de aguas arriba *m*; ~ **beam** *n* CONST cabecero *m*; ~ **box** *n* PAPER caja de cabeza de máquina *f*, caja de entrada *f*, WATER *sluices* caja de cabeza *f*; ~ **cap** *n* PRINT sobrecabeza *f*; ~ **channel** *n* TV canal alimentador *m*; ~ **clogging** *n* TV obstrucción del cabezal *f*; ~ **crash** *n* COMP&DP *disc units* avería por caída del cabezal *f*, choque de cabeza en el disco *m*; ~ **crown** *n* WATER saetín de aguas arriba *m*; ~**down display** *n* SPACE *spacecraft* representación cabeza abajo *f*, representación invertida *f*; ~ **driver** *n* RAIL jefe maquinista *m*; ~ **drum** *n* TV tambor de la cabeza *m* (*Esp*), tambor portacabeza *m* (*AmL*); ~ **end** *n* MECH ENG *engine* con admisión delantera, con admisión posterior, *of cylinder* parte delantera *f*, TEXTIL extremo inicial *m*; ~ **feed** *n* MECH ENG *machine tools* avance del cabezal *m*; ~ **frame** *n* MINE castillete de extracción *m*, bastidor del castillete de extracción *m* (*Esp*), montante del castillete de extracción *m* (*AmL*), marco de superficie *m*; ~ **gap** *n* COMP&DP entrehierro *m*, entrehierro del cabezal *m*, TV entrehierro de la cabeza *m*, entrehierro del cabezal *m*; ~ **gasket** *n* AUTO, VEH junta de culata *f*; ~ **gate** *n* WATER *before water wheel* puerta de aguas arriba *f*, compuerta de trabajo *f*, *of canal lock* compuerta de toma *f*, compuerta de cabecera *f*; ~ **house** *n* MINE caseta de bocamina *f*, caseta del filtro *f*; ~ **leader** *n* CINEMAT guía de entrada *f*; ~ **life** *n* TV vida útil de la cabeza *f*; ~ **limit** *n* HYDRAUL límite de carga de agua *m*; ~ **line** *n* TEXTIL línea del cabezal *f*; ~ **margin** *n* PRINT margen de cabeza *m*; ~ **metal** *n* PROD *founding* metal de mazarota *m*; ~ **miter sill** *AmE*, ~ **mitre sill** *BrE n* WATER *canal lock* busco de aguas arriba *m*; ~**out** *n* CINEMAT cabeza hacia afuera *f*; ~ **pipe** *n* HYDRAUL conducto de llegada *m*, WATER *of pump* conducto de llegada *m*, tubuladora de impulsión *f*; ~ **plate** *n* CONST *of a frame* placa cabecera *f*, WATER TRANSP *portable tanks* placa de fondo *f*, placa de forro *f*, plancha de fondo *f*, plancha de forro *f*; ~ **position pulse** *n* TV pulso inicial *m*; ~ **response** *n* TV respuesta inicial *f*; ~ **sea** *n* WATER TRANSP mar de proa *m*; ~ **servo lock** *n* TV servomecanismo de fijación del cabezal *m*; ~ **shot** *n* CINEMAT primer plano *m*; ~ **sluice** *n* WATER compuerta de toma *f*; ~ **smut** *n* AGRIC carbón de la inflorescencia *m*; ~ **space** *n* FOOD espacio de aire *m*, espacio de cabeza *m*; ~ **of steam** *n* HYDRAUL volumen de vapor *m*; ~ **steward** *n* WATER TRANSP *merchant navy* comisario *m*; ~**to-tape contact** *n* TV contacto de cabeza con cinta *m*; ~**to-tape speed** *n* TV velocidad de cabeza a cinta *f*; ~ **tracking** *n* TV cabeza de arrastre *f*; ~**up display** *n* (*HUD*) INSTR imagen vertical *f* (*HUD*), SPACE presentación a la altura de la vista *f*, presentación por colimador *f*; ~ **valve** *n* HYDRAUL válvula de suministro *f*; ~ **wall** *n* CONST muro de cabecera *m*, muro de fondo *m*; ~ **of water** *n* CONST naciente *m*, nacimiento de un río *m*, FUELLESS salto de agua *m*, HYDRAUL carga de agua *f*, HYDROL, WATER naciente *m*; ~ **of water pressure** *n* HYDRAUL presión de la carga de agua *f*; ~ **wear** *n* TV cascos *m pl*; ~ **wheel** *n* TV cabeza de transporte *f*; ~ **winding** *n* TV cabeza en espiral *f*, cabeza espiralada *f*

head[3] *vt* AGRIC *stage of cereal development* espigar; ~ **for** *vt* WATER TRANSP aproar a, poner la proa a

headband *n* PRINT adorno al principio de página *m*

headboard *n* MINE cabecera *f*, cuña *f*, galápago *m*, tabla de entibación del techo *f*, zapata *f*, WATER TRANSP *sailing* tabla de grátil *f*

headed: ~ **guide bush** *n* MECH ENG casquillo guía con cabeza *m*, casquillo guía encabezado *m*

header *n* COMP&DP cabecera *f*, encabezamiento *m*, CONST *masonry* travesaño *m*, HYDRAUL, NUCL colector *m*, PAPER testero *m*, PRINT cabecera *f*, PROD cabezal de tubos *m*, colector *m*, *casting* chorro de colada *m*, TELECOM cabecera *f*; ~ **course** *n* CONST hilada de tizones *f*; ~ **error control** *n* (*HEC*) TELECOM control de error de cabecera *m*; ~ **label** *n* COMP&DP etiqueta de encabezamiento *f*, etiqueta de título *f*, PACK etiqueta del soporte *f*; ~ **pipe** *n* MECH tubo colector *m*

headgate *n* AGRIC cepo de manga *m*, FUELLESS *of dam* compuerta de toma *f*

headgear *n* AIR TRANSP casco *m*, equipo del casco *m*, MINE apeo de mina *m* (*AmL*), asiento de mina *m* (*Esp*), castillete de extracción *m*

heading *n* AIR TRANSP rumbo *m*, COMP&DP encabezamiento *m*, título *m*, CONST *masonry* frente *m*, MECH ENG *driftway kept in advance* encabezamiento *m*, galería de avance *f* (*Esp*), galería del frente de ataque *f* (*AmL*), MINE avance *m*, excavación *f*, SPACE *spacecraft* rumbo *m*, orientación *f*, WATER TRANSP *direction of ship* línea de proa *f*, rumbo *m*, arrumbamiento *m*; ~ **back** *n* AGRIC poda de extremos *f*; ~ **bond** *n* CONST aparejo a tizón *m*; ~ **chisel** *n* CONST formón de perno *m*; ~ **course** *n* CONST *masonry* hilada de tizones *f*; ~ **data generator** *n* AIR TRANSP generador de información de dirección *m*; ~ **die** *n* MECH ENG troquel encabezador *m*; ~**error integrator** *n* AIR TRANSP integrador de error de rumbo *m*; ~ **error synchronizer amplifier** *n* AIR TRANSP amplificador del sincronizador de error de rumbo *m*; ~ **face** *n* MINE frente de avance *m*; ~ **hold** *n* AIR TRANSP mantenedor de rumbo *m*, mantenimiento del rumbo *m*, WATER TRANSP mantenimiento del rumbo *m*; ~ **indicator** *n* SPACE *spacecraft* indicador de rumbo *m*; ~ **information** *n* AIR TRANSP información de rumbo *f*; ~ **joint** *n* CONST *carpentry* junta a tope *f*; ~ **machine** *n* MINE excavadora de avance *f*, rozadora de galería de avance *f*; ~ **remote indicator** *n* AIR TRANSP indicador remoto de rumbo *m*; ~ **repeater** *n* AIR TRANSP repetidor de rumbo *m*; ~ **selector** *n* AIR TRANSP selector de rumbo *m*; ~ **stage** *n* AGRIC *grasses* estado de espigado *m*; ~ **synchronizer** *n* AIR TRANSP sincronizador de rumbo *m*; ~ **and vertical reference unit system** *n* SPACE unidad de sistema de referencia de avance y vertical *f*

headlamp *n* AUTO faro *m*, faro delantero *m*, VEH faro *m*, proyector de alumbrado exterior *m*; ~ **bulb** *n* AUTO bombilla del faro delantero *f*; ~ **flasher** *n* VEH emisión de ráfagas *f*; ~ **lens** *n* AUTO, VEH lente del faro delantero *f*; ~ **switch** *n* AUTO, VEH interruptor del faro delantero *m*

headland *n* OCEAN promontorio *m*, WATER TRANSP antepaís *m*

headless: ~ **guide bush** *n* MECH ENG casquillo guía sin cabeza *m*; ~ **screw** *n* MECH tornillo sin cabeza *m*

headlight: ~ **switch** *n* AUTO *electricity*, VEH interruptor del faro delantero *m*

headlights *n* BrE (*cf low beams AmE*) VEH faros inclinables *m pl*

headline *n* PRINT cabeza de página *f*, WATER TRANSP *mooring* amarra de proa *f*

headlining *n* VEH funda de tapicería *f*

headphones *n pl* ACOUST, TELECOM auriculares *m pl*

headpiece *n* MINE cumbrera *f*

headrace *n* HYDRAUL canal de carga *m*, canal de llegada *m*, canal de toma *m*, canal de trabajo *m*, WATER canal de carga *m*, canal de llegada *m*, canal de toma *m*, saetín *m*, caz de traída *m*, *of water mill* canal de alimentación *m*; ~ **canal** *n* FUELLESS canal de alimentación *m*

headrest *n* AUTO, VEH apoyacabeza *m*, reposacabeza *m*

headroom *n* CONST altura libre *f*, WATER TRANSP *shipbuilding* altura de paso *f*, altura libre *f*

headset *n* INSTR, TELECOM casco con auriculares *m*; ~ **magnifier** *n* INSTR amplificador del casco con auriculares *m*

headstock *n* AUTO cabezal *m*, MECH cabezal *m*, contrapunto *m*, MECH ENG contrapunto *m*, testera *f*, travesaño *m*, MINE castillete de extracción *m*, travesaño *m*

headwater *n* HYDRAUL nivel de aguas arriba *m*, HYDROL *mass* aguas de cabecera *f pl*, zona superior *f*; ~ **capture** *n* HYDROL *of river* captura río arriba *f*; ~ **level** *n* HYDRAUL nivel de aguas arriba *m*, carga hidráulica *f*; ~ **reach** *n* WATER tramo de cabecera *m*

headway *n* WATER TRANSP arrancada avante *f*, viada *f*; ~ **control** *n* TRANSP control de avance *m*; ~ **distribution analysis** *n* TRANSP análisis de distribución de intervalos de salida *m*; ~ **warning device** *n* TRANSP dispositivo de aviso del arranque *m*, mecanismo de advertencia para el intervalo de tiempo *m*

headwind *n* AIR TRANSP viento de frente *m*, viento en contra *m*, METEO, WATER TRANSP viento de frente *m*, viento de cara *m*

headwork *n* MINE castillete de extracción *m*

headworks *n* FUELLESS *of dam* obras de cabecera *f pl*

heald *n* TEXTIL malla de lizo *f*; ~ **wire** *n* TEXTIL alambre de malla *m*

health: ~ **food** *n* FOOD alimento natural *m*; ~ **hazard** *n* SAFE peligro sanitario *m*, riesgo sanitario *m*; ~ **physics** *n* NUCL física radiológica *f*, física sanitaria *f*, protección radiológica *f*, RAD PHYS física radiológica *f*, física sanitaria *f*; ~**related sampling** *n* SAFE muestreo con fines sanitarios *m*; ~ **and safety requirements** *n pl* SAFE normas de seguridad e higiene *f pl*; ~ **surveillance under COSHH** *n* SAFE inspección sanitaria de la COSHH *f*

Health: ~ **and Safety at Work Act** *n* BrE (*HASAWA BrE*) SAFE ley de salud y seguridad en el trabajo *f*

heap *n* COMP&DP montón de almacenamiento *m*, pila *f*, CONST pila *f*; ~ **sand** *n* PROD *founding* arena en montón *f*, arena vieja *f*

heaped *adj* CONST amontonado, apilado

heardbook *n* AGRIC libro genealógico *m*

hearing *n* ACOUST audición *f*; ~ **aid** *n* ACOUST audífono *m*, prótesis auditiva *f*; ~ **conservation** *n* SAFE conservación del oído *f*; ~ **correction** *n* ACOUST corrección auditiva *f*; ~**evoked potential** *n* ACOUST potencial evocado auditivo *m*; ~ **fatigue** *n* ACOUST fatiga auditiva *f*; ~ **loss factor index** *n* ACOUST índice del factor de pérdida auditiva *m*; ~ **test** *n* ACOUST, SAFE prueba auditiva *f*; ~ **threshold difference** *n* ACOUST diferencia en el umbral de audición *f*; ~ **threshold level** *n* ACOUST nivel del umbral de audición *m*

heart: ~ **trowel** n CONST paleta f, paletín m

hearth n CONST of fireplace fogón m, chimenea f (AmL), crisol m, hogar m, GAS crisol del horno m, fogón m, hogar m, HEAT hogar m, PROD of blast furnace suela f

heat[1]: **~-absorbing** adj THERMO endotérmico; **~-carrying** adj THERMO calorífero; **~-conducting** adj THERMO termoconductor; **~-formed** adj THERMO termoconformado; **~-fusible** adj PHYS, THERMO termofundible; **~-generating** adj PHYS, THERMO termogenerador; **~-hardened** adj THERMO termoendurecido; **~-insulated** adj HEAT ENG térmicamente aislado, MECH calorifugado, termoaislado, PETR TECH termoaislado, THERMO calorifugado, termoaislado; **~-insulating** adj MECH, PETR TECH termoaislante, PHYS termófugo, THERMO termoaislante, termófugo; **~-proof** adj HEAT, PACK resistente al calor, SAFE a prueba de calor, THERMO refractario, resistente al calor, termorresistente; **~-resistant** adj COATINGS, ELEC refractario, HEAT resistente al calor, PACK refractario, resistente al calor, PHYS calorífugo, termorresistente, SAFE refractario, termoresistente, SPACE termorresistente, THERMO resistente al calor, termorresistente; **~-resisting** adj SPACE calorífugo, refractario, termorresistente, THERMO refractario; **~-retaining** adj THERMO termoconservante; **~-sealable** adj THERMO termosellable; **~-sealed** adj THERMO termosellado; **~-seeking** adj SPACE buscador de calor, THERMO buscador por infrarrojo; **~-sensitive** adj P&R sensible al calor, termosensible, THERMO termosensible; **~-set** adj PRINT secado por calor; **~-setting** adj THERMO termofijado, termofraguante; **~-shrinkable** adj THERMO termocontraíble, termoencogible; **~-shrunk** adj MECH termocontraíble, termoencogible, termocontraído, termoencogido, THERMO termocontraído, termoencogido; **~-stabilized** adj THERMO termoestabilizado; **~-stable** adj THERMO termoestable; **~-treatable** adj THERMO keys on keyboard termotratable; **~-treated** adj THERMO programming termotratado, tratado térmicamente

heat[2] n GEN calor m; **off ~** n THERMO pipes caldo defectuoso m, calor m;

■ **a** ~ **ablation mode** n OPT modo de termoablación m; ~ **absorber** n TEXTIL, THERMO absorbente del calor m; **~-absorbing filter** n PHOTO filtro absorbente de calor m; **~-absorbing glass** n C&G vidrio absorbente de calor m; **~-absorbing glazing** n C&G vidriado absorbente de calor m; **~-absorbing power** n THERMO poder endotérmico m; ~ **absorption** n THERMO absorción de calor f; ~ **of absorption** n THERMO calor de absorción m; ~ **accumulation** n THERMO acumulación de calor f; ~ **accumulator** n HEAT ENG, THERMO acumulador de calor m; **~-activated label** n PACK etiqueta termoactivada f; ~ **of activation** n THERMO calor de activación m; **~-affected zone** n MECH zona termoafectada f, THERMO screen zona afectada por el calor f, zona termoafectada f; ~ **ageing** n P&R ensayo de deterioro por el calor m, envejecimiento en caliente m, envejecimiento por calor m; **~-and-eat food** n FOOD, PACK comida para calentar y comer f;

■ **b** ~ **balance** n REFRIG balance térmico m, THERMO balance calorífico m, equilibrio térmico m, balance térmico m; ~ **balance chart** n THERMO cuadro de balance térmico m, diagrama de balance térmico m;

~ **balance diagram** n THERMO diagrama de balance térmico m; ~ **barrier** n C&G, HEAT ENG, NUCL, SPACE, THERMO, TRANSP barrera térmica f; ~ **bonding** n P&R unión por calor f; ~ **bridge** n HEAT ENG, THERMO puente térmico m; ~ **buildup** n THERMO acumulación térmica f;

■ **c** ~ **capacity** n PHYS capacidad calorífica f, THERMO capacidad calorífica f, capacidad térmica f; ~ **caused by friction** n THERMO calor causado por fricción m; ~ **of combination** n THERMO calor de combinación m; ~ **of combustion** n CHEM of substance, THERMO calor de combustión m; ~ **compensation** n THERMO compensación térmica f, termocompensación f; ~ **of compression** n THERMO calor de compresión m; ~ **of condensation** n METEO condensación de calor f, THERMO calor de condensación m; ~ **conduction** n THERMO conducción térmica f; **~-conductivity meter** n THERMO medidor de la conductividad térmica m; ~ **conductor** n TEXTIL conductor del calor m; ~ **constant** n THERMO constante calorífica f; ~ **consumption** n THERMO consumo de calor m; ~ **content** n THERMO capacidad calorífica f; ~ **convection** n THERMO convección térmica f; ~ **cycle** n THERMO ciclo térmico m;

■ **d** ~ **dam** n AUTO represa térmica f; ~ **death** n PHYS muerte térmica f; ~ **of decomposition** n CHEM calor de descomposición m; ~ **demand** n HEAT ENG demanda de calor f, THERMO demanda calorífica f; ~ **density** n THERMO densidad calorífica f; ~ **detector** n THERMO detector térmico m; ~ **dilatation** n THERMO dilatación térmica f; ~ **discharge** n RECYCL descarga calorífica f, descarga calórica f, descarga de calor f, descarga térmica f, THERMO descarga térmica f; ~ **displacement** n THERMO desplazamiento térmico m; ~ **dissipation** n THERMO disipación térmica f, termodisipación f; ~ **of dissociation** n THERMO calor de disociación m; ~ **distortion** n THERMO termodistorsión f; ~ **drop** n THERMO caída térmica f;

■ **e** ~ **economizer** n THERMO economizador de calor m; ~ **effect** n THERMO efecto calorífico m, efecto térmico m; ~ **efficiency** n THERMO rendimiento calorífico m, rendimiento térmico m; ~ **emission** n THERMO emisión del calor f; ~ **energy** n THERMO energía calorífica f, energía térmica f; ~ **engine** n MECH, MECH ENG motor térmico m, máquina térmica f, PHYS motor térmico m, THERMO motor térmico m, máquina térmica f; ~ **engineering** n MECH ENG termotécnica f; ~ **equivalent** n THERMO equivalente térmico m; ~ **exchange** n PHYS, THERMO intercambio calorífico m, intercambio térmico m; ~ **exchanger** n AIR TRANSP termocanjeador m, FOOD intercambiador térmico m, FUELLESS, HEAT ENG intercambiador de calor m, MECH termocanjeador m, termointercambiador m, termopermutador m, termorrecuperador m, MECH ENG intercambiador de calor m, termocanjeador m, termointercambiador m, termopermutador m, termorrecuperador m, NUCL intercambiador de calor m, PETR TECH intercambiador de calor m, termointercambiador m, PROD intercambiador de calor m, termocambiador m, termopermutador m, REFRIG, THERMO termointercambiador de calor m, WATER TRANSP engine intercambiador de calor m, termocambiador m; ~ **exchanger suction accumulator** n REFRIG, THERMO

intercambiador de calor en separador de líquido *m*;
~ **exchanger tube** *n* MECH ENG tubo de termocambiador *m*, tubo de termopermutador *m*;
~**-exchanging medium** *n* THERMO medio de intercambio calorífico *m*, medio termorrecuperador *m*;
~ **expansion** *n* THERMO dilatación térmica *f*, expansión térmica *f*; ~ **of expansion** *n* THERMO calor de expansión *m*;

■~**f** ~ **filter** *n* CINEMAT filtro térmico *m*; ~**-fix tape** *n* PACK cinta que se fija por calor *f*; ~ **flow** *n* GEOL flujo calorífico *m*, HEAT ENG flujo de calor *m*, SPACE, THERMO flujo calorífico *m*; ~ **flow chart** *n* THERMO cuadro de flujo calorífico *m*, diagrama de flujo calorífico *m*, diagrama de flujo térmico *m*, gráfico de flujo térmico *m*; ~ **flow diagram** *n* THERMO diagrama de flujo calorífico *m*, diagrama de flujo térmico *m*; ~ **flow line** *n* THERMO línea de flujo calorífico *f*; ~ **flow meter** *n* THERMO medidor de flujo térmico *m*; ~ **flow rate** *n* PHYS cantidad de flujo calorífico *f*; ~ **flux** *n* SPACE flujo térmico *m*; ~ **of formation** *n* CHEM *of compound*, THERMO calor de formación *m*; ~**-forming** *n* THERMO termoformado *m*; ~ **of fusion** *n* THERMO calor de fusión *m*;

■~**g** ~ **generation** *n* PHYS, THERMO termogeneración *f*; ~ **generator** *n* PHYS, THERMO termogenerador *m*; ~ **gradient** *n* THERMO gradiente térmico *m*; ~ **gun** *n* MECH ENG pistola de aire caliente *f*;

■~**h** ~**-hardening** *n* THERMO termoendurecimiento *m*; ~ **haze** *n* THERMO calima *f*; ~ **of hydration** *n* CONST, THERMO calor de hidratación *m*;

■~**i** ~ **image** *n* THERMO termoimagen *f*; ~ **induction sealing** *n* PACK sellado por termoinducción *m*; ~ **input** *n* THERMO consumo calorífico *m*, consumo de calor *m*, gasto calorífico *m*; ~**-insulated container** *n* THERMO depósito calorifugado *m*, recipiente calorifugado *m*, recipiente termoaislado *m*; ~**-insulated lorry** *n* BrE (*cf heat-insulated truck* AmE) THERMO camión termoaislado *m*; ~**-insulated truck** *n* AmE (*cf heat-insulated lorry* BrE) THERMO camión termoaislado *m*; ~**-insulating jacket** *n* THERMO *memory* camisa termoaislante *f*; ~**-insulating wall** *n* AIR TRANSP pared termoaislante *f*; ~ **insulation** *n* CONST aislamiento térmico *m*, HEAT ENG aislación térmica *f*, aislamiento térmico *m*, MECH aislamiento térmico *m*, termoaislación *f*, termoaislamiento *m*, PACK aislamiento térmico *m*, aislamiento al calor *m*, PETR TECH aislamiento térmico *m*, termoaislación *f*, termoaislamiento *m*, RAIL aislamiento térmico *m*, THERMO aislación térmica *f*, aislamiento calorífugo *m*, aislamiento térmico *m*, calorífugo *m*, termoaislación *f*, termoaislamiento *m*; ~ **insulation effectiveness** *n* THERMO eficacia de la termoaislación *f*, rendimiento calorífugo *m*, rendimiento de aislación térmica *m*; ~ **insulation factor** *n* THERMO factor de aislación térmica *m*, factor de termoaislación *m*; ~ **insulation power** *n* THERMO poder calorífugo *m*, poder de termoaislación *m*, poder termoaislante *m*;

■~**l** ~ **lamination** *n* PACK laminado en caliente *m*; ~ **load** *n* THERMO carga térmica *f*; ~ **loss** *n* ELEC *resistor*, HEAT ENG pérdida de calor *f*, PHYS pérdida calorífica *f*, REFRIG pérdida de calor *f*, THERMO pérdida de calor *f*, pérdida térmica *f*;

■~**m** ~ **mirror** *n* FUELLESS espejo de calor *m*; ~ **of mixing** *n* THERMO calor de mezclado *m*;

■~**n** ~ **of neutralization** *n* THERMO calor de neutralización *m*;

■~**o** ~ **output** *n* THERMO calor útil *m*, energía térmica producida *f*; ~ **output density** *n* NUCL densidad calorífica de salida *f*;

■~**p** ~ **penetration time** *n* THERMO tiempo de penetración del calor *m*, tiempo de penetración térmica *m*; ~ **physicist** *n* PHYS, THERMO físico térmico *m*; ~ **pick-up** *n* REFRIG termoabsorción *f*; ~ **pipe** *n* SPACE tubo de calor *m*, tubo isotérmico *m*, TRANSP tubo isotérmico *m*; ~ **plug** *n* AUTO bujía caliente *f*, THERMO tapón fusible térmico *m*, tapón térmico *m*; ~**-proof clothing** *n* SAFE prendas antitérmicas *f pl*; ~**-protective clothing** *n* SAFE prendas termoaislantes *f pl*; ~**-protective material** *n* SAFE material protector contra el calor *m*; ~ **pump** *n* HEAT ENG, MECH, MECH ENG, PHYS, THERMO bomba calorífica *f*, bomba de calor *f*;

■~**r** ~ **radiation** *n* PACK, THERMO radiación térmica *f*; ~ **of radioactivity** *n* RAD PHYS calor de radiactividad *m*; ~ **rate** *n* THERMO consumo calorífico *m*, rendimiento térmico *m*; ~ **rate curve** *n* THERMO curva de rendimiento térmico *f*; ~ **of reaction** *n* CHEM, THERMO calor de reacción *m*; ~ **reactivation** *n* PRINT reactivación por calor *f*; ~ **recovery** *n* HEAT ENG, RECYCL recuperación del calor *f*, THERMO termorrecuperación *f*; ~ **rejection** *n* HEAT ENG rechazo de calor *m*; ~ **rejection rate** *n* NUCL tasa de eliminación de calor *f*; ~ **release** *n* NUCL liberación de calor *f*; ~**-release decal** *n* C&G calcomanía térmica *f*; ~ **removal loop** *n* NUCL lazo de evacuación de calor *m*; ~ **removed** *n* REFRIG calor cedido *m*; ~ **reservoir** *n* PHYS colector térmico *m*, REFRIG foco de calor *m*, fuente de calor *f*, THERMO foco de calor *m*, fuente de color *f*; ~ **resistance** *n* PHYS termofugacia *f*, termorresistencia *f*, SPACE termorresistencia *f*, THERMO calorifugacia *f*, termofugacia *f*, termorresistencia *f*; ~**-resistant coating** *n* COATINGS revestimiento resistente al calor *m*; ~**-resistant glass** *n* HEAT ENG vidrio resistente al calor *m*; ~**-resistant gloves** *n pl* LAB, SAFE, THERMO guantes resistentes al calor *m pl*, guantes termorresistentes *m pl*; ~**-resisting glass** *n* C&G, LAB vidrio resistente al calor *m*, THERMO vidrio pirorresistente *m*, vidrio refractario *m*; ~ **rise** *n* THERMO suministro de calor *m*; ~ **riser tube** *n* AUTO tubo elevador de calor *m*;

■~**s** ~ **screen** *n* SPACE pantalla térmica *f*; ~ **seal** *n* PRINT termosellado *m*; ~ **seal apparatus** *n* LAB aparato termosellador *m*; ~**-seal coating** *n* PACK revestido termosellable *m*; ~ **seal label** *n* PACK etiqueta termosellable *f*; ~ **seal laminating** *n* COATINGS laminación por sellado térmico *f*, sellado térmico por laminación *m*; ~ **seal tape** *n* PACK cinta termosellable *f*; ~ **seal temperature** *n* PACK temperatura de termosellado *f*; ~**-sealable paper** *n* COATINGS, PACK papel termosellable *m*; ~**-sealed wrapping** *n* THERMO envoltorio termosellado *m*; ~**-sealing** *n* PACK termosellado *m*; ~**-sealing adhesive** *n* PACK adhesivo termosellable *m*; ~**-sealing device** *n* PACK dispositivo de termosellado *m*; ~**-sealing equipment** *n* PACK equipo para el termosellado *m*; ~**-sealing machine** *n* PACK máquina de termosellado *f*; ~**-sealing and welding machine** *n* PACK máquina para termosellar y soldar *f*; ~**-sensitive material** *n* PACK material termosensible *m*; ~**-sensitive paint** *n* THERMO pintura termosensible *f*; **~-sensitive paper** *n* COMP&DP papel térmico *m*; **~ sensitivity** *n* P&R sensibilidad al calor *f*, termosensibilidad *f*; **~ sensor** *n* THERMO detector térmico *m*; **~-set adhesive paper** *n* COATINGS papel termoadherente *m*; **~-set ink** *n* COLOUR tinta de secado rápido por calor *f*; **~ setting** *n* TEXTIL fijación por calor *f*; **~ shield** *n* AIR TRANSP coraza térmica *f*, pantalla térmica *f*, pantalla de protección termoaislante *f*, ELEC ENG coraza térmica *f*, pantalla de protección termoaislante *f*, **~ sensor** *n* THERMO detector térmico *m*, SAFE blindaje térmico *m*, SPACE *spacecraft* blindaje térmico *m*, escudo térmico *m*, THERMO pantalla térmica *f*, blindaje térmico *m*; **~ shock test** *n* HEAT ENG prueba de choque de calor *f*, THERMO ensayo de resistencia al calor y a los golpes *m*, prueba de resistencia al calor y a los golpes *f*; **~ shrink fitting** *n* THERMO accesorio termoencogible *m*; **~-shrinkable film** *n* BrE (*cf heat-shrinkable wrap AmE*) PACK, THERMO película termocontraíble *f*, película termoencogible *f*; **~-shrinkable wrap** *n* AmE (*cf heat-shrinkable film BrE*) PACK, THERMO película termocontraíble *f*, película termoencogible *f*; **~ shrinking** *n* COATINGS contracción térmica *f*, THERMO termocontracción *f*; **~-shrinking foil** *n* COATINGS lámina termoencogida *f*; **~ shroud** *n* SPACE *spacecraft* cubierta térmica *f*; **~ shunt** *n* THERMO desviación térmica *f*; **~ sink** *n* ELEC disipador de calor *m*, disipador térmico *m*, elemento de disipación térmica *m*, sumidero de calor *m*, sumidero térmico *m*, ELEC ENG disipador térmico *m*, NUCL sumidero de calor *m*, PHYS sumidero de calor *m*, PROD disipador térmico *m*, sumidero de calor *m*, SPACE disipación del calor por recipiente *f*, sumidero de calor *m*, THERMO disipador de calor *m*, disipador térmico *m*, sumidero de calor *m*; **~ of solution** *n* THERMO calor de disolución *m*; **~ source** *n* REFRIG fuente de calor *f*, THERMO fuente de calor *f*; **~ spectrum** *n* THERMO espectro calorífico *m*; **~ stability** *n* P&R estabilidad al calor *f*, estabilidad térmica *f*, PACK estabilidad frente al calor *f*, THERMO estabilidad térmica *f*; **~-stretched fiber** *AmE*, **~-stretched fibre** *BrE n* TEXTIL fibra estirada por calor *f*; **~ supply** *n* THERMO suministro calorífico *m*; **~ t** **~ throughput** *n* THERMO rendimiento calorífico *m*, rendimiento térmico *m*; **~ transfer** *n* HEAT transferencia de calor *f*, P&R transferencia térmica *f*, transmisión de calor *f*, PHYS transferencia de calor *f*, REFRIG transmisión de calor *f*; **~ transfer coefficient** *n* PHYS coeficiente de transferencia de calor *m*, THERMO coeficiente de termotransferencia *m*, coeficiente de transmisión de calor *m*; **~ transfer engineer** *n* SPACE, THERMO ingeniero de termotransferencia *m*; **~ transfer engineering** *n* MECH ENG ingeniería de termotransferencia *f*, SPACE mecánica de termotransferencia *f*; **~ transfer label** *n* PACK etiqueta de termotransferencia *f*; **~ transfer surface** *n* REFRIG superficie de transmisión de calor *f*, THERMO superficie de termotransferencia *f*, superficie de transmisión de calor *f*; **~ transformation** *n* THERMO termotransformación *f*, transformación térmica *f*; **~ transition** *n* THERMO termotransición *f*, transición térmica *f*; **~ transmission** *n* HEAT ENG transmisión de calor *f*, THERMO termotransmisión *f*; **~-transmitting glass** *n* C&G vidrio transmisor de calor *m*; **~ trap** *n* NUCL trampa de calor *f*; **~ treatment** *n* AGRIC termoterapia *f*, COAL tratamiento térmico *m*, METALL termotratamiento *m*,

tratamiento térmico *m*, THERMO tratamiento térmico *m*; **~-treatment crack** *n* THERMO agrietamiento por tratamiento térmico *m*, grieta de termotratamiento *f*; **~ treatment crack sensitivity** *n* METALL, THERMO sensibilidad al agrietamiento por tratamiento térmico *f*; **~ treatment diagram** *n* THERMO diagrama de tratamiento térmico *m*;

~ v **~ of vaporization** *n* THERMO calor de vaporización *m*;

~ w **~ wave** *n* METEO ola de calor *f*, THERMO onda calorífica *f*; **~ welding** *n* PACK soldadura en caliente *f*

heat³ *vt* CHEM, PHYS, TEXTIL, THERMO calentar; **~-cure** *vt* THERMO termocurar, termomadurar, vulcanizar; **~-form** *vt* THERMO termoconformar; **~-harden** *vt* THERMO *networks* termoendurecer; **~-seal** *vt* PACK termosellar, THERMO cerrar por calor, termosellar; **~-shrink** *vt* MECH termoencoger, THERMO termocontraer, termoencoger; **~-treat** *vt* THERMO termotratar; **~ up** *vt* C&G, CHEM calentar, THERMO *programming* caldear, calentar

heat⁴: **~ up** *vi* CHEM, THERMO calentarse

heat⁵: **in ~** *phr* AGRIC en celo

HEAT *abbr* (*high explosive anti-tank*) MILIT alto explosivo anticarro *m*

heated: **~ container** *n* TRANSP contenedor caldeado *m*; **~ platen** *n* P&R platina calentada *f*; **~ windshield pane** *n* AIR TRANSP, AUTO, SPACE, TRANSP, VEH parabrisas térmico *m*

heater *n* ELEC *electronic tube* filamento *m*, resistencia de caldeo *f*, GAS, HEAT calentador *m*, HEAT ENG calorífero *m*, calentador *m*, LAB calentador *m*, MECH radiador *m*, calorífero *m*, calefactor *m*, calentador *m*, MECH ENG, PROD calentador *m*, THERMO *of node* calentador *m*, calefactor *m*, VEH calefactor *m*; **~ blower** *n* AIR TRANSP calentador de aire *m*, soplador del calentador *m*, HYDRAUL soplador del calentador *m*; **~ control** *n* AUTO control de la calefacción *m*; **~ element** *n* PHOTO elemento calentador *m*, PROD elemento calefactor *m*; **~ mat** *n* REFRIG capa calefactora *f*; **~ power supply** *n* ELEC ENG suministro de energía para calentador *m*; **~ rod** *n* NUCL calentador *m*; **~ system** *n* AUTO sistema de calefacción *m*; **~ voltage** *n* ELEC ENG *tubes* voltaje del filamento *m*

heating¹ *adj* PROD de calefacción, de calentamiento, de calorífico

heating² *n* AIR TRANSP calefacción *f*, GAS calefacción *f*, calentamiento *m*, HEAT ENG calefacción *f*, MECH calda *f*, caldeo *m*, calefacción *f*, calentamiento *m*, PROD caldeo *m*, calefacción *f*, calentamiento, TEXTIL calentamiento *m*, THERMO calefacción *f*, calentamiento *m*; **~ air** *n* AIR TRANSP, THERMO aire calentador *m*, aire de calentamiento *m*; **~ appliance** *n* HEAT ENG, THERMO aparato de calefacción *m*; **~ belt** *n* HEAT ENG cinturón de calefacción *m*; **~ blowpipe** *n* CONST soplete de calentamiento *m*; **~ body** *n* HEAT vasija interior del calentador *f*; **~ cable** *n* ELEC cable de calefacción *m*; **~ capacity** *n* HEAT ENG capacidad de calentamiento *f*, THERMO capacidad calefactora *f*, poder calorífico *m*; **~ chamber** *n* THERMO cámara de calefacción *f*, cámara de calentamiento *f*; **~ channel** *n* PACK canal de calefacción *m*; **~ circuit** *n* HEAT circuito de calefacción *m*; **~ coil** *n* HEAT ENG, REFRIG, THERMO serpentín de calefacción *m*; **~ current** *n* THERMO corriente de caldeo *f*; **~ curve** *n* P&R curva de calentamiento *f*, THERMO curva de caldeo *f*, curva de calentamiento *f*; ~ **depth** *n* THERMO penetración del calor *f*, profundidad de caldeo *f*; ~ **device** *n* HEAT artefacto de calefacción, MECH ENG artefacto de calefacción *m*, dispositivo de calefacción *m*, THERMO artefacto de calefacción *m*; ~ **element** *n* AIR TRANSP, ELEC elemento calefactor *m*, HEAT ENG elemento de calefacción *m*; ~ **engineer** *n* THERMO ingeniero calefactor *m*; ~ **furnace** *n* HEAT horno de caldeo *m*, horno de recalentar *m*, HEAT ENG horno de caldeo *m*, THERMO horno de caldeo *m*, horno de recalentar *m*; ~ **gas** *n* GAS, THERMO gas para calefacción *m*; ~ **installation** *n* HEAT, THERMO instalación de calefacción *f*; ~ **jacket** *n* THERMO camisa calefactora *f*, camisa de calefacción *f*, envuelta exterior calefactora *f*; ~ **mantle** *n* LAB canasta de calentamiento *f* (*AmL*), manto de calentamiento *m* (*Esp*); ~ **melter** *n* CONST *civil engineering* fundidor de calor *m*, fundidor por calentamiento *m*; ~ **oil** *n* THERMO aceite de calefacción *m*; ~ **panel** *n* MECH ENG panel de calefacción *m*, panel de calentamiento *m*, placa calorífica *f*; ~ **plant** *n* THERMO planta de caldeo *f*; ~ **power** *n* THERMO *programme* poder calorífico *m*, potencia calorífica *f*, potencia de caldeo *f*; ~ **resistor** *n* AIR TRANSP resistencia de calentamiento *f*, ELEC resistencia de calefacción *f*, resistencia de calentamiento *f*, resistor de caldeo *m*; ~ **surface** *n* HEAT superficie calefactora *f*, HEAT ENG superficie calefactora *f*, superficie de caldeo *f*, THERMO superficie calefactora *f*, superficie de caldeo *f*, superficie de calefacción *f*; ~ **tape** *n* LAB cinta térmica *f*; ~ **technician** *n* MECH ENG técnico de calefacción *m*; ~ **temperature curve** *n* THERMO curva de temperatura de caldeo *f*; ~ **time** *n* THERMO tiempo de caldeo *m*; ~ **tunnel** *n* PACK túnel de calefacción *m*; ~**-up** *n* C&G calentamiento *m*; ~**-up curve** *n* THERMO curva de calentamiento *f*; ~**-up time** *n* THERMO tiempo de calentamiento *m*; ~ **zone** *n* THERMO zona de caldeo *f*, zona de calefacción *f*, zona de calentamiento *f*

heat-sealing *n* COATINGS cierre térmico *m*, P&R cierre por calor *m*, resistencia al calor *f*, THERMO cierre por calor *m*, junta térmica *f*, termosellado *m*

heave[1] *n* GEOL rechazo horizontal *m*, OCEAN elevación *f*, falla *f*, PETR TECH jadeo *m*, traslación *f*; ~ **compensator** *n* PETROL compensador de movimiento vertical *m*

heave[2] *vt* WATER TRANSP *anchor* virar; ~ **in the mooring ropes** *vt* WATER TRANSP halar de las cuerdas de amarre, virar

heave[3] *vi* WATER TRANSP *in wave* oscilar verticalmente; ~ **to** *vi* WATER TRANSP *sailboat* mantenerse sobre la máquina, pairear

heaving: ~ **line** *n* WATER TRANSP *ropes* guía *f*

heavy[1] *adj* C&G *of container* pesado, MECH pesado, grueso, viscoso, denso; ~**-duty** *adj* DETERG extra-fuerte, para servicio pesado, MECH de gran capacidad, de gran potencia, para trabajo pesado, reforzado, MECH ENG de alta producción, de construcción fuerte, de gran capacidad, de gran potencia, para servicio pesado, para trabajos fuertes, para trabajos pesados, pesado, reforzado, PROD para servicio pesado

heavy[2]: ~ **anode** *n* ELEC ENG electrodo positivo compacto *m*, ánodo pesado *m*; ~ **anti-aircraft gun** *n* MILIT cañón antiaéreo de grueso calibre *m*; ~ **anti-tank gun** *n* MILIT cañón anticarro de grueso calibre

m; ~ **armament** *n* MILIT armamento de grueso calibre *m*; ~ **artillery** *n* MILIT artillería de grueso calibre *f*, artillería pesada *f*; ~**-bodied ink** *n* PRINT tinta de elevada densidad *f*; ~ **breakdown crane** *n* RAIL grúa pesada de auxilio *f*; ~ **castings** *n pl* PROD grandes piezas de fundición *f pl*; ~ **crepe** *n* PAPER crespado fuerte *m*; ~ **crude** *n* PETR TECH crudo pesado *m*, crudo viscoso *m*; ~ **crude oil** *n* PETR TECH crudo denso *m*; ~ **cut** *n* MECH ENG *machine tools* corte profundo *m*, pasada profunda *f*; ~ **displacement** *n* WATER TRANSP *of hull* desplazamiento pesado *m*; ~**-duty ball bearing** *n* MECH ENG cojinete de bolas de construcción fuerte *m*, cojinete de bolas para trabajos pesados *m*, rodamiento de bolas de construcción fuerte *m*, rulemán para trabajos pesados *m*; ~**-duty contact** *n* ELEC ENG contacto para grandes amperajes *m*; ~**-duty corrugated fiberboard** *AmE*, ~**-duty corrugated fibreboard** *BrE n* PACK cartón ondulado para trabajos pesados *m*; ~**-duty gear** *n* MECH engranaje de dentadura helicoidal *m*, MECH ENG engranaje para trabajos pesados *m*, equipo pesado *m*; ~**-duty lathe** *n* MECH ENG torno para producción pesada *m*; ~**-duty lift** *n* CONST montacargas para servicio pesado *m*; ~**-duty lock washer** *n* MECH ENG arandela de blocaje reforzada *f*; ~**-duty offset ring wrench** *n* MECH ENG llave acodada de anillo para trabajos pesados *f*; ~**-duty oil** *n* (*HD*) PETR TECH lubricante para motores de gran potencia *m*, petróleo pesado *m*; ~**-duty rectangular magnetic chuck** *n* ELECTRON, MECH ENG plato electromagnético rectangular para trabajos pesados *m*; ~ **ends** *n pl* PETR TECH colas de componentes pesados *f pl*; ~ **engineering** *n* CONST construcción pesada *f*, MECH ENG ingeniería pesada *f*; ~ **fractions** *n pl* PETR TECH fracciones densas *f pl*, fracciones pesadas *f pl*; ~ **freight vehicle traffic** *n AmE* (*cf heavy goods vehicle traffic BrE*) AUTO, TRANSP tráfico de vehículos pesados *m*; ~ **gage** *AmE*, ~ **gauge** *BrE n* TEXTIL galga gruesa *f*; ~ **goods vehicle** *n* (*HGV*) AUTO, TRANSP camión de gran tonelaje *m*; ~ **goods vehicle traffic** *n BrE* (*cf heavy freight vehicle traffic AmE*) AUTO, TRANSP tráfico de vehículos pesados *m*; ~ **group** *n* NUCL grupo pesado *m*; ~ **hydrocarbon fractions** *n pl* PETR TECH fracciones de hidrocarburo pesado *f pl*; ~ **hydrogen** *n* CHEM, NUCL, PHYS hidrógeno pesado *m*; ~ **ink** *n* PRINT tinta densa *f*; ~**-ion fusion** *n* NUCL, PART PHYS fusión de iones pesados *f*; ~ **ironwork** *n* CONST carpintería de hierro pesada *f*; ~ **jet** *n* TRANSP chorro de gran potencia *m*; ~ **lift derrick** *n* WATER TRANSP *cargo* pluma de grandes piezas *f*, pluma real *f*; ~**-lift helicopter** *n* AIR TRANSP helicóptero pesado *m*; ~ **lift launch vehicle** *n* (*HLLV*) SPACE *spacecraft* vehículo de lanzamiento de carga pesada *m*; ~**-lift vehicle** *n* SPACE *spacecraft* vehículo de carga pesada *m*; ~ **liquid test** *n* COAL ensayo por líquidos densos *m*; ~ **livestock** *n* AGRIC ganado mayor *m*; ~ **lorry** *n BrE* (*cf heavy truck AmE*) AUTO camión de gran tonelaje *m*; ~ **maintenance** *n* AIR TRANSP mantenimiento pesado *m*; ~ **medium** *n* COAL medio denso *m*; ~ **metal** *n* COAL, RAD PHYS, RECYCL metal pesado *m*; ~ **metal difference technique** *n* NUCL técnica de diferenciación de metales pesados *f*; ~ **minerals** *n pl* GEOL minerales pesados *m pl*; ~ **motor lorry** *n BrE* (*cf heavy motor truck AmE*) TRANSP camión con motor muy potente *m*; ~ **motor truck** *n AmE* (*cf heavy motor lorry BrE*) TRANSP camión con motor muy potente *m*; ~ **nut** *n* MECH ENG tuerca pesada *f*, tuerca reforzada *f*; ~-**oil engine** *n* AUTO motor de aceite pesado *m*; ~ **panel** *n* C&G panel grueso *m*; ~ **particle** *n* GAS partícula pesada *f*; ~ **rain** *n* METEO lluvia fuerte *f*; ~ **sea** *n* OCEAN ola fuerte *f*, oleada *f*; ~ **seas** *n pl* METEO, OCEAN, WATER TRANSP mar muy grueso *m*; ~-**section roll** *n* MECH ENG cilindro de gran potencia *m*, rodillo de gran potencia *m*; ~ **seed** *n* C&G demasiada semilla *f*; ~ **shower** *n* METEO chaparrón fuerte *m*, chubasco fuerte *m*; ~ **soil** *n* AGRIC terreno compactado *m*; ~ **spar** *n* MINERAL espato pesado *m*; ~ **swell** *n* METEO, WATER TRANSP mar encrespado *m*; ~ **tank** *n* MILIT carro pesado *m*; ~ **truck** *n* AmE (*cf heavy lorry BrE*) AUTO camión de gran tonelaje *m*; ~-**type plummer block** *n* PROD chumacera reforzada *f*; ~ **vehicle elevator** *n* AmE (*cf heavy vehicle lift BrE*) TRANSP elevador de vehículos pesados *m*, grúa de para vehículos pesados *f*; ~ **vehicle lift** *n* BrE (*cf heavy vehicle elevator AmE*) TRANSP elevador de vehículos pesados *m*, grúa para vehículos pesados *f*; ~ **water** *n* CHEM, NUCL, PHYS agua pesada *f*; ~ **water degasifier** *n* NUCL degasificador de agua pesada *m*; ~-**water plant** *n* NUCL planta de agua pesada *f*; ~ **water reactor** *n* NUCL reactor de agua pesada *m*, reactor moderado por agua pesada *m*; ~ **water spray nozzle** *n* NUCL boquilla de rociado con agua pesada *f*; ~ **water vapor** *AmE*, ~ **water vapour** *BrE* *n* NUCL vapor de agua pesada *m*; ~ **weather** *n* WATER TRANSP *meteorology* temporal con mucha mar *m*

heavyweight: ~ **motorcycle** *n* AUTO motocicleta de gran cilindrada *f*; ~ **paper** *n* PRINT papel de gramaje elevado *m*

hebronite *n* MINERAL ambligonita *f*, hebronita *f*

HEC *abbr* (*header error control*) TELECOM control de error de cabecera *m*

hectare *n* (*ha*) METR hectárea *f* (*ha*)

hecto *n* (*h*) METR hecto *m* (*h*)

hectogram *n* METR hectogramo *m* (*hg*)

hectogramme *n* see **hectogram**

hectolitre *n* AmE see **hectolitre** *BrE*

hectolitre *n* BrE METR hectólitro *m* (*hl*)

hectometer *n* AmE see **hectometre** *BrE*

hectometre *n* BrE METR hectómetro *m* (*hm*)

hectowatt *n* (*hW*) ELEC, ELEC ENG, METR hectovatio *m* (*hW*)

hedenbergite *n* MINERAL hedenbergita *f*

hedge *n* PROD cerca *f*; ~ **bindweed** *n* AGRIC campanilla *f*, correhuela *f*; ~ **shears** *n pl* AGRIC tijera de podar *f*; ~ **trimmer** *n* MECH ENG tijera para setos *f*

hedging *n* PROD cercado *m*

hedonic: ~ **scale** *n* FOOD escala hedónica *f*

hedyphane *n* MINERAL hedifana *f*

HEED *abbr* (*high-energy electron diffraction*) PART PHYS difracción de electrones *f*

heel[1] *n* C&G talón *m*, MECH ENG *of tool* lomo *m*, taco *m*, WATER TRANSP *of keel* parte popel *f*, *of mast* coz *f*, escora *f*, talón *m*; ~ **block** *n* MECH ENG dispositivo colocado en la parte baja *m*; ~ **plate** *n* WATER TRANSP *shipbuilding* angular *m*, cartabón *m*, cartela *f*; ~ **post** *n* WATER *of lock gate* poste de quicio *m*

heel[2] *vi* WATER TRANSP escorar

HE11: ~ **mode** *n* OPT modo HE11 *m*

heeling: ~ **moment** *n* WATER TRANSP *ship design* momento de escora *m*, momento escorante *m*

Hegman: ~ **fineness-of-grind gage** *AmE*, ~ **fine-**

ness-of-grind gauge *BrE* *n* P&R indicador de finura de grano Hegman *m*

heifer *n* AGRIC novilla *f*, vaquillona *f* (*AmL*); ~ **calf** *n* AGRIC ternera *f*

heiferette *n* AGRIC novilla que nunca ha parido *f*

height *n* GEN altitud *f*, altura *f*; ~ **above impost level** *n* CONST *of arch* altura sobre el nivel de imposta *f*; ~ **above pinch line** *n* MECH ENG *gearing* altura de la cabeza del diente *f*, saliente *f*; ~ **adjustment** *n* INSTR ajuste en altura *m*; ~ **of centers** *AmE*, ~ **of centres** *BrE* *n* MECH ENG *lathe* altura de centros *f*, altura de puntos *f*; ~ **correction** *n* GEOPHYS corrección de altura *f*; ~ **of fall** *n* PACK altura de caída *f*; ~ **gage** *AmE*, ~ **gauge** *BrE* *n* AIR TRANSP altímetro *m*, GEOPHYS altímetro *m*, indicador de altura *m*, METR escala de alturas *f*, galga de alturas *f*, PHYS, SPACE altímetro *m*; ~ **hovering** *n* TRANSP levitación en altura *f*; ~ **of instrument** *n* CONST *surveying* altura de la mira del instrumento *f*; ~-**keeping error** *n* AIR TRANSP error de mantenimiento de altura *m*; ~-**off cushion** *n* TRANSP amortiguación sin elevación *f*; ~-**on cushion** *n* TRANSP amortiguación en altura *f*, colchón amortiguador en altura *m*; ~ **position** *n* NUCL *materials* posición en el reactor *f*; ~ **of swell** *n* OCEAN, WATER TRANSP *sea* altura del oleaje *f*; ~-**to-paper** *n* PRINT altura tipográfica *f*; ~ **of type** *n* PRINT altura del tipo *f*; ~ **of withers** *n* AGRIC alzada del caballo *f*

heightening *n* CONST elevación *f*

Heisenberg: ~ **uncertainty principle** *n* PART PHYS principio de incertidumbre de Heisenberg *m*

held[1]: ~-**up** *adj* PROD en suspenso

held[2]: ~-**up order** *n* PROD orden en consigna *m*

heli: ~-**lifting** *n* AIR TRANSP helitransporte *m*, transporte por helicóptero *m*

helianthin *n* CHEM heliantina *f*

helianthine *n* CHEM heliantina *f*

helical[1] *adj* GEN helicoidal

helical[2]: ~ **aerial** *n* BrE (*cf helical antenna AmE*) TELECOM antena helicoidal *f*; ~ **antenna** *n* AmE (*cf helical aerial BrE*) TELECOM antena helicoidal *f*; ~ **coil-type heat exchanger** *n* NUCL intercambiador de calor de serpentín helicoidal *m*; ~ **dislocation** *n* CRYSTALL dislocación helicoidal *f*, METALL dislocación de tornillo *f*, dislocación helicoidal *f*; ~ **gear** *n* AUTO, MECH ENG engranaje helicoidal *m*, VEH engranaje de dientes helicoidales *m*; ~ **groove** *n* MECH ENG ranura helicoidal *f*; ~ **instability** *n* NUCL inestabilidad helicoidal *f*; ~ **potentiometer** *n* ELEC *resistance* potenciómetro helicoidal *m*; ~-**recording** *n* TV grabación helicoidal *f*; ~ **scan** *n* COMP&DP, ELECTRON, TV exploración helicoidal *f*; ~-**scan videotape recorder** *n* TV grabador de video por exploración helicoidal *m* (*AmL*), grabador de vídeo por exploración helicoidal *m* (*Esp*); ~ **scanner** *n* WATER TRANSP explorador de hélice *m*; ~ **scanning** *n* COMP&DP, ELECTRON, TV exploración helicoidal *f*; ~ **spring** *n* AUTO resorte helicoidal *m*, MECH muelle helicoidal *m*, resorte en hélice *m*, resorte helicoidal *m*, MECH ENG resorte helicoidal *m*, PHYS muelle helicoidal *m*, VEH resorte helicoidal *m*

helicin *n* CHEM helicina *f*

helicoid[1] *adj* MECH ENG helicoide, helicoideo

helicoid[2] *n* GEOM helicoide *m*; ~ **minimal surface** *n* GEOM superficie mínima helocoidal *f*

helicoidal[1] *adj* GEN helicoidal

helicoidal[2]: **~ machining** *n* MECH ENG maquinado helicoidal *m*; **~ motion** *n* NUCL movimiento helicoidal *m*

helicopter[1]: **~-lifted** *adj* AIR TRANSP, WATER TRANSP izado por helicóptero

helicopter[2] *n* AIR TRANSP helicóptero *m*; **~ avionics package** *n* AIR TRANSP conjunto electrónico del helicóptero *m*, paquete aviónico del helicóptero *m*; **~ behavior** *AmE*, **~ behaviour** *BrE n* AIR TRANSP comportamiento del helicóptero *m*; **~ gunship** *n* MILIT helicóptero armado *m*; **~ landing deck** *n* AIR TRANSP, WATER TRANSP plataforma de aterrizaje de helicópteros *f*; **~ landing surface** *n* AIR TRANSP superficie de aterrizaje de helicópteros *f*; **~ pad** *n* MAR POLL plataforma para helicópteros *f*, zona habilitada para aterrizaje de helicópteros *f*, WATER TRANSP área de anaveaje *f*; **~ shuttle service** *n* AIR TRANSP servicio de puente aéreo de helicóptero *m*; **~ station** *n* AIR TRANSP base de helicópteros *f*

helicotrema *n* ACOUST helicotrema *m*

helimagnetism *n* PHYS helimagnetismo *m*

heliodor *n* MINERAL berilo dorado *m*, heliodoro *m*

heliothermal: **~ process** *n* FUELLESS proceso heliotérmico *m*

heliotrope *n* MINERAL heliotropo *m*, piedra sangre *f*

heliotropic *adj* FUELLESS heliotrópico

heliotropin *n* CHEM heliotropina *f*, piperonal *m*

helipad *n* AIR TRANSP plataforma de despegue y aterrizaje de helicópteros *f*, PETR TECH plataforma de helipuerto *f*

heliport *n* AIR TRANSP, MAR POLL, PETR TECH helipuerto *m*; **~ deck** *n* AIR TRANSP plataforma de aterrizaje de un helipuerto *f*

helipot *n* ELEC *resistance* crisol de helio *m*

helistop *n* AIR TRANSP aparcamiento de helicópteros civiles *m*, plataforma civil de helicópteros *f*

helium *n* (*He*) CHEM, NUCL, PETR TECH, RAD PHYS, REFRIG helio *m* (*He*); **~ dehydrator unit** *n* NUCL unidad de deshidratación de helio *f*; **~-dilution refrigerator** *n* PHYS refrigerador por dilución de helio *m*; **~ leak detection** *n* NUCL detección de fugas por medio de helio *f*; **~ leak test** *n* NUCL ensayo de fugas por medio de helio *m*; **~-neon laser** *n* (*He-Ne laser*) PHYS, RAD PHYS láser de helio-neón *m* (*láser de He-Ne*)

helix *n* CHEM, GEOM hélice *f*, MECH ENG espira *f*, espiral *f*, hélice *f*, voluta *f*, OPT hélice *f*; **~ aerial** *n BrE* (*cf helix antenna AmE*) SPACE *communications* antena en hélice *f*, antena helicoidal *f*; **~ antenna** *n AmE* (*cf helix aerial BrE*) SPACE *communications* antena en hélice *f*, antena helicoidal *f*; **~ traveling-wave tube** *AmE*, **~ travelling-wave tube** *BrE n* ELECTRON tubo de ondas progresivas de helicoidal *m*; **~ waveguide** *n* ELEC ENG guiaondas por hélice *m*

helixing *n* ELEC ENG serpentín *m*

helm[1] *n* WATER TRANSP *ship* aparato de gobierno *m*, caña del timón *f*, rueda del timón *f*; **~ damage** *n* WATER TRANSP avería en el aparato de gobierno *f*; **~ indicator** *n* WATER TRANSP axiómetro *m*

helm[2] *vi* WATER TRANSP dar órdenes al timón, gobernar

helmet *n* PETR TECH, SAFE casco *m*; **~ cap lubricator** *n* PROD engrasador de casco *m*

Helmholtz: **~ coil** *n* PHYS bobina de Helmholtz *f*; **~ free energy** *n* PHYS energía libre de Helmholtz *f*; **~ galvanometer** *n* ELEC *instrument* galvanómetro de Helmholtz *m*; **~ resonator** *n* ACOUST, PHYS resonador de Helmholtz *m*

helmsman *n* WATER TRANSP timonel *m*

help: **~ directory** *n* COMP&DP, PROD directorio de ayuda *m*; **~ message** *n* COMP&DP mensaje de ayuda *m*; **~ program** *n* COMP&DP programa de ayuda *m*; **~ screen** *n* COMP&DP pantalla de ayuda *f*

helve *n* PROD astil *m*, mango *m*

helver *n* PROD mango *m*

helvine *n* MINERAL helvina *f*

hem *n* TEXTIL dobladillo *m*

hematein *AmE see haematein BrE*

hematic *AmE see haematic BrE*

hematin *AmE see haematin BrE*

hematite *AmE see haematite BrE*

hematolite *AmE see haematolite BrE*

hematoporphyrin *AmE see haematoporphyrin BrE*

hematoxylin *AmE see haematoxylin BrE*

hemi: **~-acetal** *n* CHEM semiacetal *m*

hemicellulose *n* CHEM hemicelulosa *f*

hemiellipsoidal: **~ bottom** *n* NUCL casquete inferior *m*; **~ head** *n* NUCL casquete superior *m*

hemimetallic *adj* CHEM hemimetálico

hemimorphite *n* MINERAL hemimorfita *f*

hemipinic *adj* CHEM hemipínico

hemisphere *n* GEOM hemisferio *m*

hemispherical: **~ combustion chamber** *n* AUTO cámara de combustión semiesférica *f*; **~ coverage** *n* TELECOM cobertura hemisférica *f*

hemoglobin *AmE see haemoglobin BrE*

hemolysin *n* CHEM hemolisina *f*

hemolysis *AmE see haemolysis BrE*

hemolytic *AmE see haemolytic BrE*

hemopyrrole *AmE see haemopyrrole BrE*

hemosiderin *AmE see haemosiderin BrE*

hemotoxin *AmE see haemotoxin BrE*

hemp *n* WATER TRANSP cáñamo *m*; **~ gasket** *n* PROD empaquetadura *f*, empaquetadura de cáñamo *f*, trenza de cáñamo *f*; **~ nettle** *n* AGRIC ortiga *f*; **~ packing** *n* PROD empaquetadura de cáñamo *f*, guarnición de cáñamo *f*

He-Ne: **~ laser** *n* (*helium-neon laser*) PHYS láser de He-Ne *m* (*láser de helio-neón*)

henry *n* (*H*) ELEC, ELEC ENG, METR, PHYS henrio *m* (*H*), THERMO hidrógeno *m* (*H*)

heparin *n* CHEM heparina *f*

hepatite *n* MINERAL hepatita *f*

heptad *n* CHEM héptada *f*

heptagon *n* GEOM heptágono *m*

heptagonal *adj* GEOM heptagonal

heptahedron *n* GEOM heptaedro *m*

heptane *n* CHEM heptano *m*, PETR TECH eptano *m*

heptatonic: **~ scale** *n* ACOUST escala eptavalente *f*

heptavalent *adj* CHEM heptavalente

heptene *n* CHEM hepteno *m*

heptode *n* ELECTRON heptodo *m*

heptose *n* CHEM heptosa *f*

heptyl *n* CHEM heptilo *m*

heptylene *n* CHEM heptileno *m*

heptylic *adj* CHEM heptílico

heptyne *n* CHEM heptino *m*

herbaceous: **~ perennial** *n* AGRIC planta vivaz *f*

herbicide *n* AGRIC herbicida *m*

hercynite *n* MINERAL hercinita *f*

herd *n* AGRIC manada *f* (*Esp*), piara *f*, rebaño *m* (*Esp*), rodeo *m* (*AmL*); **~ book** *n* AGRIC registro genealógico *m*; ~ **replacement** *n* AGRIC reposición de la manada *f* (*Esp*), reposición del rebaño *f* (*Esp*), reposición del rodeo *f* (*AmL*)

herder: ~ **effect** *n* MAR POLL efecto de apiaramiento *m*

herding: ~ **agent** *n* CHEM agente aglomerante *m*, MAR POLL agente aglomerante *m*, aglomerante *m*

hermaphroditic: ~ **connector** *n* ELEC ENG conector hermafrodita *m*; ~ **contact** *n* ELEC ENG contacto hermafrodita *m*, contacto macho-hembra *m*

hermetic: ~ **closure** *n* PACK cierre hermético *m*; ~ **compressor** *n* MECH ENG *for refrigerants*, REFRIG bocha *f* (*AmL*), compresor hermético *m* (*Esp*); ~ **seal** *n* PACK precinto hermético *m*, sellado hermético *m*; ~ **sealing** *n* NUCL cierre hermético *m*, sellado hermético *m*, TELECOM sellado hermético *m*

hermetically[1]: ~-**sealed** *adj* ELEC ENG, MECH herméticamente cerrado, herméticamente obturado, herméticamente sellado

hermetically[2]: ~-**sealed compressor unit** *n* MECH ENG, REFRIG bocha *f* (*AmL*), compresor hermético *m* (*Esp*); ~-**sealed unit** *n* CHEM TECH, ELEC ENG, MECH ENG, PROD, SAFE unidad herméticamente cerrada *f*

heroin *n* CHEM diacetilmorfina *f*, heroína *f*

herring: ~ **boat** *n* OCEAN caja de arenque *f*; ~ **net** *n* OCEAN red de arenque *f*

herringbone *n* MECH ENG punto espigado *m*; ~ **bar** *n* PROD *grate bar* barra de espina *f*; ~ **cross lamination** *n* GEOL laminación cruzada bidireccional *f*; ~ **gear** *n* MECH engranaje bihelicoidal *m*, engranaje de cheurón *m*, engranaje de dientes angulares *m*, engranaje de espina de pescado *m*, engranaje doble helicoidal *m*, MECH ENG engranaje de dientes angulares *m*, rueda dentada de doble hélice *f*, engranaje bihelicoidal *m*, engranaje de espina de pescado *m*; ~ **milking parlor** *AmE*, ~ **milking parlour** *BrE n* AGRIC sala de ordeño en espina de pescado *f*; ~ **pattern parquet flooring** *n* CONST suelo de parqué a espiga *m*; ~ **timbering** *n* MINE entibación armada *f* (*AmL*), entibación de muestra *f* (*Esp*); ~ **tooth** *n* MECH ENG *gears* diente angular *m*, diente bihelicoidal *m*; ~ **weave** *n* TEXTIL ligamento de espiga *m*

herringboned *adj* PRINT en forma de raspa de pescado

hertz *n* (*Hz*) GEN hercio *m*, hertz *m* (*Hz*)

Hertzian[1] *adj* C&G, ELEC, SPACE, TV herciano, hertziano

Hertzian[2]: ~ **beam** *n* ELECTRON, TV haz hertziano *m*; ~ **dipole** *n* PHYS, SPACE, TELECOM dipolo hertziano *m*; ~ **fracture** *n* C&G fractura hertziana *f*

hesperetin *n* CHEM hesperetina *f*

hesperidin *n* CHEM, FOOD hesperidina *f*

hesperitin *n* CHEM hesperitina *f*

hessian *n* TEXTIL arpillera *f*

hessite *n* MINERAL hessita *f*

hessonite *n* MINERAL hessonita *f*

heteroatom *n* CHEM heteroátomo *m*

heteroatomic *adj* CHEM heteroatómico

heteroauxin *n* CHEM heteroauxina *f*

heterocyclic *adj* CHEM heterocíclico

heterodyne *n* TV heterodino *m*; ~ **conversion** *n* ELEC ENG conversión heterodina *f*; ~ **conversion transducer** *n* ELEC ENG transductor de conversión heterodina *m*; ~ **detection** *n* TELECOM detección heterodina *f*; ~ **wavemeter** *n* WAVE PHYS medidor de ondas heterodinas *m*, ondámetro heterodino *m*

heterodyning *n* TV heterodino *m*

heterogeneous[1] *adj* METALL, NUCL heterogéneo

heterogeneous[2]: ~ **reactor** *n* NUCL reactor heterogéneo *m*

heterogenite *n* MINERAL heterogenita *f*

heterojunction *n* ELECTRON, OPT heterounión *f*, TELECOM enlace heterodino *m*; ~ **FET** *n* ELECTRON TEC heterounión *m*

heterolabeling *AmE see* heterolabelling *BrE*

heterolabelling *n BrE* NUCL heteromarcado *m*

heterometric *adj* GEOL heterométrico

heteromorphite *n* MINERAL heteromorfita *f*

heteropolar *adj* CHEM heteropolar

heteroside *n* CHEM heterósido *m*

heterosite *n* MINERAL heterosita *f*

heteroxanthine *n* CHEM heteroxantina *f*

Hettangian *adj* GEOPHYS Hetangiense *m*

heulandite *n* MINERAL heulandita *f*

heuristic *adj* COMP&DP heurístico

hew *vt* COAL cajear, desbastar, golpear, picar

hewer *n* CONST *for stone, wood* cantero *m*, picapedrero *m*

hex[1] *abbr* (*hexadecimal*) COMP&DP hexadecimal *m*

hex[2]: ~ **head wrench** *n* MECH *jackplane and trying plane* llave de cabeza hexagonal *f*; ~-**headed bolt** *n* PROD perno de cabeza hexagonal *m*; ~ **nut** *n* MECH cabeza hexagonal *f*, tuerca hexagonal *f*

hexacontane *n* CHEM hexacontano *m*

hexacosane *n* CHEM hexacosano *m*

hexad *n* CHEM héxada *f*

hexadecane *n* CHEM hexadecano *m*

hexadecimal *n* (*hex*) COMP&DP hexadecimal *m*

hexadic *adj* CHEM hexádico

hexadiene *n* CHEM hexadieno *m*

hexagon *n* GEOM hexágono *m*; ~ **head** *n* MECH ENG cabeza hexagonal *f*; ~-**head bolt and hexagon nut** *n* MECH ENG perno de cabeza hexagonal y tuerca hexagonal *m*; ~-**head screw** *n* MECH, PROD tornillo de cabeza hexagonal *m*; ~ **nut** *n* MECH ENG tuerca hexagonal *f*; ~-**socket screw** *n* MECH, MECH ENG tornillo de cabeza hueca hexagonal *m*; ~-**socket screw with flat point** *n* MECH ENG tornillo de cabeza hueca hexagonal con punto plano *m*; ~-**socket-head cap screw** *n* MECH ENG tornillo de cabeza hueca hexagonal *m*; ~-**turret lathe** *n* MECH ENG torno de torre hexagonal *m*; ~ **voltage** *n* ELEC *six-phase system* tensión hexagonal *f*

hexagonal *adj* GEOM hexagonal; ~ **close-packed lattice** *n* NUCL red hexagonal compacta *f*, retículo hexagonal compacto *m*; ~ **close-packed structure** *n* (*HCP*) CRYSTALL empaquetado hexagonal compacto *m* (*EHC*); ~ **die nut** *n* MECH ENG hembra de terraje hexagonal *f*, tuerca de aterrajar hexagonal *f*, tuerca de repasar roscas hexagonal *f*; ~-**head bolt** *n* MECH ENG bulón de cabeza hexagonal *m*, perno de cabeza hexagonal *m*; ~ **key** *n* MECH ENG llave hexagonal *f*; ~ **mesh-wired glass** *n* C&G vidrio alambrado con malla hexagonal *m*; ~ **nut** *n* MECH ENG tuerca hexagonal *f*

hexahedral *adj* GEOM hexaedral, hexaédrico

hexahedron *n* GEOM hexaedro *m*

hexahydrobenzene *n* CHEM hexahidrobenceno *m*

hexahydrobenzoic *adj* CHEM hexahidrobenzoico

hexahydrophenol *n* CHEM hexahidrofenol *m*

hexahydropyridine *n* CHEM hexahidropiridina *f*

hexamethylene: ~ **diisocyanate** *n* P&R diisocianato de hexametileno *m*

hexamethylenetetramine *n* CHEM hexametilenotetramina *f*

hexane *n* CHEM, PETR TECH hexano *m*

hexanol *n* CHEM alcohol hexílico *m*, hexanol *m*

hexatonic: ~ **scale** *n* ACOUST escala exavalente *f*

hexavalent *adj* CHEM hexavalente

hexene *n* CHEM hexeno *m*

hexidecimal: ~ **notation** *n* COMP&DP notación hexadecimal *f*

hexode *n* ELECTRON hexodo *m*

hexogen *n* CHEM hexogen *m*

hexosan *n* CHEM hexosana *f*

hexose *n* CHEM hexosa *f*

hexyl *n* CHEM hexilo *m*; ~ **alcohol** *n* CHEM alcohol hexílico *m*, hexanol *m*

hexylene *n* CHEM hexileno *m*

hexylic *adj* CHEM hexílico

hexyne *n* CHEM hexino *m*

Hf *abbr* (*hafnium*) CHEM, METALL Hf (*hafnio*)

HF[1] *abbr* (*high frequency*) ELEC, ELEC ENG, ELECTRON, TELECOM AF (*alta frecuencia*)

HF[2]: ~ **signal** *n* (*high-frequency signal*) ELECTRON señal de AF *f* (*señal de alta frecuencia*); ~ **signal generator** *n* ELECTRON generador de señal de AF *m*; ~ **spectrum** *n* ELECTRON espectro de AF *m*

hg *abbr* (*hectogram, hectogramme*) METR hg (*hectogramo*)

Hg *abbr* (*mercury*) CHEM, ELEC ENG, METALL Hg (*mercurio*)

H-girder *n* CONST viga principal en H *f*

HGV[1] *abbr* (*heavy goods vehicle*) AUTO camión de gran tonelaje *m*

HGV[2]: ~ **traffic** *n* TRANSP tráfico de vehículos pesados *m*

hi: ~**-fi sound** *n* TV sonido de alta fidelidad *m*

hiatus *n* GEOL hiato *m*, laguna estratigráfica *f*, PETR TECH hiato *m*

hidden: ~ **bar-code identification** *n* PACK identificación mediante código de barras secreto *f*; ~ **layer** *n* PETR TECH capa oculta *f*

hiddenite *n* MINERAL hiddenita *f*

hide: ~**-faced mallet** *n* MECH ENG martillo de cotillo revestido cuero *m*

hiding: ~**-power** *n* P&R capacidad encubridora *f*

hierarchical: ~ **model** *n* COMP&DP modelo jerárquico *m*; ~ **object-oriented design** *n* (*HOOD*) COMP&DP diseño jerárquico orientado al objeto *m* (*HOOD*), programa jerárquico orientado a objetos *m*; ~ **system** *n* TELECOM sistema jerárquico *m*

hierarchy *n* COMP&DP jerarquía *f*

Higgs: ~ **boson** *n* PART PHYS bosón de Higgs *m*, partícula de Higgs *f*, PHYS bosón de Higgs *m*; ~ **particle** *n* PART PHYS bosón de Higgs *m*, partícula de Higgs *f*, PHYS bosón de Higgs *m*

high[1] *adj* MECH ENG elevado, máximo; ~ **band** *adj* TV banda alta *f*; ~**-density** *adj* COMP&DP de alta densidad; ~**-fibre** *adj* FOOD alto en fibra; ~**-grade** *adj* COAL de alto nivel; ~ **in line** *adj* PRINT volado; ~**-order** *adj* COMP&DP de orden superior; ~**-performance** *adj* PHYS de alto rendimiento; ~**-pressure** *adj* GAS, PHYS, WATER de alta presión; ~**-protein** *adj* FOOD alto en proteína; ~**-speed** *adj* MECH de acción rápida, de alta velocidad, de marcha rápida, ultrarrápido, ultraveloz, MECH ENG de alta velocidad; ~**-temperature** *adj* HEAT ENG, PHYS, THERMO a

alta temperatura, de alta temperatura; ~**-tensile** *adj* MECH *bed* de gran resistencia a la tracción; ~**-torque** *adj* MECH de gran par; ~**-vacuum** *adj* MECH de alto grado de vacío, de alto vacío, de vacío casi perfecto; ~**-voltage** *adj* PHYS de alta tensión

high[2] *n* GEOL área anticiclónica *f*, METEO alta *f*, área anticiclónica *f*;

▪ **a** ~**-altitude low-opening** *n* (*HALO*) MILIT *parachute insertion technique* salto de paracaídas a gran altitud *m*; ~**-amplitude pulse** *n* ELECTRON impulso de gran amplitud *m*; ~**-angle dip** *n* PETR TECH buzamiento de gran ángulo *m*; ~**-angle shot** *n* CINEMAT toma desde un ángulo alto *f*;

▪ **b** ~ **barrier** *n* PACK protección elevada *f*; ~ **bit-rate ATM network mixer** *n* TELECOM mezclador de redes ATM de alta velocidad binaria *m*; ~**-brightness screen** *n* ELECTRON pantalla de mucho brillo *f*; ~**-bulk spun yarn** *n* TEXTIL hilado de gran volumen *m*;

▪ **c** ~**-clearance tractor** *n* AGRIC tractor de zancas *m*; **very** ~ **cliff** *n* OCEAN megacantil *m*; ~**-conductance diode** *n* ELECTRON diodo de gran conductancia *m*; ~**-contrast film** *n* CINEMAT película de gran contraste *f*; ~**-cube container** *n* (*HC*) TRANSP contenedor alto *m*; ~**-current diode** *n* ELECTRON diodo de corriente elevada *m*; ~**-current transistor** *n* ELECTRON transistor de corriente elevada *m*;

▪ **d** ~**-definition television** *n* (*HDTV*) TELECOM, TV televisión de alta definición *f* (*Esp*), televisión por definición extendida *f* (*AmL*); ~ **degree of protection** *n* PROD alto grado de protección *m*; ~**-density integrated circuit** *n* ELECTRON circuito integrado de gran densidad *m*; ~**-density logic** *n* ELECTRON circuito lógico de gran densidad *m*; ~**-density pick-up baler** *n* AGRIC prensa de alta presión *f*; ~**-density polyethylene** *n* (*HDPE*) PACK polietileno de alta densidad *m* (*PAD*); ~**-density bipolar of order 3 code** *n* (*HDB3*) TELECOM código bipolar de alta densidad del orden 3 *m*; ~**-density bipolar of order 2 code** *n* (*HDB2*) TELECOM código bipolar de alta densidad del orden 2 *m*; ~**-discharge temperature cut-out** *n* REFRIG termostato de seguridad de impulsión *m*; ~**-dose implant** *n* ELECTRON adición de dosis elevada *f*;

▪ **e** ~**-energy beam** *n* ELECTRON haz de gran potencia *m*; ~**-energy beam experiment** *n* RAD PHYS experimento con haz de alta energía *m*; ~**-energy electron** *n* ELECTRON electrón de alta energía *m*, electrón de gran potencia *m*; ~**-energy electron diffraction** *n* (*HEED*) PART PHYS difracción de electrones *f*; ~**-energy electron-positron beams** *n pl* NUCL, PART PHYS haces de electrones y positrones de alta energía *m pl*, haces electrón-positrón hiperenergéticos *m pl*; ~**-energy elemental particle** *n* PART PHYS partícula elemental de alta energía *f*; ~**-energy environment** *n* GEOL medio de alta energía *m*; ~**-energy fusion** *n* NUCL fusión hiperenergética *f*; ~**-energy ion** *n* ELECTRON ión de alta energía *m*, ión de gran potencia *m*, PART PHYS ión de alta energía *m*; ~**-energy kaon beams** *n pl* PART PHYS haces de kaones de alta energía *m pl*, haces de mesones K de alta energía *m pl*, haces mesón K hiperenergéticos *m pl*; ~**-energy laser** *n* ELECTRON láser de gran potencia *m*; ~**-energy muon beams** *n pl* PART PHYS haces de muones de alta energía *m pl*, haces muón hiperenergéticos *m pl*; **~-energy particle** *n* ELECTRON partícula de alta energía *f*, partícula de gran potencia *f*; **~-energy physics** *n* PHYS física de alta energía *f*, RAD PHYS física de altas energías *f*; **~-energy proton** *n* SPACE protón de alta energía *m*; **~-energy radiation** *n* RAD PHYS radiación de alta energía *f*; **~-energy tape** *n* TV cinta de alta energía *f*; **~ explosive** *n* MILIT alto explosivo *m*, explosivo rompedor *m*, MINE alto explosivo *m*, explosivo con base de nitroglicerina *m*, explosivo detonante *m* (*AmL*), explosivo rompedor *m*; **~ explosive anti-tank** *n* (*HEAT*) MILIT alto explosivo anticarro *m*;

~-f **~ flow rate** *n* PROD alto grado del flujo *m*; **~-flux reactor** *n* NUCL reactor de alto flujo *m*; **~ frequency** *n* (*HF*) ELEC *supply*, ELEC ENG, ELECTRON, TELECOM alta frecuencia *f* (*AF*); **very ~ frequency** *n* (*VHF*) ELEC, ELEC ENG muy alta frecuencia *f*, ELECTRON frecuencia muy alta *f* (*FMA*), frecuencia muy elevada *f* (*FME*), muy alta frecuencia *f*, SPACE frecuencia muy alta *f* (*FMA*), frecuencia muy elevada *f* (*FME*), TELECOM frecuencia muy alta *f* (*FMA*), frecuencia muy elevada *f* (*FME*), muy alta frecuencia *f*, WAVE PHYS frecuencia muy alta *f* (*FMA*), frecuencia muy elevada *f* (*FME*); **~-frequency amplification** *n* ELECTRON amplificación de alta frecuencia *f*; **~-frequency amplifier** *n* ELECTRON amplificador de alta frecuencia *m*; **~-frequency cable** *n* ELEC *AC supply* cable de alta frecuencia *m*; **~-frequency component** *n* ELECTRON componente de alta frecuencia *m*; **~-frequency current** *n* ELEC *AC* corriente de alta frecuencia *f*; **~-frequency discharge** *n* GAS descarga de alta frecuencia *f*; **~-frequency distribution frame** *n* TELECOM trama de distribución de alta frecuencia *f*; **~-frequency furnace** *n* ELEC ENG horno de alta frecuencia *m*; **~-frequency generator** *n* ELEC generador de alta frecuencia *m*; **~-frequency heating** *n* ELEC calentamiento por alta frecuencia *m*, ELEC ENG calentamiento por alta frecuencia *m*, calentador de alta frecuencia *m*; **~-frequency image** *n* SPACE *technology* imagen de alta frecuencia *f*; **~-frequency induction brazing** *n* CONST broncesoldadura de inducción de alta frecuencia *f*; **~-frequency line** *n* PHYS línea de alta frecuencia *f*; **~-frequency network analysis** *n* ELEC, ELEC ENG análisis de la red en alta frecuencia *m*; **very ~-frequency omnirange** *n* (*VHFO*) AIR TRANSP omni-alcance de muy alta frecuencia *m*, TRANSP omni-alcance de muy alta frecuencia *m*, radiofaro omnidireccional de alta frecuencia *m* (*RFMA*); **~-frequency printed circuit** *n* ELECTRON circuito impreso de alta frecuencia *m*; **~-frequency printed-circuit board** *n* ELECTRON placa de circuito impreso de alta frecuencia *f*; **~-frequency signal** *n* (*HF signal*) ELECTRON señal de alta frecuencia *f* (*señal de AF*); **~-frequency spectrum** *n* ELECTRON espectro de alta frecuencia *m*; **~-frequency switching** *n* ELEC ENG conmutación de hiperfrecuencia *f*; **~-frequency thawing** *n* REFRIG descongelación por alta frecuencia *f*; **~-frequency transformer** *n* ELEC ENG transformador de alta frecuencia *m*; **~-frequency transistor** *n* ELECTRON transistor de alta frecuencia *m*; **~-frequency welding** *n* PACK soldadura por alta frecuencia *f*; **~-frequency welding equipment** *n* PACK equipo de soldadura por alta frecuencia *m*;

~-g **~-gain amplifier** *n* ELECTRON amplificador de alta ganancia *m*; **~-gain power amplifier** *n* ELECTRON amplificador de potencia de alta ganancia *m*; **~-gamma camera tube** *n* ELECTRON tubo de cámara con gran proporción de rayos gamma *m*; **~ gear** *n* MECH alta velocidad *f*, MECH ENG alta velocidad *f*, engranaje de alta multiplicación *m*, engranaje de gran multiplicación *m*; **~ gloss** *n* COATINGS, P&R alto brillo *m*; **~-gloss foil** *n* PACK hoja de alto brillo *f*; **~ grade** *n* CHEM alto grado *m*; **~ grade heat** *n* NUCL calor de alta calidad *m*; **~-grade metamorphism** *n* GEOL metamorfismo de alto grado *m*; **~-grade ore** *n* COAL mineral de alto grado *m*; **~ gradient** *n* CONST gran pendiente *f*; **~-gravity gasoline** *n* AmE (*cf high-gravity petrol BrE*) AUTO, PETROL, VEH gasolina de alta gravedad *f*; **~-gravity petrol** *BrE n* (*cf high-gravity gasoline AmE*) AUTO, PETROL, VEH gasolina de alta gravedad *f*;

~-h **~ hat** *n* CINEMAT sombrero de copa *m*, trípode copa *m*; **~ head** *n* FUELLESS salto de agua elevado *m*;

~-i **~ impedance state** *n* ELEC ENG estado de alta impedancia *m*, estado de gran impedancia *m*; **~-intensity discharge lamp** *n* CINEMAT lámpara de descarga de alta intensidad *f*; **~-intensity electric arc** *n* ELEC, ELEC ENG arco eléctrico de alta intensidad *m*; **~-intensity ion beams** *n pl* RAD PHYS haces iónicos de elevada intensidad *m pl*; **~-intensity operation** *n* RAD PHYS operación de elevada intensidad *f*; **~-irradiance laser beam** *n* ELECTRON haz de láser de alta radiación *m*;

~-k **~ key** *n* CINEMAT iluminación de mucho contraste *f*; **~ key document** *n* PRINT documento nítido *m*;

~-l **~-level data link control** *n* (*HDLC*) COMP&DP, TELECOM control de enlace de datos de alto nivel *m*; **~ level dosimetry** *n* RAD PHYS dosimetría de alto nivel *f*, dosimetría de alto nivel energético *f*; **~-level injection** *n* ELECTRON inyección de alto nivel *f*; **~-level language** *n* COMP&DP lenguaje de alto nivel *m*; **~-level logic** *n* ELECTRON circuito lógico de alto nivel *m*; **~-level modulation** *n* ELECTRON modulación de alto nivel *f*; **~-level radioactive waste** *n* NUCL residuos radiactivos de alta actividad *m pl*; **~-level signal** *n* ELECTRON señal de alto nivel *f*; **~-level waste** *n* (*HLW*) NUCL basura de alto nivel *f*, material altamente radiactivo *m*, residuo de alto nivel *m*, residuos de gran radiactividad *m pl*, POLL basura de alto nivel *f*, RECYCL basura de alto nivel *f*, material altamente radioactivo *m*, residuo de alto nivel *m*, residuos de gran radioactividad *m pl*; **~ lift device** *n* AIR TRANSP dispositivo hipersustentador *m*; **~ lift lock** *n* HYDROL *measuring* esclusa a gran altura *f*; **~-logic level** *n* ELECTRON bloque de alto nivel *m*; **~ loss** *n* TELECOM pérdida elevada *f*;

~-m **~ modulus furnace carbon black** *n* (*HMF carbon black*) P&R negro de humo de horno y módulo alto *m*; **~-moisture corn** *n* AmE (*cf high-moisture maize BrE*) AGRIC *feeding* maíz con alto porcentaje de humedad *m*; **~-moisture maize** *n BrE* (*cf high-moisture corn AmE*) AGRIC *feeding* maíz con alto porcentaje de humedad *m*;

~-o **~-order bit** *n* COMP&DP bit a la izquierda *m*, bit de orden superior *m*; **~-order cyclic pitch** *n* AIR TRANSP *helicopter* paso cíclico de orden elevado *m*; **~-order delay** *n* ELECTRON retardo instantáneo *m*; **~-order filter** *n* ELECTRON filtro de gran capacidad *m*; **~-order harmonic** *n* ACOUST, ELECTRON, PHYS, SPACE armónico de orden superior *m*; **~-order network** *n* TELECOM red de orden superior *f*;

~ p **~-pass filter** *n* ACOUST, COMP&DP, ELECTRON, PETROL, PHYS, SPACE, TELECOM, TV filtro de paso alto *m* (*Esp*), filtro pasa-alto *m* (*AmL*); **~-pass filtering** *n* ELECTRON, TELECOM filtrado de paso alto *m*; **~-pass image** *n* SPACE imagen de paso alto *f*; **~-performance battery** *n* TRANSP batería de altas prestaciones *f*; **~-performance fan** *n* REFRIG ventilador de alto rendimiento *m*; **~-performance night vision goggles** *n pl* MILIT anteojos de alto rendimiento para visión nocturna *m pl* (*AmL*), gafas de alto rendimiento para visión nocturna *f pl* (*Esp*); **~ picture level** *n* TV alto nivel de imagen *m*; **~ pitch** *n* AIR TRANSP *helicopter* paso alto *m*, paso elevado *m*; **~-power amplifier** *n* ELECTRON, SPACE *communications* amplificador de alta potencia *m*; **~-power bipolar transistor** *n* ELECTRON transistor bipolar de gran potencia *m*; **~-power field glasses** *n pl* INSTR lente interior de gran densidad de energía *f*; **~-power laser** *n* NUCL láser de alta potencia *m*, láser de elevada densidad energética *m*; **~-power linear motor** *n* TRANSP motor lineal de gran potencia *m*; **~-power load** *n* ELEC ENG carga de gran potencia *f*; **~-power microscope** *n* INSTR microscopio de elevada potencia *m*; **~-power rectifier** *n* ELEC ENG rectificador de gran potencia *m*; **~-power SCR** *n* ELEC ENG rectificador de silicio de gran potencia *m*; **~-power transformer** *n* ELEC, ELEC ENG transformador de gran potencia *m*; **~-power transmission** *n* TELECOM transmisión de elevada potencia *f*; **~-power tube** *n* ELECTRON tubo de gran potencia *m*; **~ pressure** *n* GAS alta presión *f*, presión alta *f*, PHYS, WATER alta presión *f*; **~-pressure area** *n* METEO zona de alta presión *f*; **~-pressure blowpipe** *n* CONST soplete de alta presión *m*; **~-pressure compressor** *n* MECH ENG compresor de alta presión *m*, compresor reciprocante de alta velocidad *m*; **~-pressure controller** *n* REFRIG presostato de alta presión *m*; **~-pressure float valve** *n* REFRIG válvula de flotador de alta presión *f*; **~-pressure flushing** *n* MAR POLL descarga de agua a alta presión *f*; **~-pressure gage** *AmE*, **~-pressure gauge** *BrE n* REFRIG manómetro de alta presión *m*; **~-pressure heating system** *n* HEAT sistema de calefacción por alta presión *m*; **~-pressure hot-water system** *n* HEAT sistema de agua caliente de alta presión *m*; **~-pressure liquid chromatography** *n* (*HPLC*) CHEM, FOOD, LAB cromatografía líquida a alta presión *f* (*CLAP*); **~-pressure mercury lamp** *n* ELEC, ELEC ENG lámpara de vapor de mercurio a alta presión *f*; **~-pressure nerve syndrome** *n* OCEAN síndrome nervioso de alta presión *m*; **~-pressure nervous syndrome** *n* OCEAN síndrome nervioso de alta presión *m*; **~-pressure piston compressor** *n* MECH ENG compresor de pistón de alta presión *m*; **~-pressure safety cut-out** *n* REFRIG presostato de seguridad de alta presión *m*; **~-pressure shearer pump** *n* MINE bomba rafadora de alta presión *f*; **~-pressure tank** *n* SPACE *spacecraft* tanque de alta presión *m*; **~-pressure tire** *AmE*, **~-pressure tyre** *BrE n* TRANSP neumático de alta presión *m*; **~-pressure vacuum pump** *n* MECH ENG bomba de vacío de alta presión *f*; **~-pressure washing** *n* MAR POLL lavado a alta presión *m*; **~-pressure zone** *n* METEO zona de alta presión *f*; **~ purity pigment** *n* P&R pigmento de alta pureza *m*;

~ r **~-residue crops** *n pl* AGRIC cultivos que producen muchos residuos *m pl*; **~ resistance** *n* (*HR*) PHYS gran resistencia *f*, TELECOM alta resistencia *f*; **~ resolution** *n* (*HR*) COMP&DP alta resolución *f*, resolución de orden superior *f*; **~-resolution scan** *n* RAD PHYS barrido de alta definición *m*, barrido de alta resolución *m*, espectro de alta resolución *m*; **~-resolution study of line profiles** *n* RAD PHYS estudio de alta resolución de contornos de rayas *m*, estudio de alta resolución de contornos lineales *m*; **~ Reynolds number** *n* FLUID alto número de Reynolds *m*; **~-rise cold store** *n* REFRIG almacén con cámaras de gran altura *m*; **~-risk area of work** *n* SAFE zona de trabajo de gran riesgo *f*;

~ s **~ seas** *n pl* GEOL, OCEAN, WATER TRANSP alta mar *f*; **~-sensitivity tachometer** *n* MECH ENG tacómetro de alta precisión *m*, tacómetro de alta sensibilidad *m*, tacómetro de alta sensitividad *m*; **~ side lobe** *n* ELECTRON lóbulo lateral alto *m*, lóbulo de lado alto *m*; **~-solid mud** *n* PETR TECH lodo con alto contenido en sólidos *m*; **~-solid sludge** *n* PETR TECH lodo con alto contenido en sólidos *m*; **~ specific speed wheel** *n* FUELLESS rueda de alta velocidad específica *f*; **~ speed** *n* MECH, MECH ENG alta velocidad *f*; **~-speed auxiliary jet** *n* AUTO chorro auxiliar de alta velocidad *m*; **~-speed buffeting** *n* AIR TRANSP vibración de alta velocidad *f*; **~-speed camera** *n* CINEMAT cámara ultrarrápida *f*; **~-speed drill** *n* MECH *under a load* taladro rápido *m*; **~-speed duplication** *n* TV duplicación de alta velocidad *f* (*AmL*), tiraje de alta velocidad *m* (*Esp*); **~-speed engine** *n* MECH motor rápido *m*, WATER TRANSP *diesel* motor de gran velocidad *m*; **~-speed exit taxiway** *n* AIR TRANSP curva de salida de pista de alta velocidad *f*; **~-speed facsimile** *n* TELECOM facsímil de alta velocidad *m*; **~-speed film** *n* CINEMAT película muy sensible *f*; **~-speed film processing** *n* CINEMAT procesamiento de película muy rápida *m*; **~-speed grinding machine** *n* MECH ENG *for helicoidal machining* pulidora de alta velocidad *f*, rectificadora de alta velocidad *f*; **~-speed ground transportation** *n* TRANSP transporte terrestre de alta velocidad *m*; **~-speed inspection** *n* PACK inspección a gran velocidad *f*, inspección de alta velocidad *f*; **~-speed lens** *n* CINEMAT, OPT, PHOTO objetivo muy rápido *m*; **~-speed line** *n* RAIL línea de alta velocidad *f*, línea de gran velocidad *f*; **~-speed logic** *n* ELECTRON circuito lógico de alta velocidad *m*; **~-speed mesh** *n* ELECTRON triángulo de gran capacidad *m*; **~-speed modem** *n* ELECTRON módem de alta modulación *m*; **~-speed motor** *n* ELEC *machine* motor de alta velocidad *m*; **~-speed multirack counting system** *n* PACK sistema de contado de rejilla múltiple de alta velocidad *m*; **~-speed particle** *n* NUCL partícula de alta velocidad *f*; **~-speed passenger conveyor** *n* TRANSP pasillo rodante rápido para pasajeros *m*; **~-speed printer** *n* PRINT impresora de alta velocidad *f*; **~-speed relay** *n* ELEC relé de acción rápida *m*, relé rápido *m*; **~-speed rotary tablet compression machine** *n* PACK máquina rotativa de alta velocidad para comprimir tabletas *f*; **~-speed small tools** *n pl* MECH ENG herramientas pequeñas de alta velocidad *f pl*; **~-speed steel** *n* MECH, METALL acero de corte rápido *m*; **~-speed steel small tools** *n pl* (*HSS small tools*) MECH ENG herramientas pequeñas de acero de alta velocidad *f pl*, herramientas pequeñas de acero

de corte rápido *f pl*; **~-speed switching diode** *n*
ELECTRON diodo de gran capacidad de conmutación
m; **~-speed switching transistor** *n* ELECTRON transistor de gran capacidad de conmutación *m*; **~-stop
filter** *n* MECH ENG filtro de alta precisión *m*, filtro de
alto filtrado *m*, filtro de tamiz fino *m*; **~ sulfur
content** *AmE*, **~ sulphur content** *BrE n* CHEM,
COATINGS, PETR TECH alto contenido de azufre *m*,
contenido alto de azufre *m*;

~ t **~-tackpressure sensitive adhesive** *n* PACK
autoadhesivo con elevado tiro *m*; **~ temperature** *n*
PHYS, THERMO alta temperatura *f*; **~-temperature
alloy** *n* MECH, METALL aleación de alta temperatura *f*;
~-temperature creep *n* METALL viscofluencia a altas
temperaturas *f*; **~-temperature fuel cell** *n* TRANSP
célula de combustible para altas temperaturas *f*;
~-temperature gas radiant panel *n* HEAT panel
radiante a gas de alta temperatura *m*;
~-temperature grease *n* MECH grasa para altas
temperaturas *f*; **~-temperature insulation** *n* ELEC,
ELEC ENG aislación a alta temperatura *f*;
~-temperature molten salts fuel battery *n* TRANSP
batería de fuel de sales fundidas a alta temperatura *f*;
~ temperature short time *n* FOOD tiempo reducido a
alta temperatura *m* (*TRAT*); **~-temperature solid
electrolyte cell** *n* TRANSP electrolito sólido para alta
temperatura *m*; **~-temperature superconductivity** *n*
PHYS superconductividad a altas temperaturas *f*;
~-tenacity fiber *AmE*, **~-tenacity fibre** *BrE n* TEXTIL
fibra de alta tenacidad *f*, fibra de alta tenacidad o
alto módulo *f*, fibra de alto módulo *f*; **~-tensile steel**
n MECH, METALL acero de gran resistencia a la
tracción *m*; **~ tension** *n* ELEC, ELEC ENG, PHYS alta
tensión *f*; **~-tension detonator** *n* MINE detonador de
alta tensión *m*; **~-tension power supply** *n* ELEC ENG
alimentación de alta tensión *f*, suministro de energía
de alta tensión *m*; **~-tension terminal** *n* AUTO
terminal de alta tensión *m*; **~-test gasoline** *n* *AmE*
(*cf high-test petrol BrE*) AUTO gasolina de alto
octanaje *f*; **~-test petrol** *BrE n* (*cf high-test gasoline
AmE*) AUTO gasolina de alto octanaje *f*; **~ tide** *n*
FUELLESS marea alta *f*, OCEAN, WATER TRANSP marea
alta *f*, pleamar *f*; **~-torque motor** *n* MECH motor de
gran par de arranque *m*;

~ u **~-usage circuit group** *n* TELECOM grupo de
circuitos *m*;

~ v **~ vacuum** *n* ELECTRON, PHYS alto vacío *m*;
~-vacuum cathode ray tube *n* TV tubo de rayos
catódicos de alto vacío *m*; **~-vacuum furnace** *n*
MECH ENG horno de gran vacío *m*; **~-vacuum tube** *n*
ELECTRON, PHYS tubo de alto vacío *m*, tubo de vacío
elevado *m*; **~-velocity scanning** *n* TV exploración de
alta velocidad *f*, exploración ultrarrápida *f*;
~ voltage *n* ELEC *supply* alta tensión *f*, alto voltaje
m, ELEC ENG alta tensión *f*, PHYS alta tensión *f*, alto
voltaje *m*; **~-voltage bus** *n* ELEC *distribution* barra
colectora de alta tensión *f*, barra ómnibus de alta
tensión *f*, barra ómnibus de alto voltaje *f*; **~-voltage
cable** *n* ELEC *supply*, ELEC ENG cable de alta tensión
m, INSTR cable de alto voltaje *m*; **~-voltage circuit
breaker** *n* ELEC *switch* cortocircuito de alta tensión
m; **~-voltage electron microscope** *n* INSTR microscopio electrónico de alto voltaje *m*; **~-voltage
equipment** *n* ELEC equipo de alta tensión *m*;
~-voltage grid *n* ELEC *supply* red de distribución *f*,
red de energía eléctrica *f*; **~-voltage impulse**

generator *n* ELEC generador de impulsos de alta
tensión *m*; **~-voltage insulation** *n* ELEC, ELEC ENG
aislación a alta tensión *f*; **~-voltage motor** *n* ELEC
motor de alta tensión *m*; **~-voltage porcelain** *n* ELEC
insulation porcelana de alta tensión *f*; **~-voltage
power supply** *n* ELEC ENG suministro de energía de
alto voltaje *m*; **~-voltage rectifier** *n* ELEC rectificador
de alta tensión *m*, rectificador de alto voltaje *m*;
~-voltage switch gear *n* ELEC conmutador de alta
tensión *m*; **~-voltage system** *n* ELEC *supply* sistema
de alta tensión *m*; **~-voltage tester** *n* ELEC *instrument*
probador de hipervoltaje *m*, probador de sobretensión *m*; **~-voltage transformer** *n* ELEC
transformador de alta tensión *m*, transformador de
tensión de ánodos *m*, ELEC ENG transformador de
tensión de ánodos *m*; **~-voltage transmission line** *n*
ELEC, ELEC ENG *distribution* línea de transmisión de
alta tensión *f*; **~-voltage winding** *n* ELEC *transformer*
arrollamiento de alta tensión *m*, devanado de alto
voltaje *m*;

~ w **~ water** *n* HYDROL *river* crecida *f*, *tidal* marea
alta *f*, WATER TRANSP *tides* marea alta *f*, pleamar *f*;
~-water level *n* CONST nivel de marea alta *m*;
~-water line *n* HYDROL línea de crecida *f*; **~-water
mark** *n* HYDROL señal de la pleamar *f*, OCEAN línea de
agua alta *f*, WATER TRANSP marca de pleamar *f*;
~-water ordinary spring tide *n* (*HWOST*) FUELLESS
línea alta habitual de la marea viva *f*; **~-water
overflow** *n* WATER crecida máxima *f*, máxima avenida
f; **~ wind** *n* METEO ventarrón moderado *m*, viento
fuerte *m*;

~ y **~-yield pulp** *n* PAPER pasta de alto rendimiento *f*,
pulpa de alto rendimiento *f*

higher: **~ dimensions** *n pl* GEOM dimensiones supe-
riores *f pl*; **~ .high water** *n* OCEAN punto más alto de
pleamar *m*; **~-layer function** *n* (*HLF*) TELECOM
función de la capa superior *f*, función de nivel
superior *f*; **~-level service** *n* TELECOM servicio de
nivel superior *m*; **~-order path adaptation** *n* (*HPA*)
TELECOM adaptación de trayecto de orden superior *f*;
~-order path connection *n* (*HPC*) TELECOM conexión de trayecto de orden superior *f*; **~-order path
termination** *n* (*HPT*) TELECOM terminación de
trayecto de orden superior *f*

highest: **~ common divisor** *n* MATH máximo común
divisor *mcd*; **~ common factor** *n* (*HCF*) MATH
máximo común divisor *mcd*; **~ voltage for
equipment** *n* ELEC equipo de máxima tensión *m*

highlight *n* PHOTO alta luz *f*, PRINT zona clara de la
imagen *f*; **~ tearing** *n* TV desgarros de imagen claros
m pl

highly[1]: **~ flammable** *adj* CHEM, GAS, MINE, SAFE muy
inflamable; **~-flexible** *adj* PROD de alta flexibilidad;
~-loaded *adj* PROD de alta carga

highly[2]: **~ acid slag** *n* PROD escoria hiperácida *f*;
~ auriferous gravel *n* MINE grava hiperaurífera *f*;
~ basic slag *n* PROD escoria hiperbásica *f*;
~-flammable liquid *n* SAFE líquido muy inflamable
m; **~-inclined seam** *n* MINE capa muy inclinada *f*,
manto muy inclinado *m*; **~ plastic clay** *n* C&G, P&R
barro altamente plástico *m*; **~ seeded glass** *n* C&G
vidrio con muchas semillas *m*; **~-skilled worker** *n*
PROD trabajador de gran destreza *m*; **~ stable
oscillator** *n* ELECTRON oscilador de gran estabilidad
m; **~ visible clothing** *n* SAFE prendas visibles a gran
distancia *f pl*

highway *n* AUTO autopista *f*, COMP&DP bus *m*, conductor común *m*, enlace de comunicaciones *m*, autopista *f*, CONST, TELECOM, TRANSP, VEH autopista *f*; **~ bridge** *n* CONST puente de autopista *m*
HII: ~-type nebula *n* SPACE nebulosa de tipo HII *f*
hill: ~ agriculture *n* AGRIC cultivo de montaña *m*
hiller *n* AGRIC aporcador *m*
hillside: ~ farming *n* AGRIC cultivo en pendiente *m*
hilt *n* PROD *of pick* empuñadura *f*, mango *m*, puño *m*
hindquarter *n* AGRIC cuarto trasero *m*
hindrance *n* SAFE estorbo *m*, obstáculo *m*
hinge *n* CONST bisagra *f*, perno *m*, GEOL charnela *f*, cresta del pliegue *f*, espigón *m*, INSTR bisagra *f*, charnela *f*, gozne *m*, MECH bisagra *f*, charnela *f*, gozne *m*, articulación *f*, MECH ENG articulación *f*, bisagra *f*, charnela *f*, gozne *m*, pernio *m*; **~-and-ball joint** *n* MECH ENG articulación a rótula y pernio *f*; **~ cover** *n* PROD tapa embisagrada *f*; **~ fitting** *n* MECH ENG adaptador de bisagra *m*, conector de bisagra *m*; **~ fork** *n* AIR TRANSP forca de charnela *f*; **~ joint** *n* CONST articulación con bisagra *f*, junta con bisagra *f*; **~ with knobbed pin** *n* CONST bisagra con pasador con pomo *f*; **~ moment** *n* AIR TRANSP *helicopter* momento de charnela *m*; **~ pin** *n* CONST pasador de bisagra *m*, MECH ENG eje de articulación *m*, pasador de bisagra *m*; **~ post** *n* CONST quicial *m*; **~ shaft** *n* MECH ENG eje de bisagra *m*; **~ spindle** *n* REFRIG perno de la bisagra *m*; **~ yoke** *n* MECH ENG horquilla de bisagra *f*
hinged[1] *adj* MECH abisagrado, articulado, de charnela, MECH ENG a charnela, abatible, abisagrado, articulado, basculante, de charnela, embisagrado, engoznado, PROD abatible, TRANSP articulado
hinged[2]**: ~ body microscope** *n* INSTR microscopio de cuerpo articulado *m*; **~ bolt fitting** *n* MECH ENG *pipes* adaptador de perno articulado *m*; **~ lid** *n* PACK tapa articulada *f*; **~ panel** *n* MECH ENG panel articulado *m*, placa articulada *f*; **~ plug orifice closure** *n* PACK cierre mediante tapón articulado *m*; **~ socket wrench** *n* MECH ENG llave articulada de boca de tubo para tuercas *f*; **~ suspension** *n* MECH ENG suspensión articulada *f*; **~ valve** *n* HYDRAUL válvula de bola *f*, válvula de charnela *f*
hinging *n* MECH ENG punto de inflexión *m*; **~ post** *n* CONST quicial *m*
hinterland *n* GEOL retropaís *m*
hip *n* CONST lima *f*, faldón *m*, *of gable* cumbrera *f*; **~-and-ridge roof** *n* CONST tejado con cumbrera a cuatro aguas *m*; **~-and-valley roof** *n* CONST tejado a cuatro aguas con lima hoya *m*; **~ rafter** *n* CONST lima tesa *f*; **~ roof** *n* CONST cubierta a cuatro aguas *f*, tejado a cuatro aguas *m*; **~ roof with ridge** *n* CONST tejado a cuatro aguas con cumbrera *m*; **~ tile** *n* CONST teja de caballete *f*, teja de lima *f*
hipped: ~ ridge roof *n* CONST tejado a cuatro aguas con cumbrera *m*; **~ roof** *n* CONST tejado a cuatro aguas *m*
H-iron *n* CONST hierro en H *m*
histamine *n* CHEM histamina *f*
histogram *n* COMP&DP, MATH, PHYS, TELECOM gráfico de barras *m*, histograma *m*
histology: ~ bath *n* LAB *liquids* baño histológico *m*
histone *n* CHEM histona *f*
hit[1] *n* COMP&DP acierto *m*, impacto *m*, éxito *m*; **~-and-miss damper** *n* HEAT ENG amortiguador de impactos accidentales *m*, amortiguador de impactos aleatorios

m; **~-on-the-fly printer** *n* COMP&DP, PRINT impresora de acceso inmediato *f* (*Esp*), impresora de impacto al vuelo *f* (*AmL*); **~-or-miss governor** *n* AIR TRANSP regulador todo o nada *m*; **~-or-miss selector valve** *n* MECH ENG válvula selectora de todo o nada *f*
hit[2] *vt* COMP&DP *keys on keyboard* acertar, impactar, pulsar
hitch[1] *n* MECH *mooring* enganche *m*, MINE joroba *f*, enganche *m* (*Esp*), muesca en la roca *f* (*AmL*), filón para sostener una apea *m* (*AmL*), VEH enganche *m*, WATER TRANSP *ropes* vuelta *f*; **~ pin** *n* PROD pasador de enganche *m*; **~ roll** *n* PAPER rodillo tensor *m*
hitch[2] *vt* MECH enganchar, MINE amarrar (*Esp*), atar (*AmL*), enganchar
Hittorf: ~ dark space *n* ELECTRON espacio oscuro Hittorf *m*
hl *abbr* (*hectoliter AmE, hectolitre BrE*) METR hl (*hectólitro*)
HLF *abbr* (*higher-layer function*) TELECOM función de la capa superior *f*, función de nivel superior *f*
HLLV *abbr* (*heavy lift launch vehicle*) SPACE vehículo de lanzamiento de carga pesada *m*
HLW *abbr* (*high-level waste*) NUCL, POLL, RECYCL basura de alto nivel *f*, material altamente radioactivo *m*, residuo de alto nivel *m*, residuos de gran radioactividad *m pl*
hm *abbr* (*hectometer AmE, hectometre BrE*) METR hm *m* (*hectómetro*)
HMF: ~ carbon black *n* (*high modulus furnace carbon black*) P&R negro de humo de horno y módulo alto *m*
HMI: ~ lamp *n* CINEMAT lámpara HMI *f*
Hn *abbr* (*hahnium*) CHEM, RAD PHYS Hn (*hahnio*)
Ho *abbr* (*holmium*) CHEM Ho (*holmio*)
hoar: ~ frost *n* METEO escarcha *f*, REFRIG escarcha cristalina *f*
hob *n* MECH fresa de aplanar *f*, fresa helicoidal *f*, fresa matriz *f*, MECH ENG *for cutting screwchasers* fresa para peines *f*, macho maestro para peines de roscar *m*, *for cutting wormwheels* fresa matriz en forma de tornillo sin fin *f*, *gear-cutting machine* fresa generatriz *f*, fresa helicoidal *f*, fresa matriz *f*, *mastertap* macho maestro de roscar *m*; **~ cutting** *n* MECH ENG maquinado de engranajes con fresa matriz *m*, tallado de engranajes con fresa matriz *m*; **~ tap** *n* MECH ENG *mastertap* macho maestro de roscar *m*
hobbing *n* MECH ENG maquinado por fresa generatriz *m*, tallado de engranajes *m*, PROD maquinado por fresa generatriz *m*, talla *f*
hoe *n* CONST azada *f*
hoeing: ~ machine *n* AGRIC azada mecánica *f*
Hoffman: ~ electrometer *n* ELEC electrómetro de Hoffman *m*
hog[1]**: ~-backed bridge** *n* CONST puente con lomo *m*; **~ cholera** *n* AGRIC cólera porcino *f*; **~ crop** *n* AGRIC producción porcina *f*; **~ run** *n* AGRIC número de porcinos nacidos en un año *m*
hog[2] *vi* WATER TRANSP limpiar los fondos con escobón *m*, *ship* quebrantarse
hogback *n* GEOL cresta isoclinal *f*, crestón *m*, dique *m*, muro *m*
hogged *adj* WATER TRANSP *ship* quebrantado
hoist[1] *n* AIR TRANSP elevador *m*, grúa *f*, izador *m*, ELEC ENG *flag* vaina *f*, MECH aparejo *m*, grúa *f*, torno de izar pesos *m*, montacargas *m*, polipasto *m*, malacate *m*, MINE carrera de extracción *f* (*Esp*), cabrestante de sondeo *m*, malacate *m*, cabrestante *m*, motor de

extracción *m*, máquina de extracción *f*, torno de sondeo *m* (*AmL*), carrera de subida *f* (*AmL*), izada *f*, PROD polipasto *m*, guinche *m*, montacargas *m*, grúa *f*, SAFE montacargas *m*, WATER TRANSP eslingada *f*, montacargas *m*, polipasto *m*; ~ **arm** *n* AIR TRANSP *helicopter* brazo de grúa *m*, pescante *m*; ~ **boom** *n* AIR TRANSP *helicopter* pescante *m*; ~ **cable cutter** *n* AIR TRANSP *helicopter* cortador de cable del izador *m*; ~ **fitting** *n* AIR TRANSP *helicopter* componente del izador *m*, montaje del izador *m*; ~ **lever** *n* AIR TRANSP *helicopter* palanca del izador *f*; ~ **operator** *n* AIR TRANSP operador del izador *m*; ~ **pump** *n* AIR TRANSP *helicopter* bomba del izador *f*; ~ **room** *n* MINE cuarto del motor de extracción *m*

hoist² *vt* AIR TRANSP izar, MINE *ore* alzar, extraer, izar, PROD elevar, guindar, izar, levantar, subir, WATER TRANSP *boat with winch* izar, izar a bordo; ~ **to the surface** *vt* MINE alzar a la superficie, extraer a la superficie

hoist³: ~ **the colors** *AmE*, ~ **the colours** *BrE vi* WATER TRANSP *flag* izar la bandera nacional

hoisting *n* MINE, PROD extracción *f*, izada *f*, subida *f*; ~ **appliance** *n* PROD aparejo de izada *m*; ~ **block** *n* AIR TRANSP bloque del izador *m*, PROD cuadernal de gancho *m*, cuadernal móvil *m*; ~ **bucket** *n* PROD cuba de extracción *f*; ~ **carriage** *n* AIR TRANSP carro izador *m*; ~ **compartment** *n* CONST *of shaft* compartimiento de elevación *m*; ~ **crab** *n* PROD torno de extracción *m*; ~ **dog** *n* MINE enganchador *m*; ~ **drum** *n* MINE tambor izador *m*; ~ **engine** *n* MINE motor de extracción *m*, máquina de extracción *f*; ~ **eye** *n* AIR TRANSP anilla del izador *f*, bucle del izador *m*, hojal del izador *m*, ojo del izador *m*; ~ **gear** *n* MECH ENG aparato de extracción *m*, aparato de izar *m*, guinche *m*, PROD aparato de extracción *m*, aparato de izar *m*, mecanismo de izada *m*, SAFE aparato de izar *m*; ~ **jack** *n* PROD gato *m*; ~ **plug** *n* MINE guía de extracción *f*; ~ **pulley** *n* MINE gorrón del castillete *m* (*Esp*), polea del castillete de extracción *f* (*AmL*); ~ **reel** *n* MINE tambor de extracción *m*; ~ **ring** *n* AIR TRANSP anilla del izador *f*, argolla del izador *f*; ~ **rope** *n* MINE cable de extracción *m*, cable izador *m*, PROD *of cableway* cable izador *m*; ~ **shaft** *n* MINE pozo de extracción *m*; ~ **sling** *n* AIR TRANSP eslinga del izador *f*; ~ **system** *n* MINE equipo de extracción *m*, sistema de extracción *m*; ~ **tackle** *n* PROD aparejo izador *m*, cuadernal *m*, montón *m*

hold¹ *n* AIR TRANSP *of aircraft* agarradera *f*, agarradero *m*, asa *f*, bodega *f*, empuñadura *f*, enganche *m*, espera de instrucciones *f*, espera de permiso *f*, PROD *grip* retención *f*, sostenimiento *m*, SPACE espera de autorización para aterrizar *f*, ocupación de circuitos *f*, retención *f*, TELECOM mantenimiento de una conversación *m*, ocupación de circuitos *f*, WATER TRANSP *of ship* bodega *f*; ~ **control** *n* TV control de sincronización *m*; ~ **current** *n* ELEC *relay, thyristor* corriente de retención *f*; ~**out** *n* PRINT absorbencia *f*, rendimiento de la tinta *m*; ~**over coil** *n* REFRIG acumulador de frío *m*, serpentín acumulador *m*; ~ **point** *n* QUALITY punto de parada *m*; ~**short line** *n AmE* (*cf lead-in line BrE*) AIR TRANSP línea de sujeción corta *f*, línea guía de entrada *f*; ~ **time** *n* COMP&DP, SPACE tiempo de retención *m*

hold² *vt* COMP&DP retener, PROD *chuck, cramp* agarrar, guardar, retener, sujetar; ~ **back** *vt* RAIL retener; ~ **up**

vt MECH ENG *support* sostener, *delay* detener, immovilizar, *lift* alzar, levantar

hold³ *vi* PROD contener; ~ **fast** *vi* PROD sujetar, tener firme; ~ **up** *vi* PROD *riveting* entibar

hold⁴: **on** ~ *phr* TELECOM en espera

Holden: ~ **effect** *n* NUCL efecto de Holden *m*

holder *n* ELEC ENG *for electric lamps* casquillo *m*, portalámparas *m*, soporte *m*, MECH ENG *stand* apoyo *m*, montura *f*, portaherramientas *m*, sostén *m*

Holder: ~ **comma** *n* ACOUST coma de Holder *f*

holdfast *n* MECH ENG mordaza *f*, *cramp* mangueta *f*, prensa *f*, PROD *nail* grapa *f*

holding *n* AIR TRANSP espera *f*, fijación *f*, retención *f*, sujeción *f*, ELEC ENG mantenimiento *m*, *thyristors* sujeción *f*; ~ **anode** *n* ELEC ENG ánodo de ionización *m*; ~ **apron** *n* AIR TRANSP *airport* plataforma de espera *f*; ~ **bay** *n* AIR TRANSP *airport* compartimiento de espera *m*, área de espera *f*, área de mantenimiento *f*; ~ **beam** *n* ELECTRON haz de acumulación *m*; ~ **bin** *n* AGRIC *grading* cubo de clasificación *m*; ~ **capacity** *n* MECH ENG *of chuck* diámetro máximo de apriete *m*, volumen *m*, PACK distancia de apriete *f*, diámetro de apriete *m*, PROD diámetro de apriete *m*; ~ **coil** *n* ELEC ENG bobina de retención *f*; ~ **collet** *n* MECH ENG *machine tools* pinza de apriete *f*, pinza de fijación *f*; ~ **current** *n* ELEC ENG corriente de retención *f*; ~ **device** *n* MECH ENG dispositivo de fijación *m*, dispositivo de retención *m*; ~**down bolt** *n* PROD perno de anclaje *m*; ~ **fixture** *n* MECH ENG dispositivo de fijación *m*, dispositivo de retención *m*; ~ **path** *n* AIR TRANSP trayectoria de espera *f*; ~ **pattern** *n* AIR TRANSP circuito de espera *m*; ~ **point** *n* AIR TRANSP punto de espera *m*; ~ **power** *n* PROD potencia de sostén *f*; ~ **procedure** *n* AIR TRANSP procedimiento de espera *m*; ~ **siding** *n* RAIL, TRANSP apartadero de retención *m*; ~ **speed** *n* AIR TRANSP velocidad de espera *f*; ~ **stack** *n* AIR TRANSP pila de espera *f*; ~ **time** *n* TELECOM tiempo de espera *m*; ~ **up** *n* MECH ENG elevación *f*, inmovilización *f*, retención *f*, suspensión *f*, sustentación *f*

holdup *n* MECH ENG parada *f*

hole¹ *n* C&G agujero *m*, CONST perforación *f*, taladro *m*, orificio *m*, *well* pozo *m*, ELEC ENG *electron* laguna *f*, agujero *m*, hueco *m*, MECH ENG agujero *m*, MECH ENG *cavity* cavidad *f*, orificio *m*, hueco *m*, *in emery wheel* agujero *m*, MINE socavón *m*, NUCL orificio *m*, hueco *m*, PETR TECH pozo *m*, hueco *m*, agujero *m*, PETROL pozo *m*, PHYS *of a batch* hueco *m*, PROD abertura *f*, agujero *m*; ~ **conduction** *n* ELEC ENG *semiconductors* conducción por huecos *f*, conducción por lagunas *f*; ~ **saw** *n* MECH ENG broca cilíndrica de bordes cortantes de sierra *f*, sierra de perforación *f*; ~ **scraper** *n* MINE *blasting* cuchara de arrastre *f*

hole² *vt* CONST *dig* taladrar, *pierce* perforar, MINE hacer un hoyo, excavar, hacer un agujero, perforar, horadar (*AmL*), agujerear

holed¹ *adj* MECH agujereado, MINE perforado, rafado (*AmL*), rozado (*Esp*), PROD agujereado

holed²: ~ **nut** *n* PROD tuerca de agujeros *f*

holey: ~ **roll** *n* PAPER rodillo distribuidor *m*, rodillo perforado *m*

holing *n* MINE arranque *m*, cala *f* (*AmL*), calado *m* (*Esp*), recorte *m* (*Esp*), rompimiento *m*, roza *f*, descalce *m*, perforación *f*; ~**and-shearing machine** *n* COAL máquina rafadora y rozadora *f*; ~ **machine** *n* COAL máquina rafadora *f*; ~ **prop** *n* MINE taco de madera que se inserta en la hendidura abierta por la rozadura *m*

Hollerith: **~ card** *n* COMP&DP ficha Hollerith *f*, tarjeta Hollerith *f*; **~ code** *n* COMP&DP código Hollerith *m*

hollow[1] *n* CONST cavidad *f*, depresión *f*, hueco *m*; **~ anode** *n* ELEC *electrode* ánodo hueco *m*; **~ bolt** *n* MECH ENG perno hueco *m*; **~ cathode ion source** *n* NUCL, PHYS fuente de iones de cátodo hueco *f*; **~ circular shaft** *n* MECH ENG eje cilíndrico hueco *m*; **~ conductor** *n* ELEC conductor hueco *m*; **~ glass block** *n* C&G bloque hueco de vidrio *m*; **~ gravity dam** *n* HYDROL presa de gravedad hueca *f*; **~ neck** *n* C&G cuello hueco *m*, cuello mal soplado *m*; **~ pin** *n* MECH ENG pasador hueco *m*; **~ ram** *n* MECH ENG martinete hueco *m*, maza hueca *f*; **~ rivet** *n* MECH ENG remache hueco *m*; **~ shaft** *n* MECH ENG eje hueco *m*; **~ target** *n* NUCL blanco hueco *m*; **~ tread** *n* RAIL bandaje acanalado *m*; **~-type track girder** *n* TRANSP traviesa hueca de vía *f*; **~ ware** *n* C&G platos hondos *m pl*, soperas *f pl*; **~ ware presser** *n* C&G prensa para platos hondos *f*

hollow[2] *vt* CONST *undermine* ahuecar, MECH, MECH ENG vaciar, PROD ahondar, ahuecar, vaciar; **~ out** *vt* CONST ahuecar, *undermine* excavar, MECH, MECH ENG vaciar, PROD ahondar, ahuecar, vaciar, acanalar

hollowing *n* CONST, PROD ahuecamiento *m*; **~ out** *n* CONST formación de un hueco *f*

hollowness *n* GEN vacío *m*

holmium *n* (*Ho*) CHEM holmio (*Ho*)

Holocene *n* GEOL Holoceno *m*

hologram *n* PHYS, WAVE PHYS holograma *m*

holographic: **~ exchange** *n* TELECOM central holográfica *f*; **~ scanner** *n* COMP&DP escáner holográfico *m*, explorador holográfico *m*

holography *n* COMP&DP, PHYS, RAD PHYS, SPACE, WAVE PHYS holografía *f*

holohedral: **~ class** *n* CRYSTALL clase holoédrica *f*

holosymmetric: **~ class** *n* CRYSTALL clase holosimétrica *f*

holster *n* PROD *standard of rolling mill* castillete *m*

home[1] *adv* MECH ENG a la posición cero, a la posición de salida, al destino

home[2]: **~ appliance** *n* ELEC aparato casero *m*, aparato de uso doméstico *m*, aparato doméstico *m*, enser doméstico *m*; **~ automation** *n* GAS automatización en el hogar *f*; **~ computer** *n* COMP&DP computador de casa *m* (*AmL*), computador doméstico *m* (*AmL*), computadora de casa *f* (*AmL*), computadora doméstica *f* (*AmL*), ordenador de casa *m* (*Esp*), ordenador doméstico *m* (*Esp*), TELECOM computador doméstico *m* (*AmL*), computadora doméstica *f* (*AmL*), ordenador doméstico *m* (*Esp*); **~ electric installation** *n* ELEC, ELEC ENG instalación eléctrica doméstica *f*; **~ electronic equipment** *n* ELEC ENG conjunto electrónico doméstico *m*; **~ exchange** *n* BrE (*cf host exchange AmE*) TELECOM central primaria *f*; **~ freight** *n* WATER TRANSP flete de vuelta *m*; **~ furnishings** *n pl* TEXTIL artículos para el hogar *m pl*; **~ page** *n* COMP&DP página frontal *f*, página principal *f*; **~ port** *n* WATER TRANSP puerto con base naval *m*, *of company, navy* puerto base *m*, puerto de matrícula *m*; **~ position** *n* PROD posición de cero *f*, posición de reposo *f*, posición inicial *f*; **~-produced textile** *n* TEXTIL textil de producción casera *m*; **~ signal** *n* BrE (*cf home switch AmE*) RAIL señal de entrada *f*, señal de llegada *f*, señal de parada *f*;

~ station *n* RAIL estación base *f*; **~ switch** *n* AmE (*cf home signal BrE*) RAIL *fixed equipment* señal de entrada *f*, señal de llegada *f*, señal de parada *f*; **~ textile** *n* TEXTIL textil para el hogar *m*; **~-to-work traffic** *n* TRANSP tráfico del hogar al trabajo *m*; **~ trade** *n* WATER TRANSP cabotaje *m*

Home: **~ Office socket** *n* BrE ELEC *connection* enchufe reglamentario *m*

homeward[1]: **~-bound** *adj* WATER TRANSP *ship, cargo* en viaje de regreso

homeward[2]: **~-bound** *adv* TRANSP, WATER TRANSP en viaje de regreso

homeward[3]: **~ passage** *n* WATER TRANSP travesía de regreso *f*

homilite *n* MINERAL homilita *f*

homing *n* AIR TRANSP aterrizaje guiado *m*, vuelta a la base *f*, MILIT autoguiado *m*, radiomando *m*, recalada *f*, SPACE *spacecraft* aterrizaje guiado *m*, autoguiado *m*, radiomando *m*, recalada *f*, reposición *f*, vuelo radiogoniométrico hacia la estación de destino *m*; **~ active guidance** *n* AIR TRANSP autoguía activa *f*; **~ beacon** *n* AIR TRANSP radiofaro de recalada *m*; **~ device** *n* MILIT buscador del blanco *m*, *of missile* radiocompás *m*; **~ head** *n* MILIT, SPACE *spacecraft* cabeza buscadora *f*; **~ passive guidance** *n* AIR TRANSP autoguía pasiva *f*, guía pasiva *f*; **~ radar** *n* WATER TRANSP radar con capacidad de recalada *m*, radar de recalada *m*; **~ semi-active guidance** *n* AIR TRANSP autoguía semiactiva *f*, guía semiactiva *f*

homocentric: **~ beam** *n* PHYS haz homocéntrico *m*

homocline *n* GEOL homoclinal *m*

homocyclic *adj* CHEM homocíclico

homodyne: **~ oscillator** *n* ELECTRON oscilador homodino *m*

homogeneous[1] *adj* GEN homogéneo

homogeneous[2]: **~ cladding** *n* OPT revestimiento homogéneo *m*, TELECOM chapeado homogéneo *m*; **~ deformation** *n* GEOL deformación homogénea *f*; **~ isotropic turbulence** *n* FLUID turbulencia homogénea isótropa *f*; **~ medium** *n* PHYS medio homogéneo *m*; **~ radiation** *n* PHYS radiación homogénea *f*; **~ reactor** *n* TRANSP reactor homogéneo *m*; **~ stimulus** *n* RAD PHYS estímulo homogéneo *m*

homogenization *n* HEAT, P&R homogeneización *f*

homogenizer *n* LAB homogenizador *m*

homogenizing *n* HEAT homogeneizante *m*, METALL homogenización *f*, normalización *f*, P&R homogeneizante *m*

homograph *n* GEOM homografía *f*, homógrafo *m*

homographic *adj* GEOM homográfico

homojunction *n* ELECTRON, OPT homounión *f*, TELECOM enlace homogéneo *m*

homologation *n* VEH homologación *f*

homologous[1] *adj* CHEM, METALL, PETR TECH homólogo

homologous[2]: **~ series** *n* PETR TECH serie homóloga *f*

homometric *adj* GEOL homométrico

homopolar: **~ generator** *n* ELEC, ELEC ENG generador homopolar *m*; **~ machine** *n* ELEC ENG máquina homopolar *f*

homopolymer *n* P&R homopolímero *m*

homopolymerization *n* P&R homopolimerización *f*

homopyrrole *n* CHEM homopirrol *m*

homoterephthalic *adj* CHEM homotereftálico

homothetical *adj* PRINT homotético *m*

hone[1] *n* PROD muela de esmeril *f*, piedra de aceite *f*, piedra de afilar *f*

hone[2] *vt* MECH rectificar

honestone *n* PROD barreta abrasiva *f*, piedra de aceite *f*, piedra de repasar filos *f*

honey: ~ **stone** *n* MINERAL melita *f*

honeycomb[1] *n* AIR TRANSP alveolar de nido de abejas *m*, panal de nido de abeja *m*, pantalla enderezadora de la corriente de aire *f*, panal *m*, panel de nido de abeja *m*, PRINT sopladura *f*, SPACE panal de nido de abeja *m*, *communications* panal *m*, panel de nido de abeja *m*; ~ **material** *n* PACK material con estructura de panal *m*; ~ **protection system** *n* PACK sistema de protección con un material con estructura de panal *m*; ~ **radiator** *n* AUTO radiador de panal *m*; ~ **structure** *n* AIR TRANSP estructura de nido de abejas *f*, CONST *weathering* estructura alveolada *f*, GEOL alteración alveolar *f*, estructura alveolar *f*; ~ **texture** *n* GEOL textura alveolar *f*; ~ **winding** *n* ELEC ENG devanado de panal *m*

honeycomb[2] *vt* CONST *fill with holes* hacer huecos en forma de panel alveolar

honeycombing *n* CONST concreto celular *m* (*AmL*), hormigón celular *m* (*Esp*), venteadura *f*

honing *n* MECH *machine tools* bruñido *m*, rectificado *m*; ~ **guide** *n* MECH ENG guía de alisadora *f*, guía de bruñidora *f*; ~ **machine** *n* MECH máquina de asentar *f*, máquina de rectificar y bruñir *f*, MECH ENG rectificadora y bruñidora de interiores *f*; ~ **stone** *n* MECH piedra de afilar *f*, MECH ENG pastilla abrasiva *f*, barreta abrasiva *f*, piedra de aceite para repasar filos *f*, taco abrasivo *m*, barrita para rectificar *f*

hood *n* *AmE* (*cf bonnet BrE*) AUTO capó *m*, CONST *penthouse, porch roof* marquesina *f*, *of pile* sombrerete *m*, ELEC ENG *of lamp* caperuza *f*, MECH ENG capucha *f*, capota *f*, capó *m*, casco *m*, cubierta *f*, campana *f*, PAPER campana *f*, PHOTO caperuza *f*, tapa *f*, PROD *of forge, laboratory* campana *f*, VEH *cars* capota *f*, capó *m*; ~ **catch** *n* *AmE* AUTO enganche del capó *m*, VEH enganche del capó *m*, pestillo del capó *m*; ~ **for emery wheels** *n* PROD capucha metálica *f*; ~ **lock** *n* *AmE* AUTO cierre del capó *m*, pestillo del capó *m*

HOOD *abbr* (*hierarchical object-oriented design*) COMP&DP HOOD (*diseño jerárquico orientado al objeto*)

hook[1]: **off the** ~ *adj* TELECOM descolgado

hook[2] *n* C&G gancho *m*, CONST gancho *m*, garfio *m*, *gate hinge* corchete *m*, MECH *conduitpipe* gancho *m*, MECH ENG gancho *m*, grapón *m*, corchete macho *m*, garfio *m*, garra *f*, anzuelo *m*, PETROL gancho *m*, TEXTIL gancho de aguja *m*, WATER TRANSP garrucho *m*; ~ **block** *n* MECH ENG cuadernal de gancho *m*, polea de gancho *f*; ~ **and eye** *n* MECH ENG broche y corchete *m*, gancho y ojo *m*; ~ **with eye** *n* MECH ENG gancho con ojal *m*, tensor de gancho y ojal *m*; ~ **gear valve motion** *n* HYDRAUL distribución por mecanismo de palanca *f*; ~ **and hinge** *n* CONST gancho en ángulo *m*; ~ **load** *n* PETR TECH carga en el gancho *f*; ~ **mark** *n* C&G marca de gancho *f*; ~ **on flap** *n* CONST gancho de superficie *m*; ~ **and pin wrench** *n* MECH ENG llave de dientes *f*, llave de gancho y pasador *f*, llave de tetones *f*, llave para tuercas circulares con agujeros *f*; ~ **spanner** *n* MECH ENG llave de dientes *f*, llave de gancho y pasador *f*, llave de tetones *f*, llave para tuercas circulares con agujeros *f*; ~ **to drive** *n*

CONST gancho para clavar *m*; ~ **tooth** *n* MECH ENG *saw* diente de gancho *m*

hook[3] *vt* MECH ENG encorchetar, enganchar, garfear; ~ **on** *vt* MECH ENG unir

hooked: ~ **lid** *n* PACK tapa de gancho *f*; ~ **lock** *n* PACK cerradura de gancho *f*; ~ **tooth** *n* MECH ENG *saw* diente de gancho *m*

Hooke: ~**'s joint** *n* AUTO, MECH, MECH ENG, VEH junta cardan *f*; ~**'s law** *n* CONST, PHYS ley de Hooke *f*

hoop[1] *n* CONST *for pile* anilla *f*, aro *m*, banda *f*, fleje *m*, virola *f*, zuncho *m*, MECH aro *m*, argolla *f*, MECH ENG llanta *f*, virola *f*, fleje *m*, collar *m*, zuncho *m*, aro *m*, anilla *f*, anillo *m*, argolla *f*, collarín *m*, PACK fleje *m*, PROD anilla *f*, argolla *f*, aro *m*, collar *m*, fleje *m*, *of cask* zuncho *m*; ~ **iron** *n* CONST, PACK fleje de hierro *m*

hoop[2] *vt* MECH zunchar

hooped: ~ **concrete** *n* CONST concreto zunchado *m* (*AmL*), hormigón zunchado *m* (*Esp*)

hooping *n* PACK flejado *m*, PROD acción de poner aros *f*, zunchado *m*

hooter *n* PROD avisador acústico *m*, sirena *f*

hopcalite *n* CHEM hopcalita *f*

hopeite *n* MINERAL hopeita *f*

hopper *n* AGRIC tolva *f*, MECH, MECH ENG embudo *m*, tolva *f*, PRINT pisahojas *m*, PROD tolva *f*, *blast furnace* copa *f*, TEXTIL tolva *f*, WATER TRANSP gánguil con cántara *m*; ~ **barge** *n* WATER TRANSP draga gánguil *f*, gánguil con tolvas *m*; ~ **car** *n* *AmE* (*cf hopper wagon BrE*) RAIL vagón tolva *m*; ~ **dredger** *n* WATER TRANSP draga gánguil *f*; ~ **head** *n* CONST *of downpipe* cabeza de tolva *f*; ~ **wagon** *n* *BrE* (*cf hopper car AmE*) RAIL vagón tolva *m*

hordein *n* CHEM hordeína *f*

horizon *n* GEOL horizonte *m*, PETR TECH estrato *m*, perspectiva *f*, WATER TRANSP horizonte *m*; ~ **glass** *n* INSTR *of sextant* vidrio mitad plateado y mitad claro *m*; ~ **sensor** *n* SPACE *spacecraft* sensor del horizonte *m*, visor del horizonte *m*

horizontal[1] *adj* GEOM horizontal

horizontal[2] *n* GEOM horizontal *f*; ~ **amplifier** *n* ELECTRON amplificador horizontal *m*; ~ **arm** *n* INSTR barra horizontal *f*; ~ **axis** *n* CONST, MATH eje horizontal *m*; ~ **bar** *n* TV barra horizontal *f*; ~ **base** *n* INSTR base horizontal *f*; ~ **blanking** *n* TV supresión de la imagen *f*; ~ **blanking interval** *n* TV intervalo de supresión de la imagen *m*; ~ **carburetor** *AmE*, ~ **carburettor** *BrE n* AUTO, VEH carburador horizontal *m*; ~ **cartoning machine** *n* PACK máquina horizontal de hacer envases de cartón *f*; ~ **case loader** *n* PACK cargador de cajas en horizontal *m*; ~ **centering control** *AmE*, ~ **centring control** *BrE n* TV centrado horizontal de la imagen *m*; ~ **component** *n* PHYS componente horizontal *f*; ~ **cut longwall face** *n* MINE frente de tajo largo y horizontal *m*; ~ **deflecting plate** *n* PHYS placa de desviación horizontal *f*; ~ **deflection** *n* ELECTRON deflexión horizontal *f*, desviación horizontal *f*, TV deflexión horizontal *f*; ~ **deflection coil** *n* ELEC ENG bobina de desviación horizontal *f*; ~ **deflection control** *n* TV control de desviación horizontal de la imagen *m*; ~ **deflection plate** *n* ELECTRON, TV placa de desviación horizontal *f*; ~ **displacement** *n* GEOL desplazamiento horizontal *m*, falla horizontal *f*, GEOPHYS desplazamiento horizontal *m*; ~ **drawing-process** *n* C&G estirado horizontal *m*; ~ **dynamic convergence** *n* TV convergencia dinámica horizontal *f*; ~ **elevator** *n* TRANSP elevador en horizontal *m*; ~ **engine** *n* AUTO motor horizontal *m*, VEH motor horizontal *m*, motor transversal *m*; ~ **grinding disc** *BrE*, ~ **grinding disk** *AmE* C&G disco de esmeril horizontal *m*; ~ **hold** *n* TV sintonización horizontal *f*; ~ **hold control** *n* TV control de sincronismo horizontal *m*; ~ **lock** *n* TV sincronizado horizontal *m*; ~ **milling cutter** *n* MECH ENG fresa horizontal *f*; ~ **parity** *n* COMP&DP paridad horizontal *f*, tabulación horizontal *f*; ~ **plane** *n* GEOM plano horizontal *m*; ~ **ploughed long-wall face** *n BrE* MINE frente de tajo largo y laboreo horizontal *m*; ~ **plowed long-wall face** *AmE see horizontal ploughed long-wall face BrE*; ~ **polarization** *n* ELEC ENG, PHYS, TELECOM polarización horizontal *f*; ~ **radius** *n* CONST radio horizontal *m*; ~ **resolution** *n* TV definición horizontal *f*, resolución horizontal *f*; ~ **scanning** *n* TV exploración horizontal *f*; ~ **scanning frequency** *n* TV frecuencia de exploración horizontal *f*; ~ **seismograph** *n* GEOPHYS sismógrafo horizontal *m*; ~ **separation** *n* GEOL separación horizontal *f*; ~**-shaft Pelton Wheel** *n* FUELLESS turbina de rueda Pelton con árbol horizontal *f*; ~ **situation indicator** *n* AIR TRANSP indicador de situación horizontal *m*; ~ **spacing** *n* PROD espaciado horizontal *m*; ~ **stabilizer** *n* AIR TRANSP estabilizador horizontal *m*; ~**-stabilizer center joint bar** *n AmE* (*cf horizontal-stabilizer centre fishplate BrE*) AIR TRANSP eclisa central horizontal estabilizadora *f*; ~**-stabilizer centre fishplate** *n BrE* (*cf horizontal-stabilizer center joint bar AmE*) AIR TRANSP eclisa central horizontal estabilizadora *f*; ~ **stack** *n* PETROL pila horizontal *f*; ~ **strut** *n* AIR TRANSP puntal horizontal *m*; ~ **sweep** *n* TV barrido de izquierda a derecha *m*, barrido horizontal *m*; ~ **sync** *n* TV sincronización de línea *f* (*Esp*), sincronización horizontal *f* (*AmL*); ~ **synchronization** *n* TV sincronización de línea *f* (*Esp*), sincronización horizontal *f* (*AmL*); ~ **tabulation** *n* (*HT*) COMP&DP tabulación horizontal *f*; ~**-tangent screw** *n* INSTR tornillo de precisión horizontal *m*; ~ **and top loader cartoner** *n* PACK sistema de llenado de cajas de cartón por los laterales y por la parte superior *m*; ~ **travel** *n* PROD carrera horizontal *f*; ~**-and-vertical bar of flight direction** *n* AIR TRANSP barra horizontal y vertical de la dirección de vuelo *f*; ~ **and vertical dimensioning** *n* PROD dimensionamiento horizontal y vertical *m*; ~ **and vertical wrapping machine** *n* PACK máquina de envolver en horizontal y vertical *f*; ~ **wind shear** *n* AIR TRANSP cortador de viento horizontal *m*

horizontal[3]: **in** ~ **layers** *phr* FLUID en capas horizontales

horn *n* ACOUST bocina *f*, trompa acústica *f*, AIR TRANSP cuerno *m*, AUTO bocina *f*, claxon *m*, avisador acústico *m*, MINE brazo *m* (*AmL*), tentáculo *m* (*Esp*), SPACE *communications* balancín *m*, palanquita *f*, TRANSP claxon *m*, sirena *f*, VEH avisador acústico *m*, bocina *f*, claxon *m*, WATER TRANSP *navigation* boca de un pico de cangrejo *f*, bocina de niebla *f*; ~ **antenna** *n* SPACE *communications* antena de bocina *f*; ~ **balance** *n* AIR TRANSP compensador de cuerno *m*, compensador de herradura *m*; ~ **gate** *n* PROD *founding* canal de colada en fuente *m*; ~ **lead** *n* CHEM fosgenita *f*, MINERAL fosgenita *f*, plomo córneo *m*; ~ **loudspeaker** *n* ACOUST altavoz de bocina *m*; ~ **socket** *n* MINE

campana de pesca *f* (*Esp*), pescaherramientas abocinado *m* (*AmL*)

hornbeam *n* PAPER carpe *m*

hornblende *n* MINERAL hornblenda *f*

hornblendite *n* PETROL hornblendita *f*

hornfels *n* GEOL corneana *f*, cornubianita *f*, PETROL corneana *f*

horological: ~ **instrument** *n* INSTR instrumento de horológico *m* (*AmL*), instrumento de relojería *m* (*Esp*)

horse *n* C&G caballo *m*, macho *m*, MINE colapso *m*, cuña de tierra *f*, desplome que obstruye una galería *m*, inclusión estéril *f*, nervio *m*, PROD *in blast furnace* lobo *m*, *loam moulding* molde para chapas de figura *m*, *trestle* caballete *m*

Horsehead: ~ **nebula** *n* SPACE nebulosa del Caballete *f*

horsepower *n* (*hp*) AUTO, MECH ENG caballaje *m* (*AmL*), caballo de vapor *m* (*Esp*) (*CV*), caballos en *pl*, cabria de caballo *f*, potencia en caballos de vapor *f* (*potencia en CV*); ~ **hour** *n* MECH ENG caballaje hora *m*, caballos hora *m pl*, potencia hora *f*

horseshoe: ~ **arch** *n* CONST *structure* arco en forma de herradura *m*; ~**-fired furnace** *n* C&G horno con puertos traseros *m*; ~ **foot** *n* LAB *of liquids* pie de herradura *m* (*Esp*), pie en "U" *m* (*Esp*), pie en forma de herradura *m* (*AmL*); ~ **lifebuoy** *n* WATER TRANSP *safety* salvavidas de herradura *m*; ~ **magnet** *n* ELEC *magnetism* electroimán en herradura *m*, imán en herradura *m*, MECH ENG, PHYS imán en herradura *m*; ~ **main** *n* PROD *blast furnace* conducto circular del viento *m*, morcilla *f*; ~ **mount** *n* INSTR montaje en herradura *m*, soporte en herradura *m*; ~ **mounting** *n* INSTR montaje en herradura *m*, soporte en herradura *m*; ~ **section** *n* MECH ENG sección de herradura *f*

horticultural: ~ **cast glass** *n* C&G vidrio vaciado para horticultura *m*; ~ **glass** *n* C&G vidrio para horticultura *m*

hose *n* CONST, LAB, MECH, MECH ENG manguera *f*, PROD, SPACE *spacecraft* manguera *f*, tubo flexible *m*; ~ **clamp** *n* MECH, MECH ENG abrazadera de manguera *f*; ~ **clip** *n* MECH ENG grapa de manguera *f*; ~ **connection** *n* MECH ENG conexión de manguera *f*; ~ **coupler** *n* CONST acoplamiento de manguera *m*; ~ **coupling** *n* PROD conexión de tubería flexible *f*; ~ **hanger** *n* PROD soporte colgante de manguera *m*; ~ **knitting** *n* TEXTIL tricotado de medias *m*; ~ **nozzle** *n* MECH ENG boquilla de manguera *f*; ~ **reel** *n* PROD carretel de mangueras *m*

hosepipe *n* CONST, MECH ENG manguera *f*

hosiery *n* TEXTIL calcetería y medias *f pl*

hospital: ~ **ship** *n* WATER TRANSP buque hospital *m*

host[1] *adj* COMP&DP central, principal

host[2] *n* COMP&DP anfitrión *m*; ~ **computer** *n* COMP&DP computador anfitrión *m* (*AmL*), computador central *m* (*AmL*), computador principal *m* (*AmL*), computadora anfitrión *f* (*AmL*), computadora central *f* (*AmL*), computadora principal *f* (*AmL*), ordenador anfitrión *m* (*Esp*), ordenador central *m* (*Esp*), ordenador principal *m* (*Esp*); ~ **exchange** *n AmE* (*cf home exchange BrE*) TELECOM central primaria *f*; ~ **indexing** *n* AGRIC prueba de huésped *f*; ~ **plant** *n* AGRIC planta huésped *f*; ~ **rock** *n* GEOL roca almacén *f*

hostile: ~ **environment** *n* RAD PHYS entorno hostil *m*

hot[1]: ~**-drawn** *adj* THERMO estirado en caliente, termoestirado; ~**-forged** *adj* MECH ENG, PROD,

THERMO forjado en caliente; **~-rolled** *adj* MECH, PROD, THERMO laminado en caliente; **~-smoked** *adj* FOOD ahumado en caliente; **~-stamped** *adj* PRINT estampado en caliente

hot²: ~ **air blower** *n* HEAT, LAB soplador de aire caliente *m*; ~ **air duct** *n* AIR TRANSP conducto de aire caliente *m*; **~-air engine** *n* TRANSP motor de aire caliente *m*; **~-air finish** *n* COATINGS acabado por aire caliente *m*; ~ **air gallery** *n* AIR TRANSP colector de aire caliente *m*, galería de aire caliente *f*; ~ **air heater** *n* AGRIC quemador de aire caliente *m*; **~-air heater** *n* HEAT ENG calentador por aire caliente *m*; ~ **air heating system** *n* HEAT sistema de calefacción por aire caliente *m*; **~-air impingement dryer** *n* TEXTIL secadora por choque de aire caliente *f*; ~ **air radiation heating system** *n* SAFE sistema de calefacción por aire caliente *m*; ~ **air sizing machine** *n* TEXTIL encoladora por aire caliente *f*; ~ **air stream** *n* TEXTIL corriente de aire caliente *f*; ~ **air valve** *n* AIR TRANSP válvula de aire caliente *f*; ~ **backup** *n* PROD reserva de calor *f*; ~ **blade sealing** *n* PACK sellado mediante una cuchilla caliente *m*, termoselladora de cuchilla en caliente *f*; ~ **blast furnace** *n* PROD horno con inyección de aire caliente *m*; ~ **bonding** *n* THERMO termoadhesión *f*; ~ **box** *n* RAIL caja de grasa recalentada *f*; ~ **box detector** *n* RAIL detector de recalentamiento de la caja de grasa *m*; **~, bright and radiating nebula** *n* SPACE *type HII* nebulosa radiante, brillante y caliente *f*; **~-bulb engine** *n* AUTO motor de bulbo incandescente *m*; ~ **calendering** *n* PAPER calandrado en caliente *m*; ~ **camera** *n* TV cámara tomavistas con corriente *f*; ~ **carrier diode** *n* ELECTRON diodo portador con gran actividad *m*; ~ **cathode** *n* ELEC ENG cátodo emisor *m*; **~-cathode gas tube** *n* ELECTRON tubo de gas de cátodo incandescente *m*; ~ **cathode tube** *n* ELECTRON tubo de cátodo incandescente *m*; ~ **coating shop** *n* COATINGS taller de revestimientos en caliente *m*; ~ **creep** *n* THERMO fluencia en caliente *f*, termodeformación en caliente *f*; ~ **curing** *n* THERMO termocurado *m*; **~-cycle rotor wing** *n* AIR TRANSP, TRANSP ala de rotor de ciclo caliente *f*; ~ **cyclone** *n* COAL ciclón de alta temperatura *m*; **~-dimpling process** *n* MECH ENG proceso de abollado en caliente *m*; ~ **dip galvanised coating** *n* COATINGS galvanizado en caliente *m*; ~ **dip galvanizing** *n* COATINGS galvanizado *m*; **~-dip metal coating** *n* COATINGS revestimiento metálico por inmersión en baño caliente *m*, revestimiento metálico por inmersión en baño de metal húmedo *m*; ~ **dipping** *n* PACK inmersión en caliente *f*; ~ **drawing** *n* THERMO estirado en caliente *m*, termoestirado *m*; ~ **end coating** *n* C&G recubrimiento en el lado caliente *m*; ~ **filling** *n* PACK llenado en caliente *m*; ~ **foil** *n* PRINT lámina caliente *f*; ~ **foil carton coder** *n* PACK codificador de hojas de cajas de cartón en caliente *m*; ~ **forging** *n* MECH ENG, PROD forja en caliente *f*, forjadura en caliente *f*, THERMO forja en caliente *f*, forjadura en caliente *f*, pieza estampada en caliente *f*; ~ **forging die** *n* MECH ENG estampa de forjado en caliente *f*, troquel de forjado en caliente *m*; ~ **forming** *n* MECH, PROD conformación en caliente *f*; ~ **gas bypass regulator** *n* REFRIG regulador de derivación de gases calientes *m*; ~ **gas defrosting** *n* REFRIG desescarche por gas caliente *m*; ~ **glass wire cutting** *n* C&G corte de vidrio caliente con alambre

m; ~ **gluing** *n* PACK encolado en caliente *m*, engomado en caliente *m*; ~ **head** *n* CINEMAT cabeza caliente *f*; ~ **junction** *n* ELEC *thermocouple* unión caliente *f*, PROD unión en caliente *f*; ~ **leg** *n* NUCL rama caliente *f*; ~ **leg LOCA** *n* NUCL LOCA de rotura de la rama caliente *m*; **~-melt adhesive** *n* PACK adhesivo a base de fusiones en caliente *m*; **~-melt coated paper** *n* PAPER papel revestido con fusiones en caliente *m*; **~-melt coating** *n* PAPER revestido mediante fusiones en caliente *m*; ~ **mix** *n* CONST mezcla en caliente *f*; ~ **mold** *AmE*, ~ **mould** *BrE* *n* C&G molde caliente *m*; ~ **pass** *n* PETROL pasada en caliente *f*; ~ **pressing** *n* METALL compresión en caliente *f*, PACK prensado en caliente *m*; ~ **ration** *n* AGRIC *feedlot* ración de terminación *f*; ~ **refueling** *AmE*, ~ **refuelling** *BrE* *n* NUCL carga de combustible en condiciones de operación *f*; ~ **rolling** *n* THERMO laminado en caliente *m*; ~ **runner manifold** *n* MECH ENG *injection mould* colector de bebedero caliente *m*, colector de canal de colada caliente *m*, colector de piquera caliente *m*, colector de vaciadero caliente *m*, distribuidor de bebedero caliente *m*, distribuidor de canal de colada caliente *m*, distribuidor de piquera caliente *m*, distribuidor de vaciadero caliente *m*; ~ **runner system** *n* MECH ENG *injection mould* sistema de vaciadero caliente *m*; ~ **section** *n* AIR TRANSP *of engine* sección caliente *f*; ~ **set** *n* PROD aglomeración en caliente *f*, tajadera *f*; **~-setting adhesive** *n* P&R, PACK adhesivo de fraguado en caliente *m*, adhesivo termoendurecible *m*; **~-setting glue** *n* PACK aglomeración de goma en caliente *f*; ~ **shoe flash contact** *n* PHOTO zapata de contacto para flash *f*; ~ **shot wind tunnel** *n* AIR TRANSP túnel hipersónico de arco *m*; ~ **shrink fit** *n* MECH ENG ajustado en caliente *m*; ~ **shutdown** *n* NUCL parada caliente *f*; ~ **spark plug** *n* AUTO bujía caliente *f*; ~ **spot** *n* AGRIC zona de la parcela que florece antes *f*, C&G punto caliente *m*, PHOTO mancha por luz excesiva *f*; ~ **spring water** *n* OCEAN agua termal *f*; ~ **springs** *n* OCEAN termas *f pl*; ~ **sprue brushing** *n* MECH ENG cepillado de bebedero caliente *m*, cepillado de rebabas calientes *m*; ~ **stamp imprint** *n* PRINT estampado en caliente *m*; ~ **stamping** *n* PACK embutido en caliente *m*, PRINT estampar en caliente *m*; ~ **stamping foil** *n* PACK hoja para embutir en caliente *f*; ~ **stand-by** *n* SPACE *spacecraft* reserva en caliente *f*; ~ **stand-by system** *n* TELECOM sistema auxiliar para urgencias *m*; ~ **start** *n* AIR TRANSP arranque en caliente *m*, puesta en marcha en caliente *f*; ~ **strength** *n* MECH ENG fuerza térmica *f*, THERMO resistencia al calor *f*; ~ **tear** *n* MECH *duplicate* grieta *f*; ~ **transfer label** *n* PACK etiqueta termotransferible *f*; ~ **water** *n* HEAT ENG, THERMO agua caliente *f*; ~ **water boiler** *n* MECH ENG, THERMO caldera de agua caliente *f*; ~ **water bottle** *n* HEAT bolsa de agua caliente *f*; ~ **water heater** *n* MECH ENG calentador de agua *m*, calentador de agua caliente *m*; ~ **water heating system** *n* HEAT sistema de calefacción por agua caliente *m*; ~ **water jet** *n* GEOPHYS chorro de agua caliente *m*; ~ **water tank** *n* HEAT depósito de agua caliente *m*, tanque de agua caliente *m*; **~-water treatment** *n* AGRIC hidrotermoterapia *f*; **~-water washing** *n* MAR POLL lavado con agua caliente *m*; **~-wire ammeter** *n* ELEC, ELEC ENG amperímetro de alambre caliente *m*, amperímetro térmico *m*, INSTR amperímetro térmico *m*; ~ **wire anemometer** *n* METEO, PHYS anemómetro de hilo electrocalentado *m*; **~-wire microphone** *n* ACOUST micrófono térmico *m*; **~-wire relay** *n* ELEC relé de hilo caliente *m*; **~ wire voltmeter** *n* ELEC voltímetro de hilo caliente *m*, voltímetro térmico *m*; **~-wire wattmeter** *n* ELEC vatímetro de hilo caliente *m*, vatímetro térmico *m*; **~ wire-drawing die** *n* MECH ENG matriz de trefilar en caliente *f*; **~ working** *n* C&G trabajo en caliente *m*, METALL maquinado en caliente *m*, trabajo en caliente *m*

hot³: **~-bond** *vt* THERMO termoadherir; **~-draw** *vt* THERMO estirar en caliente, termoestirar; **~-forge** *vt* MECH ENG, PROD, THERMO forjar en caliente; **~-rivet** *vt* MECH ENG remachar en caliente; **~ roll** *vt* THERMO laminar en caliente *vt*

Hotchkiss: **~ drive** *n* VEH transmisión Hotchkiss *f*

hotel: **~ glassware** *n* C&G cristalería para hoteles *f*; **~ platform** *n* PETR TECH plataforma con alojamiento *f*; **~ rig** *n* PETR TECH plataforma-hotel *f*

hothouse *n* AGRIC invernadero *m*

hotplate *n* LAB parrilla *f* (*AmL*), placa *f* (*Esp*)

hotted: **~-up** *adj AmE* (*cf souped-up BrE*) VEH con potencia aumentada, motor preparado *m*, recalentado

Houdini: **~ eye-light** *n* ELEC *lighting* luz de ojo de Houdini *f*

hound *n* WATER TRANSP *mast* tamborete racamento *m*, zuncho de arraigada de los obenques *m*

hour *n* PHYS hora *f*; **~ circle** *n* METR círculo de declinación *m*; **~ glass** *n* C&G reloj de arena *m*; **~ of green signal indication** *n* TRANSP indicación de hora de señal verde *f*; **~ hand** *n* METR *of clock, watch* manecilla horaria *f*

hourglass: **~ calipers** *AmE*, **~ callipers** *BrE* *n* MECH ENG calibre de reloj de arena *m*, grapas de reloj de arena *f pl*; **~ screw** *n* PROD tornillo de filetes convergentes *m*, tornillo globoide *m*, tornillo glóbico *m*; **~ screw gear** *n* PROD engranaje globoide *m*; **~ spring** *n* PROD muelle de somier *m*, resorte de somier *m*

hourly: **~ output** *n* PACK producción horaria *f*, rendimiento horario *m*

house¹ *n* CONST *of crane* caseta *f*; **~ bogie** *n BrE* (*cf house trailer AmE*) VEH remolque de cabina *m*; **~ builder** *n* CONST aparejador *m* (*Esp*), constructor *m* (*AmL*), contratista *m*, maestro de obras *m* (*AmL*); **~ corrections** *n* PRINT primera corrección *f*; **~ flag** *n* WATER TRANSP *merchant navy* bandera de la naviera *f*; **~ organ** *n* PRINT publicación interna *f*; **~ paint** *n* COLOUR, CONST pintura para viviendas *f*, P&R pintura para casas *f*; **~ style** *n* PRINT estilo propio *m*; **~ trailer** *n AmE* (*cf house bogie BrE*) VEH remolque de cabina *m*; **~ wiring switch** *n* ELEC interruptor de alambre casero *m*

house² *vt* CONST *carpentry* empotrar, encajar

housed: **~ joint** *n* CONST ensambladura empotrada *f*; **~ string** *n* CONST *stair building* zanca a la francesa *f*

household: **~ coal** *n* COAL carbón doméstico *m*; **~ frozen-food storage cabinet** *n* MECH ENG, REFRIG armario casero de almacenaje de comestibles congelados *m*; **~ porcelain** *n* C&G loza de casa *f*; **~ refrigerator** *n* REFRIG, THERMO frigorífico doméstico *m*; **~ waste** *n* POLL desperdicios domésticos *m pl*, RECYCL basura casera *f*, desperdicios domésticos *m pl*, residuos domésticos *m pl*

housekeeping *n* COMP&DP preparación previa *f*, tareas de mantenimiento *f pl*, QUALITY tareas de manteni-

miento *f pl*, SPACE preparación previa *f*, *spacecraft* datos de abordos *m pl*; **~ operation** *n* COMP&DP operación de servicio *f*, operación inicial *f*, operación preparatoria *f*; **~ telemetry** *n* QUALITY telemantenimiento *m*, SPACE *spacecraft* telemetría de datos de abordo *f*, telemetría preparatoria *f*

housing *n* AUTO alojamiento *m*, CONST *putting under cover* envoltura *f*, revestimiento *m*, empotramiento *m*, FUELLESS cuadro *m*, MECH alojamiento *m*, MECH ENG *engineering* bastidor *m*, cárter *m*, cubierta protectora *f*, montante *m*, castillete *m*, caja *f*, alojamiento *m*, columna *f*, VEH alojamiento *m*; **~ lock** *n* CINEMAT bloqueo de la caja *m*

hover: **~ control** *n* AIR TRANSP *helicopter* control de vuelo estacionario *m*; **~ flight coupler** *n* AIR TRANSP *helicopter* acoplador de vuelo estacionario *m*; **~ height** *n* TRANSP altura de levitación *f*, altura en suspenso *f*; **~ pallet** *n* TRANSP plataforma levitante *f*

hovercraft *n* AIR TRANSP aerodeslizador *m*, TRANSP, WATER TRANSP aerodeslizador *m*, hovercraft *m*; **~ train** *n* TRANSP tren aerodeslizador *m*

hovering *n* AIR TRANSP *helicopter* vuelo estacionario *m*; **~ capability** *n* AIR TRANSP *helicopter* capacidad de vuelo estacionario *f*; **~ craft** *n* TRANSP embarcación neumática *f*

hoverport *n* WATER TRANSP puerto de aerodeslizadores *m*

hovertrain *n* RAIL, TRANSP aerotren *m*

howitzer *n* MILIT obús *m*

howler *n* TELECOM zumbador *m*

howling *n* ACOUST aullido *m*

hp *abbr* (*horsepower*) AUTO, MECH ENG CV (*caballo de vapor*)

HP: **~ shoe** *n* PROD zapata de AP *f*

HPA *abbr* (*higher-order path adaptation*) TELECOM adaptación de trayecto de orden superior *f*

HPC *abbr* (*higher-order path connection*) TELECOM conexión de trayecto de orden superior *f*

HPLC *abbr* (*high-pressure liquid chromatography*) CHEM, FOOD, LAB CLAP (*cromatografía líquida a alta presión*)

HPT *abbr* (*higher-order path termination*) TELECOM terminación de trayecto de orden superior *f*

HR *abbr* COMP&DP (*high resolution*) alta resolución *f*, TELECOM (*high resistance*) alta resistencia *f*

H-rate *n* PRINT porcentaje horizontal *m*

HSS: **~ small tools** *n* (*high-speed steel small tools*) MECH ENG herramientas pequeñas de acero de alta velocidad *f pl*, herramientas pequeñas de acero de corte rápido *f pl*

HT¹ *abbr* (*horizontal tabulation*) COMP&DP tabulación horizontal *f*

HT²: **~ supply** *n* ELEC, ELEC ENG fuente de alta tensión *f*

html *abbr* (*hypertext markup language*) COMP&DP lenguaje html *m*

hub *n* AIR TRANSP *helicopter* cabeza *f*, cubo *m*, plato de cubierta del cubo *m*, COMP&DP *disk* anillo central *m*, centro *m*, cubo *m*, concentrador *m*, MECH *duplicate* núcleo *m*, MINE extracción del mineral *f* (*AmL*), extracción en cubos *f* (*Esp*), mira *f*, vértice *m*, TV mira de nivelación *f*, VEH buje *m*; **~ cover plate** *n* AIR TRANSP placa que cubre el cubo *f*; **~ extractor** *n* MECH ENG extractor de cubos *m*, sacacubos *m*; **~ flange** *n* AUTO pestaña del cubo *f*, reborde del tapacubo *m*; **~-flapping stiffness** *n* AIR TRANSP *helicopter* rigidez de batimiento del cubo *f*; **~ grip** *n*

MECH ENG empuñacubos *m*, empuñadura de cubos *f*; ~ **polling** *n* COMP&DP centro de elección *m*, computador híbrido *m* (*AmL*), computadora híbrida *f* (*AmL*), cubo de elección *m*, ordenador híbrido *m* (*Esp*), sondeo del concentrador *m*; ~ **puller** *n* MECH sacacubos *m*; ~ **spacer** *n* AIR TRANSP *helicopter* separador del cubo *m*; ~ **tilt stop** *n* AIR TRANSP *helicopter* tope de inclinación del cubo *m*; ~~**-type flange** *n* MECH ENG *pipe fitting* brida de campana *f*; ~~**-type spindle** *n* MECH ENG *machine tools* eje de campana *m*, eje de cubo *m*

Hubble's: ~ **constant** *n* SPACE *communications* constante de Hubble *f*

hubcap *n* AUTO tapacubo *m*, VEH tapa de buje *f*, tapacubos *m*

hubnerite *n* MINERAL hubnerita *f*

HUD *abbr* (*head-up display*) INSTR HUD (*imagen vertical*), SPACE *craft* representación cabeza arriba *f*

hue *n* PHOTO tono *m*, PRINT tono *m*, matiz *m*; ~ **consistency** *n* PRINT uniformidad del tono *f*; ~ **control** *n* TV control de tonalidad *m*

hulk *n* WATER TRANSP pontón *m*

hull[1]: ~~**-borne** *adj* TRANSP semisumergible

hull[2] *n* AIR TRANSP, WATER casco *m*, WATER TRANSP *shipbuilding* casco *m*, plataforma *f*; ~ **drawing** *n* WATER TRANSP *shipbuilding* plano básico del casco *m*; ~ **girder** *n* WATER TRANSP *shipbuilding* buque viga *m*, viga-casco *f*; ~ **insurance** *n* WATER TRANSP seguro del casco *m*; ~~**-less barley** *n* AGRIC cebada de grano desnudo *f*; ~ **resistance** *n* WATER TRANSP *shipbuilding* resistencia del casco *f*; ~ **step** *n* AIR TRANSP rediente del casco *m*

hulled: ~ **rice** *n* AGRIC, FOOD arroz descascarillado *m*; ~ **seed** *n* AGRIC semilla descascarada *f*

huller *n* AGRIC descascaradora *f*

hum *n* ACOUST, AIR TRANSP, ELEC ENG zumbido *m*; ~ **bar** *n* TV interferencia de imagen por alimentación de la red *f*; ~~**-bucking coil** *n* CINEMAT bobina inductora de sonido *f*, bobina inductora de zumbido *f*, ELEC ENG bobina correctora de zumbido *f*, TV bobina correctora de zumbido *f*, bobina inductora de sonido *f*, bobina inductora de zumbido *f*; ~ **voltage** *n* ELEC ENG voltaje con zumbido *m*, voltaje zumbador *m*

human: ~ **error** *n* QUALITY, SAFE error humano *m*; ~ **error probability** *n* QUALITY probabilidad de error humano *f*; ~ **exposure to mechanical vibrations** *n* SAFE exposición humana a vibraciones mecánicas *f*; ~ **failure** *n* QUALITY falla humana *f*; ~ **failure cause** *n* QUALITY motivo de falla humana *m* (*AmL*), motivo de fallo humano *m* (*Esp*); ~ **reliability** *n* QUALITY fiabilidad humana *f*

humble: ~ **hook** *n* MINE *overwind gear* mantillo *m*

humboldtite *n* MINERAL humboldita *f*

humboldtine *n* MINERAL humboldtina *f*

humectant *n* CHEM humectante *m*

humic: ~ **acid** *n* CHEM ácido húmico *m*

humid: ~ **air** *n* METEO aire húmedo *m*; ~ **volume** *n* REFRIG volumen específico del aire húmedo *m*

humidification *n* THERMO humectación *f*, humidificación *f*

humidifier *n* AIR TRANSP humedecedor *m*, REFRIG humidificador *m*, THERMO cámara de reacondicionado *f*, humectador *m*, humidificador *m*

humidify *vt* CHEM humectar, FOOD humedecer, MAR POLL, MECH ENG humectar, PHYS humedecer, REFRIG humectar, humidificar, THERMO humectar, humedecer, humidificar

humidistat *n* REFRIG, THERMO higrostato *m*, humidistato *m*

humidity[1]: ~~**-resistant** *adj* THERMO higrorresistente

humidity[2] *n* GEN humedad *f*; ~ **absorber** *n* PACK absorbente de humedad *m*; ~ **of the air** *n* PACK humedad del aire *f*, THERMO humedad atmosférica *f*, humedad del aire *f*; ~ **indicator** *n* PACK indicador de humedad *m*; ~ **loss** *n* THERMO *bit* pérdida de humedad *f*; ~ **measurement** *n* METEO medición de la humedad *f*, WATER TRANSP higrometría *f*, medición de la humedad *f*

humite *n* MINERAL humita *f*

hummocked: ~ **ice** *n* OCEAN hielo en montículos *m*

hummocks *n pl* OCEAN montículos *m pl*, moqotes *m pl*

hummocky: ~ **ice** *n* OCEAN hielo en montículos *m*

hump: ~ **shunting** *n* RAIL clasificación por el método del lomo de asno *f*

humulene *n* CHEM humuleno *m*

humus *n* CHEM, COAL humus *m*, mantillo *m*, CONST humus *m*, MINE humus *m*, mantillo *m*; ~ **tank** *n* WATER tanque para cieno húmico *m*

Hund: ~ **rules** *n pl* PHYS reglas de Hund *f pl*

hundred: ~ **year storm** *phr* PETR TECH *offshore* tormenta más fuerte de los últimos 100 años

hundredweight *n BrE* METR quintal *m*

hungry[1] *adj* MINE de aspecto inútil, estéril, pobre

hungry[2]: ~ **surface** *n* PRINT superficie poco curtida *f*

hunting *n* AIR TRANSP *of helicopter rotor blade* variación *f*, penduleo *m*, funcionamiento irregular *m*, oscilación *f*, ELEC *machines* oscilaciones pendulares *f pl*, penduleo *m*, vaivén *m*, ELEC ENG oscilación *f*, *synchronous motor* variación de la velocidad corriente y tensión *f*, REFRIG fluctuación *f*, oscilación periódica anormal *f*; ~ **blade** *n* AIR TRANSP *helicopter* pala de funcionamiento irregular *f*, pala oscilante *f*

hureaulite *n* MINERAL hureaulita *f*

hurley *n* MINE vagoneta *f*

hurricane *n* METEO huracán *m*; ~ **lamp** *n* CONST farol de intemperie *m*, lámpara con costados de vidrio para proteger la llama del viento *f*, WATER TRANSP lámpara de seguridad *f*

husk[1] *n* AGRIC, FOOD chala *f*, espata *f*

husk[2] *vt* AGRIC descascarar, despellejar, pelar, FOOD descascarar, deshollejar, despellejar, pelar

husked[1] *adj* AGRIC despellejado, desvainado, FOOD despellejado, desvainado, pelado

husked[2]: ~ **rice** *n* AGRIC, FOOD arroz descascarado *m*

hutch *n* MINE artesa para lavado *f*, concentrado *m*, vagoneta *f*

Huygens': ~ **eyepiece** *n* PHYS ocular de Huygens *m*; ~ **principle** *n* PHYS principio de Huygens *m*; ~ **theory** *n* RAD PHYS teoría de Huygen *f*

hW *abbr* (*hectowatt*) ELEC, ELEC ENG, METR hW (*hectovatio*)

HWOST *abbr* (*high-water ordinary spring tide*) FUEL-LESS línea alta habitual de la marea viva *f*

hyacinth *n* MINERAL jacinto *m*

hyaline *adj* GEOL vítreo

hyalite *n* MINERAL hialita *f*, ópalo incoloro *m*

hyaloclastic: ~ **rock** *n* GEOL roca hialoclástica *f*

hyaloclastite *n* GEOL hialoclastita *f*

hyalogen *n* CHEM hialógeno *m*

hyalophane *n* MINERAL hialófana *f*

hybrid: ~ **bus** *n* TRANSP autobús mixto *m* (*Esp*), bus híbrido *m* (*AmL*), ómnibus híbrido *m* (*AmL*); ~ **call processor** *n* TELECOM procesador de llamadas híbrido *m*; ~ **circuit** *n* ELECTRON, PHYS circuito híbrido *m*; ~ **computer** *n* COMP&DP computador híbrido *m* (*AmL*), computadora híbrida *f* (*AmL*), ordenador híbrido *m* (*Esp*); ~ **corn** *n AmE* (*cf hybrid maize BrE*) AGRIC maíz híbrido *m*; ~ **electromagnetic wave** *n* ELEC *motor* onda electromagnética compuesta híbrida *f*, onda electromagnética híbrida *f*; ~ **engine** *n* TRANSP motor híbrido *m*; ~ **foil craft** *n* TRANSP barco de aleta hidrodinámica sustentadora mixta *m*; ~ **integrated circuit** *n* ELECTRON, TELECOM circuito integrado híbrido *m*; ~ **junction** *n* ELECTRON conexión híbrida *f*; ~ **maize** *n BrE* (*cf hybrid corn AmE*) AGRIC maíz híbrido *m*; ~ **microcircuit** *n* ELECTRON microcircuito híbrido *m*; ~ **mode** *n* OPT, TELECOM modo híbrido *m*; ~ **orbital** *n* CHEM *atomic* orbital híbrido *m*; ~ **parameter** *n* ELECTRON parámetro híbrido *m*; ~ **platform** *n* PETR TECH plataforma híbrida *f*; ~ **propellent** *n* SPACE propulsor híbrido *m*, propulsor mixto *m*; ~ **propulsion** *n* TRANSP propulsión híbrida *f*; ~ **scale** *n* PETROL escala híbrida *f*; ~ **switch** *n* TELECOM conmutador híbrido *m*; ~ **system** *n* TELECOM, TRANSP sistema híbrido *m*; ~ **vehicle** *n* TRANSP vehículo híbrido *m*

hybridization *n* CHEM *of atomic orbitals* hibridación *f*
hydantoic: ~ **acid** *n* CHEM ácido hidantoico *m*
hydantoin *n* CHEM hidantoina *f*
hydracid *n* CHEM hidrácido *m*
hydracrylic: ~ **acid** *n* CHEM ácido hidracrílico *m*
hydrant *n* WATER boca de riego *f*, hidrante *m*, toma de agua *f*; ~ **system** *n* PETR TECH, SAFE hidrante para repostaje *m*, sistema hidrante contra incendio *m*
hydrargillite *n* MINERAL hidrargilita *f*
hydrastic *adj* CHEM hidrástico
hydrastine *n* CHEM hidrastina *f*
hydrate[1] *n* CHEM hidrato *m*
hydrate[2] *vt* CHEM, GEOL hidratar
hydrated[1] *adj* CHEM, GEOL hidratado
hydrated[2]: ~ **layer** *n* C&G capa hidratada *f*
hydration *n* CHEM hidratación *f*, humidificación *f*, CONST, GEOL hidratación *f*
hydratropic *adj* CHEM hidratrópico
hydraucone *n* WATER cono hidráulico *m*
hydraulic[1] *adj* GEN hidráulico
hydraulic[2]: ~ **accumulator** *n* AIR TRANSP, MECH ENG, P&R acumulador hidráulico *m*; ~ **actuating cylinder** *n* HYDRAUL cilindro de funcionamiento hidráulico *m*; ~ **battery** *n* AIR TRANSP batería hidráulica *f*; ~ **bottom heave** *n* COAL hinchamiento hidráulico *m*; ~ **brake** *n* VEH freno hidráulico *m*; ~ **brake servo** *n* AUTO servofreno hidráulico *m*; ~ **brake system** *n* MECH ENG sistema de freno hidráulico *m*; ~-**bulging die** *n pl* MECH ENG estampa para indentar hidráulica *f*, matrices de bombear hidráulicas *f pl*, matrices de pandear hidráulicas *f pl*; ~ **characteristics** *n pl* HYDROL características hidráulicas *f pl*; ~ **charging** *n* HYDRAUL carga hidráulica *f*; ~ **circulation system** *n* PETR TECH sistema circulante hidráulico *m*; ~ **clamping** *n* MECH ENG apriete hidráulico *m*, fijación hidráulica *f*, sujeción hidráulica *f*; ~ **classification** *n* COAL clasificación hidráulica *f*; ~ **clutch** *n* HYDRAUL embrague hidráulico *m*; ~ **compensator** *n* PETR TECH compensador hidráulico *m*; ~ **conductivity** *n* FUELLESS, HYDROL conductividad hidráulica *f*; ~ **control system** *n*

AUTO sistema de control hidráulico *m*; ~ **conveyor ram** *n* COAL, CONST, HYDRAUL, WATER ariete hidráulico *m*; ~ **copy mill** *n* MECH ENG fresadora copiadora hidráulica *f*; ~ **cylinder** *n* MECH ENG cilindro hidráulico *m*; ~ **detector** *n* TRANSP detector hidráulico *m*; ~ **diffusivity** *n* HYDROL difusibilidad hidráulica *f*; ~ **discontinuity** *n* HYDROL discontinuidad hidráulica *f*; ~ **dredge** *n* WATER draga aspirante *f*; ~ **drive** *n* MECH ENG accionamiento hidráulico *m*, transmisión hidráulica *f*; ~ **efficiency** *n* FUELLESS rendimiento hidráulico *m*, HYDROL eficiencia hidráulica *f*; ~ **equipment** *n* MECH ENG equipo hidráulico *m*; ~ **failure** *n* SAFE falla hidráulica *f*; ~ **fitting** *n* HYDRAUL componente para máquina hidráulica *m*; ~ **fluid** *n* HYDRAUL líquido para maquinaria hidráulica *m*; ~ **fluid power** *n* MECH ENG fuerza del líquido hidráulico *f*, potencia de fluido hidráulico *f*; ~ **fluid reservoir** *n* MECH ENG depósito de fluido hidráulico *m*, depósito de líquido hidráulico *m*, recipiente de fluido hidráulico *m*, tanque de fluido hidráulico *m*, tanque de líquido hidráulico *m*; ~ **fracturing** *n* FUELLESS fisuración hidráulica *f*, GEOL, PETR TECH, PETROL fracturación hidráulica *f*; ~ **generator** *n* HYDRAUL, SPACE generador hidráulico *m*; ~ **grade line** *n* HYDROL línea de altura piezométrica hidráulica *f*; ~ **gradient** *n* HYDROL gradiente hidráulico *m*; ~ **head** *n* HYDRAUL, HYDROL, PETR TECH carga hidráulica *f*; ~ **hose** *n* P&R manguera para agua a presión *f*; ~ **impulse ram** *n* COAL, CONST, HYDRAUL, WATER ariete hidráulico *m*; ~ **impulse test** *n* MECH ENG prueba de impulso hidráulico *f*; ~ **jack** *n* CONST cric hidráulico *m*, gato hidráulico *m*, HYDRAUL gato hidráulico *m*, MECH gato hidráulico *m*, martinete hidráulico *m*, MECH ENG gato hidráulico *m*; ~ **jet propulsion** *n* TRANSP propulsión a chorro hidráulica *f*; ~ **jump** *n* HYDROL resalto hidráulico *m*; ~ **lifting jack** *n* CONST, HYDRAUL, MECH, MECH ENG gato hidráulico *m*; ~ **linkage** *n* AUTO conexión hidráulica *f*; ~ **load** *n* HYDROL carga hidráulica *f*; ~ **lock** *n* HYDRAUL agarrotamiento hidráulico *m*; ~ **locking** *n* HYDRAUL agarrotamiento hidráulico *m*; ~ **loss** *n* NUCL pérdida hidráulica *f*; ~ **machinery** *n* MECH ENG maquinaria hidráulica *f*; ~ **motor** *n* MECH ENG motor hidráulico *m*; ~-**operated valve** *n* REFRIG válvula hidráulica *f*; ~ **packing seal** *n* MECH ENG sello de empaquetadura hidráulico *m*; ~ **performance test** *n* MECH ENG prueba de efectividad hidráulica *f*; ~ **piston discharger** *n* CONST descargador con pistón hidráulico *m*; ~ **power** *n* HYDRAUL energía hidráulica *f*; ~ **power pack** *n* MINE central de energía hidráulica *f*, SPACE *spacecraft* equipo de potencia hidráulica *f*; ~ **press** *n* LAB, P&R prensa hidráulica *f*; ~ **pressure source** *n* HYDRAUL fuente de presión hidráulica *f*; ~ **pressure supply** *n* HYDRAUL suministro de presión hidráulica *m*; ~ **profile** *n* HYDROL perfil hidráulico *m*; ~ **proof pressure** *n* REFRIG presión de prueba hidráulica *f*; ~ **prop** *n* MINE accesorio hidráulico *m*, columna hidráulico *f* (*Esp*), propulsor hidráulico *m* (*AmL*); ~ **ram** *n* COAL, CONST, HYDRAUL, WATER ariete hidráulico *m*; ~ **reservoir** *n* HYDRAUL depósito hidráulico *m*; ~ **rotary percussion drilling** *n* MINE percusión hidráulica por rotación *f*, sondeo a rotorpercusión hidráulica *m* (*Esp*), sondeo hidráulico por rotación *m* (*AmL*); ~ **separation** *n* CHEM TECH separación hidráulica *f*; ~ **sheet cutter** *n* PAPER cortadora de hojas hidráulica *f*; ~ **status** *n* GAS condición hidráulica *f*; ~ **system** *n* HYDRAUL instalación hidráulica *f*, sistema hidráulico *m*, WATER TRANSP instalación hidráulica *f*; ~ **thrust** *n* FUELLESS empuje hidráulico *m*; ~ **transmission system** *n* MECH ENG sistema de transmisión hidráulica *m*; ~ **valve lifter** *n* AUTO empujaválvulas hidraúlico *m*, levantaválvulas hidraúlico *m*, VEH levantaválvulas hidraúlico *m*; ~ **winch** *n* MINE torno hidráulico para izar pesos *m*

hydraulically: ~~**operated device** *n* MECH ENG dispositivo accionado hidráulicamente *m*; ~~**operated valve** *n* MECH ENG válvula accionada hidráulicamente *f*

hydraulics *n* HYDRAUL, MECH hidráulica *f*, PETR TECH sistema hidráulico *m*, WATER hidráulica *f*

hydrazide *n* CHEM hidrazida *f*

hydrazine *n* CHEM hidracina *f*, hidrazina *f*, NUCL hidracina *f*, SPACE *propulsion* hidracina *f*, hidrazina *f*; ~ **propulsion** *n* SPACE *spacecraft* propulsión de hidracina *f*; ~ **propulsion system** *n* SPACE *spacecraft* sistema de propulsión de hidrazina *m*

hydrazoate *n* CHEM hidrazoato *m*

hydrazoic: ~ **acid** *n* CHEM ácido hidrazoico *m*

hydric *adj* CHEM hídrico

hydride *n* CHEM, METALL hidruro *m*

hydrindene *n* CHEM hidrindeno *m*

hydriodic *adj* CHEM yodhídrico

hydriodide *n* CHEM yodhidrato *m*

hydro: ~~**cooling** *n* REFRIG refrigeración por agua helada *f*; ~~**test** *n* MECH ensayo a presión hidráulica *m*

hydroaromatic *adj* CHEM hidroaromático

hydrobilirubin *n* CHEM hidrobilirrubina *f*

hydrobromide *n* CHEM bromhidrato *m*

hydrocarbon *n* CHEM, GEOL, MAR POLL, PETR TECH, VEH hidrocarburo *m*; ~ **aerosol propellant** *n* PETR TECH propulsor de aerosol de hidrocaburos *m*; ~ **fire** *n* SAFE, THERMO incendio de hidrocarburos *m*; ~ **saturation** *n* PETROL saturación de hidrocarburos *f*; ~ **slick** *n* PETR TECH mancha de hidrocarburo *f*, mancha de hidrocarburos *f*; ~ **trap** *n* PETR TECH trampa de hidrocarburo *f*

hydrocarbonate *n* CHEM hidrocarbonato *m*

hydrocarbonic *adj* CHEM hidrocarbónico

hydrocellulose *n* CHEM celulosa hidratada *f*, hidrocelulosa *f*

hydrochloric[1] *adj* CHEM, DETERG clorhídrico

hydrochloric[2]: ~ **acid** *n* CHEM, DETERG ácido clorhídrico *m*

hydrocinnamic *adj* CHEM hidrocinámico

hydrocortisone *n* CHEM hidrocortisona *f*

hydrocotarnine *n* CHEM hidrocotarnina *f*

hydrocracker *n* PETR TECH hidrocraqueador *m*

hydrocracking *n* PETR TECH hidrocraking *m*

hydrocyanic *adj* CHEM cianhídrico

hydrocyanite *n* MINERAL hidrocianita *f*

hydrocyclone *n* CHEM TECH, COAL, PETR TECH hidrociclón *m*

hydrodolomite *n* MINERAL hidrolomita *f*

hydrodynamic[1] *adj* GEN hidrodinámico

hydrodynamic[2]: ~ **bearing** *n* SPACE *spacecraft* cojinete hidrodinámico *m*; ~ **damping factor** *n* FUELLESS factor de amortiguamiento hidrodinámico *m*; ~ **drag** *n* TRANSP resistencia hidrodinámica *f*; ~ **instability** *n* FLUID, GAS inestabilidad hidrodinámica *f*; ~ **lift** *n* TRANSP elevador hidrodinámico *m*;

~ **load** *n* HYDROL carga hidrodinámica *f*; ~ **model** *n* FUELLESS modelo hidrodinámico *m*; ~ **skimmer** *n* MAR POLL rasera hidrodinámica *f*; ~ **thrust** *n* HYDROL empuje hidrodinámico *m*

hydrodynamics *n* GEN hidrodinámica *f* (*Esp*)

hydroelastic: ~ **suspension** *n* AUTO, VEH suspensión hidroelástica *f*

hydroelectric: ~ **generating station** *n* ELEC ENG central de producción hidroeléctrica *f*; ~ **generator** *n* ELEC generador hidroeléctrico *m*, alternador hidráulico *m*, ELEC ENG alternador hidráulico *m*, generador hidroeléctrico *m*; ~ **power** *n* ELEC *supply* energía hidroeléctrica *f*, potencia hidroeléctrica *f*, FUELLESS energía hidroeléctrica *f*, fuerza hidroeléctrica *f*; ~ **power plant** *n* ELEC ENG planta de energía hidroeléctrica *f*; ~ **power station** *n* ELEC *supply* central hidroeléctrica *f*, ELEC ENG central de energía hidroeléctrica *f*, HYDROL central hidroeléctrica *f*; ~ **project** *n* CONST proyecto hidroélectrico *m*

hydroelectricity *n* ELEC *supply* hidroelectricidad *f*

hydroextract *vt* TEXTIL centrifugar

hydroextraction *n* TEXTIL centrifugado *m*

hydroextractor *n* TEXTIL centrífuga *f*, *spin-dryer* centrifugadora *f*

hydrofluoric *adj* CHEM fluorhídrico

hydrofluoride *n* CHEM fluorhidrato *m*

hydrofoil *n* AIR TRANSP perfil hidrodinámico *m*, plano hidrodinámico *m*, superficie hidrodinámica *f*, TRANSP alíscafo *m*, WATER TRANSP *craft* alíscafo *m*, hidroala *f*; ~ **rudder** *n* OCEAN timón hidráulico *m*

hydrogen *n* (*H*) GEN hidrógeno *m* (*H*); ~ **bond** *n* CHEM enlace de hidrógeno *m*, CRYSTALL enlace de puente de hidrógeno *m*; ~ **cyanide** *n* CHEM cianuro de hidrógeno *m*; ~ **gas** *n* CHEM, GAS gas hidrógeno *m*; ~ **index** *n* PETROL índice de hidrógeno *m*; ~ **ion concentration** *n* CHEM concentración de ión hidrógeno *f*; ~ **liquid** *n* CHEM, THERMO hidrógeno líquido *m*; ~~**oxygen mixture** *n* OCEAN mezcla de hidrógeno-oxígeno *f*; ~ **peroxide** *n* CHEM, SPACE agua oxigenada *f*, peróxido de hidrógeno *m*; ~ **plasma** *n* GAS plasma de hidrógeno *m*; ~ **spectral line** *n* RAD PHYS espectro de rayas del hidrógeno *m*; ~ **sulfide** *AmE*, ~ **sulphide** *BrE* *n* CHEM ácido sulfhídrico *m*, hidrógeno sulfurado *m*, CHEM hidrógeno sulfurado *m*, FOOD sulfuro de hidrógeno *m*; ~ **tank** *n* SPACE *spacecraft* cuba de hidrógeno *f*, tanque de hidrógeno *m*; ~ **thyraton** *n* ELECTRON tiratrón de hidrógeno *m*; ~ **uptake** *n* NUCL captación de hidrógeno *f*

hydrogenate *vt* CHEM, COAL, DETERG, FOOD, PETR TECH hidrogenar

hydrogenated[1] *adj* CHEM, COAL, DETERG, FOOD, PETR TECH hidrogenado

hydrogenated[2]: ~ **fat** *n* FOOD grasa hidrogenada *f*

hydrogenation *n* CHEM hidrogenación *f*, COAL endurecimiento *m*, hidrogenación *f*, temple *m*, DETERG, FOOD hidrogenación *f*, PETR TECH hidrogenizado *m*

hydrogenator *n* FOOD hidrogenador *m*

hydrogenous *adj* GEOL hidrogenado, hidrogénico

hydrogeochemistry *n* CHEM, GEOL, HYDROL hidrogeoquímica *f*

hydrogeological: ~ **map** *n* HYDROL carta hidrogeológica *f*

hydrogeology *n* GEOL, HYDROL, WATER hidrogeología *f*

hydrograph *n* WATER hidrograma *m*, hidrógrafo *m*

hydrographic[1] *adj* GEOL, HYDROL, WATER TRANSP hidrográfico

hydrographic[2]: ~ **basin** n GEOL cuenca hidrográfica f; ~ **chart** n HYDROL marine, WATER TRANSP navigation carta hidrográfica f; ~ **office** n WATER TRANSP instituto hidrográfico m; ~ **signal** n OCEAN señal hidrográfica m; ~ **survey** n OCEAN investigación hidrográfica f; ~ **survey vessel** n WATER TRANSP buque hidrográfico m, buque planero m, planero m

hydrography n FUELLESS, GEOL, HYDROL, WATER TRANSP hidrografía f

hydrojet: ~ **propulsion** n TRANSP propulsión por chorro de agua f

hydrokinetic: ~ **brake** n TRANSP freno hidrocinético m

hydrologic: ~ **balance** n HYDROL equilibrio hidrológico m, WATER balance hidrológico m; ~ **cycle** n GEOL, WATER ciclo hidrológico m; ~ **investigation** n HYDROL investigación hidrológica f; ~ **study** n CONST estudio hidrológico m; ~ **year** n HYDROL año hidrológico m; ~ **yearbook** n HYDROL anuario hidrológico m

hydrologist n CONST hidrólogo m

hydrology n COAL, GEOL, HYDROL, WATER hidrología f

hydrolysis n CHEM, FOOD, GEOL, P&R hidrólisis f

hydromagnesite n MINERAL hidromagnesita f

hydromechanical: ~ **clutch** n MECH ENG embrague hidromecánico m; ~ **governor** n FUELLESS regulador hidromecánico m

hydromechanics n FLUID hidromecánica f

hydrometallurgy n COAL, METALL hidrometalurgia f

hydrometer n COAL areómetro m, densímetro m, hidrómetro m (Esp), FOOD, HYDROL densímetro m (AmL), hidrómetro m (Esp), LAB vibration test densímetro m, MECH, PETR TECH hidrómetro m (Esp), densímetro m (AmL), PHYS areómetro m, densímetro m (AmL), hidrómetro m (Esp), VEH hidrómetro m (Esp), densímetro m (AmL), WATER densímetro m (AmL), hidrómetro m (Esp)

hydrometric: ~ **degree** n METEO grado hidrométrico m; ~ **state** n HYDROL estado hidrométrico m

hydrometry n CHEM, HYDROL, PHYS, WATER hidrometría f

hydrophane n MINERAL hidrófana f

hydrophile: ~ **balance** n DETERG equilibrio hidrófilo m

hydrophilic adj AGRIC, CHEM hidrófilo, COAL hidrofílico

hydrophobic adj CHEM hidrófobo, hidrofóbico, COAL hidrofóbico, hidrófobo

hydrophone n ACOUST, OCEAN, PETR TECH, TELECOM hidrófono m

hydroplane n OCEAN hidroplano m, WATER TRANSP submarines hidroplano m, timón horizontal m

hydropneumatic: ~ **accumulator** n MECH ENG acumulador hidroneumático m; ~ **brake** n TRANSP freno hidroneumático m; ~ **suspension** n AUTO, VEH suspensión hidroneumática f

hydroponics n AGRIC hidroponía f

hydroquinone n CHEM hidroquinona f

hydroscience n WATER hidrociencia f

hydroscopic adj MECH hidroscópico

hydrosilicate n CHEM hidrosilicato m

hydrosilyation: n CHEM process hidrosiliación f

hydroskimmer n TRANSP hidroniveladora f

hydrosol n CHEM hidrosol m

hydrosopoline n CHEM hidrosopolina f

hydrosphere n HYDROL hidrosfera f

hydrostatic[1] adj GEN hidrostático

hydrostatic[2]: ~ **balance** n FLUID, HYDROL equilibrio

hidrostático m, LAB instrument balanza hidrostática f; ~ **bearing** n MECH, PROD cojinete hidrostático m; ~ **curves** n pl WATER TRANSP ship design curvas hidrostáticas f pl; ~ **equilibrium** n THERMO equilibrio hidrostático m; ~ **equipment** n MECH ENG equipo hidroestático m; ~ **head** n PETR TECH altura hidrostática f; ~ **level** n OCEAN nivel hidrostático m; ~ **load** n HYDROL carga hidrostática f; ~ **pressure** n COAL, FLUID, GAS, GEOL, HYDROL, OCEAN, PETR TECH, REFRIG presión hidrostática f; ~ **stress** n METALL carga hidrostática f, tensión hidrostática f; ~ **transmission** n MECH transmisión hidrostática f

hydrostatics n CONST, FLUID, HYDROL, PHYS, WATER hidrostática f

hydrosulfide AmE see hydrosulphide BrE

hydrosulfurous: ~ **acid** AmE see hydrosulphurous acid BrE

hydrosulphide n BrE CHEM bisulfuro m

hydrosulphurous: ~ **acid** n BrE CHEM ácido bisulfuroso m, ácido hidrosulfuroso m

hydrothermal[1] adj FUELLESS, GEOL hidrotermal, hidrotérmico

hydrothermal[2]: ~ **deposit** n GEOL sedimento acuoígneo m; ~ **ecosystem** n OCEAN ecosistema hidrotérmico m; ~ **process** n FUELLESS proceso hidrotérmico m

hydrous adj CHEM, FLUID acuoso, GEOL acuoso, hidratado, HYDROL, PETR TECH, WATER acuoso

hydroxy: ~-**capped** adj CHEM hidroxidecapado

hydroxyethylcellulose n CHEM hidroxietilcelulosa f, PETR TECH celulosa hidroxietílica f

hydroxyl n CHEM, FOOD hidróxilo m

hydroxylated adj CHEM, FOOD hidroxilado

hydrozincite n MINERAL hidrocincita f

hygrometer n GEN higrómetro m

hygrometry n GEN higrometría f

hygroscope n CHEM, CONST, HYDROL, PHYS, MECH, WATER higroscopio m

hygroscopic adj MECH hidroscópico; ~ **water** n HYDROL, WATER agua higroscópica

hygrosensibility n PAPER sensibilidad a la humedad f

hygrostability n PAPER estabilidad dimensional frente al agua f

hygrothermograph n AGRIC higrotermógrafo m

hyocholanic n CHEM hiocolánico

hyoscine n CHEM L-escopolamina f, hioscina f

hypabyssal: ~ **rock** n GEOL roca hipoabisal f

hypautomorphic adj GEOL hipautomorfo

hyperabrupt: ~ **junction** n ELECTRON conexión hiperviolenta f; ~ **varactor diode** n ELECTRON, PHYS diodo varactor hiperabrupto m

hyperapnea n OCEAN hiperafinea f

hyperballistic adj SPACE hiperbalístico

hyperballistics n SPACE hiperbalística f

hyperbaric: ~ **arthralgia** n OCEAN artnalgia hiperbárica f; ~ **atmosphere** n OCEAN atmósfera hiperbárica f; ~ **center** AmE, ~ **centre** BrE n OCEAN centro hiperbárico m; ~ **chamber** n OCEAN, PETR TECH cámara hiperbárica f; ~ **environment** n OCEAN ambiente hiperbárico m

hyperbola n GEOM hipérbola f

hyperbolic[1] adj GEOM, SPACE, WATER TRANSP hiperbólico

hyperbolic[2]: ~ **geometry** n GEOM geometría hiperbólica f; ~ **navigation** n WATER TRANSP sistema hiperbólico de navegación m; ~ **orbit** n SPACE órbita hiperbólica *f*; ~ **position-fixing system** *n* WATER TRANSP *navigation* sistema hiperbólico de determinación de la situación *m*; ~ **space** *n* GEOM espacio hiperbólico *m*

hyperboloid *n* GEOM hiperboloide *m*

hypercardioid: ~ **microphone** *n* ACOUST micrófono hipercardiode *m*

hypercharge *n* PHYS hipercarga *f*

hypereutectic *adj* METALL hipereutéctico

hypereutectoid: ~ **steel** *n* METALL acero hipereutectoide *m*

hyperfine: ~ **structure** *n* PHYS, RAD PHYS estructura hiperfina *f*

hyperfrequency *n* ELECTRON, TELECOM, TV, WAVE PHYS frecuencia ultraelevada *f*

hypergeometric: ~ **distribution** *n* MATH *statistics* distribución hipergeométrica *f*

hypergol *n* SPACE *spacecraft* hipergol *m*

hypergolic[1] *adj* SPACE *spacecraft* hipergólico

hypergolic[2]: ~ **ignition** *n* SPACE *spacecraft* ignición hipergólica *f*; ~ **property** *n* SPACE *spacecraft* propiedad hipergólica *f*

hypergroup *n* TELECOM hipergrupo *m*

hyperon *n* PART PHYS, PHYS hiperón *m*

hyperoxia *n* OCEAN hiperoxia *f*

hyperoxide *n* CHEM hiperóxido *m*

hyperplane *n* GEOM hiperplano *m*

hypersaline: ~ **water** *n* HYDROL *f*, OCEAN agua hipersalina *f*

hypersalinity *n* OCEAN hipersalinidad *f*

hypersensitize *vt* CINEMAT hipersensibilizar

hypersonic[1] *adj* FLUID, PHYS, SPACE hipersónico

hypersonic[2]: ~ **flow** *n* FLUID flujo hipersónico *m*; ~ **speed** *n* PHYS velocidad hipersónica *f*

hypersthene *n* MINERAL hiperstena *f*

hypersurface *n* GEOM hipersuperficie *f*

hypertext *n* COMP&DP hipertexto *m*; ~ **markup language** *n* (*html*) COMP&DP lenguaje html *m*

hyperthermal: ~ **field** *n* FUELLESS campo hipertérmico *m*

hyperventilation *n* OCEAN hiperventilación *f*

hyphen *n* PRINT guión *m*; ~ **ladders** *n pl* PRINT guiones conductores *m pl*

hypidiomorphic *adj* GEOL hipidiomorfo

hypo *n* CINEMAT hiposulfito *m*

hypoacusis *n* ACOUST hipoacúsia *m*

hypocenter *AmE see* hypocentre *BrE*

hypocentre *n BrE* GEOL, GEOPHYS hipocentro *m*

hypochlorate *n* CHEM hipoclorato *m*

hypochloric: ~ **acid** *n* CHEM ácido hipoclórico *m*

hypochlorite *n* CHEM hipoclorito *m*

hypochlorous: ~ **acid** *n* CHEM ácido hipocloroso *m*

hypocotyl *n* AGRIC hipocotilo *m*

hypoeutectic *adj* METALL hipoeutéctico

hypoid *n* MECH *computing* hipoide *f*; ~ **bevel gear** *n* MECH *of a terminal* engranaje cónico de dentadura hipoide *m*; ~ **gear** *n* MECH ENG engranaje hipoidal *m*, engranaje hipoide *m*; ~ **gearing** *n* AUTO, VEH engranaje hipoide *m*

hypophosphate *n* CHEM hipofosfato *m*

hypophosphite *n* CHEM hipofosfito *m*

hypophosphoric: ~ **acid** *n* CHEM ácido hipofosfórico *m*

hypophosphorous: ~ **acid** *n* CHEM ácido hipofosforoso *m*

hyposometric *adj* PHYS hipsométrico

hyposulfurous: ~ **acid** *AmE see* hyposulphurous acid *BrE*

hyposulphurous: ~ **acid** *n BrE* CHEM ácido hiposulfuroso *m*

hypotenuse *n* GEOM hipotenusa *f*

hypothermal *adj* GEOL hipotermal, hipotérmico

hypothermia *n* WATER TRANSP hipotermia *m*

hypothermic: ~ **blanket** *n* REFRIG manta hipotérmica *f*

hypothesis *n* CHEM hipótesis *f*

hypotonic *adj* CHEM hipotónico

hypsographic: ~ **curve** *n* GEOL curva hipsográfica *f*

hypsometer *n* PHYS hipsómetro *m*

hypsometric[1] *adj* COLOUR, HYDROL, PETROL hipsométrico

hypsometric[2]: ~ **map** *n* HYDROL mapa hipsométrico *m*; ~ **tint** *n* COLOUR tinta hipsométrica *f*

hystarazin *n* CHEM histarazina *f*

hysteresis *n* GEN histéresis *f*; ~ **coefficient** *n* ELEC *magnetization* coeficiente de histéresis *m*; ~ **curve** *n* ELEC *magnetism* ciclo de histéresis *m*, curva de histéresis *f*; ~ **error** *n* AIR TRANSP *altimeter* error de histéresis *m*; ~ **loop** *n* ELEC *magnetism* ciclo de histéresis *m*, curva de histéresis *f*, ELEC ENG ciclo de histéresis *m*, METALL bucle de histéresis *m*, ciclo de histéresis *m*, P&R ciclo de histéresis *m*, curva de histéresis *f*, PHYS ciclo de histéresis *m*; ~ **loss** *n* ELEC ENG, P&R, PHYS pérdida por histéresis *f*; ~ **motor** *n* ELEC ENG motor asíncrono de histéresis *m*

Hz *abbr* (*hertz*) GEN Hz (*hercio, hertz*)

I

I^1 *abbr* (*iodine*) CHEM, ELECTRON, PHOTO, TEXTIL I (*iodo, yodo*)

I^2: ~ **axis** *n* TV *project management* eje I *m*; ~ **core** *n* ELEC ENG núcleo en I *m*; ~ **demodulator** *n* TV demodulador I *m*

IALA *abbr* (*International Association of Lighthouses Authorities*) WATER TRANSP AISM (*Asociación Internacional de Señalización Marítima*)

IAS *abbr* (*immediate access store*) COMP&DP almacenamiento de acceso inmediato *m*

I-beam *n* CONST viga en doble T *f*

IBG *abbr* (*interblock gap*) COMP&DP espacio entre bloques *m*, interconexión *f*, intervalo entre bloques *m*

IC *abbr* (*integrated circuit*) AUTO, COMP&DP, ELEC, PHYS, TELECOM, TV CI (*circuito integrado*)

ICB *abbr* (*incoming calls barred*) TELECOM llamadas entrantes prohibidas *f pl*, llamadas entrantes restringidas *f pl*

ice^1: ~**-coded** *adj* THERMO enfriado con hielo, glacial

ice^2: ~ **accretion** *n* WATER acumulación de hielo *f*; ~ **bank cooler** *n* REFRIG enfriador con acumulación de hielo *m*; ~ **bank evaporator** *n* REFRIG evaporador acumulador de hielo *m*; ~ **bank tank** *n* REFRIG tanque de acumulación de hielo *m*; ~ **barrier** *n* HYDROL, OCEAN barrera de hielo *f*; ~ **block** *n* REFRIG bloque de hielo *m*; ~ **blower** *n* REFRIG lanzador de hielo *m*; ~ **breakup** *n* OCEAN rompehielos *m*; ~ **bunker** *n* REFRIG depósito para hielo *m*; ~ **cake** *n* REFRIG bloque de hielo *m*; ~ **can** *n* REFRIG molde para hielo *m*; ~ **cap** *n* OCEAN casquete glaciar *m*; ~ **cellar** *n* REFRIG almacén de hielo *m*; ~ **chunk** *n* SPACE gran pedazo de hielo *m*; ~ **condenser** *n* NUCL condensador con hielo *m*; ~ **crusher** *n* REFRIG triturador de hielo *m*; ~ **detector** *n* AIR TRANSP detector de hielo *m*; ~ **detector relay** *n* AIR TRANSP relé detector de hielo *m*; ~ **dump table** *n* REFRIG tobogán para hielo *m*; ~ **floe** *n* METEO, WATER TRANSP bandejón *m*; ~ **guard** *n* AIR TRANSP guardahielos *m*, parahielos *m*, protector antihielo *m*; ~ **island** *n* OCEAN isla de hielo *f*; ~ **jam** *n* HYDROL, OCEAN barrera de hielo suspendida *f*; ~ **lens** *n* COAL fisura del terreno relleno de hielo *f*; ~ **maker** *n* REFRIG máquina de cubitos *f*; ~**-making capacity** *n* REFRIG capacidad para producir hielo *f*; ~**-making compartment** *n* MECH ENG *of refrigerator* compartimiento de fabricación hielo *m*, congelador *m*; ~**-making machine** *n* THERMO máquina para hacer hielo *f*; ~**-making plant** *n* THERMO planta para hacer hielo *f*; ~**-melting equivalent** *n* REFRIG calor latente de hielo *m*; ~ **milk** *n* REFRIG helado de leche *m*; ~ **pack** *n* WATER TRANSP gran extensión de hielo a la deriva *f*; ~**-patterned glass** *n* C&G vidrio escarchado *m*; ~ **point** *n* PHYS temperatura de fusión del hielo *f*; ~ **probe** *n* AIR TRANSP sonda de hielo *f*; ~ **refrigerator** *n* REFRIG nevera de hielo *f*, refrigerador de hielo *m*; ~ **ridge** *n* OCEAN cordón de hielo *m*; ~ **ripple** *n* OCEAN onda de hielo *f*; ~ **sheet** *n* OCEAN manto de hielo *m*; ~ **shelf** *n* GEOL, GEOPHYS, OCEAN plataforma de hielo *f*; ~ **slab** *n* REFRIG pista de hielo *f*; ~ **storage room** *n* REFRIG cámara de almacenamiento de hielo *f*; ~ **tip** *n* REFRIG volcador de moldes de hielo *m*; ~ **warning sign** *n* SAFE, TRANSP señal de advertencia de hielo *f*; ~ **water** *n* REFRIG agua helada *f*

iceberg *n* OCEAN masa flotante *f*, WATER TRANSP gran extensión de hielo a la deriva *f*

icebound *adj* WATER TRANSP *port* cercado por el hielo, *ship* atrapado por el hielo, bloqueado por el hielo

icebreaker *n* MILIT buque rompehielos *m*, WATER TRANSP *ship* buque rompehielos *m*, rompehielos *m*

icebreaking: ~ **cargo ship** *n* WATER TRANSP buque de carga rompe-hielos *m*; ~ **oil tanker** *n* PETR TECH, PETROL, WATER TRANSP buque petrolero rompe-hielos *m*

ichnofossil *n* GEOL icnofósil *m*

icing *n* REFRIG enfriamiento con hielo *m*, WATER TRANSP enhielamiento *m*, formación de hielo *f*; ~ **probe** *n* AIR TRANSP sonda de formación de hielo *f*

icon *n* COMP&DP icono *m*

iconoscope *n* ELECTRON iconoscopio *m*

icosahedral *adj* GEOM icosaédrico

icosahedron *n* GEOM icosaedro *m*

ICRP *abbr* (*International Commission on Radiological Protection*) RAD PHYS Comisión Internacional de Protección Radiológica *f*

ID *abbr* COMP&DP (*identifier*) identificador *m*, MECH, MECH ENG (*inner diameter, inside diameter*) diámetro interior *m*, diámetro interno *m*, TELECOM (*identifier*) identificador *m*

IDD *abbr BrE* (*International Direct Dialling BrE*) TELECOM marcación directa internacional *f*

IDDD *abbr AmE* (*International Direct Distance Dialing AmE*) TELECOM marcación directa internacional *f*

ideal: ~ **bunching** *n* ELECTRON reagrupamiento óptimo *m*; ~ **conditions** *n pl* TRANSP condiciones óptimas *f pl*; ~ **filter** *n* ELECTRON filtro perfecto *m*; ~ **gas** *n* GAS gas ideal *m*, gas perfecto *m*, PHYS, THERMO gas perfecto *m*; ~ **mixture ratio** *n* AUTO proporción ideal de la mezcla *f*; ~ **rectifier** *n* ELEC ENG rectificador ideal *m*; ~ **transformer** *n* ELEC, ELEC ENG transformador ideal *m*; ~ **velocity** *n* FUEL-LESS velocidad ideal *f*

identification *n* ACOUST, COMP&DP, MECH ENG, SAFE *process* identificación *f*; ~ **beacon** *n* AIR TRANSP radiobaliza de identificación *f*; ~ **character** *n* COMP&DP carácter de identificación *m*; ~ **code** *n* COMP&DP, TELECOM código de identificación *m*; ~ **code qualifier** *n* TELECOM calificador del código de identificación *m*; ~ **of contents** *n* SAFE identificación de contenido *f*; ~ **division** *n* COMP&DP *COBOL* división de identificación *f*; ~ **light** *n* AIR TRANSP luz de identificación *f*; ~ **signal** *n* TV señal de identificación *f*; ~ **sleeve** *n* MECH ENG manguito de identificación *m*; ~ **strip** *n* PROD tira de identificación *f*; ~ **tag** *n* SAFE tarjeta de identificación *f*

identified: ~ **resources** *n pl* FUELLESS recursos identificados *m pl*

identifier *n* (*ID*) COMP&DP, TELECOM identificador *m*

identify *vt* GEN identificar
identity *n* MATH identidad *f*; **~-based security policy** *n* TELECOM norma de seguridad basada en la identidad *f*; **~ element** *n* MATH elemento identidad *m*
ideogram *n* COMP&DP ideograma *m*
IDF *abbr* (*intermediate distribution frame*) TELECOM trama de distribución intermedia *f*
IDI *abbr* (*initial-domain identifier*) TELECOM identificador de dominio inicial *m*
idioblastic *adj* GEOL euhédrico, idioblástico
idiomorphic[1] *adj* CRYSTALL, METALL, PETR TECH, PETROL idiomorfo
idiomorphic[2]: **~ crystal** *n* CRYSTALL, METALL cristal idiomórfico *m*
idiomorphous *adj* CRYSTALL, METALL, PETR TECH, PETROL idiomorfo
iditol *n* CHEM iditol *m*
idle[1] *adj* PROD *machinery, works* desocupado, inactivo, TELECOM libre
idle[2] *n* MECH ENG *guide pulley* funcionar con marcha lenta, funcionar en mínima, polea loca *f*; **~ adjustment screw** *n* AUTO tornillo de ajuste de marcha lenta *m*, tornillo de ajuste del ralentí *m*, VEH tornillo de regulación del mínimo *m*, tornillo de regulación del ralentí *m*; **~ character** *n* COMP&DP carácter de relleno *m*, carácter sin uso *m*; **~ component** *n* ELEC *alternating current*, ELEC ENG componente inactivo *m*; **~ current** *n* ELEC, ELEC ENG corriente reactiva *f*; **~ gear** *n* VEH engranaje intermedio *m*; **~ jet** *n* AUTO chicle de ralentí *m*, chorro de ralentí *m*, surtidor de marcha lenta *m*, surtidor de ralentí *m*, VEH surtidor de marcha lenta *m*, surtidor de mínimo *m*; **~ and low speed circuit** *n* AUTO circuito de ralentí y baja velocidad *m*; **~ period** *n* ELECTRON período inactivo *m*; **~ pulley** *n* MECH ENG polea de tensión *f*, polea guía *f*, polea loca *f*, polea tensora *f*; **~ return** *n* MECH ENG *machine tool work* regreso inactivo *m*, retorno en vacío *m*, retorno inactivo *m*; **~ roller** *n* TV rodillo inactivo *m*; **~ shipping** *n* WATER TRANSP tonelaje inactivo *m*, tonelaje inmovilizado *m*; **~ side** *n* PROD *of belt* ramal conducido *m*; **~ state** *n* TELECOM estado libre *m*; **~ stroke** *n* MECH ENG carrera en vacío *f*, carrera inactiva *f*, carrera muerta *f*; **~ throttle stop** *n* AIR TRANSP tope del regulador de relentí *m*; **~ time** *n* COMP&DP tiempo de inactividad *m*, tiempo pasivo *m*; **~ working channel** *n* TELECOM canal operativo libre *m*
idle[3] *vi* MECH ENG funcionar en vacío, VEH girar lentamente, ralentizar
idler *n* CINEMAT polea loca *f*, MECH polea guía *f*, polea loca *f*, polea muerta *f*, polea tensora *f*, rueda intermedia *f*, MECH ENG rueda loca *f*, piñón de transmisión *m*, piñón loco *m*, *tightening pulley* polea de tensión *f*, RAIL vagón sin carga colocado entre dos vagones cargados *m*, TV polea de transmisión *f*, polea guíafilme *f*; **~ arm** *n* AUTO brazo secundario libre *m*; **~ frequency** *n* ELECTRON frecuencia lenta *f*; **~ pulley** *n* AUTO, MECH, MECH ENG polea loca *f*
idling *n* ELEC *of motor* marcha en vacío *f*, marcha lenta *f*, marcha sin realizar ninguna función *f*, VEH marcha al ralentí *f*, marcha lenta *f*; **~ speed** *n* MECH velocidad en vacío *f*, velocidad mínima de un motor *f*
IDN *abbr* (*integrated digital network*) TELECOM red digital integrada *f*
idocrase *n* MINERAL idocrasa *f*, vesubiana *f*

idonic *adj* CHEM idónico
idosaccharic *adj* CHEM idosacárico
idose *n* CHEM idosa *f*
IDP *abbr* (*initial-domain part*) TELECOM parte de dominio inicial *f*
idranal *n* CHEM idranal *m*
idrialite *n* MINERAL idrialina *f*
IDSE *abbr* (*international data switching exchange*) TELECOM central de conmutación de datos internacionales *f*, central de conmutación para mensajes internacionales *f*
IDT *abbr* (*interdigital transducer*) TELECOM transductor interdigital *m*
IEC *abbr* (*International Electrotechnical Committee*) PROD Comité Electrotécnico Internacional *m*
IF[1] *abbr* (*intermediate frequency*) ELECTRON, TELECOM, TV FI (*frecuencia intermedia*)
IF[2]: **~ amplification** *n* ELECTRON, TELECOM amplificación de FI *f*; **~ amplifier** *n* ELECTRON, TELECOM amplificador de FI *m*; **~ filter** *n* ELECTRON, TELECOM filtro de FI *m*; **~ rejection** *n* ELECTRON supresión de FI *f*, TELECOM rechazo de FI *m*; **~ signal** *n* ELECTRON, TELECOM señal de FI *f*; **~ stage** *n* ELECTRON fase de FI *f*, momento de FI *m*, TELECOM etapa de FI *f*
IFM *abbr* (*instantaneous frequency measurement*) ELECTRON medición de frecuencia instantánea *f*
IFRB *abbr* (*International Frequency Registration Board*) SPACE *communications* IFRB (*Comité Internacional de Registro de Frecuencias*)
IFU *abbr* (*interworking functional unit*) TELECOM unidad funcional entrelazada *f*
IG *abbr* (*interpolation gain*) TELECOM ganancia de interpolación *f*
IGFET *abbr* (*insulated grid field effect transistor*) ELECTRON TECCA (*transistor de efecto de campo con circuito aislado*), TECRA (*transistor de efecto de campo con rejilla aislada*)
I-girder *n* CONST jácena en doble T *f*, viga principal en doble T *f*
igloo: **~ container** *n* TRANSP contenedor abovedado *m*
IGN *abbr* (*international gateway node*) TELECOM nodo de acceso internacional *m*, nodo de entrada internacional *m*
igneous: **~ complex** *n* GEOL complejo ígneo *m*; **~ rock** *n* FUELLESS, GEOL, PETROL roca ígnea *f*; **~ suite** *n* GEOL asociación de rocas ígneas *f*
ignimbrite *n* GEOL ignimbrita *f*
ignite[1] *vt* CHEM encender, SPACE *spacecraft* encender, incinerar, inflamar
ignite[2] *vi* CHEM encenderse, NUCL encender
igniter *n* ELEC encendedor *m*, ELEC ENG dispositivo de encendido *m*, ignitor *m*, MECH ENG encendedor *m*, SPACE *spacecraft* carga de inflamación *f*, carga de proyección *f*, dispositivo de encendido *m*, encendedor *m*, ignitor *m*, pistolete *m*
ignition *n* AIR TRANSP arranque *m*, encendido *m*, ignición *f*, inflamación *f*, AUTO encendido *m*, ignición *f*, inflamación *f*, CHEM encendido *m*, ignición *f*, CINEMAT encendido *m*, ELEC *internal combustion engine* inflamación *f*, ignición *f*, encendido *m*, ELEC ENG *of gas tube* inflamación *f*, MECH encendido *m*, ignición *f*, P&R, SAFE, SPACE ignición *f*, VEH encendido *m*, inflamación *f*; **~ advance** *n* AIR TRANSP avance automático del encendido *m*; **~ arc** *n* HEAT ENG arco de ignición *m*; **~ burner** *n* HEAT ENG quemador con

ignición *m*; ~ **capacitor** *n* AUTO condensador para encendido *m*, condensador para ignición *m*; ~ **circuit** *n* SPACE *spacecraft* circuito de ignición *m*; ~ **coil** *n* AIR TRANSP, AUTO, ELEC ENG, VEH bobina de encendido *f*; ~ **device** *n* HEAT ENG dispositivo de encendido *m*; ~ **distributor** *n* AUTO distribuidor de ignición *m*, distribuidor del encendido *m* (*Esp*), MECH ENG distribuidor *m* (*AmL*), distribuidor del encendido *m* (*Esp*); ~ **experiment** *n* NUCL experimento de ignición *m*; ~ **generator** *n* AIR TRANSP generador de encendido *m*; ~ **harness** *n* AIR TRANSP arnés de encendido *m*; ~ **key** *n* AUTO llave de encendido *f*; ~ **loss** *n* COAL pérdida de encendido *f*; ~ **magneto** *n* VEH magneto de encendido *m*; ~ **plug** *n* AUTO bujía de ignición *f*, MECH, VEH bujía de encendido *f*; ~ **point** *n* AUTO punto de ignición *m*, temperatura de encendido *f*, MECH punto de encendido *m*, temperatura de encendido *f*, PETR TECH punto de encendido *m*, temperatura de ignición *f*, PHYS temperatura de ignición *f*; ~ **poker** *n* MECH ENG atizador de ignición *m*, varilla de ignición *f*; ~ **setting** *n* AUTO ajuste de encendido *m*, reglaje de ignición *m*; ~ **starter switch** *n* AUTO interruptor de arranque *m*, interruptor de encendido *m*, VEH interruptor de arranque *m*; ~ **switch** *n* VEH interruptor de encendido *m*; ~ **system** *n* SPACE *spacecraft* sistema de ignición *m*; ~ **timing** *n* AUTO ajuste de encendido *m*, sincronizado de ignición *m*, VEH reglaje del encendido *m*; ~ **transformer** *n* ELEC, ELEC ENG transformador de encendido *m*

ignitron *n* ELEC, ELEC ENG *electronic tube* ignitrón *m*; ~ **locomotive** *n* RAIL locomotora con recticador de ignitrones *f*; ~ **rectifier** *n* ELEC ENG rectificador de ignitrones *m*

ignore: ~ **character** *n* COMP&DP carácter de omisión *m*, carácter de supresión *m*

IGSCC *abbr* (*intergranular stress corrosion cracking*) NUCL agrietamiento intergranular por tensocorrosión *m*

I-head: ~ **engine** *n* AUTO motor de culata en I *m*; ~ **valve train** *n* AUTO tren de válvulas en cabeza *m*

IHS *abbr* (*integrated home system*) COMP&DP sistema doméstico integrado *m*, sistema integrado de casa *m* (*AmL*)

IIR[1] *abbr* (*infinite impulse response*) ELECTRON, TELECOM respuesta de impulso infinito *f*

IIR[2]: ~ **digital filter** *n* ELECTRON, TELECOM filtro digital de respuesta a impulsos infinitos *m*; ~ **filter** *n* ELECTRON filtro de respuesta de impulso infinita *m*

IL *abbr* (*integrated injection logic*) ELECTRON IL (*lógica integrada a inyección*)

ILD *abbr* (*injection laser diode*) ELECTRON, OPT, TELECOM diodo láser de inyección *m*

iliac *adj* CHEM *crest* iliácico

illegal: ~ **character** *n* COMP&DP carácter ilegal *m*, carácter inválido *m*; ~ **dumping** *n* POLL, WATER vaciadura ilegal *f*; ~ **instruction** *n* COMP&DP instrucción ilegal *f*, instrucción inválida *f*; ~ **operation** *n* COMP&DP operación ilegal *f*, operación inválida *f*; ~ **op code** *n* PROD código de operación prohibido *m*; ~ **operation code** *n* PROD código de operación prohibido *m*

illite *n* COAL, GEOL, MINERAL, PETR TECH ilita *f*

illuminance *n* PHYS iluminancia *f*

illuminated[1] *adj* GEN iluminado

illuminated[2]: ~ **dial** *n* PHOTO disco iluminado *m*; ~**-dial**

instrument *n* INSTR instrumento de cuadrante iluminado *m*; ~ **folding lens** *n* INSTR, OPT lente de desdoblamiento iluminada *f*; ~ **push-button** *n* PROD pulsador iluminado *m*; ~ **source** *n* RAD PHYS fuente iluminada *f*

illuminating: ~ **apparatus** *n* LAB aparato de iluminación *m*; ~ **mirror** *n* INSTR espejo de iluminación *m*

illumination *n* CINEMAT iluminación *f*, ELEC alumbrado *m*, ELEC ENG *luminous flux intensity* alumbrado *m*, iluminación *f*, METALL brillo *m*, iluminación *f*, SPACE alumbrado *m*; ~ **angle** *n* PRINT ángulo de iluminación *m*; ~ **beam path** *n* INSTR trayectoria del haz de iluminación *f*; ~ **efficiency** *n* SPACE alumbrado eficiente *m*; ~ **mirror** *n* INSTR *for horizontal or vertical scale* espejo de iluminación *m*; ~ **mirror for vertical circle** *n* INSTR espejo de iluminación para círculo vertical *m*; ~ **optics** *n pl* INSTR, OPT óptica de iluminación *f*; ~ **path** *n* INSTR trayectoria de la iluminación *f*

illustrate *vt* PRINT ilustrar

illustrated: ~ **lettercard** *n* PAPER aerograma ilustrado *m*; ~ **postcard** *n* PAPER tarjeta postal ilustrada *f*

illustration *n* PRINT ilustración *f*

ilmenite *n* MINERAL ilmenita *f*

ILS[1] *abbr* (*instrument landing system*) AIR TRANSP, SPACE *craft* ILS (*sistema de aterrizaje por instrumentos*), sistema instrumental de aterrizaje *m*

ILS[2]: ~ **beam** *n* SPACE haz ILS *m*; ~ **glide path** *n* SPACE trayectoria de planeo con instrumentos *f*, trayectoria de planeo instrumental *f*

ilsemannite *n* MINERAL ilsemannita *f*

ilvaite *n* MINERAL ilvaita *f*, ilvaíta *f*

IM *abbr* (*interface module*) ELECTRON, SPACE, TELECOM módulo de interfaz *m*

IMA *abbr* (*input message acknowledgment*) TELECOM aviso de mensaje entrante *m*

image[1] *n* GEN imagen *f*; ~ **analyser** *n* BrE TELECOM analizador de imagen *m*; ~ **analysis** *n* TELECOM análisis de imagen *m*; ~ **analyzer** *AmE see image analyser BrE*; ~ **area** *n* CINEMAT área de la imagen *f*, PRINT área de la imagen *f*, zona de la imagen *f*; ~ **attenuation coefficient** *n* ELECTRON coeficiente de atenuación de imagen *m*; ~ **carrier** *n* TV onda portadora de imagen *f*; ~ **charge** *n* ELEC ENG carga de imagen *f*; ~ **compression** *n* ELECTRON compresión de imagen *f*; ~ **contraction** *n* TV contracción de la imagen *f*; ~**-control coil** *n* CINEMAT, TV bobina de regulación de la imagen *f*; ~ **conversion** *n* ELECTRON, TELECOM conversión de imagen *f*; ~ **converter** *n* CINEMAT, ELECTRON convertidor de imagen *m*, INSTR transformador de imagen *m*; ~ **converter tube** *n* CINEMAT, ELECTRON tubo de convertidor de imagen *m*; ~ **digitization** *n* ELECTRON, TELECOM, TV digitalización de imagen *f*, digitización de imagen *f*; ~ **digitizer** *n* ELECTRON digitalizador de imagen *m*; ~ **dislocation** *n* METALL dislocación de imagen *f*; ~ **dissector** *n* ELECTRON disector de imagen *m*; ~ **enhancement** *n* ELECTRON mejora de la imagen *f*, SPACE intensificación de imágenes *f*, TV refuerzo de la imagen *m*; ~**-erecting prism** *n* INSTR prisma de enderezamiento de imagen *m*; ~ **field** *n* CINEMAT campo de imagen *m*; ~ **file** *n* ELECTRON fichero de imagen *m*; ~ **flicker** *n* TV parpadeo de la imagen *m*, reforzador de la imagen *m*; ~ **frequency** *n* ELECTRON, TELECOM frecuencia de imagen *f*; ~**-frequency interference** *n* ELECTRON interferencia de la frecuencia de imagen *f;* ~ **iconoscope** *n* ELECTRON iconoscopio de imagen *m;* ~ **impedance** *n* ACOUST, ELEC ENG, PHYS, TELECOM impedancia de imagen *f;* ~ **intensifier** *n* ELECTRON, INSTR intensificador de imagen *m;* ~ **intensifier tube** *n* ELECTRON, INSTR, TV tubo intensificador de imagen *m;* ~ **lag** *n* TV retardo de la imagen *m,* retraso de la imagen *m;* ~ **orthicon** *n* ELECTRON, TV orticonoscopio de imagen *m;* ~ **phase change coefficient** *n* ELECTRON coeficiente de cambio de fase de imagen *m;* ~ **plane** *n* CINEMAT plano de imagen *m;* ~ **processing** *n* COMP&DP procesamiento de imágenes *m,* ELECTRON tratamiento de imágenes *m,* tratamiento de la imagen *m,* TELECOM procesamiento de imagen *m;* ~ **projection** *n* ELECTRON proyección de la imagen *f;* ~ **reactor** *n* NUCL reactor imagen *m;* ~ **refreshing** *n* COMP&DP regeneración de imagen *f;* ~ **restoration** *n* COMP&DP restauración de imagen *f;* ~ **retention** *n* TV retención de la imagen *f;* ~ **scale** *n* CINEMAT escala de imagen *f;* ~ **scanner** *n* TV explorador de imagen *m;* ~ **sensor** *n* TELECOM sensor de imagen *m;* ~ **sequence** *n* TELECOM secuencia de imagen *f;* ~ **setter** *n* PRINT montador de imágenes *m;* ~ **signal** *n* ELECTRON señal de imagen *f;* ~ **steadiness** *n* CINEMAT estabilidad de la imagen *f,* fijación de la imagen *f;* ~ **storage** *n* ELEC ENG almacenado de imágenes *m,* ELECTRON almacenamiento de imagen *m;* ~ **storage tube** *n* ELECTRON tubo de almacenamiento de imagen *m;* ~ **table** *n* PROD tabla de imágenes *f;* ~ **transfer** *n* TELECOM transferencia de imagen *f;* ~ **transfer coefficient** *n* ELECTRON coeficiente de transferencia de imagen *m;* ~ **transfer exponent** *n* ACOUST exponente de transferencia entre imágenes *m;* ~ **transmission** *n* TELECOM transmisión de imagen *f;* ~ **and waveform monitor** *n* TV monitor de imagen y configuración de onda *m,* monitor de imagen y forma de onda *m*

image² *vt* COMP&DP representar por imágenes

imager *n* COMP&DP creador de imágenes *m,* dispositivo de imagen *m*

imaginary: ~ **number** *n* MATH número imaginario *m*

imaging *n* ELECTRON formación de imágenes *f,* PRINT copiado de la imagen *m;* ~ **array** *n* ELECTRON agrupación de imágenes *f;* ~ **chip** *n* ELECTRON chip reproductor de imágenes *m;* ~ **mechanism** *n* OPT mecanismo de formación de imágenes *m;* ~ **system** *n* OPT sistema de formación de imágenes *m,* PRINT sistema de copiado de imágenes *m*

Imax: ~ **process** *n* CINEMAT proceso Imax *m*

imbalance *n* PRINT desproporción *f*

imbibition *n* HYDROL imbibición *f*

imbricate *adj* CONST, GEOL imbricado

imbricated¹ *adj* CONST, GEOL imbricado

imbricated²: ~ **structure** *n* GEOL estructura imbricada *f*

Imhoff: ~ **sedimentation cone** *n* LAB cono de sedimentación de Imhoff *m*

imide *n* CHEM imida *f*

imido *n* CHEM imido *m*

imidogen *n* CHEM imidógeno *m*

imine *n* CHEM imina *f*

imitation¹ *adj* PAPER simili, símil

imitation²: ~ **art paper** *n* PAPER papel supersatinado *m*

imitative: ~ **deception** *n* ELECTRON falsa imitación *f*

immature: ~ **grain** *n* AGRIC cereal verde *m*

immediate: ~ **access** *n* COMP&DP acceso inmediato *m;* ~ **access storage** *n* *AmE* (*IAS*) COMP&DP almacena-

miento de acceso inmediato *m;* ~ **access store** *n* *BrE* (*IAS*) COMP&DP almacenamiento de acceso inmediato *m;* ~ **address** *n* COMP&DP direccional inmediato *m,* dirección inmediata *f;* ~ **addressing** *n* COMP&DP direccional inmediato *m,* direccionamiento inmediato *m;* ~ **data** *n pl* COMP&DP datos inmediatos *m pl;* ~ **input** *n* PROD entrada inmediata *f;* ~ **input date** *n* PROD fecha de entrada inmediata *f;* ~ **I/O** *n* PROD E/S directa *f;* ~ **I/O update instruction** *n* PROD instrucción de actualización de E/S directa *f;* ~ **output** *n* PROD salida inmediata *f;* ~ **output date** *n* PROD fecha de salida inmediata *f;* ~ **update** *n* PROD actualización inmediata *f*

immerse *vt* CHEM, PHYS sumergir

immersed *adj* CHEM, PHYS sumergido

immersion *n* GEN inmersión *f;* ~ **cooling** *n* REFRIG refrigeración por inmersión *f;* ~ **freezing** *n* PACK, REFRIG congelación por inmersión *f;* ~ **heater** *n* ELEC *heating* calentador de inmersión *m,* termoinmersor *m,* ELEC ENG calentador sumergible *m,* calentador de inmersión *m,* HEAT, LAB calentador de inmersión *m,* MECH calentador de inmersión *m,* termoinmersor *m,* MECH ENG calentador de inmersión *m;* ~ **lens** *n* INSTR lente de inmersión *f,* LAB lente de inmersión *f,* lente seca *f;* ~ **milk cooler** *n* AGRIC, REFRIG enfriador de leche por inmersión *m;* ~ **muffle** *n* C&G mufla de inmersión *f;* ~ **objective** *n* INSTR objetivo de inmersión *m,* METALL objeto de inmersión *m,* objetivo de inmersión *m,* PHYS objetivo de inmersión *m;* ~ **oil** *n* LAB *microscope,* METALL aceite de inmersión *m;* ~ **plating** *n* COATINGS depósito por inmersión *m,* recubrimiento por inmersión *m;* ~ **well** *n* PROD pozo de inmersión *m*

immiscible *adj* CHEM, FLUID, FOOD, PETR TECH inmiscible

immobile: ~ **dislocation** *n* METALL dislocación fija *f,* dislocación inmóvil *f*

IMO *abbr* (*International Maritime Organization*) WATER TRANSP OMI (*Organización Marítima Internacional*)

IMP *abbr* (*interface message processor*) TELECOM procesador de mensajes de interfaz *m*

impact *n* ACOUST impacto *m,* COAL choque *m,* colisión *f,* impacto *m,* influjo *m,* repercusión *f,* CONST, MECH, PHYS choque *m,* impacto *m;* ~ **breaker** *n* MECH ENG machacadora de impactos *f,* quebrantadora de martillos *f;* ~ **crater** *n* SPACE cráter de impacto *m;* ~ **crusher** *n* MECH ENG machacadora de impactos *f,* quebrantadora de martillos *f;* ~ **energy** *n* METALL energía de impacto *f,* potencia de impacto *f;* ~ **excitation** *n* RAD PHYS excitación por impacto *f;* ~ **fluorescence** *n* TV fluorescencia de impacto *f;* ~ **fracture** *n* NUCL fractura por impacto *f;* ~ **ionization** *n* PHYS, RAD PHYS ionización por choque *f,* ionización por colisión *f;* ~ **ionization avalanche transit-time diode** *n* (*IMPATT diode*) ELECTRON, PHYS diodo de tiempo de tránsito por avalancha con ionización por choque *m;* ~ **load** *n* AIR TRANSP carga de impacto *f;* ~ **parameter** *n* PHYS parámetro de impacto *m;* ~ **plate** *n* COAL placa de impacto *f;* ~ **polystyrene** *n* P&R poliestireno de impacto *m;* ~ **pressure** *n* AIR TRANSP presión de impacto *f;* ~ **printer** *n* COMP&DP, PRINT impresora de impacto *f;* ~ **resistance** *n* PACK, TRANSP resistencia al impacto *f;* ~ **ripper** *n* MINE desfondadora hidráulica *f;* ~ **screen** *n* COAL criba de percusión *f,* criba vibradora *f,* PROD criba de percusión *f,* criba vibratoria *f;*

~ **screwdriver** n MECH ENG destornillador de golpe m, destornillador de impacto m; ~ **sound transmission level** n ACOUST nivel de transmisión del sonido de impacto m; ~ **sound-reducing material** n ACOUST material amortiguador de sonidos de impacto m; ~ **strength** n MECH resistencia al choque f, NUCL, P&R resistencia al impacto f, PHYS resistencia al choque f; ~ **stress** n PACK tensión de impacto f; ~ **study** n GAS, WATER estudio de impacto m; ~ **test** n COATINGS ensayo de impacto m, METALL prueba de impacto f, METR prueba al choque f, prueba de fragilidad f, prueba de resiliencia f, PACK ensayo de impacto m, PHYS prueba al choque f, TRANSP ensayo de impacto m, prueba de impacto f; ~ **theory of line broadening** n RAD PHYS teoría del ensanchamiento de rayas por colisión f; ~ **velocity** n METALL velocidad de impacto f; ~ **wrench** n MECH ENG llave de choque f, llave de impacto f

impairment: ~ **of hearing index** n ACOUST índice de trastorno auditivo m

impart vt MECH ENG rotary motion comunicar, impartir, transmitir, PHYS screen transmitir; ~ **energy to** vt PHYS, THERMO transmitir energía a

IMPATT: ~ **diode** n (impact ionization avalanche transit-time diode) ELECTRON, PHYS diodo de TTAICH m; ~ **oscillator** n ELECTRON oscilador de TTAICH m

impedance n ELEC, ELEC ENG, PHYS, TELECOM impedancia f; ~ **bond** n RAIL conexión inductiva f; ~ **bridge** n ELEC ENG puente para medir impedancias m; ~ **characteristic** n ELEC ENG característica de impedancia f; ~ **coil** n ELEC bobina de reactancia f, ELEC ENG bobina de reactancia f, reactor m, PHYS bobina de reactancia f; ~ **conversion** n ELEC ENG conversión de impedancia f; ~ **corrector** n ELEC compensador de impedancia m, corrector de impedancia m; ~ **coupling** n ELEC ENG acoplamiento por impedancia m; ~ **drop** n ELEC of voltage caída de tensión debida a la impedancia f; ~ **earthed neutral system** n BrE (cf impedance grounded neutral system AmE) ELEC sistema con neutro a tierra m; ~ **grounded neutral system** n AmE (cf impedance earthed neutral system BrE) ELEC sistema con neutro a tierra m; ~ **matching** n ELEC ENG adaptación de impedancias f, equilibrado de impedancias m, PHYS equilibrado de impedancias m; ~~-**matching network** n ELEC ENG red de igualación de impedancias f, PHYS red de equilibrado de impedancias f; ~~-**matching transformer** n ELEC ENG transformador de adaptación de impedancias m; ~ **mismatch** n ELEC ENG desadaptación de impedancias f, desequilibrio de impedancias m; ~ **network** n PROD red por impedancia f; ~ **ratio** n PROD relación de impedancia f; ~ **recorder** n INSTR grabador por impedancia m; ~ **relay** n ELEC relé de impedancia m; ~ **transformer** n PHYS transformador de impedancias m; ~ **voltage** n ELEC ENG voltaje de impedancia m; ~ **voltage at rated current** n ELEC of transformer tensión de cortocircuito a corriente de régimen f, tensión de cortocircuito a corriente nominal f

impedor n ELEC ENG impedancia f

impeller n AIR TRANSP of turbine engine impulsor m, propulsor m, rotor m, rotor de compresor centrífugo m, AUTO, COAL impulsor m, propulsor m, HYDRAUL rueda de paletas f, MECH rueda motriz f, propulsor m, rotor m, soplador m, rueda móvil f, NUCL impulsor m, PROD of centrifugal pump rueda móvil f, VEH rotor m, WATER TRANSP rueda de paletas f; ~ **backplate** n REFRIG disco posterior del rodete m

imperative adj COMP&DP imperativo

imperfect: ~ **dielectric** n ELEC dieléctrico con pérdida m, dieléctrico imperfecto m

impermeability n GEN impermeabilidad f

impermeable[1] adj GEN impermeable

impermeable[2]: ~ **layer** n GAS capa impermeable f

impervious adj COATINGS, CONST, GAS impermeable, GEOL impenetrable, impermeable, HYDROL impermeable, MECH impenetrable, impermeable, inatacable, P&R, PACK, PAPER impermeable, PETR TECH impenetrable, impermeable, PETROL, TEXTIL, WATER impermeable

imperviousness n FUELLESS impermeabilidad f, PROD of joint estanqueidad f, hermeticidad f

impetus n MECH fuerza f, ímpetu m, MECH ENG fuerza f, impulsión f, impulso m, ímpetu m, PHYS ímpetu m

impinge: ~ **on** vt MECH, MECH ENG chocar con, golpear contra, tocar contra

impingement n MECH, MECH ENG choque m, colisión f, golpe m, impacto m, incidencia f, METALL colisión f; ~ **drying** n CINEMAT secado por choque m

impinger n CHEM aparato de incidencia m

impinging: ~ **particle** n NUCL partícula incidente f

implant[1] n AGRIC implante m, ELECTRON acoplamiento m; ~ **and anneal** n ELECTRON acoplamiento y fijación m; ~ **dose** n ELECTRON dosis acumulada f

implant[2] vt GEN implantar

implantation n ELECTRON acoplamiento m

implanted adj ELECTRON motor acoplado

implement[1] n GEN instrumento m; ~ **carrier** n AGRIC tractor porta-aperos m

implement[2] vt MECH ENG implementar, instrumentar, llevar a cabo, poner en práctica, TELECOM implementar

implementation n GEN estructuración f, implementación f, puesta en aplicación f

implicit: ~ **differentiation** n MATH diferenciación implícita f; ~ **function** n MATH función implícita f

implied: ~ **addressing** n COMP&DP direccionamiento implícito m

implode[1] vt ELECTRON condensar, implosionar

implode[2] vi CHEM, NUCL, PROD implosionar

implosion n CHEM implosión f, ELECTRON aplastamiento m, implosión f, NUCL implosión f, PROD aplastamiento m, implosión f; ~ **weapon** n MILIT, NUCL arma de implosión f, arma nuclear de implosión f

import: ~ **licence** n BrE TRANSP licencia de importación f, WATER TRANSP licencia de importación f, permiso de importación m; ~ **license** AmE see import licence BrE

impose vt PRINT imponer

imposed: ~ **pressure gradient** n FLUID gradiente de presión impuesto m

imposing: ~ **surface** n PRINT superficie de imposición f; ~ **table** n PRINT platina f

imposition n PRINT imposición f

impost n CONST imposta f

impounding: ~ **reservoir** n WATER depósito de captación m, embalse de retención m

impoverishment n AGRIC of soil, NUCL empobrecimiento m

impregnant n GEN impregnante m

impregnate *vt* CHEM impregnar, saturar, COATINGS, CONST, ELEC ENG, PACK, PAPER, TEXTIL impregnar
impregnated[1] *adj* CHEM, COATINGS, ELEC ENG, PACK, PAPER, TEXTIL impregnado
impregnated[2]: ~ **cable** *n* ELEC cable impregnado *m*; ~ **cathode** *n* ELEC ENG cátodo impregnado *m*; ~ **coil** *n* ELEC ENG bobina impregnada *f*; ~ **fabric** *n* PACK tejido impregnado *m*; ~ **paper** *n* PACK papel impregnado *m*; ~ **paper insulation** *n* ELEC *cable conductor*, ELEC ENG aislación de papel impregnado *f*
impregnating: ~ **agent** *n* PACK agente de impregnación *m*; ~ **machine** *n* PACK máquina impregnadora *f*; ~ **varnish** *n* COATINGS barniz de impregnación *m*, barniz impregnado *m*, ELEC barniz de impregnación *m*, *insulation* barniz impregnado *m*; ~ **wax** *n* PACK cera para impregnar *f*
impregnation *n* GEN impregnación *f*
impress *vt* TEXTIL imprimir
impressed: ~ **voltage** *n* ELEC tensión aplicada *f*, voltaje aplicado *m*
impression *n* C&G, PROD, TEXTIL impresión *f*; ~ **blanket** *n* PRINT mantilla de impresión *f*; ~ **cylinder** *n* P&R cilindro impresor *m*, PRINT cilindro de impresión *m*; ~ **pad** *n* PACK almohadilla de impresión *f*; ~ **roller** *n* P&R rodillo impresor *m*
imprint[1] *n* PRINT sobreimpresión *f*
imprint[2] *vt* PRINT sobreimprimir
imprinting *n* PRINT sobreimpresión *f*; ~ **unit** *n* PRINT dispositivo de impresión suplementaria *m*
improper: ~ **time** *n* PHYS *materials* tiempo impropio *m*
improved: ~ **diesel engine** *n* TRANSP motor diesel preparado *m*; ~ **pattern** *n* PROD diseño perfeccionado *m*; ~ **type** *n* PROD tipo mejorado *m*
improvement: ~ **notice** *n* SAFE notificación de mejora *f*; ~ **of soil structure** *n* AGRIC mejoramiento estructural de suelo *m*
improver *n* FOOD, PETR TECH mejorador *m*
impulse *n* MECH impulsión *f*, impulso *m*, sobretensión *f*, sobrevoltaje *m*, MECH ENG *of force* estímulo *m*, impulso *m*, impulsión *f*, PETROL, PHYS, SPACE, TELECOM impulso *m*; ~ **counter** *n* ELEC, INSTR contador de impulsos *m*; ~ **coupling** *n* MECH ENG acoplamiento impulsor *m*, acoplamiento por impulso *m*; ~ **current** *n* ELEC corriente de choque *f*; ~ **dispersion** *n* OPT dispersión por pulsos *f*; ~ **excitation** *n* RAD PHYS excitación por pulsos *f*, TELECOM excitación por impulsos *f*; ~ **function** *n* ELECTRON función de impulsos *f*; ~ **generator** *n* ELEC *test equipment* generador de impulsos *m*, ELEC ENG generador Marx *m*, generador de impulsos *m*; ~ **heat sealer** *n* PACK termosellado por impulsos *m*; ~ **noise** *n* ACOUST ruido impulsivo *m*, COMP&DP ruido de impulsos *m*, TELECOM ruido impulsivo *m*; ~ **regenerator** *n* ELECTRON, RAD PHYS regenerador de impulsos *m*; ~ **relay** *n* ELEC ENG relé de impulsión *m*; ~ **response** *n* OPT, PETROL, TELECOM respuesta de impulsos *f*; ~ **test** *n* ELEC ENG prueba de impulsión *f*; ~ **turbine** *n* FUELLESS turbina de impulsión *f*, turbina tipo Pelton *f*, HYDRAUL turbina motriz *f*, MECH turbina de acción *f*, turbina de impulsión *f*, PROD rueda Pelton *f*, turbina de acción *f*, turbina de impulsión *f*; ~ **voltage** *n* ELEC tensión de choque *f*, ELEC ENG sobrevoltaje *m*; ~ **wheel** *n* PROD rueda de acción *f*, rueda de impulsión *f*
impulsion *n* MECH ENG impulsión *f*, impulso *m*
impulsive[1] *adj* MECH ENG impulsivo, propulsivo

impulsive[2]: ~ **noise** *n* ACOUST ruido impulsivo *m*
impulsiveness: ~ **ratio** *n* TELECOM relación de impulsividad *f*
impurify *vt* CHEM impurificar
impurity *n* CHEM, ELECTRON, METALL, MINERAL, QUALITY impureza *f*; ~ **atom** *n* CRYSTALL átomo de impureza *m*; ~ **concentration** *n* ELECTRON concentración de impurezas *f*; ~ **concentration profile** *n* ELECTRON perfil de concentración de impurezas *m*; ~ **diffusion** *n* ELECTRON difusión de impurezas *f*; ~ **level** *n* ELECTRON nivel de impurezas *m*; ~ **scattering** *n* ELECTRON dispersión de impurezas *f*
In *abbr* (*indium*) CHEM, METALL In (*indio*)
inaccuracy: ~ **of measurement** *n* METR inexactitud de la medida *f*
inactivation *n* CHEM inactivación *f*
inactive[1] *adj* AIR TRANSP en la reserva, CHEM, COMP&DP, ELECTRON inactivo, MECH ENG, PROD en la reserva, WATER TRANSP *warship* en la reserva, inactivo
inactive[2]: ~ **inventory** *n* PROD inventario inmovilizado *m*
inadequate: ~ **core cooling** *n* NUCL refrigeración inadecuada del núcleo *f*
in-and-out: ~ **bolt** *n* MECH ENG perno de entrada y salida *m*, perno pasante *m*; ~ **calipers** *AmE*, ~ **callipers** *BrE n pl* MECH ENG calibradores de entrada y salida *m pl*, calibradores de máxima y mínima *m pl*, calibrador de máxima y mínima *m*
inarching *n* AGRIC apuntalamiento *m*
in-band: ~ **signaling** *AmE*, ~ **signalling** *BrE n* SPACE *communications* señalización dentro de banda *f*, señalización por frecuencias vocales *f*
in-betweener *n* CINEMAT intermediario *m*
inboard[1] *adj* AIR TRANSP cerca del fuselaje, hacia adentro, interior
inboard[2]: ~ **binding** *n* PRINT encuadernación en cartoné *f*
inbound[1]: ~~**heading** *adj* AIR TRANSP hacia la base
inbound[2]: ~ **stock point** *n* PROD punto de existencias de llegada *m*; ~ **traffic** *n* TRANSP tráfico interior *m*
inbred: ~ **variety cross** *n* AGRIC híbrido línea variedad *m*
inbreeding *n* AGRIC consanguinización *f*
in-call: ~ **modification** *n* TELECOM modificación de llamada entrante *f*
in-camera: ~ **effect** *n* CINEMAT efecto en cámara *m*
incandescence *n* CHEM, ELEC ENG, RAD PHYS incandescencia *f*
incandescent[1] *adj* CHEM, ELEC ENG, RAD PHYS incandescente
incandescent[2]: ~ **lamp** *n* ELEC, ELEC ENG lámpara de incandescencia *f*, lámpara incandescente *f*
incendiary *adj* MILIT incendiario
in-center *AmE see in-centre BrE*
in-centre *adj BrE* GEOM centrado, céntrico, del centro
inch *n* METR pulgada *f*; ~ **screw thread** *n* MECH ENG filete de tornillo de una pulgada *m*, hilo de tornillo de una pulgada *m*, rosca de tornillo de una pulgada *f*
inches: ~ **per second** *n pl* (*IPS*) COMP&DP pulgadas por segundo *f pl* (*PPS*)
inching *n* CINEMAT avance lento *m*, PROD avance lento *m*, marcha lenta *f*; ~ **knob** *n* CINEMAT botón de avance lento *m*
incidence *n* ACOUST, AGRIC, AIR TRANSP, OPT, PHYS *element* incidencia *f*; ~ **angle** *n* AIR TRANSP, CINEMAT,

FUELLESS, OPT, PHYS, PROD, TELECOM, WAVE PHYS ángulo de incidencia *m*; ~ **oscillation** *n* AIR TRANSP oscilación de incidencia *f*; ~ **probe** *n* AIR TRANSP sonda de incidencia *f*

incident *n* AIR TRANSP, MAR POLL, OPT, POLL, TRANSP incidente *m*; ~ **beam** *n* CRYSTALL haz incidente *m*, rayo incidente *m*, PHYS haz incidente *m*; ~ **data reporting** *n* AIR TRANSP informe de datos de incidente *m*; ~ **illumination** *n* INSTR iluminación incidente *f*; ~ **light** *n* CINEMAT, PHOTO, RAD PHYS luz incidente *f*; ~**-light attachment** *n* PHOTO accesorio de luz incidente *m*; ~ **particle** *n* NUCL partícula incidente *f*; ~ **ray** *n* PHYS, WAVE PHYS rayo incidente *m*; ~ **signal** *n* ELECTRON señal incidente *f*; ~ **top lighting** *n* INSTR alumbrado vertical incidente *m*; ~ **warning sign** *n* TRANSP señal de advertencia de incidente *f*, señalización de aviso de incidente *f*; ~ **wave** *n* PHYS, WAVE PHYS onda incidente *f*

incidental: ~ **amplitude modulation** *n* ELECTRON modulación de amplitud imprevista *f*; ~ **frequency modulation** *n* ELECTRON modulación de frecuencia imprevista *f*; ~ **modulation** *n* ELECTRON modulación imprevista *f*

incinerate *vt* HEAT, THERMO incinerar
incinerated *adj* THERMO incinerado
incinerator *n* CONST, HEAT, THERMO incinerador *m*
incipient: ~ **crack** *n* AIR TRANSP fisura incipiente *f*, NUCL grieta incipiente *f*; ~ **fatigue failure** *n* AIR TRANSP fallo de fatiga incipiente *m*
incised: ~**-leaf-type camouflage net** *n* MILIT red de camuflaje de tipo hoja cortada *f*
inclination *n* CONST buzamiento *m*, inclinación *f*, ángulo *m*, GEOM, PHYS inclinación *f*, SPACE disposición *f*, inclinación *f*, pendiente *f*
incline *n* CONST *rising gradient* rampa *f*, *falling* declive *m*, *plane* plano inclinado *m*, MECH ENG plano inclinado automotor *m*; ~ **hole** *n* MINE galería inclinada *f*, perforación inclinada *f*, pozo inclinado *m*; ~ **shaft** *n* MINE pozo inclinado *m*
inclined[1] *adj* GEOL, GEOM inclinado
inclined[2]: ~ **channel** *n* NUCL canal en pendiente *m*; ~ **drive shaft** *n* AIR TRANSP *of helicopter* eje conductor inclinado *m*; ~ **fold** *n* GEOL pliegue inclinado *m*; ~ **hole** *n* MINE galería inclinada *f*, pozo inclinado *m*; ~ **plane** *n* CONST, GEOM, PHYS plano inclinado *m*; ~ **ramp** *n* PETR TECH, PETROL plano inclinado *m*; ~ **shaft** *n* MINE chiflón *m* (*AmL*), inclinación del eje en un coladero *f*, pozo inclinado *m*
inclining: ~ **test** *n* WATER TRANSP *naval architecture* experiencia de estabilidad *f*
inclinometer *n* COAL brújula de inclinación *f*, clinómetro *m*, inclinómetro *m*, GEOPHYS, INSTR, PETROL, PHYS inclinómetro *m*
included *adj* MECH ENG *angle* comprendido, incluido
inclusion *n* CRYSTALL *in crystal* inclusión *f*, imperfección *f*, METALL, MINERAL, NUCL, PETROL, QUALITY inclusión *f*
inclusive: ~ **AND circuit** *n* ELECTRON circuito Y *m*; ~ **AND gate** *n* ELECTRON puerta Y *f*; ~ **OR circuit** *n* ELECTRON circuito O lógico *m*; ~ **OR gate** *n* COMP&DP puerta O inclusiva *f*, puerta OR inclusiva *f*, ELECTRON circuito O lógico *m*, circuito lógico mezclador *m*, puerta O lógica *f*, puerta lógica mezcladora *f*; ~ **OR operation** *n* COMP&DP operación O inclusiva *f*, operación OR inclusiva *f*

incoherence *n* METALL, OPT, PHYS, TELECOM, WAVE PHYS incoherencia *f*
incoherent[1] *adj* METALL, OPT, PHYS, TELECOM, WAVE PHYS incoherente
incoherent[2]: ~ **light** *n* TELECOM, WAVE PHYS luz incoherente *f*; ~ **radiation** *n* PHYS, TELECOM radiación incoherente *f*; ~ **twin** *n* METALL macla incoherente *f*
incoming: ~ **call** *n* TELECOM llamada entrante *f*; ~ **calls barred** *n* (*ICB*) TELECOM llamadas entrantes prohibidas *f pl*, llamadas entrantes restringidas *f pl*; ~ **calls barred line** *n* TELECOM línea restringida de llamadas entrantes *f*; ~ **circuit** *n* TELECOM circuito entrante *m*; ~ **feed** *n* TV alimentación de entrada *f*; ~ **freight** *n* PROD flete de llegada *m*; ~ **group** *n* TELECOM grupo entrante *m*; ~ **line** *n* TELECOM línea entrante *f*; ~ **line fuse** *n* MECH ENG, PROD fusible de línea de entrada *m*; ~ **line voltage** *n* PROD voltaje de línea de entrada *m*; ~ **message** *n* COMP&DP mensaje entrante *m*; ~ **power terminal** *n* PROD terminal de potencia de entrada *m*; ~ **procedure** *n* TELECOM procedimiento entrante *m*; ~ **register** *n* TELECOM registro entrante *m*; ~ **signal** *n* ELECTRON señal de llegada *f*, TELECOM señal entrante *f*; ~ **traffic** *n* TELECOM tráfico entrante *m*; ~ **trunk circuit** *n* TELECOM circuito de enlace entrante *m*; ~ **voltage monitor** *n* PROD monitor de voltaje de entrada *m*; ~ **web** *n* PRINT banda entrante *f*
incommensurable *adj* MATH inconmensurable
incompatible: ~ **element** *n* GEOL elemento incompatible *m*
incomplete: ~ **rung** *n* PROD escalón incompleto *m*
incompressibility *n* AIR TRANSP, CHEM, FLUID, PHYS incompresibilidad *f*
incompressible[1] *adj* AIR TRANSP incompresible, no compresible, CHEM, FLUID, PHYS incompresible
incompressible[2]: ~ **flow** *n* FLUID, PHYS flujo incompresible *m*
inconclusive: ~ **test** *n* PHYS prueba no concluyente *f*
in-connector *n* TELECOM conector de entrada *m*
in-core: ~ **fuel cycle** *n* NUCL ciclo intranuclear del combustible *m*; ~ **fuel life** *n* NUCL permanencia del combustible en el núcleo *f*; ~ **instrument assembly** *n* NUCL conjunto de instrumentación intranuclear *m*; ~ **ionization chamber** *n* NUCL cámara de ionización intranuclear *f*; ~ **power manipulator** *n* NUCL elemento intranuclear de control de la potencia *m*
incorporate: ~ **into** *vt* HYDROL incorporar
incorporated *adj* HYDROL incorporado
incorrodible *adj* CHEM, METALL incorrosible
increase: ~ **in contrast** *n* PHOTO aumento de contraste *m*
increased: ~**-resistance rotor** *n* ELEC *generator* rotor de resistencia aumentada *m*
increasing: ~ **flow** *n* HYDROL *of river* caudal en aumento *m*
increment[1] *n* COMP&DP, ELEC incremento *m*, ELECTRON incremento *m*, paso *m*, MATH, TEXTIL incremento *m*; ~**-decrement counter** *n* ELECTRON contador arriba-abajo *m*, contador de aumento-disminución *m*, contador reversible *m*
increment[2] *vt* COMP&DP, ELEC, ELECTRON, MATH, TEXTIL incrementar
incremental[1] *adj* COMP&DP, ELEC, ELECTRON, MATH, TEXTIL incremental
incremental[2]: ~ **capacitance** *n* ELEC capacitancia incremental *f*; ~ **compiler** *n* COMP&DP compiladora

incremental *f*; ~ **digital recorder** *n* INSTR registrador de datos numéricos incremental *m*; ~ **inductance** *n* ELEC inductancia incremental *f*; ~ **plotter** *n* COMP&DP plotter incremental *m*, trazador incremental *m*; ~ **tape recorder** *n* INSTR magnetófono incremental *m*; ~ **tuning** *n* ELECTRON sintonización en avance progresivo *f*

incrompressibility *n* PHYS incompresibilidad *f*

incrustation *n* CHEM, GEOL incrustación *f*

incubator *n* HEAT incubadora *f*, LAB *for cable* incubador *m*

incunabulum *n* PRINT incunable *m*

in-cup: ~ **powder-filling machine** *n* PACK máquina para llenar vasos con productos en polvo *f*

Ind *abbr* (*indication*) TELECOM indicación *f*

indamine *n* CHEM indamina *f*

indane *n* CHEM hidrindeno *m*, indano *m*

indanthrene *n* CHEM indantreno *m*

indanthrone *n* CHEM indantrona *f*

indazine *n* CHEM indazina *f*

indazole *n* CHEM indazol *m*

indefinite: ~ **integral** *n* MATH integral indefinida *f*

indehiscent *adj* AGRIC indehiscente

indelible: ~ **ink** *n* COLOUR tinta indeleble *f*

indene *n* CHEM indeno *m*

indent[1] *n* CONST *carpentry* muesca *f*, PRINT sangría *f*

indent[2] *vt* CONST *carpentry* dentar, PRINT sangrar

indentation *n* MECH indentación *f*, mella *f*, MECH ENG indentación *f*, mella *f*, muesca *f*, METALL indentación *f*, mella *f*, PROD huella *f*, indentación *f*, muesca *f*; ~ **hardness** *n* P&R dureza a la melladura *f*, resistencia al impacto con entalla *f*

indented[1] *adj* MECH, MECH ENG, METALL, PROD indentado

indented[2]: ~ **bill of material** *n* PROD lista de materiales de compra *f*; ~ **chain** *n* MECH ENG cadena dentada *f*, cadena indentada *f*; ~ **wheel** *n* MECH ENG *cupped chain sheave* polea de cadena dentada *f*

indenter: ~ **tectonics** *n* GEOL tectónica penetrante *f*

independent[1] *adj* SPACE *system* independiente, libre

independent[2]: ~ **control** *n* NUCL control independiente *m*; ~ **crane** *n* CONST grúa independiente *f*; ~ **cutoff valve** *n* PROD distribuidor de teja de expansión *m*; ~ **excitation** *n* ELEC excitación independiente *f*; ~ **feeder** *n* ELEC *supply* alimentador independiente *m*; ~ **film-maker** *n* CINEMAT cineasta independiente *m*; ~ **front suspension** *n* AUTO suspensión delantera independiente *f*, suspensión independiente de las ruedas delanteras *f*, VEH suspensión delantera suficiente *f*, suspensión independiente de las ruedas delanteras *f*; ~ **navigation** *n* SPACE navegación independiente *f*; ~ **particle model** *n* NUCL, PHYS modelo de partículas independientes *m*; ~ **rear suspension** *n* AUTO, VEH suspensión independiente de las ruedas traseras *f*, suspensión trasera independiente *f*; ~ **sideband modulation** *n* ELECTRON modulación de banda lateral independiente *f*; ~ **system** *n* SPACE sistema autónomo *m*, sistema independiente *m*

indeterminate: ~ **waste** *n* POLL desechos indefinidos *m pl*, desperdicios no determinados *m pl*, desperdicios indefinidos *m pl*, RECYCL basura indeterminada *f*, desechos indefinidos *m pl*, desperdicios indefinidos *m pl*, desperdicios no determinados *m pl*

index[1] *n* CHEM, COMP&DP índice *m*, MECH ENG signo indicador *m*, cabezal divisor *m*, exponente *m*, fiel divisor *m*, graduador *m*, índice *m*, SPACE aguja *f*, índice *m*; ~ **of aridity** *n* HYDROL índice de aridez *m*; ~ **bar** *n* WATER TRANSP *of sextant* línea de fe de la alidada *f*; ~ **contrast** *n* OPT contraste de índice *m*; ~ **dial** *n* MECH ENG *machine tools* plato divisor *m*; ~ **dip** *n* OPT índice de horizonte *m*, índice de profundidad *m*, TELECOM gozo de índice *m*; ~ **fossil** *n* GEOL fósil característico *m*, fósil guía *m*, fósil indicador *m*; ~ **hole** *n* COMP&DP *of floppy disk* orificio de índice *m*; ~ **of humidity** *n* HYDROL índice de humedad *m*; ~ **of infiltration** *n* HYDROL índice de infiltración *m*; ~**matching material** *n* OPT material con ajuste índices *m*; ~ **mineral** *n* GEOL mineral guía *m*, mineral índice *m*; ~ **mirror** *n* INSTR *of sextant* sextante *m*; ~ **plate** *n* MECH ENG *machine tools* placa divisora *f*, placa graduadora *f*, plato divisor *m*, plato graduador *m*; ~ **profile** *n* OPT, TELECOM perfil de índice *m*; ~ **of refraction** *n* CINEMAT, OPT, PHOTO, PHYS, SPACE, TELECOM, WAVE PHYS índice de refracción *m*; ~ **register** *n* COMP&DP registro de índice *m*; ~ **tab** *n* PRINT pestaña del índice *f*; ~ **table** *n* MECH tabla indicadora *f*; ~ **tube** *n* TV tubo indicador *m*, válvula indicador *f*; ~ **value** *n* NUCL valor de índice *m*

index[2] *vt* COMP&DP indexar, poner en un índice, MECH catalogar, clasificar, SPACE clasificar, graduar

indexable: ~ **hard metal insert** *n* MECH ENG *cutting tool* inserto de metal duro graduable *m*, inserto de metal duro rotatorio *m*

indexed: ~ **addressing** *n* COMP&DP direccionamiento indexado *m*, direccionamiento indicado *m*; ~ **file** *n* COMP&DP archivo indexado *m*, archivo indicado *m*, fichero indexado *m*; ~ **sequential access** *n* COMP&DP acceso secuencial indexado *m*, acceso secuencial indicado *m*; ~ **sequential file** *n* COMP&DP archivo secuencial indexado *m*, fichero secuencial indexado *m*

indexing *n* COMP&DP indexación *f*, indicación *f*

india: ~ **rubber** *n* P&R caucho *m*, goma elástica *f*, PRINT caucho *m*

Indian: ~ **ink** *n* COLOUR, PRINT tinta china *f*; ~ **meal** *n* BrE (*cf corn meal AmE*) AGRIC harina de maíz *f* (*Esp*), polenta *f* (*AmL*)

indic *adj* CHEM índico

indican *n* CHEM indicán *m*

indicated: ~ **airspeed** *n* AIR TRANSP velocidad anemométrica indicada *f*; ~ **flight path** *n* AIR TRANSP trayectoria de vuelo indicada *f*; ~ **horsepower** *n* MECH ENG potencia bruta nominal *f*, potencia indicada *f*, potencia nominal *f*; ~ **pitch angle** *n* AIR TRANSP *of helicopter* ángulo de paso indicado *m*; ~ **value** *n* NUCL valor indicado *m*

indicating: ~ **instrument** *n* INSTR instrumento indicador *m*; ~ **stop** *n* MECH ENG tope indicador *m*; ~ **thermometer** *n* REFRIG termómetro de lectura directa *m*

indication *n* (*Ind*) TELECOM indicación *f*

indicator *n* AIR TRANSP *light signal* indicador *m*, AUTO *accessories* indicador *m*, interruptor intermitente *m*, COMP&DP indicador *m*, ELEC interruptor intermitente *m*, HYDRAUL, MECH ENG indicador *m*, VEH indicador *m*, interruptor intermitente *m*, WATER indicador *m*; ~ **color** AmE, ~ **colour** BrE *n* COLOUR colorante indicador *m*; ~ **diagram** *n* PHYS diagrama indicador *m*; ~ **gate** *n* ELECTRON impulso de sensibilización *m*; ~ **lamp** *n* ELEC luz indicadora *f*, lámpara indicadora *f*, PROD lámpara indicadora *f*, RAIL faro testigo *m*, lámpara testigo *f*, faro *m*; ~ **light** *n* AIR TRANSP, PROD luz indicadora *f*; ~ **needle** *n* ELEC, ELEC ENG, LAB, MECH ENG, PHOTO aguja indicadora *f*; ~ **paper** *n* PHOTO papel indicador *m*; ~ **plant** *n* MECH ENG instalación indicadora *f*, maquinaria indicadora *f*, material indicador *m*; ~ **plate** *n* SAFE, SPACE placa de identificación e instrucciones *f*; ~ **tube** *n* ELECTRON tubo indicador *m*

indicatrix *n* CRYSTALL indicatriz *f*

indices *n pl* CRYSTALL índices *m pl*

indicial: ~ **response** *n* ELECTRON respuesta indicativa *f*

indicolite *n* MINERAL indicolita *f*

indifference *n* CHEM indiferencia *f*

indigo *n* CHEM, COLOUR índigo *m*

indigolite *n* MINERAL indigolita *f*

indirect: ~ **addressing** *n* COMP&DP direccionamiento indirecto *m*; ~ **color separation** *AmE*, ~ **colour separation** *BrE n* PRINT selección de colores por proceso indirecto *f*; ~ **control** *n* ELEC ENG control indirecto *m*; ~ **control system** *n* TELECOM sistema de control indirecto *m*; ~ **expansion refrigeration system** *n* REFRIG sistema de enfriamiento por transmisión indirecta *m*; ~ **fire** *n* MILIT tiro indirecto *m*; ~ **frequency modulation** *n* ELECTRON modulación de frecuencia indirecta *f*; ~ **frequency synthesis** *n* ELECTRON síntesis de frecuencia indirecta *f*; ~ **frequency synthesizer** *n* ELECTRON sintetizador de frecuencia indirecta *m*; ~ **gap semiconductor** *n* ELECTRON semiconductor de separación indirecta *m*; ~ **heater-type cathode** *n* ELEC ENG cátodo de calentamiento indirecto *m*; ~ **illumination** *n* ELEC ENG iluminación indirecta *f*; ~ **initiation** *n* MINE comienzo indirecto *m*, inicio indirecto *m*; ~~**injection diesel engine** *n* TRANSP motor diesel de inyección indirecta *m*; ~ **leaching** *n* GAS lixiviación indirecta *f*; ~ **light reflector** *n* INSTR reflector de luz indirecta *m*; ~ **lighting** *n* CINEMAT, PHOTO iluminación indirecta *f*; ~ **man-hour** *n* MECH ENG hora-hombre indirecta *f*; ~ **man-hour ratio** *n* MECH ENG razón invertida hombre-hora *f*; ~ **over-current release** *n* ELEC *circuit breaker* aparato de máximo de corriente indirecta *m*; ~ **overhead camshaft** *n* AUTO eje de levas en cabeza indirecto *m*; ~ **photoconductivity** *n* ELEC fotoconductividad indirecta *f*; ~ **priming** *n* MINE cebado indirecto *m*, cebadura indirecta *f*; ~ **process** *n* PRINT proceso indirecto *m*; ~ **rectifier** *n* ELEC rectificador indirecto *m*

indirectly: ~~**heated cathode** *n* ELEC ENG cátodo caldeado indirectamente *m*

indirubin *n* CHEM, COLOUR indirrubina *f*

indiscriminate: ~ **dumping** *n* RECYCL vertido indiscriminado *m*

indistinguishability *n* PHYS indistinguibilidad *f*

indium *n* (*In*) CHEM, METALL indio *m* (*In*)

individual: ~ **channel flow control** *n* NUCL control del caudal por canales individuales *m*; ~ **control** *n* TRANSP control individual *m*; ~ **drive** *n* MECH ENG *for machine tools* accionamiento individual *m*, transmisión independiente *f*; ~ **dust removal apparatus** *n* SAFE aparatos individuales para remoción de polvos *m pl*; ~ **protection equipment** *n* (*IPE*) MILIT *chemical warfare* equipo de protección individual *m*; ~ **risk** *n* QUALITY riesgo individual *m*; ~ **section machine** *n* C&G máquina de secciones individuales *f*; ~ **store** *n* TELECOM almacén individual *m*; ~ **tool range alarm**

bit *n* PROD bit de alarma del rango individual de herramientas *m*; ~ **water supply** *n* HYDROL, WATER abastecimiento de agua individual *m*

indogen *n* CHEM indógeno *m*

indogenide *n* CHEM indogenido *m*

indole *n* CHEM indol *m*

indoleacetic *adj* CHEM indolacético

indolin *n* CHEM indolina *f*

indoline *n* CHEM indolina *f*

indone *n* CHEM indona *f*

indoor: ~ **aerial** *n BrE* (*cf indoor antenna AmE*) ELEC ENG, TV antena interior *f*; ~ **antenna** *n AmE* (*cf indoor aerial BrE*) ELEC ENG, TV antena interior *f*; ~ **cable** *n* ELEC cable interior *m*; ~ **installation** *n* ELEC instalación bajo techo *f*, instalación interior *f*; ~ **insulation** *n* ELEC, ELEC ENG aislación interior *f*, aislamiento interior *m*; ~ **lighting** *n* ELEC, ELEC ENG iluminación interior *f*; ~ **wiring** *n* ELEC ENG cableado interior *m*, montaje interior *m*

indophenin *n* CHEM, COLOUR indofenina *f*

indophenol *n* CHEM, COLOUR indofenol *m*; ~ **dye** *n* COLOUR colorante indofenólico *m*, tinte indofenólico *m*

indoxyl *n* CHEM indoxilo *m*

indoxylic *adj* CHEM indoxílico

indoxylsulfuric *AmE see indoxylsulphuric BrE*

indoxylsulphuric *adj BrE* CHEM indoxilsulfúrico

indraft *AmE see indraught BrE*

indraught *n BrE* MECH ENG absorción *f*, aspiración *f*, aspiración de aire *f*, corriente hacia adentro *f*, succión *f*; ~ **of air** *n BrE* MECH ENG absorción *f*, aspiración *f*, corriente hacia adentro *f*, flujo de aire aspirado *m*

in-drum: ~ **drying** *n* NUCL secado en bidón *m*

induce *vt* CHEM inducir, ELEC *current, voltage, charge* causar, inducir, provocar, ELEC ENG, PHYS inducir

induced: ~ **air** *n* MECH ENG aire aspirante *m*, aire inducido *m*; ~ **angle of attack** *n* AIR TRANSP, PHYS ángulo de ataque inducido *m*; ~ **charge** *n* CHEM, ELEC, ELEC ENG carga inducida *f*; ~ **current** *n* ELEC *electromagnetism*, TELECOM corriente inducida *f*; ~ **draft** *AmE see induced draught BrE*; ~~**draft burner** *AmE see induced-draught burner BrE*; ~~**draft fan** *AmE see induced-draught fan BrE*; ~ **draught** *n BrE* HEAT corriente inducida *f*, MECH ENG *chimneys* aspiración inducida *f*, corriente de aire inducida *f*, tiro aspirado *m*, tiro por aspiración *m*, *ventilation* tiro inducido *m*, ventilación por aspiración *f*; ~~**draught burner** *n BrE* MECH ENG quemador de corriente inducida *m*, quemador de tiro por aspiración *m*; ~~**draught fan** *n BrE* MECH ENG ventilador aspirador *m*, ventilador de corriente inducida *m*, ventilador de tiro inducido *m*, ventilador extractor *m*; ~ **electromotive force** *n* ELEC *electromagnetism*, ELEC ENG, PHYS fuerza electromotriz inducida *f*; ~ **failure** *n* COMP&DP avería inducida *f*, fallo inducido *m*; ~ **field** *n* ELEC *electromagnetism* campo de inducción *m*; ~ **noise current** *n* PROD ruido inducido por la corriente *m*; ~ **nuclear reaction** *n* NUCL reacción nuclear inducida *f*; ~ **over-voltage test** *n* ELEC *transformer* prueba de sobretensión inducida *f*; ~ **radioactivity** *n* PART PHYS radiactividad inducida *f*; ~ **voltage** *n* ELEC *electromagnetism* tensión inducida *f*, TELECOM voltaje inducido *m*

inducer *n* AIR TRANSP inductor *m*

inducing: ~ **flow** n CONST *of well* caudal de alimentación m; ~ **system** n PHYS sistema inductor m
in-duct: ~ **method** n REFRIG ensayo en conducto m
inductance n ELEC *electromagnetism* inductancia f, ELEC ENG inductancia f, bobina de autoinducción f, PHYS, TELECOM inductancia f; ~ **box** n ELEC ENG caja de inductancias f; ~ **bridge** n ELEC *measurement* puente de inductancias m, puente para medidas de inductancia m, ELEC ENG puente para medidas de inductancia m; ~-**capacitance filter** n ELECTRON filtro de inductancia-capacitancia m; ~ **coil** n ELEC *electromagnetism* bobina de inductancia f, inductor m, ELEC ENG bobina de inductancia f; ~ **coupling** n ELEC, ELEC ENG, PHYS acoplamiento por inductancia m; ~ **meter** n ELEC henrímetro m, inductancímetro m, ELEC ENG inductancímetro m, INSTR henrímetro m
induction n GEN inducción f; ~ **accelerator** n RAD PHYS acelerador por inducción m; ~ **coil** n AUTO bobina de inducción f, ELEC bobina de Ruhmkorff f, carrete de inducción m, ELEC ENG, GEOPHYS, VEH bobina de inducción f; ~ **current** n ELEC, ELEC ENG corriente de inducción f; ~ **displacement** n ELEC *alternating current* desplazamiento por inducción m; ~ **field** n ELEC ENG, TV campo inductor m; ~ **flux** n ELEC flujo de inducción m; ~ **frequency converter** n ELEC convertidor de frecuencia de inducción m; ~ **furnace** n ELEC ENG, PHYS, PROD horno de inducción m; ~ **generator** n ELEC, ELEC ENG alternador asincrónico m, alternador de inducción m, generador de inducción m; ~ **hardening** n ELEC ENG endurecimiento por inducción m, temple por corrientes de inducción m, METALL endurecimiento por inducción m; ~ **heater** n ELEC ENG calentador por corrientes de inducción m; ~ **heating** n ELEC ENG inductotermia f, MECH *transformer, electrical machine* calentamiento por inducción m, inductotermia f, P&R calentamiento por inducción m, THERMO inductotermia f; ~ **inner seal** n PACK sellado por inducción interna m; ~ **instrument** n ELEC ENG, INSTR instrumento de inducción m; ~ **log** n PETR TECH, PETROL perfil de inducción m; ~ **loop detector** n TRANSP detector del bucle de inducción m; ~ **motor** n ELEC motor asincrónico m, motor de inducción m, ELEC ENG, PHYS, PROD, TRANSP motor de inducción m; ~ **period** n METALL período de inducción m; ~ **pickup** n MECH ENG alimentación de inducción f, toma de inducción f; ~ **pipe** n HYDRAUL tubo de admisión m; ~ **port** n HYDRAUL lumbrera de admisión f, orificio de admisión m; ~ **pump** n ELEC ENG bomba de inducción f; ~ **regulator** n ELEC *transformer* regulador de inducción m; ~ **relay** n ELEC relé de inducción m, relé inductivo m, ELEC ENG relé inductivo m; ~ **sealer** n PACK selladora por inducción f; ~ **stroke** n VEH carrera de aspiración f, tiempo de admisión m; ~ **valve** n AUTO válvula de inducción f, HYDRAUL válvula de admisión f, válvula de entrada f; ~ **voltage** n ELEC ENG tensión de inducción f; ~ **voltage regulator** n ELEC ENG regulador del voltaje de inducción m; ~ **welding** n ELEC *process* soldadura por inducción f, PROD soldadura por corriente de inducción f
inductive: ~ **capacitor** n ELEC ENG condensador inductor m; ~ **circuit** n ELEC circuito inductivo m; ~ **coordination** n ELEC ENG coordinación inductiva f; ~ **coupling** n ELEC *inductor* acoplamiento inductivo

m, acoplamiento por inducción m, ELEC ENG, PHYS acoplamiento por inducción m, acoplamiento inductivo m; ~ **drop** n ELEC *of voltage* caída inductiva f; ~ **feedback** n ELEC reacción inductiva f, realimentación inductiva f, ELECTRON realimentación inductiva f; ~ **heating** n THERMO calentamiento inductivo m; ~ **load** n ELEC *alternating current*, ELEC ENG, TELECOM carga inductiva f; ~ **plasma** n GAS plasma inductor m; ~ **potential divider** n ELEC *autotransformer* divisor de potencial inductivo m; ~ **proximity switch** n ELEC, ELEC ENG interruptor de proximidad inductivo m; ~ **reactance** n ELEC, ELEC ENG, PHYS reactancia inductiva f; ~ **resistor** n ELEC ENG resistencia inductiva f; ~ **wirewound resistor** n ELEC ENG resistencia de alambre f, resistencia de hilo bobinado inductiva f
inductometer n ELEC, ELEC ENG inductancímetro m, inductímetro m, inductómetro m, INSTR inductómetro m
inductor n ELEC, ELEC ENG bobina de inductancia f; ~ **alternator** n ELEC, ELEC ENG *generator* alternador de hierro giratorio m; ~ **generator** n ELEC, ELEC ENG generador inductor m; ~ **machine** n ELEC ENG máquina inductora f
indulin n CHEM indulina f
induration n GEOL endurecimiento m
industrial: ~ **accident** n SAFE accidente industrial m; ~ **alcohol** n FOOD alcohol industrial m; ~ **automation** n MECH ENG automatización industrial f; ~ **bulk container system** n PACK sistema de contenedores industriales para productos a granel m; ~ **carrier** n TRANSP transporte industrial m; ~ **cleaning material** n DETERG limpiador industrial m; ~ **clothing** n SAFE ropa de trabajo f; ~ **controller** n PROD controlador industrial m; ~ **crop** n AGRIC cultivo industrial m; ~ **diamond** n MINE *drilling* diamante industrial m; ~ **discharge** n WATER descarga industrial f; ~ **dispute** n PROD conflicto laboral m; ~ **effluent** n HYDROL, WATER efluente industrial m; ~ **electronic equipment** n ELEC ENG equipamiento electrónico industrial m; ~ **electronic tube** n ELECTRON tubo electrónico industrial m; ~ **electronics** n ELEC ENG electrónica industrial f; ~ **engineering** n PROD planificación de programas de producción f; ~ **eye protectors** n pl LAB, PROD, SAFE anteojos industriales m pl (AmL), gafas industriales f pl (Esp); ~ **fishery** n FOOD, OCEAN industria pesquera f; ~ **footwear** n (cf protective footwear) SAFE calzado de trabajo m; ~ **furnace** n GAS horno industrial m; ~ **gloves** n pl SAFE guantes industriales m pl; ~ **hearing protector** n SAFE protector auditivo para el trabajo m; ~ **hygiene** n SAFE higiene industrial f; ~ **injury** n SAFE lesión industrial f; ~ **injury benefit** n SAFE compensación por lesiones de trabajo f; ~ **insurance** n SAFE seguro laboral m; ~ **interference** n ELEC ENG interferencia industrial f; ~ **irradiator** n NUCL irradiador industrial m; ~ **isotope** n NUCL, PART PHYS, PHYS isótopo industrial m; ~ **lorry** n BrE (cf industrial truck AmE) TRANSP camión industrial m; ~ **magnetron** n ELECTRON magnetrón industrial m; ~ **oven** n MECH ENG horno industrial m; ~ **overalls** n pl BrE (cf coveralls AmE) SAFE bata de trabajo f (Esp), mono m (infrml), mono de trabajo m (Esp), overoles m pl (AmL); ~ **packing** n PACK embalaje industrial m; ~ **process water** n HYDROL agua de proceso industrial f; ~ **robot** n

SAFE robot industrial *m*; ~ **safety** *n* SAFE seguridad industrial *f*; ~ **safety helmet** *n* SAFE casco industrial de seguridad *m*; ~ **standard** *n* COMP&DP norma del sector *f*, norma industrial *f*; ~ **truck** *n* AmE (cf *industrial lorry BrE*) TRANSP camión industrial *m*; ~ **valve** *n* MECH ENG válvula industrial *f*; ~ **waste** *n* POLL desechos industriales *m pl*, desperdicios industriales *m pl*, RECYCL desechos industriales *m pl*, desperdicios industriales *m pl*, residuos industriales *m pl*, WATER desperdicios industriales *m*; ~ **waste water** *n* HYDROL agua de desechos industriales *f*, POLL agua residual industrial *f*, agua de desperdicios industriales *f*, RECYCL agua residual industrial *f*, aguas de descarga industrial *f pl*, WATER agua de desperdicios industriales *f*; ~ **water** *n* HYDROL, WATER agua para la industria *f*; ~ **X-ray apparatus** *n* INSTR aparato de rayos X industrial *m*

inedible *adj* FOOD incomestible, incomible

in-edit *n* TV punto de entrada *m*

ineffective: ~ **airtime** *n* TELECOM tiempo inefectivo en el aire *m*; ~ **call** *n* TELECOM llamada inefectiva *f*

inelastic: ~ **collision** *n* PHYS choque inelástico *m*, RAD PHYS colisión inelástica *f*; ~ **neutron scattering** *n* PHYS dispersión inelástica de neutrones *f*; ~ **scattering** *n* PHYS dispersión inelástica *f*

inequality *n* COMP&DP desigualdad *f*

inert[1] *adj* GEN inerte

inert[2]: ~ **carrier** *n* AGRIC materia inerte *f*; ~ **gas** *n* GAS, NUCL gas inerte *m*; ~ **gas blanketing** *n* NUCL atmósfera de gas inerte *f*, cobertura de gas inerte *f*, protección con gas inerte *f*; ~ **gas generator** *n* GAS generador de gas inerte *m*; ~ **gas welding** *n* MECH ENG soldadura por gas inerte *f*, soldadura por gas noble *f*, PROD soldadura en atmósfera de gas inerte *f*; ~ **matter** *n* AGRIC material inerte *m*

inertia *n* MECH, MECH ENG, PHYS inercia *f*; ~ **drive** *n* AUTO volante de inercia *m*; ~ **governor** *n* MECH ENG regulador de inercia *m*; ~ **reel** *n* MECH ENG carrete de inercia *m*; ~ **switch** *n* ELEC ENG conmutador de inercia *m*

inertial[1] *adj* GEN de inercia, inercial

inertial[2]: ~ **accelerometer** *n* SPACE *spacecraft* acelerómetro de inercia *m*, acelerómetro inercial *m*; ~ **confinement** *n* PHYS confinamiento inercial *m*; ~ **force** *n* MECH, PHYS fuerza de inercia *f*; ~ **frame** *n* PHYS sistema de referencia inercial *m*, SPACE referencia inercial *f*; ~ **guidance** *n* SPACE *spacecraft* guiado por inercia *m*, guía inercial *f*; ~ **mass** *n* PHYS masa inercial *f*; ~ **navigation** *n* AIR TRANSP, SPACE navegación inercial *f*; ~ **navigation platform** *n* SPACE *spacecraft* plataforma inercial de navegación *f*; ~ **navigation system** *n* (*INS*) AIR TRANSP sistema de navegación por inercia *m*, WATER TRANSP sistema inercial de navegación *m*; ~ **platform** *n* MECH ENG plataforma estable *f*, plataforma inercial *f*; ~ **reference frame** *n* SPACE *communications* marco de referencia inercial *m*; ~ **reference system** *n* SPACE *communications* sistema de referencia inercial *m*; ~ **sensor** *n* SPACE *spacecraft* sensor inercial *m*; ~ **separator** *n* NUCL separador inercial *m*; ~ **starter** *n* MECH arrancador de inercia *m*, arrancador de volante *m*; ~ **unit** *n* SPACE *spacecraft* unidad inercial *f*; ~ **upper stage** *n* (*IUS*) SPACE última fase inercial *f*

inerting *n* NUCL, PETR TECH, SAFE inertización *f*; ~ **system** *n* NUCL sistema de inertización *m*, sistema inercial *m*

INF *abbr* (*information message*) TELECOM mensaje de información *m*

infall *n* WATER *of reservoir* orificio de llegada *m*

infantry *n* MILIT infantería *f*

infeed *n* MECH ENG *machine tools* alimentación *f*, avance normal *m*, avance radial *m*, profundidad de avance *f*, profundidad de pasada *f*, PRINT avance *m*, PROD alimentación *f*, avance *m*; ~ **roller** *n* PRINT rodillo alimentador *m*

inference *n* COMP&DP inferencia *f*; ~ **engine** *n* COMP&DP dispositivo de inferencia *m*, máquina de inferencia *f*, ELEC ENG mecanismo de interferencia *m*

inferior: ~ **character** *n* PRINT exponente *m*, subíndice *m*; ~ **coal** *n* COAL carbón ordinario *m*; ~ **figure** *n* PRINT subíndice *m*; ~ **letter** *n* PRINT exponente *m*, subíndice *m*

infilling *n* GEOL material de relleno *m*

infiltrate *vt* HYDROL infiltrar

infiltration *n* COAL infiltración *f*, HYDROL infiltración *f*, percolación *f*, WATER infiltración *f*; ~ **basin** *n* HYDROL depósito de captación de aguas *m*; ~ **gallery** *n* WATER galería de captación *f*, galería de infiltración *f*; ~ **rate** *n* HEAT caudal de infiltración *m*, velocidad de infiltración *f*; ~ **water** *n* HYDROL agua de infiltración *f*

infinite: ~ **attenuation** *n* ELECTRON atenuación infinita *f*; ~ **impulse response** *n* (*IIR*) ELECTRON, TELECOM respuesta de impulso infinito *f*; ~**-impulse-response digital filter** *n* ELECTRON, TELECOM filtro digital de respuesta a impulsos infinitos *m*; ~**-impulse-response filter** *n* ELECTRON filtro de respuesta de impulso infinito *m*; ~ **loop** *n* COMP&DP bucle infinito *m*, lazo infinito *m*

infinitely: ~ **thick layer** *n* RAD PHYS capa infinitamente gruesa *f*

infinitesimal *adj* GEOM infinitesimal

infix: ~ **notation** *n* COMP&DP notación infix *f*, notación por infijos *f*

inflammability *n* GEN inflamabilidad *f*

inflammable *adj* GEN inflamable

inflatable[1] *adj* AIR TRANSP, MAR POLL, NUCL, REFRIG, WATER TRANSP inflable

inflatable[2]: ~ **boat** *n* AIR TRANSP, WATER TRANSP bote inflable *m*; ~ **coldroom** *n* REFRIG cámara frigorífica inflable *f*; ~ **dinghy** *n* AIR TRANSP bote inflable *m*, bote salvavidas inflable *m*, neumático salvavidas *m*, SAFE bote salvavidas inflable *m*, WATER TRANSP bote auxiliar inflable *m*, bote inflable *m*, bote salvavidas inflable *m*, chinchorro inflable *m*; ~ **seal** *n* NUCL cierre hinchable *m*, cierre inflable *m*; ~ **slide** *n* AIR TRANSP tobogán inflable *m*; ~ **weir** *n* WATER vertedero inflable *m*

inflate *vt* CONST, PHYS inflar

inflated: ~ **structure** *n* CONST estructura inflada *f*

inflation *n* MAR POLL, PROD inflación *f*; ~ **cuff** *n* MAR POLL manguito de inflación *m*; ~ **pressure** *n* PROD presión de inflación *f*

inflected: ~ **arch** *n* CONST arco invertido *m*

in-flight: ~ **operation** *n* SPACE . *spacecraft* funcionamiento en vuelo *m*; ~ **operational planning** *n* AIR TRANSP *meteorology* plan operacional en vuelo *m*; ~ **refueling** AmE see *in-flight refuelling BrE*; ~ **refueling probe** AmE see *in-flight refuelling probe BrE*; ~ **refuelling** BrE *n* AIR TRANSP reabastecimiento en vuelo *m*, repostado en vuelo *m*; ~ **refuelling probe** *n* BrE TRANSP estilete para repostado en vuelo *m*;

~ **sequence** *n* SPACE secuencia en vuelo *f*; ~ **thrust vectoring** *n* SPACE vectorización de empuje en vuelo *f*
inflorescence *n* AGRIC inflorescencia *f*
inflow *n* AIR TRANSP entrada de flujo *f*, toma de flujo *f*, HYDROL afluencia *f*, WATER afluencia *f*, aflujo *m*, caudal afluente *m*; ~ **angle** *n* AIR TRANSP ángulo de entrada del flujo *m*; ~ **canal** *n* WATER canal de entrada *m*; ~ **ratio** *n* AIR TRANSP proporción de entrada del flujo *f*; ~ **of water** *n* HYDROL avenida de agua *f*, WATER aportación de agua *f*, avenida de agua *f*
influence *n* CHEM influencia *f*, COAL influjo *m*, CONST influencia *f*; ~ **line** *n* CONST línea de influencia *f*
influent: ~ **stream** *n* HYDROL curso de agua entrante *m*; ~ **water** *n* HYDROL, WATER agua de entrada *f*
influx: ~ **of water** *n* HYDROL, WATER avenida de agua *f*
informatics *n* COMP&DP informática *f*
information *n* COMP&DP, ELECTRON información *f*, TELECOM información *f*, información del directorio *f*; ~ **bit** *n* COMP&DP bit de información *m*; ~ **content** *n* COMP&DP contenido informático *m*; ~ **flow** *n* COMP&DP flujo de información *m*; ~ **hiding** *n* COMP&DP ocultación de información *f*, ocultamiento de información *m*; ~ **highway** *n* COMP&DP infopista *f*, infovía *f*; ~ **message** *n* (*INF*) TELECOM mensaje de información *m*; ~ **processing** *n* (*IP*) COMP&DP, ELECTRON procesamiento de información *m* (*PI*), tratamiento de la información *m* (*PI*); ~-**processing system** *n* COMP&DP, TELECOM sistema de tratamiento de la información *m*; ~ **product data** *n* PROD información sobre datos de productos *f*; ~ **receiver station** *n* (*IRS*) POLL, TELECOM estación receptora de información *f*; ~-**receiving station** *n* (*IRS*) POLL, TELECOM estación receptora de información *f*; ~ **request message** *n* (*INR*) TELECOM mensaje de petición de información *m*; ~ **retrieval** *n* COMP&DP recuperación de información *f*; ~ **retrieval system** *n* COMP&DP sistema de recuperación de información *m*; ~-**sending station** *n* TELECOM estación de envío de información *f*; ~ **separator** *n* (*IS*) COMP&DP separador de información *m* (*SI*); ~ **sign** *n* RAIL señal de información *f*; ~ **source** *n* COMP&DP fuente de información *f*; ~ **storage** *n* *AmE* (*cf information store BrE*) COMP&DP almacenamiento de la información *m*, TV almacenamiento de información *m*; ~ **store** *BrE* *n* (*cf information storage AmE*) COMP&DP almacenamiento de la información *m*, TV almacenamiento de información *m*; ~ **system** *n* (*IS*) COMP&DP sistema de información *m*; ~ **technology** *n* (*IT*) COMP&DP, TELECOM tecnología de la información *f*; ~ **theory** *n* COMP&DP, ELECTRON teoría de la información *f*; ~ **transfer rate** *n* TELECOM velocidad de transferencia de la información *f*; ~ **type** *n* (*IT*) TELECOM tipo de información *m*
in-frame: ~ **coding** *n* TELECOM codificación de trama entrante *f*
infraprotein *n* CHEM infraproteína *f*
infrared[1] *adj* (*IR*) COMP&DP, OPT, P&R, PHYS, RAD PHYS, WAVE PHYS infrarrojo (*IR*); ~ **sensitive** *adj* RAD PHYS sensible a infrarrojos
infrared[2] *n* (*IR*) GEN infrarrojo *m* (*IR*); ~ **burner** *n* GAS quemador infrarrojo *m*; ~ **cinematography** *n* CINEMAT cinematografía infrarroja *f*; ~ **detector** *n* ELECTRON, PHYS, TRANSP detector de infrarrojos *m*; ~ **dryer** *n* PRINT secador de infrarrojos *m*; ~ **element** *n* HEAT ENG elemento infrarrojo *m*; ~ **emulsion** *n* PHOTO emulsión infrarroja *f*; ~ **exhaust-gas**

analyser *n* *BrE* AUTO analizador infrarrojo de gases de escape *m*; ~ **exhaust-gas analyzer** *AmE* *see infrared exhaust-gas analyser BrE*; ~ **film** *n* PHOTO película infrarroja *f*; ~ **filter** *n* RAD PHYS filtro de infrarrojos *m*; ~ **heating** *n* HEAT ENG calefacción por infrarrojos *f*, RAD PHYS calentamiento por rayos infrarrojos *m*; ~ **image converter** *n* TV conversor de imagen por rayos infrarrojos *m*; ~ **laser** *n* ELECTRON láser de infrarrojos *m*; ~ **light** *n* RAD PHYS luz infrarroja *f*; ~ **link** *n* TV enlace por rayos infrarrojos *m*; ~ **microscope** *n* INSTR microscopio de rayos infrarrojos *m*; ~ **motion alarm** *n* SAFE alarma infrarroja detectora de movimiento *f*; ~ **movement-sensing alarm** *n* SAFE alarma infrarroja detectora de movimiento *f*; ~ **oven** *n* PROD estufa de secado de rayos infrarrojos *f*, horno de caldeo por rayos infrarrojos *m*; ~ **panel heating** *n* HEAT calefacción por panel de infrarrojos *f*; ~ **photography** *n* PHOTO fotografía infrarroja *f*; ~ **process ink** *n* PRINT tinta que seca por infrarrojos *f*; ~ **radiant panel** *n* GAS panel radiante infrarrojo *m*; ~ **radiation** *n* FUELLESS, PHYS, RAD PHYS, SPACE, WAVE PHYS radiación infrarroja *f*; ~ **remote control** *n* MECH ENG control infrarrojo a distancia *m*, control infrarrojo remoto *m*, control remoto infrarrojo *m*; ~-**sensitive emulsion** *n* PHOTO emulsión sensible al infrarrojo *f*; ~ **sensor** *n* MILIT, SPACE sensor de rayos infrarrojos *m*; ~ **spectrometer** *n* RAD PHYS espectrómetro de rayos infrarrojos *m*; ~ **spectrophotometer** *n* CHEM, LAB espectrofotómetro de infrarrojo *m*; ~ **spectrophotometry** *n* CHEM, LAB espectrofotometría de infrarrojo *f*; ~ **spectroscopy** *n* CHEM, PHYS espectroscopía infrarroja *f*; ~ **spectrum** *n* PHYS, RAD PHYS espectro infrarrojo *m*; ~ **therapy** *n* RAD PHYS terapia por infrarrojos *f*
infrasonic: ~ **frequency** *n* ACOUST, PHYS frecuencia infrasónica *f*; ~ **speed** *n* PHYS velocidad infrasónica *f*
infrasound *n* ACOUST, PHYS infrasonido *m*
infusion *n* C&G, FOOD infusión *f*; ~ **bottle** *n* C&G botella para infusión *f*
infusorial: ~ **earth** *n* FOOD kieselguhr *m*, MINERAL tierra de infusorios *f*
ingate *n* PROD entrada *f*
ingoing: ~ **air current** *n* MINE corriente de aire entrante *f*
ingot *n* COAL barra *f*, galápago *m*, lingote *m*, lingote de reducción directa *m*, tejo *m*, tocho *m*, MECH barra *f*, lingote *m*, tocho *m*, PROD barra *f*, galápago *m*, lingote *m*, tocho *m*; ~ **mold** *AmE*, ~ **mould** *BrE* *n* MECH materials, PROD lingotera *f*
ingredient *n* CHEM, FOOD, P&R ingrediente *m*
ingress *n* CONST acceso *m* (*Esp*), ingreso *m* (*AmL*), water entrada *f*; ~ **protection** *n* PROD protección contra el ingreso *f*; ~ **of water** *n* PROD ingreso de agua *m*
inherent: ~ **addressing** *n* COMP&DP direccionamiento inherente *m*; ~ **availability** *n* AIR TRANSP disponibilidad inherente *f*; ~ **color** *AmE*, ~ **colour** *BrE* *n* COLOUR colorante inherente *m*; ~ **feedback** *n* ELEC ENG, ELECTRON, NUCL realimentación intrínseca *f*, autorrealimentación *f*; ~ **noise pressure** *n* ACOUST *of microphone* presión del ruido inherente *f*, presión del ruido proprio *f*; ~ **regulation** *n* ELECTRON autorregulación *f*
inherently: ~ **stable reactor** *n* NUCL reactor intrínsecamente estable *m*

inheritance *n* COMP&DP herencia *f*
inhibit *vt* GEN inhibir
inhibiting: ~ **input** *n* ELECTRON alimentación inhibidora *f*; ~ **pulse** *n* ELECTRON impulso inhibidor *m*; ~ **signal** *n* ELECTRON señal inhibidora *f*
inhibition *n* CHEM inhibición *f*, ELECTRON *of vehicle* impedimento *m*, inhibición *f*
inhibitor *n* CHEM *of reaction*, DETERG, FOOD, P&R inhibidor *m*, WATER inhibidor *m*, retardador *m*; ~ **dye** *n* COLOUR agente supresor *m*
inhomogeneity *n* C&G inhomogeneidad *f*
inhomogeneous: ~ **broadening** *n* RAD PHYS ensanchamiento inhomogéneo *m*
in-house: ~ **software** *n* COMP&DP software propio *m*, soporte lógico de producción propia *m*; ~ **standard** *n* NUCL *of liquids* norma interna *f*
initial *n* PRINT inicial *f*; ~ **advance** *n* AUTO avance inicial *m*; ~ **approach** *n* AIR TRANSP aproximación inicial *f*; ~ **approach fix** *n* AIR TRANSP posición de aproximación inicial *f*; ~ **approach path** *n* AIR TRANSP trayectoria de aproximación inicial *f*; ~ **approach point** *n* AIR TRANSP punto de aproximación inicial *m*; ~ **climb-out** *n* AIR TRANSP ascenso inicial *m*, elevación inicial *f*, toma de altura inicial *f*; ~ **connection charge** *n* TELECOM cargo de conexión inicial *m*; ~ **crack growth** *n* NUCL crecimiento inicial de una grieta *m*; ~ **criticality** *n* NUCL criticidad inicial *f*; ~ **current** *n* ELEC, ELEC ENG corriente inicial *f*; ~ **dip** *n* GEOL buzamiento inicial *m*, inclinación inicial *f*; ~**domain identifier** *n* (*IDI*) TELECOM identificador de dominio inicial *m*; ~**domain part** *n* (*IDP*) TELECOM parte de dominio inicial *f*; ~ **feed** *n* AUTO avance inicial *m*; ~ **fissile charge** *n* NUCL carga inicial de material fisionable *f*; ~ **forming charge** *n* AUTO carga de formación inicial *f*; ~ **fusion temperature** *n* REFRIG temperatura de fusión incipiente *f*; ~ **gross weight** *n* AIR TRANSP peso bruto inicial *m*; ~ **inverse voltage** *n* ELEC tensión inversa inicial *f*; ~ **magnetization curve** *n* PHYS curva de imanación inicial *f*, curva de magnetización inicial *f*; ~ **program load** *n* (*IPL*) COMP&DP carga de programa inicializado *f*; ~ **ratio** *n* GEOL porcentaje inicial *m*, proporción inicial *f*; ~ **reservoir pressure** *n* PETROL presión inicial del yacimiento *f*; ~ **settlement** *n* COAL sedimento inicial *m*; ~ **stability** *n* WATER TRANSP *naval architecture* estabilidad inicial *f*; ~ **stage** *n* METALL fase inicial *f*; ~ **state** *n* COMP&DP estado inicial *m*; ~ **velocity** *n* SPACE velocidad inicial *f*; ~ **verification** *n* METR verificación inicial *f*
initialization *n* COMP&DP, ELECTRON inicialización *f*
initialize *vt* COMP&DP inicializar, ELECTRON dar nombre a, inicializar
initiating: ~ **electrode** *n* ELEC ENG electrodo primario *m*; ~ **event** *n* NUCL suceso iniciador *m*; ~ **explosive** *n* MINE explosivo iniciador *m*; ~ **particle** *n* NUCL partícula iniciadora *f*; ~ **spark** *n* ELEC ENG chispa de encendido *f*
initiation *n* CHEM iniciación *f*, MINE comienzo *m*, iniciación *f*; ~ **of fracture** *n* NUCL iniciación de la fractura *f*
initiator *n* CHEM, FOOD iniciador *m*
inject *vt* GAS, PROD, SPACE inyectar
injected: ~ **gas** *n* GAS, PETROL gas inyectado *m*
injection *n* GEN inyección *f*; ~ **blow molding** *AmE see injection blow moulding BrE*; ~ **blow molding machine** *AmE see injection blow moulding machine*

BrE; ~ **blow moulding** *BrE n* P&R *process* moldeo por inyección-soplado *m*; ~ **blow moulding machine** *n BrE* PACK moldeadora por inyección *f*, máquina de moldeo por inyección *f*; ~ **borehole** *n* NUCL orificio de inyección *m*; ~ **cock** *n* HYDRAUL grifo de inyección *m*, toma de vapor del inyector *f*; ~ **condenser** *n* HYDRAUL condensador de inyección *m*; ~ **filling** *n* PACK llenado por inyección *m*; ~ **gneiss** *n* GEOL gneis de inyección *m*; ~ **grid** *n* AIR TRANSP, ELECTRON rejilla de inyección *f*; ~ **laser** *n* ELECTRON láser inyector *m*; ~ **laser diode** *n* (*ILD*) ELECTRON, OPT, TELECOM diodo láser de inyección *m*; ~ **level** *n* ELECTRON nivel de inyección *m*; ~**-locked laser** *n* ELECTRON, OPT, TELECOM láser sincronizado por inyección *m*; ~**-locked oscillator** *n* ELECTRON oscilador de cierre de inyección *m*, oscilador sincronizado por inyección *m*, SPACE *communications* oscilador sincronizado por inyección *m*; ~**-locked oscillator demodulator** *n* SPACE *communications* demodulador oscilador sincronizado por inyección *m*; ~ **locking** *n* ELECTRON interrupción de la inyección *f*; ~ **logic** *n* ELECTRON circuito lógico de inyección *m*; ~ **machine** *n* SAFE máquina de inyección *f*; ~ **mold** *AmE see injection mould BrE*; ~ **mold for rubber** *AmE see injection mould for rubber BrE*; ~ **mold for thermoplastics** *AmE see injection mould for thermoplastics BrE*; ~ **mold for thermosetting resins** *AmE see injection mould for thermosetting resins BrE*; ~ **molding** *AmE see injection moulding BrE*; ~ **molding compound** *AmE see injection moulding compound BrE*; ~ **molding machine** *AmE see injection moulding machine BrE*; ~ **molding press** *AmE see injection moulding press BrE*; ~ **molding pressure** *AmE*, ~ **mould** *BrE n* C&G molde de inyección *m*; ~ **mould for rubber** *n BrE* MECH ENG molde de inyección para caucho *m*, molde de inyección para goma *m*, moldeado de inyección para goma *m*, P&R molde de inyección para caucho *m*, molde de inyección para goma *m*; ~ **mould for thermoplastics** *n BrE* MECH ENG molde de inyección para resinas *m*, molde de inyección para termoplásticos *m*, moldeado de inyección para termoplásticos *m*; ~ **mould for thermosetting resins** *n BrE* MECH ENG molde de inyección para resinas termoestables *m*, molde de inyección para resinas termofraguables *m*, molde de inyección para resinas termoindurantes *m*, termoestables *m pl*, termofraguables *m pl*, termoindurantes *m pl*; ~ **moulding** *n BrE* P&R, PROD moldeo por inyección *m*; ~ **moulding compound** *n BrE* PACK compuesto para moldear por inyección *m*, PROD compuesto para moldeo por inyección *m*; ~ **moulding machine** *n BrE* SAFE máquina de moldear por inyección *f*; ~ **moulding press** *n BrE* P&R prensa de moldeo por inyección *f*; ~ **moulding pressure** *n BrE* PACK presión del moldeo por inyección *f*; ~ **nozzle** *n* AUTO boquilla de inyección *f*, VEH tobera de inyección *f*; ~ **nozzle holder** *n* AUTO portaboquilla de inyección *f*; ~ **orbit** *n* SPACE puesta en órbita *f*; ~ **pipe** *n* HYDRAUL tubo de inyección *m*; ~ **procedure** *n* WATER TRANSP método de inyección *m*; ~ **pump** *n* CONST, MECH ENG, WATER TRANSP *of engine* bomba de inyección *f*; ~ **valve** *n* LAB válvula de inyección *f*; ~ **well** *n* PETR TECH, PETROL, WATER pozo de inyección *m*
injector *n* AUTO, ELECTRON, GAS, HYDRAUL, MECH, VEH

inyector *m*; ~ **test pump** *n* AUTO bomba de prueba del inyector *f*; ~ **throttle** *n* HYDRAUL toma de vapor del inyector *f*

injurious *adj* SAFE lesivo

injury *n* GEN lesión *f*

ink[1] *n* COLOUR, COMP&DP, INSTR, PAPER, PRINT tinta *f*; ~ **blade** *n* PRINT rasqueta de la tinta *f*; ~ **coverage** *n* PAPER capacidad de recubrimiento de la tinta *f*, PRINT poder cubriente de la tinta *m*; ~ **creep** *n* PRINT deslizamiento de la tinta *m*; ~-**drying curl** *n* PRINT combado del impreso al secarse la tinta *m*; ~ **duct** *n* COLOUR tintero *m*; ~ **ductor** *n* PRINT tintero *m*; ~ **flow** *n* PRINT fluencia de la tinta *f*; ~-**form roller** *n* PRINT rodillo entintador *m*; ~ **fountain** *n* COLOUR, PRINT tintero *m*; ~ **fountain roller** *n* PRINT rodillo del tintero *m*; ~ **gloss** *n* PRINT brillo de la tinta *m*; ~ **holdout** *n* PRINT poca absorbencia de la tinta *f*; ~-**jet printing paper** *n* PAPER papel para imprimir por chorro de tinta *m*; ~ **knife** *n* PRINT espátula para la tinta *f*; ~ **lay-down** *n* PRINT sedimentación de la tinta *f*; ~ **maker** *n* PRINT fabricante de tinta *m*; ~ **mixer** *n* PRINT mezclador de tinta *m*; ~ **recorder** *n* INSTR registrador escribiente *m* (*AmL*), registrador por tinta *m* (*Esp*); ~ **rub resistance test** *n* PRINT ensayo de la tinta al frotamiento *m*; ~ **setting** *n* PRINT secado de la tinta *m*; ~-**setting time** *n* PRINT tiempo de secado de la tinta *m*; ~ **tank** *n* PRINT reserva de tinta *f*; ~ **transfer** *n* PRINT transferencia de la tinta *f*; ~ **writer** *n* INSTR receptor impresor de tinta *m*

ink[2] *vt* COLOUR entintar

inked: ~ **ribbon** *n* COMP&DP cinta entintada *f*

inkjet: ~ **printer** *n* COMP&DP, PRINT impresora de chorro de tinta *f* (*Esp*), impresora de inyección de tinta *f* (*Esp*), sistema de inyección de tinta *m*; ~ **system** *n* COMP&DP sistema a chicler de tinta *m*

inky *n* CINEMAT protector de iluminación de 250 watt *m*; ~-**dink** *n* CINEMAT protector de iluminación de 250 watt *m*

inland: ~ **call** *n* TELECOM llamada nacional *f*; ~ **haulage** *n* TRANSP arrastre tierra adentro *m*; ~ **navigation** *n* WATER TRANSP navegación interior *f*; ~ **sea** *n* HYDROL, METEO, OCEAN mar interior *m*; ~ **water transport** *n* TRANSP transporte acuático interior *m*, transporte por vías navegables interiores *m*; ~ **waters** *n pl* WATER aguas del interior *f pl*; ~ **waterway** *n* WATER TRANSP vía de navegación interior *f*

inlay: ~ **graft** *n* AGRIC *pest control* injerto de incrustación *m*

inlet *n* AUTO admisión *f*, entrada *f*, HYDRAUL canalización *f*, HYDROL boca de entrada *f*, bocatoma *f* (*AmL*), ensenada *f*, MECH boca de entrada *f*, entrada *f*, orificio de entrada *m*, tubo de entrada *m*, MECH ENG entrada *f*, orificio de admisión *m*, orificio de entrada *m*, oído *m*, tragante *m*, MINE caleta *f*, entrada *f*, orificio de entrada *m*, OCEAN caleta *f*, PROD admisión *f*, entrada *f*, *of fan*, *of centrifugal pump* oído *m*, TELECOM entrada *f*, WATER admisión *f*, entrada *f*, toma *f*, bocatoma *f*, WATER TRANSP *geography* angostura *f*, ancón *m*; ~ **case** *n* MECH ENG caja de admisión *f*, caja de entrada *f*; ~ **connection** *n* PROD conexión de entrada *f*; ~ **end** *n* NUCL lado de admisión *m*; ~ **jumper** *n* NUCL conexión en puente de entrada *f*; ~ **manifold** *n* BrE (*cf intake manifold AmE*) AIR TRANSP colector de admisión *m*, distribuidor de entrada *m*, AUTO colector de admisión *m*, colector de entrada *m*, MECH colector de admisión *m*, MECH ENG colector de admisión *m*, colector de entrada *m*, múltiple *m*, múltiple de admisión *m*, tubulador de admisión *m*, VEH *of engine* colector de admisión *m*; ~ **pipe** *n* PROD tubo de entrada *m*; ~ **port** *n* (*cf intake port*) AUTO abertura de entrada *f*, lumbrera de admisión *f*, C&G puerto de entrada *m*, VEH abertura de entrada *f*, lumbrera de admisión *f*; ~ **pressure** *n* COAL presión de entrada *f*; ~ **silencer** *n* MECH silenciador de la admisión *m*; ~ **strainer** *n* PROD filtro de entrada *m*; ~ **throat** *n* AIR TRANSP *of engine* garganta de entrada *f*, gollete de entrada *m*; ~ **valve** *n* AUTO válvula de admisión *f*, válvula de entrada *f*, HYDRAUL válvula de admisión *f*, válvula de aspiración *f*, VEH válvula de admisión *f*; ~ **velocity** *n* HYDRAUL velocidad de admisión *f*, velocidad de entrada *f*

inlier *n* GEOL afloramiento de rocas antiguas *m*

in-line[1] *adj* CINEMAT, CONST alineado, MECH alineado, en serie, MECH ENG alineado, en línea, PHOTO, PRINT, TELECOM, TV alineado

in-line[2]: ~ **contact coding** *n* PACK codificación de contacto instalada en línea *f*; ~ **cylinder engine** *n* MECH ENG motor de cilindros en línea *m*; ~ **cylinders** *n pl* AUTO cilindros en línea *m*; ~ **engine** *n* AUTO motor en línea *m*, MECH ENG motor de cilindros en línea *m*, WATER TRANSP motor con los cilindros en línea *m*; ~ **finishing equipment** *n* PACK equipo de acabado en línea *m*; ~ **position** *n* PRINT posición en línea *f*; ~ **pressure connection** *n* PROD conexión a presión en línea *f*; ~ **processing** *n* COMP&DP procesamiento en línea *m*, procesamiento secuencial *m*; ~ **variation** *n* C&G variación en la línea *f*; ~ **web press** *n* PRINT prensa de banda en línea *f*

inner: ~ **bottom** *n* WATER TRANSP *naval architecture* tapa del doble fondo *f*; ~ **bottom longitudinal** *n* WATER TRANSP longitudinal del fondo interior *m*; ~ **bottom plating** *n* WATER TRANSP chapa del fondo *f*; ~ **conductor** *n* TELECOM conductor interior *m*; ~ **core** *n* GEOL núcleo interno *m*; ~ **covering** *n* ELEC *cable insulation* cubierta interior *f*, mufla *f*; ~ **diameter** *n* (*ID*) MECH, MECH ENG diámetro interior *m*, diámetro interno *m*; ~ **electron** *n* RAD PHYS electrón interno *m*; ~ **form** *AmE*, ~ **forme** *BrE* *n* PRINT plana interior *f*; ~ **harbor** *AmE*, ~ **harbour** *BrE* *n* WATER TRANSP puerto interior *m*; ~ **lining** *n* WATER TRANSP *of hull* forro interior *m*, revestimiento interior *m*; ~ **margin** *n* PRINT margen interior *m*; ~ **marker** *n* AIR TRANSP baliza interna *f*; ~ **orbital complex** *n* RAD PHYS complejo de un orbital interno *m*; ~ **planet** *n* SPACE planeta interior *m*; ~ **planet mission** *n* SPACE misión a un planeta interior *f*; ~ **port** *n* WATER TRANSP puerto interior *m*; ~ **shell electron** *n* RAD PHYS electrón de capas internas del núcleo *m*; ~ **shroud** *n* AIR TRANSP corona de refuerzo interior *f*, recubrimiento interior *m*; ~ **skin** *n* WATER TRANSP *of hull* forro interior *m*, revestimiento interior *m*; ~ **tube** *n* VEH cámara *f*; ~ **wall** *n* TELECOM pared interior *f*

inoculation *n* NUCL inoculación *f*

inorganic[1] *adj* CHEM, COLOUR, ELECTRON inorgánico

inorganic[2]: ~ **chemistry** *n* CHEM química inorgánica *f*; ~ **chromium compound** *n* CHEM compuesto inorgánico de cromo *m*; ~ **liquid laser** *n* ELECTRON láser de líquido inorgánico *m*; ~ **zinc paint** *n* COLOUR pintura de zinc inorgánico *f*

inosine *n* CHEM, FOOD inosina *f*
inositol *n* CHEM, FOOD inositol *m*
inoxidizable *adj* CHEM inoxidable
in-package: ~ **desiccation** *n* PACK, REFRIG desecación dentro de paquetes *f*
in-phase[1] *adj* ELEC, ELECTRON, PHYS, TV, WAVE PHYS en fase
in-phase[2]: ~ **component** *n* ELECTRON componente en fase *m*; ~ **current** *n* ELEC corriente en fase *f*; ~ **signal** *n* ELECTRON señal en fase *f*
in-pile: ~ **experiment** *n* NUCL experimento en caliente *m*, experimento en el interior del reactor *m*
in-place: ~ **topping** *n* AGRIC *sugar beetroot* deshojado en el suelo *m*
INPO *abbr* (*Institute of Nuclear Power Operations*) NUCL Instituto de Operaciones Nucleares *m*
in-process: ~ **gaging** *AmE*, ~ **gauging** *BrE n* METR en vías de calibrado *f*; ~ **inspection** *n* QUALITY control durante la fabricación *m*; ~ **inspection in manufacturing** *n* QUALITY control durante la fabricación *m*; ~ **inventory** *n* PROD inventario durante la producción *m*
input[1]: ~-**limited** *adj* COMP&DP limitado por entrada
input[2] *n* COMP&DP *data* entrada de datos *f*, introducción *f*, ELEC *of current, voltage* entrada *f*, ELECTRON alimentación *f*, entrada de datos *f*, GEOL entrada *f*, HYDRAUL admisión *f*, toma de vapor *f*, PHYS entrada *f*, RAD PHYS valor de entrada *m*, TV entrada *f*; ~ **admittance** *n* ELEC, ELEC ENG, PHYS admitancia de entrada *f*; ~ **amplifier** *n* ELECTRON amplificador de alimentación *m*; ~ **area** *n* COMP&DP área de entrada *f*; ~ **attenuator** *n* ELECTRON atenuador de potencia de entrada *m*; ~ **back-off** *n* SPACE *space communications of TWT* nivel de entrada por debajo de saturación *m*; ~ **bevel pinion shaft** *n* AIR TRANSP *of helicopter* eje de entrada de piñones cónicos *m*; ~ **buffer** *n* COMP&DP búfer de entrada *m*, memoria intermedia de entrada *f*, registro intermedio de entrada *m*; ~ **buffer amplifier** *n* ELECTRON amplificador compensador de potencia de entrada *m*; ~ **capacitance** *n* ELEC ENG capacitancia de entrada *f*; ~ **capacitor** *n* ELEC ENG condensador de entrada *m*; ~ **cavity** *n* ELECTRON cavidad de entrada *f*; ~ **circuit** *n* ELEC circuito de entrada *m*, circuito interno de entrada *m*, ELEC ENG circuito de entrada *m*; ~ **circuit terminal** *n* PROD terminal del circuito de entrada *m*; ~ **connection diagram** *n* PROD diagrama de conexiones de entrada *m*; ~ **control** *n* ELECTRON control de entrada *m*; ~ **current** *n* ELEC corriente de entrada *f*; ~ **data** *n pl* COMP&DP datos de entrada *m pl*; ~ **device** *n* COMP&DP dispositivo de entrada *m*, dispositivo de introducción de datos *m*, órgano de entrada *m*, ELEC ENG dispositivo de entrada *m*, órgano de entrada *m*, ELECTRON órgano de entrada *m*, PROD, TELECOM órgano de entrada *m*; ~ **electrode** *n* ELEC ENG electrodo de entrada *m*; ~ **file** *n* COMP&DP archivo de entrada *m*, archivo de lectura *m*; ~ **filter** *n* ELECTRON, SPACE *communications* filtro de entrada *m*; ~-**filter time delay** *n* PROD relé temporizador del filtro de entrada *m*; ~ **filtering** *n* ELECTRON, TELECOM filtrado de entrada *m*; ~ **gap** *n* ELECTRON espacio de entrada *m*; ~ **gas** *n* GAS gas de entrada *m*, gas de inyección *m*, PETROL gas de inyección *m*; ~ **gate** *n* ELECTRON circuito de entrada *m*, puerta de entrada *f*; ~ **image table** *n* PROD tabla de imágenes de entrada *f*; ~ **impedance** *n* ELEC, ELEC ENG, PHYS, TELECOM, TV impedancia de entrada *f*; ~ **instruction** *n* COMP&DP instrucción de entrada *f*; ~ **lead** *n* ELEC ENG cable conductor de entrada *m*; ~ **level** *n* TELECOM, TV nivel de entrada *m*; ~ **message acknowledgement** *n* (*IMA*) TELECOM aviso de mensaje entrante *m*; ~ **power** *n* ELEC ENG potencia de entrada *f*, PROD potencia absorbida *f*, potencia de entrada *f*, TELECOM, TV potencia de entrada *f*; ~ **power factor** *n* PROD factor de potencia absorbida *m*; ~ **power fuse** *n* PROD fusible de potencia absorbida *m*; ~ **pulse** *n* ELECTRON impulso de entrada *m*; ~ **queue** *n* COMP&DP cola de entrada *f*, entrada en espera *f*; ~ **record** *n* COMP&DP registro de entrada *m*; ~ **resistance** *n* ELEC ENG resistencia de entrada *f*; ~ **resonator** *n* ELECTRON resonador de entrada *m*; ~ **response** *n* ELECTRON respuesta de entrada *f*; ~ **satisfied status bit** *n* COMP&DP, PROD bit de entrada ejecutada *m*; ~ **section** *n* PROD sección de entrada *f*; ~ **section indicator** *n* PROD indicador de la sección de entrada *m*; ~ **sensor** *n* PROD sensor de la entrada *m*; ~ **shaft** *n* MECH ENG eje de entrada *m*, eje de salida *m*, eje del impulsor *m*, eje primario *m*, VEH eje de entrada *m*, eje primario *m*; ~ **shaft bearing** *n* VEH rodamiento de eje primario *m*; ~ **shell** *n* AUTO cárter de entrada *m*; ~ **signal** *n* ELECTRON, TV señal de entrada *f*; ~ **signal conditioning** *n* ELECTRON acondicionamiento de señales de entrada *m*; ~ **signal power** *n* ELECTRON potencia de señal de entrada *f*; ~ **signal quantization** *n* ELECTRON cuantificación de señal de entrada *f*; ~ **signal-to-noise ratio** *n* ELECTRON relación señal-ruido en el circuito de entrada *f*; ~ **simulator strip** *n* PROD tira del estimulador de la entrada *f*, tira del simulador de la entrada *f*; ~ **stage** *n* ELECTRON fase de entrada *f*; ~-**stage gain** *n* ELECTRON ganancia en fase de entrada *f*; ~ **of steam** *n* HYDRAUL toma de vapor *f*; ~ **stimulator** *n* PROD estimulador de la entrada *m*; ~ **tapping** *n* ELEC acometida de entrada *f*, ELEC ENG acometida de entrada *f*, ramificación de entrada *f*; ~ **terminal** *n* ELEC *connection*, ELEC ENG terminal de entrada *m*; ~-**terminal strip** *n* PROD regleta de terminales de entrada *f*; ~ **transaction accepted for delivery** *n* (*ITD*) TELECOM transacción de entrada aceptada para ejecución *f*; ~ **transaction rejected** *n* (*ITR*) TELECOM transacción de entrada rechazada *f*; ~ **transductor** *n* ELEC ENG transductor de entrada *m*; ~ **transformer** *n* ELEC ENG, PHYS transformador de entrada *m*; ~ **transient protection** *n* PROD protección transitoria de la entrada *f*; ~ **voltage** *n* ELEC tensión de entrada *f*, tensión primaria *f*, ELEC ENG tensión de entrada *f*, voltaje de entrada *m*, PROD voltaje de alimentación *m*, voltaje de entrada *m*
input[3] *vt* ELECTRON alimentar, introducir
input/output[1]: ~ **limited** *adj* COMP&DP limitado por entrada/salida
input/output[2] *n* (*I/O*) COMP&DP, ELEC, PROD entrada/salida *f* (*E/S*); ~ **buffer** *n* COMP&DP registro intermedio de entrada/salida *m*; ~ **bus** *n* COMP&DP bus de entrada/salida *m*, conductor común de entrada/salida *m*; ~ **channel** *n* COMP&DP canal de entrada/salida *m*; ~ **control** *n* COMP&DP control de entrada/salida *m*; ~ **device** *n* COMP&DP dispositivo de entrada/salida *m*; ~ **file** *n* COMP&DP archivo de entrada/salida *m*, archivo de lectura/escritura *m*; ~ **instruction** *n* COMP&DP instrucción de entrada/salida *f*; ~ **interrupt** *n* COMP&DP interrupción de

entrada/salida *f*; ~ **port** *n* COMP&DP portilla de entrada/salida *f*, puerto de entrada/salida *m*; ~ **processor** *n* COMP&DP procesador de entrada/salida *m*; ~ **register** *n* COMP&DP registro de entrada/salida *m*; ~ **scan time** *n* (*I/O scan time*) PROD tiempo de exploración de entrada/salida *m* (*tiempo de exploración de E/S*); ~ **switching** *n* COMP&DP conmutación de entrada/salida *f*

inputting *n* ELECTRON energía de entrada *f*

inquiry *n* COMP&DP *data* consulta *f*, petición *f*, pregunta *f*; ~ **control** *n* COMP&DP control de consultas *m*, control de petición *m*; ~ **processing** *n* COMP&DP procesamiento de consultas *m*, procesamiento de petición *m*; ~ **station** *n* COMP&DP estación de consulta *f*, estación de petición *f*

INR *abbr* (*information request message*) TELECOM mensaje de petición de información *m*

in-reactor: ~ **experiment** *n* NUCL experimento en caliente *m*

inrush *n* FLUID erupción *f*, irrupción *f*, HYDROL *of water* irrupción *f*; ~ **current** *n* ELEC ENG corriente de entrada *f*; ~ **current limiter** *n* ELEC, ELEC ENG limitador de corriente de entrada *m*; ~ **current protection** *n* ELEC ENG protección de la corriente de entrada *f*

INS *abbr* (*inertial navigation system*) AIR TRANSP, WATER TRANSP sistema inercial de navegación *m*

insaturation *n* CHEM insaturación *f*

inscattering *n* NUCL dispersión inelástica *f*

inscribed: ~ **circle** *n* GEOM círculo inscrito *m*

in-seam: ~ **miner** *n* MINE máquina para abrir galerías *f*, máquina rafadora para carbón *f*

insect[1]: ~**proof** *adj* PACK resistente al ataque de los insectos

insect[2] *n* AGRIC insecto *m*; ~ **control** *n* AGRIC lucha contra los insectos *f*; ~ **damage** *n* AGRIC daño de insectos *m*; ~ **screen** *n* TEXTIL mosquitera *f*

insert[1] *n* AUTO enganche *m*, inserción *f*, inserto *m*, CINEMAT, COMP&DP inserción *f*, MECH engaste *m*, pieza intercalada *f*, pieza postiza *f*, separador *m*, MECH ENG encastre *m*, inserto *m*, intercalado *m*, PACK separador *m*, PRINT inserción *f*, PROD inserto *m*; ~ **bit** *n* PETR TECH barrena de insertos *f* (*Esp*), trépano de insertos *m* (*AmL*); ~ **camera** *n* TV cámara de montaje *f*; ~ **cavity** *n* MECH ENG *of die-casting die* cavidad de encastre *f*; ~ **earphone** *n* ACOUST audífono inserto *m*; ~ **edit** *n* TV insertado de edición *m*; ~ **editing** *n* TV insertado de edición *m*; ~ **nut** *n* MECH tuerca de inserción *f*; ~ **production** *n* PRINT producción intercalada *f*; ~ **shot** *n* CINEMAT toma de inserción *f*; ~ **spring** *n* AUTO muelle de inserción *m*, resorte de inserción *m*

insert[2] *vt* CINEMAT, COMP&DP insertar, MECH ENG encastrar, intercalar, introducir en, PAPER insertar, PROD insertar, intercalar

insertable: ~ **sack** *n* PACK saco para insertar *m*

inserted[1] *adj* MECH ENG encastrado, insertado, intercalado

inserted[2]: ~ **blade milling cutter** *n* MECH ENG fresa de cuchillas insertadas *f*, fresa de cuchillas postizas *f*; ~ **jaws** *n pl* MECH ENG *of vice* mordazas de quita y pon *f pl*, mordazas postizas *f pl*; ~ **joint** *n* PROD junta de inserción *f*; ~**joint casing** *n* PROD entubado de junta de inserción *m*; ~ **scram rod** *n* NUCL barra de parada insertada *f*; ~**tooth broach** *n* MECH ENG *of broaching machine* brocha de dientes insertados *f*,

mandril de dientes insertados *m*; ~**tooth milling cutter** *n* MECH ENG fresa de dientes insertados *f*, fresa de dientes postizos *f*

inserting *n* PAPER *of sheets* inserción *f*

insertion *n* PRINT, PROD inserción *f*; ~ **gain** *n* PHYS ganancia por inserción *f*; ~ **loss** *n* ACOUST, OPT, PHYS, TELECOM pérdida por inserción *f*; ~ **schedule** *n* PRINT planificación de inserciones *f*

inset *n* PRINT inserción *f*; ~ **insert** *n* PRINT inserción intercalada *f*; ~ **joint** *n* MECH ENG conexión insertada *f*

inshore[1] *adj* WATER TRANSP costanero, costero, de bajura, interior

inshore[2] *adv* WATER TRANSP cerca de la costa

inshore[3]: ~ **current** *n* OCEAN corriente costera *f*; ~ **fishery** *n* OCEAN pesca costera *f*; ~ **pilot** *n* WATER TRANSP práctico de costa *m*; ~ **pilotage** *n* WATER TRANSP practicaje en aguas costeras *m*; ~ **waters** *n pl* HYDROL, OCEAN, WATER, WATER TRANSP aguas costeras *f pl*

inside: ~ **amalgamation plate** *n* MECH ENG placa de amalgamación interna *f*, placa de unión interna *f*; ~**and-outside calipers** *AmE*, ~**and-outside callipers** *BrE* *n* MECH ENG compás de interiores y exteriores *m*; ~ **back cover** *n* PRINT cubierta posterior interna *f*; ~ **calipers** *AmE*, ~ **callipers** *BrE* *n pl* MECH ENG calibradores de interiores *m pl*, compases de calibrar interiores *m pl*, compases de interiores *m pl*; ~**clearance slide valve** *n* HYDRAUL válvula de corredera con huelgo interior *f*; ~ **corner edge** *n* PACK borde de la esquina interior *m*; ~ **corner tool** *n* MECH ENG herramienta de aristas interiores *f*; ~ **cover** *n* HYDRAUL recubrimiento de escape *m*, recubrimiento interior *m*; ~ **diameter** *n* (*ID*) MECH, MECH ENG diámetro interior *m*, diámetro interno *m*; ~**fired boiler** *n* PROD caldera de hogar interior *f*; ~ **form** *n* PRINT forma interior *f*; ~ **gear** *n* AUTO, MECH ENG engranaje interior *m*, engranaje interno *m*; ~ **lap** *n* HYDRAUL recubrimiento de escape *m*; ~**lap slide valve** *n* HYDRAUL válvula de corredera con recubrimiento al escape *f*; ~**lead slide valve** *n* HYDRAUL válvula de corredera de avance a la evacuación *f*; ~**measuring faces** *n pl* MECH ENG *of calliper* superficies de medir interiores *f pl*; ~ **screw** *n* MECH ENG rosca interior *f*, tornillo interior *m*; ~ **thread** *n* MECH ENG rosca interior *f*; ~**threading tool** *n* MECH ENG herramienta de roscar interiores *f*, terraja macho *f*; ~ **tool** *n* MECH herramienta para interiores *f*; ~ **vapor phase oxidation** *AmE*, ~ **vapour phase oxidation** *BrE* *n* (*IVPO*) TELECOM oxidación interior en fase de vapor *f*, oxidación interna en fase de vapor *f*; ~ **welding** *n* MECH soldadura interna *f*

insolation *n* FUELLESS insolación *f* (*Esp*), soleamiento *m* (*AmL*), GEOPHYS, METEO, PHYS insolación *f*, PRINT exposición *f*, REFRIG insolación *f*

insoluble *adj* CHEM, FOOD, PETR TECH insoluble; ~ **in water** *adj* CHEM, FOOD, PETR TECH insoluble en agua

inspect *vt* MECH, QUALITY inspeccionar, SPACE examinar, inspeccionar, revisar

inspection *n* C&G inspección *f*, MECH inspección *f*, verificación *f*, PROD inspección *f*, reconocimiento *m*, verificación *f*, QUALITY control *m*, inspección *f*, SAFE, SPACE inspección *f*; ~ **by attributes** *n* QUALITY control por atributos *m*; ~ **by variables** *n* QUALITY control por parámetros *m*; ~ **card** *n* PROD ficha de inspección

f, QUALITY carta de control *f*, carta de inspección *f*;
~ **chamber** *n* CONST cámara de visita *f*; ~ **cover** *n*
PROD agujero de inspección *m*; ~ **cycle** *n* AIR TRANSP
ciclo de inspección *m*; ~ **door** *n* MECH puerta de visita
f, trampilla de inspección *f*, PROD puerta de visita *f*;
~ **equipment** *n* PACK equipo de inspección *m*, QUA-
LITY equipo de control *m*, equipo de inspección *m*;
~ **fitting** *n* PROD caja de inspección *f*; ~ **following
notifiable accidents** *n* SAFE inspección después de
accidentes reportables *f*; ~ **for disease** *n* AGRIC
inspección fitosanitaria *f*; ~ **gage** *AmE see inspection
gauge BrE*; ~ **gallery** *n* HYDROL, MINE galería de
inspección *f* (*AmL*), galería de visita *f* (*Esp*); ~ **gauge**
n BrE MECH ENG calibrador de inspección *m*; ~ **hatch**
n ELEC registro *m*, SPACE *spacecraft* compuerta de
inspección *f*, escotilla de inspección *f*; ~ **hole** *n* MECH
ENG agujero de inspección *m*, SPACE mirilla *f*; ~ **lamp**
n ELEC ENG lámpara de inspección *f*; ~ **level** *n*
QUALITY nivel de control *m*; ~ **lot** *n* QUALITY lote de
control *m*; ~ **pit** *n* AUTO foso de inspección *m*, PROD
foso de inspección *m*, foso de reparaciones *m*, VEH
foso de inspección *m*; ~ **platform** *n* CONST plataforma
de inspección *f*; ~ **procedure** *n* METR proceso de
inspección *m*; ~ **record** *n* METR registro de inspección
m; ~ **specification** *n* QUALITY especificación de control *f*; ~ **stamp** *n* PROD punzón de garantía *m*, sello de
la inspección *m*; ~ **window** *n* PACK ventana de
inspección *f*
inspector *n* MECH inspector *m*, QUALITY controlador
m, inspector *m*
inspirator *n* MECH ENG inspirador *m*, inyector aspirador *m*, inyector aspirante *m*, mezclador *m*
inspissation *n* CHEM inspisación *f*
instability *n* CHEM, ELEC ENG, PACK, RAIL inestabilidad
f; ~ **phenomena** *n pl* FLUID fenómenos de inestabilidad *m pl*; ~ **of rotating Couette flow** *n* FLUID
inestabilidad de un flujo rotatorio de Couette *f*
install *vt* COMP&DP instalar, MECH ENG introducir en,
PRINT *basic term* conectar, PROD instalar, WATER
TRANSP instalar, *locks on canal* construir, montar
installation *n* COMP&DP, CONST instalación *f*, PROD
instalación *f*, montaje *m*, TELECOM instalación *f*;
~ **accessory** *n* PROD accesorio para la instalación *m*;
~ **error** *n* PROD error de instalación *m*; ~ **for reducing
sulfur emissions** *AmE*, ~ **for reducing sulphur
emissions** *BrE n* POLL, SAFE instalación para reducir
las emisiones de azufre *f*; ~ **switch** *n* ELEC conmutador de instalación *m*
installed: ~ **capacity** *n* ELEC *supply* potencia instalada
f; ~ **power** *n* VEH potencia nominal *f*
instance *n* COMP&DP ejemplo *m*, instancia *f*
instant: ~ **flowmeter** *n* WATER fluidímetro instantáneo
m; ~ **gamma radiation** *n* RAD PHYS radiación gamma
instantánea *f*; ~ **replay** *n* TV recuperación inmediata *f*
instantaneous: ~ **acoustic energy per unit volume** *n*
ACOUST energía acústica instantánea por unidad de
volumen *f*; ~ **acoustic kinetic energy per unit
volume** *n* ACOUST energía cinética acústica instantánea por unidad de volumen *f*; ~ **acoustic potential
energy per unit volume** *n* ACOUST energía potencial
acústica instantánea por unidad de volumen *f*;
~ **current** *n* ELEC, ELEC ENG corriente instantánea *f*;
~ **detonator** *n* MINE detonador instantáneo *m*;
~ **electric blasting-cap** *n* MINE cebo eléctrico instantáneo *m*; ~ **electric dipole momentum** *n* RAD
PHYS momento instantáneo del dipolo eléctrico *m*;

~ **exposure** *n* PHOTO exposición instantánea *f*; ~ **failure intensity** *n* QUALITY *of material* intensidad de
rompimiento instantáneo *f*; ~ **failure rate** *n* QUALITY
ritmo de fallas instantáneas *m*; ~ **firing** *n* MINE
disparo instantáneo *m*; ~ **frequency** *n* ELECTRON,
SPACE *communications* frecuencia instantánea *f*;
~ **frequency estimation demodulator** *n* SPACE *communications* demodulador de estimación de
frecuencia instantánea *m*; ~ **frequency
measurement** *n* (*IFM*) ELECTRON medición de
frecuencia instantánea *f*; ~ **motor data** *n pl* PROD
datos de motor instantáneo *m pl*; ~ **recording** *n*
ACOUST grabación instantánea *f*; ~ **relay** *n* ELEC relé
de acción instantánea *m*, relé extrarrápido *m*, ELEC
ENG relé extrarrápido *m*; ~ **release** *n* ELEC *switch*
desenganche rápido *m*, escape de acción instantánea
m, MECH ENG desenganche instantáneo *m*, desenganche ultra rápido *m*; ~ **sound power** *n* ACOUST
potencia sonora instantánea *f*; ~ **sound power per
unit area** *n* ACOUST potencia sonora instantánea por
unidad de área *f*; ~ **sound pressure** *n* ACOUST
presión sonora instantánea *f*; ~ **speech power** *n*
ACOUST potencia vocal instantánea *f*; ~~**tracking
error** *n* SPACE *communications* error de seguimiento
instantáneo *m*; ~ **value** *n* ELEC *of voltage*, PHYS valor
instantáneo *m*; ~ **voltage** *n* ELEC tensión instantánea
f; ~ **water heater** *n* HEAT calentador instantáneo de
agua *m*
instar *n* AGRIC instar *m*
in-step *adj* PRINT sincronizado
Institute: ~ **of Nuclear Power Operations** *n* (*INPO*)
NUCL Instituto de Operaciones Nucleares *m*
instroke *n* HYDRAUL carrera de vuelta *f*
instruction *n* MECH ENG, PACK, PROD instrucción *f*;
~ **book** *n* MECH ENG libreto de instrucciones *m*, libro
de instrucciones *m*, PROD manual de instrucciones *m*;
~ **code** *n* COMP&DP código de instrucción *m*; ~ **cycle**
n COMP&DP ciclo de instrucción *m*; ~ **decoder** *n*
COMP&DP decodificador de instrucciones *m*;
~ **execution** *n* COMP&DP ejecución de instrucciones
f; ~~**fetching** *n* COMP&DP extracción de instrucciones
f, traída de la instrucción *f*; ~ **format** *n* COMP&DP
formato de instrucción *m*; ~ **length** *n* COMP&DP
longitud de instrucción *f*; ~ **manual** *n* PROD manual
de instrucciones *m*; ~ **panel** *n* PROD panel de
instrucciones *m*; ~ **plate** *n* PROD placa de instrucciones *f*; ~ **register** *n* COMP&DP registro de instrucción
m; ~ **repertoire** *n* COMP&DP juego de instrucciones *m*,
repertorio de instrucciones *m*; ~ **set** *n* COMP&DP
conjunto de instrucciones *m*, PROD juego de instrucciones *m*; ~ **stream** *n* COMP&DP corriente de
instrucciones *f*, flujo de instrucciones *m*; ~ **syntax** *n*
PROD sintaxis de instrucciones *f*
instructions: ~ **for opening** *n* PACK instrucciones de
apertura *f pl*; ~ **for use** *n pl* PACK instrucciones de uso
f pl, modo de empleo *m*, PROD instrucciones de
empleo *f pl*
instructor *n* AIR TRANSP, ELECTRON, SAFE, TRANSP, VEH
instructor *m*
instrument[1]: ~ **restricted** *adj* AIR TRANSP reservado a
instrumentos
instrument[2] *n* GEN instrumento *m*; ~ **approach** *n* AIR
TRANSP aproximación a ciegas *f*, aproximación por
instrumentos *f*; ~ **approach chart** *n* AIR TRANSP carta
de aproximación por instrumentos *f*; ~ **approach
procedure** *n* AIR TRANSP procedimiento de aproxi-

mación por instrumentos *m*; ~ **approach runway** *n* AIR TRANSP pista de aproximación por instrumentos *f*; ~ **basin** *n* INSTR artesa instrumental *f*; ~ **board** *n* INSTR cuadro de instrumentos *m*; ~ **cord** *n* TELECOM cordón del instrumento *m*; ~ **dial** *n* INSTR cuadrante instrumental *m*; ~ **error** *n* INSTR, MECH ENG, WATER TRANSP error de instrumento *m*, error instrumental *m*; ~ **flight** *n* AIR TRANSP vuelo mediante instrumentos *m*; ~ **flight rules** *n pl* AIR TRANSP instrucciones de vuelo por instrumentos *f pl*, reglas de vuelo por instrumentos *f pl*; ~ **flying** *n* AIR TRANSP vuelo por instrumentos *m*; ~ **landing** *n* AIR TRANSP aterrizaje a ciegas *m*, aterrizaje por instrumentos *m*; ~ **landing system** *n* (*ILS*) AIR TRANSP sistema de aterrizaje por instrumentos *m* (*ILS*), SPACE *spacecraft* sistema instrumental de aterrizaje *m*; ~ **lighting** *n* INSTR alumbrado instrumental *m*; ~ **maker** *n* INSTR aparatista *m* (*AmL*), instrumentista *m*, MECH ENG instrumentista *m*; ~**-mounting plate** *n* INSTR placa de montaje instrumental *f*; ~ **panel** *n* AIR TRANSP panel de instrumentos *m*, tablero de instrumentos *m*, AUTO tablero de instrumentos *m*, panel de instrumentos *m*, PROD tablero de instrumentos *m*, VEH panel de instrumentos *m*, WATER TRANSP tablero de instrumentos *m*; ~ **range** *n* INSTR escala instrumental *f*; ~ **rating** *n* AIR TRANSP diploma de vuelo por instrumentos *m*, permiso de vuelo por instrumentos *m*; ~ **shunt** *n* ELEC ENG resistencia de derivación para instrumento *f*; ~ **switch** *n* ELEC ENG conmutador de instrumento *m*, interruptor de instrumento *m*; ~ **transformer** *n* ELEC transformador de instrumentos *m*, transformador de medida *m*, transformador para aparatos de medida *m*, ELEC ENG transformador de instrumentos *m*, transformador de medida *m*; ~**-type relay** *n* ELEC ENG relé instrumental *m*

instrumentation *n* ELECTRON, INSTR instrumentación *f*; ~ **amplifier** *n* ELECTRON amplificador de instrumentación *m*, amplificador instrumental *m*

insulant *n* CHEM, ELEC, PROD, REFRIG aislante *m*

insular: ~ **shelf** *n* GEOL, GEOPHYS, OCEAN plataforma continental insular *f*

insulate *vt* CHEM, CONST, ELEC, ELEC ENG aislar, MINE aislar, cerrar, empotrar, encastrar, estancar, impermeabilizar, ocluir, sellar, PHYS aislar, PROD aislar, cerrar, cerrar herméticamente, hacer estanco, obturar, ocluir, precintar, sellar, REFRIG, SAFE aislar

insulated[1] *adj* GEN aislado

insulated[2]: ~ **body** *n* REFRIG caja aislada *f*, caja isoterma *f*; ~ **cable** *n* ELEC, ELEC ENG cable aislado *m*; ~ **conductor** *n* AmE (*cf insulated core BrE*) ELEC *cable* alma aislada *f*, conductor aislado *m*, ELEC ENG cable conductor electroaislado *m*, conductor aislado *m*, TELECOM conductor aislado *m*; ~ **conduit** *n* ELEC *installation* conducto aislado *m*; ~ **container** *n* THERMO recipiente aislado *m*, TRANSP contenedor aislado *m*; ~ **core** *n* BrE (*cf insulated conductor AmE*) ELEC *cable* alma aislada *f*, conductor aislado *m*, ELEC ENG cable conductor electroaislado *m*, conductor aislado *m*, TELECOM conductor aislado *m*; ~**-grid field effect transistor** *n* (*IGFET*) ELECTRON transistor de efecto de campo con circuito aislado *m* (*TECCA*), transistor de efecto de campo con rejilla aislada *m* (*TECRA*); ~ **lorry** *n* BrE (*cf insulated truck AmE*) REFRIG camión isotermo *m*, vagón isotermo *m*, THERMO camión aislado *m*; ~ **opening** *n* REFRIG abertura aislada *f*; ~ **rail** *n* RAIL carril aislado *m*, riel

aislado *m*; ~ **tooling** *n* SAFE herramental aislado *m*; ~ **tools** *n pl* SAFE herramientas aisladas *f pl*; ~ **truck** *n* AmE (*cf insulated lorry BrE*) REFRIG camión isotermo *m*, vagón isotermo *m*, THERMO camión aislado *m*; ~ **wire** *n* ELEC, ELEC ENG alambre aislado *m*, hilo electroaislado *m*

insulating[1] *adj* GEN aislante

insulating[2]: ~ **board** *n* ELEC cuadro aislado *m*, tablero aislado *m*, HEAT ENG panel aislante *m*, PACK cartón aislante *m*; ~ **brick** *n* HEAT ENG ladrillo aislante *m*; ~ **cement** *n* REFRIG cemento aislante *m*; ~ **compound** *n* ELEC ENG compuesto aislante *m*, constitución aislante *f*, PACK compuesto aislante *m*; ~ **covering** *n* ELEC ENG, PROD revestimiento aislante *m*; ~ **film** *n* COATINGS película aislante *f*; ~ **fishplate** *n* BrE (*cf insulating joint bar AmE*) RAIL eclisa aislante *f*; ~ **glass for fire protection** *n* SAFE vidrio aislante contra incendios *m*; ~ **gloves** *n pl* SAFE guantes aislantes *m pl*; ~ **jacketing** *n* PROD envuelta aisladora *f*, envuelta aislante *f*; ~ **joint** *n* AUTO, ELEC ENG, VEH junta aislante *f*; ~ **joint bar** *n* AmE (*cf insulating fishplate BrE*) RAIL eclisa aislante *f*; ~ **lacquer** *n* COATINGS laca aislante *f*; ~ **lagging** *n* PROD cubierta aislante *f*, envuelta aislante *f*; ~ **layer** *n* COATINGS, ELEC ENG, PACK capa aislante *f*; ~ **mastic** *n* REFRIG masilla aislante *f*, mástico aislante *m*; ~ **mat** *n* ELEC alfombra aisladora *f*; ~ **material** *n* CONST material aislante *m*, material de aislamiento *m*, ELEC ENG, MECH, PACK material aislante *m*; ~ **oil** *n* ELEC aceite aislador *m*, aceite aislante *m*, ELEC ENG, PETR TECH aceite aislante *m*, aceite aislador *m*; ~ **paper** *n* ELEC papel aislador *m*, papel aislante *m*, PAPER papel aislante *m*; ~ **plate** *n* ELEC ENG lámina aislante *f*, placa aislante *f*; ~ **properties** *n pl* PACK propiedades aislantes *f pl*; ~ **sheath** *n* ELEC ENG vaina aislante *f*; ~ **sheet** *n* PACK hoja aislante *f*, lámina aislante *f*; ~ **sleeve** *n* ELEC ENG, PROD manguito aislador *m*; ~ **substrate** *n* ELEC ENG, SPACE substrato aislante *m*; ~ **tape** *n* ELEC, ELEC ENG cinta aisladora *f*, cinta aislante *f*; ~ **varnish** *n* COATINGS, ELEC barniz aislador *m*, barniz aislante *m*; ~ **wall panel** *n* CONST panel aislante para pared *m*; ~ **washer** *n* ELEC, ELEC ENG arandela aisladora *f*, arandela aislante *f*; ~ **wax** *n* ELEC ENG cera aislante *f*

insulation *n* GEN aislamiento *m*; ~ **against heat and cold** *n* SAFE aislante contra calor y frío *m*; ~ **against heat gain** *n* THERMO aislamiento frigorífico *m*, aislamiento para evitar la ganancia térmica *m*; ~ **against heat loss** *n* THERMO aislamiento para evitar la pérdida de calor *m*; ~ **breakdown** *n* ELEC rotura de la aislación *f*, rotura del aislamiento *f*, aislante comunicado *m*, ELEC ENG aislante comunicado *m*, paso de la corriente por el aislante *m*; ~ **bush** *n* MECH ENG *for welding equipment* buje de aislamiento *m*, manguito de aislamiento *m*; ~ **cap** *n* MECH ENG casquillo de aislamiento *m*; ~ **class** *n* ELEC clase de aislación *f*, clase de aislamiento *f*, condición de aislación *f*; ~ **defect** *n* ELEC ENG aislamiento defectuoso *m*; ~ **distance** *n* ELEC ENG distancia de aislamiento *f*, distancia entre aislamientos *f*; ~ **finish** *n* REFRIG acabado aislante *m*; ~ **pipe** *n* MECH ENG tubo de aislamiento *m*; ~ **reference curve** *n* ACOUST curva de referencia de aislamiento *f*; ~ **resistance** *n* ELEC ENG, PHYS resistencia de aislamiento *f*; ~ **resistance meter** *n* ELEC ohmímetro *m*; ~ **screen** *n* ELEC *of cable conductor* pantalla de aislamiento *f*; ~ **tester** *n* ELEC *instrument* verificador de aislamiento *m*, verificador de electroaislación *m*; ~ **withstand voltage** *n* ELEC tensión no disruptiva de aislamiento *f*, voltaje no disruptivo de aislación *m*, PROD voltaje no disruptivo de aislación *m*

insulator *n* ACOUST aislador *m*, CHEM, CONST aislante *m*, ELEC aislador *m*, aislante *m*, ELEC ENG *electric, thermal* aislante *m*, aislador *m*, OPT, PHYS aislador *m*, PROD *material* aislante *m*, aislador *m*, REFRIG aislante *m*, TELECOM aislador *m*, aislante *m*; ~ **cap** *n* ELEC casquete aislador *m*, casquete aislante *m*; ~ **clamp** *n* ELEC ENG abrazadera aislante *f*; ~ **pin** *n* PROD vástago de aislador *m*

insulin *n* CHEM insulina *f*

INT: ~ **TR** *abbr* (*international transit exchange*) TELECOM central de tránsito internacional *f*

intact: ~ **stability** *n* WATER TRANSP *ship design* estabilidad sin avería *f*

intaglio *n* C&G camafeo *m*, grabado *m*, PRINT huecograbado *m*; ~ **cylinder** *n* PRINT cilindro para huecograbado *m*; ~ **printing** *n* PRINT impresión en huecograbado *f*

intake *n* AIR TRANSP toma de aire *f*, *of engine* entrada *f*, toma *f*, admisión *f*, HYDRAUL entrada *f*, toma *f*, aspiración *f*, HYDROL cuenca hidrográfica *f*, toma *f* (*Esp*), arranque *m*, cabecera *f*, MECH entrada *f*, admisión *f*, toma *f*, MECH ENG toma *f*, admisión *f*, entrada *f*, WATER admisión *f*, cabecera *f*, cuenca hidrográfica *f*, toma *f*; ~ **airway** *n* COAL, MINE galería de entrada de aire *f*; ~ **canal** *n* WATER canal de toma *m*; ~ **chamber** *n* HYDROL cámara de toma *f*; ~ **gate** *n* WATER compuerta de toma *f*; ~ **guide vane** *n* AIR TRANSP aleta de guía de entrada *f*; ~ **guide vane ram** *n* AIR TRANSP presión dinámica de la aleta de guía de entrada *f*; ~ **manifold** *n AmE* (*cf inlet manifold BrE*) AIR TRANSP *of engine* colector de admisión *m*, distribuidor de entrada *m*, AUTO colector de admisión *m*, colector de entrada *m*, MECH *equipment* colector de admisión *m*, MECH ENG colector de admisión *m*, múltiple *m*, colector de entrada *m*, múltiple de admisión *m*, tubulador de admisión *m*, VEH *of engine* colector de admisión *m*; ~ **port** *n* (*cf inlet port*) HYDRAUL lumbrera de admisión *f*, orificio de admisión *m*, VEH *engine* lumbrera de admisión *f*; ~ **shaft** *n* MINE pozo de toma *m*; ~ **sluice** *n* WATER esclusa de toma *f*; ~ **stroke** *n* VEH *engine* carrera de admisión *f*; ~ **structure** *n* WATER estructura de toma *f*; ~ **system** *n* MECH ENG *for fluid* sistema de admisión *m*, sistema de toma *m*; ~ **tower** *n* HYDROL torre de toma de agua *f*; ~ **valve** *n* HYDRAUL válvula de admisión *f*, válvula de aspiración *f*, VEH *of engine* válvula de admisión *f*

integer *n* COMP&DP entero *m*, número entero *m*, MATH entero *m*; ~ **type** *n* COMP&DP tipo entero *m*

integral[1] *adj* MECH ENG integral, integrante, solidario, íntegro

integral[2] *n* MATH *surveying* integral *f*; ~ **aluminium foil forming plant** *n BrE* PROD fábrica de láminas de aluminio integrales *f*; ~ **aluminum foil forming plant** *AmE see integral aluminium foil forming plant BrE*; ~ **injection** *n* AUTO, VEH inyección integral *f*; ~ **power supply** *n* PROD suministro de potencia íntegra *m*; ~ **reinforced handle** *n* PACK asidero reforzado que forma parte del envase *m*; ~ **runner** *n* FUELLESS *turbines* rueda con aletas integral *f*; ~ **sampling** *n* TELECOM muestreo integral *m*; ~ **spin**

n PHYS espín entero *m*; ~ **tank** *n* MECH ENG *aeronautical* depósito estructural *m*, depósito integral *m*; ~ **tripack** *n* CINEMAT película tripack integral *f*; ~ **water management** *n* WATER administración integral de aguas *f*; ~~**way columns** *n pl* MECH ENG *machine tools* columnas de forma integral *f pl*

integrally: ~ **cast** *adj* MECH *transformer, machine* fundido en una sola pieza

integrate *vt* ELECTRON, MATH, MECH ENG, SPACE integrar

integrated[1] *adj* GEN integrado

integrated[2]: ~ **access** *n* COMP&DP, TELECOM acceso integrado *m*; ~ **bipolar transistor** *n* ELECTRON transistor bipolar integrado *m*; ~ **capacitor** *n* ELEC ENG condensador integrado *m*; ~ **charge** *n* ELEC ENG carga integrada *f*; ~ **circuit** *n* (*IC*) AUTO, COMP&DP, ELEC, PHYS, TELECOM, TV circuito integrado *m* (*CI*); ~~**circuit connection** *n* ELEC ENG conexión de circuito integrado *f*; ~ **circuit design** *n* ELECTRON diseño de circuito integrado *m*; ~ **circuit element** *n* ELECTRON elemento de circuito integrado *m*; ~ **circuit fabrication** *n* ELECTRON fabricación de circuito integrado *f*; ~~**circuit layout** *n* ELECTRON instalación de un circuito integrado *f*; ~ **circuit mask** *n* ELECTRON máscara de circuito integrado *f*; ~ **circuit package** *n* ELECTRON bloque de circuito integrado *m*; ~ **circuit substrate** *n* ELECTRON substrato de circuito integrado *m*; ~~**circuit wafer** *n* ELECTRON pastilla de circuito integrado *f*; ~ **circuitry** *n* ELECTRON circuitería integrada *f*, conjunto de circuitos integrados *m*; ~ **data processing** *n* COMP&DP informática integrada *f*; ~ **digital exchange** *n* TELECOM central digital integrada *f*; ~ **digital network** *n* (*IDN*) TELECOM red digital integrada *f*; ~ **digital services exchange** *n* TELECOM central de servicios digitales integrados *f*; ~ **filter** *n* ELECTRON filtro integrado *m*; ~ **function** *n* ELECTRON función completa *f*; ~ **home system** *n* (*IHS*) COMP&DP sistema doméstico integrado *m*, sistema integrado de casa *m* (*AmL*); ~ **hybrid component** *n* ELECTRON componente híbrido integrado *m*; ~ **hybrid resistor** *n* ELEC ENG resistencia híbrida integrada *f*; ~ **injection logic** *n* (*IL*) ELECTRON lógica integrada a inyección *f* (*IL*); ~ **logic circuit** *n* ELECTRON circuito lógico integrado *m*; ~ **logic gate** *n* ELECTRON puerta lógica integrada *f*; ~ **modem** *n* COMP&DP módem integrado *m*; ~ **MOS transistor** *n* ELECTRON transistor de SOM integrado *m*; ~ **office system** *n* (*IOS*) COMP&DP, TELECOM sistema de oficina integrado *m* (*SOI*); ~ **optical circuit** *n* (*IOC*) OPT, TELECOM circuito óptico integrado *m*; ~ **optical switch** *n* TELECOM conmutador óptico integrado *m*; ~ **optical switching matrix** *n* TELECOM matriz de conmutación óptica integrada *f*; ~ **optoelectronic circuit** *n* (*IOC*) TELECOM circuito opticoelectrónico integrado *m*; ~ **safety** *n* SPACE seguridad integrada *f*; ~ **services digital network** *n* (*ISDN*) TELECOM red digital de servicios integrados *f* (*RDSI*); ~ **services exchange** *n* TELECOM central de servicios integrados *f*; ~ **services private automatic branch exchange** *n* TELECOM centralita telefónica automática privada de servicios integrados *f*; ~ **system** *n* TELECOM sistema integrado *m*; ~ **tank** *n* TRANSP tanque incorporado *m*; ~ **transit time** *n* (*ITT*) PETR TECH tiempo de tránsito integrado *m*; ~ **voice-data private automatic branch exchange** *n* TELECOM centralita telefónica automática privada de voz-datos integrados *f*; ~ **voice-data switch** *n* TELE-COM conmutador de voz-datos integrados *m*; ~ **weapon system** *n* AIR TRANSP sistema integrado de armamento *m*

integrating: ~ **capacitor** *n* ELEC ENG condensador integrador *m*; ~ **circuit** *n* ELEC ENG circuito de integración *m*; ~ **flowmeter** *n* AIR TRANSP fluxómetro de integración *m*; ~ **meter** *n* ELEC ENG contador totalizador *m*, medidor de integración *m*; ~ **network** *n* AIR TRANSP red de integración *f*

integration *n* ELEC ENG, ELECTRON, MATH, SPACE, TELECOM integración *f*; ~ **density** *n* ELECTRON densidad de integración *f*; ~ **gain** *n* ELECTRON ganancia de integración *f*; ~ **model** *n* SPACE *trials* modelo de integración *m*; ~ **period** *n* ELEC ENG ciclo de integración *m*, período de integración *m*; ~ **time** *n* ELEC ENG tiempo de integración *m*, ELECTRON duración de integración *f*, tiempo de integración *m*

integrator *n* AIR TRANSP, CHEM, ELEC ENG, ELECTRON integrador *m*, TRANSP totalizador *m*; ~ **amplifier** *n* AIR TRANSP amplificador integrador *m*

integrity *n* TELECOM integridad *f*

intelligent: ~ **terminal** *n* COMP&DP terminal inteligente *m*

intelligibility *n* ACOUST, TELECOM inteligibilidad *f*; ~ **index** *n* ACOUST índice de inteligibilidad *m*

INTELSAT *abbr* (*International Communication Satellite*) SPACE INTELSAT (*Satélite para Comunicaciones Internacionales*)

Intelsat: ~ **Operations Center** *n AmE* SPACE *communications* Centro de Operaciones Intelsat *m*; ~ **Operations Centre** *BrE n* SPACE Centro de Operaciones Intelsat *m*

intended: ~ **flight path** *n* AIR TRANSP trayectoria de vuelo prevista *f*

intense: ~ **light** *n* WAVE PHYS luz intensa *f*

intensification *n* ELECTRON, PHOTO intensificación *f*

intensifier *n* HYDRAUL multiplicador de presión *m*; ~ **electrode** *n* TV electrodo de posaceleración *m*; ~ **ring** *n* TV anillo de intensificación *m*; ~ **tube** *n* ELECTRON tubo intensificador *m*; ~ **vidicon** *n* ELECTRON vidicón intensificador *m*

intensify *vt* ELECTRON, PHOTO intensificar

intensity *n* CHEM intensidad *f*, ELEC *electromagnetic field* fuerza *f*, intensidad *f*, ELECTRON, GAS, OPT intensidad *f*; ~ **distribution** *n* CRYSTALL, RAD PHYS distribución de intensidad *f*; ~ **level** *n* ACOUST, ELEC ENG nivel de intensidad *m*; ~ **of light** *n* RAD PHYS intensidad de la luz *f*; ~ **modulation** *n* ELECTRON modulación de la intensidad *f*

intensive: ~ **projector** *n* ELEC *lighting* proyector convergente *m*; ~ **quantity** *n* PHYS cantidad intensiva *f*

intentional: ~ **discharge** *n* MAR POLL descarga deliberada *f*

interact *vi* CHEM interactuar, obrar entre sí, RAD PHYS interactuar

interaction *n* CHEM *between substances*, COMP&DP interacción *f*, MECH ENG acción recíproca *f*, interacción *f*, acción interior *f*, METALL interacción *f*; ~ **energy** *n* METALL energía de interacción *f*; ~ **gap** *n* ELECTRON intervalo de interacción *m*; ~ **space** *n* ELECTRON espacio de interacción *m*

interactive[1] *adj* COMP&DP, OPT interactivo

interactive[2]: ~ **compact disc** *BrE*, ~ **compact disk** *AmE n* OPT disco compacto interactivo *m*; ~ **disc**

BrE, ~ **disk** *AmE n* OPT disco interactivo *m*; ~ **graphics** *n* COMP&DP gráficos interactivos *m pl*; ~ **mode** *n* COMP&DP modo interactivo *m*; ~ **network** *n* TELECOM red interactiva *f*; ~ **primary link** *n* (*IPL*) TELECOM enlace primario interactivo *m*; ~ **system** *n* TELECOM sistema interactivo *m*; ~ **television** *n* TV televisión interactiva *f*; ~ **terminal** *n* TELECOM terminal interactivo *m*; ~ **videodisc** *BrE*, ~ **videodisk** *AmE n* OPT videodisco interactivo *m*; ~ **videography** *n* TELECOM videografía interactiva *f*; ~ **videotext** *n* TELECOM videotexto interactivo *m*

interatomic[1] *adj* CRYSTALL *distance*, RAD PHYS interatómico

interatomic[2]: ~ **forces** *n pl* RAD PHYS fuerzas interatómicas *f pl*

interblock: ~ **gap** *n* (*IBG*) COMP&DP espacio entre bloques *m*, interconexión *f*, intervalo entre bloques *m*

intercalated *adj* ELEC intercalado

intercalation *n* ELEC intercalación *f*

intercell: ~ **switching** *n* TELECOM conmutación de entre celdas *f*

intercept[1] *n* AIR TRANSP intercepción *f*, interceptación *f*, GEOM corte *m*, intersección *f*, SPACE intercepción *f*, interceptación *f*; ~ **announcer** *n* TELECOM avisador de intercepción *m*; ~ **bearing** *n* AIR TRANSP marcación de intercepción *f*; ~ **point** *n* SPACE punto de intercepción *m*

intercept[2] *vt* TELECOM interceptar

interception: ~ **equipment** *n* TELECOM equipo de intercepción *m*

interceptor: ~ **sewer** *n* HYDROL interceptador de alcantarillado *m*, sifón en la acometida a la alcantarilla *m*

interchange *n* CONST cruce de carreteras *m*, intercambio *m*, nudo de carretera *m*, RAIL intercambio *m*, transbordo *m*; ~ **control reference** *n* TELECOM referencia del control de intercambios *f*; ~ **date** *n* TELECOM fecha de intercambio *f*; ~ **header** *n* TELECOM cabecera de intercambio *f*; ~ **receiver identification** *n* TELECOM identificación del receptor del intercambio *f*; ~ **recipient** *n* TELECOM receptor del intercambio *m*; ~ **sender** *n* TELECOM emisor del intercambio *m*; ~ **sender identification** *n* TELECOM identificación del emisor del intercambio *f*; ~ **time** *n* TELECOM tiempo de intercambio *m*; ~ **track** *n* RAIL vía de intercambio *f*

interchangeability *n* INSTR, MECH ENG, PHOTO intercambiabilidad *f*

interchangeable[1] *adj* INSTR, MECH ENG, PHOTO intercambiable

interchangeable[2]: ~ **focusing screen** *n* PHOTO pantalla de enfoque intercambiable *f*; ~ **lens** *n* INSTR, OPT, PHOTO lente intercambiable *f*; ~ **objectives** *n* INSTR, OPT objetivos intercambiables *m pl*; ~ **part** *n* MECH ENG parte intercambiable *f*; ~ **waist-level finder** *n* PHOTO visor al nivel de cintura intercambiable *m*

interchannel: ~ **interference** *n* ELEC ENG interferencia entre canales *f*

interchip: ~ **signal delay** *n* ELECTRON retardo de señal entre pastillas electrónicas *m*

intercircuit: ~ **signal delay** *n* ELECTRON retardo de señal entre circuitos *m*

intercity: ~ **air service** *n* AIR TRANSP puente aéreo *m*; ~ **transport** *n* TRANSP transporte entre ciudades *m*, transporte interurbano *m*

intercom *n* TELECOM sistema de intercomunicación *m*;

~ **microphone** n CINEMAT, TV micrófono de intercomunicación m

interconnected: ~ **controls** n pl AIR TRANSP controles interconectados m pl; ~ **systems** n pl ELEC sistemas interconectados m pl

interconnecting: ~ **cable** n CONST cable de interconexión m; ~ **feeder** n ELEC alimentador de interconexión m; ~ **line** n ELEC supply línea de interconexión f; ~ **pipework** n PROD tubería interconecta f

interconnection n AIR TRANSP, COMP&DP, ELEC, ELEC ENG interconexión f; ~ **cable** n ELEC ENG cable de interconexión m; ~ **layer** n ELECTRON estratificador de interconexión m; ~ **network** n TELECOM red de interconexión f; ~ **topology** n COMP&DP topología de interconexión f

intercooler n PROD of air compressor termocambiador intermedio m

intercropping n AGRIC cultivo intercalado m

intercutting n CINEMAT, TV montaje por medio de escenas de unión m

interdigital: ~ **capacitor** n PHYS capacitor interdigital m; ~ **line** n PHYS línea interdigital f; ~ **magnetron** n ELECTRON magnetrón interdigital m; ~ **transducer** n (IDT) TELECOM transductor interdigital m

interdigitation n COMP&DP, ELEC ENG, GEOL interdigitación f

interdupe n CINEMAT interduplicado m

interelectrode: ~ **capacitance** n ELEC ENG capacitancia entre electrodos f, capacitancia interelectródica f

interexchange n BrE (cf interoffice AmE) TELECOM intercambio entre centrales m, interoficinal m

interface[1] n COMP&DP interfase f, interfaz m, ELECTRON dispositivo para conectar dos sistemas m, zona de contacto f, MECH ENG acoplamiento mutuo m, interconexión f, interfaceta f, interfase f, interfaz m, superficie de contacto f, superficie de separación f, METALL interfase f, superficie de contacto f, PETROL superficie de contacto f, TELECOM interfaz m; ~ **boundary** n METALL contorno de la superficie de contacto m, límite de interfase m; ~ **card** n ELECTRON tarjeta de contacto f, tarjeta de interconexión f; ~ **chip** n ELECTRON chip de interconexión m; ~ **circuit** n ELECTRON circuito de enlace m, TELECOM circuito de interfaz m; ~ **connector socket** n PROD conector de interfaces m; ~ **energy** n METALL capacidad de la superficie de contacto f, energía de interfase f; ~ **level** n MECH ENG grado de acoplamiento m, grado de interfaz m, nivel de interfase m, nivel de interfaz m; ~ **logic** n ELECTRON circuito lógico de enlace m; ~ **message processor** n (IMP) TELECOM procesador de mensajes de interfaz m; ~ **module** n (IM) ELECTRON, SPACE, TELECOM módulo de interfaz m; ~ **requirement** n COMP&DP requisito de interfase m, requisito de interfaz m; ~ **suppression** n PROD supresión de interfase f; ~ **unit** n COMP&DP unidad de interfase f, unidad de interfaz f

interface[2] vt COMP&DP acoplar mutuamente, hacer interfase, interconectar, PROD conectar, unir, SPACE interconectar

interfaced adj COMP&DP interconectado

interfacial: ~ **angle** n CRYSTALL ángulo entre caras m, ángulo interfacial m; ~ **tension** n MAR POLL tensión interfacial f

interfacing n SPACE adaptación f

interfere vi ELECTRON, PHYS interferir

interference n GEN interferencia f; ~ **area** n TV zona de interferencia f; ~ **band** n WAVE PHYS banda de interferencia f; ~ **color** AmE, ~ **colour** BrE n COLOUR colorante de interferencia m; ~ **eliminator** n TV eliminador de interferencias m; ~ **figure** n CRYSTALL, OPT figura de interferencia f; ~ **filter** n ELEC of circuit, ELECTRON, OPT, PHYS, TELECOM filtro de interferencia m, filtro eliminador de interferencias m; ~ **fit** n MECH ENG ajuste con apriete m, ajuste entre piezas m; ~ **fringes** n pl PHYS, WAVE PHYS franjas de interferencia f pl; ~ **generator** n ELECTRON generador de interferencias m; ~ **method** n MECH ENG of measurement método de interferencia m; ~ **microscope** n INSTR microscopio de interferencia m, METALL microscopio interferencial m, PHYS microscopio de interferencia m; ~ **noise** n ELECTRON ruido parásito m; ~ **pattern** n WAVE PHYS espectro de interferencia m, patrón de interferencia m, reflejo m; ~ **reduction factor** n SPACE communications factor de reducción de interferencia m; ~ **rejection** n ELECTRON eliminación de interferencias f, WATER TRANSP radar, radio supresión de las interferencias f; ~ **ripple** n GEOL riple de interferencia m; ~ **signal** n ELECTRON señal de interferencia f; ~ **suppression** n TELECOM eliminación de interferencias f

interfering: ~ **signal** n ELECTRON señal parásita f, SPACE señal parásita f, señal perturbadora f

interferometer n GEN interferómetro m

interfield: ~ **cut** n TV corte entre campos m

interfingering n GEOL interdigitación f

interfoliated adj GEOL interfoliada

interformational: ~ **conglomerate** n PETROL conglomerado interformacional m

interframe: ~ **coding** n TELECOM codificación intertrama f

interglacial: ~ **phase** n GEOL fase interglacial f; ~ **stage** n GEOL etapa interglacial f

intergranular[1] adj GEOL intergranular, METALL intercristalino, intergranular

intergranular[2]: ~ **stress corrosion cracking** n (IGSCC) NUCL agrietamiento intergranular por tensocorrosión m

intergrowth n GEOL intercrecimiento m

interhalogen: ~ **compound** n CHEM compuesto interhalógeno m

interim: ~ **orbit** n SPACE órbita intermedia f, órbita provisional f

interionic adj CHEM distance interiónico

interior n AUTO, VEH habitáculo m; ~ **angle** n GEOM ángulo interior m; ~ **coating** n PACK revestimiento interior m; ~ **lining** n PACK forrado interior m; ~ **packaging** n PACK embalaje interior m; ~ **strengthening bar** n PACK barra de refuerzo interior f; ~ **wrapping** n PACK envoltura interior f

interlace[1] n TV entrelazado m; ~ **sequence** n TV secuencia entrelazada f

interlace[2] vt COMP&DP entrelazar, ELECTRON entrelazar, entremezclar, TEXTIL entrelazar

interlaced: ~ **scanning** n ELECTRON, TV exploración entrelazada f

interlacing n TEXTIL entrelazamiento m; ~ **and crimping** n TEXTIL entrelazamiento y rizado m

interlayer adj GEOL, PETR TECH intercalador

interleaf n PRINT hoja intercalada f

interleave *vt* COMP&DP entrelazar, interfoliar, ELEC-TRON intercalar

interleaving *n* COMP&DP *nesting* entrelazado *m*, interfolición *f*, ELECTRON intercalación *f*, PAPER intercalado *m*

interlimb: ~ **angle** *n* GEOL ángulo interlabial *m*

interline *vt* TEXTIL entretelar

interlining *n* AIR TRANSP interrevestimiento *m*, TEXTIL entretela *f*; ~ **material** *n* TEXTIL género para entretelas *m*

interlock[1] *n* CINEMAT interbloqueo *m*, COMP&DP *of channel* bloqueo *m*, interbloqueo *m*, ELEC ENG bloqueo *m*, interbloqueo *m*, dispositivo cortacorriente *m*, NUCL enclavamiento *m*, PROD enclavamiento *m*, interbloqueo *m*, TV enclavamiento *m*; ~ **circuit** *n* ELEC ENG circuito de bloqueo *m*, circuito de entrecierre *m*; ~ **contact** *n* ELEC ENG contacto de blocaje *m*; ~ **control** *n* AIR TRANSP conexión *f*, enclavamiento, inmovilización *f*, control de enclavamiento *m*, control de interconexión *m*; ~ **device** *n* CINEMAT dispositivo de interbloqueo *m*; ~ **relay** *n* ELEC relé de enclavamiento *m*, ELEC ENG relé cortacorriente *m*; ~ **switch** *n* ELEC, ELEC ENG interruptor corta-corriente *m*

interlock[2] *vt* AIR TRANSP inmovilizar, ELEC ENG *control* enclavar, interbloquear, MECH inmovilizar, MECH ENG interconectar, enclavar, interbloquear, TEXTIL trabar

interlocked *adj* PROD enclavado

interlocking *n* AIR TRANSP interconexión *f*, MECH acoplamiento *m*, enclavamiento *m*, entrelazado *m*, inmovilización *f*, interbloqueo *m*, interconexión *f*, MECH ENG enclavamiento *m*, entrecruzado *m*, entrelazado *m*, inmovilización *f*, interbloqueo *m*, interconexión *f*; ~ **device** *n* PACK sistema de cierre *m*; ~ **guard** *n* SAFE dispositivo protector de enclavamiento *m*; ~ **milling cutter** *n* MECH ENG fresa entrecruzada *f*, fresa entrelazada *f*; ~ **relay** *n* ELEC relé de acoplamiento *m*, relé de enclavamiento *m*; ~ **system** *n* SAFE sistema de bloqueo *m*

intermediate: ~ **approach** *n* AIR TRANSP aproximación intermedia *f*; ~ **approach fix** *n* AIR TRANSP posición de aproximación intermedia *f*; ~ **approach point** *n* AIR TRANSP punto intermedio de aproximación *m*; ~ **bulk container** *n* PACK contenedor de productos a granel semielaborados *m*; ~ **case** *n* AIR TRANSP caja intermedia *f*; ~ **chemical** *n* PETR TECH químico intermedio *m*; ~ **coat** *n* COATINGS revestimiento intermedio *m*; ~-**cylinder steam engine** *n* HYDRAUL motor de vapor con cilindro intermedio *m*; ~ **design review** *n* SPACE revisión del diseño intermedio *f*, revista de diseño intermedio *f*; ~ **distribution frame** *n* *(IDF)* TELECOM trama de distribución intermedia *f*; ~ **exposure** *n* PRINT exposición intermedia *f*; ~ **frame** *n* TEXTIL bastidor intermedio *m*; ~ **frequency** *n* *(IF)* ELECTRON, TELECOM, TV frecuencia intermedia *f* *(FI)*; ~-**frequency amplification** *n* ELECTRON, TELECOM amplificación de frecuencia intermedia *f*; ~-**frequency amplifier** *n* ELECTRON, TELECOM, WATER TRANSP *radar* amplificador de frecuencia intermedia *m*; ~ **frequency filter** *n* ELECTRON, TELECOM filtro de frecuencia intermedia *m*; ~ **frequency rejection** *n* ELECTRON, TELECOM supresión de frecuencia intermedia *f*; ~ **frequency signal** *n* ELECTRON, TELECOM, TV señal de frecuencia intermedia *f*; ~ **frequency stage** *n* ELECTRON fase de frecuencia intermedia *f*, supresión de frecuencia

intermedia *f*, TELECOM etapa de frecuencia intermedia *f*; ~ **gear** *n* MECH ENG engranaje intermedio *m*; ~ **gearbox** *n* AIR TRANSP *of helicopter* caja de engranajes intermedia *f*; ~ **image** *n* PHYS imagen intermedia *f*; ~ **image screen** *n* INSTR pantalla de imagen intermedia *f*; ~ **layer** *n* COATINGS capa intermedia *f*; ~ **lens** *n* INSTR lente intermedia *f*; ~ **level radioactive waste** *n* NUCL residuos radiactivos de actividad media *m pl*; ~ **negative** *n* CINEMAT negativo intermedio *m*; ~ **positive** *n* CINEMAT positivo intermedio *m*; ~ **pressure cylinder** *n* HYDRAUL cilindro de media presión *m*; ~ **reversal negative** *n* CINEMAT negativo reversible intermedio *m*; ~ **rock** *n* GEOL roca intermedia *f*; ~ **satellite band** *n* TELECOM banda satélite intermedia *f*; ~ **shaft** *n* MECH ENG eje intermedio *m*, eje secundario *m*; ~ **storage** *n* AmE (*cf intermediate store BrE*) COMP&DP almacenamiento intermedio *m*; ~ **store** *BrE n* (*cf intermediate storage AmE*) COMP&DP almacenamiento intermedio *m*; ~ **system** *n* *(IS)* TELECOM sistema intermedio *m* *(SI)*; ~ **trunk** *n* *(IT)* TELECOM enlace intermedio *m*; ~ **type of soil** *n* COAL tipo de terreno intermedio *m*; ~ **vector boson** *n* PART PHYS, PHYS bosón vectorial intermedio *m*; ~ **voltage winding** *n* ELEC devanado de tensión intermedia *m*; ~ **water level** *n* WATER nivel del agua de zona de transición *m*; ~ **waters** *n pl* OCEAN aguas intermedias *f pl*; ~ **wheel** *n* MECH ENG *gearing* rueda intermedia *f*

intermeshed: ~ **loops** *n* TEXTIL bucles enredados *m pl*

intermetallic: ~ **compound** *n* METALL compuesto intermetálico *m*

intermingled: ~ **yarn** *n* TEXTIL hilado tangleado *m*

intermittent: ~ **agitation** *n* PHOTO agitación intermitente *f*; ~ **board machine** *n* PAPER máquina intermitente para cartón *f*; ~ **claw** *n* CINEMAT garfio intermitente *m*; ~ **contact printer** *n* CINEMAT positivadora intermitente por contacto *f*; ~ **duty** *n* ELEC *of equipment* funcionamiento intermitente *m*, trabajo intermitente *m*; ~ **fault** *n* ELEC error intermitente *m*, falla intermitente *f*; ~ **flow** *n* HYDROL corriente intermitente *f*; ~ **light** *n* CINEMAT luz intermitente *f*; ~ **load** *n* ELEC *of generator* carga intermitente *f*; ~ **noise** *n* ACOUST ruido intermitente *m*; ~ **prism** *n* CINEMAT prisma intermitente *m*; ~ **production** *n* PROD producción intermitente *f*; ~ **spring** *n* WATER manantial intermitente *m*

intermodal: ~ **container** *n* TRANSP contenedor entre módulos *m*, contenedor intermodal *m*; ~ **distortion** *n* TELECOM distorsión intermodal *f*; ~ **traffic** *n* RAIL tráfico intermodal *m*; ~ **transport** *n* REFRIG transporte combinado *m*

intermodulation *n* ELECTRON, SPACE, TELECOM, TV intermodulación *f*; ~ **distortion** *n* ELECTRON distorsión de intermodulación *f*; ~ **noise** *n* SPACE *communications* ruido de intermodulación *m*; ~ **product** *n* ELECTRON, SPACE, TELECOM producto de intermodulación *m*

intermolecular *adj* CHEM intermolecular

intermontane: ~ **basin** *n* GEOL cuenca intermontañosa *f*, cuenca intramontaña *f*

internal: ~ **angle** *n* GEOM ángulo interior *m*, ángulo interno *m*; ~ **battery** *n* ELEC ENG batería interior *f*, batería interna *f*; ~ **blocking** *n* TELECOM bloqueo interno *m*; ~ **breakdown** *n* REFRIG avería interna *f*; ~ **burner** *n* C&G quemador interno *m*; ~ **caliper gage** *AmE*, ~ **calliper gauge** *BrE n* MECH ENG calibrador de compás interior *m*, calibrador macho *m*; ~ **circuit fault** *n* PROD fallo interno de circuito *f*; ~ **clock** *n* TELECOM reloj interno *m*; ~ **combustion engine** *n* ELEC ENG motor a gasoil *m*, motor de combustión interna *m*, motor diesel *m*, MECH, MECH ENG, PETR TECH, PROD, VEH motor de combustión interna *m*; ~ **combustion turbine** *n* AIR TRANSP, GAS, MECH, PROD, THERMO, WATER TRANSP turbina de combustión interna *f*; ~ **conversion** *n* PHYS *communications, equipment* conversión interna *f*; ~ **crack** *n* METALL fisura interna *f*, grieta interna *f*; ~ **cylindrical gage** *AmE*, ~ **cylindrical gauge** *BrE n* MECH ENG calibrador cilíndrico de interiores *m*, calibrador de tapón *m*; ~ **damping** *n* AIR TRANSP amortiguación interna *f*; ~ **defrosting** *n* REFRIG desescarche desde el interior *m*; ~ **delivery slip** *n* PROD albarán de entrega *m*; ~ **demand** *n* PROD demanda interna *f*; ~ **diagnostic test** *n* PROD prueba interna de diagnóstico *f*; ~ **diameter** *n* MECH ENG, PROD *of pipe* diámetro interior *m*; ~ **energy** *n* PHYS, RAD PHYS energía interna *f*; ~ **erosion** *n* COAL erosión interna *f*; ~ **expanding brake** *n* MECH ENG freno de expansión interno *m*; ~ **extension** *n* TELECOM extensión interna *f*; ~ **and external simultaneous grinding** *n* MECH ENG *machine tools* rectificado simultáneo interior y exterior *m*; ~ **friction** *n* C&G fricción interior *f*, fricción interna *f*, tornillo interno *m*, MECH ENG fricción interior *f*, fricción interna *f*, METALL fricción interior *f*, fricción interna *f*, rozamiento interno *m*; ~ **gain** *n* ELECTRON ganancia interna *f*; ~ **gas pressure cable** *n* ELEC cable con gas a presión interna *m*; ~ **gear** *n* AUTO engranaje interior *m*, engranaje interno *m*, mecanismo interior *m*, MECH ENG engranaje interno *m*, engranaje interior *m*; ~ **graticule** *n* ELECTRON cuadrícula interna *f*; ~ **grinder** *n* MECH ENG rectificadora de interiores *f*; ~ **grinding-wheel** *n* PROD muela para rectificar interiores *f*; ~ **input signal** *n* TELECOM señal de entrada interna *f*; ~ **installation** *n* ELEC ENG instalación interna *f*; ~ **lacquering** *n* COATINGS, PACK lacado interior *m*; ~ **logic signal** *n* PROD señal interna lógica *f*; ~ **magnetism** *n* SPACE magnetismo interno *m*; ~ **magnetosphere** *n* SPACE magnetosfera interna *f*; ~ **memory** *n* COMP&DP, ELEC ENG memoria interna *f*; ~ **micrometer** *n* MECH ENG micrómetro para interiores *m*; ~ **mirror lamp** *n* CINEMAT, PHOTO, TV lámpara con recubrimiento especular interno *f*; ~ **noise** *n* ELECTRON ruido interno *m*; ~ **oxidation** *n* METALL oxidación interna *f*; ~ **photoelectric effect** *n* ELECTRON, OPT, TELECOM efecto fotoeléctrico interno *m*; ~ **plasticizer** *n* P&R plastificante interno *m*; ~ **pole dynamo** *n* ELEC *generator*, ELEC ENG dinamo de polos interiores *f*; ~**pole generator** *n* ELEC generador de polos interiores *m*; ~ **pressure** *n* WATER presión interior *f*, presión interna *f*; ~ **priority** *n* PROD prioridad interna *f*; ~ **program error flag** *AmE*, ~ **programme error flag** *BrE n* PROD banderín de error del programa interno *m*; ~ **reference point** *n* (*IRP*) TELECOM punto de referencia interna *m*; ~ **reflection** *n* RAD PHYS reflexión interna *f*; ~ **resistance** *n* ELEC *cell* resistencia interna *f*; ~ **scour** *n* COAL socavación interna *f*; ~ **screw** *n* PROD tornillo hembra *m*; ~ **setup** *n* PROD reglaje interno *m*; ~ **shaft** *n* MINE pozo interior *m*; ~ **shield** *n* ELECTRON blindaje interno *m*, pantalla interna *f*; ~ **sort** *n* COMP&DP clasificación interna *f*; ~ **storage**

AmE, ~ **store** *BrE n* COMP&DP almacenamiento interno *m*, conexión entre redes *f*, PROD almacenamiento interno *m*, memoria interna *f*; ~ **stress** *n* METALL esfuerzo interno *m*; ~ **structure** *n* PART PHYS estructura interna *f*; ~ **temperature** *n* PACK temperatura interna *f*; ~ **thread fastener** *n* MECH ENG *threaded sockets, nuts* fijador de rosca interior *m*; ~ **timing mechanism** *n* PROD mecanismo interno de sincronización *m*; ~ **traffic** *n* TELECOM tráfico interno *m*; ~ **waters** *n* OCEAN aguas interiores *f pl*; ~ **wave** *n* OCEAN onda interna *f*; ~ **wheel case** *n* AIR TRANSP caja de ruedas interna *f*; ~ **wiring** *n* TELECOM cableado interno *m*

international: ~ **air route** *n* AIR TRANSP ruta aérea internacional *f*; ~ **airport** *n* AIR TRANSP aeropuerto internacional *m*; ~ **data switching exchange** *n* (*IDSE*) TELECOM central de conmutación de datos internacionales *f*, central de conmutación para mensajes internacionales *f*; ~ **date line** *n* WATER TRANSP línea internacional de cambio de fecha *f*; ~ **gateway exchange** *n* TELECOM central de acceso internacional *f*; ~ **gateway node** *n* (*IGN*) TELECOM nodo de acceso internacional *m*, nodo de entrada internacional *m*; ~ **hydrological program** *AmE*, ~ **hydrological programme** *BrE n* HYDROL, WATER programa hidrológico internacional *m*; ~ **operations service** *n* TELECOM servicio de operaciones internacionales *m*; ~ **packet-switched data network** *n* TELECOM red de datos internacional de conmutación de paquetes *f*; ~ **packet-switching gateway exchange** *n* TELECOM central internacional de acceso a la conmutación de paquetes *f*; ~ **radioactivity standard** *n* POLL norma international de radiactividad *f*; ~ **soundtrack** *n* ACOUST, CINEMAT banda sonora internacional *f*; ~ **standard** *n* CONST norma internacional *f*; ~ **standard thread** *n* MECH ENG rosca de estándar internacional *f*; ~ **switching center** *AmE*, ~ **switching centre** *BrE n* TELECOM centro de conmutación internacional *m*; ~ **system unit** *n* (*SI unit*) ELEC, METR, PART PHYS, PHYS unidad del sistema internacional *f* (*unidad SI*); ~ **system of units** *n* (*SI*) METR, sistema internacional de unidades *m* (*SI*); ~ **telegraph alphabet** *n* AIR TRANSP, TELECOM, WATER TRANSP alfabeto telegráfico internacional *m*; ~ **transit exchange** *n* (*INT TR*) TELECOM central de tránsito internacional *f*; ~ **unit** *n* ELEC, PHYS unidad internacional *f*; ~ **waters** *n pl* OCEAN, WATER TRANSP *sea areas* aguas internacionales *f pl*

International: ~ **Association of Lighthouses Authorities** *n* (*IALA*) WATER TRANSP *navigation marks* Asociación Internacional de Señalización Marítima *f* (*AISM*); ~ **Commission on Illumination** *n* PHYS Comisión Internacional de Iluminación *f*; ~ **Commission on Radiological Protection** *n* (*ICRP*) RAD PHYS Comisión Internacional de Protección Radiológica *f*; ~ **Communication Satellite** *n* (*INTELSAT*) SPACE Satélite para Comunicaciones Internacionales *m* (*INTELSAT*); ~ **Direct Dialling** *n* *BrE* (*cf International Direct Distance Dialing AmE*) TELECOM marcación directa internacional *f*; ~ **Direct Distance Dialing** *n AmE* (*cf International Direct Dialling BrE*) TELECOM marcación directa internacional *f*; ~ **Electrotechnical Committee** *n* (*IEC*) PROD Comité Electrotécnico Internacional *m*; ~ **Frequency Registration Board** *n* (*IFRB*) SPACE Comité Internacional de Registro de Frecuencias *m* (*IFRB*); ~ **Maritime Organization** *n* (*IMO*) WATER TRANSP Organización Marítima Internacional *f* (*OMI*); ~ **Register of Potentially Toxic Chemicals** *n* (*IRPTC*) POLL, SAFE Registro Internacional de Compuestos Químicos Potencialmente Tóxicos *m*; ~ **Standards Organization** *n* (*ISO*) ELEC, MECH ENG, TELECOM Organización Internacional de Normalización *f* (*OIN*); ~ **Subscriber Dialing** *AmE*, ~ **Subscriber Dialling** *BrE* *n* TELECOM Marcación de Abonado Internacional *f*; ~ **Telegraph and Telephone Consultative Committee** *n* (*CCITT*) TELECOM Comité Consultivo Internacional de Telefonía y Telegrafía *m* (*CCITT*); ~ **Transit Center** *AmE*, ~ **Transit Centre** *BrE* *n* SPACE Centro de Tránsito Internacional *m*

internegative *n* CINEMAT, PRINT internegativo *m*

Internet *n* COMP&DP Internet *m*, la Red *f*, TELECOM Internet *m*

internetting *n* COMP&DP funcionamiento de interredes *m*, interconexión de redes *f*, TELECOM interconexión de redes *f*

internides *n pl* GEOL arco primario *m*, orogenia primaria *f*

interocean: ~ **channel** *n* OCEAN canal interoceánico *m*

interoffice *n AmE* TELECOM intercambio entre centrales *m*, interoficinal *m*

interoperation: ~ **time** *n* PROD tiempo interoperational *m*

interoperative: ~ **time** *n* PROD tiempo interoperativo *m*

inter-PABX: ~ **tie circuit** *n* TELECOM circuito de enlace entre centralitas telefónicas automáticas privadas *m*

interparticle: ~ **spacing** *n* METALL separación entre partículas *f*

interpenetration: ~ **twin** *n* CRYSTALL macla de compenetración *f*

interpersonal: ~ **messaging system** *n* TELECOM sistema de mensajería interpersonal *m*

interphase: ~ **short circuit** *n* ELEC *fault* cortocircuito interfásico *m*

interpile: ~ **sheeting** *n* COAL entibación apoyada en los pilotes *f*, forro de tablas entre pilotes *m*

interplanetary[1] *adj* SPACE interplanetario

interplanetary[2]: ~ **flight** *n* SPACE vuelo interplanetario *m*; ~ **mission** *n* SPACE misión interplanetaria *f*; ~ **probe** *n* SPACE sonda interplanetaria *f*; ~ **travel** *n* SPACE viaje interplanetario *m*

interplant *n* AGRIC *maize* intercalación de machos y hembras *f*, PROD interplanta *f*

interpolating *adj* ELECTRON interpolador

interpolation *n* COMP&DP, ELEC, MATH, OPT, TELECOM interpolación *f*; ~ **gain** *n* (*IG*) TELECOM ganancia de interpolación *f*; ~ **of speech signals** *n* TELECOM interpolación de señales vocales *f*

interpolator *n* MATH, TELECOM interpolador *m*

interpole *n* ELEC *of DC motor* polo auxiliar *m*, polo de conmutación *m*; ~ **machine** *n* ELEC máquina de polo auxiliar *f*, máquina de polo de conmutación *f*

interpret *vt* COMP&DP, GEOM interpretar

interpretative: ~ **language** *n* COMP&DP lenguaje interpretativo *m*

interpreter *n* COMP&DP intérprete *m*

interprocessor: ~ **link** *n* TELECOM enlace entre procesadores *m*

interrogate *vt* COMP&DP, TELECOM interrogar

interrogation *n* COMP&DP barrido *m*, interrogación *f*, TELECOM interrogación *f*; ~ **mode** *n* ELECTRON función de interrogación *f*

interrogator: ~ **transponder** *n* TELECOM transpondedor interrogador *m*

interrupt[1]: ~ **mask** *n* COMP&DP máscara de interrupción *f*; ~ **period** *n* PROD período de interrupción *m*; ~ **priority** *n* COMP&DP prioridad de interrupción *f*; ~ **signal** *n* COMP&DP señal de interrupción *f*; ~ **value** *n* PROD valor de interrupción *m*; ~ **vector** *n* COMP&DP vector de interrupción *m*

interrupt[2] *vt* ELEC ENG interrumpir

interrupted: ~ **ageing** *n* P&R envejecimiento interrumpido *m*; ~ **flow** *n* TRANSP circulación interrumpida *f*; ~ **tooth tap** *n* MECH ENG macho de roscar de dentadura interrumpida *m*

interrupter *n* ELEC *switch* interruptor *m*, ruptor *m*, ELEC ENG, TELECOM interruptor *m*

interrupting: ~ **voltage** *n* ELEC ENG tensión de ruptura *f*, voltaje de interrupción *m*

interruption *n* ELEC ENG, GAS, TELECOM interrupción *f*

intersatellite: ~ **link** *n* SPACE *communications* enlace entre satélites *m*; ~ **link acquisition** *n* SPACE captación del enlace entre satélites *f*; ~ **service** *n* SPACE *communications* servicio entre satélites *m*

intersect *vt* GEOL cortar, cruzar, GEOM cortar, intersecar, intersectar, MATH, MECH ENG intersecar, intersectar

intersecting[1] *adj* GEOM, MATH, MECH ENG intersectado

intersecting[2] *n* GEOM, MATH, MECH ENG intersectado *m*; ~ **arcs** *n pl* GEOM arcos intersectantes *m pl*, arcos que se cortan *m pl*; ~ **lines** *n pl* GEOM líneas intersectantes *f pl*, líneas que se cortan *f pl*; ~ **planes** *n pl* GEOM planos intersectantes *m pl*, planos que se cortan *m pl*; ~ **vein** *n* GEOL vena cruzada *f*

intersection *n* CHEM, COMP&DP, CONST, GEOM intersección *f*; ~ **angle** *n* CONST ángulo de intersección *m*; ~ **point** *n* CONST punto de intersección *m*

interstage: ~ **cooler** *n* REFRIG enfriador intermedio *m*; ~ **transformer** *n* ELEC, ELEC ENG transformador de enlace *m*

interstellar[1] *adj* SPACE interestelar

interstellar[2]: ~ **matter** *n* SPACE materia interestelar *f*; ~ **space** *n* SPACE espacio interestelar *m*

interstice *n* COAL, CONST, HYDROL intersticio *m*

interstitial: ~ **atom** *n* CRYSTALL átomo intersticial *m*; ~ **compound** *n* CHEM compuesto intersticial *m*; ~ **solid solution** *n* CRYSTALL solución sólida intersticial *f*; ~ **water** *n* COAL, HYDROL, OCEAN, PETR TECH, WATER agua intersticial *f*

interswitchboard: ~ **tie-circuit** *n* TELECOM circuito de enlace intercentral *m*

intersymbol: ~ **interference** *n* ELECTRON perturbación entre símbolos *f*, TELECOM interferencia entre símbolos *f*

intertidal: ~ **deposits** *n pl* GEOL depósitos intermareales *m pl*; ~ **zone** *n* MAR POLL zona intermareal *f*

interturn: ~ **capacitance** *n* ELEC *of coil* capacitancia de entreturno *f*; ~ **insulation** *n* ELEC *of coil* aislación de entreturno *f*, aislamiento de entreturno *m*

interval *n* ACOUST, COMP&DP, GEOL, PETR TECH intervalo *m*; ~ **difference** *n* ACOUST diferencia de intervalo *f*; ~ **timer** *n* COMP&DP marcador de intervalo *m*, temporizador de intervalos *m*; ~ **velocity** *n* PETR TECH velocidad de intervalo *f*

intervention *n* COMP&DP intervención *f*

interworking n TELECOM entrelazado m; ~ **functional unit** n (*IFU*) TELECOM unidad funcional entrelazada f; ~ **protocol** n (*IWP*) TELECOM protocolo de entrelazado m

interwoven adj PROD, TEXTIL entretejido

intonation n ACOUST entonación f

intraclast n GEOL intraclasto m

intracratonic adj GEOL intracratónico

intrados n CONST *of arch* intradós m

intraesparite n PETR TECH intraesparita f

intragranular adj GEOL, METALL intragranular

intramicrite n PETR TECH, PETROL intramicrita f

intramodal: ~ **distortion** n OPT, TELECOM distorsión intramodal f

intramolecular adj CHEM intramolecular

intraoffice: ~ **junctor circuit** n TELECOM circuito de conexión intraoficinal m

intraplate[1] adj GEOL entre placas

intraplate[2]: ~ **volcanism** n GEOL vulcanismo entre placas m

in-tray n PROD bandeja de entrada f

intricate adj MECH ENG complicado, confuso, enredado, intrincado

intrinsic[1] adj GEN intrínseco

intrinsic[2]: ~ **angular momentum** n PART PHYS momento angular intrínseco m; ~ **barrier diode** n ELECTRON diodo de barrera intrínseca m; ~ **conductivity** n ELEC, ELEC ENG conductividad intrínseca f; ~ **curvature** n GEOM curvatura intrínseca f; ~ **distribution** n RAD PHYS *of frequencies* distribución intrínseca f; ~ **error** n INSTR, METR error intrínseco m; ~ **forecast** n PROD previsión intrínseca f, pronóstico intrínseco m; ~ **impedance** n ELEC *electromagnetism*, ELEC ENG impedancia intrínseca f; ~ **joint loss** n OPT atenuación por unión intrínseca f, TELECOM pérdida intrínseca de empalme f; ~ **noise** n ELECTRON ruido intrínseco m; ~ **permeability** n ELEC *electromagnetism* permeabilidad intrínseca f; ~ **photoconductivity** n ELEC fotoconductividad intrínseca f; ~ **semiconductor** n COMP&DP, ELECTRON, PHYS semiconductor intrínseco m; ~ **stability** n FLUID estabilidad intrínseca f; ~ **temperature** n ELECTRON temperatura intrínseca f; ~ **temperature range** n ELECTRON ámbito de temperatura intrínseca m; ~ **viscosity** n FLUID viscosidad intrínseca f

intrinsically: ~ **safe** adj ELEC ENG intrínsecamente seguro

introscopy n NUCL introscopia f

intruder: ~ **presence detector** n TELECOM detector de presencia de intrusos m

intrusion n AIR TRANSP intrusión f, GEOL dolomitización f, intrusión f, PETROL, TELECOM intrusión f

intrusive[1] adj FUELLESS, GEOL intruso

intrusive[2]: ~ **sheet** n GEOL lámina intrusiva f

intumescent[1] adj COLOUR, P&R intumescente

intumescent[2]: ~ **paint** n COATINGS, COLOUR pintura intumescente f

inulin n CHEM, FOOD inulina f

inundation n HYDROL inundación f, WATER anegación f, desbordamiento m, inundación f

invaded: ~ **zone** n PETR TECH zona invadida f

invalid adj TELECOM *metal plate, iron wire* inválido

invariant[1] adj GEOM invariable, invariante

invariant[2] n ELECTRON invariante f, GEOM constante f, invariante f, MECH, PHYS invariante f

invasive: ~ **technique** n RAD PHYS técnica invasiva f

in-vehicle: ~ **aural communication system** n TRANSP sistema de comunicación auditiva en vehículo m; ~ **visual display** n TRANSP exposición visual en vehículo f, pantalla de representación visual en vehículo f, visualización en vehículo f

inventory n PACK, PETR TECH inventario m, PROD existencias de almacén f pl, gestión de existencias f, inventario m; ~ **change** n PROD cambio de inventario m; ~ **control** n PROD control de inventario m; ~ **profile** n PROD historia de inventario f; ~ **receipt** n PROD recibo de inventario m; ~ **reporting** n PROD informe de existencias m; ~ **turnover** n PROD rotación de las existencias f; ~ **valuation** n PROD valuación de existencias f; ~ **wipe-off** n PROD cancelación de existencias f

inverse[1] adj COMP&DP, ELEC ENG, ELECTRON, GEOM, MATH inverso, MECH ENG inverso, invertido, MINE, PHYS, PROD inverso

inverse[2] n MATH inversa f, MECH ENG invertido m, recíproco m; ~ **Compton effect** n PHYS efecto Compton inverso m; ~ **direction** n ELEC ENG dirección inversa f, dirección invertida f; ~ **dovetail cutter** n MECH ENG fresa de colas de milano invertida f, fresa de machiembrar invertida f; ~ **feedback** n ELEC ENG intrarreacción f, realimentación inversa f, realimentación negativa f, ELECTRON realimentación inversa f; ~ **feedback filter** n ELECTRON filtro de realimentación inversa m; ~ **gain** n ELECTRON ganancia inversa f; ~ **image** n MATH imagen inversa f; ~ **initiation** n MINE iniciación inversa f; ~ **limiter** n ELECTRON limitador inverso m; ~ **modulation** n ELECTRON modulación invertida f; ~ **photoelectric effect** n ELECTRON efecto fotoeléctrico inverso m; ~ **piezoelectric effect** n ELEC ENG, PHYS efecto piezoeléctrico inverso m; ~ **primary creep** n METALL fluencia primaria invertida f; ~ **ratio** n MATH relación inversa f, MECH ENG razón inversa f, relación recíproca f; ~ **square law** n ACOUST ley del inverso del cuadrado de la distancia f, ley del inverso del cuadrado f, PHYS ley del inverso del cuadrado f, ley del inverso del cuadrado de la distancia f; ~ **time relay** n ELEC relé de retardo dependiente m; ~ **variation** n MATH variación inversa f; ~ **video** n COMP&DP vídeo inverso m (*AmL*), vídeo inverso m (*Esp*); ~ **voltage** n PROD voltaje inverso m; ~ **voltage rating** n PROD régimen de voltaje inverso m

inverse[3]: **in ~ proportion to** phr MECH ENG en proporción inversa a

inversely: ~ **proportional numbers** n pl MATH números inversamente proporcionales n pl

inversion n GEN inversión f; ~ **axis** n CRYSTALL eje de inversión m; ~ **center** AmE, ~ **centre** BrE n CRYSTALL centro de inversión m; ~ **layer** n ELECTRON estratificador de inversión m, METEO, POLL capa de inversión f, inversión de temperatura f, TELECOM capa de inversión f, THERMO inversión de temperatura f; ~ **temperature** n ELEC *of thermocouple*, PHYS temperatura de inversión f

invert[1] n COAL *arch* lecho m, zampeado m, HYDROL parte interior f; ~ **sugar** n CHEM, FOOD azúcar invertido m

invert[2] vt CINEMAT, COMP&DP, ELEC, ELEC ENG, PHYS, TELECOM invertir

invertase n CHEM invertasa f, sucrasa f, FOOD invertasa f

inverted¹ *adj* CINEMAT, COAL invertido

inverted²: ~ **arch** *n* CONST *curve described* contrabóveda *f*, *structure itself* arco invertido *m*; ~ **burner** *n* PROD *for gas* quemador invertido *m*; ~ **commas** *n pl* PRINT comillas *f pl*; ~ **converter** *n* ELEC convertidor invertido *m*; ~ **cylinder engine** *n* PROD máquina de cilindro invertido *f*; ~ **file** *n* COMP&DP archivo inverso *m*, archivo invertido *m*; ~ **fold** *n* GEOL pliegue invertido *m*; ~ **image** *n* CINEMAT, PHOTO, PHYS, TV imagen invertida *f*; ~ **microscope** *n* INSTR microscopio invertido *m*; ~-**pattern accumulator** *n* HYDRAUL acumulador de estructura invertida *m*; ~ **pleat** *n* TEXTIL pliegue invertido *m*; ~ **population** *n* ELECTRON parque invertido *m*; ~ **rectifier** *n* ELECTRON rectificador inversor de CC/CA *m*; ~ **T-shaped track girder** *n* TRANSP traviesa en forma de T invertida *f*

inverter *n* CINEMAT, COMP&DP, ELEC inversor *m*, ELEC ENG convertidor *m*, inversor *m*, ELECTRON convertidor *m*, PHYS, TELECOM inversor *m*; ~ **gate** *n* ELECTRON circuito invertidor *m*; ~ **knob** *n* INSTR botón inversor *m*; ~ **oscillator** *n* ELECTRON oscilador invertidor *m*

inverting: ~ **amplifier** *n* ELECTRON amplificador de inversión *m*, amplificador inversor *m*; ~ **input** *n* ELECTRON entrada de corriente invertida *f*; ~ **mirror** *n* INSTR espejo inversor *m*; ~ **prism** *n* INSTR prisma inversor *m*; ~ **transistor** *n* ELECTRON transistor funcionando como inversor *m*

investigate *vti* SAFE investigar

investigation *n* MECH ENG investigación *f*; ~ **of brazability** *n* MECH ENG investigación de cobresoldabilidad *f*; ~ **field** *n* COAL campo de investigación *m*; ~ **test** *n* SPACE prueba de investigación *f*

investment: ~-**casting die** *n* MECH ENG matriz de colada a la cera perdida *f*, molde de colada a la cera perdida *m*; ~ **mold for casting** *AmE*, ~ **mould for casting** *BrE n* MECH ENG molde a la cera perdida para colada *m*

inviscid: ~ **flow distribution** *n* FLUID distribución de flujos no viscosos *f*; ~ **motion** *n* FLUID movimiento no viscoso *m*

invisible: ~ **cursor** *n* PROD cursor invisible *m*; ~ **ink** *n* COLOUR tinta invisible *f*

invitation: ~ **to send** *n* COMP&DP invitación al envío *f*; ~ **to transmit** *n* TELECOM invitación a transmitir *f*

invoice *n* PRINT, PROD, TEXTIL factura *f*; ~ **weight** *n* TEXTIL peso en factura *m*

invoiced: ~ **mass** *n* PAPER *of pulp* pasta que se factura *f*

involute¹ *adj* GEOM enrollado en espiral, involuto

involute² *n* GEOM involuta *f*; ~ **arc** *n* GEOM arco de involuta *m*, arco involuto *m*; ~ **cam** *n* MECH ENG leva de espiral *f*, leva de evolvente de círculo *f*; ~ **of a circle** *n* GEOM involuta de un círculo *f*; ~ **gear** *n* MECH ENG engranaje de perfil de evolvente en círculo *m*; ~ **gear cutters** *n pl* MECH ENG fresas para tallar engranajes de evolvente en círculos *f pl*, fresas para entallar engranajes de perfil evolvente *f pl*, máquinas para tallar engranajes de evolvente en círculos *f pl*, máquinas para tallar engranajes de perfil evolvente *f pl*; ~ **gearing** *n* MECH ENG fresado de engranajes de evolvente en círculos *m*, fresado de engranajes de perfil de evolvente *m*, maquinado de engranajes de evolvente en círculos *m*, maquinado de engranajes de perfil evolvente *m*; ~ **serration** *n* MECH ENG acanalado de involuta *m*, acanalado en espiral *m*, dentado de involuta *m*, dentado en espiral *m*, estriado de

involuta *m*, estriado en espiral *m*; ~ **spline** *n* MECH ENG ranura de involuta *f*, ranura en espiral *f*; ~ **splinemetric module** *n* MECH ENG módulo de ranurado métrico evolvente *m*

involution *n* GEOM involución *f*, MATH involución *f*, elevación a una potencia *f*

inward: ~-**flow turbine** *n* PROD turbina centrípeta *f*; ~ **flux** *n* PHYS flujo entrante *m*; ~ **propagating wave** *n* TELECOM onda de propagación hacia dentro *f*; ~ **traffic** *n* TRANSP tráfico de entrada *m*

inwardbound *adj* WATER TRANSP *port traffic* de arribada, que llega

I/O¹ *abbr* (*input/output*) COMP&DP, ELEC, PROD E/S (*entrada/salida*)

I/O²: ~ **adaptor** *n* PROD adaptador de E/S *m*; ~ **channel communication** *n* PROD comunicación entre canales de E/S *f*; ~ **chassis** *n* PROD chasis de E/S *m*; ~ **chassis module slot** *n* PROD ranura para módulo de chasis E/S *f*; ~ **designation** *n* PROD designación E/S *f*; ~ **device status** *n* PROD estado dispositivo de E/S *m*; ~ **hardware** *n* PROD equipamiento de E/S *m*; ~ **image table** *n* PROD mesa de imágenes de E/S *f*; ~ **module** *n* PROD módulo de E/S *m*; ~ **module group** *n* PROD grupo módulo de E/S *m*; ~ **module placement** *n* PROD emplazamiento para módulos de E/S *m*; ~ **rack** *n* PROD bastidor de E/S *m*; ~ **scan time** *n* PROD tiempo de exploración de E/S *m*; ~ **scanner** *n* PROD analizador de E/S *m*; ~ **status indicator** *n* PROD indicador del estado de E/S *m*; ~ **terminal location address** *n* PROD dirección de la ubicación de terminales de E/S *f*

IOC *abbr* OPT (*integrated optical circuit*) circuito óptico integrado *m*, TELECOM (*integrated optoelectronic circuit*, *integrated optical circuit*) circuito opticoelectrónico integrado *m*, circuito óptico integrado *m*

iodargyrite *n* MINERAL yodargirita *f*

iodate *n* CHEM yodato *m*

iodembolite *n* MINERAL yodembolita *f*

iodic *adj* CHEM yódico

iodide *n* CHEM yoduro *m*

iodine *n* (*I*) CHEM, ELECTRON, PHOTO, TEXTIL iodo *m* (*I*), yodo *m* (*I*); ~ **flask** *n* LAB frasco de yodo *m*; ~ **laser** *n* ELECTRON láser de yodo *m*; ~ **number** *n* (*cf iodine value*) FOOD número de yodo *m*, índice de yodo *m*; ~ **spiking** *n* NUCL formación de picos de yodo *f*; ~ **value** *n* P&R índice de yodo *m*

iodize *vt* CHEM, CHEM TECH yodar

iodoaurate *n* CHEM yodoaurato *m*

iodobenzene *n* CHEM yodobenceno *m*

iodobromite *n* MINERAL yodobromito *m*

iodoform *n* CHEM yodoformo *m*

iodohydrin *n* CHEM yodohidrina *f*

iodomercurate *n* CHEM yodomercurato *m*

iodometric *adj* CHEM yodométrico

iodometry *n* CHEM yodometría *f*

iodonium *n* CHEM yodonio *m*

iodopsin *n* CHEM yodopsina *f*

iodosobenzene *n* CHEM yodosobenceno *m*

iodous *adj* CHEM yodoso

iodyrite *n* MINERAL yodrita *f*

iolite *n* MINERAL cordierita *f*, dicroíta *f*, iolita *f*

ion *n* CHEM, ELEC, ELECTRON, GAS ión *m*, PART PHYS átomo ionizado *m*, átomo excitado *m*, ión *m*, PETR TECH ión *m*, PHYS ión *m*, átomo excitado *m*; ~ **accelerator** *n* ELECTRON, NUCL acelerador de iones *m*, acelerador iónico *m*, sincrotrón *m*, PART PHYS acelerador de iones *m*, acelerador iónico *m*, ciclotrón *m*, sincrotrón *m*, PHYS acelerador de iones *m*, sincrotrón *m*; ~ **beam** *n* ELECTRON, RAD PHYS haz de iones *m*, haz iónico *m*; ~ **beam focusing column** *n* RAD PHYS columna de enfoque de haces iónicos *f*; ~-**beam lithography** *n* ELECTRON litografía por haz de iones *f*; ~ **beam optical system** *n* RAD PHYS sistema óptico de haces iónicos *m*; ~ **bombardment** *n* ELECTRON bombardeo de iones *m*, METALL bombardeo de iones *m*, irradiación iónica *f*; ~ **budget** *n* POLL balance de cargas *m*, balance iónico *m*; ~ **burn** *n* ELECTRON mancha iónica *f*; ~ **chromatograph** *n* LAB cromatografía de iones *f*; ~ **cluster** *n* RAD PHYS cluster de iones *m*; ~ **current** *n* RAD PHYS corriente iónica *f*; ~ **emission microscope** *n* INSTR microscopio de emisión iónica *m*; ~ **engine** *n* SPACE *spacecraft* motor iónico *m*; ~ **exchange** *n* CHEM, HYDROL intercambio de iones *m*; ~ **exchange capacity** *n* GEOL capacidad de intercambio iónico *f*; ~ **exchange isotherm** *n* RAD PHYS isoterma de intercambio iónico *f*; ~ **exchange technique** *n* OPT técnica de intercambio iónico *f*, TELECOM técnica intercambiadora de iones *f*; ~-**exchange water purifier** *n* LAB purificador de agua por intercambio iónico *m*; ~ **gun** *n* PROD cañón electrónico *m*, fuente iónica *f*; ~ **implantation** *n* ELECTRON implantación de iones *f*, implantación iónica *f*, PART PHYS implantación iónica *f*, implantación de iones *f*; ~-**ion collision** *n* PART PHYS colisión ión-ión *f*; ~ **laser** *n* ELECTRON, MECH ENG láser iónico *m*; ~ **pair** *n* CHEM *of electrolyte*, RAD PHYS par iónico *f*; ~ **propulsion** *n* SPACE *spacecraft* propulsión iónica *f*; ~ **pump** *n* MECH ENG, PHYS bomba iónica *f*; ~ **rocket** *n* SPACE *spacecraft* cohete de propulsión iónica *m*; ~-**rocket engine** *n* MECH ENG motor de cohete de propulsión iónica *m*; ~ **selective electrode** *n* (*ISE*) LAB *electrochemistry* electrodo selectivo de iones *m* (*ESI*); ~ **source** *n* PHYS fuente de iones *f*; ~ **spectrum** *n* RAD PHYS espectro iónico *m*; ~ **spot** *n* TV mancha iónica *f*; ~ **sputtering** *n* CHEM *of specimen* bombardeo iónico *m*; ~ **thruster** *n* SPACE *spacecraft* empuje iónico *m*; ~ **trap** *n* ELECTRON captador de iones *m*, TV captador de iones *m*, trampa de iones *f*

ionic[1] *adj* GEN iónico *m*

ionic[2]: ~ **atmosphere** *n* RAD PHYS atmósfera iónica *f*; ~ **bombardment** *n* ELECTRON bombardeo iónico *m*; ~ **bond** *n* CHEM, CRYSTALL, RAD PHYS enlace iónico *m*; ~ **concentration** *n* GEOPHYS concentración iónica *f*; ~ **conductance** *n* RAD PHYS conductancia iónica *f*; ~ **loudspeaker** *n* ACOUST altavoz iónico *m*; ~ **mobility** *n* RAD PHYS movilidad iónica *f*; ~ **polarization** *n* PHYS polarización iónica *f*; ~ **product** *n* CHEM producto iónico *m*; ~ **propulsion** *n* SPACE *spacecraft* propulsión iónica *f*; ~ **radius** *n* CRYSTALL, RAD PHYS radio iónico *m*; ~ **strength** *n* RAD PHYS fuerza iónica *f*, intensidad iónica *f*; ~ **yield** *n* RAD PHYS campo iónico *m*, rendimiento en pares de iones *m*, rendimiento iónico *m*

ionium *n* CHEM ionio *m*

ionization *n* GEN ionización *f*; ~ **by collision** *n* PHYS, RAD PHYS ionización por choque *f*, ionización por colisión *f*; ~ **chamber** *n* PART PHYS cámara de ionización *f*, cámara de niebla *f*, PHYS, WAVE PHYS cámara de ionización *f*; ~ **counter** *n* RAD PHYS contador de destello *m*, contador de ionización *m*;

~ **current** *n* ELECTRON corriente de ionización *f*; ~ **detector** *n* RAD PHYS detector de ionización *m*; ~ **energy** *n* GAS, PHYS, RAD PHYS energía de ionización *f*; ~ **gage** *AmE*, ~ **gauge** *BrE* *n* PHYS manómetro de ionización *m*; ~ **loss** *n* PART PHYS, RAD PHYS pérdida por ionización *f*; ~ **potential** *n* PHYS, RAD PHYS potencial de ionización *m*; ~ **rate** *n* PART PHYS razón de ionización *f*, velocidad específica de ionización *f*; ~ **threshold** *n* GAS, PHYS umbral de ionización *m*; ~ **unit** *n* PRINT ionizadora *f*; ~ **vacuum gage** *AmE*, ~ **vacuum gauge** *BrE* *n* REFRIG manómetro de ionización *m*

ionize *vt* GEN ionizar

ionized[1] *adj* GEN ionizado

ionized[2]: ~ **argon laser** *n* ELECTRON láser de argón ionizado *m*; ~ **atom** *n* PART PHYS átomo excitado *m*, átomo ionizado *m*, PHYS átomo excitado *m*; ~ **environment** *n* SPACE entorno ionizado *m*; ~ **state** *n* PART PHYS estado ionizado *m*

ionizing: ~ **layer** *n* ELEC *charge* capa ionizante *f*; ~ **particle** *n* RAD PHYS partícula ionizante *f*; ~ **radiation** *n* ELEC, PHYS, POLL radiación ionizante *f*, WAVE PHYS radiación de ionización *f*, radiación ionizante *f*; ~ **wet washer** *n* SAFE arandela húmeda ionizante *f*

ionographic *adj* COMP&DP *printer*, PRINT ionográfico

ionone *n* CHEM ionona *f*

ionosphere *n* GEOPHYS, PHYS, WAVE PHYS ionosfera *f*; ~ **layer** *n* GEOPHYS capa de la ionosfera *f*

ionospheric: ~ **recorder** *n* GEOPHYS registrador ionosférico *m*; ~ **substorm** *n* GEOPHYS subtormenta ionosférica *f*

ionotropy *n* CHEM ionotropía *f*

IOS *abbr* COMP&DP (*integrated office system*) SOI (*sistema de oficina integrado*), SPACE *AmE* (*Intelsat Operations Cente*) Centro de Operaciones Intelsat *m*

IP *abbr* (*information processing*) COMP&DP, ELECTRON PI (*procesamiento de información, tratamiento de la información*)

IPA *abbr* (*isopropyl acid*) CHEM, DETERG IPA (*ácido isopropílico*)

IPE *abbr* (*individual protection equipment*) MILIT *chemical warfare* equipo de protección individual *m*

ipecac *n* CHEM, FOOD ipecac *f*, ipecacuana *f*

ipecacuanha *n* CHEM, FOOD ipecac *f*, ipecacuana *f*

ipecacuanic *adj* CHEM, FOOD ipecacuánico *m*

IPL *abbr* COMP&DP (*initial program load*) carga de programa inicializado *f*, TELECOM (*interactive primary link*) enlace primario interactivo *m*

IPS *abbr* (*inches per second*) COMP&DP PPS (*pulgadas por segundo*)

Ir *abbr* (*iridium*) CHEM Ir (*iridio*)

IR[1] *abbr* (*infrared*) GEN IR (*infrarrojo*)

IR[2]: ~-**drop** *n* ELEC *resistance* caída de voltaje *f*; ~ **radiation** *n* RAD PHYS radiación IR *f*

iraser *n* ELECTRON iraser *m*

iridescence *n* C&G, MAR POLL iridiscencia *f*, irisación *f*

iridescent *adj* C&G *glass* tornasolado

iridic *adj* CHEM irídico *m*

iridite *n* CHEM iridito *m*

iridium *n* (*Ir*) CHEM iridio *m* (*Ir*); ~ **osmine** *n* MINERAL iridosmio *m*

iridizing *n* C&G tornasolado *m*

iridosmine *n* MINERAL iridosmio *m*

iris *n* CINEMAT, PHYS, TV iris *m*; ~ **control button** *n* TV botón de control del iris *m*; ~ **diaphragm** *n* INSTR

diafragma del iris *m*; ~ **fade** *n* CINEMAT desvanecimiento por iris *m*; **--out** *n* CINEMAT abertura del iris *f*
Irish: ~ **moss** *n* MAR POLL musgo marino de Irlanda *m*
iron[1] *n* (*Fe*) CHEM hierro *m* (*Fe*), COAL chapa *f*, cuchilla
f, fierro *m* (*AmL*), fundición *f*, férreo *m*, hierro *m*
(*Esp*) (*Fe*), lingote de hierro *m*, plancha *f*, METALL
hierro *m* (*Fe*), TEXTIL *machine* plancha manual *f*;
~ **alum** *n* CHEM alumbre de hierro *m*, sulfato de
potasio y hierro *m*; ~ **band cutter** *n* PACK cortadora
de flejes de hierro *f*; ~ **black** *n* COATINGS hierro negro
m; ~ **blue pigment** *n* COLOUR pigmento azul de
hierro *m*; ~ **bridge** *n* CONST puente de hierro *m*;
~ **carbonate** *n* CHEM carbonato de hierro *m*;
~ **chromate** *n* CHEM cromato férrico *m*; ~ **core** *n*
ELEC ENG núcleo de hierro *m*, núcleo ferromagnético
m; ~ **core ammeter** *n* ELEC *instrument*, ELEC ENG,
INSTR amperímetro de núcleo de hierro *m*; ~ **core
transformer** *n* ELEC, ELEC ENG transformador de
núcleo de hierro *m*, transformador de núcleo ferromagnético *m*; ~ **core voltmeter** *n* ELEC *instrument*
voltímetro con núcleo de hierro *m*, voltímetro de
núcleo de hierro *m*; ~ **deposit** *n* MINE yacimiento de
hierro *m*; ~ **filings** *n pl* CHEM, PHYS limaduras de
hierro *f pl*; ~ **founding** *n* PROD fundición de hierro *f*;
~ **foundry** *n* PROD fundería de hierro *f*, fundicíon de
hierro *f*; ~ **garnet** *n* MINERAL granate férrico *m*;
~ **girder** *n* CONST viga principal de hierro *f*; ~ **loss** *n*
ELEC *of transformer* pérdida en el hierro *f*, pérdida en
el núcleo de hierro *f*, PHYS pérdida en el hierro *f*;
~ **ore** *n* CHEM mineral de hierro *m*; ~ **oxide** *n* CHEM,
P&R óxido de hierro *m*; ~ **oxide pigment** *n* COLOUR
pigmento de óxido de hierro *m*; ~ **pig** *n* PROD arrabio
m; ~ **pigment** *n* COLOUR pigmento de hierro *m*;
~ **piping** *n* CONST *wrought iron* sistema de tuberías de
hierro *m*; ~ **plate** *n* METALL, PROD *cast, wrought*
hierro en chapas *m*, hierro en láminas *m*, hierro en
planchas *m*, placa de fundición *f*; ~ **pyrite** *n* MINE
pirita amarilla *f*, pirita de hierro *f*, MINERAL pirrotina
f, pirita de hierro *f*, pirita amarilla *f*; ~ **rod** *n* PROD
vara de hierro *f*, varilla de hierro *f*; ~ **salt** *n* DETERG
sal de hierro *f*; ~ **scales** *n pl* PROD batiduras de hierro
f pl; ~ **sheeting** *n* PROD lámina de hierro *f*; ~ **wire** *n*
PROD alambre de hierro *m*; ~ **wire gauze** *n* PROD tela
de alambre de hierro *f*; ~ **wire rope** *n* PROD cuerda de
alambre de hierro *f*
iron[2] *vt* TEXTIL planchar; ~ **out** *vt* TEXTIL allanar
ironbound[1] *adj* PROD aherrojado, con zuncho de
hierro, guarnecido de hierro
ironbound[2]: ~ **mallet** *n* PROD mazo de madera zunchado *m*
ironclad: ~ **headstock** *n* MECH ENG cabezal blindado
m; ~ **shaft** *n* MINE pozo blindado *m*
irone *n* CHEM irona *f*
ironing *n* TEXTIL planchado *m*
ironshod *adj* PROD herrado
ironstone *n* CHEM siderita *f*, GEOL roca ferruginosa *f*
ironwork *n* CONST *heavy iron constructional work* obra
de hierro *f*, *parts made of iron* herrajes *m pl*, METALL
obra de hierro *f*, PROD *work in wrought iron*
carpintería de hierro *f*, obra de hierro *f*
ironworking *n* CONST *light* cerrajería *f*, *heavy* herrería *f*,
MECH ENG, PROD herrería *f*
ironworks *n* COAL, HEAT, MECH ENG fundería *f*, PROD
foundry, metallurgical works fundería *f*, fundicíon de
hierro *f*, fábrica siderúrgica *f*

IRP *abbr* (*internal reference point*) TELECOM punto de
referencia interna *m*
IRPTC *abbr* (*International Register of Potentially Toxic
Chemicals*) POLL, SAFE Registro Internacional de
Compuestos Químicos Potencialmente Tóxicos *m*
irradiance *n* OPT, PHYS irradiancia *f*
irradiated *adj* FOOD, NUCL, PHYS irradiado
irradiation *n* GEN radiación *f*, irradiación *f*; ~ **chamber**
n RAD PHYS cámara de irradiación *f*; ~ **of food** *n*
FOOD, PACK, RAD PHYS irradiación de alimentos *f*;
~ **hardening** *n* METALL endurecimiento por irradiación *m*, endurecimiento por radiación *m*; ~ **loop** *n*
RAD PHYS ciclo de irradiación *m*
irrational[1] *adj* COMP&DP, MATH irracional
irrational[2]: ~ **number** *n* COMP&DP, MATH número
irracional *m*
irrecoverable[1] *adj* COMP&DP *error* irrecobrable, irrecuperable
irrecoverable[2]: ~ **error** *n* COMP&DP error irrecuperable
m
irreducible: ~ **water saturation** *n* PETR TECH saturación irreducible de agua *f*
irreductible *adj* COMP&DP *polynomial* irreductible
irregular: ~ **edge** *n* C&G borde irregular *m*;
~ **polyhedron** *n* GEOM poliedro irregular *m*; ~ **yarn**
n TEXTIL hilo irregular *m*
irreversible[1] *adj* CHEM, PHYS irreversible
irreversible[2]: ~ **colloid** *n* CHEM coloide irreversible *m*
irrigate *vt* AGRIC abrevar, irrigar, regar, CONST regar,
HYDROL abrevar, irrigar, WATER abrevar, aguar,
irrigar, regar
irrigation *n* AGRIC irrigación *f*, riego *m*, HYDROL
irrigación *f*, WATER irrigación *f*, regadío *m*, riego *m*;
~ **by surface flooding** *n* AGRIC, HYDROL, WATER
irrigación por inundación de la superficie *f*, irrigación por inundación superficial *f*; ~ **canal** *n* WATER
canal de riego *m*, conducto de irrigación *m*;
~ **controller** *n* AGRIC programador de riego *m*;
~ **cooler** *n* REFRIG enfriador de cortina *m*;
~ **project** *n* HYDROL proyecto de regadío *m*;
~ **shovel** *n* AGRIC reja de irrigación *f*; ~ **water
wheel** *n* WATER azud *m*
irritant[1] *adj* SAFE irritante
irritant[2]: ~ **substance** *n* SAFE substancia irritante *f*
irrotational[1] *adj* FLUID, MATH, PHYS irrotacional
irrotational[2]: ~ **field** *n* PHYS campo irrotacional *m*;
~ **flow** *n* FLUID, PHYS flujo irrotacional *m*
irruption *n* HYDROL avenida de agua *f*, WATER avenida
de agua *f*, irrupción *f*
IRS *abbr* (*information-receiving station, information
receiver station*) POLL TELECOM estación receptora
de información *f*
IS[1] *abbr* COMP&DP (*information system*) sistema de
información *m*, (*information separator*) SI (*separador
de información*), TELECOM (*intermediate system*) SI
(*sistema intermedio*)
IS[2]: ~ **machine** *n* C&G máquina IS *f*
ISA: ~ **segment** *n* TELECOM segmento ISA *m*
isallobar *n* METEO catalobara *f*, isalobara *f*
isatic *adj* CHEM isático
isatin *n* CHEM isatina *f*
isatogenic *adj* CHEM isatogénico
isatropic *adj* CHEM isatrópico
ISC *abbr* (*international switching center AmE, international switching centre BrE*) TELECOM centro de
conmutación internacional *m*

ISCP[1] *abbr* (*international signaling control part AmE, international signalling control part BrE*) TELECOM parte de control de la señalización internaciónal *f*; ~ **AE** *abbr* (*ISCP application entity*) TELECOM entidad para aplicaciones ISCP *f*

ISCP[2]: ~ **application entity** *n* (*ISCP AE*) TELECOM entidad para aplicaciones ISCP *f*

ISD *abbr* (*International Subscriber Dialing AmE, International Subscriber Dialling BrE*) TELECOM Marcación de Abonado Internacional *f*

ISDN[1] *abbr* (*integrated services digital network*) TELECOM RDSI (*red digital de servicios integrados*)

ISDN[2]: ~ **access** *n* TELECOM acceso a la RDSI *m*; ~ **exchange** *n* TELECOM central de la RDSI *f*; ~ **primary rate access** *n* TELECOM acceso en velocidad primaria a la RDSI *m*; ~ **switch** *n* TELECOM conmutador de la RDSI *m*; ~ **user part** *n* TELECOM parte del usuario de la RDSI *f*

ISE *abbr* (*ion selective electrode*) LAB *electrochemistry* ESI (*electrodo selectivo de iones*)

isentropic[1] *adj* PHYS, THERMO isentrópico, isoentrópico

isentropic[2]: ~ **compressibility** *n* PHYS compresibilidad isentrópica *f*

isethionate *n* CHEM isetionato *m*

isethionic *adj* CHEM isetiónico

isinglass *n* FOOD cola de pescado *f*, ictiocola *f*

island *n* HYDROL, OCEAN isla *f*; ~ **arc** *n* GEOL arco-isla *m*, OCEAN arco insular *m*, arco-isla *m*; ~ **platform** *n* RAIL andén de entrevía *m*

islet *n* HYDROL isleta *f*, islote *m*, WATER TRANSP *geography* isleo *m*, isleta *f*, islote *m*

ISO[1] *abbr* (*International Standards Organization*) ELEC, MECH ENG, TELECOM OIN (*Organización Internacional de Normalización*)

ISO[2]: ~ **metric thread** *n* MECH ENG paso de rosca métrico estándar *m*, paso de rosca métrico normalizado *m*; ~ **miniature metric thread** *n* MECH ENG paso de rosca métrico para tornillos de diámetros muy pequeños *m*

isoallyl *n* CHEM isoalilo *m*

isoamyl *n* CHEM isoamilo *m*

isoamylic *adj* CHEM isoamílico

isoanomaly *n* GEOL isoanomalía *f*

isoapiol *n* CHEM isoapiol *m*

isobar *n* METEO, PETROL, PHYS, WATER TRANSP isóbara *f*

isobaric: ~ **line** *n* THERMO línea isóbara *f*; ~ **map** *n* METEO mapa isobárico *m*; ~ **process** *n* THERMO proceso isobárico *m*; ~ **spin** *n* PHYS *sheet of paper* espín isobárico *m*

isobath *n* GEOL, PETROL, WATER TRANSP isobata *f*, isóbata *f*

isoborneol *n* CHEM isoborneol *m*

isobutane *n* CHEM, PETR TECH, PETROL isobutano *m*

isobutene *n* CHEM isobuteno *m*

isobutyl *n* CHEM isobutilo *m*; ~ **alcohol** *n* CHEM alcohol isobutílico *m*

isobutylene *n* CHEM isobutileno *m*

isobutylic *adj* CHEM isobutílico

isobutyric *adj* CHEM isobutírico

isochemical: ~ **metamorphism** *n* GEOL metamorfismo isoquímico *m*

isochor *n* CHEM, GEOL, PHYS isocora *f*, THERMO línea isócora *f*

isochore *n* CHEM, GEOL, PHYS isocora *f*, THERMO línea isócora *f*

isochoric: ~ **process** *n* THERMO proceso isócoro *m*

isochronal: ~ **annealing** *n* METALL esmaltación isócrona *f*, recocido isócrono *m*; ~ **surface** *n* GEOL superficie isócrona *f*; ~ **time line** *n* GEOL línea de tiempo isócrona *f*

isochrone *n* GEOL isócrona *f*; ~ **diagram** *n* GEOL diagrama isócrono *m*

isochronism *n* PETROL isocronismo *m*

isochronous[1] *adj* COMP&DP isócrono

isochronous[2]: ~ **transmission** *n* COMP&DP transmisión isócrona *f*

isocinchomeronic *adj* CHEM isocincomerónico

isoclinal[1] *adj* GEOL, GEOPHYS, PETR TECH isóclino

isoclinal[2]: ~ **fold** *n* PETROL pliegue isoclinal *m*; ~ **line** *n* GEOPHYS, PHYS línea isoclinal *f*

isocline *n* GEOL, GEOPHYS, PETR TECH isóclino *m*

isoclinic: ~ **line** *n* GEOPHYS, PHYS línea isóclina *f*

isocracking *n* PETR TECH isocraqueo *m*

isocrotonic *adj* CHEM isocrotónico

isocyanate *n* CHEM, P&R isocianato *m*

isocyanic *adj* CHEM isociánico

isocyanide *n* CHEM isocianuro *m*

isocyclic *adj* CHEM isocíclico

isodulcital *n* CHEM isodulcital *m*

isodynamic: ~ **flux line** *n* GEOPHYS línea de flujo isodinámico *f*; ~ **line** *n* GEOPHYS línea isodinámica *f*

isoelectric[1] *adj* CHEM *point* isoeléctrico

isoelectric[2] *n* TRANSP isoeléctrico; ~ **vehicle** *n* TRANSP vehículo isoeléctrico *m*

isofacies *n* GEOL isofacies *f*

isofenchol *n* CHEM isofencol *m*

isoflavone *n* CHEM isoflavona *f*

isoformate *n* CHEM isoformato *m*

isoforming *n* CHEM isoforming *m*

isogal *n* GEOL línea isogala *f*

isogam *n* GEOL isogama *f*

isogonal *adj* GEOM, GEOPHYS, MATH isogonal, isogónico

isogonic: ~ **line** *n* GEOPHYS línea isógona *f*

isograd *n* GEOL línea isograda *f*

isogram *n* METEO, PETR TECH isograma *m*

isohaline *n* GEOL isohalina *f*

isohel *n* METEO isohelia *f*

isohypse *n* GEOL, METEO isoipsa *f*

isokinetic: ~ **sampling** *n* QUALITY muestreo isocinético *m*

isolable *adj* CHEM aislable

isolac *n* COATINGS laca uniforme *f*

isolate *vt* CHEM, CONST, ELEC aislar, ELEC ENG aislar, separar, MINE, PHYS, PROD, REFRIG, SAFE aislar

isolated: ~ **danger mark** *n* WATER TRANSP *navigation marks* señal de peligro aislado *f*; ~ **feed through input** *n* ELEC ENG alimentación aislada de la entrada *f*; ~ **neutral system** *n* ELEC sistema con neutro aislado *m*; ~ **system** *n* PHYS sistema aislado *m*

isolating: ~ **switch** *n* ELEC conmutador aislado *m*, ELEC ENG desconectador *m*, seccionador *m*; ~ **valve** *n* LAB *equipment* válvula de aislamiento *f*, PROD válvula de aislamiento *f*, válvula de seccionamiento *f*

isolation *n* GEN aislamiento *m*; ~ **amplifier** *n* ELECTRON amplificador de aislamiento *m*; ~ **diode** *n* ELECTRON diodo de aislamiento *m*; ~ **filter** *n* ELECTRON filtro de aislamiento *m*; ~ **transformer** *n* ELEC ENG, PROD transformador de aislamiento *m*; ~ **valve** *n* SPACE *spacecraft* válvula de aislamiento *f*

isolator *n* ACOUST aislador *m*, CHEM aislante *m*, ELEC aislador *m*, mal conductor *m*, material aislante *m*, aislante *m*, ELEC ENG, OPT, PHYS aislador *m*, PROD aislador *m*, aislante *m*, REFRIG aislante *m*, TELECOM aislador *m*

isoleucine *n* CHEM isoleucina *f*

isolog *AmE see* isologue *BrE*

isologous *adj* CHEM isologo

isologue *n BrE* CHEM isologo *m*

isomer *n* CHEM isómera *f*, PETR TECH isómera *f*, isómero *m*, RAD PHYS isómero *m*

isomeric: ~ **transition** *n* RAD PHYS transición isomérica *f*

isomeride *n* CHEM isomérido *m*

isomerism *n* CHEM isomería *f*, PHYS isomerismo *m*

isomerization *n* CHEM, PETR TECH isomerización *f*

isometric *adj* CHEM, CRYSTALL, MATH isométrico

isomorphism *n* CHEM, CRYSTALL, MATH isomorfismo *m*

isomorphous[1] *adj* CRYSTALL, GEOL, MATH isomorfo, isomórfico

isomorphous[2]: ~ **replacement** *n* CRYSTALL reemplazamiento isomórfico *m*; ~ **series** *n* CRYSTALL serie isomórfica *f*

isonicotinic *adj* CHEM isonicotínico

isonitrile *n* CHEM carbilamina *f*, isonitrilo *m*

isooctane *n* CHEM isooctano *m*

isopach *n* GEOL isopaca *f*; ~ **map** *n* GEOL, PETR TECH mapa de isópacas *m*

isoparaffin *n* CHEM isoparafina *f*

isopelletierine *n* CHEM isopeletierina *f*

isopentane *n* CHEM isopentano *m*

isopleth *n* CHEM, GEOL, MATH isopleta *f*

isopoly: ~ **acid** *n* CHEM isopoliácido *m*

isoprene *n* CHEM isopreno *m*

isoprenoid *n* CHEM isoprenoide *m*

isopropanol *n* CHEM alcohol isobutílico *m*, isopropanol *m*, alcohol isopropílico *m*, DETERG isopropanol *m*, FOOD alcohol isopropílico *m*

isopropenyl *n* CHEM isopropenilo *m*

isopropyl[1] *adj* CHEM, DETERG, FOOD isopropílico

isopropyl[2] *n* CHEM isopropilo *m*; ~ **acid** *n* (*IPA*) CHEM, DETERG ácido isopropílico *m* (*IPA*); ~ **alcohol** *n* CHEM, FOOD alcohol isopropílico *m*

isopropylbenzene *n* CHEM cumeno *m*, isopropilbenceno *m*

isopropylcarbinol *n* CHEM isopropilcarbinol *m*

isoquinoline *n* CHEM isoquinolina *f*

isosceles: ~ **triangle** *n* GEOM triángulo isósceles *m*

isoseismal *adj* GEOPHYS isosísmica

isoseismic: ~ **line** *n* GEOL línea isosísmica *f*

isosophic: ~ **index** *n* ACOUST índice isosófico *m*

isospin *n* PHYS *rotating fluids* isoespín *m*

isostasy *n* FUELLESS equilibrio de la corteza terrestre *m*, GEOL isostasía *f*

isostatic: ~ **adjustment** *n* GEOL ajuste isostático *m*

isosteric *adj* CHEM isostérico

isosterism *n* CHEM isosterismo *m*

isostress *n* AIR TRANSP isoestrés *m*

isotactic *adj* CHEM *polymer* isotáctico

isotherm *n* GEN isoterma *f*

isothermal[1] *adj* GEOL isotérmico, MECH isotermo, isotérmico, METALL, METEO, PETROL, PHYS, WATER TRANSP isotérmico

isothermal[2] *n* THERMO línea isoterma *f*; ~ **annealing** *n* METALL esmaltación isotérmica *f*, recocido isotérmico *m*; ~ **compressibility** *n* PHYS compresibilidad

isotérmica *f*; ~ **curve** *n* PHYS curva isotérmica *f*; ~ **expansion** *n* PHYS expansión isotérmica *f*; ~ **layer** *n* METEO capa isotérmica *f*; ~ **quenching** *n* METALL temple isotérmico *m*; ~ **reaction** *n* METALL reacción isotérmica *f*; ~ **test** *n* METALL prueba isotérmica *f*

isothermic: ~ **process** *n* THERMO proceso isotérmico *m*

isotone *n* NUCL, PHYS isótono *m*

isotope *n* CHEM *of element*, GEOL, NUCL, PART PHYS, PHYS isótopo *m*; ~ **dosage** *n* COAL dosificación de isótopos *f*; ~ **geology** *n* GEOL geología isotópica *f*; ~ **measurement** *n* COAL dosificación de isótopos *f*; ~ **separation** *n* PHYS separación de isótopos *f*

isotopic: ~ **abundance** *n* NUCL, PHYS abundancia isotópica *f*; ~ **analysis** *n* RAD PHYS análisis isotópico *m*; ~ **anomaly** *n* PHYS anomalía isotópica *f*; ~ **enrichment** *n* PART PHYS enriquecimiento isotópico *m*; ~ **generator** *n* SPACE *spacecraft* generador isotópico *m*; ~ **number** *n* PART PHYS, PHYS *rotating fluids* número isotópico *m*; ~ **spin** *n* PHYS *measuring* espín isotópico *m*; ~ **tracer** *n* NUCL trazador isotópico *m*

isotopically: ~-**tagged compound** *n* NUCL compuesto marcado isotópicamente *m*

isotopy *n* CHEM isotopia *f*

isotropic[1] *adj* CRYSTALL isótropo, ELECTRON isotrópico, GEOL, OPT isótropo, SPACE *communications*, TELECOM isotrópico

isotropic[2] *n* FLUID isótropo *m*; ~ **aerial** *n BrE* (*cf isotropic antenna AmE*) SPACE antena isotrópica *f*; ~ **antenna** *n AmE* (*cf isotropic aerial BrE*) SPACE antena isotrópica *f*; ~ **gain** *n* SPACE *communications* aumento absoluto *m*, aumento isotrópico *m*, ganancia isotrópica *f*, incremento absoluto *m*, incremento isotrópico *m*; ~ **turbulence** *n* FLUID turbulencia isótropa *f*

isotropy *n* CRYSTALL, GEOL, MATH isotropía *f*

isovalerone *n* CHEM isovalerona *f*

isovanilline *n* CHEM isovainillina *f*

isoweight: ~ **curve** *n* AIR TRANSP curva de isopeso *f*

isoxazole *n* CHEM isoxazolo *m*

issue *n* NUCL emisión *f*, salida *f*

isthmus *n* WATER TRANSP *geography* istmo *m*

IT *abbr* COMP&DP, TELECOM (*information technology*) tecnología de la información *f*, TELECOM (*intermediate trunk*) enlace intermedio *m*, (*information type*) tipo de información *m*

itaconic *adj* CHEM *acid* itacónico

italic: ~ **character** *n* COMP&DP carácter en cursiva *m*; ~ **type** *n* PRINT letra cursiva *f*

italicize *vt* PRINT componer en cursivas

italics *n pl* PRINT cursivas *f pl*

ITD *abbr* (*input transaction accepted for delivery*) TELECOM transacción de entrada aceptada para ejecución *f*

item *n* COMP&DP dato *m*, elemento *m*, unidad de datos *f*, ítem *m*, MECH ENG artículo *m*, elemento *m*, pieza *f*, unidad *f*, TEXTIL artículo *m*; ~ **number** *n* MECH ENG número de pieza *m*, número de unidad *m*

itemize *vt* TELECOM detallar

itemized: ~ **billing** *n* TELECOM facturación detallada *f*

iterate *vt* COMP&DP, MATH iterar

iteration *n* COMP&DP, MATH iteración *f*, POLL iteración *f*, repetición *f*

iterative[1] *adj* ACOUST, COMP&DP, ELEC ENG, PHYS, SPACE, TELECOM iterativo

iterative[2]: ~ **guidance** *n* SPACE *spacecraft* guía iterativa *f*; ~ **impedance** *n* ACOUST, ELEC, ELEC ENG, PHYS impedancia iterativa *f*; ~ **method** *n* COMP&DP método iterativo *m*; ~ **process** *n* COMP&DP proceso iterativo *m*

itinerary *n* WATER TRANSP itinerario *m*

ITR *abbr* (*input transaction rejected*) TELECOM transacción de entrada rechazada *f*

ITT *abbr* (*integrated transit time*) PETR TECH tiempo de tránsito integrado *m*

i-type: ~ **semiconductor** *n* ELECTRON semiconductor con caracteres completos *m*

IUS *abbr* (*inertial upper stage*) SPACE última fase inercial *f*

ivory: ~ **board** *n* PAPER cartulina bristol *f*

IVPO *abbr* (*inside vapor phase oxidation AmE, inside vapour phase oxidation BrE*) TELECOM oxidación interna en fase de vapor *f*

IWP *abbr* (*interworking protocol*) TELECOM protocolo de entrelazado *m*

ixora *n* AGRIC ixora *f*

J

J¹ *abbr* (*joule*) ELEC, FOOD, MECH, METR, PHYS, THERMO J (*julio*)

J²: ~ **particle** *n* PHYS partícula J *f*

jacinth *n* MINERAL jacinto *m*

jack¹ *n* CINEMAT enchufe hembra *m*, COMP&DP conector hembra *m*, CONST cric *m*, gato *m*, ELEC, ELEC ENG enchufe hembra *m*, *plugboard* enchufe hembra múltiple *m*, LAB elevador *m*, soporte regulable de altura *m*, enchufe hembra *m*, MECH martinete *m*, gato *m*, MECH ENG *screw-type* gato *m*, MINE blenda *f*, cuña de madera para separar rocas fracturadas por voladuras *f* (*AmL*), gato *m*, unidad de bombeo *f*, mena de zinc *f*, pizarra bituminosa *f* (*Esp*), gato elevador *m*, pizarra carbonosa candeloide *f* (*AmL*), PROD enchufe hembra *m*, gato *m*, TELECOM clavija de conexión *f*, enchufe hembra *m*, VEH soporte regulable de altura *m*, gato *m*, WATER TRANSP gato *m*; ~ **box** *n* MECH ENG caja de conexión *f*; ~ **bush** *n* ELEC ENG casquillo de enchufe *m*; ~ **field** *n* CINEMAT panel de conmutación *m*; ~ **flag** *n* WATER TRANSP torrotito *m*; ~ **leg** *n* MINE filón de roca *m*, poste extensible *m*; ~**-off screw** *n* MECH ENG gato a husillo *m*, husillo de gato *m*; ~ **panel** *n* BrE (*cf patch panel AmE*) COMP&DP, TV panel de acoplamiento *m*; ~ **plane** *n* CONST garlopa *f*; ~ **plug** *n* CINEMAT enchufe macho *m*, ELEC ENG clavija hembra de toma de corriente *f*, *plugboard* clavija de enchufe *f*; ~ **rafter** *n* CONST cabio corto *m*; ~ **rod** *n* PROD varilla de gatear *f*; ~ **socket** *n* CINEMAT, ELEC, ELEC ENG, LAB, PROD, TELECOM enchufe hembra *m*; ~ **strip** *n* ELEC ENG regleta de clavijas *f*; ~**-up platform** *n* PETROL plataforma autolevadiza *f*; ~**-up rig** *n* PETR TECH equipo autoelevable *m*, plataforma autoelevable *f*

jack² *vt* AUTO levantar con el gato, VEH levantar con el gato, mover con el gato

jacked¹: ~ **in** *adj* ELEC ENG enchufado

jacked²: ~ **pile** *n* COAL pilote hincado por medio de gatos hidráulicos *m*

jacket¹ *n* AmE (*cf sheath BrE*) ELEC *of cable* forro *m*, envoltura *f*, funda *f*, ELEC ENG camisa *f*, HEAT revestimiento exterior *m*, LAB, MECH camisa *f*, chaqueta *f*, MECH ENG *insulation* camisa *f*, envoltura *f*, chaqueta *f*, armazón *m*, NUCL camisa *f*, envoltura *f*, PETR TECH plataforma de producción metálica *f*, plataforma protectora de pozo *f*, PHYS *of clay* forro *m*, PROD *clothing plate* camisa *f*, cubierta *f*, chaqueta *f*, *non-conducting material* envoltura *f*, envuelta *f*; ~ **brush** *n* PAPER cepillo de la camisa *m*; ~ **coldroom** *n* REFRIG cámara frigorífica de doble pared *f*; ~ **cooling** *n* NUCL enfriamiento de la camisa *m*, refrigeración de un contenedor de combustible nuclear *f*; ~ **heating system** *n* NUCL sistema de calentamiento por camisa calefactora *m*; ~ **platform** *n* PETR TECH plataforma fija metálica *f*

jacket² *vt* MECH, PROD enchaquetar, envolver, forrar, guarnecer

jacketed *adj* MECH, PROD con camisa exterior, enchaquetado

jacketing *n* NUCL encamisado *m*, envainado *m*, TEXTIL tejido para chaquetas *m*

jackhammer *n* MINE *rock drilling, earth boring* martillo perforador *m*, martillo picador *m*, trépano *m*

jackleg: ~ **drill** *n* MINE martillo perforador *m*

jackscrew *n* MECH ENG gato de tornillo *m*, tornillo extractor *m*, tornillo nivelador *m*; ~ **with self-adjusting head** *n* MECH ENG tornillo nivelador de cabeza autoajustable *m*

jackshaft *n* MECH ENG contraeje *m*, eje intermedio *m*, eje secundario *m*, eje transversal *m*, árbol de contramarcha *m*, PROD *stamp mill* eje intermedio *m*

Jackson: ~ **model** *n* NUCL modelo de Jackson *m*

jacquard: ~ **board** *n* PAPER cartón jacquard *m*; ~ **fabric** *n* TEXTIL tejido jacquard *m*; ~ **paper** *n* PACK, PAPER papel jacquard *m*

jad *n* MINE roza *f*

jadeite *n* MINERAL jadeíta *f*

jag¹: ~ **bolt** *n* CONST perno arponado *m*

jag² *vt* PROD *caulking* calafatear

jagged¹ *adj* MECH dentado, mellado, SAFE dentado, raído, rallado

jagged²: ~ **bolt** *n* CONST perno arponado *m*; ~ **edge** *n* SAFE *on blade, paper* borde serrado *m*; ~ **edge trimmer** *n* PHOTO cortapruebas con bordes dentellados *m*

jagging *n* PROD *caulking* calafateo *m*

jalapic *adj* CHEM jalápico

jalapin *n* CHEM jalapina *f*

jalousie *n* C&G enrejado *m*

jalpaite *n* MINERAL jalpaíta *f*

jam¹ *n* CINEMAT atasco *m*, MECH atoramiento *m*, MECH ENG acuñamiento *m*, agarrotamiento *m*, atascamiento *m*, atoramiento *m*, obstrucción *f*, PRINT atascamiento *m*; ~ **cleat** *n* WATER TRANSP *deck fittings* cornamusa atochante *f*; ~ **nut** *n* MECH ENG contratuerca *f*, tuerca de inmovilización *f*

jam² *vt* AIR TRANSP agarrotar, AUTO agarrotar, encasquillarse, C&G, COAL agarrotar, ELECTRON interferir, HYDRAUL acuñarse, agarrotarse en su asiento, agarrotar, MECH acuñar, atorar, trabar, MECH ENG acuñar, agarrotar, atascar, atorar, encasquillarse, obstruir, MILIT encasquillarse, interferir, PROD agarrotar, SPACE agarrotar, *communications* encasquillarse, agarrotarse, interferir, enmascarar, TELECOM interferir, WATER TRANSP *emission* meter en facha, perturbar con intención de interferir

jam³ *vi* MECH, HYDRAUL acuñarse, trabarse

jamb *n* C&G sostén *m*, CONST *doorway* montante *m*, *window-opening* jamba *f*, pared de chimenea *f*; ~ **lining** *n* CONST chambrana *f*; ~ **post** *n* CONST *doorway* montante *m*, *window-opening* jamba *f*; ~ **stone** *n* CONST jamba de piedra *f*

jamesonite *n* MINERAL jamesonita *f*

jammed *adj* GEN agarrotado, encasquillado,

jammer *n* ELECTRON interferencia intencionada *f*, perturbación *f*, MILIT emisión interferente *f*, emisión perturbadora *f*, emisor perturbador *m*; ~ **oscillator** *n* ELECTRON oscilador de interferencias *m*

jamming *n* AUTO atasco *m*, encasquillamiento *m*, gripado *m*, ELECTRON interferencia intencionada *f*, perturbación *f*, MECH ENG agarrotamiento *m*, apriete *m*, encasquillamiento *m*, parada *f*, MILIT encasquillamiento *m*, interferencia intencionada *f*, SPACE encasquillamiento *m*, TELECOM perturbación por interferencia de ondas extrañas *f*, interferencia intencionada *f*; ~ **signal** *n* ELECTRON señal interferente *f*

japan *n* COATINGS, COLOUR barniz japonés *m*, laca japonesa *f*; ~ **work** *n* COATINGS lacado con barniz japonés *m*, lacado japonés *m*, COLOUR charolado *m*, lacado con barniz japonés *m*, lacado japonés *m*

Japanese: ~ **lacquer** *n* COATINGS, COLOUR laca japonesa *f*

japanic *adj* CHEM japánico

japanning *n* COATINGS, COLOUR lacado japonés *m*, PROD barnizado con laca *m*, charolamiento *m*

jar *n* FOOD tarro *m*, MINE barra de perforación *f*, corredera *f*, martillo *m* (*Esp*), percutor *m* (*AmL*), PROD barra de perforación *f*, choque *m*, corredera *f*, sacudida *f*, vibración *f*

jargon *n* MINERAL circón incoloro *m*, jargón *m*

jarosite *n* MINERAL jarosita *f*

jarring[1] *adj* PROD trepidante, vibrante

jarring[2] *n* PROD trepidación *f*, vibración *f*; ~ **table** *n* PACK mesa vibrante *f*; ~ **test** *n* PACK ensayo de vibración *m*

jasp: ~ **yarn** *n* TEXTIL hilo jaspeado *m*

jasper *n* GEOL, MINERAL jaspe *m*

jasperite *n* GEOL jasperita *f*

jaspilite *n* GEOL jaspilita *f*

JATO *abbr AmE* (*jet-assisted takeoff AmE*) AIR TRANSP despegue asistido por cohete *m*, despegue con ayuda de reactores *m*, despegue con cohetes auxiliares *m*

javellization *n* CHEM javelización *f*

jaw *n* COAL garganta *f*, horquilla *f*, MECH *generator motor* mordaza *f*, boca *f*, MECH ENG quijada *f*, garra *f*, boca *f*, mandíbula *f*, mordaza *f*, horquilla *f*, garganta *f*, NUCL mordaza *f*, WATER TRANSP quijada *f*; ~ **breaker** *n* MECH ENG machacadora de mandíbulas *f*, machacadora de mordazas *f*, machacadora de quijadas *f*; ~ **chuck** *n* MECH ENG *of machine tool* plato de garras *m*; ~ **clutch** *n* MECH ENG embrague de mordazas *m*; ~ **clutching** *n* AUTO embrague de mandíbulas *m*, embrague de mordazas *m*; ~ **crusher** *n* COAL machacadora de mordazas *f*, quebrantadora de mandíbulas *f*, trituradora de mandíbulas *f*, LAB quebradora de quijadas *f*, MECH ENG machacadora de mandíbulas *f*, machacadora de mordazas *f*, machacadora de quijadas *f*, PROD quebrantadora de mandíbulas *f*, trituradora de mandíbulas *f*; ~ **dog** *n* MECH ENG *lathe carrier with two jaws* perro de cojinete *m*; ~ **fold** *n* PRINT plegado con plegadora de mordaza *m*, plegado paralelo *m*; ~ **holder** *n* MECH ENG soporte de mandíbula *m*, soporte de mordaza *m*; ~ **plate** *n* COAL pala de mordaza *f*; ~ **steady rest** *n* MECH ENG *of machine tool* luneta de cojinetes *f*

JCL *abbr* (*job control language*) COMP&DP definición de tareas *f*, lenguaje de control de tareas *m*

JDF *abbr* (*junction distribution frame*) TELECOM repartidor de conexiones *m*, repartidor de enlace *m*

jellification *n* CHEM TECH, FOOD gelificación *f*

jemmy *n BrE* MECH palanca corta *f*, palanqueta *f*; ~ **bar** *n* MECH ENG barra corta *f*, palanqueta *f*

jenkinsite *n* MINERAL jenkinsita *f*

jenny *n* CINEMAT grúa *f*, PROD *overhead travelling crane* carro *m*

jeremejevite *n* MINERAL jeremejevita *f*

jerky: ~ **flow** *n* METALL deformación por sacudidas *f*, fluencia brusca *f*

jeroboam *n* C&G jeroboam *f*

jerrican *n* MILIT depósito portátil para gasolina *m*

jerry: ~ **can** *n* MILIT depósito portátil para gasolina *m*, TRANSP bidón de reserva de gasolina *m*, depósito portátil para gasolina *m*, lata de reserva de gasolina *f*, bidón de gasolina de 20 litros *m*

jervine *n* CHEM jervina *f*

jet[1] *n* AIR TRANSP chorro *m*, inyector *m*, reactor *m*, AUTO chorro *m*, surtidor *m*, COAL azuche *m*, FLUID chorro *m*, GEOL azabache *m*, chorro *m*, METALL buza *f*, chorro de colada *m*, haz *m*, MINERAL azabache *m*, NUCL *element of lathe-spindle which holds chuck* chorro *m*, PETR TECH azabache *m*, chorro *m*, tobera *f*, PHYS chorro *m*, *vehicles* boquilla *f*, PROD *metal left in sprue hole after casting* chorro de colada *m*, *pouring gate in mould* bebedero *m*, SPACE motor de reacción *m*, WATER *nozzle* boquilla *f*, *emission of fluid* chorro *m*; ~ **aeroplane** *n BrE* AIR TRANSP avión a reacción *m*; ~ **airplane** *AmE see jet aeroplane BrE*; ~-**assisted takeoff** *n AmE* (*JETO, cf rocket-assisted takeoff BrE*) AIR TRANSP despegue asistido por cohete *m*, despegue con ayuda de reactores *m*, despegue con cohetes auxiliares *m*; ~ **bit** *n* PETR TECH trépano de chorro *m*; ~ **bit drilling** *n* PETR TECH perforación con trépano de chorro *f*; ~ **body** *n* SPACE fuselaje a chorro *m*; ~ **cock** *n* WATER grifo de aspersión *m*; ~ **condenser** *n* HYDRAUL condensador de inyección *m*, condensador de mezcla *m*; ~ **cooling** *n* REFRIG enfriamiento por chorro de aire frio *m*; ~ **deflector** *n* SPACE deflector del chorro *m*; ~ **diameter** *n* FUELLESS diámetro de chorro *m*; ~ **drilling** *n* COAL perforación a presión *f*; ~ **engine** *n* AIR TRANSP motor a reacción *m*, MECH motor de chorro *m*, motor de reacción *m*, propulsor de chorro *m*, reactor *m*, SPACE motor de chorro *m*, THERMO motor de chorro *m*, reactor *m*; ~ **engine fuel** *n* AIR TRANSP combustible de motor a reacción *m*; ~-**flapped rotor** *n* AIR TRANSP *helicopter* rotor a palas de motor a reacción *m*, rotor alado de motor a reacción *m*; ~ **freezing** *n* REFRIG congelación por chorro de aire *f*; ~ **fuel** *n* AIR TRANSP combustible de motor a reacción *m*, combustible de reactor *m*; ~ **helicopter** *n* AIR TRANSP helicóptero a reacción *m*; ~ **instability** *n* FLUID inestabilidad del chorro *f*; ~ **noise** *n* ACOUST ruido de chorro *m*; ~ **noise suppressor** *n* AIR TRANSP supresor de ruido del reactor *m*; ~ **nozzle** *n* AIR TRANSP tobera del reactor *f*, SPACE tobera de chorro *f*; ~ **piercing** *n* COAL barrenado por chorro de fueloil con oxígeno *m*, perforación por fusión de la roca mediante un soplete *f*, perforación térmica *f*; ~ **pipe** *n* SPACE tubo inyector *m*; ~ **pipe temperature** *n* AIR TRANSP temperatura de los tubos del reactor *f*; ~ **plane** *n* AIR TRANSP avión a reacción *m*; ~ **propulsion** *n* AIR TRANSP propulsión del reactor *f*, MILIT propulsión por chorro *f*, propulsión por reacción *f*, SPACE propulsión del reactor *f*; ~ **pump** *n* NUCL, WATER bomba de chorro *f*; ~ **sled** *n* PETR TECH patín de chorro *m*; ~ **stream** *n* AIR TRANSP chorro del reactor *m*, METEO corriente en chorro *f*; ~ **turbine** *n* TRANSP turbina de chorro *f*; ~ **turbine engine** *n* TRANSP turbina de gas *f*; ~ **velocity** *n* SPACE velocidad del reactor *f*; **~ wash** *n* AIR TRANSP flujo del motor *m*

jet ² *vt* FLUID lanzar en chorro

JET¹ *abbr* (*Joint European Torus*) NUCL, RAD PHYS JET (*Consejo Europeo de Investigación Nuclear*)

JET²: **~ Tokamac** *n* NUCL, RAD PHYS Tokamac JET *m*

jetfoil *n* WATER TRANSP hidroala a reacción *m*, jetfoil *m*

JETO *abbr* AmE (*jet-assisted takeoff AmE, cf RATO BrE*) AIR TRANSP despegue asistido por cohete *m*, despegue con ayuda de reactores *m*, despegue con cohetes auxiliares *m*

jetsam *n* OCEAN echazón *f*, WATER TRANSP echazón *f*, echazón hundida *f*

jettison¹ *n* AIR TRANSP lanzamiento *m*, OCEAN echazón *f*; **~ valve** *n* AIR TRANSP válvula de lanzamiento *f*, SPACE *spacecraft* válvula de vaciado rápido de depósitos *f*

jettison² *vt* OCEAN echar mercancías al mar, SPACE *spacecraft* arrojar por la borda, lanzar, WATER TRANSP *goods* echar al mar, *for floating off* alijar

jettisonable¹ *adj* AIR TRANSP eyectable, SPACE arrojable, desprendible, lanzable

jettisonable²: **~ canopy** *n* AIR TRANSP cúpula desprendible *f*, cúpula lanzable *f*; **~ window** *n* AIR TRANSP ventana desprendible *f*, ventana lanzable *f*

jetty *n* CONST espigón *m*, espolón *m*, malecón *m*, muelle *m*, rompeolas *m*, terraplén *m* (*Esp*), vuelo *m*, OCEAN espolón, muelle *m*, rompeolas *m*, WATER TRANSP pantalán *m*, rompeolas *m*

jeweled *AmE see jewelled BrE*

jeweler *AmE see jeweller BrE*

jewelled *adj BrE* MECH de piedra dura, de piedra preciosa

jeweller *n BrE* MECH joyero *m*; **~'s eyepiece** *n BrE* INSTR pieza ocular de joyero *f*

jib *n* AIR TRANSP *helicopter* viga *f*, CINEMAT brazo *m*, CONST *of crane*, MECH aguilón *m*, NUCL pescante *m*, WATER TRANSP *sail* foque *m*; **~ boom** *n* MAR POLL *sailing boat* botalón de foque *m*; **~ crane** *n* CONST grúa de brazo *f*, NUCL grúa de pescanté *f*; **~ post** *n* CONST *crane* eje de grúa *m*

jig *n* MINE caja hidráulica *f*, criba hidráulica *f*, enganche de vagonetas *m*, lavador de sacudidas *m*, plantilla para taladrar *f*, MECH plantilla posicionadora *f*, portapiezas *m*, MECH ENG horma *f*, plantilla *f*, plantilla para taladrar *f*, posicionador *m*, METR utensilio *m*, MINE plantilla *f*, criba hidráulica *f*, lavador de sacudidas *m* (*Esp*), clasificadora hidráulica *f* (*AmL*), plano inclinado de criba *m* (*Esp*), criba de pistón *f*, plano inclinado *m* (*AmL*), enganche de vagonetas *m*, plano inclinado automotor para criba de minerales *m*, SAFE plantilla *f*; **~ bed** *n* COAL plano inclinado automotor para criba de minerales *m*; **~ borer** *n* MECH taladradora de plantillas *f*; **~ boring** *n* MECH ENG punteadora barrenadora *f*, taladro de plantilla *m*; **~-boring machine** *n* MECH ENG punteadora barrenadora *f*, taladro de plantilla *m*; **~-boring vice** *n BrE* MECH ENG tornillo de taladradora de plantilla *m*; **~-boring vise** *AmE see jig-boring vice BrE*; **~ brow** *n* MINE plano inclinado automotor de simple efecto *m*; **~ bush** *n* MECH ENG casquillo conductor para taladrar *m*, casquillo guía *m*; **~ dyeing** *n* COLOUR teñido con máquina de teñir al ancho *m*; **~ grinding** *n* MECH ENG rectificado de punteadora *m*; **~ mill** *n* MINE taller de concentración de fangos *m*; **~ milling** *n* MECH ENG fresado por

plantilla *m*; **~ pit** *n* AIR TRANSP plantilla de recesos *f*, plataforma de montaje *f*; **~ plane** *n* MINE plano inclinado de vía única y contrapeso *m*; **~ routing** *n* SAFE desbastado con plantilla *m*; **~ sieve** *n* COAL cribón oscilante *m*

jigger *n* TEXTIL botón de cruce *m*; **~ screen** *n* MINE criba de sacudidas *f*, tamiz para criba *m*

jigging *n* COAL depuración en caja *f*, fabricación de plantillas *f*, lavado en caja *m*, lavado sobre cribas de sacudida *m*, separación por medios densos *f*, MINE cribado hidráulico *m*, lavadero *m* (*Esp*), lavado sobre cribas de sacudida *m*, separación por medios densos *f* (*AmL*)

jigsaw¹ *n* CONST sierra alternativa vertical *f*, sierra de vaivén *f*; **~ blade** *n* MECH ENG, PROD hoja de sierra alternativa vertical *f*, hoja de sierra de contornear *f*, hoja de sierra de vaivén *f*

jigsaw² *vt* CONST serrar con sierra de vaivén

jigsawing *n* CONST serrado con sierra vertical de vaivén *m*

jim: **~ crow** *n* CONST *clawbar* curvadora de rieles *f*

jimmy *AmE see jemmy BrE*

jimson: **~ weed** *n* AGRIC chamico *m*

J-integral: **~ method** *n* NUCL método de integrales *m*

JIT *abbr* (*just-in-time*) PACK justo a tiempo

jitter¹: **~-free** *adj* ELECTRON sin fluctuación, sin variación

jitter² *n* COMP&DP fluctuación *f*, salto pequeño *m*, temblor *m*, ELECTRON inestabilidad *f*, TELECOM perturbación oscilatoria *f*, temblor *m*, TV inestabilidad de la imagen *f*

j-j: **~ coupling** *n* PHYS acoplamiento j-j *m*

job: **~ accounting** *n* COMP&DP contabilidad de tareas *f*; **~ batch** *n* COMP&DP lote de tareas *m*; **~ control** *n* COMP&DP control de tareas *m*, gestión de tareas *f*; **~ control language** *n* (*JCL*) COMP&DP definición de tareas *f*, lenguaje de control de tareas *m*; **~ cycle safety audit** *n* CONST control de seguridad del ciclo de trabajo *m*; **~ definition** *n* COMP&DP definición de tareas *f*; **~-oriented terminal** *n* COMP&DP terminal orientado hacia las tareas *m*; **~-processing system** *n* COMP&DP sistema de procesamiento de tareas *m*; **~ request** *n* COMP&DP petición de trabajo *f*, solicitud de tarea *f*; **~ scheduler** *n* COMP&DP organizador de tareas *m*, planificador de trabajo *m*; **~ sequence list** *n* PROD lista de trabajos *f*; **~ shop** *n* PROD taller organizado por secciones homogéneas *m*; **~ stack** *n* COMP&DP pila de tareas *f*, pila de trabajos *f*; **~ step** *n* COMP&DP paso de tarea *m*, paso de trabajos *m*; **~ stream** *n* COMP&DP corriente de trabajos *f*, flujo de tareas *m*, sistema de procesamiento de tareas *m*; **~ ticket** *n* PROD bono de trabajo *m*, ticket de trabajo *m*

jobber: **~ drill** *n* MECH ENG broca corriente *f*

jobbing *n* PRINT impresión de remiendos *f*; **~ contractor** *n* CONST contratista *m*; **~ face** *n* PRINT tipo de remiendo *m*; **~ ink** *n* PRINT tinta para remiendo *f*; **~ type** *n* PRINT tipo de remiendo *m*

jockey *n* MECH ENG *tightening-pulley* polea tensora *f*; **~ pulley** *n* MECH polea de tensión *f*, polea tensora *f*, MECH ENG polea tensora *f*; **~-roller** *n* MECH ENG *tightening-pulley* polea tensora *f*, rodillo de tensión *m*; **~-wheel** *n* MECH ENG *tightening-pulley* polea tensora *f*, rodillo de tensión *m*

Jodel: **~ detector** *n* NUCL detector Jodel *m*

jog[1] *n* CRYSTALL *in a dislocation* codo *m*, METALL desplazamiento por sacudidas *m*

jog[2] *vt* PRINT igualar, emparejar

jogged: ~ **screw dislocation** *n* METALL dislocación por tornillo desplazado *f*

joggle[1] *n* CONST engrapado *m*, *dowel, coak* ensamblaje *m*; ~ **joint** *n* CONST *carpentry* junta de ranura y lengüeta *f*, traba *f*; ~ **piece** *n* MECH ENG *king post* pendolón de una cercha *m*; ~ **post** *n* MECH ENG *king post* pendolón *m*

joggle[2] *vt* CONST *fit by means of shoulder to prevent slipping* ensamblar, *with dowel* empalmar

joggling: ~ **table** *n* MINE mesa de sacudidas *f*

Johannite *n* MINERAL, NUCL Johannita *f*

Johansson: ~ **gage** *AmE*, ~ **gauge** *n* *BrE* MECH calibrador Johansson *m*, plantilla Johansson *f*

Johnson: ~ **noise** *n* ELECTRON, PHYS ruido Johnson *m*

join[1] *n* CINEMAT unión *f*, GEOM acoplo *m*

join[2] *vt* CINEMAT, CONST unir; ~ **on** *vt* CONST *add to* empalmar; ~ **up** *vt* CONST *pipes* montar

join[3]: ~ **a traffic stream** *vi* TRANSP incorporar a una ruta principal, incorporar al tráfico

joinable: ~ **container** *n* TRANSP contenedor empalmable *m*, contenedor enganchable *f*

joiner *n* CINEMAT encoladora *f*, CONST *person* ebanista *mf*, ensamblador *m*; ~'**s bench** *n* CONST banco de ebanista *m*; ~'**s bevel** *n* CONST escuadra de ebanista *f*; ~'**s cramp** *n* CONST *sash-cramp* grapa de unión *f*; ~'**s gage** *AmE*, ~'**s gauge** *BrE* *n* CONST ancho de vía *m* (*Esp*), compás de carpintero *m*, gramil *m* (*AmL*)

joinery *n* CONST ebanistería *f*

joining: ~ **process** *n* PROD proceso de agrupación *m*

joint *n* CINEMAT junta articulada *f*, COAL diaclasa *f*, CONST junta *f*, *hinge* acoplamiento *m*, bisagra *f*, ELEC *connection* conexión *f*, unión *f*, empalme *m*, ELEC ENG junta *f*, enganche *m*, conexión *f*, GEOL diaclasa *f*, grieta *f*, fisura *f*, MECH ENG bisagra *f*, conexión *f*, junta *f*, gozne *m*, charnela *f*, empalme *m*, NUCL junta *f*, unión *f*, OPT unión *f*, PETROL junta *f*, unión *f*, conexión *f*, PRINT, TELECOM empalme *m*; ~ **bar** *n* *AmE* (*cf fishplate BrE*) RAIL eclisa *f*; ~ **box** *n* CONST caja de empalme *f*, ELEC *connection* caja de empalme *f*, caja de unión *f*; ~ **coating** *n* PETROL revestimiento de la junta *m*; ~ **cramp** *n* CONST grapa de conexión *f*; ~ **efficiency** *n* CONST eficiencia de la unión soldada *f*; ~ **line** *n* P&R junta encolada *f*; ~ **plane** *n* GEOL fractura *f*, plano de diaclasa *m*; ~ **preparation** *n* CONST preparación de la superficie a soldar *f*; ~ **ring** *n* NUCL anillo de junta *m*; ~ **riveting** *n* PROD remachado de empalme *m*, remachado de junta *m*; ~ **set** *n* GEOL conjunto de diaclasas *m*; ~ **strength** *n* PACK resistencia de la junta *f*; ~**-twisting pliers** *n pl* PROD alicates torcedores para empalmes *m pl*; ~ **user** *n* TELECOM usuario en conjunto *m*; ~ **water** *n* COAL agua mancomunada *f*

Joint: ~ **European Torus** *n* (*JET*) NUCL, RAD PHYS Consejo Europeo de Investigación Nuclear *m* (*JET*)

jointed: ~ **rule** *n* *BrE* (*cf zigzag rule AmE*) CONST metro plegable *m*, regla plegable *f*; ~ **tool-holder** *n* MECH ENG portaherramientas articulado *m*

jointer *n* CONST , PROD, TELECOM *cables* manguito de empalme *m*, ensambladora *f*, empalmadora *f*, empalmador *m*, *walls* marcador de juntas *m*, juntera *f*

jointing *n* GEOL diaclasado *m*, fisuración *f*, MINE diaclasado *m*, NUCL articulación *f*, empalme *m*, unión *f*, PROD empalme *m*, junta *f*, juntura *f*,

rejuntado *m*, unión *f*, TELECOM empalme *m*; ~ **machine** *n* PROD máquina de hacer juntas *f*; ~ **plane** *n* CONST garlopa *f*, juntura *f*

joist *n* CONST viga *f*, vigueta *f*

joisting *n* CONST viguería *f*

Jominy: ~ **test** *n* MECH *of screw* prueba de Jominy *f*

Josephson: ~ **constant** *n* PHYS constante de Josephson *f*; ~ **effect** *n* ELECTRON, NUCL, PHYS efecto de Josephson *m*; ~ **junction** *n* ELECTRON conexión Josephson *f*, PHYS empalme de Josephson *m*

Jost: ~ **function** *n* NUCL función Jost *f*

joule *n* (*J*) ELEC, FOOD, MECH, METR, PHYS, THERMO julio *m* (*J*)

Joule: ~ **effect** *n* ELEC, ELEC ENG, PHYS efecto Joule *m*; ~'**s equivalent** *n* ELEC, MECH, THERMO equivalente de Joule *m*; ~ **expansion** *n* PHYS expansión Joule *f*; ~'**s heat loss** *n* ELEC *resistance* pérdida de Joule *f*, pérdida de calor por efecto Joule *f*; ~ **heating** *n* NUCL efecto Joule *m*; ~'**s law** *n* PHYS ley de Joule *f*

Joule-Kelvin: ~ **expansion** *n* PHYS expansión de Joule-Kelvin *f*

Joule-Thomson: ~ **expansion** *n* PHYS expansión de Joule-Thomson *f*

journal *n* AUTO chumacera *f*, cojinete *m*, gorrón *m*, macho *m*, muñón *m*, pezón *m*, MECH chumacera *f*, cojinete *m*, gorrón *m*, muñón *m*, MECH ENG chumacera *f*, cojinete *m*, cuello *m*, macho *m*, manga *f*, mangueta *f*, muñón *m*, NUCL *for cable* chumacera *f*, mango *m* (*AmL*), VEH cojinete *m*, mangueta *f*; ~ **bearing** *n* MECH ENG *bearing block* chumacera *f*, cojinete liso *m*, NUCL cojinete liso *m*; ~ **box** *n* *AmE* (*cf axle box BrE*) MECH ENG *bearing block* cojinete *m*, *box enclosing bearing* caja de grasas *f*, chumacera *f*, caja de engranajes *f*, RAIL caja de grasas *f*, cojinete *m*; ~ **cross** *n* MECH muñón de cruz *m*; ~ **turbine** *n* HYDRAUL turbina axial *f*, turbina de flujo axial *f*

journey: ~ **logbook** *n* AIR TRANSP libro de a bordo *m*, libro de navegación *m*, libro de vuelo *m*

Joy: ~'**s valve-gear** *n* HYDRAUL mecanismo de distribución tipo Joy *m*

joystick *n* CINEMAT palanca de mando *f*, COMP&DP joystick *m* (*Esp*), palanca de control *f* (*Esp*), palanca de juego *f* (*AmL*), SPACE palanca de mando *f*, palanca omnidireccional *f*; ~ **selector** *n* ELEC *switch* selector por palanca universal *m*

judder *n* AIR TRANSP, SPACE oscilación aeroelástica de hipofrecuencia *f*, salto *m*, trepidación *f*

jug: ~ **hustler** *n* PETR TECH persona encargada de extenser y recoger los geófonos *f*

juglone *n* CHEM juglona *f*

juice: ~ **content** *n* FOOD contenido de zumo *m*

jukebox *n* OPT memoria de discos *f*; ~ **filing system** *n* OPT sistema de llenado de la memoria de discos *m*

jumbo[1]: ~**-size** *adj* PROD de tamaño gigante

jumbo[2] *n* PROD *water chamber round a nozzle* caja refrigerante *f*, manguito de enfriamiento *m*; ~ **including boom** *n* MINE carro de perfordoras múltiples *m* (*AmL*), grúa con brazo *f*, grúa jumbo *f*, pluma *f*, vagón perforador *m*; ~ **jet** *n* AIR TRANSP Boeing 747 *m*, avión jumbo *m*; ~ **roll** *n* PAPER bobina jumbo *f*, bobina madre *f*

jump[1] *n* COMP&DP bifurcación *f*, salto *m*, METALL recalcado *m*; ~ **cut** *n* CINEMAT corte con discontinuidad *m*; ~ **drilling** *n* CONST perforación con desviación *f*; ~ **instruction** *n* COMP&DP instrución de bifurcación *f*, instrucción de salto *f*, juntura *f* (*AmL*), unión *f*; ~ **lead** *n* ELEC *connection* conductor de cierre *m*, conductor de empalme *m*, conductor de puente *m*, VEH *electrical system* cable de alto voltaje *m*; ~ **rate** *n* METALL coeficiente de recalcado *m*; ~ **routine** *n* PROD rutina de bifurcación *f*; ~ **takeoff** *n* AIR TRANSP *helicopter* despegue de salto *m*; ~ **weld** *n* PROD soldadura a tope en ángulo recto *f*, soldadura por aproximación *f*; ~ **welding** *n* PROD soldadura a tope en ángulo recto *f*, soldadura por aproximación *f*

jump² *vt* MECH ENG triscar, MINE abrir, vibrar, PROD *wheel-tyre, head of bolt* recalcar

jump³ *vi* ELEC *arc* saltar, PROD *saw* triscar

jumper *n* ELEC *connection* conexión en puente *f*, puente de conexión *m*, puente conector *m*, puente *m*, cable de puente *m*, cable de cierre *m*, ELEC ENG cable de conexión *m*, puente *m*, MECH ENG triscador *m*, MINE taladro de sondeo *m*, barrena de percusión *f*, barreno *m* (*Esp*), pistolete de mina *m* (*AmL*), sonda de percusión *f*, broca de sondeo *f*, PROD *saw set* triscador *m*, TELECOM puente de conexión *m*, VEH cable de empalme *m*; ~ **bar** *n* PROD pistolete de mina *m* (*AmL*); ~ **boring** *n* COAL barrena de percusión *f*, pistolete de mina *m* (*AmL*); ~ **drill** *n* MINE barreno *m* (*Esp*), pistolete de mina *m* (*AmL*), taladro mecánico *m*; ~ **ring** *n* TELECOM anillo de conexión *m*; ~ **stay** *n* WATER TRANSP *rigging* boza de mal tiempo *f*, contraestay *m*, falso estay *m*; ~ **strut** *n* WATER TRANSP *mast* cruceta *f*, violín *m*; ~ **wire** *n* TELECOM cable de acoplamiento *m*

jumping: ~ **bolt heads** *n* PROD recalcado de cabezas de pernos *m*; ~ **drill** *n* MINE barra de mina *f* (*AmL*), barra de percusión *f*, barreno *m* (*Esp*), pistolete de mina *m* (*AmL*); ~ **sheet** *n* SAFE *appliance, mechanism* lona de salvamento *f*

junction *n* COMP&DP juntura *f* (*AmL*), unión *f*, CONST *roads, rivers* confluencia *f*, cruce *m*, empalme *m*, ELEC *connection* conexión *f*, empalme *m*, unión *f*, PROD bifurcación *f*, conexión *f*, confluencia *f*, empalme *m*, enlace *m*, unión *f*, TELECOM unión *f*; ~ **box** *n* ELEC, ELEC ENG, SPACE caja de conexiones *f*, caja de derivaciones *f*, caja de empalmes *f*, caja de unión *f*; ~ **cable** *n* ELEC, ELEC ENG cable de empalme *m*; ~ **capacitance** *n* ELEC ENG capacitancia de la juntura *f*; ~ **capacitor** *n* ELEC ENG condensador de empalme *m*; ~ **diode** *n* ELEC *semi-conductor*, ELECTRON diodo de unión *m*; ~ **distribution frame** *n* (*JDF*) TELECOM repartidor de conexiones *m*, repartidor de enlace *m*; ~ **FET** *n* ELECTRON unión de TEC *f*; ~ **leakage** *n* ELEC ENG dispersión de junta *f*, fuga por la junta *f*; ~ **leakage current** *n* ELEC ENG corriente de dispersión en empalme *f*; ~ **pipe** *n* CONST tubería en T *f*; ~ **plate** *n* ELEC ENG placa de junta *f*, PROD chapa de recubrimiento *f*, cubrejunta *f*; ~ **point** *n* ELEC ENG punto de unión *m*; ~ **points** *n* RAIL puntos de enlace *m pl*; ~ **station** *n* RAIL estación de transbordo *f*, estación de enlace *f*; ~ **tandem exchange** *n* TELECOM central telefónica intermedia de enlace *f*; ~ **transistor** *n* ELECTRON, PHYS transistor de uniones *m*

junctor *n* TELECOM conjuntor *m*, unidad de conexión *f*

junk *n* PETR TECH chatarra *f*; ~ **packing** *n* PROD guarnición de estopa *f*; ~ **remover** *n* PAPER eliminador de impurezas gruesas *m*; ~ **ring** *n* PROD anillo de empaquetadura *m*

Jurassic¹ *adj* GEOL, PETR TECH Jurásico

Jurassic²: ~ **period** *n* GEOL, PETR TECH período Jurásico *m*

jury: ~ **rudder** *n* WATER TRANSP timón de fortuna *m*

just¹: ~ **stage** *n* SPACE etapa justa *f*

just²: ~**-in-time** *phr* (*JIT*) PACK justo a tiempo

justification *n* COMP&DP, PRINT, TELECOM justificación *f*; ~ **key** *n* PRINT tecla de justificación *f*

justify *vt* COMP&DP, PRINT justificar

justifying: ~ **scale** *n* PRINT escala de justificación *f*

jute *n* TEXTIL yute *m*; ~ **covering** *n* ELEC ENG revestimiento de yute *m*; ~ **spinning** *n* TEXTIL hilatura del yute *f*; ~ **yarn** *n* TEXTIL hilo de yute *m*

juvenile¹ *adj* GEOL juvenil

juvenile²: ~ **water** *n* GEOL, WATER agua juvenil *f*, agua magmática *f*

juxtaposition: ~ **twin** *n* CRYSTALL macla de contacto *f*, macla de yuxtaposición *f*

K

k *abbr* (*kilo*) METR, PHYS k (*kilo*)
K *abbr* CHEM, METALL (*potassium*) K potasio, METR, PHYS, THERMO (*kelvin*) K (*Kelvin*)
K-absorption: ~ **edge** *n* NUCL borde de absorción K *m*
kaempferide *n* CHEM kaempferida *f*
kaempferol *n* CHEM kaempferol *m*
kainite *n* MINERAL cainita *f*
KALC: ~ **process** *n* (*krypton absorption in liquid carbon dioxide*) NUCL absorción de criptón en anhídrico carbónico líquido *f*
kale *n* AGRIC col común *f*
kali *n* CHEM cali *m*, kali *m*
Kalman: ~ **filter** *n* ELECTRON filtro Kalman *m*; ~ **filtering** *n* ELECTRON filtración Kalman *f*
Kanne: ~ **chamber** *n* NUCL cámara de Kanne *f*
kaolin *n* CHEM, MINERAL, P&R caolín *m*
kaolinite *n* COAL, MINERAL, PETR TECH caolinita *f*
kaolinization *n* CHEM, FUELLESS, GEOL caolinización *f*
kaon *n* PART PHYS, PHYS kaón *m*, mesón *m*
kapnite *n* MINERAL kapnita *f*
kapok *n* HEAT ENG miraguano *m*; ~ **oil** *n* CHEM esencia de capoc *f*, esencia de kapoc *f*
K-Ar: ~ **dating** *n* GEOL datación K-Ar *f*
karaya: ~ **gum** *n* CHEM goma karaya *f*, tragacanto de la India *m*, FOOD goma karaya *f*
Karnaugh: ~ **map** *n* COMP&DP mapa de Karnaugh *m*
karst *n* GEOL *limestone region* Karst *m*; ~ **hydrology** *n* WATER hidrología kárstica *f*
karstenite *n* MINERAL carstenita *f*
karstic: ~ **aquifer** *n* GEOL, HYDROL, WATER acuífero cárstico *m*; ~ **conduit** *n* HYDROL conducto cárstico *m*; ~ **spring** *n* WATER manantial kárstico *m*
karyocerite *n* NUCL cariocerita *f*
katabatic: ~ **front** *n* METEO catafrente *m*, frente catabático *m*
katathermometer *n* HEAT ENG catatermómetro *m*
Kazanian *adj* GEOL Kazaniense
kb *abbr* (*kilobyte*) COMP&DP kilo-octeto *m*, kilobyte *m*
Kcal *abbr* (*kilocalorie*) FOOD Kcal (*kilocaloría*)
K-capture *n* PHYS captura en la capa K *f*
kCi *abbr* (*kilocurie*) CHEM kCi (*kilocurie*)
kedge[1]: ~ **anchor** *n* WATER TRANSP anclote *m*
kedge[2] *vt* WATER TRANSP *ship* espiar, espiarse
K-edge: ~ **gamma densitometry** *n* NUCL densitometría gamma de borde K *f*
keel *n* AIR TRANSP, WATER TRANSP *shipbuilding* quilla *f*; ~ **laying** *n* WATER TRANSP colocación de la quilla *f*, puesta de quilla *f*; ~ **plate** *n* WATER TRANSP *shipbuilding* chapa de quilla *f*; ~ **strake** *n* WATER TRANSP *shipbuilding* traca de quilla *f*
keelson *n* WATER TRANSP *shipbuilding* sobrequilla *f*
keen: ~ **edge** *n* CONST *of tool* borde afilado *m*, borde cortante *m*, borde penetrante *m*, filo cortante *m*
keenness *n* CONST *of cutting edge* agudeza *f*, penetración *f*
keep[1]: ~~**alive electrode** *n* ELEC ENG electrodo cebador *m*, electrodo excitador *m*; ~~**alive oscillator** *n* ELECTRON oscilador de excitación *m*;

~~**alive voltage** *n* ELEC ENG voltaje de entretenimiento *m*
keep[2]: ~ **the work area tidy** *phr* SAFE mantener el lugar de trabajo ordenado
keep[3]: ~ **at open width** *vt* TEXTIL mantener al ancho; ~ **cool** *vt* PACK mantener frío; ~ **cool and dry** *vt* PACK mantener frío y seco; ~ **down** *vt* PRINT componer con minúsculas; ~ **out** *vt* PRINT extender; ~ **upright** *vt* PACK mantener siempre de pie, mantener vertical
keep[4]: ~ **its center** *vi AmE*, ~ **its centre** *vi BrE* CONST *of air-bubble in levelling-instrument* centrar la burbuja; ~ **a lookout** *vi* WATER TRANSP mantener un servicio de vigilancia; ~ **watch** *vi* MILIT, WATER TRANSP estar de guardia; ~ **the work area tidy** *vi* SAFE mantener el lugar de trabajo ordenado
keeper *n* CONST *of gate-latch* cerrojo *m*, encintado de cerrojo *m*, *lock-staple* abrazadera *f*, ELEC *magnet* armadura *f*, shunt magnético *m*, MECH ENG *lock-nut* hembra del cerrojo *f*, cerradero *m*, cuña *f*, encastre receptor del cerrojo *m*, *pawl, click* dedo de enganche *m*, saliente del cerrojo *m*, trinquete *m*, linguete *m*, retén *m*, fiador *m*, PHYS *founding* armadura *f*
keeping: ~ **quality** *n* FOOD calidad de conservación *f*, REFRIG conservación de la calidad *f*; ~ **time** *n* REFRIG periodo de conservación *m*
keg *n* CHEM barril *m*
keilhauite *n* MINERAL keilhauita *f*
kelly *n* PETR TECH cuadrante *m*, kelly *m*, varilla de arrastre *f*, vástago de perforación *m*; ~ **bushing** *n* PETR TECH buje de kelly *m* (*AmL*), buje del cuadrante *m* (*AmL*), buje del vástago *m* (*Esp*)
kelp *n* FOOD alga marina *f*, laminaria *f*
Kelvin *n* (*K*) METR, PHYS, THERMO Kelvin *m* (*K*); ~ **balance** *n* ELEC *measurement* balanza de Kelvin *f*; ~ **bridge** *n* ELEC, ELEC ENG, INSTRUM, PHYS puente de Kelvin *m*; ~ **effect** *n* AIR TRANSP, ELEC *thermoelectrics* efecto de Kelvin *m*; ~ **scale** *n* CHEM, CINEMAT, CONST, SPACE escala de Kelvin *f*, escala absoluta de temperatura *f*; ~ **statement** *n* PHYS *founding* enunciado de Kelvin *m*; ~ **temperature** *n* CINEMAT, SPACE temperatura Kelvin *f*, THERMO temperatura en grados Kelvin *f*
kelvinometer *n* CINEMAT, PHOTO termocolorímetro *m*
K-emitter *n* NUCL emisor K *m*
kemsolene *n* CHEM kemsoleno *m*
kennel: ~ **coal** *n* COAL, MINE hulla de llama larga *f*, hulla seca *f*
Kennelly-Heaviside: ~ **layer** *n* PHYS capa de Kennelly-Heaviside *f*
kep *n* MINE retén *m* (*Esp*), tope *m* (*AmL*), trinquete *m*
Keplerian: ~ **orbit** *n* SPACE órbita de Kepler *f*
Kepler: ~ **'s law of areas** *n* PHYS, SPACE ley de las áreas de Kepler *f*; ~ **'s laws** *n pl* PHYS leyes de Kepler *f pl*
kerargyrite *n* MINERAL querargirita *f*
keratin *n* CHEM queratina *f*
keratinization *n* CHEM queratinización *f*
keratinous *adj* CHEM queratinoso
keratogenous *adj* CHEM queratogenoso
kerb *n* BrE (*cf curb AmE*) CONST declive lateral de la

carretera *m*, bordillo *m*, bordillo de la acera *m*, MINE cuadro portador *m*

kerbstone *n* BrE (*cf curbstone AmE*) CONST loseta del bordillo *f*, piedra para bordillo *f*

kerf *n* COAL corte *m*, corte horizontal en una capa de carbón *m*, cráter *m*, entalla *f*, entalladura *f*, ranura *f*

kerma *n* (*kinetic energy released in matter*) NUCL, PHYS kerma *f*; ~ **rate** *n* NUCL, PHYS tasa de kerma *f*

kermanite *n* MINERAL kermanita *f*

kermes: ~ **mineral** *n* MINERAL quermes mineral *m*

kermesite *n* MINERAL quermesita *f*

kern *n* PRINT saliente *m*

kernel *n* AGRIC grano *m*, pepita *f*, COMP&DP kernel *m*, núcleo *m*, núcleo primitivo *m*, NUCL núcleo *m*

kerning *n* PRINT composición con las letras apretadas *f*

kerogen *n* CHEM querógeno *m*, GEOL, PETR TECH kerógeno *m*, PETROL querógeno *m*

kerogenite *n* GEOL kerogenita *f*

kerosene *n* AmE (*cf paraffin BrE*) AIR TRANSP, CHEM, PETR TECH, PETROL, THERMO, TRANSP keroseno *m*, parafina *f*, petróleo lampante *m*; ~ **coating** *n* AmE (*cf paraffin coating BrE*) PACK cobertura de parafina *f*; ~ **oil** *n* AmE (*cf paraffin oil BrE*) CHEM, PETR TECH, PETROL, THERMO aceite de parafina *m*, petróleo lampante *m*; ~ **series** *n* AmE (*cf paraffin series BrE*) PETR TECH serie de parafina *f*; ~ **wax** *n* AmE (*cf paraffin wax BrE*) CHEM cera de parafina *f*, ELEC *insulator* cera de parafina *f*, parafina sólida *f*

Kerr: ~ **cell** *n* PHYS célula de Kerr *f*; ~ **electro-optical effect** *n* PHYS efecto electroóptico de Kerr *m*; ~ **magneto-optical effect** *n* OPT, PHYS efecto magnetoóptico de Kerr *m*

kersantite *n* PETR TECH kersantita *f*

kerving *n* MINE rafado *m*, roza *f*, socave *m*

keryl *n* CHEM cerilo *m*

ketazine *n* CHEM quetazina *f*

ketch *n* WATER TRANSP queche *m*

ketene *n* CHEM cetena *m*

ketimine *n* CHEM cetimina *f*

keto: ~-**acid** *n* CHEM cetoácido *m*; ~-**enol tautomerism** *n* CHEM tautomerismo ceto-enólico *m*; ~-**form** *n* CHEM forma cetónica *f*

ketol *n* CHEM cetol *m*

ketone *n* CHEM, P&R cetona *f*

ketonic *adj* CHEM cetónico

ketose *n* CHEM cetosa *f*

ketotic *adj* AGRIC acetonémico

kettle *n* CHEM marmita *f*, reactor *m*, PROD *for skin drying* estufa para machos *f*; ~ **dyeing** *n* COLOUR teñido en tina *m*

keV *abbr* (*kilo-electronvolt*) CHEM keV (*kiloelectronvoltio*)

Kevlar *n* WATER TRANSP Kevlar *m*

key[1]: ~-**driven** *adj* COMP&DP accionado a tecla, controlado mediante teclas

key[2] *n* ACOUST clave *f*, tecla *f*, CINEMAT carácter de la imagen *m*, tonalidad *f*, gradación *f*, COMP&DP clave *f*, tecla *f*, CONST *keystone of arch* clave de un arco *f*, *locksmithing* llave *f*, *of door* pasador *m*, ELEC ENG llave *f*, MECH chaveta *f* (*AmL*), llave *f*, pasador *m*, cuña *f*, MECH ENG *engineering components* clavija *f*, chaveta *f* (*AmL*), pasador *m*, *spanner* llave *f*, PRINT guía *f*, PROD, TELECOM, TV tecla *f*; ~-**and-lamp unit** *n* TELECOM portalámparas de llave *m*; ~ **bed** *n* GEOL capa de guía *f*, NUCL capa de referencia *f*, estrato índice *m*; ~ **bit** *n* CONST paletón de llave *m*; ~ **bolt** *n*

MECH ENG perno de chaveta *m*; ~ **coating on film** *n* PRINT capa básica sobre la película *f*; ~ **drift** *n* MECH ENG bota de chavetas *f*, botador de chavetas *m*, punzón cilíndrico *m*; ~ **drop** *n* CONST placa de guarda *f*; ~ **field** *n* COMP&DP campo clave *m*; ~ **file** *n* MECH ENG lima de cerrajero *f*, lima de guardas *f*; ~ **horizon** *n* GEOL horizonte de referencia *m*; ~ **joint** *n* MECH ENG empalme de llave *m*, junta muescada *f*; ~ **level** *n* TV nivel de tecleado *m*; ~ **light** *n* CINEMAT, PHOTO luz principal *f*; ~ **lighting** *n* CINEMAT luz principal *f*; ~-**locked starting system** *n* MECH ENG sistema de arranque con llave *m*; ~ **management** *n* TELECOM gestión por teclado *f*; ~ **number** *n* PRINT número guía *m*; ~ **on flat** *n* MECH ENG enchavetado plano *m*; ~-**opening can** *n* PACK bote con abertura automática *m*; ~-**opening lid** *n* PACK tapa de abertura automática *f*; ~-**operated selector switch** *n* PROD conmutador selector activado por teclado (o botón) *m*; ~-**operated switch** *n* ELEC conmutador operado con teclas *m*; ~-**per-line console** *n* BrE (*cf key-per-trunk console AmE*) TELECOM consola con una clave por línea principal *f*; ~-**per-trunk console** *n* AmE (*cf key-per-line console BrE*) TELECOM consola con una clave por línea principal *f*; ~ **plate** *n* CONST bocallave *f*, chapa del ojo de la llave *f*, escudo de cerradura *m*; ~ **seating** *n* PETR TECH desarrollo de un key seat *m*, desarrollo de un ojo de cerradura *m*, key seating *m*; ~ **signature** *n* ACOUST clave musical *f*; ~ **slot** *n* MECH chavetero *m*; ~ **station** *n* TV estación base *f*; ~ **telephone set** *n* TELECOM equipo telefónico con teclado *m*; ~ **telephone system** *n* TELECOM sistema telefónico con teclado *m*

key[3] *vt* CONST, MECH, MECH ENG, PROD enchavetar, TV teclear; ~ **in** *vt* CINEMAT, COMP&DP introducir gradualmente, introducir información mediante el teclado

keyboard[1] *n* GEN teclado *m*; ~ **encoder** *n* COMP&DP codificador de teclado *m*; ~ **entry** *n* COMP&DP introducción mediante el teclado *f*; ~ **lockout** *n* COMP&DP bloqueo del teclado *m*; ~ **mask** *n* COMP&DP máscara del teclado *f*; ~ **sender** *n* TELECOM manipulador dactilográfico *m*; ~ **send-receive** *n* (*KSR*) COMP&DP transmisor-receptor a teclado *m* (*KSR*), transmisor-receptor mediante teclado *m*; ~ **template** *n* COMP&DP plantilla del teclado *f*

keyboard[2] *vt* GEN *information, text* teclear

keycap *n* PRINT capuchón del teclado *m*

keyed *adj* CONST enchavetado, MECH acuñado, con pasador, enchavetado, MECH ENG acuñado, enchavetado, PROD enchavetado

keyer *n* TV manipulador *m*

keyhole *n* CONST *locksmithing* ojo de la cerradura *m*; ~ **guard** *n* CONST tapa para el ojo de la cerradura *f*; ~ **mask** *n* CINEMAT máscara de tipo bocallave *f*; ~ **saw** *n* CONST serrucho de calar *m*

keying *n* CONST *of arch*, MECH enchavetado *m*, MECH ENG unión por chavetas *f*, enchavetado *m*, PROD enchavetado *m*, tecleado *m*, unión por chavetas *f*, acuñamiento *m*, TELECOM manipulación *f*, transmisión *f*; ~ **band** *n* PROD banda de acuñamiento *f*; ~ **error** *n* COMP&DP, TELECOM error de tecleado *m*; ~ **error rate** *n* COMP&DP frecuencia de errores por manipulación *f*; ~ **hammer** *n* PROD *platelayer's* martillo de acuñar *m*; ~ **in** *n* CONST enchavetado interior *m*; ~ **signal** *n* TV señal de tecleado *f*; ~ **up** *n*

CONST *of arch* dovela superior *f*; ~ **wedge** *n* MECH ENG cuña de apriete *f*

keynote *n* ACOUST tónica *f*

keypad *n* COMP&DP *telephone* botonera de discado *f* (*AmL*), teclado numérico *m*, PHYS, TELECOM, TV teclado numérico *m*

keypunch *n* COMP&DP perforadora *f*, perforadora de tecla *f*

keyslot *n* PROD chavetero *m*

keystone *n* CONST *of arch* clave *f*, llave *f*; ~ **distortion** *n* CINEMAT, ELECTRON distorsión trapezoidal *f*

keyswitch *n* ELEC ENG llave de contacto *f*

keytop: ~ **overlay** *n* PROD máscara de teclado *f*

keyway *n* MECH chavetero *m*, ranura de chaveta *f*, MECH ENG bocallave *f*, chavetero *m*, cuñero *m*, ranura de chaveta *f*, NUCL chavetero *m*; ~-**cutting machine** *n* PROD máquina de ranurar *f*, mortajadora para muescas *f*, *of milling type* máquina para fabricar cajas de cartón *f*, máquina de fresar chaveteros *f*; ~-**cutting tool** *n* PROD máquina de ranurar portátil *f*

keyword *n* COMP&DP palabra cable *f*; ~ **in context** *n* (*KWIC*) COMP&DP palabra clave en el contexto *f* (*KWIC*); ~ **out of context** *n* (*KWOC*) COMP&DP palabra clave fuera de contexto *f* (*KWOC*); ~ **parameter** *n* COMP&DP parámetro de palabra clave *m*; ~ **retrieval** *n* COMP&DP recuperación de palabra clave *f*

kg *abbr* (*kilogram, kilogramme*) METR, PHYS kg (*kilogramo*)

khlopinite *n* NUCL clopinita *f*

kHz *abbr* (*kilohertz*) ELEC, TRANSP kHz (*kilohertz*)

kibble *n* MINE caldero *m* (*AmL*), cuba *f* (*AmL*), espuerta *m* (*Esp*), jaula *f* (*Esp*)

kibbler *n* FOOD triturador *m*

kick *n* PETR TECH arremetida *f*, patada *f*; ~ **copy** *n* PRINT copia rechazada *f*; ~ **down** *n* AUTO reducción de marcha *f*, reducción de velocidad *f*, VEH desconectador *m*; ~-**down switch** *n* AUTO, VEH interruptor del reductor de velocidad *m*; ~-**off mechanism** *n* SPACE mecanismo de arranque *m*; ~ **rocket** *n* SPACE cohete de despegue *m*; ~ **stage** *n* SPACE etapa de despegue *f*; ~-**starter** *n* VEH arranque por pedal *m*

kickback *n* ELEC ENG tensión de retroceso *f*; ~ **power supply** *n* ELEC ENG suministro de energía de retroalimentación *m*

kicker: ~ **actuator** *n* MECH ENG *diecasting* eyector *m*; ~ **box** *n* MECH ENG caja accionadora *f*; ~ **light** *n* CINEMAT luz adicional *f*

kicking: ~ **strap** *n* WATER TRANSP *boom* trapa de la botavara *f*

kickoff *n* SPACE despegue *m*

kidney: ~-**shaped slot** *n* MECH ENG hendidura arriñonada *f*, ranura con forma de riñón *f*, ranura de riñón *f*; ~ **stone** *n* GEOL nefrita *f*; ~ **welch** *n* AGRIC vulneraria *f*

kier *n* TEXTIL autoclave *f*

kieselguhr *n* GEOL, MINERAL, THERMO diatomita *f*

kieserite *n* MINERAL kieserita *f*

kieve *n* MINE cuba *f*

Kikuchi: ~ **line** *n* NUCL línea Kikuchi *f*

kill[1] *vt* CINEMAT apagar, PETR TECH matar, neutralizar, PRINT suprimir

kill[2]: ~ **a set** *vi* CINEMAT desarmar la escenografía; ~ **a well** *vi* PETR TECH matar un pozo

killed *adj* COATINGS calmado

killing: ~ **agent** *n* CHEM agente de desoxidación *m*, METALL agente de desoxidación *m*, agente tranquilizador del baño líquido *m*

kiln[1]: ~-**dried** *adj* THERMO secado en horno

kiln[2] *n* CONST horno *m*, FOOD horno *m*, secadero *m*, tostadero *m*, HEAT horno de secado *m*, LAB horno *m*; ~ **drying** *n* CONST, PROD secado al horno *m*, secado en estufa *m*; ~ **malt** *n* FOOD malta tostada *f*

kiln[3] *vt* C&G hornear, PROD estufar, hornear, secar al horno; ~-**dry** *vt* THERMO secar en horno

kilning *n* C&G horneado *m*

kilo *n* (*k*) METR, PHYS kilo *m* (*k*); ~-**electronvolt** *n* (*keV*) CHEM kiloelectronvoltio *m* (*keV*)

kilobyte *n* (*kb*) COMP&DP kilo-octeto *m*, kilobyte *m*

kilocalorie *n* (*Kcal*) FOOD kilocaloría *f* (*Kcal*)

kilocurie *n* (*kCi*) CHEM kilocurie *m* (*kCi*)

kilogram *n* (*kg*) METR, PHYS kilogramo *m* (*kg*); ~ **meter** *AmE*, ~ **metre** *BrE* *n* METR kilográmetro *m*

kilogramme *see* kilogram

kilohertz *n* (*kHz*) ELEC, TRANSP kilohertz *m* (*kHz*)

kilometer *AmE*, **kilometre** *n* *BrE* (*km*) METR kilómetro *m* (*km*)

kilonem *n* (*kn*) CHEM kilonem *m* (*kn*)

kilovolt *n* (*kV*) ELEC ENG, MECH kilovoltio *m* (*kV*)

kilowatt *n* (*kW*) ELEC, ELEC ENG, PHYS kilovatio *m* (*kW*), kilowatio *m* (*kW*); ~-**hour** *n* (*kWh*) ELEC, ELEC ENG, PHYS kilovatio-hora *m* (*kWh*)

kimberlite *n* GEOL, PETROL kimberlita *f*

Kimmeridgian[1] *adj* GEOL, PETR TECH Kimmeridgiense

Kimmeridgian[2] *n* GEOL, PETR TECH Kimeridgio *m*

kindling: ~ **point** *n* THERMO punto de inflamación *m*, temperatura de ignición *f*, temperatura de inflamación *f*

kinematic: ~ **chain** *n* MECH cadena cinemática *f*; ~ **diagram** *n* MECH ENG diagrama cinemático *m*; ~ **envelope** *n* RAIL envoltura cinemática *f*; ~ **gage** *AmE*, ~ **gauge** *BrE* *n* RAIL medidor cinemático *m*; ~ **viscosity** *n* FLUID, FUELLESS, MECH, PHYS, REFRIG viscosidad cinemática *f*

kinematics *n* MECH, PHYS cinemática *f*

kinescope *n* ELECTRON cinescopio *m*

kinetic[1] *adj* SPACE cinética

kinetic[2]: ~ **energy** *n* GEOPHYS, MECH, MECH ENG, PHYS, SPACE energía cinética *f*; ~ **energy density** *n* ACOUST, PHYS densidad de energía cinética *f*; ~ **energy released in matter** *n* (*kerma*) NUCL, PHYS kerma *f*; ~ **heating** *n* PHYS calentamiento cinético *m*, SPACE calentamiento aerodinámico *m*, calentamiento cinético *m*; ~ **isotope effect** *n* NUCL efecto cinetoisotópico *m*; ~ **pump** *n* MECH ENG bomba cinética *f*, bomba dinámica *f*; ~ **separation** *n* NUCL separación cinética *f*; ~ **spectrophotometry** *n* RAD PHYS espectrofotometría cinética *f*; ~ **theory** *n* PHYS teoría cinética *f*; ~ **vacuum pump** *n* MECH bomba de vacío cinética *f*

kinetically: ~-**induced buoyancy** *n* POLL flotación inducida cinéticamente *f*

kinetics *n* CHEM, GAS, MECH, METALL, PHYS, THERMO cinética *f*

king[1]: ~ **plank** *n* WATER TRANSP *ship building* tablero de crujía *m*; ~ **post** *n* WATER TRANSP *deck fitting* palo macho *m*; ~ **rod** *n* CONST *of roof-truss* pendolón *m*; ~ **roll** *n* PAPER rodillo inferior *m*

king[2]: ~ **the image** *vi* PRINT entintar la imagen; ~ **the plate** *vi* PRINT entintar la plancha

kingbolt *n* MECH ENG clavija maestra *f*, perno

formando pivote *m*, perno maestro *m*, pivote central *m*, pivote de la dirección *m*, pivote de orientación de la rueda *m*

kingpin *n* MECH eje de giro de la mangueta de la rueda *m*, pivote de la dirección *m*, pivote de orientación de la rueda *m*, MECH ENG clavija maestra *f*, perno formando pivote *m*, pivote central *m*, pivote de la dirección *m*, pivote de orientación de la rueda *m*; ~ **inclination** *n* AUTO inclinación transversal del pivote de la rueda *f*, salida del pivote *f*

Kingsbury: ~ **bearing** *n* MECH cojinete Kingsbury *m*

kink[1] *n* CRYSTALL *in dislocation* doblez *m*, METALL deformación *f*, PROD ensortijamiento *m*, nudo *m*, torcedura *f*, coca de un cable *f*, WATER TRANSP *in rope* coca *f*; ~ **band** *n* GEOL, METALL banda de deformación *f*; ~ **fold** *n* GEOL pliegue muy agudo y flanco plano *m*; ~ **instability** *n* NUCL inestabilidad en cáscara *f*, inestabilidad por retorcimiento *f*

kink[2]: ~ **out of line** *vti* PROD alabearse

kip *n* AGRIC piel ligera *f*

Kipp: ~'s **apparatus** *n* CHEM, LAB aparato de Kipp *m* (*Esp*), sulfhidrador *m* (*AmL*)

Kirchhoff: ~'s **law** *n* ELEC, ELEC ENG, PHYS, RAD PHYS ley de Kirchhoff *f*

kirving *n* MINE rafado *m*, roza *f*, socave *m*, rafadura *f*, socava *f*

kiss: ~ **impression** *n* PRINT impresión realizada con poca presión *f*; ~ **roll coating** *n* COATINGS capa rizada *f*

kissing: ~ **circle** *n* GEOM círculo contiguo *m*

kit *n* MECH ENG bolsa de herramientas *f*, caja de herramientas *f*, equipo *m*, juego de herramientas *m*, NUCL aparejo *m*, conjunto para ensamblar *m*, PROD aparejo *m*, conjunto *m*, juego *m*

Kitasato: ~ **vessel** *n* CHEM TECH matraz de Kitasato *m*

kitchen: ~ **garden** *n* AGRIC huerta casera *f*; ~ **salt** *n* FOOD sal de cocina *f*; ~ **waste** *n* FOOD, POLL, RECYCL basura de cocina *f*, desperdicio *m*

kite *n* AIR TRANSP, GEOM cometa *f*

Kjeldahl: ~ **digestion apparatus** *n* LAB *for protection against particles* aparato de digestión de Kjeldahl *m*; ~ **method** *n* CHEM, NUCL método de Kjeldahl *m*

K-Jetronic: ~ **fuel injection** *n* AUTO, HEAT ENG, THERMO, VEH inyección de combustible K Jetronic *f*

Klein: ~ **bottle** *n* GEOM botella de Klein *f*

Klein-Gordon: ~ **equation** *n* PHYS ecuación de Klein-Gordon *f*

klippe *n* GEOL clipe *m*

klystron *n* ELECTRON, PHYS, RAD PHYS, SPACE, TELECOM klistron *m*; ~ **amplifier** *n* ELECTRON amplificador klistron *m*; ~ **frequency multiplier** *n* ELECTRON multiplicador de frecuencia klistron *m*; ~ **oscillator** *n* ELECTRON oscilador klistron *m*

km *abbr* (*kilometer AmE, kilometre BrE*) METR km (*kilómetro*) ,

K-meson *n* PART PHYS kaón *m*, mesón K *m*, PHYS kaón *m*

kmmererite *n* MINERAL kmmererita *f*

kn *abbr* (*kilonem*) CHEM kn (*kilonem*)

knapsack: ~ **duster** *n* AGRIC espolvoreador de mochila *m*; ~ **seeder** *n* AGRIC sembradora manual de mochila *f*; ~ **sprayer** *n* AGRIC pulverizador de mochila *m*

kneader: ~ **pulper** *n* PAPER triturador de pulpa *m*

kneading *n* C&G, CHEM TECH, FOOD amasado *m*, PROD amasadura *f*, amasamiento *m*

knebelite *n* MINERAL knebelita *f*

knee *n* MECH ENG portacarros *m*, rótula *f* (*Esp*), brazo con garras para sujetar el tronco del árbol *m*, codo *m*, curva *f*, *of curve* consola de escuadra *f*, WATER TRANSP *metal* angular *m*, curva *f*, rótula *f* (*Esp*); ~ **bend** *n* MECH acodo *m*; ~ **bracket** *n* CONST angular *m*, soporte de consola *m*; ~ **fold** *n* GEOL pliegue en rodilla *m*; ~ **mounting** *n* INSTR montaje de refuerzo *m*; ~ **pad** *n* SAFE rodillera *f*; ~-**type milling machine** *n* MECH ENG fresadora de rótula *f*

knickpoint *n* BrE GEOL ruptura de interrupción *f*, ruptura de pendiente *f*

knife: ~ **back** *n* AGRIC portasección de barra guadañadora *f*; ~ **coater** *n* PAPER estucadora de cuchilla *f*; ~ **cutter** *n* AGRIC cuchilla *f*; ~ **cylinder** *n* PAPER rodillo de cuchilla *m*; ~ **edge** *n* METR, PROD *of balance* soporte de cuchilla *m*; ~-**edge file** *n* MECH ENG lima de filo de cuchillo *f*; ~-**edge rule** *n* METR regla precisa *f*; ~-**edge switch** *n* ELEC, NUCL interruptor de contacto de cuchilla *m*; ~ **file** *n* MECH ENG lima de filo de cuchillo *f*; ~-**grinding machine** *n* MECH ENG amolador de cuchillos *m*, PROD afiladora de cuchillos *f*, amolador de cuchillos *m*; ~ **holder** *n* PAPER portacuchillas *m*; ~ **pleat** *n* TEXTIL pliegue cosido *m*; ~ **spreading** *n* COATINGS, P&R aplicación de revestimiento con cuchilla *f*; ~ **switch** *n* ELEC conmutador de cuchilla *m*, interruptor de palanca *m*; ~ **tool** *n* MECH ENG herramienta de corte *f*; ~-**tooth harrow** *n* AGRIC grada de púas *f*

knifecut *n* PRINT inserción larga y fina *f*

knit *vt* TEXTIL tejer género de punto, tricotar

knitted: ~ **fabric** *n* TEXTIL tejido de punto *m*; ~ **glass fabric** *n* C&G tela de vidrio tejida *f*

knitting *n* TEXTIL tejedura de punto *f*, tricotado *m*

knob: ~ **lever operator** *n* PROD operador de palanca de pomo *m*; ~ **tools** *n pl* C&G herramientas para desbastar *f pl*

knock[1] *n* PETR TECH autoencendido *m*; ~-**off** *n* MECH ENG cese *m*, parada *f*, suspensión *f*; ~-**off cam** *n* MECH ENG excéntrica de paro *f*, leva de paro *f*; ~-**off link** *n* MECH ENG enlace de paro *m*, unión de paro *f*; ~-**off shower** *n* PAPER rociador de alta presión *m*; ~-**on** *n* NUCL *communications* percusión *f*; ~-**out rod** *n* MECH ENG varilla de expulsión *f*, varilla de extracción *f*, varilla de eyección *f*, varilla de paro *f*

knock[2]: ~ **up** *vt* PAPER igualar

knock[3] *vi* MECH ENG autoencender, golpear, golpetear, hacer ruido; ~ **out** *vi* PROD *rivet* botar

knocked: ~-**on atom** *n* NUCL, PART PHYS átomo percutado *m*

knocking *n* AUTO, MECH ENG, VEH detonación *f*, golpeteo *m*, topetazo *m*

knoll *n* CONST cima de una loma *f*

knot[1] *n* C&G, FUELLESS nudo *m*, PAPER nudo *m*, pastilla *f*, TEXTIL nudo *m*, WATER TRANSP cote *m*, nudo *m*; ~ **breaker** *n* PAPER desintegrador de nudos *m*; ~ **extensibility** *n* TEXTIL extensibilidad del nudo *f*; ~ **grass** *n* AGRIC grama rastrera *f*; ~ **head** *n* AGRIC ternero de mala calidad con síndrome de fiebre de embarque *m*; ~ **strength** *n* TEXTIL resistencia del nudo *f*; ~ **theory** *n* GEOM teoría de nudos *f*; ~ **theory comprising several closed curves** *n* GEOM teoría de nudos que comprende varias curvas cerradas *f*; ~ **varnish** *n* COATINGS, COLOUR barniz de relleno *m*

knot[2] *vt* TEXTIL anudar

knotless[1] *adj* TEXTIL sin nudos

knotless[2]: ~ **yarn length** *n* TEXTIL longitud de hilo sin nudos *f*

knotter: ~ **screen** *n* PAPER depurador de nudos *m*, separanudos *m*

knotting *n* TEXTIL anudadura *f*, anudamiento *m*

knotty *adj* TEXTIL nudoso

knowledge: ~ **base** *n* COMP&DP base de conocimiento *f*; ~ **engineering** *n* COMP&DP ingeniería de conocimiento *f*, representación de conocimiento *f*; ~ **representation language** *n* (*KRL*) COMP&DP lenguaje de representación de conocimiento *m*

known: ~ **coal deposit** *n* COAL depósito de carbón conocido *m*, reserva de carbón *f*

knuckle *n* AUTO articulación tipo rótula *f*, charnela *f*, nudillo *m*, rótula *f* (*Esp*), CONST *of hinge* charnela *f*, junta de charnela *f*, MECH articulación *f*, MECH ENG articulación *f*, charnela *f*, junta de charnela *f*, rótula *f* (*Esp*); ~ **bearing** *n* MECH ENG cojinete de rótula *m*; ~ **joint** *n* MECH, MECH ENG articulación de rótula *f*, junta articulada *f*, junta de charnela *f*; ~**-jointed connecting rod** *n* MECH ENG biela articulada *f*

Knuckle: ~ **joint** *n* CONST junta de charnela *f*

Knudsen: ~ **effect** *n* NUCL *of gear or rack* efecto Knudsen *m*

knurl *n* MECH ENG moleta *f*, moleteado *m*, moleteador *m*

knurled[1] *adj* MECH estriado, moleteado

knurled[2]: ~**-head fastener** *n* MECH ENG fijador de cabeza moleteada *m*, perno de cabeza moleteada *m*, sujetador de cabeza moleteada *m*, tornillo de cabeza moleteada *m*; ~ **nut** *n* MECH ENG tuerca moleteada *f*, tuerca estriada *f*; ~ **operating shaft** *n* PROD eje motriz moleteado *m*; ~ **screw** *n* MECH ENG tornillo de cabeza moleteada *m*

knurling *n* C&G grafilado *m*, moleteado *m*, MECH ENG estriado *m*, moleteado *m*, porta moleta *f*, tuerca *f*; ~ **tool** *n* MECH moleta estriadora *f*, MECH ENG moleta *f*, moleteadora *f*, PAPER moleta *f*

kollergang *n* PAPER molino de muelas *m*, molino de piedras *m*

koninckite *n* MINERAL coninquita *f*

Kossel: ~ **line** *n* NUCL línea Kossel *f*

kotschubeite *n* MINERAL kotschubeyita *f*

Kr *abbr* (*krypton*) CHEM Kr (*criptón*)

kraft: ~ **face liner** *n* PAPER papel para caras con una capa de kraft *m*; ~ **liner** *n* PAPER papel kraft para caras *m*; ~ **paper** *n* PACK, PAPER papel kraft *m*; ~ **pulp** *n* PAPER pulpa kraft *f*, pasta kraft *f*

krarup: ~ **loading** *n* ELEC ENG carga continua submarina *f*

kremersite *n* MINERAL kremersita *f*

krennerite *n* MINERAL krennerita *f*

KRL *abbr* (*knowledge representation language*) COMP&DP lenguaje de representación de conocimiento *m*

Kruskal: ~ **limit** *n* NUCL límite de Kruskal *m*

krypton *n* (*Kr*) CHEM criptón *m* (*Kr*); ~ **absorption in liquid carbon dioxide** *n* (*KALC process*) NUCL absorción de criptón en anhídrido carbónico líquido *f*

kryptonate: ~ **of cadmium amalgam** *n* NUCL amalgama de criptonato de cadmio *f*

K-shell *n* NUCL, PHYS *vehicles* capa K *f*

KSR *abbr* (*keyboard send-receive*) COMP&DP KSR (*transmisor-receptor a teclado*)

K-state *n* NUCL estado K *m*

Kuhn-Thomas-Reich: ~ **sum rule** *n* NUCL regla de sumas de Kuhn-Thomas-Reich *f*

Kundt: ~**'s tube** *n* ACOUST, PHYS tubo de Kundt *m*

kupfernickel *n* MINERAL níquel arsenical *m*

Kutter: ~**'s formula** *n* HYDROL fórmula de Kutter *f*

kV *abbr* (*kilovolt*) ELEC ENG, MECH kV (*kilovoltio*)

kW *abbr* (*kilowatt*) ELEC, ELEC ENG, PHYS kW (*kilovatio, kilowatio*)

kWh *abbr* (*kilowatt-hour*) ELEC, ELEC ENG, PHYS kWh (*kilovatio-hora*)

KWIC *abbr* (*keyword in context*) COMP&DP KWIC (*palabra clave en el contexto*)

KWOC *abbr* (*keyword out of context*) COMP&DP KWOC (*palabra clave fuera de contexto*)

kyanite *n* MINERAL cianita *f*, distena *f*

Kynch: ~**'s separation theory** *n* NUCL teoría de la separación de Kynch *f*

L

l *abbr* (*liter AmE, litre BrE*) METR, PHYS l (*litro*)
L[1] *abbr* (*luminosity*) PART PHYS L (*luminosidad*)
L[2]: **~ section** *n* ELECTRON sección en L *f*; **~ shell** *n* PHYS capa L *f*; **~ split system** *n* AUTO sistema de ranurado en L *m*
La *abbr* (*lanthanum*) CHEM La (*lantano*)
lab *n* (*laboratory*) CHEM, CINEMAT, LAB, PHOTO, PHYS, PROD laboratorio *m*; **~-data sheet** *n* CINEMAT hoja de datos de laboratorio *f*; **~ report** *n* CINEMAT informe de laboratorio *m*, parte de laboratorio *f*
label[1] *n* COMP&DP etiqueta *f*, PACK etiqueta *f*, TEXTIL etiqueta *f*, marbete *m*; **~ area** *n* ACOUST área del radiómetro *f*; **~-coding machine** *n* PACK codificadora de etiquetas *f*; **~ dispenser** *n* PACK distribuidor automático de etiquetas *m*; **~ film** *n* PACK película para etiquetas *f*; **~-overprinting machine** *n* PACK máquina de sobreimpresión de etiquetas *f*; **~ record** *n* COMP&DP registro de etiqueta *m*; **~ stamper** *n* PROD máquina etiquetadora *f*, rotuladora mecánica *f*
label[2] *vt* COMP&DP, TEXTIL etiquetar
labeled *AmE see* **labelled** *BrE*
labeler *AmE see* **labeller** *BrE*
labeling *AmE see* **labelling** *BrE*
labelled[1] *adj BrE* CHEM, NUCL marcado
labelled[2]: **~ atom** *n BrE* NUCL átomo marcado *m*; **~ compound** *n BrE* NUCL compuesto marcado *m*
labeller *n BrE* PACK etiquetador *m*, rotulador *m*
labelling *n BrE* COMP&DP etiquetado *m*, PACK etiquetado *m*, rotulación *f*, PROD *of wiring* etiquetado *m*, etiquetaje *m*, marcaje *m*, rotulación *f*, RAD PHYS *of radioactive material* marcado, TEXTIL etiquetado *m*; **~ by chemical exchange** *n BrE* NUCL marcado por intercambio químico *m*; **~ machine** *n BrE* PACK etiquetadora mecánica *f*, máquina etiquetadora *f*, rotuladora mecánica *f*; **~ technique** *n BrE* NUCL técnica de activación con isótopos *f*, técnica de marcación *f*, técnica de radioactivación con isótopos *f*
labile *adj* CHEM, ELECTRON, GEOL alterable, inestable, lábil
labor *AmE see* **labour** *BrE*
laboratory *n* (*lab*) CHEM, CINEMAT, LAB, PHOTO, PHYS, PROD laboratorio *m*; **~ clothing** *n* LAB, SAFE ropa de laboratorio *f*; **~ coat** *n* LAB, SAFE bata de laboratorio *f*; **~ compaction** *n* COAL compactación de laboratorio *f*, consolidación de laboratorio *f*; **~ frame** *n* PHYS sistema de laboratorio *m*; **~ microscope** *n* INSTR, LAB microscopio de laboratorio *m*; **~ reactor** *n* NUCL reactor de laboratorio *m*; **~ standard** *n* NUCL norma de laboratorio *f*; **~ stool** *n* LAB banco *m*, taburete de laboratorio *m*
labour *n BrE* MINE faena *f*, mano de obra *f*, quehacer *m*, tarea *f*, trabajo *m*; **~ cost** *n BrE* PROD coste de la mano de obra *m*, costo de la mano de obra *m*; **~ productivity** *n BrE* PROD productividad laboral *f*; **~ rate** *n BrE* PROD jornales *m pl*; **~-saving machinery** *n BrE* PROD maquinaria para economizar el trabajo *f*

labradorite *n* MINERAL labradorita *f*
labyrinth *n* ACOUST, MINE laberinto *m*; **~ packing** *n* PROD *for turbines* empaquetadora de laberinto *f*; **~ seal** *n* MECH ENG, NUCL cierre laberíntico *m*, sellado laberíntico *m*, PACK precinto laberinto *m*, sello dédalo *m*
lac *n* PROD goma laca *f*; **~ dye** *n* COLOUR colorante de laca *m*; **~ varnish** *n* COLOUR barniz de laca *m*, laca *f*
laccaic *adj* CHEM lacaico
laccol *n* CHEM laccol *m*, lacol *m*
laccolith *n* GEOL, GEOPHYS, PETROL lacolito *m*
lace[1] *n* PROD *for belts* correílla *f*, tireta *f*, TEXTIL encaje *m*, puntilla *f*; **~ punching** *n* MECH ENG perforado en cadena *m*
lace[2] *vt* PROD *belt* coser con tiretas
laced: **~ cable fan** *n* ELEC ENG ventilador de cable entretejido *m*
Lacey: **~'s formula** *n* HYDROL fórmula de Lacey *f*
lachrymator *n* CHEM lacrimógeno *m*
lacing *n* C&G encaje *m*; **~ cord** *n* AIR TRANSP cordón de cableado *m*
lacker *n* COATINGS, COLOUR, CONST barniz *m*, MECH barniz *m*, laca *f*
lacquer[1] *n* GEN barniz *m*, laca *f*, PROD barniz de China *m*, laca *f*; **~ disc** *BrE*, **~ disk** *AmE n* ACOUST disco de laca *m*; **~ fumes** *n pl* SAFE emanaciones de barniz *f pl*; **~ sealing** *n* PACK sellado mediante lacado *m*
lacquer[2] *vt* GEN lacar, laquear
lacquered[1] *adj* GEN lacado, laqueado
lacquered[2]: **~ work** *n* COLOUR artículo lacado *m*
lacquering *n* CINEMAT *gas ionization* barnizado *m*, COATINGS, COLOUR, PACK lacado *m*; **~ machine** *n* PACK máquina lacadora *f*
lactam *n* CHEM lactama *f*
lactamide *n* CHEM lactamida *f*
lactate *n* CHEM lactato *m*
lactenin *n* CHEM lactenina *f*
lactic[1] *adj* CHEM láctico
lactic[2]: **~ acid** *n* CHEM, FOOD ácido láctico *m*; **~ acid fermentation** *n* AGRIC fermentación láctica *f*
lactide *n* CHEM lactida *f*
lactobutyrometer *n* FOOD lactobutirómetro *m*
lactometer *n* FOOD lactómetro *m*
lactone *n* CHEM lactona *f*
lactonic *adj* CHEM lactónico
lactonitrile *n* CHEM lactonitrilo *m*
lactonization *n* CHEM lactonización *f*
lactose *n* CHEM lactosa *f*
lacustrine *adj* GEOL lacustre
ladder *n* CONST, SAFE escalera *f*, WATER TRANSP *of dredge* escala *f*; **~ adder** *n* ELECTRON sumador de circuito electrónico en escalera *m*; **~ attenuator** *n* ELECTRON atenuador en escalera *m*; **~ chain** *n* PROD cadena Vaucanson *f*; **~ diagram** *n* PROD diagrama de escalones *m*; **~ diagram display** *n* PROD presentación en diagrama de escalones *f*; **~ diagram format** *n* PROD formato de diagrama de escalones *m*; **~ diagram rung** *n* PROD escalón de diagrama *m*; **~ dredge** *n* WATER TRANSP draga de rosario *f*; **~ filter** *n* ELEC-

TRON filtro de escalera *m*; ~ **network** *n* ELEC ENG red de cuadripolos *f*, red en cascada *f*, PHYS red de cuadripolos *f*, red en escalera *f*; ~ **polymer** *n* P&R polímero en escalera *m*; ~ **road** *n* MINE escalera de pozo *f* (*Esp*), pozo de las escalas *m* (*AmL*); ~ **shaft** *n* MINE escalera de pozo *f* (*Esp*), pozo de las escalas *m* (*AmL*); ~ **way** *n* MINE escala de mina *f*, pozo de las escalas *m* (*AmL*)

ladle[1] *n* C&G cucharón *m*, CONST *spoon-type* cuchara *f*, cucharón *m*, FOOD cazo *m*, PROD *pot-type* cucharón *m*, cuchara *f*; ~ **crane** *n* PROD puente grúa para la cuchara de colada *m*

ladle[2] *vt* C&G sacar con cucharón

ladler *n* C&G sacador-alimentador *m*

ladling *n* C&G cuchareado *m*

ladybird *n* AGRIC mariquita de San Antonio *f*, vaquita de San Antonio *f*

lady: ~**'s bedstraw** *n* FOOD amor de hortelano *m*, cuajaleches *m*

laevorotatory *adj BrE* CHEM, PHYS levógiro

laevulose *n BrE* CHEM, FOOD fructosa *f*, levulosa *f*

lag[1] *n* ELEC *alternating current* componente reactiva *f*, desfase *m*, retardo *m*, retraso *m*, ELEC ENG retardo *m*, desfase *m*, retraso *m*, componente reactiva *f*, ELECTRON retardo *m*, componente reactiva *f*, desfase *m*, retraso *m*, MECH ENG deformación elástica *f*, PROD retardo *m*, retraso *m*, revestimiento calorífugo *m*, TV, WATER retardo *m*, retraso *m*; ~ **deposit** *n* GEOL residuo de denudación *m*; ~ **fault** *n* GEOL hiato tectónico *m*; ~ **screw** *n* CONST tirafondo *m*, tornillo de fijación *m*; ~ **of the tide** *n* OCEAN retraso de la marea *m*; ~ **time** *n* PETR TECH tiempo que tarda el lodo desde el fondo del pozo hasta la superficie

lag[2] *vi* ELEC estar desfasado, PHYS estar desfasado, retardar, revestir

lagged *adj* COMP&DP retardado

lagging *n* AIR TRANSP *of helicopter rotor blade* retardo *m*, amortiguamiento *m*, ELEC atraso *m*, FUELLESS *of the tide* retraso *m*, HEAT ENG forro calorífugo *m*, HYDRAUL revestimiento calorifugado *m*, envuelta termoaislante *f*, MECH movimiento retardado *m*, revestimiento *m*, atraso *m*, retardo *m*, retraso *m*, MECH ENG atraso *m*, MINE entablonado *m* (*AmL*), revestimiento *m*, paralización *f*, atraso *m*, forro *m* (*Esp*), entibo provisional *m*, avance con tablestacas *m*, forro de tablas *m*, PETR TECH retardo *m*, retraso *m*, PROD *lathing* listonaje *m*, forro calorífugo *m*, enlistonado *m*, SPACE atraso *m*, THERMO forro calorífugo *m*, revestimiento aislante *m*, revestimiento calorifugado *m*, TRANSP atraso *m*; ~ **chrominance** *n* TV crominancia retrasada *f*; ~ **piece** *n* MINE aguja *f*, revestimiento *m* (*Esp*), tabla de forro *f* (*AmL*), tablestaca *f*; ~ **system** *n* AIR TRANSP sistema de amortiguamiento *m*, sistema de revestimiento *m*

lagoon *n* CONST laguna *f*, GEOL albufera *f*, HYDROL laguna *f*, OCEAN albufera *f*, WATER laguna *f*; ~ **channel** *n* OCEAN canal de albufera *m*

lagooning *n* POLL encharcamiento *m*, estancamiento *m* (*Esp*)

Lagrange's: ~ **equations** *n pl* PHYS ecuaciones de Lagrange *f pl*

Lagrangian *n* PHYS lagrangiano *m*; ~ **drifter** *n* OCEAN, WATER TRANSP *research* rastra lagrangiana *f*

lahar *n* GEOL corriente de lodo y cantos rodados *f*

laid[1]: ~**-up** *adj* WATER TRANSP *ship* amarrado

laid[2]: ~ **grain** *n* AGRIC cultivo de cereal encamado *m*;

~ **lines** *n pl* PAPER verjuras *f pl*; ~ **paper** *n* PAPER papel verjurado *m*; ~ **paper with rubber appearance** *n* PACK papel verjurado con acabado imitando a la goma *m*

laitance *n* CONST lechada de cemento *f*

lake *n* COATINGS, COLOUR laca *f*, HYDROL, WATER lago *m*; ~ **liming** *n* POLL encalamiento de lagos *m*; ~ **pigment** *n* COLOUR pigmento de laca colorante *m*; ~ **water** *n* POLL agua de lago *f*, agua lacustre *f*

Lamb: ~ **shift** *n* PHYS desplazamiento de Lamb *m*

lambda: ~ **particle** *n* PHYS partícula lambda *f*; ~ **point** *n* PHYS punto lambda *m*; ~ **probe** *n* AUTO sonda lambda *f*

lambertian: ~ **radiator** *n* OPT, TELECOM radiador de Lambert *m*, radiador lambertiano *m*; ~ **reflector** *n* OPT, TELECOM reflector de Lambert *m*, reflector lambertiano *m*; ~ **source** *n* OPT, TELECOM fuente de Lambert *f*, fuente lambertiana *f*

Lambert: ~**'s cosine law** *n* OPT, PHYS ley de Lambert del coseno *f*; ~**'s law** *n* OPT, PHYS ley de Lambert *f*

lamb: ~**'s quarter** *n* AGRIC quinoa *f*

lamella *n* METALL laminilla *f*

lamellar[1] *adj* GEOL, MECH, MINERAL laminar, laminoso

lamellar[2]: ~ **graphite cast iron** *n* MECH fundición de grafito laminar *f*; ~ **perlite** *n* METALL perlita laminar *f*; ~ **structure** *n* METALL estructura laminar *f*

lamina *n* CHEM, GEOL lámina *f*

laminar[1] *adj* CHEM, FLUID laminado, laminar

laminar[2]: ~ **flow** *n* GEN flujo laminar *m*; ~ **flow theory** *n* FLUID teoría del flujo laminar *f*; ~ **pipe flow** *n* FLUID flujo laminar en tuberías *m*; ~ **separation** *n* FLUID separación laminar *f*; ~ **structure** *n* GEOL estructura laminar *f*; ~ **transistor** *n* ELECTRON transistor laminar *m*

laminarin *n* CHEM laminarana *f*, laminarina *f*

laminate[1] *n* ELECTRON material laminar *m*, MECH estratificado *m*, madera lamenar *f*, material laminar *m*

laminate[2] *vt* GEN laminar

laminated[1] *adj* ELEC *capacitor* en forma de lámina, laminado, laminar, GEOL laminado, P&R laminado, formado por capas superpuestas, formado de chapas, PAPER laminado, PROD formado de chapas, formado por capas superpuestas, laminado, WATER TRANSP laminado

laminated[2]: ~ **armature** *n* ELEC *motor* armadura laminar *f*; ~ **brush** *n* ELEC *electrical machine*, ELEC ENG contacto laminar *m*, escobilla de láminas *f*, escobilla laminar *f*; ~ **core** *n* ELEC *generator* núcleo de chapas en mazo *m*, núcleo de laminación *m*, núcleo laminado *m*, ELEC ENG núcleo de chapas adosadas *m*; ~ **glass** *n* C&G vidrio sandwich *m*, TRANSP vidrio laminado *m*; ~ **magnet** *n* ELEC imán laminado *m*; ~ **pack** *n* PACK paquete mediante laminado *m*; ~ **plastic** *n* ELEC *insulator*, P&R plástico armado *m*, plástico formado por capas superpuestas *m*, plástico lamelado *m*, plástico laminado *m*, WATER TRANSP plástico laminado *m*; ~ **safety glass** *n* C&G, SAFE vidrio de seguridad laminado *m*; ~ **section** *n* P&R sección laminada *f*; ~ **sheet** *n* CONST chapa laminada *f*, P&R chapa de plástico laminado *f*, hoja laminada *f*, lámina *f*, plancha *f*, plancha laminada *f*; ~ **strip** *n* P&R tira laminada *f*; ~ **torsion bar** *n* AIR TRANSP barra de torsión laminada *f*; ~ **tube** *n* PACK tubo laminado *m*; ~ **windscreen** *n BrE* (*cf laminated windshield AmE*) AIR TRANSP, AUTO, C&G, SPACE,

TRANSP, VEH parabrisas laminado *m*; ~ **windshield** *n* *AmE* (*cf laminated windscreen BrE*) AIR TRANSP, AUTO, C&G, SPACE, TRANSP, VEH parabrisas laminado *m*

laminating *n* C&G laminado *m*; ~ **machine** *n* PACK laminadora *f*; ~ **resistance** *n* TEXTIL resistencia al laminado *f*; ~ **strength** *n* PACK resistencia de laminado *f*

lamination *n* GEN laminación *f*; ~ **mold** *AmE*, ~ **mould** *BrE* *n* MECH ENG, P&R molde de laminación *m*; ~ **sheet** *n* COATINGS chapa de laminación *f*

lamp *n* AUTO, CINEMAT lámpara *f*, ELEC linterna *f*, ELEC ENG bombilla eléctrica *f*, farol *m*, linterna *f*, lámpara *f*, PHOTO lámpara *f*, PROD *drying kettle* plataforma *f*, VEH lámpara *f*; ~ **base** *n* CINEMAT base de la lámpara *f*; ~ **bulb** *n* C&G foco *m*; ~ **cap** *n* ELEC ENG casquillo de lámpara *m*; ~ **chimney** *n* C&G tubo del quinqué *m*; ~ **holder** *n* CINEMAT portalámparas *m*, ELEC ladrón de bombilla *m*, ELEC ENG *socket* ladrón de bombilla *m*, casquillo-enchufe de lámpara *m*, *support* portalámparas *m*, casquillo-soporte de la lámpara *m*; ~ **house** *n* CINEMAT, INSTR cabina *f*, lampistería *f*; ~ **housing** *n* PHOTO portalámparas *m*; ~ **oil** *n* PETR TECH petróleo de alumbrado *m*, petróleo de lámparas *m*, petróleo lampante *m*; ~ **replacement** *n* PHOTO reemplazo de lámpara *f*; ~ **room** *n* MINE lamparería *f*, lampistería *f*; ~ **socket** *n* PHOTO casquillo para lámparas *m*

lampadite *n* MINERAL lampadita *f*

Lampard: ~ **and Thomson capacitor** *n* PHYS capacitor de Lampard y Thomson *m*

lamprophyre *n* PETROL lamprófido *m*

lampshade *n* ELEC ENG pantalla *f*, tulipa *f*

LAN *abbr* (*local area network*) COMP&DP, TELECOM red de área local *f*

lanarkite *n* MINERAL lanarkita *f*

land[1] *adj* SPACE de tierra

land[2] *n* MECH ENG *of drill* faja de corte *f*, parte plana entre acanaladuras *f*, P&R superficie plana entre acanaladuras *f*, WATER TRANSP tierra *f*; ~ **accretion** *n* WATER acumulación de tierra *f*; ~ **air-cushion vehicle** *n* TRANSP aerodeslizador terrestre *m*; ~ **breeze** *n* METEO, WATER TRANSP brisa de tierra *f*, terral *m*, viento de la costa *m*, viento de tierra *m*; ~ **cable** *n* TELECOM cable terrestre *m*; ~ **capability** *n* AGRIC capacidad productiva de la tierra *f*; ~ **classification** *n* AGRIC clasificación de terrenos *f*; ~ **clearing** *n* AGRIC desmonte de terrenos *m*; ~ **container** *n* TRANSP contenedor terrestre *m*; ~ **degradation** *n* POLL degradación del suelo *f*, degradación del terreno *f*; ~ **development** *n* AGRIC aprovechamiento de tierras *m*; ~ **disturbance** *n* POLL alteración del suelo *f*, alteración del terreno *f*; ~ **freight** *n* AGRIC flete terrestre *m*; ~ **line** *n* TELECOM línea terrestre *f*; ~ **management** *n* AGRIC explotación de tierras *f*; ~ **measure** *n* CONST, METR medida del terreno *f*; ~ **measuring** *n* CONST, METR medición del terreno *f*; ~ **measuring chain** *n* CONST, METR cadena para medición del terreno *f*; ~ **mobile station** *n* (*LMS*) TELECOM estación móvil terrestre *f*; ~ **packer** *n* AGRIC rodillo compactador *m*; ~ **pollutant** *n* POLL *element* contaminante de la tierra *m*, contaminante terrestre *m*; ~ **pollution** *n* POLL contaminación del suelo *f*, contaminación terrestre *f*; ~ **reclamation** *n* AGRIC recuperación de tierras *f*, WATER terrenos ganados al mar *m pl*; ~ **reform** *n* AGRIC reforma

agraria *f*; ~ **register** *n* AGRIC catastro *m*; ~ **roller** *n* AGRIC rodillo desmenuzador *m*; ~ **survey** *n* AGRIC agrimensura *f*, reconocimiento topográfico *m*, CONST agrimensura *f*; ~ **surveying** *n* AGRIC, CONST topografía *f*; ~ **surveyor** *n* AGRIC, CONST agrimensor *m*; ~ **tenure** *n* AGRIC régimen de tenencia de tierras *m*; ~ **use pattern** *n* AGRIC régimen de aprovechamiento de la tierra *m*; ~ **value** *n* AGRIC valor de la tierra *m*; ~ **vehicle** *n* SPACE vehículo terrestre *m*

land[3] *vt* WATER TRANSP *cargo* descargar, *on water* amarrar, *passengers* desembarcar

land[4] *vi* AIR TRANSP aterrizar, MINE cubrir, descargar, verter, SPACE aterrizar, WATER TRANSP *on deck* anavear, tomar cubierta

Landé: ~ **factor** *n* PHYS factor de Landé *m*

landed: ~ **price** *n* PETR TECH precio puesto en destino *m*

lander *n* SPACE módulo aterrizador *m*, módulo de aterrizaje *m*, módulo de descenso *m*; ~ **stage** *n* SPACE etapa de aterrizaje *f*

landfall *n* WATER TRANSP *navigation* punto de recalada *m*, recalada *f*

landfill *n* COAL, POLL, RECYCL relleno de tierra *m*, soterramiento *m*, terraplén *m*, vertedero público *m*, vertido controlado *m*; ~ **site** *n* POLL, RECYCL escombrera *f*

landfilling *n* COAL, CONST terraplenado *m*, POLL, RECYCL soterramiento *m*, terraplenado *m*, VEH terraplenado *m*

L&ILW *abbr* (*low and intermediate level waste*) NUCL RBMA (*residuos de baja y mediana actividad*)

landing *n* AIR TRANSP aterrizaje *m*, aterrizaje *m*, COAL descarga *f*, enganche superior *m*, llegada de la jaula al exterior *f*, vertedero *m*, CONST *of stairs* rellano *m*, MINE descarga *f*, llegada de la jaula al exterior *f*, vertedero *m*, PROD *of furnace* plataforma *f*, SPACE aterrizaje *m*, WATER TRANSP *of people, fishing, riveting* gramil *m*, captura *f*, desembarque *m*, aterraje *m*; ~ **approach speed** *n* AIR TRANSP, SPACE velocidad de aproximación de aterrizaje *f*; ~ **area** *n* AIR TRANSP, SPACE área de aterrizaje *f*; ~ **barge** *n* MILIT, TRANSP barcaza de desembarco *f*; ~ **capsule** *n* SPACE cápsula de aterrizaje *f*; ~ **charges** *n pl* *BrE* (*cf landing fees AmE*) AIR TRANSP impuestos de aterrizaje *m pl*, WATER TRANSP gastos de desembarque *m pl*; ~ **chart** *n* AIR TRANSP carta de aterrizaje *f*, WATER TRANSP *navigation* carta de desembarco *f*; ~ **craft** *n* MILIT lancha de desembarco *f*, WATER TRANSP embarcación de desembarco *f*; ~ **deck** *n* TRANSP cubierta de desembarco *f*; ~**-direction indicator** *n* AIR TRANSP indicador de dirección de aterrizaje *m*; ~ **distance** *n* AIR TRANSP distancia de aterrizaje *f*; ~ **distance available** *n* AIR TRANSP distancia disponible de aterrizaje *f*; ~ **fees** *n pl* *AmE* (*cf landing charges BrE*) AIR TRANSP impuestos de aterrizaje *m pl*, WATER TRANS gastros de desembarque *m pl*; ~ **flap** *n* AIR TRANSP flap de aterrizaje *m*, TRANSP aleta hipersustentadora de aterrizaje *f*, flap de aterrizaje *m*; ~ **gear** *n* AIR TRANSP, SPACE aterrizador *m*, tren de aterrizaje *m*, TRANSP rodamen de apoyo *m*; ~**-gear bay** *n* AIR TRANSP compartimento del tren de aterrizaje *m*; ~**-gear boot retainer** *n* AIR TRANSP fiador de la rueda del tren de aterrizaje *m*, retenedor de la rueda del tren de aterrizaje *m*; ~**-gear bracing installation** *n* AIR TRANSP instalación de abrazaderas del tren de aterrizaje *f*; ~**-gear bumper** *n* AIR TRANSP parachoques del tren de aterrizaje *m*; **~-gear compensation rod** *n* AIR TRANSP barra de compensación del tren de aterrizaje *f*; **~-gear control unit** *n* AIR TRANSP unidad de control del tren de aterrizaje *f*; **~-gear diagonal truss** *n* AIR TRANSP armazón diagonal del tren de aterrizaje *m*; **~-gear door latch** *n* AIR TRANSP cerrojo de la portezuela del tren de aterrizaje *m*, enganche de la compuerta del tren de aterrizaje *m*, retén de la compuerta del tren de aterrizaje *m*; **~-gear door unlatching** *n* AIR TRANSP apertura del cierre de la puerta del tren de aterrizaje *f*; **~-gear door uplock** *n* AIR TRANSP cierre de la compuerta del tren de aterrizaje *m*; **~-gear downlock** *n* AIR TRANSP fijación de apertura del tren de aterrizaje *f*; **~-gear downlock visual check installation** *n* AIR TRANSP instalación para la comprobación visual de la bajada del tren de aterrizaje *f*; **~-gear drop test** *n* AIR TRANSP prueba de la bajada del tren de aterrizaje *f*; **~-gear extension** *n* AIR TRANSP extensión del tren de aterrizaje *f*; **~-gear fork rod** *n* AIR TRANSP barra de horquilla del tren de aterrizaje *f*; **~-gear hinge beam** *n* AIR TRANSP faro de charnela del tren de aterrizaje *m*; **~-gear hinge beam fitting** *n* AIR TRANSP componente del faro de charnela del tren de aterrizaje *m*; **~-gear leg** *n* AIR TRANSP pata del tren de aterrizaje *f*, columna del tren de aterrizaje *f*; **~-gear leg support** *n* AIR TRANSP soporte de la columna del tren de aterrizaje *m*; **~-gear lock pin** *n* AIR TRANSP pasador de retención del tren de aterrizaje *m*; **~-gear main shock strut** *n* AIR TRANSP soporte de choque principal del tren de aterrizaje *m*; **~-gear manual release** *n* AIR TRANSP bajada del tren de aterrizaje *f*, suelta manual del tren de aterrizaje *f*; **~-gear master brake cylinder** *n* AIR TRANSP cilindro principal del freno del tren de aterrizaje *m*; **~-gear optical inspection system** *n* AIR TRANSP sistema de inspección visual del tren de aterrizaje *m*; **~-gear position indicator** *n* AIR TRANSP indicador de posición del tren de aterrizaje *m*; **~-gear retraction lock** *n* AIR TRANSP inmovilización del retractor del tren de aterrizaje *f*; **~-gear safety lock** *n* AIR TRANSP cierre de seguridad del tren de aterrizaje *m*, inmovilizador de seguridad del tren de aterrizaje *m*; **~-gear safety override** *n* AIR TRANSP contramando de seguridad del tren de aterrizaje *m*; **~-gear shaft** *n* AIR TRANSP eje del tren de aterrizaje *m*; **~-gear shock strut compression** *n* AIR TRANSP compresión del puntal de choque del tren de aterrizaje *f*; **~-gear sliding valve** *n* AIR TRANSP válvula corrediza del tren de aterrizaje *f*; **~-gear track** *n* AIR TRANSP vía del tren de aterrizaje *f*; **~-gear unlocking** *n* AIR TRANSP desenganche del tren de aterrizaje *m*; **~-gear uplock** *n* AIR TRANSP blocaje del tren de aterrizaje *m*, enganche del tren de aterrizaje *m*; **~-gear uplock box** *n* AIR TRANSP caja de blocaje del tren de aterrizaje *f*; **~-gear well** *n* AIR TRANSP alojamiento del tren de aterrizaje *m*; **~-light** *n* AIR TRANSP luz de aterrizaje *f*; **~ on water** *n* AIR TRANSP amerizaje *m*; **~ path** *n* TRANSP trayectoria de aterrizaje *f*; **~ pattern turn** *n* AIR TRANSP giro patrón de aterrizaje *m*, viraje estándar de aterrizaje *m*; **~ pier** *n* WATER TRANSP muelle de desembarque *m*; **~ place** *n* WATER TRANSP *mooring* desembarcadero *m*, embarcadero *m*; **~ pontoon** *n* TRANSP pontón de desembarco *m*; **~ procedure** *n* AIR TRANSP procedimiento de aterrizaje *m*; **~ riser** *n* CONST *of stairs* pilar del rellano *m*; **~ run** *n* AIR TRANSP carrera de

aterrizaje *f*, recorrido de aterrizaje *m*; **~ sequence** *n* AIR TRANSP secuencia de aterrizaje *f*; **~ skid** *n* AIR TRANSP deslizamiento de aterrizaje *m*, patín de aterrizaje *m*; **~ speed** *n* AIR TRANSP velocidad de aterrizaje *f*; **~ stage** *n* MINE desembarcadero *m*, embarcadero flotante *m*, enganche superior *m*, plataforma de carga *f*, SPACE desembarcadero *m*; **~ station** *n* MINE estación de desembarco *f*, estación de desembarque *f*, plataforma de carga *f*; **~ step** *n* CONST *of stairs* peldaño *m*; **~ strip** *n* AIR TRANSP pista de aterrizaje *f*, pista semipreparada de aterrizaje *f*; **~-strip marker** *n* AIR TRANSP *radio* baliza de pista de aterrizaje *f*; **~ switch** *n* ELEC *of a lift, elevator* conmutador de aterrizaje *m*; **~ trimmer** *n* CONST *of stairs* viga de rellano *f*; **~ weight** *n* AIR TRANSP peso de aterrizaje *m*; **~ zone** *n* (*LZ*) MILIT zona de aterrizaje *f*

landings *n pl* OCEAN desembarco *m*

landmark *n* AIR TRANSP marca de referencia de tierra *f*, punto de referencia *m*, CONST hito *m*, mojón *m*, MILIT señal *f*, OCEAN marca *f*, WATER TRANSP *navigation* marca en tierra *f*

landscape: **~ conservation** *n* AGRIC conservación del paisaje *f*; **~ format** *n* COMP&DP, PAPER, PRINT formato apaisado *m*; **~ gardening** *n* AGRIC jardinería ornamental *f*; **~ photographer** *n* PHOTO fotógrafo de paisajes *m*; **~ size** *n* PRINT tamaño apaisado *m*

landscaping *n* AGRIC conformación del paisaje *f*, CONST paisajismo *m*, panorámica *f*

landside *n* AGRIC *plough* costanera *f*

landslide *n* CONST desprendimiento *m*, GEOL, RAIL deslizamiento de tierras *m*; **~ block** *n* GEOL bloque deslizado *m*

landslip *n* GEOL desplazamiento *m*, desprendimiento de tierras *m*, RAIL corrimiento de tierras *m*

landward *adv* GEOL, WATER TRANSP hacia tierra

lane *n* TRANSP banda de tránsito viario *f*, carril *m*, pasillo *m*, ruta de navegación *f*, vía de tráfico *f*; **~ switching** *n* TRANSP cambio de carril *m*

Langelier's: **~ index** *n* HYDROL índice de Langelier *m*

langite *n* MINERAL langita *f*

Langmuir: **~ effect** *n* METEO *safety* efecto de Langmuir *m*

language: **~ construct** *n* COMP&DP lenguaje de invención conceptual *m*; **~ statement** *n* COMP&DP declaración de lenguaje *f*; **~ translator** *n* COMP&DP conversor de lenguaje *m*, traductor de lenguaje *m*

lanolin *n* CHEM lanolina *f*

lanoline *n* CHEM lanolina *f*

lanosterol *n* CHEM lanosterol *m*

lantern *n* PROD *drying kettle, core barrel* linterna *f*; **~ casing** *n* WATER TRANSP *light* armazón *m*, armazón del farol *m*; **~ gear** *n* MECH ENG engranaje de linterna *m*, piñón de linterna *m*; **~ gearing** *n* MECH ENG engranaje de linterna *m*, piñón de linterna *m*; **~ slide** *n* CINEMAT diapositiva proyectable *f*

lanthanide *n* CHEM lantánido *m*; **~ contraction** *n* CHEM *atomic or ionic radii* contracción lantanoidea *f*

lanthanite *n* MINERAL lantanita *f*

lanthanum *n* (*La*) CHEM lantano *m* (*La*)

lanyard *n* WATER TRANSP *ship building* acollador *m*, cabo acollador *m*, piola *f*

lap[1] *n* C&G doblez *m*, pulidor *m*, traslape *m*, COATINGS pliegue *m*, CONST *roofing* solape *m*, junta de solape *f*, HYDRAUL recubrimiento *m*, TEXTIL faldón *m*, napa *f*; **~ dissolve** *n* CINEMAT desaparición gradual *f*, desvanecimiento gradual *m*; **~ joint** *n* CONST *end of one piece lying on top of another* junta de solape *f*, *halved joint* empalme *m*, MECH reborde *m*; **~ and lead lever** *n* HYDRAUL palanca con recubrimiento de plomo *f*; **~ machine** *n* PAPER máquina de pasta en hojas plegadas *f*; **~ mark** *n* C&G marca del pulidor *f*; **~ riveting** *n* PACK remachado solapado *m*, PROD remachado de recubrimiento *m*; **~ valve** *n* HYDRAUL distribuidor con recubrimiento *m*; **~ weld** *n* NUCL, PACK, PROD soldadura a solape *f*, soldadura de recubrimiento *f*, soldadura solapada *f*; **~ welding** *n* PROD soldadura por superposición *f*; **~ winding** *n* ELEC *electrical machine*, ELEC ENG devanado imbricado *m*

lap^2 *vt* MECH, PROD alisar, pulimentar, pulir, rectificar

LAP *abbr* (*line access protocol*) TELECOM protocolo de acceso a la línea *m*

lapel: **~ microphone** *n* ACOUST micrófono de solapa *m*

lapilli *n pl* GEOL lapilli *m pl*

Laplace: **~ transform** *n* MATH, PHYS transformación de Laplace *f*, transformada de Laplace *f*; **~ transformation** *n* ELECTRON, PHYS transformación de Laplace *f*; **~'s equation** *n* PHYS ecuación de Laplace *f*

Laplacian *n* NUCL *communications*, PHYS laplaciano *m*

lapless: **~ valve** *n* HYDRAUL distribuidor sin recubrimiento *m*

lappaconitine *n* CHEM lapaconitina *f*

lapped: **~ insulation** *n* ELEC *cable conductor*, ELEC ENG aislamiento con recubrimiento *m*; **~ scarf** *n* CONST rebajo superpuesto *m*

lapping *n* PROD lapeado *m*, rectificado *m*, recubrimiento *m*, solape *m*; **~ compound** *n* PROD compuesto lapidado *m*; **~ fixture** *n* MECH ENG *machine tools* accesorio para lapidado *m*, sujetador para pulido *m*; **~ machine** *n* MECH, PROD ajustadora *f*, máquina de rectificación *f*, máquina lapidadora *f*, máquina pulidora *f*; **~ rib** *n* C&G costilla de pulido *f*; **~ tool** *n* PROD herramienta para lapear *f*

laptop: **~ computer** *n* COMP&DP computador de falda *m* (*AmL*), computador laptop *m* (*AmL*), computador portátil *m* (*AmL*), computadora de falda *f* (*AmL*), computadora laptop *f* (*AmL*), computadora portátil *f* (*AmL*), ordenador de falda *m* (*Esp*), ordenador laptop *m* (*Esp*), ordenador portátil *m* (*Esp*)

lardite *n* MINERAL lardita *f*

large^1: **~-scale** *adj* GEOL a gran escala

large^2: **~-angle scattering** *n* NUCL dispersión a gran ángulo *f*; **~ animal unit** *n* AGRIC unidad de ganado mayor *f*; **~-aperture lens** *n* PHOTO lente de gran abertura *f*; **~ body** *n* MINE *of ore* macizo de mineral *m*; **~ break LOCA** *n* (*LBLOCA*) NUCL LOCA grande *m* (*LBLOCA*); **~-capacity motorcycle** *n* TRANSP motocicleta de gran capacidad *f*; **~-capacity truck** *n* TRANSP camión de gran capacidad *m*; **~-case erector** *n* PACK montador de grandes cajas *m*; **~ coal** *n* COAL carbón grueso *m*; **~-core glass fiber** *AmE*, **~-core glass fibre** *BrE n* ELEC ENG fibra de vidrio para núcleo grande *f*, vitrofibra de núcleo grande *f*; **very ~ crude carrier** *n* (*VLCC*) PETR TECH super-transportador de crudo *m*, superpetrolero *m*; **~ eddies** *n pl* FLUID grandes remolinos *m pl*; **~ electron-positron collider** *n* (*LEP*) PART PHYS gran cámara de reacción electrón-positrón *f* (*LEP*); **~ end of connecting rod** *n* MECH ENG cabeza de biela *f*; **~-format camera** *n* INSTR cámara de formato

ancho *f*; **~-format folding camera** *n* PHOTO cámara plegable de formato grande *f*, cámara plegable de gran formato *f*; **~ hadron collider** *n* (*LHC*) PART PHYS gran cámara de reacción para hadrones *f* (*LHC*); **~-hole boring** *n* COAL perforación de amplio diámetro *f*; **~ hole-cut** *n* MINE barrena de grueso calibre *f*; **~ inflow** *n* HYDROL *of water*, WATER gran afluencia *f*; **~ orifice** *n* HYDROL orificio de grandes dimensiones *m*; **~ plate molds** *AmE*, **~ plate moulds** *BrE n pl* MECH ENG *for rubber seals and gaskets* moldes planos de grandes dimensiones *m pl*; **~ post paper** *n* PRINT papel de tamaño 41,9 x 53,3 cm *m*; **~-scale chart** *n* WATER TRANSP *chart* carta en punto mayor *f*; **~-scale integrated circuit** *n* PHYS, TELECOM circuito integrado en gran escala *m*; **very ~-scale integrated circuit** *n* PHYS, TELECOM circuito integrado en muy gran escala *m*; **~-scale integration** *n* (*LSI*) COMP&DP, ELECTRON, PHYS, TELECOM, WATER TRANS *computers on board ship* integración a gran escala *f* (*IGE*); **very ~-scale integration** *n* (*VLSI*) COMP&DP, ELECTRON, PHYS, TELECOM, WATER TRANS *computers on board ship* integración en muy gran escala *f* (*IMGE*); **~-scale integration circuit** *n* COMP&DP circuito integrado en gran escala *m*, PHYS, TELECOM circuito de integración a gran escala *m*; **~ signal** *n* ELECTRON señal de gran amplitud *f*; **~-signal bandwidth** *n* ELECTRON ancho de banda con señal ampliada *m*; **~-signal conditions** *n pl* ELECTRON condiciones de amplitud de señal *f pl*; **~-signal operation** *n* ELECTRON operación de amplitud de señal *f*; **~-size container** *n* PACK contenedor de gran tamaño *m*; **~-value capacitor** *n* ELEC ENG condensador de gran valor *m*; **~-value resistor** *n* ELEC ENG resistencia de gran valor *f*

Larmor: **~ frequency** *n* PHYS frecuencia de Larmor *f*; **~ precession** *n* PHYS precesión de Larmor *f*

larry: **~ car** *n* MINE vagoneta *f*

larsen: **~ effect** *n* CINEMAT efecto larsen *m*

laser^1: **~-guided** *adj* ELECTRON dirigido por láser

laser^2 *n* ELECTRON, OPT, PHYS, PRINT, RAD PHYS, WAVE PHYS láser *m*; **~ action** *n* ELECTRON acción con láser *f*; **~ alignment** *n* ELECTRON, MECH ENG alineación láser *f*; **~ annealing** *n* ELECTRON esmaltación por láser *f*; **~ bandwidth** *n* ELECTRON ancho de banda con láser *m*; **~ beam** *n* ELECTRON, NUCL, RAD PHYS, TELECOM, WAVE PHYS haz de láser *m*, haz lasérico *m*, rayo láser *m*; **~-beam energy** *n* ELECTRON energía por haz láser *f*; **~-beam modulation** *n* ELECTRON modulación por haz láser *f*; **~-beam recording** *n* COMP&DP grabación mediante láser *f*, registro por haz de láser *m*, ELECTRON, TV grabación por haz láser *f* (*AmL*), grabación por láser *f* (*Esp*); **~-beam welding** *n* CONST soldadura de viga por láser *f*; **~ burst** *n* ELECTRON impulso con rayos láser *m*; **~ cavity** *n* ELECTRON cavidad de láser *f*; **~ code** *n* ELECTRON código láser *m*; **~ communications** *n pl* ELECTRON comunicaciones con láser *f pl*; **~-controlled machine** *n* CONST máquina controlada por láser *f*; **~ cutting** *n* CONST, ELECTRON corte por láser *m*; **~ designation** *n* ELECTRON designación por láser *f*; **~ designation system** *n* MILIT designación de objetivos por láser *f*; **~ diode** *n* ELECTRON, OPT, PHYS, TELECOM diodo láser *m*; **~ disc** *BrE*, **~ disk** *AmE n* OPT, TV disco láser *m*; **~ drill** *n* ELECTRON taladradora de láser *f*; **~-driven fusion** *n* ELECTRON, NUCL fusión inducida por haz lasérico *f*; **~-effect threshold** *n* OPT, PHYS umbral de

efecto láser *m*; ~ **emission** *n* ELECTRON emisión de láser *f*; ~ **excitation** *n* RAD PHYS excitación por láser *f*; ~ **fusion** *n* ELECTRON, NUCL fusión por haz lasérico *f*; ~ **glass** *n* C&G vidrio láser *m*; ~ **grading system** *n* CONST sistema de graduación láser *m*; ~ **guidance** *n* ELECTRON asesoramiento por láser *m*; ~**-guided bomb** *n* (*LGB*) MILIT bomba guiada por láser *f*; ~ **gyro** *n* SPACE *craft* giroscopio láser *m*; ~ **head** *n* OPT cabezal láser *m*; ~ **illumination** *n* ELECTRON iluminación por láser *f*; ~ **impact surface ionization** *n* NUCL *pipelines* ionización superficial por impacto láser *f*; ~ **interferometer** *n* ELECTRON, MECH ENG interferómetro láser *m*; ~ **light beam** *n* RAD PHYS haz de luz láser *m*; ~ **machining** *n* MECH maquinación láser *f*; ~ **measuring instrument** *n* INSTR, METR instrumento de medición láser *m*; ~ **mechanism** *n* OPT mecanismo láser *m*; ~ **medium** *n* OPT, TELECOM medio láser *m*; ~ **melting** *n* ELECTRON fusión con láser *f*; ~ **monitoring system** *n* RAD PHYS sistema de vigilancia por láser *m*, sistema lasérico de medición *m*, sistema lasérico de monitorización *m*, sistema lasérico de vigilancia *m*; ~**-optic card** *n* OPT tarjeta laseróptica *f*; ~**-optic disc** *BrE*, ~**-optic disk** *AmE n* COMP&DP, OPT disco óptico láser *m*; ~**-optic memory** *n* (*LO-M*) OPT memoria laseróptica *f*; ~**-optic recording** *n* OPT grabación laseróptica *f*; ~**-optic tape** *n* OPT cinta laseróptica *f*; ~ **optical recorder** *n* ELECTRON grabador óptico por láser *m*; ~ **pick-up head** *n* OPT cabezal de captación láser *m*, fonocaptor láser *m*; ~ **population mechanisms** *n pl* RAD PHYS mecanismos de población lasérica *m pl*; ~ **printer** *n* COMP&DP, OPT, PRINT impresora láser *f*; ~ **printer-copier** *n* OPT, PRINT impresora y copiadora láser *f*; ~ **printing** *n* COMP&DP, OPT, PRINT impresión láser *f*; ~ **probe mass spectrography** *n* NUCL espectrografía de masas por sonda lasérica *f*; ~**-produced printing plate** *n* PRINT plancha de impresión producida por láser *f*; ~ **propulsion** *n* SPACE *craft* propulsión por haz láser *f*; ~ **pulse** *n* ELECTRON impulso por láser *m*; ~ **radiation** *n* ELECTRON, RAD PHYS radiación láser *f*; ~ **radiation hazard** *n* ELECTRON, RAD PHYS, SAFE peligro de radiación láser *m*, riesgo de radiación láser *m*; ~ **rangefinder** *n* ELECTRON telémetro por láser *m*; ~ **retroflector experiment** *n* RAD PHYS experimento con retroflector lasérico *m*; ~ **scriber** *n* ELECTRON trazador por láser *m*; ~ **scribing** *n* ELECTRON trazado por láser *m*; ~ **sensor** *n* ELECTRON sensor láser *m*; ~ **spectral line** *n* RAD PHYS espectro de rayas de láser *m*; ~ **spectroscopy** *n* RAD PHYS espectroscopía láser *f*; ~ **target designator** *n* (*LTD*) MILIT designador de objetivo por láser *m*; ~ **target marker** *n* MILIT marcador de objetivos por láser *m*; ~ **telemetry** *n* TELECOM telemetría por láser *f*; ~ **tracker** *n* ELECTRON seguidor láser *m*; ~ **tracking** *n* ELECTRON seguimiento por láser *m*; ~ **transition** *n* RAD PHYS transición lasérica *f*; ~ **treatment** *n* ELECTRON tratamiento por láser *m*; ~ **trimming** *n* ELECTRON desbastado por láser *m*, recorte por láser *m*; ~ **vaporization** *n* RAD PHYS vaporización por láser *f*; ~ **videodisc** *BrE*, ~ **videodisk** *AmE n* OPT videodisco láser *m*; ~ **warning receiver** *n* ELECTRON receptor de alarma por láser *m*; ~ **weapon** *n* ELECTRON defensa por láser *f*, proyectil por láser *m*; ~ **welding** *n* CONST, ELECTRON soldadura por láser *f*
LASER *abbr* (*light amplification by stimulated emission of radiation*) ELECTRON, RAD PHYS, WAVE PHYS

LASER (*amplificación de la luz por estímulo en la emisión de radiaciones*)
lasercard® *n* OPT tarjeta láser *f*
Laserjet® *n* OPT Laserjet® *m*
laservision: ~ **disc** *BrE*, ~ **disk** *AmE n* OPT disco de visión láser *m*, disco láser *m*; ~ **player** *n* (*LV player*) OPT reproductor de visión láser *m*; ~ **videodisc** *BrE*, ~ **videodisk** *AmE n* OPT videodisco de visión láser *m*
lash[1] *n* MECH ENG holgura *f*, huelgo *m*, juego *m*
lash[2] *vt* WATER TRANSP *helm* bloquear, *ropework* abarbetar, amarrar, trincar, coser, *waves* batir, azotar
LASH[1] *abbr* (*lighter aboard ship*) WATER TRANSP buque para transporte de barcazas *m*
LASH[2]: ~ **carrier** *n* (*lighter aboard ship carrier*) TRANSP buque portagabarras *m*
lashing *n* MINE remoción *f*, PROD *of wires, of cables* amarre *m*, WATER TRANSP *stowage* amarra *f*, cordaje de amarre *m*, ligada *f*, trinca *f*; ~ **plan** *n* WATER TRANSP *stowage* plan de trincaje *m*
lasing *n* ELECTRON tratamiento por láser *m*; ~ **medium** *n* ELECTRON aplicación con láser *f*; ~ **threshold** *n* OPT, PHYS, TELECOM umbral de acción láser *m*
last[1]: ~**-choice circuit group** *n* TELECOM grupo de circuitos de última alternativa *m*; ~**-choice group** *n* TELECOM grupo de última alternativa *m*; ~**-emergency action** *n* AIR TRANSP acción de emergencia final *f*; ~ **feedback** *n* PROD retroalimentación anterior *f*; ~**-feedback rate** *n* PROD velocidad de retroalimentación anterior *f*; ~ **and maintenance** *n* TELECOM monitorización *f*, supervisión y mantenimiento; ~**-number recall** *n* TELECOM rellamada al último número *f*; ~**-number redial** *n* TELECOM marcación automática del último número *f*; ~**-stage treatment** *n* PROD tratamiento final *m*; ~ **state** *n* PROD estado final *m*
last[2]: ~**-in-first-out** *phr* COMP&DP, PROD último en entrar, primero en salir (*LIFO*)
lasting: ~ **color** *AmE*, ~ **colour** *BrE n* P&R color permanente *m*, color sólido *m*; ~ **pigment** *n* P&R pigmento sólido *m*
latch[1] *n* COMP&DP cerrojo *m*, enclavamiento *m*, pestillo *m*, CONST, MECH, MECH ENG *of door, gate, window* aldaba *f*, sujetador *m*, cerrojo *m*, pestillo *m*, picaporte *m*, NUCL *for protection against particles* trinquete *m*, TEXTIL lengüeta *f*; ~ **address** *n* PROD dirección de retenida *f*; ~ **bit** *n* PROD broca de retenida *f*; ~ **bolt** *n* CONST pestillo de resorte *m*; ~ **catch** *n* CONST pasador *m*; ~ **circuit** *n* PROD circuito de enganche *m*; ~ **instruction** *n* PROD orden de retenida *f*; ~ **key** *n* PROD llavín *m*; ~ **lock** *n* CONST cerrojo *m*; ~ **needle** *n* TEXTIL aguja de lengüeta *f*; ~ **pin** *n* CONST pasador de barra *m*; ~ **rung** *n* PROD peldaño de retenida *m*; ~**-up** *n* SPACE cierre *m*
latch[2] *vt* COMP&DP enclavar, PETR TECH enganchar
latched: ~ **bit** *n* PROD broca enganchada *f*; ~ **lever** *n* MECH ENG palanca enganchada *f*
latching *n* ELEC ENG *relays* mecanismo de enganche *m*; ~ **current** *n* ELEC ENG corriente de retención *f*; ~ **electromagnet** *n* ELEC electroimán de enganche *m*; ~ **position** *n* PROD posición de bloqueo *f*; ~ **relay** *n* ELEC relé de enclavamiento *m*, relé enganchador *m*, ELEC ENG relé de retenida *m*; ~ **transistor** *n* ELECTRON transistor de enganche *m*
late[1] *adj* GEOL superior, tardío; ~**-stage** *adj* GEOL etapa tardía; ~**-stage magmatic** *adj* GEOL magmático superior, magmático tardío

late^2: **~-admission slide valve** *n* HYDRAUL válvula de corredera con retardo a la admisión *f*; **~ blight** *n* AGRIC añublo *m*, muerte generalizada tardía *f*; **~-break contact** *n* PROD contacto de ruptura final *m*; **~-maturing crop** *n* AGRIC cultivo de maduración tardía *m*; **~ maturity** *n* AGRIC maduración tardía *f*; **~-release slide valve** *n* HYDRAUL válvula de corredera con retardo al escape *f*

latency *n* ACOUST latencia *f*, COMP&DP latencia *f*, cadencia *f*

latensification *n* CINEMAT, PHOTO intensificación de la imagen latente *f*

latent: **~ evaporation** *n* HYDROL evaporación latente *f*; **~ heat** *n* CONST, HEAT ENG, MECH, METEO, PETR TECH, PHYS, REFRIG, THERMO calor latente *m*; **~ heat of compression** *n* THERMO calor latente de compresión *m*; **~ heat of evaporation** *n* THERMO calor latente de evaporación *m*; **~ heat of expansion** *n* THERMO calor latente de expansión *m*; **~ heat of fusion** *n* PHYS, THERMO calor latente de fusión *m*; **~ heat of solidification** *n* THERMO calor latente de solidificación *m*; **~ heat of transformation** *n* THERMO calor latente de transformación *m*; **~ heat of vaporization** *n* PHYS, THERMO calor latente de evaporación *m*; **~ image** *n* CINEMAT, OPT, PHOTO, PHYS, PRINT, TV imagen latente *f*; **~ modulus** *n* METALL módulo latente *m*

lateral^1 *adj* PETROL lateral

lateral^2 *n* MINE galería principal paralela al frente *f*; **~ accelerometer** *n* AIR TRANSP acelerómetro lateral *m*; **~ area** *n* GEOM área lateral *f*; **~ axis** *n* AIR TRANSP eje lateral *m*; **~-beam coupler** *n* AIR TRANSP acoplador lateral de vigas *m*; **~ clearance** *n* TRANSP espacio libre lateral *m*; **~ contraction** *n* METALL contracción lateral *f*; **~ crater** *n* GEOL cráter lateral *m*; **~ cyclic control support** *n* AIR TRANSP *helicopter* soporte de control cíclico lateral *m*; **~ cyclic pitch** *n* AIR TRANSP *helicopter* paso cíclico lateral *m*; **~ diffusion** *n* ELECTRON difusión lateral *f*; **~ divergence** *n* AIR TRANSP divergencia lateral *f*; **~-drift landing** *n* AIR TRANSP aterrizaje con desviación lateral *m*; **~ force** *n* TRANSP fuerza lateral *f*; **~-force coefficient** *n* AIR TRANSP coeficiente de fuerza lateral *m*; **~ guidance** *n* TRANSP dirección lateral *f*, guía lateral *f*; **~ inversion** *n* TV inversión lateral *f*; **~ magnification** *n* INSTR, PHYS amplificación lateral *f*, aumento lateral *m*, magnificación lateral *f*; **~-noise measurement point** *n* AIR TRANSP punto de medición de ruido lateral *m*; **~ offset loss** *n* OPT, TELECOM pérdida por desplazamiento lateral *f*; **~-path integrator** *n* AIR TRANSP integrador de paso lateral *m*; **~ planation** *n* GEOL ablación lateral *f*; **~ plasma deposition** *n* TELECOM deposición lateral de plasma *f*; **~ play** *n* MECH ENG juego lateral *m*; **~ recording** *n* ACOUST grabación de modulación lateral *f*; **~ separation** *n* GEOL separación lateral *f*; **~ shift** *n* GEOL desplazamiento lateral *m*; **~ stability** *n* TRANSP estabilidad lateral *f*; **~ stapling** *n* PACK grapado lateral *m*; **~ structure** *n* ELECTRON estructura lateral *f*; **~ system** *n* WATER TRANSP *navigation* sistema lateral *m*; **~-tracking angle error** *n* ACOUST error angular del registro lateral *m*; **~ transistor** *n* ELECTRON transistor lateral *m*; **~ trim** *n* AIR TRANSP compensado lateral *m*, equilibrado lateral *m*; **~ variation** *n* GEOL *dynamic memories* variación lateral *f*; **~ view** *n* INSTR vista lateral *f*; **~ yielding** *n*

NUCL *solids from liquids* cesión lateral *f*, deformación lateral *f*

laterally: **~-inverted image** *n* CINEMAT, PHOTO, PHYS, TV imagen invertida lateralmente *f*

laterite *n* CONST, GEOL, PETROL arcilla laterítica *f*, laterita *f*

latex *n* P&R látex *m*; **~ backing** *n* TEXTIL refuerzo de látex *m*; **~ foam** *n* P&R caucho esponjoso *m*, espuma de látex *f*; **~ paint** *n* COLOUR pintura al látex *f*

lath *n* CONST *plaster* varilla *f*, *slate* listón *m*, GEOL *of information* listón *m*; **~ breast** *n* PAPER caja de entradas con regletas de nivel *f*; **~ nail** *n* CONST clavo de listón *m*; **~ wood** *n* CONST madera para listón *f*

lathe *n* MECH, PROD *for turning* torno *m*; **~ bed** *n* MECH, MECH ENG *machine tools* bancada del torno *f*, banco de torno *m*; **~ bed braced by cross-girths** *n* MECH, MECH ENG banco de torno asegurado con cinchas cruzadas *m*; **~ carrier** *n* MECH ENG perro de arrastre *m*; **~ center** *AmE*, **~ centre** *BrE* *n* MECH ENG punto del torno *m*; **~ chuck** *n* MECH mandril de torno *m*; **~ dog** *n* MECH ENG perno de arrastre *m*, perro de arrastre *m*, trinquete de mandril *m*; **~ head** *n* MECH ENG cabezal de torno *m*; **~ headstock** *n* MECH ENG *machine tools* cabezal del torno *m*, cabezal fijo de torno *m*; **~ operator** *n* MECH ENG tornero *m*; **~ saddle** *n* MECH soporte del torno *m*; **~ slide** *n* MECH carro del torno *m*; **~ tool** *n* MECH ENG herramienta de torno *f*; **~ tool post** *n* MECH ENG portaherramientas del torno *m*; **~ work** *n* PROD trabajo de torno *m*

lather: **~ booster** *n* FOOD impulsador de espuma *m*

lathing *n* CONST enlistonado *m*

latitude *n* WATER TRANSP *navigation* latitud *f*; **~ coarse-motion clamp** *n* INSTR pinza de amplitud por movimiento rápido *f*

lattice *n* CHEM red cristalina *f*, CONST enrejado *m*, *frame* celosía *f*, ELECTRON *of transformer* malla *f*, red *f*, MATH grafo *m*, reticulado *m* (*AmL*), látice *m*, red *f*, retículo *m* (*Esp*), NUCL *atomic pile*, SPACE *spacecraft* reticulado *m* (*AmL*), retículo *m* (*Esp*); **~ beam** *n* CONST *frame* viga de celosía *f*; **~ bracing** *n* CONST arriostramiento de celosía *m*; **~ bridge** *n* CONST puente de celosía *m*; **~ constant** *n* METALL constante de red *f*, constante de retículo *f*, parámetro de red *m*; **~ correspondence** *n* METALL correspondencia reticular *f*; **~ defect** *n* ELECTRON *of a transformer* defecto de la red cristalina *m*, METALL defecto reticular *m*; **~ deformation** *n* METALL deformación reticular *f*; **~ filter** *n* ELECTRON filtro de red *m*; **~ girder** *n* CONST *frame*, MECH viga de celosía *f*; **~-girder arch** *n* CONST arco de viga de celosía *m*; **~ network** *n* ELEC ENG red en puente *f*, red puenteada *f*; **~ parameter** *n* CRYSTALL parámetro de la red *m*, parámetro reticular *m*; **~ pitch** *n* NUCL módulo del retículo *m*; **~-pitch spacing** *n* NUCL espaciado del retículo *m*; **~ plan** *n* TELECOM plan reticular *m*; **~ plane** *n* CRYSTALL plano reticular *m*; **~ point** *n* CRYSTALL nudo reticular *m*, METALL punto reticular *m*; **~ rib** *n* AIR TRANSP costilla enrejada de celosía *f*; **~ row** *n* CRYSTALL fila reticular *f*; **~-sided container** *n* TRANSP contenedor enrejado *m*; **~ spacing** *n* METALL espaciado reticular *m*, espaciamiento reticular *m*; **~ tower** *n* CONST, ELEC *overhead supply line* castillete de celosía *m*, torre de celosía *f*; **~ truss** *n* CONST *frame* estructura de celosía *f*; **~ work** *n* CONST trabajo de enrejado *m*; **~-wound coil** *n* ELEC, ELEC ENG bobina de panal *f*

laudanosine *n* CHEM laudanosina *f*

laudanum *n* CHEM láudano *m*

Laue: ~ **diagram** *n* CRYSTALL, RAD PHYS diagrama de Laue *m*, lauegrama *m*, patrón de Laue *m*; ~ **method** *n* CRYSTALL método de Laue *m*; ~ **pattern** *n* CRYSTALL, RAD PHYS diagrama de Laue *m*, patrón de Laue *m*, registro de Laue *m*

laumontite *n* MINERAL laumontita *f*

launch[1] *n* MECH ENG *promotion* lanzamiento *m*, WATER TRANSP lancha *f*; ~ **area** *n* SPACE área de lanzamiento *f*; ~ **azimuth** *n* SPACE acimut de lanzamiento *m*; ~ **environment** *n* SPACE entorno del lanzamiento *m*; ~ **escape motor** *n* SPACE motor de escape de lanzamiento *m*; ~ **escape system** *n* SPACE sistema de escape de lanzamiento *m*; ~ **numerical aperture** *n* (*LNA*) OPT, TELECOM apertura numérica de lanzamiento *f*, apertura numérica de salida *f*; ~ **pad** *n* SPACE pedestal para el lanzamiento *m*; ~ **platform** *n* SPACE plataforma de lanzamiento *f*; ~ **ramp shelter** *n* SPACE resguardo de la rampa de lanzamiento *m*; ~ **readiness review** *n* SPACE revisión de la disponibilidad de lanzamiento *f*; ~ **site** *n* SPACE emplazamiento de lanzamiento *m*, lugar de lanzamiento *m*; ~ **station** *n* MILIT *of rocket* estación de lanzamiento *f*, plataforma de lanzamiento *f*; ~ **success probability** *n* SPACE *craft* probabilidad de éxito del lanzamiento *f*; ~ **vehicle** *n* MILIT lanzador *m*, SPACE vehículo de lanzamiento *m*; ~ **window** *n* SPACE ventana de lanzamiento *f*

launch[2] *vt* MILIT *missile* lanzar, WATER TRANSP *vessel* botar, poner a flote

launcher *n* SPACE dispositivo de lanzamiento *m*, lanzador *m*; ~ **release gear** *n* SPACE dispositivo de disparo del lanzamiento *m*

launching *n* TELECOM emisión *f*, puesta en servicio *f*, WATER TRANSP *of boat* arriado *m*, puesta a flote *f*; ~ **aircraft** *n* SPACE nave de lanzamiento *f*; ~ **base** *n* SPACE base de lanzamiento *f*; ~ **complex** *n* SPACE complejo de lanzamiento *m*; ~ **configuration** *n* SPACE configuración de lanzamiento *f*; ~ **fiber** *AmE*, ~ **fibre** *BrE n* OPT, TELECOM fibra de lanzamiento *f*, fibra emisora *f*; ~ **gantry** *n* CONST pórtico de lanzamiento *m*; ~ **ramp** *n* MILIT *for guided missiles*, SPACE rampa de lanzamiento *f*; ~ **site** *n* SPACE emplazamiento de lanzamiento *m*, lugar de lanzamiento *m*; ~ **tower** *n* SPACE torre de lanzamiento *f*; ~ **trap** *n* PETROL trampa de diablos *f*, trampa de raspatubos *f*

launder *vt* TEXTIL lavar

laundering *n* TEXTIL lavado *m*

lauric *adj* CHEM láurico

laurionite *n* MINERAL laurionita *f*

lauryl: ~ **alcohol** *n* CHEM, DETERG alcohol laurílico *m*

lava[1]: ~-**like** *adj* GEOL lávica

lava[2]: ~ **flow** *n* GEOL corriente de lava *f*, flujo de lava *m*; ~ **plateau** *n* GEOL campo' de lava *m*, PETROL meseta de lava *f*; ~ **shield** *n* GEOL escudo de lava *m*; ~ **stream** *n* GEOL corriente de lava *f*, flujo de lava *m*

lavender *n* CINEMAT copia intermedia *f*; ~ **print** *n* PHOTO copia intermedia *f*, positivo intermedio *m*

law: ~ **of corresponding states** *n* PHYS ley de estados correspondientes *f*; ~ **of mass action** *n* CHEM, PHYS ley de acción de masas *f*; ~ **of radioactive decay** *n* NUCL, PHYS, RAD PHYS ley de desintegración radiactiva *f*; ~ **of thermodynamics** *n* PHYS, THERMO ley de la termodinámica *f*, principio de la termodinámica *m*

LAW *abbr* (*light anti-armor weapon AmE, light anti-*

armour weapon BrE) MILIT, NUCL arma de pequeño calibre contra blindaje *f*

lawn: ~ **cut** *n* AGRIC corte de césped *m*; ~ **disease** *n* AGRIC enfermedad del césped *f*; ~ **mower** *n* CONST segadora de césped *f*; ~ **rake kit** *n* CONST equipo de herramientas para jardín *m*; ~ **seed** *n* AGRIC semilla de césped *f*; ~ **sprinkler** *n* AGRIC, HYDROL, WATER aspersor para césped *m*

lawrencium *n* (*Lr*) CHEM, RAD PHYS laurencio *m* (*Lr*)

laws: ~ **of reflection** *n pl* PHYS leyes de la reflexión *f pl*; ~ **of refraction** *n pl* PHYS leyes de la refracción *f pl*; ~ **of vibration of a fixed string** *n pl* PHYS, WAVE PHYS leyes de vibración de una cuerda fija *f pl*

lawsone *n* CHEM lawsona *f*

lawsonite *n* MINERAL lawsonita *f*

laxmannite *n* MINERAL laxmannita *f*

lay[1] *n* CONST *of the country* contorno *m*, ELEC *cable component* cableado *m*, paso *m*, ELEC ENG paso de torsión *m*, MECH ENG configuración *f*, plan *m*, cableado *m*, proyecto *m*, PRINT guía *f*, tope *m*; ~ **barge** *n* PETR TECH, PETROL barcaza para tender oleoductos submarinos *f*, chata para la colocación de oleoductos submarinos *f*, gabarra para tender oleoductos submarinos *f*; ~-**by** *n* CONST aparcamiento *m*, estacionamiento *m*; ~ **of the case** *n* PRINT situación relativa de la caja *f*; ~ **day** *n* PETR TECH, TRANSP día de estadías *m*, estadía *f*; ~ **edge** *n* PRINT lado guía *m*, guía lateral *f*; ~-**flat film bag** *n* P&R, PACK bolsa plana de plástico *f*; ~-**flat tubing** *n* PACK tubo plano *m*; ~ **marks** *n pl* PRINT registros *m pl*; ~-**on roller** *n* PRINT rodillo aplicador *m*; ~ **ratio** *n* ELEC *cable component* relación de cableado *f*; ~ **shaft** *n* MECH ENG eje intermedio *m*, árbol auxiliar con engranajes *m*

lay[2] *vt* CONST colocar, situar, *pipes* instalar, MINE asentar, TELECOM disponer en capas, WATER TRANSP *rope, cable* colchar; ~ **aback** *vt* WATER TRANSP *sails* echar por delante, fachear; ~ **down** *vt* GEOL marcar, trazar; ~ **off** *vt* PROD *belt* dejar inactivo, desacoplar, desconectar; ~ **on** *vt* PROD *belt* acoplar, instalar; ~ **out** *vt* MINE *mine* acondicionar, *shaft* construir, trazar; ~ **up** *vt* WATER TRANSP *warship* amarrar, desaparejar, desarmar, desmantelar

lay[3]: ~ **down the lines** *vi* WATER TRANSP *naval architecture* galibar; ~ **the foundations** *vi* CONST *of house* cimentar, poner los cimientos

layer *n* COAL capa *f*, estrato rocoso *m*, filón *m*, yacimiento *m*, COMP&DP capa *f*, nivel *m*, CONST capa *f*, *road* tongada *f*, ELECTRON estratificador *m*, GEOL filón *m*, METALL capa delgada *f*, estratificación *f*, P&R capa *f*, PETROL estrato *m*, SPACE *spacecraft* apuntador de elevación *m*, capa *f*, TEXTIL capa de tejido *f*, capa *f*, WATER capa *f*, estrato *m*, WATER TRANSP capa *f*, tongada *f*; ~ **deposition** *n* ELECTRON deposición del estratificador *f*; ~ **insulation** *n* ELEC, ELEC ENG aislación de capas *f*, aislamiento de capas *m*; ~ **line** *n* CRYSTALL línea límite *f*; ~ **management entity** *n* (*LME*) TELECOM entidad para la gestión de capas *f*; ~ **sequence** *n* COAL secuencia de capas *f*, secuencia de estratos *f*; ~ **structure** *n* CRYSTALL estructura en capas *f*; ~ **thickness gaging** *AmE*, ~ **thickness gauging** *BrE n* NUCL medición de grosores de capas *f*, medición de grosores de estratos *f*; ~ **winding** *n* ELEC ENG devanado por capas *m*

layered: ~ **igneous rock** *n* GEOL roca ígnea estratificada *f*; ~ **structure** *n* GEOPHYS estructura estratificada *f*

layering *n* AGRIC acodo *m*, GEOL estratificación *f*, separación por capas *f*

laying *n* CONST *of piping* tendido *m*, *putting in position* colocación *f*, TELECOM disposición en capas *f*; ~ **barge** *n* PETR TECH gabarra de tendido *f*; ~ **on cloth** *n* C&G depositado en tela *m*; ~ **on plaster** *n* C&G depositado en yeso *m*; **~-up** *n* WATER TRANSP desaparejo *m*; ~ **yard** *n* C&G patio de tendido *m*

layout *n* COMP&DP *configuration* disposición *f*, plan *m*, *memory* organización *f*, *of circuit board* distribución *f*, *scheme* esquema *m*, ELEC *circuit* plano de recorrido *m*, MECH, MECH ENG *drawing* diagrama de colocación *m*, esquema de montaje *m*, disposición *f*, croquis *m*, plano *m*, trazado *m*, PACK croquis de montaje *m*, PRINT trazado *m*, boceto *m*, PROD disposición *f*, instalación *f*, trazado *m*, *design* distribución en planta *f*; ~ **character** *n* COMP&DP carácter de formato *m*; ~ **drawing** *n* MECH diagrama de distribución *m*; ~ **dye** *n* PROD tinte de trazado *m*

lazarette *n* WATER TRANSP *store* lazareto *m*, pañol pequeño *m*

lazulite *n* MINERAL espato azul *m*, lazulita *f*

lazurite *n* MINERAL lazurita *f*

lazy: ~ **coil** *n* ELEC *motor* bobina perezosa *f*; ~ **H aerial** *n* BrE (*cf lazy H antenna AmE*) TV antena colineal de dipolos *f*; ~ **H antenna** *n* AmE (*cf lazy H aerial BrE*) TV antena colineal de dipolos *f*

L-band *n* ELECTRON, SPACE, WATER TRANSP banda L *f*; ~ **frequency** *n* ELECTRON, SPACE banda L de las frecuencias *f*, WATER TRANSP *satellite communications* banda L de las frecuencias *f*, frecuencia de banda L *f*

LBLOCA *abbr* (*large break LOCA*) NUCL LBLOCA (*LOCA grande*)

L-block *n* C&G bloque en L *m*

LC[1] *abbr* (*liquid crystal*) GEN CL (*cristal líquido*)

LC[2]: ~ **filter** *n* ELECTRON filtro de CL *m*

LCA *abbr* (*loopback command "audio loop request"*) TELECOM señal para la alimentación del bucle "petición bucle acústico" *f*

LCD[1] *abbr* (*liquid crystal display*) COMP&DP, ELEC, ELECTRON, PHYS, TELECOM, TV VCL (*visualización en cristal líquido*)

LCD[2]: ~ **module** *n* COMP&DP, ELEC, ELECTRON, PHYS, TELECOM, TV módulo de imágen por cristal líquido *m*, módulo de VCL *m*; ~ **panel** *n* ELECTRON panel de VCL *m*

LCM *abbr* (*least common multiple*) COMP&DP, MATH mcm (*mínimo común múltiplo*)

LCV *abbr* (*loopback command "video loop request"*) TELECOM señal para la alimentación del bucle "petición bucle por video" *f*

L-D: ~ **ratio** *n* (*lift-drag ratio*) AIR TRANSP coeficiente de planeo *m*, coeficiente de rendimiento aerodinámico *m*

LD50 *abbr* (*mean lethal dose*) NUCL, PHYS dosis letal del 50%, dosis letal mediana

LE *abbr* (*local exchange*) TELECOM central local *f*

leach[1] *n* HYDROL desalación *f*, filtración *f*; ~ **liquor** *n* CHEM TECH licor de lixiviación *m*

leach[2] *vt* AGRIC, C&G lixiviar, CHEM *lixiviate* lixiviar, *percolate* percolar, COAL, FOOD, GAS lixiviar, GEOL lixiviar, disolver, HYDROL filtrar, infiltrar, MAR POLL escurrir, POLL, TELECOM lixiviar

leach[3] *vi* HYDROL filtrarse, escurrir, MINE escurrir

leachability *n* GEN lixiviabilidad *f*

leachant *n* NUCL lixiviador *m*

leaching *n* AGRIC, C&G lixiviación *f*, CHEM *lixiviation* lixiviación *f*, *percolation* percolación *f*, FOOD, GAS lixiviación *f*, HYDROL infiltración *f*, POLL filtración *f*, lixiviación *f*, TELECOM lixiviación *f*; ~ **agent** *n* NUCL agente lixiviador *m*; ~ **coefficient** *n* NUCL coeficiente de lixiviación *m*; ~ **plant** *n* COAL planta de lixiviación *f*; ~ **time** *n* COAL tiempo de lixiviación *m*; ~ **trench** *n* WATER zanja de lixiviación *f*

lead[1]: **~-bearing** *adj* MINE plumbífero

lead[2] *n* (*Pb*) CHEM plomo *m* (*Pb*), ELEC ENG *of brushes* conductor de suministro *m*, conductor *m*, *current supply wire* toma de alimentación *f*, cable *m*, *wire attached to device* toma de conexión *f*, ELECTRON *of a transformer* cable *m*, conductor *m*, HYDRAUL avance *m*, HYDROL sonda *f*, MECH ENG *of screw* paso *m*, *of ignition* avance *m*, METALL plomo *m* (*Pb*), MINE filón *m*, veta *f*, MINERAL plomo *m* (*Pb*), PRINT interlínea *f*; ~ **accumulator** *n* PHYS acumulador de plomo *m*; **~-acid accumulator** *n* ELEC, ELEC ENG, TRANSP, VEH acumulador de plomo *m*; **~-acid battery** *n* AUTO, ELEC, ELEC ENG, PHYS, SPACE, TELECOM, TRANSP, VEH, WATER TRANS acumulador de plomo *m*, batería de acumuladores *f*, batería de plomo *f*, batería de plomo-ácido *f*; ~ **additive** *n* POLL aditivo de plomo *m*; ~ **block** *n* WATER TRANSP *deck fittings* motón de reenvío *m*, motón de retorno *m*; ~ **button** *n* CHEM granalla de plomo *f*; ~ **control at work** *n* SAFE control de plomo en el trabajo *m*; **~-covered cable** *n* ELEC, ELEC ENG cable bajo plomo *m*, cable con cubierta de plomo *m*, cable emplomado *m*, cable envainado en plomo *m*, cable forrado de plomo *m*; ~ **crystal glass** *n* C&G cristal de plomo *m*; ~ **deposit** *n* MINE yacimiento de plomo *m*; ~ **dresser** *n* PROD *plumber's mallet* mazo de fontanero *m* (*Esp*), mazo de plomero *m* (*AmL*); ~ **filter** *n* TRANSP filtro de plomo *m*; ~ **frame** *n* ELEC, ELEC ENG bastidor de conductores *m*; **~-frame tooling** *n* MECH ENG herramientas del bastidor de conductores *f pl*; **~-free gasoline** *n* AmE (*cf lead-free petrol BrE*) PETR TECH, POLL gasolina libre de plomo *f*; **~-free paint** *n* COLOUR, CONST pintura sin plomo *f*; **~-free petrol** *n* BrE (*cf lead-free gasoline AmE*) PETR TECH, POLL gasolina libre de plomo *f*; ~ **glance** *n* MINERAL galena *f* (*Esp*); ~ **glazing** *n* COATINGS barnizado de base plomo *m*, embotamiento de plomo *m*; **~-in cable** *n* ELEC cable de acometida *m*; **~-in groove** *n* ACOUST surco inicial *m*; **~-in line** *n* BrE (*cf hold-short line AmE*) AIR TRANSP *apron marking* línea de sujeción corta *f*, línea guía de entrada *f*; **~-in wire** *n* ELEC ENG hilo conductor principal *m*; ~ **joint** *n* CONST junta de plomo *f*; ~ **jointing** *n* CONST junta de plomo *f*; ~ **lap** *n* PROD taco abrasivo de plomo *m*, taco de plomo *m*; ~ **line** *n* WATER TRANSP sondaleza *f*; ~ **matte** *n* PROD mata de plomo *f*; ~ **naphthenate** *n* P&R naftenato de plomo *m*; ~ **ore** *n* MINE galena *f* (*Esp*), mena de plomo *f* (*AmL*); **~-out groove** *n* ACOUST surco final *m*; **~-out line** *n* AIR TRANSP *apron marking* línea guía de salida *f*; **~-over groove** *n* ACOUST surco intermedio *m*; ~ **packing** *n* CONST junta de plomo *f*; ~ **paint** *n* COLOUR pintura con plomo *f*; ~ **piping** *n* CONST cañería de plomo *f* (*AmL*), tubería de plomo *f* (*Esp*); ~ **plug** *n* HYDRAUL tapón fusible *m*; ~ **printing letter** *n* PRINT letra fundida en plomo *f*; ~ **refining** *n* PROD afino del plomo *m*; ~ **roll** *n* PRINT rodillo de plomo *m*; ~ **screw** *n* MECH, MECH ENG, PROD husillo *m*, tornillo de avance *m*, tornillo patrón *m*, tornillo regulador *m*;

~ **seal** *n* PACK precinto de plomo *m*; ~-**seal wire** *n* PROD alambre para precinto de plomo *m*; ~-**sealing pliers** *n pl* PACK alicates para colocar precintos de plomo *m pl*; ~ **sheath** *n* ELEC *cable* envoltura de plomo *f*, forro de plomo *m*, ELEC ENG vaina de plomo *f*; ~-**sheathed cable** *n* ELEC, ELEC ENG cable bajo plomo *m*, cable emplomado *m*, cable envainado en plomo *m*; ~ **sheathing** *n* ELEC *cable* envoltura de plomo *f*, forro de plomo *m*; ~ **shot** *n* PROD granalla de plomo *f*; ~ **silicate** *n* C&G silicato de plomo *m*; ~-**smelting works** *n* PROD fundición de plomo *f*; ~ **sulfate** *AmE see lead sulphate BrE*; ~ **sulfide** *AmE see lead sulphide BrE*; ~ **sulphate** *n BrE* CHEM sulfato de plomo *m*, sulfato plumboso *m*; ~ **sulphide** *n BrE* CHEM sulfuro de plomo *m*; ~ **time** *n* ELECTRON tiempo de espera *m*, MECH ENG demora de entrega *f*, plazo de entrega *m*, tiempo de adelanto *m*, tiempo de avance *m*, tiempo desde la orden de pedido hasta la entrega *m*, tiempo requerido para iniciar algún proceso *m*, PRINT tiempo de preparación *m*, PROD plazo de entrega *m*, tiempo de aprovisionamiento *m*, tiempo de espera *m*, TEXTIL tiempo de avance *m*; ~ **time deviation** *n* PROD desviación del plazo de entrega *f*; ~-**tin alloy** *n* MECH ENG, METALL aleación de plomo y estaño *f*; ~ **tree** *n* CHEM árbol de plomo *m*; ~ **wire** *n* ELEC ENG hilo de plomo conductor *m*

lead[3] *vt* CONST *plumb* emplomar

lead[4] *vti* COMP&DP, PRINT interlinear

lead[5]: ~ **in phase by half pi** *vi* PHYS estar en avance de fase de medio pi

leader *n* ACOUST concertino *m*, CINEMAT guía *f*, COMP&DP *tape* cabecera de guía *f*, CONST *downpipe* bajante de aguas *m*, MECH ENG *master wheel* rueda maestra *f*, rueda matriz *f*, MILIT jefe *m*, PAPER punta para pasar la hoja *f*, TV tira sin imágenes que precede al filme *f*, WATER *pipe* bajante de aguas *m*; ~ **cloth** *n* TEXTIL tela acompañante *f*; ~ **dots** *n pl AmE* (*cf dot leaders BrE*) PRINT puntos conductores *m pl*; ~ **line** *n* MECH ENG línea guía *f*

leaders *n pl* PRINT filete puntillado *m*

leadership *n* MILIT dotes de mando *f pl*

leadhillite *n* MINERAL leadhillita *f*

leading *n* COMP&DP *printing*, PRINT interlineado *m*, PROD emplomadura *f*; ~ **block** *n* WATER TRANSP *deck fittings* motón de reenvío *m*, motón de retorno *m*; ~ **chamfer** *n* MECH ENG bisel anterior *m*; ~ **edge** *n* AIR TRANSP, CINEMAT, ELECTRON, PHYS, PROD, TELECOM borde de ataque *m*, borde de entrada *m*, borde delantero *m*, borde entrante *m*; ~-**edge flap** *n* AIR TRANSP flap-borde de ataque *m*, TRANSP aleta hipersustentadora del borde de ataque *f*, flap-borde de ataque *m*; ~-**edge glove** *n* AIR TRANSP guante del borde de ataque *m*, recubrimiento del borde de ataque *m*; ~-**edge one shot** *n* PROD borde de ataque único *m*; ~-**edge one-shot programming** *n* PROD programación única de borde de ataque *f*; ~-**edge pulse time** *n* TV duración del establecimiento del frente del impulso *f*; ~-**edge rib** *n* AIR TRANSP arista del borde de ataque *f*; ~-**edge slat** *n* AIR TRANSP aleta de ranura del borde de ataque *f*; ~-**in roll** *n* PAPER, PRINT rodillo de entrada *m*; ~-**in tape** *n* PRINT cinta de entrada *f*; ~ **light** *n* WATER TRANSP *navigation* luz de enfilación *f*; ~ **line** *n* WATER TRANSP *navigation* enfilación *f*; ~ **mark** *n* WATER TRANSP *navigation* marca de enfilación *f*; ~ **matter** *n* PRINT texto de cabecera *m*; ~ **note** *n* ACOUST tónica *f*; ~-**on pulley** *n*

MECH ENG polea guía *f*; ~-**out wire** *n* ELEC *circuit* hilo entre el cebo eléctrico y el explosor *m*; ~ **roll** *n* PAPER rodillo conductor *m*, rodillo guía *m*; ~ **wire** *n* MINE hilo conductor entre el cebo eléctrico y el explosor *m* (*AmL*), línea de tiro *f* (*Esp*); ~ **zero** *n* PROD cero a la izquierda *m*

leadless: ~ **chip carrier** *n* ELEC ENG, ELECTRON soporte para chip sin patillas *m*

leaf *n* COMP&DP nodo del árbol *m*, CONST *of T-hinge, strap-hinge, etc* contrabisagra *f*, *of door* hoja *f*, PRINT lámina *f*, PROD *moulder's tool* palustrín de hoja de laurel *m*; ~-**and-pod spot of pea** *n* AGRIC antracnosis del guisante *f*; ~ **axil** *n* AGRIC axila de la hoja *f*; ~ **blade** *n* AGRIC lámina foliar *f*; ~ **blight** *n* AGRIC añublo de la hoja *m*, muerte generalizada de la hoja *f*; ~ **blotch** *n* AGRIC septoriasis de la hoja *f*; ~ **bud** *n* AGRIC yema foliar *f*; ~ **chain** *n* MECH ENG cadena de láminas *f*, serie de láminas *f*; ~ **curl** *n* AGRIC rizamiento foliar *m*; ~-**cutting ant** *n* AGRIC hormiga cortadora *f*; ~ **damage** *n* AGRIC daño foliar *m*; ~ **margin** *n* AGRIC borde de la hoja *m*; ~ **miner** *n* AGRIC mosca minadora *f*; ~ **mold** *AmE*, ~ **mould** *BrE* *n* AGRIC moho de la hoja *m*; ~ **roller** *n* AGRIC enrollador de la hoja *m*; ~ **rust** *n* AGRIC roya de la hoja *f*, roya foliar *f*; ~ **scar** *n* AGRIC cicatriz de la hoja *f*; ~ **scorch** *n* AGRIC quemadura de hoja *f*; ~-**shaped trowel** *n* PROD *moulder's tool* palustrín de hoja de laurel *m*; ~ **sheath** *n* AGRIC vaina foliar *f*; ~ **shutter** *n* PHOTO obturador de hoja *m*; ~ **spot** *n* AGRIC mancha de hoja *f*; ~ **spring** *n* MECH ENG resorte de hojas *m*, resorte de lámina flexible *m*, resorte de planchuela *m*, VEH ballesta de hojas *f*; ~ **stripper** *n* AGRIC deshojador *m*; ~ **tendril** *n* AGRIC zarcillo foliar *m*; ~ **valve** *n* HYDRAUL válvula de charnela *f*; ~ **vein** *n* AGRIC nerviadura foliar *f*

leaflet *n* AGRIC folíolo *m*; ~ **insertor** *n* PACK dispositivo para insertar hojas *m*

leak[1]: ~-**free** *adj* REFRIG estanco; ~-**tight** *adj* MECH a prueba de filtraciones, estanco, hermético, sin fugas

leak[2] *n* C&G fuga *f*, poro *m*, CONST fuga *f*, filtración *f*, ELEC *of current, charge* pérdida *f*, fuga *f*, escape *m*, FUELLESS fuga *f*, GAS escape *m*, fuga *f*, pérdida *f*, PHYS fuga *f*; ~-**before-break criterion** *n* NUCL criterio de fuga antes de rotura *m*; ~ **detection** *n* GAS detección de escapes *f*, detección de fugas *f*, detección de pérdidas *f*; ~ **detector** *n* HEAT, LAB, PACK, SAFE detector de fugas *m*; ~-**free product** *n* PROD producto a prueba de fugas *m*, producto estanco *m*; ~ **light** *n* CINEMAT luz de fuga *f*; ~-**off pressure** *n* PETR TECH presión de leak-off *f*, presión sin pérdidas *f*; ~-**off test** *n* (*LOT*) PETR TECH prueba de integridad de la formación *f*, prueba de leak-off *f*; ~ **rate** *n* NUCL tasa de fugas *f*; ~ **test** *n* CONST, NUCL, REFRIG prueba de fugas *f*; ~ **testing** *n* CONST, NUCL, REFRIG prueba de fugas *f*; ~-**tightness** *n* NUCL estanqueidad *f*; ~ **water** *n* HYDROL, WATER agua de infiltración *f*

leak[3] *vti* CONST filtrar

leak[4] *vi* CONST *allow to escape* dejar escapar el agua, escurrirse, FUELLESS gotear, WATER TRANSP gotear, rezumar, perder

leakage *n* ELEC, ELEC ENG dispersión *f*, escape *m*, fuga *f*, pérdida *f*, FUELLESS escapes *m pl* (*AmL*), fuga *f*, goteo *m*, GAS escape *m*, fuga *f*, pérdida *f*, MAR POLL fuga *f*, PHYS dispersión *f*, fuga *f*, SAFE, TELECOM fuga *f*, WATER *of water* escape *m*, fuga *f*, infiltración *f*; ~ **current** *n* ELEC, ELEC ENG corriente de descarga espontánea *f*, corriente de dispersión *f*, corriente de fuga *f*, TELECOM corriente de fuga *f*; **~ detection** *n* PACK detección de escapes *f*; **~ field** *n* TELECOM campo de fugas *m*; **~ flux** *n* ELEC ENG, PHYS flujo de dispersión *m*; **~ indicator** *n* ELEC, ELEC ENG indicador de defectos de aislamiento *m*, indicador de fugas *m*; **~ indicator system** *n* SAFE sistema indicador de fugas *m*; **~ interception vessel** *n* NUCL vasija de recogida de fugas *f*; **~ loss** *n* ELEC *current* disipación por fuga *f*; **~ meter** *n* INSTR medidor de pérdida *m*; **~ path** *n* ELEC, ELEC ENG camino de fuga *m*, línea de fuga *f*; **~ radiation** *n* ELEC ENG radiación por fugas *f*; **~ resistance** *n* PHYS resistencia de fuga *f*; **~ test** *n* PACK ensayo de fugas *m*; **~ warning** *n* SAFE aviso de fugas *m*; **~ water pump** *n* NUCL bomba de fugas *f*

leaking: **~ fuel assembly** *n* NUCL elemento de combustible con fugas *m*

leaky: **~ capacitor** *n* ELEC ENG condensador con pérdidas *m*; **~ mode** *n* OPT, TELECOM modo con fugas *m*; **~ ray** *n* OPT, TELECOM rayo con fugas *m*

lean[1]: **--burn** *adj* THERMO de quemado escaso, de quemado pobre

lean[2]: **--burn** *n* AUTO combustión pobre *f*, mezcla pobre *f*; **--burn engine** *n* THERMO motor de quemado pobre *m*; **~ coal** *n* COAL, THERMO carbón de gas *m*, carbón magro *m*, hulla magra *f*; **~ concrete** *n* CONST concreto pobre *m* (*AmL*), hormigón pobre *m* (*Esp*); **~ die-out** *n* AIR TRANSP apagado por mezcla pobre *m*; **~ gas** *n* GAS, PETROL, PROD gas pobre *m*; **~ mixture** *n* AIR TRANSP *engine*, VEH mezcla pobre *f*; **--plasticity clay** *n* C&G barro de plasticidad pobre *m*; **--to** *n* CONST tejado de una sola agua *m*; **--to roof** *n* CONST tejadillo *m*

lean[3] *vi* CONST inclinar

leaner *n* C&G botella inclinada *f*

leaning *adj* CONST *out of perpendicular* inclinado

leap *n* CRYSTALL *in a dislocation* salto de falla *m*, GEOL accidente *m*, MINE accidente *m*, salto *m*

leapfrog: **~ test** *n* COMP&DP prueba de fil derecho *f*, prueba selectiva interna por saltos *f*, verificación por saltos *f*

leaping: **~ weir** *n* NUCL vertedero de aguas sobrantes *m*

LEAR *abbr* (*low-energy antiproton ring*) PART PHYS LEAR (*anillo antiprotón de baja energía*)

learning: **~ machine** *n* ELECTRON máquina de aprendizaje *f*; **~ phase** *n* ELECTRON fase de aprendizaje *f*

lease: **~ band** *n* TEXTIL cinta para hacer la cruz *f*; **~ rod** *n* TEXTIL barra para hacer la cruz *f*

leased: **~ line** *n* COMP&DP, TELECOM línea alquilada *f*; **~ line network** *n* COMP&DP red con línea alquilada *f*, red de líneas arrendadas *f*

leasing: **~ reed** *n* TEXTIL peine de la cruz *m*

least[1]: **~ significant** *adj* COMP&DP menos significativo

least[2]: **~ common denominator** *n* MATH mínimo común denominador *m*; **~ common multiple** *n* (*LCM*) COMP&DP, MATH mínimo común múltiplo *m* (*mcm*); **~ significant bit** *n* (*LSB*) COMP&DP, PROD, TELECOM bit de menor significación *m* (*BMS*), bit menos significativo *m* (*BMS*); **~ significant digit** *n* (*LSD*) COMP&DP, MATH, PROD dígito de menor peso *m*, dígito menos significativo *m* (*DMS*); **~ squares method** *n* CRYSTALL, MATH, PHYS método de mínimos cuadrados *m*

leat *n* PROD, WATER canal de derivación *m*, canal de llegada *m*, canal de molino *m*, canal de toma *m*, caz *m*, saetín *m*

leather: **~ apron** *n* SAFE delantal de cuero *m*; **~ bellows** *n pl* PHOTO fuelle de cuero *m*; **~ belt** *n* PROD correa de cuero *f*; **~ belting** *n* PROD correaje de cuero *m*, correas de cuero *f pl*; **~ case** *n* PHOTO estuche de cuero *m*; **~ cutting** *n* PROD venta de cuero al por menor *f*; **~ gasket** *n* PROD empaquetadura de cuero *f*; **~ gauntlets** *n pl* SAFE guanteletas de cuero *f pl*; **--link belting** *n* PROD correaje de cuero articulado *m*, correas de cuero articulado *f pl*; **~ packer** *n* PROD guarnición de cuero *f*, junta de cuero *f*; **~ pulp** *n* PAPER pulpa de cuero *f*

leatherette *n* P&R cuerina *f* (*AmL*), cuero artificial *m* (*Esp*)

leave *n* MILIT permiso *m*

leaven *n* FOOD levadura *f*

leavings *n pl* MINE estériles *m pl*

Leavitt: **~ clippers** *n pl* AGRIC descornador para animales de uno a dos años *m*

Leblanc: **~ connection** *n* ELEC *transformer* conexión Leblanc *f*; **~ process** *n* DETERG proceso de Leblanc *m*

lecithin *n* FOOD lecitina *f*

Leclanch: **~ cell** *n* ELEC ENG elemento Leclanch *m*, LAB *diaphragm* pila Leclanché *f*

LED *abbr* (*light-emitting diode*) GEN DEL (*diodo electroluminiscente, diodo emisor de luz*)

ledeburite *n* METALL ledeburita *f*

ledge *n* CONST *projection* peinazo *m*, retallo *m*, MECH ENG reborde *m*, resalto *m*, saliente *f*

ledger *n* CONST *scaffolding* puente *m*, MINE bordes de filones *m pl* (*Esp*), muro *m* (*AmL*); **~ wall** *n* MINE muro *m* (*AmL*), piso *m*

lee *n* WATER TRANSP socaire *m*, sotavento *m*; **~ canvas** *n* WATER TRANSP *in small yachts* lona antiescora *f*; **~ depression** *n* METEO depresión a sotavento *f*, depresión orográfica *f*; **~ lurch** *n* WATER TRANSP *sailing* bandazo a sotavento *m*; **~ shore** *n* WATER TRANSP *sailing* costa a sotavento *f*

leeboard *n* WATER TRANSP *boat building* gualdera de litera *f*, orza de deriva *f*

leeward[1] *adj* METEO, WATER TRANSP *navigation* de sotavento

leeward[2] *adv* METEO, WATER TRANSP *navigation* a sotavento

leeward[3]: **~ side** *n* METEO, WATER TRANSP lado de sotavento *m*

leeway *n* WATER TRANSP *sailing* abatimiento *m*, ángulo de deriva *m*; **~ track** *n* WATER TRANSP *navigation* derrota indicada por la estela *f*

left[1]: **--handed** *adj* CHEM, PHYS *ring winding* levógiro

left[2]: **--hand circular polarization** *n* (*LHCP*) PHYS, SPACE *communications* polarización circular a izquierda *f*; **--hand page** *n* PAPER, PRINT página izquierda *f*, página par *f*; **--hand rule** *n* ELEC *electromagnetism*, PHYS regla de la mano izquierda *f*; **--hand side** *n* PHYS *coil* primer miembro *m*; **~ justification** *n* COMP&DP, PRINT justificación a la izquierda *f*; **~ margin** *n* PRINT margen izquierdo *m*; **~ shift** *n* COMP&DP desplazamiento a la izquierda *m*; **--turn phase** *n* TRANSP fase de giro a la izquierda *f*; **--turning traffic** *n* TRANSP tráfico de giro a la izquierda *m*

left[3]: **--justify** *vt* COMP&DP, PRINT justificar a la izquierda

leg *n* MECH ENG pata *f*, pie *m*, soporte *m*, sostén *m*, NUCL *diaphragm* ramal *m*, tramo *m*, TELECOM rama

local *f*, WATER TRANSP *tack* bordada *f*, bordo *m*;
~ **vice** *n* BrE PROD tornillo de mesa con pie *m*; ~ **vise**
AmE see leg vice BrE; ~ **wire** *n* MINE alambre del
detonador *m*

Legendre: ~ **polynomial** *n* PHYS polinomio de Legendre *m*

legroom *n* AUTO, TRANSP, VEH espacio para las piernas
m

legume *n* FOOD legumbre *f*; ~ **inoculation** *n* AGRIC
nitrogen fixation inoculación de legumbres *f*

lehr: ~ **assistant** *n* C&G ayudante de templador *m*;
~ **attendant** *n* C&G operador de templador *m*; ~ **belt**
n C&G banda de templador *f*

Leitz: ~ **system** *n* INSTR sistema Leitz *m*

lemon: ~ **chrome** *n* COLOUR cromo limón; ~ **color**
AmE, ~ **colour** *BrE n* COLOUR colorante limón *m*

length *n* GEOM *of a chord*, METR, PAPER *of reel or roll*,
PHYS, TELECOM longitud *f*; ~ **bar** *n* METR barra
longitudinal *f*; ~ **between perpendiculars** *n* WATER
TRANSP *ship design* eslora entre perpendiculares *f*;
~ **of bore** *n* MILIT longitud de ánima *f*; ~ **of channel**
n FUELLESS longitud de canal *f*; ~ **contraction** *n* PHYS
mass contracción de longitud *f*; ~ **gage** *AmE*,
~ **gauge** *BrE n* METR calibrador de longitud *m*;
~ **grader** *n* AGRIC *seed grading* máquina alveolar *f*;
~ **indicator** *n* (*LI*) TELECOM indicador de longitud *m*;
~ **of the interval** *n* METR longitud del intervalo *f*; ~ **of
lay** *n* ELEC *cable component* longitud del cableado *f*;
~ **margin** *n* MECH ENG margen de distancia *m*;
~-**measuring instrument** *n* INSTR, MECH ENG, METR
instrumento de medición de longitudes *m*; ~ **meter**
AmE, ~ **metre** *n* BrE METR metro longitudinal *m*;
~ **overall** *n* MECH ENG *of screw, bolt* longitud cabeza
comprendida *f*, longitud total *f*, WATER TRANSP *boat
building* eslora total *f*; ~ **of page** *n* PRINT longitud de
la página *f*; ~ **of piston stroke** *n* CONST longitud del
paso del pistón *f*; ~ **of step** *n* CONST *stair building*
longitud del paso *f*; ~ **of stroke** *n* MECH ENG *of tool*
carrera del pistón *f*, recorrido de trabajo *m*, NUCL
recorrido *m*; ~ **under head to point** *n* MECH ENG *of
screw, bolt* longitud cabeza no comprendida *f*

lengthening: ~ **bar** *n* MECH ENG *for box spanner*
alargadera *f*; ~ **piece** *n* MECH ENG empalme *m*;
~ **rod** *n* MECH ENG alargadera de sonda *f*, barra de
alargamiento *f*; ~ **tube** *n* MECH ENG alargadera *f*

lengthways *adv* MECH ENG a lo largo, longitudinal-
mente

lengthwise *adv* MECH ENG a lo largo, en sentido
longitudinal

lens[1]: ~-**shaped** *adj* PHOTO lenticular

lens[2] *n* CINEMAT lente *f*, objetivo *m*, HYDROL depósito
m, yacimiento *m*, INSTR, LAB, OPT lente *f*, PHOTO lente
f, objetivo *m*, PHYS lente *f*, PROD cristal *m*, SPACE
communications lente *f*, objetivo *m*; ~ **aerial** *n* BrE (*cf
lens antenna AmE*) SPACE *communications*, TELECOM
antena de lente *f*; ~ **antenna** *n* AmE (*cf lens aerial
BrE*) SPACE *communications*, TELECOM antena de
lente *f*; ~ **aperture** *n* CINEMAT, PHOTO, PHYS, TV
abertura del objetivo *f*; ~ **with aperture
preselector** *n* CINEMAT, OPT, PHOTO objetivo con
preselector de abertura *m*; ~ **barrel** *n* CINEMAT,
PHOTO tubo donde se montan las lentes *m*; ~ **cap** *n*
CINEMAT, PHOTO protector de lente *m*, protector de
objetivo *m*, tapa del objetivo *f*; ~ **case** *n* PHOTO
estuche portaobjetivos *m*; ~ **coating** *n* PHOTO revestimiento del objetivo *m*; ~ **cover slide** *n* PHOTO guía

para el protector del objetivo *f*; ~ **coverage** *n* CINE-
MAT campo de imagen nítida *m*, cobertura del
objetivo *f*; ~ **flange** *n* PHOTO brida del objetivo *f*;
~ **flare** *n* CINEMAT resplandor del objetivo *m*, PHOTO
luz parásita del objetivo *f*; ~ **holder** *n* C&G sostén del
lente *m*; ~ **hood** *n* CINEMAT, PHOTO parasol *m*;
~ **hood bellows** *n* CINEMAT fuelle de parasol *m*;
~ **magnification** *n* INSTR lente de aumento *f*;
~ **mount** *n* PHOTO montura del objetivo *f*, portaobjetivos *m*; ~ **mounting plate** *n* PHOTO placa de montura
del objetivo *f*; ~ **movement** *n* PHOTO movimiento del
objetivo *m*; ~ **panel** *n* INSTR panel lenticular *m*,
PHOTO portaobjetivo *m*; ~ **set** *n* CINEMAT juego de
objetivos *m*; ~ **shutter** *n* CINEMAT, PHOTO obturador
m; ~ **squeeze ratio** *n* CINEMAT relación de compresión de la lente *f*; ~ **stop** *n* CINEMAT, PHOTO abertura
f; ~ **turret** *n* CINEMAT torreta rotativa *f*, OPT porta-
lentes *f*, portaobjetivos giratorio *m*, portaobjetivos
rotativo *m*, torreta portaobjetivos *f*, PRINT portaobjetivos giratorio *m*; ~ **vertex** *n* PHOTO vértice de la
lente *m*

lensing *adj* GEOL lenticular

lenticular[1] *adj* GEOL lenticular

lenticular[2]: ~ **twin** *n* METALL macla lenticular *f*

lenzinite *n* MINERAL lencinita *f*

Lenz: ~**'s law** *n* ELEC *induction*, PHYS ley de Lenz *f*

LEP[1] *abbr* (*large electron-positron collider*) PART PHYS
LEP (*gran cámara de reacción electrón-positrón*)

LEP[2]: ~ **detector** *n* PART PHYS detector LEP *m*

lepidolite *n* MINERAL lepidolita *f*

lepidomelane *n* MINERAL lepidomelana *f*

leptochlorite *n* MINERAL leptoclorita *m*

lepton *n* NUCL, PART PHYS, PHYS leptón *m*; ~ **number** *n*
PHYS número leptónico *m*

less: ~-**than-carload freight** *n* AmE (*cf less-than-
carload goods BrE*) RAIL cargo de vagones incompletos *f*; ~-**than-carload freight shipment** *n* AmE (*cf
less-than-carload goods shipment BrE*) RAIL transporte convagón de carga parcial *f*; ~-**than-carload
goods** *BrEn* (*cf less-than-carload freight AmE*) RAIL
carga de vagones incompletos *f*; ~-**than-carload
goods shipment** *n* BrE (*cf less-than-carload freight
shipment AmE*) RAIL transporte con vagón de carga
parcial *m*

lessening *n* METEO disminución *f*

let: ~-**down** *n* AIR TRANSP descenso *m*; ~-**off motion** *n*
TEXTIL desarrollador de urdimbre *m*

lethal: ~ **concentration** *n* POLL concentración letal *f*,
concentración mortal *f*; ~ **dose** *n* PHYS, POLL dosis
letal *f*, dosis mortal *f*; ~ **effect** *n* POLL efecto letal *m*,
efecto mortal *m*

lethargy *n* RAD PHYS letargia *f*, letargia neutrónica *f*

letter *n* COMP&DP carta *f*, letra *f*, PRINT letra *f*; ~-**press
printing machine** *n* PRINT impresora tipográfica *f*;
~ **quality** *n* (*LQ*) COMP&DP calidad de carta *f* (*LQ*),
calidad de letra *f* (*LQ*), PRINT calidad de letra *f* (*LQ*);
~ **shift** *n* TELECOM cambio a letras *m*; ~ **spacing** *n*
PRINT espaciado entre letras *m*, espacio de la letra *m*

lettercard *n* PAPER aerograma *f*

letterfit *n* PRINT distribución de espacios entre letras *f*

letterhead *n* PRINT membrete de carta *m*

lettering *n* PRINT rotulación *f*; ~ **on bottom** *n* C&G
grabado en fondo *m*

letterpress[1] *adj* PRINT tipográfico

letterpress[2] *n* PRINT tipografía *f*; ~ **printing** *n* PRINT
tipografía *f*

letters: ~ **shift** n COMP&DP desplazamiento de letras m, inversor de letras m, tecla de letras Baudot f
lettsomite n MINERAL lettsomita f
leuchtenbergite n MINERAL leuchtenbergita f
leucite n MINERAL, PETROL leucita f
leuco n COLOUR leuco m; ~ **compound** n CHEM of dye compuesto leuco m
leucocratic adj GEOL leucocrático
leucophane n MINERAL leucófana f
leucopyrite n MINERAL leucopirita f
leucosome n GEOL leucosoma f
leucoxene n MINERAL leucoxeno f
levan n CHEM levana f
levee n GEOL dique m
level[1]: ~ **with the ground** adj CONST a nivel del suelo
level[2] n GEN nivel m; ~ **above threshold** n ACOUST nivel por encima del umbral m; ~ **adjustment** n ELECTRON ajuste de nivel m; ~ **book** n CONST libreta de nivelación f; ~ **control** n PACK control de nivel m; ~ **crossing** n BrE (cf grade crossing AmE) CONST, RAIL paso a nivel m; ~ **cruise** n AIR TRANSP crucero nivelado m; ~ **difference** n ACOUST diferencia de nivel f; ~ **displacement** n NUCL desplazamiento de nivel m; ~ **drop** n MECH ENG caída de nivel f; ~ **dyeing** n COLOUR teñido parejo m, TEXTIL tintura de igualación f; ~ **flight** n AIR TRANSP vuelo horizontal m, vuelo nivelado m; ~ **gage** AmE, ~ **gauge** BrE n HYDROL indicador de nivel m; ~ **holding** n NUCL mantenimiento de nivel m; ~ **in the seam** n MINE galería en capa f; ~ **indicator** n COAL, INSTR, MECH ENG, NUCL indicador de nivel m, RAIL piquete indicador de rasante m, WATER indicador de nivel m; ~ **of intensity** n RAD PHYS nivel de intensidad m; ~ **keel** n WATER TRANSP quilla a nivel f; ~ **magnetic tape** n ACOUST cinta magnética uniforme f; ~ **meter** n CINEMAT, NUCL solids from liquids medidor de nivel m; ~ **recorder** n ACOUST registrador de nivel m; ~ **road** n MINE galería principal f; ~ **sensor** n SPACE sensor de nivel m, sensor de volumen m; ~ **shift** n NUCL desfase de nivel m; ~ **shifting** n ELECTRON defasaje de nivel m, desfase m; ~ **small caps** n pl PRINT versalitas f pl; ~ **switch** n PROD interruptor de nivel m; ~ **terrace** n AGRIC terraza a nivel f
level[3] vt AGRIC aplanar, CINEMAT, CONST surveying nivelar, MECH aplanar, emparejar, igualar, nivelar, PROD nivelar; ~ **out** vt AIR TRANSP nivelar
level[4]: **on a ~ with the water** phr WATER a flor del agua, a nivel del agua
leveled AmE see levelled BrE
leveling AmE see levelling BrE
levelled adj BrE CONST nivelado
levelling n BrE CONST nivelación f, surveying explanación f, ELECTRON nivelación f, MECH enrase m, enrasamiento m, nivelación f, igualación f, explanación f, PROD enrasamiento m, igualación f, explanación f, nivelación f, enrase m; ~ **agent** n BrE CHEM, TEXTIL agente igualador m; ~ **alidade** n BrE CONST, INSTR alidada de nivelación f; ~ **amplifier** n BrE ELECTRON amplificador de nivelación m; ~ **compass** n BrE CONST compás de nivelación m; ~ **harrow** n BrE AGRIC grada niveladora f; ~ **instrument** n BrE CONST equipo de nivelación m; ~ **machine** n BrE CONST public works explanadora f, aplanadora f; ~ **mark** n BrE AIR TRANSP marca de nivelación f; ~ **motor** n BrE CONST motoniveladora f, motor nivelador m; ~ **point** n BrE CONST punto de

nivelación m; ~ **pole** n BrE CONST surveying mira de nivelación f; ~ **rod** n BrE CONST surveying mira de nivelación m; ~ **screw** n BrE INSTR tornillo de nivelado m, tornillo nivelante m, MECH ENG tornillo de nivelado m, tornillo nivelador m, tornillo nivelante m; ~ **staff** n BrE CONST surveying personal de topografía m; ~ **unit** n BrE AIR TRANSP unidad de nivelación f
levelness n PROD horizontalidad f, nivel m, planeidad f, regularidad f, regularidad de superficie f
lever[1] n AIR TRANSP helicopter brazo m, palanca f, ELEC ENG dispositivo de apoyo m, palanca f, MECH ENG manecilla f, barra f, brazo m, palanca f, balancín m, PHYS heat unit palanca f, brazo m, VEH palanca f; ~ **arm** n CONST, MECH ENG brazo de palanca m; ~ **balance** n MECH ENG romana f; ~ **brake** n MECH ENG freno de palanca m; ~ **commutator switch** n ELEC conmutador de palanca m; ~ **draft machine** AmE, ~ **draught machine** BrE n PROD founding desmoldeadora de palanca f, máquina de desmoldear de palanca f; ~ **escapement** n MECH ENG ratchet mechanism escape de áncora m; ~ **feed** n MECH ENG avance por palanca m, presión con palanca f; ~**-feed drilling machine** n MECH ENG máquina de taladrar con avance manual por palanca f; ~ **of the first kind** n MECH ENG palanca de primer orden f, palanca de primer tipo f; ~ **grip tongs** n pl PROD tenazas articuladas para manejar sillares f pl; ~ **handle** n CONST of a shop door latch mango de palanca m; ~ **jack** n PROD gato de palanca m; ~ **lid** n PACK tapa de balancín f; ~ **on-off switch** n ELEC conmutador de palanca de conexión y desconexión m; ~ **press** n MECH ENG prensa de palanca f; ~ **punching machine** n PROD punzonadora de palanca f; ~ **punching-and-shearing machine** n PROD tijera punzonadora y azalladora de palanca f; ~ **ratchet motion** n MECH ENG mecanismo de trinquete de palanca m; ~ **ring** n PACK aro de balancín m; ~ **scales** n pl MECH ENG romana f; ~ **of the second kind** n MECH ENG palanca de segundo orden f, palanca de segundo tipo f; ~**-shearing machine with counterweight** n PROD máquina tijera de palanca con contrapeso f; ~ **switch** n ELEC ENG interruptor de palanca m, NUCL maneta f, manivela f; ~ **of the third kind** n MECH ENG palanca de tercer orden f, palanca de tercer tipo f; ~ **valve** n HYDRAUL válvula de palanca f; ~ **weir** n WATER vertedero de palanca m
lever[2] vt MECH ENG accionar con palanca, apalancar, levantar con palanca, palanquear; ~ **up** vt MECH ENG apalancar, levantar con palanca
leverage n CONST brazo de palanca m, MECH ENG brazo de palanca m, efecto de palanca m, juego de palancas m, sistema de palancas m, tren de palancas m; ~ **of a force** n MECH ENG brazo de fuerza m
levigation n PROD levigación f
levitation n PHYS, SPACE, TRANSP levitación f; ~ **by permanent magnets** n PHYS, TRANSP levitación por imanes permanentes f
levorotatory AmE see laevorotatory BrE
levulin n CHEM levulina f
levulinic adj CHEM levulínico
levulose AmE see laevulose BrE
levyne n MINERAL levyna f
levynite n MINERAL levynita f
lexical: ~ **access** n COMP&DP, TELECOM acceso léxico m; ~ **analysis** n COMP&DP análisis léxico m

lexicographic: ~ **order** n COMP&DP orden lexicográfico m
ley n AGRIC forage pastura de rotación f
Leyden: ~ **jar** n ELEC ENG botella de Leyden f
LF abbr COMP&DP (line feed) alimentación interlineal f, avance de línea m, espacio interlineal m, salto de línea m, ELEC, ELEC ENG, ELECTRON, PHYS (low frequency) BF (baja frecuencia), PRINT (line feed) avance de línea m, RAD PHYS, TELECOM, WAVE PHYS (low frequency) BF (baja frecuencia)
LFA abbr (loss of frame alignment) TELECOM pérdida de alineación de cuadros f
LFC abbr (local function capabilities) TELECOM capacidad de las funciones locales f
LGB abbr (laser-guided bomb) MILIT bomba guiada por láser f
LHC abbr (large hadron collider) PART PHYS LHC (gran cámara de reacción para hadrones)
LHCP abbr (left-hand circular polarization) PHYS, SPACE polarización circular a izquierdas f
L-head: ~ **engine** n AUTO motor de culata en L m
LI abbr (length indicator) TELECOM indicador de longitud m
Li abbr (lithium) CHEM, ELEC ENG Li (litio)
liability n MAR POLL responsabilidad f
liberate vt PHYS of compound liberar
liberation n CHEM liberación f
libethenite n MINERAL libethenita f
librarian: ~ **program** n COMP&DP programa bibliotecario m
library: ~ **automation** n COMP&DP automatización de biblioteca f, informatización de biblioteca f; ~ **program** n COMP&DP programa de biblioteca m
licareol n CHEM licareol m
licence n BrE PETR TECH concesión f, licencia f, QUALITY licencia f; ~ **block** n BrE PETR TECH autorización f
license AmE see licence BrE
Lichtenberg: ~ **figure** n PHYS, WAVE PHYS figura de Lichtenberg f
lick: ~**-up** n PAPER fieltro arrancador m; ~**-up overfelt** n PAPER fieltro separador superior m
licker n MECH ENG lubrication lubricador automático m
licking: ~ **block** n AGRIC piedra de sal f
lid n LAB, MECH cubierta f, tapa f, MINE cuña de madera f, PACK, POLL tapa f; ~**-sealing compound** n PACK material empleado para sellar la tapa m
lidar n OPT, SPACE lidar
lie[1]: ~ **of the land** n CONST trazado del terreno m
lie[2]: ~ **alongside** vi WATER TRANSP abarloarse; ~ **idle** vi MECH ENG estar parado, estar paralizado
lie[3]: ~ **at anchor** phr WATER TRANSP estar al ancla
lieberenite n MINERAL lieberenita f, nefelina meteorizada f, ilvaita f, ilvaíta f
lievrite n MINERAL lievrita f
life n MECH ENG duración f, existencia f, vida f, vida útil f, MINE longevidad f, vida de la explotación f (Esp), QUALITY vida f; ~**-cycle cost** n QUALITY costo de operación y de mantenimiento m; ~ **expectancy** n CONST, TELECOM esperanza de vida f; ~ **jacket** n AIR TRANSP, SAFE, WATER TRANSP chaleco salvavidas m; ~**-load curve** n PROD curva duración-carga f; ~ **preserver** n AIR TRANSP chaleco salvavidas m, CONST derrick protector m, SAFE chaleco salvavidas m; ~ **raft** n SAFE, WATER TRANSP emergency balsa

salvavidas f; ~**-saving apparatus** n SAFE, WATER TRANSP aparato salvavidas m, artefacto de salvamento m, equipo salvavidas m; ~ **support system** n OCEAN sistema de supervivencia m, SAFE, SPACE sistema de apoyo a la vida m; ~ **support technician** n OCEAN técnico en supervivencia m; ~ **table** n MATH tabla de mortalidad f; ~ **test** n ELEC ENG ensayo de duración m
lifebelt n SAFE, WATER TRANSP chaleco salvavidas m
lifeboat n AIR TRANSP, SAFE, WATER TRANSP bote de rescate m, bote salvavidas m; ~ **station** n SAFE, WATER TRANSP on board puesto de embarque en los botes salvavidas m, on land estación del servicio de salvamento de náufragos f
lifeboatman n SAFE, WATER TRANSP marinero de bote salvavidas m, marinero de embarcación de salvamento m
lifebuoy n SAFE, WATER TRANSP aro salvavidas m
lifeline n SAFE, WATER TRANSP cabo salvavidas m
lifetime n ELEC ENG duración f, vida útil f, MINE longevidad f, vida de la explotación f, PART PHYS vida media f, PHYS duración de vida f, mass longevidad f, SPACE spacecraft vida f, TELECOM duración de vida f; ~ **expectancy** n TELECOM esperanza de vida f
LIFO abbr (last-in-first-out) COMP&DP, PROD LIFO (último en entrar, primero en salir)
lift[1] n BrE (cf elevator AmE) AGRIC montacargas m, AIR TRANSP elevación f, sustentación f, CONST for goods elevador m, montacargas m, ascensor m, transportador vertical m, piling block elevación f, FUELLESS sustentación f, HYDRAUL carrera f, HYDROL diferencia de niveles f, MECH for goods transportador vertical m, elevador m, montacargas m, ascensor m, MECH ENG of cone, of cone pulley escalón m, MINE set of pumps tren de bombas de mina m, thickness of ore altura de extracción f, dispositivos para levantar grandes pesos m pl, section of mine escalón m (AmL), NUCL movimiento en sentido de apertura m, extracción f, apertura f, PHYS fuerza ascensional f, elevación f, WATER altura de elevación f, altura de impulsión f; ~**-and-force pump** n WATER bomba aspirante-impelente f; ~ **bridge** n TRANSP puente levadizo m; ~ **center** AmE, ~ **centre** BrE n AIR TRANSP centro de sustentación m; ~ **coefficient** n AIR TRANSP aerodynamics, FUELLESS, PHYS coeficiente de sustentación m; ~ **component** n AIR TRANSP componente de sustentación m; ~ **curve slope** n AIR TRANSP pendiente de la curva de sustentación f; ~**-drag ratio** n (L-D ratio) AIR TRANSP coeficiente de rendimiento aerodinámico m, aircraft efficiency coeficiente de planeo m, PHYS rendimiento aerodinámico m, WATER TRANSP naval architecture rendimiento hidrodinámico m; ~ **drive** n MECH ENG mecanismo de trasmisión vertical m; ~ **effect** n WATER TRANSP naval architecture efecto de sustentación m; ~ **fan** n TRANSP hélice elevadora f, soplante para despegue vertical m; ~ **gate** n AUTO puerta elevadiza f, puerta trasera f, CONST puerta levadiza f; ~ **gripper** n NUCL of control rod drive mechanism trinquete de elevación m; ~ **latch** n CONST pestillo vertical m; ~ **lock** n WATER esclusa elevadora f; ~ **magnet** n TRANSP imán elevador m; ~**-on/lift-off vessel** n WATER TRANSP buque de transbordo vertical m, buque de transbordo vertical por izada m; ~ **on-off ship** n TRANSP barco reflotador m; ~ **on-off system** n

TRANSP sistema de reflote *m*, sistema para transporte de mercancías *m*; ~ **pipe** *n* CONST tubería elevada *f*; ~ **piston** *n* PROD pistón elevador *m*; ~**-pull-and-push jack and cramp** *n* MECH ENG jack conmutador en contrafase *m*; ~ **pump** *n* HYDRAUL, WATER bomba impelente *f*; ~ **shaft** *n* AIR TRANSP eje de elevación *m*; ~**-to-drag ratio** *n* FUELLESS fineza *f*, rendimiento aerodinámico *m*; ~ **truck** *n* PACK carretilla elevadora *f*; ~**-type device** *n* FUELLESS dispositivo de elevación vertical *m*; ~**-up furnace** *n* HEAT horno elevado *m*; ~**-up table** *n* MECH ENG mesa de costados abatibles *f*, mesa de faldón *f*; ~ **valve** *n* HYDRAUL válvula de movimiento vertical *f*; ~ **wall** *n* WATER *of canal lock* muro de caída *m*

lift[2] *vt* MECH alzar, elevar, levantar, subir, transportar; ~ **incorrectly** *vt* SAFE levantar incorrectamente

lifted: ~ **load** *n* AIR TRANSP carga levantada *f*

lifter *n* AGRIC elevador-arrancador *m*, CONST elevador *m*, MECH ENG elevador *m*, leva *f*, MINE barreno de pie *m*, elevador *m*, PROD *foundry* tenazas *f pl*, *mould making* clavo de moldeador *m*, espátula de ganchos *f*; ~ **hole** *n* MINE barreno para desprender trozos secundarios de la cara del frente *m* (*AmL*), saneo de frentes *m* (*Esp*); ~ **windrower** *n* AGRIC arrancadora-hileradora *f*

lifting *n* MECH ENG, MINE, TRANSP alza *f*, elevación *f*, izada *f*, levantamiento *m*; ~ **accident** *n* SAFE accidente al levantar algo *m*; ~ **apparatus** *n* MECH ENG aparato de elevación *m*, aparato para elevar *m*; ~ **bag** *n* AIR TRANSP bolsa elevadora *f*; ~ **beam** *n* PROD *founding* balancín *m*, vigueta de izada de pesos *f*; ~ **bow** *n* CONST *of hoisting-bucket* asa para elevación *f*; ~ **bridge** *n* CONST, WATER TRANSP *locks, inland waterways* puente levadizo *m*; ~ **capacity with hook** *n* NUCL capacidad de izado del gancho *f*; ~ **chain** *n* CONST *of pulley block or hoist* cadena para levantar *f*, PROD *tackles* cadena de elevación de pesos *f*, cadena de carga *f*, SAFE cadena para izar *f*, cadena para levantar *f*; ~ **dog** *n* MINE gancho de elevación *m*, llave de suspensión *f*; ~ **equipment** *n* MECH ENG equipo para elevar *m*; ~ **eye** *n* WATER TRANSP *deck fitting* argolla de izada *f*, cáncamo de maniobra *m*; ~ **eyebolt** *n* MECH ENG cáncamo para izar *m*; ~ **force** *n* PHYS fuerza ascensional *f*, fuerza sustentadora *f*; ~ **gear** *n* CONST cambio de elevación *m*, MECH mecanismo elevador *m*, MECH ENG aparato de extracción *m*, mecanismo elevador *m*, PROD aparato de extracción *m*, RAIL mecanismo elevador *m*, SAFE aparatos para izar *m pl*, aparatos para levantar *m pl*; ~ **hook** *n* CONST, MECH ENG gancho de alza *m*, gancho de izar *m*, gancho de suspensión *m*, gancho para levantar *m*; ~ **injector** *n* MECH ENG inyector aspirador *m*, inyector aspirante *m*; ~ **jack** *n* MECH ENG *for replacing bogies* cric para elevar pesos *m*, gato de palanca *m*, gato mecánico *m*, *rack-type* gato *m*, *screw-type* gato de rosca *m*; ~ **lug** *n* CONST orejeta para izar *f*, MECH ENG agarradera *f*, orejeta para izar *f*; ~ **machinery** *n* MECH ENG máquinas elevadoras *f pl*; ~ **magnet** *n* ELEC, MECH ENG electroimán de elevación *m*, electroimán de suspensión *m*, electroimán elevador *m*, electroimán levantador *m*, electroimán portador *m*; ~ **piston** *n* PROD pistón elevador *m*; ~ **platform** *n* AIR TRANSP plataforma de elevación *f*; ~ **point** *n* MINE parte del cable unido a la polea del castillete *f*; ~ **power** *n* MECH ENG capacidad de levantamiento *f*, fuerza de sostén *f*, fuerza

elevadora *f*, poder portante *m*, TRANSP fuerza ascensional *f*, fuerza elevadora *f*; ~ **pressure** *n* TRANSP presión ascensional *f*; ~ **rod** *n* HYDRAUL vástago elevador *m*; ~ **rotor** *n* AIR TRANSP *of helicopter* rotor de elevación *m*; ~ **screw** *n* MECH ENG cric *m*, gato *m*, gato de tornillo *m*; ~ **shaft** *n* MECH ENG *link gear* eje de cambio *m*, eje de marcha *m*; ~ **table** *n* PROD *of rolling mill* mesa elevadora *f*; ~ **tackle** *n* MECH ENG aparato de izar *m*, aparejo para elevar *m*, aparejo para levantar *m*, PROD aparato de izar *m*, SAFE aparato de izar *m*, aparato para levantar *m*, WATER TRANSP aparejo de amantillo *m*; ~ **truck** *n* MECH camioneta montacargas *f*, carretilla de alzamiento *f*; ~ **valve** *n* HYDRAUL válvula de movimiento vertical *f*; ~ **vehicle** *n* PACK vehículo elevador *m*; ~ **wheel** *n* MECH ENG rueda elevadora *f*

liftoff *n* CONST *aviation* despegue vertical *m*, SPACE despegue *m*; ~ **speed** *n* AIR TRANSP velocidad de despegue *f*, velocidad de elevación *f*; ~ **weight** *n* SPACE peso de despegue *m*

ligand *n* CHEM ligando *m*, METALL grupo coordinador *m*; ~ **field theory** *n* CHEM *of compounds* teoría del campo de ligandos *f*

ligature *n* PRINT letras enlazadas *f pl*

light[1] *adj* MECH ENG en vacío, ligero, liviano; ~**-colored** *AmE*, ~**-coloured** *BrE adj* GEOL claro; ~**-duty** *adj* DETERG para servicio ligero; ~**-fast** *adj* COLOUR resistente a la luz; ~**-negative** *adj* PHOTO fotorresistente; ~**-positive** *adj* ELEC, ELECTRON, OPT, PHOTO, PHYS, TELECOM fotoconductor; ~**-running** *adj* MECH ENG de marcha de máquina aislada, de marcha en vacío; ~**-sensitive** *adj* C&G, CINEMAT, COLOUR, ELECTRON, PHOTO, PHYS, PRINT fotosensible; ~**-struck** *adj* CINEMAT velado por la luz; ~**-tight** *adj* CINEMAT hermético a la luz, opaco

light[2] *n* OPT, PHOTO, PHYS luz *f*, PRINT luz actínica *f*, VEH, WATER TRANSP luz *f*; ~**-activated silicon-controlled rectifier** *n* ELEC ENG rectificador controlado de silicio activado a la luz *m*; ~ **air defence gun** *BrE*, ~ **air defense gun** *AmE n* MILIT cañón antiaéreo de pequeño calibre *m*; ~ **airs** *n pl* METEO, WATER TRANSP ventolinas *f pl*; ~ **alloy** *n* MECH, METALL aleación liviana *f*; ~ **amplification by stimulated emission of radiation** *n* (*LASER*) ELECTRON, RAD PHYS, WAVE PHYS amplificación de la luz por estímulo en la emisión de radiaciones *f* (*LASER*); ~ **amplifier** *n* ELECTRON amplificador de luz *m*; ~ **anti-armor weapon** *AmE*, ~ **anti-armour weapon** *BrE n* (*LAW*) MILIT, NUCL arma de pequeño calibre contra blindaje *f*; ~ **anti-tank gun** *n* MILIT cañón anticarro de pequeño calibre *m*; ~ **armament** *n* MILIT armamento de pequeño calibre *m*; ~ **artillery** *n* MILIT artillería de pequeño calibre *f*; ~**-balancing filter** *n* CINEMAT filtro fotoequilibrante *m*; ~ **beam** *n* CINEMAT, ELECTRON, OPT, PHOTO, PHYS, TELECOM haz luminoso *m*; ~**-beam galvanometer** *n* RAD PHYS galvanómetro de haz luminoso *m*; ~**-bodied ink** *n* PRINT tinta de baja densidad *f*; ~ **box** *n* CINEMAT cajetín de iluminación *m*, PHOTO caja de luz *f* (*Esp*), cajeta de iluminación *f* (*AmL*), mesa de luz *f* (*Esp*), negatoscopio *m* (*Esp*); ~ **breeze** *n* METEO brisa ligera *f*, brisa muy débil *f*; ~ **buoy** *n* WATER TRANSP *navigation marks* boya luminosa *f*; ~ **cable** *n* ELEC ENG cable luminoso *m*; ~ **center** *AmE*, ~ **centre** *BrE n* CINEMAT centro de iluminación *m*; ~ **chopper**

n ELECTRON interruptor de luz *m*; ~ **crown** *n* C&G corona delgada *f*; ~ **crude** *n* PETR TECH crudo ligero *m*; ~ **crude oil** *n* PETR TECH petróleo ligero *m*; ~ **current** *n* OPT, TELECOM corriente luminosa *f*; ~ **detection and ranging** *n* METEO, SPACE radar por radiación óptica *m*; ~ **detector** *n* RAD PHYS fotodetector *m*, TELECOM detector luminoso *m*; ~ **displacement** *n* WATER TRANSP *of a ship* desplazamiento en rosca *m*, *yacht* desplazamiento ligero *m*; ~ **distillates** *n pl* CHEM, PETR TECH destilados ligeros *m pl*; ~ **dues** *n pl* WATER TRANSP *navigation* derechos de faros y balizas *m pl*; ~**-emitting diode** *n* (*LED*) GEN diodo electroluminiscente *m* (*DEL*), diodo emisor de luz *m* (*DEL*); ~ **energy** *n* RAD PHYS energía de la luz *f*; ~ **engine** *n* RAIL locomotora ligera *f*; ~ **engineering** *n* MECH ENG ingeniería lumínica *f*; ~ **exposure** *n* PHYS exposición luminosa *f*; ~ **face** *n* PRINT tipo de letra fino *m*; ~ **fastness** *n* P&R resistencia a cambiar de color por acción de la luz *f*; ~ **filter** *n* INSTR, PRINT filtro de luz *m*; ~ **fishing** *n* OCEAN pesca liviana *f*; ~ **fitting** *n* ELEC ENG adecuación de iluminación *f*; ~ **fractions** *n pl* PETR TECH fracciones ligeras *f pl*; ~ **gasoline** *n* AmE (*cf light petrol BrE*) AUTO, PETROL, VEH gasolina ligera *f*; ~ **guide** *n* PHYS guía luminosa *f*; ~ **gun** *n* COMP&DP pincel luminoso *m*; ~ **hydrocarbon fractions** *n pl* PETR TECH fracciones de hidrocarburos ligeras *f pl*; ~ **loading** *n* ELEC ENG carga para alumbrado *f*; ~ **locomotive** *n* RAIL locomotora ligera *f*; ~ **lorry** *n* BrE (*cf light truck AmE*) AUTO camioneta *f*, camión ligero *m*; ~ **meson spectrum** *n* RAD PHYS espectro de mesones ligeros *m*; ~ **meter** *n* CINEMAT, PHOTO, PHYS fotómetro *m*; ~ **-meter cell** *n* PHOTO célula del fotómetro *f*; ~ **-meter probe** *n* PHOTO sonda del fotómetro *f*; ~ **-meter scale** *n* PHOTO escala del fotómetro *f*; ~ **microscopy** *n* METALL microscopia óptica *f*; ~ **modulation** *n* ACOUST, ELECTRON modulación de la luz *f*; ~ **modulator** *n* ACOUST, ELECTRON modulador de luz *m*; ~ **motorcycle with kickstarter** *n* AUTO motocicleta ligera con arranque a pedal *f*; ~ **multi-role helicopter** *n* AIR TRANSP helicóptero ligero multimisión *m*; ~ **observation helicopter** *n* AIR TRANSP helicóptero de observación ligero *m*; ~ **output** *n* PHOTO potencia luminosa *f*; ~ **panel** *n* C&G panel de luz *m*, panel delgado *m*; ~ **pen** *n* COMP&DP, PHYS, TV lápiz fotosensible *m*, lápiz luminoso *m*; ~ **pen detection** *n* COMP&DP detección mediante lápiz fotosensible *f*; ~ **petrol** *n* BrE (*cf light gasoline AmE*) AUTO, PETROL, VEH gasolina ligera *f*; ~ **pipe** *n* ELEC ENG tubo luminoso *m*; ~ **pulse** *n* ELECTRON impulso luminoso *m*; ~**-rail motor tractor** *n* RAIL mototractor de vía estrecha *m*; ~ **rail transit** *n* AmE (*cf light rail transport BrE*) transporte por ferrocarril de vía estrecha *m*; ~ **rail transport** *BrE n* (*cf light rail transit AmE*) RAIL transporte por ferrocarril de vía estrecha *m*; ~ **railroad** *n* AmE (*cf light railway BrE*) RAIL ferrocarril de vía estrecha *m*; ~ **railway** *BrE n* (*cf light railroad AmE*) RAIL ferrocarril de vía estrecha *m*; ~ **ray** *n* CINEMAT, OPT, PHYS rayo luminoso *m*; ~ **scale switch** *n* PHOTO botón de escala luminosa *m*; ~ **section microscope** *n* INSTR microscopio de sección iluminada *m*; ~ **section tube** *n* INSTR tubo de sección iluminada *m*; ~**-sensitive plate** *n* PRINT plancha sensible a la luz *f*; ~ **sensor** *n* ELECTRON sensor luminoso *m*, PROD detector de luz *m*; ~ **setting**

PRINT composición fotográfica *f*; ~ **shade** *n* TEXTIL tono claro *m*; ~ **ship** *n* WATER TRANSP *cargo* buque en rosca *m*; ~ **signal** *n* ELECTRON, RAIL señal luminosa *f*; ~ **softener** *n* CINEMAT suavizador de la luz *m*; ~ **source** *n* ELECTRON fuente de luz *f*; ~ **spectrum** *n* WAVE PHYS espectro de luz *m*; ~ **spot** *n* ELECTRON mancha luminosa *f*, punto luminoso *m*; ~ **spot galvanometer** *n* INSTR galvanómetro de punto explorador *m*, galvanómetro de punto luminoso *m*, galvanómetro de punto móvil *m*; ~ **switch** *n* ELEC interruptor de luz *m*; ~ **table** *n* CINEMAT mesa de control de iluminación *f*; ~ **tone** *n* COLOUR tono claro *m*; ~ **trap** *n* CINEMAT trampa de luz *f*; ~ **truck** *n* AmE (*cf light lorry BrE*) AUTO camioneta *f*, camión ligero *m*; ~ **value** *n* PHOTO valor luminoso *m*; ~ **value setting ring** *n* CINEMAT, PHOTO anillo de ajuste del valor luminoso *m*; ~ **valve** *n* CINEMAT relé óptico *m*, válvula de haz de luz *f*; ~ **vessel** *n* WATER TRANSP buque faro *m*, buque vacío *m*; ~ **wall socket** *n* ELEC *lighting* enchufe mural de luz *m*; ~**-water hybrid reactor** *n* (*LWHR*) NUCL reactor híbrido de agua ligera *m* (*Esp*), reactor híbrido de agua liviana *m* (*AmL*); ~**-water-cooled reactor** *n* NUCL reactor refrigerado por agua ligera *m* (*Esp*), reactor refrigerado por agua liviana *m* (*AmL*); ~ **waterline** *n* WATER TRANSP flotación sin carga *f*; ~ **wave** *n* ELECTRON onda de luz *f*, WAVE PHYS onda luminosa *f*; ~ **weather** *n* METEO, WATER TRANSP tiempo de ventolinas y brisas ligeras *m*; ~ **weight paper** *n* PAPER papel de bajo gramaje *m*; ~ **weld** *n* NUCL soldadura ligera *f*; ~ **year** *n* PHYS año luz *m*

lightening *n* MAR POLL aligeramiento *m*; ~ **hole** *n* AIR TRANSP, MECH agujero de aligeramiento *m*, orificio de aligeramiento *m*

lighter *n* HEAT ENG encendedor *m*, PETROL, TRANSP, WATER TRANSP gabarra *f*; ~ **aboard ship** *n* (*LASH*) WATER TRANSP buque para transporte de barcazas *m*; ~ **aboard ship carrier** *n* (*LASH carrier*) TRANSP buque portagabarras *m*; ~ **carrier** *n* TRANSP buque remolcador de gabarras *m*

lighterage *n* WATER TRANSP transporte en gabarras *m*; ~ **charges** *n pl* WATER TRANSP derechos de alijo *m pl*

lightering *n* MAR POLL alijo *m*; ~ **vessel** *n* MAR POLL embarcación de descarga *f*

lighterman *n* WATER TRANSP gabarrero *m*

lighthouse *n* WATER TRANSP faro *m*; ~ **keeper** *n* WATER TRANSP farero *m*

lighting *n* CINEMAT, ELECTRON iluminación *f*; ~ **cable** *n* ELECTRON cable de iluminación *m*; ~ **cameraman** *n* CINEMAT, PHOTO, TV iluminador *m*; ~ **circuit** *n* ELEC circuito de alumbrado *m*; ~ **console** *n* CINEMAT consola de iluminación *f*; ~ **contrast** *n* CINEMAT contraste luminoso *m*; ~ **effect** *n* CINEMAT efecto de iluminación *m*; ~ **efficiency** *n* AIR TRANSP *helicopter* eficacia de la iluminación *f*; ~ **engineer** *n* CINEMAT, OPT luminotécnico *f*; ~ **equipment** *n* PHOTO equipo de iluminación *m*; ~ **ratio** *n* CINEMAT relación de iluminación *f*; ~ **stand** *n* PHOTO soporte para iluminación *m*; ~ **system** *n* ELEC ENG sistema de descarga eléctrica *m*, sistema de iluminación *m*, SPACE sistema de alumbrado *m*; ~ **and vision control room** *n* TV sala de control de luz e imagen *f*

lightly: ~**-doped semiconductor** *n* ELECTRON semiconductor ligeramente alterado *m*

lightness *n* PRINT claridad *f*

lightning[1]: **~-resistant** *adj* ELEC ENG resistente a descarga eléctrica

lightning[2] *n* ELEC rayo *m*, relampagueo *m*, relámpago *m*, ELEC ENG relampagueo *m*, METEO relámpago *m*; **~ arrester** *n* ELEC, ELEC ENG, GEOPHYS, SAFE, SPACE, WATER TRANSP *deck fitting* pararrayos *m*; **~ arrester for high voltage** *n* SAFE pararrayos de alto voltaje *m*; **~ brace** *n* MECH ENG plataforma del pararrayos *f*, tensores del pararrayos *m pl*; **~ conductor** *n* ELEC ENG cable conductor del rayo *m*, GEOPHYS pararrayos atmosférico *m*, SAFE material conductor de descargas eléctricas *m*; **~ conductor material** *n* SAFE material conductor de descargas eléctricas *m*; **~ current** *n* ELEC ENG corriente del relámpago *f*; **~ discharge** *n* ELEC, ELEC ENG descarga del rayo *f*, descarga eléctrica *f*; **~ flash counter** *n* GEOPHYS contador de relámpagos *m*; **~ path** *n* ELEC trayectoria de un rayo *f*; **~-proof transformer** *n* ELEC, ELEC ENG transformador a prueba de descargas atmosféricas *m*, transformador a prueba de rayos *m*; **~ protection** *n* ELEC ENG, GEOPHYS protección contra descarga eléctrica *f*, protección contra rayos *f*; **~ protection and earthing installation** *n* BrE (*cf lightning protection and grounding installation AmE*) SAFE instalación contra rayos e instalación de tierras *f*, instalación de pararrayos y puesta a tierra *f*; **~ protection fuse** *n* GEOPHYS, MECH ENG fusible de protección contra rayos *m*; **~ protection and grounding installation** *n* AmE (*cf lightning protection and earthing installation BrE*) SAFE instalación contra rayos e instalación de tierras *f*, instalación de pararrayos y puesta a tierra *f*; **~ protector** *n* SAFE pararrayos *m*; **~-resistant power line** *n* ELEC *supply* línea de alimentación resistente a los rayos *f*, línea eléctrica resistente a los rayos *f*; **~ rod** *n* ELEC *safety* barra pararrayos *f*, pararrayos de barra *m*, ELEC ENG varilla de pararrayos *f*, GEOPHYS varilla de pararrayos *f*, asta de pararrayos *f*, SAFE barra pararrayos *f*, pararrayos *m*; **~ strike** *n* METEO rayo *m*; **~ stroke** *n* ELEC rayo *m*; **~ surge** *n* ELEC *in conductor, equipment*, GEOPHYS sobretensión inducida por el rayo *f*, sobretensión por descarga atmosférica *f*; **~ surge arrester** *n* GEOPHYS pararrayos *m*

lightproof *adj* PACK protegido contra la luz

lightship *n* WATER TRANSP *navigation marks* buque faro *m*, buque vacío *m*

lightweight[1] *adj* MECH liviano

lightweight[2]: **~ apparel fabric** *n* TEXTIL tejido ligero para prendas *m*; **~ concrete** *n* CONST concreto ligero *m* (*AmL*), hormigón ligero *m* (*Esp*); **~ furnishing fabric** *n* TEXTIL tejido ligero para tapicería *m*; **~ honeycomb structure** *n* PACK estructura tipo panal de bajo peso *f*

lignan *n* CHEM lignana *f*

ligneous *adj* PAPER leñoso

lignin *n* CHEM, P&R lignina *f*

lignite *n* COAL, GEOL, MINERAL, PETROL, THERMO lignito *m*

lignum: **~ vitae** *n* MECH, WATER TRANSP guayacán *m*

ligroin *n* CHEM bencina *f*, ligroína *f*

ligurite *n* MINERAL ligurita *f*

like: **~ charges** *n pl* ELEC, PHYS cargas de igual polaridad *f pl*, cargas del mismo signo *f pl*, cargas iguales *f pl*; **~ poles** *n pl* ELEC *magnetism*, PHYS polos del mismo nombre *m pl*, polos semejantes *m pl*

likelihood *n* COMP&DP, MATH *statistics* probabilidad *f*, verosimilitud *f*

limb *n* GEOL flanco *m*, labio *m*, MATH *under a load* borde *m*, limbo *m*; **~ top** *n* INSTR cúspide del limbo *f*

limber: **~ hole** *n* WATER TRANSP *shipbuilding* groera *f*, imbornal *m*

lime *n* CHEM, COAL cal viva *f*, CONST, FOOD cal *f*; **~ burning** *n* PROD cocción de cal *f*; **~-burning industry** *n* PROD industria de la cocción de cal *f*; **~ defecation** *n* FOOD defecación de cal *f*; **~ harmotome** *n* GEOL, MINERAL harmotoma cálcico *m*; **~ kiln** *n* HEAT, PROD horno de cal *m*; **~ mortar** *n* PROD mortero de cal *m*; **~ mud** *n* PETR TECH lodo con cal *m*; **~ mudrock** *n* GEOL lutita *f*; **~ paint** *n* COATINGS pintura de cal *f*; **~ pigment** *n* COLOUR pigmento calizo *m*; **~ pit** *n* MINE, PROD calera *f*, cantera de caliza *f*, cantera de piedra de cal *f*; **~ rock** *n* CHEM piedra caliza *f*; **~ sandstone** *n* GEOL arenisca caliza *f*; **~ sludge** *n* PETR TECH lodo con cal *m*; **~ slurry** *n* C&G lechada de cal *f*; **~ stabilization** *n* CONST estabilización con cal *f*; **~-treated mud** *n* PETR TECH lodo tratado con cal *m*; **~-treated sludge** *n* PETR TECH lodo tratado con cal *m*; **~ washing** *n* COATINGS blanqueado *m*, CONST lechada

limen *n* TV limen *m*

limescale *n* FOOD, HYDROL, WATER depósito calcáreo *m*

limestone *n* C&G, CHEM, CONST, GEOL, PETROL caliza *f*, piedra caliza *f*; **~ quarry** *n* MINE calera *f* (*AmL*), cantera de caliza *f* (*Esp*), cantera de piedra de cal *f*

limewashing *n* CONST lechada *f*

limewater *n* CHEM, COATINGS agua de cal *f*

limework *n* COATINGS obra realizada en cal *f*

limey *adj* GEOL calcáreo

liming *n* AGRIC encalado *m*, CONST tratamiento alcalino *m*

limit[1] *n* MATH límite *m*, MECH ENG límite *m*, tolerancia de fabricación *f*, TRANSP límite *m*; **~ of consistency** *n* COAL límite de consistencia *m*; **~ of error** *n* METR límite de error *m*; **~ external gage** *AmE*, **~ external gauge** *BrE n* MECH ENG anillo de tolerancias *m*; **~ gage** *AmE*, **~ gauge** *BrE n* MECH ENG, METR calibre de límites *m*, calibre de tolerancia *m*, galga de tolerancia *f*, galga para límites *f*, gálibo de tolerancia *f*; **~ internal gage** *AmE*, **~ internal gauge** *BrE n* MECH ENG tapón de tolerancias *m*; **~ load** *n* AIR TRANSP *of blade*, ELEC carga límite *f*; **~ load factor** *n* AIR TRANSP factor de carga límite *m*; **~ rate of descent at touchdown** *n* AIR TRANSP velocidad de descenso límite en la toma de tierra *f*; **~ setting** *n* NUCL punto de tarado *m*, valor límite *m*; **~ size** *n* MECH tamaño límite *m*; **~ strip** *n* MECH ENG banda límite *f*, franja límite *f*; **~ switch** *n* ELEC, ELEC ENG, MECH, PROD disyuntor automático *m*, disyuntor de seguridad *m*, interruptor de fin de carrera *m*, interruptor limitador *m*, SAFE disyuntor de seguridad *m*; **~ test** *n* PROD prueba de límite *f*; **~ of tolerance** *n* MECH, METR, QUALITY límite de tolerancia *m*; **~ turbine** *n* HYDRAUL turbina de limitación *f*

limit[2] *vt* ELEC, ELEC ENG, ELECTRON limitar

limited: **~-authority autopilot** *n* AIR TRANSP piloto automático de autoridad limitada *m*; **~-presence detector** *n* TRANSP detector de presencia limitada *m*; **~ progressive system** *n* TRANSP sistema progresivo limitado *m*; **~ signal** *n* ELECTRON señal limitada *f*; **~-slip differential** *n* AUTO, VEH diferencial de deslizamiento limitado *m*, diferencial de desplazamiento limitado *m*; ~ **tightness** *n* MECH ENG *pipework* apriete limitado *m*, tensión limitada *f*; ~ **train** *n* AmE (*cf semifast train BrE*) RAIL tren de puntos de parada limitados *m*, tren semidirecto *m*, tren semiexpreso *m*, tren semirrápido *m*; ~ **waiting queue** *n* TELECOM cola de espera limitada *f*

limiter *n* ELEC fusible *m*, ELEC ENG, ELECTRON fusible *m*, limitador *m*, MECH ENG *machine tools* limitador *m*, tope *m*, SPACE separador *m*, circuito limitador *m*, limitador zonal *m*, fusible *m*, TELECOM limitador *m*, TV fusible *m*, limitador *m*; ~ **diode** *n* ELECTRON, TV diodo limitador *m*

limiting *n* ELECTRON limitación *f*; ~ **amplifier** *n* ELECTRON amplificador de limitación *m*; ~ **current** *n* ELEC corriente limitadora *f*; ~ **fuel assembly** *n* NUCL elemento de combustible limitador *m*; ~ **overload current** *n* ELEC *transformer* corriente de sobrecarga limitadora *f*; ~ **resistor** *n* ELEC resistencia limitadora *f*, resistor limitador *m*; ~ **value** *n* TELECOM valor límite *m*; ~ **viscosity number** *n* FLUID número limitador de la viscosidad *m*

limits *n pl* GAS cordillera *f*, límites *m pl*, rango *m*, PAPER finos *m pl*; ~ **and fits** *n pl* MECH ENG tamaño máximo y mínimo especificado y ajustes *m*

limnic *adj* GEOL límnico

limnimeter *n* HYDROL limnímetro *m*

limonite *n* MINE, MINERAL limonita *f*

limp¹: ~**-bound** *adj* PRINT encuadernado flexible

limp²: ~ **binding** *n* PRINT encuadernación de tapas flexibles *f*

LINAC *abbr* (*linear accelerator*) ELECTRON, NUCL, PART PHYS, PHYS acelerador lineal *m*

linalool *n* CHEM linalol *m*

linarite *n* MINERAL linarita *f*

lindane *n* CHEM lindano *m*

line¹ *n* C&G, COMP&DP línea *f*, CONST cuerda *f*, línea *f*, tubería *f*, CRYSTALL *of spectrum or diffraction pattern*, ELEC *supply network*, ELEC ENG, ELECTRON *to heap or pile up*, GEOM línea *f*, HYDRAUL canalización *f*, MECH ENG línea *f*, *contour* contorno *m*, raya *f*, *row* fila *f*, *straight* recta *f*, trazo *m*, hilera *f*, NUCL línea *f*, PACK cadena *f*, PRINT línea *f*, PROD *rope* cordel *m*, raya *f*, *straight* trazo *m*, línea *f*, RAD PHYS raya *f*, línea *f*, TELECOM línea *f*, TRANSP *AmE* (*cf queue BrE*) *traffic* fila *f*, TV trama *f*, WATER TRANSP *rope* cordel *m*, cabo *m*, línea *f*, *to throw* bota *f*, línea ecuatorial *f*; ~ **access protocol** *n* (*LAP*) TELECOM protocolo de acceso a la línea *m*; ~ **of action** *n* MECH ENG *gearing* línea de acción *f*, línea generatriz *f*, normal común a los perfiles *f*, normal de contacto *f*; ~ **adaptor** *n* COMP&DP adaptador de línea *m*; ~ **amplifier** *n* ELECTRON amplificador de línea *m*; ~ **amplitude control** *n* TV control de amplitud de la línea *m*; ~ **of apsides** *n* SPACE línea de los ápsides *f*; ~ **of bearing** *n* GEOL línea de orientación *f*, trayectoria *f*; ~ **blanking** *n* TV supresión de línea *f*; ~ **blanking level** *n* TV nivel de supresión de la línea *m*; ~ **block** *n* PRINT grabado de línea *m*; ~ **break** *n* ELEC *supply network* caída de la línea *f*; ~ **breaker** *n* ELEC *switch* conjuntor-disyuntor *m*, seccionador *m*; ~ **broadening** *n* CRYSTALL ensanchamiento Doppler *m*, ensanchamiento de una línea espectral *m*; ~ **of buckets** *n* CONST *elevator or conveyor* línea de cangilones *f*; ~ **of cars** *n* AmE (*traffic queue BrE*) AUTO, TRANSP, VEH caravana *f*; ~ **of centers** *AmE*, ~ **of centres** *BrE* *n* MECH ENG eje

m, línea de centros *f*; ~**-choking coil** *n* ELEC, ELEC ENG bobina de reactancia de línea *f*; ~ **circuit** *n* TELECOM circuito de señal *m*; ~ **clear** *n* RAIL vía libre *f*; ~**-clear signal** *n* RAIL señal de vía libre *f*; ~ **code** *n* PACK código de la línea *m*, TELECOM código en línea *m*; ~ **commutator** *n* ELEC *switch* conmutador de líneas *m*; ~ **concentrator** *n* TELECOM concentrador de líneas *m*; ~ **configuration** *n* ELEC ENG configuración de línea *f*; ~ **connection** *n* ELEC *consumer supply* conexión de línea *f*; ~ **connection unit** *n* TELECOM unidad de conexión de líneas *f*; ~ **of contact** *n* MECH ENG, PRINT línea de contacto *f*; ~ **controller** *n* ELEC ENG controlador de línea *m*; ~ **copy** *n* PRINT original de línea *m*; ~ **coupling** *n* ELEC ENG acoplamiento de línea *m*; ~ **current** *n* ELEC ENG corriente de línea *f*; ~ **cut** *n* PRINT clisé de línea *m*; ~ **diffusion** *n* TV difusión de líneas *f*; ~ **of dip** *n* GEOL línea de buzamiento *f*, línea de inclinación *f*; ~ **divider** *n* TV divisor de frecuencia para obtener la señal de línea *m*; ~ **drawing** *n* GEOM dibujo lineal *m*; ~ **drive connector** *n* PROD conector de amplificador de potencia *m*, módulo de control de línea *m*; ~ **drive signal** *n* TV señal de exploración *f*; ~ **driver** *n* COMP&DP controlador de línea *m*, impulsor de línea *m*; ~**-driver output** *n* PROD salida de amplificador de potencia *f*; ~ **drop** *n* ELEC *voltage*, ELEC ENG caída de tensión de línea *f*, caída de voltaje en línea *f*, pérdida de voltaje *f*, PROD caída de tensión en una línea *f*; ~ **engraving** *n* PRINT fotograbado de línea *m*, grabado al buril *m*; ~ **fault** *n* ELEC ENG falla en la línea *f*, TELECOM fallo de línea *m*; ~ **feed** *n* (*LF*) COMP&DP alimentación interlineal *f*, avance de línea *m*, PRINT avance de línea *m*, TELECOM alimentación de la línea *f*; ~**-feeding equipment** *n* PACK equipo de alimentación en cadena *m*; ~ **filter** *n* ELECTRON filtro antiparasitario *m*, filtro de línea *m*; ~ **flax** *n* TEXTIL lino para cordel *m*; ~ **of flux** *n* ELEC, ELEC ENG línea de flujo eléctrico *f*; ~ **flyback** *n* TV retorno de línea *m*; ~ **focus** *n* TV foco lineal *m*; ~ **of force** *n* ELEC *magnetism*, PHYS línea de fuerza *f*; ~ **frequency** *n* TV frecuencia de línea *f*; ~**-graduated master scales** *n pl* METR regla patrón graduada *f*; ~ **graph** *n* COMP&DP gráfico cartesiano *m*, gráfico lineal *m*; ~ **group** *n* TELECOM grupo de líneas *m*; ~ **impedance** *n* ELEC, ELEC ENG impedancia de línea *f*; ~ **of impression** *n* PRINT línea de impresión *f*; ~**-in** *n* TV entrada de línea *f*; ~ **in service** *n* RAIL vía en servicio *f*; ~ **input power** *n* PROD potencia de entrada a la línea *f*; ~ **insulator** *n* ELEC, ELEC ENG aislante de línea *m*; ~ **integral** *n* PHYS integral de línea *f*; ~ **interface** *n* ELEC ENG interface de línea *m*, interfaz de línea *f*; ~ **interface module** *n* TELECOM módulo de interfaz de líneas *m*; ~ **interfacing** *n* ELEC ENG interfaces de línea *f pl*; ~**-interlaced scanning** *n* TV exploración de entrelazado de líneas *f*; ~**-isolating switch** *n* ELEC *supply network* conmutador de aislación de línea *m*; ~ **level** *n* TV nivel de línea *m*; ~ **of level** *n* CONST línea de nivelación *f*; ~ **linearity control** *n* TV control de linealidad *m*; ~ **loss** *n* ELEC *supply network* pérdida de líneas *f*; ~ **module** *n* TELECOM módulo de líneas *m*; ~ **monitor** *n* TV monitor de líneas *m*; ~ **of nodes** *n* SPACE *communications* línea de nodos *f*, línea de nódulos *f*; ~ **noise** *n* ELEC ENG, ELECTRON ruido de circuito *m*, ruido de línea *m*; ~ **number** *n* COMP&DP número de línea *m*; ~ **occupied** *n* RAIL vía ocupada *f*; ~**-of-sight signal** *n* ELECTRON señal de línea visual *f*;

~-out n TV salida de línea f; **~ output** n TV base de tiempo de línea f; **~ pin** n CONST soporte de cuerda m; **~ plate** n PRINT plancha de línea f; **~ printer** n COMP&DP, PRINT impresora de línea f; **~ profile measurements** n pl RAD PHYS mediciones de los contornos de rayas f pl; **~ protection** n ELEC supply network, GEOPHYS protección de línea f; **~ protector** n ELEC, GEOPHYS protector eléctrico m; **~ protector cutout** n GEOPHYS protector eléctrico de cortacircuito m; **~ rate** n PRINT tarifa por línea f; **on ~ real time** n (OLRT) COMP&DP tiempo real en línea m (OLRT); **~ recorder** n INSTR registrador de líneas m; **~ relay** n ELEC relé de línea m; **~ rental** n TELECOM alquiler de líneas m; **~ repeater** n TELECOM repetidor de líneas m; **~ replaceable unit** n (LRU) ELEC ENG unidad reemplazable en línea f, unidad sustituible en línea f; **~ reversal** n TELECOM inversión de líneas f; **~ scanning** n COMP&DP, ELECTRON exploración de línea f, PRINT barrido de línea m, TELECOM exploración por líneas f; **~ of section** n GEOL línea de corte f; **~ segment** n GEOM segmento de recta m; **~ seizure button** n TELECOM pulsador de toma de líneas m; **~ serving a siding** n RAIL vía que da servicio a un apartadero f; **~ of shafting** n MECH ENG línea de ejes f, línea de transmisión f; **~ of sight** n TELECOM línea de visión f; **~ signal** n ELECTRON señal de línea f; **~ signaling equipment** AmE, **~ signalling equipment** BrE n TELECOM equipo de señalización de líneas m; **~ slip** n TV deslizamiento de línea m; **~ source** n POLL foco lineal m, fuente de radiación lineal f, fuente lineal f, RAD PHYS fuente de radiación puntal f; **~ space** n PRINT espacio de línea m; **~ spacing** n PRINT espaciado de línea m; **~ spectrum** n ACOUST, OPT, PHYS, RAD PHYS, TELECOM espectro de líneas m, espectro de rayas m, espectro lineal m; **~ speed** n PACK velocidad de la línea f; **~-stabilized oscillator** n ELECTRON oscilador de línea estabilizada m; **~ starter** n AmE (cf starter BrE) ELEC switch arrancador de línea m; **~ stretcher** n PHYS mass extensor de línea m; **~ of strike** n GEOL, MINE línea de dirección f, rumbo de dirección m; **~ style** n COMP&DP estilo de línea m; **~ sweep** n TV barrido lineal m; **~ switching** n COMP&DP conmutación de línea f; **~ system** n TELECOM sistema de líneas m; **~ tear** n TV rotura de línea f; **~ tension** n METALL tensión de línea f; **~ terminal** n ELEC connection, PROD, TELECOM terminal de línea m, borne de línea m; **~ terminated by an impedance** n PHYS línea terminada con una impedancia f; **~-terminating equipment** n TELECOM equipo de terminación de línea m; **~ termination** n (LT) PRINT, TELECOM terminación de línea f (TL); **~ termination equipment** n (LTE) COMP&DP equipo de terminación de línea m (ETL); **~ tester** n PAPER comprobador de línea m, cuentahilos m; **~ thrower** n WATER TRANSP lanzacabos m; **~ tilt** n TV compensación de línea f; **~-to-earth voltage** n BrE (cf line-to-ground voltage AmE) ELEC supply network voltaje de línea a tierra m; **~-to-ground voltage** n AmE (cf line-to-earth voltage BrE) ELEC supply network voltaje de línea a tierra m; **~-to-line voltage** n ELEC three-phase supply tensión entre fases f, voltaje entre fases m; **~-to-neutral voltage** n ELEC supply network tensión de línea-neutro f; **~ of traffic** n AmE (cf traffic queue BrE) AUTO, TRANSP, VEH caravana f, fila de coches f; **~ transient** n ELEC perturbaciones transitorias de

línea f pl; **~-up** n GEOL software agrupación f, PETROL alineación f, hilera f, PRINT alineación f; **~-up clamp** n PETROL abrazadera de alineación f, grapa de alineación f; **~-up slide** n CINEMAT diapositiva de referencia f; **~-up tape** n TV cinta de alineación f; **~ voltage** n ELEC supply network tensión de línea f; **~ voltage in** n ELEC, PROD voltaje de entrada de línea m; **~ width** n RAD PHYS anchura de raya f; **~ wiring** n PROD cableado de línea m; **~ work** n PRINT grabado de línea m

line² vt COATINGS revestir, forrar, CONST well alinear, revestir, trazar, MINE blindar, entubar, PROD bearing block recubrir, revestir, forrar; **~ with metal** vt MINE blindar; **~ out** vt CONST delinear, marcar con rayas; **~ with tin** vt PROD box revestir de estaño; **~ up** vt CINEMAT alinear

lineals n pl PRINT lineales f pl
lineament n GEOL alineamiento m
linear¹ adj PHYS lineal
linear²: **~ absorption coefficient** n PHYS coeficiente de absorción lineal m; **~ accelerator** n (LINAC) ELECTRON, NUCL, PART PHYS, PHYS acelerador lineal m; **~-accelerator-driven reactor** n (LADR) NUCL reactor activado por acelerador lineal m; **~ activity** n NUCL circular, divided actividad lineal f; **~ algebra** n COMP&DP, MATH álgebra lineal m; **~ amplification** n ELECTRON, TELECOM amplificación lineal f; **~ amplifier** n ELECTRON, TELECOM amplificador lineal m; **~ approximation** n TELECOM aproximación lineal f; **~ array** n ELECTRON to heap or pile up sistema lineal m; **~ attenuation coefficient** n PHYS coeficiente de atenuación lineal m; **~-beam amplifier** n ELECTRON amplificador de haz lineal m; **~-beam backward-wave oscillator** n ELECTRON oscilador de onda de retorno con haz lineal m; **~-beam tube** n ELECTRON tubo de haz lineal m; **~ bearing** n HEAT ENG soporte lineal m; **~ behavior** AmE, **~ behaviour** BrE n ELECTRON funcionamiento lineal m; **~ channel** n TELECOM canal lineal m; **~ characteristic** n ELECTRON característica lineal f; **~ charge density** n ELEC, PHYS, RAD PHYS densidad de carga lineal f; **~ circuit** n ELEC, ELECTRON, TELECOM circuito lineal m; **~ circuit element** n ELECTRON elemento de circuito lineal m; **~ code** n TELECOM código lineal m; **~ concentrator** n FUELLESS concentrador lineal m; **~ control** n ELEC control lineal m, regulación lineal f; **~ current network** n ELEC red lineal de corriente f; **~ defect** n METALL defecto lineal m; **~ detection** n ELECTRON detección lineal f; **~ detector** n ELECTRON detector lineal m; **~ digital-voice scrambler** n TELECOM encriptador de voz digital lineal m; **~ disc** BrE, **~ disk** AmE n OPT disco lineal m; **~ dispersion** n RAD PHYS dispersión lineal f; **~ distortion** n CINEMAT, TELECOM distorsión lineal f; **~-divided machine tool scale** n MECH ENG balanza de máquina herramienta dividida en líneas f; **~ energy transfer** n PHYS, RAD PHYS transferencia de energía lineal f, transferencia lineal de energía f; **~ expansion coefficient** n PHYS coeficiente de expansión lineal m; **~ filter** n ELECTRON, TELECOM filtro lineal m; **~ filtering** n ELECTRON, TELECOM filtrado lineal m; **~ four-terminal network** n ELEC cuadrípolo lineal m, red lineal de cuatro polos f, red tetrapolar lineal f; **~ gray scale** AmE, **~ grey scale** BrE n CINEMAT escala de grises lineal f; **~ induction motor** n ELEC, TRANSP motor de inducción lineal m, motor lineal asincrónico m,

motor lineal de inducción *m*; ~ **integrated circuit** *n* ELECTRON circuito integrado lineal *m*; ~ **interpolation** *n* TELECOM interpolación lineal *f*; ~ **ionization** *n* PHYS, RAD PHYS ionización lineal *f*; ~ **kinetic energy** *n* MECH ENG energía cinética lineal *f*; ~ **lead** *n* HYDRAUL avance lineal a la admisión *m*; ~ **list** *n* COMP&DP lista lineal *f*; ~ **magnification** *n* OPT, PHYS aumento lineal *m*; ~ **matrix** *n* TV matriz lineal *f*; ~ **modulation** *n* ELECTRON modulación lineal *f*; ~ **modulator** *n* ELECTRON modulador lineal *m*; ~ **motor** *n* ELEC, TRANSP motor lineal *m*; ~ **network** *n* PHYS red lineal *f*; ~ **oscillation** *n* MECH ENG, TELECOM oscilación lineal *f*; ~ **polarization** *n* TELECOM polarización lineal *f*; ~ **polymer** *n* P&R polímero lineal *m*; ~ **power amplifier** *n* ELECTRON, TELECOM amplificador de potencia lineal *m*, amplificador lineal de potencia *m*; ~ **predicting coding** *n* (*LPC*) TELECOM codificación predictiva lineal *f*; ~ **predicting coding vocoder** *n* TELECOM codificación predictiva vocoder lineal *f*; ~ **predictive coding** *n* ELECTRON codificación de predicción lineal *f*; ~ **pressure** *n* PAPER presión lineal *f*; ~ **programming** *n* COMP&DP, ELECTRON programación lineal *f*; ~**-pulse amplifier** *n* ELECTRON amplificador de impulso lineal *m*; ~ **register** *n* PRINT registro lineal *m*; ~ **resistance** *n* ELEC resistencia de variación lineal *f*, PHYS resistencia lineal *f*; ~ **resistor** *n* ELEC resistor de variación lineal *m*; ~ **scale** *n* ELECTRON, INSTR, METR escala lineal *f*; ~ **scaling calculation** *n* TELECOM cálculo de escalas lineales *m*; ~ **scan** *n* ELECTRON exploración lineal *f*; ~ **Stark effect** *n* PHYS efecto Stark lineal *m*; ~ **thermodynamics** *n* THERMO termodinámica lineal *f*; ~ **time base** *n* ELECTRON base de tiempo lineal *f*; ~ **timed acceleration** *n* PROD aceleración lineal temporizada *f*; ~ **transducer** *n* ACOUST transductor lineal *m*; ~ **tube** *n* ELECTRON tubo lineal *m*; ~ **turbine** *n* TRANSP turbina lineal *f*; ~ **work hardening** *n* METALL endurecimiento por acritud lineal *m*, endurecimiento por medios mecánicos lineales *m*

linearity *n* ELEC linealidad *f*, proporcionalidad *f*, ELECTRON, TELECOM linealidad *f*; ~ **control** *n* TV control de linealidad *m*; ~ **error** *n* TV error de linealidad *m*

linearization: ~ **function** *n* PROD función de linealización *f*

linearize *vt* CHEM, SPACE linear, linearizar

linearizer *n* CHEM, SPACE linearizador *m*

linearly: ~**-polarized mode** *n* (*LP mode*) OPT, TELECOM modo polarizado linealmente *m*; ~**-polarized wave** *n* ACOUST, PHYS *mass* onda linealmente polarizada *f*

lineation *n* GEOL lineación *m*

lined: ~ **bag** *n* PACK bolsa recubierta *f*; ~ **chipboard** *n* PAPER cartón gris forrado *m*; ~ **clamp** *n* MECH ENG abrazadera revestida *f*, agarradera revestida *f*, mordaza revestida *f*; ~ **paper** *n* GEOM papel de líneas *m*

linefinder *n* TELECOM localizador de líneas *m*

lineman *n* RAIL vigilante de vía *m*

linen *n* PRINT hilo *m*, TEXTIL tejido de lino *m*; ~ **clothing** *n* TEXTIL ropa de hogar *f*; ~ **counter** *n* PRINT contador de hilos *m*; ~ **tester** *n* PRINT cuentahilos *m*

liner *n* AIR TRANSP forro *m*, revestimiento *m*, forro inhibidor *m*, COAL camisa interior *f*, revestimiento *m*, separador *m*, MECH camisa interior *f*, forro *m*, revestimiento *m*, revestimiento protector interior *m*, MECH ENG cuña *f*, *for cylinders and bores* revestidor *m*, PAPER papel para caras *m*, PETR TECH liner *m*, tubería de revestimiento *f*, camisa *f*, PETROL forro *m*, cañería perdida *f*, tubo revestidor de fondo *m*, revestimiento *m*, PRINT alineador *m*, REFRIG cuba interior *f*, WATER TRANSP buque de línea *m*, buque de pasaje *m*; ~ **cylinder** *n* PAPER cilindro del formato *m*; ~ **hanger** *n* PETROL anclaje para cañería perdida *m*, sujeción de tubería auxiliar de revestimiento *f*; ~ **paper** *n* PAPER papel para capas lisas interiores *m*

lines: ~ **drawing** *n* WATER TRANSP *ship design* plano de formas *m*; ~ **of force** *n pl* GEOPHYS líneas de fuerza *f pl*; ~ **per minute** *n pl* (*LPM*) COMP&DP, PRINT líneas por minuto *f pl* (*LPM*); ~ **plan** *n* WATER TRANSP *ship design* plano de formas *m*

lingoid *adj* GEOL lingoide

linguiform *adj* GEOL lingüiforme

lining *n* AUTO forro *m*, COATINGS forro *m*, revestimiento *m*, CONST revestimiento interior *m*, MECH alineación *f*, camisa interior *f*, estrías *f pl*, forro *m*, revestimiento *m*, revestimiento protector interior *m*, MINE entibación *f*, revestimiento *m*, PAPER contracolado *m*, forrado *m*, PRINT forro *m*, PROD *act* forro *m*, revestimiento interior *m*, *covering* recubrimiento *m*, *of blast furnace* revestimiento *m*, *of fire bricks* camisa *f*, WATER *of pump* camisa *f*; ~ **fabric** *n* TEXTIL tela de forro *f*; ~ **plate** *n* HYDRAUL chapa de envuelta del revestimiento calorífugo *f*, PROD chapa de forro *f*, chapa de revestimiento *f*; ~ **segment** *n* CONST segmento de revestimiento *m*; ~ **sight** *n* MINE línea de mira *f* (*Esp*), línea visual *f*, niveleta *f* (*AmL*); ~ **tube** *n* MINE tubo de revestimiento *m*; ~**-up** *n* PRINT *of screw* enlomado *m*

link[1] *n* (*cf trunk AmE*) COMP&DP tronco *m*, eslabón de comunicación *m*, enlace *m*, canal de comunicación *m* (*AmL*), conexión *f*, ELEC *in system* puente de conexión *m*, conectador acoplador *m*, pieza corta de conexión *f*, MECH eslabón *m*, vínculo *m*, articulación *f*, biela de acoplamiento *f*, unión *f*, enlace *m*, conexión *f*, MECH ENG balancín *m*, acoplamiento *m*, *general term* vínculo *m*, conexión *f*, enlace *m*, enganche *m*, lazo *m*, articulación *f*, puente de conexión *m*, tirante *m*, *of cable chain* unión *f*, ligamento *m*, varilla *f*, *of chain* eslabón *m*, TELECOM enlace *m*, WATER TRANSP *of chain* eslabón *m*; ~ **bearing** *n* MECH ENG cojinete de suspensión de la corredera *m*; ~ **belting** *n* P&R correas articuladas *f pl*; ~ **block** *n* MECH ENG corredera del sector Stephenson *f*, taco del sector de la excéntrica *m*; ~ **block guide** *n* RAIL guía obturadora *f*; ~ **block pin** *n* MECH ENG pasador del sector de la excéntrica *m*; ~ **budget** *n* SPACE *communications* balance de enlace *m*; ~**-by-link encipherment** *n* TELECOM cifrado enlace por enlace *m*; ~**-by-link traffic routing** *n* TELECOM enrutamiento del tráfico enlace por enlace *m*; ~ **chain** *n* MECH ENG cadena de eslabones *f*, cadena ordinaria de eslabones *f*; ~ **editing** *n* COMP&DP edición de enlace *f*; ~ **editor** *n* COMP&DP editor de enlace *m*; ~ **fuse** *n* ELEC fusible de cinta *m*, fusible de hilo descubierto *m*, ELEC ENG fusible de cinta *m*, MECH ENG fusible de hilo descubierto *m*; ~ **gear** *n* MECH ENG distribución por corredera *f*, transmisión por corredera *f*; ~ **grinder** *n* PROD máquina de rectificar las correderas *f*; ~ **hanger** *n* MECH ENG biela de suspensión de la corredera *f*; ~ **layer** *n* TELECOM capa de enlace *f*; ~ **loader** *n* COMP&DP cargador del enlace *m*;

~ **margins** *n pl* TELECOM márgenes de enlace *m pl*; ~ **mechanism** *n* MECH ENG mecanismo de enlace *m*, mecanismo de unión *m*; ~ **motion** *n* MECH ENG distribución por corredera *f*, distribución por sector Stephenson *f*; ~ **motion with crossed rods** *n* MECH ENG corredera de barras cruzadas *f*; ~ **motion with open rods** *n* MECH ENG corredera de barras abiertas *f*; ~ **plate** *n* MECH ENG cacha de la corredera *f*; ~ **power budget** *n* TELECOM cálculo de la potencia de enlace *m*; ~ **protocol** *n* COMP&DP protocolo de comunicación *m*, protocolo de enlace *m*; ~ **rod** *n* MECH ENG biela articulada *f*, bieleta *f*, varilla de acoplamiento *f*; ~ **support** *n* MECH ENG biela de suspensión de la corredera *f*; ~ **system** *n* TELECOM sistema de enlaces *m*; ~ **valve motion** *n* MECH ENG distribución por corredera *f*

link² : ~ **together** *vt* TELECOM enlazar; ~ **up** *vt* TELECOM enlazar

linkage *n* AUTO varillaje de mando *m*, CHEM *between atoms* enlace *m*, COMP&DP enlazamiento *m*, enlace *m*, MECH vínculo *m*, encadenamiento *m*, enlace *m*, articulación *f*, eslabonamiento *m*, unión *f*, MECH ENG eslabonamiento *m*, articulación *f*, encadenamiento *m*, enlace *m*, unión *f*, sistema articulado *m*, sistema de eslabones *m*, acoplamiento *m*, varillaje *m*, NUCL *of sea* acoplamiento *m*, articulación *f*, P&R afinidad *f*, enlace *m*, unión *f*, VEH tirantería *f*, varillaje de mando *m*; ~ **editor** *n* COMP&DP editor de enlace *m*; ~ **path** *n* COMP&DP curso de enlace *m*, ruta de enlace *f*, trayectoria de enlace *f*; ~ **power steering system** *n* AUTO sistema de servodirección de unión *m*

linked : ~ **circuit** *n* ELEC circuito conectado *m*, circuito enlazado *m*, circuito unido *m*; ~ **traffic signal control** *n* TRANSP control de señalización de tráfico concatenada *m*

linker *n* COMP&DP enlazador *m*

linking *n* CHEM enlace *m*, ligadura *f*, P&R, TELECOM enlace *m*

linnaeite *n* MINERAL linneita *f*

linocut *n* PRINT grabado en linóleo *m*

linoleate *n* CHEM linoleato *m*

linoleic¹ *adj* CHEM linoleico

linoleic² : ~ **acid** *n* CHEM, FOOD, P&R ácido linoleico *m*

linoleine *n* CHEM linoleína *f*

linolenate *n* CHEM linolenato *m*

linolenic *adj* CHEM linolénico

linotype® *n* PRINT linotipia® *f*

linseed *n* AGRIC semilla de lino *f*; ~ **cake** *n* AGRIC torta de linaza *f*; ~ **oil** *n* CHEM, COATINGS, CONST, WATER TRANSP aceite de linaza *m*; ~ **oil lacquer** *n* COATINGS laca de aceite de linaza *f*

lint *n* AGRIC fibras de algodón *f pl*, OCEAN red *f*, PRINT pelusa *f*

lintel *n* CONST dintel *m*

linting *n* PAPER repelado *m*

lion's : ~ **claw** *n* CONST mordaza *f*

lip *n* C&G labio *m*, CONST *of bucket, of elevator-bucket* borde *m*, reborde *m*, LAB borde *m*, MECH arista de corte *f*, MECH ENG *of drill* arista de corte *f*, filo *m*, PROD *of crucible* pico de descarga *m*; ~ **bolt** *n* PROD perno de reborde *m*; ~ **joint pliers** *n pl* MECH ENG alicates de junta de labios *m pl*, pinzas de junta de labios *f pl*, tenaza de junta de labios *f*; ~ **microphone** *n* ACOUST micrófono labial *m*; ~ **reading** *n* ACOUST lectura labial *f*; ~ **seal** *n* MECH ENG junta de labios *f*,

sello de labios *m*, obturador para ejes en rotación *m*; ~ **sync** *n* CINEMAT sincronización labial *f*; ~ **synchronization** *n* CINEMAT sincronización labial *f*; ~ **type seal** *n* MECH ENG junta de labios *f*

lipase *n* CHEM lipasa *f*

lipid *n* CHEM lípido *m*

lipoid *adj* CHEM lipoide

lipophile *n* CHEM lipófilo *m*

lipophilic *adj* CHEM lipofílico

lipopolysaccharide *n* CHEM lipopolisacárido *m*

lipositol *n* CHEM lipositol *m*

liposoluble *adj* CHEM liposoluble

lipped : ~ **table scarf with key** *n* CONST junta rebordeada de mesa con llave *f*

liquation *n* CHEM, GAS, PHYS, REFRIG, THERMO licuación *f*

liquefaction *n* CHEM, GAS, PHYS, REFRIG, THERMO licuefacción *f*

liquefied¹ *adj* CHEM, GAS, PHYS, REFRIG, THERMO licuado

liquefied² : ~ **gas** *n* GAS gas licuado *m*; ~ **natural gas** *n* (*LNG*) GAS, PETR TECH, THERMO gas natural licuado *m* (*GNL*); ~ **natural-gas carrier** *n* (*LNG carrier*) WATER TRANSP buque gasero *m*, metanero *m*; ~ **natural-gas and liquefied-petroleum-gas carrier** *n* (*LNG-LPG carrier*) THERMO, WATER TRANSP buque para transporte de gas natural licuado y gas de petróleo licuado *m*; ~ **petroleum gas** *n* (*LPG*) AUTO, GAS, HEAT ENG, PETR TECH, THERMO, TRANSP, VEH gas licuado de petróleo *m* (*Esp*) (*GLP*), supergás *m* (*AmL*)

liquefier *n* GEN licuefactor *m*

liquefy *vt* GEN licuar

liquescence *n* GEN licuescencia *f*

liquescent *adj* GEN licuescente

liquid¹ *adj* GEN líquido; ~ **cooled** *adj* THERMO enfriado con líquido, refrigerado por líquido; ~ **metal-cooled** *adj* THERMO refrigerado por metal líquido; ~ **proof** *adj* PACK resistente a los líquidos

liquid² *n* GEN líquido *m*; ~ **air** *n* THERMO aire líquido *m*; ~ **ammonia** *n* CHEM, THERMO amoníaco líquido *m*; ~ **bipropellant propulsion** *n* SPACE *craft* propulsión con líquido bipropulsor *f*; ~ **charge** *n* REFRIG carga líquida *f*; ~ **chiller** *n* REFRIG enfriador de líquido *m*; ~ **chlorine** *n* THERMO cloro líquido *m*; ~ **chromatography** *n* POLL cromatografía de líquidos *f*; ~ **compass** *n* WATER TRANSP aguja de líquido *f*, compás de líquido *m*; ~ **coolant** *n* THERMO refrigerante líquido *m*; ~ **cooled engine** *n* AUTO motor de refrigeración líquida *m*; ~ **cooler** *n* MECH ENG enfriador de líquido *m*, refrigerante líquido *m*; ~ **cooling** *n* THERMO refrigeración por líquido *f*; ~ **crystal** *n* (*LC*) COMP&DP, CRYSTALL, ELEC, ELECTRON, NUCL, PETR TECH, PHYS, TELECOM, TV cristal líquido *m* (*CL*); ~ **crystal display** *n* (*LCD*) COMP&DP, ELEC, ELECTRON, PHYS, TELECOM, TV pantalla de cristal líquido *f*, visualización en cristal líquido *f* (*VCL*); ~ **crystal display module** *n* (*LCD module*) COMP&DP, ELEC, ELECTRON, PHYS, TELECOM, TV módulo de visualización por cristal líquido *m* (*IML*); ~ **drop model** *n* PHYS modelo de la gota líquida *m*; ~ **droplet** *n* POLL gotita de líquido *f*, gotícula de líquido *f*; ~ **effluent** *n* GAS efluente líquido *m*; ~ **flow** *n* FLUID flujo de líquidos *m*, NUCL caudal líquido *m*, corriente líquida *f*; ~ **flow indicator** *n* REFRIG visor de líquido *m*; ~ **fuel** *n*

THERMO combustible líquido *m*; **~-fuel engine** *n*
THERMO motor de combustible líquido *m*; **~-fuel
rocket** *n* THERMO cohete de combustible líquido *m*;
~ gas *n* GAS gas líquido *m*, THERMO gas líquido *m*;
~-gas engine *n* TRANSP motor de gas licuado *m*;
~ gate *n* CINEMAT ventanilla líquida *f*; **~-gate
printing** *n* CINEMAT copiado de ventanilla líquida
m; **~ gold** *n* C&G oro líquido *m*; **~ helium** *n* THERMO
helio líquido *m*; **~ hydrocarbons** *n pl* CHEM hidrocarburos líquidos *m pl*; **~ hydrogen** *n* CHEM, SPACE
hidrógeno líquido *m*; **~ injection valve** *n* REFRIG
válvula de inyección de líquido *f*; **~ laser** *n* ELEC-
TRON láser líquido *m*; **~ lasing medium** *n* ELECTRON
procedimiento de aplicación de laser líquido *m*;
~ level *n* PACK, PETR TECH nivel de líquido *m*;
~-level control *n* PACK control del nivel de líquido
m; **~-level indicator** *n* PACK indicador del nivel de
líquido *m*; **~ limit** *n* COAL tope de líquido *m*, CONST
límite líquido *m*; **~ limit device** *n* COAL aparato para
el tope de líquidos *m*, enrase *m*; **~-manure plant** *n*
AGRIC instalación para purines *f*; **~-manure
spreader** *n* AGRIC distribuidor de purín *m*;
~ measure *n* METR medición de líquidos *f*; **~ metal**
n COAL metal líquido *m*; **~-metal heat exchanger** *n*
HEAT ENG, THERMO intercambiador de calor con
metal líquido *m*; **~-metal ion source** *n* RAD PHYS
fuente de iones de metal líquido *f*; **~ monopropellant**
n THERMO monergol líquido *m*, monopropulsante
líquido *m*; **~-natural-gas bus** *n* (*LNG bus*) TRANSP
autobús de gas natural licuado *m* (*Esp*), bus de gas
natural licuado *m* (*AmL*); **~-natural-gas carrier** *n*
(*LNG carrier*) TRANSP transporte de gas natural
licuado *m*; **~ nitrogen** *n* SPACE nitrógeno líquido *m*;
~-only phase *n* THERMO fase sólo líquida *f*;
~ oxygen *n* CHEM, SPACE, THERMO oxígeno líquido
m; **~-oxygen explosive** *n* MINE explosivo de oxígeno
líquido *m*; **~-packaging line** *n* PACK cadena para
envasar líquidos *f*; **~ paraffin** *n* CHEM aceite de
parafina *m*, parafina líquida *f*, THERMO aceite de
parafina *m*, parafina líquida *f*, vaselina líquida *f*;
~ petroleum gas *n* (*LPG*) AUTO, GAS, HEAT ENG,
PETR TECH, THERMO, TRANSP, VEH gas licuado de
petróleo *m* (*GLP*) (*Esp*), supergás *m* (*AmL*);
~-petroleum-gas bus *n* TRANSP autobús de gas
licuado de petróleo *m* (*Esp*), bus de gas-petróleo
líquido *m*, ómnibus *m* (*AmL*); **~-petroleum-gas
engine** *n* (*LPG engine*) AUTO motor de gas *m*, motor
de gas licuado de petróleo *m*; **~-phase epitaxy** *n*
ELECTRON epitaxia en fase líquida *f*; **~-proof carton** *n*
PACK envase de cartón a prueba de líquidos *m*;
~ propellant *n* SPACE, THERMO combustible líquido
m, propulsante líquido *m*, propulsor líquido *m*;
~-propellant rocket *n* THERMO cohete con propulsante líquido *m*; **~ propellant systems** *n pl* SPACE
craft sistema de combustible líquido *m*; **~ receiver** *n*
REFRIG recipiente de líquido *m*; **~ rheostat** *n* ELEC
resistance reóstato de resistencia líquida *m*;
~ sloshing *n* SPACE *spacecraft* bailoteo del líquido
m; **~ slug** *n* REFRIG bolsa de líquido *f*; **~ starter
resistance** *n* ELEC resistencia líquida de arranque *f*,
reóstato de resistencia líquida de arranque *m*;
~ starting resistance *n* ELEC resistencia líquida de
arranque *f*; **~ suction heat exchanger** *n* REFRIG
cambiador de calor *m*; **~ thermometer** *n* THERMO
termómetro líquido *m*; **~ trap** *n* REFRIG dispositivo
de retención de líquido *m*; **~ tripropellant** *n* THERMO

boat building tripropulsante líquido *m*; **~ vapor
equilibrium diagram** *AmE*, **~ vapour equilibrium
diagram** *BrE* *n* THERMO diagrama de equilibrio
líquido-vapor *m*; **~ waste** *n* POLL desechos líquidos
m pl, RECYCL desechos líquidos *m pl*, residuos
líquidos *m pl*
liquidity: **~ index** *n* COAL índice de liquidez *m*
liquidus *n* CHEM *phase diagram* liquidus *m*; **~ line** *n*
METALL línea de fase líquida *f*, línea de liquidus *f*,
línea de principio de solidificación *f*
liquor *n* CHEM licor *m*; **~-to-goods ratio** *n* TEXTIL
relación del baño *f*
liroconite *n* MINERAL liroconita *f*
L-iron *n* CONST angular de hierro *m*
LISP *abbr* (*list processing language*) COMP&DP lenguaje
de procesamiento de listas *m*
Lissajous: **~ figures** *n pl* ELECTRON, PHYS figuras de
Lissajous *f pl*
list[1] *n* COMP&DP lista *f*, WATER TRANSP escora estética *f*;
~ of lights *n* WATER TRANSP libro de faros *m*;
~ processing *n* COMP&DP procesamiento de listados
m, procesamiento de listas *m*; **~ processing
language** *n* (*LISP*) COMP&DP lenguaje de procesamiento de listas *m*; **~ structure** *n* COMP&DP
estructura de listado *f*
list[2] *vt* COMP&DP enumerar, hacer listados de, hacer una
lista
list[3] *vi* WATER TRANSP *ship* ir escorado, llevar escora
listening: **~ in** *n* TELECOM escucha *f*
lister *n* AGRIC implemento lister *m*
listing *n* COMP&DP listado *m*
listric: **~ fault** *n* GEOL falla lístrica *f*
liter *n* *AmE see* litre *BrE*
literal *n* COMP&DP literal *m*, PRINT error tipográfico *m*;
~ error *n* PRINT error tipográfico *m*
litharge *n* CHEM litarge *m*, litargirio *m*, P&R almártaga
f, litarge *m*, litargirio *m*
lithergol *n* SPACE litergol *m*
lithic[1] *adj* GEOL lítico
lithic[2]: **~ tuff** *n* GEOL toba lítica *f*
lithification *n* GEOL petrificación *f*
lithionite *n* MINERAL lithionita *f*
lithium *n* (*Li*) CHEM, ELEC ENG litio *m* (*Li*); **~-chlorine
storage battery** *n* ELEC ENG, TRANSP batería de
acumuladores de litio-cloro *f*
lithoclast *n* GEOL litoclasto *m*
lithofacies *n* GEOL litofacies *f*
lithogenous *adj* GEOL litógeno
lithograph *vt* PRINT litografiar
lithographic: **~ color** *AmE*, **~ colour** *BrE* *n* COLOUR
colorante litográfico *m*; **~ mask** *n* ELECTRON recubrimiento litográfico *m*, RAD PHYS máscara
litográfica *f*, plantilla litográfica *f*; **~ oil** *n* COATINGS
aceite litográfico *m*; **~ print** *n* PRINT copia litográfica
f; **~ process** *n* ELECTRON proceso litográfico *m*;
~ slate *n* CHEM pizarra litográfica *f*; **~ stone** *n*
CHEM piedra litográfica *f*; **~ varnish** *n* COATINGS,
COLOUR barniz litográfico *m*
lithography *n* ELECTRON, PRINT litografía *f*, offset *m*
lithologic *adj* GEOL litológico
lithological *adj* GEOL litológico
lithomarge *n* MINERAL litomarga *f*
lithophile: **~ element** *n* GEOL elemento litófilo *m*
lithoplate *n* PRINT plancha litográfica *f*
lithopone *n* CHEM, MINERAL litopón *m*

lithosphere n FUELLESS, GEOL, GEOPHYS, POLL litosfera f

lithostatic: ~ **pressure** n GEOL presión litostática f

lithostratigraphic: ~ **unit** n GEOL grupo litoestratigráfico m

litmus n CHEM tornasol m; ~ **paper** n CHEM papel tornasol m

litre n BrE (l) METR, PHYS litro m (l)

Littleton: ~ **softening point** n C&G punto de ablandamiento Littleton m

littoral: ~ **current** n OCEAN corriente litoral f; ~ **drift** n HYDROL arrastre litoral m, corrientes litorales f pl; ~ **zone** n GEOL recording zona litoral f

live[1] adj ELEC activo, bajo tensión, cargado, con corriente, MILIT grenade, round, shell cargado, PHYS con corriente, PROD vivo, electricity con corriente, en tensión, projectile cargado, air a presión, load móvil, TV vivo

live[2]: ~ **action** n CINEMAT, TV acción en vivo f; ~ **axle** n MECH ENG, VEH eje del diferencial m, eje giratorio m, eje impulsor m, eje motor m; ~ **bait** n OCEAN carmada viva f; ~ **bait fishing** n OCEAN pesca con carnada viva f; ~ **broadcast** n TV emisión en directo f (Esp), emisión en vivo f (AmL); ~ **camera** n TV cámara con corriente f, cámara directa f; ~ **center** AmE, ~ **centre** BrE n MECH ENG of lathe punta giratoria f, punto fijo m; ~ **coal** n COAL ascua f, brasa f, carbón ardiente m; ~ **coverage** n TV cobertura en directo f; ~ **grades** n pl AGRIC clasificación de los animales vivos f; ~ **head** n MECH ENG of lathe cabeza giratoria del torno f; ~ **line** n ELEC supply línea activa f, línea electrizada f; ~-**line indicator** n AIR TRANSP, ELEC, SAFE safety, overhead line indicador de línea activa m; ~ **load** n CONST carga variable f; ~ **matter** n PRINT composición todavía válida f; ~ **oil** n THERMO petróleo crudo m; ~ **spindle** n MECH ENG of lathe eje del punto fijo m, huso de la cabeza movible m; ~ **steam** n HYDRAUL, NUCL, THERMO vapor a presión m, vapor vivo m; ~-**steam injector** n HEAT ENG, HYDRAUL inyector de vapor a presión m; ~ **storage** n WATER embalse útil m; ~ **weight** n AGRIC peso vivo m

lively: ~ **handle** n TEXTIL tacto vivo m

livery n AIR TRANSP airline librea f

livestock: ~ **adviser** n AGRIC asesor en producción animal m, asesora en producción animal f; ~ **breeding** n AGRIC cría de ganado f; ~ **farm** n AGRIC cabaña f (AmL), explotación ganadera f (Esp); ~ **husbandry** n AGRIC ganadería f; ~ **loading ramp** n AGRIC embarcadero m (AmL), rampa para ganado f (Esp); ~ **show** n AGRIC concurso de ganado m

living: ~ **community** n POLL comunidad vital f, comunidad viva f

lixiviation n CHEM, POLL lixiviación f

LLC abbr (logical link control) TELECOM control de enlace lógico m, control lógico de enlace m

Lloyd's: ~ **mirror** n PHYS espejo de Lloyd m

LLV abbr (lunar logistics vehicle) SPACE LLV (vehículo logístico lunar)

lm abbr (lumen) METR lm (lumen)

LMS abbr (land mobile station) TELECOM estación móvil terrestre f

LNA abbr ELECTRON (low-noise amplifier) amplificador con bajo nivel de ruidos m, OPT (launch numerical aperture) apertura numérica de lanzamiento f, apertura numérica de salida f, SPACE (low-noise amplifier) amplificador con bajo nivel de ruidos m, TELECOM (launch numerical aperture), apertura numérica de lanzamiento f, apertura numérica de salida f, (low-noise amplifier) amplificador con bajo nivel de ruidos m

L-network n ELEC ENG red L f

LNG[1] abbr (liquefied natural gas) GAS, PETR TECH, THERMO GNL (gas natural licuado)

LNG[2]: ~ **bus** n (liquid-natural-gas bus) TRANSP autobús de gas natural licuado m (Esp), bus de gas natural licuado m (AmL); ~ **carrier** n TRANSP (liquid-natural-gas carrier) transporte de gas natural licuado m, WATER TRANSP (liquefied-natural-gas carrier) buque gasero m, metanero m

LNG-LPG: ~ **carrier** n (liquefied-natural-gas and liquefied-petroleum-gas carrier) THERMO boat building, WATER TRANSP buque para transporte de gas natural licuado y gas de petróleo licuado m

LO abbr (local oscillator) ELECTRON, PHYS, SPACE, TELECOM oscilador local m

load[1]: ~-**coupled** adj COMP&DP acoplado por carga

load[2] n GEN carga f; ~-**and-trim sheet** n AIR TRANSP aircraft hoja de carga y centrado f; ~ **angle** n ELEC electrical machine ángulo de carga m; ~ **application** n AIR TRANSP aplicación de carga f; ~ **at break** n P&R carga al romperse f, tensión de tracción a la rotura f; ~-**bearing capacity** n COAL capacidad de carga f; ~-**bearing wall** n CONST muro de carga m, pared que soporta la carga f; ~ **capacity** n AIR TRANSP of circuit breaker capacidad de carga f; ~-**carrying balloon system** n MILIT sistema de globo aerostático para transporte de carga m; ~ **cast** n GEOL estructura de molde de carga m; ~ **chain** n MECH ENG of pulley-block, hoist, etc cadena de carga f, PROD trunks cadena apiladora f, cranes, pulleys cadena de carga f, SAFE cadena de carga f; ~ **characteristic** n AIR TRANSP características de carga f pl; ~ **circuit** n ELEC circuito de carga m, circuito de utilización m, TELECOM circuito en carga m; ~-**commutated converter** n ELEC convertidor conmutado de carga m; ~ **conveyor** n MINE transportador de carga m; ~ **coupling** n COMP&DP acoplamiento por carga m; ~ **curve** n ELEC supply network curva de carga f, diagrama de carga m; ~ **diagram** n ELEC ENG, MECH diagrama de carga m; ~ **dispatch office** n NUCL despacho de cargas m; ~ **dispatcher** n ELEC supply network despachador de carga m, distribuidor de carga m, repartidor de la carga m; ~ **displacement** n WATER TRANSP ship design desplazamiento en carga m; ~ **distribution** n AIR TRANSP, CONST distribución de carga f; ~ **duration curve** n ELEC supply network curva de duración de la carga f; ~ **factor** n AIR TRANSP factor de carga m, MECH coeficiente de carga m, factor de carga m, factor de utilización m, PETR TECH, REFRIG factor de carga m; ~ **fluctuation** n ELEC fluctuación de la carga f, variación de la carga f; ~ **fluctuation pattern** n SPACE modelo de fluctuación de carga m; ~ **frequency control** n ELEC electrical machine control de frecuencia de la carga m, mando de frecuencia de la carga m, regulación de frecuencia de la carga f; ~ **hook-up** n AIR TRANSP helicopter enganche de carga m; ~ **impedance** n PHYS, TELECOM impedancia de carga f; ~ **in suspension** n HYDROL carga en suspensión f; ~-**indicating bolt** n MECH ENG perno indicador de la carga m; ~ **line** n AIR TRANSP, WATER TRANSP línea de carga f; ~ **loss** n ELEC pérdida de la carga f; ~ **metamorphism** n GEOL metamorfismo de carga *m*; **~-no charge ratio** *n* TRANSP tara *f*; **~ on top** *n* MINE, PETR TECH carga de crudo sobre residuos de limpieza de tanques *f*; **~ on top process** *n* POLL *materials* proceso de carga de crudo sobre residuos de limpieza de tanques *m*; **~ peak** *n* ELEC *supply network* carga de punta *f*, carga máxima *f*, pico de carga *m*; **~ point** *n* COMP&DP punto de carga *m*; **~ potato digger** *n* AGRIC arrancadora-cargadora de papas *f* (*AmL*), arrancadora-cargadora de patatas *f* (*Esp*); **~ release** *n* AIR TRANSP suelta de carga *f*; **~ resistance** *n* PHYS resistencia de carga *f*; **~ resistor** *n* ELEC resistor de carga *m*, resistor regulador de la carga *m*; **~ rope** *n* MINE cable de contrapeso *m* (*AmL*), cable de tracción *m* (*Esp*); **~-sensitive braking** *n* TRANSP frenado en función de la carga *m*; **~-sharing system** *n* TELECOM sistema de reparto de la carga *m*; **~ shedding** *n* ELEC *supply* separación de la carga *f*; **~ switch** *n* ELEC conmutador de carga *m*, seccionador de potencia *m*; **~ tap changer** *n* ELEC cambiador de toma de carga *m*, conmutador de tomas de carga *m*; **~ terminal** *n* PROD estación de carga *f*, terminal de carga *f*; **~ test** *n* ELEC prueba de carga *f*; **~ transfer** *n* ELEC *supply*, TELECOM transferencia de cargas *f*; **~ value** *n* TRANSP valor de la carga *m*; **~ waterline** *n* WATER TRANSP *boat building* flotación con carga completa *f*

load³ *vt* CINEMAT, COMP&DP, CONST, PRINT, WATER TRANSP cargar

loaded¹ *adj* COMP&DP cargado, WATER TRANSP *cargo ship* a plena carga, cargado

loaded²: **~ cable** *n* ELEC ENG, TELECOM cable cargado *m*; **~ capacity** *n* COAL capacidad cargada *f*; **~ displacement** *n* WATER TRANSP *of ship* desplazamiento en carga *m*; **~ governor** *n* MECH ENG regulador de mesa central *m*, regulador recargado *m*; **~ impedance** *n* ACOUST impedancia cargada *f*; **~ wheel** *n* PROD muela abrasiva sucia *f*

loader *n* COMP&DP cargador *m*, PROD *machine, person* cargador *m*, cargadora *f*, pala cargadora *f*, TRANSP cargador *m*, transportista *m*; **~ back hoe** *n* CONST *road building* escarificador trasero de la cargadora *m*

loading *n* COMP&DP carga *f*, cargado *m*, HYDROL *of sonic boom* carga *f*, MINE cargamento *m*, embarque *m*, PHYS carga *f*, SPACE *craft* cargamento *m*, exceso de gasolina *m*, WATER TRANSP carga *f*; **~ area** *n* AIR TRANSP *of airport* área de carga *f*; **~ belt** *n* MINE cargador de banda *m* (*Esp*), cargador de cinta *m* (*AmL*); **~ boom** *n* WATER TRANSP *fishing* pluma de carga *f*; **~ bridge** *n* TRANSP puente de carga *m*; **~ capacity** *n* TRANSP capacidad de carga *f*; **~ chute** *n* AGRIC manga para cargar animales *f*, MINE canaleta de carga *f*, tolva de carga *f*; **~ coil** *n* ELEC, PHYS bobina de carga *f*; **~ conveyor** *n* TRANSP transportador de carga *m*; **~ crane** *n* RAIL grúa de carga *f*; **~ density** *n* MINE volumen de carga *m*; **~ dock** *n* TRANSP embarcadero *m*, malecón de carga *m*, muelle de carga *m*, muelle para carga y descarga *m*, puerto *m*; **~ door** *n* AIR TRANSP puerta de carga *f*; **~ factor** *n* AIR TRANSP, PETR TECH factor de carga *m*, SPACE *communications* factor de cargamento *m*; **~ fork** *n* AGRIC horquilla para cargar *f*; **~ function** *n* METALL función de relleno *f*; **~ gage** *AmE*, **~ gauge** *BrE* *n* RAIL gálibo de carga *m*; **~ platform** *n* CONST, RAIL, TRANSP andén de carga *m*, muelle de carga *m*, plataforma de carga *f*; **~ pocket** *n* MINE depósito para cargamento *m* (*Esp*), receptáculo para carga-

mento *m* (*AmL*); **~ ramp** *n* AIR TRANSP rampa de carga *f*; **~ room** *n* CINEMAT cuarto oscuro *m*; **~ shovel** *n* CONST *civil engineering* pala cargadora *f*; **~ siding** *n* RAIL, TRANSP apartadero de carga *m*; **~ slot** *n* TV ranura de carga *f* (*AmL*), ranura para introducir la cinta de video *f* (*Esp*); **~ spool** *n* CINEMAT bobina de carga *f*; **~ stick** *n* MINE listón de carga *m*; **~ system** *n* MINE instalación para cargamento *f*; **~ test** *n* CONST prueba de carga *f*; **~ wagon** *n* AGRIC remolque *m*

loam *n* C&G barro de fundición *m*, CONST limo *m*, *soil* tierra vegetal *f*, GEOL limo *m*, PROD barro de fundición *m*, tierra de moldeo *f*, WATER fango *m*, marga *f*, greda *f*; **~ board** *n* PROD *founding* terraja giratoria *f*; **~ cake** *n* PROD *founding* terrón de arcilla *m*; **~ core** *n* PROD *founding* macho de arcilla *m*, macho de tierra *m*; **~ mold** *AmE*, **~ mould** *BrE* *n* PROD *founding* molde de tierra *m*; **~ plate** *n* PROD *founding* armadura para moldeo al barro *f*

loamy *adj* AGRIC franco

loan: **~ capital** *n* PETR TECH capital ajeno *m*

lob *n* MINE filón en escalones *m*

lobe *n* MECH orejeta *f*, SPACE *communications* lóbulo *m*, saliente *m*

lobelia: **~ alkaloid** *n* CHEM alcaloide de lobelia *m*

lobeline *n* CHEM lobelina *f*

lobinine *n* CHEM lobinina *f*

lobster: **~ boat** *n* OCEAN bote langostero *m*

LOCA *abbr* (*loss of coolant accident*) NUCL, REFRIG, SAFE LOCA (*accidente de pérdida de refrigerante*)

local¹ *adj* COMP&DP, TELECOM local

local²: **~ alignment** *n* ELECTRON alineación local *f*; **~ area network** *n* (*LAN*) COMP&DP, TELECOM red de área local *f*; **~ call** *n* TELECOM llamada local *f*; **~ capacity** *n* TRANSP capacidad local *f*; **~ charge rate call** *n* TELECOM llamada de tarifa local *f*; **~ communications network** *n* TELECOM red de comunicaciones urbanas *f*; **~ control** *n* MECH mando directo *m*; **~ controller** *n* TRANSP controlador local *m*; **~ copy** *n* TELECOM copia local *f*; **~ distribution cable** *n* TELECOM cable de distribución local *m*; **~ distribution network** *n* TELECOM red de distribución local *f*; **~ emission source** *n* POLL fuente de emisión local *f*, fuente de emisión urbana *f*; **~ exchange** *n* (*LE*) TELECOM central local *f*, central urbana *f*; **~ exchange area** *n* TELECOM zona de central urbana *f*; **~ function capabilities** *n pl* (*LFC*) TELECOM capacidad de las funciones locales *f*; **~ intersection controller** *n* TRANSP controlador de intersecciones locales *m*; **~ I/O PC** *n* PROD PC de entrada y salida local *m*; **~ junction** *n* TELECOM unión local *f*; **~ line concentrator** *n* TELECOM distribuidor de líneas urbanas *m*; **~ maintenance** *n* TELECOM mantenimiento local *m*; **~ mean time** *n* WATER TRANSP *astronomical navigation* hora media local *f*; **~ operation** *n* TELECOM operación local *f*; **~ oscillator** *n* (*LO*) ELECTRON, PHYS, SPACE, TELECOM oscilador local *m*; **~ oscillator frequency** *n* ELECTRON frecuencia local del oscilador *f*; **~ oscillator signal** *n* ELECTRON señal local del oscilador *f*; **~ oscillator tube** *n* ELECTRON tubo de oscilador local *m*; **~ oxidation** *n* ELECTRON oxidación local *f*; **~ program** *AmE*, **~ programme** *BrE* *n* TRANSP programa de zona *m*, programa de área *m*, programa local *m*; **~ reference** *n* TELECOM referencia local *f*; **~ standards and code of practice** *n pl* PROD normas y código de práctica locales *f pl*; ~ **stress** *n* METALL esfuerzo local *m*; ~ **switch** *n* TELECOM conmutador local *m*; ~ **traffic** *n* CONST, TRANSP tráfico local *m*; ~ **traffic information** *n* TRANSP información del tráfico local *f*; ~ **train** *n* RAIL, VEH tren de cercanías *m*, tren local *m*; ~ **user terminal** *n* (*LUT*) TELECOM terminal de usuario local *m*, WATER TRANSP *satellite location* terminal local de usuario *f*; ~ **variable** *n* COMP&DP variable local *f*; ~ **yielding** *n* METALL deformación local *f*

localize *vt* COMP&DP localizar

localized: ~ **disturbance** *n* FLUID perturbación localizada *f*; ~ **dyeing** *n* COLOUR teñido localizado *m*; ~ **fringes** *n pl* PHYS franjas localizadas *f pl*

localizer *n* TRANSP localizador *m*; ~ **beam** *n* AIR TRANSP *radio* haz localizador *m*; ~ **beam heading** *n* AIR TRANSP rumbo del haz localizador *m*

locally: ~-**high vorticity** *n* FLUID vorticidad localmente grande *f*; ~-**homogeneous geometry** *n* GEOM geometría localmente homogénea *f*; ~-**oxided junction** *n* ELECTRON unión localmente oxidada *f*

locate *vt* CONST, ELEC ENG localizar, PROD colocar, establecer el emplazamiento de, localizar, poner, situar, TELECOM localizar, WATER TRANSP *ship, mark, man overboard* localizar, situar

locating *n* CONST, ELEC ENG localización *f*, ubicación *f*, MECH ENG, PETROL localización *f*, PROD, TELECOM, WATER TRANSP localización *f*, ubicación *f*; ~ **arbor** *n* MECH ENG eje posicionador *m*, árbol posicionador *m*; ~ **device** *n* MECH ENG dispositivo de marcación de cranes *m*, dispositivo localizador *m*, dispositivo posicionador *m*; ~ **disc** *BrE*, ~ **disk** *AmE n* MECH ENG disco indicador *m*; ~ **hole** *n* MECH ENG agujero de referencia *m*; ~ **key** *n* MECH saliente posicionador *m*; ~ **pin** *n* MECH clavija de situación *f*, clavija posicionadora *f*, espiga posicionadora *f*, MECH ENG *die set* espiga posicionadora *f*, clavija de buena coincidencia *f*, clavija posicionadora *f*, PHOTO clavija posicionadora *f*; ~ **rib** *n* PROD nervio de fijación *m*; ~ **screw** *n* MECH ENG perno posicionador *m*, prisionero guiador *m*; ~ **spigot** *n* MECH ENG espiga posicionadora *f*; ~ **stud** *n* MECH ENG prisionero posicionador *m*

location *n* CINEMAT exterior fuera del estudio *m*, interior fuera del estudio *m*, COMP&DP *memory* ubicación *f*, dirección *f*, posición *f*, emplazamiento *m*, CONST *act* localización *f*, *position* situación *f*, ubicación *f*, ELEC ENG localización *f*, MECH ENG *act* colocación *f*, situación *f*, localización *f*, PETROL localización *f*, ubicación *f* (*AmL*), PROD, TELECOM, WATER TRANSP localización *f*; ~ **address** *n* PROD dirección en memoria *f*; ~ **management** *n* PROD gestión de emplazamiento de posición *f*, gestión de emplazamiento de ubicación *f*; ~ **shooting** *n* CINEMAT rodaje fuera del estudio *m*; ~ **spigot** *n* MECH ENG espiga posicionadora *f*; ~ **unit** *n* CINEMAT unidad de rodaje fuera del estudio *f*

locator *n* ACOUST localizador *m*, MECH ENG indicador de posición *m*, localizador *m*

lock¹ *n* AGRIC *cotton* válvula de la cápsula madura *f*, COAL compuerta *f*, COMP&DP bloqueo *m*, cierre *m*, CONST compuerta *f*, esclusa *f*, cerradura *f*, cerrojo *m*, fijación *f*, ELECTRON *planting* bloqueo *m*, sincronización *f*, HYDROL esclusa *f*, PRINT bloqueo *m*, SAFE *coated with abrasive* cerradura *f*, chapa *f*, VEH cerradura *f*, WATER *canal*, WATER TRANSP *inland*

waterways, harbours, fastening esclusa *f*; ~-**and-block** *n* RAIL sistema bloqueador controlado a mano *m*; ~-**and-block system** *n* RAIL sistema de bloqueo automático *m*, sistema de bloqueo con accionamiento de paso *m*; ~-**and-inland-lake canal** *n* WATER canal de esclusa y de lago interior *m*; ~ **bolt** *n* CONST pasador de cerrojo *m*; ~ **bush** *n* CONST casquillo de cerrojo *m*; ~ **casing** *n* CONST caja de la cerradura *f*; ~ **chamber** *n* WATER, WATER TRANSP *canal, harbour* cuenco *m*, cuenco de esclusa *m*, cámara de esclusa *f*; ~ **cup** *n* CONST escudo de la cerradura *m*; ~-**down switch** *n* ELEC conmutador de retención en reposo *m*; ~ **dues** *n pl* WATER TRANSP *inland waterways* derechos de esclusa *m pl*; ~ **fitting** *n* CONST ajuste de cerradura *m*; ~ **gate** *n* HYDROL, WATER, WATER TRANSP *of canal, harbour* puerta de esclusa *f*; ~-**grip pliers** *n pl* *BrE* (*cf locking pliers AmE*) MECH ENG alicates de sujeción *m pl*, tenazas de sujeción *f pl*; ~-**grip wrench** *n* MECH ENG llave de enclavamiento *f*; ~ **groove** *n* AUTO ranura cerrada *f*; ~ **house** *n* WATER casa de esclusas *f*; ~-**in amplifier** *n* ELECTRON amplificador sincronizado *m*; ~-**in range** *n* ELECTRON gama de señales de sincronización *f*; ~ **keeper** *n* WATER TRANSP esclusero *m*; ~ **key** *n* CONST cerrojo *m*, llave de cerradura *f*; ~-**mortise chisel** *n* CONST formón de mortaja de cerradura *m*; ~-**on** *n* AIR TRANSP captación *f*, captura *f*, enganche *m*; ~ **rail** *n* CONST *of door* peinazo de cerradura *m*; ~ **ring** *n* MECH ENG *for ball bearings* anillo de seguridad *m*, aro de freno *m*, aro de seguridad *m*; ~ **saw** *n* CONST serrucho de punta *m*; ~ **screw** *n* MECH ENG tornillo de fijación *m*, tornillo de seguridad *m*, tornillo de traba *m*; ~ **sill** *n* WATER umbral de esclusa *m*; ~ **staple** *n* CONST grapa de la cerradura *f*; ~ **stop** *n* MECH ENG retén *m*; ~-**up relay** *n* ELEC ENG relé de cierre con llave *m*; ~ **washer** *n* AUTO arandela de presión *f*, MECH, MECH ENG arandela Groover *f*, arandela de presión *f*, arandela de seguridad *f*, PROD, VEH arandela de presión *f*; ~ **wire** *n* MECH ENG alambre de seguridad *m*, alambre fijador *m*, alambre freno *m*, SAFE alambre de seguridad *m*; ~ **wire twist** *n* MECH ENG torsión del alambre fijador *f*; ~ **work** *n* CONST cerrajería *f*

lock² *vt* AIR TRANSP inmovilizar, CINEMAT, COMP&DP bloquear, CONST cerrar, MECH cerrar, enclavar, engranar, inmovilizar, MECH ENG *clamp* enclavar, enganchar, fijar, inmovilizar, RAIL enclavar, WATER *boat* salvar el desnivel de; ~ **off** *vt* CINEMAT separar; ~ **up** *vt* PRINT ajustar la forma de

lock³ *vi* CONST *become stuck* cerrarse, sujetarse, MECH ENG *become clamped* cerrarse, unirse

lockable: ~ **connector** *n* ELEC ENG conector bloqueable *m*

lockage *n* WATER *of boat* derechos de esclusa *m pl*, esclusaje *m*

locked¹: ~ **down** *adj* PROD cerrado

locked²: ~ **canal** *n* WATER canal con esclusas *m*; ~ **in-phase quadrature** *n* ELECTRON cuadratura de fase sincronizada *f*; ~ **loop** *n* TELECOM bucle enganchado *m*; ~ **oscillator** *n* ELECTRON oscilador sincronizado *m*; ~-**rotor current** *n* ELEC *asynchronous machine* corriente con rotor en reposo *f*, corriente con rotor enclavado *f*; ~-**rotor impedance characteristic** *n* ELEC *asynchronous machine* característica de impedancia con rotor enclavado *f*; ~-**rotor torque** *n* ELEC *machine* par inicial de arranque *m*

locker *n* WATER TRANSP *shipbuilding* taquilla *f*

locking *n* CONST cerradura *f*, enclavamiento *m*, MECH ENG *clamping* fijación *f*, enclavamiento *m*, METALL cierre *m*, fijación *f*, RAIL *of wheels* bloqueo *m*, TV acoplamiento de la frecuencia del campo con la de la red *m*, sincronización con la red *f*, WATER *of boat* esclusada *f*; ~ **attachment** *n* PROD dispositivo de bloqueo *m*, dispositivo de enclavamiento *m*, dispositivo de inmovilización *m*; ~ **bar** *n* RAIL barra de bloqueo *f*, palanca de bloqueo *f*, varilla de enclavamiento *f*; ~ **bolt** *n* CONST perno de enclavamiento *m*; ~ **cam** *n* MECH ENG leva de seguridad *f*; ~ **cover** *n* PROD tapa de cierre *f*; ~ **device** *n* ELEC *safety* dispositivo de cierre *m*, dispositivo de fijación *m*, dispositivo trabador *m*, MECH ENG dispositivo de cierre *m*, dispositivo inmovilizador *m*, dispositivo sujetador *m*, dispositivo trabador *m*, SAFE dispositivo trabador *m*; ~ **device for fire-resisting doors** *n* SAFE aparato para cerrar puertas resistentes al fuego *m*; ~ **handle** *n* CONST manija *f* (*AmL*), tirador *m*, tirador con cerradura *m* (*Esp*); ~ **knob** *n* INSTR perilla de trabazón *f*; ~ **lab** *n* PROD laboratorio de cierre *m*; ~ **latch** *n* PROD cerrojo de cierre *m*; ~ **mechanism** *n* CINEMAT mecanismo de bloqueo *m*, MECH ENG mecanismo de cierre *m*; ~ **pin** *n* MECH ENG chaveta de seguridad *f*, chaveta hendida *f*, clavija de cierre *f*, pasador de seguridad *m*; ~ **plate** *n* MECH ENG chapa de trinca *f*, placa de seguridad *f*, placa de sujeción *f*; ~ **pliers** *n pl AmE* (*cf lock-grip pliers BrE*) MECH ENG *tool* alicates de sujeción *m pl*, tenazas de sujeción *f pl*; ~ **plunger** *n* MECH ENG *gearbox* pistón inmovilizador *m*; ~ **ring** *n* CINEMAT anillo de retención *m*, aro de retención *m*; ~ **stud** *n* MECH ENG pasador de retención *m*; ~ **washer** *n* MECH, MECH ENG arandela de seguridad *f*, arandela fiador *f*, arandela fiadora *f*, arandela trabante *f*

locknit *n* TEXTIL tejido de punto charmés *m*

locknut *n* MECH ENG, PROD contratuerca *f*, tuerca de apriete *f*, tuerca de fijación *f*, tuerca de seguridad *f*, tuerca inaflojable *f*

lockout *n* COMP&DP bloqueado *m*, bloqueo *m*; ~ **coil** *n* PROD bobina de cierre *f*; ~ **power sources** *n pl* PROD recursos energéticos no utilizados *m pl*; ~ **solenoid** *n* PROD solenoide de cierre *m*; ~ **valve** *n* AIR TRANSP *speed brake* válvula de bloqueo *f*, válvula de cierre *f*

lockpin *n* MECH ENG chaveta de seguridad *f*, clavija de cierre *f*, pasador de seguridad *m*

lockplate *n* MECH ENG chapa de trinca *f*, placa de seguridad *f*, placa de sujeción *f*, platillo fijador *m*

locksmith *n* CONST cerrajero *m*

locksmithery *n* CONST cerrajería *f*

locksmithing *n* CONST cerrajería *f*

lockwire: ~ **pliers** *n pl* MECH ENG tenazas para alambre de fijación *f pl*

locomotive *n* RAIL locomotora *f*; ~ **boiler** *n* HEAT caldera de locomotora *f*; ~ **depot** *n AmE* (*cf engine shed BrE*) RAIL depósito de locomotoras *m*, depósito de máquinas *m*; ~ **-holding siding** *n* RAIL, TRANSP apartadero para locomotoras *m*

loctal: ~ **base** *n* ELECTRON base loctal *f*; ~ **tube** *n* ELECTRON tubo loctal *m*

locus *n* GEOM *disc units* lugar *m*, lugar geométrico *m*

locust: ~ **control** *n* AGRIC lucha contra langosta *f*

lode *n* MINE filón *m*, veta *f*; ~ **channel** *n* MINE canal filoniano *m*; ~ **drive** *n* MINE avance filoniano *m*; ~ **filling** *n* MINE relleno filoniano *m*; ~ **mining** *n* MINE laboreo de filones *m*; ~ **tin** *n* MINE estaño de roca *m*

lodestone *n* MINERAL piedra imán *f*

lodge *n* MINE galería de carga *f*, galería de desagüe *f*; ~ **room** *n* MINE cámara de enganche *f*

lodging *n* AGRIC encamado *m*, vuelco *m*

loess *n* AGRIC loess *m*

loeweite *n* MINERAL loweíta *f*

LOF *abbr* (*loss of frame*) TELECOM pérdida de trama *f*

lofting *n* WATER TRANSP *ship building* montea *f*

loftsman *n* WATER TRANSP *ship building* galibador *m*, monteador *m*

log^1 *n* COMP&DP registro *m*, logaritmo *m*, FUELLESS, GAS diagrafía *f*, GEOL diagrafía *f*, perfil *m*, registro *m*, MATH logaritmo *m*, PAPER tronco *m*, PETR TECH perfil *m*, registro *m*, diagrafía *f*, PETROL diagrafía *f*, perfil *m*, registro *m*, TELECOM registro de operaciones *m*; ~ **band mill** *n* PROD sierra de cinta para madera en rollo *f*; ~ **conveyer** *n* PROD transportador de rollizos *m*; ~ **cross-cutting machine** *n* PROD sierra alternativa para trocear madera en rollo *f*; ~ **frame** *n* PROD sierra vertical alternativa de varias hojas *f*; ~**-in** *n* COMP&DP conexión con el sistema *f*, entrada en el sistema *f*, inicio de la sesión *m*, registro de entrada *m*, TELECOM iniciación de registro *f*; ~ **line** *n* WATER TRANSP cordel de corredera *m*; ~**-normal distribution** *n* MATH distribución logarítmico-normal *f*; ~**-normal shadowing** *n* TELECOM distribución logarítmica normal *f*; ~**-off** *n* COMP&DP desconexión del sistema *f*, fin de la sesión *m*, registro de salida *m*, salida del sistema *f*; ~**-on** *n* COMP&DP conexión con el sistema *f*, entrada en el sistema *f*, inicio de la sesión *m*, registro de entrada *m*; ~**-out** *n* COMP&DP desconexión del sistema *f*, fin de la sesión *m*, registro de salida *m*, salida del sistema *f*; ~**-periodic aerial** *n BrE* (*cf log-periodic antenna AmE*) TV antena de período logarítmico *f*, antena logarítmica *f*; ~**-periodic antenna** *n AmE* (*cf log-periodic aerial BrE*) TV antena de período logarítmico *f*, antena logarítmica *f*; ~ **roller** *n* AGRIC rodillo de troncos *m*

log^2 *vt* CINEMAT, COMP&DP, PETR TECH registrar, WATER TRANSP *events* registrar, *fault* denunciar

log^3: ~ **in** *vi* COMP&DP conectarse al sistema, entrar en el sistema, iniciar la sesión, registrar la entrada, PROD abrir, ejecutar el procedimiento de entrada en comunicación, entrar en el sistema, entrar en el sistema usuario, identificarse; ~ **off** *vi* COMP&DP desconectarse del sistema (*AmL*), registrar la salida, salir del sistema, terminar la sesión; ~ **on** *vi* COMP&DP conectarse al sistema, entrar en el sistema, iniciar la sesión, registrar la entrada; ~ **out** *vi* COMP&DP desconectarse del sistema (*AmL*), registrar la salida, salir del sistema, terminar la sesión

logarithm *n* COMP&DP, MATH, TELECOM logaritmo *m*

logarithmic^1 *adj* COMP&DP, MATH logarítmico

logarithmic^2: ~ **amplifier** *n* ELECTRON amplificador logarítmico *m*; ~ **characteristic** *n* ELECTRON característica logarítmica *f*; ~ **creep** *n* METALL deformación progresiva logarítmica *f*; ~ **decrement** *n* ELECTRON disminución logarítmica *f*, PHYS decrecimiento logarítmico *m*; ~ **potentiometer** *n* ELEC ENG potenciómetro de variación logarítmica *m*; ~ **scale** *n* ELEC, ELECTRON, INSTR, METR escala logarítmica *f*; ~ **sweep** *n* ELECTRON barrido logarítmico *m*; ~ **video amplifier** *n* ELECTRON amplificador logarítmico de imagen *m*

logatom n ACOUST logátomo m; ~ **articulation** n TELE-COM articulación de logátomos f
logbook n TRANSP cuaderno de bitácora m, diario de operaciones m
logged: ~ **distance** n WATER TRANSP distancia registrada por la corredera f
logger n COMP&DP registrador m, ELEC measurements, INSTR indicador múltiple m, registrador m, registrador automático m, registrador de datos m, tabulador electrónico m
loggia n CONST logia f
logging n PETR TECH perfilaje m, PROD explotación forestal f, transporte de troncos cortados m, TELE-COM anotación cronológica f, registro m; ~ **head** n MECH ENG balancín m
logic n COMP&DP lógica f, ELECTRON circuito lógico m, lógica f, TELECOM lógica f; ~ **addition** n ELECTRON circuito lógico sumador m, suma lógica f; ~ **algebra** n ELECTRON circuito lógico algebraico m, álgebra de proposiciones lógicas f; ~ **analyser** n BrE COMP&DP, ELECTRON analizador de lógica m, analizador lógico m; ~ **analysis** n COMP&DP, ELECTRON análisis de lógica m (AmL), análisis lógico m (Esp); ~ **analyzer** AmE see logic analyser BrE; ~ **array** n ELECTRON bloques lógicos m pl, conjunto de unidades lógicas m; ~ **card** n COMP&DP, ELECTRON placa lógica f, tarjeta de lógica f (AmL), tarjeta lógica f (Esp); ~ **circuit** n COMP&DP, ELECTRON, TELECOM circuito de lógica m, circuito lógico m; ~ **component** n ELECTRON componente lógico m; ~ **control** n ELECTRON control lógico m; ~ **design** n COMP&DP, ELECTRON diseño lógico m; ~ **device** n COMP&DP, ELECTRON dispositivo de lógica m, dispositivo lógico m; ~ **diagram** n COMP&DP, ELECTRON diagrama lógico m, PROD esquema lógico m; ~ **element** n COMP&DP, ELECTRON elemento lógico m; ~ **family** n COMP&DP, ELECTRON familia lógica f; ~ **gate** n COMP&DP, ELECTRON, PHYS puerta lógica f; ~ **high** n ELECTRON nivel lógico alto m; ~ **input signal** n ELECTRON señal de entrada de circuito lógico f; ~ **instruction** n COMP&DP instrucción lógica f; ~ **integrated circuit** n ELECTRON circuito lógico integrado m; ~ **level** n COMP&DP, ELECTRON nivel de lógica m, nivel lógico m; ~ **level signal** n PROD señal de nivel lógico f; ~ **level voltage** n ELEC, PROD voltaje de nivel lógico m; ~ **low** n ELECTRON nivel lógico bajo m; ~ **microcircuit** n ELECTRON microcircuito lógico m; ~ **operation** n COMP&DP, ELECTRON operación lógica f; ~ **operator** n COMP&DP, ELECTRON operador lógico m; ~ **output signal** n ELECTRON señal de salida de circuito lógico f; ~ **pattern** n ELECTRON configuración lógica f; ~ **reed block** n PROD bloque lógico de láminas m; ~ **reed contact** n PROD contacto lógico de láminas m; ~ **signal** n ELECTRON señal lógica f; ~ **signal converter** n NUCL convertidor de señales lógicas m; ~ **simulation** n ELECTRON simulación lógica f; ~ **simulator** n ELECTRON simulador lógico m; ~ **state** n ELECTRON estado lógico m, fase lógica f; ~ **state analysis** n ELECTRON análisis lógico de estado m, análisis lógico de fase m; ~ **state and timing analyser** BrE, ~ **state and timing analyzer** AmE n ELECTRON analizador lógico de estado y temporización m; ~ **symbol** n COMP&DP símbolo de lógica m (AmL), símbolo lógico m (Esp); ~ **test** n ELECTRON verificación lógica f; ~ **tester** n ELECTRON verificador lógico m; ~ **timing** n ELECTRON tempori-

zación lógica f; ~ **timing analysis** n ELECTRON análisis lógico de temporización m; ~ **unit** n ELEC unidad lógica f
logical[1] adj COMP&DP lógico
logical[2]: ~ **addressing** n COMP&DP direccionamiento lógico m; ~ **block** n COMP&DP bloque de lógica m, bloque lógico m; ~ **fault indication** n PROD indicación lógica de anomalías f, indicación lógica de averías f, indicación lógica de defectos f, indicación lógica de fallos f; ~ **file** n COMP&DP archivo lógico m, fichero lógico m; ~ **function** n ELECTRON función lógica f; ~ **link control** n (LLC) TELECOM control de enlace lógico m, control lógico de enlace m; ~ **machine** n ELECTRON máquina lógica f; ~ **operation** n COMP&DP operación con valores lógicos f, operación lógica f; ~ **operator** n COMP&DP operador lógico m; ~ **page length** n PRINT longitud de página lógica f; ~ **record** n COMP&DP registro lógico m; ~ **sensor** n COMP&DP detector lógico m, sensor lógico m; ~ **shift** n COMP&DP cambio lógico m, desplazamiento lógico m; ~ **type** n COMP&DP tipo lógico m; ~ **value** n COMP&DP valor lógico m; ~ **variable** n COMP&DP variable lógica f
logistic: ~ **support** n AIR TRANSP apoyo logístico m
logistics n COMP&DP logística f
logo n COMP&DP, CONST, TELECOM logo m
LOM abbr (loss of multiframe) TELECOM pérdida de multitrama f
LO-M abbr (laser-optic memory) OPT memoria laseróptica f
lone: ~ **pair** n CHEM of electrons par suelto m
long[1]: ~**life** adj FOOD de larga duración, de larga vida, PROD de gran duración; ~ **normal** adj GEOPHYS de longitud normal; ~**range** adj MILIT de gran alcance
long[2]: ~ **acceleration** n PROD aceleración larga f; ~**address acceptance** n TELECOM aceptación de direcciones extensas f; ~ **blast** n WATER TRANSP sound signals pitada larga f; ~ **compass** n CONST compás largo m; ~ **descender** n PRINT carácter descendente m; ~**distance cable** n ELEC ENG cable a larga distancia m; ~**distance flight** n AIR TRANSP vuelo de larga distancia m; ~**distance freight traffic** n AmE (cf long-distance goods traffic BrE) TRANSP tráfico de mercancías de larga distancia m; ~**distance gas transport** n TRANSP transporte de gas de larga distancia m; ~**distance goods traffic** n BrE (cf long-distance freight traffic AmE) TRANSP tráfico de mercancías de larga distancia m; ~**distance line** n ELEC ENG línea a gran distancia f, TELECOM línea de larga distancia f; ~**distance road train** n TRANSP convoy en carretera de larga distancia m; ~**fed animals** n pl AGRIC vacunos terminados con concentrados m pl; ~**fluted machine reamer** n MECH ENG escariador mecánico de ranuras profundas m; ~**focus lens** n CINEMAT, PHOTO objetivo de foco largo m; ~**haul carriage** n TRANSP transporte de larga distancia m; ~**haul lorry driver** n BrE (cf long-haul truck driver AmE) AUTO conductor de camión de largo recorrido m; ~**haul service** n AIR TRANSP air transport, TRANSP servicio de larga distancia m; ~**haul truck driver** n AmE (cf long-haul lorry driver BrE) AUTO conductor de camión de largo recorrido m; ~**hole blasting** n MINE pega de pozos profundos f, voladura de pozos profundos f; ~**life battery** n ELEC ENG batería de larga duración f; ~ **line** n OCEAN línea larga f; ~**line effect** n ELECTRON efecto de línea

larga *m*; **~-lived radioisotope** *n* RAD PHYS radioisótopo de larga vida *m*; **~ loop** *n* TRANSP circuito cerrado extenso *m*; **~ measure** *n* METR medida de longitud *f*, medida lineal *f*; **~ mission** *n* SPACE misión de largo plazo *f*; **~-necked flask** *n* LAB matraz aforado *m*, matraz de cuello largo *m*, matraz volumétrico *m*; **~-nose pliers** *n pl* MECH ENG, PROD alicates de punta larga *m pl*; **~-nosed pliers** *n pl* MECH ENG, PROD alicates de punta larga *m pl*; **~-oil alkyd** *n* P&R resina alquílica de alto contenido en aceite *f*, resina alquílica larga en aceite *f*; **~-oil varnish** *n* COATINGS, COLOUR barniz largo en aceite *m*; **~ period** *n* OCEAN periodo extenso *m*; **~-persistence screen** *n* TV pantalla de larga persistencia *f*; **~ pitch** *n* CINEMAT paso grande *m*; **~-pitch screw** *n* MECH ENG tornillo de paso grande *m*, tornillo de paso rápido *m*; **~-pitch winding** *n* ELEC *coil*, ELEC ENG devanado de paso largo *m*; **~-playing video** *n* (*VLP*) OPT video de larga duración *m* (*AmL*), vídeo de larga duración *m* (*Esp*); **~ pulse** *n* WATER TRANSP *radar* impulso largo *m*; **~-radius curve** *n* GEOM curva radial larga *f*; **~-range order** *n* CRYSTALL orden a larga distancia *m*, orden de largo alcance *m*; **~-range radar** *n* MILIT radar de gran alcance *m*, radar de largo alcance *m*; **~-range transport** *n* TRANSP transporte a largas distancias *m*; **~-range weapon** *n* MILIT proyectil de gran alcance *m*; **~ saw** *n* PROD sierra larga *f*; **~ screw** *n* MECH ENG *pipe fitting* tornillo de paso grande *m*, tornillo de paso rápido *m*; **~-shank top** *n* MECH ENG remache de cuerpo largo *m*; **~ shot** *n* CINEMAT plano lejano *m*, toma a distancia *f*; **~ splice** *n* WATER TRANSP *ropework* costura larga *f*; **~-tail pair** *n* ELECTRON par de gran persistencia *m*; **~ take** *n* CINEMAT toma larga *f*; **~-term stability** *n* ELECTRON estabilidad de larga duración *f*; **~ ton** *n* METR tonelada larga *f*; **~-wall extraction** *n* MINE extracción por tajos largos *f*; **~ wave** *n* ELEC *radiation*, WAVE PHYS onda larga *f*; **~-way signal** *n* ELECTRON señal de largo alcance *f*
longboat *n* WATER TRANSP lancha *f*
longifolene *n* CHEM longifoleno *m*
longitude *n* SPACE, WATER TRANSP *geography, navigation* longitud *f*
longitudinal[1] *adj* AIR TRANSP, ELECTRON, WATER TRANSP *ship design* longitudinal
longitudinal[2]: **~-arch kiln** *n* HEAT horno de arco longitudinal *m*; **~ axis** *n* AIR TRANSP, MECH ENG, SPACE *craft* eje longitudinal *m*; **~-beam coupler** *n* AIR TRANSP acoplador de haz longitudinal *m*; **~ chromatic aberration** *n* OPT, PHYS, RAD PHYS, TELECOM, TV aberración cromática longitudinal *f*; **~ component** *n* PHYS componente longitudinal *f*; **~ current** *n* C&G corriente logitudinal *f*; **~ cyclic stick load** *n* AIR TRANSP *helicopter* carga longitudinal de la barra cíclica *f*; **~ divergence** *n* AIR TRANSP divergencia longitudinal *f*; **~ filter** *n* ELECTRON filtro longitudinal *m*; **~ framing** *n* WATER TRANSP *shipbuilding* estructura longitudinal *f*; **~ gap loss** *n* OPT pérdida longitudinal en el entrehierro *f*; **~ magnetic recording** *n* ACOUST grabación magnética longitudinal *f*; **~ magnification** *n* INSTR amplificación longitudinal *f*, PHYS magnificación longitudinal *f*; **~ member** *n* AIR TRANSP miembro longitudinal *m*; **~ metacenter** *AmE*, **~ metacentre** *BrE* *n* WATER TRANSP *naval architecture* metacentro longitudinal *m*; **~ offset loss** *n* OPT, TELECOM pérdida por

desplazamiento longitudinal *f*, pérdida por desviación longitudinal *f*; **~ recording** *n* TV registro longitudinal *m*; **~ redundancy check** *n* (*LRC*) COMP&DP comprobación de redundancia longitudinal *f*, verificación de redundancia longitudinal *f*; **~ reinforcement** *n* CONST refuerzo longitudinal *f*, armadura longitudinal *f*; **~ scratch** *n* CINEMAT raya longitudinal *f*; **~ section** *n* CONST perfil longitudinal *m*, RAIL sección longitudinal *f*; **~ slot** *n* TELECOM ranura longitudinal *f*; **~ stability** *n* TRANSP estabilidad longitudinal *f*; **~ stress** *n* METALL esfuerzo longitudinal *m*; **~-traction test** *n* MECH ENG ensayo de tensión longitudinal *m*; **~ traverse** *n* MECH ENG *lathe work* avance longitudinal *m*, movimiento longitudinal *m*; **~ wave** *n* ACOUST, WAVE PHYS onda longitudinal *f*; **~-wind component** *n* AIR TRANSP componente de viento longitudinal *f*
longitudinals: **~ plan** *n* WATER TRANSP *ship design* plano de longitudinales *m*
longshore: **~ bar** *n* GEOL, OCEAN, WATER TRANSP barra costera *f*, barra litoral *f*; **~ current** *n* OCEAN corriente costera *f*
longshoreman *n* *AmE* (*cf docker BrE*) WATER TRANSP cargador de muelle *m*, estibador *m*, obrero portuario *m*
longtime: **~ constant** *n* ELECTRON *locksmithing* constante de larga duración *f*
longwall: **~ face** *n* MINE frente de tajo largo *m*; **~ stoping** *n* MINE explotación por tajos largos *f*; **~ system** *n* COAL laboreo por arranque del filón entero *m*, laboreo por grandes tajos *m*, laboreo por hundimiento *m*, laboreo sin dejar pilares *m*, sistema de laboreo por grandes tajos *m*
look[1]: **~-through** *adj* PAPER transparente
look[2] *n* TEXTIL aspecto *m*; **~ ahead** *n* COMP&DP adelantamiento *m*, anticipación *f*, previsión de acarreo *f*; **~-up** *n* COMP&DP búsqueda *f*, consulta *f*; **~-up table** *n* COMP&DP tabla de consulta *f*
looking: **~ glass** *n* INSTR cristal de observación *m*
lookout *n* WATER TRANSP *navigation* serviola *f*, vigía *m*
loom *n* TEXTIL telar *m*, WATER TRANSP *of light* resplandor *m*; **~ speed** *n* TEXTIL velocidad del telar *f*; **~ state** *n* TEXTIL salido de telar; **~ state weft** *n* TEXTIL trama salida de telar *f*
loop *n* ACOUST antinodo *m*, bucle *m*, C&G aro *m*, CINEMAT, COMP&DP bucle *m*, ELEC *circuit* antinodo *m*, bucle *m*, lazo *m*, ELEC ENG bucle *m*, circuito cerrado *m*, antinodo *m*, ELECTRON circuito de iteración *m*, lazo *m*, bucle *m*, GEOM lazo *m*, HYDROL meandro *m*, PETROL desvío auxiliar *m*, bucle *m*, tramo de cañería doble *m*, desvío suplementario *m*, PHYS antinodo *m*, PROD circuito *m*, bucle *m*, *oscillations* antinodo *m*, TELECOM bucle *m*, TEXTIL bucle *m*, lazada *f*, malla *f*, WATER TRANSP *of rope* seno *m*, WAVE PHYS antinodo *m*; **~ aerial** *n* *BrE* (*cf loop antenna AmE*) TELECOM antena de cuadro *f*; **~ antenna** *n* *AmE* (*cf loop aerial BrE*) TELECOM antena de cuadro *f*; **~ back connector** *n* PROD conector en bucle *m*; **~ coil** *n* ELEC bobina de bucle *f*; **~ coupling** *n* ELEC ENG *networks* acoplamiento en malla *m*; **~ divider** *n* AGRIC *harvester* divisor de arco *m*; **~ fault** *n* PROD anomalía del bucle *f*, avería del bucle *f*, fallo del bucle *m*; **~ feedback signal** *n* ELECTRON señal de realimentación en circuito cerrado *f*; **~ former** *n* CINEMAT formador de bucles *m*; **~ galvanometer** *n* ELEC, ELEC ENG galvanómetro de bucle *m*, galvanómetro de

cuadro m; ~ **lever** n PROD palanca de lazo f; ~ **line** n RAIL circuito en bucle m, ferrocarril de circunvalación m, vía apartadero f, vía de derivación f; ~ **lock** n ELECTRON bloqueo del circuito m; ~ **network** n COMP&DP red en bucle f; ~-**pile carpet** n TEXTIL alfombra de felpa de bucle f; ~ **printing** n CINEMAT copiado en bucle m; ~ **test** n ELEC prueba de lazo f, prueba del bucle f, prueba en bucle f; ~-**through operation** n PROD operación a conexión derivada f

LOOP: ~ **statement** n COMP&DP instrucción LOOP f, sentencia LOOP f

loopback: ~ **command "audio loop request"** n (LCA) TELECOM señal para la alimentación del bucle "petición bucle por audio" f; ~ **command "digital loop request"** n TELECOM señal para la alimentación del bucle "petición bucle digital" f; ~ **command "video loop request"** n (LCV) TELECOM señal para la alimentación del bucle "petición bucle por vídeo" f

looped[1] adj ELEC circuit en bucle

looped[2]: ~ **rod** n PROD barra ojalada f; ~ **signal** n TELECOM señal en bucle f; ~ **yarn** n TEXTIL hilado en bucle m

looping: ~ **mill** n PROD tren de alambre m

loose[1] adj COAL rock incoherente, ELEC terminal libre, MECH ENG pulley, reel, sleeve libre, loco, suelto, PROD nut flojo, suelto, wheel loco

loose[2]: ~ **accent** n BrE (cf piece accent AmE) PRINT acento postizo m; ~ **ballasting** n RAIL balastaje suelto m, balasto suelto m; ~ **buffer** n OPT protección flotante f; ~ **buffering** n OPT tampón variable m; ~ **cable** n PROD cable suelto m; ~-**cable structure** n OPT, TELECOM estructura de cables flotantes f, estructura de cables sueltos f; ~ **construction cable** n OPT cable construido flotante m; ~ **coupling** n COMP&DP conexión suelta f, ELEC acoplamiento inductivo m, ELEC ENG acoplamiento flojo m, acoplamiento inductivo m, PHYS acoplamiento débil m, acoplamiento inductivo m; ~ **dyeing** n COLOUR teñido suelto m; ~ **fit** n MECH ENG ajuste con holgura m, ajuste con huelgo m, ajuste flojo m, ajuste holgado m; ~-**freezing** n REFRIG congelación de productos meltos f; ~ **glass** n C&G vidrio suelto m; ~ **head** n MECH ENG of lathe, horizontal miller contrapunto m; ~ **headstock** n MECH ENG of lathe, horizontal miller contrapunto m; ~-**leaf** n PRINT hoja cambiable f; ~ **pick** n TEXTIL pasada floja f; ~ **piece** n PROD pieza desmontable f, pieza suelta f; ~-**pin hinge** n CONST bisagra de pasador suelto f; ~ **plant** n MECH ENG instalación móvil f; ~ **reel** n MECH ENG carrete suelto m; ~-**ribbon cable** n OPT cable plano flotante m; ~ **seat** n HYDRAUL asiento vibrante m; ~ **sleeve** n MECH ENG manguito desconectable m; ~ **tongue** n CONST carpentry lengüeta postiza f; ~-**tongue joint** n CONST unión de lengüeta postiza f; ~-**tube cable** n OPT cable tubo flotante m; ~-**tube structure** n TELECOM estructura de tubos sueltos f; ~ **wool** n C&G lana suelta f

loosely: ~-**wound turns** n pl ELEC ENG espiras del bobinado flojas f pl

loosen vt PROD nut, WATER TRANSP rope aflojar

looseness n PROD of nut desapriete m

loosening n RAIL acoplamiento flojo m; ~ **bar** n PROD founding barra para despegar del molde f; ~ **wedge** n MECH ENG cuña de desapriete f

LOP abbr (loss of pointer) TELECOM pérdida de apuntador f, pérdida de puntero f

lophine n CHEM lofina f

lopolith n GEOL lopolito m

Loran: ~ **chain** n AIR TRANSP cadena Loran f

Lorentz: ~ **force** n ELEC, ELEC ENG, PHYS fuerza de Lorentz f; ~ **gage** AmE, ~ **gauge** BrE n PHYS indicador de Lorentz m; ~ **transformation** n PHYS transformación de Lorentz f

Lorentz-Fitzgerald: ~ **contraction** n PHYS contracción de Lorentz-Fitzgerald f

Lorentz-Lorenz: ~ **formula** n PHYS fórmula de Lorentz-Lorenz f

Lorenz: ~ **constant** n PHYS constante de Lorenz f

lorried: ~ **troops** n pl BrE (cf trucked troops AmE) MILIT tropas transportadas por camión f pl

lorry n BrE (cf truck AmE) AUTO, CONST, MECH, REFRIG, TRANSP m, VEH camión m, vagón m; ~ **factor** n BrE (cf truck factor AmE) TRANSP factor de camión m

LOS abbr (loss of signal) TELECOM pérdida de señal f

Los Angeles: ~ **abrasion test** n CONST ensayo de abrasión de Los Angeles m

losing: ~ **stream** n HYDROL corriente de agua decreciente f

loss[1]: ~-**free** adj ELEC dielectric exento de pérdidas, libre de pérdidas, sin pérdidas

loss[2] n ELEC of synchronism pérdida f, ELEC ENG atenuación f, FUELLESS of heat, HYDRAUL of heat pérdida f, MECH ENG pérdida f, trabajo perjudicial m, energía disipada sin efectuar trabajo útil f, OPT atenuación f, pérdida f, PETR TECH, TELECOM pérdida f; ~ **angle** n ELEC, PHYS ángulo de pérdidas m; ~ **caused by fire** n SAFE pérdida causada por incendio f; ~ **of color** AmE, ~ **of colour** BrE n C&G pérdida de color f; ~ **of compactness of track** n RAIL pérdida de la compacidad de la vía f; ~ **of coolant accident** n (LOCA) NUCL, REFRIG, SAFE accidente de pérdida de refrigerante m (LOCA); ~ **due to friction** n MECH ENG merma debida a la fricción f, pérdida debida a la fricción f, pérdida por fricción f; ~ **factor** n ELEC energy factor de disipación m, factor de pérdidas m, PHYS factor de disipación m; ~ **of frame** n (LOF) TELECOM pérdida de trama f; ~ **of frame alignment** n (LFA) TELECOM pérdida de alineación de cuadros f; ~ **of heat** n HYDRAUL pérdida de calor f; ~ **of heat sink** n NUCL pérdida de sumidero de calor f; ~ **of multiframe** n (LOM) TELECOM pérdida de multitrama f; ~ **of off-site power** n NUCL pérdida del suministro del exterior f, pérdida total de corriente alterna f; ~ **of picture lock** n TV pérdida de imagen fija f; ~ **of pointer** n (LOP) TELECOM pérdida de apuntador f, pérdida de puntero f, pérdida del apuntador f; ~ **of power** n MECH ENG pérdida de potencia f; ~ **of pressure** n HYDRAUL disminución de la presión f, pérdida de carga f, pérdida de presión f; ~ **prevention** n QUALITY prevención de pérdidas f; ~ **of returns** n PETR TECH pérdida de circulación f, pérdida de retornos f; ~ **of sheet** n C&G caída del listón f; ~ **of signal** n (LOS) TELECOM pérdida de señal f

lossless adj ELEC ENG sin fugas, sin pérdidas

lossy[1] adj ELEC ENG con pérdidas, disipativo, ELECTRON, TELECOM disipativo

lossy[2]: ~ **dielectric** n ELEC dieléctrico disipativo m; ~ **line** n ELEC ENG, PHYS línea con fugas f, línea con pérdidas f; ~ **material** n ELEC dielectric, line, etc material disipador *m*, material disipativo *m*, material que disipa mucha energía *m*, substancia disipativa *f*

lost: ~ **bullet** *n* MILIT bala perdida *f*; ~ **circulation** *n* PETR TECH pérdida de circulación *f*, pérdida de lodo *f*, pérdida de retornos *f*, PETROL circulación perdida *f*; ~ **ends** *n pl* TEXTIL cabos perdidos *m pl*; ~ **hole** *n* PETR TECH hueco perdido *m*; ~ **time** *n* PETR TECH tiempo perdido *m*; ~ **traffic** *n* TELECOM tráfico perdido *m*; ~ **wax** *n* C&G cera perdida *f*; ~~**wax casting** *n* PROD moldeo a la cera perdida *m*; ~~**wax mold for casting** *AmE*, ~~**wax mould for casting** *BrE n* MECH ENG molde de cera perecedero *m*, molde para moldeo a la cera perdida *m*

lot *n* CINEMAT *of electrode* plató *m*; ~ **size** *n* PROD número de piezas de la serie a fabricar *m*; ~ **sizing** *n* PROD determinación de la dimensión de un pedido *f*, fijación del número de piezas de una serie *f*; ~ **splitting** *n* PROD división de lote *f*

LOT *abbr* (*leak-off test*) PETR TECH prueba de integridad de la formación *f*, prueba de leak-off *f*

loudness *n* ACOUST, PHYS intensidad de sonido *f*, sonoridad *f*; ~ **level** *n* ACOUST, PHYS nivel de sonido *m*, nivel de sonoridad *m*

loudspeaker *n* ACOUST altavoz *m*, altoparlante *m*, parlante *m*, CINEMAT altavoz *m*, ELEC *radio*, PHYS, TELECOM altavoz *m*, altoparlante *m*, parlante *m*, TV altavoz *m*; ~ **system** *n* ACOUST sistema de altavoces *m*

louver *AmE see louvre BrE*

louvre *n BrE* C&G persiana *f*, MECH celosía *f*, claraboya *f*, persiana *f*, MECH celosía *f*, claraboya *f*, rejilla de ventilación *f*, VEH abertura *f*

low[1]: **as** ~ **as reasonably achievable** *adj* (*ALARA*) NUCL ALARA; ~ **calorie** *adj* FOOD bajo en calorías; ~~**fat** *adj* FOOD bajo en grasas; ~~**key** *adj* CINEMAT claro, de poco contraste; ~ **order** *adj* COMP&DP de orden inferior; ~ **power** *adj* ELEC ENG poca potencia

low[2] *n* GEOL mínimo *m*, METEO baja *f*;

▶ **a** ~~**alloy steel** *n* METALL acero de baja aleación *m*; ~~**altitude orbit** *n* SPACE órbita de baja altitud *f*; ~~**amplitude signal** *n* ELECTRON señal de baja amplitud *f*; ~~**angle shot** *n* CINEMAT toma desde un ángulo bajo *f*, PHOTO toma de ángulo bajo *f*;

▶ **b** ~~**band recording** *n* TV registro de banda baja *m*; ~~**band standard** *n* TV norma de banda baja *f*; ~ **beams** *n pl AmE* (*cf dipped headlights BrE*) VEH *lighting* faros inclinables *m pl*, luces cortas *f pl*; ~~**bed trailer** *n* CONST remolque de plataforma baja *m*; ~ **boy trailer** *n* CONST plataforma de transporte *f*, remolque *m*;

▶ **c** ~ **capacitance** *n* ELEC ENG baja capacidad *f*, baja capacitancia *f*; ~~**carbon steel** *n* MECH ENG, METALL acero bajo en carbono *m*, acero suave *m*; ~ **concentration** *n* ELECTRON baja concentración *f*; ~~**contrast original** *n* CINEMAT original de bajo contraste *m*; ~~**cost automation technique** *n* MECH ENG técnica de automatización de bajo costo *f*; ~~**cost conversion** *n* RAD PHYS conversión a bajo costo *f*; ~~**cycle fatigue** *n* CRYSTALL fatiga con pocos ciclos *f*;

▶ **d** ~~**density pick-up baler** *n* AGRIC prensa de baja presión *f*; ~ **depression** *n* METEO depresión baja *f*, depresión poco profunda *f*; ~~**distortion modulation** *n* ELECTRON modulación de baja distorsión *f*; ~~**drift oscillator** *n* ELECTRON oscilador de baja derivación *m*;

▶ **e** ~~**energy antiproton ring** *n* (*LEAR*) PART PHYS

anillo antiprotón de baja energía *m* (*LEAR*); ~~**energy beam** *n* ELECTRON haz de baja potencia *m*; ~~**energy environment** *n* GEOL medio de baja energía *m*; ~~**energy focused ion beam** *n* ELECTRON, RAD PHYS haz iónico convergente de baja energía *m*; ~~**energy laser** *n* ELECTRON láser de baja energía *m*; ~~**energy nuclear physics** *n* NUCL, PART PHYS, RAD PHYS física nuclear de baja energía *f*; ~~**energy radiation** *n* RAD PHYS radiación de baja energía *f*; ~~**energy single-frequency laser** *n* ELECTRON, RAD PHYS láser de monofrecuencia de baja energía *m*; ~~**energy transverse jet** *n* RAD PHYS haz transversal de baja energía *m*; ~ **explosive** *n* MINE explosivo lento *m*, explosivo no detonante *m*;

▶ **f** ~~**freezing dynamite** *n* MINE dinamita de temperatura de congelación baja *f*; ~ **frequency** *n* (*LF*) ELEC, ELEC ENG, ELECTRON, RAD PHYS, TELECOM, WAVE PHYS baja frecuencia *f* (*BF*); ~~**frequency amplification** *n* ELECTRON amplificación de baja frecuencia *f*; ~~**frequency amplifier** *n* ELECTRON amplificador de baja frecuencia *m*; ~~**frequency compensation** *n* ELECTRON compensación de baja frecuencia *f*; ~~**frequency furnace** *n* ELEC ENG horno de baja frecuencia *m*; ~~**frequency generator** *n* ELEC, ELECTRON generador de baja frecuencia *m*; ~~**frequency image** *n* SPACE imagen de baja frecuencia *f*; ~~**frequency induction heater** *n* ELEC ENG calentador de inducción de baja frecuencia *m*; ~~**frequency induction heating** *n* ELEC ENG calentamiento por inducción de baja frecuencia *m*; ~~**frequency oscillator** *n* ELECTRON oscilador de baja frecuencia *m*; ~~**frequency response** *n* ELECTRON respuesta de baja frecuencia *f*; ~~**frequency signal** *n* ELECTRON señal de baja frecuencia *f*;

▶ **g** ~~**gain amplifier** *n* ELECTRON amplificador de poca ganancia *m*; ~ **gear** *n* MECH ENG multiplicación pequeña *f*; ~~**grade metamorphism** *n* GEOL metamorfismo de bajo grado *m*; ~~**grade ore** *n* MINE mineral de calidad inferior *m*, mineral de poca ley *m*, mineral pobre *m*; ~ **gradient** *n* CONST pendiente pequeña *f*; ~~**gravity gasoline** *n AmE* (*cf low-gravity petrol BrE*) AUTO, VEH gasolina de baja gravedad *f*; ~~**gravity petrol** *BrE n* (*cf low-gravity gasoline AmE*) AUTO, VEH gasolina de baja gravedad *f*;

▶ **h** ~ **head** *n* FUELLESS salto bajo *m*; ~~**high-low doping profile** *n* ELECTRON perfil de alteración variable *m*;

▶ **i** ~~**impedance path** *n* PROD circuito de baja impedancia *m*; ~~**insertion force connector** *n* ELEC ENG conector de baja fuerza de inserción *m*; ~ **insertion loss** *n* TELECOM bajas pérdidas de inserción *f pl*; ~ **and intermediate level waste** *n* (*L&ILW*) NUCL residuos de baja y mediana actividad *m pl* (*RBMA*);

▶ **k** ~ **kiln** *n* COAL horno lento *m*;

▶ **l** ~ **lead gasoline** *n AmE* (*cf low lead petrol BrE*) AUTO, PETROL, VEH gasolina baja en plomo *f*; ~ **lead petrol** *n BrE* (*cf low lead gasoline AmE*) AUTO, PETROL, VEH gasolina baja en plomo *f* (*Esp*), nafta baja en plomo *f* (*AmL*); ~~**leakage diode** *n* ELECTRON diodo de baja dispersión *m*; ~~**level amplification** *n* ELECTRON amplificación de bajo nivel *f*; ~~**level amplifier** *n* ELECTRON amplificador de bajo nivel *m*; ~~**level DC I/O line** *n* PROD línea E/S de CC de bajo nivel *f*; ~~**level DC out** *n* PROD salida de CC de bajo nivel *f*; ~~**level DC voltage** *n* ELEC, PROD tensión de CC de bajo nivel *f*, voltaje de CC de pequeña intensidad *m*; ~-**level device** *n* ELECTRON dispositivo de bajo nivel *m*; ~-**level fault** *n* PROD fallo de bajo nivel *m*; ~-**level injection** *n* ELECTRON inyección de bajo nivel *f*; ~-**level language** *n* COMP&DP lenguaje de bajo nivel *m*; ~-**level modulation** *n* ELECTRON modulación de bajo nivel *f*; ~-**level radioactive waste** *n* NUCL residuos radiactivos de baja actividad *m pl*; ~-**level signal** *n* ELECTRON, PROD señal de bajo nivel *f*; ~-**level transistor** *n* ELECTRON transistor de bajo nivel *m*; ~ **level of twist** *n* TEXTIL nivel bajo de torsión *m*; ~-**level video** *n* TV video de bajo nivel *m* (*AmL*), vídeo de bajo nivel *m* (*Esp*); ~-**level warning light** *n* MECH ENG luz de advertencia de bajo nivel *f*, luz de advertencia débil *f*; ~-**level waste** *n* POLL, RECYCL desperdicios de bajo nivel *m pl*, residuos de escasa actividad *m pl*, residuos de escasa radiactividad *m pl*; ~-**level waste package** *n* NUCL bulto de residuos de baja actividad *m*; ~ **logic level** *n* ELECTRON nivel bajo de circuito lógico *m*; ~ **loss** *n* TELECOM bajas pérdidas *f pl*; ~-**loss cable** *n* ELEC *supply* cable de pequeñas pérdidas *m*, cable poco disipativo *m*, TELECOM cable de pequeñas pérdidas *m*; ~-**loss dielectric** *n* ELEC dieléctrico de pequeñas pérdidas *m*; ~-**loss fiber** *AmE*, ~-**loss fibre** *BrE n* OPT, TELECOM fibra de baja atenuación *f*, fibra de pequeñas pérdidas *f*; ~-**loss insulator** *n* ELEC, ELEC ENG aislante de poca pérdida *m*;

▣ **n** ~-**noise amplification** *n* ELECTRON, SPACE, TELECOM ampliación con bajo nivel de ruidos *f*; ~-**noise amplifier** *n* (*LNA*) ELECTRON, SPACE, TELECOM amplificador con bajo nivel de ruidos *m*; ~-**noise engineering** *n* ACOUST, MECH ENG ingeniería de bajo nivel de ruido *f*, técnica de bajo nivel de ruido *f*; ~-**noise preamplifier** *n* ELECTRON, RAD PHYS preamplificador con bajo nivel de ruidos *m*;

▣ **o** ~-**order filter** *n* ELECTRON filtro de paso bajo *m*; ~-**order harmonic** *n* ELECTRON armónico de bajo nivel *m*; ~-**order position** *n* COMP&DP posición de orden inferior *f*;

▣ **p** ~ **pass** *n* AIR TRANSP pasabajos *m*; ~-**pass band** *n* TELECOM banda de paso bajo *f*; ~-**pass filter** *n* ACOUST, COMP&DP, ELEC, ELECTRON, PETROL, PHYS, TELECOM filtro de paso bajo *m*, filtro de paso de banda *m*; ~-**pass filtering** *n* ACOUST, COMP&DP, ELEC, ELECTRON, PETROL, PHYS, TELECOM filtración de paso bajo *f*, filtración de paso de banda *f*; ~-**pass image** *n* SPACE imagen de paso bajo *f*; ~-**pass response** *n* ELECTRON respuesta de paso bajo *f*; ~-**pass sampled data filter** *n* ELECTRON filtro de información de muestra de paso bajo *m*; ~-**pass section** *n* ELECTRON sección de paso bajo *f*; ~-**plasticity clay** *n* C&G barro de plasticidad baja *m*; ~-**power diode** *n* ELECTRON diodo de baja potencia *m*, diodo de poca potencia *m*; ~-**power distress transmitter** *n* (*LPDT*) TELECOM transmisor de socorro de baja potencia *m*; ~-**power laser diode** *n* TELECOM diodo láser de baja potencia *m*; ~ **pressure** *n* GAS, PHYS presión baja *f*; ~-**pressure alarm** *n* PROD alarma por baja presión *f*; ~-**pressure area** *n* GEOL área de baja presión *f*, METEO zona de baja presión *f*, área de baja presión *f*; ~-**pressure blowpipe** *n* CONST soplete de baja presión *m*; ~ **pressure casting** *n* MECH ENG fundición de baja presión *f*; ~-**pressure compressor** *n* MECH ENG compresor de baja presión *m*, compresor de pequeña presión *m*; ~-**pressure controller** *n* REFRIG presostato de baja presión *m*; ~-**pressure**

core spray *n* (*LPCS*) NUCL aspersión del núcleo a baja presión *f* (*LPCS*); ~-**pressure filter** *n* PROD filtro de baja presión *m*; ~-**pressure float valve** *n* REFRIG válvula de flotador de baja presión *f*; ~-**pressure flushing** *n* MAR POLL limpieza con descarga a baja presión *f*, limpieza con descarga de agua a baja presión *f*; ~-**pressure fuel filter** *n* AIR TRANSP filtro de combustible de baja presión *m*; ~-**pressure gas burner** *n* HEAT ENG quemador de gas a baja presión *m*; ~-**pressure heating** *n* HEAT ENG calefacción a baja presión *f*; ~-**pressure hot-water boiler** *n* HEAT caldera de agua caliente a baja presión *f*; ~-**pressure hot-water system** *n* HEAT sistema de agua caliente a baja presión *m*; ~-**pressure mercury lamp** *n* ELEC, ELEC ENG lámpara de vapor de mercurio a poca presión *f*; ~-**pressure piston compressor** *n* MECH ENG compresor de pistón de baja presión *m*; ~-**pressure safety cutout** *n* REFRIG presostato de seguridad de baja presión *m*; ~-**pressure vacuum pump** *n* MECH ENG bomba de vacío de baja presión *f*; ~-**profile bezel** *n* PROD bisel de bajo perfil *m*; ~-**profile open-end wrench** *n* MECH, MECH ENG *tool* llave de boca de perfil bajo *f*, llave española de perfil bajo *f*;

▣ **r** ~-**rank graywacke** *AmE*, ~-**rank greywacke** *BrE n* GEOL, PETROL grauwaka de bajo grado *f*; ~-**rate encoding** *n* (*LRE*) TELECOM codificación a baja velocidad *f*; ~ **reset** *n* PROD reposición baja *f*; ~ **resistance** *n* PHYS, TELECOM baja resistencia *f*; ~ **Reynolds number** *n* FLUID bajo número de Reynolds *m*; ~ **ring to ground** *n* TELECOM anillo bajo a tierra *m*;

▣ **s** ~-**shaft furnace** *n* COAL horno castellano *m*, horno de cuba baja *m*; ~ **shot** *n* CINEMAT toma desde un ángulo bajo *f*; ~-**shrink base** *n* CINEMAT soporte de bajo encogimiento contracción *m*; ~ **signal level** *n* ELECTRON nivel de señal bajo *m*; ~-**solid mud** *n* PETR TECH lodo con bajo contenido en sólidos *m*; ~-**solid sludge** *n* PETR TECH lodo con bajo contenido en sólidos *m*; ~ **speed** *n* MECH ENG, TELECOM baja velocidad *f*; ~-**speed camera** *n* CINEMAT cámara de baja velocidad *f*; ~-**speed diesel engine** *n* WATER TRANSP motor diesel lento *m*; ~-**speed electric motor** *n* ELEC ENG motor eléctrico de baja velocidad *m*; ~-**speed engine** *n* WATER TRANSP *diesel* motor poco revolucionado *m*; ~-**speed modem** *n* ELECTRON módem de acción lenta *m*; ~-**speed photography** *n* CINEMAT, PHOTO fotografía a baja velocidad *f*; ~ **spot** *n* PRINT zona que no imprime en los procesos offset *f*; ~-**stop filter** *n* MECH ENG filtro de tope inferior *m*; ~ **sulfur content** *n* *AmE*, ~ **sulphur content** *BrE n* PETR TECH contenido bajo de azufre *m*, contenido bajo de sulfuro *m*; ~ **superheat** *n* REFRIG pequeño recalentamiento *m*;

▣ **t** ~ **temperature** *n* PHYS, REFRIG, THERMO baja temperatura *f*; ~-**temperature compartment** *n* REFRIG, THERMO compartimiento congelador *m*; ~-**temperature cooling installation** *n* MECH ENG *for ships and transporters* instalación de enfriamiento de baja temperatura *f*; ~-**temperature display case** *n* REFRIG, THERMO mueble de exposición a bajas temperaturas *m*; ~-**temperature insulation** *n* REFRIG, THERMO aislamiento para baja temperatura *m*; ~-**temperature resistance** *n* P&R resistencia a la baja temperatura *f*; ~-**temperature sinking** *n* THERMO perforación a baja temperatura *f*, profundización a baja temperatura *f*; **~-temperature technique** *n* REFRIG, THERMO técnica a baja temperatura *f*; **~-temperature thermometer** *n* REFRIG, THERMO termómetro para baja temperatura *m*; **~ tenor of ore** *n* MINE mineral de baja ley *m*, mineral pobre *m*; **~-tensile carbon steel tube** *n* HEAT, METALL tubo de acero al carbono de baja tensión de rotura *m*; **~ tension** *n* ELEC, ELEC ENG baja tensión *f*, bajo voltaje *m*, TELECOM baja tensión *f*; **~-tension detonator** *n* MINE detonador eléctrico de bajo voltaje *m*; **~ test gasoline** *n* (*cf low test petrol BrE*) *AmE* AUTO, PETROL, VEH gasolina de bajo octanaje *f*; **~ test petrol** *BrE* *n* (*cf low test gasoline AmE*) AUTO, PETROL, VEH gasolina de bajo octanaje *f*; **~-thrust motor** *n* SPACE motor con pequeño empuje *m*; **~ tide** *n* FUELLESS, HYDROL, OCEAN, WATER, WATER TRANSP bajamar *m*, marea baja *f*; **~-to-high transition** *n* ELECTRON flanco de subida *m*, transición de bajo a alto *f*; **~-torque operation** *n* PROD funcionamiento con par motor pequeño *m*, operación con torque pequeño *f* (*AmL*); **~-traffic road** *n* CONST carretera de poco tráfico *f*;

~ v **~ vacuum** *n* PHYS bajo vacío *m*; **~-velocity layer** *n* PETROL capa de velocidad baja *f*; **~-visibility landing** *n* AIR TRANSP aterrizaje con baja visibilidad *m*, aterrizaje con visibilidad pobre *m*; **~-volatile coal** *n* COAL carbón materias volátiles *m*; **~ voltage** *n* ELEC, ELEC ENG, TELECOM baja tensión *f*, bajo voltaje *m*; **~-voltage cable** *n* ELEC *supply*, ENG ELEC, cable de baja tensión *m*; **~-voltage installation** *n* ELEC, ELEC ENG instalación de baja tensión *f*, instalación de bajo voltaje *f*; **~-voltage network** *n* ELEC red de baja tensión *f*; **~-voltage winding** *n* ELEC devanado de baja tensión *m*, devanado de bajo voltaje *m*;

~ w **~ water** *n* FUELLESS, HYDROL *at sea* marea baja *f*, *in river or lake* estiaje *m*, bajamar *m*, OCEAN, WATER bajamar *m*, WATER TRANSP *tide* bajamar *m*, marea baja *f*; **~-water discharge** *n* WATER descarga de aguas bajas *f*; **~-water level** *n* WATER nivel de bajamar *m*, nivel de estiaje *m*; **~-water mark** *n* CONST marca de nivel inferior de agua *f*, HYDROL *of river* línea de nivel mínimo *f*, *tide* línea de bajamar *f*, OCEAN línea de nivel mínimo *f*, WATER TRANSP *tide* línea de bajamar *f*; **~-weight coating** *n* (*LWC*) PAPER capa de estucado de bajo gramaje *f*; **~-wing plane** *n* AIR TRANSP avión de ala baja *m*;

~ y **~-yield clay** *n* GEOL arcilla de bajo rendimiento *f*; **~-yield region** *n* ELECTRON zona de bajo rendimiento *f*

Lowell: **~ light** *n* CINEMAT lámpara Lowell *f*

lower[1] *adj* GEOL inferior

lower[2]: **~ annealing temperature** *n* C&G temperatura mínima de revenido *f*, temperatura mínima de templado *f*; **~ bainite** *n* METALL bainita inferior *f*; **~ case** *n* PRINT minúscula *f*; **~ control limit** *n* QUALITY límite inferior de control *m*; **~ deck** *n* WATER TRANSP cubierta inferior *f*; **~ harmonic** *n* ELECTRON armónico inferior *m*; **~-level service** *n* TELECOM servicio de bajo nivel *m*; **~ limit** *n* TELECOM límite inferior *m*; **~ limit of detectability** *n* POLL límite inferior de detectabilidad *m*, límite mínimo de detección *m*; **~ link** *n* AIR TRANSP *of rotor shaft* conexión inferior *f*; **~ loop** *n* CINEMAT bucle inferior *m*; **~ nibble** *n* PROD cuarteto inferior *m*; **~-order path adaptation** *n* (*LPA*) TELECOM adaptación de camino de menor orden *f*; **~-order path connection** *n* (*LPC*)

TELECOM conexión de camino de menor orden *f*; **~-order path termination** *n* (*LPT*) TELECOM terminación de camino de menor orden *f*; **~ pantograph final warning sign** *n* RAIL señal de alarma inferior final del pantógrafo *f*; **~ ply** *n* COATINGS capa inferior *f*; **~ printing** *n* PRINT impresión en minúscula *f*; **~ quality of service** *n* QUALITY, TELECOM calidad inferior de servicio *f*; **~ roll** *n* MECH ENG *rolling mill* rodillo inferior *m*; **~ shaft** *n* AUTO eje inferior *m*; **~ shroud** *n* WATER TRANSP *rigging* obenque del palo macho *m*; **~ side** *n* PRINT lado inferior *m*; **~ sideband** *n* COMP&DP, ELECTRON, PHYS, TELECOM, TV banda lateral inferior *f*; **~-sideband filter** *n* ELECTRON, TELECOM filtro de banda lateral inferior *m*; **~ sieve** *n* AGRIC zaranda inferior de granos *f*; **~ spool** *n* CINEMAT carrete inferior *m*; **~-storage basin** *n* FUELLESS embalse de almacenamiento inferior *m*; **~ subfield** *n* TELECOM subcampo inferior *m*; **~ surface** *n* AIR TRANSP superficie baja *f*, PHYS superficie inferior *f*; **~ tank** *n* AUTO depósito inferior *m*; **~ track** *n* HYDROL *of river* tramo inferior *m*; **~ workings** *n pl* MINE labores mineras inferiores *f pl*; **~ yield point** *n* METALL límite de elasticidad *m*

lower[3] *vt* CONST rebajar, ELEC ENG *voltage*, SAFE *antennas, waveguides* bajar, WATER TRANSP *boats* arriar, amainar

lowering *n* PHYS descenso *m*

lowest: **~ achievable emission rate** *n* POLL mínima velocidad de emisión *f*; **~ hourly traffic** *n* TRANSP tráfico mínimo por hora *m*; **~ usable frequency** *n* (*LUF*) SPACE mínima frecuencia empleada *f* (*LUF*)

lox *n* CHEM oxígeno líquido *m*, SPACE lox *m*, oxígeno líquido *m*, THERMO oxígeno líquido *m*

loxodromics *n* SPACE loxodromía *f*

LP: **~ mode** *n* (*linearly-polarized mode*) OPT, TELECOM modo linealmente polarizado *m*

LPA *abbr* (*lower-order path adaptation*) TELECOM adaptación de camino de menor orden *f*

LPC *abbr* TELECOM (*lower-order path connection*) conexión de camino de menor orden *f f*, TELECOM (*linear predicting coding*) codificación predictiva lineal *f*

LPCS *abbr* (*low pressure core spray*) NUCL LPCS (*aspersión del núcleo a baja presión*)

LPDT *abbr* (*low-power distress transmitter*) TELECOM transmisor de socorro de baja potencia *m*

LPG[1] *abbr* (*liquefied petroleum gas, liquid petroleum gas*) GEN GLP (*gas licuado de petróleo*)

LPG[2]: **~ carrier** *n* WATER TRANSP buque tanque para el transporte de GLP *m*; **~ engine** *n* (*liquid-petroleum-gas engine*) AUTO motor de GLP *m*

LPM *abbr* (*lines per minute*) COMP&DP, PRINT LPM (*líneas por minuto*)

LPT *abbr* (*lower-order path termination*) TELECOM terminación de camino de menor orden *f*

LQ *abbr* (*letter quality*) COMP&DP, PRINT LQ (*calidad de carta, calidad de letra*)

Lr *abbr* (*lawrencium*) CHEM, RAD PHYS Lr (*laurencio*)

LRC *abbr* (*longitudinal redundancy check*) COMP&DP comprobación de redundancia longitudinal *f*, verificación de redundancia longitudinal *f*

LRE *abbr* (*low-rate encoding*) TELECOM codificación a baja velocidad *f*

LRT *abbr* (*light rail transport BrE*) RAIL transporte por ferrocarril de vía estrecha *m*

LRU *abbr* (*line replaceable unit*) ELEC ENG unidad reemplazable en línea *f*, unidad sustituible en línea *f*

L-S: ~ **coupling** *n* PHYS acoplamiento L-S *m*

LSB *abbr* (*least significant bit*) COMP&DP, PROD, TELECOM BMS (*bit de menor significación, bit menos significativo*)

LSD *abbr* (*least significant digit*) COMP&DP, MATH, PROD DMS (*dígito menos significativo*)

LSI[1] *abbr* (*large-scale integration*) COMP&DP, ELECTRON, PHYS, TELECOM IGE (*integración a gran escala*)

LSI[2]: ~ **circuit** *n* COMP&DP, PHYS, TELECOM circuito IGE *m*

LT *abbr* (*line termination*) PRINT terminación de línea *f*, TELECOM TL (*terminación de línea*)

LTD *abbr* (*laser target designator*) MILIT designador de objetivo por láser *m*

LTE *abbr* (*line termination equipment*) COMP&DP ETL (*equipo de terminación de línea*)

Lu *abbr* (*lutetium*) CHEM, METALL Lu (*lutecio*)

lubber: ~ **line** *n* AIR TRANSP, SPACE, WATER TRANSP *of compass* línea de base *f*, línea de fe *f*, línea de referencia *f*, índice de referencia de la brújula *m*

lubricant *n* GEN lubricante *m*

lubricate *vt* GEN lubricar

lubricated[1] *adj* GEN lubricado

lubricated[2]: ~ **thread torque** *n* MECH ENG torsión de rosca lubricada *f*

lubricating: ~ **nipple** *n* MECH boquilla de lubricación *f*; ~ **oil** *n* AUTO, PROD, VEH aceite de lubricación *m*, aceite lubricante *m*; ~ **pump** *n* MECH, PROD bomba de lubricación *f*; ~ **pump and pipe connections** *n pl* PROD *lathe* bomba de lubricación con sus tuberías *f*; ~ **rack** *n* PROD rampa de engrase *f*; ~ **system** *n* AUTO, MECH ENG sistema de lubricación *m*; ~ **unit** *n* CONST equipo de lubricación *m*

lubrication *n* GEN lubricación *f*; ~ **chart** *n* MECH cuadro de lubricación *m*, guía de lubricación *f*; ~ **fitting** *n* MECH ENG accesorio lubricante *m*; ~ **system** *n* PROD sistema de lubricación *m*

lubricator *n* ELEC ENG engrasador *m*, PROD engrasador *m*, lubricador *m*

lubrifaction *n* PROD lubricación *f*

lubrification *n* PROD lubricación *f*, REFRIG engrase *m*, lubricación *f*

lucerne *n* BrE (*cf alfalfa AmE*) AGRIC alfalfa *f*

Lucite® *n* P&R Lucita® *f*

LUF *abbr* (*lowest usable frequency*) SPACE LUF (*mínima frecuencia empleada*)

luff[1] *n* WATER TRANSP *sail* amura *f*, caída de proa *f*; ~ **tackle** *n* CONST aparejo de combés *m*

luff[2] *vi* WATER TRANSP meter de orza, orzar

luffing: ~ **crane** *n* CONST grúa de brazo amantillable *f*

lug *n* MECH, MECH ENG, PROD *part* agarradera *f*, lóbulo *m*, PROD *spike* anillo *m*, casquillo *m*, saliente *m*, *tug, pull* estirón *m*, argolla *f*, tirón *m*, WATER TRANSP *shipbuilding* chapa cáncamo *f*, orejeta *f*, tojino *m*; ~ **kit** *n* PROD juego de conexiones *m*, juego de lengüetas *m*; ~ **nut** *n* AmE (*cf wheelnut BrE*) AUTO tuerca de la rueda *f*, tuerca de orejetas *f*, tuerca de palomilla *f*

luggage: ~ **compartment** *n* BrE (*cf baggage room AmE*) RAIL maletero *m*, departamento de equipaje *m*, pañol de equipajes *m*, compartimiento de equipaje *m*, sala de equipaje *f*, compartimiento de equipajes *m*; ~ **trolley** *n* TRANSP carrito porta-equipajes *m*; ~ **van** *n*

BrE (*cf baggage car AmE*) RAIL, VEH furgón de equipajes *m*

lumachelle *n* PETROL lumaquela *f*

lumberjack: ~ **checks** *n pl* TEXTIL cuadros tipo cazadora canadiense *m pl*

lumen *n* (*lm*) METR lumen *m* (*lm*)

lumenized: ~ **lens** *n* INSTR, OPT lente de flujo luminoso *f*

lumenizing *n* COATINGS luminización *f*

lumenmeter *n* PHYS medidor de flujo luminoso *m*

luminaire *n* ELEC *lighting* luminaria *f*

luminance *n* GEN luminancia *f*; ~ **amplifier** *n* ELECTRON amplificador de luminancia *m*; ~ **carrier output** *n* TV intensidad de la portadora de luminancia *f*; ~ **delay** *n* TV retardo de la luminosidad *m*, retraso de la luminancia *m*; ~ **difference signal** *n* TV señal de diferencia de luminancia *f*; ~ **ratio** *n* RAD PHYS razón de luminancia *f*; ~ **signal** *n* (*Y-signal*) SPACE *communications*, TV señal de luminancia *f*

luminescence *n* CHEM, COLOUR, ELEC ENG, PHYS, RAD PHYS, TV luminiscencia *f*; ~ **quantum yield** *n* RAD PHYS rendimiento cuántico de la luminiscencia *m*; ~ **threshold** *n* OPT, PHYS, TV umbral de luminiscencia *m*

luminescent[1] *adj* GEN luminiscente

luminescent[2]: ~ **diode** *n* ELECTRON diodo luminiscente *m*; ~ **discharge** *n* GAS descarga luminiscente *f*; ~ **glass** *n* C&G vidrio luminiscente *m*; ~ **paint** *n* COLOUR pintura luminiscente *f*; ~ **pigment** *n* COLOUR pigmento luminiscente *m*

luminosity *n* (*L*) PART PHYS, PHYS luminosidad *f* (*L*); ~ **coefficient** *n* RAD PHYS coeficiente de luminosidad *m*; ~ **factor** *n* RAD PHYS factor de luminosidad *m*; ~ **lifetime** *n* RAD PHYS duración de la luminosidad *f*, vida media de la luminosidad *f*

luminous: ~ **cloud** *n* METEO nube luminosa *f*; ~ **and coloured protective clothing** *n* SAFE prendas protectoras de colores vivos *f pl*; ~ **efficacy** *n* PHYS eficacia luminosa *f*; ~ **efficiency** *n* PHYS eficiencia luminosa *f*; ~ **energy** *n* WAVE PHYS energía luminosa *f*; ~ **exitance** *n* PHYS emisividad luminosa *f*; ~ **flux** *n* ELEC ENG, PHYS flujo luminoso *m*; ~ **intensity** *n* ELEC ENG, PHYS, RAD PHYS intensidad luminosa *f*; ~ **paint** *n* COLOUR pintura luminosa *f*; ~ **source** *n* LAB, OPT, PHOTO, PHYS, RAD PHYS, WAVE PHYS fuente luminosa *f*

Lummer-Brodhun: ~ **photometer** *n* LAB, PHYS fotómetro de Lummer-Brodhun *m*

lumnite *n* CHEM lumnita *f*

lump *n* CONST terrón *m*, PAPER grumo *m*, pastilla *f*; ~ **breaker roll** *n* PAPER rodillo superior de la prensa del manchón *m*, rompegrumos *m* (*AmL*); ~ **coal** *n* COAL, MINE carbón grueso *m*, hulla en trozos gruesos *f*; ~ **limestone** *n* GEOL caliza granular *f*; ~ **ore** *n* MINE mineral en terrones *m*, mineral en trozos *m*; ~ **sugar** *n* FOOD azúcar en cubitos *m*, cortadillo *m*, cuadradillo *m*, terrón de azúcar *m*; ~ **sum freight** *n* PETR TECH, WATER TRANSP flete fijo *m*

lumped: ~ **capacitance** *n* ELEC capacitancia centralizada *f*, capacitancia localizada *f*, ELEC ENG capacitancia concentrada *f*; ~ **capacitor** *n* ELEC ENG condensador compuesto *m*; ~ **element** *n* ELEC ENG elemento concentrado *m*; ~**element circuit** *n* ELEC ENG circuito de elementos localizados *m*

lumpless: ~ **small coal** *n* COAL cisco *m*

lumpy: ~ **demand** *n* PROD demanda corta *f*

lunar: ~ **logistics vehicle** *n* (*LLV*) SPACE *craft* vehículo logístico lunar *m* (*LLV*); ~ **orbit** *n* SPACE órbita lunar *f*; ~ **probe** *n* SPACE sonda lunar *f*; ~ **wave** *n* OCEAN onda lunar *f*

lunisolar: ~ **potential** *n* SPACE potencial lunisolar *m*; ~ **wave** *n* OCEAN onda lunisolar *f*

lunnite *n* MINERAL lunnita *f*

lupuline *n* CHEM lupulina *f*

lurch[1] *n* WATER TRANSP *motion of ship* bandazo *m*

lurch[2] *vi* WATER TRANSP *ship* dar un bandazo

lure *n* OCEAN añagaza *f*, señuelo *m*

lussatite *n* MINERAL lussatita *f*

luster *AmE see* lustre *BrE*

lusterless *AmE see* lustreless *BrE*

lustre *n BrE* C&G, COLOUR lustre *m*, GEOL, MINERAL brillo *m*, P&R, PROD, TEXTIL lustre *m*; ~ **finish** *n BrE* COATINGS acabado de lustre *m*, brillo *m*

lustreless *adj BrE* TEXTIL deslustrado

lustrous[1] *adj* TEXTIL brillante

lustrous[2]: ~ **schist** *n* GEOL esquisto lustroso *m*

LUT *abbr* (*local user terminal*) TELECOM terminal de usuario local *m*

lutation *n* PROD lutación *f*

lute *n* PROD arandela *f*, arcilla para junturas *f*, luten *m*, mástique *m*, potea *f*

lutein *n* CHEM luteína *f*

luteocobaltic *adj* CHEM luteocobáltico

luteol *n* CHEM luteol *m*

luteolin *n* CHEM luteolina *f*

luteoline *n* CHEM luteolina *f*

lutetium *n* (*Lu*) CHEM, METALL lutecio *m* (*Lu*)

lutidine *n* CHEM lutidina *f*

lutidinic *adj* CHEM lutidínico

lutidone *n* CHEM lutidona *f*

lutite *n* GEOL *text* lutita *f*

lux *n* (*lx*) METR, PHOTO, PHYS lux *m* (*lx*); ~ **value** *n* PHOTO valor en lux *m*

LV: ~ **disc** *BrE*, ~ **disk** *AmE n* (*laservision disc BrE*, *laservision disk AmE*) OPT disco de visión láser *m*, disco láser *m*; ~ **player** *n* (*laservision player*) OPT reproductor de visión láser *m*

LV-Rom® *abbr* (*Laservision read-only memory*) OPT LV-Rom® (*memoria de solo lectura laservisión*)

LWC[1] *abbr* (*low-weight coating*) PAPER capa de estucado de bajo gramaje *f*

LWC[2]: ~ **paper** *n* PAPER papel con capa estucado de bajo gramaje *m*

LWHR *abbr* (*light-water hybrid reactor*) NUCL reactor híbrido de agua ligera *m* (*Esp*), reactor híbrido de agua liviana *m* (*AmL*)

lx *abbr* (*lux*) METR, PHOTO, PHYS lx (*lux*)

lye *n* CHEM lejía *f*

lying: ~ **shaft** *n* MECH ENG árbol acamado *m*

Lyman: ~ **series** *n* PHYS, RAD PHYS serie de Lyman *f*

lyogel *n* CHEM liogel *m*

lyophilic *adj* CHEM liofílico

lyophilizate *n* AGRIC, CHEM TECH, FOOD, PACK, REFRIG liofilizado *m*

lyophilization *n* AGRIC liofilización *f*, CHEM TECH criodeshidratación *f*, liofilización *f*, secado por congelación *m*, FOOD criodeshidratación *f*, liofilización *f*, PACK liofilización *f*, REFRIG criodeshidratación *f*, liofilización *f*, THERMO liofilización *f*; ~ **flask** *n* C&G frasco para liofilización *m*

lyophily *n* CHEM liofilia *f*

lyophobic *adj* CHEM liófobo

lyosol *n* CHEM liosol *m*

lyre: --**shaped bellcrank** *n* AIR TRANSP *flight controls* palanca acodada en forma de lira *f*

lysergic *adj* CHEM *acid* lisérgico

lysine *n* CHEM lisina *f*

lysolecithin *n* CHEM lisolecitina *f*

lysophosphatide *n* CHEM lisofosfatida *f*

lyxonic *adj* CHEM lixónico

lyxose *n* CHEM lixosa *f*

LZ *abbr* (*landing zone*) MILIT zona de aterrizaje *f*

M

m *abbr* (*milli-*) METR m (*mili-*)

M^1 *abbr* (*mega-*) METR M (*mega-*)

M^2: ~ **bit** *n* COMP&DP, TELECOM bit M *m*; ~ **and E track** *n* (*music and effects track*) CINEMAT banda de música y efectos sonoros *f*; ~ **shell** *n* PHYS capa M *f*, capa de electrón *f*; ~ **wrap** *n* TV revestimiento de electrón *m*

mA *abbr* (*milliampere*) ELEC, ELEC ENG, PHYS mA (*miliamperio*)

MA *abbr* ELECTRON (*maintenance contract*) CM (*contrato de mantenimiento*), TELECOM (*medium adaptor*) adaptador intermedio *m*, adaptador medio *m*

maar *n* GEOL cráter-lago *m*, maar *m*

MAC *abbr* AIR TRANSP (*mean aerodynamic chord*) cuerda aerodinámica media *f*, TELECOM (*medium access control*) control de acceso medio *m*

macadam *n* CONST *roads* macádam *m*; ~ **spreader** *n* TRANSP esparcidora macadán *f*

macadamization *n* CONST colocación de macadam *f*

mace: ~ **oil** *n* FOOD aceite de macis *m*

maceral *n* GEOL maceral *m*

macerate *vt* CHEM, FOOD macerar

maceration *n* CHEM, FOOD maceración *f*

macerator *n* CHEM, FOOD macerador *m*

Mach: ~ **compensator** *n* ACOUST, AIR TRANSP compensador de Mach *m*; ~ **number** *n* ACOUST, AIR TRANSP, PHYS número de Mach *m*; ~ **principle** *n* PHYS principio de Mach *m*

machinability *n* MECH facilidad de maquinado *f*, MECH ENG maquinabilidad *f*, trabajabilidad *f*

machine^1: **~-coated** *adj* PACK recubierto a máquina; **~-dependent** *adj* COMP&DP dependiente de la computadora (*AmL*), dependiente de la máquina, dependiente del ordenador (*Esp*); **~-independent** *adj* COMP&DP independiente de la computadora (*AmL*), independiente de la máquina (*AmL*), independiente del ordenador (*Esp*); **~-oriented** *adj* COMP&DP basado en máquina, basado en ordenador (*Esp*), específico para máquina, orientado hacia la computadora (*AmL*); **~-readable** *adj* COMP&DP legible por computador (*AmL*), legible por ordenador (*Esp*)

machine^2 *n* AUTO máquina *f*, C&G máquina *f*, *for making handles* torno *m*, COMP&DP ordenador *m* (*Esp*), computadora *f* (*AmL*), computador *m* (*AmL*), ELEC ENG mecanismo *m*, máquina *f*, PROD máquina *f*; ~ **bolt** *n* MECH ENG bulón ordinario *m*, perno común *m*, perno hecho a máquina *m*, perno torneado *m*, tornillo hecho a máquina *m*; ~ **cage** *n* SAFE *gearwheels* jaula para máquina *f*; ~ **center** *AmE*, ~ **centre** *BrE n* MECH ENG centro de maquinado *m*; ~ **check** *n* COMP&DP verificación automática *f*; ~ **chest** *n* PAPER tina de máquina *f*; ~ **with closed-circuit ventilation** *n* MECH ENG máquina con circulación de circuito cerrado *f*, máquina con ventilación de circuito cerrado *f*; ~ **code** *n* COMP&DP código de máquina *m*, código interno *m*; ~ **cutting** *n* MECH ENG, MINE fresado *m*; ~ **cycle** *n* COMP&DP ciclo automatizado *m*, ciclo de máquina *m*; ~ **deckle** *n* PAPER ancho de tela utilizado *m*; ~ **die plate** *n* MECH ENG dado de terraje automático *m*; ~ **direction** *n*

PAPER sentido longitudinal *m*, dirección de fabricación *f*, PRINT sentido de máquina *m*; **~-divided machine-tool scale** *n* MECH ENG regla de máquina herramienta dividida a máquina *f*; ~ **drilling** *n* MINE perforadora mecánica *f*, taladradora mecánica *f*; ~ **error** *n* COMP&DP error de máquina *m*, error informático *m*; ~ **fence** *n* SAFE cerca protectora para máquina *f*, valla protectora para máquina *f*; ~ **fill** *n* PAPER ancho máximo de fabricación *m*; **~-finished paperboard** *n* (*MF paperboard*) PAPER cartón alisado *m*; ~ **finishing** *n* MECH ENG acabado mecánico *m*; ~ **flaw** *n* PAPER costero de máquina *m*; **~-glazed board** *n* (*MG board*) PAPER cartón satinado en una cara *m*; **~-glazed cylinder** *n* (*MG cylinder*) PAPER cilindro satinado *m*; **~-glazed paper** *n* (*MG paper*) PACK papel abrillantado en máquina *m*, PAPER papel satinado en una cara *m*; ~ **guard** *n* SAFE guardamáquinas *m*; ~ **gun** *n* MILIT ametralladora *f*; ~ **instruction** *n* COMP&DP instrucción automática *f*; ~ **instruction code** *n* COMP&DP código de instrucción de máquina *m*; ~ **language** *n* COMP&DP lenguaje de máquina *m*; ~ **leader** *n* CINEMAT, TV guía de máquina *f*; ~ **learning** *n* COMP&DP aprendizaje asistido por ordenador *m* (*Esp*), aprendizaje con ayuda de computadora *m* (*AmL*); ~ **lying idle** *n* MECH ENG máquina parada *f*, máquina paralizada *f*; **~-made nut** *n* MECH ENG tuerca hecha a máquina *f*; ~ **motion** *n* PROD movimiento a máquina *m*; ~ **with open-circuit ventilation** *n* MECH ENG máquina con circulación de circuito abierto *f*, máquina con ventilación de circuito abierto *f*; ~ **operation** *n* COMP&DP operación automatizada *f*; ~ **processor** *n* PHOTO procesador en máquina *m*; ~ **punch** *n* MECH ENG sacabocados mecánico *m*; **~-readable data** *n pl* COMP&DP datos legibles por computador *m pl* (*AmL*), datos legibles por ordenador *m pl* (*Esp*); ~ **run** *n* MECH ENG corrida de máquina *f*; ~ **running empty** *n* PROD máquina sin carga *f*; ~ **running light** *n* MECH ENG máquina funcionando en vacío *f*; ~ **running on no load** *n* MECH ENG máquina funcionando en vacío *f*, máquina funcionando sin carga *f*; ~ **running under load** *n* MECH ENG máquina funcionando con carga *f*; ~ **screw** *n* MECH ENG tornillo mecánico *m*, tornillo para metales *m*; ~ **shutdown** *n* PROD paro de máquina *m*; ~ **shutdown circuit** *n* PROD circuito de paro de la máquina *m*; ~ **speed** *n* C&G velocidad de la máquina *f*; ~ **splicer** *n* CINEMAT máquina empalmadora *f*; ~ **start-up** *n* C&G arranque de la máquina *m*; ~ **status** *n* MECH ENG estado de la máquina *m*; ~ **stop** *n* C&G paro de la máquina *m*; **~-system shutdown** *n* PROD paro del sistema de la máquina *m*; ~ **tap** *n* MECH ENG macho de roscar a máquina *m*, macho girado mecánicamente *m*; ~ **time** *n* COMP&DP tiempo de computador *m* (*AmL*), tiempo de computadora *m* (*AmL*), tiempo de máquina *m*, tiempo de ordenador *m* (*Esp*); ~ **tool** *n* MECH, MECH ENG máquina herramienta *f*; **~-tool brake** *n* MECH ENG freno de máquina herramienta *m*; ~ **tool design** *n* MECH ENG *in field of ergonomics* diseño de máquina herramienta *m*; ~ **tool scales** *n pl* MECH ENG *circular, divided* romana de máquina herramienta *f*; ~ **tool spindle** *n* MECH ENG husillo de la máquina herramienta *m*; ~ **tray** *n* C&G bandeja de la máquina *f*, charola de la máquina *f* (*AmL*), placa de la máquina *f* (*Esp*); ~ **utilization degree** *n* PROD grado de utilización de la máquina *m*, nivel de eficacia de la máquina *m*; ~ **vice** *BrE* ~ **vise** *AmE* MECH ENG *working in parallel slides* morsa de máquina *f*, morsa de máquina herramienta *f*; ~ **vision verification** *n* PACK verificación visual de la máquina *f*; ~ **width** *n* PRINT anchura de la máquina *f*; ~ **work** *n* MECH ENG trabajo hecho a máquina *m*

machine³ *vt* MECH maquinar, trabajar, PROD labrar, *casting* mecanizar; ~**-flush** *vt* MECH ENG lavar a máquina

machined¹ *adj* MECH maquinado, trabajado en la máquina; ~**-all-over** *adj* MECH maquinado por completo

machined²: ~ **casting** *n* PROD fundición mecanizada *f*; ~ **circular plate** *n* MECH ENG chapa circular maquinada *f*; ~ **rectangular plate** *n* MECH ENG chapa rectangular maquinada *f*; ~ **surface** *n* MECH superficie maquinada *f*

machinery *n* MECH ENG conjunto de máquinas *m*, maquinaria *f*, mecanismos *m pl*, máquinas *f pl*; ~ **hazard** *n* SAFE peligro originado por la maquinaria *m*, riesgo originado por la maquinaria *m*

machining *n* MECH, MECH ENG fabricación a máquina *f*, fresado *m*, maquinado *m*, trabajo mecánico *m*, PROD mecanización *f*; ~ **allowance** *n* PROD *founding* sobreespesor para el mecanizado *m*; ~ **center** *AmE*, ~ **centre** *n BrE* MECH centro de maquinado *m*

machinist *n* PROD *person* maquinista *m*, operario de máquina herramienta *m*

machmeter *n* AIR TRANSP medidor de número de Mach *m*

Mach: ~ **'s number** *n* ACOUST número de Mach *m*; ~ **principle** *n* PHYS principio de Mach *m*

macle *n* MINERAL macla *f*

maclurin *n* CHEM maclurina *f*

MacPherson: ~ **strut** *n* AUTO, VEH puntal MacPherson *m*, tirante MacPherson *m*; ~ **strut front suspension** *n* AUTO, VEH suspensión frontal de puntal MacPherson *f*

macro *n* COMP&DP macro *m*; ~ **assembler** *n* COMP&DP ensamblador de macros *m*, macroensamblador *m*; ~ **lens** *n* CINEMAT, INSTR, OPT, PHOTO objetivo macro *m*; ~ **particle** *n* CHEM TECH macropartícula *f*; ~ **processor** *n* COMP&DP macroprocesador *m*, procesador de macros *m*

macrobend *n* ELEC ENG macrocurva *f*; ~ **loss** *n* OPT pérdida por macrodoblado *f*, TELECOM pérdida de macroflexión *f*

macrobending *n* OPT macrodoblado *m*, TELECOM macroflexión *f*

macroclimate *n* METEO macroclima *m*

macrocontrol *n* TRANSP macrocontrol *m*

macrocyclic *adj* CHEM macrocíclico

macroelement *n* AGRIC macroelemento *m*

macrohardness *n* MECH ENG macrodureza *f*

macroinstruction *n* COMP&DP macroinstrucción *f*

macromodular: ~ **steam generator** *n* NUCL generador de vapor macromodular *m*

macromolecular¹ *adj* CHEM, P&R macromolecular

macromolecular²: ~ **dispersion** *n* FOOD dispersión macromolecular *f*

macromolecule *n* CHEM, P&R macromolécula *f*

macronutrient *n* AGRIC macronutriente *m*

macropolymer *n* CHEM macropolímero *m*

macroprogram *n* AmE, **macroprogramme** *n BrE* TRANSP macroprograma *m*

macroradiography *n* NUCL macrorradiografía *f*

macroscopic: ~ **cross-section** *n* NUCL sección eficaz macroscópica *f*; ~ **flux variation** *n* NUCL mapa de flujo *m*, variación de flujo macroscópica *f*; ~ **variables** *n pl* PHYS variables macroscópicas *f pl*

macroseismic *adj* GEOPHYS macrosísmica *f*

macrostructural *adj* CHEM macroestructural

macrostructure *n* CHEM macroestructura *f*

macrowaste *n* POLL desechos a gran escala *m pl*, desperdicio mayor *m*, macrodesecho *m*

mad: ~ **cow disease** *n* AGRIC encefalopatía espongiforme bovina *f* (*BSE*), enfermedad de la vaca loca *f*; ~ **itch** *n* AGRIC pseudo rabia *f*, *animal disease* picazón loca *f*, seudorabia *f*

made¹: ~ **in sections** *adj* PROD desmontable; ~**-to-measure** *adj* TEXTIL hecho a medida

made²: ~ **block** *n* MECH ENG cuadernal de piezas *m*, PROD polea de ensamblaje *f*

MAF *abbr* (*management applications function*) TELECOM función de aplicaciones de gestión *f*

mafic *adj* GEOL, PETROL máfico

mag: ~ **card** *n* PRINT tarjeta magnética *f*; ~**-dyno** *n* ELEC *automotive* dino magnético *m*; ~**-optical print** *n* CINEMAT copia magnetoóptica *f*

MAG: ~ **welding** *n* (*metal active-gas welding*) CONST, THERMO soldadura MAG *f* (*Esp*) (*soldadura con gas activo de metal*), soldeo MAG *m* (*AmL*) (*soldeo con gas activo de metal*)

magamp *abbr* (*magnetic amplifier*) ELEC ENG, ELECTRON, PHYS, SPACE amplificador magnético *m*

magazine *n* CINEMAT chasis *m*, MECH ENG depósito alimentador *m*, MINE depósito de municiones *m*; ~ **back** *n* PHOTO soporte para placas *m*; ~ **camera** *n* CINEMAT cámara con chasis *f*; ~ **creel** *n* TEXTIL fileta de almacenamiento *f*

magenta *n* COLOUR, PRINT magenta *f*

magic: ~ **eye** *n* ELECTRON, TELECOM ojo mágico *m*; ~ **number** *n* PHYS número mágico *m*

magmatic: ~ **differentiation** *n* GEOL diferenciación magmática *f*; ~ **stoping** *n* GEOL excavación magmática *f*

magnesia *n* CHEM, HEAT ENG magnesia *f*

magnesian¹ *adj* CHEM magnesiano, GEOL magnésico

magnesian²: ~ **limestone** *n* GEOL caliza magnésica *f*

magnesic *adj* CHEM magnésico

magnesioferrite *n* MINERAL magnesioferrita *f*

magnesite *n* CHEM, MINERAL, P&R magnesita *f*; ~ **brick** *n* CONST ladrillo de refractario de magnesita *m*; ~ **chrome refractory** *n* C&G refractario básico *m*

magnesium *n* (*Mg*) CHEM, ELEC ENG, METALL magnesio *m* (*Mg*); ~ **carbonate** *n* HEAT ENG carbonato de magnesio *m*; ~ **silver chloride cell** *n* ELEC ENG elemento clorídico de plata y magnesio *m*; ~ **sulfate** *AmE*, ~ **sulphate** *BrE n* DETERG sulfato de magnesio *m*

magnesol *n* CHEM magnesol *m*

magnet *n* ELEC imán *m*, ELEC ENG electroimán *m*, LAB imán *m*, magneto *m*, PHYS imán *m*; ~ **coil** *n* ELEC, ELEC ENG bobina de electroimán *f*; ~ **core** *n* ELEC ENG núcleo del electroimán *m*; ~ **crane** *n* PROD grúa de electroimán *f*, grúa de electroimán portador *f*, grúa portador *f*; ~ **spheric cavity** *n* GEOPHYS, SPACE *geophysics* imán de cavidad esférica *m*

magnetic[1] *adj* GEN magnético

magnetic[2]:

▪ **a** ~ **adjustable link** *n* MECH ENG conexión ajustable magnética *f*; ~ **amplifier** *n* (*magamp*) ELEC ENG, ELECTRON, PHYS, SPACE amplificador magnético *m*; ~ **anomaly** *n* GEOL, GEOPHYS anomalía magnética *f*; ~ **arc blowout contact** *n* MECH ENG contacto de soplado magnético de arco *m*; ~ **attraction** *n* ELEC, ELEC ENG, PHYS, SPACE atracción magnética *f*; ~ **axis** *n* GEOPHYS, SPACE eje magnético *m*; ~ **azimuth** *n* AIR TRANSP, GEOPHYS, MECH, SPACE azimut magnético *m*;

▪ **b** ~ **balance** *n* GEOPHYS balanza magnética *f*; ~ **balance track** *n* CINEMAT banda magnética de balance *f*; ~ **bay** *n* GEOPHYS recinto magnético *m*; ~ **beam compressor** *n* PART PHYS compresor de haz magnético *m*; ~ **bearing** *n* AIR TRANSP marcación magnética *f*, azimut magnético *m*, GEOPHYS azimut magnético *m*, dirección magnética *f*, MECH azimut magnético *m*, marcación magnética *f*, SPACE *craft* azimut magnético *m*, rumbo magnético *m*; ~ **bearing momentum wheel** *n* SPACE *craft* rueda de inercia con rodamiento magnético *f*; ~ **bias** *n* ELEC ENG, TV polarización magnética *f*; ~ **blowout** *n* ELEC ENG soplado magnético *m*; ~ **blowout circuit breaker** *n* ELEC, ELEC ENG disyuntor de inyección magnética *m*, disyuntor de soplado magnético *m*; ~ **blowout contacts** *n pl* MECH ENG contactos de soplado magnético *m pl*; ~ **bottle** *n* PHYS botella magnética *f*; ~ **bubble memory** *n* COMP&DP, ELEC ENG memoria de burbuja magnética *f*;

▪ **c** ~ **card** *n* COMP&DP tarjeta magnética *f*; ~-**card reader** *n* COMP&DP lector de tarjetas magnéticas *m*; ~ **cell** *n* COMP&DP célula magnética *f*; ~ **center track** *AmE see magnetic centre track BrE*; ~ **centering ring** *AmE see magnetic centring ring BrE*; ~ **centre track** *n BrE* CINEMAT banda magnética central *f*; ~ **centring ring** *n BrE* SPACE anillo de centraje magnético *m*; ~ **circuit** *n* ELEC, ELEC ENG, PHYS, SPACE circuito magnético *m*; ~ **clutch** *n* ELEC, ELEC ENG, MECH ENG, VEH embrague electromagnético *m*, embrague magnético *m*; ~ **coating** *n* CINEMAT recubrimiento magnético *m*, TV revestimiento magnético *m*; ~ **compass** *n* AIR TRANSP, GEOPHYS, INSTR aguja magnética *f*, brújula *f*, brújula magnética *f*, compás magnético *m*, MECH ENG, PHYS aguja magnética *f*, WATER TRANSP aguja magnética *f*, brújula *f*; ~ **confinement** *n* PHYS confinamiento magnético *m*; ~ **constant** *n* ELEC ENG, PHYS constante magnética *f*; ~ **cooling** *n* REFRIG enfriamiento magnético *m*; ~ **core** *n* COMP&DP núcleo magnético *m*, ELEC ENG *circuit* núcleo de ferrita *m*, núcleo magnético *m*, *memory* núcleo de memoria magnética *m*; ~-**core memory** *n* ELEC ENG memoria de núcleo magnético *f*; ~ **coupling** *n* ELEC *of a transformer* acoplamiento magnético *m*; ~ **coupling coefficient** *n* ELEC *of a transformer* coeficiente de acoplamiento electromagnético *m*, coeficiente de acoplamiento magnético *m*; ~ **course** *n* WATER TRANSP *navigation* rumbo de la aguja *m*, rumbo magnético *m*; ~ **crack detector** *n* MECH ENG detector magnético para grietas *m*; ~ **cushion** *n* TRANSP amortiguación magnética *f*, colchón amortiguador magnético *m*; ~-**cushion**

train *n* TRANSP tren de amortiguación magnética *m*; ~ **cycle** *n* GEOPHYS ciclo magnético *m*;

▪ **d** ~ **daily variation** *n* GEOPHYS variación magnética diaria *f*; ~ **damping** *n* ELEC ENG amortiguación magnética *f*, GEOPHYS amortiguamiento magnético *m*; ~ **declination** *n* GEOPHYS, PHYS, WATER TRANSP *navigation* declinación magnética *f*; ~ **deflection** *n* GEOPHYS, NUCL, PART PHYS desviación magnética *f*; ~ **depolarization of resonance radiation** *n* RAD PHYS depolarización magnética de la radiación de resonancia *f*; ~ **detector** *n* TRANSP detector magnético *m*; ~ **deviation** *n* GEOPHYS desviación magnética *f*; ~ **dip** *n* GEOL, GEOPHYS, PETR TECH, PETROL inclinación magnética *f*; ~ **dipole** *n* PHYS dipolo magnético *m*; ~ **dipole moment** *n* PHYS momento magnético dipolar *m*; ~ **dipole transition** *n* RAD PHYS transición de dipolo magnético *f*; ~ **disc** *n BrE* ELEC, ELEC ENG disco magnético *m*; ~ **discontinuity** *n* GEOPHYS discontinuidad magnética *f*; ~ **disk** *AmE see magnetic disc BrE*; ~ **domain** *n* ELEC ENG dominio magnético *m*; ~ **doorstop** *n* CONST tope magnético para la puerta *m*; ~ **drag** *n* TRANSP deriva magnética *f*; ~ **drain plug** *n* MECH ENG tapón de desagüe magnético *m*, tapón de purga magnético *m*, tapón de vaciado magnético *m*; ~ **drum** *n* COMP&DP, ELEC ENG tambor magnético *m*; ~ **drum memory** *n* COMP&DP, ELEC ENG memoria de cilindro magnético *f*;

▪ **e** ~ **energy** *n* ELEC, ELEC ENG, PHYS energía magnética *f*; ~ **epitaxial layer** *n* ELECTRON estratificador magnético epitaxial *m*; ~ **equator** *n* GEOPHYS, PHYS ecuador magnético *m*; ~ **erasing head** *n* COMP&DP, TV cabeza magnética borradora *f*;

▪ **f** ~ **face** *n* MECH ENG cara magnética *f*, embrague magnético *m*, superficie magnética *f*; ~ **field** *n* ELEC, ELEC ENG, GEOL, PHYS, TELECOM, TV campo magnético *m*; ~-**field aerial** *n BrE* (*cf magnetic-field antenna AmE*) GEOPHYS antena de campo magnético *f*; ~-**field antenna** *n AmE* (*cf magnetic-field aerial BrE*) GEOPHYS antena de campo magnético *f*; ~-**field configuration** *n* NUCL, RAD PHYS configuración del campo magnético *f*; ~-**field gradient** *n* ELEC, ELEC ENG, PHYS gradiente del campo magnético *m*; ~-**field intensity** *n* ELEC, ELEC ENG, PETROL, PHYS, RAD PHYS intensidad del campo magnético *f*; ~-**field lines** *n pl* RAD PHYS líneas de campo magnético *f pl*, líneas de fuerza del campo magnético *f pl*; ~-**field strength** *n* ELEC, ELEC ENG, PETROL, PHYS, RAD PHYS intensidad del campo magnético *f*; ~ **film** *n* CINEMAT, COATINGS película magnética *f*; ~ **film projector** *n* CINEMAT proyector de película magnética *m*; ~ **filter** *n* MECH ENG filtro magnético *m*; ~ **fishing tool** *n* PETR TECH herramienta de pesca magnética *f*; ~ **flux** *n* ELEC, ELEC ENG, FUELLESS, PHYS, RAD PHYS, TV flujo magnético *m*; ~-**flux density** *n* ELEC, GEOPHYS, PHYS, SPACE densidad de flujo magnético *f*; ~-**flux density meter** *n* GEOPHYS medidor de flujo de densidad magnética *m*; ~-**flux linkage** *n* FUELLESS enlace de flujo magnético *m*; ~ **flywheel** *n* ELEC ENG circuito compensador magnético *m*; ~ **focusing** *n* ELEC ENG concentración magnética *f*, enfoque magnético *m*; ~ **force** *n* ELEC, GEOPHYS, PETROL fuerza magnética *f*; ~-**force welding** *n* NUCL soldadura por fuerza magnética *f*;

▪ **h** ~ **head** *n* ACOUST cabeza magnética *f*, COMP&DP cabeza magnética *f*, cabezal magnético *m*, TV cabeza magnética *f*; **~-head core** *n* TV núcleo de cabeza magnética *m*; **~-head gap** *n* TV entrehierro de cabeza magnética *m*, entrehierro del cabezal *m*, intervalo de cabeza magnética *m*; **~ heading** *n* AIR TRANSP dirección magnética *f*; **~ holdfast** *n* MECH ENG gancho de seguridad magnético *m*, grapa magnética *f*; **~ holding** *n* MECH ENG sujeción magnética *f*; **~ hysteresis** *n* ELEC, ELEC ENG histéresis magnética *f*; **~ hysteresis loop** *n* ELEC bucle de histéresis magnética *m*, ciclo de histéresis magnética *m*;

~ i **~ inclination** *n* GEOL, GEOPHYS, PETR TECH, PETROL inclinación magnética *f*; **~ inclinometer** *n* GEOPHYS inclinómetro magnético *m*; **~ indicator** *n* MECH ENG indicador magnético *m*; **~ induction** *n* ELEC, ELEC ENG, PETROL, PHYS, TELECOM inducción magnética *f*; **~ induction current loop** *n* TELECOM bucle de corriente de inducción magnética *m*; **~ induction density** *n* ELEC densidad de inducción magnética *f*; **~ induction flux** *n* ELEC ENG flujo de inducción magnética *m*; **~ ink** *n* COMP&DP, PRINT tinta magnética *f*; **~ ink character reader** *n* (*MICR*) COMP&DP lector de caracteres en tinta magnética *m*, reconocimiento de caracteres en tinta magnética *m*; **~ intensity** *n* GEOPHYS intensidad magnética *f*; **~ interference** *n* GEOPHYS interferencia magnética *f*; **~ interference field** *n* GEOPHYS campo de interferencia magnética *m*; **~ interval** *n* GEOL intervalo magnético *m*; **~ isotope separation** *n* NUCL, PHYS separación magnética de isótopos *f*;

~ l **~ lag** *n* MECH ENG histéresis magnética *f*, retardo de imanación *m*, retardo de imantación *m*, retardo de magnetización *m*; **~ latching relay** *n* ELEC ENG relé de conexión magnética *m*; **~ latitude** *n* GEOPHYS, PHYS latitud magnética *f*; **~-latitude effect** *n* GEOPHYS efecto de latitud magnética *m*; **~ leakage** *n* ELEC ENG dispersión magnética *f*, escape magnético *m*, pérdida magnética *f*; **~ lens** *n* INSTR, PHYS, RAD PHYS lente magnética *f*; **~ levitation** *n* PHYS, TRANSP levitación magnética *f*; **~ line of force** *n* ELEC ENG línea de fuerza magnética *f*; **~ loop detector** *n* TRANSP detector de bucle magnético *m*; **~ lunar daily variation** *n* GEOPHYS variación magnética lunar diaria *f*;

~ m **~ map** *n* GEOPHYS mapa magnético *m*; **~ master** *n* CINEMAT copia maestra magnética *f*; **~ material** *n* ACOUST, ELEC ENG material magnético *m*; **~ media** *n pl* ACOUST medio magnético *m*, COMP&DP medio magnético *m*, soporte magnético *m*, ELEC ENG medio magnético *m*; **~ meridian** *n* GEOPHYS, PHYS meridiano magnético *m*; **~ method** *n* GEOPHYS método magnético *m*; **~ mine** *n* MILIT mina magnética *f*; **~ mirror** *n* PHYS espejo magnético *m*; **~ moment** *n* ELEC, PHYS momento magnético *m*; **~ momentum** *n* PART PHYS momento magnético *m*, número cuántico *m*; **~ monopole** *n* PHYS monopolo magnético *m*;

~ n **~ needle** *n* AIR TRANSP, GEOPHYS, INSTR, MECH ENG, PHYS, WATER TRANSP aguja imantada *f*, aguja imanada *f*; **~ North** *n* GEOPHYS, PHYS, WATER TRANSP Norte magnético *m*; **~ north pole** *n* GEOPHYS, PHYS polo norte magnético *m*;

~ o **~ objective** *n* ELECTRON, INSTR, NUCL objetivo magnético *m*; **~ order** *n* METALL orden magnético *m*; **~ overload relay** *n* ELEC, ELEC ENG relevador electromagnético de sobrecarga *m*, relé electromagnético de sobrecarga *m*;

~ p **~ particle** *n* MECH, MECH ENG, NUCL, TV partícula magnética *f*; **~ particle examination** *n* MECH examen por partículas magnéticas *m*; **~ particle inspection** *n* MECH ENG, NUCL inspección por partículas magnéticas *f*; **~ particle orientation** *n* TV orientación de partículas magnéticas *f*; **~ permeability** *n* ELEC, PETROL permeabilidad magnética *f*; **~ polarization** *n* ACOUST, ELEC ENG polarización magnética *f*; **~ pole** *n* ELEC, GEOPHYS, PHYS polo magnético *m*; **~ pole strength** *n* GEOPHYS intensidad de polo magnético *f*; **~ potential** *n* ELEC ENG potencial magnético *m*; **~ printing effect** *n* ACOUST efecto de impresión magnética *m*; **~ probe** *n* NUCL sonda magnética *f*; **~ prospecting** *n* GEOPHYS prospección magnética *f*; **~ pyrite** *n* MINERAL pirita magnética *f*;

~ q **~ quantum number** *n* PHYS número cuántico magnético *m*;

~ r **~ rack** *n* MECH ENG bastidor magnético *m*; **~ recorder** *n* ACOUST, COMP&DP grabador magnético *m*; **~ recording** *n* ACOUST, COMP&DP grabación magnética *f*, TELECOM, TV registro magnético *m*; **~ recording medium** *n* TV soporte de registro magnético *m*; **~ reproducer** *n* TV reproductor magnético *m*; **~ repulsion** *n* ELEC ENG repulsión magnética *f*; **~ resistance** *n* ELEC, ELEC ENG reluctancia *f*, resistencia magnética *f*, PHYS resistencia magnética *f*; **~ resonance** *n* ELEC ENG, PHYS resonancia magnética *f*; **~ resonance spectroscopy** *n* RAD PHYS espectroscopía de resonancia magnética *f*; **~ reversal** *n* GEOL inversión magnética *f*;

~ s **~ saturation** *n* ELEC, ELEC ENG saturación magnética *f*; **~ scalar potential** *n* PHYS potencial escalar magnético *m*; **~ screening** *n* ELEC *field* blindaje antimagnético *m*, coraza magnética *f*; **~ separator** *n* COAL, MINE, NUCL, PROD separador magnético *m*; **~ shell** *n* PHYS capa magnética *f*; **~ shielding** *n* ELEC ENG blindaje magnético *m*; **~ solar-quiet-day variation** *n* GEOPHYS variación magnética solar de un día en calma *f*, variación magnética solar de un día tranquilo *f*; **~ sound stripe** *n* CINEMAT banda magnética de sonido *f*; **~ soundtrack** *n* CINEMAT banda magnética de sonido *f*; **~ south** *n* GEOPHYS Sur magnético *m*; **~ South Pole** *n* GEOPHIS, PHYS polo sur magnético *m*; **~ spectrograph** *n* GEOPHYS espectrógrafo magnético *m*; **~ starter** *n* AUTO, ELEC, ELEC ENG, PROD, VEH arrancador electromagnético *m*; **~ stirrer** *n* LAB agitador magnético *m*; **~ stock** *n* CINEMAT película magnética *f*; **~ storage medium** *n* ELEC ENG medio de almacenaje magnético *m*; **~ storm** *n* GEOPHYS, SPACE tormenta magnética *f*; **~ strip sound head** *n* CINEMAT cabezal de sonido para banda magnética *m*; **~ stripe** *n* GEOL banda magnética *f*; **~-striped film** *n* CINEMAT película con banda magnética *f*; **~ striping** *n* CINEMAT colocación de banda magnética *f*; **~ survey** *n* GEOPHYS estudio magnético *m*, levantamiento magnético *m*, prospección magnética *f*; **~ susceptibility** *n* ELEC coeficiente de imanación *m*, susceptibilidad magnética *f*, PETROL, PHYS susceptibilidad magnética *f*; **~ suspension** *n* TRANSP suspensión magnética *f*;

~ t **~ tape** *n* ACOUST, COMP&DP, ELEC, GEOPHYS, PRINT, TELECOM cinta magnética *f*, TV cinta magnetofónica *f*, cinta magnética *f*; **~ tape cartridge** *n* COMP&DP cartucho de cinta magnética *m*; **~ tape unit** *n* COMP&DP unidad de cinta magnética *f*;

~ **thermometer** *n* REFRIG termómetro magnético *m*; ~ **thickness gage** *AmE*, ~ **thickness gauge** *BrE n* LAB medidor magnético de espesor *m*; ~ **thin film** *n* ELECTRON película magnética delgada *f*; ~ **tool rack** *n* CONST herramienta magnética *f*; ~ **transfer** *n* CINEMAT transferencia magnética *f*; ~ **transition** *n* METALL transición magnética *f*;

■ **v** ~ **variation** *n* GEOPHYS variación magnética *f*, WATER TRANSP declinación magnética *f*, variación de la aguja *f*, variación magnética *f*; ~ **variometer** *n* GEOPHYS inductor ajustable magnético *m*, variómetro magnético *m*; ~ **vector potential** *n* ELEC *of a field* potencial vector magnético *m*, PHYS potencial magnético vectorial *m*;

■ **w** ~ **wave** *n* ELEC ENG onda magnética *f*; ~ **wire** *n* ACOUST hilo magnetofónico *m*

magnetism *n* GEN magnetismo *m*

magnetite *n* MINERAL, NUCL magnetita *f*

magnetization *n* GEN , imantación *f*, magnetización *f*, imanación *f*; ~ **curve** *n* ELEC ENG curva de imanación *f*, curva de magnetización *f*, PHYS curva de magnetización *f*

magnetize *vt* CHEM magnetizar, ELEC, ELEC ENG imanar, imantar, magnetizar, GEOL, PETROL imantar, PHYS imanar, imantar, magnetizar, TELECOM, TV imantar

magnetized[1] *adj* GEN magnetizado

magnetized[2]: ~ **plasma** *n* NUCL plasma imantado *m*

magnetizing: ~ **coil** *n* ELEC, ELEC ENG bobina de excitación *f*, bobina imanante *f*, bobina magnetizante *f*; ~ **current** *n* ELEC ENG corriente magnetizante *f*; ~ **field** *n* ELEC ENG campo magnetizante *m*; ~ **force** *n* ELEC fuerza magnetizante *f*

magneto *n* AUTO magneto *m*, máquina magnetoeléctrica *f*, ELEC magneto *m*, ELEC ENG magneto *m*, máquina magnetoeléctrica *f*, VEH, WATER TRANSP magneto *m*; ~ **bearing** *n* MECH ENG cojinete de magneto *m*, palier de magneto *m*; ~ **ignition** *n* AUTO, VEH encendido por magneto *m*, ignición por magneto *f*; **~-optic disk** *n* (*m-o disk*) COMP&DP disco magnetoóptico *m* (*disco m-o*); **~-optic memory** *n* OPT memoria magnetoóptica *f*; **~-optical disc** *BrE* (*m-o disc*), **~-optical disk** *AmE* (*m-o disk*) *n* OPT disco magnetoóptico *m* (*disco m-o*); **~-optical effect** *n* OPT, PHYS efecto magnetoóptico *m*; ~ **switchboard** *n* TELECOM cuadro de conmutadores magnético *m*; **~-telluric prospecting** *n* GEOPHYS prospección magneto-telúrica *f*

magnetoconductivity *n* TELECOM magnetoconductividad *f*

magnetodiode *n* ELECTRON diodo electromagnético *m*

magnetoelectric: ~ **generator** *n* ELEC, ELEC ENG generador magnetoeléctrico *m*

magnetoelectricity *n* ELEC ENG magnetoelectricidad *f*

magnetogasdynamics *n* (*MGD*) NUCL magnetodinámica de los gases *f*, magnetogasodinámica *f* (*MGD*)

magnetogram *n* GEOPHYS magnetógrama *m*

magnetograph *n* GEOPHYS magnetógrafo *m*

magnetographic: ~ **printer** *n* COMP&DP, PRINT impresora magnetográfica *f*

magnetohydrodynamic: ~ **conversion** *n* ELEC ENG, GEOPHYS conversión magnetohidrodinámica *f*; ~ **converter** *n* ELEC ENG, NUCL, SPACE convertidor magnetohidrodinámico *m*; ~ **generation** *n* ELEC ENG producción magnetohidrodinámica *f*; ~ **generator** *n* ELEC, ELEC ENG generador magnetohidrodinámico

m; ~ **instability** *n* GEOPHYS inestabilidad magnetohidrodinámica *f*; ~ **pump** *n* ELEC ENG bomba magnetohidrodinámica *f*; ~ **wave** *n* GEOPHYS onda magnetohidrodinámica *f*

magnetohydrodynamics *n* (*MHD*) ELEC ENG, FLUID, GEOPHYS, PHYS, SPACE magnetohidrodinámica *f*

magnetometer *n* AIR TRANSP, ELEC, GEOPHYS, INSTR, PETROL, PHYS magnetómetro *m*; ~ **boom** *n* SPACE *craft* brazo del magnetómetro *m*; ~ **survey** *n* GEOPHYS, PETR TECH exploración magnetométrica *f*

magnetometry *n* ELEC ENG, GEOPHYS, PETR TECH magnetometría *f*

magnetomotive: ~ **force** *n* (*mmf*) ELEC, PHYS fuerza magnetomotriz *f* (*fmm*)

magneton *n* PHYS magnetón *m*

magnetophone *n* GEOPHYS magnetófono *m*

magnetoplasma *n* NUCL magnetoplasma *m*, plasma magnético *m*

magnetoresistance *n* PHYS magnetoresistencia *f*

magnetoresistor: ~ **potentiometer** *n* ELEC, INSTR potenciómetro magnetorresistor *m*

magnetoscope *n* GEOPHYS, TELECOM magnetoscopio *m*

magnetosphere *n* GEOPHYS, SPACE esfera magnética *f*, magnetosfera *f*; ~ **bow shock** *n* SPACE frente de choque de la magnetosfera *m*

magnetostatic *adj* NUCL magnetostático

magnetostriction *n* ACOUST, ELEC ENG, PHYS magnetoestricción *f*; ~ **loudspeaker** *n* ACOUST altavoz de magnetoestricción *m*; ~ **microphone** *n* ACOUST micrófono de magnetoestricción *f*

magnetostrictive: ~ **material** *n* ELEC ENG material magnetoestrictivo *m*; ~ **transductor** *n* ELEC ENG transductor magnetoestrictivo *m*

magnetotail *n* SPACE cola magnética *f*

magnetron *n* ELECTRON, MECH ENG, PHYS magnetrón *m*; ~ **amplifier** *n* ELECTRON amplificador de magnetrón *m*; ~ **arcing** *n* ELEC ENG formación de arco en el magnetrón *f*; ~ **oscillator** *n* ELECTRON oscilador de magnetrón *m*

magnetting *n* C&G inmantado *m*

magnification *n* INSTR amplificación *f*, aumento *m*, PHYS magnificación *f*; ~ **changer** *n* INSTR conmutador de aumento *m*; ~ **effectiveness** *n* INSTR eficacia del aumento *f*; ~ **factor** *n* CINEMAT factor de amplificación *m*, factor de aumento *m*, ELECTRON factor de amplificación *m*, INSTR factor de amplificación *m*, factor de aumento *m*; ~ **scale** *n* INSTR graduación de aumento *f*

magnified: **~-viewfinder image** *n* PHOTO imagen aumentada del visor *f*

magnifier *n* INSTR amplificador *m*, lupa *f*; ~ **enlargement** *n* INSTR, PHOTO ampliación fotográfica *f*

magnify *vt* CINEMAT, INSTR, PHYS magnificar

magnifying[1] *adj* INSTR amplificador, de aumento

magnifying[2] *n* INSTR amplificación *f*; ~ **glass** *n* LAB, MECH, PHYS cristal de aumento *m*, lupa de aumento *f*, vidrio de aumento *m*; ~ **lens** *n* INSTR lente de aumento *f*; ~ **picture viewer** *n* INSTR visualizador ampliador de diapositivas *m*; ~ **power** *n* PHYS poder de magnificación *m*

magnitude *n* PHYS magnitud *f*; **~-frequency curve** *n* ACOUST curva magnitud-frecuencia *f*

magnon *n* PHYS magnón *m*

magnox: ~ **reactor** *n* NUCL reactor magnox *m*

Magnum: ~ **terrace** n AGRIC *conservation* terraza Magnum *f*

Magnus: ~ **effect** n PHYS efecto Magnus *m*

mag-optical: ~ **print** n CINEMAT copia magnetoóptica *f*

maiden: ~ **flight** n AIR TRANSP vuelo inaugural *m*; ~ **heifer** n AGRIC novilla no cubierta *f*, vaquillona sin servicio *f* (*AmL*); ~ **nut** n MECH ENG tuerca de apriete *f*; ~ **voyage** n WATER TRANSP *of ship* viaje inaugural *m*

mail[1]: ~ **order-packed** adj PACK embalado para enviar por correo, empaquetado para enviar por correo

mail[2]: ~ **and cargo terminal** n TRANSP terminal de carga y correo *f*; ~ **server** n TELECOM servidor de correo *m*; ~ **train** n RAIL tren correo *m*; ~ **van** n AUTO, VEH furgoneta de correo *f*

mailing n COMP&DP correo *m*; ~ **sleeve** n PACK funda para envíos postales *f*; ~ **tube** n AmE (*cf postal tube BrE*) PACK tubo para envíos postales *m*

main n CONST *conduitpipe* tubería principal *f*, WATER canalización principal *f*; ~ **air-supply hose** n RAIL manguera principal de inyección de aire *f*; ~ **air-supply pipe** n RAIL manguera principal de inyección de aire *f*; ~ **anode** n ELEC ENG ánodo principal *m*; ~ **bar** n ELEC ENG segmento principal *m*; ~ **battery** n AIR TRANSP *of aircraft* batería principal *f*; ~ **beam** n CONST viga maestra *f*, SPACE *communications* haz principal *m*, luz de carretera *f*, WATER TRANSP bao maestro *m*; ~ **bearing** n AUTO, CONST cojinete principal *m*, VEH, WATER TRANSP *of engine* cojinete del cigüeñal *m*, cojinete principal *m*; ~**-bearing bushing** n AUTO buje de cojinete principal *m*, casquillo del cojinete principal *m*, collar del cojinete principal *m*, manguito del cojinete principal *m*; ~ **brake hose** n AmE (*cf main brake pipe BrE*) RAIL manguera de acoplamiento de la cañería del freno *f*; ~ **brake pipe** BrE n (*cf main brake hose AmE*) RAIL manguera de acoplamiento de la cañería del freno *f*; ~ **branch** n AGRIC rama principal lateral *f*; ~ **burner** n HEAT ENG quemador principal *m*; ~ **busbar** n ELEC, TELECOM barra colectora principal *f*; ~ **casting** n PROD *forge* cazoleta del pivote *f*, placa para colocar un moldeo en el torno *f*; ~ **chute** n COAL alcancía principal *f* (*AmL*), tolua principal *f* (*Esp*), MINE alcancía principal *f* (*AmL*), chimenea principal *f*, coladero principal *m* (*Esp*), paso principal *m* (*AmL*), puerta principal *f* (*Esp*), tolua principal *f* (*Esp*), THERMO alcancia principal *f* (*AmL*), puerta principal *f* (*Esp*); ~ **circuit** n ELEC *of network* circuito principal *m*; ~ **conductor** n ELEC ENG conductor principal *m*; ~ **contacts** n pl ELEC contactos principales *m pl*; ~ **coolant pump** n NUCL bomba del refrigerante del reactor *f*, bomba principal *f*; ~ **crack** n METALL grieta principal *f*; ~ **deck** n WATER TRANSP cubierta principal *f*; ~ **distribution frame** n (*MDF*) TELECOM repartidor principal *m*, trama principal de distribución *f*; ~ **drain** n AGRIC colector *m*, CONST desagüe principal *m*; ~ **drive** n MECH ENG accionamiento principal *m*, mecanismo de transmisión principal *m*; ~ **drive gear** n AUTO engranaje de mando principal *m*; ~ **drive shaft** n AIR TRANSP *of helicopter* eje conductor principal *m*; ~ **drive unit** n INSTR, MECH ENG, PROD unidad de transmisión principal *f*; ~ **exchange** n TELECOM central principal *f*; ~ **exposure** n PRINT exposición principal *f*; ~ **feed motion** n MECH ENG movimiento de avance principal *m*; ~ **feedwater system** n (*MFWS*) NUCL sistema de agua de alimentación principal *m* (*MFWS*); ~ **forage area** n AGRIC zona forrajera principal *f*; ~ **gap** n ELEC ENG espacio interelectródico principal *m*, separación principal *f*; ~ **gate** n COAL canal de colada *m*, entrada principal *f*, PROD *foundry* bebedero *m*, canal de colada *m*, reguera *f*; ~**-gear axle beam** n AIR TRANSP viga del eje del engranaje principal *f*; ~**-gear sliding door** n AIR TRANSP puerta corrediza del engranaje principal *f*; ~ **gearbox** n AIR TRANSP caja de engranajes principal *f*; ~**-gearbox support** n AIR TRANSP *of helicopter* soporte de la caja de cambios principal *m*; ~ **girder** n CONST viga principal *f*; ~ **intake airway** n COAL, MINE galería de entrada de aire principal *f*; ~ **international switching center** AmE, ~ **international switching centre** BrE n TELECOM centro principal de conmutación internacional *m*, centro principal de distribución internacional *m*; ~ **international trunk-switching center** AmE, ~ **international trunk-switching centre** BrE n TELECOM centro principal de conmutación de enlaces internacionales *m*; ~ **intervals on the diatonic scale** n pl ACOUST intervalos principales en la escala diatónica *m pl*; ~ **isolating valve** n NUCL válvula principal de aislamiento *f*; ~ **jet** n AUTO, VEH chorro principal *m*, surtidor principal *m*; ~ **landing gear** n AIR TRANSP *of helicopter* tren de aterrizaje principal *m*; ~ **landing gear brace strut** n AIR TRANSP puntal oblicuo del tren de aterrizaje principal *m*; ~ **landing gear door** n AIR TRANSP portezuela del tren de aterrizaje principal *f*; ~ **leg** n NUCL lazo principal *m*; ~ **line** n CONST vía férrea troncal *f*, RAIL línea principal *f*, vía principal *f*, TELECOM línea principal *f*; ~ **load** n CONST carga principal *f*; ~ **lode** n MINE filón principal *m*, veta madre *f* (*AmL*), veta principal *f* (*Esp*); ~ **memory** n COMP&DP memoria central *f*; ~ **mirror** n INSTR espejo principal *m*; ~ **pin** n MECH ENG *kingbolt* perno maestro *m*, perno pinzote *m*; ~ **pole** n ELEC *of a terminal* polo principal *m*; ~**-power disconnect** n PROD desconexión de la potencia principal *f*; ~ **press** n PAPER prensa principal *f*; ~ **quantum number** n AIR TRANSP número cuántico principal *m*; ~ **reflector** n SPACE *communications* reflector principal *m*; ~ **regulator valve** n AUTO válvula reguladora principal *f*; ~ **reinforcement** n CONST armadura principal *f*, refuerzo principal *m*; ~ **repeater distribution frame** n TELECOM trama de distribución principal de repetición *f*; ~ **return airway** n MINE galería principal de retorno del aire *f*; ~ **rib** n AIR TRANSP costilla principal *f*; ~ **road** n CONST, TRANSP *highway* camino principal *m*, carretera principal *f*; ~ **roadway** n COAL galería principal *f*; ~ **rod** n MECH ENG varilla maestra *f*; ~ **root** n AGRIC raíz principal *f*; ~ **rotor** n AIR TRANSP *of helicopter* rotor principal *m*; ~**-rotor blade** n AIR TRANSP *of helicopter* pala de rotor principal *f*; ~**-rotor head** n AIR TRANSP *of helicopter* cabeza de rotor principal *f*; ~**-rotor hub** n AIR TRANSP *of helicopter* cubo del rotor principal *m*; ~**-rotor shaft** n AIR TRANSP *of helicopter* eje del rotor principal *m*; ~ **scope tube** n INSTR tubo de alcance principal *m*; ~ **sewer** n CONST cloaca maestra *f* (*AmL*), colector maestro *m* (*Esp*), HYDROL alcantarilla principal *f*, RECYCL cañería cloacal *f*, colector *m*, WATER alcantarilla principal *f*; ~ **shaft** n AIR TRANSP, AUTO eje principal *m*, MECH cigüeñal *m*, eje motor *m*, eje principal *m*, MECH ENG *engines* árbol de manivelas *m*, eje motor *m*, cigüeñal *m*, eje principal *m*, MINE pozo maestro *m*, pozo principal *m*, VEH *of gearbox* eje primario *m*, eje principal *m*; **~-shaft bearing** *n* CONST, WATER TRANSP *shipbuilding* chumacera del eje *f*; **~-sheet track** *n* WATER TRANSP *deck fittings* barraescota de la mayor *f*, escotero *m*; **~ shroud** *n* WATER TRANSP *rigging* obenque mayor *m*; **~ solar generator** *n* SPACE *craft* generador solar principal *m*; **~ spillway** *n* HYDROL, WATER aliviadero principal *m*; **~ spring** *n* MECH ENG, MILIT resorte motor *m*, resorte principal *m*; **~ steam** *n* NUCL *metal, cell* vapor principal *m*; **~-steam isolation valve** *n* NUCL válvula de aislamiento de vapor principal *f*; **~ steam pipe** *n* HYDRAUL conducto principal de vapor *m*, válvula de cuello *f*, válvula principal del vapor *f*; **~-steam system** *n* NUCL sistema de vapor principal *m*; **~-steamline break** *n* NUCL (*MSLB*) rotura de la línea de vapor principal *f* (*MSLB*); **~ storage** *n* AmE (*cf main store BrE*) COMP&DP almacenamiento central *m*, almacenamiento principal *m*, memoria central *f*, memoria principal *f*, unidad de almacenamiento central *f* (*AmL*), unidad de almacenamiento principal *f*; **~ store** *n* BrE (*cf main storage AmE*) COMP&DP almacenamiento central *m*, almacenamiento principal *m*, memoria central *f*, memoria principal *f*, unidad de almacenamiento central *f* (*AmL*), unidad de almacenamiento principal *f*; **~ switch** *n* ELEC interruptor general *m*, interruptor principal *m*, ELEC ENG interruptor principal *m*, TELECOM conmutador principal *m*; **~ switching contacts** *n pl* ELEC contactos del interruptor general *m pl*, contactos del interruptor principal *m pl*; **~ tap** *n* MECH ENG canilla principal *f*, grifo maestro *m*; **~ terminal** *n* AUTO borne principal *m*, terminal principal *m*; **~ track** *n* RAIL vía principal *f*; **~ trading route** *n* WATER TRANSP *shipping* principal ruta comercial *f*; **~ transformer** *n* NUCL transformador principal *m*; **~ trunk-exchange area** *n* TELECOM centro de enlace principal *m*; **~ trunk-switching center** AmE, **~ trunk-switching centre** *n* BrE TELECOM centro de conmutación de enlace principal *m*; **~ unit** *n* MECH ENG unidad principal *f*; **~ valve** *n* HEAT válvula principal *f*; **~ wall** *n* CONST *of building* pared maestra *f*

mainbrace *n* WATER TRANSP *rigging* braza mayor *f*

mainframe *n* COMP&DP gran computador *m* (*AmL*), gran ordenador *m* (*Esp*), unidad central *f* (*AmL*), unidad principal *f*

mainmast *n* WATER TRANSP palo mayor *m*

mainplane *n* AIR TRANSP *of aircraft* plano principal *m*

mains[1]: **~-operated** *adj* BrE (*cf current-operated AmE*) ELEC *appliance*, ELEC ENG accionado por la corriente, alimentado por la red, enchufado a la red

mains[2] *n* BrE (*cf current AmE*) ELEC *supply network* red *f*, alimentación eléctrica *f*, alimentación por la red *f*, red eléctrica *f*, corriente *f*, ELEC ENG red de distribución eléctrica *f*, alimentación eléctrica *f*, TV red eléctrica *f*, corriente *f*, suministro principal *m* (*AmL*), WATER tubería principal *f*, canalización principal *f*, red de distribución *f*; **~ cable** *n* BrE (*cf current cable AmE*) ELEC, ELEC ENG cable de la corriente *m*, cable de la red eléctrica *m*; **~ current** *n* BrE (*cf current AmE*) ELEC ENG corriente de la red eléctrica *f*; **~ frequency** *n* BrE (*cf current frequency AmE*) ELEC, ELEC ENG frecuencia de alimentación eléctrica *f*, frecuencia de la corriente *f*, frecuencia de la red eléctrica *f*, frecuencia de red *f*; **~ hum** *n* BrE (*cf*

current hum AmE) ELEC *supply*, ELEC ENG murmullo de la corriente *m*, zumbido de corriente *m*, zumbido de la red *m*; **~ lead** *n* BrE (*cf current lead AmE*) ELEC, ELEC ENG cable conductor de corriente *m*, cable conductor de la red *m*, cable de corriente *m*; **~ lead cleat** *n* BrE (*cf current lead cleat AmE*) ELEC, ELEC ENG mordaza del cable de toma de corriente *f*; **~ plug** *n* BrE (*cf current plug AmE*) ELEC, ELEC ENG clavija de conexión a la red *f*, enchufe de conexión a la red *m*, enchufe de la corriente *m*, enchufe tomacorriente *m*; **~ rectifier** *n* BrE (*cf current rectifier AmE*) ELEC, ELEC ENG rectificador de corriente *m*, rectificador de red *m*, rectificador de voltaje de la red *m*; **~ socket** *n* BrE (*cf current socket AmE*) ELEC, ELEC ENG clavija hembra de corriente *f*, enchufe de corriente *m*, clavija de corriente *f*; **~ supply** *n* BrE (*cf current supply AmE*) ELEC *network* red *f*, alimentación eléctrica *f*, alimentación por la red *f*, red eléctrica *f*, corriente *f*, ELEC ENG suministro de la red *m*, *network* alimentación eléctrica *f*; **~ switch** *n* BrE (*cf current switch AmE*) ELEC, ELEC ENG interruptor de corriente *m*, interruptor de red *m*, interruptor de voltaje de la red *m*, llave de la corriente *f*; **~ transformer** *n* BrE (*cf current transformer AmE*) ELEC *supply* transformador de alimentación *m*, transformador de corriente *m*, transformador de intensidad *m*, transformador de la red de corriente eléctrica *m*, transformador de la red principal *m*, ELEC ENG transformador de amperaje *m*, transformador de intensidad *m*, transformador de la red de corriente eléctrica *m*, ELECTRON transformador de corriente *m*, transformador de la red principal *m*, transformador en serie *m*; **~ voltage** *n* BrE (*cf current voltage AmE*) *supply* ELEC, ELEC ENG, TV voltaje de la red *m*, voltaje de alimentación *m*, voltaje de la corriente *m*, tensión de la corriente *f*; **~ water** *n* BrE (*cf city water AmE*) HYDROL, WATER agua industrial *f*, canalización principal de aguas *f*

mainsail *n* WATER TRANSP mayor *f*, vela mayor *f*

mainsheet *n* WATER TRANSP escota de la mayor *f*

mainstay *n* WATER TRANSP *rigging* estay mayor *m*

maintain[1]: **~ aseptic area conditions** *vi* SAFE mantener condiciones de zona aséptica; **~ course and speed** *vi* WATER TRANSP mantener rumbo y velocidad

maintainability *n* MECH, PROD, QUALITY, SPACE conservabilidad *f*, facilidad de mantenimiento *f*

maintained: **~-contact push-button** *n* PROD pulsador de contacto sostenido *m*; **~ oscillation** *n* PHYS oscilación sostenida *f*

maintainer *n* CONST *civil engineering* encargado de mantenimiento *m*

maintenance *n* COMP&DP mantenimiento *m*, MECH conservación *f*, mantenimiento *m*, PROD, SAFE, SPACE, TV mantenimiento *m*; **~ cell description** *n* (*MCD*) TELECOM descripción de la célula de mantenimiento *f*; **~ contract** *n* (*MA*) ELECTRON contrato de mantenimiento *m* (*CM*); **~ cost** *n* QUALITY costo de mantenimiento *m*; **~ current** *n* ELEC *of relay, thyristor* corriente de conservación *f*, corriente de mantenimiento *f*; **~ data card** *n* PROD ficha de mantenimiento *f*; **~ function** *n* TELECOM función de mantenimiento *f*; **~ level** *n* RAIL nivel de gastos de entretenimiento *m*, nivel de gastos de mantenimiento *m*; **~ manual** *n* AIR TRANSP, PROD, SAFE manual de mantenimiento *m*; **~ period** *n* CONST período de mantenimiento *m*; **~ processor** *n* TELECOM procesador de mantenimiento *m*; **~ record** *n* AIR TRANSP registro de mantenimiento *m*; **~ service provider** *n* (*MSP*) TELECOM proveedor del servicio de mantenimiento *m*; **~ shop** *n* CONST taller de mantenimiento *m*, taller de reparaciones *m*; **~ unit** *n* AIR TRANSP, PROD unidad de mantenimiento *f*

Maintenance: **~ Operation Protocol** *n* (*MOP*) TELECOM Protocolo de Operación para Mantenimiento *m*

mainway *n* MINE galería principal *f*

maisonette *n* CONST casita *f*, dúplex *m*

maize *n* BrE (*cf corn AmE*) AGRIC maíz *m*; **~ binder** *n* BrE (*cf corn binder AmE*) AGRIC cortadora-empacadora de maíz *f*; **~-borer** *n* BrE (*cf corn-borer AmE*) AGRIC barrenador del maíz *m*; **~ breeding** *n* BrE (*cf corn breeding AmE*) AGRIC mejoramiento genético de maíz *m*; **~ drill** *n* BrE (*cf corn drill AmE*) AGRIC sembradora de maíz *f*; **~ drying shed** *n* BrE (*cf corn crib AmE*) AGRIC secadero de maíz *m*, criba de maíz *f*; **~ flake** *n* BrE (*cf corn flake AmE*) AGRIC copo de maíz *m*; **~ germ meal** *n* BrE (*cf corn germ meal AmE*) AGRIC harina de germen de maíz *f*; **~ gluten feed** *n* BrE (*cf corn gluten feed AmE*) AGRIC alimento de gluten de maíz *m*; **~ grower** *n* BrE (*cf corn grower AmE*) AGRIC agricultor de maíz *m*, productor de maíz *m*; **~-growing area** *n* BrE (*cf corn-growing area AmE*) AGRIC región productora de maíz *f*; **~ husk** *n* BrE (*cf corn husk AmE*) AGRIC chala de maíz *f* (*AmL*), espata de maíz *f* (*Esp*); **~ husker** *n* BrE (*cf corn husker AmE*) AGRIC deschaladora de maíz *f* (*AmL*), deshojadora de maíz *f* (*Esp*); **~ picker** *n* BrE (*cf corn picker AmE*) AGRIC cosechadora de maíz *f*; **~ picker-husker** *n* BrE (*cf corn picker-husker AmE*) AGRIC cosechadora-deshojadora de maíz *f* (*Esp*), espigadora-deschaladora de maíz *f* (*AmL*); **~ picker-sheller** *n* BrE (*cf corn picker-sheller AmE*) AGRIC cosechadora-desgranadora de maíz *f* (*Esp*), espigadora-desgranadora de maíz *f* (*AmL*); **~ sheller** *n* BrE (*cf corn sheller AmE*) AGRIC desgranadora de maíz *f*; **~ silage** *n* BrE (*cf corn silage AmE*) AGRIC ensilado de maíz *m*; **~ snapper** *n* BrE (*cf corn snapper AmE*) AGRIC espigadora de maíz *f*; **~ stalk** *n* BrE (*cf corn stalk AmE*) AGRIC tallo del maíz *m*; **~ stunt** *n* BrE (*cf corn stunt AmE*) AGRIC enanismo del maíz *m*; **~ syrup** *n* BrE (*cf corn syrup AmE*) AGRIC jarabe de maíz *m*; **~ thresher** *n* BrE (*cf corn thresher AmE*) AGRIC trilladora de maíz *f*

majolica *n* C&G mayólica *f*; **~ colors** *AmE*, **~ colours** *BrE* *n pl* C&G colores de mayólica *m pl*; **~ painter** *n* C&G decorador de mayólica *m*; **~ tile** *n* C&G mosaico de mayólica *m*; **~ ware** *n* C&G loza de mayólica *f*

major: **~ account holder** *n* TELECOM titular principal de la cuenta *m*; **~ alarm** *n* TELECOM alarma importante *f*; **~ arc** *n* GEOM arco mayor *m*; **~ axis** *n* GEOM eje mayor *m*; **~ common chord** *n* ACOUST acorde perfecto mayor *m*; **~ fault bit** *n* COMP&DP, PROD bit de ruptura a nivel superior *m*; **~ hazard** *n* QUALITY, SAFE peligro mayor *m*, riesgo mayor *m*; **~ inspection** *n* AIR TRANSP inspección general *f*; **~ overhaul** *n* NUCL revisión general *f*; **~ railway junction** *n* RAIL empalme ferroviario principal *m*; **~ road** *n* CONST, TRANSP carretera principal *f*; **~ scale** *n* ACOUST escala mayor *f*; **~ scale of equal temperament** *n* ACOUST escala mayor de igual temperamento *f*; **~ second** *n* ACOUST segunda mayor *f*; **~ seventh** *n* ACOUST séptima mayor *f*; **~ sixth** *n* ACOUST sexta mayor *f*; **~ source** *n* POLL fuente mayor *f*, fuente principal *f*,

origen principal *m*; **~ third** *n* ACOUST tercera mayor *f*; **~ whole tone** *n* ACOUST tono completo mayor *m*

Majorana: **~ force** *n* NUCL fuerza de Majorana *f*

majority: **~ carrier** *n* ELECTRON vector mayoritario *m*, PHYS portadora principal *f*; **~-carrier diode** *n* ELECTRON diodo de vector mayoritario *m*; **~-carrier transistor** *n* ELECTRON transistor de vector mayoritario *m*; **~ gate** *n* ELECTRON circuito eléctrico principal *m*; **~ logic** *n* ELECTRON circuito eléctrico principal *m*

make[1] *n* ELEC ENG *in circuit* cierre *m*, conexión *f*, MECH ENG *contact* cierre *m*, conexión *f*, contacto *m*, MINE irrupción *f*, PROD marca *f*, nombre *m*, *manufacture* fabricación *f*, manufactura *f*, procedimiento de fabricación *m*, proceso de fabricación *m*, producción *f*; **~-and-break** *n* ELEC, ELEC ENG conjuntor-disyuntor *m*; **~-and-break coil** *n* ELEC bobina de apertura-cierre *f*; **~-and-break contact** *n* ELEC ENG contacto reposo-trabajo *m*; **~-and-break device** *n* ELEC *switch* dispositivo de apertura-cierre *m*; **~-and-break ignition** *n* AUTO, VEH encendido por apertura y cierre *m*, ignición de apertura y cierre *f*; **~-break time** *n* ELEC *of relay* duración de apertura/cierre *f*; **~ contact** *n* ELEC *relay*, ELEC ENG contacto de trabajo *m*; **~ current** *n* ELEC ENG corriente de trabajo *f*; **~-make contact** *n* ELEC *relay* contacto de trabajo-trabajo *m*; **~ pulse** *n* ELEC ENG impulso de trabajo *m*; **~-ready** *n* PRINT arreglo *m*, alzado *m*; **~-ready sheet** *n* PRINT hoja para arreglos *f*; **~-ready time** *n* PRINT tiempo de arreglo *m*; **~ relay** *n* ELEC relé de cierre *m*; **~ time** *n* ELEC *relay* duración de cierre *f*; **~-up** *n* PRINT compaginación *f*, ajuste *m*, WATER aportación *f*, reposición *f*; **~-up fuel** *n* NUCL combustible de reposición *m*; **~-up gas** *n* GAS gas de reposición *m*; **~-up mirror** *n* INSTR espejo de reposición *m*; **~-up rate** *n* MECH ENG coeficiente de compensación *m*; **~-up water** *n* FOOD agua necesaria *f*, HYDROL, REFRIG agua de relleno *f*

make[2] *vt* CONST *joint* unir, *road* construir, fabricar, *reinforced concrete* confeccionar, elaborar, ELEC ENG *circuit* conectar, cerrar, PROD *joint* ejecutar, *tools* elaborar, fabricar, construir; **~ fast** *vt* WATER TRANSP *boom* hacer firme, asegurar, *line, boat* amarrar, *load* trincar; **~ flush** *vt* MECH ENG hacer fluir, hacer salir; **~ good** *vt* PROD *wear and tear* corregir, reparar; **~ impermeable** *vt* CONST impermeabilizar; **~ ready** *vt* PRINT poner a punto; **~ up** *vt* PRINT compaginar

make[3]: **~ foam** *vi* CHEM TECH hacer espuma; **~ a joint** *vi* CONST unir; **~ a port** *vi* WATER TRANSP estar en un puerto, llegar a un puerto; **~ a round trip** *vi* PETR TECH hacer un viaje; **~ sail** *vi* WATER TRANSP *ship* dar la vela, hacer vela; **~ a survey** *vi* CONST hacer un levantamiento topográfico, hacer una investigación, investigar; **~ a tack** *vi* WATER TRANSP *sailing* correr un bordo, dar un bordo; **~ a tight joint** *vi* PROD hacer una junta hermética, sellar herméticamente; **~ a turn round winch with line** *vi* WATER TRANSP tomar una vuelta al cabo con el chigre; **~ water** *vi* WATER TRANSP hacer agua

maker *n* GEN fabricante *m*; **~'s mark** *n* PROD *essayer's mark* marca del fabricante *f*, punzón de garantía del fabricante *m*

makeshift[1] *adj* PROD, SPACE provisional (*Esp*), provisorio (*AmL*)

makeshift² *n* PROD, SPACE instalación provisional *f* (*Esp*), instalación provisoria *f* (*AmL*)

making: ~ **capacity** *n* ELEC *of relay* capacidad de cierre *f*, poder de cierre *m*, ELEC ENG capacidad de conexión *f*; ~ **on blowpipe** *n* C&G trabajo con la caña de soplo *m*; **~-up** *n* PETR TECH *of a joint* ajuste *m*, PHOTO *process* preparación *f*, TEXTIL confección *f*

malachite *n* MINERAL malaquita *f*

malacolite *n* MINERAL malacolita *f*

malacon *n* MINERAL, NUCL malacón *m*

malate *n* CHEM malato *m*

malaxage *n* MECH ENG malaxación *f*

malaxator *n* MECH ENG malaxador *m*, máquina de amasar y mexclar *f*

maldonite *n* MINERAL maldonita *f*

male: ~ **caliper gage** *AmE*, ~ **calliper gauge** *n BrE* MECH ENG calibre interior plano *m*, calibre macho plano *m*; ~ **cone** *n* MECH ENG cono macho *m*; ~ **connector** *n* ELEC ENG enchufe macho *m*; ~ **esterile** *n* AGRIC androestéril *m*; ~ **plug** *n* TELECOM enchufe macho *m*; ~ **screw** *n* MECH ENG tornillo *m*; ~ **thread** *n* MECH ENG *tooling* rosca macho *f*

maleic: ~ **acid** *n* CHEM ácido maleico *m*; ~ **ester** *n* DETERG éster maleico *m*

maleimide *n* CHEM maleimida *f*

malfunction¹ *n* GEN funcionamiento incorrecto *m*, disfunción *f*, fallo *m*, malfuncionamiento *m*, funcionamiento defectuoso *m*

malfunction² *vi* ELEC ENG, ELECTRON, MECH, MECH ENG, TELECOM fallar, funcionar mal

malic¹ *adj* CHEM málico

malic²: ~ **acid** *n* CHEM, FOOD ácido málico *m*

malicious: ~ **call** *n* TELECOM llamada maliciosa *f*; **~-call tracing** *n* TELECOM localización de llamadas maliciosas *f*

mallardite *n* MINERAL mallardita *f*

malleability *n* MECH, METALL maleabilidad *f*

malleable¹ *adj* MECH, METALL maleable

malleable²: ~ **cast iron** *n* MECH fundición maleable *f*

malleablizing *n* HEAT maleabilización *f*

malleation *n* PROD martillaje *m*

mallet *n* C&G mazo *m*, MECH maza de hierro *f*, PROD maceta *f*, mazo *m*

malleus *n* ACOUST martillo *m*

malonamide *n* CHEM malonamida *f*

malonate *n* CHEM malonato *m*

malonic *adj* CHEM malónico

malonitrile *n* CHEM malonitrilo *m*

malt¹ *n* CHEM, FOOD malta *f*; ~ **extract** *n* FOOD extracto de malta *m*; ~ **house** *n AmE* (*cf maltings BrE*) FOOD fábrica de malta *f*, maltería *f*; ~ **sprout** *n* AGRIC brote de cebada germinada *m*

malt² *vt* FOOD maltear

maltase *n* CHEM, FOOD maltasa *f*

Maltese: ~ **cross** *n* MECH cruz de Malta *f*; ~ **cross assembly** *n* CINEMAT mecanismo de cruz de Malta *m*; ~ **cross mechanism** *n* MECH ENG mecanismo de cruz de Malta *m*; ~ **cross movement** *n* CINEMAT movimiento de cruz de Malta *m*

maltha *n* MINERAL brea mineral *f*, maltenos *m pl*

malthacite *n* MINERAL maltacita *f*

malting: ~ **barley** *n* FOOD cebada para maltear *f*

maltings *n pl BrE* (*cf malt house AmE*) FOOD fábrica de malta *f*, maltería *f*

maltose *n* CHEM maltosa *f*

Malus: ~ **law** *n* PHYS ley de Malus *f*

mammillary *adj* MINERAL mamilar

mammoth: ~ **tanker** *n* TRANSP cisterna pesada *f*

man¹: **~-day** *n* PROD hombre-día *m*; **~-hour** *n* CONST hora de mano de obra *f*, hora-hombre *f*, PROD hombre-hora *m*; **~-machine interaction** *n* (*MMI*) COMP&DP interacción hombre-máquina *f* (*MMI*); **~-machine interface** *n* SPACE *craft* contacto hombre-máquina *m*; **~-machine ratio** *n* PROD relación hombre-máquina *f*; **~-machine relationship** *n* TELECOM relación hombre-máquina *f*; **~-made earth tremor** *n* POLL temblor de tierra ocasionado por el hombre *m*; **~-made earthquake** *n* POLL temblor de tierra ocasionado por el hombre *m*; **~-made fiber** *AmE*, **~-made fibre** *n BrE* HEAT ENG, PACK, TEXTIL fibra artificial *f*; **~-made noise** *n* SPACE ruido industrial *m*; **~-of-war** *n* MILIT, WATER TRANSP buque de guerra *m*; **~-week** *n* PROD hombre-semana *m*; **~-year** *n* PROD hombre-año *m*

man² *vt* WATER TRANSP *ship* dotar, tripular

MAN *abbr* (*metropolitan area network*) TELECOM red de área metropolitana *f*

managed: ~ **object class** *n* (*MOC*) TELECOM clase de objetos controlados *f*

management: ~ **applications function** *n* (*MAF*) TELECOM función de aplicaciones de gestión *f*; ~ **center** *AmE*, ~ **centre** *n BrE* TELECOM centro de gestión *m*; ~ **chart** *n* PROD organigrama de gerencia *f* (*AmL*), organigrama de gestión *f* (*Esp*); ~ **domain** *n* (*MD*) TELECOM dominio de gestión *m*; ~ **information** *n* TELECOM información para administración de empresas *f*; ~ **information base** *n* (*MIB*) TELECOM base de información para dirección de empresas *f*; ~ **information system** *n* (*MIS*) COMP&DP sistema integrado de administración *m* (*SIG*), sistema integrado de gestión *m*, TELECOM sistema integrado de administración *f* (*SIG*); ~ **report** *n* PROD informe de administración *m*, informe de gerencia *m* (*AmL*), informe de gestión *m* (*Esp*)

Management: ~ **Integrated System** *n* TELECOM condición secundaria de indicación para varios puntos *f*

mandatory¹ *adj* TELECOM forzoso, preceptivo

mandatory²: ~ **sign** *n* SAFE letrero obligatorio *m*, señal obligatoria *f*; ~ **standard** *n* QUALITY norma obligatoria *f*

mandelic *adj* CHEM mandélico

mandrel *n* C&G mandril *m*, COAL mandril *m*, mandrín *m*, pico de minero de dos puntas *m*, CONST mandrín *m*, MECH ENG *spindle* husillo *m*, eje *m*, mandril *m*, mandrín *m*, MINE mandril *m*, mandrín *m*, pico de minero de dos puntas *m*, P&R husillo *m*, mandril *m*, tornillo *m*, PROD mandrín *m*; ~ **nose** *n* MECH ENG *of lathe* nuez del mandrín *f*; ~ **running in bearings** *n* MECH ENG mandril funcionando con cojinetes *m*

maneuver *n AmE see* manoeuvre *BrE*

maneuverability *n AmE see* manoeuvrability *BrE*

maneuverable *adj AmE see* manoeuvrable *BrE*

maneuvering: ~ **valve** *n AmE see* manoeuvring valve *BrE*

manganese *n* (*Mn*) C&G, CHEM, MECH, METALL manganeso *m* (*Mn*); ~ **bronze** *n* MECH bronce manganoso *m*; ~ **dioxide** *n* ELEC ENG *in batteries* dióxido de manganeso *m*; ~ **nodule** *n* GEOL nódulo de manganeso *m*; ~ **steel** *n* MECH, METALL, PROD acero al manganeso *m*

manganic *adj* CHEM mangánico

manganiferous *adj* GEOL manganífero

manganite *n* CHEM, MINERAL manganita *f*
manganocalcite *n* MINERAL manganocalcita *f*
manganous[1] *adj* CHEM manganoso
manganous[2]: ~ **sulfate bath method** *AmE*, ~ **sulphate bath method** *n BrE* NUCL método del baño de sulfato de manganeso *m*
manhole *n* CONST *shelter* refugio *m*, pozo de inspección *m*, nicho *m*, ELEC *supply* caja subterránea *f*, cámara *f*, registro *m*, HYDROL registro *m*, galería de inspección *f* (*AmL*), galería de visita *f* (*Esp*), MECH registro *m*, pozo de visita *m*, MECH ENG registro *m*, entrada de hombre *f*, cámara de visita *f*, boca de inspección *f*, pozo de visita *m*, boca de acceso *f*, MINE boca de inspección *f*, arqueta *f*, galería de inspección *f* (*AmL*), galería de visita *f* (*Esp*), paso para los hombres *m*, pozo de inspección *m*, registro *m*, NUCL boca de hombre *f*, SPACE boca de inspección *f*; ~ **cover** *n* MECH tapa de agujero de hombre *f*, tapa de registro *f*; ~ **door** *n* CONST puerta de acceso *f*, tapa de pozo *f*; ~ **gasket** *n* MECH obturador de agujero de hombre *m*; ~ **plate** *n* CONST placa de registro *f*
manifold[1] *adj* GEOM múltiple
manifold[2] *n* AIR TRANSP colector múltiple *m*, ramificador múltiple *m*, GEOM variedad *f*, LAB distribuidor *m*, múltiple *m*, MECH distribuidor *m*, diversidad *f*, MECH ENG *of superheater* colector *m*, colector de vapor *m*, múltiple *m*, NUCL colector *m*, distribuidor *m*, PETR TECH manifold *m*, múltiple de distribuición *m*, múltiple de tuberías *m*, plano de las válvulas de cubierta *m*, PRINT copia *f*, PROD colector *m*, distribuidor *m*; ~ **drying apparatus** *n* REFRIG cámara de vacío con conexiones múltiples *f*; ~ **pressure** *n* AIR TRANSP presión del colector *f*; ~ **system** *n* MAR POLL sistema de colectores *m*
Manila: ~ **hemp** *n* AGRIC, PAPER abacá *m*
manipulating *n* PROD manejo *m*, maniobra *f*, manipulación *f*; ~ **device** *n* MECH ENG *for technical components* manipulador *m*; ~ **industrial robot** *n* MECH ENG robot industrial manipulador *m*, robot industrial para manipulación *m*, PROD manipulador *m*
manipulation *n* PROD manejo *m*, manipulación *f*; ~ **detection** *n* TELECOM detección por manipulación *f*
manned: ~ **flight** *n* SPACE vuelo asistido *m*, vuelo tripulado *m*; ~ **helicopter** *n* AIR TRANSP helicóptero tripulado *m*; ~ **maneuvering unit** *AmE*, ~ **manoeuvring unit** *n BrE* SPACE unidad de maniobra asistida *f*; ~ **module** *n* SPACE módulo asistido *m*, módulo tripulado *m*; ~ **orbital space flight** *n* SPACE vuelo en órbita espacial tripulado *m*; ~ **orbiting laboratory** *n* (*MOL*) SPACE laboratorio orbital tripulado *m* (*MOL*); ~ **space research** *n* SPACE investigación espacial tripulada *f*; ~ **workshop** *n* SPACE taller asistido *m*
mannide *n* CHEM manida *f*
manning *n* WATER TRANSP *of ship* dotación *f*
Manning's: ~ **formula** *n* HYDROL fórmula de Manning *f*
mannitan *n* CHEM manita *f*
mannite *n* CHEM manita *f*
mannitol *n* CHEM manitol *m*; ~ **hexanitrite** *n* CHEM hexanitrito de manitol *m*
mannonic *adj* CHEM manónico
mannose *n* CHEM manosa *f*
manoeuvrability *n BrE* AIR TRANSP maniobrabilidad *f*, MECH ENG manejabilidad *f*, maniobrabilidad *f*, NUCL, TRANSP, WATER TRANSP *of ship* maniobrabilidad *f*
manoeuvrable *adj BrE* WATER TRANSP maniobrable
manoeuvre[1] *n BrE* MECH ENG manejo *m*, maniobra *f*, WATER TRANSP maniobra *f*
manoeuvre[2] *vti BrE* MECH ENG, PROD, RAIL, SPACE, TRANSP maniobrar, WATER TRANSP hacer una maniobra, maniobrar
manoeuvring: ~ **valve** *n BrE* HYDRAUL válvula de control *f*, válvula de estrangulación *f* (*AmL*), válvula de maniobra *f*, válvula reguladora *f* (*Esp*)
manometer *n* GEN manómetro *m*
manometric: ~ **switch** *n* ELEC interruptor manométrico *m*
manpack: ~ **radio** *n* MILIT radio de mochila *f*
manpower *n* PROD fuerza de trabajo *f*, mano de obra *f*, personal *m*, recursos humanos *m pl*
manrider *n* CONST vagoneta *f*
manriding: ~ **car** *n* MINE vehículo para transporte de personal *m*
mansard: ~ **roof** *n BrE* (*cf gambrel roof AmE*) CONST cubierta de la mansarda *f*
mantissa *n* COMP&DP, MATH mantisa *f*
mantle *n* GEOL manto *m*, GEOPHYS capa *f*, manto *m*, PROD *of blast furnace* camisa exterior *f*, cuba *f*; ~ **plume** *n* GEOL pluma mantélica *f*
manual[1] *adj* CONST, MECH, PROD manual
manual[2] *n* PROD *handbook* manual *m*; ~ **arc welding** *n* CONST, MECH soldadura por arco manual *f*; ~ **attempt** *n* TELECOM prueba manual *f*; ~ **blowpipe** *n* MECH ENG *for cutting, welding* soplete manual *m*; ~ **bypass** *n* PROD derivación manual *f*; ~ **choke control** *n* AUTO mando manual de la mariposa *m*, mando manual del estrangulador *m*; ~ **cocking** *n* PHOTO montaje manual *m*; ~ **control** *n* AIR TRANSP, CONST control manual *m*, ELEC accionamiento manual *m*, control manual *m*, mando manual *m*, MECH, PHOTO control manual *m*; ~–**control indicator** *n* PHOTO indicador de control manual *m*; ~ **damper** *n* HEAT ENG amortiguador manual *m*, regulador manual *m*; ~ **defrost** *n* REFRIG desescarche manual *m*; ~ **dimmer** *n* CINEMAT atenuador manual *m*; ~ **disarming** *n* SPACE *craft* desarme manual *m*; ~ **editing** *n* TV edición manual *f*; ~ **exchange** *n* TELECOM central telefónica manual *f*, oficina central manual *f*; ~ **gain control** *n* ELECTRON control de ganancia manual *m*; ~ **gearbox** *n* AUTO, VEH cambio de velocidades manual *m*; ~ **handling** *n* NUCL manejo manual *m*; ~ **handling equipment** *n* MECH ENG equipo de manejo manual *m*; ~ **input** *n* COMP&DP entrada manual *f*, ingreso manual *m*, introducción manual *f*; ~ **labor** *AmE*, ~ **labour** *BrE n* PROD mano de obra *f*, trabajo a mano *m*, trabajo manual *m*; ~ **lift truck** *n* PACK carretilla elevadora manual *f*; ~ **lifting technique** *n* SAFE técnica para levantar pesos a mano *f*; ~ **lubricating equipment** *n* MECH ENG equipo de lubricación manual *m*; ~ **metal arc welding** *n* MECH ENG soldadura manual con electrodo consumible *f*, soldadura por arco con electrodo consumible *f*; ~ **operation** *n* COMP&DP funcionamiento manual *m*, operación manual *f*, TELECOM funcionamiento manual *m*; ~ **override** *n* PROD anulación manual *f*; ~ **remote control** *n* AIR TRANSP control remoto manual *m*; ~ **reset** *n* ELEC *of controls* reposición a mano *f*, reposición manual *f*; ~ **shutdown** *n* NUCL parada manual *f*; ~ **switchboard** *n* TELECOM cuadro

conmutador manual *m*, cuadro manual *m*;
~ **switching** *n* ELEC ENG conmutación manual *f*;
~ **system** *n* TELECOM sistema manual *m*; ~ **threading**
n CINEMAT enhebramiento manual *m*;
~ **transmission** *n* AUTO transmisión manual *f*;
~ **working** *n* TELECOM explotación manual *f*
manually: ~**-controlled** *adj* ELEC ENG controlado a
mano
manufacture[1] *n* C&G, CONST, MECH ENG, PROD elaboración *f*, fabricación *f*, manufactura *f*
manufacture[2] *vt* C&G, CONST, MECH ENG, PROD elaborar
manufactured: ~ **edible fat** *n* FOOD grasa comestible
fabricada *f*; ~ **gas** *n* GAS gas sintético *m*
manufacturer *n* GEN fabricante *m*; ~**'s discretion** *n*
MECH ENG criterio del fabricante *m*
manufacturing *n* C&G, MECH ENG, PROD elaboración *f*,
fabricación *f*, manufactura *f*; ~ **bill of material** *n*
PROD lista de materiales para la fabricación *f*; ~ **cycle**
n PROD ciclo de fabricación *m*; ~ **documents** *n pl*
PROD documentación de la fabricación *f*, documentos
de fabricación *m pl*; ~ **follow-up** *n* PROD seguimiento
de fabricación *m*; ~ **lead time** *n* PROD tiempo para
aprovisionamiento *m*; ~ **location** *n* PROD lugar de
fabricación *m*; ~ **papers** *n pl* PROD documentación de
la fabricación *f*, documentos de fabricación *m pl*;
~ **resource planning** *n* PROD planeamiento de los
recursos para la fabricación *m*
manure[1] *n* AGRIC estiércol *m*; ~ **crane** *n* AGRIC
cargador de estiércol *m*; ~ **spreader** *n* AGRIC espar-
ciador de estiércol *m*
manure[2] *vt* AGRIC abonar, estercolar, POLL, RECYCL
abonar
manuscript *n* PRINT original *m*
manway *n* MINE galería de circulación del personal *f*,
pozo de las escalas *m* (*AmL*), PETR TECH pasarela *f*,
rampa de paso del personal *f*
many: ~**-body problem** *n* SPACE problema pluriperso-
nal *m*; ~**-nuclear transfer reaction** *n* NUCL reacción
de transferencia polinuclear *f*
manyplies *n* AGRIC omaso *m*
map *n* PAPER plano topográfico *m*; ~ **paper** *n* PAPER
papel cartográfico *m*
mapper *n* CONST cartógrafo *m*
mapping *n* CONST encuadre *m*
maraging: ~ **steel** *n* METALL acero para la producción
de martensita exenta de carbono *m*
marble *n* GEOL, MINE mármol *m*; ~ **quarry** *n* MINE
cantera de mármol *f*
marbling *n* AGRIC *of meat* marmoleado *m*, PAPER,
PRINT jaspeado *m*
marcasite *n* MINERAL marcasita *f*
margarate *n* CHEM margarato *m*
margaric *adj* CHEM margárico
margarine *n* CHEM, FOOD margarina *f*
margarite *n* MINERAL margarita *f*
margarodite *n* MINERAL margarodita *f*
margin *n* COMP&DP, CONST *of roofing-slate, shingle*
margen *m*, GEOL borde *m*, margen *m*, HYDROL orilla *f*,
margen *m*, MECH ENG *tolerance, limit* tolerancia *f*,
margen *m*, PRINT margen *m*; ~ **gluer** *n* PACK engo-
mador de márgenes *m*; ~ **over** *n* MECH ENG margen
por exceso *m*, tolerancia en más *f*; ~ **settings** *n pl*
PRINT definición de márgenes *f*; ~ **under** *n* MECH ENG
margen por defecto *m*, tolerancia en menos *f*
marginal: ~ **check** *n* COMP&DP comprobación margi-

nal *f*, verificación marginal *f*; ~ **field** *n* PETR TECH
campo marginal *m*; ~ **plateau** *n* OCEAN meseta
marginal *f*; ~ **relay** *n* ELEC relé de estrecho margen
funcional *m*; ~ **sea** *n* GEOL aguas territoriales *f pl*,
OCEAN mar marginal *m*; ~ **test** *n* COMP&DP prueba
marginal *f*; ~ **trench** *n* GEOL, GEOPHYS, OCEAN fosa
periférica *f*
marialite *n* MINERAL marialita *f*
marigram *n* FUELLESS mareograma *m*
marigraph *n* OCEAN mareógrafo *m*
marina *n* WATER TRANSP puerto deportivo *m*
marinade *n* OCEAN escabeche *m*
marine[1] *adj* CHEM *acid*, GEOL marino, WATER TRANSP
marino, de marina, marítimo
marine[2]: ~ **acoustics** *n* ACOUST, OCEAN acústica
submarina *f*; ~ **aggregate** *n* OCEAN agregado de
mar *m*; ~ **air-cushion vehicle** *n* TRANSP aerodeslizador marítimo *m*; ~ **aquaculture** *n* OCEAN
acuacultura marina *f*, acuicultura marina *f*; ~ **architect and engineer** *n* WATER TRANSP arquitecto naval
e ingeniero de máquinas *m*, ingeniero naval superior e
ingeniero de máquinas *m*; ~ **band** *n* GEOL banda
marina *f*; ~ **biological laboratory** *n* LAB, OCEAN
laboratorio de biología marina *m*; ~ **boiler** *n* HEAT
caldera marina *f*; ~ **diesel oil** *n* WATER TRANSP gasoil
para motores marinos *m*; ~ **disposal** *n* RECYCL
eliminación marina *f*; ~ **drilling rig** *n* CONST equipo
de sondeo marítimo *m*; ~ **engineer** *n* WATER TRANSP
aboard ship maquinista naval *m*, *merchant navy* jefe
maquinista *m*; ~ **engineering** *n* WATER TRANSP *on
board activity* ingeniería naval *f*, mecánica naval *f*;
~ **environment** *n* POLL entorno marino *m*, medio
ambiente marino *m*; ~ **farm** *n* OCEAN criadero de
productos del mar *m*; ~ **fish farming** *n* OCEAN
piscicultura marina *f*; ~ **grazing** *n* OCEAN ramoneo
bentónico *m*; ~ **insurance** *n* WATER TRANSP seguro
marítimo *m*; ~ **loss** *n* WATER TRANSP pérdida en el
mar *f*; ~ **propeller** *n* TRANSP hélice marina *f*; ~ **radar
band** *n* WATER TRANSP banda del radar marino *f*,
banda del radar náutico *f*; ~**-radar frequency** *n*
WATER TRANSP frecuencia del radar náutico *f*; ~ **radiant boiler** *n* HEAT, HEAT ENG, THERMO caldera
radiante marina *f*; ~ **radiant reheat boiler** *n* HEAT,
HEAT ENG, THERMO caldera radiante de recalentamiento marina *f*; ~ **refrigeration plant** *n* REFRIG,
THERMO, WATER TRANSP instalación frigorífica
marina *f*; ~ **riser** *n* PETR TECH riser *m*, tubería marina
f, tubo ascendente *m*; ~ **safety** *n* SAFE seguridad en el
mar *f*; ~ **sediment** *n* OCEAN sedimento marino *m*
mariner's: ~ **compass** *n* WATER TRANSP aguja de
marear *f*, compás de navegación *m*; ~ **needle** *n*
GEOPHYS aguja de marinero *f*, brújula *f*
maritime[1] *adj* METEO, WATER TRANSP marítimo
maritime[2]: ~ **air** *n* METEO aire marítimo *m*; ~ **air-
cushion vehicle** *n* WATER TRANSP aerodeslizador
marítimo *m*; ~ **climate** *n* METEO clima marino *m*,
clima marítimo *m*; ~ **community** *n* WATER TRANSP
comunidad marítima *f*; ~ **equatorial air** *n* METEO aire
ecuatorial marítimo *m*; ~ **industry** *n* WATER TRANSP
sector marítimo *m*; ~ **law** *n* WATER TRANSP derecho
marítimo *m*; ~ **mobile satellite service** *n* WATER
TRANSP *satcom, navcom* servicio móvil marítimo
por satélite *m*; ~ **peril** *n* WATER TRANSP peligro de
mar *m*; ~ **radio beacon** *n* WATER TRANSP radiofaro
marítimo *m*; ~ **safety** *n* SAFE, WATER TRANSP seguridad marítima *f*; ~ **satellite** *n* SPACE *communications*

satélite marítimo *m*; ~ **switching center** *n AmE*, ~ **switching centre** *n BrE* (*MSC*) TELECOM centro de conmutación marítima *m*

mark[1] *n* COMP&DP marca *f*, referencia *f*, PROD *line, scratch* referencia *f*, marca *f*, trazo *m*, *of assayer* punzón de garantía *m*, WATER TRANSP marca *f*; ~ **point** *n* CONST punto de referencia *m*; ~ **reader** *n* COMP&DP lector de marcas *m*, lector de referencias *m*; ~ **reading** *n* COMP&DP lectura de marcas *f*, lectura de referencias *f*; ~ **scanning** *n* COMP&DP escaneo de marcas *m*, escaneo de referencias *m*, exploración de marcas *f*; ~ **sensing** *n* COMP&DP detección de marcas *f*, detección de referencias *f*

mark[2] *vt* MAR POLL balizar, PROD *with marking gauge, scribing gauge* marcar; ~ **out** *vt* CONST *route* amojonar, estaquillar, marcar, trazar

marked: ~ **idle channel** *n* TELECOM canal libre marcado *m*; ~ **yarn** *n* TEXTIL hilo comercializado *m*

marker *n* AIR TRANSP baliza *f*, COMP&DP marcador *m*, referente *m*, GEOL capa de referencia *f*, MECH ENG indicador *m*, marcador *m*, referencia *f*, TELECOM marcador *m*, TRANSP baliza *f*, radiobaliza automática *f*, radiofaro *m*; ~ **beacon** *n* AIR TRANSP radiobaliza de demarcación *f*; ~ **bed** *n* GEOL capa *f*, formación de referencia *f*; ~ **buoy** *n* WATER TRANSP *navigation* boya marcadora *f*, boya para marcar *f*; ~ **control system** *n* TELECOM sistema de control del marcador *m*; ~ **lamp** *n* VEH lámpara marcadora del contorno *f*; ~ **light** *n* CINEMAT luz indicadora *f*, luz marcadora *f*; ~ **system** *n* TELECOM sistema del marcador *m*

market: ~ **closeness** *n* TEXTIL proximidad del mercado *f*; ~ **garden** *n* AGRIC explotación hortícola *f*; ~ **outlet** *n* PROD mercado *m*; ~ **price** *n* TEXTIL precio de mercado *m*; ~ **pulp** *n* PAPER pasta de mercado *f*, pasta para vender *f*; ~ **research** *n* PROD, QUALITY investigación de mercados *f*

marketability *n* TEXTIL comercialidad *f*

marketable: ~ **gas** *n* GAS gas comercializable *m*

marking *n* CONST *levelling operations* marca *f*, PROD marca *f*, marcado *m*, referencia *f*, señal *f*, TELECOM marcación *f*, TEXTIL marcada *f*; ~ **awl** *n* PROD punzón de marcar *m*; ~ **equipment** *n* PACK equipo para marcar *m*; ~ **felt** *n* PAPER fieltro marcador *m*; ~ **gage** *AmE*, ~ **gauge** *BrE n* GEOL, MECH ENG, PROD, WATER TRANSP gramil *m*; ~ **ink** *n* COLOUR tinta de marcar *f*; ~ **label** *n* PACK etiqueta de marcado *f*; ~ **machine** *n* PACK máquina marcadora *f*; ~ **press** *n* PAPER, PRINT prensa marcadora *f*; ~ **sequence** *n* TELECOM secuencia de marcación *f*

marl *n* WATER marga *f*

marlaceous *adj* GEOL margoso

marlinspike *n* WATER TRANSP *ropework* pasador *m*

marly[1] *adj* GEOL margoso

marly[2]: ~ **clay** *n* WATER arcilla margosa *f*; ~ **loam** *n* GEOL fango margoso *m*, tierra de moldeo *f*; ~ **soil** *n* AGRIC suelo margoso *m*

marmolite *n* MINERAL marmolita *f*

maroon *n* COLOUR, P&R marrón *m*

marquetry *n* C&G marquetería *f*

married: ~ **print** *n* CINEMAT copia sincronizada *f*; ~ **sound** *n* CINEMAT sonido sincronizado *m*

marring *n* PRINT *of impression* adaptación *f*

marry: ~ **up** *vt* CINEMAT sincronizar

Mars: ~ **segment** *n* SPACE *communications* segmento de Marte *m*

marsh *n* HYDROL marisma *f*, zona pantanosa *f*, WATER cenegal *m*, ciénaga *f*, marisma *f*, pantano *m*; ~ **gas** *n* MINE gas de los pantanos *m*, metano *m*; ~ **island** *n* OCEAN isla pantanosa *f*, isla salobre *f*

marshaling *AmE see* **marshalling** *BrE*

Marshall: ~ **test** *n* CONST ensayo Marshall *m*

marshalling *n* *BrE* RAIL, TRANSP clasificación *f*, colocación ordenada *f*, ordenamiento *m*; ~ **area** *n* *BrE* RAIL, TRANSP área de clasificación *f*, área de ordenamiento *f*; ~ **track** *n* *BrE* RAIL, TRANSP vía de clasificación *f*, vías de maniobra *f pl*; ~ **yard** *n* *BrE* (*cf switching yard AmE, cf classification yard AmE*) RAIL, TRANSP estación de clasificación *f*

marshy[1] *adj* GEOL, HYDROL cenagoso, pantanoso

marshy[2]: ~ **environment** *n* GEOL terreno pantanoso *m*

Martens: ~ **test** *n* P&R ensayo de Martens *m*

martensite *n* CRYSTALL martensita *f*

martensitic: ~ **transformation** *n* CRYSTALL transformación martensítica *f*

martingale *n* COAL amarra *f*, brida *f*, fijación *f*, soporte giratorio *m*

martite *n* MINERAL martita *f*

marver *n* C&G mármol de sacador *m*; ~ **mark** *n* C&G marca de marmol *f*

marvering *n* C&G rolado de vela en el mármol *m*

Marx: ~ **generator** *n* NUCL generador Marx *m*

maser *n* PHYS, TELECOM máser *m*

MASER *abbr* (*microwave amplification by stimulated emission of radiation*) ELECTRON, SPACE MASER (*amplificador de microondas por emisión estimulada de radiación*)

mash *n* AGRIC *feed* mezcla de granos molidos *f*, FOOD malta empastada *f*, malta remojada *f*; ~ **liquor** *n* FOOD licor de maceración *m*; ~ **tun** *n* FOOD cuba de maceración *f*

masher *n* FOOD cuba de maceración *f*

mashing[1]: ~-**programmable** *adj* COMP&DP programable mediante máscaras

mashing[2] *n* CHEM, FOOD macerado *m*

mask[1]: ~ **programmable** *adj* COMP&DP programable mediante máscaras

mask[2] *n* CINEMAT, COMP&DP máscara *f*, ELECTRON máscara *f*, rejilla *f*, PHOTO, SAFE, TELECOM máscara *f*; ~ **alignment** *n* ELECTRON posicionamiento de la rejilla *m*; ~ **attachment** *n* CINEMAT aditamento de la máscara *m*; ~ **carrier** *n* ELECTRON transmisor de rejilla *m*; ~ **data** *n* PROD datos de enmascaramiento *m pl*, datos de filtración *m pl*, formulario de datos *m*; ~ **generation** *n* ELECTRON generador de filtraciones *m*; ~ **microphone** *n* ACOUST micrófono de careta *m*; ~-**programmable array** *n* ELECTRON distribución de filtros programables *f*; ~-**programmable filter** *n* ELECTRON filtro de recubrimiento programable *m*; ~ **run-out** *n* ELECTRON recorrido de filtración *m*; ~ **set** *n* ELECTRON conjunto de elementos de filtración *m*; ~ **shot** *n* CINEMAT toma con máscara *f*

masked: ~ **lithography** *n* ELECTRON, PRINT litografía enmascarada *f*

masking *n* ACOUST, COMP&DP enmascaramiento *m*, ELECTRON enmascaramiento *m*, filtrado *m*, PRINT enmascarado *m*; ~ **effect** *n* ACOUST efecto enmascarador *m*; ~ **frame** *n* PHOTO soporte de enmascaramiento *m*; ~ **lacquer** *n* COATINGS, COLOUR laca de enmascarar *f*; ~-**level audiogram** *n* ACOUST audiograma de nivel de enmascaramiento *m*; ~ **lithography** *n* COATINGS litografía enmascarada *f*; ~ **noise** *n* ACOUST ruido enmascarador *m*; ~ **paint** *n*

COLOUR pintura de cobertura *f*; ~ **paste** *n* COLOUR pasta para enmascarar *f*; ~ **tape** *n* CONST, PACK cinta adhesiva *f*

maskless: ~ **lithography** *n* ELECTRON, PRINT litografía descubierta *f*

mason *n* CONST albañil *m*

masonite *n* MINERAL masonita *f*

masonry *n* C&G, CONST albañilería *f*, mampostería *f*; ~ **dam** *n* HYDROL presa de mampostería *f*; ~ **drill** *n* MECH ENG taladro de albañilería *m*, taladro de hormigón *m*; ~-**earth dam** *n* HYDROL presa de tierra en mampostería *f*; ~ **nail** *n* CONST clavo para mampostería *m*; ~ **work** *n* CONST obra de albañilería *f*, obra de mampostería *f*

mass[1]: ~-**colored** *AmE*, ~-**coloured** *BrE adj* COLOUR teñido en la masa; **of a ~ on a vertical spring** *adj* MECH ENG de una masa sobre un resorte vertical

mass[2] *n* CHEM, GEOPHYS, PHYS masa *f*; ~ **absorption coefficient** *n* PHYS coeficiente de absorción de masa *m*; ~ **airflow** *n* AIR TRANSP flujo de la masa de aire *m*; ~ **assignment** *n* NUCL asignación de masas *f*; ~ **attenuation coefficient** *n* NUCL coeficiente másico de atenuación *m*; ~ **balance** *n* NUCL balance de masas *m*; ~ **budget** *n* SPACE *communications* balance de masas *m*; ~ **concentration** *n* SAFE concentración masiva *f*; ~ **concrete** *n* CONST concreto en masa *m* (*AmL*), hormigón en masa *m* (*Esp*); ~ **defect** *n* PHYS defecto de masa *m*; ~ **discharge coefficient** *n* SPACE coeficiente de descarga de masa *m*; ~ **energy absorption coefficient** *n* NUCL coeficiente másico de absorción de energía *m*; ~-**energy equivalence** *n* PHYS equivalencia de masa y energía *f*; ~ **energy transfer coefficient** *n* NUCL coeficiente másico de transferencia de energía *m*, PHYS coeficiente de transferencia de masa-energía *m*; ~ **excess** *n* PHYS exceso de masa *m*; ~ **flow** *n* AIR TRANSP flujo de la masa *m*, GEOL flujo masivo *m*, NUCL flujo másico *m*; ~ **flow rate** *n* REFRIG caudal másico *m*; ~ **flux** *n* FLUID flujo de masa *m*; ~-**impregnated paper insulation** *n* ELEC *of cable conductor*, ELEC ENG aislamiento de papel impregnado *m*; ~ **number** *n* (*A*) PART PHYS *of element* masa atómica *f* (*A*), PHYS número másico *m*; ~ **per unit length** *n* PHYS masa por unidad de longitud *f*; ~ **per unit volume** *n* PHYS masa por unidad de volumen *f*; ~ **production** *n* PROD fabricación en serie *f*, producción a gran escala *f*, producción en serie *f*, producción masiva *f*, WATER TRANSP *shipbuilding* producción en serie *f*; ~ **rate** *n* PHYS flujo de masa *m*; ~ **resistivity** *n* ELEC resistencia específica de masas *f*, resistividad de masas *f*; ~ **spectrograph** *n* PHYS, RAD PHYS espectrógrafo de masas *m*; ~ **spectrometer** *n* LAB, PHYS, RAD PHYS espectrómetro de masas *m*; ~ **spectrometer-type leak detector** *n* MECH ENG *vacuum technology* buscafugas espectrómetro de masa *m*; ~ **spectrometry** *n* CHEM, PHYS espectrometría de masas *f*; ~ **spectrum** *n* CHEM, PHYS, RAD PHYS espectro de masas *m*; ~ **spectrum analysis** *n* CHEM, PHYS, RAD PHYS análisis del espectro masa *m*; ~ **stopping power** *n* NUCL poder de frenado másico total *m*; ~ **storage** *n AmE* (*cf mass store AmE*) COMP&DP almacenamiento masivo *m*, memoria de gran capacidad *f*, memoria de masa *f*, memoria masiva *f*; ~ **store** *n BrE* (*cf mass storage AmE*) COMP&DP almacenamiento masivo *m*, memoria de gran capacidad *f*, memoria de masa *f*, memoria

masiva *f*; ~ **sulfur dioxide concentration** *AmE*, ~ **sulphur dioxide concentration** *BrE n* SAFE concentración masiva de bióxido de azufre *f*; ~-**terminated cable** *n* ELEC ENG cable acabado en masa *m*; ~ **termination** *n* ELEC ENG terminación en masa *f*; ~ **transfer** *n* GAS transferencia de masa *f*

massicot *n* CHEM, MINERAL masicote *m*, protóxido de plomo *m*

massive[1] *adj* GEOL masivo, sólido

massive[2]: ~ **reaction** *n* METALL reacción masiva *f*

mast *n* CONST *of derrick crane* mástil *m*, PETROL pluma *f*, asta *f*, árbol *m*, mástil *m*, WATER TRANSP palo *m*; ~ **aerial** *n BrE* (*cf mast antenna AmE*) TELECOM antena de mástil *f*; ~ **antenna** *n AmE* (*cf mast aerial BrE*) TELECOM antena de mástil *f*; ~ **crane** *n* WATER TRANSP cargo loading grúa de mástil *f*, palo de carga *m*; ~ **foot** *n* WATER TRANSP pie de palo *m*; ~ **foot safety rail** *n* WATER TRANSP *boat building, deck fittings* baranda de seguridad al pie del palo *f* (*AmL*), barandilla de seguridad al pie del palo *f* (*Esp*); ~ **rake** *n* WATER TRANSP caída del palo *f*; ~ **step** *n* WATER TRANSP carlinga *f*; ~ **tabernacle** *n* WATER TRANSP fogonadura *f*

master *n* ACOUST director *m*, maestro *m*, registro principal *m*, COMP&DP maestro *m*, modelo *m*, OPT galvano *m*, negativo *m*, original *m*; ~ **builder** *n* CONST aparejador *m* (*Esp*), constructor *m* (*AmL*), maestro de obras *m* (*AmL*); ~ **card** *n* COMP&DP tarjeta maestra *f*; ~ **change** *n* (*MC*) TRANSP cambio principal *m*; ~ **clock** *n* COMP&DP, TELECOM reloj maestro *m*, reloj patrón *m*, reloj principal *m*; ~ **console** *n* COMP&DP consola principal *f*; ~ **control** *n* TV control maestro *m*, control principal *m*; ~ **control desk** *n* PRINT mesa de control principal *f*; ~ **control fader** *n* TV control maestro del fundido *m*, control principal del fundido *m*; ~ **control panel** *n* TV panel del control maestro *m* (*AmL*), tablero de control principal *m* (*Esp*); ~ **control relay** *n* PROD relé de control principal *m*; ~ **control reset** *n* (*MCR*) PROD reposición de control principal *f*; ~ **control room** *n* (*MCR*) TELECOM comando multiplo de señal de liberación *m*; ~ **controller** *n* TRANSP controlador principal *m*; ~ **cylinder** *n* AIR TRANSP *of brake* cilindro principal *m*, AUTO, VEH cilindro maestro *m*, cilindro principal *m*; ~ **disc** *BrE*, ~ **disk** *AmE n* OPT disco original *m*; ~ **disk** *n* COMP&DP *CD ROM mastering* disco maestro *m*, disco principal *m*; ~ **engine** *n* AIR TRANSP motor principal *m*; ~ **file** *n* COMP&DP archivo maestro *m*, fichero maestro *m*; ~ **frequency** *n* ELECTRON frecuencia principal *f*; ~ **fuse** *n* MINE cebo de mando *m*, espoleta de mando *m*, mecha de mando *f*; ~ **gage** *AmE see master gauge BrE*; ~ **gain control** *n* ELECTRON control de ganancia principal *m*; ~ **gauge** *n BrE* MECH ENG calibre de comparación *m*, calibre de referencia *m*, calibre maestro *m*, calibre patrón *m*; ~ **group** *n* TELECOM grupo maestro *m*; ~ **help directory** *n* PROD directorio de consulta principal *m*; ~ **indicator** *n* MECH ENG indicador maestro *m*; ~ **key** *n* CONST, PROD llave de paso *f*, llave maestra *f*; ~ **leaf** *n* AUTO hoja maestra *f*; ~ **lode** *n* MINE filón principal *m*; ~ **mariner** *n* WATER TRANSP *merchant navy* oficial de la marina mercante con título de capitán *m*; ~ **mask** *n* ELECTRON recubrimiento de origen *m*; ~ **monitor** *n* TV monitor maestro *m* (*AmL*), monitor principal *m*; ~ **negative** *n* CINEMAT negativo original *m*; ~ **oscillator** *n* (*MO*)

ELECTRON, PHYS oscilador maestro *m*, oscilador patrón *m*, oscilador principal *m*, TELECOM oscilador maestro *m*; ~ **pattern** *n* ELECTRON patrón original *m*; ~ **positive** *n* CINEMAT copia positiva maestra *f*; ~ **processor** *n* TELECOM procesador maestro *m*; ~ **production schedule** *n* PROD programa principal de producción *m*; ~ **program** *AmE*, ~ **programme** *BrE* *n* TRANSP programa maestro *m*; ~ **pulse** *n* ELECTRON impulso principal *m*; ~ **record** *n* COMP&DP registro maestro *m*; ~ **scheduler** *n* PROD programador principal *m*; ~~**slave flip-flop** *n* ELECTRON biestable ordenador-seguidor *m*; ~~**slave system** *n* COMP&DP sistema maestro-esclavo *m*, sistema principal-subordinados *m*; ~ **spline** *n* MECH ENG estría principal *f*, ranura principal *f*; ~ **station** *n* COMP&DP estación maestra *f*, estación principal *f*, puesto principal *m*; ~ **switch** *n* ELEC conmutador de gobierno *m*, disyuntor magistral *m*, interruptor maestro *m*, interruptor principal *m*, ELEC ENG interruptor maestro *m*, interruptor principal *m*, TV interruptor principal *m*; ~ **tap** *n* MECH ENG macho maestro de roscar *m*, macho patrón de roscar *m*; ~ **tape** *n* COMP&DP, TV cinta maestra *f*; ~ **wheel** *n* MECH ENG rueda maestra *f*
mastering *n* OPT generación de originales *f*
master's: ~ **certificate** *n* WATER TRANSP título de capitán de la marina mercante *m*
masthead *n* WATER TRANSP calcés *m*, tope *m*; ~ **light** *n* WATER TRANSP *navigation* luz de tope *f*
mastic *n* PETROL, WATER TRANSP cemento *m*, masilla *f*, mástique *m*, zulaque *m*
mastication *n* P&R malaxación *f*, masticación *f*, trituración *f*
mastitis *n* AGRIC mastitis *f*
mastoid *n* ACOUST mastoide *f*
mat[1] *adj* COLOUR, TEXTIL mate
mat[2] *n* COAL losa continua de cimentación *f*, placa *f*, placa de sustentación *f*, PRINT matriz *f*; ~ **enameling** *AmE*, ~ **enamelling** *n* *BrE* COATINGS esmalte mate *m*; ~ **formation** *n* C&G formación de colchoneta *f*; ~ **ink** *n* COLOUR tinta mate *f*; ~ **lacquer** *n* COATINGS, COLOUR laca mate *f*; ~ **reinforcement** *n* CONST armadura de malla *f*, mallazo *m*
mat[3] *vt* TEXTIL esterar
match[1]: ~ **cut** *n* TV adaptación de corte *f*; ~ **dissolve** *n* TV adaptación del desvanecido de imagen *f*; ~ **hooks** *n pl* CONST ganchos gemelos *m pl*; ~ **photometer** *n* PHOTO fotómetro de contraste *m*; ~ **plate** *n* PROD *moulding, casting* falsa de madera *f*, placa portamodelo *f*
match[2] *vt* CINEMAT igualar, CONST *joinery* coincidir, empalmar, unir, PROD adaptar, cotejar, emparejar, TV adaptar
matchboard *n* CONST *carpentry* tabla machihembrada *f*, PROD *founding* placa modelo de madera *f*
matched: ~ **cladding** *n* OPT revestimiento ajustado *m*, TELECOM revestimiento adaptado *m*; ~ **conics technique** *n* SPACE técnica cónica equilibrada *f*; ~ **diodes** *n pl* ELECTRON diodos coincidentes *m pl*; ~ **filter** *n* ELECTRON filtro adaptado *m*; ~ **filtering** *n* ELECTRON filtración equilibrada *f*; ~ **impedance** *n* ELEC ENG impedancia equilibrada *f*; ~ **load** *n* ELEC ENG carga compensada *f*, PHYS carga ajustada *f*; ~ **resistor** *n* ELEC ENG resistencia apareada *f*; ~ **transistors** *n pl* ELECTRON transistores emparejados *m pl*; ~ **tubes** *n pl* ELECTRON tubos adaptados *m*

pl; ~ **waveguide** *n* ELEC, ELEC ENG guía de ondas adaptadas *f*
matching *n* PRINT *of inks* ajuste *m*; ~ **amplifier** *n* ELECTRON amplificador de adaptación *m*; ~ **attenuation** *n* ELECTRON atenuación de armonía *f*; ~ **machine** *n* CONST *joinery* machihembradora *f*; ~ **plane** *n* CONST *carpentry* cepillo de machihembrar *m*; ~ **transformer** *n* ELEC, ELEC ENG transformador de adaptación *m*
mated: ~ **contacts** *n pl* ELEC ENG contactos acoplados *m pl*
material *n* CHEM, CONST material *m*, MECH ENG ingrediente *m*, materia *f*, material *m*, substancia *f*; ~ **buckling** *n* NUCL curratura del material *f*; ~ **defects** *n pl* MECH ENG defectos del material *m pl*; ~ **dispersion** *n* OPT, TELECOM dispersión del material *f*; ~ **dispersion coefficient** *n* OPT, TELECOM coeficiente de dispersión material *m*; ~ **dispersion parameter** *n* ÓPT, TELECOM parámetro de dispersión material *m*; ~ **flow** *n* PACK tránsito de material *m*; ~~**handling crane** *n* PACK grúa para mover materiales *f*; ~ **issue** *n* PROD expedición de materiales *f*; ~ **issue note** *n* PROD albarán de expedición de materiales *m*; ~ **item file** *n* PROD archivo de partidas de material *m*; ~ **pollution** *n* POLL contaminación de materiales *f*, contaminación material *f*; ~ **quantity per unit** *n* PROD cantidad de materiales por unidad *f*; ~ **requirement planning** *n* PROD planeamiento de los requerimientos de materiales *m*; ~ **scattering** *n* OPT esparcimiento material *m*, TELECOM dispersión del material *f*; ~ **testing** *n* MECH ENG ensayo de materiales *m*, prueba de materiales *f*
materials *n pl* CONST, SAFE, TEXTIL materiales *m pl*; ~ **handling** *n* NUCL manejo de materiales *m*, movimiento de materiales *m*; ~ **reclamation** *n* RECYCL recuperación de materiales *f*; ~ **specification** *n* QUALITY especificación de materias *f*; ~ **testing reactor** *n* (*MTR*) NUCL reactor de ensayo de materiales *m*; ~ **testing system** *n* TEXTIL sistema de ensayo de materiales *m*
mate's: ~ **receipt** *n* WATER TRANSP *merchant navy* admítese *m*, recibo del piloto *m*
math: ~ **package** *n* PRINT paquete matemático *m*
mathematical: ~ **chance** *n* MATH probabilidad matemática *f*; ~ **induction** *n* COMP&DP inducción matemática *f*; ~ **model** *n* COMP&DP, ELECTRON, GAS modelo matemático *m*; ~ **particle** *n* NUCL partícula matemática *f*; ~ **physics** *n* PHYS física matemática *f*; ~ **probability** *n* MATH probabilidad matemática *f*; ~ **programming** *n* COMP&DP programación matemática *f*
mathematics *n* COMP&DP, MATH matemática *f*, matemáticas *f pl*
mating *n* MECH acoplamiento *m*; ~ **connector** *n* PROD conectador de acoplamiento *m*; ~ **flanges** *n pl* MECH bridas que casan *f pl*, NUCL bridas de contacto *f pl*; ~ **surfaces** *n pl* MECH ENG superficies coincidentes *f pl*, superficies de acoplamiento *f pl*
matlockite *n* MINERAL matlockita *f*
matrass *n* *AmE* (*cf bolt-head flask BrE*) LAB *glassware* matraz *m*
matrix *n* COMP&DP matriz *f*, CONST *civil engineering* matriz *f*, pasta *f*, GEOL, MATH, METALL, PROD, TV matriz *f*; ~ **circuit** *n* TELECOM circuito de transformación de coordenadas cromáticas *m*, circuito matricial *m*; ~ **configuration** *n* TELECOM configura-

ción matriz f; ~ **display** n TELECOM display matricial m, presentación de matrices f, visualizador matricial m; ~ **fuel** n NUCL combustible matricial m; ~ **hairline** n PRINT rebarba f; ~ **magazine** n PRINT depósito de matrices m; ~ **mechanics** n MECH, PHYS mecánica matricial f; ~ **printer** n COMP&DP, PRINT impresora matricial f; ~ **signalization** n TRANSP señalización con matriz luminosa f, señalización matriz f, señalización primaria f

matrixing n TV matrizado m, transmisión con matrices f

matt[1] *adj* COLOUR, TEXTIL mate

matt[2]: ~ **cutting** n C&G corte de colchoneta m; ~ **finish** n COLOUR acabado mate m; ~ **glaze** n C&G vidriado de colchoneta m; ~ **paper** n PRINT papel mate m; ~ **screen** n INSTR pantalla mate f

matte n CINEMAT trama f, METALL *coarse metal* mata f; ~ **box** n CINEMAT parasol m, PHOTO caja de deslustrado f; ~ **and counter-matte** n CINEMAT trama y contratrama f; ~ **roll** n CINEMAT rollo de tramas m; ~ **shot** n CINEMAT toma con viñeta f

matter n PRINT composición f, texto m

matting n P&R acabado mate m; ~ **amplifier** n ELECTRON, TV amplificador de matrizado m

mattock n CONST piqueta f, zapapico m, PROD zapapico m

mattress n TEXTIL colchón m; ~ **cover** n TEXTIL funda de colchón f; ~ **ticking** n TEXTIL tela de colchón f

maturation n PETR TECH, WATER maduración f; ~ **pond** n WATER estanque de maduración m

mature: ~ **river** n HYDROL río natural m

maturing: ~ **temperature** n C&G temperatura de maduración f

matzo n FOOD pan ázimo m

maul n CONST maza de pilotes f, mazo m

mauveine n CHEM mauveína f

maximal: ~ **stress** n PRINT tracción máximal f; ~ **sustainable yield** n OCEAN máximo rendimiento sostenible m

maximization n TELECOM maximización f

maximum n NUCL valor máximo m; ~ **admissible power** n TELECOM máxima potencia admisible f, potencia admisible máxima f; ~ **allowable belt stress** n MECH ENG carga de cinta máxima permisible f, carga de correa máxima admisible f; ~ **allowable pressure** n PROD presión máxima admisible f; ~ **available power** n ELEC, ELEC ENG *supply* potencia disponible f, potencia máxima disponible f, potencia útil f; ~ **axial thrust** n FUELLESS empuje axial máximo m; ~ **beam** n WATER TRANSP *boat building* manga máxima f; ~ **bending moment** n SPACE *craft* momento máximo de flexión m; ~ **capacity** n NUCL potencia máxima f, potencia máxima posible f; ~ **consumption** n HYDROL consumo máximo m; ~ **continuous power** n AIR TRANSP potencia máxima continua f; ~ **credible accident** n NUCL máximo accidente creíble m; ~ **current** n ELEC, ELEC ENG corriente máxima f, máxima corriente f; ~ **current rating** n ELEC, ELEC ENG máxima corriente permisible f; ~ **cutout** n ELEC ENG automático de sobreintensidad máxima m, disyuntor de máxima m; ~ **daily runoff** n HYDROL escurrimiento máximo diario m; ~ **deckle** n PAPER ancho útil de la tela m; ~ **demand** n ELEC *supply*, ELEC ENG consumo máximo m, demanda máxima f, potencia máxima instalada f, punta de carga f; ~ **depth** n OCEAN profundidad máxima f;

~ **design speed** n VEH velocidad específica máxima f; ~**-dressed width of warp** n TEXTIL anchura máxima de urdimbre encolada f; ~ **effective range** n MILIT alcance máximo eficaz m; ~ **emission concentration** n (*MEC*) POLL concentración máxima de emisión f (*CME*); ~ **engine overspeed** n AIR TRANSP sobrevelocidad máxima del motor f; ~ **entropy principle** n RAD PHYS principio de máxima entropía m; ~ **except takeoff power** n (*METO power*) AIR TRANSP potencia máxima excepto al despegue f; ~ **exposure limit** n SAFE límite máximo de exposición m; ~ **flap-extended speed** n AIR TRANSP velocidad máxima con flaps extendidos f; ~ **flood level** n HYDROL nivel máximo de caudal m; ~ **flux heat** n NUCL máximo flujo de calor m; ~ **fuel-central temperature** n NUCL temperatura máxima en el centro del combustible f; ~ **hourly runoff** n HYDROL escurrimiento máximo horario m; ~ **hourly volume** n TRANSP volumen máximo por hora m; ~ **instantaneous power** n SPACE potencia instantánea máxima f; ~ **landing gear-extended speed** n AIR TRANSP velocidad máxima con el tren de aterrizaje extendido f; ~ **landing gear-operating speed** n AIR TRANSP velocidad máxima con el tren de aterrizaje operando f; ~ **lift** n AIR TRANSP sustentación máxima f; ~ **likelihood** n MATH máxima probabilidad f, máxima verosimilitud f; ~ **load** n AIR TRANSP carga máxima f, WATER TRANSP *cargo* carga hasta la línea de carga máxima f; ~ **melting rate** n C&G razón máxima de fundido f; ~**-minimum thermometer** n HEAT ENG, LAB, PHYS, THERMO termómetro de máxima y mínima m; ~ **numerical aperture** n OPT, TELECOM apertura numérica máxima f; ~**-operating altitude** n AIR TRANSP altitud de operación máxima f; ~ **output** n ELEC *of generator* potencia máxima f, rendimiento máximo m; ~ **output mixture ratio** n AUTO proporción de mezcla ideal f; ~ **payload** n AIR TRANSP carga máxima f; ~ **permissible deviation** n MECH desviación máxima admisible f; ~ **permissible dose** n RAD PHYS dosis máxima admisible f; ~ **permissible error** n METR error máximo permisible m; ~ **permissible Mach number** n AIR TRANSP número de Mach permisible máximo m; ~ **permissible occupational whole-body dose** n NUCL, RAD PHYS máxima dosis corporal admisible para personas profesionalmente expuestas f; ~ **permissible operating speed** n AIR TRANSP velocidad de operación permisible máxima f; ~ **power** n ELEC *supply* potencia máxima f; ~ **power at rated wind speed** n FUELLESS fuerza máxima a la velocidad nominal del viento f; ~ **power input** n ELEC ENG entrada de potencia máxima f; ~ **power requirement** n PROD demanda máxima de potencia f; ~ **power transmission** n ELEC ENG transmisión de potencia máxima f; ~**-rated step voltage** n ELEC *tap changer* tensión máxima nominal en escalón f; ~**-rated through-current** n ELEC corriente de tránsito máxima nominal f; ~ **relative time interval error** n (*MRTIE*) TELECOM error máximo de intervalo relativo m; ~ **ripple current** n PROD máxima corriente con fluctuaciones f; ~ **rotor speed** n AIR TRANSP velocidad de rotor máxima f; ~ **shaft speed** n FUELLESS *wind power* velocidad máxima del árbol f; ~ **signal** n ELECTRON señal de máxima f; ~**-signal amplitude** n ELECTRON amplitud de señal de máxima f; ~ **sound pressure** n ACOUST presión sonora máxima *f*; ~ **speed** *n* AIR TRANSP *of aircraft*, TRANSP, VEH, WATER TRANSP *of ship* velocidad máxima *f*; ~ **speed in level flight with rated power** *n* AIR TRANSP velocidad máxima en vuelo nivelado con potencia nominal *f*; ~ **spring back load** *n* AIR TRANSP fuerza de resorte máxima *f*; ~ **theoretical numerical aperture** *n* TELECOM máxima apertura numérica teórica *f*; ~ **threshold speed** *n* AIR TRANSP velocidad de umbral máxima *f*; ~ **time interval error** *n* (*MTIE*) TELECOM error máximo de intervalo *m*; ~ **total load** *n* CONST carga máxima total *f*; ~ **total weight** *n* VEH peso total máximo *m*; ~ **trimmed-machine width** *n* PACK ancho máximo de máquina tras cortar *m*, PAPER ancho útil máximo de máquina *m*; ~ **usable frequency** *n* (*MUF*) ELEC, ELEC ENG, TELECOM frecuencia máxima de consumo *f*, frecuencia máxima utilizable *f*; ~ **voltage** *n* ELEC tensión máxima *f*; ~-**voltage relay** *n* ELEC relé de máxima *m*, relé de máximo de tensión *m*; ~ **water-holding capacity** *n* AGRIC capacidad máxima de retención de agua *f*; ~ **weight** *n* PACK peso máximo *m*; ~ **welding current** *n* CONST corriente máxima de soldadura *f*; ~ **wheel vertical load** *n* AIR TRANSP carga máxima vertical de la rueda *f*; ~ **width** *n* PAPER *untrimmed* anchura máxima *f*

maxite *n* MINERAL maxita *f*

maxwell *n* (*Mx*) ELEC, ELEC ENG *unit of magnetic flux* maxvelio *m* (*Mx*), maxwell *m* (*Mx*)

Maxwell: ~ **distribution** *n* PHYS distribución de Maxwell *f*; ~'**s equations** *n pl* ELEC *electromagnetism*, PHYS ecuaciones de Maxwell *f pl*

Mayday *n* WATER TRANSP *radio distress signal* Mayday *f*

Mb *abbr* (*megabyte*) COMP&DP, ELECTRON Mb (*megabyte*)

MBE *abbr* (*molecular-beam epitaxy*) ELECTRON, RAD PHYS epitaxia por haz molecular *f*

MC *abbr* (*master change*) TRANSP cambio principal *m*

MCC *abbr* (*multipoint command conference*) TELECOM conferencia de mando para varios puntos *f*

MCD *abbr* (*maintenance cell description*) TELECOM descripción de la célula de mantenimiento *f*

MCF *abbr* (*message communication function*) TELECOM función de comunicación de mensajes *f*

MCFD *abbr* (*millions of cubic feet per day*) PETR TECH millones de pies cúbicos de gas por día *m pl*

MCN *abbr* (*multipoint command negating MCS*) TELECOM comando multipunto para inversión MCS *m*

MCR *abbr* PROD (*master control reset*) reposición de control principal *f*, TELECOM (*master control room*) comando multiplo de señal de liberación *m*

MCT *abbr* (*multipoint command token claim*) TELECOM comando multipunto de petición de autorización *m*

MCV *abbr* (*multipoint command visualization forcing*) TELECOM comando multipunto de forzamiento de visualización *m*

Md *abbr* (*mendelevium*) CHEM, NUCL, RAD PHYS Md (*mendelevio*)

MD *abbr* TELECOM (*management domain*) dominio de gestión *m*, TELECOM (*message dropping*) dispositivo de mediación *m*

MDF *abbr* (*main distribution frame*) TELECOM repartidor principal *m*, trama principal de distribución *f*

MDI *abbr* (*diphenylmethane diisocyanate*) P&R MDI (*diisocianato de difenilmetano*)

MDR *abbr* (*memory data register*) COMP&DP registro de datos de la memoria *m*

ME *abbr* (*metabolizable energy*) AGRIC energía metabolizable *f*

meadow: ~ **ore** *n* MINE, MINERAL limonita *f*

meager: ~ **clay** *AmE see* meagre clay *BrE*

meagre: ~ **clay** *n BrE* C&G barro magro *m*

mean *n* COMP&DP, MATH media *f*, promedio *m*; ~ **absolute deviation** *n* PROD desviación media absoluta *f*; ~ **aerodynamic chord** *n* (*MAC*) AIR TRANSP cuerda aerodinámica media *f*; ~ **annual variation** *n* WATER TRANSP *of tide* variación anual media *f*; ~ **anomaly** *n* SPACE anomalía principal *f*, fallo principal *m*; ~ **bond energy** *n* NUCL energía de enlace media *f*; ~ **busy hour** *n* TELECOM hora cargada media *f*; ~ **chord of the control surface** *n* AIR TRANSP cuerda media de la superficie de control *f*; ~ **daily flow** *n* WATER caudal medio diario *m*; ~ **deviation** *n* ELEC, MATH desviación media *f*; ~ **draft** *AmE*, ~ **draught** *BrE n* WATER TRANSP *ship design* calado medio *m*; ~ **error** *n* ELEC error medio *m*, error medio cuadrático *m*; ~ **free path** *n* ACOUST recorrido libre medio *m*, METALL camino medio libre *m*, PHYS recorrido libre medio *m*; ~ **geometric chord** *n* GEOM cuerda media geométrica *f*; ~ **glide path error** *n* AIR TRANSP media del error de trayectoria de planeo *f*; ~ **hourly runoff** *n* HYDROL escorrentía media por hora *f*; ~ **lethal dose** *n* (*LD50*) NUCL, PHYS dosis letal del 50% *f*, dosis letal mediana *f*; ~ **life** *n* PHYS vida media *f*, QUALITY duración de vida media *f*, duración media *f*; ~ **opinion score** *n* TELECOM media de opinión *f* (*AmL*), puntuación media de opinión *f* (*Esp*), resultado de opinión media *m* (*Esp*); ~ **pitch angle** *n* AIR TRANSP ángulo de paso medio *m*; ~ **sea level** *n* OCEAN, WATER TRANSP *navigation* nivel medio del mar *m*; ~ **solar time** *n* SPACE hora media solar *f*, tiempo solar medio *m*; ~ **speed** *n* TRANSP velocidad media *f*; ~ **square error** *n* (*MSE*) COMP&DP, MATH error medio cuadrático *m* (*EMC*); ~ **square value** *n* ELEC valor cuadrático medio *m*, valor eficaz *m*; ~ **square velocity** *n* PHYS promedio del cuadrado de la velocidad *m*; ~ **steam isolation valve** *n* (*MSIV*) NUCL MSIV; ~ **stress** *n* METALL esfuerzo medio *m*; ~ **temperature difference** *n* HEAT, REFRIG diferencia de las temperaturas medias *f*, diferencia media de temperatura *f*; ~ **tidal range** *n* FUELLESS, GEOPHYS, HYDROL, WATER TRANSP amplitud media de las mareas *f*; ~ **time between failures** *n* (*MTBF*) COMP&DP, ELEC ENG, MECH, QUALITY, SPACE tiempo medio entre fallos *m*; ~ **time between removals** *n* (*MTBR*) SPACE tiempo medio entre desmontaje *m* ; ~ **time to failure** *n* QUALITY duración media antes de fallas *f*; ~ **time to repair** *n* COMP&DP, ELEC ENG, MECH, SPACE tiempo medio de reparación *m* (*MTTR*); ~ **trajectory** *n* MILIT trayectoria media *f*; ~ **value** *n* PHYS valor promedio *m*; ~ **value recorder** *n* INSTR registrador de valor medio *m*; ~ **wind speed** *n* FUELLESS velocidad media del viento *f*

meander *n* HYDROL meandro *m*

meandering *n* CONST *surveying* serpenteo *m*; ~ **stream** *n* GEOL corriente meandriforme *f*

meaningless: ~ **data** *n pl* COMP&DP datos sin sentido *m pl*

means: ~ **of detecting and suppressing explosions** *n pl* SAFE medios de detección y supresión de explosiones *m pl*; ~ **of escape** *n* SAFE medio de salvamento *m*

measurable: ~ **quantity** *n* METR cantidad mensurable *f* measurand *n* ELECTRON medidor *m*, METR magnitud sometida a medición *f*

measure¹ *n* CHEM *certain proportion, percentage* medida *f*, METR dimensión *f*, medida *f*, *instrument for measuring dimensions* cinta métrica *f*, *size, number* medición *f*

measure² *vt* CHEM medir, MECH ENG *to calibrate* calibrar, METR *land* estimar, medir, evaluar, tarar, cubicar, comparar, mensurar (*AmL*)

measured: ~ current *n* ELEC corriente medida *f*; ~ quantity *n* ELECTRON cantidad medida *f*; ~ ton *n* WATER TRANSP tonelada de arqueo *f*; ~ voltage *n* ELEC *current* tensión medida *f*, voltaje medido *m*

measurement *n* CHEM, ELECTRON *of atomic density* medición *f*, medida *f*, METR medida *f*, *size, number* medición *f*, RAD PHYS *of atomic density* medición *f*, medida *f*, SAFE *communications* medición *f*, WAVE PHYS *of wavelength* medida *f*, medición *f*; ~ of air pollution *n* POLL, SAFE medición de la contaminación del aire *f*; ~ and evaluation of vibration severity *n* SAFE medición y evaluación de la intensidad de las vibraciones *f*; ~ process *n* METR procedimiento de medida *m*; ~ of quantities *n* CONST cubicación *f*, medición de cantidades *f*; ~ range selector *n* INSTR, METR selector de rango *m*; ~ standard *n* METR medida estándar *f*; ~ unit *n* METR, PETR TECH unidad de medida *f*

measurements: ~ while drilling *n pl* (*MWD*) PETR TECH mediciones durante la perforación *f pl* (*MWD*)

measuring *n* CHEM medición *f*, medida *f*, METR *in metres* mensuración *f* (*AmL*), *size, number* medición *f*, SAFE medición *f*; ~ amplifier *n* ELECTRON amplificador de medición *m*; ~ apparatus *n* CONST, ELEC, ELEC ENG, ELECTRON, INSTR, METR aparato de medición *m*, aparato de medida *m*, medidor *m*; ~ block *n* MECH ENG *tool-setting gauge* bloque de medición *m*; ~ bridge *n* MECH ENG puente de medidas *m*; ~ chain *n* CONST cadena de agrimensor *f*; ~ cylinder *n* LAB probeta *f*, PHOTO cilindro de medición *m*; ~ desk *n* NUCL mesa de mediciones *f*; ~ device *n* CONST, ELEC, ELEC ENG, INSTR, METR aparato de medida *m*, dispositivo de medida *m*; ~ equipment *n* ELEC, METR instrumental de medida *m*; ~ error *n* METR error de medida *m*; ~ instrument *n* CONST, ELEC, ELEC ENG, INSTR, METR aparato de medida *m*, instrumento de medición *m*, instrumento de medida *m*; ~ machine *n* METR máquina de medir *f*; ~ microscope *n* INSTR microscopio de medidas *m*; ~ oscilloscope *n* ELEC osciloscopio medidor *m*; ~ relay *n* ELEC ENG relé de mediciones *m*; ~ rod *n* METR metro de medir *m*, varilla para medir la profundidad del líquido *f*; ~ spark gap *n* ELEC ENG chispómetro *m*; ~ system *n* ELEC, INSTR banco de mediciones *m*, sistema de medida *m*; ~ tape *n* CONST, METR cinta de medir *f*; ~ transducer *n* METR transductor de medida *m*; ~ tube *n* CHEM probeta *f*; ~ weir *n* AGRIC vertedor medidor *m*, HYDROL, WATER vertedero de aforo *m*

meat: ~-and-bone meal *n* AGRIC harina de huesos y carne *f*; ~-fat ratio *n* AGRIC proporción carne-grasa *f*; ~ hook *n* FOOD gancho de carne *m*

meatus *n* ACOUST meato *m*

MEC *abbr* (*maximum emission concentration*) POLL *legislation* CME (*concentración máxima de emisión*)

mechanic *n* PROD *person* mecánico *m*

mechanical: ~ admittance *n* ACOUST, ELEC, ELEC ENG, MECH, PHYS admitancia mecánica *f*; ~ air filter *n* HEAT ENG filtro mecánico de aire *m*; ~ analysis *n* GEOL análisis mecánico *m*; ~ behavior test *AmE*, ~ behaviour test *BrE n* GAS prueba de comportamiento mecánico *f*; ~ bond *n* NUCL cohesión mecánica *f*; ~ boy *n* C&G carretilla mecánica *f*; ~ broom *n* CONST escoba mecánica *f*; ~ chopper *n* NUCL monocromador mecánico de neutrones *m*; ~ classifier *n* COAL clasificador mecánico *m*; ~ collector *n* POLL colector mecánico *m*, electrodo mecánico *m*; ~ component *n* MECH ENG componente mecánico *m*; ~ concentration *n* PROD concentración mecánica *f*; ~ contactor *n* ELEC *of relay* contactor mecánico *m*; ~ cutter *n* PETROL cortador mecánico *m*; ~ decanning *n* NUCL desenvainado mecánico *m*; ~ decladding *n* NUCL desenvainado mecánico *m*; ~ dividing head *n* MECH ENG cabezal divisor mecánico *m*; ~ draftsman *AmE*, ~ draughtsman *BrE n* PROD delineante mecánico *m* (*Esp*), dibujante mecánico *m* (*AmL*); ~ drawing *n* PROD dibujo mecánico *m*; ~ drive *n* MECH accionamiento mecánico *m*, MECH ENG accionamiento mecánico *m*, mecanoaccionamiento *m*, transmisión mecánica *f*; ~ editing *n* TV edición mecánica *f*; ~ efficiency *n* FUELLESS, MECH ENG eficiencia mecánica *f*, rendimiento mecánico *m*; ~ end stop *n* ELEC *tap changer* tope de extremo mecánico *m*; ~ endurance *n* PROD resistencia mecánica *f*; ~ energy *n* MECH ENG energía mecánica *f*; ~ engineer *n* MECH ENG, PROD ingeniero mecánico *m*; ~ engineering *n* MECH ENG, PROD ingeniería mecánica *f*; ~ equivalent of heat *n* MECH, THERMO equivalente mecánico del calor *m*; ~ error *n* TV error mecánico *m*; ~ exhaust air installations *n pl* SAFE instalaciones mecánicas para extracción del aire *f pl*; ~ filter *n* ELECTRON filtro mecánico *m*; ~ firing *n* MECH ENG *stoking* encendido mecánico *m*; ~ fuel pump *n* AUTO, VEH bomba de gasolina mecánica *f*, bomba mecánica de combustible *f*; ~ grab *n* CONST gancho mecánico *m*; ~ hazard *n* MECH, SAFE peligro mecánico *m*, riesgo mecánico *m*; ~ impedance *n* ACOUST, ELEC, ELEC ENG impedancia mecánica *f*; ~ instability *n* METALL inestabilidad mecánica *f*; ~ interlock *n* PROD enclavamiento mecánico *m*; ~ isolation *n* SAFE aislamiento mecánico *m*; ~ latch *n* PROD cerrojo mecánico *m*; ~ life *n* ELEC ENG, PROD duración mecánica *f*, existencia mecánica *f*, vida mecánica *f*; ~ locking *n* MECH ENG bloqueo mecánico *m*, enclavamiento mecánico *m*; ~ milking *n* AGRIC ordeño mecánico *m*; ~ modulation *n* ELECTRON modulación mecánica *f*; ~ operation *n* MECH ENG *of valve* operación mecánica *f*; ~ optical switch *n* OPT, TELECOM conmutador óptico mecánico *m* (*Esp*), dispositivo de conmutación óptico mecánico *m* (*AmL*); ~ oscillation *n* ACOUST oscilación mecánica *f*; ~ overlay *n* PRINT superposición mecánica *f*; ~ piping *n* HYDROL canalización automática *f*; ~ polishing *n* MECH ENG, METALL abrillantado mecánico *m*, pulido mecánico *m*; ~ properties *n pl* CONST, FLUID, MECH ENG, P&R características mecánicas *f pl*, propiedades mecánicas *f pl*; ~ pulp *n* PACK, PAPER pasta mecánica *f*; ~-pulp board *n* PACK tablero de pasta mecánica *m*, PAPER cartón conteniendo pulpa mecánica *m*; ~ reactance *n* ACOUST reactancia mecánica *f*; ~ recorder *n* ACOUST registrador mecánico *m*; ~ recording *n* ACOUST grabación mecánica *f*; ~ refrigeration *n* MECH ENG, REFRIG refrigeración mecánica *f*; ~ **resistance** *n* ACOUST resistencia mecánica *f*; ~ **resonance** *n* PHYS resonancia mecánica *f*; ~ **sample** *n* COAL muestra mecánica *f*; ~ **setting** *n* PRINT composición mecánica *f*; ~ **shearing** *n* AGRIC esquila mecánica *f*; ~ **shock test** *n* METR ensayo al choque mecánico *m*; ~ **spin attachment** *n* CINEMAT aditamento mecánico giratorio *m*; ~ **splice** *n* OPT, TELECOM, TV conexión mecánica *f*, empalme mecánico *m*, junta mecánica *f*, unión mecánica *f*; ~ **stability** *n* P&R estabilidad mecánica *f*; ~ **stage** *n* INSTR, PHOTO etapa mecánica *f*; ~ **stage control** *n* INSTR, PHOTO control de etapa mecánica *m*; ~ **stoker** *n* HEAT cargador mecánico *m*; ~ **stop unit** *n* MECH ENG dispositivo de parada mecánico *m*; ~ **system** *n* ACOUST, MECH ENG *cooling, lubricating, power transmission systems* sistema mecánico *m*; ~ **testing** *n* MECH ENG ensayo mecánico *m*, prueba mecánica *f*; ~ **tint** *n* PRINT *broadcasting* láminas de grisar *f pl*; ~ **transmission** *n* FUELLESS, MECH ENG transmisión mecánica *f*; ~ **transmission system** *n* FUELLESS, MECH ENG sistema de transmisión mecánica *m*; ~ **trencher** *n* PETROL excavadora mecánica de zanjas *f*; ~ **tripping device** *n* ELEC *circuit breaker* dispositivo de disyunción mecánica *m*, disyuntor mecánico *m*; ~ **vibration** *n* ACOUST vibración mecánica *f*; ~ **wave** *n* ELEC ENG onda mecánica *f*; ~ **wear** *n* CONST, PROD desgaste mecánico *m*; ~ **weathering** *n* GEOL alteración mecánica *f*, PETROL erosión mecánica *f*; ~ **woodpulp** *n* PAPER pasta mecánica *f*; ~ **woodpulp board** *n* PAPER cartón conteniendo pasta mecánica *m*; ~ **woodpulp paper** *n* PAPER papel conteniendo pasta mecánica *m*; ~ **zero adjustment** *n* ELEC, INSTR ajuste mecánico de cero *m*, regulación del cero mecánico *f*

mechanically: ~**-blocked electrical impedance** *n* ACOUST, ELEC, ELEC ENG impedancia eléctrica bloqueada mecánicamente *f*; ~**-propelled ship** *n* WATER TRANSP buque de propulsión mecánica *m*, buque de vapor *m*; ~ **refrigerated vehicle** *n* REFRIG, TRANSP, VEH vehículo frigorífico *m*; ~**-tuned magnetron** *n* ELECTRON magnetrón sintonizado mecanicamente *m*; ~**-tuned oscillator** *n* ELECTRON oscilador sintonizado mecánicamente *m*

mechanics *n* MATH, MECH, MECH ENG, PHYS mecánica *f*

mechanism *n* ELEC, ELECTRON, LAB, MECH aparato *m*, MECH ENG aparato *m*, dispositivo *m*, maquinaria *f*, mecanismo *m*, técnica *f*, PHOTO, WATER TRANSP aparato *m*

mechanization: ~ **of farms** *n* AGRIC mecanización de explotaciones agrícolas *f*

mechanized: ~ **coal-winning** *n* COAL, MINE arranque de carbón mecánico *m*

mechanothermal: ~ **effect** *n* THERMO efecto mecanotérmico *m*

meconate *n* CHEM meconato *m*

meconic *adj* CHEM mecónico

meconin *n* CHEM meconina *f*

meconine *n* CHEM meconina *f*

media *n* TV medios *m pl*; ~ **access control** *n* TELECOM control de acceso al medio *m*, control de acceso al soporte *m*

mediamarimeter *n* OCEAN mediamarímetro *m*

median *n* COMP&DP, GEOM, MATH mediana *f*; ~ **lethal concentration** *n* POLL concentración letal media *f*; ~ **lethal dose** *n* POLL, RAD PHYS dosis media letal *f*, valor medio de dosis letal *m*; ~ **line** *n* PETR TECH mediana *f*; ~ **valley** *n* GEOL valle intermedio *m*

mediant *n* ACOUST mediante *m*

mediation: ~ **device** *n* TELECOM dispositivo de mediación *m*; ~ **function** *n* TELECOM función de mediación *f*

mediator *n* PART PHYS mediador *m*

medicinal *adj* CHEM *oil* medicinal

Mediterranean: ~ **climate** *n* METEO clima mediterráneo *m*

medium[1]: ~**-early** *adj* AGRIC semi-precoz; ~ **grade** *adj* MINE de calidad media, de clase media; ~**-graded** *adj* COAL *soil* de clase media; ~**-grained** *adj* GEOL *programme* de grano medio; ~**-late** *adj* AGRIC semi-tardío

medium[2] *n* GEN agente *m*, caldo *m*, medio *m*, vehículo *m*; ~ **access control** *n* (*MAC*) TELECOM control de acceso medio *m*; ~ **adaptor** *n* (*MA*) TELECOM adaptador intermedio *m*, adaptador medio *m*; ~**-angle lens** *n* CINEMAT, PHOTO objetivo de ángulo medio *m*; ~ **close-up** *n* CINEMAT primer plano medio *m*; ~ **distillates** *n pl* PETR TECH destilados medios *m pl*; ~**-energy nuclear physics** *n* NUCL física nuclear de energías intermedias *f*; ~ **frequency** *n* ELEC ENG, HEAT frecuencia media *f*; ~**-frequency furnace** *n* ELEC ENG, HEAT horno de frecuencias medias *m*; ~**-frequency heating** *n* ELEC ENG, HEAT calentamiento de media frecuencia *m*; ~ **grade** *n* PROD *of emery wheel* grado de dureza media *m*, nivel medio de dureza *m*; ~**-grade metamorphism** *n* GEOL metamorfismo de grado intermedio *m*; ~ **grain** *n* CINEMAT, GEOL, METALL, MINE, PAPER, PHOTO, PRINT grano medio *m*; ~ **grinding** *n* PROD *between coarse and fine* rectificado medio *m*; ~ **head** *n* FUELLESS salto medio *m*, salto de agua medio *m*; ~**-power amplifier** *n* ELECTRON amplificador de potencia media *m*; ~**-range aircraft** *n* AIR TRANSP avión de alcance medio *m*; ~**-range airliner** *n* AIR TRANSP avión de pasajeros de alcance medio *m*; ~ **rate** *n* TELECOM precio medio *m*, tarifa media *f*; ~**-scale integration** *n* (*MSI*) COMP&DP, ELECTRON, PHYS, TELECOM integración a media escala *f* (*IME*), integración de mediana escala *f* (*IME*); ~ **shot** *n* CINEMAT plano medio *m*; ~**-soft grade** *n* PROD *of emery wheel* grado medio suave *m*, nivel de blandura intermedia *m*; ~**-speed engine** *n* WATER TRANSP *diesel* motor medianamente revolucionado *m*; ~**-type ball bearing** *n* PROD cojinete de bolas de tipo medio *m*; ~**-volatile coal** *n* COAL carbón medio en volátiles *m*; ~ **voltage** *n* ELEC ENG voltaje medio *m*; ~**-voltage system** *n* ELEC ENG sistema de voltaje medio *m*; ~**-voltage vacuum contactor** *n* PROD contactor en vacío de tensión media *m*; ~ **wave** *n* WAVE PHYS onda media *f*

meerschaum *n* MINERAL espuma de mar *f*, sepiolita *f*

meet[1] *n* GEOM intersección *f*; ~**-me bridge** *n* TELECOM puente de encuentro *m*; ~**-me conference call** *n* TELECOM comunicación para conferencia de encuentro *f*, comunicación telefónica colectiva de encuentro *f*, conferencia colectiva de encuentro *f*, llamada múltiple *f*

meet[2] *vt* QUALITY, SAFE *regulations* cumplir con

meet[3] *vi* WATER *conflow* confluir; ~ **with a serious accident** *vi* SAFE sufrir un accidente grave

meeting *n* CONST *act, place* unión *f*; ~ **post** *n* WATER *of lock gate* montante de encuentro *m*

megabit n ELECTRON megabit m
megabyte n (Mb) COMP&DP, ELECTRON megabyte m (Mb)
megachip n COMP&DP, ELECTRON megachip m
megacycle n ELEC frequency megaciclo m
megadoc n OPT megadoc m
megadyne n METR megadina f
megahertz n ELEC frequency, ELECTRON, PETROL, TV megahertz m, megahertzio m
megascale adj GEOL a gran escala
megastream: ~ **circuit** n TELECOM circuito de megaflujo m
megawatt n (MW) ELEC power, ELEC ENG megavatio m (MW)
Megger n ELEC, ELEC ENG, ELECTRON, GEOPHYS, INSTR Megger m, megaóhmetro m, megóhmetro m
megohm n ELEC, ELECTRÓN, ELEC ENG, GEOPHYS megaohmio m, megohm m, megohmio m
megohmmeter n ELEC, ELECTRON, ELEC ENG, ELECTRON, GEOPHYS, INSTR megaóhmetro m, megóhmetro m
meionite n MINERAL meionita f
Meissner: ~ **effect** n ELECTRON, PHYS efecto Meissner m
Meker: ~ **burner** n LAB mechero de Meker m
mel n ACOUST melio m
melaconite n MINERAL melaconita f
melamine n CHEM, TEXTIL melamina f; ~ **formaldehyde resin** n (MF) P&R resina de melamina-formaldehído f; ~ **resin** n ELEC insulation resina de melamina f
melanin n CHEM melanina f
melanite n MINERAL andradita f, melanita f, topazolita f
melanocratic adj GEOL melanocrático
melanosome n GEOL melanosoma m
melanterite n MINERAL melanterita f
Melde's: ~ **experiment** n PHYS experimento de Melde m
melding n PRINT combinación f
melibiose n CHEM melibiosa f
melilite n MINERAL melilita f
melinite n MINERAL melinita f
meliphane n MINERAL melifana f
meliphanite n MINERAL melifanita f
mellite n MINERAL melita f
mellitic adj CHEM melítico
mellitose n CHEM melitosa f
melody n ACOUST melodía f
melt[1] n PROD colada f; ~ **flow rate** n FLUID velocidad del flujo de fusión f
melt[2] vt CHEM, HEAT fundir, METEO appliance, mechanism derretir, PROD, TEXTIL fundir, THERMO ablandar, derretir, fundir; ~ **down** vt THERMO fundir
melter n PROD caldera de fusión f, cazo de plomero m, crisol m
melting n HEAT,METEO, PHYS, PROD, TEXTIL, THERMO fusión f; ~ **bath** n THERMO baño de fusión m; ~ **core catcher** n NUCL colector del núcleo fundido m; ~ **crucible** n THERMO crisol de fusión m; ~ **furnace** n COAL, THERMO horno de fusión m; ~ **heat** n THERMO calor de fusión m; ~ **point** n CHEM punto de fusión m, METEO punto de gota m, P&R punto de congelación m, punto de fusión m, PHYS, REFRIG, TEXTIL punto de fusión m, THERMO temperatura de fusión f, fixed equipment punto de fusión m; ~ **point curve** n THERMO curva del punto de fusión f; ~ **pot** n

CHEM crisol de fusión m, recipiente refractario m, PROD caldera de fusión f, cazo de plomero m, crisol m, THERMO caldera de fusión f, crisol m; ~ **range** n THERMO gama de temperaturas de fusión f, intervalo de temperatura de fusión m, rango de temperatura de fusión m; ~ **test** n THERMO ensayo de fusión m, experimento de fusión m, prueba de fusión f; ~ **time** n THERMO tiempo de fusión m
member n COMP&DP miembro m, CONST of frame pieza f, GEOL, MATH miembro m, MECH ENG parte f, pieza f, órgano m
membership n COMP&DP calidad de miembro f, membrecía f (AmL), pertenencia f, pertenencia a un grupo f
membrane n SPACE craft bóveda laminar f, membrana f; ~ **filter** AmE, ~ **filtre** n BrE CHEM TECH, LAB filtro de membrana m; ~ **keyboard** n ELEC ENG, PROD teclado de membrana m; ~ **keyswitch** n ELEC ENG cierre de contacto-membrana m; ~ **loudspeaker** n ACOUST altavoz de membrana m
memory[1]: ~**-resident** adj COMP&DP residente en memoria
memory[2] n COMP&DP, ELEC ENG memoria f; ~ **access** n COMP&DP, ELEC ENG acceso a la memoria m; ~ **backup** n PROD respaldo de memoria m; ~ **bank** n COMP&DP banco de memoria m; ~ **bit location** n PROD posición de celda binaria f, posición de memoria binaria f; ~ **capacity** n COMP&DP, ELEC ENG capacidad de la memoria f; ~ **card** n COMP&DP tarjeta de memoria f; ~ **cartridge** n PROD cartucho de memoria m; ~ **chip** n COMP&DP chip de memoria m; ~ **circuit** n TELECOM circuito de memoria m; ~ **compaction** n COMP&DP compactación de la memoria f; ~ **compression** n COMP&DP compresión de la memoria f; ~ **controller** n ELEC ENG controlador de la memoria m; ~ **cycle** n COMP&DP ciclo de memoria m; ~ **data register** n (MDR) COMP&DP registro de datos de la memoria m; ~ **dump** n COMP&DP volcado de memoria m, vuelco de memoria m; ~ **hierarchy** n COMP&DP jerarquía de la memoria f; ~ **location** n COMP&DP dirección de memoria f, posición de memoria f, ubicación de memoria f; ~ **management** n COMP&DP administración de memoria f, gestión de la memoria f; ~ **map** n COMP&DP mapa de memoria m, topografía de memoria f (AmL), PROD mapa de memoria m, tarjeta de memoria f; ~ **module** n COMP&DP, PROD módulo de memoria m; ~ **module socket** n PROD enchufe para módulo de memoria m; ~ **parity error** n COMP&DP error de paridad de la memoria m; ~ **protect keyswitch** n COMP&DP, PROD cerradura de contactos para la protección de la memoria f; ~ **protection** n COMP&DP protección de la memoria f; ~ **random access** n COMP&DP acceso aleatorio a la memoria m; ~ **store** n TV almacenamiento de datos m, memoria f; ~ **store switch** n PROD conmutador de memoria m; ~ **system** n TV sistema de memoria m; ~ **tracking** n PROD rastreo de memoria m; ~ **transistor** n ELECTRON transistor de memoria m; ~ **tube** n ELECTRON tubo de memoria m
mend vt TEXTIL remendar, repasar
mendelevium n (Md) CHEM, NUCL, RAD PHYS mendelevio m (Md)
mending n PROD reparación f, TEXTIL remiendo m, repasado m; ~ **link** n MECH ENG malla suelta f
mendipite n MINERAL mendipita f

mendozite *n* MINERAL mendocita *f*

menilite *n* MINERAL menilita *f*

meniscus *n* CONST menisco *m*, GEOM media luna *f*, PHYS menisco *m*, THERMO meniscal *m*, menisco *m*; ~ **lens** *n* CINEMAT objetivo menisco *m*, INSTR lente de menisco *f*, objetivo menisco *m*, OPT lente de menisco *f*, PHOTO objetivo menisco *m*, PHYS lente menisco *f*

mensuration *n* GEOM cálculo de magnitudes *m*, medida *f*

menthane *n* CHEM mentano *m*

menthanediamine *n* CHEM mentanodiamina *f*

menthanol *n* CHEM mentanol *m*

menthanone *n* CHEM mentanona *f*

menthene *n* CHEM menteno *m*

menthenol *n* CHEM mentenol *m*

menthenone *n* CHEM mentenona *f*

menthofuran *n* CHEM mentofurano *m*

menthol *n* CHEM mentol *m*

menthone *n* CHEM mentona *f*

menthyl *n* CHEM mentilo *m*

menu[1]: **~-driven** *adj* COMP&DP controlado por menús, regido por menús

menu[2] *n* COMP&DP menú *m*, menú drop down *m*; **~-driven application** *n* COMP&DP aplicación gestionada por menús *f*, aplicación regida por menús *f*; ~ **screen** *n* COMP&DP pantalla menú *f*

mepacrine *n* CHEM mepacrina *f*

meprobamate *n* CHEM meprobamato *m*

merbromin *n* CHEM merbromina *f*

mercantile: ~ **marine** *n* WATER TRANSP marina mercante *f*

mercaptal *n* CHEM mercaptal *m*

mercaptan *n* CHEM, P&R, PETR TECH, POLL mercaptano *m*

mercaptide *n* CHEM mercaptido *m*

mercaptoacetic *adj* CHEM mercaptoacético

mercaptol: ~ **process** *n* CHEM proceso del mercaptol *m*

mercaptomerin *n* CHEM mercaptomerina *f*

Mercator: ~ **chart** *n* WATER TRANSP *navigation* carta Mercator *f*, carta mercatoriana *f*; ~ **plotting chart** *n* OCEAN red de coordenadas de Mercator *f*, retícula cartográfica mercatoriana *f*; ~ **projection** *n* SPACE, WATER TRANSP *navigation* proyección de Mercator *f*, proyección mercatoriana *f*

Mercator-Holder: ~ **scale** *n* ACOUST escala Mercator-Holder *f*

mercerization *n* CHEM mercerización *f*

merchant: ~ **fleet** *n* WATER TRANSP flota mercante *f*; ~ **haulage** *n* TRANSP transporte de mercancías *m*, transporte mercante *m*; ~ **marine** *n* WATER TRANSP marina mercante *f*; ~ **navy** *n* WATER TRANSP marina civil *f*; ~ **ship** *n* WATER TRANSP buque mercante *m*, navío mercante *m*

merchantman *n* WATER TRANSP buque mercante *m*, navío mercante *m*

mercuration *n* CHEM mercuración *f*

mercurial *adj* CHEM mercurial

mercuric *adj* CHEM mercúrico

mercurification *n* CHEM mercurificación *f*

mercury *n* (*Hg*) CHEM, ELEC ENG, METALL mercurio *m* (*Hg*); ~ **arc** *n* ELEC, ELEC ENG arco de mercurio *m*; **~-arc converter** *n* ELEC *alternating current*, ELEC ENG convertidor de arco de mercurio *m*; **~-arc lamp** *n* ELEC, ELEC ENG, RAD PHYS *lighting* lámpara de arco de mercurio *f*, lámpara de vapor de mercurio *f*; **~-arc**

rectifier *n* ELEC ENG rectificador de arco mercurial *m*; ~ **barometer** *n* METEO, METR, PHYS barómetro de mercurio *m*; ~ **battery** *n* ELEC ENG batería seca de mercurio *f*; ~ **bromide laser** *n* ELECTRON láser de mercurio y bromuro *m*; ~ **cell** *n* ELEC ENG pila de mercurio *f*; ~ **delay line** *n* ELECTRON línea de retardo de mercurio *f*; ~ **fulminate** *n* CHEM cianato mercúrico *m*, fulminato de mercurio *m*; ~ **intensification** *n* PHOTO intensificación con mercurio *f*; ~ **interrupter** *n* ELEC ENG conmutador de mercurio *m*, interruptor de mercurio *m*; ~ **laser** *n* ELECTRON láser de mercurio *m*; ~ **ore** *n* MINE, MINERAL cinabrio *m*; ~ **pool cathode** *n* ELEC ENG cátodo de charco de mercurio *m*; ~ **pool tube** *n* ELEC ENG, ELECTRON tubo con depósito de mercurio *m*, tubo de charco de mercurio *m*; ~ **rectifier** *n* ELEC ENG rectificador de mercurio *m*; ~ **relay** *n* ELEC relé de mercurio *m*; ~ **switch** *n* ELEC, ELEC ENG interruptor de mercurio *m*; ~ **thermometer** *n* PHYS, REFRIG termómetro de mercurio *m*; ~ **vapor** *AmE see mercury vapour BrE*; ~ **vapor rectifier** *AmE see mercury vapour rectifier BrE*; ~ **vapor turbine** *AmE see mercury vapour turbine BrE*; ~ **vapour** *n BrE* CHEM, CONST, MECH ENG vapor de mercurio *m*; ~ **vapour rectifier** *n BrE* ELEC ENG rectificador de vapor de mercurio *m*; ~ **vapour turbine** *n BrE* MECH ENG turbina de vapor de mercurio *f*; **~-wetted contacts** *n pl* ELEC ENG contactos impregnados en mercurio *m pl*; **~-wetted reed relay** *n* ELEC ENG relé reed con contactos de mercurio *m*

merge[1] *n* COMP&DP fusión *f*; ~ **volume** *n* TRANSP volumen de la fusión *m*, volumen en la incorporación *m*

merge[2] *vt* COMP&DP fusionar

merged: ~ **bipolar technology** *n* ELECTRON tecnología bipolar combinada *f*; ~ **transistor logic** *n* (*MTL*) ELECTRON circuito lógico transistorizado combinado *m* (*CLTC*)

merging *n* COMP&DP fusión *f*, TRANSP fusión *f*, intercalación *f*; ~ **control** *n* TRANSP control de la fusión *m*

meridian *n* SPACE meridiano *m*; ~ **circle** *n* INSTR *of a telescope* círculo meridiano *m*; ~ **gyro** *n* SPACE giromeridiano *m*; ~ **ray** *n* OPT rayo meridiano *m*; ~ **telescope** *n* INSTR, OPT telescopio meridiano *m*; ~ **transit** *n* SPACE paso por el meridiano *m*

meridional *adj* SPACE meridional, TELECOM meridiano

meristem *n* AGRIC meristema *m*

merogenesis *n* GAS merogénesis *f*

meroxene *n* MINERAL meroxeno *m*

mesa: ~ **diode** *n* ELECTRON diodo mesa *m*; ~ **process** *n* ELECTRON proceso mesa *m*; ~ **transistor** *n* ELECTRON transistor mesa *m*

mesaconic *adj* CHEM mesacónico

MESFET *abbr* (*metal semiconductor field-effect transistor*) ELECTRON EEMTEC (*especificación de equipos mezclados en transistores de efecto de campo*)

mesh[1] *n* COAL malla *f*, mallazo *m*, retícula *f*, ELEC *of system* malla *f*, anillo *m*, ELEC ENG, ELECTRON *network*, FOOD malla *f*, MECH ENG *engagement, gearing* engrane *m*, OCEAN, PAPER, PHYS malla *f*, PROD malla *f*, engrane *m*, SPACE *craft* engrane *m*, retícula *f*, TEXTIL, WATER malla *f*; ~ **connection** *n* ELEC acoplamiento en triángulo *m*, conexión en anillo *f*, conexión en polígono *f*, conexión en triángulo *f*, montaje en triángulo *m*, ELEC ENG *of* *storage tube terminals* conexión en triángulo *f*, PHYS conexión de malla *f*, conexión en triángulo *f*; **~ current** *n* ELEC ENG corriente en la malla *f*; **~ network** *n* ELEC *supply* red mallada *f*, red poligonal *f*, SPACE *communications* red poligonal *f*, red reticular *f*; **~ pin** *n* OCEAN molde *m*; **~ sandwich** *n* SPACE panel de malla *m*; **~ size** *n* COAL malla del tamiz *f*, tamaño de la retícula *m*, tamaño de malla *m*, MECH, OCEAN tamaño de la malla *m*; **~ storage tube** *n* ELECTRON tubo de almacenamiento mallado *m*

mesh² *vt* MECH ENG *gear teeth* endentar, engranar
mesh³ *vi* MECH ENG *gear teeth* engranarse
meshed: **~ loops** *n pl* TEXTIL bucles engarzados *m pl*; **~ network** *n* COMP&DP, ELEC *supply* red de mallas *f*; **~ stitch** *n* TEXTIL puntada engarzada *f*
meshing *n* MECH, MECH ENG engrane *m*, toma *f*
mesidine *n* CHEM mesidina *f*
mesitylene *n* CHEM mesitileno *m*
mesitylenic *adj* CHEM mesitilénico
mesocotyl *n* AGRIC mesocótilo *m*
mesole *n* MINERAL mesolita *f*
mesolite *n* MINERAL mesolita *f*
mesolittoral *n* OCEAN mesolitoral *m*
mesomeric *adj* CHEM mesomérico
mesomerism *n* CHEM mesomería *m*
mesomorphic: **~ phase** *n* CRYSTALL fase mesomórfica *f*
meson *n* CHEM electrón pesado *m*, NUCL mesón *m*, PART PHYS, PHYS kaón *m*, mesón *m*
mesophase *n* CRYSTALL *liquid crystals* mesofase *f*
mesorcinol *n* CHEM mesorcinol *m*
mesosphere *n* GEOPHYS, SPACE mesosfera *f*
mesostructure *n* CRYSTALL *polycrystalline materials* mesoestructura *f*
mesotartaric *adj* CHEM mesotartárico
mesothorium *n* CHEM mesotorio *m*
mesotype *n* MINERAL escolecita *f*, mesotipa cálcica *f*
mesoxalic *adj* CHEM mesoxálico
mesozoic *n* GEOL, PETR TECH mesozoico *m*
mess *n* WATER TRANSP *navy* comedor de marinería *m*, sollado *m*; **~ deck** *n* WATER TRANSP *on ship* alojamiento de la marinería *m*
message *n* COMP&DP mensaje *m*, TELECOM comunicación *f*, mensaje *m*, parte *m*, aviso *m*; **~ chute** *n* AIR TRANSP *of helicopter* canal de comunicación *m*, canal de mensajes *m*; **~ communication function** *n* (*MCF*) TELECOM función de comunicación de mensajes *f*; **~ control system** *n* TELECOM comando multipunto de transmisión simétrica de datos *m*; **~ dropping** *n* (*MD*) TELECOM dispositivo de mediación *m*; **~ handling** *n* (*MH*) TELECOM manipulación de mensajes *f*; **~ handling system** *n* (*MHS*) TELECOM sistema de codificación de mensajes *m*; **~ header** *n* COMP&DP, TELECOM cabecera de mensaje *f*; **~ log** *n* TELECOM registro de llamadas *m*, registro del mensaje *m*; **~ pager** *n* TELECOM paginador de mensajes *m*; **~ processing equipment** *n* WATER TRANSP *satellite communications* equipo procesador de mensajes *m*; **~ register** *n* TELECOM registro de llamadas *m*, registro del mensaje *m*; **~ retrieval** *n* COMP&DP, TELECOM recuperación de mensajes *f*; **~ routing** *n* COMP&DP encaminamiento de mensajes *m*; **~ signal unit** *n* (*MSU*) TELECOM unidad de señal de mensajes *f*; **~ sink** *n* COMP&DP receptor de mensajes *m*; **~ slip** *n* PROD error de mensaje *m*; **~ source** *n* COMP&DP origen del mensaje *m*; **~ store** *n* (*MS*) TELECOM

almacén de mensajes *m*, memoria de mensajes *f*; **~ store area** *n* PROD zona de recepción de mensajes *f*; **~ storing** *n* (*MS*) TELECOM almacenamiento de mensajes *m*, memorización de mensajes *f*; **~ switch** *n* TELECOM conmutador de mensajes *m*; **~-switched network** *n* COMP&DP red con conmutación de mensajes *f*; **~ switching** *n* COMP&DP, TELECOM conmutación de mensajes *f*; **~-switching center** *AmE*, **~-switching centre** *BrE* *n* TELECOM centro de conmutación de mensajes *m*, centro de conmutación de tráfico *m*; **~-switching network** *n* TELECOM red de conmutación de tráfico *f*; **~-switching processor** *n* TELECOM procesador de conmutación de mensajes *m*; **~-switching system** *n* TELECOM sistema de conmutación de mensajes *m*; **~ text** *n* COMP&DP texto del mensaje *m*; **~ transfer** *n* (*MT*) COMP&DP, TELECOM transferencia de mensajes *f*; **~ transfer agent** *n* (*MTA*) TELECOM agente de transferencia de mensajes *m*; **~ transfer part** *n* TELECOM componente para transferencia de mensajes *m*; **~ transfer system** *n* TELECOM sistema de transferencia de mensajes *m*
Message: **~-master**® *n* TELECOM maestro de mensajes *m*
Message-Oriented: **~ Text Interchange Standard** *n* (*MOTIS*) TELECOM sistema de intercambio de texto orientado a mensajes *m*, sistema de manipulación de mensajes *m*, sistema normalizado *m*
messaging *n* COMP&DP mensajería *f*
messenger *n* WATER TRANSP *lines* virador *m*; **~ line** *n* WATER TRANSP guindaleza del virador *f*, guía *f*
metabasic: **~ rock** *n* GEOL roca metabásica *f*
metabasite *n* GEOL, PETROL metabasita *f*
metabisulfite *AmE see* metabisulphite *BrE*
metabisulphite *n* *BrE* CHEM metabisulfito *m*
metabolizable: **~ energy** *n* (*ME*) AGRIC energía metabolizable *f*
metaborate *n* CHEM metaborato *m*
metaboric *adj* CHEM metabórico
metacenter *AmE see* metacentre *BrE*
metacentre *n* *BrE* PHYS, WATER TRANSP *naval architecture* metacentro *m*
metacentric: **~ height** *n* WATER TRANSP *naval architecture* altura metacéntrica *f*
metachlorite *n* MINERAL metaclorito *m*
metachlorotoluene *n* CHEM metaclorotolueno *m*
metachrome: **~ dyeing** *n* COLOUR teñido metacromo *m*
metacinnabarite *n* MINERAL metacinabarita *f*
metacresol *n* CHEM metacresol *m*
metacrylic *adj* CHEM metacrílico
metadyne *n* ELECTRON metadino *m*
metal¹: **~-bodied** *adj* PROD con consistencia metálica; **~-clad** *adj* MECH, MECH ENG blindado, con revestimiento metálico, metalizado; **~-coated** *adj* COATINGS, PROD metalizado; **~-faced** *adj* COATINGS metalizado
metal² *n* C&G metal *m*, CONST *roads* macadam *m*, macadán *m*, MINE roca *f*, mineral *m*, PROD *cast iron* arrabio *m*; **~ active-gas welding** *n* (*MAG welding*) CONST, THERMO soldadura con gas activo de metal *f* (*Esp*) (*soldadura MAG*), soldeo con gas activo de metal *m* (*AmL*) (*soldeo MAG*); **~-air battery** *n* TRANSP batería metálica *f*; **~ arc welding** *n* THERMO soldeo con electrodo consumible *m*, soldeo por arco con electrodo metálico *m*; **~-bound mallet** *n* PROD martillo de cabezas desmontables *m*; **~ box** *n* PACK

caja metálica *f*; ~ **can** *n* PACK bote metálico *m*; ~-**cavity fixing umbrella** *n* CONST paraguas de fijación con cavidad de metal *m*; ~-**clad conductor** *n* ELEC *cable* conductor blindado *m*, conductor con revestimiento metálico *m*, conductor metalizado *m*; ~-**clad substrate** *n* ELECTRON substrato blindado *m*; ~ **coat** *n* COATINGS capa metálica *f*; ~-**coated conductor** *n* ELEC *of cable* conductor acorazado *m*, conductor armado *m*, conductor metalizado *m*; ~-**coated thread** *n* COATINGS hilo metalizado *m*, rosca metalizada *f*; ~ **coating** *n* COATINGS *of reflectors* capa metálica *f*, recubrimiento metálico *m*, revestimiento metálico *m*, MECH ENG metalización *f*, recubrimiento metálico *m*, revestimiento metálico *m*, PACK revestimiento metálico *m*, recubrimiento metálico *m*, PROD blindaje *m*, recubrimiento metálico *m*, revestimiento metálico *m*, TELECOM recubrimiento metálico *m*, revestimiento metálico *m*, TV metalizado *m*; ~-**conductor cable** *n* TELECOM cable de conductores metálicos *m*; ~ **cone tube** *n* ELECTRON tubo con cono metálico *m*; ~-**cutting band-saw blade** *n* MECH ENG, PROD hoja de sierra de cinta para metales *f*; ~-**cutting saw blade** *n* MECH ENG, PROD hoja de sierra para metales *f*; ~ **dark slide** *n* PHOTO chasis metálico *m*; ~ **decorating machine** *n* PRINT máquina metalgráfica *f*; ~ **detector** *n* CONST, PACK detector de metales *m*; ~ **drift** *n* COAL galería en roca *f*, galería estéril *f*, MINE galería estéril *f*; ~ **drum** *n* PACK bidón de metal *m*, tambor de metal *m*; ~ **edging case** *n* PACK caja metálica de bordes canteados *f*; ~ **enameling works** *AmE*, ~ **enamelling works** *BrE* *n* COATINGS fábrica de esmaltado metálico *f*; ~ **eyelet** *n* PROD ojete metálico *m*; ~ **fatigue** *n* CRYSTALL fatiga del metal *f*, fatiga metálica *f*; ~ **filament** *n* ELEC ENG filamento metálico *m*; ~ **film** *n* ELECTRON película metálica *f*; ~ **film resistor** *n* ELEC ENG resistencia de película metalizada *f*; ~ **foil** *n* PACK hoja de metal *f*; ~ **founding** *n* PROD fundición de metal *f*; ~ **gate** *n* ELECTRON dispositivo con puerta metálica *m*; ~ **gate CMOS integrated circuit** *n* ELECTRON circuito integrado de SCOM *m*; ~ **glaze** *n* ELECTRON esmalte metálico *m*; ~ **glaze film** *n* COATINGS capa de vidrio metálico *f*, película metálica vidriada *f*, película metálica vitrificada *f*; ~ **glaze resistor** *n* ELEC ENG resistor de metal vidriada *m*; ~ **grinding regulations** *n pl* SAFE normas sobre el esmerilado de metales *f pl*; ~ **inert-gas welding** *n* (*MIG welding*) CONST soldeo al arco en atmósfera de gas inerte con electrodo consumible *m*; ~-**lined shaft** *n* MINE pozo blindado *m*; ~ **mining** *n* MINE laboreo de minerales *m*; ~-**oxide semiconductor** *n* (*MOS*) COMP&DP semiconductor metal-óxido *m* (*SOM*); ~-**oxide semiconductor capacitor** *n* ELEC ENG condensador semiconductor de óxido metalizado *m*; ~-**oxide semiconductor delay line** *n* ELECTRON línea de retardo de semiconductor de óxido de metal *f*; ~-**oxide semiconductor driver** *n* ELECTRON excitador de semiconductor de óxido de metal *m* (*excitador de SOM*); ~-**oxide semiconductor gate** *n* ELECTRON circuito de conductor de óxido de metal *m*; ~-**oxide semiconductor logic circuit** *n* ELECTRON circuito lógico de semiconductor de óxido de metal *m*; ~-**oxide semiconductor power transistor** *n* ELECTRON transistor de potencia de semiconductor de óxido de metal *m*; ~-**oxide semiconductor technology** *n* ELECTRON tecnología de semiconduc-

tor de óxido de metal *f*; ~-**oxide semiconductor transistor** *n* ELECTRON transistor de semiconductor de óxido de metal *m*; ~ **particle** *n* PROD partícula metálica *f*; ~ **pick-up** *n* PROD captación metálica *f*; ~ **plating** *n* COATINGS metalizado *m*; ~-**position switch** *n* PROD interruptor de posición metálica *m*; ~ **powder** *n* METALL pulvimetal *m*; ~ **recovery** *n* COAL recuperación del metal *f*; ~ **rectifier** *n* ELEC célula rectificadora *f*, rectificador de disco seco *m*, rectificador de placas secas *m*, rectificador seco *m*; ~ **refinery** *n* METALL, PROD refinería metalúrgica *f*; ~ **reflector** *n* INSTR metal reflector *m*; ~ **removal** *n* MECH ENG remoción de metal *f*; ~ **saw** *n* PROD sierra para metales *f*; ~-**sawing machine** *n* PROD máquina para aserrar metales *f*; ~-**semiconductor junction** *n* ELECTRON unión metal-semiconductor *f*; ~ **shears** *n pl* PROD tijeras para metales *f pl*; ~ **sheath** *n* ELEC ENG revestimiento metálico *m*; ~-**sheathed cable** *n* ELEC ENG cable forrado de metal *m*; ~-**sheathed conductor** *n* ELEC ENG conductor forrado de metal *m*; ~-**slitting saw** *n* MECH ENG fresa de cortar metales *f*; ~-**strip closure** *n* PACK cierre de tira metálica *m*; ~-**to-metal clutch** *n* MECH ENG embrague en seco *m*; ~-**to-metal joint** *n* METALL junta metálica *f*; ~ **tube** *n* ELECTRON tubo metálico *m*; ~ **vapor laser** *AmE*, ~ **vapour laser** *BrE* *n* ELECTRON láser de vapor metálico *m*

metal[3] *vt* CONST *road* colocar macadam sobre, extender capa de base sobre; ~-**coat** *vt* COATINGS metalizar
metalanguage *n* COMP&DP metalenguaje *m*
metalation *AmE see metallation BrE*
metaldehyde *n* CHEM lustre metálico *m*, metaldehído *m*
metaled: ~ **road** *AmE see metalled road BrE*
metaling *AmE see metalling BrE*
metalization *AmE see metallization BrE*
metalized *AmE see metallized BrE*
metalizing *AmE see metallizing BrE*
metallation *n BrE* CHEM metalación *f*
metalled: ~ **road** *n BrE* CONST carretera pavimentada *f*
metallic[1] *adj* ELEC metálico
metallic[2]: ~ **bond** *n* METALL adherencia metálica *f*, junta metálica *f*; ~ **circuit** *n* ELEC ENG circuito magnético *m*; ~ **coating** *n* COATINGS, MECH ENG, PACK, PROD, TELECOM recubrimiento metálico *m*, revestimiento metálico *m*; ~ **conductor** *n* ELEC ENG conductor metálico *m*; ~ **conductor cable** *n* TELECOM cable de conductores metálicos *m*; ~ **crosspoint** *n* TELECOM punto de cruce metálico *m*; ~ **ink** *n* COLOUR tinta metálica *f*; ~ **lustre** *n* CHEM *property* brillo metálico *m*; ~ **mirror** *n* INSTR espejo metálico *m*; ~ **oxide semiconductor** *n* ELECTRON semiconductor metal-óxido *m* (*SOM*); ~ **pigment paint** *n* COLOUR pintura de pigmento metálico *f*; ~ **rectifier** *n* ELEC, ELEC ENG rectificador metálico *m*; ~ **resistor** *n* ELEC resistor metálico *m*; ~ **sheath** *n* ELEC *cable conductor* envoltura metálica *f*, funda metálica *f*, vaina metálica *f*; ~ **structure** *n* CONST estructura metálica *f*
metalliferous *adj* CHEM metalífero
metalline *n* CHEM metalino *m*
metalling *n BrE* CONST extendido de capa de rodadura *m*, pavimentación *f*
metallization *n BrE* CONST, ELECTRON, PHYS, PROD metalización *f*, SPACE metalización *f*, vulcanización *f*; ~ **layer** *n BrE* ELECTRON estratificador de metali-

zación *m*; ~ **mask** *n BrE* ELECTRON máscara de metalización *f*

metallized[1] *adj BrE* ELEC metalizado

metallized[2]: ~ **film** *n BrE* PACK película metalizada *f*; ~ **film capacitor** *n BrE* ELEC ENG capacitor para película metalizada *m*, condensador de película metalizada *m*; ~ **hole** *n BrE* ELEC *printed circuit board* hueco metalizado *m*; ~ **mica capacitor** *n BrE* ELEC ENG condensador de mica metalizada *m*; ~ **paint** *n BrE* COLOUR, P&R pintura metalizada *f*; ~ **paper** *n BrE* PACK, PAPER papel metalizado *m*; ~**-paper capacitor** *n BrE* ELEC condensador de papel metalizado *m*; ~ **screen** *n BrE* ELECTRON pantalla metalizada *f*

metallizing *n BrE* C&G metalizado *m*

metallo: ~**-organic pigment** *n* COLOUR pigmento órgano-metálico *m*

metallogenetic: ~ **province** *n* GEOL provincia metalogenética *f*

metallographic: ~ **microscope** *n* LAB, METALL microscopio metalográfico *m*

metallography *n* METALL metalografía *f*

metalloid *n* CHEM, METALL metaloide *m*

metalloidal *adj* CHEM, METALL metaloideo, metaloídico

metallurgic: ~ **coke** *n* COAL, METALL cok metalúrgico *m*

metallurgical: ~ **furnace** *n* MECH ENG, METALL horno metalúrgico *m*; ~ **waste** *n* COAL, METALL escombros metalúrgicos *m pl*

metamer *n* CHEM metámero *m*

metameric[1] *adj* CHEM, COLOUR, PRINT metamérico

metameric[2]: ~ **colors** *AmE*, ~ **colours** *BrE n pl* COLOUR, PRINT colores metaméricos *m pl*

metamerism *n* CHEM metamería *f*

metamict *adj* GEOL metamíctico

metamorphic: ~ **differentiation** *n* GEOL diferenciación metamórfica *f*; ~ **facies** *n* GEOL facies metamórfica *f*; ~ **grade** *n* GEOL grado metamórfico *m*; ~ **rock** *n* FUELLESS roca metamórfica *f*; ~ **zone** *n* GEOL zona metamórfica *f*

metamorphism *n* GEOL, PETROL metamorfismo *m*

metanil *n* CHEM metanilo *m*

metaphosphate *n* CHEM metafosfato *m*

metaphosphoric *adj* CHEM metafosfórico

metarsenious *adj* CHEM metarsenioso

metasediment *n* GEOL metasedimento *m*

metasilicate *n* CHEM metasilicato *m*

metasilicic *adj* CHEM metasilícico

metasomatism *n* GEOL metasomatismo *m*

metastable[1] *adj* RAD PHYS metaestable

metastable[2]: ~ **atom** *n* PART PHYS, RAD PHYS átomo metaestable *m*; ~ **equilibrium** *n* PHYS equilibrio metaestable *m*; ~ **loss rate** *n* RAD PHYS tasa de fugas metaestable *f*, tasa de pérdidas metaestable *f*; ~ **state** *n* METALL, PHYS estado metaestable *m*

metastannic *adj* CHEM metaestánico

metathesis *n* CHEM metátesis *f*

metavolcanic *n* GEOL metavolcánico *m*

metaxite *n* MINERAL metaxita *f*

meteor *n* METEO, SPACE estrella fugaz *f*, meteoro *m*; ~ **burst communication** *n* SPACE *communications* comunicación por ionización meteórica *f*; ~ **burst link** *n* SPACE *communications* enlace por ionización meteórica *m*; ~ **dust** *n* SPACE polvo meteórico *m*; ~ **echo** *n* SPACE *spacecraft* radioeco meteórico *m*

meteoric: ~ **water** *n* HYDROL aguas meteóricas *f pl*

meteorite *n* METEO, SPACE meteorito *m*; ~ **influx** *n* SPACE influjo meteorítico *m*

meteoroid *n* METEO, SPACE meteoroide *m*

meteorological: ~ **conditions** *n pl* METEO, POLL condiciones meteorológicas *f pl*; ~ **data** *n pl* AIR TRANSP información meteorológica *f*, METEO, POLL, SPACE datos meteorológicos *m pl*, información meteorológica *f*; ~ **inversion** *n* METEO, POLL inversión meteorológica *f*, inversión térmica *f*; ~ **satellite** *n* METEO, SPACE satélite meteorológico *m*; ~ **satellite service** *n* METEO, SPACE *space communications* servicio de satélite meteorológico *m*; ~ **sensor** *n* METEO, WATER TRANSP elemento sensible *m*; ~ **station** *n* METEO estación de observación meteorológica *f*, estación meteorológica *f*; ~ **tide** *n* METEO, OCEAN marea meteorológica *f*

meteorology *n* METEO, SPACE, WATER TRANSP meteorología *f*

meter *n* ELEC *instrument* contador *m*, medidor *m*, MECH ENG contador *m*, TELECOM medidor *m*; *AmE measurement unit see metre BrE*; ~**-calibration bench** *n* GAS banco de calibración de medidores *m*, banco para calibrar medidores *m*; ~ **cell** *n* PHOTO célula del exposímetro *f*; ~ **gage** *AmE see metre gauge BrE*; ~ **loss** *n* ELEC *instrument* pérdida del aparato de medida *f*; ~ **movement** *n* ELEC ENG *of measurement device* parte móvil del medidor *f*; ~**-type relay** *n* ELEC ENG relé para contador *m*

metering *n* GAS medición *f*, HYDRAUL aforo *m*, METR medida *f*, PRINT dosificación *f*, regulación *f*, PROD aforo *m*, TELECOM aforo *m*, calibración *f*, cómputo *m*, medición *f*, tasación *f*, WATER aforo *m*; ~ **equipment** *n* PACK equipo dosificador *m*; ~ **friction** *n* PRINT fricción de entrada *f*; ~ **hole** *n* MECH ENG orificio de medición *m*; ~ **jet** *n* MECH ENG surtidor de dosificación *m*, surtidor de regulación *m*; ~ **land** *n* PROD alcance de medida *m*, muro de sostenimiento *m*; ~ **pump** *n* LAB bomba reguladora *f*; ~ **rate** *n* TELECOM tarifa según contador *f*, tasa de mediación *f*; ~ **rod coater** *n* COATINGS, PAPER estucadora de varilla igualadora *f*; ~ **roll coater** *n* COATINGS, PAPER estucadora de rodillo igualador *f*; ~ **roller** *n* PRINT rodillo regulador *m*; ~ **valve** *n* AUTO válvula de estrangulación *f*, válvula reguladora *f* (*Esp*), MECH ENG válvula dosificadora *f*

meter/kilogram/second/ampere: ~ **system** *n AmE see metre/kilogram/second/ampere system BrE*

methacrylate *n* P&R metacrilato *m*

methacrylic *adj* CHEM metacrílico

methadone *n* CHEM metadona *f*

methanal *n* CHEM, FOOD, P&R, TEXTIL formaldehído *m*, metanal *m*

methanation *n* GAS metanación *f*

methane *n* AGRIC, CHEM, GAS, METEO, PETR TECH, SAFE metano *m*; ~ **bacterium** *n* CHEM metanobacteria *f*; ~ **carrier** *n* WATER TRANSP metanero *m*; ~ **carrier with self-supporting tank** *n* TRANSP transporte de metano con tanques autoportantes *m*; ~ **detector** *n* GAS, MINE *fire damp* detector de metano *m*; ~**-draining boring** *n* COAL perforación para la extracción de metano *f*; ~ **fermentation** *n* HYDROL fermentación metánica *f*, METEO fermentación de metano *f*; ~ **gas** *n* CHEM, GAS, SAFE gas metano *m*; ~ **indicator** *n* MINE *fire damp* indicador de metano *m*;

~ **series** n GAS serie del metano f; ~ **tanker** n PETR TECH buque tanque de metano m

methanilic adj CHEM metanílico

methanoic adj CHEM metanoico

methanol n CHEM, GAS alcohol metílico m, metanol m, P&R, THERMO alcohol metílico m; ~ **cell** n TRANSP célula de metanol f

methanometer n CHEM, CHEM TECH, GAS, INSTR, MINE grisuómetro m

methimazol n CHEM metimazol m

methionic adj CHEM metiónico

method n CHEM, PHYS método m; ~ **of costing** n MECH ENG método de estimación del costo m; ~ **of feeding** n C&G alimentación f, método de alimentar m; ~ **of measurement** n CONST método de medición m; ~ **of routing** n RAIL método de fijación de itinerarios m

methods: ~ **engineer** n MECH ENG ingeniero encargado del estudio de los métodos m; ~ **manager** n MECH ENG gerente de métodos m

methol n CHEM metol m

methoxide n CHEM metóxido m

methoxybenzene n CHEM anisol m, metoxibenceno m, FOOD anisol m

methoxyethanol n CHEM metoxietanol m

methoxyl n CHEM metoxilo m

Methuselah n C&G Matusalén m

methyl n CHEM metilo m; ~ **acetate** n CHEM, DETERG, P&R acetato de metilo m; ~ **alcohol** n CHEM, GAS, P&R, THERMO alcohol metílico m, metanol m; ~ **bromide** n CHEM bromuro de metilo m; ~ **chloride** n CHEM clorometano m, cloruro de metilo m; ~ **ester** n DETERG éster metílico m; ~ **ethyl ketone** n CHEM metiletilcetona f; ~ **ethyl ketoxime** n P&R metiletilcetoxima f; ~ **iodide** n CHEM ioduro de metilo m, yoduro de metilo m; ~ **tertiary-butyl ether** n CHEM, PETR TECH éter metílico terciariobutílico m

methylal n CHEM metilal m

methylamine n CHEM metilamina f

methylaniline n CHEM metilanilina f

methylate[1] n CHEM metilato m

methylate[2] vt CHEM metilar

methylated: ~ **spirit** n CHEM, COLOUR, FOOD alcohol desnaturalizado m, alcohol metilado m

methylation n CHEM metilación f

methylene: ~ **iodide** n CHEM yoduro de metileno m

methylic adj CHEM metílico

methylnaphthalene n CHEM metilnaftaleno m

methylpentose n CHEM metilpentosa f

methylpropane n CHEM isobutano m, metil propano m, PETR TECH, PETROL isobutano m

meticulous: ~ **inspection** n CONST, SAFE comprobación meticulosa f, verificación meticulosa f

METO: ~ **power** n (maximum except takeoff power) AIR TRANSP potencia máxima excepto al despegue f

metol n CHEM metol m

metre n BrE MECH ENG, METR, TEXTIL metro m; ~ **gauge** n BrE RAIL vía de un metro f, vía métrica f

metre/kilogram/second/ampere: ~ **system** (MKSA system) n BrE METR sistema metro/kilogramo/segundo/amperio m (sistema MKSA)

metric[1] adj METR métrico

metric[2]: ~ **carat** n METR precious stones quilate métrico m; ~ **centner** n METR quintal métrico m; ~ **fine-pitch thread** n MECH ENG rosca métrica de paso fino f; ~ **horsepower** n METR caballo métrico

m; ~ **quintal** n METR quintal métrico m; ~ **system** n METR sistema métrico m; ~ **ton** n METR, PETR TECH tonelada métrica f; ~ **tonne** n METR, PETR TECH tonelada métrica f; ~ **trapezoidal-screw thread** n MECH ENG hilo de rosca trapezoidal métrico m

metrical[1] adj METR métrico

metrical[2]: ~ **geometry** n GEOM, METR geometría métrica f

metrology n METR metrología f

metropolitan: ~ **area network** n (MAN) TELECOM red de área metropolitana f; ~ **network** n TELECOM red metropolitana f; ~ **switch** n TELECOM conmutador metropolitano m

Meyer: ~ **bar** n PRINT barra de Meyer f

MF[1] abbr (multiple frequency) TELECOM múltiples frecuencias f pl

MF[2]: ~ **paperboard** n (machine-finished paperboard) PAPER cartón alisado m; ~ **sender-receiver** (multifrequency sender-receiver) n TELECOM emisorreceptor multifrecuencia m, transmisor-receptor multifrecuencia m; ~ **telephone** n (multifrequency telephone) TELECOM teléfono multifrecuencia m

MFA abbr (multiframe alignment) TELECOM alineamiento de múltiples bastidores m

MFM abbr (modified frequency modulation) ELECTRON MFM (modulación de frecuencia modificada)

MFWS abbr (main feedwater system) NUCL MFWS (sistema de agua de alimentación principal)

mg abbr (miligram, milligramme) METR mg (miligramo)

Mg abbr (magnesium) CHEM, ELEC ENG, METALL Mg (magnesio)

MG: ~ **board** n (machine-glazed board) PAPER cartón satinado en una cara m; ~ **cylinder** n (machine-glazed cylinder) PAPER cilindro satinador m; ~ **machine** n PAPER máquina con secador yankee f; ~ **paper** n (machine-glazed paper) PAPER papel satinado una cara m

MGD abbr (magnetogasdynamics) NUCL MGD (magnetogasodinámica)

MH abbr (message handling) TELECOM manipulación de mensajes f

MHD[1] abbr (magnetohydrodynamics) ELEC ENG, FLUID, GEOPHYS, PHYS, SPACE magnetohidrodinámica f

MHD[2]: ~ **conversion** n ELEC ENG, GEOPHYS conversión MHD f; ~ **converter** n ELEC ENG, NUCL, SPACE convertidor MHD m; ~ **generation** n ELEC ENG producción MHD f; ~ **generator** n ELEC ENG generador MHD m; ~ **instability** n GEOPHYS inestabilidad MHD f; ~ **pump** n ELEC ENG bomba MHD f; ~ **wave** n GEOPHYS onda MHD f

MHS abbr (message handling system) TELECOM sistema de manipulación de mensajes m

miargyrite n MINERAL miargirita f

MIB abbr (management information base) TELECOM base de información para dirección de empresas f

MIC abbr (microwave integrated circuit) ELECTRON, PHYS CIM (circuito integrado de microondas)

mica n GEN mica f; ~ **capacitor** n ELEC, ELEC ENG condensador de mica m; ~ **dielectric capacitor** n ELEC, ELEC ENG capacitor dieléctrico de mica m; ~ **schist** n GEOL, PETROL micaesquisto m

micaceous[1] adj GEOL micáceo

micaceous[2]: ~ **iron ore** n MINERAL hematites f pl; ~ **iron oxide** n CHEM, P&R óxido de hierro micáceo m

micelle n CHEM of colloid, P&R micela f

Michelson: ~ **interferometer** n PHYS interferómetro de Michelson m

Michelson-Morley: ~ **experiment** n PHYS experimento de Michelson y Morley m

MICR abbr (magnetic ink character reader) COMP&DP lector de caracteres en tinta magnética m, reconocimiento de caracteres en tinta magnética m

micrite n GEOL, PETROL micrita f

micro[1] n COMP&DP micro m

micro-[2] pref METR micro

microammeter n ELEC ENG, ELECTRON microamperímetro m

microampere n ELEC, ELEC ENG unit of current microampere m, microamperio m

microanalysis n CHEM microanálisis m

microanalytic adj CHEM microanalítico

microanalytical adj CHEM microanalítico

microbend n ELEC ENG micro curvatura f; ~ **loss** n OPT pérdida por microdoblado f, TELECOM pérdida de microflexión f

microbending n OPT microdoblado m, TELECOM microflexión f

microbiological: ~ **hazard** n SAFE peligro microbiológico m, riesgo microbiológico m

microbubble n OPT microburbuja f

microburette n CHEM microbureta f

microcellular: ~ **rubber** n P&R caucho microcelular m

microchannel n ELECTRON microcanal m; ~ **image intensifier** n ELECTRON intensificador de imagen de microcanal m; ~ **plate** n ELECTRON placa de microcanal f

microchemistry n CHEM microquímica f

microchip n COMP&DP, ELECTRON, RAD PHYS microchip m

microcircuit n COMP&DP, ELECTRON microcircuito m

microclimate n METEO microclima m

microcline n MINERAL microclina f

microcode n COMP&DP microcódigo m

microcomputer n COMP&DP microcomputadora f (AmL), microordenador m (Esp)

microcontrol n TRANSP micro control m

microcontroller n COMP&DP microcontrolador m

microcosmic adj CHEM salt microcósmico

microcrack n METALL, OPT grieta microscópica f, microfisura f

microcreep n METALL microfluencia f

microcreping n PAPER microcrespado m

microcrystalline[1] adj CHEM, CRYSTALL microcristalino

microcrystalline[2]: ~ **limestone** n GEOL caliza microcristalina f; ~ **wax** n PETR TECH cera microcristalina f

microdevitrification n C&G, OPT microdesvitrificación f

microdistillation n CHEM microdestilación f

microelectronics n COMP&DP, ELECTRON microelectrónica f

microelement n AGRIC, CHEM microelemento m

microfarad n ELEC, ELEC ENG microfarad m, microfaradio m

microfiche n COMP&DP, PRINT microficha f; ~ **reader** n COMP&DP, PRINT lector de microfichas m

microfilm n COMP&DP microfilm m, microfilme m, micropelícula f, PHOTO, PRINT microfilm m; ~ **reader** n COMP&DP lector de microfilme m, lector de micropelícula m; ~ **recorder** n COMP&DP grabador de microfilme m, grabador de micropelícula m

microfilter n WATER microfiltro m

microfold n GEOL micropliegue m

microfossil n GEOL microfósil m

microgranite n PETROL microgranito m

microgranular adj GEOL microgranular

micrograph n CRYSTALL micrografía f

micrographic: ~ **method** n MECH ENG analysis of materials, METALL método micrográfico m; ~ **microscope** n INSTR microscopio micrográfico m

microgravity n SPACE microgravedad f, microgravitación f

microgroove n ACOUST microsurco m

microhardness n METALL, P&R microdureza f

microhenry n ELEC microhenrio m

microhm n ELEC ENG micro ohmio m

microinstruction n COMP&DP microinstrucción f

microlite n MINERAL microlita f

microlog n PETROL microperfil m

micromachining n RAD PHYS micromaquinado m, micromaquinización f

micrometer AmE see micrometre BrE

micrometre n BrE LAB, MECH, MECH ENG, METR, PHYS formerly micron micrómetro m; ~ **callipers** BrE n pl MECH ENG calibradores micrométricos m pl, compases micrométricos m pl, compases micrométricos de gruesos m pl; ~ **screw** BrE n INSTR, MECH ENG tornillo micrométrico m

micrometric[1] adj METR micrométrico

micrometric[2]: ~ **spark discharger** n ELEC descargador de chispa micrométrico m

micrometry n MECH ENG micrometría f

micromicron n METR length unit micromicrón m

micromil n METR micromil m

micromillimeter AmE see micromillimetre BrE

micromillimetre n BrE METR micromilímetro m

microminiaturization n ELECTRON microminiaturización f

micron n METR micron m; ~ **barrier** n ELECTRON barrera micrométrica f; ~ **circuit** n ELECTRON circuito micrométrico m

micronic adj MECH ENG filter micrométrico

micronize vt CHEM micronizar

micronized adj P&R pigments, fillers micronizado, pulverizado

micronutrient n HYDROL elemento micronutritivo m, oligoelemento m

microorganism n HYDROL, POLL microorganismo m

microperthite n MINERAL micropertita f

microphone n ACOUST, COMP&DP, ELEC, PHYS, TV micrófono m

microphotography n CINEMAT, PHOTO microfotografía f

microphotometer n RAD PHYS microfotómetro m

micropipette n LAB micropipeta f

micropit n C&G, METALL, OPT, P&R, QUALITY micropicadura f

microprobe n RAD PHYS microsonda f

microprocessor n COMP&DP, ELEC, ELECTRON, MECH ENG, PRINT, SPACE microprocesador m; ~ **chip** n COMP&DP, ELECTRON chip microprocesador m; ~ **control** n ELECTRON control por microprocesador m, TELECOM control del microprocesador m

microprogram n COMP&DP microprograma m

microprogramming n COMP&DP microprogramación f

micropump n MECH ENG microbomba f

microresistivity: ~ **log** n GEOPHYS registro de microresistividad m

microrheology n C&G, METALL, P&R microreología f

microrocket n SPACE microbomba f, microcohete m

microscope n CHEM, INSTR, LAB, METR, OPT, PHYS microscopio m; ~ **adaptor** n PHOTO adaptador de microscopio m; ~ **body** n INSTR cuerpo del microscopio m; ~ **camera** n INSTR cámara del microscopio f; ~ **condenser** n LAB condensador de microscopio m; ~ **eyepiece** n INSTR, LAB ocular del microscopio m; ~ **slide** n C&G, LAB portaobjetos m; ~ **slide cover slip** n LAB cubreobjeto m; ~ **stage** n INSTR platina del microscopio f; ~ **tube** n INSTR tubo electrónico del microscopio m

microscopic: ~ **dust** n SAFE polvo microscópico m; ~ **photometer** n INSTR fotómetro microscópico m; ~ **stage** n INSTR platina microscópica f; ~ **state** n RAD PHYS estado microscópico m

microscopy n CHEM, INSTR, LAB, OPT, PHYS microscopía f

microsecond n COMP&DP microsecundo m

microsegregation n METALL microsegregación f

microspheres n pl P&R microesferas f pl

microstrain n METALL microdeformación f

microstrainer n WATER microfiltro rotativo m, microtamiz m

microstrip n ELECTRON microbanda f, PHYS franja microscópica f

microstructure n GEN microestructura f

microswitch n ELEC, ELEC ENG microconmutador m, microinterruptor m, microrruptor m

microsyringe n LAB microjeringa f

microthruster n SPACE microempuje m

microtome n LAB micrótomo m

microtwin n METALL micromacla f

microvolt n ELEC unit of potential microvolt m, microvoltio m, ELEC ENG, PHYS microvoltio m, microvolt m

microwavable: ~ **packaging** n PACK embalaje para calentar en hornos de microondas m

microwave n ELEC, ELECTRON, PHYS, SPACE, TELECOM, WAVE PHYS microonda f; ~ **absorption** n TELECOM absorción de microondas f; ~ **aerial** n BrE (cf microwave antenna AmE) PHYS, SPACE antena de doble reflector f, antena de microondas f, TELECOM, TV antena de microondas f; ~ **amplification** n ELECTRON amplificación de microonda f; ~ **amplification by stimulated emission of radiation** n (MASER) ELECTRON, SPACE amplificador de microondas por emisión estimulada de radiación m (MASER); ~ **amplifier** n ELECTRON, PHYS, TELECOM amplificador de microondas m; ~**amplifier tube** n ELECTRON tubo de amplificador de microonda m; ~ **antenna** n AmE (cf microwave aerial BrE) PHYS, SPACE antena de doble reflector f, antena de microondas f, TELECOM, TV antena de microondas f; ~ **attenuation** n ELECTRON, TELECOM atenuación de microondas f; ~ **attenuator** n ELECTRON, TELECOM atenuador de microondas m; ~ **background radiation** n PHYS, RAD PHYS radiación de fondo de microondas f; ~ **bandpass filter** n ELECTRON filtro paso banda de microondas m; ~ **band-stop filter** n ELECTRON filtro de retención de banda de microondas m; ~ **beam** n TELECOM haz de microondas m; ~ **cavity** n ELECTRON cavidad de microondas f; ~ **circuit** n ELECTRON circuito de microondas m; ~ **circulator** n TELECOM circulador de microondas m; ~ **delay line** n ELECTRON línea de retardo de microondas f; ~ **diode** n ELECTRON diodo de microondas m; ~ **discharge** n GAS descarga de microondas f; ~ **filter** n ELECTRON filtro de microondas m; ~ **frequency** n ELECTRON, PHYS frecuencia de microondas f; ~ **generator** n ELECTRON generador de microondas m; ~ **integrated circuit** n (MIC) ELECTRON, PHYS circuito integrado de microondas m (CIM); ~ **inversion** n RAD PHYS inversión de microondas f; ~ **landing system** n (MLS) AIR TRANSP sistema de aterrizaje de microondas m (MLS); ~ **limiter** n ELECTRON limitador de microondas m; ~ **link** n PHYS conexión de microonda f, TV enlace por microondas m; ~ **mixer** n ELECTRON mezclador de microondas m; ~ **modulator** n TELECOM modulador de microondas m; ~ **module** n ELECTRON módulo de microondas m; ~ **oscillator** n ELECTRON oscilador de microondas m; ~ **oscillator tube** n ELECTRON tubo de oscilador de microondas m; ~ **oven** n ELEC ENG, FOOD horno de microondas m; ~ **phase shifter** n ELEC ENG, ELECTRON, TELECOM, WAVE PHYS desfasador de microondas m; ~ **power** n ELEC ENG potencia de microondas f; ~**power amplification** n ELECTRON amplificación de potencia de microondas f; ~**power amplifier** n ELECTRON amplificador de potencia de microondas m; ~**power transistor** n ELECTRON transistor de potencia de microondas m; ~ **printed circuit** n ELECTRON circuito impreso de microondas m; ~ **resonator** n ELECTRON, TELECOM resonador de microondas m; ~ **signal** n ELECTRON señal de microondas f; ~**signal generator** n ELECTRON generador de señal de microondas m; ~ **signal source** n ELECTRON fuente de señal de microondas f; ~ **spectroscopy** n PHYS, RAD PHYS espectroscopía de microondas f, espectroscopía por microondas f; ~ **spectrum** n PHYS, RAD PHYS espectro de microondas m; ~ **substrate** n ELECTRON substrato de microondas m; ~ **switch matrix** n TELECOM matriz de conmutación de microondas f; ~ **synthesizer** n ELECTRON sintetizador de microondas m; ~ **system** n TELECOM sistema de microondas m; ~ **technology** n SPACE tecnología de microondas f; ~ **thawing** n REFRIG descongelación por microondas f; ~ **tower** n TELECOM torre de microondas f; ~ **transistor** n ELECTRON transistor de microondas m; ~ **transistor amplifier** n ELECTRON amplificador de microondas transistorizado m; ~ **transmission line** n ELEC ENG línea de transmisión de microondas f; ~ **tube** n ELECTRON tubo de microondas m, MECH ENG tubo de hiperfrecuencias m, tubo de microondas m, tubo para frecuencias ultraelevadas m; ~ **tunable filter** n ELECTRON filtro sintonizable de microondas m

mid: ~**engine** n AUTO motor central m; ~**shot** n CINEMAT plano medio m; ~ **wing** n AIR TRANSP, TRANSP ala media f

midair: ~ **collision** n AIR TRANSP colisión en vuelo f

midband: ~ **frequency** n ELECTRON frecuencia en banda intermedia f; ~ **gain** n ELECTRON ganancia en banda intermedia f

middle[1] adj GEOL central, medio, PAPER of board interior

middle[2] n MECH ENG, PROD of three-part foundry flask parte central f; ~ **breaker** n AGRIC arado aporcador m; ~ **cut** n PROD files, rasps lima semidulce f; ~ **distillate** n CHEM, PETR TECH destilado medio m; ~ **ear** n ACOUST oído medio m; ~ **frequencies** n pl TELECOM broadcasting frecuencias medias f pl; ~ **ground** n WATER TRANSP in navigable waters bajo m, banco central m, medianía f; ~ **infrared** n PHYS,

RAD PHYS infrarrojo intermedio *m*; ~ **layer** *n* TEXTIL capa de tejido intermedia *f*; ~ **marker** *n* AIR TRANSP *of ILS* radiobaliza intermedia *f*; ~ **part** *n* MECH ENG, PROD *of three-part foundry flask* parte central *f*; **~-pile segment** *n* COAL segmento del pilar de en medio *m*; ~ **rail** *n* CONST *of door* travesaño intermedio *m*

middles *n pl* MINE mixtos *m pl*

middletones *n pl* PRINT tonos medios *m pl*

middlings *n pl* AGRIC subproductos de molienda del trigo *m pl*, COAL mixtos *m pl*, FOOD acemite *m*, MINE mixtos *m pl*; ~ **bran** *n* FOOD salvado de acemite *m*

midge *n* AGRIC *sorghum, alfalfa* mosquita *f*

midocean: ~ **ridge** *n* GEOL dorsal oceánica *f*

midpoint: ~ **anchor** *n* RAIL anclaje del punto medio *m*, fijación del punto medio *f*; ~ **earthing** *n* BrE (*cf midpoint grounding AmE*) ELEC *of connection* puesta a tierra del punto medio *f*; ~ **grounding** *n* AmE (*cf midpoint earthing BrE*) ELEC *of connection* puesta a tierra del punto medio *f*

midrib *n* AGRIC nerviadura central *f*, METALL nervio central *m*, resalte central *m*

midship[1] *adv* WATER TRANSP a media eslora, en crujía, en el centro, en la maestra

midship[2] *n* WATER TRANSP crujía *f*, maestra *f*; ~ **beam** *n* WATER TRANSP *naval architecture* bao maestro *m*; ~ **body** *n* WATER TRANSP cuerpo central *m*; ~ **frame** *n* WATER TRANSP *naval architecture* cuaderna maestra *f*; ~ **section** *n* WATER TRANSP *naval architecture* maestra *f*, sección media *f*

midshipman *n* WATER TRANSP *navy* guardia marina *m*

midstream *n* HYDROL zona media del río *f*

midtravel *n* MECH ENG punto medio del recorrido *m*

midwall *n* MINE muro medianero *m*, tabique *m*

MIG: ~ **welding** *n* (*metal inert-gas welding*) CONST soldeo al arco en atmósfera de gas inerte con electrodo consumible *m*

migmatite *n* GEOL, PETROL migmatita *f*

migmatization *n* GEOL, PETROL migmatización *f*

migrant: ~ **worker** *n* AGRIC trabajador migratorio *m*

migrate *vi* CHEM *of ions*, PETROL migrar

migration *n* CHEM *of ions*, COLOUR, P&R, PETR TECH migración *f*

mike: ~ **stew** *n* CINEMAT silbido del micrófono *m*; ~ **tap** *n* CINEMAT enchufe del micrófono *m*

MIL *abbr* (*multipoint indication loop*) TELECOM circuito cerrado indicador de varios puntos *m*

milarite *n* MINERAL milarita *f*

mild: ~ **steel** *n* MECH ENG, METALL acero bajo en carbono *m*, acero dulce *m*, acero suave *m*

mildew[1]: **~-proof** *adj* COATINGS resistente al moho

mildew[2] *n* AGRIC mildiú *m*, FOOD moho *m*; **~-proofing** *n* COATINGS impermeabilización al moho *f*

mile *n* METR, TRANSP milla *f*

mileage *n* TRANSP distancia en millas *f*, recorrido en millas *m*; ~ **recorder** *n* BrE AUTO cuentakilómetros *m*

mileometer *n* BrE (*cf odometer AmE*) AUTO, CONST, TRANSP, VEH cuentaki lómetros *m*, cuentapasos *m*, odómetro *m*

milepost *n* RAIL punto kilométrico *m*

miles: ~ **per gallon** *n pl* (*mpg*) TRANSP millas por galón *f pl*

milestone *n* MECH, TRANSP hito *m*, mojón *m*

military: ~ **observation satellite** *n* MILIT, SPACE satélite de observación militar *m*

milk: ~ **cattle** *n* AGRIC ganado lechero *m*, ganado

vacuno de leche *m*; ~ **collection lorry** *n* BrE (*cf milk collection truck AmE*) AGRIC cisterna recolectora de leche *f*; ~ **collection truck** *n* AmE (*cf milk collection lorry BrE*) AGRIC cisterna recolectora de leche *f*; ~ **cooler** *n* AGRIC, REFRIG enfriador de leche *m*, refrigerador de leche *m*; ~ **cow** *n* AGRIC vaca lechera *f*; ~ **fat** *n* FOOD grasa de leche *f*; ~ **fever** *n* AGRIC fiebre de la leche *f*; ~ **powder** *n* FOOD leche en polvo *f*; ~ **protein** *n* FOOD proteína láctea *f*; ~ **tank** *n* AGRIC cisterna recolectora de leche *f*; ~ **tanker** *n* AUTO camión-cisterna de leche *m*; ~ **yield** *n* AGRIC rendimiento de la leche *m*

milkiness *n* C&G, CHEM opacidad *f*

milking: ~ **ability** *n* AGRIC capacidad de ordeño *f*

mill[1] *n* MINE chimenea de mineral *f* (*AmL*), pozo vertedero *m*, taller de preparación mecánica *m*, P&R molino *m*, PAPER fábrica *f*, PROD *crushing, grinding machine* quebrantadora *f*, machacadora *f*, molino *m*, trituradora *f*, *stamp-milling machine* molino de pisones *m*; ~ **course** *n* WATER caz *m*, saetín *m*; ~ **gearing** *n* MECH ENG engranaje de fresadoras *m*; ~ **hammer** *n* AGRIC molino de martillo *m*; ~ **hole** *n* MINE chimenea de mineral *f* (*AmL*), coladero *m* (*Esp*), pozo de comunicación *m* (*AmL*), pozo vertedero *m*; ~ **race** *n* WATER caz *m*, saetín *m*; ~ **result** *n* PROD rendimiento del bocarte *m*; ~ **run** *n* PROD capacidad de un molino *f*; ~ **scale** *n* PROD batiduras de laminado *f pl*, cascarilla de laminación *f*; ~ **tail** *n* WATER caz *m*, saetín *m*

mill[2] *vt* COAL desmenuzar, moler, molturar, MECH fresar, moletear, PROD bocartear, fresar, laminar, recantear, *to knurl* moletear

millboard *n* PACK, PAPER cartón gris *m*

milled: ~ **head** *n* MECH ENG cabeza fresada *f*, cabeza moleteada *f*; ~ **knob** *n* MECH ENG botón estriado *m*; ~ **nut** *n* MECH ENG tuerca cerillada *f*, tuerca estriada *f*, tuerca rayada *f*; ~ **ore** *n* MINE mineral bocarteado *m*

miller *n* AGRIC, FOOD, MECH, MECH ENG, PROD, SAFE fresadora *f*

Miller: ~ **bridge** *n* ELEC *of circuit* puente Miller *m*; ~ **indices** *n pl* CRYSTALL, METALL índices de Miller *m*

millerayes *n* TEXTIL milrayas *m*

millerite *n* MINERAL millerita *f*

millet *n* AGRIC mijo *m*

milliammeter *n* ELEC, ELEC ENG, INSTR miliámetro *m*, miliamperímetro *m*

milliampere *n* (*mA*) ELEC, ELEC ENG, PHYS miliamperio *m* (*mA*)

millicron *n* METR milicrón *m*

milligram *AmE see* **milligramme** *BrE*

milligramme *n* BrE METR miligramo *m* (*mg*)

Millikan: ~ **conductor** *n* ELEC *cable* conductor Millikan *m*

Millikan's: ~ **experiment** *n* PHYS experimento de Millikan *m*

millimeter *AmE see* **millimetre** *BrE*

millimetre *n* BrE METR milímetro *m* (*mm*); ~ **wave** *n* BrE PHYS onda milimétrica *f*; **~-wave amplification** *n* BrE ELECTRON, TELECOM, WAVE PHYS amplificación de onda milimétrica *f*; **~-wave amplifier** *n* BrE ELECTRON, TELECOM, WAVE PHYS amplificador de onda milimétrica *m*; **~-wave magnetron** *n* BrE ELECTRON, WAVE PHYS magnetrón de onda milimétrica *m*; **~-wave source** *n* BrE ELECTRON, WAVE PHYS fuente de onda milimétrica *f*; **~-wave travelling-wave tube** *n* BrE ELECTRON, WAVE PHYS tubo de onda

de propagación milimétrica *m*, tubo de propagación de ondas milimétricas *m*; **~-wave tube** *n BrE* ELECTRON, WAVE PHYS tubo de onda milimétrica *m*; **~-wavelength emission** *n BrE* RAD PHYS emisión de ondas con longitud *f*, emisión de ondas milimétricas *f*
millimetric *adj* ELECTRON milimétrico
milling *n* AGRIC, CHEM molienda *f*, CHEM TECH fresado *m*, molienda *f*, COAL molienda *f*, molturación *f*, FOOD industria harinera *f*, molienda *f*, MINE bocarteo *m* (*AmL*), fresado *m* (*Esp*), molturación *f* (*AmL*), PROD fresado *m*, knurling moleteado *m*, TEXTIL batanado *m*, enfurtido *m*; **out-~** *n* MECH ENG fresado exterior *m*; **~ attachment** *n* MECH ENG *machine tools* accesorio para fresar *m*; **~ ball** *n* CHEM TECH molino de bolas *m* (*Esp*), triturador de bolas *m* (*AmL*); **~ by-products** *n pl* AGRIC subproductos de molienda *m pl*; **~ cutter** *n* MECH ENG cortador rotatorio de metales *m*, fresa *f*; **~ cutter with inserted teeth** *n* MECH ENG fresa con dientes insertados *f*; **~-cutter sharpening machine** *n* PROD afiladora de fresas *f*; **~ cutter with spiral teeth** *n* MECH ENG fresa de dientes en espiral *f*; **~ cutter with straight teeth** *n* MECH ENG fresa con dientes rectos *f*; **~ cutting arbor** *n* MECH ENG eje de fresa *m*; **~ file** *n* PROD lima-fresa *f*; **~ head** *n* MECH ENG cabezal para fresar *m*; **~ industry** *n* FOOD industria harinera *f*, molienda *f*; **~ jig** *n* MECH ENG plantilla de fresado *f*, útil para fresar *m*; **~ liquid** *n* CHEM TECH líquido de fresado *m*; **~ machine** *n* MECH fresa *f*, fresadora *f*, MECH ENG fresadora *f*, PROD, SAFE fresa *f*, fresadora *f*; **~-machine arbor** *n* MECH ENG husillo de fresadora *m*, PROD eje de la fresadora *m*, eje portafresas *m*, mandril portafresas *m*, portafresas de una máquina fresadora *m*; **~-machine cutter arbor** *n* PROD eje portafresas *m*, eje portafresas de una fresadora *m*, mandril portafresas *m*; **~ tool** *n* PROD *knurling tool* fresa portamoleta *f*, herramienta de fresado *f*; **~ waste** *n* AGRIC desperdicios de molienda *m pl*
millions: **~ of cubic feet per day** *n pl* (*MCFD*) PETR TECH millones de pies de gás cúbicos por día *m pl*; **~ of instructions per second** *n pl* (*MIPS*) COMP&DP, PRINT millones de instrucciones por segundo *m pl* (*MIPS*)
millisecond *n* (*ms*) COMP&DP milisegundo *m* (*ms*); **~ delay cap** *n* MINE cebo con retardo de milisegundo *m*; **~ delay detonator** *n* MINE cebo desfasado en milisegundos *m*
millivolt *n* (*mV*) ELEC *unit of potential*, ELEC ENG milivoltio *m* (*mV*)
millivoltmeter *n* ELEC, INSTR milivoltímetro *m*
milliwatt *n* (*mW*) ELEC *unit of power*, ELEC ENG milivatio *m* (*mW*)
milliwattmeter *n* ELEC, ELEC ENG, INSTR milivatímetro *m*
millstone *n* FOOD muela de molino *f*; **~ grit** *n* GEOL arenisca silícea *f*, griota *f*, piedra moleña *f*, MINERAL, PROD piedra moleña *f*
milo: **~ grain** *n* AGRIC grano de sorgo *m*
MIMD *abbr* (*multiple-instruction, multiple-data*) COMP&DP flujo de instrucciones múltiple-flujo de datos múltiple *m*
mimetene *n* MINERAL mimetesita *f*
mimetite *n* MINERAL mimetesita *f*, plomo verde *m*
mimic: **~ board** *n* ELEC cuadro de esquema *m*
mince *vt* FOOD picar
minced: **~ grass** *n* AGRIC pasto picado *m*

mincer *n* FOOD picador *m*
mine[1] *n* MILIT mina *f*, MINE mina subterránea *f*, mina terrestre *f*, mineral *m*; **~ car** *n* COAL, MINE vagoneta *f*, TRANSP vagón minero *m*; **~ chamber** *n* MINE hornillo de mina *m*; **~ detector** *n* MILIT detector de minas *m*; **~ development** *n* MINE reconocimiento de la mina *m*, trazado de la mina *m*; **~ entrance** *n* MINE bocamina *f*; **~ fan** *n* MINE ventilador de mina *m*; **~ hoist** *n* MINE torno de extracción *m*; **~ level** *n* MINE galería de mina *f*; **~ opening** *n* MINE trabajo preparatorio *m*, vía minera *f*; **~ pumping** *n* MINE bombeo de agotamiento *m*; **~ resistance** *n* MINE resistencia de la mina a la corriente de aire *f*; **~ run** *n* MINE producto todo uno *m*; **~ shaft** *n* MINE pozo de mina *m*; **~ stone** *n* MINE mineral *m*; **~ surveying compass** *n* MINE brújula de mina *f*, brújula de minero *f*; **~ timber** *n* MINE madera para apeas *f*, madera para minas *f*; **~ tin** *n* MINE estaño de roca *m*, estaño nativo *m*; **~ truck** *n* MINE vagoneta *f*, vagón de mina *m*; **~ yield** *n* COAL producción *f*
mine[2] *vt* MINE explotar, extraer
mine[3] *vi* MINE hacer trabajos de mina, volar, minar
mineability *n* MINE explotabilidad *f*, minabilidad *f*
mineable *adj* MINE explotable, minable
mined[1] *adj* MILIT minado
mined[2]: **~-out area** *n* MINE zona no minada *f*
minefield *n* MILIT campo de minas *m*
minelayer *n* MILIT, WATER TRANSP buque minador *m*, minador *m*, sembrador de minas *m*
minelaying *n* MILIT, WATER TRANSP fondeo de minas *m*; **~ ship** *n* MILIT, WATER TRANSP buque minador *m*
miner *n* AGRIC insecto minador *m*, COAL, MINE minero *m*, máquina para abrir galerías *f*, máquina rafadora de carbón *f*
mineral[1] *adj* CHEM, COAL, GEOL, MINERAL mineral; **~-matter-free** *adj* POLL exento de materia mineral, libre de materia mineral, sin materia mineral
mineral[2] *n* CHEM mineral *m*, COAL carbón mineral *m*, mineral *m*, MINERAL mineral *m*; **~ analysis** *n* CHEM, METALL, MINERAL, PETROL análisis mineral *m*; **~ assemblage** *n* GEOL asociación mineral *f*, asociación mineralógica *f*; **~ caoutchouc** *n* MINERAL caucho mineral *m*; **~ chemistry** *n* CHEM *inorganic*, MINERAL química mineral *f*; **~ coal** *n* COAL carbón mineral *m*; **~ color** *AmE*, **~ colour** *BrE n* COLOUR colorante mineral *m*; **~ deficiency** *n* AGRIC carencia de minerales *f*; **~ deposit** *n* MINE criadero mineral *m* (*AmL*), depósito de mineral *m*, yacimiento *m* (*Esp*), yacimiento mineral *m*; **~ fiber** *AmE*, **~ fibre** *BrE n* HEAT ENG fibra mineral *f*; **~-insulated cable** *n* ELEC, ELEC ENG cable aislado de minerales *m*, cable con aislamiento de material mineral *m*; **~ insulation** *n* ELEC *of cable conductor*, ELEC ENG aislamiento de minerales *m*; **~ isochrone** *n* GEOL isocrona mineral *f*; **~ jelly** *n* CHEM, PETR TECH, PETROL petrolato *m*, vaselina ® *f*; **~ naphtha** *n* COAL petróleo *m*; **~ oil** *n* AUTO, COAL aceite mineral *m*, petróleo *m*, MINERAL aceite mineral *m*, P&R aceite mineral *m*, petróleo *m*; **~ pigment** *n* COLOUR pigmento mineral *m*; **~ pitch** *n* CONST brea *f*; **~ processing** *n* COAL, MINERAL explotación de minerales *f*; **~ rights** *n pl* PETR TECH derechos para explotar yacimientos minerales *m pl*; **~ soil** *n* COAL, MINERAL terreno mineral *m*; **~ spring** *n* WATER manantial de agua mineral *m*; **~ tallow** *n* MINERAL cera mineral *f*, sebo mineral *m*; **~ water** *n* FOOD agua mineral *f*, GEOL agua juvenil *f*, HYDROL

agua mineral *f*, WATER agua juvenil *f*, agua mineral *f*;
~ **wool** *n* HEAT ENG, REFRIG lana mineral *f*
mineralization *n* CHEM, GEOL, MINERAL mineraliza-
ción *f*
mineralizer *n* CHEM, GEOL, MINERAL mineralizador *m*
mineralizing *adj* CHEM, GEOL, MINERAL mineralizante
mineralogic *AmE see mineralogical BrE*
mineralogical *adj BrE* GEOL, MINERAL mineralógico
mineralogist *n* GEOL, MINERAL, PETR TECH mineralo-
gista *m*
mineralogy *n* MINERAL, PETR TECH mineralogía *f*
minerogenic *adj* COAL minerogenético
minerogenous *adj* COAL minerógeno
miners': ~ **bar** *n* MINE barra de mina *f* (*AmL*), barra de
percusión *f*
minestuff *n* MINE ganga *f*
minesweeper *n* MILIT, WATER TRANSP barreminas *m*,
buque dragaminas *m*, dragaminas *m*
minesweeping *n* MILIT, WATER TRANSP dragado de
minas *m*, rastreo de minas *m*
mini *n* COMP&DP mini *m*; ~-**bundle cable** *n* OPT cable en
minihaz *m*
miniature *n* CINEMAT miniatura *f*; ~-**aircraft index** *n*
AIR TRANSP índice de aviones en miniatura *m*; ~ **ball
bearing** *n* MECH ENG microcojinete de bolas *m*;
~ **binoculars** *n pl* INSTR binoculares miniatura *m pl*;
~ **bottle** *n* C&G botella perfumera *f*; ~ **camera** *n*
INSTR, PHOTO cámara miniatura *f*; ~ **chemical-agent
detector** *n* MILIT microdetector de agentes químicos
m; ~ **circuit breaker** *n* ELEC, ELEC ENG interruptor
automático miniatura *m*, microdisyuntor *m*; ~ **film** *n*
PHOTO película miniatura *f*; ~ **film cassette** *n* INSTR
casette miniatura de película *f*; ~ **magnetron** *n* ELEC-
TRON magnetrón de pequeño tamaño *m*; ~ **maker** *n*
CINEMAT miniaturista *m*; ~ **relay** *n* ELEC ENG micro-
relé *m*; ~ **screw thread** *n* MECH ENG rosca de tornillo
en miniatura *f*; ~ **traveling-wave tube** *AmE*, ~ **travelling-wave tube** *n BrE* ELECTRON microtubo de
propagación de ondas *m*
miniaturization *n* COMP&DP miniaturización *f*
minicam *n* TV cámara miniatura *f*
minicomputer *n* COMP&DP minicomputadora *f* (*AmL*),
miniordenador *m* (*Esp*)
minimal: ~ **submanifolds** *n pl* GEOM submúltiples
mínimos *m pl*, subvariedades mínimas *f pl*;
~ **surface** *n* GEOM superficie mínima *f*
minimum: ~-**access programming** *n* COMP&DP programación de acceso mínimo *f*; ~ **calibrated speed** *n*
AIR TRANSP *during normal stall* velocidad calibrada
mínima *f*; ~ **circuit breaker** *n* ELEC ENG interruptor
de mínima *m*; ~ **consumption** *n* HYDROL consumo
mínimo *m*; ~ **control speed during landing
approach** *n* AIR TRANSP velocidad mínima de control
durante aproximación al aterrizaje *f*; ~ **control
speed in the air** *n* AIR TRANSP velocidad de control
mínima en el aire *f*; ~ **control speed on the ground** *n*
AIR TRANSP velocidad de control mínima en tierra *f*;
~ **current relay** *n* ELEC relé de mínima *m*, relé de
mínimo de corriente *m*; ~ **daily runoff** *n* HYDROL
escurrimiento mínimo diario *m*; ~ **demonstrated
threshold speed** *n* AIR TRANSP velocidad de umbral
demostrada mínima *f*; ~ **descent altitude** *n* AIR
TRANSP altitud de descenso mínima *f*; ~ **descent
height** *n* AIR TRANSP altura de descenso mínima *f*;
~ **detectable signal** *n* ELECTRON señal detectable
mínima *f*; ~ **deviation** *n* PHYS desviación mínima *f*;

~-**dressed width of warp** *n* TEXTIL anchura mínima
de urdimbre encolada *f*; ~ **energy level** *n* PART PHYS
estado fundamental *m*, situación de mínima energía
f; ~ **error-free pad** *n* (*MEFP*) TELECOM línea artificial mínima sin errores *f*; ~ **focusing distance** *n*
CINEMAT distancia mínima de enfoque *f*; ~ **glide
path** *n* AIR TRANSP trayectoria de planeo mínima *f*;
~ **hourly runoff** *n* HYDROL escurrimiento mínimo por
hora *m*; ~ **irradiation** *n* RAD PHYS irradiación mínima
f; ~ **low water** *n* WATER estiaje mínimo *m*; ~ **payable**
n TELECOM mínimo cotizable *m*; ~-**power relay** *n*
ELEC relé de mínima *m*, relé de mínimo de potencia
m; ~ **rate** *n* TELECOM tasa mínima *f*; ~ **safe altitude** *n*
AIR TRANSP altitud de seguridad mínima *f*; ~-**shift
keying** *n* (*MSK*) ELECTRON teclado de desplazamiento mínimo *m* (*TDM*), TELECOM manipulación
por desplazamiento número *f*; ~ **signal** *n* ELECTRON
señal mínima *f*; ~ **stress** *n* METALL esfuerzo mínimo
m; ~ **takeoff safety speed** *n* AIR TRANSP velocidad
mínima de seguridad de despegue *f*; ~ **theoretical
thickness** *n* WATER TRANSP *of hull* espesor mínimo
teórico *m*; ~ **tillage** *n* AGRIC laboreo mínimo *m*;
~ **unstick speed** *n* AIR TRANSP velocidad de despegue
mínima *f*; ~ **voltage** *n* ELEC mínimo de tensión *m*,
tensión mínima *f*; ~ **weather conditions** *n pl* AIR
TRANSP condiciones atmosféricas mínimas *f pl*;
~ **weight** *n* PACK peso mínimo *m*; ~ **welding
current** *n* CONST corriente mínima de soldadura *f*
mining *n* COAL, HYDROL minería *f*, MINE colocación de
minas *f* (*AmL*), explotación de minas *f* (*Esp*),
industria minera *f*, laboreo de minas *m*, minería *f*,
zapa *f*; ~ **appliance** *n* MINE accesorio de minas *m*
(*Esp*), material de minas *m* (*AmL*); ~ **area** *n* MINE
distrito minero *m*, dominio minero *m*, pertenencia
minera *f*, zona minera *f*, área minera *f*; ~ **bucket** *n*
MINE jaula de extracción *f*, vagoneta *f*; ~ **claim** *n*
MINE concesión minera *f* (*AmL*), pertenencia minera
f (*Esp*); ~ **concession** *n* MINE concesión minera *f*;
~ **cradle** *n* MINE *ore dressing* criba lavadora *f*;
~ **engineer** *n* MINE ingeniero minero *m*;
~ **engineering** *n* MINE ingeniería minera *f*, tecnología
minera *f*; ~ **hole** *n* MINE hornillo de mina *m* (*AmL*),
perforación de producción *f* (*Esp*); ~ **machine** *n*
MINE máquina de arranque *f* (*AmL*), máquina de
mina *f* (*Esp*); ~ **timber** *n* MINE madera para ademas *f*
(*AmL*), madera para apeas *f*, madera para entibas *f*
(*Esp*), madera para minas *f*
minisubmersible *n* OCEAN escúter submarino *m*, mini-
submarino *m*, minitractor submarino individual *m*
minium *n* CHEM, MINERAL minio *m*, tetróxido de
plomo *m*, óxido de plomo rojo *m*
minivan *n* TRANSP mini-furgoneta *f*
Minkowski: ~ **space** *n* PHYS espacio de Minkowski *m*
minor: ~ **alarm** *n* TELECOM alarma menor *f*; ~ **arc** *n*
GEOM *memory* arco menor *m*; ~ **axis** *n* GEOM *of an
ellipse* eje menor *m*; ~ **base check** *n* AIR TRANSP
servicio menor de base *m*; ~ **check** *n* AIR TRANSP
revisión menor *f*; ~ **diameter** *n* MECH ENG diámetro
menor *m*; ~ **diameter error** *n* METR error de diámetro
menor *m*; ~ **elements** *n pl* AGRIC microelementos *m
pl*; ~ **and major servicing operations** *n pl* AIR
TRANSP operaciones de servicio mayores y menores
f pl; ~ **planet** *n* SPACE asteroide *m*; ~ **repairs** *n pl*
PROD, RAIL reparaciones pequeñas *f pl*; ~ **road** *n*
CONST carretera secundaria *f*; ~ **second** *n* ACOUST
segunda menor *f*; ~ **semitone** *n* ACOUST semitono

menor *m*; ~ **seventh** *n* ACOUST séptima menor *f*; ~ **sixth** *n* ACOUST sexta menor *f*; ~ **third** *n* ACOUST tercera menor *f*; ~ **watershed** *n* AGRIC cuenca hidrográfica menor *f*; ~ **whole tone** *n* ACOUST tono completo menor *m*

minority: ~ **carrier** *n* ELECTRON portador minoritario *m*, PHYS portadora secundaria *f*

minus: ~ **acceleration** *n* MECH, MECH ENG aceleración negativa *f*; ~ **correction** *n* PRINT corrección menor *f*; ~ **sight** *n* CONST *surveying* visual de frente *f*; ~ **tapping** *n* ELEC bifurcación negativa *f*, derivación negativa *f*, toma negativa *f*; ~ **terminal** *n* AUTO terminal negativo *m*

minute *n* CONST, METR, PHYS minuto *m*; ~ **examination** *n* PROD examen minucioso *m*; ~ **hand** *n* METR *of clock, watch* manecilla minutera *f*

miogeosyncline *n* GEOL miogeosinclinal *m*

mionite *n* MINERAL mionita *f*

MIPS *abbr* (*millions of instructions per second*) COMP&DP, PRINT MIPS (*millones de instrucciones por segundo*)

mirabilite *n* MINERAL mirabilita *f*

mirbane *n* CHEM mirbano *m*

mirror *n* PHYS, VEH espejo *m*; **~-coated lamp** *n* PHOTO lámpara con recubrimiento especular *f*; ~ **condenser lamp** *n* CINEMAT lámpara condensadora con recubrimiento especular *f*; ~ **configuration** *n* NUCL configuración especular *f*; ~ **electron microscope** *n* INSTR microscopio electrónico especular *m*; ~ **finish** *n* MECH, MECH ENG, PROD acabado a espejo *m*, acabado especular *m*; ~ **galvanometer** *n* ELEC, ELEC ENG, INSTR galvanómetro de espejo *m*; ~ **image** *n* CHEM *of molecule*, CINEMAT imagen especular *f*; ~ **lens** *n* PHOTO catadrióptico *m*, lente de espejos *f*; **~-making** *n* C&G fabricación de espejos *f*; ~ **nucleus** *n* PHYS núcleo espejo *m*; ~ **nuclides** *n pl* PHYS núclidos espejo *m pl*; ~ **plane** *n* CRYSTALL *of symmetry* plano de reflexión *m*, plano de simetría *m*; **~-plating** *n* C&G plateado de espejos *m*; ~ **shot** *n* CINEMAT toma especular *f*; ~ **shutter** *n* CINEMAT, PHOTO obturador de espejo *m*

MIS[1] *abbr* (*management information system*) COMP&DP, TELECOM SIG (*sistema integrado de administración*)

MIS[2]: ~ **transistor** *n* (*multipoint indication secondary-status transistor*) ELECTRON transistor de PSID *m* (*transistor de posición secundaria con indicación diversa*)

misalignment *n* MECH ENG defecto de alineación *m*, defecto de alineamiento *m*, desalineación *f*, desalineamiento *m*, mal alineamiento *m*, mala alineación *f*, PRINT desalineación *f*; ~ **loss** *n* OPT, TELECOM pérdida por desalineación *f*

miscibility: ~ **gap** *n* METALL cadencia de miscibilidad *f*, intervalo de miscibilidad *m*

miscible[1] *adj* CHEM, PETR TECH mezclable, miscible

miscible[2]: ~ **substance** *n* POLL substancia miscible *f*

MISD *abbr* (*multiple-instruction single-data*) COMP&DP MISD (*multiflujo de instrucciones monoflujo de datos*)

misfire *n* ELEC ENG descebado *m*, fallo de encendido *m*, MINE bocazo *m* (*Esp*), fallo en el tiro *m* (*AmL*)

misfit *n* CRYSTALL *defect* desajuste *m*, METALL desajuste *m*, desequilibrio *m*

mismatch *n* ELEC ENG desajuste *m*, MECH ENG desadaptación *f*, desajuste *m*, desarreglo *m*, falta de adaptación *f*, inadaptación *f*, mal acoplamiento *m*,

mala colocación *f*, VEH *engine* fallo de encendido *m*; ~ **factor** *n* ELEC ENG coeficiente de pérdidas por reflexión *m*

mismatched[1] *adj* PHYS desajustado

mismatched[2]: ~ **camera** *n* TV cámara desacoplada *f*; ~ **seams** *n pl* TEXTIL costuras no casadas *f pl*

mispickel *n* MINERAL mispíquel *m*

misplaced: ~ **size** *n* COAL tamaño mal clasificado *m*

misprint *n* PRINT errata *f*

misregistration *n* PRINT falta de registro *f*, TV registro defectuoso *m*

missed: **~-approach procedure** *n* AIR TRANSP procedimiento de aproximación abortada *m*, procedimiento de aproximación frustrada *m*

missile *n* MILIT misil *m*, proyectil *m*; ~ **cradle** *n* MILIT cuna del misil *f*

missing: ~ **cap detector** *n* PACK detector de la falta de cápsula *m*; ~ **dots** *n pl* PAPER, PRINT puntos faltantes *m pl*; ~ **pill equipment** *n* PACK equipo para detectar si faltan píldoras en los envases *m*

missorting *n* MECH ENG mala clasificación *f*

mist[1] *n* METEO bruma *f*, neblina *f*, niebla *f*, PETR TECH mezcla de agua y aire *f*, neblina *f*, vapor *m*, POLL bruma *f*, neblina *f*, REFRIG niebla *f*; ~ **blower** *n* AGRIC atomizador *m*; ~ **propagation** *n* AGRIC multiplicación con niebla artificial *f*; ~ **sprayer** *n* AGRIC nebulizador *m*

mist[2] *vi* POLL lloviznar, nebulizar

misting *n* PRINT nube de tinta *f*

mite *n* AGRIC ácaro *m*

miter *AmE see* mitre *BrE*

mitigation *n* MAR POLL mitigación *f*

mitre *n BrE* C&G, CONST inglete *m*, PRINT bisel *m*, inglete *m*; ~ **bevel** *n BrE* C&G biselado a inglete *m*; ~ **bevel both sides** *n BrE* C&G biselado por ambos lados *m*; ~ **board** *n BrE* CONST tablero a inglete *m*; ~ **box** *n BrE* CONST caja a inglete *f*; ~ **cutting machine** *n BrE* CONST cortadora de inglete *f*; ~ **fence** *n BrE* CONST *of saw bench* protección de inglete *f*; ~ **gear** *n BrE* CONST engranaje de inglete *m*; ~ **grinding machine** *n BrE* C&G máquina esmeriladora de ingletes *f*; ~ **joint** *n BrE* CONST junta a inglete *f*; ~ **machine** *n BrE* CONST máquina de inglete *f*; ~ **post** *n BrE* WATER *of lock gate* batiente *m*, batiente de puerta *m*, busco *m*; ~ **sill** *n BrE* WATER batiente *m*, batiente de puerta *m*, busco *m*; ~ **square** *n BrE* CONST falsa escuadra *f*

MIV *abbr* (*multipoint indication visualization*) TELECOM visualización de indicación para varios puntos *f*

mix[1] *n* C&G, FOOD, P&R mezcla *f*; **~-and-dispense storage system** *n* PACK PROD sistema de almacenado, mezcla y distribución *m*; ~ **design** *n* CONST selección de la dosificación *f*; ~ **dissolve** *n* TV mezcla de desvanecido de imagen *f*; **~-in-place** *n* CONST *civil engineering* mezcla en el lugar *f*, mezcla en la obra *f*; ~ **proportion** *n* CONST proporción de la mezcla *f*

mix[2] *vt* CHEM *substances* mezclar, CONST *mortar* amasar, mezclar, TV mezclar

mixed: ~ **adhesive** *n* PACK mezcla de adhesivos *f*; ~ **average sample** *n* HYDROL promedio de muestreo mixto *m*; **~-base notation** *n* COMP&DP notación de base mixta *f*; **~-batch store** *n* C&G almacén de mezclas *m*; ~ **boards** *n pl* PAPER *sorted wastepaper* mezcla de papeles clasificados *f*, *unsorted wastepaper* mezcla de papeles sin clasificar *f*; ~ **cargo ship** *n* WATER TRANSP buque de carga mixta *m*;

~ **dislocation** *n* CRYSTALL, METALL dislocación mixta *f*; ~ **farming** *n* AGRIC explotación mixta *f*; ~ **feed** *n* AGRIC pienso compuesto *m*; ~**-flow fan** *n* REFRIG ventilador centrífugo helicoidal *m*; ~**-flow pump** *n* MECH ENG, MINE bomba de flujo mixto *f*; ~**-flow turbine** *n* HYDRAUL turbina mixta *f*; ~ **forest** *n* AGRIC bosque mixto *m*; ~ **gage track** *AmE see mixed gauge track BrE*; ~ **gas** *n* GAS gas mezclado *m*; ~ **gauge track** *n BrE* RAIL, TRANSP vía de anchura mixta *f*; ~ **grazing** *n* AGRIC pastoreo mixto *m*; ~ **levitation** *n* PHYS, TRANSP levitación mixta *f*; ~ **light** *n* PHOTO luz combinada *f*, luz mixta *f*; ~ **light-coloured printer shavings** *n pl* PAPER *wastepaper* blanco 2ª con pasta mecánica *m*; ~ **liquor** *n* WATER licor mezclado *m*; ~**-logic board** *n* ELECTRON placa de lógica mixta *f*; ~ **magazines** *n pl* PAPER *wastepaper* papeles e impresos leídos *m pl*; ~ **papers** *n pl* PAPER papeles e impresos leídos *m pl*, *sorted wastepaper* mezcla de papeles clasificados *f*, *unsorted wastepaper* mezcla de papeles sin clasificar *f*; ~ **path** *n* SPACE rumbo mixto *m*, trayectoria mixta *f*; ~ **power supply** *n* TRANSP alimentación mixta *f*; ~ **process** *n* ELECTRON proceso mixto *m*; ~ **radiation** *n* RAD PHYS radiación mixta *f*; ~**-radix notation** *n* COMP&DP notación de base mixta *f*; ~ **refrigerant cascade** *n* REFRIG cascada integrada *f*; ~ **sewage and waste water treatment** *n* WATER tratamiento mixto de aguas negras y residuales *m*; ~ **strawboard** *n* PAPER cartón de paja mixto *m*; ~ **strawpaper** *n* PAPER papel de paja mixto *m*; ~ **syncs** *n pl* TV mezcla de sincronismos *f* (*AmL*), sincronismos mixtos *m pl* (*Esp*); ~ **technology** *n* ELECTRON tecnología mixta *f*; ~ **terrain** *n* TELECOM terreno mixto *m*; ~ **tide** *n* OCEAN marea mixta *f*; ~ **white shavings** *n pl* PAPER blanco 1ª bis *m*

mixer *n* C&G *batch plant operator* mezclador *m*, CHEM TECH amasadora *f*, mezcladora *f*, CINEMAT mezclador *m*, COAL difusor *m*, mezclador *m*, hormigonera *f*, CONST hormigonera *f*, mezcladora *f*, ELECTRON mezclador *m*, MECH ENG, P&R mezclador *m*, mezcladora *f*, PHYS mezclador *m*, SPACE *communications* mezcladora *f*, difusor *m*, TV mezclador *m*; ~**-amplifier** *n* TV amplificador-mezclador *m*; ~ **bellcrank** *n* AIR TRANSP *of helicopter* palanca acodada del mezclador *f*; ~ **diode** *n* ELECTRON diodo mezclador *m*; ~**-preamplifier** *n* ELECTRON preamplificador mezclador *m*; ~ **rod** *n* AIR TRANSP *of helicopter* varilla del mezclador *f*; ~ **stage** *n* ELECTRON etapa mezcladora *f*; ~ **truck** *n* CONST camión hormigonera *m*, concretera *f* (*AmL*); ~ **tube** *n* ELECTRON tubo mezclador *m*, MECH ENG tubo mezclador *m*, válvula mezcladora *f*

mixing *n* ACOUST mezcla *f*, mezcla de sonidos *f*, C&G amasado *m*, CHEM TECH amasado *m*, mezclado *m*, CONST mezclado *m*, FOOD amasado *m*, PETR TECH mezcla *f*, PROD mezcla *f*, mezcladura *f*; ~ **amplifier** *n* ELECTRON amplificador de mezcla *m*; ~**-and-blending equipment** *n* PACK equipo de mezcla y combinación *m*; ~ **basin** *n* HYDROL depósito mezclador *m*, WATER pileta de mezcla *f*; ~ **box** *n* C&G caja de mezclas *f*; ~ **chamber** *n* AUTO, GAS, VEH cámara de mezcla *f*, cámara de mezclado *f*; ~ **chest** *n* PAPER tina de mezcla *f*; ~ **cylinder** *n* PROD cilindro mezclador *m*; ~ **desk** *n* TV mesa mezcladora *f*; ~ **mill** *n* CHEM TECH amasadora de cilindros *f*, PROD molino mezclador *m*, trituradora mezcladora *f*; ~ **pan mill** *n* CHEM TECH

amasadora de platos *f*, mezcladora de platos *f*; ~ **plant** *n* PROD instalación mezcladora *f*; ~ **propeller** *n* CHEM TECH hélice mezcladora *f*; ~ **pump** *n* PAPER bomba mezcladora *f*; ~ **rate** *n* CONST proporción de la mezcla *f*; ~ **room** *n* C&G casa de mezclas *f*; ~ **sieve** *n* CHEM TECH manga de mezclado *f*; ~ **tank** *n* CHEM TECH, CINEMAT tanque de mezclado *m*, tanque de mezclar *m*; ~ **technique** *n* CHEM TECH técnica de mezclado *f*; ~ **time** *n* CONST, PETROL tiempo de mezcla *m*, tiempo de mezclado *m*; ~ **transistor** *n* ELECTRON transistor de mezcla *m*; ~ **trough** *n* C&G mezclado *m*; ~ **unit** *n* AIR TRANSP *of helicopter*, CHEM TECH, PROD unidad del mezclador *f*; ~ **vessel** *n* CHEM TECH cuba de mezclado *f*

mixture *n* CHEM, FOOD, PETR TECH mezcla *f*, mixtura *f*; ~ **composition** *n* SPACE composición de la mezcla *f*; ~ **control** *n* AIR TRANSP *of engine* control de mezcla *m*; ~ **ratio** *n* AUTO proporción de la mezcla *f*

MIZ *abbr* (*multiple indication zero communication*) TELECOM comunicación nula de indicación para varios puntos *f*

mizzen *n* WATER TRANSP *sail, mast* cangreja *f*, cangrejo *m*; ~ **mast** *n* WATER TRANSP palo de mesana *m*, palo mayor *m*; ~ **sail** *n* WATER TRANSP *mast* cangreja *f*, cangrejo *m*

mizzonite *n* MINERAL mizzonita *f*

MKSA: ~ **system** *n* (*meter/kilogram/second/ampere system AmE, metre/kilogram/second/ampere system BrE*) METR sistema MKSA *m* (*sistema metro/kilogramo/segundo/amperio*)

MLM *abbr* (*multilongitudinal modes*) TELECOM modos multilongitudinales *m pl*

MLS *abbr* (*microwave landing system*) AIR TRANSP MLS (*sistema de aterrizaje de microondas*)

mm *abbr* (*millimeter AmE, millimetre BrE*) METR mm (*milímetro*)

mmf *abbr* (*magnetomotive force*) ELEC, PHYS fmm (*fuerza magnetomotriz*)

MMI *abbr* (*man-machine interaction*) COMP&DP MMI (*interacción hombre-máquina*)

MMIC *abbr* (*monolithic microwave integrated circuit*) PHYS CMIM (*circuito monolítico integrado de microondas*)

Mn *abbr* (*manganese*) C&G, CHEM, MECH, METALL Mn (*manganeso*)

mnemonic *adj* COMP&DP *code, symbol* nemónico

m-o: ~ **disc** *BrE* (*magneto-optical disc*), ~ **disk** *AmE n* (*magneto-optical disk*) OPT disco m-o *m* (*disco magnetoóptico*)

MO *abbr* (*master oscillator*) TELECOM oscilador maestro *m*

Mo *abbr* (*molybdenum*) AGRIC, CHEM, METALL Mo (*molibdeno*)

mobile: ~ **aeronautical station** *n* SPACE estación aeronáutica móvil *f*; ~ **belt** *n* GEOL cinturón móvil *m*; ~ **camera** *n* TV cámara móvil *f*; ~ **component** *n* POLL componente móvil *m*, elemento móvil *m*; ~ **control unit** *n* CINEMAT, TV unidad de control móvil *f*; ~ **crane** *n* CONST grúa móvil *f*; ~ **crusher** *n* COAL trituradora móvil *f*; ~ **data-processing terminal equipment** *n* TELECOM equipo terminal móvil de procesamiento de datos *m*; ~ **fire-extinguisher** *n* SAFE extintor de incendios móvil *m*; ~ **hose reel** *n* SAFE carrete de manguera móvil *m*; ~ **installation** *n* TELECOM instalación móvil *f*; ~ **land station** *n* SPACE estación terrestre móvil *f*; ~ **location registration** *n*

TELECOM registro de localizaciones móviles *m*; ~ **logging unit** *n* GAS unidad móvil de registro *f*; ~ **maritime station** *n* SPACE estación marítima móvil *f*; ~ **mounting** *n* INSTR montaje móvil *m*; ~ **radio cell** *n* TELECOM radio móvil celular *f*; ~ **radio station** *n* TELECOM emisora de radio móvil *f*, estación de radio móvil *f*, estación de radiocomunicación móvil *f*, estación móvil radioeléctrica *f* (*AmL*), radioemisora de servicio móvil *f*, radioestación móvil *f*; ~ **satellite communications** *n* WATER TRANSP servicio móvil de comunicaciones por satélite *m*; ~ **satellite service** *n* SPACE *communications* servicio de satélite móvil *m*; ~ **station** *n* (*MS*) PRINT, SPACE, TELECOM estación móvil *f* (*MS*); ~ **switching center** *n AmE*, ~ **switching centre** *n BrE* (*MSC*) TELECOM centro de conmutación móvil *m*; ~ **telephone service** *n* TELECOM servicio móvil telefónico *m*; **~-to-base relay** *n* TELECOM estación repetidora para enlace móvil-base *f*; ~ **unit** *n* CINEMAT, MILIT unidad móvil *f*

mobility *n* CHEM *ionic*, PETROL, PHYS movilidad *f*; ~ **ratio** *n* PETROL relación de movilidad *f*

Möbius: ~ **strip** *n* GEOM *text* banda de Moebius *f*, banda de Möbius *f*

MOC *abbr* (*managed object class*) TELECOM clase de objetos controlados *f*

mock[1] *adj* TEXTIL falso

mock[2]: ~ **cake** *n* TEXTIL corona para tintura *f*; **~-up** *n* PRINT maqueta del libro *f*, PROD maqueta *f*, modelo *m*, SPACE maqueta *f*, modelo *m*, patrón *m*, simulador *m*, WATER TRANSP *boat design* maqueta *f*

modacrylic *adj* TEXTIL modacrílico

modal: ~ **dispersion** *n* OPT dispersión modal *f*; ~ **distortion** *n* TELECOM distorsión modal *f*; ~ **noise** *n* OPT, TELECOM ruido modal *m*; ~ **note** *n* ACOUST nota modal *f*

mode *n* ACOUST, COMP&DP modo *m*, ELECTRON función *f*, GEOL *process* composición mineralógica *f*, PROD modo *m*, método *m*; ~ **change** *n* COMP&DP cambio de modo *m*; ~ **coupling** *n* OPT, TELECOM acoplamiento de modos *m*; ~ **distortion** *n* TELECOM distorsión de modos *f*; ~ **field diameter** *n* OPT, TELECOM diámetro de campo de modos *m*; ~ **filter** *n* ELECTRON filtro de función *m*, filtro de modos *m*, OPT, TELECOM filtro de modos *m*; ~ **hopping** *n* OPT, TELECOM inestabilidad de modos *f*, salto de modos *m*; ~ **jump** *n* ELECTRON interrupción de función *f*; ~ **jumping** *n* OPT, TELECOM inestabilidad de oscilación *f*, salto de modos *m*; **~-locked laser** *n* ELECTRON láser de función estabilizada *m*; ~ **locking** *n* ELECTRON fijación de función *f*; ~ **mixer** *n* OPT, TELECOM mezclador de modos *m*, perturbador *m*; ~ **of operation** *n* TELECOM modalidad de explotación *f*, modalidad de funcionamiento *f*, modalidad de utilización *f*, modo de funcionamiento *m*, modo de utilización *m*; ~ **scrambler** *n* OPT distorsionador de modos *m*, TELECOM codificador de modos *m*, dispositivo de transmisión secreta de modos *m*; ~ **selector switch** *n* AIR TRANSP interruptor selector de modo *m*; ~ **separation** *n* ELECTRON separación de función *f*; **~-setting knob** *n* PROD conmutador selector de modo *m*; ~ **stripper** *n* ELECTRON, OPT, TELECOM separador de modos *m*; ~ **volume** *n* OPT, TELECOM volumen de modos *m*

model *n* COMP&DP, SPACE, TELECOM, WATER TRANSP *naval architecture* modelo *m*; ~ **builder** *n* CINEMAT maquetista *m*; ~ **calibration** *n* POLL modelo de calibración *m*, patrón de calibración *m*, patrón de comprobación *m*, patrón de verificación *m*; ~ **railroad** *n AmE* (*cf model railway BrE*) RAIL ferrocarril modelo *m*; ~ **railway** *n BrE* (*cf model railroad AmE*) RAIL ferrocarril modelo *m*; ~ **set** *n* CINEMAT maqueta *f*; ~ **shot** *n* CINEMAT toma con maquetas *f*; ~ **test** *n* WATER TRANSP *naval architecture* ensayo con modelos *m*, ensayo con un modelo *m*

modeling *AmE see modelling BrE*

modelling *n BrE* COMP&DP modelado *m*, modelismo *m*, GEOL modelado *m*, PROD modelación *f*, modelado *m*, QUALITY modelado *m*; ~ **clay** *n BrE* C&G arcilla de modelar *f*, PROD arcilla de modelar *f*, arcilla plástica *f*; ~ **light** *n BrE* CINEMAT, PHOTO, TV iluminación de realce *f*

modem *n* (*modulator-demodulator*) COMP&DP, ELECTRON, PRINT, TELECOM módem *m* (*modulador-demodulador*); ~ **board** *n* ELECTRON cuadro de modem *m*; ~ **interchange** *n* COMP&DP, TELECOM intercambio por modem *m*; ~ **interface** *n* COMP&DP interfaz de modem *m*, ELECTRON separador de módem *m*, TELECOM interfaz de modem *m*; ~ **interfacing** *n* ELECTRON separación de módem *f*; ~ **link** *n* PROD enlace mediante modem *m*; ~ **receiver** *n* ELECTRON receptor de modem *m*; ~ **transmitter** *n* ELECTRON transmisor de modem *m*

moderate: ~ **gale** *n* METEO, WATER TRANSP ventarrón moderado *m*, viento fresco *m*; ~ **weather** *n* METEO, WATER TRANSP tiempo bonancible *m*; ~ **wind** *n* METEO ventarrón moderado *m*, viento fresco *m*

moderator *n* ELECTRON, PHYS, RAD PHYS moderador *m*

modern: ~ **construction** *n* CONST edificación moderna *f*; ~ **face** *n* PRINT estilo moderno *m*; ~ **figures** *n pl* PRINT números estilo moderno *m*

modification: ~ **indicator** *n* TELECOM indicador de modificaciones *m*; ~ **kit** *n* PROD lote de modificación *m*; ~ **proposal** *n* PROD propuesta de modificación *f*

modified: ~ **cotton system** *n* TEXTIL sistema de algodón modificado *m*; ~ **frequency modulation** *n* (*MFM*) ELECTRON modulación de frecuencia modificada *f* (*MFM*); ~ **starch** *n* FOOD almidón modificado *m*; ~ **system** *n* TEXTIL sistema modificado *m*

modifier *n* COAL modificador *m*

modify *vt* COMP&DP, ELECTRON, GEOM modificar

moding *n* ELECTRON gama de funciones *f*, gama de modos *f*

modular[1] *adj* GEN modular

modular[2]: ~ **arithmetic** *n* COMP&DP, MATH aritmética modular *f*; ~ **gaging system** *AmE*, ~ **gauging system** *BrE* *n* METR sistema de calibrado modular *m*; ~ **labeling system** *AmE*, ~ **labelling system** *BrE* *n* PACK sistema de etiquetado modular *m*, sistema de rotulado modular *m*; ~ **machine tool construction** *n* MECH ENG construcción de máquinas *f*; ~ **programming** *n* COMP&DP programación modular *f*; ~ **surface cleaner** *n* PACK limpiador de superficie modular *m*; ~ **unit** *n* MECH ENG unidad modular *f*

modularity *n* COMP&DP, QUALITY modularidad *f*

modulate *vt* ELECTRON modular, variar, PHYS, TELECOM, TV modular

modulated: ~ **beam** *n* ELECTRON haz modulado *m*; ~ **carrier** *n* ELECTRON portador modulado *m*, TV portadora modulada *f*; ~ **continuous wave** *n* TV onda continua modulada *f*; ~ **groove** *n* ACOUST surco modulado *m*; ~ **oscillator** *n* ELECTRON oscilador modulado *m*; ~ **signal** *n* TELECOM señal modulada *f*; ~ **space** *n* ACOUST espacio modulado *m*; ~ **structure** *n* METALL estructura modulada *f*; ~ **wave** *n* ELECTRON onda modulada *f*

modulating: ~ **signal** *n* ELECTRON señal de modulación *f*; ~ **wave** *n* ELECTRON onda de modulación *f*, TV onda moduladora *f*

modulation *n* GEN modulación *f*; ~ **amplifier** *n* ELECTRON amplificador de modulación *m*; ~ **angle** *n* ACOUST ángulo de modulación *m*; ~ **band** *n* ELECTRON banda de modulación *f*; ~ **depth** *n* ELECTRON, PHYS amplitud de modulación *f*, profundidad de modulación *f*; ~ **electrode** *n* TV electrodo de modulación *m*; ~ **factor** *n* ELECTRON, PHYS factor de modulación *m*; ~ **frequency** *n* ELEC *alternating current*, ELECTRON, TELECOM *broadcasting* frecuencia de modulación *f*; ~ **grid** *n* TV grilla de modulación *f* (*AmL*), rejilla de modulación *f* (*Esp*); ~ **index** *n* ELECTRON índice de modulación *m*; ~ **level** *n* WAVE PHYS nivel de modulación *m*; ~ **noise** *n* ACOUST ruido de modulación *m*, ELECTRON perturbación de modulación *f*, ruido de modulación *m*, TELECOM ruido de modulación *m*, TV ruido modulado *m* (*AmL*), ruido producido por la señal *m* (*Esp*); ~ **transfer function** *n* ELECTRON función de propagación de modulación *f*; ~ **wave** *n* ELECTRON onda de modulación *f*

modulator *n* COMP&DP, ELECTRON, TELECOM, TV modulador *m*; ~ **-demodulator** *n* (*modem*) COMP&DP, TELECOM modulador-demodulador *m* (*módem*); ~ **diode** *n* ELECTRON diodo modulador *m*; ~ **driver** *n* ELECTRON preamplificador de modulación *m*; ~ **logic board** *n* PROD tablero lógico de modulador *m*

module *n* COMP&DP módulo *m*, ELEC *equipment* dispositivo modular *m*, elemento modular *m*, unidad de construcción modular *f*, módulo *m*, ELECTRON, HYDRAUL módulo *m*, MECH ENG *gearing* módulo *m*, unidad de construcción modular *f*, PETR TECH módulo *m*, PROD unidad de construcción modular *f*, SPACE módulo *m*; ~ **extraction pad** *n* PROD panel de extracción modular *m*; ~ **group** *n* PROD grupo modular *m*; ~ **set** *n* ELECTRON unidad modular *f*

modulus *n* MATH, PETROL, PHYS módulo *m*; ~ **of compression** *n* WATER TRANSP *GRP construction* coeficiente de compresión *m*; ~ **of elasticity** *n* AIR TRANSP, COAL, CONST, MECH, MECH ENG, METALL, P&R, PETR TECH, PHYS, WATER TRANSP *GRP construction* coeficiente de elasticidad *m*, módulo de Young *m*, módulo de elasticidad *m*; ~ **of elongation** *n* P&R coeficiente de alargamiento *m*, módulo de alargamiento *m*, módulo de elongación *m*; ~ **of rigidity** *n* PHYS módulo de rigidez *m*

modus: ~ **operandi** *n* PROD modo de funcionar *m*, modus operandi *m*

mofette *n* FUELLESS *hot spring* mofeta *f*

Moho: ~ **discontinuity** *n* GEOL discontinuidad de Moho *f*

Mohorovicic: ~ **discontinuity** *n* GEOL discontinuidad de Moho *f*

Mohr: ~**'s clips** *n pl* LAB pinzas de Mohr *f pl* (*Esp*), presillas de Mohr *f pl* (*AmL*)

moiety *n* CHEM *of molecule* parte de una molécula *f*

moiré: ~ **effect** *n* TV efecto muaré *m*; ~ **pattern** *n* ACOUST diagrama muaré *m*

Moiré: ~ **fringes** *n pl* PHYS franjas de Moiré *f pl*

moist: ~ **corn** *n* AmE AGRIC, ~ **maize** *n* BrE maíz húmedo *m*

moisten *vt* CHEM humectar, FOOD humedecer, MAR POLL, MECH ENG humectar, PHYS humedecer, REFRIG humidificar, THERMO embeber, humectar, humedecer, humidificar, impregnar, mojar

moistened *adj* THERMO impregnado de caucho

moistening *n* CHEM humectación *f*, THERMO impregnación *f*; ~ **device** *n* PACK mecanismo de humidificación *m*; ~ **equipment** *n* PACK equipo de humidificación *m*

moisture[1]: ~**-proof** *adj* PACK protegido frente a la humedad; ~**-repellent** *adj* PACK repelente de la humedad; ~**-resistant** *adj* PACK resistente a la humedad; ~**-retaining** *adj* AGRIC, CHEM hidrófilo

moisture[2] *n* CHEM humedad *f*; ~**-absorbent bag** *n* PACK bolsa que contiene un producto absorbente de la humedad *f*; ~ **absorber** *n* CONST deshumificador *m*; ~**-and-temperature detector** *n* TRANSP termómetro-higrómetro *m*; ~ **content** *n* AGRIC contenido de agua *m*, CHEM contenido de humedad *m*, COAL contenido de humedad *m*, humedad específica *f*, porcentaje de humedad *m*, CONST, FOOD contenido de humedad *m*, PACK contenido de humedad *m*, contenido húmedo *m*, PAPER, PHYS contenido de humedad *m*, REFRIG contenido de agua *m*, contenido de humedad *m*, TEXTIL contenido de humedad *m*, WATER contenido de humedad *m*, estado higrométrico *m*; ~ **deficiency** *n* AGRIC carencia de humedad *f*; ~ **detector** *n* PROD hidoscopio *m*, hidróscopo *m*; ~ **determination** *n* PACK determinación de la humedad *f*; ~ **expansion** *n* PAPER aumento de volumen debido a la humedad *m*; ~ **index** *n* METEO índice de humedad *m*; ~ **regain** *n* TEXTIL tasa legal de humedad *f*; ~ **separator-reheaters** *n* NUCL separadores de humedad-recalentadores *m pl*; ~**-set ink** *n* COLOUR tinta de fraguado al vapor *f*; ~ **test** *n* PACK medida de humedad *f*; ~ **transfer** *n* REFRIG, TEXTIL transferencia de humedad *f*

mol *abbr* (*mole*) CHEM *of element, compound*, METR, PHYS, WATER mol *f*

MOL *abbr* (*manned orbiting laboratory*) SPACE MOL (*laboratorio orbital tripulado*)

molal *adj* CHEM molal

molality *n* CHEM *of solution* molalidad *f*

molar[1] *adj* CHEM molar

molar[2]: ~ **gas constant** *n* PHYS constante molar de los gases *f*; ~ **heat capacity** *n* PHYS capacidad calórica molar *f*; ~ **internal energy** *n* PHYS energía interna molar *f*; ~ **volume** *n* PHYS volumen molar *m*

molarity *n* CHEM molaridad *f*

mold *AmE see* **mould** *BrE*

moldboard *AmE see* **mouldboard** *BrE*

molded *AmE see* **moulded** *BrE*

molder *AmE see* **moulder** *BrE*

molding *AmE see* **moulding** *BrE*

mole *n* (*mol*) CHEM *of element, compound* mol *f*, CONST dique rompeolas *m*, malecón *m*, muelle *m*, terraplén *m* (*Esp*), METR mol *f*, OCEAN malecón *m*, terraplén *m*, PHYS mol *f*, WATER dique rompeolas *m*, malecón *m*, mol *f*, terraplén *m*, WATER TRANSP malecón *m* (*AmL*), terraplén *m*; ~ **drainage** *n* CONST drenaje topero *m*; ~ **fraction** *n* CHEM, METALL fracción molecular *f*, REFRIG fracción molar *f*; ~ **head** *n* OCEAN morro de malecón *m*; ~ **plough** *n* BrE AGRIC arado topo de drenaje *m*; ~ **plow** *AmE see* **mole plough** *BrE*; ~ **titer** *AmE*, ~ **titre** *BrE n* REFRIG título molar *m*

molecular: ~**-beam epitaxy** *n* (*MBE*) ELECTRON, RAD PHYS epitaxia por haz molecular *f*; ~ **conductivity** *n*

THERMO conductividad molecular *f*; ~ **depression of freezing point** *n* THERMO depresión molecular del punto de congelamiento *f*; ~ **electronics** *n* ELECTRON electrónica molecular *f*; ~ **elevation of boiling point** *n* THERMO elevación molecular del punto de ebullición *f*; ~ **field** *n* PHYS campo molecular *m*; ~ **gas laser** *n* ELECTRON, GAS láser de gas molecular *m*; ~ **heat** *n* THERMO calor molecular *m*; ~ **laser** *n* ELECTRON láser molecular *m*; ~ **orbital** *n* CHEM *of atoms*, PHYS, RAD PHYS orbital molecular *m*; ~ **pump** *n* PHYS bomba molecular *f*; ~ **refractivity** *n* PHYS refractividad molecular *f*; ~ **sieve** *n* CHEM criba molecular *f*, malla molecular *f*; ~ **spectroanalysis** *n* RAD PHYS espectroanálisis molecular *m*; ~ **spectrum** *n* RAD PHYS espectro molecular *m*; ~ **vibrational energy level** *n* RAD PHYS nivel de energía vibracional de la molécula *m*; ~ **weight** *n* PETR TECH peso molecular *m*

molecule *n* GEN molécula *f*; ~ **beam** *n* TELECOM haz molecular *m*

molleton *n* TEXTIL muletón *m*

mollusc: ~ **detacher** *n* OCEAN rasqueta de mariscador *f*; ~ **detaching** *n* OCEAN despegamiento de molusco *m*; ~ **harvesting** *n* OCEAN marisqueo *m*, recolección de mariscos *f*

molten[1] *adj* C&G, MECH, THERMO fundido

molten[2]: ~ **core** *n* SPACE núcleo fundido *m*, núcleo licuado *m*; ~ **glass** *n* C&G vidrio fundido *m*; ~ **materials** *n pl* SAFE materiales fundidos *m pl*; ~ **metal** *n* METALL, SAFE metal fundido *m*; ~-**metal splash** *n* SAFE salpicadura de metal fundido *f*; ~ **pool** *n* PROD *welding* baño de fusión *m*

molybdate *n* CHEM molibdato *m*

molybdenite *n* MINERAL molibdenita *f*

molybdenum *n* (*Mo*) AGRIC, CHEM, METALL molibdeno *m* (*Mo*)

molybdic: ~ **ocher** *AmE*, ~ **ochre** *BrE* *n* MINERAL molibdita *f*, ocre de molibdeno *m*

molybdite *n* MINERAL molibdita *f*

molysite *n* MINERAL molysita *f*

moment *n* CONST momento *m*, MECH momento *m*, momento de par *m*, MECH ENG *tendency* momento *m*, par *m*, torque *m*, PHYS momento *m*; ~ **about an axis** *n* PHYS momento alrededor de un eje *m*; ~ **arm** *n* MECH ENG brazo del momento *m*; ~ **coefficient** *n* MECH ENG coeficiente del momento *m*; ~ **of inertia** *n* CONST, PHYS, WATER TRANSP *naval architecture* momento de inercia *m*

momentaneous: ~ **capacity** *n* TRANSP capacidad momentánea *f*

momentary: ~ **action** *n* ELEC ENG acción momentánea *f*; ~ **action switch** *n* ELEC ENG interruptor de proceso momentáneo *m*; ~-**close push-button** *n* PROD pulsador de cierre momentáneo *m*; ~-**contact push-button** *n* PROD pulsador de contacto momentáneo *m*; ~-**contact switch** *n* ELEC, ELEC ENG, PROD interruptor de contacto momentáneo *m*; ~-**overload protection** *n* ELEC, PROD protección contra sobrecarga momentánea *f*; ~ **push-key** *n* PROD tecla-pulsadora momentánea *f*

momentum *n* MECH, MECH ENG cantidad de movimiento *f*, impulsión *f*, impulso *m*, velocidad adquirida *f*, ímpetu *m*, PHYS momento lineal *m*, velocidad adquirida *f*, ímpetu *m*; ~ **wheel** *n* SPACE rueda de inercia *f*, volante de inercia *m*

monadic[1] *adj* COMP&DP monádico

monadic[2]: ~ **operation** *n* COMP&DP operación monádica *f*

monatomic: ~ **gas** *n* CHEM, GAS, PHYS gas monoatómico *m*

monaural *adj* ACOUST monoaural, monoauricular

monazite *n* MINERAL monazita *f*

monheimite *n* MINERAL monheimita *f*

monitor[1] *n* COMP&DP monitor *m*, ELEC *instrument* dispositivo monitor *m*, equipo de control *m*, monitor *m*, INSTR detector *m*, regulador *m*, monitor *m*, PROD *capstan head* torre revólver *f*, portaherramientas revólver *m*, RAD PHYS, TELECOM, TV monitor *m*; ~ **lathe** *n* PROD torno con cabezal revólver *m*; ~ **record** *n* PETROL registro monitor *m*; ~ **unit** *n* CINEMAT, COMP&DP unidad monitora *f*, TELECOM aparato monitor *m*, unidad monitora *f*, TV unidad monitora *f*

monitor[2] *vt* CINEMAT controlar el sonido de, regular, COMP&DP monitorear (*AmL*), supervisar, MAR POLL vigilar, PROD comprobar, contrastar, observar, supervisar, verificar, vigilar, SPACE observar, contrastar, TEXTIL controlar

monitored: ~ **retrievable storage** *n* (*MRS*) NUCL almacenamiento vigilado con posibilidad de recuperación *m* (*AVR*)

monitoring[1] *n* ACOUST monitorado *m*, PROD contrastación *f*, escucha *f*, monitoreo *m*, observación *f*, regulación *f*, verificación *f*, vigilancia *f*, SPACE comprobación *f*, contrastación *f*, control *m*, observación *f*, regulación *f*, verificación *f*, vigilancia *f*, TELECOM monitorización *f*, TEXTIL control *m*, TV control *m*, monitoreo *m* (*AmL*); ~ **controller** *n* PROD controlador de comprobación *m*; ~ **loudspeaker** *n* ACOUST, CINEMAT altavoz de control *m*; ~ **satellite** *n* SPACE satélite de comprobación *m*, satélite de contrastación *m*; ~ **service** *n* TELECOM servicio de monitorización *m*; ~ **system** *n* RAD PHYS sistema de monitorización *m*, sistema de vigilancia *m*

monitoring[2] ~ **and maintenance** *phr* TELECOM monitorización *f*, supervisión y mantenimiento

monkey *n* CONST maza *f*; ~ **block** *n* PROD cuadernal giratorio *m*, motón giratorio *m*; ~ **board** *n* BrE (*cf footboard AmE*) PETR TECH encuelladero *m*, plataforma del encuellador *f*, tabla de piso *f*, zona de madera en la planchada del taladro *f*, PETROL plataforma astillero *f*, plataforma de la torre *f*; ~ **carriage** *n* PROD *of overhead travelling crane* carro de rodadura *m*; ~ **wrench** *n* MECH llave de tuercas *f*, MECH ENG llave de cremallera *f*, llave de tuercas *f*, llave inglesa *f*, llave inglesa de cremallera *f*, llave universal *f*, VEH llave de tuercas *f*, llave inglesa *f*

mono: ~ **crystalline silicon** *n* SPACE *craft* silicona monocristalina *f*; ~ **key** *n* TV llave de comprobación *f*

monoaccelerator: ~ **CRT** *n* ELECTRON tubo de rayos catódicos con monoacelerador *m*

monoacetin *n* CHEM monoacetina *f*

monoacid *n* CHEM monoácido *m*

monoacidic *adj* CHEM monoácido

monoalcoholic *adj* CHEM monoalcohólico

monoamide *n* CHEM monoamida *f*

monoamine *n* CHEM monoamina *f*

monoamino *adj* CHEM monoamino

monoatomic[1] *adj* CHEM monoatómico

monoatomic[2]: ~ **fluid** *n* GAS fluido monoatómico *m*

monoazo: ~ **dye** *n* COLOUR colorante monoazoico *m*, tinte monoazoico *m*

monobasic *adj* CHEM monobásico
monobath *n* CINEMAT monobaño *m*
monobeam: ~ **system** *n* TRANSP sistema de haz único *m*
monobloc: ~ **concrete sleeper** *n* BrE (*cf monobloc concrete tie AmE*) RAIL traviesa de hormigón *f*; ~ **concrete tie** *n* AmE (*cf monobloc concrete sleeper BrE*) RAIL traviesa de hormigón *f*
monochord *n* ACOUST monocordio *m*
monochromatic[1] *adj* CINEMAT, OPT, PHYS, PRINT monocromático
monochromatic[2]: ~ **lens** *n* INSTR, OPT lente monocromática *f*; ~ **light** *n* METALL aspecto monocromático *m*, WAVE PHYS luz monocromática *f*; ~ **radiation** *n* OPT, RAD PHYS, TELECOM radiación monocromática *f*
monochromator *n* OPT, PHYS, TELECOM monocromador *m*
monochrome[1] *adj* COMP&DP, PRINT monocromo
monochrome[2] *n* CINEMAT monocromo *m*, monocromía *f*; ~ **dyeing** *n* COLOUR teñido monocromo *m*; ~ **receiver** *n* TV receptor monocromo *m*; ~ **signal** *n* SPACE *communications* señal monocroma *f*
monocline *n* GEOL monoclinal *m*; ~ **fold** *n* PETROL pliegue monoclinal *m*
monoclinic[1] *adj* CHEM, CRYSTALL monoclínico
monoclinic[2]: ~ **system** *n* METALL sistema monoclínico *m*
monocoque[1] *adj* SPACE monocasco
monocoque[2]: ~ **structure** *n* SPACE estructura monocasco *f*
monocular: ~ **telescope** *n* INSTR telescopio monocular *m*
monoculture *n* AGRIC monocultivo *m*
monoecious *adj* AGRIC monoico
monoenergetic *adj* PHYS monoenergético
monoethylenic *adj* CHEM monoetilénico
monofilament *n* P&R monofilamento *m*; ~ **yarn** *n* TEXTIL monofilamento *m*
monogenetic *adj* GEOL monogenético
monohalogenated *adj* CHEM monohalogenado
monohydrate *n* CHEM monohidrato *m*
monohydrated *adj* CHEM monohidratado
monohydric *adj* CHEM monohídrico
monolayer *n* CHEM monocapa *f*, monoestrato *m*
monolithic: ~ **amplifier** *n* ELECTRON amplificador monolítico *m*; ~ **array** *n* ELECTRON conjunto monolítico *m*; ~ **filter** *n* ELECTRON, TELECOM filtro monolítico *m*; ~ **integrated circuit** *n* ELECTRON, TELECOM circuito integrado monolítico *m*; ~ **microwave integrated circuit** *n* (*MMIC*) PHYS circuito monolítico integrado de microondas *m* (*CMIM*)
monomer *n* CHEM, P&R, PETR TECH monómero *m*
monomeric *adj* CHEM, P&R, PETR TECH monomérico
monomial *n* MATH monomio *m*
monomict *adj* GEOL monomíctico
monomineralic *adj* GEOL, MINERAL monomicta, monomineralógico
monomode: ~ **fiber** AmE, ~ **fibre** BrE *n* OPT, TELECOM fibra monomodo *f*, fibra unimodo *f*; ~ **optical fiber** AmE, ~ **optical fibre** BrE *n* OPT, TELECOM fibra óptica monomodo *f*
monomolecular: ~ **layer** *n* CHEM capa monomolecular *f*; ~ **reaction** *n* CHEM reacción monomolecular *f*
monomotor: ~ **bogie** *n* BrE (*cf monomotor truck AmE*) AUTO carretilla con motor *f*; ~ **truck** *n* AmE

(*cf monomotor bogie BrE*) AUTO carretilla con motor *f*
monophase[1] *adj* ELEC *supply* de una sola fase, monofásico
monophase[2]: ~ **reaction** *n* METALL reacción monofásica *f*
monophonic: ~ **pick-up** *n* ACOUST captador monofónico *m*, fonocaptor monofónico *m*; ~ **recording** *n* ACOUST grabación monofónica *f*
monopolar[1] *adj* ELEC *supply* monopolar, unipolar
monopolar[2]: ~ **line** *n* ELEC, ELEC ENG *supply* línea monopolar *f*
monopole: ~ **aerial** *n* BrE (*cf monopole antenna AmE*) TELECOM antena monopolo *f*; ~ **antenna** *n* AmE (*cf monopole aerial BrE*) TELECOM antena monopolo *f*
monopropellant *n* CHEM monopropulsante *m*, monopropulsor *m*; ~ **thruster** *n* SPACE *craft* propulsor monopropelante *m*, propulsor monopropulsante *m*
monorail *n* CONST, MINE, RAIL, TRANSP monocarril *m*, monorraíl *m*; ~ **conveyor** *n* MINE, TRANSP transportador monocarril *m*, transportador monorraíl *m*; ~ **grab trolley** *n* TRANSP vagoneta sobre monocarril *f*
monosaccharide *n* CHEM monosacárido *m*
monosaccharoses *n pl* CHEM monosacarosas *f pl*
monosodium: ~ **glutamate** *n* (*MSG*) CHEM, FOOD glutamato monosódico *m*
monostable[1] *adj* COMP&DP, ELECTRON, PHYS monoestable
monostable[2] *n* ELECTRON, PHYS monoestable *m*; ~ **multivibrator** *n* ELECTRON multivibrador monoestable *m*
monostearin *n* CHEM monoestearina *f*
monosubstituted *adj* CHEM monosubstituido, monosustituido
monotron *n* ELECTRON monotrón *m*
monotropic *adj* METALL monotrópica
monovalence *n* CHEM monovalencia *f*
monovalency *n* CHEM monovalencia *f*
monovalent *adj* CHEM monovalente
monoxide *n* CHEM monóxido *m*
monsoon *n* METEO monzón *m*; ~ **circulation** *n* METEO circulación del monzón *f*; ~ **climate** *n* METEO clima del monzón *m*; ~ **rain** *n* METEO lluvia del monzón *f*
Monte: ~ **Carlo method** *n* COMP&DP método Montecarlo *m*
montebrasite *n* MINERAL montebrasita *f*
monticellite *n* MINERAL monticellita *f*
montmorillonite *n* COAL, MINERAL, PETR TECH montmorillonita *f*
monument *n* CONST *surveying* hito *m*, mojón *m*
monumenting *n* CONST *surveying* amojonamiento *m*, marcado *m*
monzonite *n* PETROL monzonita *f*
mood: ~ **lighting** *n* CINEMAT iluminación especial *f*
moon: ~ **pool** *n* PETR TECH moon pool *m*; ~ **segment** *n* SPACE *communications* segmento lunar *m*
Mooney: ~ **viscosity** *n* P&R, PHYS viscosidad de Mooney *f*
moonstone *n* MINERAL ortoclasa *f*, piedra de la luna *f*
moor *vt* MAR POLL amarrar, fondear, METEO fondear, WATER TRANSP amarrar, fondear
moored ~ **buoy** *n* WATER TRANS boya de amarre *f*
mooring *n* MAR POLL, PETR TECH amarre *m*, WATER TRANSP *equipment, line rope* amarre *m*, *of equipment, line, rope* amarradura *f*; ~ **berth** *n* WATER TRANSP fondeadero de amarre *m*, puerto de amarre *m*; ~ **bitt**

n WATER TRANSP bita de amarre *f*; ~ **bracket** *n* MAR
POLL, WATER TRANSP puntal de amarre *m*; ~ **buoy** *n*
MAR POLL, PETROL, WATER TRANSP *navigation* boya de
amarre *f*, boya de anclaje *f*, cuerpo muerto *m*;
~ **chain** *n* MAR POLL, WATER TRANSP cadena de
amarre *f*; ~ **cleat** *n* WATER TRANSP *boat-building,
deck fittings* cornamusa de amarre *f*; ~ **gear** *n* WATER
TRANSP *of ship* equipo de fondeo y amarre *m*;
~ **harness** *n* AIR TRANSP arnés de amarre *m*; ~ **lane**
n COAL amarra *f*; ~ **line** *n* WATER TRANSP estacha *f*,
estacha de amarre *f*; ~ **pile** *n* WATER TRANSP duque de
alba *m*; ~ **post** *n* WATER TRANSP muerto *m*; ~ **ring** *n*
AIR TRANSP anilla de amarre *f*; ~ **rope** *n* WATER
TRANSP cordaje de amarre *m*
mop[1]: ~ **board** *n* AmE (*cf skirting board* BrE) CONST
skirting rodapié de madera *m*; ~~**end brush** *n* PROD
for polishing pulidora de trapo *f*
mop[2]: ~ **up** *vt* AGRIC *forest* apagar
MOP *abbr* (*Maintenance Operation Protocol*) TELECOM
local area network Protocolo de Operación para
Mantenimiento *m*
moraine *n* COAL, GEOL morrena *f*
mordant *n* CHEM mordiente *m*; ~ **dyeing** *n* PHOTO
teñido con mordente *m*
more: ~ **bit** *n* TELECOM bit adicional *m*
morenosite *n* MINERAL morenosita *f*
morin *n* CHEM morina *f*
morindin *n* CHEM morindina *f*
morion *n* MINERAL morión *m*
morning: ~ **glory** *n* AGRIC enredadera de campanillas *f*
morphine *n* CHEM morfina *f*
morpholine *n* CHEM, DETERG morfolina *f*
morphometric *adj* GEOL *circuits* morfométrico
morphotropic *adj* CHEM morfotrópico
morphotropism *n* CHEM morfotropismo *m*
morphotropy *n* CHEM morfotropía *f*
Morse: ~ **taper** *n* MECH ENG cono Morse *m*; ~ **taper
center** *AmE*, ~ **taper centre** *BrE n* MECH ENG punto
de cono Morse *m*; ~ **taper pin** *n* MECH ENG pasador
para cono Morse *m*; ~ **taper shank** *n* MECH ENG
espiga de cono Morse *f*; ~ **taper shank drill** *n* MECH
ENG broca con espiga de cono Morse *f*; ~ **taper
shank twist drill** *n* MECH ENG broca salomónica con
espiga de cono Morse *f*
mortar *n* CHEM, CHEM TECH argamasa *f*, mortero *m*,
CONST *mixture of plaster, lime, sand, cement* argamasa
f, *mixture of lime, sand, water* mortero *m*, LAB, MILIT,
PROD *of stamp mill* mortero *m*; ~ **bed** *n* CONST, PROD
of stamp mill fundación del mortero *f*, lecho de
mortero *m*; ~ **block** *n* PROD *stamp mill* bloque de
fundación del mortero *m*; ~ **box** *n* PROD *of stamp mill*
mortero *m*; ~ **mill** *n* PROD quebrantadora de mortero
f; ~ **mixer** *n* CONST amasadora *f*
mortise[1] *n* CONST mortaja *f*, PRINT muesca *f*, PROD *of
tackle block* mortaja *f*; ~~**and-tenon heel joint** *n*
CONST junta embutida de mortaja y espiga *f*; ~~**and-
tenon joint** *n* CONST junta de mortaja y espiga *f*;
~ **block** *n* MECH ENG, PROD polea de mortaja *f*;
~~**boring bit** *n* CONST barrena de perforación de
mortaja *f*; ~ **chisel** *n* CONST *for mortising machine*
formón de mortaja *m*; ~ **gage** *AmE*, ~ **gauge** *BrE n*
CONST gramil de mortaja *m*; ~ **joint** *n* CONST junta de
mortaja *f*; ~ **lock** *n* CONST cerradura embutida *f*;
~ **wheel** *n* PROD *with inserted wooden clogs* rueda con
dentadura postiza de madera *f*
mortise[2] *vt* PRINT escoplear

mortising *n* CONST cajeado *m*; ~~**and-boring machine**
n PROD máquina de mortajar y taladrar *f*; ~ **machine**
n CONST cajeadora *f*, MECH ENG mortajadora *f*, PROD
cajeadora *f*, escopleadora *f*, mortajadora *f*;
~ **machine with oscillating tool action** *n* MECH
ENG mortajadora con acción de herramienta oscilante *f*
mortuary *n* REFRIG depósito de cadáveres *m*
morvenite *n* MINERAL morvenita *f*
morvin *n* CHEM morvina *f*
MOS[1] *abbr* COMP&DP (*metal-oxide semiconductor*),
ELECTRON (*metallic oxide semiconductor*) SOM
(*semiconductor metal-óxido*)
MOS[2]: ~ **capacitor** *n* ELEC ENG condensador SOM *m*;
~ **delay line** *n* ELECTRON línea de retardo SOM *f*;
~ **driver** *n* ELECTRON preamplificador SOM *m*;
~ **gate** *n* ELECTRON circuito de SOM *m*; ~ **logic
circuit** *n* ELECTRON circuito lógico de SOM *m*;
~ **power transistor** *n* ELECTRON transistor de potencia SOM *m*; ~ **technology** *n* ELECTRON tecnología de
SOM *f*; ~ **transistor** *n* ELECTRON transistor SOM *m*,
transistor de semiconductor de óxido de metal *m*
mosaic *n* AGRIC *disease*, ELECTRON, FOOD mosaico *m*
mosandrite *n* MINERAL mosandrita *f*
Moseley's: ~ **law** *n* PHYS ley de Moseley *f*
mosquito: ~ **net** *n* TEXTIL mosquitera *f*; ~ **netting** *n*
TEXTIL confección de mosquiteras *f*
mosquitocide *n* CHEM culicida *m*, mosquitocida *m*
moss: ~ **agate** *n* C&G, MINERAL ágata musgosa *f*
Mössbauer: ~ **effect** *n* PHYS efecto Mösbauer *m*
most[1]: ~ **significant** *adj* COMP&DP más significativo
most[2]: ~ **significant bit** *n* (*MSB*) COMP&DP, PROD,
TELECOM bit de mayor significación *m* (*BMS*), bit
más significativo *m* (*BMS*); ~ **significant character**
n COMP&DP carácter más significativo *m*; ~ **significant digit** *n* (*MSD*) COMP&DP, MATH, PROD dígito
más significativo *m* (*DMS*)
moth *n* AGRIC polilla *f*
mother *n* ACOUST disco matriz *m*, maestro *m*, matriz *f*;
~ **crystal** *n* ELECTRON cristal madre *m*; ~ **liquor** *n*
FOOD licor madre *m*; ~ **lode** *n* MINE filón madre *m*;
~~**of-pearl bead** *n* C&G gota de madreperla *f*; ~~**of-
pearl culture** *n* OCEAN cultivo del nácar *m*; ~ **ship** *n*
SPACE, WATER TRANSP buque nodriza *m*
motherboard *n* COMP&DP, ELECTRON placa base *f*,
placa matriz *f*
motion *n* MECH desplazamiento *m*, marcha *f*, movimiento *m*, PHYS movimiento *m*; ~ **analysis** *n*
CINEMAT análisis de movimientos *m*; ~ **analysis
camera** *n* CINEMAT cámara para análisis de movimientos *f*; ~ **blur** *n* PHOTO imagen borrosa por
movimiento *f*; ~ **detector** *n* TRANSP tacómetro *m*;
~ **in a straight line** *n* MECH, MECH ENG, PHYS
movimiento en línea recta *m*, movimiento rectilíneo
m; ~ **indicator** *n* MECH ENG indicador de velocidad
m, tacómetro *m*; ~ **picture** *n* CINEMAT película
cinematográfica *f*; ~ **picture camera** *n* CINEMAT
cámara cinematográfica *f*; ~ **pictures** *n pl* CINEMAT
cine *m*; ~ **plate** *n* MECH ENG soporte de resbaladeras
m; ~ **unsharpness** *n* CINEMAT falta de nitidez debido
al movimiento *f*
motional *adj* ACOUST *impedance* cinética, mocional
MOTIS *abbr* (*Message-Oriented Text Interchange
Standard*) TELECOM sistema de intercambio de texto
orientado a mensajes *m*

motive: ~ **force** *n* WATER TRANSP *ship design* fuerza motriz *f*

motor[1]: ~-**driven** *adj* ELEC, ELEC ENG accionado por electromotor, MECH accionado por electromotor, accionado por motor, de propulsión mecánica, motorizado, MECH ENG, PROD accionado por motor

motor[2] *n* AUTO motor *m*, ELEC, ELEC ENG electromotor *m*, motor *m*, MECH *electrical machine* automóvil *m*, coche *m*, motor *m*, MECH ENG *of mechanical power* máquina *f*, motor de combustión *m*, automóvil *m*, motor *m*, auto *m*, coche *m*, electromotor *m*, SPACE motor *m*, máquina *f*; ~ **armature** *n* ELEC armadura del motor *f*; ~-**assisted bicycle** *n* AUTO, TRANSP bicicleta con motor *f*; ~-**body panels tooling** *n* MECH ENG herramientas del panel de la carrocería del automóvil *f pl*; ~ **bogie** *n* BrE (*cf motor truck AmE*) RAIL bogie motor *m* (*Esp*), boje motor *m* (*AmL*), carretón de motor *m*; ~ **branch circuit** *n* PROD circuito derivado de motor *m*; ~ **case** *n* SPACE caja del motor *f*, envoltura del motor *f*; ~ **control** *n* TV control de motor *m* (*AmL*), control por motor *m*; ~ **controller** *n* PROD controlador de motor *m*; ~ **converter** *n* ELEC ENG convertidor de electromotor *m*; ~ **cruiser** *n* TRANSP crucero a motor *m*; ~ **drive** *n* ELEC ENG, PHOTO accionamiento por motor *m*; ~-**drive mechanism** *n* ELEC mecanismo de accionamiento motorizado *m*; ~-**driven conveyor** *n* PROD transportador accionado por motor *m*; ~-**driven fan** *n* SAFE abanico movido por motor *m*; ~-**driven level** *n* INSTR cuadro de contactos motorizado *m*; ~-**driven system** *n* TELECOM sistema de accionamiento motorizado *m*, sistema de accionamiento por motor *m*; ~ **generator** *n* ELEC ENG motor generatriz *m*; ~-**generator set** *n* ELEC ENG, MECH ENG grupo convertidor *m*, grupo electrógeno *m*, grupo motor-generador *m*; ~ **grader** *n* CONST, TRANSP motoniveladora *f*, niveladora de motor *f*; ~ **home** *n* TRANSP carcasa del motor *f*; ~ **nameplate** *n* PROD placa de características del motor *f*; ~ **oil** *n* PETR TECH, VEH lubricante de motor *m*; ~ **phase current** *n* PROD corriente de fase del motor *f*; ~ **power loss** *n* PROD pérdida de potencia del motor *f*; ~-**propelled patrol boat** *n* MILIT buque patrullero impulsado por motor *m*; ~ **pump** *n* MAR POLL bomba motorizada *f*; ~ **rating** *n* PROD potencia del motor *f*; ~ **rewind** *n* CINEMAT rebobinado a motor *m*; ~ **sailer** *n* WATER TRANSP yate velero motorizado *m*; ~ **shaft** *n* MECH ENG *of machine tool* eje del motor *m*; ~ **ship** *n* WATER TRANSP motonave *f*; ~ **spirit** *n* PETR TECH gasolina para motores *f*; ~ **starter** *n* ELEC ENG reóstato de arranque del motor *m*; ~ **switching** *n* PROD interruptor del motor *m*; ~ **truck** *n* AmE (*cf motor bogie BrE*) RAIL bogie motor *m* (*Esp*), boje motor *m* (*AmL*), carretón de motor *m*; ~ **vessel** *n* WATER TRANSP motonave *f*; ~ **winding** *n* PROD devanado del motor *m*

motorboat *n* WATER TRANSP embarcación a moto *f*

motorboating *n* ELECTRON embarcación a motor *f*

motorcar *n* AUTO, VEH automóvil *m*, coche *m*; ~ **parts** *n pl* AUTO, VEH piezas de recambio del automóvil *f pl*, recambios del automóvil *m pl*

motorized: ~ **driving pulley** *n* MECH ENG polea conductora *f*, polea de tracción mecánica *f*, polea impulsora *f*, polea motorizada *f*, polea motriz *f*; ~ **unit** *n* MILIT unidad motorizada *f*; ~ **zoom lens** *n* CINEMAT, OPT objetivo zoom motorizado *m*

motorway *n* BrE (*cf freeway AmE, cf roadway AmE*) AUTO, CONST, TRANSP, VEH autopista *f*, calzada *f*, carretera *f*

mottled *adj* PRINT moteado

mottramite *n* MINERAL mottramita *f*

mould[1]: ~-**resistant** *adj* BrE PACK resistente a la acción de los mohos

mould[2] *n* BrE AGRIC moho *m*, MECH ENG molde *m*, P&R matriz *f*, molde *m*, PAPER forma *f*, PROD *founding* molde *m*, matriz *f*, WATER TRANSP *casting* moho *m*, molde de fundición *m*, *shipbuilding, wood, steel* molde *m*, gálibo *m*; ~ **blowing** *n* BrE C&G soplado con molde *m*; ~ **coating** *n* BrE C&G recubrimiento del molde *m*; ~ **dryer** *n* BrE PROD *founding* estufa de secar moldes *f*; ~-**emptier** *n* BrE C&G sacador de molde *m*; ~ **engraving** *n* BrE MECH ENG grabado con molde *m*; ~ **for casting** *n* BrE MECH ENG molde para fundición *m*; ~ **for food products** *n* BrE MECH ENG molde para productos alimenticios *m*; ~ **for glass-reinforced polyester** *n* BrE (*mould for GRP BrE*) MECH ENG molde para poliester reforzado con fibra de vidrio *m*; ~ **for glassware** *n* BrE MECH ENG molde para cristalería *m*; ~ **for GRP** *n* BrE (*mould for glass-reinforced polyester BrE*) MECH ENG molde para poliester reforzado con fibra de vidrio *m*; ~ **for mineral materials** *n* BrE MECH ENG *glass, ceramics, concrete* molde para materiales minerales *m*; ~ **for plastics** *n* BrE MECH ENG, P&R molde para plásticos *m*; ~ **for rubber** *n* BrE MECH ENG, P&R molde para caucho *m*; ~ **for structural foam** *n* BrE MECH ENG molde para espuma estructural *m*; ~ **for thermoplastics** *n* BrE MECH ENG, P&R molde para termoplásticos *m*; ~ **for thermoset plastics** *n* BrE MECH ENG, P&R molde para plásticos endurecidos *m*, molde para plásticos termofraguados *m*; ~ **holder** *n* BrE C&G, P&R soporte del molde *m*; ~ **loft** *n* BrE WATER TRANSP *shipbuilding* sala de gálibos *f*; ~ **maker** *n* BrE C&G moldero *m*; ~ **mark** *n* BrE C&G marca de molde *f*; ~ **oil** *n* BrE CONST aceite de encofrado *m*; ~ **plate** *n* BrE MECH ENG chapa para moldes *f*; ~ **shrinkage** *n* BrE P&R contracción en el molde *f*; ~ **texturing** *n* BrE MECH ENG textura del molde *f*

mould[3] *vt* BrE C&G *clay* moldear

mouldboard *n* BrE AGRIC vertedera *f*

moulded[1]: **not** ~ *adj* BrE C&G no moldeado

moulded[2]: ~ **board** *n* BrE PACK, PAPER cartón moldeado *m*; ~ **breadth** *n* BrE WATER TRANSP *ship design* manga de trazado *f*; ~ **casting** *n* BrE PROD pieza moldeada *f*; ~ **contact block** *n* BrE PROD bloque de contacto moldeado *m*; ~ **depth** *n* BrE WATER TRANSP *naval architecture* puntal de trazado *m*; ~ **displacement** *n* BrE WATER TRANSP *ship design* desplazamiento de trazado *m*; ~ **draught** *n* BrE WATER TRANSP *ship design* calado de trazado *m*; ~ **hose** *n* BrE P&R manguera moldeada *f*; ~ **plastic** *n* BrE P&R plástico moldeado *m*; ~ **printing plate** *n* BrE PRINT plancha de impresión de matriz *f*; ~ **pulp products** *n pl* BrE PAPER productos de celulosa moldeada *m pl*

moulder *n* BrE PROD *person* moldeador *m*

moulding *n* BrE ACOUST lengüeta *f*, moldeado *m*, pieza moldeada *f*, CONST *ornamental strip* moldura *f*, ELEC ENG cajetín *m*, cajetín de madera *m*, P&R moldeado *m*, moldeo *m*, PROD moldeo *m*, pieza moldeada *f*, WATER TRANSP *shipbuilding* galón *m*, moldeo *m*, verduguillo *m*; ~ **bench** *n* BrE PROD banco de moldear *m*, banco de moldeo *m*; ~ **box** *n* BrE PROD caja de moldear *f*; ~ **cycle** *n* BrE P&R ciclo de moldeado *m*, ciclo de moldeo *m*; ~ **flask** *n* BrE PROD caja de moldear *f*; ~ **floor** *n* BrE PROD taller de moldeo *m*; ~ **frame** *n* BrE WATER TRANSP *shipbuilding* bastidor de moldeo *m*, espiche *m*; ~ **hole** *n* BrE PROD foso de moldear *m*, foso de moldeo *m*, pozo de colada *m*; ~ **machine** *n* BrE CONST *woodworking* máquina de moldear *f*, PROD *founding* máquina de moldear *f*, máquina de moldurar *f*; ~ **powder** *n* BrE P&R polvos para moldeo *m pl*; ~ **sand** *n* BrE PROD arena de fundición *f*, arena de moldear *f*, arena de moldurar *f*; ~ **shop** *n* BrE PROD taller de moldeo *m*

mount[1] *n* CINEMAT montura *f*, montura del objetivo *f*, MECH ENG bancada *f*, soporte *m*, soporte elástico *m*, suspensión *f*, PHOTO montura *f*; ~ **of front element** *n* PHOTO montaje del elemento frontal *m*

mount[2] *vt* COMP&DP montar, ELECTRON, OCEAN instalar, montar, PROD armar, instalar, montar

mountain: ~ **breeze** *n* METEO brisa de montaña *f*; ~ **chain** *n* GEOL cadena de montañas *f*; ~ **climate** *n* METEO clima de montaña *m*; ~ **cork** *n* MINERAL corcho de montaña *m*, corcho fósil *m*; ~ **flesh** *n* MINERAL carne fósil *f*; ~ **leather** *n* MINERAL cuero de montaña *m*; ~ **mass** *n* COAL macizo *m*; ~ **railroad** *n* AmE (*cf mountain railway BrE*) RAIL ferrocarril de montaña *m*; ~ **railway** *n* BrE (*cf mountain railroad AmE*) RAIL ferrocarril de montaña *m*; ~ **road** *n* CONST carretera de montaña *f*; ~ **soap** *n* MINERAL jabón de montaña *m*, jabón mineral *m*; ~ **tallow** *n* MINERAL hatchetina *f*; ~ **and valley winds** *n pl* METEO vientos de montaña y de valle *m pl*; ~ **wood** *n* MINERAL madera de montaña *f*

mounted[1]: ~ **on frictionless bearings** *adj* MECH ENG montado sobre cojinetes sin rozamiento

mounted[2]: ~ **artillery** *n* MILIT artillería a caballo *f*; ~ **filter** *n* PHOTO filtro montado *m*

mounting *n* ELECTRON instalación *f*, montaje *m*, MECH ENG soporte *m*, PHOTO soporte *m*, montaje *m*, PROD *of equipment, machinery* instalación *f*, montaje *m*; ~ **base** *n* MECH ENG base de instalación *f*, base de montaje *f*; ~ **bath** *n* LAB *of a microscope* baño de montaje *m*; ~ **bezel** *n* PROD guía de montaje *f*; ~ **bolt** *n* MECH ENG tornillo de montaje *m*; ~ **bracket** *n* PHOTO soporte de montaje *m*, PROD consola para el montaje *f*; ~ **foot** *n* PHOTO pie de montaje *m*; ~ **hardware set** *n* PROD equipamiento de montaje *m*; ~ **layout** *n* PROD esquema de montaje *m*; ~ **pad** *n* MECH ENG asiento de montaje *m*; ~ **polarization** *n* ELEC ENG polarización de montaje *f*; ~ **rail** *n* PROD carril de montaje *m*

mourning: ~ **flag** *n* WATER TRANSP bandera de luto *f*

mouse *n* COMP&DP ratón *m*; ~ **hole** *n* ELEC ENG hueco ratón *f* (*Esp*), vaina *f* (*AmL*), FUELLESS *geothermal drilling equipment* ratonera *f*, PETR TECH hueco ratón *m* (*Esp*); ~ **software** *n* COMP&DP software de ratón *m*

mouth *n* ACOUST abertura *f*, boca *f*, CONST *of plane* boca *f*, *of rock-breaker* entrada *f*, HYDROL *of river* desembocadura *f*, MINE entrada *f*, agujero de colada *m*, desembocadura *f*, gola *f*, embocadura *f*, boca *f*, tragante *m*, PROD *of blast furnace* boca *f*, *taphole of furnace* agujero de colada *m*, *of converter* tragante *m*, WATER TRANSP *of river, strait* boca *f*, desembocadura *f*; ~ **blowing** *n* C&G soplado con la boca *m*; ~ **blown glass** *n* C&G vidrio soplado a mano *m*; ~ **tool** *n* C&G boquilla *f*

mouthpiece *n* TELECOM boca *f*

move: ~ **out correction** *n* GEOL corrección dinámica *f*; ~ **time** *n* PROD tiempo de desplazamiento *m*, tiempo de mantenimiento *m*, tiempo de transferencia *m*, tiempo de transporte *m*

moveable[1] *adj* AIR TRANSP, ELEC, MECH ENG, PROD, WATER TRANSP móvil

moveable[2]: ~ **bridge** *n* WATER TRANSP *locks, inland waterways* puente móvil *m*; ~ **contact** *n* ELEC, PROD contacto móvil *m*, cursor *m*; ~ **contact crossbar** *n* AIR TRANSP, PROD barra cruzada de contacto móvil *f*; ~ **core** *n* ELEC *of transformer* núcleo móvil *m*; ~ **rotor blade** *n* AIR TRANSP pala de rotor movible *f*; ~ **stop** *n* MECH ENG tope movible *m*, tope móvil *m*

movement *n* ACOUST, GAS movimiento *m*, MECH ENG acción *f*, circulación *f*, desplazamiento *m*, impulso *m*, marcha *f*, movimiento *m*, traslado *m*; ~ **file** *n* COMP&DP archivo de movimientos *m*, archivo de transacciones *m*, fichero de transacciones *m*

mover *n* MECH ENG *moving power* fuerza motriz *f*, motor *f*, máquina tractora *f*, móvil *m*

movie *n* CINEMAT película cinematográfica *f*; ~ **projector** *n* AmE (*cf cinema projector BrE*) CINEMAT, ELEC *lighting* proyector cinematográfico *m*, proyector de cine *m*

moving: ~ **armature** *n* ACOUST, ELEC armadura móvil *f*; ~ **background** *n* CINEMAT fondo móvil *m*; ~ **belt flat box** *n* PAPER caja plana de banda móvil *f*; ~ **carpet** *n* TRANSP alfombra móvil *f*; ~ **charge** *n* ELEC ENG carga de impulso *f*, carga móvil *f*; ~ **coil** *n* ELEC, ELEC ENG *of galvanometer* cuadro móvil *m*, bobina móvil *f*; ~ **coil ammeter** *n* ELEC, ELEC ENG amperímetro de cuadro móvil *m*; ~ **coil galvanometer** *n* ELEC, ELEC ENG, PHYS galvanómetro de bobina móvil *m*, galvanómetro de cuadro móvil *m*; ~ **coil meter** *n* ELEC, ELEC ENG medidor de núcleo móvil *m*; ~ **coil microphone** *n* ACOUST micrófono magnetodinámico *m*, PHYS micrófono de bobina móvil *m*; ~ **coil relay** *n* ELEC relé galvanométrico *m*; ~ **coil voltmeter** *n* ELEC, INSTR voltímetro de cuadro móvil *m*; ~ **contact** *n* ELEC ENG contacto móvil *m*; ~ **fiber switch** *AmE*, ~ **fibre switch** *BrE n* TELECOM conmutador móvil aislado con fibra *m*; ~ **floor** *n* TRANSP suelo móvil *m*; ~ **formwork** *n* CONST encofrado móvil *m*; ~ **grate** *n* HEAT rejilla móvil *f*; ~ **gripper** *n* NUCL *of control rod drive mechanism* trinquete móvil *m*; ~ **iron instrument** *n* ELEC, ELEC ENG aparato de hierro móvil *m*, INSTR instrumento de imán móvil *m*; ~ **iron meter** *n* ELEC, ELEC ENG medidor de hierro móvil *m*, medidor electromagnético *m*, INSTR medidor de imán móvil *m*; ~ **load** *n* CONST *live load* sobrecarga dinámica *f*, sobrecarga móvil *f*; ~ **magnet galvanometer** *n* ELEC, ELEC ENG, INSTR galvanómetro de imán móvil *m*; ~ **magnet instrument** *n* INSTR instrumento de imán móvil *m*; ~ **magnet medium** *n* ELEC ENG medio de imán móvil *m*; ~ **pavement** *n* BrE (*cf moving sidewalk AmE*) TRANSP acera móvil *f* (*Esp*), andén móvil *m*, pavimento móvil *m*, pavimento rodante *m*, vereda móvil *f* (*AmL*); ~ **platform** *n* BrE (*cf moving sidewalk AmE*) CONST acera para transporte *f* (*Esp*), plataforma móvil *f*, vereda para transporte *f* (*AmL*); ~ **saw** *n* SAFE sierra móvil *f*; ~ **sidewalk** *n* AmE (*cf passenger conveyor BrE*) AIR TRANSP cinta transportadora de pasajeros *f*, pasillo mecánico *m*, CONST (*cf moving platform BrE*) acera para transporte *f* (*Esp*), plata-

forma móvil *f*, vereda para transporte *f* (*AmL*), TRANSP (*cf moving pavement BrE*) acera móvil *f* (*Esp*), andén móvil *m*, pavimento móvil *m*, pavimento rodante *m*, vereda movíl *f* (*AmL*); **~ staircase** *n* BrE (*cf moving stairway AmE*) CONST, TRANSP escalera mecánica *f*, escalera móvil *f*; **~ stairway** *n* AmE (*moving staircase AmE*) CONST, TRANSP escalera móvil *f*, escalera mecánica *f*; **~ table** *n* C&G mesa móvil *f*; **~ traffic** *n* TRANSP tráfico en movimiento *m*
mow *vt* AGRIC cortar
mower *n* AGRIC segador *m*
mowing: **~ attachment** *n* AGRIC mecanismo de siega *m*
Moy: **~ head** *n* CINEMAT cabeza Moy *f*
mpg *abbr* (*miles per gallon*) TRANSP millas por galón *f pl*
MRS *abr* (monitored retrievable storage) NUCL AVR (*almacenamiento vigilado con posibilidad de recuperación*)
MRTIE *abbr* (*maximum relative time interval error*) TELECOM error máximo de intervalo relativo *m*
ms *abbr* (*millisecond*) COMP&DP ms (*milisegundo*)
MS *abbr* PRINT, SPACE (*mobile station*) MS (*estación móvil*), TELECOM (*message storing*) almacenamiento de mensajes *m*, memorización de mensajes *f*, (*multiplex section*) sección de múltiplex *f*, (*message store*) almacén de mensajes *m*, memoria de mensajes *f*, (*mobile station*) MS (*estación móvil*)
MSB *abbr* (*most significant bit*) COMP&DP, PROD, TELECOM BMS (*bit de mayor significación, bit más significativo*)
MSC *abbr* TELECOM (*mobile switching center AmE, mobile switching centre BrE*) centro de conmutación móvil *m*, TELECOM (*maritime switching center AmE, maritime switching centre BrE*) centro de conmutación marítima *m*
MSD *abbr* (*most significant digit*) COMP&DP, MATH, PROD DMS (*dígito más significativo*)
MSE *abbr* (*mean square error*) COMP&DP, MATH EMC (*error medio cuadrático*)
MSG *abbr* (*monosodium glutamate*) CHEM, FOOD glutamato monosódico *m*
MSI[1] *abbr* (*medium-scale integration*) COMP&DP, ELECTRON, PHYS, TELECOM IME (*integración a media escala, integración de mediana escala*)
MSI[2]: **~ circuit** *n* TELECOM circuito MSI *m*
MSIV *abbr* (*mean steam isolation valve*) NUCL MSIV
MSK *abbr* (*minimum-shift keying*) ELECTRON TDM (*teclado de desplazamiento mínimo*), TELECOM manipulación por desplazamiento mínimo *f*
MSLB *abbr* (*main-steamline break*) NUCL MSLB (*rotura de la línea de vapor principal*)
MSN *abbr* (*multiple subscriber number*) TELECOM número de abonado múltiple *m*
MSP *abbr* TELECOM (*maintenance service provider*) proveedor del servicio de mantenimiento *m*, TELECOM (*multiplex section protection*) protección de la sección de múltiplex *f*
MST *abbr* (*multiplex section termination*) TELECOM terminación de la sección múltiplex *f*
MSU *abbr* (*message signal unit*) TELECOM unidad de señal de mensajes *f*
mSv: **~year** *n* RAD PHYS mSv-año *m*
MSV *abbr* (*multiservice vessel*) PETR TECH, WATER TRANSP buque multiservicios *m*
MT *abbr* (*message transfer*) TELECOM transferencia de mensajes *f*

MTA *abbr* (*message transfer agent*) TELECOM agente de transferencia de mensajes *m*
MTBF *abbr* (*mean time between failures*) COMP&DP, ELEC ENG, MECH, QUALITY, SPACE tiempo medio entre fallos *m*
MTBR *abbr* (*mean time between removals*) SPACE tiempo medio entre desmontaje *m*
MTIE *abbr* (*maximum time interval error*) TELECOM error máximo de intervalo *m*
MTL *abbr* (*merged transistor logic*) ELECTRON CLTC (*circuito lógico transistorizado combinado*)
MTPI *abbr* (*multiplexer timing physical interface*) TELECOM interfase física para sincronismo del multiplexor *f*
MTR *abbr* (*materials testing reactor*) NUCL reactor de ensayo de materiales *m*
MTS *abbr* (*multiplexer timing source*) COMP&DP, TELECOM fuente de señales de sincronismo del multiplexor *f*
MTTR *abbr* (*mean time to repair*) tiempo medio de reparación *m*
M-type: **~ microwave tube** *n* ELECTRON tubo de microondas tipo M *m*; **~ tube** *n* ELECTRON tubo tipo M *m*
mucic *adj* CHEM múcico
muciferous *adj* CHEM mucilaginoso
muciform *adj* CHEM muciforme
mucin *n* CHEM mucina *f*
mucipheric *adj* CHEM muciférico
mucoitin: **~~sulfuric** *AmE*, **~~sulphuric** *BrE adj* CHEM mucoitin-sulfúrico
muconic *adj* CHEM mucónico
mucoprotein *n* CHEM mucoproteína *f*
mud *n* CHEM lodo *m*, MINE lodo de inyección *m*, lodo de perforación *m*, OCEAN, PETR TECH barro *m*, cieno *m*, fango *m*, lodo *m*, PETROL, PROD, RECYCL lodo *m*, WATER barro *m*, cieno *m*, fango *m*, lodo *m*; **~ analysis log** *n* PETR TECH diagrama de análisis del lodo *m*, registro de análisis del lodo *m*; **~ bit** *n* MINE lodo de perforación *m*; **~ bottom** *n* MINE cenagal *m*, fondo de fango *m*, suelo de cieno *m*; **~ box** *n* PETR TECH compartimiento de lodo *m*, *perforation* balsa de lodos *f*, PETROL balsa de lodos *f*, piscina de lodos *f*, PROD *sluices* caja de fangos *f*; **~ cake** *n* PETROL costra de lodo *f*, revoque de inyección *m*, revoque de lodo *m*; **~ circulation** *n* PETROL circulación de inyección *f*; **~ coal** *n* COAL carbón de pantanos *m*; **~ cock** *n* PROD *of boiler* grifo de vaciamiento *m*; **~ column** *n* PETR TECH altura hidrostática *f*, circulación del lodo *f*; **~ content** *n* WATER contenido de fango *m*; **~ crack** *n* GEOL grieta de desecación *f*; **~ density** *n* PETROL densidad del lodo *f*; **~ door** *n* PROD *of boiler* agujero de limpieza *m*; **~ engineer** *n* PETR TECH ingeniero de lodo *m*; **~ filtrate** *n* PETROL filtrado de lodo *m*; **~ flow** *n* GEOL corriente de fango *f*, flujo de lodo *m*; **~ hose** *n* PETROL manguera de inyección de lodos *f*; **~ line** *n* PETR TECH fondo del mar *m*; **~ log** *n* GEOPHYS registro con lodo *m*, registro de fango *m*, PETR TECH diagrama del lodo *m*, registro del lodo *m*, PETROL perfil de inyección *m*; **~ logging** *n* PETROL perfil de inyección *m*; **~ loss** *n* PETR TECH pérdida de lodo *f*; **~ pit** *n* PETR TECH tanque de lodo *m*, *perforation* balsa de lodos *f*; **~ plug** *n* PROD *boiler* tapón roscado de limpieza *m*; **~ pump** *n* MINE bomba del lodo *f*, bomba para fangos *f*, PETR TECH bomba de lodo *f*, PETROL bomba de inyección de lodos *f*; **~ pump valve** *n* PETR TECH

válvula de la bomba de lodo *f*; ~ **return line** *n* PETR TECH conducto de retorno del lodo *m*; ~ **ring** *n* PETR TECH colector de lodo *m*; ~ **system** *n* PETR TECH sistema de lodo *m*; ~ **tank** *n* PETR TECH tanque de lodo *m*; ~ **volcano** *n* FUELLESS, PETR TECH volcán de lodo *m*; ~ **weight** *n* PETR TECH densidad del lodo *f*, peso del lodo *m*, PETROL peso de la inyección *m*

mudflap *n* VEH aleta guardabarros *f*

mudflat *n* WATER TRANSP *geography* lodazal blando *m*, marisma *f*

mudguard *n* BrE (*cf fender AmE*) AUTO, TRANSP, VEH aleta *f*, guardabarros *m*

mudsill *n* CONST durmiente *m*, solera *f*

mudstone *n* GEOL *circuits* caliza micrítica *f*, fangolita *f*, roca carbonatada micrítica *f*

MUF *abbr* (*maximum usable frequency*) ELEC ENG, TELECOM frecuencia límite superior *f*, frecuencia máxima de consumo *f*, frecuencia máxima utilizable *f*

muff *n* MECH ENG manguito *m*, manguito de acoplamiento *m*; ~ **coupling** *n* MECH ENG embrague de manguito *m*, manguito de acoplamiento *m*

muffle *n* C&G, HEAT, PROD *pulley block* mufla *f*; ~ **furnace** *n* HEAT, LAB horno de mufla *m*, PROD horno de copela *m*, horno de mufla *m*; ~ **support** *n* C&G soporte de la mufla *m*

muffler *n* AmE (*cf silencer BrE*) ACOUST, AUTO, TRANSP, VEH silenciador *m*; ~ **jacket** *n* AUTO chaqueta del silenciador *f*; ~ **shell** *n* AUTO revestimiento del silenciador *m*

mulch *n* AGRIC cobertura de rastrojo *f*

mulcher: ~-**transplanter** *n* AGRIC desenrolladora de película plástica *f*

mulching *n* AGRIC acolchonamiento de suelos *m*

Mullen: ~ **tester** *n* PAPER aparato Mullen para medir la resistencia al estallido *m*

muller *n* PROD *of amalgamating pan* moleta *f*

Mullin's: ~ **effect** *n* P&R efecto de Mullin *m*

mullion: ~ **structure** *n* GEOL estructura columelar *f*

mullite *n* MINERAL mullita *f*

mullock *n* MINE escombros *m pl*, estériles *m pl*, roca no aurífera *f*

mullocking *n* MINE trabajos en roca *m pl*

multi: ~-**emitter transistor** *n* ELECTRON transistor de emisor múltiple *m*; ~ **frequency** *n* TELECOM múltiples frecuencias *f pl*; ~-**image lens** *n* CINEMAT lente de imagen múltiple *f*; ~-**impression hot runner mold** *n* AmE, ~-**impression hot runner mould** *n* BrE MECH ENG molde que produce más de una pieza por ciclo de moldeo *m*; ~-**impression mold** AmE, ~-**impression mould** BrE *n* MECH ENG *plastic moulding*, P&R molde de impresión múltiple *m*; ~-**impression unscrewing tools** *n pl* MECH ENG herramientas de desatornillar de impresión múltiple *f pl*

multiaccess: ~ **system** *n* COMP&DP sistema de acceso múltiple *m*

multiaddress: ~ **instruction** *n* COMP&DP instrucción de direccionamiento múltiple *f*

multiaddressing *n* TELECOM direccionamiento múltiple *m*, multidireccionamiento *m*, múltiples direcciones *f pl*

multiagent: ~ **munitions** *n pl* MILIT municiones de agentes múltiples *f pl*

multianode: ~ **rectifier** *n* ELEC ENG rectificador polianódico *m*

multiaxle: ~ **heavy freight vehicle** *n* AmE (*cf multiaxle heavy goods vehicle BrE*) TRANSP vehículo de mer-

cancías pesadas multieje *m*; ~ **heavy goods vehicle** BrE *n* (*cf multiaxle heavy freight vehicle AmE*) TRANSP vehículo de mercancías pesadas multieje *m*

multiband: ~ **aerial** *n* BrE (*cf multiband antenna AmE*) antena multibanda *f*; ~ **antenna** *n* AmE (*cf multiband aerial BrE*) PHYS antena multibanda *f*; ~ **filter** *n* ELECTRON, TELECOM filtro multibanda *m*

multibeam: ~ **aerial** *n* BrE (*cf multibeam antenna AmE*) PHYS, SPACE *communications*, TELECOM antena de haces múltiples *f*, antena multihaz *f*; ~ **antenna** *n* AmE (*cf multibeam aerial BrE*) PHYS, SPACE *communications*, TELECOM antena de haces múltiples *f*, antena multihaz *f*; ~ **cathode ray tube** *n* (*multibeam CRT*) ELECTRON tubo de rayos catódicos de haces múltiples *m* (*TRC de haces múltiples*); ~ **CRT** *n* (*multibeam cathode ray tube*) ELECTRON TRC de haces múltiples *m* (*tubo de rayos catódicos de haces múltiples*); ~ **echo sounder** *n* OCEAN ecosonda de haces múltiples *f*, ecosonda de canal múltiple *f*; ~ **sounder** *n* OCEAN sondeador de haces múltiples *m*, resonador acústico *m*

multibearer: ~ **service** *n* TELECOM servicio de múltiples portadores *m*, servicio de varios portadores *m*

multibreak: ~ **circuit breaker** *n* ELEC disyuntor de múltiples desconexiones *m*

multibroad *n* CINEMAT batería de lámparas múltiples *f*

multiburst *n* TV señal de sincronismo de color múltiple *f*

multicavity: ~ **klystron** *n* ELECTRON, PHYS, RAD PHYS klistron de cavidad múltiple *m*; ~ **magnetron** *n* ELECTRON, PHYS magnetrón de cavidad múltiple *m*

multicellular *adj* ACOUST *loudspeaker* multicelular

multichannel[1] *adj* WATER TRANSP *radio, satellite communications* multicanal

multichannel[2]: ~ **amplifier** *n* ELECTRON amplificador multicanal *m*; ~ **analyser** BrE, ~ **analyzer** AmE *n* PHYS analizador multicanal *m*; ~ **carrier** *n* SPACE *communications* onda portadora multicanal *f*, portadora multicanálica *f*; ~ **elementary loudspeaker** *n* ACOUST, TELECOM altavoz elemental multicanal *m*; ~ **filter** *n* ELECTRON, TELECOM filtro multicanal *m*; ~ **monitoring** *n* WATER TRANSP *radio* comprobación multicanal *f*; ~ **protocol** *n* COMP&DP protocolo multicanal *m*; ~ **selector** *n* TV selector de canales múltiples *m*

multicollector: ~ **transistor** *n* ELECTRON transistor de colector múltiple *m*

multicolor: ~ **printing** AmE *see multicolour printing BrE*; ~ **rotary printing machine** AmE *see multicolour rotary printing machine BrE*

multicolored AmE *see multicoloured BrE*

multicolour: ~ **printing** *n* BrE PRINT impresión multicolor *f*; ~ **rotary printing machine** *n* BrE PRINT rotativa de varios colores *f*

multicoloured *adj* BrE COLOUR multicolor, polícromo

multicomponent[1] *adj* CHEM multicomponente

multicomponent[2]: ~ **glass fiber** AmE, ~ **glass fibre** BrE OPT fibra de vidrio de multicomponentes *f*

multiconductor: ~ **cable** *n* ELEC, ELEC ENG cable de múltiples conductores *m*, cable policonductor *m*, TV cable de múltiples conductores *m*; ~ **locking plug** *n* ELEC *connection* tomacorriente enclavado de múltiples conductores *m*, tomacorriente enclavado policonductor *m*, tomacorriente trabado policonductor *m*

multicopy: ~ **business forms** n pl PAPER formularios para copias múltiples m pl

multicore: ~ **cable** n ELEC, ELEC ENG, TV cable de varios conductores no concéntricos m, cable multiconductor m, cable multifilar m

multicylinder: ~ **dryer section** n PAPER sección de secado de varios cilindros f; ~ **engine** n AUTO motor multicilíndrico m; ~ **injection pump** n AUTO bomba de inyección multicilíndrica f

multidecking: ~ **system** n TRANSP sistema de varias cubiertas m

multidentate adj CHEM ligand multidentado

multidestination: ~ **carrier** n SPACE communications portadora a multidestinación f; ~ **mode** n TELECOM modo de múltiples destinos m, modo de varios destinos m

multidimensional: ~ **filtering** n TELECOM filtrado multidimensional m, filtraje multidimensional m

multidrill: ~ **head** n MECH ENG taladro múltiple m

multidrop: ~ **link** n COMP&DP enlace multipunto m, enlace tipo margarita m

multielectrode: ~ **tube** n ELECTRON tubo multielectródico m

multiengine: ~ **helicopter** n AIR TRANSP helicóptero multimotor m, helicóptero polimotor m

multifiber: ~ **cable** AmE see multifibre cable BrE; ~ **joint** AmE see multifibre joint BrE

multifibre: ~ **cable** n BrE ELEC ENG, OPT, TELECOM cable de muchas fibras m, cable de múltiples fibras m, cable de varias fibras m, cable multifibra m, ; ~ **joint** n BrE ELEC ENG, OPT, TELECOM unión de múltiples fibras f, unión multifibra f

multifilament: ~ **machine** n TEXTIL máquina multifilamento f; ~ **yarn** n TEXTIL multifilamento m

multiflue: ~ **boiler** n PROD caldera multitubular f

multifocal: ~ **finder** n CINEMAT visor multifocal m; ~ **glasses** n pl INSTR, OPT anteojos multifocales m pl (AmL), gafas multifocales f pl (Esp), lentes multifocales f pl

multiframe: ~ **alignment** n (MFA) TELECOM alineamiento de múltiples bastidores m

multifrequency: ~ **aerial** n BrE (cf multifrequency antenna AmE) TELECOM antena multifrecuencia f; ~ **antenna** n AmE (cf multifrequency aerial BrE) TELECOM antena multifrecuencia f; ~ **generator** n TELECOM generador multifrecuencia m; ~ **receiver** n TELECOM receptor multifrecuencia m; ~ **sender-receiver** n TELECOM emisor-receptor multifrecuencia m; ~ **telephone** n (MF telephone) TELECOM teléfono multifrecuencia m

multifuel: ~ **engine** n AUTO, THERMO motor multicarburante m, motor multicombustible m, motor policombustible m; ~ **heater** n MECH ENG calentador de varias clases de combustibles m

multifunction: ~ **tester** n ELEC ENG probador multifuncional m

multigage AmE see multigauge BrE

multigauge n BrE CINEMAT proyector m, PROD desconectador m; ~ **isolator** n BrE PROD desconectador múltiple m; ~ **projector** n BrE CINEMAT proyector de paso múltiple m, proyector multipaso m

multigrade: ~ **oil** n AUTO, COAL, VEH aceite multigrado m

multigrid: ~ **tube** n ELECTRON tubo de rejillas múltiples m

multigrip: ~ **pliers** n pl MECH ENG alicates estriados m pl, tenazas estriadas f pl

multigun: ~ **tube** n ELECTRON equipo de tubos m

multihull n WATER TRANSP multicasco m

multihulled: ~ **ship** n WATER TRANSP buque multicasco m

multilane: ~ **labeling system** AmE, ~ **labelling system** BrE n PACK sistema de etiquetado múltiple m; ~ **machine** n PACK máquina multivía f

multilayer[1] adj CHEM de varias capas, multicapa

multilayer[2] n SPACE craft capas múltiples f pl; ~ **aquifer** n GEOL, HYDROL, WATER acuífero de varias capas m; ~ **board** n PAPER cartón multicapas m; ~ **coil** n ELEC bobina de varias capas f; ~ **color film** AmE, ~ **colour film** BrE n CINEMAT película multicapa en color f; ~ **filtration** n WATER filtración multicapa f; ~ **headbox** n PAPER caja de entrada multicapa f; ~ **paper** n PAPER papel multicapas m; ~ **printed circuit** n ELECTRON, TELECOM circuito impreso de capas múltiples m, circuito impreso de multicapa m; ~ **resist** n ELECTRON protector de multicapas m; ~ **thick films** n pl ELECTRON multicapa de película gruesa f; ~ **thin films** n pl ELECTRON multicapa de película delgada f

multileaf: ~ **damper** n REFRIG registro de persianas m

multilevel: ~ **bill of material** n PROD lista de materiales múltiples f; ~ **modulation** n ELECTRON modulación a varios niveles f; ~ **system** n TELECOM sistema de multinivel m

multilongitudinal: ~ **modes** n pl (MLM) TELECOM modos multilongitudinales m pl

multimedia[1] adj COMP&DP multimedia

multimedia[2]: ~ **filter** n HYDROL filtro para varios usos m

multimetal: ~ **plate** n PRINT plancha polimetálica f

multimeter n ELEC ENG, TV multímetro m, polímetro m, voltiamperímetro m

multimicroprocessor: ~ **system** n TELECOM sistema multimicroprocesador m

multimodal: ~ **traffic** n RAIL tráfico multimodal m

multimode: ~ **distortion** n OPT, TELECOM distorsión multimodal f, distorsión multimodo f; ~ **fiber** AmE, ~ **fibre** n BrE OPT, PHYS, TELECOM fibra multimodo f; ~ **group delay** n OPT, TELECOM retardo de grupo multimodal m, retardo grupal multimodo m; ~ **laser** n ELECTRON, OPT, TELECOM láser multimodo m; ~ **optical fiber** AmE, ~ **optical fibre** n BrE OPT, TELECOM fibra óptica multimodal f

multinomial n MATH polinomio m; ~ **distribution** n MATH distribución polinomial f

multioctave: ~ **tunable filter** n ELECTRON filtro sintonizable de varias octavas m; ~ **tunable oscillator** n ELECTRON oscilador sintonizable de varias octavas m; ~ **tuning** n ELECTRON sintonización de varias octavas f

multipack n PACK conjunto formado por varios paquetes m

multipath: ~ **fading** n TELECOM desvanecimiento por multitrayectoria m, desvanecimiento por trayectoria de propagación múltiple m; ~ **propagation** n TELECOM propagación por multitrayecto f, propagación por trayectoria múltiple f; ~ **reflection** n TELECOM reflexión por multitrayecto f, reflexión por multitrayectoria f; ~ **signals** n pl TV señales de doble imagen f pl

multiphase[1] *adj* ELEC *motor*, ELECTRON, GEOL polifásico, multifásico

multiphase[2]: ~ **controller** *n* TRANSP controlador polifásico *m*; ~ **digital model** *n* GAS modelo digital de fases múltiples *m*

multiplane: ~ **animation** *n* CINEMAT animación multiplano *f*

multiplate: ~ **clutch** *n* MECH ENG embrague de discos múltiples *m*, embrague pluridisco *m*, embrague polidisco *m*

multiplay *n* ACOUST reproducción múltiple *f*

multiple[1] *adj* GEN múltiple

multiple[2] *n* METR, PETROL múltiple *m*; ~ **access** *n* COMP&DP, SPACE, TELECOM acceso múltiple *m*; ~ **barge convoy set** *n* TRANSP convoy de barcazas *m*; ~ **beam** *n* TELECOM multihaz *m*; ~-**beam aerial** *n* BrE (*cf multiple beam antenna AmE*) PHYS, TELECOM antena de haces múltiple *f*, antena multihaz *f*; ~ **beam antenna** *n AmE* (*cf multiple-beam aerial BrE*) PHYS, TELECOM antena de haces múltiple *f*, antena multihaz *f*; ~ **beam interference** *n* PHYS interferencia entre múltiples haces *f*; ~ **beam sizing** *n* TEXTIL encolado de la urdimbre en plegador múltiple *m*; ~ **beam slashing** *n* TEXTIL encolado de la urdimbre en plegador múltiple *m*; ~ **blade spring** *n* MECH ENG resorte de hojas múltiples *m*; ~ **contact switch** *n* ELEC conmutador de múltiples contactos *m*, conmutador selector *m*, selector *m*, ELEC ENG combinador *m*, integrador *m*; ~ **current generator** *n* ELEC ENG generador polimórfico *m*; ~ **daylight press** *n* P&R prensa de abertura múltiple *f*; ~ **development** *n* FUELLESS desarrollo múltiple *m*; ~ **diffraction** *n* TELECOM difracción múltiple *f*; ~ **disc clutch** *BrE*, ~ **disk clutch** *n AmE* AUTO, MECH ENG embrague de discos múltiples *m*, embrague pluridisco *m*, embrague polidisco *m*; ~ **drilling machine** *n* MECH, PROD taladradora múltiple *f*; ~ **earthing connection** *n BrE* (*cf multiple grounding connection AmE*) PROD conexión a tierra múltiple *f*; ~ **echo** *n* ACOUST, OCEAN eco múltiple *m*; ~ **expansion engine** *n* PROD máquina de poliexpansión *f*; ~ **exposure** *n* CINEMAT, PHOTO exposición múltiple *f*; ~ **feed rack** *n* PROD cremallera de avance múltiple *f*, rampa de engrase de múltiples salidas *f*; ~ **feeder** *n* ELEC *supply* alimentador múltiple *m*; ~ **frame printing** *n* CINEMAT copiado multicuadro *m*; ~ **frequency** *n* (*MF*) TELECOM múltiples frecuencias *f pl*; ~-**frequency generator** *n* TELECOM generador multifrecuencia *m*; ~-**frequency sender-receiver** *n* TELECOM emisor-receptor multifrecuencia *m*; ~-**frequency telephone** *n* TELECOM teléfono multifrecuencia *m*; ~ **of gearing** *n* MECH ENG accionamiento múltiple *m*; ~ **glazing unit** *n* C&G unidad de vidriado múltiple *f*; ~ **grounding connection** *n AmE* (*cf multiple earthing connection BrE*) PROD conexión a tierra múltiple *f*; ~ **hearth furnace** *n* HEAT, THERMO horno con hogares múltiples *m*; ~-**instruction multiple-data** *n* (*MIMD*) COMP&DP flujo de instrucciones múltiple-flujo de datos múltiple *m*; ~-**instruction single-data** *n* (*MISD*) COMP&DP flujo de instrucciones múltiple-flujo de datos único *m* (*MISD*); ~-**layer color film** *AmE*, ~-**layer colour film** *BrE n* PRINT película de color de múltiples capas *f*; ~-**leaf damper** *n* MECH ENG amortiguador de múltiples ballestas *m*; ~ **machining** *n* PROD mecanización en serie *f*; ~ **microphone** *n* ACOUST micrófono múltiple *m*;

~ **milling** *n* PROD fresado en serie *m*; ~ **mode transportation system** *n* TRANSP sistema de transporte múltiple *m*; ~ **modulation** *n* ELECTRON modulación múltiple *f*; ~-**operator welding set** *n* PROD equipo de soldadura para varios operarios *m*; ~ **order filter** *n* ELECTRON filtro de tipo múltiple *m*; ~ **outlet plug** *n* TV toma de corriente múltiple *f*, toma macho de dispositivo de conexión múltiple *m*; ~ **path** *n* SPACE trayectoria múltiple *f*; ~ **pile-up** *n* TRANSP apilado múltiple *m*, choque múltiple *m*, colisión múltiple *f*; ~ **plate capacitor** *n* ELEC capacitor de múltiples placas *m*, condensador de múltiples placas *m*; ~ **plate clutch** *n* MECH ENG embrague de discos múltiples *m*, embrague pluridisco *m*, embrague polidisco *m*; ~ **plug** *n* ELEC, ELEC ENG ladrón *m*; ~ **proportions** *n pl* CHEM porporciones múltiples *f pl*; ~ **punching machine** *n* PROD punzonadora múltiple *f*; ~-**ram broaching machine** *n* MECH ENG brochadora de correderas múltiples *f*; ~ **reflector aerial** *n* BrE (*cf multiple reflector antenna AmE*) TELECOM antena con reflector múltiple *f*, antena multireflector *f*; ~ **reflector antenna** *n AmE* (*cf multiple reflector aerial BrE*) TELECOM antena con reflector múltiple *f*, antena multireflector *f*; ~ **regression** *n* AGRIC regresión múltiple *f*; ~ **row blasting** *n* MINE explosiones sucesivas *f pl*, voladuras sucesivas *f pl*; ~ **rung display** *n* PROD dispositivo visualizado de niveles múltiples *m*, expositor de múltiples niveles *m*; ~ **sampling** *n* TELECOM muestreo múltiple *m*; ~ **seizure** *n* TELECOM toma múltiple *f*; ~ **server queue** *n* TELECOM cola multiservidor *f*; ~ **skirt system** *n* TRANSP sistema de plinto múltiple *m*, sistema multiplinto *m*; ~-**skirted plenum chamber** *n* TRANSP cámara impelente multiplinto *f*; ~ **socket** *n* ELEC *connection* enchufe hembra múltiple *m*, toma-corriente múltiple *m*; ~ **special electrical logging** *n* PETR TECH diagrafía eléctrica especial múltiple *f*, perfilaje eléctrico especial múltiple *m*, registro eléctrico especial múltiple *m*; ~-**speed camera** *n* CINEMAT cámara de velocidades múltiples *f*; ~ **spindle drill** *n* PROD taladradora de polihusillos *f*; ~-**spindle drilling head** *n* MECH ENG cabezal de taladrar de husillos múltiples *m*, cabezal de taladrar de polihusillos *m*; ~ **splitting** *n* NUCL desdoblamiento múltiple *m*, escisión múltiple *f*; ~-**stranded conductor** *n* ELEC *cable* conductor cableado múltiple *m*, conductor de hilos retorcidos múltiple *m*, conductor trenzado múltiple *m*; ~ **subscriber number** *n* (*MSN*) TELECOM número de abonado múltiple *m*; ~ **switch** *n* ELEC conmutador múltiple *m*, interruptor múltiple *m*; ~ **switchboard** *n* TELECOM conmutador múltiple *m*, cuadro conmutador múltiple *m*, cuadro múltiple *m*; ~-**threaded screw** *n* PROD tornillo plurirroscas *m*; ~ **tool lathe** *n* MECH ENG torno de herramientas múltiples *m*; ~ **twin quad** *n* ELEC ENG cuádruple de pares retorcidos *m*, maclado múltiple *m*; ~ **unit tube** *n* ELECTRON tubo de unidad múltiple *m*; ~-**use carbonizing base paper** *n* PAPER papel soporte carbón de varios usos *m*; ~ **V-belt drive** *n* MECH ENG transmisión por correa en V múltiple *f*, transmisión por correa trapezoidal múltiple *f*; ~ **wedge** *n* MINE cuña múltiple *f*; ~ **winding** *n* ELEC *of transformer*, ELEC ENG arrollamiento múltiple *m*, devanado de varias capas *m*, devanado múltiple *m*; ~ **wire system** *n* ELEC sistema multifilar *m*

multiplet *n* PHYS, RAD PHYS multiplete *m*

multiplex[1] *n* COMP&DP, ELECTRON múltiplex *m*, SPACE *communications* transmisión simultánea sobre el mismo hilo *f*, transmisión simultánea sobre la misma onda *f*, TELECOM múltiplex *m*, transmisión simultánea sobre el mismo hilo *f*, transmisión simultánea sobre la misma onda *f*; ~ **channel** *n* ELECTRON multicanal *m*; ~ **circuit** *n* PROD circuito en multiplex *m*; ~ **lap winding** *n* ELEC devanado paralelo múltiple *m*; ~ **operation** *n* ELECTRON funcionamiento con varios canales *m*; ~ **section** *n* (*MS*) TELECOM sección de múltiplex *f*; ~-**section alarm indication signal** *n* TELECOM señal de indicación de alarma de la sección de múltiplex *f*; ~ **section overhead** *n* TELECOM sobrecarga de la sección múltiplex *f*; ~ **section protection** *n* (*MSP*) TELECOM protección de la sección de múltiplex *f*; ~ **section termination** *n* (*MST*) TELECOM terminación de la sección múltiplex *f*; ~ **timing generator** *n* TELECOM generador de sincronismo de múltiplex *m*; ~ **transmission** *n* TV transmisión en múltiplex *f*
multiplex[2] *vt* COMP&DP multiplexar, ELECTRON transmitir simultáneamente, TELECOM multiplexar, transmitir simultáneamente
multiplexer *n* (*mux*) COMP&DP, ELECTRON, TELECOM, TV multiplexor *m*; ~ **channel** *n* COMP&DP canal multiplexor *m*; ~ **timing physical interface** *n* (*MTPI*) TELECOM interfase física para sincronismo del multiplexor *f*; ~ **timing source** *n* (*MTS*) COMP&DP, TELECOM fuente de señales de sincronismo del multiplexor *f*
multiplexing *n* COMP&DP multiplexación *f*, multiplexión *f*, SPACE *communications* correlación múltiple *f*, transmisión simultánea *f*, transmisión simultánea de muchas informaciones *f*, TELECOM multiplexación *f*, multiplexión *f*, transmisión simultánea *f*, transmisión simultánea de muchas informaciones *f*; ~ **frequency** *n* ELECTRON frecuencia de transmisión simultánea *f*; ~ **identification** *n* TELECOM identificación de multiflexión *f*
multiplicand *n* COMP&DP, MATH multiplicando *m*
multiplication *n* MATH multiplicación *f*
multiplicative *adj* MATH multiplicativo
multiplicator *n* TELECOM multiplicador *m*
multiplicity *n* PHYS multiplicidad *f*
multiplier *n* COMP&DP, ELECTRON, TELECOM multiplicador *m*; ~ **phototube** *n* ELECTRON fototubo multiplicador *m*, INSTR célula fotoeléctrica multiplicadora *f*, fotocélula multiplicadora *f*, fototubo multiplicador *m*
multiplug: ~ **adaptor** *n* ELEC ladrón *m*, ELEC ENG adaptador multiclavija *m*, ladrón *m*
multiply[1]: ~ **sack** *n* PACK saco de varias hojas *m*
multiply[2]: ~ **by** *vt* MATH multiplicar por
multiplying: ~ **gear** *n* MECH ENG engranaje multiplicador *m*; ~ **gearing** *n* MECH ENG engranaje multiplicador *m*; ~ **glass** *n* INSTR lente amplificadora *f*; ~ **wheel** *n* MECH ENG engranaje multiplicador *m*
multipoint: ~ **command assign token** *n* (*MCA*) TELECOM señal de mando asignada para varios puntos *f*; ~ **command conference** *n* (*MCC*) TELECOM conferencia de mando para varios puntos *f*; ~ **command negating MCS** *n* (*MCN*) TELECOM transmisión de datos simétricos de anulación de mando para varios puntos *f*; ~ **command release token** *n* TELECOM señal de liberación de mando para varios puntos *f*; ~ **command symmetrical data transmission** *n*

TELECOM transmisión de datos simétricos de mando para varios puntos *f*; ~ **command token claim** *n* (*MCT*) TELECOM demanda de señal de mando para varios puntos *f*; ~ **command visualization forcing** *n* (*MCV*) TELECOM corrección forzada de visualización de mando para varios *f*; ~ **gluing machine** *n* PACK engomadora por puntos múltiples *f*; ~ **indication loop** *n* (*MIL*) TELECOM circuito cerrado indicador de varios puntos *m*; ~ **indication secondary-status transistor** *n* (*MIS transistor*) ELECTRON transistor de posición secundaria con indicación diversa *m* (*transistor de PSID*); ~ **indication visualization** *n* (*MIV*) TELECOM visualización de indicación para varios puntos *f*; ~ **indication zero communication** *n* (*MIZ*) TELECOM comunicación nula de indicación para varios puntos *f*; ~ **link** *n* COMP&DP enlace multipunto *m*; ~ **modem link** *n* PROD enlace con varios puntos mediante módem *m*, enlace multiterminal mediante módem *m*; ~ **recorder** *n* INSTR grabador de multipuntos *m*
multipolar[1] *adj* ELEC *machine* multipolar
multipolar[2]: ~ **armature** *n* ELEC *generator, motor* armadura multipolar *f*
multipole *n* PHYS multipolo *m*; ~ **filter** *n* ELECTRON filtro multipolar *m*
multipolling *n* TELECOM interrogación múltiple *f*
multiport *adj* COMP&DP multipuerto
multiported: ~ **valve** *n* PROD distribuidor de lumbreras múltiples *m*
multiposition: ~ **relay** *n* ELEC relevador multiposición *m*, relé de múltiples posiciones *m*; ~ **switch** *n* ELEC ENG conmutador selector multiposicional *m*
multiprocessing *n* COMP&DP multiprocesamiento *m*, procesamiento múltiple *m*; ~ **system** *n* COMP&DP sistema de multiprocesamiento *m*, sistema de procesamiento múltiple *m*
multiprocessor *n* COMP&DP, TELECOM multiprocesador *m*; ~ **system** *n* TELECOM sistema multiprocesador *m*
multiprogramming *n* COMP&DP multiprogramación *f*; ~ **system** *n* COMP&DP sistema de multiprogramación *m*
multipurpose: ~ **carrier** *n* TRANSP carguero polivalente *m*, WATER TRANSP buque de carga para usos varios *m*; ~ **cold store** *n* REFRIG, THERMO almacén frigorífico polivalente *m*; ~ **helicopter** *n* AIR TRANSP helicóptero de aplicación general *m*, helicóptero polivalente *m*, helicóptero todo uso *m*; ~ **material pipeline** *n* TRANSP tubería de material polivalente *f*; ~ **ship** *n* WATER TRANSP *merchant navy* buque polivalente *m*; ~ **vessel** *n* PETR TECH barco multiusos *m*
multirange: ~ **meter** *n* ELEC, INSTR aparato de medida de varias sensibilidades *m*, aparato de varias sensibilidades *m*, medidor de varias escalas *m*
multirate: ~ **switching system** *n* TELECOM sistema de conmutación de múltiple tarifa *m*, sistema de conmutación de tarifas múltiples *m*
multiscreen *n* TV pantalla múltiple *f*
multisection: ~ **filter** *n* ELECTRON filtro multiseccional *m*; ~ **prefilter** *n* ELECTRON prefiltro multiseccional *m*
multisegment: ~ **magnetron** *n* ELECTRON magnetrón plurisectorial *m*
multisensor: ~ **image** *n* SPACE imagen de multisensores *f*
multiservice: ~ **switching system** *n* TELECOM sistema de conmutación de servicios múltiples *m*; ~ **vessel** *n*

(*MSV*) PETR TECH, WATER TRANSP buque multiservicios *m*

multiskirt: ~ **system** *n* TRANSP sistema de plinto múltiple *m*, sistema multiplinto *m*

multisnack: ~ **bagging** *n* PACK embolsado de comida diversa *m*

multispan: ~ **greenhouse** *n* AGRIC invernadero multicuerpo *m*

multispiral: ~ **scanning disc** *BrE*, ~ **scanning disk** *AmE n* TV disco de lectura multiespiral *m*

multistage: ~ **amplifier** *n* ELECTRON amplificador multigradual *m*; ~ **circuit** *n* TELECOM circuito de varias etapas *m*, circuito multietapa *m*; ~ **compression** *n* REFRIG compresión en varios escalonamientos *f*, compresión múltiple *f*; ~ **compressor** *n* MECH ENG compresor multigradual de varias etapas *m*, compresor multigradual de varios pasos *m*; ~ **network** *n* TELECOM red multietapa *f*; ~ **progression tooling** *n* MECH ENG herramientas de progresión de varias etapas *f pl*; ~ **pumping** *n* MINE agotamiento repetido *m*; ~ **refrigerating plant** *n* REFRIG, THERMO instalación frigorífica múltiple *f*; ~ **rocket** *n* SPACE *craft* cohete multietapa *m*

multistandard *adj* TV multiestandar, multinorma

multistrand *n* WATER TRANSP *rope* cable multitorónico *m*, cabo multitorónico *m*

multistringer *n* MECH ENG larguero múltiple *m*

multitasking *n* COMP&DP multitarea *f*

multithreading *n* COMP&DP multiposicionamiento *m*, subprocesamiento múltiple *m*

multithroat: ~ **vane** *n* AIR TRANSP álabe de entrada múltiple *m*, álabe de garganta múltiple *m*

multitool: ~ **lathe** *n* MECH ENG torno de herramientas múltiples *m*

multitrack: ~ **recorder** *n* INSTR grabador de multipistas *m*; ~ **recording** *n* ACOUST grabación multipistas *f*

multitube: ~ **heat exchanger** *n* HEAT ENG, THERMO intercambiador de calor multitubo *m*; ~ **nozzle** *n* AIR TRANSP tobera de tubo múltiple *f*

multiturn: ~ **encoder** *n* PROD codificador multiespiras *m*; ~ **potentiometer** *n* ELEC, ELEC ENG potenciómetro helicoidal *m*, potenciómetro multivuelta *m*; ~ **valve actuator** *n* MECH ENG servoválvula de múltiples espiras *f*

multiunit: ~ **container** *n* PACK contenedor múltiple *m*; ~ **developing tank** *n* PHOTO tanque de revelado de unidades múltiples *m*; ~ **tank spiral** *n* PHOTO bobina del tanque de unidades múltiples *f* (*AmL*), espiral del tanque de unidades múltiples *m* (*Esp*)

multiuser: ~ **system** *n* COMP&DP sistema multiusuario *m*

multi-V: ~ **belt** *n* MECH ENG correa en V múltiple *f*, correa trapezoidal múltiple *f*

multivalence *n* CHEM multivalencia *f*

multivariable: ~ **recorder** *n* INSTR grabador de variables múltiples *m*

multivat: ~ **board machine** *n* PAPER máquina de cartón de formas redondas *f*

multivibrator *n* ELECTRON, PHYS, TELECOM multivibrador *m*

multiwall: ~ **sack** *n* PACK saco de varias hojas *m*

multiwinding: ~ **transformer** *n* ELEC transformador de arrollamiento múltiple *m*, transformador de devanado múltiple *m*

multiwire *adj* MECH ENG de múltiples hilos

mu-metal *n* PHYS mu-metal *m*

mummies *n pl* AGRIC frutas secas *f pl*

municipal: ~ **dump** *n* POLL, RECYCL basurero municipal *m*, escombrera municipal *f*, vaciadero municipal *m*, vertedero municipal *m*; ~ **waste** *n* POLL, RECYCL, WATER desechos municipales *m pl*; ~ **water** *n* HYDROL, WATER agua de uso local *f*

muon *n* NUCL, PART PHYS, PHYS muón *m*; ~ **decay track** *n* RAD PHYS seguimiento de la desintegración del muón *m*, vía de desintegración del muón *f*; ~ **magnetic momentum** *n* RAD PHYS momento magnético del muón *m*; ~ **neutrino** *n* PART PHYS, PHYS neutrino muón *m*, neutrino muónico *m*

murchisonite *n* MINERAL murchisonita *f*

murexide *n* CHEM murexida *f*

muriated *adj* CHEM muriatado

muscarine *n* CHEM muscarina *f*

muscovite *n* MINERAL moscovita *f*

mush: ~ **winding** *n* ELEC *of small alternating current machine* devanado de confusión *m*, devanado de interferencia *m*

mushroom: ~ **anchor** *n* WATER TRANSP ancla de hongo *f*, hongo *m*; ~ **head** *n* MECH ENG, PROD cabeza redonda *f*; ~**-head bolt** *n* MECH ENG, PROD perno de cabeza de hongo *m*, perno de cabeza redonda *m*; ~ **insulator** *n* ELEC, ELEC ENG aislante de campana *m*; ~ **stopper** *n* C&G tapón de hongo *m*; ~ **valve** *n* AUTO válvula de hongo *f*, válvula de seta *f*; ~ **ventilator** *n* WATER TRANSP *deck fittings* hongo *m*, hongo de ventilación *m*, manguerote *m*

music: ~ **and effects track** *n* (*M and E track*) CINEMAT banda de música y efectos sonoros *f*

musical: ~ **interval** *n* ACOUST, WAVE PHYS intervalo de música *m*; ~ **scale** *n* ACOUST escala musical *f*

mussel: ~ **bed** *n* OCEAN criadero de mejillones *m*, mejillonero *m*; ~ **boat** *n* OCEAN barco mejillonero *m*; ~ **breeding** *n* OCEAN cría de mejillones *f*, reproducción del mejillón *f*; ~ **culture** *n* OCEAN miticultura *f*

mustard: ~ **gas** *n* CHEM, GAS gas mostaza *m*; ~ **oil** *n* FOOD aceite de mostaza *m*; ~**-seed oil** *n* FOOD aceite de semilla de mostaza *m*

mutagenic *adj* AGRIC mutágeno *m*

mutarotation *n* CHEM mutarotación *f*

mutation: ~ **breeding** *n* AGRIC mejoramiento por mutación *m*

mute[1] *adj* PRINT apagado

mute[2]: ~ **film** *n* CINEMAT película muda *f*; ~ **shot** *n* CINEMAT toma sin sonido *f*

muteness *n* ACOUST mudez *f*, mutismo *m*, silencio *m*

mutilated: ~ **gear** *n* MECH ENG engranaje parcialmente dentado *m*; ~ **wheel** *n* MECH ENG rueda parcialmente dentada *f*

muting *n* PETROL borrado *m*; ~ **device** *n* TELECOM dispositivo silenciador *m*

mutual: ~ **coupling** *n* TELECOM acoplamiento mutuo *m*; ~ **impedance** *n* TELECOM impedancia mutua *f*; ~ **inductance** *n* ELEC, ELEC ENG, PHYS inductancia mutua *f*; ~ **inductance coupling** *n* ELEC, ELEC ENG, PHYS acoplamiento de inductancia mutua *m*; ~ **induction** *n* ELEC, ELEC ENG, PHYS inducción mutua *f*; ~ **inductive coupling** *n* ELEC, ELEC ENG, PHYS acoplamiento por inducción mutua *m*; ~ **inductor** *n* ELEC, ELEC ENG, PHYS bobina de acoplamiento *f*, inductor mutuo *m*; ~ **sync** *n* TELECOM sincronización mutua *f*; ~ **synchronization** *n* TELECOM sincronización mutua *f*

mux *n* (*multiplexer*) COMP&DP, ELECTRON, TELECOM, TV multiplexor *m*

muzzle *n* MILIT boca *f*

mV *abbr* (*millivolt*) ELEC, ELEC ENG mV (*milivoltio*)

mW *abbr* (*milliwatt*) ELEC, ELEC ENG mW (*milivatio*)

MW *abbr* (*megawatt*) ELEC, ELEC ENG MW (*megavatio*)

MWD *abbr* (*measurements while drilling*) PETR TECH MWD (*mediciones durante la perforación*)

Mx *abbr* (*maxwell*) ELEC, ELEC ENG *unit of magnetic flux* Mx (*maxvelio, maxwell*)

mycelium *n* AGRIC micelio *m*

mycoprotein *n* FOOD micoproteína *f*

mycotoxin *n* FOOD micotoxina *f*, toxina fúngiga *f*

mylar: **~ base** *n* TV base de Mylar *f*

mylonite *n* GEOL, PETROL milonita *f*

myocin *n* CHEM miocina *f*

myrcene *n* CHEM mirceno *m*

myria- *pref* METR miria

myriagram *n* METR miriágramo *m*

myriagramme *n see myriagram*

myristic[1] *adj* CHEM mirístico

myristic[2]: **~ alcohol** *n* CHEM, DETERG alcohol mirístico *m*

myristin *n* CHEM miristina *f*

myristyl *adj* CHEM miristilo

myronic *adj* CHEM mirónico

myrosin *n* CHEM mirosina *f*

mytilotoxine *n* CHEM mitilotoxina *f*

N

n *abbr* METR (*nano*) n (*nano*), PART PHYS (*neutron*) n (*neutrón*)

n+: **~-type semiconductor** *n* ELECTRON semiconductor tipo n+ *m*

N *abbr* ACOUST (*neper*) N (*neperio*), CHEM (*nitrogen*) N (*nitrógeno*), ELEC, METR, PHYS (*newton*) N (*newton*)

N₂ *abbr* (*nitrogen gas*) GAS N₂ (*gas de nitrógeno*)

N₂O *abbr* (*nitrous oxide*) CHEM, POLL óxido de nitrógeno III *m*

N₂O₅ *abbr* (*nitrogen pentoxide*) CHEM, POLL N₂O₅ (*óxido de nitrógeno V*)

NA *abbr* (*numerical aperture*) CONST, OPT, TELECOM apertura numérica *f*

Na *abbr* (*sodium*) CHEM, METALL Na (*sodio*)

nacelle *n* AIR TRANSP góndola *f*; **~ intake ring** *n* AIR TRANSP aro de admisión de la góndola *m*

nacreous: **~ pigment** *n* COLOUR, P&R pigmento nacarado *m*

nacrite *n* MINERAL nacrita *f*

NAD *abbr* (*noise amplitude distribution*) TELECOM distribución de amplitud de ruido *f*

nagatelite *n* NUCL *materials* nagatelita *f*

nagyagite *n* MINERAL nagyagita *f*, telurio foliado *m*, telurio hojoso nagyagita *m*

nail¹ *n* CONST clavo *m*, chimenea *f* (*Esp*), MECH clavo *m*, MINE aguja de mina *f*, *chute raise* chimenea *f* (*Esp*), clavo *m* (*AmL*), clavo de chimenea *m*, columna rica *f*; **~ claw** *n* CONST chimenea *f* (*Esp*), punta *f*; **~ extractor** *n* CONST extractor de clavos *m*; **~ puller** *n* PACK extractor de clavos *m*; **~ punch** *n* CONST punzón *m*; **~ set** *n* CONST embutidor de clavos *m*

nail² *vt* CONST clavar

nailing *n* CONST clavadura *f*; **~ machine** *n* PACK máquina para clavar clavos *f*

nailmaking *n* PROD fabricación de clavos *f*

NAK *abbr* (*negative acknowledgement*) COMP&DP acuse de recibo negativo *m*, reconocimiento negativo *m*

name: **~ server** *n* TELECOM servidor designado *m*

nameplate *n* ELEC *of appliance* etiqueta *f*, letrero *m*, rótulo *m*, MECH, MECH ENG chapa de fabricante *f*, placa de identificación *f*, placa del constructor *f*, placa identificadora del nombre *f*, placa rotulada *f*

NAND: **~ circuit** *n* ELECTRON circuito NO-Y *m*, circuito NY *m*; **~ gate** *n* COMP&DP puerta NAND *f*, ELECTRON circuito NI *m*, puerta NAND *f*, PHYS puerta NAND *f*; **~ operation** *n* COMP&DP operación NAND *f*

nannofossil *n* GEOL nanofosil *m*

nano *pref* (n) METR nano (n)

nanosecond *n* COMP&DP, METR, PHYS, TV nanosegundo *m*

nantokite *n* MINERAL nantocoíta *f*

nap¹ *n* TEXTIL vello *m*

nap² *vt* TEXTIL perchar

Naperian: **~ logarithm** *n* MATH logaritmo natural *m*, logaritmo neperiano *m*

naphtha *n* CHEM, THERMO nafta *f* (*AmL*)

naphthacene *n* CHEM, P&R naftaceno *m*

naphthalene *n* CHEM, DETERG naftaleno *m*

naphthalenedisulfonic *AmE see naphthalenedisulphonic BrE*

naphthalenedisulphonic *adj BrE* CHEM naftalendisulfónico

naphthalenic *adj* CHEM, DETERG, P&R naftalénico

naphthane *n* CHEM naftano *m*

naphthenate *n* P&R naftenato *m*

naphthene *n* CHEM nafteno *m*

naphthenic *adj* CHEM, P&R nafténico

naphthionic *adj* CHEM, P&R naftiónico

naphthoic *adj* CHEM naftoico

naphthol *n* CHEM naftol *m*; **~ dyeing** *n* COLOUR teñido azoico *m*

naphtholate *n* CHEM naftolato *m*

naphtholsulfonic *AmE see naphtholsulphonic BrE*

naphtholsulphonic *adj BrE* CHEM naftolsulfónico

naphthoquinone *n* CHEM naftoquinona *f*

naphthoyl *n* CHEM naftoilo *m*

naphthyl *n* CHEM naftil *m*, naftilo *m*

naphthylamine *n* CHEM naftilamina *f*

naphthylene *n* CHEM naftileno *m*

naphthylic *adj* CHEM naftílico

nappe *n* GEOM capa *f*, hoja *f*, HYDRAUL, HYDROL capa de agua *f*, lámina vertiente *f*

napping *n* TEXTIL perchado *m*

narceine *n* CHEM narceína *f*

narcotic¹ *adj* CHEM, OCEAN narcótico

narcotic² *n* CHEM narcótico *m*

narcotine *n* CHEM narcotina *f*

narghile *n* OCEAN narguile *m*

naringenin *n* CHEM naringenina *f*

naringin *n* CHEM naringina *f*

narration: **~ track** *n* CINEMAT banda de narración *f*

narrative *n* COMP&DP narrativa *f*

narrow¹: **~-band** *adj* COMP&DP, ELECTRON, TELECOM, TV de banda estrecha; **~-leaved** *adj* AGRIC acicular

narrow²: **~-angle lens** *n* CINEMAT, PHOTO objetivo angular *m*; **~-band amplifier** *n* ELECTRON amplificador de banda estrecha *m*; **~-band circuit** *n* ELECTRON circuito de banda estrecha *m*; **~-band demodulation** *n* ELECTRON demodulación de banda estrecha *f*; **~-band filter** *n* ELECTRON, TELECOM filtro de banda estrecha *m*; **~-band filtering** *n* ELECTRON, TELECOM filtración de banda estrecha *f*; **~-band frequency modulation** *n* (*NBFM*) ELECTRON, TELECOM modulación de frecuencia de banda estrecha *f* (*MFBE*); **~-band interference** *n* ELECTRON interferencia de banda estrecha *f*; **~-band low-pass filter** *n* ELECTRON, TELECOM, filtro de paso de banda estrecha *m*; **~-band low-pass filtering** *n* ELECTRON, TELECOM filtrado de paso banda estrecha *m*; **~-band noise** *n* ELECTRON, TELECOM interferencia de banda angosta *f*, ruido de banda estrecha *m*; **~-band phase shift keying** *n* (*NBPSK*) TELECOM codificación por desplazamiento de fase en banda estrecha *f*; **~-band receiver** *n* TELECOM receptor de banda estrecha *m*; **~-band rejection filter** *n* ELECTRON filtro de eliminación de banda estrecha *m*; **~-band response spectrum** *n* NUCL espectro de respuesta de banda estrecha *m*; **~-band signal** *n* ELECTRON, TELECOM señal de banda estrecha *f*; **~-band switch** *n* TELECOM conmutador de banda estrecha *m*; **~-band switching network** *n* TELECOM red de conmutación de banda estrecha *f*; **~-band tube** *n* ELECTRON tubo de banda estrecha *m*; **~-band voice modulation** *n* (*NBVM*) TELECOM modulación vocal de banda angosta *f*; **~-bandsaw hazard** *n* SAFE peligro originado por sierra de cinta *m*, riesgo originado por sierra de cinta *m*; **~-based terrace** *n* AGRIC *conservation* terraza de base angosta *f*; **~-bore tube** *n* LAB tubo de calibre angosto *m*; **~-fabric** *n* TEXTIL cintería *f*; **~-gage diesel locomotive** *AmE see narrow-gauge diesel locomotive BrE*; **~-gage film** *AmE see narrow-gauge film BrE*; **~-gage lighting system** *AmE see narrow-gauge lighting system BrE*; **~-gage railroad** *n AmE* (*cf narrow-gauge railway BrE*) RAIL ferrocarril de vía estrecha *m*; **~-gage track system** *AmE see narrow-gauge track system BrE*; **~-gauge diesel locomotive** *n BrE* RAIL, TRANSP locomotora diesel de vía estrecha *f*; **~-gauge film** *n BrE* CINEMAT película de paso estrecho *f*; **~-gauge lighting system** *n BrE* AIR TRANSP *runway* sistema de alumbrado de vía estrecha *m*, sistema de iluminación de vía estrecha *m*; **~-gauge railway** *n BrE* (*cf narrow-gage railroad AmE*) RAIL ferrocarril de vía estrecha *m*; **~-gauge track system** *n BrE* RAIL infraestructura de vía angosta *f*; **~-neck container** *n* C&G recipiente de cuello angosto *m*; **~-necked bottle** *n* C&G botella de cuello angosto *f*, LAB botella de cuello angosto *f*, frasco de cuello angosto *m*; **~-necked flask** *n* LAB matraz de cuello angosto *m*; **~ pulse** *n* ELECTRON impulso breve *m*, impulso corto *m*, pulso de corta duración *m*; **~ weir** *n* HYDRAUL aliviadero en pared delgada *m*, vertedero de cresta aguda *m*, vertedero de cresta delgada *m*, vertedero en pared delgada *m*, WATER aliviadero en pared delgada *m*

narrowcasting *n* TV selección reducida de artistas *f*

narrows *n* OCEAN angostura *f*, bocal *m*, pasa *f*, WATER TRANSP *of river* paso *m*

NASA *abbr AmE* (*National Aeronautics and Space Administration*) SPACE NASA (*Administración Nacional de Aeronáutica y del Espacio*)

nascent: **~ neutron** *n* NUCL neutrón naciente *m*

nasse *n* OCEAN nasa *f*

national: **~ code** *n* TELECOM clave nacional *f*, código nacional *m*; **~ destination code** *n* (*NDC*) TELECOM código nacional de destino *m*; **~ grid** *n* ELEC, NUCL red eléctrica nacional *f*; **~ identification digits** *n* (*NID*) TELECOM dígitos de identificación nacional *m pl*; **~ navy** *n* MILIT, WATER TRANSP armada nacional *f*, marina nacional *f*; **~ number** *n* (*NN*) TELECOM número nacional *m*; **~ pipe thread** *n* (*NPT*) MECH ENG rosca para tubos cónicos *f*; **~ significant number** *n* (*NSN*) TELECOM número nacional significativo *m*

National: **~ Aeronautics and Space Administration** *n AmE* (*NASA*) SPACE Administración Nacional de Aeronáutica y del Espacio *f* (*NASA*); **~ Television Standards Committee** *n AmE* (*NTSC*) TV Comité Nacional de Normas de Televisión *m* (*NTSC*)

native[1] *adj* GEOL, MINERAL nativo

native[2]: **~ mode** *n* COMP&DP modo nativo *m*; **~ pasture** *n* AGRIC pastura nativa *f*

NATM *abbr* (*new Austrian tunnelling method*) CONST nuevo método austríaco de perforación de túneles *m*

natrium *n* CHEM (*Na*) sodio *m* (*Na*)

natrolite *n* MINERAL natrolita *f*

natron *n* CHEM, MINERAL natrón *m*

natural *n* ACOUST nota natural *f*; **~ acidification** *n* POLL acidificación natural *f*; **~ adhesive** *n* PACK, SAFE adhesivo natural *m*; **~ ageing** *n* METALL, P&R, THERMO envejecimiento natural *m*; **~ circulation** *n* NUCL circulación natural *f*; **~ circulation boiling-water reactor** *n* NUCL reactor de agua en ebullición de circulación natural *m*; **~ color** *AmE*, **~ colour** *n BrE* COLOUR colorante natural *m*, TEXTIL color natural *m*; **~ convection** *n* FLUID, HEAT ENG, PHYS convección natural *f*; **~-convection air-cooled condenser** *n* REFRIG condensador de aire por convección natural *m*; **~-convection cooling** *n* NUCL enfriamiento por convección natural *m*; **~ cooling** *n* THERMO enfriamiento natural al aire libre *m*; **~ draft** *AmE see natural draught BrE*; **~-draft cooling** *AmE see natural-draught cooling BrE*; **~ drainage** *n* WATER drenaje natural *m*; **~ draught** *n BrE* HEAT corriente de aire natural *f*; **~-draught cooling** *n BrE* THERMO enfriamiento con tiro natural *m*, refrigeración con tiro natural *f*; **~ dry gas** *n* GAS, PETROL gas seco natural *m*; **~ environment** *n* POLL, WATER ambiente natural *m*, medio ambiente natural *m*; **~ erosion** *n* AGRIC erosión natural *f*; **~ fiber** *AmE*, **~ fibre** *BrE n* TEXTIL fibra natural *f*; **~ frequency** *n* ACOUST, ELEC, ELECTRON, MECH ENG, PETROL, PHYS, RAD PHYS, SPACE, WAVE PHYS frecuencia natural *f*, frecuencia propia *f*; **~ frequency oscillation** *n* ELECTRON oscilación de frecuencia propia *f*; **~ gas** *n* GAS, HEAT ENG, PETR TECH, POLL, THERMO gas natural *m*; **~ gas deposit** *n* GAS depósito de gas natural *m*, yacimiento de gas natural *m*; **~-gas engine** *n* TRANSP, VEH motor de gas natural *m*; **~ gas liquid** *n* (*NGL*) GAS, PETR TECH, TRANSP líquido de gas natural *m* (*LGN*); **~-gas liquids tanker** *n* (*NGL tanker*) PETR TECH buque tanque de gas natural líquido *m*; **~ groundwater recharge** *n* WATER relleno natural de aguas freáticas *m*; **~ harbor** *AmE*, **~ harbour** *BrE n* WATER TRANSP puerto natural *m*; **~ harmonic** *n* ACOUST, WAVE PHYS armónico natural *m*; **~ language** *n* COMP&DP lenguaje natural *m*; **~ light** *n* CINEMAT, PHOTO luz natural *f*; **~ line width** *n* RAD PHYS anchura de raya natural *f*; **~ logarithm** *n* MATH logaritmo natural *m*, logaritmo neperiano *m*; **~ mode of vibration** *n* ACOUST, SPACE modo de vibración natural *m*, modo de vibración propio *m*; **~ nuclear reactor** *n* NUCL reactor nuclear natural *m*; **~ number** *n* COMP&DP, MATH número natural *m*; **~ oscillation** *n* MECH ENG oscilación fundamental *f*, oscilación libre *f*, oscilación natural *f*, oscilación propia *f*; **~ period** *n* ELECTRON período propio *m*; **~ radioactivity** *n* PHYS, RAD PHYS radiactividad natural *f*; **~ radionuclide** *n* PHYS, RAD PHYS radionucleido natural *m*; **~ resources** *n pl* AGRIC recursos naturales *m pl*; **~ rubber** *n* P&R caucho *m*, goma elástica *f*, poliisopreno *m*; **~ shade** *n* TEXTIL tono natural *m*; **~ sine** *n* GEOM seno natural *m*; **~-uranium fuel** *n* NUCL combustible de uranio natural *m*; **~-uranium slug** *n* NUCL cartucho de uranio natural *m*; **~ ventilation** *n* NUCL ventilación natural *f*; **~ void** *n* GAS vacío natural *m*; **~ whole number** *n* GEOM número entero natural *m*, número natural *m*, MATH número entero *m*, número entero natural *m*; **~ width** *n* NUCL anchura natural *f*

naturally[1]: **~ aged** *adj* THERMO de envejecimiento natural

naturally[2]: **~-acid lake** *n* POLL lago de agua natural ácida *m*; **~-occurring element** *n* NUCL elemento de origen natural *m*

naumannite *n* MINERAL naumannita *f*

nautical[1] *adj* OCEAN, WATER TRANSP náutico

nautical[2]: **~ almanac** *n* WATER TRANSP almanaque náutico *m*; **~ celestial globe** *n* OCEAN esfera celeste náutica *f*; **~ mile** *n* METEO, OCEAN, SPACE, WATER TRANSP milla marina *f*, milla náutica *f*

naval[1] *adj* MILIT, WATER TRANSP naval

naval[2]: **~ architect** *n* WATER TRANSP arquitecto naval *m*, ingeniero naval superior *m*; **~ architecture** *n* WATER TRANSP arquitectura naval *f*; **~ base** *n* MILIT, WATER TRANSP base naval *f*; **~ brass** *n* MECH, MECH ENG latón naval *m*; **~ dockyard** *n* MILIT, WATER TRANSP arsenal naval *m*; **~ maneuvers zone** *AmE*, **~ manoeuvres zone** *n BrE* MILIT, OCEAN zona de ejercicios navales *f*

Naval: **~ Air Service** *n AmE* (*cf Fleet Air Arm BrE*) MILIT, WATER TRANSP *forces* Arma Aérea Naval *f*, Fuerza Aeronaval *f*, Fuerza Aérea Naval *f*

Navier-Stokes: **~ equation** *n* PHYS ecuación de Navier-Stokes *f*

navigability *n* MAR POLL, WATER TRANSP navegabilidad *f*

navigable[1] *adj* WATER TRANSP navegable; **in ~ condition** *adj* WATER TRANSP *ship* en buen estado para navegar

navigable[2]: **~ channel** *n* HYDROL, WATER TRANSP canal navegable *m*; **~ river** *n* HYDROL, WATER TRANSP río navegable *m*

navigate *vt* WATER TRANSP *vessel* gobernar

navigating: **~ bridge** *n* WATER TRANSP puente de navegación *m*

navigation *n* AIR TRANSP, HYDROL, OCEAN, SPACE, TRANSP, WATER TRANSP navegación *f*; **~ aid** *n* WATER TRANSP ayuda a la navegación *f*; **~ by dead reckoning** *n* OCEAN, WATER TRANSP navegación a la estima *f*; **~ by sounding** *n* OCEAN, WATER TRANSP navegación con la sonda en la mano *f*; **~ channel** *n* HYDROL, OCEAN, TRANSP canal *m*, canal de navegación *m*, paso *m*; **~ light** *n* AIR TRANSP, WATER TRANSP luz de navegación *f*; **~ lock** *n* HYDROL, WATER, WATER TRANSP esclusa de cuenco *f*, esclusa de navegación *f*; **~ officer** *n* MILIT, WATER TRANSP *navy* oficial de derrota *m*; **~ radar** *n* WATER TRANSP radar náutico *m*; **~ warning signal** *n* TELECOM, WATER TRANSP señal de alarma navegacional *f*, señal de aviso navegacional *f*; **~ zone** *n* OCEAN, WATER TRANSP zona de navegación *f*

navigational[1] *adj* AIR TRANSP, TRANSP, WATER TRANSP náutico

navigational[2]: **~ aid** *n* AIR TRANSP dispositivo de ayuda de navegación *m*; **~ instruments** *n pl* WATER TRANSP instrumentos náuticos *m pl*

navigator *n* AIR TRANSP, TRANSP, WATER TRANSP navegante *m*

naviplane *n* TRANSP hidroavión *m*

navy *n* MILIT, WATER TRANSP *of a nation* armada *f*, marina *f*, marina de guerra *f*; **~ task force** *n* MILIT, WATER TRANSP agrupación naval *f*, división naval con atribuciones especiales *f*

NB *abbr* (*nominal bore*) NUCL *of pipe or tube* diámetro interno nominal *m*

Nb *abbr* (*niobium*) CHEM, METALL Nb (*niobio*)

NBFM *abbr* (*narrow-band frequency modulation*) ELECTRON, TELECOM MFBE (*modulación de frecuencia de banda estrecha*)

NBPSK *abbr* (*narrow-band phase shift keying*) TELECOM codificación por desplazamiento de fase en banda estrecha *f*

NBVM *abbr* (*narrow-band voice modulation*) TELECOM modulación vocal de banda angosta *f*

NC[1] *abbr* (*numerical control*) COMP&DP, ELEC, MECH, MECH ENG, PROD CN (*control numérico*)

NC[2]: **~ contact** *n* CONST, ELEC, PROD contacto normalmente cerrado *m*; **~ jig borer** *n* MECH ENG taladradora de plantillas de CN *f*; **~ machine** *n* MECH ENG máquina de CN *f*; **~ machine tool** *n* MECH ENG máquina herramienta de CN *f*

NCC *abbr* (*network control center AmE, network control centre BrE*) TELECOM centro de control de red *m*

n-channel *n* ELECTRON canal n *m*; **~ device** *n* ELECTRON aparato equipado de canal n *m*; **~ discrete FET** *n* ELECTRON TEC discreto de canal n *m*; **~ integrated MOS transistor** *n* ELECTRON transistor SOM integrado de canal n *m*; **~ pulldown transistor** *n* ELECTRON transistor de tracción con canal n *m*; **~ silicon gate MOS process** *n* ELECTRON proceso SOM con circuito de silicio con canal n *m*; **~ technology** *n* ELECTRON tecnología de canal n *f*

n-core: **~ cable** *n* ELEC ENG cable de varios núcleos *m*

NCR[1] *abbr* PAPER (*no carbon required*) NCR (*autocopiativo no carbonado*), TV (*network control room*) sala de control de la cadena *f*

NCR[2]: **~ papers** *n pl* PAPER papeles autocopiativos no carbonados *m pl*

NCS *abbr* (*network coordination station*) SPACE estación de coordinación de redes *f*

Nd *abbr* (*neodymium*) CHEM, ELECTRON, METALL Nd (*neodimio*)

NDC *abbr* (*national destination code*) TELECOM código nacional de destino *m*

NDF *abbr* (*new data flag*) COMP&DP, TELECOM bandera de datos nuevos *f*, señalizador de nuevos datos *m*

NDM *abbr* (*normal disconnected mode*) TELECOM modo desconectado normal *m*

NDN *abbr* (*nondelivery notification*) TELECOM notificación de falta de entrega *f*

NDR *abbr* (*normalized drilling rate*) PETR TECH régimen de perforación normalizado *m*, tasa de penetración normalizada *f*, velocidad de avance normalizada *f*

NDT *abbr* (*nondestructive testing*) MECH ENG, PHYS, SPACE ensayo no destructivo *m*

NE *abbr* (*net energy*) AGRIC energía neta *f*, TELECOM (*network element*) elemento de red *m*

Ne *abbr* (*neon*) CHEM, ELEC ENG Ne (*neón*)

neap: **~ tide** *n* FUELLESS, HYDROL, OCEAN, WATER TRANSP marea equinoccial *f*, marea muerta *f*

near[1]: **~ collision** *n* AIR TRANSP casi colisión *f*, cuasicolisión *f*; **~-critical reactor** *n* NUCL reactor cuasicrítico *m*, reactor en condiciones próximas a la criticidad *m*; **~-end crosstalk** *n* ELEC ENG paradiafonia *f*; **~ field** *n* OPT, TELECOM campo próximo *m*; **~-field analysis** *n* OPT, TELECOM análisis de campo próximo *m*; **~-field diffraction pattern** *n* OPT, TELECOM diagrama de difracción de campo próximo *m*, figura de difracción de campo próximo *f*; **~-field intensity** *n* SPACE *communications* intensidad de campo cercano *f*; **~-field pattern** *n* OPT, TELECOM diagrama de campo próximo *m*; **~-field radiation pattern** *n* OPT, TELECOM diagrama de radiación de campo próximo *m*; **~-field region** *n* OPT, TELECOM región de campo próximo *f*; **~-field scanning technique** *n* OPT, TELECOM técnica de barrido de campo próximo *f*, técnica de exploración de campo próximo *f*; **~ infrared** *n* PHYS banda cercana al infrarrojo *f*, infrarrojo cercano *m*, RAD PHYS infrarrojo cercano *m*; **~-letter-quality** *n* (*NLQ*) COMP&DP calidad cercana a la de carta *f* (*NLQ*); **~ mesh** *n* COAL cuasireticuloide *m*; **~ miss** *n* AIR TRANSP casi colisión *f*, cuasicolisión *f*, SPACE bomba que explota cerca del blanco *f*; **~ parabolic orbit** *n* SPACE órbita parabólica cercana *f*; **~ range** *n* SPACE alcance próximo *m*, campo cercano *m*, margen próximo *m*; **~ ultraviolet** *n* PHYS banda cercana al ultravioleta *f*, ultravioleta cercano *m*, RAD PHYS radiación ultravioleta cercana *f*, rango de ultravioleta cercano *m*, ultravioleta cercano *m*

near²: **at the ~ end** *adv* TELECOM al principio

nearest: **~-neighbor interaction** *AmE see nearest-neighbour interaction BrE*; **~ neighbors** *n AmE see nearest neighbours BrE*; **~-neighbour interaction** *n BrE* CRYSTALL interacción con el vecino más cercano *f*; **~ neighbours** *n pl BrE* CRYSTALL primeros vecinos *m pl*, próximos vecinos *m pl*, vecinos más cercanos *m pl*

nearing: **~-up pulley** *n* MECH ENG *endless rope haulage* polea de acercamiento *f*

nearly: **~ perfect crystal** *n* CRYSTALL, METALL cristal casi perfecto *m*

nearshore *adj* GEOL a lo largo de la costa, litoral

neat *adj* MAR POLL puro, sin mezcla

nebula *n* SPACE nebulosa *f*

nebulium *n* CHEM nebulio *m*

nebulizer *n* CHEM, CHEM TECH atomizador *m*, nebulizador *m*, LAB, PACK, PETR TECH, TRANSP atomizador *m*

neck *n* AUTO cuello *m*, gollete *m*, C&G cuello *m*, CONST *of chisel* collarín *m*, cuello *m*, ELECTRON collarín *m*, LAB, MECH boca *f*, cuello *m*, METALL garganta *f*, PROD *of metallurgical furnace* cuello *m*, *of rolling-mill roll* gorrón *m*; **~ chain** *n* AGRIC *animal production* cadena de identificación de ganado *f*; **~ flange** *n* MECH ENG *pipe fitting* brida de collar *f*; **~ mold** *AmE see neck mould BrE*; **~ molding** *AmE see neck moulding BrE*; **~ molding plane** *AmE see neck moulding plane BrE*; **~ mould** *n BrE* CONST molde de collarín *m*, moldeado de collarín *m*; **~ moulding** *n BrE* CONST molde de collarín *m*, moldeado de collarín *m*; **~ moulding plane** *n BrE* CONST cepillo para la moldura del collarín *m*; **~ ring** *n* C&G orificio *m*; **~ ring holder** *n* C&G portaorificio *m*; **~ shield** *n* SAFE escudo para cuello *m*

necking *n* MECH ENG anillo de apriete *m*, rebajo *m*, METALL corrosión circunferencial de los tubos cerca de la placa *f*, estricción *f*, rebajo *m*, PHYS collarín *m*

necrosis *n* AGRIC necrosis *f*

necrotic *adj* AGRIC necrosado

nectar: **~ gland** *n* AGRIC glándula nectarífera *f*

needle¹: **~-shaped** *adj* METALL acicular, aguzado

needle² *n* CONST viga de recalzo *f*, ELEC aguja indicadora *f*, LAB *pointer of instrument*, MECH ENG aguja *f*, aguja indicadora *f*, MINE aguja de mina *f*, TEXTIL aguja *f*, VEH válvula de aguja *f*; **~ bar** *n* TEXTIL barra de agujas *f*; **~ bearing** *n* MECH ENG cojinete de

agujas *m*, cojinete de rodillos *m*, rodamiento de agujas *m*, rulemán de agujas *m*; **~ bed** *n* TEXTIL fontura de agujas *f*; **~ dam** *n* WATER compuerta de agujas *f*, presa de agujas *f*; **~ dial** *n* LAB carátula de aguja *f*; **~ etching** *n* C&G grabado con agujas *m*; **~ file** *n* MECH ENG lima de aguja *f*; **~ follower** *n* MECH ENG *surface texture examination* seguidor de aguja *m*; **~ galvanometer** *n* ELEC, INSTR galvanómetro de aguja *m*; **~ jet** *n* VEH calibre por aguja *m*; **~ lubricator** *n* PROD lubricador de aguja *m*; **~-nose pliers** *n pl* MECH ENG *tool* pinzas de punta de aguja *f pl*; **~ roller bearing** *n* MECH ENG cojinete de rodillos en aguja *m*; **~-shaped particle** *n* METALL partícula en forma de aguja *f*; **~ valve** *n* AUTO, CHEM, FUELLESS, HYDRAUL, LAB, MECH ENG, NUCL, REFRIG válvula cónica *f*, válvula de aguja *f*, válvula de espiga *f*; **~ valve guide** *n* AUTO, VEH guía de válvula de aguja *f*

needled: **~ felt** *n* PAPER fieltro agujado *m*

needling *n* TEXTIL punzonado *m*; **~ code** *n* TEXTIL código para el punzonado *m*; **~ penetration** *n* TEXTIL penetración del punzonado *f*

needloom: **~ carpet** *n* TEXTIL alfombra de telar de agujas *f*

Néel: **~ point** *n* PHYS, REFRIG punto de Néel *m*

NEF *abbr* (*noise exposure forecast*) ACOUST NEF (*predicción de exposición al ruido*)

negative¹ *adj* ELEC, MATH negativo

negative² *n* CINEMAT, MATH, PHOTO, PHYS, PRINT negativo *m*; **~ acknowledgement** *n* (*NAK*) COMP&DP acuse de recibo negativo *m*, reconocimiento negativo *m*; **~ air cushion** *n* TRANSP amortiguador de aire inverso *m*; **~ angle** *n* GEOM ángulo negativo *m*; **~ bank** *n* AUTO inclinación negativa *f*; **~ battery** *n* TELECOM batería negativa *f*; **~ bias** *n* ELEC ENG polarización negativa *f*; **~ booster** *n* ELEC transformador rebajador del voltaje *m*, ELEC ENG reductor *m*, transformador rebajador del voltaje *m*; **~ carrier** *n* PHOTO portanegativos *m*; **~ charge** *n* ELEC, ELEC ENG, PHYS carga negativa *f*; **~-cold chamber** *n* REFRIG cámara de frío negativo *f*; **~ conductance** *n* ELEC *semiconductor* ELEC ENG conductancia negativa *f*; **~ conductor** *n* ELEC, ELEC ENG conductor negativo *m*; **~-copying process** *n* PRINT proceso de copiado de negativo *m*; **~ curvature** *n* GEOM curvatura negativa *f*; **~ cutter** *n* CINEMAT, PHOTO cortador de negativos *m*; **~ cutting** *n* CINEMAT corte de negativos *m*; **~ earthed terminal** *n BrE* (*cf negative grounded terminal AmE*) AUTO terminal a tierra negativo *m*; **~ echo** *n* TV eco negativo *m*; **~ electrode** *n* ELEC, ELEC ENG electrodo negativo *m*; **~ feedback** *n* ELEC ENG, ELECTRON realimentación inversa *f*, realimentación negativa *f*, WAVE PHYS retroalimentación negativa *f*; **~ feeder** *n* ELEC *supply* alimentador negativo *m*; **~-flux image reactor** *n* NUCL reactor imagen de flujo negativo *m*; **~ Gauss curvature** *n* GEOM curvatura de Gauss negativa *f*, curvatura negativa de Gauss *f*; **~ glow** *n* PHYS brillo negativo *m*; **~ grounded terminal** *n AmE* (*cf negative earthed terminal BrE*) AUTO terminal a tierra negativo *m*; **~ image** *n* PHOTO imagen negativa *f*; **~ impedance** *n* ELEC ENG impedancia negativa *f*; **~-impedance converter** *n* ELEC ENG conversor de impedancia negativa *m*; **~ integer** *n* MATH entero negativo *m*; **~ ion** *n* ELEC *charged particle*, ELEC ENG, ELECTRON, PART PHYS, PHYS, RAD PHYS anión *m*, ión negativo *m*; **~ lens** *n* INSTR, OPT lente negativa *f*;

~-**lens surface** *n* INSTR, OPT superficie de lente negativa *f*; ~ **logic** *n* ELECTRON lógica negativa *f*; ~ **magnetostriction** *n* ELEC ENG magnetoestricción negativa *f*; ~-**meniscus lens** *n* INSTR, OPT lente de menisco negativo *f*; ~ **meson** *n* PART PHYS mesón negativo *m*; ~ **modulation** *n* ELECTRON modulación negativa *f*; ~ **notification** *n* (*NN*) TELECOM notificación negativa *f*; ~ **number** *n* CINEMAT número de negativo *m*; ~ **perforation** *n* CINEMAT perforación del negativo *f*; ~ **photoresist** *n* ELECTRON fotoprotector negativo *m*; ~-**picture phase** *n* TV fase de la imagen negativa *f*; ~ **plate** *n* AUTO placa negativa *f*, PRINT plancha negativa *f*; ~ **pole** *n* ELEC *terminal*, ELEC ENG, PHYS polo negativo *m*; ~ **power supply** *n* ELEC ENG fuente negativa *f*; ~ **pressure** *n* MECH ENG presión negativa *f*; ~ **pressure signs** *n pl* SAFE señales de presión negativa *f pl*; ~ **print** *n* PHOTO copia negativa *f*; ~ **rake** *n* MECH ENG *of cutting tool* ángulo de rebaje negativo *m*; ~ **reactance** *n* ELEC ENG reactancia negativa *f*; ~ **reactivity** *n* NUCL antirreactividad *f*, reactividad negativa *f*, PHYS antirreactividad *f*; ~ **reactor** *n* NUCL reactor negativo *m*; ~ **resist** *n* ELEC, ELEC ENG, ELECTRON protector negativo *m*; ~ **resistance** *n* ELEC, ELEC ENG, ELECTRON resistencia negativa *f*; ~-**resistance amplifier** *n* ELEC, ELEC ENG, ELECTRON amplificador de resistencia negativa *m*; ~-**resistance characteristic** *n* ELEC ENG característica de resistencia negativa *f*; ~-**resistance diode** *n* ELECTRON, PHYS, diodo de resistencia negativa *m*; ~-**resistance oscillator** *n* ELECTRON, PHYS oscilador de resistencia negativa *m*; ~ **scanning** *n* TV lectura negativa *f*; ~ **skin friction** *n* COAL rozamiento superficial negativo *m*; ~ **sleeve** *n* PHOTO portanegativos *m*; ~ **terminal** *n* AUTO, ELEC, ELEC ENG, VEH borne negativo *m*, terminal negativo *m*; ~ **track** *n* CINEMAT banda del negativo *f*; ~ **video signal** *n* TV señal negativa de video *f* (*AmL*), señal negativa de vídeo *f* (*Esp*); ~ **viewer** *n* PHOTO visor de negativos *m*; ~ **voltage** *n* ELEC ENG tensión negativa *f*, voltaje negativo *m*; ~-**voltage supply** *n* ELEC ENG suministro de tensión negativa *m*, suministro de voltaje negativo *m*; ~ **working plate** *n* PRINT plancha negativa *f*

negatively[1]: ~ **skewed** *adj* GEOM desviado negativamente

negatively[2]: ~ **doped region** *n* PHYS región con dopado negativo *f*

negator *n* COMP&DP negador *m*

negatron *n* ELECTRON, PART PHYS electrón negativo *m*, negatrón *m*

negotiate *vt* RAIL *a curve* tomar

Nel: ~ **temperature** *n* ELEC *antiferromagnetism* temperatura Nel *f*

nematic: ~ **liquid crystals** *n pl* CRYSTALL, ELECTRON cristales líquidos nemáticos *m pl*; ~ **phase** *n* CRYSTALL fase nemática *f*

nematicide *n* AGRIC nematicida *m*

nematode *n* AGRIC nemátodo *m*; ~ **disease** *n* AGRIC anguilulosis *f*

N-entity *n* TELECOM entidad N *f*

neoabietic *adj* CHEM neoabiético

neoclassical: ~-**pinch effect** *n* NUCL efecto de estricción neoclásica *m*

neodymium *n* (*Nd*) CHEM, ELECTRON, METALL neodimio *m* (*Nd*); ~ **laser** *n* ELECTRON láser de neodimio *m*

neoergosterol *n* CHEM neoergosterol *m*

neon *n* (*Ne*) CHEM, ELEC ENG neón *m* (*Ne*); ~ **fluor**-escent tube *n* RAD PHYS tubo fluorescente de neón *m*; ~ **glow lamp** *n* ELEC lámpara de efluvios de neón *f*, lámpara luminiscente de neón *f*; ~ **indicator** *n* ELEC ENG indicador de neón *m*; ~ **lamp** *n* ELEC, ELEC ENG, PHYS lámpara de neón *f*; ~ **tube** *n* ELEC *lighting* ENG, ELEC, PHYS lámpara de neón *f*, lámpara luminiscente de neón *f*, tubo de neón *m*

neoprene *n* CHEM, CONST, P&R, PACK neopreno *m*; ~ **molded seal** *AmE*, ~ **moulded seal** *BrE n* P&R sello moldeado de neopreno *m*

neotectonic *adj* GEOL neotectónico

neovolcanic *adj* GEOL neovolcánico

nep *n* TEXTIL botón *m*

NEP *abbr* (*noise equivalent power*) OPT, TELECOM potencia equivalente de ruido *f*

neper *n* (*N*) ACOUST neperio *m* (*N*), ELECTRON, PHYS neper *m*

nepheline *n* MINERAL nefelina *f*

nephelinite *n* PETROL nefelinita *f*

nephelinyte *n* PETROL nefelinita *f*

nephelite *n* MINERAL nefelita *f*

nepheloid: ~ **transparency** *n* PAPER transparencia nubosa *f*

nephelometer *n* CHEM, INSTR, LAB nefelómetro *m*

nephelometry *n* CHEM, INSTR, LAB, nefelometría *f*

nephrite *n* GEOL, MINERAL nefrita *f*

neptunium *n* (*Np*) CHEM, RAD PHYS neptunio *m* (*Np*)

NERF *abbr* (*network element function*) TELECOM función del elemento de red *f*

neritic: ~ **water** *n* OCEAN agua nerítica *f*; ~ **zone** *n* GEOL zona nerítica *f*

Nernst: ~ **bridge** *n* ELEC ENG puente de Nernst *m*

nerol *n* CHEM nerol *m*

nerve: ~ **agent** *n* MILIT gas agente nervioso *m*

nest[1] *n* MECH ENG *of gear wheels* engranaje *m*, MINE montaje en serie *m*

nest[2] *vt* MATH encajar

nest[3] *vti* COMP&DP anidar

nested[1] *adj* COMP&DP anidado, jerarquizado, MATH encajado

nested[2]: ~ **intervals** *n pl* MATH intervalos encajados *m pl*; ~ **loop** *n* COMP&DP bucle anidado *m*

nesting *n* COMP&DP anidamiento *m*, jerarquización *f*; ~ **box** *n* PACK caja telescópica *f*; ~ **form** *n* PRINT montaje combinado *m*; ~ **magazine** *n* PACK almacén telescópico *m*

net *n* PETR TECH neto *m*; ~ **area** *n* FUELLESS *of collector* superficie neta *f*; ~ **assimilation rate** *n* AGRIC tasa neta de asimilación *f*; ~ **blotch** *n* AGRIC mancha reticulada *f*; ~ **breeding rate** *n* NUCL tasa neta de reproducción *f*; ~ **calorific value** *n* HEAT ENG valor calórico neto *m*; ~ **charge** *n* ELEC ENG carga neta *f*; ~ **control station** *n* ELEC estación de control de la red *f*, estación de dirección de la red *f*; ~ **depth** *n* OCEAN altura de la red *f*; ~ **donator** *n* POLL donador de red *m*; ~ **drum** *n* OCEAN tambor *m*; ~ **energy** *n* (*NE*) AGRIC energía neta *f* (*EN*); ~ **frame** *n* OCEAN armadura *f*, armazón *m*; ~ **heat loss** *n* HEAT ENG, THERMO pérdida de calor neta *f*; ~ **horsepower** *n* MECH ENG potencia de red *f*, potencia neta *f*; ~ **income** *n* PETR TECH ingresos netos *m pl*, renta neta *f*; ~ **making** *n* OCEAN elaboración de redes *f*; ~ **mender** *n* OCEAN redero *m*; ~ **mending** *n* OCEAN remiendo de redes *m*, reparación de redes *f*; ~ **mouth** *n* OCEAN boca de la red *f*, gola *f*; ~ **output** *n* GEOPHYS potencial neto *m*; ~-**pay zone** *n* PETROL zona de

producción neta *f*; **~-positive-suction head** *n* NUCL carga de aspiración neta positiva *f*; **~ receiver** *n* POLL colector de red *m*; **~ refrigerating effect** *n* REFRIG potencia refrigeradora neta *f*; **~ register** *n* WATER TRANSP *tonnage* registro neto *m*; **~ repairer** *n* OCEAN reparador de redes *m*; **~ roller** *n* OCEAN bola *f*, diábolo *m*, esfera *f*, rueda *f*; **~ sling** *n* WATER TRANSP *for loading cargo* red de carga *f*; **~ time interval** *n* TRANSP intervalo de tiempo neto *m*; **~ ton** *n* METR tonelada neta *f*; **~ tonnage** *n* PETR TECH tonelaje neto *m*, WATER TRANSP arqueo neto *m*; **~ weight** *n* FOOD, METR, TEXTIL peso neto *m*; **~ wing area** *n* AIR TRANSP área del ala neta *f*
Net: **the ~** *n* COMP&DP la Net *f*, la Red *f*
netsonde *n* OCEAN netsonde *m*, sonda de red *f*
netting *n* CONST malla *f*, *wire* red *f*, OCEAN paño de red *m*, confección *f*, enredar *m*, red protectora *f*, construcción *f*; **~ frame** *n* OCEAN armadura *f*, armazón *m*; **~ needle** *n* OCEAN lanzadera de malla *f*, lanzadera de redero *f*
network[1]: **~-like** *adj* AIR TRANSP estilo red
network[2] *n* COMP&DP, CONST red *f*, ELEC *supply* red *f*, malla *f*, ELEC ENG *of circuit elements, telecommunications* red *f*, *of stations* red eléctrica *f*, interconexión *f*, *transmitters, television etc* cadena *f*, P&R retículo *m* (*Esp*), red *f*, reticulado *m* (*AmL*), PHYS, PROD, SPACE red *f*, TRANSP cadena *f*, red *f*, TV cadena *f*, red de televisoras *f*; **~ access control** *n* COMP&DP control de acceso a la red *m*; **~ analyser** *n* BrE COMP&DP analizador de redes *m*, ELEC, ELEC ENG analizador de redes *m*, analizador de redes eléctricas *m*, TELECOM analizador de redes *m*; **~ analysis** *n* ELEC, ELEC ENG análisis de redes *m*; **~ analyzer** *AmE see network analyser BrE*; **~ architecture** *n* ELEC ENG arquitectura de red *f*; **~ breakdown** *n* TELECOM corte de red *m*, interrupción en el servicio de red *f*, ruptura de red *f*; **~ broadcast repeater station** *n* TV estación repetidora de la cadena *f*; **~ cable** *n* TELECOM cable de red *m*; **~ constant** *n* ELEC ENG constante de una red *f*; **~ control center** *n* AmE, **~ control centre** BrE *n* (*NCC*) TELECOM centro de control de red *m*; **~ control channel** *n* COMP&DP canal de control de la red *m*; **~ control room** *n* (*NCR*) TV sala de control de la cadena *f*; **~ controller** *n* COMP&DP controlador de redes *m*; **~ coordination station** *n* (*NCS*) SPACE *communications* estación de coordinación de redes *f*; **~ coverage** *n* TV cobertura de la cadena *f*; **~ cue** *n* TV aviso sonoro de la cadena *m*; **~ database** *n* COMP&DP, ELECTRON, TELECOM base de datos de red *f*; **~ delay** *n* COMP&DP demora de red *f*, retardo de la red *m*; **~ discard indicator** *n* TELECOM indicador de abandono de red *m*; **~ element** *n* (*NE*) TELECOM elemento de red *m*; **~ element function** *n* (*NERF*) TELECOM función del elemento de red *f*; **~ former** *n* C&G formador de redes *m*; **~ gateway** *n* TELECOM dispositivo de acceso a la red *m*; **~ identification** *n* TV identificación de la cadena *f*; **~ interconnection** *n* COMP&DP, TELECOM interconexión de redes *f*; **~ interface card** *n* COMP&DP tarjeta de interfaz de red *f*; **~ layer** *n* COMP&DP nivel de red *m*; **~ layer relay** *n* (*NLR*) TELECOM relé de capa de red *m*; **~ load analysis** *n* COMP&DP análisis de carga de la red *m*; **~ management** *n* COMP&DP, TELECOM administración de red *f*; **~ management application service element** *n* (*NM-ASE*) TELECOM elemento de red del servicio de aplicación de gestión *m*, solicitud de

administración de la red *f*; **~ management center** *n* AmE, **~ management centre** BrE *n* (*NMC*) TELECOM centro de gestión de red *m*; **~ manager** *n* COMP&DP, TELECOM administrador de red *m*; **~ map** *n* TELECOM mapa de red *m*; **~ model** *n* COMP&DP modelo de red *m*; **~ modifier** *n* C&G modificador de redes *m*; **~-node interface** *n* TELECOM interfaz rednodo *m*; **~ operating system** *n* (*NOS*) COMP&DP sistema operativo de red *m* (*NOS*); **~ operators maintenance channel** *n* (*NOMC*) TELECOM canal de mantenimiento de operadores de red *m*; **~ parameter** *n* PHYS parámetro de red *m*; **~ performance** *n* (*NP*) COMP&DP funcionamiento de la red *m*, TELECOM calidad de servicio de la red *f*, características de la red *f pl*, comportamiento de la red *m*, funcionamiento de la red *m*; **~ protection** *n* ELEC protección de la red *f*; **~ protocol data unit** *n* (*NPDU*) TELECOM unidad de datos del protocolo de la red *f*; **~ service** *n* (*NS*) TELECOM mantenimiento de la red *m*; **~ service access point** *n* (*NSAP*) TELECOM punto de acceso al mantenimiento de la red *m*; **~ simulator** *n* COMP&DP simulador de red *m*; **~ software** *n* COMP&DP software de red *m*; **~ specialist** *n* COMP&DP especialista en redes *m*; **~ spur** *n* ELEC ENG derivación de red *f*; **~ station** *n* COMP&DP estación de red *f*; **~ supervision and management** *n* TELECOM gestión y supervisión de la red *f*; **~ supervisor** *n* TELECOM supervisor de la red *m*; **~ synthesis** *n* ELEC síntesis de redes *f*, síntesis del cuadripolo *f*, ELEC ENG síntesis de redes *f*; **~ terminal equipment** *n* (*NTE*) TELECOM equipo terminal de la red *m*; **~ termination** *n* (*NT*) TELECOM terminación de la red *f*; **~ theory** *n* ELEC ENG teoría de redes *f*; **~ topology** *n* COMP&DP topología de red *f*; **~ virtual terminal** *n* (*NVT*) COMP&DP terminal virtual en red *m* (*NVT*)
Network: **~ Switching Center** *n* AmE, **~ Switching Centre** BrE *n* TELECOM Centro de Conmutación de la Red *m*
networked *adj* TELECOM interconectado, reticular
networking *n* COMP&DP conexión en red *f*, integración en red *f*
neural: **~ network** *n* COMP&DP red neural *f*, red neurológica *f*, red neuronal *f*
neuraminic *adj* CHEM neuramínico
neurodine *n* CHEM neurodina *f*
neuron *n* COMP&DP neurona *f*
neutral[1] *adj* CHEM, PHYS neutro
neutral[2] *n* AUTO posición neutra *f*, MECH conductor neutro *m*, punto neutro *m*, VEH posición neutra *f*, punto muerto *m*; **~ amber glass** *n* C&G vidrio ambar neutro *m*; **~ armature** *n* ELEC *relay* armadura neutra *f*; **~ atom** *n* PART PHYS átomo neutro *m*; **~-atom beam injection** *n* NUCL inyección de haz atómico neutral *f*, inyección de haz atómico sin carga *f*; **~ axis** *n* CONST eje neutral *m*, eje neutro *m*, fibra neutra *f*; **~ burn-out** *n* NUCL abrasamiento neutral *m*, quemado neutral *m*; **~ compensator** *n* ELEC ENG compensador neutral *m*; **~ conductor** *n* ELEC ENG *multiple-wire distributing system* conductor neutral *m*; **~ currents** *n pl* PHYS corrientes neutras *f pl*; **~-density filter** *n* CINEMAT filtro de densidad neutra *m*, PHOTO, PRINT filtro de densidad neutra *m*, filtro neutro *m*; **~ flame** *n* CONST llama neutra *f*; **~ gas** *n* SPACE gas neutro *m*; **~ glass** *n* C&G vidrio neutro *m*; **~ gray** *AmE*, **~ grey** BrE *n* PRINT gris neutro *m*;

~ **particle** n NUCL, PART PHYS, PHYS partícula neutra f; ~ **particle detector** n NUCL detector de partículas neutrales m, detector de partículas neutras m; ~ **point** n PHYS punto neutro m; ~ **point displacement voltage** n ELEC supply network tensión de desplazamiento de punto neutro f; ~ **polar relay** n ELEC ENG relé polar neutral m; ~ **relay** n ELEC relevador neutral m, relevador neutro m, relé neutral m, relé neutro m, relé no polarizado m, ELEC ENG relé neutro m; ~ **section** n RAIL contact line sección neutra f; ~ **shade** n TEXTIL tono neutro m; ~ **state** n PART PHYS estado neutro m; ~ **sulfite pulp** AmE, ~ **sulphite pulp** n BrE PAPER pulpa al sulfito neutro f; ~ **terminal** n ELEC connection, ELEC ENG borne neutro m, terminal neutro m; ~ **test card** n CINEMAT cartulina neutra de prueba f; ~ **tint** n COLOUR tono neutro m; ~ **-tinted glass** n C&G vidrio neutro de color m; ~ **transmission** n COMP&DP transmisión neutral f; ~ **wedge** n CINEMAT cuña neutra f; ~ **white glass** n C&G vidrio neutro blanco m; ~ **wire** n ELEC circuit alambre neutro m, conductor neutro m, hilo neutro m, ELEC ENG, PROD alambre neutro m; ~ **zone** n ELEC ENG zona neutra f

neutrality n CHEM, ELEC, PHYS neutralidad f

neutralization n GEN neutralización f; ~ **pond** n NUCL piscina de neutralización f

neutralized: ~ **amplifier** n ELECTRON amplificador neutralizado m

neutralizer n CHEM, SPACE neutralizador m

neutralizing[1] adj CHEM neutralizador

neutralizing[2] n CHEM neutralizador m; ~ **agent** n CHEM, SAFE agente neutralizador m, agente neutralizante m

neutrino n PART PHYS, PHYS neutrino m

neutron n (n) ELEC, PART PHYS, PETROL, PHYS, RAD PHYS neutrón m (n); ~ **absorber** n NUCL absorbente de neutrones m; ~ **-absorbing reaction** n NUCL reacción absorbente de neutrones f; ~ **activation logging** n NUCL medición de la activación neutrónica f, registro de la activación neutrónica m; ~ **beam** n PART PHYS haz de neutrones m; ~ **burst** n NUCL ráfaga de neutrones f; ~ **capture** n PHYS captura de neutrones f; ~ **counter tube** n NUCL tubo contador de neutrones m; ~ **diffraction** n CRYSTALL difracción de neutrones f; ~ **excess** n PHYS exceso de neutrones m; ~ **-gamma log** n PETR TECH diagrafía de neutrón-gamma f, perfil neutrón-gamma m, registro neutrón-gamma m; ~ **log** n FUELLESS, GAS, PETR TECH, PETROL diagrafía neutrón f, perfil de neutrones m, perfil gamma m, perfil neutrón m, perfilaje neutrónico m, registro neutrón m, registro neutrónico m; ~ **logging** n FUELLESS, GAS, PETR TECH, PETROL diagrafía neutrón f, perfil de neutrones m, perfil gamma m, perfil neutrón m, perfilaje neutrónico m, registro de neutrones m, registro neutrón m, registro neutrónico m; ~ **mass** n RAD PHYS masa del neutrón f; ~ **-neutron log** n PETR TECH diagrafía de neutrón-neutrón f, perfil neutrón-neutrón m, registro neutrón-neutrón m; ~ **number** n PHYS número de neutrones m; ~ **radiative capture** n RAD PHYS captura radiante de neutrones f, captura radiativa de neutrones f; ~ **scattering** n PART PHYS dispersión de neutrones f; ~ **source reactor** n NUCL reactor emisor de neutrones m; ~ **star** n SPACE estrella de neutrones f; ~ **thermalization** n RAD PHYS termalización de

neutrones f; ~ **yield** n PART PHYS, PHYS producción de neutrones f, rendimiento en neutrones m

never: ~ **-exceed Mach number** n AIR TRANSP aviation número de Mach nunca a exceder m

nevyanskite n MINERAL newjanskita f

new[1] adj CHEM, COMP&DP, MECH ENG, NUCL, TELECOM nuevo

new[2]: ~ **Austrian tunnelling method** n CONST nuevo método austríaco de perforación de túneles m; ~ **data flag** n (NDF) COMP&DP bandera de datos nuevos f, TELECOM bandera de datos nuevos f, señalizador de nuevos datos m; ~ **-element storage drum** n NUCL bidón de almacenamiento de elementos nuevos m; ~ **fuel** n NUCL combustible nuevo m; ~ **-fuel assembly** n NUCL elemento de combustible nuevo m; ~ **-fuel element** n NUCL elemento de combustible nuevo m; ~ **products** n MECH ENG productos nuevos m pl

New Zealand: ~ **flax** n AGRIC formio m

Newcastle: ~ **disease** n AGRIC neumoencefalitis aviar f

newel n CONST at top of stairs pilarote m, MECH ENG of Archimedean screw espigón m, PROD core núcleo m; ~ **post** n CONST at top of stairs pilarote m

news: ~ **network** n TV cadena de noticias f

newscast n TV boletín informativo m (Esp), noticiero de televisión m (AmL), noticioso de televisión m (AmL), programa de noticias m (Esp)

newsgroup n COMP&DP foro de interés m, grupo de discusión m, grupo de interés m, newsgroup m

newspaper: ~ **rotary press** n PRINT rotativa de periódicos f

newsprint n PAPER papel prensa m

newsreel: ~ **camera** n CINEMAT, TV cámara para documentales de actualidades f; ~ **cameraman** n CINEMAT, TV operador de cámara de actualidades m

newsroom n TV sala de redacción f

newton n (N) ELEC, METR, PHYS newton m (N)

Newtonian[1] adj PHYS newtoniano

Newtonian[2]: ~ **aberration** n PHYS aberración newtoniana f; ~ **mechanics** n PHYS, SPACE mecánica Newtoniana f; ~ **telescope** n PHYS telescopio newtoniano m

Newton: ~ **'s ring** n PHOTO, PHYS anillo de Newton m

next: ~ **nearest neighbors** AmE, ~ **nearest neighbours** BrE n METALL vecindad más próxima f

N-facility n TELECOM instalación N f

NFE abbr (nitrogen-free extract) AGRIC extracto no nitrogenado m

NGL[1] abbr (natural gas liquid) GAS, PETR TECH, TRANSP LGN (líquido de gas natural)

NGL[2]: ~ **tanker** n (natural-gas liquids tanker) PETR TECH buque cisterna de LGN m, buque tanque de gas natural líquido m, WATER TRANSP buque cisterna de LGN m

NH₃ abbr (ammonia) GEN NH_3 (amoníaco)

Ni abbr (nickel) CHEM, ELEC ENG, METALL, MINERAL Ni (níquel)

niacinamide n CHEM nicotinamida f

nialamide n CHEM nialamida f

nibble n COMP&DP cuarteto m, media palabra f

nibbler n MECH ENG recortadora de chapa de uña vibratoria f

nibbling: ~ **machine** n MECH ENG tool cizalla de uña vibrante f, recortadora de chapa de uña vibratoria f

Nicad: ~ **battery** n PHOTO pila de níquel y cadmio f

niccolum *n* CHEM nicolo *m*
nick¹ *n* AGRIC *maize* complementaridad *f*, encaje *m*, PROD *in screw head* ranura *f*, *notch* muesca *f*
nick² *vt* PROD ranurar
nicked: **~-tooth milling cutter** *n* MECH ENG fresa de dientes interrumpidos *f*
nickel¹ *n* (*Ni*) CHEM, ELEC ENG, METALL, MINERAL níquel *m* (*Ni*); **~ arsenide** *n* CHEM arseniuro de níquel *m*; **~ bloom** *n* MINERAL annabergita *f*, flores de níquel *f*; **~-cadmium battery** *n* CINEMAT, ELEC ENG, SPACE, TRANSP acumulador de níquel-cadmio *m*, batería de níquel-cadmio *f*; **~ hydroxide** *n* CHEM, SPACE hidróxido de níquel *m*; **~-iron battery** *n* ELEC ENG, SPACE, TRANSP acumulador de níquel-hierro *m*, batería de níquel-hierro *f*, batería ferroníquel *f*; **~-iron storage battery** *n* ELEC ENG, TRANSP batería de acumuladores de níquel-hierro *f*; **~-ocher** *AmE*, **~-ochre** *n* *BrE* MINERAL niquelocre *m*; **~ plating** *n* ELEC *process*, PROD niquelado *m*; **~-silver** *n* ELEC ENG niquelado-plateado *m*; **~-zinc storage battery** *n* ELEC ENG, TRANSP batería de acumuladores de zinc-níquel *f*
nickel²: **~-plate** *vt* COATINGS niquelar
nickelage *n* PROD niquelado *m*
nickelic *adj* CHEM niquelado
nickeline *n* MINERAL niquelina *f*
nickeling *n* PROD niquelación *f*, niqueladura *f*
nickelocene *n* CHEM niqueloceno *m*
nickelous *adj* CHEM niqueloso
nickelure *n* PROD niqueluro *m*
nicker *n* MECH ENG *of centre bit* muescador *m*
nicking *n* PROD ranurado *m*; **~ machine** *n* COAL máquina entalladora *f*, PROD ranurado *m*
nickpoint *AmE see knickpoint BrE*
Nicol: **~ prism** *n* PHYS prisma de Nicol *m*
nicopyrite *n* MINERAL nicopirita *f*
nicotinamide *n* CHEM nicotinamida *f*
nicotine *n* CHEM nicotina *f*
nicotinic *adj* CHEM nicotínico
nicotyrine *n* CHEM nicotirina *f*
NID *abbr* (*national identification digits*) TELECOM dígitos de identificación nacional *m pl*
niggles *n pl* OCEAN molestia progresiva *f*
night: **~ effect** *n* CINEMAT efecto nocturno *m*; **~ flight** *n* AIR TRANSP vuelo nocturno *m*; **~ range** *n* AIR TRANSP alcance nocturno *m*, radio de acción nocturno *m*; **~ service** *n* TELECOM servicio nocturno *m*; **~ sight** *n* MILIT alza nocturna *f*; **~ soil** *n* AGRIC abono de excrementos humanos *m*, abono de excrementos pútridos *m*, HYDROL material de desecho *m*, RECYCL abono de excrementos humanos *m*, abono de excrementos pútridos *m*; **~ storage heater** *n* HEAT, HEAT ENG, THERMO acumulador de calor nocturno *m*, calentador para almacenamiento térmico nocturno *m*; **~ tariff** *n* ELEC *supply* tarifa nocturna *f*; **~ telescope** *n* INSTR telescopio de noche *m*; **~ vision goggles** *n pl* (*NVG*) MILIT, OPT anteojos de visión nocturna *m pl* (*AmL*), gafas de visión nocturna *f pl* (*Esp*); **~ watch** *n* MILIT guardia nocturna *m*; **~ wave** *n* AIR TRANSP onda nocturna *f*
nil: **~-ductility transition temperature** *n* NUCL temperatura de transición de ductilidad nula *f*
nill *n* PROD batiduras de forja *f pl*
nimbostratus *n* (*Ns*) METEO nimbostratus *m* (*Ns*)
nine: **~'s complement** *n* COMP&DP complemento a

nueve *m*; **~-digit counter** *n* PACK contador de nueve dígitos *m*
ninety: **~ degree error** *n* TV error de noventa grados *m*
niobite *n* CHEM, MINERAL columbita *f*, niobita *f*
niobium *n* (*Nb*) CHEM, METALL niobio *m* (*Nb*)
nip *n* MINE *vein, lode* contracción *f*, derrumbe *m*, estrechamiento *m*, hundimiento *m*, mordisco *m*, OCEAN desmoronamiento *m*, socavón *m*, PAPER línea de tangencia *f*, PRINT línea de tangencia de dos cilindros *f*; **~-and-tuck folder** *n* PRINT plegadora de martillo *f*; **~ pressure** *n* PAPER presión en la línea de tangencia *f*
nippers *n pl* CONST, MECH ENG alicates de corte *m pl*, PROD alicates de corte *m pl*, mordazas de retención *f pl*, pinzas de retención *f pl*, tenazas de corte *f pl*
nipple *n* CONST, MECH ENG *plumbing* boquilla *f*, boquilla acopladora *f*, conectador *m*, entrerrosca *f*, manguito roscado *m*, niple *m*, unión roscada *f*; **~-drinker** *n* AGRIC bebedero de boquilla *m*
niter: **~-blued steel** *AmE see nitre-blued steel BrE*
nitramine *n* CHEM nitramina *f*
nitrate¹ *n* CHEM, POLL nitrato *m*; **~ base** *n* CINEMAT, PHOTO soporte de nitrato *m*; **~-based explosive** *n* MINE explosivo a base de nitrato *m*; **~ film** *n* CINEMAT película de nitrato *f*; **~ paper** *n* PAPER papel nitrado *m*
nitrate² *vt* CHEM nitrar
nitratine *n* CHEM nitratina *f*, nitro de Perú *m*, salitre de Perú *m*
nitration *n* CHEM nitración *f*
nitratite *n* MINERAL nitratita *f*
nitrazine *n* CHEM nitracina *f*
nitre: **~-blued steel** *n* *BrE* MECH, MECH ENG, METALL acero azulado con nitrato potásico *m*
nitric¹ *adj* CHEM nítrico
nitric²: **~ acid** *n* CHEM, POLL ácido nítrico *m*; **~ oxide** *n* (*NO*) CHEM, POLL pentaóxido de dinitrógeno *m*, óxido de nitrógeno V *m*, óxido nítrico *m*
nitridation *n* CHEM nitruración *f*
nitride¹ *n* CHEM nitruro *m*; **~ hardening** *n* MECH endurecimiento con nitruro *m*
nitride² *vt* CHEM, MECH ENG nitrurar
nitrided: **~ steel** *n* MECH ENG, METALL acero nitrurado *m*
nitriding *n* CHEM, MECH ENG nitruración *f*
nitrification *n* CHEM, HYDRAUL, HYDROL nitrificación *f*
nitrify¹ *vt* CHEM, HYDRAUL, HYDROL nitrificar
nitrify² *vi* CHEM, HYDRAUL, HYDROL nitrificar, nitrificarse
nitrifying *adj* CHEM, HYDRAUL, HYDROL nitrificante
nitrile *n* CHEM nitrilo *m*; **~ rubber** *n* P&R caucho de nitrilo *m*, caucho nitrílico *m*; **~ seal** *n* PROD obturador de nitrilo *m*
nitrin *n* CHEM nitrina *f*
nitrite *n* CHEM nitrito *m*
nitritoid *adj* CHEM nitritoide
nitro *n* CHEM nitro *m*; **~-compound** *n* CHEM nitroderivado *m*
nitroamine *n* CHEM nitroamina *f*
nitroaniline *n* CHEM nitroanilina *f*
nitrobenzene *n* CHEM nitrobenceno *m*
nitrocellulose *n* CHEM nitrato de celulosa *m*, nitroalgodón *m*, nitrocelulosa *f*; **~ lacquer** *n* COATINGS, COLOUR, CONST laca de nitrocelulosa *f*
nitrocellulosic *adj* CHEM nitrocelulósico
nitrochloroform *n* CHEM nitrocloroformo *m*

nitrocotton: ~ **explosive** *n* MINE algodón pólvora *m*
nitroethane *n* CHEM nitroetano *m*
nitroform *n* CHEM nitroformo *m*
nitrogelatine *n* MINE nitrogelatina *f*
nitrogen *n* (*N*) CHEM, GAS, PETR TECH nitrógeno *m* (*N*);
~~**-cooled reactor** *n* NUCL reactor refrigerado por
nitrógeno *m*; ~ **cover gas** *n* NUCL cobertura de gas
nitrógeno *f*, nitrógeno gaseoso protector *m*;
~ **deficiency** *n* AGRIC deficiencia de nitrógeno *f*;
~ **dioxide** *n* CHEM, POLL, SAFE dióxido de nitrógeno
m; ~~**-free extract** *n* (*NFE*) AGRIC extracto no
nitrogenado *m* (*ENN*); ~ **gas** *n* (*N₂*) CHEM nitrógeno
gaseoso *m*, GAS gas de nitrógeno *m* (*N₂*); ~ **narcosis**
n OCEAN narcosis causada por nitrógeno *f*, narcosis
por nitrógeno *f*; ~ **oxide** *n* CHEM, POLL (*NO₂*) óxido
de nitrógeno *m* (*NO₂*); ~ **pentoxide** *n* CHEM (*N₂O₅*)
óxido de nitrógeno V *m* (*N₂O₅*), POLL pentaóxido de
dinitrógeno *m*, óxido de nitrógeno V *m* (*N₂O₅*);
~ **peroxide** *n* CHEM, POLL peróxido de nitrógeno *m*;
~ **purging** *n* SPACE *of tank on spacecraft* vaciado del
nitrógeno *m*; ~ **requirement** *n* AGRIC necesidad de
nitrógeno *f*
nitrogenous *adj* CHEM nitrogenoso
nitroglucose *n* CHEM nitroglucosa *f*
nitroglycerine *n* CHEM, MILIT nitroglicerina *f*, MINE
glonoina *f* (*AmL*), nitroglicerina *f* (*Esp*)
nitroindole *n* CHEM nitroindol *m*
nitromannitol *n* CHEM hexanitrito de manitol *m*
nitrometer *n* CHEM azotímetro *m*, nitrómetro *m*
nitromethane *n* CHEM nitrometano *m*
nitron *n* CHEM nitrón *m*
nitronaphthalene *n* CHEM nitronaftaleno *m*
nitronium *n* CHEM nitronio *m*
nitroparaffin *n* CHEM nitroparafina *f*
nitrophenol *n* CHEM nitrofenol *m*
nitrosate *n* CHEM nitrosato *m*
nitrosation *n* CHEM nitrosación *f*
nitrosifying *adj* CHEM nitrosificante
nitrosite *n* CHEM nitrosito *m*
nitrosochloride *n* CHEM nitrosocloruro *m*
nitrosubstituted *adj* CHEM nitrosubstituido, nitrosustituido
nitrosulfuric *AmE see* nitrosulphuric *BrE*
nitrosulphuric *adj BrE* CHEM nitrosulfúrico
nitrosyl *n* CHEM nitrosil *m*, nitrosilo *m*
nitrotartaric *adj* CHEM nitrotartárico
nitrotoluene *n* CHEM nitrotolueno *m*
nitrous[1] *adj* CHEM nitroso
nitrous[2]: ~ **oxide** *n* (*N₂O*) CHEM, POLL trióxido de
dinitrógeno *m*, óxido de nitrógeno III *m*, óxido
nitroso *m*
nitrox *n* OCEAN nitrox *m*
nitryl *n* CHEM nitrilo *m*
nivation *n* CHEM nivación *f*
nivenite *n* NUCL nivenita *f*
Nixie: ~ **tube** *n* ELECTRON tubo Nixie *m*
N-layer *n* TELECOM capa N *f*
NLQ *abbr* (*near-letter-quality*) COMP&DP NLQ (*calidad
cercana a la de carta*)
NLR *abbr* (*network layer relay*) TELECOM relé de capa
de red *m*
NM-ASE *abbr* (*network management application service
element*) TELECOM solicitud de administración de la
red *f*
NMC *abbr* (*network management centre BrE*) TELECOM
centro de gestión de red *m*

NMOS: ~ **component** *n* ELECTRON componente SOM
de canal N *m*; ~ **integrated circuit** *n* ELECTRON
circuito integrado SOM de canal N *m*; ~ **logic** *n*
ELECTRON circuito lógico SOM de canal N *m*;
~ **transistor** *n* ELECTRON transistor SOM de canal
N *m*
NMR[1] *abbr* (*nuclear magnetic resonance*) CHEM, NUCL,
PETR TECH, PHYS, RAD PHYS resonancia magnética
nuclear *f*
NMR[2]: ~ **log** *n* PETR TECH diagrafía de resonancia
magnética nuclear *f*, perfil de resonancia magnética
nuclear *m*, registro de resonancia magnética nuclear
m
NN *abbr* (*national number*) TELECOM número nacional
m
NNE *abbr* (*non-SDH network element*) TELECOM elemento de red sin jerarquía digital sincrónica *m*
NNI *abbr* (*noise and number index*) ACOUST NNI (*índice
de ruido y número de operaciones*)
No *abbr* (*nobelium*) CHEM, RAD PHYS No (*nobelio*)
NO[1] *abbr* (*nitric oxide*) CHEM, POLL NO (*óxido nítrico*)
NO[2]: ~ **contact** *n* CONST, ELEC, PROD contacto normalmente abierto *m*; ~ **early-make contact** *n*
(*normally-open early-make contact*) PROD contacto
de cierre inmediato normalmente abierto *m*; ~ **late-break contact** *n* PROD contacto de ruptura retardada
normalmente abierto *m*
NO₂ *abbr* (*nitrogen oxide*) CHEM, POLL NO₂ (*óxido de
nitrógeno*)
nobelium *n* (*No*) CHEM, RAD PHYS nobelio *m* (*No*)
noble[1] *adj* CHEM *gas* noble
noble[2]: ~ **gas** *n* CHEM, GAS gas noble *m*; ~ **metal** *n*
METALL, POLL metal estable *m*, metal noble *m*
no-break: ~ **power supply** *n* SPACE suministro de
energía de continuidad absoluta *m*, suministro de
energía ininterrumpida *m*
noctilucent: ~ **cloud** *n* METEO nube noctilucente *f*
noctuid *n* AGRIC noctuido *m*
nocturnal: ~ **phase** *n* SPACE fase nocturna *f*
nodal[1] *adj* CHEM nodal
nodal[2]: ~ **current** *n* ELEC corriente nodal *f*; ~ **expansion method** *n* NUCL método de expansión nodal *m*;
~ **head** *n* CINEMAT cabeza nodal *f*; ~ **line** *n* ACOUST
línea nodal *f*; ~ **plane** *n* PHOTO, PHYS plano nodal *m*;
~ **points** *n pl* PHYS puntos nodales *m pl*; ~ **voltage** *n*
ELEC *of circuit* tensión nodal *f*
node *n* ACOUST nodo *m*, AGRIC *culm* nudo *m*, COMP&DP
nodo *m*, CRYSTALL, ELEC nudo *m*, ELEC ENG nodo *m*,
nudo *m*, ELECTRON nodo *m*, vértice *m*, GEOM nodo *m*,
METALL nodo *m*, nudo *m*, PHYS, SPACE, TELECOM
nodo *m*, WAVE PHYS nodo *m*, nudo *m*; ~ **processor**
n COMP&DP procesador de nodos *m*
nodular: ~ **corrosion** *n* NUCL *boat fitting* corrosión
nodular *f*; ~ **limestone** *n* GEOL caliza nodular *f*;
~ **marls** *n pl* GEOL margas nodulares *f pl*
nodule *n* C&G *nodulated blowing wool*, CHEM, COAL,
GEOL, NUCL, PETROL nódulo *m*
no-fines: ~ **concrete** *n* CONST cemento sin finos *m*,
concreto sin finos *m* (*AmL*), hormigón sin finos *m*
(*Esp*)
noggin *n BrE* CONST encajadura de ladrillos *f*, tabique
de ladrillo *m*
nogging *AmE see* noggin *BrE*
no-go: ~ **gage** *AmE*, ~ **gauge** *BrE n* MECH ENG
calibrador de huelgo mínimo *m*, calibrador mínimo
m, calibrador no pasa *m*, calibrador que no pasa *m*

noise *n* ACOUST, COMP&DP, ELECTRON, PHYS, SAFE ruido *m*, SPACE *communications* estrépito *m*, ruido *m*, sonido *m*, TELECOM perturbación oscilatoria *f*, ruido *m*, TV ruido *m*, WAVE PHYS interferencias *f pl*, ruido *m*; ~ **abatement** *n* SAFE supresión de ruido *f*; ~ **abatement door** *n* SAFE puerta amortiguadora de ruidos *f*; ~-**abating foam panel** *n* SAFE panel de espuma amortiguador de ruidos *m*; ~-**abating wall** *n* SAFE pared amortiguadora de ruido *f*; ~ **absorption device** *n* MECH ENG dispositivo para absorción de ruidos *m*, silenciador *m*; ~ **amplitude distribution** *n* (*NAD*) TELECOM distribución de amplitud de ruido *f*; ~ **analysis** *n* ACOUST, PETROL análisis del ruido *m*; ~-**and-vibration measuring equipment** *n* INSTR, SAFE equipo para medir ruidos y vibraciones *m*; ~-**and-vibration protection** *n* SAFE *diodes* protección contra ruidos y vibraciones *f*; ~ **barrier** *n* ACOUST barrena acústica *f*, CONST barrena acústica *f*, capa de insonorización *f*; ~ **bund** *n* CONST núcleo de ruido *m*; ~ **certification** *n* ACOUST certificación de ruido *f*; ~ **contour** *n* ACOUST curva de nivel de ruido *f*; ~ **control** *n* SAFE *diodes* control de ruidos *m*; ~ **diode** *n* ELECTRON diodo de ruidos *m*; ~ **emission value** *n* MECH ENG *of machinery* valor de sonoemisión *m*; ~ **equivalent power** *n* (*NEP*) OPT, TELECOM potencia equivalente de ruido *f*; ~ **exposure forecast** *n* (*NEF*) ACOUST predicción de exposición al ruido *f* (*NEF*); ~ **factor** *n* ELECTRON, PHYS, PRINT, SPACE *communications* factor de ruido *m*; ~ **field** *n* TELECOM, TV campo de ruido *m*, campo perturbador *m*; ~ **figure** *n* ELECTRON coeficiente de ruidosidad *m*; ~ **generator** *n* ELECTRON, TELECOM generador de ruido *m*; ~ **immunity** *n* COMP&DP inmunidad a los ruidos *f*; ~ **index** *n* ACOUST, TELECOM índice de ruido *m*; ~-**induced hearing impairment** *n* SAFE deterioro auditivo producido por ruidos *m*; ~-**insulating equipment** *n* SAFE equipo aislador de ruidos *m*; ~ **labeling** *AmE*, ~ **labelling** *n BrE* INSTR clasificación de ruido *f*, MECH ENG clasificación de ruido *f*, marcación de ruido *f*; ~ **level** *n* POLL, TELECOM, WAVE PHYS nivel de ruido *m*; ~ **masking** *n* TELECOM enmascaramiento de ruido *m*; ~ **modulation** *n* ACOUST, TV limitación de ruidos *f*; ~ **nuisance** *n* ACOUST molestia sonora *f*; ~ **and number index** *n* (*NNI*) ACOUST índice de ruido y número de operaciones *m* (*NNI*); ~ **pollution** *n* ACOUST, POLL, SAFE contaminación acústica *f*, contaminación por ruido *f*, contaminación sonora *f*, perturbación por ruido *f*; ~ **pollution level** *n* (*NPL*) ACOUST, POLL, SAFE nivel de contaminación sonora *m* (*LNP*); ~ **power** *n* ELECTRON, NUCL *motor* potencia de salida de ruido *f*; ~ **prediction** *n* ACOUST predicción de ruido *f*; ~-**protection booth** *n* SAFE caseta protectora contra ruidos *f*; ~ **protection for compressors** *n* SAFE protección contra ruidos de compresores *f*; ~-**protective capsule** *n* SAFE cápsula protectora contra ruidos *f*; ~-**protective hood** *n* SAFE campana protectora contra ruidos *f*, capucha protectora contra ruidos *f*; ~-**protective insulating glass** *n* ACOUST, SAFE vidrio para aislamiento acústico *m*; ~-**protective plug** *n* SAFE tapón para aislamiento acústico *m*; ~ **reducer** *n* ACOUST, TELECOM reductor de ruidos *m*; ~ **reduction** *n* ACOUST, INSTR, SAFE, TELECOM reducción de ruidos *f*; ~-**reduction index** *n* ACOUST, SAFE índice de reducción de ruido *m*; ~ **shield** *n* ACOUST pantalla anti-ruido *f*; ~ **signal** *n*

TV señal de ruidos *f*; ~ **source** *n* ELECTRON, POLL fuente de ruidos *f*; ~ **suppression** *n* ELEC ENG eliminación de parásitos *f*; ~ **temperature** *n* ELEC ENG, SPACE *communications* temperatura de ruido *f*; ~ **transmission impairment** *n* (*NTI*) TELECOM deterioro de la calidad de transmisión debido al ruido *m*; ~ **voltage** *n* ELEC ENG voltaje de ruido *m*

noiseless[1] *adj* SAFE sin ruido

noiseless[2]: ~ **timing chain** *n* AUTO cadena de sincronización silenciosa *f*

noisy: ~ **blacks** *n pl* TV alteración del negro por parásitos *f*

no-knock: ~ **mixture** *n* AUTO mezcla antidetonante *f*

no-load[1] *adj* AIR TRANSP libre de carga, sin carga, vacío

no-load[2]: ~ **characteristic** *n* AIR TRANSP características sin carga *f pl*; ~ **current** *n* ELEC corriente en vacío *f*, corriente sin carga *f*; ~ **direct voltage** *n* ELEC tensión directa en circuito abierto *f*, tensión directa en vacío *f*, tensión directa sin carga *f*; ~ **force** *n* NUCL fuerza sin carga *f*; ~ **heat consumption** *n* C&G consumo de calor sin carga *m*; ~ **loss** *n* ELEC pérdida sin carga *f*, pérdidas en vacío *f pl*; ~ **operation** *n* AIR TRANSP operación en vacio *f*, ELEC ENG funcionamiento en vacío *m*, operatividad sin carga *f*; ~ **start** *n* ELEC *of motor* arranque en vacío *m*; ~ **test** *n* ELEC prueba en vacío *f*, prueba sin carga *f*

NOMC *abbr* (*network operators maintenance channel*) TELECOM canal de mantenimiento de operadores de red *m*

nomenclature *n* CHEM *of substances* nomenclatura *f*

nominal: ~ **bore** *n* (*NB*) NUCL diámetro interno nominal *m*; ~ **capacitance** *n* PROD capacitancia nominal *f*; ~ **capacity** *n* C&G capacidad nominal *f*; ~ **content** *n* PACK, PRINT contenido nominal *m*; ~ **diameter** *n* MECH ENG diámetro nominal *m*; ~ **freezing time** *n* REFRIG tiempo de congelación nominal *m*; ~ **gust velocity** *n* AIR TRANSP velocidad de ráfaga nominal *f*; ~ **operating conditions** *n pl* SPACE condiciones de funcionamiento nominal *f pl*; ~ **size** *n* MECH ENG, PACK medida nominal *f*, tamaño nominal *m*; ~ **stress** *n* METALL carga de régimen *f*, tensión nominal *f*; ~ **thickness** *n* QUALITY espesor nominal *m*; ~ **thrust** *n* SPACE *of spacecraft in vacuum* propulsor nominal *m*; ~ **value** *n* ELEC valor nominal *m*; ~ **voltage** *n* ELEC *of system* tensión nominal *f*

no-mixing: ~ **cascade** *n* NUCL cascada sin mezcla *f*

non: ~ **freeze liquid** *n* REFRIG líquido incongelable *m*; ~ **irretentive output** *n* PROD salida no retentiva *f*

nonabsorbable *adj* CHEM no absorbible

nonacceptance *n* QUALITY rechazo *m*

nonacidic: ~ **lake** *n* POLL lago no acídico *m*, lago no ácido *m*

nonacosane *n* CHEM nonacosano *m*

nonane *n* CHEM nonano *m*

nonapproved *adj* QUALITY, SAFE, TELECOM no aprobado

nonaqueous[1] *adj* CHEM no acuoso

nonaqueous[2]: ~ **electrolyte battery** *n* TRANSP batería con electrólito anhidro *f*, batería seca *f*

nonarching *adj* ELEC ENG que no forma arco

nonassociated: ~ **gas** *n* GAS, PETR TECH gas no asociado *m*

nonautomatic: ~ **loom** *n* TEXTIL telar no automático *m*

nonbinary: ~ **code** *n* TELECOM código no binario *m*

nonbituminous: ~ coal *n* COAL carbón no bituminoso *m*

nonblocking: ~ concentrator *n* ELEC ENG concentrador antibloqueo *m*; ~ network *n* ELEC ENG sistema antibloqueo *m*, TELECOM red de no bloqueo *f*; ~ switch *n* ELEC ENG conmutador antibloqueo *m*

nonbonding: ~ electron *n* NUCL electrón no enlazante *m*

nonboosted: ~ antenna repeater system *n* TELECOM sistema de repetidores sin amplificador de antena *m*

nonbridging: ~ contacts *n pl* ELEC ENG contactos no simultáneos *m pl*

nonbroadcast: ~ rights *n pl* TV derechos de no emisión *m pl*

noncaking[1] *adj* COAL inaglutinable

noncaking[2]: ~ coal *n* COAL carbón inaglutinable *m*

noncapacitive[1] *adj* ELEC, ELEC ENG *of load* incapacitivo, no capacitivo

noncapacitive[2]: ~ load *n* ELEC ENG carga sin capacidad *f*

noncarbonate: ~ hardness *n* HYDROL grado de dureza no carbonatada *m*

noncircularity *n* TELECOM no circularidad *f*

noncoherent: ~ swept-tone modulation *n* TELECOM modulación no coherente por barrido de frecuencia *f*

noncohesive: ~ soil *n* COAL suelo incohesivo *m*

noncoking *adj* COAL, MINE no coquizable

noncombustibility: ~ test *n* SAFE prueba de incombustibilidad *f*

noncompensated: ~ motor *n* ELEC ENG motor descompensado *m*

nonconcentrator: ~ solar cell *n* ELEC ENG elemento solar desconcentrador *m*

noncondensed: ~ discharge *n* ELEC ENG descarga incondensable *f*

nonconducting: ~ state *n* ELEC ENG estado aislante *m*, estado dieléctrico *m*

nonconductive *adj* ELEC ENG no conductor

nonconfirmed: ~ service *n* TELECOM servicio no confirmado *m*

nonconflicting: ~ traffic flow *n* TRANSP afluencia de tráfico no conflictivo *f*

nonconformance *n* PROD incumplimiento de especificación *m*

nonconformity *n* QUALITY inconformidad *f*

nonconjugated *adj* CHEM *bond, compound* no conjugado

nonconservation: ~ of parity *n* PHYS violación de paridad *f*

nonconsumable: ~ electrode *n* CONST, ELEC ENG electrodo no consumible *m*

noncontact: ~ suspension *n* TRANSP suspensión sin contacto *f*

noncrystalline *adj* CHEM, COAL, CRYSTALL, ELECTRON, GEOL, P&R amorfo

noncutting: ~ return *n* MECH ENG *of tool* vuelta inactiva de vacío *f*; ~ stroke *n* MECH ENG carrera de vacío inactiva *f*

nondairy *adj* FOOD no lácteo

nondedicated: ~ signaling channel *AmE*, ~ signalling channel *n BrE* TELECOM canal de señalización no dedicado *m*

nondegradable *adj* PACK, RECYCL no degradable

nondelivery: ~ notification *n (NDN)* TELECOM notificación de falta de entrega *f*

nondepositional: ~ gap *n* GEOL gap no deposicional *m*

nondestructive: ~ materials testing *n* NUCL ensayo no destructivo de materiales *m*; ~ read *n* COMP&DP lectura no destructiva *f*; ~ test *n* MECH ENG, PHYS, SPACE ensayo no destructivo *m (NDT)*, prueba no destructiva *f*, test no destructivo *m*; ~ testing *n (NDT)* MECH ENG, PHYS, SPACE ensayo no destructivo *m*; ~ testing system *n* MECH ENG, PHYS, SPACE sistema de ensayos no destructivos *m*; ~ ultrasonic testing *n* MECH ENG, NUCL ensayo ultrasónico no destructivo *m*

nondimensional: ~ diameter *n* FUELLESS diámetro adimensional *m*

nondispersive: ~ medium *n* PHYS medio no dispersivo *m*

nondroppable: ~ blocks *n pl* TELECOM bloques no separables *m pl*

nonelution *adj* CHEM *chromatography* ineluible

nonencapsulated: ~~winding dry-type reactor *n* ELEC reactor de tipo seco de devanado no encapsulado *m*; ~~winding dry-type transformer *n* ELEC, ELEC ENG transformador de tipo seco no encapsulado *m*

nonequilibrium: ~ mode distribution *n* OPT, TELECOM distribución en modo no equilibrado *f*, distribución modal de no equilibrio *f*

non-equivalence: ~ gate *n* COMP&DP puerta de no equivalencia *f*; ~ operation *n* COMP&DP operación de no equivalencia *f*

nonerasable: ~ data disc *BrE*, ~ data disk *AmE n* OPT disco de datos no borrable *m*; ~ storage *AmE*, ~ store *BrE n* COMP&DP almacenamiento no borrable *m*, memoria indeleble *f*

non-Euclidean: ~ geometry *n* GEOM geometría no euclídea *f*

nonexpansion: ~ engine *n* MECH ENG motor de no expansión *m*

nonfading: ~ color *AmE*, ~ colour *BrE n* COLOUR color permanente *m*, colorante que no desvanece *m*

nonfat *adj* FOOD sin grasa

nonferric *adj* CHEM no férrico

nonferrous[1] *adj* CHEM no ferroso

nonferrous[2]: ~ metals regulations *n pl* SAFE reglamento para metales no ferrosos *m*

nonfiery *adj* MINE no ardiente

nonflammable[1] *adj* GEN incombustible, ininflamable, no inflamable, ignífugo

nonflammable[2]: ~~liquid extinguisher *n* SAFE extintor de líquidos no inflamables *m*

non-food: ~ product *n* PACK producto que no puede estar en contacto con alimentos *m*; ~ packaging *n* PACK envase no utilizable para alimentos *m*

non-frost-susceptible: ~ soil *n* COAL terreno no susceptible de helarse *m*

non-Gaussian: ~ noise *n* TELECOM ruido no gausiano *m*

nongraded *adj* GEOL mal clasificado

nonhalation *n* PHOTO, PRINT antihalo *m*

nonhierarchical: ~ system *n* TELECOM sistema no jerárquico *m*

nonimpact: ~ printer *n* COMP&DP, PRINT impresora sin impacto *f*; ~ printing system *n* PRINT sistema de impresión sin impacto *m*

noninductive[1] *adj* ELEC *load*, ELEC ENG no inductivo

noninductive[2]: ~ circuit *n* ELEC circuito no inductivo *m*; ~ load *n* ELEC *alternating current* carga no inductiva *f*; ~ resistor *n* CONST resistencia no inductiva *f*, ELEC resistencia no inductiva *f*, resistencia óhmica *f*, resistor no inductivo *m*, resistor óhmico *m*; ~ **winding** *n* CONST, ELEC bobina no inductiva *f*; ~ **wirewound resistor** *n* CONST resistencia inalámbrica no inductiva *f*

noninstrument: ~ **runway** *n* AIR TRANSP pista sin instrumentos *f*

noninverting: ~ **input** *n* CONST entrada de bucle cerrado *f*

nonionic *adj* GEN no iónico

nonionizing: ~ **radiation** *n* RAD PHYS radiación no ionizante *f*

noniron *adj* TEXTIL que no necesita plancha

non-iron: ~ **finish** *n* COATINGS acabado estucado *m*

nonisentropic *adj* PHYS, THERMO anisentrópico

nonisotropic: ~ **materials** *n pl* MECH ENG materiales no isotrópicos *m pl*

nonkinking: ~ **rope** *n* WATER TRANSP cabo que no hace cocas *m*

nonlamellar: ~ **perlite** *n* METALL perlita no laminar *f*

nonlinear[1] *adj* ELEC alineal, no lineal, no proporcional

nonlinear[2]: ~ **amplification** *n* ELECTRON, TELECOM amplificación alineal *f*, amplificación no lineal *f*; ~ **amplifier** *n* ELECTRON, TELECOM amplificador alineal *m*; ~ **circuit** *n* TELECOM circuito alineal *m*; ~ **conditions** *n pl* CONST condiciones no lineales *f pl*; ~ **digital speech** *n* TELECOM señal de frecuencia vocal no lineal *f*, señal vocal no lineal *f*; ~ **distortion** *n* ELECTRON, TELECOM distorsión alineal *f*, distorsión no lineal *f*; ~ **element** *n* CONST elemento no lineal *m*; ~ **filtering** *n* ELECTRON filtrado no lineal *m*, TELECOM filtrado alineal *m*, filtrado no lineal *m*; ~ **interpolation** *n* TELECOM interpolación no lineal *f*; ~ **network** *n* CONST red no lineal *f*; ~ **oscillation** *n* MECH ENG, TELECOM oscilación no lineal *f*; ~ **potentiometer** *n* CONST potenciómetro no lineal *m*; ~ **programming** *n* COMP&DP programación no lineal *f*; ~ **resistance** *n* ELEC, TELECOM resistencia alineal *f*; ~ **resistor** *n* ELEC, TELECOM resistencia alineal *f*, resistor alineal *m*; ~ **scale** *n* CONST, METR escala no lineal *f*; ~ **scattering** *n* OPT esparcimiento no lineal *m*, TELECOM dispersión no lineal *f*; ~ **Stark effect** *n* PHYS efecto Stark no lineal *m*

nonlocalized: ~ **fringes** *n pl* PHYS franjas no localizadas *f pl*

nonmagnetic[1] *adj* CHEM no magnético, ELEC, ELEC ENG amagnético, antimagnético, diamagnético, no magnético, GEOPHYS antimagnético, PHYS *lathe* no magnético

nonmagnetic[2]: ~ **steel** *n* ELEC, ELEC ENG, METALL acero diamagnético *m*

nonmandatory *adj* TELECOM no obligatorio, no perceptivo

nonmechanical: ~ **hazard** *n* SAFE *steam engine* peligro no mecánico *m*, riesgo no mecánico *m*

nonmeridian: ~ **ray** *n* OPT rayo no meridiano *m*

nonmetal *adj* CHEM no metálico

nonmetallic: ~ **coating** *n* COATINGS, METALL recubrimiento no metálico *m*; ~ **inclusion** *n* METALL, QUALITY inclusión no metálica *f*

nonmigratory: ~ **plasticizer** *n* P&R plastificante no migratorio *m*

nonoccluded: ~ **front** *n* METEO frente no ocluido *m*

nonodorous *adj* PACK inodoro

nonoperating *adj* PROD inoperativo

nonose *n* CHEM nonosa *f*

nonoxidizing *adj* CHEM, GEOL, METALL, SAFE no oxidante

nonplastic *adj* CONST, P&R no plástico

non-plug-in: ~ **position switch** *n* PROD interruptor de posición no enchufable *m*, interruptor sin enchufe *m*, interruptor sin toma de corriente *m*; ~ **switch** *n* PROD interruptor no enchufable *m*, interruptor sin enchufe tomacorriente *m*

nonpolar[1] *adj* CHEM, P&R, PHYS *bond, molecule* no polar

nonpolar[2]: ~ **dielectric** *n* PHYS dieléctrico no polar *m*; ~ **solvent** *n* P&R solvente no polar *m*

nonpolarized: ~ **electrolytic capacitor** *n* CONST capacitador electrolítico no polarizado *m*; ~ **plug** *n* ELEC *connection* clavija impolarizada *f*, clavija no polarizada *f*; ~ **relay** *n* CONST, ELEC relé neutro *m*, relé no polarizado *m*

nonporous *adj* GAS no poroso

nonpressure: ~ **pipeline** *n* MECH ENG tubería sin presión *f*

nonpressurized: ~ **refiner** *n* PAPER refinador no presurizado *m*; ~ **section** *n* AIR TRANSP *fuselage* sección no presurizada *f*

nonprocedural: ~ **language** *n* COMP&DP lenguaje sin procedimientos *m*

nonreactive[1] *adj* CHEM no reactivo

nonreactive[2]: ~ **load** *n* ELEC *alternating current* carga no reactiva *f*

nonreciprocal: ~ **circuit** *n* TELECOM circuito no recíproco *m*; ~ **wave guide** *n* TELECOM guía de ondas no recíproca *f*

nonrecurrent: ~ **parent** *n* AGRIC padre donante *m*; ~ **pulse** *n* ELECTRON impulso no cíclico *m*

nonrecurring: ~ **cost** *n* SPACE costos circunstanciales *m pl*, costos imprevistos *m pl*, costos no recurrentes *m pl*, costos ocasionales *m pl*

nonrecursive: ~ **filter** *n* ELECTRON, TELECOM filtro no recurrente *m*, filtro no recursivo *m*; ~ **pulse** *n* ELECTRON impulso no recursivo *m*

nonreflecting: ~ **glass** *n* C&G vidrio no reflejante *m*

non-reflective: ~ **glass** *n* C&G vidrio con muchas semillas *m*, vidrio no reflejante *m*

nonrefractory: ~ **material** *n* OPT, PHYS material no refractario *m*

nonregenerative: ~ **repeater** *n* ELECTRON repetidor no regenerativo *m*

nonrenewable: ~ **fuse** *n* ELEC, MECH ENG fusible no restaurable *m*

nonrepeatable: ~ **measurement** *n* METR medida no repetible *f*

nonreproductible *adj* PACK irreproducible

nonreserved: ~ **space** *n* TRANSP espacio libre *m*, espacio sin reservar *m*

non-resonant: ~ **line** *n* ELECTRON línea sin resonancia *f*

nonrestricted: ~ **valve** *n* CONST válvula no restringida *f*

nonretentive: ~ **latch** *n* PROD cerrojo no retentivo *m*; ~ **output** *n* PROD salida no retentiva *f*; ~ **timer** *n* PROD temporizador no retentivo *m*

nonreturn[1]: ~~**-to-zero** *adj* (*NRZ*) COMP&DP, TELECOM sin retorno a cero; ~~**-to-zero-inverted** *adj* (*NRZI*) TELECOM sin retorno al cero invertido

nonreturn[2]: ~ **modulation** *n* TELECOM modulación sin retorno *f*; ~~**-to-zero recording** *n* COMP&DP grabación sin retorno a cero *f*; ~ **valve** *n* CONST, FUELLESS,

HYDRAUL, MECH ENG, PROD válvula de retención f, válvula de retenida f

nonreturnable[1] *adj* FOOD no retornable

nonreturnable[2]: ~ **bottle** *n* PACK, RECYCL botella sin retorno f; ~ **pallet** *n* PACK, RECYCL paleta sin retorno f

nonreusable *adj* COMP&DP desechable, no reutilizable

nonreversible: ~ **motor** *n* ELEC motor irreversible *m*; ~ **plug** *n* ELEC *connection* clavija irreversible f

nonrotating: ~ **star** *n* AIR TRANSP *helicopter* estrella antigiratoria f, estrella fija f

non-rust: ~ **paper** *n* PAPER papel no oxidante *m*

nonsalient: ~ **pole** *n* ELEC polo no saliente *m*

nonsaturated: ~ **logic** *n* ELECTRON circuito lógico no saturado *m*

nonscheduled: ~ **outage** *n* NUCL parada no programada f

non-SDH: ~ **network element** *n* (*NNE*) TELECOM elemento de red sin jerarquía digital sincrónica *m*

non-self-sustained: ~ **discharge** *n* CONST descarga no autónoma f

nonsequence *n* GEOL *graphics* interrupción f

nonshorting: ~ **switch** *n* CONST interruptor de contactos aislados *m*

nonshrink: ~ **treatment** *n* TEXTIL tratamiento inencogible *m*

nonsimple: ~ **closed curve** *n* GEOM curva cerrada no simple f

nonsincronizado *adj* CINEMAT, TV no sincronizado

nonskid: ~ **coating** *n* COATINGS revestimiento antideslizante *m*

nonslip[1] *adj* WATER TRANSP *deck surface* antideslizante, antirresbaladizo

nonslip[2]: ~ **deck paint** *n* COATINGS, WATER TRANSP *boat building* pintura antideslizante f; ~ **differential** *n* AUTO diferencial autoblocante *m*; ~ **sole** *n* SAFE suela antideslizante f

nonsoapy: ~ **detergent** *n* DETERG detergente no jabonoso *m*

nonsorted *adj* GEOL inclasificado, mal clasificado

nonspill: ~ **battery** *n* BrE (*cf sealed battery AmE*) VEH batería hermética f

nonstaining *adj* P&R que no mancha

nonstandard: ~ **control track** *n* TV pista de control especial f; ~ **diamond crossing** *n* RAIL cruzamiento oblicuo no normalizado *m*

nonstochastic: ~ **radiation effects** *n pl* NUCL efectos no estocásticos de la radiación *m pl*

nonstoichiometric *adj* CHEM *proportions* no estequiométrico

nonstop: ~ **flight** *n* AIR TRANSP vuelo sin escalas *m*; ~ **rapid transit system** *n* TRANSP sistema de tránsito rápido sin paradas *m*; ~ **urban transportation** *n* TRANSP transporte urbano sin paradas *m*

nonswiveling *AmE see* **nonswivelling** *BrE*

nonswivelling *adj* BrE MECH ENG nogiratorio

nonsync *adj* CINEMAT, TV asincrónico, asíncrono, no sincronizado

non-synchronous: ~ **satellite** *n* SPACE satélite asíncrono *m*, satélite no fijo *m*

non-tarnish: ~ **paper** *n* PAPER papel no empañante *m*

nonterminating: ~ **decimal** *n* MATH decimal infinito *m*, decimal no finalizador *m*

nontoxic *adj* SAFE no tóxico

nontransparent: ~ **bearer service** *n* TELECOM servicio no transparente del portador *m*

nontrorlite *n* MINERAL nontrorlita f

nonuniform: ~ **motion** *n* PHYS movimiento no uniforme *m*; ~ **source of radiation** *n pl* RAD PHYS fuente no uniforme de radiación f

nonvolatile[1] *adj* COMP&DP, CONST, P&R no volátil

nonvolatile[2]: ~ **content** *n* P&R contenido no volátil *m*; ~ **memory** *n* COMP&DP memoria no volátil f, memoria remanente f, CONST memoria estable f

non-wirewound: ~ **potentiometer** *n* ELEC potenciómetro no bobinado *m*; ~ **resistor** *n* CONST resistencia inalámbrica f

nonwound: ~ **rotor** *n* CONST rotor no devanado *m*

nonyellowing: ~ **paint** *n* COATINGS, P&R pintura que no amarillea f

nonyl: ~ **alcohol** *n* CHEM, DETERG alcohol nonílico *m*

nonylene *n* CHEM nonileno *m*

nonylic *adj* CHEM nonílico

noon: ~ **sight** *n* WATER TRANSP *celestial navigation* punto de mediodía *m*

no-operation: ~ **instruction** *n* (*no op*) COMP&DP instrucción no operativa f (*no op*)

NOR: ~ **circuit** *n* ELECTRON circuito NO-O *m*; ~ **gate** *n* COMP&DP puerta NO f, puerta NO-O f, puerta NOR f, ELECTRON puerta NO-O f, PHYS puerta NOR f; ~ **operation** *n* COMP&DP operación NO f, operación NO-O f, operación NOR f

noradrenalin *n* CHEM noradrenalina f

norbergite *n* MINERAL norbergita f

norbornadiene *n* CHEM norbornadieno *m*

norbornane *n* CHEM norbornano *m*

norbornylene *n* CHEM norbornileno *m*

no-reflux *adj* CHEM sin reflujo

norephedrine *n* CHEM norefedrina f

norepinephrina *n* CHEM noradrenalina f, norepinefrina f

no-return: ~ **bottle** *n* PACK botella no retornable f

norite *n* PETROL norita f

norm *n* GEOL *network* norma f

normal[1] *adj* PHYS *of gear or rack* normal

normal[2] *n* GEOM, PETROL normal f; ~ **auditory sensation area** *n* ACOUST zona de sensación auditiva normal f; ~ **axis** *n* AIR TRANSP eje normal *m*; ~ **bed** *n* HYDROL *of river* lecho normal *m*; ~ **brake application** *n* RAIL aplicación normal de frenos f, frenado normal *m*; ~ **conditions** *n pl* MECH ENG condiciones normales f *pl*; ~ **coordinates** *n pl* PHYS coordenadas normales f *pl*; ~ **coupling** *n* NUCL acoplamiento normal *m*; ~ **cubic meter** *AmE see* **normal cubic metre** *BrE*; ~ **cubic metre** *BrE n* PETROL metro cúbico normal *m*; ~ **curve distribution** *n* COMP&DP, MATH, PHYS distribución normal f; ~ **descent angle** *n* AIR TRANSP ángulo de descenso normal *m*; ~ **disconnected mode** *n* (*NDM*) TELECOM modo desconectado normal *m*; ~ **distribution** *n* COMP&DP, MATH, PHYS distribución normal f; ~ **distribution curve** *n* MATH curva de distribución normal f; ~ **energy level** *n* NUCL nivel energético fundamental *m*, nivel energético normal *m*; ~ **fault** *n* GEOL falla normal f; ~ **flow** *n* TRANSP afluencia normal f; ~ **form** *n* COMP&DP forma normal f; ~ **formation pressure** *n* PETROL presión normal de la formación f; ~ **hearing threshold** *n* ACOUST umbral auditivo normal *m*; ~ **horizontal separation** *n* GEOL separación horizontal normal f; ~ **inspection** *n* QUALITY control normal *m*, inspección normal f; ~ **level** *n* NUCL nivel fundamental *m*, nivel normal *m*;

~ **listener** *n* ACOUST oyente normal *m*; ~ **mode** *n* ACOUST, PHYS modo normal *m*; ~ **mode acquisition** *n* SPACE modo de captación normal *m*; ~ **move-out corrections** *n pl* PETR TECH correcciones normales de move-out *f pl*; ~ **operating conditions** *n* NUCL condiciones de operación normales *f pl*; ~ **pressure** *n* GEOL, PETR TECH, PETROL presión normal *f*; ~ **reaction** *n* PHYS reacción normal *f*; ~**response modes** *n* (*NRM*) TELECOM modos de respuesta normal *m pl*; ~ **reverse switch** *n* TV llave normal-reversa *f*; ~ **rupture** *n* METALL rotura normal *f*; ~ **salt** *n* CHEM sal normal *f*; ~ **sea water** *n* OCEAN agua de referencia de mar *f*, agua normal de mar *f*; ~ **situation class** *n* TELECOM clase de situación normal *f*; ~ **solution** *n* CHEM solución normal *f*; ~ **stress** *n* COAL tensión normal *f*; ~ **threshold of painful hearing** *n* ACOUST umbral normal de audición dolorosa *m*; ~ **throw** *n* GEOL altura de salto *f*, altura en perpendicular *f*; ~ **traffic** *n* TRANSP tráfico normal *m*; ~ **trend** *n* GEOL dirección normal *f*, PETR TECH curso normal *m*, tendencia normal *f*; ~ **vacuum-brake application** *n* RAIL aplicación normal del freno de vacío *f*, aplicación normal del vacuofreno *f*; ~ **voltage** *n* CONST voltaje normal *m*; ~ **water** *n* NUCL agua normal *f*; ~ **working conditions** *n pl* MECH ENG condiciones normales de funcionamiento *f pl*, régimen de marcha normal *m*; ~ **Zeeman effect** *n* PHYS efecto Zeeman normal *m*

normality *n* CHEM, QUALITY normalidad *f*

normalization *n* COMP&DP estandarización *f*, MECH, METALL normalización *f*

normalize *vt* COMP&DP, MECH, METALL normalizar, regular

normalized: ~ **detectivity** *n* OPT detectividad normalizada *f*; ~ **drilling rate** *n* (*NDR*) PETR TECH régimen de perforación normalizado *m*, tasa de penetración normalizada *f*, velocidad de avance normalizada *f*; ~ **frequency** *n* OPT, TELECOM frecuencia normalizada *f*; ~ **impact sound level** *n* ACOUST nivel sonoro de impactos normalizado *m*

normalizing *n* HEAT normalización *f*

normally: ~~**closed contact** *n* CONST, ELEC, PROD contacto normalmente cerrado *m*; ~~**open contact** *n* CONST, ELEC, PROD contacto normalmente abierto *m*; ~~**open early-make contact** *n* (*NO early-make contact*) PROD contacto de cierre inmediato normalmente abierto *m*; ~~**open late-break contact** *n* PROD contacto de ruptura retardada normalmente abierto *m*

normanite *n* MINE normanita *f*

normative: ~ **mineral** *n* GEOL, MINERAL mineral normativo *m*

normorphine *n* CHEM normorfina *f*

nornarceine *n* CHEM nornarceina *f*

nornicotine *n* CHEM nornicotina *f*

noropianic *adj* CHEM noropiánico

north[1]: ~~**up** *adj* WATER TRANSP *radar* norte arriba

north[2]: ~ **by east** *adv* WATER TRANSP *compass point* norte cuarta al nordeste; ~ **by west** *adv* WATER TRANSP *compass point* norte cuarta al noroeste

north[3] *n* WATER TRANSP *compass point* norte *m*; ~~**northeast** *n* WATER TRANSP *compass point* nornordeste *m*; ~~**northwest** *n* WATER TRANSP *compass point* nornoroeste *m*; ~ **pole** *n* PHYS polo norte *m*; ~ **wind** *n*, METEO, WATER TRANSP nortazo *m*, norte *m*, viento del norte *m*

North: ~ **Atlantic Current** *n* GEOL, OCEAN Corriente del Atlántico Norte *f*; ~ **Atlantic Drift** *n* GEOL, OCEAN deriva del Atlántico Norte *f*; ~ **Pacific Current** *n* GEOL, OCEAN Corriente del Pacífico Norte *f*; ~ **Pacific Drift** *n* GEOL, OCEAN deriva del Pacífico Norte *f*

northeast[1] *adj* WATER TRANSP *wind* del nordeste, nordestal

northeast[2] *adv* WATER TRANSP *wind* en el nordeste, nordeste; ~ **by east** *adv* WATER TRANSP *wind* nordeste cuarta al este; ~ **by north** *adv* WATER TRANSP *wind* nordeste cuarta al norte

northeaster *n* WATER TRANSP *wind* nordestada *f*, nordeste *m*

northeasterly[1] *adj* WATER TRANSP del nordeste

northeasterly[2] *adv* WATER TRANSP del nordeste, hacia el nordeste

northerly[1] *adj* WATER TRANSP del norte, procedente del norte

northerly[2] *adv* WATER TRANSP que sopla del norte, del norte, hacia el norte, que va hacia el norte

northern: ~ **latitude** *n* WATER TRANSP *navigation* latitud norte *f*; ~ **lights** *n pl* GEOPHYS, METEO, SPACE, WATER TRANSP aurora boreal *f*

northwest[1]: ~ **by north** *adv* WATER TRANSP *wind* noroeste cuarta al norte; ~ **by west** *adv* WATER TRANSP *wind* noroeste cuarta al oeste

northwest[2]: ~ **wind** *n* WATER TRANSP noroeste *m*, viento del noroeste *m*

northwester *n* WATER TRANSP *wind* noroeste *m*

northwesterly *adj* WATER TRANSP del noroeste, hacia el noroeste

Norton's: ~ **theorem** *n* PHYS teorema de Norton *m*

norvaline *n* CHEM norvalina *f*

Norwegian: ~ **trench** *n* GEOL, GEOPHYS fosa noruega *f*, PETR TECH fosa noruega *f*, trinchera noruega *f*

NOS *abbr* (*network operating system*) COMP&DP NOS (*sistema operativo de red*)

noscapine *n* CHEM noscapina *f*

nose[1] *n* AIR TRANSP *of planes* proa *f*, C&G *of blowpipe* nariz *f*, MECH ENG *of mandrel, drilling-spindle* parte roscada del husillo del cabezal *f*, nariz *f*, *of tool* punta *f*, boca *f*, MILIT cono de choque *m*, PROD *of bellows* pico *m*, *of lifter* boca *f*, *of a casting ladle* vertedera *f*, *of tuyere* busa *f*, morro *m*; ~ **cone** *n* AIR TRANSP cono de morro *m*, SPACE cono del morro *m*, cono de la ojiva *m*, ojiva *f*; ~ **gear** *n* AIR TRANSP tren de aterrizaje del morro *m*; ~ **gear door** *n* AIR TRANSP portezuela del tren de aterrizaje del morro *f*; ~ **gear leg** *n* AIR TRANSP columna del tren de aterrizaje del morro *f*, pata del tren de aterrizaje del morro *f*; ~ **gear saddle** *n* AIR TRANSP soporte del tren de aterrizaje del morro *m*; ~ **gear steer lock** *n* AIR TRANSP bloqueo del control del tren de aterrizaje del morro *m*; ~ **gear steering** *n* AIR TRANSP control del tren de aterrizaje del morro *m*, dirección del tren de aterrizaje del morro *f*; ~ **gear wheel** *n* AIR TRANSP rueda del tren de aterrizaje del morro *f*; ~ **heaviness** *n* AIR TRANSP pesadez de morro *f*; ~~**in positioning** *n* AIR TRANSP posición de morro contra el viento *f*, posición morro de entrada *f*; ~ **key** *n* MECH ENG contrachaveta *f*; ~~**out positioning** *n* AIR TRANSP posición de morro a favor del viento *f*, posición morro de salida *f*; ~ **sill** *n* PROD solera de frente *f*; ~~**wheel steering** *n* AIR TRANSP control de la rueda del morro *m*, dirección de la rueda del morro *f*; ~~**wheel steering bar** *n* AIR TRANSP barra de control de la rueda del morro *f*; **~-wheel steering control wheel** *n* AIR TRANSP volante de control de dirección de la rueda del morro *m*

nose[2]: **in a ~-up attitude** *phr* AIR TRANSP con el morro levantado, en actitud encabritada

nosean *n* MINERAL noseana *f*

noseband *n* WATER TRANSP *deck equipment* defensa de proa *f*

noselite *n* MINERAL noselita *f*

nosepiece *n* CONST *stud union for pipes* lengüeta *f*, PROD *of bellows* busa *f*, *of pipe* boquerel *m*

nosing *n* CONST *latch catch, keeper of gate latch* tajamar *m*, *lock staple, keeper of door bolt* vuelo *m*, *of step, stair building* mampirlán *m*; **~ line** *n* CONST *stair building* fin de tramo *m*; **~ plane** *n* CONST cepillo con protección *m*

no-slip: **~ condition** *n* FLUID condición de no deslizamiento *f*

NOT: **~ circuit** *n* ELECTRON circuito NOT *m*; **~ gate** *n* COMP&DP, ELECTRON, PHYS puerta NOT *f*; **~ operation** *n* COMP&DP operación NOT *f*

notation *n* COMP&DP, PROD, TELECOM anotación *f*, notación *f*; **~ convention** *n* PROD convenio sobre anotaciones *m*

notch[1] *n* C&G, CINEMAT muesca *f*, CONST *in lock bolt, to receive bit of key* entalladura *f*, muesca *f*, ranura *f*, MECH corte *m*, entalla *f*, ranura *f*, rebaje *m*, rebajo *m*, muesca *f*, entalladura *f*, hendidura *f*, incisión *f*, MECH ENG rebajo *m*, METALL corte *m*, ranura *f*, rebaje *m*, rebajo *m*, incisión *f*, muesca *f*, entalla *f*, entalladura *f*, hendidura *f*, PROD corte *m*, entalla *f*, ranura *f*, rebaje *m*, rebajo *m*, muesca *f*, entalladura *f*, hendidura *f*, incisión *f*, WATER entalladura *f*, orificio abierto en la parte superior *m*, hendidura *f*, muesca *f*, entalla *f*; **~ angle** *n* METALL ángulo de la entalla *m*; **~ bending test** *n* MECH ENG prueba de flexión en probeta entallada *f*; **~ effect** *n* MECH ENG efecto de muesca *m*; **~ filter** *n* COMP&DP filtro de banda eliminada *m*, filtro de entalla *m*, ELECTRON filtro de entalla *m*, filtro de banda eliminada *m*, GEOPHYS filtro supresor de banda escalonada *m*, TELECOM filtro de banda eliminada *m*, filtro de entalla *m*, filtro de hendidura *m*; **~ gaging** *AmE*, **~ gauging** *BrE* *n* HYDRAUL aforo en vertedero *m*; **~ impact test** *n* NUCL ensayo de impacto en probeta entallada *m*; **~ joint** *n* CONST junta de ranura *f*, unión de escotadura *f*; **~ toughness** *n* NUCL resistencia a la propagación de grietas *f*, tenacidad a la entalla *f*

notch[2] *vt* CINEMAT hacer muescas, CONST, MECH entallar, MECH ENG dentellar, entallar, mellar, muescar, ranurar, METALL, PROD, WATER entallar

notched[1] *adj* MECH ENG con dientes, con muesca, dentado, dentellado, entallado, mellado

notched[2]: **~ band** *n* MECH ENG cinta dentada *f*; **~-bar impact test** *n* MECH *tools* prueba de resiliencia en probeta entallada *f*; **~ belt** *n* VEH correa dentada *f*; **~-belt timing** *n* AUTO sincronizador de correa dentada *m*; **~ hole** *n* MECH ENG *of screw plate* agujero rayado *m*; **~ nozzle** *n* AIR TRANSP tobera coronada *f*, tobera dentada *f*; **~ nut** *n* MECH ENG tuerca almenada *f* (*Esp*), tuerca castilla *f* (*AmL*); **~ stem** *n* MECH ENG espiga roscada *f*; **~ weir** *n* HYDROL, WATER aliviadero entallado *m*

notcher *n* CINEMAT muescadora *f*

notching *n* PROD entalla *f*, entalladura *f*, muesca *f*, ranura *f*; **~ die** *n* MECH ENG *press tool* troquel de ranurar *m*; **~ process** *n* PROD proceso de entallar *m*, proceso de muescar *m*

note *n* ACOUST nota *f*

notifiable: **~ accident** *n* SAFE accidente reportable *m*

notification *n* MAR POLL notificación *f*

no-tillage *n* AGRIC no laboreo *m*

no-twist: **~ roving** *n* C&G arqueado sin torcedura *m*

noy *n* ACUST noy *m*

noumeaite *n* MINERAL noumeaíta *f*

novocaine *n* CHEM novocaina *f*

novolac *n* P&R novolaca *f*

no-volt: **~ release** *n* ELEC ENG desconexión por falta de corriente *f*

no-voltage *n* ELEC, ELEC ENG voltaje nulo *m*; **~ release relay** *n* ELEC relé de apertura sin tensión *m*, relé de desexcitación sin tensión *m*

now: **~ printing** *adv* PRINT en impresión

nowel *n* PROD *of foundry-flask* parte inferior *f*, rastra *f*

noxious *adj* CHEM nocivo

nozzle *n* AIR TRANSP tobera *f*, AUTO, C&G boquilla *f*, CHEM TECH tobera *f*, COAL boquilla *f*, buza *f*, inyector *m*, tobera *f*, CONST, FUELLESS boquilla *f*, GAS boquilla *f*, inyector *m*, HYDRAUL tobera *f*, LAB *type of fixing of rail to rail* boquilla *f*, MECH tobera *f*, boquilla *f*, MECH ENG pitón *m*, boca *f*, boquilla *f*, inyector *m*, lanza *f*, nariz *f*, boquerel *m*, tobera *f*, P&R pico *m*, PHYS tobera *f*, PROD *of branch pipe* lanza *f*, *of impulse turbine, diesel* tobera *f*, boca *f*, *of bellow, injector, oxyacetylene blowpipe* boquilla *f*, lanza de agua *f*, inyector *m*, SPACE boquilla *f*, orificio *m*, tobera *f*, inyector *m*, embocadura *f*; **~ adaptor** *n* MECH ENG adaptador de boquilla *m*; **~ area** *n* SPACE área de la tobera *f*, área del depósito de difusión *f*, área del inyector *f*; **~ cowl** *n* AIR TRANSP capó de tobera *m*; **~ efficiency** *n* SPACE eficiencia del depósito de difusión *f*; **~ exit** *n* PHYS salida del inyector *f*; **~ expansion area ratio** *n* SPACE coeficiente del área de expansión de la tobera *m*; **~ holder** *n* AUTO portainyector *m*; **~ holder spindle** *n* AUTO pivote de sujeción de la boquilla *m*; **~ temperature indicator** *n* AIR TRANSP indicador de la temperatura de la boquilla *m*, indicador de la temperatura de la tobera *m*; **~ throat** *n* SPACE garganta de la tobera *f*; **~ tip** *n* PROD boquilla de la tobera *f*; **~ velocity coefficient** *n* FUELLESS coeficiente de la velocidad en la boquilla *m*

NP *abbr* (*network performance*) COMP&DP, TELECOM calidad de servicio de la red *f*, características de la red *f pl*, comportamiento de la red *m*

Np *abbr* (*neptunium*) CHEM, RAD PHYS Np (*neptunio*)

NPDU *abbr* (*network protocol data unit*) TELECOM unidad de datos del protocolo de la red *f*

NPI *abbr* TELECOM (*null pointer indication*) indicación de puntero nulo *f*, TELECOM (*numbering-plan identification*) identificación del plan de numeración *f*

NPL *abbr* (*noise pollution level*) ACOUST, POLL, SAFE LNP (*nivel de contaminación sonora*),

npn: **~ transistor** *n* ELECTRON transistor npn *m*

n-position: **~ switch** *n* ELEC ENG interruptor de varias posiciones *m*

N-protocol *n* TELECOM protocolo N *m*; **~ data unit** *n* TELECOM unidad N de datos del protocolo *f*

NPT[1] *abbr* (*national pipe thread*) MECH ENG rosca para tubos cónicos *f*

NPT[2]: **~ screw thread** *n* MECH ENG rosca de tornillo NPT *f*

N-relay *n* TELECOM relé N *m*, retransmisión N *f*

NRM *abbr* (*normal-response modes*) TELECOM modos de respuesta normal *m pl*

NRZ[1] *abbr* (*nonreturn-to-zero*) COMP&DP, TELECOM sin retorno a cero

NRZ[2]: ~ **recording** *n* COMP&DP grabación NRZ *f*

NRZI *abbr* (*nonreturn-to-zero-inverted*) TELECOM sin retorno al cero invertido

NS *abbr* (*network service*) TELECOM mantenimiento de la red *m*

Ns *abbr* (*nimbostratus*) METEO Ns (*nimbostratus*)

NSAP *abbr* (*network service access point*) TELECOM punto de acceso al mantenimiento de la red *m*

NSC *abbr* (*Network Switching Center AmE, Network Switching Centre BrE*) TELECOM Centro de Conmutación de la Red *m*

N-service *n* TELECOM servicio N *m*; ~ **data unit** *n* TELECOM unidad de datos de protocolo N *f*

NSN *abbr* (*national significant number*) TELECOM número nacional significativo *m*

NSSS *abbr* (*nuclear steam supply system*) NUCL NSSS (*sistema de producción nuclear de vapor*)

n-step: ~ **starter** *n* ELEC arrancador de n pasos *m*

NT *abbr* (*network termination*) TELECOM terminación de la red *f*

NTE *abbr* (*network terminal equipment*) TELECOM equipo terminal de la red *m*

nth: ~**-order filter** *n* ELECTRON filtro de tipo nth *m*

NTI *abbr* (*noise transmission impairment*) TELECOM deterioro de la calidad de transmisión debido al ruido *m*

NT-LB *abbr* (*B-ISDN network termination*) TELECOM T-RDSI (*terminación de la red digital de servicios integrados*)

NT1-LB *abbr* (*B-ISDN network termination 1*) TELECOM terminación 1 de RDSI-BA *f* (*terminación 1 de red digital de servicios integrados de banda ancha*)

NTSC[1] *abbr AmE* (*National Television Standards Committee AmE*) TV NTSC (*Comité Nacional de Normas de Televisión*)

NTSC[2]: ~ **color television system** *AmE*, ~ **colour television system** *BrE n* TV sistema de televisión color NTSC *m*

NT2-LB *abbr* (*B-ISDN network termination 2*) TELECOM terminación 2 de RDSI-BA *f* (*terminación 2 de red digital de servicios integrados de banda ancha*)

n-type *n* ELECTRON tipo n *m*; ~ **component** *n* ELECTRON componente de tipo n *m*; ~ **epitaxial layer** *n* ELECTRON estratificador epitaxial de tipo n *m*; ~ **impurity** *n* ELECTRON impureza de tipo n *f*; ~ **semiconductor** *n* ELECTRON, PHYS semiconductor tipo n *m*; ~ **silicon** *n* ELECTRON silicio de tipo n *m*; ~ **substrate** *n* ELECTRON substrato tipo n *m*

nuance *n* COLOUR gradación de matiz *f*

nuclear[1] *adj* ELEC, MILIT , NUCL, PHYS nuclear; ~**-powered** , *adj* SPACE nucleopropulsado WATER TRANSP *ship* con propulsión nuclear

nuclear[2]: ~ **abundance** *n* NUCL, PHYS abundancia nuclear *f*; ~ **activity** *n* NUCL, RAD PHYS actividad nuclear *f*; ~ **battery** *n* CONST, NUCL batería nuclear *f*; ~ **cell** *n* CONST celda nuclear *f*; ~ **cement log** *n* PETROL perfil de cemento nuclear *m*; ~ **charge** *n* NUCL, PART PHYS carga nuclear *f*; ~ **cooling** *n* NUCL, REFRIG enfriamiento nuclear *m*; ~ **deformation** *n* NUCL deformación nuclear *f*; ~**-detection satellite** *n* SPACE satélite de detección nuclear *m*; ~ **energy** *n* ELEC, PHYS energía nuclear *f*; ~ **equation of state** *n*

RAD PHYS ecuación de estado del núcleo *f*, ecuación nuclear *f*; ~ **explosion** *n* MILIT, NUCL explosión nuclear *f*; ~ **fission** *n* NUCL, PART PHYS, PHYS fisión nuclear *f*; ~ **force** *n* NUCL, PART PHYS, PHYS fuerza nuclear *f*, interacción nuclear *f*; ~ **fuel** *n* MILIT, NUCL combustible nuclear *m*; ~ **fusion** *n* NUCL, PART PHYS fusión nuclear *f*; ~ **isomerism** *n* NUCL, PHYS isomerismo nuclear *m*; ~ **log** *n* PETR TECH diagrafía nuclear *f*, perfil radiactivo *m*, registro radiactivo *m*; ~ **magnetic log** *n* PETROL perfil por magnetismo nuclear *m*; ~ **magnetic resonance** *n* (*NMR*) CHEM *analysis*, NUCL, PETR TECH, PHYS, RAD PHYS resonancia magnética nuclear *f*; ~ **magnetic resonance log** *n* PETR TECH diagrafía de resonancia magnética nuclear *f*, perfil de resonancia magnética nuclear *m*, registro de resonancia magnética nuclear *m*; ~ **model** *n* PHYS modelo nuclear *m*; ~ **physicist** *n* NUCL, PART PHYS, PHYS físico nuclear *m*; ~ **physics** *n* NUCL, PART PHYS, PHYS física nuclear *f*; ~ **poison removal** *n* MAR POLL, NUCL, SAFE eliminación de venenos del reactor *f*; ~ **potential** *n* NUCL potencial de núcleo *m*, potencial nuclear *m*, RAD PHYS potencial del núcleo *m*, potencial nuclear *m*; ~ **power** *n* NUCL, PHYS energía nuclear *f*, SPACE propulsión nuclear *f*; ~ **power plant** *n* CONST, NUCL central nuclear *f*; ~ **power station** *n* CONST, ELEC, NUCL, PHYS central nuclear *f*, central nucleoeléctrica *f*; ~ **power supply** *n* NUCL abastecimiento de energía nuclear *m*, SPACE abastecimiento de energía nuclear *m*, suministro de energía nuclear *m*; ~ **propulsion** *n* SPACE propulsión nuclear *f*; ~ **quadrupole moment** *n* NUCL, PHYS momento cuadrupolar nuclear *m*; ~ **radiation** *n* NUCL, POLL, RAD PHYS, SAFE radiación nuclear *f*; ~ **radiation spectrum** *n* RAD PHYS, SPACE espectro de radiaciones nucleares *m*; ~ **reaction** *n* CHEM, NUCL, PHYS, RAD PHYS reacción nuclear *f*; ~ **reactor** *n* CONST, ELEC, NUCL, PHYS reactor nuclear *m*; ~ **reactor poison removal** *n* NUCL, POLL, SAFE eliminación de venenos del reactor nuclear *f*; ~ **research** *n* NUCL, RAD PHYS investigación nuclear *f*; ~ **safety** *n* SAFE seguridad nuclear *f*; ~ **shell** *n* MILIT, NUCL proyectil nuclear *m*; ~ **shock wave** *n* NUCL, RAD PHYS onda de choque nuclear *f*; ~ **spin** *n* PHYS, RAD PHYS espín nuclear *m*; ~ **steam supply system** *n* (*NSSS*) NUCL sistema de producción nuclear de vapor *m* (*NSSS*); ~ **symmetry energy** *n* NUCL, RAD PHYS energía de simetría nuclear *f*; ~ **tranche** *n* ELEC, NUCL tranche nuclear *m*; ~ **waste** *n* NUCL, POLL, RECYCL, SAFE basura nuclear *f*, residuos nucleares *m pl*

nucleate: ~ **boiling** *n* REFRIG ebullición nucleada *f*

nucleation *n* CRYSTALL *crystal growth*, METALL, METEO, NUCL cristalización *f*, germinación *f*, nucleación *f*; ~ **rate** *n* CHEM índice de nucleación *m*, METALL porcentaje de nucleación *m*, índice de nucleación *m*

nucleic *adj* CHEM nucleico

nuclein *n* CHEM nucleína *f*

nucleohistone *n* CHEM nucleohistona *f*

nucleolin *n* CHEM nucleolina *f*

nucleon *n* NUCL, PHYS *proton or neutron* nucleón *m*; ~ **number** *n* NUCL, PHYS número nucleónico *m*

nucleonics *n* NUCL, PHYS nucleónica *f*

nucleophilic *adj* CHEM nucleofílico

nucleophilicity *n* CHEM nucleofilia *f*

nucleus *n* C&G, COMP&DP, NUCL, PART PHYS, PHYS, PROD núcleo *m*; ~ **breeding herd** *n* AGRIC ganado básico *m*, plantel *m* (*AmL*)

nuclide *n* NUCL nucleido *m*, PART PHYS, PHYS núclido *m*

nudging *n* SPACE *of spacecraft* sacudida *f*

nugget *n* MINE, PETROL pepita *f*

nuisance: ~ **call** *n* TELECOM llamada con interferencia *f*

null¹ *adj* CHEM *points* nulo

null² *n* COMP&DP *character* null *m*, nulo *m*; ~ **flux suspension** *n* TRANSP suspensión de flujo nulo *f*; ~ **galvanometer** *n* ELEC, ELEC ENG, INSTR galvanómetro de cero *m*, galvanómetro de señal nula *m*; ~ **instruction** *n* COMP&DP instrucción nula *f*; ~ **method** *n* ELEC *of measurement* método de ajuste a cero *m*, método de cero *m*, método de lectura cero *m*, PHYS método nulo *m*; ~ **pointer indication** *n* (*NPI*) TELECOM indicación de cero con aguja *f*, indicación de puntero nulo *f*; ~ **string** *n* COMP&DP cadena nula *f*, cadena vacía *f* (*Esp*), serie vacía *f* (*AmL*); ~ **voltage** *n* ELEC tensión de anulación *f*

nullator *n* PHYS anulador *m*

number¹ *n* GEN número *m*; ~ **of passes** *n* CONST número de pasadas *m*; ~ **plate** *n* BrE (*cf license plate AmE*) AUTO matrícula *f*, MECH ENG placa de matrícula *f*, plaquita numeradora *f*, chapa de número *f*, VEH chapa de matrícula *f*, placa de matrícula *f*; ~ **of repeats** *n* TEXTIL número de cursos *m*; ~ **representation** *n* COMP&DP representación numérica *f*; ~ **system** *n* COMP&DP sistema numérico *m*; ~ **theory** *n* MATH teoría de números *f*

number² *vt* PROD numerar

numbered: ~ **copy** *n* PRINT copia numerada *f*

numbering *n* PHOTO, PRINT numeración *f*; ~ **apparatus** *n* PACK numerador *m*; ~ **machine** *n* PRINT numeradora *f*; ~**-plan identification** *n* (*NPI*) TELECOM identificación del plan de numeración *f*; ~**-plan indicator** *n* TELECOM indicador del plan de numeración *m*

numerator *n* MATH numerador *m*

numeric: ~ **keypad** *n* COMP&DP teclado numérico *m*; ~ **literal** *n* COMP&DP literal numérico *m*; ~ **representation** *n* COMP&DP representación numérica *f*

numerical¹ *adj* MATH numérico

numerical²: ~ **analysis** *n* COMP&DP análisis numérico *m*; ~ **aperture** *n* (*NA*) CONST, OPT, TELECOM apertura numérica *f*; ~ **code** *n* COMP&DP código numérico *m*; ~ **control** *n* (*NC*) COMP&DP, ELEC, MECH, MECH ENG, PROD control numérico *m* (*CN*); ~ **control machine** *n* MECH ENG máquina de control numérico *f*; ~ **control machine tool** *n* MECH ENG máquina herramienta de control numérico *f*; ~ **value** *n* METR valor numérico *m*

nummulitic: ~ **limestone** *n* GEOL caliza numulítica *f*

nurling: ~ **tool** *n* PROD moleta de tornero *f*

nursery: ~ **cold store** *n* REFRIG cámara frigorífica para plantas de vivero *f*; ~ **refrigerator** *n* REFRIG, THERMO frigorífico para biberones *m*

N-user: ~ **data** *n* TELECOM datos de mantenimiento N para el usuario *m pl*

nut *n* CONST, MECH, MECH ENG, PROD, VEH tuerca *f*; ~**-and-bolt works** *n pl* CONST trabajos con tuercas y pernos *m pl*; ~ **cage** *n* MECH ENG separador de tuercas *m*; ~ **lock** *n* MECH ENG contratuerca *f*, fiador de tuerca *m*, freno para tuerca *m*, inmovilizador de tuerca *m*; ~**-sizing screen** *n* COAL criba de clasificación de menudos *f*; ~ **spinner** *n* MECH ENG destornillador para tuercas *m*; ~ **splitter** *n* MECH ENG rajatuercas *m*, rompetuercas *m*

nutation *n* PHYS, SPACE nutación *f*; ~ **damper** *n* SPACE *of spacecraft* amortiguación de la nutación *f*, amortiguador *m*

nutrient *n* FOOD nutriente *m*, MAR POLL elemento nutritivo *m*, nutriente *m*; ~ **content** *n* FOOD contenido en nutriente *m*; ~ **loss** *n* FOOD pérdida de nutriente *f*; ~ **removal** *n* HYDROL evacuación de elementos nutritivos *f*; ~ **requirements** *n pl* FOOD demanda de nutrientes *f*; ~ **salts** *n pl* HYDROL sales nutritivas *f pl*

nutrition *n* FOOD nutrición *f*

nutritional: ~ **supplement** *n* FOOD suplemento nutritivo *m*

nutritious *adj* FOOD alimenticio, nutritivo

nutritive *adj* FOOD alimenticio, nutritivo

nuts: ~ **and bolts** *phr* CONST tuercas y pernos *m*

NVG *abbr* (*night vision goggles*) MILIT, OPT anteojos de visión nocturna *m pl* (*AmL*), gafas de visión nocturna *f pl* (*Esp*)

NVT *abbr* (*network virtual terminal*) COMP&DP NVT (*terminal virtual en red*)

n-way: ~ **switch** *n* ELEC conmutador intermedio-n *m*, conmutador secundario-n *m*, interruptor de n posiciones *m*, interruptor intermedio-n *m*, interruptor secundario-n *m*

nydrazid *n* CHEM nidrazida *f*

nylon¹: ~**-reinforced** *adj* PACK nailon reforzado

nylon² *n* CHEM, P&R, TEXTIL nailon *m*, nilón *m*, nylon *m*; ~ **brush** *n* P&R cepillo con cerdas de naylon *m*; ~ **line** *n* WATER TRANSP cabo de nylon *m*; ~ **rope** *n* MECH ENG cuerda de nylon *f*; ~ **thread** *n* P&R, TEXTIL hilo de nylon *m*

nylstop: ~ **self-locking nut** *n* MECH ENG tuerca autotrabadora con tope de nylon *f*

Nyquist: ~ **demodulator** *n* TV demodulador de Nyquist *m*; ~ **frequency** *n* PETROL frecuencia de Nyquist *f*

nystatin *n* CHEM nistatina *f*

O

O *abbr* (*oxygen*) GEN O (*oxígeno*)

OA *abbr* (*office automation*) COMP&DP, PROD OA (*automatización de oficina, ofimática*)

oakum *n* WATER TRANSP *ropes* estopa *f*

OAM *abbr* (*organization and maintenance*) TELECOM explotación y mantenimiento *f*

OAMC *abbr* (*operation administration and maintenance center AmE, operation administration and maintenance centre BrE*) TELECOM centro de mantenimiento y administración de la explotación *m*

OAMP *abbr* (*operation administration maintenance and provisioning*) TELECOM provisión y mantenimiento de la administración explotadora *f*

oarlock *n AmE* (*cf rowlock BrE*) WATER TRANSP *boat fitting* chumacera *f*, chumacera de horquilla *f*, escalamera *f*

oat: ~ **bin** *n* AGRIC cajón de avena *m*; ~ **panicle** *n* AGRIC panícula de avena *f*

obduction *n* GEOL obducción *f*

obedience: ~ **level** *n* TRANSP grado de cumplimiento *m*

obelisk *n* GEOM, PRINT obelisco *m*

object: ~ **code** *n* COMP&DP, PHYS código objeto *m*; ~ **in space** *n* SPACE objeto en el espacio *m*; ~ **language** *n* COMP&DP lenguaje objeto *m*; ~ **machine** *n* COMP&DP máquina objeto *f*; ~ **module** *n* COMP&DP módulo objeto *m*; ~**-oriented architecture** *n* COMP&DP arquitectura orientada al objeto *f*; ~**-oriented design** *n* (*OOD*) COMP&DP diseño orientado al objeto *m*; ~**-oriented programming system** *n* COMP&DP sistema de programación orientado al objeto *m*; ~ **program** *n* COMP&DP programa objeto *m*; ~ **stage** *n* INSTR portaobjetos *m*

objective *n* INSTR, PHYS objetivo *m*; ~ **aperture** *n* INSTR diafragma del objetivo *m*; ~ **detector** *n* TRANSP detector del objetivo *m*; ~ **lens** *n* INSTR lente del objetivo *f*, LAB, METALL objetivo *m*; ~ **nose-piece** *n* INSTR *microscope* portaobjetivo *m*; ~ **pole piece** *n* INSTR masa polar del objetivo *f*; ~ **turret** *n* INSTR cabezal de portaobjetivos *m*

oblate[1] *adj* GEOM achatado

oblate[2]: ~ **ellipsoid** *n* GEOM elipsoide achatado *m*, PHYS elipsoide oblato *m*; ~ **nucleus** *n* NUCL núcleo achatado *m*, núcleo oblato *m*; ~ **spheroid** *n* GEOM esferoide achatado *m*

obligate: ~ **aerobe** *n* FOOD aerobio obligado *m*

obligatory: ~ **well** *n* PETR TECH pozo obligatorio *m*

oblimak *n* NUCL oblimak *m*

oblique[1] *adj* GEOM oblicuo

oblique[2]: ~ **angle** *n* GEOM ángulo oblicuo *m*; ~ **arch** *n* CONST *architecture* arco oblicuo *m*; ~ **axes** *n pl* MATH ejes oblicuos *m pl*; ~ **bridge** *n* CONST puente oblicuo *m*; ~ **cone** *n* GEOM cono oblicuo *m*; ~ **illumination** *n* METALL iluminación oblicua *f*; ~ **serif** *n* PRINT serif oblicua *f*; ~ **stroke** *n* GEOM *screen* trazo oblicuo *m*; ~ **triangle** *n* GEOM triángulo oblicuo *m*

oblong[1] *adj* GEOM alargado

oblong[2] *n* GEOM figura alargada *f*; ~ **page** *n* PRINT

página apaisada *f*; ~ **size** *n* PRINT formato alargado *m*

OBO: ~ **carrier** *n* (*oil-bulk-ore carrier*) TRANSP transporte marítimo combinado *m*, WATER TRANSP buque de transporte mixto *m*, buque transportador mixto *m*

obscene: ~ **call** *n* TELECOM llamada indecente *f*, llamada obscena *f*

observation *n* AIR TRANSP detector de radar *m*, CONST *sight*, WATER TRANSP *celestial navigation* observación *f*; ~ **chamber** *n* OCEAN cámara de observación *f*, PETR TECH cápsula marina de observación *f*; ~ **hole** *n* C&G mirilla de observación *f*; ~ **mirror** *n* INSTR reflector de observación *m*; ~ **satellite** *n* SPACE satélite de observación *m*; ~ **service** *n* TELECOM servicio de observación *m*; ~ **telephone** *n* TELECOM teléfono de escucha *m*; ~ **tower** *n* MILIT torre de observación *f*; ~ **well** *n* GAS, WATER *gearing* pozo de observación *m*

observed: ~ **altitude** *n* WATER TRANSP *sextant* altura observada *f*; ~ **position** *n* OCEAN punto observado *m*, WATER TRANSP *navigation* situación observada *f*; ~ **threshold** *n* ELECTRON, NUCL, OPT, PHYS umbral observado *m*

observer *n* AIR TRANSP observador *m*

obsidian *n* C&G, MINERAL, PETROL obsidiana *f*

obsolescence *n* PROD caducidad *f*

obstacle *n* METALL obstáculo *m*; ~ **gain** *n* ELECTRON ganancia impeditiva *f*; ~ **hardening** *n* METALL endurecimiento por obstaculización *m*; ~ **in rotating fluid** *n* FLUID obstáculo en un fluido en rotación *m*; ~ **in stratified fluid** *n* FLUID obstáculo en un fluido estratificado *m*

obstruction *n* CONST *general term* obstrucción *f*, *in pipe* obstáculo *m*

obturating: ~ **plug** *n* MECH ENG tapón obturador *m*

obturator *n* HEAT, MECH ENG, PROD obturador *m*

obtuse[1] *adj* GEOM obtuso; ~**-angled** *adj* GEOM de ángulo obtuso; ~**-angular** *adj* GEOM obtusángulo

obtuse[2]: ~ **angle** *n* GEOM ángulo obtuso *m*; ~ **triangle** *n* GEOM triángulo obtuso *m*

obtuseness *n* GEOM *data* obtusidad *f*

OCB *abbr* (*outgoing calls barred*) TELECOM comunicaciones de salida no permitidas *f pl*, comunicaciones de salida prohibidas *f pl*, llamadas de salida bloqueadas *f pl*

occlude *vt* CHEM *metal* ocluir

occluded[1] *adj* CHEM, METEO, MINE, PAPER, PROD ocluido, sellado

occluded[2]: ~ **front** *n* METEO frente ocluido *m*, oclusión frontal *f*

occlusion *n* CHEM, METEO, PAPER oclusión *f*, sellado *m*

occulting: ~ **light** *n* WATER TRANSP *navigation marks* luz de ocultaciones *f*

occupancy: ~ **detector** *n* TRANSP detector de ocupación *m*; ~ **rate** *n* CONST tasa de ocupación *f*, TRANSP grado de ocupación *m*, índice de ocupación *m*

occupational: ~ **hazard** *n* SAFE peligro profesional *m*, riesgo profesional *m*; ~ **MAC** *n* POLL CMA ocupacional *f*; ~ **maximum allowable concentration** *n*

POLL concentración máxima permisible ocupacional *f*; ~ **noise** *n* ACOUST ruido ocupacional *m*; ~ **noise exposure** *n* SAFE exposición al ruido ocupacional *f*; ~ **safety** *n* SAFE seguridad en el trabajo *f*; ~ **safety cream** *n* SAFE crema de seguridad ocupacional *f*; ~ **threshold limit value** *n* POLL valor límite umbral ocupacional *m*; ~ **TLV** *n* POLL TLV ocupacional *m*

occupationally: ~ **exposed** *adj* NUCL profesionalmente expuesto

occupied: ~ **track** *n* RAIL vía ocupada *f*

ocean: ~ **basin** *n* GEOL, OCEAN cuenca oceánica *f*; ~ **crust** *n* GEOL, OCEAN corteza oceánica *f*; ~ **current** *n* METEO, OCEAN, WATER TRANSP corriente oceánica *f*; ~~**data acquisition system** *n* (*ODAS*) OCEAN sistema de adquisición de datos oceánicos *m* (*SADO*); ~ **deeps** *n pl* OCEAN, WATER TRANSP *geography* fosa submarina *f*; ~ **depths** *n pl* OCEAN, WATER TRANSP *geography* grandes profundidades oceánicas *f pl*; ~ **dynamics** *n* OCEAN, WATER TRANSP dinámica oceánica *f*; ~ **floor** *n* OCEAN lecho oceánico *m*; ~ **floor spreading** *n* GEOL expansión del fondo oceánico *f*, OCEAN renovación de los fondos oceánicos *f*; ~~**going ship** *n* WATER TRANSP buque de altura *m*; ~ **liner** *n* WATER TRANSP transatlántico *m*; ~ **navigation** *n* OCEAN, WATER TRANSP navegación de altura *f*, navegación oceánica *f*; ~ **survey vessel** *n* WATER TRANSP buque oceanográfico *m*; ~ **thermal conversion** *n* FUELLESS, OCEAN, THERMO conversión térmica oceánica *f*; ~ **thermal energy** *n* OCEAN, THERMO energía térmica oceánica *f*; ~ **trench** *n* GEOL, GEOPHYS, OCEAN fosa oceánica *f*

oceanic: ~ **basin** *n* GEOL, OCEAN cuenca oceánica *f*; ~ **crust** *n* GEOL, OCEAN corteza oceánica *f*; ~ **current** *n* METEO, OCEAN, WATER TRANSP corriente oceánica *f*; ~ **ridge** *n* OCEAN *especially mid-ocean* dorsal oceánica *f*; ~ **routing chart** *n* WATER TRANSP *navigation* carta de derrotas óptimas *f*

oceanographer *n* METEO, OCEAN, WATER TRANSP oceanógrafo *m*

oceanographic: ~ **buoy** *n* OCEAN boya oceanográfica *f*; ~ **dredge** *n* OCEAN rastra oceanográfica *f*; ~ **laboratory** *n* OCEAN, WATER TRANSP laboratorio oceanográfico *m*; ~ **research ship** *n* OCEAN, WATER TRANSP barco de investigaciones oceanográficas *m*, barco oceanográfico *m*, buque de investigaciones oceanográficas *m*; ~ **research vessel** *n* OCEAN, WATER TRANSP barco de investigaciones oceanográficas *m*, barco oceanográfico *m*

Oceanographic: ~ **Data Acquisition System** *n* OCEAN sistema de información oceanográfica *m*

oceanographical *adj* METEO, OCEAN, WATER TRANSP oceanográfico

oceanography *n* METEO, OCEAN, WATER TRANSP oceanografía *f*

oceanology *n* METEO, OCEAN, WATER TRANSP oceanología *f*

OCO: ~ **carrier** *n* (*oil-coal-ore carrier*) TRANSP barco de transporte de materiales mixtos *m*, transporte mixto *m*, WATER TRANSP buque de transporte combinado *m*

OCR[1] *abbr* (*optical character recognition*) COMP&DP, PRINT OCR (*lector óptico de caracteres, reconocimiento óptico de caracteres*)

OCR[2]: ~ **paper** *n* PAPER papel para lectura óptica *m*; ~ **system** *n* (*optical character reading system*) PACK sistema OCR *m* (*sistema de lectura óptica de caracteres*)

o-cresol *n* CHEM o-cresol *m*

octacosane *n* CHEM octacosano *m*

octadecane *n* CHEM octadecano *m*

octagon *n* GEOM octágono *m*, octógono *m*

octagonal: ~ **nut** *n* MECH ENG tuerca ochavada *f*, tuerca octogonal *f*; ~ **nut angle gage** *AmE*, ~ **nut angle gauge** *BrE* *n* MECH ENG calibre para ángulos de tuercas octogonales *m*, galga para ángulos de tuercas octogonales *f*; ~ **reamer** *n* MECH avellanador *m*, MECH ENG avellanador *m*, escariador *m*, PROD avellanador *m*

octahedral *adj* CHEM, CRYSTALL, GEOM octaédrico

octahedrite *n* MINERAL octahedrita *f*

octahedron *n* CHEM, CRYSTALL, GEOM octaedro *m*

octal[1] *adj* COMP&DP octal

octal[2]: ~ **base** *n* MECH ENG base octal *f*, casquillo con ocho pistones *m*, casquillo octal *m*; ~ **notation** *n* COMP&DP notación octal *f*; ~ **tube** *n* ELECTRON tubo octal *m*

octamer *n* CHEM octámero *m*

octanal *n* CHEM octanal *m*, octilaldehído *m*, PETR TECH octanal *m*

octane *n* CHEM, PETR TECH, VEH octano *m*; ~ **index** *n* AUTO, PETROL, PETR TECH, VEH octanaje *m*, índice de octano *m*; ~ **number** *n* (*ON*) PETR TECH, VEH número de octano *m*, octanaje *m*; ~ **number rating** *n* (*ONR*) AUTO clasificación del número de octano *f*; ~ **rating** *n* AUTO, PETROL índice de octano *m*, PETR TECH octanaje *m*, VEH graduación octánica *f*, octanaje *m*, índice de octano *m*

octant: ~ **mirror** *n* INSTR reflector octante *m*

octavalent *adj* CHEM octavalente

octave: ~ **band** *n* ACOUST, ELECTRON banda de octava *f*; ~~**band filter** *n* ELECTRON filtro de banda de octava *m*; ~~**band oscillator** *n* ELECTRON oscilador de banda de octava *m*

octene *n* CHEM octeno *m*

octet *n* CHEM, COMP&DP octeto *m*

octode *n* ELECTRON octodo *m*

octose *n* CHEM octosa *f*

octovalent *adj* CHEM octovalente

octyl *n* CHEM octilo *m*; ~ **aldehyde** *n* CHEM octanal *m*, octilaldehído *m*, PETR TECH octanal *m*

octyne *n* CHEM octina *f*

OCU *abbr* (*operational conversion unit*) AIR TRANSP unidad de conversión operacional *f*

OD *abbr* HYDROL (*oxygen deficit*) DO (*déficit en oxígeno*), MECH, MECH ENG (*outside diameter*) diámetro exterior *m*

O-D: ~ **equation** *n* (*origin and destination equation*) TRANSP ecuación de origen y destino *f*; ~ **survey** *n* (*origin and destination survey*) TRANSP *traffic* estudio sobre origen y destino *m*

ODAS *abbr* (*ocean-data acquisition system*) OCEAN SADO (*sistema de adquisición de datos oceánicos*)

odd: ~ **container** *n* TRANSP contenedor singular *m*; ~~**even check** *n* COMP&DP comprobación de paridad par-impar *f*, verificación de paridad par-impar *f* (*AmL*); ~~**even nucleus** *n* PHYS, RAD PHYS núcleo par-impar *m*; ~ **harmonic** *n* ELECTRON, PHYS *of clay* armónico impar *m*; ~~**odd nucleus** *n* PHYS, RAD PHYS núcleo impar-impar *m*; ~~**odd spin** *n* NUCL espín impar-impar *m*; ~~**order filter** *n* ELECTRON filtro de orden impar *m*; ~ **page** *n* PRINT página derecha *f*, página impar *f*; ~ **parity** *n* COMP&DP, PHYS *wave* *function* paridad impar *f*; ~ **pitch** *n* MECH ENG *screws* paso bastardo *m*

oddments *n pl* PRINT página accesoria *f*

odds *n pl* MATH probabilidades *f pl*

odometer *n AmE* (*cf mileometer BrE, trip counter BrE*) AUTO, CONST, TRANSP VEH cuentakilómetros *m*, cuentapasos *m*, odómetro *m*

odontograph *n* MECH ENG *for gear teeth* odontógrafo *m*

odontolite *n* MINERAL odontolita *f*

odor[1]: ~-**proof** *AmE see odour-proof BrE*

odor[2]: ~ **control** *AmE see odour control BrE*; ~ **threshold** *AmE see odour threshold BrE*

odorant *n* PETR TECH odorante *m*

odoriferous *adj* CHEM oloroso

odoriphore *n* CHEM odorífero *m*

odorization *n* GAS odorización *f*

odorizer *n* CHEM TECH agente odorante *m*, odorante *m*

odorless *AmE see odourless BrE*

odorous *adj* CHEM TECH oloroso, POLL odorífero (*Esp*), oloroso (*AmL*)

odour[1]: ~-**proof** *adj BrE* PACK que evita el paso de olores

odour[2]: ~ **control** *n BrE* CHEM TECH, POLL control de olores *m*; ~ **threshold** *n BrE* HYDROL *sewage*, RECYCL, WATER límite crítico de olores *m*

odourless *adj BrE* CHEM, CHEM TECH inodoro, sin olor

ODP *abbr* (*open distribution processing*) TELECOM procesamiento de distribución abierta *m*

O-E *abbr* (*optical-electrical*) TELECOM O-E (*óptico-eléctrico*)

oersted *n* CONST, ELEC, PHYS oersted *m*, oerstedio *m*

off *n* MECH ENG desconexión *f*, rebaja *f*, reducción *f*

OFF *abbr* (*optical flexibility frame*) OPT, TELECOM bastidor de flexibilidad óptica *m*

off-air[1] *adj* TELECOM de señal en el aire, TV fuera del aire, que no transmite

off-air[2]: ~ **call setup** *n* TELECOM establecimiento de una comunicación de señal en el aire *m*; ~ **period** *n* CONST período de interrupción *m*; ~ **pick-up** *n* TV captador fuera del aire *m*, captador que no transmite *m*

offals *n pl* AGRIC residuos de matadero *m pl*

off-board *adj* ELECTRON de placa inferior, fuera de la placa

off-camera *adj* CINEMAT fuera del campo visual de la cámara

off-center *AmE see off-centre BrE*

off-centre *adj BrE* MECH ENG descentrado, desnivelado, desplazado, desviado, excéntrico, fuera de centro, fuera de su lugar, fuera del eje, no paralelo, SPACE excéntrico

off-color: ~ **shade** *AmE see off-colour shade BrE*

off-colour: ~ **shade** *n BrE* COLOUR matiz fuera de color *m*

off-course *adv* SPACE fuera de trayectoria, a la deriva

off-critical: ~ **amount** *n* NUCL cantidad no crítica *f*, masa no crítica *f*

offcut[1] *n* PAPER cabo *m*, PRINT inserción *f*

offcut[2] *vt* PRINT intercalar

offcuts *n pl* CINEMAT recortes *m pl*

off-cycle: ~ **defrosting** *n* REFRIG desescarche natural cíclico *m*

off-delay: ~ **relay** *n* ELEC ENG relé de retardo en desconexión *m*

offer *n* TELECOM oferta *f*, presentación *f*

off-flavor *AmE see off-flavour BrE*

off-flavour *n BrE* FOOD aroma desagradable *m*, defecto de aroma *m*

off-gas *n* GAS gas residual *m*, NUCL, SPACE *launching of spacecraft* gases de descarga *m pl*; ~ **condenser** *n* NUCL condensador de descargas gaseosas *m*

office: ~ **automation** *n* (*OA*) COMP&DP, PROD automatización de oficina *f* (*OA*), ofimática *f* (*OA*); ~ **printing machine** *n* PRINT impresora offset de oficina *f*

Office: ~ **for Research and Experiments** *n* (*ORE*) RAIL Oficina para la Investigación y Experimentos *f*

official: ~ **timetable** *n* RAIL guía oficial de horarios *f*, horario oficial *m*, tabla oficial de horarios *f*

offing[1]: **in the** ~ *adj* WATER TRANSP *navigation* en franquía, fuera de puntas, mar afuera

offing[2]: **in the** ~ *adv* WATER TRANSP en franquía, fuera de puntas, mar afuera

offing[3] *n* WATER TRANSP franquía *f*

offlap *n* GEOL solapamiento regresivo *m*

off-line[1] *adj* COMP&DP, TELECOM desconectado, fuera de línea

off-line[2] *adv* COMP&DP, TELECOM fuera de línea, no acoplado al sistema

off-line[3]: ~ **computer** *n* COMP&DP, NUCL computador autónomo *m* (*AmL*), computador fuera de línea *m* (*AmL*), computadora autónoma *f* (*AmL*), computadora fuera de línea *f* (*AmL*), ordenador autónomo *m* (*Esp*), ordenador fuera de línea *m* (*Esp*); ~ **docking station** *n* TRANSP muelle-dársena independiente *m*; ~ **editing** *n* TV edición fuera de línea *f*; ~ **processing** *n* COMP&DP procesamiento fuera de línea *m*; ~ **working** *n* CONST funcionamiento manual *m*, TELECOM funcionamiento fuera de línea *m*, funcionamiento por línea independiente *m*

off-load *n* PROD descargamento *m*; ~ **charging** *n* NUCL *project management* recarga de combustible en condiciones de parada *f*

off-machine: ~ **coater** *n* PAPER estucadora fuera de máquina *f*; ~ **coating** *n* PAPER estucado fuera de máquina *m*; ~ **creping** *n* PAPER crespado fuera de máquina *m*

off-normal: ~ **operating conditions** *n pl* NUCL condiciones de operación anormales *f pl*

off-peak: ~ **energy storage** *n* ELEC, ELEC ENG, NUCL, THERMO almacenamiento de energía en horas de baja demanda *m*; ~ **load** *n* ELEC ENG carga fuera de la hora punta *f*; ~ **period** *n* ELEC *supply* período de carga reducida *m*, período de marcha a potencia reducida *m*, período fuera de puntas *m*; ~ **power** *n* NUCL potencia de carga base *f*

off-period *n* ELEC ENG período de bloqueo *m*, período de corte *m*

off-position *n* MECH ENG posición "no" *f*, posición de abierto *f*, posición de cortar *f*, posición de desconexión *f*, posición de parada *f*, posición de reposo *f*

off-prints *n pl* PRINT reimpresiones separadas *f pl*

off-quality *adj* TEXTIL falto de calidad

offset[1] *adj* MECH ENG desviado, PRINT repintado, VEH desfasado

offset[2] *n* AGRIC bulbo lateral *m*, hijuelo *m*, CINEMAT descentramiento *m*, CONST *projection* desplazamiento *m*, retallo *m*, ELECTRON offset *m*, GEOL *mountains* desplazamiento horizontal *m*, desviación ortogonal *f*, estribación *f*, GEOPHYS disposición de sensores desplazados *f*, componente horizontal de desplazo *f*,

desplazamiento horizontal *m*, zona desplazada *f*, retranqueo *m*, acodo *m*, MECH descentramiento *m*, compensación *f*, desviación *f*, desplazamiento horizontal *m*, MECH ENG balance *m*, desnivel *m*, deformación *f*, margen *m*, compensación *f*, saliente *f*, rebaje *m*, MINE desviación *f*, pozo de compensación *m*, desplazamiento *m*, perforación enfrentada *f*, labor atravesada *f*, recorte *m* (*Esp*), PRINT impresión litográfica *f*, offset *m*, TV regulación a cero voltios *f*, WATER enclave *m*; ~ **aerial** *n* BrE (*cf offset antenna AmE*) SPACE antena con alimentador descentrado *f*; ~ **antenna** *n* (*AmE cf offset aerial BrE*) SPACE *communications* antena con alimentador descentrado *f*; ~ **blade** *n* AIR TRANSP *helicopter* pala descentrada *f*, pala excéntrica *f*; ~ **carrier system** *n* TV sistema de portador desplazado *m*; ~ **coater** *n* PAPER estucadora offset *f*; ~ **connecting rod** *n* AUTO, VEH biela excéntrica *f*; ~ **deep printing** *n* PRINT impresión en hueco-offset *f*; ~ **disc harrow** BrE, ~ **disk harrow** AmE *n* AGRIC grada de discos excéntricos *f*; ~ **drive** *n* MINE galería de labor atravesada *f* (*AmL*), galería de recorte *f*, transversal *f* (*Esp*); ~ **flapping hinge** *n* AIR TRANSP *helicopter* charnela de aleteo descentrada *f*; ~ **lens** *n* CINEMAT lente de descentramiento *f*; ~ **paper** *n* PAPER papel offset *m*; ~ **printing press** *n* PRINT prensa para impresión offset *f*; ~ **reflector** *n* SPACE *communications* reflector descentrado *m*; ~ **ring wrench** *n* MECH ENG llave inglesa acodada *f*; ~ **roller** *n* PROD rodillo no radial *m*; ~ **signal method** *n* TV método de señal desplazada *m*; ~ **viewfinder** *n* CINEMAT visor descentrado *m*
offset³ *vt* PRINT reimprtir
offsets *n pl* WATER TRANSP *naval construction* cartilla de trazado *f*
off-setting *n* MECH ENG, PROD descentramiento *m*, desviación *f*
off-shade *n* PAPER fuera de tono; ~ **dyeing** *n* COLOUR teñido fuera de matiz *m*
offshoot *n* AGRIC rebrote lateral *m*
offshore¹ *adj* GEOL, OCEAN, PETR TECH, WATER TRANSP costa-fuera, fuera costa, en alta mar
offshore² *adv* GEOL, OCEAN, PETR TECH, WATER TRANSP mar adentro, en alta mar
offshore³ *n* GEOL, OCEAN, PETR TECH, WATER TRANSP alta mar *f*, mar abierto *m*; ~ **bar** *n* GEOL, HYDROL, OCEAN, WATER TRANSP cordón litoral *m*, barra de arena de alta mar *f*, banco de arena de alta mar *m*; ~ **breeze** *n* METEO viento de la costa *m*; ~ **drilling** *n* PETR TECH perforación costa-fuera *f*, sondeo en mar abierto *m*; ~ **field** *n* PETR TECH campo petrolero costa-fuera *m*, campo petrolífero marino *m*; ~ **fishery** *n* OCEAN pesca de altura *f*, pesca de gran altura *f*, pesquería en aguas lejanas *f*; ~ **fishing** *n* OCEAN pesca de altura *f*, pesca de gran altura *f*; ~ **oil industry** *n* PETR TECH industria petrolífera costa-fuera *f*, industria petrolífera marina *f*; ~ **platform** *n* PETR TECH plataforma costa-fuera *f*, plataforma marina *f*; ~ **trough** *n* OCEAN surco sublitoral *m*; ~ **well** *n* PETR TECH pozo costa-fuera *m*, perforación petrolífera no costera situada en la plataforma continental *f*, pozo marítimo *m*; ~ **wind** *n* WATER TRANSP viento de tierra *m*, viento terral *m*
offtake *n* MINE tubo de descarga *m*, *mine pits* galería de desagüe *f*, recardación *f*, galería de extracción *f*, reservas *f pl* (*Esp*), *of coal* existencias *f pl* (*AmL*),

WATER *canals* toma de agua *f*, galería de extracción *f*, tubo de descarga *m*, galería de desagüe *f*
off-the-shelf: ~ **information** *n* PACK información de las existencias *f*
off-tune: ~ **frequency** *n* ELECTRON frecuencia desintonizada *f*
OFS *abbr* (*out-of-frame second*) TELECOM segundo fuera *m*
ogee *n* CONST *moulds* cimacio *m*, talón *m*; ~ **plane** *n* CONST cepillo de talón *m*
OHA *abbr* (*overhead access*) TELECOM acceso de cabecera *m*, acceso inicial *m*
OHC *abbr* (*overhead camshaft*) AUTO, MECH, VEH ALC (*árbol de levas en culata*), eje de levas en la culata *m*
ohm *n* ELEC *unit*, ELEC ENG, METR, MINE, PHYS, TELECOM ohm *m*, ohmio *m*
ohmic¹ *adj* ELEC *resistance*, ELEC ENG, METR, MINE, PHYS, TELECOM óhmico
ohmic²: ~ **conductor** *n* PHYS conductor óhmico *m*; ~ **contact** *n* ELEC ENG contacto eléctrico de característica óhmica *m*, contacto óhmico *m*, FUELLESS, PHYS contacto óhmico *m*; ~ **drop** *n* ELEC *resistance* caída óhmica *f*; ~ **loss** *n* ELEC *heating*, ELEC ENG pérdida por efecto Joule *f*, pérdida óhmica *f*, PHYS pérdida óhmica *f*; ~ **resistance** *n* ELEC, ELEC ENG resistencia real *f*, resistencia óhmica *f*; ~ **value** *n* ELEC ENG valor óhmico *m*
ohmmeter *n* GEN ohmímetro *m*, óhmetro *m*
Ohm's: ~ **law** *n* ELEC, ELEC ENG, PHYS ley de Ohm *f*
OHV¹ *abbr* AUTO (*overhead valve, overhead valves*) válvula en culata *f*, válvulas en culata *f pl*, METALL, PETR TECH, PETROL, THERMO (*overhead valve*) válvula en culata *f*, VEH (*overhead valves*), válvulas en culata *f pl*
OHV²: ~ **engine** *n* AUTO motor de válvulas en cabeza *m*, motor de válvulas en culata *m*
oil¹: ~**-bearing** *adj* PETR TECH, PETROL con petróleo, contenido petróleo, oleaginoso, petrolífero; ~**-burning** *adj* THERMO caldeado con fueloil; ~**-cooled** *adj* THERMO enfriado con aceite, refrigerado con aceite; ~**-fired** *adj* THERMO caldeado con fueloil; ~**-forming** *adj* CHEM formador de aceite; ~**-hardened** *adj* METALL templado en aceite, templado en fueloil, THERMO templado en aceite; ~**-painted** *adj* COLOUR pintado al óleo; ~**-quenched** *adj* METALL, THERMO templado en aceite; ~**-resistant** *adj* P&R resistente al aceite; ~**-soluble** *adj* CHEM, P&R soluble en aceite
oil² *n* GEN aceite *m*; ~ **absorption** *n* P&R absorción de aceite *f*; ~**-based ink** *n* PRINT tinta al aceite *f*; ~**-based mud** *n* PETR TECH, PETROL lodo a base de petróleo *m*, lodo con base de petróleo *m*; ~**-based sludge** *n* PETR TECH, PETROL lodo con base petróleo *m*; ~ **basin** *n* GEOL, PETR TECH, PETROL bolsa de petróleo *f*; ~ **bath** *n* LAB *device* baño de aceite *m*; ~ **bath air cleaner** *n* AUTO filtro de aire en baño de aceite *m*; ~ **bath air filter** *n* AUTO filtro de aire en baño de aceite *m*; ~**-bound distemper** *n* COLOUR diluyente al aceite *m*; ~**-bound paint** *n* COLOUR pintura al aceite *f*; ~**-bound water paint** *n* COLOUR pintura al agua al aceite *f*; ~ **box** *n* PROD *axes* caja de engrase *f*, caja de grasa *f*, depósito de aceite *m*; ~ **break switch** *n* PROD interruptor en baño de aceite *m*; ~**-bulk-ore carrier** *n* (*OBO carrier*) TRANSP transporte marítimo combinado *m*, transporte mixto por mar *m*, WATER TRANSP buque de transporte mixto

m, buque transportador mixto *m*; ~ **burner** *n* AGRIC quemador de aceite *m*, MECH ENG quemador de petróleo *m*, THERMO quemador de fueloil *m*; ~ **burner motor** *n* MECH ENG motor de combustión de petróleo *m*; ~-**carbon deposit** *n* AUTO sedimento carbonoso del aceite *m*; ~ **change** *n* VEH cambio de aceite *m*; ~ **change shop** *n* AUTO taller de cambio de aceite *m*; ~ **channel** *n* AUTO conducto de aceite *m*, MECH ENG *drilling-machine tables* ranura de engrase *f*; ~ **circuit breaker** *n* ELEC, ELEC ENG disyuntor en aceite *m*, interruptor en aceite *m*; ~-**clearance vessel** *n* MAR POLL embarcación dedicada a la remoción de hidrocarburos *f*, POLL contenedor evacuador de aceites *m*, recipiente evacuador de aceites *m*; ~-**coal-ore carrier** *n* (*OCO carrier*) TRANSP barco de transporte de materiales mixtos *m*, transporte mixto *m*, WATER TRANSP buque de transporte combinado *m*; ~ **cock** *n* MECH ENG grifo de aceite *m*, llave de aceite *f*, llave de grasa *f*; ~-**concentrating agent** *n* POLL agente concentrador de aceite *m*, agente recogedor de aceite *m*; ~ **conservator** *n* ELEC ENG conservador de aceite *m*; ~ **control ring** *n* AUTO anillo de cojinete falso *m*, anillo de control de engrase *m*, anillo rascador de aceite *m*, segmento de control de engrase *m*, segmento de engrase *m*, VEH anillo de control de engrase *m*, anillo rascador de aceite *m*, segmento rascador de aceite *m*; ~-**cooled transformer** *n* ELEC, ELEC ENG transformador enfriado por aceite *m*, transformador refrigerado por aceite *m*; ~ **cooler** *n* ELEC *transformer* enfriador de aceite *m*, radiador del aceite *m*, refrigerador de aceite *m*, REFRIG enfriador de aceite *m*, THERMO enfriador de aceite *m*, refrigerador de aceite *m*, VEH refrigerante de aceite *m*; ~ **cooling** *n* ELEC *transformer* enfriamiento del aceite *m*, refrigeración del aceite *f*, MECH ENG enfriamiento por aceite *m*, oleoenfriamiento *m*; ~ **crops** *n pl* AGRIC cultivos de oleaginosas *m pl*; ~ **cup** *n* MECH ENG aceitador *m*, aceitadora *f*, copa de aceite *f*, copa de lubricación *f*, engrasador de copa *m*, lubricadora *f*; ~ **dashpot** *n* MECH ENG amortiguador hidráulico *m*, freno de aceite *m*, oleoamortiguador *m*, RAIL freno de aceite *m*; ~ **dipstick** *n* AUTO, VEH varilla del nivel del aceite *f*; ~ **discovery** *n* PETR TECH descubrimiento de petróleo *m*; ~ **distributor** *n* MECH ENG distribuidor de aceite *m*; ~ **drain** *n* REFRIG purgador de aceite *m*; ~ **drain hole** *n* AUTO agujero de drenaje del aceite *m*; ~ **drain plug** *n* AUTO tapón de drenaje del aceite *m*, MECH tapón de purga de aceite *m*, VEH tapón roscado de purga del aceite *m*, tapón roscado del cárter de aceite *m*; ~ **drop** *n* PHYS gota de aceite *f*; ~-**eating bacterium** *n* RECYCL bacteria olefaga *f*; ~-**expander ring** *n* AUTO segmento de engrase con expansores *m*; ~ **exploration** *n* PETR TECH exploración petrolífera *f*, prospección, petrolífera *f*; ~ **feed** *n* AUTO, VEH alimentación de aceite *f*; ~-**filled cable** *n* ELEC cable con aceite circulante *m*, cable de aceite *m*, cable de aceite fluido *m*, ELEC ENG cable eléctrico impregnado de aceite *m*; ~-**filled pipe-type cable** *n* ELEC cable tipo tubo de lubricación de aceite *m*; ~ **filler pipe** *n* AUTO tubo de llenado del aceite *m*; ~ **filter** *n* AUTO, MECH, MECH ENG, VEH filtro de aceite *m*; ~ **filter cap** *n* AUTO tapón del filtro de aceite *m*; ~-**fired boiler** *n* HEAT, HEAT ENG caldera de gasóleo *f*; ~-**fired central heating system** *n* HEAT, HEAT ENG sistema de calefacción central por gasóleo *m*; ~-**fired furnace**

n HEAT, HEAT ENG horno de gasóleo *m*; ~-**fired heating** *n* HEAT, HEAT ENG calefacción por gasóleo *f*; ~-**fired installation** *n* HEAT, MECH ENG, PETROL, THERMO instalación de caldeado con petróleo *f*, instalación de calefacción con petróleo *f*; ~-**fired power plant** *n* NUCL central eléctrica de fueloil *f*; ~-**fired power station** *n* ELEC *supply* central eléctrica activada con aceite *f*, HEAT ENG central eléctrica alimentada por gasóleo *f*, THERMO central de fuerza motriz caldeada por gasoil *f*, central energética caldeada con petróleo *f*; ~-**fired rotary dryer** *n* HEAT *asphalt plant* secadora rotativa alimentada por gasóleo *f*; ~ **firing** *n* CONST, PETROL alimentación con petróleo *f*; ~ **flow** *n* PROD flujo de aceite *m*; ~ **formation volume factor** *n* PETROL factor de volumen de la formación petrolífera *m*; ~-**free compressor** *n* REFRIG compresor sin aceite *m*; ~ **fuel** *n* THERMO petróleo combustible *m*; ~ **gage** *AmE see oil gauge BrE*; ~ **gallery** *n* AUTO conducto de aceite *m*; ~ **gasification** *n* PETR TECH gasificación del crudo *f*; ~ **gauge** *n BrE* MECH ENG manómetro de aceite *m*, nivel para aceite *m*, oleómetro *m*, PROD manómetro de aceite *m*; ~ **groove** *n* MECH ENG *in bearings* canal de engrase *m*, conducto de lubricación *m*, muescas aceitadas *f pl*, ranura de lubricación *f*; ~ **hydraulic starter** *n* ELEC arrancador hidráulico de aceite *m*; ~-**immersed capacitor** *n* ELEC capacitor en baño de aceite *m*, condensador en baño de aceite *m*; ~-**immersed transformer** *n* ELEC ENG transformador en baño de aceite *m*; ~ **immersion lens** *n* INSTR, LAB *knot* lente de inmersión en aceite *f*; ~ **in place** *n* PETR TECH, PETROL petróleo in situ *m*; ~ **inlet** *n* AUTO entrada de aceite *f*; ~ **insulator** *n* ELEC, ELEC ENG aislador de aceite *m*; ~ **interrupter** *n* PROD interruptor en baño de aceite *m*; ~ **length** *n* P&R longitud de aceite *f*; ~-**level mark** *n* VEH marca del nivel de aceite *f*, señal del nivel de aceite *f*; ~-**level stick** *n* AUTO, VEH varilla del nivel del aceite *f*; ~ **line** *n* AUTO, VEH marca del nivel de aceite *f*, nivel de aceite *m*; ~ **mill** *n* AGRIC molino aceitero *m*; ~ **mop** *n* MAR POLL material absorbente *m*; ~-**ore carrier** *n* (*OO carrier*) TRANSP transporte combinado crudo-mineral *m*, transporte combinado petróleo-mineral *m*, transporte de material petrolífero *m*; ~-**packing paper** *n* PACK, PAPER papel para envases de aceite *m*; ~ **paint** *n* COLOUR pintura al óleo *f*; ~ **pan** *n* AUTO cárter de aceite *m*, depósito de aceite *m*, MECH depósito de aceite *m*, recogedor de aceite *m*; ~-**pan gasket** *n* AUTO, VEH junta del cárter de aceite *f*; ~-**paper capacitor** *n* ELEC ENG condensador de papel aceitado *m*; ~ **pier** *n* TRANSP muelle petrolero *m*; ~ **pipe** *n* PROD *lubrication* tubería de engrase *f*, tubo de lubricación *m*; ~ **pipeline** *n* CONST, MECH ENG oleoducto *m*, PETR TECH conducto petrolero *m*, oleoducto *m*, PETROL, TRANSP oleoducto *m*; ~ **pressostat** *n* REFRIG presostato de aceite *m*; ~-**pressure gage** *AmE*, ~-**pressure gauge** *BrE n* AUTO indicador de presión de aceite *m*, manómetro de aceite *m*, VEH indicador de presión de aceite *m*; ~-**pressure safety cutout** *n* REFRIG presostato de seguridad de aceite *m*; ~-**pressure switch** *n* AIR TRANSP interruptor de la presión del aceite *m*; ~-**pressure warning light** *n* AUTO luz de aviso de la presión del aceite *f*; ~ **pump** *n* AUTO, CONST, REFRIG, VEH bomba de aceite *f*; ~-**pump gasket** *n* REFRIG junta de la bomba de aceite *f*; ~ **pump spindle** *n* AUTO eje de la bomba del aceite *m*, pivote de la bomba del aceite *m*; ~ **quenching** *n* METALL temple general instantáneo en aceite *m*, THERMO enfriamiento en aceite *m*, temple general instantáneo en aceite *m*; ~ **reclaiming** *n* MECH ENG recuperación de lubricantes usados *f*; ~**recovery skimmer** *n* MAR POLL, POLL succionador para la extracción de petróleo *m*; ~**recovery vessel** *n* MAR POLL embarcación dedicada a la recuperación de hidrocarburos *f*, POLL barco recuperador de aceites *m*, buque para la extracción de petróleo *m*; ~ **regeneration plant** *n* RECYCL planta de regeneración de aceite *f*, planta de transformación de aceites *f*, planta de óleo-transformación *f* (*AmL*); ~ **relief valve plunger** *n* AUTO pistón de la válvula de descarga de aceite *m*; ~**removing system** *n* GAS sistema de separación de petróleo *m*; ~ **reservoir** *n* MINE depósito de aceite *m*, depósito de petróleo *m*, reservorio oleífero *m*, PETR TECH, PETROL yacimiento petrolífero *m*; ~**resisting hose** *n* P&R manguera resistente al aceite *f*; ~ **ring** *n* AUTO, MECH ENG, PROD, VEH anillo aceitador *m*, anillo de control de engrase *m*, anillo de engrase *m*, anillo de lubricación *m*, anillo lubricante *m*; ~ **sand** *n* PETROL arena petrolífera *f*; ~ **saturation** *n* PETROL saturación de petróleo *f*; ~ **scrubbing** *n* PETR TECH eliminado del agua del crudo *m*; ~ **seal** *n* MECH, MECH ENG cierre de aceite *m*, obturador de aceite *m*, sello de aceite *m*, sello de lubricación *m*; ~ **seed** *n* FOOD aceite de semilla *m*; ~ **self-sufficiency** *n* PETR TECH autosuficiencia de petróleo *f*; ~ **separator** *n* HYDROL, REFRIG separador de aceite *m*; ~ **shale** *n* GEOL esquisto bituminoso *m*, PETR TECH, PETROL esquisto bituminoso *m*, pizarra bituminosa *f*; ~ **show** *n* PETR TECH indicio de petróleo *m*, señal de existencia de petróleo *f*; ~ **show analyser** *n BrE* PETR TECH analizador de señales de petróleo *m*; ~ **show analyzer** *AmE see oil show analyser BrE*; ~ **sight glass** *n* REFRIG indicador de nivel de aceite *m*; ~**sight o-ring** *n* REFRIG orificio del visor del indicador del nivel de aceite *m*; ~ **slick** *n* PETR TECH, POLL mancha de aceite flotando en el agua *f*, mancha de aceite flotante *f*; ~ **slick sinking** *n* POLL hundimiento de mancha de aceite por corrientes marinas *m*; ~ **slinger** *n* MECH ENG arandela para impedir el paso del lubricante al eje *f*, deflector de aceite *m*, salpicador de aceite *m*; ~**softened rubber** *n* P&R caucho reblandecido con aceite *m*, caucho suavizado con aceite *m*; ~ **spill** *n* MAR POLL derrame de hidrocarburos *m* (*Esp*), POLL derrame petrolero *m*; ~ **spill response** *n* MAR POLL respuesta dada en casos de derrames de hidrocarburos *f*; ~ **still** *n* REFRIG rectificador de aceite *m*; ~ **stimulation** *n* PETROL estimulación petrolífera *f*; ~ **sump** *n* AIR TRANSP cárter de aceite *m*, cárter de lubricante *m*; ~ **switch** *n* ELEC, ELEC ENG conmutador en baño de aceite *m*, disyuntor de aceite *m*, disyuntor en baño de aceite *m*, interruptor en aceite *m*, PROD disyuntor en baño de aceite *m*, interruptor en baño de aceite *m*; ~ **tank** *n* CONST tanque de aceite *m*, tanque de petróleo *m*, ELEC ENG cuba para petróleo *f*, tanque de aceite *m*; ~ **tanker** *n* PETR TECH buque tanque petrolero *m*, WATER TRANSP *ship* petrolero *m*; ~ **temperature cutout** *n* REFRIG termostato de seguridad de aceite *m*; ~ **temperature indicator** *n* AIR TRANSP indicador de la temperatura del aceite *m*; ~ **temperature probe**

n AIR TRANSP sonda de temperatura del aceite *f*; ~ **tracing paper** *n* PAPER papel de calco aceitado *m*; ~ **transformer** *n* ELEC transformador en baño de aceite *m*; ~ **trap** *n* HYDROL separador de aceite *m*, PETR TECH trampa de petróleo *f*, WATER colector de aceite *m*, interceptor de aceite *m*, separador de aceite *m*; ~ **tube twist drill** *n* MECH ENG broca helicoidal con canal lubricador *f*; ~ **of vitriol** *n* CHEM aceite de vitriolo *m*; ~ **waste** *n* POLL desperdicio de aceite *m*, residuos de aceite *m pl*, residuos petrolíferos *m pl*; ~**water contact** *n* PETROL contacto petróleo-agua *m*; ~**water interface** *n* MAR POLL interfaz hidrocarburos-agua *m*; ~ **well** *n* PETROL pozo petrolífero *m*

oil³ *vt* AUTO, MECH, MECH ENG engrasar, PROD engrasar, fundir, VEH engrasar; ~ **quench** *vt* METALL templar en aceite, THERMO enfriar en aceite, templar en aceite

oilcake *n* AGRIC torta oleaginosa *f*; ~ **breaker** *n* AGRIC trituradora de tortas oleaginosas *f*

oilcan *n* PROD aceitera *f*

oilcloth *n* CHEM caucho *m*, goma elástica *f*, P&R, TEXTIL caucho *m*, goma elástica *f*, hule *m*

oiled: ~ **bearing** *n* MECH ENG cojinete aceitado *m*

oiler *n* MINE buque petrolero *m*, copa de lubricación *f* (*AmL*), engrasador *m* (*Esp*), PROD *cup* copa de lubricación *f*, *person* engrasador *m*, *can* aceitera *f*, TEXTIL engrasador *m*, WATER TRANSP buque petrolero *m*

oilfield *n* PETROL, PETR TECH campo petrolífero *m*, yacimiento petrolífero *m*

oilhole *n* MECH ENG agujero de lubricación *m*, boquilla de engrase *f*

oiling *n* PROD embadurnamiento con aceite *m*, engrase *m*, TEXTIL engrase *m*

oilless: ~ **bearing** *n* MECH ENG cojinete autolubricado *m*, cojinete con lubricante sólido *m*, cojinete grafitado *m*, cojinete sin aceite *m*, cojinete sin lubricación *m*

oilmeter *n* MECH ENG depósito de petróleo *m*, oleómetro *m*

oilproof: ~ **protective gloves** *n pl* SAFE guantes protectores a prueba de aceite *m pl*

oilseed *n* AGRIC semilla oleaginosa *f*

oilskin *n* P&R encerado *m*, tela aceitada *f*, tela impermeable *f*, TEXTIL encerado *m*, WATER TRANSP *sailing clothes* ropa aceitada *f*

oilstone *n* MECH ENG *abrasives* piedra afiladora *f*, piedra de aceite *f*, piedra de repasar filos *f*, PROD piedra de aceite *f*, piedra de afilar *f*

oiltight *adj* PROD estanco al aceite, estanco al petróleo

OK: ~**signal** *n* TELECOM señal de OK *f*

okenite *n* MINERAL okenita *f*

okra *n* AGRIC kimbombó *m* (*Esp*), okra *f*, quingombó *m* (*AmL*)

old: ~ **corrugated cartons** *n pl* (*OCC*) PAPER cajas de cartón ondulado usadas *f pl*; ~ **ground level** *n* CONST nivel original del terreno *m*; ~ **number** *n* TELECOM número antiguo *m* (*Esp*), número viejo *m* (*AmL*); ~ **style** *n AmE* PRINT tipo antiguo *m*

Oldham: ~ **coupling** *n* MECH acoplamiento Oldham *m*

oldland *n* GEOL zócalo *m*

oleander *n* AGRIC adelfa *f*

oleandrin *n* CHEM oleandrina *f*

oleate *n* CHEM oleato *m*

olefin *n* CHEM, DETERG, PETR TECH, PETROL olefina *f*

olefinic¹ *adj* CHEM, DETERG, PETR TECH, PETROL olefínico

olefinic[2]: ~ **content** n CHEM contenido olefínico m

oleic[1] adj CHEM oléico

oleic[2]: ~ **acid** n CHEM, DETERG, FOOD, PROD ácido oléico m; ~ **ink** n COLOUR tinta de aceite f, tinta oléica f

olein n CHEM oleína f

oleo: ~ **oil** n CHEM oleomargarina f

oleometer n CHEM, INSTR oleómetro m

oleophilic[1] adj CHEM oleofílico, MAR POLL olefilo

oleophilic[2]: ~ **belt** n MAR POLL cinta olefila f; ~ **belt skimmer** n MAR POLL rasera con cinta olefila f

oleophosphoric adj CHEM oleofosfórico

oleoresin n CHEM oleoresina f

oleoresinous[1] adj CHEM oleoresinoso

oleoresinous[2]: ~ **paint** n CONST pintura oleoresinosa f; ~ **varnish** n COATINGS, COLOUR barniz oleoresinoso m

oleovitamin n CHEM oleovitamina f

oleum n CHEM, DETERG ácido sulfúrico fumante m, óleum m

oligoclase n MINERAL oligoclasa f

oligomer n CHEM oligómero m

oligomeric adj CHEM oligomérico

oligomerization n CHEM oligomerización f

oligomycyn n CHEM oligomicina f

oligonite n MINERAL dialogita f, oligonita f

olistolith n GEOL olistolito m

olive: ~ **grower** n AGRIC olivicultor m

olivenite n MINERAL olivenita f

olivine n MINERAL olivino m, pesidoto m

OLRT abbr (on line real time) COMP&DP OLRT (tiempo real en línea)

omega: ~ **loop** n TV lazo omega m; ~ **minus particle** n PHYS partícula omega menos f

Omega: ~ **wrap** n TV revestimiento Omega m

omnibearing: ~ **indicator** n AIR TRANSP indicador de marcación omnidireccional m; ~ **selector** n AIR TRANSP selector omnidireccional m

omnidirectional: ~ **aerial** n BrE (cf omnidirectional antenna AmE) SPACE, TELECOM antena omnidireccional f; ~ **antenna** n AmE (cf omnidirectional aerial BrE) SPACE, TELECOM antena omnidireccional f; ~ **microphone** n ACOUST micrófono omnidireccional m; ~ **radiorange** n AIR TRANSP radiofaro omnidireccional m

omnirange: ~ **indicator** n AIR TRANSP indicador de radiofaro omnidireccional m

omphacite n MINERAL omfacita f

OMR abbr (optical mark reading) COMP&DP OMR (lectura óptica de marcas)

OMS abbr (orbital manoeuvring system BrE) SPACE sistema de maniobra orbital m

on adj MECH ENG en funcionamiento

ON abbr (octane number) PETR TECH OCTN, número de octano m, VEH número de octano m, octanaje m

on-air: ~ **period** n ELEC ENG período de conducción m; ~ **time** n TV tiempo en emisión m, tiempo en el aire m

on-board[1] adj ELECTRON sobre la placa, SPACE spacecraft a bordo

on-board[2]: ~ **circuitry** n ELECTRON circuito sobre la placa m; ~ **communication station** n TELECOM estación de comunicaciones a bordo f; ~ **computer** n SPACE spacecraft computador de a bordo m (AmL), computadora de a bordo f (AmL), ordenador de a bordo m (Esp); ~ **equipment** n SPACE equipo de a bordo m; ~ **processing** n SPACE communications proceso de señal a bordo m, proceso de transformación a bordo m, sistematización a bordo f; ~ **subscriber** n TELECOM abonado a bordo m; ~ **switching** n SPACE communications conmutación a bordo f, interconexión a bordo f; ~ **system** n SPACE sistema de a bordo m

on-call: ~ **bus system** n TRANSP sistema de autobuses mediante aviso m

once: ~-**through boiler** n HEAT caldera de entrada única f; ~-**through charge** n NUCL carga de agotamiento f, carga de un solo paso f; ~-**through steam generator** n (OTSG) NUCL generador de vapor de un solo paso m; ~-**through-then-out** n (OTTO) NUCL ciclo de agotamiento y descarga m

on-chip: ~ **amplification** n ELECTRON amplificador en chip m; ~ **analog-to-digital conversion** n ELECTRON conversión analógico-digital en chip f; ~ **capacitor** n ELEC ENG condensador en chip m; ~ **circuit** n ELECTRON circuito en chip m; ~ **filter** n ELECTRON chip de filtro m; ~ **processing** n ELECTRON tratamiento de la información en microplaca m; ~ **transistor** n ELECTRON transistor en chip m

oncolith n GEOL oncolito m

on-delay: ~ **phase** n ELEC, ELEC ENG etapa de retardo f; ~ **relay** n ELEC, ELEC ENG relé de retardo m

one[1]: ~-**dimensional** adj PHYS unidimensional; ~-**phase** adj ELEC ENG monofásico; **in ~ piece** adj PROD todo de una pieza; ~-**point letter-spaced** adj PRINT espaciado fino; ~-**pole** adj ELECTRON monopolar

one[2]: ~-**address instruction** n COMP&DP instrucción de una dirección f; ~-**and-one lease** n TEXTIL pasado de la cruz uno y uno m; ~-**bath development** n PRINT revelado de un baño m; ~-**coil transformer** n ELEC transformador de una bobina m; ~'**s complement** n COMP&DP complemento a uno m; ~-**crop farming** n AGRIC monocultivo m; ~-**cycle reactor** n NUCL reactor de ciclo de agotamiento m, reactor de ciclo único m; ~-**cylinder engine** n AUTO, MECH ENG motor de cilindro único m, motor de un cilindro m, motor monocilíndrico m; ~-**digit adder** n ELECTRON semisumador m, sumador de un bit m, sumador de un solo dígito m; ~-**digit subtractor** n COMP&DP substractor de un solo dígito m, ELECTRON restador de un bit m, semirrestador m, substractor de un solo dígito m; ~-**element cell** n ELEC ENG célula unielemental f; ~-**feed ration** n AGRIC pienso completo m; ~-**furrow tractor** n AGRIC tractor monosurco m; ~-**light print** n CINEMAT copia monoiluminada f; ~-**off tooling** n MECH ENG herramienta de encargo f, herramienta no en serie f; ~-**part die** n MECH ENG troquel de una parte m; ~-**part screwplate** n MECH ENG terraja de una pieza f; ~-**phase controller** n TRANSP controlador monofásico m; ~-**piece base** n PROD base enteriza f; ~-**piece connector** n ELEC ENG conector monobloque m; ~-**plus-one address instruction** n COMP&DP instrucción de una más una direcciones f; ~-**plus-one carrier system** n TELECOM sistema de onda portadora de uno más uno m; ~-**second theodolite** n INSTR teodolito de un segundo m; ~-**shot circuit** n ELECTRON circuito único m; ~-**shot multivibrator** n ELECTRON multivibrador monoestable m; ~-**shot programming** n PROD programación en una sola operación f; ~-**shot signal** n ELECTRON señal monoestable f; ~-**third octave band** n ACOUST banda de tercio de octava f; ~-**time carbonizing**

base paper *n* PAPER papel soporte carbón de un solo uso *m*; **~-to-one printing** *n* CINEMAT copiado uno a uno *m*; **~-track recording** *n* ACOUST grabación monopista *f*; **~-up** *n* PRINT impresión a molde sencillo *f*; **~-way bottle** *n* PACK, RECYCL botella sin retorno *f*; **~-way container** *n* PACK contenedor sin retorno *m*; **~-way pack** *n* PACK paquete sin retorno *m*; **~-way pallet** *n* PACK, TRANSP bandeja de un solo acceso *f*, bandeja no retornable *f*, paleta de un solo acceso *f* (*Esp*), paleta no retornable *f* (*Esp*), pálet de un solo acceso *m* (*AmL*), pálet no retornable *m* (*AmL*); **~-way repeater** *n* ELECTRON repetidor unidireccional *m*; **~-way roller** *n* PROD rodillo unidireccional *m*

one[3]: **~ engine inoperative** *phr* AIR TRANSP un motor inoperativo

ONE: **~ state** *n* ELECTRON ONE (según arquitectura de la red Olivetti), estado UNO *m*

ongoing: **~ qualification test** *n* NUCL prueba continua de cualificación *f*

on-hook: **~ condition** *n* TELECOM condición de colgado *f*, condición en reposo *f*; **~ dialing** *AmE*, **~ dialling** *BrE n* TELECOM marcación en reposo *f* (*AmL*), marcado en reposo *m* (*Esp*)

onion *n* C&G cebolla *f*; **~ harvester** *n* AGRIC cosechadora de cebollas *f*; **~ maggot** *n* AGRIC mosca de las cebollas *f*; **~ salt** *n* CHEM sal de cebolla *f*; **~ set** *n* AGRIC cebollita para plantar *f*

onionskin: **~ paper** *n* PAPER papel cebolla *m*, papel de copias *m*, papel superfino *m*

onlap *n* GEOL desborde transgresivo *m*, solapamiento expansivo *m*

on-line[1] *adj* COMP&DP conectado, en línea, online, TELECOM en línea

on-line[2]: **~ data charge** *n* PROD cobro directo *m*, gastos de datos en línea *m pl*; **~ database** *n* COMP&DP, ELECTRON, TELECOM base de datos en línea *f*; **~ measurement** *n* NUCL medición en línea *f*; **~ processing** *n* COMP&DP procesamiento en línea *m*; **~ programming** *n* PROD programación en línea *f*; **~ quality monitoring** *n* TEXTIL control de calidad a tiempo real *m*

on-load: **~ charging** *n* NUCL carga de combustible en condiciones de operación *f*; **~ current** *n* ELEC ENG corriente en carga *f*; **~ fueling** *AmE*, **~ fuelling** *BrE n* NUCL carga de combustible en condiciones de operación *f*; **~ refueling** *AmE*, **~ refuelling** *BrE n* NUCL carga de combustible en condiciones de operación *f*; **~ tap changer** *n* ELEC combinador de regulación en carga *m*, combinador en carga *m*, graduador de regulación en carga *m*; **~ tap changing** *n* ELEC *transformer* combinación de regulación en carga *f*, combinación de toma *f*, graduación de regulación en carga *f*; **~ voltage** *n* ELEC tensión de servicio *f*, tensión de trabajo *f*, voltaje de régimen *m*, voltaje de servicio *m*, ELEC ENG voltaje en carga *m*

on-machine: **~ coating** *n* PAPER estucado en máquina *m*; **~ creping** *n* PAPER crespado en máquina *m*

on-off[1] *adj* MECH ENG de encendido y apagado, de marcha y parada, enchufado-desenchufado

on-off[2] *n* CINEMAT encendido y apagado *m*; **~ control** *n* ELEC control de cierre o apertura *m*, control de conexión y desconexión *m*, regulación por todo o nada *f*, SPACE control de cierre o apertura *m*, control de conexión y desconexión *m*, control de todo o nada *m*, mando de puesta en marcha *m*, regulación

discontinua *f*; **~ pilot light** *n* CINEMAT luz piloto de encendido y apagado *f*; **~ service indicator** *n* PROD indicador de servicio de conexión y desconexión *m*; **~ switch** *n* CINEMAT botón de encendido y apagado *m*, conmutador de encendido y apagado *m*, interruptor *m*, ELEC conmutador conectador-desconectador *m*, interruptor *m*, interruptor de alimentación *m*, interruptor de corriente *m*, interruptor de entrada *m*, interruptor de red *m*, interruptor encendido-apagado *m*, interruptor general *m*, interruptor para conectar y desconectar la alimentación *m*, ELEC ENG conmutador conectador-desconectador *m*, interruptor *m*, interruptor de alimentación *m*, interruptor de corriente *m*, interruptor de red *m*, interruptor encendido-apagado *m*, interruptor general *m*, MECH ENG conmutador conectador-desconectador *m*, interruptor de alimentación *m*, interruptor de encendido *m*, interruptor de puesta en marcha *m*, interruptor general *m*, PHOTO botón de encendido y apagado *m*, PHYS interruptor on-off *m*; **~ switch indicator** *n* PROD indicador de interruptor apagado-encendido *m*

ONP *abbr* (*open network provision*) TELECOM provisión de la red abierta *f*

on-peak: **~ conditions** *n pl* ELEC *supply* condiciones máximas *f pl*

ONR *abbr* (*octane number rating*) AUTO clasificación del número de octano *f*

on-scene: **~ commander** *n* MAR POLL jefe en lugar del siniestro *m*; **~ communications** *n pl* TELECOM comunicaciones en escena *f pl*

onset *n* CHEM inicio *m*; **~ of magnetic field** *n* RAD PHYS iniciación del campo magnético *f*

onsetter *n* *BrE* (*cf platman AmE*) MINE enganchador *m*, pocero *m*

onsetting *n* MINE carga de vagones en la jaula *f*, enganche *m*; **~ station** *n* MINE estación de carga *f*, estación de enganche *f*

on-shift: **~ operator** *n* NUCL operador de turno *m*

onshore[1] *adj* PETR TECH de tierra firme, en litoral de costa, WATER TRANSP de mar, sobre la costa, sobre tierra

onshore[2] *adv* GEOL hacia la costa

onshore[3]: **~ base** *n* PETR TECH base costera *f*; **~ breeze** *n* METEO brisa de lago *f*, brisa de mar *f*, virazón *f*; **~ wind** *n* METEO viento de tierra *m*, WATER TRANSP marero *m*, viento a la tierra *m*

on-site: **~ maintenance tools** *n pl* CONST herramientas de mantenimiento in situ *f pl*; **~ storage** *n* NUCL almacenamiento en el emplazamiento del reactor *m*; **~ waste disposal** *n* NUCL almacenamiento de residuos en el emplazamiento *m*

on-state: **~ conductivity** *n* ELEC ENG conductividad activada *f*; **~ current** *n* ELEC ENG corriente activada *f*

ontogeny *n* AGRIC ontogenia *f*

onyx *n* MINERAL ónice *m*, ónix *m*

OO: **~ carrier** *n* (*oil-ore carrier*) TRANSP transporte combinado crudo-mineral *m*, transporte combinado petróleo-mineral *m*, transporte de material petrolífero *m*

oolith *n* PETR TECH, PETROL oolito *m*

oolitic: **~ limestone** *n* GEOL caliza oolítica *f*

oosparite *n* PETR TECH, PETROL oosparita *f*

ooze[1] *n* GEOL fango *m*, HYDROL *slimy mud* infiltración *f*, cieno *m*, rezumamiento *m*, OCEAN barros arenosos *m pl*

ooze² *vt* HYDROL infiltrar

oozing *n* HYDROL fuga *f*

oozue *n* GEOL fango pelágico rico en oozoos *m*

op¹: **no ~** *abbr* (*no-operation instruction*) COMP&DP no op (*instrucción no operativa*)

op²: **~ amp** *n* (*operational amplifier*) COMP&DP, ELECTRON, PHYS, TELECOM amplificador operacional; **~ code** *n* (*operation code*) COMP&DP código de operación *m*, código de información *m*, PROD cifrado de operación *m*, código de información *m*, código de operación *m*

OPA *abbr* (*optoelectronic pulse amplifier*) TELECOM amplificador optoelectrónico de impulsos *m*

opacified: **~ silica aerogel** *n* HEAT ENG, REFRIG aerogel de sílice opalizado *m*

opacifier *n* C&G opacador *m*

opacifying *adj* CHEM *agent*, DETERG opacificante

opacimeter *n* CHEM, PAPER opacímetro *m*

opacity *n* CHEM, PHYS, PRINT, WAVE PHYS opacidad *f*; **~ paper backing** *n* PAPER opacidad sobre fondo de papel *f*; **~ tester** *n* PAPER aparato para medir la opacidad *m*; **~ white backing** *n* PAPER opacidad sobre fondo blanco *f*

opal *n* MINERAL ópalo *m*; **~ glass** *n* C&G vidrio opalino *m*; **~ printing** *n* CINEMAT copiado opalino *m*

OPAL: **~ detector** *n* PART PHYS detector OPAL *m*

opalescence *n* HYDROL opalescencia *f*

opalescent: **~ glass** *n* C&G vidrio opalescente *m*

opaline *n* C&G opalino *m*

opaque *n* COATINGS cubriente *m*; **~ color** *AmE*, **~ colour** *BrE* *n* COLOUR colorante opaco *m*; **~ glass** *n* C&G vidrio opaco *m*; **~ leader** *n* CINEMAT, TV guía opaca *f*; **~ medium** *n* PHYS medio opaco *m*; **~ pigment** *n* COLOUR pigmento opaco *m*; **~ substance** *n* OPT suspensión opaca *f*, RAD PHYS sustancia opaca *f*

opaquing *n* CINEMAT retoque de negativos *m*

OPC *abbr* (*originating point code*) TELECOM código de punto de origen *m*

opcimeter *n* INSTR opacímetro *m*

OPEC *abbr* (*Organization of Petroleum-Exporting Countries*) PETR TECH OPEP (*Organización de Países Exportadores de Petróleo*)

open¹ *adj* WATER TRANSP *boat* abierto, sin cubierta; **~-cast** MINE a cielo abierto, al aire libre; **~-ended** *adj* TEXTIL a cabo abierto; **~-type** *adj* MECH ENG *machine specification* abierto, de tipo abierto

open²: **~ east** *adv* COAL hacia el este

open³: **~ angle** *n* GEOM ángulo abierto *m*; **~ arc** *n* ELEC ENG arco descubierto *m*; **~ assembly time** *n* P&R tiempo de montaje abierto *m*; **~ belt** *n* PAPER correa recta *f*, PROD correa abierta *f*, correa recta *f*; **~-cast mining** *n* MINE explotación a cielo abierto *f*, laboreo al aire libre *m*; **~ cell** *n* P&R célula abierta *f*; **~-cell cellular plastic** *n* P&R plástico celular de célula abierta *m*; **~-cell foamed plastic** *n* P&R, REFRIG plástico celular de celdillas abiertas *m*; **~ chain** *n* CHEM cadena abierta *f*; **~ channel** *n* HYDRAUL canal descubierto *m*; **~ channel flow** *n* FLUID flujo en canal abierto *m*; **~ circuit** *n* COAL circuito abierto *m*, ELEC circuito abierto *m*, circuito cortado *m*, circuito interrumpido *m*, ELEC ENG circuito abierto *m*, circuito al aire *m*, circuito de hilo desnudo *m*, PHYS circuito abierto *m*; **~-circuit characteristics** *n pl* ELEC *equipment* características en circuito abierto *f pl*; **~-circuit crushing** *n* COAL compresión de circuito

abierto *f*; **~-circuit current** *n* ELEC corriente en circuito abierto *f*; **~-circuit impedance** *n* ELEC, ELEC ENG impedancia en circuito abierto *f*; **~-circuit operation** *n* ELEC *equipment* funcionamiento en circuito abierto *m*, trabajo en circuito abierto *m*, utilización en circuito abierto *f*; **~-circuit test** *n* ELEC prueba en circuito abierto *f*; **~-circuit voltage** *n* ELEC tensión de circuito abierto *f*, ELEC ENG voltaje en vacío *m*, FUELLESS tensión de circuito abierto *f*; **~-circuit winding** *n* ELEC *transformer, machine* arrollamiento en circuito abierto *m*, devanado en circuito abierto *m*; **~-coil armature** *n* ELEC, ELEC ENG inducido en circuito abierto *m*; **~-coil spring** *n* HYDRAUL muelle de compresión *m*, resorte de compresión *m*, MECH ENG resorte de compresión *m*; **~ condition** *n* PROD situación libre *f*; **~ conductor** *n* ELEC ENG conductor descubierto *m*; **~ contact** *n* ELEC *relay* contacto abierto *m*; **~ core** *n* ELEC *transformer* núcleo abierto *m*; **~-core transformer** *n* ELEC, ELEC ENG transformador de núcleo abierto *m*; **~-cut mining** *n* MINE explotación a cielo abierto *f*; **~-cycle gas turbine** *n* TRANSP turbina de gas de ciclo abierto *f*; **~-delta connection** *n* ELEC conexión Scott *f*, conexión de transformador monofásico sobre línea trifásica *f*, conexión en V *f*, conexión en delta abierta *f*, conexión en triángulo abierto *f*; **~-die forging** *n* MECH ENG, PROD forja con estampa abierta *f*; **~ digging** *n pl* MINE excavación a cielo abierto *f*, explotación a cielo abierto *f*; **~ distribution processing** *n* (*ODP*) TELECOM procesamiento de distribución abierta *m*; **~ drain** *n* CONST, POLL, RECYCL, WATER albañal *m*; **~ dump** *n* RECYCL escombrera al aire libre *f*, vertedero al aire libre *m*; **~-end wrench** *n* MECH llave de boca *f*, llave española *f*, MECH ENG llave de boca *f*, llave de maquinista *f*, llave española *f*; **~-face calender** *n* PAPER calandra de construcción abierta *f*; **~-face spotlight** *n* CINEMAT proyector de luz abierto *m*; **~ fiber** *AmE*, **~ fibre** *BrE* *n* TEXTIL fibra abierta *f*; **~ flap valve** *n* HYDRAUL válvula de bola *f*, válvula de charnela *f*; **~ flume** *n* PROD *hydroturbine* cámara de agua abierta *f*; **~ fold** *n* PETROL pliegue abierto *m*; **~-frame calender** *n* PAPER calandra de bastidor abierto *f*; **~-frame linear power supply** *n* ELEC ENG suministro de energía lineal a bastidor abierto *m*; **~-frame power supply** *n* ELEC ENG suministro de energía con armazón abierto *m*; **~-frame super calender** *n* PAPER supercalandra de bastidor abierto *f*; **~-frame switching power supply** *n* ELEC ENG suministro de energía conmutando a armazón abierto *m*; **~ front** *n* HYDRAUL sección frontal abierta *f*; **~-front bin** *n* PROD depósito de frente abierto *m*; **~-front mechanical power press** *n* MECH ENG prensa mecánica de frente abierto *f*; **~ fuel cycle** *n* NUCL *type of fixing of rail to rail* ciclo abierto *m*; **~ fuse** *n* ELEC fusible de tipo descubierto *m*; **~ headbox** *n* PAPER caja de entrada abierta *f*; **~ heap** *n* PROD *copper smelting* montón de tostación *m*; **~-hearth furnace** *n* COAL horno de solera *m*, HEAT horno de hogar abierto *m*, PROD horno de solera *m*, THERMO horno de hogar abierto *m*; **~ hole** *n* PETROL pozo abierto *m*, pozo sin entubar *m*; **~-hole completion** *n* PETROL terminación a pozo abierto *f*; **~-hole drilling** *n* PETR TECH perforación en hueco no revestido *f*; **~ hood** *n* PAPER campana abierta *f*; **~-jointed clayware pipe** *n* CONST tubería de arcilla con juntas abiertas *f*; **~-jointed porous pipe** *n* CONST

tubería porosa con juntas abiertas *f*; **~-link chain** *n* PROD cadena de eslabones abiertos *f*; **~ loop** *n* AIR TRANSP círculo abierto *m*, ELEC *circuit* bucle abierto *m*, circuito abierto *m*, lazo abierto *m*; **~-loop oscillator** *n* ELECTRON oscilador con circuito de reacción abierto *m*; **~-loop transfer function** *n* NUCL función de transferencia en lazo abierto *f*; **~ mill** *n* P&R molino abierto *m*, molino de dos rodillos *m*; **~ mouth sack** *n* PACK saco de boca abierta *m*; **~ network provision** *n* (*ONP*) TELECOM provisión de la red abierta *f*; **~-newel stair** *n* CONST escalera de eje abierto *f*; **~ order** *n* PROD orden de compra a un precio concreto *f*; **~ pass** *n* PROD *rolling mill* acanaladura abierta *f*; **~ pit** *n* MINE excavación a cielo abierto *f*, explotación a cielo abierto *f*, foso descubierto *m*; **~-pit mine** *n* COAL, MINE excavación a cielo abierto *f*, mina a cielo abierto *f*; **~-pit mining** *n* COAL, MINE, NUCL minería a cielo abierto *f*; **~ position** *n* ELEC *relay* posición abierta *f*; **~ propeller** *n* TRANSP hélice abierta *f*; **~ quarry** *n* MINE cantera a cielo abierto *f*; **~ resonator** *n* ELECTRON resonador exterior *m*; **~ roadstead** *n* OCEAN, WATER TRANSP rada abierta *f*; **~-sand molding** *AmE*, **~-sand moulding** *BrE n* PROD molde de arena al descubierto *m*; **~ sea** *n* GEOL, OCEAN, WATER TRANSP alto mar *m*, mar abierto *m*; **~ seas** *n pl* OCEAN mar libre *m*; **~-side planing machine** *n* MECH ENG, PROD cepilladora con un costado abierto *f*, cepilladora monomontante *f*; **~-sight alidade** *n* CONST, INSTR alidada con mira de ranura *f*; **~-slot armature** *n* ELEC *generator, motor* armadura de ranura abierta *f*; **~-socket ratchet** *n* MECH ENG trinquete de tubo abierto *m*; **~-spiral** *n* HYDRAUL muelle de compresión *m*, resorte de compresión *m*; **~-spiral spring** *n* MECH ENG resorte de compresión *m*; **~ string** *n* CONST *stairbuilding* zanca inglesa *f*; **~ system** *n* COMP&DP, TELECOM, THERMO sistema abierto *m*; **~ systems architecture** *n* (*OSA*) COMP&DP, TELECOM arquitectura de sistemas abiertos *f*; **~ systems interconnection** *n* (*OSI*) COMP&DP, TELECOM interconexión de sistemas abiertos *f* (*OSI*); **~ systems interconnection layer** *n* (*OSI layer*) TELECOM capa de interconexión de sistemas abiertos *f*; **~ systems interconnection resource** *n* (*OSI resource*) TELECOM recurso de interconexión de sistemas abiertos *m*; **~-top container** *n* TRANSP contenedor descubierto *m*; **~-turbine chamber** *n* WATER cámara de agua abierta *f*; **~-type compressor unit** *n* REFRIG compresor de grupo abierto *m*; **~-wafer rotary switch** *n* ELEC ENG interruptor rotatorio de sectores *m*; **~ wagon** *n* BrE (*cf gondola car AmE*) RAIL vagón abierto *m*, vagón batea *m*, vagón de bordes bajos *m*; **~-wall container** *n* TRANSP contenedor abierto *m*; **~ wall string** *n* CONST *stairbuilding* escalera abierta *f*; **~ water** *n* OCEAN aguas abiertas *f pl*, PETROL aguas libres *f pl*, WATER TRANSP mar libre *m*; **~-web girder** *n* CONST viga de alma abierta *f*; **~ winding** *n* ELEC *transformer, reactor* devanado abierto *m*; **~ wire** *n* ELEC ENG alambre descubierto *m*, alambre desnudo *m*, PROD alambre descubierto *m*, alambre desnudo *m*, hilo aéreo *m*, hilo desnudo *m*; **~-wire feeder** *n* ELEC ENG cable de alimentación aéreo *m*; **~-wire line** *n* ELEC ENG línea abierta *f*; **~-wire transmission line** *n* ELEC, ELEC ENG línea de transmisión abierta *f*
open[4] *vt* PHOTO *diaphragm* abrir; **~ up** *vt* CINEMAT abrir, MINE abrir, explotar

open[5]: **~ here** *phr* PACK abrir por aquí; **~ this end** *phr* PACK abrir por este extremo
opencast: **~ mine** *n* COAL mina a cielo abierto *f*
opener *n* TEXTIL abridora *f*
opening *n* C&G *of cylinder* abertura *f*, agujero *m*, corte *m*, CONST *aperture* apertura *f*, orificio *m*, abertura *f*, ELEC ENG apertura *f*, agujero *m*, ELECTRON apertura *f*, HYDRAUL *in thin partition* orificio *m*, INSTR apertura *f*, MECH agujero *m*, MECH ENG agujero *m*, brecha *f*, abertura *f*, orificio *m*, hueco *m*, luz *f*, salida *f*, vano *m*, MINE excavación *f*, trabajo preparatorio *m*, PROD agujero *m*, REFRIG abertura *f*; **~ bit** *n* MECH ENG barrena de ensanchar *f*, escariador *m*; **~ instructions** *n pl* PACK instrucciones de apertura *f pl*; **~ mechanism** *n* PACK mecanismo de apertura *m*; **~ shot** *n* CINEMAT toma inicial *f*, MINE barreno de excavación *m*, excavación con trépano de granalla de acero *f*; **~ stock** *n* PROD existencias iniciales *f pl*; **~ time** *n* ELEC *relay*, ELEC ENG tiempo de apertura *m*; **~ travel** *n* PROD carrera de apertura *f*; **~ up** *n* MINE apertura *f*, preparación *f* (*AmL*)
openwork *n* MINE explotación a cielo abierto *f*, explotación a roza abierta *f* (*AmL*), explotación en trinchera *f* (*Esp*)
operand *n* COMP&DP operando *m*
operate[1]: **~ current** *n* ELEC ENG corriente de funcionamiento *f*; **~ lag** *n* ELEC ENG tiempo de funcionamiento *m*; **~ relay** *n* ELEC ENG relé de funcionamiento *m*; **~ time** *n* ELEC ENG tiempo de funcionamiento *m*, tiempo de maniobra *m*; **~ voltage** *n* ELEC ENG tensión de funcionamiento *f*
operate[2] *vt* MINE explotar, PHOTO *safety* utilizar, PROD *business* dirigir, *machines* accionar, explotar, impulsar, manejar, maniobrar, hacer funcionar, utilizar, manipular; **~ lut** *vt* COAL explotar
operate[3] *vi* MECH ENG funcionar, trabajar
operating[1] *adj* MECH ENG de funcionamiento
operating[2]: **~ altitude** *n* SPACE altitud operacional *f*; **~ condition** *n* METR condición de funcionamiento *f*; **~ conditions** *n pl* ELEC *equipment* régimen *m*, condiciones de funcionamiento *f pl*, condiciones de trabajo *f pl*, régimen de funcionamiento *m*, condiciones de utilización *f pl*, ELEC ENG condiciones de funcionamiento *f pl*; **~ console** *n* TELECOM consola de operador *f*, consola de operadores *f*, consola de trabajo *f*; **~ cost** *n* QUALITY costo de funcionamiento *m*; **~ current** *n* ELEC, ELEC ENG corriente de funcionamiento *f*, corriente de servicio *f*, corriente de trabajo *f*; **~ cycle** *n* TRANSP ciclo de funcionamiento *m*; **~ depth** *n* OCEAN profundidad de servicio *f*; **~ error** *n* COAL error de operación *m*; **~ force** *n* PROD eficacia de funcionamiento *f*; **~ frequency** *n* MECH ENG frecuencia de empleo *f*, frecuencia de servicio *f*, frecuencia de trabajo *f*, frecuencia de utilización *f*, TELECOM frecuencia de trabajo *f*; **~ handwheel** *n* MECH ENG volante de mando *m*, volante de maniobra *m*; **~ head** *n* HYDRAUL caída efectiva *f*, caída útil *f*, PROD altura útil *f*, carga motriz *f*, caída útil *f*; **~ hours** *n pl* PROD horas de funcionamiento *f pl*, horas de servicio *f pl*; **~ hours indicator** *n* WATER TRANSP *of engine* registrador de horas de funcionamiento *m*; **~ instructions** *n pl* MECH ENG instrucciones de empleo *f pl*, instrucciones de manejo *f pl*, instrucciones de operación *f pl*, instrucciones de utilización *f pl*, NUCL instrucciones de operación *f pl*; **~ lever** *n* MECH ENG palanca de mando *f*, palanca de

maniobra *f*; ~ **life** *n* ELEC ENG vida en funcionamiento *f*; ~ **lifetime** *n* NUCL *device* vida de servicio *f*; ~ **limitations** *n pl* PROD limitaciones de operación *f pl*; ~ **magnet** *n* PROD imán de maniobra *m*; ~ **and maintenance application part** *n* TELECOM solicitud de mantenimiento y explotación *f*; ~ **manual** *n* MECH ENG manual de operaciones *m*; ~ **method** *n* TEXTIL método operatorio *m*; ~ **mode** *n* ELEC ENG modo de funcionamiento *m*; ~ **overload** *n* PROD sobrecarga en funcionamiento *f*; ~ **permit** *n* AIR TRANSP *air transport* permiso de operación *m*; ~ **point** *n* ELEC ENG punto de funcionamiento *m*; ~ **position** *n* TELECOM puesto de operador *m*, puesto de operadora *m*; ~ **pressure** *n* REFRIG presión de funcionamiento *f*, SPACE *craft* presión de trabajo *f*; ~ **procedure** *n* PROD maniobra *f*; ~ **radius** *n* PROD autonomía *f*; ~ **range** *n* AIR TRANSP radio de acción de operaciones *m*, radio de operaciones *m*, MILIT *of missile* alcance eficaz *m*, radio de acción *m*; ~ **shaft** *n* PROD eje de maniobra *m*; ~ **side** *n* PAPER lado del conductor *m*; ~ **speed** *n* TRANSP velocidad de funcionamiento *f*; ~ **switch** *n* ELEC conmutador de funcionamiento *m*, interruptor de funcionamiento *m*, ELEC ENG interruptor de funcionamiento *m*; ~ **system** *n* (*OS*) COMP&DP, TELECOM sistema operativo *m* (*SO*); ~ **system function** *n* (*OSF*) TELECOM función del sistema operativo *f* (*FSO*); ~ **system kernel** *n* COMP&DP núcleo del sistema operativo *m*; ~ **temperature** *n* AIR TRANSP temperatura de operación *f*, REFRIG temperatura de funcionamiento *f*, SPACE temperatura de trabajo *f*, temperatura funcional *f*; ~ **time** *n* PROD tiempo de comunicación *m*, tiempo de funcionamiento *m*, tiempo de maniobra *m*; ~ **voltage** *n* ELEC *of system* voltaje de trabajo *m*, tensión de trabajo *f*, voltaje de funcionamiento *m*, voltaje de régimen *m*, tensión de servicio *f*, voltaje de servicio *m*, ELEC ENG voltaje de funcionamiento *m*, PROD voltaje de régimen *m*, tensión de funcionamiento *f*, voltaje de servicio *m*; ~ **weight** *n* SPACE peso funcional *m*; ~ **well** *n* GAS pozo en operación *m*

operation¹: **in ~** *adj* PROD en servicio

operation²: ~ **administration and maintenance center** *AmE*, ~ **administration and maintenance centre** *n BrE* (*OAMC*) TELECOM centro de mantenimiento y administración de la explotación *m*; ~ **administration maintenance and provisioning** (*OAMP*) TELECOM provisión y mantenimiento de la administración explotadora *f*; ~ **analysis** *n* PROD análisis de operación *m*; ~ **area** *n* NUCL *process* zona de operaciones *f*; ~ **center** *AmE*, ~ **centre** *n BrE* SPACE centro de accionamiento *m*; ~ **code** *n* (*op code*) COMP&DP, PROD cifrado de operación *m*, código de información *m*, código de operación *m*; ~ **counter** *n* ELEC *tap changer* contador de funcionamiento *m*; ~ **duplex** *n* COMP&DP dúplex todo completo *m*, funcionamiento dúplex *m*, operación en dúplex *f*, sistema de transmisión bidireccional *m*, TELECOM operación duplex *f*; ~ **number** *n* PROD número de subrutina *m*; ~ **register** *n* COMP&DP registro de operación *m*; ~ **table** *n* COMP&DP tabla de operaciones *f*; ~ **temperature** *n* PROD temperatura de funcionamiento *f*; ~ **ticket** *n* PROD hoja de trabajo *f*, parte de funcionamiento *f*

operational: ~ **amplifier** *n* (*op amp*) COMP&DP, ELECTRON, PHYS, TELECOM amplificador operacional *m* (*AO*); ~ **amplifier chip** *n* COMP&DP, ELECTRON chip

de amplificador operacional *m*; ~ **amplifier comparator** *n* ELECTRON amp op funcionando como comparador *m*; ~ **availability** *n* PROD disponibilidad operacional *f*; ~ **calculus** *n* ELECTRON cálculo operacional *m*; ~ **ceiling** *n* AIR TRANSP techo operacional *m*; ~ **conversion unit** *n* (*OCU*) AIR TRANSP unidad de conversión operacional *f*; ~ **current** *n* PROD corriente operacional *f*; ~ **delay** *n* TRANSP retraso operacional *m*; ~ **depth** *n* OCEAN profundidad eficaz de operación *f*; ~ **error** *n* POLL error de explotación *m*, error de operación *m*, error operativo *m*; ~ **mine** *n* MINE mina en servicio *f*, mina operativa *f*; ~ **noise** *n* ACOUST ruido de operaciones *m*; ~ **range** *n* PROD alcance eficaz *m*; ~ **research** *n* (*OR*) COMP&DP investigación de operaciones *f* (*OR*); ~ **test** *n* METR prueba operacional *f*, PROD prueba funcional *f*, prueba operacional *f*

operations: ~ **center** *AmE*, ~ **centre** *BrE n* TELECOM centro de explotaciones *m*, centro de operaciones *m*; ~ **and maintenance** *n pl* (*OAM*) TELECOM explotación y mantenimiento *f*; ~ **manual** *n* AIR TRANSP manual de operaciones *m*; ~~**related defect** *n* NUCL defecto relacionado con la operación *m*; ~ **research** *n* COMP&DP investigación operativa *f*; ~ **room** *n* TELECOM sala de servicio *f*; ~ **sequence** *n* PROD secuencia de operaciones *f*

operative: ~ **contacts** *n pl* PROD contactos de trabajo *m pl*; ~ **management** *n* NUCL *fuel* dirección de operaciones *f*

operator¹ *n* COMP&DP operador *m*, CONST maquinista *m*, operador *m*, operario *m*, MECH ENG maquinista *m*, obrero *m*, operador *m*, operario *m*, técnico encargado *m*, MINE maquinista *m*, obrero *m*, operario *m*, PETR TECH, PRINT, TELECOM operador *m*; ~ **center** *AmE*, ~ **centre** *BrE n* TELECOM centro de operadores *m*, centro de personal de explotación *m*; ~ **command** *n* COMP&DP comando de operador *m*, instrucción del operador *f*, mandato de operador *m*; ~ **commands** *n pl* TELECOM señales de mando de operador *f pl*; ~ **console** *n* COMP&DP consola de operador *f*; ~ **message** *n* COMP&DP mensaje de operador *m*; ~**'s console** *n* TELECOM consola de operador *f*, consola de operadores *f*, consola de trabajo *f*; ~ **position** *n* TELECOM puesto de operador *m*, puesto de operadora *m*; ~ **precedence** *n* COMP&DP prioridad de operador *f*; ~**'s side** *n* PRINT lado del operador *m*; ~**'s telephone** *n* TELECOM teléfono de operador *m*; ~ **system** *n* TELECOM sistema del operador *m*

operator²: **no ~ available** *phr* TELECOM ningún operador disponible; ~ **temporarily unavailable** *phr* TELECOM falta temporaria de operador (*AmL*), operador temporalmente fuera de servicio *m* (*Esp*)

ophiolite: ~ **suite** *n* GEOL asociación ofiolítica *f*

ophite *n* PETROL ofita *f*

ophthalmic: ~ **test stand** *n* INSTR plataforma de pruebas oftálmicas *f*

ophthalmometer *n* INSTR oftalmómetro *m*

opianic *adj* CHEM opiánico

opianine *n* CHEM opianina *f*

opianyl *n* CHEM opianilo *m*

opiate *n* CHEM opiato *f*

opposed: ~ **cylinders** *n pl* AUTO cilindros opuestos *m pl*; ~ **piston engine** *n* MECH ENG motor de pistones contrapuestos *m*

opposing: ~ **field** *n* ELEC *electromagnetism* campo

opuesto *m*; ~ **green** *n* TRANSP luz verde en sentido contrario *f*

opposite: ~ **charge** *n* CHEM, ELEC carga opuesta *f*; ~ **phase** *n* ELEC *alternating current* fase opuesta *f*; ~ **sides** *n pl* GEOM lados opuestos *m pl*; ~ **text** *n* PRINT texto opuesto *m*

optic: ~ **axis** *n* CRYSTALL, OPT, PHYS, TELECOM eje óptico *m*

optical[1]: ~-**electrical** *adj* (*O-E*) TELECOM óptico-eléctrico (*O-E*)

optical[2]:

~ a ~ **aberration** *n* OPT, TELECOM aberración óptica *f*; ~ **absorption** *n* OPT, RAD PHYS absorción óptica *f*; ~ **activity** *n* CHEM *of compound*, OPT, PHYS actividad óptica *f*; ~ **amplifier** *n* ELECTRON, OPT, TELECOM amplificador óptico *m*; ~ **antipode** *n* CRYSTALL antípoda óptico *m*, enantiómero *m*; ~ **attenuator** *n* ELECTRON, OPT, TELECOM atenuador óptico *m*; ~ **axis** *n* OPT, PHOTO, TELECOM eje óptico *m*;

~ b ~ **balance** *n* OPT, PRINT equilibrio óptico *m*; ~ **bench** *n* CINEMAT, METR, OPT, PHOTO, PHYS, PRINT banco óptico *m*; ~ **bistability** *n* OPT, TELECOM biestabilidad óptica *f*; ~ **bleaching** *n* DETERG blanqueo óptico *m*; ~ **branch** *n* PHYS *of vehicle* región óptica *f*; ~ **brightener** *n* DETERG avivador de colores *m*, P&R abrillantador óptico *m*, PAPER blanqueante óptico *m*;

~ c ~ **cable** *n* OPT, TELECOM, TV cable óptico *m*; ~ **cable assembly** *n* OPT, TELECOM montaje de cable óptico *m*; ~ **carrier** *n* ELECTRON portador óptico *m*; ~ **cavity** *n* OPT, RAD PHYS, TELECOM cavidad óptica *f*; ~ **center** *AmE*, ~ **centre** *BrE n* PHYS, TELECOM centro óptico *m*; ~ **character reader** *n* (*OCR*) COMP&DP, PRINT lector óptico de caracteres *m* (*OCR*); ~ **character reading system** *n* (*OCR system*) COMP&DP, PACK sistema de lectura óptica de caracteres *m* (*sistema OCR*); ~ **character recognition** *n* (*OCR*) COMP&DP, PRINT reconocimiento óptico de caracteres *m* (*OCR*); ~ **characteristic** *n* TELECOM característica óptica *f*; ~ **circulator** *n* TELECOM circulador óptico *m*; ~ **coherence** *n* OPT, TELECOM coherencia óptica *f*; ~ **combiner** *n* OPT, TELECOM combinador óptico *m*; ~ **communications** *n* OPT, TELECOM comunicaciones ópticas *f pl*; ~ **comparator** *n* METR comparador óptico *m*; ~ **condenser** *n* CINEMAT, OPT condensador óptico *m*; ~ **connector** *n* OPT, TELECOM conectador óptico *m*, conector óptico *m*; ~ **correlator** *n* ELECTRON correlador óptico *m*; ~ **coupler** *n* ELEC ENG, OPT, TELECOM acoplador óptico *m*; ~ **coupling** *n* ELEC ENG, OPT, TELECOM acoplamiento óptico *m*;

~ d ~ **data bus** *n* OPT enlace óptico de datos *m*, TELECOM bus de datos ópticos *m*; ~ **data disk** *n* COMP&DP, OPT disco de datos ópticos *m*; ~ **data disk document filing system** *n* COMP&DP, OPT sistema de archivo de documentos del disco óptico de datos *m*; ~ **database** *n* OPT base de datos óptica *f*; ~ **density** *n* OPT densidad óptica *f*; ~ **depth** *n* OCEAN profundidad óptica *f*, SPACE óptica de profundidad *f*; ~ **detection** *n* ELECTRON, OPT, TELECOM detección óptica *f*; ~ **detector** *n* ELECTRON, OPT, TELECOM detector óptico *m*; ~ **digital data disk** *n* COMP&DP, OPT disco óptico digital de datos *m*; ~ **disk** *n* COMP&DP, OPT disco óptico *m*; ~ **disk cassette** *n* COMP&DP, OPT casete del disco óptico *f*; ~ **disk drive** *n* COMP&DP, OPT unidad de disco óptico *f*; ~ **disk exchanger** *n*

COMP&DP, OPT intercambiador de discos ópticos *m*; ~ **disk filing system** *n* COMP&DP, OPT sistema de archivo por discos ópticos *m*; ~ **disk library** *n* COMP&DP, OPT biblioteca de discos ópticos *f*; ~ **disk player** *n* COMP&DP, OPT reproductor de discos ópticos *m*; ~ **disk reader** *n* COMP&DP, OPT lector de discos ópticos *m*; ~ **disk read-only memory** *n* COMP&DP, OPT memoria de sólo lectura del disco óptico *f*; ~ **distortion** *n* C&G distorsión óptica *f*; ~ **drive** *n* COMP&DP, OPT unidad óptica *f*;

~ e ~ **effect** *n* CINEMAT, OPT efecto óptico *m*; ~ **electron** *n* RAD PHYS electrón óptico *m*; ~ **emitter** *n* OPT emisor óptico *m*; ~ **encoder** *n* SPACE *communications* codificador óptico *m*; ~ **enlargement** *n* CINEMAT ampliación óptica *f*; ~ **exchange** *n* OPT, TELECOM central óptica *f*;

~ f ~ **fiber** *AmE*, ~ **fibre** *BrE n* C&G, CINEMAT, COMP&DP, ELEC ENG, OPT, PHYS, SPACE, TELECOM fibra óptica *f*, fibróptica *f*; ~ **fibre cable** *n BrE* COMP&DP, ELEC ENG, OPT, TELECOM cable de fibra óptica *m*; ~ **fibre connector** *n BrE* COMP&DP, ELEC ENG, OPT, TELECOM conector de fibra óptica *m*; ~ **fibre coupler** *n BrE* OPT, TELECOM acoplador de fibra óptica *m*; ~ **fibre gyrometer** *n BrE* SPACE girómetro de fibra óptica *m*; ~ **fibre link** *n BrE* OPT, TELECOM enlace de fibra óptica *m*; ~ **fibre pigtail** *n* COMP&DP, ELEC ENG cable de llegada de fibra óptica *m*, cable flexible de conexión de fibra óptica *m*, OPT cable de llegada de fibra óptica *m*, cable flexible de conexión de fibra óptica *m*, fibra óptica terminal *f*, TELECOM cable de llegada de fibra óptica *m*, cable flexible de conexión de fibra óptica *m*, latiguillo de fibra óptica *m*; ~ **fibre splice** *n BrE* OPT, TELECOM empalme de fibra óptica *m*, junta de fibra óptica *f*, unión de fibra óptica *f*; ~ **fibre transmission** *n BrE* OPT, TELECOM transmisión de fibra óptica *f*, transmisión por fibras ópticas *f*; ~ **fibre transmission system** *n BrE* OPT sistema de transmisión por fibras ópticas *m*; ~ **filter** *n* ELECTRON, OPT, PRINT, TELECOM filtro óptico *m*; ~ **fine grain** *n* CINEMAT grano fino óptico *m*; ~ **flat** *n* CINEMAT cristal ópticamente plano *m*, vidrio ópticamente plano *m*, METR disco de vidrio ópticamente plano *m*, plano óptico *m*; ~ **flat filter** *n* CINEMAT filtro plano óptico *m*; ~ **flexibility frame** *n* (*OFF*) OPT, TELECOM bastidor de flexibilidad óptica *m*; ~ **flux** *n* OPT flujo óptico *m*; ~ **frequency** *n* ELECTRON, OPT frecuencia óptica *f*;

~ g ~ **gain** *n* ELECTRON ganancia óptica *f*; ~ **glass** *n* INSTR lente óptica *f*, PHOTO cristal óptico *m*; ~ **graticule** *n* METR cuadrícula óptica *f*, retícula óptica *f*; ~ **guided wave** *n* ELEC ENG onda guiada ópticamente *f*;

~ h ~ **head** *n* OPT cabezal óptico *m*; ~ **house** *n* CINEMAT, OPT alojamiento óptico *m*; ~ **hybrid circuit** *n* ELECTRON circuito híbrido óptico *m*;

~ i ~ **image** *n* ELECTRON, OPT imagen óptica *f*; ~ **input** *n* ELEC ENG entrada de energía óptica *f*; ~ **input power** *n* ELEC ENG energía de entrada óptica *f*; ~ **instrument** *n* INSTR, OPT, PHYS instrumento óptico *m*; ~ **instruments for dimensional measurement** *n pl* INSTR, METR, OPT instrumentos ópticos para medidas dimensionales *m pl*; ~ **integrated circuit** *n* ELECTRON circuito integrado óptico *m*; ~ **interference** *n* OPT, TELECOM interferencia óptica *f*; ~ **inversion** *n* CHEM, OPT inversión de Walden *f*, inversión óptica *f*; ~ **isolation** *n* ELEC,

ELEC ENG, OPT, TELECOM aislamiento óptico *m*; ~ **isolator** *n* ELEC, ELEC ENG, OPT, TELECOM aislador óptico *m*; ~ **isomer** *n* CHEM *of compound* isómero óptico *m*, CRYSTALL enantiómero *m*, isómero óptico *m*;

~ l ~ **link** *n* OPT enlace óptico *m*; ~ **lithography** *n* ELECTRON litografía óptica *f*; ~ **logic circuit** *n* ELECTRON circuito lógico óptico *m*; ~ **logic gate** *n* ELECTRON circuito lógico óptico *m*, puerta lógica óptica *f*;

~ m ~ **mark reader** *n* COMP&DP lector óptico de marcas *m*; ~ **mark reading** *n* (*OMR*) COMP&DP lectura óptica de marcas *f* (*OMR*); ~ **maser** *n* ELECTRON maser óptico *m*; ~ **mask** *n* ELECTRON máscara óptica *f*; ~ **measuring projector** *n* MECH ENG proyector de medición óptico *m*; ~ **medium** *n* COMP&DP soporte óptico *m*, OPT medio óptico *m*; ~ **memory** *n* ELEC ENG, OPT memoria óptica *f*; ~ **memory card** *n* OPT tarjeta de memoria óptica *f*; ~ **modulation** *n* ELECTRON, TELECOM modulación óptica *f*; ~ **modulator** *n* ELECTRON, TELECOM modulador óptico *m*; ~ **multiplex** *n* ELECTRON, TV multiplex óptico *m*; ~ **multiplexer** *n* ELECTRON, TV multiplexor óptico *m*; ~ **multiplexing** *n* ELECTRON, TV transmisión simultánea óptica *f*;

~ n ~ **negative** *n* CINEMAT negativo óptico *m*;

~ o ~ **oscillator** *n* ELECTRON oscilador óptico *m*; ~ **output** *n* ELEC ENG salida de energía óptica *f*; ~ **output power** *n* ELEC ENG potencia de salida óptica *f*;

~ p ~ **parametric oscillator** *n* TELECOM oscilador paramétrico óptico *m*; ~ **path** *n* PHYS camino óptico *m*, TELECOM camino óptico *m*, recorrido óptico *m*, trayectoria óptica *f*, vía de transmisión óptica *f*; ~ **path length** *n* OPT camino óptico *m*, longitud de camino óptico *f*, TELECOM longitud de la vía de transmisión óptica *f*, longitud de la vía óptica *f*; ~ **pattern** *n* ELECTRON, OPT imagen óptica *f*; ~ **plummet** *n* INSTR plomada óptica *f*; ~ **polarization** *n* TELECOM polarización óptica *f*; ~ **power** *n* ELEC ENG potencia óptica *f*, OPT poder óptico *m*, potencia óptica *f*, TELECOM potencia óptica *f*; ~ **power output** *n* TELECOM potencia óptica de salida *f*; ~ **power source** *n* ELEC, ELEC ENG generador de energía óptica *m*; ~ **print** *n* CINEMAT copia óptica *f*; ~ **printer** *n* CINEMAT positivadora óptica *f*; ~ **printing** *n* PRINT impresión por medios ópticos *f*; ~ **processing** *n* TELECOM procesamiento óptico *m*; ~-**profile grinder** *n* MECH ENG rectificadora óptica para perfiles *f*; ~ **publishing** *n* OPT publicación óptica *f*; ~ **pulse** *n* ELECTRON, OPT impulso óptico *m*; ~ **pumping** *n* ELECTRON, NUCL, PHYS, RAD PHYS bombeo óptico *m*; ~ **pyrometer** *n* PHYS, RAD PHYS pirómetro óptico *m*;

~ r ~ **radiation** *n* OPT, TELECOM radiación óptica *f*; ~ **rangefinder** *n* PHOTO telémetro óptico *m*; ~ **ray** *n* OPT rayo óptico *m*; ~ **reader** *n* METR *ship* lector óptico *m*; ~ **read-only memory** *n* (*OROM*) OPT memoria óptica de sólo lectura *f*; ~ **receiver** *n* OPT, TELECOM receptor óptico *m*; ~ **recording** *n* ACOUST, OPT grabación óptica *f*, TELECOM registro óptico *m*; ~ **refraction** *n* TELECOM refracción óptica *f*; ~ **regenerative receiver** *n* OPT receptor óptico regenerativo *m*; ~ **regenerative repeater** *n* TELECOM repetidor regenerador óptico *m*, repetidor regenerativo óptico *m*; ~ **relay** *n* ELEC ENG relé óptico *m*; ~ **repeater** *n*

OPT, TELECOM repetidor óptico *m*; ~ **resist** *n* ELECTRON protección óptica *f*; ~ **resonance** *n* ELECTRON resonancia óptica *f*; ~ **resonator** *n* RAD PHYS, TELECOM resonador óptico *m*; ~ **return loss** *n* (*ORL*) TELECOM pérdida de retorno óptica *f*, pérdidas de retorno ópticas *f pl*; ~ **ROM** *n* COMP&DP ROM óptica *f*;

~ s ~ **scanner** *n* COMP&DP escáner óptico *m*, explorador óptico *m*; ~ **scanning device** *n* (*OSD*) OPT, TV dispositivo óptico de búsqueda *m* (*AmL*), lector óptico *m*; ~ **sensing** *n* ELECTRON, OPT, SPACE sensibilidad óptica *f*; ~ **sensor** *n* ELECTRON, OPT, SPACE sensor óptico *m*; ~ **servo** *n* ELEC ENG servo óptico *m*; ~ **sight** *n* INSTR visión óptica *f*, SPACE alza óptica *f*, anteojo de puntería *m*, mira óptica *f*; ~ **signal** *n* ELEC ENG, ELECTRON, TELECOM señal óptica *f*; ~-**signal conversion** *n* ELEC ENG conversión de señal óptica *f*; ~-**signal processing** *n* ELECTRON tratamiento de señal óptica *m*, RAD PHYS procesamiento óptico de señales *m*; ~ **solar reflector** *n* (*OSR*) SPACE reflector solar óptico *m* (*OSR*); ~ **sound** *n* CINEMAT sonido óptico *m*; ~ **sound camera** *n* CINEMAT cámara de sonido óptico *f*; ~ **sound head** *n* CINEMAT cabeza de sonido óptico *f*; ~ **sound negative** *n* CINEMAT negativo de sonido óptico *m*; ~ **sound positive** *n* CINEMAT copia positiva de sonido óptico *f*; ~ **sound recording** *n* CINEMAT registro de sonido óptico *m*; ~ **sound reproducer** *n* CINEMAT reproductor de sonido óptico *m*; ~ **spectral analyser** *n* BrE ELECTRON, OPT, COMP&DP, PHYS, TELECOM analizador espectral óptico *m*; ~ **spectral analysis** *n* COMP&DP, ELECTRON, OPT, PHYS, TELECOM análisis espectral óptico *m*; ~ **spectral analyzer** *AmE see optical spectral analyser BrE*; ~ **spectrum** *n* ELECTRON, OPT, RAD PHYS, TELECOM espectro óptico *m*; ~ **speed trap detector** *n* TRANSP detector óptico de exceso de velocidad *m*; ~ **splice** *n* OPT empalme óptico *m*, TELECOM empalme óptico *m*, óptica junta *f*; ~ **stepper** *n* ELECTRON graduador óptico *m*; ~ **storage** *n* AmE (*cf optical store BrE*) COMP&DP, OPT almacenamiento óptico *m*, memoria óptica *f*; ~ **storage medium** *n* OPT medio de almacenamiento óptico *m*; ~ **store** *n* BrE (*cf optical storage AmE*) COMP&DP, OPT almacenamiento óptico *m*, memoria óptica *f*; ~ **switch** *n* ELEC, ELEC ENG, OPT interruptor óptico *m*, TELECOM conmutador óptico *m*; ~ **switching** *n* COMP&DP, ELEC ENG, TELECOM conmutación óptica *f*; ~-**switching crosspoint** *n* TELECOM contacto de conmutación óptica *m*, punto de cruce de conmutación óptica *m*; ~-**switching matrix** *n* TELECOM matriz de conmutación óptica *f*; ~-**switching network** *n* (*OSN*) TELECOM red de conmutación óptica *f*; ~-**switching system** *n* TELECOM sistema de conmutación óptica *m*; ~ **system** *n* ELECTRON sistema óptico *m*;

~ t ~ **tape** *n* OPT cinta laseróptica *f*, cinta óptica *f*; ~ **telescope** *n* SPACE telescospio óptico *m*; ~ **thickness** *n* OPT espesor óptico *m*, SPACE espesor óptico *m*, grosor óptico *m*, TELECOM espesor óptico *m*; ~ **time domain reflectometry** *n* (*OTDR*) OPT, TELECOM reflectometría óptica en el dominio temporal *f*; ~ **tool** *n* C&G, OPT herramienta óptica *f*; ~ **track** *n* CINEMAT banda óptica *f*; ~ **transfer** *n* CINEMAT transferencia óptica *f*; ~ **transition** *n* RAD PHYS transición óptica *f*; ~ **transmission line** *n* ELEC ENG línea de transmisión óptica *f*; ~ **transmission**

system *n* OPT sistema de transmisión óptica *m*; ~ **tuning** *n* TELECOM sintonización óptica *f*, sintonía óptica *f*; **~ v** ~ **videodisc** *n* BrE COMP&DP, OPT videodisco óptico *m*; ~ **videodisk** AmE *see optical videodisc BrE*; ~ **viewfinder** *n* PRINT visor óptico *m*; **~ w** ~ **wave** *n* ELEC ENG onda óptica *f*; ~ **waveguide** *n* ELEC ENG, OPT, TELECOM guiaondas óptico *m*, guía de ondas óptica *f*; ~ **window** *n* OPT ventana óptica *f*; **~ z** ~ **zoom** *n* CINEMAT zoom óptico *m*

optically[1]: ~ **flat** *adj* PHOTO ópticamente plano; ~ **letter-spaced** *adj* PRINT espaciado óptico

optically[2]: ~-**active material** *n* OPT, TELECOM material ópticamente activo *m*; ~-**coupled solid-state relay** *n* ELEC ENG relé sólido acoplado ópticamente *m*; ~-**pumped laser** *n* ELECTRON láser bombeado ópticamente *m*; ~-**smooth surface** *n* PHYS superficie ópticamente lisa *f*

optimal: ~ **control** *n* NUCL, TELECOM control óptimo *m*; ~ **controller** *n* NUCL, TELECOM controlador óptimo *m*; ~ **crushing size** *n* COAL tamaño óptimo de triturado *m*; ~ **operating method** *n* GAS método óptimo de operación *m*; ~ **path** *n* TELECOM camino óptimo *m*, recorrido óptimo *m*, trayectoria óptima *f*, vía de transmisión óptima *f*; ~ **sampling** *n* TELECOM muestreo óptimo *m*

optimization *n* COMP&DP optimización *f*

optimize *vt* COMP&DP optimizar

optimum: ~ **bunching** *n* ELECTRON agrupación óptima *f*; ~ **burn-up** *n* NUCL quemado óptimo *m*; ~ **damping** *n* ELEC ENG amortiguación óptima *f*; ~ **grind** *n* COAL molido óptimo *m*; ~ **moisture content** *n* CONST contenido óptimo de humedad *m*; ~ **object illumination** *n* RAD PHYS iluminación óptima del objeto *f*; ~ **re-entry corridor** *n* SPACE corredor de reentrada óptimo *m*

option: ~ **code** *n* COMP&DP código de opción *m*

optional: ~ **equipment** *n* MECH ENG equipo opcional *m*, equipo optativo *m*; ~ **hardware** *n* PROD equipamiento opcional *m*; ~ **word** *n* COMP&DP *COBOL* palabra opcional *f*

optionally: ~ **droppable blocks** *n pl* TELECOM bloques separables optativamente *m pl*

optocoupler *n* ELEC ENG, TELECOM optoacoplador *m*

optoelectronic[1] *adj* OPT, TELECOM optoelectrónico

optoelectronic[2]: ~ **amplifier** *n* ELECTRON, OPT, TELECOM amplificador óptico-electrónico *m*; ~ **chip** *n* ELECTRON chip óptico-electrónico *m*; ~ **coupler** *n* ELEC ENG, OPT, TELECOM acoplador optoelectrónico *m*; ~ **crosspoint** *n* TELECOM contacto optoelectrónico *m*, punto de cruce optoelectrónico *m*; ~ **device** *n* ELEC ENG dispositivo óptico-electrónico *m*, OPT dispositivo optoelectrónico *m*; ~ **pick-up** *n* MECH ENG captación optoelectrónica *f*; ~ **pulse amplifier** *n* (OPA) ELECTRON, OPT, TELECOM amplificador optoelectrónico de impulsos *m*; ~ **receiver** *n* TELECOM receptor optoelectrónico *m*; ~ **switch** *n* ELEC, ELEC ENG, OPT interruptor optoelectrónico *m*; ~ **switching matrix** *n* TELECOM matriz de conmutación optoelectrónica *f*; ~ **transducer** *n* ELEC ENG transductor optoelectrónico *m*

optoelectronics *n* COMP&DP, ELEC ENG, ELECTRON, OPT, PHYS, TELECOM optoelectrónica *f*, óptica electrónica *f*

optometer *n* INSTR optómetro *m*

optronics *n* ELECTRON, OPT optoelectrónica *f*, óptica electrónica *f*

OR[1] *abbr* (*operational research*) COMP&DP OR (*investigación de operaciones*)

OR[2]: ~ **circuit** *n* ELECTRON circuito O *m*, circuito OR *m*; ~ **gate** *n* COMP&DP, ELECTRON, PHYS puerta O *f*, puerta OR *f*; ~ **operation** *n* COMP&DP operación O *f*, operación OR *f*

orange: ~ **peel** *n* C&G cáscara de naranja *f*, P&R cáscara de naranja *f*, superficie rugosa *f*

orangite *n* MINERAL orangita *f*

orbit[1] *n* SPACE órbita *f*; ~ **control** *n* SPACE control de órbita *m*; ~ **correction** *n* SPACE corrección de órbita *f*; ~ **counter** *n* SPACE contador de órbitas *m*, cuentavueltas de órbitas *m*; ~ **determination** *n* SPACE determinación de órbita *f*; ~ **inclination** *n* SPACE inclinación de órbita *f*; ~ **modification** *n* SPACE modificación de órbita *f*; ~ **prediction** *n* SPACE predicción de órbita *f*; ~ **support** *n* SPACE soporte de órbita *m*; ~ **tracking** *n* SPACE seguimiento de órbita *m*; ~ **trimming** *n* SPACE afinamiento de órbita *m*, compensación de órbita *f*

orbit[2] *vi* SPACE orbitar, volar en círculo

orbital[1] *adj* RAD PHYS orbital, SPACE de órbita, orbital

orbital[2] *n* CHEM *of electron* orbital *m*, PHYS órbital *m*, RAD PHYS orbital *m*; ~ **angular momentum** *n* PHYS momento angular orbital *m*, RAD PHYS cantidad de movimiento angular-orbital *f*, momento angular orbital *m*; ~ **angular momentum quantum number** *n* PHYS número cuántico del momento angular orbital *m*; ~ **catch-up** *n* SPACE alcance orbital *m*; ~ **decay** *n* SPACE decaimiento orbital *m*, disminución de órbita *f*; ~ **electron** *n* RAD PHYS electrón orbital *m*; ~ **flight** *n* SPACE vuelo orbital *m*; ~ **glider** *n* SPACE planeador de órbita *m*, planeador orbital *m*, TRANSP planeador orbital *m*; ~ **injection** *n* SPACE puesta en órbita *f*; ~ **maneuvering system** *n* AmE, ~ **manoeuvring system** BrE *n* SPACE sistema de maniobra orbital *m*; ~ **momentum** *n* RAD PHYS momento orbital *m*; ~ **period** *n* SPACE intervalo de órbita *m*, período orbital *m*; ~ **quantum number** *n* PHYS, RAD PHYS número cuántico orbital *m*; ~ **rocket** *n* SPACE cohete en órbita *m*, cohete orbital *m*; ~ **sander** *n* MECH ENG lijadora orbital *f*; ~ **station** *n* SPACE estación orbital *f*; ~ **transfer vehicle** *n* (*OTV*) SPACE vehículo de transferencia entre órbitas *m* (*OTV*); ~ **vehicle** *n* SPACE vehículo orbital *m*; ~ **velocity** *n* PHYS velocidad orbital *f*; ~ **workshop** *n* SPACE taller orbital *m*

orbiter *n* SPACE satélite artificial *m*; ~ **stage** *n* SPACE etapa orbital *f*

orbiting *n* SPACE puesta en órbita *f*; ~ **astronomical observatory** *n* SPACE observatorio astronómico orbitante *m*; ~ **laboratory** *n* SPACE laboratorio orbitante *m*; ~ **object** *n* SPACE objeto en órbita *m*; ~ **satellite** *n* SPACE satélite en órbita sincrónica con la Tierra *m*

orcein *n* CHEM orceína *f*

orchardgrass *n* AGRIC pata de gallo *f*

order[1]: **out of** ~ *adj* CINEMAT averiado, descompuesto, ELEC ENG inhabilitado, MECH, PACK, PROD, QUALITY, TELECOM averiado

order[2] *n* ACOUST *of a harmonic*, CHEM *of reaction* orden *m*; ~ **of battle** *n* MILIT orden de batalla *f*; ~-**disorder** *n* METALL orden-desorden *m*; ~-**disorder model** *n* NUCL modelo de orden-desorden *m*; ~-**disorder transformation** *n* CRYSTALL transformación orden-desorden f; ~ **hardening** n METALL endurecimiento por puesta en orden m; ~ **of interference** n PHYS orden de interferencia m; ~ **of magnitude** n COMP&DP, PHYS orden de magnitud m; ~ **point** n PROD punto de pedido m; ~ **of precedence** n COMP&DP orden de prioridad m; ~ **of reaction** n METALL orden de reacción m; ~ **shop** n PROD orden de lanzamiento de fabricación f

ordered: ~ **alloy** n METALL aleación ordenada f; ~ **chain** n CHEM of polymer cadena ordenada f; ~ **pair** n MATH par ordenado m; ~ **solid solution** n METALL solución sólida ordenada f; ~ **tree** n COMP&DP árbol ordenado m

ordering: ~ **bias** n COMP&DP polarización de orden f, sesgo de ordenación m; ~ **policy** n PROD plan de pedidos m; ~ **rules** n pl PROD normas sobre ordenación de pedidos f pl; ~ **unit** n PROD unidad de pedido f

ordinal n GEOM ordinal m; ~ **number** n MATH número ordinal m

ordinary: ~ **both-way line** n TELECOM línea bidireccional ordinaria f; ~ **ceramic** n C&G cerámica ordinaria f; ~ **detonator** n MINE detonador progresivo m; ~ **fuse** n MINE cebo progresivo m, espoleta progresiva f, estopín progresivo m; ~ **hexagonal nut** n MECH ENG tuerca hexagonal común f, tuerca hexagonal ordinaria f; ~ **line** n TELECOM línea ordinaria f; ~ **network** n TELECOM red ordinaria f; ~ **points** n pl BrE (cf ordinary switch AmE) RAIL cambios de vía ordinarios m pl; ~ **Portland cement** n CONST cemento Portland normal m; ~ **ray** n PHYS rayo ordinario m; ~ **switch** n AmE (cf ordinary points BrE) RAIL cambios de vía ordinarios m pl; ~ **timber set** n MINE marco de cumbrera y dos pies m; ~ **water** n NUCL process agua normal f

ordinate n COMP&DP, MATH ordenada f, WATER TRANSP lines plan sección transversal f

ordnance: ~ **gun** n MILIT cañón de artillería m; ~ **material** n MILIT material de armamento m; ~ **survey map** n MILIT mapa topográfico m

ore[1]: ~**-bearing** adj MINE metalífero

ore[2] n COAL mena f, mineral m, GEOL yacimiento m, MINE mineral m; ~ **assaying** n NUCL ensayo de minerales m; ~ **at grass** n MINE mineral en la superficie m; ~ **bin** n MINE acumulador para mineral m, depósito para mineral m; ~ **carrier** n WATER TRANSP mineralero m; ~ **contents** n pl MINE contenido en mineral m (AmL), ley de mineral f (Esp), riqueza en mineral f; ~ **crusher** n MINE bocarte de mineral m (AmL), quebrantadora de mineral f, triturado de mineral m, trituradora de mineral f; ~ **deposit** n METALL yacimiento metalífero m, MINE criadero m (Esp), criadero menero m (AmL), depósito menero m, yacimiento metalífero m, NUCL yacimiento metalífero m; ~ **dressing** n MINE beneficio de minerales m, preparación de menas f, preparación mecánica de minerales f; ~ **dump** n MINE cancha de mineral f (AmL), cubo para mineral m, escorial m, vertedero de mineral m (Esp); ~ **enrichment plant** n NUCL planta de enriquecimiento f, planta de enriquecimiento de menas f; ~ **extraction** n MINE extracción de menas f, extracción de minerales f; ~ **feeder** n MINE filón m, guía f, ramal m (AmL); ~ **formation** n GEOL, MINE formación de minerales f, formación metalífera f; ~ **hopper** n MINE depósito para minerales m (AmL), guánguil para minerales m (AmL), silo para minerales m (Esp),

tolva para minerales f; ~ **mineral** n GEOL mena f; ~ **mining** n MINE extracción de minerales f, laboreo de minerales m, minería metalífera f; ~**-oil carrier** n WATER TRANSP mineralero-petrolero m; ~ **pass** n COAL alcancía f (AmL), tolua f (Esp), MINE chimenea para mineral f, alcancía f (AmL); ~ **process** n PROD tratamiento con mineral m, steel manufacture método de oxidación del mineral m; ~ **sampling** n MINE desmuestre m (Esp), muestreo del mineral m (AmL); ~ **separator** n MINE separador de minerales m; ~ **shoot** n GEOL zona de enriquecimiento f; ~**-slurry-oil tanker** n (OSO tanker) WATER TRANSP buque cisterna para líquidos espesos m; ~ **stamp** n MINE bocarte m, triturador de minerales m; ~ **treatment** n MINE tratamiento de minerales m; ~ **washer** n MINE lavador de minerales m

ore[3]: **be in** ~ vi MINE estar en el filón

ORE abbr (Office for Research and Experiments) RAIL Oficina para la Investigación y Experimentos f

organ: ~ **of Corti** n ACOUST órgano de Corti m; ~ **pipe** n ACOUST tubo de órgano m

organic[1] adj AGRIC, CHEM, FOOD orgánico

organic[2]: ~ **acid** n CHEM ácido orgánico m; ~ **base** n CHEM base orgánica f; ~ **chemistry** n CHEM química orgánica f; ~ **coating** n COATINGS revestimiento orgánico m; ~ **compound** n CHEM compuesto orgánico m; ~ **dye laser** n RAD PHYS láser de colorante orgánico m; ~ **fluid engine** n TRANSP motor de líquido orgánico m; ~ **glass** n C&G vidrio orgánico m; ~ **hygrometer** n REFRIG higrómetro orgánico m; ~ **liquid laser** n ELECTRON láser de líquido orgánico m; ~ **matter** n AGRIC, GEOL, HYDROL, PETR TECH, POLL materia orgánica f; ~ **matter content** n HYDROL contenido en materia orgánica m; ~ **moderator** n NUCL moderador orgánico m; ~ **pigment** n COLOUR pigmento orgánico m; ~ **refrigerant** n MECH ENG refrigerante orgánico m; ~ **resistor** n ELEC ENG resistencia orgánica f; ~ **soil** n COAL suelo orgánico m

organization: ~ **and maintenance** n (OAM) TELECOM organización y mantenimiento f

Organization: ~ **of Petroleum-Exporting Countries** n (OPEC) PETR TECH Organización de Paises Exportadores de Petróleo f (OPEP)

organochlorine[1] adj AGRIC, CHEM, RECYCL organoclorado

organochlorine[2] n RECYCL compuestos organoclorados m pl, organoclorado m; ~ **pesticide** n AGRIC pesticida organoclorado m

organogenous adj COAL organógeno

organomagnesium n CHEM organomagnesio m; ~ **compound** n CHEM compuesto organomagnésico m

organometallic adj CHEM organometálico

organophosphorus: ~ **pesticide** n AGRIC pesticida organofosforado m

organosol n CHEM organosol m

organzine n TEXTIL torzal m

orient vt CONST surveying orientar

orientable: ~ **viewfinder** n CINEMAT visor orientable m

oriental: ~ **alabaster** n MINERAL alabastro oriental m, ónix argelino m, ónix calcáreo m, ónix de Argelia m; ~ **turquoise** n MINERAL turquesa oriental f

orientated: ~ **polypropylene film** n PACK película de polipropileno orientada f; ~ **polypropylene label** n PACK etiqueta de polipropileno orientada f

orientation *n* CONST, PRINT orientación *f*; ~ **control** *n* TELECOM control de la orientación *m*; ~ **factor** *n* METALL factor de orientación *m*

orientational: ~ **polarization** *n* PHYS polarización orientacional *f*

oriented: ~ **core** *n* PETROL testigo orientado *m*; ~ **growth** *n* METALL crecimiento columnar *m*, crecimiento de granos orientados *m*; ~ **nucleation** *n* METALL nucleación de granos orientados *f*

orifice *n* C&G agujero *m*, orificio *m*, ELEC ENG agujero *m*, HYDRAUL abertura *f*, *in thick wall* orificio *m*, *under water* orificio anegado *m*, orificio sumergido *m*, MECH agujero *m*, MECH ENG abertura *f*, agujero *m*, boca *f*, orificio *m*, PETR TECH orificio *m*, PROD agujero *m*; ~ **plate** *n* REFRIG orificio calibrado *m*

origin: ~ **and destination equation** *n* (*O-D equation*) TRANSP ecuación de origen y destino *f*; ~ **and destination survey** *n* (*O-D survey*) TRANSP *traffic* estudio sobre origen y destino *m*

original *n* CINEMAT, PRINT, TV original *m*; ~ **called number** *n* TELECOM número llamado original *m*; ~ **disc** *BrE*, ~ **disk** *AmE* *n* ACOUST disco original *m*; ~ **edition** *n* PRINT edición original *f*; ~ **inspection** *n* QUALITY control en primera presentación *m*; ~ **language print** *n* CINEMAT copia en idioma original *f*; ~ **redirection reason** *n* TELECOM razón de reexpedición original *f*; ~ **seed** *n* AGRIC semilla original *f*; ~ **uncut negative** *n* CINEMAT negativo original sin cortar *m*

originating: ~ **exchange** *n* TELECOM central de procedencia *f*; ~ **junctor** *n* TELECOM conjuntor *m*; ~ **point code** *n* (*OPC*) TELECOM código de punto de origen *m*; ~ **register** *n* TELECOM registro de origen *m*; ~ **traffic** *n* TELECOM tráfico de origen *m*, TRANSP tráfico de procedencia *m*

originator *n* TELECOM expedidor *m*, remitente *m*

O-ring *n* MECH junta tórica *f*, MECH ENG *seal with circular section* aro tórico *m*, junta tórica *f*, P&R, VEH junta tórica *f*

Orion: ~ **Nebula** *n* SPACE Nebulosa de Orión *f*

ORL *abbr* (*optical return loss*) TELECOM pérdida de retorno óptica *f*

orlon *n* CHEM orlón *m*

orlop: ~ **deck** *n* WATER TRANSP *ship design* cubierta inferior *f*, sollado *m*

ornamental: ~ **border** *n* PRINT orla de adorno *f*; ~ **rule** *n* PRINT filete adornado *m*

ornithuric *adj* CHEM ornitúrico

orogen *n* GEOL orógeno *m*

orogenic[1] *adj* GEOL orogénico

orogenic[2]: ~ **belt** *n* GEOL cinturón orogénico *m*; ~ **cycle** *n* GEOL ciclo orogénico *m*; ~ **phase** *n* GEOL fase orogénica *f*; ~ **zone** *n* GEOL zona orogénica *f*

orogeny *n* GEOL orogenia *f*

orographic: ~ **depression** *n* METEO depresión orográfica *f*

OROM *abbr* (*optical read-only memory*) OPT memoria óptica de sólo lectura *f*

orotron *n* ELECTRON orotrón *m*

orphan *n* PRINT huérfano *m*

orpiment *n* MINERAL oropimente *m*

orsellic *adj* CHEM orsélico

orsellinic *adj* CHEM orselínico

orthicon *n* ELECTRON, TV orticonoscopio *m*

orthite *n* MINERAL, NUCL cerina *f*, ortita *f*

orthobasic *adj* CHEM ortobásico

orthocarbonic *adj* CHEM ortocarbónico

orthocenter *AmE see orthocentre BrE*

orthocentre *n* *BrE* GEOM ortocentro *m*

orthochemical: ~ **limestone** *n* GEOL caliza ortoquímica *f*

orthochlorite *n* MINERAL ortoclorito *m*

orthochlorotoluene *n* CHEM ortoclorotolueno *m*

orthochromatic: ~ **emulsion** *n* CINEMAT, PHOTO emulsión ortocromática *f*

orthochromatism *n* CINEMAT, PHOTO ortocromatismo *m*

orthochromatization *n* CINEMAT, PHOTO ortocromatización *f*

orthoclase *n* MINERAL ortoclasa *f*

orthodromic: ~ **projection** *n* SPACE, WATER TRANSP proyección ortodrómica *f*

orthodromy *n* SPACE, WATER TRANSP ortodromía *f*

orthoformic *adj* CHEM ortofórmico

orthoforming *adj* CHEM formador de orto

orthogonal[1] *adj* GEOM, TELECOM, TV ortogonal

orthogonal[2]: ~ **polarization** *n* TELECOM polarización ortogonal *f*; ~ **projection** *n* GEOM proyección ortogonal *f*; ~ **scanning** *n* TV exploración ortogonal *f*; ~ **signal** *n* TELECOM señal ortogonal *f*

orthohydrogen *n* CHEM ortohidrógeno *m*

orthophosphate *n* CHEM ortofosfato *m*

orthophosphoric[1] *adj* CHEM, DETERG ortofosfórico

orthophosphoric[2]: ~ **acid** *n* CHEM, DETERG ácido ortofosfórico *m*

orthoquartzite *n* GEOL ortocuarcita *f*

orthorhombic *adj* CRYSTALL rómbico

orthoscopic *adj* PHYS ortoescopico

orthosilicate *n* CHEM ortosilicato *m*

orthosilicic *adj* CHEM ortosilícico

orthotropic: ~ **materials** *n pl* MECH ENG materiales ortotrópicos *m pl*

orthotropism *n* AGRIC ortotropismo *m*

orthovanadic *adj* CHEM ortovanádico

orthoxylene *n* CHEM, PETR TECH ortoxileno *m*

OS *abbr* (*operating system*) COMP&DP, TELECOM SO (*sistema operativo*)

Os *abbr* (*osmium*) CHEM Os (*osmio*)

OSA *abbr* (*open systems architecture*) COMP&DP, TELECOM arquitectura de sistemas abiertos *f*

osazone *n* CHEM osazona *f*

oscillate[1] *vt* ELECTRON vibrar

oscillate[2] *vi* ELECTRON fluctuar, oscilar, WAVE PHYS oscilar

oscillating[1] *adj* ELEC, ELECTRON, WAVE PHYS fluctuante, oscilante, oscilatorio, vibrante

oscillating[2]: ~ **capacitor** *n* ELEC capacitor oscilante *m*, condensador oscilante *m*; ~ **circuit** *n* ELEC, TV circuito oscilador *m*, circuito oscilante *m*; ~ **conveyor** *n* MECH ENG transportador oscilante *m*; ~ **crystal method** *n* RAD PHYS método del cristal oscilante *m*; ~ **damper** *n* ELEC *alternating current, galvanometer* amortiguador de oscilaciones *m*; ~ **doctor** *n* PAPER cuchilla oscilante *f*; ~ **electron** *n* NUCL electrón oscilatorio *m*; ~ **quantity** *n* ELECTRON intensidad de oscilación *f*; ~ **shower** *n* PAPER rociador oscilante *m*; ~ **table** *n* COAL mesa oscilante *f*

oscillation *n* CONST *of level* oscilación *f*, ELEC *alternating current*, ELECTRON, MECH ENG oscilación *f*, fluctuación *f*, vibración *f*, PHYS, TELECOM, WAVE PHYS oscilación *f*; ~ **camera** *n* CRYSTALL cámara de oscilaciones *f*; ~ **frequency** *n* ELECTRON, TELECOM frecuencia de oscilación *f*; ~ **mode** *n* ELECTRON función de oscilación *f*; ~ **of a pendulum** *n* MECH ENG oscilación de un péndulo *f*; ~ **period** *n* ELECTRON período de oscilación *m*; ~ **of a spring** *n* MECH ENG oscilación de un resorte *f*

oscillator *n* GEN oscilador *m*; ~ **bank** *n* ELECTRON conjunto de osciladores *m*; ~ **circuit** *n* ELECTRON circuito oscilador *m*; ~ **coil** *n* CINEMAT, ELEC ENG bobina osciladora *f*; ~ **crystal** *n* ELECTRON cristal de oscilador *m*; ~ **drift** *n* ELEC deriva del oscilador *f*, ELECTRON cambio de frecuencia del oscilador *m*, deriva del oscilador *f*, TELECOM deriva del oscilador *f*

oscillatory[1] *adj* ELECTRON, TELECOM, TV oscilante, oscilatorio

oscillatory[2]: ~ **scanning** *n* ELECTRON, TELECOM, TV exploración oscilatoria *f*; ~ **system** *n* ELECTRON, TELECOM, TV sistema oscilatorio *m*

oscillogram *n* TV oscilograma *m*

oscillograph *n* CHEM, ELECTRON oscilógrafo *m*

oscilloscope *n* GEN osciloscopio *m*; ~ **trace** *n* ELECTRON trazo del osciloscopio *m*; ~ **tube** *n* ELECTRON tubo de osciloscopio *m*

osculating[1] *adj* GEOM osculador, osculante

osculating[2]: ~ **curve** *n* GEOM bordillo osculante *m*, curva osculante *f*

osculatory *adj* GEOM osculatorio

OSD *abbr* (*optical scanning device*) TV dispositivo óptico de búsqueda *m*, lector óptico *m*

OSF *abbr* (*operating system function*) TELECOM FSO (*función del sistema operativo*)

OSI[1] *abbr* (*open systems interconnection*) COMP&DP, TELECOM OSI (*interconexión de sistemas abiertos*)

OSI[2]: ~ **layer** *n* (*open systems interconnection layer*) TELECOM capa de interconexión de sistemas abiertos *f*; ~ **resource** *n* (*open systems interconnection resource*) TELECOM recurso de interconexión de sistemas abiertos *m*

osmate *n* CHEM osmiato *m*

osmic *adj* CHEM ósmico

osmious *adj* CHEM osmioso

osmiridium *n* MINERAL osmiridio *m*

osmium *n* (*Os*) CHEM osmio *m* (*Os*)

osmol *n* CHEM osmol *m*

osmolarity *n* CHEM osmolaridad *f*

osmole *n* CHEM osmol *m*

osmophore *n* CHEM osmóforo *m*

osmophoric *adj* CHEM osmofórico

osmosis *n* AGRIC, CHEM, CHEM TECH, HYDROL, PETR TECH, PHYS ósmosis *f*

osmotic[1] *adj* AGRIC, CHEM, CHEM TECH, HYDROL, PETR TECH, PHYS osmótico

osmotic[2]: ~ **pressure** *n* GEOPHYS, PETR TECH, PHYS, REFRIG presión osmótica *f*; ~ **process** *n* CHEM TECH proceso osmótico *m*

OSN *abbr* (*optical-switching network*) TELECOM red de conmutación óptica *f*

OSO: ~ **tanker** *n* (*ore-slurry-oil tanker*) WATER TRANSP buque cisterna para líquidos espesos *m*

osone *n* CHEM osona *f*

osotetrazine *n* CHEM osotetrazina *f*

osotriazole *n* CHEM osotriazol *m*

OSR *abbr* (*optical solar reflector*) SPACE OSR (*reflector solar óptico*)

ossein *n* CHEM oseína *f*

ossicle *n* ACOUST huesecillo *m*, osículo *m*

ossicular: ~ **chain** *n* ACOUST cadena de huesecillos *f*, cadena osicular *f*

ostein *n* CHEM osteína *f*

osteolite *n* MINERAL osteolita *f*

ostrich: ~ **breeding** *n* AGRIC cría del avestruz *f*

Ostwald: ~ **viscometer** *n* CHEM TECH, LAB viscosímetro de Ostwald *m*, viscómetro de Ostwald *m*; ~**'s dilution law** *n* CHEM *electrolyte* ley de la dilución de Ostwald *f*

OTDR *abbr* (*optical time domain reflectometry*) OPT, TELECOM reflectometría óptica en el dominio temporal *f*

otosclerosis *n* ACOUST otosclerosis *m*

otter: ~ **board** *n* OCEAN puerta de red *f*, puerta del arte de arrastre *f*

OTTO *abbr* (*once-through-then-out*) NUCL ciclo de agotamiento y descarga *m*

Otto: ~ **cycle** *n* AUTO ciclo de Otto *m*, VEH ciclo de Otto *m*, ciclo de cuatro tiempos *m*

ottrelite *n* MINERAL otrelita *f*

OTV *abbr* (*orbital transfer vehicle*) SPACE OTV, vehículo de transferencia entre órbitas *m*

O-type: ~ **carcinotron** *n* ELECTRON carcinotrón tipo O *m*; ~ **microwave tube** *n* ELECTRON tubo de microondas tipo O *m*; ~ **tube** *n* ELECTRON tubo tipo O *m*

ounce *n* METR onza *f*

out *n* PRINT omisión *f*

outage: ~ **time** *n* NUCL duración de parada *f*, período de indisponibilidad *m*, tiempo de parada *m*

outboard[1] *adj* MECH ENG, WATER TRANSP *rigging, engine* exterior, fuera de bordo, hacia el costado, hacia el exterior

outboard[2]: ~ **engine** *n* WATER TRANSP motor fueraborda *m*; ~ **inflatable** *n* TRANSP, WATER TRANSP fueraborda hinchable *m*

outbound: ~ **beam** *n* AIR TRANSP *navigation* haz de salida *m*; ~ **heading** *n* AIR TRANSP *navigation* rumbo de salida *m*; ~ **traffic** *n* TRANSP tráfico exterior *m*

outbreak *n* AGRIC *of disease* brote *m*, THERMO *broadcasting* brote *m*, estallido *m*

outbreeding *n* AGRIC cría por cruza *f*

outbuilding *n* CONST anejo *m*, anexo *m*

outcoming: ~ **particle** *n* NUCL partícula saliente *f*

outcrop *n* GEOL afloramiento *m*, MINE afloramiento *m*, crestón *m*

outdated: ~ **film** *n* CINEMAT película anticuada *f*

outdoor: ~ **cable** *n* ELEC cable de exterior *m*; ~ **crop** *n* AGRIC cultivo al aire libre *m*; ~ **electrical equipment** *n* ELEC ENG instalación eléctrica a la intemperie *f*; ~ **electrical installation** *n* ELEC *equipment* instalación eléctrica a la intemperie *f*; ~ **noise** *n* ACOUST ruido exterior *m*; ~ **paint** *n* COLOUR, CONST pintura para exteriores *f*; ~ **switchgear** *n* ELEC conmutador de exterior *m*, interruptor de exterior *m*

outer[1] *adj* MECH ENG exterior, externo, extremo, periférico

outer[2]: ~ **axis gimbal** *n* AIR TRANSP cardan del eje exterior *m*; ~ **case** *n* PACK caja externa *f*; ~ **conductor** *n* TELECOM conductor exterior *m*; ~ **contact area** *n* SPACE superficie externa de contacto *f*; ~ **distant signal** *n* RAIL señal avanzada exterior *f*; ~**-end paper** *n* PRINT hoja de guarda externa *f*; ~ **flap** *n* PACK solapa externa *f*; ~ **form** *AmE*, ~ **forme** *BrE n* PRINT plana exterior *f*; ~ **fueled zone** *AmE*, ~ **fuelled zone** *BrE n* NUCL zona periférica del núcleo *f*; ~ **harbor** *AmE*, ~ **harbour**

BrE n OCEAN, WATER TRANSP antepuerto *m*, puerto exterior *m*; ~ **hull** *n* WATER TRANSP *boat building* forro exterior *m*; ~ **insulation** *n* ELEC, ELEC ENG aislación exterior *f*, aislamiento exterior *m*; ~ **marker** *n* AIR TRANSP *of runway* radiobaliza exterior *f*; ~ **orbital complex** *n* RAD PHYS complejo de un orbital externo *m*; ~ **planet mission** *n* SPACE misión a un planeta exterior *f*; ~ **port** *n* OCEAN, WATER TRANSP antepuerto *m*, puerto exterior *m*; ~ **race** *n* MECH, MECH ENG anillo de rodadura exterior *m*, anillo exterior *m*, aro de rodamiento exterior *m*, PROD anillo de rodadura exterior *m*; ~ **side** *n* PRINT lado exterior *m*; ~ **skin** *n* WATER TRANSP *boat building* forro exterior *m*; ~ **space** *n* SPACE espacio cósmico *m*

outerwear *n* TEXTIL prendas exteriores *f pl*

outfall[1] *n* HYDROL descarga *f*, RECYCL desagüe *m*, desembocadura *f*, WATER desagüe *m*, desembocadura *f*, vertedero *m*; ~ **pipe** *n* RECYCL cañería de desagüe *f*, tubería de desagüe *f*

outfall[2]: ~ **to sea** *vi* HYDROL *rivers* desembocar en el mar, salir al mar

outfit *n* MECH ENG equipamiento *m*, equipo *m*, equipo de herramientas *m*, herramental *m*, PHOTO equipo *m*

outflow *n* PROD, WATER caudal *m*, desagüe *m*, descarga *f*, efluente *m*, gasto *m*

outgas *vt* CHEM desgasar

outgassing *n* CHEM desgasado *m*

outgoing[1] *adj* TELECOM saliente

outgoing[2]: ~ **air current** *n* MINE corriente de aire exterior *f*; ~ **call** *n* TELECOM comunicación de salida *f*, llamada saliente *f*; ~**-calls-barred line** *n* TELECOM línea de llamadas de salida bloqueadas *f*; ~ **channel** *n* TV canal de salida *m*; ~ **circuit** *n* ELEC circuito exterior *m*, TELECOM circuito saliente *m*; ~ **conveyor belt** *n* PROD cinta transportadora de salida *f*; ~ **feed** *n* TV alimentación de salida *f*; ~ **group** *n* TELECOM grupo saliente *m*; ~ **line** *n* TELECOM línea saliente *f*, TV línea de salida *f*; ~ **procedure** *n* TELECOM procedimiento saliente *m*; ~ **traffic** *n* TELECOM tráfico saliente *m*; ~ **trunk circuit** *n* TELECOM circuito de enlace de salida *m*; ~ **web** *n* PRINT banda saliente *f*

outgoing[3]: ~ **calls barred** *phr* (*OCB*) TELECOM comunicaciones de salida no permitidas, comunicaciones de salida prohibidas, llamadas de salida bloqueadas

outgrow *vt* AGRIC cubrir con vegetación

outgrowth *n* AGRIC *cereals* germinación en la espiga *f*

outhaul *n* WATER TRANSP *boom fitting* driza de fuera *f*

outlet *n* AUTO salida *f*, ELEC ENG toma de corriente *f*, HYDRAUL lumbrera de escape *f*, orificio de escape *m*, orificio de evacuación *m*, HYDROL *communications* desagüe *m*, MECH ENG *of current* tomacorriente *m*, boca de salida *f*, descarga *f*, escape *m*, desagüe *m*, orificio de salida *m*, paso *m*, orificio de descarga *m*, OCEAN desembocadura *f*, PROD descarga *f*, desagüe *m*, orificio de descarga *m*, orificio de salida *m*, salida *f*, TELECOM enchufe *m*, salida *f*, WATER boca de salida *f*, descarga *f*, orificio de descarga *m*, salida *f*; ~ **box** *n* ELEC *connection* caja de distribución *f*, caja de embutir *f*, caja de salida *f*; ~ **channel** *n* WATER canal de salida *m*; ~ **connection** *n* PROD conectador *m*, toma de corriente *f*; ~ **edge** *n* NUCL etapa de salida *f*; ~ **flow control** *n* WATER control del caudal de salida *m*; ~ **pipe** *n* WATER conducto de evacuación *m*, tubería de salida *f*, tubo de salida *m*; ~ **port** *n* C&G puerto de salida *m*; ~ **side** *n* NUCL lado de salida *m*; ~ **temperature** *n* POLL temperatura de descarga *f*;

~ **valve** *n* AUTO válvula de salida *f*, HYDRAUL compuerta de descarga *f*, válvula de escape *f*, válvula de evacuación *f*, válvula de salida *f*; ~ **works** *n pl* WATER estructuras de descarga *f pl*

outline[1] *n* CINEMAT argumento *m*, MECH ENG bosquejo *m*, configuración *f*, contorno *m*, diagrama *m*, exposición a grandes rasgos *f*, perfil *m*, plan general *m*, reseña *f*, resumen *m*, silueta *f*, traza *f*, trazado *m*, croquis *m*, dibujo a trazos *m*, esquema *m*, PRINT boceto *m*, perfil *m*; ~ **drawing** *n* MECH ENG croquis *m*, dibujo acotado *m*, dibujo de contorno aproximado y sin detalles *m*; ~ **lighting** *n* CINEMAT iluminación de contorno *f*

outline[2] *vt* PRINT delinear, perfilar

out-of-action *adj* ELEC, MECH ENG avenado, fuera de servicio, inutilizado, PROD fuera de servicio

out-of-balance[1] *adj* MECH ENG desbalanceado, desequilibrado, fuera de equilibrio

out-of-balance[2]: ~ **forces** *n pl* MECH ENG fuerzas asimétricas *f pl*, fuerzas desbalanceadas *f pl*

out-of-band: ~ **filtering** *n* ELECTRON filtración fuera de banda *f*; ~ **signaling** *AmE*, ~ **signalling** *BrE n* SPACE *communications* señalización fuera de banda *f*

out-of-course: ~ **running** *n* RAIL circulación con retraso *f*

out-of-focus[1] *adj* CINEMAT, PHOTO, TV desenfocado, fuera de foco

out-of-focus[2]: ~ **image** *n* CINEMAT, PHOTO, TV imagen desenfocada *f*

out-of-frame[1] *adj* PRINT fuera del marco

out-of-frame[2] *n* TELECOM fuera de trama de información *m*; ~ **second** *n* (*OFS*) TELECOM segundo fuera de cuadro *m*

out-of-jig: ~ **cradle** *n* MECH ENG cojinete no alineado *m*

out-of-order *adj* ELEC *fault* interrumpido, inutilizado, desordenado, en desorden, en mal estado, estropeado, fuera de servicio, descompuesto, averiado, inservible, improcedente, MECH ENG inhabilitado, fuera de servicio, en mal estado, descompuesto, inutilizado, averiado, PROD fuera de servicio

out-of-parallel *adj* MECH ENG fuera de fase, no paralelo

out-of-phase *adj* ELEC *alternating current* desfasado, fuera de fase, TELECOM, TV desfasado

out-of-pitch[1] *adj* AIR TRANSP *helicopter* fuera de paso

out-of-pitch[2]: ~ **blade** *n* AIR TRANSP *helicopter* pala fuera de paso *f*

out-of-plumb *adj* CONST desplomado, fuera de plomada

out-of-range *adj* MILIT fuera de alcance

out-of-repair *adj* ELEC, MECH ENG, PROD fuera de servicio

out-of-round[1] *adj* AUTO, MECH ENG, PETROL, PRINT ovalado, ovalizado

out-of-round[2]: ~ **finish** *n* C&G acabado no redondo *m*; ~ **wear** *n* AUTO desgaste por ovalización *m*

out-of-roundness *n* AUTO, MECH ENG, PETROL, PRINT ovalización *f*

out-of-season: ~ **breeding** *n* AGRIC reproducción fuera de la época *f*

out-of-sequence: ~ **activity** *n* PROD actividad desclasificada *f*; ~ **operation** *n* PROD operación desclasificada *f*

out-of-service: ~ **time** *n* TELECOM tiempo fuera de servicio *m*; ~ **track** *n* RAIL vía fuera de servicio *f*

out-of-shape *adj* C&G deformado
out-of-square *adj* MECH ENG, PRINT descuadrado, fuera de escuadra
out-of-stock: **~ situation** *n* PROD situación sin existencias *f*
out-of-sync[1] *adj* TV desincronizado
out-of-sync[2]: **~ error** *n* TELECOM error de desincronización *m*, error de fuera de sincronismo *m*, error de fuera de sincronización *m*
out-of-synchronization: **~ error** *n* TELECOM error de desincronización *m*, error de fuera de sincronismo *m*, error de fuera de sincronización *m*
out-of-tolerance *adj* MECH ENG fuera de tolerancias
out-of-track *adj* AIR TRANSP *helicopter* desalineado, fuera de guía
out-of-true *adj* MECH ENG desalineado, desviado, ladeado, torcido, PRINT mal cortado
out-of-use *adj* MECH ENG fuera de uso
outport *n* OCEAN, WATER TRANSP antepuerto *m*, puerto exterior *m*
outpouring *n* CONST efusión *f*
output[1]: **~-limited** *adj* COMP&DP limitado en la salida
output[2] *n* COAL extracción *f*, COMP&DP salida *f*, ELEC, ELEC ENG corriente de salida *f*, potencia de salida *f*, potencia generada *f*, potencia suministrada *f*, potencia útil *f*, rendimiento *m*, GAS salida *f*, MECH ENG capacidad *f*, caudal *m*, fabricación *f*, información de salida *f*, potencia *f*, potencia generada *f*, potencia útil *f*, producción *f*, rendimiento *m*, salida *f*, MINE extracción *f*, fabricación *f*, producción *f*, rendimiento *m*, NUCL extracción *f*, rendimiento *m*, PRINT salida *f*, PROD *pumps* capacidad *f*, potencia de salida *f*, potencia generada *f*, potencia suministrada *f*, potencia útil *f*, corriente de salida *f*, rendimiento *m*, caudal *m*, extracción *f*, producción *f*, energía suministrada *f*, TV potencia de salida *f*; **~ admittance** *n* ELEC, ELEC ENG, PHYS admitancia de salida *f*; **~ amplifier** *n* ELECTRON, TV amplificador de salida *m*; **~ angle** *n* HYDRAUL, OPT, PROD, TELECOM ángulo de salida *m*; **~ area** *n* COMP&DP zona de salida *f*; **~ attenuation** *n* ELECTRON atenuación de salida *f*; **~ attenuator** *n* ELECTRON atenuador de salida *m*; **~ back-off** *n* SPACE *communications* nivel de salida por debajo de saturación *m*; **~ biasing** *n* PROD derivación de capacidad *f*; **~ buffer** *n* COMP&DP búfer de salida *m*, memoria intermedia de salida *f*; **~ capacitance** *n* ELEC ENG capacitancia de salida *f*; **~ capacitor** *n* ELEC ENG condensador de salida *m*; **~ cavity** *n* ELECTRON cavidad de salida *f*; **~ charge** *n* ELEC ENG carga de salida *f*; **~ circuit** *n* ELEC ENG, TELECOM circuito de salida *m*; **~ control** *n* TV control de salida *m*; **~ current** *n* ELEC, ELEC ENG corriente de salida *f*; **~ data** *n* COMP&DP datos de salida *m pl*; **~ device** *n* COMP&DP dispositivo de salida *m*, PRINT dispositivo impresor *m*, PROD dispositivo de salida *m*, órgano de salida *m*; **~ divergence** *n* TELECOM divergencia de salida *f*; **~ earth short** *n BrE* (*cf output ground short AmE*) PROD cortocircuito de salida a tierra *m*; **~ electrode** *n* ELEC ENG electrodo de salida *m*; **~ file** *n* COMP&DP, PRINT archivo de salida *m*, fichero de salida *m*; **~ ground short** *n AmE* (*cf output earth short BrE*) PROD cortocircuito de salida a tierra *m*; **~ image table** *n* PROD tabla de imagen de salida *f*; **~ image table location** *n* PROD ubicación de la tabla de imagen de salida *f*; **~ impedance** *n* ELEC, ELEC ENG, PHYS, TELECOM impedancia de salida *f*;

~ level *n* TELECOM nivel de potencia *m*, nivel de salida *m*, TV nivel de salida *m*; **~-limited process** *n* COMP&DP proceso limitado en la salida *m*; **~ mirror** *n* INSTR reflector de salida *m*; **~ monitor** *n* TV monitor de salida *m*; **~ override** *n* PROD cancelación de salida *f*, derogación de salida *f*; **~ override instruction** *n* PROD mando de derogación de salida *m*; **~ phase-to-phase short** *n* PROD cortocircuito interfásico a la salida *m*; **~ port** *n* TELECOM puerta de salida *f*; **~ power** *n* ELEC, ELEC ENG potencia de salida *f*, potencia útil *f*, TELECOM potencia de salida *f*; **~ quantity** *n* ELEC ENG cantidad de salida *f*; **~ queue** *n* COMP&DP cola de salida *f*; **~ ramp control** *n* PROD control de rampa de salida *m*; **~ record** *n* COMP&DP registro de salida *m*; **~ recorder** *n* INSTR grabador de salida *m*; **~ shaft** *n* AUTO, VEH eje de salida *m*, eje propulsor *m*; **~ signal** *n* ELEC ENG, TELECOM, TV señal de salida *f*; **~ terminal** *n* ELEC borna de salida *m*, terminal de salida *m*, ELEC ENG terminal de salida *m*, PROD borna de salida *f*; **~ transducer** *n* ELEC ENG transductor de salida *m*; **~ transformer** *n* ELEC, ELEC ENG, PHYS transformador de salida *m*; **~ voltage** *n* ELEC tensión de salida *f*, tensión de salida máxima *f*, ELEC ENG voltaje de salida *m*, TELECOM tensión de salida *f*, TV voltaje en los bornes *m*; **~ winding** *n* ELEC *transformer* devanado de salida *m*
outrigger *n* AIR TRANSP larguero de soporte de plano fijo *m*
outside *n* PAPER *paper ream* hojas de protección *f pl*; **~ air temperature indicator** *n* AIR TRANSP indicador de la temperatura del aire exterior *m*; **~ air temperature probe** *n* AIR TRANSP sonda de temperatura del aire exterior *f*; **~-and-inside calipers** *AmE*, **~-and-inside callipers** *BrE n pl* MECH ENG compás de interiores y exteriores *m*; **~ broadcast** *n* TV radiodifusión en el exterior *f* (*AmL*), radioemisión en el exterior *f* (*Esp*); **~ calipers** *AmE*, **~ callipers** *BrE n pl* MECH ENG compás de espesor *m*, compás de exteriores *m*, compás de gruesos *m*; **~ circle** *n* MECH ENG *gearing* círculo de cabeza *m*, círculo exterior *m*; **~ clearance** *n* HYDRAUL recubrimiento exterior negativo *m*; **~ defective paper** *n* PAPER papel costero *m*, papel quebrado *m*; **~ diameter** *n* (*OD*) MECH, MECH ENG diámetro exterior *m*; **~ dimensions** *n pl* MECH ENG, PACK dimensiones exteriores *f pl*; **~-fired boiler** *n* PROD caldera de hogar exterior *f*; **~ gear** *n* MECH ENG engranaje exterior *m*; **~ lab** *n* CINEMAT laboratorio externo *m*; **~ lap** *n* HYDRAUL recubrimiento a la admisión *m*, recubrimiento exterior *m*; **~ lead** *n* HYDRAUL avance lineal a la admisión *m*; **~ measuring faces** *n pl* MECH ENG *caliper* compás de medición de caras externas *m*; **~ paint** *n* COLOUR pintura externa *f*; **~ pipe** *n* GAS tubería exterior *f*; **~ plant cable** *n* TV cable exterior de planta *m*; **~ screw** *n* MECH ENG tornillo macho *m*; **~ string** *n* CONST *stairbuilding* zanca exterior *f*; **~ thread** *n* MECH ENG rosca exterior *f*; **~-threading tool** *n* MECH ENG herramienta de roscar exteriormente *f*, terraja hembra *f*
outsize *n* COAL desclasificador *m*
outstanding *adj* PROD atrasado, impagado, pendiente, por pagar
outstep: **~ well** *n* PETR TECH pozo de delimitación *m*, pozo de paso exterior *m*

outstroke *n* HYDRAUL carrera de ida *f*
outturn: ~ **sheet** *n* PAPER hoja de muestra *f*
outward[1]: **~-bound** *adv* TRANSP, WATER TRANSP en viaje de ida
outward[2]: ~ **angle** *n* GEOM ángulo convexo *m*, ángulo saliente *m*; **~-flow turbine** *n* HYDRAUL turbina centrífuga *f*; ~ **flux** *n* PHYS flujo saliente *m*; ~ **passage** *n* WATER TRANSP travesía de ida *f*, viaje de ida *m*; ~ **propagating wave** *n* TELECOM onda de propagación de salida *f*; ~ **traffic** *n* TRANSP tráfico de salida *m*
oval[1] *adj* GEOM ovalado; **~-shaped** *adj* GEOM de forma ovalada
oval[2] *n* GEOM óvalo *m*; ~ **burr** *n* MECH ENG cincel ovalado *m*; ~ **compass** *n* MECH ENG compás elíptico *m*; ~ **countersunk rivet** *n* MECH ENG remache de cabeza ovalada *m*; ~ **file** *n* MECH ENG lima alméndrica *f*; **~-head fastener** *n* MECH ENG abrazadera de cabeza ovalada *f*; **~-head screw** *n* MECH ENG tornillo de cabeza ovalada *m*; ~ **knob** *n* CONST *locksmithing* pomo oval *m*; ~ **pulley** *n* MECH ENG polea ovalada *f*; ~ **window** *n* ACOUST ventana oval *f*
oven[1]: **~-dried** *adj* THERMO secado en estufa, secado en horno; **~-dry** *adj* PAPER secado en estufa, secado en horno
oven[2]: ~ **ageing** *n* P&R envejecimiento en el horno *m*; ~ **dehydration** *n* REFRIG secado en estufa *m*; **~-dry tensile strength** *n* TEXTIL resistencia a la tracción del secado al horno *f*; ~ **with forced convection** *n* LAB estufa con convección forzada *f*, horno con convección forzada *m*; ~ **with natural convection** *n* LAB estufa con convección natural *f*, horno con convección natural *m*; **~-proof glass** *n* THERMO vidrio a prueba de hornos *m*, vidrio refractario *m*
over[1]: ~ **ripe** *adj* AGRIC sobremaduro
over[2]: ~ **temperature** *n* THERMO sobretemperatura *f*
overageing *n* METALL hiperenvejecimiento *m*
overall[1] *adj* CONST general, MECH ENG de conjunto, de extremo a extremo, exterior, general, global, que incluye todo, total
overall[2] *n* TEXTIL guardapolvo *m*; ~ **dimensions** *n pl* MECH ENG, PACK dimensiones exteriores *f pl*, dimensiones extremas *f pl*, dimensiones totales *f pl*; ~ **efficiency** *n* FUELLESS rendimiento total *m*; ~ **internal height** *n* MECH ENG altura interna total *f*; ~ **length** *n* MECH ENG largo total *m*, longitud total *f*, METR longitud total *f*, TEXTIL longitud máxima *f*; ~ **protective suit** *n* SAFE traje de protección total *m*; ~ **refrigerating effect** *n* REFRIG potencia frigorífica total *f*; ~ **response curve** *n* ACOUST curva de respuesta total *f*; ~ **shade** *n* TEXTIL tonalidad máxima *f*; ~ **time interval** *n* TRANSP intervalo de tiempo total *m*; ~ **travel speed** *n* TRANSP velocidad global del viaje *f*; ~ **travel time** *n* TRANSP tiempo total de viaje *m*; ~ **width** *n* MECH ENG ancho total *m*
overalls *n pl BrE* (*cf coveralls AmE*) PROD, SAFE bata de trabajo *f* (*Esp*), mono de trabajo *m* (*Esp*), overol *m* (*AmL*)
over-and-back: ~ **fold** *n* PRINT plegado en acordeón *m*, plegado en zigzag *m*
over-and-under: ~ **current relay** *n* ELEC relé de máxima y mínima *m*, relé de máximo y mínimo de corriente *m*
overarm: ~ **machine** *n* MECH ENG *milling machine* máquina con brazo soporte *f*
overbalance *vi* SAFE perder el equilibrio, volcar

overbend *n* PETROL sobreflexión *f*
overboard *adv* WATER TRANSP al agua, al exterior, en el mar, por la borda
overbreak *n* MINE exceso de excavación *m*
overbridge *n* CONST paso superior *m*
overbunching *n* ELECTRON agrupación excesiva *f*
overburden *n* COAL, MINE montera *f*, recubrimiento *m*, terrenos de recubrimiento *m pl*, tierra de descombro *f*, PETR TECH sobrecarga *f*; ~ **drill** *n* COAL perforación del manto de recubrimiento *f*; ~ **effect** *n* PETR TECH efecto sobrecarga *m*; ~ **gradient** *n* GEOL gradiente de recubrimiento *m*, PETR TECH gradiente de sobrecarga *m*; ~ **pressure** *n* COAL presión del manto de recubrimiento *f*, PETR TECH presión de sobrecarga *f*
overcapacity *n* AIR TRANSP *air transport* sobrecapacidad *f*
overcharge *n* ELEC *of accumulator* sobrecarga *f*, REFRIG exceso de refrigerante *m*
overcompounding *n* ELEC ENG hiperexcitación *f*
overcrank *vt* CINEMAT, PHOTO, TV accionar a una velocidad mayor que la normal
overcropping *n* AGRIC cultivo abusivo *m*
overcure *n* P&R exceso de curado *m*, sobrevulcanización *f*
overcurrent *n* ELEC sobreamperaje *m*, sobrecarga de corriente *f*, sobrecorriente *f*, sobreintensidad *f*, ELEC ENG sobreamperaje *m*; ~ **blocking device** *n* ELEC *motor drive* dispositivo de bloqueo de máximo de corriente *m*, dispositivo de bloqueo de sobrecorriente *m*; ~ **circuit breaker** *n* ELEC disyuntor de sobrecorriente *m*, disyuntor de sobreintensidad *m*, interruptor de máxima *m*, ELEC ENG disyuntor de sobreintensidad *m*; ~ **protection** *n* ELEC dispositivo de protección de máximo de corriente *m*, protección contra sobrecorriente *f*, ELEC ENG protección de sobrecorriente *f*, SAFE dispositivo de protección de máximo de corriente *m*; ~ **relay** *n* ELEC relé de máxima *m*, relé de sobrecorriente *m*; ~ **switch** *n* ELEC conmutador de sobrecorriente *m*, disyuntor de sobrecorriente *m*, interruptor de sobrecorriente *m*; ~ **trip** *n* ELEC ENG disyuntor de máxima *m*
overcut: ~ **margins** *n pl* PRINT márgenes sobrecortados *m pl*
overcutting *n* ACOUST sobrecorte *m*
overdamping *n* PHYS sobreatenuación *f*
overdevelop *vt* CINEMAT, PHOTO revelar con exceso
overdevelopment *n* CINEMAT, PHOTO exceso de revelado *m*, sobrerevelado *m*
overdeviation *n* SPACE sobredesviación *f*
overdischarging *n* ELEC ENG agotamiento *m*
overdosage *n* CHEM sobredosificación *f*
overdrive *n* AUTO sobremarcha *f*, supermarcha *f*, MECH multiplicador de velocidad *m*, sobremarcha *f*, sobremultiplicación *f*, VEH supermarcha *f*, velocidad sobremultiplicada *f*
overdry *vt* PAPER sobresecar
overdye *vt* TEXTIL sobreteñir
overexpose *vt* CINEMAT sobreexponer, PHOTO dar exceso de exposición, sobreexponer, RAD PHYS sobreexponer
overexposed *adj* CINEMAT, PHOTO *film, picture*, RAD PHYS sobreexpuesto
overexposure *n* CINEMAT, PHOTO, RAD PHYS sobreexposición *f*
overextraction *n* HYDROL sobreextracción *f*

overfall: ~ **type fish pass** n FUELLESS escalera de peces tipo vertedero f

overfeed[1] n AGRIC, MECH ENG, REFRIG, TEXTIL sobrealimentación f; ~ **stoker** n AGRIC, MECH ENG, REFRIG hogar mecánico de alimentación superior m

overfeed[2] vt AGRIC, MECH ENG, PROD, REFRIG, TEXTIL sobrealimentar

overfeeding n AGRIC, MECH ENG, REFRIG, TEXTIL sobrealimentación f

overfishing n OCEAN pesca en exceso f, sobrepesca f

overflow[1] n CHEM derrame m, COAL desbordamiento m, finos m pl, inundación f, mineral triturado fino m, rebose m, COMP&DP desbordamiento m, desborde m, exceso m, CONST aliviadero m, HYDRAUL aliviadero m, alza f, HYDROL aliviadero m, desbordamiento m, inundación f, MECH desagüe m, desbordamiento m, MECH ENG compuerta f, corriente de la superficie f, desagüe m, desbordamiento m, exceso m, inundación f, rebosadura f, rebose m, superabundancia f, vertedero de superficie m, of injector derrame m, TELECOM desbordamiento m, WATER aliviadero m, derrame m, desbordamiento m, rebose m, pipe tubo de desbordamiento m; ~ **accept** n TELECOM aceptación de sobrecarga f; ~ **area** n COMP&DP zona de desbordamiento f; ~ **dam** n HYDROL presa con compuerta de rebosamiento f, presa de desagüe f, WATER presa de rebose f, presa de vertedero f; ~ **hole** n AUTO, VEH agujero de derrame m, agujero de desagüe de seguridad m, agujero de desbordamiento m, agujero de rebose m; ~ **pipe** n AUTO, VEH tubo de desagüe m, tubo de rebose m, WATER tubo de desbordamiento m; ~ **process** n C&G proceso de sobreflujo m; ~ **of a screen** n COAL cribado m; ~ **valve** n HYDRAUL válvula de caudal sobrante f, válvula de derrame f, válvula de rebose f, válvula de sobrante f, RAIL válvula de derrame f, válvula de rebose f

overflow[2] vi HYDROL desbordarse, inundarse

overfold n GEOL pliegue invertido m, pliegue tumbado m

overgage: ~ **hole** AmE see overgauge hole BrE

overgauge: ~ **hole** n BrE PETR TECH, PETROL agujero de diámetro excesivo m

overglazing n C&G sobrevidriado m

overgrazing n AGRIC sobrepastoreo m

overgrinding n COAL molienda excesiva f

overground adj COAL aéreo

overgrowth n AGRIC sobrecrecimiento m

overhand: ~ **knot** n WATER TRANSP nudo simple m; ~ **stope** n MINE destroza de cabeza f (Esp), escalón de cielo m, escalón de testero m, grada al revés f, grada invertida f, rebaje de cabeza m (AmL); ~ **stoping** n MINE arranque por realce m (Esp), explotación por frentes invertidas f (Esp), explotación por gradas al revés f (AmL), explotación por gradas invertidas f, labor de realce f (AmL), trabajo por testeros m

overhang n CONST bovedilla f, VEH alerón m, saliente m

overhanging n CONST voladizo m, ~ **arm** n PROD of milling machine soporte portafresas en saliente m; ~ **crank** n MECH ENG manivela saliente f; ~ **face** n MINE frente inclinado m; ~ **wall** n CONST pared en voladizo f

overhaul[1] n AIR TRANSP of equipment servicio m

overhaul[2] vt AIR TRANSP equipment revisar, WATER TRANSP maintenance recorrer, repasar, revisar, tirarmollar, navigation hacer un recorrido, alcanzar, ship maintenance limpiar fondos, carenar

overhead n TELECOM sobrecarga f; ~ **access** n (OHA) TELECOM acceso de cabecera m, acceso inicial m; ~ **bank** n CINEMAT, TV banco de luces de techo m; ~ **bit** n TELECOM bit de cabeza m, bit inicial m; ~**-bunker refrigerated truck** n REFRIG vagón refrigerante con depósito de hielo en el techo m; ~ **cable** n ELEC supply network, ELEC ENG cable aéreo m; ~ **camshaft** n (OHC) AUTO, MECH, VEH eje de levas en la culata m, árbol de levas colocado en la culata m, árbol de levas en culata m (ALC); ~**-cone** n MECH ENG contracono m; ~ **cone pulley** n MECH ENG polea de contracono f; ~ **conveyor** n PACK transportador elevado m; ~ **crane** n CINEMAT grúa móvil f, CONST grúa aérea f, MECH, PROD puente-grúa m; ~ **crossover** n RAIL paso elevado m; ~ **drum car** n AmE (cf overhead drum wagon BrE) RAIL vagón para la colocación de catenaria m; ~ **drum wagon** BrE (cf overhead drum car AmE) RAIL vagón para la colocación de catenaria m; ~ **electrical monorail conveyor** n MECH ENG transportador monocarril eléctrico aéreo m; ~ **engine** n PROD steam máquina pilón f; ~ **guard** n SAFE to fail protección superior f, protector elevado m; ~ **light** n AIR TRANSP luz alta f; ~ **line** n CONST, ELEC línea aérea f, línea eléctrica f, ELEC ENG, TELECOM línea aérea f; ~ **line knuckle** n RAIL junta articulada de línea aérea f; ~ **network** n TELECOM red aérea f; ~ **panel** n AIR TRANSP panel alto m; ~ **pilot bar** n MECH ENG of lathe barra de guía al aire libre f, barra de guía alta f; ~ **power line** n ELEC ENG conducción de energía aérea f; ~ **power line fitting** n ELEC ENG accesorio de conducción de energía aérea m; ~ **runway** n PROD transportador aéreo m, vía aérea f; ~ **system** n ELEC ENG sistema aéreo m; ~ **track** n PROD vía aérea f; ~ **transmission** n MECH ENG countershaft transmisión superior f; ~ **traveling crane** AmE, ~ **travelling crane** BrE n PACK grúa puente f; ~ **valve** n (OHV) AUTO, METALL, PETR TECH, PETROL, THERMO mechanics válvula en culata f; ~**-valve engine** n AUTO, VEH motor de válvulas en cabeza m; ~ **valves** n pl (OHV) AUTO, VEH válvulas en culata f pl; ~ **water tank** n HYDROL depósito de agua elevado m

overheat[1]: ~ **thermoresistor** n AIR TRANSP termorresistor de recalentamiento m

overheat[2] vt THERMO recalentar, sobrecalentar

overheat[3] vi THERMO of ribbed bulkheads recalentarse

overheating n ELEC ENG calentamiento anormal m, recalentamiento m, MECH ENG, PROD recalentamiento m, sobrecalentamiento m, SAFE recalentamiento m, THERMO recalentamiento m, sobrecalentamiento m, VEH recalentamiento m

overlap n COMP&DP solapamiento m, superposición f, CONST solape m, GEOL solapamiento m, PRINT superposición f, solapa f, TV jobs, programmes solapamiento m, WATER TRANSP construction solape m; ~ **contact** n PROD contacto de recubrimiento m; ~ **joint** n CONST unión con solape f; ~ **section** n RAIL sección solapada f

overlapping n COATINGS solapado m, CONST solape m, ELEC ENG oscilación independiente f, superposición f, METALL solapamiento m, superposición f, PHYS superposición f; ~ **flaps** n pl PACK solapas solapadas f pl

overlay[1] n COMP&DP superposición f, CONST capa

superpuesta *f*, PRINT cama *f*, TV capa superpuesta *f*;
~ cladding *n* MECH *paint-burning lamp* revestimiento
protector *m*
overlay² *vt* TV superponer
overlaying *n* AmE (*cf flashing BrE*) C&G recubrimiento
m
overleap: **~ joint** *n* CONST *halved joint of wood* junta de
solape *f*
overload¹ *n* GEN sobrecarga *f*; **~ channel** *n* TELECOM
canal de sobrecarga *m*; **~ current** *n* ELEC *supply,
equipment*, ELEC ENG corriente de sobrecarga *f*;
~ factor *n* ELEC *supply* factor de sobrecarga *m*;
~ indicator *n* ELEC *supply, equipment* indicador de
sobrecarga *m*; **~ level** *n* ELEC ENG nivel de sobrecarga
m, nivel límite *m*; **~ protection** *n* ELEC *circuit,
equipment*, ELEC ENG protección contra sobrecarga
f; **~ protection device** *n* ELEC ENG, SAFE dispositivo
de protección contra sobrecarga *m*; **~ relay** *n* ELEC
relé de máxima *m*, relé de sobrecarga *m*, ELEC ENG
relé de sobrecarga *m*, PROD relé de máxima *m*, relé de
sobrecarga *m*; **~ running** *n* PROD marcha con sobrecarga *f*; **~ test** *n* ELEC prueba de sobrecarga *f*;
~ voltage *n* ELEC *circuit, equipment* tensión de
sobrecarga *f*
overload² *vt* GEN sobrecargar
overloaded *adj* GEN sobrecargado
overloading *n* GEN sobrecarga *f*
overlock *vt* TEXTIL sobreorillar
overlook *vt* SAFE inspeccionar, pasar por alto
overmating *n* AGRIC exceso de machos en un rodeo *m*
overoxidize *vt* CHEM sobreoxidar
overpass *n* RAIL paso elevado *m*
overplacement *n* GEOL, MINE montera *f*, superposición *f*, terrenos de recubrimiento *m pl*
overpotential: **~ protection** *n* ELEC ENG protección
sobrepotencial *f*
overpower *vt* WATER controlar
overpressure *n* AIR TRANSP, PETR TECH sobrepresión *f*,
PROD sobrepresión *f*, sobretensión *f*, sobrevoltaje *m*;
~ test *n* PROD prueba de sobrepresión *f*, prueba de
sobretensión *f*
overprint¹ *n* CINEMAT, PHOTO sobreimpresión *f*;
~ colors AmE, **~ colours** BrE *n pl* PRINT colores
para sobreimprimir *m pl*; **~ lacquer** *n* PRINT laca
para aplicar sobre la impresión *f*; **~ varnish** *n*
COATINGS, PRINT barniz de sobreimpresión *m*
overprint² *vt* CINEMAT, PHOTO, PRINT sobreimprimir
overprinting *n* GEOL *geochronology* sobreposición *f*,
superposición *f*, MECH ENG sobreimpresión *f*, superposición de renglones *f*, obliteración *f*, PRINT
sobreimpresión *f*, obliteración *f*, PROD sobreimpresión *f*
overproduction *n* PROD sobreproducción *f*
overrange *n* PROD desbordamiento de capacidad *m*
overrefining *n* PROD *metals* sobrerrefinado *m*
override¹: **~ control** *n* AIR TRANSP conmutación de
mando *f*, neutralización de control *f*, prioridad de
mando *f*, transferencia de mando *f*; **~ switch** *n* ELEC
interruptor de paso de mando *m*, interruptor de
transferencia de mando *m*
override² *vt* MECH sobrepasar, PROD cancelar el efecto
de, substituir a
overrider *n* VEH contrapeso *m*
overriding¹ *adj* MECH esencial, sobrepasado, PROD
primordial, prioritario, privilegiado

overriding² *n* MECH solapamiento *m*; **~ impression** *n*
TEXTIL impresión principal *f*
overripeness *n* AGRIC exceso de madurez *m*
overrun¹ *n* AIR TRANSP exceso *m*, rebase *m*, AUTO
arrastre del motor *m*, PRINT tirada excesiva *f*, VEH
arrastre del motor *m*, rebasamiento de la velocidad
límite *m*
overrun² *vt* RAIL *station, stop signal* sobrepasar
overrun³ *vi* TV excederse
overrunning: **~ clutch** *n* AIR TRANSP embrague de
rueda libre *m*, embrague de sobremarcha *m*, AUTO
embrague de rotación libre *m*, embrague de rueda
libre *m*
overs *n pl* PRINT hojas sobrantes *f pl*
oversaturated *adj* GEOL sobresaturado
oversaturation *n* TV sobresaturación *f*
overscan *n* TV sobreexploración *f*
overscore *vt* PRINT subrayar por arriba
overseas¹ *adj* WATER TRANSP de ultramar, ultramarino
overseas²: **~ container** *n* TRANSP contenedor de
ultramar *m*; **~ packaging** *n* PACK embalaje para el
transporte marítimo *m*
oversee *vt* PROD inspeccionar, vigilar
oversewing *n* TEXTIL sobrehilado *m*
oversheath *n* ELEC *of cable* sobreenvoltura *f*, sobre-
funda *f*, sobrevaina *f*
overshipment *n* PROD sobreembarque *m*
overshoot¹ *n* AIR TRANSP entrada larga *f*, sobremodulación *f*, ELEC ENG punta *f*, sobreimpulso *m*, METALL
sobretensión *f*; **~ distortion** *n* TV distorsión por
sobremodulación *f*
overshoot² *vt* AIR TRANSP *runway* rebasar, salirse de,
MECH excederse, ir más allá de, exceder, RAIL rebasar
overshooting *n* AIR TRANSP entrada larga *f*
overshot *n* PETR TECH campana de pesca *f*, enchufe de
pesca *m*, overshot *m*; **~ water-wheel** *n* WATER rueda
hidráulica de admisión superior *f*; **~ wheel** *n* WATER
rueda de arcaduces *f*, rueda hidráulica de alimentación superior *f*
oversize¹ *adj* MECH ENG de mayor tamaño que el
especificado, de sobremedida, extragrande, sobredi-
mensionado
oversize² *n* COAL desechos de cribado *m pl*, gruesos *m
pl*, rechazos *m pl*, sobredimensión *f*, tamaños grandes
m pl, MECH sobredimensión *f*, sobretamaño *m*, MINE
desechos de cribado *m pl*, gruesos *m pl*, rechazos *m
pl*, sobredimensión *f*
oversized *adj* MECH, MECH ENG de sobreespesor
oversizing *n* MECH, MECH ENG sobredimensión *f*,
sobreespesor *m*, sobretamaño *m*
overspeed *n* MECH, MECH ENG, PROD exceso de
velocidad *m*, sobrevelocidad *f*, velocidad excesiva *f*,
VEH embalamiento *m*; **~ brake** *n* MECH ENG freno
para sobrevelocidad *m*; **~ control** *n* FUELLESS regulador por velocidad excesiva *m*; **~ gear** *n* MECH ENG
limitador de embalamiento *m*, moderador de sobrevelocidad *m*; **~ protection** *n* MECH ENG protector de
sobrevelocidad *m*; **~ test** *n* ELEC *machine* prueba de
embalamiento *f*, prueba de exceso de velocidad *f*,
prueba de sobrevelocidad *f*, prueba de velocidad
excesiva *f*
overspeeder *n* MECH ENG moderador de sobrevelocidad *m*
oversquare: **~ engine** *n* AUTO motor supercuadrado *m*
oversteer¹ *n* AUTO, VEH giro en exceso *m*, sobreviraje *m*
oversteer² *vi* AUTO, VEH sobrevirar

overstocking _n_ AGRIC sobrecarga de ganado por unidad de superficie _f_

overstowage _n_ WATER TRANSP _of cargo_ apilamiento _m_, peso de las cargas apiladas _m_

overstress _n_ PROD _machines_ sobrecarga _f_, sobrefatiga _f_

overstressing _n_ METALL exceso de tensión _m_, sobrecarga _f_, PROD deformación permanente por esfuerzos que sobrepasan el límite elastico _f_, exceso de tensión _m_, sobrecarga _f_

overstrike _n_ PRINT superposición _f_

overtaking: ~ **lane** _n_ CONST carril de adelantamiento _m_, vía de alcance _f_, TRANSP vía de alcance _f_

over-the-road: ~ **system** _n_ REFRIG sistema de enfriamiento en ruta _m_

overthrust _n_ GEOL, PETR TECH cabalgamiento _m_, corrimiento _m_, pliegue geológico _m_; ~ **block** _n_ GEOL bloque corrido _m_; ~ **fold** _n_ GEOL pliegue cobijante _m_; ~ **sheet** _n_ GEOL manto de cabalgamiento _m_

overtime _n_ PROD horas extraordinarias _f pl_

overtone _n_ ELECTRON armónico superior _m_, PHYS armónico de orden superior _m_

overtop[1] _vti_ HYDROL verter por la cresta

overtop[2]: ~ **its banks** _vi_ HYDROL _river_ rebosar

overtravel _n_ PROD sobrecarrera _f_; ~ **detection** _n_ PROD detección de sobrecarrera _f_

overturn[1] _vti_ MECH ENG forzar, invertir, tumbar, volcar, voltear

overturn[2] _vi_ SAFE zozobrar

overturned: ~ **fold** _n_ GEOL pliegue invertido _m_; ~ **limb** _n_ GEOL flanco invertido _m_

overturning _n_ SAFE, TRANSP capotaje _m_, vuelco _m_, zozobra _f_; ~ **moment** _n_ CONST momento de giro _m_

overvoltage _n_ CHEM, ELEC, ELEC ENG, PHYS sobretensión _f_, sobrevoltaje _m_, tensión excesiva _f_, voltaje excesivo _m_, sobrecarga de voltaje _f_; ~ **breakdown** _n_ ELEC ENG paso de corriente por aislante de sobrevoltaje _m_; ~ **protection** _n_ ELEC, ELEC ENG, SAFE dispositivo de protección de máximo de tensión _m_, protección contra la sobretensión _f_; ~ **protection device** _n_ ELEC, ELEC ENG, SAFE dispositivo de protección contra la sobretensión _m_; ~ **relay** _n_ ELEC relé de máxima _m_, relé de máximo de tensión _m_, relé de sobretensión _m_, ELEC ENG relé de sobretensión _m_; ~ **release** _n_ ELEC _circuit breaker_ aparato de máximo de tensión _m_

overweight _n_ METR sobrepeso _m_

overwind _n_ MINE acción de sobrepasar el fin de carrera _f_; ~ **gear** _n_ MINE mecanismo para evitar que se rebasen los enganches _m_ (_AmL_), moderador de velocidad de fin de carrera _m_, topes _m pl_ (_Esp_)

overwinder _n_ MINE freno de jaula _m_ (_Esp_), mecanismo moderador de velocidad al final de la carrera _m_ (_AmL_); ~ **and overspeeder** _n_ MINE mecanismo moderador de velocidad y de sobrevelocidad _m_

overwinding _n_ MINE acción de sobrepasar el fin de carrera _f_, rebase de los enganches _m_; ~ **allowance** _n_ MINE, SAFE altura de seguridad _f_; ~ **gear** _n_ MINE mecanismo para evitar que se rebasen los enganches _m_ (_AmL_), moderador de velocidad de fin de carrera _m_, topes _m pl_ (_Esp_)

overwinter _vi_ AGRIC invernar

overworking _n_ PROD trabajo excesivo _m_

overwrap _n_ PACK sobreenvoltura _f_

overwrapping: ~ **machinery** _n_ PACK maquinaria para sobreenvolver _f_

overwrite _vt_ PRINT sobreescribir

overwriting _n_ COMP&DP sobreescritura _f_, sobregrabación _f_

ovipositor _n_ AGRIC oviscapto _m_

ovoglobulin _n_ CHEM ovoglobulina _f_

ovoid _n_ COAL ovoide _m_

ovolo _n_ CONST _quarter circle shape_ óvolo _m_; ~ **plane** _n_ CONST cepillo de óvolo _m_

Owen: ~ **bridge** _n_ ELEC _circuit_ circuito de puente Owen _m_, puente Owen _m_

own: ~ **coding** _n_ COMP&DP codificación propia _f_; ~-**exchange supervisory circuit** _n_ TELECOM circuito de supervisión de central propia _m_

oxalate _n_ CHEM oxalato _m_

oxalated _adj_ CHEM oxalatado

oxalic[1] _adj_ CHEM oxálico

oxalic[2]: ~ **acid** _n_ CHEM, PHOTO ácido oxálico _m_

oxaloacetic _adj_ CHEM oxaloacético

oxaluric _adj_ CHEM oxalúrico

oxalylurea _n_ CHEM oxalilurea _f_

oxamic _adj_ CHEM oxámico

oxamide _n_ CHEM oxamida _f_

oxanilic _adj_ CHEM oxanílico

oxanilide _n_ CHEM oxanilida _f_

oxazine _n_ CHEM oxazina _f_

oxazole _n_ CHEM oxazol _m_

Oxberry: ~ **optical printer** _n_ CINEMAT positivadora óptica Oxberry _f_

oxbow _n_ HYDROL recodo _m_

oxetone _n_ CHEM oxetona _f_

Oxford: ~ **gray** _AmE_, ~ **grey** _BrE_ _n_ COLOUR gris Oxford _m_

oxidability _n_ CHEM oxidabilidad _f_

oxidable _adj_ CHEM oxidable

oxidation _n_ CHEM, CINEMAT, ELEC, HYDROL, POLL oxidación _f_; ~ **ditch** _n_ HYDROL, WATER zanja de oxidación _f_; ~ **dye** _n_ COLOUR colorante por oxidación _m_; ~ **pond** _n_ HYDROL, RECYCL, WATER fosa séptica de oxidación _f_; ~-**reduction** _n_ (_redox_) CHEM, LAB oxidación-reducción _f_, óxido-reducción _m_, oxidorreducción _m_ (_redox_); ~-**reduction cell** _n_ LAB _switch_ celda de óxido-reducción _f_; ~ **reduction potential** _n_ POLL potencial de oxido-reducción _m_, potencial de reducción de oxidación _m_, potencial redox _m_

oxidative: ~ **coupling** _n_ GAS junta oxidativa _f_

oxide _n_ CHEM, TV óxido _m_; ~ **buildup** _n_ CINEMAT, TV acumulación de óxido _f_; ~-**ceramic lathe tools** _n pl_ MECH ENG herramientas para torno de óxido cerámico _f pl_; ~-**coated cathode** _n_ ELEC ENG cátodo recubierto con óxido _m_, cátodo revestido de óxido _m_; ~ **film** _n_ COATINGS película de óxido _f_; ~ **layer** _n_ COMP&DP capa de óxido _f_; ~ **ore** _n_ CHEM óxido mineral _m_; ~ **shedding** _n_ TV desprendimiento del óxido _m_; ~ **side** _n_ CINEMAT, TV lado del óxido _m_

oxidic: ~ **waste** _n_ COAL materia estéril _f_

oxidizability _n_ CHEM oxidabilidad _f_

oxidizable _adj_ CHEM oxidable

oxidize[1] _vt_ CHEM oxidar

oxidize[2] _vi_ CHEM oxidarse

oxidizer _n_ AIR TRANSP, CHEM, POLL oxidante _m_, SPACE comburente oxidante _m_, oxidante _m_, THERMO oxidante _m_

oxidizing[1] _adj_ CHEM, GEOL, SAFE oxidante

oxidizing[2]: ~ **agent** _n_ AIR TRANSP oxidante _m_, CHEM agente oxidante _m_, compuesto oxidante _m_, oxidante _m_, POLL agente oxidante _m_, oxidante _m_, SPACE,

THERMO oxidante *m*; **~ flame** *n* CHEM llama azul *f*, llama oxidante *f*, CONST llama oxidante *f*; **~ substance** *n* SAFE substancia oxidante *f*

oxidoreduction *n* (*redox*) CHEM LAB oxidación-reducción *f*, óxido-reducción *m*, oxidoreducción *f* (*redox*)

oximation *n* CHEM oximación *f*

oxime *n* CHEM oxima *f*

oximeter *n* CHEM oxímetro *m*

oximetric *adj* CHEM oximétrico

oximetry *n* CHEM oximetría *f*

oxo: **~ acid** *n* CHEM oxoácido *m*; **~ alcohol** *n* DETERG oxo-alcohol *m*; **~ process** *n* DETERG proceso oxo *m*; **~ synthesis** *n* DETERG oxo-síntesis *f*

oxonium *n* CHEM oxonio *m*

oxozone *n* CHEM oxozono *m*

oxyacetylene: **~ blowpipe** *n* CONST, PROD soplete de oxiacetileno *m*, soplete oxiacetilénico *m*; **~ welding** *n* CONST, MECH, PROD, THERMO soldadura con oxiacetileno *f*, soldadura oxiacetilénica *f*, soldeo oxiacetilénico *m*; **~ welding equipment** *n* PROD equipos de soldadura oxiacetilénica *m pl*

oxyacid *n* CHEM oxiácido *m*, oxoácido *m*

oxycellulose *n* CHEM oxicelulosa *f*

oxychloride *n* CHEM oxicloruro *m*

oxycutting *n* MECH *process* oxicorte *m*

oxycyanide *n* CHEM oxicianuro *m*

oxyfluoride *n* CHEM oxifluoruro *m*

oxygen *n* (*O*) CHEM, HYDROL, MAR POLL, METALL, SAFE, SPACE oxígeno *m* (*O*); **~ arc cutting** *n* CONST corte por arco con oxígeno *m*, corte por arco *m*, PROD corte oxieléctrico *m*, corte por arco eléctrico y chorro de oxígeno *m*, oxicorte por arco *m*; **~ bottom blowing** *n* METALL soplado de fondo con oxígeno *m*; **~ breathing apparatus** *n* SAFE aparato para respirar oxígeno *m*; **~ cylinder** *n* PROD botella de oxígeno *f*, SPACE *craft* botellón de oxígeno *m*; **~ deficit** *n* (*OD*) HYDROL déficit en oxígeno *m* (*DO*); **~ depletion of the air** *n* MINE agotamiento del aire en oxígeno *m*, empobrecimiento del aire en oxígeno *m*; **~ enrichment** *n* C&G enriquecimiento con oxígeno *m*; **~ furnace** *n* COAL horno a oxígeno *m*; **~ generator** *n* CONST generador de oxígeno *m*; **~-helium mixture** *n* OCEAN mezcla heliox *f*; **~ index** *n* AIR TRANSP índice de oxígeno *m*; **~ lance** *n* CONST soplete perforador *m*; **~ lancing** *n* METALL afino por corriente de oxigeno *m*, PROD *welding* afino por corriente de oxigeno *m*, soplado de oxígeno *m*; **~ mask** *n* AIR TRANSP, SAFE, SPACE máscara de oxígeno *f*; **~ outlet** *n* PROD salida de oxígeno *f*; **~ poisoning** *n* OCEAN hiperoxia *f*, intoxicación por exceso de oxígeno *f*; **~ regulator** *n* SPACE regulador de oxígeno *m*; **~ respirator** *n* SPACE respirador de oxígeno *m*; **~-salinity diagram** *n* OCEAN diagrama oxígeno-salinidad *m*; **~ self-rescue apparatus** *n* SAFE aparato de autorrescate con oxígeno *m*; **~ self-rescuer** *n* SAFE aditamento de autorrescate con oxígeno *m*; **~ supply** *n* SAFE dotación de oxígeno *f*, SPACE *craft* suministro de oxígeno *m*; **~ value** *n* AIR TRANSP índice de oxígeno *m*

oxygenase *n* CHEM oxigenasa *f*

oxygenate *vt* CHEM, HYDROL oxigenar

oxygenated[1] *adj* CHEM, HYDROL oxigenado

oxygenated[2]: **~ water** *n* HYDROL, WATER agua oxigenada *f*

oxygenation *n* CHEM, HYDROL oxigenación *f*; **~ capacity** *n* HYDROL capacidad de oxigenación *f*

oxygenic *adj* CHEM oxigénico

oxygenizable *adj* CHEM oxigenable

oxyhaemography *n* BrE CHEM oxihemografía *f*

oxyhemography *AmE see oxyhaemography BrE*

oxyhydric *adj* CHEM oxhídrico

oxyhydrogen *adj* CHEM oxhídrico

oxylene *n* CHEM oxileno *m*

oxyphilic *adj* CHEM oxifílico

oxyphilous *adj* CHEM oxifiloso

oxyphosphate *n* CHEM oxifosfato *m*

oxysalt *n* CHEM oxisal *f*

oxysulfide *AmE see oxysulphide BrE*

oxysulphide *n* BrE CHEM oxisulfuro *m*

oxytetracycline *n* CHEM oxitetraciclina *f*

oxytocic *adj* CHEM oxitócico

oyster: **~ bed** *n* OCEAN criadero de ostras *m*; **~ culture** *n* OCEAN ostricultura *f*; **~ dredger** *n* WATER TRANSP embarcación dedicada a la pesca de ostras con rastro *f*; **~ farm** *n* OCEAN parque de cultivo de ostras *m*; **~ farmer** *n* OCEAN ostricultor *m*; **~-fattening pond** *n* OCEAN estanque de engorde *m*

oystershell: **~ scale** *n* AGRIC serpeta del manzano *f*

ozalid *n* PRINT copia ozalida *f*; **~ process** *n* PRINT proceso ozalida *m*

ozocerite *n* MINERAL ozocerita *f*

ozone *n* CHEM, CHEM TECH, METEO, SPACE ozono *m*; **~ absorption** *n* RAD PHYS absorción ozónica *f*; **~ concentration** *n* POLL concentración de ozono *f*; **~ layer** *n* METEO, POLL, SPACE capa de ozono *f*, ozonosfera *f*; **~ resistance** *n* P&R resistencia al ozono *f*

ozonide *n* CHEM ozonuro *m*

ozonization *n* CHEM, CHEM TECH, METEO ozonización *f*; **~ plant** *n* HYDROL planta de ozonización *f*

ozonize *vti* CHEM, CHEM TECH, METEO ozonizar

ozonized[1] *adj* CHEM, CHEM TECH, METEO ozonizado

ozonized[2]: **~ water** *n* HYDROL, WATER agua ozonizada *f*

ozonizer *n* CHEM, CHEM TECH, METEO ozonizador *m*

ozonolysis *n* CHEM, CHEM TECH ozonólisis *f*

ozonoscope *n* CHEM, INSTR ozonoscopio *m*

ozonoscopic *adj* CHEM ozonoscópico

ozonosphere *n* METEO ozonosfera *f*, POLL capa de ozono *f*, ozonosfera *f*, SPACE ozonosfera *f*

P

p *abbr* METR (*peta, pico*) p (*peta, pico*), NUCL, PART PHYS, RAD PHYS (*proton*) p (*protón*)

p⁺¹ *abbr* (*positron*) PART PHYS, PHYS p⁺ (*positrón*)

p⁺²: ~ **region** *n* ELECTRON región p⁺ *f*; ~ **semiconductor** *n* ELECTRON semiconductor p⁺ *m*

p⁻: ~ **region** *n* ELECTRON región p⁻ *f*; ~ **semiconductor** *n* ELECTRON semiconductor p⁻ *m*

P¹ *abbr* CHEM, ELECTRON, METALL, PHYS (*phosphorus*) P (*fósforo*)

P²: ~ **operation** *n* PART PHYS operación de transformación de la paridad *f*; ~ **wave** *n* GEOL onda P *f*, onda primaria *f*, PHYS onda P *f*

Pa *abbr* ACOUST (*pascal*) Pa (*pascal*), CHEM, METEO, METR, PETR TECH, PHYS, RAD PHYS (*pascal, protactinium*) Pa (*pascal, protactinio*)

PA¹ *abbr* (*polyamide*) CHEM, ELECTRON, P&R, TEXTIL PA (*poliamida*)

PA²: ~ **container** *n* TRANSP contenedor PA *m*; ~ **system** *n* (*public address system*) AIR TRANSP sistema de megafonía *m*, sistema público de altavoces *m*

PABX *abbr* (*private automatic branch exchange*) TELECOM centralita privada automática conectada a la red pública *f*

pace *n* CINEMAT ritmo *m*

pachnolite *n* MINERAL pachnolita *f*

pack¹ *n* MINE muro de sostén *m*, pilar de sostén *m*, relleno de galerías *m*, PACK, PHOTO paquete *m*; ~-**handling equipment** *n* PACK equipo de manipulado de paquetes *m*; ~ **ice** *n* WATER TRANSP hielo a la deriva *m*; ~ **system** *n* MINE mecanismo de relleno *m*, procedimiento de relleno *m*; ~ **wall** *n* MINE murete de piedra en seco para relleno *m*, murete de piedra para relleno *m*

pack² *vt* COMP&DP comprimir, empaquetar, MECH empaquetar, MINE hundir, macizar (*AmL*), rellenar (*Esp*), PAPER empaquetar

package *n* COMP&DP, ELEC ENG paquete *m*, PACK envase *m*, paquete *m*, SPACE *craft* embalaje *m*, envase *m*, TEXTIL envase *m*; ~ **dyeing** *n* COLOUR teñido en bobinas *m*; ~ **for standardization** *n* PACK normalización de envases *f*; ~ **freight** *n* AmE (*cf package goods BrE*) TRANSP carga por lotes *f*; ~ **goods** *n* BrE (*cf package freight AmE*) TRANSP carga por lotes *f*; ~ **lacquer** *n* COATINGS empaquetada *f*, laca en paquete *f*; ~ **reactor** *n* NUCL reactor prefabricado *m*; ~ **sleeve** *n* TEXTIL funda de bobina *f*; ~ **test** *n* PACK ensayo del paquete *m*

packaged: ~ **boiler** *n* HEAT ENG caldera unitaria *f*

packaging *n* FOOD empaquetado *m*, envasado *m*, PACK embalaje *m*, envasado *m*, envase *m*, PAPER embalaje *m*, envase *m*, PROD embalaje *m*, empacado *m*, empaquetado, envasado *m*, envase *m*, *machinery* empaquetadura *f*, TEXTIL embalaje *m*; ~ **area** *n* PROD zona de empaquetado *f*; ~ **line** *n* PACK cadena de embalaje *f*; ~ **printing** *n* PRINT impresión de envases *f*; ~ **profile** *n* PACK perfil de embalaje *m*

packed: ~-**bed scrubber** *n* POLL lavador de lecho compacto *m*, lavador de lecho fijo *m*; ~ **column** *n* CHEM, CHEM TECH, PETR TECH columna de relleno *f*, columna empacada *f*; ~ **decimal** *n* COMP&DP decimal empaquetado *m*; ~ **tower** *n* CHEM TECH columna de empaquetamiento *f*

packer *n* MECH ENG embalador *m*, empacador *m*, empaquetador *m*, enfardador *m*, PETROL obturador anular *m*, TEXTIL empaquetador *m*; ~'**s bay** *n* C&G bodega de empaque *f*

packet *n* COMP&DP, PROD, TELECOM, TEXTIL paquete *m*; ~ **assembler-disassembler** *n* (*PAD*) COMP&DP, TELECOM ensamblador-desensamblador de paquetes *m* (*PAD*); ~ **broadcasting** *n* TELECOM radiodifusión de paquetes *f*, radiodifusión por paquetes *f*; ~-**data-transmission network** *n* TELECOM red de transmisión de datos por paquetes *f*; ~ **delay** *n* COMP&DP retardo de paquete *m*; ~-**mode bearer service** *n* TELECOM servicio portador en modos por paquete *m*; ~-**mode terminal** *n* COMP&DP terminal en modo de paquetes *m*; ~ **port** *n* TELECOM acceso al paquete *m*, puerto de paquetes *m*; ~ **radio** *n* TELECOM radio del paquete *f*; ~ **sequencing** *n* COMP&DP secuencia de paquetes *f*; ~ **switch** *n* (*PS*) ELEC interruptor de empaquetado *m*, TELECOM conmutador de paquete *m*, interruptor de empaquetado *m*; ~-**switched bearer service** *n* TELECOM servicio portador con conmutación de paquetes *m*; ~-**switched network** *n* (*PSN*) COMP&DP, ELECTRÓN, TELECOM red de conmutación por paquetes *f*, red de transmisión por paquetes *f*; ~ **switching** *n* COMP&DP, ELEC ENG, TELECOM conmutación por paquetes *f*, transmisión por paquetes *f*; ~-**switching exchange** *n* (*PSE*) COMP&DP, TELECOM central de conmutación de paquetes *f* (*CCP*); ~-**switching network** *n* COMP&DP, TELECOM red de conmutación de paquetes *f*; ~-**switching node** *n* (*PSN*) COMP&DP, TELECOM nodo de conmutación de paquetes *m*; ~-**switching processor** *n* COMP&DP, TELECOM procesador de conmutación de paquetes *m*; ~ **transmission** *n* COMP&DP transmisión de paquetes *f*, TELECOM transmisión por paquetes *f*

packetizer: ~-**depacketizer** *n* TELECOM empaquetador-desempaquetador *m*

packing *n* MECH empaquetadura *f*, envasado *m*, envase *m*, MECH ENG *act* embalaje *m*, relleno *m*, empaque *m*, envase *m*, envasado *m*, obturación *f*, apisonado *m*, aglomeración *f*, MINE rellenado *m* (*Esp*), macizado *m* (*AmL*), relleno *m*, OCEAN embalaje *m*, PROD *of sand of a mould* compacción *f*, compactación *f*, apisonado *m*, TEXTIL empaquetado *m*; ~ **case** *n* TEXTIL caja de embalaje *f*; ~ **density** *n* COMP&DP densidad de almacenamiento *f*, CRYSTALL densidad de empaquetado *f*, ELECTRON densidad de registro *f*, P&R densidad de masa comprimida *f*, densidad de relleno *f*, TEXTIL densidad de empaquetado *f*, TV densidad de grabación *f*; ~ **effect** *n* NUCL efecto de masa *m*; ~ **fraction** *n* OPT, PHYS, TELECOM fracción de empaquetado *f*; ~ **gland** *n* MECH ENG corona de empaquetadura *f*, portaempaquetadura *m*, prensaestopas *m*, PROD, SPACE prensaestopas *m*; ~ **piece** *n*

C&G pieza para empaquetar *f*, MECH ENG calzo *m*, espaciador *m*; ~ **retainer** *n* MECH ENG retenedor de la empaquetadura *m*; ~ **ring** *n* MECH ENG *of piston* aro de guarnición *m*, aro empaquetador *m*; ~ **seal** *n* NUCL cierre de prensaestopas *m*; ~ **with siccative** *n* PACK empaquetado con un agente secante *m*; ~ **slip** *n* PROD funda de empaquetamiento *f*; ~ **station** *n* PACK sección de empaquetado *f*; ~ **stick** *n* C&G vara de empaque *f*; ~ **type** *n* PROD tipo de empaquetado *m*

packstone *n* GEOL roca carbonatada de granos y matriz micrítica *f*

pad[1] *n* AUTO forro *m*, pastilla *f*, pastilla de fricción *f*, C&G papel separador *m*, ELEC ENG, ELECTRON adaptador *m*, reductor *m*, MECH almohadilla *f*, cojinete *m*, portabrocas *m*, MECH ENG almohadilla *f*, MILIT *of tracked vehicle* amortiguador *m*, OCEAN canastilla *f*, PACK, PETR TECH, PRINT, PROD almohadilla *f*, atenuador fijo *m*, TELECOM adaptador *m*, atenuador *m*, TEXTIL relleno *m*, VEH forro *m*, pastilla *f*, pastilla de fricción *f*; ~ **dyeing** *n* COLOUR teñido mediante impregnación *m*, TEXTIL tintura en foulard *f*; ~ **foundation** *n* COAL zapata de cimentación *f*; ~ **inside rubber boot** *n* CONST amortiguador de neopreno *m*; ~ **mangle** *n* TEXTIL fulard de aprestar *m*; ~ **roller** *n* CINEMAT rodillo amortiguado *m*

pad[2] *vt* COMP&DP, PRINT rellenar, TEXTIL fulardar, poner hombreras, rellenar

PAD *abbr* (*packet assembler-disassembler*) COMP&DP, TELECOM PAD (*ensamblador-desensamblador de paquetes*)

padded[1] *adj* MECH acolchado, almohadillado, rellenado, MECH ENG acolchado, almohadillado, PACK acolchado, almohadillado, rellenado, PETR TECH, PRINT, PROD almohadillado

padded[2]: ~ **bridge** *n* INSTR puente de medida de varias tomas *m*; ~ **clothing** *n* SAFE prendas acolchadas *f pl*

padding *n* COMP&DP relleno *m*, MECH acolchado *m*, almohadillado *m*, MECH ENG acolchado *m*, almohadillado *m*, guata *f*, relleno *m*, PACK acolchado *m*, relleno *m*, almohadillado *m*, PAPER costura en bloc *f*, papel teñido en calandra *m*, PETR TECH, PRINT, PROD almohadillado *m*, SPACE acolchonado, TEXTIL foulardado *m*, picado *m*; ~ **emulsion** *n* PRINT emulsión para blocs *f*; ~ **press** *n* PRINT prensa para hacer blocs *f*

paddle *n* C&G, CINEMAT paleta *f*, HYDRAUL rueda de paletas *f*, MECH ENG *of fan, of water wheel* paleta *f*; ~ **board** *n* MECH ENG *of fan, of water wheel* paleta de rueda hidráulica *f*; ~ **boat** *n* WATER TRANSP buque de rueda *m*; ~ **mixer** *n* HYDRAUL amasadora *f*, mezclador de paletas *m*, MINE batidora de paletas *f*, mezclador de paletas *m*; ~ **wheel** *n* WATER rueda de palas *f*, WATER TRANSP *boat building* rueda de paletas *f*

padlock *n* CONST candado *m*

pads *n* PACK cartón ondulado para envasado *m*

Pag: ~ **belt** *n* CINEMAT correa Pag *f*

page[1] *n* COMP&DP, PRINT página *f*; ~ **bearer** *n* PRINT sujetador de la página *m*; ~ **bursting** *n* PRINT desborde de página *m*; ~ **depth** *n* PRINT altura de página *f*; ~ **frame** *n* COMP&DP marco de página *m*; ~ **number** *n* PRINT número de la página *m*; ~ **printer** *n* COMP&DP, PRINT impresora de páginas *f*; ~ **proof** *n* PRINT prueba de página *f*; ~ **shoe** *n* PRINT prueba de página *f*; ~ **table** *n* COMP&DP tabla de páginas *f*

page[2] *vt* COMP&DP paginar

pager *n* TELECOM paginador *m*

pages: ~ **per minute** *n pl* (*PPM*) COMP&DP páginas por minuto *f pl* (*PPM*)

paginate *vt* COMP&DP paginar, PRINT foliar, paginar, numerar páginas

pagination *n* PRINT numeración *f*, paginación *f*

paging *n* COMP&DP *display*, TELECOM paginación *f*; ~ **channel** *n* TELECOM canal de paginación *m*; ~ **service** *n* TELECOM servicio de paginación *m*

pail *n* COMP&DP balde de acero *m*, CONST cubo *m*, MAR POLL balde de acero *m*

pailful *n* CONST baldada *f*

paint *n* CONST, MECH, P&R, VEH pintura *f*; ~ **burning lamp** *n* CONST lámpara quemadora de pintura *f*; ~ **fumes** *n pl* SAFE emanaciones de pintura *f pl*; ~ **mill** *n* C&G molino para pintura *m*; ~ **remover** *n* COLOUR quitapinturas *m*; ~ **spray** *n* MECH ENG pulverizador de pintura *m*; ~ **spraying apparatus ventilation system** *n* SAFE sistema de ventilación para aspersores de pintura *m*; ~ **stripper** *n* CONST decapante de pintura *m*; ~ **thinner** *n* COATINGS, COLOUR diluyente de pintura *m*

paintbox *n* TV *communications* caja de pinturas *f*

paintbrush *n* P&R brocha *f*, pincel *m*

painted: ~ **matte** *n* CINEMAT trama pintada *f*

painter *n* WATER TRANSP *mooring* boza *f*

painting: ~ **on glass** *n* C&G pintura en vidrio *f*; ~ **on porcelain** *n* C&G pintura en porcelana *f*; ~ **varnish** *n* COATINGS pintura de barniz *f*

paintwork *n* CONST pintura *f*

pair *n* CINEMAT junta articulada *f*, ELEC ENG par *m*; ~ **annihilation** *n* NUCL *switch*, PART PHYS aniquilación de pares *f*; ~ **of dividers** *n* MECH ENG compás de dividir *m*, compás de puntas secas *m*; ~ **peaks** *n pl* RAD PHYS picos de pares *m pl*; ~ **production** *n* PART PHYS, PHYS producción de pares *f*

paired[1] *adj* CHEM *electrons*, ELEC ENG, ELECTRON, PHYS *electrons* apareado

paired[2]: ~ **cable** *n* ELEC cable de pares *m*, ELEC ENG cable de conductores pareados *m*, cable de pares *m*, TV cable de pares *m*, cable gemelo *m*; ~ **electrons** *n pl* RAD PHYS electrones pareados *m pl*

pairing *n* ELEC *cable* ELEC ENG pareado *m*, apareamiento *m*, emparejado *m*, formación de pares *f*, TV solapado de líneas *m*

pairs: ~ **of high-mass jets** *n pl* RAD PHYS pares de haces de elevada masa *m pl*

PAL[1] *abbr* COMP&DP, TELECOM (*programmable array logic*) PAL (*lógica de matriz programable, array lógico preformable, arreglo lógico programable*), TV (*programmable array logic*) sistema de línea con alternación de fase *m*

PAL[2]: ~ **color system** *AmE*, ~ **colour system** *BrE n* TV sistema de televisión en color PAL *m*

palaeoceanography *n BrE* GEOL, OCEAN paleoceanografía *f*

palaeocurrent: ~ **direction** *n BrE* GEOL dirección paleocorriente *f*

palaeogeographic: ~ **province** *n BrE* GEOL provincia paleogeográfica *f*

palaeomagnetism *n BrE* GEOL, PHYS paleomagnetismo *m*

palaeopressure *n BrE* PETR TECH paleopresión *f*

palaeoslope *n BrE* GEOL paleopendiente *f*

palaeozoic[1] *adj BrE* GEOL, PETR TECH paleozoico

palaeozoic[2] *n BrE* GEOL, PETR TECH paleozoico *m*

palagonite n PETROL palagonita f
palatability n AGRIC palatabilidad f
pale n CONST *paling, stake* valla f
paleoceanography AmE see palaeoceanography BrE
paleocurrent: ~ **direction** AmE see *palaeocurrent direction* BrE
paleogeographic: ~ **province** AmE see *palaeogeographic province* BrE
paleomagnetism AmE see palaeomagnetism BrE
paleopressure AmE see palaeopressure BrE
paleoslope AmE see palaeoslope BrE
paleozoic AmE see palaeozoic BrE
palette n TV caja de pinturas f; ~ **knife** n LAB, MECH ENG cuchillo de espátula m (AmL), espátula f (Esp)
paling n CONST *fence* estacada f, *pale, picket* palizada f
palisade n CONST empalizada f
palladic adj CHEM, METALL paládico
palladious adj CHEM, METALL paladioso
palladium n (Pd) CHEM, METALL paladio m (Pd)
pallet n AIR TRANSP bandeja f (Esp), paleta f, bandeja de carga f, plataforma para mercancías f, pálet de carga m (AmL), C&G *for glass containers* tarima f, PACK, TRANSP bandeja f, paleta f, pálet m (AmL); ~ **collar** n TRANSP collarín de la bandeja de carga m (Esp), collarín de la pálet m (AmL), collarín de paleta m (Esp); ~ **container** n TRANSP contenedor de bandejas m (Esp), contenedor de paletas m (Esp), contenedor de pálets m (AmL); ~ **for anvil** n PROD *power hammer* espiga de apoyo para el yunque f, estampa inferior f; ~**-for-tup** n PROD *power hammer* calzo de maza m; ~ **hood** n PACK cubierta para bandeja f (Esp), cubierta para paleta f (Esp), cubierta para pálet f (AmL); ~ **load** n PACK carga de la bandeja f, carga de la paleta f, carga de la pálet f (AmL); ~ **loader** n PACK cargadora de bandejas f, cargadora de paletas f, cargadora de pálets f (AmL); ~ **loading** n PACK carga de bandejas f, carga de paletas f, carga de pálets f (AmL); ~ **with loose partition** n TRANSP bandeja con separación desmontable f, paleta con separación desmontable f, paleta de una sola cara f, pálet con separación desmontable m (AmL), pálet de una sola cara m (AmL); ~ **ship** n TRANSP barco de bandejas de carga m, barco de paletas de carga m, TRANSP, barco de pálets de carga m (AmL); ~ **shrink-wrapping** n PACK envoltura de la bandeja con un material retráctil f, envoltura de la paleta con un material retráctil f, envoltura de la pálet con un material retráctil f (AmL); ~ **strapping material** n PACK flejado de la bandeja m, flejado de la paleta m, flejado de la pálet m (AmL); ~ **stretch-wrapping machine** n PACK máquina para envolver bandejas con un material estirable f (Esp), máquina para envolver paletas con un material estirable f (Esp), máquina para envolver pálets con un material estirable f (AmL); ~ **truck** n AGRIC transportador de bandejas m, transportador de paletas m, transportador de pálets m (AmL); ~ **unloading** n PACK descarga de bandejas f, descarga de paletas f, descarga de pálets f (AmL); ~ **wrapper** n PACK retractiladora de bandejas f, retractiladora de paletas f, retractiladora de pálets f (AmL)
palleting n C&G entarimado m
palletizable adj PACK, TRANSP paletalizable
palletization n PACK, TRANSP paletización f
palletize vt PACK, TRANSP paletizar
palletized: ~ **board** n PACK paletizado m; ~**-cargo**

carrier n PACK, TRANSP transporte de carga en bandeja m (Esp), transporte de carga en palét m (AmL)
palletizing n TRANSP paletizado m; ~ **adhesive** n PACK adhesivo de paletizado m
palm: ~**-kernel oil** n FOOD aceite de palmiste m; ~ **nut oil** n CHEM, FOOD aceite de palma m; ~ **oil** n CHEM, FOOD aceite de palma m
palmic adj CHEM pálmico
palmitate n CHEM palmitato m
palmitic adj CHEM palmítico
palmitin n CHEM palmitato de glicerilo m
palmitone n CHEM palmitona f
paludal: ~ **environment** n GEOL ambiente palustre m, ambiente pantanoso m
PAM[1] abbr COMP&DP, ELECTRON, SPACE (*pulse-amplitude modulation*) PAM (*modulación de amplitud de impulso, modulación de impulsos en amplitud*), SPACE, TELECOM (*pass-along message*) PAM (*modulación de amplitud de impulso, modulación de impulsos en amplitud*), transmisión de mensaje f, TELECOM (*pulse-amplitude modulation*) transmisión de mensaje f, PAM (*modulación de amplitud de impulso, modulación de impulsos en amplitud*)
PAM[2]: ~ **network** n (*pulse-amplitude modulation network*) TELECOM red con modulación de amplitud de impulsos f
pamphlet: ~ **stitching** n PRINT costura de folletos f
pan[1] n C&G bandeja f charola f (AmL), placa f, pálet m (AmL), CINEMAT toma panorámica f, COAL artesa f, batea de carga f, cuba de amalgamación f, cubeta f, cárter m, depósito m, gamella f, hoja f, losa f, tacho m, traílla f, LAB *eliquated metals* platillo m, MECH ENG bandeja f, bantea de carga f, platillo m, cárter m, patín m, caldera f, vasija f, plato m, recipiente m, perol m, MINE gamella f, traílla f, PROD cuba de amalgamación f; ~ **amalgamator** n PROD amalgamador en cubetas m; ~**-and-tilt handle** n CINEMAT barra de panorámica horizontal y vertical f; ~**-and-tilt head** n CINEMAT, PHOTO cabezal de panorámica horizontal y vertical m; ~ **filter** n COAL filtro de gamella m, INSTR filtro del patín m; ~ **handle** n CINEMAT barra de panorámica f; ~ **head** n CONST, MECH ENG, PROD *of rivet* cabeza chanfleada f, cabeza troncocónica f; ~**-head rivet** n CONST, MECH ENG, PROD remache de cabeza troncocónica m; ~**-head screw** n CONST, MECH ENG, PROD tornillo de cabeza troncocónica m; ~**-head tripod** n PHOTO trípode con cabezal panorámico horizontal m; ~ **mill** n PROD cuba de amalgamación f; ~ **roller** n PRINT rodillo de cola de la matriz m; ~ **scales** n pl LAB *eliquated metals*, METR báscula f; ~ **and scan** n TV *fixed equipment* panorámica y exploración f
pan[2] vt CINEMAT hacer panorámicas, hacer una toma panorámica; ~ **down** vt CINEMAT cabecear, hacer panorámicas hacia abajo
PAN (*peroxyacetylnitrate*) abbr CHEM, POLL PAN (*peroxoacetilnitrato, peroxiacetilnitrato*)
panabase n MINERAL cobre gris antimonial m, tetraedrita f
panaglide n CINEMAT steadicam de Panavision® m
panary: ~ **fermentation** n FOOD fermentación de masa panaria f
Panavision: ~ **system** n CINEMAT sistema Panavisión m
pancake: ~ **coil** n ELEC, ELEC ENG bobina de induc-

tancia con devanado *f*, bobina plana *f*, devanado espiral en forma de disco plano *m*; ~ **ice** *n* OCEAN tortas de hielo *f pl*; ~ **motor** *n* ELEC ENG motor con devanado en espiral *m*

panchromatic[1] *adj* CHEM, CINEMAT, PHOTO, PRINT pancromático

panchromatic[2]: ~ **emulsion** *n* CINEMAT, PHOTO emulsión pancromática *f*; ~ **film** *n* CINEMAT, PHOTO película pancromática *f*

pancreatin *n* CHEM pancreatina *f*

pandermite *n* MINERAL pandermita *f*

pane *n* CONST *of glass* cristal *m*, hoja de vidrio *f*, MECH ENG *face or side* cara *f*, PROD *of hammer* boca *f*, peña *f*

panel *n* COAL compartimiento *m*, cámara aislada *f*, CONST *of door*, ELEC *control*, GAS panel *m*, MINE compartimiento *m*, cámara aislada *f*, REFRIG panel *m*, TEXTIL tablero *m*, pieza *f*; ~ **cooler** *n* REFRIG panel de enfriamiento *m*; ~ **fabric** *n* TEXTIL tejido en paneles *m*; ~ **heater** *n* THERMO calentador de panel *m*; ~ **heating** *n* THERMO calentamiento de panel *m*; ~ **mounting** *n* ELEC *instrument, control*, PROD montaje en panel *m*; ~ **shears** *n pl* MECH ENG cizallas de mano *f pl*; ~ **system** *n* TELECOM sistema automático panel *m*, sistema panel *m*

panflavine *n* CHEM panflavina *f*

panic: ~ **bolts** *n pl* SAFE falleba de emergencia *f*

panicle *n* AGRIC panoja *f*

panne *n* TEXTIL pana *f*

panning *n* CHEM lavado en batea *m*, COMP&DP panorámica *f*

panorama: ~ **periscope** *n* NUCL periscopio panorámico *m*

panoramic: ~ **camera** *n* PHOTO cámara panorámica *f*; ~ **lens** *n* CINEMAT, OPT, PHOTO objetivo panorámico *m*; ~ **photograph** *n* PHOTO fotografía panorámica *f*; ~ **sight** *n* INSTR vista panorámica *f*; ~ **telescope** *n* INSTR telescopio panorámico *m*

pantellerite *n* PETROL pantelerita *f*

pantile *n* CONST teja canalón *f*

panting *n* OCEAN jadeo *m*, palpitación *f*

pantograph *n* ELEC, MECH ENG *drawing*, RAIL pantógrafo *m*; ~ **contact-strip** *n* MECH ENG, RAIL barra de contacto del pantógrafo *f*; ~ **dresser** *n* MECH ENG, RAIL *grinding wheels* enderezador pantógrafo *m*; ~ **slippage** *n* MECH ENG, RAIL deslizamiento del pantógrafo *m*; ~ **slipper** *n* MECH ENG, RAIL patín del pantógrafo *m*; ~ **tie-bar** *n* RAIL varilla de unión del pantógrafo *f*

pantonal: ~ **scale** *n* ACOUST escala pantonal *f*

pantothenate *n* CHEM pantotenato *m*

papain *n* CHEM, FOOD papaína *f*

papaveraldine *n* CHEM papaveraldina *f*

papaverine *n* CHEM papaverina *f*

paper *n* PAPER papel *m*; ~ **bag** *n* PACK, PAPER bolsa de papel *f*; ~**-banding machine** *n* PACK enfajadora *f*, máquina para colocar fajas de papel *f*; ~ **binding** *n* PRINT encuadernación en rústica *f*; ~ **board in the flat** *n* PAPER cartón en hojas *m*; ~ **capacitor** *n* ELEC, ELEC ENG capacitor de papel *m*, condensador con dieléctrico de papel *m*, condensador de papel *m*; ~ **chromatography** *n* CHEM cromatografía en papel *f*; ~**-chromatography apparatus** *n* CHEM, LAB aparato de cromatografía sobre papel *m*; ~**-chromatography tank** *n* CHEM, LAB tanque de cromatografía sobre papel *m*; ~ **coal** *n* COAL lignito en láminas delgadas *m*; ~ **collar** *n* TEXTIL cuello en

papel *m*; ~ **conditioning** *n* PAPER acondicionado del papel para ensayos *m*; ~**-converting industry** *n* PACK, PAPER industria de la conversión del papel *f*; ~ **core** *n* PACK mandril de papel *m*; ~ **covering** *n* COATINGS empapelado *m*; ~ **cutter** *n* PRINT guillotina *f*; ~ **for conductor insulation** *n* ELEC, PAPER papel aislante para cables eléctricos *m*; ~ **for laminated insulators** *n* ELEC, PAPER papel para aislantes laminados *m*; ~ **for long storage documents** *n* PAPER papel para documentos de larga duración *m*; ~ **for punched cards** *n* PAPER papel para fichas perforadas *m* (*Esp*), papel para tarjetas perforadas *m* (*AmL*); ~ **for textile paper tubes** *n* PAPER papel para conos de hilatura *m*, papel para tubos de hilatura *m*; ~**-forming cylinder** *n* PAPER cilindro formador *m*; ~ **gasket** *n* MECH ENG papel de empaquetadura *m*; ~ **grade** *n* PHOTO grado del papel *m*; ~ **grain** *n* PAPER grano del papel *m*; ~ **hum** *n AmE* (*cf paper stain BrE*) C&G mancha de papel *f*; ~**-insulated cable** *n* ELEC, ELEC ENG cable aislado con papel *m*; ~ **insulation** *n* ELEC, ELEC ENG aislación de papel *f*, aislamiento de papel *m*; ~ **lining** *n* COATINGS revestimiento de papel *m*; ~ **low** *n* COMP&DP falta de papel *f*; ~ **machine** *n* PAPER máquina de papel *f*; ~**-machine clothings** *n pl* PAPER *wires, felts* vestiduras *f pl*; ~**-machine drive** *n* PAPER accionamiento de la máquina de papel *m*; ~ **making** *n* PAPER fabricación de papel *f*; ~ **mill** *n* PAPER fábrica de papel *f*, RECYCL fábrica de papel *f*, papelera *f*; ~ **moisture-content** *n* PRINT contenido de humedad del papel *m*; ~ **negative** *n* PHOTO negativo en papel *m*; ~ **plate** *n* PRINT plancha de papel *f*; ~ **polisher** *n* C&G pulidor de papel *m*; ~ **pull** *n* PRINT tracción del papel *f*; ~ **pulp** *n* RECYCL pasta de madera *f*, pasta de papel *f*, pulpa de madera *f*; ~ **roll** *n* PAPER bobina de papel *f*; ~**-roll cutter** *n* PRINT cortadora de bobinas de papel *f*; ~ **run** *n* PRINT pasada del papel *f*; ~ **sack** *n* PACK saco de papel *m*; ~ **side-air permeability measurement** *n* PAPER medida de la permeabibilidad mediante flujo lateral de aire *f*; ~ **size** *n* PRINT tamaño del papel *m*; ~ **skip** *n* COMP&DP salto de papel *m*; ~ **slew** *n AmE* (*cf paper throw BrE*) COMP&DP salto de papel *m*; ~ **stain** *n BrE* (*cf paper hum AmE*) C&G mancha de papel *f*; ~ **strength** *n* PAPER, PRINT resistencia mecánica del papel *f*; ~ **swelling** *n* PAPER dilatación del papel *f*; ~ **tape** *n* COMP&DP, ELEC *insulation* cinta de papel *f*; ~**-tape loop** *n* COMP&DP bucle de cinta de papel *m*; ~**-tape punch** *n* COMP&DP perforadora de cinta de papel *f*; ~**-tape reader** *n* COMP&DP lector de cinta de papel *m*; ~ **throw** *n BrE* (*cf paper slew AmE*) COMP&DP salto de papel *m*; ~ **wallcovering** *n* COATINGS empapelado *m*; ~ **web** *n* PRINT banda de papel *f*; ~ **without finish** *n* PAPER papel sin acabado *m*; ~ **wrapping** *n* PACK envoltura de papel *f*

paperback *n* PRINT libro de tapas blandas *m*

paperclip *n* PACK clip *m*, sujetapapeles *m*

papyraceous: ~ **lignite** *n* COAL lignito papiráceo *m*

para: ~**-autochthonous unit** *n* GEOL *OR operation* unidad para-autóctona *f*

parabanic[1] *adj* CHEM parabánico

parabanic[2]: ~ **acid** *n* CHEM ácido parabánico *m*

parabenzene *n* CHEM parabenceno *m*

parabola *n* GEOM parábola *f*

parabolic: ~ **aerial** *n BrE* (*cf parabolic antenna AmE*) SPACE, TELECOM, TV antena parabólica *f*; ~ **antenna** *n AmE* (*cf parabolic aerial BrE*) SPACE, TELECOM, TV antena parabólica f; ~ **creep** n METALL estiramiento parabólico m, fluencia parabólica f; ~ **index fiber** AmE, ~ **index fibre** BrE n OPT, PHYS, TELECOM fibra de variación parabólica de índice f, fibra de índice parabólico f; ~ **mesh antenna** n SPACE *communications* red de antenas parabólicas f; ~ **mirror** n PHYS espejo parabólico m; ~ **profile** n OPT, TELECOM perfil parabólico m; ~ **profile index** n OPT, TELECOM índice de perfil parabólico m; ~ **reflector** n CINEMAT, MILIT, PHOTO reflector parabólico m; ~ **reflector aerial** n BrE (*cf parabolic reflector antenna* AmE) TELECOM antena de reflector parabólico f; ~ **reflector antenna** n AmE (*cf parabolic reflector aerial* BrE) TELECOM antena de reflector parabólico f; ~ **shading** n TV sombreado parabólico m; ~ **trough conveyor** n (*PTC*) INSTR transportador de cinta cóncava parabólico m (*PTC*); ~ **velocity** n SPACE velocidad parabólica f

paraboloidal: ~ **aerial** n BrE (*cf paraboloidal antenna* AmE) SPACE antena paraboloidal f; ~ **antenna** n AmE (*cf paraboloidal aerial* BrE) SPACE antena paraboloidal f

parabrake n SPACE *craft* paracaídas frenante de cola m

paracetaldehyde n CHEM paracetaldehído m

parachor n CHEM paracoro m

parachute n AIR TRANSP, SPACE *craft* paracaídas m; ~ **cluster** n MILIT conjunto de paracaídas m; ~ **drop** n MILIT salto en paracaídas m; ~ **flare** n MILIT, WATER TRANSP *pyrotechnic, distress signal* bengala con paracaídas f; ~ **landing** n AIR TRANSP, MILIT aterrizaje en paracaídas m; ~ **pack** n MILIT bolsa del paracaídas f; ~ **with pilot** n MILIT paracaídas con piloto m; ~ **release handle** n AIR TRANSP anilla de apertura del paracaídas f

parachutist n MILIT paracaidista m

parachymosin n CHEM pararenina f

paracresol n CHEM paracresol m

paracusis n ACOUST paracusia f

paracyanogen n CHEM paracianógeno m

paradichlorobenzene n CHEM paradiclorobenceno m

paradigm n COMP&DP paradigma m

paradrop n AIR TRANSP lanzamiento en paracaídas m

paraffin n BrE (*cf kerosene* AmE) AIR TRANSP, CHEM, PETR TECH, PETROL, THERMO, TRANSP parafina f; ~ **coating** n BrE (*cf kerosene coating* AmE) PACK cobertura de parafina f; ~ **oil** n BrE (*cf kerosene oil* AmE) CHEM, PETR TECH, PETROL, THERMO aceite de parafina m, petróleo lampante m; ~ **series** n BrE (*cf kerosene series* AmE) PETR TECH serie de parafina f; ~ **wax** n BrE (*cf kerosene wax* AmE) CHEM cera de parafina f, ELEC *insulator* cera de parafina f, parafina sólida f

paraffinic *adj* CHEM parafínico

parafoil n SPACE parapista f

paragenesis n GEOL paragénesis f

paragonite n MINERAL paragonita f

paragraph n PRINT párrafo m

parahydrogen n CHEM parahidrógeno m

paraisomer n CHEM paraisómero m

paraldehyde n CHEM paraldehído m

paralic *adj* GEOL *floppy disc* parálico

parallax n CINEMAT, MECH ENG, PHOTO, PHYS paralaje m; ~ **correction** n CINEMAT corrección de paralaje f; ~**-free viewfinder** n CINEMAT visor sin paralaje m

parallel[1]: ~ *adj* COMP&DP, ELEC *circuit*, GEOM, TEXTIL *circuit* paralelo; **in** ~ *adj* GEOM, TEXTIL en paralelo;

~**-connected** *adj* ELEC, ELEC ENG, PHYS acoplado en paralelo, conectado en derivación, conectado en paralelo; ~**-fed** *adj* AIR TRANSP alimentado en paralelo

parallel[2] *adv* GEOM paralelamente

parallel[3]: ~ **access** n COMP&DP acceso en paralelo m; ~ **adder** n COMP&DP, ELECTRON sumador paralelo m; ~ **algorithm** n COMP&DP, MATH, SPACE algoritmo paralelo m; ~ **arithmetic** n COMP&DP, MATH aritmética en paralelo f; ~ **arm-type suspension** n AUTO suspensión de tipo brazo paralelo f, VEH suspensión de tipo brazo paralelo; ~ **arrangement** n ELEC ENG disposición en paralelo f, instalación en paralelo f; ~ **band** n RAD PHYS banda paralela f; ~ **beam** n ELECTRON, PHYS haz paralelo m; ~ **circuit** n ELEC, MINE, TELECOM circuito en derivación m, circuito en paralelo m; ~ **computer** n COMP&DP computador en paralelo m (*AmL*), computadora en paralelo f (*AmL*), ordenador en paralelo m (*Esp*); ~ **condition** n PROD disposición en paralelo f; ~**-connected resistance** n ELEC resistencia conectada en paralelo f; ~ **connection** n ELEC, ELEC ENG conexión en derivación f, conexión en cantidad f, conexión en paralelo f, conexión en shunt f, acoplamiento en paralelo m, MINE acoplamiento en cantidad m, acoplamiento en derivación m, PHYS conexión en paralelo f; ~ **control device** n ELEC *tap-changer* dispositivo de control en paralelo m; ~ **conversion** n ELECTRON conversión paralela f; ~ **converter** n ELECTRON convertidor paralelo m; ~ **cut** n MINE excavación paralela f, rafadura paralela f, socavación paralela f; ~ **digital signal** n ELECTRON señal digital paralela f; ~ **dowel** n MECH ENG pasador paralelo m; ~ **feeder** n ELEC alimentador en paralelo m, alimentador en shunt m; ~ **fence** n PROD *of saw bench* guía rectilínea f; ~ **file** n MECH ENG lima de bordes paralelos f; ~**-flow heat-exchanger** n HEAT ENG intercambiador de calor de flujos paralelos m, NUCL cambiador de calor de caudales en paralelo m, intercambiador de calor de flujos paralelos m, REFRIG, THERMO intercambiador de calor de flujos paralelos m; ~ **flow turbine** n HYDRAUL turbina axial f, turbina de caudal paralelo f; ~ **fold** n GEOL *computer* pliegue paralelo m; ~ **form** n ELEC ENG, GEOM forma en paralelo f; ~**-free viewfinder** n CINEMAT visor sin paralaje m; ~ **gluing** n PACK aplicación del adhesivo en líneas paralelas f; ~ **gutter** n CONST *building* cuneta paralela f; ~ **input-output** n COMP&DP entrada/salida en paralelo f; ~ **interface** n PRINT interfaz en paralelo m; ~ **involute gear** n MECH ENG dispositivo evolvente paralelo m; ~ **jaw capacity** n MECH ENG capacidad de mordaza paralela f; ~ **lay** n ELEC ENG colocación en paralelo f; ~ **lines** n pl GEOM líneas paralelas f pl, rectas paralelas f pl; ~ **magazine camera** n CINEMAT cámara de chasis paralelo f; ~ **mark** n PRINT signo igual m; ~ **milling cutter** n MECH ENG fresa paralela f; ~ **mounting** n ELEC *circuit* montaje en paralelo m; ~ **mouse** n COMP&DP ratón paralelo m; ~ **mouse-adaptor** n COMP&DP adaptador de ratón paralelo m; ~ **multiplier** n ELECTRON multiplicador paralelo m; ~ **operation** n PRINT operación paralela f; ~ **pin** n MECH ENG pasador paralelo m; ~ **pin with internal thread** n MECH ENG pasador paralelo con rosca interna m; ~ **pipe-thread** n MECH ENG rosca para tuberías paralela f; ~**-plate capacitor** n ELEC ENG,

PHYS condensador de placas paralelas *m*, condensador de planos paralelos *m*; ~ **port** *n* COMP&DP puerto paralelo *m*; ~ **positioning** *n* AIR TRANSP posicionamiento paralelo *m*; ~ **processing** *n* COMP&DP, ELECTRON, TELECOM procesamiento en paralelo *m*; ~ **resistance** *n* ELEC ENG resistencia en paralelo *f*; ~ **resonance** *n* ELECTRON, PHYS resonancia paralela *f*; ~ **resonant circuit** *n* ELECTRON circuito de resonancia paralelo *m*; ~ **rule** *n* MECH ENG regla paralela *f*; ~ **ruler** *n* MECH ENG, WATER TRANSP *navigation* regla de paralelas *f*, regla para trazar paralelas *f*; ~ **search storage** *AmE*, ~ **search store** *BrE* COMP&DP memoria de búsqueda en paralelo *f*; ~-**shank tools** *n pl* MECH ENG herramientas de mango paralelo *f pl*; ~-**shank twist drill** *n* MECH ENG broca helicoidal de cola cilíndrica *f*; ~ **spark gap** *n* ELEC abertura de chispas en paralelo *f*, distancia interelectródica *f*, ELEC ENG abertura de chispas en paralelo *f*; ~ **storage** *n* ELEC ENG memoria magnética de registro en paralelo *f*; ~ **synchronous system** *n* TELECOM sistema síncrono en paralelo *m*; ~-**to-serial conversion** *n* ELEC ENG conversión de paralelo a serie *f*; ~-**to-serial converter** *n* ELEC ENG conversor de paralelo a serie *m*; ~ **transfer** *n* COMP&DP transferencia en paralelo *f*; ~ **transmission** *n* COMP&DP, TELECOM transmisión en paralelo *f*; ~ **vane-attenuator** *n* ELECTRON atenuador de álabe en paralelo *m*; ~ **vice** *n* *BrE* MECH ENG tornillo de banco de movimiento paralelo *m*, tornillo de banco paralelo *m*; ~ **vise** *AmE see parallel vice BrE*; ~-**wire line** *n* ELEC línea bifilar *f*, ELEC ENG línea bifilar *f*, línea de conductores paralelos *f*; ~-**wound yarn** *n* TEXTIL hilo enrollado en paralelo *m*

paralleling *n* ELEC ENG acoplamiento en derivación *m*, conexión en paralelo *f*, montaje en paralelo *m*, puesta en paralelo *f*

parallelism *n* GEOM, MECH ENG, TEXTIL paralelismo *m*

parallelization: ~ **of fibers** *AmE*, ~ **of fibres** *BrE n* TEXTIL disposición en paralelo de las fibras *f*

parallelogram *n* GEOM, MECH paralelogramo *m*; ~ **of forces** *n* GEOM, PHYS paralelogramo de fuerzas *m*; ~ **of velocities** *n* PHYS paralelogramo de velocidades *m*

paramagnetic[1] *adj* ELEC *material*, PHYS paramagnético

paramagnetic[2]: ~ **amplifier** *n* ELECTRON amplificador paramagnético *m*; ~ **Curie point** *n* RAD PHYS punto paramagnético de Curie *m*; ~ **material** *n* PETROL material paramagnético *m*; ~ **rail** *n* TRANSP carril paramagnético *m*, rail paramagnético *m*, riel paramagnético *m*; ~ **resonance** *n* ELEC, ELECTRON, PHYS *of transformer* resonancia paramagnética *f*

paramagnetism *n* ELEC, PHYS paramagnetismo *m*

parameter *n* COMP&DP, ELECTRON, PHYS parámetro *m*; ~ **out-of-range class** *n* TELECOM parámetro de categoría fuera de rango *m*; ~ **passing** *n* COMP&DP transmisión de parámetros *f*; ~ **profile** *n* TELECOM perfil del parámetro *m*; ~ **substitution** *n* COMP&DP sustitución de parámetros *f*; ~ **value** *n* (*PV*) TELECOM valor de parámetro *m*

parameterization *n* COMP&DP parametrización *f*

parametric[1] *adj* COMP&DP paramétrico

parametric[2]: ~ **amplification** *n* ELECTRON, PHYS, SPACE, TELECOM amplificación paramétrica *f*; ~ **amplifier** *n* (*paramp*) ELECTRON, PHYS, SPACE, TELECOM amplificador paramétrico *m*; ~ **amplifier diode**

n ELECTRON diodo de amplificador paramétrico *m*; ~ **analysis** *n* ELECTRON análisis paramétrico *m*; ~ **coordinates** *n pl* GEOM coordenadas paramétricas *f pl*; ~ **laser** *n* ELECTRON láser paramétrico *m*; ~ **oscillator** *n* TELECOM oscilador paramétrico *m*; ~ **test** *n* TELECOM prueba paramétrica *f*

paramp *n* (*parametric amplifier*) ELECTRON, PHYS, SPACE, TELECOM amplificador paramétrico *m*

paranthine *n* MINERAL parantina *f*

parapet *n* CONST parapeto *m*; ~ **gutter** *n* CONST canalón de pretil *m*

paraphase: ~ **amplifier** *n* ELECTRON, TV amplificador desfasador *m*

pararennin *n* CHEM pararenina *f*

pararosaniline *n* CHEM pararosanilina *f*

parasite *n* MINERAL parasita *f*

parasitic[1] *adj* ELECTRON parásito

parasitic[2]: ~ **aerial** *n* *BrE* (*cf parasitic antenna AmE*) PHYS antena parásita *f*; ~ **antenna** *n* *AmE* (*cf parasitic aerial BrE*) PHYS antena parásita *f*; ~ **capacitance** *n* ELEC ENG capacitancia parásita *f*; ~ **capture** *n* NUCL *eliquated metals* captura parásita *f*; ~ **component** *n* ELEC ENG componente parásita *f*; ~ **coupling** *n* ELEC ENG, TELECOM acoplamiento parásito *m*; ~ **crater** *n* GEOL *communications, antennas, aircraft* cráter parásito *m*; ~ **current** *n* ELEC ENG corriente de Foucault *f*, corriente parásita *f*; ~ **diode** *n* ELECTRON diodo parásito *m*; ~ **drag** *n* AIR TRANSP resistencia aerodinámica parasítica *f*, retardo parasítico *m*; ~ **element** *n* PHYS elemento parásito *m*; ~ **inductance** *n* ELEC, ELEC ENG inductancia parásita *f*; ~ **oscillation** *n* PHYS, TELECOM oscilación parásita *f*; ~ **radiation** *n* TV radiación parásita *f*; ~ **suppressor** *n* ELECTRON eliminador de ruidos parásitos *m*; ~ **transistor** *n* ELECTRON transistor parásito *m*

paratartaric *adj* CHEM paratartárico

paratypical *adj* CHEM paratípico

paraxial: ~ **ray** *n* OPT, PHYS, TELECOM rayo paraxial *m*

paraxylene *n* CHEM, PETR TECH paraxileno *m*

parboil *vt* FOOD cocer parcialmente

parcel *n* TRANSP bulto *m*, fardo *m*, paquete *m*; ~ **of ore** *n* MINE cantidad de minerales *f* (*AmL*), porción de minerales *f* (*Esp*); ~ **registration card** *n* TRANSP tarjeta de identificación de paquete *f*

parcelled: ~ **goods** *n* PACK mercancías empaquetadas *f pl*

parcelling: ~ **machine** *n* PACK empaquetadora *f*

parcels: ~ **chute** *n* TRANSP tobogán de paquetes *m*; ~ **counter** *n* TRANSP mostrador de paquetes *m*; ~ **depot** *n* TRANSP depósito de paquetes *m*; ~ **office** *n* TRANSP oficina de paquetería *f*

parchment: ~ **paper** *n* FOOD papel encerado *m*, PACK papel pergamino *m*, PAPER papel encerado *m*, papel pergamino *m*

pare *vt* PRINT recortar

parent *n* COMP&DP *node* padre *m*; ~ **acid** *n* CHEM ácido precursor *m*; ~ **fraction** *n* NUCL fracción de precursores *f*; ~ **mass peak** *n* NUCL pico másico de precursores *m*; ~ **nuclide** *n* NUCL nucleido padre *m*, nucleido precursor *m*, RAD PHYS nucleido padre *m*; ~ **peak** *n* NUCL pico de precursores *m*; ~ **phase** *n* METALL fase generatriz *f*; ~ **roll** *n* CINEMAT rollo matriz *m*

parenthesis: ~-**free notation** *n* COMP&DP notación sin paréntesis *f*

pargasite n MINERAL pargasita f
paring: ~ **chisel** n CONST, MECH ENG formón m;
~ **machine** n CONST, MECH ENG *wood trimmer* formón
m
parison n C&G vela f; ~ **check** n C&G estrellada en la
vela f; ~ **gatherer** n C&G recogedor de velas m;
~ **mold** AmE, ~ **mould** BrE n C&G bombillo m
parity n COMP&DP, PHYS, RAD PHYS paridad f; ~ **bit** n
COMP&DP bit de paridad m; ~ **check** n COMP&DP
verificación de paridad f; ~ **conservation law** n
RAD PHYS ley de conservación de la paridad f;
~ **control** n TELECOM control de paridad m; ~ **digit**
n COMP&DP dígito de paridad m; ~ **error** n COMP&DP
error de paridad m; ~ **transformation operation** n
PART PHYS operación de transformación de la paridad
f
park vt TV aparcar, estacionar (AmL)
parked[1] adj TELECOM estacionado
parked[2]: ~ **line** n TELECOM línea estacionada f
parking: ~ **area** n AIR TRANSP área de aparcamiento f,
CONST plaza de aparcamiento f (Esp), plaza de
estacionamiento f (AmL), zona de aparcamiento f
(Esp), zona de estacionamiento f (AmL), SPACE área
de aparcamiento f; ~ **brake** n AIR TRANSP freno de
aparcamiento m, AUTO freno de estacionamiento m,
MECH *brazing lamp* freno de estacionamiento m,
freno de parada m, RAIL, VEH freno de estacionamiento m; ~-**brake lever** n VEH palanca de freno de
estacionamiento f; ~ **gear** n AUTO engranaje de
aparcamiento m, engranaje de estacionamiento m,
marcha de aparcamiento f; ~ **lock-gear** n AUTO
engranaje de bloqueo para estacionamiento m,
marcha de bloqueo para estacionamiento f; ~ **orbit**
n MILIT *of satellite* órbita de aparcamiento f, SPACE
órbita de aparcamiento f, órbita de espera f, órbita de
estabilización f; ~ **pawl** n AUTO trinquete de aparcamiento m, trinquete del freno de estacionamiento m
parrot: ~-**nose pipe wrench** n CONST llave curva de
tubería f
parse vt COMP&DP analizar sintácticamente
parsec n PHYS parsec m
parser n COMP&DP programa de análisis sintáctico m
parsing n COMP&DP análisis sintáctico m
part[1] n AUTO pieza de repuesto f, COMP&DP pieza f,
MECH ENG componente m, elemento m, fragmento m,
parte f, pieza f, pieza de repuesto f, porción f, PROD *of
a mould* coquilla f, TEXTIL parte f, VEH pieza de
repuesto f; ~ **load** n AUTO carga parcial f; ~-**load
consignment** n TRANSP envío de carga parcial m;
~-**load efficiency** n MECH ENG eficiencia de carga
reducida f; ~-**load freight** n AmE (cf part-load goods
BrE) TRANSP carga parcial de mercancías f; ~-**load
goods** BrE n pl (cf part-load freight AmE) TRANSP
carga parcial de mercancías f; ~-**load traffic** n RAIL
tráfico de cargas parciales m; ~ **loads** n pl TRANSP
cargas parciales f pl; ~ **number** n PACK número de la
pieza m; ~ **owner** n WATER TRANSP *of ship* copropietario m, socio m; ~-**turn actuator attachment** n
MECH ENG accesorio actuador de giro parcial m;
~-**winding starting** n AUTO arranque del devanado
de piezas m, ELEC *motor* arranque del devanado de
piezas m, puesta en marcha del arrollamiento de
piezas f, ELEC ENG, MECH ENG arranque del devanado
de piezas m
part[2] vi MECH ENG desprenderse, partirse, romperse,
zafarse

partial[1] adj ACOUST parcial
partial[2] n ACOUST parcial m; ~ **carry** n COMP&DP
acarreo parcial m; ~ **coating** n COATINGS revestimiento parcial m; ~ **coherence** n OPT, TELECOM
coherencia parcial f; ~ **discharge** n ELEC *condenser*
descarga parcial f; ~-**discharge inception test** n
ELEC prueba inicial de descarga parcial f;
~ **dislocation** n CRYSTALL, METALL dislocación parcial f; ~ **exposure** n PRINT exposición parcial f;
~ **node** n ACOUST nodo parcial m, ELEC ENG nodo
imperfecto m; ~ **plating** n COATINGS chapado parcial
m; ~ **pressure** n CHEM *vapour*, PHYS presión parcial f;
~-**recovery refrigeration system** n REFRIG sistema
de enfriamiento con refrigerante parcialmente recuperado m; ~ **reflection** n WAVE PHYS reflexión parcial
f; ~-**response code** n TELECOM código de respuesta
parcial m; ~ **time to date** n PROD plazo parcial a la
fecha m; ~ **trip** n NUCL disparo parcial m; ~-**voltage
starting** n ELEC *motor* arranque por tensión parcial
m, puesta en marcha por tensión parcial f
particle n ACOUST, ELECTRON, PART PHYS, PHYS partícula f, RAD PHYS partícula de fuga f, partícula ilesa f,
SAFE, TELECOM, TEXTIL partícula f; ~ **acceleration** n
ACOUST, ELECTRON, NUCL, PART PHYS, PHYS aceleración de partículas f; ~ **accelerator** n ACOUST,
ELECTRON, NUCL, PART PHYS, PHYS acelerador de
partículas m; ~ **beam** n ELECTRON, PART PHYS haz de
partículas m; ~-**beam technology** n ELECTRON, PART
PHYS tecnología de haz de partículas f; ~ **board** n
MECH *brazing-lamp* tabla de partículas f, PAPER
tablero de partículas m; ~ **classification** n CHEM
TECH clasificación de partículas f; ~ **collision** n
PART PHYS colisión de partículas m; ~ **dynamics** n
NUCL dinámica de las masas en movimiento f,
dinámica de partículas f, PART PHYS dinámica de
partículas f; ~ **fluence** n PART PHYS, PHYS fluencia de
partículas f; ~-**fluence rate** n PART PHYS, PHYS tasa de
fluencia de partículas f; ~ **leakage** n NUCL fuga de
partículas f; ~ **number** n METALL número de partículas m; ~ **number conservation law** n NUCL ley de
conservación numérica de partículas f; ~ **physics** n
PART PHYS, PHYS física de partículas f;
~ **reinforcement** n METALL reforzamiento de partículas m; ~ **separation** n PART PHYS separación de
partículas f; ~-**shape factor** n CHEM TECH factor de
forma de partículas m; ~ **siever** n CHEM TECH
tamizador de gránulos m; ~ **size** n CHEM, CHEM
TECH, METALL, NUCL, P&R tamaño de la partícula
m; ~-**size analyser** n CHEM TECH aparato de
granulometría m; ~-**size curve** n C&G curva granulométrica f; ~-**size distribution** n CHEM *of powder*
CONST distribución del tamaño de partículas f; ~-**size
measurement** n P&R medida del tamaño de partículas f; ~-**size reduction** n CHEM TECH reducción del
tamaño de partículas f, reducción granulométrica f,
COAL reducción del tamaño de partículas f; ~ **sizing** n
CHEM TECH medición de partículas f; ~ **storage** n
PART PHYS almacenamiento de partículas m; ~ **tra-
jectories buffeted by turbulent molecules** n pl RAD
PHYS trayectorias de partículas sacudidas por molé-
culas turbulentas f pl; ~ **velocity** n ACOUST velocidad
de partículas f
particles: ~ **identified as having spins 0, 1/2, 1, 3/2, 2**
n pl PART PHYS partículas identificadas con spin 0, 1/
2, 1, 3/2, 2 f pl
particulate n CHEM TECH particulado m; ~-**fluidized**

bed *n* CHEM TECH, HEAT lecho fluidizado particulado *m*; ~ **materials** *n pl* POLL materia granulosa *f*, materia particulada *f*; ~ **matter** *n* POLL materia granulosa *f*, materia particulada *f*, partículas *f pl*; ~ **removal of air pollutants** *n* POLL eliminación de partículas contaminantes del aire *f*, remoción de partículas contaminantes del aire *f*, retirada de partículas contaminantes del aire *f*, separación de partículas contaminantes del aire *f*

parting *n* CHEM separación de metales nobles *f*, MECH ENG plano de junta *m*, plano de separación *m*, ruptura *f*, separación *f*, bifurcación *f*, división *f*, tabique *m*, PROD *of mould* junta *f*; ~ **blade** *n* MECH ENG cuchilla de trocear *f*; ~ **dust** *n* PROD *foundry* arena de espolvorear *f*; ~ **line** *n* PROD *foundry, moulding box* junta *f*; ~-**off blade** *n* MECH ENG *for tool holder* cuchilla de trocear *f*; ~ **pulley** *n* MECH ENG polea desmontable *f*; ~ **sand** *n* PROD arena para espolvorear moldes *f*; ~ **tool** *n* MECH ENG bedano *m*, escoplo triangular *m*, herramienta de trocear *f*, tronzador *m*; ~ **tools** *n pl* MECH ENG *of lathe* herramientas de sangrar *f pl*; ~ **of the waters** *n* HYDROL división de las aguas *f*

partition[1] *n* COMP&DP partición *f*, CONST tabique divisorio *m*, mediana *f*, NUCL *colours in clothes* partición *f*; ~ **chromatography** *n* CHEM cromatografía de partición *f*, cromatografía de reparto *f*; ~ **coefficient** *n* CHEM *between phases* coeficiente de distribución *m*, coeficiente de partición *m*, coeficiente de reparto *m*, METALL coeficiente de partición *m*; ~ **density** *n* COAL densidad de partición *f*; ~ **function** *n* PHYS función de partición *f*; ~ **gate** *n* ELEC ENG entrada de distribución *f*; ~ **noise** *n* ELECTRON ruido de partición *m*; ~ **size** *n* COAL tamaño de partición *m*; ~ **wall** *n* CONST pared divisoria *f*, PACK pieza de separación *f*

partition[2] *vt* COMP&DP partir

partitioned[1] *adj* COMP&DP dividido, partido

partitioned[2]: ~ **charge** *n* ELEC, ELEC ENG carga repartida *f*

partitioning *n* CHEM partición *f*, reparto *m*, COMP&DP partición *f*, CONST *placing partitions* tabiquería *f*, *placing walls* medianería *f*, ELEC ENG reparto *m*; ~ **insert** *n* PACK inserción de medianerías *f*

parton *n* PHYS partón *m*

parts: ~ **list** *n* PROD nomenclatura *f*; ~ **per million** *n pl* (*ppm*) CHEM partes por millón *f* (*ppm*); ~ **requisition** *n* PROD petición de piezas *f*

party: ~ **address** *n* TELECOM dirección compartida *f*; ~ **wall** *n* CONST pared medianera *f*

parvoline *n* CHEM parvolina *f*

pascal *n* (*Pa*) GEN pascal *m* (*Pa*)

Pascal: ~'s **principle** *n* PHYS principio de Pascal *m*

Paschen: ~'s **law** *n* PHYS ley de Paschen *f*; ~ **series** *n* PHYS series de Paschen *f pl*; ~ **series lines** *n pl* RAD PHYS líneas de Paschen *f pl*

Paschen-Back: ~ **effect** *n* PHYS efecto Paschen-Back *m*

pass[1] *n* COMP&DP paso *m*, MINE chimenea *f* (*AmL*), coladero *m* (*Esp*), paso *m*, PROD pasada *f*, canal *m*, WATER TRANSP *geography* paso *m*; ~-**along message** *n* (*PAM*) SPACE, TELECOM transmisión de mensaje *f*; ~ **band** *n* COMP&DP banda de paso *f*, banda pasante *f*, ELECTRON paso banda *m*, MECH ENG banda de paso *f*, banda de transmisión libre *f*, banda pasante *f*, PHYS pasabanda *m*, TELECOM banda de paso *f*, banda

pasante *f*; ~-**band attenuation** *n* ELECTRON atenuación paso banda *f*; ~-**band response** *n* ELECTRON respuesta paso banda *f*; ~ **transistor** *n* ELECTRON transistor de paso *m*

pass[2] *vt* PRINT aprobar, RAIL pasar

pass[3]: ~ **through a lock** *vi* WATER TRANSP pasar por una esclusa

passage *n* AUTO conducto *m*, PROD conducto tubular *m*, WATER TRANSP *navigation* pasaje *m*, travesía *f*, tránsito *m*; ~ **bed** *n* GEOL capa de transición *f*; ~ **detector** *n* TRANSP detector de tránsito *m*; ~ **of water** *n* PROD agujero de agua *m*, paso de agua *m*

passageway *n* MINE galería *f* (*AmL*), galería de servicio *f* (*Esp*), pasadizo *m* (*AmL*), pasarela *f*, transversal *f* (*Esp*)

passenger *n* AIR TRANSP, RAIL, SPACE, TRANSP pasajero *m*, viajero *m*, viajera *f*; ~ **automobile** *n* AmE (*cf passenger car BrE*) TRANSP coche de viajeros *m*, VEH coche de turismo *m*, coche para uso particular *m*; ~ **bridge** *n* AIR TRANSP aeropuente de pasajeros *m*, puente aéreo de pasajeros *m*; ~ **cabin** *n* TRANSP cabina de pasajeros *f*, camarote de pasaje *m*; ~ **car** *n* (*cf passenger automobile AmE*) TRANSP vagón de pasajeros *m*, cabina de ascensor *f*, coche de pasajeros *m*, coche de viajeros *m*, VEH coche de turismo *m*, coche para uso particular *m*; ~ **car equivalent** *n* TRANSP equivalente a coche de pasajeros *m*; ~ **car unit** *n* (*PCU*) TRANSP unidad de pasajeros *f*, unidad de viajeros *f*; ~ **coach** *n* TRANSP coche de viajeros *m*; ~ **compartment** *n* TRANSP compartimiento de pasajeros *m*; ~ **conveyor** *n* BrE (*cf moving sidewalk AmE*) AIR TRANSP *at airport* cinta transportadora de pasajeros *f*, pasillo mecánico *m*; ~ **elevator** *n* AmE (*cf passenger lift BrE*) TRANSP ascensor de pasajeros *m*; ~ **hall** *n* TRANSP sala de pasajeros *f*; ~ **information center** AmE, ~ **information centre** BrE *n* RAIL centro de información para los viajeros *m*; ~ **kilometer** AmE, ~ **kilometre** BrE *n* TRANSP pasajero-kilómetro *m*; ~ **lift** *n* BrE (*cf passenger elevator AmE*) TRANSP ascensor de pasajeros *m*; ~ **reservation system** *n* TRANSP sistema de reservaciones de pasajeros *m* (*AmL*), sistema de reservas de pasajeros *m* (*Esp*); ~ **ropeway** *n* TRANSP funicular de pasajeros *m*; ~ **seat** *n* AIR TRANSP asiento de pasajero *m*; ~ **service** *n* TRANSP servicio de pasajeros *m*; ~ **ship** *n* WATER TRANSP buque de pasaje *m*, corredera mecánica *f*, malva india *f*; ~ **terminal** *n* TRANSP terminal de pasajeros *f*; ~ **transport** *n* TRANSP transporte de pasajeros *m*

passing: ~ **aid** *n* TRANSP ayuda en carretera *f*; ~ **lane** *n* CONST camino para pasar *m*; ~ **light** *n* VEH luz de cruce *f*; ~ **point** *n* RAIL punto de paso *m*; ~ **sight distance** *n* TRANSP distancia de visibilidad en adelantamiento *f*; ~ **track** *n* RAIL vía apartadero *f*; ~ **track in station** *n* RAIL vía apartadero en la estación *f*

passivate *vt* CHEM, ELECTRON, PHYS, SPACE neutralizar, pasivar

passivated[1] *adj* CHEM, ELECTRON, PHYS, SPACE pasivado

passivated[2]: ~ **transistor** *n* ELECTRON transistor pasivado *m*

passivation *n* CHEM, ELECTRON, PHYS, SPACE neutralización *f*, pasivación *f*; ~ **layer** *n* ELECTRON estratificador de pasivación *m*

passive[1] *adj* COMP&DP pasivo, ELECTRON estático, pasivo

passive[2]: ~ **aerial** *n* BrE (*cf passive antenna AmE*) PHYS antena pasiva *f*; ~ **air defence** *n* BrE MILIT defensa antiaérea pasiva *f*; ~ **air defense** *AmE see passive air defence BrE*; ~ **alerting** *n* TELECOM alarma pasiva *f*, alerta pasiva *f*; ~ **antenna** *n* AmE (*cf passive aerial BrE*) PHYS antena pasiva *f*; ~ **band-pass filter** *n* ELECTRON filtro de paso de banda estático *m*, filtro de paso de banda pasivo *m*; ~ **band-stop filter** *n* ELECTRON filtro eliminador de banda pasivo *m*; ~ **circuit** *n* PHYS, TELECOM circuito pasivo *m*; ~ **component** *n* ELECTRON, NUCL, PHYS componente pasivo *m*, TELECOM componente pasivo *m*, elemento pasivo *m*; ~ **control** *n* SPACE control pasivo *m*; ~ **dipole** *n* ELEC ENG, PHYS, TELECOM dipolo pasivo *m*; ~ **earth pressure** *n* COAL empuje de tierras pasivo *m*, CONST empuje pasivo *m*; ~ **electrodynamic damper** *n* SPACE *craft* amortiguador electrodinámico pasivo *m*; ~ **element** *n* ELECTRON elemento pasivo *m*; ~ **filter** *n* ELECTRON, TELECOM filtro estático *m*, filtro pasivo *m*; ~ **filtering** *n* ELECTRON, TELECOM filtro estático *m*, filtro pasivo *m*; ~ **flat car** *n* TRANSP camión de plataforma estática *m*, camión de plataforma pasiva *m*, vagón plataforma *m*; ~ **infrared detector** *n* GAS, PHYS, TRANSP detector pasivo de infrarrojos *m*; ~ **load** *n* ELEC ENG carga pasiva *f*; ~ **mode** *n* ELECTRON función pasiva *f*, modo pasivo *m*; ~ **motor-vehicle safety** *n* TRANSP seguridad pasiva de vehículos de motor *f*; ~ **network** *n* ELEC, ELEC ENG red pasiva *f*; ~ **occupant-restraint system** *n* TRANSP sistema pasivo de sujeción del pasajero *m*; ~ **optical network** *n* (*PON*) TELECOM red óptica pasiva *f*; ~ **quadripole** *n* ELEC ENG cuadrípolo pasivo *m*; ~ **satellite** *n* SPACE, TV satélite pasivo *m*; ~ **seatbelt system** *n* TRANSP sistema pasivo de cinturón de seguridad *m*; ~ **sensor** *n* ELECTRON, SPACE sensor pasivo *m*; ~ **solar system** *n* CONST sistema solar pasivo *m*; ~ **star** *n* COMP&DP *network topology* estrella pasiva *f*; ~ **substrate** *n* ELECTRON substrato pasivo *m*; ~ **system** *n* ACOUST, FUELLESS sistema pasivo *m*; ~ **thermal control** *n* (*PTC*) SPACE control térmico pasivo *m* (*PTC*); ~ **threat** *n* TELECOM amenaza pasiva *f*; ~ **transducer** *n* ELEC ENG transductor pasivo *m*; ~ **transport unit** *n* TRANSP unidad de transporte no motora *f*

password *n* COMP&DP, TELECOM contraseña *f*; ~ **protection** *n* COMP&DP protección por contraseña *f*

paste[1] *n* SPACE *spacecraft* engrudo *m*, materia activa *f*, pasta *f*; ~ **fuel** *n* NUCL combustible en pasta *m*; ~ **ink** *n* COLOUR tinta en pasta *f*; ~ **mold** *AmE see paste mould BrE*; ~**-mold blowing** *AmE see paste-mould blowing BrE*; ~**-mold press-and-blow process** *AmE see paste-mould press-and-blow process BrE*; ~ **mould** *n* BrE C&G molde empastado *m*; ~**-mould blowing** *n* BrE C&G soplado en molde empastado *m*, soplo en molde empastado *m*; ~**-mould press-and-blow process** *n* BrE C&G proceso de prensa con molde empastado *m*, proceso de soplo con molde empastado *m*; ~**-up** *n* PRINT montaje de originales *m*

paste[2] *vt* PAPER contracolar; ~ **up** *vt* PRINT montar originales

pasted[1] *adj* PRINT pegado

pasted[2]: ~ **board** *n* PAPER cartón contracolado *m*; ~**-ivory board** *n* PAPER cartulina marfil *f*; ~ **lined board** *n* PAPER cartón forrado *m*; ~ **paper** *n* PAPER papel contracolado *m*, papel pegado *m*; ~ **sack** *n* PACK saco pegado *m*

paster *n* PAPER empalmadora *f*

Pasteur: ~ **pipette** *n* LAB *process* pipeta Pasteur *f*

pasteurization *n* CHEM, FOOD, QUALITY, THERMO pasteurización *f*

pasteurize *vt* CHEM, FOOD, QUALITY, THERMO pasteurizar

pasteurized *adj* CHEM, FOOD, QUALITY, THERMO pasteurizado

pasting *n* PAPER laminado *m*, contracolado *m*, *sacks* pegado *m*; ~ **machine** *n* PAPER máquina encoladora *f*

pasture *n* AGRIC pastura *f*

patch[1] *n* COAL bolsada de mineral *f*, COMP&DP parche *m*, ELEC ENG conexión provisional *f*, MAR POLL mancha de hidrocarburos pequeña *f*, MINE bolsada de mineral *f*, bolsón de mineral *m* (*AmL*), parcela de mineral *f* (*Esp*), PETR TECH mancha de hidrocarburos pequeña *f*, PRINT recorte *m* (*Esp*), sobreimpresión tapando *f*; ~ **bay** *n* CINEMAT empalme de bastidor *m*; ~ **board** *n* BrE (*cf patch panel AmE*) COMP&DP, TV panel de acoplamiento *m*, panel de conexiones *m*; ~ **budding** *n* AGRIC injerto de parche *m*; ~ **cord** *n* COMP&DP, ELEC ENG cable de conexión *m*; ~ **field** *n* CINEMAT campo de acoplamiento *m*; ~ **panel** *n* AmE (*cf patch board BrE*) COMP&DP, TV panel de conexiones *m*, panel de acoplamiento *m*; ~**-pocket form** *n* PRINT forma de bolsillo sobreimpresa *f*; ~ **splice** *n* CINEMAT empalme de acoplamiento *m*

patch[2] *vt* CINEMAT acoplar, COMP&DP corregir programas, corregir provisionalmente, parchear, ELEC ENG conectar, empalmar, PRINT sobreimprimir, sobreimprimir tapando, TV conectar

patching *n* ELEC ENG remiendo *m*, PROD bacheo *m*, parcheo *m*, remiendo *m*; ~**-up** *n* PROD bacheo *m*, parcheo *m*, remiendo *m*

patchwork *n* PROD obra hecha con diversos trozos *f*, remiendo *m*

patent *n* MECH ENG patente *f*, patente de invención *f*, TEXTIL patente *f*; ~ **agent** *n* MECH ENG agente de patentes *m*; ~ **flour** *n* FOOD harina patentada *f*; ~ **of improvement** *n* MECH ENG patente de perfeccionamiento *f*

patented *adj* MECH ENG, TEXTIL patentado

patents: ~ **applied for** *phr* TEXTIL patentes solicitadas *fra*

paternoster: ~ **pump** *n* WATER bomba de cadena sin fin *f*, bomba de rosario *f*

path *n* AIR TRANSP trayecto *m*, trayectoria *f*, CINEMAT trayectoria *f*, COMP&DP trayecto *m*, ruta de acceso *f*, vía de acceso *f*, CONST sendero *m*, ELEC trayectoria *f*, ELEC ENG circuito *m*, trayecto *m*, GEOM, PHYS camino *m*, trayectoria *f*, PROD *of flame in boiler* trayecto *m*, trayectoria *f*, SPACE recorrido *m*, trayectoria *f*, TELECOM vía *f*, vía de transmisión *f*, TRANSP, WATER TRANSP *of ship* trayectoria *f*; **by-~** *n* CONST senda *f*, vereda *f* (*AmL*); ~ **attenuation** *n* TV atenuación de la trayectoria *f*; ~ **correction** *n* MILIT *of rocket*, SPACE *of craft* corrección de trayectoria *f*; ~ **difference** *n* PHYS diferencia de caminos *f*; ~ **length** *n* NUCL *process* longitud de la trayectoria *f*; ~ **memory** *n* TELECOM memoria de la vía de transmisión *f*; ~ **overhead** *n* (*POH*) TELECOM acceso superior *m*, vía de transmisión aérea *f*

pathfinder *n* MILIT *parachuting* localizador de trayectoria *m*

pathogenic[1] *adj* HYDROL patógeno
pathogenic[2]: ~ **hazard** *n* SAFE peligro patógeno *m*, riesgo patógeno *m*; ~ **waste** *n* RECYCL desechos patógenos *m pl*, residuos patógenos *m pl*
pathological: ~ **waste** *n* RECYCL desechos patógenos *m pl*, residuos patológicos *m pl*
patina *n* CHEM pátina *f*
patio: ~ **door** *n* C&G puerta de vidrio *f*
patouillet *n* MECH ENG *washer* máquina para lavar minerales *f*
patrimonial: ~ **sea** *n* OCEAN mar patrimonial *m*
patrol: ~ **boat** *n* MAR POLL buque patrullero *m*, lancha patrullera *f*, MILIT buque patrullero *m*, OCEAN escampavía pesquera *f*, WATER TRANSP *police* embarcación patrullera *f*, lancha patrullera *f*, patrullera *f*; ~ **craft** *n* MILIT buque patrullero *m*, embarcación patrullera *f*; ~ **inspection** *n* QUALITY inspección volante *f*; ~ **vessel** *n* MILIT buque patrullero *m*, embarcación patrullera *f*
patron *n* PROD *template* modelo *m*, patrón *m*, plantilla *f*
pattern[1] *n* COMP&DP modelo *m*, motivo *m*, patrón *m*, trama *f*, ELECTRON estructura *f*, PROD modelo *m*, *templet* plantilla *f*, SPACE *communications* diagrama *m*, dispersión *f*, modelo *m*, patrón *m*, representación *f*, TEXTIL muestra *f*, patrón *m*; ~ **generation** *n* ELECTRON generación estructural *f*; ~ **generator** *n* TV generador de imagen de prueba *m*, generador patrón *m* (*AmL*); ~ **length** *n* TEXTIL bandera de dibujo *f*; ~ **maker** *n* PROD *person* fabricante de modelos *mf*, machero *m*, modelador *m*, modelista *m*, plantillero *m*; ~ **making** *n* PROD fabricación de modelos *f*, modelaje *m*, modelería *f*; ~ **matching** *n* PROD concordancia con un modelo *f*; ~ **molder** *AmE*, ~ **moulder** *BrE n* PROD *person* modelista *m*; ~ **plate** *n* PROD *founding* placa portamodelo *f*; ~ **plating** *n* COATINGS normativa de chapada *f*; ~ **projector** *n* CINEMAT proyector de imágenes patrón *m*; ~ **recognition** *n* COMP&DP reconocimiento de tramas *m*, ELECTRON reconocimiento de la configuración *m*, reconocimiento de la estructura *m*, TELECOM reconocimiento de patrones *m*; ~ **registration** *n* ELECTRON *of a field* referencia de la estructura *f*; ~ **shop** *n* PROD *founding* taller de modelos *m*
pattern[2] *vt* TEXTIL adornar con dibujos
patterned[1] *adj* TEXTIL labrado
patterned[2]: ~ **glass** *n AmE* (*cf figured rolled glass BrE*) C&G vidrio rolado *m*; ~ **marble** *n* GEOL mármol modelado *m*
patterning *n* ELECTRON configuración *f*, estructuración *f*, TEXTIL realización de muestras *f*, TV imagen patrón *f*; ~ **capacities** *n* TEXTIL capacidades para realizar muestras *f pl*
Pauli: ~ **exclusion principle** *n* PART PHYS, PHYS principio de exclusión de Pauli *m*; ~ **principle** *n* CHEM, PART PHYS principio de Pauli *m*
pause *n* TV pausa *f*; ~ **control** *n* TV control de pausas *m*
paved: ~ **road** *n AmE* (*cf metalled road BrE*) CONST camino asfaltado *m*
pavement *n BrE* (*cf sidewalk AmE*) COAL pavimento *m* (*AmL*), piso *m*, adoquinado *m* (*Esp*), calzada *f*, muro *m*, CONST vereda *f* (*AmL*), acera *f* (*Esp*), adoquinado *m* (*Esp*), piso *m*, empedrado *m*, pavimento *m* (*AmL*), andén *m*, calzada *f*, MINE muro *m*, piso *m*, TRANSP adoquinado *m* (*Esp*), pavimento *m* (*AmL*); ~ **design** *n* CONST diseño de pavimento *m*; ~-**quality concrete** *n* (*PQC*) CONST concreto para pavimento *m* (*AmL*),

hormigón para pavimento *m* (*Esp*); ~-**spreading machine** *n* CONST asfaltadora *f*, TRANSP asfaltadora *f*, pavimentadora *f*; ~ **surface evenness** *n* CONST uniformidad del pavimento *f*
paver *n* CONST empedrador *m*
paving *n* CONST pavimentación *f*, SAFE material para pavimentos *m*; ~ **block** *n* C&G bloque de piso *m*; ~ **material** *n AmE* (*cf road metal BrE*) CONST balasto *m*, macadam *m*, macadán *m*, piedra triturada para caminos *f*; ~ **stone** *n* CONST losa *f*, adoquín *m*, *single stone* loseta de pavimento *f*
pavior *AmE see paviour BrE*
paviour *n BrE* CONST *person* empedrador *m*, solador *m*; ~'**s hammer** *n BrE* CONST maza de solador *f*
pawl *n* MECH fiador *m*, uña *f*, MECH ENG dedo de enganche *m*, diente de encaje *m*, fiador *m*, fiador de rueda *m*, fiador giratorio *m*, linguete *m*, paleta de reloj *f*, retén de uña *m*, seguro *m*, trinquete *m*, uña *f*; ~-**and-ratchet motion** *n* MECH ENG movimiento de rueda dentada y trinquete *m*; ~ **bitt** *n* MECH ENG *of capstan* bita de los linguetes *f*; ~ **coupling** *n* MECH ENG acoplamiento de trinquete *m*; ~ **head** *n* MECH ENG *of capstan* pie del cabrestante *m*; ~ **rim** *n* MECH ENG *of capstan* freno del molinete *m*, rueda dentada de los linguetes *f*; ~ **ring** *n* MECH ENG *of capstan* anillo de trinquete *m*
pay[1]: ~-**by-use basis** *n* TELECOM base de pago por uso *f*; ~ **cable** *n* TV televisión por cable privada *f*; ~ **dirt** *n* MINE aluvión explotable *m*, aluvión productivo *m* (*Esp*), aluvión remunerador *m* (*AmL*), terreno aurífero *m* (*AmL*), terreno productivo *m* (*Esp*); ~ **television** *n* TELECOM, TV televisión de pago *f* (*Esp*), televisión para abonados *f* (*Esp*), televisión por subscripción *f* (*AmL*); ~-**television network** *n* TELECOM, TV red de televisión de pago *f* (*Esp*), red de televisión por abono *f* (*AmL*); ~ **TV** *n* TV TV paga *f*, compañía de televisión privada *f*; ~ **zone** *n* GEOL, PETR TECH formación productora *f*, PETROL complejo petrolífero explotable *m*, formación petrolífera *f*, zona productiva *f*
pay[2]: ~ **off** *vt* WATER TRANSP *sailors* desembarcar, desenrolar; ~ **out** *vt* WATER TRANSP *the cable* filar
paying: ~ **off** *n* WATER TRANSP *of crew* desenrole *m*
payload *n* AIR TRANSP carga *f*, MAR POLL carga útil *f*, SPACE *craft* carga de pago *f*, instrumentos colocados en los satélites *m pl*, material científico *m*, tripulación e instrumentos *m pl*, TELECOM, VEH carga útil *f*; ~ **bay** *n* SPACE *spacecraft* compartimiento de carga *m*
payoff *n* SPACE resultado final *m*
payphone *n* TELECOM teléfono de pago previo *m*, teléfono público *m*
PB *abbr* (*polybutylene*) P&R PB (*polibutileno*)
Pb *abbr* (*lead*) CHEM, METALL, MINERAL Pb (*plomo*)
PBX[1] *abbr* (*private branch exchange*) TELECOM PBX (*central telefónica privada*)
PBX[2]: ~ **switchboard** *n* TELECOM panel de control de la centralita privada *m*, tablero conmutador de la centralita privada *m*
PC[1] *abbr* COMP&DP (*personal computer*) PC (*computador personal AmL, computadora personal AmL, ordenador personal Esp*), CONST, ELECTRON, PHYS (*printed circuit*) CI (*circuito impreso*), TELECOM (*personal computer*) PC (*computador personal AmL, computadora personal AmL, ordenador personal Esp*)
PC[2]: ~ **board** *n* (*printed-circuit board*) ELEC, ELECTRON placa de CI (*placa de circuito impreso*)

PCB *abbr* (*printed-circuit board*) COMP&DP, ELEC, ELECTRON, TELECOM, TV PCI (*placa de circuito impreso, tablero de circuito impreso, tarjeta de circuito impreso*)

p-channel *n* ELECTRON canal p *m*; ~ **depletion-mode MOS transistor** *n* ELECTRON transistor SOM en modo de transición a canal p *m*; ~ **device** *n* ELECTRON dispositivo de canal p *m*; ~ **enhancement-mode MOS transistor** *n* ELECTRON transistor SOM en modo de intensificación del canal p *m*; ~ **FET** *n* ELECTRON TEC de canal p *m*; ~ **integrated FET** *n* ELECTRON TEC integrado de canal p *m*; ~ **integrated-junction FET** *n* ELECTRON TEC de unión integrada de canal p *m*

PCI *abbr* (*protocol control information*) TELECOM información para el control del protocolo *f*

PCM[1] *abbr* (*pulse-code modulation*) GEN PCM (*modulación por códigos de pulsos, modulación por impulsos codificados*)

PCM[2]: ~ **filter** *n* ELECTRON filtro de MCI *m*; ~ **multiplexer** *n* ELECTRON multiplexor de MCI *m*; ~ **multiplexing** *n* ELECTRON, TELECOM transmisión simultánea de MCI *f*; ~ **switching system** *n* TELECOM sistema de conmutación por modulación de impulsos codificados *m*; ~ **system** *n* TELECOM sistema con modulación por impulsos codificados *m*

PCM-FM: ~ **modulation** *n* ELECTRON modulación MCI-FM *f*

p-cresol *n* CHEM p-cresol *m*

PCS: ~ **fiber** *AmE*, ~ **fibre** *BrE* *n* (*plastic-clad silica fibre BrE*) OPT, TELECOM fibra PCS *f* (*fibra de sílice con revestimiento plástico*)

PCT *abbr* (*peak cladding temperature*) NUCL temperatura máxima de la vaina *f*

PCU *abbr* (*passenger car unit*) TRANSP unidad de pasajeros *f*, unidad de viajeros *f*

PCV[1] *abbr* (*positive crankcase ventilation*) AUTO ventilación cerrada de cárter *f*, ventilación positiva del cárter *f*

PCV[2]: ~ **sleeve** *n* PROD manguito de PCV *m*

PCVD *abbr* (*plasma-activated chemical vapor deposition AmE, plasma-activated chemical vapour deposition BrE*) ELECTRON, OPT, TELECOM DVQPA (*deposición de vapor químico de plasma activado*)

pd *abbr* (*potential difference*) ELEC, ELEC ENG, PHYS, TELECOM diferencia de potencial *f*

PD *abbr* (*protocol discriminator*) TELECOM discriminador de protocolo *m*

Pd *abbr* (*palladium*) CHEM, METALL Pd (*paladio*)

PDA *abbr* (*pulse-distribution amplifier*) ELECTRON, TELECOM amplificador de distribución de impulsos *m*

PDAU *abbr* TELECOM (*pulse-distribution amplifier unit*) unidad amplificadora de distribución de impulsos *f*, TELECOM (*physical-delivery access unit*) unidad de acceso a la entrega física *f*

PDF *abbr* (*probability density function*) MATH FDP (*función de densidad de probabilidad*)

PDH *abbr* (*plesiochronous digital hierarchy*) TELECOM jerarquía digital plesiocrónica *f*

PDM *abbr* (*pulse-duration modulation*) SPACE PDM (*modulación de impulsos en duración, modulación por duración de los impulsos*)

PDN *abbr* (*public data network*) COMP&DP RPD (*red pública de datos*)

PDR *abbr* ELEC (*power-directional relay*) relé para sentido de fuerza *m*, SPACE (*preliminary-design review*) PDR (*revisión del anteproyecto, revisión preliminar de diseño*)

PDS *abbr* (*physical delivery system*) TELECOM sistema de entrega física *m*

PDU *abbr* (*protocol data unit*) TELECOM unidad de datos de protocolo *f*

PE *abbr* COMP&DP (*phase encoding*) PE (*codificación de fase*), MILIT, MINE (*plastic explosive*) explosivo moldeable *m* (*AmL*), explosivo plástico *m* (*Esp*)

pea: ~ **coal** *n* COAL carbón granza *m*, carbón menudo *m*, grancilla *f*, menudos *m pl*

peak[1]: ~**-to-peak** *adv* TV pico a pico *m*

peak[2] *n* CHEM *in spectrum*, NUCL *process* pico *m*, WATER TRANSP *picks* pico de loro *m*, *gaff sail* puño de pico *m*; ~ **amplitude** *n* ELECTRON amplitud máxima *f*; ~ **arc voltage** *n* ELEC tensión máxima de arco *f*; ~ **brightness** *n* TV luminosidad máxima *f*, picos de brillo *m pl* (*AmL*); ~ **busy hour** *n* TELECOM hora cargada máxima *f*, hora punta cargada *f*; ~ **capacity** *n* CONST capacidad máxima *f*; ~ **cladding temperature** *n* (*PCT*) NUCL *position of spacecraft* temperatura máxima de la vaina *f*; ~ **clipping** *n* ELECTRON descrestado de ondas *m*, recorte de onda *m*, TELECOM, TV descrestado de ondas *m*; ~ **concentration** *n* POLL concentración máxima *f*; ~ **current** *n* ELEC *of supply network* corriente de cresta *f*, corriente de pico *f*, corriente máxima *f*, ELEC ENG corriente de punta *f*, PHYS corriente máxima *f*; ~ **demand** *n* GAS demanda pico *f*; ~ **distortion** *n* TV distorsión máxima *f*; ~ **engine speed** *n* VEH velocidad punta del motor *f*; ~ **envelope power** *n* TELECOM pico de potencia de la envolvente *m*, potencia de pico de la envolvente *f*; ~ **factor** *n* ELECTRON, SPACE *communications* factor de máxima *m*, factor de punta *m*; ~ **flow** *n* HYDROL caudal máximo *m*; ~ **frequency deviation** *n* SPACE *communications*, TELECOM desviación de frecuencia máxima *f*; ~ **heat flux** *n* NUCL flujo térmico máximo *m*; ~ **hour** *n* RAIL, TRANSP hora punta *f*; ~**-hour factor** *n* (*PHF*) RAIL, TRANSP factor hora punta *m*; ~**-hour traffic** *n* RAIL, TRANSP tráfico de hora punta *m*; ~ **indicator** *n* ELECTRON indicador de máxima *m*; ~ **intensity wavelength** *n* OPT longitud de onda de la cresta de intensidad *f*, longitud de onda del pico de intensidad *f*, TELECOM longitud de onda de intensidad de cresta *f*, longitud de onda de intensidad máxima *f*; ~ **inverse voltage** *n* ELEC tensión inversa de cresta *f*, tensión máxima inversa *f*, voltaje inverso máximo *m*; ~ **limiter** *n* CINEMAT, TV limitador del valor de pico *m*, limitador del valor máximo *m*; ~ **load** *n* ELEC *of supply network* carga de punta *f*, pico de carga *m*, ELEC ENG carga máxima *f*, punta de carga *f*; ~**-load nuclear-power plant** *n* NUCL central nuclear de carga de pico *f*; ~**-load power plant** *n* ELEC *supply network* central eléctrica con carga máxima *f*; ~**-load traffic** *n* TRANSP tráfico pesado *m*; ~ **luminosity** *n* RAD PHYS luminosidad de pico *f*, luminosidad máxima *f*; ~ **meter** *n* TV medidor de valor de pico *m*; ~**-period traffic** *n* TRANSP tráfico hora punta *m*; ~ **power** *n* ELEC ENG potencia de cresta *f*, potencia máxima *f*, TV pico máximo de potencia *m*; ~ **programme meter** *n* TV medidor de picos de programas *m*; ~ **pulse amplitude** *n* ELECTRON amplitud máxima de impulso *f*; ~ **rate** *n* HYDROL régimen máximo *m*, TELECOM tasa máxima *f*; ~ **revs** *n* VEH número máximo de revoluciones *m*;

~ **signal** *n* TV señal de picos *f*; ~ **signal amplitude** *n* ELECTRON amplitud máxima de señal *f*; ~ **sound pressure** *n* ACOUST nivel sonoro de pico *m*; ~ **speech power** *n* ACOUST potencia vocal de pico *f*; ~ **time** *n* TV hora pico *f*; ~-**to-average power ratio** *n* NUCL relación de potencia máxima-media *f*; ~-**to-peak amplitude** *n* ELECTRON amplitud de cresta a cresta *f*; ~-**to-peak signal amplitude** *n* TV amplitud de señales pico a pico *f*; ~-**to-peak value** *n* ACOUST valor pico a pico *m*, PHYS diferencia entre el máximo y el mínimo *f*; ~ **traffic flow** *n* TRANSP volumen de tráfico en horas punta *m*; ~ **traffic volume** *n* TRANSP volumen de tráfico en horas punta *m*; ~ **value** *n* ELEC *of current, of voltage* valor de cresta *m*, valor máximo *m*, ELECTRON valor máximo *m*, valor de pico *m*, PHYS valor máximo *m*, valor de cresta *m*, TELECOM valor de cresta *m*, valor máximo *m*; ~ **velocity** *n* WATER velocidad máxima *f*; ~ **voltage** *n* ELEC ENG tensión en cresta *f*, voltaje máximo *m*, PHYS, TV voltaje máximo *m*; ~ **voltmeter** *n* ELEC *instrument* voltímetro de cresta *m*, voltímetro indicador del valor de cresta *m*; ~ **water demand** *n* WATER demanda máxima de agua *f*; ~ **water flow** *n* WATER caudal máximo de agua *m*; ~ **white** *n* TV cresta del blanco *f*

peaking *n* ELECTRON momento de máxima *m*; ~ **capacity** *n* ELEC *of supply network* capacidad agudizadora *f*, capacidad de corrección *f*; ~ **circuit** *n* ELECTRON circuito diferenciador de crestas *m*, TV circuito diferenciador *m*; ~ **control** *n* TV control de picos *m*; ~ **network** *n* TV red de picos *f*; ~ **transformer** *n* ELEC, ELEC ENG transformador de núcleo saturable *m*

peaks *n pl* TV picos *m pl*

pean: ~ **hammer** *n* PROD martillo de bola *m*, martillo de peña *m*

peanut: ~ **oil** *n* AGRIC, CHEM, FOOD aceite de cacahuete *m* (*Esp*), aceite de maní *m* (*AmL*)

pear: ~-**shaped vessel** *n* LAB *process* pera *f*

pearl: ~ **ash** *n* DETERG perlasa *f*, potasa purificada *f*; ~ **screen** *n* CINEMAT pantalla perlada *f*

pearlstone *n* PETROL perlita *f*

peat *n* CHEM, COAL turba *f*

pebble *n* CONST piedrecita *f*, PETROL canto rodado pequeño *m*, guijarro *m*, piedrecita *f*; ~ **bed** *n* NUCL *spacecraft* lecho de bolas *m*; ~ **mill** *n* COAL molino de guijarros *m*, molino de piedras *m*, molino de piedras de sílex *m*, PROD molino de bolos *m*, molino de guijarros *m*; ~ **paving** *n* CONST pavimento de piedras *m*

PEC *abbr* (*photoelectric cell*) GEN célula fotoeléctrica *f*

peck *n* METR celemín *m*

pectase *n* CHEM pectasa *f*

pectate *n* CHEM pectato *m*

pectic *adj* CHEM péctico

pectin *n* CHEM, FOOD pectina *f*; ~ **jelly** *n* FOOD gelatina de pectina *f*

pectinose *n* CHEM pectinosa *f*

pectizable *adj* CHEM pectizable

pectization *n* CHEM pectización *f*

pectize *vt* CHEM pectizar

pectolite *n* MINERAL pectolita *f*

pectose *n* CHEM pectosa *f*

pectous *adj* CHEM pectoso

pedal *n* AUTO, VEH pedal *m*; ~ **adjuster** *n* VEH regulador del pedal *m*; ~-**damper assembly** *n* AIR TRANSP montaje de amortiguador de pedal *m*;

~-**operated control** *n* MECH ENG control de pedal *m*, pedal autoregulado *m*

pedestal *n* MECH caballete *m*, pedestal *m*, soporte *m*, MECH ENG *upright standard* basamento *m*, caballete *m*, pedestal *m*, soporte *m*, *plummer block, bearing* portacojinetes *m*, PROD *barrel of boiler* peana *f*, soporte *m*, zócalo *m*, TRANSP peana *f*, TV pedestal *m*; ~ **adjustment** *n* TV adaptación del pedestal *f*; ~ **base** *n* INSTR base del pedestal *f*; ~ **box** *n* MECH ENG *box enclosing bearing* caja de engrase *f*, caja de grasa *f*; ~ **cover** *n* MECH ENG *of bearing block* sombrerete del portacojinetes *m*; ~ **level control** *n* TV control del nivel del pedestal *m*

pedestrian: ~-**actuated signal** *n* TRANSP señal activada por peatones *f*; ~ **area** *n* TRANSP zona peatonal *f*; ~ **conveyor** *n* TRANSP cinta transportadora de pasajeros *f*, pasillo mecánico *m*, transportador peatonal *m*; ~-**only crossing zone** *n* TRANSP cruce peatonal solamente *m*; ~ **phase** *n* TRANSP fase peatonal *f*; ~ **push-button** *n* TRANSP pulsador de semáforo para peatones *m*, pulsador para abrir semáforo *m*; ~ **subway** *n* CONST paso subterráneo de peatones *m*; ~ **zone** *n* TRANSP zona peatonal *f*

pedometer *n* PHYS pedómetro *m*

peel[1]: ~-**off wrapping** *n* PACK envoltura repelable *f*; ~ **shim** *n* MECH ENG película de separación *f*

peel[2] *vt* FOOD pelar

peel[3]: ~ **off** *vi* PROD *welding, paints* descascarillarse, descortezarse, exfoliarse; ~ **off in flakes** *vi* CHEM exfoliarse

peelable: ~ **protective coating** *n* PACK recubrimiento protectora repelable *m*; ~ **system** *n* PACK sistema por repelado *m*

peeled *adj* FOOD pelado

peeling *n* ACOUST negativo *m*, PAPER repelado *m*, TEXTIL peladura *f*; ~-**off** *n* CHEM exfoliación *f*; ~ **test** *n* PROD prueba de descascarillado *f*, prueba de exfoliación *f*

peen *n* PROD *of hammer* peña *f*

peening *n* PROD chorreo con granalla *m*, martillado *m*

peephole *n* PROD *of furnace* mirilla *f*, SPACE *of craft* mirilla *f*, ventanillo *m*

peer[1]: ~-**to-peer** *adj* COMP&DP al mismo nivel, de igual a igual

peer[2]: ~ **entities** *n pl* TELECOM entidades nobles *f pl*; ~-**entity authentication** *n* TELECOM autenticación por entidades nobles *f*; ~-**to-peer master** *n* PROD sistema principal de una red en la que los sistemas están interconectados *m*; ~-**to-peer slave** *n* PROD sistema subsidiario de una red de sistemas interconectados *m*

peg[1] *n* CONST espiga *f*, estaca *f*, MECH chaveta *f* (*AmL*), clavija *f*, espiga *f*, pasador *m*; ~ **tooth** *n* MECH ENG *of saw* diente común *m*, diente recto *m*

peg[2] *vt* CONST colocar clavijas, enclavijar, PROD enclavijar

pegboard *n* CINEMAT bastidor de montaje *m*

pegged: ~ **tenon joint** *n* CONST junta de espiga *f*

pegging *n* CONST, PROD enclavijamiento *m*, estaqueado *m*, jalonamiento *m*; ~ **peen** *n* PROD *founding* pisón de punta *m*; ~ **rammer** *n* PROD *founding* atacador cónico *m*, pisón de punta *m*

pelagic: ~ **waters** *n pl* OCEAN aguas pelágicas *f pl*

pelargonate *n* CHEM pelargonato *m*

pelargonic *adj* CHEM pelargónico

pelite *n* GEOL pelita *f*

pelitic *adj* GEOL pelítico
pellet *n* AGRIC píldora *f*, COAL balín *m*, bolo *m* (*AmL*), gragea *f*, gránulo *m*, metralla *f*, pastilla *f* (*Esp*), pastilla de combustible nuclear *f*, pella *f* (*AmL*), pellet *m*, perdigón *m*, píldora *f* (*Esp*), P&R bolita *f*, granza *f*, gránulo *m*; **~-clad chemical interaction** *n* NUCL interacción química pastilla-vaina *f*; **~-clad mechanical interaction** *n* NUCL interacción mecánica pastilla-vaina *f*; **~ limestone** *n* GEOL caliza peloide *f*; **~ stack** *n* NUCL columna de pastillas *f*
pelleted: **~ seed** *n* AGRIC semilla peleteada *f*
pelletierine *n* CHEM peletierina *f*
pelletizing *n* P&R formación de bolitas *f*, formación de granza *f*, granulación *f*, peletización *f*
pellicular: **~ water** *n* COAL agua pelicular *f*
pelorus *n* WATER TRANSP *navigation* taxímetro *m*
Peltier: **~ coefficient** *n* PHYS coeficiente de Peltier *m*; **~ effect** *n* ELEC, PHYS efecto Peltier *m*
Pelton: **~ turbine** *n* FUELLESS turbina tipo Pelton *f*; **~ wheel** *n* FUELLESS rueda tipo Pelton *f*
pen *n* GEOPHYS lápiz *m*; **~ light** *n* ELEC, ELEC ENG lámpara de haz eléctrico filiforme *f*, lápiz especial fotosensible *m*; **~ plotter** *n* AmE (*cf pen recorder BrE*) COMP&DP trazador de plumas *m*, ELEC, INSTR, LAB registrador estilográfico *m* (*AmL*), registrador gráfico *m* (*Esp*); **~ recorder** *n* BrE (*cf pen plotter AmE*) COMP&DP trazador de plumas *m*, ELEC, INSTR, LAB registrador estilográfico *m* (*AmL*), registrador gráfico *m* (*Esp*); **~-ruling machine** *n* PRINT máquina de rayado a pluma *f*
pencil: **~ beam** *n* ELECTRON haz electrónico estrecho *m*, RAD PHYS haz filiforme *m*; **~ glide** *n* METALL deslizamiento de la muestra obtenida de acero líquido *m*, deslizamiento de planos en una deformación *m*, deslizamiento del haz *m*; **~ test** *n* CINEMAT prueba del lápiz *f*
pendant: **~ bracket** *n* MINE silleta colgante *f* (*AmL*), soporte colgante *m* (*Esp*); **~ group** *n* CHEM *in polymer* grupo pendiente *m*; **~ switch control** *n* SAFE interruptor de control colgante *m*
pending *adj* PROD colgante, pendiente, suspendido
pendular *adj* MECH pendular
pendulum *n* GEOPHYS péndulo *m*, MECH balancín *m*, péndulo *m*, PHYS péndulo *m*; **~ bob** *n* PHYS péndulo de movimiento vertical *m*; **~ floater** *n* C&G flotador de péndulo *m*; **~ hardness** *n* P&R dureza de péndulo *f*, resistencia al impacto con péndulo *f*; **~ motion** *n* MECH ENG movimiento pendular *m*; **~ suspension** *n* TRANSP suspensión pendular *f*; **~ suspension-spring** *n* GEOPHYS muelle de suspensión del péndulo *m*; **~ vehicle suspension** *n* TRANSP vagón con suspensión pendular *m*
penecontemporaneous *adj* GEOL penecontemporáneo
penetrant: **~-liquids inspection** *n* NUCL inspección por líquidos penetrantes *f*
penetrating: **~ paint** *n* COLOUR pintura penetrante *f*; **~ power** *n* RAD PHYS poder de penetración *m*
penetration *n* ELECTRON, MECH penetración *f*; **~ CRT** *n* ELECTRON nivel de penetración del TRC *m*; **~ depth** *n* CONST, ELECTRON profundidad de penetración *f*; **~ grade** *n* CONST nivel de penetración *m*; **~ method** *n* NUCL *rail* método de penetración *m*; **~ test** *n* COAL ensayo de penetración *m*, prueba de penetración *f*; **~ tester** *n* P&R penetrómetro *m*; **~ twin** *n* CRYSTALL

interpenetration twin macla de compenetración *f*; **~ unit** *n* NUCL conjunto de penetración *m*
penetrometer *n* CONST penetrómetro *m*, LAB cualímetro *m*, penetrómetro *m*
penicillin: **~ phial** *n* BrE (*cf penicillin vial AmE*) C&G ampolleta para penicilina *f*, frasco para penicilina *m*; **~ vial** *n* AmE (*cf penicillin phial BrE*) C&G ampolleta para penicilina *f*, frasco para penicilina *m*
peninsula *n* HYDROL, WATER TRANSP *geography* península *f*
pennant *n* WATER TRANSP *signals* gallardete *m*, grímpola *f*; **~ line** *n* PETROL línea de banderines *f*
pennine *n* MINERAL pennina *f*
penninite *n* MINERAL penninita *f*
penny: **~-shaped crack** *n* METALL grieta en forma de monedas *f*
pennyweight *n* METR pennyweight *m*
penstock *n* FUELLESS *dams* conducto forzado *m*, HYDROL *spacecraft* compuerta de esclusa *f*, WATER compuerta de esclusa *f*, canal de llegada *m*, canal de toma *m*, tubería forzada *f*, conducto forzado *m*, canal de aguas arriba *m*
pent: **~ roof** *n* CONST tejadillo *m*
pentachloride *n* CHEM pentacloruro *m*
pentadiene *n* CHEM pentadieno *m*
pentagon *n* GEOM pentágono *m*
pentagonal *adj* GEOM pentagonal
pentagrid: **~ converter** *n* ELEC ENG conversor pentarrejilla *m*
pentahedral *adj* GEOM pentahédrico, pentaédrico
pentahedron *n* GEOM pentahedro *m*, pentaédro *m*
pentamethylendiamine *n* CHEM pentametilendiamina *f*
pentane *n* CHEM, PETR TECH pentano *m*
pentanoic *adj* CHEM, PETR TECH pentanoico
pentanol *n* CHEM pentanol *m*
pentanone *n* CHEM pentanona *f*
pentaprism *n* PHOTO pentaprisma *m*
pentasulfide *AmE see pentasulphide BrE*
pentasulphide *n* BrE CHEM pentasulfuro *m*
pentathionate *n* CHEM pentationato *m*
pentathionic *adj* CHEM pentatiónico
pentatomic *adj* CHEM pentatómico
pentatonic: **~ scale** *n* ACOUST escala pentatónica *f*
pentavalence *n* CHEM pentavalencia *f*
pentavalent[1] *adj* CHEM pentavalente
pentavalent[2]: **~ element** *n* CHEM elemento pentavalente *m*
pentene *n* CHEM penteno *m*
penthiophene *n* CHEM pentiofeno *m*
pentite *n* CHEM pentita *f*
pentitol *n* CHEM pentitol *m*
pentlandite *n* MINERAL pentlandita *f*
pentode *n* ELECTRON, PHYS péntodo *m*
pentosan *n* CHEM pentosan *m*
pentosazon *n* CHEM pentosazona *f*
pentose *n* CHEM pentosa *f*
pentosid *n* CHEM pentósido *m*
pentosuric *adj* CHEM pentosúrico
pentothal *n* CHEM pentotal *m*
pentoxide *n* CHEM pentóxido *m*
pentrough *n* WATER canal de alimentación *m*, canal de carga *m*
pentyl *n* CHEM pentilo *m*
pentylentetrazol *n* CHEM pentilentetrazol *m*
penumbra *n* PHYS penumbra *f*

peonin *n* CHEM peonina *f*
pepper: ~ **alkaloid** *n* CHEM alcaloide de pimienta *m*
pepsin *n* CHEM, FOOD pepsina *f*
pepsinogen *n* CHEM pepsinógeno *m*
pepsinum *n* CHEM pepsino *m*
peptide: ~ **link** *n* CHEM *in compound* enlace peptídico *m*
peptizable *adj* CHEM, DETERG, FOOD, P&R peptizable
peptizate *vt* CHEM, DETERG, FOOD, P&R peptizar
peptization *n* CHEM, DETERG, FOOD, P&R peptización *f*
peptize *vt* CHEM, DETERG, FOOD, P&R peptizar
peptizer *n* CHEM, DETERG, FOOD, P&R peptizador *m*
peptolysis *n* CHEM peptólisis *f*
peptonizable *adj* CHEM peptonizable
per[1]: ~-**capita consumption** *n* WATER consumo por habitante *m*
per[2]: ~ **unit area** *phr* PHYS por unidad de area; ~ **unit length** *phr* PHYS por unidad de longitud; ~ **unit mass** *phr* PHYS por unidad de masa; ~ **unit volume** *phr* PHYS por unidad de volumen
peracetic *adj* CHEM peracético
peracid[1] *adj* GEOL perácido
peracid[2] *n* CHEM perácido *m*
peralkaline *adj* CHEM, GEOL peralcalino
peraluminous *adj* GEOL peraluminoso
perborate *n* CHEM, DETERG perborato *m*
perbromide *n* CHEM perbromuro *m*
percarbonate *n* CHEM percarbonato *m*
perceived: ~ **color** *AmE*, ~ **colour** *BrE n* COLOUR color percibido *m*
percentage *n* TEXTIL porcentaje *m*; ~ **awaiting repair** *n* RAIL porcentaje en espera de reparación *m*; ~ **determination** *n* METR dosificación *f*; ~ **modulation** *n* ELECTRON porcentaje de modulación *m*; ~ **of nonconforming items** *n* QUALITY porcentaje de unidades inconformes *m*; ~ **synchronization** *n* TV porcentaje de sincronización *m*; ~ **tilt** *n* TV porcentaje de la deformación del cuadro *m*
percentile: ~ **level** *n* ACOUST nivel percentil *m*
perception: ~-**reaction time** *n* TRANSP tiempo entre percepción y reacción *m*
perch *n* METR percha *f*, WATER TRANSP *navigation marks* espeque *m*
perched: ~ **water** *n* WATER aguas colgadas *f pl*; ~ **water table** *n* HYDROL nivel de aguas colgadas *m*; ~ **watercourse** *n* HYDROL curso de agua aislado *m*
perchlorate *n* CHEM perclorato *m*; ~ **explosive** *n* MINE explosivo de perclorato *m*
perchloric *adj* CHEM perclórico
perchloride *n* CHEM percloruro *m*
perchlorinated *adj* CHEM perclorado
perchromate *n* CHEM percromato *m*
perchromic *adj* CHEM percrómico
percolate[1] *vt* AGRIC infiltrar, FOOD percolar, HYDROL infiltrar, percolar, WATER percolar
percolate[2] *vi* CHEM percolar, HYDROL rezumar
percolating: ~ **water** *n* HYDROL agua de infiltración *f*, agua filtrada *f*, agua infiltrada *f*, WATER agua de infiltración *f*
percolation *n* CHEM filtración *f*, percolación *f*, FOOD percolación *f*, HYDROL infiltración *f*, percolación *f*
percussion: ~ **cap** *n* MILIT cápsula del cartucho *f*; ~ **drill** *n* MINE barra de mina *f* (*AmL*), barra de percusión *f*, barreno *m* (*Esp*), martillo perforador de percusión *m*, pistolete de mina *m* (*AmL*), sonda de percusión *f*; ~ **drilling** *n* COAL sondeo por percusión

m, taladro por percusión *m*, PETR TECH perforación por percusión *f*, sondeo de percusión *m*; ~ **fuse** *n* MILIT cebo fulminante *m*, MINE espoleta de percusión *f*, estopín de percusión *m*; ~ **mortar** *n* LAB *process* mortero de percusión *m*; ~ **needle** *n* MILIT percutor *m*; ~ **plate** *n* MECH ENG *die set* chapa de percusión *f*; ~ **pressure** *n* MILIT presión de percusión *f*; ~ **priming** *n* MILIT cebo fulminante *m*; ~ **rig** *n* MINE equipo perforador de percusión *m*; ~ **rivet** *n* MECH ENG remache percusivo *m*; ~ **sieve** *n* PROD criba de percusión *f*
percussive: ~ **drill** *n* MECH ENG *hammer drill* martillo perforador de percusión *m*, perforadora de percusión *f*, sonda de percusión *f*; ~ **drilling** *n* COAL sondeo por percusión *m*, taladro por percusión *m*; ~ **force** *n* MECH ENG fuerza de percusión *f*; ~-**rope boring** *n* COAL sondeo a la cuerda por percusión *m*; ~-**rope drilling** *n* COAL sondeo a la cuerda por percusión *m*
percylite *n* MINERAL percylita *f*
pereirine *n* CHEM pereirina *f*
perennial[1] *adj* AGRIC perenne
perennial[2]: ~ **spring** *n* HYDROL, WATER fuente perenne *f*, manantial perenne *m*
perfect[1]: ~-**bound** *adj* PRINT encuadernado sin costura
perfect[2]: ~ **binder** *n* PRINT encuadernadora sin costura *f*; ~ **binding** *n* PRINT encuadernación americana *f*, encuadernación sin costura *f*; ~ **crystal** *n* METALL cristal perfecto *m*, cristal sin defectos *m*; ~ **dielectric** *n* ELEC *capacitor* dieléctrico ideal *m*, dieléctrico perfecto *m*; ~ **dislocation** *n* CRYSTALL dislocación perfecta *f*; ~ **fifth** *n* ACOUST quinta perfecta *f*; ~ **fluid** *n* PHYS fluido perfecto *m*; ~ **fourth** *n* ACOUST cuarta perfecta *f*; ~ **gas** *n* GAS, PHYS gas perfecto *m*, THERMO gas ideal *m*, gas perfecto *m*; ~-**gas scale** *n* PHYS escala del gas perfecto *f*; ~ **mixture ratio** *n* AUTO proporción perfecta de la mezcla *f*; ~ **reflecting diffuser** *n* PAPER difusor perfecto reflectante *m*; ~ **square** *n* MATH cuadrado perfecto *m*
perfect[3] *vt* PRINT imprimir por la segunda cara, retirar
perfecting *n* PRINT retiración *f*; ~ **machine** *n* PRINT máquina de retiración *f*; ~ **unit** *n* PRINT cuerpo impresor de retiración *m*
perfectly: ~-**set page** *n* PRINT página de composición perfecta *f*
perforate *vt* COAL perforar
perforated: ~ **angle** *n* MECH *for plastics* ángulo perforado *m*; ~ **bag on a roll** *n* PACK bolsa perforada formando una bobina *f*; ~ **brick** *n* CONST ladrillo perforado *m*; ~ **casing** *n* PETROL tubo de revestimiento perforado *m*; ~ **disc anode** *AmE*, ~ **disk anode** *BrE n* TV ánodo de disco perforado *m*; ~ **line** *n* PRINT línea troquelada *f*; ~ **overlap** *n* PACK sobrevuelta perforada *f*; ~ **pipe** *n* PETROL cañería perforada *f*, tubería perforada *f*; ~ **plate** *n* NUCL placa soporte *f*, *metal plate, iron wire* placa perforada *f*; ~ **reel** *n* PACK bobina perforada *f*; ~ **tape** *n* COMP&DP, TELECOM cinta perforada *f*
perforating[1] *adj* PROD perforador
perforating[2]: ~ **ejector-punch** *n* MECH ENG punzón eyector de perforación *m*; ~ **gun** *n* PETR TECH cañón perforador *m*; ~ **machine** *n* PACK, PRINT perforadora *f*
perforation *n* C&G, PHOTO, PROD perforación *f*; ~ **blade** *n* PRINT cuchilla de perforación *f*; ~ **pitch** *n* CINEMAT paso de la perforación *m*; ~ **wheel** *n* PRINT rueda de perforación *f*

perforator *n* COMP&DP perforadora *f*, MECH ENG perforador *m*, PROD barrena *f*, perforadora *f*, taladro *m*

performance *n* COMP&DP funcionamiento *m*, rendimiento *m*, MECH ENG capacidad *f*, cumplimiento *m*, ejecución *f*, funcionamiento *m*, potencia *f*, producción *f*, rendimiento *m*, QUALITY ejecución *f*, funcionamiento *m*; ~ **data** *n* TELECOM características de operación *f pl*, datos sobre la calidad de servicio *m pl*, datos sobre las características de funcionamiento *m pl*; ~ **efficiency** *n* PROD eficacia de funcionamiento *f*; ~ **index** *n* CHEM índice de rendimiento *m*; ~ **properties** *n pl* MECH ENG características de funcionamiento *f pl*, características funcionales *f pl*, cualidades técnicas *f pl*; ~ **specification** *n* MECH ENG características funcionales *f pl*, especificaciones de funcionamiento *f pl*; ~ **test** *n* ELEC prueba de funcionamiento *f*, prueba de rendimiento *f*; ~ **testing** *n* QUALITY control de ejecución *m*, control de funcionamiento *m*

performing: ~ **CMISE service user** *n* TELECOM usuario del servicio de calidad de transmisión de CMISE *m*

perhydride *n* CHEM perhidruro *m*

perhydrol *n* CHEM perhidrol *m*

periapsis *n* SPACE periapsis *f*

periastron *n* SPACE estrella binaria *f*, periastro *m*, periastrón *m*

periclase *n* CHEM *mineral* periclase *f*, MINERAL periclasa *f*

periclasite *n* MINERAL periclasa *f*

pericline *n* GEOL, MINERAL periclina *f*

peridot *n* MINERAL olivino *m*, peridoto *m*

peridotite *n* PETROL peridotita *f*

peridotyte *n* PETROL peridotita *f*

perigee *n* PHYS, SPACE perigeo *m*; ~ **kick motor** *n* SPACE motor de impulsión en perigeo *m*; ~ **stage** *n* SPACE etapa en perigeo *f*

perihelion *n* FUELLESS, PHYS, SPACE perihelio *m*

perilla: ~-**seed oil** *n* CHEM aceite de menta perilla *m*

perilymph *n* ACOUST perilinfa *f*

perimeter *n* CONST, GEOM perímetro *m*; ~ **blasting** *n* MINE perímetro de explosión *m*; ~ **frame** *n* AUTO bastidor *m*; ~ **track** *n* AIR TRANSP derrota perimétrica *f*, pista perimétrica *f*, ruta perimétrica *f*

period *n* ACOUST período *m*, AGRIC época *f*, ELECTRON período *m*, GEOL, PETROL período *m*, época *f*, PHYS período *m*; **off** ~ *n* ELEC ENG período de bloqueo *m*, período de corte *m*; **on** ~ *n* ELEC ENG intervalo por conducción *m*, período de conducción *m*; ~ **of lowest flow** *n* HYDROL período de caudal mínimo *m*; ~-**measuring channel** *n* NUCL canal de medición del período *m*, canal periodimétrico *m*; ~ **of oscillation** *n* ELEC *alternating current* período de oscilación *m*; ~ **pulse** *n* ELECTRON período de impulso *m*, tiempo de impulso *m*; ~ **range** *n* NUCL intervalo de período *m*

periodate *n* CHEM peryodato *m*

periodic¹ *adj* ACOUST periódico, ELEC *alternating current* cíclico, intermitente, periódico, ELECTRON, PHYS periódico

periodic²: ~ **acid** *n* CHEM ácido periódico *m*; ~ **damping** *n* ELEC ENG detención momentánea periódica *f*; ~ **function** *n* ELECTRON función periódica *f*; ~ **inspection** *n* MECH ENG inspección periódica *f*; ~ **polarity inversion** *n* TV inversión de polaridad periódica *f*; ~ **pulse** *n* ELECTRON impulso periódico *m*; ~ **quantity** *n* ACOUST magnitud periódica *f*, ELECTRON cantidad periódica *f*; ~ **refresh** *n* ELECTRON reposo periódico *m*; ~ **shutdown** *n* NUCL parada periódica *f*; ~ **signal** *n* ELECTRON, TELECOM señal periódica *f*; ~ **sound-wave** *n* WAVE PHYS onda periódica de sonido *f*; ~ **table** *n* CHEM *of elements* tabla periódica *f*; ~ **time** *n* ELECTRON período *m*; ~ **tone** *n* ACOUST tono periódico *m*; ~ **variation** *n* GEOPHYS variación periódica *f*; ~ **wave** *n* ELEC ENG onda periódica *f*

periodical: ~ **winds** *n pl* METEO vientos periódicos *m pl*

periodicity *n* CRYSTALL periodicidad *f*, ELECTRON frecuencia *f*, periodicidad *f*

periodide *n* CHEM perioduro *m*

peripheral¹: ~-**limited** *adj* COMP&DP limitado por los periféricos

peripheral² *n* COMP&DP periférico *m*, unidad periférica *f*, TELECOM periférico *m*; ~ **control element** *n* NUCL elemento de control periférico *m*; ~ **device** *n* COMP&DP, ELEC ENG, TELECOM dispositivo periférico *m*; ~ **fuel assembly** *n* NUCL elemento de combustible periférico *m*; ~ **hem** *n* MILIT *of parachute* costura periférica *f*; ~ **interface adaptor** *n* (*PIA*) COMP&DP adaptador de interfaz de periféricos *m* (*PIA*); ~-**jet air cushion** *n* TRANSP amortiguación de aire por chorros periféricos *f*, colchón amortiguador por chorros de aire periféricos *m*; ~-**length checking** *n* MECH ENG verificación de longitud periférica *f*; ~ **management** *n* TELECOM gestión periférica *f*; ~ **module** *n* TELECOM módulo periférico *m*; ~ **nucleon** *n* NUCL, PHYS nucleón periférico *m*; ~ **port** *n* PROD acceso de periféricos *m*; ~ **processor** *n* (*PP*) COMP&DP, TELECOM procesador periférico *m*; ~ **skirt** *n* TRANSP plinto periférico *m*; ~ **transfer** *n* COMP&DP transferencia de periféricos *f*; ~ **unit** *n* COMP&DP unidad periférica *f*; ~ **velocity** *n* FUELLESS velocidad periférica *f*; ~ **wheel speed** *n* MECH ENG rueda de velocidad periférica *f*

periphery *n* CONST periferia *f*

periscope *n* CINEMAT, PHYS, SPACE, WATER TRANSP periscopio *m*; ~ **aerial** *n* BrE (*cf periscope antenna AmE*) PHYS antena periscópica *f*; ~ **antenna** *n* AmE (*cf periscope aerial BrE*) PHYS antena periscópica *f*

periscopic: ~ **lens** *n* OPT, PHOTO objetivo periscópico *m*; ~ **sextant** *n* SPACE sextante periscópico *m*

perishable: ~ **goods** *n pl* AGRIC productos perecederos *m pl*

peristaltic: ~ **pump** *n* LAB *position of spacecraft* bomba peristáltica *f*

peritectic: ~ **reaction** *n* METALL reacción peritéctica *f*

peritectoid *n* METALL peritectoide *m*

perlic *adj* PETROL perlítico

perlite *n* PETROL perlita *f*; ~ **plaster** *n* HEAT ENG enyesado de perlita *m*

perlon *n* CHEM perlón *m*

permafrost *n* COAL capa subterránea de hielo *f*, gelisuelo *m*, permahielo *m*, GEOL permahielo *m*, PETR TECH capa subterránea de hielo *f*, gelisuelo *m*, permahielo *m*

permalloy *n* ELEC *magnetism*, PHYS permalloy *m*

permanence: ~ **of irrotational motion** *n* FLUID permanencia del movimiento irrotacional *f*

permanent: ~ **anticyclone** *n* METEO alta de Ogasawara *f*, anticiclón permanente *m*; ~ **color** *AmE*, ~ **colour** *BrE n* COLOUR colorante permanente *m*; ~ **concrete**

shuttering *n* CONST cerramiento permanente de cemento *m* (*Esp*), cerramiento permanente de concreto *m pl* (*AmL*); ~ **current** *n* OCEAN corriente permanente *f*; ~ **deformation** *n* METALL deformación permanente *f*; ~ **disability** *n* SAFE incapacidad permanente *f*; ~ **echo** *n* SPACE eco permanente *m*; ~ **error** *n* COMP&DP error permanente *m*; ~ **flow** *n* HYDROL corriente de agua permanente *f*; ~ **guide base** *n* PETROL base estructural permanente *f*; ~ **guide structure** *n* PETROL base estructural permanente *f*, bastidor permanente *m*; ~ **ink** *n* COLOUR tinta permanente *f*; ~ **irrigation** *n* AGRIC riego permanente *m*; ~ **load** *n* COAL carga permanente *f*; ~ **magnet** *n* ELEC, ELEC ENG, MECH ENG, PHYS, TELECOM, TRANSP imán permanente *m*; ~-**magnet centering** *AmE*, ~-**magnet centring** *BrE n* TV centrado de imán permanente *m*; ~-**magnet electron microscope** *n* INSTR microscopio electrónico de imán permanente *m*; ~-**magnet flowmeter** *n* NUCL flujómetro de imán permanente *m*; ~-**magnet focusing** *n* ELEC ENG concentración de imanes permanentes *f*; ~-**magnet generator** *n* ELEC ENG, FUELLESS generador de imán permanente *m*; ~-**magnet loudspeaker** *n* ACOUST altavoz de imán permanente *m*; ~-**magnet relay** *n* ELEC relé de imán permanente *m*; ~-**magnet split-capacitor motor** *n* ELEC ENG motor con condensador hendido de imán permanente *m*; ~-**magnet stepper motor** *n* ELEC ENG motor de velocidad gradual de imanes permanentes *m*; ~-**magnet synchronous motor** *n* ELEC ENG motor síncrono de imán permanente *m*; ~ **memory** *n* COMP&DP, ELEC ENG memoria permanente *f*; ~ **pasture** *n* AGRIC pastura permanente *f*; ~ **set** *n* MECH ENG deformación permanente *f*, deformación remanente *f*; ~-**sheen finish** *n* COATINGS acabado con lustre permanente *m*; ~ **stress** *n* C&G estrés permanente *m*; ~ **structure** *n* CONST estructura fija *f*; ~ **threshold shift** *n* ACOUST desplazamiento permanente del umbral *m*; ~ **virtual circuit** *n* (*PVC*) COMP&DP, TELECOM circuito virtual permanente *m* (*PVC*); ~-**way installation** *n* RAIL instalación de vías permanentes *f*; ~ **work** *n* CONST trabajo constante *m*

permanently: ~-**pleated** *adj* TEXTIL indesplisable
permanganate *n* CHEM, HYDROL permanganato *m*
permanganic *adj* CHEM permangánico
permeability *n* GEN permeabilidad *f*; ~ **coefficient** *n* COAL coeficiente de permeabilidad *m*; ~ **of free space** *n* ELEC ENG permeabilidad de espacio libre *f*, PHYS permeabilidad del vacío *f*; ~ **logging** *n* PETR TECH diagrama de la permeabilidad *m*, perfilaje de permeabilidad *m*, registro de permeabilidad *m*
permeable[1] *adj* GEN permeable; ~ **to grease** *adj* PACK permeable a la grasa
permeable[2]: ~ **layer** *n* GAS capa permeable *f*, estrato permeable *m*; ~ **primer** *n* P&R pintura de imprimación permeable *f*
permeameter *n* COAL permeámetro *m*
permeance *n* ELEC *magnetism* permeancia *f*, penetración *f*, infiltración *f*, permeación *f*, ELEC ENG permeación *f*, permeancia *f*
Permian: ~ **Period** *n* PETR TECH período Pérmico *m*
permissible: ~ **current** *n* ELEC ENG corriente admisible *f*; ~ **explosive** *n* *AmE* (*cf permitted explosive BrE*) MINE explosivo admisible *m*, explosivo autorizado *m*, explosivo de seguridad *m*; ~ **level of interference** *n* SPACE *communications* nivel de interferencia admisi-

ble *m*; ~ **load** *n* COAL carga admisible *f*; ~ **residual unbalance** *n* MECH ENG *of stiff shafts* desequilibrio residual admisible *m*, desequilibrio residual permitido *m*; ~ **voltage** *n* ELEC ENG tensión admisible *f*
permissive: ~ **block** *n* RAIL enclavamiento condicional *m*
permitted: ~ **explosive** *n* *BrE* (*cf permissible explosive AmE*) MINE explosivo admisible *m*, explosivo autorizado *m*, explosivo de seguridad *m*
permittivity *n* ELEC *capacitor* ELEC ENG, PHYS, SPACE, TELECOM permitividad *f*, capacitancia inductiva específica *f*, constante dieléctrica *f*; ~ **of air** *n* ELEC ENG permitividad del aire *f*; ~ **of free space** *n* ELEC ENG permitividad del vacío *f*
permittor *n* COAL condensador *m*
permonosulfuric *AmE see permonosulphuric BrE*
permonosulphuric *adj BrE* CHEM permonosulfúrico
permutation *n* COMP&DP, MATH permutación *f*
pernitrate *n* CHEM pernitrato *m*
pernitric *adj* CHEM pernítrico
peroxidation *n* CHEM peroxidación *f*
peroxide *n* CHEM peróxido *m*
peroxidize *vt* CHEM peroxidar
peroxoacetylnitrate *n* (*PAN*) CHEM peroxoacetilnitrato *m* (*PAN*)
peroxophosphate *n* CHEM peroxofosfato *m*
peroxy: ~ **acid** *n* CHEM peroxiácido *m*
peroxyacetylnitrate *n* (*PAN*) POLL peroxiacetilnitrato *m* (*PAN*)
peroxydisulfuric *AmE see peroxydisulphuric BrE*
peroxydisulphuric *adj BrE* CHEM peroxidisulfúrico
perpend *n* CONST *masonry* perpiaño *m*, tizón *m*; ~ **stone** *n* CONST piedra de perpiaño *f*
perpendicular[1] *adj* GEOM perpendicular; ~ **to each other** *adj* METR *brazing lamp* perpendiculares entre sí
perpendicular[2] *n* GEOM perpendicular *f*; ~ **amidships** *n* WATER TRANSP *ship design* perpendicular media *f*; ~ **lines** *n pl* GEOM líneas perpendiculares *f pl*, rectas perpendiculares *f pl*; ~ **magnetic recording** *n* ACOUST grabación magnética perpendicular *f*; ~ **magnetization** *n* TV imantación perpendicular *f*
perpetual: ~ **inventory** *n* PROD inventario continuo *m*, inventario permanente *m*; ~ **screw** *n* MECH ENG tornillo sin fin *m*
perrhenate *n* CHEM perrenato *m*
perrhenic *adj* CHEM perrénico
persalt *n* CHEM persal *f*
perseulose *n* CHEM perseulosa *f*
persistence *n* COMP&DP persistencia *f*, ELEC *cathode ray tube* continuidad *f*, persistencia *f*, ELECTRON persistencia *f*; ~ **characteristic** *n* ELECTRON característica de persistencia *f*; ~ **of vision** *n* CINEMAT persistencia de la visión *f*
personal: ~ **call** *n* TELECOM comunicación personal *f*; ~ **computer** *n* (*PC*) COMP&DP, TELECOM computador doméstico *m* (*AmL*), computador personal *m* (*AmL*) (*PC*), computadora doméstica *f* (*AmL*), computadora personal *f* (*AmL*) (*PC*), ordenador doméstico *m* (*Esp*), ordenador personal *m* (*Esp*) (*PC*); ~ **dosimetry** *n* RAD PHYS dosimetría personal *f*; ~ **eye-protector** *n* SAFE protector ocular personal *m*; ~ **eye-protector for welding** *n* SAFE protector ocular personal para soldar *m*; ~ **identification number** *n* (*PIN*) ELECTRON número de identificación personal *m* (*NIP*); ~-**location beacon** *n* WATER TRANSP radiobaliza de localización de náufragos *f*;

~-locator beacon n WATER TRANSP *satellite rescue* radiobaliza de localización de náufragos *f*; **~ protection** n SAFE protección personal *f*; **~ rapid transport** n (*PRT*) TRANSP transporte privado rápido *m*; **~ sound-exposure meter** n SAFE medidor acústico personal *m*

Perspex® n P&R Perspex® *m*, polimetacrilato de metilo *m*, WATER TRANSP metacrilato *m*

persulfate *AmE see* persulphate *BrE*

persulphate n *BrE* CHEM persulfato *m*

PERT[1] *abbr* (*program evaluation and review technique AmE, programme evaluation and review technique BrE*) SPACE PERT (*método para planificar y controlar proyectos, técnica de revisión y evaluación de programas*)

PERT[2]: **~ chart** n COMP&DP diagrama PERT *m*, gráfica PERT *f*

perthite n MINERAL, PETROL pertita *f*

perthitic *adj* MINERAL, PETROL pertítico

perturbation n FLUID, SPACE perturbación *f*; **~ of orbit** n SPACE perturbación de órbita *f*

perturbed: **~ frequency** n RAD PHYS frecuencia perturbada *f*

Peru: **~ saltpeter** *AmE*, **~ saltpetre** *BrE* n CHEM nitro de Perú *m*, salitre de Perú *m*

perveance n ELEC ENG, TELECOM perveancia *f*

perviousness n FUELLESS permeabilidad *f*

perylene n CHEM perileno *m*

pest n AGRIC plaga *f*; **~ control** n AGRIC lucha contra las plagas *f*; **~ incidence** n AGRIC incidencia de plagas *f*

pesticide n AGRIC, CHEM pesticida *m*

pestle n CHEM mano de mortero *f*, CHEM TECH majadero *m*, mano de mortero *f*, LAB pistilo *m*

pet: **~ cock** n HYDRAUL grifo de descompresión *m*; **~ valve** n HYDRAUL válvula de desahogo *f*, válvula de equilibrio *f*, válvula equilibrada *f*

PET[1]: **~ bottle** n PACK botella de polietileno *f*; **~ film** n (*polyethylene film*) PACK película de polietileno *f*

peta *pref* (*p*) METR peta (*p*)

petalite n MINERAL petalita *f*

Petri: **~ dish** n AGRIC caja Petri *f*, LAB *bacteriology* caja Petri *f*, placa de cultivo *f*; **~ net** n COMP&DP red Petri *f*

petrochemical[1] *adj* PETR TECH, PETROL petroquímico

petrochemical[2]: **~ plant** n CHEM, PETR TECH, PETROL instalación petroquímica *f*, planta petroquímica *f*

petrochemicals n *pl* CHEM, PETR TECH, PETROL petroquímicos *m pl*, productos petroquímicos *m pl*

petrofabric: **~ analysis** n GEOL análisis petrofábrico *m*

petrogenetic: **~ grid** n GEOL *ring network* red petrogenética *f*

petrol n *BrE* (*cf gas AmE, cf gasoline AmE*) AUTO, P&R, PETR TECH, PETROL, THERMO, VEH gasolina *f* (*Esp*), nafta *f* (*AmL*); **~-and-oil-resistant hose** n *BrE* (*cf gasoline-and-oil-resistant hose AmE*) P&R manguera resistente a la gasolina y al aceite *f* (*Esp*), manguera resistente a la nafta y al aceite *f* (*AmL*); **~ consumption** n *BrE* (*cf gasoline consumption AmE*) AUTO, VEH consumo de gasolina *m* (*Esp*), consumo de nafta *m* (*AmL*); **~ dump** n *BrE* (*cf gasoline dump AmE*) MILIT depósito provisional de gasolina *m* (*Esp*), depósito provisional de nafta *m* (*AmL*); **~ engine** n *BrE* (*cf gasoline engine AmE*) AUTO, THERMO, VEH, WATER TRANSP motor de gasolina *m* (*Esp*), motor de nafta *m* (*AmL*); **~-engine vehicle** n *BrE* (*cf gasoline-engine vehicle*

AmE) AUTO, POLL, VEH vehículo con motor de gasolina *m* (*Esp*), vehículo con motor de nafta *m* (*AmL*); **~ filter** n *BrE* (*cf gasoline filter AmE*) AUTO, VEH filtro de gasolina *m* (*Esp*), filtro de nafta *m* (*AmL*); **~-fuelled bus** n *BrE* (*cf gas-fueled bus AmE*) AUTO, VEH autobús de gasolina *m*; **~-fuelled car** n *BrE* (*cf gas-fueled car AmE*) AUTO coche de gasolina *m* coche de gasolina *m* (*Esp*), coche de nafta *m* (*AmL*); **~ hose** n *BrE* (*cf gasoline hose AmE*) AUTO, P&R, VEH manguera de gasolina *f* (*Esp*), manguera de nafta *f* (*AmL*), tubo flexible de gasolina *m* (*Esp*), tubo flexible de nafta *m* (*AmL*); **~ mixture** n (*cf gasoline mixture AmE*) AUTO, VEH mezcla de gasolina *f* (*Esp*), mezcla de nafta *f* (*AmL*); **~-oil contact** n *BrE* (*cf gasoline-oil contact AmE*) PETR TECH, PETROL contacto gas-petróleo *m*; **~-oil mixture** n *BrE* (*cf gasoline-oil mixture AmE*) AUTO, VEH mezcla aceite-gasolina *f* (*Esp*), mezcla aceite-nafta *f* (*AmL*), mezcla de aceite y gasolina *f* (*Esp*), mezcla de aceite y nafta *f* (*AmL*); **~ pump** n *BrE* (*cf gasoline pump AmE*) GEN bomba de alimentación *f*, bomba de combustible *f*, bomba de gasolina *f* (*Esp*), bomba de nafta *f* (*AmL*); **~ resistance** n *BrE* (*cf gasoline resistance AmE*) P&R resistencia a la gasolina *f* (*Esp*), resistencia a la nafta *f* (*AmL*); **~ station** n *BrE* (*cf gasoline station AmE*) AUTO, TRANSP, VEH estación de gasolina *f* (*Esp*), estación de nafta *f* (*AmL*), estación de servicio *f*, gasolinera *f*; **~ tank** n *BrE* (*cf gasoline tank AmE*) AUTO, VEH depósito de gasolina *m* (*Esp*), depósito de nafta *m* (*AmL*); **~ tank cap** n *BrE* (*cf gasoline tank cap AmE*) AUTO, VEH tapón del depósito de gasolina *m* (*Esp*), tapón del depósito de nafta *m* (*AmL*)

petrolatum n CHEM, PETR TECH, PETROL *jelly* petrolato *m*, vaselina ® *f*

petrolene n CHEM petroleno *m*

petroleum n PETR TECH, PETROL petróleo *m*; **~ basin** n PETR TECH, PETROL cuenca petrolífera *f*, estanque de petróleo *m*, región petrolífera *f*; **~ company** n PETR TECH, PROD empresa petrolífera *f*; **~ engineer** n PETR TECH, PETROL ingeniero petrolero *m*, ingeniero petrolífero *m*; **~ field** n PETROL TECH, PETROL campo petrolífero *m*, yacimiento petrolífero *m*, yacimiento petrolífero *m*; **~ gas** n GAS, PETR TECH, PETROL gas de petróleo *m*; **~ geology** n GEOL, PETR TECH geología del petróleo *f*; **~ jelly** n CHEM, PETR TECH, PETROL petrolato *m*, vaselina ® *f*; **~ naphtha** n PETROL nafta de petróleo *f* (*AmL*); **~, oil and lubricants** n *pl* (*POL*) MILIT, PETROL petróleo, aceite y lubricants *m pl*; **~ product** n PETR TECH, PETROL, POLL producto petrolero *m*, producto petrolífero *m*; **~ province** n PETR TECH campo de petróleo *m*; **~ wax** n PETR TECH cera de petróleo *f*

petrolic *adj* CHEM *ether* petrolero

petrology n COAL, PETR TECH, PETROL petrología *f*

petrosilex n PETROL felsita *f*

petrosulfur *AmE see* petrosulphur *BrE*

petrosulphur n *BrE* PETR TECH sulfuro de petróleo *m*; **~ compounds** n *pl BrE* PETR TECH compuestos petrosulfúricos *m pl*

petticoat: **~ insulator** n ELEC, ELEC ENG aislador de campana *m*

petty: **~ officer** n WATER TRANSP *navy* suboficial *m*

petzite n MINERAL petcita *f*

Petzval: **~ lens** n CINEMAT lente Petzval *f*

pey: **~ sand** n PETROL arena productiva *f*

PFM *abbr* (*pulse frequency modulation*) COMP&DP, ELECTRON modulación de frecuencia de impulsos *f*

PFR *abbr* (*power-fail restart*) COMP&DP reinicio tras fallo en alimentación *m*

Pfund: ~ **series** *n* PHYS series de Pfund *f pl*

PGM *abbr* (*precision-guided munition*) MILIT munición guiada *f*

ph *abbr* (*phase*) TELECOM fase *f*

pH[1] *abbr* (*potential of hydrogen*) CHEM, HYDROL pH (*potencial hidrógeno*)

pH[2]: ~ **control** *n* COAL control de pH *m*; ~ **controller** *n* COAL controlador de pH *m*; ~ **depression** *n* POLL bajada del pH *f*, depresión del pH *f*, disminución del pH *f*, bajada del potencial hidrógeno *f*, depresión del potencial hidrógeno *f*, disminución del potencial hidrógeno *f*; ~ **drop** *n* CHEM caída del pH *f*, POLL bajada del pH *f*, bajada del potencial hidrógeno *f*, caída del pH *f*, descenso del pH *m*, disminución del pH *f*; ~ **meter** *n* COAL medidor de pH *m*, LAB *feather-edged brick* medidor de pH *m*, pHmetro *m*, METR pHmetro *m*; ~ **number** *n* HYDROL coeficiente pH *m*; ~ **value** *n* AGRIC, HYDROL valor de pH *m*

phacolite *n* GEOL, MINERAL facolita *f*

phacolith *n* GEOL, MINERAL facolito *m*

Phanerozoic *adj* GEOL Fanerozoico

phanite *n* PETROL fenita *f*

phantom *n* NUCL *simulation model* fantoma *m*, maniquí *m*; ~ **circuit** *n* ELEC ENG circuito fantasma *m*, circuito virtual *m*, TELECOM circuito fantasma *m*; ~ **coil** *n* ELEC ENG bobina fantasma *f*; ~ **horizon** *n* GEOPHYS espectro de Brocken *m*, horizonte fantasma *m*

pharmacolite *n* MINERAL farmacolita *f*

pharmacosiderite *n* MINERAL farmacosiderita *f*

phase[1]: **in** ~ *adj* ELECTRON, TV en fase; **out of** ~ *adj* ELEC, ELECTRON defasado; **in** ~ **opposition** *adj* ELECTRON en oposición de fase; **~-shifted** *adj* ELECTRON desfasado

phase[2]: **in** ~ *adv* ELEC, ELECTRON, PHYS, TV, WAVE PHYS en fase

phase[3] *n* (*ph*) GEN fase *f*; ~ **adaptor** *n* ELEC *alternating current* adaptador de fase *m*; ~ **adjustment** *n* ELECTRON, TV ajuste de fase *m*; ~ **advancer** *n* ELEC *motor* adelantador de fase *m*, modificador de fase *m*; ~ **alignment** *n* TELECOM alineamiento de fase *m*; ~ **alternation line** *n* (*PAL*) TV sistema de línea con alternación de fase *m*; **~-ambiguity resolution** *n* SPACE *communications* definición de la fase de ambigüedad *f*; **~-amplitude characteristic** *n* TELECOM característica de fase y amplitud *f*, característica fase-amplitud *f*; ~ **angle** *n* AIR TRANSP ángulo de desfasaje *m*, ELEC *alternating current* desfasaje *m*, distancia angular de fase *f*, ángulo de adelanto de fase *m*, ángulo de desfasaje *m*, ángulo de desfasamiento *m*, ángulo de retraso de fase *m*, ELECTRON ángulo de defasaje *m*, FUELLESS ángulo de retraso de fase *m*, PHYS ángulo de desfasaje *m*, WAVE PHYS decalaje de fase *m*, ángulo de desfasaje *m*; **~-balance relay** *n* ELEC relé de equilibrio de fases *m*; ~ **boundary** *n* METALL contorno de fase *m*, límite de fase *m*; **~-change velocity** *n* TELECOM velocidad de cambio de fase *f*, velocidad de variación de fase *f*; ~ **changer** *n* ELEC *alternating current* desfasador *m*, ELECTRON desfasador *m*, convertidor de fase *m*, TELECOM, WAVE PHYS desfasador *m*; ~ **coefficient** *n* TELECOM coeficiente de fase *m*; ~ **comparator** *n*

ELECTRON, TV comparador de fase *m*; ~ **compensation** *n* ELEC *alternating current*, TELECOM compensación de fase *f*, corrección de fase *f*; ~ **constant** *n* ACOUST, ELECTRON, OPT, PHYS, TELECOM, TV fase constante *f*, constante de fase *f*; **~-contrast microscope** *n* LAB, PHYS microscopio de contraste de fase *m*; ~ **control** *n* ELECTRON, TELECOM, TV control de fase *m*; ~ **converter** *n* ELEC *alternating current*, ELECTRON, TV convertidor de fase *m*; ~ **current** *n* ELEC corriente de fase *f*, ELEC ENG corriente activa *f*, corriente de fase *f*; ~ **delay** *n* TV retardo de fase *m*; **~-delay keying** *n* ELECTRON conmutador de retardo de fase *m*; ~ **demodulation** *n* ELECTRON, TELECOM desmodulación de fase *f*; ~ **demodulator** *n* ELECTRON desmodulador de fase *m*; ~ **detector** *n* ELECTRON comparador de fase *m*, detector de fase *m*, TELECOM, TV detector de fase *m*; ~ **diagram** *n* CHEM *of system* diagrama de fases *m*, METALL diagrama de constitución *m*, NUCL, TRANSP diagrama de fases *m*; ~ **difference** *n* ACOUST, ELEC *transformer*, ELECTRON, PETROL, PHYS, TELECOM, TV, WAVE PHYS diferencia de fase *f*, desfasamiento *m*, desfase *m*, desfasaje *m*; **~-difference angle** *n* ELEC ángulo de diferencia de fases *m*; ~ **discriminator** *n* ELECTRON discriminador de fase *m*; ~ **displacement** *n* ELEC *alternating current* desfasado *m*, desfasaje *m*, desfasamiento *m*, desfase *m*, desplazamiento de fase *m*; **~-displacement induction-loop detector** *n* TRANSP detector de núcleo de inducción de desfase *m*; ~ **distortion** *n* ACOUST, ELECTRON, PHYS, TELECOM, TV distorsión de fase *f*; ~ **distribution** *n* METALL distribución de fase *f*; ~ **encoding** *n* (*PE*) COMP&DP codificación de fase *f* (*PE*); ~ **equalizer** *n* ELEC *alternating current* compensador de fase *m*, ecualizador de fase *m*, igualador de fase *m*; ~ **equilibrium** *n* THERMO equilibrio de fases *m*; ~ **error** *n* ELECTRON, TV error de fase *m*; ~ **failure** *n* TV interrupción de fase *f*; **~-failure protection** *n* PROD protección contra interrupción de una fase *f*; **~-frequency response curve** *n* ACOUST curva de respuesta fase-frecuencia *f*; ~ **generator** *n* ELECTRON generador de fase *m*; ~ **grid** *n* ELEC *alternating current* rejilla de fase *f*; ~ **insulation** *n* ELEC *alternating current*, ELEC ENG aislación de fase *f*, aislamiento de fase *m*; ~ **integral** *n* SPACE fase integral *f*; ~ **inversion** *n* COAL, ELEC, PETROL, PROD inversión de fase *f*; ~ **inverter** *n* ELEC *AC/DC circuit* inversor de fase *m*; ~ **jitter** *n* SPACE *communications* fase de fluctuación *f*, fase de variaciones cíclicas *f*; ~ **lag** *n* ELEC *alternating current* retardo de fase *m*, retraso de fase *m*, ELECTRON, OCEAN, PHYS retardo de fase *m*; ~ **lead** *n* ELEC *alternating current* adelanto de fase *m*, avance de fase *m*, ELECTRON avance de fase *m*, PHYS conducción de fase *f*; ~ **lock** *n* TV sincronización de fase *f*; **~-locked demodulator** *n* SPACE *communications* detector de enganche de fase *m*; **~-locked loop** *n* (*PLL*) ELECTRON circuito de fase sincronizada *m*, SPACE bucle de enganche de fase *m*, circuito de bloqueo de fase *m*, circuito de fase sincronizada *m*, TELECOM bucle de enganche de fase *m*, TV lazo de enganche de fase *m*; **~-locked oscillator** *n* ELECTRON oscilador de sincronización de fase *m*; ~ **locking** *n* ELECTRON bloqueo de fase *m*, sincronización de fase *f*, TELECOM enclavamiento de fase *m*, enganche de fase *m*, TV fijación de fase *f*; ~ **loss** *n* PROD pérdida de fase *f*; ~ **margin** *n* ELECTRON margen de fase *m*;

~ **modulation** *n* (*PM*) COMP&DP, ELECTRON, PHYS, TELECOM, TV modulación de fase *f* (*MF*); ~ **modulator** *n* COMP&DP, ELECTRON, PHYS, TELECOM, TV modulador de fase *m*; ~ **non-linear distortion** *n* SPACE *communications* dispersión de fase no lineal *f*; ~ **opposition** *n* ELECTRON, PHYS oposición de fase *f*; **~-out** *n* WAVE PHYS desfasaje *m*; ~ **quadrature** *n* ELECTRON cuadratura de fase *f*; ~ **reference** *n* TV referencia de fase *f*; ~ **regulation** *n* TELECOM regulación de fase *f*; ~ **response** *n* ELECTRON respuesta de fase *f*; ~ **reversal** *n* COAL, ELEC, PETROL, PROD, TV inversión de fase *f*; **~-reversal switch** *n* ELEC ENG interruptor de inversión de fase *m*; **~-reversed secondaries** *n pl* ELEC ENG secundarios de fase invertida *m pl*; ~ **sequence** *n* ELEC, ELECTRON *three-phase system* secuencia de fases *f*; **~-sequence rectifier** *n* ELEC *three-phase system* ELECTRON rectificador de secuencia de fases *m*; **~-shaped QPSK** *n* TELECOM transmisión por desplazamiento de fase cuaternaria *f*; ~ **shift** *n* ELEC *alternating current* desfase *m*, corrimiento de fase *m*, desplazamiento de fase *m*, cambio de fase *m*, desfasaje *m*, variación de fase *f*, ELECTRON desplazamiento de fase *m*, NUCL *of transformer* desviación de fase *f*, PHYS corrimiento de fase *m*, SPACE *communications* variación de fase *f*, TRANSP cambio de fase *m*, TV desfasaje *m*; **~-shift keying** *n* (*PSK*) ELECTRON conmutación de desplazamiento de fase *f* (*CDF*), conmutación de retardo de fase *f* (*CRF*), TELECOM codificación por desplazamiento mínima *f*; **~-shift keying modulation** *n* (*PSK*) COMP&DP modulación por desviación de fase *f* (*PSK*), SPACE *communications* modulación por variación de fase *f* (*PSK*); **~-shift microphone** *n* ACOUST micrófono de desviación de fase *m*; **~-shift oscillator** *n* ELECTRON oscilador de variación de fase *m*; ~ **shifter** *n* ELEC *alternating current*, ELECTRON, TELECOM, WAVE PHYS desfasador *m*, variador de fase *m*; **~-shifting capacitor** *n* ELEC capacitor desfasador *m*, condensador desfasador *m*; **~-shifting element** *n* ELECTRON elemento de variación de fase *m*; **~-shifting network** *n* ELEC *alternating current* red cambiadora de fase *f*, red desfasadora *f*, red desplazadora de fase *f*, PHYS red de corrimiento de fase *f*; **~-shifting transformer** *n* ELEC *alternating current* transformador desfasador *m*; ~ **skipping** *n* TRANSP salto de fase *m*; ~ **space** *n* PHYS espacio de fase *m*; ~ **splitter** *n* ELEC *alternating current*, ELECTRON desfasador múltiple *m*, divisor de fase *m*; **~-splitter amplifier** *n* ELEC, ELECTRON amplificador de partición de fase *m*; ~ **splitting** *n* ELEC *alternating current*, ELECTRON división de fase *f*, separación de fases *f*; ~ **stability** *n* ELEC *alternating current*, TELECOM estabilidad de fase *f*; ~ **terminal** *n* ELEC *connection* borne de fase *m*, terminal de fase *m*, ELEC ENG borne de fase *m*; ~ **to ground** *n* PROD fase a tierra *f*; **~-to-earth fault** *n* BrE (*cf phase-to-ground fault AmE*) ELEC *alternating current* tierra accidental a fase *f*; **~-to-ground fault** *n* AmE (*cf phase-to-earth fault BrE*) ELEC *alternating current* tierra accidental a fase *f*; **~-to-neutral voltage** *n* ELEC *system* tensión neutra a fase *f*; **~-to-phase voltage** *n* ELEC *three phase system* tensión entre fases *f*; ~ **transformation** *n pl* THERMO transformación de fase *f*; ~ **tuning** *n* TELECOM sintonización de fase *f*; ~ **unbalance** *n* PROD desequilibrio de fases *m*; ~ **variation** *n* ELEC *alternating current* variación de fase *f*; ~ **velocity** *n*

PETROL, PHYS velocidad de fase *f*; ~ **voltage** *n* ELEC *system* tensión de fase *f*, tensión por fase *f*; ~ **winding** *n* ELEC devanado de fase *m*; **~-wound rotor motor** *n* ELEC rotor con devanado en fase *m*
phase[4]: **~-shift** *vt* ELEC ENG, ELECTRON, TELECOM, WAVE PHYS desfasar, variar la fase
phase[5]: **be in** ~ *vi* ELEC *AC supply* estar en fase
phased[1] *adj* TV en fase
phased[2]: **~-array aerial** *n* BrE (*cf phased-array antenna AmE*) SPACE *communications* antena con elementos controlados por face *f*, antena de elementos múltiples desfasados *f*; **~-array antenna** *n* AmE (*cf phased-array aerial BrE*) SPACE *communications* antena con elementos controlados por face *f*, antena de elementos múltiples desfasados *f*; ~ **ignition** *n* SPACE ignición sincronizada *f*
phaseolin *n* CHEM faseolina *f*
phaseolunatin *n* CHEM faseolunatina *f*
phaser *n* TV sincronizador *m*
phasing *n* ELEC, ELECTRON, TRANSP, TV ajuste de fase *m*, fasaje *m*, puesta en fase *f*, sincronización *f*; ~ **diagram** *n* TRANSP diagrama de ajuste de fases *m*, diagrama de sincronización *m*; ~ **signal** *n* ELECTRON señal de ajuste de fase *f*, TV señal de fase *f* (*AmL*), señal de puesta en fase *f* (*Esp*); ~ **unit** *n* AIR TRANSP *helicopter* unidad de puesta en fase *f*
phasor *n* ELEC *waveform* fasor *m*, vector de corriente *m*; ~ **representation** *n* ELEC ENG representación vectorial *f*
pheelgite *n* MINERAL pheelgita *f*
phellandrene *n* CHEM felandreno *m*
phenacetin *n* CHEM fenacetina *f*
phenaceturic *adj* CHEM fenacetúrico
phenacyl *n* CHEM fenacil *m*, fenacilo *m*
phenadone *n* CHEM fenadona *f*
phenakite *n* MINERAL fenaquita *f*
phenanthraquinone *n* CHEM fenantraquinona *f*
phenanthrazine *n* CHEM fenantrazina *f*
phenanthridine *n* CHEM fenantridina *f*
phenanthridone *n* CHEM fenantridona *f*
phenanthrol *n* CHEM fenantrol *m*
phenanthroline *n* CHEM fenantrolina *f*
phenanthryl *n* CHEM fenantril *m*, fenantrilo *m*
phenate *n* CHEM fenato *m*
phenazine *n* CHEM fenacina *f*
phenazocine *n* CHEM fenazocina *f*
phenazone *n* CHEM fenazona *f*
phenetidine *n* CHEM fenetedina *f*
phenetole *n* CHEM fenetol *m*
pheniramine *n* CHEM feniramina *f*
phenoclast *n* GEOL, PETROL fenoclasto *m*
phenocryst *n* GEOL, PETROL fenocristal *m*
phenocrystalline *adj* GEOL, PETROL fenocristalino
phenol *n* CHEM, HYDROL fenol *m*
phenolate *n* CHEM fenolato *m*
phenolic[1] *adj* CHEM fenólico
phenolic[2]: ~ **plastic** *n* P&R plástico fenólico *m*; ~ **resin** *n* ELEC *insulation*, P&R resina fenólica *f*
phenolphthalein *n* CHEM fenolftaleína *f*
phenolsulfonic AmE *see* phenolsulphonic BrE
phenolsulphonic *adj* BrE CHEM fenolsulfónico
phenomenal: ~ **wave** *n* OCEAN ola excepcional *f*, ola fenomenal *f*
phenosafranine *n* CHEM fenosafranina *f*
phenothiazine *n* CHEM fenotiazina *f*
phenotype *n* AGRIC fenotipo *m*

phenoxazine *n* CHEM fenoxazina *f*
phenoxide *n* CHEM fenóxido *m*
phenoxybenzene *n* CHEM fenoxibenceno *m*
phenyl *n* CHEM fenil *m*, fenilo *m*
phenylacetamide *n* CHEM fenilacetamida *f*
phenylacetic *adj* CHEM fenilacétivo
phenylalanine *n* CHEM fenilalanina *f*
phenylamine *n* CHEM fenilamina *f*
phenylated *adj* CHEM fenilado
phenylenediamine *n* CHEM fenilendiamina *f*
phenylethylamine *n* CHEM feniletilamina *f*
phenylethylene *n* CHEM feniletileno *m*
phenylglycine *n* CHEM fenilglicina *f*
phenylglycol *n* CHEM fenilglicol *m*
phenylglycolic *adj* CHEM fenilglicólico
phenylhydrazine *n* CHEM fenilhidrazina *f*
phenylhydrazone *n* CHEM fenilhidrazona *m*
phenylhydroxyacetic *adj* CHEM fenilhidroxiacético
phenylhydroxylamine *n* CHEM fenilhidroxilamina *f*
phenylic *adj* CHEM fenílico
phenylmethane *n* CHEM fenilmetano *m*
phenylpropiolic *adj* CHEM fenilpropiólico
phenylpyrazole *n* CHEM fenilpirazol *m*
phenylurea *n* CHEM fenilurea *f*
PHF *abbr* (*peak-hour factor*) RAIL, TRANSP factor hora punta *m*
phi: **~-meson** *n* PART PHYS mesón fi *m*
phial *n* *BrE* (*cf vial AmE*) C&G ampolleta *f*, botellita *f*, CHEM ampolleta *f*, frasco pequeño *m*, LAB *rail* ampolleta *f* (*AmL*), frasco pequeño *m*
Phillips: **~ screw** *n* MECH ENG tornillo Phillips *m*, tornillo de cabeza Phillips *m*
phillipsite *n* MINERAL filipsita *f*
phlobaphene *n* CHEM flobafeno *m*
phlogopite *n* MINERAL flogopita *f*
phloretic *adj* CHEM florético
phloretin *n* CHEM floretina *f*
phlorhizin *n* CHEM florizina *f*
phloridzin *n* CHEM floridizina *f*
phlorol *n* CHEM florol *m*
phlorrhizin *n* CHEM florizina *f*
PHMA *abbr* (*polyhexylmethacrylate*) P&R PHMA (*polihexilmetacrilato*)
phoenicite *n* MINERAL fenicita *f*
phoenicochroite *n* MINERAL fenicrocoíta *f*
phon *n* ACOUST, PHYS fonio *m*
phonation *n* ACOUST fonación *f*
phonecard *n* TELECOM tarjeta telefónica *f*
phonetic: **~ power** *n* ACOUST potencia fonética *f*
phonolite *n* GEOL, PETROL, PROD fonolita *f*
phonolyte *n* GEOL, PETROL, PROD fonolita *f*
phonon *n* PHYS fonón *m*; **~-gas model** *n* PHYS modelo de gas de fonones *m*
phonovision *n* OPT fonovisión *f*
phorone *n* CHEM forona *f*
phosgene *n* CHEM, MILIT *chemical warfare* fosgeno *m*
phosgenite *n* CHEM fosgenita *f*, MINERAL fosgenita *f*, plomo córneo *m*
phospham *n* CHEM fosfamo *m*
phosphatase *n* CHEM fosfatasa *f*
phosphate *n* CHEM, DETERG, HYDROL fosfato *m*; **~ chemistry regime** *n* NUCL régimen de control químico por fosfatos *m*; **~ coating** *n* COATINGS fosfatación *f*, revestimiento de fosfato *m*; **~ ester** *n* DETERG éster fosfático *m*; **~ of lime** *n* CHEM fosfato de cal *m*; **~ rock** *n* PETROL roca fosfática *f*

phosphated *adj* CHEM, COATINGS fosfatado
phosphatic[1] *adj* AGRIC, CHEM, GEOL fosfático
phosphatic[2]: **~ deposits** *n pl* GEOL depósitos fosfáticos *m pl*; **~ fertilizer** *n* AGRIC abono fosfatado *m*
phosphation *n* DETERG fosfatización *f*
phosphatization *n* CHEM fosfatación *f*, fosfatado *m*, COATINGS fosfatado *m*
phosphide *n* CHEM fosfuro *m*
phosphine *n* CHEM *compound* fosfina *f*
phosphite *n* CHEM fosfito *m*
phosphocatalysis *n* CHEM fosfocatálisis *f*
phosphochalcite *n* MINERAL fosforocalcita *f*
phosphoglyceric *adj* CHEM fosfoglicérico
phospholipid *n* CHEM, FOOD fosfolípido *m*
phosphomolybdic *adj* CHEM fosfomolíbdico
phosphonium *n* CHEM fosfonio *m*
phosphor *n* CHEM fósforo *m*, luminóforo *m*, ELECTRON, METALL, PHYS fósforo *m*; **~ bronze** *n* CHEM, ELEC, ELEC ENG bronce fosforoso *m*; **~-dot faceplate** *n* TV punto fosforescente de fondo *m*; **~ screen** *n* TV pantalla fluorescente *f*; **~ strip** *n* TV banda fosforescente *f*
phosphorated *adj* CHEM fosforado
phosphorescence *n* COMP&DP, ELECTRON, PHYS, RAD PHYS, SPACE, WATER TRANSP *in sea* fosforescencia *f*
phosphorescent: **~ material** *n* ELECTRON material fosforescente *m*; **~ safety-sign** *n* SAFE letrero de seguridad fosforescente *m*, señal de seguridad fosforescente *f*
phosphoric[1] *adj* CHEM fosfórico
phosphoric[2]: **~ acid** *n* CHEM ácido fosfórico *m*
phosphorite *n* MINERAL fosforita *f*
phosphorize *vt* CHEM fosforizar
phosphorized *adj* CHEM fosforado
phosphorochalcite *n* MINERAL fosforocalcita *f*
phosphorogenic *adj* CHEM fosforogénico
phosphorus *n* (*P*) CHEM, ELECTRON, METALL, PHYS fósforo *m* (*P*); **~ doping** *n* ELECTRON alteración mediante fósforo *f*
phosphoryl *n* CHEM fosforil *m*
phosphorylase *n* CHEM fosforilasa *f*
phosphorylated *adj* CHEM fosforilado
phosphotungstate *n* CHEM fosfotungstato *m*
photicon *n* ELECTRON foticón *m*
photo: **~-chamber** *n* INSTR recámara fotográfica *f*; **~-coupled solid-state relay** *n* ELEC ENG relé de estado sólido foto-acoplado *m*; **~ page** *n* PRINT página gráfica *f*; **~ reconnaissance** *n* AIR TRANSP reconocimiento fotográfico *m*; **~-typesetting** *n* COMP&DP, PRINT fotocomposición *f*
photoactivation: **~ analysis** *n* RAD PHYS análisis por fotoactivación *m*
photoactive: **~ transducer** *n* ELEC ENG transductor fotoactivo *m*
photocathode *n* ELEC fotocátodo *m*, ELEC ENG cátodo de célula fotoeléctrica *m*, fotocátodo *m*, PHYS, TV fotocátodo *m*
photocell *n* GEN célula fotoeléctrica *f*, fotocelda *f*, fotocélula *f*
photochemical[1] *adj* CHEM, PHOTO, POLL fotoquímico
photochemical[2]: **~ effect** *n* FUELLESS efecto fotoquímico *m*; **~ smog** *n* POLL esmog fotoquímico *m*, humo-niebla fotoquímica *f*
photochemistry *n* CHEM, PHOTO, POLL fotoquímica *f*
photoclinometer *n* INSTR, PETROL fotoclinómetro *m*

photocomposer n AmE (cf **filmset** BrE) PRINT fotocompositora f

photoconducting: ~ **drum** n OPT tambor foto-conductor m; ~ **layer** n OPT capa fotoconductora f

photoconductive[1] adj ELEC, ELECTRON, OPT, PHOTO, PHYS, TELECOM fotoconductivo, fotoconductor

photoconductive[2]: ~ **cell** n ELECTRON, PHYS célula fotoconductiva f; ~ **gain** n ELECTRON ganancia fotoconductiva f

photoconductivity n ELEC, ELECTRON, OPT, PHOTO, PHYS, TELECOM fotoconductividad f

photocurrent n ELEC, ELECTRON, OPT, PHOTO, PHYS, TELECOM corriente fotoeléctrica f, fotocorriente f

photodetachment n NUCL of a transformer fotodesprendimiento m

photodetection n ELEC, ELECTRON, OPT, RAD PHYS, TELECOM fotodetección f

photodetector n ELEC, ELECTRON, OPT, RAD PHYS, TELECOM fotodetector m

photodiode n ELEC, ELECTRON, OPT, PHOTO, PHYS, TELECOM fotodiodo m; ~ **array** n ELECTRON conjunto de fotodiodos m

photodisintegration n OPT, PHYS fotodesintegración f

photodissociation n CHEM fotodisociación f

photoelectric[1] adj ELEC, ELECTRON fotoeléctrico

photoelectric[2]: ~ **amplifier** n ELECTRON amplificador fotoeléctrico m; ~ **cell** n (PEC) CHEM, CINEMAT, ELEC, ELECTRON, PHOTO, PHYS, RAD PHYS, SPACE, TV célula fotoeléctrica f; ~ **current** n ELEC corriente fotoeléctrica f; ~ **detector** n TRANSP célula fotoeléctrica f, detector fotoeléctrico m; ~ **device** n ELECTRON dispositivo fotoeléctrico m; ~ **effect** n ELECTRON, OPT, PHYS, RAD PHYS, TELECOM efecto fotoeléctrico m; ~ **emission** n ELECTRON emisión fotoeléctrica f; ~ **guard** n SAFE dispositivo protector fotoeléctrico m; ~ **layer** n COATINGS capa fotoeléctrica f; ~**light barriers and scanners** n pl PACK barreras y escáners fotoeléctricos m pl; ~ **microscope** n INSTR microscopio fotoeléctrico m; ~ **receiver** n OPT receptor fotoeléctrico m; ~ **register control** n PACK control fotoeléctrico del registro m; ~ **relay** n ELEC, ELEC ENG relé fotoeléctrico m; ~ **threshold** n PHYS umbral fotoeléctrico m; ~ **transducer** n ELEC ENG transductor fotoeléctrico m; ~ **tube** n ELECTRON tubo fotoeléctrico m

photoelectrically: ~**operated relay** n ELEC ENG relé accionado fotoeléctricamente m

photoelectron n ELEC, ELECTRON fotoelectrón m

photoelectronic adj ELEC, ELECTRON fotoelectrónico

photoemission n ELEC, ELECTRON, OPT, PHOTO, TV fotoemisión f; ~ **electron microscope** n INSTR microscopio electrónico de fotoemisión m

photoemissive[1] adj ELEC, ELECTRON, OPT, PHOTO, TV fotoemisor

photoemissive[2]: ~ **effect** n OPT, RAD PHYS, TELECOM efecto fotoemisivo m; ~ **layer** n ELECTRON estratificador fotoemisivo m

photoengrave vt ELECTRON, PRINT fotograbar

photoengraving n ELECTRON, PRINT fotograbado m

photoetching n PRINT proceso de grabado al ácido m

photoflood n CINEMAT fotorreflector m; ~ **bulb** n PHOTO bombilla fotoflood f

photofluorography n NUCL, RAD PHYS, SPACE fotofluorografía f

photogalvanic: ~ **cell** n FUELLESS célula fotogalvánica f

photogenerator n ELEC ENG, ELECTRON fotogenerador m

photogrammetric: ~ **camera** n INSTR cámara fotogramétrica f

photogrammetry n CONST, SPACE craft fotogrametría f

photograph[1] n CINEMAT, PHOTO, TV fotografía f

photograph[2]: ~ **with a tripod** vt PHOTO fotografiar con trípode

photographer n PHOTO fotógrafa f, fotógrafo m

photographic: ~ **apparatus** n PHOTO equipo fotográfico m; ~ **base-paper** n PAPER papel soporte fotográfico m; ~ **exposure** n ACOUST exposición fotográfica f; ~ **grain** n PHOTO, PRINT grano de la fotografía m; ~ **paper** n PHOTO papel fotográfico m; ~ **plate** n INSTR, PRINT placa fotográfica f; ~ **print** n PRINT copia fotográfica f; ~ **proof** n PRINT prueba fotográfica f

photography n CINEMAT, PHOTO, TV fotografía f

photogravure: ~ **ink** n COLOUR tinta para huecograbado f

photohalides n pl PHOTO fotohaluros m pl

photoinitiator n P&R, PHYS fotoiniciador m

photoionization n P&R, PHYS fotoionización f

photolithography n ELECTRON, PRINT fotolitografía f

photoluminescence n CHEM, RAD PHYS fotoluminiscencia f

photolysis n CHEM reaction, FUELLESS fotólisis f

photolytic adj CHEM reaction fotolítico

photomask n ELECTRON fotomáscara f

photomechanical[1] adj PRINT fotomecánico

photomechanical[2]: ~ **transfer** n PRINT transferencia por difusión f

photometer n CINEMAT, INSTR, P&R, PHOTO, PHYS fotómetro m

photometric: ~ **brightness** n RAD PHYS brillo fotométrico m; ~**light source** n INSTR fuente de luz fotométrica f

photometry n PHYS fotometría f

photomicrogram n METALL fotomicrograma m

photomicrograph n METALL fotomicrografía f

photomicroscope n INSTR, METALL fotomicroscopio m

photomounting n PHOTO fotomontaje m

photomultiplier n ELECTRON, PART PHYS, PHYS, RAD PHYS fotomultiplicador m

photon n OPT, PART PHYS, PHYS, RAD PHYS fotón m; ~ **amplification** n PART PHYS, RAD PHYS amplificación de fotones f, amplificación fotónica f; ~**counting camera** n cámara de recuento de fotones f; ~ **detector** n PART PHYS detector de fotones m; ~ **energy** n PART PHYS energía de fotones f, energía fotónica f; ~ **log** n PETROL perfil fotónico m; ~ **noise** n OPT ruido fotónico m, TELECOM ruido de fotones m; ~**photon absorption** n PART PHYS absorción fotón-fotón f

photoplotter n COMP&DP, ELECTRON fototrazador m

photopolymer n CHEM, PHYS, PRINT fotopolímero m; ~ **coating** n PRINT recubierto de fotopolímero m

photopolymerization n CHEM, PHYS, PRINT fotopolimerización f

photoreaction n CHEM, PHOTO fotoreacción f

photoresist n ELECTRON fotoprotector m; ~ **coating** n ELECTRON revestimiento fotoprotector m

photoresistant: ~ **pigment** n COLOUR pigmento fotoresistente m, sustancia fotoendurecible f

photoresistor *n* METALL, PHOTO, RAD PHYS fotoresistor *m*

photosensitive[1] *adj* GEN fotosensible

photosensitive[2]: ~ **glass** *n* C&G vidrio fotosensible *m*; ~ **resist** *n* COLOUR reserva fotosensible *f*; ~ **tube** *n* ELECTRON tubo fotosensible *m*

photosensitivity *n* CINEMAT, ELECTRON, PHOTO, PHYS, PRINT fotosensibilidad *f*

photosensor *n* ELECTRON, OPT, PHOTO fotosensor *m*

photosphere *n* RAD PHYS, SPACE fotosfera *f*

photospheric: ~ **absorption** *n* RAD PHYS absorción fotosférica *f*

photosynthesis *n* CHEM, FUELLESS, HYDROL fotosíntesis *f*

photosynthetic: ~ **layer** *n* OCEAN capa de fotosíntesis *f*, capa eufótica *f*

phototelegraphy *n* TELECOM fototelegrafía *f*

phototheodolite *n* INSTR fototeodolito *m*

phototransistor *n* COMP&DP, ELECTRON, RAD PHYS fototransistor *m*

phototube *n* ELECTRON fototubo *m*, tubo fotoeléctrico *m*, INSTR fototubo *m*; ~ **relay** *n* ELEC ENG relé de tubo fotoeléctrico *m*

photovaristor *n* ELEC ENG fotovaristor *m*

photovoltaic[1] *adj* ELECTRON, PHYS, SPACE fotovoltaico *m*

photovoltaic[2]: ~ **cell** *n* ELEC ENG, FUELLESS, PHYS, SPACE *craft* célula fotovoltaica *f*; ~ **current** *n* ELEC ENG corriente fotovoltaica *f*; ~ **effect** *n* ELEC ENG, FUELLESS, OPT, PHYS, SPACE, TELECOM efecto fotovoltaico *m*; ~ **generator** *n* ELEC ENG generador fotovoltaico *m*; ~ **solar-power plant** *n* ELEC ENG, FUELLESS planta de energía solar fotovoltaica *f*

phreatic: ~ **bed** *n* WATER capa freática *f*; ~ **ground water** *n* GEOL capa freática *f*; ~ **level** *n* WATER nivel freático *m*

phthalamide *n* CHEM ftalamida *f*

phthalate *n* CHEM ftalato *m*

phthalein *n* CHEM ftaleína *f*

phthalic[1] *adj* CHEM ftálico *m*

phthalic[2]: ~ **anhydride** *n* CHEM, P&R anhídrido ftálico *m*

phthalide *n* CHEM ftálido *m*

phthalin *n* CHEM ftalina *f*

phthalocyanine *n* P&R ftalocianina *f*

phugoid *n* AIR TRANSP fugoide *m*; ~ **effect** *n* AIR TRANSP efecto fugoide *m*; ~ **oscillation** *n* AIR TRANSP oscilación fugoide *f*

phycology *n* OCEAN ficología *f*

phyllite *n* GEOL, PETROL filita *f*

phyllitic: ~ **marble** *n* GEOL mármol filítico *m*

phyllonite *n* GEOL filonita *f*

phyric[1] *adj* GEOL *programming* fírico

phyric[2] *n* PETROL fírico *m*

physalite *n* MINERAL fisalita *f*

physical: ~ **agent** *n* POLL agente físico *m*; ~ **balance** *n* LAB balanza física *f*; ~ **circuit** *n* ELEC ENG circuito metálico *m*, parfísico *m*; ~ **connection** *n* (*PhC*) TELECOM conexión física *f*; ~ **delivery** *n* TELECOM entrega física *f*; ~ **delivery access unit** *n* (*PDAU*) TELECOM unidad de acceso a la entrega física *f*; ~ **delivery system** *n* (*PDS*) TELECOM sistema de entrega física *m*; ~ **file** *n* COMP&DP archivo físico *m*, fichero físico *m*; ~ **helical editing** *n* TV edición físico-helicoidal *f*; ~ **interface** *n* (*PI*) TELECOM interfaz físico *m*; ~ **layer** *n* COMP&DP *open systems interconnection* capa física *f*, nivel físico *m*, TELECOM capa

física *f*; ~ **layer operations and maintenance** *n pl* (*PL-OAM*) TELECOM explotación y mantenimiento de la capa física *f*; ~ **layer protocol** *n* COMP&DP protocolo del nivel físico *m*; ~ **layer service** *n* (*PLS*) TELECOM servicio de la capa física *m*; ~ **medium sublayer** *n* TELECOM subcapa física media *f*; ~ **memory** *n* ELEC ENG memoria física *f*; ~ **optics** *n* OPT, PHYS, TELECOM óptica física *f*; ~ **property** *n* P&R, PHYS propiedad física *f*; ~ **quadruplex editing** *n* TV edición por cuadruplex física *f*; ~ **record** *n* COMP&DP registro físico *m*; ~ **security** *n* TELECOM seguridad física *f*; ~ **service** *n* (*PhS*) TELECOM servicio físico *m*; ~ **water treatment** *n* WATER tratamiento físico del agua *m*

physico: ~ **chemical environment** *n* POLL entorno físico-químico *m*, medio ambiente físico-químico *m*

physiochemistry *n* CHEM fisioquímica *f*

physiological: ~ **effects** *n pl* SAFE *nuclear power plant* efectos fisiológicos *m pl*; ~ **noise** *n* ACOUST acústica fisiológica *f*

physostigmine *n* CHEM fisostigmina *f*

phytase *n* FOOD fitasa *f*

phytic: ~ **acid** *n* CHEM, FOOD ácido fítico *m*

phytin *n* CHEM, FOOD fitina *f*

phytocidal *adj* AGRIC, CHEM fitocídico

phytopathologist *n* AGRIC fitopatólogo *m*

phytoplankton: ~ **bloom** *n* OCEAN florescencia del fitoplancton *f*, florescencia fitoplanctónica *f*

phytotoxic *adj* AGRIC, CHEM fitotóxico

pi: ~ **bond** *n* CHEM *covalent* enlace pi *m* enlace *m* ligadura pi *f*; ~ **characters** *n pl* PRINT caracteres raros *m pl*; ~ **network** *n* ELEC ENG, PHYS red pi *f*; ~ **types** *n pl* PRINT tipos raros *m pl*; ~ **winding** *n* ELEC ENG devanado en pi *m*

PI *abbr* TELECOM (*physical interface*) interfaz físico *m*, TELECOM (*presentation indicator*), indicador de presentación *m*

PIA *abbr* (*peripheral interface adaptor*) COMP&DP PIA (*adaptador de interfaz de periféricos*)

piano: ~ **wire** *n* MECH ENG cable con hilos desnudos *m*, cuerda de piano *f*

piazetta *n* CONST *planning* plazoleta *f*

pica *n* PRINT pica *f*

pick[1] *n* C&G pico *m*, HYDRAUL martillo para desincrustar calderas *m*, MINE escogimiento *m*, PROD martillo de desincrustar *m*, pico *m*, piocha *f*, TEXTIL pasada *f*; ~ **and-claw crowbar** *n* CONST palanca de pie de cabra *f*; ~ **breaker** *n* COAL rozadora de percusión *f*; ~ **hammer** *n* PROD martillo picador *m*; ~ **handle** *n* CONST piqueta *f*, PROD mango de pico *m*; ~ **list** *n* PROD lista de pedido *f*; ~ **mattock** *n* CONST, PROD zapapico *m*; ~ **rate** *n* TEXTIL proporción de pasadas *f*; ~ **resistance** *n* PAPER resistencia al arrancado *f*; ~ **up** *n* ACOUST captador *m*, AUTO reprise *m*, ELEC *measurement* lector electromagnético *m*, MECH ENG toma *f*, captación *f*, recepción *f*, NUCL captación *f*, PAPER tomador *m*, TELECOM captación *f*, captador *m*; ~ **up angle** *n* MECH ENG ángulo de acoplamiento *m*, PRINT ángulo tomador *m*; ~ **up arm** *n* ACOUST brazo del fonocaptor *m*; ~ **up baler** *n* AGRIC recogedora-enfardadora *f*; ~ **up fitting** *n* MECH ENG accesorio de captación *m*; ~ **up for contact meter** *n* MECH ENG captador para medidor de contacto *m*; ~ **up freight train** *n* AmE (*cf pick-up goods train BrE*) RAIL tren de recogida de carga *m*; ~ **up gear** *n* MECH ENG dispositivo captador *m*; ~ **up**

goods train *n BrE* (*cf pick-up freight train AmE*) RAIL tren de recogida de carga *m*; **~-up head** *n* ACOUST cabeza del fonocaptor *f*; **~-up lorry** *n BrE* (*cf pick-up truck AmE*) AGRIC camioneta *f*, AUTO, VEH camioneta *f*, furgoneta *f*; **~-up roll** *n* PAPER rodillo tomador *m*; **~-up transmitter** *n* TV transmisor de imágenes *m*; **~-up truck** *n AmE* (*cf pick-up lorry BrE*) AGRIC camioneta *f*, AUTO, VEH camioneta *f*, furgoneta *f*; **~-up tube** *n* ELECTRON tubo receptor *m*, TV tubo captador *m*, tubo tomavistas *m*; **~-up voltage** *n* ELEC ENG voltaje de captación *m*

pick[2] *vt* CONST picar, *lock* forzar, MINE escoger, PAPER arrancar, repelar; **~ up a mooring** *vt* WATER TRANSP *manoeuvre, yachts* tomar un muerto, tomar una boya de amarre

pickax *AmE see* **pickaxe** *BrE*

pickaxe *n BrE* CONST pico *m*, piqueta *f*, zapapico *m*, PROD zapapico *m*

picked: **~ ore** *n* MINE minerales escogidos *m pl*, minerales seleccionados *m pl*

picker *n* MINE aguja de mina *f*, aguja de polvorero *f*, destarcador *m* (*Esp*), disparador de barrenos *m* (*Esp*), martillo para clasificar *m*, pico de minero *m*, polvorero *m* (*AmL*)

picket *n* CONST *surveying* estaca *f*, piquete *m*

picking *n* AGRIC recolección *f*, CONST estaquillado *m*, PAPER arrancado *m*, arrancado superficial *m*, PRINT repelado *m*, TEXTIL picada *f*; **~ of arrivals** *n* GEOL clasificación de llegadas *f*; **~ belt** *n* MINE cinta de escogido *f* (*AmL*), cinta de recogida *f* (*Esp*); **~ list** *n* PROD lista de pedido *f*; **~ resistance** *n* PAPER resistencia al arrancado *f*; **~ season** *n* AGRIC época de recolección *f*; **~ stock** *n* PROD existencia de pedido *f*; **~ table** *n* MINE mesa de clasificación *f*, mesa de cribado *f*

pickle *n* OCEAN adobo *m*

pickling *n* CHEM decapado *m*, decapaje *m*, CONST limpieza de metales *f*, WATER TRANSP *ship maintenance* decapado *m*, solución ácida *f*; **~ brine** *n* FOOD, OCEAN preparación *f*

picks: **~ per inch** *n pl* TEXTIL pasadas por pulgada *f pl*

pico *n* (*p*) METR pico (*p*)

picoline *n* CHEM picolina *f*

picosecond *n* COMP&DP, NUCL, PHYS picosegundo *m*; **~ pulse** *n* PART PHYS pulso en picosegundos *m*

picotite *n* MINERAL picotita *f*

picrate *n* CHEM picrato *m*

picric *adj* CHEM pícrico

picrite *n* PETROL picrita *f*

picrol *n* CHEM picrol *m*

picrolite *n* MINERAL picrolita *f*

picromerite *n* MINERAL picromerita *f*

picrotin *n* CHEM picrotina *f*

PICS *abbr* (*protocol-implementation conformance statement*) TELECOM declaración de conformidad en el cumplimiento del protocolo *f*

pictograph *n* PRINT pictograma *m*

pictorial: **~ symbol** *n* SAFE pictograma *m*

picture *n* CINEMAT, COMP&DP, PHOTO, TV imagen *f*; **~ amplitude** *n* TELECOM amplitud de imagen *f*; **~ black** *n* TELECOM nivel de negro *m*, señal de densidad máxima *f*; **~ book** *n* PRINT libro ilustrado *m*; **~ bounce** *n* TELECOM temblor de la imagen *m*; **~ break-up** *n* TV desgarro de imagen *m*; **~ brightness** *n* TELECOM brillo de la imagen *m*; **~ carrier** *n* ELECTRON, TELECOM, TV portadora de

imagen *f*; **~-carrier frequency** *n* ELECTRON, TELECOM, TV frecuencia de la portadora de imagen *f*; **~ circuit** *n* TELECOM circuito de imagen *m*; **~ clap** *n* CINEMAT imagen de la claqueta *f*; **~ compression** *n* TELECOM, TV compresión de imagen *f*; **~ contrast** *n* TELECOM contraste de imagen *m*; **~-control coil** *n* TELECOM bobina de encuadre de la imagen *f*; **~-cuing mark** *n* CINEMAT marca de sincronización de la imagen *f*; **~ definition** *n* TELECOM definición de la imagen *f*; **~ dot** *n* PRINT punto de la imagen *m*, TELECOM elemento de imagen *m*; **~ drift** *n* TV deslizamiento de la imagen *m*; **~-fading** *n* CINEMAT desvanecimiento de la imagen *m*, fundido de imagen *m*, TV fundido de imagen *m*; **~ failure** *n* TV interrupción de imagen *f*; **~ filter** *n* TELECOM filtro de imagen *m*; **~ flutter** *n* TV fluctuación de imagen *f*; **~ gate** *n* CINEMAT ventanilla de proyección *f*; **~ glass** *n* C&G vidriera *f*; **~ head** *n* CINEMAT cabezal de proyección *m*; **~ library** *n* PHOTO biblioteca de fotografías *f*, fototeca *f*; **~ lock** *n* TELECOM, TV fijación de imagen *f*; **~ match** *n* TV adaptación de imagen *f*; **~-modulated generator** *n* TELECOM generador modulado por la imagen *m*; **~ monitor** *n* TV monitor de imagen *m*; **~ pass band** *n* TELECOM banda de paso de video *f* (*AmL*), banda de paso de vídeo *f* (*Esp*); **~ processing** *n* COMP&DP procesamiento de imágenes *m*; **~-quality control** *n* TELECOM control de la calidad de la imagen *m*; **~ ratio** *n* CINEMAT formato de la imagen *m*, relación de las dimensiones de la imagen *f*; **~ reel** *n* CINEMAT, TV bobina de imagen *f*; **~ safety area** *n* CINEMAT área de seguridad de la imagen *f*; **~ shift** *n* TV desplazamiento de imagen *m*; **~ signal** *n* ELECTRON señal de imagen *f*, TELECOM señal de video *f* (*AmL*), señal de vídeo *f* (*Esp*); **~ size** *n* PHOTO tamaño de fotografía *m*; **~ slip** *n* CINEMAT deslizamiento de la imagen *m*; **~ strip** *n* PRINT tira de imágenes *f*; **~ synchronizer** *n* CINEMAT sincronizador de la imagen *m*; **~ tube** *n* ELECTRON, TELECOM tubo de imagen *m*; **~ white** *n* TELECOM nivel de blanco *m*, señal de densidad mínima *f*

pie *n* PRINT conjunto de tipos desordenados *m*; **~ chart** *n* COMP&DP gráfico de sectores *m*, MATH ciclograma *m*, diagrama de sectores *m*, gráfico de sectores *m*; **~ section** *n* ELEC ENG sección circular *f*; **~ winding** *n* ELEC ENG bobinado en disco aplanado *m*

piece[1]: **~-dyed** *adj* TEXTIL teñido en pieza

piece[2] *n* C&G pieza *f*; **~ accent** *n AmE* (*cf loose accent BrE*) PRINT acento postizo *m*; **~ goods** *n pl* TEXTIL géneros en pieza *m pl*

piedmontite *n* MINERAL piamontita *f*

pier *n* CONST *masonry support of arch* pilar *m*, *of stone bridge* estribo *m*, *of timber bridge* pilote *m*, WATER TRANSP *jetty, breakwater* embarcadero *m*, escollera *f*, espigón *m*

pierce *vt* PROD *holes* perforar, ventear, *moulds* agujerear

Pierce: **~ oscillator** *n* ELECTRON oscilador Pierce *m*

piercer *n* MECH ENG *bow-drill* perforadora *f*, punzón *m*, taladrador *m*, taladro de mano *m*, PROD *moulds* aguja de ventear *f*, punzón *m*

piercing *n* PROD venteo *m*; **~-die** *n* MECH ENG *press tools* estampa perforadora *f*, troquel de punzonar *m*

pierhead *n* OCEAN morro *m*, WATER TRANSP morro de la escollera *m*

piezoelectric[1] *adj* GEN piezoeléctrico

piezoelectric[2]: **~ crystal** *n* ELEC ENG, TELECOM cristal

piezoeléctrico *m*; ~ **detector** *n* TRANSP detector piezoeléctrico *m*; ~ **effect** *n* ELEC ENG, PHYS efecto piezoeléctrico *m*; ~ **element** *n* ELEC ENG elemento piezoeléctrico *m*; ~ **microphone** *n* ACOUST micrófono piezoeléctrico *m*; ~ **oscillator** *n* ELEC, ELEC ENG, PHYS oscilador piezoeléctrico *m*; ~ **pick-up** *n* MECH ENG captador piezoeléctrico *m*, fonocaptor piezoeléctrico *m*; ~ **properties** *n pl* ELEC ENG propiedades piezoeléctricas *f pl*; ~ **resonator** *n* ELEC ENG resonador piezoeléctrico *m*; ~ **sensor** *n* ELEC, OPT sensor piezoeléctrico *m*; ~ **substrate** *n* ELEC ENG substrato piezoeléctrico *m*; ~ **transducer** *n* ELEC ENG transductor piezoeléctrico *m*; ~**-tuned magnetron** *n* ELEC ENG magnetrón modulado piezo-eléctricamente *m*
piezoelectricity *n* GEN piezoelectricidad *f*
piezometer *n* COAL, CONST piezómetro *m*
piezometric: ~ **head** *n* PETR TECH altura piezométrica *f*; ~ **map** *n* PETR TECH mapa piezométrico *m*
piezomicrophone *n* ACOUST micrófono piezoeléctrico *m*
pig *n* PETR TECH diablo *m*, marrano *m*, raspador de tuberías *m*, PETROL diablo *m*, taco limpiador *m*, limpiador *m*, raspatubos *m*, PROD *founding* galápago *m*, lingote *m*, pan *m*, *general term* taco de limpiar *m*, trineo de aparejo *m*, *pipes* raspador *m*; ~**-and-ore process** *n* PROD procedimiento de fundición y mineral *m*; ~ **bed** *n* METALL, PROD era de colada *f*; ~ **boiling** *n* PROD pudelación húmeda *f*, pudelaje caliente *m*; ~ **iron** *n* METALL, PROD arrabio *m*, fundición bruta de primera fusión *f*, hierro en lingotes *m*; ~ **of iron** *n* PROD *founding* lingote de hierro *m*; ~**-iron breaker** *n* METALL, PROD rompelingotes *m*; ~**-iron yard** *n* METALL, PROD *foundry* parque de arrabio *m*; ~ **lead** *n* PROD plomo en lincotes *m*, plomo en panes *m*; ~ **of lead** *n* PROD *founding* galápago de plomo *m*; ~ **metal** *n* METALL, PROD metal de colada *m*; ~ **mold** *AmE*, ~ **mould** *BrE* *n* PROD molde de lingote *m*; ~ **yard** *n* METALL, PROD *foundry* parque de arrabio *m*
pigeonite *n* MINERAL pigeonita *f*
piggyback: ~ **satellite** *n* SPACE satélite secundario en el lanzador *m*, satélite transportado sobre otro satélite *m*; ~ **traffic** *n* RAIL tráfico de remolques sobre vagón de ferrocarril *m*; ~ **transport** *n* TRANSP transporte de remolques en vagón plataforma *m*
pigment¹ *n* C&G, CHEM, COLOUR, P&R, TEXTIL pigmento *m*; ~ **dyeing** *n* COLOUR teñido con pigmentos *m*
pigment² *vt* COLOUR, TEXTIL pigmentar
pigmentation *n* COLOUR, TEXTIL pigmentación *f*
pigmented *adj* COLOUR, TEXTIL pigmentado
pigtail *n* ELEC cable flexible de conexión *m*, ELEC ENG acoplamiento metálico flexible *m*, cable conductor de llegada *m*, cable flexible de conexión *m*, clavija macho sobresaliente *f*, enrollado en espiral *m*; ~ **hook** *n* PROD gancho de cola de cerdo *m*
pile¹ *n* COAL montón *m*, pila *f*, CONST *pointed timber* pilote *m*, *heap* pila *f*, ELEC ENG pila eléctrica *f*, NUCL pila *f*, PRINT pila de hojas *f*, PROD *faggot* paquete *m*, TEXTIL montón *m*, pelo *m*, WATER TRANSP *ryepeck* pilote *m*, tablaestaca *f*; ~ **block** *n* COAL falso pilote *m*; ~ **board** *n* PRINT mesa de la pila *f*; ~ **cap** *n* COAL encepado de cabezas de pilotes *m*, sombrerete del pilote *m*, CONST cabezal *m*; ~ **cutoff level** *n* COAL, CONST nivel de corte del pilote *m*; ~ **drawer** *n* CONST cajón de apilar *m*; ~**-driver** *n* COAL hincadora de

pilotes *f*, martinete *m*, CONST martinete de hinca *m*, martillo pilón *m*; ~**-driving** *n* COAL hinca de pilotes *f*, CONST hincado de pilotes *m*, MINE hinca de pilotes *f*; ~**-driving formula** *n* COAL fórmula para la hincadura de los pilotes *f*; ~**-driving record** *n* COAL registro de hincadura de los pilotes *m*; ~ **extractor** *n* CONST arrancapilotes *m*; ~ **ferrule** *n* CONST zuncho de pilote *m*; ~ **footing** *n* COAL zapata sobre pilotes *f*; ~ **groin** *AmE see pile groyne BrE*; ~ **group** *n* COAL grupo de pilotes *m*; ~ **groyne** *n BrE* WATER estacada de pilotes *f*; ~ **hammer** *n AmE* (*cf piling hammer BrE*) COAL martillo pilón *m*, CONST martillo pilón *m*, maza *f*, hincadora de pilotes *f*; ~ **head** *n* COAL cabeza de pilote *f*; ~ **height** *n* TEXTIL altura de pelo *f*; ~ **hood** *n* CONST capuchón *m*; ~ **hoop** *n* CONST cincho de pilote *m*; ~ **jogger** *n* PRINT igualador de pilas *m*; ~ **joint** *n* COAL diaclasa *f*; ~ **length** *n* COAL longitud del pilote *f*; **in ~ loop** *n* NUCL lazo intranuclear *m*; ~ **plank** *n* CONST tablestaca *f*; ~ **point** *n* COAL azabache *m*, azuche *m*; ~ **ram** *n* COAL martinete *m*; ~ **scanner** *n* PRINT escáner de pilas *m*; ~ **segment** *n* COAL segmento del pilote *m*; ~ **shoe** *n* COAL, CONST azuche *m*; ~ **situation plan** *n* COAL plan de situación de pilotes *m*; ~ **splice** *n* COAL refuerzo de pilotes *m*; ~ **tip** *n* COAL extremidad del pilote *f*, inclinación del pilote *f*; ~**-up** *n* ELEC ENG contactos apilados *m pl*; ~ **weight** *n* TEXTIL peso de pelo *m*; ~ **work** *n* CONST pilotaje *m*; ~**-wound coil** *n* ELEC bobina en pilas *f*, bobinado en pilas *m*
pile² *vt* COAL amontonar (*AmL*), hacer una bola de, taluzar (*Esp*), CONST *stack* apilar, PROD empaquetar
pilfer¹: ~**-proof** *adj* PACK a prueba de robos
pilfer²: ~**-proof seal** *n* PACK precinto a prueba de robos *m*
piling *n* COAL avance con agujas *m*, empaquetado *m*, COMP&DP apilamiento *m*, CONST *of piles collectively* pilotaje *m*, *stacking* amontonamiento *m*, *driving piles* apilamiento *m*, CRYSTALL, ELEC ENG, GEOM apilamiento *m*, MINE berlingado *m*, reverzo *m*, avance con agujas *m*, blindaje *m*, entibación *f*, PETR TECH pilotaje *m*, PRINT espesamiento de la tinta *m*, PROD recalzo con pilotes *m*, amontonamiento *m*, empaquetado *m*, pilotaje *m*, apilamiento *m*; ~ **frame** *n* CONST estructura de pilotaje *f*; ~ **hammer** *n BrE* (*cf pile hammer AmE*) COAL martillo pilón *m*, CONST martillo pilón *m*, maza *f*, hincadora de pilotes ; ~ **up** *n* COMP&DP, CONST, CRYSTALL, ELEC ENG, GEOM, PROD apilamiento *m*
pill *vt* TEXTIL pildear
pillar *n* C&G pilar *m*, CONST poste *m*, *pier of arch* columna *f*, GEOPHYS puntal *m*, columna *f*, soporte *m*, pilar *m*, MINE montón *m* (*Esp*), terreno estéril *m* (*AmL*), TELECOM pilar *m*, WATER TRANSP *shipbuilding* puntal *m*; ~ **balance** *n* CONST equilibrio de la columna *m*; ~ **buoy** *n* WATER TRANSP *navigation mark* boya luminosa de castillete *f*; ~ **drawing** *n* COAL demolición de macizos *f*, despilaramiento *m*, MINE despilaramiento *m*; ~ **drill** *n* MECH ENG taladro de columna *m*; ~**-drilling machine** *n* MECH ENG perforadora de columna *f*, taladradora de columna *f*; ~ **extraction** *n* COAL extracción de los pilares *f*; ~ **fire-hydrant** *n* SAFE hidrante contra incendio tipo pilar *m*; ~ **hydrant** *n* MECH ENG, WATER hidrante de columna *m*; ~ **scales** *n pl* LAB báscula de columna *f*; ~ **stand** *n* INSTR estand de columna *m*; ~ **working** *n*

COAL demolición de pilares *f*, despilaramiento *m*, explotación por pilares *f*, MINE despilaramiento *m*

pillbox *n* MILIT blocao de cemento *m*, línea de transmisión de placas paralelas *f*

pilling *n* TEXTIL pildeo *m*

pillion *n* VEH asiento trasero *m*

pillow *n* MECH ENG gorrón *m*, rangua *f*, tejuelo *m*, buje *m*, *of bearing-brush* cojinete *m*; ~ **block** *n* MECH ENG chumacera *f*, cojinete *m*, soporte *m*; ~ **distortion** *n* CINEMAT distorsión cóncava *f*; ~ **lava** *n* GEOL diabasa esferoidal *f*, lava almohadillada *f*

pilocarpidine *n* CHEM pilocarpidina *f*

pilocarpine *n* CHEM pilocarpina *f*

pilot¹ *n* AIR TRANSP aviador *m*, piloto *m*, RAIL máquina exploradora *f*, quitapiedras *m*, TELECOM onda piloto *f*, piloto *m*, TV piloto *m*, WATER TRANSP *navigation* práctico *m*, piloto *m*; ~ **balloon** *n* AIR TRANSP globo piloto *m*, globo sonda *m*; ~ **bearing** *n* AUTO cojinete piloto *m*; ~ **bit** *n* PETR TECH barrena de arrastre *f*, broca *f*, mecha piloto *f*, trépano piloto *m*; ~ **boat** *n* WATER TRANSP embarcación de práctico *f*; ~ **bushing** *n* AUTO casquillo piloto *m*, cojinete piloto *m*, manguito piloto *m*; ~ **carrier** *n* TELECOM onda portadora piloto *f*, portadora piloto *f*; ~ **chart** *n* WATER TRANSP *navigation* carta de navegación *f*; ~ **claw** *n* CINEMAT garfio auxiliar *m*; ~ **cutter** *n* WATER TRANSP lancha de práctico *f*; ~ **flag** *n* WATER TRANSP bandera de práctico *f*; ~ **flame** *n* MECH ENG llama auxiliar *f*, llama de encendido *f*, llama piloto *f*; ~ **frequency** *n* CINEMAT frecuencia auxiliar *f*; ~ **hole** *n* MECH ENG agujero guía *m*, agujero piloto *m*, orificio guía *m*, PETROL agujero guía *m*; ~ **lamp** *n* AmE (*cf pilot light BrE*) CINEMAT lámpara indicadora *f*, ELEC ENG lámpara indicadora *f*, lámpara piloto *f*, GAS lámpara indicadora *f*, lámpara testigo *f*, VEH lámpara testigo *f*, lámpara piloto *f*; ~ **light** *n* BrE (*cf pilot lamp AmE*) CINEMAT lámpara indicadora *f*, ELEC ENG lámpara indicadora *f*, lámpara piloto *f*, GAS lámpara indicadora *f*, lámpara testigo *f*, VEH lámpara testigo *f*, lámpara piloto *f*; ~ **network** *n* ELEC *supply* red de distribución del conductor auxiliar *f*; ~ **operated check valve** *n* PROD válvula de retención accionada por piloto *f*; ~ **plant** *n* COAL planta piloto *f*; ~ **pressure chamber** *n* AIR TRANSP cámara de presión piloto *f*; ~ **project** *n* PETR TECH proyecto experimental *m*; ~ **signal** *n* TV señal piloto *f*; ~ **switch** *n* ELEC interruptor piloto *m*; ~ **test** *n* COAL ensayo piloto *m*, prueba piloto *f*; ~ **tone** *n* TV onda piloto *f*, tono piloto *m*; ~ **tone cable** *n* CINEMAT cable de la señal de identificación *m*; ~ **tone generator** *n* CINEMAT generador de la señal de identificación *m*; ~ **tone sound** *n* CINEMAT señal sonora de identificación *f*; ~ **valve** *n* MECH ENG válvula auxiliar *f*, válvula de mando *f*, válvula piloto *f*; ~ **waters** *n pl* WATER TRANSP zona de practicaje *f*; ~ **wheel** *n* MECH ENG volante de maniguetas radiales *m*; ~ **wire** *n* ELEC ENG hilo auxiliar *m*

pilot² *vt* AIR TRANSP, TRANSP, WATER TRANSP pilotar (*Esp*), pilotear (*AmL*)

pilotage *n* OCEAN, WATER TRANSP practicaje *m*; ~ **waters** *n pl* OCEAN zona de practicaje *f*; ~ **zone** *n* OCEAN zona de practicaje *f*

pilotless: ~ **target aircraft** *n* AIR TRANSP, MILIT avión blanco sin piloto *m*

pilotone *n* CINEMAT señal de identificación *f*

pimaric *adj* CHEM pimárico

pimelic *adj* CHEM pimélico

pimelite *n* MINERAL pimelita *f*

pi-meson *n* PART PHYS, PHYS mesón pi *m*, pión *m*

pin *n* CINEMAT clavija *f*, CONST *of hinge* pasador *m*, *of lock* clavija *f*, ELEC ENG clavija *f*, chaveta *f*, patilla *f*, HYDRAUL *valves* vástago *m*, MECH, MECH ENG, PROD gozne *m*, púa *f*, *valves* espiga *m*, vástago *f*, *connectors* alfiler de contacto *m*; ~ **assignment** *n* PROD asignación de clavijas *f*; ~ **chain** *n* CONST pasador con cadena *m*; ~ **connector** *n* CINEMAT conector de puntas *m*; ~ **coupling** *n* MECH ENG acoplamiento por pasador *m*, empalme con manguito y pasadores *m*; ~ **drift** *n* MECH ENG botapasador *m*, sacapasador *m*; ~ **drill** *n* MECH ENG broca con guía *f*, broca de punzón *f*, broca de tetón cilíndrico *f*; ~ **driver** *n* MECH, MECH ENG botador *m*; ~ **extractor** *n* MECH ENG botapasador *m*, sacapasador *m*; ~ **frame** *n* TEXTIL bastidor de clavijas *m*; ~ **insulator** *n* ELEC, ELEC ENG aislante de clavija *m*, aislador rígido *m*, aislante rígido *m*; ~ **movement** *n* CINEMAT movimiento del garfio *m*; ~ **punch** *n* CONST punzón de clavo *m*; ~ **register** *n* PRINT registro de botonera *m*; **shearing** ~ *n* PRINT alfiler de corte *m*; ~ **shears** *n pl* CONST tijeras de espiga *f pl*; ~ **spanner** *n* CONST llave de gancho con espiga *f*; ~ **stenter** *n* TEXTIL rame de agujas *m*; ~ **termination** *n* PROD terminación en clavija *f*; ~**-to-pin breakdown** *n* ELEC ENG ruptura entre patillas *f*; ~**-to-pin capacitance** *n* ELEC ENG capacitancia entre patillas *f*; ~ **valve** *n* CONST válvula de aguja *f*; ~ **vice** *n* BrE CONST tornillo de carpintero de mano *m*, tornillo de mano *m*; ~ **vise** *AmE see pin vice BrE*; ~ **weir** *n* WATER vertedero de aguja *m*; ~ **wrench** *n* CONST llave de espiga *f*, MECH ENG llave de pitones *f*, llave para tuercas redondas *f*

PIN¹ *abbr* (*personal identification number*) ELECTRON NIP (*número de identificación personal*)

PIN²: ~ **assignment** *n* PROD asignación del número de identidad personal *f*; ~ **attenuator diode** *n* ELECTRON diodo atenuador NIP *m*; ~ **diode** *n* ELECTRON, TELECOM diodo PIN *m*; ~**-diode attenuator** *n* ELECTRON atenuador de diodo NIP *m*; ~**-diode modulation** *n* ELECTRON modulación de diodo NIP *f*; ~**-diode phase shifter** *n* ELECTRON variador de fase de diodo NIP *m*; ~ **photodiode** *n* ELECTRON fotodiodo NIP *m*, fotodiodo PIN *m*, fotodiodo positivo-intrínseco-negativo *m*

pinacol *n* CHEM pinacol *m*

pinacolic *adj* CHEM pinacólico

pinacoline *n* CHEM pinacolina *f*

pinacolone *n* CHEM pinacolona *f*

pinacone *n* CHEM pinacona *f*

pinboard *n* ELEC ENG cuadro de conexiones *m*, tablero de control *m*

pincers *n pl* CONST alicates *m pl*, tenazas *f pl*, MECH, MECH ENG, PROD, VEH alicates *m pl*

pinch¹ *n* MINE *vein, lode* adelgazamiento *m*, contracción *f*; ~ **cock** *n* CHEM válvula por estrechamiento *f*, CONST apretadora *f*; ~ **effect** *n* ACOUST irregularidad del surco *f*; ~ **nut** *n* MECH ENG contratuerca *f*; ~**-off effect** *n* ELECTRON efecto de punto de contacto *m*; ~**-out trap** *n* PETR TECH trampa por acuñamiento *f*; ~ **point** *n* MECH ENG *mechanical handling equipment* punta de espolón *f*; ~ **roller** *n* CINEMAT, PRINT rodillo de presión *m*; ~ **and swell** *n* GEOL contracción e hinchamiento *f*

pinch[2] *vt* MECH ENG apretar, contraer, estrechar, morder

pinched: ~ **resistor** *n* ELEC ENG resistencia reostrictiva *f*

pinchers *n pl* C&G pinzas *f pl*

pinching: ~ **bar** *n* CONST palanca de pie de cabra *f*; ~ **tools** *n pl* C&G herramientas para pinchar *f pl*

pincushion: ~ **distortion** *n* CINEMAT, PHOTO, PHYS distorsión en corsé *f*

pine: ~ **oil** *n* DETERG aceite de pino *m*

pinene *n* CHEM pineno *m*

PIN-FET: ~ **integrated receiver** *n* OPT receptor integrado PIN-FET *m*

pinger *n* OCEAN percutor del sonar *m*

pinging *AmE see pinking BrE*

pinhole *n* CINEMAT perforación *f*, OPT agujero puntual *m*, P&R pequeña burbuja ocluida *f*, PAPER agujero de alfiler *m*, microagujero *m*, PHOTO punto transparente *m*, PHYS *spacecraft* agujero puntual *m*; ~ **camera** *n* PHOTO estenoscopio *m*; ~ **photography** *n* PHOTO estenopetografía *f*, fotografía sin objetivo *f*

pinic *adj* CHEM pínico

pinion *n* AUTO, MECH ENG, VEH piñón *m*; ~-**cutting machine** *n* MECH ENG máquina de tallar piñones *f*; ~ **gear** *n* AUTO engranaje de piñón *m*, VEH piñón diferencial *m*; ~ **shaft flange** *n* AUTO plato del eje del piñón *m*, VEH plato del eje del piñón de ataque *m*; ~ **web** *n* MECH ENG brazo de piñón *m*; ~ **wheel** *n* MECH ENG rueda de piñón *f*

pinite *n* MINERAL pinita *f*

pink[1]: ~ **coloration** *AmE*, ~ **colouration** *BrE* *n* COLOUR coloración rosada *f*; ~ **glass** *n* C&G vidrio rosa *m*; ~ **noise** *n* ACOUST, PHYS ruido rosa *m*; ~ **salt** *n* CHEM sal rosada *f*; ~ **topaz** *n* MINERAL topacio rosa *m*

pink[2] *vt* MECH ENG cortar los bordes, dentellar, festonear, perforar, picar el motor

pinked[1] *adj* MECH ENG dentellado

pinked[2]: ~ **edge** *n* MECH ENG borde festoneado *m*, borde recortado *m*

pinking *n BrE* AUTO autoencendido *m*, detonación *f*, golpeo por autoencendido *m*, picado por autoencendido *m*, MECH ENG festoneado *m*, VEH autoencendido *m*, detonación *f*, golpeo por autoencendido *m*, picado por autoencendido *m*; ~ **shears** *n pl* MECH ENG tijeras de festonear *f pl*, tijeras picafestones *f pl*

pinned: ~ **key** *n* CONST *locksmithing* llave de pasador *f*; ~-**key lock** *n* CONST pasador con llave de empernada *m*; ~ **tenon joint** *n* CONST junta de espiga empernada *f*

pinning *n* CRYSTALL dislocación andada por obstáculos discretos *f*, METALL fijación *f*, partícula de metal adheridas *f*; ~-**up device** *n* TEXTIL dispositivo de sujeción *m*

pinonic *adj* CHEM pinónico

pinpoint: ~ **acoustic source** *n* ACOUST fuente acústica de precisión *f*

pint *n* METR *imperial liquid measure* pinta *f*

pintle *n* CONST *of lock* pasador de cadena *m*, *of gate-lock* clavija *f*, MECH ENG *king-pin* perno pinzote *m*, pivote central *m*, WATER TRANSP *of rudder* macho *m*; ~ **injection nozzle** *n* AUTO boquilla de inyección de aguja *f*

pion *n* PART PHYS, PHYS mesón pi *m*, pión *m*

pip *n* TELECOM cresta de señal *f*, imagen de un eco *f*, pip *m*

pipage *n* CONST *carriage through pipes* transporte por tuberías *m*, *system of pipes* red de tuberías *f*, sistema de tuberías *m*

pipe[1] *n* CONST caño *m*, tubería *f*, *of key* conducto *m*, cuerpo *m*, fuste *m*, FLUID tubería *f*, MECH tubería *f*, cañería *f*, conducto *m*, tubo *m*, caño *m*, MECH ENG conducto *m*, PETR TECH conducción *f*, tubo *m*, tubería *f*; ~ **anchor** *n* MECH ENG anclaje de tubería *m*, tirante de tubería *m*; ~ **bend** *n* MECH ENG curvatubos *m*; ~ **bender** *n* CONST curvadora de tubos *f*; ~ **bends screwed and socketed** *n pl* MECH ENG curvas de tubos atornilladas y enchufadas *f pl*; ~ **box** *n* PROD *founding* caja para tubos *f*; ~ **cap** *n* MECH ENG tapón hembra roscado *m*; ~ **casing** *n* COAL cajillo para tuberías *m*; ~ **clamp** *n* MINE abrazadera para sujetar tubos *f*; ~-**clamping elements** *n pl* MECH ENG elementos de sujeción de tubos *m pl*; ~ **clamps** *n pl* MINE grapa para tubos *f*; ~ **clip** *n* MECH ENG abrazadera para tubos *f*; ~ **collar** *n* CONST abrazadera *f*, anilla para tubos *f*; ~ **component** *n* MECH ENG componente de tubo *m*; ~-**coning tool** *n* CONST herramienta cónica para tuberías *f*; ~ **connection** *n* CHEM TECH unión de tuberías *f*, CONST empalme de tuberías *m*, unión de tuberías *f*, GAS unión de tuberías *f*, MECH ENG conexión de tubo *f*, unión de tuberías *f*, METALL, PETR TECH, WATER unión de tuberías *f*; ~-**cooling grid** *n* REFRIG red de tubos refrigerantes *f*; ~ **cot** *n* WATER TRANSP *collapsible* litera de bastidor tubular *f*; ~ **coupling** *n* CONST, MECH ENG, PROD acoplamiento de tuberías *m*, manguito para tubos *m*, acoplamiento de tubos *m*; ~ **cross** *n* MECH ENG cruz de tubos *f*; ~ **cutter** *n* CONST *device* cortadora de tubos *f*, cortatubos *m*; ~ **deck** *n* PETROL plataforma de tuberías *f*; ~ **diffusion** *n* METALL difusión tubular *f*; ~ **flow** *n* FLUID flujo en tuberías *m*; ~ **grab** *n* CONST agarradera de tubería *f*; ~ **hook** *n* CONST gancho soportatubos *m*; ~ **joint** *n* CONST abrazadera de tubos *f*, junta de tuberías *f*, manguito *m*, MECH ENG, MINE junta de tuberías *f*; ~ **junction** *n* MECH ENG unión de tubo *f*; ~ **key** *n BrE* (*cf barrel key AmE*) CONST *locksmithing* llave principal *f*; ~ **manifold** *n* PETR TECH colector *m*, múltiple de tubería *m*; ~ **plug** *n* MECH ENG tapón de tubo *m*, tapón macho roscado *m*; ~ **rack** *n* PETR TECH guardatuberías *m*; ~ **reducer** *n* CONST reductor de tubería *m*; ~ **screwing** *n* CONST atornillado de tubería *m*; ~ **slick** *n* PROD *founding* alisador de tubo *m*; ~ **smoother** *n* PROD *founding* alisador de tubo *m*; ~ **strap** *n* CONST correa para tubería *f*; ~ **string** *n* PETROL columna de tuberías *f*; ~ **support** *n* MECH ENG apoyo para caños *m*, soportatubos *m*; ~ **tap** *n* CONST macho para rosca de tubería *m*; ~ **tee** *n* MECH ENG conector en T para tubos *m*, unión en T para tubos *f*; ~ **thread** *n* MECH ENG rosca de tubo *f*; ~ **threader** *n* CONST roscadora de tubos *f*; ~ **threading** *n* CONST rosca de tubo *f*; ~ **tongs** *n pl* CONST tenazas para tubería *f pl*, PETR TECH llaves de tubería *f pl*; ~ **twister** *n* CONST pinza para apretar tuberías *f*; ~-**type cable** *n* ELEC cable entubado *m*; ~ **union** *n* CONST unión de tubería *f*, MECH ENG conexión de tubos *f*, unión de tubos *f*; ~ **vice** *n BrE* CONST tornillo para tubos *m*, prensa para tubos *f*; ~ **vise** *AmE see pipe vice BrE*; ~ **wrench** *n* MECH ENG llave aprietatubos *f*, llave de tubista *f*, llave para tubos *f*

pipe² *vt* CONST *conveyance* conducir por tubería, *furnish or equip with* montar tuberías, TV transmitir por cable coaxial

pipeclay *n* C&G barro para tubos *m*, CONST arcilla de tubería *f*; ~ **triangle** *n* LAB triángulo de tubo de arcilla *m*

pipecoline *n* CHEM pipecolina *f*

piped: ~ **key** *n* CONST *locksmithing* llave tubular *f*; ~ **key lock** *n* CONST cerradura tubular *f*; ~ **television** *n* TV televisión por cable *f*

pipefitter *n* CONST *person* montador de tuberías *m*

pipefitting *n* MECH ENG accesorio de cañería *m*, accesorio para tubos *m*

pipelayer *n* CONST *person* instalador de tuberías *m*, montador de tuberías *m*, MECH ENG *person* instalador de tuberías *m*, tubista *m*

pipelaying *n* CONST tendido de tuberías *m*; ~ **barge** *n* PETR TECH barcaza para tendido de tuberías *f*, gabarra para tendido de tuberías *f*, PETROL barcaza para tendido de tuberías *f*

pipeline *n* COMP&DP conducto *m*, CONST conducto *m*, oleoducto *m*, tubería *f*, FUELLESS conducto *m*, tubería *f*, HYDRAUL canalización *f*, MECH ENG *system of pipes* acueducto *m*, canalización *f*, cañería *f*, tubería *f*, PETR TECH, PETROL oleoducto *m*, POLL conducto *m*, tubería *f*, cañería *f*, TRANSP, WATER TRANSP *for oil* oleoducto *m*; ~ **processor** *n* COMP&DP procesador de conducto *m*; ~ **system** *n* TELECOM sistema de cable coaxial *m*, sistema de línea coaxial *m*, sistema de línea concéntrica *m*; ~ **transportation** *n* TRANSP línea de desplazamiento *f*, transporte por oleoducto *m*, transporte por tubería *m*

pipeliner *n* TRANSP transportista *m*

pipelining *n* COMP&DP encauzamiento *m*, ELECTRON canalización *f*

piperazine *n* CHEM piperacina *f*

piperic *adj* CHEM pipérico

piperidine *n* CHEM piperidina *f*

piperonal *n* CHEM piperonal *m*

piperylene *n* CHEM piperileno *m*

pipes: ~ **and fittings** *n pl* CONST tuberías y accesorios *m pl*

pipette *n* LAB pipeta *f*; ~ **stand** *n* LAB portapipetas *m*

pipetting: ~ **bulb** *n* LAB pera de succión *f*

pipework *n* HYDRAUL canalización *f*, MECH cañería *f*; ~ **system** *n* MECH ENG *valves, fittings, etc* sistema de canalización *m*, sistema de tuberías *m*

pipeworks *n pl* CONST sistema de tuberías *m*, tendido de tuberías *m*

piping *n* COAL arrastre hidráulico *m*, cavidad de contracción *f*, explotación hidráulica *f*, formación de veneros interiores *f*, laboreo por el método hidráulico *m*, rechupe *m*, tubería *f*, tubos conductores *m pl*, CONST sistema de tuberías *f*, GAS cañería *f*, caño *m*, tubería *f*, HYDROL canalización *f*, MINE laboreo por el método hidráulico *m*, PETR TECH entubación *f*; ~ **network** *n* CONST red de tuberías *f*; ~ **plan** *n* WATER TRANSP *shipbuilding* diagrama de la instalación de tuberías *m*; ~ **seepage** *n* WATER infiltración de tubería *f*

Pirani: ~ **gage** *AmE*, ~ **gauge** *BrE n* PHYS medidor de Pirani *m*; ~ **vacuum gage** *AmE*, ~ **vacuum gauge** *BrE n* LAB indicador de vacío Pirani *m*

pirate: ~ **recording** *n* ACOUST, TV grabación pirata *f*

pirn *n* C&G bobina de telar *f*, TEXTIL canilla *f*; ~**winding machine** *n* TEXTIL canillera *f*

pisciculteur *n* OCEAN piscicultor *m*

pisciculture *n* OCEAN piscicultura *f*

pisolite: ~ **limestone** *n* GEOL caliza de pisolita *f*

pisolitic: ~ **limestone** *n* GEOL caliza pisolítica *f*

pistil *n* AGRIC pistilo *m*

pistol: ~**-grip with shutter release** *n* PHOTO empuñadura de pistola con disparador *f*; ~ **light** *n* ELEC *lighting* luz de pistola *f*

piston *n* AUTO *of engine* pistón *m*, HYDRAUL, MECH, MECH ENG émbolo *m*, pistón *m*, MINE disco flotante *m*, émbolo *m*, pistón *m*, PHYS, VEH, WATER TRANSP *of engine* pistón *m*; ~ **area** *n* MECH ENG área del pistón *f*; ~**-attenuator** *n* ELECTRON, PHYS atenuador de pistón *m*; ~**-blower** *n* MECH ENG máquina soplante de pistón *f*; ~ **body** *n* AUTO cuerpo del pistón *m*; ~ **boss** *n* AUTO protuberancia del pistón *f*; ~**-boss bushing** *n* AUTO buje soporte del pie de biela *m*; ~ **with clack-valve** *n* MECH ENG pistón con válvula de charnela bola *m*; ~ **clearance** *n* AUTO holgura del pistón *f*, juego del pistón *m*, tolerancia del pistón *f*, MECH ENG espacio nocivo *m*, espacio perjudicial *m*, VEH holgura del pistón *f*, juego del pistón *m*, tolerancia del pistón *f*; ~ **compressor** *n* GAS compresor de pistón *m*, compresor de émbolo *m*, MECH ENG compresor de pistón *m*, compresor reciprocante *m*; ~ **crown** *n* VEH corona del pistón *f*; ~ **engine** *n* AIR TRANSP motor de pistones *m*, motor de émbolo *m*, AUTO motor de pistones *m*, MECH ENG motor de émbolo *m*, máquina de pistón *f*; ~ **with extended rod** *n* MECH ENG contravarilla del pistón *f*; ~ **freezing** *n* AUTO, VEH agarrotamiento del pistón *m*; ~ **head** *n* AUTO cabeza del émbolo *f*, MECH ENG cabeza del pistón *f*, cuerpo del émbolo *m*; ~ **jig** *n* COAL caja de pistón *f*; ~ **knock** *n* AUTO, VEH golpeo del pistón *m*; ~ **locked to connecting rod** *n* AUTO, VEH pistón unido a la biela *m*; ~ **packing** *n* MECH ENG *hemp, rubber, leather, etc* empaquetadura del pistón *f*; ~ **pin** *n* AUTO bulón del pistón *m*, pasador del émbolo *m*, pasador del pistón *m*, perno del émbolo *m*, VEH bulón del pistón *m*, eje de pie de biela *m*; ~**-pin bushing** *n* AUTO, VEH casquillo del bulón del pistón *m*, casquillo del pie de biela *m*; ~**-pin locked to piston** *n* AUTO, VEH bulón del pie de biela unido al pistón *m*; ~ **pump** *n* PROD, WATER bomba de pistón *f*; ~ **relief-duct** *n* CONST conducto de salida del pistón *m*; ~ **ring** *n* AUTO, MECH, MECH ENG, VEH anillo de pistón *m*, anillo de émbolo *m*, aro de émbolo *m*, aro del pistón *m*, segmento del pistón *m*; ~**-ring clamp** *n* AUTO, VEH abrazadera del rodamiento de bolas *f*; ~**-ring compressor** *n* AUTO, VEH compresor de segmentos del pistón *m*; ~**-ring groove** *n* AUTO, VEH alojamiento del segmento *m*, ranura del segmento *f*; ~**-ring pliers** *n pl* MECH ENG tenazas de aros de pistón *f pl*; ~ **rod** *n* AUTO, MECH ENG, PROD, RAIL, VEH barra del pistón *f*, biela del pistón *f*, vástago del pistón *m*; ~ **sampler** *n* COAL muestreador de pistón *m*; ~**-seal housings** *n pl* MECH ENG empaquetadura del obturador del pistón *f*; ~ **skirt** *n* AUTO, VEH falda del pistón *f*, falda del émbolo *f*; ~ **slap** *n* AUTO, VEH golpe del pistón *m*, golpeteo del pistón *m*; ~ **stroke** *n* AUTO pistonada *f*, MECH ENG embolada *f*, pistonada *f*, *length of stroke* carrera del pistón *f*, carrera del émbolo *f*, VEH pistonada *f*; ~ **surface** *n* MECH ENG superficie del pistón *f*; ~ **with tailrod** *n* MECH ENG pistón con contravástago *m*; ~ **top** *n* AUTO cabeza del pistón *f*; ~**-type preforming unit** *n* MECH ENG unidad de preformado de émbolo *f*; ~ **valve** *n* MECH ENG válvula del pistón *f*

pistonphone *n* ACOUST, HYDRAUL auricular de pistón *m*, cámara de comprensión *f*, pistonófono *m*

pit *n* COAL pozo *m*, CONST cantera *f*, excavación *f*, foso *m*, pozo *m*, MAR POLL hoya *f*, MECH ENG *for turntable* depósito *m*, MINE pozo *m*, cantera *f*, PETR TECH balsa *f*, tanque *m*, WATER foso *m*, hoya *f*, hoyo *m*; ~ **bank** *n* MINE enganche superior *m*, patio de la mina *m*; ~ **bottom** *n* COAL muro *m*, MINE fondo del piso *m*, muro *m*; ~ **coal** *n* COAL, MINE carbón bituminoso *m*, carbón mineral *m*, carbón de piedra *m*, hulla *f*; ~ **cock** *n* HYDRAUL distribuidor rotativo de vapor *m*, grifo de purga *m*; ~ **eye** *n* MINE boca del pozo *f*, enganche de la calle *m*; ~ **gas** *n* COAL, MINE, THERMO grisú *m*; ~**-gas detector** *n* CHEM, CHEM TECH, GAS, INSTR, MINE grisuscopio *m*, grisuómetro *m*; ~**-gas indicator** *n* CHEM, CHEM TECH, GAS, INSTR, MINE gasoscopio *m*, grisuscopio *m*, grisuómetro *m*; ~ **guides** *n pl* MINE guías de la jaula *f pl*; ~ **heap** *n* MINE escorial *m*; ~ **landing** *n* MINE anchurón de enganche *m* (*AmL*), plataforma de enganche *f* (*Esp*); ~ **lever** *n* PETR TECH brazo del indicador del nivel en las balsas de lodo *m*; ~ **mouth** *n* MINE boca del pozo *f*, enganche de la calle *m*; ~ **prop** *n* MINE estemple *m*, puntal de mina *m*; ~ **sand** *n* MINE arena de cantera *f*, arena de mina *f*; ~ **silo** *n* AGRIC silo cuba *m*; ~ **wood** *n* MINE estemple *m*, puntal de madera *m*

PIT[1] *abbr* (*programmable interval timer*) ELECTRON temporizador de intervalos programable

PIT[2]: ~**-forming mode** *n* OPT modo de formación PIT *m*

pitch[1] *n* ACOUST altura tonal *f*, *scale* altura *f*, AIR TRANSP cabeceo *m*, paso *m*, CINEMAT *antennae, waveguides*, COMP&DP paso *m*, CONST *of roof* pendiente *f*, *inclination or slope* declive *m*, *natural bitumen* betún *m*, ELEC *coil* paso *m*, ELEC ENG declive *m*, GEOL *in fuel pellet* inclinación *f*, sesgo *m*, MECH *blast furnace* paso *m*, MECH ENG *of rivet-centres* separación *f*, paso *m*, paso geométrico *m*, paso de los dientes *m*, espaciado *m*, OPT tono *m*, PAPER brea depositable *f*, grumo de resina depositable *m*, PHOTO paso *m*, PHYS *steel* elevación *f*, *on ship* cabeceo *m*, tono *m*, SPACE grado de elevación *m*, cabeceo *m*, WATER TRANSP *of propeller* paso *m*, cabezada *f*, WAVE PHYS timbre *m*, tono *m*; ~ **angle** *n* AIR TRANSP *helicopter* ángulo de cabeceo *m*, ángulo de paso *m*, FUELLESS *airscrew, orbit* ángulo de inclinación *m*, WATER TRANSP ángulo de cabeceo *m*; ~ **arc** *n* MECH ENG arco de engrane *m*; ~ **attitude** *n* AIR TRANSP actitud de cabeceo *f*, SPACE *of craft* ángulo de inclinación longitudinal *m*; ~ **axis** *n* AIR TRANSP eje de paso *m*, eje del cabeceo *m*, SPACE *of craft* eje de cabeceo *m*; ~ **center diameter** *AmE*, ~ **centre diameter** *BrE* *n* AIR TRANSP diámetro del centro del cabeceo *m*, diámetro del centro del paso *m*; ~ **chain** *n* MECH ENG cadena Galle *f*, cadena articulada *f*; ~**-change axis** *n* AIR TRANSP *helicopter* eje de cambio de paso *m*; ~**-change beam** *n* AIR TRANSP *helicopter* viga de cambio de paso *f*; ~**-change rod** *n* AIR TRANSP *helicopter* barra de cambio de paso *f*; ~**-change spider** *n* AIR TRANSP *helicopter* araña de cambio de paso *f*; ~ **channel** *n* AIR TRANSP canal de cabeceo *m*, canal de paso *m*; ~ **circle** *n* MECH ENG círculo primitivo de contacto *m*; ~**-circle diameter** *n* AIR TRANSP diámetro del círculo de cabeceo *m*,

diámetro del círculo del paso *m*; ~ **circumference** *n* MECH ENG *gearing* circunferencia primitiva *f*; ~ **coal** *n* COAL azabache *m*, lignito bituminoso *m*; ~ **compensation** *n* AIR TRANSP *helicopter* compensación de cabeceo *f*, compensación de paso *f*; ~ **cone** *n* MECH ENG *gearing* cono de contacto *m*, cono primitivo *m*; ~ **control** *n* AIR TRANSP control de cabeceo *m*, control de paso *m*; ~**-control arm** *n* AIR TRANSP *helicopter* brazo de control de cabeceo *m*, brazo de control de paso *m*; ~**-control lever** *n* AIR TRANSP *helicopter* palanca de control del paso *f*; ~**-control load** *n* AIR TRANSP *helicopter* carga de control del cabeceo *f*, carga de control del paso *f*; ~**-control rod angle** *n* AIR TRANSP ángulo de la barra de control del cabeceo *m*, ángulo de la barra de control del paso *m*; ~**-correcting unit** *n* AIR TRANSP *flight controls* unidad correctora de cabeceo *f*; ~ **damper** *n* AIR TRANSP amortiguador del cabeceo *m*; ~**-detector synchro** *n* AIR TRANSP sincronizador detector de cabeceo *m*, sincronizador detector del paso *m*; ~**-detector synchronizer** *n* AIR TRANSP sincronizador detector de cabeceo *m*, sincronizador detector del paso *m*; ~ **diameter** *n* AIR TRANSP diámetro del cabeceo *m*, diámetro del paso *m*, MECH ENG *gearing* diámetro del círculo primitivo *m*, diámetro primitivo *m*; ~**-diameter error** *n* METR *sailing* error en el diámetro del paso *m*; ~**-diameter ratio** *n* AIR TRANSP *propeller* relación del diámetro del cabeceo *f*, relación del diámetro del paso *f*; ~**-excited vocoder** *n* TELECOM vocoder de tono excitado *m*; ~ **of fins** *n* REFRIG paso de aletas *m*; ~ **gyro** *n* SPACE giroscopio de cabeceo *m*; ~ **increase** *n* AIR TRANSP *helicopter* incremento del cabeceo *m*, incremento del paso *m*; ~ **information** *n* AIR TRANSP información de cabeceo *f*, información del paso *f*; ~ **of lead screw** *n* MECH ENG paso del tornillo de avance *m*, paso del tornillo regulador *m*; ~ **line** *n* MECH ENG círculo de contacto *m*, círculo primitivo *m*, *of gearing* círculo de engrane *m*; ~**-locking system** *n* AIR TRANSP *helicopter* sistema bloqueador del paso *m*, sistema de blocaje del paso *m*; ~ **pine** *n* CONST, WATER TRANSP *timber* pino negral *m*; ~ **point** *n* MECH ENG *gearing* punto de contacto de los círculos primitivos *m*; ~ **radius** *n* AIR TRANSP radio del cabeceo *m*, radio del paso *m*, MECH ENG *gearing* radio primitivo *m*; ~**-rate gyro** *n* AIR TRANSP giróscopo de régimen del cabeceo *m*; ~ **reversing** *n* AIR TRANSP *of propeller* inversión del cabeceo *f*, inversión del paso *f*, TRANSP inversión del paso *f*; ~**, roll and yaw axes** *n pl* AIR TRANSP ejes de cabeceo, balanceo y guiñada *m pl*, SPACE ejes de cabeceo, inclinación y guiñada *m pl*; ~ **of roof** *n* CONST *architecture* pendiente del tejado *f*; ~ **roof** *n* CONST tejado a dos aguas *m*; ~ **setting** *n* AIR TRANSP *propeller* ajuste del paso *m*; ~ **stop** *n* AIR TRANSP *helicopter* tope del paso *m*; ~ **surface** *n* MECH ENG *gearing* superficie primitiva de rodadura *f*; ~ **synchro** *n* AIR TRANSP sincronizador de cabeceo *m*, sincronizador de paso *m*; ~ **synchronization** *n* AIR TRANSP sincronizador de cabeceo *m*, sincronizador de paso *m*; ~**-throttle synchronizer** *n* AIR TRANSP sincronizador del regulador de paso *m*; ~**-thruster** *n* SPACE propulsor de tiro *m*; ~ **to be cut** *n* MECH ENG *screwcutting* paso de corte *m*; ~ **trim** *n* AIR TRANSP regulación de cabeceo *f*; ~**-up** *n* AIR TRANSP cabeceo del morro hacia arriba *m*, encabritamiento *m*;

~ **wheel** *n* MECH ENG rueda de engranaje *f*; ~-**zone location** *n* MECH ENG *V-belts* lugar de paso *m*

pitch²: ~-**up** *vt* AIR TRANSP levantar el morro

pitch³ *vi* GEOL inclinarse, MECH ENG *gear-wheels* engranar, engranar con, WATER TRANSP *ship motion* cabecear, dar cabezadas

pitchblende *n* CHEM, GEOL pechblenda *f*, MINERAL pechblenda *f*, uraninita *f*

pitched: ~ **chain** *n* MECH ENG cadena Galle *f*, cadena articulada *f*

pitchfork *n* AGRIC horquilla para heno *f*

pitching *n* AIR TRANSP cabeceo *m*, MECH ENG *gearing* engrane *m*, engranaje *m*, PHYS *surveying* inclinación *f*, WATER TRANSP cabeceo *m*; ~ **moment** *n* FUELLESS momento de cabeceo *m*

pitchstone *n* MINERAL vidrio volcánico *m*

pith *n* AGRIC médula *f*; ~ **ray** *n* AGRIC radio medular *m*

pithead *n* MINE boca del pozo *f*, bocamina *f*; ~ **building** *n* MINE relleno de minas *m*; ~ **frame** *n* MINE castillete de extracción *m*; ~ **gear** *n* MINE gorrón del castillete *m* (*Esp*), polea del castillete de extracción *f* (*AmL*); ~ **pulley** *n* MINE polea del castillete de extracción *f*; ~ **works** *n pl* MINE labor de extracción *f*, sistema de extracción *m*

pitman *n* MECH ENG barra de conexión *f*, biela *f*; ~ **arm** *n* AUTO, VEH biela de mando de la dirección *f*, brazo de mando *m*, brazo de pitman *m* ~ **head** *n* MECH ENG cabeza de biela *f*

Pitot: ~ **tube** *n* AIR TRANSP, PHYS tubo de Pitot *m*

pitsaw *n* PROD sierra abrazadera *f*

pitticite *n* MINERAL pittizita *f*

pittizite *n* MINERAL pittizita *f*

pivalic *adj* CHEM piválico

pivot *n* INSTR centro de giro *m*, pivote *m*, MECH centro de rotación *m*, charnela *f*, eje de rotación *m*, espiga *f*, gorrón *m*, pivote *m*, MECH ENG centro de giro *m*, charnela *f*, eje de rotación *m*, espiga *f*, gorrón *m*, pivote *m*, NUCL centro de giro *m*, pivote *m*; ~ **axle** *n* VEH eje de pivote *m*; ~ **bridge** *n* CONST puente giratorio *m*, puente pivotante *m*; ~-**hung sash** *n* CONST *window* hoja basculante *f*; ~-**hung window** *n* CONST *pivoted horizontally* ventana corredera *f*, ventana corrediza *f*, *pivoted vertically* ventana de hoja basculante *f*; ~ **pin** *n* VEH pasador de pivote *m*; ~ **ring** *n* AUTO anillo de pivote *m*; ~ **valve** *n* HYDRAUL válvula de mariposa *f*

pivoted¹ *adj* MECH articulado, basculante, montado sobre pivote, oscilante, MECH ENG, TRANSP articulado

pivoted²: ~ **armature** *n* ELEC, ELEC ENG inducido articulado *m*; ~ **lever** *n* MECH ENG palanca articulada *f*

pixel *n* COMP&DP pixel *m*, punto *m*, PRINT pixel *m*; ~ **carrier** *n* COMP&DP, PRINT portador de pixeles *m*

pixels: ~ **per inch** *n pl* COMP&DP pixeles por pulgada *m pl*

pixlock *n* TV fijación de imágenes *f*

PJC *abbr* (*pointer justification-count*) TELECOM cálculo justificativo del puntero *m*

PJE *abbr* (*pointer justification-event*) TELECOM evento justificativo del puntero *m*

PL *abr* (*private line*) TELECOM enlace de acceso *m*, línea privada *f*

PLA *abbr* (*programmed logic array*) COMP&DP PLA (*matriz lógica programada*)

placard *n* MECH ENG afiche *m*, anuncio *m*, cartel *m*, letrero *m*, rótulo *m*

placer *n* MINE guía retenida *f*, mecanismo guiador *m*, placer *m*; ~ **deposit** *n* GEOL, MINE yacimiento de aluvión *m*; ~ **dirt** *n* MINE aluvión aurífero *m*, placer *m*; ~ **gold** *n* MINE gravas auríferas *f pl*, oro corrido *m*, oro de aluvión *m*, placeres de oro *m pl* (*Esp*); ~ **ground** *n* MINE terreno de aluviones *m*, terreno de placeres *m*; ~ **mine** *n* MINE mina aurífera *f*, mina de placeres *f*; ~ **workings** *n pl* MINE explotación aurífera *f*, explotación de placeres *f*

plagioclase *n* MINERAL plagioclasa *f*

plain¹ *adj* C&G *undecorated glass* simple, TEXTIL liso

plain²: ~ **bearing** *n* MECH ENG, VEH cojinete de contacto plano *m*, cojinete liso *m*; ~-**bed lathe** *n* MECH ENG torno de bancada recta *m*; ~ **bit** *n* MINE barreno liso *m*; ~ **color** *AmE*, ~ **colour** *BrE n* COLOUR colorante puro *m*; ~ **column** *n* CONST *architecture* columna simple *f*; ~ **conductor** *n* ELEC *cable* conductor plano *m*; ~ **cylindrical boiler** *n* HYDRAUL caldera uniformemente cilíndrica *f*; ~ **dyeing** *n* COLOUR teñido puro *m*; ~ **fabric** *n* TEXTIL tejido liso *m*, tejido tafetán *m*; ~ **fitting** *n* MECH ENG accesorio plano *m*, accesorio sencillo *m*, ajuste simple *m*; ~ **gage** *AmE see plain gauge BrE*; ~ **gage for pipe threads** *AmE see plain gauge for pipe threads BrE*, ~ **gauge** *BrE n* MECH ENG calibre simple *m*, galga simple *f*; ~ **gauge for pipe threads** *n BrE* MECH ENG galga simple para roscas de tubos *f*; ~-**grinder** *n* MECH ENG rectificadora de superficies planas *f*; ~ **hub-flange** *n* MECH ENG plato de rueda plano *m*; ~ **lathe** *n* MECH ENG torno de cilindrar *m*, torno simple *m*; ~ **length** *n* MECH ENG *of screw* distancia plana *f*, longitud común *f*; ~ **milling cutter** *n* MECH ENG fresa cilíndrica *f*, fresa de cepillar *f*, fresa de planear *f*, fresa de refrentar *f*, fresa de un corte *f*; ~-**press roll** *n* PAPER rodillo de prensa simple *m*; ~-**rib interlock** *n* TEXTIL interlock acanalado *m*, interlock de canalé plano *m*; ~ **roll** *n* PROD cilindro liso *m*; ~-**rolled glass** *n* C&G vidrio rolado sin grabado *m*; ~ **sandblast** *n* C&G esmerilado con chorro de arena *m*; ~ **slide valve** *n* HYDRAUL distribuidor de concha *m*; ~ **socket** *n* MECH ENG tomacorriente sencillo *m*; ~ **surface** *n* MECH ENG superficie lisa *f*, superficie plana *f*; ~ **thrust-bearing** *n* MECH ENG cojinete de empuje liso *m*; ~ **tile** *n* CONST teja plana *f*; ~ **traveling wheel** *AmE*, ~ **travelling wheel** *BrE n* MECH ENG rueda de traslación simple *f*; ~-**tread tire** *AmE*, ~-**tread tyre** *BrE n* VEH neumático con poco dibujo *m*, neumático con relieve desgastado *m*; ~ **tube** *n* CONST tubo plano *m*; ~ **turning-lathe** *n* MECH ENG torno de cilindros *m*; ~ **ungeared lathe** *n* MECH ENG torno acoplado directamente *m*; ~ **washer** *n* MECH ENG arandela común *f*, arandela plana *f*, VEH arandela plana *f*; ~ **washer for metric bolts, screws and nuts** *n* MECH ENG arandela plana para tornillos y tuercas métricas *f*; ~ **weave** *n* PAPER tela de tejido liso *f*, TEXTIL ligamento tafetán *m*

plan *n* WATER TRANSP *naval architecture, navigation* plan *m*, plano *m*, proyecto *m*; ~ **view** *n* MECH ENG proyección horizontal *f*, vista desde arriba *f*, vista en planta *f*

planar¹ *adj* GEOL plano, GEOM llano, planar, plano

planar²: ~ **bipolar transistor** *n* ELECTRON transistor bipolar de tecnología planar *m*; ~ **diffusion** *n* ELECTRON difusión planar *f*; ~ **diode** *n* ELECTRON diodo planar *m*; ~ **epitaxial diode** *n* ELECTRON diodo epitaxial planar *m*; ~ **integrated circuit** *n* ELECTRON circuito integrado planar *m*; ~ **reflector** *n* INSTR reflector planar *m*; ~ **triode** *n* ELECTRON triodo planar *m*; ~ **waveguide** *n* ELEC ENG guía de ondas plana *f*

Planck's: ~ **constant** *n* (*h*) PHYS constante de Planck *f* (*h*); ~ **formula** *n* PHYS fórmula de Planck *f*; ~ **law** *n* PHYS, RAD PHYS *radiation, distribution law* ley de Planck *f*; ~ **radiation formula** *n* RAD PHYS fórmula de Plank para la radiación *f*

plane[1] *n* AIR TRANSP avión *m*, CONST *joiner's tool* cepillo *m*, GEOM plano *m*, MECH ENG *engineers' surface-plate* superficie plana *f*, PHYS *jackplane, trying plane* plano *m*; ~ **angle** *n* GEOM ángulo plano *m*; ~ **bit** *n* CONST fresadora de cepillo *f*; ~ **figures** *n pl* GEOM figuras planas *f pl*; ~ **geometry** *n* GEOM geometría del plano *f*, geometría plana *f*; ~ **of incidence** *n* PHYS plano de incidencia *m*; ~ **iron** *n* CONST *of hand-plane* cepillo de hierro *m*, MECH ENG *of planing machine* cuchillas de cepilladora *f pl*, hierros de cepillo *m pl*; ~-**milling** *n* MECH ENG fresado en plano *m*; ~-**milling machine** *n* MECH ENG fresadora en plano *f*; ~ **mirror** *n* INSTR, PHYS espejo plano *m*; ~ **parallel waves** *n pl* WAVE PHYS ondas planas paralelas *f*; ~ **of polarization** *n* OPT plano de polarización *m*; ~-**polarized wave** *n* PHYS onda polarizada plana *f*, WAVE PHYS onda de polarizada en el plano *f*; ~ **polygon** *n* GEOM polígono plano *m*; ~ **of shear** *n* METALL plano de cortadura *m*, plano de corte *m*; ~ **stock** *n* CONST caja de cepillo *f*; ~ **of symmetry** *n* MECH ENG, METALL plano de simetría *m*; ~ **table** *n* CONST *surveying* plancheta *f*, MINE mesa inclinada de superficie plana *f*; ~ **triangle** *n* GEOM triángulo plano *m*; ~ **trigonometry** *n* GEOM trigonometría plana *f*; ~ **wave** *n* ACOUST, ELEC ENG, OPT, PHYS, SPACE, TELECOM onda plana *f*

plane[2] *vt* MECH alisar, aplanar, cepillar, desbastar

planer *n* AmE (*cf planing machine BrE*) C&G aplanador *m*, CONST cepillo mecánico *m*, MECH cepilladora *f*, aplanador *m*, MECH ENG aplanador *m*

planet *n* SPACE planeta *m*; ~-**action spindle** *n* MECH ENG eje de movimiento planetario *m*; ~ **carrier** *n* AUTO, VEH portador del planetario *m*; ~ **gear** *n* AIR TRANSP, AUTO engranaje planetario *m*, MECH ENG *sun-and-planet motion* engranaje planetario *m*, rueda satélite *f*, VEH engranaje planetario *m*; ~ **gearing** *n* MECH ENG *sun-and-planet motion* engranaje planetario *m*; ~-**pinion cage** *n* AIR TRANSP *helicopter* caja del piñón planetario *f*; ~ **spindle** *n* MECH ENG eje de movimiento planetario *m*; ~ **wheel** *n* AUTO piñón planetario *m*, MECH ENG rueda planetaria *f*, rueda satélite *f*, VEH piñón planetario *m*

planetary[1] *adj* MECH *machinery*, SPACE planetario

planetary[2]: ~ **boundary layer** *n* METEO capa de fricción *f*, capa límite atmosférica *f*, capa límite planetaria *f*; ~-**gear differential** *n* AUTO, VEH diferencial de engranaje planetario *m*; ~ **gear set** *n* AUTO equipo de engranaje planetario *m*; ~-**gear system** *n* AUTO sistema de engranaje planetario *m*; ~-**gear train** *n* MECH ENG tren de engranaje planetario *m*; ~ **gears** *n* AUTO engranajes planetarios *m pl*; ~ **interior** *n* SPACE interior planetario *m*; ~ **mill** *n* LAB *appliance, mechanism* desintegrador planetario *m*; ~ **nebula** *n* SPACE nebulosa planetaria *f*; ~ **pinion** *n* AUTO, MECH ENG piñón planetario *m*; ~ **probe** *n* SPACE sonda planetaria *f*

planimeter *n* CONST, GEOM planímetro *m*

planimetry *n* GEOM planimetría *f*

planing *n* C&G aplanado *m*, CONST cepilladura *m*, proceso de cepillado *m*, MECH, MECH ENG aplanado *m*; ~ **hull-type ship** *n* TRANSP barco con casco tipo hidroavión *m*; ~ **machine** *n* BrE (*cf planer AmE*) C&G aplanador *m*, CONST cepillo mecánico *m*, MECH cepilladora *f*, aplanador *m*, MECH ENG aplanador *m*; ~ **and thicknessing machine** *n* CONST cepilladora y esgualador *f*, MECH ENG máquina de cepillar y sacar a gruesos *f*; ~ **tool** *n* CONST cepilladora *f*

planisher *n* MECH bruñidor *m*, MECH ENG *machine* planador *m*, *person* alisador *m*, *tool* bruñidor *m*, martillo de aplanar *m*

planishing *n* MECH ENG aplanamiento *m*, pulido *m*, pulido por laminación en frío *m*; ~ **roll** *n* MECH ENG cilindro pulidor *m*; ~ **stake** *n* MECH ENG tas de aplanar *m*; ~ **tool** *n* MECH ENG herramienta de pulir *f*

plank *n* CONST madero *m*, tablón *m*, WATER TRANSP *shipbuilding* madero *m*, tabla *f*, tablón *m*; ~ **partition** *n* CONST tabique de madera *m*

planking *n* COAL forro de madera *m*, maderos *m pl*, tablazón *m*, CONST entarimado *m*

plankton: ~ **microscope** *n* INSTR microscopio de plancton *m*

planned: ~ **environment** *n* POLL medio ambiente planificado *m*; ~ **maintenance** *n* QUALITY mantenimiento planificado *m*, mantenimiento programado *m*; ~-**projected available stock** *n* PROD existencias disponibles según planificación y previsión *f pl*; ~ **stock movements** *n pl* PROD movimientos de existencias planeados *m*; ~ **year** *n* PROD año planificado *m*, programado *m*

planning *n* TELECOM planificación *f*, programación *f*; ~ **bill of material** *n* PROD planeamiento de listas de materiales *m*; ~ **board** *n* PROD junta de planeamiento *f*; ~ **horizon** *n* PROD perspectiva de planificación *f* (*Esp*), planeación *f* (*AmL*); ~ **interval** *n* PROD intervalo de planeamiento *m*; ~ **permission** *n* CONST licencia de construcción *f*, licencia de edificación *f*

planoconcave: ~ **lens** *n* INSTR, OPT, PHYS lente planocóncava *f*

planoconvex: ~ **lens** *n* INSTR, OPT, PHYS lente planoconvexa *f*

planomiller *n* MECH ENG cepilladora *f*

plant *n* CONST planta *f*, fábrica *f*, PROD *equipment* planta *f*, fábrica *f*, maquinaria *f*, instalación *f*, REFRIG planta *f*; ~ **association** *n* AGRIC comunidad de plantas *f*; ~ **breeder** *n* AGRIC experto en fitomejoramiento *m*, mejorador vegetal *m*; ~ **breeding** *n* AGRIC mejora genética de plantas *f*; ~ **density** *n* AGRIC densidad de siembra *f*; ~ **disease** *n* AGRIC enfermedad de las plantas *f*; ~ **licensing** *n* NUCL licenciamiento de la planta *m*, proceso de concesión de la licencia de operación *m*; ~-**lifetime extension** *n* NUCL extensión de la vida de la central *f*; ~ **louse** *n* AGRIC áfido *m*; ~ **pathologist** *n* AGRIC fitopatólogo *m*; ~ **physiologist** *n* AGRIC fisiólogo vegetal *m*, fitofisiólogo *m*; ~ **pigment** *n* COLOUR pigmento vegetal *m*; ~ **production** *n* AGRIC fitotécnia *f*, producción vegetal *f*; ~-**recovery phase** *n* NUCL fase de recuperación de la central *f*; ~ **sample** *n* AGRIC muestra de material vegetal *f*; ~ **spacing** *n* AGRIC distanciamento entre las plantas *m*; ~ **start-up** *n* NUCL arranque de la central *m*; ~ **switchyard** *n* NUCL parque de intemperie *m*, parque de interruptores de la planta *m*

plantation n AGRIC plantación f
planter n AGRIC sembradora f
planting n AGRIC plantación f, siembra f, PROD puesta en obra f; ~ **rate** n AGRIC densidad de siembra f; ~ **scheme** n AGRIC plan de cultivo m; ~ **season** n AGRIC época de siembra f
plasma n ELECTRON plasma m, GAS gas caliente ionizado m, plasma m, MINERAL, NUCL, PART PHYS, PHYS plasma m, SPACE gas caliente ionizado m, plasma m, protoplasma m; ~**-activated chemical vapor deposition** AmE, ~**-activated chemical vapour deposition** BrE n (PCVD) ELECTRON, OPT, TELECOM deposición de vapor químico de plasma activado f (DVQPA); ~ **arc-cutting** n CONST corte de arco eléctrico con plasma m; ~ **arc-power collector** n TRANSP recopilador de potencia de arco de plasma m; ~ **cloud** n GEOPHYS nube de plasma f; ~ **cutting** n CONST corte con plasma m; ~**-developed resist** n ELECTRON protección por plasma desarrollado f; ~ **display** n COMP&DP pantalla de plasma f, visualización de plasma f; ~ **engine** n SPACE motor de plasma m; ~ **environment** n SPACE ambiente de plasma m, proximidad del plasma f; ~ **etching** n ELECTRON grabado químico por plasma m; ~ **particle** n GEOPHYS partícula plasma f; ~ **radiation** n GAS radiación de plasma f; ~ **thruster** n SPACE impulsor de plasma m
plasmagene: ~ **gas** n GAS gas de plasmagén m
plasmatron n GAS plasmatrón m
plast: ~ **spraying** n COATINGS rociado de yeso para estucado m
plaster[1] n CONST yeso m; ~ **coating** n COATINGS revestimiento de yeso m; ~ **of Paris** n CONST yeso de París m, yeso fino m; ~ **rock** n CONST roca de yeso f; ~ **stone** n CONST piedra de yeso f
plaster[2] vt CONST enlucir
plastering n CONST enlucido m; ~ **trowel** n CONST, MECH ENG cuchara de albañil f (AmL), llana de albañil f (Esp), llana para enlucir f (Esp)
plasterwork n CONST enlucido m
plastic[1]: ~**-coated** adj COATINGS plastificado
plastic[2] n CHEM, P&R, PETR TECH, REFRIG plástico m; ~**-based laminate** n P&R laminado plástico m, plástico laminado m; ~ **blunting** n METALL, P&R despuntado plástico m; ~ **bottle** n P&R, PHOTO botella plástica f; ~**-clad glass fiber** AmE, ~**-clad glass fibre** n BrE OPT fibra de vidrio con revestimiento plástico f; ~**-clad silica fiber** AmE, ~**-clad silica fibre** BrE n (PCS fibre BrE) OPT, TELECOM fibra de sílice con revestimiento plástico f (fibra PCS); ~ **cladding** n ELEC ENG chapado plástico m, recubrimiento plástico m; ~ **clay** n C&G, GEOL arcilla plástica f; ~ **coating** n COATINGS revestimiento plástico m, TELECOM cobertura plástica f, recubrimiento de plástico m; ~ **covering** n COATINGS, P&R cubierta plástica f; ~ **deformation** n CONST, CRYSTALL, METALL, P&R, PHYS deformación plástica f; ~ **developing-tank** n PHOTO tanque plástico de revelado m; ~ **dish** n P&R, PHOTO cubeta plástica f; ~ **explosive** n (PE) MILIT, MINE explosivo moldeable m (AmL), explosivo plástico m (Esp); ~ **fiber** AmE see plastic fibre BrE; ~**-fiber cable** AmE see plastic-fibre cable BrE; ~ **fibre** n BrE OPT, TELECOM fibra de plástico f, fibra plástica f; ~**-fibre cable** n BrE ELEC ENG cable de fibra plástica m, cable fibroplástico m; ~**-film capacitor** n ELEC ENG condensador de película

plástica m; ~ **flow** n METALL fluencia plástica f, P&R deformación plástica f; ~**-flow properties** n P&R propiedades de la deformación plástica f pl; ~**-foam packaging** n PACK envase de espuma plástica endurecida m; ~**-foil tooling** n MECH ENG herramientas de hoja plástica f pl; ~ **instability** n METALL inestabilidad plástica f; ~**-insulated cable** n ELEC ENG, TELECOM cable aislado con plástico m; ~**-laminate covering** n COATINGS, P&R cubierta con lámina plástica f; ~ **limit** n COAL, CONST, P&R límite de plasticidad m, límite plástico m; ~ **materials** n pl SAFE materiales plásticos m pl; ~**-molded footwear** AmE, ~**-moulded footwear** BrE n SAFE calzado de plástico moldeado m; ~ **mount** n PHOTO montura plástica f; ~ **pipeline** n MECH ENG tuberías de plástico f pl; ~ **plug** n PACK tapón de plástico m; ~ **properties** n pl FLUID propiedades plásticas f pl; ~ **protective elements** n pl SAFE elementos protectores hechos de plástico m pl; ~ **sheeting** n PACK obtención de hojas de plástico f; ~ **welding** n MECH ENG soldadura por forja f, soldeo de plásticos m, P&R soldeo de plásticos m; ~**-welding machine** n MECH ENG, P&R soldadora de plásticos f; ~ **yield** n NUCL deformación plástica f, límite elástico con deformación plástica m, P&R deformación plástica f
plasticity n C&G, COAL, METALL, P&R plasticidad f; ~ **index** n COAL, CONST, GEOPHYS, P&R índice de plasticidad m
plasticize vt P&R plastificar
plasticizer n CHEM, CONST, P&R plastificante m; ~ **admixture** n CONST concrete mezcla plastificante f; ~ **migration** n P&R migración del plastificante f
plastid n CHEM cromatóforo m, plastidio m
plastifying: ~ **admixture** n CONST mezcla plastificante f
plastimeter n P&R plastómetro m
plastisol n P&R plastisol m
plastomer n CHEM, PETR TECH plastómero m
plastometer n PRINT plastómetro m
plat n MINE cámara de enganche de vagonetas f, enganche inferior m, piso de cargar m, plano de la superficie de los trabajos subterráneos m, cámara de enganche f
platband n CONST flat arch platabanda f
plate[1]: ~**-glazed** adj PAPER paper, board satinado entre placas
plate[2] n C&G placa f, CHEM of distillation column plato m, CONST head-plate of frame placa f, wall-plate plancha f, ELEC cell electrodo m, capacitor placa f, GEOL placa f, MECH placa f, chapa f, lámina f, platillo m, platina f, plancha f, MECH ENG chapa f, lámina f, plancha f, placa f, riel m, carril m, plato m, mesa f, bastidor m, METALL placa f, chapa f, PRINT plancha f, PROD cast iron lámina f, placa f, WATER TRANSP shipbuilding chapa f, plancha f; ~ **amalgamation** n COAL amalgamación de placa f; ~ **anemometer** n INSTR, METEO, PHYS anemómetro de placa m; ~**-backing** n PRINT termoendurecido de las planchas m; ~**-bending roller** n MECH ENG rodillo para curvar chapas m; ~**-bending rolls** n pl MECH ENG curvadora de chapas f; ~ **boundary** n GEOL límite de placa m; ~ **camera** n PHOTO cámara de placas f; ~ **capacitor** n ELEC capacitor de placa m; ~ **changeover** n PRINT cambio de plancha m; ~ **circuit** n ELEC ENG circuito anódico m; ~ **clutch** n MECH ENG embrague de discos m; ~ **column** n PETR TECH columna de placas f;

~-**column scrubber** n POLL lavador de columna de platos m, lavador de placas m; ~ **coupling** n MECH ENG acoplamiento de bridas m, acoplamiento de discos m, acoplamiento de platillos m, acoplamiento de platos m; ~ **cylinder** n PRINT cilindro portaplanchas m; ~-**edge planing machine** n MECH ENG cepilladora de bordes de chapas f; ~-**flattening-and-bending machine** n MECH ENG aplanadora y curvadora de chapas f, máquina de enderezar y curvar chapas f; ~-**folding machine** n PRINT plegadora a bolsillo f; ~-**folding-and-bending machine** n MECH ENG plegadora y curvadora de chapas f; ~-**freezer** n REFRIG congelador de placas m; ~ **gage** AmE, ~ **gauge** BrE n MECH ENG calibrador para espesores de chapas m, galga para espesores de chapas f, METR calibrador de clisés m, calibrador para clisés m, galga para espesores de chapas f; ~ **girder** n CONST viga armada f; ~ **glass** n C&G polished flat glass cristal m, luna f, CONST vidrio plano pulido m; ~ **glazing** n PAPER satinado entre placas m; ~ **glazing-calender** n PAPER calandra satinadora de placas f; ~ **hoist** n PROD polipasto para chapas m; ~-**holder** n PHOTO portaplacas m; ~ **ice** n REFRIG hielo en placas m; ~ **iron** n METALL, PROD hierro en chapas m, hierro en láminas m, hierro en planchas m, placa de fundición f; ~ **iron girder** n CONST viga de hierro f; ~ **laying** n RAIL colocación de la vía f, tendido de vía m; ~ **level** n INSTR nivel de vía m; ~ **link** n MECH ENG gear corredera de chapa f; ~ **lockup system** n PRINT sistema de cierre de la plancha m; ~-**making** n PRINT pasado de planchas m; ~ **margin** n GEOL margen de placa m; ~ **mill** n MECH ENG laminador de chapas m, tren de chapas m; ~ **molding** AmE, ~ **moulding** BrE n PROD founding moldeado con placa intermedia m; ~ **printing** n PRINT impresión con plancha f; ~-**printing machine** n PRINT prensa de talla dulce f; ~-**processing** n PRINT procesado de planchas m; ~-**processor** n PRINT procesador para planchas m; ~ **roll** n MECH ENG cilindro de chapa m; ~ **saw** n MECH ENG sierra para chapa f; ~ **shears** n pl MECH ENG cizalla para chapa f, tijera para chapa f; ~ **spring** n MECH ENG leaf-spring ballesta f, muelle de hojas m; ~-**straightening machine** n RAIL máquina aplanadora de chapas f; ~ **strap** n AUTO abrazadera de plato f; ~ **tectonics** n GEOL tectónica de placas f; ~ **web** n WATER TRANSP shipbuilding bulárcama f; ~-**web girder** n CONST viga de alma llena f; ~-**works** n pl PROD taller de laminación de chapas m

plate[3] vt ELEC ENG platear, MECH machinery blindar, enchapar, metalizar, MILIT acorazar, WATER TRANSP shipbuilding, navy acorazar, cubrir con planchas, dar un baño de metal a, forrar con planchas, planchear

plateau n GEOL, OCEAN, PETR TECH meseta f; ~ **level** n PETR TECH nivel de la meseta m

plated[1] adj MILIT acorazado

plated[2]: ~-**through hole** n ELECTRON, SPACE perforación metalizada f

platelet n P&R plaqueta f; ~ **structure** n METALL estructura de laminilla f

platen n CINEMAT platina f, COMP&DP rodillo m, MECH ENG mesa f, placa gruesa f, platina f, plato m, P&R platina f; ~ **press** n P&R prensa de platina f

plater n PROD chapista m; ~'**s shop** n WATER TRANSP taller de conformado m

platform n CONST andén m, plataforma f, MECH ENG explanada f, plataforma f, PETR TECH, PROD plataforma f, RAIL andén m, muelle m, plataforma f; ~ **awning** n RAIL marquesina del andén f; ~ **car** n RAIL vagón plataforma m; ~ **equipment** n PETR TECH equipamiento de plataforma m; ~ **lift** n PROD plataforma elevadora f; ~ **lorry** n BrE (cf platform truck AmE) AUTO camión plataforma m; ~ **truck** n AmE (cf platform lorry BrE) AUTO camión plataforma m

platforming n PETR TECH plataformación f, proceso de formación catalítica m, proceso de reformación catalítica m

plating n ELEC ENG recubrimiento electrolítico m, PROD plaqueado m, revestimiento electrolítico m, manufacture of iron plates fabricación de chapas f, WATER TRANSP of gangway forro m; ~-**out test** n PROD prueba de plegado f

platinic adj CHEM platínico

platiniridium n CHEM platinoiridio m

platinochloride n CHEM platinocloruro m

platinum n (Pt) CHEM, ELEC, METALL platino m (Pt); ~ **crucible** n LAB crisol platinado m; ~-**iridium** n CHEM platinoiridio m; ~-**resistance thermometer** n PHYS termómetro de resistencia de platino m; ~ **sponge** n CHEM esponja de platino f; ~ **wire** n LAB alambre de platino m

platman n AmE (cf onsetter BrE) MINE enganchador m, pocero m

platoon n TRANSP sección f; ~ **dispersion** n TRANSP dispersión sectorial f

platt n MINE anchurón de enganche m (AmL), plataforma de enganche f (Esp)

platter n COMP&DP disco m, placa f, plato m

plattnerite n MINERAL plattnerita f

play[1] n MECH ENG carrera f, room to move huelgo m, juego m, holgura f

play[2] vt TV reproducir

playback n ACOUST reproducción f, sonido pregrabado m, TV lectura f; ~ **head** n CINEMAT cabeza lectora f, cabeza reproductora f, TV cabeza reproductora f; ~ **loss** n TV pérdida de reproducción f; ~ **video-tape recorder** n TV grabador reproductor de video m (AmL), grabador reproductor de vídeo m (Esp)

playing: ~ **time** n CINEMAT tiempo de registro m

pleat[1] n TEXTIL pliegue m

pleat[2] vt TEXTIL plisar

pleated adj TEXTIL plisado

pleater n TEXTIL plisadora f

pleating n TEXTIL plisado m; ~ **machine** n TEXTIL máquina de plisar f

plenum: ~ **chamber** n ACOUST cámara plenum f, AIR TRANSP cámara de distribución f, cámara de pleno f, cámara distribuidora de aire f, cámara impelente f, AUTO cámara de distribución f, cámara de sobrepresión f, cámara distribuidora de aire f, cámara impelente f; ~-**chamber air-cushion system** n TRANSP sistema colchón de aire por cámara impelente m; ~ **fan** n MECH ENG ventilador impelente m; ~ **ventilator** n MECH ENG ventilador impelente m

plesiochronous: ~ **digital hierarchy** n (PDH) TELECOM jerarquía digital plesiocrónica f

plesiosynchronous: ~ **line terminal** n TELECOM terminal de línea plesiosincrónico m; ~ **transmission equipment** n TELECOM equipo de transmisión plesiosincrónico m

plexiglass: ~ **fairing** n AIR TRANSP carenado de plexiglas m

plied: ~ **yarn** *n* TEXTIL hilo doblado *m*

plier: ~~-**saw set** *n* CONST juego de alicates *m*

pliers *n pl* AUTO, CONST alicates *m pl*, ELEC *tool* alicates *m pl*, tenacillas *f pl*, MECH alicates *m pl*, MECH ENG *tool* pinzas *f pl*, alicates *m pl*, tenacillas *f pl*, PROD, VEH alicates *m pl*

plimsoll: ~ **line** *n* WATER TRANSP línea de máxima carga *f*

pliofilm *n* CHEM pliopelícula *f*

pliolit *n* CHEM pliolito *m*

PLL *abbr* (*phase-locked loop*) ELECTRON circuito de fase sincronizada *m*, SPACE bucle de enganche de fase *m*, circuito de bloqueo de fase *m*, circuito de fase sincronizada *m*, TELECOM bucle de enganche de fase *m*, TV lazo de enganche de fase *m*

PL-OAM *abbr* (*physical-layer operations and maintenance*) TELECOM explotación y mantenimiento de la capa física *f*

plot[1] *n* AGRIC *of land* parcela *f*, AIR TRANSP *navigation* trazado *m*, representación gráfica *f*, COMP&DP trazado *m*, WATER TRANSP *navigation course* trazado de la derrota *m*

plot[2] *vt* CONST trazar, GEOM delinear, trazar, MATH *graph* dibujar (*Esp*), graficar (*AmL*), WATER TRANSP *course* puntear, trazar, *position* cartear; ~ **a bearing** *vt* WATER TRANSP tomar y trazar marcaciones

plotter *n* COMP&DP, ELEC plotter *m*, trazador *m*, INSTR trazador *m*

plotting *n* COMP&DP trazado *m*, MILIT *radar* fijación de la posición *f*, *topography* trazado de planos *m*, WATER TRANSP *navigation* punteo *m*; ~ **board** *n* COMP&DP mesa trazadora *f*, tablero de trazado *m*; ~ **chart** *n* WATER TRANSP *navigation* carta de punteo de la derrota *f*; ~ **ground** *n* CONST *surveying* zona de trazado *f*; ~ **paper** *n* CONST papel para dibujo técnico *m*; ~ **sheet** *n* WATER TRANSP *navigation* carta de arrumbamiento *f*; ~ **table** *n* WATER TRANSP *navigation* mesa de derrota *f*

plough[1] *n BrE* AGRIC arado *m*, CONST *joinery* cepillo ranurador *m*; ~ **anchor** *n BrE* WATER TRANSP ancla de arado *f*; ~ **belt** *n BrE* MECH ENG cinta de ranurar *f*; ~ **folder** *n BrE* PRINT doblador de ingenio *m*, plegadora de lengüeta de encuadernador *f*; ~ **plane** *n BrE* CONST *joinery* cepillo ranurador *m*; ~ **and press** *n BrE* PRINT cortadora de los cantos del libro *f*, ingenio *m*; ~ **share** *n BrE* AGRIC reja de arado *f*

plough[2]: ~ **in** *vt BrE* AGRIC enterrar con arado; ~ **out** *vt BrE* AGRIC arrancar con arado; ~ **under** *vt BrE* AGRIC enterrar con arado; ~ **up** *vt BrE* AGRIC arrancar con arado

ploughed: ~~-**and-feathered joint** *n BrE* CONST junta ranurada y con lengüeta *f*, unión ranurada y embadurnada *f*; ~~-**and-tongued joint** *n BrE* CONST *insert between two ploughed boards* unión ranurada y con lengüeta *f*, *on edge of one board* junta ranurada y machihembrada *f*

ploughshare *n BrE* WATER TRANSP *anchor* ancla de arado *f*

ploughsole *n BrE* AGRIC piso de arado *m*

plow *AmE see plough BrE*

plowed: ~~-**and-feathered joint** *AmE see ploughed-and-feathered joint BrE*; ~~-**and-tongued joint** *AmE see ploughed-and-tongued joint BrE*

plowshare *n AmE see ploughshare BrE*

plowsole *AmE see ploughsole BrE*

PLS *abbr* (*physical-layer service*) TELECOM servicio de la capa física *m*

plucking *n* TEXTIL despinzado *m*

plug[1] ~~-**in** *adj* PROD conectable, enchufable

plug[2] *n* AUTO bujía *f*, C&G tapón *m*, CINEMAT enchufe *m*, tomacorriente *m*, CONST *of cock* tapón obturador *m*, enchufe *m*, *stopper* tapón *m*, *wedge* cuña de calzo *f*, *for quarrying and stone-working* cuña *f*, clavija *f*, taco *m*, ELEC *connection* clavija de conexión *f*, enchufe macho *m*, clavija *f*, clavija de contacto *f*, ELEC ENG enchufe macho *m*, HYDRAUL tapón fusible *m*, MECH obturador *m*, tarugo *m*, bujía *f*, tapador *m*, tapón *m*, PETR TECH tapón *m*, PHYS *plane, trying-plane* enchufe *m*, PRINT relleno *m*, PROD enchufe macho *m*, *at bottom of reservoir* obturador *m*, tapón de arcilla para parar la colada *m*, TELECOM clavija *f*, toma *f*, TV conector macho *m*, VEH bujía *f*, tapón *m*, WATER *hydrant* hidrante *m*, boca de agua *f*; ~ **adaptor** *n* ELEC, ELEC ENG adaptador de enchufe *m*; ~~-**and-cord switchboard** *n* TELECOM cuadro conmutador con clavija y cordón *m*, cuadro de conmutación con clavija y cordón *m*, tablero de conmutación con clavija y cordón *m*; ~ **box** *n* ELEC ENG caja de enchufes *f*; ~ **center bit** *AmE*, ~ **centre bit** *BrE n* MECH ENG berbiquí de clavija *m*; ~ **cock** *n* CONST llave de paso *f*; ~ **compatibility** *n* ELEC ENG compatibilidad de enchufes *f*; ~ **connection** *n* ELEC ENG conexión por enchufe *f*; ~ **connector** *n* ELEC ENG conector de clavija *m*; ~ **door** *n* PROD puerta empernada *f*; ~ **drill** *n* MECH ENG perforadora de percusión a mano *f*, perforadora de percusión manual *f*; ~ **gage** *AmE*, ~ **gauge** *BrE n* CONST calibrador macho *m*, MECH ENG calibrador de tapón para agujeros *m*, calibre cilíndrico *m*, calibre de macho *m*, calibre macho cilíndrico *m*, galga de clavija *f*, METR calibre cilíndrico *m*, calibre de tapón *m*, galga de clavija *f*; ~ **hole** *n* CONST *of cock* orificio con tapón *m*; ~~-**in coil** *n* ELEC ENG bobina de clavija *f*, bobina reemplazable *f*; ~~-**in component** *n* ELEC ENG componente enchufable *m*; ~~-**in module** *n* ELEC ENG módulo enchufable *m*; ~~-**in relay** *n* ELEC ENG relé enchufable *m*; ~~-**in switch** *n* PROD enchufe tomacorriente *m*, interruptor enchufable *m*; ~~-**in termination** *n* ELEC *cable accessory* clavija de terminación *f*; ~~-**in unit** *n* ELEC unidad enchufable *f*, unidad recambiable *f*, ELEC ENG elemento enchufable *m*, unidad conectable *f*; ~ **pin** *n* ELEC *connection* dispositivo enchufable *m*, elemento enchufable *m*, unidad enchufable *f*; ~ **receptacle** *n* ELEC *connection* caja de contacto *f*, receptáculo de clavija *m*, toma de enchufe *m*, tomacorriente de clavija *m*; ~ **seat** *n* MECH ENG asiento de clavija *m*, asiento de tapón *m*, repisa para clavija *f*; ~ **and socket** *n* TELECOM clavija y enchufe *f*; ~ **socket** *n* CINEMAT hembra para tomacorriente *f*, VEH base de enchufe *f*; ~ **switch** *n* ELEC ENG conmutador de clavijas *m*; ~ **tap** *n* MECH ENG *bottoming tap* macho semicónico *m*, *second tap* macho de roscar final *m*, macho intermedio para roscar *m*, macho de acabar *m*; ~~-**tenon joint** *n* CONST junta de tapón de espiga *f*; ~~-**timer** *n* ELEC ENG temporizador de clavijas *m*, temporizador de enchufe *m*; ~~-**type connection** *n* ELEC conexión tipo enchufe *f*, conexión tipo toma de corriente *f*; ~~-**type connector** *n* TELECOM conectador tipo clavija *m*; ~~-**type outlet** *n* ELEC *connection* tomacorriente de clavija tipo enchufe *m*; ~ **wire** *n* ELEC ENG hilo de clavija *m*

plug³ *vt* ELEC ENG enchufar, WATER TRANSP *shipbuilding* taponar; ~ **in** *vt* CINEMAT enchufar, ELEC *connection*, ELEC ENG, TELECOM conectar, enchufar, TV enchufar

plugboard *n* COMP&DP tablero de conexiones *m*, ELEC ENG cuadro de contactos enchufables *m*, regleta de clavijas enchufables *f*

pluggable *adj* ELEC ENG conectable, enchufable

plugger *n* MECH ENG perforadora de percusión *f*, perforadora de percusión a mano *f*

plugging *n* ELEC *of wall* enchufes *m pl*, ELEC ENG frenado por inversión de las conexiones *m*, frenado por inversión de la secuencia de fases *m*, MECH ENG colocación de tarugos *f*, taponamiento *m*, obturación *f*, MINE cuarteamiento de rocas *m*, PETR TECH obturación *f*, taponamiento *m*, taponado *m*, PRINT cegado de los puntos *m*, TEXTIL abrochado con cierre *m*; ~ **bar** *n* MECH ENG barra de obturación *f*, barra de taponamiento *f*

plumb¹: **off** ~ *adj* CONST desplomado

plumb² *n* CONST plomada *f*, vertical *f*; ~ **bob** *n* CONST plomada *f*; ~ **line** *n* CONST hilo de plomada *m*

plumb³ *vt* CONST *to seal* nivelar, *to test* aplomar

plumbago *n* AGRIC plombagina *f*, CHEM grafito *m*, plombagina *f*; ~ **crucible** *n* PROD crisol de grafito *m*

plumbate *n* CHEM plumbato *m*

plumber *n* CONST *person* fontanero *m* (*Esp*), plomero *m* (*AmL*); ~'**s joint** *n* CONST junta de fontanero *f* (*Esp*), junta de plomero *f* (*AmL*); ~'**s solder** *n* CONST soldador de fontanero *m* (*Esp*), soldador de plomero *m* (*AmL*)

plumbic *adj* CHEM plúmbico

plumbicon *n* ELECTRON plumbicón *m*

plumbing *n* CONST fontanería *f* (*Esp*), plomería *f* (*AmL*)

plumbite *n* CHEM plumbita *f*

plumbous *adj* CHEM plomboso

plume *n* FLUID pluma *f*, OCEAN *computer* defluviación *f*, defluviación formando penacho *f*, POLL penacho *m*; ~ **opacity** *n* C&G opacidad de la pluma de humo *f*; ~ **rise** *n* POLL altura del penacho de humos *f*, elevación del penacho de humos *f*

plummer: ~ **block** *n* MECH ENG cojinete *m*, PROD chumacera *f*; ~-**block bearing** *n* MECH ENG cojinete *m*

plummet *n* CONST plomada *f*

plump: ~ **gate** *n* PROD *founding* canal de colada en caída directa *m*

plunge *n* GEOL *programming* hundimiento *m*

plunger *n* C&G pistón *m*, ELEC ENG ampolla hermética *f*, núcleo móvil *m*, solenoide *m*, MECH pistón *m*, émbolo *m*, MECH ENG contacto de presión *m*, golpeador *m*, macho *m*, percutor *m*, pistón *m*, pulsador *m*, émbolo macizo *m*, PROD pistón *m*, émbolo *m*, VEH émbolo *m*; ~-**assist mechanism** *n* C&G mecanismo del pistón *m*; ~ **elevator** *n AmE* (*cf plunging lift BrE*) CONST ascensor hidráulico *m*; ~ **fuel-pump** *n* AUTO, VEH bomba de combustible de pistón *f*, bomba de combustible de émbolo *f*; ~ **jig** *n* PROD criba filtrante *f*, criba hidráulica de pistón *f*; ~ **lift** *n* MINE bombeo neumático *m*, tubería de impulsión *f*; ~ **piston** *n* MECH ENG pistón de faldilla *m*, pistón tubular *m*; ~ **pump** *n* WATER bomba de pistón tubular *f*, bomba de émbolo buzo *f*, bomba impelente *f*; ~ **relay** *n* ELEC ENG relé de núcleo móvil

m; ~ **ring** *n* C&G aro del pistón *m*; ~ **set** *n* MINE equipo impelente *m*, grupo impelente *m*; ~-**type jig** *n* COAL caja de pistón *f*, caja de émbolo *f*

plunging *n* CONST inmersión *f*; ~ **lift** *n BrE* (*cf plunger elevator AmE*) CONST ascensor hidráulico *m*

plurivalent *adj* CHEM plurivalente

plus: ~ **diopter** *AmE*, ~ **dioptre** *BrE n* CINEMAT dioptría positiva *f*; ~ **sign** *n* CONST *surveying* signo plus *m*; ~ **tapping** *n* ELEC derivación positiva *f*; ~ **terminal** *n* AUTO terminal positivo *m*

pluton *n* GEOL *programme* plutón *m*

plutonic: ~ **magma** *n* PETROL magma plutónico *m*; ~ **rock** *n* GEOPHYS roca plutónica *f*

plutonium *n* (*Pu*) CHEM, GEOL, MINERAL, NUCL, PHYS, RAD PHYS plutonio *m* (*Pu*)

ply *n* AUTO capa *f*, pliegue *m*, MECH ENG doblez *m*, huelgo *m*, pliegue *m*, tolerancia *f*, SPACE chapa *f*, pliegue *m*, TEXTIL capa *f*, VEH tejido *m*, textura *f*; ~ **glass** *n* C&G *of hollow glass* vidrio sandwich *m*; ~ **separation** *n* P&R separación en capas *f*, separación en pliegues *f*

plybond: ~ **strength** *n* P&R fuerza de adherencia de las capas *f*, fuerza de adherencia de los pliegues *f*

plywood *n* CONST, PACK, WATER TRANSP madera contrachapada *f* (*Esp*), madera terciada *f* (*AmL*), contrachapado *m* (*AmL*), madera laminada *f*; ~ **adhesive** *n* PACK adhesivo para madera contrachapada *m*; ~ **case** *n* PACK caja de madera contrachapada *f*; ~ **drum** *n* PACK tambor de madera contrachapada *m*

Pm *abbr* (*promethium*) CHEM, NUCL Pm (*promecio*)

PM¹ *abbr* (*phase modulation*) COMP&DP, ELECTRON, PHYS, TELECOM, TV MF (*modulación de fase*)

PM²: ~ **conversion coefficient** *n* SPACE *communications* coeficiente de conversión de modulación de fase *m*; ~ **transfer coefficient** *n* SPACE *communications* coeficiente de transferencia de modulación de fase *m*

PMBX *abbr* (*private manual branch exchange*) TELECOM central privada manual *f*

PMMA *abbr* (*polymethyl methacrylate*) P&R PMMA (*metacrilato de polimetilo, polimetacrilato de metilo*)

p-n: ~ **homojunction diode** *n* ELECTRON diodo de homounión p-n *m*; ~ **junction** *n* PHYS juntura p-n *f*; ~ **rectifier** *n* ELEC ENG rectificador de positivo-negativo *m*

PN¹ *abbr* (*positive notification*) TELECOM notificación positiva *f*

PN²: ~ **junction diode** *n* ELEC *semi-conductor* diodo de unión NP *m*, ELECTRON diodo de unión PN *m*

pneumatic¹ *adj* PHYS, VEH neumático *m*

pneumatic²: ~ **assembly-tool** *n* MECH ENG herramienta de ensamblar neumática *f*; ~ **brake** *n* VEH freno neumático *m*; ~ **brake system** *n* MECH ENG sistema de frenado por aire comprimido *m*; ~ **cell** *n* COAL balonet neumático *m*, jaula neumática *f*, subespacio neumático *m*; ~ **clutch** *n* MECH ENG embrague neumático *m*; ~ **conveying of bulk materials** *n* MECH ENG transporte neumático de materiales a granel *m*; ~ **coupling** *n* MECH ENG *power transmission* acoplamiento neumático *m*; ~ **cylinder** *n* AIR TRANSP *helicopter*, MECH ENG cilindro neumático *m*; ~ **detector** *n* TRANSP detector neumático *m*; ~ **drill** *n* CONST *rock drill* taladro neumático *m*; ~ **equipment** *n* MECH ENG equipo neumático *m*; ~ **extraction-pump** *n* CHEM TECH bomba de extracción neumática *f*; ~ **filter** *n* CHEM TECH filtro

neumático *m*; ~ **fluid power** *n* MECH ENG potencia del fluido neumático *f*; ~ **gage** *AmE*, ~ **gauge** *BrE n* METR comparador de aire comprimido *m*; ~ **hammer** *n* MINE martinete de aire comprimido *m*; ~ **hammerdrill** *n* CONST martillo de aire comprimido *m*; ~ **handling** *n* COAL removido neumático *m*; ~ **impact-wrench** *n* MECH ENG aprietatuercas neumático de percusión *m*; ~ **jig** *n* COAL caja de pulsación neumática *f*, MECH ENG criba de aire comprimido *f*; ~ **loudspeaker** *n* ACOUST altavoz neumático *m*; ~ **motor** *n* MECH ENG motor de aire comprimido *m*, neumomotor *m*; ~ **pick** *n* MINE martillo picador de aire comprimido *m*; ~ **pipe conveyor** *n* TRANSP transportador mediante tubería neumática *m*; ~ **power-hammer** *n* CONST martillo neumático *m*; ~ **pump** *n* MECH ENG, PHYS bomba neumática *f*; ~ **ram** *n* COAL pisón de aire comprimido *m*; ~ **rammer** *n* PROD *founding* pisón de aire comprimido *m*; ~ **release** *n* PHOTO disparador neumático *m*; ~ **riveter** *n* PROD remachadora de aire comprimido *f*; ~ **suspension** *n* TRANSP suspensión neumática *f*; ~ **table** *n* COAL mesa neumática *f*; ~ **tire** *AmE see pneumatic tyre BrE*; ~**-tired roller** *AmE see pneumatic-tyred roller BrE*; ~ **tool** *n* MECH ENG herramienta de aire comprimido *f*, herramienta neumática *f*; ~ **transmission system** *n* MECH ENG *power transmission* sistema de transmisión neumática *m*; ~ **treatment** *n* COAL tratamiento por aire comprimido *m*; ~ **tyre** *n BrE* VEH neumático *m*; ~**-tyred roller** *n BrE* CONST apisonadora con neumáticos *f*; ~ **valve** *n* MECH ENG válvula neumática *f*
pneumatically: ~**-operated switch** *n* ELEC interruptor accionado neumáticamente *m*; ~**-operated valve** *n* MECH ENG válvula accionada por aire comprimido *f*, válvula neumoaccionada *f*
pneumatics *n* PHYS neumáticos *m pl*
pneumatolysis *n* GEOL neumatolisis *f*
p-n-p[1] *abbr* (*positive-negative-positive*) ELECTRON, PHYS, RAD PHYS p-n-p (*positivo-negativo-positivo*)
p-n-p[2]: ~ **transistor** *n* ELECTRON, PHYS tránsistor p-n-p *m*
PNP *abbr* (*private-numbering plan*) TELECOM plan de numeración privado *m*
p-n-p-n: ~ **component** *n* ELECTRON componente p-n-p-n *m*; ~ **device** *n* ELECTRON dispositivo p-n-p-n *m*
PNX *abbr* (*private network exchange*) TELECOM central de red privada *f*
Po *abbr* (*polonium*) CHEM, RAD PHYS Po (*polonio*)
pocket *n* COAL bolsada *f*, bolsón *m*, cavidad rellena de agua *f*, cavidad rellena de gas *f*, poceta de recogida de aguas *f*, MINE bolsada *f*, bolsón *m*, cavidad rellena de agua *f*, cavidad rellena de gas *f*, MINERAL bolsada *f*; ~ **calculator** *n* TELECOM calculadora de bolsillo *f*; ~ **compass** *n* MILIT brújula de bolsillo *f*; ~**-dryer ventilation roll** *n* PAPER rodillo de ventilación de las bolsas secadoras *m*; ~ **folding-machine** *n* PRINT plegadora a bolsillo *f*; ~ **grinder** *n* PAPER desfibrador de cajones *m*; ~ **terminal** *n* TELECOM terminal de bolsillo *m*
pocketbook *n* PRINT libro de bolsillo *m*
pocking *n* C&G viruelas *f pl*
pockmarks *n pl* C&G marcas de viruelas *f pl*
pod *n* AGRIC marlo *m* (*AmL*), mazorca *f* (*Esp*), vaina *f*, SPACE *for exterior load* receptáculo aerodinámico *m*, *spacecraft* compartimiento desprendible de carga *m*, compartimiento múltiple para cohetes *m*, cápsula

expulsable *f*, MILIT receptáculo para una ametralladora *m*
podocarpic *adj* CHEM podocárpico
podophyllin *n* CHEM podofilina *f*
POGO: ~ **effect** *n* SPACE efecto POGO *m*
POH *abbr* (*path overhead*) TELECOM acceso superior *m*, vía de transmisión aérea *f*
point[1] *adj* PHYS puntual; **in-**~ *adj* TV en punto; **out-**~ *adj* TV fuera de punto; ~**-to-point** *adj* COMP&DP, ELEC, ELEC ENG, PROD, TRANSP punto a punto
point[2] *n* CONST *glaziers' diamond* punta *f*, puntero *m*, GEOM punto *m*, MECH ENG *sharp end of thing* punta *f*, *of gear-tooth* saliente *f*, PHYS *under a load*, PRINT punto *m*, VEH punto *m*, momento de encendido *m*, WATER TRANSP *on chart* punto *m*, *cape* punta *f*; ~ **charge** *n* ELEC *electrostatics* carga de punta *f*, carga puntual *f*, PHYS carga puntual *f*; ~ **chuck** *n* MECH ENG portabrocas *m*; ~ **circle** *n* MECH ENG *gearing* circunferencia de la corona *f*, círculo de la corona *m*, círculo exterior *m*; ~ **code** *n* TELECOM código de puntos fijos *m*; ~ **of concurrence** *n* GEOM punto de coincidencia *m*, punto de concurrencia *m*; ~ **contact** *n* ELEC ENG, ELECTRON contacto de punta *m*; ~**-contact detector diode** *n* ELECTRON diodo detector de contacto de punta *m*; ~**-contact diode** *n* ELECTRON diodo de contacto de punta *m*; ~**-contact mixer diode** *n* ELECTRON diodo mezclador de contacto de punta *m*; ~**-contact silicon diode** *n* ELECTRON diodo de silicio de contacto de punta *m*; ~**-contact transistor** *n* ELECTRON transistor de contacto de punta *m*; ~ **defect** *n* CRYSTALL defecto puntual *m*, METALL laguna *f*; ~ **group** *n* CRYSTALL grupo puntual *m*; ~ **group symmetry** *n* CRYSTALL simetría de grupos *f*; ~ **of intersection** *n* GEOM punto de intersección *m*; ~**-lock plunger** *n* RAIL palanca de maniobra de la aguja *f*; ~ **of no return** *n* AIR TRANSP punto de no retorno *m*, punto límite de retorno *m*; ~**-of-sale display** *n* PACK expositor en el punto de venta *m*; ~**-of-sale terminal** *n* PACK terminal en el punto de venta *m*; ~ **of osculation** *n* GEOM punto de osculación *m*; ~**-plate rectifier** *n* ELEC rectificador de placas puntuales *m*; ~ **recorder** *n* INSTR grabador puntual *m*; ~ **resistance** *n* COAL resistencia en un punto *f*; ~ **of sale** *n* (*POS*) COMP&DP punto de venta *m* (*PV*); ~**-set geometry** *n* GEOM geometría de conjunto de puntos *f*, geometría de puntos *f*; ~ **source** *n* CINEMAT, NUCL, PHOTO, PHYS, POLL fuente puntual *f*, RAD PHYS foco puntual *m*, fuente puntual *f*; ~**-source light** *n* PHOTO iluminación proveniente de una fuente puntual *f*; ~**-source radio transmitter** *n* TRANSP punto radio-transmisor *m*; ~ **of support** *n* MECH ENG punto de apoyo *m*; ~ **switch** *n* RAIL aguja de cambio de vía *f*; ~ **system** *n* PRINT sistema de medida por puntos tipográficos *m*; ~ **of tangency** *n* GEOM punto de tangencia *m*; ~ **tool** *n* MECH ENG *lathe* herramienta de punta *f*; ~**-to-point communication** *n* PROD comunicación punto a punto *f*; ~**-to-point line** *n* COMP&DP línea punto a punto *f*; ~**-to-point link** *n* ELEC ENG enlace de punto a punto *m*; ~**-to-point transport** *n* TRANSP transporte de puerta a puerta *m*; ~**-to-point wiring** *n* ELEC alambrado de punto a punto *m*, ELEC ENG cableado de punto a punto *m*, montaje de punto a punto *m*; ~ **vacuum-cleaning system** *n* SAFE sistema modular de aspiración *m*
point[3] *vt* CONST *wall* afilar, apuntar
pointable: ~ **generator** *n* SPACE generador dirigible *m*

pointed: ~ **square-head coach-screw** n CONST tornillo puntiagudo de cabeza cuadrada m

pointer n COMP&DP graphics puntero m, ELEC on instrument puntero m, aguja indicadora f, apuntador m, ELEC ENG on instrument, LAB aguja indicadora f, MECH ENG of meter aguja indicadora f, aguja f, METR fiel m, PHOTO aguja indicadora f, PRINT puntero m, RAIL palanca de maniobra de agujas f, TELECOM on instrument aguja f, apuntador m, puntero m; ~ **chain** n COMP&DP cadena puntero f; ~ **instrument** n INSTR instrumento de medida de lectura directa m; ~ **jack** n MECH ENG palanquita de indicación f; ~ **justification-count** n (PJC) TELECOM cálculo justificativo del puntero m; ~ **justification-event** n (PJE) TELECOM evento justificativo del puntero m; ~ **knob** n MECH ENG botón con índice m, perilla con flecha f, perilla con índice f

pointing n CONST rejuntado m, SPACE dirección f, puntería f; ~ **accuracy** n SPACE precisión en la puntería f; ~ **error** n SPACE error de apuntamiento m, error de puntería m; ~ **loss** n SPACE communications pérdida de puntería f, TELECOM pérdida por apartamento f

pointless: ~ **ignition** n AmE (cf contactless ignition BrE) AUTO, VEH encendido sin platinos m, ignición sin contactos f, ignición sin platinos f; ~ **pickup** n AmE (cf contactless pickup BrE) ELEC transductor sin contactos m; ~ **transistorized ignition** n AmE (cf contactless transistorized ignition BrE) AUTO, VEH arranque transistorizado sin platinos m, ignición transistorizada sin platinos f

points n pl BrE AUTO (cf contact breaker-point AmE) platino del ruptor m, CONST (cf switch AmE) aguja f, cambios de vía m pl, juego de agujas m, cambiavía m, RAIL aguja f, cambiavía m, juego de agujas m, VEH (cf contact breaker-point AmE) punto de interrupción de contacto m, ruptor m, platino del ruptor m; ~ **of the compass** n pl WATER TRANSP cuartas f pl, rumbos de la aguja m pl; ~ **heating** n RAIL calentamiento de agujas m; ~ **rod** n RAIL palanca de las agujas f; ~ **switching** n RAIL cambio de agujas m

poise n METR poise m

Poiseuille: ~ **flow** n FLUID flujo de Poiseuille m; ~'s **law** n PHYS ley de Poiseuille f

poison n CHEM TECH, NUCL, POLL, SAFE veneno m; ~ **plant** n AGRIC planta venenosa f

poisoning n CHEM of catalyst envenenamiento m, POLL empobrecimiento m, envenenamiento m

poisons: ~ **cupboard** n LAB spacecraft, SAFE armario de sustancias tóxicas m

Poisson: ~ **distribution** n COMP&DP, MATH, PHYS distribución de Poisson f; ~'s **equation** n ELEC potential problems, PHYS ecuación de Poisson f; ~'s **law** n PHYS, SPACE ley de Poisson f; ~'s **ratio** n COAL, CONST, MECH, PETROL coeficiente de Poisson m, PHYS razón de Poisson f; ~ **traffic** n TELECOM tráfico Poisson m

poker n GAS obturador m, PROD picafuegos m; ~ **vibrator** n CONST vibrador m

poking n PROD gas generators acción de limpiar f

POL abbr (petroleum, oil and lubricants) MILIT petróleo, aceite y lubricantes m pl

polar[1] adj CHEM compound, GEOM polar; ~-**orbiting** adj SPACE de órbita sobre el polo

polar[2]: ~ **air** n METEO aire polar m; ~ **aurora** n GEOPHYS, METEO, SPACE, WATER TRANSP aurora polar f; ~ **axis** n INSTR eje polar m; ~-**axis circle** n INSTR círculo del eje polar m; ~ **climate** n METEO clima polar m; ~ **coordinates** n pl PHYS coordenadas polares f pl; ~ **diagram** n PHYS diagrama polar m; ~ **dielectric** n PHYS dieléctrico polar m; ~ **front** n METEO frente polar m; ~ **molecule** n P&R molécula polar f; ~ **orbit** n SPACE órbita polar f; ~ **triangle** n GEOM triángulo polar m

polarimeter n CHEM, LAB, PHYS, RAD PHYS polarímetro m

polarimetric adj CHEM, LAB, PHYS, RAD PHYS polarimétrico

polarimetry n CHEM, LAB, PHYS, RAD PHYS polarimetría f

polariscope n CHEM, LAB, PHYS, RAD PHYS polariscopio m

polarity n CHEM, ELEC, ELEC ENG, ELECTRON, PHYS, TV polaridad f; ~ **control** n TV control de la polaridad m; ~ **epoch** n GEOL época de polaridad f; ~ **reversal** n ELEC, ELEC ENG, SPACE inversión de polaridad f, inversión de polos f; ~ **reverser** n ELEC switch, ELEC ENG inversor de polaridad m; ~-**reversing switch** n ELEC, ELEC ENG conmutador inversor de la polaridad m; ~ **sign** n ELEC cell signo de polaridad m; ~ **tester** n ELEC connections buscapolos m

polarizability n CHEM, LAB, PHYS, RAD PHYS polarizabilidad f

polarizable adj CHEM, LAB, PHYS, RAD PHYS polarizable

polarization n GEN polarización f; ~ **angle** n OPT ángulo de polarización m; ~ **charge** n PHYS carga de polarización f; ~-**coupling loss** n TELECOM pérdida por acoplamiento de polarización f; ~ **current** n PHYS corriente de polarización f; ~ **diplexer** n SPACE, TELECOM diplexor de polarización m; ~ **filter** n CINEMAT, INSTR, PHOTO filtro de polarización m; ~ **grid** n SPACE rejilla de polarización f; ~ **isolation** n SPACE aislamiento de polarización m, separación de polarización f; ~ **microscope** n LAB microscopio polarizador m; ~ **purity** n SPACE pureza de polarización f

polarize vt LAB, METALL, OPT, SPACE, TELECOM polarizar

polarized[1] adj LAB, METALL, OPT, SPACE, TELECOM polarizado

polarized[2]: ~ **capacitor** n ELEC ENG condensador polarizado m; ~ **connector** n ELEC ENG conector polarizado m; ~ **electrolytic capacitor** n ELEC ENG condensador electrolítico polarizado m; ~ **light** n CINEMAT, PHOTO, PHYS, RAD PHYS, WAVE PHYS luz polarizada f; ~ **plug** n ELEC ENG clavija polarizada f, enchufe polarizado m; ~ **relay** n ELEC, ELEC ENG relevador polarizado m, relé polarizado m; ~ **wave** n WAVE PHYS onda polarizada f

polarizer n LAB, METALL, OPT, PHYS, SPACE, TELECOM polarizador m

polarizing: ~ **angle** n OPT ángulo polarizante m; ~ **filter** n CINEMAT, INSTR, PHOTO filtro polarizador m; ~ **microscope** n C&G microscopio polarizante m, CRYSTALL microscopio de polarización m, INSTR, LAB microscopio polarizador m, PHYS microscopio polarizante m; ~ **prism** n INSTR prisma polarizador m; ~ **spectacles** n pl PHOTO for stereo viewing anteojos polarizantes m pl (AmL), gafas polarizantes f pl (Esp); ~ **sun prism** n INSTR helioscopio de polarización m

polarogram n CHEM polarograma m

polarographic *adj* CHEM polarográfico
polarography *n* CHEM polarografía *f*
Polaroid® *n* PHOTO, PHYS, RAD PHYS polaroide *m*;
~ **fade** *n* CINEMAT desvanecimiento polaroid *m*
polaron *n* PHYS polarón *m*
pole *n* CONST *post, mast* palo *m*, poste *m*, *surveyor's
levelling-pole* jalón *m*, mira *f*, CRYSTALL, ELEC, ELEC
ENG, GEOM, GEOPHYS polo *m*, METR *linear measure*
polar *m*, PETR TECH, PHYS polo *m*; ~ **arrangement** *n*
PROD disposición de polos *f*; ~**-box** *n* MINE caja de
sonda *f*; ~**-changer switch** *n* ELEC conmutador
cambiador de polos *m*; ~**-changing starter** *n* AUTO,
ELEC, ELEC ENG, VEH arrancador por cambio del
número de polos *m*; ~ **face** *n* TV superficie polar *f*;
~ **figure** *n* CRYSTALL *X-ray pattern* figura polar *f*;
~ **hook** *n* MINE caracola *f* (*AmL*), gancho *m* (*Esp*);
~ **lathe** *n* MECH ENG torno al aire *m*, torno de puntos
m; ~**-mounted transformer** *n* ELEC *overhead line*
transformador de distribución para montaje en poste
m, transformador para montaje en poste *m*, ELEC
ENG transformador para montaje en poste *m*;
~**-mounting** *n* PROD montaje sobre polos *m*;
~ **piece** *n* ELEC ENG, MECH ENG ensanchamiento
polar *m*, masa polar *f*, pieza polar *f*, PHYS pieza polar
f; ~ **plate** *n* CONST *building* carrera inferior *f*; ~ **route**
n TELECOM ruta de líneas sobre postes *f*, ruta de
postes *f*; ~**-shading** *n* ELEC *generator* sombreado de
polo *m*; ~ **shoe** *n* ELEC ENG expansión polar *f*, TV
pieza polar *f*; ~ **slip** *n* ELEC *machine* deslizamiento de
polos *m*; ~ **strength** *n* PHYS fuerza polar *f*; ~ **tips** *n pl*
TV cuernos polares *m pl*; ~**-type transformer** *n* ELEC,
ELEC ENG transformador para poste *m*
poleman *n* CINEMAT microfonista *m*
polianite *n* MINERAL polianita *f*
polish[1] *n* COATINGS barniz *m*, brillo *m*
polish[2] *vt* C&G *first stage of polishing process*, COAL
pulir, MECH dar lustre, pulimentar, encerar, bruñir,
lustrar, MECH ENG, P&R bruñir, PROD lustrar, pulimentar, pulir, bruñir; ~ **with emery** *vt* COAL
esmerilar, picar; ~ **till dry** *vt* C&G pulir hasta secar
Polish: ~ **notation** *n* COMP&DP notación por sufijos *f*
polished: ~ **edge** *n* C&G borde pulido *m*; ~ **rod** *n*
FUELLESS *windmill pump* vástago pulido *m*; ~ **wired
glass** *n* C&G vidrio acorazado y pulido *m*
polisher *n* C&G pulidor *m*, PROD *person* bruñidor *m*,
pulidor *m*, pulidora *f*
polishing *n* COATINGS pulido *m*, MECH ENG abrillantado *m*, METALL pulido *m*, abrillantado *m*, P&R
abrillantado *m*, bruñido *m*, pulido *m*, PAPER abrillantado *m*, PROD bruñido *m*, pulido *m*,
pulimentación *f*, pulimentado *m*; ~ **agent** *n* C&G
agente pulidor *m*; ~ **head** *n* MECH ENG cabezal
pulidor *m*, torno para pulidoras *m*; ~ **lathe** *n* MECH
ENG torno pulidor *m*; ~ **machine** *n* PROD pulidora *f*;
~ **paper** *n* C&G papel para pulir *m*; ~ **shop** *n* C&G
taller de pulido *m*; ~ **unit** *n* C&G unidad pulidora *f*;
~ **wheel** *n* C&G rueda pulidora *f*, MECH ENG, METALL
disco de pulir *m*, pulidora *f*, PROD disco de pulir *m*
poll[1]: ~ **adze** *n* CONST azada *f*; ~ **pick** *n* CONST pico con
martillo *m*
poll[2] *vt* COMP&DP sondear, TELECOM interrogar
pollen *n* AGRIC polen *m*
pollination *n* AGRIC polinización *f*
polling *n* COMP&DP escrutinio *m*, llamada selectiva *f*,
sondeo *m*, TELECOM interrogación *f*, llamada selectiva *f*; ~ **key** *n* TELECOM clave de interrogación *f*,

pulsador de interrogación *m*; ~ **system** *n* TELECOM
sistema de interrogación *m*
pollucite *n* MINERAL polucita *f*
pollutant *n* MAR POLL, POLL, SAFE contaminante *m*,
substancia contaminante *f*; ~ **deposition** *n* MAR
POLL, POLL precipitación de contaminante *f*, sedimentación de contaminante *f*
pollute *vt* AGRIC, POLL, QUALITY, SAFE, WATER contaminar, polucionar
polluted[1] *adj* AGRIC, MAR POLL, POLL, QUALITY, SAFE,
WATER contaminado, poluto
polluted[2]: ~ **rainwater** *n* HYDROL, MAR POLL, POLL,
WATER agua de lluvia contaminada *f*, agua de lluvia
impura *f*; ~ **water** *n* HYDROL, MAR POLL, POLL, WATER
agua contaminada *f*, agua impura *f*
polluter: ~ **pays principle** *n* POLL canon de emisiones
m, principio de que el contaminador paga *m*, tasas
por contaminación *f pl*
polluting: ~ **agent** *n* CHEM, MAR POLL, POLL, SAFE
agente contaminante *m*
pollution *n* GEN contaminación *f*, polución *f*; ~ **control**
n POLL control de la contaminación *m*; ~ **emitter** *n*
POLL emisor de contaminantes *m*; ~ **research** *n* MAR
POLL, POLL investigación de la contaminación *f*;
~ **source** *n* POLL emisor de contaminantes *m*, fuente
de contaminación *f*
polonium *n* (*Po*) CHEM, RAD PHYS polonio *m* (*Po*)
polyacrylamide *n* CHEM, PETR TECH poliacrilamida *f*
polyacrylate *n* CHEM, P&R poliacrilato *m*
polyacrylonitrile *n* CHEM poliacrilonitrilo *m*
polyamide *n* (*PA*) AGRIC, CHEM, ELECTRON, P&R, TEX-
TIL poliamida *f* (*PA*); ~ **printed circuit** *n* ELECTRON
circuito impreso en poliamida *m*
polyamine *n* CHEM, P&R poliamina *f*
polyatomic *adj* CHEM, GAS poliatómico
polybasite *n* MINERAL polibasita *f*
polybutadiene *n* SPACE polibutadieno *m*
polybutylene *n* (*PB*) P&R polibutileno *m* (*PB*)
polycarbonate *n* CHEM, ELEC, P&R policarbonato *m*
polycarpic *adj* AGRIC policárpico
polychloroprene *n* CHEM policloropreno *m*
polychromatic *adj* C&G *glass* policromático
polychrome *adj* PRINT polícromo
polycondensation *n* CHEM policondensación *f*
polycrase *n* MINERAL policrasa *f*
polycrystalline: ~ **semiconductor** *n* ELECTRON semiconductor policristalino *m*; ~ **silicon** *n* ELECTRON
silicio policristalino *m*; ~ **solid** *n* CRYSTALL sólido
policristalino *m*
polycyclic[1] *adj* CHEM policíclico
polycyclic[2]: ~ **aromatic hydrocarbon** *n* POLL hidrocarburo aromático policíclico *m*
polydentate *adj* CHEM polidentado
polydimethylsiloxane *n* CHEM polidimetilsiloxano *m*
polyene *n* CHEM polieno *m*
polyenic *adj* CHEM poliénico
polyester *n* GEN poliéster no saturado *m*, poliéster *m*;
~ **base** *n* CINEMAT soporte de poliéster *m*; ~ **foam** *n*
P&R espuma de poliéster *f*; ~ **paint** *n* CONST pintura al
poliéster *f*; ~ **resin** *n* CHEM resina poliéster *f*
polyesterification *n* CHEM poliesterificación *f*
polyether: ~ **foam** *n* P&R espuma de poliéster *f*
polyethylene *n* GEN polietileno *m*; ~ **bags on the roll** *n
pl* PACK bobina de bolsas de polietileno *f*;
~ **container** *n* PACK contenedor de polietileno *m*;
~ **film** *n* (*PET film*) PACK película de polietileno *f*;

~ **glycol** *n* CHEM, DETERG polietilenglicol *m*; ~ **pallet-covers and liners** *n pl* PACK tapas y envolturas de polietileno para paletas *f pl*; ~ **self-adhesive tape** *n* PACK cinta de polietileno autoadhesiva *f*; ~ **terephthalate** *n* ELEC *dielectric*, P&R polietilentereftalato *m*, tereftalato de polietileno *m*

polyfunctional *adj* CHEM polifuncional

polygenetic: ~ **conglomerate** *n* GEOL conglomerado poligenético *m*

polygon *n* GEOM, METALL, PHYS *under a load* polígono *m*; ~ **connection** *n* ELEC conexión en polígono *f*

polygonal[1] *adj* GEOM, METALL, PHYS poligonal

polygonal[2]: ~ **delay line** *n* ELECTRON línea de retardo poligonal *f*; ~ **dislocation** *n* METALL dislocación poligonal *f*; ~ **mirror** *n* INSTR, OPT espejo poligonal *m*

polygonization *n* METALL poligonización *f*

polygorskite *n* GEOL, PETR TECH poligorskita *f*

polyhalite *n* GEOL, MINERAL polihalita *f*

polyhedral[1] *adj* CRYSTALL, GEOM, METALL poliédrico

polyhedral[2]: ~ **angle** *n* GEOM ángulo poliédrico *m*

polyhedron *n* CRYSTALL, GEOM, METALL poliedro *m*

polyhexylmethacrylate *n* (*PHMA*) P&R polihexilmetacrilato *m* (*PHMA*)

polyiamide *n* P&R poliamida *f*; ~ **printed circuit** *n* ELECTRON circuito impreso en poliamida *m*

polyisoprene *n* CHEM, P&R poliisopreno *m*

polymer *n* GEN polímero *m*

polymeria *n* CHEM polimería *f*

polymeric *adj* CHEM polimérico

polymerism *n* CHEM polimerismo *m*

polymerization *n* GEN *glass fibre-reinforced plastic construction* polimerización *f*

polymerize *vt* GEN polimerizar

polymerized: ~ **enamel** *n* MECH ENG *production* esmalte polimerizado *m*

polymerizer *n* TEXTIL polimerizador *m*

polymethacrylate *n* P&R polimetacrilato *m*

polymethyl: ~ **methacrylate** *n* (*PMMA*) P&R metacrilato de polimetilo *m* (*PMMA*), polimetacrilato de metilo *m* (*PMMA*)

polymethylene *n* CHEM polimetileno *m*

polymictic: ~ **conglomerate** *n* GEOL conglomerado polimíctico *m*

polymignite *n* MINERAL polimignita *f*

polymorphic: ~ **transformation** *n* CRYSTALL transformación polimórfica *f*

polymorphism *n* CHEM, CRYSTALL, METALL alotropía *f*, polimorfismo *m*

polynomial *n* COMP&DP, MATH, PHYS polinomio *m*; ~ **filter** *n* ELECTRON filtro polinómico *m*

polynucleotide *n* CHEM polinucleotido *m*

polyol *n* CHEM, P&R poliol *m*

polyolefin *n* CHEM, P&R, TEXTIL poliolefina *f*; ~ **barrier-film** *n* PACK película tipo barrera de poliolefina *f*; ~ **container** *n* PACK contenedor de poliolefina *m*

polyoxyethylene *n* CHEM polioxietileno *m*

polyoxymethylene *n* (*POM*) CHEM polioximetileno *m* (*POM*), P&R polióxido de metileno *m* (*POM*)

polypeptide *n* CHEM polipéptido *m*

polyphase[1] *adj* ELEC *AC network motor* polifásico, ELEC ENG multifasado, polifásico, GEOL *of liquids* multifase

polyphase[2]: ~ **circuit** *n* ELEC, ELEC ENG circuito polifásico *m*; ~ **current** *n* ELEC, ELEC ENG corriente polifásica *f*; ~ **generator** *n* ELEC, ELEC ENG generador polifásico *m*, generatriz multifásica *f*; ~ **induction-**

motor *n* ELEC ENG motor de inducción polifásico *m*; ~ **motor** *n* ELEC, ELEC ENG motor polifásico *m*; ~ **network** *n* ELEC, ELEC ENG *supply* red polifásica *f*; ~ **synchronous motor** *n* ELEC, ELEC ENG motor síncrono polifásico *m*; ~ **transformer** *n* ELEC, ELEC ENG transformador polifásico *m*

polyphenol *n* CHEM polifenol *m*

polyphosphoric: ~ **acid** *n* DETERG ácido polifosfórico *m*

polyploid *adj* AGRIC poliploide

polypnea *n* OCEAN polipnea *f*

polypropylene *n* GEN polipropileno *m*; ~ **closure** *n* PACK cierre de polipropileno *m*; ~ **strap** *n* PACK correa de polipropileno *f*

polysaccharide *adj* AGRIC, CHEM polisacárido *m*

polysilicon *n* ELECTRON polisilicio *m*; ~ **gate** *n* ELECTRON circuito de polisilicio *m*; ~ **layer** *n* ELECTRON estratificador de polisilicio *m*

polysiloxane *n* CHEM, P&R polisiloxano *m*

polystyrene *n* (*PS*) CHEM, P&R, PACK poliestireno *m* (*PS*)

polysulfide *AmE see* polysulphide *BrE*

polysulfone *AmE see* polysulphone *BrE*

polysulphide *n* *BrE* CHEM, P&R polisulfuro *m*

polysulphone *n* *BrE* CHEM polisulfona *f*

polyterpene *n* CHEM politerpeno *m*

polytetrafluoroethylene *n* (*PTFE*) CHEM, P&R politetrafluoretileno *m* (*PTFE*)

polythene *n* CHEM, FOOD, PETR TECH, WATER TRANSP *ship parts, equipment* politeno *m*

polythermal: ~ **cargo ship** *n* TRANSP buque de carga politérmica *m*

polyunsaturated *adj* CHEM, FOOD poliinsaturado

polyurethane *n* (*PUR*) CHEM, CONST, P&R, TEXTIL poliuretano *m* (*PUR*); ~ **foam** *n* P&R, WATER TRANSP espuma de poliuretano *f*; ~ **resin** *n* CONST resina de poliuretano *f*

polyvalence *n* CHEM polivalencia *f*

polyvalency *n* CHEM polivalencia *f*

polyvalent *adj* CHEM polivalente

polyvinyl *n* CHEM, TEXTIL polivinilo *m*; ~ **acetal** *n* CHEM, P&R acetal de polivinilo *m*; ~ **acetate** *n* P&R acetato de polivinilo *m*; ~ **alcohol** *n* CHEM alcohol polivinílico *m*, P&R alcohol polivinílico *m*, polialcohol vinílico *m*; ~ **alcohol size** *n* TEXTIL apresto de alcohol de polivinilo *m*; ~ **butyral** *n* CHEM, P&R polivinilbutiral *m*; ~ **chloride** *n* (*PVC*) COMP&DP, CONST, ELEC, ELEC ENG, P&R, PACK, TELECOM cloruro de polivinilo *m* (*PVC*); ~ **ether** *n* CHEM poliviniléter *m*, P&R poliviniléter *m*, éter polivinílico *m*; ~ **fluoride** *n* P&R fluoruro de polivinilo *m*, fluoruro de vinilo *m*

polyvinylbenzene *n* CHEM polivinilbenceno *m*

polyvinylidene: ~ **chloride** *n* (*PVDC*) P&R cloruro de polivinilideno *m* (*PVDC*), policloruro de vinilideno *m*

polyvinylpyrrolidone *n* (*PVP*) DETERG polivinilpirrolidona *f* (*PVP*)

POM *abbr* (*polyoxymethylene*) CHEM, P&R POM (*polioximetileno, polióxido de metileno*)

pomace *n* FOOD residuo seco *m*

pomaceous: ~ **fruit** *n* FOOD fruta de pepitas *f*

pome: ~ **fruit** *n* FOOD fruto pomoideo *m*

pomology *n* AGRIC fruticultura *f*

PON *abbr* (*passive optical network*) TELECOM red óptica pasiva *f*

pond *n* CHEM TECH alberca *f*, COAL alberca *f*, balsa *f*, charca *f*, embalse *m*, estanque *m*, pantano *m*, tramo de canal entre dos esclusas *m*, CRYSTALL alberca *f*, PAPER embalse *m*, WATER tramo de canal entre dos esclusas *m*; ~ **depth** *n* PAPER profundidad del embalse *f*

pondage *n* FUELLESS acopio *m*, almacenamiento *m*

pontoon *n* CONST, PETROL, WATER TRANSP pontón *m*; ~ **bridge** *n* MILIT, TRANSP puente de barcas *m*, puente de pontones *m*, WATER TRANSP puente de barcas *m*; ~ **crane** *n* WATER TRANSP grúa flotante *f*; ~ **dock** *n* TRANSP dique flotante *m*

pool *n* GAS acumulación *f*, charco *m*, depósito *m*, yacimiento *m*, PETROL acumulación *f*, depósito *m*, yacimiento *m*; ~ **boiling** *n* REFRIG ebullición libre *f*; ~ **cathode** *n* ELEC ENG cátodo líquido *m*

poop: ~ **deck** *n* WATER TRANSP *boat building* cubierta de toldilla *f*

poor: ~ **conductor** *n* ELEC ENG mal conductor *m*; ~ **grade** *n* MINE *of ore* mineral de baja ley *m*; ~ **insulant** *n* ELEC ENG mal aislante *m*; ~ **insulation** *n* ELEC ENG mal aislamiento *m*, mala aislación *f*; ~ **mixture** *n* AUTO mezcla pobre *f*; ~-**reception area** *n* TV zona de recepción insuficiente *f*; ~ **resolution** *n* CINEMAT resolución pobre *f*

pop[1]: ~ **gate** *n* PROD *founding* canal de colada en caída directa *m*; ~ **rivet** *n* PROD remache tubular de forma especial *m*; ~-**up menu** *n* COMP&DP menú desplegable *m*; ~-**up type** *n* PROD tipo de acción rápida *m*; ~-**up window** *n* COMP&DP ventana desplegable *f*

pop[2] *vt* COMP&DP desplegar

pope: ~ **reel** *n* PAPER enrolladora pope *f*

poplar *n* PAPER álamo *m*

poplin *n* TEXTIL popelín *m*

poppet *n* PROD castillete de extracción *m*, *lathe* contrapunto *m*; ~ **head** *n* MECH ENG *lathe* cabeza móvil de torno *f*, contrapunto *m*; ~ **holes** *n* MECH ENG *capstan* bocabarras *f*; ~ **valve** *n* AUTO válvula accionada por leva *f*, válvula de asiento cónico *f*, válvula de disco con movimiento vertical *f*, válvula de elevación *f*, válvula de resortes *f*, válvula de seta *f*, válvula de vástago *f*, HYDRAUL distribuidor de válvula *m*, válvula de asiento cónico *f*, PROD *of steam engine* distribuidor de válvula *m*, válvula de asiento cónico *f*, válvula de resortes *f*; ~ **valve gear** *n* HYDRAUL distribución por válvulas *f*

population: ~ **density of excited atoms** *n* RAD PHYS densidad de la población de átomos excitados *f*; ~ **dose** *n* POLL dosis universal *f*; ~ **equivalent** *n* WATER equivalente de poblaciones *m*, equivalente demográfica *m*; ~ **inversion** *n* ELECTRON, PHYS, RAD PHYS inversión de población *f*; ~-**inversion mechanisms** *n pl* RAD PHYS mecanismos de inversión de población *m pl*

populin *n* CHEM populina *f*

porcelain *n* C&G, ELEC, ELEC ENG, TEXTIL porcelana *f*; ~-**borer** *n* C&G perforador de porcelana *m*; ~ **button** *n* C&G botón de porcelana *m*; ~-**calcining furnace** *n* C&G horno calcinificador de porcelana *m*; ~ **capsule** *n* CHEM TECH cápsula de porcelana *f*; ~ **clay** *n* C&G caolín *m*; ~ **color** *AmE*, ~ **colour** *BrE n* C&G color de porcelana *m*; ~ **conduit-box** *n* C&G caja registro de porcelana *f*; ~ **crucible** *n* C&G, LAB crisol de porcelana *m*; ~ **cup** *n* C&G taza de porcelana *f*; ~ **decoration** *n* C&G decorado de porcelana *m*; ~-**driller** *n* C&G perforador de porcelana *m*; ~ **enamel** *n* COATINGS esmalte de porcelana *m*;

~ **evaporating-basin** *n* C&G evaporador de porcelana *m*; ~ **filter-plate** *n* C&G filtro plano de porcelana *m*; ~ **finish** *n* COATINGS terminación en porcelana *f*; ~ **funnel** *n* C&G embudo de porcelana *m*; ~ **gilder** *n* C&G decorador de porcelana *m*; ~ **goods** *n pl* C&G porcelanas *f pl*; ~ **industry** *n* C&G industria de la porcelana *f*; ~ **insulation** *n* C&G, ELEC, ELEC ENG aislamiento de porcelana *m*; ~ **insulator** *n* C&G, ELEC, ELEC ENG aislador de porcelana *m*, aislante de porcelana *m*; ~ **junction-box** *n* C&G caja de registro de porcelana *f*; ~-**maker** *n* C&G fabricante de porcelana *m*; ~-**piercer** *n* C&G perforador de porcelana *m*; ~ **plate** *n* C&G placa de porcelana *f*, plato de porcelana *m*; ~ **polisher** *n* C&G pulidor de porcelana *m*; ~ **reject** *n* C&G porcelana rechazada *f*; ~ **thread-guide** *n* C&G guía de hilatura de porcelana *f*; ~ **tooth** *n* C&G diente de porcelana *m*; ~ **tube** *n* C&G tubo de porcelana *m*; ~ **utensil** *n* C&G utensilio de porcelana *m*; ~ **varnish** *n* C&G, COATINGS barniz de porcelana *m*

porch *n* TV pórtico *m*; ~ **roof** *n* CONST *penthouse* porche *m* (*AmL*), techo del porche *m* (*Esp*)

pore *n* GAS poro *m*; ~-**gas pressure** *n* COAL presión del gas embebido *f*, presión del gas intersticial *f*; ~ **overpressure** *n* COAL sobrepresión intersticial *f*; ~ **pressure** *n* COAL presión intersticial *f*, subpresión *f*, PETR TECH presión de poro *f*, presión intersticial *f*; ~ **space** *n* GEOL espacio poroso *m*, espacio vacío *m*; ~ **volume** *n* COAL, PETROL volumen de poro *m*; ~ **water** *n* COAL, HYDROL, OCEAN, PETR TECH, PETROL, WATER agua intersticial *f*; ~-**water pressure** *n* COAL presión del agua embebida *f*, presión del agua intersticial *f*

poromeric: ~ **coated fabric** *n* P&R tela revestida poromérica *f*

porosimeter *n* CHEM TECH, PAPER porosímetro *m*

porosity *n* GEN porosidad *f*; ~ **log** *n* PETR TECH diagrafía de la porosidad *f*, perfil de porosidad *m*, registro de la porosidad *m*

porous[1] *adj* COAL poroso, porífero, FUELLESS poroso

porous[2]: ~ **absorber** *n* ACOUST material absorbente poroso *m*; ~ **extracting cup** *n* CHEM TECH capa porosa de extracción *f*; ~ **layer** *n* COAL capa porosa *f*, espacio vacío *m*, poro *m*, GAS capa porosa *f*, estrato poroso *m*; ~ **material** *n* ACOUST material poroso *m*; ~ **media** *n* GAS medios porosos *m pl*

porpezite *n* MINERAL porpezita *f*

porphin *n* CHEM porfina *f*

porphyraceous *adj* GEOL porfídico

porphyritic *adj* GEOL *screen* porfirítico

porphyroblastic *adj* GEOL porfidoblástico

porphyroclast *adj* GEOL porfidoclasto

porphyropsin *n* CHEM porfiropsina *f*

Porro: ~ **prism** *n* INSTR prisma Porro *m*

port *n* C&G puerto *m*, COMP&DP puerto *m*, punto de acceso *m*, ELEC ENG acceso *m*, puerto *m*, HYDRAUL, MECH abertura *f*, lumbrera *f*, orificio *m*, MECH ENG abertura *f*, acceso *m*, lumbrera *f*, orificio *m*, portillo *m*, puerto *m*, NUCL abertura *f*, PHYS, PRINT puerto *m*, PROD acceso *m*, SPACE *craft* babor *m*, aeropuerto *m*, costado izquierdo *m*, puerto *m*, TELECOM puerto *m*, VEH lumbrera *f*, abertura *f*, WATER TRANSP porta *f*, portillo *m*, puerto *m*, *part of a ship* babor *m*; ~ **apron** *n* C&G pretil del puerto *m*; ~ **authority** *n* WATER TRANSP autoridad rectora del puerto *f*; ~ **backwall** *n BrE* (*cf port endwall AmE*) C&G pared trasera del puerto *f*; ~ **of call** *n* WATER TRANSP puerto de escala *m*; **~ charges** *n pl* WATER TRANSP derechos portuarios *m pl*; **~ coldstore** *n* REFRIG acceso de almacén frigorífico *m*; **~ of commissioning** *n* WATER TRANSP puerto de entrega de mando *m*; **~ crown** *n* BrE (*cf uptake crown AmE*) C&G corona del puerto *f*; **~ of documentation** *n AmE* (*cf port of registry BrE*) WATER TRANSP puerto de matrícula *m*; **~ door** *n* REFRIG puerta cortafuga de frío *f*; **~ endwall** *AmE* (*cf port backwall BrE*) C&G pared trasera del puerto *f*; **~ facilities** *n pl* WATER TRANSP instalaciones portuarias *f pl*; **~ mouth** *n* C&G boca del puerto *f*; **~ neck** *n* C&G cuello del puerto *m*; **~ opening** *n* HYDRAUL abertura de la lumbrera *f*; **~ of registration** *n* WATER TRANSP puerto de inscripción *m*, puerto de registro *m*; **~ of registry** *n* BrE (*cf port of documentation AmE*) WATER TRANSP puerto de matrícula *m*; **~ sidewall** *n* C&G pared lateral del puerto *f*; **~ sill** *n* C&G dintel del puerto *m*; **~-to-throat area ratio** *n* SPACE relación entre el área de garganta y la abertura *f*; **~ of transit** *n* WATER TRANSP puerto de tránsito *m*; **~ watch** *n* WATER TRANSP *personnel* guardia de babor *f*; **~ width** *n* MECH ENG *cylinder* ancho de la abertura *m*

portable[1] *adj* COMP&DP portátil
portable[2]: **~ appliance** *n* ELEC aparato portátil *m*, enser portátil *m*; **~ coldroom** *n* REFRIG cámara frigorífica desmontable *f*; **~ crane** *n* CONST grúa móvil *f*; **~ drilling-machine** *n* MECH ENG perforadora portátil *f*, taladradora portátil *f*; **~ fan** *n* MECH ENG ventilador portátil *m*; **~ fire-extinguisher** *n* SAFE extintor de incendios portátil *m*; **~ hoisting-platform** *n* CONST plataforma de elevación portátil *f*; **~ ladder** *n* SAFE escalera portátil *f*; **~ lamp** *n* ELEC *lighting*, ELEC ENG linterna *f*, lámpara portátil *f*; **~ light** *n* CONST .luz portátil *f*, lámpara portátil *f*; **~ machine** *n* SAFE máquina portátil *f*; **~ mold** *AmE*, **~ mould** *BrE n* P&R molde portátil *m*; **~ pack** *n* TV unidad de alimentación portátil *f*; **~ plant** *n* MECH ENG instalación móvil *f*; **~ power tool** *n* ELEC, MECH ENG herramienta eléctrica portátil *f*; **~ pump** *n* LAB *of colloid* bomba portátil *f*; **~ receiver** *n* TELECOM receptor portátil *m*; **~ relay** *n* TV repetidor portátil *m*; **~-socket outlet** *n* ELEC *connection* base portátil *f*, enchufe portátil *m*, zócalo de tomacorriente portátil *m*; **~ terminal** *n* WATER TRANSP *satellite communications, computers* terminal portátil *m*; **~ transmitter** *n* TELECOM, TV transmisor portátil *m*; **~-vice bench** *n BrE* CONST banco portátil de tornillo *m*; **~-vice stand** *n BrE* CONST soporte portátil de tornillo *m*; **~-vice stand with leg vice** *n BrE* CONST soporte portátil de tornillo con tornillo de pie *m*; **~-vise bench** *AmE see portable-vice bench BrE*; **~-vise stand** *AmE see portable-vice stand BrE*; **~-vise stand with leg vise** *AmE see portable-vice stand with leg vice BrE*; **~ water-storage tank** *n* MILIT depósito portátil de agua *m*
portal *n* CONST embocadura *f*, portal *m*, vestíbulo *m*; **~ crane** *n* CONST grúa pórtica *f*; **~ mast** *n* WATER TRANSP *derrick* grúa pórtico-castillete *f*
portface *n* HYDRAUL espejo del distribuidor *m*
porthole *n* MECH ENG lumbrera *f*, orificio *m*, WATER TRANSP *deck equipment* portilla *f*, portillo *m*; **~ fan** *n* MECH ENG ventilador aspirante colocado sobre una ventana *m*
portion: **~ pack** *n* PACK paquete de ración *m*

portioning: **~ machine** *n* PACK máquina de envasar en porciones *f*
Portland: **~ sulfate-resisting cement** *AmE*, **~ sulphate-resisting cement** *BrE n* CONST cemento Portland resistente a los sulfatos *m*
portrait *n* PRINT orientación vertical *f*; **~ attachment** *n* CINEMAT, OPT, PHOTO lente para retratos *f*; **~ format** *n* COMP&DP formato vertical *m*; **~ lens** *n* INSTR, PHOTO lente de retrato *f*
POS *abbr* (*point of sale*) COMP&DP PV (*punto de venta*)
Posidriv: **~ screw** *n* MECH ENG tornillo Posidriv *m*
position *n* CINEMAT posición *f*, MECH ENG posición *f*, ubicación *f*; **on ~** *n* ELEC ENG posición de cierre *f*, posición de conectado, posición de funcionamiento *f*; **~ exchange force** *n* NUCL fuerza de intercambio espacial *f*; **~-finding** *n* MILIT determinación de la posición *f*; **~-fixing** *n* MILIT fijación de la posición *f*; **~ indicator** *n* PROD indicador de posición *m*; **~-indicator plan** *n* PHYS plano indicador de posiciones *m*; **~ light** *n* SPACE alumbrado de posición *m*, encendido de posición *m*, luz de posición *f*, VEH luz de posición *f*, luz de situación *f*, WATER TRANSP *navigation* luz de situación *f*; **~ reference system** *n* PETROL sistema de referencia de posición *m*; **~ switch** *n* ELEC conmutador de posición *m*, contactor de posición *m*, interruptor de posición *m*, ruptor de posición *m*, ELEC ENG, PROD interruptor de posición *m*; **~ vector** *n* GEOM, PHYS vector de posición *m*
positional: **~ crosstalk** *n* TV diafonía posicional *f*
positioner *n* CINEMAT posicionador *m*, regulador de posición *m*, MECH ENG posicionador *m*, situador en posición *m*, útil giratorio para soldar *m*
positioning *n* MECH ENG *drill* situación *f*, colocación *f*, posicionamiento *m*, control posicional *m*, WATER TRANSP posicionamiento *m*; **~ block** *n* MECH ENG bloque de posicionamiento *m*, polea de colocación *f*; **~ repeatability** *n* MECH ENG *machine tool* repetibilidad de posicionamiento *f*; **~ screw jack** *n* MECH ENG cric para posicionar *m*, gato para posicionar *m*
positive[1] *adj* ELEC *electrode* positivo; **~-negative-positive** *adj* (*p-n-p*) ELECTRON, PHYS, RAD PHYS positivo-negativo-positivo (*p-n-p*); **~-reading** *adj* PRINT al derecho
positive[2] *n* PHOTO *vibration test* prueba positiva *f*; **~ abnormal-pressure** *n* PETR TECH presión anormal positiva *f*; **~ acknowledgement** *n* COMP&DP carácter de acuse positivo de recepción *m*, reconocimiento positivo *m*; **~ angle** *n* GEOM ángulo positivo *m*; **~ bank** *n* AUTO inclinación positiva *f*; **~ battery** *n* TELECOM batería positiva *f*; **~ bias** *n* ELEC ENG polarización de rejilla positiva *f*, sesgo positivo *m*; **~ charge** *n* ELEC *electrostatics*, ELEC, PHYS carga positiva *f*; **~ cold chamber** *n* REFRIG cámara de frío positivo *f*; **~ column** *n* ELECTRON, PHYS columna positiva *f*; **~ crankcase ventilation** *n* (*PCV*) AUTO ventilación cerrada de cárter *f*, ventilación positiva del cárter *f*, VEH cárter motor con ventilación directa *m*; **~ curvature** *n* GEOM curvatura positiva *f*; **~-displacement compressor** *n* MECH ENG compresor que comprime aire desplazándolo mecánicamente *m*; **~-displacement pump** *n* HYDRAUL bomba con aumento y disminución de volumen *f*, bomba volumétrica *f*, MECH ENG bomba de desplazamiento positivo *f*, bomba volumétrica *f*, PROD bomba volumétrica *f*; **~-displacement**

vacuum pump *n* MECH ENG bomba de vacío de desplazamiento positivo *f*; ~ **distortion** *n* CINEMAT distorsión en barril *f*, distorsión positiva *f*; ~ **drive** *n* AUTO transmisión directa *f*, transmisión por ejes y engranajes *f*; ~ **drive of Morse tapers** *n* MECH ENG conexión directa de cono Morse *f*; ~ **earthed terminal** *n* BrE (*cf positive grounded terminal AmE*) AUTO, ELEC, ELEC ENG, VEH borne positivo de tierra *m*; ~ **feedback** *n* RAD PHYS retroalimentación positiva *f*; ~ **film** *n* CINEMAT película positiva *f*; ~ **Gauss curvature** *n* GEOM curvatura de Gauss positiva *f*, curvatura positiva de Gauss *f*; ~ **grounded terminal** *n* AmE (*cf positive earthed terminal BrE*) AUTO, ELEC, ELEC ENG, VEH borne positivo de tierra *m*; ~ **image** *n* PHOTO imagen positiva *f*; ~ **ion** *n* CHEM, ELEC, ELECTRON, PART PHYS, PHYS, RAD PHYS catión *m*, ión positivo *m*; **--ionized atom** *n* CHEM, ELEC, ELECTRON, PART PHYS, PHYS, RAD PHYS ión positivo *m*; ~ **lens** *n* INSTR, OPT lente positiva *f*; **--lens surface** *n* INSTR, OPT superficie de lente positiva *f*; ~ **logic** *n* ELECTRON, lógica positiva *f*; ~ **magnetostriction** *n* ELEC ENG magnetoestricción positiva *f*; **--meniscus lens** *n* INSTR, OPT lente de menisco positivo *f*; ~ **meson** *n* PART PHYS mesón positivo *m*; ~ **modulation** *n* ELECTRON modulación positiva *f*; ~ **mold** AmE, ~ **mould** BrE *n* P&R molde positivo *m*; **--negative rectifier** *n* ELEC ENG rectificador de positivo-negativo *m*; ~ **notification** *n* (*PN*) TELECOM notificación positiva *f*; ~ **perforation** *n* CINEMAT perforación positiva *f*; **--phase sequence** *n* ELEC *generator* secuencia de fases positivas *f*; **--phase sequence reactance** *n* ELEC reactancia de la secuencia de fases positivas *f*; **--phase sequence resistance** *n* ELEC resistencia de la secuencia de fases positivas *f*; ~ **photoresist** *n* ELECTRON fotoprotector positivo *m*; ~ **picture phase** *n* TV fase de imagen positiva *f*; ~ **pitch** *n* CINEMAT paso positivo *m*; ~ **plate** *n* AUTO placa positiva *f*; ~ **pole** *n* ELEC *connection*, ELEC, PHYS polo positivo *m*; **--power supply** *n* ELEC ENG suministro de energía positiva *m*; ~ **ray** *n* ELECTRON rayo positivo *m*; ~ **resist** *n* ELECTRON protección positiva *f*; ~ **rewinder** *n* CINEMAT rebobinadora positiva *f*; ~ **separation** *n* CINEMAT separación positiva *f*; ~ **sequence** *n* ELEC *AC* secuencia positiva *f*; ~ **stress** *n* MECH ENG esfuerzo de compresión *m*; ~ **terminal** *n* AUTO, ELEC, ELEC ENG, VEH borne positivo *m*, terminal positivo *m*; **--type valve rotator** *n* AUTO rotador de válvula tipo positivo *m*, rotador forzado *m*

positively[1]: ~ **skewed** *adj* GEOM positivamente inclinado

positively[2]: **--skewed doped region** *n* PHYS región dopada positivamente *f*

positron *n* (p^+) PART PHYS, PHYS positrón *m* (p^+)

possible: ~ **capacity** *n* TRANSP capacidad posible *f*; ~ **reserves** *n pl* PETR TECH, PETROL reservas posibles *f pl*

post[1] *n* AUTO borna *f*, poste *m*, puntal *m*, COAL adema *f*, CONST *of door* pilar *m*, jamba *f*, montante *m*, *upright* poste *m*, *of crane* puntal *m*, MECH ENG columna *f*, MINE pilar macizo *m* (*AmL*), poste *m* (*Esp*), adema *f*, WATER TRANSP *mooring, marker* pilote *m*, noray *m*; ~ **bracket** *n* RAIL mástil con cruceta para señal *m*; **--emergence application** *n* AGRIC aplicación en postemergencia *f*; **--flying check** *n* AIR

TRANSP *aviation* revisión postvuelo *f*; **--harvest** *n* AGRIC postcosecha *f*; **--hole digger** *n* AGRIC cavadora de hoyos *f*; ~ **insulator** *n* ELEC aislante del borne del acumulador *m*, ELEC ENG aislante del borne del acumulador *m*, aislante del poste *m*; ~ **pallet** *n* TRANSP bandeja de sujeción *f*, paleta de sujeción *f*, pálet de sujeción *m* (*AmL*); **--sowing application** *n* AGRIC aplicación después de siembra *f*

post[2]: ~ **hours** *vt* PROD contabilizar horas; ~ **to stock** *vt* PROD contabilizar como existencias

postaccelerator: ~ **CRT** *n* ELECTRON TRC intensificador *m*

postal: ~ **tube** *n* BrE (*cf mailing tube AmE*) PACK tubo para envíos postales *m*

postamble *n* COMP&DP postámbulo *m*

postcombustion: ~ **chamber** *n* COAL cámara de poscombustión *f*

postcrane *n* CONST grúa de puntal *f*

postdialing: ~ **delay** *AmE see postdialling delay BrE*

postdialling: ~ **delay** *n* BrE TELECOM retardo después del discado *m*, retardo postdiscado *m*, retardo posterior al discado *m*

postdriver *n* CONST hincadora de postes *f*

posted: **be** ~ **to a ship** *vi* WATER TRANSP estar destinado en un buque, ser destinado a un buque

poster: ~ **paper** *n* PAPER papel para carteles *m*; ~ **stick** *n* PRINT componedor para carteles *m*

postfix: ~ **notation** *n* COMP&DP notación por sufijos *f*

postforming *adj* P&R posmoldeado *m*

postglacial: ~ **clay** *n* COAL, GEOL arcilla posglaciar *f*

postheating *n* PROD poscalentamiento *m*

posting *n* PROD contabilización *f*, envío por correo *m*, fijación de carteles o anuncios *f*, inscripción *f*

postkinematic *adj* GEOL *networks* postcinemático

postmortem: ~ **program** *n* COMP&DP programa post mortem *m*

postprocessing *n* ELECTRON proceso posterior *m*

postprocessor *n* COMP&DP postprocesador *m*

postscoring *n* ACOUST sonorización *f*

poststaff *n* CONST jalón *m*, mira *f*, poste *m*

postsync: ~ **field-blanking interval** *n* TV posincronización del intervalo del campo de borrado *f*

postsynchronize *vt* CINEMAT postsincronizar

postulate *n* GEOM axioma *m*, MATH axioma *m*, postulado *m*

pot[1] *n* OCEAN nasa *f*; ~ **arch** *n* C&G horno de precalentado de crisoles *m*; ~ **arching** *n* C&G precalentamiento de crisoles *m*; ~ **carriage** *n* C&G carro para crisoles *m*; ~ **clay** *n* C&G barro para crisoles *m*; ~ **cooling** *n* C&G enfriamiento en el crisol *m*; ~ **furnace** *n* THERMO horno de crisoles *m*, horno de sales *m*; ~ **insulator** *n* ELEC, ELEC ENG aislador de crisol *m*, aislante de crisol *m*; ~ **life** *n* P&R tiempo para transformación *m*, vida útil *f*; ~ **mouth** *n* C&G boca del crisol *f*; ~ **opal** *n* C&G ópalo de crisol *m*; ~ **room** *n* C&G cuarto de crisoles *m*; ~ **ruby** *n* C&G rubí de crisol *m*; ~ **scrap** *n* PROD restos de crisoles viejos *m pl*; ~ **spout** *n* C&G pico del crisol *m*; **--type field rheostat** *n* ELEC *resistance* reóstato de campo tipo crisol *m*, reóstato de excitación tipo crisol *m*

pot[2]: ~ **anneal** *vt* THERMO recocer en crisol, recocer en horno

potable *adj* WATER potable

potash *n* C&G potasa *f*, CHEM carbonato potásico *m*, potasa *f*, PETROL potasa *f*; ~ **alum** *n* CHEM alumbre potásico *m*, kalinita *f*, sulfato de aluminio y potasio *m*; ~ **bulb** *n* LAB, PHOTO bulbo desecador *m*, tubo desecador *m*

potassic *adj* GEOL potásico

potassium *n* (*K*) CHEM, METALL potasio *m* (*K*); ~ **carbonate** *n* DETERG carbonato de potasio *m*; ~ **chlorate** *n* CHEM clorato de potasio *m*, clorato potásico *m*; ~ **chloride** *n* CHEM cloruro de potasio *m*, cloruro potásico *m*; ~ **cyanide** *n* CHEM cianuro de potasio *m*, cianuro potásico *m*; ~ **hydroxide** *n* CHEM hidróxido de potasio *m*, hidróxido potásico *m*; ~ **nitrate** *n* CHEM nitrato de potasio *m*, nitrato potásico *m*, FOOD nitrato potásico *m*; ~ **permanganate** *n* CHEM permanganato de potasio *m*; ~ **sulfate** *AmE*, ~ **sulphate** *BrE n* DETERG sulfato de potasio *m*

potato: ~ **blight** *n* FOOD añublo de la papa *m* (*AmL*), añublo de la patata *m* (*Esp*); ~ **digger** *n* AGRIC cosechadora de papas *f* (*AmL*), cosechadora de patatas *f* (*Esp*); ~ **planter** *n* AGRIC sembradora de papas *f* (*AmL*), sembradora de patatas *f* (*Esp*)

potential *n* ELEC, ELEC ENG, PHYS, SPACE *communications* potencial *m*, voltaje *m*; ~ **accident** *n* SAFE accidente potencial *m*; ~ **barrier** *n* ELEC ENG, PHYS, POLL, TELECOM barrera de potencial *f*; ~ **difference** *n* (*pd*) ELEC, ELEC ENG, PHYS, TELECOM diferencia de potencial *f*; ~ **divider** *n* ELEC, PHYS dividor de potencia *m*; ~ **drop** *n* ELEC, ELEC ENG caída de potencial *f*, caída de tensión *f*, caída de voltaje *f*, PHYS caída de potencial *f*; ~ **energy** *n* PHYS energía potencial *f*; ~ **evapotranspiration** *n* HYDROL, WATER evapotranspiración potencial *f*; ~ **function** *n* PHYS *cabin* función de potencial *f*; ~ **geodesic head** *n* NUCL carga geodésica potencial *f*; ~ **gradient** *n* ELEC, PHYS gradiente de potencial *m*; ~ **hazard** *n* SAFE peligro potencial *m*, riesgo potencial *m*; ~ **of hydrogen** *n* (*pH*) CHEM, HYDROL potencial hidrógeno *m* (*pH*); ~ **loop** *n* ELEC *voltage* vientre de tensión *m*, vientre de voltaje *m*; ~ **temperature-salinity diagram** *n* OCEAN diagrama de la relación temperatura-salinidad *m*, diagrama de temperatura potencial-salinidad *m*; ~ **transformer** *n* ELEC, ELEC ENG transformador de potencial *m*, transformador de tensión *m*, transformador de voltaje *m*, PROD transformador de voltaje *m*; ~ **well** *n* PHYS pozo de potencial *m*

potentially: ~ **explosive atmosphere** *n* COAL atmósfera potencialmente explosiva *f*

potentiometer *n* CINEMAT, CONST, ELEC potenciómetro *m*, ELEC ENG medidor de diferencia de voltaje *m*, potenciómetro *m*, LAB, PHYS potenciómetro *m*; ~ **rheostat** *n* ELEC *resistor* reóstato en puente *m*, reóstato potenciométrico *m*; ~ **slider** *n* ELEC *resistor* corredera de potenciómetro *f*, cursor de potenciómetro *m*

potentiometric: ~ **head** *n* PETR TECH altura potenciométrica *f*, cabeza potenciométrica *f*; ~ **level** *n* PETR TECH nivel potenciométrico *m*; ~ **map** *n* PETR TECH mapa potenciométrico *m*; ~ **recorder** *n* INSTR registrador potenciométrico *m*

potherb *n* AGRIC hortaliza de hoja *f*

pothole *n* CONST *cavity in mine-roof* pozo *m*, *in road* bache *m*, HYDROL *in watercourse caused by stones* poza *f*, VEH *in road* bache *m*

potter: ~'**s clay extraction** *n* C&G extracción de barro para alfarería *f*; ~'**s earth** *n* C&G tierra para alfarería

f; ~'**s ore** *n* C&G mineral para alfarería *f*; ~'**s wheel** *n* C&G torno de alfarero *m*, torno de alfarería *m*

pottery *n* C&G alfarería *f*, loza de barro *f*, vasijas de barro *f pl*, PROD *place* alfarería *f*; ~ **clay** *n* C&G, CONST arcilla de alfarería *f*; ~ **decorator** *n* C&G decorador de alfarería *m*; ~ **kiln** *n* THERMO horno de alfarería *m*; ~ **maker** *n* C&G alfarero *m*; ~ **raw materials** *n pl* C&G materias primas para alfarería *f pl*

potting *n* PROD, SPACE encapsulación *f*, encapsulado *m*; ~ **compound** *n* SPACE material de relleno *m*

pouch: ~-**making machine** *n* PACK máquina de fabricar bolsas *f*

poultry: ~ **farm** *n* AGRIC granja avícola *f*; ~ **keeper** *n* AGRIC avicultor *m*; ~ **manure** *n* AGRIC gallinaza *f*

pound[1] *n* METR libra *f*; ~ **avoirdupois** *n* METR libra avoirdupois *f*; ~ **net** *n* OCEAN corral *m*, garlito *m*

pound[2] *vt* FOOD *to grind* machacar, moler, PROD *to pulverize with pestle* picar

pounder *n* PROD maza *f*

pounds: ~ **per hour** *n pl* METR libras por hora *f pl*; ~ **per square inch** *n pl* (*psi*) METR, PETR TECH libras por pulgada cuadrada *f pl* (*lb/pulg*[2], *LPPC*)

pour *n* C&G vaciado *m*; ~ **point** *n* FLUID punto de fluidez *m*, PETR TECH punto de fluidez *m*, punto de licuefacción *m*, REFRIG punto de goteo *m*, VEH temperatura de descongelación *f*, temperatura de fluidez *f*; ~ **spout** *n* PACK derrame *m*; ~-**spout closure** *n* PACK cierre antiderrame *m*; ~-**spout seal** *n* PACK precinto antiderrame *m*

pourable: ~ **slurry** *n* MINE fangos de lavado colables *m pl*, lodo colable *m*

pourer *n* PROD *person* fundidor *m*

pouring *n* PRINT vaciado *m*, PROD *founding* colada *f*, SAFE *founding* colada en lingotera *f*, vaciado *m*; ~-**gate** *n* PROD bebedero alimentador *m*, *mould* agujero de colada *m*; ~-**hole** *n* PROD *mould* agujero de colada *m*, bebedero alimentador *m*; ~-**sleeve** *n* MECH ENG *diecasting die* manguito para colada *m*

powder[1]: ~ **filled** *adj* ELEC ENG rellenado con polvo

powder[2] *n* CHEM, P&R polvo *m*; ~ **camera** *n* CRYSTALL cámara de polvo *f*; ~ **coating** *n* COATINGS capa pulverizada *f*, recubrimiento pulvimetalúrgico *m*, COLOUR revestimiento en polvo *m*, P&R recubrimiento con pintura en polvo *m*; ~ **diffractometer** *n* CRYSTALL, INSTR difractómetro de polvo *m*; ~ **explosive** *n* MINE explosivo de pólvora *m*; ~ **fire extinguisher** *n* SAFE extintor de incendios de polvo *m*; ~-**metal die** *n* MECH ENG matriz pulvimetalúrgica *f*; ~ **mill** *n* PROD fábrica de pólvoras *f*, *machine* molino de pólvora *m*; ~ **pattern** *n* CRYSTALL diagrama de polvo *m*; ~ **photograph** *n* CRYSTALL fotografía de polvo *f*; ~ **store** *n* MINE polvorín *m*; ~ **works** *n* PROD fábrica de pólvoras *f*, molino de pólvora *m*

powdered: ~ **color** *AmE*, ~ **colour** *BrE n* COLOUR colorante en polvo *m*; ~ **dye** *n* COLOUR tintura en polvo *f*; ~ **glass** *n* C&G vidrio molido *m*; ~ **gold** *n* C&G oro en polvo *m*, oro molido *m*; ~ **insulant** *n* REFRIG aislante en polvo *m*; ~-**iron core** *n* ELEC ENG núcleo de hierro pulverizado *m*

powdering *n* P&R resistencia a la grasa *f*, trituración *f*; ~ **ink** *n* COLOUR tinta pulverizada *f*

powdery[1] *adj* GEOL pulverulento

powdery[2]: ~ **mildew** *n* AGRIC oidio *m*, FOOD moho polvoriento *m*

power[1] *n* AUTO fuerza *f*, potencia *f*, ELEC, ELEC ENG energía *f*, potencia *f*, MATH exponente *m*, potencia *f*,

MECH, MECH ENG energía *f*, energía eléctrica *f*, fuerza *f* poder *m*, potencia *f*, *energy supply* suministro de energía *m*, *electricity supply* suministro eléctrico *m*, *f*, OPT potencia *f*, PHYS *bed* potencia *f*, aumento *m*, SPACE *craft* aumento *m*, energía *f*, potencia *f*, TELECOM energía eléctrica *f*; ~ **adaptor** *n* CINEMAT adaptador de potencia *m*; ~ **amplification** *n* ELECTRON amplificación de potencia *f*; ~ **amplifier** *n* ELEC ENG, ELECTRON, PHYS, PROD, SPACE, TELECOM amplificador de potencia *m*; ~**-amplifier transistor** *n* ELECTRON transistor de amplificación de potencia *m*; ~**-amplifier tube** *n* ELECTRON tubo de amplificador de potencia *m*; ~**-and-interlock relay box** *n* AIR TRANSP caja de relé de fuerza e interconexión *f*; ~**-assisted brake** *n* VEH servofreno *m*; ~**-assisted steering** *n* AUTO, VEH dirección asistida *f*, servodirección *f*; ~ **bandwidth** *n* ELECTRON magnitud de ancho de banda *f*; ~ **belt** *n* CINEMAT correa de potencia *f*; ~ **boiler** *n* HYDRAUL caldera de vapor *f*, generador de vapor *m*; ~ **booster** *n* AUTO amplificador de voltaje *m*, sobrealimentador de potencia *m*; ~ **brake** *n* AUTO servofreno *m*; ~ **bus** *n* SPACE colector de energía *m*; ~ **cable** *n* ELEC *supply network* cable alimentador *m*, cable de alimentación *m*, cable tomacorriente *m*, ELEC ENG cable para transporte de energía *m*, cable tomacorriente *m*; ~ **capacitor** *n* ELEC, ELEC ENG capacitor de energía *m*, condensador de potencia *m*; ~ **circuit** *n* ELEC circuito de alimentación *m*, circuito de potencia *m*; ~ **coefficient** *n* FUELLESS *wind* coeficiente de energía *m*, coeficiente de fuerza *f*; ~**-collection system** *n* TRANSP sistema de concentración de potencia *m*; ~**-conditioning unit** *n* SPACE *craft* unidad de tratamiento de energía *f*, unidad de tratamiento de potencia *f*; ~ **constriction** *n* METALL potencia de contracción *f*; ~ **consumption** *n* ELEC *supply network*, ELEC ENG consumo de energía *m*; ~ **converter** *n* ELEC ENG convertidor de energía *m*, SPACE convertidor de energía *m*, red distribuidora de energía *f*, transformador de energía *m*; ~ **curves** *n pl* FUELLESS gráficos de energía *m pl*, gráficos de fuerza *m pl*; ~ **cylinder** *n* AUTO cilindro mecánico *m*; ~ **density** *n* FUELLESS densidad de energía *f*, TELECOM densidad de potencia *f*; ~ **diode** *n* ELECTRON diodo de potencia *m*; ~**-directional relay** *n* (*PDR*) ELEC relé para sentido de fuerza *m*; ~ **dissipation** *n* PROD ergodisipación *f*; ~ **distribution** *n* PROD distribución de fuerza *f*; ~ **distribution network** *n* SPACE red de distribución de potencia *f*; ~ **divider** *n* ELEC *supply* divisor de potencia *m*, ELEC ENG divisor de energía *m*, TELECOM divisor de potencia *m*; ~**-down** *n* ELEC ENG reducción de potencia *f*, baja de potencia *f*, PROD pérdida de potencia *f*; ~**-down feature** *n* ELEC ENG característica de descenso de potencia *f*; ~ **drill** *n* CONST *rock-drill* taladro mecánico *m*; ~ **drop** *n* CINEMAT pérdida de potencia *f*; ~ **energy** *n* METALL potencia de impacto *f*; ~ **factor** *n* ELEC, ELEC ENG, P&R, PHYS, PROD factor de potencia *m*; ~**-factor correction** *n* ELEC ENG corrección del factor de potencia *f*; ~ **fail** *n* TELECOM caída de tensión *f*, fallo de tensión *m*; ~**-fail restart** *n* (*PFR*) COMP&DP reinicio tras fallo en alimentación *m*; ~ **failure** *n* CINEMAT caída de tensión *f*, ELEC avería de la energía *f*, ELEC ENG fallo de potencia *m*, avería de la energía *f*; ~ **fan** *n* AUTO electroventilador *m*, ventilador eléctrico *m*; ~ **feed** *n* MECH ENG *machine-tools* alimentación mecánica *f*, avance automático *m*, TELECOM actuador

m, alimentación *f*, suministro de energía *m*; ~**-feeding** *n* TELECOM alimentación *f*; ~**-flux density** *n* (*cf radiant flux density*) OPT densidad de flujo de potencia *f*, SPACE *craft* densidad de flujo de energía *f*, densidad de flujo de potencia *f*; ~ **frequency** *n* ELEC *supply network*, ELEC ENG frecuencia de la red eléctrica *f*, frecuencia de red *f*; ~ **frequency heating** *n* HEAT calefacción acoplada a la red eléctrica *f*; ~ **gain** *n* ELECTRON, PHYS ganancia de potencia *f*; ~ **gas** *n* GAS gas energético *m*; ~ **generation** *n* ELEC ENG producción de energía *f*; ~ **grid** *n* ELEC ENG rejilla de potencia *f*; ~ **hacksaw** *n* MECH ENG sierra alternativa mecánica para metales *f*; ~ **hammer** *n* MECH ENG, PROD pilón *m*, martillo pilón *m*, martinete *m*; ~ **indicator** *n* PROD indicador de potencia *m*; ~ **inductor** *n* ELEC ENG inductor de potencia *m*; ~ **input** *n* ELEC ENG potencia de entrada *f*; ~**-interlock bar** *n* PROD cerrojo de enclavamiento de energía *m*; ~**-interlock relay** *n* PROD relé de enclavamiento de potencia *m*; ~**-law index fiber** *AmE*, ~**-law index fibre** *BrE* *n* OPT, TELECOM fibra de perfil de índice potencial *f*; ~**-law index profile** *n* OPT perfil de índice potencial *m*; ~ **lead** *n* ELEC alimentación *f*, conductor de alimentación *m*, línea de alimentación *f*, PROD conectador de alimentación *m*; ~ **level** *n* ACOUST nivel de potencia *m*; ~ **limiter** *n* MECH ENG ergolimitador *m*, limitador de potencia *m*; ~ **line** *n* ELEC, ELEC ENG línea de alto voltaje *f*, PROD línea de alta tensión *f*, línea de transporte de energía *f*; ~ **loader** *n* CONST cargador de energía *m*, pala cargadora *f*; ~ **loading** *n* METR carga por unidad de potencia *f*; ~ **loss** *n* ELEC ENG pérdida de potencia *f*; ~ **loss ride-through** *n* ELEC regulación de pérdida de potencia *f*, PROD pérdida de potencia durante la marcha *f*; ~ **module** *n* ELEC ENG, PROD módulo de potencia *m*; ~ **nibbler** *n* *BrE* (*cf power nibbling machine AmE*) MECH ENG *tool* cizalla de uña vibrante *f*, recortadora de chapa *f*; ~ **nibbling machine** *n* *AmE* (*cf power nibbler BrE*) MECH ENG *tool* cizalla de uña vibrante *f*, recortadora de chapa *f*; ~**-operated lathe chuck** *n* MECH ENG mandril de torno accionado mecánicamente *m*, mandril de torno mecanoaccionado *m*, mandril de torno motorizado *m*; ~ **oscillator** *n* ELECTRON oscilador de potencia *m*; ~ **outage** *n* PROD corte de energía *m*, interrupción de potencia *f*; ~ **outlet** *n* ELEC *connection* enchufe con energía de alimentación *m*, receptáculo de alimentación *m*, receptáculo de suministro eléctrico *m*, tomacorriente *m*; ~ **output** *n* ELEC ENG capacidad *f*, potencia disponible *f*, FUELLESS rendimiento de energía *f*, GAS rendimiento energético *m*; ~ **pack** *n* CINEMAT unidad de alimentación *f*, ELEC ENG fuente de energía *f*, unidad de alimentación *f*, bloque de alimentación *m*, MAR POLL equipo motor *m*; ~**-pack unit** *n* PHOTO unidad de potencia *f*; ~ **per unit area** *n* SPACE energía por unidad de superficie *f*; ~ **plant** *n* AIR TRANSP grupo motopropulsor *m*, grupo motor *m*, planta motriz *f*, sistema propulsor *m*, ELEC *supply* central de energía *f*, planta de energía *f*, central de luz y fuerza *f*, instalación de energía *f*, planta generadora *f*, planta central *f*, ELEC ENG sistema de propulsión *m*, planta de generación *f*, SPACE central energética *f*, sistema propulsor *m*, TELECOM planta de energía *f*, instalación de fuerza *f*, central eléctrica *f*, central de energía *f*, planta generadora *f*, planta de fuerza *f*, planta eléctrica *f*, instalación de energía *f*, WATER

TRANSP *engines* instalación energética *f*, grupo electrógeno *m*, sistema propulsor *m*; ~ **plug** *n* ELEC ENG clavija de toma de corriente *f*; ~ **press** *n* SAFE prensa mecánica *f*; ~ **producer** *n* MECH ENG fuente de energía *f*, productor de energía *m*; ~-**range monitor** *n* NUCL monitor de rango de potencia *m*; ~ **rapid traverse** *n* MECH ENG *machine tools* avance transversal rápido automático *m*; ~ **rating** *n* ELEC ENG clasificación de potencia *f*, potencia de salida *f*; ~ **rectifier** *n* ELEC rectificador de alimentación *m*, rectificador de potencia *m*, rectificador para aplicaciones de corrientes fuertes *m*, rectificador para aplicaciones de potencia *m*, válvula rectificadora de alimentación *f*; ~-**reflection coefficient** *n* OPT coeficiente de reflexión de potencia *m*; ~ **relay** *n* ELEC ENG, PROD relé de potencia *m*; ~ **required by machine tools** *n* MECH ENG potencia requerida por máquinas herramientas *f*; ~ **resistor** *n* ELEC ENG resistencia de gran disipación *f*; ~ **rewinder** *n* CINEMAT rebobinadora de potencia *f*; ~ **saw** *n* AGRIC, MECH ENG sierra mecánica *f*; ~ **shape** *n* NUCL configuración de la potencia *f*, distribución de la potencia *f*; ~ **shovel** *n* CONST *civil engineering* pala mecánica *f*; ~ **source** *n* ELEC ENG generador *m*; ~ **spectral density** *n* SPACE *communications* densidad del espectro de energía *f*, densidad espectral de energía *f*; ~ **spectrum** *n* ELEC ENG espectro energético *m*; ~ **station** *n* MECH ENG, MINE, PHYS, TELECOM central de energía *f*, central de fuerza motriz *f*, central eléctrica *f*, estación generadora *f*; ~ **steering** *n* AUTO, VEH servodirección *f*, dirección asistida *f*; ~-**steering pump** *n* AUTO, VEH bomba de servodirección *f*; ~ **stroke** *n* AUTO carrera de trabajo *f*, carrera motriz *f*; ~ **sub-system** *n* SPACE subsistema de potencia *m*; ~ **supply** *n* CINEMAT suministro eléctrico *m*, ELEC, ELEC ENG, ELECTRON *network* alimentación de corriente *f*, fuente de alimentación, fuente de energía *f*, suministro de energía *m*, PHYS suministro de potencia *m*, RAIL *vehicles, fixed equipment* suministro de energía *m*, TELECOM alimentación de corriente *f*, alimentación *f*, alimentación de fuerza *f*, fuente de alimentación *f*, fuente de energía *f*, fuente de potencia *f*, suministro de energía *m*, TV fuente de alimentación *f*; ~-**supply circuit** *n* ELEC ENG circuito de alimentación de energía eléctrica *m*; ~-**supply duct** *n* RAIL conducto para el suministro de energía *m*; ~-**supply filter** *n* ELECTRON filtro de alimentación de energía *m*, filtro de suministro de energía *m*; ~-**supply input fuse** *n* MECH ENG, PROD fusible de entrada de suministro de energía *m*; ~-**supply interrupt** *n* COMP&DP interrupción del suministro eléctrico *f*; ~-**supply unit** *n* (*PSU*) ELEC, ELEC ENG fuente de alimentación eléctrica *f*, MILIT unidad de energía *f*, PROD fuente de alimentación eléctrica *f*, unidad de alimentación *f*; ~ **surge** *n* ELEC ENG sobretensión de energía *f*; ~ **switch** *n* ELEC, ELEC ENG interruptor de alimentación *m*, PROD interruptor de potencia *m*; ~-**switching transistor** *n* ELECTRON transistor de conmutación de potencia *m*; ~ **system** *n* ELEC ENG red de energía eléctrica *f*, REFRIG tren termostático *m*; ~ **take-off** *n* AIR TRANSP despegue propulsado *m*; ~ **terminal bloc** *n* PROD tablero de bornas de potencia *m*; ~ **thyristor** *n* TELECOM tiristor de potencia *m*; ~ **tool** *n* AGRIC herramienta mecánica *f*, MECH herramienta mecánica *f*, herramienta motorizada *f*; ~-**torquing** *n* PROD par motor *m*; ~ **tower** *n* FUELLESS *solar energy* torre

solar *f*; ~ **train** *n* AIR TRANSP tren de fuerza *m*, tren de suministro de energía *m*, AUTO tren de fuerza *m*, tren motor *m*; ~ **transformer** *n* ELEC ENG transformador de energía *m*, PROD transformador de energía *m*, transformador de fuerza *m*; ~ **transistor** *n* ELECTRON transistor de potencia *m*; ~ **transmission** *n* ELEC ENG transmisión de energía *f*; ~ **transmission by belt drive** *n* MECH ENG transmisión de energía por correa *f*; ~ **transmission line** *n* ELEC ENG línea de transporte de energía *f*; ~-**transmission network** *n* ELEC ENG red conductora de energía *f*; ~-**transmission system** *n* MECH ENG sistema de transmisión de energía *m*; ~ **tube** *n* ELECTRON tubo de potencia *m*; ~ **unit** *n* PROD aparato mecánico *m*, bloque motor *m*, grupo electrógeno *m*, grupo motor *m*, unidad de motor *f*, unidad de potencia *f*, unidad motriz *f*, TRANSP unidad de motor *f*, unidad motriz *f*, VEH grupo motopropulsor *m*, grupo motor *m*; ~-**weight ratio** *n* AIR TRANSP coeficiente de potencia-peso *m*, MECH ENG potencia másica *f*, relación potencia-masa *f*; ~ **wirewound resistor** *n* ELEC ENG resistencia devanada de potencia *f*; ~ **wiring** *n* PROD cableado de fuerza *m*, línea de transporte de energía *f*; ~-**wiring kit** *n* PROD kit para cableado de fuerza *m*

power² *vt* MECH ENG impulsar; ~ **down** *vt* ELEC ENG bajar la potencia; ~ **up** *vt* ELEC, ELEC ENG, PROD, RAD PHYS energizar

powerhouse *n* FUELLESS central eléctrica *f* (*Esp*), usina *f* (*AmL*)

Poynting: ~'s **theorem** *n* PHYS teorema de Poynting *m*; ~ **vector** *n* PHYS vector de Poynting *m*

pozzolanic: ~ **cement** *n* CONST cemento puzolánico *m*

pp *abbr* (*pages*) PRINT págs. (*páginas*)

PP *abbr* COMP&DP, TELECOM (*peripheral processor*) procesador periférico *m*

PPDU *abr* (*presentation protocol data unit*) TELECOM unidad de presentación de datos del protocolo *f*

ppm *abbr* (*parts per million*) CHEM ppm (*partes por millón*)

PPM *abbr* (*pages per minute*) COMP&DP PPM (*páginas por minuto*)

pps *abbr* (*pulses per second*) TELECOM impulsos por segundo *m pl*

PQC *abbr* (*pavement-quality concrete*) CONST concreto para pavimento *m* (*AmL*), hormigón para pavimento *m* (*Esp*)

Pr *abbr* (*praseodymium*) CHEM Pr (*praseodimio*)

PRA *abbr* NUCL (*probabilistic risk assessment*) APR (*análisis probabilista de riesgo*), TELECOM *primary rate access* acceso a la tarifa primaria

practical: ~ **capacity** *n* TRANSP capacidad práctica *f*; ~ **capacity under rural conditions** *n* TRANSP capacidad real en el medio rural *f*; ~ **capacity under urban conditions** *n* TRANSP capacidad real en el medio urbano *f*; ~-**test method** *n* OPT método de pruebas prácticas, TELECOM método práctico de prueba *m*; ~ **unit** *n* MECH ENG unidad conveniente *f*, unidad práctica *f*

practician *n* PROD profesional *m*

pragma *n* COMP&DP pragma *m*

pragmatics *n* COMP&DP pragmática *f*

prase *n* MINERAL cuarzo verde *m*, prasio *m*

praseodymium *n* (*Pr*) CHEM praseodimio *m* (*Pr*)

praseolite *n* MINERAL praseolita *f*

pratique *n* WATER TRANSP libre plática *f*

PRBS *abbr* (*pseudo-random binary sequence*) TELECOM secuencia binaria pseudoaleatoria *f*

pre-acidification: ~ **alkalinity** *n* POLL alcalinidad preacidificación *f*, alcalinidad previa acidificación *f*

preadmission *n* HYDRAUL avance a la admisión *m*, preadmisión *f*

preaeration *n* HYDROL *of horizontal stationary engine* preaireación *f*

preageing *n* TELECOM preenvejecimiento *m*

preamble *n* SPACE *communications* preámbulo *m*

preamplification *n* GEN preamplificación *f*

preamplifier *n* GEN preamplificador *m*

preblowing *n* C&G soplo primario *m*

pre-bored: ~ **pile** *n* COAL pilote pretaladrado *m*

Precambrian *n* GEOL Precámbrico *m*

precast[1] *adj* CONST prefabricado, premoldeado

precast[2]: ~ **concrete** *n* CONST concreto prefabricado *m* (*AmL*), hormigón prefabricado *m* (*Esp*); ~ **unit** *n* CONST unidad prefabricada *f*

precast[3] *vt* CONST, WATER TRANSP prefabricar

precasting: ~ **works** *n pl* CONST prefabricados *m pl*

precautionary: ~ **measure** *n* SAFE medida preventiva *f*

precautions *n pl* SAFE precauciones *f pl*; ~ **against dust** *n pl* SAFE precauciones contra el polvo *f pl*; ~ **to be taken** *n pl* SAFE precauciones que deben tomarse *f pl*

precedence *n* COMP&DP prioridad *f*

precession *n* PHYS precesión *f*, SPACE precedencia *f*, precesión *f*; ~ **camera** *n* CRYSTALL cámara de precesión *f*; ~ **rate** *n* SPACE velocidad de precesión *f*

prechamber *n* VEH precámara *f*

precharge: ~ **contactor** *n* PROD contactor de precarga *m*

precipitability *n* CHEM precipitabilidad *f*

precipitable: ~ **water** *n* METEO agua precipitable *f*

precipitant *n* CHEM precipitante *m*

precipitate[1] *n* CHEM, CHEM TECH, METALL, PETR TECH precipitado *m*

precipitate[2] *vi* CHEM, CHEM TECH, METALL, PETR TECH precipitar

precipitated[1] *adj* CHEM, CHEM TECH, METALL, PETR TECH precipitado

precipitated[2]: ~ **silica** *n* P&R sílice precipitada *f*

precipitating: ~ **agent** *n* CHEM, CHEM TECH agente de precipitación *m*, agente precipitante *m*, precipitador *m*, precipitante *m*; ~ **tank** *n* CHEM, CHEM TECH cuba de precipitación *f*, tanque de precipitación *m*

precipitation[1] *n* CHEM, CONST precipitación *f*, METALL precipitación *f*, solubilización *f*, METEO precipitación *f*; ~ **anneal** *n* THERMO *of ribbed bulkheads* recocido por precipitación *m*; ~ **annealing** *n* CHEM TECH precipitación recocida *f*; ~ **area** *n* CHEM TECH superficie de precipitación *f*, área de precipitación *f*, METEO, WATER área de precipitación *f*; ~ **collector** *n* POLL *gas treatment* colector de depósito radiactivo *m*, colector de precipitación *m*, electrodo receptor *m*, precipitador electrostático *m*; ~ **event** *n* POLL precipitación *f*, resultado de precipitación *m*; ~ **gage** *AmE*, ~ **gauge** *BrE n* METEO, WATER pluviómetro acumulativo *m*; ~ **hardening** *n* CRYSTALL endurecimiento estructural *m*, METALL endurecimiento por solubilización de un componente *m*, PROD endurecimiento estructural *m*, THERMO *in fuel pellet* endurecimiento por precipitación *m*; ~ **heat-treatment** *n* PROD termotratamiento para endurecimiento estructural *m*; ~ **tank** *n* CHEM TECH cuba de precipitación *f*, tanque de precipitación *m*; ~ **vessel** *n* CHEM TECH vaso de precipitados *m*

precipitation[2]: ~ **harden** *vt* THERMO *in fuel pellet* endurecer estructuralmente, endurecer por precipitación, endurecer por solubilización

precipitator *n* CHEM precipitador *m*

precision *n* COMP&DP, MECH, MECH ENG, METR, PHYS precisión *f*; ~ **approach** *n* AIR TRANSP *aviation* aproximación de precisión *f*; ~-**approach procedure** *n* AIR TRANSP procedimiento de aproximación de precisión *m*; ~-**approach radar rating** *n* AIR TRANSP clasificación del radar de aproximación de precisión *f*; ~ **engineering** *n* MECH ENG ingeniería de precisión *f*, técnica de precisión *f*; ~ **grinding** *n* PROD *machine tools* rectificado de precisión *m*; ~-**guided munition** *n* (*PGM*) MILIT munición guiada *f*; ~ **instrument** *n* INSTR, PHYS instrumento de precisión *m*; ~ **machine-tools** *n pl* MECH ENG máquinas herramientas de precisión *f pl*; ~ **machining** *n* MECH ENG maquinado de precisión *m*; ~ **micrometer** *n* MECH ENG micrómetro de precisión *m*; ~ **milling** *n* MECH ENG fresadora de precisión *f*; ~ **roller-chain and chain-wheel** *n* MECH ENG cadena calibrada de rodillos y polea de cadena *f*; ~ **seeder** *n* AGRIC sembrador de precisión *m*; ~ **setting** *n* MECH ENG ajuste de precisión *m*; ~ **shim** *n* MECH ENG calza de precisión *f*; ~ **slide** *n* MECH ENG *for machine tool* carro de precisión *m*; ~ **tachometer** *n* MECH ENG tacómetro de precisión *m*; ~ **wirewound resistor** *n* ELEC ENG resistencia devanada de precisión *f*

precoating *n* COAL revestimiento primario *m*, PAPER preestucado *m*

precoded: ~ **tag survey** *n* TRANSP comprobación por tarjeta precodificada *f*

precombustion *n* THERMO precombustión *f*; ~ **chamber** *n* THERMO *project management*, VEH cámara de precombustión *f*

precommissioning: ~ **checks** *n pl* NUCL verificaciones previas a la puesta en marcha *f pl*

preconcentrate *n* COAL preconcentrado *m*

preconsolidation: ~ **pressure** *n* COAL presión de preconsolidación *f*

precooked *adj* FOOD precocido

precooled *adj* FOOD preenfriado

precooler *n* REFRIG preenfriador *m*

precooling *n* RAIL, REFRIG prerefrigeración *f*

precrushing *n* COAL trituración primaria *f*

precursor: ~ **pollutant** *n* POLL contaminante precursor *m*

predelivery: ~ **reminder** *n* PROD aviso previo de entrega *m*

pre-delta: ~ **slope** *n* OCEAN pendiente predeltaica *f*

predicate *n* COMP&DP predicado *m*

predicted: ~ **reliability** *n* SPACE fiabilidad prevista *f*

predictive: ~ **capability** *n* POLL capacidad de predicción *f*

predistortion *n* ACOUST predistorsión *f*; ~ **technique** *n* TELECOM técnica de predistorsión *f*

predryer *n* PAPER presecador *m*

predub *vt* CINEMAT efectuar el predoblaje de

pre-edit *vt* CINEMAT preeditar

pre-emergence: ~ **application** *n* AGRIC aplicación en preemergencia *f*

pre-emphasis *n* ACOUST acentuación de los contrastes *f*, pre-énfasis *m*, preacentuación *f*, preamplificación *f*,

PHYS pre-énfasis *m*, SPACE *communications* acentuación de los contrastes *f*, preacentuación *f*, preamplificación *f*, TV pre-énfasis *m*, preacentuación *f*; ~ **improvement factor** *n* SPACE *communications* factor de mejora de la preacentuación *m*

pre-employment: ~ **health screening** *n* SAFE examen médico de admisión *m*

pre-expediting *n* PROD preseguimiento *m*

prefabricate *vt* CONST, WATER TRANSP prefabricar

prefabricated: ~ **package** *n* PACK envase prefabricado *m*; ~ **panel** *n* REFRIG panel prefabricado *m*; ~ **unit** *n* CONST unidad prefabricada *f*

prefabrication *n* CONST, WATER TRANSP *shipbuilding* prefabricación *f*

preferential: ~ **list** *n* SPACE lista preferencial *f*, lista preferente *f*; ~ **process** *n* COMP&DP proceso preferencial *m*

preferred: ~ **frequencies** *n pl* ACOUST frecuencias preferentes *f pl*; ~ **orientation** *n* CRYSTALL, GEOL orientación predominante *f*, orientación preferente *f*

prefilter *n* ELECTRON prefiltro *m*

prefiltering *n* ELECTRON prefiltrado *m*

prefiring *n* SPACE predisparo *m*

prefix *n* TELECOM desconexión *f*, prefijo *m*; ~ **notation** *n* COMP&DP notación por prefijos *f*

preflash *vt* CINEMAT utilizar un preflash

preflashing *n* CHEM preflashing *m*

preflight: ~ **information** *n* AIR TRANSP información prevuelo *f*; ~ **planning** *n* AIR TRANSP planificación previa al vuelo *f*

prefocusing *n* CINEMAT preenfoque *m*

prefog *vt* CINEMAT prevelar

preform[1] *n* C&G preforma *f*, P&R compuesto premoldeado *m*, preforma *f*

preform[2] *vt* TELECOM preformar

pre-formed: ~ **fiber** *AmE*, ~ **fibre** *BrE n* OPT, TELECOM fibra preformada *f*; ~ **spray scrubber** *n* POLL lavador por aspersión preformada *m*, lavador por pulverización en contracorriente *m*, lavador spray *m*

preforming *n* P&R premodelado *m*; ~ **press** *n* P&R prensa de premoldeado *f*

pregnane *n* CHEM pregnano *m*

prehardener *n* CINEMAT preendurecedor *m*

preheat *vt* GEN precalentar

preheater *n* GEN precalentador *m*

preheating *n* GEN precalentamiento *m*; ~ **oven** *n* P&R horno de precalentamiento *m*

preheptatonic: ~ **scale** *n* ACOUST escala preeptavalente *f*

prehnite *n* MINERAL prehnita *f*

prehnitene *n* CHEM pregnitano *m*

prehnitic *adj* CHEM pregnítico

preignition *n* VEH encendido prematuro *m*, preencendido *m*

preimpregnate *n* P&R material preimpregnado *m*, prepreg *m*

preimpregnation *n* C&G preimpregnación *f*

preionization *n* RAD PHYS preionización *f*

preliminary: ~ **bath** *n* CINEMAT, PHOTO baño preliminar *m*; ~ **cost-estimate** *n* CONST presupuesto preliminar *m*; ~ **design** *n* CONST anteproyecto *m*; ~**-design review** *n* (*PDR*) SPACE revisión del anteproyecto *f* (*PDR*), revisión preliminar de diseño *f* (*PDR*); ~ **seating** *n* MECH ENG asentamiento preliminar *m*; ~ **sedimentation** *n* HYDROL sedimentación

preliminar *f*; ~ **treatment** *n* WATER tratamiento preliminar *m*

preload *n* MECH ENG carga previa *f*

premachined: ~ **condition** *n* MECH ENG premaquinado *m*

premake: ~**-ready** *n* PRINT puesta a punto previa *f*

premature: ~ **ignition** *n* AUTO, VEH encendido prematuro *m*, ignición prematura *f*

premetalized: ~ **dye** *AmE see premetallized dye BrE*

premetallized: ~ **dye** *n BrE* TEXTIL colorante premetalizado *m*

premium: ~ **fuel** *n BrE* (*cf premium gasoline AmE*) AUTO combustible de alto octanaje *m*, gasolina de alto octanaje *f*; ~ **gas** *n AmE* (*cf premium petrol BrE*) AUTO combustible de alto octanaje *m*, gasolina de alto octanaje *f*; ~ **gasoline** *n AmE* (*cf premium fuel BrE, premium petrol BrE*) AUTO combustible de alto octanaje *m*, gasolina de alto octanaje *f*; ~**-grade gas** *n AmE* (*cf premium-grade petrol BrE*) AUTO, PETR TECH, PETROL, VEH gasolina super *f*; ~**-grade gasoline** *AmE* (*cf premium-grade petrol BrE*) AUTO, PETR TECH, PETROL, VEH gasolina super *f*; ~**-grade petrol** *n BrE* (*cf premium-grade gas AmE, premium-grade gasoline AmE*) AUTO, PETR TECH, PETROL, VEH, gasolina super *f*; ~ **petrol** *n BrE* (*cf premium gas AmE, premium gasoline AmE*) AUTO combustible de alto octanaje *m*, gasolina de alto octanaje *f*

premuffler *n* AUTO presilenciador *m*

preplanting *n* AGRIC presiembra *f*

preplasticizing *n* P&R *plastics* preplastificación *f*

prepower: ~ **check** *n* PROD chequeo prepotencial *m*

prepreg *n* P&R material preimpregnado *m*, prepreg *m*

prepress: ~ **proof** *n* PRINT prueba sin utilizar el proceso de impresión *f*

prepricing *n* PACK pre-precio *m*

preprint *n* PRINT preimpresión *f*

preprinted: ~ **label** *n* PACK etiqueta preimpresa *f*

preprocessed *adj* ELECTRON preprocesado, pretratado

preprocessing *n* ELECTRON pretratamiento *m*

preprocessor *n* COMP&DP preprocesador *m*

preproduction *n* PROD preproducción *f*; ~ **aircraft** *n* AIR TRANSP avión de preproducción *m*; ~ **tooling** *n* MECH ENG herramientas pre-producción *f pl*; ~ **train** *n* RAIL tren prototipo *m*

preprogrammed *adj* COMP&DP preprogramado

prerecord *vt* ACOUST grabar, COMP&DP, TV pregrabar

prerecorded[1] *adj* ACOUST, COMP&DP, TV pregrabado

prerecorded[2]: ~ **message** *n* TELECOM mensaje pregrabado *m*, mensaje prerregistrado *m*; ~ **tape** *n* TV cinta pregrabada *f*

presbyacusis *n BrE* ACOUST presbiacusia *f*

presbycusis *AmE see presbyacusis BrE*

prescreening *n* COAL cribado primario *m*, depuración primaria *f*, filtrado primario *m*

preseizure: ~ **dialing** *AmE*, ~ **dialling** *BrE n* TELECOM marcación de pretoma *f*, marcación de toma previa *f*

preselection: ~ **gear change** *n* VEH cambio con preselección de marchas *m*

preselector *n* ELECTRON, HEAT, VEH preselector *m*

presence: ~ **loop** *n* TRANSP cuadro de actividad presente *m*

presentation: ~ **graphics** *n pl* COMP&DP gráficos de presentación *m pl*; ~ **indicator** *n* (*PI*) TELECOM indicador de presentación *m*; ~ **layer** *n* COMP&DP capa de presentación *f*, nivel de presentación *m*;

~ **protocol data unit** *n* (*PPDU*) TELECOM unidad de presentación de datos del protocolo *f*

preservative *n* AGRIC, PACK, PROD conservante *m*

preserve[1] *n* AGRIC conserva de fruta *f*, FOOD conserva *f*

preserve[2] *vt* FOOD conservar, preservar

preserved: ~ **latex** *n* P&R látex preservado *m*

preserving: ~ **industry** *n* AGRIC, FOOD, PACK industria conservera *f*; ~ **jar** *n* BrE (*cf canning jar AmE*) C&G, FOOD, PACK botella para conserva *f*, jarro para conservas *m*

preset[1] *n* ELECTRON ajuste previo *m*, preselección *f*; ~ **frequency** *n* ELECTRON frecuencia de preselección *f*; ~ **pot** *n* ELEC *resistance* crisol de ajuste *m*; ~ **shutter** *n* PHOTO obturador preajustado *m*; ~ **value** *n* PROD valor prefijado *m*

preset[2] *vt* COMP&DP preajustar, preconfigurar, predeterminar

presetting *n* ELECTRON preselección *f*; ~ **of channels** *n* TV prefijación de canales *f* (*Esp*), presintonía de canales *f* (*AmL*); ~ **gage** *AmE*, ~ **gauge** *BrE n* METR calibración de ajuste previo *f*

pre-signaling: ~ **distance** *AmE see pre-signalling distance BrE*

pre-signalling: ~ **distance** *n* BrE RAIL distancia anterior a la señalización *f*

pre-sowing: ~ **application** *n* AGRIC aplicación en presiembra *f*

pre-split: ~ **basting** *n* MINE embaste *m*

press[1] *n* C&G, PACK, PAPER, PRINT prensa *f*, PROD prensa *f*, estampadora *f*, TEXTIL prensa *f*; ~ **-button** *n* TELECOM pulsador *m*, tecla *f*; ~ **camera** *n* PHOTO cámara de reportero de prensa *f*; ~ **cutting** *n* PROD recorte de prensa *m*; ~ **fabric** *n* PAPER fieltro de prensa *m*; ~ **felt** *n* PAPER fieltro de prensa *m*, fieltro húmedo *m*; ~ **-finishing machine** *n* TEXTIL máquina de planchado final *f*; ~ **fit** *n* PROD ajuste forzado *m*, encastre a presión *m*; ~ **-hardening** *n* METALL presión de endurecimiento *f*; ~ **nut** *n* MECH ENG tuerca de apriete *f*; ~ **proof** *n* PRINT capilla *f*, hoja de prueba *f*, prueba de prensa *f*; ~ **roll** *n* PAPER, PRINT rodillo de la prensa *m*; ~ **stack** *n* PAPER conjunto de rodillos que forman la prensa *m*; ~ **stud** *n* TEXTIL botón a presión *m*; ~ **-through packaging sheet** *n* PACK obtención del envase prensado la hoja *f*; ~ **tool** *n* MECH ENG estampa *f*, troquel *m*; ~ **-type vertical broaching machine** *n* MECH ENG brochadora vertical por presión *f*

press[2] *vt* COAL presionar, PAPER prensar, PROD embutir en la prensa, estampar, prensar, *key, button* pulsar

pressboard *n* ELEC *insulation* cuadro de pulsadores *m*, PAPER cartón compacto para cajas *m*, cartón prensado *m*

pressed: ~ **bimetallic half-thrust washer** *n* MECH ENG arandela bimetálica de semi-empuje prensada *f*; ~ **glass** *n* BrE (*cf pressware AmE*) C&G loza prensada *f*, vidrio prensado *m*; ~ **-steel bucket** *n* PROD cangilón de acero embutido *m*

presser *n* C&G prensista *m*; ~ **bar** *n* TEXTIL barra prensatelas *f*

pressing *n* C&G *glass*, PACK prensado *m*, TEXTIL planchado *m*, prensado *m*; ~ **pump** *n* HYDRAUL bomba impelente *f*

pressostat *n* REFRIG presostato *m*

presspahn: ~ **-transformer board** *n* PAPER cartón prensado *m*, prespan *m*

presspaper *n* PAPER papel prensado *m*

pressure[1]: ~ **-locked** *adj* HYDRAUL bajo presión

pressure[2] *n* GAS, HYDRAUL presión *f*, MECH *fixed equipment* carga *f*, impulso *m*, presión *f*, tensión *f*, PHYS, POLL, REFRIG, SPACE presión *f*; ~ **-air system** *n* AIR TRANSP sistema de aire comprimido *m*; ~ **alarm** *n* PROD alarma por presión *f*; ~ **altimeter** *n* AIR TRANSP altímetro de presión *m*, baroaltímetro *m*, LAB, METEO, PHYS baroaltímetro *m*; ~ **altitude** *n* AIR TRANSP altitud barométrica *f*; ~ **amplitude** *n* ACOUST amplitud de presión *f*; ~ **anemometer** *n* INSTR, METEO, PHYS anemómetro de presión *m*; ~ **angle** *n* MECH, MECH ENG *gearing* ángulo de presión *m*; ~ **bomb** *n* PETROL bomba de presión *f*; ~ **-boost valve** *n* AUTO válvula de incremento de presión *f*, válvula de sobrepresión *f*; ~ **box** *n* PROD caja de presión *f*; ~ **broadening** *n* PHYS ensanchamiento por presión *m*, RAD PHYS ensanchamiento de las líneas espectrales debido a la presión *m*; ~ **buildup** *n* AIR TRANSP acumulación de presión *f*; ~ **bulkhead** *n* AIR TRANSP mampara de presión *f*, mampara estanca *f*, MECH ENG mamparo estanco *m*; ~ **cable** *n* ELEC cable a presión *m*; ~ **cap** *n* AUTO casquillo de presión *m*; ~ **cell** *n* COAL cavidad a presión *f*, célula *f*; ~ **change** *n* GAS cambio de presión *m*; ~ **characteristic** *n* METEO característica de la presión *f*; ~ **check** *n* C&G estrellada por presión *f*, prueba de presión *f*; ~ **cloth** *n* PHOTO paño de presión *m*; ~ **coefficient** *n* AIR TRANSP *aerodynamics*, FUELLESS, PHYS coeficiente de presión *m*; ~ **control** *n* HEAT control de presión *m*; ~ **-control emergency** *n* PROD control a presión en emergencia *m*; ~ **-control normal** *n* PROD control a presión normal *m*; ~ **-controlled valve** *n* REFRIG válvula presostática *f*; ~ **-controller** *n* REFRIG presostato *m*; ~ **cooker** *n* FOOD olla a presión *f*, olla de cierre hermético *f*, olla de presión *f*, olla exprés *f*, MECH ENG autoclave *f*, olla de cierre hermético *f*, olla a presión *f*, olla exprés *f*; ~ **-cooling** *n* REFRIG refrigeración por presión de aire *f*; ~ **curve** *n* HYDRAUL curva de presiones *f*, curva piezométrica *f*; ~ **decay** *n* HYDRAUL pérdida de presión *f*; ~ **declination** *n* HYDRAUL caída de presión *f*, pérdida de carga *f*; ~ **delivery** *n* HYDRAUL entrega de presión *f*, suministro de presión *m*; ~ **detector** *n* GAS detector de presión *m*; ~ **diecasting die** *n* MECH ENG matriz para fundición inyectada de presofusión *f*, matriz para fundición por inyección a presión *f*; ~ **difference** *n* HYDRAUL diferencia de presión *f*; ~ **differential cutout** *n* REFRIG presostato diferencial *m*; ~ **-differential warning valve** *n* AUTO válvula de presión diferencial *f*, válvula de seguridad por diferencia de presión *f*; ~ **draft** *AmE see pressure draught BrE*; ~ **drag** *n* AIR TRANSP resistencia aerodinámica por presión *f*, retardo por la resistencia del aire *m*; ~ **draught** *n* BrE MECH ENG *ventilation* ventilación mecánica por insuflación *f*; ~ **drop** *n* FUELLESS, HEAT caída de presión *f*, HYDRAUL, PETR TECH caída de presión *f*, pérdida de carga *f*, PROD caída de presión *f*; ~ **-dyeing** *n* COLOUR teñido a presión *m*; ~ **equalization** *n* OCEAN igualación de presión *f*; ~ **equipment** *n* MECH ENG, PETR TECH equipo de presión *m*, equipo de presurizado *m*; ~ **-feed** *n* AUTO alimentación por inyección *f*; ~ **-filling** *n* PACK llenado a presión *m*; ~ **-filter** *n* CHEM TECH, COAL, WATER filtro de presión *m*; ~ **-forming** *n* P&R moldeado a presión *m*; ~ **-forming machine** *n* PACK termoformadora a presión *f*; ~ **front**

n MILIT *of explosion* frente de presión *m*; ~ **gage** *AmE see pressure gauge BrE*; ~ **gate** *n* CINEMAT ventanilla de presión *f*, PHOTO compuerta de presión *f*; ~ **gauge** *n BrE* AGRIC manómetro *m*, AIR TRANSP barómetro *m*, COAL manómetro *m*, medidor de presiones *m*, medidor de presión *m*, CONST barómetro *m*, indicador de presión *m*, manómetro *m*, HYDRAUL, INSTR indicador de presión *m*, manómetro *m*, LAB barómetro *m*, indicador de presión *m*, manómetro *m*, piezómetro *m*, MECH manómetro *m*, MECH ENG indicador de presión *m*, manómetro *m*, METR barómetro *m*, PETR TECH manómetro *m*, PHYS barómetro *m*, indicador de presión *m*, manómetro *m*, PROD, RAIL, REFRIG manómetro *m*, WATER TRANSP barómetro *m*; ~ **gradient** *n* FLUID, PETR TECH gradiente de presión *m*; ~ **graph** *n* INSTR diagrama de presiones *m*; ~ **guide** *n* CINEMAT guía de presión *f*; ~ **hank dyeing** *n* COLOUR teñido en madeja a presión *m*; ~ **head** *n* COAL altura piezométrica *f*, carga de agua *f*, carga hidrostática debida a la presión *f*, tubo de Pitot con toma estática *m*, tubo de Pitot presostático *m*, HYDRAUL carga de agua *f*; ~ **height** *n* AIR TRANSP altura de la presión *f*; ~ **indicator** *n* AGRIC, COAL manómetro *m*, CONST, HYDRAUL, INSTR, LAB indicador de presión *m*, manómetro *m*, MECH manómetro *m*, MECH ENG indicador de presión *m*, manómetro *m*, PETR TECH, PHYS, PROD, RAIL, REFRIG manómetro *m*; ~ **indicator card** *n* VEH *engine* diagrama del ciclo *m*; ~ **inlet** *n* AIR TRANSP *air-conditioning* entrada de presión *f*; ~ **intensification** *n* PROD intensificación de la presión *f*, manointensificación *f*; ~ **jet** *n* HEAT ENG chorro a presión *m*; ~ **level** *n* ACOUST nivel de presión *m*; ~ **loss** *n* HYDRAUL disminución de la presión *f*, pérdida de carga *f*, pérdida de presión *f*; ~ **lubrication** *n* AUTO lubricación con alimentación a presión *f*; ~ **main line** *n* MECH ENG línea de presión principal *f*; ~ **maintenance** *n* PETROL conservación de la presión *f*; ~ **measurement** *n* SPACE medida de la presión *f*; ~ **microphone** *n* ACOUST micrófono de presión *m*; ~**monitoring** *n* PROD regulación de la presión *f*; ~**mould for casting** *n* MECH ENG molde para fundición por presión *m*; ~ **pad** *n* AUTO pastilla de presión *f*, taco de presión *m*, CINEMAT, PHOTO taco de presión *m*; ~ **pin** *n* MECH ENG *die set* pasador de presión *m*; ~ **pipe** *n* MECH ENG tubo de presión *m*; ~ **plate** *n* AUTO placa de presión *f*, plato de presión *m*, CINEMAT placa de presión *f*, MECH ENG plato de presión *m*, PHOTO placa de presión *f*, PROD plato de presión *m*, VEH plato de empuje *m*; ~**plate drive strap** *n* AUTO abrazadera de conducción de plato de presión *f*; ~**plate release lever** *n* AUTO palanca de desembrague del plato de presión *f*, VEH palanca del plato de empuje *f*; ~**plate spring** *n* VEH muelle del plato de empuje *m*; ~ **pump** *n* COAL, HYDRAUL, WATER bomba de presión *f*; ~ **rate-of-change regulating** *n* AIR TRANSP regulación del régimen de cambio de presión *f*; ~ **rate-of-change switch** *n* AIR TRANSP interruptor del régimen de cambio de presión *m*; ~ **ratio** *n* SPACE relación entre dos presiones *f*; ~ **reducer** *n* AIR TRANSP reductor de presión *m*, HYDRAUL regulador manorreductor *m*, válvula manorreductora *f*, SPACE *craft* válvula manorreductora *f*; ~**reducing valve** *n* CONST válvula reductora de presión *f*, HYDRAUL válvula manorreductora *f*, MECH ENG válvula manorreductora *f*, válvula reduc-

tora de presión *f*, PROD válvula manorreductora *f*, REFRIG válvula reductora de presión *f*; ~ **reduction** *n* PHYS reducción de presión *f*; ~**reflection coefficient** *n* ACOUST coeficiente de reflexión de presión *m*; ~ **regulator** *n* CONST regulador de presión *m*, ELEC ENG regulador manorreductor *m*, HYDRAUL regulador de presión *m*; ~**relief duct** *n* RAIL conducto para aliviar la presión *m*; ~**relief valve** *n* HYDRAUL válvula de seguridad *f*, válvula de desahogo *f*, válvula equilibrada *f*, MECH ENG válvula de alivio *f*, válvula de desahogo *f*, válvula de seguridad *f*, PROD válvula de reducción de presión *f*, válvula de seguridad *f*; ~ **ridge** *n* OCEAN cresta barométrica *f*, cresta de presión *f*; ~ **roller** *n* ACOUST cilindro de presión *m*, rodillo de presión *m*, rodillo prensador *m*, C&G rodillo prensador *m*, CINEMAT rodillo de presión *m*, MECH ENG cilindro de presión *m*, rodillo de presión *m*, rodillo prensador *m*; ~ **screw** *n* MECH ENG tornillo de presión *m*; ~ **seal** *n* HYDRAUL cierre a presión *m*, cierre autoclave *m*, cierre estanco a la presión *m*; ~**sealed car** *n* AmE (*cf pressure-sealed wagon BrE*) RAIL vagón presurizado *m*; ~**sealed wagon** *BrE n* (*cf pressure-sealed car AmE*) RAIL vagón presurizado *m*; ~**sensitive detector** *n* TRANSP *traffic* detector piezo-sensible *m*; ~**sensitive hot-melt adhesive** *n* PACK producto autoadhesivo que se aplica fundido *m*; ~**sensitive labeler** *AmE*, ~**sensitive labeller** *BrE n* PACK etiquetadora con etiquetas autoadhesivas *f*; ~**sensitive tape** *n* PACK cinta sensible a la presión *f*; ~**set ink** *n* COLOUR tinta de secado por presión *f*; ~ **setting** *n* PROD ajuste de la presión *m*; ~ **shadow** *n* GEOL cola de presión *f*, sombra de presión *f*; ~ **side** *n* HYDRAUL pared de carga *f*; ~ **sleeve** *n* MECH ENG manguito de presión *m*; ~ **stage** *n* HYDRAUL escalón de presión *m*; ~**suppression pool** *n* NUCL piscina de supresión de la presión *f*; ~ **surge** *n* HYDRAUL aumento brusco de la presión *m*; ~ **swing adsorption** *n* (*PSA*) GAS adsorción por cambios de presión *f* (*ACP*); ~ **switch** *n* ELEC, ELEC ENG interruptor automático por caída de presión *m*, HYDRAUL conmutador activado por presión *m*, disyuntor de aire comprimido *m*, presostato *m*, PROD disyuntor de aire comprimido *m*, presostato *m*; ~ **system** *n* AIR TRANSP sistema de presión *m*; ~ **tank** *n* OCEAN tanque de presión *m*; ~ **tendency** *n* METEO tendencia de presión *f*; ~ **test** *n* HYDRAUL ensayo manométrico *m*, prueba de presión *f*; ~**tight joint** *n* MECH ENG *pipe-threading* junta hermética *f*, junta que no pierde *f*; ~ **transducer** *n* PROD transductor para medir presiones *m*; ~ **transmitter** *n* HYDRAUL multiplicador de presión *m*, transmisor de presión *m*; ~ **tube** *n* AUTO tubo de presión *m*; ~ **tunnel** *n* FUELLESS *hydroelectric power* túnel a presión *m*; ~ **turbine** *n* HYDRAUL turbina de reacción *f*; ~ **valve** *n* HYDRAUL válvula de suministro *f*; ~ **variation** *n* GAS, WAVE PHYS variación de presión *f*; ~ **vessel** *n* CONST recipiente a presión *m*, MECH, MECH ENG recipiente a presión *m*, vasija de presión *f*, REFRIG recipiente a presión *m*; ~**vs-depth plot** *n* PETR TECH gráfico presión-profundidad *m*; ~ **wave** *n* TELECOM onda de presión *f*; ~**welded safety grating** *n* SAFE rejilla de seguridad soldada a presión *f*; ~ **welding** *n* CONST soldadura de presión *f*, PROD, THERMO soldeo por presión *m*; ~ **wheel** *n* WATER pozo de inyección *m*, rueda de reacción *f*

pressurestat *n* CHEM manostato *m*, piezostato *m*

pressurization *n* AIR TRANSP presionización *f* (*AmL*), presurización *f* (*Esp*)

pressurize *vt* REFRIG presurizar

pressurized[1] *adj* MECH comprimido, con presión interior, de presión regulada, presionizado

pressurized[2]: ~ **connection** *n* ELEC ENG conexión a presión *f*, conexión presurizada *f*; ~ **floor** *n* AIR TRANSP suelo presurizado *m*; ~ **glue feed** *n* PACK sistema de alimentación a presión de la goma *m*; ~ **hot-water tank** *n* HEAT depósito de agua caliente presurizada *m*, tanque presurizado de agua caliente *m*; ~ **natural gas** *n* GAS, TRANSP gas natural presurizado *m*; ~ **natural-gas bus** *n* TRANSP autobús de gas natural a presión *m* (*Esp*), bus por gas natural a presión *m*, ómnibus *m* (*AmL*); ~ **steam** *n* HYDRAUL vapor a presión *m*, vapor vivo *m*; ~ **thermal shock** *n* NUCL choque térmico a presión *m*; ~ **water reactor** *n* NUCL, PHYS reactor de agua presurizada *m*

pressurizer: ~ **pressure control** *n* NUCL control de la presión del primario por medio del presurizador *m*; ~ **relief-tank** *n* NUCL depósito de alivio del presionador *m*; ~ **relief-valve** *n* NUCL válvula de alivio del presionador *f*; ~ **surge-line** *n* NUCL línea de compensación del presionador *f*

pressurizing: ~ **gas** *n* SPACE gas de presurización *m*; ~ **gas tank** *n* SPACE tanque de gas de presurización *m*; ~ **manifold** *n* AIR TRANSP colector presurizado *m*; ~ **valve** *n* AIR TRANSP válvula presurizada *f*

pressware *n* *AmE* (*cf pressed glass BrE*) C&G loza prensada *f*, vidrio prensado *m*

presswork *n* PRINT impresión *f*, tirada *f*

pre-start: ~ **warning** *n* MECH ENG advertencia prearranque *f*

prestore *vt* COMP&DP prealmacenar

prestrain *n* METALL predeformación *f*

prestressed: ~ **concrete** *n* CONST concreto pretensado *m* (*AmL*), hormigón pretensado *m* (*Esp*)

prestriped: ~ **film** *n* CINEMAT película con banda sonora previamente colocada *f*

prestriping *n* CINEMAT colocación previa de la banda sonora *f*

pretimed: ~ **signal** *n* TRANSP señal pre-programada *f*

pretravel *n* ELEC ENG carrera *f*

pretreating *n* CHEM pretratamiento *m*

pretreatment *n* COAL tratamiento preliminar *m*, tratamiento previo *m*

pretzel *n* GEOM *text* brezel *m*, figura ocho *f*, pretzel *m*

prevailing: ~ **torque-type hexagon-nut** *n* MECH ENG tuerca hexagonal de torsión dominante *f*; ~ **wind** *n* METEO viento dominante *m*, viento predominante *m*, viento prevaleciente *m*

prevent *vt* SAFE *accidents* prevenir

prevention: ~ **of atmospheric pollution** *n* POLL prevención de contaminación atmosférica *f*; ~ **cost** *n* QUALITY costo de prevención *m*; ~ **of noise pollution** *n* ACOUST, POLL prevención de contaminación acústica *f* (*Esp*), prevención de contaminación sonora *f* (*AmL*); ~ **of water pollution** *n* MAR POLL, POLL prevención de contaminación del agua *f*

preventive: ~ **action** *n* QUALITY acción impeditiva *f*; ~ **fire protection** *n* SAFE protección preventiva contra incendios *f*; ~ **maintenance** *n* COMP&DP, CONST, TELECOM mantenimiento preventivo *m*

preview[1] *n* TV avance *m*; ~ **monitor** *n* TV monitor de cámara *m*

preview[2] *vt* TV ver antes de transmitir

prevulcanized: ~ **latex** *n* P&R *rubber* látex prevulcanizado *m*

PRF *abbr* (*pulse-repetition frequency*) COMP&DP, ELECTRON, PHYS, TELECOM frecuencia de repetición de impulsos *f*

price: ~ **marking** *n* PACK marcador de precios *m*; ~ **tag** *n* PACK tarjeta colgante del precio *f*

priceite *n* MINERAL priceíta *f*

prick: ~ **bar** *n* PROD *furnace-poker* hurgón *m*, picafuegos *m*; ~ **punch** *n* MECH ENG punzón de marcar *m*, punzón de mecánico *m*

pricker *n* MINE aguja de polvorero *f*, lanzasondas *m* (*AmL*), punzón *m* (*Esp*), PROD *furnace-poker* hurgón *m*, picafuegos *m*, *loam mould* buril *m*, *moulds* aguja para hacer agujeros *f*

pricking *n* PROD *clinkering* limpieza de la parrilla *f*

prills: ~-**and-oil** *n* MINE pepitas de mineral y combustible líquido *f pl*

primacord *n* MINE cuerda detonante *f*, mecha detonante *f*, mecha rápida *f*; ~ **fuse** *n* SPACE espoleta de la mecha detonante *f*

primary *n* ELEC ENG inductor *m*; ~ **access** *n* TELECOM acceso primario *m*; ~ **armature** *n* ELEC *generator-motor* armadura primaria *f*; ~ **barrel** *n* AUTO cuba primaria *f*; ~ **battery** *n* ELEC ENG batería de pilas *f*; ~ **blasting** *n* MINE explosión primaria *f*; ~ **carbide** *n* METALL carburo metálico primario *m*; ~ **cell** *n* ELEC ENG elemento *m*; ~ **chaincase** *n* VEH cárter principal de la cadena *m*; ~ **circuit** *n* ELEC circuito primario *m*; ~ **clarification** *n* WATER clarificación primaria *f*; ~ **coating** *n* OPT, TELECOM revestimiento primario *m*; ~ **collision** *n* TRANSP choque importante *m*, colisión importante *f*; ~ **color** *AmE*, ~ **colour** *BrE* *n* CINEMAT, COLOUR, PHYS, RAD PHYS color primario *m*; ~ **creep** *n* METALL componente primario de la termofluencia *m*; ~ **crusher** *n* COAL molienda primaria *f*, MINE triturador primario *m*; ~ **crushing** *n* MINE molienda primaria *f*; ~ **cup** *n* AUTO casquillo primario *m*; ~ **current** *n* ELEC, ELEC ENG *transformer* corriente inductora *f*, corriente primaria *f*; ~ **cyclic variation** *n* AIR TRANSP *helicopter* variación cíclica primaria *f*; ~ **emission** *n* ELECTRON emisión primaria *f*; ~ **explosive** *n* MINE explosivo primario *m*; ~ **extinction** *n* CRYSTALL extinción primaria *f*; ~ **fiber** *AmE*, ~ **fibre** *BrE* *n* C&G fibra primaria *f*; ~ **filter** *n* WATER filtro primario *m*; ~ **fuel cell** *n* TRANSP célula de combustible principal *f*; ~ **grinding** *n* COAL molienda primaria *f*; ~ **headbox** *n* PAPER caja de entrada principal *f*; ~ **heat exchanger** *n* AIR TRANSP intercambiador de calor primario *m*, permutador térmico primario *m*, termocanjeador primario *m*, termointercambiador primario *m*, termopermutador primario *m*; ~ **index** *n* COMP&DP índice principal *m*; ~ **inductance** *n* ELEC *transformer*, ELEC ENG inductancia primaria *f*; ~ **interference** *n* RAD PHYS interferencia primaria *f*; ~ **ionization** *n* PHYS, RAD PHYS ionización primaria *f*; ~ **letdown** *n* NUCL descarga de agua del primario *f*; ~ **makeup** *n* HYDROL, NUCL, WATER aporte de agua al primario *m*; ~ **memory** *n* COMP&DP memoria central *f*, memoria principal *f*; ~ **mirror** *n* INSTR espejo primario *m*; ~ **piston** *n* AUTO pistón primario *m*; ~ **precipitation** *n* HYDROL precipitación primaria *f*; ~ **processor chassis** *n* PROD chasis de procesador primario *m*; ~-**rate access** *n* (*PRA*) TELECOM acceso a la tarifa primaria *m*; ~ **recovery** *n* PETR TECH, PETROL recuperación primaria *f*; ~ **refrigerant** *n* REFRIG fluido frigorígeno *m*, refrigerante primario *m*; ~ **runway** *n* AIR TRANSP pista principal *f*; ~ **sampling** *n* COAL muestreo primario *m*; ~~**secondary leakage** *n* NUCL *across steam generator* fugas primario-secundario *f pl*; ~ **settlement** *n* COAL sedimentación primaria *f*; ~ **shaft** *n* AUTO eje primario *m*; ~ **shoe** *n* AUTO zapata primaria *f*; ~ **standard** *n* PHYS principales estándar *m pl*; ~ **storage** *AmE*, ~ **store** *BrE n* COMP&DP almacenamiento central *m*, almacenamiento principal *m*, memoria principal *f*; ~ **structure** *n* AIR TRANSP estructura primaria *f*; ~ **tap** *n* ELEC ENG ramal primario *m*; ~ **treatment** *n* HYDROL *lathe* tratamiento primario *m*; ~ **voltage** *n* ELEC *transformer*, ELEC ENG tensión primaria *f*; ~ **winding** *n* AUTO arrollamiento primario *m*, bobinado primario *m*, ELEC *transformer* arrollamiento primario *m*, devanado inductor *m*, devanado primario *m*, ELEC ENG devanado inductor *m*, arrollamiento primario *m*, PHYS bobinado primario *m*, VEH arrollamiento primario *m*

prime[1]: ~ **coat** *n* CONST capa de imprimación *f*; ~ **contractor** *n* SPACE adjudicatario principal *m*, contratista principal *m*; ~ **factor** *n* MATH divisor primo *m*, factor primo *m*; ~ **lens** *n* CINEMAT, OPT, PHOTO objetivo principal *m*; ~ **mover** *n* MECH ENG fuente de energía primaria *f*, fuente energética *f*, fuente natural de energía *f*, máquina generadora de energía *f*, máquina motriz *f*, primer móvil *m*; ~ **number** *n* MATH número primo *m*; ~~**time slot** *n* TV pequeño espacio de publicidad en horas de máxima audiencia *m*

prime[2] *vt* COATINGS imprimar, HYDRAUL *boiler* llenar con agua, cebar, MINE cebar, PROD *painting* imprimar, WATER *pump* cebar

primer *n* CHEM cebo *m*, COATINGS imprimación *f*, imprimador *m*, COLOUR imprimación *f*, CONST imprimador *m*, tapaporos *m*, MILIT cebo *m*, MINE cebador *m* (*AmL*), cebo *m* (*Esp*), cápsula fulminante *f* (*AmL*), estopín *m* (*AmL*), iniciador *m* (*Esp*), P&R pintura de imprimación *f*, aprestador *m*, imprimador *m*, PROD *paint* pintura de imprimación *f*; ~ **cartridge** *n* MINE cartucho-cebo *m*; ~ **charge** *n* SPACE carga iniciadora *f*; ~ **pump** *n* AIR TRANSP bomba de cebado *f*

priming *n* AIR TRANSP, HYDRAUL cebado *m*, MINE acción de cebar *f*, cebado *m*, cebadura *f*, OCEAN *counter* adelanto *m*, PROD *of painting* imprimación *f*, primera mano *f*, WATER *to wet valve of pump* cebado *m*; ~ **charge** *n* MINE, SPACE *craft* carga de cebado *f*, carga iniciadora *f*, carga-cebo *f*; ~ **coat** *n* PROD *painting* capa de imprimación *f*; ~ **cock** *n* WATER grifo cebador *m*; ~ **explosive** *n* MINE explosivo de cebado *m*; ~ **paint** *n* COLOUR, CONST pintura de imprimación *f*; ~ **pipe** *n* WATER *of pump* tubo de cebado *m*; ~ **power** *n* COAL cebador *m*

primuline *n* CHEM primulina *f*

principal *n* CONST *frame or roof* par *m*; ~ **axe** *n* PHYS *mooring* eje principal *m*; ~ **axis** *n* CRYSTALL, PHYS eje principal *m*; ~ **color** *AmE*, ~ **colour** *BrE n* COLOUR color principal *m*; ~ **component** *n* MATH componente principal *f*; ~ **curvature** *n* C&G curvatura principal *f*; ~ **maxima** *n pl* PHYS máximos principales *m pl*; ~ **member** *n* CONST *of frame* elemento principal *m*; ~ **photography** *n* CINEMAT, PHOTO fotografía principal *f*; ~ **planes** *n pl* PHYS *theory of origin of*

universe planos principales *m pl*; ~ **points** *n pl* PHYS *conduit, pipe* puntos principales *m pl*; ~ **quantum number** *n* PHYS número cuántico principal *m*; ~ **rafter** *n* CONST par *m*; ~ **ray** *n* PHYS rayo principal *m*; ~ **tapping** *n* ELEC *connection* conexión intermedia principal *f*, toma intermedia principal *f*

principle *n* PHYS principio *m*; ~ **of maximum entropy** *n* RAD PHYS principio de máxima entropía *m*; ~ **of superposition** *n* WAVE PHYS principio de superposición *m*

principles: ~ **of farm management** *n pl* AGRIC teoría de explotación agrícola *f*

print[1] *n* CINEMAT copia *f*, COMP&DP impresión *f*, PHOTO copia *f*, prueba positiva *f*, PROD *of moulding* impresión *f*, *projection on core* portamacho *m*; ~~**and-apply labeling machine** *AmE*, ~~**and-apply labelling machine** *BrE n* PACK máquina que imprime y coloca la etiqueta *f*; ~ **buffer** *n* PRINT memoria intermedia de impresión *f*; ~~**cutter** *n* PRINT guillotina *f*; ~ **drum** *n* COMP&DP tambor de impresión *m*; ~~**dryer** *n* PHOTO secadora de pruebas *f*; ~ **file** *n* PRINT fichero de impresión *m*; ~ **film** *n* CINEMAT película para copia *f*; ~ **format** *n* COMP&DP formato de impresión *m*; ~ **head** *n* COMP&DP cabezal de impresión *m*; ~~**maker** *n* PRINT impresor *m*; ~ **pitch** *n* CINEMAT paso de la copia *m*; ~ **position** *n* COMP&DP posición de impresión *f*; ~~**server** *n* COMP&DP servidor de impresión *m*; ~ **shop** *n* PRINT imprenta *f*; ~ **speed** *n* COMP&DP velocidad de impresión *f*; ~~**through** *n* TV distorsión por capa adyacente *f*; ~~**through level** *n* TV nivel de distorsión por capa adyacente *m*; ~ **tongs** *n pl* PHOTO pinzas para pruebas *f pl*; ~~**viewer** *n* CINEMAT visor de copias *m*; ~ **wheel** *n* COMP&DP rueda de impresión *f*

print[2] *vt* CINEMAT copiar, COMP&DP imprimir, PHOTO positivar, PRINT imprimir, reproducir, tirar, TEXTIL estampar; ~ **recto** *vt* PRINT imprimir en blanco; ~~**up** *vt* CINEMAT hacer copias

printability *n* PAPER, PRINT aptitud para la impresión *f*, imprimibilidad *f*

printed: ~ **book** *n* PRINT libro impreso *m*; ~ **circuit** *n* (*PC*) COMP&DP, CONST, ELECTRON, PHYS circuito impreso *m* (*CI*); ~~**circuit board** *n* (*PC board*, *PCB*), COMP&DP, ELEC, ELECTRON, PHYS placa de circuito impreso *f* (*PCI, placa de CI*), tablero de circuito impreso *m* (*PCI, tablero de CI*), tarjeta de circuito impreso *f* (*PCI, tarjeta de CI*); ~~**circuit connector** *n* ELEC ENG conector de circuito impreso *m*; ~~**circuit laminate** *n* ELECTRON laminado de circuito impreso *m*; ~~**circuit substrate** *n* ELECTRON substrato de circuito impreso *m*; ~ **dirt** *n* CINEMAT suciedad impresa *f*; ~ **fabric** *n* TEXTIL tejido estampado *m*; ~ **folding-carton** *n* PACK caja plegable impresa *f*; ~ **matter** *n* PRINT impresos *m pl*; ~ **sheet** *n* PRINT hoja impresa *f*; ~~**wiring board** *n* ELECTRON placa de circuito impreso *f*

printer *n* CINEMAT positivadora *f*, COMP&DP impresora *f*, PHOTO positivadora *f*, PRINT, TELECOM impresor *m*, impresora *f*; ~ **aperture** *n* CINEMAT, PHOTO, TV abertura de la positivadora *f*; ~~**applicator** *n* PACK aplicador-impresor *m*; ~'s **black** *n* COLOUR negro de imprenta *m*; ~'s **color** *AmE*, ~'s **colour** *BrE n* COLOUR colorante de imprenta *m*; ~ **commands** *n pl* PRINT órdenes de impresión *f pl*; ~ **designed for narrow fabric** *n* TEXTIL estampadora diseñada para cintería *f*; ~ **directory** *n* COMP&DP, PRINT directorio de impresión *m*; ~'s **ink** *n* PRINT tinta de imprenta *f*; ~ **light** *n* CINEMAT luz de la positivadora *f*; ~ **machine** *n* COMP&DP impresora *f*, PRINT impresora *f*, máquina de imprimir *f*, TELECOM impresora *f*; ~ **output** *n* PRINT impresión *f*; ~ **point** *n* CINEMAT luz de positivado *f*; ~ **port** *n* PRINT puerto de impresora *m*; ~ **scale** *n* CINEMAT escala de la positivadora *f*; ~-**slotter** *n* PACK impresora ranuradora *f*; ~ **start-mark** *n* CINEMAT marca de inicio de la positivadora *f*; ~'s **supply** *n* PRINT consumibles de imprenta *m pl*; ~ **sync** *n* CINEMAT sincronización de la positivadora *f*; ~ **synchronization** *n* CINEMAT sincronización de la positivadora *f*

printing *n* C&G, COMP&DP impresión *f*, PHOTO impresión *f*, tiraje de pruebas *m*, preimpresión *f*, PRINT impresión *f*, tirada *f*, TEXTIL estampación *f*, estampado *m*; ~ **area** *n* PRINT zona de impresión *f*; ~ **black** *n* COLOUR negro de imprenta *m*; ~ **by machine** *n* PRINT impresión por máquina *f*; ~ **cam** *n* PRINT leva impresora *f*; ~ **color** *AmE*, ~ **colour** *BrE n* COLOUR color de impresión *m*; ~ **cylinder** *n* PRINT cilindro de impresión *m*; ~ **disc** *BrE*, ~ **disk** *AmE n* PRINT disco de impresión *m*; ~ **down** *n* CINEMAT, PRINT insolación *f*; ~ **echo** *n* PRINT eco de impresión *m*, imagen fantasma *f*; ~ **fly press** *n* PRINT prensa de abanico *f*; ~ **form** *n* PRINT forma impresora *f*; ~ **with four colors** *AmE*, ~ **with four colours** *BrE n* PRINT cuatricromía *f*; ~ **frame** *n* PRINT prensa neumática *f*; ~ **gate** *n* CINEMAT ventanilla de impresión *f*; ~ **head** *n* PRINT cabeza de impresión *f*; ~ **implements** *n pl* PRINT elementos de impresión *m pl*; ~ **in black** *n* PRINT impresión en negro *f*; ~ **ink** *n* P&R tinta de imprimir *f*, PRINT tinta de imprenta *f*; ~ **lab** *n* CINEMAT laboratorio de copias *m*; ~ **lake** *n* COLOUR, PRINT laca de impresión *f*; ~ **loss** *n* CINEMAT pérdida por copiado *f*; ~ **machine** *n* COMP&DP impresora *f*, PRINT impresora *f*, máquina de imprimir *f*, TELECOM impresora *f*, TEXTIL máquina de estampar *f*; ~ **mask** *n* PHOTO máscara de impresión *f*; ~ **off-line** *n* PACK, PRINT impresión fuera de máquina *f*; ~ **on site** *n* PACK impresión in situ *f*; ~ **on-line** *n* PACK, PRINT impresión en máquina *f*; ~ **opacity** *n* PAPER opacidad de impresión *f*; ~-**out emulsion** *n* PHOTO emulsión para imágenes directas *f*; ~ **paper** *n* PHOTO papel para copias *m*; ~ **press** *n* PRINT prensa de imprimir *f*; ~ **pressure** *n* PRINT presión de impresión *f*; ~ **process** *n* PRINT proceso de impresión *m*; ~ **roll** *n* P&R cilindro de impresión *m*; ~ **roller** *n* PRINT rodillo impresor *m*; ~ **sheet** *n* PRINT hoja de impresión *f*; ~ **stage** *n* PHOTO etapa de impresión *f*, tiraje de pruebas *m*; ~ **stock** *n* CINEMAT película para duplicados *f*; ~ **technique** *n* PHOTO técnica de impresión *f*; ~ **time** *n* PHOTO tiempo de impresión *m*; ~ **trade** *n* PRINT industria gráfica *f*; ~-**trade worker** *n* PRINT trabajador de la industria gráfica *m*; ~ **type** *n* PRINT tipo de imprenta *m*; ~ **varnish** *n* COATINGS, COLOUR, PRINT barniz de impresión *m*; ~ **works** *n* PRINT imprenta *f*

printjob *n* PRINT trabajo de impresión *m*

printout *n* COMP&DP copia impresa *f*, impresión de salida *f*, impreso *m*, TELECOM salida de impresión *f*

printstyle *n* PRINT estilo de impresión *m*

prior: ~ **distribution** *n* MATH distribución a priori *f*

priority *n* COMP&DP prioridad *f*; ~ **encoder** *n* ELECTRON codificador de prioridad *m*; ~ **interrupt** *n* COMP&DP interrupción prioritaria *f*; ~ **order** *n* PROD orden de prioridad *m*; ~ **processing** *n* COMP&DP procesamiento prioritario *m*; ~ **queue** *n* COMP&DP cola prioritaria *f*; ~ **sequencing** *n* COMP&DP secuencia prioritaria *f*; ~ **valve** *n* HYDRAUL válvula prioritaria *f*

prise *vt BrE* (*cf pry AmE*) CONST apalancar

prism *n* GEN prisma *m*; ~-**beam splitter** *n* CINEMAT divisor del haz con prisma *m*; ~ **binoculars** *n pl* INSTR binoculares prismáticos *m pl*

prismatic: ~ **binoculars** *n pl* INSTR binoculares prismáticos *m pl*; ~ **glass** *n* C&G vidrio prismático *m*; ~ **jointing** *n* GEOL disyunción prismática *f*; ~ **slip** *n* CRYSTALL deslizamiento prismático *m*; ~ **spectrograph** *n* RAD PHYS espectrógrafo prismático *m*; ~ **spectrum** *n* RAD PHYS espectro prismático *m*

pristine: ~ **fiber** *AmE*, ~ **fibre** *BrE n* C&G fibra pristina *f*; ~ **glass** *n* C&G vidrio pristino *m*

privacy *n* ACOUST privacidad *f*, COMP&DP carácter privado *m*, confidencialidad *f*, TELECOM privacidad *f*, secreto de la comunicación *m*

private: ~ **automatic branch exchange** *n* (*PABX*) TELECOM centralita privada automática conectada a la red pública *f*; ~ **automatic exchange** *n* TELECOM central automática privada *f*, central privada automática *f*, centralita automática *f*; ~ **branch exchange** *n* (*PBX*) TELECOM central telefónica privada *f* (*PBX*), centralita privada *f*; ~ **car** *n* *AmE* (*cf private wagon BrE*) RAIL vagón particular *m*, vagón privado *m*; ~ **dial-up port** *n* TELECOM puerto de marcación privado *m*; ~ **line** *n* TELECOM enlace de acceso *m*, línea privada *f*; ~-**management domain** *n* (*PRMD*) TELECOM dominio de gestión privada *m*; ~ **manual branch exchange** *n* (*PMBX*) TELECOM central privada manual *f*; ~ **manual exchange** *n* TELECOM central manual privada *f*; ~ **network** *n* TELECOM red privada *f*; ~ **network exchange** *n* (*PNX*) TELECOM central de red privada *f*; ~-**numbering plan** *n* (*PNP*) TELECOM plan de numeración privado *m*; ~ **telephone network** *n* TELECOM red telefónica privada *f*; ~ **type** *n* COMP&DP tipo privado *m*; ~ **vehicle** *n* VEH coche para uso privado *m*, coche particular *m*; ~ **wagon** *n* *BrE* (*cf private car AmE*) RAIL vagón particular *m*, vagón privado *m*; ~ **wire** *n* (*PW*) TELECOM circuito privado *m*

privileged: ~ **instruction** *n* COMP&DP instrucción privilegiada *f*; ~ **operation** *n* COMP&DP operación privilegiada *f*

prize *vt* CONST *with lever* forzar

PRM *abbr* (*protocol-reference model*) TELECOM modelo de referencia del protocolo *m*

PRMD *abbr* (*private-management domain*) TELECOM dominio de gestión privada *m*

probabilistic: ~ **risk assessment** *n* (*PRA*) NUCL análisis probabilista del riesgo *m* (*APR*); ~ **safety assessment** *n* (*PSA*) NUCL análisis probabilista de la seguridad *m* (*APS*)

probability *n* COMP&DP, MATH probabilidad *f*; ~ **curve** *n* MATH curva de probabilidad *f*; ~ **density** *n* PHYS densidad de probabilidad *f*; ~ **density function** *n* (*PDF*) MATH *statistics* función de densidad de probabilidad *f* (*FDP*); ~ **distribution** *n* COMP&DP distribución de probabilidad *f*; ~ **of excess delay** *n* TELECOM probabilidad de retraso excedente *f*; ~ **theory** *n* MATH teoría de probabilidad *f*

probable: ~ **reserves** *n pl* PETR TECH, PETROL reservas probables *f pl*

probe *n* AIR TRANSP sonda *f*, COAL cabezal medidor *m*, sonda *f*, ELEC *measurement* cabezal medidor *m*, probeta *f*, sonda *f*, GAS exploración *f*, MINE sonda *f*, OCEAN registrador *m*, sonda *f*, PHYS prueba *f*, REFRIG ensayo *m*, SPACE sonda *f*; ~ **electrode** *n* GAS electrodo explorador *m*; ~ **microphone** *n* ACOUST micrófono sonda *m*

problem: ~ **definition** *n* COMP&DP definición de problemas *f*; ~ **description** *n* COMP&DP descripción de problemas *f*; ~~**oriented language** *n* COMP&DP lenguaje orientado al problema *m*; ~~**oriented software** *n* COMP&DP software orientado al problema *m*

procaine *n* CHEM procaína *f*

procedure *n* MECH ENG marcha a seguir *f*, modo operatorio *m*, proceso *m*, PROD método *m*, procedimiento *m*, QUALITY procedimiento *m*; ~ **division** *n* COMP&DP división de procedimientos *f*; ~ **library** *n* COMP&DP biblioteca de procedimientos *f*; ~ **name** *n* COMP&DP nombre de procedimiento *m*; ~~**oriented language** *n* COMP&DP lenguaje orientado a los procedimientos *m*

process[1]: **in ~ gaging** *AmE*, **in ~ gauging** *BrE adv* METR en vías de calibrado

process[2] *n* CHEM proceso *m*, COAL elaboración *f*, manipulación *f*, operación *f*, procedimiento *m*, procesado *m*, procesamiento *m*, proceso *m*, transformación *f*, MECH ENG procedimiento *m*, proceso *m*, PHOTO, PRINT procedimiento *m*, PROD *artificial* procedimiento *m*, proceso *m*, QUALITY, TEXTIL proceso *m*; ~ **automation** *n* COMP&DP automatización de procesos *f*, informatización *f*; ~ **camera** *n* CINEMAT cámara para reproducción fotomecánica *f*; ~ **chart** *n* PROD ordinograma de programación *m*; ~ **colors** *AmE*, ~ **colours** *BrE n pl* PRINT colores para cuatricromía *m pl*; ~ **control** *n* ELEC ENG control de proceso *m*, QUALITY control de proceso *m*, maestría de procesos *f*, TELECOM control de proceso *m*; ~ **controller** *n* ELEC ENG controlador de procesos *m*; ~ **control system** *n* COMP&DP sistema de control de procesos *m*; ~ **engineering** *n* COMP&DP ingeniería de procesos *f*, PETR TECH ingeniería de procesos *f*, tecnología de procesos *f*; ~ **engraver** *n* ELECTRON, PRINT fotograbador *m*; ~ **industry** *n* PROD industria de transformación *f*; ~ **ink** *n* PRINT tinta para tricromía *f*; ~ **printing** *n* PRINT impresión en colores *f*, impresión policroma *f*, impresión a varios colores *f*; ~ **quality control** *n* QUALITY control de calidad durante el proceso *m*, maestría de la calidad durante fabricación *f*; ~ **specification** *n* QUALITY especificación de proceso *f*; ~ **state** *n* COMP&DP estado de procesos *m*; ~ **suspension** *n* COMP&DP suspensión de procesos *f*; ~ **water** *n* HYDROL, WATER agua de elaboración *f*

process[3] *vt* CHEM tratar, CINEMAT revelar, COMP&DP, FOOD procesar

processed: ~ **data** *n* COMP&DP datos procesados *m*; ~ **disc** *BrE*; ~ **disk** *AmE n* ACOUST disco elaborado *m*; ~ **ice** *n* REFRIG hielo fraccionado *m*

processing *n* COAL enganche de la calle *m*, proceso de fabricación *m*, COMP&DP procesamiento *m*, PETR TECH procesado *m*, refinado *m*, PHOTO revelado *m*, TELECOM procesamiento *m*; ~ **card** *n* TELECOM ficha de procesamiento *f*, tarjeta de procesamiento *f*;

~ **drum** *n* PHOTO tambor de revelado *m*; ~ **equipment** *n* CINEMAT equipo de revelado *m*; ~ **error** *n* COMP&DP, PRINT error de procesado *m*; ~ **facility** *n* GAS instalación de procesamiento *f*, planta de procesamiento *f*; ~ **installation** *n* GAS instalación de procesamiento *f*; ~ **laboratory** *n* CINEMAT laboratorio de revelado *m*; ~ **load** *n* COMP&DP carga de procesamiento *f*; ~ **machine** *n* PHOTO máquina para revelado *f*, PRINT máquina procesadora *f*; ~ **marks** *n pl* CINEMAT marcas de revelado *f pl*; ~ **mode** *n* COMP&DP modo de procesamiento *m*; ~ **plant** *n* MINE planta de transformación *f* (*AmL*), planta de tratamiento *f* (*Esp*); ~ **power** *n* TELECOM capacidad procesamiento *f*, potencia de procesamiento *f*; ~~**priority code** *n* TELECOM código de prioridad de procesamiento *m*; ~ **time** *n* COMP&DP tiempo de procesamiento *m*

processor[1]: ~~**limited** *adj* COMP&DP limitado por el procesador

processor[2] *n* COMP&DP, PRINT, TELECOM procesador *m*; ~ **chassis** *n* PROD chasis de procesador *m*; ~ **hardware fault** *n* PROD anomalía del equipo procesador *f*, avería del equipo procesador *f*, fallo del equipo procesador *f*; ~ **status word** *n* COMP&DP palabra de estado del procesador *f*

Proctor: ~ **compaction test** *n* COAL prueba de resistencia a la compactación *f*; ~ **test** *n* CONST ensayo Proctor *m*

procurement: ~ **lead time** *n* PROD plazo entre la iniciación de una compra y el recibo del material *m*; ~ **request** *n* PROD petición de compra *f*, solicitud de compra *f*; ~ **requisition** *n* PROD petición de compra *f*, solicitud de compra *f*; ~ **specification** *n* SPACE especificación de las adquisiciones *f*

prod *n* MECH ENG punta de contacto *f*, punta de prueba *f*, varilla de contacto *f*, PROD *of loam plate, loam mould* varilla de refuerzo *f*

prodelta: ~ **clay** *n* GEOL arcilla prodeltaica *f*

prodigiosin *n* CHEM prodigiosina *f*

produce *vt* CINEMAT, TV producir

producer *n* GAS productor *m*; ~ **coal** *n* COAL carbón pobre *m*

producing: ~ **horizon** *n* GEOL, PETR TECH horizonte productivo *m*

product: ~ **accounting** *n* PROD contabilización de productos *f*; ~~**and-process mixes** *n pl* TEXTIL combinaciones de productos y procesos *f pl*; ~ **cost** *n* PROD coste de productos *m*; ~ **family** *n* PROD familia de productos *f*; ~ **group** *n* PROD grupo de productos *m*; ~ **liability** *n* QUALITY responsabilidad por producto *f*; ~ **load** *n* REFRIG carga térmica debida al producto *f*; ~ **range** *n* PROD gama de productos *f*; ~ **specification** *n* QUALITY especificación del producto *f*; ~ **test** *n* QUALITY prueba de producto *f*; ~ **tree** *n* PROD árbol de productos *m*; ~ **type** *n* QUALITY tipo de producto *m*; ~ **variant** *n* PROD variante de producto *f*; ~~**variant option descriptions** *n pl* PROD descripciones para la elección entre variantes de productos *f pl*

production *n* COAL producción *f*, MINE obtención *f*, producción *f*, TEXTIL producción *f*; ~ **aircraft** *n* AIR TRANSP avión de producción en serie *m*; ~ **batch** *n* QUALITY lote de producción *m*; ~ **code** *n* CINEMAT código de producción *m*; ~ **console** *n* TV consola de producción *f*; ~ **control** *n* PROD control de la producción *m*; ~ **control room** *n* TV sala de control de producción *f*; ~ **date** *n* PROD fecha de producción *f*; ~ **day** *n* PROD día de producción *m*; ~ **drawing** *n* PROD dibujo de producción *m* (*Esp*), plano de fabricación *m*, plano de producción *m* (*AmL*); ~ **drilling** *n* PETR TECH perforación por percusión *f*, sondeo de producción *m*; ~ **expenses** *n pl* CINEMAT gastos de producción *m pl*; ~ **facilities** *n pl* PETROL instalaciones de producción *f pl*, PROD equipos de producción *m pl*, instalaciones de producción *f pl*, TV instalaciones de producción *f pl*; ~ **flow** *n* TEXTIL flujo de producción *m*; ~ **layer** *n* PETR TECH capa con hidrocarburos *f*, capa de producción *f*, capa productiva *f*; ~ **licence** *n BrE* PETR TECH concesión para producción *f*, licencia de producción *f*; ~ **license** *AmE see production licence BrE*; ~ **line** *n* MECH ENG cadena de producción en serie *f*, circuito de producción *m*, línea de montaje en serie *f*, proceso de fabricación *m*, tren de montaje *m*, PACK cadena de producción *f*, cadena de producción en serie *f*, PROD cadena de producción en serie *f*, línea de montaje en serie *f*, WATER TRANSP *ship building* línea de fabricación *f*, tren de montaje *m*; ~ **mode** *n* GAS modalidad de producción *f*; ~ **order** *n* PROD orden de producción *m*; ~**order issue** *n* PROD emisión de la orden de fabricación *f*; ~ **overheads** *n pl* CINEMAT gastos fijos de producción *m pl*; ~ **per unit area** *n* C&G producción por unidad de área *f*; ~ **phase** *n* PETR TECH fase de producción *f*; ~ **plan** *n* PROD plan de producción *m*; ~ **planning** *n* PROD, QUALITY planificación de la producción *f*; ~ **platform** *n* PETR TECH, PETROL plataforma de producción *f*; ~ **recorder** *n* INSTR registrador de producción *m*; ~ **rule** *n* COMP&DP regla de producción *f*; ~ **schedule** *n* CINEMAT plan de producción *m*, PROD programa de fabricación *m*, programa de producción *m*, TV plan de producción *m*; ~ **scheduling** *n* PROD programación de la producción *f*; ~ **scheduling and control** *n* PROD programación y verificación de la producción *f*; ~ **smoothing** *n* PROD estabilización de la producción *f*; ~ **still** *n* CINEMAT, PHOTO fotografía de producción *f*; ~ **string** *n* PETR TECH sarta de producción *f*, tubería de producción *f*, PETROL columna de producción *f*, tubería de producción *f*; ~ **test** *n* PETROL ensayo de producción *m*, prueba de producción *f*; ~ **time** *n* PROD tiempo de fabricación *m*; ~ **tubing** *n* PETR TECH tubería de producción *f*, tubing *m*; ~ **unit of measure** *n* PROD unidad de medida de la fabricación *f*; ~ **well** *n* GAS, PETR TECH, PETROL pozo de producción *m*

productive: ~ **time** *n* COMP&DP tiempo productivo *m*
productiveness *n* PROD productividad *f*
productivity *n* PROD productividad *f*; ~ **index** *n* PETROL índice de productividad *m*
professional: ~ **deafness** *n* ACOUST sordera profesional *f*
profile: ~ **dispersion** *n* OPT, TELECOM dispersión del perfil *f*; ~**dispersion factor** *n* OPT factor de dispersión de perfil *m*; ~**dispersion parameter** *n* TELECOM parámetro de dispersión del perfil *m*; ~ **drag** *n* AIR TRANSP resistencia aerodinámica del perfil *f*; ~ **grinder** *n* MECH ENG rectificadora de plantillas *f*; ~ **grinding** *n* MECH ENG rectificado con plantillas *m*; ~ **parameter** *n* OPT parámetro del perfil *m*; ~ **projector** *n* METR comparador óptico de proyección para verificar perfiles *m*, proyector de perfiles *m*

profiles: ~ **of spectral lines** *n pl* RAD PHYS contornos de las rayas espectrales *m pl*
profiling *n* MECH ENG perfilado *m*; ~ **roller** *n* MECH ENG *of milling machine* rodillo de perfilar *m*
progesterone *n* CHEM progesterona *f*
progradation *n* OCEAN progradación *f*
prograde[1]: ~ **metamorphism** *n* GEOL metamorfismo progresivo *m*
prograde[2] *vi* GEOL progradar
program[1] *n* COMP&DP programa *m*, PROD, TELECOM, TV *AmE* (*see programme BrE*); ~ **body** *n* COMP&DP cuerpo del programa *m*; ~ **checkout** *n* COMP&DP comprobación de programas *f*; ~ **control** *n* COMP&DP control de programas *m*; ~ **counter** *n* COMP&DP contador de instrucciones *m*; ~ **design** *n* COMP&DP diseño de programas *m*; ~ **development** *n* COMP&DP desarrollo de programas *m*; ~ **execution** *n* COMP&DP ejecución de programas *f*; ~ **file** *n* COMP&DP archivo de programa *m*, fichero de programa *m*; ~ **instruction** *n* COMP&DP instrucción de programa *f*; ~ **library** *n* COMP&DP biblioteca de programas *f*; ~ **linking** *n* COMP&DP enlace de programas *m*; ~ **listing** *n* COMP&DP listado de programa *m*; ~ **parameter** *n* COMP&DP parámetro de programa *m*; ~ **part** *n* COMP&DP parte de programa *f*; ~ **scheduling** *n* COMP&DP planificación de programas *f*; ~ **specification** *n* COMP&DP especificación de programas *f*; ~ **status word** *n* (*PSW*) COMP&DP palabra de estado de programa *f*; ~ **storage** *n* COMP&DP almacenamiento de programas *m*; ~ **structure** *n* COMP&DP estructura de programa *f*; ~ **testing** *n* COMP&DP prueba de programa *f*; ~ **unit** *n* COMP&DP unidad de programa *f*; ~ **verification** *n* COMP&DP verificación de programa *f*
program[2] *vt* COMP&PD programar, PROD, TELECOM, TV *AmE* (*see programme BrE*)
programmable[1] *adj* COMP&DP, PROD, TELECOM, TV programable
programmable[2]: ~ **array logic** *n* (*PAL*) COMP&DP lógica de matriz programable *f* (*PAL*), TELECOM, TV array lógico preformable *m* (*PAL*), arreglo lógico programable *m* (*PAL*); ~ **box** *n* CONST elemento programable *m*; ~ **control** *n* TELECOM control programable *m*; ~ **controller** *n* PROD controlador programable *m*; ~**controller system** *n* PROD sistema de controlador programable *m*; ~ **controls** *n pl* PROD controles programables *m*; ~ **device** *n* COMP&DP, TELECOM dispositivo programable *m*; ~**encoder position switch** *n* PROD interruptor de posición de codificador programable *m*; ~ **interval timer** *n* (*PIT*) ELECTRON temporizador de intervalos programable *m* (*TIP*); ~ **logic array** *n* COMP&DP matriz lógica programable *f*; ~ **logic controller** *n* PROD controlador lógico programable *m*; ~**motor protector** *n* PROD protector de motor programable *m*; ~ **oscillator** *n* ELECTRON oscilador programable *m*; ~ **read-only memory** *n* (*PROM*) COMP&DP memoria programable de solo lectura *f* (*PROM*); ~ **sequencer** *n* TELECOM secuenciador programable *m*; ~**signal generator** *n* ELECTRON generador de señal programable *m*; ~ **uni-junction transistor** *n* ELECTRON transistor de una sola unión programable *m*
programme[1] *n BrE* PROD, TELECOM, TV programa *m*; ~ **audio-track** *n BrE* TV pista de audio de programas *f*; ~ **cost** *n BrE* TV costo del programa *m*; ~ **error flag** *n BrE* PROD banderín de errores del programa *m*;

~ evaluation and review technique *n BrE* (*PERT*) SPACE método para planificar y controlar proyectos *m* (*PERT*); **~ for computer-processing wire-line logs** *n BrE* PETR TECH programa para proceso por ordenador de los registros eléctricos *m*; **~-identification signal** *n BrE* TV señal de identificación del programa *f*; **~ monitor** *n BrE* TV monitor de programa *m*; **~ repeater** *n BrE* TV repetidor de programas *m*; **~ rung** *n BrE* PROD pase de programa *m*; **~ scan time** *n BrE* PROD tiempo de exploración del programa *m*; **~ scanning** *n BrE* PROD exploración de programa *f*, programa de exploración *m*; **~ selector** *n BrE* TELECOM selector de programas *m*; **~ timer** *n BrE* LAB dispositivo de accionamiento por tiempos programados *m* (*AmL*), temporizador programable *m* (*Esp*)

programme[2] *vt BrE* PROD, TELECOM, TV programar

programmed[1] *adj* COMP&DP, PROD, TELECOM, TV programado

programmed[2]: **~ control** *n* TV control programado *m*; **~ logic array** *n* (*PLA*) COMP&DP matriz lógica programada *f* (*PLA*); **~ servo-system** *n* SPACE servomecanismo programado *m*, servosistema programado *m*

programmer *n* COMP&DP, PROD programador *m*; **~ unit** *n* COMP&DP unidad de programador *f*

programming *n* COMP&DP programación *f*; **~ language** *n* COMP&DP lenguaje de programación *m*; **~ logic** *n* PROD lógica de programación *f*; **~ unit** *n* COMP&DP unidad de programa *f*

progress *n* PROD avance *m*, progreso *m*; **~ control** *n* PROD control del avance *n*

progression *n* MATH progresión *f*; **~ die** *n* MECH ENG *press tools* estampa progresiva *f*, troquel progresivo *m*; **~ speed** *n* TRANSP aumento de la velocidad *m*, velocidad de avance *f*

progressive: **~ ageing** *n* P&R envejecimiento progresivo *m*; ; **~ failure** *n* COAL rotura progresiva *f*; **~ interlace** *n* TV entrelazado progresivo *m*; **~ metamorphism** *n* GEOL metamorfismo progresivo *m*; **~ proof** *n* PRINT prueba de gama *f*; **~ switching magazine** *n* TELECOM almacén de conmutación progresiva *m*; **~ system** *n* TRANSP sistema progresivo *m*; **~ transition** *n* TELECOM transición progresiva *f*; **~ unconformity** *n* GEOL discordancia progresiva *f*

prohibited: **~ area** *n* MILIT, WATER TRANSP *navigation* zona prohibida *f*

prohibition: **~ notice** *n* SAFE *paper, board* notificación de prohibición *f*; **~ sign** *n* SAFE *civil engineering* letrero de prohibición *m*

project[1]: **~ controller** *n* SPACE controlador de proyecto *m*; **~-design manager** *n* MECH ENG gerente de diseño de proyectos *m*; **~ manager** *n* CONST, PROD director de proyecto *m*; **~ monitoring** *n* CONST control del proyecto *m*; **~ production** *n* PROD ejecución del proyecto *f*

project[2] *vt* CINEMAT, GEOM proyectar

projected: **~ available stock** *n* PROD existencias previstas disponibles *f*; **~ background** *n* CINEMAT fondo proyectado *m*

projectile *n* MILIT proyectil *m*; **~ energy** *n* MILIT energía del proyectil *f*

projecting: **~ hairs** *n pl* TEXTIL pelos salientes *m pl*

projection *n* CONST saliente *m*, vuelo *m*, *of stone, gutter beyond wall* proyección *f*, CRYSTALL, GEOM, PHOTO, PHYS proyección *f*; **~ along the c-axis** *n* CRYSTALL proyección a lo largo del eje c *f*; **~ axis** *n* CINEMAT eje de proyección *m*; **~ box** *n* CINEMAT proyector *m*; **~ electron-beam lithography** *n* ELECTRON litografía por proyección de haz de electrones *f*; **~ head** *n* CINEMAT cabezal de proyección *m*; **~ lamp** *n* CINEMAT, PHOTO lámpara de proyección *f*; **~ length** *n* CONST longitud del saliente *f*; **~ lens** *n* INSTR lente de proyección *f*, PHOTO lente de proyección *f*, objetivo de proyección *m*; **~ lithography** *n* ELECTRON litografía por proyección *f*; **~ microscope** *n* INSTR microscopio de proyección *m*; **~ port** *n* CINEMAT ventanilla de proyección *f*; **~ printer** *n* CINEMAT impresor a proyección *m*; **~ screen** *n* CINEMAT, INSTR pantalla de proyección *f*; **~ speed** *n* CINEMAT velocidad de proyección *f*; **~ television** *n* TV televisión proyectada una pantalla *f*; **~ welding** *n* CONST, PROD soldadura con saliente *f*

projectionist *n* CINEMAT proyeccionista *m*

projective: **~ geometry** *n* GEOM geometría proyectiva *f*

projector *n* CINEMAT, PHOTO proyector *m*; **~ attachment** *n* INSTR acoplamiento proyector *m*; **~ compass** *n* WATER TRANSP aguja de proyección *f*; **~ lamp** *n* CINEMAT, PHOTO lámpara del proyector *f*; **~ lens** *n* INSTR lente proyectora *f*; **~-lens pole piece** *n* INSTR pieza polar de la lente proyectora *f*

prolate[1] *adj* GEOM alargado hacia los polos

prolate[2]: **~ ellipsoid** *n* PHYS elipsoide prolate *m*; **~ spheroid** *n* GEOM esferoide alargado *m*

PROM[1] *abbr* (*programmable read-only memory*) COMP&DP PROM (*memoria programable de solo lectura*)

PROM[2]: **~ programmer** *n* COMP&DP programador de PROM *m*

promenade: **~ deck** *n* WATER TRANSP cubierta de paseo *f*

promethium *n* (*Pm*) CHEM, NUCL promecio *m* (*Pm*)

prominence *n* SPACE prominencia *f*, protuberancia *f*

prominent: **~ joint** *n* C&G junta prominente *f*

promontory *n* WATER TRANSP *of land* promontorio *m*

promoter *n* CHEM promotor *m*

promoting *n* CHEM promoción *f*

prompt *n* COMP&DP apremio *m*, mensaje *m*, orientación *f*, PROD apremio *m*; **~ critical** *n* NUCL crítico con neutrones inmediatos *m* (*Esp*), crítico con neutrones no retardados *m* (*AmL*); **~ neutron** *n* PHYS traza de neutrones *f*, RAD PHYS neutrón inmediato *m*

prompter *n* TV analizador *m*

prong *n BrE* (*cf tine AmE*) CONST diente *m*, púa *f*, MECH diente *m*, MECH ENG diente *m*, garra *f*, punta *f*, púa *f*; **~ center** *AmE*, **~ centre** *BrE n* MECH ENG *lathe* punto de tres dientes *m*; **~ chuck** *n* MECH ENG plato de garras *m*, plato de puntas *m*, plato de púas *m*

pronged: **~ shovel** *n* CONST excavadora con púas *f*

prontosil *n* CHEM prontosil *m*

Prony: **~ brake** *n* AUTO, VEH freno de Prony *m*

proof *n* PHOTO prueba *f*, PRINT prueba de imprenta *f*, PROD *trial* ensayo *m*, experimento *m*, prueba *f*; **~-correction marks** *n* PRINT signos de corrección de pruebas *m pl*; **~ load** *n* AIR TRANSP *airworthiness*, MECH ENG *of fasteners* carga de prueba *f*; **~ marks** *n pl* PRINT signos de corrección de pruebas *m pl*; **~ pressure** *n* HYDRAUL presión de prueba *f*, MECH ENG presión de prueba *f*, voltaje de prueba *m*, REFRIG presión de prueba *f*; **~ test** *n* ELEC prueba *f*

proofing: **~ system** *n* PRINT sistema para obtener pruebas *m*

proofreading *n* PRINT corrección de pruebas *f*
prop *n* COAL adema *f*, amparo *m*, apea *f*, apoyo *m*, estemple *m* (*AmL*), estípula *f*, mamposta *f* (*AmL*), pilar *m*, puntal *m*, tutor *m*, vela *f*, CONST apea *f*, apoyo *m*, puntal *m*, MECH ENG apoyo *m*, contrafuerte *m*, puntal *m*, soporte *m*, sostén *m*, MINE adema *f*, apea *f*, apoyo *m* (*AmL*), cercha *f* (*Esp*), columna *f* (*Esp*), estemple *m* (*AmL*), mamposta *f* (*AmL*), poste *m* (*Esp*), puntal *m*, taco *m* (*AmL*), tope *m*, topes de fin de carrera *m pl*, trinquete *m*; ~ **drawing** *n* MINE arranca-apeas *m*, arranca-estemples *m*
propadiene *n* CHEM propadieno *m*
propagate[1] *vt* WAVE PHYS propagar
propagate[2] *vi* OPT propagarse
propagation *n* COMP&DP, TELECOM, WAVE PHYS propagación *f*; ~ **anomaly** *n* TV anomalía de propagación *f*; ~ **coefficient** *n* ACOUST, TELECOM coeficiente de propagación *m*; ~ **constant** *n* OPT, PHYS, TELECOM constante de propagación *f*; ~ **delay** *n* COMP&DP retardo de propagación *m*, SPACE *communications* demora de propagación *f*, retardo de propagación *m*; ~ **equation** *n* PHYS ecuación de propagación *f*; ~ **loss** *n* PHYS pérdida por propagación *f*; ~ **medium** *n* ELEC ENG medio de propagación *m*; ~ **mode** *n* OPT modo de propagación *f*; ~ **path** *n* ELEC ENG vía de propagación *f*; ~ **sensitivity** *n* MINE sensibilidad de propagación *f*; ~ **speed** *n* ACOUST, WAVE PHYS velocidad de propagación *f*; ~ **velocity** *n* TELECOM, WAVE PHYS velocidad de propagación *f*
propane *n* CHEM, PETR TECH propano *m*; ~ **tanker** *n* PETR TECH, WATER TRANSP buque-cisterna de propano *m*
propanoic *adj* CHEM propanóico
propanol *n* CHEM propanol *m*
propanone *n* CHEM acetona *f*, propanona *f*, COATINGS, FOOD acetona *f*, P&R *solvent* acetona *f*, propanona *f*
propargyl *n* CHEM propargílico *f*
propedeutics *n* CHEM propedéutica *f*
propellant *n* CHEM propelente *m*, propulsante *m*, POLL propelente *m*, propergol *m*; ~ **force** *n* MILIT *of rocket* fuerza del propulsante *f*; ~ **fuel** *n* SPACE combustible propulsante *m*, combustible propulsor *m*; ~ **grain** *n* SPACE grano propulsor *m*; ~ **mass** *n* SPACE masa propulsora *f*
propelled: ~ **charge** *n* MILIT carga impulsada *f*
propellent: ~ **fuel** *n* SPACE combustible propulsante *m*, combustible propulsor *m*
propeller *n* AIR TRANSP, MAR POLL hélice *f*, MECH ENG impulsor *m*, inyector *m*, propulsor *m*, *screw-propeller* propulsor de hélice *m*, WATER TRANSP *of boat* hélice *f*; ~ **boss** *n* WATER TRANSP cubo de la hélice *m*, núcleo de la hélice *m*; ~ **bracket** *n* WATER TRANSP arbotante *m*; ~ **drive** *n* TRANSP propulsión por hélice *f*; ~ **fan** *n* HEAT ENG, MECH ENG, REFRIG ventilador de hélice *m*, ventilador helicoidal *m*; ~ **governor** *n* AIR TRANSP gobernador de hélice *m*, regulador de hélice *m*; ~ **hub** *n* AIR TRANSP cubo de la hélice *m*, WATER TRANSP cubo de la hélice *m*, núcleo de la hélice *m*; ~ **pitch** *n* AIR TRANSP paso de la hélice *m*; ~ **relay unit** *n* AIR TRANSP unidad de relé de la hélice *f*; ~ **shaft** *n* BrE (*cf drive shaft AmE*) AIR TRANSP eje de la hélice *m*, AUTO árbol de mando *m*, árbol de transmisión *m*, eje de la transmisión *m*, eje impulsor *m*, eje motriz *m*, árbol impulsor *m*, MECH ENG eje motor *m*, árbol de transmisión *m*, eje conductor *m*, VEH árbol impulsor *m*, eje de la transmisión *m*, eje propulsor *m*, árbol de

mando *m*, árbol de transmisión *m*, WATER TRANSP *boat building* eje de cola *m*, eje portahélice *m*; ~**-shaft tunnel** *n* BrE (*cf drive-shaft tunnel AmE*) AUTO, VEH alojamiento del árbol de mando *m*, túnel del árbol de transmisión *m*; ~ **thrust** *n* TRANSP empuje de la hélice *m*, tracción de la hélice *f*; ~**-thrust coefficient** *n* TRANSP coeficiente de propulsión de la hélice *m*; ~ **torque** *n* AIR TRANSP par de la hélice *m*; ~ **turbine** *n* FUELLESS turbina de hélice *f*; ~**-turbine plane** *n* AIR TRANSP, TRANSP avión turbo-hélice *m*; ~ **wash** *n* AIR TRANSP *slipstream* flujo de la hélice *m*, torbellino de la hélice *m*
propelling: ~ **charge** *n* MILIT carga propulsora *f*; ~ **force** *n* MECH ENG fuerza de propulsión *f*, fuerza motriz *f*; ~ **gear** *n* MECH ENG aparato de propulsión *m*, dispositivo transportador *m*; ~ **nozzle** *n* AIR TRANSP tobera propulsora *f*
propene *n* CHEM, PETR TECH propeno *m*
propenoic *adj* CHEM propenóico
propenylic *adj* CHEM propenílico
proper: ~ **shutdown** *n* NUCL parada segura *f*; ~ **subset** *n* COMP&DP subconjunto correcto *m*; ~ **time** *n* PHYS tiempo propio *m*
property *n* CHEM *characteristic*, GAS, GEOM propiedad *f*
propfan *n* AIR TRANSP *propeller* propfan *m*
propjet: ~ **engine** *n* TRANSP motor de propulsión a chorro *m*
proportion: ~ **of nonconforming items** *n* QUALITY proporción de unidades inconformes *f*
proportional: ~**-control valve** *n* PROD válvula de control proporcional *f*; ~ **counter** *n* PHYS contador proporcional *m*; ~ **pressure-reducing valve** *n* PROD válvula de reducción de presión proporcional *f*; ~ **reducer** *n* PHOTO reductor proporcional *m*; ~ **sampling** *n* QUALITY muestreo proporcional *m*; ~ **valve** *n* PROD válvula proporcional *f*; ~ **weir** *n* HYDROL vertedero proporcional *m*; ~ **width** *n pl* PRINT anchura proporcional *f*
proportionate: ~ **arm** *n* ELEC *bridge* brazo proporcionado *m*
proportioning *n* CHEM proporcionamiento *m*; ~ **valve** *n* AUTO válvula de control *f*, válvula de dosificación *f*, válvula de regulación *f*
propping *n* CONST entibación *f*, sistema de apuntalamiento *m*; ~ **agent** *n* PETROL material de apoyo *m*
proprietary: ~ **information** *n* PROD información específica *f*
propulsion *n* CHEM propulsión *f*, MECH ENG impulsión *f*, impulso *m*, propulsión *f*, SPACE, WATER TRANSP propulsión *f*; ~ **by air pressure** *n* TRANSP propulsión por presión de aire *f*; ~ **by reaction** *n* SPACE propulsión por reacción *f*; ~ **by spiral-drive with varying pitch** *n* TRANSP propulsión por accionamiento espiral con paso variable *f*; ~ **by stationary drive-wheels** *n* TRANSP propulsión por ruedas motrices estacionarias fijas *f*; ~ **engine** *n* WATER TRANSP motor propulsor *m*, máquina propulsora *f*; ~ **magnet** *n* TRANSP imán de propulsión *m*; ~ **system** *n* SPACE sistema de propulsión *m*; ~ **unit** *n* AIR TRANSP, SPACE unidad de propulsión *f*
propulsive: ~ **force** *n* MECH ENG fuerza de propulsión *f*, fuerza motriz *f*
propwood *n* CONST madera para entibación *f*
propyl *n* CHEM propilo *m*
propylamine *n* CHEM propilamina *f*

propylene n CHEM, PETR TECH propileno m; ~ **oxide** n CHEM, DETERG óxido propilénico m

propylic adj CHEM propílico

propyne n CHEM propino m

propynoic adj CHEM propinóico

prosopite n MINERAL prosopita f

prospect: ~ **hole** n MINE agujero de prospección m, agujero de sondeo m, pozo de cateo m (AmL), pozo de prospección m (Esp); ~ **tunnel** n MINE socavón de cateo m, túnel de prospección m

prospecting n MINE busca de minerales f (AmL), calicata f, cata f (Esp), cateo m (AmL), exploración f, prospección f (Esp), sondeo m, PETR TECH exploración f, prospección f (Esp), sondeo m; ~ **dredge** n MINE draga de prospección f; ~ **level** n MINE galería de cateo f (AmL), galería de exploración f (Esp), galería de prospección f (Esp), galería de reconocimiento f (AmL)

prospection n MINE cateo m (AmL), prospección f (Esp)

protactinium n (Pa) CHEM, RAD PHYS protactinio m (Pa)

protagon n CHEM protágono m

protease n CHEM proteasa f

protected: ~ **area** n CONST zona protegida f; ~ **field** n COMP&DP campo protegido m; ~ **location** n COMP&DP emplazamiento protegido m, posición protegida f (Esp), ubicación protegida f (AmL); ~ **screw** n MECH ENG of vice tornillo de seguridad m

protecting: ~ **chamfer** n MECH ENG bisel de protección m; ~ **lacquer** n COATINGS laca protectora f

protection n ELEC ENG, SAFE, SPACE protección f; ~ **against dripping water** n PROD protección contra goteo de agua f; ~ **against exposure at work** n SAFE protección contra la exposición a riesgos en el trabajo f; ~ **against gas** n MILIT chemical warfare protección contra gases f; ~ **against heavy seas** n PROD protección contra mar gruesa f; ~ **cage** n OCEAN jaula protectora f; ~ **capacitor** n ELEC ENG condensador protector m; ~ **circuit** n ELEC ENG, TELECOM circuito de protección m; ~ **coat** n PACK recubrimiento protector m; ~ **coating** n PROD capa protectora f; ~ **copy** n CINEMAT copia de protección f; ~ **diode** n ELECTRON diodo de protección m; ~ **helmet** n PETROL casco protector m; ~ **layer** n PACK capa de protección f; ~ **master** n CINEMAT copia maestra de protección f; ~ **of pinch points on idlers** n MECH ENG protección de punta de espolón en las ruedas locas f; ~ **resistor** n ELEC ENG resistencia protectora f; ~ **sleeve** n MECH ENG manguito de protección m; ~ **time** n PROD tiempo de protección m

Protection: ~ **and Indemnity Association** n MAR POLL Asociación de Protección e Indemnización f

protective[1] adj SAFE, TEXTIL protector

protective[2]: ~ **agent** n PACK, SAFE agente protector m; ~ **apron** n SAFE delantal protector m; ~ **armor** AmE, ~ **armour** BrE n MILIT blindaje protector m; ~ **bonnet** n COATINGS sombrerete de protección m, sombrero de protección m; ~ **cap** n MECH ENG cubierta protectora f, tapa protectora f; ~ **circuit** n ELEC circuito de protección m; ~ **clothing** n MILIT chemical warfare vestimenta protectora f, SAFE prendas protectoras f pl; ~ **clothing against heat and fire** n SAFE prendas protectoras antitérmicas e ignífugas f pl; ~ **clothing for cold-storage work** n

SAFE prendas protectoras termoaislantes f pl; ~ **clothing for rescue services** n SAFE prendas protectoras para trabajos de salvamento f pl; ~ **coat of paint** n COATINGS capa protectora de pintura f; ~ **coating** n AmE (cf fibre coating BrE) COATINGS, OPT revestimiento protector m, P&R capa protectora f, PAPER recubrimiento protector m, recubrimiento tipo barrera m, PHYS revestimiento protector m; ~ **coating of paint** n COATINGS capa protectora de pintura f; ~ **colloid** n CHEM coloide protector m; ~ **conductor** n ELEC ENG conductor de protección m; ~ **cover** n COATINGS, PACK, SAFE cubierta protectora f; ~ **covering** n COATINGS, PACK, SAFE envoltura protectora f; ~ **cream** n SAFE crema protectora f; ~ **film** n COATINGS, PACK película protectora f; ~ **finish** n COATINGS acabado protector m; ~ **footwear** n SAFE calzado protector m; ~ **gaiters** n SAFE polainas protectoras f pl; ~ **glass** n SAFE cristal protector m, vidrio protector m; ~ **glass for welder's goggles** n SAFE cristal protector de gafas de soldador m; ~ **glasses** n pl LAB, MECH ENG, OPT, PROD, SAFE anteojos de protección m pl (AmL), gafas protectoras f pl (Esp); ~ **gloves** n pl SAFE guantes protectores m pl; ~ **gown** n LAB, SAFE bata protectora f; ~ **helmet** n SAFE casco protector m; ~ **hood** n INSTR campana protectora f, MILIT chemical warfare capucha protectora f, SAFE campana protectora f, capucha protectora f; ~ **lacquer** n COATINGS laca protectora f; ~ **layer** n COATINGS capa protectora f; ~ **multiple earthing** n BrE (cf protective multiple grounding AmE) ELEC installation puesta a tierra de protección múltiple f; ~ **multiple grounding** n AmE (cf protective multiple earthing BrE) ELEC installation puesta a tierra de protección múltiple f; ~ **oxide coat** n COATINGS revestimiento protector antióxido m; ~ **paint** n C&G, COATINGS pintura protectora f; ~ **relay** n ELEC ENG relé protector m; ~ **restraint system** n SAFE sistema protector de sujeción m; ~ **screen** n PROD pantalla protectora f, SAFE mampara protectora f, communications pantalla protectora f, rejilla protectora f; ~ **sheathing** n COATINGS forro protector m, revestimiento protector m; ~ **spark discharger** n ELEC chispero protector m, descargador de chispa protector m, saltachispas protector m; ~ **spectacles** n pl LAB, MECH ENG, OPT, PROD, SAFE anteojos de protección m pl (AmL), gafas protectoras f pl (Esp); ~ **strip** n PROD cinta protectora f; ~ **suit** n SAFE traje protector m; ~ **wrapper** n PACK envoltura protectora f

protein n CHEM proteína f; ~ **fibers** AmE, ~ **fibres** BrE n pl TEXTIL fibras proteínicas f pl; ~ **size** n TEXTIL apresto proteínico m

proteinic adj CHEM proteínico

proterozoic n GEOL proterozoico m

protid n CHEM compound prótido m

protide n CHEM compound prótido m

protobastite n MINERAL protobastita f

protocol n CHEM, COMP&DP, SPACE, TELECOM protocolo m; ~ **class** n TELECOM clase de protocolo f; ~ **control indicator** n TELECOM indicador de control del protocolo m; ~ **control information** n (PCI) TELECOM información para el control del protocolo f; ~ **converter** n COMP&DP, TELECOM convertidor de protocolo m; ~ **data unit** n (PDU) TELECOM unidad de datos de protocolo f; ~ **discriminator** n (PD) TELECOM discriminador de protocolo m; ~ **error**

class *n* TELECOM clase de error del protocolo *f*; **~-implementation conformance statement** *n* (*PICS*) TELECOM declaración de conformidad en el cumplimiento del protocolo *f*; **~-reference model** *n* (*PRM*) TELECOM modelo de referencia del protocolo *m*; **~ unit** *n* (*PU*) TELECOM unidad de protocolo *f*

protolith *n* GEOL protolito *m*

protolysis *n* CHEM protólisis *f*

proton *n* (*p*) CHEM, ELEC ENG, NUCL, PART PHYS, PHYS, RAD PHYS protón *m* (*p*); **~-absorptive capacity** *n* POLL, RAD PHYS capacidad de absorción de protones *f*, capacidad de absorción protónica *f*; **~-antiproton collider** *n* PART PHYS cámara de reacción protón-antiprotón *f*; **~-antiproton collision** *n* PART PHYS colisión protón-antiprotón *f*; **~-antiproton collision at 500 GeV** *n* PART PHYS colisión de protones antiprotones con energía de 500 GeV *f*; **~ beam** *n* ELECTRON, PART PHYS haz de protones *m*; **~ irradiation** *n* SPACE irradiación de protones *f*, irradiación protónica *f*; **~ microscope** *n* INSTR microscopio protónico *m*; **~ number** *n* PART PHYS número de protones *m*; **~-proton collision** *n* PART PHYS colisión protón-protón *f*; **~ resonance magnetometer** *n* PETROL magnetómetro por resonancia protónica *m*; **~ supersynchrotron** *n* PART PHYS super sincrotrón de protones *m*; **~ synchrotron** *n* (*PS*) PART PHYS sincrotrón de protones *m*; **~ telescope** *n* INSTR telescopio protónico *m*

prototype *n* WATER TRANSP *naval architecture* prototipo *m*; **~ stage** *n* RAD PHYS etapa del prototipo *f*; **~ tooling** *n* MECH ENG herramientas prototipo *f pl*

protoxide *n* CHEM protóxido *m*

protractor *n* GEOM graduador *m*, transportador *m*, METR *assayer's mark* goniómetro *m*, protractor *m*, transportador *m*, WATER TRANSP *for navigation* transportador de ángulos *m*

proustite *n* MINERAL proustita *f*

prove *vt* MINE examinar, probar (*Esp*), reconocer (*AmL*)

proven: **~ area** *n* PETR TECH área comprobada *f*; **~ reserves** *n pl* PETR TECH, PETROL reservas comprobadas *f pl*

provide: **~ an oxygen supply** *vt* CHEM TECH, PHYS suministrar una reserva de oxígeno; **~ power** *vt* PROD suministrar energía; **~ spontaneous emission of light** *vt* RAD PHYS proporcionar una fuente de emisión espontánea de luz

proving: **~ cabinet** *n* FOOD armario de fermentación *m*, cámara de fermentación *f*; **~ flight** *n* AIR TRANSP vuelo de demostración *m*, vuelo de pruebas *m*; **~ run** *n* NUCL prueba funcional *f*; **~ trial** *n* NUCL prueba funcional *f*

provision *n* TELECOM prestación *f*

prow *n* WATER TRANSP obra muerta de proa *f*, proa de un bajel *f*

proximate: **~ analysis** *n* CHEM, GEOL análisis inmediato *m*

proximity: **~ effect** *n* ELEC ENG efecto de proximidad *m*; **~ lithography** *n* ELECTRON litografía de proximidad *f*; **~ log** *n* PETR TECH diagrafía de proximidad *f*, diagrama de proximidad *m*, perfil de resistividad *m*, PETROL perfil de proximidad *m*, perfil de resistividad *m*; **~ mask** *n* ELECTRON máscara de proximidad *f*; **~ switch** *n* ELEC, ELEC ENG conmutador de proximidad *m*, interruptor de proximidad *m*, PROD

conmutador de proximidad *m*; **~-warning indicator** *n* AIR TRANSP indicador de aviso de proximidad *m*

projection: **~ lens** *n* CINEMAT, OPT objetivo de proyección *m*

PRT *abbr* (*personal rapid transport*) TRANSP transporte privado rápido *m*

prulaurasin *n* CHEM prulaurasina *f*

pruner *n* AGRIC, MECH ENG podador *m*

pruning: **~ saw** *n* MECH ENG serrucho para podar *m*

Prussian: **~ blue** *n* CHEM azul de Prusia *m*

prussiate *n* CHEM prusiato *m*

prussic: **~ acid** *n* CHEM ácido prúsico *m*

pry *vt AmE* (*cf prise BrE*) CONST apalancar

PS *abbr* CHEM, P&R, PACK (*polystyrene*) PS (*poliestireno*), PART PHYS (*proton synchrotron*) sincrotrón de protones *m*, TELECOM (*packet switch*) conmutador de paquete *m*

PSA *abbr* GAS (*pressure swing adsorption*) ACP (*adsorción por cambios de presión*), NUCL (*probabilistic safety assessment*) APS (*análisis probabilista de la seguridad*)

psalterium *n* AGRIC omaso *m*

psamite *n* PETROL psamita *f*

PSE *abbr* (*packet-switching exchange*) COMP&DP, TELECOM CCP (*central de conmutación de datos*)

pseudo[1]: **~-random** *adj* TELECOM pseudoaleatorio, semialeatorio

pseudo[2]: **~-acid** *n* CHEM pseudoácido *m*; **~-elliptic filter** *n* SPACE *communications* filtro pseudoelíptico *m*; **~-instruction** *n* COMP&DP pseudoinstrucción *f*, sentencia declarativa *f*; **~-ionone** *n* CHEM pseudoionona *f*; **~-language** *n* COMP&DP pseudolenguaje *m*; **~-lock** *n* TV pseudofijación *f*; **~-plastic** *n* CHEM pseudoplástico *m*; **~-potentiometric head** *n* PETR TECH altura pseudopotenciométrica *f*, cabezal pseudopotenciométrico *m*; **~-random binary sequence** *n* (*PRBS*) TELECOM secuencia binaria pseudoaleatoria *f*; **~-random noise** *n* TELECOM ruido pseudoaleatorio *m*; **~-random noise code** *n* TELECOM código de ruidos pseudoaleatorios *m*; **~-random number** *n* COMP&DP número pseudoaleatorio *m*; **~-random signal** *n* TELECOM señal pseudoaleatoria *f*; **~-sonic log** *n* PETR TECH diagrafía pseudosónica *f*, perfil pseudosónico *m*, registro pseudosónico *m*; **~-sonic profile** *n* PETR TECH perfil pseudosónico *m*, registro pseudosónico *m*

pseudocode *n* COMP&DP pseudocódigo *m*

pseudomalachite *n* MINERAL pseudomalaquita *f*

pseudomer *n* CHEM pseudómero *m*

pseudomeric *adj* CHEM pseudomérico

pseudomerism *n* CHEM pseudomería *f*

pseudomorph *n* GEOL pseudoamorfo *m*

pseudonitrole *n* CHEM pseudonitrol *m*

pseudonoise *n* TELECOM pseudorruido *m*; **~ sequence** *n satellite communications* secuencia de pseudorruido *f*

pseudosphere *n* GEOM pseudoesfera *f*

psi *abbr* (*pounds per square inch*) METR, PETR TECH LPPC (*libras por pulgada cuadrada*)

psilomelane *n* MINERAL psilomelana *f*

PSK *abbr* (*phase-shift keying, phase-shift keying modulation*) COMP&DP, ELECTRON, SPACE, TELECOM PSK (*conmutación de desplazamiento de fase, conmutación de retardo de fase, modulación por desviación de fase, modulación por variación de fase*)

PSN *abbr* COMP&DP, ELECTRON, TELECOM (*packet-*

switched network) m, red de conmutación por paquetes *f*, red de transmisión por paquetes *f*, COMP&DP, TELECOM (*packet-switching node*) nodo de conmutación de paquetes *m*

psophometric: ~ **power** *n* TELECOM potencia sofométrica *f*; ~-**weighting factor** *n* SPACE *communications* factor ponderado sofométrico *m*

PSTN *abbr* (*public switched telephone network*) TELECOM red telefónica conmutada *f*

PSU *abbr* (*power-supply unit*) ELEC, ELEC ENG fuente de alimentación eléctrica *f*, MILIT unidad de energía *f*, PROD fuente de alimentación eléctrica *f*, unidad de alimentación *f*

PSW *abbr* (*program status word*) COMP&DP palabra de estado de programa *f*

psychotrine *n* CHEM sicotrina *f*

psychrometer *n* LAB psicrómetro *m*, sicrómetro *m*, REFRIG sicrómetro *m*

psychrometry *n* PHYS psicometría *f*

Pt *abbr* (*platinum*) CHEM, ELEC, METALL Pt (*platino*)

PTC *abbr* INSTR (*parabolic trough conveyor*) PTC (*transportador de cinta cóncava parabólico*), SPACE (*passive thermal control*) PTC (*control térmico pasivo*)

pterin *n* CHEM pterina *f*

PTFE *abbr* (*polytetrafluoroethylene*) CHEM, P&R PTFE (*politetrafluoretileno*)

ptomaine *n* CHEM ptomaína *f*

ptygmatic: ~ **fold** *n* GEOL pliegue ptigmático *m*

p-type: ~ **base** *n* ELECTRON base tipo p *f*; ~ **collector** *n* ELECTRON colector tipo p *m*; ~ **conductivity** *n* ELEC ENG conductividad por portadores positivos *f*; ~ **diffusion** *n* ELECTRON difusión tipo p *f*; ~ **epitaxial layer** *n* ELECTRON estratificador epitaxial tipo p *m*; ~ **implanted layer** *n* ELECTRON estratificador añadido tipo p *m*; ~ **impurity** *n* ELECTRON impureza de tipo p *f*; ~ **semiconductor** *n* ELECTRON semiconductor de tipo p *m*, PHYS semiconductor tipo p *m*; ~ **silicon** *n* ELECTRON silicio de tipo p *m*; ~ **silicon substrate** *n* ELECTRON substrato de silicio de tipo p *m*

PU *abbr* (*protocol unit*) TELECOM unidad de protocolo *f*

Pu *abbr* (*plutonium*) CHEM, GEOL, MINERAL, NUCL, PHYS, RAD PHYS Pu (*plutonio*)

public: ~ **address system** *n* (*PA system*) ACOUST, AIR TRANSP sistema de megafonía *m*, sistema público de altavoces *m*; ~ **address system amplifier** *n* ACOUST, AIR TRANSP, ELECTRON amplificador del sistema público de altavoces *m*; ~ **data network** *n* (*PDN*) COMP&DP red pública de datos *f* (*RPD*); ~ **dial-up port** *n* TELECOM puerto para discado público *m*, puerto para marcación pública *m*; ~ **health** *n* SAFE higiene pública *f*, sanidad pública *f*, WATER higiene pública *f*, sanidad pública *f*, salud pública *f*; ~ **mobile network** *n* TELECOM red de servicio público móvil *f*, red pública móvil *f*; ~ **network** *n* TELECOM red de servicio público *f*, red pública *f*; ~ **road** *n* CONST vía pública *f*; ~ **switched telephone network** *n* (*PSTN*) TELECOM red telefónica conmutada *f*, red telefónica pública de líneas conmutadas *f*; ~ **telephone** *n* TELECOM teléfono público *m*; ~ **telephone exchange** *n* TELECOM central telefónica pública *f*; ~ **telephone network** *n* TELECOM red telefónica pública *f*; ~ **water supply** *n* WATER abastecimiento público de agua *m*; ~ **works** *n pl* CONST, WATER obras públicas *f pl*

pucker *n* PRINT contracción por secado defectuoso *f*

puddle *n* HYDROL argamasa *f*, charco *m*; ~ **ball** *n* PROD lupia *f*; ~ **bar** *n* PROD barra de hierro pudelado *f*; ~-**bar train** *n* PROD tren de pudelar barras *m*; ~ **roll** *n* PROD cilindro desbastador *m*; ~ **rolls** *n pl* PROD tren de pudelaje *m*; ~ **train** *n* PROD tren de pudelar *m*

puddler's: ~ **rabble** *n* PROD gancho de pudelador *m*, pudelador mecánico *m*

puddling *n* HYDRAUL arcilla batida *f*; ~ **trough** *n* MINE artesa de barro trabajado *f*, artesa de encofrado *f*, artesa de pudelado *f*

puff[1] *n* C&G resoplo *m*

puff[2] *vt* FOOD soplar

pug *n* HYDRAUL arcilla batida *f*, MINE locomotora de maniobra *f*, *clay* arcilla amasada *f*, arcilla batida *f*, salbanda arcillosa *f*, veta de arcilla entre la roca madre y las paredes *f*; ~ **mill** *n* HYDRAUL amasadora *f*, mezclador de paletas *m*

pugging *n* CONST *deadening* mezcla insonorizante *f*

pulegone *n* CHEM pulegona *f*

Pulfrich: ~ **refractometer** *n* PHYS refractómetro de Pulfrich *m*

pull[1] *n* C&G estirón *m*, MECH ENG *tractive effort* esfuerzo de tracción *m*, tiro *m*, tracción *f*, SPACE combate *m*, contienda *f*, fuerza portante *f*, tracción *f*; ~-**apart basin** *n* GEOL cuenca asociada a fallas direccionales *f*; ~ **box** *n* ELEC *installation* caja de acceso *f*, caja de derivación *f*, caja de paso *f*; ~ **current** *n* BrE (*cf withdrawal current AmE*) C&G corriente de estiraje *f*; ~-**down** *n* CINEMAT tracción *f*; ~-**down claw** *n* CINEMAT garfio de tracción *m*; ~-**down menu** *n* COMP&DP, PRINT menú desplegable *m*; ~-**down test** *n* REFRIG ensayo de puesta en régimen *m*; ~-**in wire** *n* ELEC, ELEC ENG hilo de tracción *m*; ~-**off closure** *n* PACK cierre que se abre estirando de un extremo *m*; ~-**off coupling** *n* ELEC *connection*, ELEC ENG acoplamiento desviador *m*; ~-**ring** *n* PACK anilla de tirar *f*; ~ **rod** *n* MECH ENG tirante de reglaje *m*, varilla de maniobra *f*, varilla de tracción *f*; ~ **roller** *n* PRINT rodillo de arrastre *m*; ~ **switch** *n* ELEC interruptor de cordón *m*; ~-**through winding** *n* ELEC devanado de hilos sacados *m*

pull[2] *vt* PRINT sacar; ~ **out** *vt* CONST *nail* arrancar, extraer, sacar

pull[3]: ~ **back** *vi* CINEMAT, TV *of light* alejarse; ~ **focus** *vi* CINEMAT enfocar constantemente

pulled: ~-**in selvage** *n* TEXTIL orillo con tensión *m*

pulley *n* MECH ENG cuadernal *m*, motón *m*, polea *f*, roldana *f*, MINE carrucha *f* (*Esp*), garrucha *f* (*AmL*), polea *f*, PHYS polea *f*, WATER TRANSP roldana *f*, cuadernal *m*, motón *m*, polea *f*; ~ **block** *n* MECH ENG cuadernal *m*, SAFE aparejo de poleas *m*, WATER TRANSP *purchases* cuadernal *m*, motón *m*; ~-**block hook** *n* MECH ENG gancho de cuadernal *m*; ~ **coupling** *n* MECH ENG acoplamiento de platos con pernos a paño *m*; ~ **for gut band** *n* MECH ENG polea para cinta de tripa *f*; ~ **key-seating machine** *n* MECH ENG máquina de cajera de polea *f*; ~ **lathe** *n* MECH ENG torno para poleas *m*; ~ **sheave** *n* MECH ENG roldana *f*; ~ **shell** *n* MECH ENG cuerpo de la polea *m*; ~-**turning lathe** *n* MECH ENG torno de polea *m*; ~ **wheel** *n* MECH ENG roldana *f*

pulleying *n* MINE acción de rebasar los topes de fin de carrera *f*

pulling *n* MECH ENG arrastre *m*, desgarramiento *m*, tiro *m*, tracción *f*, TV alargamiento de la imagen *m*; ~ **casing** *n* WATER *well-boring* camisa de extracción *f*; ~-**in** *n* TELECOM tracción *f*; ~ **out** *n* MECH ENG *nail* extracción *f*; ~ **rope** *n* MECH ENG cable de tracción *m* (*Esp*), cable tractor *m* (*AmL*)

pulp *n* COAL pasta de madera *f*, producto molido *m*, raíz *f*, PAPER pasta *f*, pulpa *f*, PROD pasta de madera *f*, pulpa *f*, WATER pulpa *f*; ~**-and-paper contraries** *n pl* PAPER impurezas *f pl*; ~ **batch** *n* PAPER carga de pasta en la pila holandesa *f*; ~ **machine** *n* PAPER seca-pastas *f*; ~ **mill** *n* PAPER, RECYCL fábrica de pasta *f*; ~**-molding system** *AmE*, ~**-moulding system** *BrE n* PACK sistema de moldeo de la pasta *m*

pulper *n* PAPER desintegrador *m*, desfibrador *m*

pulping *n* PAPER desfibrado *m*, proceso de cocción *m*

pulpit *n* WATER TRANSP *deck equipment* balcón *m*, batayola *f*, plataforma arponera *f*, púlpito *m*

pulpwood *n* PAPER madera para pasta *f*

pulsatance *n* PHYS pulsancia *f*

pulsating: ~ **address** *n* PROD dirección pulsátil *f*, ~ **current** *n* ELEC, ELEC ENG corriente ondulatoria *f*, corriente pulsatoria *f*; ~ **flow** *n* FLUID, REFRIG flujo pulsátil *m*; ~ **jet engine** *n* AIR TRANSP motor a reacción pulsatorio *m*, motor a reacción pulsátil *m*, pulsorreactor *m*; ~ **pressure** *n* PROD presión pulsátil *f*

pulsation *n* ELEC ENG pulsación *f*

pulsator: ~ **jig** *n* COAL caja de pulsación *f*

pulsatory: ~ **current** *n* ELEC, ELEC ENG corriente pulsatoria *f*

pulse¹: ~**-modulated** *adj* ELECTRON impulso modulado

pulse² *n* COMP&DP, ELEC impulso *m*, ELECTRON impulso *m*, pulso *m*, impulso electrónico de microsegundos *m*, FOOD legumbre *f*, OPT, PHYS pulso *m*, SPACE *communications* alteración en el valor de una variable *f*, impulso *m*, vibración *f*, ritmo *m*, señal de duración muy corta *f*, impulso electrónico de microsegundos *m*, TV pulso *m*, WAVE PHYS pulso *m*, impulso *m*, vibración *f*, emisión *f*; ~**-accelerator** *n* ELECTRON, RAD PHYS acelerador por pulsos *m*; ~ **amplification** *n* ELECTRON, TELECOM amplificación de impulso *f*, amplificación de pulsos *f*; ~ **amplifier** *n* ELECTRON, TELECOM amplificador de impulsos *m*; ~ **amplitude** *n* ELECTRON amplitud de impulso *f*, amplitud del pulso *f*; ~**-amplitude modulation** *n* (*PAM*) COMP&DP, ELECTRON, SPACE, TELECOM modulación de amplitud de impulso *f* (*PAM*), ~**-amplitude modulation network** *n* (*PAM network*) TELECOM red con modulación de amplitud de impulsos *f*; ~ **broadening** *n* OPT, TELECOM dispersión de impulsos *f*, ensanchamiento de pulsos *m*; ~ **capacitor** *n* ELEC capacitor de impulsos *m*, condensador de impulsos *m*; ~ **carrier** *n* ELECTRON portadora de impulsos *f*, TV portadora de pulsos *f*; ~ **characteristics** *n pl* ELECTRON características de impulso *f pl*, características del pulso *f pl*; ~ **circuit** *n* ELEC ENG, ELECTRON circuito de impulsos *m*; ~ **clipper** *n* TV limitador de pulsos *m* (*Esp*), recortador de pulsos *m* (*AmL*); ~ **code** *n* ELECTRON código de impulsos *m*; ~**-code modulation** *n* (*PCM*) COMP&DP, ELECTRON, PHYS, RAD PHYS, SPACE, TELECOM, TV modulación por códigos de pulsos *f*; ~ **coder** *n* ELECTRON, RAD PHYS codificador de impulsos *m*, codificador de pulsos *m*; ~ **compression** *n* TELECOM compresión de impulso *f*; ~ **counter** *n* ELECTRON contador de impulsos *m*; ~**-counting technique** *n* TELECOM técnica de recuento de impulsos *f*; ~ **decay-time** *n* TELECOM tiempo de amortiguamiento del impulso *m*, tiempo

de bajada del impulso *m*, tiempo de caída del impulso *m*; ~ **dispersion** *n* OPT, TELECOM dispersión de pulsos *f*, dispersión de impulsos *f*; ~**-distribution amplifier** *n* (*PDA*) ELECTRON, TELECOM amplificador de distribución de impulsos *m*; ~**-distribution amplifier unit** *n* (*PDAU*) TELECOM unidad amplificadora de distribución de impulsos *f*; ~**-duration modulation** *n* (*PDM*) ELECTRON modulación de la duración del impulso *f*, SPACE modulación de impulsos en duración *f* (*PDM*), modulación por duración de los impulsos *f* (*PDM*); ~ **frequency** *n* ELECTRON frecuencia de impulsos *f*; ~ **frequency modulation** *n* (*PFM*) COMP&DP, ELECTRON modulación de frecuencia de impulsos *f*; ~ **generation** *n* ELECTRON generación de impulsos *f*; ~ **generator** *n* COMP&DP, ELEC, ELECTRON generador de impulsos *m*, PHYS, RAD PHYS generador de pulsos *m*, TELECOM generador de impulsos *m*; ~ **height** *n* COMP&DP altura del impulso *f*, ELECTRON altura del impulso *f*, amplitud del impulso *f*; ~ **interleaving** *n* TELECOM intercalación de impulsos *f*; ~ **interval** *n* ELECTRON intervalo de impulso *m*; ~**-interval modulation** *n* TV intervalo de modulación de pulsos *m*, modulación de pulsos en intervalo *f*; ~ **jet** *n* AIR TRANSP pulsorreactor *m*; ~ **jitter** *n* TELECOM fluctuación de impulsos *f*; ~ **leading-edge** *n* TELECOM flanco anterior del impulso *m*, frente del impulso *m*; ~ **length** *n* ELECTRON, TELECOM duración del impulso *f*, duración del pulso *f*, longitud del impulso *f*; ~ **modulation** *n* ELEC *regulation*, ELECTRON modulación del impulso *f*, modulación de impulsos *f*; ~ **modulator** *n* ELECTRON modulador de impulsos *m*; ~ **noise** *n* SPACE *communications* ruido del impulso *m*; ~ **phase** *n* ELECTRON fase de impulso *f*; ~**-phase modulation** *n* ELECTRON modulación de fase de impulso *f*; ~ **phasing** *n* TV sincronización de pulsos *f*; ~ **polarity** *n* ELECTRON polaridad del impulso *f*; ~ **position** *n* ELECTRON posición de los impulsos *f*; ~**-position modulation** *n* ELECTRON modulación de la posición del impulso *f*, SPACE modulación por posición de impulsos *f*; ~ **profile** *n* TELECOM perfil de impulso *m*; ~ **rate** *n* ELECTRON porcentaje de impulsos *m*; ~**-rate factor** *n* TV factor de frecuencia de pulsos *m*; ~ **regeneration** *n* ELECTRON regeneración de impulsos *f*, PHYS, TV regeneración de pulsos *f*; ~**-repetition frequency** *n* (*PRF*) COMP&DP, ELECTRON, PHYS, TELECOM frecuencia de repetición de impulsos *f*; ~**-repetition interval** *n* ELECTRON intervalo de repetición de impulsos *m*; ~**-repetition period** *n* ELECTRON período de repetición de impulsos *m*; ~**-repetition rate** *n* PHYS *computing* tasa de repetición de pulsos *f*; ~ **restoration** *n* TV restauración de pulsos *f*; ~ **separation** *n* ELECTRON separación de impulsos *f*; ~ **separator** *n* TV separador de pulsos *m*; ~ **sequence** *n* ELECTRON secuencia de impulsos *f*; ~ **shape** *n* ELECTRON forma del impulso *f*; ~ **shaping** *n* COMP&DP conformación de impulsos *f*, formación de impulsos *f*; ~ **signal** *n* ELECTRON señal de impulso *f*; ~ **spacing** *n* ELECTRON intervalo de impulsos *m*; ~ **spike** *n* ELEC *voltage* impulso parásito *m*, sobreimpulso *m*, ELEC ENG *voltage* impulso parásito *m*; ~ **spreading** *n* OPT, TELECOM ensanchamiento de pulsos *m*, dispersión de impulsos *f*; ~ **sync** *n* TV sincronización de pulsos *f*; ~ **synchronization** *n* TV sincronización de pulsos *f*; ~ **synthesizer** *n* ELECTRON sintetizador de impulsos *m*; ~ **tilt** *n* ELECTRON parte horizontal del impulso *f*; **~-time modulation** *n* ELECTRON modulación de la duración del impulso *f*, TELECOM modulación de impulsos en posición *f*, modulación por impulsos de duración variable *f*; **~ trailing-edge** *n* TELECOM flanco posterior del impulso *m*; **~ train** *n* COMP&DP ráfaga de impulsos *f*, serie de impulsos *f*, tren de impulsos *m*, ELECTRON tren de impulsos *m*; **~ transformer** *n* ELEC, ELEC ENG transformador de impulsos *m*, PHYS transformador de pulsos *m*; **~ widening** *n* TELECOM ensanchamiento de impulso *m*, prolongación de duración de impulso *f*; **~ width** *n* COMP&DP anchura de impulso *f*, ELECTRON magnitud del impulso *f*, PHYS anchura del pulso *f*, TELECOM ancho del impulso *m*, anchura de impulso *f*, duración del impulso *f*, TV ancho del pulso *m*; **~-width modulation** *n* (*PWM*) ELECTRON modulación de la magnitud del impulso *f* (*PWM*), SPACE modulación de la anchura del impulso *f* (*PWM*)

pulse³: **~ off** *vi* PROD emitir impulsos; **~ on** *vi* PROD pulsar

pulsed: **~-afterglow technique** *n* RAD PHYS técnica de la posluminiscencia pulsada *f*; **~ current** *n* ELEC corriente pulsada *f*; **~-electron gun** *n* ELECTRON, RAD PHYS cañón de electrones pulsados *m*, haz pulsado de electrones *m*; **~ lamp** *n* CINEMAT lámpara pulsatoria *f*; **~ laser** *n* ELECTRON láser de impulsos *m*, RAD PHYS láser pulsado *m*; **~ magnetron** *n* ELECTRON magnetrón de impulsos *m*; **~ maser** *n* ELECTRON maser de impulsos *m*; **~ mode** *n* ELEC ENG modo de pulsado *m*, ELECTRON función de impulsos *f*, modo de impulsos *m*; **~-neutron log** *n* PETR TECH diagrafía de neutrón impulsado *f*, perfil neutrón impulsado *m*, registro neutrón impulsado *m*; **~ operation** *n* ELECTRON operación de impulsos *f*; **~ oscillator** *n* ELECTRON oscilador de impulsos *m*; **~ radar detector** *n* TRANSP detector radárico de impulsos *m*; **~ ultrasonic detector** *n* TRANSP detector ultrasónico de impulsos *m*

pulser *n* ELECTRON generador de impulsos *m*

pulses: **~ per second** *n pl* (*pps*) TELECOM impulsos por segundo *m pl*

pulsojet *n* TRANSP pulsorreactor *m*

pulverization *n* CHEM, COAL pulverización *f*; **~ burner** *n* MECH ENG quemador de pulverización *m*

pulverize *vt* CHEM moler, pulverizar, CHEM TECH, COAL, CONST pulverizar, PROD triturar

pulverized¹ *adj* CHEM TECH pulverizado

pulverized²: **~ charcoal** *n* COAL carbón vegetal pulverizado *m*; **~ coal** *n* COAL carbón pulverizado *m*

pulverizer *n* CHEM TECH, CONST, WATER pulverizador *m*

pulverizing: **~ chamber** *n* CHEM TECH cámara de pulverización *f*; **~ equipment** *n* CHEM TECH equipo de pulverización *m*, pulverizador *m*; **~ water** *n* WATER agua pulverizada *f*

pulverulent *adj* CHEM TECH polvoriento, pulverulento

pulvimixer *n* PROD, TRANSP máquina para mezclar la nieve y apisonarla *f*

pumice *n* C&G, GEOL piedra pómez *f*; **~ soap** *n* DETERG jabón de piedra pómez *m*; **~-stone** *n* MINERAL piedra pómez *f*, pumita *f*

pumicing *n* PROD apomazado *m*

pump¹ *n* GEN bomba *f*; **~ barrel** *n* WATER cuerpo de bomba *m*; **~ coast-down** *n* NUCL parada por inercia de una bomba *f*; **~ compartment** *n* WATER *of shaft* compartimiento de bombas *m*; **~ connection** *n* WATER conexión de bomba *f*; **~ and connections** *n pl* MECH ENG *for machine-tool* bomba y conexiones *f pl*; **~ cylinder** *n* WATER cilindro de bomba *m*; **~ dispenser system** *n* PACK, PROD sistema distribuidor mediante bomba *m*; **~ dredge** *n* CONST, WATER TRANSP draga de bombeo *f*; **~ dredger** *n* CONST, WATER TRANSP draga de bombeo *f*, draga de succión *f*; **~-fed evaporator** *n* REFRIG evaporador alimentado por bomba *m*; **~ frequency** *n* SPACE frecuencia de bombeo *f*; **~ gear** *n* PROD, WATER armadura de la bomba *f*, mecanismo de la bomba *m*; **~ head** *n* HEAT altura de la bomba *f*; **~ house** *n* WATER casa de bombas *f*; **~ housing** *n* AUTO, VEH alojamiento de la bomba *m*; **~ line** *n* PHYS línea longitudinal *f*; **~ pressure** *n* PETR TECH presión de bomba *f*; **~ rod** *n* WATER varilla de bombeo *f*; **~ room** *n* WATER cámara de bombas *f*, sala de bombas *f*; **~ rundown** *n* NUCL parada por inercia de una bomba *f*; **~ shaft** *n* WATER pozo de bombas *m*; **~ spring-bow** *n* MECH ENG compás de muelle para bomba *m*; **~ station** *n* WATER estación de bombas *f*; **~ sump** *n* WATER sumidero de bomba *m*; **~ turbine** *n* FUELLESS turbina de bomba *f*; **~ valve** *n* PETR TECH válvula de bomba *f*; **~ water** *n* HYDRAUL, HYDROL, WATER agua bombeada *f*

pump² *vt* CONST, MECH ENG bombear, PETR TECH agotar, PROD, WATER, WATER TRANSP bombear; **~ out** *vt* CONST bombear, extraer, vaciar, MECH vaciar, MECH ENG, PROD, WATER bombear, extraer, vaciar, WATER TRANSP achicar, agotar

pumpdown *n* REFRIG evacuación de recipiente *f*

pumped: **~ storage scheme** *n* FUELLESS *hydroelectric power* proyecto de almacenamiento bombeado *m*

pumping *n* MINE, PETR TECH, WATER agotamiento *m*, bombeo *m*, bombeo de desagüe *m*, desagüe *m*, extracción de agua *f*; **~ depression cone** *n* WATER cono de depresión de bombeo *m*; **~ engine** *n* MINE, PETR TECH, WATER bomba de agotamiento *f*, bomba mecánica *f*, máquina de agotamiento *f*, máquina de desagüe *f*; **~ equipment** *n* WATER equipo de bombeo *m*; **~ light** *n* ELECTRON luz indicadora de inestabilidad *f*; **~ out** *n* MINE, PETR TECH extracción de agua *f*, WATER, WATER TRANSP agotamiento *m*, bombeo *m*, extracción de agua *f*; **~ pit** *n* COAL pozo de aspiración *m*; **~ plant** *n* HYDROL instalación de bombas *f*, WATER estación de bombeo *f*, instalación de bombas *f*, WATER TRANSP instalación de bombas *f*; **~ rate** *n* PETR TECH, PETROL rata de agotamiento *f* (*AmL*), ritmo de agotamiento *m*, tasa de agotamiento *f* (*Esp*), PETROL ritmo de agotamiento *m*, tasa de agotamiento *f*; **~ schedule** *n* PETR TECH, PETROL programa de bombeo *m*; **~ shaft** *n* WATER pozo de bombeo *m*; **~ sleeper** *n* BrE (*cf dancing tie AmE*) RAIL traviesa oscilante *f*; **~-station** *n* CONST estación de bombeo *f*, casa de bombas *f*, HYDROL instalación de bombeo *f*, MINERAL, PETR TECH, PETROL estación de bombeo *f*, WATER estación de bombeo *f*, instalación de bombeo *f*, WATER TRANSP *drydock* instalación de bombeo *f*; **~ test** *n* COAL, HYDRAUL, WATER ensayo de bombeo *m*, prueba de bombeo *f*; **~ unit** *n* MAR POLL grupo motobomba *m*, unidad de bombeo *f*, PROD unidad de bombeo *f*; **~ well** *n* COAL pozo bombeo *m*

punch¹ *n* CINEMAT perforación *f*, COMP&DP perforadora *f*, CONST punzón *m*, MECH embutidor *m*, granete *m*, sacabocados *m*, *for driving nails* botador *m*, *for making holes* punzón *m*, MECH ENG sacabocados *m*, granete *m*, *for driving nails* botador *m*, embutidor *m*, *for making holes* punzón *m*; ~ **card** *AmE see punched card BrE*; ~-**card reader** *AmE see punched-card reader BrE*; ~-**card reproducer** *AmE see punched-card reproducer BrE*; ~ **holder** *n* MECH, MECH ENG portapunzón *m*; ~ **mark** *n* MECH, MECH ENG referencia de perforación *f*; ~ **plate** *n* MECH, MECH ENG chapa de punzonar *f*; ~ **prop** *n* MINE puntal *m* (*Esp*), vela *f* (*AmL*); ~ **shank** *n* MECH, MECH ENG barrena de punzonar *f*; ~ **tape** *AmE see punched tape BrE*; ~-**tape reader** *AmE see punched-tape reader BrE*; ~-**tape reproducer** *AmE see punched-tape reproducer BrE*; ~-**through** *n* ELECTRON perforación *f*

punch[2] *vt* CONST, MECH, MECH ENG, PROD punzonar, taladrar; ~ **out** *vt* MECH, MECH ENG, PROD botar, cortar

punched: ~ **card** *n BrE* COMP&DP ficha perforada *f*, tarjeta perforada *f*; ~-**card reader** *n BrE* COMP&DP lector de fichas perforadas *m*, lector de tarjetas perforadas *m*; ~-**card reproducer** *n BrE* COMP&DP reproductor de fichas perforadas *m*, reproductor de tarjetas perforadas *m*; ~ **plate** *n* COAL chapa perforadora *f*, CONST placa perforada *f*; ~-**plate screen** *n* CONST pantalla perforada *f*; ~ **tape** *n BrE* COMP&DP, TELECOM cinta perforada *f*; ~-**tape reader** *n BrE* COMP&DP, TELECOM lector de cinta perforada *m*; ~-**tape reproducer** *n BrE* COMP&DP, TELECOM reproductor de cinta perforada *m*

punching *n* COMP&DP perforación *f*, MECH ENG, PROD *with hollow punch* troquelado *m*, *with solid punch* punzonado *m*; ~-**and-shearing machine** *n* MECH ENG máquina de punzonar y cizallar *f*; ~ **machine** *n* MECH ENG *solid-punch type* prensa de recortar *f*, punzonadora *f*, PROD *hollow-punch type* punzonadora *f*, *solid-punch type* prensa de recortar *f*, recortadora *f*; ~ **out** *n* MECH ENG, PROD *with hollow punch* taladro *m*; ~ **track** *n* COMP&DP pista de perforación *f*

punctuation: ~ **marks** *n pl* PRINT signos de puntuación *m pl*

puncture *n* ELECTRON, PAPER perforación *f*; ~ **strength** *n* PAPER resistencia a la perforación *f*; ~ **test** *n* ELEC *high-voltage equipment* prueba de descarga disruptiva *f*, prueba de tensión disruptiva *f*; ~ **tester** *n* PAPER aparato para medir la resistencia a la perforación *m*

punnet: ~ **tray** *n* PACK bandeja-envase *f*

punty *n* C&G varilla separadora *f*

puntying *n* C&G separación *f*

PUR *abbr* (*polyurethane*) CHEM, CONST, P&R, TEXTIL PUR (*poliuretano*)

purchase *n* MECH ENG aparejo *m*; ~ **block** *n* MECH ENG polea del aparejo *f*; ~ **fall** *n* MECH ENG beta de aparejo *f*; ~ **rig** *n* WATER TRANSP *lifting gear* aparejo compuesto *m*

pure: ~-**chance traffic** *n* TELECOM tráfico ideal *m*, tráfico puramente aleatorio *m*; ~ **coal** *n* COAL, MINE carbón puro *m*; ~ **resistance** *n* ELEC ENG resistencia pura *f*; ~ **spectrum** *n* RAD PHYS espectro puro *m*; ~ **tone** *n* ACOUST tono puro *m*; ~-**tone audiogram** *n* ACOUST audiograma de tonos puros *m*; ~-**tone audiometry** *n* ACOUST audiometría tonal *f*; ~ **water** *n* HYDROL, WATER agua pura *f*

purge: ~ **cock** *n* WATER grifo de purga *m*; ~ **recovery system** *n* REFRIG grupo de purga *m*; ~ **valve** *n* FUELLESS *geothermal drilling equipment* válvula purgadora *f*

purging *n* COMP&DP purga *f*, PETR TECH depuración *f*,

purgado *m*, saneamiento *m*; ~ **cock** *n* WATER grifo de vaciamiento *m*

purification *n* GEN depuración *f*, purificación *f*; ~ **plant** *n* CHEM, CHEM TECH, GAS instalación de depuración *f*, HYDROL instalación de depuración *f*, planta de depuración *f*, planta de purificación *f*, planta depuradora *f*, PETR TECH instalación de depuración *f*, RECYCL, WATER instalación de depuración *f*, planta de depuración *f*, planta de purificación *f*, planta depuradora *f*

purified: ~ **gas** *n* GAS gas purificado *m*; ~ **water** *n* HYDROL, WATER agua purificada *f*; ~-**water reservoir** *n* HYDROL, WATER depósito de agua purificada *m*; ~-**water tank** *n* HYDROL, WATER depósito de agua purificada *m*

purifier *n* CHEM depurador *m*, purificador *m*, CHEM TECH purificador *m*

purify *vt* CHEM, CHEM TECH, GAS, HYDROL depurar, purificar, PETR TECH purificar, refinar, RECYCL, THERMO, WATER depurar, purificar

purifying: ~ **agent** *n* CHEM, CHEM TECH, GAS, HYDROL, PETR TECH, WATER agente purificador *m*; ~ **apparatus** *n* CHEM, CHEM TECH, LAB aparato de purificación *m*; ~ **plant** *n* CHEM, CHEM TECH, GAS, HYDROL, PETR TECH instalación de depuración *f*, planta de depuración *f*, planta de purificación *f*, RECYCL, WATER instalación de depuración *f*

purine *n* CHEM purina *f*

purity *n* GAS pureza *f*

purlin *n* CONST correa *f*; ~ **post** *n* CONST larguero *m*

purple[1]: ~ **plague** *n* ELEC ENG compuesto frágil de aluminio y oro *m*, contaminación púrpura *f*

purple[2] *vt* COLOUR purpurar

purpose[1]: ~-**designed** *adj* PACK diseñado expresamente para un fin determinado

purpose[2]: ~-**formulated adhesive** *n* P&R, PACK adhesivo formulado para un fin determinado *m*

purpurin *n* CHEM, COLOUR purpurina *f*

purpuroxanthin *n* CHEM purpuroxantina *f*

purse: ~-**fastener** *n* OCEAN cierre de la bolsa *m* (*AmL*), embolsado *m* (*Esp*); ~ **line** *n* OCEAN jareta *f*; ~ **seine** *n* OCEAN red de cerco con jareta *f*

purser *n* WATER TRANSP *merchant navy* comisario *m*, sobrecargo *m*

pursing *n* OCEAN cierre por jalado de la jareta *m* (*AmL*), embolsado de la captura *m*, cierre de la bolsa *m* (*AmL*), embolsado *m* (*Esp*)

pursuit: ~ **plane** *n* AIR TRANSP, MILIT avión de caza *m*; ~ **radar** *n* MILIT radar de perseguimiento *m*

purity *n* COAL pureza *f*

push[1]: ~-**pull** *adj* ELEC balanceado, TELECOM balanceado, en contrafase, equilibrador, simétrico, TRANSP equilibrado, simétrico

push[2]: ~ **back** *n* AIR TRANSP retroceso *m*; ~-**button** *n* CHEM *oiler* botón de presión *m*, pulsador *m*, CINEMAT botón de contacto *m*, ELEC *control* botón pulsador *m*, botón de contacto *m*, ELEC ENG botón pulsador *m*, botón de contacto *m*, conmutador de botón *m*, conmutador pulsador *m*, pulsador *m*, MECH ENG conmutador de botón *m*, pulsador *m*, botón impulsor *m*, conmutador pulsador *m*, botón de contacto *m*, PHOTO botón de contacto *m*, TELECOM botón pulsador *m*, botón de contacto *m*, conmutador de botón *m*, conmutador pulsador *m*, pulsador *m*, TV botón pulsador *m*; ~-**button control panel** *n* ELEC panel de control por botones de contacto *m*, panel de control por botón *m*, panel de control por botón de presión *m*, panel de control por pulsador *m*; **~-button dial** *n* TELECOM discado de marcación con pulsador *m*; **~-button faucet** *n* AmE (*cf* push-button tap *BrE*) CONST canilla de botón *f* (*AmL*), grifo de botón *m* (*Esp*), llave con interruptor de botón *f*; **~-button machine** *n* MECH ENG máquina con pulsador *f*; **~-button operation** *n* PHOTO accionamiento con disparador *m*; **~-button starter** *n* ELEC puesta en marcha mediante pulsador *f*; **~-button switch** *n* ELEC, ELEC ENG, PROD interruptor de botón de presión *m*, interruptor de pulsador *m*; **~-button tap** *n BrE* (*cf* push-button faucet *AmE*) CONST canilla de botón *f* (*AmL*), grifo de botón *m* (*Esp*), llave con interruptor de botón *f*; **~-button telephone** *n* TELECOM teléfono de botonera *m* (*AmL*), teléfono de teclado *m* (*Esp*); **~-down blasting machine** *n* MINE explosor de pulsador *m*; **~-down list** *n* COMP&DP lista de desplazamiento descendente *f*; **~-down stack** *n* COMP&DP pila de desplazamiento descendente *f*; **~ fit** *n* MECH ENG ajuste sin holgura *m*, ajuste sin huelgo *m*, ajuste suave *m*, montaje a frotamiento dulce *m*; **~ net** *n* OCEAN red pequeña unida a un mango largo *f*; **~-off wipe** *n* CINEMAT, TV transición donde una imagen quita a otra de la pantalla *f*; **~-on mount** *n* PHOTO montaje de presión *m*; **~-on-push-off operation** *n* PROD operación de aceleración-desaceleración *f*; **~-plate conveyor** *n* PROD transportador de paletas *m*; **~-pull** *n* ELEC, ELECTRON, TELECOM contrafase *f*, TRANSP compresión-tracción *f*; **~-pull amplifier** *n* ELEC, ELECTRON, TELECOM amplificador en contrafase *m*, amplificador en push-pull *m*, amplificador simétrico *m*; **~-pull circuit** *n* ELEC, ELECTRON, TELECOM circuito en contrafase *m*, circuito simétrico *m*; **~-pull oscillator** *n* ELEC, ELECTRON, TELECOM oscilador en contrafase *m*, oscilador simétrico *m*; **~-pull scanning** *n* ELEC, ELECTRON, OPT exploración en contrafase *f*; **~-pull switch** *n* ELEC, ELECTRON interruptor de configuración simétrica *m*, interruptor de disposición simétrica *m*; **~-pull transformer** *n* ELEC, ELECTRON, TELECOM transformador simétrico *m*; **~ rod** *n* AUTO, MECH, MECH ENG, VEH varilla de empuje *f*, varilla empujadora *f*, varilla impulsora *f*; **~-rod switch** *n* PROD conmutador de pulsador de varilla *m*; **~ screen** *n* PROD criba de sacudidas *f*; **~ stick** *n* SAFE empujador *m*; **~-through connection** *n* PROD junta a medio hierro *f*; **~-to-test indicating light** *n* PROD lámpara indicadora del pulsador de pruebas *f*; **~-to-test pilot light** *n* PROD lámpara piloto del pulsador de pruebas *f*; **~ tow** *n* TRANSP remolque por empuje *m*; **~ towing** *n* TRANSP remolque empujado *m*; **~ tug** *n* TRANSP remolque mediante empuje *m*; **~-up** *n* C&G empujón *m*; **~-up list** *n* COMP&DP lista de desplazamiento ascendente *f*; **~-up stack** *n* COMP&DP pila de desplazamiento ascendente *f*

push[3] *vt* CINEMAT forzar; **~ back** *vt* TRANSP eliminar, retirar

push[4] *vti* COMP&DP desplazar

push[5]: **~-to-talk** *phr* TELECOM con botón de apretar para hablar, pulsar para hablar

pusher: **~ furnace** *n* HEAT horno con impulsor *m*; **~ locomotive** *n* AmE (*cf* banking locomotive *BrE*) RAIL locomotora de refuerzo para subida de rampas *f*, locomotora empujadora *f*, locomotora trasera *f*; **~ operation** *n* RAIL doble tracción con unidad tractora en cola *f*, subida de rampas con tracción

en cola *f*; **~ propeller** *n* AIR TRANSP hélice impulsora *f*; **~ tug** *n* WATER TRANSP empujador *m*, remolcador empujador *m*

pushing: **~ jack** *n* PROD gato de empuje *m*

pushpit *n* WATER TRANSP *yachts* balcón de popa *m*, púlpito de popa *m*

put[1]: **~ on file** *adj* TELECOM archivado

put[2]: **~ byte** *n* PROD transferido por octeto *m*

put[3]: **~ down** *vt* MINE *bore hole* profundizar; **~ in** *vt* ELEC instalar; **~ into commission** *vt* WATER TRANSP armar, dar de alta, hacer entrega de, poner en servicio activo; **~ into operation** *vt* PROD poner en funcionamiento; **~ on board** *vt* WATER TRANSP meter a bordo; **~ on hold** *vt* TELECOM colocar en espera, poner en espera; **~ on stand-by** *vt* MAR POLL poner en situación de espera; **~ out** *vt* SAFE *fire* apagar; **~ pressure on** *vt* COAL presionar; **~ through** *vt* TELECOM comunicar, conectar, poner en comunicación; **~ under cover** *vt* CONST poner a cubierto; **~ up** *vt* CONST edificar

put[4]: **~ to sea** *vi* WATER TRANSP hacerse a la mar

putlock *n* CONST almojaya *f*, almojaya del andamio *f*

putlog *n* CONST almojaya *f*, almojaya del andamio *f*

putrefy *vi* FOOD descomponer, podrir, pudrir

putrescent *adj* FOOD putrefacto

putrid *adj* FOOD podrido, putrefacto

putty[1] *n* C&G, COLOUR masilla *f*, CONST masilla *f*, plaste *m*; **~-joint** *n* CONST junta de unión *f*; **~ knife** *n* CONST cuchilla de vidriero *f*, espátula *f*; **~-powder** *n* CONST polvo de yeso *m*

putty[2] *vt* CONST enmasillar, rellenar con masilla

puttying *n* CONST masillado *m*

puzolan *n* PETROL puzolana *f*

puzzle: **~ lock** *n* CONST cerradura de combinación *f*

PV *abbr* (*parameter value*) TELECOM valor de parámetro *m*

PVC[1] *abbr* COMP&DP (*permanent virtual circuit*) PVC (*circuito virtual permanente*), CONST, ELEC, ELEC ENG, P&R, PACK (*polyvinyl chloride*) PVC (*cloruro de polivinilo*), TELECOM (*permanent virtual circuit*) PVC (*circuito virtual permanente*)

PVC[2]: **~ bottle** *n* PACK botella de PVC *f*; **~ insert-fitment** *n* PACK elemento intercalable de PVC *m*; **~ insulation** *n* ELEC, ELEC ENG aislación de PVC *f*, aislamiento de PVC *m*; **~ pressure-sensitive tape** *n* PACK cinta de PVC autoadhesiva *f*; **~ sheath** *n* ELEC ENG cable de PVC *m*, funda de PVC *f*, placa de PVC *f*

PVDC *abbr* (*polyvinylidene chloride*) P&R PVDC (*cloruro de polivinilideno*)

PVP *abbr* (*polyvinylpyrrolidone*) DETERG PVP (*polivinilpirrolidona*)

PVT: **~ analysis** *n* PETROL análisis de presión, volumen y temperatura *m*

PW *abbr* (*private wire*) TELECOM circuito privado *m*

PWM *abbr* (*pulse-width modulation*) ELECTRON, SPACE PWM (*modulación de la anchura del impulso*)

p-xylene *n* CHEM p-xileno *m*

pycnite *n* MINERAL picnita *f*

pycnometer *n* INSTR, LAB, PETR TECH, PHYS picnómetro *m*

pyelogram: **~ cassette** *n* INSTR casete para pielograma *f*

pyelography *n* INSTR pielografía *f*

pylon *n* AIR TRANSP pilón *m*, soporte *m*, voladizo *m*, CONST pilón *m*, ELEC castillete *m*, pilón *m*, torre *f*, ELEC ENG castillete *m*, torre *f*

pyramid *n* GEOM pirámide *f*; **~ cut** *n* MINE corte piramidal *m*, franqueo en forma de cono *m*

pyramidal: **~ plane** *n* METALL plano piramidal *m*; **~ slip** *n* METALL deslizamiento piramidal *m*

pyran *n* CHEM pirano *m*

pyranometer *n* FUELLESS, INSTR radiómetro solar *m*

pyranose *n* CHEM piranosa *f*

pyrargyrite *n* MINERAL pirargirita *f*

pyrazine *n* CHEM pirazina *f*

pyrazol *n* CHEM pirazol *m*

pyrazoline *n* CHEM pirazolina *f*

pyrazolone *n* CHEM pirazolona *f*

pyrene *n* CHEM pireno *m*

pyrgom *n* MINERAL fassaita *f*, pyrgom *m*

pyrheliometer *n* FUELLESS radiómetro del sol *m*

pyridazin *n* CHEM piridazina *f*

pyridine *n* CHEM piridina *f*

pyridone *n* CHEM piridona *f*

pyrimidine *n* CHEM pirimidina *f*

pyrite *n* GEOL, MINE, MINERAL pirita *f*

pyrites *n* MINERAL pirita *f*

pyritic *adj* MINE, MINERAL pirítico

pyroacetic *adj* CHEM piroacético

pyroarsenate *n* CHEM piroarsenato *m*

pyroboric *adj* CHEM pirobórico

pyrocatechin *n* CHEM pirocatequina *f*

pyrochlore *n* MINERAL pirocloro *m*

pyrochroite *n* MINERAL pirocroíta *f*

pyroclastic[1] *adj* GEOL, GEOPHYS, PETROL piroclástico

pyroclastic[2]: **~ rock** *n* GEOL, GEOPHYS, PETROL roca piroclástica *f*

pyroelectric *adj* CRYSTALL, ELEC, THERMO piroeléctrico

pyroelectricity *n* CRYSTALL, ELEC, THERMO piroelectricidad *f*

pyrogallic *adj* CHEM, PHOTO pirogálico

pyrogallol *n* CHEM, PHOTO pirogalol *m*

pyrogenic[1] *adj* GEOPHYS, THERMO pirogénico

pyrogenic[2]: **~ reaction** *n* GEOPHYS, THERMO reacción pirogénica *f*

pyrolusite *n* MINERAL pirolusita *f*

pyrolysis *n* CHEM, FOOD, GAS, THERMO pirólisis *f*

pyrolytic *adj* CHEM, FOOD, GAS, THERMO pirolítico

pyromeconic *adj* CHEM piromecónico

pyromellitic *adj* CHEM piromelítico

pyrometer *n* GEN pirómetro *m*; **~ probe** *n* ELEC sonda pirométrica *f*; **~ protection-tube** *n* SAFE tubo protector del pirómetro *m*

pyrometric *adj* GEN pirométrico

pyrometry *n* GEN pirometría *f*

pyromorphite *n* MINERAL piromorfita *f*

pyromucic *adj* CHEM piromúcico

pyrone *n* CHEM pirona *f*

pyrope *n* COLOUR, MINERAL piropo *m*

pyrophoric *adj* CHEM, METALL pirofórico

pyrophosphate *n* CHEM pirofosfato *m*

pyrophosphoric[1] *adj* CHEM pirofosfórico

pyrophosphoric[2]: **~ acid** *n* CHEM, DETERG ácido pirofosfórico *m*

pyrophosphorous *adj* CHEM pirofosforoso

pyrophyllite *n* MINERAL, PETR TECH pirofilita *f*

pyrorthite *n* MINERAL pirortita *f*

pyrosclerite *n* MINERAL pirosclerita *f*

pyroscope *n* PHYS piroscopio *m*

pyrostat *n* PHYS piroestato *m*

pyrostibite *n* MINERAL pirostibita *f*

pyrosulfate *AmE see* pyrosulphate *BrE*

pyrosulfite *AmE see* pyrosulphite *BrE*

pyrosulfuric *AmE see* pyrosulphuric *BrE*

pyrosulfuryl *AmE see* pyrosulphuryl *BrE*

pyrosulphate *n* *BrE* CHEM pirosulfato *m*

pyrosulphite *n* *BrE* CHEM pirosulfito *m*

pyrosulphuric *adj* *BrE* CHEM pirosulfúrico

pyrosulphuryl *n* *BrE* CHEM pirosulfuril *m*

pyrotechnic: **~ delay** *n* SPACE retraso pirotécnico *m*; **~ valve** *n* SPACE válvula pirotécnica *f*

pyrotechnical: **~ shock** *n* SPACE *spacecraft* choque pirotécnico *m*

pyrotechnics *n* SPACE pirotecnia *f*

pyroxene *n* MINERAL piroxeno *m*

pyroxenite *n* GEOL, MINERAL, PETROL piroxenita *f*

pyroxyline *n* CHEM piroxilina *f*; **~ lacquer** *n* COATINGS, COLOUR laca de piroxilina *f*

pyrrhotine *n* MINERAL pirrotina *f*

pyrrhotite *n* MINERAL pirrotita *f*

pyrrole *n* CHEM pirrol *m*

pyrrolidine *n* CHEM pirrolidina *f*

pyrrolidone *n* CHEM pirrolidona *f*

pyrroline *n* CHEM pirrolina *f*

pyruvate *n* CHEM piruvato *m*

pyruvic *adj* CHEM pirúvico

Pythagoras': **~ theorem** *n* GEOM teorema de Pitágoras *m*

Pythagorean: **~ comma** *n* ACOUST coma de Pitágoras *f*; **~ scale** *n* ACOUST escala de Pitágoras *f*

Q

Q: ~ **flag** n WATER TRANSP bandera alfabética Q f
QA abbr (quality assurance) GEN garantía de calidad f
QAM abbr (quadrature amplitude modulation) COMP&DP, ELECTRON, TELECOM MAC (modulación de amplitud en cuadratura)
QC abbr (quality control) GEN control de calidad m
QCD abbr (quantum chromodynamics) PART PHYS, PHYS cromodinámica cuántica f
Q-channel n ELECTRON canal Q m
Q-demodulator n ELECTRON demodulador Q m
Q-device n NUCL dispositivo Q m
QED abbr (quantum electrodynamics) ELEC, ELECTRON, PART PHYS, PHYS electrodinámica cuántica f
Q-electron n ELECTRON, NUCL electrón Q m
Q-factor n PHYS factor calidad m
QL abbr (query language) COMP&DP QL (lenguaje de consulta)
Q-percentile: ~ **life** n NUCL vida de percentil Q f
QPSK abbr (quaternary phase-shift keying) ELECTRON, TELECOM conmutación de variación de fase cuaternaria
QSG abbr (quasi-stellar galaxy) SPACE QSG (galaxia cuasiestelar)
Q-shell n NUCL capa Q f; ~ **electron** n ELECTRON, NUCL electrón de la capa Q m
Q-signal n ELECTRON, TV señal Q f
QSO abbr (quasi-stellar object) SPACE QSO (cuerpo cuasiestelar)
QSS abbr (quasi-stellar radio source) SPACE QSS (radiofuente cuasiestelar)
Q-switched: ~ **laser** n ELECTRON, NUCL láser Q conmutado m, láser conectado en Q m
Q-switching n ELECTRON conexión Q f
QTOL: ~ **aircraft** n (quiet take-off and landing aircraft) AIR TRANSP QTOL (avión de despegue y aterrizaje silencioso)
quackgrass n AGRIC grama f
quad n ELEC ENG cable con 4 conductores aislados m, cuadrete m, ELECTRON cuadrete m, PRINT cuadrado m; ~ **carburetor** AmE, ~ **carburettor** BrE n AUTO, VEH carburador cuádruple m; ~-**in-line package** n (QUIP) ELECTRON pastilla con cuatro hileras de conexiones f (PCHC); ~ **operational amplifier** n ELECTRON amplificador cuádruple m, cuádruple amplificador operacional m
quadded: ~ **cable** n ELEC ENG cable cuádruple de pares m, cable en cuadretes m
quadding n ELEC ENG cuadruplete m
quadrac n ELEC ENG, MATH cuadrático m
quadrangle n GEOM cuadrilátero m, cuadrángulo m
quadrangular adj GEOM cuadrangular
quadrant n GEOM cuadrante m, MECH ENG of sector-gear sector dentado m, of steam-engine sector del cambio de marcha m, of compass, callipers cuadrante m, cuarto de círculo m, of screw-cutting lathe balancín de escuadra m, MINE balancín de escuadra m, cartabón m; ~ **electrometer** n ELEC ENG, INSTR electrómetro de cuadrantes m; ~ **plate** n MECH ENG of screw-cutting lathe chapa del cuadrante f

quadrantal: ~ **error** n AIR TRANSP error cuadrantal m; ~ **height rule** n AIR TRANSP ley de altura cuadrantal f
quadraphony n ACOUST cuadrafonía f
quadratic[1] adj MATH cuadrático
quadratic[2]: ~ **profile** n OPT perfil cuadrático m
quadrature[1]: **in** ~ adj ELECTRON, PHYS en cuadratura
quadrature[2] n GEN cuadratura f; ~ **amplitude modulation** n (QAM) COMP&DP, ELECTRON, TELECOM modulación de amplitud en cuadratura f (MAC); ~ **amplitude modulator** n COMP&DP, ELECTRON, TELECOM modulador de amplitud de la cuadratura m; ~ **axis** n ELEC machine eje en cuadratura m; ~ **axis component** n ELEC alternating current componente transversal f; ~ **component** n ELEC alternating current, ELECTRON componente en cuadratura m; ~ **control** n ELEC alternating current control en cuadratura m; ~ **demodulator** n ELEC, ELECTRON demodulador de cuadratura m; ~ **displacement** n TV desplazamiento por cuadratura m; ~ **error** n TV error por cuadratura m; ~ **mirror filter** n ELECTRON, TELECOM filtro de espejo en cuadratura m; ~ **phase** n ELECTRON fase en cuadratura f; ~ **phase subcarrier signal** n TV señal subportadora de fase en cuadratura f; ~ **power** n ELEC alternating current energía en cuadratura f, potencia en cuadratura f; ~ **signal** n ELECTRON señal de cuadratura f; ~ **voltage** n ELEC alternating current tensión en cuadratura f, voltaje en cuadratura m
quadribasic adj CHEM tetrabásico
quadricone: ~ **bit** n PETR TECH barrena tetracónica f (Esp), mecha tetracónica f (AmL), trépano tetracónico m (AmL)
quadricycle n CHEM tetraciclo m
quadrilateral adj GEOM cuadrilateral
quadripole n ELEC, ELEC ENG, PHYS, RAD PHYS cuadrípolo m
quadrivalence n CHEM cuadrivalencia f, tetravalencia f
quadrivalent adj CHEM cuadrivalente, tetravalente
quadroxide n CHEM tetróxido m
quadruple: ~-**pair cable** n ELEC ENG cable de cuatro pares m; ~ **scanning** n TV exploración cuádruple f
quadruplex adj TV cuadruplexo
quadrupolar: ~ **configuration** n NUCL configuración cuadripolar f, configuración tetrapolar f
quadrupole n ELEC, ELEC ENG, PHYS, RAD PHYS cuadrípolo m; ~ **electric momentum** n ELEC, ELEC ENG, PHYS, RAD PHYS momento eléctrico cuadripolar m; ~ **field** n NUCL campo cuadripolar m; ~ **moment** n PHYS momento cuadripolar m; ~ **potential** n NUCL potencial del cuadripolo m; ~ **resonance** n NUCL resonancia del cuadripolo f
quaint: ~ **character** n PRINT carácter doble m
qualification: ~ **approval** n QUALITY aprobación de calificación f; ~ **model** n SPACE modelo de calificación m; ~ **test** n NUCL, QUALITY, SPACE prueba de calificación f; ~ **test review** n SPACE revisión de la prueba de calificación f
qualified: ~ **name** n COMP&DP nombre cualificado m
qualitative: ~ **analysis** n CHEM, WATER análisis cuali-

tativo *m*; ~ **autoradiography** *n* NUCL autorradiografía cualitativa *f*; ~ **characteristic** *n* QUALITY característica cualitativa *f*

quality *n* GEN calidad *f*; ~ **acceptance criteria** *n pl* GEN criterios de aceptación de calidad *m pl*; ~ **of aggregate** *n* CONST calidad de los áridos *f*; ~ **assessment** *n* METR *of a joint* valoración de la calidad *f*; ~ **assurance** *n* (*QA*) GEN garantía de calidad *f*; ~~**assurance certificate** *n* GEN certificado de garantía de calidad *m*; ~~**assurance examination** *n* GEN inspección de garantía de calidad *f*; ~~**assurance in final inspection and test** *n* QUALITY garantía de calidad en control y pruebas definitivas *f*; ~~**assurance procedure to BS5750** *n* MECH ENG procedimiento de garantía de calidad para BS5750 *m*; ~ **audit** *n* QUALITY comprobación de calidad *f*; ~ **auditor** *n* QUALITY controlador de calidad *m*; ~ **check** *n* GEN comprobación de calidad *f*; ~ **control** *n* (*QC*) GEN control de calidad *m*; ~ **cost** *n* QUALITY costo de la calidad *m*; ~ **degradation** *n* TV degradación de calidad *f*; ~ **economics** *n* QUALITY economía de la calidad *f*; ~ **engineering** *n* QUALITY técnica de dirección de la calidad *f*; ~ **factor** *n* GEN factor de calidad *m*, índice de calidad *m*; ~ **grading** *n* AGRIC, QUALITY clasificación por calidad *f*; ~ **guarantee** *n* GEN garantía de calidad *f*; ~ **improvement** *n* QUALITY mejoramiento de la calidad *m*; ~ **label** *n* PACK, QUALITY etiqueta de calidad *f*; ~ **loop** *n* QUALITY presilla de la calidad *f*; ~ **loss** *n* GEN pérdida de la calidad *f*; ~ **management** *n* GEN administración de calidad *f*, dirección de calidad *f*; ~ **manual** *n* GEN manual de calidad *m*; ~ **mark** *n* GEN marca de calidad *f*; ~ **monitoring of ambient air** *n* SAFE control de calidad del aire ambiente *m*; ~ **plan** *n* QUALITY proyecto de calidad *m*; ~ **planning** *n* QUALITY planificación de la calidad *f*; ~ **policy** *n* QUALITY política de la calidad *f*; ~ **record** *n* QUALITY registro de la calidad *m*; ~~**related cost** *n* QUALITY costo relacionado con la calidad *m*; ~ **of reproduction** *n* CINEMAT, PHOTO, QUALITY, TV calidad de reproducción *f*; ~ **of service** *n* QUALITY, TELECOM calidad del servicio *f*; ~ **spiral** *n* QUALITY espiral de calidad *f*; ~ **surveillance** *n* QUALITY control de la calidad *m*; ~ **system** *n* QUALITY sistema de calidad *m*; ~ **through design** *n* MECH ENG, PROD, QUALITY calidad a través del diseño *f*

quantification *n* GEN cuantificación *f*

quantifier *n* CONST, MATH cuantificador *m*

quantify *vt* CONST, MATH cuantificar

quantitative: ~ **analysis** *n* CHEM, WATER análisis cuantitativo *m*; ~ **characteristic** *n* QUALITY característica cuantitativa *f*

quantity: ~ **back-order** *n* PROD cantidad pendiente *f*; ~ **completed** *n* PROD cantidad entregada por completo *f*; ~ **declared unfit** *n* PROD cantidad declarada defectuosa *f*; ~ **fuse** *n* MINE cebo eléctrico de incandescencia *m*; ~ **packing** *n* PACK, PROD empaquetamiento a cantidad *m*; ~ **recorder** *n* INSTR registrador de cantidades *m*, registrador de dimensiones *m*; ~ **surveyor** *n* CONST estimador *m*, inspector que controla las mediciones *m*

quantization *n* GEN cuantificación *f*; ~ **distortion** *n* ELECTRON distorsión de cuantificación *f*; ~ **error** *n* ELECTRON, TELECOM error de cuantificación *m*; ~ **level** *n* COMP&DP, ELECTRON nivel de cuantificación *m*; ~ **noise** *n* COMP&DP, SPACE, TELECOM ruido de

cuantificación *m*; ~ **pulse modulation** *n* ELECTRON, TELECOM modulación de impulsos cuantificados *f*

quantize *vt* GEN cuantificar

quantized: ~ **delay line** *n* TV línea de retardo cuantificada *f*; ~ **gate** *n* TV puerta cuantificada *f*; ~~**pulse modulation** *n* ELECTRON, TELECOM modulación de impulso cuantificado *f*; ~ **quantity** *n* ELECTRON cantidad cuantificada *f*; ~ **signal** *n* ELECTRON señal cuantificada *f*

quantizer *n* GEN cuantificador *m*, dispositivo de cuantificación *m*

quantum[1] *adj* GEN cuántico

quantum[2] *n* GEN cuanto *m*, paquete de energía *m*, quántum *m*; ~ **chromodynamics** *n* (*QCD*) PART PHYS, PHYS cromodinámica cuántica *f*; ~ **efficiency** *n* ELECTRON, NUCL, OPT, PART PHYS, PHYS, RAD PHYS, TELECOM eficiencia cuántica *f*, rendimiento cuántico *m*; ~ **electrodynamics** *n* (*QED*) ELEC, ELECTRON, PART PHYS, PHYS electrodinámica cuántica *f*; ~~**field theory** *n* PART PHYS, PHYS teoría cuántica de campos *f*; ~ **Hall effect** *n* PHYS efecto Hall cuántico *m*; ~ **leap** *n* PART PHYS, PHYS salto cuántico *m*; ~~**limited operation** *n* OPT procedimiento cuánticamente limitado *m*; ~ **mechanical line shape** *n* RAD PHYS contorno de raya mecánica cuántico *m*; ~ **mechanics** *n* PART PHYS, PHYS mecánica cuántica *f*; ~ **noise** *n* ELECTRON, OPT, PHYS, TELECOM ruido cuántico *m*; ~~**noise-limited operation** *n* OPT procedimiento limitado por ruido cuántico *m*; ~ **number** *n* CHEM, ELECTRON, NUCL, PART PHYS, PHYS número cuántico *m*; ~ **physics** *n* PART PHYS, PHYS física cuántica *f*; ~ **state** *n* PART PHYS, PHYS estado cuántico *m*, SPACE estado cuántico *m*, nivel de energía *m*; ~ **statistics** *n* PHYS estadística cuántica *f*; ~ **theory** *n* CHEM, ELECTRON, NUCL, PART PHYS, PHYS, RAD PHYS, SPACE, TELECOM, TV teoría cuántica *f*; ~ **transistor** *n* ELECTRON transistor cuántico *m*; ~ **yield** *n* PHYS resultado cuántico *m*

quarantine[1] *n* AGRIC, SAFE, WATER TRANSP cuarentena *f*; ~ **flag** *n* WATER TRANSP bandera de sanidad *f*

quarantine[2] *vt* AGRIC, SAFE, WATER TRANSP poner en cuarentena

quark *n* NUCL, PART PHYS, PHYS cuark *m*, quark *m*; ~ **color** *AmE*, ~ **colour** *BrE* *n* PART PHYS, PHYS color del quark *m*; ~ **confinement** *n* PART PHYS, PHYS confinamiento del quark *m*, limitación del quark *f*; ~~**lepton scheme** *n* PART PHYS, PHYS esquema quark-leptón *m*

quarried *adj* CONST, GEOL, MINE explotado en una cantera

quarry *n* CONST, GEOL, MINE cantera *f*; ~ **bar** *n* MINE gravera *f*; ~ **face** *n* MINE lecho de cantera *m*; ~ **head** *n* MINE frente de cantera *m*; ~ **stripping** *n* MINE desbroce de la cantera *m*

quarrying *n* MINE cantería *f*, explotación de canteras *f*, extracción de piedra *f*; ~ **machine** *n* MINE máquina de acanalar *f*, rafadora de cantera *f*

quarryman *n* MINE cantero *m* (*AmL*), cortador de piedra *m*, obrero de cantera *m* (*Esp*)

quart *n* METR cuartillo *m*

quarter[1]: ~~**bound** *adj* PRINT encuadernado a media piel, encuadrado a media piel

quarter[2] *n* METR *avoirdupois weight* cuarto *m*, WATER TRANSP *ship design* aleta *f*, costado de popa *m*; ~ **belt** *n* PROD correa semicruzada *f*; ~ **berth** *n* WATER TRANSP litera del patrón *f*; ~~**binding** *n* PRINT encuadración a media piel *f*; **~ fold** *n* PRINT tres pliegues *m pl*; **~ horse** *n* AGRIC caballo americano *m*; **~ light** *n BrE* (*cf quarter window AmE*) AIR TRANSP, AUTO ventanilla *f*; **~ mask** *n* SAFE mascarilla *f*; **~ round** *n* CONST, MECH ENG cuarto bocel *m*; **~-round milling cutter** *n* CONST, MECH ENG fresa de cuarto bocel *f*; **~ tone** *n* PRINT grabado directo de trama gruesa *m*; **~-turn belt** *n* PROD correa semicruzada *f*; **~-twist belt** *n* PROD correa semicruzada *f*; **~ wave line** *n* PHYS línea de cuarto de onda *f*; **~-wave plate** *n* PHYS placa de cuarto de onda *f*; **~-wave whip aerial** *n BrE* (*cf quarter-wave whip antenna AmE*) PHYS, TELECOM, TV antena de látigo de cuarto de onda *f*; **~-wave whip antenna** *n AmE* (*cf quarter-wave whip aerial BrE*) PHYS, TELECOM, TV antena de látigo de cuarto de onda *f*; **~ wavelength** *n* ELECTRON amplitud de un cuarto de onda *f*; **~ wind** *n* WATER TRANSP viento a un largo *m*; **~ window** *n AmE* (*cf quarter light BrE*) AIR TRANSP, AUTO ventanilla *f*

quartered: **~ belt** *n* PROD correa semicruzada *f*

quartermaster *n* WATER TRANSP cabo de maniobra *m* (*Esp*), cabo de mar *m* (*Esp*), timonel de combate *m* (*AmL*)

quartet *n* PHYS cuarteto *m*; **~ model** *n* NUCL *pipelines* modelo de cuartetes *m*

quarto *n* PRINT libro en cuarto *m*

quartz *n* ELECTRON, MINERAL, PHYS cuarzo *m*; **~ crystal** *n* CINEMAT, COMP&DP, CRYSTALL, ELEC, ELECTRON cristal de cuarzo *m*; **~-crystal clock** *n* ELEC, ELECTRON reloj de cristal de cuarzo *m*; **~-crystal filter** *n* ELEC, ELECTRON filtro de cristal de cuarzo *m*; **~-crystal oscillator** *n* CINEMAT, ELEC, ELECTRON, PHYS, TELECOM oscilador de cristal de cuarzo *m*; **~ delay line** *n* ELECTRON, TV línea de retardo de cuarzo *f*; **~ halogen lamp** *n* CINEMAT, ELEC lámpara halógena de cuarzo *f*; **~ iodine** *n* CINEMAT lámpara de vapor de yodo con cubierta de cuarzo *f*; **~ iodine lamp** *n* CINEMAT lámpara de vapor de yodo con cubierta de cuarzo *f*; **~ light** *n* CINEMAT luz de cuarzo *f*; **~ monochromator** *n* NUCL monocromador de cuarzo *m*; **~ oscillator** *n* CINEMAT, ELEC, ELECTRON, PHYS, TELECOM oscilador de cuarzo *m*; **~ resonator** *n* ELECTRON resonador de cuarzo *m*; **~ sandstone** *n* MINERAL arenisca de cuarzo *f*; **~ vein** *n* GEOL, MINE, MINERAL filón de cuarzo *m*; **~ wedge** *n* CRYSTALL cuña de cuarzo *f*

quartzarenite *n* GEOL cuarzoarenita *f*

quartzdiorite *n* PETROL cuarzodiorita *f*

quartzite *n* CONST, GEOL, PETROL cuarcita *f*

quartzitic: **~ sandstone** *n* GEOL arenisca cuarcítica *f*

quartzose *adj* GEOL cuarcítico (*Esp*), cuarzoso (*AmL*)

quasar *n* SPACE cuásar *m*, estrella con intensidad luminosa pulsante *f*

quasi[1]: **~-statical** *adj* SPACE cuasiestático

quasi[2]: **~-adiabatic calorimeter** *n* NUCL calorímetro cuasiadiabático *m*; **~-breeder reactor** *n* NUCL reactor cuasirreproductor *m*; **~-chemical approximation** *n* METALL aproximación cuasiquímica *f*; **~-constant slip** *n* NUCL deslizamiento cuasiconstante *m*; **~-particle** *n* PHYS cuasi-partícula *f*; **~-peak voltage** *n* TELECOM tensión de cuasicresta *f*, voltaje de cuasicresta *f*; **~-statical loading** *n* SPACE carga cuasiestática *f*, cargamento cuasiestático *m*; **~-steady state** *n* PHYS estado cuasiestacionario *m*; **~-steady-state distribution** *n* METALL distribución de estado cuasiconstante *f*; **~-stellar decoupling** *n* SPACE desacoplo cuasiestelar *m*, desconexión cuasiestelar *f*; **~-stellar galaxy** *n* (*QSG*) SPACE galaxia cuasiestelar *f* (*QSG*); **~-stellar object** *n* (*QSO*) SPACE cuerpo cuasiestelar *m* (*QSO*); **~-stellar radio source** *n* (*QSS*) SPACE radiofuente cuasiestelar *f* (*QSS*)

quassin *n* CHEM cuasina *f*

quaternary[1] *adj* CHEM, GEOL, NUCL, PETR TECH cuaternario

quaternary[2] *n* CHEM, GEOL, NUCL, PETR TECH cuaternario *m*; **~ fission** *n* NUCL, PART PHYS, PHYS fisión cuaternaria *f*; **~ phase-shift keying** *n* (*QPSK*) ELECTRON, TELECOM conmutación de variación de fase cuaternaria *f* (*CVFC*); **~ physics** *n* NUCL, PART PHYS, PHYS física cuaternaria *f*

Quaternary: **~ era** *n* GEOL, PETR TECH era Cuaternaria *f*

quaternion *n* MATH cuaternio *m*

quay *n* WATER TRANSP muelle *m*, muelle de atraque *m*; **~ crane** *n* TRANSP grúa de muelle *f*

quayside: **~ conveyor** *n* TRANSP transportador en muelle *m*; **~ roadway** *n* AUTO muelle *m*

quench[1] *n* METALL templado brusco en agua *m*; **~ ageing** *n* METALL, NUCL envejecimiento por temple *m*; **~ hardening** *n* METALL, NUCL endurecimiento por temple *m*

quench[2] *vt* C&G, CHEM, CRYSTALL templar, MECH *of tyre* ahogar, enfriar repentinamente, sumergir, templar, METALL, PROD, THERMO templar

quenched: **~ cullet** *n BrE* (*cf shredded cullet AmE*) C&G cullet enfriado en agua *m* (*AmL*), fundente enfriado en agua *m* (*Esp*)

quenching *n* C&G, CHEM, CRYSTALL templado en agua *m*, METALL enfriamiento rápido *m*, temple instantáneo *m*, NUCL, PHYS extinción *f*, REFRIG enfriamiento rápido *m*; **~ bath** *n* METALL baño de enfriamiento *m*, baño de temple *m*; **~ of luminescence** *n* RAD PHYS extinción de la luminiscencia *f*

quercetin *n* CHEM quercetina *f*

quercitannic *adj* CHEM quercitánico

quercite *n* CHEM quercita *f*

quercitin *n* CHEM quercitina *f*

query[1] *n* COMP&DP consulta *f*, interrogación *f*; **~ language** *n* (*QL*) COMP&DP lenguaje de consulta *m* (*QL*); **~ processing** *n* COMP&DP procesamiento de consultas *m*, procesamiento de interrogaciones *m*

query[2] *vt* COMP&DP consultar, interrogar

quetch: **~ roller** *n* TEXTIL rodillo impregnador *m*; **~ unit** *n* TEXTIL dispositivo de impregnación *m*

queue *n* COMP&DP cola *f*, fila en espera *f*, TELECOM cola *f*, cola de llamadas *f*, TRANSP *BrE* (*cf line AmE*) *traffic* fila *f*; **~ of cars** *n BrE* (*cf line of cars AmE*) AUTO, TRANSP, VEH caravana *f*, fila de coches *f*; **~ control** *n* TELECOM control de espera *m*; **~ detector** *n* TRANSP detector de retenciones *m*; **~ management** *n* COMP&DP, TELECOM administración de colas *f*, gestión de colas *f*; **~ of traffic** *n BrE* (*cf line of traffic AmE*) AUTO, TRANSP, VEH caravana *f*, fila de coches *f*; **~ warning sign** *n* TRANSP señal de aviso de retención *f*

queued: **~ access** *n* COMP&DP acceso mediante cola *m*, acceso por fila en espera *m*

queueing[1] *adj* TELECOM puesto en cola, puesto en cola de espera

queueing[2] *n* TELECOM puesta en cola *f*, puesta en cola de espera *f*; **~ device** *n* TELECOM dispositivo de puesta en cola *m*; **~ network** *n* TELECOM red de sistema de espera *f*; ~ **theory** *n* COMP&DP teoría de esperar *f*, teoría de colas *f*; ~ **time** *n* TELECOM tiempo de espera en cola *m* (*Esp*), tiempo de espera en línea *m* (*AmL*), TV tiempo de espera *m*

quick[1]: **~-drying** *adj* PACK, TEXTIL de secado rápido; **~-freezing** *adj* FOOD, REFRIG, THERMO de congelamiento rápido; **~-frozen** *adj* FOOD, REFRIG, THERMO congelado rápidamente; **~-release** *adj* PRINT de salida inmediata

quick[2]: **~-acting fuse** *n* MILIT cebo de acción rápida *m*; **~-action chuck** *n* MECH ENG mandril de acción rápida *m*, mandril de cambio rápido *m*; **~-break switch** *n* ELEC, ELEC ENG interruptor de corte rápido *m*, interruptor de ruptura brusca *m*, interruptor instantáneo *m*, interruptor rápido *m*, interruptor ultrarrápido *m*; **~-change aircraft** *n* AIR TRANSP avión de cambio rápido *m*; **~-change drill chuck** *n* MECH ENG portabrocas de cambio rápido *m*; ~ **charge** *n* TRANSP carga disponible *f*; ~ **chilling** *n* REFRIG, THERMO refrigeración rápida *f*; ~ **clay** *n* COAL arcilla moviente *f*; **~-closing valve** *n* WATER válvula de cierre rápido *f*; ~ **coupler** *n* SPACE acoplador rápido *m*; ~ **disconnect** *n* AIR TRANSP, HYDRAUL desconexión rápida *f*; **~-donning oxygen mask** *n* AIR TRANSP mascarilla de oxígeno de colocación rápida *f*; **~-flashing light** *n* WATER TRANSP luz centelleante *f*; **~-freezer** *n* FOOD, REFRIG, THERMO congelador rápido *m*; **~-freezing** *n* FOOD, REFRIG, THERMO congelación rápida *f*; **~-freezing installation** *n* FOOD, MECH ENG, REFRIG instalación para congelación rápida *f*, instalación para congelado rápido *f*; **~-freezing plant** *n* FOOD, MECH ENG, REFRIG instalación para congelación rápida *f*, instalación para congelado rápido *f*; ~ **release** *n* MECH ENG, PROD, SPACE aflojamiento rápido *m*, desembrague rápido *m*; **~-release clamping system** *n* MECH ENG, PROD sistema de aflojamiento rápido *m*; **~-release coupling** *n* MECH ENG, PROD acoplamiento de desembrague rápido *m*; **~-release die** *n* MECH ENG, PROD molde de aflojamiento rápido *m*, troquel de suelta rápida *m*; **~-release fastener** *n* MECH ENG, PROD sujetador de desenganche rápido *m*; **~-release pipe coupling** *n* MECH ENG, PROD acoplamiento de tubos de desembrague rápido *m*; **~-release taper** *n* MECH ENG chaflán de aflojamiento rápido *m*; **~-setting cement** *n* CONST cemento rápido *m*; ~ **throwover switch** *n* ELEC conmutador rápido *m*, conmutador rápido de dos direcciones *m*, conmutador rápido de dos vías *m*

quick[3]: **~-freeze** *vt* FOOD, REFRIG, THERMO congelar rápidamente

quicklime *n* C&G, CHEM, CONST, MAR POLL cal viva *f*
quicksand *n* COAL, HYDROL, OCEAN arena fluyente *f*, arena movediza *f*
quicksilver *n* CHEM, ELEC ENG, METALL mercurio *m* (*Hg*)
quicksilvering *n* COATINGS, PROD *for mirrors* amalgama para espejos *f*, revestimiento con mercurio *m*
quickweed *n* AGRIC albahaca silvestre *f*

quickwork *n* WATER TRANSP *ship design* carena *f*, fondo del buque *m*, fondo interior del buque *m*, fondos *m pl*, obra viva *f*
quiesce *vi* COMP&DP estar en estado de reposo, reposar
quiescent *adj* CHEM inactivo, COMP&DP quieto, en reposo, ELEC, ELEC ENG estático, inactivo
quiescing *adj* COMP&DP en reposo, quiescente
quiet: ~ **mode** *n* PRINT modo silencioso *m*; ~ **running** *n* AUTO, MECH ENG, VEH funcionamiento silencioso *m*, funcionamiento suave *m*, marcha silenciosa *f*, marcha suave *f*; ~ **take-off and landing aircraft** *n* (*QTOL aircraft*) AIR TRANSP avión de despegue y aterrizaje silencioso *m* (*QTOL*); ~ **water** *n* HYDROL, WATER agua dormida *f*
quilt[1] *n* TEXTIL colcha *f*
quilt[2] *vt* TEXTIL acolchar
quilter *n* TEXTIL acolchador *m*
quinacrine *n* CHEM quinacrina *f*
quinaldic *adj* CHEM quináldico
quinaldine *n* CHEM quinaldina *f*
quinaldinic *adj* CHEM quinaldínico
quinalizarin *n* CHEM quinalizarina *f*
quinamine *n* CHEM quinamina *f*
quincite *n* MINERAL quincita *f*
quincy: ~ **cutter** *n* AGRIC cuchilla recta de arado de doble filo *f*
quinhydrone *n* CHEM quinhidrona *f*
quinic *adj* CHEM quínico
quinicine *n* CHEM quinicina *f*
quinidine *n* CHEM quinidina *f*
quinine *n* CHEM quinina *f*
quininic *adj* CHEM quinínico
quinite *n* CHEM quinita *f*
quinitol *n* CHEM quinitol *m*
quinoa *n* CHEM quinoa *f*
quinoid *adj* CHEM quinoide
quinol *n* CHEM hidroquinona *f*, quinol *m*
quinoline *n* CHEM, COAL quinolina *f*
quinolinic *adj* CHEM, COAL quinolínico
quinone *n* CHEM quinona *f*
quinonoid *adj* CHEM quinonoide
quinovin *n* CHEM quinovina *f*
quinoxalin *n* CHEM quinoxalina *f*
quinoxaline *n* CHEM quinoxalina *f*
quintal *n* METR quintal *m*
quintet *n* PHYS quinteto *m*
QUIP *abbr* (*quad-in-line package*) ELECTRON PCHC (pastilla con cuatro hileras de conexiones)
quire *n* PAPER, PRINT mano *f*
quirk *n* CONST *joinery* caveto *m*
quoin *n* CONST sillar de esquina *f*, MECH ENG *wedge* cuña *f*, PROD piedra angular *f*; ~ **post** *n* WATER *of lock gate* montante de giro *m*, poste de quicio *m*
quotation: ~ **marks** *n pl* PRINT comillas *f pl*; ~ **request** *n* PROD petición de cotización *f*
quotes *n pl* PRINT comillas *f pl*
quotient *n* COMP&DP cociente *m*
Q-value *n* PHYS calor de reacción *m*
QWERTY: ~ **keyboard** *n* COMP&DP teclado QWERTY *m*

R

R[1] *abbr* (*Reynolds number, roentgen*) AIR TRANSP, FLUID FUELLESS, PHYS, RAD R (*número de Reynolds, renguenio, roentgen*)

R[2]: **~ factor** *n* CRYSTALL factor R *m*

Ra *abbr* (*radium*) CHEM, RAD PHYS Ra (*radio*)

rabbet *n* CONST rebajo *m*, renvalso *m*; **~ draft** *AmE*, **~ draught** *BrE n* WATER TRANSP *ship design* calado de trazado *m*; **~ iron** *n* CONST hierro de rebajo *m*; **~ plane** *n* CONST guillame *m*, rebajador *m*, cepillo de ranurar *m*

rabbeted: ~ joint *n* CONST junta por rebajo *f*

rabbit: ~ breeding *n* AGRIC cunicultura *f*

rabbittite *n* NUCL rabitita *f*

rabbling *n* PROD *furnace* limpieza del fondo *f*, remoción del caldo *f*

rabies *n* AGRIC rabia *f*

Racah: ~ coupling *n* NUCL acoplamiento Racah *m*

race *n* HYDRAUL, HYDROL canal de trabajo *m*, corriente de agua *f*, MECH, MECH ENG anillo de bolas *m*, anillo de rodadura *m*, anillo guía *m*, aro de rodaduras *m*, aro de rodamiento *m*, jaula *f*, OCEAN hilero *m*, PROD anillo de rodadura *m*, WATER caz *m*, saetín *m*, WATER TRANSP hilero *m*, *current* corriente de marea *f*, escarceo *m*

racemate *n* CHEM racemato *m*

racemic *adj* CHEM racémico *m*

racemization *n* CHEM racemización *f*

racemize *vt* CHEM racemizar

racemizing *adj* CHEM racemizado

racetrack: ~ holding pattern *n* AIR TRANSP sistema de espera de velódromo *m*

raceway *n* ELEC, ELEC ENG conducto eléctrico *m*, HYDRAUL, HYDROL canal de conducción *m*, canal de trabajo *m*, canalización *f*, MECH, MECH ENG, PROD *of ball bearings* anillo de rodadura *m*, canal de conducción *m*, saetín *m*

rachis *n* AGRIC raquis *m*

racing *n* MECH ENG embalado *m*

rack[1]: **~-mounted** *adj* ELEC ENG montado-cremallera

rack[2] *n* AGRIC pesebre *m*, ELEC ENG cremallera *f*, MECH caballete *m*, cremallera *f*, rejilla *f*, sector dentado *m*, soporte *m*, MECH ENG sector dentado *m*, atril *m*, bastidor *m*, batiente *m*, caballete *m*, consola *f*, cremallera *f*, soporte *m*, *unscrewing device* dispositivo para desenroscar *m*, MILIT *for weapons* bastidor *m*, PRINT chibalete *m*, PROD bastidor *m*, cremallera *f*, TELECOM armario metálico *m*, soporte *m*, TRANSP, VEH cremallera *f*; **~-and-pin processing** *n* CINEMAT revelado en cremallera y clavija *m*; **~-and-pinion** *n* MECH cremallera y piñón *f*; **~-and-pinion drive gear** *n* NUCL tren de accionamiento por cremallera y piñón *m*; **~-and-pinion gear** *n* MECH ENG mecanismo de engranaje de cremallera y piñón *m*; **~-and-pinion jack** *n* MECH ENG gato de cremallera y piñón *m*; **~-and-pinion railroad** *n AmE* (*cf rack-and-pinion railway BrE*) AUTO, RAIL ferrocarril de cremallera y piñón *m*; **~-and-pinion railway** *n BrE* (*cf rack-and-pinion railroad AmE*) AUTO, RAIL ferrocarril de cremallera y piñón *m*; **~-and-pinion steering** *n*

AUTO, VEH dirección de piñón y cremallera *f*, engranaje de cremallera *m*; **~ body lorry** *n BrE* (*cf rack body truck AmE*) RAIL locomotora de cremallera *f*, TRANSP camión con estanterías *m*; **~ body truck** *n AmE* (*cf rack body lorry BrE*) RAIL locomotora de cremallera *f*, TRANSP camión con estanterías *m*; **~ engine** *n* RAIL, TRANSP locomotora de cremallera *f*; **~ feed** *n* MECH ENG avance por cremallera *m*; **~ gearing** *n* TRANSP transmisión por cremallera *f*; **~ line** *n* CINEMAT grupo de cremalleras *m*; **~ mark** *n* C&G marca del estante *f*; **~ mount** *n* PACK bastidor *m*; **~ and pinion** *n* INSTR, MECH, MECH ENG, PROD, RAIL, TRANSP cremallera y piñón *f*, engranaje de cremallera *m*; **~ rail** *n* RAIL rail de cremallera *m*; **~-rail locomotive** *n* RAIL locomotora de ferrocarril de cremallera *f*; **~ railroad** *n AmE* (*cf rack railway BrE*) NUCL sistema de adición de boro *m*, RAIL, TRANSP ferrocarril de cremallera *m*; **~-railroad trailer** *n AmE* (*cf rack-railway trailer BrE*) RAIL, TRANSP remolque por cremallera *m*; **~ railway** *n BrE* (*cf rack railroad AmE*) NUCL sistema de adición de boro *m*, RAIL, TRANSP ferrocarril de cremallera *m*; **~-railway trailer** *n BrE* (*cf rack-railroad trailer AmE*) RAIL, TRANSP remolque por cremallera *m*; **~ wheel** *n* MECH ENG piñón de la cremallera *m*, rueda de escape *f*, rueda dentada *f*; **~ which engages with a pinion** *n* MECH ENG cremallera que engancha con un piñón *f*; **~ wiring** *n* ELEC ENG hilo-cremallera *m*

rack[3] *vt* CINEMAT enganchar; **~ the carriage of a traveling crane** *AmE*, **~ the carriage of a travelling crane** *BrE n* MECH ENG trasladar el carro de un puente grúa

rack[4]: **~ focus** *vi* CINEMAT enfocar con cremallera

racking *n* AGRIC embotellado *m*, FOOD embotellado *m*, trasiego *m*; **~ pipe** *n* PETR TECH tubo para estibado *m*

racon *n* WATER TRANSP baliza de radar *f*, racón *m*

radar[1]: **~-controlled** *adj* AIR TRANSP, PHYS, TELECOM, TRANSP, WATER TRANSP controlado por radar

radar[2] *n* GEN radar *m*; **~ aerial** *n BrE* (*cf radar antenna AmE*) AIR TRANSP, PHYS, RAD PHYS, TELECOM, TRANSP, TV, WATER TRANSP antena de radar *f*, antena radárica *f*; **~ altimeter** *n* AIR TRANSP altímetro radárico *m*; **~ antenna** *n AmE* (*cf radar aerial BrE*) AIR TRANSP, PHYS, RAD PHYS, TELECOM, TRANSP, TV, WATER TRANSP antena de radar *f*, antena radárica *f*; **~ approach** *n* AIR TRANSP, TRANSP, WATER TRANSP aproximación por radar *f*; **~ approach control center** *AmE*, **~ approach control centre** *BrE n* TRANSP centro de control de aproximación por radar *m*; **~ beacon** *n* AIR TRANSP, MILIT, PHYS, RAD PHYS, TELECOM, TRANSP, WATER TRANSP baliza de radar *f*, baliza radárica *f*, faro de radar *m*; **~ beam** *n* AIR TRANSP, PHYS, RAD PHYS, TRANSP, WATER TRANSP haz de radar *m*, haz radárico *m*; **~ bearing** *n* AIR TRANSP, TRANSP, WATER TRANSP marcación de radar *f*; **~ blip** *n* AIR TRANSP eco radárico *m*, traza radárica *f*, WATER TRANSP impulso del radar *m*; **~ calibration** *n* RAD PHYS, WAVE PHYS calibración de radar *f*; **~ coast image** *n* TRANSP, WATER TRANSP imagen de las costas por radar *f*; ~ **with coherent pulse** *n* AIR TRANSP, PHYS, RAD PHYS, TRANSP, WATER TRANSP radar de impulsos sincronizados *m*; ~ **contact** *n* TRANSP contacto por radar *m*; ~ **control** *n* AIR TRANSP, TRANSP, WATER TRANSP control de radar *m*; ~ **controller** *n* AIR TRANSP, TRANSP, WATER TRANSP controlador de radar *m*; ~ **detection** *n* AIR TRANSP, TRANSP, WATER TRANSP detección de objetos por el radar *f*, detección radárica *f*; ~ **dish** *n* AIR TRANSP reflector parabólico de radar *m*; ~ **display** *n* AIR TRANSP, MILIT, PHYS, RAD PHYS, TRANSP, WATER TRANSP pantalla de radar *f*; ~ **dome** *n* WATER TRANSP radomo *m*; ~ **echo** *n* AIR TRANSP, TRANSP, WATER TRANSP eco radárico *m*; ~ **equipment** *n* MILIT accesorio de radar *m*, TRANSP equipo de radar *m*; ~ **heading** *n* AIR TRANSP, TRANSP, WATER TRANSP rumbo radárico *m*; ~ **homing** *n* AIR TRANSP, TRANSP, WATER TRANSP aproximación por radar *f*, guiado por radar *m*; ~ **identification** *n* AIR TRANSP, MILIT, TRANSP, WATER TRANSP identificación radárica *f*; ~ **image** *n* SPACE imagen por radar *f*; ~ **imager** *n* WATER TRANSP radar con panel de retención de imagen *m*; ~ **interference** *n* WATER TRANSP interferencia *f*; ~ **marker beacon** *n* AIR TRANSP, MILIT, TRANSP, WATER TRANSP radiobaliza marcadora de transmisión constante *f*, radiobaliza marcadora de transmisión secuencial *f*, ramark *m*; ~ **marker float** *n* TRANSP, WATER TRANSP marcador flotante de radar *m*; ~ **mast** *n* AIR TRANSP, TRANSP, WATER TRANSP mástil de radar *m*; ~ **monitoring** *n* AIR TRANSP, MILIT, TRANSP, WATER TRANSP vigilancia por radar *f*; ~ **navigation** *n* AIR TRANSP, RAD PHYS, TRANSP, WATER TRANSP navegación por radar *f*; ~ **operator** *n* AIR TRANSP, MILIT, TRANSP, WATER TRANSP operador de radar *m*, radarista *m*; ~ **picket station** *n* TRANSP estación repetidora de radar *f*; ~ **plotting** *n* AIR TRANSP, MILIT, TRANSP, WATER TRANSP marcación radárica *f*, punteo de radar *m*; ~ **range** *n* AIR TRANSP, MILIT, TRANSP, WATER TRANSP alcance del radar *m*; ~ **rating** *n* AIR TRANSP, RAD PHYS, TRANSP, WATER TRANSP clasificación del radar *f*; ~ **reflector** *n* AIR TRANSP, MILIT, SAFE, TRANSP, WATER TRANSP reflector de radar *m*; ~ **reflector buoy** *n* TRANSP, WATER TRANSP boya reflector de radar *f*; ~ **relay station** *n* AIR TRANSP, MILIT, TRANSP, WATER TRANSP estación relé de radar *f*; ~ **response** *n* AIR TRANSP, MILIT, TRANSP, WATER TRANSP respuesta de radar *f*; ~ **scan** *n* AIR TRANSP, MILIT, RAD PHYS, TRANSP, WATER TRANSP exploración por radar *f*, exploración radárica *f*; ~ **scan pattern** *n* AIR TRANSP, MILIT, RAD PHYS, TRANSP, WATER TRANSP diagrama de exploración por radar *m*; ~ **scanner** *n* AIR TRANSP, MILIT, RAD PHYS, TRANSP, WATER TRANSP antena de barrido radar *f*, sondador radar *m*; ~ **scope** *n* AIR TRANSP, MILIT, RAD PHYS, TRANSP, WATER TRANSP pantalla de radar *f*; ~ **screen** *n* AIR TRANSP, MILIT, WATER TRANSP pantalla de radar *f*; ~ **sensor** *n* AIR TRANSP, MILIT, RAD PHYS, TRANSP, WATER TRANSP detector de radar *m*; ~ **sonde** *n* AIR TRANSP, RAD PHYS, TRANSP, WATER TRANSP observación por sonda radárica *f*; ~ **speed meter** *n* AIR TRANSP, RAD PHYS, TRANSP, WATER TRANSP contador de velocidad por radar *m*; ~ **station** *n* AIR TRANSP, MILIT, TRANSP, WATER TRANSP instalación de radar *f*; ~ **surveillance** *n* AIR TRANSP, MILIT, TRANSP, WATER TRANSP vigilancia con radar *f*; ~ **surveillance system** *n* AIR TRANSP, MILIT, TRANSP, WATER TRANSP

sistema de vigilancia con radar *m*; ~ **telemeter** *n* AIR TRANSP, MILIT, TRANSP, WATER TRANSP telémetro de radar *m*; ~ **tracking** *n* (*RT*) AIR TRANSP, MILIT, TRANSP, WATER TRANSP seguimiento con radar *m*, seguimiento por radar *m*; ~ **tracking station** *n* AIR TRANSP, MILIT, TRANSP, WATER TRANSP estación de seguimiento con radar *f*; ~ **transponder beacon** *n* AIR TRANSP, MILIT, TRANSP, WATER TRANSP baliza respondedora radar *f*; ~ **tube** *n* ELECTRON, RAD PHYS tubo de radar *m*; ~ **unit** *n* AIR TRANSP, TRANSP, WATER TRANSP unidad de radar *f*; ~ **vectoring** *n* AIR TRANSP, MILIT, TRANSP, WATER TRANSP guía vectorial por radar *f*; ~ **wave** *n* PHYS, RAD PHYS, WAVE PHYS onda radárica *f*

radial[1] *adj* GEN radial

radial[2]: ~ **and axial turbocompressor** *n* MECH ENG turbocompresor radial y axial *m*; ~-**chart recorder** *n* INSTR registrador de gráfico radial *m*; ~ **component** *n* PHYS componente radial *f*; ~ **compressor** *n* AIR TRANSP compresor radial *m*; ~ **control** *n* OPT control radial *m*; ~ **cylindrical roller bearing** *n* MECH ENG cojinete cilíndrico radial *m*, cojinete de rodillos de acción radial *m*, rodamiento de rodillos de acción radial *m*; ~-**deflecting electrode** *n* TV electrodo de desviación radial *m*; ~ **diehead** *n* MECH ENG cabezal para roscar radial *m*, portacojinetes radial *m*; ~-**distribution function** *n* PHYS, RAD PHYS función de la distribución radial *f*; ~ **drilling-machine** *n* MECH taladradora radial *f*; ~ **electrical fields** *n pl* ELEC, RAD PHYS campos eléctricos radiales *m pl*; ~ **feeder** *n* ELEC *supply* alimentador radial *m*; ~-**flow fan** *n* HEAT ENG ventilador de flujo radial *m*; ~-**flow tank** *n* HYDROL depósito de flujo radial *m*; ~ **gate** *n* FUELLESS compuerta radial *f*; ~ **internal clearance** *n* MECH ENG *roller bearings* holgura radial interna *f*, huelgo interno radial *m*; ~ **lead** *n* ELEC ENG conexión perpendicular *f*, conexión radial *f*; ~-**lead capacitor** *n* ELEC ENG condensador de conexión perpendicular *m*; ~-**lead resistor** *n* ELEC ENG resistencia de conexión perpendicular *f*; ~ **neutron flux** *n* NUCL flujo neutrónico radial *m*; ~ **part** *n* RAD PHYS parte radial *f*; ~-**ply tire** *AmE*, ~-**ply tyre** *BrE n* AUTO, P&R, VEH cubierta con pliegues radiales *f*, neumático con pliegues radiales *m*; ~ **positioning time** *n* OPT tiempo de posicionado radial *m*; ~ **power distribution** *n* NUCL distribución radial de potencia *f*; ~ **shift** *n* NUCL desviación radial *f*; ~ **shuffling** *n* NUCL redistribución radial del combustible *f*; ~-**sludge tank** *n* HYDROL depósito de sedimentos radiales *m*; ~ **system** *n* ELEC, ELEC ENG sistema en estrella *m*, sistema radial *m*; ~-**threading die** *n* MECH ENG cojinete de roscar radial *m*; ~ **tire** *AmE*, ~ **tyre** *BrE n* AUTO, P&R, VEH neumático radial *m*; ~ **velocity** *n* FUELLESS, RAD PHYS velocidad radial *f*

radian *n* ELEC, ELECTRON, GEOM, PHYS radián *m*

radiance *n* GEN radiación *f*, radiancia *f*

radiant[1] *adj* GEN radiante

radiant[2]: ~ **boiler** *n* HEAT, HEAT ENG, THERMO caldera radiante *f*; ~ **cooler** *n* REFRIG, THERMO enfriador radiante *m*, refrigerador radiante *m*; ~ **cooling** *n* REFRIG, THERMO enfriamiento radiante *m*; ~ **dryer** *n* PAPER secador de infrarrojos *m*, secador radiante *m*; ~ **efficiency** *n* PHYS, RAD PHYS eficiencia radiante *f*; ~ **emittance** *n* OPT, TELECOM emitancia de radiación *f*, emitancia radiante *f*; ~ **energy** *n* PHYS, RAD PHYS, TELECOM energía radiante *f*; ~-**energy density** *n*

PHYS, RAD PHYS, TELECOM densidad de energía radiante *f*; **~-energy fluence rate** *n* PHYS, RAD PHYS, TELECOM tasa de flujo de energía radiante *f*; **~ exitance** *n* OPT, PHYS, RAD PHYS, TELECOM exitancia radiante *f*; **~ exposure** *n* PHYS, RAD PHYS exposición a la radiación *f*; **~ flux** *n* OPT, PHYS, RAD PHYS, TELECOM flujo energético *m*, flujo radiante *m*; **~ flux density** *n* OPT, PHYS, RAD PHYS, TELECOM densidad de flujo radiante *f*; **~ heat** *n* HEAT, HEAT ENG, RAD PHYS, THERMO calor radiante *m*; **~ heater** *n* HEAT ENG, MECH ENG, RAD PHYS, THERMO calefactor de calor radiante *m*, calefactor por radiación *m*, calentador de calor radiante *m*, calentador radiante *m*; **~ heating** *n* HEAT, HEAT ENG, RAD PHYS, THERMO calefacción radiante *f*, calentamiento radiante *m*; **~ intensity** *n* OPT, PHYS, RAD PHYS, TELECOM intensidad radiante *f*; **~ power** *n* OPT, PHYS, RAD PHYS, TELECOM potencia radiante *f*; **~ quantity** *n* NUCL cantidad radiante *f*; **~ superheater** *n* HEAT, HEAT ENG, RAD PHYS, THERMO sobrecalentador radiante *m*
radiate[1] *vt* GEN irradiar, radiar
radiate[2] *vi* GEN desprender rayos, emitir rayos
radiated: **~ energy** *n* RAD PHYS energía radiada *f*; **~ interference** *n* ELEC ENG, RAD PHYS interferencia radiada *f*; **~ output** *n* RAD PHYS potencia radiada *f*; **~ power** *n* ELEC, NUCL, RAD PHYS, TELECOM, TV potencia radiada *f*
radiating[1] *adj* OPT, RAD PHYS, TELECOM, TV emisor, irradiante, radiante
radiating[2]: **~-cable communication system** *n* RAD PHYS, TELECOM sistema de comunicación por cable radiante *m*; **~ circuit** *n* TV circuito radiante *m*; **~ particle** *n* PART PHYS partícula radiactiva *f*
radiation[1]: **~-proof** *adj* RAD PHYS a prueba de radiaciones, protegido contra las radiaciones
radiation[2] *n* GEN irradiación *f*, radiación *f*; **~-absorption analysis** *n* NUCL, RAD PHYS análisis de la absorción de radiaciones *m*; **~ angle** *n* ELECTRON, OPT, RAD PHYS, TELECOM ángulo de radiación *m*; **~ belt** *n* RAD PHYS, SPACE cinturón de irradiación *m*, cinturón de radiación *m*; **~ burn** *n* RAD PHYS quemadura por radiación *f*; **~ catalysis** *n* RAD PHYS catálisis por radiación *f*; **~ channel** *n* CHEM, NUCL, RAD PHYS canal de radiación *m*; **~ chemistry** *n* CHEM, NUCL, RAD PHYS química de las radiaciones *f*; **~ constant** *n* HEAT ENG constante de radiación *f*; **~ counter** *n* RAD PHYS contador de radiación *m*, WAVE PHYS contador de centelleo *m*, contador de destellos *m*, medidor de radiación *m*, radiómetro *m*; **~ counter tube** *n* ELECTRON, RAD PHYS tubo contador de irradiación *m*, tubo contador de radiación *m*; **~ cross-linking** *n* P&R, RAD PHYS reticulación por irradiación *f*, reticulación por radiación *f*; **~ damage** *n* RAD PHYS daños por irradiación *m pl*, deterioro por irradiación *m*; **~ degradation** *n* RAD PHYS degradación por irradiación *f*; **~ density** *n* PHYS, RAD PHYS, TELECOM densidad de radiación *f*; **~ detector** *n* LAB, RAD PHYS detector de radiación *m*; **~ dose** *n* POLL, RAD PHYS, SPACE dosis de irradiación *f*, dosis de radiación *f*; **~ dosimeter** *n* RAD PHYS dosímetro de radiación *m*; **~ dosimetry** *n* RAD PHYS dosimetría de radiación *f*; **~ effects reactor** *n* NUCL reactor de vigilancia de los efectos de irradiación *m*; **~ excitation** *n* ELECTRON, RAD PHYS excitación de radiación *f*; **~ field** *n* RAD PHYS campo de radiación *m*; **~-flux density** *n* NUCL, RAD PHYS densidad del

flujo de radiación *f*; **~ frequency** *n* RAD PHYS frecuencia de radiación *f*; **~ hardening** *n* ELEC ENG, NUCL, RAD PHYS endurecimiento por radiación *m*; **~ hardness** *n* ELEC ENG, NUCL dureza de la radiación *f*, poder de penetración de la radiación *m*, resistencia a la radiación *f*, PHYS poder de penetración de la radiación *m*, RAD PHYS, TELECOM dureza de la radiación *f*, poder de penetración de la radiación *m*, resistencia a la radiación *f*; **~ hazard** *n* NUCL peligro de radiación *m*, SAFE, TELECOM peligro de radiación *m*, riesgo de radiación *m*; **~-heat transfer coefficient** *n* HEAT ENG, RAD PHYS, THERMO coeficiente de transferencia del calor de irradiación *m*; **~ heating** *n* HEAT ENG, RAD PHYS, THERMO caldeo por radiación *m*, calor de radiación *m*; **~ impedance** *n* RAD PHYS, TELECOM impedancia de radiación *f*; **~-induced activation** *n* RAD PHYS activación inducida por irradiación *f*, activación inducida por radiación *f*; **~-induced mutation** *n* NUCL, RAD PHYS mutación inducida por radiación *f*; **~-induced reaction** *n* RAD PHYS reacción inducida por radiación *f*; **~ intensity** *n* RAD PHYS, SPACE intensidad de irradiación *f*, intensidad de radiación *f*; **~ ionization** *n* GEOPHYS, PHYS, RAD PHYS ionización de radiación *f*; **~ laws** *n pl* RAD PHYS leyes de la radiación *f pl*; **~ loss** *n* PART PHYS, RAD PHYS pérdida por radiación *f*; **~ measurement** *n* RAD PHYS medición de radiación *f*; **~ meter** *n* INSTR, MILIT, NUCL, RAD PHYS medidor de radiación *m*; **~ mode** *n* OPT, RAD PHYS, TELECOM modo de radiación *m*; **~ monitor** *n* NUCL, RAD PHYS, SPACE monitor de radiación *m*; **~ monitoring** *n* NUCL monitorización de radiación *f*, RAD PHYS, SPACE detección de radiación *f*, monitorización de radiación *f*, seguimiento de radiación *m*, vigilancia de radiación *f*; **~ pattern** *n* OPT, PHYS, RAD PHYS, SPACE, TELECOM, TV característica de radiación *f*, diagrama de radiación *m*, patrón de radiación *m*; **~ physics** *n* NUCL, RAD PHYS física de radiación *f*; **~ pressure** *n* ACOUST, PART PHYS, PHYS, RAD PHYS presión de radiación *f*; **~ processing** *n* NUCL, RAD PHYS procesamiento por irradiación *m*, tratamiento por irradiación *m*; **~ protection** *n* ELEC ENG protección contra radiación *f*, protección radiológica *f*, MILIT *nuclear warfare* protección contra radiación *f*, POLL, RAD PHYS, SAFE protección contra radiación *f*, protección radiológica *f*; **~ pyrometer** *n* GEOPHYS, INSTR, LAB, PHYS, RAD PHYS pirómetro de radiación *m*; **~ resistance** *n* NUCL, PHYS, RAD PHYS resistencia a la radiación *f*; **~ shield** *n* RAD PHYS, SAFE escudo contra la radiación *m*; **~ shielding** *n* RAD PHYS, SAFE pantalla contra la radiación *f*; **~-shielding glass** *n* C&G, RAD PHYS, SAFE vidrio opaco a la radiación *m*; **~ sickness** *n* RAD PHYS malestar producido por la radiación *m*, radiopatía *f*; **~ source** *n* ELECTRON, NUCL, RAD PHYS emisor de radiación *m*, fuente de radiación *f*; **~ spectrum** *n* GEOPHYS, RAD PHYS espectro de radiación *m*; **~ treatment** *n* INSTR, RAD PHYS radioterapia *f*; **~ unit** *n* RAD PHYS unidad de la radiación *f*, unidad de radioterapia *f*
radiationless: **~ transition** *n* RAD PHYS transición sin emisión de radiación *f*, transición sin radiación *f*
radiative[1] *adj* ELEC, RAD PHYS, SPACE, THERMO radiante, radiativo
radiative[2]: **~ capture** *n* RAD PHYS captura radiativa *f*; **~ cascade** *n* RAD PHYS cascada radiativa *f*; **~ collision** *n* RAD PHYS colisión radiativa *f*;

~ **experiment** n RAD PHYS experimento radiativo m; ~ **heat transfer** n RAD PHYS, SPACE transferencia de calor por radiación f, transferencia de calor radioactivo f; ~ **recombination** n ELECTRON, RAD PHYS recombinación radiativa f; ~ **transfer** n RAD PHYS transferencia radiativa f; ~ **transition** n RAD PHYS transición radiativa f

radiator n AUTO radiador m, HEAT ENG calorífero m, MECH radiador m, THERMO for heating calorífero m, mechanism radiador m, VEH radiador m; ~ **blind** n AUTO, VEH rejilla del radiador f; ~ **cap** n AUTO, VEH tapón del radiador m; ~ **core** n AUTO, VEH elemento del radiador m, núcleo del radiador m; ~ **drain cock** n AUTO, VEH espita de drenaje del radiador f; ~ **drain tap** n AUTO, VEH tapón de vaciado del radiador m; ~ **draining** n AUTO, VEH drenaje del radiador m; ~ **element** n AUTO, VEH elemento del radiador m; ~ **filler cap** n AUTO, VEH tapón del radiador m; ~ **filler neck** n AUTO, VEH cuello del radiador m; ~ **fin** n AUTO, VEH aleta del radiador f; ~ **flange** n AUTO, VEH brida del radiador f, pestaña del radiador f, saliente del radiador m; ~ **frame** n AUTO, VEH armazón del radiador m, cuerpo del radiador m, marco del radiador m; ~ **grille** n AUTO, VEH rejilla del radiador f; ~ **header** n AUTO, VEH depósito superior del radiador m; ~ **hose** n AIR TRANSP, AUTO, VEH manguito del radiador m, tubo del radiador m; ~**-pressure cap** n AUTO, VEH tapón de presión del radiador m; ~ **support** n AUTO, VEH soporte del radiador m; ~**-vent hose** n AUTO, VEH manguito de ventilación del radiador m

radical n CHEM, GAS, MATH, P&R radical m; ~ **process** n P&R proceso de radicales m

radicle n AGRIC radícula f

radio¹: ~**-controlled** adj RAD PHYS, TELECOM, TRANSP dirigido por radio

radio²: ~ **aerial** n BrE (cf radio antenna AmE) AUTO, TELECOM, TRANSP, VEH antena de radio f; ~ **altimeter** n AIR TRANSP altímetro radioeléctrico m, radioaltímetro m; ~ **amateur** n TELECOM radioaficionado m; ~ **antenna** n AmE (cf radio aerial BrE) AUTO, TELECOM, TRANSP, VEH antena de radio f; ~**-approach aid** n AIR TRANSP, TELECOM ayuda de aproximación por radio f; ~ **astrometry** n PHYS, SPACE radioastrometría f; ~ **astronomy** n PHYS, SPACE radioastronomía f; ~ **beacon** n AIR TRANSP at sea radiobaliza f, on land radiofaro m, MILIT, TRANSP on land radiofaro m, at sea radiobaliza f, WATER TRANSP at sea radiobaliza f, on land radiofaro m; ~ **beam** n RAD PHYS enlace de radio m; ~ **bearing** n AIR TRANSP, TELECOM, WATER TRANSP marcación radiogoniométrica f, radiodemora f, radiomarcación f; ~**-broadcast satellite** n SPACE, TELECOM satélite de radiodifusión m; ~ **broadcasting** n TELECOM radiodifusión f; ~**-cassette deck** n AUTO, PROD, VEH alojamiento para radio-casete m; ~ **channel** n AIR TRANSP, TELECOM canal de radio m; ~ **code message** n MILIT radiograma en código m; ~ **compass** n AIR TRANSP, WATER TRANSP brújula radiogoniométrica f, radiobrújula f, radiocompás m, radiogoniómetro de navegación m; ~ **control system** n TELECOM sistema de control por radio m, sistema de mando por radio m, sistema de radiocontrol m, sistema de telemando por radio m; ~**-determination satellite system** n AIR TRANSP, SPACE, WATER TRANSP sistema de radiodeterminación por satélite m, sis-

tema satelitario de radiodeterminación m; ~ **direction finder** n AIR TRANSP, INSTR, TRANSP, WATER TRANSP radiogoniómetro m; ~ **direction finding** n AIR TRANSP, PHYS, TELECOM, TRANSP, WATER TRANSP radiogoniometría f, radiolocalización direccional f; ~ **direction-finding station** n AIR TRANSP, TELECOM, TRANSP, WATER TRANSP estación radiogoniométrica f; ~ **engineer** n AIR TRANSP, WATER TRANSP técnico del servicio radioeléctrico m; ~ **equipment** n AIR TRANSP, TELECOM, TRANSP, WATER TRANSP equipo de radio m; ~ **facilities** n pl AIR TRANSP, TELECOM, TRANSP, WATER TRANSP servicios de radio m pl; ~ **facility** n AIR TRANSP, TELECOM, WATER TRANSP aparato de radiocomunicación m, instalación radioeléctrica f; ~ **fix** n AIR TRANSP, TELECOM, WATER TRANSP determinación de posición por radio f, localización radiogoniométrica f, situación radiogoniométrica f; ~ **frequency** n (RF) GEN frecuencia de radio f (RF), frecuencia radioeléctrica f, radiofrecuencia f (RF); ~**-frequency generator** n ELEC ENG generador de radiofrecuencia m; ~**-guided flight** n AIR TRANSP, MILIT vuelo radiodirigido m, vuelo radioguiado m; ~ **homing** n TELECOM radioconducción desde el punto de destino f, recalada por radio f, TRANSP recalada por radio f, radioconducción desde el punto de destino f; ~ **homing beacon** n AIR TRANSP, TRANSP, WATER TRANSP radiofaro de recalado m, radiofaro direccional m; ~ **interference** n ELECTRON, RAD PHYS, WAVE PHYS interferencia radioeléctrica f, radiointerferencia f; ~ **interferometer** n GEOPHYS, INSTR, RAD PHYS interferómetro de radio m; ~ **labeling** AmE, ~ **labelling** BrE n CHEM of compound, group, atom marcado radioactivo m; ~ **link** n AIR TRANSP contacto por radio m, enlace radiofónico m, TELECOM cable hertziano m, enlace de microondas m, radioenlace de microondas m, TV cadena de estaciones de radio f, WATER TRANSP enlace radioeléctrico m; ~ **marker** n TRANSP radiofaro de rumbo m; ~ **navigation** n AIR TRANSP, RAD PHYS, WATER TRANSP navegación radiogoniométrica f, radionavegación f; ~**-navigation mobile station** n TELECOM estación móvil de radionavegación f; ~ **noise** n ELECTRON ruido radioeléctrico m; ~ **officer** n WATER TRANSP oficial radiotelegrafista m; ~ **operator** n WATER TRANSP radiooperador m; ~ **paging** n TELECOM llamada sin hilos f, llamadas por radio f pl; ~**-paging system** n TELECOM sistema de llamada sin hilos m, sistema de llamadas por radio m; ~**-patrol car** n AUTO coche radio-patrulla m; ~ **position fixing** n TRANSP determinación radioeléctrica de la posición f; ~ **range** n AIR TRANSP, TELECOM, WATER TRANSP alcance de radio m; ~ **receiver** n PHYS, RAD PHYS radiorreceptor m; ~ **relay** n ELEC ENG radioestación repetidora f; ~ **remote-control** n RAD PHYS, TRANSP control remoto por radio m; ~ **room** n WATER TRANSP cuarto de radiotelegrafía m; ~ **sensitivity** n RAD PHYS radiosensibilidad f, sensibilidad radioeléctrica f; ~ **signal** n ELEC ENG, ELECTRON radioseñal f, señal de radio f, señal transmitida por radio f; ~ **sonobuoy** n WATER TRANSP radio sonoboya f, radiocomunicación f; ~ **source** n RAD PHYS, SPACE fuente radioeléctrica f, radiofuente f; ~ **spectrum** n ELECTRON, RAD PHYS espectro de ondas de radiocomunicación m, espectro radioeléctrico m; ~ **star** n RAD PHYS, SPACE estrella radioeléctrica f, radioestrella f; ~ **station** n TELECOM estación de radio f;

~ steering *n* TRANSP dirección por radio *f*; **~ subsystem** *n* TELECOM subsistema radioeléctrico *m*; **~ system** *n* TELECOM red radioeléctrica *f*; **~ taxicab** *n* TRANSP taxi con radio *m*; **~ telecontrol** *n* TELECOM, TRANSP control remoto por radio *m*, telecontrol por radio *m*; **~ telescope** *n* INSTR, PHYS radiotelescopio *m*; **~ tracking** *n* MILIT seguimiento radioeléctrico *m*; **~ transmitter** *n* PHYS, RAD PHYS, TELECOM radiotransmisor *m*; **~ wave** *n* ELEC, ELEC ENG, ELECTRON, GEOPHYS, PHYS, RAD PHYS, WAVE PHYS onda de radio *f*, onda hertziana *f*, onda radioeléctrica *f*; **~~wave hazard** *n* SAFE peligro causado por ondas radioeléctricas *m*, riesgo causado por ondas radioeléctricas *m*; **~~wave propagation** *n* RAD PHYS, WAVE PHYS propagación de ondas de radio *f*; **~ window** *n* PHYS, RAD PHYS región de transmisiones por radio *f*, ventana de radio *f*, ventana radioeléctrica *f*

radioactinium *n* CHEM, RAD PHYS, WATER TRANSP actinio radioactivo *m*, radiactinio *m*

radioactivation: ~ analysis *n* RAD PHYS análisis por radiactivación *m*

radioactive[1] *adj* GEN radiactivo, radioactivo

radioactive[2]**: ~ body** *n* PHYS, RAD PHYS cuerpo radiactivo *m*; **~ contamination** *n* PHYS, POLL, RAD PHYS contaminación radiactiva *f*; **~ dating** *n* PHYS, RAD PHYS datación radiactiva *f*; **~ decay** *n* PART PHYS, RAD PHYS desintegración radiactiva *f*; **~~decay rate** *n* PART PHYS, RAD PHYS velocidad de desintegración radiactiva *f*; **~~decay series** *n* PART PHYS, RAD PHYS cadena de desintegración radiactiva *f*, familia de desintegración radiactiva *f*; **~ dust** *n* MILIT, NUCL, POLL, RAD PHYS polvo radiactivo *m*; **~ element** *n* RAD PHYS elemento radiactivo *m*; **~ emanation** *n* RAD PHYS emanación radiactiva *f*; **~ equilibrium** *n* PHYS, RAD PHYS equilibrio radiactivo *m*; **~ fallout** *n* AGRIC, NUCL, PHYS, POLL, RAD PHYS cenizas radiactivas *f pl*, deposición radiactiva *f* (*AmL*), lluvia radioactiva *f*, poso radiactivo *m*, precipitación radiactiva *f* (*Esp*); **~ half-life** *n* NUCL, RAD PHYS período de semidesintegración *m*, vida media radiactiva *f*; **~~ion implantation** *n* ELECTRON, PART PHYS, RAD PHYS implantación de ion radiactivo *f*; **~ isotope** *n* PART PHYS, PHYS, RAD PHYS isótopo radiactivo *m*; **~ log** *n* PETR TECH diagrafía radioactiva *f*, perfil radiactivo *m*, registro radiactivo *m*; **~~point source** *n* CINEMAT fuente puntual *f*, NUCL foco puntual *m*, fuente de radiación puntual *f*, fuente puntual *f*, PHOTO, PHYS fuente puntual *f*, POLL, RAD PHYS foco puntual *m*, fuente de radiación puntual *f*, fuente puntual *f*; **~ pollution** *n* NUCL, PHYS, POLL, RAD PHYS, SAFE contaminación radiactiva *f*; **~ purity** *n* RAD PHYS pureza radiactiva *f*, pureza radionucléidica *f*; **~ series** *n* PHYS, RAD PHYS serie radiactiva *f*; **~ standard** *n* RAD PHYS patrón radiactivo *m*; **~ substance** *n* POLL, RAD PHYS, SAFE substancia radiactiva *f*; **~ tracer** *n* PHYS, RAD PHYS indicador de radioactividad *m*, radiotrazador *m*, trazador radiactivo *m*; **~ transformation** *n* RAD PHYS transformación radiactiva *f*; **~ transmutation** *n* RAD PHYS transmutación radiactiva *f*; **~ waste** *n* NUCL, PHYS, POLL, RAD PHYS residuos radiactivos *m pl*; **~~waste evaporator** *n* NUCL, PHYS, POLL, RAD PHYS evaporador de residuos radiactivos *m*; **~~waste management** *n* NUCL, POLL, RAD PHYS gestión de residuos radiactivos *f*

radioactivity *n* GEN radiactividad *f*, radioactividad *f*; **~ in the environment** *n* AGRIC radioactividad de ambiente *f*; **~ meter** *n* INSTR, NUCL, RAD PHYS medidor de radiactividad *m*

radioanalysis *n* RAD PHYS radioanálisis *m*

radioastronomical: ~ aerial *n* BrE (*cf radioastronomical antenna AmE*) TELECOM antena radioastronómica *f*; **~ antenna** *n* AmE (*cf radioastronomical aerial BrE*) TELECOM antena radioastronómica *f*

radiocaesium *n* BrE RAD PHYS radiocesio *m*

radiocarbon *n* GEOPHYS, PHYS, RAD PHYS radiocarbono *m*; **~ dating** *n* GEOPHYS, PHYS, RAD PHYS determinación de edades por medio del radiocarbono *f*

radiocesium *AmE see radiocaesium BrE*

radiochemical *adj* CHEM, RAD PHYS radioquímico

radiochemistry *n* CHEM, RAD PHYS radioquímica *f*

radiochromatography *n* CHEM, RAD PHYS radiocromatografía *f*

radiocobalt *n* CHEM, RAD PHYS cobalto radioactivo *m*, radiocobalto *m*

radiocommunication *n* TELECOM comunicación por radio *f*, comunicación radioeléctrica *f*, radiocomunicación *f*

radiodiagnosis *n* RAD PHYS radiodiagnóstico *m*

radiogenic[1] *adj* GEOL, RAD PHYS radiogénico

radiogenic[2]**: ~ isotope** *n* GEOL, PHYS, RAD PHYS isótopo radiogénico *m*

radiogoniometer *n* AIR TRANSP, INSTR, PHYS, RAD PHYS, WATER TRANSP radiogoniómetro *m*

radiogoniometry *n* AIR TRANSP, PHYS, RAD PHYS, WATER TRANSP radiogoniometría *f*

radiograph[1] *n* INSTR, PHYS, RAD PHYS radiógrafo *m*

radiograph[2] *vt* INSTR, PHYS, RAD PHYS radiografiar

radiographer *n* INSTR, PHYS, RAD PHYS radiógrafo *m*, radiólogo *m*, técnico radigráfico *m*

radiographic: ~ examination *n* MECH ENG, PHYS, RAD PHYS inspección radiográfica *f*

radiography *n* INSTR, PHYS, RAD PHYS radiografía *f*

radioguidance *n* TELECOM, TRANSP radioguía *f*

radioguide *vt* TELECOM, TRANSP dirigir por radio

radioiodine *n* CHEM, RAD PHYS iodo radioactivo *m*, radioyodo *m*, yodo radioactivo *m*

radioisomer *n* CHEM, RAD PHYS radioisómero *m*

radioisotope *n* AGRIC, CHEM, PART PHYS, PHYS, RAD PHYS radioisótopo *m*; **~ power generator** *n* SPACE grupo electrógeno radioisótopo *m*; **~ tracer technique** *n* AGRIC técnica de marcadores radioisotópicos *f*

radiolarian: ~ chert *n* GEOL sílex de radiolarios *m*

radiolite *n* MINERAL radiolita *f*

radiolocation *n* AIR TRANSP, MILIT, RAD PHYS, TRANSP, WATER TRANSP radiolocalización *f*

radiology *n* RAD PHYS radiología *f*

radioluminescence *n* RAD PHYS radioluminiscencia *f*

radiolysis *n* CHEM, RAD PHYS radiólisis *f*

radiomechanic *n* MECH, MILIT, RAD PHYS radiomecánico *m*

radiometer *n* CHEM, FUELLESS, GEOPHYS, INSTR, PHYS, RAD PHYS radiómetro *m*

radiometric[1] *adj* CHEM, FUELLESS, GEOL, GEOPHYS, RAD PHYS radiométrico

radiometric[2]**: ~ age determination** *n* GEOL, GEOPHYS, RAD PHYS determinación radiométrica de la edad *f*; **~ analysis** *n* RAD PHYS análisis radiométrico *m*; **~ log** *n* PETROL perfil radiométrico *m*

radiometry *n* CHEM, FUELLESS, GEOL, GEOPHYS, METEO, RAD PHYS radiometría *f*
radiomicrometer *n* MECH ENG radiomicrómetro *m*
radiomimetic *adj* CHEM radiomimético
radionuclide *n* PHYS radionuclido *m*, RAD PHYS radionucleido *m*
radiophone[1] *n* TELECOM, TRANSP, WATER TRANSP radioteléfono *m*
radiophone[2] *vt* TELECOM, TRANSP, WATER TRANSP radiotelefonear
radiosonde *n* GEOPHYS, RAD PHYS, TELECOM radiosonda *f*
radiostrontium *n* CHEM, RAD PHYS estroncio radioactivo *m*, radioestroncio *m*
radiotelephone *n* TELECOM, TRANSP, WATER TRANSP radioteléfono *m*; ~ **link** *n* TELECOM, TRANSP, WATER TRANSP enlace radiotelefónico *m*
radiotelephony *n* (*RT*) TELECOM, TRANSP, WATER TRANSP radiotelefonía *f* (*RT*)
radiotherapy *n* INSTR, RAD PHYS radioterapia *f*
radiotive: ~ **lifetime** *n* RAD PHYS vida media radiativa *f*
radiotoxicity *n* INSTR, RAD PHYS radiotoxicidad *f*
radium *n* (*Ra*) CHEM, RAD PHYS radio *m* (*Ra*); ~ **emanation** *n* CHEM, RAD PHYS emanación de radio *f*, emanación rádica *f*
radius *n* CONST *of crane*, GEOM radio *m*, MECH ENG *under the head of bolts, screws, etc* curva de unión *f*, curva de acuerdo *f*, OPT, PHYS radio *m*; ~ **arm** *n* AUTO, VEH biela de empuje *f*; ~ **of curvature** *n* GEOM radio de curvatura *m*; ~ **of gyration** *n* CONST, MECH ENG radio de giro *m*
radix *n* COMP&DP, PRINT base *f*; ~ **complement** *n* COMP&DP complemento de base *m*; ~~-**minus-one complement** *n* COMP&DP complemento de base menos uno *m*; ~ **notation** *n* COMP&DP notación de base *f*
radome *n* AIR TRANSP, RAD PHYS, SPACE, TELECOM, WATER TRANSP cúpula de radar *f*, radomo *m*
radon *n* (*Rn*) CHEM, PHYS, RAD PHYS radón *m* (*Rn*)
raffinose *n* CHEM rafinosa *f*
raft *n* COAL balsa *f*, losa *f*, losa continua de cimentación *f*, masa flotante *f*, WATER TRANSP armadía *f*, *flat craft* balsa *f*, batayola *f*, jangada *f* (*AmL*)
rafter *n* CONST cabio *m*, viga *f*
rag[1]: ~~-**left** *adj* AmE (*cf ragged-left BrE*) PRINT *assayer's mark* sin justificar por la izquierda; ~~-**right** *adj* AmE (*cf ragged-right BrE*) PRINT *assayer's mark* sin justificar por la derecha
rag[2] *n* PAPER trapo *m*; ~ **bolt** *n* CONST perno de anclaje *m*; ~ **breaker** *n* PAPER pila filochadora *f*; ~ **cutter** *n* PAPER cortadora de trapos *f*; ~ **duster** *n* PAPER cedazo para trapos *m*; ~ **pulp** *n* PAPER pasta de trapos *f*, pulpa de trapos *f*; ~ **shredder** *n* PAPER cortadora de trapos *f*, matraca *f*; ~ **sorter** *n* PAPER clasificador de trapos *m*; ~ **thrasher** *n* PAPER cedazo para trapos *m*, diablo *m*; ~ **wheel** *n* MECH ENG piñón de cadena *m*, PROD *calico mop* disco de trapo para pulir *m*
ragged[1]: ~~-**left** *adj* BrE (*cf rag-left AmE*) PRINT *assayer's mark* sin justificar por la izquierda; ~~-**right** *adj* BrE (*cf rag-right AmE*) PRINT *assayer's mark* sin justificar por la derecha
ragged[2]: ~ **fire** *n* MILIT *artillery* tiro irregular *m*; ~ **setting** *n* PRINT composición sin justificar *f*
ragger *n* PAPER eliminador de cuerdas *m*
ragging *n* MINE concentración de fangos *f*, desbaste *m*, lavado previo *m*, trituración a mano *f*

RAI *abbr* (*remote-alarm indication*) TELECOM indicación de alarma remota *f*, teleindicación de alarma *f*
rail[1]: ~ **mounted** *adj* TRANSP montado sobre raíles
rail[2] *n* CONST *carpentry* travesaño *m*, *of fence or other structure* barandilla *f* (*Esp*), baranda *f* (*AmL*), *fencina* riel *m*, carril *m*, *bar* riel *m*, ELEC ENG, RAIL carril *m*, rail *m*, riel *m*; ~ **base** *n* RAIL base del carril *f*; ~~-**bending device** *n* RAIL aparato para curvar carriles *m*; ~~-**bending machine** *n* RAIL máquina curvadora de carriles *f*; ~ **bond** *n* BrE (*cf rail splice AmE*) RAIL brida de carril *f*, conexión de carril *f*; ~ **brake** *n* RAIL freno sobre el carril *m*; ~ **break** *n* RAIL rotura de rail *f*; ~~-**carrying car** *n* AmE (*cf rail carrying wagon BrE*) RAIL vagón para transporte de carriles *m*; ~~-**carrying wagon** *BrE n* (*cf rail-carrying car AmE*) RAIL vagón para transporte de carriles *m*; ~ **clip** *n* RAIL sujetacarril *m*; ~ **coach** *n* RAIL vagón de ferrocarril *m*; ~ **crane** *n* TRANSP grúa sobre carriles *f*; ~ **crossover** *n* RAIL cruzamiento de vías *m*; ~~-**cutting machine** *n* RAIL máquina cortacarriles *f*; ~~-**drilling machine** *n* RAIL máquina de taladrar carriles *f*; ~ **ferry** *n* TRANSP transbordador sobre carriles *m*; ~ **flange** *n* RAIL pestaña del carril *f*; ~ **foot** *n* RAIL zapata del carril *f*; ~ **gage** *AmE*, ~ **gauge** *BrE n* RAIL anchura de vía *f*, entrevía *f*, galga de la vía *f*; ~~-**grinding train** *n* RAIL tren de rectificar carriles *m*; ~ **head** *n* RAIL cabeza de carril *f*, término de la vía *m*; ~ **inspection** *n* RAIL inspección ferroviaria *f*; ~ **joint** *n* RAIL junta de carril *f*; ~ **junction** *n* RAIL empalme ferroviario *m*; ~ **laying** *n* RAIL tendido de carriles *m*; ~ **lifter** *n* RAIL levantacarriles *m*; ~ **mill** *n* RAIL laminador de carriles *m*; ~ **motor unit** *n* TRANSP automotor *m*, autovía *f*, tren-tranvía *m*; ~~-**planing machine** *n* RAIL cepilladora de carriles *f*; ~ **profile** *n* RAIL perfil de carril *m*; ~ **safety** *n* RAIL, SAFE seguridad en vías férreas *f*; ~ **section** *n* RAIL sección de carril *f*; ~ **splice** *n* AmE (*cf rail bond BrE*) RAIL brida de carril *f*, conexión de carril *f*; ~ **tank car** *n* AmE (*cf rail tank wagon BrE*) RAIL, TRANSP vagón cisterna *m*; ~ **tank wagon** *BrE n* (*cf rail tank car AmE*) RAIL, TRANSP vagón cisterna *m*; ~ **tongs** *n pl* RAIL tenazas portacarriles *f pl*; ~ **track** *n* MINE, RAIL, TRANSP vía férrea *f*; ~ **transport** *n* RAIL, TRANSP transporte por vía férrea *m*; ~~-**wear tolerance** *n* RAIL tolerancia del carril al desgaste *f*; ~ **wheel** *n* MECH ENG *of overhead travelling crane* rueda de riel *f*, rueda de traslación *f*
railbed *n* RAIL base del carril *f*
railcar *n* RAIL automotor *m*
railing *n* CONST balaustrada *f*, baranda *f* (*AmL*), barandilla *f* (*Esp*)
railroad: ~ **arch** *n* AmE (*cf railway arch BrE*) CONST, RAIL arco de ferrocarril *m*; ~ **bridge** *n* AmE (*cf railway bridge BrE*) CONST, RAIL puente ferroviario *m*; ~ **center** *n* AmE (*cf railway centre BrE*) RAIL centro de ferrocarriles *m*, estación de ferrocarril *f*; ~ **container** *n* AmE (*cf railway container BrE*) RAIL contenedor ferriviario *m*; ~ **cutting** *n* AmE (*cf railway cutting BrE*) RAIL cortacarriles *m*; ~ **embankment** *n* AmE (*cf railway embankment BrE*) RAIL vías en terraplén *f pl*; ~ **inspection trolley** *n* AmE (*cf railway inspection trolley BrE*) CONST vagón de inspección de vía *m*; ~ **junction** *n* AmE (*cf railway junction BrE*) RAIL empalme ferroviario *m*, estación de empalme *f*, nudo ferroviario *m*; ~ **regulations** *n pl* AmE (*cf railway regulations BrE*) RAIL reglamento ferroviario *m*; ~ **semitrailer** *n*

AmE (*cf railway semitrailer BrE*) RAIL sistema de rociado del núcleo de alta presión *m*; ~ **tie screw** *n AmE* (*cf railway sleeper screw BrE*) RAIL tirafondo de traviesas *m*; ~ **tie screwdriver** *n AmE* (*cf railway sleeper screwdriver BrE*) RAIL destornillador de traviesas *m*; ~ **tie-adzing machine** *n AmE* (*cf railway tie-adzing machine BrE*) RAIL máquina azoladora de traviesa *f*; ~ **tunnel** *n AmE* (*cf railway tunnel BrE*) CONST, RAIL túnel ferroviario *m*

railway: ~ **arch** *n BrE* (*cf railroad arch AmE*) CONST, RAIL arco de ferrocarril *m*; ~ **bridge** *n BrE* (*cf railroad bridge AmE*) CONST, RAIL puente ferroviario *m*; ~ **centre** *n BrE* (*cf railroad center AmE*) RAIL centro de ferrocarriles *m*, estación de ferrocarril *f*; ~ **container** *n BrE* (*cf railroad container AmE*) RAIL contenedor ferroviario *m*; ~ **cutting** *n BrE* (*cf railroad cutting AmE*) RAIL cortacarriles *m*; ~ **embankment** *n BrE* (*cf railroad embankment AmE*) RAIL vías en terraplén *f pl*; ~ **inspection trolley** *n BrE* (*cf railroad inspection trolley AmE*) CONST vagón de inspección de vía *m*; ~ **junction** *n BrE* (*cf railroad junction AmE*) RAIL empalme ferroviario *m*, estación de empalme *f*, nudo ferroviario *m*; ~ **regulations** *n pl BrE* (*cf railroad regulations AmE*) RAIL reglamento ferroviario *m*; ~ **semitrailer** *n BrE* (*cf railroad semitrailer AmE*) RAIL sistema de rociado del núcleo de alta presión *m*; ~ **sleeper screw** *n BrE* (*cf railroad tie screw AmE*) RAIL tirafondo de traviesas *m*; ~ **sleeper screwdriver** *n BrE* (*cf railroad tie screwdriver AmE*) RAIL destornillador de traviesas *m*; ~ **tie-adzing machine** *n BrE* (*cf railroad tie-adzing machine AmE*) RAIL máquina azoladora de traviesa *f*; ~ **tunnel** *n BrE* (*cf railroad tunnel AmE*) CONST, RAIL túnel ferroviario *m*

rain[1]: ~**-eroded** *adj* GEOL, GEOPHYS, METEO erosionado por la lluvia

rain[2]: ~ **area** *n* HYDROL, METEO, WATER zona lluviosa *f*; ~ **attenuation** *n* SPACE atenuación por lluvia *f*; ~ **clutter** *n* WATER TRANSP perturbación por lluvia *f*; ~ **erosion** *n* GEOL, GEOPHYS, METEO erosión por la lluvia *f*; ~**-fed agriculture** *n* AGRIC agricultura de secano *f*; ~**-free period** *n* AGRIC, METEO, POLL, WATER TRANSP período sin lluvias *m*; ~ **gage** *AmE*, ~ **gauge** *BrE n* CONST pluviógrafo *m*, pluviómetro *m*, FUEL-LESS pluviógrafo *m*, pluviómetro *m*, udómetro *m*, HYDROL, INSTR, LAB, METEO, WATER pluviógrafo *m*, pluviómetro *m*; ~ **scatter** *n* SPACE dispersión por lluvia *f*

rainbow[1]: ~**-effect** *adj* COLOUR esfumado

rainbow[2] *n* METEO, PHYS arco iris *m*; ~ **cattle** *n* AGRIC ganado de distinto pelaje *m*

rainfall *n* AGRIC, FUELLESS, HYDROL, METEO, WATER pluviosidad *f*, precipitación *f*; ~ **area** *n* METEO, WA-TER zona de lluvias *f*; ~ **intensity** *n* METEO intensidad de la precipitación *f*; ~ **pattern** *n* AGRIC, METEO, WATER, WATER TRANSP régimen pluvial *m*; ~ **station** *n* AGRIC, METEO estación pluviométrica *f*

rainforest *n* AGRIC selva tropical húmeda *f*

rainout *n* POLL cenizas radiactivas *f pl*, precipitación radiactiva *f*

rainwater *n* AGRIC, COAL, HYDROL, METEO, WATER agua de lluvia *f*; ~ **catchment** *n* AGRIC, WATER captación de agua de lluvia *f*; ~ **downpipe** *n BrE* (*cf rainwater downspout AmE*) CONST bajante de aguas *m*; ~ **downspout** *n AmE* (*cf rainwater down-pipe BrE*) CONST bajante de aguas *m*; ~ **head** *n* CONST cabezal de la bajante de aguas *m*; ~ **pipe** *n* CONST tubería para agua pluvial *f*

rainy: ~ **season** *n* AGRIC, GEOL, METEO, WATER estación de lluvias *f*

raise[1] *n* MINE alzamiento *m*, chimenea *f* (*Esp*), coladero *m* (*Esp*), contracielo *m* (*AmL*), pozo de comunicación *m* (*AmL*); ~ **stope** *n* MINE chimenea en bancos *f* (*Esp*), contracielo escalonado *m* (*AmL*), laboreo ascendente *m* (*Esp*), laboreo escalonado *m* (*AmL*)

raise[2] *vt* MINE elevar, excavar hacia arriba, izar, *ore* extraer, PROD *steam* generar, producir, TEXTIL per-char, WATER TRANSP *flag* arbolar; ~ **to a power** *vt* MATH elevar a una potencia

raised: ~ **beach** *n* GEOPHYS playa elevada *f*; ~ **countersunk-rivet** *n* MECH remache de cabeza avellanada elevada *m*; ~ **deck** *n* WATER TRANSP *ship* saltillo *m*; ~ **edge** *n* TEXTIL borde perchado *m*; ~ **head** *n* MECH ENG cabeza elevada *f*; ~**-head screw** *n* MECH ENG tornillo de cabeza elevada *m*; ~**-roof van** *n* VEH furgoneta con techo alzado *f*

raising *n* AGRIC cría *f*, CONST, HYDROL elevación *f*, MINE ejecución de un realce *f*, alzamiento *m*, PHYS elevación *f*, TEXTIL perchado *m*; ~ **agent** *n* FOOD agente leudante *m*; ~ **machine** *n* TEXTIL percha *f*; ~ **power** *n* FOOD potencia leudante *f*; ~ **steam** *n* HYDRAUL generación de vapor *f*, producción de vapor *f*, PROD producción de vapor *f*; ~ **table** *n* MECH ENG mesa ascendente *f*

rake *n* ACOUST *of stylus* peine *m*, inclinación *f*, rastrillo *m*, AGRIC rastrillo *m*, CINEMAT inclinación *f*, CONST rastrillo *m*, MINE *of hutches* tren *m*, rama *f*, PROD *poker with flat blade at right angles* rodo *m*, WATER TRANSP *of mast* caída *f*; ~**-bar loader** *n* AGRIC rastrillo recolector-cargador *m*

raker *n* CONST puntal inclinado *m*

raking *n* AGRIC rastrillado *m*; ~ **fire** *n* MILIT tiro de enfilada *m*; ~ **shore** *n* CONST puntal *m*; ~ **stem** *n* WATER TRANSP *shipbuilding* roda con lanzamiento *f*

ralstonite *n* MINERAL ralstonita *f*

ram[1] *n* CONST cabezal *m*, apisonadora *f*, martinete *m*, ariete *m*, MECH corredera *f*, ariete *m*, carro portaherramienta *m*, MECH ENG *of shaper* carro portaherramienta *m*, *plunger* vástago *m*, MINE *pile* martinete de hinca *m*, P&R, PHYS pistón *m*, PROD, WATER ariete *m*, WATER TRANSP *hydraulics, collision* abordaje de proa *m*, abordaje deliberado *m*, drao *m*, empuje hidráulico *m*; ~ **air** *n* MECH ENG aire admitido en sentido de la marcha *m*, REFRIG aire a presión *m*; ~ **bow** *n* TRANSP proa curva entrante *f*; ~ **drag** *n* TRANSP resistencia dinámica *f*; ~ **effect** *n* AIR TRANSP efecto de presión dinámica *m*; ~ **penetration test** *n* COAL prueba de penetración del pistón *f*; ~ **pump** *n* COAL ariete hidráulico *m*, compuerta *f*, deshornadora *f*, maza *f*, pistón *m*, tapón de arcilla *m*, CONST *of power hammer* ariete hidráulico *m*, HYDRAUL bomba impelente *f*, ariete hidráulico *m*, WATER ariete hidráulico *m*, bomba impelente *f*; ~ **recovery** *n* AIR TRANSP recuperación de presión dinámica *f*

ram[2] *vt* CONST apisonar, MINE apisonar, atacar (*Esp*), atracar (*AmL*), hincar, PROD apisonar, *founding* apretar, WATER TRANSP *hydraulics* abordar de proa, impeler con fuerza; ~ **home** *vt* MINE *a charge* atracar

RAM *abbr* (*random-access memory*) COMP&DP, ELEC, ELEC ENG, PRINT RAM (*memoria de acceso aleatorio*)

Raman: ~ **effect** *n* PHYS, RAD PHYS efecto de Raman *m*;

~ **scattering** *n* PHYS, RAD PHYS difusión de Raman *f*;
~ **spectroscopy** *n* PHYS, RAD PHYS espectroscopía de Raman *f*
ramark *n* RAD PHYS, WATER TRANSP radiofaro para radar *m*, ramark *m*
Rameau-Bach: ~ **scale** *n* ACOUST escala de Rameau-Bach *f*
ramjet *n* AIR TRANSP estatorreactor *m*; ~ **engine** *n* THERMO estatorreactor *m*
rammer *n* CONST *for paving slabs* compactador de suelos *m*, *paviors' beetle* pisón de adoquinador *m*, *ramming* apisonador *m*, MILIT *artillery* atacador *m*, baqueta *f*, PROD martinete *m*
ramming *n* CONST *tamping*, MINE apisonamiento *m*, PROD *founding* apisonamiento *m*, *of sand* compacción *f*, compactación *f*, apisonado *m*; ~ **bar** *n* MINE atacadera de barrenos *f*
ramp¹ *n* AIR TRANSP, ELEC ENG, rampa *f*, GEOPHYS plano inclinado *m*, MINE, NUCL, PETROL, SPACE, TRANSP rampa *f*; ~ **change of load** *n* NUCL cambio de carga en rampa *m*; ~-**closure sign** *n* TRANSP señal de cierre de rampa *f*; ~ **generator** *n* ELEC ENG generador de rampa *m*; ~ **metering** *n* TRANSP medición de rampa *f*; ~ **status** *n* AIR TRANSP estado de plataforma *m*; ~-**to-ramp time** *n* AIR TRANSP tiempo de rampa a rampa total del viaje *m*; ~ **voltage** *n* ELEC, ELEC ENG, PHYS, WATER TRANSP, WAVE PHYS voltaje diente de sierra *m*; ~ **waveform** *n* ACOUST, ELEC, ELEC ENG, ELECTRON, PHYS, WAVE PHYS forma de onda en diente de sierra *f*; ~ **weight** *n* AIR TRANSP peso en plataforma *m*
ramp² *vt* ELEC ENG lanzar
rampant *adj* AGRIC rastrero, CONST *architecture* rampante
Ramsden: ~ **eyepiece** *n* PHYS ocular de Ramsden *m*; ~ **'s chain** *n* CONST cadena de Ramsden *f*
ranch *n* AGRIC establecimiento ganadero *m*, rancho *m*
ranching *n* AGRIC pradera pobre *f*
Rand: ~ **tablet** *n* COMP&DP tableta Rand *f*
random¹ *adj* GEN aleatorio
random²: ~ **access** *n* COMP&DP acceso aleatorio *m*, acceso casual *m*, acceso directo *m*, acceso fortuito *m*, ELEC ENG, ELECTRON acceso aleatorio *m*, SPACE acceso aleatorio *m*, acceso casual *m*, acceso directo *m*, acceso fortuito *m*; ~-**access device** *n* COMP&DP dispositivo de acceso aleatorio *m*; ~-**access file** *n* COMP&DP archivo de acceso aleatorio *m*; ~-**access memory** *n* (*RAM*) COMP&DP, ELEC, ELEC ENG, PRINT memoria de acceso aleatorio *f* (*RAM*); ~ **arrangement** *n* METALL distribución fortuita *f*; ~ **channel** *n* TELECOM canal aleatorio *m*, canal probabilístico *m*; ~ **distribution** *n* METALL distribución fortuita *f*; ~ **error** *n* COAL, METR error accidental *m*, error aleatorio *m*, error casual *m*, PHYS, TELECOM error aleatorio *m*; ~ **event** *n* ELECTRON acontecimiento fortuito *m*, circunstancia imprevista *f*, suceso aleatorio *m*; ~ **excitation** *n* COMP&DP, TELECOM excitación aleatoria *f*; ~ **failure** *n* ELEC ENG fallo fortuito *m*; ~ **field** *n* TELECOM campo de propiedades estadísticas *m*; ~ **file** *n* COMP&DP archivo aleatorio *m*; ~ **loading** *n* METALL carga distribuida de forma arbitraria *f*; ~ **logic** *n* COMP&DP, ELECTRON circuito lógico aleatorio *m*; ~-**logic chip** *n* COMP&DP, ELECTRON chip lógico aleatorio *m*; ~-**logic circuit** *n* COMP&DP, ELECTRON circuito lógico aleatorio *m*; ~ **multiple access** *n* COMP&DP, TELECOM acceso

múltiple aleatorio *m*; ~ **noise** *n* ACOUST, ELECTRON, GEOPHYS, PHYS, SPACE, TELECOM ruido aleatorio *m*, ruido casual *m*, ruido complejo *m*, ruido errático *m*, ruido estadístico *m*; ~-**noise generator** *n* ELECTRON, PHYS, SPACE, TELECOM generador de ruidos complejos *m*; ~-**noise signal** *n* ELECTRON, PHYS, SPACE, TELECOM señal de ruidos complejos *f*; ~-**noise source** *n* ELECTRON, PHYS, SPACE, TELECOM fuente de ruidos complejos *f*; ~ **number** *n* COMP&DP, MATH, TELECOM número aleatorio *m*; ~-**number generation** *n* COMP&DP, MATH, TELECOM generación de números aleatorios *f*; ~-**number generator** *n* COMP&DP, MATH, TELECOM generador de números aleatorios *m*; ~-**phase error** *n* TV error de fase aleatoria *m*, error de fase casual *m*; ~ **pulse** *n* ELECTRON, TELECOM impulso aleatorio *m*, impulso fortuito *m*; ~ **sample** *n* AGRIC, COAL, FOOD, MATH, QUALITY, TELECOM muestra al azar *f*, muestra aleatoria *f*; ~-**sample reading** *n* PRINT lectura de una hoja al azar *f*; ~ **sampling** *n* AGRIC, COAL, FOOD, MATH, QUALITY, TELECOM muestreo al azar *m*, muestreo aleatorio *m*; ~ **scan** *n* COMP&DP exploración aleatoria *f*; ~-**scan device** *n* COMP&DP dispositivo de exploración aleatoria *m*; ~ **scattering** *n* NUCL dispersión aleatoria *f*; ~ **signal** *n* ELECTRON, TELECOM, WATER TRANSP señal aleatoria *f*, señal casual *f*, señal estadística *f*, señal fortuita *f*; ~ **solution** *n* METALL solución aleatoria *f*; ~ **thermal motion** *n* RAD PHYS, THERMO movimiento térmico aleatorio *m*; ~ **variable** *n* COMP&DP, ELECTRON, MATH variable aleatoria *f*, variable estadística *f*; ~ **voltage** *n* ELEC, ELEC ENG, ELECTRON tensión aleatoria *f*; ~ **walk** *n* COMP&DP caminata aleatoria *f* (*AmL*), trayectoria aleatoria *f* (*Esp*); ~ **winding** *n* ELEC *small AC machines* bobina de arrollamiento al azar *f*, bobina de arrollamiento desordenado *f*, ELEC ENG devanado casual *m*
range¹ *n* AGRIC extensión de tierra con pastizales naturales *f*, AIR TRANSP alcance *m*, radio de acción *m*, COMP&DP, ELECTRON, GEOM, MECH, MECH ENG alcance *m*, extensión *f*, gama *f*, margen *m*, rango *m*, MILIT alcance *m*, alza *f*, autonomía *f*, *of missiles* polígono de lanzamiento *m*, radio de acción *m*, recorrido *m*, PHYS rango *m*, PROD alcance *m*, SPACE período *m*, polígono de lanzamiento *m*, campo de variabilidad *m*, *of instruments* capacidad *f*, campo de aplicación *m*, escala *f*, *sphere of activity* esfera de actividad *f*, *life* duración *f*, intervalo *m*, *size* magnitud *f*, *of stress* margen *m*, *of temperature, speed* gama *f*, alcance *m*, transcurso *m*, *sweep* recorrido *m*, *operating range* radio de acción *m*, TELECOM gama *f*, recorrido *m*, campo *m*, margen *m*, TEXTIL serie *f*, alcance *m*, gama *f*, TV rango *m*, WATER TRANSP *of cable, navigation, tide, electron equipment* amplitud *f*, bitadora *f*, distancia *f*, alcance *m*, enfilación *f*; ~ **of action per charge** *n* TRANSP actuación según carga *f*; ~ **adjustment** *n* PROD reglaje del alza *m*; ~ **card** *n* MILIT *artillery* croquis de fuegos *m*, plancheta *f*; ~ **dial** *n* MILIT *artillery* cuadrante de alcances *m*, indicador de distancias *m*, nivel de puntería en elevación *m*; ~ **finding** *n* ELECTRON búsqueda de radio de acción *f*, SPACE localización de señal *f*; ~ **of half-life** *n* RAD PHYS gama de períodos de semidesintegración *f*; ~ **indicator** *n* AUTO, VEH indicador de distancias *m*; ~ **management** *n* AGRIC manejo de pastizales naturales *m*; ~ **of movement** *n* NUCL *antennae, waveguides* banda de desplazamiento *f*,

recorrido *m*; ~ **of points** *n* GEOM margen de puntos *m*, rango de puntos *m*; ~ **pole** *n* CONST *surveying* jalón *m*, vara de agrimensor *f*; ~ **resolution** *n* SPACE resolución en alcance *f*, resolución en distancia *f*; ~ **switch** *n* ELEC, ELEC ENG conmutador de gamas *m*, conmutador de márgenes *m*; ~ **table** *n* MILIT tabla de tiro *f*; ~ **of vision** *n* MILIT alcance visual *m*

range^2 *vt* MILIT *gun* ahorquillar; ~ **from** *vt* TELECOM variar desde; ~ **to** *vt* MILIT telemetrar

rangefinder *n* CINEMAT, ELECTRON, MILIT, PHOTO, TV localizador de señal *m*, telémetro *m*; ~ **window** *n* CINEMAT, ELECTRON, PHOTO, TV ventana del telémetro *f* (*AmL*), visor del telémetro *m* (*Esp*)

ranging *n* AIR TRANSP exploración a gran distancia *f*, SPACE determinación de distancia *f*, exploración a gran distancia *f*, referencia *f*, reglaje en alcance *m*, replanteo *m*; ~ **fire** *n* MILIT *artillery* tiro de horquilla *m*, tiro de reglaje *m*; ~ **magnifier** *n* INSTR amplificador de distancias *m*; ~ **pole** *n* CONST *surveying* jalón *m*, vara de agrimensor *f*; ~ **rod** *n* CONST vara de agrimensor *f*

rank *n* MATH, MILIT rango *m*

Rankine: ~ **cycle** *n* HEAT, THERMO, TRANSP ciclo de Rankine *m*; ~~**cycle engine** *n* HEAT, THERMO, TRANSP motor de ciclo Rankine *m*

rap *vt* PROD desprender el modelo

rapeseed *n* AGRIC colza *f*; ~ **oil** *n* AGRIC, FOOD aceite de colza *m*

rapid: ~ **air cooling** *n* REFRIG, THERMO enfriamiento rápido por aire *m*, refrigeración rápida por aire *f*; ~ **annealing** *n* C&G templado rápido *m*; ~ **automatic transport** *n* TRANSP transporte rápido automático *m*; ~~**change tool holder** *n* MECH ENG portaherramientas de cambio rápido *m*; ~ **chilling** *n* REFRIG, THERMO refrigeración rápida *f*; ~ **cooling** *n* REFRIG refrigeración rápida *f*, THERMO enfriamiento rápido *m*, refrigeración rápida *f*; ~~**exit taxiway** *n* AIR TRANSP, TRANSP, VEH pista de rodaje de salida rápida *f*; ~~**fatigue test** *n* METALL prueba de fatiga rápida *f*; ~ **film-advance lever** *n* PHOTO control de avance de la película *m*; ~ **filter plant** *n* HYDROL planta filtradora de rápidos *f*; ~ **fire** *n* MILIT tiro rápido *m*; ~~**fire gun** *n* MILIT cañón de tiro rápido *m*; ~ **hardener** *n* REFRIG endurecedor rápido *m*; ~~**hardening cement** *n* CONST cemento rápido *m*; ~ **heat-up cathode** *n* THERMO, TV cátodo de calentamiento rápido *m*; ~~**loading system** *n* PHOTO sistema de carga rápida *m*; ~~**transit railroad** *n* AmE (*cf rapid-transit railway* BrE) NUCL, RAIL, TRANSP ferrocarril de tránsito rápido *m*, vía férrea de tránsito rápido *f*; ~~**transit railway** BrE *n* (*cf rapid-transit railroad* AmE) NUCL, RAIL, TRANSP ferrocarril de tránsito rápido *m*, vía férrea de tránsito rápido *f*; ~~**transit system** *n* (*RTS*) RAIL sistema de circulación rápida *m*, sistema de transporte rápido *m*

rapping *n* POLL golpeo *m*, sacudida *f*, PROD *founding* sacudidas ligeras para desprender un modelo *f*

rapture: ~ **of the deep** *n* OCEAN embriaguez de las profundidades *f*

rare: ~ **earths** *n pl* CHEM tierras raras *f pl*; ~~**gas tube** *n* CHEM, ELECTRON, GAS tubo de gas raro *m*

rarefaction *n* ACOUST, PHYS, WAVE PHYS enrarecimiento *m*, rarefacción *f*, rarificación *f*

Raschel: ~ **knitting machine** *n* TEXTIL máquina Raschel de punto por urdimbre *f*

rasp *n* CONST escofina *f*; ~ **cut** *n* CONST escofina *f*

rasping *n* CONST escofinado *m*, limado *m*, raspado *m*

raster *n* COMP&DP barrido *m*, presentación de líneas *f*, trama *f*, ELECTRON formación de líneas *f*, trama *f*, PRINT *data processing*, TV trama *f*; ~ **display** *n* COMP&DP presentación visual de líneas *f*, visualización de barrido *f*, visualización de tramas *f*, visualización por puntos *f*; ~ **generator** *n* COMP&DP, TV generador de tramas *m*; ~ **graphics** *n pl* COMP&DP dibujo con líneas *m*, gráficos de barrido *m pl*, gráficos formados por puntos *m pl*; ~ **pitch** *n* TV trama exploradora *f*; ~ **scan** *n* COMP&DP escudriñado de líneas *m*, exploración de barrido *f*, exploración de trama *f*, exploración por puntos *f*, TV exploración de trama *f*; ~~**scan cathode ray tube** *n* ELECTRON tubo de rayos catódicos de exploración de la imagen *m*; ~~**scan device** *n* COMP&DP dispositivo de escudriñado de líneas *m*, dispositivo de exploración de tramas *m*, dispositivo de exploración por puntos *m*; ~~**scan electron-beam lithography** *n* ELECTRON litografía por haz electrónico para exploración de la imagen *f*; ~~**scanned beam** *n* ELECTRON haz de exploración de imagen *m*; ~ **scanning** *n* COMP&DP exploración de trama *f*, ELECTRON exploración de la imagen *f*, PROD exploración total de imagen *f*, TV exploración de trama *f*

rat: ~ **hole** *n* ELEC ENG hueco rata *m* (*Esp*), vaina *f* (*AmL*), PETR TECH hueco del cuadrante *m* (*Esp*), hueco del kelly *m* (*Esp*), hueco rata *m* (*Esp*), PETROL pozo de diámetro reducido *m*, pozo para vástago de perforación *m*, pozo piloto *m*, ratonera *f*; ~~**tail file** *n* MECH ENG lima cola de ratón *f*, lima de cola de rata *f*, lima redonda *f*

ratch^1 *n* MECH ENG cremallera *f*, rueda dentada con fiador *f*, rueda dentada con trinquete *f*

ratch^2 *vt* MECH ENG trinquetar, endentar

ratchet *n* CONST trinquete *m*, MECH, MECH ENG, carrete *m*, catraca *f*, chicharra *f*, cric *m*, gatillo *m*, retén *m*, trinquete *m*, uña *f*; ~~**and-pawl motion** *n* MECH ENG mecanismo de trinquete *m*; ~ **brace** *n* CONST, MECH ENG berbiquí de trinquete *m*, carraca *f*, catraca *f*; ~ **flare-nut wrench** *n* MECH ENG llave para tuercas salientes de trinquete *f*; ~ **lever** *n* MECH ENG carraca *f*, catraca *f*, palanca de gatillo *f*, palanca de trinquete *f*; ~ **motion** *n* MECH ENG mecanismo de trinquete *m*; ~ **screwing stock** *n* MECH ENG cabezal roscador de catraca *m*; ~ **spanner** *n* MECH ENG chicharra *f*, llave de apriete de trinquete *f*; ~ **stop** *n* MECH ENG cabeza moleteada *f*; ~ **wheel** *n* MECH ENG rueda de estrella *f*, rueda de trinquete *f*; ~ **wrench** *n* MECH ENG chicharra *f*, llave de apriete de trinquete *f*

ratchetting *n* NUCL *gearwheels* tableteo *m* (*AmL*), trinqueteo *m* (*Esp*)

rate *n* COMP&DP frecuencia *f*, tasa *f*, velocidad *f*, METR porcentaje *m*, variación *f*, PHYS tasa *f*; ~ **of absorption** *n* WATER velocidad de absorción *f*; ~ **of air change** *n* HEAT cambio en la velocidad del aire *m*; ~ **of climb** *n* (*RC*) AIR TRANSP, SPACE régimen de ascenso *m*, velocidad ascensional *f*, velocidad de ascenso *f*; ~ **of combustion** *n* HEAT ENG, THERMO velocidad de combustión *f*; ~ **constant** *n* METALL constante nominal *f*; ~ **of cooling** *n* REFRIG, THERMO velocidad de enfriamiento *f*; ~ **of cure** *n* P&R velocidad de vulcanización *f*, velocidad de endurecimiento *f*, THERMO velocidad de endurecimiento *f*, velocidad de vulcanización *f*; ~ **of curing** *n* CONST grado de curado *m*; ~ **of current rise** *n* ELEC ENG grado de elevación de corriente *m*; ~ **of decay** *n* ACOUST velocidad de caída *f*; ~ **of descent** *n* AIR TRANSP, NUCL, SPACE velocidad de descenso *f*; ~ **of drying** *n* THERMO velocidad de secado *f*; ~ **of emergence** *n* AGRIC tasa de emergencia *f*; ~ **of fire** *n* MILIT cadencia de fuego *f*, cadencia de tiro *f*; ~ **of flow** *n* COAL caudal medio *m*, gasto *m*, velocidad de descarga *f*, velocidad de movimiento *f*, velocidad de paso *f*, P&R régimen de flujo *m*, velocidad de flujo *f*, REFRIG caudal *m*, WATER caudal medio *m*, régimen de corriente *m*, régimen de descarga *m*, velocidad del gasto *f*; ~ **of gain** *n* AGRIC ritmo de ganancia de peso *m*; ~ **of germination** *n* AGRIC vigor germinativo *m*; ~ **gyro** *n* PHYS tasa de giro *f*; ~ **of heat release** *n* HEAT ENG, THERMO termodifusividad *f*, velocidad de desprendimiento de calor *f*, velocidad de liberación de calor *f*; ~ **of heat transfer** *n* HEAT, THERMO régimen de transferencia de calor *m*, tasa de transferencia de calor *f*; ~ **of heating** *n* HEAT, THERMO velocidad de calentamiento *f*; ~ **of loading** *n* METALL porcentaje de carga *m*; ~ **of milking** *n* AGRIC flujo lácteo *m*; ~**-of-climb indicator** *n* AIR TRANSP, SPACE indicador de la velocidad del ascenso *m*, indicador del régimen de ascenso *m*; ~**-of-rise detector** *n* THERMO detector de porcentaje de aumento *m*; ~ **of penetration** *n* (*ROP*) PETR TECH tasa de penetración *f* (*ROP*); ~ **of progress** *n* CONST nivel de avance *m*, nivel de progreso *m*; ~ **of rise** *n* ELEC ENG grado de elevación *m*, velocidad de crecimiento *f*; ~ **of sailing** *n* WATER TRANSP andar de un velero *m*; ~ **of shear** *n* P&R velocidad de corte *f*; ~ **of spread** *n* CONST velocidad de difusión *f*, THERMO *equipment* velocidad de alcance *f*, velocidad de propagación *f*; ~ **of travel** *n* NUCL *of electrode* velocidad de desplazamiento *f*; ~ **of turn** *n* AIR TRANSP régimen de viraje *m*; ~ **of voltage rise** *n* ELEC ENG grado de elevación del voltaje *m*

rated[1]: ~ **altitude** *n* AIR TRANSP altitud nominal *f*, altura calculada *f*; ~ **capacity** *n* COAL, WATER capacidad asignada *f*, capacidad de régimen *f*, capacidad estipulada *f*, capacidad indicada *f*, capacidad nominal *f*; ~ **conditions** *n pl* ELEC ENG condiciones evaluadas *f pl*, condiciones nominales *f pl*; ~ **current** *n* ELEC, ELEC ENG corriente de régimen *f*, corriente nominal *f*; ~ **engine speed** *n* AUTO, VEH velocidad nominal del motor *f*; ~ **frequency** *n* ELEC frecuencia de régimen *f*, frecuencia de servicio *f*, frecuencia nominal *f*; ~ **horsepower** *n* AUTO, VEH potencia nominal *f*; ~ **insulation level** *n* ELEC *test voltages* nivel nominal de aislación *m*; ~ **insulation voltage** *n* ELEC, ELEC ENG, PROD tensión nominal de aislación *f*, voltaje nominal de aislamiento *m*; ~ **load** *n* ELEC, ELEC ENG carga máxima admisible *f*; ~ **operational current** *n* PROD intensidad nominal de funcionamiento *f*; ~ **output** *n* COMP&DP salida nominal *f*; ~ **power** *n* ELEC potencia de régimen *f*, potencia nominal *f*, potencia normal *f*; ~ **power capacity** *n* NUCL potencia nominal *f*; ~ **range** *n* NUCL campo nominal de medida *m*, rango nominal *m*; ~ **sensing distance** *n* PROD distancia nominal de detección *f*; ~ **short-time current** *n* ELEC corriente máxima momentánea *f*; ~ **step voltage** *n* ELEC tensión nominal por pasos *f*; ~ **stop** *n* PROD parada nominal *f*; ~ **thermal current** *n* PROD, THERMO corriente térmica nominal *f*; ~ **through-current** *n* ELEC corriente nominal de tránsito *f*; ~ **value** *n* ELEC

appliance valor nominal *m*; ~ **voltage** *n* ELEC, ELEC ENG, PROD tensión de régimen *f*, tensión especificada *f*, tensión nominal *f*, voltaje de régimen *m*; ~**-voltage ratio** *n* ELEC, ELEC ENG, PROD relación de tensión nominal *f*; ~ **welding current** *n* CONST corriente nominal de soldadura *f*; ~ **wind speed** *n* FUELLESS, METEO velocidad nominal del viento *f*

rated[2]: **at ~ operational current** *phr* PROD a la corriente de régimen, a la corriente operacional

rating *n* ELEC *appliance* régimen *m*, ELEC ENG potencia de servicio *f*, MECH potencia de régimen *f*, condición de trabajo *f*, régimen de trabajo *m*, potencia de servicio *f*, METR tarado *m*, PHYS tasación *f*, PROD régimen normal *m*, régimen nominal *m*, régimen de trabajo *m*, TV clasificación *f*; ~ **curve** *n* ACOUST curva de clasificación *f*; ~ **pressure** *n* HYDRAUL presión de régimen de trabajo *f*, presión efectiva *f*

ratio *n* MATH, METR, PHYS, REFRIG cociente *m*, proporción *f*, razón *f*, relación *f*, tasa *f*; ~ **arm** *n* ELEC brazo de relación *m*

ratioed: ~ **capacitors** *n pl* ELEC ENG condensadores de amperaje de servicio *m pl*

rational: ~ **fish stock management** *n* OCEAN gestión racional de los recursos pesqueros *f*; ~ **fishery management** *n* OCEAN explotación pesquera racional *f*; ~ **mechanics** *n* MECH, MECH ENG mecánica racional *f*; ~ **number** *n* COMP&DP, MATH número racional *m*

RATO *abbr* BrE (*rocket-assisted takeoff* BrE, *cf JETO* AmE) AIR TRANSP despegue asistido por cohete *m*, despegue con ayuda de reactores *m*, despegue con cohetes auxiliares *m*

rattle[1] *n* PAPER carteo *m*

rattle[2] *vt* PROD *founding* desrebabar en el tonel

rattler *n* PROD tambor desarenador *m*

rattling *n* PROD desarenación al tonel *f*, *founding* limpieza en tambor giratorio *f*; ~ **barrel** *n* PROD tonel desarenador *m*

raw[1] *adj* COAL crudo, en bruto, no refinado, HYDROL sin depurar

raw[2]: ~ **agricultural products** *n pl* AGRIC productos agrícolas sin elaborar *m pl*; ~ **coal** *n* COAL, MINE carbón no lavado *m*; ~**-coal bunker** *n* COAL, MINE carbonera de carbón no lavado *f*, carbonera de carbón todouno *f*; ~**-coal screen** *n* COAL, MINE filtro de carbón bruto *m*; ~ **cotton** *n* AGRIC, TEXTIL algodón en rama *m*; ~ **data** *n* COMP&DP, ELECTRON datos no analizados *m pl*, datos sin procesar *m pl*; ~ **film** *n* CINEMAT película virgen *f*, TV película en rama *f*; ~ **gas** *n* GAS gas crudo *m*; ~ **material** *n* C&G, COAL, P&R, PAPER, PETR TECH, PROD, TEXTIL materia prima *f*; ~ **rubber** *n* P&R caucho crudo *m*; ~ **sewage** *n* HYDROL, POLL, RECYCL, WATER aguas negras crudas *f pl*, aguas negras sin depurar *f pl*, aguas residuales no tratadas *f pl*, residuos brutos *m pl*, residuos no tratados *m pl*, residuos sin depurar *m pl*; ~ **sludge** *n* POLL, RECYCL, WATER cieno no tratado *m*, cieno sin tratar *m*, fango no tratado *m*, fango sin tratar *m*, lodo no tratado *m*, lodo sin tratar *m*, sedimento no tratado *m*, sedimento sin tratar *m*; ~ **stock** *n* CINEMAT, PHOTO película virgen *f*; ~**-stock dyeing** *n* COLOUR teñido de fibras en rama *m*; ~ **sugar** *n* AGRIC azúcar sin refinar *m*; ~ **tape** *n* CINEMAT, TV cinta no elaborada *f*; ~ **water** *n* HYDROL, WATER agua bruta *f*, agua cruda *f*; ~ **wool** *n* AGRIC, TEXTIL lana en rama *f*

ray *n* GEN radiación *f*, rayo *m*; ~ **optics** *n* OPT, TELECOM óptica de rayos *f*; **~ path** *n* GEOL rayo sísmico *m*, PETROL trayectoria de rayos *f*

Rayl *n* ACOUST Rayl *m*

Rayleigh: **~ criterion** *n* PHYS criterio de Rayleigh *m*; **~ disc** *BrE*, **~ disk** *n* AmE ACOUST disco de Rayleigh *m*; **~ fading** *n* TELECOM desvanecimiento de Rayleigh *m*; **~ interferometer** *n* PHYS interferómetro de Rayleigh *m*; **~ refractometer** *n* PHYS refractómetro de Rayleigh *m*; **~ scattering** *n* OPT, RAD PHYS, TELECOM difusión de Rayleigh *f*, dispersión de Rayleigh *f*, esparcimiento de Rayleigh *m*; **~ wave** *n* OPT, PHYS, RAD PHYS, TELECOM, WAVE PHYS onda de Rayleigh *f*

Rayleigh-Jeans: **~ formula** *n* PHYS fórmula de Rayleigh-Jeans *f*

rayon *n* P&R, TEXTIL rayón *m*

Rb *abbr* (*rubidium*) CHEM Rb (*rubidio*)

RBE *abbr* (*relative biological effectiveness*) NUCL EBR (*eficacia biológica relativa*)

RBT *abbr* (*remote batch terminal*) COMP&DP terminal de teleproceso por lotes *m*

RC[1] *abbr* AIR TRANSP (*rate of climb*) régimen de ascenso *m*, velocidad de ascenso *f*, ELEC, ELEC ENG, ELECTRON (*resistance-capacitance*) RC (*resistencia-capacitancia*), SPACE (*rate of climb*) régimen de ascenso *m*, velocidad de ascenso *f*

RC[2]: **~ circuit** *n* ELEC ENG, ELECTRON circuito RC *m*; **~ coupling** *n* ELEC ENG, ELECTRON acoplamiento RC *m*; **~ filter-circuit** *n* ELEC ENG, ELECTRON circuito con filtro RC *m*; **~ ladder filter** *n* ELEC ENG, ELECTRON filtro en escalera RC *m*; **~ oscillator** *n* ELEC ENG, ELECTRON, PHYS, TELECOM oscilador RC *m*, oscilador resistencia-capacitancia *m*

RCS *abbr* (*reactor coolant system*) NUCL RCS (*sistema del refrigerante del reactor*)

RCTL: **~ logic** *n* ELECTRON circuito lógico RCTL *m*

RCU *abbr* (*remote control unit*) TELECOM unidad para control a distancia *f*

RDB *abbr* (*relational database*) COMP&DP base de datos relacional *f*

RDR *abbr* (*reflection density reference*) PRINT referencia de densidad óptica externa *f*

Re *abbr* (*rhenium*) CHEM Re (*renio*)

reach *n* AIR TRANSP, COMP&DP, ELECTRON alcance *m*, HYDROL parte recta entre dos curvas *f*, MECH ENG *of hand*, MILIT, PROD, SPACE, TEXTIL alcance *m*, WATER tramo *m*, parte recta entre dos curvas *f*, WATER TRANSP alcance *m*, tramo *m*

reacquisition: **~ mode** *n* SPACE *spacecraft* modo de readquisición *m*

reactance *n* ELEC, ELEC ENG, ELECTRON, PHYS reactancia *f*; **~ attenuator** *n* ELEC, ELEC ENG, ELECTRON, PHYS atenuador de reactancia *m*; **~ bond** *n* RAIL unión de reactancias *f*; **~ circuit** *n* ELEC, ELEC ENG, ELECTRON, PHYS circuito de reactancia *m*; **~ coil** *n* ELEC, ELEC ENG, PHYS bobina de reactancia *f*; **~ drop** *n* ELEC, ELEC ENG caída de tensión en la reactancia *f*, caída en la reactancia *f*; **~-frequency multiplier** *n* ELEC, ELEC ENG, ELECTRON multiplicador de frecuencia-reactancia *m*; **~ relay** *n* ELEC ENG, ELECTRON relé de reactancia *m*

reactant *n* CHEM, PHYS reactivo *m*

reaction *n* CHEM, PHYS reacción *f*; **~ bomb** *n* LAB bomba de reacción *f*; **~ and impulse turbine** *n* HYDRAUL, WATER turbina de acción y de impulsión *f*, turbina mixta *f*; **~ jet propulsion** *n* AIR TRANSP propulsión del motor a reacción *f*; **~ motor** *n* ELEC motor de reacción *m*; **~ primer** *n* COATINGS imprimador de reacción *m*; **~ rail** *n* RAIL carril de reacción *m*; **~ rate** *n* CHEM, METALL velocidad de reacción *f*; **~-sintering process** *n* NUCL proceso de sinterización por reacción *m*; **~ time** *n* TRANSP tiempo de reacción *m*; **~ turbine** *n* FUELLESS, HYDRAUL, MECH, WATER turbina de reacción *f*, turbina tipo Francis *f*; **~ waterwheel** *n* WATER rueda hidráulica de reacción *f*; **~ wheel** *n* SPACE rueda de inercia *f*, rueda de reacción *f*, volante de inercia *m*, WATER rueda de reacción *f*; **~ zone** *n* COAL zona de reacción *f*

reactivate *vt* CHEM, COAL, GEOL reactivar

reactivation *n* CHEM, COAL, GEOL reactivación *f*

reactive: **~ circuit** *n* ELEC, ELEC ENG circuito reactivo *m*; **~ component** *n* ELEC, ELEC ENG componente reactivo *m*; **~ current** *n* ELEC, ELEC ENG corriente reactiva *f*; **~ dye** *n* COLOUR, TEXTIL colorante reactivo *m*, tinte reactivo *m*; **~ element** *n* ELEC, ELEC ENG elemento reactivo *m*; **~ energy** *n* ELEC, ELEC ENG energía reactiva *f*; **~ load** *n* ELEC, ELEC ENG, ELECTRON, PHYS, TELECOM carga reactiva *f*; **~-plasma etching** *n* ELECTRON aplicación de plasma reactivo *f*; **~ power** *n* ELEC *AC circuit*, ELEC ENG, PHYS potencia reactiva *f*; **~ site** *n* CHEM *in molecule* sitio de reacción *m*; **~ voltage** *n* ELEC, ELEC ENG, ELECTRON, PHYS tensión reactiva *f*, voltaje reactivo *m*

reactivity *n* CHEM, NUCL, PHYS reactividad *f*; **~ feedback** *n* NUCL realimentación de reactividad *f*; **~ surge** *n* NUCL pico de reactividad *m*

reactor *n* AUTO, CHEM, ELEC, ELEC ENG, ELECTRON, NUCL reactor *m*; **~ art** *n* NUCL diseño de reactores *m*; **~ behavior** *AmE*, **~ behaviour** *BrE n* NUCL comportamiento del reactor *m*; **~-charging face** *n* NUCL zona de carga del reactor *f*; **~ component** *n* NUCL componente del reactor *m*; **~ control** *n* AIR TRANSP, NUCL control del reactor *m*; **~ control board** *n* NUCL panel de control del reactor *m*; **~-coolant drain tank** *n* NUCL, REFRIG depósito de drenajes del refrigerante del reactor *m*; **~-coolant inlet nozzle** *n* NUCL, REFRIG tobera de entrada del primario *f*, tobera de entrada del refrigerante del reactor *f*; **~-coolant pump** *n* NUCL, REFRIG bomba del refrigerante del reactor *f*, tobera de entrada del primario *f*, tobera de entrada del refrigerante del reactor *f*, THERMO bomba del refrigerante del reactor *f*; **~-coolant system** *n* (*RCS*) NUCL sistema del refrigerante del reactor *m* (*RCS*); **~ design** *n* NUCL diseño de reactores *m*, diseño del reactor *m*, tipo de reactor *m*; **~ engineering** *n* NUCL ingeniería de reactores *f*; **~ hall** *n* NUCL sala del reactor *f*; **~ loop** *n* NUCL lazo del primario *m*, lazo del refrigerante del reactor *m*; **~ operator** *n* NUCL operador de reactor *m*; **~ pressure vessel** *n* NUCL, PHYS reactor presurizado *m*; **~ protection system** *n* (*RPS*) NUCL sistema de protección del reactor *m* (*RPS*); **~ trip** *n* NUCL disparo del reactor *m*, parada de emergencia del reactor *f*; **~ vessel** *n* NUCL vasija del reactor *f*; **~-vessel beltline region** *n* NUCL región intermedia de la vasija del reactor *f*; **~ vessel level-indicating system** *n* NUCL sistema indicador del nivel de la vasija del reactor *m*

read[1]: **~ only** *adj* COMP&DP de lectura fija, sólo de lectura

read[2] *n* COMP&DP lectura *f*; **~-after-write** *n* COMP&DP lectura después de escritura *f*, lectura tras escritura *f*; **~ amplifier** *n* ELECTRON amplificador de lectura *m*; **~ beam** *n* COMP&DP, ELECTRON, OPT, TELECOM haz de lectura *m*; ~ **error** *n* COMP&DP error de lectura *m*; ~ **head** *n* COMP&DP, OPT cabeza de lectura *f*, cabezal de lectura *m*, lector *m*, PRINT lector *m*; ~ **laser** *n* ELECTRON, OPT láser de exploración *m*, láser de lectura *m*; ~**mostly memory** *n* COMP&DP memoria principalmente de lectura *f*; ~**only disc** *BrE*, ~**only disk** *AmE* *n* OPT disco de sólo lectura *m*; ~**only medium** *n* OPT medio de sólo lectura *m*; ~**only memory** *n* (*ROM*) COMP&DP, ELEC, ELEC ENG memoria de sólo lectura *f* (*ROM*); ~**out** *n* CHEM lectura *f*, COMP&DP extracción mediante lectura *f*, lectura de salida *f*, ELEC dispositivo de lectura *m*, escala *f*, indicación *f*, indicador *m*, interpretación de la indicación *f*, lectura *f*, INSTR interpretación de la indicación *f*, TELECOM lectura de salida *f*; ~**out potentiometer** *n* ELEC potenciómetro de lectura *m*; ~**out system** *n* MECH ENG sistema de lectura *m*; ~ **time** *n* COMP&DP, PRINT tiempo de lectura *m*; ~ **transistor** *n* ELECTRON transistor de lectura *m*; ~**write** *n* COMP&DP, OPT lectura-escritura *f*; ~**write channel** *n* COMP&DP, OPT canal de lectura-escritura *m*; ~**write drive** *n* COMP&DP, OPT unidad de lectura-escritura *f*; ~**write head** *n* COMP&DP, OPT cabezal de lectura-escritura *m*; ~**write memory** *n* COMP&DP, OPT memoria de lectura-escritura *f*; ~**write optical drive** *n* COMP&DP, OPT unidad óptica de lectura y escritura *f*, unidad óptica de lectura-escritura *f*

read[3]: ~ **out** *vt* COMP&DP extraer mediante lectura, extraer por lectura

read[4]: ~**while-write** *phr* COMP&DP lectura durante la escritura *f*

reader *n* COMP&DP corrector *m*, lector *m*, OPT lector *m*, PRINT corrector *m*, lector *m*

reading *n* CHEM, COMP&DP, CONST, ELEC, ELECTRON lectura *f*; ~ **glasses** *n pl* INSTR, OPT anteojos de lectura *m pl* (*AmL*), gafas de lectura *f pl* (*Esp*), lentes de lectura *f pl*; ~ **gun** *n* ELECTRON cañón de lectura *m*; ~ **microscope** *n* INSTR microscopio de lectura *m*; ~ **rate** *n* COMP&DP velocidad de lectura *f*; ~ **spectacles** *n pl* INSTR, OPT anteojos de lectura *m pl* (*AmL*), gafas de lectura *f pl* (*Esp*)

ready[1] *adj* COMP&DP, TELECOM listo, preparado; ~**for-sending** *adj* COMP&DP, TELECOM listo para ser transmitido; ~**made** *adj* PHOTO comercial; ~**to-activate** *adj* COMP&DP, TELECOM listo para activar; ~**to-send** *adj* COMP&DP, TELECOM listo a transmitir, preparado para enviar, preparado para transmitir

ready[2]: ~ **meal** *n* FOOD comida preparada *f*; ~**mixed concrete** *n* CONST concreto preamasado *m* (*AmL*), hormigón preamasado *m* (*Esp*), concreto amasado en fábrica *m* (*AmL*), hormigón amasado en fábrica *m* (*Esp*)

reaeration *n* WATER reaireación *f*

reafforestation *n* AGRIC reforestación *f*, repoblación forestal *f*

reagent *n* AGRIC, CHEM, COAL, P&R, PHOTO reactivo *m*; ~ **bottle** *n* LAB botella de reactivo *f*, frasco de reactivo *m*

real[1]: ~**time** *adj* CINEMAT, COMP&DP, ELEC ENG, ELECTRON, TELECOM, TV de tiempo real, en tiempo real

real[2]: ~ **address** *n* COMP&DP direccional real *m*, dirección real *f*; ~ **component** *n* ELEC, ELEC ENG componente activo *m*; ~ **density** *n* COAL densidad relativa *f*; ~ **gap length** *n* TV tiempo real de intervalo *m*; ~ **image** *n* PHYS imagen real *f*; ~ **memory** *n*

COMP&DP memoria real *f*; ~ **minor scale** *n* ACOUST escala real menor *f*; ~ **number** *n* COMP&DP, MATH número real *m*; ~ **power** *n* ELEC, ELEC ENG potencia activa *f*; ~ **sound source** *n* ACOUST fuente acústica real *f*; ~ **time** *n* CINEMAT, COMP&DP, ELECTRON, TELECOM, TV tiempo real *m*; ~**time analyser** *n* *BrE* ACOUST, COMP&DP, ELECTRON, TELECOM analizador en tiempo real *m*; ~**time analysis** *n* ACOUST, COMP&DP, ELECTRON, TELECOM análisis en tiempo real *m*; ~**time analyzer** *AmE see real-time analyser BrE*; ~**time control** *n* COMP&DP, ELECTRON, TELECOM, TRANSP control en tiempo real *m*; ~**time data** *n* (*RTD*) COMP&DP, ELECTRON, PROD, TELECOM datos en tiempo real *m pl* (*RTD*); ~**time input** *n* COMP&DP, ELECTRON, TELECOM entrada en tiempo real *f*; ~**time language** *n* CINEMAT, COMP&DP, ELECTRON, TELECOM, TV lenguaje en tiempo real *m*; ~**time monitor** *n* COMP&DP, ELECTRON, TELECOM monitor en tiempo real *m*; ~**time output** *n* CINEMAT, COMP&DP, ELECTRON, TELECOM, TV salida en tiempo real *f*; ~**time processing** *n* CINEMAT, COMP&DP, ELECTRON, TELECOM, TV procesamiento en tiempo real *m*, tratamiento de la señal en tiempo real *m*; ~**time repeater satellite** *n* CINEMAT, COMP&DP, ELECTRON, TELECOM, TV satélite repetidor en tiempo real *m*; ~**time signal processing** *n* COMP&DP, ELECTRON, TELECOM, TV tratamiento de la señal en tiempo real *m*; ~**time simulation** *n* COMP&DP, ELECTRON, TELECOM simulación en tiempo real *f*; ~**time simulator** *n* COMP&DP, ELECTRON, TELECOM simulador en tiempo real *m*; ~**time spectral analyser** *BrE n* COMP&DP, ELECTRON, TELECOM analizador espectral en tiempo real *m*; ~**time spectral analysis** *n* COMP&DP, ELECTRON, TELECOM análisis espectral en tiempo real *m*; ~**time spectral analyzer** *AmE see real-time spectral analyser BrE*; ~**time system** *n* CINEMAT, ELECTRON, TELECOM, TV sistema en tiempo real *m*; ~ **type** *n* COMP&DP tipo real *m*

realgar *n* CHEM, MINERAL rejalgar *m*

realized: ~ **production time** *n* PROD tiempo de producción realizado *m*

ream[1] *n* C&G bandas de estrías paralelas *f pl*, PACK, PRINT resma *f*

ream[2] *vt* MECH, MECH ENG avellanar, escariar, mandrilar, rectificar, PETROL ensanchar, escariar, rectificar, PROD avellanar

reamer *n* C&G escariador *m*, herramienta para escariar *f*, MECH, MECH ENG avellanador *m*, ensanchador *m*, escariador *m*, fresa cónica para escariar *f*, herramienta para escariar *f*, MINE escariador *m*, PETR TECH herramienta para ensanchar *f*, PROD avellanador *m*, fresa cónica para escariar *f*, herramienta para escariar *f*, máquina de escariar *f*, VEH escariador *m*; ~ **cutter** *n* MECH, MECH ENG, METALL, PROD fresa para escariador *f*; ~ **with spiral flutes** *n* MECH ENG, PROD fresa con estrías espirales *f*; ~ **tap** *n* MECH ENG, PROD macho escariador *m*

reaming *n* GEN avellanado *m*, escariado *m*; ~ **bit** *n* PETR TECH barrena de arrastre *f*, broca *f*, mecha para escariar *f*, trépano para escariado *m*; ~ **iron** *n* CONST hierro escariador *m*; ~**out** *n* CONST, MECH, MECH ENG, MINE, PETR TECH, PROD escariado *m*

reaper *n* AGRIC segadora de rastrillos *f*; ~**binder** *n* AGRIC segadora-atadora *f*

reaping: ~ **scythe** *n* AGRIC guadaña para cereales *f*

rear[1]: **~-mounted** *adj* AGRIC de montaje trasero

rear[2] *n* AUTO, TRANSP, VEH parte trasera *f*; **~ axle** *n* AUTO, MECH, VEH eje posterior *m*, eje trasero *m*; **~-axle assembly** *n* AUTO, MECH, VEH montaje del puente trasero *m*; **~-axle drive shaft** *n* AUTO, MECH, VEH semieje trasero *m*; **~-axle flared tube** *n* AUTO, MECH, VEH trompeta del eje trasero *f*; **~-axle housing** *n* AUTO, MECH, VEH alojamiento del eje trasero *m*, cárter del eje trasero *m*; **~-axle housing assembly** *n* AUTO, MECH, VEH montaje del alojamiento del eje trasero *m*; **~-axle shaft** *n* AUTO, MECH, VEH eje trasero *m*, puente trasero *m*; **~-brake van** *n* RAIL vagón con freno posterior *m*; **~ bumper** *n* AUTO, VEH parachoques trasero *m*; **~ door** *n* AUTO, VEH puerta trasera *f*; **~-dump car** *n* AmE RAIL vagón basculante con descarga hacia atrás *m*, vagón basculante hacia atrás *m*; **~ end** *n* AUTO, TRANSP, VEH extremo posterior *m*, parte posterior *f*; **~-end collision** *n* AUTO, TRANSP, VEH choque por detrás *m*, colisión por detrás *f*; **~-end torque** *n* AUTO, MECH, VEH par trasero *m*; **~ engine** *n* AUTO, VEH motor trasero *m*; **~-engine rear-wheel drive** *n* AUTO, VEH tracción por ruedas traseras con motor trasero *f*; **~-facing roller** *n* PROD rodillo hacia atrás *m*; **~ fender** *n* AmE (*cf rear wing BrE*) AUTO, TRANSP, VEH aleta trasera *f*, guardabarros trasero *m*; **~ focal plane** *n* CINEMAT, PHOTO plano focal posterior *m*; **~ focus** *n* PHOTO foco posterior *m*; **~-furrow wheel** *n* AGRIC rueda de cola *f*, rueda de talón *f*; **~ lamp** *n* AUTO, VEH lámpara de señalización posterior *f*, lámpara posterior *f*; **~ license-plate lamp** *n* AmE (*cf rear number-plate lamp BrE*) AUTO, VEH luz de matrícula trasera *f*; **~ light** *n* AUTO, CONST, VEH luz trasera *f*; **~ marker-plate lamp** *n* (*cf rear number-plate lamp BrE*) AUTO, VEH luz de matrícula trasera *f*; **~-mounted engine** *n* AUTO, VEH motor de montaje trasero *m*, motor trasero *m*; **~-mounted ripper** *n* AUTO, TRANSP, VEH desfondeadora montada detrás *f*, disgregadora montada detrás *f*; **~ number-plate lamp** *n* BrE (*cf rear license-plate lamp AmE, rear marker-plate lamp AmE*) AUTO, VEH luz de matrícula trasera *f*; **~ pillar** *n* MECH ENG columna posterior *f*; **~ projection** *n* CINEMAT proyección por transparencia *f*; **~-projection screen** *n* CINEMAT pantalla de retroproyección *f*; **~ propeller** *n* TRANSP, WATER TRANSP hélice trasera *f*; **~ reflector** *n* AUTO, TRANSP, VEH, WATER TRANSP reflectante trasero *m*; **~ shutter** *n* CINEMAT, PHOTO obturador posterior *m*; **~ spring** *n* MILIT *of firearm* ballesta posterior *f*; **~ suspension** *n* AUTO, VEH suspensión trasera *f*; **~ suspension** *n* VEH suspensión trasera *f*; **~-tipping trailer** *n* TRANSP remolque basculante trasero *m*; **~-view mirror** *n* AUTO, C&G, INSTR, TRANSP, VEH espejo retrovisor *m*; **~-view system** *n* AUTO, TRANSP, VEH sistema retrovisor *m*; **~ wheel** *n* AUTO, TRANSP, VEH rueda trasera *f*; **~-wheel drive** *n* AUTO, TRANSP, VEH arriate marginal *m*, tracción a las ruedas traseras *f*, tracción efectiva de ruedas *f*, tracción trasera *f*; **~ window** *n* AUTO, TRANS, VEH ventanilla posterior *f*; **~ wing** *n* BrE (*cf rear fender AmE*) AUTO,TRANSP, VEH aleta trasera *f*, guardabarros trasero *m*

rearing *n* AGRIC cría *f*; **~ by hand** *n* AGRIC cría artificial *f*; **~ pond** *n* AGRIC laguna de cría *f*; **~ proportion** *n* AGRIC porcentaje de animales criados *m*

rearrangeable: **~ non-blocking network** *n* TELECOM red no bloqueante de reordenamiento *f*

rearrangement *n* CHEM *molecular* rearreglo *m*

rearward: **~ takeoff** *n* AIR TRANSP *helicopter* despegue hacia atrás *m*

reason: **~ for hold** *n* PROD motivo de retención *m*

reassemble *vt* CONST rearmar, volver a montar

reattachment *n* FLUID readherencia *f*

rebate *n* CONST, MECH ENG ranura *f*, rebaje *m*; **~ plane** *n* CONST, MECH ENG cepillo ranurador *m*

rebated: **~ joint** *n* CONST, MECH ENG junta de rebajo *f*

reboil *n* C&G sobrecalentamiento *m*; **~ bubble** *n* C&G burbuja de sobrecalentamiento *f*

reboiler *n* PETR TECH calderín *m*

rebore *vt* AUTO, MECH ENG, VEH rectificar

reboring *n* AUTO, MECH ENG, VEH agujero rectificado *m*, rectificado de cilindros *m*

rebound[1] *n* AUTO, MILIT, P&R rebote *m*; **~ clip** *n* AUTO brida de rebote *f*, retén de rebote *m*, VEH brida de rebote *f*

rebound[2] *vi* AUTO, MILIT, P&R rebotar

rebroadcast *vt* TELECOM, TV retransmitir

rebuild *vt* CONST reconstruir

rebuilding *n* CONST reconstrucción *f*

recalescence *n* PHYS recalescencia *f*

recalibrated *adj* NUCL, RAD PHYS recalibrado

recalibration *n* NUCL, RAD PHYS recalibración *f*, recalibrado *m*

recall *n* TELECOM repetición de llamada *f*

recast *vt* PROD refundir

recede *vi* HYDROL, WATER descender, retroceder

receding: **~ flood** *n* HYDROL, WATER caudal descendente *m*; **~ water table** *n* AGRIC, GEOPHYS, HYDROL, WATER nivel freático descendente *m*

receipt *n* COMP&DP recepción *f*; **~ for goods** *n* QUALITY recibo de productos *m*; **~ of goods** *n* QUALITY aceptación de productos *f*; **~ ticket** *n* PROD recibo *m*

receive[1]: **~-only** *adj* COMP&DP, TELECOM sólo para recepción, sólo para recibir

receive[2]: **~ crystal** *n* ELECTRON, OPT, TELECOM cristal de recepción *m*; **~ fiber optic terminal device** *AmE*, **~ fibre optic terminal device** *BrE n* ELECTRON, OPT, TELECOM dispositivo terminal de recepción de fibra óptica *m*; **~ filter** *n* ELECTRON, TELECOM filtro de recepción *m*; **~ machine** *n* ELECTRON, TELECOM máquina de recepción *f*

receive[3] *vt* COMP&DP, ELECTRON, TELECOM recibir

received: **~ data** *n* COMP&DP, TELECOM datos recibidos *m pl*, información recibida *f*; **~ signal** *n* COMP&DP, ELECTRON, TELECOM señal recibida *f*

receiver *n* GEN receptor *m*; **~ band pass** *n* TV paso de banda del receptor *m*; **~ board** *n* ELECTRON cuadro receptor *m*; **~ diode** *n* ELECTRON diodo receptor *m*; **~ gage** *AmE see receiver gauge BrE*; **~ gain** *n* ELECTRON ganancia receptora *f*; **~ gauge** *n* BrE METR galga receptora *f*, indicador del recipiente *m*; **~ inset** *n* TELECOM inserción del receptor *f*; **~ signal** *n* ELEC ENG, ELECTRON, RAD PHYS, TELECOM radioseñal *f*, señal de radio *f*, señal transmitida por radio *f*; **~-signal element timing** *n* TELECOM temporización del elemento de señal del receptor *f*; **~-space** *n* MECH ENG *of an expansion engine* recipiente intermedio *m*

receiving: **~ address** *n* PROD dirección receptora *f*; **~ aerial** *n* BrE (*cf receiving antenna AmE*) RAD PHYS, TELECOM, TV antena de recepción *f*, antena receptora *f*; **~ antenna** *n* AmE (*cf receiving aerial BrE*) RAD PHYS, TELECOM, TV antena de recepción *f*, antena receptora *f*; **~ assembly** *n* NUCL conjunto receptor *m*; ~ **channel** *n* TELECOM canal de recepción *m*; ~ **department** *n* PROD departamento receptor *m*; ~-**dish aerial** *n* BrE (*cf receiving-dish antenna AmE*) TELECOM, TV antena parabólica receptora *f*; ~-**dish antenna** *n* AmE (*cf receiving-dish aerial BrE*) TELECOM, TV antena parabólica receptora *f*; ~ **drum** *n* PETR TECH tambor receptor *m*; ~ **earth station** *n* SPACE, TELECOM, TV estación terrestre receptora *f*; ~ **inspection** *n* PROD inspección de recepción *f*, QUALITY control de aceptación *m*; ~ **range** *n* RAD PHYS, TELECOM, TV alcance de recepción *m*; ~ **trap** *n* PETROL trampa receptora *f*; ~ **trunk** *n* TRANSP enlace de recepción *m*; ~ **tube** *n* ELECTRON tubo receptor *m*; ~ **water** *n* HYDROL, WATER agua de recepción *f*

recent *n* GEOL reciente *m*; ~ **water** *n* HYDROL, WATER agua reciente *f*

receptacle *n* CHEM, PROD receptáculo *m*

reception *n* COMP&DP, PROD recepción *f*; ~ **aerial** *n* BrE (*cf reception antenna AmE*) TELECOM, TV antena de recepción *f*; ~ **antenna** *n* AmE (*cf reception aerial BrE*) TELECOM, TV antena de recepción *f*; ~ **channel** *n* TELECOM, TV canal de recepción *m*; ~ **department** *n* PROD departamento de recepción *m*; ~ **frequency** *n* ELECTRON, TELECOM, TV frecuencia de recepción *f*; ~ **level** *n* ELECTRON nivel de recepción *m*

receptor *n* POLL colector *m*, electrofiltro *m*, receptor *m*; ~ **region** *n* POLL región receptora *f*, zona receptora *f*

recess[1] *n* CONST entrante de pared *m*, escotadura *f*

recess[2] *vt* CONST ranurar, rebajar

recessed: ~-**flange coupling** *n* MECH ENG acoplamiento de platos con pernos de cabeza embutida *m*; ~-**head fastener** *n* MECH ENG sujetador de cabeza con ranuras en cruz *m*; ~ **switch** *n* ELEC interruptor embutido *m*, interruptor empotrado *m*

recessing *n* CONST rebaje *m*; ~ **machine** *n* CONST máquina de ranurar *f*, máquina de rebajar *f*

recession *n* HYDROL *of flood*, WATER retroceso *m*; ~ **curve** *n* HYDROL, WATER curva de retroceso *f*

recessive *adj* AGRIC recesivo

recharge[1] *n* HYDROL, WATER recarga *f*; ~ **time** *n* PHOTO tiempo de recarga *m*; ~ **well** *n* HYDROL, WATER pozo de recarga *m*, pozo de restablecimiento *m*

recharge[2] *vt* GEN recargar

rechargeable[1] *adj* CINEMAT, ELEC, ELEC ENG, PHOTO, PHYS, TV recargable

rechargeable[2]: ~ **battery** *n* CINEMAT, ELEC, ELEC ENG, PHOTO, PHYS, TV acumulador recargable *m*, batería recargable *f*, pila recargable *f*; ~ **cell** *n* PHYS célula recargable *f*

recharging *n* GEN recargado *m*; ~ **battery** *n* CINEMAT, ELEC ENG, PHOTO, PHYS, TV batería recargable *f*

recheck *vt* METR verificar de nuevo, volver a comprobar

recifal: ~ **slope** *n* OCEAN pendiente de arrecife *f*

recipient *n* CHEM recipiente *m*, TELECOM receptor *m*, recibidor *m*, recipiente *m*; ~ **identification code** *n* TELECOM código de identificación del receptor *m*, código de identificación del recibidor *m*; ~ **reference** *n* TELECOM referencia del receptor *f*, referencia del recibidor *f*; ~ **reference qualifier** *n* TELECOM calificador de referencia del recibidor *m*

reciprocal[1] *adj* GEN recíproco

reciprocal[2] *n* COMP&DP, GEOM, MATH recíproco *m*; ~ **bearing** *n* AIR TRANSP azimut inverso *m*, marcación inversa *f*, marcación recíproca *f*, WATER TRANSP marcación recíproca *f*; ~ **circuit** *n* TELECOM circuito

recíproco *m*; ~ **course** *n* WATER TRANSP rumbo opuesto *m*, vuelta encontrada *f*; ~ **gear** *n* MECH ENG engranaje alternativo *m*, mecanismo alternativo *m*; ~ **lattice** *n* CRYSTALL red recíproca *f*; ~ **leg** *n* AIR TRANSP trayecto recíproco *m*; ~ **movement** *n* PETR TECH movimiento recíproco *m*; ~ **period** *n* NUCL período de reciprocidad *m*; ~ **probe** *n* PETROL sondeo recíproco *m*; ~ **ratio** *n* MECH ENG razón inversa *f*; ~ **space** *n* CRYSTALL espacio recíproco *m*; ~ **spiral** *n* MECH ENG espiral hiperbólica *f*; ~ **transducer** *n* ACOUST transductor recíproco *m*

reciprocating[1] *adj* MECH, MECH ENG alternativo, de vaivén, oscilante, reciprocante

reciprocating[2]: ~ **blade** *n* PRINT cuchilla oscilante *f*; ~ **charger** *n* C&G cargador recíproco *m*; ~ **compressor** *n* REFRIG compresor alternativo *m*; ~ **engine** *n* AIR TRANSP, MECH ENG, VEH, WATER TRANSP motor alternativo *m*, motor de funcionamiento alternativo *m*, motor de pistones *m*, motor de émbolos *m*, máquina alternativa *f*; ~ **internal-combustion engine** *n* AIR TRANSP, MECH ENG, TRANSP, VEH, WATER TRANSP motor alternativo de combustión interna *m*; ~ **mill** *n* PROD laminador de vaivén *m*; ~ **motion** *n* MECH, MECH ENG movimiento alternativo *m*, movimiento de vaivén *m*, movimiento recíproco *m*; ~ **parts** *n pl* MECH, MECH ENG partes oscilantes *f pl*; ~-**piston engine** *n* AIR TRANSP motor de pistones alternativos *m*; ~ **pump** *n* WATER bomba aspirante e impelente *f*, bomba de movimiento alternativo *f*; ~ **saw** *n* MECH ENG, PROD sierra alternativa *f*; ~-**saw blade** *n* MECH ENG, PROD hoja de sierra alternativa *f*; ~-**shaft seal** *n* MECH ENG obturador laberíntico del eje alternativo *m*

reciprocation *n* GEOM reciprocidad *f*

reciprocity: ~ **effect** *n* CINEMAT, PHOTO, TV efecto de reciprocidad *m*; ~ **failure** *n* CINEMAT, PHOTO, TV fallo de reciprocidad *m*; ~ **law** *n* CINEMAT, PHOTO, PHYS, TV ley de reciprocidad *f*; ~-**law failure** *n* CINEMAT, PHOTO, TV fracaso de la ley de reciprocidad *m*; ~ **theorem** *n* ELEC ENG, PHYS teorema de reciprocidad *m*

recirculate *vt* COAL reciclar, recircular

recirculating: ~-**ball steering-gear** *n* AUTO engranaje de la dirección de bola de recirculación *m*; ~ **water economy** *n* HYDROL, WATER economía de la recirculación del agua *f*

recirculation *n* C&G *of currents in glass tank furnace*, NUCL *of fission products* recirculación *f*

reclaimed: ~ **area** *n* AGRIC, POLL área recuperada *f*, área restaurada *f*, RECYCL área recuperada *f*; ~ **land** *n* AGRIC tierra saneada *f*; ~ **rubber** *n* P&R caucho recuperado *m*

reclaiming *n* PETR TECH regeneración *f*

reclamation *n* POLL, RECYCL recuperación *f*, restablecimiento *m*, restauración *f*, saneamiento *m*, transformación *f*

reclining: ~ **seat** *n* AUTO, VEH asiento abatible *m*, asiento plegable *m*, asiento reclinable *m*

reclosable: ~ **pack** *n* PACK paquete que se puede volver a cerrar *m*

recognised: ~ **private operating agency** *n* TELECOM agencia explotadora privada reconocida *f*

recognition *n* ACOUST aceptación *f*, reconocimiento *m*, COMP&DP reconocimiento *m*

recoil *n* MECH, MECH ENG, MILIT *of firearm* retroceso *m*; ~ **brake** *n* MILIT amortiguador de retroceso *m*;

~ **electron** *n* ELECTRON, PART PHYS, PHYS, RAD PHYS electrón de retroceso *m*; ~ **energy** *n* MILIT energía de retroceso *f*; ~ **nucleus** *n* PHYS núcleo de retroceso *m*; ~ **slide** *n* MILIT corredera de retroceso *f*; ~ **spring** *n* MILIT resorte recuperador *m*

recoilless: ~ **gun** *n* MILIT cañón sin retroceso *m*

recombination *n* ELECTRON, PHYS recombinación *f*; ~ **base current** *n* ELECTRON corriente de base de recombinación *f*; ~ **coefficient** *n* ELECTRON, PHYS coeficiente de recombinación *m*; ~ **process** *n* ELECTRON, PHYS proceso de recombinación *m*; ~ **rate** *n* ELECTRON, PHYS porcentaje de recombinación *m*, tasa de recombinación *f*

recommendation *n* PROD, QUALITY, SPACE, TELECOM recomendación *f*; ~ **indicator** *n* TELECOM indicador de recomendación *m*

recommended: ~ **dietary allowance** *n* AGRIC ración alimenticia recomendada *f*; ~ **production order** *n* PROD orden de producción recomendado *m*; ~ **purchase order** *n* PROD orden de compra recomendado *m*; ~ **speed** *n* AUTO, TRANSP, VEH velocidad recomendada *f*

recompression *n* OCEAN recompresión *f*

recondition *vt* MECH ENG, TRANSP reacondicionar

reconditioning *n* SPACE regeneración *f*, reparación *f*

reconfigurable *adj* COMP&DP reconfigurable

reconfiguration *n* COMP&DP reconfiguración *f*

reconfigure *vt* COMP&DP reconfigurar

reconnaissance *n* MILIT, TV reconocimiento *m*; ~ **vehicle** *n* MILIT vehículo de reconocimiento *m*

reconnect *vt* ELEC ENG, TELECOM reconectar

reconnection *n* ELEC ENG, TELECOM nueva conexión *f*, reconexión *f*

reconstruct *vt* CONST reconstruir

reconstruction *n* COMP&DP, CONST reconstrucción *f*

reconverter *n* ELECTRON reconvertidor *m*

record¹ *n* ACOUST disco *m*, grabación *f*, registro *m*, registro sonoro *m*, CHEM, COMP&DP, PETROL registro *m*, PHYS record *m*; ~ **book** *n* PROD libro registro *m*; ~ **button** *n* CINEMAT botón de grabación *m*, TV botón de grabación *m*, pulsador de grabación *m*; ~ **changer** *n* ACOUST cambiadiscos *m*; ~ **class** *n* COMP&DP clase de registro *f*; ~ **creation** *n* COMP&DP creación de registro *f*; ~ **crop** *n* AGRIC cosecha record *f*; ~ **current** *n* TV *video* corriente de grabación *f*; ~**current optimizer** *n* TV mejorador de la corriente de grabación *m*; ~ **driver** *n* TV polea motriz de grabación *f*; ~ **format** *n* COMP&DP formato de grabación *m*; ~ **head** *n* ACOUST cabezal de grabación *m*, COMP&DP, TV cabeza de registro *f*, cabezal de grabación *m*; ~ **ink** *n* COLOUR tinta de registro *f*; ~ **length** *n* COMP&DP longitud de registro *f*; ~ **player** *n* ACOUST, ELEC ENG gramófono *m*, tocadiscos *m*; ~ **separator** *n* (*RS*) COMP&DP separador de registros *m*; ~ **time** *n* PETROL tiempo de registro *m*; ~ **updating** *n* COMP&DP actualización de registros *f*

record² *vt* ACOUST, COMP&DP, GEOPHYS, PHYS, TV grabar, registrar

recorded: ~ **announcement machine** *n* TELECOM máquina de anuncios registrados *f*; ~ **dose** *n* RAD PHYS dosis registrada *f*; ~ **public information service** *n* TELECOM servicio público de información registrada *m*; ~ **velocity** *n* ACOUST velocidad de grabado *f*; ~ **wavelength** *n* ACOUST longitud de onda grabada *f*

recorder *n* ACOUST, COMP&DP, ELEC, INSTR grabadora *f*, registrador *m*, MECH ENG *self-registering apparatus* aparato grabador *m*, contador *m*, oscilógrafo *m*, registrador *m*, TELECOM, TV grabadora *f*, registrador *m*

recording *n* GEN grabación *f*, registro *m*; ~ **anemometer** *n* INSTR, METEO, PHYS anemómetro registrador *m*; ~ **barometer** *n* LAB, METEO, PHYS, WATER TRANSP barómetro registrador *m*; ~ **chain** *n* TV cadena de grabación *f*; ~ **channel** *n* CINEMAT canal de registro *m*; ~ **characteristic** *n* ACOUST, TV característica de grabación *f*; ~ **density** *n* COMP&DP densidad de grabación *f*, densidad de registro *f*; ~ **device** *n* INSTR aparato registrador *m*; ~ **head** *n* ACOUST cabezal de grabación *m*, COMP&DP, TV cabeza de registro *f*, cabezal de grabación *m*; ~ **magnetic head** *n* ACOUST cabeza magnética grabadora *f*; ~ **medium** *n* COMP&DP medio de registro *m*, soporte de grabación *m*; ~ **oscillograph** *n* ACOUST oscilógrafo registrador *m*; ~ **paper** *n* INSTR papel de grabación *m*; ~-**reproducing magnetic head** *n* ACOUST cabeza magnética reproductora o grabadora *f*; ~ **storage tube** *n* ELECTRON tubo de almacenamiento de la grabación *m*; ~ **surface** *n* COMP&DP superficie de grabación *f*, superficie de registro *f*; ~ **thermometer** *n* THERMO termógrafo *m*; ~ **tide gage** *AmE*, ~ **tide gauge** *BrE n* GEOPHYS, OCEAN mareógrafo *m*; ~ **track** *n* ACOUST, COMP&DP pista de grabación *f*, pista de registro *f*; ~ **unit** *n* INSTR unidad de grabación *f*

recover *vt* COAL cubrir de nuevo, forrar de nuevo, recobrar, recubrir, recuperar, reentelar, regenerar, rescatar, POLL recuperar, restablecer, restaurar, TELECOM desmontar, recuperar

recoverable: ~ **error** *n* COMP&DP error recuperable *m*; ~ **orbiter** *n* SPACE impulsor recuperable *m*, satélite artificial recuperable *m*; ~ **reserves** *n pl* PETR TECH, PETROL reservas recuperables *f pl*; ~ **thruster** *n* SPACE impulsor recuperable *m*

recovered: ~ **charge** *n* ELEC ENG carga recuperada *f*

recovery *n* AIR TRANSP recuperación *f*, rescate *m*, salvamento *m*, COAL producción *f*, recuperación *f*, rendimiento *m*, restablecimiento *m*, MAR POLL, METALL, OCEAN, P&R, PETROL recuperación *f*, POLL recuperación *f*, restablecimiento *m*, restauración *f*, RECYCL recuperación *f*, SPACE reactivación *f*, recuperación *f*, regeneración *f*, TEXTIL recuperación *f*, WATER TRANSP *of person or item at sea* recuperación *f*, salvamento *m*; ~ **ability** *n* AGRIC capacidad de rebrote *f*; ~ **creep** *n* METALL estiramiento de recuperación *m*; ~ **device** *n* MAR POLL, POLL aparato de recuperación *m*, dispositivo de recuperación *m*, dispositivo recuperador *m*, sistema recuperación *m*; ~ **factor** *n* PETR TECH, PETROL factor de recuperación *m*; ~ **from dynamic loads** *n* ELEC ENG recuperación de cargas dinámicas *f*; ~ **package** *n* SPACE equipo recuperable *m*; ~ **process** *n* PETR TECH, PETROL proceso de recuperación *m*; ~ **rate** *n* METALL proporción de aprovechamiento *f*; ~ **system** *n* NUCL, POLL sistema recuperación *m*; ~ **voltage** *n* ELEC *switch* tensión de restablecimiento *f*, tensión del circuito cortado *f*

recruitment *n* ACOUST, MILIT reclutamiento *m*

recrystallization *n* CHEM, CRYSTALL, METALL recristalización *f*

rectangle *n* GEOM figura alargada *f*, rectángulo *m*; ~ **die-set** *n* MECH ENG juego de matrices rectangula-

res *m*; ~ **head-fastener** *n* MECH ENG sujetador de cabeza rectangular *m*
rectangular[1] *adj* GEOM rectangular
rectangular[2]: ~ **cross-section** *n* CONST sección transversal rectangular *f*; ~ **hysteresis loop** *n* ELEC ENG ciclo de histéresis rectangular *m*; ~ **parallel keys** *n pl* MECH ENG llaves paralelas rectangulares *f pl*; ~ **pulse** *n* ELECTRON impulso rectangular *m*; ~**-to-circular transition** *n* ELEC ENG transición rectangular a circular *f*; ~ **wave** *n* ELEC ENG, WAVE PHYS onda rectangular *f*; ~ **waveguide** *n* ELEC ENG, PHYS, WAVE PHYS guía de ondas paralelepipédica *f*, guía de ondas rectangular *f*; ~ **wiring** *n* ELEC ENG cableado rectangular *m*
rectangularity *n* GEOM rectangularidad *f*
rectification *n* CHEM, ELEC, ELEC ENG rectificación *f*, MECH ENG corrección *f*, enderezamiento *m*, rectificación *f*, repaso *m*; ~ **efficiency** *n* ELEC, ELEC ENG eficacia de la rectificación *f*; ~ **lens** *n* INSTR, OPT lente de rectificación *f*
rectified[1] *adj* CHEM, ELEC, ELEC ENG, MECH ENG rectificado
rectified[2]: ~ **alternating-current** *n* ELEC, ELEC ENG corriente alterna rectificada *f*; ~ **current** *n* ELEC, ELEC ENG corriente enderezada *f*, corriente rectificada *f*; ~ **output** *n* ELEC, ELEC ENG producción rectificada *f*; ~ **voltage** *n* ELEC, ELEC ENG tensión rectificada *f*
rectifier *n* GEN rectificador *m*; ~ **anode** *n* ELEC ENG, ELECTRON ánodo rectificador *m*; ~ **bridge** *n* ELEC ENG puente rectificador *m*; ~ **cell** *n* ELEC ENG célula rectificadora *f*; ~ **diode** *n* ELEC ENG, ELECTRON diodo rectificador *m*; ~ **locomotive** *n* RAIL electrolocomotora con rectificador *f*, locomotora eléctrica de rectificador *f*; ~ **roll** *n* PAPER rodillo rectificador *m*; ~ **substation** *n* ELEC ENG, MECH subestación rectificadora *f*; ~ **transformer** *n* ELEC, ELEC ENG transformador rectificador *m*; ~ **tube** *n* ELEC ENG tubo rectificador *m*; ~ **unit** *n* ELEC, ELECTRON unidad rectificadora *f*, TELECOM conjunto rectificador *m*, unidad rectificadora *f*
rectify *vt* GEN rectificar
rectifying: ~ **circuit** *n* ELEC ENG circuito de rectificación *m*; ~ **junction** *n* ELEC ENG juntura rectificadora *f*
rectilineal: ~ **motion** *n* MECH, MECH ENG, PHYS, WAVE PHYS movimiento rectilíneo *m*
rectilinear[1] *adj* MECH, MECH ENG, PHYS, TELECOM, TV rectilíneo
rectilinear[2]: ~ **aerial** *n* BrE (*cf rectilinear antenna AmE*) TELECOM antena rectilínea *f*; ~ **antenna** *n* AmE (*cf rectilinear aerial BrE*) TELECOM antena rectilínea *f*; ~ **combing-machine** *n* TEXTIL peinadora rectilínea *f*; ~ **motion** *n* MECH, MECH ENG, PHYS, WAVE PHYS movimiento rectilíneo *m*; ~ **propagation** *n* PHYS, TV, WAVE PHYS propagación rectilínea *f*; ~ **scanning** *n* PHYS, TV, WAVE PHYS exploración por líneas *f*
recto *n* PAPER, PRINT anverso *m*, página derecha *f*, página impar *f*
recultivation *n* AGRIC, POLL recultivo *m*
recumbent: ~ **fold** *n* GEOL pliegue recumbente *m*, pliegue tumbado *m*
recuperation *n* C&G, CHEM, HEAT ENG, PROD recuperación *f*
recuperative: ~ **furnace** *n* C&G, HEAT ENG, PROD horno recuperativo *m*

recuperator *n* C&G, CHEM, HEAT, PROD recuperador *m*
recurrent: ~ **cost** *n* SPACE costo recurrente *m*; ~ **pulses** *n pl* ELECTRON impulsos recurrentes *m pl*
recurring[1] *adj* MATH cíclico, periódico, recurrente
recurring[2]: ~ **decimal** *n* MATH decimal periódico *m*; ~ **unit** *n* CHEM *in polymer* unidad de repetición *f*
recursion *n* COMP&DP, ELEC, TELECOM recursión *f*
recursive[1] *adj* COMP&DP, ELEC, TELECOM recursivo
recursive[2]: ~ **filter** *n* COMP&DP, ELECTRON, TELECOM filtro recursivo *m*; ~ **filtering** *n* COMP&DP, ELECTRON, TELECOM filtrado recursivo *m*; ~ **function** *n* COMP&DP función recursiva *f*
recyclable *adj* PACK, POLL, RECYCL reciclable, reutilizable
recycle[1]: ~ **time** *n* PHOTO tiempo de recirculación *m*
recycle[2] *vt* CONST, PACK, POLL, RECYCL reciclar, recircular, regenerar, reutilizar
recycled: ~ **material** *n* CONST, POLL, RECYCL material reciclado *m*; ~ **paper** *n* PAPER, POLL, RECYCL papel reciclado *m*
recycling *n* GEN reciclado *m*; ~ **method** *n* CONST, POLL, PROD, RECYCL método de reciclaje *m*; ~ **time** *n* PHOTO tiempo de recirculación *m*
red[1] *adj* TRANSP *traffic light* cerrado, en rojo; ~**-hot** *adj* HEAT ENG, THERMO al rojo vivo, calentado al rojo, candente, enrojecido
red[2]: ~**-abstracting filter** *n* INSTR filtro abstractivo de rayos infrarrojos *m*; ~ **adder** *n* TV circuito aditivo rojo *m*; ~ **arsenic** *n* CHEM, MINERAL arsénico rojo *m*; ~ **beam** *n* ELECTRON, TV haz rojo *m*, rayo rojo *m*; ~**-beam magnet** *n* ELECTRON, TV imán de rayos rojos *m*; ~ **bed** *n* GEOL capa roja *f*; ~**-black level** *n* TV nivel rojo-negro *m*; ~ **clay** *n* PETROL arcilla roja *f*; ~ **cobalt** *n* MINERAL cobalto rojo *m*; ~ **color difference axis** AmE *see red colour difference axis BrE*; ~ **color difference signal** AmE *see red colour difference signal BrE*; ~ **colour difference axis** BrE *n* (*R-Y axis*) TV eje R-Y *m*; ~ **colour difference signal** *n* (*R-Y signal*) TV señal R-Y *f*; ~ **copper ore** *n* CHEM, MINERAL cobre rojo *m*, cuprita *f*; ~ **ensign** *n* WATER TRANSP *flags* bandera roja *f*; ~ **green blue** *n* (*RGB*) COMP&DP, TV rojo verde azul *m* (*RGB*); ~ **laser** *n* ELECTRON láser rojo *m*; ~ **lead** *n* C&G, CHEM, MINERAL, P&R minio *m*, plomo rojo *m*, óxido de plomo rojo *m*; ~**-lead ore** *n* MINERAL crocoíta *f*, plomo rojo *m*; ~ **litmus paper** *n* CHEM papel tornasol rojo *m*; ~ **peak level** *n* TV nivel máximo del rojo *m*; ~ **phase** *n* TRANSP fase de luz roja *f*, luz roja *f*; ~ **primary** *n* TV rojo primario *m*; ~ **quark** *n* PHYS quark rojo *m*; ~ **rod** *n* FUELLESS *windmill pump* vástago rojo *m*; ~ **schorl** *n* MINERAL chorlo rojo *m*; ~**-screen grid** *n* ELECTRON, TV retícula de pantalla roja *f*; ~ **signal** *n* ELECTRON, TV señal roja *f*; ~ **tide** *n* OCEAN marea roja *f*, aguas coloradas *f pl*, agua oxidada *f*; ~ **tube** *n* ELECTRON tubo rojo *m*; ~ **waters** *n pl* OCEAN aguas rojas *f pl*
redevelopment *n* CINEMAT re-revelado *m*
redirect *vt* TELECOM reexpedir
redirecting: ~ **counter** *n* TELECOM contador de reexpedición *m*; ~ **indicator** *n* TELECOM indicador de reexpedición *m*; ~ **number** *n* TELECOM número de reexpedición *m*; ~ **reason** *n* TELECOM razón de reexpedición *f*
redirection: ~ **number** *n* TELECOM número de reexpedición *m*
redistil *vt* BrE CHEM redestilar

redistill *AmE see redistil BrE*

redistillation *n* CHEM redestilación *f*

redistribution *n* ELEC ENG redistribución *f*

redock *vi* SPACE reacoplarse

redox¹ *abbr* (*oxidation-reduction, oxidoreduction*) CHEM, LAB redox (*oxidación-reducción, óxido-reducción, oxidoreducción*)

redox²: **~ cell** *n* CHEM, LAB célula de redox *f*, celda de redox *f*

redriving *n* COAL reclavado *m*, rehincado *m*

reduce¹ *vt* CHEM, CONST reducir, MATH, MECH ENG adelgazar, reducir, PHOTO reducir, PROD adelgazar; **~ to ashes** *vt* CHEM reducir a cenizas; **~ to its lowest terms** *vt* MATH reducir a la mínima expresión; **~ to width** *vt* CONST reducir el ancho

reduce² *vi* COAL disminuir, reducir; **~ speed** *vi* MECH ENG, TRANSP reducir la velocidad

reduced: **~ coordinates** *n pl* PHYS coordenadas reducidas *f pl*; **~ fraction** *n* MATH fracción irreducible *f*; **~ inspection** *n* QUALITY control reducido *m*; **~ instruction set computer** *n* (*RISC*) COMP&DP computador con juego reducido de instrucciones *m* (*AmL*), computadora con juego reducido de instrucciones *f* (*AmL*), ordenador con juego reducido de instrucciones *m* (*Esp*); **~-load configuration** *n* SPACE configuración de carga reducida *f*; **~ mass** *n* PHYS masa reducida *f*; **~ model** *n* TELECOM modelo reducido *m*; **~ power tapping** *n* ELEC toma reducida de energía *f*, toma reducida de potencia *f*; **~ rate** *n* TELECOM tarifa reducida *f*; **~-salt food** *n* FOOD alimento bajo en sal *m*; **~ sodium** *n* FOOD sodio reducido *m*; **~ take-off and landing aircraft** *n* (*RTOL aircraft*) AIR TRANSP avión de despegue y aterrizaje reducido *m*

reducer *n* CHEM, CINEMAT, CONST, PHOTO reductor *m*

reducible: **~ polynomial** *n* COMP&DP polinomio reducible *m*

reducing *n* CHEM, CINEMAT, CONST, PHOTO, PRINT reducción *f*; **~ agent** *n* CHEM agente químico *m*, agente reductor *m*, COAL agente reductor *m*, MILIT agente químico *m*, POLL agente reductor *m*, agente químico *m*, TEXTIL agente químico *m*; **~ flame** *n* HEAT ENG, THERMO llama desoxidante *f*, llama reductora *f*; **~ furnace** *n* HEAT, PROD, THERMO horno de reducción *m*, horno reductor *m*; **~ gas** *n* GAS, HEAT ENG, THERMO gas reductor *m*; **~ gear** *n* MECH ENG engranaje desmultiplicador *m*, engranaje reductor de velocidad *m*, VEH engranaje reductor de velocidad *m*; **~ pipe fitting** *n* CONST accesorio reductor de tubería *m*; **~ valve** *n* LAB, MECH ENG, PROD válvula de escape *f*, válvula reductora *f*; **~ wheel** *n* PROD muela abrasiva de desbastar *f*

reduction *n* AGRIC *of stocks*, CHEM reducción *f*, COAL debilitamiento *m*, reducción *f*; **~ compass** *n* MECH ENG compás de reducción *m*; **~ crucible** *n* PROD crisol de reducción *m*; **~ furnace** *n* HEAT, PROD, THERMO horno de reducción *m*, horno reductor *m*; **~ gear** *n* VEH engranaje reductor *m*, par de reducción *m*; **~ mask** *n* PHOTO máscara de reducción *f*; **~ print** *n* CINEMAT, PHOTO, TV copia de reducción *f*; **~ ratio** *n* COAL factor de reducción *m*, relación desmultiplicadora *f*; **~ sleeve** *n* MECH ENG manguito reductor *m*; **~ tube** *n* GEOPHYS, LAB adaptador reductor *m*, tubo reductor *m*

reductive *adj* CHEM reductivo

redundancy *n* COMP&DP, SPACE redundancia *f*;

~ check *n* COMP&DP, SPACE verificación de redundancia *f*

redundant: **~ code** *n* COMP&DP código redundante *m*

reed *n* CONST *joinery* caña *f*, junquillo *m*, ELEC, ELEC ENG, TELECOM lámina *f*, lengüeta *f*, TEXTIL peine *m*, WATER TRANSP *navigation aid* bocina de boquilla *f* (*AmL*), nautófono *m* (*Esp*); **~ contact** *n* ELEC, PROD, TELECOM contacto de lengüetas *m*, contacto de láminas *m*; **~-contact relay** *n* ELEC, ELEC ENG, PROD relé de contacto de láminas flexibles *m*; **~ relay** *n* ELEC, ELEC ENG, PROD, TELECOM relé de láminas *m*, relé de láminas flexibles *m*, relé de láminas magnéticas *m*; **~-relay crosspoint** *n* ELEC, ELEC ENG, TELECOM contacto del relé de láminas *m*, punto de cruce del relé de láminas *m*; **~-relay electronic exchange** *n* ELEC, ELEC ENG, TELECOM central electrónica de relé de láminas *f*; **~-relay switch** *n* ELEC, ELEC ENG, TELECOM conmutador de relé de láminas *m*; **~-relay switching** *n* ELEC, ELEC ENG, TELECOM conmutación de relé de láminas *f*; **~-relay switching network** *n* ELEC, ELEC ENG, TELECOM red de conmutación de relés por láminas *f*; **~-relay system** *n* ELEC, ELEC ENG, TELECOM sistema de relé de láminas *m*; **~ switch** *n* ELEC, ELEC ENG, PHYS, TELECOM interruptor de lengüeta *m*, interruptor de láminas *m*

re-edit *vt* CINEMAT, TV reeditar, volver a editar

reef¹ *n* GEOL arrecife *m*, MINE filón de cuarzo aurífero *m*, filón tubular *m*, yacimiento vertical de oro dentro del cuarzo *m*, OCEAN arrecife *m*, WATER TRANSP *sail* rizo *m*; **~ band** *n* OCEAN faja de rizos *f*; **~ cringle** *n* WATER TRANSP *sailing boats* garrucho de la faja de rizos *m*; **~ drive** *n* MINE galería filoniana *f*; **~ effect** *n* PETR TECH efecto arrecife *m*; **~ flat** *n* GEOL, OCEAN bajío del arrecife *m*; **~ front** *n* GEOL, OCEAN reborde del arrecife *m*; **~ furrow** *n* GEOL, OCEAN surco del arrecife *m*; **~ glacis** *n* GEOL, OCEAN declive del arrecife *m*; **~ knoll** *n* GEOL, OCEAN bioihermo *m*; **~ knot** *n* WATER TRANSP nudo de rizo *m*; **~ pediment** *n* GEOL pedimento del arrecife *m*; **~ slope** *n* GEOL, OCEAN pendiente del arrecife *f*; **~ spur** *n* GEOL, OCEAN espolón coralífero *m*

reef² *vt* WATER TRANSP *sail* rizar, tomar rizos

reefer: **~ ship** *n* WATER TRANSP buque frigorífico *m*

reefing: **~ pennant** *n* WATER TRANSP *classic sailboat, yachts* amante de rizos *m*, amantillo *m*

reel¹: **~-to-reel** *adj* CINEMAT de carrete a carrete

reel² *n* CINEMAT, COMP&DP carrete *m*, ELEC ENG devanadera *f*, devanadora *f*, MAR POLL rollo *m*, OCEAN carretel *m*, PACK, PAPER bobina *f*, rollo *m*, PETROL carretel *m*, carrete *m*, PRINT bobina *f*, PROD, TEXTIL devanadora *f*, devanadora *f*, TV bobina *f*, carrete *m*; **~ capacity** *n* CINEMAT, TV capacidad del carrete *f*; **~ drum** *n* PAPER tambor de la enrolladora *m*; **~ end** *n* CINEMAT, TV final del carrete *m*; **~-fed press** *n* PRINT prensa alimentada por bobinas *f*; **~-feed** *n* PRINT alimentación por bobina *f*; **~ feed bag** *n* PACK bolsa que se suministra en bobinas *f*; **~-feed press** *n* PRINT rotativa *f*; **~ insulator** *n* ELEC, ELEC ENG aislante de carrete *m*; **~ lifter** *n* PACK elevador de bobinas *m*; **~ mower** *n* AGRIC cortadora de césped de cuchillas helicoidales *f*; **~ overwrapper** *n* PACK sobreembalado de la bobina *m*; **~ sample** *n* PAPER muestra tomada en la bobina *f*; **~ spindle** *n* CINEMAT husillo del carrete *m*; **~ spool** *n* PAPER carrete de la bobina *m*; **~-wrapping-and-handling**

equipment *n* PACK equipo para embalar y manejar bobinas *m*

reel[3] *vt* ELEC ENG, PAPER, PRINT bobinar; **~ in** *vt* MAR POLL enrollar

reelcore *n* PRINT mandril *m*

reeled: **~ capacitor** *n* ELEC ENG condensador devanado *m*; **~ contact** *n* ELEC ENG contacto bobinado *m*; **~ resistor** *n* ELEC ENG resistencia enrollada *f*

reeling *n* ELEC ENG, P&R devanado *m*, enrollado *m*, enrolladora *f*, PAPER enrolladora *f*, enrollado *m*; **~ end** *n* PAPER extremo de la enrolladora *m*; **~ machine** *n* P&R, PAPER mecanismo de enrollar *m*, máquina de devanado *f*; **~-off** *n* PAPER desenrollado *m*

re-embark *vi* WATER TRANSP *passengers* reembarcar

re-entrant[1] *adj* COMP&DP reentrante, GEOM cóncavo, entrante, reentrante

re-entrant[2] *n* COMP&DP reentrante *m*, GEOM reentrante *m*, ángulo cóncavo *m*, ángulo entrante *m*; **~ beam tube** *n* ELECTRON tubo de haz ondulado *m*

re-entry: **~ vehicle** *n* SPACE, VEH vehículo de reentrada *m*

re-etching *n* PRINT regrabado *m*

reeve *vt* WATER TRANSP hacer pasar por un motón, laborear en un motón

re-extraction *n* COAL nueva extracción *f*

reference: **~ atmosphere** *n* SPACE atmósfera de referencia *f*; **~ audio level** *n* ACOUST, TV nivel de referencia del audio *m*; **~ axis** *n* ACOUST, TV eje de referencia *m*; **~ black** *n* TV negro de referencia *m*; **~ burst** *n* SPACE *communications* descarga de referencia *f*; **~ capacitor** *n* ELEC, ELEC ENG capacitor de referencia *m*, condensador de referencia *m*; **~ clock** *n* TELECOM reloj de referencia *m*; **~ conditions** *n pl* METR condiciones de referencia *f pl*; **~ coupling** *n* ELEC, ELEC ENG acoplamiento de referencia *m*; **~ edge** *n* TV borde de referencia *m*; **~ electrode** *n* ELEC, ELECTRON, LAB electrodo de referencia *m*; **~ energy** *n* ACOUST energía de referencia *f*; **~ frequency** *n* TELECOM frecuencia de referencia *f*; **~-friction condition** *n* AIR TRANSP *of runway* condición de fricción de referencia *f*; **~ fuel** *n* PETR TECH combustible de referencia *m*; **~ gage** *AmE*, **~ gauge** *BrE n* MECH ENG calibre de comprobación *m*, calibre patrón *m*, patrón de referencia *m*; **~ landing approach speed** *n* AIR TRANSP velocidad de aproximación de aterrizaje de referencia *f*; **~ level** *n* ELECTRON nivel de referencia *m*; **~ line** *n* GEOM línea de referencia *f*; **~ mark** *n* CONST *surveying* hito *m*, marca de referencia *f*, mojón *m*; **~ noise** *n* ACOUST, ELECTRON ruido de referencia *m*; **~ phase** *n* TV fase de referencia *f*; **~ plant** *n* NUCL central de referencia *f*; **~ point** *n* ACOUST, GEOM punto de referencia *m*; **~ print** *n* CINEMAT, TV copia de referencia *f*; **~ sensibility** *n* TELECOM sensibilidad de referencia *f*; **~ sensor** *n* AUTO sensor de referencia *m*; **~ signal** *n* ELECTRON señal de referencia *f*; **~-signal input** *n* ELECTRON entrada de señal de referencia *f*; **~-signal phase** *n* ELECTRON fase de señal de referencia *f*; **~ sound acceleration** *n* ACOUST aceleración acústica de referencia *f*; **~ sound intensity** *n* ACOUST, PHYS intensidad sonora de referencia *f*; **~ sound power** *n* ACOUST potencia sonora de referencia *f*; **~ sound pressure** *n* ACOUST, POLL presión acústica de referencia *f*, presión sonora de referencia *f*; **~ sound velocity** *n* ACOUST velocidad acústica de referencia *f*;

~ standard *n* METR referencia estándar *f*; **~ station** *n* SPACE estación de referencia *f*, estación testigo *f*; **~ strip** *n* CINEMAT tira de referencia *f*; **~ surface** *n* OPT, TELECOM superficie de referencia *f*; **~-surface diameter** *n* OPT, TELECOM diámetro de la superficie de referencia *m*; **~-surface tolerance field** *n* OPT, TELECOM campo de tolerancia de la superficie de referencia *m*; **~ tape** *n* ACOUST, TV cinta de referencia *f*; **~ temperature** *n* METEO, METR temperatura de referencia *f*; **~ test method** *n* (*RTM*) OPT, TELECOM método de prueba de referencia *m*; **~ voltage** *n* ELEC, ELEC ENG voltaje de referencia *m*; **~ volume** *n* ACOUST volumen de referencia *m*; **~ white** *n* TV blanco de referencia *m*

refill[1] *n* FOOD llenado *m*

refill[2] *vt* RAIL *the brake* rellenar

refine *vt* C&G, MAR POLL, PAPER, POLL refinar

refined[1] *adj* C&G, MAR POLL, PAPER, POLL refinado

refined[2]: **~ product** *n* MAR POLL, POLL producto de refinación *m*, refinado *m*

refinement *n* CHEM mejora *f*, COMP&DP refinación *f*, CRYSTALL refinamiento *m*

refiner: **~ bar** *n* PAPER cuchilla del refino *f*; **~ mechanical pulp** *n* (*RMP*) PAPER pasta mecánica de refino *f* (*RMP*)

refinery *n* PETR TECH, PROD *for cast iron* refinería *f*; **~ gas** *n* GAS, PETR TECH, THERMO gas de refinería petrolera *m*

refining *n* C&G, CHEM, PAPER, PETR TECH, PROD refinación *f*, refinado *m*, refino *m*; **~ furnace** *n* HEAT, PROD, THERMO horno de afinación *m*, horno de afino *m*, horno de refinación *m*; **~ glass** *n* C&G, CHEM TECH, SAFE cristal de refinación *m*; **~ zone** *n* C&G zona de refino *f*

refinishing *n* COATINGS, P&R aplicación de un acabado nuevo *f*

refit[1] *n* WATER TRANSP *of ship* recorrida *f*, reparación *f*

refit[2] *vt* WATER TRANSP *of ship* recorrer, reparar

refitting *n* MECH ENG transformación *f*

reflect *vt* GEN reflejar

reflectance *n* GEN reflectancia *f*; **~ density** *n* OPT densidad de reflectancia *f*; **~ energy factor** *n* OPT factor de energía de reflectancia *m*; **~ factor** *n* OPT, PAPER, RAD PHYS factor de reflectancia *m*

reflected: **~ beam** *n* OPT, PHYS, TRANSP haz reflejado *m*; **~-beam photoelectric detector** *n* OPT, PHYS, TRANSP detector fotoeléctrico de haz reflejado *m*; **~ heat** *n* OPT, THERMO calor reflejado *m*; **~ impedance** *n* ELEC ENG, OPT impedancia reflejada *f*; **~ light** *n* CINEMAT, INSTR, OPT, PHOTO luz reflejada *f*; **~-light microscope** *n* INSTR, OPT microscopio de luz reflejada *m*; **~-light mirror** *n* INSTR, OPT espejo de luz reflejada *m*; **~-light reading** *n* CINEMAT, OPT, PHOTO lectura de luz reflejada *f*; **~ power** *n* ELEC ENG, OPT potencia reflejada *f*; **~ ray** *n* OPT, PHYS, WAVE PHYS rayo reflejado *m*; **~ resistance** *n* ELEC ENG, OPT resistencia reflejada *f*; **~ signal** *n* ELEC ENG, ELECTRON, OPT señal reflejada *f*; **~ voltage** *n* ELEC ENG, OPT tensión reflejada *f*; **~ wave** *n* ELEC ENG, OCEAN, OPT, PHYS, WAVE PHYS onda de eco *f*, onda reflejada *f*

reflecting[1] *adj* ACOUST, ELEC ENG, OPT reflectante

reflecting[2]: **~ electrode** *n* ELEC ENG, OPT electrodo de emisión secundaria *m*, electrodo de reflexión *m*; **~ goniometer** *n* GEOM goniómetro de reflexión *m*; **~ instrument** *n* INSTR, OPT instrumento reflector *m*;

~ **microscope** n INSTR, OPT microscopio reflector m; ~-**mirror galvanometer** n ELEC, ELEC ENG, INSTR galvanómetro de espejo cóncavo m, galvanómetro de espejo ustorio m; ~ **prism** n INSTR, OPT prisma reflector m; ~ **satellite** n OPT, SPACE satélite reflector m; ~ **screen** n CINEMAT, OPT, PHOTO pantalla reflectora f; ~ **stud** n CONST poste reflectante m; ~ **telescope** n INSTR, OPT, PHYS telescopio de reflexión m, telescopio reflector m; ~ **viewfinder** n CINEMAT, OPT, PHOTO visor de cámara oscura m

reflection n GEN reflexión f; ~ **coefficient** n ACOUST, ELECTRON, OPT, PHYS coeficiente de reflexión m; ~ **density reference** n (RDR) PRINT referencia de densidad óptica externa f; ~ **electron microscope** n ELECTRON, INSTR, OPT microscopio electrónico de reflexión m; ~ **factor** n ELECTRON, OPT, PHYS factor de reflexión m; ~ **from ionosphere** n WAVE PHYS reflexión en la ionosfera f; ~ **grating** n OPT, PHYS, WAVE PHYS gratícula reflectora f, red reflectora f, rejilla reflectora f; ~ **loss** n ELECTRON pérdida de potencia f, pérdida de reflexión f; ~ **method** n NUCL método de reflexión m; ~ **peak** n PETROL pico de reflexión m; ~ **print** n PRINT impresión por reflexión f; ~ **shooting** n GEOPHYS disparo de fuente de energía m, disparo de reflexión m; ~ **wave** n GEOPHYS onda de reflexión f

reflective: ~ **coat** n COATINGS capa reflectante f, capa reflectora f; ~ **disc** BrE, ~ **disk** AmE n OPT disco reflector m; ; ~ **insulant** n HEAT ENG, REFRIG, THERMO aislante reflector m; ~ **insulation** n HEAT ENG, REFRIG, THERMO aislación reflectora f, aislamiento reflector m; ~ **LCD** n ELECTRON VCL reflectante m

reflectivity n FUELLESS, HEAT ENG, OPT, SPACE reflectancia f, reflectividad f, reflexividad f; ~ **coefficient** n SPACE coeficiente de reflectividad m, coeficiente de reflexión m

reflectometer n P&R, PAPER reflectómetro m

reflector n GEN espejo m, reflector m; ~ **aerial** n BrE (cf reflector antenna AmE) SPACE, TELECOM, TV antena de reflector f, antena reflectora f; ~ **antenna** n AmE (cf reflector aerial BrE) SPACE, TELECOM, TV antena de reflector f, antena reflectora f; ~ **electrode** n ELEC ENG, TV electrodo de reflexión m; ~ **lamp** n CINEMAT, PHOTO, TV lámpara con reflector f; ~ **space** n ELECTRON espacio reflector m; ~ **stand** n CINEMAT, PHOTO, TV soporte del reflector m; ~ **telescope** n INSTR, OPT telescopio reflector m

reflectorized: ~ **board** n RAIL cuadro luminoso m, cuadro reflectante m

reflex[1] adj GEOM reflejado

reflex[2] n GEOM reflejo m; ~ **angle** n GEOM ángulo cóncavo m, ángulo saliente m; ~ **baffle** n ACOUST caja acústica reflectora f, pantalla reflectora f; ~ **bunching** n ELECTRON agrupación de reflejos f; ~ **camera** n CINEMAT, PHOTO, TV cámara reflex f; ~ **housing** n CINEMAT, PHOTO caja reflex f; ~ **klystron** n ELECTRON, PHYS, RAD PHYS klistron de reflexión m; ~ **mirror** n PHOTO espejo reflex m; ~ **printing method** n PHOTO, PRINT método de impresión reflex m; ~ **projection** n CINEMAT, PHOTO, TV proyección reflex f; ~ **reflector** n OPT, VEH catadióptrico m, catafaro m; ~ **shutter** n CINEMAT, PHOTO, TV obturador reflex m; ~ **viewfinder** n CINEMAT, PHOTO, TV visor reflex m

refloat vt WATER TRANSP ship desencallar, desvarar

reflow: ~ **soldering** n ELEC ENG soldadura por reflujo f

reflux n CHEM, CHEM TECH, NUCL, PETR TECH reflujo m;

~ **boiling** n CHEM TECH ebullición por reflujo f; ~ **condenser** n LAB, NUCL condensador de reflujo m; ~ **valve** n HYDRAUL válvula de contención f, válvula de retención f

refolding n GEOL repliegue m

reforestation n AGRIC reforestación f, repoblación forestal f

reformatting n COMP&DP reformateado m

reforming n PETR TECH conversión f, reformado m

refract vt ACOUST, OPT, PHYS, TELECOM refractar

refracted[1] adj ACOUST, OPT, PHYS, TELECOM refractado

refracted[2]: ~ **near-end method** n TELECOM método local refractado m; ~ **near-field method** n OPT método de campo próximo refractado m; ~ **ray** n OPT, PHYS, TELECOM rayo refractado m; ~-**ray method** n OPT, PHYS, TELECOM método de rayos refractados m

refracting: ~ **prism** n OPT, PHYS prisma refringente m; ~ **telescope** n INSTR, OPT, PHYS telescopio de refracción m, telescopio refractante m, telescopio refringente m

refraction n ACOUST, OPT, PHYS, TELECOM, WATER TRANSP, WAVE PHYS refracción f; ~ **grating** n LAB, OPT red de refracción f, rejilla de refracción f; ~ **shooting** n GEOPHYS disparo de refracción m; ~ **wave** n GEOPHYS, PETROL, WAVE PHYS onda de refracción f

refractive: ~ **index** n GEN índice de refracción m; ~-**index contrast** n CINEMAT, OPT, PHOTO, PHYS, SPACE, TELECOM contraste del índice de refracción m; ~-**index profile** n CINEMAT, OPT, PHOTO, PHYS, SPACE, TELECOM, WAVE PHYS perfil del índice de refracción m; ~ **power** n PHOTO poder de refracción m

refractivity n GEN refractividad f

refractometer n INSTR, LAB, PHYS, RAD PHYS refractómetro m

refractor n GEOPHYS, INSTR, OPT, PHYS refractor m; ~ **telescope** n INSTR, OPT telescopio refractante m, telescopio refringente m

refractory[1] adj C&G, CHEM, HEAT, SPACE, THERMO pirorresistente, refractario

refractory[2] n C&G, CHEM, HEAT, PROD, THERMO producto refractario m, refractario m; ~ **brick** n HEAT, LAB, THERMO ladrillo refractario m; ~ **coating** n COATINGS, HEAT, THERMO revestimiento refractario m; ~ **lining** n COATINGS, HEAT, THERMO forro refractario m, revestimiento refractario m; ~ **material** n COAL, GAS, HEAT, THERMO material refractario m; ~ **metal** n METALL metal refractario m; ~ **tube** n HEAT, THERMO tubo refractario m; ~ **wash** n COATINGS baño refractario m

reframe vt CINEMAT reencuadrar, volver a encuadrar

refreeze vt REFRIG, THERMO recongelar

refresh[1] n COMP&DP, ELECTRON regeneración f; ~ **cycle** n COMP&DP, ELECTRON ciclo de refresco m, ciclo de regeneración m; ~ **mode** n COMP&DP, ELECTRON función de regeneración f, modo de generación m; ~ **rate** n COMP&DP, ELECTRON velocidad de regeneración f; ~ **signal** n COMP&DP, ELECTRON señal de regeneración f

refresh[2] vt COMP&DP, ELECTRON refrescar, regenerar

refreshed: ~ **image** n COMP&DP, ELECTRON imagen regenerada f

refrigerant[1] adj GEN refrigerante

refrigerant[2] n GEN refrigerante m; ~ **capacity** n

REFRIG capacidad de refrigerante *f*; ~ **charge** *n* REFRIG carga de refrigerante *f*; ~ **circuit** *n* REFRIG circuito del refrigerante *m*; ~ **compressor** *n* MECH ENG, REFRIG compresor de refrigerante *m*, compresor refrigerante *m*; ~ **connection** *n* REFRIG conexión para el refrigerante *f*; ~~**-cooled compressor** *n* REFRIG compresor refrigerado por refrigerante *m*; ~ **distributor** *n* REFRIG distribuidor de fluido frigorífico *m*; ~ **liquefying set** *n* MECH ENG, REFRIG aparato licuante refrigerante *m*; ~ **metering device** *n* REFRIG dispositivo de regulación *m*

refrigerate *vt* FOOD, MECH ENG, REFRIG, THERMO enfriar, refrigerar; ~ **by compression** *vt* MECH ENG, REFRIG, THERMO refrigerar por compresión

refrigerated[1] *adj* AUTO, FOOD, REFRIG, THERMO, VEH refrigerado

refrigerated[2]: ~ **bakery slab** *n* FOOD, REFRIG mesa refrigerada para pastelería *f*; ~ **cabinet** *n* FOOD, MECH ENG, REFRIG, THERMO armario frigorífico *m*; ~ **car** *n* *AmE* (*cf refrigerated wagon BrE*) RAIL, REFRIG vagón refrigerado *m*; ~ **cargo** *n* REFRIG, TRANSP cargamento refrigerado *m*; ~~**-cargo ship** *n* REFRIG, TRANSP, WATER TRANSP buque de carga refrigerada *m*; ~~**-cargo vessel** *n* REFRIG, TRANSP, WATER TRANSP barco frigorífico *m*; ~ **container** *n* REFRIG, TRANSP contenedor frigorífico *m*; ~ **counter** *n* REFRIG vitrina frigorífica *f*; ~ **display cabinet** *n* REFRIG gabinete de exhibición refrigerado *m*; ~ **display case** *n* REFRIG vitrina frigorífica *f*; ~ **farm tank** *n* REFRIG tanque enfriador de granja *m*; ~ **incubator** *n* LAB, REFRIG incubador refrigerado *m*; ~ **lorry** *n* *BrE* (*cf refrigerated truck AmE*) AUTO, REFRIG, TRANSP camión frigorífico *m*, camión refrigerante *m*; ~ **showcase** *n* REFRIG vitrina frigorífica *f*; ~ **trailer** *n* REFRIG, TRANSP camión frigorífico articulado *m*; ~ **transport** *n* FOOD, REFRIG, TRANSP transporte frigorífico *m*; ~ **truck** *n* *AmE* (*cf refrigerated lorry BrE*) AUTO, REFRIG, TRANSP camión frigorífico *m*, camión refrigerante *m*; ~ **vehicle** *n* REFRIG, TRANSP, VEH vehículo refrigerado *m*; ~ **wagon** *n* *BrE* (*cf refrigerated car AmE*) RAIL, REFRIG vagón refrigerado *m*; ~ **warehouse** *n* FOOD, MECH ENG, REFRIG, THERMO almacén frigorífico *m*; ~ **window** *n* REFRIG escaparate frigorífico *m*

refrigerating[1] *adj* FOOD, MECH ENG, REFRIG enfriador, refrigerador

refrigerating[2]: ~ **capacity** *n* REFRIG potencia frigorífica *f*; ~ **circuit** *n* REFRIG circuito frigorífico *m*; ~ **compressor** *n* REFRIG compresor frigorífico *m*; ~ **hold** *n* REFRIG, TRANSP bodega refrigerada *f*; ~ **machine** *n* REFRIG máquina frigorífica *f*; ~ **plant** *n* MECH ENG, REFRIG, THERMO instalación frigorífica *f*, planta frigorífica *f*; ~ **system** *n* MECH ENG, REFRIG sistema frigorífico *m*, sistema refrigerante *m*; ~ **unit** *n* REFRIG grupo frigorífico *m*

refrigeration *n* FOOD, REFRIG, THERMO enfriamiento *m*, enfriamiento artificial *m*, frío artificial *m*, refrigeración *f*; ~ **contractor** *n* REFRIG instalador frigorista *m*; ~ **cycle** *n* REFRIG, THERMO ciclo frigorífico *m*; ~ **engineer** *n* REFRIG, THERMO frigorista *m*, ingeniero frigorista *m*, mecánico frigorista *m*; ~ **engineering** *n* FOOD, REFRIG, THERMO ingeniería de refrigeración *f*; ~ **output** *n* REFRIG producción frigorífica *f*; ~ **service engineer** *n* REFRIG técnico frigorista de mantenimiento *m*; ~ **system** *n* REFRIG, THERMO sistema de refrigeración *m*, sistema frigorífico *m*;

~ **test** *n* FOOD, REFRIG, THERMO ensayo de enfriamiento *m*, ensayo frigorífico *m*

refrigerator *n* ELEC, FOOD, MECH ENG, REFRIG, THERMO frigorífico *m*, heladera *f*, nevera *f*, refrigerador *m*

refuel *vt* AIR TRANSP, MILIT, TRANSP, VEH repostar

refueler *AmE see refueller BrE*

refueling *AmE see refuelling BrE*

refueller *n BrE* AIR TRANSP avión para repostar en vuelo *m*, repostador *m*, VEH camión repostador *m*, repostador *m*, WATER TRANSP buque repostador *m*

refuelling *n BrE* AIR TRANSP reabastecimiento *m*, repostado *m*, MAR POLL toma de combustible *f*, MECH ENG reabastecimiento *m*, reaprovisionamiento *m*; ~ **aircraft** *n BrE* AIR TRANSP, MILIT avión de repostaje *m*; ~ **boom** *n BrE* AIR TRANSP brazo de carga para combustibles *m*, sonda de avión nodriza para aprovisionar en vuelo a otros aviones *f*; ~ **craft** *n BrE* TRANSP navío de repostaje *m*, navío para repostar combustible *m*; ~ **in-flight system** *n BrE* AIR TRANSP, TRANSP sistema de repostaje en vuelo *m*; ~ **outage critical path** *n BrE* NUCL camino crítico de la recarga de combustible *m*; ~ **tanker** *n BrE* AIR TRANSP avión de reaprovisionamiento en vuelo *m*, TRANSP camión-cisterna de combustible *f*; ~ **water storage tank** *n BrE* NUCL depósito de almacenamiento de agua de recarga *m*

refuge: ~ **hole** *n* CONST orificio de seguridad *m*

refurbishing *n* SPACE *spacecraft* reacondicionamiento *m*

refuse *n* COAL basura *f*, desechos *m pl*, desperdicios *m pl*, despojos *m pl*, detritos *m pl*, detritus *m*, residuos *m pl*, NUCL basura *f*, PACK basura *f*, desechos *m pl*, desperdicios *m pl*, despojos *m pl*, detritos *m pl*, detritus *m*, residuos *m pl*, POLL detritos *m pl*, PROD, RECYCL basura *f*, desechos *m pl*, desperdicios *m pl*, despojos *m pl*, detritos *m pl*, detritus *m*, residuos *m pl*, SAFE basura *f*, WATER basura *f*, desechos *m pl*, desperdicios *m pl*, despojos *m pl*, detritos *m pl*, detritus *m*, residuos *m pl*; ~ **collection** *n* RECYCL colecta de basuras *f*, recogida de basuras *f*, recolección de basuras *f*; ~~**-collection lorry** *n* (*cf refuse-collection truck AmE*) RECYCL camión de recolección de basura *m*, VEH camión de recogida de basuras *m*; ~~**-collection truck** *n AmE* (*cf refuse-collection lorry BrE*) RECYCL camión de recolección de basura *m*, VEH camión de recogida de basuras *m*; ~~**-collection vehicle** *n* RECYCL vehículo de recogida de basura *m*, VEH camión de recolección de basura *m*, vehículo de recogida de basura *m*; ~ **dump** *n* POLL basurero *m*, RECYCL, WATER basurero *m*, escombrera *f*, vertedero de basura *m*; ~ **dumping** *n AmE* (*cf refuse tipping BrE*) RECYCL, WATER vertido de basuras *m*; ~ **sack** *n BrE* (*cf garbage bag AmE*) PACK saco de basura *m*; ~ **tipping** *n BrE* (*cf refuse dumping AmE*) RECYCL, WATER vertido de basuras *m*

regasification *n* GAS regasificación *f*

regelation *n* PHYS, REFRIG recongelación *f*

regenerate *vt* GEN regenerar

regenerated: ~ **pulse** *n* ELECTRON impulso regenerado *m*; ~ **rubber** *n* P&R caucho regenerado *m*

regeneration *n* CHEM, CINEMAT, COMP&DP, ELECTRON, GAS regeneración *f*, SPACE depuración *f*, reconstitución *f*, regeneración *f*, TELECOM, WATER regeneración *f*; ~ **mode** *n* GAS modalidad de regeneración *f*

regenerative[1] *adj* SPACE *communications* de reacción, reactivo, regenerador, regenerativo

regenerative[2]: **~ airheater** *n* HEAT, SAFE, THERMO calentador de aire regenerativo *m*; **~ amplification** *n* ELECTRON amplificación reactiva *f*, amplificación regenerativa *f*; **~ amplifier** *n* ELECTRON amplificador de reacción *m*, amplificador regenerativo *m*; **~ braking** *n* RAIL frenado regenerativo *m*; **~ cell** *n* TRANSP acumulador regenerable *m*, batería regenerable *f*; **~ circuit** *n* ELECTRON circuito reactivo *m*, circuito regenerativo *m*; **~ cooling** *n* REFRIG, THERMO enfriamiento por recuperación *m*, refrigeración regenerativa *f*; **~ feedback** *n* ELECTRON reacción *f*; **~ furnace** *n* C&G horno regenerativo *m*; **~ heating** *n* HEAT, REFRIG, THERMO calefacción por recuperación *f*; **~ repeater** *n* ELECTRON repetidor reactivo *m*

regenerator *n* ELECTRON recuperador *m*, SPACE regenerador *m*, termorrecuperador *m*, TELECOM regenerador *m*; **~ section** *n* TELECOM sección del regenerador *f*; **~-section overhead** *n* TELECOM línea aérea de la sección del regenerador *f*; **~-section termination** *n* TELECOM terminación de la sección del regenerador *f*; **~ test method** *n* TELECOM generador de temporización del regenerador *m*; **~ timing generator** *n* TELECOM generador de sincronización del regenerador *m*

regime *n* HYDROL régimen *m*

regional: **~ airport** *n* AIR TRANSP aeropuerto regional *m*; **~ carrier** *n* AIR TRANSP, TRANSP línea aérea regional *f*; **~ metamorphism** *n* FUELLESS metamorfismo regional *m*; **~ planning** *n* AGRIC planificación rural *f*; **~-planning policy** *n* AGRIC ordenación de territorio *f*; **~ processor** *n* (*RP*) TELECOM procesador regional *m*; **~ radio-warning system** *n* TELECOM, TRANSP sistema regional de advertencia por radio *m*

register[1] *n* CINEMAT, COMP&DP, ELEC ENG registro *m*, MECH ENG contador *m*, registrador *m*, PRINT registro *m*, impresión a registro *f*, PROD *of furnace* registro *m*, TELECOM contador *m*, registrador *m*; **analog shift ~** *n* AmE, **analogue shift ~** *n* BrE COMP&DP registro de desplazamiento analógico *m*; **~ bar** *n* CINEMAT barra registradora *f*; **clock ~** *n* COMP&DP registro cronométrico *m*; **~-controlled system** *n* TELECOM sistema de control por registradores *m*; **~ gage** *AmE*, **~ gauge** *BrE n* PRINT guía de registro *f*; **~ length** *n* COMP&DP longitud de registro *f*; **~ mount** *n* CINEMAT montura registradora *f*; **~ peg** *n* CINEMAT garfio *m*; **~ pin** *n* CINEMAT garfio *m*; **~ print** *n* CINEMAT copia de registro *f*; **temporary ~** *n* COMP&DP registro provisorio *m*, registro temporal *m*; **~ ton** *n* WATER TRANSP tonelada de arqueo *f*; **~ tonnage** *n* WATER TRANSP arqueo de registro *m*; **~ translator** *n* TELECOM registrador traductor *m*

register[2] *vt* COMP&DP registrar, MECH ENG hacer coincidir exactamente, hacer corresponder, MILIT *artillery* corregir, PHOTO, TELECOM registrar

registered[1] *adj* AGRIC *in the herdbook* inscripto

registered[2]: **~ depth** *n* WATER TRANSP *ship design* puntal de registro *m*; **~ seed** *n* AGRIC semilla de primera multiplicación *f*, semilla registrada *f*

registration *n* AGRIC inscripción *f*, registro *m*, AIR TRANSP matrícula *f*, registro *m*, CINEMAT, COMP&DP, TV registro *m*; **~ accuracy** *n* CINEMAT, TV exactitud del registro *f*; **~ of artwork** *n* CINEMAT, TV registro del diseño gráfico *m*; **~ control** *n* CINEMAT, TV control del

registro *m*; **~ drift** *n* CINEMAT, TV deslizamiento del registro *m*; **~ feed** *n* AGRIC derecho de inscripción *m*; **~ fire** *n* MILIT *artillery* tiro de reglaje *m*; **~ holes** *n* CINEMAT, TV perforaciones de registro *f pl*

regolith *n* GEOL regolito *m*

regrazing *n* AGRIC revegetación *f*

regression *n* COMP&DP, GEOL, MATH regresión *f*

regressive: **~ overlap** *n* GEOL estratificación regresiva *f*

regrind *vt* COAL, PROD reafilar, reamolar, rectificar, remoler

regrinding *n* COAL, PROD re-rectificado *m*, reafilado *m*, rectificación *f*

regrowth *n* AGRIC rebrote *m*

regular: **~ gas** *n* AmE (*cf regular petrol BrE*) AUTO, PETROL, VEH *fuel* gasolina normal *f*, gasolina regular *f*, gasolina sin aditivo *f*; **~ gasoline** *n* AmE (*cf regular petrol BrE*) AUTO, PETROL, VEH gasolina normal *f*, gasolina regular *f*, gasolina sin aditivo *f*; **~ part-load car** *n* AmE (*cf regular part-load wagon BrE*) RAIL vagón normal de carga parcial *m*; **~ part-load wagon** *n* BrE (*cf regular part-load car AmE*) RAIL vagón normal de carga parcial *m*; **~ petrol** *n* BrE (*cf regular gas AmE*, *cf regular gasoline AmE*) AUTO, PETROL, VEH gasolina normal *f*, gasolina regular *f*, gasolina sin aditivo *f*; **~ polygon** *n* GEOM polígono regular *m*; **~ share** *n* AGRIC reja común americana *f*; **~ tetrahedron** *n* GEOM tetraedro regular *m*

regularization *n* WATER regularización *f*

regulate *vt* ELEC ENG, POLL, PROD, SPACE regular

regulated: **~ bus system** *n* SPACE sistema de colector regulado *m*; **~ deposition** *n* POLL deposición regulada *f*, electrodeposición regulada *f*, precipitación regulada *f*, sedimentación regulada *f*; **~-output current** *n* ELEC ENG corriente de salida regulada *f*; **~-output voltage** *n* ELEC ENG tensión de salida regulada *f*; **~ power supply** *n* ELEC fuente de alimentación regulada *f*, ELEC fuente de alimentación regulada *f*, suministro de energía regulado *m*; **~ voltage** *n* ELEC ENG voltaje regulado *m*

regulating *n* MECH ajuste *m*, MECH ENG ajuste *m*, regulación *f*, regularización *f*, MINE, NUCL regulación *f*; **~ door** *n* MINE puerta de regulación *f*; **~ dynamo** *n* ELEC, ELEC ENG dinamo reguladora *f*; **~ nut** *n* MECH ENG tuerca de regulación *f*; **~ resistance** *n* ELEC ENG resistencia de reglaje *f*; **~ screw** *n* MECH ENG tornillo de regulación *m*, tornillo regulador *m*; **~ sluice** *n* HYDRAUL, WATER compuerta de toma de agua *f*, compuerta reguladora *f*; **~ starter** *n* ELEC arrancador regulador *m*; **~ transformer** *n* LAB transformador regulador *m*; **~ valve** *n* HYDRAUL, LAB válvula de estrangulación *f* (*AmL*), válvula reguladora *f* (*Esp*)

regulation *n* ACOUST reglamento *m*, AGRIC disposición *f*, CHEM control *m*, ELEC ENG reglaje *m*, regulación *f*, MECH ENG regulación *f*, regularización *f*, SAFE normativa *f*, reglamento *m*, TELECOM norma *f*, ordenanza *f*, reglamento *m*, regulación *f*; **~ range** *n* ELEC ENG rango de regulación *m*; **~ strategy** *n* TRANSP estrategia de reglamentación *f*; **~ transformer** *n* ELEC, ELEC ENG transformador de regulación *m*

regulator *n* AUTO, ELEC, ELEC ENG, LAB regulador *m*, MECH ENG regulador *m*, registro *m*, cronómetro regulador *m*, TELECOM regulador *m*; **~ cutout** *n* AUTO, ELEC, ELEC ENG escape libre regulador *m*, válvula reguladora de escape libre *f*; **~ door** *n* COAL puerta de regulación *f*; ~ **gate** *n* HYDRAUL compuerta de toma de agua *f*, compuerta reguladora *f*

regulatory: ~ **agency** *n* WATER TRANSP organismo regulador *m*; ~ **body** *n* NUCL organismo regulador *m*

rehabilitation *n* POLL rehabilitación *f*, restablecimiento *m*, restauración *f*

reheat[1] *n* C&G recalentado *m*, HEAT ENG, REFRIG, TRANSP recuperación del calor *f*, recalentamiento *m*

reheat[2] *vt* HEAT ENG, REFRIG recalentar

reheater *n* HEAT ENG, REFRIG recalentador *m*

reheating *n* C&G, HEAT ENG, REFRIG, TRANSP recalentamiento *m*, recuperación del calor *f*, recalentado *m*

reignition *n* SPACE recebado del arco eléctrico *m*, reencendido *m*, reignición *f*

reinfestation *n* AGRIC reinfestación *f*

reinforced: ~ **board** *n* PAPER cartón reforzado *m*; ~ **concrete** *n* CONST, MILIT concreto armado *m* (*AmL*), hormigón armado *m* (*Esp*); ~ **packaging material** *n* PACK material reforzado para embalar *m*; ~ **paper** *n* PAPER papel reforzado *m*; ~ **plastic** *n* C&G, P&R, PACK plástico armado *m*, plástico reforzado *m*; ~ **timbering** *n* MINE entibación armada *f* (*AmL*), entibación de muestra *f* (*Esp*), entibado reforzado *m*; ~ **union paper** *n* PAPER papel alquitranado reforzado *m* (*Esp*), papel embreado reforzado *m* (*AmL*)

reinforcement *n* CONST armadura *f*, act refuerzo *m*, *system using iron* reforzamiento *m*, ELEC *cable* zunchado *m*

reinforcing *n* CONST armado *m*, refuerzo *m*; ~ **agent** *n* CHEM, P&R agente de refuerzo *m*; ~ **filler** *n* P&R carga de refuerzo *f*

reinjection *n* PETR TECH reinyección *f*

reintegration *n* CHEM reintegración *f*

Reissner's: ~ **membrane** *n* ACOUST membrana de Reissner *f*

reject[1] *n* CINEMAT, COAL, PROD, QUALITY, TEXTIL desecho *m*, rechazo *m*; ~ **disposal** *n* COAL evacuación de desechos *f*

reject[2] *vt* CINEMAT, MECH ENG, PROD, QUALITY, TEXTIL desechar, rechazar

rejected: ~ **frequency** *n* ELECTRON frecuencia excluida *f*, frecuencia rechazada *f*; ~ **quantity** *n* PROD, QUALITY cantidad rechazada *f*

rejection *n* COMP&DP, ELECTRON, QUALITY exclusión *f*, rechazamiento *m*, rechazo *m*; ~ **band** *n* ELECTRON banda de supresión *f*; ~ **filter** *n* ELECTRON filtro de supresión *m*; ~ **note** *n* PROD notificación de rechazo *f*

rejector *n* ELECTRON supresor *m*

rejuvenation *n* GEOL rejuvenecimiento *m*, PETR TECH reactivación *f*

REL *abbr* (*release message*) TELECOM liberación del mensaje *f*

relation *n* COMP&DP relación *f*

relational[1] *adj* CINEMAT, COMP&DP, TELECOM relacional

relational[2]: ~ **database** *n* (*RDB*) COMP&DP base de datos relacional *f*; ~ **editing** *n* CINEMAT, TV montaje relacional *m*; ~ **model** *n* COMP&DP modelo relacional *m*; ~ **operator** *n* COMP&DP operador de relación *m*, operador relacional *m*; ~ **processor** *n* COMP&DP procesador de relación *m*, procesador relacional *m*

relative: ~ **abundance** *n* NUCL, PHYS abundancia relativa *f*; ~ **addressing** *n* COMP&DP direccionamiento relativo *m*; ~ **altitude** *n* AIR TRANSP altitud relativa *f*; ~ **angular-deviation gain** *n* ACOUST ganancia de desviación angular relativa *f*; ~ **angular-deviation loss** *n* ACOUST pérdida de desviación

angular relativa *f*; ~ **aperture** *n* PHYS apertura relativa *f*; ~ **atomic mass** *n* PHYS masa atómica relativa *f*; ~ **bearing** *n* AIR TRANSP, OCEAN, RAD PHYS, WATER TRANSP marcación relativa *f*; ~ **biological effectiveness** *n* (*RBE*) NUCL eficacia biológica relativa *f* (*EBR*); ~ **density** *n* COAL densidad real *f*, densidad relativa *f*, P&R peso específico *m*, PHYS densidad relativa *f*; ~ **differential threshold** *n* ACOUST umbral diferencial relativo *m*; ~ **dryness** *n* HYDRAUL, HYDROL porcentaje relativo de vapor seco *m*; ~ **efficiency** *n* ACOUST eficacia relativa *f*; ~ **error** *n* COMP&DP error relativo *m*; ~ **evaporation** *n* HYDROL evaporación relativa *f*; ~ **evapotranspiration** *n* HYDROL, WATER evapotranspiración relativa *f*; ~ **frequency** *n* COMP&DP frecuencia relativa *f*; ~ **gain** *n* SPACE aumento relativo *m*, ganancia relativa *f*, incremento relativo *m*; ~ **grain area** *n* COAL área de exfoliación relativa *f*; ~ **harmonic content** *n* ACOUST, ELECTRON contenido armónico relativo *m*; ~ **humidity** *n* HEAT, HEAT ENG, HYDROL, METEO, P&R, PAPER, PHYS, REFRIG, TEXTIL, WATER humedad relativa *f*; ~ **molecular mass** *n* PHYS masa molecular relativa *f*; ~ **motion** *n* PHYS movimiento relativo *m*; ~ **permeability** *n* ELEC, ELEC ENG, PHYS permeabilidad específica *f*, permeabilidad relativa *f*; ~ **permittivity** *n* ELEC, ELEC ENG, PHYS constante dieléctrica relativa *f*, permitividad relativa *f*; ~ **power** *n* ELEC ENG, PHYS potencia aparente *f*; ~ **pressure coefficient** *n* PHYS coeficiente de presión relativa *m*; ~ **risk** *n* MATH riesgo relativo *m*; ~ **signal amplitude** *n* ELECTRON amplitud de señal relativa *f*; ~ **slip** *n* ELEC deslizamiento relativo *m*; ~ **tone** *n* ACOUST tono relativo *m*; ~ **velocity** *n* MECH ENG, PHYS velocidad relativa *f*; ~ **viscosity** *n* FLUID viscosidad relativa *f*; ~ **water velocity** *n* FUELLESS, HYDROL, WATER velocidad de agua relativa *f*

relatively: ~ **negative voltage** *n* ELEC ENG voltaje relativamente negativo *m*; ~ **positive voltage** *n* ELEC ENG voltaje relativamente positivo *m*

relativistic[1] *adj* SPACE relativista

relativistic[2]: ~ **mechanics** *n* PHYS, SPACE mecánica relativista *f*; ~ **particle** *n* PART PHYS, PHYS, SPACE partícula relativista *f*

relativity *n* PHYS, SPACE relatividad *f*; ~ **effect** *n* PHYS, SPACE efecto relativista *m*

relax *vt* ELEC, METALL, P&R, TEXTIL relajar

relaxation *n* ELEC, METALL, P&R, TEXTIL relajación *f*; ~ **center** *AmE*, ~ **centre** *BrE* *n* METALL centro de relajación *m*; ~ **oscillation** *n* ELECTRON, PHYS oscilación de relajación *f*; ~ **oscillator** *n* ELECTRON, PHYS oscilador de relajación *m*; ~ **time** *n* ELEC, METALL tiempo de relajación *m*

relaxed: ~ **fiber** *AmE*, ~ **fibre** *BrE* *n* TEXTIL fibra relajada *f*

relay *n* GEN relé *m*; ~ **armature** *n* ELEC, ELEC ENG armadura magnética *f*; ~ **coil** *n* ELEC ENG bobina de disyuntor *f*, PROD bobina de relé *f*; ~ **contact** *n* ELEC, ELEC ENG, PROD contacto de relé *m*; ~ **core** *n* ELEC ENG núcleo del relé *m*; ~ **hum** *n* ELEC ENG zumbido del relé *m*; ~ **interrupter** *n* ELEC, ELEC ENG relé interruptor *m*; ~ **ladder rung** *n* PROD travesaño de escala de relés *m*; ~ **logic** *n* PROD lógica de relé *f*; ~ **magnet** *n* ELEC, ELEC ENG electroimán de relé *m*; ~ **rod** *n* AUTO varilla del relé *f*; ~ **satellite** *n* SPACE, TV satélite de retransmisión *m*, satélite repetidor *m*; ~ **set** *n* TELECOM grupo de relevadores *m*, grupo de relés *m*, juego de relés *m*; ~ **station** *n* TELECOM, TV estación repetidora *f*; ~ **switch** *n* CINEMAT conmutador relé *m*; ~**-switching system** *n* ELEC ENG sistema de conmutación *m*; ~ **system** *n* TELECOM sistema de relé hertziano *m*, sistema de retransmisión *m*; ~ **transmitter** *n* TELECOM, TV transmisor repetidor *m*; ~ **winding** *n* ELEC, TELECOM bobina de relevador *f*, bobinado de relé *m*, carrete de relevador *m*

relaying: ~ **and routing function** *n* TELECOM función de encaminamiento y de relevo *f*

release¹ *n* COMP&DP emisión *f*, lanzamiento *m*, liberación *f*, versión *f*, ELEC, ELEC ENG desconexión *f*, interrupción *f*, liberación *f*, HYDRAUL distribución *f*, emisión *f*, escape *m*, salida *f*, MECH ENG *tripping device* disparador *m*, mecanismo de disparo *m*, liberación *f*, relevador *m*, PAPER antiadhesivo *m*, PROD *of steam* escape *m*, TELECOM liberación *f*; ~ **agent** *n* CHEM, P&R agente de desmoldeado *m*; ~ **bearing** *n* AUTO cojinete de desembrague *m*; ~**-bearing hub** *n* AUTO cubo del cojinete de desenganche *m*; ~**-bearing sleeve** *n* AUTO manguito del cojinete de desembrague *m*; ~ **button** *n* CINEMAT, PHOTO, TV botón del disparador *m*, pulsador de desconexión *m*; ~**-coated paper** *n* PAPER papel revestido antiadherente *m*, papel revestido no adherente *m*; ~ **current** *n* ELEC, ELEC ENG corriente de desconexión *f*, corriente de liberación *f*; ~ **horizon** *n* PROD horizonte de lanzamiento *m*; ~ **indicator** *n* TELECOM indicador de liberación *m*; ~ **lag** *n* ELEC ENG tiempo de reposición *m*; ~ **level** *n* COMP&DP nivel de emisión *m*, nivel de versión *m*; ~ **lever** *n* AGRIC, AUTO palanca de desengrane *f*; ~**-lever pin** *n* AGRIC, AUTO pasador de palanca de desenganche *m*; ~**-lever spring** *n* AGRIC, AUTO muelle de palanca de desenganche *m*, resorte de palanca de desenganche *m*; ~ **mesh** *n* COAL retícula de arranque *f*; ~ **message** *n* (*REL*) TELECOM liberación del mensaje *f*; ~ **negative** *n* CINEMAT negativo para copias *m*; ~ **period** *n* HYDRAUL período de escape *m*; ~ **point** *n* HYDRAUL principio de escape *m*, punto de suelta *m*; ~ **positive** *n* CINEMAT copia definitiva *f*; ~ **printing** *n* CINEMAT, PRINT impresión de copias definitivas *f*; ~ **relay** *n* ELEC relé de apertura *m*, relé de desexcitación *m*, relé de vuelta al reposo *m*; ~ **rod** *n* AUTO, VEH varilla de desenganche *f*; ~ **switch** *n* ELEC, ELEC ENG disyuntor *m*, interruptor *m*; ~ **time** *n* AIR TRANSP hora de relevo *f*, tiempo de emisión *m*, ELEC ENG duración de liberación *f*; ~ **valve** *n* HYDRAUL válvula de descarga *f*, válvula de seguridad *f*

release² *vt* AUTO, CHEM soltar, CINEMAT disparar, ELEC ENG interrumpir, GAS aflojar, desacoplar, emitir, liberar, soltar, MECH, MECH ENG desconectar, desembragar, desengranar, soltar, PHYS desprender, PROD desconectar, desembragar, desenganchar, disparar, VEH soltar

released: ~ **order** *n* PROD orden de desenganche *f*

releaser: ~ **milking installation** *n* AGRIC instalación de ordeño por aspiración *f*

releasing *n* RAIL desembrague *m*; ~ **hook** *n* CONST gancho de liberación *m*

releveling *AmE see* **relevelling** *BrE*

relevelling *n BrE* CONST renivelación *f*

reliability *n* GEN confiabilidad *f*, fiabilidad *f*, seguridad *f*; ~ **analysis** *n* SAFE análisis de fiabilidad *m*, SPACE análisis de fiabilidad *m*, análisis funcional *m*; ~ **index** *n* CRYSTALL índice de fiabilidad *m*; ~ **test** *n* ELEC ENG

prueba de confiabilidad *f*; ~ **testing** *n* ELEC ENG ensayo de funcionamiento *m*

reliable: ~ **transfer server** *n* (*RTS*) TELECOM portador de transferencias fiable *m*

relict¹ *adj* GEOL, SPACE residual

relict²: ~ **radiation** *n* GEOL, SPACE radiación antigua *f*, radiación primitiva *f*, radiación residual *f*

relictual *adj* GEOL relictual

relief *n* MECH, MECH ENG alivio *m*, desahogo *m*, descompresión *f*, destalonado *m*, rebajado *m*, rebajo *m*, METALL rebajo *m*, PROD alivio *m*; ~ **angle** *n* MECH ENG ángulo de destalonado *m*, ángulo de incidencia *m*; ~ **crew** *n* AIR TRANSP tripulación de relevo *f*; ~ **gap** *n* ELEC *spark* distancia del salto de la chispa de seguridad *f*; ~ **hole** *n* MINE barreno auxiliar *m*, barreno de alivio *m* (*AmL*), barreno de descarga *m* (*Esp*); ~ **printing** *n* PRINT impresión tipográfica *f*, tipografía *f*; ~ **track** *n* RAIL vía auxiliar de paso *f*; ~ **train** *n* RAIL tren de socorro *m*; ~ **valve** *n* AUTO, FUELLESS, HYDRAUL, MECH, PETR TECH, PROD, REFRIG, VEH válvula de alivio *f*, válvula de descarga *f*, válvula de seguridad *f*; ~ **weaves** *n pl* TEXTIL ligamentos en relieve *m pl*; ~ **well** *n* PETROL pozo de auxilio *m*, WATER pozo de alivio *m*, pozo de drenaje *m*

relieve *vt* HYDRAUL, MECH, MECH ENG, PROD aflojar, aliviar, descargar, destalonar, rebajar, soltar

relieved: ~ **milling cutter** *n* MECH ENG fresa de dientes destalonados *f*; ~ **teeth** *n pl* MECH ENG dientes destalonados *m pl*

reliever *n* MINE barreno auxiliar *m*, barreno de alivio *m* (*AmL*), barreno de descarga *m* (*Esp*)

relieving: ~ **lathe** *n* MECH ENG torno de despojar *m*, torno de destalonar *m*

reline *vt* AUTO, VEH poner forros nuevos

relining *n* COATINGS, PROD recubrimiento *m*, revestimiento *m*

relinquishment: ~ **requirement** *n* PETR TECH requerimiento de renuncia *m*

reload *vt* CINEMAT, COMP&DP, PHOTO, PROD, TV recargar, volver a cargar

reloading *n* CINEMAT, COMP&DP, PHOTO, PROD, TV recarga *f*

relocatable: ~ **program** *n* COMP&DP programa reubicable *m*

relocate *vt* COMP&DP reubicar

relocation *n* COMP&DP reubicación *f*

reluctance *n* ELEC, ELEC ENG, PHYS reluctancia *f*, resistencia magnética *f*; ~ **motor** *n* ELEC, ELEC ENG, TRANSP motor síncrono de reluctancia *m*

reluctivity *n* ELEC, ELEC ENG, PHYS reluctancia específica *f*, reluctividad *f*, resistencia magnética específica *f*

rem *n* (*roentgen equivalent for man*) RAD PHYS rem *m* (*dosis equivalente en renguenios en el hombre*)

remainder *n* COMP&DP, MATH remanente *m*, residuo *m*, resto *m*

remaking *n* PROD *joints* rehacimiento *m*

remanence *n* ELEC, ELEC ENG, PETROL, PHYS imanación remanente *f*, imanación residual *f*, remanencia *f*

remanent: ~ **charge** *n* ELEC, ELEC ENG, PETROL, PHYS carga remanente *f*; ~ **flux density** *n* ELEC, ELEC ENG, PHYS densidad de flujo remanente *f*; ~ **induction** *n* ELEC, ELEC ENG, PHYS inducción remanente *f*; ~ **magnetization** *n* ELEC, ELECTRON, PETROL, PHYS magnetización remanente *f*

remedial: ~ **maintenance** *n* COMP&DP mantenimiento remediador *m*, mantenimiento reparador *m*

remelting: ~ **machine** *n* C&G cortadora de oxígeno *f*

remetal *vt BrE (cf repave AmE)* CONST repavimentar

remetalling *n BrE (cf repaving AmE)* CONST *roads* repavimentación *f*

reminder: ~~-**alarm service** *n* TELECOM servicio de alarma de advertencia *m*; ~ **call** *n* TELECOM llamada recordatoria *f*

remodulation *n* ELECTRON remodulación *f*

remolded: ~ **sample** *AmE see remoulded sample BrE*

remolding *AmE see remoulding BrE*

remote[1] *adj* COMP&DP, TELECOM, TV a distancia, remoto; ~~-**controlled** *adj* AUTO, MECH ENG, MILIT, TV por control remoto

remote[2]: ~ **access** *n* COMP&DP acceso a distancia *m*, acceso remoto *m*, TELECOM acceso remoto *m*; ~~-**alarm indication** *n (RAI)* TELECOM indicación de alarma remota *f*, teleindicación de alarma *f*; ~ **amplifier** *n* ELECTRON amplificador remoto *m*; ~ **arming and safety unit** *n* SPACE unidad de activación de armas y seguridad a distancia *f*; ~ **batch processing** *n* COMP&DP procesamiento por lotes remoto *m*, teleproceso por lotes *m*; ~ **batch terminal** *n (RBT)* COMP&DP terminal de teleproceso por lotes *m*, terminal por lotes remoto *m (AmL)*; ~ **broadcast** *n* TV radiodifusión remota *f*, radiodifusión telemandada *f*; ~~-**bulb thermostat** *n* REFRIG, THERMO termostato de bulbo remoto *m*; ~ **channel** *n* PROD canal remoto *m*; ~ **concentrator** *n* TELECOM concentrador remoto *m*; ~ **control** *n* GEN accionamiento a distancia *m*, control a distancia *m*, control remoto *m*, dirección a distancia *f*, gobierno a distancia *m*, mando a distancia *m*, maniobra a distancia *f*, regulación a distancia *f*, teleaccionamiento *m*, telecontrol *m*, teledirección *f*, telegobierno *m*, telemando *m*, telemaniobra *f*, telerregulación *f*; ~~-**control by television camera** *n* TRANSP, TV control remoto por cámara de televisión *m*; ~~-**control focusing** *n* TV enfoque por control remoto *m*, enfoque por mando a distancia *m*; ~ **control sign** *n* TRANSP señal de control remoto *f*; ~ **control system** *n* SAFE sistema de control remoto *m*; ~ **control unit** *n (RCU)* TELECOM unidad de control a distancia *f*; ~~-**controlled camera** *n* CINEMAT, PHOTO, TV cámara con mando a distancia *f*, cámara de control remoto *f*; ~~-**controlled flight** *n* AIR TRANSP vuelo teledirigido *m*, MILIT vuelo teledirigido *m*, vuelo telemaniobrado *m*; ~~-**controlled pneumatic valve** *n* MECH ENG válvula neumática por control remoto *f*, válvula neumática por telemando *f*; ~~-**cut-off tube** *n* ELECTRON tubo de desconexión remoto *m*; ~ **data processing** *n* COMP&DP, TELECOM teleprocesamiento de datos *m*; ~ **detection** *n* TELECOM teledetección *f*; ~ **electronics** *n* ELECTRON, INSTR electrónica remota *f*; ~~-**handling device** *n* SAFE aditamento para manejo remoto *m*; ~ **job entry** *n (RJE)* COMP&DP entrada de trabajos a distancia *f*; ~~-**line concentrator** *n* COMP&DP, TELECOM concentrador de línea remota *m*; ~ **loading** *n* COMP&DP carga a distancia *f*, carga remota *f*, TELECOM carga a distancia *f*, carga remota *f*, volumen de tráfico remoto *m*; ~ **maintenance** *n* TELECOM telemantenimiento *m*; ~ **management** *n* TELECOM teledirección *f*; ~ **manipulator** *n* OCEAN telemanipulador *m*; ~ **manipulator arm** *n* SPACE brazo de manipulación a distancia *m*; ~ **metering** *n*

NUCL medición remota *f*; ~ **mode** *n* PROD modo remoto *m*; ~~-**mode selection** *n* PROD selección de modo a distancia *f*; ~ **monitoring** *n* COMP&DP, TELECOM, TV monitorización a distancia *f*, telecomprobación *f*, televigilancia *f*, vigilancia a distancia *f*; ~~-**operating terminal** *n* COMP&DP, TELECOM terminal teleaccionada *f*, terminal telemandada *f*, terminal telemaniobrada *f*; ~ **operation** *n* COMP&DP, TELECOM, TV funcionamiento remoto *m*, operación remota *f*; ~~-**operation service element** *n (ROSE)* TELECOM elemento del servicio de operación remota *m*; ~ **operator** *n* COMP&DP, OCEAN, TELECOM teleoperador *m*; ~ **pickup point** *n* TV lugar de recogida por mando a distancia *m*; ~~-**piloted vehicle** *n* AIR TRANSP, MILIT vehículo pilotado a distancia *m*; ~ **power supply** *n* ELEC, ELEC ENG suministro de energía a distancia *m*; ~ **program mode** *n* PROD modo de teleprogramación *m*; ~~-**reading thermometer** *n* INSTR, REFRIG, THERMO termómetro de lectura a distancia *m*; ~ **reset** *n* PROD reposición remota *f*; ~ **RTD module** *n* PROD módulo RTD remoto *m*; ~ **sensing** COMP&DP, GEOL, MAR POLL, SPACE, TELECOM, TV detección a distancia *f*, detección remota *f*, lectura a distancia *f*, teledetección *f*; ~ **sensing satellite** *n* SPACE satélite de detección a distancia *m*, satélite de detección remota *m*, satélite de teledetección *m*; ~ **sensor** *n* CONST sensor a distancia *m*, sensor remoto *m*; ~ **shutdown** *n* NUCL parada remota *f*; ~~-**shutdown circuit** *n* PROD circuito de cierre remoto *m*; ~ **switching** *n* TELECOM, TV interruptor de accionamiento remoto *m*, interruptor telemandado *m*, teleconmutación *f*; ~~-**switching stage** *n* TELECOM, TV etapa de teleconmutación *f*; ~~-**switching system** *n* TELECOM, TV sistema de teleconmutación *m*; ~~-**switching unit** *n (RSU)* TELECOM, TV unidad de teleconmutación *f*; ~ **temperature gage** *AmE*, ~ **temperature gauge** *BrE n* HEAT ENG, INSTR, REFRIG calibrador remoto de temperatura *m*, indicador de temperatura por acción remota *m*, termómetro por acción remota *m*; ~ **temperature monitoring** *n* REFRIG, THERMO control remoto de temperatura *m*, vigilancia remota de temperatura *f*; ~ **terminal** *n* COMP&DP terminal a distancia *m*, terminal remoto *m*; ~ **test** *n* COMP&DP prueba a distancia *f*, PROD prueba por control a distancia *f*; ~ **test mode** *n* PROD modo de prueba por control a distancia *m*; ~ **unit** *n (RU)* COMP&DP, TELECOM, TV unidad remota *f*

remoulded: ~ **sample** *n BrE* COAL muestra de remoldeado *f*

remoulding *n BrE* PROD remoldeo *m*

removable[1] *adj* GEN cambiable, desmontable, móvil, removible, separable

removable[2] *n* AIR TRANSP componente desmontable *m*; ~ **back** *n* PHOTO tapa posterior desmontable *f*; ~ **coupling link** *n* RAIL brida de enganche desmontable *f*; ~ **disc** *BrE*, ~ **disk** *AmE n* COMP&DP disco extraíble *m*, disco separable *m*; ~ **insert** *n* MECH ENG pieza cambiable *f*, pieza desmontable *f*, pieza móvil *f*, pieza removible *f*, pieza separable *f*, PROD accesorio de inserción *m*, accesorio desmontable *m*; ~ **part** *n* ELEC, ELEC ENG parte removible *f*

removal *n* CONST eliminación *f*, retirada *f*, supresión *f*, MAR POLL remoción *f*, MECH ENG *of machinery* desmontaje *m*, traslado *m*, MINE separación *f*, desmontaje *m*, POLL eliminación *f*, evacuación *f*, retirada *f*, separación *f*, remoción *f*, WATER TRANSP extracción *f*; ~ **from pasture** *n* AGRIC retirada de ganado de los pastos *f*; ~ **of iron** *n* C&G eliminación de hierro *f*; ~ **of locomotive rods** *n* RAIL desmontaje de las varillas de la locomotora *m*; ~ **of stalk from fruit** *n* AGRIC despezonado *m*; ~ **truck** *n* AmE (*cf removal van BrE*) AUTO, VEH camión de mudanzas *m*; ~ **van** *n* BrE (*cf removal truck AmE*) AUTO, VEH camión de mudanzas *m*

remove *vt* HYDROL trasladar, MECH ENG desmontar, remover, *wire edge from edge of knife* descantear, MINE retirar, PROD *burr from casting* desbarbar, SAFE quitar, eliminar, TRANSP desplazar, transportar, WATER TRANSP *cast from mould* extraer; ~ **the side shoots of** *vt* AGRIC despimpollar

removing *n* CONST eliminación *f*, retirada *f*

remreed: ~ **crosspoint** *n* TELECOM contacto de lengüeta rem *m*, punto de cruce de lengüeta rem *m*

rendered: ~ **fat** *n* FOOD grasa derretida *f*, grasa fundida *f*

rendering *n* CONST enlucido *m*, revoque *m*; ~ **plant** *n* AGRIC planta extractora de grasa *f*

rendezvous *n* SPACE cita espacial *f*, reunión en órbita *f*, reunión espacial *f*; ~ **maneuver** AmE, ~ **manoeuvre** BrE *n* TRANSP maniobra de acoplamiento *f*, maniobra de agrupamiento *f*; ~ **procedure** *n* SPACE procedimiento para el encuentro espacial *m*; ~ **radar** *n* SPACE radar de cita *m*; ~ **trajectory** *n* SPACE trayectoria de cita *f*

renewable: ~ **source** *n* FUELLESS, PHYS fuente renovable *f*; ~ **source of energy** *n* FUELLESS, PHYS fuente de energía renovable *f*, fuente renovable *f*

renewal: ~ **parts list** *n* PROD lista de recambios *f*, lista de refacciones *f* (*AmL*), lista de repuestos *f* (*Esp*)

Re900 *abbr* (*Reynolds number 900*) FLUID Re900 (*número de Reynolds 900*)

rennet *n* AGRIC, FOOD cuajo *m*; ~ **casein** *n* AGRIC, FOOD caseína de cuajo *f*

rennin *n* AGRIC, FOOD renina *f*

renovated: ~ **pasture** *n* AGRIC pastura renovada *f*

renovation *n* AGRIC, PROD renovación *f*

rental: ~ **payment** *n* PETR TECH pago de la renta *m*

reorder: ~ **period** *n* PROD período de hacer nuevos pedidos *m*; ~ **point** *n* PROD punto de rehacer pedidos *m*; ~ **quantity** *n* PROD cantidad pedida de nuevo *f*, cantidad vuelta a pedir *f*

reoxidation *n* CHEM, POLL reoxidación *f*

repack *vt* MECH ENG *piston* reguarnecer

repair[1] *n* MECH ENG, PROD, WATER TRANSP *ship* reparación *f*; ~ **link** *n* MECH ENG eslabón para reparar cadenas *m*; ~ **outfit** *n* PROD bolsa de reparaciones *f*; ~ **shop** *n* PROD taller de reparaciones *m*; ~ **time** *n* COMP&DP tiempo de reparación *m*; ~ **track** *n* BrE (*cf rip track AmE*) RAIL vía para reparaciones de vagones *f*

repair[2] *vt* ELECTRON reparar, restablecer, PROD corregir, reparar, WATER TRANSP *of a ship* carenar, reparar; ~**, inspect and paint** *vt* RAIL reparar, inspeccionar y pintar

repairing *n* ELECTRON, MECH ENG, PROD, WATER TRANSP reparación *f*

repave *vt* AmE (*cf remetal BrE, resurface BrE*) CONST repavimentar

repaving *n* AmE (*cf remetalling BrE*) CONST *roads* repavimentación *f*

repeat *n* COMP&DP, PRINT, TV repetición *f*; ~ **key** *n*

COMP&DP, TV tecla de repetición *f*; ~ **matter** *n* PRINT composición conservada para reimpresión *f*

repeatability *n* AGRIC repetibilidad *f*, METR repetibilidad *f*, reproductibilidad *f*

repeatable: ~ **measurement** *n* METR medición repetible *f*

repeated: ~**-call attempt** *n* TELECOM intento de llamada repetida *m*; ~ **loading** *n* METALL carga cíclica *f*; ~ **signal** *n* ELECTRON, WATER TRANSP señal repetida *f*; ~ **yield point** *n* METALL límite de estirado cíclico *m*

repeater *n* COMP&DP, ELECTRON, PHYS repetidor *m*, SPACE amplificador *m*, repetidor *m*, TELECOM, TV, WATER TRANSP repetidor *m*; ~ **compass** *n* SPACE, WATER TRANSP compás repetidor *m*; ~ **lamp** *n* ELEC ENG, GAS lámpara indicadora *f*; ~ **satellite** *n* SPACE, TV satélite repetidor *m*; ~ **signal** *n* ELECTRON, WATER TRANSP señal repetidora *f*

repeating: ~ **coil** *n* ELEC ENG bobina de repetición *f*; ~ **decimal** *n* MATH decimal periódico *m*, decimal recurrente *m*; ~ **signal** *n* RAIL señal repetidora *f*

repeller *n* ELEC ENG reflector *m*

repertoire *n* COMP&DP repertorio *m*

repetition: ~ **fire** *n* MILIT tiro de repetición *m*; ~ **rate** *n* ELECTRON frecuencia de repetición *f*

repetitive: ~ **flight plan** *n* AIR TRANSP plan de vuelo repetitivo *m*; ~ **signal** *n* ELECTRON señal repetitiva *f*; ~ **sweep** *n* ELECTRON barrido repetitivo *m*; ~ **work** *n* PROD trabajo en serie *m*

replacement: ~ **battery assembly** *n* PROD recambio del conjunto de la batería *m*; ~ **cost valuation** *n* PROD estimación del coste de amortización *f*, estimación del coste de reposición *f*; ~ **price** *n* PROD precio de reposición *m*; ~ **programer interconnect cable** AmE, ~ **programmer interconnect cable** BrE *n* PROD cable interconector del programador de reposición *m*

replant *vt* AGRIC replantar

replay *n* TV repetición *f*; ~ **characteristic** *n* TV característica de la repetición *f*

replenisher *n* CINEMAT, PHOTO, TV baño reforzador *m*, baño regenerador *m*

replenishing: ~ **solution** *n* CINEMAT, PHOTO, TV solución reforzadora *f*, solución regeneradora *f*

replenishment *n* CINEMAT, PHOTO, TV refuerzo *m*, regeneración *f*, WATER regeneración *f*; ~ **lead time** *n* PROD plazo de reaprovisionamiento *m*; ~ **order** *n* PROD orden de reaprovisionamiento *f*

replicated: ~ **pattern** *n* ELECTRON configuración reiterada *f*

reply *n* COMP&DP, ELECTRON, TELECOM, TV respuesta *f*

repoint *vt* CONST reapuntalar

report[1] *n* AIR TRANSP, COMP&DP, METEO informe *m*, MINE detonación *f*, estallido *m*, explosión *f*, SPACE boletín de información *m*, detonación *f*, estallido *m*, explosión *f*, fallo *m*, parte *m*; ~ **for landing** *n* AIR TRANSP, METEO informe de aterrizaje *m*; ~ **for take off** *n* AIR TRANSP, METEO informe de despegue *m*, llamada de despegue *f*; ~ **generation** *n* COMP&DP generación de informes *f*; ~**-program generator** *n* COMP&DP generador de programas de informes *m*; ~ **sheet** *n* CINEMAT nómina *f*

report[2]: ~ **to the port authorities** *phr* WATER TRANSP ir a la autoridad portuaria, presentarse ante la autoridad portuaria

reportable: ~ **accident** *n* SAFE accidente reportable *m*

repository n COMP&DP, NUCL, POLL depósito m, repositorio m
representation n COMP&DP representación f
reprint vt CINEMAT, PHOTO, PRINT reimprimir
repro: ~ **proof** n PRINT prueba para reproducción f
reprocess vt PROD, RECYCL reprocesar, retratar, transformar
reprocessing n PROD, RECYCL proceso de retratamiento m, reacondicionamiento m, reelaboración f, regeneración f, reprocesado m, reprocesamiento m, reproceso m, reutilización f, transformación f; ~ **plant** n PROD, RECYCL instalación de regeneración f, planta de reacondicionamiento f, planta transformadora f
reproducibility n COAL, METR reproducibilidad f, reproductibilidad f
reproducing n ACOUST copiado m, lectura f, reproducción f; ~ **chain** n TV cadena reproductora f; ~ **characteristic** n ACOUST característica de reproducción f; ~ **head** n CINEMAT, TV cabeza reproductora f; ~ **loss** n ACOUST pérdida de lectura f; ~ **magnetic-head** n ACOUST cabeza magnética reproductora f; ~ **network** n TV cadena reproductora f; ~**-recording characteristic** n ACOUST característica de reproducción o de grabación f
reproduction n ACOUST copiado m, reproducción f; ~ **camera** n PHOTO, PRINT cámara de reproducción f; ~ **characteristics** n pl CINEMAT, TV características de reproducción f pl; ~ **level** n CINEMAT, TV nivel de reproducción m; ~ **loss** n CINEMAT, TV pérdida de reproducción f; ~ **pull** n PRINT prueba de reproducción f; ~ **of tonal values** n PHOTO reproducción de valores tonales f
reproductive: ~ **ability** n AGRIC capacidad reproductora f; ~ **efficiency** n AGRIC índice de prolificidad m
reprofiling n CONST reperfilado m
reprographics n COMP&DP reprografía f
repudiation n TELECOM rechazo m
repulsion n ELEC, ELEC ENG, PHYS rechazo m, repulsión f; ~**-induction motor** n ELEC, ELEC ENG motor de inducción por repulsión m; ~ **motor** n ELEC, ELEC ENG motor de repulsión m
repulsive: ~ **force** n ELEC, ELEC ENG, PHYS fuerza de repulsión f, fuerza repulsiva f; ~ **junction** n METALL unión repulsiva f
req n COMP&DP, TELECOM pedido m, petición f, solicitud f
request[1] n COMP&DP, TELECOM pedido m, petición f, solicitud f; ~ **channel** n SPACE petición de canal f; ~ **for quotation** n PROD solicitud de cotización f; ~ **for service** n TELECOM pedido de servicio m, solicitud de servicio f; ~ **stack** n COMP&DP, TELECOM pila de solicitudes f; ~ **to send** n COMP&DP, TELECOM solicitud para enviar f
request[2] vt COMP&DP, PROD, TELECOM solicitar
required[1]: ~ **flightpath** n AIR TRANSP trayectoria de vuelo requerida f; ~ **frequency** n FUELLESS frecuencia necesaria f
required[2]: **as** ~ phr PROD tal como se requiere
requirement n COMP&DP requisito m, SAFE norma f, requisito m; ~ **explosion** n PROD explosión de la demanda f
rerecording n ACOUST re-registro m, regrabación f, transcripción f, transferencia de la banda sonora de una grabación a otra f

reroute vt WATER TRANSP shipping cambiar la derrota habitual de, cambiar la ruta habitual de
rerouting n TELECOM desvío m (Esp), reencaminamiento m (AmL), WATER TRANSP cambio de la derrota habitual m, cambio de la ruta habitual m
rerun[1] n COMP&DP reejecución f, PRINT reimpresión f
rerun[2] vt COMP&DP volver a ejecutar, reejecutar
RES abbr (reserved field) TELECOM campo reservado m
rescheduling n PROD reprogramación f
rescue[1] n AIR TRANSP, MILIT, SAFE, WATER TRANSP rescate m, salvamento m; ~ **apparatus** n AIR TRANSP, SAFE, WATER TRANSP dispositivos de salvamento m pl; ~ **blanket** n SAFE cobija de rescate f (AmL), manta de rescate f (Esp); ~ **boat** n AIR TRANSP, SAFE, WATER TRANSP bote de rescate m, bote salvavidas m, embarcación de salvamento f, lancha de salvamento f; ~ **chute** n AIR TRANSP, SAFE, WATER TRANSP rampa de salvamento f; ~ **coordination center** AmE, ~ **coordination centre** BrE n AIR TRANSP, SAFE, WATER TRANSP centro coordinador de salvamento m, centro de coordinación de rescate m; ~ **dump** n COMP&DP copia de memoria para restauración del sistema f, vaciado de rescate m; ~ **equipment** n AIR TRANSP, SAFE, WATER TRANSP equipo de rescate m; ~ **and fire fighting service** n AIR TRANSP, SAFE servicio de rescate e incendios m; ~ **helicopter** n AIR TRANSP, MILIT, SAFE helicóptero de rescate m, helicóptero de salvamento m; ~ **operation** n AIR TRANSP, MILIT, SAFE, WATER TRANSP operación de salvamento f; ~ **party** n SAFE grupo de rescate m; ~ **services** n pl SAFE servicios de salvamento m pl; ~ **station** n SAFE cuartel de rescate m, estación de rescate f; ~ **strap** n AIR TRANSP, SAFE, WATER TRANSP correa de rescate f; ~ **vehicle** n AIR TRANSP, SAFE, WATER TRANSP vehículo de rescate m; ~ **work** n SAFE operación de salvamento f
rescue[2] vt AIR TRANSP, SAFE, WATER TRANSP rescatar, salvar
research: ~ **area** n COAL campo de investigación m; ~ **center** AmE, ~ **centre** BrE n TELECOM centro de investigación m; ~ **with colliders** n PART PHYS investigación con cámaras de reacción f; ~ **development engineer** n MECH ENG ingeniero de desarrollo de investigación m; ~ **station** n AGRIC centro de investigaciones m
reseat vt AUTO, VEH hacer asientos nuevos
reseeding n AGRIC resiembra f
reserve: ~ **battery** n ELEC ENG batería de reserva f; ~ **buoyancy** n WATER TRANSP ship design buque de salvamento m, reserva de flotabilidad f; ~ **capacity** n TRANSP capacidad de reserva f
reserved[1]: ~ **for special use** adj PROD reservado para uso especial
reserved[2]: ~ **field** n (RES) TELECOM campo reservado m; ~ **word** n COMP&DP palabra reservada f
reserves n pl AIR TRANSP reservas f pl
reservoir n FLUID depósito m, GEOL yacimiento m, HYDROL depósito m, PETR TECH, PETROL depósito m, represa f, reservorio m, yacimiento de petróleo m, VEH depósito m, WATER balsa f, embalse m, estanque m, lago artificial m, pantano m, represa f; ~ **basin** n WATER cuenco del embalse m, vaso del embalse m; ~ **capacitor** n ELEC ENG condensador de cubeta m; ~ **conditions** n pl PETR TECH, PETROL condiciones del depósito f pl, condiciones del yacimiento f pl; ~ **energy** n PETR TECH, PETROL energía del yacimiento

f; ~ **lining** *n* WATER forro del embalse *m*; ~ **pressure** *n* PETR TECH, PETROL presión del yacimiento *f*; ~ **rock** *n* GAS, GEOL roca almacén *f*, roca de almacenamiento *f*, roca productiva *f*

reset[1] *n* CINEMAT, COMP&DP reajuste *m*, reinicialización *f*, reposición *f*, restauración *f*, MECH ENG restauración *f*, PROD, TV reajuste *m*, reinicializacion *f*, reposición *f*, restauración *f*; ~ **button** *n* COMP&DP botón de reposición *m*, botón de reset *m*, botón de restauración *m*, pulsador de reinicio *m*; ~ **knob** *n* CINEMAT, TV botón de reajuste *m*, botón de reseteado *m*, pulsador de reposición *m*; ~ **push** *n* PROD pulsador de reposición *m*; ~ **rung** *n* PROD etapa de reposición *f*

reset[2] *vt* CINEMAT reajustar, reinicializar, COMP&DP *counter* poner a cero, reponer, *computer* reinicializar, ELECTRON poner a cero, borrar, poner condiciones iniciales, MECH, MECH ENG reajustar, reafilar, rearmar, PROD poner a cero, reajustar, rearmar, poner en condición inicial, reponer, TV reinicializar; ~ **to zero** *vt* MECH ENG *instrument* volver a poner a 0

resetting *n* GEOL *geochronology* recomposición *f*, MECH ENG, PROD reposicionamiento *m*, reajuste *m*, puesta a cero *f*, reposición *f*, restauración *f*, reengaste *m*

resharpening *n* MECH ENG reafilado *m*

reshipment *n* WATER TRANSP reembarque *m*

reshipping *n* WATER TRANSP acción de reembarcar *f*

reshoot *vt* CINEMAT, TV volver a rodar

reside *vt* COMP&DP residir

resident: ~ **program** *n* COMP&DP programa residente *m*

residual[1] *adj* CHEM, ELEC, ELEC ENG, METALL, PETR TECH, PROD residual

residual[2]: ~ **austenite** *n* METALL austenita residual *f*; ~ **capacitance** *n* ELEC, ELEC ENG capacidad residual *f*, capacitancia residual *f*; ~ **charge** *n* ELEC *electrostatics* carga remanente *f*, carga residual *f*, ELEC ENG, TV carga remanente *f*, carga residual *f*; ~ **current** *n* ELEC, ELEC ENG corriente remanente *f*, corriente residual *f*; ~ **discharge** *n* ELEC, ELEC ENG descarga residual *f*; ~ **energy** *n* HEAT energía residual *f*; ~ **flux density** *n* ELEC, ELEC ENG, PHYS densidad de flujo remanente *f*; ~ **frequency modulation** *n* ELECTRON modulación de frecuencia residual *f*; ~ **fuel oil** *n* PETR TECH fueloil para calderas *m*; ~ **gap** *n* ELEC ENG intervalo aislante residual *m*; ~ **gas** *n* ELECTRON gas residual *m*, GAS gas sobrante *m*, POLL gas residual *m*, gas sobrante *m*; ~ **magnetism** *n* ELEC, ELEC ENG, PROD magnetismo remanente *m*; ~ **magnetization** *n* RAD PHYS imanación residual *f*, imantación remanente *f*, magnetización residual *f*; ~ **moisture** *n* PACK, REFRIG humedad residual *f*; ~ **noise** *n* COMP&DP ruido residual *m*; ~ **oil saturation** *n* (*ROS*) PETROL saturación de aceite residual *f*; ~ **radioactivity** *n* RAD PHYS radiactividad residual *f*; ~ **relay** *n* ELEC, ELEC ENG relé residual *m*; ~ **resistance** *n* ELEC, ELEC ENG resistencia residual *f*; ~ **set** *n* P&R endurecimiento residual *m*, solidificación residual *f*; ~ **shrinkage** *n* TEXTIL encogimiento residual *m*; ~ **sideband** *n* COMP&DP, ELECTRON, PHYS, TELECOM, TV banda lateral residual *f*; ~ **silver** *n* METALL, PHOTO plata residual *f*; ~ **strength** *n* COAL fuerza residual *f*; ~ **stress** *n* C&G esfuerzo residual *m*, CONST tensión residual *f*; ~ **water content** *n* HYDROL, OPT contenido de agua residual *m*; ~ **water saturation** *n* HYDROL, PETROL saturación de agua residual *f*

residue *n* AGRIC, CHEM, COMP&DP, FOOD, MAR POLL residuo *m*, PETR TECH residuo *m*, sobrante *m*, POLL desecho *m*, residuo *m*, WATER residuo *m*; ~ **arithmetic** *n* COMP&DP aritmética del residuo *f*; ~**refining process** *n* PETR TECH proceso de refino del sobrante *m*

residues: ~ **of oil manufacture** *n pl* AGRIC residuos de aceiterías *m pl*; ~ **of the starch industry** *n pl* AGRIC residuos de almidonería *m pl*

resilience *n* COMP&DP resiliencia *f*, resistencia *f*, MECH ENG elasticidad *f*, resiliencia *f*, P&R, PAPER, PROD, TEXTIL resiliencia *f*

resilient: ~ **isolator** *n* AIR TRANSP, SAFE, SPACE aislador resilente *m*; ~ **rail** *n* TRANSP rail elástico *m*; ~ **shaft-coupling** *n* MECH ENG acoplamiento de eje flexible *m*

resin *n* CHEM, MECH resina *f*, P&R colofonia *f*, resina *f*, PACK, TEXTIL, WATER TRANSP resina *f*; ~**bonded plywood** *n* P&R madera conglomerada *f* (*Esp*), madera terciada pegada con adhesivo resinoso *f* (*AmL*); ~**bonded wheel** *n* MECH ENG muela de resina sintética *f*; ~**oil varnish** *n* COATINGS barniz de aceite de resina *m*; ~ **roof bolting** *n* MINE bulonado *m*, sistema de empedernado del techo *m*

resist *n* COATINGS capa protectora *f*, capa resistente *f*, ELECTRON protección *f*, PRINT reserva *f*, capa protectora *f*; ~**coated wafer** *n* COATINGS, ELECTRON pastilla con revestimiento de protección *f*; ~ **coating** *n* COATINGS, P&R resistencia *f*, revestimiento resistente *m*

resistance *n* GEN fuerza contraria *f*, oposición *f*, resistencia *f*; **on** ~ *n* ELEC ENG estado-resistencia *m*; ~ **box** *n* ELEC, ELEC ENG caja de resistencia *f*; ~ **butt welding** *n* CONST soldadura a tope por resistencia *f*; ~**capacitance** *n* (*RC*) ELEC, ELEC ENG, ELECTRON resistencia-capacitancia *f* (*RC*), resistencia-condensador *f* (*RC*); ~**capacitance coupling** *n* ELEC, ELEC ENG, ELECTRON acoplamiento por capacitancia y resistencia *m*, acoplamiento por resistencia-capacitancia *m*; ~ **coating** *n* COATINGS, P&R resistencia *f*, revestimiento resistente *m*; ~ **coil** *n* ELEC, ELEC ENG bobina de resistencia *f*; ~ **drop** *n* ELEC, ELEC ENG caída de tensión por resistencia *f*, caída de voltaje por resistencia *f*; ~ **furnace** *n* ELEC ENG, THERMO horno de resistencia *m*; ~ **heating** *n* ELEC, ELEC ENG, THERMO caldeo por resistencia *m*, calentamiento por efecto Joule *m*, calentamiento por resistencia *m*; ~ **material** *n* ELEC, ELEC ENG material de resistencia *m*; ~ **meter** *n* ELEC, ELEC ENG, INSTR, METR, MINE, PHYS, TELECOM medidor de resistencia *m*, ohmímetro *m*, óhmetro *m*; ~ **seam welding** *n* CONST soldadura de costura por resistencia *f*; ~ **spot welding** *n* ELEC, MECH ENG soldadura de punto por resistencia *f*, soldadura eléctrica por resistencia por puntos *f*; ~ **thermometer** *n* INSTR, PHYS, REFRIG, THERMO termómetro de resistencia *m*; ~ **to bending** *n* MECH ENG resistencia a la flexión *f*, rigidez *f*, PAPER, PHYS rigidez *f*; ~ **to buckling** *n* MECH ENG resistencia a la flexión *f*, resistencia al pandeo *f*; ~ **to crushing** *n* MECH ENG resistencia a la compresión *f*; ~ **to flow** *n* FLUID resistencia al flujo *f*; ~ **to forward motion** *n* TRANSP resistencia al avance *f*; ~ **to heat** *n* HEAT ENG, THERMO resistencia al calor *f*, resistencia térmica *f*; ~ **to impact** *n* MECH ENG resistencia al choque *f*, resistencia al impacto *f*; ~ **to lodging** *n* AGRIC resistencia al encamado *f*; ~ **to motion** *n* MECH ENG resistencia al movimiento *f*; ~ **to shattering** *n* PACK resistencia a ser desmenuzado *f*; ~ **to shearing** *n* MECH ENG resistencia al corte *f*, resistencia al esfuerzo cortante *f*; ~ **to shock** *n* MECH ENG resistencia al choque *f*; ~ **to sliding** *n* MECH ENG resistencia al deslizamiento *f*; ~ **to soiling** *n* TEXTIL resistencia al ensuciado *f*; ~ **to tearing** *n* MAR POLL resistencia al desgarramiento *f*, MECH ENG resistencia al rasgado *f*; ~ **to tension** *n* MECH ENG resistencia a la tracción *f*; ~ **to thermal shock** *n* THERMO resistencia al cambio brusco de temperatura *f*, resistencia al choque térmico *f*; ~ **to trampling** *n* AGRIC resistencia a la pisada *f*; ~ **to twisting** *n* MECH ENG resistencia a la torsión *f*; ~ **welding** *n* CONST, ELEC, ELEC ENG, MECH ENG, THERMO soldadura por resistencia *f*, soldadura por resistencia eléctrica *f*; ~~**welding equipment** *n* CONST, ELEC, ELEC ENG, MECH ENG, THERMO equipo de soldadura por resistencia *m*, equipo de soldeo por resistencia *m*; ~ **wire** *n* ELEC, ELEC ENG, METALL alambre de resistencia *m*, hilo de resistencia *m*

resistant[1] *adj* CONST, ELEC, MECH ENG, P&R resistente; ~ **to impact** *adj* MECH ENG, METR resistente al choque

resistant[2]: ~ **coating** *n* COATINGS, P&R capa protectora *f*; ~ **variety** *n* AGRIC variedad resistente *f*

resisting: ~ **torque** *n* AUTO par de resistencia *m*

resistive[1] *adj* ELEC, ELEC ENG, TELECOM resistente, resistivo

resistive[2]: ~ **attenuator** *n* ELEC, ELEC ENG, ELECTRON, TELECOM atenuador resistivo *m*; ~ **circuit** *n* ELEC, ELEC ENG, TELECOM circuito resistivo *m*; ~ **coupling** *n* ELEC, ELEC ENG, TELECOM acoplamiento por resistencia eléctrica *m*; ~ **element** *n* ELEC, ELEC ENG, TELECOM elemento resistente *m*; ~ **load** *n* ELEC, ELEC ENG, TELECOM carga resistiva *f*; ~ **thin film** *n* ELECTRON película delgada resistente *f*; ~ **voltage divider** *n* ELEC divisor de tensión resistivo *m*

resistivity *n* GEN resistencia específica *f*, resistividad *f*; ~ **index** *n* PETROL índice de resistividad *m*; ~ **log** *n* FUELLESS, GEOPHYS registro de resistencia *m*, registro de resistividad *m*, PETR TECH, PETROL perfil de resistividad *m*, registro de resistencia *m*, registro de resistividad *m*; ~ **logging** *n* PETR TECH, PETROL perfilado de resistividad *m*; ~ **meter** *n* GEOPHYS, INSTR, PETR TECH medidor de resistividad *m*

resistojet *n* SPACE reactor resistor *m*

resistor *n* AUTO, ELEC, ELEC ENG, PHYS resistencia eléctrica *f*, resistor *m*; ~ **core** *n* ELEC ENG núcleo de la resistencia *m*; ~ **ink** *n* COLOUR tinta de protección *f*; ~ **ladder** *n* ELEC ENG escala de resistencias *f*; ~ **network** *n* ELEC ENG red de resistencias *f*; ~ **string** *n* ELEC ENG fibras de resistencia *f pl*; ~ **trimming** *n* ELEC ENG ajuste de resistencia *m*; ~~**type spark plug** *n* AUTO bujía de incandescencia *f*; ~ **voltage divider** *n* ELEC ENG divisor de tensión por resistencias *m*

resite *n* P&R resina termoendurecible en su fase final *f*, resita *f*

resol *n* P&R resina termoendurecible en estado inicial *f*, resol *m*

resoldering *n* PROD resoldadura *f*, resoldeo *m*

resolution *n* ACOUST, CHEM, CINEMAT, ELECTRON, MATH, PRINT resolución *f*, TV definición *f*, resolución *f*; ~ **chart** *n* CINEMAT carta de resolución *f*; ~ **enhancement technology** *n* (*RET*) PRINT tecnología que mejora la resolución *f*

resolved: ~ **shear stress** *n* METALL esfuerzo cortante descompuesto *m*

resolving: ~ **power** *n* CINEMAT, ELECTRON, METALL, PHOTO, PHYS poder de resolución *m*, poder resolutivo *m*

resonance *n* GEN resonancia *f*; ~ **bridge** *n* ELEC puente de resonancia *m*; ~ **broadening** *n* RAD PHYS ensanchamiento debido a una resonancia *m*; ~ **curve** *n* TV curva de resonancia *f*; ~ **damper** *n* AUTO amortiguador de resonancia *m*; ~ **filter** *n* ELECTRON, RAD PHYS filtro de resonancia *m*; ~ **frequency** *n* ACOUST, ELECTRON, PHYS, RAD PHYS, TELECOM, WAVE PHYS frecuencia resonante *f*; ~ **line** *n* ELECTRON, RAD PHYS raya de resonancia *f*; ~ **neutron detector** *n* ELECTRON, RAD PHYS detector de neutrones de resonancia *m*; ~ **peak** *n* ELECTRON, RAD PHYS pico de resonancia *m*; ~ **radiation** *n* ELECTRON, RAD PHYS radiación resonante *f*; ~ **screen** *n* COAL pantalla de resonancia *f*; ~ **silencer** *n* SAFE silenciador de resonancia *m*; ~ **spectrum** *n* WAVE PHYS espectro de resonancia *m*

resonant[1] *adj* GEN resonante

resonant[2]: ~ **absorption** *n* TELECOM absorción de resonancia *f*; ~ **burning** *n* THERMO quemado por resonancia *m*; ~ **cavity** *n* ELECTRON, OPT, PHYS, TELECOM cavidad resonante *f*; ~ **circuit** *n* ELEC, ELECTRON, PHYS, TELECOM, TRANSP circuito resonante *m*; ~~**circuit induction loop detector** *n* TRANSP detector del núcleo de inducción del circuito resonante *m*; ~~**earthed neutral system** *n* BrE (*cf resonant-grounded neutral system AmE*) ELEC sistema con neutro a tierra resonante *m*; ~~**energy transfer** *n* RAD PHYS transferencia de energía resonante *f*; ~ **frequency** *n* ACOUST, ELECTRON, PHYS, RAD PHYS, TELECOM, WAVE PHYS frecuencia resonante *f*; ~~**grounded neutral system** *n* AmE (*cf resonant-earthed neutral system BrE*) ELEC sistema con neutro a tierra resonante *m*; ~ **line** *n* ELECTRON línea resonante *f*; ~~**line oscillator** *n* ELECTRON oscilador de línea resonante *m*; ~ **modes** *n pl* RAD PHYS modos resonantes *m pl*; ~ **optical cavity** *n* OPT cavidad óptica resonante *f*; ~~**reed relay** *n* ELEC ENG relé de láminas resonantes *m*

resonator *n* ACOUST, ELECTRON, TELECOM caja de resonancia *f*, resonador *m*; ~ **grid** *n* ELECTRON rejilla resonante *f*

resorcinol *n* CHEM resorcinol *m*; ~ **resin** *n* P&R resina de resorcinol *f*

resorcylic *adj* CHEM resorcílico

resource *n* COMP&DP, MAR POLL, PROD recurso *m*; ~ **allocation** *n* COMP&DP asignación de recursos *f*; ~ **sharing** *n* COMP&DP compartimento de recursos *m*, recursos compartidos *m pl*; ~~**sharing network** *n* COMP&DP red de compartimiento de recursos *f*, red de recursos compartidos *f*; ~ **unavailable class** *n* TELECOM clase no disponible de recursos *f*, clase no obtenible de recursos *f*; ~ **unit** *n* PROD unidad de recursos *f*

resowing *n* AGRIC resiembra *f*

respirator *n* OCEAN equipo respiratorio *m*, SAFE mascarilla de respiración *f*

respiratory[1] *adj* COAL, SAFE respiratorio

respiratory[2]: ~ **filter** *n* SAFE filtro para respirador *m*; ~~**protection workshop** *n* SAFE taller con protección respiratoria *m*; ~ **protective equipment** *n* SAFE equipo de protección al aparato respiratorio *m*; ~ **system** *n* COAL, MINE, OCEAN, PETR TECH, SAFE aparato respiratorio *m*

responder *n* AIR TRANSP *communications* contestador *m*, respondedor *m*; ~ **beacon** *n* AIR TRANSP radiofaro contestador *m*, radiofaro respondedor *m*

response *n* ACOUST, COMP&DP, ELECTRON, TELECOM, TV respuesta *f*; ~ **characteristic** *n* TV característica de respuesta *f*; ~ **curve** *n* ELECTRON curva de respuesta *f*; ~ **time** *n* COMP&DP, ELECTRON, METR, TELECOM tiempo de respuesta *m*; ~ **to current** *n* ACOUST respuesta de corriente *f*; ~ **to power** *n* ACOUST respuesta de potencia *f*; ~ **to voltage** *n* ACOUST respuesta de voltaje *f*

responsibility *n* MECH ENG responsabilidad *f*

responsivity *n* TELECOM responsividad *f*

rest *n* ACOUST atril *m*, pausa *f*, MECH ENG *supporting device* soporte *m*, MINE barra de apoyo *f*, sustentáculo *m*; ~ **mass** *n* PART PHYS, PHYS masa en reposo *f*; ~ **period** *n* AGRIC tiempo de reposo *m*, AIR TRANSP período de descanso *m*, período de reposo *m*; ~ **skid** *n* TRANSP patín de soporte *m*

restackability *n* PACK aptitud a volver a ser apilado *f*

restart[1] *n* AIR TRANSP *engine* reanudamiento *m*, rearranque *m*, reencendido *m*, COMP&DP reanudación *f*, reinicio *m*, TV reinicio *m*; ~ **point** *n* COMP&DP punto de reanudación *m*, punto de reinicio *m*

restart[2] *vt* AIR TRANSP *engine* reencender, reanudar, COMP&DP reanudar, volver a comenzar, reiniciar, MECH ENG *machinery* rearrancar, recebar, poner en marcha, TELECOM reiniciar

restarting: ~ **injector** *n* MECH ENG inyector automático *m*, inyector de autocebado *m*

resting: ~ **contact** *n* ELEC *relay* contacto de reposo *m*; ~ **land** *n* AGRIC tierra en descanso *f*; ~ **stage** *n* AGRIC etapa de reposo *f*

restitution: ~ **coefficient** *n* PHYS coeficiente de restitución *m*

restocking *n* PROD regeneración natural *f*, renovación de existencias *f*

restoration *n* COAL restablecimiento *m*, PETR TECH restauración *f*, PROD renovación *f*, restablecimiento *m*; ~ **mode** *n* SPACE modo restaurador *m*

restore[1] *n* COMP&DP restauración *f*

restore[2] *vt* COMP&DP restaurar

restoring: ~ **force** *n* MECH, PHYS fuerza de restauración *f*, fuerza repositora *f*; ~ **moment** *n* AIR TRANSP momento enderezador *m*; ~ **torque** *n* MECH par antagonista *m*, par de llamada *m*, par de reposición *m*

restrainer *n* CINEMAT, PHOTO retardador *m*

restricted: ~ **information-transfer service** *n* TELECOM servicio restringido de transferencia de información *m*; ~ **service** *n* TELECOM servicio restringido *m*; ~ **solubility** *n* METALL solubilidad restringida *f*

restrictor *n* PROD estrangulador *m*, válvula reductora *f*, TELECOM reductor *m*, restrictor *m*; ~ **valve** *n* REFRIG válvula limitadora *f*

restructuring *n* PROD reestructuración *f*

restyle *vt* MECH ENG, TRANSP reacondicionar

restyling *n* MECH ENG, TRANSP reacondicionamiento *m*, recomposición *f*

result *n* METR resultado *m*

resultant *n* MATH, MECH ENG, PHYS resultante *f*

resurface *vt* BrE (*cf repave* AmE) CONST repavimentar

resurfacing *n* BrE (*cf repaving* AmE) CONST *roads* repavimentación *f*

resurgence *n* HYDROL, WATER resurgencia *f*

resurgent *adj* HYDROL, WATER resurgente

resurvey *n* CONST *of land* nuevo levantamiento topográfico *m*

resuscitation: ~ **equipment** *n* SAFE equipo para resucitación *m*

resuscitator *n* SAFE aparato reanimador *m*

resynchronize *vt* TELECOM resincronizar

RET *abbr* (*resolution enhancement technology*) PRINT tecnología que mejora la resolución *f*

retail: ~ **package** *n* PACK envase para la venta al por menor *m*

retailer *n* PROD comerciante al por menor *mf*, detallista *mf*

retainer *n* MINE aro de tope *m*, dispositivo de retenida *m*

retaining: ~ **dam** *n* WATER presa de retención *f*; ~ **plate** *n* MECH ENG *injection mould* placa de contención *f*, placa de retención *f*; ~ **ring** *n* MECH, MECH ENG anillo de retención *m*, anillo retenedor *m*, anillo sujetador *m*, PHOTO anillo de sujeción *m*; ~ **spring** *n* MECH ENG, MINE muelle de retenida *m*, resorte de retención *m*; ~ **structure** *n* WATER estructura de retención *f*; ~ **valve** *n* HYDRAUL, WATER válvula de contención *f*, válvula de retención *f*; ~ **wall** *n* CONST dique *m*, muro de contención *m*, muro de soporte *m*, presa *f*, WATER dique *m*, presa *f*

retake *n* CINEMAT, TV repetición *f*

retard[1]: ~-**and-impact fuse** *n* MILIT espoleta de percusión y retardo *f*

retard[2] *vt* CHEM, ELEC, MECH ENG, SPACE, TRANSP retardar, retrasar

retardation *n* CHEM, ELEC, MECH, MECH ENG, SPACE, TRANSP atraso *m*, retardación *f*, retardo *m*, retraso *m*; ~ **coil** *n* ELEC bobina de retardo *f*; ~ **rocket** *n* TRANSP cohete de frenado *m*, cohete de retardo *m*

retarded: ~ **acceleration** *n* MECH aceleración negativa *f*, MECH ENG aceleración negativa *f*, aceleración retardada *f*, aceleración retardatriz *f*; ~ **admission** *n* HYDRAUL, HYDROL admisión retardada *f*; ~ **flow** *n* HYDROL, WATER caudal retardado *m*; ~ **motion** *n* MECH ENG movimiento de retardo *m*; ~ **potentials** *n pl* PHYS potenciales retardados *m pl*; ~ **release** *n* HYDRAUL retardo de escape *m*; ~ **velocity** *n* MECH ENG velocidad de retardo *f*, velocidad negativa *f*

retarder *n* P&R, TRANSP retardador *m*; ~ **parachute** *n* MILIT paracaídas retardador *m*

retarding: ~ **agent** *n* CONST agente retardante *m*, retardador de fraguado *m*, TEXTIL agente retardante *m*

retention *n* GEN retención *f*; ~ **aid** *n* PAPER agente favorecedor de la retención *m*; ~ **of rights** *n* PETR TECH retención de derechos *f*; ~ **time** *n* ELEC ENG tiempo de retención *m*; ~ **valve** *n* MECH ENG válvula de retención *f*

retentive: ~ **capacity** *n* HYDROL capacidad de retención *f*

retentivity *n* PHYS, TV capacidad de retener *f*, retentividad *f*

rethreading: ~ **file** *n* MECH ENG repasadora de roscas *f*

rethreshing *n* AGRIC trilla de retorno *f*

reticle *n* CINEMAT, ELECTRON, INSTR retículo *m* (*Esp*), reticulado *m* (*AmL*); ~ **illumination knob** *n* INSTR botón de iluminación reticular *m*

reticulated: ~ **mirror** *n* SPACE espejo reticulado *m*

reticulation *n* CINEMAT, ELECTRON, PHOTO, PRINT reticulación *f*; reticulado *m*

reticulum *n* AGRIC reticulado *m* (*AmL*), retículo *m* (*Esp*)

retinalite *n* MINERAL retinalita *f*

retinasphalt *n* MINERAL retinasfalto *m*

retinellite *n* MINERAL retinalita *f*

retinite *n* MINERAL retinita *f*

retinning *n* PROD reestañado *m*

retonation: ~ **wave** *n* MINE onda de retroceso *f*, onda retrógada *f*

retort *n* CHEM, CHEM TECH, FOOD, HEAT, LAB, PETR TECH alambique *m*, retorta *f*; ~ **clamp** *n* LAB pinza de retorta *f*; ~ **coal** *n* COAL carbón de retorta *m*; ~ **stand** *n* LAB soporte de retorta *m*

retouch *vt* C&G, COLOUR, PHOTO, PRINT retocar

retouching *n* C&G, COLOUR, PHOTO, PRINT retocado *m*, retoque *m*; ~ **ink** *n* COLOUR tinta de retocar *f*

retrace *n* ELECTRON retroceso *m*

retractable[1] *adj* MECH retractible, retraíble, retráctil

retractable[2]: ~ **aerial** *n* BrE (*cf retractable antenna AmE*) TV antena retractible *f*, antena retráctil *f*; ~ **antenna** *n* AmE (*cf retractable aerial BrE*) TV antena retractible *f*, antena retráctil *f*; ~**-blade knife** *n* MECH ENG cuchillo de hoja retráctil *m*; ~ **filter** *n* PHOTO filtro retraíble *m*; ~ **wheel** *n* AUTO, VEH rueda retráctil *f*

retracting: ~ **spring** *n* AUTO muelle de recuperación *m*, muelle retráctil *m*, resorte de recuperación *m*, resorte retráctil *m*

retransfer *n* PRINT transporte litográfico *m*

retransmit *vt* TELECOM retransmitir

retreaded: ~ **tire** *AmE*, ~ **tyre** *BrE n* AUTO, P&R, VEH neumático recauchutado *m*

retreat[1] *n* CONST *recess* empotramiento *m*, encastre *m*, PROD retratamiento *m*, tratamiento adicional *m*; ~ **mining** *n* MINE trabajo explotado en retirada *m*

retreat[2] *vt* COAL, PROD retratar, tratar de nuevo

retreating: ~ **blade** *n* AIR TRANSP *helicopter* pala en retroceso *f*; ~ **blade stall** *n* AIR TRANSP *helicopter* entrada en pérdida de la pala en retroceso *f*

retree *n* PAPER papel de desperdicio *m*

retrieval *n* COMP&DP, TEXTIL recuperación *f*, reparación *f*

retrieve *vt* COMP&DP, TEXTIL recuperar

retroaction *n* COMP&DP reacción *f*

retroactive: ~ **tenacity** *n* MECH ENG resistencia al aplastamiento *f*

retrofit[1] *n* COMP&DP actualización retroactiva *f*, puesta en nivel *f*, retroinstalación *f*, FUELLESS *by manufacturer* colocación de instalaciones solares *f*

retrofit[2] *vt* FUELLESS colocar una instalación solar

retrofocus: ~ **lens** *n* CINEMAT, OPT, PHOTO lente de retroenfoque *f*

retrogradation *n* FOOD retrogradación *f*

retrograde[1] *adj* FUELLESS, GEOL, SPACE retrógrado

retrograde[2]: ~ **metamorphism** *n* FUELLESS, GEOL metamorfismo retrógrado *m*, retrometamorfismo *m*; ~ **orbit** *n* SPACE órbita retrógrada *f*

retrogressive: ~ **metamorphism** *n* FUELLESS, GEOL metamorfismo retrógrado *m*, retrometamorfismo *m*

retropack *n* SPACE carga retrógrada *f*

retroreflection *n* RAD PHYS retrorreflexión *f*

retroreflective: ~ **marker** *n* AIR TRANSP *airport* baliza retrorreflectiva *f*

retrorocket *n* SPACE, TRANSP retrocohete *m*; ~ **sequence** *n* SPACE, TRANSP secuencia de retrocohete *f*

retrosequence *n* SPACE retrosecuencia *f*

retry *n* COMP&DP reintento *m*, repetición *f*

retting *n* AGRIC enriaje de cáñamo *m*, TEXTIL enriado *m*

return[1] *n* COMP&DP retorno *m*, MINE, NUCL rendimiento *m*, PROD ganancia *f*, rendimiento *m*; ~ **address** *n* COMP&DP direccional de retorno *m*, dirección de retorno *f*; ~ **airway** *n* MINE galería de retorno del aire *f*; ~ **block** *n* MECH ENG pasteca *f*; ~ **cargo** *n* WATER TRANSP flete de retorno *m*; ~ **channel** *n* COMP&DP canal de retorno *m*; ~ **circuit** *n* ELEC ENG circuito de retorno *m*; ~ **code** *n* COMP&DP código de retorno *m*; ~ **conductor** *n* ELEC, ELEC ENG conductor de retorno *m*; ~ **current** *n* ELEC, ELEC ENG, HYDROL corriente de retorno *f*, corriente inversa *f*; ~ **current coefficient** *n* ELEC, ELEC ENG coeficiente de adaptación *m*, coeficiente de corrientes reflejadas *m*; ~ **factor** *n* SPACE factor de retorno *m*; ~ **filter** *n* PROD filtro de retorno *m*; ~**-flow compressor** *n* REFRIG compresor de flujo alterno *m*, compresor en contracorriente *m*; ~ **flue** *n* HEAT, PROD humero de retorno *m*; ~**-flue boiler** *n* PROD caldera con humero de retorno *f*; ~ **instruction** *n* COMP&DP instrucción de retorno *f*; ~ **interval** *n* TV tiempo de retorno *m*; ~ **label** *n* PACK etiqueta retornable *f*; ~**-line filtration** *n* PROD filtración de línea de retorno *f*; ~ **on asset** *n* (*ROA*) PETR TECH beneficio sobre recursos *m*; ~ **path** *n* TELECOM vía de retorno *f*; ~ **pulley** *n* MECH ENG polea de retorno *f*; ~ **roller** *n* MECH ENG rodillo de retorno *m*; ~ **rope** *n* MECH ENG soga de retorno *f*; ~ **scanning-beam** *n* ELECTRON, TV haz explorador de retorno *m*; ~ **spring** *n* AUTO, MECH ENG, PROD, VEH muelle de recuperación *m*, muelle recuperador *m*, resorte de retorno *m*; ~ **stroke** *n* MECH ENG *of piston* carrera de retorno *f*, PHYS golpe de retorno *m*; ~ **to service** *n* TELECOM retorno al servicio *m*; ~ **tube** *n* PROD tubo de retorno *m*; ~ **tube boiler** *n* PROD caldera tubular con retorno de llama *f*; ~ **tubular boiler** *n* PROD caldera tubular con retorno de llama *f*; ~ **valve** *n* MECH ENG válvula de escape *f*, válvula del sobrante *f*; ~ **wall** *n* CONST pared de vuelta *f*; ~ **wheel** *n* MECH ENG rueda de retorno *f*; ~ **wire** *n* ELEC *circuit*, ELEC ENG hilo de retorno *m*, hilo de vuelta *m*

return[2] *vt* COMP&DP regresar, retornar, volver

return[3]: ~ **to surface** *vi* WATER TRANSP *submarine* subir a la superficie

returnable: ~ **bottle** *n* PACK, RECYCL botella retornable *f*; ~ **container** *n* PACK, RECYCL contenedor retornable *m*; ~ **packaging** *n* PACK, RECYCL embalaje retornable *m*

returns *n pl* PROD *founding* desperdicios de colada *m pl*; ~ **and allowances** *n pl* PROD rendimientos y reducciones *m pl*

reurbanization *n* AGRIC reurbanización *f*

reusable[1] *adj* COMP&DP, PACK, RECYCL reutilizable

reusable[2]: ~ **box** *n* PACK, RECYCL caja reutilizable *f*; ~ **optical disc** *BrE*, ~ **optical disk** *AmE n* OPT disco óptico reutilizable *m*; ~ **packaging** *n* PACK, RECYCL embalaje reutilizable *m*

reuse[1] *n* RECYCL reutilización *f*, uso repetido *m*, utilización de nuevo *f*

reuse[2] *vt* RECYCL emplear de nuevo, reemplear, reutilizar, usar de nuevo, utilizar de nuevo, volver a usar, volver a utilizar

rev[1] *n* VEH revolución *f*, vuelta *f*; ~ **counter** *n* INSTR, VEH cuentarrevoluciones *m*, tacómetro *m*

rev[2]: ~ **up** *vt* VEH acelerar, embalar

revamping *n* PETR TECH reestructuración *f*, remodelación *f*

reveal *n* CONST distancia del marco de la ventana hasta la pared *f*, telar *m*

revealed: ~ **failure** *n* QUALITY falla revelada *f*

revenue: ~ **cutter** *n* WATER TRANSP *customs* guardacostas *m*; ~-**earning train** *n* RAIL tren que produce ingresos *m*, tren rentable *m*

reverberant: ~ **field** *n* ACOUST campo reverberante *m*

reverberation *n* ACOUST, GEOPHYS, PHYS, WAVE PHYS eco *m*, reverberación *f*; ~ **chamber** *n* SPACE cámara de reverberación *f*; ~ **room** *n* ACOUST cámara reverberante *f*; ~ **time** *n* ACOUST tiempo de reverberación *m*

reverberatory *n* PROD horno de reverbero *m*; ~ **chamber** *n* PROD *of furnace* laboratorio *m*; ~ **flame** *n* PROD llama de reverbero *f*; ~ **furnace** *n* PROD horno de reverbero *m*

reversal *n* CINEMAT película reversible *f*, TELECOM, TRANSP inversión *f*; ~ **control channel** *n* TELECOM canal de control por inversión *m*; ~ **development** *n* CINEMAT, PHOTO revelado por inversión *m*; ~ **dupe** *n* CINEMAT dupe reversible *m*; ~ **film** *n* CINEMAT, PHOTO película reversible *f*; ~ **finder** *n* CINEMAT, PHOTO visor de inversión *m*, visor enderezador *m*; ~ **master print** *n* CINEMAT, PRINT copia maestra reversible *f*; ~ **print** *n* CINEMAT, PRINT copia reversible *f*; ~ **process** *n* CINEMAT, PHOTO, PRINT proceso de inversión *m*; ~ **processing** *n* CINEMAT, PHOTO, PRINT revelado por inversión *m*; ~ **of the sphere** *n* GEOM inversión de la esfera *f*; ~-**type color film** *AmE*, ~-**type colour film** *BrE n* CINEMAT, PHOTO película reversible a color *f*

reverse[1] *adj* CINEMAT, COMP&DP inverso

reverse[2] *n* MECH contramarcha *f*, marcha atrás *f*, PRINT dorso *m*, reverso *m*, VEH marcha atrás *f*; ~ **action** *n* CINEMAT, TV acción inversa *f*; ~ **angle** *n* CINEMAT, TV ángulo inverso *m*; ~ **authentication** *n* COMP&DP autentificación inversa *f*; ~ **bias** *n* ELEC ENG, PHYS polarización inversa *f*; ~ **braking** *n* TRANSP frenado inverso *m*; ~ **channel** *n* COMP&DP canal de retorno *m*, canal inverso *m*; ~-**charge call** *n* *BrE* (*cf collect call AmE*) TELECOM llamada a cobro revertido *f* (*Esp*), llamada pagadera en destino *f* (*AmL*); ~ **clipping** *n* COMP&DP recortado inverso *m*, recorte inverso *m*; ~ **combustion** *n* PETROL combustión inversa *f*; ~ **compatibility** *n* TV compatibilidad inversa *f*; ~ **contact** *n* ELEC ENG, PROD contacto de inversión *m*; ~ **contactor** *n* ELEC ENG, PROD contactor de inversión *m*; ~ **current** *n* ELEC, ELEC ENG corriente invertida *f*, inversión de corriente *f*; ~-**current circuit breaking** *n* ELEC *switch*, ELEC ENG disyuntor de contracorriente *m*; ~-**current relay** *n* ELEC, ELEC ENG relevador de corriente inversa *m*, relé de corriente inversa *m*, relé de inversión de corriente *m*; ~-**cycle defrosting** *n* REFRIG, THERMO desescarche por inversión de ciclo *m*; ~ **direction** *n* COMP&DP, ELEC ENG dirección inversa *f*; ~-**direction flow** *n* COMP&DP, ELEC dirección inversa de flujo *f*, flujo en dirección inversa *m*; ~ **emission** *n* ELECTRON emisión inversa *f*; ~ **fault** *n* GEOL falla inversa *f*; ~-**flow turbine** *n* FUELLESS turbina de contraflujo *f*; ~ **gear** *n* AUTO, VEH engranaje de marcha atrás *m*; ~ **idler gear** *n* AUTO, VEH engranaje intermedio de contramarcha *m*, engranaje intermedio de retroceso *m*, engranaje intermedio inversor de marchas *m*; ~ **idler shaft** *n*

AUTO, VEH eje intermedio de marcha atrás *m*, eje intermedio inversor *m*, árbol de marcha atrás *m*, árbol intermedio de marcha atrás *m*; ~-**image switch** *n* TV interruptor de imagen en negativo *m*; ~ **light** *n* *AmE* (*cf reversing light BrE*) AUTO, VEH luz de marcha atrás *f*; ~ **mask** *n* CINEMAT máscara inversa *f*; ~ **motion** *n* TV marcha atrás *f*; ~ **osmosis** *n* CHEM TECH, CONST, HYDROL ósmosis inversa *f*; ~-**phase relay** *n* ELEC relé de inversión de fases *m*; ~ **pitch** *n* AIR TRANSP *propeller* paso invertido *m*; ~ **Polish notation** *n* COMP&DP notación inversa por sufijos *f*, notación polaca inversa *f*; ~-**press felt** *n* PAPER fieltro de la prensa invertida *m*; ~ **printing** *n* CINEMAT, PHOTO, PRINT copiado inverso *m*, copiado por inversión *m*, impresión en negativo *f*; ~ **reaction** *n* NUCL reacción inversa *f*; ~-**recovery time** *n* ELECTRON tiempo de recuperación inversa *m*; ~-**roll coater** *n* PAPER estucadora de rodillo invertido *f*; ~-**roll coating** *n* COATINGS revestimiento interior de superficies cilíndricas *m*; ~ **routing** *n* TELECOM encaminamiento inverso *m*; ~-**routing address** *n* TELECOM dirección de encaminamiento inverso *f*; ~ **scan** *n* TV exploración inversa *f*; ~-**side printing** *n* PACK, PRINT impresión del reverso *f*; ~ **thrust** *n* AIR TRANSP empuje invertido *m*, tracción inversa *f*; ~ **traveling wave** *AmE*, ~ **travelling wave** *BrE n* ELEC ENG, WAVE PHYS onda progresiva inversa *f*; ~ **video** *n* COMP&DP vídeo inverso *m*, vídeo invertido *m*; ~ **voltage** *n* ELEC, ELEC ENG tensión inversa *f*, voltaje inverso *m*; ~-**voltage protection** *n* ELEC, ELEC ENG protección contra voltaje inverso *f*

reverse[3] *vt* ELECTRON, HYDRAUL invertir, MECH ENG dar contramarcha a, dar marcha atrás a, invertir la marcha de

reverse[4]: ~ **the motion** *vi* MECH ENG dar contramarcha, dar marcha atrás, dar máquina atrás, invertir

reversed: ~ **arch** *n* CONST *architecture*, HYDRAUL arco invertido *m*; ~ **controls** *n pl* AIR TRANSP mandos invertidos *m pl*; ~ **image** *n* CINEMAT, PHOTO, PHYS, TV imagen invertida *f*; ~ **ogee** *n* CONST cima invertida *f*; ~ **press** *n* PAPER prensa invertida *f*; ~ **profile** *n* GEOPHYS perfil inverso *m*; ~ **steam** *n* HYDRAUL contravapor *m*

reverser *n* ELECTRON inversor *m*

reversibility *n* CHEM, ELEC ENG, MECH ENG, PHYS, TRANSP reversibilidad *f*

reversible[1] *adj* CHEM, ELEC ENG, MECH ENG, PHYS, TRANSP reversible

reversible[2]: ~ **booster** *n* ELEC ENG elevador-reductor *m*, generador regulador *m*; ~ **furniture** *n* PRINT composición reversible *f*; ~ **gear** *n* MECH ENG mecanismo de inversión *m*; ~ **motor** *n* ELEC ENG, TRANSP motor de dos sentidos de rotación *m*, motor reversible *m*; ~ **pallet** *n* TRANSP bandeja reversible *f* (*Esp*), paleta reversible *f*, pálet invertible *m* (*AmL*); ~-**pitch propeller** *n* AIR TRANSP, WATER TRANSP hélice de paso reversible *f*; ~ **plough** *n* *BrE* AGRIC arado reversible *m*; ~ **plow** *AmE see reversible plough BrE*; ~ **ratchet** *n* MECH ENG matraca invertible *f*, trinquete reversible *m*; ~ **switch** *n* ELEC ENG conmutador reversible *m*; ~ **transducer** *n* ACOUST. transductor reversible *m*, ELEC ENG transductor bilateral *m*

reversing *n* ELECTRON inversión *f*, MECH ENG *motion* retroceso *m*, contramarcha *f*, media vuelta *f*, cambio de marcha *m*, inversión de marcha *f*, inversión *f*,

MINE, RAIL inversión de marcha *f*; ~ **bath** *n* CINEMAT, PHOTO baño de inversión *m*; ~ **braking switchgroup** *n* TRANSP conmutaciones de frenado inverso *f pl*; ~ **current** *n* OCEAN corriente alternativa *f*; ~-**drum switch** *n* ELEC conmutador de tambor inversor *m*, interruptor de tambor inversor *m*; ~ **frame** *n* OCEAN bastidor reversible *m*; ~ **gear** *n* CINEMAT engranaje de inversión *m*, MECH ENG mecanismo de cambio de marcha *m*, mecanismo de inversión *m*; ~ **lever** *n* MECH ENG palanca de cambio de marcha *f*; ~ **lever rod** *n* MECH ENG, RAIL barra de cambio de marcha *f*; ~ **light** *n BrE* (*cf reverse light AmE*) AUTO, VEH luz de marcha atrás *f*; ~ **link** *n* MECH ENG sector de Stephenson *m*, sector del cambio de marcha *m*; ~ **mill** *n* PROD laminador reversible *m*; ~ **motion** *n* MECH ENG *of lathe* marcha atrás *f*, retroceso *m*; ~ **motor** *n* ELEC motor de inversión rápida de marcha *m*; ~ **ring** *n* PHOTO anillo inversor *m*; ~ **rod** *n* MECH ENG *valve gear*, RAIL barra de cambio de marcha *f*; ~ **screw** *n* MECH ENG tornillo de inversión *m*; ~-**sequencer step operation** *n* PROD operación gradual de secuenciador reversible *f*; ~ **shaft** *n* MECH ENG *valve gear* cambio de marcha *m*; ~ **steam** *n* HYDRAUL vapor de inversión *m*; ~ **switch** *n* ELEC ENG conmutador inversor *m*; ~ **valve** *n* HYDRAUL válvula de cambio de marcha *f*, válvula de inversión *f*

revertive: ~ **control system** *n* TELECOM sistema de control por impulsos inversos *m*

revetment *n* CONST revestimiento *m*

review *n* CHEM repaso *m*, PRINT revisión *f*, SPACE análisis *m*, revisión *f*

revise *vt* PRINT revisar

revised: ~ **edition** *n* PRINT edición revisada *f*

revolution *n* GEOM, MECH ENG, SPACE giro *m*, revolución *f*, rotación *f*, vuelta *f*, VEH revolución *f*; ~ **counter** *n* INSTR, MECH ENG contador de vueltas *m*, cuentarrevoluciones *m*, cuentavueltas *m*, tacómetro *m*; ~ **indication** *n* MECH ENG indicación de vueltas *f*

revolutions: ~ **per minute** *n pl* AUTO, CINEMAT, PHYS, VEH revoluciones por minuto *f pl*

revolving: ~ **armature** *n* ELEC, ELEC ENG inducido giratorio *m*; ~ **back** *n* PHOTO tapa posterior giratoria *f*; ~-**bottom spreader** *n* AGRIC distribuidor de fondo giratorio *m*; ~ **cutter** *n* MECH ENG disco cortante *m*; ~-**cylinder engine** *n* TRANSP motor de cilindros giratorios *m*; ~-**cylinder sorter** *n* AGRIC clasificadora de cilindros giratorios *f*; ~ **die-head** *n* MECH ENG portaluneta revólver *m*; ~ **head punch** *n* MECH ENG punzón revólver *m*; ~ **nosepiece** *n* INSTR, LAB, MECH ENG portaobjetivo revólver *m*, portaobjetivo rotativo *m*; ~-**packer-type tiller** *n* AGRIC cultivador tipo compactador giratorio *m*; ~ **punch pliers** *n pl* MECH ENG alicates punzonadores revólver *m pl*, sacabocados revólver *m*; ~ **screen** *n* COAL criba giratoria *f*, criba rotatoria *f*, tromel *m*, CONST criba giratoria *f*, criba rotatoria *f*, MINE criba giratoria *f*, criba rotatoria *f*, tromel *m*, PROD criba giratoria *f*, criba rotatoria *f*; ~ **shutter** *n* CINEMAT, OPT, PHOTO, TV obturador giratorio *m*; ~ **stage** *n* LAB platina giratoria *f*; ~ **table** *n* MECH ENG mesa rotativa *f*; ~ **tool holder** *n* MECH ENG portaherramientas revólver *m*

rewind[1] *n* CINEMAT, COMP&DP, PAPER, PHOTO, TEXTIL, TV rebobinado *m*; ~ **handle** *n* CINEMAT, PHOTO, TV

palanca de rebobinado *f*; ~ **speed** *n* CINEMAT, COMP&DP, PHOTO, TV velocidad de rebobinado *f*; ~ **tension** *n* CINEMAT tensión de rebobinado *f*

rewind[2] *vt* CINEMAT, COMP&DP, PAPER, PHOTO, TEXTIL rebobinar, reenrollar

rewinder *n* CINEMAT, COMP&DP, PAPER, PHOTO, TEXTIL, TV rebobinadora *f*

rewinding *n* GEN rebobinado *m*

rewiring *n* ELEC, ELEC ENG *supply* realambrado *m*

rework: ~ **center** *AmE*, ~ **centre** *BrE n* PROD centro de reprocesado *m*; ~ **routing** *n* PROD recorrido del regenerado *m*

rewrite[1] *n* COMP&DP reescritura *f*

rewrite[2] *vt* COMP&DP reescribir

Reynolds: ~ **number** *n* (*R*) AIR TRANSP, FLUID, FUELLESS, PHYS, RAD PHYS número de Reynolds *m*; ~ **number 900** *n* (*Re900*) FLUID número de Reynolds 900 *m* (*Re900*); ~ **stress** *n* FLUID esfuerzo de Reynolds *m*

RF[1] *abbr* (*radio frequency*) ACOUST, ELEC, TELECOM, TV, WATER TRANSP RF (*frecuencia de radio, radiofrecuencia*)

RF[2]: ~ **alternator** *n* ELEC ENG, ELECTRON, TELECOM alternador de RF *m*; ~ **amplification** *n* ELEC ENG, ELECTRON, TELECOM amplificación de RF *f*; ~ **amplifier** *n* ELEC ENG, ELECTRON, TELECOM amplificador de RF *m*; ~ **carrier** *n* ELEC ENG, ELECTRON, TELECOM portador de RF *m*; ~ **coil** *n* ELEC, ELEC ENG, ELECTRON, TELECOM bobina de RF *f*; ~ **current** *n* ELEC, ELEC ENG, ELECTRON, TELECOM corriente de RF *f*; ~ **current source** *n* ELEC ENG, ELECTRON, TELECOM generador de corriente de RF *m*; ~ **dub** *n* TV doblaje de RF *m*; ~ **generator** *n* ELEC ENG, ELECTRON, TELECOM generador de RF *m*; ~ **heating** *n* ELECTRON, HEAT, P&R, THERMO calentamiento por RF *m*; ~ **interference** *n* ELECTRON, TELECOM, TV interferencia de RF *f*; ~ **oscillator** *n* ELECTRON, TELECOM, TV oscilador de RF *m*; ~ **pulse** *n* ELECTRON, TELECOM, TV pulso de RF *m*; ~ **section** *n* ELEC, ELEC ENG, ELECTRON sección de RF *f*; ~ **section-generator** *n* ELEC, ELEC ENG, ELECTRON generador de sección de RF *m*; ~ **sensor** *n* SPACE, TELECOM sensor de RF *m*; ~ **shielding** *n* ELECTRON, TELECOM, TV protección de RF *f*; ~ **stage** *n* ELEC ENG, ELECTRON fase de RF *f*; ~ **transformer** *n* ELEC ENG, ELECTRON transformador de RF *m*; ~ **transistor** *n* ELEC, ELEC ENG, ELECTRON transistor de RF *m*

Rf *abbr* (*rutherfordium*) RAD PHYS Rf (*ruterfordio*)

RGB[1] *abbr* (*red green blue*) COMP & DP, TV RGB (*rojo verde azul*)

RGB[2]: ~ **input** *n* COMP&DP, TV entrada RGB *f*; ~ **monitor** *n* COMP&DP, TV monitor RGB *m*, monitor de rojo verde azul *m*

Rh *abbr* (*rhodium*) CHEM Rh (*rodio*)

rhaetizite *n* MINERAL reticita *f*, rhäticita *f*

rhenic *adj* CHEM rénico

rhenium *n* (*Re*) CHEM renio *m* (*Re*)

rheological: ~ **properties** *n pl* FLUID propiedades reológicas *f pl*; ~ **variable** *n* METALL variable reológica *f*

rheology *n* COAL, FLUID, GAS, METALL, P&R, PHYS reología *f*

rheostat *n* AUTO, ELEC, ELEC ENG, LAB, PHYS reóstato *m*; ~ **slider** *n* ELEC, ELEC ENG contacto corredizo de reóstato *m*, cursor de reóstato *m*; ~-**sliding contact** *n*

AUTO contacto deslizante del reóstato *m*; ~ **starter** *n*
ELEC, ELEC ENG arrancador reostático *m*

rheostatic: ~ **brake** *n* TRANSP freno reostático *m*;
~ **braking** *n* RAIL, VEH frenado reostático *m*

rhizome *n* AGRIC rizoma *m*

rhizosphere *n* AGRIC *soils* rizósfera *f*

rho: ~-**meson** *n* PART PHYS mesón ro *m*

rhodite *n* MINERAL rodita *f*

rhodium *n* (*Rh*) CHEM rodio *m* (*Rh*)

rhodizite *n* MINERAL rodicita *f*

rhodochrosite *n* MINERAL rodocrosita *f*

rhodonite *n* MINERAL rodonita *f*

rhomb *n* GEOM rombo *m*

rhombohedral *adj* CRYSTALL romboédrico

rhomboid[1] *adj* GEOM romboide

rhomboid[2] *n* GEOM romboide *m*

rhomboidal *adj* GEOM romboidal, rómbico

rhombus *n* GEOM rombo *m*

rhumb: ~ **line** *n* WATER TRANSP loxodrómica *f*; ~-**line**
navigation *n* WATER TRANSP navegación loxodrómica
f

rhumbatron *n* ELECTRON rumbotrón *m*

rhyolite *n* PETROL riolita *f*

rhythm *n* ACOUST ritmo *m*

rhythmic: ~ **bedding** *n* GEOL estratificación *f*

RI *abbr* (*routing indicator*) COMP&DP, TELECOM indicador de encaminamiento *m*, indicador de radar *m*,
indicador de ruta *m*

rib *n* AIR TRANSP montante *m*, nervadura *f*, *on wing of*
plane costilla *f*, COAL *angled edge* arista *f*, costilla *f*,
nervio *m*, varilla *f*, *passageway in mine* pilar de
seguridad *m*, *geological feature* dique *m*, nervadura *f*,
MECH saliente *m*, lomo *m*, reborde *m*, costilla *f*,
acanalado *m*, PRINT, PROD nervadura *f*, SPACE costilla
f, nervadura *f*, arco *m*, TEXTIL bordón *m*, acanalado
m, WATER TRANSP *shipbuilding* costilla *f*; ~ **eye area** *n*
AGRIC área de músculo dorsal *f*; ~ **grass** *n* AGRIC
llantén lanceolado *m*; ~ **hole** *n* MINE pilar de
seguridad *m*; ~ **mark** *n* C&G marca de costilla *f*,
marca de ranura del molde *f*

ribband *n* WATER TRANSP *of hull* cintón *m*

ribbed[1] *adj* CONST, MECH, MECH ENG acanalado, con
nervaduras, estriado, nervado, TEXTIL acanalado

ribbed[2]: ~ **frame** *n* CONST estructura nervada *f*; ~ **G-**
cramp *n* MECH ENG grapa G acanalada *f*, grapa G
estriada *f*; ~ **piston** *n* AUTO pistón estriado *m*, pistón
ranurado *m*; ~ **radiator** *n* HEAT radiador de elementos *m*; ~ **stitch** *n* TEXTIL punto acanalado *m*; ~ **V-belt**
n MECH ENG correa acanalada *f*, correa trapezoidal *f*

ribbing *n* MECH, MECH ENG, TEXTIL acanalado *m*

ribbon *n* ACOUST cinta *f*, C&G listón *m*, COMP&DP, METR
cinta *f*; ~ **brake** *n* MECH, MECH ENG freno de banda
m; ~ **cable** *n* ELEC, OPT, PROD, TELECOM cable cinta
m, cable de tiras *m*, cable plano *m*; ~ **cellular radiator**
n AUTO radiador celular de bandas *m*, radiador
celular de cintas *m*; ~ **guide** *n* TV alimentador de la
cinta *m*; ~ **ice** *n* REFRIG hielo en cintas *m*;
~ **loudspeaker** *n* ACOUST altavoz de cinta *m*;
~ **machine** *n* C&G máquina de vaciado continuo *f*;
~ **microphone** *n* ACOUST micrófono de cinta *m*; ~ **rail**
n RAIL carril soldado *m*

riboflavin *n* CHEM *compound*, FOOD riboflavina *f*

ribonucleic *adj* CHEM *acid* ribonucleico

rice: ~ **binder** *n* AGRIC agavilladora de arroz *f*; ~ **field** *n*
AGRIC arrozal *m*; ~ **flour** *n* AGRIC, FOOD harina de

arroz *f*; ~ **hull** *n* AGRIC cáscara del grano de arroz *f*;
~ **mill** *n* AGRIC, FOOD molino de arroz *m*

riceland: ~ **plough** *n* BrE AGRIC arado para arrozales
m; ~ **plow** AmE see riceland plough BrE

rich: ~ **clay** *n* C&G barro rico *m*; ~ **coal** *n* COAL carbón
graso *m*; ~ **gas** *n* GAS, PETROL gas rico *m*; ~ **mixture** *n*
AUTO, VEH mezcla rica *f*

Richter: ~ **scale** *n* CONST, GEOL, GEOPHYS escala de
Richter *f*

ricinoleic *adj* CHEM *acid* ricinoleico

rickets *n* AGRIC raquitismo *m*

ricochet *n* MILIT rebote *m*

riddle *n* COAL, PROD cedazo *m*, criba *f*, criba de lavado
f, tamiz *m*

riddler *n* COAL, PROD cribador *m*, máquina cribadora *f*

riddling *n* COAL, PROD cribado *m*

riddlings *n pl* COAL, PROD desperdicios del cribado *m pl*

ride[1] *n* CONST recorrido *m*

ride[2]: ~ **at anchor** *vi* WATER TRANSP estar fondeado a la
gira, estar surto al ancla

rideability *n* CONST posibilidad de recorrido *f*

rider *n* LAB jinetillo *m* (*AmL*), reiter *m* (*Esp*); ~ **arch** *n*
C&G arco de la cámara *m*; ~ **plate** *n* WATER TRANSP
shipbuilding chapa horizontal de la sobrequilla *f*,
sobrequilla *f*; ~ **roll** *n* PAPER rodillo prensor *m*

ridge[1] *n* AGRIC camellón *m*, CONST cumbrera *f*, *of dust*
montón *m*, OCEAN dorsal submarina *f*, reborde *m*,
cresta *f*, PROD *over surface* estría *f*, saliente *m*, WATER
TRANSP dorsal *f*, dorsal anticiclónica *f*, cuña *f*;
~ **beam** *n* CONST viga de cumbrera *f*; ~ **buster** *n*
AGRIC rompedor de camellón *m*; ~ **capping** *n* CONST
lead or tiles caballete *m*; ~ **drill** *n* AGRIC sembradora
en camellones *f*; ~ **line** *n* CONST *of roof* cumbrera *f*;
~ **roof** *n* CONST cubierta a dos aguas *f*; ~ **terrace** *n*
AGRIC terraza de borde *f*; ~ **tile** *n* CONST cobija *f*, teja
de caballete *f*; ~ **waveguide** *n* ELEC ENG guía de
ondas con resalte *f*, guía de ondas tabicada *f*

ridge[2] *vt* CONST *roof* colocar el caballete

ridged: ~ **roof** *n* CONST tejado a dos aguas *m*

ridgepiece *n* CONST cumbrera *f*

ridgeplate *n* CONST placa de caballete *f*

ridger *n* AGRIC alomador *m*, aporcador *m*

ridging[1] *adj* AGRIC acaballonado, alomado, aporcado

ridging[2]: ~ **cultivator** *n* AGRIC cultivador de asiento *m*

riding: ~ **cut-off valve** *n* HYDRAUL distribuidor de teja
de expansión *m*, máquina alternativa de vapor *f*;
~ **light** *n* WATER TRANSP *navigation* luz de fondeo *f*

riebeckite *n* MINERAL riebeckita *f*

Rieke: ~ **diagram** *n* ELECTRON diagrama de Rieke *m*

Riemann: ~ **geometry** *n* GEOM, MATH geometría de
Riemann *f*, geometría riemanniana *f*; ~ **integral** *n*
GEOM, MATH integral de Riemann *f*

Riemannian: ~ **geometry** *n* GEOM, MATH geometría de
Riemann *f*, geometría riemanniana *f*

riffle: ~ **sampler** *n* COAL divisor de muestra *m*,
separador de mineral *m*

riffler *n* MECH ENG *file* escofina encorvada *f*, PAPER
arenero *m*

rifle *n* MILIT rifle *m*, fusil *m*, raya *f*; ~ **barrel** *n* MILIT
cañón del fusil *m*; ~ **bullet** *n* MILIT bala del fusil *f*;
~ **butt** *n* MILIT culata del fusil *f*; ~ **grenade** *n* MILIT
granada del fusil *f*; ~ **grip** *n* CINEMAT, PHOTO
empuñadura tipo fusil *f*; ~ **range** *n* MILIT alcance
del fusil *m*, polígono de tiro del fusil *m*; ~ **stock** *n*
MILIT caja del fusil *f*; ~ **telescope** *n* INSTR telescopio
de fusil *m*, MILIT mira telescópica del fusil *f*

rifled: ~ **gun** n MILIT *firearms* cañón rayado m
rifling n MILIT rayado m
rift: ~ **tectonics** n GEOL tectónica de rift f; ~ **valley** n
GEOL valle tectónico m
rig[1] n MECH ENG mecanismo de maniobra m, OCEAN
aparejo m, jarcia f, jarcia firme y de labor f, PETR
TECH equipo de formación m, equipo de perforación
m, plataforma de sondeo f, sondeadora f, taladro m,
PROD *outfit* instalación de prueba f, tren de sondeo m,
for loam work caballete m, WATER TRANSP aparejo m,
arboladura f; ~ **floor** n PETR TECH piso de la torre m,
piso del taladro m, piso-base de trabajo m, planchada
f
rig[2] vt PROD *cables, wires* aparejar, *machines* instalar,
montar, equipar, *with pulley blocks* montar con
cabría, WATER TRANSP *mast* aparejar, enjarciar;
~ **out** vt PROD equipar; ~ **up** vt PETROL montar,
PROD equipar, instalar
rigger n WATER TRANSP aparejador m
rigging n MECH ENG *working mechanism* mecanismo de
maniobra m, mecanismo de sondeo m, OCEAN jarcia
f, aparejo m, WATER TRANSP arboladura f, cabuyería f,
palos y jarcia m pl; ~ **drawing** n WATER TRANSP
croquis de arboladura y de jarcia m; ~ **position** n
AIR TRANSP posición de montaje f; ~ **screw** n WATER
TRANSP *boat building* acollador m, tornillo de ajustar
m; ~**up** n PETR TECH montaje de la torre de sondeo m
right[1]: ~**angled** adj GEOM de ángulo recto, PHYS
angulado recto; ~**hand** adj MECH dextroso, hacia
la derecha; ~**handed** adj PHYS orientado segun la
regla de la mano derecha
right[2]: ~**and-left coupling** n MECH ENG *turnbuckle*
manguito roscado apriete m; ~**and-left screw** n
MECH ENG tornillo de pasos contrarios m, tornillo de
roscas a derechas y a izquierdas m; ~**and-left screw
link** n MECH ENG *turnbuckle* junta roscada a izquierda
y derecha f; ~ **angle** n GEOM ángulo recto m; ~**angle
finder** n PHOTO visor de ángulo recto m; ~**angle
triangle** n GEOM triángulo de ángulo recto m,
triángulo rectángulo m; ~**angled bend** n MECH
ENG codo en ángulo recto m; ~**angled bend
coupling** n MECH ENG acoplamiento de codo en
ángulo recto m; ~ **ascension** n SPACE ascensión recta
f; ~**circular cone** n GEOM cono circular recto m;
~**circular cylinder** n GEOM cilindro circular recto m;
~**hand circular polarization** n SPACE *communications* polarización circular a derechas f, polarización
circular dextrógira f; ~**hand knife-tool** n MECH ENG
lathe herramienta de corte a derechas f; ~**hand lock**
n CONST cerradura a derechas f; ~**hand milling
cutter** n MECH ENG fresa a derechas f; ~**hand page**
n PRINT página impar f; ~**hand
rule** n ELEC, ELEC ENG, PHYS regla de la mano derecha
f, regla de los tres dedos f, regla del tirabuzón f;
~**hand screw** n MECH ENG tornillo dextrógiro m;
~**hand side** n PHYS miembro de la derecha m;
~**hand tap** n MECH ENG macho roscador a derechas
m; ~**hand thread** n MECH ENG rosca derecha f, rosca
hacia la derecha f; ~**hand turnoff** n RAIL cambio de
vía a la derecha m; ~**handed screw** n MECH ENG
tornillo de rosca a derechas m, tornillo de rosca
dextrógira m; ~**handed spiral** n MECH ENG espiral
hacia la derecha f; ~ **justification** n COMP&DP, PRINT
justificación a la derecha f; ~ **margin** n PRINT margen
derecho m; ~ **shift** n COMP&DP desplazamiento a la
derecha m, tecla de mayúsculas derecha f; ~**turning**

traffic n TRANSP tráfico de giro a la derecha m; ~ **of
way** n AGRIC derecho de paso m, AIR TRANSP *airport*
preferencia de paso f, *air traffic* prioridad de paso f,
CONST derecho de paso m, servidumbre de paso f,
WATER TRANSP *navigation* prioridad de paso f
right[3]: ~**justify** vt COMP&DP, PRINT justificar a la
derecha
right[4]: **at ~ angles** phr GEOM en ángulos rectos
righting: ~ **lever** n WATER TRANSP *naval architecture*
brazo adrizante m; ~ **moment** n WATER TRANSP *naval
architecture* momento de adrizamiento m
rigid: ~ **automatic coupling** n AUTO, TRANSP, VEH
acoplamiento automático rígido m; ~ **axle** n AUTO,
VEH eje rígido m; ~ **body** n PHYS sólido rígido m;
~ **box** n PACK caja rígida f; ~ **coaxial line** n ELEC ENG,
PHYS, TELECOM línea coaxial rígida f; ~ **construction**
n CONST firme rígido m; ~ **coupling** n MECH ENG *gear
drive* acoplamiento rígido m; ~ **and folding cartons**
n pl PACK cajas de cartón rígidas y plegables f pl;
~ **leg** n PHOTO pie rígido m; ~ **pipe** n MECH ENG
tubería rígida f; ~ **plastic** n P&R plástico rígido m;
~ **PVC** n PACK PVC rígido m; ~ **reflector** n SPACE
reflector rígido m; ~ **rotor** n AIR TRANSP *of helicopter*,
MECH ENG rotor rígido m; **sidewall air cushion** n
TRANSP amortiguación rígida por aire lateral f,
amortiguador de aire con costados rígidos m; ~ **sidewall hovercraft** n TRANSP, WATER TRANSP
aerodeslizador de costados rígidos m; ~ **skirt** n
TRANSP plinto rígido m; ~**skirt hovercraft** n
TRANSP, WATER TRANSP aerodeslizador de plinto
rígido m; ~ **stinger** n PETROL espolón rígido m
rigidity n ACOUST, MECH ENG, PAPER, PHYS rigidez f;
~ **modulus** n COAL, PHYS módulo de rigidez m
rill n GEOL arroyo m, HYDROL arroyo m, riachuelo m;
~ **erosion** n AGRIC erosión asurcada f
rim n VEH llanta f, cerco m; ~ **cementation** n GEOL
cemento sintaxial m; ~ **flange** n VEH talón de la llanta
m; ~ **syncline** n GEOL sinclinal periférico m
rime n REFRIG escarcha opaca f
rimmed adj COATINGS efervescente
rinderpest n AGRIC peste bovina f
ring[1]: ~**shaped** adj GEOM, MECH, MECH ENG anillado,
en forma de anillo
ring[2] n AIR TRANSP aro m, AUTO anillo m, aro m,
segmento m, C&G, CHEM anillo m, COMP&DP aro m
(*Esp*), círculo m (*AmL*), *network* anillo m, HYDRAUL
anillo m, arandela f, corona f, MECH anillo m,
arandela f, argolla f, segmento m, segmento de pistón
m, corona f, MECH ENG argolla f, PETR TECH aro m,
PHOTO anillo m, PROD círculo m, SPACE estruendo m,
anillo m, TELECOM anillo m, TEXTIL anillo m, aureola
f, círculo m, TRANSP aro m, VEH anillo m, segmento
m; ~**and-pinion gearing** n AUTO, VEH engranaje de
corona y piñón m; ~ **armature** n ELEC *generator*
armadura de anillo f; ~ **bolt** n WATER TRANSP *deck
fittings* cáncamo de argolla m, perno con argolla m;
~ **burner** n CONST quemador de anillo m;
~ **configuration** n TELECOM configuración en anillo
f; ~ **core** n NUCL núcleo anular m; ~ **counter** n TV
anillo contador m, contador en anillo m; ~ **current** n
AmE (*cf ring main BrE*) ELEC, ELEC ENG cable anular
m, canalización circular f, circuito anular m, circuito
de anillo m; ~ **end** n AUTO extremo del segmento m;
~ **feeder** n ELEC *supply network* alimentador en anillo
m; ~ **of flame** n GAS, THERMO anillo de llama m;
~ **flash** n PHOTO flash anular m; · ~ **frame** n AIR

TRANSP cuaderna *f*; ~ **fuselage** *n* AIR TRANSP cuaderna *f*; ~ **gage** *AmE see ring gauge BrE*; ~ **gap** *n* AUTO, VEH separación de anillo *f*; ~ **gauge** *n* BrE METR calibre anular *m*, calibre de anillo *m*, compuerta cilíndrica *f*; ~ **gear** *n* AUTO, VEH anillo dentado *m*, corona dentada *f*, engranaje anular *m*, engranaje de anillo *m*; ~ **head** *n* TV cabeza de anillo *f*; ~ **joint** *n* AUTO, VEH junta anular *f*, junta de anillo *f*; ~ **laser** *n* PHYS láser de anillo *m*; ~ **magnet** *n* PHYS imán anular *m* (*Esp*), imán con forma de anillo *m* (*AmL*), TV imán anular *m*; ~ **main** *n* BrE (*cf ring circuit AmE, ring current AmE*) ELEC, ELEC ENG cable anular *m*, canalización circular *f*, circuito anular *m*, circuito de anillo *m*; ~-**main system** *n* ELEC, ELEC ENG sistema en circuito de anillo *m*, sistema en circuito de canalización circular *m*; ~ **network** *n* COMP&DP, TELECOM red en anillo *f*, red en círculo *f*; ~ **and pinion** *n* AUTO, VEH corona y piñón *f*; ~ **pliers** *n pl* MECH ENG alicates anulares *m pl*; ~-**roll crusher** *n* COAL trituradora de cilindros anulares *f*, trituradora de rodillos *f*; ~ **seal** *n* GAS sello anular *m*; ~ **shears** *n pl* MECH ENG tijeras anulares *f pl*; ~ **spanner** *n* BrE (*cf ring wrench AmE*) AUTO, MECH ENG, VEH llave de anillo *f*; ~ **spinning** *n* TEXTIL hilatura de anillos *f*; ~-**spinning frame** *n* TEXTIL continua de hilar de anillos *f*; ~-**spun yarn** *n* TEXTIL hilado de continua de anillos *m*; ~ **supply system** *n* ELEC, ELEC ENG sistema de canalización circular *m*, sistema de circuito de anillo *m*; ~ **topology** *n* COMP&DP topología de anillo *f*; ~ **translator** *n* TELECOM translador de anillo *m*; ~ **tube** *n* TEXTIL tubo de anillos *m*; ~-**type thrust washer** *n* MECH ENG arandela de presión del tope anular *f*, arandela de presión de anillo *f*; ~ **weld** *n* NUCL soldadura anular *f*; ~ **winding** *n* ELEC *coil* arrollamiento anular *m*, arrollamiento en anillo *m*, devanado en anillo *m*, devanado toroidal *m*; ~ **wrench** *n* AmE (*cf ring spanner BrE*) AUTO, MECH ENG, VEH llave de anillo *f*

ring³ *vt* TEXTIL anillar

ring⁴ *vi* TELECOM dar timbre (*AmL*), llamar, telefonear, tocar el timbre (*Esp*)

Ring: ~ **Nebula** *n* SPACE Nebulosa en Anillo *f*

ringer *n* TELECOM dispositivo de llamada *m*, llamador *m*, timbre *m*

ringing *n* CONST, ELEC ENG, ELECTRON llamada *f*, oscilación transitoria *f*, señal de llamada *f*, TELECOM llamada *f*, llamada de timbre *f*; ~ **current** *n* TELECOM corriente de llamada *f*, corriente de repique *f*; ~ **machine** *n* TELECOM generador de corriente de llamada *m*, generador de llamada *m*, máquina de llamada *f*, máquina de repique *f*; ~ **period** *n* TELECOM período de la llamada *m*; ~ **test** *n* ELEC, ELEC ENG prueba por excitación de oscilaciones transitorias *f*

rink: ~ **floor** *n* REFRIG pavimento soporte de pista *m*

rip¹: ~ **current** *n* OCEAN, WATER TRANSP corriente de arranque *f*, corriente de resaca *f*; ~ **pin** *n* AIR TRANSP, MILIT *parachute* perno para apertura manual *m*; ~ **tide** *n* OCEAN, WATER TRANSP corriente de resaca *f*; ~ **track** *n* AmE (*cf repair track BrE*) RAIL vía para reparaciones de vagones *f*

rip² *vt* CONST rasgar, romper

riparian *adj* HYDROL, OCEAN, WATER, WATER TRANSP ribereño

ripcord *n* AIR TRANSP, MILIT *parachute* cable de apertura manual *m*

ripening *n* PHOTO, PRINT maduración *f*

ripidolite *n* MINERAL ripidolita *f*

ripper *n* AGRIC escarificadora *f*, CONST escarificador *m*, rompedor de caminos *m*, máquina escarificadora *f*, MINE aparato disgregador de suelos *m* (*AmL*), desfondadora de terrenos *f* (*AmL*), desgarrador *m*, escariador de terrenos *m* (*Esp*), escarificador *m* (*Esp*)

ripping *n* CONST desgarro *m*, rasgado *m*

ripple *n* ACOUST armónico de orden superior *m*, fluctuación *f*, ondulación *f*, rizado *m*, CONST ondulación *f*, onda *f*, rizo de agua *m*, ELECTRON armónico de orden superior *m*, HYDROL onda *f*, PHYS armónico de orden superior *m*, SPACE armónico de orden superior *m*, fluctuación *f*, rizado *m*, serie de ondas *f*, variación pequeña del voltaje *f*, TV interferencia de imagen por variaciones de la red *f*; ~ **attenuation** *n* CONST atenuación de onda *f*; ~-**carry adder** *n* COMP&DP sumador de acarreo variable *m* (*Esp*), sumador de llevar por onda *m* (*AmL*); ~ **factor** *n* CONST factor de ondulación *m*; ~ **filter** *n* CONST filtro de impulsos *m*, filtro de ondulación *m*, filtro de pulsaciones *m*, filtro de zumbido *m*, filtro para fluctuaciones *m*, *civil engineering* filtro de grava *m*, RAD PHYS filtro de impulsos *m*, filtro de ondulación *m*, filtro de pulsaciones *m*, filtro de zumbido *m*, filtro para fluctuaciones *m*; ~ **frequency** *n* CONST, RAD PHYS frecuencia de onda *f*, frecuencia de ondulación *f*, frecuencia de zumbido *f*; ~ **mark** *n* GEOL riple *f*, riple de corriente *f*, HYDROL señales de marea fósil *f pl*, OCEAN pliegue *m*; ~ **paper** *n* PAPER papel ondulado sencillo *m*; ~ **tank** *n* WAVE PHYS canal hidrodinámico de oscilación *m*; ~ **voltage** *n* CONST, ELECTRON tensión de ondulación *f*, tensión ondulatoria *f*, voltaje ondulado *m*

ripples *n pl* OCEAN cabrilleo *m*

riprap *n* CONST pedraplén *m*, escollera *f*

RISC *abbr* (*reduced instruction set computer*) COMP&DP computador con juego reducido de instrucciones *m* (*AmL*), computadora con juego reducido de instrucciones *f* (*AmL*), ordenador con juego reducido de instrucciones *m* (*Esp*)

rise¹ *n* CONST *of arch* altura *f*, HYDROL, OCEAN ascenso *m*, aumento *m*, crecida *f*, WATER TRANSP *of tide* altura de pleamar *f*; ~ **face** *n* COAL chimenea *f* (*AmL*); ~ **of floor** *n* WATER TRANSP *ship design* astilla muerta *f*; ~ **time** *n* AIR TRANSP *sonic boom* tiempo de propagación *m*, COMP&DP tiempo de ascenso *m*, tiempo de subida *m*, CONST tiempo de elevación *m*, PETROL tiempo de formación *m*, PHYS tiempo de ascenso *m*; ~ **workings** *n pl* COAL, MINE labor a cielo abierto *f*

rise² *vi* HYDROL *waters* crecer, *source* nacer, MINE trabajar, WATER *source* nacer, WATER TRANSP *pressure* subir, *wind* levantarse

riser *n* CONST *vertical part of step* contrapeldaño *m*, montante ascendente *m*, ELEC *supply* conductor ascendente *m*, PETR TECH, PETROL conducto elevador *m*, elevador *m*, tubo ascendente *m*, tubo de subida *m*, PROD *moulds* alimentador *m*, mazarota *f*, bebedero *m*; ~ **pin** *n* PROD *founding* pasador para abrir respiraderos *m*; ~ **pipe** *n* CONST tubería vertical *f*, PETR TECH, PETROL caño de subida *m*; ~ **pipeline** *n* PETR TECH, PETROL tubería vertical de subida *f*; ~ **stick** *n* PROD *founding* pasador para abrir respiraderos *m*; ~ **tensioner** *n* PETR TECH, PETROL tensor del tubo de subida *m*

rising *n* MINE labor a cielo *f*, subida del petróleo *f*;

~ **arch** *n* CONST *curve described* arco ascendente *m*, *structure* arco elevadizo *m*; ~ **gradient** *n* CONST pendiente ascendente *f*, rampa *f*; ~ **main** *n* CONST *building* conducto ascendente *m*, ELEC *supply* canalización ascendente *f*, conducto ascendente *m*, línea de subida *f*, tubería ascendente *f*; ~ **sun magnetron** *n* CONST magnetrón ascendente *m*; ~ **tide** *n* FUELLESS, OCEAN, WATER TRANSP marea ascendente *f*, marea creciente *f*, marea entrante *f*

risk *n* QUALITY, SAFE riesgo *m*; ~ **assessment** *n* MAR POLL, POLL, QUALITY, SAFE apreciación de los riesgos *f*, evaluación del riesgo *f*, valoración de los riesgos *f*; ~ **criteria** *n* QUALITY, SAFE criterios de los riesgos *m pl*; ~ **evaluation** *n* MAR POLL, POLL, QUALITY, SAFE apreciación de los riesgos *f*, evaluación del riesgo *f*, valoración de los riesgos *f*; ~ **of exposure** *n* RAD PHYS, SAFE *radiation* riesgo de exposición *m*; ~ **management** *n* QUALITY, SAFE manejo de riesgos *m*; ~ **quantification** *n* QUALITY, SAFE cuantificación de riesgos *f*; ~ **of suffocation** *n* SAFE peligro de asfixia *m*

Ritz: ~ **combination principle** *n* PHYS principio de combinación de Ritz *m*

river: ~ **authority** *n* WATER autoridad fluvial *f*; ~ **bar** *n* HYDROL franja arenosa *f*; ~ **basin** *n* AGRIC, HYDROL, WATER, WATER TRANSP cuenca fluvial *f*; ~ **bed** *n* HYDROL, WATER cauce del río *m*, cuenca del río *f*, fondo del río *m*, lecho del río *m*, madre del río *f*; ~ **boat** *n* WATER TRANSP embarcación fluvial *f*; ~ **capture** *n* HYDROL, WATER aprovechamiento de un río *m*, captura de un río *f*; ~ **channel** *n* AGRIC, HYDROL, WATER, WATER TRANSP río canalizado *m*; ~ **dam** *n* HYDROL, WATER, WATER TRANSP presa de río *f*; ~ **dredge** *n* AGRIC, HYDROL, WATER draga fluvial *f*; ~ **erosion** *n* HYDROL erosión fluvial *f*; ~ **fleet** *n* WATER TRANSP flota de transporte fluvial *f*; ~ **mouth** *n* HYDROL, MINE, OCEAN, WATER, WATER TRANSP boca del río *f*, desembocadura del río *f*; ~ **port** *n* WATER TRANSP puerto fluvial *m*; ~ **safety** *n* SAFE, WATER TRANSP seguridad fluvial *f*; ~ **traffic** *n* WATER TRANSP tráfico fluvial *m*; ~ **training** *n* AGRIC, HYDROL, WATER regulación de ríos *f*; ~ **user** *n* AGRIC, HYDROL, WATER, WATER TRANSP usuario de un río *m*; ~ **wall** *n* CONST, HYDROL, WATER muro de contención del río *m*, muro de encauzamiento *m*; ~ **water** *n* AGRIC, HYDROL, WATER agua fluvial *f*; ~ **works** *n pl* WATER obras fluviales *f pl*

riverbank *n* CONST, HYDROL, WATER, WATER TRANSP orilla *f*, orilla del río *f*, ribera *f*

riverside[1] *adj* HYDROL, OCEAN, WATER, WATER TRANSP ribereño

riverside[2] *n* HYDROL, OCEAN, WATER, WATER TRANSP ribereño *m*

rivet *n* CONST, MECH, MECH ENG, PROD remache *m*, roblón *m*; ~ **cold press** *n* MECH ENG prensa de remachar *f*; ~ **dolly** *n* CONST contrarremachador *m*; ~**-heating furnace** *n* CONST, PROD, THERMO horno calientarremaches *m*; ~ **joint** *n* CONST junta de remache *f*; ~ **knocking-off hammer** *n* CONST, MECH ENG martillo de remachar *m*, martillo de remache *m*; ~ **set** *n* CONST buterola *f*; ~ **shank diameter** *n* MECH ENG diámetro del cuerpo del remache *m*; ~ **snap** *n* CONST embutidor *m*

riveted: ~ **lap joint** *n* MECH ENG junta de solapa remachada *f*; ~ **plate** *n* CONST placa con remaches

f, placa roblonada *f*; ~ **seam** *n* PACK cosido remachado *m*

riveter *n* CONST, MECH, MECH ENG, PROD remachadora *f*

riveting *n* CONST, MECH, MECH ENG, PROD remachado *m*, remache *m*, roblonado *m*, roblonadura *f*; ~ **hammer** *n* CONST martillo de remachar *m*; ~ **machine** *n* CONST máquina remachadora *f*; ~ **set** *n* CONST juego de remaches *m*

riving: ~ **knife** *n* SAFE guarda para rajar *f*

rivulet *n* GEOL, HYDROL arroyuelo *m*

RJE *abbr* (*remote job entry*) COMP&DP entrada de trabajos a distancia *f*

RMP *abbr* (*refiner mechanical pulp*) PAPER RMP (*pasta mecánica de refino*)

RMS[1] *abbr* (*root-mean-square*) CONST, ELEC, ELECTRON, MATH, TELECOM media cuadrática *f*, raíz cuadrada media *f*

RMS[2]: ~ **current** *n* ELEC ENG corriente eficaz *f*; ~ **deviation** ELEC, MATH desviación característica *f*, desviación media cuadrática *f*, desviación normal *f*, desviación típica *f*; ~ **frequency deviation** *n* SPACE desviación de frecuencia eficaz *f*; ~ **value** *n* CONST, OPT valor cuadrático medio *m*, valor efectivo *m*, valor eficaz *m*, PHYS raíz cuadrada del valor cuadrático medio *f*; ~ **water level** *n* FUELLESS promedio cuadrático del nivel de agua *m*

Rn *abbr* (*radon*) CHEM, PHYS, RAD PHYS Rn (*radón*)

ROA *abbr* (*return on asset*) PETR TECH beneficio sobre recursos *m*

road[1]: ~**-bound** *adj* TRANSP limitado a carretera

road[2] *n* AUTO, CONST, TRANSP, VEH calzada *f*, camino *m*, carretera *f*; ~ **bed** *n* RAIL *fixed equipment* explanación *f*, infraestructura de la vía férrea *f*, lecho de vía *m*; ~ **bridge** *n* AUTO, CONST, TRANSP, VEH puente de carretera *m*; ~ **building** *n* AUTO, CONST, TRANSP, VEH construcción de carreteras *f*; ~**-building machinery** *n* AUTO, CONST, TRANSP, VEH maquinaria para construcción de carreteras *f*; ~ **camber** *n* VEH cambio de rasante *m*; ~ **clearance** *n* AUTO, TRANSP, VEH permiso de circulación *m*; ~ **grader** *n* AUTO motoniveladora de carreteras *f*; ~ **haulage** *n* AUTO, TRANSP, VEH transporte por carretera *m*; ~ **hauler** *AmE*, ~ **haulier** *n BrE* AUTO, TRANSP, VEH transportista *m*; ~ **head** *n* COAL cabeza de línea *f*, frente del camino en construcción *m*; ~ **identification sign** *n* AUTO señal de identificación de carretera *f*; ~ **jam** *n* AUTO, TRANSP, VEH atasco *m*; ~ **junction** *n* AUTO, TRANSP, VEH cruce de carreteras *m*; ~ **locomotive** *n* AUTO apisonadora *f*; ~ **making** *n* CONST, TRANSP, VEH construcción de carreteras *f*; ~ **map** *n* AUTO, TRANSP, VEH mapa de carreteras *m*, mapa vial *m*; ~ **marker cone** *n* AUTO, VEH cono señalizador de carreteras *m*; ~ **message** *n* AUTO, TRANSP, VEH mensaje en carretera *m*; ~ **metal** *n BrE* (*cf paving material AmE*) CONST balasto *m*, macadam *m*, macadán *m*, piedra triturada para caminos *f*; ~**-metal-spreading machine** *n BrE* (*cf asphalt-spreading machine AmE*) CONST, TRANSP asfaltadora *f*, máquina asfaltadora *f*; ~ **news** *n* AUTO, TELECOM, TRANSP, TV, VEH noticias de carreteras *f pl*; ~ **over railway** *n* AUTO, CONST, RAIL, TRANSP, VEH paso a nivel de ferrocarril *m*; ~ **painting** *n* CONST pintado de la carretera *m*; ~ **plough** *n BrE* AUTO, CONST, VEH roturadora *f*; ~ **plow** *AmE see road plough BrE*; ~**-rail** *n* TRANSP tren-camión *m*; ~**-rail bus** *n* TRANSP, VEH autobús-

ferrobús *m* (*Esp*), bus-ferrobús *m* (*AmL*), omnibús-
ferrobús *m* (*AmL*); ~ **resistance** *n* VEH resistencia a
la rodadura *f*; ~ **ripper** *n* CONST, TRANSP escarificadora para carreteras *f*; ~ **roller** *n* AUTO, CONST,
TRANSP, VEH apisonadora *f*; ~ **safety** *n* CONST, SAFE
seguridad en la carretera *f*, seguridad vial *f*, seguridad
viaria *f*; ~-**safety device** *n* AUTO, SAFE, TRANSP, VEH
aditamento de seguridad en el camino *m*; ~ **sign** *n*
AUTO, CONST, TRANSP, VEH señal de carretera *f*, señal
de tráfico *f*; ~ **tank car** *n* (*RTC*) camión cisterna *m*;
~ **tanker** *n* MAR POLL camión cisterna *m*, vehículo
tanque de carreta *m*; ~-**tarring machine** *n* AUTO,
CONST, TRANSP, VEH máquina asfaltadora *f*; ~ **tractor**
n AUTO, VEH tractor *m*; ~ **traffic** *n* AUTO, TRANSP, VEH
tráfico rodado *m*; ~ **traffic radar** *n* AUTO, RAD PHYS,
TELECOM, TRANSP, VEH radar para tráfico *m*; ~ **trailer**
n AUTO, VEH remolque de carretera *m*; ~ **train** *n*
TRANSP convoy en carretera *m*; ~ **transport** *n* AUTO,
CONST, TRANSP, VEH transporte por carretera *m*
roadheader *n* MINE excavadora de galerías *f* (*AmL*),
minador *m* (*Esp*), topo *m* (*Esp*), barreno de techo *m*
roads *n pl* OCEAN, WATER TRANSP fondeadero *m*, rada *f*
roadside: ~ **radio transmitter** *n* AUTO, RAD PHYS,
TELECOM, TRANSP, VEH radio-transmisor de carretera
m
roadstead *n* OCEAN rada *f*, fondeadero *m*, WATER
TRANSP fondeadero *m*, rada *f*
roadstones *n pl* CONST balasto *m*, grava *f*, macadam *m*
roadway *n* AUTO, CONST *AmE* (*cf motorway BrE*)
autopista *f*, calzada *f*, carretera *f*, MINE vía *f*, galería *f*
(*AmL*), galería de transporte *f* (*Esp*), TRANSP, VEH
AmE (*cf motorway BrE*) autopista *f*, calzada *f*,
carretera *f*
roaming: ~ **subscriber** *n* TELECOM abonado de vaga-
bundeo *m*
roaring: ~ **forties** *n pl* OCEAN cuarenta rugientes *m pl*
roaster *n* AGRIC pollo asadero *m* (*Esp*), pollo parrillero
m (*AmL*), C&G horno de calcinación *m*, COAL horno
m, horno de calcinación *m*, HEAT, PROD, THERMO
calcín *m*, horno de calcinación *m*, horno de tostación
m; ~ **ear** *n* AGRIC mazorca de maíz para asar *f*
roasting *n* COAL calcinación *f*, FOOD tostado *m*, PROD
calcinación *f*; ~ **furnace** *n* C&G, COAL, HEAT, PROD,
THERMO calcín *m*, horno de calcinación *m*, horno de
tostación *m*; ~ **kiln** *n* C&G, COAL, HEAT, PROD,
THERMO calcín *m*, horno de calcinación *m*, horno
de tostación *m*; ~ **oven** *n* C&G, COAL horno de
calcinación *m*, HEAT, PROD, THERMO calcín *m*, horno
de calcinación *m*, horno de tostación *m*
robot *n* COMP&DP robot *m*; ~ **gripping device** *n* MECH
ENG dispositivo de fijación automática *m*, dispositivo
de sujeción automática *m*
robotic: ~ **arm** *n* PROD brazo robótico *m*; ~ **palletizing
and stretch system** *n* PACK sistema robotizado de
paletización y retractilado *m*
robotics *n* COMP&DP robótica *f*
Rochelle: ~ **salt** *n* CHEM, ELEC ENG, FOOD sal de
Rochelle *f*, sal de ácido tartárico *f*, tartrato sódico-
potásico *m*
rock *n* WATER TRANSP durmiente *m*, escollo *m*;
~ **asphalt** *n* GEOL, PETR TECH, PETROL asfalto mineral
m; ~ **association** *n* GEOL asociación de rocas *f*; ~ **bit**
n PETR TECH barrena *f* (*Esp*), broca *f*, mecha *f* (*AmL*),
trépano *m* (*AmL*); ~ **bolt** *n* CONST perno para roca *m*;
~ **borer** *n* CONST *machine* perforadora *f*; ~ **breaker** *n*
CONST quebrantarrocas *m*; ~ **capping** *n* MINE recu-

brimiento de rocas *m*, terreno de recubrimiento *m*;
~ **channeler** *AmE*, ~ **channeller** *BrE* *n* CONST, MINE
acanaladora de rocas *f*, acanaladora para roca *f*;
~-**cutting dredger** *n* WATER TRANSP draga rompe-
rrocas *f*; ~ **dowel** *n* CONST taco para roca; ~ **drift** *n*
MINE galería en roca *f*; ~ **drill** *n* COAL, CONST, MINE
martillo perforador de roca *m*, perforadora *f*,
perforadora para roca *f*, taladradora *f*, taladro *m*;
~ **fill** *n* CONST escollera *f*, WATER enrocamiento *m*,
escollera *f*, pedraplén *m*, rocalla *f*; ~-**fill dam** *n* WATER
dique de escollera *m*; ~ **fracture** *n* GEOL fractura de
roca *f*; ~ **layer** *n* WATER estrato rocoso *m*; ~ **lever** *n*
CONST *equalizing-bar* palanca para piedra *f*; ~ **meal** *n*
MINERAL roca desintegrada *f*; ~ **mechanics** *n* COAL,
GEOL mecánica de rocas *f*; ~ **milk** *n* MINERAL caliza
terrosa *f*, leche de montaña *f*; ~ **oil** *n* COAL, PETROL
petróleo *m*; ~ **pressure** *n* COAL presión de falla *f*;
~ **rubble** *n* HYDRAUL brecha de fricción *f*; ~ **salt** *n*
CHEM sal de roca *f*, FOOD sal gorda *f*, GAS sal gema *f*,
MINERAL halita *f*, sal común *f*, sal gema *f*; ~ **shoe** *n*
COAL pedestal de roca *m*; ~ **slip** *n* GEOL deslizamiento
de roca *m*; ~ **sounding** *n* COAL sondeo de roca *m*;
~ **tar** *n* PETR TECH, PETROL alquitrán de petróleo *m*;
~ **tip** *n* COAL cargadero de rocas *m*; ~ **type** *n* COAL,
PETROL tipo de roca *m*; ~ **wool** *n* HEAT ENG lana de
roca *f*; ~ **work** *n* MINE pedraplén *m*, rocalla *f*, trabajo
en roca *m*; ~-**work explosive** *n* MINE explosivo para
trabajo en roca *m*
rocker *n* AUTO, C&G balancín *m*, MECH, MECH ENG
balancín *m*, basculador *m*, oscilador *m*, MINE criba
lavadora *f*, pedestal de oscilación *m*; ~ **arm** *n* AUTO,
VEH balancín *m*, brazo basculante *m*, brazo empujaválvulas *m*, brazo oscilante *m*, empujador *m*; ~-**arm
assembly** *n* AUTO, VEH montaje del brazo basculante
m; ~-**arm shaft** *n* AUTO, VEH eje de balancines *m*, eje
del balancín *m*; ~-**arm support** *n* AUTO, VEH soporte
del brazo del balancín *m*; ~ **bearing** *n* MECH ENG
apoyo de oscilación *m*; ~ **box** *n* AUTO, VEH culata de
balancines *f*, eje portabalancines *m*; ~ **cover** *n* AUTO,
VEH tapa de balancines *f*; ~ **shaft** *n* AUTO, VEH eje de
balancines *m*; ~ **switch** *n* CINEMAT, ELEC, ELEC ENG
conmutador basculante *m*, interruptor oscilante *m*
rocket *n* AIR TRANSP, MILIT, SPACE cohete *m*, WATER
TRANSP *propeller* bengala *f*, cohete *m*; ~-**assisted
projectile** *n* MILIT proyectil cohético *m*; ~-**assisted
takeoff** *n* BrE (*RATO*, *cf jet-assisted takeoff AmE*)
AIR TRANSP despegue asistido por cohete *m*, despegue
con ayuda de reactores *m*, despegue con cohetes
auxiliares *m*; ~ **engine** *n* MECH ENG motor cohete *m*,
motor cohético *m*, SPACE motor del cohete *m*;
~ **igniter** *n* MILIT carga de ignición *f*; ~ **launcher** *n*
MILIT, SPACE lanzacohetes *f*; ~-**launching site** *n*
MILIT, SPACE plataforma lanzacohetes *f*; ~ **motor** *n*
MILIT, SPACE motor cohético *m*, propulsor de cohete
m; ~ **pistol** *n* MILIT espoleta cohética *f*; ~ **plume** *n*
MILIT estela del cohete *f*; ~ **propellant** *n* MILIT, SPACE
propulsante cohético *m*; ~ **propulsion** *n* MILIT, SPACE
propulsión del cohete *f*; ~ **signal** *n* MILIT, SPACE señal
con cohetes *f*
rocketry *n* AIR TRANSP, MILIT, SPACE cohetería *f*
rocking: ~ **table** *n* C&G mesa mecedora *f*
rockslide *n* GEOL deslizamiento de rocas *m*
Rockwell: ~ **hardness test** *n* MECH ENG ensayo de
dureza Rockwell *m*, prueba de dureza Rockwell *f*;
~ **hardness-testing machine** *n* MECH ENG máquina
para prueba de dureza Rockwell *f*

rod n C&G *optical blank* varilla f, CONST *surveyors' level staff* vara de medir f, jalón m, varilla f, HYDRAUL vástago m, biela f, LAB varilla f, MINE barra f, maestra f, medida para muros de ladrillo f, barra maestra f, vástago m, mira f, WATER *of pump* vástago m; **~ actuator** n PROD actuador de varillas m; **~ consolidation** n NUCL consolidación de barras f; **~ coupling** n MINE acoplamiento de vástago m, enganche de barras m; **~-end plain eye** n MECH ENG ojo de cabeza de biela m; **~-end spherical eye** n MECH ENG ojo redondo de cabeza de biela m; **~ guide** n PROD guía para varillas f; **~-in-tube technique** n OPT, TELECOM técnica de varilla en tubo f; **~ joint** n MINE enganche de barra m; **~ lever** n PROD palanca de varillas f; **~ linkage** n MECH ENG sistema de palancas m, sistema de varillas articuladas m, varillaje m; **~ mill** n COAL laminador para redondos m, molino de barras m, tren de laminar redondos m, PROD *rolling mill* laminador para redondos m; **~-operated disconnect switch** n PROD desconectador accionado por varillas m; **~ seal** n MECH ENG varilla de obturación f; **~-seal housing** n MECH ENG caja de la varilla de obturación f; **~ support** n MINE llave de retenida f; **~-turning tool** n MINE herramienta de giro f, mango de maniobra m (*AmL*); **~ weeder** n AGRIC barra escardadora f

rodding n MINE separación de guiaderas f

rodenticide n AGRIC raticida m

rods n pl MINE varillas de sonda f pl, VEH varillaje m

roentgen n (R) PHYS, RAD PHYS renguenio m, roentgen m (R); **~ equivalent for man** n (*rem*) RAD PHYS dosis equivalente en renguenios en el hombre f (*rem*)

roentgenoluminescence n NUCL, PHYS, RAD PHYS renguenoluminiscencia f

roentgenometallography n METALL, NUCL, PHYS, RAD PHYS renguenometalografía f

roguing n AGRIC depuración f

roll[1] n AIR TRANSP *aerobatic flight* tonel m, CINEMAT rollo m, PAPER cilindro m, rodillo m, PHYS rodamiento m, PROD cilindro m, rodillo m, SPACE balanceo m, desplazamiento sobre ruedas en la pista m, tonel m, TEXTIL rodillo m; **~ attitude** n SPACE posición de balanceo f, situación de balanceo f; **~ baler** n AGRIC empacadora de pacas cilíndricas f, enfardadora de fardos cilíndricos f; **~ boiling** n TEXTIL ebullición en rollo f; **~ call polling** n COMP&DP elección por pasado de lista f, sondeo nominal m; **~ channel** n AIR TRANSP *automatic pilot* canal de alabeo m; **~ coating** n COATINGS revestimiento de bobinas m; **~ crusher** n COAL trituradora de cilindros f; **~ cue** n CINEMAT indicación de rollo f; **~ diameter** n TEXTIL diámetro del rodillo m; **~ film** n CINEMAT película en bobina f, película en carrete f, película en rollo f (*Esp*), PHOTO película a granel f (*AmL*), película en bobina f, película en carrete f, película en rollo f (*Esp*), PRINT, TV película en bobina f, película en carrete f, película en rollo f (*Esp*); **~-forming equipment** n PROD equipo para formación de perfiles estampados m; **~ head** n PAPER cubre testero m; **~ headbox** n PAPER rodillo de la caja de entrada m; **~-in** n COMP&DP carga en la memoria principal f, restauración en memoria principal f; **~-in refrigerator** n REFRIG recinto frigorífico para carretillas m; **~ in-roll out** n COMP&DP carga-descarga de la RAM f, carga-descarga de la memoria principal f, intercambio de

programas m; **~ label printing** n PACK impresión de etiquetas formando bobinas f; **~ length** n TEXTIL longitud del rodillo f; **~ mark** n AmE (cf *roller mark* BrE) C&G marca de rodillo f, marca de piel f; **~ marking** n MECH ENG defectos superficiales producidos por los cilindros m pl, marcas superficiales producidas por los cilindros f pl; **~ number** n CINEMAT número de rollo m; **~-on vessel** n TRANSP, WATER TRANSP buque de transbordo rodado m, buque rolón m; **~-on/roll-off** n (*ro-ro*) TRANSP, WATER TRANSP embarque por propulsión propia m; **~-on/roll-off depot** n TRANSP, WATER TRANSP depósito de cargas rodadas m; **~-on/roll-off port** n TRANSP, WATER TRANSP puerto de transbordo rodado m; **~-on/roll-off ship** n TRANSP, WATER TRANSP buque transportador de vehículos carreteros y vagones cargados m; **~-on/roll-off system** n TRANSP, WATER TRANSP sistema de embarque y desembarque autopropulsado m; **~-on/roll-off vessel** n TRANSP, WATER TRANSP buque de transbordo rodado m, buque rolón m; **~-out** n COMP&DP descarga de la memoria principal f, registro en memoria auxiliar m; **~-out Fourdrinier** n PAPER mesa de formación en voladizo f; **~-over** n TRANSP capotaje m, vuelco m, zozobra f; **~-over anticline** n GEOL anticlinal de inversión m; **~-over bar** n VEH barra antivuelco f, barra transversal f; **~-over draft machine** AmE, **~-over draught machine** BrE n PROD moldeadora basculante de sacudidas f, máquina de desmoldear de inversión f; **~-over drop machine** n PROD máquina de desmoldear de inversión f; **~-over plough** n BrE AGRIC arado de ida y vuelta m; **~-over plow** AmE see *rollover plough* BrE; **~-over scraper** n AGRIC pala de buey f; **~-over table** n PROD mesa de inversión f; **~-rate gyro** n SPACE giroscopio que mide la velocidad angular de balanceo m; **~ scale** n PROD cascarilla de laminación f; **~ screen** n COAL filtro de placas m; **~ shell** n PROD envolvente de cilindros m; **~ sulfur** AmE, **~ sulphur** BrE n CHEM azufre cilindrado m; **~ test** n WATER TRANSP *ship design* prueba de balance f; **~ train** n PROD tren de rodillos m; **~-up** n PRINT entintar

roll[2]: **~ in** vt COMP&DP cargar en la memoria principal, restaurar en memoria principal; **~ ink** n COLOUR, PRINT untar la tinta; **~ out** vt COMP&DP descargar de la memoria principal, registrar en memoria auxiliar

roll[3]: **~ over** vi TRANSP zozobrar

rolled[1]: **as ~** adj PROD en estado tosco de laminación

rolled[2]: **~ glass** n C&G vidrio rolado m; **~ oats** n pl AGRIC copos de avena m pl; **~ section** n WATER TRANSP *shipbuilding* perfil laminado m

roller n AGRIC, C&G, CINEMAT rodillo m, CONST *road* apisonadora f, *operator* tambor m, rodillo m, DETERG, ELEC tambor m, MECH cilindro m, rodillo m, OCEAN rompiente m, P&R, PRINT cilindro m, rodillo m, PROD cilindro laminador m, WATER TRANSP *sea* rompiente m; **~ bearing** n MECH ENG cojinete de rodillos m, cojinete de rulemán m, descanso de rodamiento m, rodamiento de rodillos m, rulemán m, VEH rodamiento de rodillos m; **~ bit** n PETR TECH barrena de arrastre f, broca f, broca de rodillos f, mecha de cola de pescado f, trépano en cola de carpa m; **~-blind dark slide** n PHOTO chasis de cortinilla m; **~-blind shutter** n PHOTO obturador de cortinilla m; **~ boom** n WATER TRANSP botavara con dispositivo de arrollamiento f; **~ bridge** n CONST puente corredizo *m*; **~ chain** *n* MECH ENG cadena de rodillos *f*; **~ clutch** *n* AUTO embrague de rodillos *m*; **~ coating** *n* COATINGS, PAPER estucado con rodillo *m*; **~ dryer** *n* PRINT rodillo secador *m*; **~ dust collector** *n* ELEC ENG aspirador del polvo por rodillos *m*; **~ fairlead** *n* WATER TRANSP *deck fittings* alabante de rodillos *m*, guía de rolete *f*; **~ gage** *AmE see roller gauge BrE*; **~ gate** *n* HYDROL compuerta cilíndrica *f*, compuerta de rodillos *f*; **~ gauge** *n BrE* C&G calibrador de rodillos *m*; **~ lever** *n* PROD palanca de rodillos *f*; **~ mark** *n BrE* (*cf roll mark AmE*) C&G marca de rodillo *f*, marca de piel *f*; **~ mill** *n* AGRIC azadón rodante *m*, cuchilla circular *f*, molino aplastador *m*, FOOD molino de rodillos *m*, PROD triturador de muelas horizontales *m*; **~ operator** *n* CONST maquinista de apisonadora *m*, operador de apisonadora *m*; **~ paint** *n* COLOUR, CONST pintura de rodillo *f*; **~ painting** *n* COLOUR, CONST pintura a rodillo *f*; **~ pallet** *n* TRANSP bandeja cilíndrica *f*, paleta cilíndrica *f*, pálet cilíndrico *m* (*AmL*); **~ pin** *n* PROD eje portarrodillo *m*; **~ printing** *n* PRINT estampado a máquina *f*, TEXTIL estampación con rodillos *f*; **~ and rotary cutting press** *n* PACK prensa cortadora rotativa *f*; **~-rusher** *n* AGRIC molino aplastador *m*; **~ setting** *n* TEXTIL reglaje del rodillo *m*; **~ shaft** *n* AUTO eje de rodillos *m*; **~ shoe** *n* PROD zapata de rodillo *f*; **~ tappet** *n* AUTO, VEH levantaválvulas de rodillos *m*; **~ timing chain** *n* AUTO cadena sincronizadora de rodillos *f*; **~ tool chest** *n* MECH ENG mango de herramienta con rodillos *m*; **~ transport** *n* CINEMAT, TRANSP transporte por rodillo *m*; **~ tray** *n* C&G bandeja del rodillo *f*; **~ weir** *n* WATER vertedero de rodillos *m*

rolling *n* CONST *of metalled roads* canto rodado *m*, grava *f*, rodamiento *m*, PROD *of metal* laminación *f*, WATER TRANSP *of ship* balance *m*; **~ bearing** *n* MECH ENG cojinete de bolas *m*, cojinete de rodillos *m*, cojinete de rulemán *m*; **~ bridge** *n* CONST puente corredizo *m*; **~ circle** *n* GEOM círculo generador *m*; **~ code band splitting** *n* TELECOM corte por rodadura de las bandas de código *m*; **~ door** *n* CONST puerta arrolladiza *f*; **~ fork** *n* AGRIC máquina cultivadora *f*; **~ friction** *n* PHYS rozamiento debido al rodamiento *m*; **~-friction coefficient** *n* PHYS coeficiente de rozamiento debido al rodamiento *m*; **~ furnace** *n* HEAT, PROD, THERMO horno basculante *m*; **~ hitch** *n* WATER TRANSP *knots* nudo de boza *m*; **~ landside** *n* AGRIC costanera giratoria *f*; **~ load** *n* CONST tren de cargas *m*; **~ mill** *n* MECH ENG, PROD *establishment* fábrica de laminación *f*, taller de laminación *m*, taller de láminas *m*, *for metal* laminador *m*, RAIL laminador *m*; **~-mill roll** *n* MECH ENG, PROD, RAIL cilindro de laminador *m*; **~-mill train** *n* MECH ENG, PROD, RAIL tren laminador *m*; **~ moment** *n* AIR TRANSP momento de balanceo *m*; **~ over** *n* PROD *founding* inversión *f*; **~ press** *n* CHEM TECH, PROD calandria *f*, prensa de cilindros *f*, prensa de rodillos *f*; **~ process** *n* C&G rolado *m*; **~ resistance** *n* VEH resistencia a la rodadura *f*; **~ shutter** *n* CONST cortina enrollable *f*; **~ stability** *n* AIR TRANSP *aircraft* estabilidad transversal *f*; **~ stock** *n* CONST, RAIL material móvil *m*, material rodante *m*; **~-stock label** *n* CONST, RAIL etiqueta para material móvil *f*

rolls *n pl* MECH ENG molino de cilindros *m*, tren laminador *m*

rollup: **~ door** *n* VEH puerta levadiza *f*

ROM *abbr* (*read-only memory*) COMP&DP, ELEC, ELEC ENG ROM (*memoria de sólo lectura*)

Roman: **~ arch** *n* CONST arco de medio punto *m*; **~ numeral** *n* MATH, PRINT número romano *m*; **~ type** *n* PRINT redondilla *f*

romeite *n* MINERAL romeíta *f*

rood *n* METR rood *m*

roof *n* COAL bóveda *f*, roca del techo *f*, CONST *of tunnel, cave* techumbre *f*, *top of building* techo *m*, *exterior upper covering of building* tejado *m*, MINE bóveda *f*, roca del techo *f*, PROD *of fire box* cielo *m*, RAIL, VEH techo *m*; **~-bolting drilling machine** *n* MINE máquina colocadora de pernos *f* (*Esp*), máquina colocadora de redondos *f* (*AmL*), máquina para el empernado del techo *f*; **~ frame** *n* CONST armazón del tejado *m*, estructura del tejado *f*; **~ light** *n* C&G claraboya *f*, luz de techo *f*; **~ pitch** *n* CONST *architecture* inclinación del tejado *f*, pendiente del tejado *f*; **~ plate** *n* CONST losa del techo *f*; **~ prism** *n* PHYS prisma triangular *m*; **~ rack** *n* AUTO, VEH baca *f*; **~-shielding plate** *n* NUCL placa protectora del techo *f*; **~ truss** *n* CONST armadura de cubierta *f*, par *m*

roofer *n* CONST *person* constructor de tejados *m*, techador *m*

roofer's: **~ hammer** *n* CONST martillo de techador *m*

roofing *n* CONST cubierta *f*, techado *m*; **~ felt** *n* CONST fieltro impermeable *m*

rooftop: **~ air-conditioning unit** *n* CONST, HEAT, REFRIG, THERMO acondicionador de techo *m*; **~ heliport** *n* AIR TRANSP helipuerto de azotea *m*

room *n* COAL anchurón *m* (*AmL*), cámara *f*, emplazamiento *m* (*Esp*), medida de carbón *f*, sala *f*, CONST cuarto *m*, espacio *m*, habitación *f*, pieza *f*, MINE anchurón *m* (*AmL*), cámara *f*, espacio *m*, sala *f*; **~ acoustics** *n pl* ACOUST acústica de salas *f*; **~ air-conditioning unit** *n* CONST, HEAT, REFRIG, THERMO acondicionador de habitaciones *m*; **~ temperature** *n* PACK, PHYS, THERMO temperatura ambiente *f*; **~-temperature setting adhesive** *n* PACK adhesivo que se fija a temperatura ambiente *m*; **~ thermostat** *n* REFRIG, THERMO termostato ambiente *m*, termostato de habitación *m*

root *n* C&G raíz *f*, COMP&DP base *f*, raíz *f*, CONST podedumbre *f*, MECH *motor vehicles* raíz *f*; **~ activity** *n* AGRIC actividad radicular *f*; **~ bead** *n* PETROL cordón de raíz *m*; **~-crop farm** *n* AGRIC explotación dedicada al cultivo de raíces y tubérculos *f*; **~-crop tractor** *n* AGRIC tractor para cultivos en línea *m*; **~ file system** *n* PROD sistema de ficheros de raíz *m*; **~ frequency deviation** *n* SPACE raíz cuadrada de frecuencia eficaz *f*; **~-mean-square** *n* (*RMS*) CONST, ELEC, ELECTRON, MATH, TELECOM media cuadrática *f*, raíz cuadrada media *f*; **~-mean-square current** *n* ELEC ENG corriente eficaz *f*; **~-mean-square deviation** ELEC, MATH desviación característica *f*, desviación media cuadrática *f*, desviación normal *f*, desviación típica *f*; **~-mean-square value** *n* CONST, OPT valor cuadrático medio *m*, valor efectivo *m*, valor eficaz *m*, PHYS raíz cuadrada del valor cuadrático medio *f*; **~-mean-square water level** *n* FUELLESS promedio cuadrático del nivel de agua *m*; **~ pass** *n* MECH *motor vehicles* cordón del fondo *m*, PETROL cordón de raíz *m*; **~ of weld** *n* CONST base de la soldadura *f*; **~ zone** *n* GEOL zona de raíces *f*

rooter *n* AGRIC escarificador *m*

rootstock n AGRIC patrón m

ROP abbr (rate of penetration) PETR TECH ROP (tasa de penetración)

rope n MECH cable m, cabo m, soga f, PAPER cuerda f, SAFE cuerda f, mecate m, soga f, TEXTIL cuerda f, WATER TRANSP cabo m, cordaje m, for rigging cabo de jarcia m; ~ **carrier** n PAPER cuerda para pasar la banda de papel en la sequería f; ~ **cleat** n MECH ENG abrazadera para cables f; ~ **dyeing** n COLOUR teñido en cuerda m; ~ **hauling** n COAL arrastre por cable m; ~ **marking** n TEXTIL marcado en cuerda m; ~ **skimmer** n MAR POLL rasera con maroma absorbente f, rasera de maroma continua f; ~**-type sling** n SAFE eslinga de cuerda f, estrobo de cuerda m; ~ **yarn** n TEXTIL hilo de cable m

ropeless: ~ **hoisting apparatus** n MINE máquina de extracción sin cables f

ropiness n FOOD viscosidad f

ro-ro[1] abbr (roll-on/roll-off) TRANSP, WATER TRANSP embarque por propulsión propia m

ro-ro[2]: ~ **depot** n TRANSP, WATER TRANSP depósito de cargas rodadas m; ~ **port** n TRANSP, WATER TRANSP puerto de transbordo rodado m; ~ **ship** n TRANSP, WATER TRANSP buque transportador de vehículos carreteros y vagones cargados m; ~ **system** n TRANSP, WATER TRANSP sistema de embarque y desembarque autopropulsado m; ~ **vessel** n TRANSP, WATER TRANSP buque de transbordo rodado m, buque rolón m

ROS abbr (residual-oil saturation) PETROL saturación de aceite residual f

rose n ELEC ENG alcachofa de toma f, WATER strainer at foot of pump alcachofa f; ~ **burner** n CONST gas quemador con varias salidas m; ~ **chafer** n AGRIC cultivo de raíces m

ROSE abbr (remote-operation service element) TELECOM elemento del servicio de operación remota m

rosette n C&G roseta f, PRINT adorno floral m, florón m

rosin n P&R esencia de trementina f, resina de trementina f

rot[1]: ~**-proof** adj PAPER resistente a la pudrición

rot[2] n AGRIC, CONST, WATER TRANSP in wood podredumbre f

rot[3] vt AGRIC, CONST, WATER TRANSP corromperse, pudrirse

rotameter n INSTR, LAB, PETR TECH, PHYS rotámetro m

rotary n AmE (cf roundabout BrE) AUTO, CONST, TRANSP, VEH glorieta f, rotonda f; ~ **air heater** n HEAT, THERMO calentador de aire giratorio m; ~ **amplifier** n ELEC ENG, ELECTRON amplificador giratorio m; ~ **bit** n PETR TECH barrena m (Esp), broca f, mecha f (AmL), trépano m (AmL); ~ **capacitor** n ELEC, ELEC ENG capacitor rotativo m, condensador rotativo m; ~ **cleaner** n AGRIC cernedor giratorio m; ~ **compressor** n MECH ENG, REFRIG, THERMO compresor rotativo m; ~**-compressor single shaft stationary** n MECH ENG compresor rotativo monoeje estacionario m; ~ **continuous-core drilling** n MINE sondeo continuo con extracción continua de muestras m; ~ **converter** n ELEC, ELEC ENG convertidor m, convertidor de potencia rotativo m, convertidor giratorio m, convertidor rotativo m, convertidor sincrónico m; ~ **crane** n CONST grúa giratoria f; ~ **current** n OCEAN corriente circular f; ~**-current armature** n ELEC, ELEC ENG generator armadura de corriente trifásica f; ~ **cutter** n PRINT

cuchilla giratoria f; ~ **cutting tool** n GAS herramienta cortadora giratoria f, herramienta cortadora rotatoria f; ~**-disc valve** n BrE AUTO, VEH válvula de disco rotatorio f; ~ **discharger** n ELEC spark, ELEC ENG descargador giratorio m, explosor giratorio m; ~**-disk valve** AmE see rotary-disc valve BrE; ~ **dividing table** n MECH ENG mesa divisoria giratoria f, mesa divisoria rotatoria f; ~ **drill** n COAL, CONST, MINE, PETR TECH, PETROL perforadora a rotación f; ~ **drilling** n COAL, MINE, PETR TECH, PETROL perforación rotativa f, sondeo rotativo m; ~**-drum feeder** n MECH ENG, TEXTIL alimentador de tambor rotativo m; ~ **dryer** n PROD secador rotativo m; ~ **engine** n AUTO, VEH motor Wankel m, motor rotativo m; ~ **evaporator** n INSTR, LAB rotavapor m; ~ **exchange** n TELECOM central rotativa f; ~ **feeder** n MECH ENG alimentador rotatorio m; ~ **feeder and collecting table** n PACK alimentador rotativo y mesa de recogida m; ~ **field** n ELEC, ELEC ENG campo magnético giratorio m; ~**-field converter** n ELEC, ELEC ENG convertidor de campo giratorio m; ~ **filling** n PACK sistema rotativo de llenado m; ~ **filter** n COAL, WATER filtro rotativo m; ~ **frequency-converter** n ELEC, ELEC ENG convertidor de frecuencia rotativo m; ~ **furnace** n C&G, COAL, HEAT, PROD, THERMO horno giratorio m; ~ **grate** n PROD parrilla giratoria f; ~ **heading machine** n COAL rozadora f, rozadora rotativa de galería de avance f; ~**-hearth kiln** n HEAT, THERMO horno con hogar giratorio m; ~ **hoe** n AGRIC azadón rotativo m, rotoazada f; ~ **hose** n PETR TECH manguera de lodo f; ~ **joint** n ELEC ENG junta rotativa f; ~ **kiln** n C&G, COAL, HEAT, PROD, THERMO horno giratorio m, horno rotativo m; ~ **knob** n ELEC ENG botón giratorio m; ~ **magazine** n PHOTO, SPACE chasis giratorio m; ~ **molding of fiber and rollercoat varnishing** AmE, ~ **moulding of fibre and rollercoat varnishing** BrE n PACK moldeado rotativo de fibras y barnizado m; ~ **movement** n CINEMAT movimiento giratorio m; ~ **orbital sander** n MECH ENG lijadora orbital rotatoria f; ~ **percussive masonry drill** n MECH ENG taladro de albañilería rotativo por percusión m, taladro de albañilería rotopercutiente m; ~**-piston engine** n AUTO motor de pistón rotativo m; ~**-piston meter** n GAS medidor de pistón giratorio m, medidor de pistón rotatorio m; ~ **plough** n BrE AGRIC arado rotativo m; ~ **plow** AmE see rotary plough BrE; ~ **pneumatic engine** n MECH ENG motor de aire comprimido rotativo m; ~ **potentiometer** n ELEC, ELEC ENG, INSTR potenciómetro giratorio m, potenciómetro rotativo m; ~ **printer** n PRINT maquinista de rotativa m; ~ **printing** n PRINT impresión en rotativa f; ~ **printing machine** n PRINT rotativa f; ~ **printing press** n PACK, PRINT prensa rotativa f; ~ **pump** n PHYS, WATER bomba de rotación f, bomba rotativa f; ~ **scraper** n AGRIC raspador giratorio m; ~ **screen** n COAL, CONST, MINE, PROD criba giratoria f, criba rotatoria f, rotocriba f; ~**-screen printing** n PRINT impresión serigráfica rotativa f; ~**-screw compressor** n PROD compresor de tornillos rotatorios m; ~ **seal** n REFRIG cierre rotativo m; ~ **selector switch** n ELECTRON conmutador selector rotativo m; ~ **shaft lip-type seal** n MECH ENG obturador para ejes en rotación m; ~ **shaft seal** n MECH ENG obturador para ejes en rotación m; ~**-shear blade** n MECH ENG cuchilla de tijera rotatoria f; ~ **slasher** n AGRIC cortadora rotativa f; ~ **subsoiler** n AGRIC subsolador rotativo *m*; ~ **switch** *n* CINEMAT, ELEC, ELEC ENG, PROD, TELECOM conjuntor rotatorio *m*, conmutador giratorio *m*, conmutador rotativo *m*, conmutador rotatorio *m*; ~ **system** *n* TELECOM sistema automático de conmutadores rotativos *m*, sistema conmutador rotatorio *m*; ~ **table** *n* MECH ENG, METR, PETR TECH, PETROL, PROD mesa rotativa *f*, mesa rotatoria *f*; ~**-table sandblast machine** *n* PROD *founding* chorreadora de arena de mesa rotatoria *f*; ~ **tidal current** *n* OCEAN corriente giratoria de marea *f*; ~ **tiller** *n* AGRIC cultivador rotativo *m*; ~ **transformer** *n* ELEC, ELEC ENG transformador rotatorio *m*; ~ **unit** *n* PRINT rotativa *f*; ~ **valve** *n* FUELLESS, HYDRAUL válvula giratoria *f*, válvula rotativa *f*; ~ **vane feeder** *n* MECH ENG *handling equipment* alimentador rotativo de paletas *m*; ~ **video head** *n* CINEMAT cabeza rotativo de vídeo *f*, TV cabeza rotativa de vídeo *f*; ~ **wafer switch** *n* ELEC, ELEC ENG conmutador de sectores rotatorio *m*; ~ **wall crane** *n* CONST grúa de pared rotatoria *f*; ~ **washer** *n* PROD lavador rotativo *m*; ~ **washing machine** *n* PROD lavadora rotatoria *f*; ~ **weed screen** *n* AGRIC cernedor rotativo *m*; ~**-wing aircraft** *n* AIR TRANSP avión de ala rotatoria *m*

rotatable: ~ **aerial** *n* *BrE* (*cf rotatable antenna AmE*) TELECOM, TV antena giratoria *f*, antena orientable *f*; ~ **antenna** *n* *AmE* (*cf rotatable aerial BrE*) TELECOM, TV antena giratoria *f*, antena orientable *f*; ~ **arm** *n* MAR POLL brazo girable *m*; ~ **nozzle** *n* SPACE boquilla giratoria *f*, tobera giratoria *f*; ~ **water jet** *n* TRANSP chorro de agua giratorio *m*

rotate *vt* COMP&DP girar

rotating: ~ **annulus** *n* FLUID anillo rotatorio *m*; ~**-annulus convection** *n* FLUID convección por anillo rotatorio *f*; ~**-anode tube** *n* CONST tubo de ánodo giratorio *m*; ~ **armature** *n* ELEC *generator* armadura giratoria *f*; ~ **beacon** *n* AIR TRANSP baliza giratoria *f*; ~ **bending test** *n* METALL prueba de flexión rotativa *f*; ~ **bowl** *n* C&G vasija rotatoria *f*; ~ **Couette flow** *n* FLUID flujo rotatorio de Couette *m*; ~**-crystal method** *n* RAD PHYS método del cristal giratorio *m*; ~ **drum** *n* CINEMAT, GEOPHYS tambor giratorio *m*; ~**-drum streak camera** *n* CINEMAT, PHOTO, TV cámara de tambor rotatorio para imágenes unidimensionales *f*; ~ **electrical machine** *n* ELEC, ELEC ENG máquina eléctrica de rotación *f*; ~ **field** *n* ELEC, ELEC ENG, PHYS, TELECOM campo giratorio *m*; ~**-field instrument** *n* ELEC, ELEC ENG, INSTR, PHYS, TELECOM instrumento de campo rotativo *m*, instrumento de campo rotatorio *m*; ~ **fluids** *n pl* FLUID fluidos rotatorios *m pl*; ~ **machine** *n* C&G máquina rotatoria *f*; ~ **mirror** *n* CINEMAT, INSTR, PHYS espejo giratorio *m*, espejo rotatorio *m*; ~**-mirror streak camera** *n* CINEMAT, PHOTO, TV cámara de espejo rotativo para imágenes unidimensionales *f*; ~ **part** *n* MECH ENG elemento giratorio *m*, pieza giratoria *f*; ~**-piston engine** *n* TRANSP motor de pistón giratorio *m*; ~ **prism** *n* OPT prisma giratorio *m*, prisma rotatorio *m*; ~ **shower** *n* PAPER rociador giratorio *m*; ~ **shutter** *n* CINEMAT, PHOTO, TV obturador rotativo *m*; ~ **speed** *n* PETR TECH velocidad de rotación *f*; ~ **sprayer** *n* WATER *boat building* aspersor giratorio *m*; ~ **system of out-of-balance masses** *n* MECH ENG sistema rotativo de desequilibrio de masas *m*; ~**-wing aircraft** *n* AIR TRANSP aparato de ala rotatoria *m*

rotation *n* AGRIC rotación de cultivos *f*, CHEM,

CRYSTALL, GEOM, OPT, PHYS, RAD PHYS rotación *f*, SPACE cambio *m*, giro *m*, rotación *f*; ~ **axis** *n* CRYSTALL eje de rotación *m*; ~ **of coordinate axes** *n* GEOM rotación de ejes coordenados *f*; ~ **firing** *n* MINE pega por rotación *f*, voladura por rotación *f*; ~ **photography** *n* CINEMAT fotografía de rotación *f*, fotografía de rotación *f*, CRYSTALL, PHOTO fotografía de rotación *f*; ~ **position sensing** *n* COMP&DP detección de posición de rotación *f*; ~ **spectrum** *n* RAD PHYS espectro de rotación *m*; ~ **speed** *n* AIR TRANSP, PETR TECH velocidad de rotación *f*, velocidad rotatoria *f*

rotational[1] *adj* GEN rotacional, rotativo

rotational[2]: ~ **compass** *n* MECH ENG compás rotacional *m*, compás rotativo *m*; ~ **delay** *n* COMP&DP, OPT demora rotacional *f*, retardo rotacional *m*, retraso rotacional *m*; ~ **elasticity** *n* MECH ENG elasticidad de torsión *f*; ~ **energy** *n* PROD energía rotacional *f*; ~ **inertia** *n* MECH ENG inercia de rotación *f*, inercia rotacional *f*; ~ **mold** *AmE*, ~ **mould** *BrE* *n* MECH ENG, PROD matriz rotativa *f*, molde rotativo *m*; ~ **quantum-number** *n* PHYS número cuántico rotacional *m*; ~ **spectrum** *n* PHYS espectro rotacional *m*; ~ **speed** *n* FUELLESS velocidad de rotación *f*; ~ **symmetry** *n* GEOM, MATH simetría de rotación *f*, simetría rotativa *f*; ~ **wave** *n* ACOUST onda rotacional *f*

rotatory: ~ **power** *n* PHYS poder de rotación *m*

rotavator *n* AGRIC arado rotativo *m*

rotenone *n* CHEM rotenona *f*

rothoffite *n* MINERAL rotofita *f*

rotogravure: ~ **printing** *n* P&R, PRINT impresión en huecograbado *f*

rotor *n* AIR TRANSP *of a helicopter*, AUTO rotor *m*, COAL rueda móvil *f*, rotor *m*, ELEC *generator*, ELEC ENG, PHYS, VEH rotor *m*; ~ **arm** *n* AUTO, VEH brazo del rotor *m*; ~ **blade** *n* AIR TRANSP *of a helicopter* pala de rotor *f*; ~ **diameter** *n* FUELLESS diámetro del rotor *m*; ~ **disc** *BrE*, ~ **disk** *AmE* *n* AIR TRANSP *of helicopter* disco del rotor *m*; ~ **efficiency** *n* AIR TRANSP eficiencia de rotor *f*; ~ **field** *n* ELEC *of a generator* campo rotórico *m*; ~ **head** *n* AIR TRANSP cabeza de rotor *f*; ~ **hub** *n* AIR TRANSP cubo de rotor *m*; ~ **inflow** *n* AIR TRANSP entrada de flujo del rotor *f*; ~ **lamination** *n* ELEC ENG laminación del inducido *f*; ~ **mast** *n* AIR TRANSP mástil de rotor *m*; ~ **overspeed** *n* AIR TRANSP sobrevelocidad del rotor *f*; ~ **plate** *n* ELEC ENG, TRANSP placa móvil *f*; ~ **radius** *n* AIR TRANSP radio del rotor *m*; ~ **shaft** *n* ELEC *of a generator* eje de rotor *m*; ~ **speed** *n* AIR TRANSP velocidad del rotor *f*; ~ **starter** *n* ELEC, ELEC ENG arrancador del rotor *m*; ~ **stream** *n* AIR TRANSP chorro del rotor *m*, corriente del rotor *f*, flujo del rotor *m*; ~ **thrust** *n* AIR TRANSP empuje del rotor *m*, tracción del rotor *f*; ~ **tip velocity** *n* AIR TRANSP velocidad circunferencial *f*, velocidad de las puntas de las palas del rotor *f*, velocidad periférica *f*; ~ **torque** *n* AIR TRANSP par del rotor *m*; ~ **weight** *n* FUELLESS peso del rotor *m*; ~ **winding** *n* ELEC, ELEC ENG devanado del inducido *m*, devanado rotórico *m*

rotoscope *vt* CINEMAT rotoscopio *m*

rotting *n* CONST *of timber* pudrición *f*

rouge *n* C&G cosmético de pulir *m*, PROD *chemistry* rojo de Inglaterra *m*, rojo de pulir *m*, óxido férrico finamente dividido *m*

rough[1]: ~**-forged** *adj* PROD forjado en tosco;

~-**grained** *adj* CONST granulado de áspero; ~-**hewn** *adj* CONST labrado áspero; ~-**machined** *adj* MECH maquinado con medidas aproximadas, maquinado en basto; ~-**rolled** *adj* PROD laminado en tosco; ~-**stamped** *adj* PROD estampado en tosco

rough²: ~ **anode** *n* ELEC ENG ánodo rígido *m*; ~-**capacity load table** *n* PROD tabla de cargas de capacidad bruta *f*; ~ **cast** *n* CONST revestimiento tosco *m*; ~ **cast gear** *n* PROD engranaje tosco de fundición *m*; ~ **casting** *n* CONST revestimiento basto *m*, PROD pieza bruta de fundición *f*; ~ **coal** *n* COAL, MINE hulla a granel *f*; ~ **cut** *n* CINEMAT montaje preliminar *m*, MECH ENG, PROD picadura basta *f*, picadura gruesa *f*, talla basta *f*, TV montaje preliminar *m*; ~-**cut capacity planing** *n* MECH ENG, PROD alisado de picadura basta *m*; ~-**cut planing** *n* MECH ENG, PROD, cepillado tosco *m*; ~ **cutting** *n* C&G corte burdo *m*; ~ **dressing** *n* CONST *of building stone* desbaste *m*; ~ **edge** *n* C&G borde burdo *m*; ~ **file** *n* MECH ENG lima basta *f*, lima gruesa *f*; ~ **grinding** *n* C&G esmerilado burdo *m*; ~ **grinding wheel** *n* MECH ENG muela abrasiva de desbastar *f*; ~ **landing** *n* AIR TRANSP aterrizaje violento *m*; ~-**pea coal** *n* COAL carbón granza a granel *m*; ~ **pigweed** *n* AGRIC yuyo colorado *m*; ~ **road** *n* AUTO, CONST, VEH carretera rústica *f*; ~-**rolled glazing** *n* C&G vidriado burdo rolado *m*; ~ **sea** *n* METEO, WATER TRANSP mar grueso *m*; ~ **surface** *n* MECH ENG superficie rugosa *f*, superficie áspera *f*; ~ **vacuum** *n* PHYS vacío aproximado *m*; ~ **weather** *n* METEO, WATER TRANSP borrasca *f*, tiempo borrascoso *m*; ~ **wood** *n* CONST madera rústica *f*

rough³: ~ **down** *vt* CONST *timber* cepillar

roughage *n* AGRIC forraje basto *m*

roughed: ~ **forging** *n* MECH ENG, PROD forja en tosco *f*

rougher *n* COAL, PROD fresadora para desbastar *f*, rastrillador *m*, tren de desbaste *m*

roughing *n* COAL, PROD desbastado *m*, desbaste *m*; ~-**down** *n* COAL, PROD desbaste *m*; ~-**down roll** *n* COAL, PROD cilindro desbastador *m*; ~ **mill** *n* PROD tren desbastador *m*; ~ **pass** *n* COAL, PROD *through rolls* paso de desbaste *m*, canal de desbaste *m*; ~ **roll** *n* PROD cilindro desbastador *m*; ~ **slot mill** *n* MECH ENG fresa de desbastar chaveteros *f*; ~ **tank** *n* WATER sedimentador desbastador *m*; ~ **tool** *n* MECH ENG cincel de debastar *m*, *lathe* herramienta de debastar *f*, herramienta gruesa *f*; ~ **wheel** *n* INSTR *for preliminary surfacing* rueda de desbaste *f*, PROD muela abrasiva de desbastar *f*

roughneck *n* PETR TECH, PETROL ayudante de perforación *m*, cuñero *m*, cuñero de perforación *m*, peón de perforación *m*

roughness *n* MECH, MECH ENG aspereza *f*, dureza *f*, irregularidad *f*, rugosidad *f*, PAPER rugosidad *f*; ~ **profile** *n* MECH, MECH ENG perfil de aspereza *m*; ~ **tester** *n* PAPER aparato para medir la rugosidad *m*

roulette *n* GEOM ruleta *f*

round¹: ~-**nosed** *adj* MECH ENG de punta redonda

round² *n* CONST *of ladder* peldaño *m*, GEOL voladura *f*, MILIT descarga *f*, andanada *f*, disparo completo *m*, salva *f*, MINE carga completa de mineral *f*, barrote redondo *m*, serie de barrenos *f*, pega *f*, disparo completo *m*, WATER TRANSP *of beam* brusca *f*; ~ **of ammunition** *n* MILIT disparo completo *m*; ~ **bale** *n* AGRIC fardo cilíndrico *m*; ~-**bottomed flask** *n* LAB matraz de fondo redondo *m*; ~ **cell** *n* PRINT celda

circular *f*; ~ **distance piece** *n* MECH ENG pieza de separación redonda *f*, separador redondo *m*; ~-**edge corner smoother** *n* PROD *moulder's tool* alisador de escuadra de bordes redondos *m*; ~-**edge file** *n* MECH ENG lima de cantos redondeados *f*; ~-**edge milling cutter** *n* MECH ENG fresa de cantos redondeados *f*; ~-**ended pouch** *n* PACK bolsa de fondo redondo *f*; ~-**faced pulley** *n* MECH ENG polea bombeada *f*; ~ **file** *n* MECH ENG lima cilíndrica *f*, limatón *f*; ~-**head bolt** *n* MECH ENG perno de cabeza hemisférica *m*, perno de cabeza redonda *m*, perno de cabeza redondeada *m*, perno de cabeza semiesférica *m*; ~-**headed bolt** *n* MECH ENG perno de cabeza hemisférica *m*, perno de cabeza redonda *m*, perno de cabeza redondeada *m*, perno de cabeza semiesférica *m*; ~-**headed screw** *n* MECH ENG tornillo con cabeza gota de cebo *m*, tornillo de cabeza redonda *m*, tornillo de cabeza semiesférica *m*; ~-**hole perforating** *n* PRINT perforación redonda *f*; ~-**nose chisel** *n* MECH ENG cincel de pico redondo *m*, formón de punta redonda *m*; ~-**nose tool** *n* MECH ENG herramienta de punta redonda *f*; ~-**nosed cold chisel** *n* MECH ENG cortafríos de pico redondo *m*; ~-**nosed pliers** *n pl* MECH, MECH ENG, PROD alicates de boca redonda *m pl*, alicates de punta redonda *m pl*; ~ **nut** *n* MECH ENG tuerca cilíndrica *f*; ~ **pinch plate** *n* PROD chapa de pliegues redondos *f*; ~ **punch with conical head** *n* MECH ENG sacabocados cilíndrico con cabeza cónica *m*; ~-**section coil spring** *n* MECH ENG sector redondo del muelle en espiral *m*, sector redondo del muelle helicoidal *m*; ~ **stern** *n* WATER TRANSP popa redonda *f*; ~ **trip** *n* PETR TECH, PETROL carrera completa *f*, carrera de sacada y bajada *f*, entrada y salida de la tubería de revestimiento *f*, SPACE, TRANSP, WATER TRANSP viaje de ida y vuelta *m*; ~ **window** *n* ACOUST ventana redonda *f*

round³: ~ **turn and two half hitches** *phr* WATER TRANSP vuelta redonda y medio cote doble

round⁴ *vt* COMP&DP, MATH, PROD redondear, PROD contornear, *to make cylindrical* redondear, WATER TRANSP *cape* doblar; ~ **down** *vt* COMP&DP, MATH, PROD redondear por defecto; ~ **off** *vt* COMP&DP, MATH, PROD redondear; ~ **up** *vt* COMP&DP, MATH, PROD redondear por exceso

roundabout *n BrE* (*cf rotary AmE, cf traffic circle AmE*) AUTO, CONST, TRANSP, VEH glorieta *f*, rotonda *f*

rounded: ~-**approach orifice** *n* HYDRAUL orificio de entrada redondeada *m*; ~ **back** *n* PRINT lomo redondeado *m*; ~ **edge** *n* C&G borde redondeado *m*

rounding *n* COMP&DP, MATH, PRINT, PROD redondeo *m*; ~ **and backing** *n* PRINT redondeo y enlomado *m*; ~ **and binding** *n* PRINT redondeo y encuadernación *m*; ~ **code** *n* PROD código de redondeo *m*; ~ **error** *n* COMP&DP, MATH, PROD error de redondeo *m*; ~ **machine** *n* PROD máquina para redondear *m*; ~ **pulley** *n* MECH ENG polea redonda *f*; ~ **wooden rollers** *n pl* PROD *lathe* cilindrado de rodillos de madera *m*

roundness *n* GEOL redondeamiento *m*, redondez *f*; ~-**measuring instrument** *n* INSTR, METR instrumento de medida esférica *m*

roustabout *n* PETR TECH limpiador *m*, operario no especializado *m*, peón de patio *m*

route *n* AIR TRANSP, COMP&DP ruta *f*, RAIL itinerario *m*, recorrido *m*, TELECOM arteria *f*, itinerario *m*, línea *f*, ruta *f*, trayecto *m*, trayectoria *f*, trazado *m*, vía *f*,

WATER TRANSP *commercial, mercantile* derrota *f*, itinerario *m*, ruta *f*; **~ description** *n* AIR TRANSP, TRANSP, WATER TRANSP descripción de ruta *f*; **~-familiarization flight** *n* AIR TRANSP vuelo de familiarización de ruta *m*; **~ guidance by radio** *n* TRANSP derrotero por radio *m*; **~ licence** *n* BrE AIR TRANSP licencia de ruta *f*; **~ license** *AmE see route licence BrE*; **~ locking** *n* RAIL enclavamiento del itinerario *m*; **~ sheet** *n* PROD hoja de ruta *f*

router *n* COMP&DP encaminador *m*, MECH ENG *of centre bit* buriladora *f*, encaminador *m*

routine *n* COMP&DP rutina *f*; **~ analysis** *n* COMP&DP, QUALITY *of quantitative data* análisis rutinario *m*; **~ inspection** *n* AIR TRANSP inspección rutinaria *f*

routing *n* COMP&DP encaminamiento *m*, enrutamiento *m*, PROD circulación de los materiales *f*, TELECOM curso *m*, despacho *m*, encaminamiento *m*, trazado *m*, arteria *f*, línea *f*, vía *f*; **~ address** *n* TELECOM dirección de encaminamiento *f*; **~ block** *n* PRINT bloque de fresado *m*; **~ chart** *n* WATER TRANSP *navigation* carta de arrumbamiento *f*; **~ code for part-load traffic** *n* RAIL hoja de ruta para el tráfico de carga parcial *f*; **~ control** *n* TELECOM control de encaminamiento *m*; **~ indicator** *n* (*RI*) COMP&DP, TELECOM indicador de encaminamiento *m*, indicador de radar *m*, indicador de ruta *m*; **~ information** *n* COMP&DP, TELECOM información de encaminamiento *f*, información sobre enrutamiento *f*; **~ list** *n* PROD lista de operaciones *f*; **~ machine** *n* MECH ENG acanaladora *f*, ranuradora *f*, recanteadora de chapa *f*; **~ system** *n* WATER TRANSP *navigation* organización del tráfico marítimo *f*, sistema de la organización del tráfico marítimo *m*

rove *n* TEXTIL madeja *f*, torzal *m*

rover *n* SPACE blanco *m*, blanco colocado a una distancia alejada *m*

roving *n* C&G arqueado *m*, P&R fibra continua *f*, hebra *f*, TEXTIL mecha *f*; **~ dyeing** *n* TEXTIL tintura de mechas *f*; **~ frame** *n* TEXTIL mechera *f*, vaivén *m*

row[1] *n* COMP&DP fila *f*, hilera *f*; **~-binder** *n* AGRIC segadora de cultivos en líneas *f*; **~ crop** *n* AGRIC cultivo en líneas separadas *m*; **~-crop cultivator** *n* AGRIC cultivador en hileras *m*; **~-crop seeder** *n* AGRIC sembradora para cultivos en hilera *f*; **~ of piles** *n* COAL serie de pilotes *f*; **~ pitch** *n* COMP&DP grado de separación entre filas *m*, interlínea *f*, paso longitudinal *m*

row[2] *vi* WATER TRANSP bogar, remar

rower *n* AGRIC hilerador *m*

Rowland: **~ circle** *n* PHYS círculo de Rowland *m*; **~'s experiment** *n* PHYS experimento de Rowland *m*; **~ mounting** *n* PHYS montaje de Rowland *m*

rowlock *n* BrE (*cf oarlock AmE*) WATER TRANSP *boat fitting* chumacera *f*, chumacera de horquilla *f*, escalamera *f*

royalty *n* PETR TECH derechos de licencia de explotación *m pl*, gastos de licencia de explotación *m pl*

RP *abbr* (*regional processor*) TELECOM procesador regional *m*

RPS *abbr* (*reactor protection system*) NUCL RPS (*sistema de protección del reactor*)

RS[1] *abbr* (*record separator*) COMP&DP separador de registros *m*

RS[2]: **~ flip-flop** *n* CONST interruptor de seguridad *m*

RSU *abbr* (*remote-switching unit*) TELECOM, TV unidad de teleconmutación *f*

RT *abbr* AIR TRANSP, MILIT, TRANSP, WATER TRANSP (*radar tracking*) seguimiento con radar *m*, seguimiento por radar *m*, TELECOM, TRANSP, WATER TRANSP (*radiotelephony*) RT (*radiotelefonía*)

RTC *abbr* (*road tank road*) TRANSP camión-cisterna *m*

RTD[1] *abbr* (*real-time data*) COMP&DP, ELECTRON, PROD, TELECOM datos en tiempo real

RTD[2]: **~ input terminal** *n* PROD terminal de entrada de datos en tiempo real *m*; **~ output terminal** *n* PROD terminal de salida de datos en tiempo real *m*

RTM *abbr* (*reference test method*) OPT, TELECOM método de prueba de referencia *m*

RTOL: **~ aircraft** *n* (*reduced take-off and landing aircraft*) AIR TRANSP avión de despegue y aterrizaje reducido *m*

RTS *abbr* RAIL (*rapid-transit system*) sistema de circulación rápida *m*, sistema de transporte rápido *m*, TELECOM (*reliable transfer server*) portador de transferencias fiable *m*

RU *abbr* (*remote unit*) COMP&DP, TELECOM, TV unidad remota *f*

Ru *abbr* (*ruthenium*) CHEM Ru (*rutenio*)

rub[1]: **~ bar cylinder** *n* AGRIC cilindro de listones *m*

rub[2]: **~ down** *vt* PROD *surface with emery cloth* pulimentar; **~ the rust off** *vt* PROD desoxidar por frote

rubber[1]: **~-coated** *adj* COATINGS, P&R revestido de caucho; **~-covered** *adj* COATINGS, P&R recubierto de caucho; **~-lined** *adj* COATINGS, P&R forrado de caucho

rubber[2] *n* CHEM caucho *m*, P&R caucho *m*, goma elástica *f*, PRINT caucho *m*; **~ belting** *n* MECH ENG, P&R correaje de goma *m*, correas de transmisión de caucho *f pl*; **~ blanket** *n* P&R, PRINT mantilla de caucho *f*; **~ boat** *n* P&R, WATER TRANSP bote de caucho *m*, bote de goma *m*; **~ boots** *n pl* P&R botas de goma *f pl*; **~ buffer** *n* MECH ENG *die set*, P&R amortiguador de caucho *m*; **~ bulb** *n* LAB, P&R bulbo de caucho *m* (*AmL*), pera de caucho *f* (*Esp*); **~ cable** *n* ELEC, ELEC ENG, P&R cable con aislamiento de caucho *m*; **~ coating** *n* COATINGS, P&R revestimiento de caucho *m*; **~ dinghy** *n* MILIT, P&R balsa de caucho *f*, chinchorro de caucho *m*, chinchorro de goma *m*, WATER TRANSP chinchorro de caucho *m*, chinchorro de goma *m*, balsa de caucho *f*; **~ engine mounting** *n* AUTO, P&R, VEH soporte de goma del motor *m*; **~ extruder** *n* MECH ENG, P&R extrusor de caucho *m*; **~ gloves** *n pl* P&R, SAFE *circuit* guantes de caucho *m pl*, guantes de goma *m pl*, guantes de hule *m pl*; **~ hose for steam** *n* MECH ENG, P&R manguera de caucho para vapor *f*; **~-insulated cable** *n* COATINGS, ELEC, ELEC ENG, P&R cable aislado por caucho *m*; **~ insulation** *n* COATINGS, ELEC, ELEC ENG, P&R aislamiento de caucho *m*, aislante de caucho *m*; **~ latex** *n* P&R látex de caucho *m*; **~ lining** *n* P&R, SAFE revestimiento de caucho *m*; **~ mark** *n* PAPER filigrana *f*; **~ mold** *AmE*, **~ mould** *BrE n* MECH ENG, P&R molde de caucho *m*; **~ mounting** *n* VEH montaje sobre tacos elásticos *m*; **~ number** *n* CINEMAT número de caucho *m*; **~ pad** *n* AUTO, P&R taco de goma *m*; **~ squeegee** *n* CINEMAT escurridor de caucho *m*; **~ stopper** *n* LAB, P&R tapón de caucho *m* (*Esp*), tapón de hule *m* (*AmL*); **~ suction hose** *n* P&R, WATER manguera de succión de caucho *f*; **~ tip** *n* CINEMAT, PHOTO *for cable* punta de caucho *f*; **~-tired roller** *AmE see rubber-tyred roller BrE*; **~ tubing** *n*

LAB, P&R manguera *f*, tubo de caucho *m*; **~-tyred roller** *n BrE* CONST apisonadora de neumáticos *f*; **~ varnish** *n* COATINGS, P&R barniz de caucho *m*; **~ weather seal** *n* VEH junta de estanqueidad de goma *f*

rubberize *vt* COATINGS, P&R engomar, impregnar de caucho

rubberized[1] *adj* COATINGS, P&R engomado, impregnado de caucho

rubberized[2]: **~ cloth** *n* COATINGS, P&R paño engomado *m*

rubberizing *n* COATINGS, P&R impregnación *f*

rubbing: **~-off of rust** *n* PROD desoxidación por frote *f*; **~ strake** *n* WATER TRANSP verduguillo *m*; **~ surface** *n* PROD superficie de frotamiento *f*, superficie de rozamiento *f*

rubbish *n BrE* (*cf garbage AmE*) NUCL basura *f*, PACK, PROD basura *f*, desechos *m pl*, desperdicios *m pl*, despojos *m pl*, residuos *m pl*, RECYCL basura *f*, desechos *m pl*, desperdicios *m pl*, despojos *m pl*, escombros *m pl*, residuos *m pl*, SAFE basura *f*; **~ bag** *n BrE* (*cf garbage bag AmE*) PACK bolsa de basura *f*; **~ chute** *n BrE* (*cf garbage chute AmE*) RECYCL colector de basura *m*, vertedero de basura *m*; **~ pulley** *n* MECH ENG polea para escombros *f*; **~ wheel** *n* MECH ENG rueda para escombros *f*

rubble *n* CONST *for building* escombro *m*, piedra de machaqueo *f*, piedra machacada *f*, GEOL detritos *m pl*, material detrítico *m*, detritus *m*, PETROL ripio *m*; **~ masonry** *n* CONST mampostería ordinaria *f*; **~ stone** *n* CONST *for building* piedra en bruto *f*, piedra sin labrar *f*

rubbly *adj* CONST de cascotes, tosco

rubellite *n* MINERAL rubelita *f*, turmalina roja *f*

ruberythric *adj* CHEM ruberítrico

rubicelle *n* MINERAL espinela rojo-amarillenta *f*

rubidium *n* (*Rb*) CHEM rubidio *m* (*Rb*)

ruby *n* CONST, GEOL, MINERAL rubí *m*; **~-crystal laser** *n* ELECTRON, RAD PHYS láser de cristal de rubí *m*; **~ laser** *n* ELECTRON, RAD PHYS láser de rubí *m*

rudaceous: **~ rocks** *n pl* GEOL rocas rudíticas *f pl*

rudder *n* AIR TRANSP, PHYS, WATER TRANSP timón *m*, timón de dirección *m*; **~-angle indicator** *n* AIR TRANSP, PHYS, WATER TRANSP axiómetro *m*; **~ bar** *n* AIR TRANSP, WATER TRANSP barra del timón de dirección *f*; **~ brace** *n* AIR TRANSP, WATER TRANSP hembra del timón *f*; **~ control** *n* AIR TRANSP, WATER TRANSP control del timón de dirección *m*; **~ pedal** *n* AIR TRANSP, WATER TRANSP pedal del timón de dirección *m*; **~ plane** *n* WATER TRANSP *shipbuilding* azafrán *m*, pala del timón *f*; **~ post** *n* AIR TRANSP poste del timón de dirección *m*, WATER TRANSP codaste *m*; **~-power unit** *n* AIR TRANSP, WATER TRANSP unidad de fuerza del timón de dirección *f*; **~ quadrant** *n* AIR TRANSP, WATER TRANSP sector del timón *m*; **~ travel** *n* AIR TRANSP, WATER TRANSP recorrido del timón de dirección *m*; **~ trim** *n* AIR TRANSP, WATER TRANSP reglaje del timón de dirección *m*; **~-trim light** *n* AIR TRANSP luz del regulador del timón de dirección *f*; **~ trunk** *n* WATER TRANSP *shipbuilding* bocina de la limera *f*

rudites *n pl* GEOL ruditas *f pl*

ruffle *n* TEXTIL volante *m*

rugosity *n* PETROL rugosidad *f*

rule[1] *n* INSTR, MECH ENG cartabón *m*, regla graduada *f*,

PRINT filete *m*; **~ base** *n* COMP&DP fundamento de la norma *m*

rule[2] *vt* PRINT delinear

ruler *n* GEOM regla *f*

rules *n pl* MECH ENG, PROD, SAFE normas *f pl*; **~ of the air** *n pl* AIR TRANSP reglamentos del aire *m pl*

ruling *n* MECH ENG decisión *f*, rayado *m*

rumble *n* ACOUST vibración de baja frecuencia *f*, AUTO golpeteo del motor *m*, picado de las bielas *m*, ronquido *m*, VEH golpeteo del motor *m*; **~ seat** *n* AUTO, VEH asiento trasero descubierto *m*

rumbler *n* PROD *founding* tonel desarenador *m*

rumbling *n* MINE ruido sondeo *m* (*Esp*), subterráneo *m* (*AmL*)

rumen *n* AGRIC rumen *m*

run[1] *n* COMP&DP *process* ejecución *f*, *sequence* pasada *f*, vuelta *f*, HYDROL *streamlet* riachuelo *m*, MECH ENG carrera *f*, período de marcha continua *m*, recorrido *m*, sección *f*, tramo *m*, movimiento *m*, pasada *f*, ciclo *m*, curso *m*, funcionamiento *m*, marcha *f*, MINE vena *f* (*AmL*), rumbo del filón *m* (*Esp*), OCEAN remonte *m*, arribazón *f*, PROD *of blast furnace* campaña *f*; **~ bearing** *n* AUTO cojinete ablandado *m*; **~ color** *AmE*, **~ colour** *BrE n* COLOUR color superpuesto *m*; **~ current limit** *n* PROD límite corriente de ciclo *m*; **~ distance** *n* WATER TRANSP *navigation* distancia recorrida *f*; **~ of ground** *n* MINE corrimiento de tierras *m*, derrumbamiento de tierras *m*, desplome del terreno *m*, desprendimiento de tierras *m*, hundimiento de tierras *m*; **~ indicator** *n* PROD indicador de marcha *m*; **~ of mine** *n* COAL mineral bruto *m*, producto bruto extraído de la mina *m*, material bruto *m*; **~ mode** *n* PROD modo de marcha *m*; **~ number** *n* TEXTIL número de carreras *m*; **~-of-mine coal** *n* MINE carbón bruto *m*, carbón todo en uno *m* (*AmL*), carbón todouno *m* (*Esp*); **~-of-river scheme** *n* FUELLESS, HYDRAUL proyecto de energía sin almacenamiento *m*; **~-of-river station** *n* FUELLESS, HYDRAUL instalación de energía sin almacenamiento *f*; **~-out leader** *n* CINEMAT guía de fin de cinta *f*; **~-out signal** *n* CINEMAT señal de fin de cinta *f*; **~ of sluices** *n* WATER esclusaje *m*; **~ time** *n* COMP&DP, PROD período de ejecución *m*, tiempo de ejecución *m*, tiempo de pasada *m*; **~ time error** *n* COMP&DP, PROD error de período de ejecución *m*; **~-time output** *n* COMP&DP salida de tiempo de ejecución *f*, salida de tiempo de pasada *f*; **~-up area** *n* AIR TRANSP *airport* zona de embalamiento *f*, zona de recorrido *f*, *engine* calentamiento *m*, funcionamiento *m*

run[2] *vt* CINEMAT accionar, poner en funcionamiento, CONST *machinery* manejar, *moulding, bead on joint* vaciar, ELEC *solder* soldar, MECH ENG recorrer, correr, trazar, manejar, tender, girar, *load* accionar, PROD *business* dirigir, *machinery* manipular, explotar, hacer funcionar, accionar, tender, utilizar, manejar, *programmes* ejecutar, *eliquated metals* colar; **~ back** *vt* PRINT pasar texto a la línea anterior; **~ down** *vt* WATER TRANSP *ship* abordar accidentalmente, embestir deliberadamente; **~ in** *vt* VEH hacer funcionar, poner en marcha, rodar; **~ off** *vt* PROD *metal from furnace* colar; **~ through** *vt* HYDROL atravesar

run[3]: **~ off** *vti* WATER *water from tank* escaparse, vaciar

run[4] *vi* MECH ENG derramarse, derretirse, desplazarse, verterse, MINE derrumbarse, explotar, PROD *colours* desteñirse, *traffic* circular, WATER TRANSP *of ship* gobernar; **~ aground** *vi* OCEAN, WATER TRANSP embarrancar, encallar, varar; ~ **ashore** *vi* OCEAN, WATER TRANSP embarrancar, encallar, varar, zabordar; ~ **before the wind** *vi* WATER TRANSP navegar con el viento a un largo; ~ **down** *vi* HYDROL *water* correr, PRINT pasar a la línea siguiente; ~ **dry** *vi* HYDROL, OCEAN, WATER agotarse, secarse; ~ **hot** *vi* MECH ENG calentarse; ~ **light** *vi* MECH ENG marchar en vacío; ~ **off** *vi* AIR TRANSP descarrilar, salirse de; ~ **on** *vi* PRINT componer continuamente; ~ **on no load** *vi* MECH ENG funcionar en vacío; ~ **out** *vi* WATER *liquid* derramarse, escurrirse, salirse; ~ **out of true** *vi* MECH ENG ovalizar; ~ **out of the vertical** *vi* MECH ENG salirse de la vertical; ~ **over** *vi* WATER rebosar; ~ **to waste** *vi* HYDROL perderse; ~ **under load** *vi* MECH ENG funcionar en carga, marchar en carga

runaway[1] *adj* RAIL incontrolado

runaway[2]: ~ **car** *n* AmE (*cf runaway wagon BrE*) RAIL vagón incontrolado *m*, vagón que se ha cortado de un tren en marcha *m*; ~ **speed** *n* FUELLESS *turbines* velocidad de embalamiento *f*; ~ **wagon** *n* BrE (*cf runaway car AmE*) RAIL vagón incontrolado *m*, vagón que se ha cortado de un tren en marcha *m*

rung *n* CONST, PROD escalón *m*, peldaño *m*

runnability *n* PAPER paso de la banda sin problemas *m*, paso del papel sin problemas *m*

runner *n* AGRIC abresurcos *m*, FUELLESS *turbines* rodete *m*, HYDRAUL rueda de paletas *f*, MECH guía de deslizamiento *f*, rodillo de rodadura *m*, polea fija *f*, carro transversal *m*, polea guía *f*, MECH ENG aparejo de motón movible *m*, patín *m*, corredera *f*, rotor *m*, rueda intermedia *f*, polea fija *f*, cuadernal móvil *m*, polea guía *f*, rodete *m*, rueda parásita *f*, PROD rodete *m*, *foundry* reguera *f*, cavidad que se deja en un molde para sacar probeta *f*, canal de colada *m*, polea guía *f*, rodillo de rodadura *m*, rueda de paletas *f*, bebedero *m*, WATER TRANSP *running rigging* aparejo de fuerza de un solo motón *m*; ~ **basin** *n* PROD *founding* piso de colada *m*; ~ **blade** *n* FUELLESS *turbines*, HYDRAUL paleta de rotor *f*, paleta del rodete *f*, paleta móvil *f*, paleta receptora *f*; ~ **pin** *n* PROD barra para romper el tapón de la piquera *f*; ~ **stick** *n* PROD mandril de colada *m*; ~ **vane** *n* HYDRAUL paleta móvil *f*, álabe del rodete *m*

runnerless: ~ **mold plate** *AmE*, ~ **mould plate** *BrE n* MECH ENG placa matriz sin bebedero *f*, placa matriz sin canal de colada *f*

running *n* COMP&DP ejecución *f*, proceso *m*, CONST *line* trazado *m*, MECH ENG funcionamiento *m*, marcha *f*, P&R corrimiento *m*, deslizamiento *m*, PAPER, TEXTIL funcionamiento *m*; ~ **block** *n* MECH ENG polea móvil *f*; ~ **bridge** *n* CONST puente de estribo *m*; ~ **brook** *n* GEOL, HYDROL arroyo en movimiento *m*; ~ **costs** *n pl* MECH ENG, PAPER, PROD, TEXTIL costes de funcionamiento *m pl*; ~-**down cutter** *n* MECH ENG fresa hueca *f*; ~ **end** *n* MECH ENG *of tackle* parte móvil *f*; ~ **fit** *n* MECH ajuste corredizo *m*, MECH ENG ajuste corredizo *m*, ajuste de deslizamiento *m*, ajuste deslizante *m*, ajuste suelto *m*; ~ **fix** *n* WATER TRANSP *navigation* situación por dos marcaciones sucesivas *f*, situación por marcaciones sucesivas *f*; ~ **foot** *n* METR pie de rodadura *m*; ~ **gate** *n* PROD *founding* agujero de colada *m*, bebedero *m*; ~ **gear** *n* MECH ENG aparato de rodadura *m*, tren de rodaje *m*, tren rodante *m*, WATER TRANSP *engine* mecanismo móvil *m*; ~ **ground** *n* COAL terreno movedizo *m*; ~-**in** *n* AUTO rodaje *m*, MECH ENG puesta en marcha *f*; ~ **jig** *n* COAL criba de

escurrido *f*; ~ **light** *n* RAIL luz de funcionamiento *f*, luz indicadora de funcionamiento sin carga *f*, MECH ENG luz indicadora de funcionamiento *f*, luz de marcha *f*; ~ **mold** *AmE*, ~ **mould** *BrE n* PROD *pouring* molde que pierde por las grietas *m*; ~-**off over the surface** *n* HYDROL recorrido del agua en superficie *m*; ~ **on no load** *n* MECH ENG funcionamiento en vacío *m*, marcha en vacío *f*; ~ **on overload** *n* MECH ENG funcionamiento en sobrecarga *m*, marcha en sobrecarga *f*; ~ **on wrong line** *n* RAIL circulación a contravía *f*; ~ **rail** *n* MECH ENG, RAIL carril de la vía *m*, carril de translación *m*; ~ **rigging** *n* WATER TRANSP jarcia de labor *f*, jarcia móvil *f*; ~ **sand** *n* COAL, HYDROL, OCEAN arena fluyente *f*, arena movediza *f*; ~ **soil** *n* COAL terreno movedizo *m*; ~ **speed** *n* TRANSP velocidad de marcha *f*; ~ **surface** *n* RAIL superficie de rodadura *f*, superficie ondulada *f*; ~ **test** *n* MECH ENG prueba de funcionamiento *f*; ~ **time** *n* C&G tiempo de operación *m*, CINEMAT duración *f*, TRANSP duración de funcionamiento *f*, tiempo de funcionamiento *m*; ~ **title** *n* PRINT título repetido *m*; ~ **torque** *n* PROD par motor de servicio *m*; ~ **trap** *n* CONST *plumbing* sifón en U *m*, válvula corredera *f*; ~ **under load** *n* MECH ENG funcionamiento con carga *m*; ~ **wheel** *n* MECH ENG rueda de traslación *f*

runoff *n* AGRIC escorrentía *f*, AIR TRANSP descarrilamiento *m*, CONST derrame *m*, desagüe *m*, FUELLESS, HYDROL, MAR POLL, POLL derrame *m*, escurrimiento *m*, recorrido *m*, WATER aflujo *m*, derrame *m*, escape *m*, escorrentía *f*, escurrimiento *m*, recorrido *m*; ~ **coefficient** *n* CONST coeficiente de desagüe *m*, HYDROL, MAR POLL, POLL, WATER coeficiente de escorrentía *m*, coeficiente de escurrimiento *m*

runout *n* PROD carrera *f*, *axes* descentramiento *m*, *from mould, furnace* escape de metal fundido *m*

runway *n* AIR TRANSP pista *f*, MECH ENG carrilera *f*; ~ **alignment** *n* AIR TRANSP orientación de pista *f*; ~-**alignment indicator** *n* AIR TRANSP indicador de orientación de pista *m*; ~ **basic length** *n* AIR TRANSP longitud básica de pista *f*; ~ **centerline** *AmE see runway centreline BrE*; ~-**centerline light** *AmE see runway-centreline light BrE*; ~-**centerline marking** *AmE see runway-centreline marking BrE*; ~ **centreline** *n BrE* AIR TRANSP eje de la pista *m*, línea central de la pista *f*; ~-**centreline light** *n BrE* AIR TRANSP luz de la línea central de la pista *f*, luz del eje de la pista *f*; ~-**centreline marking** *n BrE* AIR TRANSP balizado del eje de la pista *m*, marcado de la línea central de la pista *m*, marcaje del eje de la pista *m*; ~ **crossing light** *n* AIR TRANSP luz de cruce de pista *f*; ~ **designator** *n* AIR TRANSP designador de pista *m*; ~-**end light** *n* AIR TRANSP luz de final de pista *f*; ~-**end safety area** *n* AIR TRANSP zona de seguridad de final de pista *f*; ~ **gradient** *n* AIR TRANSP inclinación de pista *f*; ~ **in use** *n BrE* (*cf active runway AmE*) AIR TRANSP pista en activo *f*, pista en servicio *f*; ~ **number** *n* AIR TRANSP número de pista *m*; ~ **threshold** *n* AIR TRANSP umbral de pista *m*; ~-**threshold marking** *n* AIR TRANSP balizaje del umbral de pista *m*; ~ **touchdown zone light** *n* AIR TRANSP luces de la zona de contacto con la pista *f pl*; ~ **visual range** *n* AIR TRANSP alcance visual de pista *m*

rupture[1] *n* CHEM *of bond*, METALL rotura *f*, ruptura *f*; ~ **member** *n* REFRIG dispositivo de ruptura *m*; ~ **strength** *n* METALL resistencia a la rotura *f*

rupture^2 *vt* CHEM *bond*, METALL romper
rural: ~ **automatic exchange** *n* TELECOM central automática rural *f*; ~ **district** *n* ELEC ENG distrito rural *m*; ~ **exchange** *n* TELECOM central rural *f*; ~ **network** *n* TELECOM red rural *f*; ~ **sector** *n* AGRIC agro *m*; ~ **switch** *n* TELECOM conmutador rural *m*; ~ **water supply** *n* AGRIC, HYDROL, WATER abastecimiento de agua rural *m*
rush *n* CONST junquillo *m*, torrente *m*; ~ **of air** *n* MINE aflujo de aire *m*; ~ **hour** *n* AUTO, RAIL, TRANSP *traffic* hora punta *f*; ~~**hour factor** *n* RAIL, TRANSP *traffic* factor hora punta *m*; ~~**hour traffic** *n* RAIL, TRANSP tráfico hora punta *m*; ~ **order** *n* PRINT orden urgente *f*
rushes *n pl* CINEMAT, TV copión *m*
Russell-Saunders: ~ **coupling** *n* PHYS acoplamiento de Russell-Saunders *m*
Russian: ~ **thistle** *n* AGRIC cardo ruso *m*
rust *n* AGRIC roya *f*, AUTO, CHEM, FOOD, MECH, VEH, WATER TRANSP herrumbre *f*, oxidación *f*, óxido *m*; ~ **film** *n* COATINGS película de óxido *f*; ~ **inhibitor** *n* AUTO, MECH, VEH, WATER TRANSP sustancia antioxidante *f*; ~~**preventive packaging** *n* PACK embalaje que evita la oxidación *m*; ~~**proofing** *n* MECH ENG ensayo de oxidación *m*; ~~**proofing paint** *n* COATINGS pintura antioxidante *f*; ~ **protection** *n* PACK protección frente a la oxidación *f*; ~~**protective paint** *n* COLOUR pintura protectora contra óxido *f*; ~ **remover** *n* MECH ENG desoxidante *m*, disolvente del óxido *m*; ~ **of wheat** *n* AGRIC roya parda *f*
rustiness *n* AUTO, CHEM, FOOD, MECH, VEH, WATER TRANSP herrumbrosidad *f*
rut *n* CONST bache *m*, rodada *f*
rutabaga *n* AGRIC mostaza negra *f*
ruthenic *adj* CHEM, METALL ruténico
ruthenium *n* (*Ru*) CHEM, METALL rutenio *m* (*Ru*)
Rutherford: ~ **scattering** *n* PHYS difusión de Rutherford *f*
rutherfordium *n* (*Rf*) RAD PHYS ruterfordio *m* (*Rf*)
rutile *n* CHEM, MINERAL rutilo *m*
R-wire *n* TELECOM cable R *m*
R-Y: ~ **axis** *n* (*red color difference axis AmE, red colour difference axis BrE*) TV eje R-Y *m*; ~ **signal** *n* (*red color difference signal AmE, red colour difference signal BrE*) TV señal R-Y *f*
Rydberg: ~ **constant** *n* PHYS constante de Rydberg *f*; ~ **energy** *n* PHYS energía de Rydberg *f*
ryegrass *n* AGRIC ballico *m*

S

s *abbr* GEN (*second*) s (*segundo*), PART PHYS (*spin*) s (*espín*)

S *abbr* CHEM, METALL (*sulfur AmE, sulphur BrE*) S (*azufre*), METR (*siemens*) S (*siemens, siemensio*), P&R, PETR TECH (*sulfur AmE, sulphur BrE*) S (*azufre*), PHYS (*siemens*) S (*siemens, siemensio*)

S: ~ **band** *n* ELECTRON banda S *f*; ~ **distortion** *n* TV distorsión S *f*; ~ **hook** *n* MECH ENG gancho en S *m*; ~ **stage** *n* TELECOM etapa S *f*; ~ **trap** *n* CONST *plumbing* sifón en S *m*; ~ **wave** *n* PHYS onda S *f*; ~ **wrench** *n* MECH ENG llave inglesa curvada en S *f*

SA *abbr* (*section adaptation*) TELECOM adaptación de sección *f*

Sabattier: ~ **effect** *n* CINEMAT efecto Sabattier *m*, solarización *f*

sabin *n* ACOUST sabine *m*

Sabine: ~ **absorption** *n* ACOUST absorción Sabine *f*; ~ **coefficient** *n* ACOUST coeficiente Sabine *m*

saccharate *n* CHEM sacarato *m*

saccharic *adj* CHEM sacárico

saccharide *n* CHEM glúcido *m*, sacárido *m*

saccharimeter *n* INSTR, PHYS medidor de sacarina *m*

saccharin *n* CHEM sacarina *f*

saccharose *n* FOOD sacarosa *f*

saccoblast *n* CHEM sacoblasto *m*

sachet *n* PACK bolsita *f*; ~ **form fill seal unit** *n* PACK unidad para formar, llenar y cerrar bolsitas *f*

sack *n* PACK saco *m*; ~ **barrow** *n* PACK carretilla para sacos *f*; ~**closing machine** *n* PACK cerradora de sacos *f*; ~**filling line** *n* PACK cadena de llenado de sacos *f*; ~**filling machine** *n* PACK llenadora de sacos *f*; ~ **knife** *n* PACK cuchillo para sacos *m*; ~ **scales** *n* PACK escalas de sacos *f pl*; ~ **sealer** *n* PACK precintadora de sacos *f*; ~**sewing machine** *n* PACK cosedora de sacos *f*; ~ **type seeder** *n* AGRIC sembradora centrífuga manual *f*

sacker *n* AGRIC embolsador *m*, ensacador *m*

sacrificial: ~ **anode** *n* PETR TECH ánodo de sacrificio *m*

SACSE *abbr* (*signaling association control service element AmE, signalling association control service element BrE*) TELECOM elemento de control de la asociación de señalización *m*

sadden *vt* COLOUR oscurecer

saddle *n* MECH ENG *machine tool* carro portaherramienta *m*; ~**back harrow** *n* AGRIC grada de dientes para caballones *f*; ~**bottomed car** *n* TRANSP vagón con fondo en tolva *m*; ~**bottomed self-discharging car** *n* TRANSP vagón tolva autodescargable *m*; ~ **clamp terminal** *n* PROD terminal de la sujeción del carro portaherramientas *m*; ~**feed rate** *n* MECH ENG velocidad de avance del carro portaherramienta *f*; ~ **key** *n* MECH ENG chaveta cóncava *f*, chaveta de fricción *f*, chaveta hueca *f*; ~ **mount combination** *n* TRANSP combinación suspensión-vagón *f*; ~ **point** *n* METALL punto de equilibrio *m*, punto del mínimo *m*; ~ **stitching** *n* PRINT costura por el lomo *f*; ~ **tile** *n* CONST teja de albardilla *f*, teja sillín *f*; ~ **unit** *n* REFRIG grupo frigorífico en caballete *m*

saddlebag: ~ **monorail** *n* TRANSP monoraíl-alforja *m*

saddled: ~ **finish** *n* C&G corona sentada *f*

safe *n* PROD arca *f*, caja de caudales *f*, caja de seguridad *f*, caja fuerte *f*, SAFE caja de caudales *f*, caja de seguridad *f*, caja fuerte *f*; ~ **action area** *n* CINEMAT área de acción segura *f*, TV zona de acción de seguridad *f*, zona de seguridad *f*; ~**area generator** *n* TV generador en zona de seguridad *m*; ~ **concentration** *n* NUCL concentración segura *f*; ~**edge file** *n* MECH ENG lima de canto liso *f*; ~ **ground** *n* WATER TRANSP *mooring* fondeadero limpio *m*; ~ **ironing temperature** *n* TEXTIL temperatura de seguridad para el planchado *f*; ~ **limit** *n* SAFE límite de seguridad *m*; ~ **load** *n* COAL carga admisible *f*, MECH ENG carga admisible *f*, carga de seguridad admisible *f*, carga límite *f*; ~ **load indicator** *n* SAFE indicador de carga segura *m*; ~ **methods of working** *n pl* SAFE seguridad en los métodos de trabajo *f*; ~ **shutdown earthquake** *n* NUCL seísmo de parada segura *m*; ~ **storage of flammable liquids** *n* SAFE almacén seguro de líquidos inflamables *m*; ~ **stress under bending** *n* MECH ENG resistencia límite a la flexión *f*; ~ **use** *n* SAFE *communications* uso sin riesgos *m*; ~ **water** *n* OCEAN aguas navegables *f pl*, WATER TRANSP aguas navegables *f pl*, aguas seguras *f pl*; ~**water mark** *n* WATER TRANSP baliza de fondos limpios *f*; ~ **working load** *n* SAFE carga segura de trabajo *f*; ~ **working practices** *n pl* SAFE prácticas para trabajar con seguridad *f pl*

safeguarding *n* SAFE *stranded ship* defensas *f pl*, salvaguardia *f*

safekeeping *n* POLL custodia *f*

safelight *n* CINEMAT, PHOTO luz de seguridad *f*, luz inactínica *f*; ~ **filter** *n* PHOTO pantalla de blindaje *f*, pantalla de seguridad *f*

safety[1] *n* MECH, QUALITY, SAFE seguridad *f*; ~ **advisor** *n* CONST, SAFE asesor sobre seguridad *m*, asesora sobre seguridad *f*; ~ **apparatus** *n* MECH ENG, MINE, SAFE aparato de seguridad *m*, aparato protector *m*; ~ **appliance** *n* MECH ENG, MINE, SAFE dispositivo de seguridad *m*; ~ **arch** *n* CONST arco de descarga *m*; ~ **at work** *n* SAFE seguridad en el trabajo *f*; ~ **barrier** *n* SAFE barrera de seguridad *f*; ~ **base** *n* CINEMAT soporte de seguridad *m*; ~ **belt anchorage** *n* BrE (*cf seat belt attachment AmE*) AUTO, SAFE, VEH anclaje del cinturón de seguridad *m*; ~ **boiler** *n* PROD caldera de seguridad *f*; ~ **bolt** *n* MECH ENG *of wall plug* seguro *m*; ~ **bonnet** *n* BrE (*cf safety hood AmE*) TRANSP capó de seguridad *m*; ~ **boot** *n* SAFE bota de seguridad *f*; ~ **catch** *n* AUTO cierre de seguridad *m*, MECH ENG cerrojo de seguridad *m*, fiador *m*, retén *m*, MILIT *of gun* seguro *m*, VEH cierre de seguridad *m*; ~ **chain** *n* MECH ENG, SAFE cadena de seguridad *f*; ~ **clamp** *n* SAFE grapa de seguridad *f*; ~ **closure** *n* PACK cierre de seguridad *m*; ~ **cock** *n* MECH ENG llave con seguro *f*; ~ **code** *n* MECH ENG, SAFE código de seguridad *m*; ~ **colors** *AmE*, ~ **colours** *BrE n pl* SAFE colores de seguridad *m pl*; ~ **committee** *n* SAFE comisión de seguridad *f*, comité de seguridad *m*; ~ **container** *n* LAB recipiente de seguridad *m*;

~ **cover** n PROD tapa de seguridad f; ~ **curtain** n SAFE cortina de seguridad f; ~ **cutout** n REFRIG general use, SAFE dispositivo de seguridad por corte m; ~ **device** n MECH ENG, MINE aparato de seguridad m, aparato protector m, dispositivo de seguridad m, SAFE aditamento de seguridad m, aparato de seguridad m, aparato protector m, dispositivo de seguridad m; ~ **door** n CONST puerta de seguridad f; ~ **drag bar** n MINE safety-dog or backstay of mine-car barrera de seguridad f (Esp), paradera f (AmL), puntal de seguridad m (Esp), tentemozo m (AmL); ~ **earth** n BrE (cf safety ground AmE) ELEC tierra de seguridad f; ~ **earth symbol** n BrE (cf safety ground symbol AmE) PROD símbolo de puesta a tierra de seguridad m; ~ **education** n SAFE educación para la seguridad f; ~ **engineering** n SAFE ingeniería para seguridad f; ~ **equipment** n SAFE with grinding disc equipo de seguridad m; ~ **explosive** n MINE explosivo de seguridad m; ~ **factor** n COAL, ELEC coeficiente de seguridad m, factor de seguridad m, SAFE factor de seguridad m, WATER TRANSP elemento de seguridad m, factor de seguridad m; ~ **film** n CINEMAT película de soporte de seguridad f, PHOTO película de seguridad f, película ininflamable f, PRINT película no inflamable f; ~ **first campaign** n SAFE campaña "La Seguridad Primero" f; "~ **first" training** n SAFE entrenamiento para la campaña "La Seguridad Primero" m; ~ **fittings** n pl SAFE spacecraft dispositivos de seguridad m pl, herrajes de seguridad m pl; ~ **funnel** n LAB paper, board embudo antirebase m (AmL), embudo de seguridad m (Esp); ~ **fuse** n MINE espoleta de seguridad f, estopín de seguridad m, fusible de seguridad m, mecha de Bickford f, mecha de seguridad f, mecha lenta f, SAFE fusible de seguridad m; ~ **fuse initiation** n MINE, SAFE iniciación de la mecha de seguridad f; ~ **gas tank** n TRANSP cisterna de seguridad para gas f; ~ **gasoline tank** n AmE (cf safety petrol tank BrE); ~ **glass** n C&G cristal blindado m, vidrio templado m, CONST cristal blindado m, cristal de seguridad m, cristal inastillable m, SAFE cristal de seguridad m, cristal inastillable m, vidrio de seguridad m, cristal blindado m, TRANSP cristal de seguridad m; ~ **glasses** n pl C&G, INSTR, LAB, OPT, PROD, SAFE anteojos de seguridad m pl (AmL), gafas de seguridad f pl (Esp), lentes de seguridad f pl (Esp); ~ **goggles** n pl C&G, INSTR, LAB, OPT, PROD, SAFE anteojos de seguridad m pl (AmL), gafas de seguridad f pl (Esp), lentes de seguridad f pl (Esp); ~ **ground** n AmE see safety earth BrE; ~ **ground symbol** n AmE see safety earth symbol BrE; ~ **guard plate** n PROD mango de seguridad f; ~ **handle** n pl SAFE placa de defensa m; ~ **harness** n AIR TRANSP, CINEMAT, SAFE arnés de seguridad m, WATER TRANSP correaje de seguridad m; ~ **hazard** n SAFE riesgo m; ~ **headway** n SAFE avance de seguridad m, TRANSP avance de seguridad m, intervalo de seguridad entre trenes y autobuses m; ~ **helmet** n SAFE, TRANSP casco de seguridad m; ~ **hood** n AmE see safety bonnet BrE; ~ **hook** n MECH ENG gancho de seguridad m; ~ **in the home** n SAFE seguridad en el hogar f; ~ **instructions** n pl SAFE instrucciones de seguridad f pl; ~ **interlock** n MECH ENG enclavamiento de seguridad m; ~ **island** n TRANSP isleta f; ~ **jack** n CINEMAT enchufe hembra de seguridad m; ~ **ladder** n SAFE escalera de seguridad f; ~ **lock** n CONST cerradura de seguridad

f, dispositivo de seguridad m; ~ **management** n QUALITY manejo de la seguridad m; ~ **margin** n SAFE margen de seguridad m; ~ **measure** n QUALITY prevención f, SAFE medida de seguridad f; ~ **mixing tap** n MECH ENG canilla mezcladora de seguridad f; ~ **net** n SAFE red de seguridad f; ~ **nut** n MECH ENG contratuerca f, tuerca de seguridad f; ~ **officer** n SAFE encargado de seguridad en el trabajo m; ~ **paper** n PAPER papel de seguridad m; ~ **petrol tank** n BrE (cf safety gasoline tank AmE) TRANSP cisterna de seguridad para gasolina f; ~ **pin** n CINEMAT, WATER TRANSP of shackle pasador de seguridad m; ~ **placard** n LAB aviso de seguridad m, letrero de seguridad m, placa de aviso f, PROD, SAFE aviso de seguridad m; ~ **plug** n HYDRAUL tapón de seguridad m, tapón fusible m; ~ **precautions** n SAFE medidas de seguridad f pl; ~ **pulley block** n SAFE aparejo de poleas de seguridad m; ~ **recommendations** n pl AIR TRANSP recomendaciones de seguridad f pl; ~ **record** n CONST registro de seguridad m; ~ **regulations** n pl SAFE normas de seguridad f pl; ~**-relief valve** n HYDRAUL grifo de purga m, válvula de seguridad f; ~ **representative** n SAFE delegado de seguridad m; ~ **requirement** n SAFE norma de seguridad f; ~ **requirements and supervision** n pl SAFE requisitos y supervisión de seguridad m pl; ~ **risk** n SAFE riesgo m; ~ **rules** n pl SAFE normas de seguridad f pl; ~ **screen** n LAB pantalla de blindaje f (AmL), pantalla de seguridad f (Esp); ~ **sign** n LAB señal de seguridad f, SAFE letrero de seguridad m, señal de seguridad f; ~ **specifications** n pl TRANSP especificaciones de seguridad f pl; ~ **spectacles** n pl C&G, INSTR, LAB, OPT, PROD, SAFE anteojos de seguridad m pl (AmL), gafas de seguridad f pl (Esp), lentes de seguridad f pl (Esp); ~ **spring** n MILIT resorte de seguridad m; ~ **stock** n PROD existencias de seguridad f pl; ~ **stop cable** n TRANSP cable de parada de seguridad m; ~ **storage tank** n SAFE depósito de seguridad m; ~ **switch** n ELEC conmutador de seguridad m, ELEC ENG interruptor de seguridad m; ~ **time** n PROD tiempo de seguridad m; ~ **tube** n LAB boat building tubo de seguridad m; ~ **unit** n PROD, SPACE spacecraft unidad de seguridad f; ~ **valve** n GAS, HYDRAUL, MECH, PROD, SAFE válvula de seguridad f; ~ **valves and fittings** n pl SAFE válvulas y accesorios de seguridad f pl; ~ **vessel** n SAFE materials recipiente de seguridad m; ~ **warning** n LAB, PROD, SAFE aviso de seguridad m

safety[2]: **be a** ~ **risk** phr SAFE ser un peligro

safflorite n MINERAL safflorita f

safflower n AGRIC cártamo m; ~ **oil** n FOOD aceite de cártamo m

safranin n CHEM safranina f

safrol n CHEM azafrol m, safrol m

sag[1] n NUCL flecha f; ~ **bend** n PETR TECH curvatura de pandeo f

sag[2] vi WATER TRANSP keel curvarse hacia abajo

sagenite n MINERAL sagenita f

sagging n P&R corrimiento descolgado m, WATER TRANSP shipbuilding deformación cóncava del centro del buque f, momento flector de arrufo m

sagittal: ~ **focal line** n PHYS línea focal sagital f

sahlite n MINERAL sahlita f

sail[1] n WATER TRANSP vela f; ~ **area** n WATER TRANSP área vélica f; ~ **locker** n WATER TRANSP pañol de velas m; ~ **loft** n WATER TRANSP pañol de velas m; ~ **plan** n

WATER TRANSP plano de velamen *m*; ~ **reaper** *n* AGRIC segadora de rastrillos *f*

sail² *vi* WATER TRANSP navegar a vela

sailboard *n* WATER TRANSP tabla de velas *f*

sailcloth *n* WATER TRANSP paños *m pl*

sailing *n* WATER TRANSP travesía *f*, *practice* navegación *f*, *vessels* salida programada *f*; ~ **directions** *n pl* WATER TRANSP *navigation* derrotero *m*, instrucciones náuticas *f pl*

sailmaker *n* WATER TRANSP maestro velero *m*

sailor *n* SAFE marinero de embarcación de salvamento *m*, WATER TRANSP marinero de embarcación de salvamento *m*, marinero novel *m*, marinero

sal: ~ **ammoniac** *n* CHEM sal amoníaco *f*

salacetol *n* CHEM salacetol *m*

saleable: ~ **coal** *n* COAL carbón vendible *m*; ~ **mass** *n* PAPER *of pulp* peso comercial de una pasta *m*

sales: ~ **engineer** *n* PROD técnico de ventas *m*; ~ **yarn spinning** *n* TEXTIL hilatura para rebajas *f*

salicin *n* CHEM salicina *f*

salicyl *n* CHEM salicilo *m*

salicylaldehyde *n* CHEM salicilaldehído *m*

salicylate *n* CHEM salicilato *m*

salicylated *adj* CHEM salicilado

salicylic *adj* CHEM salicílico

salient: ~ **pole** *n* ELEC *electrical machines*, ELEC ENG polo saliente *m*; ~ **pole generator** *n* ELEC *electrical machines* generador de polos salientes *m*; ~ **pole rotor** *n* ELEC, ELEC ENG inducido de polos salientes *m*; ~ **pole stator** *n* ELEC ENG estator de polos salientes *m*

salifiable *adj* CHEM salificable

saligenin *n* CHEM saligenol *m*

saline¹ *adj* HYDROL, WATER salino

saline²: ~ **solution** *n* NUCL solución salina *f*; ~ **spring** *n* HYDROL, WATER manantial salino *m*; ~ **water** *n* AGRIC, GEOL, HYDROL, WATER agua salada *f*, agua salobre *f*; ~ **water conversion** *n* WATER destilación del agua salada *f*

salinity *n* CHEM, FUELLESS, HYDROL, PETR TECH, WATER, WATER TRANSP salinidad *f*

salinization *n* HYDROL salinización *f*

salinometer *n* COAL, INSTR, OCEAN salinómetro *m*

salite *n* MINERAL salita *f*

salmon: ~ **breeder** *n* OCEAN salmonicultor *m*, salmonicultora *f*; ~ **culture** *n* OCEAN salmonicultura *f*; ~ **farmer** *n* OCEAN salmonicultor *m*, salmonicultora *f*

salol *n* CHEM salol *m*

saloon *n* TRANSP sedán *m*, WATER TRANSP *ships* cámara *f*, salón *m*; ~ **coach** *n* TRANSP coche restaurante *m*

salt¹: ~–**bearing** *adj* GEOL salino; ~–**glazed** *adj* COLOUR barnizado a la sal

salt² *n* CHEM sal *f*; ~ **balance** *n* OCEAN balance salino *m*; ~ **bath brazing** *n* CONST soldadura con baño de sal *f*; ~–**bath furnace** *n* HEAT horno de baño salino *m*; ~ **bubble** *n* C&G burbuja de sal *f*; ~ **cake** *n* C&G sal en bruto *f*, FOOD bloque de sal *m*, sal en bloque *f*; ~ **cavity** *n* GAS cavidad de sal *f*; ~ **column** *n* GEOL, PETR TECH columna de sal *f*; ~ **content** *n* GAS contenido de sal *m*, contenido salino *m*, OCEAN contenido de sales *m*; ~ **curing** *n* OCEAN salazón *f*; ~ **deposit** *n* GAS depósito de sal *m*; ~ **diapirism** *n* GEOL, PETR TECH diapirismo salino *m*; ~ **dome** *n* GEOL, PETR TECH domo salino *m*, domo salífero *m*; ~ **glaze** *n* COATINGS vidriado común *m*; ~ **lick** *n* AGRIC piedra de sal *f*, salgar *m*; ~ **liquor** *n* NUCL licor salino *m*; ~ **marsh** *n* OCEAN marisma *f*; ~ **pillow** *n*

GEOL, PETR TECH intumescencia salina *f*; ~ **refinery** *n* PROD refinería de sal *f*, salinas *f pl*; ~ **rock** *n* GEOL roca de sal *f*, roca salina *f*; ~ **spray** *n* P&R niebla salina *f*, rocío salino *m*; ~ **spray test** *n* C&G prueba del agua salada *f*; ~ **substitute** *n* FOOD substituto de sal *m*; ~ **swamp** *n* WATER pantano salobre *m*; ~ **tectonics** *n* GEOL, PETR TECH tectónica salina *f*; ~ **water** *n* AGRIC, GEOL, HYDROL, WATER agua salada *f*; ~ **water drilling mud** *n* PETR TECH lodo de perforación a base de agua salada *m*; ~ **water drilling sludge** *n* PETR TECH lodo de perforación a base de agua salada *m*; ~ **water infiltration** *n* HYDROL infiltración de agua salada *f*; ~ **water invasion** *n* HYDROL invasión de agua salada *f*; ~ **water mud** *n* PETR TECH lodo de agua salada *m*; ~ **water plant** *n* WATER instalación para tratamiento de agua salada *f*; ~ **water sludge** *n* PETR TECH lodo de agua salada *m*; ~ **works** *n* PROD refinería de sal *f*, salinas *f pl*

salt³: ~ **out** *vt* CHEM *soap* desalar, extraer por salado

saltation *n* HYDROL saltación *f*

saltbed *n* HYDROL cauce salino *m*

salted: ~ **atmosphere** *n* REFRIG atmósfera salada *f*

saltern *n* FOOD, OCEAN salina *f*

salting *n* FOOD salazón *f*; ~ **agent** *n* NUCL agente salino *m*

saltpeter *AmE see* **saltpetre** *BrE*

saltpetre *n BrE* C&G nitrato de potasio *m*, salitre *m*, CHEM, FOOD salitre *m*

saltwater: ~ **wedge** *n* OCEAN cuña de agua de mar *f*

salty *adj* CHEM, HYDROL, WATER, WATER TRANSP salado

salvage¹ *n* WATER TRANSP salvamento *m*, bienes salvados *m pl*, *payment* prima de salvamento *f*; ~ **award** *n* WATER TRANSP recompensa por el salvamento *f*; ~ **crane** *n* TRANSP grúa de salvamento *f*, grúa-cesta de salvamento *f*; ~ **lorry** *n BrE* (*cf salvage truck AmE*) AUTO camión de salvamento *m*, TRANSP camión de salvamento *m*, vehículo de salvamento *m*; ~ **truck** *n AmE* (*cf salvage lorry BrE*) AUTO camión de salvamento *m*, TRANSP camión de salvamento *m*, vehículo de salvamento *m*; ~ **tug** *n* WATER TRANSP remolcador de salvamento *m*; ~ **vessel** *n* WATER TRANSP buque de salvamento *m*

salvage² *vt* RECYCL reciclar, recuperar

salvaged: ~ **material** *n* RECYCL material reciclado *m*, material recuperado *m*

salvaging *n* RECYCL reciclado *m*, recuperación *f*

salvarsan *n* CHEM salvarsán *m*

salvo *n* MILIT *gun* descarga *f*, salva *f*

SAM *abbr* (*surface-to-air missile*) MILIT misil de tierra a aire *m*, misil tierra-aire *m*

samarium *n* (*Sm*) CHEM samario *m* (*Sm*); ~ **effect** *n* NUCL efecto del samario *m*

samarskite *n* MINERAL samarsquita *f*

sample¹ *n* GEN muestra *f*, testigo *m*; ~ **admission vessel** *n* NUCL *vehicles* recipiente de admisión de la muestra *m*; ~–**and-hold circuit** *n* ELEC ENG circuito porta-muestra *m*; ~ **captor** *n* QUALITY *water* prueba de muestreo *f*; ~ **changer** *n* NUCL cambiador de muestras *m*; ~ **divider** *n* LAB *general equipment* distribuidor de muestras *m*; ~ **holder** *n* NUCL porta-muestras *m*; ~ **period** *n* PETR TECH período de muestreo *m*; ~ **size** *n* ELECTRON volumen de la muestra *m*, METR tamaño de muestra *m*; ~ **stabilization** *n* QUALITY estabilización de muestra *f*; ~ **strip** *n* TEXTIL tira de muestra *f*; ~ **surveillance** *n*

QUALITY control de muestras *m*; ~ **time** *n* PROD tiempo de muestreo *m*

sample[2] *vt* AGRIC, COAL, COMP&DP muestrear, ELECTRON obtener muestras, FOOD, MATH muestrear, PHYS probar, QUALITY, SPACE muestrear, TELECOM tomar muestras, muestrear, enviar muestras, WATER muestrear

sampled: ~**-data filtering** *n* ELECTRON filtración de datos discontinuos *f*; ~**-data size filter** *n* ELECTRON filtro de volumen de datos discontinuos *m*; ~ **signal** *n* ELECTRON señal de prueba *f*, TELECOM señal muestreada *f*; ~ **value** *n* ELECTRON valor de muestra *m*

sampler *n* COAL, PROD muestreador *m*, tomamuestras *m*, TELECOM discriminador cromático *m*, tomamuestras *m*, muestreador *m*, TV *colour content* discriminador cromático *m*

sampling *n* COAL toma de muestras *f*, ELECTRON discriminación selectiva cromática *f*, muestreo *m*, FOOD demuestre *m*, PETR TECH toma de muestras *f*, PHYS muestra *f*, PROD, SPACE, TELECOM muestreo *m*, WATER muestreo *m*, catadura *f*, toma de muestras *f*; ~ **amplifier** *n* ELECTRON amplificador de muestreo *m*; ~ **device** *n* LAB dispositivo de muestreo *m*, muestreador *m*; ~ **frequency** *n* COMP&DP, ELECTRON, PETROL, TELECOM frecuencia de muestreo *f*; ~ **inspection** *n* QUALITY control por muestreo *m*; ~ **line** *n* QUALITY *water* tubería de muestreo *f*; ~ **method** *n* QUALITY método de muestreo *m*; ~ **network** *n* QUALITY red de muestreo *f*; ~ **plan** *n* METR plan de muestreo *m*; ~ **point** *n* COAL punto de muestreo *m*, QUALITY punto de escogimiento *m*, punto de muestreo *m*; ~ **probe** *n* QUALITY *water* prueba de muestreo *f*; ~ **pump** *n* LAB bomba de muestreo *f*; ~ **rate** *n* COMP&DP frecuencia de muestreo *f*, tasa de muestreo *f*, ELECTRON, PETROL, TELECOM frecuencia de muestreo *f*; ~ **spectrum analyser** *n* BrE ELECTRON, TELECOM analizador del espectro de la muestra *m*; ~ **spectrum analyzer** *AmE see sampling spectrum analyser BrE*; ~ **theorem** *n* PETR TECH teorema de muestreo *m*; ~ **tube** *n* LAB tubo de muestreo *m*; ~ **vertical amplifier** *n* ELECTRON amplificador vertical de muestreo *m*

SAMSARS *abbr* (*satellite-aided maritime search and rescue system*) TELECOM sistema de búsqueda y rescate marítimos mediante satélite *m*

samson: ~ **post** *n* WATER TRANSP *ship building* puntal *m*

sand[1] *n* COAL, PETR TECH, PROD *for foundry* arena *f*; ~ **bar** *n* GEOL, HYDROL, OCEAN, WATER TRANSP barra de arena *f*; ~ **bath** *n* LAB baño de arena *m*; ~ **casting** *n* PROD moldeo en arena *m*; ~ **equivalent** *n* CONST equivalente de arena *m*; ~ **filter** *n* COAL, HYDROL, WATER filtro de arena *m*; ~ **floor** *n* PROD *foundry* taller de moldeo en arena *m*; ~ **and gravel trap** *n* HYDROL colector de arena y grava *m*, purgador de arena y grava *m*; ~ **hole** *n* PROD *casting* escarabajo *m*; ~ **jet** *n* PROD chorro de arena *m*; ~ **line** *n* PETR TECH cable de cuchareo *m*; ~ **mold** *AmE*, ~ **mould** *BrE* *n* PROD molde de arena *m*; ~ **ribbon** *n* OCEAN cinta de arena *f*; ~ **riddler** *n* PROD *founding* criba para arena *f*; ~ **ripple** *n* OCEAN arruga *f*; ~ **seal** *n* CONST capa fina de arena *f*; ~**-shale ratio** *n* PETR TECH proporción de arena a lutita *f*; ~ **shop** *n* PROD *foundry* taller de preparación de arenas *m*; ~ **sifter** *n* PROD *founding* criba para arena *f*; ~ **trap** *n* HYDROL depósito de arenas *m*, depósito de fangos *m*, PETR TECH trampa

de arena *f*, WATER desarenador *m*, guardaarenas *m*, trampa de arena *f*; ~ **vent** *n* PROD *of mould* respiradero *m*; ~**-washing** *n* PETR TECH lavado por arena *m*; ~ **wave** *n* OCEAN ola de arena *f*

sand[2] *vt* PROD enarenar, lijar

sandbag *n* SAFE bolsa de arena *f*

sandbank *n* GEOL, HYDROL banco de arena *m*, barra de arena *f*, OCEAN banco de arena *m*, encalladero *m*, barra de arena *f*, WATER TRANSP encalladero *m*, banco de arena *m*, barra de arena *f*

sandblast[1] *n* COAL chorro de arena *m*; ~ **apparatus** *n* C&G aparato para pulir con chorro de arena *m*; ~ **cleaning room** *n* PROD cámara de limpieza con chorro de arena *f*; ~ **machine** *n* PROD chorreadora de arena *f*; ~ **obscuring** *n* C&G pulido con chorro de arena *m*

sandblast[2] *vt* CONST, MECH chorrear con arena, limpiar con chorro de arena

sandblasting *n* C&G pulido con chorro de arena *m*, MAR POLL, MECH, PROD, WATER TRANSP limpieza con chorro de arena *f*; ~ **nozzle** *n* C&G boquilla para pulir con chorro de arena *f*

sandbur *n* AGRIC roseta *f*

sanding *n* C&G lijado *m*, CONST *civil engineering* pulimento *m*, engravillado *m*, lijado *m*, formación de una barra de arena *f*, MECH lijado *m*, P&R lijado *m*, pulido *m*, limpieza con arena *f*, PROD lijado *m*, enarenado *m*

sandow *n* TRANSP cable elástico *m*, elemento de suspensión elástica *m*

sandpaper[1] *n* MECH, PROD papel de lija *m*

sandpaper[2] *vt* MECH, PROD lijar

sandpapering *n* C&G, CONST, MECH, P&R, PROD lijado *m*; ~ **machine** *n* PROD lijadora *f*

sandstone *n* CONST, GEOL arenisca *f*, OCEAN arenisca *f*, arenita *f*, roca de playa *f*, PETR TECH arenisca *f*

sandtable *n* PAPER arenero *m*

sandwich *n* PRINT intercalación *f*, uso de dos o más tipos de tintas en impresión multicolor *m*; ~**-paned insulating panel** *n* REFRIG panel aislante tipo sandwich *m*; ~**-panel insulation** *n* REFRIG aislamiento mediante paneles en sandwich *m*; ~ **winding** *n* ELEC devanado alternado *m*

sandy[1] *adj* GEOL arenoso, arenífero; ~ **loam** *adj* AGRIC francoarenoso

sandy[2]: ~ **bed** *n* HYDROL lecho arenoso *m*; ~ **chalk** *n* GEOL creta arenosa *f*; ~ **clay** *n* C&G, CONST, GEOL arcilla arenosa *f*; ~ **ground** *n* COAL tierra arenácea *f*; ~ **limestone** *n* GEOL caliza arenosa *f*; ~ **loam** *n* C&G, CONST arcilla arenosa *f*, GEOL arcilla arenosa *f*, marga arenosa *f*

sanidine *n* MINERAL sanidina *f*

sanitary: ~ **engineering** *n* WATER ingeniería sanitaria *f*, técnica sanitaria *f*; ~ **paint** *n* COLOUR pintura para entorno húmedo *f*; ~ **ware** *n* C&G aparatos sanitarios *m pl*; ~ **waste water** *n* HYDROL, RECYCL, WATER aguas de alcantarillado *f pl*

sanitation *n* WATER higienización *f*, saneamiento *m*, sanidad pública *f*

sanitization *n* COMP&DP esterilización *f*, higienización *f*, sanitarizado *m*

sanserif *n* PRINT tipo de palo seco *m*; ~ **face** *n* PRINT tipo de palo seco *m*

santonic *adj* CHEM santónico

santonin *n* CHEM santonina *f*

SAP *abbr* (*service access point*) TELECOM punto de acceso al servicio *m*

sapele *n* WATER TRANSP *boat building* caoba de Guinea *f*, sapeli *m*

SAPI *abbr* (*service access point identifier*) TELECOM identificador del punto de acceso al servicio *m*

sapogenin *n* CHEM sapogenina *f*

saponification *n* CHEM saponificación *f*; ~ **number** *n* FOOD número de saponificación *m*, índice de saponificación *m*

saponifier *n* CHEM saponificador *m*

saponify *vt* CHEM saponificar

saponifying *adj* CHEM saponificante

saponin *n* CHEM saponina *f*

saponite *n* MINERAL piedra jabón *f*, saponita *f*

sapphire *n* ELECTRON zafiro *m*, MINERAL zafirita *f*; ~ **quartz** *n* MINERAL cuarzo azul *m*; ~ **substrate** *n* ELECTRON substrato de zafiro *m*

sapphirine *n* MINERAL zafirino *m*

sapping *n* MINE socavón *m*

sapropel *n* OCEAN sapropel *m*; ~ **deposit** *n* GEOL depósito sapropélico *m*

sapropelic: ~ **deposit** *n* GEOL sedimento sapropélico *m*

SAR *abbr* (*search and rescue*) AIR TRANSP, MILIT, TELECOM SAR (*búsqueda y rescate*)

sarcine *n* CHEM sarcina *f*

sarcolactic *adj* CHEM sarcoláctico

sarcolite *n* MINERAL sarcolita *f*

sarcosine *n* CHEM sarcosina *f*

sard *n* MINERAL sarda *f*

sardonyx *n* MINERAL calcedonia parda *f*, sardónica *f*

sarkinite *n* MINERAL sarcinita *f*

sartorite *n* MINERAL sartorita *f*

sash *n* CONST hoja de ventana *f*; ~ **bar** *n* CONST *iron* separador de ventana *m*, *wood* montante *m*; ~ **bar iron** *n* CONST *rolled sections* montante de hierro *m*; ~ **clamp** *n* CONST grapa para ventana *f*; ~ **cramp** *n* CONST grapa de bastidor *f*; ~ **fastener** *n* CONST cerrojo de ventana *m*, falleba de ventana *f*; ~ **gate** *n* WATER contrapuerta de corredera *f*; ~ **iron** *n* CONST bastidor de hierro *m*; ~ **window** *n* CONST ventana de guillotina *f*

sassoline *n* MINERAL sassolina *f*

sassolite *n* MINERAL sassolita *f*

SATCOM *abbr* (*satellite communications*) TELECOM, WATER TRANSP SATCOM (*comunicaciones por satélite, telecomunicaciones vía satélite*)

satellite *n* PHYS, PRINT, SPACE *communications* satélite *m*; ~-**aided maritime search and rescue system** *n* (*SAMSARS*) TELECOM sistema de búsqueda y rescate marítimos mediante satélite *m*; ~-**apogee motor combination** *n* SPACE combinación satélite-motor de apogeo *f*; ~ **channel** *n* TV canal por satélite *m*; ~ **communications** *n pl* (*SATCOM*) TELECOM comunicaciones mediante satélites *f pl*, comunicaciones por satélite *f pl* (*SATCOM*), WATER TRANSP comunicaciones por satélite *f pl* (*SATCOM*), telecomunicaciones vía satélite *f pl* (*SATCOM*); ~ **computer** *n* COMP&DP computador satélite *m* (*AmL*), computadora satélite *f* (*AmL*), ordenador satélite *m* (*Esp*); ~ **control center** *AmE*; ~ **control centre** *BrE* *n* TELECOM centro de control de satélites *m*; ~ **coverage area** *n* TV zona de cobertura por satélite *f*; ~ **dish** *n* TV parabólica *f*, reflector parabólico *m*; ~ **emergency position-indicating radio**

beacon *n* TELECOM radiofaro indicador de posición de emergencia mediante satélite *m*; ~ **exchange** *n* TELECOM central auxiliar *f*, central satélite *f*, oficina satélite *f*; ~ **link** *n* SPACE, TV enlace por satélite *m*; ~ **meteorology** *n* SPACE meteorología por observaciones de satélite *f*; ~ **navigation** *n* AIR TRANSP navegación por satélite *f*; ~ **navigator** *n* (*SATNAV*) SPACE, WATER TRANSP sistema de radionavegación por satélite *m* (*SATNAV*); ~ **switching** *n* SPACE centro de conmutación del satélite *m*; ~ **system monitor** *n* (*SSM*) SPACE monitor del sistema de satélites *m* (*SSM*); ~ **telecast** *n* TV programa de televisión por satélite *m*; ~ **track** *n* SPACE trayectoria del satélite *f*; ~ **transmission** *n* TELECOM transmisión por satélite *f*; ~ **valve** *n* AUTO válvula satélite *f*; ~ **well** *n* PETR TECH pozo satélite *m*

Satellite: ~ **System Operation Guide** *n* (*SSOG*) SPACE Guía de Explotación del Sistema de Satélites *f* (*SSOG*)

satin *n* TEXTIL raso *m*, satén *m*; ~ **etch** *n* C&G grabado satinado *m*; ~ **finish** *n* COATINGS, COLOUR acabado satinado *m*; ~ **finish glass** *n* C&G vidrio biselado *m*; ~-**finishing wheel** *n* MECH ENG muela de satinado *f*, muela de satinar *f*; ~ **spar** *n* MINERAL espato lustroso *m*

SATNAV *abbr* (*satellite navigator*) SPACE, WATER TRANSP SATNAV (*sistema de radionavegación por satélite*)

Satstream: ~ **circuit** *n* TELECOM circuito Satstream *m*

saturable: ~ **reactor** *n* ELEC ENG reactor de núcleo magnético saturable *m*, PHYS reactor saturable *m*; ~ **transformer** *n* ELEC, ELEC ENG transformador saturable *m*

saturant *n* CHEM saturante *m*

saturate *adj* CHEM saturado

saturated[1] *adj* CHEM, CINEMAT, PAPER, REFRIG saturado

saturated[2]: ~ **air** *n* METEO, REFRIG aire saturado *m*; ~ **boiling** *n* NUCL ebullición en condiciones de saturación *f*; ~ **core** *n* ELEC ENG núcleo saturado *m*; ~ **diving** *n* PETR TECH buceo por saturación *m*; ~ **hydrocarbon** *n* CHEM, PETR TECH hidrocarburo saturado *m*; ~ **layer** *n* METEO capa saturada *f*; ~ **logic** *n* ELECTRON circuito lógico saturado *m*; ~ **mode** *n* ELECTRON función saturada *f*; ~ **polyester** *n* P&R poliéster saturado *m*; ~ **soil** *n* COAL terreno saturado *m*, tierra rica *f*; ~ **solution** *n* CHEM solución saturada *f*; ~ **steam** *n* HEAT, HEAT ENG, THERMO vapor saturado *m*; ~ **steam-cooled heater** *n* NUCL calentador refrigerado por vapor saturado *m*; ~ **toroidal transformer** *n* ELEC, ELEC ENG transformador toroidal saturado *m*; ~ **transformer** *n* ELEC, ELEC ENG transformador saturado *m*; ~ **transistor** *n* ELECTRON transistor saturado *m*; ~ **vapor** *AmE see saturated vapour BrE*; ~ **vapor pressure** *AmE see saturated vapour pressure BrE*; ~ **vapour** *n BrE* PHYS vapor saturado *m*; ~ **vapour pressure** *n BrE* PHYS presión de vapor saturado *f*

saturating: ~ **signal** *n* ELECTRON señal de saturación *f*

saturation *n* GEN saturación *f*; ~ **back-scattering correction** *n* NUCL corrección de la retrodispersión por saturación *f*; ~ **banding** *n* TV saturación de bandas *f*; ~ **characteristics** *n pl* RAD PHYS características de saturación *f pl*; ~ **conditions** *n pl* ELEC ENG condiciones de saturación *f pl*; ~ **current** *n* ELECTRON, PHYS corriente de saturación *f*; ~ **deficit** *n* METEO déficit de saturación *m*; ~ **dive** *n* OCEAN buceo a saturación *m*; ~ **diver** *n* PETR TECH buzo de saturación *m*; ~ **diving** *n* OCEAN buceo en saturación *m*, PETR TECH inmersión por saturación *f*; ~ **hardening** *n* METALL endurecimiento por saturación *m*; ~ **induction** *n* ELEC, ELEC ENG inducción de saturación *f*, inducción magnética máxima *f*; ~ **magnetization** *n* ELEC ENG magnetización de saturación *f*; ~ **output power** *n* ELECTRON potencia de salida de saturación *f*; ~ **output state** *n* ELECTRON volumen de flujo de saturación *m*; ~ **point** *n* SPACE punto de saturación *m*; ~ **region** *n* ELECTRON zona de saturación *f*; ~ **temperature** *n* REFRIG temperatura de saturación *f*; ~ **voltage** *n* ELEC ENG voltaje de saturación *m*

saucer: **~-head screw** *n* MECH ENG tornillo de cabeza semiredonda *m*

save[1]: **~-all** *n* PAPER recogepastas *m*, recupera-pastas *m*; **~-all tray** *n* PAPER bandeja de aguas blancas *f*

save[2] *vt* COMP&DP escribir en el disco, guardar, salvar, PAPER recuperar

saw[1] *n* MECH, MECH ENG serrucho *m*, sierra *f*; ~ **arbor** *n* MECH ENG eje de la sierra *m*, eje de sierra circular *m*; ~ **bench** *n* CONST banco de sierra *m*, sierra circular de mesa *f*; ~ **blade** *n* MECH ENG, PROD hoja de sierra *f*; ~ **clamp** *n* MECH ENG brida de sierra *f*, cepo de sierra *m*; ~ **cut** *n* CONST corte de sierra *m*; ~ **file** *n* MECH ENG lima de sierra *f*, lima para dientes de sierra *f*; ~ **frame** *n* MECH ENG arco de la sierra *m*, armadura de la sierra *f*, bastidor de sierra *m*; ~ **guide** *n* MECH ENG guía de sierra *f*; ~ **kerf** *n* MECH ENG anchura del corte *f*; ~ **log** *n* CONST tronco para aserrar *m*; ~ **pulley** *n* MECH ENG *of band sawing machine* polea de sierra *f*; ~ **set** *n* MECH ENG composición de los dientes de la sierra *f*, tenazas de triscar *f pl*; **~-sharpening machine** *n* MECH, MECH ENG, PROD afiladora de sierra *f*; ~ **with teeth** *n* MECH ENG sierra con dientes *f*; ~ **timber** *n* CONST madera para aserrar *f*; ~ **tooth oscillation** *n* ELEC oscilación en diente de sierra *f*; ~ **tooth roof** *n* CONST tejado dentado *m*

saw[2] *vt* AGRIC, CONST, MECH, MINE aserrar

SAW[1] *abbr* (*surface acoustic wave*) ACOUST, ELECTRON, PHYS, TELECOM, WAVE PHYS onda acústica de superficie

SAW[2]: ~ **compression filter** *n* ELECTRON filtro de compresión de OAS *m*; ~ **delay line** *n* ELECTRON línea de retardo de OAS *f*; ~ **device** *n* ELECTRON, TELECOM dispositivo OAS *m*; ~ **expansion filter** *n* ELECTRON filtro de expansión de OAS *m*; ~ **filter** *n* ELECTRON filtro de OAS *m*; ~ **filtering** *n* ELECTRON filtrado de OAS *m*

sawbuck *n* CONST caballete de aserrar *m*

sawdust *n* CONST aserrín *m*, serrín *m*

sawfly *n* FOOD nombre genérico de las avispas del género tentredínidos *m*

sawhorse *n* CONST caballete de aserrar *m*

sawing *n* AGRIC, CONST, MECH, MINE aserradura *f*; ~ **list** *n* PROD lista de aserrado *f*; ~ **machine** *n* CONST máquina de aserrar *f*, MECH ENG sierra mecánica *f*; ~ **out** *n* C&G corte *m*

sawmill *n* AGRIC, CONST, MECH, MINE aserradero *m* (*Esp*), serrería mecánica *f* (*AmL*)

sawn: **~-in back** *n* PRINT lomo aserrado *m*

sawtooth: ~ **current** *n* TV corriente en diente de sierra *f*; ~ **generator** *n* TV generador de dientes de sierra *m*; ~ **signal wave** *n* RAD PHYS onda en diente de sierra *f*, señal en diente de sierra *f*; ~ **voltage** *n* ELEC ENG

voltaje en diente de sierra *m*; ~ **waveform** *n* ACOUST, ELEC, ELEC ENG, ELECTRON, PHYS, WAVE PHYS forma de onda en diente de sierra *f*

Sb *abbr* (*antimony*) C&G, CHEM, METALL Sb (*antimonio*)

SBA *abbr* (*slurry blasting agent*) MINE explosivo fluidizado *m*

S-band: ~ **diode** *n* ELECTRON diodo de banda S *m*

SBLOCA *abbr* (*small break LOCA*) NUCL SBLOCA (*LOCA pequeño*)

SBM *abbr* (*single-buoy mooring*) PETR TECH SBM (*anclaje a boya simple*)

SBR *abbr* (*styrene butadiene rubber*) P&R SBR (*caucho butadieno-estireno*)

SBST *abbr* (*single bituminous surface treatment*) CONST tratamiento superficial bituminoso simple *m*

Sc *abbr* CHEM (*scandium*) Sc (*escandio*), METEO (*stratocumulus*) Sc (*estratocúmulo*)

scab *n* FOOD costra *f*, roña *f*, PROD *founding* darta *f*

scabbard *n* MILIT funda *f*

scaffold *n* CINEMAT practicable *m*, CONST, PROD andamio *m*; ~ **board** *n* CONST tablón del andamio *m*; ~ **pole** *n* CONST alma del andamio *f*

scaffolding *n* CONST, PROD, SAFE andamiaje *m*; ~ **protective net** *n* SAFE red de seguridad para andamiajes *f*

scala: ~ **timpani** *n* ACOUST rampa timpánica *f*; ~ **vestibuli** *n* ACOUST rampa vestibular *f*

scalable: ~ **font** *n* PRINT tipo de letra dimensionable *m*; ~ **fount** *n* PRINT tipo de letra dimensionable *m*

scalar[1] *adj* COMP&DP escalado (*AmL*)

scalar[2] *n* MATH, PHYS escalar *m*; ~ **measurement** *n* ELEC ENG medición escalar *f*; **~-network analyser** *n* BrE ELEC, ELEC ENG analizador de red escalar *m*; **~-network analysis** *n* ELEC, ELEC ENG análisis de red escalar *m*; **~-network analyzer** AmE *see scalar-network analyser BrE*; ~ **potential** *n* ELEC ENG, PHYS potencial escalar *m*; ~ **product** *n* PHYS producto escalar *m*; ~ **resistor** *n* ELEC ENG resistencia escalar *f*; ~ **type** *n* COMP&DP tipo escalar *m*

scald[1] *n* FOOD, SAFE, THERMO escaldadura *f*; ~ **mark** *n* FOOD marca de escaldado *f*

scald[2] *vt* FOOD, SAFE, THERMO escaldar

scalding *adj* FOOD, SAFE, THERMO escaldado

scale[1] *n* ACOUST *of frequencies*, CONST escala *f*, DETERG *in boiler* escama *f*, incrustación *f*, ELEC *instrument*, GEOM *continuous paper* escala *f*, HEAT *in boilers*, HYDRAUL *in boiler* incrustación *f*, MECH *cohetes* capa de óxido *f*, rebaba *f*, oxidación *f*, MECH ENG *for weighing, measuring, spring* romana *f*, balanza *f*, escuadra *f*, báscula *f*, METR *anything graduated, means of comparison, relative dimensions* escala *f*, *weighing machine* báscula *f*, PRINT escala *f*, PROD *in boilers* incrustación *f*, *exfoliation* escama *f*, *on castings* rebaba *f*, cascarilla de óxido *f*; ~ **beam** *n* MECH ENG brazo de la balanza *m*; ~ **of charges** *n* CONST escala de cargas *f*; ~ **dial** *n* CINEMAT cuadrante graduado *m*; ~ **division** *n* ELEC *instruments* división de escala *f*; ~ **drawing** *n* GEOM dibujo a escala *m*; ~ **factor** *n* COMP&DP factor de escala *m*; ~ **formation** *n* WATER formación de incrustaciones *f*; ~ **illumination** *n* WATER TRANSP *radar* iluminación de la escala *f*; ~ **of image** *n* PHOTO escala de la imagen *f*; ~ **inhibitor** *n* REFRIG antiincrustante *m*; ~ **interval** *n* METR intervalo de la escala *m*; ~ **length** *n* METR longitud de la escala *f*; ~ **mark** *n* METR *air bubble in a casting, etc* marca graduada *f*; ~ **model** *n* CINEMAT maqueta a escala *f*, GEOM, WATER TRANSP *of ship* modelo a escala *m*; ~ **numbering** *n* METR numeración de la escala *f*; ~ **pan** *n* MECH ENG platillo de balanza *m*; ~ **paper** *n* PAPER papel milimetrado *m*; ~ **of radial wavefunctions** *n* RAD PHYS escala de funciones de onda radiales *f*; ~ **range** *n* METR amplitud de la escala *f*; ~ **solvent** *n* HEAT, RAIL disolvente de incrustaciones *m*; ~ **spacing** *n* METR longitud de una división de la escala *f*; ~ **switch** *n* ELEC interruptor de escala *m*; ~ **trap** *n* REFRIG separador de impurezas *m*

scale^2 *vt* COMP&DP cambiar de proporción, escalar, graduar, PROD desescamar, desoxidar, *drawings* trazar a escala

scalene: ~ **cone** *n* GEOM cono escaleno *m*; ~ **triangle** *n* GEOM triángulo escaleno *m*

scaler *n* ELECTRON desmultiplicador de impulsos *m*

scales *n* LAB báscula *f*, MECH ENG *balance* graduación *f*, *weighing machine* balanza *f*, báscula *f*

scaling *n* COMP&DP cambio de escala *m*, CONST *closing* descascarillado *m*, METR tarado *m*, PROD exfoliación *f*, oxidación *f*, *flaking* descamación *f*, desescamado *m*, escamación *f*; ~ **bar** *n* MINE barreno limpiador *m*, desincrustador *m*, bulón de saneo *m* (*Esp*), redondo de saneado del techo *m* (*AmL*); ~ **circuit** *n* ELECTRON circuito desmultiplicador de impulsos *m*; ~ **factor** *n* ELECTRON factor de desmultiplicación de impulsos *m*; ~ **hammer** *n* PROD martillo de picar calderas *m*, martillo desincrustador *m*; ~ **a spring** *n* METR reducción de muelle *f*; ~ **value** *n* PROD valor desmultiplicador *m*

scallop *n* TV festoneado *m*; ~ **culture** *n* OCEAN cultivo de pecten *m*, pectinicultura *f*

scalloped: ~ **rail** *n* RAIL carril festoneado *m*

scalloping *n* TV festoneado *m*

scalpel *n* LAB bisturí *m*, escalpelo *m*; ~ **blade** *n* LAB hoja de escalpelo *f*

scalper *n* AGRIC máquina de despelusar *f*

scalping *n* AGRIC *forest* despastaje *m*, COAL desconchado *m*, desprendimiento violento de vapor *m*, ganga *f*; ~ **screen** *n* COAL criba para remover la ganga *f*

scan^1 *n* AIR TRANSP barrido *m*, exploración *f*, COMP&DP escaneo *m*, exploración *f*, PETR TECH barrido *m*, PRINT escaneo *m*, TV, WATER TRANSP exploración *f*, WAVE PHYS adquisición de un espectro *f*, barrido *m*, toma de datos *f*; ~ **burn** *n* TV barrido de remanencia de la imagen *m*; ~ **converter** *n* ELECTRON convertidor de exploración *m*; ~ **line** *n* SPACE línea de exploración *f*; ~ **platform** *n* SPACE plataforma de exploración *f*; ~ **rate** *n* COMP&DP frecuencia de exploración *f*, velocidad de exploración *f*, velocidad de escaneo *f*; ~ **registration** *n* TV registro de exploración *m*; ~ **ring** *n* TV anillo de exploración *m*; ~ **time** *n* PROD tiempo de examen *m*, tiempo de observación *m*

scan^2 *vt* COMP&DP, PRINT escanear, explorar, PROD, TRANSP barrer, examinar, explorar, TV, WATER TRANSP, WAVE PHYS explorar

scandium *n* (*Sc*) CHEM escandio *m* (*Sc*)

scanner *n* CHEM, COAL analizador *m*, COMP&DP analizador *m*, escáner *m*, ELEC dispositivo de exploración *m*, explorador *m*, ELECTRON analizador *m*, dispositivo explorador *m*, GEOL, MECH ENG, METALL, PHYS analizador *m*, PRINT escáner *m*, QUALITY analizador *m*, RAD PHYS antena direccional giratoria *f*, dispositivo analizador de barrido *m*, tomógrafo

axial computarizado por rayos x *m*, TELECOM analizador *m*, dispositivo de exploración *m*, explorador *m*, TEXTIL analizador *m*, TV *programme* antena exploradora *f*, analizador *m*, WATER analizador *m*, WAVE PHYS dispositivo analizador de barrido *m*; ~ **distributor** *n* TELECOM distribuidor de exploración *m*; ~ **printer** *n* INSTR, PRINT impresor analizador *m*

scanning *n* COMP&DP escaneo *m*, exploración *f*, ELECTRON exploración *f*, PETR TECH barrido *m*, escrutación *f*, exploración *f*, PHYS exploración *f*, PRINT escaneo *m*, RAD PHYS barrido *m*, toma de datos *f*, SPACE análisis *m*, examen minucioso *m*, exploración *f*, TELECOM barrido *m*, TV exploración *f*, barrido *m*, búsqueda *f*, lectura *f*, WATER TRANSP *radar* exploración *f*; ~ **area** *n* TV campo de lectura *m*, área de búsqueda *f*; ~ **Auger microscopy** *n* NUCL microscopía de barrido Auger *f*; ~ **beam** *n* ELECTRON, TV haz explorador *m*; ~ **coil** *n* CINEMAT, TV bobina de exploración *f*; ~ **cycle** *n* TV ciclo de exploración *m*; ~ **device** *n* TV dispositivo de barrido *m*; ~ **dot** *n* TV punto de exploración *m*; ~ **drum** *n* TV tambor de exploración *m*; ~ **electron beam** *n* ELECTRON haz electrónico de exploración *m*; ~ **electron microscope** *n* (*SEM*) ELEC microscopio electrónico de barrido *m* (*MEB*), ELECTRON, INSTR microscopio electrónico de exploración *m*, LAB microscopio electrónico de barrido *m* (*MEB*), PHYS microscopio de electrones *m*, RAD PHYS microscopio electrónico de barrido *m* (*MEB*); ~ **electron-beam lithography** *n* ELECTRON litografía por haz electrónico explorador *f*; ~ **electron-beam system** *n* ELECTRON sistema de exploración por haz electrónico *m*; ~ **error** *n* TV error de exploración *m*; ~ **field** *n* TV campo de exploración *m*; ~ **gap** *n* TV intervalo de exploración *m*; ~ **gate** *n* TV puerta de exploración *f*; ~ **head** *n* PRINT cabezal explorador *m*, TV cabezal de exploración *m*; ~ **ion microscopy** *n* (*SIM*) RAD PHYS microscopía iónica de barrido *f* (*MIB*); ~ **laser** *n* ELECTRON, OPT láser de exploración *m*, láser de lectura *m*; ~ **laser beam** *n* ELECTRON, OPT haz lasérico de exploración *m*, haz láser de exploración *m*; ~ **line** *n* ELECTRON, TV línea de exploración *f*; ~ **-mirror electron microscope** *n* INSTR microscopio electrónico de espejo exploratorio *m*; ~ **printing** *n* CINEMAT copiado por exploración de imagen *m*; ~ **process** *n* TV proceso de exploración *m*; ~ **rate** *n* AIR TRANSP frecuencia de barrido *f*, velocidad de exploración *f*; ~ **sequence** *n* PROD secuencia de exploración *f*; ~ **sonar** *n* OCEAN sonar explorador *m*; ~ **spectrometer** *n* RAD PHYS espectrómetro de barrido *m*; ~ **speed** *n* AIR TRANSP velocidad de barrido *f*, TV velocidad de exploración *f*; ~ **spot** *n* TV punto de exploración *m*; ~ **spot control** *n* TV control del punto de exploración *m*; ~ **standard** *n* TV norma de exploración *f*; ~ **switch** *n* ELEC ENG conmutador explorador *m*; ~ **yoke** *n* TV bobina reguladora de la exploración *f*, yugo *m*

scantling *n* CONST *dimensions* cuartón *m*, escantillón *m*, WATER TRANSP *boat building* escantillón *m*

scapolite *n* MINERAL wernerita *f*

scar *n* GEOL roca escarpada *f*

scarf *n* CONST empalme *m*, rebajo *m*, PROD escarpe *m*; ~ **joint** *n* CONST junta biselada *f*, junta de diente de sierra *f*; ~ **jointing** *n* CONST empalme biselado *m*; ~ **weld** *n* PROD soldadura en bisel *f*; ~ **welding** *n* PROD soldadura en bisel *f*

scarfing *n* PROD biselado *m*, corte oblicuo *m*

scarification *n* CONST escarificación *f*

scarifier *n* AGRIC, CONST escarificador *m*, TRANSP escarificadora *f*

scarify *vt* CONST escarificar

scarlet: ~ **lake** *n* COATINGS, COLOUR laca escarlata *f*

scarp *n* OCEAN escarpa *f*

scatter *n* SPACE dispersión *f*, esparcimiento *m*; ~ **load** *n* COMP&DP carga de dispersión *f*, carga dispersa *f*; ~ **proof** *n* PRINT prueba de dispersión *f*; ~ **read** *n* COMP&DP lectura dispersa *f*, lectura por dispersión *f*

scatterable: ~ **mine** *n* MILIT mina de dispersión de efectos *f*

scattered: ~ **light** *n* RAD PHYS luz dispersada *f*; ~ **neutron** *n* NUCL neutrón difuso *m*; ~ **radiation** *n* RAD PHYS radiación dispersada *f*

scattering *n* ACOUST, CINEMAT, COAL dispersión *f*, CRYSTALL dispersión *f*, difusión *f*, ELECTRON dispersión de la radiación *f*, re-radiación *f*, reflexión difusa *f*, difusión *f*, dispersión *f*, FUELLESS dispersión *f*, METALL partículas diseminadas *f pl*, salpicaduras de acero líquido *f pl*, NUCL dispersión *f*, OPT difusión *f*, esparcimiento *m*, PETR TECH, RAD PHYS dispersión *f*, SPACE difusión *f*, diseminación *f*, dispersión *f*, TELECOM difusión *f*, dispersión *f*; ~ **angle** *n* PHYS ángulo de difusión *m*; ~ **coefficient** *n* TELECOM coeficiente de dispersión *m*; ~ **cross-section** *n* PHYS sección eficaz de difusión *f*; ~ **factor** *n* CRYSTALL factor de dispersión *m*; ~ **foil** *n* NUCL lámina de dispersión *f*; ~ **medium** *n* NUCL medio de dispersión *m*; ~ **meter** *n* OCEAN difusiómetro *m*

scatterometer *n* OCEAN difusiómetro *m*

scavenge: ~ **pump** *n* PROD bomba de barrido *f*; ~ **system** *n* PROD sistema de barrido *m*

scavenger: ~ **cell** *n* COAL célula de barrido *f*, cámara limpiadora *f*

scavenging *n* CHEM depuración *f*, MECH barrido *m*, expulsión *f*, NUCL arrastre *m*, barrido *m*, PETR TECH barrido *m*, expulsión *f*, WATER barrido *m*, retirada de las basuras *f*, WATER TRANSP barrido *m*

SCC *abbr* ELEC (*single-cotton-covered*) conductor forrado con una capa de algodón, TELECOM (*satellite control center AmE*, *satellite control centre BrE*) centro de control de satélites *m*

SCCP: ~ **method indicator** *n* TELECOM indicador del método SCCP *m*

scenario *n* CINEMAT guión *m*, PROD simulación de planificaciones *f*

scene: ~-**to-scene color grading** *AmE*, ~-**to-scene colour grading** *BrE* *n* CINEMAT gradación de color de una escena a la otra *f*

scenery: ~ **lamp** *n* ELEC lámpara de decoración *f*

schedule[1] *n* CINEMAT plan *m*, PROD *of criteria* programa *m*, horario *m*, baremo *m*, plan *m*, TRANSP horario *m*, TV programación *f*; ~ **of machinery** *n* PROD inventario de maquinaria *m*; ~ **speed** *n* TRANSP velocidad del programa *f*

schedule[2] *vt* PROD hacer una lista de, inventariar, programar, TELECOM fijar plazos, planear, programar

scheduled: ~ **flight** *n* AIR TRANSP vuelo regular *m*; ~ **maintenance** *n* COMP&DP, NUCL mantenimiento programado *m*; ~ **operating time** *n* TELECOM horario fijo de servicio *m*, tiempo de programación programada *m*; ~ **outage** *n* NUCL parada programada *f*; ~ **receipt** *n* PROD recepción programada *f*; ~ **reporting signal** *n* TELECOM señal para informes

programados *f*; ~ **service** *n* CONST servicio programado *m*, TRANSP servicio con horario fijo *m*

scheduler *n* COMP&DP *jobs, programs* organizador *m*, *programs* planificador *m*

scheduling *n* TV programación *f*; ~ **algorithm** *n* COMP&DP, MATH, SPACE algoritmo de planificación *m*; ~ **option** *n* PROD opción según programa *f*

scheelite *n* MINERAL scheelita *f*

scheelitine *n* MINERAL scheelitina *f*

scheererite *n* MINERAL scheererita *f*

schefferite *n* MINERAL schefferita *f*

schematic: ~ **wiring diagram** *n* NUCL diagrama esquemático del cableado *m*

scheme *n* COMP&DP esquema *m*, MECH ENG *diagram* bosquejo *m*, diagrama *m*, esquema *m*, plan *m*, plano *m*, programa *m*, proyecto *m*; ~ **arch** *n* CONST *curve* arco de diseño *m*, *structure* arco proyectado *m*

Schering: ~ **bridge** *n* ELEC ENG, PHYS puente de Schering *m*

Schfftan: ~ **process** *n* CINEMAT proceso Schfftan *m*

schiller: ~ **spar** *n* MINERAL bastita *f*, espato tornasolado *m*

schistose *adj* GEOL pizarroso

schistosity *n* GEOL esquistosidad *f*, pizarrosidad *f*

schistous: ~ **coal** *n* COAL carbón esquistoso *m*

Schlieren: ~ **photography** *n* PHOTO, PHYS fotografía de Schlieren *f*

Schlueter: ~ **equation of motion** *n* NUCL ecuación Schlueter del movimiento *f*

Schmidt: ~ **number** *n* PHYS número de Schmidt *m*; ~ **optical system** *n* CINEMAT sistema óptico Schmidt *m*; ~ **system** *n* INSTR sistema Schmidt *m*

Schmitt: ~ **trigger** *n* ELECTRON, PHYS trigger de Schmitt *m*

Schnabel: ~ **car** *n* *BrE* RAIL vagón Schnabel *m*

schorl *n* MINERAL chorlo *m*, turmalina negra *f*

Schottel: ~ **propeller** *n* TRANSP hélice Schottel *f*, propulsor Schottel *m*

Schottky: ~ **barrier** *n* ELECTRON aislante Schottky *m*, barrera de Schottky *f*, PHYS barrera de Schottky *f*; ~-**barrier detector diode** *n* ELECTRON diodo detector con aislante Schottky *m*; ~-**barrier diode** *n* ELECTRON diodo con aislante Schottky *m*; ~-**barrier FET** *n* ELECTRON TEC con aislante Schottky *m*; ~-**barrier mixer diode** *n* ELECTRON diodo mezclador con aislante Schottky *m*; ~-**barrier rectifier diode** *n* ELECTRON diodo rectificador con aislante Schottky *m*; ~ **bipolar integrated circuit** *n* ELECTRON circuito integrado bipolar Schottky *m*; ~ **clamped transistor** *n* ELECTRON transistor estabilizado Schottky *m*; ~ **clamping diode** *n* ELECTRON diodo de bloqueo Schottky *m*; ~ **defect** *n* CRYSTALL defecto de Schottky *m*; ~ **device** *n* ELECTRON dispositivo Schottky *m*; ~ **diode** *n* ELECTRON, PHYS diodo de Schottky *m*; ~ **effect** *n* ELECTRON efecto Schottky *m*; ~ **noise** *n* PHYS ruido de Schottky *m*; ~ **TTL** *n* ELECTRON SLTT Schottky *m*

schreibersite *n* MINERAL schreibersita *f*

Schrödinger: ~ **equation** *n* PHYS ecuación de Schrödinger *f*

schwartzembergite *n* MINERAL schwartzembergita *f*

Schwarzschild: ~ **radius** *n* PHYS radio de Schwarzschild *m*

schwatzite *n* MINERAL schwatzita *f*

science: ~ **of heat** *n* THERMO calorimetría *f*

scintillation *n* PHYS centelleo *m*, SPACE centelleo *m*, escintilación *m*, TELECOM titilación *f*, TEXTIL centelleo *m*; ~ **coincidence spectrometer** *n* NUCL espectrómetro de centelleo *m*; ~ **counter** *n* PART PHYS contador de centelleo *m*, contador de destello *m*, PHYS contador de centelleo *m*, RAD PHYS contador de centelleo *m*, detector de centelleo *m*, detector de destellos *m*, WAVE PHYS radiómetro *m*; ~ **noise** *n* SPACE ruido de escintilación *m*; ~ **spectrometer** *n* RAD PHYS espectrómetro de centelleo *m*

scintillator *n* RAD PHYS escintilador *m*

scion: ~ **grafting** *n* AGRIC injerto de punta *m*

scissor: ~ **crossing** *n* RAIL vía diagonal de unión *f*; ~ **joint** *n* MECH ENG eje de tijeras *m*

scissoring *n* COMP&DP recortado *m*, recorte *m* (*Esp*)

scissors *n* MECH ENG, TEXTIL tijeras *f pl*; ~ **crossing** *n* RAIL cruzamiento *m*, vía diagonal de unión *f*

scleroclase *n* MINERAL escleroclasa *f*

scleroprotein *n* FOOD escleroproteína *f*

SCN *abbr* (*specification change notice*) TRANSP anuncio de cambio de especificación *m*, aviso de cambio de especificación *m*

scolecite *n* MINERAL escolecita *f*

scoop *n* AGRIC azadón *m*, CINEMAT reflector *m*, LAB cucharón *m*, pala *f*, MAR POLL cuchara *f*, cucharón *m*, POLL cangilón *m*, cucharón *m*; ~ **dump car** *n* AmE TRANSP vagoneta basculante de pico *f*; ~ **dump wagon** *BrE* *n* (*cf scoop dump car AmE*) TRANSP vagoneta basculante de pico *f*; ~ **net** *n* OCEAN salabardo *m*, mediomundo *m* (*AmL*), red barredera *f* (*Esp*); ~ **water-wheel** *n* WATER noria *f*; ~ **wheel** *n* WATER noria *f*; ~ **wheel elevator** *n* TRANSP elevador-noria *m*; ~ **wheel feeder** *n* TRANSP alimentador de la noria *m*

scope *n* (*cf oscilloscope*) AIR TRANSP, COMP&DP, ELECTRON alcance *m*, MECH ENG *of standard* alcance *m*, extensión *f*, gama *f*, MILIT, PROD, SPACE alcance *m*, TEXTIL amplitud *f*, alcance *m*, TV osciloscopio *m*, pantalla de tubo de rayos catódicos *f*, WATER TRANSP alcance *m*

scorch[1] *n* P&R vulcanización prematura *f*

scorch[2] *vt* THERMO abrasar, chamuscar, sobrecalentar, tostar

scorched *adj* THERMO abrasado, chamuscado, cristalizado después de un sobrecalentamiento, sobrecalentado, tostado

scorching: ~ **tendency** *n* P&R tendencia a vulcanizarse prematuramente *f*

scorchy *adj* P&R chamuscado

score[1] *n* C&G, PRINT estría *f*

score[2] *vt* C&G, PRINT estriar

score[3]: ~ **a hit** *vi* MILIT hacer blanco

scored: ~ **pulley** *n* MECH ENG polea ranurada *f*

scoria *n* GEOL escoria *f*, escoria volcánica *f*

scoring *n* C&G rayado *m*, PRINT estriado *m*

scorodite *n* MINERAL escorodita *f*

scotch *n* MECH ENG calzo *m*, cuña de bloqueo *f*, tope *m*

scotching *n* MECH acuñado *m*, MECH ENG acuñado *m*, frote *m*

scotchlight: ~ **signal** *n* RAIL señal repetidora reflectante *f*

Scott: ~ **connection** *n* ELEC conexión Scott *f*

scour[1] *n* FUELLESS derrubio *m*, socavación *f*, HYDROL socavación *f*, arrastre *m*, derrubio *m*, WATER arrastre *m*, socavación *f*; ~-**and-fill** *n* GEOL arrastre y relleno *m*

scour[2] *vt* C&G, CONST desgrasar, DETERG desgrasar,

lavar con detergentes, pulir, ELEC, FOOD desgrasar, FUELLESS derrubiar, socavar, HYDROL formar cauce, socavar, MECH, MECH ENG desgrasar, PROD *metals* decapar, desgrasar, desoxidar, limpiar por descarga de agua, WATER derrubiar, limpiar por descarga de agua, socavar

scouring *n* FUELLESS derrubios *m pl*, OCEAN socavación *f*, limpieza *f*, limpieza con descarga de agua *f*, PETR TECH erosión *f*, socavación *f*, PROD *metals* decapado *m*, desoxidación *f*, TEXTIL descrudado *m*, WATER derrubios *m pl*, limpieza *f*, descarga de agua *f*; ~ **basin** *n* OCEAN dársena de limpieza *f*; ~ **liquid** *n* C&G, CONST desgrasador *m*, DETERG descrudecedor *m*, desgrasador *m*, detergente *m*, ELEC, FOOD, MECH, MECH ENG, PROD desgrasador *m*; ~ **liquor** *n* DETERG lejía de lavado *f*; ~ **powder** *n* DETERG polvo desengrasador *m*; ~ **soap** *n* DETERG jabón desengrasador *m*; ~ **solution** *n* DETERG solución desengrasante *f*

scours *n* AGRIC diarrea del ganado *f*

SCPC *abbr* (*single channel per carrier*) SPACE, TELECOM SCPC (*un solo canal por portadora, canal único por portadora, portadora monocanal*)

SCR[1] *abbr* ELEC (*silicon rectifier*) rectificador de silicio *m*, ELEC ENG (*silicon-controlled rectifier*) RCS (*rectificador controlado de silicio*) ELEC ENG, PHYS (*silicon rectifier*) rectificador de silicio *m*, TELECOM (*silicon-controlled rectifier*) RCS (*rectificador controlado de silicio*)

SCR[2]: ~ **amplifier** *n* ELECTRON amplificador para RCS *m*; ~ **converter** *n* ELEC ENG convertidor del RCS *m*; ~ **crosspoint** *n* TELECOM punto de cruce RCS *m*; ~ **preregulation** *n* ELEC ENG pre-regulación del RCS *f*; ~ **preregulator** *n* ELEC ENG pre-regulador del RCS *m*; ~-**regulated power supply** *n* ELEC ENG suministro de energía regulado por RCS *m*; ~ **regulation** *n* ELEC ENG regulación del RCS *f*; ~ **regulator** *n* ELEC ENG regulador del RCS *m*; ~ **trimmer transformer** *n* ELEC, ELEC ENG transformador del RCS *m*

scram *n* NUCL parada de emergencia *f*; ~ **rod** *n* NUCL barra de parada *f*

scramble *vt* MILIT encriptar, escamotear, SPACE escamotear, TELECOM encriptar, mezclar, TV distorsionar

scrambled: ~ **message** *n* TELECOM transmisión secreta *f*; ~ **transmission** *n* TELECOM transmisión secreta *f*

scrambler *n* MILIT escamoteamiento *m*, SPACE dispersor de energía *m*, distorsionador *m*, escamoteamiento *m*, perturbador de conversación *m*, TELECOM dispositivo de transmisión secreta *m*, encriptador *m*, mezclador *m*, perturbador de conversación *m*, TV circuito perturbador *m*; ~ **telephone** *n* MILIT teléfono de mezclado *m*

scrambling *n* MILIT, SPACE escamoteo *m*, TELECOM encriptación *f*, mezcla *f*, transmisión secreta *f*, TV distorsionado *m*; ~ **control** *n* TELECOM control de encriptación *m*

scrammed: ~ **rod** *n* NUCL barra introducida en el núcleo *f*

scrap[1] *n* AGRIC residuo *m*, COAL chatarra *f*, residuos *m pl*, MECH *cursor* chatarra *f*, desecho *m*, METALL chatarra *f*, rebaba *f*, PROD fragmento *m*, *from foundry* desechos de fundición *m*, *metal* chatarra *f*, desechos *m pl*; ~ **factor** *n* PROD factor de desguace *m*; ~ **iron** *n* COAL metralla *f*, PROD chatarra de hierro *f*; ~ **material** *n* PACK material de desecho *m*; ~ **metal** *n* PROD chatarra de metal *f*; ~ **process** *n* PROD tratamiento con chatarra *m*; ~ **quantity** *n* PROD cantidad de chatarra *f*; ~ **return** *n* C&G banda de desperdicio *f*

scrap² *vt* MECH dar de baja, descartar, desmontar, MINE rascar, PROD descartar, desechar, desguazar, rascar, WATER TRANSP desguazar

scrape *vt* CONST rascar, raspar, MAR POLL, MINE, PROD rascar

scraped: ~-**surface freezer** *n* REFRIG congelador con rascador *m*

scraper *n* COAL cuchara de arrastre *f*, cuchara sacabarro *f*, máquina escarbadora *f*, CONST, descarnador *m*, excavadora *f*, raspador *m*, traílla *f*, FOOD raspador *m*, MAR POLL *air bubble in a casting* rasqueta *f*, MECH, MECH ENG descarnador *m*, escarbador *m*, escariador *m*, rascador *m*, raspador *m*, rasqueta *f*, MINE, cuchara de arrastre *f*, cuchara sacabarro *f*, excavadora de cable *f*, PETR TECH raspador *m*; ~ **chain assembly** *n* MINE cadena con raederas *f*, cadena con rastras *f*; ~ **chain conveyor** *n* MINE transportador con paletas rascadoras *m*, transportador de raederas *m*, transportador de rasquetas *m*; ~ **conveyor** *n* PROD transportador con paletas rascadoras *m*, transportador de raederas *m*, transportador de rasquetas *m*

scraping *n* MAR POLL, MINE, PROD raspadura *f*, rasqueteado *m*; ~ **plane** *n* CONST cepillo raspador *m*; ~ **tools** *n pl* MINE herramientas de arrastre *f pl*, herramientas de rascado *f pl*

scrapping: ~ **factor** *n* PROD factor de desguace *m*

scrapyard *n* PROD parque de desguace *m*

scratch *n* C&G raya *f*, rayón *m*, CINEMAT raya *f*, P&R estría *f*, raya *f*, PRINT rasgo diagonal *m*, TEXTIL rascadura *f*; ~ **awl** *n* CONST lezna de marcar *f*, punzón de marcar *m*; ~ **brush** *n* CONST cepillo de arañar *m*; ~ **file** *n* COMP&DP archivo borrador *m*, archivo de trabajo *m*; ~ **gage** *AmE*, ~ **gauge** *BrE n* CONST gramil *m*; ~ **pad** *n* COMP&DP libreta de borrador *f*, zona de trabajo *f*; ~ **pad memory** *n* COMP&DP memoria de trabajo *f*; ~ **resistance** *n* P&R resistencia al rayado *f*; ~ **tape** *n* COMP&DP cinta de borrador *f*, cinta de notas *f*, cinta reutilizable *f*

scratched: ~ **mold** *AmE*, ~ **mould** *BrE n* C&G molde rayado *m*

scratching *n* TEXTIL esbozo *m*

scree *n* GEOL coluviones de ladera *f pl*, talud *m*, GEOPHYS pendiente *f*, talud *m*

screed: ~ **heater** *n* CONST maestra *f*, regla maestra *f*; ~ **height** *n* CONST altura de la regla *f*; ~ **profile** *n* CONST perfil de la regla *m*

screen¹: ~-**based** *adj* COMP&DP basado en pantalla, especial para pantalla; ~-**displayed** *adj* PRINT en pantalla

screen² *n* CINEMAT pantalla *f*, COAL criba *f*, filtro *m*, pantalla *f*, COMP&DP *protection* apantallado *m*, *display* pantalla *f*, CONST tamiz *m*, criba *f*, cedazo *m*, *wall* cerca *f*, *on opening* reja *f*, ELEC, ELECTRON pantalla *f*, GEOL tamiz *m*, abrigo *m*, HYDROL defensa *f*, filtro *m*, abrigo *m*, MECH zaranda *f*, tamiz *m*, filtro *m*, pantalla *f*, MINE cedazo *m*, tamiz *m*, criba *f*, PAPER tamiz *m*, clasificador de tamiz *m*, PHYS pantalla *f*, PRINT pantalla *f*, trama *f*, PROD criba *f*, cedazo *m*, tamiz *m*, RECYCL tamiz *m*, rejilla *f*, criba *f*, cedazo *m*, SPACE filtro *m*, pantalla *f*, TV pantalla *f*, blindaje *m*; ~ **analysis** *n* (*cf granulometric analysis BrE*) C&G análisis granulométrico *m*, granulometría *f*, CHEM TECH, COAL, GEOL, NUCL análisis granulométrico *m*; ~ **angle** *n* PRINT ángulo de la trama *m*; ~ **bar** *n* CONST barrote *m*; ~ **brightness** *n* CINEMAT brillo de pantalla *m*; ~ **count** *n* PRINT contador de retícula *m*; ~ **curve** *n* PRINT curva de la trama *f*; ~ **display** *n* COMP&DP pantalla *f*, visualización de pantalla *f* (*AmL*); ~ **dump** *n* COMP&DP vuelco de pantalla *m*; ~ **effect** *n* TELECOM efecto de blindaje *m*, efecto de pantalla *m*; ~ **factor** *n* NUCL factor de pantalla *m*; ~ **grid** *n* ELECTRON rejilla de pantalla *f*; ~ **grid tube** *n* ELECTRON tubo de rejilla de pantalla *m*; ~ **image** *n* COMP&DP imagen de pantalla *f*; ~ **mask** *n* CINEMAT máscara de pantalla *f*; ~ **painter** *n* COMP&DP pintor de pantalla *m*; ~ **penetration** *n* ELECTRON penetración de la pantalla *f*; ~ **plate** *n* COAL plancha perforadora para cribas *f*, NUCL placa pantalla *f*; ~ **printing** *n* C&G proceso de impresión *m*, PRINT serigrafía *f*; ~ **printing machine** *n* PACK impresora serigráfica *f*; ~ **processing** *n* PRINT procesado serigráfico *m*; ~ **ratio** *n* CINEMAT dimensiones de pantalla *f pl*; ~ **resolution** *n* PRINT resolución de la trama *f*; ~ **roller** *n* PRINT rodillo tramado *m*; ~ **ruling** *n* PRINT línea de la trama *f*; ~ **shape** *n* PRINT forma de la trama *f*; ~ **terminal** *n* TELECOM terminal de pantalla *m*; ~ **test** *n* CINEMAT prueba cinematográfica *f*; ~ **time** *n* CINEMAT duración *f*; ~ **tint** *n* PRINT fondo tramado *m*; ~ **varnish** *n* COATINGS barniz con tratamiento químico *m*; ~ **washer** *n* PRINT lavador de pantallas serigráficas *m*

screen³ *vt* CHEM blindar, cribar, proteger, tamizar, CINEMAT proyectar, CONST cernir, cribar, tamizar, ELEC apantallar, MAR POLL cribar, NUCL, PHYS, RAD PHYS apantallar, SPACE apantallar, faradizar

screened: ~ **aerial** *n BrE* (*cf screened antenna AmE*) TV antena apantallada *f*, antena blindada *f*; ~ **antenna** *n AmE* (*cf screened aerial BrE*) TV antena apantallada *f*, antena blindada *f*; ~ **cable** *n* COMP&DP cable apantallado *m*, ELEC cable apantallado *m*, cable blindado *m*, PHYS cable apantallado *m*; ~ **coal** *n* COAL carbón tamizado *m*

screener *n* PAPER depurador de tamiz *m*

screening *n* CHEM cernidura *f*, desperdicios de criba *m pl*, CONST cribado *m*, ELEC *electromagnetic field* apantallamiento *m*, blindaje *m*, apantallado *m*, MAR POLL criba *f*, NUCL apantallamiento *m*, PAPER clasificación *f*, rechazos de depuración *m pl*, PHYS apantallamiento *m*, PROD cribado *m*, paso por la criba *m*, RAD PHYS apantallamiento *m*, SPACE faradización *f*, filtrado *m*, selección *f*, tamizado *m*, *protective* apantallamiento *m*, TV *equipment* blindaje *m*; ~ **booth** *n* CINEMAT cabina de proyección *f*; ~ **box** *n* PROD caja de cribado *f*; ~ **constant** *n* NUCL constante de apantallamiento *f*; ~ **effect** *n* ELEC efecto de blindaje *m*, efecto de pantalla *m*; ~ **efficiency** *n* COAL eficacia del filtrado *f*; ~ **indicator** *n* (*SI*) TELECOM indicador de apantallamiento *m*; ~ **inspection** *n* QUALITY control selectivo *m*; ~ **mesh** *n* COAL malla de tamiz *f*; ~ **number** *n* NUCL constante de apantallamiento *f*; ~ **plant** *n* COAL planta de filtrado *f*; ~ **room** *n* CINEMAT sala de proyección *f*; ~ **surface** *n* COAL superficie de filtrado *f*; ~ **test** *n* QUALITY ensayo de selección *m*, SPACE prueba de selección *f*; ~ **time** *n* CINEMAT duración *f*

screenings *n pl* AGRIC granos rotos *m pl*, COAL cerniduras *f pl*, desperdicios del cribado *m pl*, granzas *f pl*, HYDROL desperdicios del cribado *m pl*

screenplay *n* CINEMAT guión cinematográfico *m*

screw *vt* MECH atornillar, roscar, MECH ENG atornillar, enroscar

screwcap: ~ **tooling** *n* MECH ENG maquinado de casquillos roscados *m*, maquinado de cápsula roscada *m*, maquinado de tapones de rosca *m*

screwdriver: ~ **bit** *n* MECH ENG destornillador de berbiquí *m*; ~ **slot** *n* ELEC ENG ranura para atornillador-destornillador *f*, ranura para destornillador *f*

screwed: ~ **fitting** *n* MECH ENG *pipes* ajuste roscado *m*; ~ **joint** *n* NUCL junta atornillada *f*; **~-pipe coupling** *n* MECH ENG acoplamiento de tubo roscado *m*; ~ **and socketed bend** *n* MECH ENG *pipes* codo roscado y enchufado *m*

screwing *n* MECH atornillamiento *m*, MECH ENG *threading, tapping* roscadura *f*, atornillamiento *m*, apriete *m*, enroscado *m*, sujeción *f*, fileteado *m*, PETR TECH enroscamiento *m*, roscado *m*; **~-and-tapping machine** *n* MECH ENG máquina de roscar y aterrajar *f*, roscadora-aterrajadora *f*; ~ **chuck** *n* MECH ENG cabezal para roscar *m*; ~ **device** *n* NUCL dispositivo atornillador *m*; ~ **die** *n* MECH ENG cojinete de roscar *m*, terraja *f*; ~ **head** *n* MECH ENG cabezal roscador *m*; **~-in** *n* PETR TECH atornillado *m*, enroscamiento *m*, enrosque *m*; ~ **machine** *n* MECH ENG máquina de filetear *f*, máquina de roscar *f*; **~-out** *n* PETR TECH aflojado *m*, desatornillado *m*; **~-up** *n* MECH ENG fileteado *m*

scribe[1]: ~ **awl** *n* CONST *carpenter's* lezna de trazado *f*

scribe[2] *vti* CONST trazar

scriber *n* CONST *carpenter's* gramil *m*, *of scribing-block* punzón *m*, ELECTRON *lasers* punta de trazar *f*, MECH ENG *of centre-bit* buril *m*, gramil *m*, punta de trazar *f*, punzón de trazar *m*, aguja de marcar *f*

scribing *n* ELECTRON *with lasers* trazado *m*; ~ **awl** *n* CONST *carpenter's* lezna de trazado *f*; ~ **block** *n* MECH ENG *engineer's* gramil de escuadra *m*, gramil de trazar *m*, verificador de superficies planas *m*; ~ **gage** *AmE*, ~ **gauge** *BrE n* CONST *carpenter's* gramil *m*; ~ **step** *n* ELECTRON intervalo de trazo *m*

scrim *n* CINEMAT gasa *f*; ~ **screen** *n* TEXTIL tamiz de bucarán *m*

script *n* CINEMAT guión cinematográfico *m*, COMP&DP guión *m*, libreto *m*, PRINT manuscrito *m*, letra cursiva *f*; ~ **person** *n* CINEMAT encargada del guión *f*, encargado del guión *m*; ~ **writer** *n* CINEMAT, TV guionista *m*

scroll[1]: ~ **bar** *n* COMP&DP barra de desplazamiento *f*, barra de enrollamiento *f*; ~ **chuck** *n* MECH ENG plato autocentrante *m*, plato con ajuste espiral *m*, portaherramientas cónico *m*; ~ **clutch** *n* MECH ENG embrague cónico *m*; ~ **saw** *n* MECH ENG sierra de arco *f*, sierra de calar *f*, sierra de contornear *f*, sierra de marquetería *f*; ~ **shears** *n pl* MECH ENG cizalla de rollos *f*

scroll[2] *vt* COMP&DP desplazar por la pantalla, enrollar

scrolling *n* COMP&DP desplazamiento por pantalla *m*, enrollamiento *m*, PRINT desplazamiento *m*

scroop: ~ **finish** *n* COATINGS acabado con efecto de crujido *m*

scrub: ~ **cultivator** *n* AGRIC cultivador de matorrales *m*; ~ **mark** *n BrE* (*cf rub AmE*) C&G tallón *m*

scrubber *n* AGRIC máquina desterronadora *f*, COAL depurador *m*, MINE depurador *m* (*Esp*), separador por lavado *m* (*AmL*), torre depuradora *f*, SPACE depurador *m*, limpiador de tanques *m*, purificador *m*; ~ **walls** *n pl* POLL membranas para depuración *f pl*

scrubbing *n* CHEM TECH, PETR TECH depuración *f*, POLL depuración *f*, lavado *m*, limpieza *f*, THERMO *programming* depuración *f*; ~ **soap** *n* DETERG jabón de fregado *m*

scuba *n* OCEAN, WATER TRANSP aparato respiratorio autónomo *m*; ~ **diving** *n* PETR TECH buceo *m*, WATER TRANSP buceo con aparato respiratorio autónomo *m*; ~ **tank** *n* OCEAN botella de aire *f*

scuff: ~ **mark** *n* C&G raspón *m*, TEXTIL marca por desgaste *f*

scuffing *n* TEXTIL rasguño *m*

scull[1] *n* PROD *founding* fondo de cuchara *m*, WATER TRANSP espadilla *f*

scull[2] *vi* WATER TRANSP singlar

scum *n* C&G escoria *f*, espuma *f*, CHEM espuma *f*, impurezas flotantes *f pl*, nata *f*, COAL desechos *m pl*, escorias *f pl*, FOOD espuma *f*, HYDROL materia espumosa de aguas de cloaca *f*, MAR POLL impurezas flotantes *f pl*, PRINT velo *m*; ~ **baffle** *n* HYDROL tabique para materias flotantes *m*

scumble *n* P&R difuminación *f*

scumming *n* PRINT formación de velo *f*

scupper *n* WATER TRANSP imbornal *m*

scurvy *n* AGRIC escorbuto *m*

scutcheon *n BrE* CONST *locksmithing* escudete *m*, escudo de cerradura *m*

scuttle *vt* WATER TRANSP *ship* barrenar

scythe *n* AGRIC guadaña *f*

SD *abbr* (*signal distributor*) TELECOM distribuidor de señales *m*

SDH[1] *abbr* (*synchronous digital hierarchy*) TELECOM jerarquía digital sincrónica *f*, jerarquía digital síncrona *f*

SDH[2]: ~ **management network** *n* (*SMN*) TELECOM red de gestión de jerarquía digital síncrona *f*; ~ **management subnetwork** *n* (*SMS*) TELECOM subred de gestión de jerarquía digital síncrona *f*; ~ **physical interface** *n* (*synchronous digital hierarchy physical interface*) TELECOM interfaz físico de jerarquía digital síncrona *m*

SDLC *abbr* (*synchronous data-link control*) COMP&DP SDLC (*procedimiento de control de transmisión síncrona*)

SDR *abbr* (*system design review*) SPACE (*revisión del diseño del sistema*)

SDU *abbr* (*service data unit*) TELECOM unidad de datos de servicio *f*

SE *abbr* (*slurry explosive*) MINE explosivo fluidizado *m*

Se *abbr* (*selenium*) CHEM, ELEC ENG Se (*selenio*)

sea[1]: **~-damaged** *adj* WATER TRANSP averiado por el agua de mar; **-water-coded** *adj* THERMO enfriado por agua de mar, refrigerado por agua de mar

sea[2]: **at** ~ *adv* WATER TRANSP en el mar; **by** ~ *adv* WATER TRANSP por mar, por vía marítima

sea[3] *n* HYDROL, OCEAN mar *m*; ~ **anchor** *n* OCEAN, WATER TRANSP ancla flotante *f*; ~ **area** *n* WATER TRANSP región del mar *f*, zona de mar *f*; ~ **arm** *n* OCEAN, WATER TRANSP brazo de mar *m*; ~ **bed** *n* CONST lecho marino *m*, OCEAN lecho del mar *m*; ~ **bottom** *n* OCEAN fondo del mar *m*; ~ **breeze** *n* METEO brisa de mar *f*; ~ **buoy** *n* WATER TRANSP boya de recalada *f*; ~ **canal** *n* OCEAN canal interoceánico *m*, canal marítimo *m*; ~ **carriage** *n* WATER TRANSP transporte por mar *m*; ~ **carrier** *n* WATER TRANSP porteador *m*, transportista *m*; ~ **clutter** *n* SPACE eco parásito por reflexión marina *m*, ecos de mar *m pl*, TELECOM ecos de mar *m pl*, ecos parásitos del mar *m pl*, emborronamiento debido al mar *m*, WATER TRANSP *radar* perturbación por mar *f*; ~ **conditions** *n pl* WATER TRANSP estado de la mar *m*; ~ **damage** *n* WATER TRANSP daños causados por la mar *m pl*; ~ **deep** *n* OCEAN foso submarino *m*; ~ **defence** *n BrE* METEO antierosionante marino *m*; ~ **defense** *AmE see sea defence BrE*; ~ **dike** *AmE*, ~ **dyke** *BrE n* WATER dique de mar *m*; ~ **floor** *n* CONST, FUELLESS, OCEAN fondo del mar *m*; ~ **foam** *n* OCEAN espuma de mar *f*; ~ **grass bed** *n* OCEAN herbazal de marisma *m*; ~ **high** *n* OCEAN colina abisal *f*, región de alta presión *f*; ~ **ice** *n* REFRIG, WATER TRANSP hielo marino *m*; ~ **knoll** *n* OCEAN colina abisal *f*; ~ **lane** *n* OCEAN, WATER TRANSP ruta marítima *f*, vía marítima *f*; ~ **level** *n* CONST, FUELLESS, WATER, WATER TRANSP nivel del mar *m*; ~ **link** *n* WATER TRANSP enlace marítimo *m*; ~ **loch** *n* WATER TRANSP ría *f*; ~ **marsh** *n* OCEAN marjal marino *m*; ~ **moat** *n* OCEAN foso submarino *m*; ~ **noise** *n* OCEAN ruido del mar *m*; ~ **ranch** *n* OCEAN coto de acuicultura marina *m*, vallicultura *f*; ~ **ranching** *n* OCEAN cría y ramoneo *f*; ~ **route** *n* WATER TRANSP *navigation* derrota marítima *f*, *trade* ruta marítima *f*; ~ **salt** *n* FOOD sal de mar *f*, sal marina *f*; ~ **salt nucleus** *n* OCEAN núcleo de sal marina *m*; ~ **scarp** *n* OCEAN escarpa submarina *f*; ~ **state** *n* WATER TRANSP estado de la mar *m*; ~ **state spectrum** *n* OCEAN espectro del estado de la mar *m*; ~ **temperature** *n* WATER TRANSP temperatura del mar *f*; ~ **trade** *n* WATER TRANSP comercio marítimo *m*, tráfico marítimo *m*; ~ **transport** *n* WATER TRANSP transporte marítimo *m*; ~ **trial** *n* WATER TRANSP *ship building* prueba de mar *f*; ~ **tug** *n* WATER TRANSP remolcador de altura *m*; ~ **wall** *n* CONST muro del muelle *m*, WATER TRANSP malecón *m* (*AmL*), terraplén *m*, muro del muelle *m*; ~ **water** *n* OCEAN, WATER TRANSP agua de mar *f*; ~**water ice** *n* REFRIG hielo de agua de mar *m*; ~**water intrusion** *n* WATER intrusión de agua del mar *f*

Seabee: ~ **carrier** *n* WATER TRANSP Seabee *m*, carguero tipo Seabee *m*, buque carguero tipo Seabee *m*

seaboard *n* (*cf shore*) OCEAN cornisa *f*, cornisa marina *f*, litoral *m*, WATER TRANSP *geography* cornisa *f*, litoral *m*

seaborne[1] *adj* WATER TRANSP procedente del mar, transportado por mar

seaborne[2]: ~ **trade** *n* WATER TRANSP comercio marítimo *m*, tráfico marítimo *m*

seacock *n* WATER TRANSP *shipbuilding* toma de mar *f*, válvula de comunicación con el mar *f*, válvula de mar *f*

seafloor: ~ **renewal** *n* OCEAN renovación de los fondos oceánicos *f*; ~ **spreading** *n* GEOPHYS expansión del fondo marino *f*, OCEAN expansión de los fondos oceánicos *f*

seafront *n* OCEAN fachada marítima *f*

seagoing: ~ **vessel** *n* MAR POLL buque de navegación marítima *m*, WATER TRANSP buque de altura *m*

seakeeping: ~ **qualities** *n pl* WATER TRANSP condiciones marineras *f pl*

seal[1] *n* (*cf lipped cover tile BrE*) C&G sello *m*, ELEC *protection* cierre *m*, obturación *f*, LAB junta hermética *f*, MECH retén del lubricante *m*, sello *m*, precinto *m*, MECH ENG *for dynamic application* precinto *m*, junta

hermética *f*, sello *m*, anillo estanco *m*, MINE cerrar, aislar, PETR TECH obturación *f*, sello *m*, WATER TRANSP *shipbuilding* frisa *f*, junta estanca *f*, junta hermética *f*, obturación *f*; ~ **assembly** *n* NUCL conjunto de cierre *m*, conjunto de sellado *m*; ~ **coat** *n* CONST capa de sellado *f*; ~ **gas** *n* GAS, NUCL gas de sellado *m*; ~ **unit** *n* NUCL unidad de sellado *f*; ~ **of Viton** *n* PROD junta de Viton *f*; ~ **water** *n* NUCL *solar power* agua de cierres *f*

seal[2] *vt* MAR POLL precintar, MINE aislar, cerrar, PAPER ocluir, sellar, WATER TRANSP *shipbuilding* frisar, hacer estanco, hacer hermético, obturar; ~ **up** *vt* PROD *close* obturar

sealant *n* C&G sellador *m*, CHEM obturador *m*, sellador *m*, sustancia taponadora *f*, P&R, PRINT sellador *m*, VEH producto para obturar *m*, tapajuntas *m*; ~ **polymer** *n* PETR TECH polímero obturador *m*, polímero sellador *m*

sealed[1] *adj* MAR POLL precintado

sealed[2]: ~ **battery** *n AmE* (*cf nonspill battery BrE*) VEH *electrical system* batería hermética *f*; ~ **beam unit** *n* AUTO unidad de faro hermético *f*; ~ **contacts** *n pl* ELEC ENG contactos herméticos *m pl*; ~ **cooling system** *n* AUTO sistema de refrigeración hermético *m*; ~ **motor** *n* ELEC motor blindado *m*; ~ **power factor** *n* PROD factor de potencia sellado *m*; ~~**quench furnace** *n* HEAT, THERMO horno de templado hermético *m*; ~ **reactor** *n* ELEC reactor blindado *m*; ~ **rectifier** *n* ELEC ENG rectificador sellado *m*; ~ **source** *n* NUCL fuente sellada *f*; ~ **switch contact** *n* PROD contacto del interruptor bloqueado *m*; ~ **transformer** *n* ELEC, ELEC ENG transformador sellado *m*; ~~**wafer rotary switch** *n* ELEC ENG interruptor giratorio de sectores sellado *m*

sealer *n* COLOUR, P&R sellador *m*

sealing *n* C&G sellado *m*, CONST *fixing* estanqueidad *f*, sellado *m*, PETR TECH proceso de tapado *m*, sellamiento *m*, RAIL estanqueidad *f*; ~ **cap** *n* PACK tapón hermético *m*; ~ **compound** *n* CONST pasta de sellado *f*; ~ **edge** *n* C&G borde de sellado *m*; ~ **machine** *n* PACK máquina de cerrar *f*, máquina precintadora *f*; ~ **material** *n* NUCL material de sellado *m*; ~ **paint** *n* COLOUR, CONST pintura selladora *f*; ~ **pliers** *n pl* MECH ENG alicates de precintar *m pl*; ~ **plug** *n* MECH ENG tapón de precintado *m*, tapón de precintar *m*; ~ **ring** *n* AUTO anillo de sellado *m*, MECH ENG anillo de estanqueidad *m*, anillo de precintado *m*, anillo obturador *m*, VEH anillo de estanqueidad *m*, anillo de sellado *m*; ~ **surface** *n* C&G superficie de sellado *f*; ~ **tape** *n* PRINT cinta selladora *f*; ~~**up** *n* CONST *closing* cierre *m*; **weld** *n* NUCL soldadura de sellado *f*

seam[1] *n* C&G costura *f*, COAL capa de carbón *f*, fisura *f*, grieta *f*, línea de separación entre capas *f*, MECH *tools* costura *f*, MECH ENG costura *f*, junta *f*, reborde *m*, MINE veta *f* (*AmL*), diaclasa *f* (*Esp*), filón *m*, fisura *f*, grieta *f*, capa de carbón *f*, recubrimiento *m*, manto *m*, PAPER, PRINT, TEXTIL costura *f*; ~ **coal** *n* MINE capa de carbón *f*; ~ **line** *n* C&G, TEXTIL línea de costura *f*; ~ **nodules** *n* COAL masa caliza con fragmentos de plantas fósiles *f*; ~ **roller** *n* MECH ENG rodillo de costuras *m*, rodillo de rebabas *m*; ~ **sequence** *n* COAL secuencia de las capas *f*; ~ **weld** *n* NUCL costura soldada *f*; ~ **welding wheel blank** *n* MECH ENG primordio para ruedas de soldadura continua *m*, roldana circular para soldadura continua *f*; ~ **work** *n*

COAL, MINE trabajos en capa *m pl*, trabajos en manto *m pl*; ~ **working** *n* MINE laboreo en capas *m*, laboreo en manto *m*

seam[2] *vt* TEXTIL coser

seamanship *n* WATER TRANSP arte marinera *m*, competencia náutica *f*, pericia marinera *f*

seamark *n* OCEAN línea de máxima pleamar *f*, marca *f*, WATER TRANSP baliza *f*, línea de pleamar *f*, marca *f*

seamarking *n* OCEAN, WATER TRANSP balizamiento *m*

seamed: ~ **pipe** *n* MECH ENG caño con costura *m*, tubo con costura *m*

seaming *n* TEXTIL cosido de unión *m*

seamless[1] *adj* TEXTIL sin costuras

seamless[2]: ~ **pipe** *n* MECH ENG caño sin costura *m*, tubo sin costura *m*; ~ **pressure vessel** *n* MECH ENG depósito de presión sin costura *m*; ~ **printing** *n* PRINT impresión sin costura *f*; ~ **rolled ring** *n* MECH ENG anillo laminado sin costura *m*, anillo laminado sin soldadura *m*; ~ **wrought-copper tube** *n* MECH ENG tubo de cobre forjado sin costura *m*, tubo de cobre fundido sin costura *m*

seamount *n* GEOL, OCEAN pico submarino *m*, montaña submarina *f*

seaplane *n* AIR TRANSP hidroavión *m*; ~ **base** *n* AIR TRANSP base de hidroaviones *f*

seaport *n* WATER TRANSP puerto de mar *m*

seaquake *n* GEOPHYS, OCEAN maremoto *m*, seísmo submarino *m*, sismo submarino *m*

search *n* COMP&DP búsqueda *f*; ~ **coil** *n* ELEC *magnetism* bobina exploradora *f*, sonda magnética *f*, ELEC ENG bobina de prueba *f*, bobina exploradora *f*; ~ **key** *n* COMP&DP clave de búsqueda *f*, criterio de búsqueda *m*, tecla de búsqueda *f*; ~ **query** *n* COMP&DP interrogación de búsqueda *f*, petición de búsqueda *f*; ~ **and rescue** *n* (*SAR*) AIR TRANSP, MILIT, TELECOM búsqueda y rescate *f* (*SAR*), WATER TRANSP búsqueda y salvamento *f*; ~ **tree** *n* COMP&DP árbol de búsqueda *m*; ~ **word** *n* COMP&DP expresión de búsqueda *f*, palabra de búsqueda *f*

searching *n* COMP&DP búsqueda *f*

searchlight *n* ELEC ENG enfoque continuo *m*, iluminación *f*, proyección continuada de un haz luminoso *f*, MILIT proyector de exploración *m*

seascape *n* OCEAN perfil de la costa *m*, vista de la costa *f*

season *n* AGRIC campaña *f* (*AmL*), temporada *f*, época *f*, GEOL, PETROL época *f*; ~ **pattern code** *n* PROD código de configuración estacional *m*

seasonal: ~ **behavior** *AmE*, ~ **behaviour** *BrE n* PROD comportamiento estacional *m*; ~ **demand** *n* GAS demanda estacional *f*; ~ **factor** *n* PROD factor estacional *m*, factor temporal *m*; ~ **index** *n* PROD índice estacional *m*; ~ **pattern** *n* PROD configuración estacional *f*; ~ **pattern code** *n* PROD código de configuración estacional *m*

seasonality *n* PROD estacionalidad *f*

seasoned: ~ **timber** *n* CONST madera curada *f*, madera sazonada *f*, madera seca *f*, madera secada *f*, WATER TRANSP *boat building* madera curada *f*, madera sazonada *f*, madera seca *f*; ~ **wood** *n* CONST madera curada *f*, madera sazonada *f*, madera seca *f*, madera secada *f*, WATER TRANSP *boat building* madera curada *f*, madera sazonada *f*, madera seca *f*

seasoning *n* CONST *timber* cura *f*, desecación *f*, secado *m*

seat *n* AUTO, C&G, CONST asiento *m*, HYDRAUL alojamiento *m*, asiento *m*, MECH asiento *m*, emplazamiento *m*, superficie de apoyo *f*, superficie de contacto *f*, MECH ENG *support* asiento *m*, banco *m*, taburete *m*, MINE muro *m*, base *f*, NUCL asiento *m*, PROD asiento *m*, superficie de apoyo *f*, TRANSP, VEH asiento *m*; ~ **back** *n* VEH respaldo de asiento *m*; ~ **belt** *n* AIR TRANSP, PETR TECH, SAFE, TRANSP cinturón de seguridad *m* (*Esp*), faja de seguridad *f* (*AmL*); ~ **belt attachment** *n* *AmE* (*cf safety belt anchorage BrE*) AUTO, SAFE, VEH anclaje del cinturón de seguridad *m*; ~ **cushion** *n* VEH almohadillado del asiento *m*, cojín del asiento *m*; ~ **of slide-valve** *n* HYDRAUL asiento de válvula de corredera *m*; ~ **upholstery** *n* VEH tapicería *f*

seating *n* CONST asentamiento *m*, HYDRAUL, MECH asiento *m*, MECH ENG *support* asiento *m*, base *f*, lecho *m*, soporte *m*, NUCL asiento *m*, PROD *moulds* portamacho *m*, alojamiento del macho *m*, asiento *m*, saliente del macho *m*

seaward[1] *adj* WATER TRANSP del lado del mar, que da al mar

seaward[2] *adv* WATER TRANSP hacia afuera, hacia el mar, mar adentro

seaward[3]: ~ **defence boat** *n* WATER TRANSP embarcación para la defensa de radas y puertos *f*

seawater: ~-**in-crude oil emulsion** *n* MAR POLL, POLL emulsión de petróleo bruto en agua de mar *f*; ~ **interface** *n* HYDROL superficie de contacto con el agua de mar *f*, superficie de contacto con el agua salada *f*

seaway *n* OCEAN canal marítimo *m*, *state of sea* mar encrespado *m*; ~ **route** *n* OCEAN vía marítima *f*

seaweed *n* HYDROL, MAR POLL, PETROL alga *f*

seaworthy: ~ **packaging** *n* PACK embalaje para el transporte marítimo *m*

sebacic *adj* CHEM sebácico

sec *abbr* (*secant*) COMP&DP, CONST, GEOM, MATH *trigonometry* sec (*secante*)

SECAM[1] *abbr* (*sequential color with memory system AmE, sequential colour with memory system BrE*) TV *standard* SECAM (*sistema de color secuencial con memoria*)

SECAM[2]: ~ **system** *n* TV sistema SECAM *m*

secant *n* (*sec*) COMP&DP, CONST, GEOM, MATH *trigonometry* secante *f* (*sec*)

second[1] *adj* ACOUST segundo

second[2] *n* (*s*) ACOUST segunda parte *f*, segundo *m* (*s*), segundogrado *m*, CONST, METR, PHYS segundo *m* (*s*); ~ **anode** *n* ELEC ENG electrodo positivo secundario *m*, ánodo secundario *m*, TV segundo ánodo *m*; ~-**channel frequency** *n* ELECTRON frecuencia de segundo canal *f*; ~ **condenser lamp** *n* CINEMAT, PHOTO lente condensadora secundaria *f*; ~ **condenser lens** *n* INSTR, OPT lente condensadora secundaria *f*; ~ **cut** *n* MECH ENG *files* lima entrefina *f*, segunda pasada *f*; ~ **deck** *n* WATER TRANSP segunda cubierta *f*; ~ **dog watch** *n* MILIT segundo cuartillo *m*; ~ **engineer** *n* WATER TRANSP maquinista naval primero *m*, segundo maquinista *m*; ~ **gear** *n* AUTO segunda marcha *f*; ~ **generation** *n* COMP&DP segunda generación *f*; ~-**generation computer** *n* COMP&DP computador de segunda generación *m* (*AmL*), computadora de segunda generación *f* (*AmL*), ordenador de segunda generación *m* (*Esp*); ~ **generation copy** *n* CINEMAT copia de segunda generación *f*; ~ **generation dupe** *n* CINEMAT dupe de segunda generación *m*; ~ **hand** *n* MECH ENG *of watch* segundero *m*; ~ **harmonic** *n* ELECTRON segundo armónico *m*; ~ **harmonic distortion** *n* ELECTRON distorsión del segundo armónico *f*; ~ **harmonic injection** *n* ELECTRON inyección del segundo armónico *f*; ~ **IF amplifier** *n* ELECTRON, TELECOM amplificador de FI secundaria *m*; ~ **intermediate frequency** *n* ELECTRON, TELECOM, TV frecuencia intermedia secundaria *f*; ~ **ionization potential** *n* PHYS potencial de segunda ionización *m*; ~ **law** *n* PHYS segunda ley *f*; ~ **local oscillator** *n* ELECTRON oscilador local secundario *m*; ~ **moment of area** *n* MECH ENG *inertia* segundo momento de inercia del área *m*; ~ **motion shaft** *n* MECH ENG eje de segundo movimiento *m*; ~ **nearest neighbor** *AmE*, ~ **nearest neighbour** *BrE n* CRYSTALL segundo vecino próximo *m*; ~**-order bandpass filter** *n* ELECTRON filtro de paso de banda de segundo orden *m*; ~**-order band-stop filter** *n* ELECTRON filtro eliminador de banda de segundo orden *m*; ~**-order filter** *n* ELECTRON filtro de segundo orden *m*; ~**-order high-pass filter** *n* ELECTRON filtro de paso alto de segundo orden *m*; ~**-order low-pass filter** *n* ELECTRON filtro de paso bajo de segundo orden *m*; ~**-order prefilter** *n* ELECTRON prefiltro de segundo orden *m*; ~**-order servo** *n* ELEC ENG servo de segundo orden *m*; ~**-order transition** *n* PHYS transición de segundo orden *f*; ~ **proof** *n* PRINT segunda prueba *f*; ~ **surface mirror** *n* (*SSM*) SPACE espejo de superficie secundaria *m* (*SSM*); ~ **tap** *n* MECH ENG macho de roscar intermedio *m*, segundo macho de roscar *m*; ~**-tier trunk exchange area** *n* TELECOM segunda zona telefónica de la central de línea privada *f*; ~**-tier trunk switching center** *AmE*, ~**-tier trunk switching centre** *BrE n* TELECOM segundo centro de conexiones telefónicas de línea privada *m*; ~ **trace echo** *n* WATER TRANSP *radar* eco de segundo impulso *m*; ~ **unit** *n* CINEMAT segunda unidad *f*; ~ **window fiber** *AmE*, ~ **window fibre** *BrE n* OPT, TELECOM fibra de segunda ventana *f*

secondary: ~ **acetate** *n* TEXTIL acetato secundario *m*; ~ **air** *n* AUTO, HEAT ENG aire secundario *m*; ~ **battery** *n* AUTO, ELEC, ELEC ENG, PHYS batería de acumuladores *f*, SPACE batería de acumuladores *f*, batería secundaria *f*, TELECOM, TRANSP, VEH, WATER TRANSP batería de acumuladores *f*; ~ **blasting** *n* MINE pega secundaria *f*, voladura secundaria *f*; ~ **brake system** *n* VEH sistema de freno auxiliar *m*; ~ **cell** *n* ELEC *accumulator* celda secundaria *f*, pila secundaria *f*, ELEC ENG elemento de acumulador *m*, pila secundaria *f*; ~ **center of disturbance** *AmE see secondary centre of disturbance BrE*; ~ **center tap** *AmE see secondary centre tap BrE*; ~ **centre of disturbance** *n* ELEC WAVE PHYS centro secundario de perturbaciones *m*; ~ **centre tap** *n BrE* ELEC ENG derivación central secundaria *f*, toma central secundaria *f*; ~ **checkers** *n pl* C&G revisores secundarios *m pl*; ~ **coating** *n* OPT revestimiento secundario *m*, TELECOM cobertura secundaria *f*; ~ **coil** *n* ELEC ENG bobina secundaria *f*; ~ **collision** *n* TRANSP choque secundario *m*, colisión secundaria *f*; ~ **color** *AmE*, ~ **colour** *BrE n* COLOUR, PRINT color secundario *m*; ~ **containment** *n* NUCL contención secundaria *f*; ~ **creep** *n* METALL termofluencia secundaria *f*; ~ **crusher** *n* COAL molienda secundaria *f*; ~ **cup** *n* AUTO casquillo secundario *m*; ~ **current** *n* ELEC *transformer* corriente inducida *f*, corriente secundaria *f*, ELEC ENG corriente inducida *f*;

~ **curvature** *n* C&G curvatura secundaria *f*; ~ **duct** *n* AIR TRANSP *turbofan* canal secundario *m*, conducto secundario *m*; ~ **electrochemical generator** *n* TRANSP generador electroquímico secundario *m*; ~ **electron** *n* ELECTRON, RAD PHYS electrón secundario *m*; ~ **element** *n* CHEM elemento secundario *m*; ~ **emission** *n* ELECTRON, PHYS emisión secundaria *f*; ~ **emission multiplier** *n* TV multiplicador de emisión secundaria *m*; ~ **emission noise** *n* ELECTRON ruido de emisión secundaria *m*; ~ **emission ratio** *n* ELECTRON cadencia de emisión secundaria *f*; ~ **emission target** *n* ELECTRON blanco de emisión secundaria *m*, objetivo de emisión secundaria *m*; ~ **emission tube** *n* ELECTRON tubo de emisión secundaria *m*; ~ **explosive** *n* MINE explosivo secundario *m*; ~ **extinction** *n* CRYSTALL extinción secundaria *f*; ~ **fibers** *AmE*, ~ **fibres** *BrE n pl* PAPER fibras secundarias *f pl*; ~ **fuel cell** *n* TRANSP célula combustible secundaria *f*, célula energética secundaria *f*, elemento de combustible de acumulador *m*; ~ **gas cap** *n* PETR TECH capa gasífera secundaria *f*; ~ **grid emission** *n* ELECTRON emisión de rejilla secundaria *f*; ~ **grinding** *n* COAL molienda secundaria *f*; ~ **headbox** *n* PAPER caja de entrada secundaria *f*; ~ **high explosive** *n* MINE explosivo detonante secundario *m*, explosivo rompedor secundario *m*; ~ **index** *n* COMP&DP índice secundario *m*; ~ **inductance** *n* ELEC, ELEC ENG inductancia del secundario *f*; ~**-ion mass spectrometry** *n* (*SIMS*) PHYS espectrometría de masas de iones-secundarios *f*; ~ **ionic emission** *n* TELECOM emisión iónica secundaria *f*; ~ **ionization** *n* PHYS, RAD PHYS ionización secundaria *f*; ~ **line** *n* TRANSP línea secundaria *f*; ~ **maxima** *n pl* PHYS máximos secundarios *m pl*; ~ **memory** *n* COMP&DP memoria secundaria *f*; ~ **mirror** *n* INSTR espejo secundario *m*; ~ **nozzle** *n* AIR TRANSP *engine* tobera secundaria *f*; ~ **nuclear reaction** *n* NUCL reacción nuclear secundaria *f*; ~ **particle** *n* NUCL partícula secundaria *f*; ~ **piston** *n* AUTO pistón secundario *m*; ~ **porosity** *n* PETR TECH porosidad secundaria *f*; ~ **porosity index** *n* (*SPI*) PETR TECH índice de porosidad secundaria *m* (*IPS*); ~ **radiation** *n* (*cf X-ray fluorescence*) RAD PHYS radiación secundaria *f*; ~ **reactor** *n* NUCL reactor secundario *m*; ~ **recovery** *n* PETR TECH recuperación secundaria *f*; ~ **recrystallization** *n* METALL recristalización secundaria *f*; ~ **reflector** *n* SPACE espejo secundario *m*, reflector secundario *m*; ~ **refrigerant** *n* REFRIG refrigerante secundario *m*; ~ **relay** *n* ELEC relé secundario *m*; ~ **resistance** *n* ELEC ENG resistencia del secundario *f*; ~ **road** *n* TRANSP carretera de segundo orden *f*, carretera secundaria *f*; ~ **separation** *n* NUCL *for injection moulding* separación secundaria *f*; ~ **settlement** *n* COAL sedimentación secundaria *f*; ~ **shutdown system** *n* NUCL sistema de parada secundaria *m*; ~ **side** *n* NUCL *communications* lado secundario *m*; ~ **sleeve** *n* AUTO manguito secundario *m*; ~ **source** *n* OPT, PHYS fuente secundaria *f*; ~ **standard** *n* PHYS stándard secundario *m*; ~ **still** *n* FOOD alambique secundario *m*; ~ **storage** *AmE*, ~ **store** *BrE n* COMP&DP almacenamiento secundario *m*; ~ **structure** *n* SPACE estructura secundaria *f*; ~ **suspension** *n* TRANSP suspensión secundaria *f*; ~ **tap** *n* ELEC ENG tomas en el secundario *f pl*; ~ **terminal** *n* ELEC ENG terminal del secundario *m*; ~ **tillage** *n* AGRIC labòr complementaria *f*; ~ **viewing tube** *n* INSTR tubo de enfoque secundario *m*; ~ **voltage** *n* ELEC *transformer* tensión secundaria *f*, ELEC ENG voltaje del circuito inducido *m*, voltaje del secundario *m*; ~ **wave** *n* PHYS *seismology* onda secundaria *f*; ~ **winding** *n* AUTO arrollamiento secundario *m*, bobinado secundario *m*, devanado secundario *m*, ELEC *transformer* arrollamiento secundario *m*, devanado secundario *m*, ELEC ENG devanado secundario *m*, arrollamiento secundario *m*, PHYS bobinado secundario *m*, VEH arrollamiento secundario *m*; ~ **X-ray** *n* RAD PHYS rayo X secundario *m*

seconds *n pl* TEXTIL artículos de segunda *m pl*

secret: ~ **gutter** *n* CONST canalón oculto *m*

section *n* CONST tramo *m*, GEOL corte *m*, sección *f*, GEOM sección *f*, segmento *m*, MECH ENG corte transversal *m*, pieza *f*, sección *f*, sección transversal *f*, tramo *m*, *cut through bar* corte *m*, trayecto *m*, PETR TECH perfil *m*, corte *m*, sección *f*, PRINT cuadernillo *m*, PROD parte *f*, sección *f*, *of boiler* elemento *m*, RAIL tramo *m*, TELECOM sección *f*, TEXTIL cabezal *m*, sección *f*, WATER *boat building* tramo *m*, WATER TRANSP *shipbuilding* perfil *m*; ~ **adaptation** *n* (*SA*) TELECOM adaptación de sección *f*; ~ **drawing** *n* MECH ENG plano parcial *m*, vista parcial *f*; ~ **harrow** *n* AGRIC grada de dientes *f*; ~ **of maximum intensity of stress** *n* MECH ENG *materials* sección de intensidad máxima de esfuerzo *f*, sección de intensidad máxima de fatiga *f*; ~ **mill** *n* PROD *rolling* laminador para perfiles laminados *m*; ~ **overhead** *n* (*SOH*) TELECOM línea aérea de la sección *f*, sección de línea aérea *f*; ~ **printing** *n* CINEMAT copiado por secciones *m*; ~ **of uniform strength** *n* MECH ENG *materials* sección de resistencia uniforme *f*; ~ **warping** *n* TEXTIL urdido seccional *m*

sectional[1] *adj* GEOM seccionado, seccional, MECH ENG divisible, en secciones, por secciones, seccional, divisional, *transportable* desmontable

sectional[2]: ~ **beam** *n* TEXTIL plegador seccional *m*; ~ **boiler** *n* HEAT caldera desmontable *f*, PROD caldera de pequeños elementos *f*; ~ **chart** *n* AIR TRANSP carta local *f*; ~ **cold room** *n* REFRIG cámara frigorífica prefabricada *f*; ~ **curvature** *n* GEOM curvatura seccional *f*; ~ **drawing** *n* WATER TRANSP *ship design* trazado de secciones *m*, trazado de secciones longitudinales y transversales *m*; ~ **drive** *n* PAPER accionamiento seccional *m*; ~ **view** *n* MECH ENG vista de corte *f*, vista de sección *f*, vista seccional *f*; ~ **warp sizing** *n* TEXTIL encolado de urdimbre seccional *m*; ~ **warp slashing** *n* TEXTIL encolado de urdimbre seccional *m*; ~ **warping** *n* TEXTIL urdido seccional *m*; ~ **warping machine** *n* TEXTIL urdidor seccional *m*

sectionalization *n* ELEC seccionamiento *m*

sectionalized: ~ **busbar** *n* ELEC barra colectora subdividida *f*, barra ómnibus subdividida *f*; ~ **cross-bonding** *n* ELEC conexión blindada subdividida *f*, conexión cruzada subdividida *f*; ~ **shield-bonding** *n* ELEC conexión blindada subdividida *f*, conexión cruzada subdividida *f*

sectionalizing: ~ **joint** *n* ELEC *cable* empalme por secciones *m*, junta por secciones *f*; ~ **switch** *n* ELEC interruptor seccionador *m*, seccionador *m*

sectioning: ~ **technique** *n* NUCL *geophysics* técnica de seccionamiento *f*

sector *n* CONST, GEOM, PETR TECH, WATER TRANSP *of light* sector *m*; ~ **gate** *n* FUELLESS *dams* compuerta de

sector *f*; ~ **gear** *n* AUTO sector dentado *m*, MECH ENG engranaje de arco *m*, sector dentado *m*, VEH sector dentado *m*; ~ **light** *n* WATER TRANSP luz de sector *f*; ~ **scan** *n* MILIT *radar* exploración por sectores *f*; ~ **shaft** *n* AUTO eje de sector *m*; ~**-shaped conductor** *n* ELEC conductor perfilado de sección sectorial *m*; ~ **weir** *n* WATER compuerta sectorial *f*; ~ **wheel** *n* MECH ENG sector dentado *m*

secular[1] *adj* GEOPHYS, PHYS radiactivo, secular

secular[2]: ~ **change** *n* GEOPHYS cambio secular *m*, variación secular *f*; ~ **equilibrium** *n* PHYS equilibrio secular *m*; ~ **variation** *n* GEOPHYS variación secular *f*

secure *vt* CONST fijar, TRANSP *mooring* amarrar

security *n* PROD garantía *f*, protección *f*, seguridad *f*, QUALITY confiabilidad *f*, seguridad *f*, SAFE seguridad *f*, TELECOM protección *f*; ~ **audit** *n* TELECOM comprobación de la seguridad *f*, protección *f*; ~ **audit trail** *n* TELECOM trayectoria de la comprobación de la seguridad *f*; ~ **bolt** *n* SAFE perno de protección *m*; ~ **door** *n* SAFE puerta de protección *f*, puerta de seguridad *f*; ~ **firm** *n* SAFE compañía de seguridad *f*; ~ **kernel** *n* COMP&DP núcleo de seguridad *m*, núcleo primitivo de seguridad *m*; ~ **label** *n* TELECOM etiqueta de seguridad *f*; ~ **management information base** *n* (*SMIB*) TELECOM base de información para la gestión de la seguridad *f*; ~ **officer** *n* SAFE encargada de seguridad *f*, encargado de seguridad *m*; ~ **paper** *n* PAPER papel de seguridad *m*; ~ **policy** *n* TELECOM plan de seguridad *m*; ~ **requirements** *n pl* SAFE requisitos de protección *m pl*; ~ **service** *n* TELECOM servicio de seguridad *m*; ~ **window** *n* SAFE ventana de protección *f*

sedan *n* AmE (*cf saloon BrE*) TRANSP sedán *m*

sedentary[1] *adj* COAL sedentario

sedentary[2]: ~ **fishery** *n* OCEAN pesquería sedentaria *f*

sediment *n* CHEM, CHEM TECH, COAL sedimento *m*, PETR TECH residuo *m*, sedimento *m*, RECYCL sedimento *m*, WATER poso *m*, sedimento *m*; ~ **break** *n* OCEAN ruptura en los sedimentos *f*; ~ **chamber** *n* AUTO cámara de sedimentación *f*; ~ **discharge** *n* WATER descarga sedimentaria *f*; ~ **layer** *n* GAS capa sedimentaria *f*, estrato sedimentario *m*; ~ **probe** *n* OCEAN colector de muestras de suelo *m*, extractor de sedimentos *m*; ~ **sounder** *n* OCEAN sonda de sedimentos *f*, sondeador de sedimentos *m*; ~ **space** *n* AUTO espacio de sedimentación *m*

sedimentary: ~ **basin** *n* GAS, GEOL, PETR TECH cuenca sedimentaria *f*; ~ **cycle** *n* GEOL ciclo sedimentario *m*; ~ **deposit** *n* RECYCL cuenca de sedimentación *f*, depósito sedimentario *m*; ~ **environment** *n* GEOL ambiente sedimentario *m*; ~ **model** *n* GAS modelo sedimentario *m*; ~ **phase** *n* GEOL fase sedimentaria *f*; ~ **rock** *n* COAL, GEOL, PETR TECH roca sedimentaria *f*; ~ **rock salt** *n* GAS sal de roca sedimentaria *f*, sal gema sedimentaria *f*; ~ **sequence** *n* GEOL secuencia sedimentaria *f*; ~ **soil** *n* COAL terreno sedimentario *m*; ~ **structure** *n* GEOL estructura sedimentaria *f*

sedimentation *n* CHEM, P&R, PETR TECH, PHYS sedimentación *f*, POLL deposición *f*, precipitación *f*, sedimentación *f*, RECYCL, WATER sedimentación *f*; ~ **analysis** *n* COAL análisis de sedimentación *m*; ~ **basin** *n* CHEM TECH cámara de sedimentación *f*, RECYCL cuenca de sedimentación *f*, embalse de sedimentación *m*; ~ **break** *n* OCEAN interrupción en la sedimentación *f*; ~ **pit** *n* CHEM TECH foso de sedimentación *m*; ~ **pond** *n* COAL balsa de sedimentación *f*; ~ **potential** *n* CHEM TECH potencial de sedimentación *m*; ~ **rate** *n* PETR TECH tasa de sedimentación *f*, RECYCL régimen de sedimentación *m*, velocidad de sedimentación *f*, índice de sedimentación *m*; ~ **tank** *n* CHEM TECH cuba de sedimentación *f*, tanque de sedimentación *m*, RECYCL cisterna de sedimentación *f*, depósito de sedimentación *m*, tanque de sedimentación *m*, WATER tanque de decantación *m*; ~ **test** *n* CONST ensayo de sedimentación *m*; ~ **volume** *n* CHEM TECH volumen de sedimentación *m*

sedimented *adj* CHEM, CHEM TECH, COAL, PETR TECH, RECYCL, WATER sedimentado

see: ~**-through mirror** *n* AmE (*cf two-way mirror BrE*) C&G espejo falso *m*, falso espejo *m*; ~**-through packaging** *n* PACK embalaje transparente *m*

Seebeck: ~ **coefficient** *n* PHYS coeficiente de Seebeck *m*; ~ **effect** *n* ELEC, ELEC ENG, PHYS efecto Seebeck *m*

seed[1]: ~**-free** *adj* C&G libre de semilla

seed[2] *n* AGRIC, C&G semilla *f*; ~ **agitator** *n* AGRIC agitador de semilla *m*; ~ **assembly** *n* NUCL elemento de sembrado *m*; ~ **box** *n* AGRIC tolva *f*; ~ **company** *n* AGRIC compañía de semillas *f*; ~**-core reactor** *n* NUCL reactor de núcleo sembrado *m*; ~ **crystal** *n* CRYSTALL cristal germen *m*, germen cristalino *m*; ~ **darrow** *n* AGRIC sembradora de mano *f*; ~ **drill** *n* AGRIC sembradora *f*; ~ **element** *n* NUCL *orbitography* elemento de sembrado *m*; ~ **filling** *n* AGRIC llenado de grano *m*; ~**-free time** *n* C&G tiempo para que el vidrio esté libre de gases *m*; ~ **lac** *n* COLOUR laca resinosa granulada *f*; ~ **nursery** *n* AGRIC vivero de semillas *m*; ~ **plate** *n* AGRIC platillo distribuidor de semilla *m*; ~ **production** *n* AGRIC multiplicación de semillas *f*; ~ **tube** *n* AGRIC tubo de descarga de semilla *m*

seedbed *n* AGRIC lecho de siembra *m*, sementera *f*

seeder *n* AGRIC sembradora *f*

seeding *n* CHEM *of crystals* siembra *f*, NUCL *diodes* sembrado *m*; ~ **potential** *n* C&G capacidad de producir semillas *f*; ~ **rate** *n* AGRIC densidad de siembra *f*

seedling *n* AGRIC plántula *f*

seek[1]: ~ **area** *n* COMP&DP zona de búsqueda *f*, área de búsqueda *f*; ~ **arm** *n* COMP&DP brazo de búsqueda *m*; ~ **time** *n* (*cf radial positioning time*) COMP&DP tiempo de búsqueda *m*, OPT intervalo de posicionamiento *m*, tiempo de búsqueda *m*

seek[2] *vt* COMP&DP buscar, investigar

seeling *n* WATER TRANSP bandazo *m*

seep[1]: ~ **of sound** *n* WAVE PHYS velocidad del sonido *f*

seep[2] *vt* CONST percolar

seep[3] *vi* CHEM colarse, filtrarse, percolar, COAL gotear, percolar; ~ **through** *vi* TEXTIL rezumar

seepage *n* CHEM escurrimiento *m*, filtración *f*, infiltración *f*, percolación *f*, COAL goteo *m*, infiltración *f*, percolación *f*, rezumado *m*, GAS afloramiento *m*, emanación *f*, exudación *f*, vertiente *f*, MAR POLL infiltración *f*, WATER filtración *f*, infiltración *f*, percolación *f*, permeabilidad *f*; ~ **loss** *n* AGRIC pérdida por escurrimiento *f*; ~ **water** *n* CHEM agua infiltrada *f*

seesaw: ~ **motion** *n* MECH ENG basculación *f*, movimiento de balanceo *m*, movimiento de oscilación *m*, movimiento de vaivén *m*

seesawing *n* MECH ENG balanceo *m*, oscilación *f*, vaivén *m*

Seger: ~ **cone** *n* C&G cono Seger *m*

segment[1] *n* COMP&DP, GEOM segmento *m*, MECH ENG división *f*, sección *f*, segmento *m*, NUCL *diodes*, SPACE, TELECOM segmento *m*; ~ **gear** *n* MECH ENG cremallera en segmento *f*, engranaje de segmento *m*, sector dentado *m*; ~ **terminator** *n* TELECOM terminador del segmento *m*; ~ **type** *n* (*ST*) TELECOM tipo de segmento *m*

segment[2] *vt* COMP&DP, GEOM segmentar

segmental[1] *adj* GEOM segmental, segmentario

segmental[2]: ~ **arch** *n* CONST *structure* arco rebajado *m*, bóveda segmentada *f*; ~ **circular saw** *n* MECH ENG sierra de arco circular *f*

segmentation *n* CHEM, COMP&DP, GEOM segmentación *f*; ~ **permitted flag** *n* (*SPF*) TELECOM bandera reglamentaria de segmentación *f*; ~ **and reassembly** *n* TELECOM segmentación y rearmado *f*; ~ **and reassembly sublayer** *n* TELECOM subcapa de segmentación y rearmado *f*

segmented: ~ **approach path** *n* AIR TRANSP trayecto de aproximación segmentado *m*; ~ **fuel rod** *n* NUCL varilla de combustible segmentada *f*; ~ **multiprocessor system** *n* TELECOM sistema de multiprocesador segmentado *m*; ~ **pile** *n* COAL pilote segmentado *m*; ~ **recording** *n* TV grabación segmentada *f*; ~ **saw** *n* MECH ENG *for masonry stone* sierra segmentada *f*; ~ **scanning** *n* TV exploración segmentada *f*

Segrè: ~ **chart** *n* PART PHYS patrón de Segrè *m*

segregation *n* C&G segregación *f*, CHEM, CONST separación *f*, NUCL segregado *m*

seiche *n* FUELLESS *water level* oscilación periódica del espejo de agua *f*, OCEAN ola seca *f*, seiche *f*

seine *n* OCEAN red de cerco *f*; ~ **net** *n* WATER TRANSP *fishing* red de cerco *f*; ~ **staff** *n* OCEAN calón *m*

seiner *n* OCEAN cerquero *m*

seismic[1] *adj* CONST, GEOPHYS, PETR TECH sísmico

seismic[2]: ~ **activity** *n* GEOL actividad sísmica *f*; ~ **array** *n* GEOL formación sísmica *f*; ~ **borehole** *n* GEOPHYS barreno sísmico *m*, pozo sísmico *m*; ~ **design** *n* CONST diseño antisísmico *m*; ~ **engineering** *n* GEOPHYS ingeniería sísmica *f*; ~ **exploration** *n* COAL, GEOPHYS, PETR TECH exploración sísmica *f*; ~ **exploration method** *n* GEOPHYS método de exploración sísmica *m*; ~ **focus** *n* GEOPHYS foco sísmico *m*; ~ **mass** *n* GEOPHYS masa sísmica *f*; ~ **path** *n* GEOPHYS recorrido sísmico *m*, PETR TECH recorrido sísmico *m*, trayectoria sísmica *f*; ~ **phenomena** *n pl* GEOPHYS fenómenos sísmicos *m pl*; ~**-profile recorder** *n* INSTR, WAVE PHYS grabador del perfil sísmico *m*, medidor sísmico *m*, sismógrafo *m*; ~ **prospecting** *n* GEOPHYS prospección sísmica *f*; ~ **prospection** *n* GEOPHYS prospección sísmica *f*; ~ **spectral analysis** *n* GEOPHYS análisis del espectro sísmico *m*; ~ **station** *n* GEOPHYS estación sísmica *f*; ~ **survey** *n* CONST, GEOPHYS, PETR TECH estudio sísmico *m*; ~ **velocity** *n* GEOL, PETR TECH velocidad sísmica *f*; ~ **wave** *n* GEOL, GEOPHYS, WAVE PHYS onda sísmica *f*; ~ **wave trace** *n* GEOPHYS, PETROL diagrama de onda sísmica *m*; ~ **zone** *n* GEOPHYS zona sísmica *f*

seismicity *n* CONST, GEOPHYS, SPACE sismicidad *f*

seismogenic *adj* GEOPHYS sismogénico

seismogram *n* PETR TECH sismograma *m*

seismograph *n* CONST, GAS, GEOPHYS, PHYS sismógrafo *m*

seismological: ~ **map** *n* GEOPHYS, PHYS mapa sismológico *m*

seismologist *n* GEOPHYS, PHYS sismologista *m*

seismology *n* GEOPHYS, PHYS sismología *f*
seismometer *n* GEOPHYS, PHYS sismógrafo *m*, sismómetro *m*
seismotectonics *n* GEOPHYS, PHYS sismotectónica *f*
seize[1] *vt* WATER TRANSP *ropes* abarbetar, ligar
seize[2] *vi* AIR TRANSP, AUTO, HYDRAUL agarrotar, MECH atorarse, MECH ENG agarrotar, atascarse, atorarse, NUCL *unit* agarrotarse, PROD agarrotar
seizing *n* AUTO agarrotamiento *m*, MECH ENG aferramiento *m*, agarrotamiento *m*, atascamiento *m*, VEH agarrotamiento *m*, gripado *m*
seizure *n* TELECOM toma *f*
SELCAL *abbr* (*selective calling system*) TELECOM sistema de llamada selectiva *m*
select[1] *n* PRINT orden *m*
select[2] *vt* MINE elegir, escoger, seleccionar
selectable *adj* ELEC ENG seleccionable
selected: ~ **chunks** *n pl* C&G pedazos seleccionados *m pl*; ~ **fill** *n* CONST relleno seleccionado *m*; ~ **sizes** *n pl* MECH ENG *for bolts and nuts* medidas seleccionadas *f pl*, tamaños seleccionados *m pl*
selecting *n* TELECOM selección *f*
selection *n* C&G selección *f*; ~ **of arrivals** *n* GEOL selección de llegadas *f*; ~ **information** *n* PROD información selectiva *f*; ~ **rule** *n* NUCL, PHYS regla de selección *f*; ~ **stage** *n* TELECOM etapa de selección *f*
selective: ~ **calling system** *n* (*SELCAL*) TELECOM sistema de llamada selectiva *m*; ~ **catalytic reduction** *n* POLL reducción catalítica selectiva *f*; ~ **coating** *n* FUELLESS revestimiento selectivo *m*; ~ **collection** *n* RECYCL colecta selectiva *f* (*AmL*), recogida selectiva *f*, recolección selectiva *f*; ~ **diffusion** *n* ELECTRON difusión selectiva *f*; ~ **diversion** *n* TRANSP desviación selectiva *f*; ~ **dump** *n* COMP&DP vuelco selectivo *m*; ~ **erasure** *n* COMP&DP borrado selectivo *m*; ~ **fading** *n* TELECOM desvanecimiento selectivo *m*; ~ **feedback** *n* ELEC ENG, ELECTRON realimentación selectiva *f*; ~ **feedback amplifier** *n* ELECTRON amplificador de realimentación selectiva *m*; ~ **field protection** *n* TELECOM protección selectiva de campo *f*; ~ **quenching** *n* RAD PHYS extinción selectiva *f*; ~ **reducer** *n* PHOTO reductor selectivo *m*; ~ **reflection** *n* PHYS reflexión selectiva *f*; ~ **sequential access** *n* COMP&DP acceso secuencial selectivo *m*; ~ **solvent** *n* CHEM solvente selectivo *m*, PETR TECH disolvente selectivo *m*; ~ **surface** *n* FUELLESS superficie selectiva *f*; ~ **switch** *n* ELEC conmutador selectivo *m*; ~ **vehicle detector** *n* TRANSP detector selectivo de vehículos *m*; ~ **voltmeter** *n* ELEC voltímetro selectivo *m*
selectively: ~-**plated contacts** *n pl* ELEC ENG contactos selectivamente revestidos *m pl*
selectivity *n* ELECTRON, PHYS selectividad *f*
selector *n* COMP&DP selector *m*, ELEC ENG convertidor *m*, selector *m*, TELECOM, VEH selector *m*; ~ **channel** *n* COMP&DP canal selector *m*; ~ **lever** *n* AUTO palanca de selector *f*, VEH palanca selectora *f*; ~ **relay** *n* ELEC ENG relé selector *m*; ~ **switch** *n* ELEC conmutador *m*, conmutador selector *m*, selector *m*, ELEC ENG conmutador selector *m*, uniselector *m*, PROD conmutador selector *m*
selenate *n* CHEM selenato *m*
selenic *adj* CHEM selénico
selenide *n* CHEM seleniuro *m*, selenuro *m*

selenious *adj* CHEM selenioso
selenite *n* CHEM selenita *f*, yeso cristalizado *m*, MINERAL selenita *f*
selenitic *adj* CHEM, MINERAL selenítico
selenium *n* (*Se*) CHEM, ELEC ENG selenio *m* (*Se*); ~ **cell** *n* ELEC ENG célula de selenio *f*, pila de selenio *f*, PHYS célula de selenio *f*; ~ **rectifier** *n* ELEC, ELEC ENG, PHYS rectificador de selenio *m*; ~ **ruby glass** *n* C&G vidrio ruby selénico *m*
selenocyanate *n* CHEM selenocianato *m*
selenocyanic *adj* CHEM selenociánico
selenous *adj* CHEM selenioso
self[1]: ~-**adapting** *adj* COMP&DP autoadaptable, autoadaptado; ~-**blimped** *adj* CINEMAT autoblindado; ~-**closing** *adj* PACK autocerrado; ~-**contained** *adj* PHYS autocontenido, SPACE autónomo, independiente; ~-**documenting** *adj* COMP&DP autodocumentado; ~-**draining** *adj* WATER TRANSP autodrenante, de desagüe automático, de purga automática; ~-**healing** *adj* ELEC ENG autorregenerable; ~-**heating** *adj* ELEC ENG autocalentable; ~-**induced** *adj* AUTO, ELEC, ELEC ENG, PHYS autoinducido; ~-**inflating** *adj* MAR POLL autohinchable, autoinflable; ~-**lifting** *adj* PROD autoascensible; ~-**locking** *adj* PACK autocerrable, de autobloqueo, VEH de autobloqueo, de cierre automático; ~-**powered** *adj* ELEC ENG autoalimentado, automático; ~-**propelled** *adj* MAR POLL autopropulsado, con propulsión propia, SPACE autopropulsado, WATER TRANSP *barge, dredger* autopropulsado, con propulsión propia; ~-**righting** *adj* WATER TRANSP *lifeboat* autoadrizable; ~-**sealing** *adj* PACK autocerrable, SPACE autosoldable, de cierre automático, de cierre propio; ~-**shielding** *adj* PROD autoapantallado; ~-**threading** *adj* CINEMAT autoenhebrante
self[2]: ~-**absorption** *n* CHEM, RAD PHYS autoabsorción *f*; ~-**acting brake** *n* AUTO, VEH freno automático *m*; ~-**acting circular table** *n* MECH ENG *machine tool* mesa circular automática *f*, mesa circular de acción automática *f*, mesa circular de movimiento automático *f*; ~-**acting feed** *n* MECH ENG alimentación automática *f*, alimentación de acción automática *f*; ~-**acting incline** *n* MECH ENG inclinación automática *f*, inclinación de acción automática *f*; ~-**acting injector** *n* MECH ENG inyector automático *m*; ~-**acting plane** *n* MECH ENG plano automático *m*, rampa automática *f*; ~-**acting regulator** *n* MECH ENG regulador automático *m*; ~-**acting sliding lathe** *n* MECH ENG *for surfacing and screw-cutting* torno paralelo automático *m*; ~-**acting switch** *n* ELEC ENG conmutador automático *m*, interruptor automático *m*; ~-**adhesive film** *n* PACK película autoadhesiva *f*; ~-**adhesive label** *n* PACK etiqueta autoadhesiva *f*; ~-**adhesive laminated tape** *n* PACK cinta laminada autoadhesiva *f*, precinto laminado autoadhesivo *m*; ~-**adhesive tape** *n* P&R cinta autoadhesiva *f*, PACK cinta autoadhesiva *f*, precinto autoadhesivo *m*; ~-**adjusting brake** *n* AUTO, VEH freno autorregulable *m*, freno de ajuste automático *m*; ~-**adjusting clutch** *n* AUTO embrague automático *m*, embrague autorregulable *m*; ~-**adjusting floating weir** *n* MAR POLL aliviadero flotante autorregulado *m*; ~-**adjustment** *n* TV autoajuste *m*; ~-**advancing chock** *n* MINE entibación autoavanzante *f* (*AmL*), taco autoavanzante *m* (*Esp*); ~-**aligned gate** *n* ELECTRON puerta autoalineada *f*; ~-**aligned transistor** *n*

ELECTRON transistor autoalineado *m*; **~-aligning bearing** *n* MECH ENG cojinete autoalineable *m*, cojinete de alineación propia *m*, conector de holgura *m*, VEH cojinete autoalineable *m*; **~-balancing switch** *n* ELEC, ELEC ENG, ELECTRON interruptor autocompensado *m*; **~-bias** *n* ELEC ENG autopolarización *f*, polarización automática de rejilla *f*; **~-biased tube** *n* ELECTRON tubo autopolarizado *m*; **~-canceling** *AmE*, **~-cancelling** *BrE n* ELEC autocancelación *f*; **~-cancelling steering column switch** *n BrE* ELEC *automotive* interruptor de la columna de dirección de autocancelación *m*, interruptor de la columna de mando de autocancelación *m*; **~-cancelling turn signal switch** *n BrE* ELEC *automotive* interruptor de la señal de espira de autocancelación *m*, interruptor de la señal de giro de autocancelación *m*, interruptor de la señal de vuelta de autocancelación *m*; **~-capacitance** *n* ELEC, PHYS autocapacitancia *f*; **~-centering chuck** *AmE see self-centring chuck BrE*; **~-centering dies** *AmE see self-centring dies BrE*; **~-centering vise** *AmE see self-centring vice BrE*; **~-centring chuck** *n BrE* MECH ENG mandril autocentrador *m*, plato autocentrador *m*; **~-centring dies** *n pl BrE* MECH ENG matriz de autocentrado *f*, molde de autocentrado *m*, terrajas concéntricas *f pl*; **~-centring vice** *n BrE* MECH ENG tornillo concéntrico *m*; **~-checking code** *n* COMP&DP código autoverificante *m*, código de autocomprobación *m*; **~-cleaning air filter** *n* HEAT ENG filtro de aire autolimpiable *m*; **~-closing cock** *n BrE* (*cf self-closing faucet AmE*) CONST canilla de cierre automático *f*, grifo de cierre automático *m*; **~-closing door** *n* CONST puerta de cierre automático *f*; **~-closing faucet** *n AmE* (*cf self-closing cock BrE*) CONST canilla de cierre automático *f*, grifo de cierre automático *m*; **~-cocking shutter** *n* CINEMAT, PHOTO obturador con disparador automático *m*; **~-color** *AmE*, **~-colour** *BrE n* COLOUR armonía de tonalidades de un color *f*; **~-commutated converter** *n* ELEC convertidor de autoconmutación *m*; **~-contained accumulator** *n* HYDRAUL acumulador completo *m*; **~-contained air-conditioning unit** *n* HEAT acondicionador autónomo *m*, REFRIG acondicionador autónomo *m*, climatizador autónomo *m*, THERMO acondicionador autónomo *m*; **~-contained countershaft** *n* MECH ENG eje intermedio autónomo *m*, eje secundario completo *m*, eje secundario independiente *m*; **~-contained driving motion** *n* MECH ENG movimiento de impulsión completo *m*, movimiento de impulsión independiente *m*; **~-contained navigational aid** *n* AIR TRANSP ayuda de navegación autónoma *f*, ayuda navegacional autónoma *f*; **~-contained power steering system** *n* AUTO sistema de servodirección integral *m*; **~-contained pressure cable** *n* ELEC cable a presión autónomo *m*; **~-controlling system** *n* TV sistema autorregulado *m*; **~-coring chisel** *n* CONST *wood-mortising* formón de auto-centrado *m*; **~-destruction** *n* MILIT autodestrucción *f*; **~-discharge** *n* AUTO descarga espontánea *f*, ELEC descarga automática *f*, ELEC ENG descarga automática *f*, descarga en circuito abierto *f*, descarga espontánea *f*, SPACE autodescarga *f*, descarga en circuito abierto *f*, descarga espontánea *f*; **~-discharge freight car** *n AmE* (*cf self-discharge freight wagon BrE*) vagón de mercancías auto-descargable *m*; **~-discharge freight wagon** *n BrE*

(*cf self-discharge freight car AmE*) TRANSP vagón de mercancías auto-descargable *m*; **~-discharge time constant** *n* ELEC ENG constante de tiempo de la descarga automática *f*; **~-discharging car** *n AmE* (*cf discharging wagon BrE*) RAIL vagón de descarga automática *m*; **~-discharging wagon** *n BrE* (*cf discharging car AmE*) RAIL vagón de descarga automática *m*; **~-discharging water bucket** *n* WATER cangilón de agua de descarga automática *m*; **~-drill anchor** *n* CONST anclaje autoperforador *m*; **~-drive taxi** *n* TRANSP taxi sin conductor *m*; **~-dump rake** *n* AGRIC rastra autodescargante *f*; **~-dumping bucket** *n* CONST cubo autobasculante *m*; **~-erecting screen** *n* PHOTO pantalla automontable *f*; **~-etching primer** *n* COATINGS imprimación por auto-ataque químico *f*; **~-excitation** *n* ELEC ENG, NUCL autoexcitación *f*; **~-excited motor** *n* ELEC motor autoexcitado *m*, motor de excitación propia *m*; **~-excited oscillator** *n* ELECTRON oscilador autoexcitado *m*; **~-excited power oscillator** *n* ELECTRON oscilador de potencia autoexcitado *m*; **~ feeder** *n* AGRIC alimentador automático *m*; **~-feeding rack wagon** *n* AGRIC acoplado alimentador de comedero *m*; **~-feeding reamer** *n* MECH ENG escariador auto-alimentador *m*, fresador de avance automático *m*; **~-firing** *n* AUTO disparo automático *m*; **~-flux** *n* PHYS auto-flujo *m*; **~-generating transducer** *n* ELEC ENG transductor autogenerador *m*; **~-hardening** *n* METALL autoendurecimiento *m*; **~-healing capacitor** *n* ELEC ENG condensador autorregenerable *m*; **~-healing properties** *n pl* TEXTIL propiedades autocurativas *f pl*; **~-heating coefficient** *n* ELEC ENG coeficiente de autocalentamiento *m*; **~-holding taper** *n* MECH ENG *for tool shanks* manguito cónico *m*; **~-identification** *n* TELECOM autoidentificación *f*; **~-ignition** *n* AUTO encendido automático *m*; **~-inductance** *n* ELEC autoinductancia *f*, coeficiente de autoinducción *m*, coeficiente de inducción propia *m*, ELEC ENG, PHYS autoinductancia *f*; **~-inductance variation** *n* ELEC variación de autoinductancia *f*; **~-induction** *n* AUTO autoinducción *f*, ELEC autoinducción *f*, inducción propia *f*, ELEC ENG autoinducción *f*, inducción automática *f*, PHYS autoinducción *f*; **~-induction current** *n* ELEC ENG corriente de autoinducción *f*; **~-inspection** *n* QUALITY autocontrol *m*, autoinspección *f*; **~-learning machine** *n* COMP&DP máquina autodidáctica *f*, máquina de auto-aprendizaje *f*; **~-lifting pressure plate** *n* PROD placa de presión autoascensible *f*; **~-lifting terminal clamp** *n* PROD pinza terminal autodesprendible *f*; **~-lubricating bearing** *n* MECH ENG cojinete autoengrasado *m*, cojinete autolubricado *m*; **~-luminosity** *n* SPACE autoluminosidad *f*; **~-noise** *n* OCEAN ruido propio *m*; **~-opening die-head** *n* MECH ENG *of screwing-machine* terraja de apertura automática *f*; **~-opening screwing head** *n* MECH ENG *of screwing-machine* portaterrajas de apertura automática *m pl*; **~-organizing system** *n* COMP&DP sistema auto-organizado *m*, sistema autoestructurado *m*; **~-orthogonal convolutional coding** *n* TELECOM codificación convolucional auto-octogonal *f*; **~-phased array** *n* TV antena autoadaptable *f*; **~-pollination** *n* AGRIC autopolinización *f*; **~-potential** *n* GEOPHYS potencial espontáneo *m*, potencial propio *m*; **~-potential log** *n* GEOPHYS registro de potencial propio *m*, PETR TECH diagrafía del autopotencial *f*, perfil del autopotencial *m*, registro del autopotencial *m*; **~-priming dirty-water pump** *n* HYDRAUL, NUCL bomba autocebadora de aguas residuales *f*; **~-priming pump** *n* AUTO bomba de cebado automático *f*, HYDRAUL bomba autocebable *f*, bomba autocebadora *f*, VEH bomba de cebado automático *f*; **~-propelled barge** *n* WATER TRANSP gabarra con propulsión propia *f*; **~-propelled skimmer** *n* MAR POLL rasera autopropulsada *f*; **~-propelled turret** *n* MILIT *of tank* torreta autopropulsada *f*; **~-propulsion** *n* SPACE, WATER TRANSP autopropulsión *f*; **~-purification** *n* WATER autodepuración *f*, autopurificación *f*; **~-rake reaper** *n* AGRIC segadora de rastrillo *f*; **~-reading staff** *n* CONST *surveying* mira parlante *f*; **~-registering apparatus** *n* MECH ENG aparato autorregistrador *m*, aparato de registro automático *m*; **~-regulating maintenance system** *n* TRANSP sistema autorregulado de mantenimiento *m*; **~-relative addressing** *n* COMP&DP autodireccionamiento relativo *m*; **~-rescue apparatus** *n* SAFE *with carbon monoxide filter* aparato para autorrescate *m*; **~-resetting loop** *n* COMP&DP bucle de autorrestauración *m*, lazo de autoreposición *m*; **~-resetting relay** *n* ELEC relé de autorreposición *m*, relé de reposición automática *m*; **~-righting test** *n* WATER TRANSP *lifeboat* prueba de autoadrizamiento *f*; **~-sagging temperature** *n* C&G temperatura de autoestiramiento *f*; **~-scattering** *n* PHYS autodifusión *f*; **~-seal pocket envelope** *n* PACK, PAPER bolsa postal autocerrable *f*; **~-service station** *n* TRANSP estación de auto-servicio *f*, gasolinera auto-servicio *f*; **~-shade** *n* COLOUR matiz igual *m*; **~-starting synchronous motor** *n* ELEC ENG motor síncrono de arranque automático *m*; **~-supporting partition** *n* CONST *building* tabiquería autoportante *f*; **~-supporting rigid vehicle** *n* TRANSP vehículo rígido auto-portante *m*; **~-sustained discharge** *n* ELEC descarga autostenida *f*, ELEC ENG descarga autosostenida *f*; **~-teaching manual** *n* PROD manual autodidáctico *m*; **~-tensioning winch** *n* WATER TRANSP *deck fittings* chigre de amarre de tensión constante *m*, chigre de tensión constante *m*; **~-timer** *n* PHOTO autodisparador *m*; **~-tipping car** *n* AmE (*cf self-tipping wagon BrE*) RAIL vagón autobasculante *m*; **~-tipping wagon** *n* BrE (*cf self-tipping car AmE*) RAIL vagón autobasculante *m*; **~-tracking** *n* ELECTRON autoalineación *f*, autorreglaje *m*; **~-tracking band-pass filter** *n* ELECTRON filtro de paso banda de autorreglaje *m*; **~-venting system** *n* PACK sistema de autoventilación *m*; **~-vulcanization** *n* P&R autovulcanización *f*

sellaite *n* MINERAL sellaíta *f*

Sellers: **~ thread** *n* MECH ENG rosca Sellers *f*, rosca americana *f*

selsyn: **~ motor** *n* CINEMAT motor autosincrónico *m*

selvage *n* CONST borde *m*, orillo *m*, GEOL salbanda *f*, METALL orillo *m*, MINE salbanda *f*, P&R, PAPER, TEXTIL orillo *m*; **~ cutting process** *n* TEXTIL procedimiento para cortar los orillos *m*

SEM *abbr* ELEC, ELECTRON (*scanning electron microscope*) MEB (microscopio electrónico de barrido), microscopio electrónico de exploración *m*, microscopio de electrones *m*, INSTR (*surface electron microscope*) microscopio de exploración electrónica, *m* LAB, PHYS, RAD PHYS (*scanning electron microscope*) MEB (*microscopio electrónico de barrido*) microsco-

pio electrónico de exploración *m*, microscopio de electrones *m*

semantic: **~ analysis** *n* COMP&DP análisis semántico *m*, reconocimiento *m*

semaphoric: **~ program** *AmE*, **~ programme** *BrE n* TRANSP programa semafórico *m*

semelin *n* MINERAL semelina *f*

semeline *n* MINERAL semelín *f*

semen: **~ bank** *n* AGRIC banco de semen *m*

SEMF *abbr* (*synchronous equipment management function*) TELECOM función de gestión del equipo sincrónico *f*

semiactive: **~ landing-gear** *n* AIR TRANSP tren de aterrizaje semiactivo *m*

semiamphibious: **~ air-cushion vehicle** *n* TRANSP, WATER TRANSP aerodeslizador semi-anfibio *m*

semianthracite *n* COAL semiantracita *f*

semiautomatic[1] *adj* MECH ENG semiautomático

semiautomatic[2]: **~ labeling machine** *AmE*, **~ labelling machine** *BrE n* PACK máquina de etiquetado semiautomática *f*; **~ points switching** *n* RAIL cambio de agujas semi-automático *m*; **~ pressing** *n* C&G prensado semiautomático *m*; **~ strapping machine** *n* PACK máquina semiautomática de flejado *f*; **~ system** *n* TELECOM sistema semiautomático *m*; **~ transmission** *n* AUTO transmisión semiatomática *f*, VEH transmisión semiautomática *f*; **~ trunk working** *n* TELECOM explotación semiautomática de la línea principal *f*

semibituminous[1] *adj* COAL semibituminoso

semibituminous[2]: **~ coal** *n* COAL carbón semibituminoso *m*, carbón semigraso *m*

semibleached: **~ pulp** *n* PAPER pasta semiblanqueada *f*, pulpa semiblanqueada *f*

semibrittle: **~ fracture** *n* CRYSTALL, MECH, METALL fractura semiquebradiza *f*

semicarbazide *n* CHEM semicarbazida *f*

semicarbazone *n* CHEM semicarbazona *f*

semichemical: **~ pulp** *n* PAPER pasta semiquímica *f*, pulpa semiquímica *f*

semicircle *n* GEOM semicírculo *m*

semicircular: **~ arch** *n* CONST arco semicircular *m*; **~ beta spectrograph** *n* NUCL espectrógrafo beta semicircular *m*; **~ channel** *n* ACOUST canal semicircular *m*; **~ lens** *n* INSTR lente semicircular *f*

semiclassical: **~ approximation** *n* NUCL *steam engine* aproximación semiclásica *f*

semiconductor *n* ELECTRON, PHYS semiconductor *m*; **~ amplifier** *n* ELECTRON amplificador con dispositivos semiconductores *m*, TELECOM amplificador con dispositivos semiconductores *m*, amplificador de semiconductores *m*; **~ chip** *n* ELECTRON chip semiconductor *m*; **~ component** *n* ELECTRON componente semiconductor *m*; **~ counter** *n* PART PHYS contador de semiconductores *m*; **~ crosspoint** *n* TELECOM contacto de semiconductores *m*, punto de cruce de semiconductores *m*; **~ crystal** *n* ELECTRON cristal semiconductor *m*; **~ device** *n* COMP&DP, ELECTRON dispositivo semiconductor *m*; **~ diode** *n* COMP&DP, ELECTRON diodo semiconductor *m*; **~ doping** *n* ELECTRON dopado del semiconductor *m*; **~ fabrication** *n* ELECTRON elaboración de un semiconductor *f*; **~ integrated circuit** *n* ELECTRON circuito integrado de semiconductor *m*; **~ laser** *n* ELECTRON, OPT, RAD PHYS, TELECOM láser de semiconductor *m*; **~ layer** *n* ELECTRON estratificador de semiconductor *m*; ~ **material** *n* ELECTRON componente de semiconductor *m*, material de semiconductor *m*; ~ **memory** *n* COMP&DP, ELEC ENG memoria de semiconductores *f*; ~ **photodetector** *n* ELECTRON fotodetector de semiconductor *m*; ~ **rectifier** *n* ELEC, ELEC ENG rectificador de semiconductor *m*; ~ **relay** *n* ELEC ENG relé de semiconductor *m*; ~ **resistor** *n* ELEC ENG resistencia de semiconductor *f*; ~ **single crystal** *n* ELECTRON monocristal semiconductor *m*, semiconductor monocristalino *m*; ~ **substrate** *n* ELECTRON substrato de semiconductor *m*; ~ **switch** *n* ELEC ENG conmutador para semiconductor *m*; ~ **switching device** *n* ELEC conmutador de semiconductor *m*; ~ **technology** *n* ELECTRON tecnología de semiconductores *f*; ~ **wafer** *n* ELECTRON pastilla de semiconductor *f*

semicontinuous: ~ **casting** *n* C&G vaciado semicontinuo *m*

semicustom[1] *adj* COMP&DP semipersonalizado *m*

semicustom[2]: ~ **chip** *n* ELECTRON chip semipersonalizado *m*; ~ **circuit** *n* ELECTRON circuito semipersonalizado *m*

semi-deep: ~ **furrow drill** *n* AGRIC sembradora de granos en línea *f*

semidiesel: ~ **engine** *n* AUTO, MECH ENG motor semidiesel *m*

semi-digger: ~ **bottom** *n* AGRIC cuerpo de arado múltiple *m*

semidine *n* CHEM semidina *f*

semidirectional: ~ **microphone** *n* ACOUST micrófono semidireccional *m*

semidiurnal: ~ **tide** *n* OCEAN, WATER TRANSP marea semidiurna *f*; ~ **wave** *n* OCEAN ola semidiurna *f*

semienclosed: ~ **motor** *n* ELEC motor semicerrado *m*

semifast: ~ **train** *n* BrE (*cf limited train AmE*) RAIL tren de puntos de parada limitados *m*, tren semidirecto *m*, tren semiexpreso *m*, tren semirrápido *m*

semifinished *adj* PROD semiacabado, semielaborado

semifloating: ~ **axle** *n* AUTO eje semiflotante *m*, VEH eje semiflotante *m*, eje semiportante *m*

semigantry: ~ **crane** *n* CONST grúa semicaballete *f*

semigelatin *n* MINE semigelatina *f*; ~ **dynamite** *n* MINE dinamita semigelatinosa *f*; ~ **explosive** *n* MINE explosivo semigelatinoso *m*

semihomogeneous: ~ **fuel element** *n* NUCL elemento de combustible semihomogéneo *m*

semihot: ~ **laboratory** *n* NUCL laboratorio semicaliente *m*

semi-impermeable: ~ **layer** *n* WATER capa semiimpermeable *f*

semi-infinite: ~ **crack** *n* NUCL grieta semiinfinita *f*

semi-insulating: ~ **substrate** *n* ELECTRON substrato semiaislante *m*

semimajor: ~ **axis** *n* SPACE semieje mayor *m*

semimatt *adj* TEXTIL semi-mate

semimetal *n* CHEM semimetal *m*

semimetalic AmE *see* semimetallic BrE

semimetallic *adj* BrE CHEM semimetálico

semipermanent: ~ **anticyclone** *n* METEO anticiclón semipermanente *m*

semipermeable: ~ **membrane** *n* PHYS membrana semipermeable *f*

semipermissive: ~ **stop signal** *n* RAIL señal de parada discrecional *f*

semipolar *adj* CHEM semipolar

semiportable *adj* MECH ENG semifijo, semiportátil, semitransportable

semipositive: ~ **mold** AmE, ~ **mould** BrE *n* P&R molde semipositivo *m*

semireflecting: ~ **mirror** *n* INSTR espejo semireflector *m*; ~ **plate** *n* PHYS lámina semirreflectante *f*

semireinforcing: ~ **carbon black** *n* (*SRF carbon black*) P&R negro de humo de horno y refuerzo medio *m*

semireverberant: ~ **room** *n* ACOUST cámara semirreverberante *f*

semi-rigid: ~ **automatic coupling** *n* TRANSP acoplamiento automático semi-rígido *m*; ~ **delivery hose** *n* SAFE *heat unit* manguera semi-rígida de descarga *f*

semirotary: ~ **actuator** *n* PROD actuador oscilatorio *m*; ~ **pump** *n* WATER bomba oscilatoria *f*

semisilvered: ~ **mirror** *n* INSTR espejo semiplateado *m*

semiskimmed *adj* FOOD semidescremada

semislipper: ~ **piston** *n* AUTO pistón de media falda *m*, pistón de medio patín *m*

semisolid: ~ **combustible waste** *n* POLL desechos combustibles semisólidos *m pl*, desperdicio combustible semisólido *m*, residuos combustibles semisólidos *m pl*

semisubmersible: ~ **platform** *n* PETR TECH plataforma semisumergible *f*; ~ **rig** *n* PETR TECH plataforma semisumergible *f*

semitone *n* ACOUST, PHYS semitono *m*

semitrailer *n* TRANSP remolque de dos ruedas *m*, VEH semirremolque *m*; ~ **lorry** *n* BrE (*cf semitrailer truck AmE*) TRANSP camión semi-trailer *m*, camión semirremolque *m*; ~ **motor vehicle** *n* TRANSP vehículo de motor semi-trailer *m*; ~ **towing vehicle** *n* TRANSP vehículo remolcador semi-trailer *m*; ~ **truck** *n* AmE (*cf semitrailer lorry BrE*) TRANSP camión semi-trailer *m*, camión semirremolque *m*

semitrailing: ~ **arm** *n* AUTO, VEH barra de semiarrastre *f*

semitransparent: ~ **color** AmE, ~ **colour** BrE *n* C&G color semi-transparente *m*; ~ **photocathode** *n* ELEC, ELEC ENG, PHYS, TV fotocátodo semi-transparente *m*

senarmontite *n* MINERAL senarmontita *f*

send *vt* COMP&DP enviar, transmitir

sender *n* TELECOM emisor *m*, transmisor *m*; ~ **identification** *n* TELECOM identificación del emisor *f*; ~-**receiver** *n* COMP&DP emisor-receptor *m*, transmisor-receptor *m*

sending *n* COMP&DP envío *m*, transmisión *f*

senhouse: ~ **slip** *n* WATER TRANSP *deck fittings* gancho disparador *m*

senior: ~ **reactor operator** *n* NUCL operador jefe de reactor *m*, operadora jefe de reactor *f*

sennet *n* WATER TRANSP cajeta *f*

sensation *n* ACOUST sensación *f*

sense *n* GEOL *pipelines* dirección *f*; ~ **amplifier** *n* ELECTRON amplificador de detección *m*

sensible: ~ **cooling effect** *n* REFRIG potencia frigorífica sensible *f*; ~ **heat** *n* GEOPHYS, HEAT ENG calor sensible *m*, PHYS calor perceptible *m*; ~ **heat ratio** *n* REFRIG factor de calor sensible *m*

sensing *n* COMP&DP detección *f*, NUCL captación *f*, determinación del sentido de una indicación *f*; ~ **device** *n* MAR POLL dispositivo detector *m*; ~ **electrode** *n* ELEC ENG electrodo sensor *m*; ~ **element** *n* ELECTRON elemento detector *m*, NUCL elemento captador *m*, elemento sensor *m*; ~ **lead** *n*

ELEC ENG cable sensible *m*; ~ **relay** *n* ELEC ENG relé detector *m*; ~ **resistor** *n* ELEC ENG resistencia sensora *f*; ~ **switch** *n* ELEC ENG interruptor detector *m*

sensitive: ~ **altimeter** *n* AIR TRANSP, INSTR altímetro de precisión *m*; ~ **energy** *n* GAS energía sensible *f*; ~ **friction drill** *n* MECH ENG taladradora de fricción de precisión *f*; ~ **gang drill** *n* MECH ENG taladradora múltiple de precisión *f*, taladradora múltiple sensible *f*; ~ **heat air cooler** *n* REFRIG enfriador de aire de calor sensible *m*; ~ **paper** *n* PHOTO papel sensibilizado *m*

sensitivity *n* ACOUST, COAL, ELEC sensibilidad *f*, ELEC ENG sensitividad *f*, sensibilidad *f*, INSTR, MINE, OPT sensibilidad *f*, PHYS sensitividad *f*, SPACE *communications* sensitividad *f*, sensibilidad *f*, TELECOM sensibilidad *f*; ~ **analysis** *n* PROD análisis de sensibilidad *m*; ~ **to initiation** *n* MINE sensibilidad a la iniciación *f*; ~ **to light** *n* RAD PHYS sensibilidad a la luz *f*

sensitization *n* CINEMAT, PHOTO, PRINT sensibilización *f*

sensitize *vt* CINEMAT, PHOTO, PRINT sensibilizar

sensitized: ~ **fluorescence** *n* RAD PHYS fluorescencia sensibilizada *f*

sensitizer *n* CINEMAT, PHOTO, PRINT sensibilizador *m*

sensitizing: ~ **bath** *n* CINEMAT, PHOTO baño de sensibilización *m*

sensitometric: ~ **curve** *n* CINEMAT curva sensitométrica *f*; ~ **step wedge** *n* CINEMAT cuña escalonada sensitométrica *f*

sensitometry *n* ACOUST, CINEMAT sensitometría *f*

sensor *n* AUTO sensor *m*, COMP&DP detector *m*, ELECTRON captador *m*, detector *m*, sensor *m*, INSTR sensor *m*, sensor detector *m*, METR *of controls* captador *m*, sensor *m*, NUCL, PHYS sensor *m*, SPACE sensor detector *m*, captador *m*, sensor *m*, sonda *f*, TELECOM detector *m*, captador *m*, sensor *m*, VEH sensor *m*, WATER TRANSP *meteorology* sensor *m*, detector *m*; ~ **signal** *n* ELECTRON señal captadora *f*, señal registradora *f*; ~ **system** *n* SPACE sistema registrador *m*, sistema sensor *m*

sentence *n* COMP&DP sentencia *f*

sentinel *n* COMP&DP centinela *m*, PRINT señalizador *m*

separability *n* NUCL separabilidad *f*

separable *adj* CHEM, CHEM TECH, COAL separable

separate[1]: ~ **collection** *n* RECYCL colecta por separado *f*, recogida por separado *f*, recolección por separado *f*; ~ **excitation** *n* ELEC ENG excitación independiente *f*; ~ **excited dynamo** *n* ELEC ENG dinamo excitado independientemente *m*; ~ **excited generator** *n* ELEC, ELEC ENG generador excitado por separado *m*; ~ **lead cable** *n* (*SL cable*) ELEC cable de conductores emplomados *m*; ~ **sewerage system** *n* WATER sistema de alcantarillado separado *m*; ~ **ventilation** *n* MINE ventilación autónoma *f*; ~ **winding transformer** *n* ELEC transformador de devanado independiente *m*

separate[2] *vt* CHEM, CHEM TECH, GAS, POLL separar; ~ **out** *vt* CHEM extraer, filtrar

separate[3] *vi* CHEM, CHEM TECH, COAL separarse; ~ **out** *vi* CHEM extraerse, filtrarse

separated: ~-**braking circuits** *n pl* TRANSP circuitos de frenado independiente *m pl*, circuitos de freno individuales *m pl*

separately: ~ **excited motor** *n* ELEC motor de excitación separada *m*; ~ **lead-sheathed cable** *n* ELEC cable de conductores con vaina de plomo *m*, cable de conductores emplomados *m*

separating: ~ **agent** *n* CHEM, CHEM TECH agente de separación *m*; ~ **burette** *n* CHEM TECH, LAB bureta de separación *f*; ~ **column** *n* CHEM TECH, LAB columna de separación *f*; ~ **funnel** *n* CHEM TECH embudo de extracción *m*, LAB embudo de separación *m*; ~ **power** *n* NUCL poder de separación *m*; ~ **rod** *n* TEXTIL tirante de separación *m*; ~ **tower** *n* CHEM TECH, LAB torre de separación *f*; ~ **unit** *n* AGRIC *straw*, CHEM TECH, COAL, MECH ENG, PROD unidad separadora *f*

separation *n* CHEM, CHEM TECH, COAL, PETR TECH, PHYS separación *f*, SPACE decantación *f*, desunión *f*, separación *f*; ~ **by flocculation** *n* CHEM TECH separación por floculación *f*; ~ **by geometry** *n* NUCL separación geométrica *f*; ~ **circuit** *n* TV circuito separador *m*; ~ **density** *n* COAL densidad de separación *f*; ~ **effect** *n* CHEM TECH efecto de separación *m*; ~ **filter** *n* ELECTRON, TV filtro de separación *m*; ~ **funnel** *n* CHEM, LAB embudo de separación *m*; ~ **layer** *n* CHEM TECH capa de extracción *f*, capa de separación *f*; ~ **liquid** *n* CHEM TECH líquido de separación *m*; ~ **maneuver** *AmE*, ~ **manoeuvre** *BrE n* SPACE maniobra de separación *f*; ~ **master** *n* CINEMAT copia maestra con separación de colores *f*; ~ **mechanism** *n* SPACE mecanismo de separación *m*; ~ **motor** *n* SPACE motor de separación *m*; ~ **negative** *n* CINEMAT negativo con separación de colores *m*; ~ **positive** *n* CINEMAT copia positiva con separación de colores *f*; ~ **process** *n* CHEM TECH proceso de separación *m*; ~ **rocket** *n* SPACE cohete de separación *m*; ~ **size** *n* CHEM TECH tamaño de separación *m*

separative: ~ **effort** *n* NUCL esfuerzo de separación *m*

separator *n* CHEM TECH, CRYSTALL separador *m*, ELEC *cable* capa separadora *f*, FOOD, MAR POLL separador *m*, MECH ENG *oil* divisor *m*, partidor *m*, separador *m*, MINE embudo de decantación *m* (*AmL*), separador *m*, cono de decantación *m* (*Esp*), PETR TECH, TELECOM separador *m*, WATER colector de agua *m*, separador de agua *m*; ~ **funnel** *n* CHEM embudo separador *m*; ~ **symbol** *n* COMP&DP símbolo separador *m*

sepia: ~ **toning** *n* PHOTO viraje en sepia *m*

sepiolite *n* MINERAL sepiolita *f*

sepmag *n* CINEMAT, TV banda magnética individual *f*; ~ **lock** *n* CINEMAT, TV bloqueo de banda magnética individual *m*

sepopt *n* CINEMAT banda óptica individual *f*

septic: ~ **sludge** *n* RECYCL cieno séptico *m*, residuos sépticos *m pl*; ~ **tank** *n* HYDROL fosa séptica *f*, *planting* tanque séptico *m*, RECYCL, WATER tanque séptico *m*, fosa séptica *f*

septivalent *adj* CHEM septivalente

septum *n* ELEC ENG diafragma *m*

sequence *n* ACOUST, GEOL secuencia *f*, MATH secuencia *f*, sucesión *f*; ~ **check** *n* COMP&DP secuencia de comprobación *f*, verificador de secuencia *m*; ~ **control** *n* COMP&DP control de secuencia *m*, control secuencial *m*; ~ **control register** *n* COMP&DP registro de control de secuencia *m*, registro de control secuencial *m*; ~ **current transformer** *n* PROD transformador de intensidad secuencial *m*; ~ **number** *n* (*SN*) TELECOM número de orden *m*, número secuencial *m*; ~ **number protection** *n* (*SNP*) TELECOM protección del número de orden *f*, protección del número secuencial *f*; ~ **relay** *n* ELEC ENG relé

secundario teleaccionado *m*; ~ **valve** *n* MECH ENG
válvula secuencial *f*

sequencer *n* COMP&DP, ELEC ENG, PROD, TELECOM
computador de secuencia *m* (*AmL*), computadora
de secuencia *f* (*AmL*), dispositivo de secuencia *m*,
ordenador de secuencia *m* (*Esp*), secuenciador *m*;
~ **input** *n* PROD entrada de secuenciador *f*; ~ **input
instruction** *n* PROD instrucción de entrada de
secuenciador *f*; ~ **instruction data form** *n* PROD
estructura de datos de las instrucciones del secuenciador *f*; ~ **jump operation** *n* PROD operación de
bifurcación del secuenciador *f*; ~ **load** *n* PROD carga
del secuenciador *f*; ~ **output** *n* PROD salida del
secuenciador *f*; ~ **output instruction** *n* PROD instrucción de salida del secuenciador *f*; ~ **step instruction**
n PROD instrucción gradual del secuenciador *f*,
instrucción progresiva del secuenciador *f*

sequencing *n* COMP&DP secuencia *f*, secuenciado *m*,
ELEC ENG clasificación secuencial *f*, TELECOM clasificación *f*, control secuencial *m*, secuenciamiento *m*

sequential[1] *adj* COMP&DP, TELECOM secuencial

sequential[2]: ~ **access** *n* COMP&DP acceso secuencial
m; ~ **color with memory system** *AmE*, ~ **colour
with memory system** *BrE* *n* (*SECAM*) TV sistema de
color secuencial con memoria *m* (*SECAM*);
~ **decoding** *n* TELECOM decodificación secuencial *f*;
~ **file** *n* COMP&DP archivo secuencial *m*, fichero
secuencial *m*; ~ **input-output** *n* (*SIO*) COMP&DP
entrada-salida en serie *f* (*SIO*), entrada-salida
secuencial *f* (*SIO*); ~ **interlace** *n* TV entrelazado
secuencial *m*; ~ **numbering** *n* PRINT numeración
secuencial *f*; ~ **processing** *n* COMP&DP procesamiento secuencial *m*; ~ **scanning** *n* TV exploración
por líneas sucesivas *f*; ~ **search** *n* COMP&DP búsqueda
secuencial *f*; ~ **test** *n* TELECOM prueba secuencial *f*;
~ **tone coding** *n* TELECOM codificación por tonos
secuenciales *f*

sequester *vt* CHEM secuestrar

sequestering: ~ **agent** *n* CHEM agente acomplejante
m, agente secuestrador *m*

sequestrene *n* CHEM secuestreno *m*

serial[1] *adj* COMP&DP, PRINT en serie, TELECOM en serie,
secuencial, serial; ~-**form** *adj* ELEC ENG en forma de
serie, en serie; ~-**parallel** *adj* COMP&DP en serie-
paralelo

serial[2]: ~ **access** *n* COMP&DP acceso en serie *m*;
~ **access device** *n* COMP&DP dispositivo de acceso
en serie *m*; ~ **access storage** *n* COMP&DP memoria
de acceso en serie *f*; ~ **adder** *n* COMP&DP, ELECTRON
sumador en serie *m*; ~ **analog-to-digital conversion**
n CONST, ELECTRON conversión en serie de analógico
a digital *f*; ~ **analog-to-digital converter** *n* CONST
convertidor en serie de analógico a digital *m*, ELEC-
TRON convertidor de sistema análogo a sistema
digital en serie *m*; ~ **computer** *n* COMP&DP computador serie *m* (*AmL*), computadora serie *f* (*AmL*),
ordenador serie *m* (*Esp*); ~ **digital output** *n* COMP&DP
salida digital en serie *f*; ~ **digital signal** *n* ELECTRON
señal digital en serie *f*; ~ **interface** *n* COMP&DP, PRINT,
TELECOM interfaz en serie *m*; ~ **line** *n* ELEC ENG línea
de serie *f*; ~ **memory** *n* ELEC ENG memoria en serie *f*;
~ **number** *n* COMP&DP número de serie *m*, MECH ENG
número de fabricación *m*, número de orden *m*,
número de serie *m*, PHOTO número de serie *m*;
~ **operation** *n* COMP&DP funcionamiento en serie *m*,
operación en serie *f*; ~ **printer** *n* COMP&DP, PRINT

impresora en serie *f*; ~ **processing** *n* COMP&DP
procesamiento en serie *m*; ~ **programmable
interface** *n* TELECOM interfaz serie programable *f*;
~ **programming** *n* COMP&DP programación en serie *f*;
~ **rudders** *n pl* AIR TRANSP timones de dirección en
serie *m pl*; ~ **storage** *n* *AmE* (*cf serial store BrE*)
COMP&DP almacenamiento en serie *m*; ~ **store** *n* *BrE*
(*cf serial storage AmE*) COMP&DP almacenamiento en
serie *m*; ~ **subtractor** *n* ELECTRON restador serie *m*;
~-**to-parallel conversion** *n* ELEC ENG conversión de
serie a paralelo *f*; ~-**to-parallel converter** *n* ELEC ENG
convertidor de serie a paralelo *m*; ~ **transfer** *n*
COMP&DP transferencia en serie *f*; ~ **transmission** *n*
COMP&DP transmisión en serie *f*; ~ **wiring** *n* PROD
cableado en serie *m*

serialization *n* COMP&DP, ELEC ENG serialización *f*

serialize *vt* COMP&DP poner en serie, serializar, ELEC
ENG producir en serie, serializar

serializer *n* ELEC ENG registrador por serie *m*, seriali-
zador *m*

sericite *n* MINERAL sericita *f*; ~ **schist** *n* GEOL esquisto
de sericita *m*

series[1]: **in** ~ *adj* ELEC, MATH, PHYS en serie;
~-**connected** *adj* ELEC, ELEC ENG conectado en serie

series[2] *n* CHEM *of reactions*, COMP&DP, ELEC, GEOL,
MATH serie *f*, MECH ENG cadena *f*, serie *f*;
~ **arrangement** *n* ELEC ENG instalación en serie *f*,
montaje en serie *m*; ~ **capacitance** *n* ELEC ENG
capacitancia en serie *f*; ~ **capacitor** *n* ELEC, ELEC
ENG condensador en serie *m*; ~ **circuit** *n* ELEC ENG,
MINE, TELECOM circuito en serie *m*; ~ **coil** *n* ELEC
bobina en serie *f*; ~ **collector resistance** *n* ELEC ENG
resistencia serie de colector *f*; ~-**connected
resistance** *n* ELEC resistencia conectada en serie *f*;
~ **connection** *n* ELEC acoplamiento en serie *m*,
conexión en serie *f*, montaje en serie *m*, ELEC ENG
acoplamiento en serie *m*, conexión en serie *f*, MINE,
PHYS conexión en serie *f*; ~ **converter** *n* ELEC ENG
convertidor en serie *m*; ~ **DC motor** *n* ELEC ENG
motor CC en serie *m*; ~ **direct current motor** *n*
ELEC ENG motor de corriente continua en serie *m*;
~ **dynamo** *n* ELEC ENG dinamo excitado en serie *m*;
~ **excitation** *n* ELEC ENG excitación en serie *f*;
~ **excited machine** *n* ELEC *generator* máquina de
excitación en serie *f*; ~ **feed** *n* ELEC ENG alimentación
en serie *f*; ~ **feedback** *n* ELEC ENG, ELECTRON
realimentación en serie *f*; ~ **inductor** *n* ELEC inductor
en serie *m*; ~ **input-output** *n* (*SIO*) COMP&DP
entrada-salida en serie *f* (*SIO*), entrada-salida
secuencial *f* (*SIO*); ~ **of links** *n* TELECOM serie de
enlaces *f*; ~ **motor** *n* ELEC motor arrollado en serie *m*,
motor con arrollamientos en serie *m*, motor devanado en serie *m*, ELEC ENG motor excitado en serie *m*;
~ **mounting** *n* ELEC montaje en serie *m*; ~-**parallel
circuit** *n* ELEC ENG, MINE circuito en serie-paralelo *m*;
~-**parallel switch** *n* ELEC ENG conmutador serie-
paralelo *m*; ~-**pass power transistor** *n* ELECTRON
transistor de potencia de pasos en serie *m*; ~-**pass
transistor** *n* ELECTRON transistor de pasos en serie *m*;
~-**produced power reactor** *n* NUCL reactor comercial de construcción en serie *m*, reactor de potencia
producido en serie *m*; ~ **production** *n* WATER TRANSP
fabricación en serie *f*, producción en serie *f*;
~ **reactance** *n* ELEC ENG reactancia en serie *f*;
~-**regulated power supply** *n* ELEC ENG suministro
de energía regulado en serie *m*; ~ **regulation** *n* ELEC

ENG regulación de serie *f*; ~ **regulator** *n* ELEC ENG regulador en serie *m*; ~ **resistance** *n* ELEC, ELEC ENG resistencia en serie *f*; ~ **resistor** *n* ELEC, ELEC ENG resistor en serie *m*; ~ **resonance** *n* ELEC ENG, PHYS resonancia en serie *f*; ~ **resonant circuit** *n* ELEC ENG circuito resonante en serie *m*; ~ **starter** *n* ELEC mecanismo de arranque en serie *m*; ~ **switch** *n* ELEC conmutador en serie *m*; ~ **transformer** *n* ELEC transformador en serie *m*; ~ **winding** *n* ELEC arrollamiento en serie *m*, devanado en serie *m*, ELEC ENG devanado en serie *m*; ~**-wound dynamo** *n* ELEC dinamo serie *f*, máquina dinamoeléctrica excitada en serie *f*, ELEC ENG dinamo serie *f*, dínamo excitada en serie *f*; ~**-wound machine** *n* ELEC máquina excitada en serie *f*, máquina serie *f*; ~**-wound motor** *n* ELEC, ELEC ENG motor excitado en serie *m*

serif *n* PRINT serif *f*, trazo con remates *m*

serigraphy *n* PRINT serigrafía *f*

serotonin *n* CHEM serotonina *f*

serpent: ~ **coil** *n* LAB serpentín *m*

serpentine *n* MINERAL serpentina *f*

serpentinization *n* FUELLESS serpenteo *m*

serrated: ~ **lockwasher** *n* MECH ENG arandela de fijación acanalada *f*, arandela dentada de fijación *f*, arandela estriada de fijación *f*; ~ **pulse** *n* TV impulso fraccionado *m*, pulso diente de sierra *m*

serration *n* MECH ENG estriación *f*

serrodyne[1] *n* ELECTRON serrodina *f*; ~ **modulator** *n* ELECTRON modulador de serrodina *m*

serrodyne[2] *vt* ELECTRON serrodinar

serve *vt* PROD *boiler* calentar

server *n* COMP&DP procesador de interconexión *m*, servidor *m*

service[1]: **in** ~ *adj* PROD en servicio

service[2] *n* QUALITY, RAIL servicio *m*, SPACE acometida *f*, servicio *m*, utilidad *f*; ~ **access point** *n* (*SAP*) TELECOM punto de acceso al servicio *m*; ~ **access point identifier** *n* (*SAPI*) TELECOM identificador del punto de acceso al servicio *m*; ~ **area** *n* AIR TRANSP, SPACE área de servicio *f*; ~ **bit** *n* COMP&DP bit de servicio *m*; ~ **brake** *n* VEH freno de servicio *m*; ~ **ceiling** *n* AIR TRANSP techo de servicio *m*, techo práctico *m*; ~ **chest** *n* PAPER tina de mezcla *f*; ~ **cycle** *n* PROD ciclo de servicio *m*; ~ **data unit** *n* (*SDU*) TELECOM unidad de datos de servicio *f*; ~ **gage** *AmE*, ~ **gauge** *BrE* REFRIG manómetro de montador *m*; ~ **layer** *n* TELECOM capa de servicio *f*, nivel de servicio *m*; ~ **level** *n* PROD nivel de servicio *m*; ~ **life** *n* COAL, CONST, ELEC ENG NUCL, PACK, SPACE duración de la utilización *f*, duración del servicio *f*, vida útil *f*; ~ **line** *n* ELEC ENG cable de alimentación *m*, línea de servicio *f*, línea de suministro *f*, TELECOM línea de servicio *f*; ~ **load** *n* REFRIG carga térmica debida al servicio *f*, WATER carga de servicio *f*; ~ **or option not available class** *n* TELECOM clase no disponible de opción o servicio *f*; ~ **or option not implemented class** *n* TELECOM clase no implementada de opción o servicio *f*; ~ **oscillator** *n* ELECTRON oscilador de servicio *m*, oscilador principal *m*; ~ **pistol** *n* MILIT pistola reglamentaria *f*; ~ **program** *n* COMP&DP programa de servicio *m*; ~ **provider** *n* (*SP*) TELECOM prestador de servicios *m*; ~ **provider link** *n* (*SPL*) TELECOM enlace con el prestador de servicios *m*, vínculo con el prestador de servicios *m*; ~ **station** *n* PROD estación de servicio *f*, TRANSP estación de servicio

f, puesto de servicio *m*; ~ **steam** *n* NUCL vapor de servicios *m*; ~ **string advice** *n* TELECOM cadena de aviso de servicio *f*; ~ **time** *n* PROD, TELECOM tiempo de servicio *m*; ~ **tools** *n pl* MECH ENG herramientas de servicio *f pl*; ~ **trolley** *n* AIR TRANSP carretilla de servicio *f*; ~ **tunnel** *n* CONST galería de servicio *f*; ~ **vehicle** *n* AIR TRANSP vehículo de servicio *m*; ~ **volume** *n* TRANSP volumen de servicio *m*

serviceability *n* NUCL duración prevista *f*, facilidad de mantenimiento *f*

servicer *n* AIR TRANSP servidor *m*, servidora *f*

servicing *n* TELECOM mantenimiento *m*, servicio *m*

serving *n* ELEC *cable* forro *m*, amarraje *m*, cinta aislante *f*, barbeta *f*, TELECOM revestimiento *m*; ~ **exchange** *n* TELECOM central de servicio *f*

servo *n* TRANSP, VEH servo *m*; ~ **amplifier** *n* ELECTRON servoamplificador *m*; ~ **capstan** *n* TV servo cabrestante *m*; ~**-controlled tape mechanism** *n* TV mecanismo de cinta servocontrolada *m*, mecanismo de cinta servoregulada *m*; ~ **loop** *n* CINEMAT, TV circuito de servomecanismo *m*; ~**-modulator valve** *n* AUTO válvula servomoduladora *f*; ~**-operated valve** *n* REFRIG válvula servoaccionada *f*; ~ **system** *n* SPACE servomecanismo *m*, servosistema *m*, TV sistema de servomecanismo *m*; ~ **system drift** *n* SPACE deriva del servomecanismo *f*; ~ **wheel** *n* TV servorueda *f*

servoaltimeter *n* AIR TRANSP servoaltímetro *m*

servobrake *n* AUTO, VEH servofreno *m*

servocontrol *n* AIR TRANSP servocontrol *m*, CINEMAT servocontrol *m*, servomando *m*, ELEC ENG servocontrol *m*

servohydraulic: ~ **test equipment** *n* MECH ENG equipo de pruebas servohidráulico *m*

servomechanism *n* COMP&DP, ELEC ENG, MECH ENG, PHYS, TV servomecanismo *m*

servomotor *n* ELEC ENG, FUELLESS, NUCL servomotor *m*

servovalve *n* MECH ENG, PROD servoválvula *f*

servozoom *n* CINEMAT servozoom *m*

SES *abbr* TELECOM (*severely errored second*) segundo severamente erróneo *m*, WATER TRANSP (*surface effect ship*) *satellites* buque de sustentación hidrodinámica *m*

sesame: ~ **oil** *n* AGRIC, FOOD aceite de ajonjolí *m*

sesquiterpenoid *adj* CHEM sesquiterpenoide

sessile: ~ **dislocation** *n* CRYSTALL dislocación fija *f*

session: ~ **layer** *n* COMP&DP capa de sesión *f*, nivel de sesión *m*; ~ **protocol** *n* (*SP*) TELECOM protocolo de sesión *m*; ~ **protocol data unit** *n* (*SPDU*) TELECOM unidad de datos del protocolo de sesión *f*

set[1] *adj* MECH ENG *programmed* ajustado, establecido, invariable, prefijado, rígido, señalado

set[2] *n* CINEMAT decorado *m*, plató *m*, COMP&DP conjunto *m*, juego *m*, CONST *of rivets* lote *m*, *of tools* buterola *f*, conjunto *m*, juego *m*, *street paving* endurecimiento de la superficie *m*, ELEC ENG calaje *m*, conjunto *m*, GEOL conjunto *m*, grupo *m*, HYDRAUL batería *f*, MATH conjunto *m*, MECH ENG *saws* triscado *m*, *deformation* flecha *f*, deformación *f*, *of instruments* juego *m*, torcedura *f*, *of saw tooth* triscamiento *m*, *firmness* estabilidad *f*, P&R endurecimiento *m*, solidificación *f*, curado rápido *m*, PRINT composición *f*, TEXTIL conjunto *m*, TV decorado *m*, WATER *pumps in mine* grupo *m*, juego *m*; ~ **of box spanners** *n* MECH ENG juego de llaves de tubo *m*; ~ **of change wheels** *n*

MECH ENG *for lathe* juego de engranajes *m*, juego de ruedas *m*, *geared machine* juego de engranajes de recambio *m*; ~ **clamp** *n* CINEMAT pinza de cierre *f*; ~ **collar** *n* MECH ENG *for shafting* collar de fijación *m*; ~ **of contacts** *n* ELEC juego de contactos *m*; ~ **counter sensor** *n* PROD detector de contador *m*; ~ **of cutters** *n* PROD juego de cuchillas *m*; ~ **of gears** *n* AUTO, VEH juego de engranajes *m*, tren de engranajes *m*; ~ **grease cup** *n* MECH ENG casco de grasa consistente *m*; ~ **of instructions** *n* PROD conjunto de instrucciones *m*; ~ **key** *n* MECH ENG chaveta de fijación *f*; ~ **of lenses** *n* CINEMAT conjunto de lentes *m*, PHOTO serie de objetivos *f*; ~ **nut** *n* MECH ENG contratuerca *f*, tuerca de ajuste *f*, tuerca de fijación *f*, tuerca de inmovilización *f*; ~**-off** *n* CONST *architecture* saliente *m*, zarpa *f*, PRINT repinte *m*; ~**-on voltage-controlled oscillator** *n* ELECTRON oscilador de voltaje controlado en servicio *m*; ~ **pin** *n* MECH ENG *binding* pasador de fijación *m*; ~ **point** *n* CHEM posición de ajuste *f*, punto de ajuste *m*, punto de referencia *m*; ~ **point accuracy** *n* NUCL precisión de tarado *f*; ~ **of points** *n BrE* (*cf switch AmE*) CONST aguja *f*, cambiavía *m*, juego de agujas *m*, RAIL cambiavía *m*, juego de agujas *m*, aguja *f*; ~ **pressure** *n* PROD presión de regulación *f*; ~ **of rolls** *n* PAPER juego de rodillos *m*, PROD *rolling mill* juego de cilindros *m*; ~ **screw** *n* PROD tornillo de fijación *m*, tornillo de sujeción *m*, tornillo fijador *m*; ~ **of shores** *n* CONST *building* puntales *m pl*; ~ **solid** *n* PRINT composición apretada *f*; ~ **of spare parts** *n* PROD juego de piezas de recambio *m*, juego de piezas de repuesto *m*; ~ **of speeds** *n* MECH ENG conjunto de velocidades *m*, juego de velocidades *m*; ~ **square** *n* GEOM, MECH ENG cartabón *m*, escuadra *f*; ~ **with stretcher piece** *n* CONST juego con separadores *m*; ~ **of supplementary lenses** *n* PHOTO serie de objetivos auxiliares *f*; ~ **theory** *n* MATH teoría de conjuntos *f*; ~ **of timber** *n* CONST juego de maderas *m*; ~ **of tools** *n* MECH ENG equipo de herramientas *m*, juego de herramientas *m*; ~**-up diagram** *n* TV plano de instalación *m*; ~**-valued attribute** *n* TELECOM atributo de valor de consigna *m*, atributo de valor predeterminado *m*; ~ **of valves** *n* GAS conjunto de válvulas *m*; ~ **versus reset** *n* PROD regulación frente a la reposición *f*; ~ **of weights** *n* LAB juego de pesas *m*; ~ **of wells** *n* WATER grupo de pozos *m*; ~ **of wheels** *n* AUTO, VEH juego de ruedas *m*

set[3] *vt* CINEMAT ajustar, COMP&DP montar, *variable* poner a uno, fijar, *counter* ajustar, CONST *rivet* fijar, asentar, *to place, put, fix, plant* colocar, *stake* erigir, depositar, ELECTRON poner a uno, MECH ENG *mount* fijar, *saws* regular, instalar, *place* colocar, *tools* adaptar, establecer, engarzar, engastar, montar, poner, insertar, OCEAN armar, PRINT ajustar, componer, PROD poner a uno; ~ **ablaze** *vt* THERMO encender, incendiar; ~ **fire to** *vt* THERMO encender, incendiar; ~ **in motion** *vt* MECH ENG poner en marcha, poner en movimiento; ~ **out** *vt* CONST *stone bed* colocar; ~ **over** *vt* MECH ENG apartar, descentrar; ~ **to work** *vt* MECH ENG *machine* poner a funcionar, poner a trabajar; ~ **to zero** *vt* MECH ENG *instrument* llevar a cero, poner a cero, volver a cero; ~ **up** *vt* CINEMAT preparar, COMP&DP instalar, preparar, configurar, CONST *partitions*, OCEAN *protection against sea* montar, TELECOM establecer, TV *studio, set, editing*

room instalar, montar, WATER TRANSP *flag* arbolar; ~ **up again** *vt* MECH ENG poner de nuevo

set[4] *vi* CONST *cement* fraguar; ~ **boards edgeways** *vi* CONST bordear; ~ **in** *vi* WATER TRANSP *tide* repuntar para corriente; ~ **out** *vi* WATER TRANSP *tide* refluir, repuntar para menguante; ~ **sail** *vi* WATER TRANSP hacerse a la vela

setback *n* CONST *wall* retranqueo *m*

setscrew *n* MECH ENG perno de fijación *m*, tornillo de ajuste *m*, tornillo de apriete *m*, tornillo de fijación *m*, tornillo de presión *m*, tornillo prisionero *m*

sett *n* CONST adoquín *m*

setter: ~ **sight** *n* MILIT *artillery* alza reguladora *f*

setting *n* AIR TRANSP ajuste *m*, fijación *f*, graduación *f*, reglaje *m*, CHEM TECH congelación *f*, solidificación *f*, COAL calibración *f*, endurecimiento *m*, montaje *m*, CONST *lines and cements* ajuste *m*, *landmarks* colocación *f*, deslinde *m*, CRYSTALL solidificación *f*, MECH ENG *mounting* erección *f*, triscadura *f*, preparación *f*, regulación *f*, instalación *f*, colocación *f*, montaje *m*, METR tarado *m*, OCEAN *of a net* armado *m*, lance *m*, PROD *cores* asentamiento de refractarios en un horno *m*, montaje de refractarios en un horno *m*, reglaje de machos *m*; ~ **machine** *n* MECH ENG *saw* triscadora *f*; ~ **master** *n* MECH ENG calibrador de regulación *m*; ~ **out** *n* AGRIC corte de amelga *f*; ~**-out** *n* CONST colocación de señales *f*, deslinde *m*; ~ **over** *n* MECH ENG descentrado *m*; ~ **rate** *n* C&G razón de asentamiento *f*; ~ **stick** *n* PRINT componedor *m*; ~ **time** *n* P&R tiempo de endurecimiento *m*, tiempo de solidificación *m*; ~ **up** *n* MECH ENG *of machine* preparación *f*, puesta a punto *f*, PROD *moulds* ajuste *m*; ~**-up** *n* CRYSTALL establecimiento *m*; ~**-up machine** *n* PROD *founding* máquina de remoldear *f*; ~**-up pit** *n* PROD *founding* fosa de remoldeo *f*

settle[1] *vt* CHEM TECH sedimentar; ~ **on** *vt* CHEM TECH asentar

settle[2] *vi* COAL asentarse, *liquid* clarificarse, depositarse, estabilizarse, posarse, CONST asentarse

settleable: ~ **solids** *n pl* HYDROL *on working barge* sólidos sedimentables *m pl*

settled: ~ **sewage** *n* HYDROL, POLL, RECYCL, WATER aguas negras decantadas *f pl*; ~ **weather** *n* METEO, WATER TRANSP tiempo estable *m*, tiempo hecho *m*

settlement *n* COAL asentamiento *m*, sedimentación *f*, CONST asentamiento *m*, asiento *m*; ~ **gage** *AmE*, ~ **gauge** *BrE n* COAL calibrador de sedimentación *m*, dosis de cemento *f*; ~ **meter** *n* CHEM TECH medidor de asentamiento *m*; ~ **reference marker** *n* CHEM TECH punto de referencia de la sedimentación *m*

settler: ~ **chamber** *n* NUCL cámara de decantación *f*

settling *n* CHEM asentamiento *m*, sedimentación *f*, COAL asiento *m*, depósito *m*, hundimiento *m*, sedimento *m*, CONST *of ground* decantación *f*, GEOL asentamiento *m*, HYDROL sedimento *m*, depósito *m*, PHYS estabilización *f*; ~ **basin** *n* CHEM TECH artesa de sedimentación *f*, COAL estanque decantador *m*, balsa de decantación *f*, HYDROL estanque decantador *m*, depósito de sedimentación *m*, *of headstock, lathe or tailstock* estanque de decantación *m*, MINE balsa de decantación *f*, estanque decantador *m*, WATER depósito de sedimentación *m*, estanque decantador *m*; ~ **cone** *n* CHEM TECH cono de sedimentación *m*, COAL tolva decantadora *f*; ~ **cyclone** *n* CHEM TECH ciclón de sedimentación *m*; ~ **pit** *n* CHEM TECH foso de sedimentación *m*; ~ **pond** *n* COAL balsa de sedimentación *f*; ~ **pool** *n* CHEM TECH estanque de deposición *m*, estanque de sedimentación *m*; ~ **rate** *n* CHEM TECH velocidad de sedimentación *f*; ~ **reservoir** *n* CHEM TECH estanque de deposición *m*, estanque de sedimentación *m*; ~ **speed** *n* COAL velocidad de sedimentación *f*; ~ **sump** *n* CHEM TECH pozo de sedimentación *m*; ~ **tank** *n* COAL cuba de decantación *f*, cuba de sedimentación *f*, HYDROL depósito de decantación *m*, PETR TECH depósito de sedimentación *m*; ~ **time** *n* CHEM TECH tiempo de estabilización *m*; ~ **tub** *n* CHEM TECH cuba de sedimentación *f*; ~ **vat** *n* CHEM TECH cuba de sedimentación *f*

settlings *n pl* CHEM sólidos sedimentables *m pl*

setup *n* COMP&DP configuración *f*, preparación *f*, instalación *f*, CONST *instrument* instalación *f*, montaje *m*, PROD ajuste *m*, montaje *m*, organización *f*, estructuración *f*, instalación *f*, sistema *m*, disposición *f*, puesta en página *f*, colocación *f*, TV instalación *f*; ~ **channel** *n* TELECOM canal de ajuste inicial *m*, canal de ajuste preliminar *m*, canal de instalación *m*, canal de preparación inicial *m*; ~ **phase** *n* PROD *machine* fase de instalación *f*, fase de montaje *f*, *system* fase de organización *f*, fase de preparación *f*; ~ **time** *n* COMP&DP tiempo de configuración *m*, tiempo de preparación *m*, PROD tiempo de establecimiento *m*, tiempo de instalación *m*, tiempo de preparación *m*, TEXTIL tiempo de inutilización *m*

SEV *abbr* (*surface-effect vehicle*) TRANSP vehículo de efecto en superficie *m*

seven: ~-**layer reference model** *n* COMP&DP modelo de referencia de siete capas *m*, modelo de referencia de siete niveles *m*

seventh *n* ACOUST séptima *f*

severely: ~ **errored second** *n* (*SES*) TELECOM segundo severamente erróneo *m*

severite *n* MINERAL severita *f*

sew *vt* TEXTIL coser

sewage *n* HYDROL aguas cloacales *f pl*, POLL aguas de albañal *f pl*, aguas de alcantarilla *f pl*, aguas fecales *f pl*, aguas negras *f pl*, RECYCL, WATER aguas cloacales *f pl*, aguas de albañal *f pl*, aguas de alcantarilla *f pl*, aguas fecales *f pl*, aguas negras *f pl*; ~ **analysis** *n* WATER análisis de agua de alcantarillas *m*, análisis de aguas negras *m*; ~ **disposal** *n* RECYCL eliminación de aguas cloacales *f*, evacuación de aguas residuales *f*, evacuación de residuos *f*; ~ **disposal plant** *n* WATER estación depuradora de aguas cloacales *f*; ~ **effluent** *n* RECYCL efluente de aguas residuales *m*, WATER efluente de alcantarillas *m*; ~ **farm** *n* HYDROL, POLL, RECYCL, WATER área para disposición de aguas negras *f*; ~ **farming** *n* AGRIC irrigación con aguas cloacales *f*, RECYCL irrigación con aguas cloacales *f*, utilización de los residuos para abono de tierras *f*, WATER irrigación con aguas cloacales *f*; ~ **gas** *n* GAS gas cloacal *m*, RECYCL gas cloacal *m*, gas residual *m*; ~-**pumping station** *n* HYDROL, RECYCL, WATER instalación de bombeo de aguas residuales *f*; ~ **sludge** *n* HYDROL fango cloacal *m*, lodo de alcantarillado *m*, RECYCL lodo residual *m*, WATER cieno cloacal *m*, fango cloacal *m*, fango de alcantarilla *m*, fangos de alcantarilla *m pl*, lodo de aguas cloacales *m*, lodo residual *m*; ~ **treatment plant** *n* RECYCL instalación de depuración de aguas residuales *f*, planta de tratamiento de residuos *f*, WATER instalación de depuración de aguas residuales *f*; ~ **waste** *n* POLL desperdicios residuales *m pl*, RECYCL

basura residual *f*, desperdicios residuales *m pl*; ~ **waste water** *n* HYDROL, POLL, RECYCL, WATER aguas residuales de alcantarilla *f pl*; ~ **works** *n pl* HYDROL, RECYCL planta de depuración de aguas residuales *f*, WATER planta de depuración de aguas residuales comunitarias *f*

sewer *n* COAL alcantarilla *f*, CONST alcantarilla *f*, cloaca *f*, albañal *m*, HYDROL alcantarilla *f*, cloaca *f*, MECH ENG alcantarilla *f*, POLL albañal *m*, RECYCL, WATER alcantarilla *f*, cloaca *f*; ~ **cleaning** *n* HYDROL, RECYCL limpia de cloacas *f*, limpieza de alcantarillas *f*, WATER limpia de cloacas *f*, limpieza de alcantarillas *f*, limpieza de cloacas *f*; ~ **drain** *n* WATER conducto de desagüe *m*; ~ **network** *n* HYDROL red de alcantarillado *f*; ~ **system** *n* RECYCL sistema de alcantarillado *m*

sewerage *n* COAL, CONST aguas residuales *f pl*, HYDROL aguas residuales *f pl*, alcantarillaje *m*, POLL aguas de albañal *f pl*, alcantarillaje *m*, RECYCL aguas residuales *f pl*, desagüe *m*, alcantarillaje *m*, WATER alcantarillaje *m*; ~ **system** *n* HYDROL red de alcantarillado *f*, RECYCL red cloacal *f*, red de alcantarillado *f*, sistema de desagüe *m*

sewing *n* PRINT, TEXTIL costura *f*; ~ **machine** *n* PRINT cosedora *f*, máquina de coser *f*, TEXTIL máquina de coser *f*

sewn: ~-**in label** *n* TEXTIL etiqueta cosida *f*; ~ **sack** *n* PACK saco cosido *m*

sextant *n* OPT, PHYS, WATER TRANSP sextante *m*; ~ **altitude** *n* WATER TRANSP altura instrumental *f*

sextet *n* PHYS sexteto *m*

seybertite *n* MINERAL seibertita *f*

SF *abbr* (*signal fail*) TELECOM falla de señal *f* (*AmL*), fallo de señal *m* (*Esp*)

sferics *AmE see* spherics *BrE*

SFET *abbr* (*synchronous frequency encoding technique*) TELECOM técnica de codificación de frecuencia síncrona *f*, técnica síncrona de codificación de frecuencia *f*

SFM *abbr* (*subcarrier frequency modulation*) TELECOM modulación de frecuencia de subportadora *f*

SFU *abbr* (*store-and-forward unit*) TELECOM unidad de almacenamiento y reexpedición *f*

SGC *abbr* (*signaling grouping channel AmE, signalling grouping channel BrE*) TELECOM canal agrupador de señalización *m*, canal de agrupamiento de señalización *m*

SGML *abbr* (*Standard Generalized Markup Language*) COMP&DP, PRINT lenguaje de mercado generalizado estándar *m*, lenguaje SGML *m*

SGTR *abbr* (*steam generator tube rupture*) NUCL SGTR (*rotura de tubos en un generador de vapor*)

shackle[1] *n* AUTO argolla *f*, grillete *m*, CONST *of padlock* grillete *m*, perno de enganche *m*, MAR POLL grillete *m*, MECH *wire* collera *f*, enganche *m*, MECH ENG abrazadera *f*, grillete *m*, VEH sujeción *f*, argolla *f*, gemela *f*, WATER TRANSP *chain piece, chain side* grillete *m*; ~ **insulator** *n* ELEC, ELEC ENG aislador de parada *m*

shackle[2] *vt* WATER TRANSP engrilletar

shade *n* C&G sombra *f*, tono *m*, PHOTO sombra *f*, PRINT sombra *f*, tono *m*, TEXTIL matiz *m*

shaded[1] *adj* C&G, PHOTO, PRINT sombreado

shaded[2]: ~-**pole motor** *n* ELEC motor de inducción de polos protegidos *m*, motor de polo sombreado *m*, motor de polos protegidos *m*, ELEC ENG motor con devanados en cortocircuito *m*

shading n P&R degradación f, sombra f, TV sombreado m; ~ **corrector** n TV corrector del sombreado m; **~-off pigment** n COLOUR pigmento esfumado m; ~ **paint** n COLOUR pintura sombreadora f, P&R pintura para sombrear f; ~ **signal** n TV señal compensadora f

shadow n CINEMAT, PHOTO sombra f, PRINT sombra f, zona oscura f; ~ **area** n TV *fixed equipment* zona de sombra f; ~ **detail** n PHOTO detalle de las sombras m; ~ **key** n CINEMAT reflector difusor principal m; ~ **light** n CINEMAT reflector difusor m; ~ **mask** n ELECTRON, TV máscara de sombra f; ~ **mask tube** n ELECTRON tubo para máscara de sombra m, TV tubo de imagen de máscara de sombra m; ~ **microscope** n INSTR microscopio de sombra m; ~ **wall** n C&G pared de sombra f

shadowgraph n C&G radiografía f

shadowing n TELECOM ensombrecimiento m, TV sombra f

shaft n COAL chimenea f (*Esp*), columna f (*Esp*), estator m, pozo m, CONST *of column* fuste m, *chimney stack* tiro m, HYDRAUL chimenea f (*Esp*), cuerpo m, MECH eje m, árbol m, barra f, MECH ENG eje m, flecha f, mango m, husillo m, árbol m, MINE caña f (*AmL*), chimenea f (*Esp*), galería f (*Esp*), pozo m, VEH árbol m, WATER TRANSP árbol m, chimenea f (*AmL*), *propeller, engine* eje m; **~-bearing** n MECH ENG cojinete del eje m; ~ **bunker loading** n MINE cargamento de la carbonera m; ~ **center height** *AmE*, ~ **centre height** *BrE* n MECH ENG altura del centro del eje f; ~ **collar** n MECH ENG anillo del eje m, aro del eje m, collar del eje m, MINE marco de superficie m; ~ **coupling** n ELEC ENG, MECH ENG acoplamiento de eje m; ~ **deepening** n MINE profundización de pozos f; ~ **drive** n AUTO, VEH eje propulsor m, árbol propulsor m; ~ **furnace** n PROD horno de cuba m; ~ **in water-bearing ground** n WATER *excavation* pozo m; ~ **key** n MECH ENG chaveta del eje f, llave del eje f; ~ **kiln** n COAL vientre del alto horno m; ~ **lap** n MECH ENG revolución del eje f, vuelta del eje f; ~ **mine** n MINE mina explotada por pozos f; ~ **safety pillar** n MINE pilote de seguridad del pozo m; ~ **sinking** n MINE barrenado profundo m; **~-sinking bar** n MINE perforadora de barrenado profundo f; ~ **spillway** n WATER vertedero de pozo m; ~ **step** n MECH ENG rangua del eje f

shafting n ELEC ENG transmisión f, MECH ENG conjunto de ejes de transmisión m, sistema de transmisión m, transmisión f; ~ **lathe** n MECH ENG torno cilíndrico m

shake n CONST *timber* tabla de ripia f, MECH ENG *oscillatory movement* trepidación por huelgo f, sacudimiento m, vibración f, oscilación f

shaker n CHEM TECH agitador m, LAB agitador m, mesa vibrante f, P&R agitador m; ~ **conveyor** n PROD transportador por sacudidas m

shaking n MECH ENG agitación f, bamboleo m, oscilación f, vibración f, PROD trepidación f, vibración f; ~ **barrel** n PROD *founding* tambor de limpieza m, tambor desarenador m; ~ **grate** n PROD criba de sacudidas f, emparrillado móvil m, parrilla de vaivén f; ~ **machine** n PROD *founding* agitador para limpiar piezas m, tambor desarenador m; ~ **mill** n PROD *founding* tambor desarenador m; ~ **motion** n MECH ENG movimiento oscilatorio m, movimiento vibratorio m; ~ **screen** n COAL criba de sacudidas f, PROD cedazo sacudidor m, criba de trepidación f, criba

vibratoria f; ~ **table** n COAL mesa de sacudidas f, mesa sacudidora f, mesa vibratoria f, PROD mesa de sacudidas f, mesa trepidante f; ~ **tray** n PROD artesa de sacudidas f

shale n C&G, GEOL pizarra f, PETR TECH arcilla esquistosa f, lutita f, esquisto m; ~ **base line** n PETR TECH línea base de lutita f; ~ **density** n PETR TECH densidad de lutita f; ~ **diapirism** n GEOL, PETR TECH diapirismo esquistoso m; ~ **dome** n GEOL, PETR TECH domo esquistoso m; ~ **factor** n PETR TECH factor de lutita m; ~ **shaker** n PETR TECH vibradores m pl, zaranda f

shallow n OCEAN bajío m, bajo fondo m, WATER TRANSP bajío m; ~ **burial** n NUCL almacenamiento a poca profundidad m; ~ **depression** n METEO depresión baja f, depresión poco profunda f; ~ **descent** n AIR TRANSP descenso poco pronunciado m; ~ **draft** *AmE*, ~ **draught** *BrE* n WATER TRANSP poco calado m; ~ **ploughing** n BrE AGRIC arada superficial f; ~ **plowing** *AmE see shallow ploughing* BrE; ~ **stabilization** n COAL estabilización superficial f; ~ **water** n OCEAN aguas someras f; ~ **water blackout** n OCEAN síncope del buzo m

shallowing: **~-up sequence** n GEOL secuencia de somerización f

shallows n pl OCEAN encalladero m, WATER TRANSP encalladero m, *geology* bajo fondo m, paraje de aguas poco profundas m

shaly[1] adj COAL, GEOL esquistoso

shaly[2]: ~ **brown coal** n COAL lignito de pizarra esquistoso m

shank n AGRIC brazo del cultivador m, CONST *of rivet* espiga f, fuste m, *of key* caña f, MECH ENG *of bolt, nail* cuerpo m, caña f, *of tool* espiga f, mango m, vástago m, PROD *founding* cuchara de horquilla f, cuchara de mano f; ~ **ladle** n PROD *founding* cuchara de horquilla f, cuchara de mano f

shape[1] n TEXTIL forma f; ~ **change** n METALL cambio de forma m; **~-cutting machine** n C&G máquina cortadora de formas f; ~ **factor** n HEAT ENG factor de forma m

shape[2] vt MECH ENG conformar, dar forma, *to model* modelar, PROD conformar, modelar, dar forma

shaped[1] adj MECH ENG, PROD configurado, creado, hecho, modelado, perfilado

shaped[2]: ~ **beam** n ELECTRON haz perfilado m; ~ **beam aerial** n BrE (*cf shaped beam antenna AmE*) SPACE antena de haz conformado f, antena de haz contorneado f, antena de haz perfilado f; ~ **beam antenna** n AmE (*cf shaped beam aerial BrE*) SPACE antena de haz conformado f, antena de haz contorneado f, antena de haz perfilado f; ~ **beam tube** n ELECTRON tubo de haz perfilado m; ~ **bevel** n C&G bisel con forma m; ~ **conductor** n ELEC conductor perfilado m; ~ **pulse** n ELECTRON impulso perfilado m; ~ **reflector** n SPACE reflector conformado m

shaper n MECH cepilladora f, limadora f, máquina de tallar engranajes f, prensa de embutir f, MECH ENG cepilladora f, limadora f, máquina de tallar engranajes f, PROD *sheet metal worker* embutidor m, embutidora f; ~ **tools** n pl MECH ENG herramientas de cepilladora f pl, herramientas de limadora f pl

shaping n PROD conformación f, embutición f; ~ **amplifier** n ELECTRON amplificador de corrección m; ~ **machine** n MECH forjadora f, limadora f, MECH

ENG cepilladora *f*, limadora *f*, *sheet metal* forjadora *f*, prensa *f*, prensa de embutir *f*, conformadora *f*, estampa de forja *f*, PROD forjadora *f*; ~ **network** *n* TV red correctora *f*; ~ **planer** *n* AmE MECH ENG cepilladora *f*; ~ **tool** *n* C&G herramienta para dar forma *f*

shard *n* GEOL ripio *m*

share[1] *n* AGRIC reja de arado *f*; ~ **point** *n* AGRIC punto de reja *m*; ~ **throat** *n* AGRIC filo de la reja *m*

share[2] *vt* COMP&DP compartir

shared: ~ **file** *n* COMP&DP archivo compartido *m*; ~ **memory** *n* COMP&DP memoria compartida *f*; ~ **memory system** *n* COMP&DP sistema de memoria compartida *m*; ~ **service line** *n* ELEC ENG, TELECOM línea de servicio compartido *f*

sharing *n* COMP&DP compartición *f*

sharp[1] *adj* ACOUST afinado, CINEMAT nítido, MECH afilado, MECH ENG *angle* afilado, en punta, puntiagudo, cortante, agudo, PHOTO, PRINT, PROD afilado, nítido; ~-**edged** *adj* MECH ENG *angle* de arista cortante, de borde afilado, de canto vivo, de filo cortante, de ángulo agudo

sharp[2] *n* ACOUST sostenido *m*; ~-**crested weir** *n* HYDRAUL, WATER vertedero de cresta aguda *m*, vertedero de cresta delgada *m*, vertedero en pared delgada *m*; ~ **curve** *n* GEOM curva cerrada *f*; ~-**cutoff filter** *n* ELECTRON filtro de corte rápido *m*; ~-**cutoff tube** *n* ELECTRON tubo de corte rápido *m*; ~ **edge** *n* C&G borde filoso *m*; ~-**edged orifice** *n* HYDRAUL orificio de aristas vivas *m*, orificio en pared delgada *m*; ~-**edged tool** *n* MECH ENG herramienta afilada *f*; ~ **end** *n* COAL punta *f*; ~ **oil paint** *n* COLOUR pintura al aceite de secado rápido *f*, pintura rápida al óleo *f*; ~ **pulse** *n* ELECTRON impulso rápido *m*; ~ **ridge of steel** *n* PROD nervio vivo del acero *m*; ~ **yield point** *n* METALL límite bien definido de fluencia *m*, límite justo de estirado *m*

sharpen *vt* CHEM TECH, MECH afilar, MECH ENG afilar, aguzar, PROD afilar

sharpened *adj* CHEM TECH, MECH afilado, MECH ENG afilado, aguzado, PROD afilado

sharpener *n* CHEM TECH, MECH afilador *m*, afiladora *f*, MECH ENG afilador *m*, *instrument* muela de afilar *f*, sacapuntas *m*, *machine* afiladora *f*, amolador *m*, PROD *machine* afiladora *f*, amolador *m*

sharpening *n* MECH, MECH ENG, PROD afiladura *f*; ~ **machine** *n* MECH, MECH ENG afiladora *f*, PAPER *stone, grinders* máquina de repicar *f*, PROD afiladora *f*; ~ **steel** *n* FOOD barra de afilar *f*; ~ **wheel** *n* PROD muela abrasiva de afilar *f*

sharpness *n* CINEMAT nitidez *f*, GEOM *programming* precisión *f*, MECH ENG *of point* agudeza *f*, definición *f*, *of cutting edge* filo *m*, PHOTO nitidez *f*, PHYS *assayer's mark* agudeza *f*, PRINT nitidez *f*; ~ **control** *n* TV control de la nitidez *m*

shatter *n* MINE pedazo *m*; ~ **cut** *n* MINE labrado de fragmentos *m*, tallado de fragmentos *m*

shattering *n* AGRIC desgrane *m*

shatterproof: ~ **glass** *n* C&G, SAFE, TRANSP cristal irrompible *m*

shave: ~ **hook** *n* CONST rasqueta *f*

shaving *n* CONST cepillado *m*

shavings *n pl* PAPER recortes *m pl*

SHC *abbr* (*superhigh cube*) TRANSP hipercubo *m*

sheaf *n* PROD polea *f*, roldana *f*

shear[1] *n* GEOL cizalla *f*, MECH cizalla *f*, tijera *f*, MECH

ENG *materials* deformación debida al esfuerzo cortante *f*, deslizamiento *m*, *metal* esfuerzo cortante *m*, P&R cizalla *f*, corte *m*, esfuerzo cortante *m*, esfuerzo de cizalla *m*, PHYS corte *m*; ~ **alignment** *n* C&G alineación de las tijeras *f*; ~ **blade** *n* C&G hoja de tijeras *f*, MECH ENG cizalla *f*, cuchilla de corte *f*; ~ **cutter** *n* PRINT cortador de cizalla *m*; ~ **flow** *n* FLUID flujo de cortadura *m*; ~ **flow instability** *n* FLUID inestabilidad de flujos de cortadura *f*; ~ **folding** *n* GEOL plegamiento de cizalla *m*; ~ **force** *n* COAL fuerza tangencial *f*, resistencia al corte *f*, CONST esfuerzo cortante *m*, MECH ENG fuerza de cisión *f*, fuerza de cizallamiento *f*, fuerza de corte *f*, fuerza tangencial *f*; ~ **fracture** *n* METALL fractura por esfuerzo cortante *f*; ~-**jointed telescope** *n* INSTR telescopio articulado de cizalla *m*; ~ **layer** *n* FLUID capa de cortadura *f*; ~ **legs** *n pl* CONST cabria *f*, trípode *m*; ~ **lip** *n* METALL borde de la cortadura *m*; ~ **mark** *n* C&G marca de las tijeras *f*; ~ **modulus** *n* COAL coeficiente de rigidez *m*, MECH ENG coeficiente de corte *m*, módulo de corte *m*, PETR TECH, PHYS módulo de corte *m*; ~ **rate** *n* P&R velocidad de corte *f*; ~ **spray** *n* C&G rociado de tijeras *m*; ~ **strain** *n* PHYS esfuerzo de corte *m*; ~ **strength** *n* MECH esfuerzo de corte *m*; ~ **stress** *n* MECH ENG esfuerzo cortante *m*, P&R esfuerzo cortante *m*, esfuerzo de cizalla *m*, tensión de corte *f*, PHYS tensión de corte *f*; ~ **test** *n* MECH ENG *for rivets* prueba de cizallamiento *f*, prueba de corte *f*; ~ **wave** *n* ACOUST onda de cizalladura *f*, onda rotacional *f*; ~ **zone** *n* GEOL zona de cizalla *f*

shear[2] *vt* MECH ENG cizallar, cortar, recortar, tonsurar, TEXTIL esquilar

shearcut *n* C&G corte de cuchillas *m*

shearer *n* MINE rafadora-cargadora *f*

shearing *n* GEOL cizallamiento *m*, corte *m*, MECH ENG cizallamiento *m*, cortadura *f*, corte *m*, tonsura *f*, tronchadura *f*; ~ **die** *n* MECH ENG *press tools* estampa de corte *f*, troquel de corte *m*; ~ **effect** *n* PAPER efecto de cizallamiento *m*; ~ **machine** *n* COAL cizalla mecánica *f*, esquiladora mecánica *f*, rozadora para entalladuras verticales *f*, MECH ENG cizalla *f*, cizalladora *f*, tijera mecánica *f*, TEXTIL esquiladora *f*; ~ **pin** *n* PRINT alfiler de corte *m*; ~ **and punching machine** *n* MECH ENG cizalladora y perforadora *f*, máquina de cizallar y punzonar *f*; ~ **strain** *n* MECH ENG deformación de corte *f*, deformación por cizallamiento *f*, deformación por esfuerzo cortante *f*; ~ **strength** *n* MECH ENG resistencia al cizallamiento *f*, resistencia al corte *f*, resistencia al esfuerzo cortante *f*, METALL resistencia a la cortadura *f*, resistencia al cizallamiento *f*, P&R resistencia al corte *f*, resistencia al esfuerzo cortante *f*; ~ **stress** *n* CONST esfuerzo cortante *m*, resistencia al cizallamiento *f*, MECH ENG esfuerzo de cizallamiento *m*, esfuerzo de corte *m*; ~ **tenacity** *n* MECH ENG tenacidad de cizallamiento *f*, tenacidad de corte *f*

shears *n pl* C&G cuchillas *f pl*, tijeras *f pl*, MECH cizalla *f*, MECH ENG *shearing machine* cizallas *f pl*, banco *m*, *of lathe* bancada *f*, *scissors* tijeras *f pl*, máquina de cizallar *f*, cizalla *f*, TEXTIL cizalla *f*

sheath *n* (*cf jacket AmE*) AGRIC vaina *f*, ELEC *cable* funda *f*, envoltura *f*, forro *m*, ELEC ENG revestimiento *m*, funda *f*, MECH estuche *m*, funda *f*, revestimiento *m*, OPT pared metálica *f*, PROD *cover, case, guard* forro *m, electric cables* envoltura *f*; ~ **fold** *n* GEOL pliegue de revestimiento *m*

sheathe *vt* AGRIC, ELEC, ELEC ENG, MECH, OPT, PROD envainar

sheathed: ~ **cable** *n* ELEC cable enfundado *m*, ELEC ENG cable enfundado *m*, cable envainado *m*; ~ **deck** *n* WATER TRANSP *boat building* cubierta con revestimiento *f*, cubierta forrada *f*; ~ **thermocouple** *n* NUCL termopar blindado *m*

sheathing *n* COATINGS forro *m*, revestimiento *m*, ELEC ENG vaina *f*, PROD *lagging* envoltura *f*, guarnición *f*, revestimiento *m*

sheave *n* MECH ENG polea *f*, *grooved pulley* polea acanalada *f*, *for pitched chain* polea de cadena articulada *f*, polea de garganta *f*, *grooved pulley in pulley block* polea de cuadernal *f*, *of eccentric* disco de excéntrica *m*, WATER TRANSP *fittings* roldana *f*; ~ **block** *n* MECH ENG bloque de polea *m*; ~ **pulley block** *n* MECH ENG bloque de polea *m*, cuadernal de polea *m*

shed *n* CONST cobertizo *m*, galpón *m*, TEXTIL calada *f*; ~ **roof** *n* CONST cubierta a un agua *f*, tejadillo *m*

sheen *n* MAR POLL brillo *m*, TEXTIL viso *m*

sheep: ~'s **leap** *n* CONST salto de carnero *m*

sheepsfoot: ~ **roller** *n* CONST rodillo de pata de cabra *m*

sheepshank *n* WATER TRANSP *knot* margarita *f*

sheer[1] *adj* TEXTIL puro

sheer[2] *n* WATER TRANSP *shipbuilding* arrufo reglamentario *m*; ~ **aft** *n* WATER TRANSP *ship design* arrufo de proa *m*; ~ **draft** *n* WATER TRANSP *ship design* plano de longitudinales *m*; ~ **drawing** *n* WATER TRANSP *ship design* plano longitudinal *m*; ~ **forward** *n* WATER TRANSP *ship design* arrufo a proa *m*; ~ **line** *n* WATER TRANSP *boat building* línea de arrufo *f*; ~ **plan** *n* WATER TRANSP *ship design* plano de simetría *m*

sheer[3]: ~ **off** *vi* WATER TRANSP mudar el rumbo, separarse de la derrota

sheerstrake *n* WATER TRANSP *shipbuilding* traca de cinta *f*

sheet[1] *n* MECH chapa *f*, hoja *f*, lámina *f*, NUCL, P&R hoja *f*, lámina *f*, PAPER hoja *f*, pliego *m*, PRINT pliego *m*, TEXTIL sábana *f*, WATER TRANSP chapa *f*, escota *f*, escotín *m*, *rope, sail* trapo *m*; ~ **bend** *n* WATER TRANSP *knot* nudo de tejedor *m*, vuelta de vinatera *f*; ~ **boiling** *n* NUCL ebullición laminar *f*; ~ **calender** *n* PAPER calandra de hojas *f*; ~-**cutting machine** *n* PACK cortadora de hojas *f*; ~ **deliverer** *n* PRINT sacapliegos *m*; ~ **erosion** *n* AGRIC erosión de una capa uniforme de suelo *f*; ~-**fed carton printer** *n* PACK, PRINT impresora de cajas en troquel *f*; ~-**fed machine** *n* PRINT prensa de hojas *f*; ~ **feeder** *n* COMP&DP, PRINT alimentador de hojas *m*; ~ **feeding** *n* COMP&DP, PRINT alimentación de hojas *f*; ~ **film** *n* PHOTO película plana *f*; ~ **flow** *n* GEOL corriente laminar *f*; ~ **formation** *n* PAPER formación del papel *f*; ~ **gage** *AmE*, ~ **gauge** *BrE* *n* MECH ENG galga de chapa *f*, galga de láminas *f*, galga de plancha *f*; ~ **glass** *n* C&G vidrio plano *m*; ~ **iron gage** *AmE*, ~ **iron gauge** *BrE* *n* MECH ENG galga de chapa de hierro *f*, galga de palastro *f*, galga de plancha de hierro *f*; ~-**iron pipe** *n* CONST tubería de palastro *f*; ~-**iron works** *n* PROD taller de chapas finas *m*; ~ **lead** *n* CONST plomo en planchas *m*; ~ **lightning** *n* METEO relámpago difuso *m*; ~-**metal screw** *n* MECH ENG tornillo de plancha *m*; ~ **mill** *n* PROD laminador para chapas finas *m*; ~ **pile**

n COAL, CONST tablestaca *f*; ~ **piling** *n* COAL colocación de pilotes *f*, CONST *wood* tablestacado *m*; ~ **resistance** *n* ELEC ENG resistencia de lámina *f*; ~ **signature** *n* PRINT señal que facilita el alzado de los pliegos *f*; ~ **steel** *n* VEH chapa de acero *f*; ~ **steel case** *n* PROD caja de chapa fina de acero *f*; ~-**turning device** *n* PRINT volteador de hojas *m*; ~ **of water** *n* HYDROL capa de agua *f*, OCEAN extensión de agua *f*

sheet[2] *vt* CONST *civil engineering* forrar, revestir

sheeted: ~ **car** *n* AmE (*cf sheeted wagon BrE*) RAIL vagón con costados revestidos *m*; ~ **wagon** *BrE n* (*cf sheeted car AmE*) RAIL vagón con costados revestidos *m*

sheeter *n* PRINT cortadora de hojas *f*; ~ **box** *n* MECH ENG, TEXTIL reunidora de cintas *f*

sheeting *n* CONST *civil engineering* revestimiento *m*, TEXTIL tejido para sábanas *m*; ~ **pile** *n* CONST tablestaca *f*

sheetwise *n* PRINT disposición vertical de páginas en el pliego *f*; ~ **make-up** *n* PRINT imposición para imprimir a blanco y retiración en dos formas distintas *f*

sheetwork *n* PRINT impresión a blanco y retiración *f*

shelf *n* CONST *board* estante *m*, tabla *f*, LAB estante *m*, OCEAN bajo *m*, meseta submarina *f*, plataforma continental *f*, WATER TRANSP *geography* plataforma submarina *f*; ~ **appeal** *n* PACK aspecto tras el almacenado *m*; ~ **freezer** *n* REFRIG congelador con estanterías *m*; ~ **ice** *n* OCEAN hielo de plataforma *m*; ~ **impact** *n* PACK impacto en el estante *m*; ~ **life** *n* CINEMAT duración de almacenado *f*, duración útil en almacenaje *f*, vida útil en depósito *f*, P&R duración de almacenado *f*, duración en almacenaje *f*, duración útil en almacenaje *f*, PACK caducidad *f*, PRINT duración de almacenado *f*, duración en almacenaje *f*, duración útil en almacenaje *f*; ~ **life test** *n* PACK ensayo de caducidad *m*; ~ **space** *n* PACK espacio de almacenado *m*; ~ **stability** *n* PACK estabilidad durante el almacenado *f*

shelfback *n* PRINT lomo *m*

shell[1]: ~-**on** *adj* FOOD con caparazón

shell[2] *n* C&G cascarón *m*, concha *f*, COAL capa de roca dura *f*, corteza *f*, película delgada de metal imperfectamente unida a la superficie *f*, revestimiento *m*, MECH ENG *of pulley* caja de polea *f*, cepo de polea *f*, cuerpo de polea *m*, *of crushing roll* tambor *m*, MILIT proyectil *m*, NUCL, PAPER carcasa *f*, PROD *of boiler* cuerpo cilíndrico *m*, SPACE caparazón *m*, corteza *f*, coraza *f*, revestimiento *m*, WATER TRANSP *of tank* cuerpo *m*, forro exterior *m*; ~-**and-tube evaporator** *n* REFRIG evaporador multitubular de envolvente *m*; ~-**and-tube heat exchanger** *n* NUCL cambiador de calor de haz tubular *m*, REFRIG intercambiador multitubular de envolvente *m*; ~ **and auger** *n* MINE *boring* capa de roca dura y barrena *f*; ~ **auger** *n* MINE barrena de cuchara *f*, barreno de pola *m*; ~ **boiler** *n* HYDRAUL caldera cilíndrica *f*; ~ **breccia** *n* GEOL brecha en capa de roca dura *f*; ~ **burst** *n* MILIT explosión del proyectil *f*; ~ **chuck** *n* MECH, MECH ENG anillo sujetador *m*; ~ **and coil condenser** *n* REFRIG condensador de serpentín de envolvente *m*; ~ **course** *n* NUCL virola *f*; ~ **drill** *n* MECH ENG broca de manguito *f*, broca hueca *f*; ~ **end mill** *n* MECH ENG fresa radial hueca *f*, fresa universal hueca *f*; ~ **gimlet** *n* CONST barrena cilíndrica *f*; ~ **ice** *n* REFRIG hielo en tubos *m*; ~ **liner** *n* COAL tubo hueco *m*; ~ **mill** *n* MECH

ENG *cutter* fresa hueca *f*; ~ **model** *n* PHYS *airworthiness* modelo de capas *m*; ~-**molding resin** *AmE*, ~-**moulding resin** *BrE n* P&R resina fundida en molde de cáscara *f*, resina moldeada en cascarón *f*; ~ **plate** *n* PROD *of barrel, boiler* chapa del forro *f*, teja de chapa *f*, virola *f*; ~ **plating** *n* WATER TRANSP *shipbuilding* chapas del forro *f pl*, planchas del forro exterior *f pl*; ~ **reamer** *n* MECH ENG escariador hueco *m*; ~ **reamer with taper bore** *n* MECH ENG escariador hueco con taladro interior cónico *m*; ~ **splinter** *n* MILIT casco del proyectil *m*; ~ **strength** *n* FOOD resistencia de la cáscara *f*; ~-**type boiler** *n* HEAT caldera de casco *f*, caldera de cuerpo cilíndrico *f*; ~-**type motor** *n* ELEC motor acorazado *m*; ~-**type transformer** *n* ELEC, ELEC ENG transformador acorazado *m*

shell[3] *vt* FOOD pelar

shellac[1] *n* COLOUR goma laca *f*, CONST laca *f*, ELEC goma laca *f*, laca *f*; ~ **varnish** *n* COATINGS barniz de laca *m*

shellac[2] *vt* GEN lacar

shellack *n* COLOUR goma laca *f*

shelled[1] *adj* AGRIC desvainado, FOOD descascarado, descortezado, desvainado, pelado

shelled[2]: ~ **corn** *n* *AmE* (*cf shelled maize BrE*) AGRIC grano de maíz entero *m*; ~ **maize** *n* *BrE* (*cf shelled corn AmE*) AGRIC grano de maíz entero *m*

sheller *n* AGRIC desgranadora *f*

shellfish: ~ **basket** *n* OCEAN canasta *f*; ~ **culture** *n* OCEAN cultivo de mariscos *m*; ~ **farm** *n* OCEAN vivero de mariscos *m*; ~ **farmer** *n* OCEAN cultivador de mariscos *m*, cultivadora de mariscos *f*

shelling: ~ **cage** *n* AGRIC caja de desgranamiento *f*

shelly: ~ **limestone** *n* GEOL caliza conchífera *f*; ~ **sandstone** *n* GEOL arenisca conchífera *f*

shelter[1] *n* CONST refugio *m*, MILIT resguardo *m*, SPACE cobertizo *m*, resguardo *m*, TRANSP cochera *f*, WATER TRANSP abrigo *m*, lugar de refugio *m*, socaire *m*; ~ **deck** *n* WATER TRANSP cubierta de abrigo *f*, cubierta de paseo *f*

shelter[2] *vt* CONST, MILIT, WATER TRANSP poner al socaire

SHF[1] *abbr* (*super-high frequency*) ELECTRON, SPACE, TELECOM FSA (*frecuencia superalta*)

SHF[2]: ~ **signal generator** *n* ELECTRON, SPACE, TELECOM generador de señal de FSA *m*

shield[1] *n* COMP&DP blindaje *m*, CONST *tunnelling* escudo *m*, *wooden screen or guard* protección *f*, ELEC *cable* blindaje *m*, pantalla *f*, ELEC ENG pantalla *f*, GEOL escudo *m*, LAB protección *f*, blindaje *m*, MILIT abrigo *m*, NUCL blindaje *m*, PROD blindaje *m*, pantalla *f*, SPACE escudo *m*, pantalla *f*, resguardo *m*, TV *communications* pantalla *f*, blindaje *m*; ~-**bonding** *n* ELEC *cable* conexión blindada *f*, conexión cruzada *f*, ligadura blindada *f*; ~ **cooling system** *n* NUCL sistema de refrigeración del blindaje *m*; ~ **drain wire** *n* ELEC hilo de drenaje blindado *m*, hilo de retorno por tierra *m*, ELEC ENG hilo de retorno por tierra *m*, PROD alambre de blindaje *m*, hilo de blindaje *m*; ~-**driven anchor** *n* CONST anclaje perforado con escudo *m*; ~ **support** *n* MINE apoyo protector *m*; ~ **volcano** *n* GEOL volcán de escudo *m*

shield[2] *vt* ELEC, NUCL, PHYS, RAD PHYS apantallar, SPACE apantallar, resguardar

shielded: ~ **cable** *n* ELEC, ELEC ENG, PHYS cable blindado *m*, PROD cable armado *m*, TV cable blindado *m*; ~-**cable connection** *n* PROD conexión con cable armado *f*; ~ **coffin** *n* NUCL contenedor blindado *m*; ~ **enclosure** *n* ELEC ENG cierre blindado *m*; ~ **pair** *n* ELEC ENG par apantallado *m*, par blindado *m*; ~ **transformer** *n* ELEC ENG transformador blindado *m*; ~ **transmission line** *n* ELEC, ELEC ENG línea de transmisión armada *f*; ~ **wire** *n* ELEC, ELEC ENG hilo conductor armado *m*

shielding *n* ELEC *cable* apantallamiento *m*, blindaje *m*, NUCL, PHYS apantallamiento *m*, RAD PHYS protección *f*, pantalla *f*, apantallamiento *m*, SAFE *of compound* blindaje *m*, SPACE protección *f*, armado *m*, protectivo *m*, apantallamiento *m*; ~ **conductor** *n* ELEC *cable* conductor blindado *m*; ~ **effect** *n* ELEC *electromagnetic field* efecto de apantallamiento *m*, efecto de blindaje *m*, efecto de pantalla *m*

shift[1] *n* COMP&DP cambio *m*, desplazamiento *m*, GEOL desplazamiento *m*, NUCL desviación *f*, PETR TECH turno de trabajo *m*, PROD relevo *m*, turno *m*, SPACE *communications* desvío *m*, fluctuación *f*, TEXTIL vestido-camisa *m*, turno *m*, TV desplazamiento *m*; ~ **character** *n* COMP&DP carácter de desplazamiento *m*; ~ **clock rate** *n* PROD frecuencia de turno *f*; ~ **of G** *n* WATER TRANSP centro de gravedad *m*, movimiento de G *m*; ~-**in character** *n* (*SI character*) COMP&DP carácter cambiador de código *m* (*carácter SI*), carácter de desplazamiento hacia dentro *m*; ~ **left register** *n* PROD registro izquierdo de desplazamiento *m*; ~-**out character** *n* COMP&DP carácter de desplazamiento hacia fuera *m*; ~ **pulse** *n* ELECTRON impulso variable *m*; ~ **register** *n* COMP&DP registro de desplazamiento *m*, ELECTRON registrador variable *m*, PROD registrador de impulso *m*, registro de desvíos *m*, TELECOM registrador de corrimiento *m*, registro de desplazamiento *m*; ~ **right register** *n* PROD registro derecho de desplazamiento *m*; ~ **supervisor** *n* NUCL supervisor de turno *m*; ~ **technical adviser** *n* NUCL asesor técnico de turno *m*, asesora técnica de turno *f*; ~ **work** *n* PROD trabajo por turnos *m*

shift[2] *vt* COMP&DP desplazar, cambiar, PROD cambiar velocidades, desplazar, maniobrar, TEXTIL desplazar

shift[3] *vi* COMP&DP pasar a mayúsculas, PROD desplazarse, moverse, WATER TRANSP *cargo* correrse, rolar, saltar

shifting: ~ **link** *n* MECH ENG enlace de desplazamiento *m*, enlace de desviación *m*, enlace de desvío *m*; ~ **rod** *n* MECH ENG barra de desplazamiento *f*, palanca desplazadora *f*; ~ **spanner** *n* MECH ENG llave extractora *f*, llave inglesa ajustable *f*

shim *n* MECH ENG cuña *f*, diafragma *m*, NUCL compensación *f*, RAIL cuña *f*; ~ **assembly** *n* NUCL conjunto de compensación *m*; ~ **element** *n* NUCL elemento de compensación *m*; ~ **member** *n* NUCL elemento de compensación *m*; ~ **rod bank** *n* NUCL banco de barras de compensación *m*; ~ **safety rod** *n* NUCL barra compensadora de seguridad *f*

shimming *n* MECH ENG acuñamiento *m*

shimmy: ~ **damper** *n* AIR TRANSP amortiguador de oscilaciones *m*, amortiguador de shimmy *m*, amortiguador de vibraciones *m*

shin *n* AGRIC borde cortante de la vertedera *m*

shingle *n* CONST *wood tile* teja de madera *f*, tejamanil *m*; ~ **bank** *n* OCEAN banco de grava *m*, banco de guijarros *m*, WATER banco de grava *m*, WATER TRANSP banco de guijarros *m*, *beach, bank* guijarros *m pl*, zahorra *f*, banco de grava *m*; ~ **beach** *n* OCEAN playa de grava *f*, playa de guijarros *f*; ~ **distance** *n* PRINT distancia de la graduación *f*; ~ **spit** *n* OCEAN cresta de playa *f*, restinga *f*

shingling *n* PRINT graduación de los márgenes *f*

ship[1] *n* MAR POLL, OCEAN barco *m*, buque *m*, TRANSP buque *m*, WATER TRANSP buque *m*, embarcación *f*, nave *f*, barco *m*; ~**'s articles** *n pl* PETR TECH, WATER TRANSP artículos navieros *m pl*; ~ **automation** *n* WATER TRANSP automatización del buque *f*; ~**'s boat** *n* WATER TRANSP bote de a bordo *m*, embarcación de un buque *f*; ~**'s books** *n pl* WATER TRANSP libros y cuadernos de a bordo *m pl*; ~**-borne earth station** *n* SPACE estación terrestre embarcada *f*; ~**-borne lighter** *n* TRANSP barcaza a bordo *f*; ~**'s bottom** *n* WATER TRANSP carena *f*, obra viva *f*; ~**'s bottom paint** *n* COLOUR, WATER TRANSP pintura contra incrustaciones *f*; ~**'s boy** *n* WATER TRANSP grumete *m*, marinero novel *m*, mozo *m*; ~ **broker** *n* WATER TRANSP corredor marítimo *m*; ~ **canal** *n* OCEAN canal navegable *m*, WATER TRANSP canal apto para buques de navegación marítima *m*, canal marítimo *m*; ~ **chandler** *n* WATER TRANSP abastecedor de buques *m*, proveedor de efectos navales *m*; ~ **course** *n* OCEAN *navigation* derrota *f*; ~ **designer** *n* WATER TRANSP proyectista naval *mf*; ~ **earth station** *n* WATER TRANSP estación terrestre de buque *f*; ~ **girder** *n* WATER TRANSP *shipbuilding* eslora *f*, viga *f*; ~**'s hands** *n pl* WATER TRANSP tripulación *f*; ~ **in ballast** *n* WATER TRANSP buque en lastre *m*; ~ **in distress** *n* WATER TRANSP buque en peligro *m*, buque siniestrado *m*; ~**'s log** *n* WATER TRANSP diario de navegación *m*; ~ **model towing tank** *n* WATER TRANSP *ship, boat building* canal de experiencias hidrodinámicas *m*; ~**'s papers** *n pl* WATER TRANSP documentación del buque *f*; ~**'s passport** *n* WATER TRANSP pasavante *m*; ~ **polling** *n* TELECOM interrogación de las estaciones de barco *f*; ~**'s position** *n* WATER TRANSP situación del buque *f*; ~**'s protest** *n* WATER TRANSP protesta de mar *f*; ~**'s register** *n* WATER TRANSP matrícula del buque *f*, patente de navegación *f*; ~ **reporting system** *n* TELECOM sistema de información de estación de barco *m*; ~**-station identity** *n* TELECOM identidad de la estación barco *f*; ~ **station number** *n* TELECOM número de la estación de barco *m*; ~**-to-ship alerting** *n* TELECOM, WATER TRANSP alerta entre barcos *f*; ~**-to-shore alerting** *n* TELECOM, WATER TRANSP alerta barco-tierra *f*; ~**-to-shore radio** *n* TELECOM, WATER TRANSP radiotelefonía buque a costa *f*; ~**-type rig** *n* PETR TECH barco-plataforma *m*, PETROL equipo perforador tipo barco *m*, WATER TRANSP *aerials, reflectors* instalación para buques *f*, montaje para buques *m*

ship[2] *vt* WATER TRANSP *anchor* embarcar, *goods, cargo* despachar, enviar, cargar, expedir, estibar, *oars* armar

ship[3]: ~ **water** *vi* WATER TRANSP embarcar agua

shipboard[1]: **on** ~ *adv* WATER TRANSP a bordo del buque

shipboard[2] *n* WATER TRANSP bordo del buque *m*; ~ **terminal** *n* WATER TRANSP *telecommunications* terminal de a bordo *f*

shipbreaking *n* WATER TRANSP desguace de buques *m*

shipbuilder *n* WATER TRANSP constructor de buques *m*, constructor naval *m*, constructora de buques *f*, constructora naval *f*

shipbuilding *n* WATER TRANSP construcción naval *f*

shipchandling *n* WATER TRANSP aprovisionamiento de buques *m*

shiphandling *n* WATER TRANSP arte de la maniobra *m*, manejo del buque *m*

shipload *n* WATER TRANSP carga completa de un buque *f*, cargamento entero *m*

shiploading *n* WATER TRANSP carga del buque *f*, embarque de mercancías *m*

shipmaster *n* WATER TRANSP *merchant navy* capitán *m*, patrón *m*

shipment *n* PROD embarque *m*, WATER TRANSP cargamento *m*, expedición *f*

shipowner *n* WATER TRANSP armador *m*, armadora *f*, naviera *f*, naviero *m*, propietaria del buque *f*, propietario del buque *m*

shipped: ~ **quantity** *n* PROD cantidad embarcada *f*

shipper *n* WATER TRANSP cargador *m*, cargadora *f*, expedidor *m*, expedidora *f*

shipping *n* PROD embarque *m*, WATER TRANSP *of a country* buques *m pl*, navegación *f*, tráfico marítimo *m*; ~ **agency** *n* WATER TRANSP agencia de transportes marítimos *f*, consignación de buques *f*; ~ **agent** *n* WATER TRANSP agente de transporte marítimo *m*, consignataria de buques *f*, consignatario de buques *m*; ~ **bill** *n* WATER TRANSP manifiesto de embarque *m*; ~ **channel** *n* OCEAN canal de navegación *m*; ~ **charges** *n pl* WATER TRANSP gastos de embarque *m pl*, gastos de expedición *m pl*; ~ **clerk** *n* WATER TRANSP encargada del envío y recepción de mercancías *f*, encargado del envío y recepción de mercancías *m*; ~ **company** *n* WATER TRANSP compañía naviera *f*; ~ **corridor** *n* OCEAN corredor de salida al mar *m*, vía de gran tráfico marítimo *f*; ~ **documents** *n pl* WATER TRANSP documentos de embarque *m pl*; ~ **fever** *n* AGRIC fiebre de embarque *f*; ~ **intelligence** *n* WATER TRANSP información acerca de la actividad naviera *f*, información relativa a un embarque *f*; ~ **lane** *n* WATER TRANSP vía marítima *f*; ~ **note** *n* WATER TRANSP nota de embarque *f*, nota de expedición *f*; ~ **office** *n* WATER TRANSP oficina supervisora de la contratación de marinos *f*; ~ **order** *n* WATER TRANSP orden de expedición *f*; ~ **port** *n* WATER TRANSP puerto de embarque *m*, puerto de expedición *m*; ~ **route** *n* WATER TRANSP derrota marítima *f*, ruta marítima *f*; ~ **terms** *n pl* WATER TRANSP condiciones de una expedición *f pl*, términos de embarque *m pl*; ~ **ton** *n* WATER TRANSP tonelada de flete *f*; ~ **trade** *n* WATER TRANSP actividad naviera *f*, comercio marítimo *m*; ~ **weight** *n* AGRIC, PROD peso de embarque *m*, WATER TRANSP peso de embarque *m*, peso declarado de embarque *m*

shipwright *n* WATER TRANSP *on board* carpintero *m*, carpintero de ribera *m*, constructor de botes *m*

shipyard *n* WATER TRANSP astillero *m*, factoría comercial y naval *f*

shirt *n* PROD *of furnace* revestimiento *m*; ~**-dress** *n* TEXTIL vestido-camisa *m*

shirting *n* TEXTIL tela para camisas *f*, camisería *f*

shoal *n* HYDROL banco de arena sumergido *m*, OCEAN alfaque *m*, banco de arena inundado *m*, banco de arena sumergido *m*, *of fish* banco *m*, cardumen *m*, *programme* mancha *f*, encalladero *m*, *effect* bajío *m*, PROD bajo fondo *m*, WATER banco de arena sumergido *m*

shock *n* ACOUST choque *m*, MECH ENG aceleración brusca *f*, SPACE choque *m*, golpe *m*, sacudida *f*; ~ **absorber** *n* AUTO amortiguador mecánico *m*, CONST, ELEC, MECH, SPACE, VEH amortiguador *m*;

~-absorbing body n RAIL amortiguador de choques m; **~ chilling** n REFRIG enfriamiento de choque m; **~ excitation** n TELECOM excitación parásita f, excitación por choque f; **~ mount** n SPACE montaje antigolpes m, soporte elástico m; **~ resistance** n P&R resistencia a los choques f, resistencia a los golpes f; **~ shoe** n AGRIC zapata para golpes f; **~ wave** n GEOPHYS onda de choque f, MINE onda de choque f, onda dinámica f, PETR TECH onda dinámica f, PHYS, WAVE PHYS onda de choque f; **~ wave initiator** n SPACE iniciador de la onda de choque m

Shockley: ~ diode n ELECTRON diodo Shockley m; **~ dislocation** n METALL dislocación Shockley f

shockproof[1] adj CINEMAT a prueba de golpes, PACK antichoque

shockproof[2]: **~ socket** n SAFE enchufe hembra a prueba de choques eléctricos m, enchufe hembra a prueba de sacudidas eléctricas m

shoddy: ~ fabric n TEXTIL tela de lana regenerada f; **~-type filling** n AmE (cf shoddy-type weft BrE) TEXTIL trama de lana regenerada f; **~-type weft** n BrE (cf shoddy-type filling AmE) TEXTIL trama de lana regenerada f

shoe n CONST rain water zapata f, MECH measuring zapata f, patín m, MINE anillo cortante m, caja f, abrazadera f, NUCL zapata f, PROD of amalgamating pan patín m, RAIL zapata f, TV terminal de cable m, VEH zapata f; **~ board** n PAPER cartón para calzados m; **~ brake** n VEH freno de zapata m; **~ furrow opener** n AGRIC abresurcos tipo zapata m; **~ sieve** n AGRIC zaranda de granos limpios f

shoeing: ~ bar n pl CONST barra para calzar f

shoot vt CONST ajustar el cepillado, dump, discharge vaciar, volar, descargar, OCEAN net calar, lanzar

shooter n MINE disparador m, disparador de barrenos m (Esp), pegador m, polvorero m (AmL)

shooting n CINEMAT rodaje m; **~ brake** n TRANSP camioneta con equipo de TV de exteriores f, furgoneta con equipo de TV de exteriores f; **~ distance** n PHOTO distancia de toma de la fotografía f; **~ needle** n MINE aguja de polvorero f, espigueta f; **~ range** n MILIT campo de tiro m, polígono de tiro m; **~ ratio** n CINEMAT formato de rodaje m, relación de rodaje f; **~ script** n CINEMAT guión completo m; **~ to playback** n CINEMAT rodaje con playback m, rodaje con sincronización sonora a una banda previamente grabada m

shop n C&G fábrica f, taller m, team of workers equipo m, MECH, PROD taller m; **~ arrival date** n PROD fecha de llegada al taller f; **~ crane** n PROD grúa de taller f; **~ date** n PROD fecha de taller f; **~ floor** n PROD taller m; **~ packet** n PROD paquete de taller m; **~ papers** n pl PROD documentos de taller m pl; **~ priming** n COATINGS imprimación en taller f; **~ receipt** n PROD recibo de taller m; **~ traveler** AmE, **~ traveller** BrE n PROD puente-grúa de taller m

shore[1] n COAL adema f, CONST puntal m, ribera f, GEOL costa f, litoral m, HYDROL ribera f, MINE adema f, OCEAN cornisa f, cornisa marina f, costa marina f, ribera f, WATER TRANSP litoral m, geography, shipbuilding escora f, puntal m, ribera f; **~ end** n ELEC ENG extremo a tierra m; **~ fisherman** n OCEAN pescador con artes de playa m, pescador de bajura m; **~ leave** n WATER TRANSP permiso de tierra m; **~ protection** n WATER protección de costas f; **~ reception facility** n MAR POLL instalación receptora de residuos en tierra f, instalación receptora en tierra f; **~-to-ship alerting** n TELECOM, WATER TRANSP alerta tierra-barco f

shore[2]: **~ up** vt COAL apuntalar, WATER TRANSP apuntalar, escorar

Shore: ~ hardness n P&R dureza Shore f; **~ hardness tester** n LAB stranded ship esclercscopio m, probador de dureza de Shore m

shoreline n C&G orilla f, CONST, HYDROL ribera f, MAR POLL línea de litoral f, línea de pleamar f, OCEAN línea de costa f, ribera f, WATER TRANSP geography línea de costa f, línea de pleamar f, contorno m, amarra de tierra f, línea de litoral f, ribera f; **~ clean-up** n MAR POLL limpieza de la costa desde la línea de pleamar f, limpieza del litoral f, OCEAN limpieza del litoral f

shoreward[1] adj WATER TRANSP navigation frente a la costa, que se mueve hacia la costa

shoreward[2] adv WATER TRANSP navigation hacia la costa, hacia tierra

shoring n CONST apuntalamiento m; **~-up** n COAL apuntalamiento m

short[1]: **~-circuit** adj PHYS cortocircuitado; **~-circuited** adj PHYS cortocircuitado

short[2] n CINEMAT corto m, cortometraje m, ELEC ENG corto m; **~ blast** n WATER TRANSP pitada corta f; **~ channel** n ELECTRON canal corto m; **~ channel MOS transistor** n ELECTRON transistor de SOM con canal corto m; **~ circuit** n COMP&DP, ELEC, ELEC ENG, PHYS, TELECOM cortocircuito m; **~-circuit armature** n ELEC armadura en cortocircuito f; **~-circuit flux** n ACOUST, TV flujo en cortocircuito m; **~-circuit impedance** n ELEC, ELEC ENG impedancia en cortocircuito f; **~-circuit interrupting current** n PROD corriente interruptiva de cortocircuito f; **~-circuit protection** n ELEC ENG, PROD protección contra cortocircuitos f; **~-circuit rotor** n ELEC rotor en cortocircuito m; **~-circuited armature** n ELEC ENG armazón cortocircuitado m, armazón en cortocircuito m; **~-circuited slip-ring rotor** n ELEC rotor de anillos colectores cortocircuitados m; **~-circuiting device** n ELEC, ELEC ENG dispositivo de cortocircuito m; **~ code dialing** AmE, **~ code dialling** BrE n TELECOM discado de corto código m; **~-delay detonator** n MINE detonador con retardo m; **~-delay electric detonator** n MINE detonador eléctrico con retardo m; **~-distance transport** n TRANSP transporte de cercanías m; **~ end** n CINEMAT extremo corto m; **~-flame burner** n HEAT ENG quemador de llama corta m; **~-focus lens** n CINEMAT, INSTR, OPT, PHOTO objetivo de focal corta m; **~ glass** n C&G vidrio duro m; **~ grain** n PRINT dirección longitudinal según el lado más corto f; **~-haul airliner** n AIR TRANSP avión de pasajeros de corto alcance m; **~-haul cable** n ELEC ENG cable de corriente de corto alcance m; **~-haul skidder** n TRANSP carretilla de portes f; **~-interaction tube** n ELECTRON tubo de interacción corta m; **~-lifetime particle** n PART PHYS partícula de vida corta f; **~-lived particle** n PART PHYS partícula de vida corta f; **~-lived tornado** n METEO tornado efímero m; **~-neck projection tube** n ELECTRON tubo de proyección de boca pequeña m; **~ normal** n PETR TECH perpendicular corta f; **~ oil alkyd** n P&R resina alquílica corta en aceite f, resina alquílica de bajo contenido en aceite f; **~ oil varnish** n COATINGS barniz bajo en aceite m, barniz corto en aceite m, barniz de bajo porcentaje de aceite m,

COLOUR barniz corto en aceite *m*, barniz de bajo porcentaje de aceite *m*, barniz bajo en aceite *m*; ~ **pipe** *n* HYDRAUL conducto corto *m*; ~ **pitch** *n* CINEMAT paso corto *m*; ~ **pulse** *n* ELECTRON impulso breve *m*, impulso corto *m*, impulso de pequeña duración *m*, WATER TRANSP *radar* impulso corto *m*; ~**-pulsed laser** *n* WAVE PHYS láser de pulsación corta *m*, láser de pulsos cortos *m*; ~**-range order** *n* CRYSTALL orden a pequeña distancia *m*, orden de corto alcance *m*, METALL orden de pequeño alcance *m*, PHYS orden de corto alcance *m*; ~**-range particle** *n* NUCL partícula de corto alcance *f*; ~**-range radar** *n* MILIT radar de corto alcance *m*; ~ **run** *n* PACK corta duración *f*, lote pequeño *m*, PRINT tirada corta *f*; ~**-stroke engine** *n* VEH motor de carrera corta *m*, motor de pequeña carrera *m*; ~ **take-off and landing aircraft** *n* (*STOL aircraft*) AIR TRANSP, TRANSP avión de despegue y aterrizaje corto *m*; ~**-term drift** *n* ELECTRON *oscillator* desplazamiento de corta duración *m*; ~**-term frequency stability** *n* ELECTRON estabilidad de frecuencia de corta duración *f*; ~**-term protection** *n* ELEC ENG protección breve *f*, protección de corta duración *f*; ~**-time constant filter** *n* PROD filtro constante de corta duración *m*; ~**-time rating** *n* ELEC *equipment* capacidad de carga breve *f*; ~**-time test** *n* ELEC prueba de corta duración *f*; ~ **ton** *n* METR tonelada corta *f*; ~**-wall coal-cutting machine** *n* COAL rafadora de franja pequeña *f*; ~ **wave** *n* ELEC, WAVE PHYS onda corta *f*; ~**-wavelength laser** *n* ELECTRON láser de longitud de onda corta *m*; ~ **weight** *n* METR peso deficiente *m*, PACK falta de peso *f*

short³ *vt* ELEC ENG cortocircuitar, puentear, PROD cortocircuitar; ~ **out** *vt* PROD provocar cortocircuito

shortage *n* PROD déficit *m*, escasez *f*, insuficiencia *f*

shorted: ~ **output circuit** *n* PROD circuito de salida cortocircuitado *m*; ~ **turn** *n* ELEC ENG espira corto-circuitada *f*

shorten *vt* MILIT *range*, TEXTIL acortar, WATER TRANSP amainar

shortening *n* FOOD aditivo graso *m*, manteca *f*, GEOL antiplástico *m*, encogimiento *m*

shortest: ~**-path program** *AmE*, ~**-path programme** *BrE* *n* TRANSP programa de trayectoria más corta *m*, programación de trayectoria más corta *f*; ~**-route program** *AmE*, ~**-route programme** *BrE* *n* TRANSP programa de recorrido más corto *m*, programa de ruta más corta *m*

shorting *n* ELEC ENG, PROD cortocircuitación *f*; ~ **contact** *n* ELEC ENG contacto de cortocircuitar *m*, contacto para puentear *m*; ~ **contact switch** *n* ELEC ENG conmutador de contactos cortocircuitantes *m*; ~ **switch** *n* ELEC, ELEC ENG interruptor cortocircui-tantes *m*

shot¹ *n* CINEMAT toma *f*, MILIT disparo *m*, tiro *m*, MINE disparo *m*, impacto *m*, pega *f*, tiro *m*, PETR TECH disparo *m*, tiro *m*, PHOTO toma *f*, instantánea *f*, PRINT toma instantánea *f*; ~ **bag test** *n* C&G prueba de la bolsa de municiones *f*; ~ **blasting** *n* CONST limpieza con chorro de perdigones *f*; ~ **boring** *n* MINE sondeo con trépano de granalla de acero *m*; ~ **breakdown** *n* CINEMAT descomposición en tomas *f*; ~**-by-shot firing** *n* MINE pega de barrenos *f*; ~ **drill** *n* MINE sondadora de granalla de acero *f*, sondadora de rotación *f*; ~ **drilling** *n* MINE sondeo por granalla de acero *m*, sondeo por rotación *m*, PETR TECH perfora-

ción para barrenar *f*; ~ **firer** *n* COAL barrenista *m*, dinamitero *m*, pegador *m*, polvorista *m*, CONST, MINE artillero *m*, dinamitero *m*; ~**-firing** *n* MINE pega de barrenos *f*; ~**-firing circuit** *n* MINE línea de tiro *f*; ~ **hole** *n* MINE hoyo de explosión *m*; ~**-hole drilling** *n* PETR TECH perforación de hoyo de disparo *f*; ~**-hole plug** *n* PETR TECH obturación de hoyo de disparo *f*, ratacado de los hoyos de disparo *m*; ~ **list** *n* CINEMAT, TV lista de tomas *f*; ~ **noise** *n* ELECTRON interferencia *f*, ruido de descarga *m*, OPT ruido de agitación térmica *m*, ruido de descarga *m*, ruido granular *m*, PHYS ruido de disparo *m*, SPACE ruido de agitación térmica *m*, ruido de batido *m*, ruido de descarga *m*, ruido de disparo *m*, TELECOM ruido de agitación térmica *m*, ruido granular *m*, TV interferencia por agitación térmica *f*; ~ **peening** *n* NUCL chorreado con granalla *m*

shot²: **in** ~ *phr* CINEMAT en la toma

shot³ *vt* PROD *granules* granallar, limpiar con chorro de granalla; ~**-dye** *vt* COLOUR teñir a pistola, teñir con pulverizador

shotting *n* MINE chorreado con granalla *m* (*AmL*), proyección de hormigón *f* (*Esp*)

shoulder *n* AUTO arcén *m*, C&G hombro *m*, CONST, TRANSP, VEH arcén *m*; ~ **brace** *n* CINEMAT soporte de hombro *m*; ~ **head** *n* PRINT título a lo ancho de la página *m*; ~ **hole** *n* MINE *blasting* hoyo de reborde *m* (*Esp*), hoyo de resalto *m* (*Esp*); ~ **pad** *n* TEXTIL hombrera *f*; ~ **wing** *n* AIR TRANSP, TRANSP ala semialta *f*

shouldered: ~ **tenon** *n* CONST espiga de tope *f*

shovel¹ *n* CONST, MAR POLL pala *f*; ~ **cultivator** *n* AGRIC carpidor *m*, rotoazada *f*; ~ **dredger** *n* WATER TRANSP pala mecánica *f*; ~ **work** *n* CONST trabajo a pala *m*

shovel² *vt* CONST mover con pala, palear

shovelful *n* CONST palada *f*

show *n* GEOL indicio *m*, MINE aureola *f*, PETR TECH indicio *m*; ~ **sheet** *n* PRINT capilla *f*, hoja de prueba *f*, prueba de prensa *f*

shower *n* CONST aguacero *m*, chaparrón *m* (*AmL*), lluvia *f*, lluvia de chispas (*Esp*) *f*, METEO chaparrón *m*, chubasco *m*, PAPER rociador *m*; ~ **screen** *n* C&G cortina de regadera *f*

showering: ~ **arc transient** *n* PROD corriente momen-tánea de chorro de arco *f*

shrapnel *n* MILIT granada de metralla *f*

shredded: ~ **cullet** *n* *AmE* (*cf quenched cullet BrE*) C&G cullet enfriado en agua *m* (*AmL*), fundente enfriado en agua *m*

shredder *n* AGRIC desmenuzadora *f*, PAPER desmenu-zadora en seco *f*

shredding: ~ **machine** *n* PACK trituradora *f*

shrimp: ~ **boat** *n* OCEAN, WATER TRANSP camaronero *m*; ~ **trawler** *n* WATER TRANSP camaronero *m*

shrimper *n* OCEAN camaronero *m*, embarcación cama-ronera *f*

shrimping: ~ **net** *n* OCEAN red camaronera *f*, red de arrastre de vara *f*

shrink¹: ~ **capsule** *n* PACK cápsula retráctil *f*; ~ **film** *n* *BrE* (*cf shrink wrap AmE*) FOOD envoltura de contracción *f*, PACK película contraíble *f*, película encogible *f*, película retráctil *f*, THERMO envoltorio encogible *m*, película contraíble *f*, película encogible *f*; ~ **fit** *n* MECH ajuste en caliente *m*, ajuste por contracción *m*; ~ **flow line wrappers** *n pl* PACK sistema para envolver con un material retráctil *m*;

~ **head** *n* PROD *founding* mazarota *f*; ~ **overwrapping machine** *n* PACK máquina de sobreembalaje retráctil *f*; ~ **pack** *n* PACK paquete retractilado *m*; ~ **resistance** *n* TEXTIL inencogibilidad *f*; ~ **rule** *n* PROD *founding* regla de modelista *f*; ~ **sleeve** *n* PAPER tela encogible *f*; ~-**sleeve wrapping machine** *n* PACK máquina aplicadora de fundas retráctiles *f*; ~ **tubing** *n* PROD entubación por contracción *f*, entubado por contracción *m*; ~ **tunnel for sleeve sealing** *n* PACK túnel de retractilación para el sellado de fundas *m*; ~ **tunnel for sleeving** *n* PACK túnel de retractilación para el enfundado *m*; ~ **wrap** *n AmE* (*cf shrink film BrE*) FOOD envoltura de contracción *f*, PACK película contraíble *f*, película encogible *f*, película retráctil *f*, THERMO *heat shrinkable* envoltorio encogible *m*, película contraíble *f*, película encogible *f*; ~-**wrapped pallet cover** *n* PACK paleta con envoltura retráctil *f*; ~-**wrapped product** *n* PACK producto con envoltura retráctil *m*; ~ **wrapping** *n* PACK envoltura retráctil *f*

shrink[2]: ~ **on** *vt* PROD *tools* enmangar en caliente, enmanguitar en caliente

shrink[3] *vti* C&G, TEXTIL, THERMO encoger

shrinkable *adj* C&G, TEXTIL encogible, THERMO contraíble, encogible

shrinkage *n* AGRIC *cattle* desbaste *m*, C&G, CINEMAT encogimiento *m*, CONST *of cement* contracción de secado *f*, contracción de fraguado *f*, METALL contracción *f*, encogimiento *m*, P&R contracción *f*, encogimiento *m*, contracción volumétrica *f*, PAPER encogimiento *m*, contracción *f*, PHYS encogimiento *m*, PROD *of setting* merma *f*, encogimiento *m*, retracción *f*, contracción *f*, TELECOM contracción *f*, encogimiento *m*, TEXTIL encogimiento *m*; ~ **cavity** *n* METALL rechupe *m*; ~ **crack** *n* CONST grieta por contracción *f*, GEOL, PROD *founding* grieta de contracción *f*; ~ **cracking** *n* CONST agrietamiento por contracción *m*; ~ **factor** *n* PROD coeficiente de consolidación *m*; ~ **limit** *n* COAL franja-almacén *f*; ~ **on solidification** *n* PACK contracción al solidificar *f*

shrinking *n* CONST encogimiento *m*, PAPER contracción *f*, PROD contracción *f*, encogimiento *m*, retracción *f*, TELECOM contracción *f*, encogimiento *m*; ~-**on** *n* PROD enmangado en caliente *m*, enmanguitado en caliente *m*

shrinkproof: ~ **finish** *n* COATINGS acabado a prueba de contracciones *m*

shroud *n* SPACE cubierta *f*, recubrimiento *m*, refuerzo *m*, WATER TRANSP obenque *m*; ~ **ring** *n* AIR TRANSP *of turbine engine* anillo de refuerzo *m*, arandela de refuerzo *f*

shrouded[1] *adj* PROD oculto

shrouded[2]: ~-**cover screw** *n* PROD tornillo de cabeza oculta *m*; ~ **propeller** *n* AIR TRANSP, TRANSP hélice amortajada *f*

shrouding: ~ **gear** *n* MECH ENG engranaje encerrado *m*

shroud *n* WATER TRANSP *rigging, standing* obencadura *f*

shuck *vt* OCEAN *networks* abrir, desvalvar

shunt[1] *adj* ELEC ENG derivado, PHYS desviado

shunt[2] *n* ELEC derivador *m*, ELEC ENG derivación *f*, PHYS desvío *m*, RAIL vía apartadero *f*; ~ **capacitance** *n* ELEC ENG capacitancia en derivación *f*; ~ **capacitor** *n* PHYS condensador derivado *m*; ~ **circuit** *n* ELEC ENG circuito derivado *m*; ~ **coil** *n* ELEC ENG bobina de paralelo *f*; ~ **current** *n* ELEC ENG corriente derivada *f*; ~ **dynamo** *n* ELEC ENG dinamo excitada

en derivación *f*; ~ **excitation** *n* ELEC ENG excitación en derivación *f*; ~ **feed** *n* ELEC, ELEC ENG alimentación en derivación *f*, alimentación en paralelo *f*; ~ **feedback** *n* ELEC ENG, ELECTRON realimentación en paralelo *f*; ~ **motor** *n* ELEC, ELEC ENG motor en derivación *m*; ~ **regulator** *n* ELEC ENG regulador en derivación *m*; ~ **resistance** *n* ELEC ENG resistencia en derivación *f*; ~ **resistor** *n* ELEC ENG resistencia en paralelo *f*; ~ **switch** *n* ELEC conmutador en derivación *m*; ~ **trip** *n* PROD desconexión en derivación *f*; ~ **winding** *n* ELEC devanado en derivación *m*, devanado en shunt *m*, ELEC ENG devanado en derivación *m*; ~-**wound dynamo** *n* ELEC ENG dinamo excitada en derivación *f*; ~-**wound motor** *n* ELEC ENG motor excitado en derivación *m*

shunt[3] *vt* ELEC ENG derivar

shunter *n* RAIL *engine* locomotora para maniobras *f*, *person* obrero de servicio de maniobras *m*, enganchador de vagones *m*

shunting *n* RAIL clasificación de vagones *f*, maniobras *f pl*; ~ **device** *n* ELEC dispositivo en derivación *m*, dispositivo en paralelo *m*; ~ **engine** *n BrE* (*cf switch engine AmE*) CONST, RAIL, TRANSP locomotora de maniobras *f*; ~ **on level tracks** *n* RAIL, TRANSP maniobra en vías horizontales *f*; ~ **switch** *n* ELEC interruptor de derivación *m*; ~ **winch** *n* CONST cabrestante de maniobras *m*, torno de maniobras *m*; ~ **yard** *n BrE* (*cf classification yard AmE, switching yard AmE*) RAIL estación de clasificación *f*

shut[1] *n* PROD *founding* compuerta *f*, hoja *f*, WATER compuerta *f*; ~-**in pressure** *n* PETR TECH presión de cierre *f*, PETROL presión a pozo cerrado *f*, presión hermética *f*; ~-**off** *n* C&G apagado *m*; ~-**off gate** *n* WATER compuerta de paso *f*

shut[2]: ~ **down** *vt* AIR TRANSP apagar, cerrar, derribar, parar, SPACE cerrar, cortar la potencia a, parar; ~ **off** *vt* HYDRAUL cortar, PROD *molten metal* interceptar, WATER *water-bearing strata* cortar, interrumpir; ~ **up** *vt* PROD *welding* encolar

shutdown *n* C&G apagado *m*, cerrado *m*, NUCL parada *f*, SPACE apagado *m*, cierre *m*, interrupción *f*, parada *f*; ~ **circuit** *n* ELEC ENG circuito de seguridad *m*; ~ **cooling** *n* NUCL refrigeración del núcleo en condiciones de parada *f*; ~ **margin** *n* NUCL margen de parada *m*; ~ **procedure** *n* NUCL, SPACE procedimiento de apagado *m*, procedimiento de cierre *m*; ~ **sensor** *n* SPACE sensor de apagado *m*

shutoff: ~ **valve** *n* HYDRAUL válvula de retención *f*, PROD válvula de cierre *f*, válvula de parada *f*, WATER TRANSP válvula de seccionamiento *f*

shutter *n* CINEMAT obturador *m*, CONST contraventana *f*, persiana *f*, HYDRAUL alza *f*, compuerta *f*, INSTR obturador *m*, MINE portacebo *m* (*AmL*), obturador *m* (*Esp*), PHOTO, PROD *of fan* obturador *m*, SPACE portacebo *m* (*AmL*), obturador *m* (*Esp*), portaespoleta *f*, charnela portacebo *f*; ~ **angle** *n* CINEMAT, PHOTO, TV ángulo del obturador *m*; ~ **with B setting** *n* PHOTO obturador con ajuste B *m*; ~ **blade** *n* CINEMAT, PHOTO laminilla del obturador *f*; ~ **blur** *n* CINEMAT emborronamiento por el obturador *m*; ~ **phasing device** *n* CINEMAT dispositivo de puesta en fase del obturador *m*; ~ **release** *n* CINEMAT, PHOTO disparador *m*; ~ **release button** *n* CINEMAT, PHOTO, TV botón del disparador *m*; ~ **release cable** *n* CINEMAT cable del disparador *m*; ~ **speed** *n* PHOTO velocidad del obturador *f*; ~ **speed control** *n* PHOTO control de velocidad del obturador *m*; ~ **speed setting** *n* CINEMAT, PHOTO, TV ajuste de velocidad del obturador *m*; ~ **speed setting knob** *n* PHOTO perilla de ajuste de velocidad del obturador *f*; ~ **system** *n* SPACE sistema de cierre *m*

shuttering *n* CONST encofrado *m*

shutting: ~-**off** *n* HYDRAUL cierre *m*, WATER cierre *m*, interrupción *f*, separación *f*; ~-**off water** *n* WATER cierre del agua *m*; ~ **post** *n* CONST larguero de cerradura *m*; ~ **together** *n* PROD *welding* encolado *m*; ~ **up** *n* PROD *welding* encolado *m*

shuttle *n* AIR TRANSP puente aéreo *m*, HYDRAUL manguito *m*, SPACE astronave de lanzadera *f*, bombardeo en lanzadera *m*, transbordador espacial *m*, TEXTIL, TV lanzadera *f*; ~ **armature** *n* ELEC armadura del obturador *f*; ~ **haulage** *n* COAL arrastre de vagonetas *m*; ~ **plate** *n* HYDRAUL placa del manguito *f*; ~ **service** *n* AIR TRANSP servicio de puente aéreo *m*; ~ **spindle** *n* TEXTIL broca de lanzadera *f*; ~ **tanker** *n* PETR TECH petrolero puente *m*; ~ **traffic** *n* TRANSP tráfico lanzadera *m*; ~ **train** *n* RAIL puente ferroviario *m*, tren que viaja comtinuamente entre dos puntos *m*; ~ **valve** *n* PROD válvula de doble efecto *f*

SI¹ *abbr* COMP&DP (*information separator*) SI (*separador de información*), METR (*international system of units*) SI (*sistema internacional de unidades*), TELECOM (*intermediate system*) SI (*sistema intermedio*)

SI²: ~ **character** *n* (*shift-in character*) COMP&DP carácter SI *m* (*carácter cambiador de código*); ~ **unit** *n* (*international system unit*) ELEC, METR, PART PHYS, PHYS unidad SI *f* (*unidad del sistema internacional*)

Si *abbr* CHEM (*silicon*) Si (*silicio*), GEOL (*silica*) Si (*sílice*)

siberite *n* MINERAL siberita *f*

siccative¹ *adj* THERMO secante

siccative² *n* FOOD, THERMO secante *f*

sickle: ~ **bar** *n* AGRIC barra de eorte *f*; ~ **pitman** *n* AGRIC biela de la cuchilla *f*

side¹ *n* CONST alero *m*, costado *m*, ladera *f*, lado *m*, GEOM lado *m*, INSTR cara *f*, costado *m*, flanco *m*, miembro *m*, pared *f*, pata *f*, MINE cara *f*, costero *m* (*AmL*), hastial *m* (*Esp*), pared *f*, OPT lado *m*, PROD *of crab winch* flanco *m*, WATER TRANSP costado *m*; ~-**and-face milling cutter with plain** *n* MECH ENG fresadora de tres cortes con meseta *f*; ~-**band alloy** *n* METALL aleación de banda lateral *f*; ~ **bar** *n* CONST *of ladder* baranda *f* (*AmL*), barandilla *f* (*Esp*); ~-**buffer screw coupling** *n* TRANSP acoplamiento a rosca de amortiguador lateral *m*; ~-**by-side cylinders** *n pl* MECH ENG cilindros yuxtapuestos *m pl*; ~ **casting** *n* PROD *founding* colada en talón *f*; ~ **chain** *n* CHEM cadena lateral *f*; ~ **channel** *n* OCEAN canal litoral *m*; ~ **chisel** *n* CONST *wood-turning* formón de bisel oblicuo *m*; ~ **circuit** *n* ELEC ENG circuito lateral *m*, línea real *f*; ~ **clearance** *n* MECH ENG despeje lateral *m*, espacio lateral *m*, huelgo lateral *m*, juego lateral *m*, *gearing* huelgo entre dientes *m*; ~ **collision** *n* TRANSP choque lateral *m*, colisión lateral *f*; ~ **construction** *n* WATER TRANSP *shipbuilding* construcción sobre cubierta en el costado *f*; ~ **dressing** *n* AGRIC abonamiento lateral *m*; ~ **dump car** *n AmE* (*cf side dump wagon BrE*) RAIL vagón basculante lateralmente *m*; ~ **dump wagon** *n BrE* (*cf side dump car AmE*) RAIL vagón basculante lateralmente *m*; ~ **effect** *n* COMP&DP efecto lateral *m*; ~ **entry** *n* MINE galería de ventilación lateral *f*, galería principal

lateral *f*; ~ **finder** *n* CINEMAT visor lateral *m*; ~ **fit** *n* MECH ENG ajuste lateral *m*; ~-**frame** *n* PACK larguero *m*, marco lateral *m*; ~ **frequency** *n* ELECTRON, TELECOM frecuencia lateral *f*; ~ **gate** *n* PROD *founding* canal de colada en talón *m*; ~ **gear** *n* AUTO engranaje planetario *m*, VEH transmisión del movimiento lateral *f*; ~ **girder** *n* WATER TRANSP *shipbuilding* vagra lateral *f*; ~ **hole** *n* MINE pozo de sondeo lateral *m*; ~ **index** *n* PRINT índice escalonado lateral *m*; ~ **joint** *n* INSTR articulación lateral *f*; ~ **lash** *n* MECH ENG fresa radial *f*, golpe lateral *m*, huelgo lateral *m*, juego lateral *m*; ~ **lobe** *n* ELECTRON, PHYS, SPACE, WATER TRANSP lóbulo lateral *m*; ~ **lobe cancellation** *n* ELECTRON cancelación de lóbulo lateral *f*; ~ **lock** *n* TV fijación lateral *f*; ~ **marker light** *n AmE* (*cf sidelight BrE*) VEH luz lateral *f*; ~ **member** *n* AUTO, VEH barra lateral *f*; ~ **mirror** *n* VEH retrovisor lateral *m*; ~-**mounted terminal** *n* AUTO borne de montaje lateral *m*, terminal lateral *m*, VEH borne de montaje lateral *m*; ~ **note** *n* PRINT nota marginal *f*; ~-**on collision** *n* TRANSP costado en colisión *m*; ~ **panel** *n* PACK, VEH panel lateral *m*; ~ **plane** *n* CONST cepillo lateral *m*; ~-**planing machine** *n* PROD cepilladora de escote *f*; ~ **plates** *n pl* PROD *for emery wheels, of roller chain* cartelas *f pl*; ~ **plating** *n* WATER TRANSP *shipbuilding* planchas del costado *f pl*; ~ **pocket** *n* C&G bolsa lateral *f*; ~ **product** *n* CHEM, CHEM TECH subproducto *m*; ~ **pulley** *n* CONST polea lateral *f*; ~ **push rod** *n* PROD biela de acoplamiento *f*; ~-**push roller** *n* PROD rodillo de empuje lateral *m*; ~ **rabbet plane** *n* CONST cepillo de ranura lateral *m*; ~ **reaction** *n* CHEM reacción secundaria *f*; ~ **register** *n* PRINT registro lateral *m*; ~ **run** *n* PAPER bobina cabo *f*; ~ **stay bolt** *n* RAIL perno de anclaje lateral *m*; ~ **stoping** *n* MINE arranque lateral *m*, laboreo por escalones laterales *m*; ~ **thrust** *n* ACOUST empuje lateral *m*, FUELLESS empuje horizontal *m*, MECH ENG empuje lateral *m*, fuerza lateral *f*; ~ **thruster** *n* WATER TRANSP impulsor lateral *m*; ~-**valve engine** *n* AUTO motor de válvula lateral *m*; ~ **wall** *n* MINE hastial *m*, muro lateral *m*, pared lateral *f*, pared del pozo *f*, WATER pared lateral *f*; ~ **wall with ventilation flaps** *n* TRANSP pared lateral con aletas de ventilación *f*; ~-**wipe contact** *n* ELEC ENG contacto por barrido lateral *m*; ~ **wiping** *n* ELEC ENG barrido de cable lateral *m*

side²: **this ~ up** *phr* PACK este lado siempre hacia arriba

sideband *n* COMP&DP, ELECTRON, PHYS, TELECOM, TV banda lateral *f*; ~ **attenuation** *n* ELECTRON atenuación de banda lateral *f*; ~ **frequency** *n* ELECTRON, TELECOM frecuencia de banda lateral *f*; ~ **interference** *n* ELECTRON interferencia de banda lateral *f*; ~ **suppression** *n* ELECTRON eliminación de banda lateral *f*

sidecar *n* TRANSP barquilla auxiliar suspendida *f*, sidecar *m* (*Esp*), zapato *m* (*AmL*)

sidedraft: ~ **carburetor** *AmE see sidedraught carburettor BrE*

sidedraught: ~ **carburettor** *n BrE* AUTO, VEH carburador de aspiración lateral *m*, carburador de succión lateral *m*, carburador de tiro lateral *m*

sidegrooved: ~ **specimen** *n* METALL muestra lateralmente rayada *f*, probeta con ranuras laterales *f*

sidehill: ~ **cut** *n* CONST desmonte *m*

sidelight[1] *n* BrE (*cf side marker light AmE*) VEH luz lateral *f*

sidelight[2] *vt* PHOTO iluminar lateralmente

sidereal: ~ **day** *n* PHYS, SPACE día sideral *m*; ~ **time** *n* PHYS, SPACE hora sideral *f*, hora sidérea *f*; ~ **year** *n* PHYS, SPACE año sideral *m*

siderite *n* MINERAL siderita *f*

sideritic: ~ **mudstone** *n* GEOL micrítica siderítica *f*

sideslip *n* PHYS deslizamiento lateral *m*

sidetone *n* TELECOM efecto local *m*, ruido de fondo *m*, tono lateral *m*

sidetrack: ~ **drilling** *n* PETR TECH perforación desviada *f*

sidetracking *n* PETR TECH desviación *f*

sidewalk *n* AmE (*cf pavement BrE*) COAL adoquinado *m* (*Esp*), calzada *f*, muro *m*, pavimento *m* (*AmL*), piso *m*, CONST acera *f* (*Esp*), andén *m*, calzada *f*, piso *m*, vereda *f* (*AmL*), *road surface, stone walks* adoquinado *m* (*Esp*), empedrado *m*, pavimento *m* (*AmL*), TRANSP adoquinado *m* (*Esp*), pavimento *m* (*AmL*)

sidewall[1]: ~-**coupled** *adj* ELEC ENG acoplado lateralmente

sidewall[2]: ~ **core** *n* PETR TECH núcleo de pared *m*, núcleo lateral *m*, testigo de pared *m*, testigo lateral *m*; ~ **coring** *n* PETR TECH extracción de testigos de pared *f*; ~ **neutron log** *n* PETR TECH perfil neutrónico de pared *m*; ~ **pad** *n* PETR TECH almohadilla de pared lateral *f*; ~ **sampler** *n* PETR TECH sacamuestras de pared lateral *m*

sideways: ~-**looking airborne radar** *n* (*SLAR*) AIR TRANSP, MAR POLL radar aéreo de exploración lateral *m* (*RAEL*)

siding *n* CONST forrado *m*, tinglado *m*, vía muerta *f*, RAIL apartadero *m*, desvío *m*, vía muerta *f*, TRANSP apartadero *m*

sidings *n* RAIL, TRANSP apartadero *m*

siege: ~ **artillery** *n* MILIT artillería de sitio *f*

siemens *n* (*S*) METR, PHYS siemens *m* (*S*), siemensio *m* (*S*)

sieve[1] *n* CHEM TECH tamiz *m*, COAL, CONST cedazo *m*, criba *f*, tamiz *m*, HYDROL tamiz *m*, LAB, PROD cedazo *m*, criba *f*, tamiz *m*, RECYCL cedazo *m*, cernidor *m*, colador *m*, criba *f*, tamiz *m*; ~ **analysis** *n* C&G análisis granulométrico *m*, CHEM TECH, COAL análisis granulométrico *m*, análisis por tamizado *m*, GEOL, NUCL análisis granulométrico *m*; ~ **bottom** *n* CHEM TECH fondo del tamiz *m*; ~ **diaphragm** *n* CHEM TECH diafragma de filtración *m*; ~ **drum** *n* CHEM TECH tambor cribador *m*, tambor tamizador *m*; ~ **dryer** *n* CHEM TECH secador de tamices *m*; ~ **fraction** *n* C&G cuarteo por malla *m*; ~ **frame** *n* CHEM TECH armazón de tamices *m*; ~ **grate** *n* CHEM TECH parrilla de tamiz *f*; ~ **jigger** *n* CHEM TECH vibradora de tamices *f*; ~ **mesh** *n* COAL malla del tamiz *f*; ~ **netting** *n* CHEM TECH red del tamiz *f*; ~ **plate** *n* CHEM TECH placa de criba *f*, placa de tamiz *f*; ~ **set** *n* CHEM TECH juego de tamices *m*; ~ **shaker** *n* LAB *with grinding disc* vibradora de tamices *f*; ~ **tray** *n* CHEM TECH plato perforado *m*

sieve[2] *vt* CHEM TECH, COAL, CONST cernir, cribar, tamizar, FOOD tamizar, PROD, RECYCL cernir, cribar, tamizar

sieve[3] *vti* HYDROL cribar

sievert *n* (*Sv*) NUCL, PHYS, RAD PHYS sievert *m* (*Sv*)

sieving *n* CHEM TECH cribado *m*, tamizado *m*, CONST cribado *m*, MAR POLL tamizado *m*, POLL cribado *m*; ~ **rate** *n* CHEM TECH velocidad de tamizado *f*; ~ **residue** *n* CHEM TECH residuo del tamizado *m*

sift *vt* COAL, CONST, FOOD, MAR POLL, PROD tamizar

sifted: ~ **coal** *n* COAL carbón tamizado *m*

sifter *n* PROD *founding* cedazo *m*, criba *f*; ~ **valve** *n* HYDRAUL válvula de desahogo *f*, válvula equilibrada *f*

sifting *n* CONST tamizado *m*, PROD cribado *m*, tamizado *m*

siftings *n pl* PROD granzas *f pl*

sight[1] *n* CONST *aim or observation taken* observación *f*, *line of vision* visual *f*, INSTR visor *m*, vista *f*, goniómetro *m*, WATER TRANSP observación astronómica *f*; ~ **bar** *n* WATER TRANSP alidada *f*; ~ **distance** *n* CONST distancia de visibilidad *f*, TRANSP distancia visual *f*; ~-**feed lubricator** *n* MECH ENG lubricador de gota visible *m*; ~-**feed needle valve** *n* MECH ENG válvula de aguja de alimentación visible *f*; ~ **glass** *n* PETR TECH vidrio transparente *m*, REFRIG visor *m*; ~ **hole** *n* MILIT alza *f*

sight[2] *vt* PHOTO apuntar

sighted: ~ **alidade** *n* CONST, INSTR alidada de pínulas *f*; ~ **level** *n* CONST nivel de visibilidad *m*

sighting *n* CONST, MILIT puntería *f*; ~ **board** *n* CONST tablero de mira *m*; ~ **color** AmE, ~ **colour** BrE *n* COLOUR color fugaz *m*; ~ **device** *n* INSTR aparato visor *m*; ~ **line** *n* INSTR ángulo visual *m*, MILIT sistema de puntería *m*; ~ **mirror** *n* INSTR espejo visual *m*; ~ **range** *n* MILIT distancia de puntería *f*; ~ **telescope** *n* CONST telescopio de mira *m*, INSTR telescopio visual *m*

sigma: ~ **bond** *n* CHEM enlace covalente *m*, enlace sigma *m*, enlace *m*; ~ **hyperon** *n* PART PHYS, PHYS hiperón sigma *m*; ~ **particle** *n* PHYS partícula sigma *f*; ~ **pile** *n* NUCL pila sigma *f*

sign[1] *n* COMP&DP signo *m*, VEH señal *f*; ~ **bit** *n* COMP&DP bit de signo *m*; ~ **digit** *n* COMP&DP dígito de signo *m*

sign[2]: ~ **off** *vi* COMP&DP cerrar la sesión; ~ **on** *vi* COMP&DP iniciar la sesión

signal[1] *n* GEN señal *f*, SPACE *warning* aviso *m*; ~ **agility** *n* ELECTRON agilidad de la señal *f*, rapidez en el envío de la señal *f*; ~ **amplitude** *n* ELECTRON amplitud de señal *f*; ~ **analyser** *n* BrE ELECTRON, RAD PHYS, TELECOM analizador de señales *m*; ~ **analysis** *n* ELECTRON, RAD PHYS, TELECOM análisis de señales *m*; ~ **analyzer** AmE *see signal analyser* BrE; ~ **at danger** *n* RAIL señal en caso de peligro *f*; ~ **averaging** *n* ELECTRON obtención del promedio de señal *f*; ~ **bandwidth** *n* ELECTRON ancho de banda de señal *m*; ~ **book** *n* WATER TRANSP código de señales *m*, libro de señales *m*; ~ **box** *n* BrE RAIL caja de señales *f*, puesto de señalización *m*; ~ **buried in noise** *n* ELECTRON perturbación de señal por ruido *f*; ~ **clipping** *n* ELECTRON corte de señal *m*; ~ **comparator** *n* ELECTRON comparador de señales *m*; ~ **comparison** *n* ELECTRON comparación de señal *f*; ~ **complex** *n* TV sistema de señales *m*; ~ **component** *n* ELECTRON componente de señal *m*; ~ **compression** *n* TELECOM compresión de señales *f*; ~ **conditioner** *n* ELECTRON acondicionador de señal *m*; ~ **conditioning** *n* ELECTRON acondicionamiento de señal *m*, PROD condicionamiento para señal *m*, preparación de la señal *f*; ~ **conversion** *n* ELECTRON,

TELECOM conversión de señales *f*; ~ **conversion equipment** *n* ELECTRON equipo convertidor de señal *m*, TELECOM signal conversion equipment *m*; ~ **converter** *n* ELECTRON generador de la base de tiempos *m*, TELECOM convertidor de señales *m*; ~ **delay** *n* ELECTRON retardo de señal *m*, TELECOM retardo de señal *m*, tiempo de propagación de la señal *m*; ~ **detection** *n* TELECOM detección de señales *f*; ~ **detector** *n* TELECOM detector de señales *m*; ~ **digitization** *n* ELECTRON, TELECOM, TV digitización de señal *f*; ~ **digitizer** *n* ELECTRON, TELECOM, TV digitizador de señal *m*; ~ **distortion** *n* ELECTRON distorsión de señal *f*, TELECOM deformación de señal *f*, distorsión de señal *f*; ~ **distributor** *n* (*SD*) TELECOM distribuidor de señales *m*; ~ **edge** *n* ELECTRON frente de la señal *m*; ~ **electrode** *n* ELECTRON electrodo de señal *m*; ~ **element timing** *n* TELECOM temporización del elemento de señal *f*, temporización del intervalo elemental *f*, temporización del intervalo unitario *f*; ~ **envelope** *n* TELECOM envolvente de la señal *f*; ~ **expansion** *n* TELECOM expansión de la señal *f*; ~ **extension** *n* TELECOM extensión de la señal *f*; ~ **fail** *n* (*SF*) TELECOM falla de señal *f* (*AmL*), fallo de señal *m* (*Esp*); ~ **flag** *n* WATER TRANSP bandera de señales *f*; ~ **flow-graph** *n* ELECTRON diagrama de flujo *m*; ~ **frequency** *n* ELECTRON frecuencia de señal *f*; ~ **generation** *n* ELECTRON, PHYS, TELECOM generación de señal *f*; ~ **generator** *n* ELECTRON, PHYS, TELECOM generador de señales *m*; ~ **generator calibration** *n* ELECTRON, PHYS TELECOM, calibración del generador de señal *f*; ~ **glass** *n* C&G vidrio de señales *m*; ~ **ground** *n* TELECOM retorno de tierra del circuito de señal *m*; ~ **identification plate** *n* RAIL placa de identificación *f*, señal de identificación *f*; ~ **injector** *n* ELECTRON inyector de señal *m*; ~ **input** *n* ELECTRON señal de entrada *f*; ~ **installation** *n* TRANSP instalación de señales *f*; ~ **lamp** *n* RAIL lámpara de señales *f*; ~ **level** *n* ELECTRON, TELECOM nivel de señal *m*; ~ **limiter** *n* ELECTRON limitador de señal *m*; ~ **line** *n* ELEC ENG línea de señal *f*; ~ **locker** *n* WATER TRANSP caja de banderas *f*, pañol de señales *m*, taquilla de banderas *f*; ~ **mast** *n* WATER TRANSP semáforo *m*, verga de señales *f*; ~ **modeling** *AmE*, ~ **modelling** *BrE n* ELECTRON modelación de la señal *f*; ~ **multiplexing** *n* ELECTRON, TELECOM transmisión simultánea de la señal *f*; ~**-operating rod** *n* RAIL varilla accionadora de señales *f*; ~ **phase** *n* ELECTRON fase de señal *f*; ~ **plate** *n* ELECTRON placa de señal *f*; ~ **power** *n* ELECTRON potencia de señal *f*; ~ **processing** *n* COMP&DP procesamiento de señales *m*, ELECTRON tratamiento de la señal *m*, TELECOM procesamiento de señales *m*; ~**-processing chip** *n* ELECTRON chip procesador de señales *m*; ~ **processor** *n* (*SP*) ELECTRON, TELECOM, TV procesador de señales *m*; ~ **pulse** *n* ELECTRON impulso de señal *m*; ~ **quantization** *n* TELECOM cuantificación de una señal *f*; ~ **receiver** *n* TELECOM receptor de señales *m*; ~ **regeneration** *n* ELECTRON regeneración de la señal *f*; ~ **regenerator** *n* ELECTRON regenerador de la señal *m*; ~ **restoration** *n* TELECOM restablecimiento de una señal *m*; ~ **shaping** *n* COMP&DP configuración de la señal *f*, conformación de señales *f*, ELECTRON formación de la señal *f*; ~**-shaping filter** *n* ELECTRON filtro de formación de señal *m*, TELECOM filtro de conformación de la señal *m*, filtro de formación de señal *m*; ~ **simulation** *n* ELECTRON

simulación de la señal *f*; ~ **splitter** *n* TV divisor de señal *m*; ~ **station** *n* WATER TRANSP estación de señales *f*, semáforo *m*; ~ **structure** *n* RAIL armazón de señales *m*; ~ **synthesis** *n* ELECTRON síntesis de la señal *f*; ~ **threshold** *n* ELECTRON, PHYS, SPACE, TELECOM umbral de la señal *m*; ~**-to-clutter ratio** *n* TELECOM relación señal-ecos parásitos *f*; ~**-to-noise and distortion ratio** *n* (*SINAD ratio*) TELECOM relación señal-ruido y distorsión *f* (*relación SINAD*); ~**-to-noise ratio** *n* (*SNR*) ACOUST, COMP&DP, ELECTRON, PETR TECH, PHYS, TELECOM, TV relación señal-ruido *f*; ~ **tower** *n* AmE (*cf signal box BrE*) RAIL caja de señales *f*, puesto de señalización *m*; ~ **transmission** *n* TELECOM transmisión de la señal *f*; ~ **weakening** *n* TELECOM debilitamiento de la señal *m*

signal² *vt* ELECTRON enviar una señal
signal³ *vti* WATER TRANSP comunicar por señales, dar una señal, enviar una señal, hacer una señal, señalar
signaling *AmE see* **signalling** *BrE*
signalling *n BrE* COMP&DP señalamiento *m*, señalización *f*, SPACE, TELECOM señalización *f*, transmisión de señales *f*, WATER TRANSP señalización *f*; ~ **association control service element** *n BrE* TELECOM elemento de control de la asociación de señalización *m*; ~ **channel** *n BrE* TELECOM canal de señalización *m*, canal para señalización *m*; ~ **connection control part** *n BrE* TELECOM dispositivo de control de la conexión de señalización *m*; ~ **control part** *n BrE* TELECOM dispositivo de control de señalización *m*, parte de control de la señalización *f*; ~ **detector** *n BrE* TELECOM detector de señalización *m*; ~ **distance** *n BrE* TRANSP distancia de la señalización *f*, distancia entre señales *f*; ~ **generator** *n BrE* ELEC ENG generador de señalización *m*, generador de transmisión de señales *m*; ~ **grouping channel** *n BrE* (*SGC*) TELECOM canal agrupador de señalización *m*, canal de agrupamiento de señalización *m*; ~ **information** *n BrE* TELECOM información de señalización *f*; ~ **network** *n BrE* TELECOM red de señalización *f*; ~ **point** *n BrE* TELECOM punto de señalización *m*; ~ **protocol** *n BrE* COMP&DP protocolo de señalización *m*; ~ **reliability** *n BrE* TELECOM fiabilidad de la señalización *f*; ~ **system** *n BrE* TELECOM sistema de señalización *m*; ~ **transfer point** *n BrE* (*STP*) TELECOM punto de transferencia de la señalización *m*; ~ **virtual channel** *n BrE* (*SVC*) TELECOM canal virtual de señalización *m*; ~ **wires** *n BrE* RAIL circuito de señalización *m*

signature *n* PRINT cuadernillo *m*; ~ **number** *n* PRINT número de signatura *m*
signed: ~ **magnitude representation** *n* COMP&DP representación de magnitudes con signo *f*
significance: ~ **test** *n* COMP&DP, MATH prueba de significación *f* (*Esp*), prueba de significancia *f* (*AmL*)
significant: ~ **figure** *n* MATH cifra significativa *f*, dígito significativo *m*; ~ **wave** *n* OCEAN ola significativa *f*, onda significativa *f*
SIL *abbr* (*speech interference level*) ACOUST SIL (*nivel de interferencia con la palabra*)
silage *n* AGRIC ensilaje *m*; ~ **corn** *n* AmE (*cf silage maize BrE*) AGRIC maíz para ensilaje *m*; ~ **cutter** *n* AGRIC picadora-ensiladora *f*; ~ **effluent** *n* HYDROL efluente ensilado *m*; ~ **maize** *n BrE* (*cf silage corn AmE*) AGRIC maíz para ensilaje *m*
silane *n* CHEM, P&R silano *m*

silence: ~ **elimination** *n* TELECOM eliminación de silencio *f*

silencer *n* (*cf* **muffler** *AmE*) ACOUST, AUTO, SAFE, TRANSP, VEH silenciador *m*

silhouetting *n* CINEMAT aparición en silueta *f*, silueteado *m*, TV aparición en silueta *f*

silica *n* C&G arena silícea *f*, sílice *f*, CHEM, ELECTRON, GEOL, MINERAL, PHYS sílice *f*; ~ **aerogel** *n* HEAT ENG, REFRIG aerogel de sílice *m*; ~ **coating** *n* TELECOM cobertura de sílice *f*, revestimiento de sílice *m*; ~ **content** *n* MINE contenido en silicio *m*, contenido en sílice *m*; ~ **dust** *n* SAFE polvo de sílice *m*; ~ **fiber** *AmE*, ~ **fibre** *BrE* *n* HEAT ENG, OPT, TELECOM fibra de sílice *f*; ~ **gel** *n* CHEM gel de sílice *m*, sílica gel *f*, FOOD gel de sílice *m*, PACK dióxido de silicio *m*, gel de sílice *m*; ~ **glass** *n* METALL masa de cuarzo fundido *f*, sílice fundida *f*, vidrio de sílice *m*; ~ **scum** *n* C&G espuma de sílice *f*, nata de sílice *f*; ~ **scum line** *n* C&G línea de la espuma de sílice *f*

silicate *n* CHEM silicato *m*; ~**-bearing sheet** *n* GEOL capa de silicato *f*; ~ **paint** *n* COATINGS, COLOUR pintura de silicato *f*

siliceous[1] *adj* CHEM, GEOL, GEOPHYS, PETR TECH silíceo

siliceous[2]: ~ **nondetrital rock** *n* GEOL roca silícea no detrítica *f*; ~ **sinter** *n* PETR TECH toba silícea *f*; ~ **sinter terrace** *n* GEOPHYS terraza de silíceo sinterizado *f*, terraza sinterizada de silíceo *f*

silicic: ~ **acid** *n* CHEM ácido silícico *m*

siliciclastic: ~ **rock** *n* GEOL roca siliciclástica *f*

silicide *n* CHEM siliciuro *m*

siliciuret *n* CHEM siliciuret *m*

silicoborate *n* CHEM silicoborato *m*

silicofluoride *n* CHEM fluosilicato *m*, silicofluoruro *m*

silicon *n* (*Si*) GEN sílice *f* (*Si*), silicio *m* (*Si*); ~ **avalanche diode** *n* ELECTRON diodo de avalancha de silicio *m*; ~ **avalanche photodiode** *n* ELECTRON fotodiodo de avalancha de silicio *m*; ~ **bipolar integrated circuit** *n* ELECTRON circuito integrado bipolar de silicio *m*; ~ **bipolar transistor** *n* ELECTRON transistor bipolar de silicio *m*; ~ **carbide** *n* ELEC ENG, PHYS carburo de silicio *m*; ~ **carbide varistor** *n* ELEC ENG resistencia de carburo de silicio comprimido *f*, varistor de carburo de silicio *m*; ~ **cell** *n* ELEC ENG elemento de silicio *m*, FUELLESS célula de silicio *f*; ~ **chip** *n* COMP&DP chip de silicio *m*, descantilladura de silicio *f*, plaqueta de sílice *f*, ELEC brizna de silicio *f*, descantilladura de silicio *f*, viruta de silicio *f*, ELECTRON, RAD PHYS chip de silicio *m*; ~**-controlled rectifier** *n* (*SCR*) ELEC ENG, TELECOM rectificador controlado de silicio *m* (*RCS*); ~**-controlled rectifier crosspoint** *n* TELECOM punto de cruce del rectificador controlado por silicio *m*; ~**-controlled switch** *n* ELEC, ELEC ENG interruptor controlado por silicio *m*; ~ **counters** *n pl* RAD PHYS contadores de silicio *m pl*; ~ **crystal** *n* ELECTRON cristal de silicio *m*; ~ **crystal mixer** *n* ELECTRON mezclador de cristal de silicio *m*; ~ **detector** *n* ELECTRON, RAD PHYS detector de silicio *m*; ~ **detector diode** *n* ELECTRON diodo de detector de silicio *m*; ~ **device** *n* ELEC ENG dispositivo de silicio *m*; ~ **diode** *n* ELEC, ELECTRON diodo de silicio *m*; ~ **dioxide** *n* ELECTRON dióxido de silicio *m*; ~ **dioxide layer** *n* ELECTRON estratificador de dióxido de silicio *m*; ~ **doping** *n* ELECTRON, PHYS adulteración con silicio *f*; ~ **epitaxial layer** *n* ELECTRON estratificador epitáxico de silicio *m*; ~ **epitaxial planar transistor** *n* ELECTRON transistor planar epitáxico

de silicio *m*; ~ **FET** *n* ELECTRON TEC de silicio *m*; ~ **foundry** *n* ELECTRON fundidora de silicio *f*; ~ **gate** *n* ELECTRON puerta de silicio *f*; ~ **gate technology** *n* ELECTRON tecnología de puerta de silicio *f*; ~ **gate transistor** *n* ELECTRON transistor con puerta de silicio *m*; ~ **integrated circuit** *n* ELECTRON circuito integrado de silicio *m*; ~ **intensifier target** *n* ELECTRON placa intensificadora de silicio *f*; ~**-intensifier-target camera tube** *n* ELECTRON cámara intensificadora de silicio *f*; ~ **junction diode** *n* ELECTRON diodo de unión de silicio *m*; ~ **layer** *n* ELECTRON capa de silicio *f*; ~ **mixer diode** *n* ELECTRON diodo mezclador de silicio *m*; ~ **nitride** *n* ELECTRON nitruro de silicio *m*; ~ **on sapphire** *n* (*SOS*) ELECTRON silicio con zafiro *m*; ~ **oxide** *n* CHEM, ELECTRON óxido de silicio *m*; ~ **photocell** *n* ELECTRON fotocélula de silicio *f*; ~ **photodiode** *n* ELECTRON fotodiodo de silicio *m*; ~ **phototransistor** *n* ELECTRON fototransistor de silicio *m*; ~ **rectifier** *n* (*SCR*) ELEC, ELEC ENG, PHYS rectificador de silicio *m*; ~ **solar cell** *n* ELEC ENG pila solar de silicio *f*; ~ **steel** *n* ELEC ENG, METALL acero al silicio *m*; ~ **steel core** *n* ELEC ENG núcleo de acero silicioso *m*; ~ **steel lamination** *n* ELEC ENG laminación de acero de silicio *f*; ~ **substrate** *n* ELECTRON substrato de silicio *m*; ~ **valley** *n* ELECTRON valle del silicio *m*; ~ **wafer** *n* COMP&DP oblea de silicio *f*, ELECTRON disco de silicio *m*, pastilla de silicio *f*; ~ **Zener diode** *n* ELECTRON, PHYS, TV diodo Zener de silicio *m*

silicone *n* CHEM, ELEC, ELEC ENG, P&R silicona *f*; ~ **cladding** *n* ELEC ENG revestimiento de silicona *m*; ~ **compound** *n* WATER TRANSP compuesto de silicona *m*, compuesto silicónico *m*; ~ **fluid** *n* ELEC fluido silicónico *m*; ~ **rubber** *n* ELEC caucho silicónico *m*, goma silicónica *f*

silicophenyl *n* CHEM silicofenil *m*

silicotitanate *n* CHEM silicotitanato *m*

silicotungstate *n* CHEM silicotungstato *m*

silicotungstic *adj* CHEM silicotúngstico

silk *n* C&G, TEXTIL seda *f*; ~**-like handle** *n* TEXTIL tacto sedoso *m*; ~ **screen** *n* C&G pantalla de seda *f*; ~ **spinning** *n* TEXTIL hilatura de la seda *f*; ~ **yarn** *n* TEXTIL hilo de seda *m*

silking *n* AGRIC *maize* floración femenina del maíz *f*, P&R aspecto sedoso *m*

silkscreen: ~ **printing** *n* TEXTIL estampación en tamiz de seda *f*

sill *n* CONST *of frame-house or partition* larguero *m*, *at foot of structure* solera *f*, *up from ground, in doorway* umbral *m*, HYDROL fondo *m*, MINE piso *m*, fondo *m*, filón-capa *m*, *muro transversal sumergido m (AmL)*, solera *f* (*Esp*), durmiente *m* (*AmL*), umbral *m*, OCEAN umbral *m*, PROD *of ore stamp* solera *f*, WATER *of canal lock* umbral *m*, busco *m*, reborde *m*, WATER TRANSP *port* borde inferior *m*; ~ **piece** *n* MINE arriostramiento longitudinal entre pies derechos de marcos *m*; ~ **plate** *n* CONST *of plummer block* durmiente *m*, PROD *of fire door* umbral *m*

sillimanite *n* MINERAL sillimanita *f*

silo *n* AGRIC silo *m*, MILIT, SPACE lanzador de misiles colocado en un refugio subterráneo *m*, silo *m*; ~ **filling** *n* AGRIC ensilado *m*; ~ **pressure** *n* COAL presión del silo *f*; ~ **unloader** *n* AGRIC descargador de silo *m*

siloxane *n* CHEM siloxano *m*

silt[1] *n* COAL cieno *m*, limo *m*, lodo glutinoso *m*, residuos del lavado de carbones *m pl*, sedimento *m*, GEOL limo *m*, HYDROL cieno *m*, OCEAN depósito detrítico *m*, limo *m*, WATER cieno *m*, lodo glutinoso *m*, sedimento *m*; ~ **discharge** *n* WATER descarga de sedimento *f*; ~ **plug** *n* OCEAN tapón de légamo *m*; ~ **storage space** *n* WATER deposición de limo *f*; ~ **trap** *n* WATER trampa de fangos *f*, trampa de limo *f*

silt²: ~ **up** *vt* HYDROL encenegar, obstruir con sedimentos

silt³: ~ **up** *vi* HYDROL encenegarse, obstruirse

silted: ~ **up** *adj* HYDROL obstruido

silting *n* CHEM sedimentación *f*, PROD relleno hidráulico con fangos *m*; ~ **up** *n* GEOL, HYDROL sedimentación *f*

siltstone *n* GEOL limolita *f*

silver *n* (*Ag*) C&G, CHEM, ELEC ENG, METALL, PHOTO plata *f* (*Ag*); ~ **battery** *n* ELEC ENG batería de plata *f*; ~ **bromide** *n* CHEM bromuro de plata *m*; ~ **bromide collodion plate** *n* PHOTO placa con colodión de bromuro de plata *f*; ~ **bronze powder** *n* COLOUR polvo de purpurina plateada *m*; ~~**cadmium battery** *n* ELEC ENG batería en plata y cadmio *f*; ~~**cadmium cell** *n* ELEC ENG pila de plata y cadmio *f*; ~ **case tantalum capacitor** *n* ELEC ENG condensador de tantalio recubierto en plata *m*; ~ **cell** *n* ELEC ENG elemento en plata *m*; ~ **chloride** *n* CHEM, ELEC ENG cloruro de plata *m*; ~ **chloride emulsion** *n* PHOTO emulsión de cloruro de plata *f*; ~ **color** *AmE*, ~ **colour** *BrE* *n* COLOUR colorante plateado *m*; ~ **contact** *n* ELEC ENG contacto en plata *m*; ~ **content** *n* PHOTO contenido de plata *m*; ~ **cyanide** *n* CHEM cianuro de plata *m*; ~ **electrode** *n* LAB *of light* electrodo de plata *m*; ~ **fluoride** *n* CHEM fluoruro de plata *m*; ~ **fog** *n* CINEMAT velo por la plata *m*; ~ **frost** *n* GEOL, METEO helada *f*; ~ **glance** *n* CHEM, MINERAL argentita *f*; ~ **halide** *n* PHOTO haluro de plata *m*; ~ **halide emulsion** *n* PHOTO emulsión de haluro de plata *f*; ~ **iodide** *n* CHEM, PHOTO yoduro de plata *m*; ~~**lead ore** *n* MINE plomo argentífero *m*, plomo de obra *m*; ~ **mine** *n* MINE mina de plata *f*; ~ **nitrate** *n* CHEM nitrato de plata *m*; ~ **oxide** *n* CHEM, ELEC ENG óxido de plata *m*; ~ **oxide battery** *n* ELEC ENG batería de óxido de plata *f*; ~ **oxide cell** *n* ELEC ENG pila de óxido de plata *f*; ~~**oxide storage battery** *n* ELEC ENG, TRANSP batería de acumuladores de óxido-plata *f*; ~~**plated contact** *n* ELEC ENG contacto plateado *m*; ~ **plating** *n* PROD plateado *m*; ~ **recovery** *n* CINEMAT recuperación de plata *f*; ~ **selenide** *n* CHEM seleniuro de plata *m*; ~ **solder** *n* PROD suelda de plata *f*; ~ **staining** *n* C&G manchado con plata *m*; ~~**zinc battery** *n* ELEC ENG batería de plata y zinc *f*; ~~**zinc cell** *n* ELEC ENG pila de plata y zinc *f*; ~~**zinc primary battery** *n* ELEC ENG batería primaria de plata y zinc *f*; ~~**zinc primary cell** *n* ELEC ENG pila primaria de plata y zinc *f*; ~~**zinc storage battery** *n* ELEC ENG batería de acumuladores de plata-zinc *f*, TRANSP batería de acumuladores plata-zinc *f*; ~~**zinc storage cell** *n* ELEC ENG célula de memoria de plata y zinc *f*

silvered: ~ **mica capacitor** *n* ELEC ENG condensador de mica plateada *m*; ~ **mirror** *n* INSTR espejo plateado *m*; ~ **reflector** *n* INSTR reflector plateado *m*

silvering *n* ACOUST plateado *m*, revestimiento de plata *m*, C&G plateado *m*, PROD revestimiento de plata *m*, *mirrors* azogamiento *m*, plateado *m*

silverware *n* FOOD platería *f*

SIM *abbr* (*scanning ion microscopy*) RAD PHYS MIB (*microscopía iónica de barrido*)

sima *n* GEOPHYS cavidad *f*, sima *f*

SIMD: ~ **machine** *n* COMP&DP dispositivo SIMD *m*

similar: ~ **figures** *n pl* GEOM figuras semejantes *f pl*; ~ **fold** *n* GEOL pliegue similar *m*; ~ **folding** *n* PETROL plegamiento similar *m*

SIMM *abbr* (*single in-line memory module*) COMP&DP SIMM (*módulo de memoria de una sola fila alineada, módulo simple de memoria en línea*)

simmer¹ *vti* FOOD, THERMO hervir a fuego lento

simmer² *vi* CHEM *process* ebullir suavemente

simple: ~ **beam** *n* CONST viga simplemente apoyada *f*; ~ **cubic lattice** *n* CRYSTALL red cúbica sencilla *f*; ~ **fraction** *n* MATH fracción común *f*, fracción simple *f*, quebrado común *m*; ~ **harmonic motion** *n* PHYS, WAVE PHYS movimiento armónico simple *m*; ~ **hybrid circuit** *n* ELECTRON circuito híbrido simple *m*; ~~**packaged crystal oscillator** *n* ELEC oscilador de cristal listo para funcionar *m*, ELECTRON oscilador de cristal completo *m*, oscilador de cristal listo para funcionar *m*; ~ **pendulum** *n* PHYS péndulo simple *m*; ~ **rod cylinder** *n* PROD cilindro de varilla única *m*; ~ **shear stress** *n* METALL esfuerzo cortante sencillo *m*

simplex¹ *adj* COMP&DP símplex, TELECOM simple, símplex, unidireccional

simplex²: ~ **lap winding** *n* ELEC devanado imbricado de circuito único *m*, devanado imbricado simple *m*; ~ **operation** *n* COMP&DP funcionamiento simplex *m*

simplified: ~ **representation of center holes** *n* *AmE*, ~ **representation of centre holes** *n* *BrE* MECH ENG *technical drawing* representación simplificada de agujeros de centro *f*

simply: ~~**supported** *adj* CONST simplemente apoyado

SIMS *abbr* (*secondary-ion mass spectrometry*) PHYS espectrometría de masas de iones-secundarios *f*

simulate *vt* COMP&DP, ELECTRON, GAS, RAD PHYS, TELECOM, TRANSP simular

simulated: ~ **event** *n* PART PHYS, RAD PHYS suceso simulado *m*; ~ **speech** *n* TELECOM señal vocal simulada *f*; ~ **watermark** *n* PAPER falsa filigrana *f*

simulation *n* COMP&DP, ELECTRON, GAS simulación *f*; ~ **language** *n* COMP&DP lenguaje de simulación *m*; ~ **program** *n* COMP&DP programa de simulación *m*; ~ **of traffic** *n* TRANSP simulación de tráfico *f*

simulator *n* AIR TRANSP, COMP&DP, ELECTRON, TELECOM simulador *m*

simulcast: ~ **broadcasting** *n* TV radiodifusión simultánea *f*

simultaneity *n* PHYS simultaneidad *f*

simultaneous: ~ **equations** *n pl* MATH ecuaciones simultáneas *f pl*, sistema de ecuaciones *m*; ~ **firing** *n* MINE disparos simultáneos *m pl*; ~ **shot firing** *n* MINE pega simultánea *f*; ~ **system** *n* TRANSP sistema simultáneo *m*

sin *abbr* (*sine*) COMP&DP, CONST, GEOM, MATH *trigonometry* sen (*seno*)

SINAD: ~ **ratio** *n* (*signal-to-noise and distortion ratio*) TELECOM relación SINAD *f* (*relación señal-ruido y distorsión*)

sinapic *adj* CHEM sinápico

sinapine *n* CHEM sinapina *f*

SINCGARS *abbr* (*single channel ground and airborne radio system*) MILIT sistema de radio monocanal terrestre y aéreo *m*

sine *n* (*sin*) COMP&DP, CONST, GEOM, MATH *trigonometry* seno *m* (*sen*); ~ **bar** *n* METR barra de senos *f*, regla de senos *f*; ~ **center** *AmE*, ~ **centre** *BrE n* METR seno central *m*; ~ **curve** *n* MATH sinusoide *f*; ~ **galvanometer** *n* ELEC brújula de senos *f*, PHYS galvanómetro sinusoidal *m*; ~ **rule** *n* GEOM ley de los senos *f*, regla del seno *f*; ~ **table** *n* MECH *of measuring instrument* tabla senoidal *f*; ~ **wave** *n* ACOUST, ELEC, ELECTRON, PHYS, WAVE PHYS onda senoidal *f*, onda sinusoidal *f*; ~ **wave convergence** *n* TV convergencia de la onda senoidal *f*; ~ **wave modulation** *n* ELECTRON modulación de onda sinusoidal *f*; ~ **wave oscillator** *n* ELECTRON oscilador de onda sinusoidal *m*; ~ **wave tuning** *n* ELECTRON sintonización de onda sinusoidal *f*

singe *vt* TEXTIL chamuscar

singeing *n* TEXTIL chamuscado *m*, gaseado *m*; ~ **machine** *n* TEXTIL chamuscadora *f*

singing *n* ELECTRON ondas sinusoidales *f pl*, oscilación parásita *f*, PETR TECH ondas sinusoidales *f pl*; ~ **point** *n* ELECTRON amplificación máxima *f*, punto de cebado *m*

single[1]: ~**-colored** *AmE*, ~**-coloured** *BrE adj* COLOUR de un solo color; ~**-cotton-covered** *adj* (*SCC*) ELEC forrado con una capa de algodón; ~**-hull** *adj* WATER TRANSP *vessel* de un solo casco, monocasco; ~**-layer** *adj* COATINGS de capa única, de una sola capa; ~**-paper-covered** *adj* (*SPC*) ELEC forrado con una capa de papel; ~**-phase** *adj* ELEC, ELEC ENG monofásico; ~**-pole** *adj* ELEC de un solo polo, monopolar, unipolar, TV unipolar; ~**-rubber-covered** *adj* (*SRC*) ELEC forrado con una capa de caucho

single[2]:

~ a ~ **acoustic source** *n* ACOUST fuente acústica única *f*; ~ **acting compressor** *n* REFRIG compresor de simple efecto *m*; ~ **acting servomotor** *n* FUELLESS servomotor de efecto simple *m*; ~ **address** *n* COMP&DP direccional único *m*, dirección simple *f*, dirección única *f*; ~**-address instruction** *n* COMP&DP instrucción de dirección única *f*; ~**-aisle aircraft** *n* AIR TRANSP avión de fuselaje estrecho *m*, avión de pasillo único *m*; ~**-angle cutter** *n* MECH ENG fresa cónica *f*, herramienta de ángulo fijo *f*; ~**-angular cutter** *n* MECH ENG fresa cónica *f*; ~**-anode rectifier** *n* ELEC ENG rectificador unianodal *m*; ~**-anode tube** *n* ELECTRON tubo de un solo ánodo *m*;

~ b ~ **bag** *n* PROD saco único *m*; ~**-balanced mixer** *n* ELECTRON mezclador monocompensado *m*; ~**-bath developer** *n* PHOTO revelador de baño único *m*; ~**-bay enclosure** *n* PROD encerramiento de una sola nave *m*; ~**-beam cathode ray tube** *n* ELECTRON tubo de rayos catódicos de un solo haz *m*; ~**-beam spectrophotometer** *n* RAD PHYS espectrofotómetro de haz simple *m*; ~**-beam tube** *n* ELECTRON tubo de un solo haz *m*; ~ **bituminous surface treatment** *n* (*SBST*) CONST tratamiento superficial bituminoso simple *m*; ~ **blackwall hitch** *n* WATER TRANSP vuelta de gancho simple *f*; ~ **blade shutter** *n* CINEMAT obturador de laminilla simple *m*; ~**-blast circular bellows** *n pl* MECH ENG fuelle circular de ráfaga única *m*; ~**-bolt clamping** *n* PROD fijación a perno simple *f*; ~**-break contact** *n* ELEC ENG contacto unipolar *m*; ~ **broad** *n* CINEMAT batería de lámparas simples *f*; ~**-buoy mooring** *n* (*SBM*) PETR TECH anclaje a boya simple *m* (*SBM*);

~ c ~**-camera extension** *n* PHOTO extensión de

cámara única *f*; ~**-channel amplifier** *n* ELECTRON amplificador de un solo canal *m*; ~**-channel carrier** *n* SPACE portadora monocanal *f*; ~ **channel ground and airborne radio system** *n* (*SINCGARS*) MILIT sistema de radio monocanal terrestre y aéreo *m*; ~ **channel per carrier** *n* (*SCPC*) SPACE un solo canal por portadora *m* (*SCPC*), TELECOM canal único por portadora *m* (*SCPC*), portadora monocanal *f* (*SCPC*), un solo canal por portadora *m* (*SCPC*); ~**-channel protocol** *n* COMP&DP protocolo de canal único *m*; ~**-coated paper** *n* PAPER papel estucado por una cara *m*; ~**-coil latching relay** *n* ELEC ENG relé de enlace unipolar *m*; ~**-conductor cable** *n* ELEC, ELEC ENG cable monoconductor *m*, cable monofilar *m*; ~**-conductor wire** *n* PROD cable monofilar *m*; ~**-cord switchboard** *n* TELECOM conmutador manual de monocordio *m*; ~**-core cable** *n* ELEC, ELEC ENG cable monoconductor *m*, cable monofilar *m*; ~**-crop farming** *n* AmE AGRIC cultivo en surco único *m*; ~ **crystal** *n* CRYSTALL, ELECTRON monocristal *m*; ~**-crystal growth** *n* ELECTRON ampliación de un solo cristal *f*; ~**-crystal semiconductor** *n* ELECTRON semiconductor de un solo cristal *m*; ~**-cylinder engine** *n* MECH ENG motor de cilindro único *m*, motor monocilíndrico *m*;

~ d ~ **day tide** *n* WATER TRANSP marea diurna *f*; ~**-decked pallet** *n* TRANSP bandeja sencilla *f*, paleta sencilla *f*, pálet sencillo *m* (*AmL*); ~**-decked ship** *n* WATER TRANSP buque de una cubierta *m*; ~ **delivery** *n* PROD entrega única *f*; ~ **diamond crossing with slips** *n* RAIL cruzamiento oblicuo con superficie de deslizamiento *m*; ~**-diffusion process** *n* ELECTRON proceso de difusión única *m*; ~ **digit dialing** *AmE*, ~ **digit dialling** *BrE n* TELECOM discado de dígito único *m*; ~**-distributor line-composing machine** *n* PRINT compositora para líneas de simple distribución *f*; ~**-distributor machine** *n* PRINT máquina de simple distribución *f*; ~ **drive circuit** *n* ELEC ENG circuito de accionamiento individual *m*; ~ **dry plate clutch** *n* AUTO embrague de disco único en seco *m*;

~ e ~ **earth** *n* BrE (*cf single ground AmE*) ELEC conductor de tierra único *m*; ~ **effect evaporator** *n* FOOD evaporador de efecto único *m*; ~**-element shipping cask** *n* NUCL contenedor de transporte para un único elemento de combustible *m*; ~**-end sizing** *n* TEXTIL encolado de un solo cabo *m*; ~**-ended amplifier** *n* ELECTRON amplificador sin transformador de salida *m*; ~**-ended crystal mixer** *n* ELECTRON mezclador de cristal de un solo frente *m*; ~**-ended operation** *n* PROD operación con terminación única *f*; ~**-ended output** *n* ELEC ENG salida asimétrica *f*; ~**-ended spanner** *n* MECH llave de boca única *f*, MECH ENG llave de boca única *f*, llave inglesa de horquilla *f*, llave sencilla *f*; ~**-ended tube** *n* ELECTRON tubo con una sola salida *m*; ~ **escape peak** *n* RAD PHYS pico de fugas simple *m*; ~**-expansion engine** *n* MECH ENG motor de expansión única *m*;

~ f ~**-faced pallet** *n* PACK paleta sencilla *f*, plataforma de carga sencilla *f*, pálet sencillo *m* (*AmL*), TRANSP bandeja de una sola cara *f*, paleta con separación desmontable *f*, paleta de una sola cara *f*, pálet con separación desmontable *m* (*AmL*), pálet de una sola cara *m* (*AmL*); ~ **feeder** *n* ELEC alimentador único *m*; ~**-fiber cable** *AmE see single-fibre cable BrE*; ~**-fiber line** *AmE see single-fibre line BrE*; ~**-fibre cable** *n* BrE ELEC ENG cable conductor de una fibra *m*, cable monofibra *m*; **~-fibre line** *n* BrE ELEC línea monofibra *f*, ELEC ENG línea de fibra única *f*, línea monofibra *f*; **~-flanged traveling wheel** *AmE*, **~-flanged travelling wheel** *BrE n* MECH ENG rueda de traslación de pestaña única *f*; **~ flotation** *n* COAL flotación única *f*; **~-flue boiler** *n* PROD caldera de un conducto de humos *f*; **~ frame** *n* CINEMAT cuadro individual *m*, fotograma único *m*, TV fotograma único *m*; **~-frame filming** *n* CINEMAT filmación fotograma a fotograma *f*; **~-frequency laser** *n* ELECTRON, TELECOM láser de frecuencia única *m*; **~-frequency operation** *n* TELECOM operación en una frecuencia *f*;

~ g **~-geared lathe** *n* MECH ENG torno de velocidad única *m*; **~-gob feeding** *n* (*cf single-gob process AmE*) C&G alimentación de vela sencilla *f*, alimentador de cavidad simple *m*, proceso de alimentación de vela sencilla *m*; **~-gob process** *n AmE* (*cf single-gob feeding BrE*) C&G alimentador de cavidad simple *m*, proceso de alimentación de vela sencilla *m*; **~-grid tube** *n* ELECTRON tubo de rejilla única *m*; **~ ground** *n AmE* (*cf single earth BrE*) ELEC conductor de tierra único *m*; **~-gun storage tube** *n* ELECTRON tubo de almacenamiento de un solo cañón *m*;

~ h **~ head system** *n* PACK, PROD sistema de cabeza simple *m*; **~-heterojunction laser diode** *n* ELECTRON diodo de láser en monohetero-unión *m*;

~ i **~ impression mold** *AmE*, **~ impression mould** *BrE n* MECH ENG molde de impresión única *m*; **~ inlet fan** *n* MECH ENG ventilador de un oído *m*, ventilador de una entrada *m*, REFRIG ventilador de un oído *m*; **~ in-line memory module** *n* (*SIMM*) COMP&DP módulo de memoria de una sola fila alineada *m* (*SIMM*), módulo simple de memoria en línea *m* (*SIMM*); **~ in-line package** *n* (*SIP*) COMP&DP pastilla de una fila de conexiones *f*, ELECTRON encapsulado con una sola línea de conexiones *m*, monobloque en serie *m* (*MBS*);

~ j **~ jersey** *n* TEXTIL tejido de punto de una fontura *m*; **~-jet injection nozzle** *n* AUTO boquilla de inyección de surtidor único *f*;

~ l **~-layer ceramic capacitor** *n* ELEC ENG condensador cerámico de una sola capa *m*; **~-layer film** *n* CINEMAT película de capa simple *f*; **~-leaf damper** *n* REFRIG registro de persiana simple *m*; **~ lens** *n* PHOTO lente acromática *f*; **~-lens reflex camera** *n* (*SLR*) PHOTO cámara reflex con objetivo acromático *f*, cámara reflex de un objetivo *f*; **~-level masking structure** *n* ELECTRON estructura de enmascaramiento de un solo nivel *f*; **~-level polysilicon process** *n* ELECTRON proceso de polisilicio de un solo nivel *m*; **~-level resonance** *n* NUCL resonancia a un solo nivel *f*; **~-line diagram** *n* ELEC diagrama unilineal *m*, esquema unifilar *m*, esquema unilineal *m*; **~-line token** *n* RAIL señal de vía única *f*; **~-line working** *n* RAIL circulación en vía única *f*; **~ linear inductor motor** *n* (*SLIM*) ELEC, TRANSP motor inductor lineal simple *m*; **~ lock** *n* HYDROL esclusa *f*; **~-longitudinal mode** *n* (*SLM*) TELECOM modo longitudinal único *m*;

~ m **~ Matthew Walker** *n* WATER TRANSP *knot* piña de acollador *f*; **~-mode cable** *n* ELEC ENG cable unimodal *m*; **~-mode fiber** *AmE*, **~-mode fibre** *BrE n* OPT, TELECOM fibra monomodo *f*; **~-mode optical fiber** *AmE*, **~-mode optical fibre** *BrE n* ELEC ENG fibra óptica unimodal *f*, OPT, TELECOM fibra

óptica monomodo *f*; **~-mode optical integrated circuit** *n* ELECTRON circuito integrado óptico de una sola función *m*; **~ and multilayer glass** *n* SAFE vidrio de una o varias capas *m*;

~ n **~-notch joint** *n* CONST *carpentry* junta de mortaja única *f*;

~ o **~-output power supply** *n* ELEC, ELEC ENG alimentación de energía de salida única *f*; **~-output switching power supply** *n* ELEC, ELEC ENG fuente conmutada de salida única *f*; **~ overlap** *n* MECH ENG superposición única *f*;

~ p **~-pair cable** *n* ELEC ENG cable de par único *m*; **~ perforation film** *n* CINEMAT película de perforaciones simples *f*; **~-phase bridge rectifier** *n* ELEC rectificador monofásico en puente *m*; **~-phase current** *n* CINEMAT, ELEC ENG corriente monofásica *f*; **~-phase electric current** *n* CONST corriente eléctrica monofásica *f*, corriente eléctrica monopolar *f*; **~-phase induction motor** *n* ELEC ENG motor de inducción monofásico *m*; **~-phase machine** *n* ELEC ENG máquina monofásica *f*; **~-phase motor** *n* ELEC, ELEC ENG motor monofásico *m*; **~-phase supply** *n* ELEC, ELEC ENG suministro monofásico *m*; **~-phase transformer** *n* ELEC, ELEC ENG transformador monofásico *m*; **~-phase winding** *n* ELEC ENG devanado monofásico *m*; **~ pilot instrument rating** *n* AIR TRANSP habilitación de vuelo por instrumentos para piloto único *f*; **~-pitch roof** *n* CONST tejado a un agua *m*, tejado de vertiente simple *m*; **~ plane iron** *n* CONST hierro en una capa *m*; **~-plate rudder** *n* WATER TRANSP timón de plancha sencilla *m*; **~-platform pallet** *n* TRANSP bandeja de un solo tablero *f*, paleta de un solo tablero *f*, pálet un solo tablero *m* (*AmL*); **~-ply board** *n* PAPER cartón de una capa *m*; **~-point bonding** *n* ELEC conexión de una sola punta *f*; **~-point mooring** *n* PETR TECH amarre simple *m*; **~-pole double-throw switch** *n* (*SPDT switch*) ELEC conmutador de simple polo doble tiro *m*, conmutador de un circuito y dos direcciones *m*, conmutador de un polo y dos vías *m*, ELEC ENG conmutador unipolar *m*, interruptor unipolar de doble vano *m*; **~-pole single-throw relay** *n* (*SPST relay*) ELEC ENG relé de acción unipolar *m*, relé unipolar con contacto de cambio *m*, relé unipolar de doble vano *m*, relé unipolar y univanal *m*; **~-pole single-throw switch** *n* (*SPST switch*) ELEC ENG interruptor simple *m*, interruptor unipolar y univanal *m*; **~-pole switch** *n* ELEC conmutador de un polo *m*, conmutador monopolar *m*, conmutador unipolar *m*, ELEC ENG conmutador monofásico *m*; **~ portion** *n* FOOD porción individual *f*; **~ portion packaging machine** *n* PACK embaladora de porciones simples *f*; **~ precision** *n* COMP&DP precisión sencilla *f*, precisión simple *f*; **~ primary-type linear motor** *n* TRANSP motor lineal primario simple *m*; **~-processor common-control system** *n* TELECOM sistema con procesador único y control común *m*; **~ pulse** *n* ELECTRON pulso aislado *m*; **~-pulse signal** *n* ELECTRON señal de un solo impulso *f*;

~ r **~-riveted butt joint** *n* CONST junta de soldadura a tope con remache único *f*; **~-riveted lap joint** *n* CONST junta con recubrimiento de remache único *f*; **~ rotor** *n* AIR TRANSP rotor único *m*;

~ s **~ scan key** *n* PROD tecla de ciclo único *f*; **~-screw ship** *n* WATER TRANSP buque de una sola hélice *m*; **~-seated valve** *n* HYDRAUL válvula de asiento sencillo *f*; **~-section filter** *n* ELECTRON filtro de una sola sección *m*; **~-segment message** *n* (*SSM*) TELECOM mensaje de segmento único *m* (*SSM*); **~-server queue** *n* TELECOM cola de un solo servidor *f*; **~-sheet thickness** *n* PAPER espesor de una sola hoja *m*; **~-side claw** *n* CINEMAT garfio lateral simple *m*; **~ sideband** *n* (*SSB*) ELECTRON, PHYS, TELECOM, TV banda lateral única *f* (*BLU*); **~-sideband filter** *n* ELECTRON filtro de una sola banda lateral *m*; **~-sideband modulation** *n* ELECTRON modulación de una sola banda lateral *f*; **~-sideband modulator** *n* ELECTRON modulador de una sola banda lateral *m*; **~-sideband signal** *n* ELECTRON señal de una sola banda lateral *f*; **~-sideband transmission** *n* PHYS transmisión por banda lateral única *f*, TELECOM transmisión por banda lateral única *f*, transmisión por una banda lateral *f*, TV transmisión por una banda lateral *f*, transmisión por banda lateral única *f*; **~-sided disc** *BrE*, **~-sided disk** *AmE* OPT disco de una sola cara *m*; **~-sided disk** *n* COMP&DP disco de un solo lado *m*, disco de una sola cara *m*, OPT *see single-sided disc BrE*; **~-sided distribution frame** *n* TELECOM repartidor de una sola cara *m*; **~-sided printed circuit** *n* ELECTRON circuito impreso a una sola cara *m*, circuito impreso unilateral *m*; **~-size gravel aggregate** *n* CONST árido de tamaño uniforme *m*; **~ slot** *n* PROD monorranura *f*; **~-slot module** *n* PROD módulo de ranura simple *m*; **~-stage amplifier** *n* ELEC, ELECTRON amplificador de una sola etapa *m*, amplificador de una sola fase *m*; **~-stage compression** *n* HYDRAUL, REFRIG compresión en escalonamiento *f*, compresión simple *f*; **~-stage compressor** *n* HYDRAUL compresor de una sola etapa *m*, compresor monocompresional *m*; **~-stage pumping** *n* MINE agotamiento en una sola fase *m*; **~-stage turbine** *n* HYDRAUL turbina monoepática *f*, turbina monoexpansiva *f*; **~-stamp mill** *n* PROD *ore stamp* bocarte de pilón simple *m*; **~-step operation** *n* COMP&DP operación de un solo paso *f*; **~-stroke lever** *n* PHOTO control unidireccional *m*; **~ stud** *n* PROD *founding* soporte sencillo *m*; **~ supply** *n* ELEC ENG alimentación simple *f*, alimentación única *f*, suministro único *m*; **~-supply voltage** *n* ELEC ENG voltaje de suministro único *m*; **~ system** *n* CINEMAT sistema simple *m*;

~ t **~ tackle** *n* PROD polipasto simple *m*; **~-thickness sheet glass** *n* *BrE* (*cf single-thickness window glass AmE*) C&G vidrio plano sencillo *m*; **~-thickness window glass** *n* *AmE* (*cf single-thickness sheet glass BrE*) C&G vidrio plano sencillo *m*; **~-threaded screw** *n* MECH ENG tornillo de entrada única *m*, tornillo de hilo único *m*; **~-throw relay** *n* ELEC ENG relé unipolar *m*; **~-throw switch** *n* ELEC ENG interruptor de vía única *m*, PHYS interruptor de disparo único *m*; **~-track line** *n* RAIL línea de vía única *f*; **~-trip bottle** *n* C&G botella no retornable *f*; **~ turn encoder** *n* PROD codificador de vuelta simple *m*; **~-type composing and casting machine** *n* PRINT máquina de fundición y de composición simple *f*;

~ u **~-user access** *n* COMP&DP, TELECOM acceso para un solo usuario *m*;

~ w **~-wave rectification** *n* ELEC rectificación de una alternancia *f*, rectificación de una onda *f*, rectificación monofásica *f*; **~-way modulator** *n* ELEC modulador de una dirección *m*, modulador de una

vía *m*; **~-way rectifier** *n* ELEC rectificador de una dirección *m*, rectificador de una vía *m*; **~-weight paper** *n* PHOTO papel de soporte delgado *m*; **~-wire cable conductor** *n* ELEC conductor de cable unifilar *m*, conductor sencillo *m*; **~-wire system** *n* ELEC sistema monofilar *m*, sistema unifilar *m*

single[3]: **~ up** *vt* WATER TRANSP *mooring line, ropes* aligerar

singled: **~ module** *n* PROD módulo simple *m*

singlet *n* NUCL, PHYS *of ship* singlete *m*

singularity *n* PHYS singularidad *f*

sinistral: **~ fault** *n* GEOL falla en dirección siniestral *f*, PETR TECH falla siniestra *f*

sink[1] *n* COMP&DP receptor *m*, sumidero de calor *m* (*AmL*), ELEC ENG perforación *f*, disipador *m*, GEOL depresión *f*, HYDRAUL sumidero *m*, METALL cavidad *f*, MINE cono de avance *m*, depresión *f* (*AmL*), hoyada *f* (*AmL*), hundimiento *m*, perforación descendente *f*, POLL colector *m*, pozo *m*, resumidero *m* (*AmL*), sumidero *m* (*Esp*), vertedero *m*; **~ hole** *n* CONST sumidero *m*, GEOL dolina *f*, hayada *f*, MINE colector de agua *m*, dolina *f*, embudo de contracción *m*, hayada *f*, rechupe *m*, sumidero *m*; **~ trap** *n* HYDROL colector de sumidero *m*

sink[2] *vt* CONST hundir

sink[3] *vi* MINE asentarse, WATER TRANSP irse a pique

sinkage *n* PRINT cortesía *f*, WATER TRANSP incremento de carena *m*

sinker *n* TEXTIL platina *f*; **~ bar** *n* MINE barra de hinca *f*, barra maestra *f*, barra perforadora *f*, barra unida al cable *f*, TEXTIL barra de platinas *f*

sinking *n* MINE abertura *f*, profundización *f*, subsidencia *f*, hundimiento *m*, PROD *casting* asentamiento *m*; **~ agent** *n* MAR POLL agente hundidor *m*; **~ head** *n* PROD *founding* mazarota *f*; **~ trestle** *n* COAL cuadro de pozo *m*

sinter[1] *n* GEOL incrustación sobre rocas *f*; **~ terrace** *n* GEOPHYS terraza sinterizada *f*

sinter[2] *vt* CHEM, CHEM TECH, COAL sinterizar

sintered[1] *adj* CHEM, CHEM TECH, COAL sinterizado, MECH aglomerado, sinterizado

sintered[2]: **~ anode** *n* ELEC ENG ánodo sinterizado *m*; **~ brake** *n* RAIL freno sinterizado *m*; **~ density ratio** *n* CHEM TECH relación de densidades de sinterizado *f*; **~ glass** *n* C&G vidrio sinterizado *m*; **~ glass filter crucible** *n* LAB crisol de Gooch *m*, crisol de filtro de vidrio sinterizado *m*; **~ glass filter funnel** *n* LAB embudo de filtro de vidrio sinterizado *m*; **~ hard metal pellet** *n* MECH ENG nódulo de metal duro sinterizado *m*; **~ metal material** *n* MECH ENG material de metal sinterizado *m*; **~ refractory** *n* C&G refractario sinterizado *m*

sintering *n* C&G sinterizado *m*, CHEM TECH sinterización *f*, sinterizado *m*, COAL aglomeración *f*, aglutinación *f*, sinterización *f*, sinterizado *m*, HEAT, METALL sinterización *f*, RAIL sinterizante *m*, TELECOM sinterización *f*; **~ activator** *n* CHEM TECH activador de la sinterización *m*; **~ coal** *n* COAL, MINE carbón sinterizado *m*, hulla grasa de llama larga *f*, hulla semigrasa *f*; **~ density** *n* CHEM TECH densidad de sinterización *f*; **~ furnace** *n* CHEM TECH horno de sinterización *m*, mufla de sinterización *f*; **~ and infiltration technique** *n* CHEM TECH técnica de sinterizado e infiltración *f*; **~ inhibitor** *n* CHEM TECH inhibidor de la sinterización *m*; **~ pan** *n* CHEM TECH cuba de sinterización *f*; **~ plant** *n* CHEM TECH planta de sinterización *f*; ~ **platform** *n* CHEM TECH plataforma de sinterización *f*; ~ **powder** *n* CHEM TECH polvo sinterizante *m*; ~ **technique** *n* CHEM TECH técnica de sinterización *f*; ~ **temperature** *n* CHEM TECH temperatura de sinterización *f*; ~ **time** *n* CHEM TECH tiempo de sinterización *m*; ~ **under pressure** *n* CHEM TECH sinterización a presión *f*

sinusoid *n* COMP&DP, GEOM, MATH sinusoide *f*

sinusoidal[1] *adj* GEN senoidal, sinusoidal

sinusoidal[2]: ~ **conditions** *n pl* ELEC ENG condiciones sinusoidales *f pl*; ~ **current** *n* ELEC ENG, PHYS corriente sinusoidal *f*; ~ **field** *n* ELEC ENG campo sinusoidal *m*; ~ **function** *n* ELEC ENG, MATH función sinusoidal *f*; ~ **motion** *n* PHYS movimiento sinusoidal *m*; ~ **oscillation** *n* ELECTRON oscilación sinusoidal *f*; ~ **quantity** *n* ELEC ENG, ELECTRON cantidad sinusoidal *f*; ~ **signal** *n* ELECTRON, TELECOM señal sinusoidal *f*; ~ **-signal generator** *n* ELECTRON generador de señales sinusoidales *m*; ~ **voltage** *n* ELEC ENG tensión sinusoidal *f*, PHYS voltaje sinusoidal *m*; ~ **wave** *n* ACOUST, ELEC, ELECTRON, PHYS onda senoidal *f*, onda sinusoidal *f*

SIO *abbr* (*series input-output*) COMP&DP SIO (*entrada-salida en serie, entrada-salida secuencial*)

SIP *abbr* (*single in-line package*) COMP&DP pastilla de una fila de conexiones *f*, ELECTRON MBS (*monobloque en serie*)

siphon *AmE see* syphon *BrE*

sipping *n* NUCL detección de fugas por recogida y análisis de los gases de escape *f*

sire *n* AGRIC semental *m*

siren *n* PROD, SAFE, WATER TRANSP sirena *f*

sisal *n* WATER TRANSP sisal *m*; ~ **rope** *n* MECH ENG cable de henequén *m*, cuerda de sisal *f*, soga de sisal *f*

SISD: ~ **machine** *n* COMP&DP dispositivo SISD *m*

sister: ~ **ship** *n* WATER TRANSP buque con las mismas características *m*, buque de iguales características *m*, buque gemelo *m*

site[1]: ~ **-delivered** *adj* CONST entregado en obra

site[2]: **on** ~ *adv* CONST del lugar; en el lugar, en el emplazamiento, in situ

site[3] *n* CONST obra *f*; ~ **code** *n* PACK código de situación *m*; ~ **concrete** *n* CONST concreto mezclado en obra *m* (*AmL*), hormigón mezclado en obra *m* (*Esp*); ~ **criteria** *n pl* POLL criterio de emplazamiento *m*, criterio de situación *m*, criterio de ubicación *m*; ~ **diversity** *n* SPACE emplazamiento variado *m*; ~ **emergency plan** *n* NUCL plan de emergencia de la central *m*, plan de emergencia del emplazamiento *m*; ~ **meeting** *n* CONST reunión a pie de obra *f*, reunión en la obra *f*; ~ **weld** *n* NUCL soldadura en obra *f*

situ[1]: **in** ~ *adv* CONST, MECH en el mismo sitio, in situ

situ[2]: **in** ~ **combustion** *n* PETR TECH combustión in situ *f*; **in** ~ **concrete** *n* CONST concreto fabricado a pie de obra *m* (*AmL*), concreto in situ *m* (*AmL*), hormigón fabricado a pie de obra *m* (*Esp*), hormigón in situ *m* (*Esp*); **in** ~ **monitoring** *n* NUCL monitorización in situ *f*; **in** ~ **pile** *n* COAL carbón autóctono *m*

six: ~ **carbon ring** *n* CHEM anillo de seis carbonos *m*; ~ **-channel monitor** *n* INSTR monitor de seis canales *m*, monitor de seis pistas *m*; ~ **-fold rotation axis** *n* CRYSTALL eje de rotación senario *m*; ~ **-membered ring** *n* CHEM anillo de seis miembros *m*; ~ **-phase current** *n* ELEC ENG corriente exafásica *f*; ~ **-phase**

rectifier *n* ELEC ENG rectificador exafásico *m*; ~ **-ply belting** *n* PROD correas de seis pliegues *f pl*

sixmo *n* PRINT pliego doblado para formar seis hojas *m*

sixteenmo *n* PRINT dieciseisavo *m*

sixth[1] *n* ACOUST sexta *f*

size[1] *n* GEN apresto *m*, cola *f*, talla *f*; ~ **bath** *n* TEXTIL baño de apresto *m*; ~ **circulator unit** *n* TEXTIL dispositivo para circular la cola *m*; ~ **color** *AmE*, ~ **colour** *BrE n* COLOUR color de apresto *m*, colorante de apresto *m*; ~ **distribution** *n* COAL distribución por tamaños *f*; ~ **fraction** *n* COAL fraccionado por tamaños *m*; ~ **grading** *n* C&G, COAL clasificación por tamaños *f*; ~ **paint** *n* COLOUR pintura de apresto *f*; ~ **press** *n* PAPER prensa encoladora *f*; ~ **-press coated paper** *n* PAPER papel estucado en prensa encoladora *m*; ~ **-press coating** *n* PAPER estucado en prensa encoladora *m*; ~ **-press pigmented coated paper** *n* PAPER papel pigmentado en prensa encoladora *m*; ~ **reduction** *n* CHEM TECH reducción de tamaño *f*; ~ **roll** *n* PAPER rodillo encolador *m*

size[2] *vt* COAL ajustar, calibrar, clasificar por dimensiones, TEXTIL encolar

size[3]: **be to** ~ *phr* CONST tener la medida

sized: ~ **coal** *n* COAL carbón clasificado *m*; ~ **ice** *n* REFRIG hielo calibrado *m*; ~ **paper** *n* PAPER papel encolado *m*; ~ **rolled flat iron** *n* METALL plancha pasada por rodillos conformados *f*; ~ **warp** *n* TEXTIL urdimbre encolada *f*

sizing *n* COAL calibración *f*, clasificación *f*, dimensionamiento *m*, granulometría *f*, COMP&DP ajuste de dimensión *m*, dimensionamiento *m*, METR calibrado *m*, PACK clasificación volumétrica *f*, PAPER encolado *m*, TEXTIL apresto *m*, encolado *m*; ~ **agent** *n* CHEM, COLOUR agente de apresto *m*, TEXTIL agente encolador *m*; ~ **machine** *n* TEXTIL encoladora *f*; ~ **preparation** *n* COLOUR preparación de apresto *f*; ~ **screen** *n* PROD criba clasificadora *f*; ~ **tester** *n* PAPER aparato para medir el grado de encolado *m*

skatole *n* CHEM escatol *m*

skatolecarboxylic *adj* CHEM escatolcarboxílico

skatoxysulfate *AmE see* skatoxysulphate *BrE*

skatoxysulfuric *AmE see* skatoxysulphuric *BrE*

skatoxysulphate *n BrE* CHEM escatoxisulfato *m*

skatoxysulphuric *adj BrE* CHEM escatoxisulfúrico

skeg *n* WATER TRANSP *boat building* aleta de popa *f*, enquilladura *f*, falso codaste *m*, zapata *f*

skeletal: ~ **coding** *n* COMP&DP codificación esquemática *f*, código esquemático *m*

skeleton *n* CONST armazón *m*; ~ **black** *n* PRINT diapositiva negra *f*; ~ **container** *n* TRANSP contenedor con armadura *m*; ~ **girder** *n* CONST viga de armazón *f*

skene: ~ **arch** *n* CONST arco escarzano *m*, arco rebajado *m*

sketch *n* CONST boceto *m*, croquis *m*, esbozo *m*, trazado *m*

skew[1] *adj* COMP&DP sesgado, CONST oblicuo, sesgado

skew[2] *n* COMP&DP inclinación *f*, PETR TECH desalineamiento *m*, TV distorsión oblicua *f*; ~ **bridge** *n* CONST puente oblicuo *m*; ~ **error** *n* TV error de distorsión oblicua *m*; ~ **ray** *n* OPT rayo no meridional *m*, TELECOM rayo oblicuo *m*, rayo sesgado *m*

skew[3] *vt* PRINT escalonar la composición

skewed: ~ **curve** *n* GEOM curva alabeada *f*, curva oblicua *f*

skewing *n* CONST posición oblicua *f*, sesgadura *f*, sesgo *m*

skewness *n* CONST, GEOM oblicuidad *f*

skiatron *n* ELECTRON skiatrón *m*

skid[1] *n* MECH patín *m*, zapata de aterrizaje *f*, PETR TECH paquete *m*, patín *m*, skid *m*, TRANSP calzo *m*; **~ base** *n* PACK base de calzo *f*; **~ pad** *n* VEH calzo *m*; **~ track** *n* CONST deslizadera *f*; **~ wire** *n* ELEC alambre deslizante *m*

skid[2] *vt* AIR TRANSP, TRANSP patinar

skid[3] *vi* VEH derrapar, patinar

skidder *n* TRANSP carretilla *f*

skidding *n* AIR TRANSP deslizamiento *m*, patinazo *m*, TRANSP, VEH patinazo *m*; **~ conditions** *n pl* TRANSP condiciones de deslizamiento *f pl*

skidproof *adj* CHEM antideslizante

skim[1] *n* PROD desperdicios *m pl*, escoria *f*; **~ bar** *n* C&G barra desnatadora *f*; **~ gate** *n* PROD *founding* bebedero de despumar *m*, cámara de depuración *f*

skim[2] *vt* PROD despumar, espumar; **~ off** *vt* POLL desescoriar, desnatar, espumar, PROD desescoriar, despumar, espumar

skimmed: **~ latex** *n* P&R látex desescoriado *m*, látex filtrado *m*; **~ milk powder** *n* FOOD leche en polvo descremada *f*

skimmer *n* AGRIC raedera *f*, C&G desnatador *m*, MAR POLL espumadera *f*, rasera *f*, PETR TECH limpiador de gas *m*, POLL desescoriador *m*, desnatador *m*, espumador *m*, succionador *m*, PROD *blast furnace casting* desescoriador *m*, espumadera *f*, sifón espumador *m*, succionador *m*; **~ block** *n* C&G bloque desnatador *m*; **~ missile** *n* MILIT misil de trayectoria rasante *m*

skimming *n* C&G, FOOD desnatado *m*, PROD desescoriado *m*, despumación *f*, espumado *m*; **~ barge** *n* MAR POLL gabarra de limpieza con rasera *f*; **~ barrier** *n* MAR POLL barrera superficial *f*; **~ chamber** *n* PROD *founding* cámara de depuración *f*; **~ head** *n* MAR POLL cabeza de la rasera *f*; **~ ladle** *n* PROD cuchara espumadora *f*; **~ rod** *n* C&G barra desnatadora *f*

skin[1] *n* AIR TRANSP revestimiento del avión *m*, superficie *f*, COAL corteza *f*, costra *f*, cáscara *f*, piel *f*, P&R capa exterior delgada *f*, película membranosa *f*, SPACE capa exterior *f*, corteza *f*, envuelta *f*, revestimiento metálico *m*, WATER TRANSP forro *m*; **~ blemish** *n* FOOD marca de piel *f* ; **~ blister** *n* C&G ampolla de superficie *f*; **~ cream** *n* SAFE crema para la piel *f*; **~ depth** *n* PHYS profundidad de la corteza *f*; **~ dive** *n* OCEAN buceo *m*; **~ diving** *n* OCEAN buceo sin traje *m*; **~-drying** *n* PROD *founding* secado superficial *m*; **~ effect** *n* AIR TRANSP efecto Kelvin *m*, efecto de superficie *f*, ELEC ENG efecto Kelvin *m*, efecto pelicular *m*, PETR TECH efecto pelicular *m*, PETROL, PHYS efecto superficial *m*; **~ film** *n* PACK película para termoconformar *f*; **~ friction** *n* PHYS rozamiento laminar *m*; **~ pack** *n* PACK paquete termoconformado *m*; **~ resistance** *n* COAL resistencia friccional *f*; **~-to-skin timbering** *n* MINE entibación adosada *f*, entibado adosado *m* (*AmL*), entibado ajustado *m* (*Esp*), entibado hasta el frente de ataque *m*

skin[2] *vt* OCEAN *fish* despellejar

skinning *n* PROD *founding* desescoriado *m*

skip[1] *n* COMP&DP omisión *f*, salto *m*, MAR POLL cajón *m*, volquete *m*, TRANSP *cranes* cajón *m*, cesta *f*, cubo *m*, cucharón *m*; **~ distance** *n* WAVE PHYS distancia de salto *f*, zona de silencio *f*; **~ extraction** *n* COAL extracción intermitente *f*; **~ lorry** *n* BrE (*cf skip truck AmE*) MAR POLL camión portavolquetes *m*, TRANSP camión de caja basculante *m*, camión-espuerta *m*; **~ truck** *n* AmE (*cf skip lorry BrE*) MAR POLL camión portavolquetes *m*, TRANSP camión de caja basculante *m*, camión-espuerta *m*; **~ wagon** *n* RAIL vagón tolva *m*; **~-winding system** *n* MINE sistema de extracción no continua *m*

skip[2] *vt* CINEMAT *frame*, PRINT saltar

skirt *n* C&G faldón *m*, CONST faldón *m*, guardaaguas *m*, MAR POLL falda *f*, faldilla *f*, MILIT *of rocket* falda *f*, TRANSP plinto *m*; **~ board** *n* CONST *carpentry* tabla delantal *f*

skirting *n* CONST *carpentry* zócalo *m*; **~ board** *n* BrE (*cf base board AmE, mopboard AmE*) CONST *carpentry* rodapié *m*, zócalo *m*

skiver *n* PRINT cuchilla de encuadernador *f*

skull *n* PROD *founding* fondo de cuchara *m*, lobo *m*

skutterudite *n* MINERAL skutedurita *f*

sky: **~ noise temperature** *n* SPACE temperatura de ruido de fondo *f*, temperatura de ruido espacial *f*; **~ wave** *n* PHYS onda celeste *f*

skylight *n* CONST tragaluz *m*, WATER TRANSP lumbrera *f*, tragaluz *m*

skylite *n* CINEMAT luz del cielo *f*

skypan *n* CINEMAT panorámica desde el cielo *f*

SL: **~ cable** *n* (*separate lead cable*) ELEC cable de conductores emplomados *m*

slab *n* C&G loza *f*, COAL desbaste *m*, losa *f*, primera talla *f*, CONST *of timber* plancha *f*, tabla *f*, *of concrete, stone* losa *f*, losa de hormigón *f*, PRINT superficie de imposición *f*; **~ coil** *n* ELEC bobina chata *f*, bobina extraplana *f*, bobina plana *f*, ELEC ENG bobina plana *f*; **~ interferometry** *n* OPT interferometría de placas *f*, TELECOM interferometría plana *f*; **~ pile** *n* NUCL pila de placas *f*; **~ reactor** *n* NUCL reactor de placas *m*; **~ serifs** *n pl* PRINT tipo palo seco plano *m*; **~ shears** *n pl* PROD cizallas para desbastes *f pl*, tijeras para desbastes *f pl*

slabber *n* PROD fresadora horizontal *f*, fresadora-cepillo *f*

slabbing *n* PROD desbaste plano *m*, laminado de desbastes planos *m*, petaca *f*; **~ mill** *n* PROD *rolling* tren de laminación de desbastes planos *m*; **~ miller** *n* PROD fresadora horizontal *f*

slack *n* COAL carbón menudo *m*, cisco *m*, MECH ENG *play* huelgo *m*, juego *m*, soltura *f*, MINE finos *m pl*, TELECOM, WATER TRANSP *of rope, belt* seno *m*; **~ coal** *n* COAL menudos de carbón *m pl*; **~ heap** *n* MINE montón de finos *m*; **~ length** *n* PROD *of belt, transmission rope* seno *m*; **~ portion** *n* PROD *of belt, transmission rope* seno *m*; **~ side** *n* PROD *of belt, transmission rope* ramal conducido *m*; **~ tide** *n* OCEAN repunte de la marea *m*, estoa *f*; **~ time** *n* PROD tiempo de demora previsible *m*, tiempo de retardo estimable *m*; **~ water** *n* HYDROL agua tranquila *f*, OCEAN agua represada *f*, agua tranquila *f*, estoa *f*, remanso *m*, WATER agua tranquila *f*, WATER TRANSP estoa *f*, remanso *m*, repunte *m*

slackening *n* MECH ENG juego *m*

slacking *n* PROD *of blast furnace* enfriamiento *m*

slag *n* COAL, CONST, GEOL, HEAT ENG, PETR TECH escoria *f*; **~ dump** *n* PROD escombrera para escorias *f*, escorial *m*; **~ formation period** *n* PROD *Bessemer process* período de escorificación *m*; **~ glass** *n* C&G escoria *f*; **~ heap** *n* MINE, PROD escorial *m*; **~ pot** *n* PROD depósito de escorias *m*; **~ tap furnace** *n* HEAT

ENG horno con salida de escoria *m*; ~ **tip** *n* PROD escombrera para escorias *f*; ~ **wool** *n* HEAT ENG lana de escoria *f*

slake *vt* CHEM apagar

slaked: ~ **lime** *n* CHEM, CONST cal apagada *f*

slamming *n* WATER TRANSP machetazo *m*, macheteo *m*, pantocazo *m*

slant[1] *n* CONST, GEOM inclinación *f*, pendiente *f*, PRINT inclinación *f*; ~ **angle** *n* MILIT alcance inclinado *m*; ~ **course line** *n* AIR TRANSP *landing* línea de curso oblicuo *f*; ~ **fracture** *n* METALL fractura sesgada *f*; ~ **height** *n* GEOM altura inclinada *f*; ~ **polarization** *n* ELEC ENG polarización oblicua *f*

slant[2] *vi* CONST inclinar

slanted: ~ **letters** *n pl* PRINT caracteres inclinados *m pl*

slanter: ~ **engine** *n* AUTO motor inclinado *m*

slanting *adj* CONST *oblique* inclinado, oblicuo, *sloping* pendiente

SLAR *abbr* (*sideways-looking airborne radar*) AIR TRANSP, MAR POLL RAEL (*radar aereo de exploración lateral*)

slash *n* AGRIC broza *f*; ~ **disposal** *n* AGRIC distribución de residuos *f*; ~ **print** *n* CINEMAT copia de trabajo *f*

slashed: ~ **zero** *n* PRINT cero cruzado *m*

slasher[1]: ~-**dyed** *adj* TEXTIL teñido de encoladora

slasher[2]: ~ **sizing** *n* TEXTIL apresto por encoladora *m*

slat: ~ **dryer** *n* PAPER secadora de listones *f*

slate *n* CINEMAT claqueta *f*, CONST, GEOL, PETR TECH pizarra *f*; ~ **ax** *AmE*, ~ **axe** *BrE* *n* CONST hacha para cortar pizarra *f*; ~-**foliated lignite** *n* COAL lignito de pizarra esquistoso *m*, lignito pizarroso *m*; ~ **industry** *n* MINE industria de pizarra *f*; ~ **knife** *n* CONST cuchilla para pizarra *f*; ~ **lath** *n* CONST listón para pizarra *m*; ~ **nail** *n* MECH ENG clavo de pizarrero *m*; ~ **quarry** *n* MINE cantera de pizarra *f*; ~ **splitting** *n* CONST hendidura de la pizarra *f*

slater: ~'s **hammer** *n* CONST martillo de pizarrero *m*

Slatis-Siegbahn: ~ **spectrometer** *n* NUCL espectrómetro Slatis-Siegbahn

slaty: ~ **cleavage** *n* GEOL exfoliación pizarrosa *f*

slave: ~ **application** *n* COMP&DP aplicación esclava *f*, aplicación subordinada *f*; ~ **cylinder** *n* AUTO cilindro auxiliar *m*, VEH cilindro secundario *m*; ~ **processor** *n* COMP&DP procesador esclavo *m*, procesador subordinado *m*; ~ **relay** *n* ELEC relé plano *m*; ~ **station** *n* COMP&DP estación esclava *f*, estación subordinada *f*; ~ **unit** *n* TV monitor encadenado *m*, unidad esclava *f*; ~ **video cassette recorder** *n* TV grabador de cintas de video esclavo *m* (*AmL*), grabador de cintas de vídeo encadenado *m* (*Esp*)

slavelock *n* TV fijación de encadenados *f*

slaving *n* TV monitor encadenado *m*, unidad esclava *f*

SLC *abbr* (*subscriber line circuit*) TELECOM circuito de línea de abonado *m*

SLD *abbr* (*superluminescent diode*) TELECOM diodo superluminiscente *m*

sledge[1] *n* CONST martillo de dos manos *m*

sledge[2] *vt* CONST golpear con un martillo

sledgehammer *n* CONST maza *f*, PROD martillo de dos manos *m*, martillo de fragua *m*

sleek *adj* TEXTIL impecable

sleeper *n* RAIL *fixed equipment* traviesa *f*, TRANSP coche-litera *m*, coche cama *m*, WATER TRANSP durmiente *m*; ~ **bed** *n* RAIL lecho para la traviesa *m*; ~ **drilling machine** *n* RAIL taladradora de traviesas *f*; ~ **screw** *n* *BrE* (*cf tie screw AmE*) RAIL

tirafondo de traviesa *m*; ~-**screw extractor** *n* *BrE* (*cf spike puller AmE*) RAIL *fixed equipment* extractor de tirafondos *m*; ~ **screwdriver** *n* *BrE* (*cf tie screwdriver AmE*) RAIL destornillador de tirafondos *m*, destornillador de traviesas *m*

sleeping: ~ **car** *n* RAIL coche cama *m*; ~ **car attendant** *n* RAIL encargada del coche cama *f*, encargado del coche cama *m*

sleeve *n* AUTO eje *m*, huso *m*, manguito *m*, árbol *m*, C&G manga *f*, MECH camisa *f*, manguito *m*, MECH ENG manguito *m*, MILIT *of parachute* manga *f*, PACK funda *f*, PRINT manguito *m*, PROD camisa *f*, manguito *m*; ~ **anchor** *n* CONST anclaje de manguito *m*; ~ **pattern** *n* HYDRAUL diseño del manguito *m*; ~-**valve engine** *n* AUTO motor de válvula de camisa *m*

slenderness: ~ **ratio** *n* CONST coeficiente de esbeltez *m*

slew[1]: ~ **speed** *n* PROD velocidad de salto *f*

slew[2] *vi* MECH balancearse

slewing *n* CONST *of crane* rotación *f*; ~ **round** *n* CONST *of crane* giro *m*

slice *n* COMP&DP *bit* porción *f*, sector *m*, tajada *f*, FOOD porción *f*, GEOL lámina *f*, PAPER regleta de nivel *f*; ~ **architecture** *n* COMP&DP arquitectura de porciones *f*, arquitectura por registros encadenados *f*; ~ **lip** *n* PAPER labio de la regleta *m*

slicing *n* PROD corte *m*, seccionamiento *m*

slick *n* MAR POLL mancha *f*, mancha de hidrocarburos *f*, PROD *founding* herramienta para alisar *f*

slickenside *n* GEOL espejo de falla *m*, plano de deslizamiento *m*

slicker *n* PROD *founding* alisador *m*

slide[1] *n* CINEMAT diapositiva *f*, COAL atierre *m*, corrimiento *m*, pliegue-falla *m*, HYDRAUL distribuidor *m*, LAB cursor *m*, portaobjetos *m*, MECH carro *m*, deslizamiento *m*, guía de deslizamiento *f*, tapa corrediza *f*, PHOTO diapositiva *f*, PRINT diapositiva *f*, deslizador *m*; ~ **bar** *n* CINEMAT *of oil* barra de guía *f*, barra deslizante *f*, MECH ENG *for crosshead of piston* barra corrediza *f*, resbaladera de la cruceta *f*; ~ **box** *n* HYDRAUL caja del distribuidor *f*, PHOTO caja para examinar diapositivas *f*; ~ **bridge** *n* ELEC ENG puente de cursor *m*; ~ **changer** *n* PHOTO cambiador de diapositivas *m*; ~-**copying attachment** *n* PHOTO accesorio para copiado de diapositivas *m*; ~-**copying device** *n* PHOTO equipo para copiado de diapositivas *m*; ~ **damper** *n* HEAT ENG amortiguador de deslizamiento *m*, REFRIG registro de guillotina *m*; ~ **duplication** *n* PHOTO duplicado de diapositivas *m*; ~ **holder** *n* PHOTO marquito portadiapositivas *m*, portadiapositivas *m*; ~ **pickup** *n* TV transductor de transparencias a televisión *m*; ~ **potentiometer** *n* ELEC ENG potenciómetro del cursor *m*; ~ **projector** *n* PHOTO proyector de diapositivas *m*; ~-**rest tools** *n pl* MECH ENG *lathe* herramientas de tornear *f pl*; ~ **rheostat** *n* ELEC resistencia variable *f*, reóstato de cursor *m*; ~ **rod** *n* HYDRAUL barra del distribuidor *f*, biela del distribuidor *f*, vástago del distribuidor *m*; ~ **rule** *n* COMP&DP regla de cálculo *f*, regla deslizante *f*; ~ **scanner** *n* TV explorador de transparencias *m*; ~ **switch** *n* ELEC conmutador corredizo *m*, conmutador de botón deslizante *m*, conmutador deslizante *m*, ELEC ENG interruptor deslizante *m*; ~-**throttle valve** *n* HYDRAUL regulador del distribuidor *m*; ~ **valve** *n* HYDRAUL distribuidor de concha *m*, válvula de corredera *f*, VEH distribuidor *m*, válvula de corredera *f*; ~ **valve gear** *n* HYDRAUL mecanismo de válvula de corredera *m*; ~ **viewer** *n* PHOTO visor de diapositivas *m*; ~ **wire bridge** *n* ELEC ENG puente de hilo y cursor *m*

slide² *vi* MECH desplazarse, resbalarse

sliding *n* MECH ENG *lathe work* avance *m*, METALL deformación del contorno del grano *f*, desplazamiento *m*; ~ **base plate** *n* CINEMAT base deslizante *f*; ~ **caliper gage** *AmE see* sliding calliper gauge *BrE*; ~ **calipers** *AmE see* sliding callipers *BrE*; ~ **calliper gauge** *n BrE* MECH ENG calibrador de cursor de corredera *m*, galga de nonio de avance *f*; ~ **callipers** *n pl BrE* MECH ENG nonio de avance *m*; ~ **contact** *n* ELEC ENG frotador *m*, PHYS contacto por deslizamiento *m*; ~ **door** *n* CONST puerta corredera *f*, puerta corrediza *f*; ~ **filter drawer** *n* PHOTO cajonera para filtros *f*; ~ **fit** *n* MECH ajuste corredizo *m*, ajuste suave *m*, MECH ENG ajuste corredizo *m*; ~ **formwork** *n* CONST encofrado deslizante *m*; ~ **fracture** *n* NUCL fractura por deslizamiento *f*; ~ **frequency** *n* TV frecuencia de deslizamiento *f*; ~ **friction** *n* PHYS rozamiento por deslizamiento *m*; ~ **friction coefficient** *n* PHYS coeficiente de rozamiento por deslizamiento *m*; ~ **gate** *n* CONST compuerta corrediza *f*, compuerta deslizante *f*; ~ **gear** *n* VEH engranaje desplazable *m*; ~**gear starting motor** *n* ELEC motor de arranque por engranajes deslizantes *m*; ~**gear transmission** *n* AUTO transmisión de engranajes deslizantes *f*; ~ **leg** *n* PHOTO *of liquids* palanca de arrastre *f*, pasador de película *m*; ~ **lid** *n* PACK tapa deslizante *f*; ~ **load** *n* ELEC ENG carga de cursor *f*; ~ **parallel vice** *n BrE* MECH ENG tornillo paralelo desplazable *m*; ~ **parallel vise** *AmE see* sliding parallel vice *BrE*; ~ **sash** *n* CONST *of window* hoja corredera *f*; ~ **scale** *n* PROD escala de aumentos *f*, *salaries* escala gradual *f*, escala móvil *f*; ~ **shutter** *n* CONST persiana corredera *f* (*Esp*), persiana corrediza *f* (*AmL*), MINE charnela portacebo *f*; ~ **sleeve** *n* AUTO manguito deslizante *m*, manguito desplazable *m*; ~ **sluice gate** *n* FUELLESS *dams* compuerta de desagüe deslizable *f*; ~ **switch** *n* ELEC ENG conmutador del cursor *m*; ~ **tee socket wrench** *n* MECH ENG *tool* llave de tubo con palanca en T *f*; ~ **window** *n* CONST ventana corredera *f*, ventana corrediza *f*, ventana de hoja basculante *f*

slim: ~ **hole** *n* PETR TECH agujero de diámetro pequeño *m*, hueco de diámetro pequeño *m*, pozo de diámetro reducido *m*, PETROL agujero de diámetro pequeño *m*

SLIM *abbr* (*single linear inductor motor*) ELEC, TRANSP motor inductor lineal simple *m*

slime *n* C&G lama *f*, COAL babaza *f*, cieno *m*, fango *m*, lodo *m*, HYDROL cieno *m*, babaza *f*, PAPER lodo *m*, REFRIG capa pegajosa *f*, capa viscosa *f*, WATER babaza *f*, cieno *m*, fango *m*

slimes *n pl* COAL fangos *m pl*, finos *m pl*

sling *n* C&G estrobo *m*, MAR POLL braga *f*, eslinga *f*, PROD *chain* eslinga *f*, WATER TRANSP *of yard, goods, rigging* braga *f*, cruz *f*, eslinga *f*, eslingada *f*, honda *f*; ~ **beam** *n* PROD *foundry* balancín *m*; ~ **dog** *n* PROD pata de eslinga *f*; ~ **hanger** *n* PROD *shaft hanger* silleta de transmisión *f*, transportador con soportes colgantes *m*; ~ **hygrometer** *n* REFRIG higrómetro de honda *m*, sicrómetro de honda *m*; ~ **identification tag** *n* SAFE etiqueta de identificación para eslingas *f*; ~ **transport** *n* AIR TRANSP transporte de cabestrillo *m*, transporte de eslinga *m*

slingshot *n* SPACE tirachinas *m*, tirador *m*

slip¹ *n* AIR TRANSP *of propeller* resbalamiento *m*, CRYSTALL *crystal defect*, ELEC *machine*, ELEC ENG deslizamiento *m*, PAPER lechada *f*, PETR TECH cuña *f*, WATER TRANSP *boat building* puesto de atraque en una marina *m*, grada *f*, varadero *m*, *of propeller* torbellino *m*, deslizamiento de la hélice *m*, retroceso de la hélice *m*; ~ **band** *n* CRYSTALL banda de deslizamiento *f*; ~ **box** *n* MINE gancho de deslizamiento *m*; ~ **case** *n* PACK caja deslizante *f*; ~ **circle** *n* CONST círculo de deslizamiento *m*; ~ **cleavage** *n* GEOL esquistosidad de cizalla *f*, esquistosidad de crenulación *f*, esquistosidad superpuesta *f*; ~ **cylinder** *n* METALL cilindro de deslizamiento *m*; ~ **form** *n* CONST molde deslizante *m*; ~ **gage** *AmE*, ~ **gauge** *BrE n* METR calibrador de espesores *m*, galga de bloques *f*; ~ **jacket** *n* PROD *for snap moulding* camisa de colada *f*; ~ **joint** *n* AUTO junta deslizante *f*, HYDRAUL junta de dilatación *f*, VEH junta deslizante *f*; ~ **line** *n* CRYSTALL línea de deslizamiento *f*; ~ **marking** *n* METALL señal de deslizamiento *f*; ~**on sleeve** *n* PHOTO funda protectora *f*; ~ **plane** *n* CRYSTALL plano de deslizamiento *m*; ~ **proof** *n* PRINT prueba en galera *f*; ~**proof finish** *n* COATINGS acabado antideslizante *m*, acabado a prueba de deslizamiento *m*; ~ **resistant sole** *n* SAFE *ring winding* suela antideslizante *f*; ~ **ring** *n* ELEC motor anillo rozante *m*, ELEC ENG anillo deslizante *m*, PHYS anillo de acceso *m*, VEH anillo colector *m*, anillo de fricción *m*, colector *m*; ~**ring induction motor** *n* ELEC ENG motor de inducción por anillo deslizante *m*; ~**ring motor** *n* ELEC motor de anillo colector *m*, motor de anillo rozante *m*; ~**ring rotor** *n* ELEC *generator* rotor de anillo colector *m*, rotor de anillo rozante *m*; ~ **road** *n BrE* (*cf access road AmE*) CONST, TRANSP calle de acceso *f*, camino de acceso *m*, carretera de acceso *f*; ~ **road census** *n BrE* TRANSP carretera de entrada censada *f*, censo de carreteras de acceso *m*, censo de vías de acceso *m*; ~ **road control** *n BrE* TRANSP control de carretera de acceso *m*, control del camino de acceso *m*; ~ **road count** *n BrE* TRANSP carretera de acceso válida *f*, recuento de carreteras de acceso *m*, recuento de vías de acceso *m*; ~ **road metering** *n BrE* TRANSP medición de carretera de acceso *f*, medición de la vía de acceso *f*; ~ **scar** *n* GEOL roca escarpada en pendiente *f*; ~ **share** *n* AGRIC reja *f*; ~ **step height** *n* METALL altura de la línea de deslizamiento *f*; ~ **surface** *n* COAL superficie de deslizamiento *f*; ~**tongue joint** *n* CONST junta con lengüeta postiza *f*

slip² *vt* WATER TRANSP *for repairs* subir a la grada, varar, *ropes* largar, arriar, filar

slip³: ~ **one's cable** *vi* WATER TRANSP abandonar el ancla, filar la cadena hasta la malla, largar por ojo la cadena del ancla

slippage *n* CONST deslizamiento *m*

slipperiness *n* TRANSP resbalabilidad *m*, untuosidad *f*

slipping *n* PROD *of rolls of rolling-mill* deslizamiento *m*

slipstream *n* AIR TRANSP *of propeller* chorro *m*, flujo de la hélice *m*, torbellino de la hélice *m*

slipway *n* WATER TRANSP *fishing ship* rampa *f*, *repairs* grada *f*, varadero *m*

slit *n* PACK corte longitudinal *m*, ranura *f*, PHOTO, PHYS rendija *f*, PROD grieta *f*, hendidura *f*, raja *f*, rendija *f*, SPACE abertura *f*, grieta *f*, hendidura *f*, raja *f*, ranura *f*, rendija *f*, WAVE PHYS ranura *f*; ~ **diaphragm** *n* PHOTO diafragma de rendija *m*; ~ **mortise joint** *n* CONST junta de mortaja estrecha *f*; ~ **resonator** *n* ACOUST resonador de rendija *m*; ~ **scanning** *n* TV exploración de la línea del sonido *f*; ~ **shutter** *n* TV obturador en ranura *m*; ~ **system** *n* SPACE sistema de ranuras *m*, sistema de refugio *m*

slitter *n* C&G ranuradora *f*, PAPER, PRINT cortadora longitudinal *f*; ~ **rewinder** *n* PAPER cortadora-rebobinadora *f*

slitting *n* PACK corte longitudinal *m*, PAPER corte longitudinal *m*, hendido *m*, PROD cortado en tiras *m*, ranurado; ~ **disc** *BrE*, ~ **disk** *AmE n* C&G disco ranurador PAPER; ~ **and printing machine** *n* PACK cortadora longitudinal-impresora *f*; ~ **and rewinding machine** *n* PACK cortadora longitudinal-rebobinadora *f*; ~ **time** *n* PROD tiempo de ranurado *m*

sliver *n* C&G astilla *f*, TEXTIL mecha *f*

SLM *abbr* (*single-longitudinal mode*) TELECOM modo longitudinal único *m*

sloop *n* WATER TRANSP balandra *f*, balandro *m*

slope *n* COAL pendiente *f*, plano inclinado *m*, talud *m*, CONST *downward* pendiente *f*, *of hill* vertiente *f*, *of hill, slant or incline* ladera *f*, talud *m*, falda *f*, declive *m*, *upward* rampa *f*, GEOM declive *m*, pendiente *f*, MINE inclinación *f*, galería inclinada *f*, chiflón *m*, plano inclinado *m*, talud *m*, PHYS pendiente *f*; ~ **current** *n* OCEAN corriente de gradiente *f*; ~ **failure** *n* COAL derrabe *m*, derrumbe de galería *m*; ~ **level** *n* CONST ángulo de la pendiente *m*; ~ **protection** *n* CONST defensa de taludes *f*; ~ **shaft** *n* PETR TECH buzamiento *m*; ~ **stability** *n* COAL estabilidad de la galería *f*; ~ **toe** *n* COAL pie del talud *m*; ~ **top** *n* COAL coronamiento *m*, coronamiento del talud *m*, punta *f*, tragante *m*

sloshing *n* SPACE bailoteo del líquido *m*, desplazamiento de la carga de combustible líquido *m*, movimiento de un líquido en el interior de un tanque *m*

slot *n* C&G ranura *f*, ELEC ENG ranura *f*, muesca *f*, NUCL ranura *f*, PROD chavetero *m*, encaje *m*, muesca *f*, ranura *f*, SPACE pista *f*, ranura *f*, rastro *m*, rendija *f*, segmentos lisos *m pl*, TELECOM hendidura *f*, ranura *f*, rendija *f*, TV ranura *f*; ~ **aerial** *n BrE* (*cf slot antenna AmE*) SPACE, TELECOM antena de ranura *f*, antena ranurada *f*; ~ **antenna** *n AmE* (*cf slot aerial BrE*) SPACE, TELECOM antena de ranura *f*, antena ranurada *f*; ~ **die** *n* PRINT molde de ranura *m*; ~ **diffuser** *n* REFRIG difusor lineal *m*; ~ **feeding** *n* PRINT alimentación por ranura *f*; ~ **flap** *n* AIR TRANSP, TRANSP flap ranurado *m*; ~ **line** *n* PHYS ranura *f*; ~ **lip** *n* C&G labio de la ranura *m*; ~ **mortise joint** *n* CONST *carpentry* junta con ranura *f*

slotted: ~ **ALOHA system** *n* TELECOM sistema ALOHA de línea ranurada *m*; ~ **armature** *n* ELEC armadura dentada *f*, ELEC ENG armazón con ranuras *m*; ~ **clinch rivet** *n* CONST remache de redoblar *m*, remache ranurado *m*; ~**core cable** *n* OPT cable de núcleo ranurado *m*; ~ **line** *n* ELEC ENG línea artificial calibrada *f*, línea ranurada *f*; ~ **line probe** *n* ELEC ENG sonda de línea ranurada *f*; ~ **oil control ring** *n* AUTO segmento de engrase *m*; ~ **rivet** *n* CONST remache ranurado *m*; ~ **system** *n* TELECOM sistema de línea ranurada *m*; ~ **waveguide** *n* ELEC, ELEC ENG, WAVE PHYS guía de ondas calibrada *f*; ~ **wing** *n* AIR TRANSP, TRANSP ala con ranura *f*, ala ranurada *f*

sloughing: ~ **shale** *n* PETR TECH lutita de desprendimiento *f*

slow¹: ~ **ahead** *adv* WATER TRANSP avante poca; ~ **astern** *adv* WATER TRANSP atrás a poca

slow²: ~**acting relay** *n* ELEC relé de acción diferida *m*, relé de acción lenta *m*, relé de acción retardada *m*, relé lento *m*; ~**blow fuse** *n* CINEMAT, ELEC ENG, PROD fusible de acción retardada *m*; ~**break switch** *n* ELEC conmutador de cierre retardado *m*, conmutador lento normalmente cerrado *m*; ~**burning fuse** *n* MINE cebo de combustión lenta *m*; ~ **combustion** *n* AUTO combustión lenta *f*; ~**down cylinder** *n* PRINT cilindro ralentizador *m*; ~**freezing** *n* FOOD, REFRIG congelación lenta *f*; ~ **match** *n* MINE mecha lenta *f*; ~ **motion** *n* CINEMAT, TV acción lenta *f*; ~**motion control knob** *n* INSTR botón de control de movimiento lento *m*; ~**motion disc** *BrE*, ~**motion disk** *AmE* TV disco de movimiento lento *m*; ~**moving percentage** *n* PROD porcentaje de movimiento lento *m*; ~ **neutron** *n* PHYS neutrón lento *m*; ~**operate relay** *n* ELEC ENG relé retardado *m*; ~ **quenching** *n* METALL, REFRIG enfriamiento lento *m*; ~**running diesel engine** *n* TRANSP motor diesel poco revolucionado *m*; ~ **sand filter** *n* HYDROL, WATER filtro de arena lento *m*; ~ **sand filtration** *n* WATER filtración lenta de arena *f*; ~**scan television** *n* TELECOM televisión de exploración lenta *f*; ~**scan television system** *n* TV sistema de televisión de barrido lento *m*, sistema de televisión de pequeña velocidad de escansión *m*; ~**scan videoconferencing** *n* TELECOM videoconferencia de exploración lenta *f*; ~**setting cement** *n* CONST cemento de fraguado lento *m*; ~**speed compressor** *n* HYDRAUL compresor de pequeña velocidad *m*; ~ **train** *n* RAIL tren local *m*; ~ **wave** *n* ELEC ENG onda lenta *f*; ~**wave structure** *n* ELEC ENG, PHYS estructura de onda lenta *f*; ~**wave tube** *n* ELECTRON tubo de onda lenta *m*

slowing: ~ **down** *n* NUCL moderación *f*; ~**down area** *n* PHYS *air-bubble in casting* área de frenado *f*; ~**down density** *n* PHYS *air-bubble in casting* densidad de frenado *f*; ~**down length** *n* PHYS *of controls* longitud de frenado *f*; ~**down power** *n* PHYS poder de frenado *m*

slowly: ~ **varying voltage** *n* ELEC ENG voltaje de variación lenta *m*

SLR *abbr* (*single-lens reflex camera*) PHOTO cámara reflex con objetivo acromático *f*, cámara reflex de un objetivo *f*

slub *n* TEXTIL gata *f*

slubbing¹: ~**dyed** *adj* TEXTIL teñido en mecha

slubbing²: ~ **frame** *n* TEXTIL bastidor de mecha *m*

sludge *n* CHEM barro *m*, lodo *m*, COAL cieno *m*, CONST lodo *m*, FOOD barro *m*, lodo *m*, HYDROL fango *m*, lodo *m*, sedimento *m*, PETR TECH, PETROL lodo *m*, POLL cieno *m*, lodo *m*, PROD *ore dressing* barros *m pl*, fango *m*, lodo *m*, RECYCL lodo *m*, sedimento *m*, cieno *m*, fango de aguas cloacales *m*, barro *m*, cieno cloacal *m*, REFRIG fango *m*, WATER cieno *m*, cieno cloacal *m*, lodo *m*; ~ **bulking** *n* HYDROL aumento de la masa de lodo *m*, WATER abultamiento de cienos *m*; ~ **conditioning** *n* HYDROL tratamiento de sedimentos *m*, WATER acondicionamiento de cienos *m*; ~ **dewatering** *n* HYDROL achique de sedimentos *m*, eliminación de fangos *f*, WATER achique de sedimentos *m*; ~ **digestion** *n* HYDROL, RECYCL digestión de lodos *f*; ~ **digestion gas** *n* GAS, HYDROL gas de digestión de lodos *m*; ~ **disposal** *n* WATER disposición de cienos *f*; ~**drying bed** *n* HYDROL lecho para el secado de lodos de alcantarilla *m*; ~ **formation test** *n* ELEC prueba de formación de lodo *f*; ~ **gas** *n* GAS, RECYCL gas de digestión de fangos cloacales *m*, gas de pantanos *m*; ~ **gulper** *n* RECYCL contenedor de lodos *m*; ~ **incineration** *n* WATER incineración de cienos *f*; ~ **lancing** *n* NUCL eliminación de lodos por chorro de agua y aspiración *f*; ~ **liquor** *n* HYDROL fango líquido *m*, WATER licor de cienos *m*; ~ **press** *n* HYDROL prensa de lodos *f*; ~ **processing** *n* RECYCL depuración del lodo *f*, tratamiento del lodo *m*; ~ **pump** *n* MINE bomba de arena *f*, cuchara de arena *f*; ~ **ripening** *n* WATER maduración de cienos *f*; ~ **scraper** *n* HYDROL arrastrador de lodos *m*; ~ **stabilization** *n* HYDROL estabilización de sedimentos *f*; ~ **thickening** *n* HYDROL espesamiento del lodo *m*, WATER espesamiento de cienos *m*

sludger *n* MINE bomba centrífuga para arenas y lodos *f*, bomba de arena *f*, cubeta sacalodos *f*, cuchara *f*, cucharilla *f*, rasqueta para limpiar barrenos *f*

slug *n* C&G cuello caído *m*, COAL criba *f*, pepita *f*, tarugo *m*, ELEC ENG espira de cortocircuito *f*, espiral *f*, relantizador *m*, retardador *m*, sintonizador de guía de ondas *m*; ~ **in neck** *n* C&G cuello caído *m*; ~ **tuning** *n* ELEC ENG sintonía por barra *f*, sintonía nuclear *f*

slugged: ~ **bottom** *n* C&G fondo caído *m*

slugging *n* CHEM agitación *f*, efervescencia *f*, hervor *m*, REFRIG golpe de líquido *m*

sluice *n* FUELLESS *dams* conducto de evacuación *m*, MINE esclusa *f*, aparato de lavado *m* (*AmL*), canal de lavado *m* (*Esp*), RECYCL esclusa *f*, canal de desagüe *m*, conducto de desagüe *m*, compuerta *f*, WATER compuerta *f*, esclusa *f*, WATER TRANSP *canal* compuerta *f*, esclusa *f*, aguas retenidas en el cuenco *f pl*; ~ **box** *n* WATER caja de esclusa *f*; ~ **valve** *n* HYDRAUL válvula de compuerta *f*, válvula de corredera *f*, WATER válvula de compuerta *f*, válvula de desagüe *f*

sluicegate *n* FUELLESS compuerta de desagüe *f*, WATER compuerta de desagüe *f*, compuerta de descarga *f*, compuerta de esclusa *f*, WATER TRANSP *lock* compuerta *f*, puerta *f*

sluiceway *n* WATER conducto de evacuación *m*, descargador de fondo *m*

sluicing *n* WATER acarreo hidráulico *m*, arrastre con chorros de agua *m*, esclusaje *m*, transporte hidráulico *m*

slump: ~ **cone** *n* CONST cono de asentamiento *m*; ~ **test** *n* CONST ensayo de asentamiento *m*

slumping *n* OCEAN desmoronamiento *m*, socavón *m*

slung: ~ **bucket** *n* MAR POLL balde embragado *m*; ~ **pump** *n* MINE bomba de eslinga *f* (*AmL*), bomba de tiro *f* (*Esp*)

slur *n* PRINT remosqueo *m*

slurry *n* C&G lechada *f*, COAL fango de lavado *m*, lechada *f*, lodo *m*, mortero *m*, DETERG barro líquido *m*, fango de lavado *m*, FOOD papilla *f*, MINE barro *m*, fango de lavado *m*, lodo *m*, *explosive* dinamita semigelatinosa *f*, PAPER *pigments, coating* suspensión de pigmentos *f*, suspensión de cargas *f*, suspensión *f*, RECYCL materia insoluble acuosa *f*, suspensión acuosa espesa *f*; ~ **basin** *n* COAL balsa de lodos *f*, capa fangosa *f*, intercalación de roca estéril *f*, MINE intercalación de roca estéril *f*; ~ **blasting agent** *n* (*SBA*) MINE explosivo fluidizado *m*; ~ **explosive** *n* (*SE*) MINE explosivo fluidizado *m*; ~ **pond** *n* COAL estanque decantador *m*; ~ **pump** *n* MINE bomba para

lodos *f*; ~ **seal** *n* CONST sellado con lechada *m*; ~ **tanker** *n* TRANSP cisterna de líquidos semipastosos *f*; ~ **trench wall** *n* COAL foso decantador *m*; ~ **trough** *n* PETR TECH batea de lodo *f*

slush *n* HYDROL fango *m*, MINE barro *m*, fango *m*, lodo *m*, relleno hidráulico *m*, REFRIG nieve fundente *f*; ~ **ice** *n* REFRIG hielo nieve humedecido *m*; ~ **molding** *AmE*, ~ **moulding** *BrE n* P&R moldeado en hueco *m*, moldeo rotacional *m*; ~ **propellant** *n* SPACE propulsor de líquidos densos *m*; ~ **pump** *n* PETR TECH bomba del lodo *f*

slusher *n* MINE cabrestante portátil *m*, cuchara de arrastre *f*, excavadora de arrastre *f*, traílla portadora *f*

slushing *n* PAPER desintegración *f*

SM *abbr* (*synchronous multiplexer*) TELECOM multiplexor síncrono *m*

Sm *abbr* (*samarium*) CHEM Sm (*samario*)

SMAE *abbr* (*system management application entity*) TELECOM entidad de aplicación para la gestión del sistema *f*

small[1]: ~**-scale** *adj* GEOL a pequeña escala, WATER TRANSP *chart* de punto menor

small[2] *n* MINE menudo de carbón *m*; ~**-angle prism** *n* PHYS prisma de ángulo pequeño *m*; ~**-angle scattering** *n* CRYSTALL difusión a bajo ángulo *f*; ~ **arms** *n pl* MILIT armas ligeras *f pl*; ~ **bar mill** *n* PROD *rolling* laminador pequeño *m*, tren laminador pequeño para perfiles *m*; ~ **break LOCA** *n* (*SBLOCA*) NUCL LOCA pequeño *m* (*SBLOCA*); ~ **cap** *n* PRINT mayúscula pequeña *f*, versalitas *f pl*; ~ **coal** *n* COAL, MINE carbón menudo *m*; ~ **coal without fines** *n* COAL carbón menudo sin finos de minerales *m*; ~ **end** *n* AUTO, VEH pie de biela *m*; ~ **end bush** *n* VEH casquillo de pie de biela *m*; ~ **end bushing** *n* AUTO buje del pie de biela *m*, cojinete del pie de biela *m*; ~**-gain amplifier** *n* ELECTRON amplificador de poca ganancia *m*; ~ **grain** *n* AGRIC cereal *m*; ~**-scale integration** *n* (*SSI*) COMP&DP, ELECTRON, PHYS, TELECOM integración a pequeña escala *f*; ~ **signal** *n* ELECTRON señal pequeña *f*; ~**-signal amplification** *n* ELECTRON amplificación de pequeña señal *f*; ~**-signal amplifier** *n* ELECTRON amplificador de pequeña señal *m*; ~**-signal parameter** *n* ELECTRON parámetro de pequeña señal *m*; ~**-signal transistor** *n* ELECTRON transistor de pequeña señal *m*; ~ **stream** *n* HYDROL arroyo pequeño *m*; ~ **stuff** *n* WATER TRANSP *ropes* jarcia menuda *f*; ~ **tip car** *n AmE* (*cf small tip wagon BrE*) RAIL vagoneta basculante pequeña *f*; ~ **tip wagon** *BrE n* (*cf small tip car AmE*) RAIL vagoneta basculante pequeña *f*

smalls *n pl* COAL menudos *m pl*

smaltite *n* MINERAL esmaltina *f*

smaragdite *n* MINERAL esmeraldita *f*

smart: ~ **bomb** *n* MILIT bomba inteligente *f*; ~ **card** *n* COMP&DP módulo inteligente *m*, tarjeta con microprocesador *f*, tarjeta inteligente *f*; ~**-card reader** *n* TELECOM lector de tarjetas inteligentes *m*; ~ **shell** *n* MILIT proyectil inteligente *m*; ~ **terminal** *n* COMP&DP terminal inteligente *m*; ~ **weapon** *n* MILIT arma inteligente *f*

SMC *abbr* (*surface-mounted component*) TELECOM componente de montaje superficial *m*

SMDS *abbr* (*switched multimegabit data service*) TELECOM servicio de conmutación de datos de multimegabits *m*, servicio de líneas conmutadas de datos de multimegabits *m*

smearing *n* PRINT remosqueo *m*, TV borrosidad *f*

smectic: ~ **liquid crystals** *n pl* ELECTRON cristales líquidos esmécticos *m pl*; ~ **phase** *n* CRYSTALL fase esméctica *f*

smectite *n* CHEM, COAL, GEOL, PETR TECH esmectita *f*

smelt *vt* HEAT fundir

smelter *n* METALL, PROD obrero metalúrgico *m*

smelting *n* COAL fundición *f*, HEAT fusión *f*; ~ **furnace** *n* ELEC ENG horno de fusión *m*

SMF *abbr* (*submultiframe*) TELECOM bastidor auxiliar múltiple *m*

SMIB *abbr* (*security management information base*) TELECOM base de información para la gestión de la seguridad *f*

smith *n* CONST, MECH ENG herrero *m*; ~**'s pliers** *n pl* CONST tenazas para forja *f pl*

Smith: ~ **chart** *n* PHYS carta de Smith *f*

smithery *n* CONST *girder work*, MECH ENG, PROD herrería *f*

smithsonite *n* BrE (*cf calamine AmE*) COAL, MINE smithsonita *f*, MINERAL esmitsonita *f*, smithsonita *f*

smithy *n* CONST forja *f*, fragua *f*, MECH, MECH ENG, PROD forja *f*

SMN *abbr* (*SDH management network*) TELECOM red de gestión de jerarquía digital síncrona *f*

smog *n* METEO, POLL bruma cargada de humo *f*, esmog *m*, humo-niebla *f*

smoke[1]: ~ **alarm** *n* SAFE alarma contra humos *f*; ~**-and-gas-alarm installation** *n* SAFE instalación de alarmas contra humos y gases *f*; ~ **arch** *n* HEAT ENG arco de humo *m*, bóveda colectora de humos *f*; ~ **bomb** *n* MILIT bomba fumígena *f*; ~ **box** *n* CONST cámara de humos *f*, HEAT ENG, RAIL caja de humos *f*; ~ **candle** *n* CINEMAT bote de humo *m*; ~ **chart** *n* SAFE gráfica de humos *f*; ~ **control** *n* SAFE control de humos *m*; ~ **detector** *n* SAFE detector de humos *m*; ~ **gas desulfurization installation** *AmE*, ~ **gas desulphurization installation** *BrE n* POLL, SAFE instalación para desulfurizar humos y gases *f*; ~ **grenade** *n* MILIT granada fumígena *f*; ~ **and heat exhaust installation** *n* SAFE instalación para la extracción de humos y calor *f*; ~ **and heat extraction system** *n* SAFE sistema de extracción de humos y calor *m*; ~ **helmet** *n* SAFE casco contra humos *m*; ~ **mask** *n* AIR TRANSP mascarilla de humo *f*, máscara de humo *f*; ~ **protection doors** *n pl* SAFE puerta de protección contra humos *f*; ~ **screen** *n* MILIT cortina de humo *f*; ~ **tube** *n* HEAT ENG tubo de humos *m*

smoke[2] *vt* FOOD ahumar

smoked: ~ **glass** *n* C&G vidrio ahumado *m*

smokeless[1] *adj* FUELLESS sin humos

smokeless[2]: ~ **zone** *n* SAFE zona con prohibición de fumar *f*

smoking *n* FOOD ahumado *m*

smoky: ~ **quartz** *n* MINERAL cuarzo ahumado *m*

smolder *AmE see smoulder BrE*

smoldering: ~ **fire** *AmE see smouldering fire BrE*

smooth[1] *adj* C&G, PAPER, PROD alisado

smooth[2]: ~ **blasting** *n* MINE voladura suave *f*; ~**-bore gun** *n* MILIT cañón de ánima lisa *m*; ~ **braking** *n* RAIL, VEH frenado suave *m*; ~ **core armature** *n* ELEC *generator* armadura de núcleo liso *f*, armadura suave del núcleo *f*; ~ **finish** *n* PAPER alisado *m*; ~ **grinding** *n* C&G esmerilado fino *m*; ~ **operation** *n* PROD opera-

ción uniforme *f*; ~ **plain packing** *n* PACK empaque con papel sencillo *m*; ~ **roller** *n* CONST rodillo de alisar *m*, rodillo liso *m*; ~ **traffic** *n* TELECOM tráfico regularizado *m*; ~ **wall blasting** *n* MINE voladura de muros suave *f*

smooth[3] *vt* COAL pulir

smoothed: ~ **edge** *n* C&G borde alisado *m*

smoothing *n* C&G *of hollow glass* alisado *m*, COMP&DP alisamiento *m*, aplanamiento *m*, ELEC, ELEC ENG filtraje *m*, ELECTRON nivelación *f*, PROD alisado *m*, alisadura *f*, aplanamiento *m*; ~ **capacitor** *n* ELEC capacitor de aplanamiento *m*, condensador de aplanamiento *m*; ~ **choke** *n* ELEC *inductor* obturador de filtraje *m*, bobina de reactancia de absorción *f*, bobina de impedancia de filtrado *f*, inductancia de filtraje *f*, ELEC ENG bobina de impedancia de filtrado *f*, bobina de reactancia de absorción *f*; ~ **circuit** *n* ELEC circuito de filtrado *m*, circuito estabilizador *m*, circuito nivelador *m*, circuito supresor de ondulaciones residuales *m*; ~ **factor** *n* PROD factor aplanador *m*, factor de filtrado *m*, factor de nivelación familiar *m*, factor de pulimentación familiar *m*; ~ **filter** *n* ELEC ENG filtro de nivelación *m*, ELECTRON filtro de nivelación *m*, filtro eléctrico *m*; ~ **harrow** *n* AGRIC rastra *f*; ~ **press** *n* PAPER prensa alisadora *f*; ~ **resistor** *n* ELEC resistor de aplanamiento *m*, resistor de filtro *m*; ~ **roll** *n* PAPER rodillo alisador *m*; ~**-roll coating** *n* PAPER estucado con rodillos alisadores *m*

smoothness *n* PAPER lisura *f*; ~ **tester** *n* PAPER aparato para medir la lisura *m*

smother *vt* THERMO apagar, cegar, sofocar, tapar

smoulder *vi* BrE THERMO arder sin llama, humear sin llama

smouldering: ~ **fire** *n* BrE AGRIC incendio de rescoldo *m*, SAFE, THERMO fuego latente *m*, fuego sin llama *m*

SMPTE[1] *abbr* (*Society of Motion Picture Technicians*) CINEMAT SMPTE (*Sociedad de Técnicos Cinematográficos*)

SMPTE[2]: ~ **projection leader** *n* CINEMAT guía de proyección SMPTE *f*; ~ **time code** *n* CINEMAT, TV código de tiempos de la SMPTE *m*

SMS *abbr* (*SDH management subnetwork*) TELECOM subred de gestión de jerarquía digital síncrona *f*

smudge *n* PRINT mancha *f*

smudging: ~ **print** *n* PRINT impresión manchada *f*

smut *n* AGRIC tizón *m*

smutter *n* AGRIC máquina para desinfectar semillas contra tizón *f*

SN *abbr* (*sequence number*) TELECOM número de orden *m*, número del abonado *m*, número secuencial *m*

Sn *abbr* (*tin*) CHEM, METALL, MINE, PROD Sn (*estaño*)

SNA *abbr* (*systems network architecture*) COMP&DP, TELECOM arquitectura de sistemas de redes *f*

snag *n* TEXTIL enganchón *m*

snake *n* C&G serpiente *f*

snaking *n* AIR TRANSP serpenteo *m*; ~ **column** *n* PRINT columna deformada *f*

snap[1]: ~**-action** *adj* PROD de acción rápida; ~**-on** *adj* PROD a presión, encajado a presión

snap[2]: ~**-action switch** *n* ELEC interruptor de acción rápida *m*, ELEC ENG conmutador ultrarrápido *m*, interruptor de acción rápida *m*; ~**-action valve** *n* REFRIG barostato *m*, válvula de acción instantánea *f*; ~ **cap** *n* PACK cápsula roscada que se rompe al abrirse por primera vez *f*; ~ **gage** *AmE*, ~ **gauge** *BrE n*

METR calibre de herradura *m*, calibre de horquilla *m*, calibre de mordaza *m*; ~ **hinge closure** *n* PACK cierre con charnela que se rompe al abrirse por primera vez *m*; **~-in socket** *n* ELEC ENG enchufe hembra de acción inmediata *m*; **~-in switch** *n* ELEC ENG interruptor inmediato *m*; ~ **lock** *n* PROD cerradura de funcionamiento ultrarrápido *f*; **~-off closure** *n* PACK cierre apertura rápida *m*; **~-off diode** *n* ELECTRON diodo de ruptura brusca *m*; **~-on closure** *n* PACK cierre de presión *m*; **~-on lid** *n* PACK tapón que se rompe al abrirse por primera vez *m*; **~-out** *n* PRINT talón de formularios con intercalación de papel carbón *m*; **~-out perforation** *n* PRINT perforación para facilitar el desgarro *f*; ~ **shackle** *n* WATER TRANSP *fittings, rigging* grillete automático *m*, mosquetón con sacavueltas *m*

snap³ *vi* PROD desconectar rápidamente, desenganchar bruscamente, estallar, romperse bruscamente, saltarse

snapped: ~ **corn** *n* AmE (*cf snapped maize BrE*) AGRIC maíz cosechado a mano que permanece con la espata *m*; ~ **maize** *n* BrE (*cf snapped corn AmE*) AGRIC maíz cosechado a mano que permanece con la espata *m*

snapshot *n* COMP&DP imagen instantánea *f*, instantánea *f*, PHOTO imagen instantánea *f*; ~ **dump** *n* COMP&DP vuelco instantáneo *m*

snarl¹ *n* TEXTIL maraña *f*

snarl² *vt* TEXTIL enmarañar, ensortijar

SNDCF *abbr* (*subnetwork dependent convergence function*) TELECOM función de convergencia dependiente de la red secundaria *f*

Snell: **~'s law** *n* PHYS ley de Snell *f*

SNG *abbr* (*synthetic natural gas*) GAS, PETR TECH GNS (*gas natural sintético*)

sniffer: ~ **device** *n* GAS dispositivo olfateador *m*

sniper *n* MILIT tirador emboscado *m*

snoot *n* CINEMAT aditamento cónico *m*

snorkel *n* CINEMAT periscopio *m*, OCEAN tubo de respiración atmosférica *m*, tubo para toma de aire libre *m*

snorkle *n* CINEMAT esnorkel *m*

snow¹: **~-capped** *adj* METEO coronado de nieve

snow² *n* ELECTRON nieve *f*, parásitos *m pl*, METEO, REFRIG, TV nieve *f*; ~ **barrier** *n* CONST valla de contención de nieve *f*; ~ **belt** *n* METEO cinturón de nieve *m*; ~ **blindness** *n* METEO ceguera de la nieve *f*; ~ **blower** *n* TRANSP máquina quitanieves *f*; ~ **cover** *n* METEO capa de nieve *f*, suelo nevado *m*; ~ **detector** *n* TRANSP detector de nieve *m*; ~ **flurry** *n* METEO ráfaga de nieve *f*; ~ **gun** *n* REFRIG proyector de nieve *m*; ~ **ice** *n* REFRIG hielo nieve *m*; ~ **line** *n* METEO límite de la nieve *m*; ~ **machine** *n* CINEMAT máquina de nieve *f*; ~ **melt** *n* AmE (*cf snow water BrE*) WATER deshielo de la nieve *m*, fusión de nieves *f*; ~ **plough** *n* BrE AGRIC quitanieves *m*; ~ **plow** *n* AmE *see snow plough BrE*; ~ **storage** *n* HYDROL depósito de nieve *m*; ~ **tire** *n* AmE, ~ **tyre** *n* BrE *n* VEH neumático para nieve *m*; ~ **water** *n* BrE WATER deshielo de la nieve *m*, fusión de nieves *f*

snowdrift *n* METEO banco de nieve *m*, nieve acumulada *f*

snowed: **~-up** *adj* METEO aprisionado por la nieve

snowfall *n* METEO caída de nieve *f*, nieve caída *f*

snowflake *n* METEO copo de nieve *m*; ~ **curve** *n* GEOM curva de copo de nieve *f*; ~ **topology** *n* COMP&DP topología en estrella *f*, topología en forma de copo de nieve *f*

SNP *abbr* (*sequence number protection*) TELECOM protección del número de orden *f*, protección del número secuencial *f*

SNR *abbr* (*signal-to-noise ratio*) GEN relación señal-ruido *f*

snubber *n* MECH, SPACE amortiguador *m*, tambor de frenado *m*; ~ **capacitor** *n* ELEC ENG condensador de retención *m*; ~ **circuit** *n* ELEC ENG circuito de seguridad *m*; ~ **resistor** *n* ELEC ENG resistencia de seguridad *f*

SO: ~ **character** *n* COMP&DP carácter SO *m*

soak¹ *vt* C&G, FOOD, TEXTIL remojar

soak² *vi* C&G, FOOD, TEXTIL empaparse

soaking *n* C&G, FOOD, TEXTIL remojo *m*; **~-drying cycle** *n* C&G, CONST, FOOD ciclo de secado por impregnación *m*; **~ pit** *n* HEAT, THERMO, WATER horno de termodifusión *m*

soapstone *n* MINERAL saponita *f*

societal: ~ **risk** *n* QUALITY riesgo social *m*

Society: ~ **of Motion Picture Technicians** *n* (*SMPTE*) CINEMAT Sociedad de Técnicos Cinematográficos *f* (*SMPTE*)

socket¹ *n* CINEMAT enchufe hembra *m*, CONST *of shovel* casquillo *m*, ELEC *connection* toma de corriente *f*, tomacorriente *m*, enchufe hembra *m*, ELEC ENG enchufe hembra a rosca *m*, enchufe hembra *m*, LAB enchufe hembra *m*, MECH manguito *m*, portalámparas *m*, enchufe *m*, tomacorriente *m*, MECH ENG *drill* tomacorriente *m*, MINE pescaherramientas abocinado *m* (*AmL*), campana de pesca *f* (*Esp*), PHYS enchufe *m*, PROD casquillo adaptador *m*, receptáculo *m*, caja de enchufe *f*, enchufe hembra *m*, portalámparas *m*, tomacorriente *m*, manguito *m*, TELECOM caja de enchufe *f*, enchufe hembra *m*, base de enchufe *f*, TV tomacorriente *m*; ~ **adaptor** *n* ELEC, ELEC ENG adaptador de bayoneta *m*, adaptador de enchufe *m*; ~ **board** *n* ELEC ENG regleta de clavijas bipolares hembra *f*; ~ **contact** *n* ELEC ENG contacto de clavija *m*; ~ **coupler** *n* ELEC *connection* acoplador de enchufe hembra *m*; ~ **joint** *n* MECH junta de rótula *f*, junta esférica *f*; ~ **outlet** *n* TELECOM enchufe *m*; ~ **pipe** *n* CONST tubería de enchufe *f*; ~ **plug** *n* ELEC *connection* clavija *f*, conector macho *m*; ~ **punch** *n* PROD sacabocados a golpe *m*; ~ **with shrouded contacts** *n* ELEC *connection* enchufe macho con contactos blindados *m*; ~ **wrench** *n* MECH llave de cubo *f*

socket² *vt* CONST *pipes* empalmar con junta de enchufe

sod *n* AGRIC césped *m*; ~ **seeder** *n* AGRIC sembradora bajo cubierta *f*

soda *n* C&G, CHEM sosa *f*; ~ **acid fire-extinguisher** *n* SAFE extintor de soda-ácido *m*; ~ **alum** *n* CHEM alumbre potásico *m*, alumbre sódico *m*; ~ **ash** *n* DETERG ceniza de sosa *f*, sosa comercial *f*, PAPER carbonato sódico *m*; **~-chlorine pulp** *n* PAPER pulpa al cloro-sosa *f*; ~ **lime** *n* CHEM *lime sodium hydroxide* cal soda *f*; ~ **niter** *n* AmE, ~ **nitre** *n* BrE *n* C&G nitrato de sodio *m*, MINERAL nitro sódico *m*; ~ **pulp** *n* PAPER pasta a la sosa *f*, pulpa a la sosa *f*

sodalite *n* MINERAL sodalita *f*

sodamide *n* CHEM sodamida *f*

sodic *adj* CHEM, GEOL sódico

sodium *n* (*Na*) CHEM, METALL sodio *m* (*Na*); ~ **alginate** *n* FOOD alginato sódico *m*;

~ **bicarbonate** *n* CHEM, DETERG, FOOD bicarbonato de sodio *m*, bicarbonato sódico *m*; ~ **borate** *n* CHEM borato sódico *m*; ~ **carbonate** *n* CHEM carbonato de sodio *m*, carbonato sódico *m*, DETERG, PAPER carbonato de sodio *m*; ~ **caseinate** *n* FOOD caseinato sódico *m*; ~ **chloride** *n* CHEM cloruro sódico *m*; ~**-cooled reactor** *n* NUCL reactor refrigerado por sodio *m*; ~**-cooled valve** *n* AUTO válvula de refrigeración por sodio *f*; ~ **D-line** *n* PHYS línea D del sodio *f*; ~ **hydroxide** *n* CHEM hidróxido de sodio *m*, sosa cáustica *f*; ~ **lamp** *n* ELEC *lighting* lámpara de sodio *f*; ~ **nitrate** *n* C&G nitrato de sodio *m*, CHEM nitrato sódico *m*; ~ **polyphosphate** *n* CHEM, FOOD polifosfato sódico *m*; ~ **salt** *n* CHEM sal de sodio *f*; ~ **sesquicarbonate** *n* DETERG sesquicarbonato de sodio *m*; ~ **silicate** *n* DETERG silicato de sodio *m*; ~ **sulfate** *AmE see sodium sulphate BrE*; ~ **sulfur storage battery** *AmE see sodium sulphur storage battery BrE*; ~ **sulphate** *n BrE* CHEM sulfato sódico *m*, DETERG sulfato de sodio *m*; ~ **sulphur storage battery** *n BrE* ELEC ENG, TRANSP batería de acumuladores de azufre-sodio *f*, batería de reserva sulfurosódica *f*; ~ **tetraborate** *n* CHEM, DETERG tetraborato de sodio *m*; ~ **thiosulfate** *AmE*, ~ **thiosulphate** *BrE* *n* CHEM hiposulfito de sodio *m*, tiosulfato sódico *m*; ~ **vapor lamp** *AmE*, ~ **vapour lamp** *BrE n* ELEC, ELEC ENG, RAD PHYS lámpara de vapor de sodio *f*
soffit *n* CONST *of arch* intradós *m*, *underside of floor* sofito *m*
soft[1]: ~**-bound** *adj* PRINT encuadernado con tapas blandas; ~**-sectored** *adj* COMP&DP dividido en sectores por software, sectorizado blando
soft[2]: ~ **anneal** *n* THERMO *materials* recocido blando *m*, recocido suave *m*; ~ **annealing** *n* METALL recocido blando *m*; ~**-brazing solder** *n* PROD soldadura de latón dulce *f*; ~ **bromide paper** *n* PHOTO papel bromuro suave *m*; ~ **coal** *n* COAL, MINE carbón bituminoso *m*, hulla grasa *f*; ~ **copy** *n* COMP&DP copia blanda *f*, copia en pantalla *f*; ~ **corn** *n AmE* (*cf soft maize BrE*) AGRIC maíz blando *m*; ~**-cover binding** *n* PRINT encuadernación de tapas blandas *f*; ~ **cut** *n* CINEMAT transición suave *f*; ~ **decision decoding** *n* TELECOM decodificación de la decisión blanda *f*; ~ **developer** *n* PHOTO revelador suave *m*; ~ **dot** *n* PRINT punto débil *m*; ~ **fire** *n* C&G fuego suave *m*; ~ **focus** *n* CINEMAT, PHOTO, TV imagen ligeramente difusa *f*; ~**-focus lens** *n* CINEMAT lente difusora *f*, objetivo anacromático *m*, INSTR, OPT objetivo anacromático *m*, PHOTO lente difusora *f*, objetivo anacromático *m*, PHYS objetivo anacromático *m*; ~ **glass** *n* C&G vidrio suave *m*; ~ **grade** *n* PROD *emery wheels* grado de dureza blando *m*, nivel de blandura *m*; ~ **ground** *n* CONST suelo blando *m*, terreno suave *m*; ~ **handle** *n* TEXTIL tacto suave *m*; ~ **iron** *n* ELEC ENG hierro de bobina móvil *m*, hierro dulce *m*, METALL hierro blando *m*, hierro de bobina móvil *m*, hierro dulce *m*, PHYS hierro blando *m*; ~**-iron core** *n* ELEC ENG núcleo de hierro fácilmente imanado por inducción *m*; ~ **key** *n* COMP&DP tecla blanda *f*, tecla programable *f*; ~ **keyboard** *n* COMP&DP teclado blando *m*, teclado programable *m*; ~ **landing** *n* AIR TRANSP, SPACE aterrizaje suave *f*; ~ **light** *n* CINEMAT, PHOTO, TV iluminación difusa *f*; ~ **magnetic material** *n* ELEC ENG material de gran permeabilidad y pequeña histéresis *m*, PHYS material magnético blando *m*; ~ **maize** *n BrE* (*cf soft corn*

AmE) AGRIC maíz blando *m*; ~ **metal hammer** *n* PROD martillo de metal dúctil *m*; ~ **mock-up** *n* SPACE maqueta blanda *f*, simulador suave *m*; ~ **nip** *n* PAPER línea de contacto blanda *f*; ~ **nip roll** *n* PAPER rodillo de línea de contacto blanda *m*; ~ **porcelain** *n* C&G porcelana suave *f*; ~ **proof** *n* PRINT prueba electrónica *f*; ~ **radiation** *n* RAD PHYS radiación blanda *f*; ~ **return** *n* PRINT nueva línea transitoria *f*; ~**-sectored disk** *n* COMP&DP disco dividido en sectores por software *m*; ~ **sectoring** *n* COMP&DP división en sectores por software *m*, sectorización blanda *f*; ~ **snow** *n* METEO nieve blanda *f*, nieve dura *f*; ~ **solder** *n* ELEC *connection* soldadura blanda *f*, soldante blando *m*; ~ **soldering** *n* ELEC *connection* soldadura blanda *f*, soldadura blanda con estaño y plomo *f*; ~ **source** *n* CINEMAT fuente de iluminación difusa *f*, fuente difusa *f*; ~ **start** *n* PROD arranque suave *m*; ~ **superconductor** *n* ELEC, ELECTRON, PHYS superconductor débil *m*; ~ **tissue** *n* PAPER papel tisú guata *m*; ~ **tube** *n* ELECTRON tubo de escaso vacío *m*; ~ **water** *n* HYDROL, WATER agua blanda *f*; ~**-water generator** *n* CHEM TECH generador de agua dulce *m*; ~ **wheel** *n* PROD muela dulce *f*; ~ **X-ray** *n* RAD PHYS rayo X blando *m*
soften *vt* GEN ablandar
softener *n* CHEM TECH, CONST, GAS, P&R, PRINT ablandador *m*, TEXTIL suavizante *m*
softening *n* CHEM TECH, CONST, GAS, HEAT ENG, P&R, PRINT ablandamiento *m*; ~ **agent** *n* TEXTIL agente suavizante *m*; ~ **furnace** *n* C&G horno de ablandamiento *m*; ~ **point** *n* P&R, REFRIG punto de reblandecimiento *m*, TEXTIL punto de suavizado *m*; ~ **range** *n* C&G rango de ablandamiento *m*
softness *n* PAPER, PRINT blandura *f*
software *n* COMP&DP software *m*, soporte lógico *m*, ELEC *computing* elementos de programación *m pl*, software *m*, PETR TECH componente lógico *m*, dotación lógica *f*, software *m*, PHYS software *m*; ~ **adaptation** *n* COMP&DP adaptación del software *f*, adaptación del soporte lógico *f*; ~ **configuration** *n* COMP&DP configuración del software *f*, configuración del soporte lógico *f*; ~ **design** *n* COMP&DP diseño de soporte lógico *m*, diseño del software *m*; ~ **development** *n* COMP&DP desarrollo de software *m*, desarrollo de soporte lógico *m*; ~ **engineering** *n* COMP&DP ingeniería de software *f*, ingeniería de soporte lógico *f*, técnica de programación *f*; ~ **error** *n* COMP&DP error de software *m*; ~ **methodology** *n* COMP&DP metodología de soporte lógico *f*, metodología del software *f*; ~ **package** *n* COMP&DP paquete de programas *m*, paquete de software *m*, paquete de soporte lógico *m*, PHYS paquete de software *m*; ~ **products** *n pl* COMP&DP productos de producción *m pl*, TELECOM productos de producción *m pl*, productos software *m pl*; ~ **resources** *n pl* COMP&DP recursos de software *m pl*, recursos de soporte lógico *m pl*; ~ **tool** *n* COMP&DP dispositivo de soporte lógico *m*, herramienta de software *f*
softwood *n* CONST madera blanda *f*, madera de coníferas *f*, madera de resinosas *f*, PAPER madera de coníferas *f*, WATER TRANSP madera de coníferas *f*, madera de resinosas *f*; ~ **pulp** *n* PAPER pulpa de coníferas *f*, pasta de coníferas *f*
SOH *abbr* COMP&DP (*start of header*) comienzo de cabecera *m*, comienzo de título *m*, inicio de encabe-

zamiento *m*, TELECOM (*section overhead*) línea aérea de la sección *f*, sección de línea aérea *f*

soil *n* AGRIC, COAL suelo *m*, terreno *m*, GEOPHYS suelo *m*, tierra *f*; **~ amendment** *n* AGRIC enmienda del suelo *f*; **~ building** *n* AGRIC restauración de suelo *f*; **~ exploration** *n* COAL exploración del suelo *f*; **~ freezing** *n* REFRIG congelación del suelo *f*; **~ management** *n* AGRIC manejo de suelos *m*; **~ mechanics** *n pl* COAL geomecánica *f*, geotecnia *f*, mecánica de suelos *f*, CONST geotecnia *f*, mecánica del suelo *f*, GEOL geotecnia *f*, mecánica de suelos *f*; **~ pipe** *n* WATER bajante de aguas sucias *m*, tubería de evacuación *f*, tubo de acometida a la alcantarilla *m*; **~ pollutant** *n* POLL contaminante de la tierra *m*, contaminante del suelo *m*, contaminante del terreno *m*; **~ pollution** *n* POLL contaminación de la tierra *f*, contaminación del suelo *f*; **~ pressure** *n* COAL geopresión *f*; **~ profile pit** *n* AGRIC calicata *f*; **~ pulverizer** *n* AGRIC rodillo pulverizador *m*; **~-release finish** *n* COATINGS acabado granulado *m*; **~ science** *n* AGRIC edafología *f*, COAL edafología *f*, pedología *f*, WATER geotecnia *f*; **~ stabilization** *n* CONST estabilización del suelo *f*; **~ surgeon** *n* AGRIC grada rodillo *f*; **~ water** *n* WATER suelo agua *m*

soilage *n* AGRIC verdeo *m*

soiling *n* AGRIC suministro de verdeo *m*

solanidine *n* CHEM solanidina *f*

solar[1] *adj* CONST solar; **~-powered** *adj* ELEC, ELEC ENG alimentado por energía solar, FUELLESS impulsado por la energía del sol, alimentado por energía solar

solar[2]: **~ absorbency** *n* FUELLESS absorbencia solar *f*; **~ absorber** *n* SPACE absorbedor solar *m*, atenuador solar *m*; **~ absorptivity** *n* FUELLESS absorbencia solar *f*; **~ absorption coefficient** *n* FUELLESS coeficiente de absorción solar *m*; **~ activity** *n* METEO, PHYS actividad solar *f*; **~ altitude** *n* FUELLESS, SPACE altura del sol *f*; **~ altitude angle** *n* FUELLESS, SPACE altura del sol sobre el horizonte *f*; **~ azimuth** *n* FUELLESS, SPACE acimut solar *m*; **~ battery** *n* FUELLESS, TV batería solar *f*; **~ cell** *n* ELEC célula solar *f*, heliopila *f*, pila solar *f*, ELEC ENG célula fotovoltaica solar *f*, pila solar *f*, FUELLESS, PHYS, RAD PHYS célula solar *f*, SPACE celdilla solar *f*, célula fotovoltaica solar *f*, célula solar *f*, heliopila *f*, pila solar *f*, TELECOM célula solar *f*, heliopila *f*, pila solar *f*; **~-cell panel** *n* ELEC ENG panel de células solares *m*; **~ collector** *n* CONST panel solar *m*, FUELLESS colector solar *m*; **~ concentrator** *n* FUELLESS dispositivo concentrador solar *m*, INSTR concentrador solar *m*; **~ constant** *n* FUELLESS, GEOPHYS, SPACE constante solar *f*; **~ control glass** *n* C&G vidrio antisolar *m*; **~ corona** *n* GEOPHYS corona solar *f*; **~ distillation** *n* FUELLESS destilación solar *f*; **~ dynamics** *n* FUELLESS dinámica solar *f*; **~ electric power plant** *n* ELEC ENG, FUELLESS planta de potencia eléctrica solar *f*; **~ electric power station** *n* ELEC ENG central de fuerza eléctrica solar *f*; **~ electricity** *n* ELEC ENG electricidad solar *f*; **~ energy** *n* ELEC ENG, FUELLESS, PHYS energía solar *f*; **~ energy conversion** *n* ELEC ENG conversión de la energía solar *f*; **~ engineering** *n* FUELLESS ingeniería solar *f*; **~ farm** *n* FUELLESS instalación solar *f*; **~ flare** *n* GEOPHYS destello solar *m*, fulguración solar *f*, SPACE centelleo solar *m*, erupción cromosférica *f*, erupción solar *f*, llamarada solar *f*; **~ furnace** *n* FUELLESS horno solar *m*; **~ generator** *n* ELEC ENG generador helioeléctrico *m*, SPACE generador helioeléctrico *m*,

generador solar *m*; **~ heat** *n* FUELLESS calor solar *m*; **~ heating system** *n* FUELLESS sistema de calefacción solar *m*; **~ panel** *n* FUELLESS, PHYS, SPACE, TELECOM panel solar *m*; **~ pond** *n* FUELLESS laguna solar *f*; **~ power** *n* FUELLESS, PHYS poder solar *m*; **~ power farm** *n* ELEC ENG central de energía solar *f*; **~ proton** *n* GEOPHYS protón solar *m*; **~ radiation** *n* FUELLESS, GEOPHYS, POLL, RAD PHYS radiación solar *f*; **~ radiation pressure** *n* SPACE presión de la radiación solar *f*; **~ sail** *n* SPACE vela solar *f*; **~-sail propulsion** *n* SPACE propulsión por vela solar *f*; **~ sensor** *n* SPACE sensor solar *m*; **~ storm** *n* GEOPHYS tormenta solar *f*; **~ technology** *n* FUELLESS tecnología solar *f*; **~ telescope** *n* INSTR telescopio solar *m*; **~ telescope tower** *n* INSTR torre de telescopio solar *f*; **~ thermal conversion** *n* FUELLESS conversión termica solar *f*; **~ tide** *n* GEOPHYS marea solar *f*; **~ tower** *n* FUELLESS torre solar *f*; **~ wind** *n* GEOPHYS, PHYS, SPACE viento solar *m*

solarimeter *n* FUELLESS solarímetro *m*

solarization *n* CINEMAT, PHOTO solarización *f*

solder[1] *n* ELEC ENG soldadura *f*; **~ joint** *n* PROD junta estañosoldada *f*; **~ tag** *n* PROD terminal para estañosoldar *m*; **~ termination** *n* PROD terminación de soldadura *f*

solder[2] *vt* CONST, ELEC, ELEC ENG, PROD soldar

solderability *n* PROD soldabilidad *f*

solderable[1] *adj* PROD soldable

solderable[2]: **~ lacquer** *n* COATINGS laca con capacidad de unirse *f*, laca soldable *f*

soldered: **~ seam** *n* FOOD borde soldado *m*; **~ side** *n* TELECOM lateral soldado *m*

solderer *n* MECH, MECH ENG, METALL soldador *m*

soldering *n* CONST soldadura *f*, PROD soldeo con aleaciones de estaño y plomo *m*; **~ bit** *n* PROD *tool* soldador de cobre *m*; **~ blowpipe** *n* CONST soplete de soldadura *m*; **~ copper** *n* PROD soldador de cobre *m*; **~ flux** *n* ELEC fundente para soldar *m*; **~ gun** *n* ELEC pistola de soldar *f*; **~ iron** *n* CONST hierro de soldar *m*, ELEC cautín *m*, hierro de soldar *m*, soldador *m*, PROD soldador *m*; **~ joint** *n* PROD junta estañosoldada *f*

sole *n* AGRIC fondo del surco *m*, CONST *of plane* base *f*, solera *f*, GEOL base de capa *f*, base de un glaciar *f*, MINE durmiente *m* (*AmL*), muro transversal sumergido *m* (*AmL*), suelo *m*, solera *f* (*Esp*), PROD *of furnace* solera *f*, *of plummer block* patín *m*; **~ furrow** *n* AGRIC gleba del surco muerto *f*; **~ piece** *n* CONST solera *f*; **~ plate** *n* CONST solera *f*, PROD *of plummer block* placa de base *f*, SPACE placa de cimentación *f*, zapata *f*

solenoid *n* AUTO interruptor magnético *m*, ELEC *coil*, ELEC ENG, PHYS, PROD, REFRIG, TV solenoide *m*, VEH interruptor magnético *m*, solenoide *m*; **~ actuation** *n* ELEC ENG fuerza solenoide *f*; **~ coil** *n* REFRIG bobina de solenoide *f*; **~-operated shutoff valve** *n* PROD válvula de parada accionada por solenoide *f*; **~ relay** *n* ELEC relé de núcleo buzo *m*, ELEC ENG relé solenoide *m*; **~ stepper motor** *n* ELEC ENG motor de paso solenoide *m*; **~ valve** *n* HYDRAUL, PROD, REFRIG válvula de solenoide *f*

solenoidal: **~ field** *n* PHYS campo solenoidal *m*

solicited: **~-information indicator** *n* TELECOM indicador de información solicitada *m*

solid[1] *adj* CHEM sólido, COAL macizo, CONST *firm ground* macizo, sólido, ELECTRON compacto, GEOL,

MINE macizo, PROD compacto; **~-state** *adj* COMP&DP, TV de estado sólido

solid[2] *n* GEOM, PHYS sólido *m*, PROD *gold, silver* puro, sólido *m*; **~ aluminium capacitor** *n* BrE ELEC ENG condensador de aluminio sólido *m*; **~ aluminum capacitor** *AmE see solid aluminium capacitor BrE*; **~ angle** *n* ELEC, GEOM, PHYS ángulo sólido *m*; **~ bifocals** *n pl* C&G bifocales sólidos *m pl*; **~ blank** *n* PROD pieza maciza *f*; **~ block** *n* PROD bloque macizo *m*; **~ board** *n* PAPER cartón homogéneo *m*; **~ bond** *n* ELEC ligadura sólida *f*; **~ brick** *n* CONST ladrillo compacto *m*, ladrillo macizo *m*; **~ casting** *n* PROD pieza maciza de fundición *f*; **~ color** *AmE*, **~ colour** *BrE n* COLOUR color liso *m*; **~ conductor** *n* ELEC conductor de cable unifilar *m*, conductor sencillo *m*, ELEC ENG hilo único *m*; **~ content** *n* PRINT contenido sólido *m*; **~-core-type insulator** *n* ELEC, ELEC ENG aislante por núcleo sólido *m*; **~ dielectric** *n* ELEC ENG dieléctrico de papel impregnado en aceite *m*; **~-electrolyte capacitor** *n* ELEC ENG condensador de electrólito sólido *m*; **~ exchanger** *n* COAL pérdida sólida *f*; **~ expansion thermometer** *n* REFRIG termómetro de dilatación de sólidos *m*; **~-fuel booster** *n* SPACE impulsor de combustible sólido *m*; **~-fuelled rocket** *n* SPACE cohete aprovisionado de combustible sólido *m*; **~ geometry** *n* GEOM geometría de sólidos *f*, geometría sólida *f*; **~ hydrocarbons** *n pl* CHEM hidrocarburos sólidos *m pl*; **~ ink density** *n* PRINT densidad de la tinta en las masas *f*; **~ letter** *n* PRINT letra llena *f*; **~ matter** *n* HYDROL materias sólidas *f pl*, PRINT composición sin interlinear *f*, RECYCL materias sólidas *f pl*; **~ measure** *n* METR medida sólida *f*; **~-newel stair** *n* CONST escalera de pilares macizos *f*; **~ nuclear fuel** *n* NUCL combustible nuclear sólido *m*; **~ object** *n* PROD objeto sólido *m*; **~ particle** *n* POLL partícula sólida *f*; **~ phase** *n* THERMO fase sólida *f*; **~ piston** *n* HYDRAUL émbolo tubular *m*; **~ propellant** *n* SPACE propelente sólido *m*, propulsor sólido *m*; **~-propellant rocket** *n* SPACE cohete de propelente sólido *m*, cohete de propulsor sólido *m*; **~-propellant system** *n* SPACE sistema de propelentes sólidos *m*; **~ of revolution** *n* GEOM sólido de revolución *m*; **~ rotor** *n* ELEC rotor macizo *m*; **~ solution** *n* CHEM, CRYSTALL, GEOL solución sólida *f*; **~ state** *n* COMP&DP, ELEC, PART PHYS, RAD PHYS estado sólido *m*; **~-state amplifier** *n* ELECTRON, TELECOM amplificador de estado sólido *m*; **~-state camera** *n* ELECTRON cámara compacta *f*, cámara de estado sólido *f*; **~-state component** *n* PROD componente de estado sólido *m*; **~-state controls** *n pl* PROD mandos de estado sólido *m pl*; **~-state detector** *n* RAD PHYS detector de estado sólido *m*; **~-state device** *n* ELEC dispositivo de estado sólido *m*, ELECTRON aparato compacto *m*, dispositivo de estado sólido *m*, equipo compacto *m*, PHYS aparato de estado sólido *m*, TELECOM dispositivo de estado sólido *m*; **~-state effect** *n* NUCL efecto de estado sólido *m*; **~-state electronics** *n* ELECTRON electrónica del estado sólido *f*; **~-state laser** *n* ELECTRON láser compacto *m*; **~-state maser** *n* ELECTRON maser compacto *m*; **~-state memory** *n* ELEC ENG memoria de semiconductores *f*; **~-state module** *n* PROD módulo de estado sólido *m*; **~-state motor controller** *n* PROD controlador de circuito impreso para motor *m*, controlador de motor de estado sólido *m*, controlador transisto-

rizado *m*; **~-state physics** *n* PART PHYS física del estado sólido *f*; **~-state rectifier** *n* ELECTRON rectificador de estado sólido *m*; **~-state relay** *n* ELEC ENG relé de estado sólido *m*; **~-state surge arrester** *n* ELEC ENG protector de sobretensión de carácter sólido *m*; **~ synchrotransformer** *n* ELEC ENG sincrotransformador sólido *m*; **~ tantalum capacitor** *n* ELEC ENG condensador de tantalio sólido *m*, MECH ENG condensador de tantalio sólido *m*; **~ waste** *n* POLL desechos sólidos *m pl*, desperdicios sólidos *m pl*, residuos sólidos *m pl*, RECYCL desperdicios sólidos *m pl*; **~ wire** *n* ELEC conductor alambre macizo *m*, hilo sencillo *m*, ELEC ENG *conductor* alambre macizo *m*

Solid: ~ Spinning Upper Stage *n* (*SSUS*) SPACE última fase rotatoria sólida *f* (*SSUS*); **~ State Interlocking** *n* BrE (*SSI*) RAIL enclavamiento de estado sólido *m*

solidification *n* PHYS solidificación *f*; **~ point** *n* REFRIG punto de solidificación *m*

solidified: ~ fat *n* FOOD grasa solidificada *f*

solidifier *n* MAR POLL solidificador *m*

solidifying *n* METALL solidificación *f*

solidity *n* AIR TRANSP *propeller* consistencia *f*, solidez *f*, FUELLESS solidez *f*

solidly: ~-earthed neutral system *n* BrE (*cf solidly-grounded neutral system AmE*) ELEC sistema con neutro puesto directamente a tierra *m*; **~-grounded neutral system** *n* AmE (*cf solidly-earthed neutral system BrE*) ELEC sistema con neutro puesto directamente a tierra *m*

solids *n pl* PRINT masas *f pl*, masas llenas *f pl*

solifluction: ~ lobe *n* GEOL lóbulo de solifluxión *m*, GEOPHYS lóbulo de soliflucción *m*; **~ tongue** *n* GEOPHYS lengua de soliflucción *f*

soling *n* P&R solado *m*

solo: ~ flight time *n* AIR TRANSP tiempo de vuelo en solitario *m*; **~-piston pump** *n* HYDRAUL bomba de un solo émbolo *f*

solstitial: ~ period *n* SPACE período de los solsticios *m*, época solsticial *f*; **~ point** *n* SPACE punto solsticial *m*

solubility *n* CHEM, COAL, P&R solubilidad *f*; **~ product** *n* CHEM *of electrolyte* producto de solubilidad *m*

soluble[1] *adj* CHEM, PETR TECH soluble

soluble[2]: **~ deposit extraction** *n* CHEM TECH extracción de los depósitos solubles *f*; **~ glass** *n* DETERG vidrio soluble *m*; **~ poison control** *n* NUCL control por venenos solubles *m*; **~ sachet** *n* PACK bolsita soluble *f*

solute[1] *adj* CHEM soluto

solute[2] *n* FOOD soluto *m*

solution *n* CHEM, CHEM TECH solución *f*, GEOM *theory, entity* resultado *m*, MATH solución *f*; **~ annealing** *n* METALL recocido por solubilización *m*; **~ gas drive** *n* PETR TECH empuje del gas en solución *m*, empuje por gas en disolución *m*; **~ gas-oil ratio** *n* PETR TECH relación petróleo-gas en solución *f*; **~ mixer** *n* P&R mezclador de soluciones *m*; **~ polymerization** *n* P&R polimerización en solución *f*

solvate *n* CHEM solvato *m*

solvated *adj* CHEM solvatado

solvation *n* CHEM solvatación *f*

Solvay: ~'s ammonia soda process *n* DETERG proceso de sosa amoniacal de Solvay *m*; **~'s process** *n* DETERG proceso de Solvay *m*

solvent[1] *adj* CHEM disolvente, POLL disolvente, solvente

solvent[2] *n* CHEM disolvente *m*, solvente *m*, CINEMAT disolvente *m*, COAL, DETERG disolvente *m*, solvente *m*, FOOD, METALL disolvente *m*, P&R disolvente *m*, solvente *m*, PACK disolvente *m*, POLL disolvente *m*, solvente *m*, TEXTIL disolvente *m*; **~-based ink** *n* PRINT tinta a base de disolventes *f*; **~-coated paper** *n* PAPER papel revestido por medio de disolventes *m*; **~ dyeing** *n* COLOUR teñido al disolvente *m*; **~ extraction** *n* FOOD extracción disolvente *f*; **~ leaching** *n* COAL extracción con disolventes *f*; **~ recovery** *n* FOOD recuperación de disolvente *f*; **~ refining** *n* PETR TECH refino con disolvente *m*; **~ welding** *n* P&R soldadura con solvente *f*

SOM *abbr* (*start of message*) COMP&DP comienzo del mensaje *m*

Sommerfield: **~ number** *n* FUELLESS *tidal power constant* número Sommerfield *m*

sonar *n* ACOUST, MILIT, OCEAN, WATER TRANSP, WAVE PHYS sonar *m*; **~ hole** *n* OCEAN nicho del sonar *m*; **~ signal** *n* ELECTRON señal sonárica *f*; **~ transducer** *n* ACOUST transductor sonar *m*

sone *n* ACOUST sonio *m*, PHYS sone *m*

sonic[1] *adj* ACOUST acústico, sónico

sonic[2]: **~ bang** *n* SAFE golpe sónico *m*; **~ boom** *n* ACOUST, AIR TRANSP, PHYS, SAFE estampido sónico *m*; **~ cleaner** *n* CINEMAT limpiador sónico *m*; **~ depth finder** *n* MILIT detector sónico de profundidad *m*, sonda acústica *f*, OCEAN, WATER TRANSP detector sónico de profundidad *m*; **~ detector** *n* TRANSP detector sónico *m*; **~ fatigue** *n* METALL fatiga acústica *f*; **~ log** *n* PETR TECH diagrafía sónica *f*, perfil sónico *m*, registro sónico *m*

sonometer *n* PHYS, WAVE PHYS sonómetro *m*

soot: **~-and-whitewash print** *n* CINEMAT copia con efecto de sombreado *f*

sorbent *n* MAR POLL sorbente *m*; **~ wick** *n* MAR POLL mecha absorbente *f*

sorbic: **~ acid** *n* CHEM ácido sórbico *m*

sorbite *n* CHEM sorbita *f*

sorbitol *n* CHEM sorbitol *m*

sorbose *n* CHEM sorbosa *f*

sorghum: **~ stalk field** *n* AGRIC rastrojo del sorgo *m*

sorption *n* CHEM, WATER sorción *f*; **~ pump** *n* PHYS bomba de absorción *f*

sort[1] *n* COMP&DP clasificación *f*; **~ field** *n* COMP&DP campo de clasificación *m*; **~ generator** *n* COMP&DP generador de clasificación *m*; **~ program** *n* COMP&DP programa de clasificación *m*

sort[2] *vt* COMP&DP clasificar, MINE entresacar, escoger, triar; **~ by color** *AmE*, **~ by colour** *BrE vt* TEXTIL clasificar por colores; **~ by hand** *vt* COAL clasificar a mano, seleccionar a mano; **~ by shade** *vt* TEXTIL clasificar por matices

sorter *n* C&G clasificador *m*

sorting *n* C&G clasificación *f*, COAL clasificación *f*, elección *f*, separación *f*, COMP&DP clasificación *f*, GEOL clasificación *f*, separación *f*, PAPER selección *f*; **~ belt** *n* PROD banda clasificadora *f*, cinta clasificadora *f*; **~ line** *n* RAIL línea de clasificación *f*; **~ machine** *n* PACK máquina clasificadora *f*; **~ siding** *n* RAIL apartadero de clasificación *m*, ramal de clasificación *m*, TRANSP apartadero de clasificación *m*

sorts *n pl* PRINT suertes *f pl*

SOS *abbr* (*silicon on sapphire*) ELECTRON silicio con zafiro

sound[1] *n* ACOUST sonido *m*, OCEAN brazo de mar *m*,

estrecho *m*, PHYS sonido *m*, WATER TRANSP *navigation* brazo de mar *m*, estrecho *m*, sonda *f*; **~-absorbent ceiling** *n* SAFE cielo falso absorbente de sonidos *m*; **~-absorbent door** *n* SAFE puerta amortiguadora de sonido *f*; **~-absorbent foam panel** *n* SAFE panel de espuma amortiguador de sonidos *m*; **~-absorbent wall** *n* SAFE pared acústica *f*; **~ absorber** *n* ACOUST absorbedor de sonido *m*; **~-absorbing machine** *n* SAFE máquina insonizadora *f*; **~ absorption** *n* ACOUST absorción sonora *f*; **~ acceleration** *n* ACOUST aceleración sonora *f*; **~ acceleration level** *n* ACOUST nivel de aceleración sonora *m*; **~ alarm radiation dosimeter** *n* RAD PHYS dosímetro de alarma acústica *m*; **~ analyser** *n* *BrE* ACOUST analizador sonoro *m*; **~ analyzer** *AmE see sound analyser BrE*; **~ booth** *n* CINEMAT cabina insonorizada *f*; **~ broadcast transmitter** *n* TELECOM emisor de radiodifusión de sonido *m*, transmisor de radiodifusión de sonido *m*; **~ broadcasting** *n* TELECOM radiodifusión sonora *f*; **~ camera** *n* CINEMAT cámara insonora *f*; **~ carrier** *n* ELECTRON portadora de sonido *f*; **~ channel** *n* OCEAN canal sonoro *m*, canal acústico *m*, canal limpia *m*, TV canal de sonido *m*; **~ column** *n* ACOUST columna sonora *f*; **~ control desk** *n* CINEMAT tablero de control sonoro *m*; **~ control room** *n* CINEMAT cabina de control sonoro *f*; **~-deadening paint** *n* COLOUR pintura antiacústica *f*; **~ detector** *n* MILIT ecodetector *m*, sonodetector *m*; **~ diffusion** *n* ACOUST difusión sonora *f*; **~ direct positive** *n* CINEMAT copia positiva con sonido directo *f*; **~ effects** *n pl* CINEMAT efectos sonoros *m pl*, TV efectos de sonido *m pl*, efectos sonoros *m pl*; **~ energy** *n* ACOUST energía acústica *f*, energía sonora *f*, ELEC ENG energía acústica *f*; **~ energy density** *n* ACOUST, PHYS densidad de energía sónica *f*; **~ energy density level** *n* ACOUST nivel de densidad de energía sonora *m*; **~ energy flux** *n* PHYS flujo de energía sónica *m*; **~ exposure meter** *n* SAFE exposímetro acústico *m*; **~ field** *n* ACOUST campo sonoro *m*; **~ film head** *n* CINEMAT cabezal sonoro *m*; **~ film lamp** *n* CINEMAT lámpara insonorizada *f*; **~ frequency** *n* ELECTRON frecuencia de sonido *f*; **~ head** *n* TV lector del sonido *m*; **~-insulated door** *n* SAFE puerta insonorizadora *f*; **~ insulation** *n* ACOUST aislamiento acústico *m*, aislamiento fónico *m*, aislamiento sónico *m*, AIR TRANSP, VEH insonorización *f*, WATER TRANSP aislamiento acústico *m*, insonorización *f*; **~ intensity** *n* ACOUST, PHYS intensidad sonora *f*, intensidad sónica *f*; **~ intensity level** *n* ACOUST nivel de intensidad sonora *m*, PHYS nivel de intensidad de sonido *m*; **~ isolation** *n* ACOUST aislamiento fónico *m*, aislamiento sónico *m*; **~ level** *n* ACOUST nivel sonoro *m*; **~ level meter** *n* ACOUST sonómetro *m*, SAFE medidor acústico *m*; **~ locator** *n* ACOUST fonogoniómetro *m*, fonolocalizador *m*, localizador acústico *m*, sonolocalizador *m*, WAVE PHYS fonogonióometro *m*, fonolocalizador *m*; **~ modulation** *n* ACOUST modulación sonora *f*; **~ negative** *n* CINEMAT negativo de sonido *m*; **~ on vision** *n* TV sonido sobre imagen *m*; **~ path** *n* OCEAN recorrido ideal *m*; **~ positive** *n* CINEMAT copia positiva de sonido *f*; **~ power** *n* ACOUST *of source* potencia sonora *f*; **~ power level** *n* ACOUST nivel de potencia sonora *m*, PHYS nivel de potencia sónica *m*; **~ pressure** *n* ACOUST presión acústica *f* (*Esp*), presión sonora *f* (*AmL*), PHYS presión de sonido *f*, POLL presión acústica *f* (*Esp*), presión sonora *f* (*AmL*); ~ **pressure level** *n* (*SPL*) ACOUST nivel de presión acústica *m*, nivel de presión de sonido *m*, nivel de presión sonora *m*, PHYS nivel de presión de sonido *m*, POLL nivel de presión acústica *m*, nivel de presión de sonido *m*, nivel de presión sonora *m*; ~ **pressure spectrum** *n* ACOUST, POLL espectro de la presión acústica *m* (*Esp*), espectro de la presión sonora *m* (*AmL*); ~ **quality** *n* TELECOM calidad del sonido *f*; ~ **ranging** *n* ACOUST fonolocalización *f*, fonotelemetría *f*, WAVE PHYS fonolocalización *f*, fonotelemetría *f*, localización acústica *f*, radar acústico *m*; ~ **ray curve** *n* OCEAN deformación de los rayos acústicos *f*; ~ **recorder** *n* INSTR grabador de sonidos *m*, registrador de sonidos *m*; ~ **recording** *n* CINEMAT grabación *f*, registro sonoro *m*, grabación de sonido *f*, TELECOM grabación de sonido *f*, registro de sonido *m*, registro sonoro *m*, TV grabación de sonido *f*; ~~**reduction index** *n* PHYS índice de reducción de sonido *m*; ~ **signal** *n* ELECTRON, RAIL señal acústica *f*, TELECOM señal acústica *f*, señal de audio *f*, señal de sonido *f*, WATER TRANSP señal acústica *f*; ~ **source** *n* ACOUST, POLL fuente acústica *f*, fuente de sonido *f*, fuente sonora *f*; ~ **spectrograph** *n* ACOUST espectrógrafo acústico *m*; ~ **stage** *n* CINEMAT sala insonorizada *f*; ~~**sync generator** *n* CINEMAT, TV generador de sincronismo sonoro *m*; ~ **take** *n* ACOUST, CINEMAT toma de sonido *f*; ~ **take desk** *n* ACOUST consola de toma de sonido *f*; ~ **transfer** *n* CINEMAT transferencia sonora *f*; ~ **transmission** *n* ACOUST transmisión de sonido *f*, transmisión del sonido *f*, TELECOM propagación del sonido *f*, transmisión acústica *f*, transmisión de sonido *f*, transmisión sonora *f*; ~ **velocity** *n* ACOUST velocidad del sonido *f*; ~ **wave** *n* PHYS onda de sonido *f*, WAVE PHYS onda acústica *f*, onda de sonido *f*

sound² *vt* OCEAN escandallar, sondear

sound³ *vi* CONST sondar, WATER TRANSP escandallar, sondear

sounder *n* WATER TRANSP batómetro *m*, sonda *f*, sonda acústica *f*

sounding *n* OCEAN sondeo *m*, escandallada *f*, PROD sonda acústica *f*, sondaje *m*, sondeo *m*, WATER TRANSP escandallada *f*, *in chart* sonda *f*; ~ **balloon** *n* METEO, SPACE globo sonda *m*; ~ **board** *n* WAVE PHYS mesa de sonido *f*; ~ **datum** *n* OCEAN cero hidrográfico *m*; ~ **datum level** *n* OCEAN nivel de reducción de sondas *m*; ~ **lead** *n* OCEAN, WATER TRANSP escandallo *m*; ~ **lidar** *n* SPACE lidar sonda *m*, sondeador lidar *m*; ~ **line** *n* OCEAN línea de sonda *f*, WATER TRANSP sondaleza *f*; ~ **pole** *n* WATER TRANSP pértiga sonda *f*; ~ **pool** *n* OCEAN colección *f*; ~ **profile** *n* OCEAN perfil batimétrico *m*; ~ **record** *n* COAL informe de sondeo *m*; ~ **rocket** *n* MILIT cohete de sondeo *m*, SPACE cohete sonda *m*

soundings *n pl* WATER TRANSP *of sea bottom* fondos aplacerados *m pl*, paraje sondable con escandallo *m*

soundproof: ~ **booth** *n* SAFE caseta a prueba de sonidos *f*; ~ **capsule** *n* SAFE cápsula a prueba de sonidos *f*; ~ **door** *n* SAFE puerta insonorizada *f* ~ **hood** *n* SAFE capucha a prueba de sonidos *f*; ~ **insulating glass** *n* ACOUST, SAFE vidrio aislante insonorizador *m*; ~ **plug** *n* SAFE tapón insonorizador *m*; ~ **tile** *n* C&G azulejo a prueba de sonidos *m*, SAFE azulejo a prueba de sonidos *m*, mosaico insonizado *m*

soundproofing *n* ACOUST, CINEMAT, SAFE insonoriza-

ción *f*; ~ **material** *n* ACOUST material de insonorización *m*

soundtrack *n* ACOUST banda sonora *f*, pista de sonido *f*, pista sonora *f*, CINEMAT banda sonora *f*, TV pista de sonido *f*, pista sonora *f*, banda sonora *f*

soundwave *n* ACOUST onda sonora *f*, TELECOM onda acústica *f*, onda sonora *f*

souped: ~~**up** *adj BrE* (*cf hotted-up AmE*) VEH *engine*, *colloquial* con potencia aumentada, con motor preparado , recalentado

sour: ~ **crude** *n* PETR TECH crudo con mucho azufre *m*, crudo sulfuroso *m*; ~ **gas** *n* GAS, PETR TECH, PETROL gas con azufre *m*, gas corrosivo *m*, gas ácido *m*

source *n* ELEC ENG fuente *f*, generador de fuerza *m*, ELECTRON fuente *f*, generador *m*, HYDRAUL fuente *f*, HYDROL *of river* nacimiento *m*, fuente *f*, PHYS *tools* fuente *f*, WATER fuente *f*, nacimiento *m*; ~ **address** *n* COMP&DP direccional de la fuente *m*, dirección original *f*; ~ **area** *n* GEOL área de la fuente *f*, POLL campo sonoro *m*, zona de influencia de la fuente *f*, área de la fuente *f*; ~ **code** *n* COMP&DP código fuente *m*; ~ **contact** *n* ELEC ENG contacto del generador *m*; ~ **document** *n* COMP&DP documento fuente *m*, documento original *m*; ~ **impedance** *n* ELEC ENG impedancia del generador *f*; ~ **language** *n* COMP&DP lenguaje fuente *m*; ~ **machine** *n* COMP&DP máquina fuente *f*; ~ **power efficiency** *n* OPT eficiencia de potencia de la fuente *f*, TELECOM eficiencia de la fuente de alimentación *f*, eficiencia de la fuente de energía *f*; ~ **program** *n* COMP&DP programa fuente *m*; ~ **range monitor** *n* NUCL monitor de rango de fuente *m*; ~ **reactor** *n* NUCL reactor-fuente *m*; ~ **region** *n* GEOL región de origen *f*; ~ **rock** *n* GEOL reservorio *m* (*AmL*), PETR TECH roca madre *f*

South: ~ **geomagnetic Pole** *n* GEOPHYS polo sur geomagnético *m*

sow *n* PROD cuesco *m*, lobo *m*, marrano *m*, metal madre *m*, *foundry* canal de colada *m*, reguera *f*, bebedero *m*

Soxhlet: ~ **extraction equipment** *n* LAB equipo de extracción Soxhlet *m*

SP *abbr* ELECTRON (*signal processor*) procesador de señales *m*, TELECOM (*service provider*) prestador de servicios *m*, (*session protocol*) protocolo de sesión *m*, (*signaling point AmE, signalling point BrE*) punto de señalización *m*, (*signal processor*) procesador de señales *m*, TV (*signal processor*) procesador de señales *m*

space¹: ~~**centred** *adj* METALL de cuerpos centrados; ~~**saving** *adj* PACK de tamaño reducido

space² *n* COMP&DP *characters*, GEOM espacio *m*, HYDRAUL intersticio *m*, espacio *m*, PHYS espacio *m*, SPACE espacio *m*, intersticio *m*, intervalo *m*; ~ **age** *n* SPACE era espacial *f*; ~ **agency** *n* SPACE agencia espacial *f*; ~ **astronomy** *n* SPACE astronomía espacial *f*; ~ **capsule** *n* SPACE cápsula espacial *f*; ~ **center** *AmE*, ~ **centre** *BrE n* SPACE centro espacial *m*; ~ **character** *n* COMP&DP carácter de espacio *m*; ~ **charge** *n* AIR TRANSP carga espacial *f*; ~ **coherence** *n* TELECOM coherencia de espacio *f*; ~ **communications** *n pl* TELECOM comunicaciones espaciales *f pl*; ~ **curve** *n* GEOM curva en el espacio *f*, curva espacial *f*; ~ **detection and tracking system** *n* (*SPADATS*) MILIT sistema de detección y seguimiento espacial *m*; ~~**division switching** *n* COMP&DP conmutación espacial *f*, conmutación por división de espacio *f*; **~ engineering** *n* SPACE ingeniería espacial *f*; **~ environment** *n* SPACE ambiente espacial *m*, entorno espacial *m*; **~ flight** *n* SPACE vuelo espacial *m*; **~ group** *n* CRYSTALL grupo espacial *m*; **~ heating** *n* GAS calefacción del ambiente *f*; **~ lattice** *n* CRYSTALL red espacial *f*; **~ launch** *n* SPACE lanzamiento espacial *m*, tiro espacial *m*; **~ observatory** *n* SPACE observatorio espacial *m*; **~ plane** *n* SPACE plano espacial *m*; **~ probe** *n* SPACE sonda espacial *f*; **~ program** *AmE*, **~ programme** *BrE* *n* SPACE programa espacial *m*; **~ qualification** *n* SPACE cualificación espacial *f*; **~ rendezvous** *n* SPACE cita espacial *f*, encuentro espacial *m*; **~ research** *n* SPACE investigación espacial *f*; **~ research service** *n* SPACE servicio de investigación espacial *m*; **~ saving** *n* PACK ahorro de espacio *m*; **~ segment** *n* SPACE segmento espacial *m*; **~ shot** *n* SPACE tiro espacial *m*; **~ shuttle** *n* SPACE, TELECOM lanzadera espacial *f*, transbordador espacial *m*; **~ sickness** *n* SPACE indisposición espacial *f*, malestar espacial *m*, mareo espacial *m*; **~ simulation chamber** *n* SPACE cámara de simulación espacial *f*; **~ stage** *n* TELECOM etapa espacial *f*; **~ station** *n* SPACE estación espacial *f*; **~ step-out** *n* SPACE salida espacial *f*; **~ switch** *n* TELECOM conmutación espacial *f*; **~ technology** *n* TRANSP tecnología espacial *f*; **~-time** *n* PHYS, SPACE tiempo espacial *m*; **~-time continuum** *n* PHYS, SPACE tiempo espacial continuo *m*; **~-time correlation** *n* TELECOM correlación espacio-temporal *f*; **~-time-space network** *n* TELECOM red espacio-tiempo-espacio *f*; **~ tracking** *n* MILIT, SPACE seguimiento espacial *m*; **~ tracking and data acquisition network** *n* (*STADAN*) MILIT red de seguimiento espacial y adquisición de datos *f*; **~ travel** *n* SPACE viaje espacial *m*; **~ tug** *n* SPACE remolcador espacial *m*; **~ vehicle** *n* SPACE vehículo espacial *m*; **~ workshop** *n* SPACE taller espacial *m*

Space: **~ Transportation System** *n* (*STS*) SPACE Sistema de Transporte Espacial *m*

spacecraft *n* SPACE aeronave *f*, artefacto espacial *m*, astronave *f*, cosmonave *f*

spaced[1]: **~-out** *adj* TELECOM alejado, espaciado, separado

spaced[2]: **~ division switching** *n* TELECOM conmutación por divisiones espaciadas *f*; **~ division switching system** *n* TELECOM sistema de conmutación por divisiones espaciadas *m*; **~ division system** *n* TELECOM sistema por divisiones espaciadas *m*

spacelab *n* SPACE vehículo-lanzadera espacial *m*

spacer *n* C&G separador *m*, PROD distanciador *m*, espaciador *m*, separador *m*, SPACE espaciador *m*, intermediario *m*, separador *m*; **~ block** *n* CONST bloque separador *m*

spaceship *n* SPACE cosmonave *f*, vehículo espacial *m*

spacesuit *n* SPACE traje espacial *m*

spacewalk *n* SPACE paseo espacial *m*

spacing *n* AIR TRANSP distancia *f*, separación *f*, CINEMAT espaciado *m*, CRYSTALL distancia interplanar *f*, OPT distancia interplanar *f*, espaciamiento *m*, PHYS separación *f*, TRANSP espaciamiento *m*, separación *f*; **~ loss** *n* TV pérdida de espacios *f*

SPADATS *abbr* (*space detection and tracking system*) MILIT sistema de detección y seguimiento espacial *m*

spade *n* CONST azada *f*, pala *f*; **~ lug** *n* PROD perno de pala *m*; **~ rudder** *n* WATER TRANSP timón colgado *m*

spalling *n* C&G astillamiento *m*, CONST desbaste *m*, desprendimiento *m*

span *n* AIR TRANSP *of wings* envergadura *f*, CONST *of girder, roof* luz *f*, vano *m*, vuelo *m*, eslinga *f*, METR intervalo de medida *m*, PHYS *tools* envergadura *f*; **~ piece** *n* CONST *collar beam* eslinga *f*; **~ pole** *n* ELEC poste del vano *m*; **~ roof** *n* CONST cubierta a dos aguas *f*

spandrel *n* CONST *architecture* tímpano *m*

spaniolite *n* MINERAL spaniolita *f*

Spanish: **~ burton** *n* WATER TRANSP aparejo de estrinque *m*, candeletón *m*

spanner *n* (*cf wrench*) MECH, MECH ENG llave de tuercas *f*, VEH llave de gancho *f*, llave de tetones *f*, llave de tuercas *f*

spar *n* AIR TRANSP larguero *m*, PETR TECH esparto *m*, SPACE larguero *m*, WATER TRANSP *boom, mast* berlinga *f*, percha *f*; **~ buoy** *n* WATER TRANSP baliza de espeque *f*, boya de espeque *f*

spare: **~ bulb** *n* PHOTO lámpara de repuesto *f*; **~ ends** *n pl* TEXTIL hilos sobrantes *m pl*; **~ line** *n* TELECOM línea de reserva *f*, línea libre *f*; **~ number** *n* TELECOM número desocupado *m*, número disponible *m*; **~ part** *n* AUTO pieza de recambio *f*, repuesto *m*, VEH pieza de recambio *f*, recambio *m*, WATER TRANSP pieza de repuesto *f*, recambio *m*, repuesto *m*; **~ tire** *n* AmE (*see spare tyre BrE*) AUTO, VEH neumático de recambio *m*, neumático de repuesto *m*, rueda de recambio *f*, rueda de repuesto *f*; **~ track** *n* COMP&DP pista de reserva *f*, pista libre *f*; **~ tyre** *n* BrE AUTO (*cf spare wheel BrE*) neumático de recambio *m*, neumático de repuesto *m*, rueda de recambio *f*, VEH rueda de recambio *f*, rueda de repuesto *f*; **~ wheel** *n* BrE (*cf spare tyre BrE*) AUTO neumático de recambio *m*, neumático de repuesto *m*, rueda de recambio *f*, rueda de repuesto *f*

sparge: **~ pipe** *n* FOOD rociador *m*; **~ ring cooler** *n* REFRIG enfriador del anillo batidor *m*; **~ ring type milk cooler** *n* AGRIC, REFRIG enfriador de leche con anillo de aspersión *m*

sparging *n* CHEM inyección de vapor *f*, lavado de bagazo *m*, NUCL inyección de vapor *f*

spark[1] *n* GEN chispa *f*; **~ absorber** *n* ELEC amortiguador de chispas *m*; **~ advance** *n* AIR TRANSP adelanto de la chispa de encendido *m*, avance del encendido *m*; **~ arrester** *n* ELEC amortiguador de chispas *m*, apagachispas *m*, dispositivo contra chispas *m*; **~ blowout** *n* ELEC apagachispas *m*, soplado de chispas *m*; **~ capacitor** *n* ELEC ENG condensador antiparasitario *m*; **~ chamber** *n* PHYS cámara de chispas *f*; **~ coil** *n* AUTO, ELEC bobina de inducción *f*, ELEC ENG carrete de Ruhmkorff *m*, bobina de inducción *f*, VEH bobina de inducción *f*; **~ counter** *n* RAD PHYS contador de chispas *m*; **~ discharge** *n* PHYS descarga de chispas *f*; **~ extinguisher** *n* ELEC apagachispas *m*, soplador de chispas *m*; **~ fuse** *n* MINE cebo de chispa *m* (*Esp*), cebo explosivo *m* (*AmL*); **~ gap** *n* ELEC *electrodes* distancia entre electrodos *f*, distancia interelectródica *f*, ELEC ENG descargador *m*, distancia entre electrodos *f*, PHYS separación entre chispas *f*; **~ ignition** *n* ELEC *automotive* encendido por chispa *m*; **~-out stop** *n* MINE dispositivo inmovilizador suave *m*; **~-over** *n* ELEC *voltage* formación de arco de tensión *f*; **~ plug** *n* AUTO, ELEC, VEH bujía de encendido *f*; **~ plug body** *n* AUTO, ELEC, VEH cuerpo de la bujía *m*; **~ plug cable** *n*

AUTO, ELEC, VEH cable de la bujía *m*; ~ **plug electrode** *n* AUTO, ELEC, VEH electrodo de la bujía *m*; ~ **plug gap** *n* AUTO, ELEC, VEH separación de los electrodos de la bujía *f*; ~ **plug gasket** *n* AUTO, ELEC, VEH junta de la bujía *f*; ~ **plug hole** *n* AUTO, ELEC, VEH alojamiento de la bujía *m*; ~ **plug point** *n* AUTO, ELEC punta del electrodo de la bujía *f*, VEH punta de electrodo de la bujía *f*; ~ **plug shell** *n* AUTO, ELEC, VEH carcasa de la bujía *f*; ~ **plug terminal** *n* AUTO, ELEC, VEH terminal de la bujía *m*; ~ **plug wire** *n* AUTO, ELEC, VEH cable de la bujía *m*; ~**-quencher** *n* ELEC amortiguador de chispas *m*, apagachispas *m*, apagador de chispas *m*; ~ **quenching** *n* ELEC ENG enfriamiento de la chispa *m*; ~ **recorder** *n* INSTR registrador del encendido *m*; ~ **spectrum** *n* RAD PHYS espectro de chispas *m*; ~ **suppression** *n* ELEC ENG supresión de la chispa *f*; ~ **suppressor** *n* ELEC ENG supresor de la chispa *m*; ~ **timing** *n* AUTO reglaje de la chispa *m*, sincronización de la chispa *f*

spark² *vi* ELEC ENG chisporrotear

sparker *n* GEOPHYS sparker *m*

sparking *n* ELEC ENG chisporroteo *m*, descarga disruptiva *f*, TV chispeo *m*; ~ **distance** *n* ELEC ENG distancia máxima chispeante *f*

sparkling *n* PROD *engine* encendido *m*; ~ **heat** *n* PROD calda sudante *f*, calor del soldeo *m*

sparse: ~ **matrix** *n* COMP&DP matriz dispersa *f*, matriz escasa *f*

spartalite *n* MINERAL espartalita *f*

spartein *n* CHEM esparteína *f*

spate *n* HYDROL *flood* crecida *f*, *freshet* torrente *m*

spatial: ~ **coherence** *n* PHYS, TELECOM coherencia espacial *f*; ~ **distribution** *n* POLL distribución espacial *f*, distribución en el espacio *f*; ~ **domain** *n* ELECTRON dominio espacial *m*; ~ **frequency** *n* ELEC ENG, PHYS frecuencia espacial *f*; ~ **modulation** *n* ELECTRON modulación espacial *f*; ~ **pattern** *n* POLL modelo espacial *m*, patrón espacial *m*; ~ **period** *n* ELECTRON período espacial *m*; ~ **quantization** *n* PHYS cuantización espacial *f*; ~ **rendezvous** *n* SPACE cita espacial *f*; ~ **resolution** *n* POLL análisis espacial *m*, resolución espacial *f*, separación espacial *f*; ~ **response** *n* ELECTRON respuesta espacial *f*; ~ **trend** *n* POLL evolución espacial *f*, tendencia espacial *f*; ~ **variability** *n* POLL variabilidad espacial *f*

spatter *n* CONST salpicadura *f*; ~ **work** *n* MINE laboreo hidráulico *m* (*AmL*), laboreo por avalancha *m* (*Esp*)

spatula *n* LAB espátula *f*

spawning: ~ **ground** *n* OCEAN lugar de desove *m*, zona de freza *f*

SPC *abbr* ELEC (*single-paper-covered*) *conductor* forrado con una capa de papel, TELECOM (*stored program control AmE, stored programme control BrE*) control de programa almacenado *m*

SPDT: ~ **relay** *n* ELEC ENG relé unipolar con contacto de cambio *m*, relé unipolar de doble vano *m*; ~ **switch** *n* (*single pole double-throw switch*) ELEC ENG conmutador unipolar *m*, interruptor unipolar de doble vano *m*

SPDU *abbr* (*session protocol data unit*) TELECOM unidad de datos del protocolo de sesión *f*

speaking: ~ **clock** *n* TELECOM reloj parlante *m*, reloj telefónico *m*; ~ **rod** *n* CONST *surveying* mira parlante *f*

spear *n* WATER *pump rod* varilla de bomba *f*, vástago de bomba *m*; ~**-headed railing** *n* CONST baranda con punta de flecha *f* (*AmL*), barandilla con punta de

flecha *f* (*Esp*); ~ **pyrites** *n* MINERAL marcasita *f*; ~ **rod** *n* MINE arpón pescador *m*, arpón pescaherramientas *m*, grapa de sondeo *f*

special: ~ **character** *n* COMP&DP carácter especial *m*; ~ **edition** *n* PRINT edición extraordinaria *f*; ~ **effects** *n pl* CINEMAT, TV efectos especiales *m pl*; ~ **effects bus** *n* TV bus de efectos especiales *m*; ~ **effects department** *n* CINEMAT, TV departamento de efectos especiales *m*; ~ **effects generator** *n* CINEMAT, TV generador de efectos especiales *m*; ~ **effects person** *n* CINEMAT, TV especialista en efectos especiales *m*; ~ **precautions** *n pl* SAFE precauciones especiales *f pl*; ~**-purpose computer** *n* COMP&DP computador especializado *m* (*AmL*), computadora especializada *f* (*AmL*), ordenador especializado *m* (*Esp*); ~ **regulations** *n pl* SAFE reglamentos especiales *m pl*; ~ **surface** *n* INSTR superficie específica *f*; ~ **theory** *n* PHYS teoría especial *f*

specialized: ~ **cold store** *n* REFRIG, THERMO almacén frigorífico especializado *m*; ~ **support group** *n* RAD PHYS grupo de apoyo especializado *m*

specific¹ *adj* PHYS específico

specific²: ~ **absorption** *n* METEO absorción específica *f*; ~ **acoustic impedance** *n* ACOUST, ELEC ENG, PHYS impedancia acústica específica *f*; ~ **activity** *n* NUCL, PHYS actividad específica *f*; ~ **adhesion** *n* P&R adherencia específica *f*, adhesión específica *f*; ~ **attenuation** *n* SPACE atenuación específica *f*; ~ **capacitance** *n* ELEC *of condensor* capacitancia específica *f*; ~ **capacity** *n* FUELLESS *of well* capacidad específica *f*; ~ **charge** *n* PART PHYS, PHYS carga específica *f*; ~ **conductance** *n* ELEC conductancia específica *f*; ~ **detectivity** *n* OPT, TELECOM detectividad específica *f*; ~ **efficiency** *n* ACOUST eficacia específica *f*; ~ **emission** *n* ELEC ENG emisión específica *f*; ~ **energy** *n* GAS, SPACE energía específica *f*; ~ **enthalpy** *n* PHYS entalpía específica *f*; ~ **entropy** *n* PHYS entropía específica *f*; ~ **Gibbs function** *n* PHYS función específica de Gibbs *f*; ~ **gravity** *n* GEOPHYS gravedad específica *f*, P&R peso específico *m*, PETR TECH densidad *f*, gravedad específica *f*, PHYS, TEXTIL gravedad específica *f*, WATER TRANSP *of sea water* peso específico *m*; ~ **gravity curve** *n* COAL curva densimétrica *f*; ~ **gravity fraction** *n* COAL fracción densimétrica *f*; ~ **heat** *n* HEAT ENG, P&R, REFRIG, SPACE, THERMO calor específico *m*; ~ **heat at constant pressure** *n* THERMO calor específico a presión constante *m*; ~ **heat capacity** *n* PHYS capacidad calórica específica *f*; ~ **heat capacity at constant pressure** *n* PHYS capacidad calórica específica a presión constante *f*; ~ **heat capacity at constant volume** *n* PHYS capacidad calórica específica a volumen constante *f*; ~ **Helmholtz function** *n* PHYS función Helmholtz específica *f*; ~ **humidity** *n* METEO humedad específica *f*; ~ **impulse** *n* SPACE impulso específico *m*; ~ **index** *n* PAPER, PRINT cuerpo del papel *m*; ~ **inductive capacity** *n* ELEC ENG, TV capacidad inductiva específica *f*; ~ **internal energy** *n* PHYS energía específica interna *f*; ~ **latent heat** *n* PHYS calor latente específico *m*; ~ **pathogen free pig** *n* AGRIC cerdo libre de ciertas enfermedades específicas *m*; ~ **peak flow** *n* HYDROL caudal máximo específico *m*; ~ **power** *n* SPACE energía específica *f*, potencia específica *f*; ~ **resistance** *n* ELEC, ELEC ENG resistencia específica *f*, resistividad *f*; ~ **rotation** *n* PHYS rotación específica *f*; ~ **speed** *n* FUELLESS velocidad

específica *f*; ~ **stiffness** *n* SPACE rigidez específica *f*;
~ **surface area** *n* P&R superficie específica *f*;
~ **volume** *n* PHYS volumen específico *m*
specification *n* PROD especificación *f*, pliego de
condiciones *m*, TEXTIL especificación *f*, WATER
TRANSP *building contract* pliego de condiciones *m*,
of rule especificación *f*; ~ **change notice** *n* (*SCN*)
TRANSP anuncio de cambio de especificación *m*, aviso
de cambio de especificación *m*; ~ **and description**
language *n* COMP&DP, TELECOM lenguaje de descripción y especificación *m*; ~ **language** *n* COMP&DP
lenguaje de especificación *m*; ~ **limit** *n* QUALITY límite
de especificación *m*; ~ **sheet** *n* CINEMAT, TV hoja de
especificaciones *f*
specifications *n pl* CONST especificaciones *f pl*; ~ **sheet**
n VEH ficha técnica *f*
specimen *n* CHEM, COAL, CRYSTALL espécimen *m*,
muestra *f*, MECH ejemplar *m*, muestra *f*, P&R espécimen *m*, probeta *f*, PAPER hoja de muestra *f*;
~ **chamber** *n* INSTR recámara de muestras *f*;
~ **holder** *n* NUCL portaprobetas *m*; ~ **insertion**
airlock *n* INSTR compartimiento estanco para introducción de muestras *m*; ~ **stage** *n* INSTR etapa de
muestreo *f*; ~ **test** *n* METALL probeta de ensayo *f*
speckle[1] *n* PRINT pérdida de puntos *f*, SPACE mancha *f*,
mácula *f*, TEXTIL lunar *m*; ~ **noise** *n* OPT ruido por
moteado *m*, TELECOM ruido de mácula *m*
speckle[2] *vt* PAPER, TEXTIL motear
specks *n pl* PAPER defectos *m pl*, motas *f pl*
spectacle: ~ **frame** *n* INSTR montura de gafas *f*;
~ **glass** *n* C&G vidrio óptico *m*; ~ **lens** *n* INSTR cristal
de gafas *m*; ~ **magnifier** *n* INSTR lupa *f*
spectral: ~ **analysis** *n* (*cf spectrum analysis*) COMP&DP,
ELECTRON, PHYS, TELECOM análisis espectral *m*;
~ **bandwidth** *n* TELECOM ancho de banda espectral
m, anchura de banda espectral *f*; ~ **characteristic** *n*
ELECTRON característica espectral *f*; ~ **colors** *AmE*,
~ **colours** *BrE n pl* RAD PHYS colores espectrales *m pl*;
~ **density** *n* ACOUST, ELECTRON, PHYS densidad
espectral *f*; ~ **emissivity** *n* PHYS emisividad espectral
f; ~ **energy distribution** *n* FUELLESS distribución de
energías espectrales *f*; ~ **energy irradiance** *n* OPT
irradiancia de energía espectral *f*; ~ **irradiance** *n*
OPT irradiancia espectral *f*, TELECOM irradiación
espectral *f*; ~ **line** *n* OPT, PHYS línea espectral *f*, RAD
PHYS, TELECOM línea espectral *f*, raya espectral *f*;
~ **line profile** *n* RAD PHYS contorno de raya espectral
m; ~ **line width** *n* CRYSTALL anchura de línea
espectral *f*, OPT ancho de línea espectral *m*, anchura
de línea espectral *f*, RAD PHYS anchura de raya
espectral *f*, TELECOM ancho de raya espectral *m*,
anchura de línea espectral *f*; ~ **luminance** *n* PHYS
luminancia espectral *f*; ~ **luminous efficiency** *n* PHYS
eficiencia luminosa espectral *f*; ~ **map** *n* SPACE mapa
espectral *m*; ~ **occupancy** *n* TELECOM ocupancia
espectral *f*; ~ **pyranometer** *n* FUELLESS radiómetro
espectral *m*; ~ **radiance** *n* TELECOM radiancia espectral *f*; ~ **range** *n* PHYS rango espectral *m*;
~ **reflectance** *n* PHYS reflectancia espectral *f*;
~ **responsivity** *n* TELECOM responsividad espectral
f; ~ **sensibility** *n* OPT sensibilidad espectral *f*;
~ **sensitivity** *n* CINEMAT sensibilidad espectral *f*;
~ **terms** *n pl* PHYS términos espectrales *m pl*;
~ **transmittance** *n* PHYS transmitancia espectral *f*;
~ **width** *n* OPT, TELECOM anchura espectral *f*;

~ **window** *n* OPT ventana espectral *f*, TELECOM
ventana de prueba espectral *f*
spectrochemical *adj* CHEM espectroquímico
spectrograph *n* ACOUST, GEOPHYS, NUCL, OPT, PHYS,
RAD PHYS espectrógrafo *m*
spectrographic: ~ **analysis** *n* PHYS, RAD PHYS análisis
espectrográfico *m*
spectrometer *n* GEN espectrómetro *m*
spectrometric: ~ **analysis** *n* RAD PHYS análisis espec-
trométrico *m*
spectrometry *n* CHEM, GAS, PETR TECH, PHYS, RAD
PHYS, TELECOM espectrometría *f*
spectrophotometer *n* CHEM, LAB, PHYS, RAD PHYS
espectrofotómetro *m*
spectrophotometry *n* CHEM, LAB, PHYS, RAD PHYS
espectrofotometría *f*
spectroradiometer *n* FUELLESS espectroradiómetro *m*
spectroscope *n* CHEM, PHYS, RAD PHYS, WAVE PHYS
espectroscopio *m*; ~ **collimator** *n* INSTR colimador
espectroscópico *m*
spectroscopy *n* CHEM, PHYS, RAD PHYS, WAVE PHYS
espectroscopía *f*
spectrum *n* GEN espectro *m*; ~ **allocation** *n* WATER
TRANSP asignación de espectro *f*; ~ **analyser** *n* *BrE*
ELECTRON, TELECOM analizador de espectro *m*;
~ **analysis** *n* COMP&DP, ELECTRON, PHYS análisis
espectral *m*, RAD PHYS análisis espectroscópico *m*,
TELECOM análisis espectral *m*; ~ **analyzer** *AmE see*
spectrum analyser BrE; ~ **ban** *n* PHYS, WAVE PHYS
banda *f*; ~ **projector** *n* RAD PHYS proyector espectral
m; ~ **of turbulence** *n* FLUID espectro de turbulencia
m
specular: ~ **density** *n* ACOUST densidad especular *f*;
~ **reflection** *n* CINEMAT, PHYS, TELECOM reflexión
especular *f*
speech *n* ACOUST palabra *f*; ~ **activity factor** *n* TELE-
COM factor de actividad vocal *m*; ~ **analysis** *n*
TELECOM análisis de voz *m*; ~ **audiogram** *n* ACOUST
audiograma vocal *m*; ~ **audiometer** *n* ACOUST audiómetro vocal *m*; ~ **audiometry** *n* ACOUST audiometría
vocal *f*; ~ **channel** *n* COMP&DP canal de voz *m*; ~ **chip**
n COMP&DP chip de voz *m*, plaqueta de voz *f*; ~ **circuit**
n TELECOM circuito de conversación *m*; ~ **coding** *n*
TELECOM codificación de la voz *f*; ~**-data network** *n*
TELECOM red de transmisión de voz y datos *f*;
~ **detection** *n* ELECTRON, SPACE, TELECOM detección
vocal *f*; ~ **detector** *n* ELECTRON detector de las
frecuencias vocales *m*, TELECOM detector de la
palabra *m*, detector de las frecuencias vocales *m*;
~ **encoding** *n* COMP&DP codificación vocal *f*, TELECOM
codificación de la voz *f*; ~ **generation** *n* TELECOM
generación de la palabra *f*; ~**-grade private wire** *n*
TELECOM circuito telefónico privado escalonado *m*;
~ **interference level** *n* (*SIL*) ACOUST nivel de interferencia con la palabra *m* (*SIL*); ~ **interpolation** *n* (*SI*)
SPACE interpolación vocal *f*, TELECOM *data transmis-*
sion interpolación de señales vocales *f*; ~ **memory** *n*
TELECOM memoria de señales vocales *f*; ~ **mod-**
ulation *n* TELECOM modulación por la palabra *f*;
~ **module** *n* PROD módulo de voz *m*; ~ **path** *n* TELE-
COM canal de conversación *m*, vía de conversación *f*;
~ **processing** *n* COMP&DP procesamiento de la voz *m*,
TELECOM procesamiento de la palabra *m*;
~ **production** *n* TELECOM producción de la palabra
f, producción de voz *f*; ~ **recognition** *n* COMP&DP
reconocimiento de la voz *m*; ~ **scrambler** *n* TELECOM

codificador de la voz para comunicación secreta *m*, codificador para telefonía secreta *m*; ~ **service** *n* TELECOM servicio de transmisión de la palabra *m*; ~ **signal** *n* TELECOM señal de frecuencia vocal *f*, señal vocal *f*; ~ **synthesis** *n* COMP&DP síntesis de sonidos vocales *f*, síntesis de voz *f*, ELECTRON síntesis acústica *f*, síntesis de sonidos vocales *f*, síntesis de voz *f*, TELECOM síntesis de sonidos vocales *f*; ~ **synthesizer** *n* COMP&DP sintetizador de voz *m*; ~ **understanding** *n* COMP&DP comprensión de la voz *f*

speed *n* CINEMAT velocidad *f*, PHYS rapidez *f*, TEXTIL, TRANSP, WAVE PHYS velocidad *f*; ~ **brake** *n* AIR TRANSP, TRANSP flap desacelerador *m*; ~ **control** *n* ELEC control de velocidad *m*, regulador de velocidad *m*, TEXTIL control de velocidad *m*; ~ **control by beacons** *n* RAIL control de velocidad por baliza *m*; ~ **control device** *n* FUELLESS regulador de velocidad *m*; ~ **control with track magnets** *n* RAIL control de velocidad por imanes de seguimiento *m*; ~ **-density relationship** *n* TRANSP relación velocidad-densidad *f*; ~ **detector** *n* TRANSP detector de la velocidad *m*; ~ **flow diagram** *n* TRANSP diagrama del flujo de la velocidad *m*; ~ **-flow relationship** *n* TRANSP relación velocidad-flujo *f*; ~ **lathe** *n* MECH ENG torno rápido *m*; ~ **of light** *n* PHYS, WAVE PHYS velocidad de la luz *f*; ~ **limit** *n* TRANSP límite de velocidad *m*; ~ **limiter** *n* AUTO, VEH limitador de velocidad *m*; ~ **over the ground** *n* WATER TRANSP *of ship* velocidad con respecto al fondo *f*; ~ **pot** *n* PROD potenciómetro de velocidad *m*; ~ **of propagation** *n* WAVE PHYS velocidad de propagación *f*; ~ **recorder** *n* INSTR registrador de velocidad *m*, TEXTIL registro de velocidad *m*; ~ **recording tape** *n* RAIL cinta registradora de velocidad *f*; ~ **restriction** *n* RAIL limitación de velocidad *f*, límite de velocidad *m*; ~ **selector** *n* CINEMAT selector de velocidades *m*; ~ **of sound** *n* AIR TRANSP, PHYS velocidad del sonido *f*; ~ **switch** *n* PROD conmutador velociselector *m*; ~ **through the water** *n* WATER TRANSP velocidad de avance por el agua *f*; ~ **trap** *n* TRANSP trampa de velocidad *f*; ~ **variation frequency** *n* ACOUST frecuencia de variación de velocidad *f*; ~ **-volume curve** *n* TRANSP curva de volumen por velocidad *f*

speedometer *n* AUTO, VEH velocímetro *m*, WATER TRANSP corredera electrónica *f*; ~ **cable** *n* AUTO, VEH cable del velocímetro *m*; ~ **drive gear** *n* AUTO, VEH engranaje de mando del tacómetro *m*

spend: ~ **ground** *vi* MINE agotar el frente de arranque

spent[1] *adj* CHEM agotado, gastado

spent[2]: ~ **acid** *n* DETERG ácido agotado *m*, TEXTIL ácido empleado *m*; ~ **capacity** *n* PROD capacidad agotada *f*; ~ **-fuel rack** *n* NUCL bastidor de almacenamiento de combustible gastado *m*; ~ **grinding sand** *n* C&G arena de desecho *f*

sperm: ~ **oil** *n* DETERG aceite de ballena *m*

spermaceti: ~ **oil** *n* DETERG aceite de blanco de ballena *m*

spermidine *n* CHEM espermidina *f*

spermin *n* CHEM espermina *f*

sperrylite *n* MINERAL esperrilita *f*

spessartine *n* MINERAL esperssartina *f*

SPF *abbr* PART PHYS (*superproton synchroton*) super sincrotrón de protones *m*, TELECOM (*segmentation permitted flag*) bandera reglamentaria de segmentación *f*

sphalerite *n* CHEM blenda *f*, MINE esfalerita *f*, MINERAL blenda *f*, esfalerita *f*

sphene *n* MINERAL esfena *f*

sphere *n* GEOM, PHYS esfera *f*; ~ **gap** *n* ELEC ENG explosor de esferas *m*; ~ **of reflection** *n* CRYSTALL esfera de reflexión *f*

spherical[1] *adj* GEN esférico

spherical[2]: ~ **aberration** *n* CINEMAT, PHOTO, PHYS, TELECOM aberración de esfericidad *f*, aberración esférica *f*; ~ **aerial** *n* BrE (*cf spherical antenna AmE*) TELECOM antena esférica *f*; ~ **antenna** *n* AmE (*cf spherical aerial BrE*) TELECOM antena esférica *f*; ~ **container** *n* TRANSP contenedor esférico *m*; ~ **coordinates** *n pl* PHYS coordenadas esféricas *f pl*; ~ **distortion** *n* CINEMAT distorsión esférica *f*; ~ **geometry** *n* GEOM geometría esférica *f*; ~ **harmonic** *n* SPACE armonía esférica *f*; ~ **joint** *n* VEH *steering* junta de rótula *f*; ~ **lens** *n* CINEMAT, INSTR, OPT, PHOTO objetivo esférico *m*, PHYS lentes esféricas *f pl*; ~ **mirror** *n* INSTR, LAB, OPT, PHYS, TELECOM espejo esférico *m*; ~ **sector** *n* GEOM sector esférico *m*; ~ **tank** *n* SPACE depósito esférico *m*; ~ **triangle** *n* GEOM triángulo esférico *m*; ~ **wave** *n* ACOUST, ELEC ENG, PHYS, WAVE PHYS onda esférica *f*

sphericity *n* GEOM esfericidad *f*

spherics *n pl* METEO atmosféricos *m pl*, esferas *f pl*, esféricos *m pl*, parásitos atmosféricos *m pl*

spheroid *n* GEOM elipsoide atachado *m*, elipsoide de revolución *m*, esferoide *m*, PHYS esferoide *m*

spherometer *n* PHYS esferómetro *m*

spherosiderite *n* MINERAL esferosiderita *f*

spherulite *n* GEOL, MINERAL, PETR TECH esferulita *f*

spherulitic: ~ **texture** *n* GEOL textura esferolítica *f*

sphingosine *n* CHEM esfingosina *f*

sphragidite *n* MINERAL esfragidita *f*

SPI *abbr* (*secondary porosity index*) PETR TECH IPS (*índice de porosidad secundaria*)

spider *n* C&G araña *f*, CINEMAT cangrejo *m*, PETR TECH araña *f*, grapa a cuñas *f*, PROD *for mould or core* armadura *f*, *of amalgamating pan* cursor *m*, VEH cruceta *f*; ~ **and slips** *n pl* MINE anillo de maniobra *m*; ~ **-type armature** *n* ELEC cepo de armadura *m*; ~ **unit** *n* AIR TRANSP araña *f*, cruceta *f*

spigot *n* CONST *cock or faucet* llave *f*, *plug of cock* canilla *f*, tubo *m*, *vent peg* espiga *f*; ~ **-and-faucet joint** *n* CONST empalme de enchufeo y cordón *m*; ~ **-and-faucet joint pipes** *n pl* CONST tuberías con uniones de cordón y grifo *f pl* (*Esp*), tuberías con uniones de enchufe y cordón *f pl* (*AmL*); ~ **joint** *n* CONST empalme de cordón *m*

spike *n* AGRIC espiga *f*, marlo *m* (*AmL*), mazorca *f* (*Esp*), C&G pico *m*, CINEMAT impulso *m*, CONST perno *m*, ELEC ENG corriente de fuga *f*, MINE *quarrying* escarpiador *m* (*AmL*), perno *m* (*Esp*), NUCL semilla *f*, TRANSP punta *f*, TV pico *m*, impulso de hiperamplitud *m*; ~ **driver** *n* RAIL martillo neumático para clavar *m*; ~ **nail** *n* CONST clavo *m*; ~ **puller** *n* AmE (*cf sleeper-screw extractor BrE*) RAIL extractor de tirafondos *m*; ~ **-tooth harrow** *n* AGRIC grada de dientes rígidos *f*

spikelet *n* AGRIC espiguilla *f*

spile *n* CONST cuña *f*

spiling *n* CONST *driving piles* hincado de pilotes *m*

spilite *n* PETR TECH espilita *f*

spill *n* ELEC ENG dispersión *f*, MAR POLL, POLL, WATER derrame *m*; ~ **light** *n* CINEMAT luz difusa *f*

spillage *n* GAS, MAR POLL, POLL derramamiento *m*,

derrame *m*, rebosamiento *m*, PETR TECH derramamiento *m*, derrame *m*, POLL derramamiento *m*, WATER derramamiento *m*, derrame *m*

spillings *n pl* PROD *iron founding* fugas de fundición *f pl*

spillover: ~ **loss** *n* SPACE pérdida de desbordamiento *f*

spillway *n* CONST aliviadero *m*, vertedero *m*, FUELLESS *dams* vertedor *m*, HYDRAUL aliviadero *m*, HYDROL aliviadero de crecidas *m*, aliviadero *m*, WATER aliviadero *m*, aliviadero de crecidas *m*, canal aliviadero *m*, vertedero *m*, vertedero de crecidas *m*, aliviadero evacuador de crecidas *m*; ~ **canal** *n* HYDRAUL canal de descarga *m*, canal de vertedero *m*, canal evacuador *m*; ~ **channel** *n* FUELLESS *dams* canal vertedor *m*, HYDRAUL canal evacuador *m*, canal de vertedero *m*, canal de descarga *m*, WATER caz vertedor *m*; ~ **dam** *n* WATER dique avertedero *m*

spilosite *n* PETR TECH espilosita *f*

spin[1] *n* (*s*) AIR TRANSP manoeuvre barrena *f*, tirabuzón *m*, PART PHYS espín *m* (*s*), números cuánticos *m pl*, PHYS spin *m*, RAD PHYS espín *m* (*s*), SPACE rotación *f*, giro *m*, vuelta *f*; ~ **angular momentum** *n* PHYS momento angular de spin *m*; ~ **axis** *n* SPACE eje de giro *m*, eje de rotación *m*; ~ **chiller** *n* REFRIG enfriador de tambor-agitador *m*; ~~**down** *n* SPACE giro hacia abajo *m*, reducción del giro *f*; ~ **exchange** *n* NUCL cambio de espín *m*; ~~**off** *n* SPACE derivación *f*, producto secundario *m*; ~~**orbit coupling** *n* PHYS acoplamiento spin-órbita *m*; ~ **quantum number** *n* PHYS número cuántico de spin *m*; ~ **reversal transition** *n* PART PHYS transición de la inversión del espín *f*; ~ **rocket** *n* SPACE cohete estabilizador por giro *m*, cohete giratorio *m*; ~ **stabilization** *n* SPACE estabilización por giro *f*; ~ **temperature** *n* PHYS temperatura de spin *f*; ~ **thruster** *n* SPACE impulsor de giro *m*; ~~**up** *n* SPACE acceleración del giro *f*, giro hacia arriba *m*; ~ **wave** *n* PHYS onda de spin *f*; ~ **wipe** *n* CINEMAT transición donde una imagen reemplaza otra girando *f*

spin[2] *vt* TEXTIL hilar

spin[3] *vi* AIR TRANSP, SPACE dar vueltas, descender en barrena, entrar en barrena, girar

spinasterol *n* CHEM espinasterol *m*

spindle *n* C&G *in cutting of hollow glass*, CINEMAT, MECH husillo *m*, MECH ENG *of roller* cabeza del husillo *f*, husillo *m*, PRINT mandril *m*, PROD husillo *m*, huso *m*, *of rig for loam-work* eje *m*, árbol *m*, TEXTIL huso *m*, VEH palier *m*; ~ **arm** *n* AUTO brazo del huso *m*, PROD *loam-work* brazo portaplaca *m*, VEH brazo del huso *m*; ~ **cam** *n* PROD leva de huso *f*; ~~**molding machine** *AmE*, ~~**moulding machine** *BrE n* CONST máquina de modelar con torno *f*; ~ **nose** *n* MECH ENG *lathe* cabeza del husillo *f*, unidad del husillo *f*; ~ **and sweep** *n* PROD *rig for loam-work* terraja *f*

spindrift *n* HYDROL desplazamiento rotativo *m*, movimiento rotativo *m*, METEO, OCEAN rocío del mar *m*

spine *n* PRINT lomo *m*

spinel *n* CHEM aluminato de magnesio *m*, espinel *m*, espinela *f*; ~ **refractory** *n* C&G refractario de espinela *m*

spinnaker *n* WATER TRANSP balón *m*, espí *m*; ~ **boom** *n* WATER TRANSP tangón del espí *m*

spinner *n* AIR TRANSP buje *m*, cono de hélice *m*, ojiva *f*, C&G hilandera *f*

spinning *n* AUTO *of the wheel* rotación *f*, C&G hilado *m*, TEXTIL hilatura *f*; ~ **bodies** *n pl* FLUID cuerpos rotatorios *m pl*; ~~**disk humidifier** *n* REFRIG, THERMO humidificador de disco centrífugo *m*, humidificador de disco giratorio *m*; ~ **line** *n* PETR TECH cable enroscatubos *m*, línea para enroscar tubos *f*; ~ **paper** *n* PAPER papel para hilar *m*; ~ **reserves** *n pl* FUELLESS excedente de capacidad de rotación *m*; ~ **system** *n* TEXTIL sistema de hilatura *m*; ~ **wheel** *n* TEXTIL torno de hilar *m*; ~ **yarn** *n* TEXTIL hilo hilado *m*

spinodal: ~ **decomposition** *n* METALL descomposición espinodal *f*

spiral[1] *adj* GEOM espiral, MECH ENG en espiral, espiralado, espiroidal

spiral[2] *n* ELEC ENG, GEOM espiral *f*, MECH ENG caracol *m*, embrague cónico *m*, engranaje espiral *m*, engranaje helicoidal *m*, espira *f*, espiral *f*, fresa de dientes helicoidales *f*, hélice *f*, sistema de engranaje helicoidal *m*, METALL, OPT, PHOTO, QUALITY espiral *f*; ~ **aerial** *n* BrE (*cf spiral antenna AmE*) TELECOM antena espiral *f*; ~ **antenna** *n* AmE (*cf spiral aerial BrE*) TELECOM antena espiral *f*; ~ **balance** *n* METR balanza de resorte *f*; ~ **bevel gearing** *n* AUTO engranaje cónico espiral *m*; ~ **bit** *n* PETR TECH barrena de arrastre *f*, broca *f*, mecha helicoidal *f*, trépano en espiral *m*; ~ **casing** *n* PROD *of turbine, centrifugal pump, fan* cámara de caracol *f*, cámara espiral *f*, envuelta de caracol *f*; ~ **chute** *n* MINE conducto espiral *m*, plano inclinado helicoidal *m*; ~ **classifier** *n* COAL clasificador helicoidal *m*; ~ **conveyor** *n* HYDRAUL tornillo de Arquímedes *m*; ~ **corkscrew** *n* TEXTIL sacacorchos en espiral *m*; ~ **dive** *n* AIR TRANSP picado en espiral *m*; ~ **felt roll** *n* PAPER rodillo desplegador *m*; ~ **fracture** *n* C&G fractura en espiral *f*; ~ **glide** *n* AIR TRANSP planeo en espiral *m*; ~ **ratchet screwdriver end** *n* MECH ENG punta de destornillador de trinquete *f*; ~ **stairs** *n pl* CONST escalera de caracol *f*, escalera en espiral *f*; ~ **track** *n* OPT pista espiral *f*; ~ **turbulence** *n* FLUID turbulencia espiral *f*; ~ **waveguide** *n* TELECOM guiaondas en espiral *m*, guía de ondas en espiral *f*; ~ **wheel** *n* MECH ENG muelle helicoidal *m*, rueda espiral *f*, rueda helicoidal *f*

spirally: ~~**wound tube** *n* PACK tubo enrollado en espiral *m*

spirane *n* CHEM espirano *m*

spire *n* MECH ENG *turn* acanaladura *f*, espira *f*, estría *f*, ranura *f*, vuelta espiral *f*

spirit *n* CHEM alcohol *m*, espíritu *m*, DETERG, FOOD, P&R, PETR TECH, PHOTO, TEXTIL alcohol *m*; ~ **duplicator copy paper** *n* PAPER papel para hectografía *m*; ~ **gauge** *n* FOOD indicador de alcohol *m*; ~ **lacquer** *n* COATINGS, COLOUR laca de alcohol *f*, CONST laca al alcohol *f*; ~ **lamp** *n* LAB lámpara de alcohol *f*; ~ **level** *n* CONST nivel de aire *m*, METR nivel de burbuja de aire *m*; ~ **poise** *n* FOOD poise de alcohol *m*; ~ **of turpentine** *n* CHEM esencia de trementina *f*; ~ **varnish** *n* COATINGS, COLOUR barniz de alcohol *m*

spit *n* GEOL, HYDROL banco de arena *m*, OCEAN flecha litoral *f*, lengua de arena *f*, banco de arena *m*, WATER TRANSP banco de arena *m*

SPITE *abbr* (*switching process interworking telephony event*) TELECOM sistema de telefonía por interconexión de procesos *m*

SPL *abbr* ACOUST, POLL (*sound pressure level*) NPS (*nivel de presión acústica, nivel de presión de sonido, nivel de presión sonora*), TELECOM (*service provider* *link*) enlace con el prestador de servicios *m*, vínculo con el prestador de servicios *m*

splash *n* MINE manchón *m*; ~ **guard** *n* PROD guardasalpicaduras *m*, salpicadero *m*; ~ **lubrication** *n* AUTO, RAIL lubricación por barboteo *f*, lubricación por salpicadura *f*; ~ **lubrification** *n* REFRIG engrase por barboteo *m*; **~-proof vent cap** *n* AUTO casquillo de ventilación impermeable *m*; ~ **wing** *n* PROD guardasalpicaduras *m*, salpicadero *m*

splashback *n* CONST salpicadura *f*

splashdown *n* AIR TRANSP aterrizaje forzoso *m*, SPACE choque al amerizar *m*

splasher *n* PROD salpicadero *m*

splat: ~ **cooling** *n* C&G enfriamiento por rociado *m*

splay *vi* CONST *window frame* descantear

splayed: ~ **joint** *n* CONST junta biselada *f*; ~ **miter joint** *AmE*, ~ **mitre joint** *BrE* *n* CONST empalme a inglete *m*, empalme biselado *m*, junta a inglete *f*

splice[1] *n* C&G unión *f*, CINEMAT, OPT, PAPER, PRINT empalme *m*, TELECOM empalme *m*, junta *f*, unión *f*, TV empalme *m*, WATER TRANSP *rope* ajuste *m*; ~ **bar** *n* RAIL cubrejunta de angular *m*, eclisa *f*, travesia *f*; ~ **box** *n* ELEC *connection* caja de empalmes *f*; ~ **joint** *n* RAIL junta *f*; ~ **loss** *n* TELECOM pérdida del empalme *f*, pérdida de la unión *f*

splice[2] *vt* CINEMAT, PAPER empalmar, TELECOM empalmar, juntar, unir, TEXTIL empalmar

spliced: ~ **rope** *n* WATER TRANSP cabo ayustado *m*

splicer *n* CINEMAT empalmadora *f*, TELECOM empalmador *m*; ~ **cable** *n* TELECOM cable del soldador *m*

splicing *n* PAPER empalmado *m*, TEXTIL empalme *m*; ~ **block** *n* CINEMAT prensa de empalmar *f*; ~ **cement** *n* CINEMAT cemento de empalmar *m*; ~ **table** *n* PRINT mesa para empalmar *f*; ~ **tape** *n* CINEMAT cinta de empalmar *f*

spline *n* MECH estría *f*, ranura *f*, MECH ENG *feather key* ranura *f*, SPACE lengüeta *f*, estría *f*, ranura *f*, acanaladura *f*; ~ **gage** *AmE*, ~ **gauge** *BrE* *n* METR calibrador de ranura *f*

splined *adj* MECH ranurado

splines: ~ **and serration** *n pl* MECH ENG ranuras y estriaciones *f pl*

splining: ~ **tool** *n* MECH ENG herramienta de ranurar *f*

splinter *n* C&G astilla *f*, CONST astilla de madera *f*, brizna *f*

splintery: ~ **fracture** *n* COAL fractura astillosa *f*

split[1] *adj* C&G separado

split[2] *n* C&G hendidura *f*, CONST *crack* división *f*, hendidura *f*, MINE corriente parcial *f*, dispersión *f*, grieta de ventilación *f*, grieta *f*, PRINT rebaje *m*, división *f*, PROD grieta *f*, hendidura *f*, raja *f*, rendija *f*, *mine ventilation* bifurcación *f*, ramal *m*; ~ **anode magnetron** *n* ELECTRON magnetrón de ánodo dividido *m*; **~-beam camera** *n* CINEMAT cámara de haz dividido *f*; ¬**-beam cathode ray tube** *n* TV tubo de rayos catódicos de haz dividido *m*; ~ **core box** *n* PROD *mould making* caja de machos de dos partes *f*; ~ **cotter pin** *n* MECH ENG chaveta hendida *f*, clavija hendida *f*, pasador de aletas *m*; ~ **current** *n* MINE, PROD corriente parcial *f*; ~ **die** *n* MECH ENG estampa partida *f*, troquel partido *m*; ~ **field lens** *n* CINEMAT lente de campo dividido *f*, lente bifocal *f*, OPT, PHOTO, TV lente de campo dividido *f*; ~ **flap** *n* AIR TRANSP, TRANSP flap de intradós *m*, flap doble *m*; ~ **housing** *n* AUTO alojamiento dividido *m*, VEH alojamiento dividido *m*, cárter dividido *m*; ~ **image rangefinder**

n PHOTO telémetro de imagen dividida *m*; ~ **lens** *n* INSTR lente dividida *f*, lente partida *f*; ~ **mold** *AmE*, ~ **mould** *BrE* *n* C&G molde de varias partes *m*, P&R molde partido *m*; **~-phase motor** *n* ELEC motor de arranque por fase auxiliar *m*, motor de fase dividida *m*, ELEC ENG motor de fase abierta *m*, motor monofásico con devanado auxiliar de arranque *m*, motor monofásico de tres conductores *m*; ~ **pin** *n* MECH ENG chaveta hendida *f*, pasador de aletas *m*; **~-piston skirt** *n* AUTO, VEH falda de pistón acanalada *f*, falda de pistón dividida *f*; **~-pole motor** *n* ELEC motor de polos divididos *m*; ~ **pulley** *n* MECH ENG polea partida *f*; ~ **railroad tie** *n* *AmE* (*cf split sleeper BrE*) RAIL traviesa partida *f*; ~ **reel** *n* CINEMAT carrete dividido *m*; ~ **ring** *n* MECH ENG anillo para llaves *m*, anillo partido *m*, collar partido *m*; ~ **roller** *n* C&G rodillo de varias partes *m*; ~ **screen** *n* CINEMAT pantalla fraccionada *f*, pantalla partida *f*, COMP&DP pantalla dividida *f*; **~-set collar** *n* MECH ENG anillo de seguridad partido *m*, palanca cruciforme *f*, volante cruciforme *m*; ~ **sleeper** *n* *BrE* RAIL traviesa partida *f*; ~ **spool** *n* CINEMAT carrete dividido *m*; **~-stator variable capacitor** *n* ELEC ENG condensador variable de estator fraccionado *m*; ~ **weld** *n* PROD soldadura de boca abierta *f*; ~ **welding** *n* PROD soldadura de boca abierta *f*

split[3] *vt* CONST *slate* partir, separar, MINE cuartearse, resquebrajarse, agrietarse, TEXTIL separar

split[4] *vi* CONST rajarse, RAIL partir

splitter *n* CINEMAT separador *m*, COAL disipador de energía *m*, partidor *m*, rompedor *m*; ~ **box** *n* ELEC *cable accessory* caja divisoria de fases *f*

splitting *n* CONST hendidura *f*, CRYSTALL, NUCL desdoblamiento *m*, PHYS separación *f*, PROD hendidura *f*, rajamiento *m*, subdivisión *f*; ~ **ax** *AmE*, ~ **axe** *BrE* *n* CONST hacha hendedora *f*; ~ **of the cylinder** *n* C&G abertura del cilindro *f*; ~ **electrode** *n* TV electrodo de corte *m*

SPN *abbr* (*subscriber premises network*) TELECOM red de instalación del abonado *f*

spodumene *n* MINERAL espodumena *f*

spoil[1] *n* CONST *civil engineering* escombro *m*, PRINT pliego estropeado *m*, RAIL escombro *m*, préstamo de tierras *m*; ~ **bank** *n* MINE depósito de dragados *m* (*AmL*), depósito de ripios *m* (*Esp*), escombrera *f* (*Esp*); ~ **car** *n* *AmE* (*cf spoil wagon BrE*) RAIL vagón basculante pequeño *m*; ~ **disposal** *n* CONST vertido de escombros *m*; ~ **heap** *n* CONST *civil engineering* escombrera *f*, MINE terreno arrancado por una pala excavadora *m*; ~ **tip** *n* COAL cargadero de dragados *m*, cargadero de mineral *m*; ~ **to waste** *n* CONST desechos *m pl*; ~ **wagon** *n* *BrE* (*cf spoil car AmE*) RAIL vagón basculante pequeño *m*

spoil[2] *vt* FOOD echar a perder, estropear

spoiled: ~ **casting** *n* PROD pieza fundida defectuosa *f*; ~ **negative** *n* PHOTO negativo deteriorado *m*

spoiler *n* AIR TRANSP aleta de ranura *f*, deflector aerodinámico *m*, expoliador *m*, perturbador de filetes de aire *m*, espoiler *m*, TRANSP alerón *m*, aminorador *m*, deflector aerodinámico *m*, espoiler *m*, VEH alerón trasero *m*

spoils *n pl* PRINT pliegos para maculaturas *m pl*

spoke: ~ **wheel** *n* VEH rueda de radios *f*; ~ **wheel center** *AmE*, ~ **wheel centre** *BrE* *n* VEH cuerpo de la rueda de radios *m*

spokeshave *n* CONST cuchilla de doble mango *f*, rebajador de rayos *m*
spondee *n* ACOUST espondeo *m*
sponge: ~ **culture** *n* OCEAN cultivo de esponjas *m*; ~ **lead** *n* AUTO plomo esponjoso *m*
spongine *n* CHEM espongina *f*
spontaneous: ~ **brake application** *n* RAIL, VEH aplicación espontánea de frenos *f*, frenado espontáneo *m*; ~ **breaking** *n* C&G rotura espontánea *f*; ~ **combustion** *n* SAFE combustión espontánea *f*; ~ **decay** *n* RAD PHYS desintegración espontánea *f*; ~ **emission** *n* ELECTRON, PHYS, RAD PHYS, TELECOM emisión espontánea *f*; ~ **emission of radiation at a constant rate** *n* RAD PHYS emisión espontánea de radiación a velocidad constante *f*; ~ **excitation** *n* NUCL excitación espontánea *f*; ~ **fission** *n* NUCL, PHYS, RAD PHYS fisión espontánea *f*; ~ **fission probability** *n* NUCL, PHYS, RAD PHYS probabilidad de fisión espontánea *f*; ~ **ignition** *n* SPACE ignición espontánea *f*; ~ **log** *n* FUELLESS registro espontáneo *m*; ~ **magnetization** *n* PHYS imanación espontánea *f*, RAD PHYS imanación espontánea *f*; ~ **nucleation** *n* METALL nucleación espontánea *f*; ~ **potential log** *n* GEOPHYS registro de potencial espontáneo *m*, PETR TECH diagrafía potencial espontáneo *f*, registro de potencial espontáneo *m*; ~ **transition** *n* RAD PHYS transición espontánea *f*
spoofing *n* COMP&DP interferencia *f*; ~ **program** *n* COMP&DP programa de bromeo *m*, programa de interferencia *m*
spool[1] *n* ACOUST bobina *f*, carrete *m*, C&G carrete *m*, bobina *f*, CINEMAT bobina *f*, ELEC ENG devanadera *f*, devanadera *f*, PROD bobina *f*, carrete *m*, devanadera *f*, devanadera *f*, TEXTIL devanadera *f*, TV carrete *m*
spool[2] *vt* CINEMAT bobinar, enrollar, TV embobinar
spooler *n* COMP&DP bobinador *m*, cola de impresión *f*, spooler *m*
spooling *n* COMP&DP bobinando *m*, spooling *m*, PHOTO bobinado *m* (*AmL*), rebobinado *m* (*Esp*), TV entrada-salida diferida *f*
spoon: ~ **auger** *n* CONST barrena de cuchara *f*, sonda de cuchara *f*; ~ **bow** *n* WATER TRANSP *boat building* proa redonda *f*; ~ **dredge** *n* WATER draga de cuchara *f*; ~ **dredger** *n* WATER draga de cuchara *f*; ~ **sampler** *n* COAL palas extractoras de muestras *f pl*
sports: ~ **finder** *n* PHOTO visor para fotografías deportivas *m*
spot *n* CINEMAT reflector de lente escalonada *m*, TRANSP impacto de haz luminoso *m*; ~ **beam** *n* SPACE haz luminoso *m*, haz radioeléctrico fino *m*; ~ **beam aerial** *n* BrE (*cf spot beam antenna AmE*) SPACE antena de haz fino *f*; ~ **beam antenna** *n* AmE (*cf spot beam aerial BrE*) SPACE antena de haz fino *f*; ~ **beam coverage** *n* TELECOM cobertura del haz del punto de exploración *f*, cobertura del haz del punto de imagen *f*; ~ **color** AmE, ~ **colour** BrE *n* PRINT color de la mancha *m*, color solitario *m*; ~ **cooling** *n* REFRIG enfriamiento localizado *m*; ~ **footing** *n* COAL base de apoyo *f*, lecho de cimentación *m*; ~ **grazing** *n* AGRIC pastoreo sectorial *m*; ~ **-shape corrector** *n* TV corrector de puntos y formas *m*; ~ **speed** *n* TRANSP velocidad de exploración *f*, velocidad del punto luminoso *f*; ~ **welding** *n* CONST, ELEC soldadura por puntos *f*
spotface: ~ **cutter** *n* MECH ENG fresa de refrentar *f*, herramienta de refrentar *f*

spotlight *n* AUTO faro orientable *m*, CINEMAT luz concentrada *f*, proyector de luz *m*, ELEC luz concentrada *f*, lámpara proyectora de haz concentrado *f*, PHOTO luz concentrada *f*, proyector de luz *m*, VEH faro orientable *m*, luz auxiliar orientable *f*
spotted: ~ **slate** *n* GEOL pizarra moteada *f*
spotter: ~ **plane** *n* AIR TRANSP, MAR POLL avión explorador *m*
spotting *n* PHOTO moteado *m*; ~ **plate** *n* LAB placa de análisis de manchas *f*; ~ **tile** *n* LAB mosaico de análisis de manchas *f*
spout *n* C&G *of Owens machine* noria *f*, *in rolling process* surtidor *m*, pico *m*, LAB tubo de descarga *m*, tubo de rebose *m*, pico *m*, METEO tromba *f*, PROD canilla *f*, espita *f*, pico *m*, tubo de descarga *m*, WATER *of pump* pico de salida *m*; ~ **cover** *n* AmE (*cf cover tile BrE*) C&G cubierta de la noria *f*, tapón *m*, CONST tapón *m*; ~ **hole** *n* WATER *of pump* agujero de salida *m*
spouting *n* HYDROL chorro *m*, surtidor *m*
spray[1]: ~ **-dried** *adj* DETERG deshidratado por aspersión
spray[2] *n* HYDROL agua pulverizada *f*, PROD agua pulverizada *f*, nebulizador *m*, pulverización *f*, pulverizador *m*, WATER TRANSP *of sea* rocío *m*; ~ **aperture** *n* MAR POLL abertura de aspersión *f*; ~ **boom** *n* AGRIC aguilón de la pulverizadora *m*, MAR POLL tangón de aspersión *m*; ~ **cellulose paint** *n* COLOUR pintura a la celulosa en aerosol *f*; ~ **chamber** *n* REFRIG cámara de pulverización *f*; ~ **coater** *n* PAPER estucadora por rociado *f*; ~ **coating** *n* COATINGS revestimiento por aspersión *m*, revestimiento por rociado *m*; ~ **compressor** *n* HYDRAUL, PROD compresor de inyección de agua *m*; ~ **condenser** *n* GAS condensador de rociado *m*; ~ **cooling** *n* REFRIG enfriamiento por aspersión *m*; ~ **cutter** *n* PAPER cortadora mediante chorros de agua *f*; ~ **diffuser** *n* CHEM TECH atomizador *m*; ~ **drag** *n* AIR TRANSP *at takeoff* resistencia de rociado *f*; ~ **-drying** *n* DETERG deshidratación por aspersión *f*; ~ **freezer** *n* REFRIG congelador por aspersión *m*; ~ **freezing** *n* REFRIG congelación por pulverización *f*; ~ **gun** *n* MAR POLL pistola aspersora *f*; ~ **hood** *n* WATER TRANSP capota contra rociones *f*; ~ **irrigation** *n* HYDROL riego por aspersión *m*; ~ **paint** *n* COLOUR, CONST pintura a pistola *f*; ~ **painting** *n* COLOUR, CONST pintura por pulverización *f*; ~ **producer** *n* PROD pulverizador *m*; ~ **tap** *n* MECH ENG canilla atomizadora *f*, canilla pulverizadora *f*; ~ **-type cooler** *n* REFRIG enfriador por pulverización *m*; ~ **-type evaporator** *n* REFRIG evaporador de lluvia *m*
spray[3] *vt* CHEM asperjar, COLOUR pulverizar, CONST asperjar, MAR POLL asperjar, rociar, WATER asperjar; ~ **down** *vt* CINEMAT rociar; ~ **with shotcrete** *vt* CONST rociado con hormigón proyectado *m*
sprayer *n* CHEM atomizador *m*, pulverizador *m*, rociador *m*, CHEM TECH, LAB, PACK atomizador *m*, PAPER rociador *m*, PETR TECH, TRANSP atomizador *m*; ~ **nozzle** *n* AGRIC pico de pulverizadora *m*, MECH ENG boquilla de regadera *f*, boquilla pulverizadora *f*, boquilla rociadora *f*
spraying *n* HYDROL aspersión *f*, pulverización *f*, WATER aspersión *f*; ~ **paint** *n* CONST, P&R pintura de rociar *f*; ~ **screen** *n* COAL filtración por proyección *f*
spraypath *n* MAR POLL recorrido de aspersión *m*, trayectoria de aspersión *f*
spread[1] *n* C&G extensión *f*, COMP&DP dispersión *f*,

planilla *f*, GAS distribución *f*, REFRIG amplitud *f*, SPACE envergadura *f*; **~-spectrum modulation** *n* ELECTRON modulación de la propagación del espectro *f*, TELECOM modulación de espectro expandido *f*; **~-spectrum modulator** *n* ELECTRON modulador de la propagación del espectro *m*; **~ spectrum multiple access** *n* (*SSMA*) SPACE acceso múltiple por espectro ensanchado *m*; **~ spectrum signal** *n* ELECTRON señal de propagación del espectro *f*, WATER TRANSP *satellite communications* señal de espectro ensanchado *f*

spread[2] *vt* MAR POLL, SPACE ensanchar

spread[3] *vi* MAR POLL extenderse

spreader *n* AGRIC esparcidor *m*, CINEMAT cangrejo *m*, MECH travesaño *m*, MINE esparcidora *f*, TRANSP repartidor *m*, esparcidora *f*, WATER *jet of water* esparcidor *m*; **~ bar** *n* PAPER barra esplegadora *f*, barra eliminadora de arrugas *f*; **~-finisher** *n* P&R paleta para esparcir *f*; **~ jet** *n* WATER *for branch pipe* chorro en abanico *m*; **~ roll** *n* PAPER rodillo desplegador *m*

spreadhead *n* PRINT título a dos o más columnas *m*

spreading *n* CHEM diseminado *m*, esparcido *m*, extendido *m*, MAR POLL dispersión *f*, ensanchamiento *m*; **~ field** *n* WATER campo de esparcimiento *m*; **~ lens** *n* CINEMAT, INSTR, OPT, PHOTO, PHYS lente divergente *f*; **~ machine** *n* COATINGS esparcedora *f*, máquina de expansión *f*; **~ table** *n* PROD mesa de distribución *f*

spreadsheet *n* COMP&DP hoja de cálculo *f*, hoja electrónica *f*, planilla electrónica *f*

sprig *n* PROD clavo de moldeador *m*; **~ bolt** *n* CONST perno arponado *m*

spring[1]: **~-loaded** *adj* PROD accionado por muelle, accionado por resorte, cargado por muelle, cargado por resorte

spring[2] *n* ACOUST muelle *m*, CONST *of arch* arranque *m*, HYDROL *source* fuente *f*, MECH muelle *m*, resorte *m*, MECH ENG resorte *m*, muelle *m*, PHYS resorte *m*, VEH muelle *m*, resorte *m*, WATER manantial *m*, fuente *f*, WATER TRANSP *mooring* esprín *m*; **~ adjusting caliper** *AmE*, **~ adjusting calliper** *BrE* *n* METR calibrador de ajuste por resorte *m*; **~ balance** *n* MECH ENG *for weighing* balanza de resorte *f*, pesón *m*, romana de muelle *f*, PHYS punto de equilibrio de un resorte *m*; **~ bolt** *n* CONST cerrojo de resorte *m*, PROD perno de resorte *m*; **~ buffer** *n* *BrE* (*cf spring bumper AmE*) RAIL tope de resorte *m*, tope seco *m*; **~ bumper** *n* *AmE* (*cf spring buffer BrE*) RAIL tope de resorte *m*, tope seco *m*; **~ cage press** *n* C&G prensa con jaula con resortes *f*; **~ clip** *n* MECH ENG abrazadera de resorte *f*, presilla *f*, soporte antivibratorio *m*, sujetador de resortes *m*; **~ commutator** *n* ELEC *switch* conmutador con contactos elásticos *m*, interruptor de resorte *m*; **~ corn sheller** *n* *AmE* (*cf spring maize sheller BrE*) AGRIC desgranadora de maíz a resorte *f*; **~ cotter** *n* MECH ENG chaveta de resorte *f*; **~ dividers** *n pl* MECH ENG separadores de resortes *m pl*; **~-drive camera** *n* CINEMAT cámara accionada por resorte *f*, cámara de cuerda *f*; **~ ejector** *n* MECH ENG eyector de resortes *m*; **~ governor** *n* MECH ENG chaveta de resorte *f*, gancho de seguridad *m*, gobernador de resorte *m*, mosquetón *m*, regulador del resorte *m*; **~ grease lubricator** *n* PROD engrasador a compresión *m*, engrasador de resorte *m*; **~ guide** *n* PROD guía de resorte *f*; **~ hanger pin** *n* CONST pasador de muelle

suspensor m; **~ head** *n* HYDROL cabecera de un manantial *f*, origen de un manantial *m*, WATER origen de un manantial *m*; **~ jack** *n* ELEC ENG jack de enlace *m*; **~ latch** *n* PROD cerrojo de resorte *m*; **~ leaf** *n* VEH hoja de ballesta *f*; **~ line** *n* OCEAN esprín *m*; **~-loaded core** *n* P&R macho accionado por resorte *m*; **~-loaded pressure-relief valve** *n* REFRIG válvula de seguridad de resorte *f*; **~-loaded valve** *n* HYDRAUL regulador de resorte *m*, válvula accionada por muelle *f*, válvula accionada por resorte *f*; **~ lock** *n* CONST cerradura de muelle *f*, cerradura de resorte *f*; **~ maize sheller** *n* *BrE* (*cf spring corn sheller AmE*) AGRIC desgranadora de maíz a resorte *f*; **~ manometer** *n* PHYS manómetro de muelle *m*; **~-mounted pressure plate** *n* PHOTO placa de presión montada sobre resortes *f*; **~ neap cycle** *n* FUELLESS *tides* ciclo periódico de catorce días de las mareas *m*, OCEAN ciclo periódico de catorce días de las mareas *m*; **~ power hammer** *n* PROD martinete de resorte *m*; **~ pressure plate** *n* CINEMAT placa de presión con muelle *f*; **~-release device** *n* SPACE aparato de disparo a resorte *m*, aparato de liberación por resorte *m*; **~ retainer** *n* AUTO retén de resorte *m*; **~ return force** *n* PROD fuerza de retroceso por muelle *f*; **~ return lever** *n* PROD palanca de resorte *f*; **~ return switch** *n* ELEC conmutador de retorno elástico *m*, conmutador de retorno por muelle *m*; **~ seat** *n* AUTO, VEH asiento de resorte *m*; **~ stop** *n* MECH ENG paro de resorte *m*, tope de resorte *m*; **~ subjected to bending** *n* MECH ENG resorte bajo flexión *m*, resorte flexionado *m*; **~ subjected to torsion** *n* MECH ENG resorte bajo torsión *m*; **~ switch** *n* ELEC conmutador con contactos elásticos *m*, interruptor de resorte *m*; **~-tensioned pressure lever** *n* PHOTO control de presión tensionada por resortes *m*; **~ tide** *n* FUELLESS, HYDROL, OCEAN , WATER TRANSP marea muerta *f*, marea equinoccial *f*, marea viva *f*; **~ and toggle mechanism** *n* PROD mecanismo de resorte y fiador *m*; **~-tooth harrow** *n* AGRIC vibrocultivador *m*; **~ valve** *n* HYDRAUL válvula de resorte *f*; **~ washer** *n* MECH ENG arandela de resorte *f*, arandela elástica *f*, brida de ballestas *f*, estribo de ballestas *m*, muñón de resorte *m*; **~ water** *n* GEOL, HYDROL, WATER agua de manantial *f*; **~ zone** *n* C&G zona de rebote *f*

springer *n* CONST salmer *m*; **~ stone** *n* CONST piedra de arranque de un arco *f*, salmer *m*

springing *n* CONST *architecture* arranque *m*, MINE cuarteamiento *m*, ensanchamiento del fondo por explosión de una carga *m*; **~ course** *n* CONST *of arch* recorrido del arranque *m*; **~ line** *n* CONST *of arch* imposta *f*, línea de arranque *f*

sprinkle *vt* AGRIC aspersar, CHEM *dust* asperjar, rociar, CONST aspersar, asperjar, HYDROL aspersar, MAR POLL asperjar, SAFE aspersar, WATER *water* asperjar, aspersar, esparcir, pulverizar, rociar

sprinkled: **~ edges** *n* PRINT bordes jaspeados *m pl*

sprinkler *n* CONST rociador *m*, regadera *f*, aspersor *m*, HYDROL, SAFE, WATER aspersor *m*, instalación automática de extinción por aspersor *f*, rociador *m*; **~ and water spray fire-extinguishing installations** *n pl* SAFE instalaciones para extinguir el fuego por medio de aspersores y rocío *f pl*

sprinkling *n* CHEM *dusting* rociado *m*, HYDROL aspersión *f*, WATER *watering* aspersión *f*, rociado *m*, rociadura *f*

sprite *n* COMP&DP duendecillo *m*, sprite *m*

sprocket *n* AUTO rueda dentada *f*, CINEMAT engranaje *m*, COMP&DP rueda de cadena *f*, rueda dentada *f*, VEH rueda dentada para cadena articulada *f*; ~ **chain** *n* MECH cadena articulada *f*; ~ **and chain timing** *n* AUTO sincronizador de cadena y rueda dentada *m*; ~ **drive** *n* CINEMAT transmisión por engranajes *f*; ~ **hole** *n* CINEMAT perforación *f*, COMP&DP perforación marginal *f*, perforación de arrastre *f*, PHOTO perforación *f*; ~ **noise** *n* CINEMAT ruido de engranaje *m*; ~ **tooth** *n* CINEMAT diente de engrane *m*; ~ **wheel** *n* MECH piñón para cadena *m*, rueda catalina *f*, MECH ENG piñón de cadena de Galle *m*, rueda catalina *f*, rueda de cadena *f*, rueda dentada para cadena articulada *f*, PROD rueda catalina *f*, rueda dentada para cadena articulada *f*

sprue *n* P&R canal de colada *m*, PROD *foundry* rebaba *f*, chatarra de bebederos *f*, *runner pin* barra para romper el tapón de la piquera *f*; ~ **bush** *n* MECH ENG casquillo de inyección de colada *m*, casquillo del canal de colada *m*, guía del husillo eyector del casquillo de colada *f*, P&R bebedero *m*; ~ **cutter** *n* PROD cortabebederos *m*, desbarbador *m*; ~ **hole** *n* PROD agujero de colada *m*; ~ **opening** *n* P&R abertura de colada *f*, agujero de colada *m*; ~ **pin** *n* MECH ENG *diecasting die* muñón de colada *m*; ~ **puller pin** *n* MECH ENG *injection mould* husillo eyector *m*

sprung: ~ **gear** *n* VEH engranaje montado sobre muelles *m*; ~ **weight** *n* VEH soporte por muelles

SPST: ~ **relay** *n* (*single-pole single-throw relay*) ELEC ENG relé de acción unipolar *m*, relé unipolar y univanal *m*; ~ **switch** *n* (*single-pole single-throw switch*) ELEC ENG interruptor simple *m*, interruptor unipolar y univanal *m*

spud[1]: ~ **mud** *n* PETR TECH lodo del hueco de superficie *m*; ~ **sludge** *n* PETR TECH lodo del hueco de superficie *m*

spud[2]: ~ **in** *vt* PETR TECH iniciar la perforación

spudding: ~ **bit** *n* PETR TECH broca *f*, mecha de un pozo *f*, primera barrena *f*, trépano iniciador *m*; ~ **in** *n* PETR TECH inicio de la perforación *m*, inicio del sondeo *m*

spun[1] *adj* P&R hilado; ~-**dyed** *adj* TEXTIL teñido en hilado

spun[2]: ~ **cable** *n* OPT cable hilado *m*; ~ **concrete** *n* CONST concreto centrifugado *m* (*AmL*), hormigón centrifugado *m* (*Esp*); ~ **glass** *n* C&G vidrio hilado *m*; ~ **roving** *n* C&G arqueado alrededor *m*; ~ **yarn sizing** *n* TEXTIL apresto del hilado *m*; ~ **yarn winch** *n* TEXTIL barca de torniquete para hilados *f*

spunbond *n* TEXTIL no tejidos de filamentos *m pl*

spur *n* CONST *strut, brace* puntal *m*, ELEC *system* cilindro recto *m*, zanca *f*; ~ **chuck** *n* MECH ENG plato de tres mordazas *m*, plato de tulipa *m*; ~ **dike** *n* OCEAN dique para regeneración de costas *m*, escolleras *f pl*; ~ **gear** *n* MECH ENG engranaje cilíndrico de dientes rectos *m*; ~-**geared pulley block** *n* MECH ENG cuadernal de engranaje recto *m*; ~ **tenon joint** *n* CONST junta de espiga *f*; ~ **wheel** *n* MECH ENG rueda dentada de dientes rectos *f*

spurious: ~ **emission level** *n* SPACE nivel de emisión espúreos *m*, nivel de emisión falso *m*; ~ **signal** *n* SPACE señal espúrea *f*, señal falsa *f*, señal parásita *f*

spurt *n* SPACE aumento *m*, esfuerzo *m*, explosión *f*

spurting: ~ **out** *n* HYDROL brote *m*, chorro *m*

sputter *vi* CHEM *liquid* barbotar, chisporrotear, metalizar

sputtering *n* CHEM *of liquid* barboteo *m*, chisporroteo *m*, ELEC ENG deposición catódica *f*, deposición electrónica *f*

spy: ~ **glass** *n* INSTR anteojos *m pl*, gemelos *m pl*; ~ **hole** *n* MECH ENG agujero de observación *m*

squalene *n* CHEM escualeno *m*

squall *n* METEO, OCEAN turbonada *f*

squalling: ~ **wind** *n* METEO viento a ráfagas *m*, viento rafagoso *m*

square[1] *adj* GEOM, MATH, MECH ENG cuadrado

square[2] *n* CONST, GEOM, MATH cuadrado *m*, MECH ENG *drawing instrument* escuadra *f*, cuadrado *m*, cartabón *m*, METR escuadra *f*; ~ **back** *n* PRINT lomo plano *m*; ~ **bag with gussets** *n* PACK bolsa de fondo cuadrado de fuelle *f*; ~-**ball lock retainer** *n* MECH ENG *die set* retén de seguridad de muñón cuadrado *m*; ~-**bellows camera** *n* PHOTO cámara fotográfica de fuelle cuadrado *f*; ~ **bit drive** *n* MECH ENG *tools* portabrocas de mango cuadrado *m*, portaherramientas cuadradas *m*; ~ **centimeter** *AmE*, ~ **centimetre** *BrE n* METR centímetro cuadrado *m*; ~ **decimeter** *AmE*, ~ **decimetre** *BrE n* METR decímetro cuadrado *m*; ~ **drift** *n* MECH ENG punzón cónico cuadrado *m*; ~ **driftpin** *n* MECH ENG pasador cónico cuadrado *m*; ~ **drive** *n* MECH ENG portaherramientas de mango cuadrado *m*; ~-**edge preparation** *n* CONST preparación del canto escuadrado *f*; ~ **file** *n* MECH ENG lima cuadrada *f*, lima de cuatro caras *f*; ~ **foot** *n* METR pie cuadrado *m*; ~ **head** *n* CONST cabeza cuadrada *f*; ~-**head screw** *n* MECH ENG tornillo de cabeza cuadrada *m*; ~ **inch** *n* METR pulgada cuadrada *f*; ~ **joint** *n* CONST junta cuadrada *f*; ~-**jointed floor** *n* CONST suelo con juntas en ángulo recto *m*; ~ **law** *n* PHYS ley de cuadrado *f*; ~-**law detector** *n* ELEC ENG detector cuadrático *m*; ~ **loop** *n* ELEC ENG núcleo rectangular *m*; ~-**loop ferrite** *n* ELEC ENG núcleo rectangular de ferrita *m*; ~ **matter** *n* PRINT composición llena *f*; ~ **measure** *n* METR medida cuadrada *f*; ~ **measures** *n pl* METR *tools* medidas cuadradas *f pl*; ~ **meter** *AmE*, ~ **metre** *BrE n* METR metro cuadrado *m*; ~ **mile** *n* METR milla cuadrada *f*; ~-**mouthed rabbet** *n* CONST ranura con forma cuadrada *f*; ~ **neck bolt** *n* MECH ENG cerrojo acodado cuadrado *m*; ~ **parallel keys** *n pl* MECH ENG chavetas paralelas cuadradas *f pl*; ~ **rabbet plane** *n* CONST cepillo de ranurar cuadrado *m*; ~ **root** *n* MATH raíz cuadrada *f*; ~ **root and edge angles** *n pl* METR raíz cuadrada y ángulos de costado *f*; ~-**shank drill** *n* MECH ENG broca de mango cuadrado *f*; ~ **thread** *n* MECH ENG *of a screw* filete cuadrado *m*, hilo cuadrado *m*; ~-**thread screw** *n* MECH ENG tornillo de hilo cuadrado *m*, tornillo de paso cuadrado *m*, tornillo de rosca cuadrada *m*; ~-**thread tap** *n* MECH ENG tornillo de hilo cuadrado *m*; ~-**threaded screw** *n* MECH ENG tornillo de rosca cuadrada *m*; ~ **timber** *n* CONST madera cuadrada *f*; ~-**to roof** *n* CONST albardilla *f*; ~ **transom stern** *n* WATER TRANSP *boat building* popa llana *f*; ~ **washer** *n* MECH ENG arandela cuadrada *f*; ~ **wave** *n* ELECTRON onda cuadrada *f*, onda rectangular *f*, PHYS onda cuadrada *f*; ~-**wave generation** *n* ELECTRON generación de onda cuadrada *f*, generación de onda rectangular *f*; ~-**wave generator** *n* ELECTRON generador de onda cuadrada *m*, generador de onda rectangular *m*, TV generador de onda cuadrada *m*; ~-**wave voltage** *n* TV voltaje de onda cuadrada *m*; ~ **waveform** *n* TELECOM onda cuadrada *f*; ~ **yard** *n* METR yarda cuadrada *f*

square[3]: **be** ~ *vi* PROD ser cuadrado

square[4] *vt* MATH elevar al cuadrado, PROD escuadrar

squared[1] *adj* CONST, GEOM, MATH, MECH ENG, PRINT, PROD cuadrado

squared[2]: ~ **indentation** *n* PRINT sangría recta *f*; ~ **timber** *n* CONST madera cuadrada *f*

squareness *n* CONST cuadratura *f*, forma cuadrada *f*; ~ **cylinder** *n* METR cilindro cubicado *m*

squaring *n* CONST escuadra *f*, PAPER escuadrado *m*; ~ **the circle** *n* GEOM cuadratura del círculo *f*; ~ **circuit** *n* TV circuito de cuadratatura de la onda *m*

s-quark *n* PART PHYS quark extrañeza *m*

squat *n* TRANSP asentamiento de popa debido a la velocidad *m*

squealing *n* TELECOM chillido *m*, enganche acústico *m*, interferencia *f*

squeegee[1] *n* C&G *for enamelling* raspador *m*, CINEMAT, PHOTO escurridor *m*, PRINT regleta de goma *f*, TEXTIL enjugador *m*; ~ **roller** *n* PRINT rodillo escurridor *m*

squeegee[2] *vt* CINEMAT, PHOTO escurrir

squeeze[1] *n* MINE apretamiento *m* (*Esp*), asentamiento *m* (*AmL*), estrechamiento *m*, *of cement* inyección forzada de cemento *f*, PETR TECH forzamiento de cemento *m*; ~ **gate** *n* AGRIC *chute* aprietavacío *m*; ~ **roll** *n* PAPER rodillo escurridor *m*; ~-**roll coater** *n* PAPER estucadora de rodillo escurridor *f*

squeeze[2] *vt* CINEMAT, PROD *to compress* comprimir; ~ **out** *vt* PROD exprimir

squeeze[3] *vi* MINE asentarse el terreno, bocartear, triturar, troquelar

squeezer *n* PROD *moulding machine* moldeadora mecánica *f*

squeezing *n* MINE apiñamiento *m* (*Esp*), asiento del terreno *m*, distorsión del agujero taladrado *f* (*AmL*), extracción por presión *f*; ~ **roller** *n* TEXTIL rodillo exprimidor *m*

squelch *n* TELECOM reglaje silencioso *m*, silenciador en ausencia de señal *m*, supresión de ruido *f*

squib *n* CONST carretilla eléctrica *f*, MINE detonador *m* (*Esp*), mecha *f* (*AmL*), SPACE buscapiés *m*, carga explosiva dentro de un recipiente de paredes *f*, carga iniciadora *f*

squid *n* PHYS *for plastics* squid *m*

squirrel: ~ **cage** *n* ELEC ENG jaula de ardilla *f*; ~-**cage motor** *n* ELEC motor de armadura de barras *m*, motor de armadura de jaula *m*, motor de armadura de jaula de ardilla *m*, motor de jaula de ardilla *m*, ELEC ENG motor de rotor en cortocircuito *m*, PROD motor con rotor de jaula *m*, motor con rotor en jaula de ardilla *m*, motor de rotor en cortocircuito *m*; ~-**cage rotor** *n* ELEC ENG rotor en cortocircuito *m*; ~-**cage winding** *n* ELEC ENG devanado en barras *m*

squirt: ~ **hose** *n* WATER manguera de aspersión *f*

squitter *n* NUCL disparo accidental *m*, funcionamiento accidental *m*

Sr *abbr* (*strontium*) CHEM Sr (*estroncio*)

SRAM *abbr* (*static RAM*) COMP&DP RAM estática *f*

SRC *abbr* (*single-rubber-covered*) ELEC *conductor* forrado con una capa de caucho

SRD *abbr* OPT, TELECOM (*superluminescent diode*) diodo superluminiscente *m*, (*superradiant diode*) diodo superradiante *m*

SRF: ~ **carbon black** *n* (*semireinforcing carbon black*) P&R negro de humo de horno y refuerzo medio *m*

SRP *abbr* (*sustained release pellet*) AGRIC píldora de efecto retardado *f*

SSB *abbr* (*single sideband*) ELECTRON, PHYS, TELECOM, TV BLU (*banda lateral única*)

SSC *abbr* (*sudden storm commencement*) SPACE inicio repentino de tormenta *m*

S-shaped: ~ **hook** *n* MECH ENG gancho en forma de S *m*; ~ **spanner** *n* MECH ENG llave de apretar tuercas en forma de S *f*

SSI *abbr* COMP&DP, ELECTRON, PHYS (*small-scale integration*) IPE (*integración a pequeña escala*), RAIL (*Solid State Interlocking*) *fixed equipment* enclavamiento de estado sólido *m*, TELECOM (*small-scale integration*) IPE (*integración a pequeña escala*)

SSM *abbr* SPACE (*second surface mirror*) SSM (*espejo de superficie secundaria*) TEC ESP (*surface-to-surface missile*) SSM (*misil superficie-superficie*), TEC ESP (*satellite system monitor*) SSM (*monitor del sistema de satélites*), TELECOM (*single-segment message*) SSM (*mensaje del segmento único*)

SSMA *abbr* (*spread spectrum multiple access*) SPACE acceso múltiple por espectro ensanchado *m*

SSOG *abbr* (*Satellite System Operation Guide*) SPACE SSOG (*Guía de Explotación del Sistema de Satélites*)

SST *abbr* (*supersonic transport aircraft*) AIR TRANSP avión de transporte supersónico *m*

SSUS *abbr* (*Solid Spinning Upper Stage*) SPACE SSUS (*última fase rotatoria sólida*)

St *abbr* (*stratus*) METEO St (*stratus*)

ST *abbr* (*segment type*) TELECOM tipo de segmento *m*

stab: ~ **stitching** *n* PRINT costura en bloque *f*, engrapado talonario *m*; ~ **terminal** *n* PROD borne de perforaciones *m*

stabbing *n* PETR TECH enchufado *m*; ~ **awl** *n* MECH ENG lezna *f*, punzón *m*; ~ **board** *n* PETR TECH encuelladero *m*, plataforma del encuellador *f*; ~ **machine** *n* PRINT taladradora de pliegos para su costura *f*; ~ **sheet** *n* PRINT hoja para puntura *f*

stability *n* CHEM *of compound* estabilidad *f*, COAL estabilidad *f*, resistencia a la floculación *f*, COMP&DP, MINE, TELECOM, WATER TRANSP *ship design* estabilidad *f*; ~ **curtain** *n* TRANSP cortina de estabilidad *f*; ~ **curve** *n* WATER TRANSP *boat design* curva de estabilidad *f*; ~ **skirt** *n* TRANSP plinto de estabilidad *m*

stabilization *n* GEN *ship design* estabilización *f*; ~ **by low center of gravity** *AmE*, ~ **by low centre of gravity** *BrE* *n* TRANSP estabilización mediante centro de gravedad bajo *f*, estabilización por centro inferior de gravedad *f*; ~ **device** *n* TRANSP dispositivo de estabilización *m*, instrumento de estabilización *m*; ~ **rail** *n* TRANSP rail de estabilización *m*; ~ **of rotation** *n* SPACE estabilización de la rotación *f*; ~ **time** *n* OPT tiempo de estabilización *m*

stabilize *vt* CHEM estabilizar

stabilized[1] *adj* CHEM estabilizado

stabilized[2]: ~ **latex** *n* P&R látex estabilizado *m*; ~ **material** *n* CONST material estabilizado *m*; ~ **platform** *n* SPACE plataforma estabilizada *f*

stabilizer *n* GEN estabilizador *m*; ~ **bar** *n* AUTO, VEH *suspension* barra estabilizadora *f*; ~ **tower** *n* PETR TECH torre estabilizadora *f*

stabilizing: ~ **agent** *n* CHEM agente estabilizante *m*; ~ **bath** *n* CINEMAT, PHOTO baño estabilizador *m*; ~ **fin** *n* WATER TRANSP aleta estabilizadora *f*; ~ **wheel** *n*

TRANSP rueda estabilizadora *f*; ~ **winding** *n* ELEC devanado estabilizador *m*, devanado terciario *m*

stable[1] *adj* CHEM *compound* estable; **~-to-light** *adj* PACK estable a la luz

stable[2]: ~ **air** *n* METEO aire estable *m*; ~ **current** *n* OCEAN corriente permanente *f*; ~ **equilibrium** *n* PHYS equilibrio estable *m*; ~ **field** *n* METEO campo estable *m*; ~ **flow** *n* TRANSP flujo estable *m*; ~ **fly** *n* AGRIC mosca de establo *f*; ~ **isotope** *n* PHYS isótopo estable *m*; ~ **noise** *n* ACOUST ruido estable *m*

stabling *n* RAIL depósitos cubiertos para equipos móviles *m pl*

stachydrine *n* CHEM cadabina *f*, estaquidrina *f*

stachyose *n* CHEM estaquiosa *f*

stack[1] *n* AIR TRANSP conducto de escape *m*, C&G estiba *f*, COMP&DP apilado *m*, pila *f*, CONST chimenea *f* (*Esp*), HEAT ENG chimenea *f*, MINE apilado *m*, chimenea *f* (*Esp*), PACK apilado *m*, PAPER apilado *m*, conjunto de rodillos *m*, PETR TECH chimenea *f* (*Esp*), pilar de erosión *m*, PRINT apilado *m*; ~ **architecture** *n* COMP&DP arquitectura de pila *f*; ~ **gas** *n* NUCL gases de descarga por la chimenea *m pl*; ~ **pipe** *n* CONST *rainwater downpipe* bajante *m*; ~ **plume** *n* C&G pluma de chimenea *f*; ~ **silo** *n* AGRIC silo parva *m*

stack[2] *vt* COMP&DP, CONST apilar, PROD amontonar, apilar; **~ up** *vt* PAPER apilar

stackable[1] *adj* PACK apilable

stackable[2]: ~ **container** *n* TRANSP contenedor apilable *m*

stacked: **~-dryer section** *n* PAPER sección de secadores superpuestos *f*; ~ **heads** *n pl* TV cabezas apiladas *f pl*; ~ **presses** *n pl* PAPER prensas superpuestas *f pl*

stacker *n* C&G estibador *m*; ~ **arm** *n* C&G brazo del estibador *m*

stacking *n* C&G acomodo en estibas *m*, COMP&DP apilado *m*, apilamiento *m*, CONST apilamiento *m*, CRYSTALL apilamiento *m*, superposición *f*, ELEC ENG, GEOM apilamiento *m*, MINE, PACK, PAPER, PRINT apilado *m*, PROD acumulación *f*, amontonamiento *m*, apilamiento *m*; ~ **box** *n* PACK caja apilable *f*; ~ **conveyor** *n* PACK transportador de objetos apilados *m*; ~ **fault** *n* CRYSTALL fractura de apilamiento *f*; ~ **height** *n* PACK altura de la pila *f*; ~ **pallet** *n* PACK paleta para apilar *f*, TRANSP bandeja apilable *f*, paleta apilable *f*, pálet apilable *m* (*AmL*); ~ **sequence** *n* CRYSTALL secuencia de apilamiento *f*; ~ **truck** *n* PACK carretilla motorizada para apilar *f*; **~-up** *n* PACK escalonado vertical *m*

STADAN *abbr* (*space tracking and data acquisition network*) MILIT red de seguimiento espacial y adquisición de datos *f*

stadia: ~ **surveying** *n* CONST taquimetría *f*

stadimeter *n* CONST anteojo estadiómetro *m*

stadiometer *n* CONST estadiómetro *m*

staff *n* CONST mira *f*, PROD gancho de pudelar *m*, herramienta portaocho *f*; **~-calling installation** *n* SAFE *element* sistema de megafonía *m*; ~ **holder** *n* CONST *person* portamiras operarios *m pl*, soporte de la vara *m*; ~ **reading** *n* CONST *surveying* lectura de la mira *f*

stage *n* CINEMAT escenario *m*, CONST *scaffold* andamio *m*, GEOL etapa *f*, INSTR platina *f*, fase *f*, plataforma *f*, expansión *f*, LAB *heat unit* platina *f*, MINE altura de impulsión *f*, escalón *m*, piso de reposo *m*, PAPER etapa *f*, PROD etapa *f*, fase *f*, paso *m*, andamio *m*; ~ **base** *n* INSTR portaobjetos *m*; ~ **clip** *n* INSTR pinzas porta-

objetos *f pl*, LAB *graphic display* sujetador sobre platina *m*; ~ **compression** *n* PROD *of air* compresión en etapas *f*, compresión escalonada *f*; ~ **compressor** *n* PROD compresor de fases escalonadas *m*; ~ **coupling** *n* ELEC ENG acoplamiento escalonado *m*; ~ **efficiency** *n* ELECTRON rendimiento de fase *m*; ~ **integrator** *n* SPACE integrador de etapa *m*, totalizador de etapa *m*; ~ **loader** *n* MINE cargador gradual *m*, cargador por etapas *m*; ~ **pumping** *n* MINE agotamiento por repeticiones *m*

stagger: **~-tuned amplifier** *n* ELECTRON amplificador de sintonía escalonada *m*

staggered: ~ **air bar** *n* PRINT barra de aire escalonada *f*; ~ **fin** *n* REFRIG aleta al tresbolillo *f*; ~ **heads** *n pl* TV cabezas escalonadas *f pl*; ~ **locks** *n pl* HYDROL *network* esclusas escalonadas *f pl*

staggering *n* TV escalonamiento *m*

staging[1] *adv* COMP&DP por etapas

staging[2] *n* CONST andamiaje *m*, PROD andamiaje *m*, graduación *f*, SAFE andamiaje *m*

stagnation: ~ **point** *n* AIR TRANSP *aerodynamics* punto de estancamiento *m*, FLUID punto de remanso *m*, PHYS punto estático *m*; ~ **pressure** *n* FLUID presión de remanso *f* (*Esp*)

stain[1] *n* PAPER, QUALITY mancha *f*

stain[2] *vt* CHEM colorar, descolorar, mancharse, teñir, COLOUR aplicar tintura, decolorar, descolorar, teñir, P&R manchar, PAPER manchar, teñir, QUALITY manchar, TEXTIL decolorar, descolorar

stained: ~ **glass window** *n* C&G ventana con emplomado *f*, vitral *m*

stainer *n* COLOUR tintura *f*; ~ **pigment** *n* COLOUR pigmento de tintura *m*

staining *n* C&G *method of decorating glass* manchado *m*, CHEM coloración *f*, descoloración *f*, teñido *m*, tinción *f*, COLOUR, TEXTIL descoloración *f*

stainless[1] *adj* METALL, PHOTO inoxidable

stainless[2]: ~ **steel** *n* AUTO, MECH ENG, METALL, PROD, VEH acero inoxidable *m*; ~ **steel beaker** *n* LAB *heat unit* vasija de acero inoxidable *f*; ~ **steel dust** *n* COAL limaduras *f pl*; ~ **steel tube** *n* MECH ENG tubo de acero inoxidable *m*

stair *n* CONST escalera *f*; ~ **rod dislocation** *n* METALL dislocación articulada en escalera *f*

staircase *n* CONST estructura de la escalera *f*, escalera con armazón *f*, TV escalera *f*; ~ **signal** *n* TV señal en forma de escalera *f*

stairs *n pl* CONST escaleras *f pl*; ~ **interrupted by landings** *n* CONST escaleras con descansillos *f pl*

stake *n* CONST *stick or post* estaca *f*, *surveying* bigorneta *f*; ~ **net** *n* OCEAN arte de estacas *m*, red estacada *f*, WATER TRANSP arte de estacas *m*

staking *n* CONST *surveying* estacado *m*, estaquillado *m*; ~ **out** *n* CONST, PROD jalonamiento *m*

stalagmometer *n* PHYS estalagmómetro *m*

stall[1] *n* AIR TRANSP *compressor, turbine engine* pérdida *f*, COAL pérdida de sustentación *f*, anchurón *m* (*AmL*), cámara de tostación *f* (*AmL*), emplazamiento *m* (*Esp*), sala *f*, cámara *f*, FUELLESS parada *f*, MINE caseta de tostación *f* (*Esp*), galería de tostación *f* (*AmL*), cámara *f* (*AmL*), anchurón *m* (*AmL*), emplazamiento *m* (*Esp*), galería atascada *f* (*Esp*), pesebre *m*, sala *f*, cámara de tostación *f* (*AmL*); ~ **load** *n* PROD carga de calada *f*; ~ **road** *n* MINE galería de avance *f* (*Esp*), galería del frente de ataque *f* (*AmL*); ~ **warning device** *n* AIR TRANSP dispositivo de aviso de entrada en pérdida *m*

stall[2] *vti* AUTO calar, calarse, FUELLESS ahogar, pararse, VEH calar, calarse, parar, pararse

stamp[1] *n* PROD bocarte *m*, martinete *m*, pisón *m*, *mill for stamping ore* molino de bocartes *m*, molino de pisones *m*, *steel metal* embutido *m*, estampado *m*; ~ **battery** *n* PROD batería de bocartes *f*; ~ **boss** *n* PROD *ore mill* cabeza de pilón *f*; ~ **etching paste** *n* C&G pasta para grabar *f*; ~ **guide** *n* PROD estructura de forja *f*, guía de pilón *f*; ~ **head** *n* PROD cabeza de pilón *f*, pisón de almadeneta *m*; ~ **house** *n* MINE cámara de bocarte *f*; ~ **mill** *n* COAL molino de bocartes *m*, molino de pisones *m*, triturador *m*, PROD molino de bocartes *m*, molino de pisones *m*; ~ **milling** *n* PROD bocarteo *m*; ~ **shoe** *n* PROD zapata de pilón *f*; ~ **stem** *n* PROD vástago de estampa *m*

stamp[2] *vt* PROD *crush* machacar, triturar, bocartear, *mark*, estampar, timbar, timbrar, estampillar, marcar, sellar

stamped[1]: **as ~** *adj* PROD según estampado

stamped[2]: ~ **bucket** *n* CONST caldero estampado *m*

stamper *n* ACOUST negativo para hacer discos *m*, OPT matriz *f*, PROD *person* estampador *m*

stamping *n* ELEC ENG chapa magnética *f*, PRINT estampado *m*, estampación *f*, sellado *m*, PROD *branding* punzonamiento *m*, estampado *m*, estampación *f*, *crushing* machacamiento *m*, trituración *f*; ~ **machine** *n* PROD *steel metal working* estampadora *f*, prensa de estampar *f*, prensa estampadora *f*, troqueladora *f*; ~ **mill** *n* PROD *for crushing ore* molino de bocartes *m*, molino de pisones *m*; ~ **press** *n* PRINT prensa de estampado en relieve *f*, PROD *sheet metal working* prensa de estampar *f*, prensa estampadora *f*, prensa troqueladora *f*; ~ **test** *n* PROD *of metals* ensayo de estampación *m*, prueba de estampación *f*; ~ **varnish** *n* COATINGS, COLOUR barniz de estampación *m*

stanchion *n* CONST *prop* junta metálica de ventana *f*, puntal *m*, RAIL poste *m*, columna *f*, WATER TRANSP *deck fitting* candelero *m*, puntal *m*

stand[1]: ~-**by working** *adj* TELECOM de explotación de reserva, de trabajo de reserva

stand[2] *n* ACOUST *music* atril *m*, CHEM estante *m*, soporte *m*, CINEMAT soporte *m*, INSTR estand *m*, equipo completo *m*, plataforma *f*, LAB *heat unit*, VEH soporte *m*; ~-**alone** *n* COMP&DP computador autónomo *m* (*AmL*), computador solo *m* (*AmL*), computadora autónoma *f* (*AmL*), computadora sola *f* (*AmL*), ordenador autónomo *m* (*Esp*), ordenador solo *m* (*Esp*); ~-**alone controller** *n* PROD controlador independiente *m*; ~-**alone exchange** *n* TELECOM central autónoma *f*, central independiente *f*; ~-**alone system** *n* SPACE sistema autónomo *m*, sistema independiente *m*; ~-**alone unit** *n* PROD unidad independiente *f*; ~-**by** *n* PROD reserva *f*; ~-**by processor** *n* TELECOM procesador auxiliar *m*, procesador de reserva *m*; ~-**by supply** *n* ELEC suministro de reserva *m*; ~-**by system** *n* TELECOM sistema de reserva *m*; ~ **on wheels** *n* PROD base de ruedas *f*; ~ **of pipe** *n* PETR TECH parada *f* (*AmL*), pareja *f* (*AmL*), triple *m* (*Esp*); ~ **with rising table** *n* PROD soporte de plataforma de altura variable *m*; ~ **of tide** *n* OCEAN, WATER TRANSP estoa *f*; ~-**up capitals** *n pl* PRINT mayúsculas rectas *f pl*

stand[3] *vt* PROD *rough handling* resistir

stand[4]: ~ **for** *vi* WATER TRANSP *navigation* aproar a, gobernar hacia; ~ **inshore** *vi* WATER TRANSP *navigation* recalar a tierra; ~ **to the north** *vi* WATER TRANSP *navigation* navegar hacia el norte

standage *n* MINE colector de agua *m*, depósito de bomba *m*, pozo de desagüe *m*

standard[1] *adj* COMP&DP común, estándar, normal, normalizado, MECH ENG de referencia, de uso corriente, estándar, normal, normalizado, reglamentario, típico, uniforme, usual, METR estándar, PHYS stándard, POLL, SPACE, TV estándar

standard[2] *n* ACOUST norma *f*, COMP&DP estándar *m*, CONST *scaffold pole* soporte *m*, puntal *m*, poste *m*, MECH caballete *m*, MECH ENG modelo *m*, apoyo *m*, caballete *m*, columna *f*, prototipo *m*, pilar *m*, poste *m*, soporte *m*, montante *m*, pie *m*, norma *f*, patrón *m*, patrón de medida *m*, estándar *m*, METR estándar *m*, MINE ley *f*, PHYS stándard *m*, POLL estándar *m*, PROD *tower or trellis post, as for aerial ropeway* pilón *m*, *of planing machine* pie *m*, QUALITY norma *f*, SPACE estándar *m*, TELECOM estándar *m*, marco *m*, modelo *m*, norma *f*, patrón *m*, pauta *f*, tipo *m*, TV estándar *m*, norma *f*; ~ **altimeter setting** *n* AIR TRANSP reglaje del altímetro normal *m*; ~ **ambient temperature** *n* REFRIG temperatura ambiente normal *f*; ~ **atmosphere** *n* METEO atmósfera de referencia *f*, atmósfera tipo *f*; ~ **capacitor** *n* ELEC ENG condensador estándar *m*; ~ **cell** *n* ELEC pila patrón *f*, ELEC ENG elemento estándar *m*, PHYS celda standard *f*; ~ **color specification** *AmE*, ~ **colour specification** *BrE n* PRINT especificación normalizada de colores *f*; ~ **compass** *n* WATER TRANSP aguja magistral *f*, compás magistral *m*; ~ **compliance test** *n* GAS prueba de homologación *f*; ~ **container** *n* TRANSP contenedor estándar *m*; ~ **control equipment** *n* PROD equipo de control reglamentario *m*; ~ **deviation** *n* COMP&DP desviación estándar *f*, desviación típica *f*, ELECTRON desviación normalizada *f*, MATH desviación estándar *f*, desviación típica *f*, PHYS desviación stándard *f*, PROD desviación característica *f*, desviación típica *f*; ~ **division** *n* MATH desviación normalizada *f*; ~ **error** *n* MATH error estándar *m*; ~ **form** *n* MATH forma estándar *f*, forma normal *f*, formulario estándar *m*, formulario normal *m*; ~ **gage** *AmE see standard gauge BrE*; ~ **gage film** *AmE see standard gauge film BrE*; ~ **gauge** *BrE n* CONST calibre normal *m*, MECH ENG *instrument for measuring wire or drills* plantilla *f*, calibrador patrón *m*, calibre *m*, vitola *f*, galga patrón *f*, RAIL ancho normal de vía *m*; ~ **gauge film** *n BrE* CINEMAT película de paso normal *f*; ~ **gray card** *AmE*, ~ **grey card** *BrE n* CINEMAT carta de grises estándar *f*; ~ **height** *n* PRINT altura normal *f*; ~ **ink** *n* PRINT tinta normal *f*; ~ **interface** *n* COMP&DP, TELECOM interfaz normalizada *f*; ~ **item** *n* PROD material reglamentario *m*; ~ **knob selector** *n* PROD selector normalizado *m*; ~ **leader** *n* CINEMAT, TV guía estándar *f*; ~ **legs** *n* CINEMAT trípode alto *m*; ~ **lens** *n* CINEMAT, OPT, PHOTO objetivo normal *m*; ~ **light source** *n* ELEC ENG generador de luz estándar *m*; ~ **measures** *n pl* METR medidas estándar *f pl*; ~ **measuring signal** *n* TV señal de mediciones estándar *f*; ~ **meter** *AmE*, ~ **metre** *BrE n* PHYS metro patrón *m*; ~ **microphone** *n* ACOUST micrófono patrón *m*; ~ **multigaging elements** *AmE*, ~ **multigauging elements** *BrE n pl* METR elementos de calibración múltiple estándar *m pl*; ~ **nut** *n* MECH ENG tuerca normalizada *f*, tuerca reglamentaria *f*; ~ **ohm** *n* ELEC *unit* ohmio patrón *m*; ~ **orifice** *n* HYDRAUL orificio de aristas vivas *m*, orificio en pared delgada *m*; ~ **part** *n* MECH ENG *for tooling* parte reglamentaria *f*, pieza normalizada *f*, pieza reglamentaria *f*; ~ **pattern** *n* TV patrón de normas *m*, patrón estándar *m*; ~ **pitch** *n* AIR TRANSP *of propeller* paso nominal *m*; ~ **pressure** *n* PETR TECH presión normal *f*; ~ **of quality** *n* METR estándar de calidad *m*; ~ **rail gage** *AmE*, ~ **rail gauge** *BrE n* RAIL vía de ferrocarril de ancho normal *f*; ~ **rating cycle** *n* REFRIG ciclo de referencia *m*; ~ **reference atmosphere** *n* MECH ENG atmósfera de referencia estándar *f*; ~ **solution** *n* CHEM solución estándar *f*, solución patrón *f*; ~ **specification** *n* MECH ENG, PROD especificación estándar *f*, especificación normal *f*, especificación reglamentaria *f*; ~ **tape** *n* TV cinta de referencia *f*; ~ **temperature** *n* (*STP*) PETR TECH temperatura normal *f*, PHYS temperatura stándard *f*; ~ **test piece** *n* PROD probeta normalizada *f*, probeta tipo *f*, probeta unificada *f*; ~ **time** *n* PROD hora legal *f*, hora oficial *f*, WATER TRANSP hora legal *f*; ~ **track** *n* RAIL vía normal *f*; ~ **tuning frequency** *n* ACOUST frecuencia de sintonización normalizada *f*; ~ **weights** *n pl* METR pesos estándar *m pl*

Standard: ~ **Generalized Markup Language** *n* (*SGML*) COMP&DP, PRINT lenguaje de marcado generalizado estándar *m*, lenguaje SGML *m*

standardization *n* CHEM, CHEM TECH estandarización *f*, normalización *f*, uniformización *f*, COMP&DP estandarización *f*, ELEC, ELEC ENG, ELECTRON uniformización *f*, GAS estandarización *f*, normalización *f*, MECH ENG uniformización *f*, PHYS standarización *f*, PROD uniformización *f*, QUALITY normalización *f*, uniformización *f*, TELECOM estandarización *f*, normalización *f*, regularización *f*, tipificación *f*, uniformización *f*, TV normalización *f*; ~ **of test methods** *n* INSTR, LAB, MECH ENG normalización de métodos de prueba *f*, reglamentación de métodos de prueba *f*, uniformación de métodos de prueba *f*

standardize *vt* CHEM, CHEM TECH, ELEC, ELEC ENG, ELECTRON, MECH ENG estandarizar, normalizar, uniformizar, PROD uniformizar, *specifications* normalizar, QUALITY normalizar, uniformizar, TELECOM uniformizar

standardized: ~ **impact-sound** *n* ACOUST ruido de impactos normalizado *m*; ~ **sound insulation** *n* ACOUST aislamiento acústico normalizado *m*; ~ **threshold hearing** *n* ACOUST umbral de audición normalizado *m*

standards: ~ **conversion** *n* TV conversión de normas *f*; ~ **converter** *n* TV convertidor de normas *m*; ~ **selector** *n* TV seleccionador de normas *m*

standby[1] *adj* COMP&DP auxiliar, de reserva, en espera, PROD, MILIT, QUALITY a la espera en reserva, de reserva, TELECOM a la escucha, en espera; **on** ~ *adj* MAR POLL a la espera, en modalidad de espera

standby[2]: ~ **boat** *n* PETR TECH embarcación de apoyo *f*; ~ **boiler** *n* HEAT ENG caldera auxiliar *f*, caldera de reserva *f*; ~ **mode** *n* SPACE modo auxiliar *m*, modo de reserva *m*; ~ **redundancy** *n* SPACE redundancia de reserva *f*; ~ **set** *n* ELEC ENG grupo auxiliar *m*, grupo de reserva *m*; ~ **time** *n* COMP&DP tiempo de espera *m*; ~ **unit** *n* ELEC ENG, MILIT, PROD unidad de reserva *f*

standing: ~ **block** *n* MECH ENG polea fija *f*, prensa de torno *f*, WATER TRANSP *fittings* cuadernal fijo *m*,

montón fijo *m*; ~ **end** *n* MECH ENG cabeza fija *f*; ~ **knife cutter** *n* AGRIC cuchilla recta de arado *f*; ~ **matter** *n* PRINT composición pendiente de impresión *f*; ~ **rigging** *n* WATER TRANSP jarcia firme *f*, jarcia muerta *f*; ~ **timber** *n* CONST madera en pie *f*; ~ **type** *n* PRINT composición pendiente de impresión *f*; ~ **vice** *n BrE* PROD tornillo con pie *m*; ~ **vise** *AmE see standing vice BrE*; ~ **water** *n* HYDROL, WATER agua estancada *f*; ~ **wave** *n* ACOUST, ELEC ENG, PHYS, TELECOM, WAVE PHYS onda estacionaria *f*; ~~**wave ratio** *n* (*SWR*) PHYS, SPACE relación de onda estacionaria *f* (*ROE*), TELECOM coeficiente de onda estacionaria *m*, relación de amplitud de ondas estacionarias *m*, relación de onda estacionaria *f* (*ROE*)

standpipe *n* PETR TECH bastidor de la manguera *m*, columna reguladora *f*, standpipe *m*, tubo vertical *m*, WATER *in street* tubo vertical *m*

standstill *n* MECH ENG parada *f*, alto *m*

stannate *n* CHEM estanato *m*

stannic[1] *adj* CHEM estánico

stannic[2]: ~ **oxide** *n* CHEM dióxido de estaño *m*, óxido estánico *m*

stannite *n* MINERAL estannina *f*

stannous *adj* CHEM estannoso, estañoso

stapes *n* ACOUST estribo *m*

staple[1] *n* CONST grapa *f*, argolla *f*, presilla *f*, MINE pozo ciego *m* (*Esp*), pozo de ventilación *m* (*AmL*), PACK grapa *f*, PROD *stem chaplet* soporte sencillo *m*; ~ **fiber** *AmE*, ~ **fibre** *BrE n* TEXTIL fibra cortada *f*; ~ **fiber yarn** *AmE*, ~ **fibre yarn** *n BrE* TEXTIL hilo de fibra discontinua *m*; ~ **food** *n* FOOD alimento básico *m*, alimento principal *m*, materia prima *f*; ~ **length** *n* TEXTIL longitud de fibra *f*; ~ **pit** *n* MINE chimenea *f* (*Esp*), pozo interior de comunicación *m*; ~ **post** *n* WATER *of sluice gate* poste de quicio *m*; ~ **remover** *n* MECH ENG extractor de grampas *m* (*AmL*), extractor de grapas *m* (*Esp*); ~ **shaft** *n* MINE chimenea *f* (*Esp*), pozo interior de comunicación *m*; ~ **vice** *n BrE* PROD tornillo con pie *m*; ~ **vise** *AmE see staple vice BrE*

staple[2] *vt* PACK grapar

stapling: ~ **equipment** *n* PACK equipo de grapado *m*; ~ **machine** *n* PACK grapadora *f*; ~ **pliers** *n pl* PACK alicates de grapar *m pl*; ~ **wire** *n* PACK alambre para grapar *m*

star[1]: ~~**connected** *adj* TELECOM con conexión en estrella, conectado en estrella; ~~**wired** *adj* TELECOM conexionado en estrella

star[2] *n* AUTO, COMP&DP, ELEC, METEO, OPT estrella *f*, SPACE estrella *f*, lucero *m*, TELECOM estrella *f*; ~ **bit** *n* MINE trépano de corona *m*, trépano de corte en cruz *m*, trépano en estrella *m*; ~ **chart** *n* SPACE, WATER TRANSP carta celeste *f*, WATER TRANSP carta celeste *f*, planisferio *m*; ~ **configuration** *n* TELECOM configuración en estrella *f*; ~~**connected armature** *n* ELEC armadura con conexión en estrella *f*, armadura conectada en estrella *f*; ~ **connection** *n* ELEC *reactor, transformer* conexión en estrella *f*, montaje en estrella *m*, ELEC ENG, PHYS, TELECOM conexión en estrella *f*; ~ **coupler** *n* OPT, TELECOM acoplador en estrella *m*; ~ **crack** *n* C&G astillado en estrella *m*; ~~**delta connection** *n* ELEC ENG conexión estrella-triángulo *f*; ~~**delta starter** *n* ELEC *switch*, ELEC ENG arrancador de estrella-triángulo *m*; ~~**delta starting switch** *n* ELEC conmutador de arranque estrella-triángulo *m*; ~~**delta switch** *n* ELEC ENG interruptor estrella-triángulo *m*; ~-**delta transformation** *n* PHYS transformación estrella-delta *f*; ~ **diagonal** *n* INSTR diagonal de cruz *f*; ~ **distribution** *n* TELECOM distribución en estrella *f*; ~ **dyeing** *n* COLOUR teñido en estrella *m*; ~ **filter** *n* CINEMAT filtro de estrella *m*; ~ **fracture** *n* C&G fractura en estrella *f*; ~ **network** *n* COMP&DP, SPACE, TELECOM red en estrella *f*; ~ **quad** *n* ELEC ENG cuadrete estrella *m*, PHYS cable de estrella *m*; ~-**quad cable** *n* ELEC ENG cable estrella-cuadrete *m*; ~ **sensor** *n* SPACE sensor estelar *m*, sensor sidéreo *m*; ~-**star connection** *n* ELEC conexión Y-Y *f*, conexión estrella-estrella *f*; ~ **structure** *n* TELECOM estructura en estrella *f*; ~ **switch** *n* TELECOM conmutador en estrella *m*; ~-**to-delta conversion** *n* ELEC conversión de estrella a delta *f*, conversión de estrella a triángulo *f*; ~-**to-delta transformation** *n* ELEC transformación de estrella a delta *f*, transformación de estrella a triángulo *f*; ~ **topology** *n* COMP&DP topología en estrella *f*; ~ **tracker** *n* SPACE seguidor de estrellas *m*; ~ **transit detector** *n* SPACE detector del tránsito de estrellas *m*; ~ **voltage** *n* ELEC tensión de una fase *f*, tensión de una fase de la estrella *f*, tensión entre fase y neutro *f*, tensión entre fases *f*; ~ **washer** *n* PROD arandela de estrella *f*; ~ **wheel** *n* AUTO rueda estrellada *f*, MECH ENG rueda de estrella *f*

starboard *n* SPACE, WATER TRANSP estribor *m*

starch *n* CHEM, FOOD, PAPER, PRINT, TEXTIL almidón *m*; ~ **slurry** *n* FOOD lechada de almidón *f*, papilla de almidón *f*

starchy *adj* CHEM feculoso, FOOD amiláceo

Stark: ~ **effect** *n* PHYS efecto Stark *m*

starred: ~ **roll** *n* PAPER bobina estropeada en los bordes *f*

start[1] *n* COMP&DP arranque *m*, comienzo *m*, inicio *m*, TELECOM comienzo *m*, inicio *m*, principio *m*; ~ **address field** *n* PROD campo de dirección de arranque *m*; ~ **bit** *n* COMP&DP bit de arranque *m*, bit de comienzo *m*; ~ **button** *n* CINEMAT botón de arranque *m*; ~ **element** *n* COMP&DP elemento de arranque *m*, elemento inicial *m*; ~ **fence** *n* PROD barrera inicial *f*; ~ **of header** *n* (*SOH*) COMP&DP comienzo de cabecera *m*, comienzo de título *m*, inicio de encabezamiento *m*; ~ **mark** *n* CINEMAT marca de inicio *f*, TV punto de arranque *m*; ~ **of message** *n* (*SOM*) COMP&DP comienzo del mensaje *m*; ~ **rung** *n* PROD eslabón inicial *m*; ~ **statement** *n* PROD enunciado inicial *m*, situación inicial *f*; ~ **of text** *n* (*STX*) COMP&DP comienzo de texto *m*; ~ **time** *n* COMP&DP tiempo de arranque *m*

start[2] *vt* AUTO poner en marcha, C&G *cut* empezar, COMP&DP arrancar, HYDRAUL cebar, MECH ENG echar a andar, poner en marcha, activar, *an injector* comenzar, cebar, iniciar, PROD *pumps, injectors* cebar, iniciar, poner en marcha, poner en movimiento, arrancar, VEH poner en marcha; ~ **in operation** *vt* WATER *a pump* cebar; ~ **up** *vt* MECH ENG *set machine in motion* arrancar, poner en movimiento

start[3] *vti* COMP&DP comenzar, iniciar

start[4]: ~ **the flow of water in a siphon** *phr* WATER cebar un sifón

starter *n* (*cf line starter AmE*) AUTO arrancador *m*, motor de arranque *m*, COAL cebador *m*, ELEC *motor* arrancador *m*, artefacto de arranque *m*, *switch* arrancador de línea *m*, ELEC ENG arrancador *m*,

electrodo de encendido *m*, FOOD iniciador *m*, VEH mecanismo de puesta en marcha *m*, arranque *m*, arrancador *m*; ~ **bar** *n* CONST barra de arranque *f*; ~ **battery** *n* ELEC *automotive*, ELEC ENG, TRANSP batería de arranque *f*; ~ **brush** *n* AUTO escobilla del arrancador *f*; ~ **button** *n* VEH botón de arranque *m*, pulsador de arranque *m*; ~ **cable** *n* AUTO, VEH cable del estárter *m*; ~ **collector ring** *n* AUTO anillo del collector del arrancador *m*; ~ **commutator** *n* AUTO conmutador del arrancador *m*; ~ **control** *n* AUTO mando del arrancador *m*; ~ **drive assembly** *n* AUTO montaje del arrancador *m*, montaje del propulsor del arrancador *m*; ~ **electrode** *n* ELEC ENG electrodo de encendido *m*, electrodo del arranque *m*; ~ **field coil** *n* AUTO bobina inductora del arrancador *f*; ~ **field winding** *n* AUTO devanado del estátor del arrancador *m*, devanado del inductor del arrancador *m*; ~ **gear** *n* AUTO engranaje del arrancador *m*, MECH ENG engranaje de arranque *m*; ~ **jet** *n* AUTO chorro de arranque *m*, surtidor de arranque *m*; ~ **motor** *n* AUTO, ELEC ENG motor de arranque *m*, MECH ENG burro de arranque *m* (*AmL*), motor de arranque *m* (*Esp*), VEH motor de arranque *m*; ~ **motor pinion** *n* AUTO, VEH piñón de puesta en marcha *m*; ~ **pole shoe** *n* AUTO pieza polar del arrancador *f*; ~ **ring gear** *n* AUTO, VEH anillo elástico para piñón de puesta en marcha *m*; ~ **slip ring** *n* AUTO anillo rozante del arrancador *m*, VEH muelle de retroceso del motor de arranque *m*

starting *n* MECH ENG arranque *m*, comienzo *m*, inicio *m*, principio *m*, puesta en marcha *f*, salida *f*, MINE arranque *m*; ~ **capacitor** *n* ELEC capacitor de arranque *m*, condensador de arranque *m*; ~ **change-over switch** *n* ELEC conmutador de arranque *m*, conmutador inversor de arranque *m*, inversor de arranque *m*, inversor de corriente de arranque *m*, ELEC ENG inversor de arranque *m*, inversor de corriente de arranque *m*; ~ **crank** *n* VEH manivela de arranque *f*; ~ **device** *n* ELEC motor dispositivo de arranque *m*; ~ **friction** *n* MECH ENG fricción de arranque *f*; ~ **gear** *n* MECH ENG engranaje de arranque *m*; ~ **handle** *n* AUTO, MECH ENG palanca de arranque *f*; ~ **hum** *n* TV zumbido de arranque *m*; ~ **jet** *n* AUTO chorro de arranque *m*, surtidor de arranque *m*; ~ **lever** *n* AUTO, MECH ENG palanca de arranque *f*; ~ **motor** *n* ELEC motor de arranque *m*, motor de puesta en marcha *m*; ~ **rheostat** *n* ELEC, ELEC ENG reóstato de arranque *m*, PROD par motor al arranque *m*, par motor de arranque *m*; ~ **torque** *n* MECH ENG momento de par de arranque *m*, PROD par motor al arranque *m*, par motor de arranque *m*; ~ **transformer** *n* ELEC ENG transformador de arranque *m*

startup: ~ **burner** *n* C&G mechero de arranque *m*; ~ **circuit** *n* TELECOM circuito de arranque *m*; ~ **zero power test** *n* NUCL prueba de arranque a cero potencia *f*

starvation *n* PRINT falta de alimentación *f*

starving *n* REFRIG subalimentación *f*

stassfurtite *n* MINERAL stassfurtita *f*

stat *n* PRINT copia fotostática *f*

state *n* COMP&DP, PHYS, WATER TRANSP estado *m*; **off** ~ *n* ELEC ENG estado de desactivado *m*; **on** ~ *n* ELEC ENG estado de activado *m*; ~ **of the art** *n* PROD estado actual de la tecnología *m*; ~ **diagram** *n* COMP&DP diagrama de estado *m*; ~ **of equilibrium** *n* THERMO estado de equilibrio *m*; ~-**of-the-art technique** *n*

CONST tecnología al día *f*; ~ **transition diagram** *n* TELECOM diagrama de transición de estados *m*

statement *n* COMP&DP *programming* instrucción *f*, sentencia *f*, PROD estado de cuentas *m*, presentación *f*, memoria *f*, declaración *f*; ~ **label** *n* COMP&DP etiqueta de instrucción *f*, etiqueta de la declaración *f*

static[1] *adj* COMP&DP, ELEC ENG estático

static[2] *n* ELEC ENG electricidad estática *f*, TV ruido atmosférico *m*, ruido de estática *m*; ~ **air cushion** *n* TRANSP amortiguación por aire estático *f*, colchón amortiguador de aire estático *m*; ~ **allocation** *n* COMP&DP asignación estática *f*; ~ **balance** *n* MECH ENG equilibrio estático *m*; ~ **balance of grinding wheels** *n* MECH ENG equilibrio estático de las muelas *m*; ~ **balancer** *n* ELEC ENG equilibrador estático *m*; ~ **characteristic** *n* ELEC ENG característica estática *f*; ~ **charge** *n* ELEC ENG carga estática *f*; ~ **conditions** *n pl* ELEC ENG condiciones estáticas *f pl*; ~ **converter** *n* ELEC, ELEC ENG convertidor estático *m*, SPACE convertidor estático *m*, mutador *m*; ~ **correction** *n* PETR TECH corrección estática *f*; ~ **discharge head** *n* WATER altura de impulsión *f*; ~ **dump** *n* COMP&DP vuelco estático *m*; ~ **electric field** *n* ELEC ENG campo eléctrico estático *m*; ~ **electrical machine** *n* ELEC ENG máquina electroestática *f*; ~ **electricity** *n* CONST, TEXTIL electricidad estática *f*; ~ **eliminator** *n* TEXTIL eliminador de electricidad estática *m*; ~ **error** *n* TV error estático *m*; ~ **field** *n* ELEC ENG, TELECOM campo estático *m*; ~ **fluid level** *n* PETR TECH nivel de fluido en reposo *m*; ~ **focus** *n* TV enfoque estático *m*; ~ **friction** *n* MECH ENG fricción estática *f*, PHYS rozamiento estático *m*; ~ **friction coefficient** *n* PHYS coeficiente de rozamiento estático *m*; ~ **head** *n* HY-DRAUL altura manométrica *f*, carga de agua *f*, WATER altura de elevación *f*, altura manométrica *f*; ~ **hovering** *n* TRANSP levitación estática *f*; ~ **inverter** *n* ELEC ENG invertidor estático *m*, SPACE inversor estático *m*; ~ **lift** *n* HYDRAUL *pumps* altura manométrica *f*, WATER altura de elevación *f*, altura manométrica *f*; ~ **mark** *n* CINEMAT marca estática *f*; ~ **memory** *n* COMP&DP, ELEC ENG memoria estática *f*; ~ **on film** *n* PHOTO electricidad estática sobre la película *f*; ~ **operation** *n* ELEC ENG funcionamiento estático *m*; ~ **pin** *n* MILIT *of parachute* espiga estática *f*; ~ **pressure** *n* ACOUST, AIR TRANSP, REFRIG presión estática *f*; ~ **RAM** *n* (*SRAM*) COMP&DP RAM estática *f*; ~ **relay** *n* ELEC, TELECOM relé estático *m*; ~ **screen** *n* ELEC pantalla estática *f*; ~ **stability** *n* AIR TRANSP estabilidad estática *f*; ~ **strain test** *n* MECH ENG prueba de deformación estática *f*; ~ **suction lift** *n* WATER altura estática de aspiración *f*; ~ **test** *n* SPACE ensayo estático *m*, verificación estática *f*; ~ **thrust** *n* AIR TRANSP, MILIT empuje estático *m*; ~ **transformer** *n* ELEC, ELEC ENG transformador estático *m*; ~ **voltmeter** *n* ELEC, INSTR voltímetro estático *m*

statics *n* ELEC ENG, PHYS estática *f*

station *n* COMP&DP puesto *m*, ELEC, ELEC ENG, FUELLESS, GAS, HEAT ENG central *f*, SPACE estación *f*, posición *f*, THERMO central *f*, TRANSP emisora *f*, estación *f*, estación almacén *f*, estación-depósito *f*, WATER TRANSP *lines plan* cuadernas de trazado *f pl*, sección transversal *f*; ~ **acquisition function** *n* SPACE función de adquisición de órbita *f*; ~ **area** *n* RAIL zona de la estación *f*; ~ **barred** *n* TELECOM estación bloqueada *f*; ~ **blackout** *n* NUCL pérdida total de corriente alterna *f*, apagón de la central *m*; ~ **correc-**

tion mode *n* SPACE modo de corrección de posición *m*; ~ **coverage** *n* TV cobertura de la emisora *f*; ~ **identification** *n* TV identificación de la emisora *f*; ~ **keeping** *n* SPACE control de posición *m*, mantenimiento de órbita *m*, mantenimiento en posición *m*, mantenimiento en órbita *m*; ~~**keeping satellite** *n* SPACE satélite de mantenimiento en órbita *m*; ~ **radar** *n* MILIT radar central *m*; ~ **sync generator** *n* ELECTRON, TV generador de señales de sincronización de la emisora *m*; ~ **time** *n* TV tiempo de emisora *m*; ~ **timing** *n* TV cadencia de la emisora *f*; ~ **wagon** *n* AmE (*cf estate car BrE*) AUTO, VEH furgoneta *f*

stationary: ~ **aerial wave** *n* WAVE PHYS onda aérea estacionaria *f*; ~ **armature** *n* ELEC *generator* armadura estacionaria *f*, ELEC ENG armazón fijo *m*; ~ **blade** *n* HYDRAUL paleta directriz *f*, paleta fija *f*; ~ **boiler** *n* PROD caldera fija *f*; ~ **charger** *n* TRANSP cargador permanente *m*; ~ **contact** *n* PROD contacto fijo *m*; ~ **emission source** *n* POLL fuente de emisión constante *f*, fuente estacionaria de emisión *f*; ~ **field** *n* ELEC ENG campo constante *m*, campo estacionario *m*; ~ **firefighting installation** *n* SAFE instalación estacionaria para combate de incendios *f*; ~ **front** *n* METEO frente casi estacionario *m*, frente estacionario *m*; ~ **gripper** *n* NUCL *of control rod drive mechanism* trinquete estacionario *m*; ~ **hydraulic riveter** *n* PROD remachadora hidráulica fija *f*; ~ **light wave** *n* WAVE PHYS onda luminosa estacionaria *f*; ~ **link** *n* MECH ENG *valve gear* unión estacionaria *f*; ~ **longitudinal wave** *n* ACOUST, WAVE PHYS onda longitudinal estacionaria *f*; ~ **orbit** *n* SPACE órbita estacionaria *f*; ~ **phase** *n* TELECOM fase estacionaria *f*; ~ **plate** *n* MECH ENG plato estacionario *m*, plato fijo *m*; ~ **point** *n* SPACE punto estacionario *m*; ~ **portion** *n* PROD parte fija *f*; ~ **state** *n* PHYS, RAD PHYS, THERMO estado estacionario *m*; ~ **traffic** *n* TRANSP tráfico constante *m*; ~ **transverse wave** *n* WAVE PHYS onda transversal estacionaria *f*; ~ **vane** *n* HYDRAUL encauzador *m*, paleta directriz *f*, paleta fija *f*, álabe fijo *m*; ~ **wave** *n* PHYS, TELECOM, WAVE PHYS onda estacionaria *f*; ~ **wave pattern** *n* WAVE PHYS patrón de ondas estacionarias *m*, red de ondas estacionarias *f*; ~~**wave tube** *n* ACOUST tubo de ondas estacionarias *m*; ~ **waves in electron orbit** *n* WAVE PHYS onda estacionaria en la órbita del electrón *f*

stationery *n* COMP&DP artículos de papelería *m pl*

statistic *n* MATH estadística *f*

statistical[1] *adj* MATH, QUALITY estadístico

statistical[2]: ~ **analysis** *n* COMP&DP análisis estadístico *m*; ~ **check** *n* METR comprobación estadística *f*; ~ **data** *n* COMP&DP datos estadísticos *m pl*; ~ **description of turbulent motion** *n* FLUID descripción estadística del movimiento turbulento *f*; ~ **forecasting** *n* PROD previsión estadística *f*; ~ **multiplexer** *n* COMP&DP multiplexor estadístico *m*; ~ **physics** *n* PHYS física estadística *f*; ~ **quality control** *n* QUALITY control estadístico de la calidad *m*; ~ **sample of decay data** *n* RAD PHYS muestra estadística de los datos de desintegración *f*; ~ **table** *n* QUALITY tabla estadística *f*

statistics *n* MATH estadísticas *f pl*

statmux *n* COMP&DP estamux *m* (*AmL*), multiplexación estadística *f*

stator *n* AIR TRANSP, AUTO, ELEC estator *m*, ELEC ENG estator *m*, láminas fijas *f pl*, PHYS estator *m*; ~ **coil** *n* ELEC ENG bobina del estator *f*; ~ **frame** *n* ELEC ENG

armadura del estator *f*; ~ **lamination** *n* ELEC ENG
chapa del estator *f*; ~ **plate** *n* ELEC ENG placa del
estator *f*; ~**-rotor starter motor** *n* ELEC motor de
arranque por rotor estatórico *m*; ~ **vane** *n* AIR
TRANSP aleta de estátor *f*; ~ **winding** *n* ELEC ENG
devanado estatórico *m*

status *n* COMP&DP categoría *f*, estado *m*; ~ **character** *n*
COMP&DP carácter de estado *m*, carácter de la
categoría *m*; ~ **data** *n* TELECOM datos condición *m*
pl, datos de estado *m pl*, datos situación *m pl*, datos
status *m pl*; ~ **indication** *n* TELECOM indicación de
situación *f*, indicación de status *f*; ~ **indicator** *n* PROD
indicador de estado *m*; ~ **lamp** *n* TELECOM lámpara
de estado *f*, piloto de estado *m*; ~ **register** *n*
COMP&DP registro de categoría *m*, registro de estado
m; ~ **word** *n* COMP&DP palabra de estado *f*, palabra
de la categoría *f*

statutory: ~ **regulations** *n pl* SAFE normativa legal *f*
staunch *adj* PROD de impermeabilización
staunchness *n* PROD impermeabilización *f*
staurolite *n* MINERAL estaurolita *f*
staurotide *n* MINERAL estaurotida *f*
stave *n* PROD *mine pit* escalón *m*, *of barrel* duela *f*;
~ **silo** *n* AGRIC silo hecho con duelas de madera *m*
stay *n* CONST estancia *f* (*Esp*), permanencia *f* (*Esp*),
estadía *f* (*AmL*), *prop* riostra *f*, *tie rod in building*
tirante *m*, MECH ENG estay *m*, PROD *bar of foundry
flask* travesaño *m*, WATER TRANSP estay *m*; ~ **block** *n*
REFRIG arriostramiento *m*; ~ **bolt** *n* CONST perno de
puntal *m*; ~ **pole** *n* ELEC *overhead line* poste de línea
m; ~ **rod** *n* CONST tirante *m*; ~ **tube** *n* PROD *of boiler*
tubo atirantador *m*
staying *n* PROD *bolting* apuntalamiento *m*, arriostramiento *m*
stayput: ~ **agent** *n* CHEM agente de permanencia *m*
stays: **in** ~ *adv* WATER TRANSP *sailing* con el viento por
la proa, orzando a fil de roda
STD *abbr* (*subscriber trunk dialing AmE, subscriber
trunk dialling BrE*) TELECOM selección automática
interurbana *f*
Steadicam *n* CINEMAT Steadicam *f*
steadiness: ~ **test** *n* CINEMAT prueba de estabilidad *f*,
prueba de fijación *f*
steady[1]: ~**-state** *adj* PHYS regular
steady[2] *n* MECH ENG *lathe* luneta *f*; ~ **approach** *n* AIR
TRANSP aproximación continuada *f*; ~ **bearing** *n*
WATER TRANSP *navigation* rumbo franco *m*;
~ **breeze** *n* WATER TRANSP viento hecho *m*;
~ **current** *n* PHYS corriente continua *f*; ~ **flight** *n*
AIR TRANSP vuelo uniforme *m*; ~ **flow** *n* AIR TRANSP
flujo estable *m*, flujo uniforme *m*, FLUID flujo
estacionario *m*, flujo uniforme *m*, PHYS flujo constante *m*; ~ **noise** *n* ACOUST ruido constante *m*, ruido
continuo *m*; ~ **pin** *n* MECH ENG *shaft key* pasador de
fijación *m*, PROD *core print* portamacho *m*, *of
moulding-box* pasador de fijación *m*; ~ **rest** *n* MECH
ENG *lathe* centrador fijo *m*, luneta fija *f*, soporte fijo
m; ~ **state** *n* ELEC estado estacionario *m*, estado
permanente *m*, ELEC ENG régimen permanente *m*,
PHYS estado regular *m*, TELECOM estado estacionario
m, régimen permanente *m*; ~**-state condition** *n* ELEC
ENG condición de estado estacionario *f*, OPT condición de estado estacionario *f*, condición estacionaria
f, TELECOM condición de régimen permanente *f*,
condición estacionaria *f*; ~**-state creep** *n* METALL
viscofluencia de estado permanente *f*; ~**-state**

inversion *n* RAD PHYS inversión en régimen estacionario *f*; ~**-state launching conditions** *n pl* TELECOM
condiciones de puesta en establecimiento del estado
estacionario *f pl*; ~**-state pressure** *n* MECH ENG
presión de estado constante *f*, presión de estado
estacionario *f*, presión de estado permanente *f*,
presión de régimen permanente *f*
steam[1]: **in** ~ *adj* MECH ENG a régimen de vaporización
steam[2] *n* FUELLESS, HEAT, HYDRAUL, PHYS, TEXTIL
vapor *m*, vapor de agua *m*; ~ **accumulator** *n* HY-
DRAUL acumulador de vapor de agua *m*,
vapoacumulador *m*; ~ **admission** *n* HYDRAUL admisión de vapor *f*; ~ **blowing** *n* C&G soplado con vapor
m; ~ **boiler** *n* HYDRAUL caldera de vapor *f*, generador
de vapor *m*, THERMO caldera de vapor *f*; ~ **box** *n*
HYDRAUL cámara de distribución de vapor *f*; ~ **brake**
n HYDRAUL freno de vapor *m*, vapofreno *m*; ~ **bus** *n*
VEH autobús de vapor *m* (*Esp*), ómnibus de vapor *m*
(*AmL*); ~ **calender** *n* TEXTIL calanda de vaporización
f; ~ **car** *n* TRANSP vagón a vapor *m*, unidad de vapor
f; ~ **case** *n* HYDRAUL cámara de distribución de
vapor *f*; ~ **casing** *n* HYDRAUL revestimiento de vapor
m; ~ **chamber** *n* HYDRAUL cámara de distribución *f*,
cámara de vapor *f*; ~ **chest** *n* HYDRAUL cámara de
distribución *f*, depósito de vapor *m*; ~ **cleaning** *n*
MAR POLL limpieza con vapor *f*; ~ **coal** *n* COAL
carbón térmico *m*; ~ **cock** *n* HYDRAUL grifo rotativo
de vapor *m*; ~ **coil** *n* HEAT ENG serpentín de vapor *m*;
~ **cone** *n* HYDRAUL tobera de vapor *f*; ~ **cracking** *n*
PETR TECH escisión del hidrocarburo por vapor *f*;
~ **cylinder** *n* HYDRAUL cilindro de vapor *m*;
~ **distillation** *n* CHEM destilación al vapor *f*, destilación con vapor *f*, CHEM TECH destilación por arrastre
de vapor *f*; ~ **dome** *n* HYDRAUL cúpula de vapor *f*,
bóveda de vapor *f*; ~ **dryer** *n* HYDRAUL secadero de
vapor *m*, secador de vapor *m*; ~ **dumping system** *n*
NUCL sistema de alivio de vapor *m*, sistema de
descarga atmosférica de vapor *m*; ~ **edge** *n* HY-
DRAUL arista exterior *f*; ~ **ejector** *n* HYDRAUL
eyector de vapor *m*; ~**-electric generator** *n* ELEC,
ELEC ENG generador eléctrico de vapor *m*; ~**-electric
power plant** *n* ELEC ENG instalación de energía
eléctrica a vapor *f*; ~**-electric power station** *n* ELEC
ENG central de energía eléctrica a vapor *f*; ~ **emission**
n POLL desprendimiento de vapor *m*, emisión de
vapor *f*; ~ **engine** *n* AUTO motor de vapor *m*, HY-
DRAUL máquina de vapor de agua *f*, PHYS motor de
vapor *m*; ~ **engine indicator** *n* HYDRAUL indicador
de máquina de vapor *m*; ~ **entraining** *n* CHEM TECH
arrastre de vapor *m*; ~ **extraction** *n* FOOD extracción
con vapor *f*; ~ **gage** *AmE*, ~ **gauge** *BrE n* HYDRAUL
manómetro de vapor *m*, PHYS medidor de vapor *m*;
~ **generation** *n* WATER TRANSP *engine* generación de
vapor *f*; ~ **generator** *n* HEAT generador de vapor *m*;
~ **generator overfill** *n* NUCL llenado excesivo de un
generador de vapor *m*; ~ **generator tube plugging** *n*
NUCL taponado de tubos en un generador de vapor
m; ~ **generator tube rupture** *n* (*SGTR*) NUCL rotura
de tubos en un generador de vapor *f* (*SGTR*);
~ **governor** *n* HYDRAUL regulador de vapor *m*;
~ **heating** *n* CONST calefacción por vapor *f*; ~ **heating system** *n* HEAT sistema de calefacción por vapor
m; ~ **hose** *n* HYDRAUL manguera de vapor *f*;
~ **humidifier** *n* REFRIG, THERMO humidificador de
vapor *m*; ~ **injector** *n* HEAT ENG, HYDRAUL inyector
de vapor *m*; ~ **inlet** *n* HYDRAUL orificio de admisión

de vapor *m*; ~ **jacket** *n* HEAT ENG camisa de vapor *f*, HYDRAUL camisa exterior de vapor *f*; ~ **jet** *n* GEOPHYS chorro de vapor *m*, HYDRAUL chorro de vapor de agua *m*; ~**-laden emission** *n* POLL emisión cargada de vapor *f*; ~ **lap** *n* HYDRAUL recubrimiento exterior *m*; ~ **line** *n* HYDRAUL tubería de vapor *f*; ~ **loop** *n* HYDRAUL tubería de vapor *f*; ~ **nozzle** *n* HYDRAUL tobera de vapor *f*; ~ **outlet** *n* HYDRAUL evacuador de vapor *m*; ~ **packing** *n* HYDRAUL guarnición de vapor *f*; ~ **pipe** *n* HYDRAUL tubería de vapor *f*; ~ **pipeline** *n* HYDRAUL conducción de vapor *f*; ~ **piping** *n* HYDRAUL tubería de vapor *f*; ~ **piston** *n* HYDRAUL émbolo accionado por vapor *m*; ~ **plant** *n* HEAT planta generadora de vapor *f*; ~ **port** *n* HYDRAUL lumbrera de admisión *f*, orificio de admisión de vapor *m*; ~ **power** *n* HYDRAUL accionamiento por vapor *m*; ~ **pressure** *n* HEAT, TEXTIL presión de vapor *f*; ~ **quality** *n* HEAT ENG título de vapor *m*, HYDRAUL calidad del vapor *f*; ~ **raising** *n* HYDRAUL generación de vapor *f*, producción de vapor *f*; ~ **reforming** *n* PETR TECH reformado de la vaporización *m*, reformado por vapor *m*; ~**-relief valve** *n* HYDRAUL válvula de seguridad de vapor *f*; ~ **separator** *n* HYDRAUL colector de agua condensada *m*, purificador de vapor *m*, separador de vapor *m*; ~ **space** *n* HYDRAUL volumen de vapor *m*; ~ **stop valve** *n* HYDRAUL válvula de cierre de vapor *f*, válvula de interrupción de vapor *f*, válvula de retención de vapor *f*; ~ **superheater** *n* HEAT ENG sobrecalentador de vapor *m*; ~ **supply pipe** *n* HYDRAUL tubería de entrada de vapor *f*, tubería de llegada del vapor *f*; ~ **trap** *n* HEAT ENG trampa de vapor *f*, HYDRAUL purgador del vapor *m*, PETR TECH separador de vapor *m*, trampa de vapor *f*; ~ **turbine** *n* HEAT turbina de vapor *f*, vapoturbina *m*, HYDRAUL, WATER TRANSP *engine* turbina de vapor *f*; ~ **valve** *n* HYDRAUL distribuidor del vapor *m*, válvula de admisión del vapor *f*, válvula de paso de vapor *f*; ~**-water cycle** *n* NUCL ciclo de agua-vapor *m*
steam³ *vt* FOOD cocer al vapor, TEXTIL limpiar con vapor, vaporizar; ~ **distil** *vt* BrE CHEM destilar al vapor; ~ **distill** *AmE see steam distil BrE*; ~ **set** *vt* TEXTIL fijar con vapor
steamed *adj* WATER TRANSP *wood* tratado al vapor
steamer *n* HYDRAUL caldera de vapor *f*, generador de vapor *m*
steaming: ~ **light** *n* WATER TRANSP luz de tope *f*
steamtight *adj* HEAT ENG estanco al vapor, HYDRAUL vapohermético
steamway *n* HYDRAUL conducto de vapor *m*, orificio de admisión de vapor *m*, tubería de toma del vapor *f*
stearate *n* CHEM estearato *m*
stearic *adj* CHEM esteárico
stearin *n* CHEM, FOOD estearina *f*
stearyl *n* CHEM estearilo *m*
steatite *n* MINERAL esteatita *f*, jaboncillo de sastre *m*, talco *m*, TEXTIL jaboncillo de sastre *m*
steel¹: ~**-colored** *AmE*, ~**-coloured** *BrE adj* COLOUR de color de acero, HEAT ENG de color del acero
steel² *n* METALL acero *m*; ~ **alloy** *n* COAL, MECH ENG aleación de acero *f*; ~ **alloy dust** *n* COAL limaduras *f pl*; ~ **band chain** *n* CONST *land measuring* cadena con cinta de acero *f*; ~ **band strapping** *n* PACK sujeción con flejes de acero *f*; ~ **beam** *n* CONST viga de acero *f*; ~ **bridge** *n* CONST puente de acero *m*; ~ **casting** *n* WATER TRANSP pieza de acero fundido *f*; ~ **chimney** *n* CONST chimenea de acero *f*; ~ **construction** *n* CONST

estructura de acero *f*; ~ **fixer** *n* CONST montador de estructuras metálicas *m*; ~ **fixing** *n* CONST montaje de estructuras metálicas *m*; ~ **form** *n* CONST encofrado metálico *m*, molde de acero *m*; ~ **furnace** *n* PROD horno de fabricar acero *m*; ~ **pile** *n* COAL pilote de acero *m*, tablestaca de acero *f*; ~ **pipe** *n* CONST tubería de acero *f*; ~ **platform** *n* PETR TECH plataforma de acero *f*; ~ **section** *n* WATER TRANSP perfil de acero *m*, perfil de acero laminado *m*; ~ **straight edge** *n* METR regla de acero *f*; ~ **wheel on steel rail system** *n* TRANSP rueda de acero en sistema de rail de acero *f*
steelworks *n* METALL, PROD acería *f*
steelyard *n* PHYS romana *f*
Steenbeck *n* CINEMAT mesa de montaje Steenbeck *f*
steep¹: ~ **bevel** *n* C&G bisel agudo *m*; ~ **coast** *n* OCEAN costa escarpada *f*; ~ **gradient** *n* CONST pendiente empinada *f*; ~ **turn** *n* AIR TRANSP viraje pronunciado *m*; ~ **vein** *n* MINE filón de fuerte pendiente *m*
steep² *vt* C&G empapar, remojar, FOOD empapar, macerar, remojar, PRINT escalonar, TEXTIL remojar
steeple: ~**-head rivet** *n* CONST remache de cabeza cónica *m*
steer¹ *n* AGRIC novillo *m*; ~ **angle** *n* AUTO, VEH ángulo de giro *m*
steer² *vt* TRANSP *car* conducir, cruzar, gobernar, WATER TRANSP *sailing* gobernar; ~ **clear of** *vt* WATER TRANSP *navigation* gobernar apartándose de, gobernar poniéndose en franquía de; ~ **for** *vt* WATER TRANSP *navigation* arrumbarse, poner rumbo a
steerable: ~ **beam aerial** *n* BrE (*cf steerable beam antenna AmE*) TELECOM antena de haz orientable *f*; ~ **beam antenna** *n* AmE (*cf steerable beam aerial BrE*) TELECOM antena de haz orientable *f*
steered: ~ **wheel** *n* VEH rueda orientada *f*
steering *n* AUTO, MILIT, TELECOM, TRANSP, VEH dirección *f*; ~ **angle** *n* WATER TRANSP ángulo del timón *m*; ~ **arm** *n* AUTO, VEH brazo de mando *m*; ~**-axis inclination** *n* AUTO, VEH inclinación de la columna de la dirección *f*, inclinación del eje de la dirección *f*; ~ **axle** *n* VEH eje de la dirección *m*; ~ **chain** *n* WATER TRANSP cadena para guardines *f*, guardín *m*; ~ **circle** *n* VEH radio de giro *m*; ~ **column** *n* AUTO, VEH columna de dirección *f*; ~**-column lock** *n* AUTO, VEH bloqueo de la columna de dirección *m*; ~ **compass** *n* WATER TRANSP aguja de gobierno *f*, compás de gobierno *m*; ~ **gear** *n* AUTO engranaje de la dirección *m*, VEH mecanismo de mando de la dirección *m*, sistema de mando de la dirección *m*, WATER TRANSP mecanismo de gobierno *m*; ~ **gearbox** *n* AUTO caja de engranajes de la dirección *f*, caja de la dirección *f*, VEH caja de engranajes de la dirección *f*, caja de la dirección *f*, cárter de la dirección *m*; ~ **geometry** *n* AUTO geometría de la dirección *f*; ~ **head** *n* VEH mecanismo de la dirección *m*; ~ **idler arm** *n* AUTO, VEH brazo intermedio de la dirección *m*; ~ **knuckle** *n* AUTO rótula de dirección *f*, VEH pivote de la dirección *m*; ~ **knuckle pin** *n* AUTO, VEH pivote de la rótula de dirección *m*; ~ **linkage** *n* AUTO varillaje de la dirección *m*, VEH varillaje de la dirección *m*; ~ **lock** *n* AUTO, VEH ángulo máximo de giro de las ruedas delanteras *m*; ~ **play** *n* AUTO, VEH holgura de la dirección *f*, juego de la dirección *m*; ~ **rod** *n* AUTO, VEH barra de la dirección *f*; ~ **shaft** *n* AUTO, VEH árbol de la dirección *m*; ~ **system** *n* AUTO sistema de dirección *m*; ~ **wheel** *n* AUTO volante *m*, VEH volante de dirección *m*, WATER TRANSP rueda de gobierno *f*,

rueda del timón *f*; ~ **wire** *n* WATER TRANSP alambre de acero para guardines *m*, guardín *m*

Stefan-Boltzmann: ~ **constant** *n* PHYS constante de Stefan-Boltzman *f*; ~ **law** *n* PHYS, RAD PHYS ley de Stefan-Boltzmann *f*

Stefan: ~'s **constant** *n* HEAT ENG constante de Stefan *f*; ~'s **law** *n* PHYS, RAD PHYS ley de Stefan *f*

steinmannite *n* MINERAL steinmannita *f*

Steinmetz: ~'s **coefficient** *n* PHYS coeficiente de Steinmetz *m*; ~'s **law** *n* PHYS ley de Steinmetz *f*

stellar[1] *adj* SPACE estelar

stellar[2]: ~ **guidance** *n* SPACE guiado estelar *m*; ~ **navigation** *n* SPACE navegación estelar *f*

stem[1] *n* C&G pie de copa *m*, CONST *of key* caña *f*, espiga *f*, alma *f*, vástago *m*, HYDRAUL vástago *m*, PHYS *machinery* capilar *m*, WATER *of sluice gate* cola *f*, WATER TRANSP *boat building* roda *f*; ~ **carrier** *n* C&G acarreador de pie de copa *m*; ~ **fitting** *n* WATER TRANSP *yachts, decks* guarnimiento del tope de roda *m*; ~ **rake** *n* WATER TRANSP *ship design* lanzamiento de roda *m*

stem[2] *vt* MINE atacar (*Esp*), atracar (*AmL*), tapar

stemmer *n* MINE atacadera de cobre o madera *f*

stemming *n* MINE atacado *m* (*Esp*), atraque *m* (*AmL*), retacado *m* (*AmL*); ~ **material** *n* MINE material de atraque *m*; ~ **rod** *n* MINE barra de ataque *f* (*Esp*), barra de atraque *f* (*AmL*); ~ **stick** *n* MINE barra de ataque *f* (*Esp*), barra de atraque *f* (*AmL*)

stemware *n* C&G copas con pie alto *f pl*

stench: ~ **trap** *n* CONST *plumbing* sifón guardaolores *m*

stencil *n* C&G estarcido *m*, PRINT clisé *m*, PROD estarcido *m*, patrón para duplicar *m*; ~ **duplicator copy paper** *n* PAPER papel para ciclostilo *m*, papel para mimiógrafo *m* (*AmL*); ~ **plate** *n* PROD cliché *m*, negativo *m*; ~ **silk** *n* C&G seda para estarcir *f*

stenter: ~ **frame** *n* TEXTIL bastidor de rame *m*

step[1] *adj* PROD gradual

step[2] *n* C&G paso *m*, CONST *of stairway* escalón *m*, paso *m*, *on monument* estribo *m*, *of ladder* peldaño *m*, grada *f*, CRYSTALL *dislocation* salto *m*, escalón de crecimiento *m*, METALL paso *m*, PRINT escala *f*, PROD barrote *m*, peldaño *m*, etapa *f*, intervalo *m*, fase *f*, paso *m*, RAIL escalón *m*, WATER TRANSP *mast* carlinga *f*; ~-**and-repeat** *n* PRINT copia y repetición *f*; ~ **box** *n* MECH ENG rangua *f*, tejuelo *m*; ~-**by-step control** *n* ELEC *motor drive* control paso a paso *m*, mando paso a paso *m*; ~-**by-step system** *n* TELECOM sistema paso a paso *m*; ~ **completion bit** *n* COMP&DP, PROD bit de fin de ejecución *m*, bit de fin de instrucciones *m*; ~ **cone** *n* MECH ENG polea de escalones *f*, polea escalonada *f*; ~ **cone drive** *n* MECH ENG accionamiento por polea escalonada *m*, conductor de polea escalonada *m*; ~ **contact printer** *n* CINEMAT positivadora por contacto escalonado *f*; ~ **counter** *n* COMP&DP contador de pasos *m*; ~ **data** *n* PROD datos de instrucciones *m pl*; ~-**down autotransformer** *n* ELEC, ELEC ENG autotransformador reductor *m*; ~-**down ring** *n* CINEMAT anillo reductor *m*, aro reductor *m*; ~-**down station** *n* ELEC *transformer* estación reductora *f*; ~-**down transformer** *n* ELEC transformador rebajador *m*, transformador rebajador de tensión *m*, transformador rebajador de voltaje *m*, transformador reductor *m*, ELEC ENG transformador rebajador *m*, transformador rebajador de tensión *m*, transformador rebajador de voltaje *m*, PHYS transformador de

reducción *m*, PROD transformador reductor *m*; ~ **drill** *n* MECH ENG broca de múltiples diámetros *f*, broca escalonada *f*; ~ **function** *n* COMP&DP función escalonada *f*, función por pasos *f*, ELECTRON función escalonada *f*; ~ **function generator** *n* ELECTRON generador de función escalonada *m*; ~ **function response** *n* ELECTRON respuesta de función escalonada *f*; ~ **increment** *n* TEXTIL aumento de pasos *m*; ~ **index fiber** *AmE*, ~ **index fibre** *BrE* *n* OPT, TELECOM fibra con índice de pasos *f*, fibra de índice escalonado *f*; ~ **index profile** *n* OPT perfil de índice escalonado *m*, TELECOM perfil con índice de pasos *m*, perfil de índice escalonado *m*; ~ **joint** *n* CONST junta escalonada *f*, MECH ENG junta de recubrimiento *f*; ~ **lens** *n* CINEMAT lente escalonada *f*; ~-**out well** *n* PETR TECH pozo de delimitación *m*; ~ **printing** *n* CINEMAT copiado escalonado *m*; ~ **recovery diode** *n* ELECTRON diodo de recuperación escalonada *m*; ~ **switch** *n* ELEC conmutador de avance por pasos *m*, conmutador de contactos escalonados *m*, conmutador por pasos *m*; ~ **tooth gear** *n* MECH ENG engranaje de dientes cruzados *m*; ~ **track system** *n* SPACE sistema de comportamiento de trayectoria *m*; ~ **transformer** *n* PROD transformador reductor-elevador *m*; ~-**up autotransformer** *n* ELEC, ELEC ENG autotransformador elevador *m*; ~-**up ring** *n* CINEMAT anillo de aumento *m*, aro de aumento *m*, PHOTO anillo de aumento *m*; ~-**up station** *n* ELEC estación elevadora *f*; ~-**up transformer** *n* ELEC, ELEC ENG transformador elevador *m*, PHYS transformador de amplificación *m*, TV transformador elevador de voltaje *m*; ~ **wedge** *n* CINEMAT, PHOTO cuña escalonada *f*, PRINT escala de grises *f*

step[3]: **in** ~ *phr* ELEC ENG en sincronismo, sincronizado

stephanite *n* MINERAL estefanita *f*

stepladder *n* CONST escalera de mano *f*

stepless: ~ **control** *n* ELEC control progresivo *m*, regulación continua *f*

stepped[1] *adj* MECH ENG dentado, en escalones, escalonado

stepped[2]: ~ **climb** *n* AIR TRANSP ascenso escalonado *m*, SPACE ascenso escalonado *m*, ascenso inicial *m*; ~ **gear** *n* MECH ENG engranaje cruzado *m*, engranaje escalonado *m*; ~ **grate** *n* PROD parrilla a etapas *f*; ~ **roll** *n* MECH ENG cilindro escalonado *m*

stepper: ~ **controller** *n* PROD controlador gradual *m*; ~ **motor** *n* CINEMAT motor de velocidad gradual *m*, motor paso a paso *m*, COMP&DP *disk drive actuator* motor de avance por pasos *m*, motor paso a paso *m*, ELEC motor paso a paso *m*, ELEC ENG motor de velocidad gradual *m*

stepping: ~ **motor** *n* ELEC motor paso a paso *m*; ~ **switch** *n* ELEC relé de cascada *m*, relé de múltiples posiciones *m*, ELEC ENG interruptor temporizado *m*

stepwise: ~ **refinement** *n* COMP&DP ajustes sucesivos *m pl*, aproximaciones sucesivas *f pl*, refinamiento por pasos *m*

steradian *n* ELECTRON esteroradian *m*, GEOM esterorradián *m*, PHYS esteroradian *m*

stercorite *n* MINERAL estercorita *f*

stereo: ~ **video cassette recorder** *n* TV grabador de video en estéreo *m* (*AmL*), grabador de vídeo en estéreo *m* (*Esp*); ~ **viewer** *n* PHOTO visor estereoscópico *m*

stereochemistry *n* CHEM estereoquímica *f*

stereographic: ~ **projection** *n* CRYSTALL, METALL proyección estereográfica *f*
stereoisomer *n* CHEM estereoisómero *m*
stereometric: ~ **camera** *n* INSTR cámara estereométrica *f*
stereomicroscope *n* INSTR estereomicroscopio *m*, LAB estereomicroscopio *m*, microscopio estereoscópico *m*
stereophonic[1] *adj* ACOUST estereofónico
stereophonic[2]: ~ **pick-up** *n* ACOUST captador estereofónico *m*; ~ **recording** *n* ACOUST grabación estereofónica *f*
stereophony *n* ACOUST estereofonía *f*
stereoplate *n* PRINT plancha de estereotipia *f*
stereoscope *n* PHOTO estereoscopio *m*
stereoscopic: ~ **camera** *n* PHOTO cámara estereoscópica *f*; ~ **film** *n* CINEMAT película estereoscópica *f*; ~ **pair** *n* PHOTO par estereoscópico *m*
stereoscopy *n* PHOTO estereoscopía *f*
stereospecific *adj* CHEM estereoespecífico
stereotype: ~ **plate** *n* PRINT plancha de estereotipia *f*
stereovision *n* TV estereovisión *f*, visión en estereo *f*
steric *adj* CHEM estérico
stern *n* WATER TRANSP *of boat* hacia popa, popa *f*; ~ **flag** *n* WATER TRANSP bandera de popa *f*; ~ **frame** *n* WATER TRANSP marco del codaste *m*, peto *m*; ~ **light** *n* WATER TRANSP luz de alcance *f*; ~ **line** *n* WATER TRANSP largo de popa *m*; ~ **post** *n* WATER TRANSP codaste *m*; ~ **pulpit** *n* WATER TRANSP balcón de popa *m*, púlpito de popa *m*; ~ **thruster** *n* WATER TRANSP impulsor de popa *m*, impulsor lateral de popa *m*; ~ **tube** *n* WATER TRANSP bocina *f*
sternbergite *n* MINERAL sternbergita *f*
Stern-Gerlach: ~ **experiment** *n* PHYS experimento de Stern-Gerlach *m*
steroid *n* CHEM esteroide *m*
sterol *n* CHEM esterol *m*
stevedore *n* WATER TRANSP estibador *m*; ~**-type pallet** *n* TRANSP bandeja estiba *f*, paleta estiba *f*, pálet estiba *m* (*AmL*)
Stevens: ~**'s phon** *n* ACOUST, PHYS fonio Stevens *m*
stibiconite *n* MINERAL estibiconita *f*
stibilite *n* MINERAL estibilita *f*
stibious *adj* CHEM estibioso
stibnite *n* CHEM antimonita *f*, estibnita *f*, sulfuro de antimonio *m*, MINERAL antimonita *f*, estibina *f*, estibnita *f*
stick[1] *n* C&G vara *f*, CONST *of timber* palo *m*; ~ **lack** *n* COATINGS, COLOUR laca colorante *f*; ~ **of sulfur** *AmE*, ~ **of sulphur** *BrE n* CHEM barra de azufre *f*
stick[2] *vt* CONST *joinery* clavar, pegar, ELEC ENG interrumpir
stick[3] *vi* PROD adherirse, pegarse
sticking *n* ELEC ENG retención *f*, bloqueo *m*, interrupción *f*, PROD *piston, bearings* adherencia *f*, adhesión *f*, agarrotamiento *m*; ~ **contacts** *n pl* ELEC *relay* contactos adhesivos *m pl*, contactos que se pegan *m pl*
stiffen *vt* TEXTIL almidonar
stiffener *n* MECH ENG contrafuerte *m*, larguero *m* (*Esp*), montante de refuerzo *m*, nervio *m*, reforzador *m*, SPACE contrafuerte *m*, refuerzo *m*, rigidizador *m*, TEXTIL almidonador *m*, refuerzo *m*, WATER TRANSP rigidizador *m*
stiffening *n* CONST refuerzo *m*, rigidización *f*, MECH ENG atirantamiento *m*, nervadura *f*, refuerzo *m*, SPACE reforzador *m* (*AmL*), rigidización *f*; ~ **dope** *n*

COLOUR aditivo endurecedor *m*; ~ **plate** *n* MECH ENG placa de refuerzo *f*; ~ **varnish** *n* COATINGS, COLOUR barniz endurecedor *m*
stiffness *n* ACOUST rigidez *f*, MECH ENG atirantamiento *m*, dureza *f*, resistencia *f*, rigidez *f*, PAPER, PHYS, TEXTIL rigidez *f*
stigmasterol *n* CHEM estigmasterol *m*
stigmatic: ~ **lens** *n* PHOTO lente estigmática *f*
stilbene *n* CHEM estilbeno *m*
stilbite *n* MINERAL estilbita *f*
stile *n* CONST *of door or sash* montante *m*
still *n* CHEM, CHEM TECH, FOOD, HEAT, LAB, PETR TECH alambique *m*; ~ **air** *n* FUELLESS aire quieto *m*; ~**-air freezing** *n* REFRIG congelación en aire en reposo *f*; ~ **camera** *n* PHOTO cámara de fotografía fija *f*; ~ **frame** *n* CINEMAT, TV imagen fija *f*; ~**-life photography** *n* PHOTO fotografía de naturaleza muerta *f*; ~ **water** *n* FOOD agua sin gas *f*, HYDROL agua estancada *f*, agua tranquila *f*, OCEAN agua tranquila *f*, WATER agua estancada *f*, agua tranquila *f*
stilling: ~ **basin** *n* HYDROL *disc* estanque de amortiguación *m*
stilpnomelane *n* MINERAL estilpnomelana *f*
stilted: ~ **arch** *n* CONST arco peraltado *m*, *structure* arco realzado *m*
stimulate *vt* PROD, RAD PHYS estimular
stimulated: ~ **emission** *n* ELECTRON, OPT, PHYS, RAD PHYS, TELECOM emisión estimulada *f*
stimulation *n* PETR TECH, PETROL estimulación *f*
stimulus *n* ACOUST, RAD PHYS estímulo *m*
stinger *n* PETR TECH, PETROL espiga *f*, espolón *m*, obturador *m*
stink: ~ **trap** *n* CONST *plumbing* sifón guardaolores *m*
stirred: ~ **reactor** *n* CHEM TECH reactor con agitación *m*
stirrer *n* CHEM TECH agitador *m*, LAB agitador *m*, mezclador *m*, P&R agitador *m*; ~ **blade** *n* LAB *coil* paleta de mezclador *f*
stirring *n* C&G meneado *m*, remosión *f*, CHEM agitación *f*, mezclado *m*; ~ **equipment** *n* CHEM TECH equipo agitador *m*; ~ **rod** *n* CINEMAT varilla para agitar los baños *f*
stirrup *n* ACOUST estribo *m*, CONST cerco *m*, estribo *m*, brida *f*, MECH ENG brida *f*, estribo *m*; ~ **bolt** *n* MECH ENG perno de brida *m*; ~ **hanger** *n* CINEMAT soporte de estribo *m*, MECH ENG colgante de brida *m*; ~ **joint** *n* MECH ENG junta de brida *f*; ~ **piece** *n* MECH ENG pieza de brida *f*; ~ **pump for water** *n* HYDROL, SAFE, WATER bomba de estribo para agua *f*; ~ **strap** *n* MECH ENG abrazadera de brida *f*, cinta de brida *f*
stirruped: ~ **concrete** *n* CONST concreto zunchado *m* (*AmL*), hormigón zunchado *m* (*Esp*)
stitch[1] *n* TEXTIL puntada *f*, punto *m*, malla *f*; ~ **detail** *n* TEXTIL detalle de la puntada *m*
stitch[2] *vt* TEXTIL coser; ~ **down** *vt* TEXTIL coser abajo
stitched[1] *adj* PACK, PRINT, PROD, TEXTIL cosido
stitched[2]: ~ **box** *n* PACK caja cosida con grapas *f*
stitching *n* WATER TRANSP cosido *m*; ~ **wire** *n* PACK, TEXTIL alambre para máquina de coser con grapas *m*
STM *abbr* TELECOM (*synchronous transfer mode*) modo de transferencia síncrona *m*, TELECOM (*synchronous transport module*) módulo de transporte síncrono *m*
STM-n *abbr* (*synchronous transport module-n*) TELECOM módulo-n de transporte síncrono *m*
stochastic[1] *adj* COMP&DP estocástico, MATH *statistics* aleatorio, estocástico

stochastic²: ~ **cooling** *n* PART PHYS enfriamiento aleatorio *m*, enfriamiento estocástico *m*; ~ **loading** *n* METALL carga estocástica *f*; ~ **model** *n* COMP&DP modelo estocástico *m*; ~ **process** *n* PHYS proceso estocástico *m*

stock¹: ~-**dyed** *adj* TEXTIL teñido en rama

stock² *n* CINEMAT película virgen *f*, COAL batolito pequeño *m*, intrusión de roca ígnea *f*, macizo magmático *m*, GEOL intrusión de roca ígnea *f*, MECH ENG *of plane* caja del cepillo *f*, cojinete de roscar *m*, terraja *f*, material en bruto *m*, MINE berbiquí de barrena *m*, cimentación del yunque *f*, tubo *m*, PAPER pasta en suspensión *f*, PETR TECH existencias *f pl*, PRINT material para imprimir *m*, PROD *blast furnace* carga *f*, existencias *f pl*; ~ **anchor** *n* WATER TRANSP ancla con cepo *f*; ~ **at inspection** *n* PROD existencias bajo inspección *f pl*; ~ **chest** *n* PAPER tina de mezcla *f*; ~ **coal** *n* COAL carbón almacenado *m*; ~ **control** *n* PROD control de existencias *m*, RAIL control de existencias *m*, control del material móvil *m*; ~ **diameter** *n* TELECOM diámetro normal *m*; ~ **distributor** *n* PROD *blast furnace* aparato distribuidor de la carga *m*; ~ **indicator** *n* PROD *blast furnace* indicador de carga *m*; ~ **issue status** *n* PROD estado de salida de existencias *m*; ~ **line** *n* PROD *blast furnace* nivel de la carga *m*; ~ **location** *n* PROD ubicación de existencias *f*; ~ **movements** *n pl* PROD movimientos de las existencias *m*; ~ **on hand** *n* PROD existencias disponibles *f pl*; ~ **on order** *n* PROD existencias en pedido *f pl*; ~-**out** *n* PROD agotadas las existencias *f pl*; ~ **plant** *n* AGRIC planta para reproducción *f*; ~ **preparation** *n* PAPER preparación de pastas *f*; ~ **receipt** *n* PROD recibo de existencias *m*; ~ **record** *n* PROD registro de existencias *m*; ~ **record card** *n* PROD ficha de existencias *f*; ~ **removal** *n* MECH ENG *machining* desbastado *m*; ~ **sheets** *n pl AmE* (*cf stock sizes BrE*) C&G tamaños de vidrio plano de línea *m pl*, vidrio plano de línea *m*; ~ **shortage** *n* PROD escasez de existencias *f*; ~ **shot** *n* CINEMAT toma de archivo *f*; ~ **shot library** *n* CINEMAT archivo de imágenes *m*, archivo de tomas *m*, cinemateca *f*; ~ **sizes** *n pl BrE* (*cf stock sheets AmE*) C&G tamaños de vidrio plano de línea *m pl*, vidrio plano de línea *m*; ~ **sizing** *n* PAPER encolado en masa *m*; ~ **transaction** *n* PROD transacción de existencias *f*; ~ **transfer** *n* PROD traspaso de acciones *m*; ~ **turnover** *n* PROD rotación de las existencias *f*; ~ **unit** *n* PROD unidad de existencias *f*; ~ **valuation** *n* PROD evaluación de las existencias *f*, valuación de existencias *f*

stockade *n* HYDRAUL empalizada *f*

stocker: ~ **cattle** *n* AGRIC vacuno joven alimentado normalmente *m pl*

stocking *n* OCEAN *OR operation* repoblación íctica *f*, *programme* cultivo de alevinos *m*; ~ **rate** *n* AGRIC carga ganadera *f*

stockless: ~ **anchor** *n* WATER TRANSP ancla sin cepo *f*

stockpile *vt* CONST almacenar

stocks ~ **and dies** *n pl* MECH ENG portaterrajas y terrajas *m pl*

stocktaking *n* PROD inventario de mercaderías *m*

stockyard *n* CONST acopio *m*, almacenaje *m*

stoichiometric¹ *adj* CHEM estequiométrico

stoichiometric²: ~ **composition** *n* METALL composición estequiométrica *f*; ~ **compound** *n* CRYSTALL compuesto estequiométrico *m*

stoichiometry *n* CHEM estequiometría *f*

stoke¹: ~ **hole** *n* PROD agujero de caldeo *m*, fogón *m*

stoke² *vt* PROD *furnace* aprovisionar de combustible, atizar, caldear

stokehold *n* HYDRAUL cámara de calderas *f*, sala de calderas *f*

stoker *n* PROD *machine* cargador mecánico *m*, *person* fogonero *m*

Stokes': ~ **law** *n* PHYS ley de Stokes *f*; ~ **velocity** *n* C&G velocidad de Stokes *f*

stoking *n* PROD caldeo *m*; ~ **door** *n* PROD puerta de fogón *f*, puerta de hogar *f*

STOL: ~ **aircraft** *n* (*short take-off and landing aircraft*) AIR TRANSP, TRANSP avión de despegue y aterrizaje corto *m*

stolport *n* AIR TRANSP aeropuerto de despegue y aterrizaje corto *m*

stolzite *n* MINERAL estolcita *f*

stone *n* CONST piedra *f*, roca *f*, METR *unit of weight* stone *m*, MINE hastial *m*, diamante sin tallar *m*, mineral *m*, piedra *f*, roca *f*, ganga *f* (*AmL*), pedruscos *m pl* (*Esp*), roca de los respaldos *f*, gema bruta *f*; ~ **band** *n* COAL intercalación de roca *f*; ~ **bed** *n* COAL capa rocosa *f*; ~ **bolt** *n* MECH ENG perno de empotramiento *m*; ~ **breaker** *n* CONST *machine* machacadora *f*; ~ **chippings** *n pl* CONST residuos de piedras *m pl*; ~ **coal** *n* MINE antracita *f*; ~ **crusher** *n* CONST machacadora *f*, trituradora *f*; ~ **dresser** *n* CONST *person* cantero *m*, labrador de piedras *f*; ~ **drift** *n* COAL galería en rocas *f*, MINE galería en roca *f*; ~ **dust** *n* COAL polvillo incombustible *m*, MINE polvillo incombustible *m*, polvo de talla *m*; ~ **hook** *n* CONST gancho para bloques de piedras *m*; ~ **mill** *n* CONST molino de machaqueo de piedras *m*; ~ **oil** *n* COAL petróleo *m*, PETR TECH aceite mineral *m*; ~ **pit** *n* COAL cantera *f*, MINE cantera de piedra *f*, pedrera *f*; ~ **quarry** *n* MINE cantera de piedra natural *f*; ~-**splitting hammer** *n* COAL mazo de romper piedras *m*; ~ **spreader** *n* TRANSP diseminadora de piedra *f*; ~ **tubbing** *n* COAL revestimiento de fábrica *m*, revestimiento de mampostería *m*, MINE entubado de mampostería *m*, revestimiento de mampostería *m*; ~ **wedge** *n* CONST cuña de cantera *f*; ~ **working** *n* COAL laboreo de rocas *m*

stoneware *n* C&G vasijas de barro *f pl*

stonework *n* CONST obra de mampostería *f*

stop¹ *n* COMP&DP parada *f*, CONST *for chamfer* parada *f*, tope *m*, MECH tope *m*, trinquete *m*, fiador *m*, seguro *m*, MECH ENG interrupción *f*, alto *m*, pausa *f*, paro *m*, detención *f*, cesación *f*, PHOTO diafragma *m*, punto *m*, obturador *m*, paso *m*, PHYS parada *f*, TEXTIL paro *m*, VEH detención *f*, parada *f*; ~-**and-go traffic** *n* TRANSP tráfico de parada y continuación alternativas *m*; ~ **bath** *n* CINEMAT, PHOTO baño de paro *m* (*Esp*), baño detenedor *m* (*AmL*); ~ **belt** *n* C&G banda de paro *f*; ~ **bit** *n* COMP&DP bit de detenida *m*, bit de parada *m*; ~ **brake** *n* RAIL freno de parada *m*; ~ **code** *n* COMP&DP código de detenida *m*, código de parada *m*; ~ **collar** *n* MECH ENG collar de retén *m*, collar de tope *m*; ~-**cylinder press** *n* PRINT prensa de cilindro de parada *f*; ~ **element** *n* COMP&DP elemento de detenida *m*, elemento de parada *m*; ~ **gap** *n* PROD boca de agujero *f*; ~ **instruction** *n* COMP&DP instrucción de detenida *f*, instrucción de parada *f*; ~ **joint** *n* ELEC *cable* empalme de retención *m*; ~ **key** *n* TV botón de parada *m*, pulsador de detención *m*; ~ **lamp** *n* VEH luz de alto *f*, luz de pare *f*; ~ **light**

switch *n* AUTO, VEH interruptor de luz de frenado *m*; ~ **log weir** *n* WATER esclusa de travesaños corredizos *f*; ~ **motion** *n* CINEMAT toma de vistas imagen por imagen *f*, MECH ENG *disengaging gear* desembrague *m*, movimiento de detención *m*, paro *m*, TEXTIL mecanismo de paro *m*, parahilos *m*; ~ **motion on creel** *n* TEXTIL mecanismo de paro en la fileta *m*; ~ **pattern** *n* PRINT patrón suspendido *m*; ~ **pin** *n* PHOTO pasador limitador *m*; ~ **plank** *n* WATER *of dam, sluice-gate* tablón de cierre *m*; ~ **plate** *n* PHOTO placa limitadora *f*; ~ **screw** *n* PHOTO tornillo limitador *m*, PROD obturador de rosca *m*; ~ **signal disc shunting** *BrE*, ~ **signal disk shunting** *AmE* *n* maniobra de la señal de parada *f*; ~ **valve** *n* CONST válvula de cierre *f*, HYDRAUL válvula de contención *f*, válvula de retención *f*

stop^2 *vt* COMP&DP detener, MECH ENG interrumpir, PROD interrumpir, obturar, taponar, WATER *leak* tapar, WATER TRANSP *engines* parar; ~ **down** *vt* CINEMAT, PHOTO diafragmar; ~ **a leak in** *vt* WATER parar una fuga en; ~ **off** *vt* WATER TRANSP *hawser, rope* abozar delante; ~ **with putty** *vt* CONST *hole* tapar con masilla; ~ **up** *vt* PROD taponar, *tapping-hole* tapar, obturar

stop^3 *vti* C&G *crack*, COMP&DP, TEXTIL parar

stopbutton: ~ **switch** *n* PROD pulsador de parada *m*

stopclock *n* PHYS cronómetro *m*

stopcock *n* CONST llave de paso *f*, LAB llave *f*, llave de paso *f*, válvula de cierre *f*

stope^1 *n* MINE banco *m* (*AmL*), destroza *f* (*Esp*), escalón *m* (*Esp*), grada *f* (*AmL*), tajo de arranque *m*, labor escalonada *f*; ~ **face** *n* COAL, MINE frente de arranque *m* (*AmL*); ~ **floor** *n* MINE piso escalonado *m*

stope^2 *vt* MINE arrancar (*AmL*), destrozar (*Esp*), excavar

stoped: ~**-out workings** *n pl* MINE laboreo de arranque *m*

stoping *n* MINE explotación por bancos *f*, explotación por gradas *f*, arranque *m* (*AmL*), banco ascendente *m* (*Esp*), gradería *f* (*AmL*), recorte *m* (*Esp*), compartimiento de ventilación *m* (*Esp*), explotación por escalones *f*, obstrucción *f*, tabique de ventilación *m* (*AmL*); ~ **of the seam** *n* MINE arranque de filones *m*

stopover *n* AIR TRANSP escala *f*

stoppage *n* MECH atasco *m*, PROD interrupción *f*, atasco *m*, obstrucción *f*, oclusión *f*; ~ **for repairs** *n* PROD parada por reparaciones *f*

stopped: ~ **chamfer** *n* CONST *joinery* bisel escalonado *m*; ~ **lens** *n* PHYS lentes de frenado *f pl*

stopper *n* C&G tapón *m*; ~ **knot** *n* WATER TRANSP *knot* barrilete *m*, nudo de retenida *m*, piña de acollador *f*

stoppered: ~ **bottle** *n* LAB frasco con tapón *m*; ~ **flask** *n* LAB matraz con tapón *m*; ~ **measuring cylinder** *n* LAB probeta con tapón *f*

stopping *n* CONST *for filling cracks* parada *f*, sellado *m*, MECH ENG *of injector* detención *f*; ~**-and-starting gear** *n* MECH ENG engranaje de arranque y paro *m*; ~ **knife** *n* CONST *putty-knife* cuchilla de parada *f*; ~ **marks** *n pl* TEXTIL marcas de paro *f pl*; ~ **potential** *n* PHYS potencial de frenado *m*; ~ **power** *n* PHYS poder de frenado *m*; ~ **sight distance** *n* TRANSP distancia de visibilidad en parada *f*; ~ **train** *n* RAIL tren de cercanías *m*, tren local *m*

stopway *n* AIR TRANSP *runway* zona de parada *f*; ~ **light** *n* AIR TRANSP *runway* luz de zona de parada *f*

storable: ~ **propellant** *n* SPACE propelente almacenable *m*, propulsor almacenable *m*

storage *n* (*cf store BrE*) COMP&DP *act* almacenamiento *m*, memoria *f*, MAR POLL almacenamiento *m*, PHOTO *equipment, aircraft* almacenaje *m*, PROD almacenaje *m*, almacenamiento *m*, depósito *m*, SAFE *of spacecraft* almacén *m*; ~ **allocation** *n* COMP&DP asignación de almacenamiento *f*, asignación de memoria *f*; ~ **area** *n* CONST zona de almacenamiento *f*; ~ **basin** *n* FUELLESS embalse de almacenamiento *m*, HYDROL embalse *m*; ~ **battery** *n* AUTO acumulador *m*, batería de acumuladores *f*, COMP&DP batería *f*, ELEC, ELEC ENG acumulador *m*, batería de acumuladores *f*, batería *f*, ELECTRON, HEAT ENG acumulador *m*, PHOTO batería *f*, PHYS acumulador *m*, batería *f*, batería de acumuladores *f*, SPACE acumulador *m*, batería de acumuladores *f*, TELECOM batería de acumuladores *f*, THERMO acumulador *m*, TRANSP batería de acumuladores *f*, VEH, WATER TRANSP acumulador *m*, batería de acumuladores *f*; ~ **canister** *n* NUCL contenedor de almacenamiento *m*; ~ **capacitor** *n* ELEC ENG condensador acumulador *m*; ~ **capacity** *n* COMP&DP capacidad de almacenamiento *f*, capacidad de memoria *f*, WATER capacidad de almacenamiento *f*; ~ **cell** *n* ELEC ENG célula de memoria *f*, elemento de memoria *m*, PRINT célula de memoria *f*; ~ **configuration** *n* SPACE configuración para almacenamiento *f*; ~ **dam** *n* WATER dique de embalse *m*; ~ **density** *n* COMP&DP densidad de almacenamiento *f*, densidad de grabación *f*; ~ **device** *n* COMP&DP dispositivo de almacenamiento *m*, dispositivo de memoria *m*; ~ **durability** *n* PACK caducidad *f*; ~ **effect** *n* ELEC ENG efecto-almacenamiento *m*, efecto-memoria *m*; ~ **element** *n* COMP&DP elemento de almacenamiento *m*, elemento de memoria *m*, ELEC ENG elemento de memoria *m*; ~ **entry** *n* COMP&DP entrada de almacenamiento *f*, entrada de memoria *f*; ~ **environment** *n* NUCL medio de almacenamiento *m*; ~ **facility** *n* POLL almacén *m*, depósito *m*, WATER TRANSP instalación de almacenamiento *f*; ~ **factor** *n* REFRIG coeficiente de utilización de un almacén *m*; ~ **and forwarding** *n* COMP&DP, almacenamiento y retransmición *m*, PRINT almacenamiento y conmutación hacia delante *m*; ~ **and forwarding switching center** *AmE*, ~ **and forwarding switching centre** *BrE* *n* COMP&DP centro de conmutación de almacenamiento y retransmisión *m*; ~ **fragmentation** *n* COMP&DP fragmentación de memoria *f*; ~ **head-end plant** *n* NUCL planta de preparación de residuos para el almacenamiento *f*; ~ **heater** *n* HEAT, HEAT ENG acumulador térmico *m*, MECH ENG acumulador térmico *m*, radiador de almacenamiento calorífico *m*, THERMO acumulador térmico *m*, calentador para almacenamiento térmico *m*; ~ **hierarchy** *n* COMP&DP jerarquía de almacenamiento *f*, jerarquía de la memoria *f*; ~ **lake** *n* HYDROL lago artificial *m*, PETR TECH yacimiento de petróleo *m*; ~ **lake dam** *n* HYDROL lago artificial *m*; ~ **level regulation** *n* WATER regulación del nivel del agua embalsada *f*; ~ **location** *n* COMP&DP dirección de memoria *f*, ubicación en el almacenamiento *f*, emplazamiento de almacenamiento *m*; ~ **map** *n* COMP&DP mapa de almacenamiento *m*, mapa de la memoria *m*; ~ **medium** *n* COMP&DP medio de almacenamiento *m*, soporte de memoria *m*; ~ **memory** *n* (*cf store memory AmE*) COMP&DP memoria *f*; ~ **mesh**

n ELECTRON malla de almacenamiento *f*, malla de memorización *f*; ~ **oscilloscope** *n* PHYS osciloscopio de almacenamiento *m*; ~ **period** *n* PHOTO período de almacenaje *m*; ~ **protection** *n* COMP&DP protección de almacenamiento *f*, protección de memoria *f*; ~ **rack** *n* C&G repisa de almacenaje *f*; ~ **requirement** *n* COMP&DP requisito de almacenamiento *m*, requisito de memoria *m*; ~ **reservoir** *n* PROD embalse *m*; ~ **scheme** *n* FUELLESS proyecto de almacenamiento *m*; ~ **screen** *n* ELECTRON pantalla de almacenamiento *f*, pantalla de memorización *f*; ~ **siding** *n* RAIL, TRANSP apartadero de almacenaje *m*; ~ **space** *n* PACK espacio de almacenaje *m*; ~ **tank** *n* PETR TECH tanque de almacenado *m* (*Esp*), tanque de almacenaje *m* (*AmL*), tanque de almacenamiento *m*, POLL almacén *m*, depósito *m*, tanque de almacenado *m* (*Esp*), tanque de almacenaje *m* (*AmL*), tanque de almacenamiento *m*, PROD tanque de almacenamiento *m*, depósito *m*, SPACE depósito para almacenamiento *m*; ~ **temperature** *n* PROD temperatura de almacenamiento *f*; ~ **time** *n* ELEC ENG duración de almacenaje *f*, duración de almacenaje útil *f*, duración de disipación *f*, tiempo de memorización y búsqueda *m*; ~ **tube** *n* COMP&DP tubo de almacenamiento de memoria *m*, tubo electrónico memorizador *m*, ELECTRON tubo de almacenamiento *m*; ~ **unit** *n* PROD unidad de almacenamiento *f*

store[1] *n* COMP&DP memoria *f*, almacenamiento *m*, ELEC ENG memoria *f*, almacén *m*, PROD almacén *m*, aprovisionamiento *m*, existencia *f*; **~-and-forward conversion facility** *n* TELECOM servicio de conversión por almacenamiento y reexpedición *m*; **~-and-forward facility** *n* TELECOM servicio de almacenamiento y reexpedición *m*; **~-and-forward switching network** *n* TELECOM red de conmutación con escala *f*; **~-and-forward transmission** *n* TELECOM transmisión por almacenamiento y reexpedición *f*; **~-and-forward unit** *n* (*SFU*) TELECOM unidad de almacenamiento y reexpedición *f*; ~ **bit** *n* COMP&DP, PROD bit de memoria *m*; ~ **memory** *n* BrE (*cf storage memory AmE*) COMP&DP memoria *f*

store[2] *vt* COAL almacenar, aprovisionar, COMP&DP, ELEC almacenar, ELEC ENG almacenar, memorizar, GAS almacenar

stored: ~ **energy** *n* METALL energía acumulada *f*, energía almacenada *f*, PHYS, RAD PHYS energía almacenada *f*; ~ **program** *n* COMP&DP programa almacenado *m*, programa guardado en memoria *m*; ~ **program computer** *n* COMP&DP computador con programa almacenado *m* (*AmL*), computador con programa almacenado en memoria *m* (*AmL*), computadora con programa almacenado *f* (*AmL*), computadora con programa almacenado en memoria *f* (*AmL*), computadora de programa almacenado *f* (*AmL*), ordenador con programa almacenado *m* (*Esp*), ordenador con programa almacenado en memoria *m* (*Esp*); ~ **program control** *n* AmE see *stored programme control BrE*; ~ **program control exchange** *AmE see stored programme control exchange BrE*; ~ **program control PABX** *AmE see stored-programme control PABX BrE*; ~ **program switching system** *AmE see stored programme switching system BrE*; ~ **programme control** *n* BrE TELECOM control de programa almacenado *m*; ~ **programme control exchange** *n* BrE TELECOM

central de control de programa almacenado *f*; ~ **programme control PABX** *n* BrE TELECOM PABX de control para programas almacenados *m*; ~ **programme switching system** *n* BrE TELECOM sistema de conmutación de programa almacenado *m*; **~-up energy** *n* PROD energía almacenada *f*

storeperson *n* PROD almacenista *m*

storm *n* METEO tempestad *f*, tormenta *f*; ~ **choke** *n* PETR TECH estrangulador de emergencias *m*; ~ **cloud** *n* METEO nubarrón *m*; ~ **drain** *n* CONST desagüe de aguas pluviales *m*, HYDROL colector para aguas pluviales *m*, RECYCL desagüe de aguas pluviales *m*; ~ **sail** *n* WATER TRANSP vela de capa *f*; ~ **sewage** *n* HYDROL, RECYCL, WATER aguas cloacales de lluvia *f pl*; ~ **sewer** *n* RECYCL canal de evacuación de aguas de lluvia *m* (*Esp*), canal de evacuación de aguas pluviales *m* (*AmL*); ~ **sewer system** *n* CONST sistema de drenaje pluvial *m*; ~ **surge** *n* OCEAN oleaje de temporal *m*; ~ **tide** *n* OCEAN onda de temporal *f*; ~ **warning** *n* METEO, WATER TRANSP aviso de tempestad *m*; ~ **water** *n* AGRIC agua de lluvia *f*, COAL agua de lluvia *f*, aguas pluviales *f pl*, HYDROL, METEO, WATER agua de lluvia *f*

stove[1] *n* PROD estufa *f*; ~ **enamel** *n* COATINGS esmalte secado en estufa *m*, COLOUR esmalte para horno *m*

stove[2]: ~ **enamel** *vt* COLOUR hornear al esmalte, esmaltar al horno

stoving *n* COATINGS, PROD estufación *f*, estufado *m*, secado mediante estufa *m*; ~ **enamel varnish** *n* COATINGS, P&R barniz esmaltado para secar en estufa *m*

stow *vt* AIR TRANSP almacenar, recoger, MINE rellenar, SPACE almacenar, arrizar, estibar, guardar, plegar, WATER TRANSP arrumar, estibar

stowage *n* SPACE almacenaje *m*, estibaje *m*, WATER TRANSP estibaje *m*, *of cargo* arrumazón *m*, estiba *f*, arrumaje *m*

stower *n* AGRIC estiba *f*

stowing *n* MINE relleno *m*; ~ **dirt** *n* COAL fango almacenado *m*; ~ **equipment** *n* MINE equipo de relleno *m*; ~ **material** *n* COAL fangos *m pl*, lodos *m pl*, material de estibaje *m*; ~ **tool** *n* C&G herramienta para estibar *f*

STP *abbr* (*standard temperature*) PETR TECH temperatura normal *f*, PHYS STP (*temperatura estándar*), TELECOM (*signaling transfer point AmE, signalling transfer point BrE*) punto de transferencia de la señalización *m*

straddle *vt* PROD colocar a ambos lados, montar a horcajadas

straddling *n* MECH ENG fresado con dos fresas acopladas *m*, fresado paralelo *m*

straight: ~ **chain** *n* CHEM *structure* cadena lineal *f*, cadena recta *f*; ~ **common crossing** *n* RAIL cruzamiento agudo en recta *m*; ~ **edge** *n* C&G regla *f*, MECH ENG canto en línea recta *m*, corte recto *m*, filo recto *m*, METR regla *f*; ~ **engine** *n* MECH ENG motor en línea *m*; **~-faced pulley** *n* MECH ENG polea de llanta plana *f*; ~ **fence** *n* MECH ENG *of saw bench* guía en línea *f*; **~-flank gear** *n* MECH ENG engranaje de dientes de flancos rectos *m*; **~-flow valve** *n* FUELLESS válvula de paso recto *f*; **~-fluted drill** *n* MECH ENG broca de estrías rectas *f*, broca de labios rectos *f*; ~ **hood** *n* PROD campana recta *f*; **~-in approach** *n* AIR TRANSP aproximación directa *f*; ~ **joint** *n* ELEC empalme recto *m*, MECH ENG junta a tope *f*, junta

lisa *f*; ~ **line** *n* GEOM, PHYS línea recta *f*; ~~**-line
capacitance** *n* ELEC ENG capacitancia de variación
lineal *f*; ~~**-line compressor** *n* PROD compresor con
cilindros en línea *m*; ~~**-line frequency** *n* ELEC
frecuencia rectlínea *f*, ELEC ENG frecuencia rectilínea
f; ~~**-line image reverser** *n* PRINT inversor de derecha
a izquierda *m*; ~ **negative** *n* PHOTO negativo directo
m; ~~**-nose cock** *n* CONST canilla recta *f* (*AmL*), grifo
recto *m* (*Esp*); ~ **packing** *n* C&G empaque sencillo *m*;
~~**-pane hammer** *n* CONST martillo recto *m*; ~~**-peen
hammer** *n* CONST martillo de puño recto *m*;
~ **pincers** *n pl* C&G pinzas rectas *f pl*; ~ **pressing** *n*
C&G prensado recto *m*; ~ **run** *n* PRINT tirada de doble
producción *f*; ~~**-run product** *n* PETR TECH producto
de destilación *m*; ~~**-shank twist drill** *n* MECH ENG
broca de mango cilíndrico *f*, broca de mango recto *f*;
~~**-sided spline** *n* MECH ENG *for cylindrical shafts*
estría de pared recta *f*, ranura de pared recta *f*;
~ **stem** *n* WATER TRANSP proa recta *f*; ~ **tap** *n* MECH
ENG macho de roscar de estrías rectas *m*; ~ **throat** *n*
C&G garganta recta *f*; ~~**-through can washer** *n* FOOD
lavador de latas *m*; ~~**-through press** *n* PAPER prensa
de paso recto *f*; ~~**-through traffic** *n* TRANSP tráfico en
vías preferentes *m*; ~~**-tooth meshing gear** *n* AUTO
engranaje de dientes rectos *m*; ~~**-tooth wheel** *n* MECH
ENG rueda de dientes rectos *f*; ~ **track** *n* RAIL vía
recta *f*; ~ **turning** *n* MECH ENG torneado de cilindros
m

straighten *vt* CONST *alignment of road* enderezar,
rectificar, PROD desalabear, poner derecho, rectificar,
rod enderezar

straightener *n* MECH ENG atirantador *m*, enderezador
m

straightening *n* PROD *of buckled tubes* enderezamiento
m; ~ **machine** *n* MECH ENG aplanadora *f*, enderezadora *f*

straightness: ~~**-measuring instrument** *n* INSTR, METR
instrumento de medida de rectilineidad *m*

strain[1] *n* C&G esfuerzo *m*, tensión *f*, GEOL deformación
f, MECH alargamiento *m*, deformación *f*, resistencia a
la tracción *f*, tensión *f*, MECH ENG deformación *f*,
esfuerzo de deformación *m*, estiramiento *m*, fatiga *f*,
tensión *f*, tirón *m*, *deformation or set produced by
stress* deformación por tensión *f*, *stretching; violent
effort* resistencia a la tracción *f*, METALL resistencia a
la tracción *f*, tensión *f*, P&R deformación *f*, PHYS
tensión *f*, WATER TRANSP deformación *f*; ~ **disc** *BrE*,
~ **disk** *AmE n* C&G disco de esfuerzo *m*; ~ **ellipsoid** *n*
GEOL elipsoide de deformación *m*, MECH ENG elipsoide de tensión *m*; ~ **gage** *AmE see strain gauge
BrE*; ~ **gage bridge** *AmE see strain gauge bridge
BrE*; ~ **gage technique** *AmE*, ~ **gauge** *BrE n* CONST
medidor de deformación *m*, medidor de esfuerzos *m*,
ELEC ENG electro-elongámetro *m*, extensímetro de
resistencia eléctrica *m*, galga eléctrica de deformación *f*, indicador de tensión *m*, INSTR extensómetro
m, LAB deformímetro *m*, MECH extensímetro de
resistencia eléctrica *m*, galga eléctrica de deformación *f*, medidor de deformación *m*, METR indicador
de tensión *m*, OCEAN extensímetro *m*, medidor de
deformación *m*, P&R extensómetro *m*, PHYS medidor
de tensión *m*; ~ **gauge bridge** *n BrE* ELEC ENG
puente de extensímetro *m*, puente del indicador de
tensión *m*; ~ **gauge technique** *n BrE* MECH ENG
técnica de medición de tensión *f*; ~ **hardening** *n*
METALL endurecimiento por deformación en frío *m*;

~~**-indicating lacquer** *n* COATINGS laca indicadora de
deformación *f*; ~ **modulus** *n* CONST módulo de
deformación *m*; ~ **slip cleavage** *n* GEOL clivaje por
deformación *m*, exfoliación por deformación *f*;
~ **tensor** *n* PHYS tensor de esfuerzos *m*; ~ **viewer** *n*
C&G visor de esfuerzos *m*

strain[2] *vt* CHEM *filter* filtrar, MECH ENG forzar, estirar,
tensar, deformar

strainer *n* GAS colador *m*, filtro *m*, MECH ENG *stretcher*
tensor *m*, PAPER separador de nudos *m*, PETR TECH
colador *m*, filtro *m*, PROD criba *f*, cedazo *m*, colador
m, alcachofa de aspiración *f*, purgador *m*, depurador
m, WATER *rose or snore piece of pump* alcachofa de
aspiración *f*; ~ **pump** *n* MAR POLL bomba filtrante *f*

straining *n* CHEM filtración *f*; ~ **beam** *n* CONST viga de
deformación *f*; ~ **chest** *n* PAPER caja de desgotado *f*,
tina de desgotado *f* (*AmL*); ~ **piece** *n* CONST sopanda
f; ~ **screw** *n* MECH ENG perno tensador *m*, tensor de
tornillo *m*; ~ **work** *n* COAL filtrado *m*

strake *n* COAL batea *f*, traca *f*, PROD *of boiler* virola *f*,
WATER TRANSP hilera de planchas *f*, traca *f*; ~ **drum
cam** *n* PROD leva de tambor de lengüetas *f*

strand *n* C&G hebra *f*, filamento *m*, CONST ribera *f*,
GEOL playa *f*, HYDROL ribera *f*, OCEAN playa *f*, ribera
f, cordón *m*, OPT hebra *f*, hilo *m*, torón *m*, PHYS *rolling
stock* filamento *m*, trenza de filamentos *f*, PROD torón
m, SPACE cordón *m*, filamento *m*, torón *m*, WATER
TRANSP ribera *f*; ~ **break detector** *n* C&G detector de
rotura del filamento *m*

stranded: ~ **cable** *n* ELEC, ELEC ENG *conductor* cable
trenzado *m*; ~ **conductor** *n* ELEC, ELEC ENG conductor trenzado *m*; ~ **wire** *n* PROD hilo cableado *m*,
alambre trenzado *m*, cable trenzado *m*

strange: ~ **quark** *n* PART PHYS quark extrañeja *m*,
strange quark *m*, PHYS quark extraño *m*

strap *n* AUTO abrazadera *f*, CONST *of hinge* correa *f*,
stirrup or fastening fleje *m*, *of double-strap gate hinge*
abrazadera *f*, MECH ENG *of end of connecting rod or
side rod* brida *f*, conector *m*, abrazadera *f*, *strengthening strip or band* fleje *m*, cinta metálica *f*, correa *f*,
PACK fleje *m*, PHOTO correa *f*, PROD banda *f*,
armadura *f*, tira *f*, correa *f*, fleje *m*, abrazadera *f*;
~~**-on** *n* SPACE conexión *f*; ~ **bar** *n* MECH ENG *belt-
shifting apparatus* palanca de poleas *f*; ~ **bolt** *n* CONST
perno para flejes *m*; ~ **brake** *n* MECH, MECH ENG
freno de cinta *m*; ~ **clutch** *n* MECH ENG embrague de
cinta *m*; ~ **connecting rod end** *n* MECH ENG conector
del extremo de varilla *m*; ~ **fork** *n* MECH ENG
horquilla de cinta *f*; ~ **hinge** *n* CONST bisagra *f*;
~~**-on** *n* SPACE impulsor anexo *m*; ~ **rail** *n*
RAIL brida de carriles *f*; ~ **wrench** *n* MECH ENG llave
de cinta *f*

strapdown[1]: ~~**-mounted** *adj* SPACE montaje contra el
desmontaje *phr*

strapdown[2]: ~ **equipment** *n* SPACE equipo de desmontaje *m*; ~ **inertial platform** *n* SPACE plataforma
inercial de desmontaje *f*; ~ **system** *n* SPACE sistema
de desmontaje *m*

strapper *n* PACK máquina flejadora *f*

strapping *n* PHYS fleje *m*; ~ **equipment** *n* PACK equipo
para flejar *m*; ~ **machine** *n* PACK flejadora *f*; ~ **seal** *n*
PACK precintado por flejado *m*; ~ **steel** *n* CONST, PACK
fleje de acero *m*

strategic: ~ **missile** *n* MILIT misil estratégico *m*

stratification *n* COAL, FUELLESS, GEOL estratificación *f*,

METALL estratificación *f*, capa delgada *f*, PETR TECH estratificación *f*

stratified[1] *adj* COAL, GEOL, MECH ENG, METALL, PETR TECH estratificado

stratified[2]: **~ charge engine** *n* TRANSP motor de cámara de precombustión *m*; **~ sampling** *n* COAL muestra estratificada *f*, SAFE muestreo estratificado *m*

stratify *vti* COAL estratificar, estratificarse

stratigraphic: **~ column** *n* GEOL columna estratigráfica *f*; **~ trap** *n* PETR TECH trampa estratigráfica *f*

stratigraphy *n* COAL estratigrafía *f*

stratocumulus *n* (*Sc*) METEO estratocúmulo, stratocumulus *m* (*Sc*)

stratosphere *n* METEO estratosfera *f*

stratovolcano *n* GEOPHYS volcán estratificado *m*

stratum *n* COAL estrato *m*, filón de minerales *m*, GEOL capa *f*

stratus *n* (*St*) METEO stratus *m* (*St*); **~ fractus** *n* METEO fractus stratus *m*, stratus fractus *m*

straw *n* PAPER paja *f*; **~ carrier** *n* AGRIC sacapajas *m*; **~ pulp** *n* PAPER pasta de paja *f*; **~ spreader** *n* AGRIC difusor de paja *m*

stray[1] *adj* PHYS disperso

stray[2]: **~ coupling** *n* ELEC ENG, TELECOM acoplamiento parásito *m*; **~ current** *n* ELEC ENG corriente de fuga *f*, corriente parásita *f*; **~ current corrosion** *n* ELEC ENG corrosión por corrientes de fugas *f*; **~ field** *n* ELEC campo de dispersión *m*, campo de dispersión magnética *m*, campo parásito *m*; **~ light** *n* CINEMAT luz parásita *f*; **~-light filter** *n* INSTR filtro de luz difusa *m*; **~ radiation** *n* RAD PHYS radiación perdida *f*, SPACE escape *m*, huida *f* (*AmL*), radiación parásita *f*

streak *n* MINE veta pequeña *f*, PAPER raya *f*; **~ camera** *n* CINEMAT cámara para imágenes unidimensionales *f*; **~ image converter camera** *n* CINEMAT cámara de conversión de imágenes unidimensionales *f*

streaking *n* CINEMAT formación de imágenes falsas *f*

stream[1] *n* GEOL arroyo *m*, HYDROL arroyo *m*, corriente de agua *f*; **~ bed** *n* HYDROL lecho fluvial *m*; **~ channel** *n* HYDROL canal fluvial *m*; **~ line** *n* HYDROL línea de corriente *f*

stream[2]: **~ a warp** *vi* WATER TRANSP dar una espía

streamer *n* COMP&DP cinta de serpentina *f*, cinta para copia de seguridad *f*, streamer *m*, PRINT título a toda plana *m*; **~ chamber** *n* PART PHYS cámara de chispas seguidas *f*

streaming: **~ tape drive** *n* COMP&DP dispositivo de cinta para copia de seguridad *m*, impulsor de cinta a serpentina *m*, unidad de cinta para copia de seguridad *f*

streamlet *n* GEOL arroyuelo *m*, HYDROL arroyuelo *m*, riachuelo *m*

streamline *n* PHYS corriente natural *f*

streamlined *adj* GEN aerodinámico

streamway *n* HYDROL curso de agua *m*, WATER cauce de corriente *m*

street: **~ cleaner** *n* TRANSP limpiadora de calles *f*; **~ cleaning lorry** *n* BrE (*cf street cleaning truck AmE*) AUTO camión de limpieza urbana *m*; **~ cleaning truck** *n* AmE (*cf street cleaning lorry BrE*) AUTO camión de limpieza urbana *m*

streetcar *n* AmE (*cf tram BrE*) TRANSP tranvía *m*; **~ stop** *n* AmE (*cf tram stop BrE*) TRANSP parada del tranvía *f*; **~ track** *n* AmE (*cf tram track BrE*) TRANSP vía del tranvía *f*

strength *n* CHEM *of acid* fuerza *f*, COAL fuerza *f*, riqueza *f*, GAS fuerza *f*, solidez *f*, METALL solidez *f*, resistencia *f*, MINE potencia *f*, concentración *f*, riqueza *f*, PAPER resistencia mecánica *f*, PHYS resistencia *f*, PROD potencia *f*, resistencia *f*, TEXTIL resistencia *f*, fuerza *f*

strengthen *vt* PROD reforzar

strengthened: **~ passenger compartment** *n* TRANSP compartimiento de pasajeros reforzado *m*

strengthening *n* PROD refuerzo *m*

stress[1] *n* C&G tensión *f*, COAL carga *f*, esfuerzo *m*, tensión *f*, CONST esfuerzo *m*, tensión *f*, GEOL fatiga *f*, tensión *f*, MAR POLL esfuerzo *m*, MECH carga *f*, fatiga *f*, fuerza *f*, tensión *f*, MECH ENG esfuerzo *m*, fatiga *f*, fuerza *f*, tensión *f*, resistencia a la deformación *f*, resistencia a la fatiga *f*, METALL esfuerzo repetitivo *m*, fatiga *f*, P&R carga *f*, esfuerzo *m*, fatiga *f*, tensión *f*, PETR TECH esfuerzo *m*, tensión *f*, PHYS, SPACE tensión *f*, WATER TRANSP esfuerzo *m*; **~ analysis** *n* SPACE análisis de tensión *m*; **~ coating** *n* COATINGS revestimiento de alta resistencia *m*; **~ due to temperature change** *n* MECH ENG esfuerzo debido al cambio de temperatura *m*; **~ expansion** *n* RAIL expansión por tensiones *f*; **~ marks** *n pl* CINEMAT marcas de desgaste *f pl*; **~ relaxation** *n* C&G revenido *m*; **~ relief** *n* HEAT atenuación de tensión *f*, THERMO relajación de esfuerzos interiores *f*; **~-relieving anneal** *n* THERMO recocido para relajamiento de esfuerzos interiores *m*; **~ and strain analysis** *n* MECH ENG análisis de esfuerzo y deformación *m*, análisis de esfuerzo y fatiga *m*; **~-strain curve** *n* P&R curva de esfuerzo y deformación *f*, curva de tensión-deformación *f*; **~-strain diagram** *n* WATER TRANSP *naval architecture* curva de cargas-deformaciones *f*; **~ tensor** *n* PHYS tensor de tensiones *m*

stress[2] *vt* MECH ENG sobrecargar, someter a esfuerzo, PHYS tensionar

stressed: **~ zone** *n* C&G zona en tensión *f*

stretch[1] *n* MECH ENG alargamiento *m*, dilatación *f*, estiramiento *m*, extensión *f*, tensión *f*, tirantez *f*, P&R estiramiento *m*, PAPER alargamiento *m*; **~ at break** *n* PAPER alargamiento hasta la rotura *m*; **~ at breaking point** *n* PAPER alargamiento en el punto de rotura *m*; **~ die** *n* MECH ENG molde alargador *m*; **~ film** *n* PACK película para conformar por estiramiento *f*; **~ length** *n* PAPER longitud de alargamiento *f*; **~ modulus** *n* PETR TECH módulo de elasticidad *m*; **~-out** *n* NUCL extensión del período de estancia del combustible en el reactor *f*; **~-out operation** *n* PROD operación prolongada *f*; **~ roll** *n* PAPER rodillo tensor *m*; **~ thrust** *n* GEOL cabalgamiento por cizalla en un pliegue *m*; **~ wrapping** *n* PACK envoltura conformada por estiramiento *f*; **~ of yarn in sizing** *n* TEXTIL alargamiento del hilo en el encolado *m*

stretch[2] *vt* TEXTIL estirar; **~-frame print** *vt* CINEMAT copiar descomprimiendo la imagen

stretchable *adj* PAPER extensible

stretched: **~ aircraft** *n* AIR TRANSP avión alargado *m*

stretcher *n* CONST tensor *m*, viga *f*, ladrillo al hilo *m*, soga *f*, MECH ENG *strainer* atesador *m*, extensor *m*, tensor *m*, SAFE camilla *f*, TEXTIL ensanchador *m*, horma *f*, tensor *m*; **~ cart** *n* SAFE *equipment* camilla con ruedas *f*, carro para camillas *m*; **~ piece** *n* MINE tirante *m*

stretching *n* CHEM *of bond* alargamiento *m*, CONST alargamiento *m*, estiraje *m*, estiramiento *m*; **~ course** *n* CONST *masonry* recorrido de estiramiento *m*;

~ **screw** *n* MECH ENG tornillo tensor *m*; ~ **zone** *n* TEXTIL zona de estiramiento *f*

stretchy *adj* TEXTIL elástico

striation *n* METALL estriación *f*

strickle *n* PROD *founding* terraja *f*; ~ **board** *n* CONST tablón *m*; ~ **molding** *AmE*, ~ **moulding** *BrE* *n* PROD moldeo a terraja *m*

strickled: ~ **casting** *n* PROD pieza aterrajada *f*

Strickler: ~'s **formula** *n* HYDROL fórmula de Strickler *f*

strickling *n* PROD aterrajamiento *m*

strictly: ~ **nonblocking network** *n* TELECOM red estrictamente antibloqueante *f*

striding: ~ **level** *n* MECH ENG nivel a caballo *m*, nivel principal *m*

strike[1] *n* GEOL dirección de buzamiento *f* (*Esp*), MINE arrumbamiento *m* (*AmL*), dirección de buzamiento *f* (*Esp*), encuentro *m*, *of underground lode* hallazgo *m* (*AmL*), rumbo del filón *m* (*Esp*); ~ **aircraft** *n* AIR TRANSP, MILIT avión de caza *m*; ~ **drive** *n* MINE intersección *f*; ~ **gear** *n* MECH ENG engranaje de cebado *m*; ~ **slip** *n* GEOL desplazamiento de rumbo *m* (*AmL*), desplazamiento direccional *m* (*Esp*); ~-**slip movements** *n pl* GEOL *theory, entity* movimientos de desgarre horizontal *m pl*; ~-**slip thrust** *n* GEOL cabalgamiento de desplazamiento direccional *m*

strike[2] *vt* CINEMAT copiar, MINE aflorar, encontrar, OCEAN batir, golpear

strike[3]: ~ **colors** *AmE*, ~ **colours** *BrE* *vi* WATER TRANSP *flags* arriar la bandera

striker *n* MECH ENG *belt-striking gear* cebador *m*, percutor *m*; ~ **spring** *n* MILIT *of firearm* resorte del percutor *m*

striking *n* ELEC ENG cebado *m*, ELECTRON choque *m*; ~ **the centering** *AmE*, ~ **the centring** *BrE* *n* CONST *of arch* centrado *m*; ~ **gear** *n* MECH ENG *belt-striking gear* engranaje cebador *m*; ~ **plate** *n* CONST *locksmithing* plancha de cerradura *f*; ~ **post** *n* CONST poste para descimbrado *m*

string *n* C&G hilera *f*, COMP&DP cadena *f*, CONST zanca *f*, PETR TECH sarta *f*, PRINT tira *f*; ~ **array** *n* COMP&DP *text* arreglo en serie *m*, matriz de cadenas *f*; ~ **board** *n* CONST montante *m*; ~ **of casing** *n* CONST *well-sinking* cuerda del enturbado *f*; ~ **constructions** *n pl* RAD PHYS construcciones de cadenas *f pl*, construcciones en secuencia ordenada *f pl*; ~ **length** *n* COMP&DP longitud de la cadena *f*; ~ **literal** *n* COMP&DP literal de la cadena *m*, serie literal *f*; ~ **manipulation** *n* COMP&DP *text* manipulación de cadenas *f* (*Esp*), manipulación en series *f* (*AmL*); ~ **operation** *n* COMP&DP *text* operación de cadenas *f*, operación en series *f*; ~ **piece** *n* CONST zanca *f*; ~ **proof** *n* PRINT prueba de galera *f*; ~ **rod** *n* MECH ENG barra de transmisión *f*

stringer *n* CONST *beam running longitudinally* riostra *f*, zanca *f*, *main lengthwise timber in bridge* larguero *m*, MINE larguero *m* (*Esp*), reforzador *m* (*AmL*), RAIL traviesa colocada en sentido longitudinal *f*, SPACE larguero *m*, obturador longitudinal *m*, WATER TRANSP *deck* palmejar *m*, trancanil *m*; ~ **angle** *n* WATER TRANSP *ship building* angular de trancanil *m*

stringy: ~ **knot** *n* C&G nudo fibroso *m*

strip[1] *n* AIR TRANSP banda *f*, tira *f*, CINEMAT tira *f*, COMP&DP banda *f*, cinta *f*, CONST *of wood* fleje *m*, tabla *f*, MECH ENG fleje *m*, PACK fleje *m*, tira *f*, PHOTO, PHYS tira *f*, PROD banda *f*, fleje *m*, conicidad *f*, tira *f*, cinta *f*; ~ **chart recorder** *n* ELEC registrador de banda *m*, registrador de banda de papel *m*, registrador de carta en rollo *m*, registrador gráfico en banda de papel *m*, INSTR registrador de cinta *m*; ~ **cropping** *n* AGRIC cultivo en franjas *m*; ~ **formwork** *n* CONST encofrado de tablas *m*; ~ **grazing** *n* AGRIC pastoreo en franjas *m*; ~ **gumming** *n* PRINT engomado en franjas *m*; ~ **light** *n* CINEMAT luz estrecha *f*; ~ **line** *n* ELEC ENG línea de cinta *f*, PHYS línea laminar *f*; ~ **log** *n* PETR TECH perfil de franja *m*, perfil desguarnecido *m*; ~ **mine** *n* MINE mina a cielo abierto *f*; ~ **shim** *n* MECH ENG tiras de metal *f pl*; ~-**type detector** *n* SPACE detector de tipo banda *m*; ~ **washer** *n* MECH ENG arandela rectangular *f*; ~-**wound armature** *n* ELEC, ELEC ENG inducido del devanado en bandas *m*; ~-**wound flexible metal hose** *n* MECH ENG manguera recubierta con tiras de metal flexible *f*

strip[2] *vt* COAL deslingotar, COLOUR desmontar, NUCL reextraer, PRINT *page* desmontar, PROD *founding* desmoldear, deslingotar, *thread from screw* arrancar

stripe *n* CINEMAT banda *f*, COMP&DP raya *f*, MILIT divisa *f*, galón *m*, TEXTIL raya *f*; ~ **fabric** *n* TEXTIL tela a rayas *f*

striped[1] *adj* PAPER estriado

striped[2]: ~ **film** *n* CINEMAT película con banda incorporada *f*

stripiness: ~ **in the warp** *n* TEXTIL barrado por urdimbre *m*

stripper *n* AGRIC cosechadora de peine *f*, COAL excavador *m*, extractor *m*, minero que rescata madera de entibación *m*, PRINT separadora de recortes *f*; ~ **bush** *n* MECH ENG *injection mould* casquillo de extracción *m*; ~ **plate** *n* MECH ENG *injection mould* chapa extractora *f*, placa eyectora *f*

stripping *n* C&G remoción *f*, COAL deslingotado *m*, desmonte *m*, explotación en descubierto *f*, explotación por excavadoras *f*, ELEC, ELEC ENG, MECH ENG desforramiento *m*, MINE desmonte de la montera *m*, explotación en descubierto *f*, PRINT encintado *m*, PROD desforramiento *m*, desmontaje *m*, desoxidación *f*, eliminación de la capa de metal electrodepositado *f*, explotación en descubierto *f*, rascado *m*, *foundry* deslingotado *m*, desmoldeo *m*; ~ **column** *n* REFRIG columna de agotamiento *f*; ~ **machine** *n* PROD *founding* agramadera *f*, desmoldeadora *f*; ~ **pump** *n* MAR POLL bomba de agotamiento *f*

strippings *n pl* MINE montera *f*

strobe: ~ **light** *n* CINEMAT, SPACE luz estroboscópica *f*; ~ **light projector** *n* SPACE proyector de luz estroboscópica *m*; ~ **pulse** *n* TELECOM impulso de fijación *m*

stroboscope *n* PHYS, WAVE PHYS estroboscopio *m*

stroke *n* AUTO carrera *f*, carrera del pistón *f*, CONST carrera *f*, HYDRAUL carrera *f*, desplazamiento *m*, MECH ENG *of piston* carrera *f*, golpe *m*, recorrido *m*, NUCL recorrido *m*, PHYS golpe *m*, PRINT trazo *m*; ~ **counter** *n* MECH ENG contador de carreras *m*; ~ **of drilling spindle** *n* MECH ENG carrera del husillo de la taladradora *f*; ~ **of ram** *n* MECH ENG carrera del ariete *f*, carrera del carnero *f*; ~ **of the walking beam** *n* MINE carrera del balancín de perforación *f*

stromatolite *n* GEOL estromatolito *m*

stromeyerite *n* MINERAL stromeyerita *f*

strong: ~ **breeze** *n* METEO brisa fuerte *f*; ~ **gale** *n* METEO viento muy duro *m*; ~ **interaction** *n* PART PHYS fuerza internuclear *f*, PHYS interacción fuerte *f*; ~ **inversion** *n* ELECTRON inversión pronunciada *f*; ~ **nuclear force** *n* NUCL interacción fuerte *f*, PART

PHYS fuerza fuerte *f*, fuerza internuclear *f*, interacción fuerte *f*

strontianite *n* MINERAL estroncianita *f*

strontic *adj* CHEM de estroncio, estróncico

strontium *n* (*Sr*) CHEM estroncio *m* (*Sr*); **~ chromate pigment** *n* COLOUR pigmento de cromato de estroncio *m*

strop *n* MECH ENG *of tackle block* asentador *m*, suavizador *m*

strophanthin *n* CHEM estrofantina *f*

Strowger: ~ system *n* TELECOM sistema Strowger *m*

struck: ~~-up casting *n* PROD pieza aterrajada *f*; **~~-up core** *n* PROD *founding* núcleo aterrajado *m*

structural[1] *adj* CONST estructural

structural[2]: **~ analysis** *n* CONST análisis estructural *m*, cálculo de estructuras *m*; **~ analysis software** *n* SPACE soporte lógico de análisis estructural *m*; **~ dynamics** *n* MECH ENG dinámica estructural *f*; **~ effect** *n* CONST efecto estructural *m*; **~ fire protection** *n* SAFE protección contra incendios de estructuras *f*; **~ foam mold** *AmE*, **~ foam mould** *BrE* *n* MECH ENG molde de espuma estructural *m*; **~ formula** *n* CHEM fórmula de constitución *f*, fórmula estructural *f*; **~ glass** *n* C&G vidrio estructural *m*; **~ iron** *n* CONST hierro estructural *m*; **~ isomerism** *n* CHEM isomerismo estructural *m*; **~ map** *n* GEOL mapa estructural *m*; **~ model** *n* SPACE modelo estructural *m*; **~ sound** *n* ACOUST sonido estructural *m*; **~ steel** *n* CONST, METALL acero estructural *m*; **~ tap** *n* PETR TECH sello estructural *m*; **~ varnish** *n* COATINGS barniz estructural *m*

structure *n* CONST, PHYS, RAIL estructura *f*; **~~-borne sound** *n* ACOUST sonido estructural *m*; **~ contour map** *n* GEOL mapa de contorno de estructura *m*; **~ factor** *n* CRYSTALL factor de estructura *m*; **~ index** *n* SPACE índice de estructuras *m*; **~ noise** *n* ACOUST ruido estructural *m*; **~ subsurface contour map** *n* GEOL mapa de contorno de estructura de subsuperficie *m*

structured: ~ design *n* COMP&DP diseño estructurado *m*; **~ programming** *n* COMP&DP programación estructurada *f*; **~ type** *n* COMP&DP tipo estructurado *m*

strut *n* AUTO puntal *m*, COAL contrete de apoyo *m*, larguero *m*, montante *m*, puntal grueso *m*, riostra *f*, vela *f*, CONST *placed between walls of trench* columna *f*, montante *m*, *timbering* puntal *m*, *between straining beam and tie beam in wooden frame* riostra *f*, *brace* codal *m*, *between rafter and king post, tie-beam in wooden roof truss* poste *m*, MECH, PACK poste *m*, puntal *m*, VEH montante *m*, WATER TRANSP *of shaft* arbotante *m*; **~~-action pawl motion** *n* MECH ENG movimiento del trinquete activador del puntal *m*

strutting *n* CONST apuntalamiento *m*, acoplamiento *m*

struvite *n* MINERAL struvita *f*

STS *abbr* (*Space Transportation System*) SPACE Sistema de Transporte Espacial *m*

stub *n* CONST tope *m*, *of bolt of tumbler lock* guarda *f*, ELEC ENG colilla *f*, chicote *m*, PHYS *motor vehicles* cabo *m*; **~ axle** *n* VEH mangueta *f*; **~ drill** *n* MECH ENG broca corta *f*; **~ end** *n* MECH ENG cabeza de barra de conexión *f*, cabeza de biela *f*, cabeza de muñón *f*; **~ mortise** *n* CONST mortaja ciega *f*; **~ tenon** *n* CONST espiga invisible *f*

stubble *n* AGRIC rastrojo *m*; **~ bottom** *n* AGRIC cuerpo

de arado apto para rastrojo *m*; **~ mulch tilling** *n* AGRIC labor bajo cubierta de rastrojo *f*

stubborn: ~ ore *n* MINE mineral refractario *m*

stubook *n* PRINT libro talonario *m*

stud *n* AGRIC arnés *m*, AUTO espárrago *m*, gorrón *m*, husillo *m*, pasador *m*, perno *m*, MECH clavija de conexión *f*, perno sin cabeza *m*, polea *f*, MECH ENG prisionero *m*, refuerzo de eslabón *m*, diente de retención *m*, espárrago *m*, husillo giratorio *m*, perno sin cabeza *m*, polea *f*, tachuela *f*, pasador corto *m*, resalto *m*, PROD espárrago *m*, pasador corto *m*, borna *f*, terminal *m*, clavija de conexión *f*, perno sin cabeza *m*, soporte doble *m*, prisionero *m*, VEH espárrago *m*; **~ bolt** *n* MECH ENG perno de trabante *m*, perno prisionero *m*, tornillo opresor *m*; **~ chain** *n* MECH ENG *pintle chain* cadena Galle *f*, cadena articulada *f*, cadena de gorrones *f*; **~ chaplet** *n* PROD *founding* soporte doble *m*; **~ coupling** *n* CONST *for pipes* unión de pasador *f*; **~ driver** *n* MECH ENG insertador de pernos *m*; **~ extractor** *n* MECH ENG extractor de pernos *m*; **~ link** *n* CONST unión con pernos *f*; **~~-link chain cable** *n* CONST cable de cadena de eslabones con pasador *m*; **~ mounting** *n* PROD montaje sobre perno *m*; **~ partition** *n* CONST tabique con postes *m*; **~ union** *n* CONST unión con pernos *f*, unión de entramado *f*; **~ welding** *n* CONST soldadura con pasador *f*; **~ welding gun** *n* CONST soplete de soldadura con pasador *m*; **~ wheel** *n* MECH ENG *gearing* rueda intermedia *f*, rueda parásita *f*

studded: ~ link cable chain *n* CONST cadena de cable de eslabones con pasador *f*; **~ tire** *AmE*, **~ tyre** *BrE n* VEH neumático con clavos *m*, neumático esculpido *m*

studdle *n* MINE puntal separador del ademado *m*

studio *n* CINEMAT estudio cinematográfico *m*; **~ broadcast** *n* TV programa emitido desde el estudio *m*; **~ camera** *n* PHOTO cámara de estudio *f*; **~ control room** *n* TV sala de control del estudio *f*; **~ facilities** *n pl* TV instalaciones del estudio *f pl*; **~ manager** *n* TV director del estudio *m*, gerente del estudio *mf*; **~ monitor** *n* TV monitor del estudio *m*; **~ work** *n* PHOTO trabajo de estudio fotográfico *m*

stuff[1] *n* COATINGS madera aserrada *f*, PAPER pasta en suspensión *f*, pulpa en suspensión *f*, PROD materia *f*, material *m*, materias *f pl*, TEXTIL material *m*; **~ chest** *n* PAPER tina de pasta *f*; **~ sizing** *n* PAPER encolado en masa *m*

stuff[2] *vt* TRANSP acolchar

stuffing *n* PROD empaquetado *m*, empaquetadura *f*, guarnición *f*, relleno *m*, *material* construcción *f*, material con que se rellena algo *m*, TELECOM, TRANSP relleno *m*; **~ box** *n* MECH ENG caja de empaquetadura *f*, caja de estopas de relleno *f*, prensaestopas *m*, PROD prensaestopas *m*; **~ box lid** *n* NUCL tapa de prensaestopa *f*; **~ character** *n* TELECOM carácter de empaquetadura *m*; **~ device** *n* TELECOM dispositivo de relleno *m*; **~ digit** *n* TELECOM dígito de relleno *m*; **~ rate** *n* TELECOM tasa de relleno *f*

stump *n* CONST *of bolt of tumbler lock* tocón *m*

stunted *adj* AGRIC achaparrado

stupefacient[1] *adj* CHEM estupefaciente

stupefacient[2] *n* CHEM estupefaciente *m*

STX *abbr* (*start of text*) COMP&DP comienzo de texto *m*

style *n* CONST, PRINT, TEXTIL estilo *m*; **~ attribute** *n* PRINT atributo de estilo *m*

styling *n* TEXTIL estilización *f*

stylolite *n* GEOL estilolito *m*

stylus: ~ **force** n ACOUST fuerza de la aguja f; ~ **instrument** n ACOUST estilite m; ~ **recording instrument** n INSTR instrumento de grabación por agujas m

styphnate n CHEM estifnato m

styphnic: ~ **acid** n CHEM trinitroresorcinol m, ácido estífnico m

styracitol n CHEM estiracitol m

styramate n CHEM estiramato m

styrene n CHEM, PETR TECH estireno m; ~ **butadiene rubber** n (SBR) P&R caucho butadieno-estireno m (SBR)

styrolene n CHEM estiroleno m

stythe n MINE gas carbónico m

sub: ~ **timer alarm** n LAB alarma de intervalos de tiempo f

SUB: ~ **character** n (substitute character) COMP&DP carácter de sustitución m

subacetate n CHEM subacetato m

subaddress n TELECOM señas auxiliares del destinatario f pl, subdirección f

subaddressing n TELECOM subdirección f

subambient: ~ **temperature flexibility test** n MECH ENG prueba de la flexibilidad de la temperatura subambiente f

subantomorphic adj GEOL subantomórfico

subaqueous: ~ **pump** n WATER bomba submarina f

subatomic: ~ **particle** n PHYS partícula subatómica f

sub-base n CONST subbase f

sub-basin n GEOL cubeta f

sub-bottom: ~ **profiler** n OCEAN perfilador del subsuelo marino m, sondador del subsuelo marino m

subcarbonate n CHEM subcarbonato m

subcarrier n SPACE, TV subportadora f; ~ **component** n TV componente de la subportadora m; ~ **frequency** n ELECTRON, TELECOM, TV frecuencia de la subportadora f; ~ **frequency modulation** n (SFM) TELECOM modulación de frecuencia de subportadora f; ~ **lock** n TV sujeción de la subportadora f; ~ **modulation** n TV modulación de la subportadora f; ~ **offset** n TV desplazamiento de la subportadora m; ~ **oscillator** n ELECTRON, TV oscilador de la subportadora m; ~ **phase** n TV fase de la subportadora f; ~ **rectification** n TV rectificado de la subportadora f

subchannel n ELECTRON subcanal m

subchloride n CHEM subcloruro m

sub-Clos: ~ **network** n TELECOM red sub-Clos f

subcoating n COATINGS revestimiento interior m

subcontracting: ~ **item** n PROD partida subcontratada f

subcooled: ~ **boiling** n PROD ebullición subenfriada f

subcooler n REFRIG subenfriador m

subcritical: ~ **reaction** n RAD PHYS reacción subcrítica f

subdominant[1] adj ACOUST subdominante

subdominant[2] n ACOUST cuarta nota de la escala diatónica f

subdrift n MINE galería intermedia f, subgalería f, subpiso m

subduction n PETR TECH subcanalización f, subducción f; ~ **zone** n PETR TECH zona de subducción f

suberate n CHEM suberato m

suberic adj CHEM subérico

suberification n CHEM suberificación f

suberin n CHEM suberina f

suberone n CHEM suberona f

suberyl n CHEM suberilo m

suberylic adj CHEM suberílico

subframe n VEH bastidor auxiliar m

subgrade n RAIL capa de asiento f, explanación f; ~ **reaction modulus** n COAL módulo de reacción del subsuelo m

subharmonic[1] adj ACOUST subarmónico

subharmonic[2] n ELECTRON subarmónica f

subhedral adj GEOL subhédrico

subjective: ~ **camera** n CINEMAT cámara subjetiva f; ~ **loudness** n ACOUST of sound sonoridad subjetiva f; ~ **test** n TELECOM ensayo subjetivo m, prueba subjetiva f; ~ **tone** n ACOUST tono subjetivo m

subland: ~ **twist drill** n MECH ENG broca helicoidal multidiámetro f

sublayer n TEXTIL capa inferior f

sublethal: ~ **effect** n POLL efecto sub-letal m

sublevel n MINE galería intermedia f, subnivel m, subpiso m, PHYS subnivel m

sublimable adj CHEM sublimable

sublimate n CHEM, PETR TECH sublimado m

sublimation n CHEM, PHYS sublimación f

sublimatory n CHEM sublimador m

sublime vt CHEM sublimar

sublimed adj CHEM sublimado

sublot n PROD sublote m

sub-machine: ~ **gun** n MILIT metralleta f, subfusil m

submarine[1] adj OCEAN, WATER TRANSP submarino

submarine[2] n OCEAN, WATER TRANSP submarino; ~ **cable** n ELEC ENG, PHYS, TELECOM cable submarino m, cable sumergible m, WATER TRANSP cable submarino m; ~ **earthquake** n GEOPHYS maremoto m, movimiento sísmico submarino m; ~ **plateau** n OCEAN meseta submarina f; ~ **relief** n OCEAN relieve submarino m; ~ **slope** n OCEAN pendiente submarina f; ~ **tanker** n TRANSP cisterna submarina f; ~ **topography** n OCEAN topografía submarina f; ~ **valley** n OCEAN valle submarino m

submerge vt WATER sumergir

submerged: ~ **arc welding** n CONST soldadura por arco sumergido f; ~ **bar** n HYDROL, OCEAN, WATER banco de arena inundado m, banco de arena sumergido m; ~ **combustion** n GAS combustión sumergida f; ~ **concrete** n CONST concreto sumergido m (AmL), hormigón sumergido m (Esp); ~ **condenser** n REFRIG condensador sumergido m; ~ **optical repeater** n TELECOM repetidor sumergido m; ~ **orifice** n HYDRAUL orificio anegado m, orificio sumergido m, vertedero sumergido m; ~ **overfall** n HYDRAUL vertedero sumergido m; ~ **pump** n WATER bomba que puede funcionar sumergida f; ~ **repeater** n TELECOM repetidor óptico sumergido m; ~ **spring** n WATER manantial sumergido m; ~ **turbine** n HYDRAUL turbina anegada f; ~ **weir** n HYDRAUL vertedero anegado m, vertedero sumergido m

submergence n CHEM sumergencia f, sumersión f, OCEAN inmersión f, sumersión f

submersible[1] adj OCEAN, PETR TECH sumergible

submersible[2] n OCEAN, WATER TRANSP submarino m; ~ **platform** n PETR TECH plataforma sumergible f; ~ **pump** n MINE bomba sumergible f .

submersion n CHEM sumersión f

submicron: ~ **particulate air filter** n SAFE filtro de aire para partículas submicrónicas m

subminiature: ~ **camera** n PHOTO cámara fotográfica

subminiatura *f*; ~ **relay** *n* ELEC ENG relé subminiatura *m*

submission: ~ **identifier** *n* TELECOM identificador de conformidad adjudicación *m*; ~ **time** *n* TELECOM tiempo de confirmación *m*

submultiframe *n* (*SMF*) TELECOM bastidor auxiliar múltiple *m*

submultiple *n* METR submúltiplo *m*

submultiplex *vt* TELECOM submultiplexar, transmitir por submúltiplex

submunitions *n* MILIT submuniciones *f pl*

subnetwork *n* TELECOM red secundaria *f*, subred *f*; ~ **dependent convergence function** *n* (*SNDCF*) TELECOM función de convergencia dependiente de la red secundaria *f*

subnitrate *n* CHEM subnitrato *m*

subnormal *n* GEOM subnormal *f*; ~ **pressure** *n* PETR TECH presión subnormal *f*

subpopulation: ~ **collective dose** *n* POLL dosis colectiva de la subpoblación *f*

subprogram *n* COMP&DP subprograma *m*

subreflector *n* SPACE *communications* subreflector *m*

subroutine *n* COMP&DP subrutina *f*; ~ **call** *n* COMP&DP llamada de subrutina *f*; ~ **library** *n* COMP&DP biblioteca de subrutinas *f*

subsatellite: ~ **point** *n* SPACE punto del subsatélite *m*

subscriber *n* COMP&DP abonado *m*, afiliado *m*, suscriptor *m*, ELEC abonado *m*, afiliado *m*, TELECOM abonado *m*, afiliado *m*, subscriptor *m*, titular de un abono *m*, TV abonado *m*, afiliado *m*; ~ **calling rate** *n* TELECOM promedio de llamadas del abonado *m*, tasa de llamadas del abonado *f*; ~**'s line** *n* TELECOM línea de abonado *f*; ~ **line circuit** *n* (*SLC*) TELECOM circuito de línea de abonado *m*; ~**'s meter** *n* TELECOM contador de abonado *m*; ~ **number** *n* (*SN*) TELECOM número del abonado *m*; ~ **premises network** *n* (*SPN*) TELECOM red de instalación del abonado *f*; ~**'s private meter** *n* TELECOM contador privado de abonado *m*; ~ **service** *n* TELECOM servicio de abonado *m*; ~**'s store** *n* TELECOM ˙registro del abonado *m*; ~ **trunk dialing** *AmE see subscriber trunk dialling BrE*; ~ **trunk dialing access code** *AmE see subscriber trunk dialling access code BrE*; ~ **trunk dialling** *BrE n* TELECOM selección automática interurbana *f*; ~ **trunk dialling access code** *n BrE* TELECOM código de acceso a la selección automática interurbana *m*

subscript *n* COMP&DP, PRINT subíndice *m*

subsea: ~ **completion** *n* PETR TECH completación en el fondo marino *f*, completación submarina *f*, conclusión bajo el mar *f*, terminación submarina *f*; ~ **well** *n* POLL pozo submarino *m*; ~ **wellhead** *n* GAS, PETR TECH, PETROL cabeza de pozo submarina *f*

subsequent: ~ **delivery** *n* PROD entrega posterior *f*

subset *n* COMP&DP juego parcial de caracteres *m*, subconjunto *m*, MATH subconjunto *m*

subshell *n* PHYS *cohetes* subcapa *f*

subside *vi* CONST *ground* asentar, FUELLESS *water* bajar, HYDROL *water* bajar, retirarse, WATER, WATER TRANSP *water* bajar

subsidence *n* CONST *of surface* asiento *m*, *of building, mountain* desplome *m*, GEOL hundimiento del terreno *m*, descenso *m*, asiento *m*, decrecida *f*, subsidencia *f*, HYDROL *of water level* descenso *m*, *due to action of underground streams* decrecida *f*, METEO, MINE subsidencia *f*, PETR TECH hundimiento del terreno *m*,

asiento *m*, subsidencia *f*, descenso *m*, POLL decrecida *f*, subsidencia *f*, descenso *m*, RAIL asiento *m*, desplome *m*

subsident: ~ **basin** *n* GEOL estanque subsidente *m*, PETR TECH cuenca hundida *f*, cuenca subsidente *f*, estanque subsidente *m*

subsoil: ~ **water** *n* COAL, HYDROL, POLL, WATER agua subterránea *f*

subsoiler *n* AGRIC subsolador *m*; ~ **chisel** *n* AGRIC cincel subsolador *m*; ~ **plough with mole drain** *n BrE* AGRIC arado topo *m*; ~ **plow with mole drain** *AmE see subsoiler plough with mole drain BrE*

subsonic: ~ **aircraft** *n* AIR TRANSP avión subsónico *m*; ~ **frequency** *n* ACOUST, ELECTRON, RAD PHYS frecuencia subsónica *f*; ~ **guided missile** *n* MILIT misil guiado subsónico *m*

substage *n* MINE subpiso *m*

substance *n* C&G, CHEM substancia *f*, PAPER, PRINT gramaje *m*

substandard[1] *adj* QUALITY subestándar

substandard[2]: ~ **gage** *AmE*, ~ **gauge** *n BrE* CINEMAT paso menor que el normal *m*

substantive: ~ **dye** *n* COLOUR colorante directo *m*, tinte directo *m*

substation *n* CONST subestación *f*, ELEC *supply network*, ELEC ENG subcentral *f*, subestación *f*, PROD subestación *f*; ~ **for frequency conversion** *n* ELEC, ELEC ENG subestación para la conversión de frecuencia *f*

substituent *n* CHEM substituyente *m*

substitute: ~ **character** *n* (*SUB character*) COMP&DP carácter de sustitución *m*

substitutional: ~ **solid solution** *n* CRYSTALL solución sólida sustitución *f*

substorm *n* GEOPHYS subtormenta *f*

substractive: ~ **primary colors** *AmE*, ~ **primary colours** *BrE adj* PRINT colores primarios sustractivos

substrate *n* COMP&DP substrato *m*, sustrato *m*, METALL sustrato *m*, P&R material de soporte *m*, substrato *m*, sustrato *m*, PHYS substrato *m*, sustrato *m*, PRINT base *f*, soporte *m*, TELECOM substrato *m*, sustrato *m*

substratum *n* GEOL substrato *m*, subsuelo *m*, PETR TECH substrato *m*

substring *n* COMP&DP subcadena *f*, subserie *f*

substructure *n* CONST infraestructura *f*, PETR TECH subestructura *f*

subsulfate *AmE see subsulphate BrE*

subsulphate *n BrE* CHEM subsulfato *m*

subsurface: ~ **conditions** *n pl* PETR TECH condiciones sub-superficiales *f pl*; ~ **contour** *n* GEOL curva subsuperficial *f*, isohipsa *f*, línea de contorno *f*; ~ **current** *n* OCEAN corriente subsuperficial *f*; ~ **erosion** *n* WATER erosión subsuperficial *f*; ~ **flow** *n* HYDROL curso de agua subterráneo *m*, flujo freático *m*; ~ **geologist** *n* GEOL, PETR TECH, PETROL geólogo del subsuelo *m*; ~ **irrigation** *n* AGRIC, HYDROL, WATER irrigación subsuperficial *f*; ~ **zone** *n* OCEAN zona subsuperficial *f*

subsynchronous: ~ **satellite** *n* SPACE satélite subsíncrono *m*

subsystem *n* COMP&DP, SPACE, TELECOM subsistema *m*

subtangent *n* GEOM subtangente *f*

subtask *n* COMP&DP subtarea *f*

subtend *vt* GEOM subtender

subterranean: ~ **propagation** *n* TELECOM propagación subterránea *f*; ~ **river** *n* HYDROL río subterráneo

m; ~ **volcano** *n* GEOPHYS volcán subterráneo *m*;
~ **water** *n* WATER agua subterránea *f*
subtractive: ~ **color printer** *AmE*, ~ **colour printer**
BrE n CINEMAT positivadora sustractiva a color *f*;
~ **method** *n* ELECTRON método substractivo *m*;
~ **primaries** *n pl* CINEMAT, TV colores primarios
sustractivos *m pl*; ~ **process** *n* CINEMAT proceso
sustractivo *m*; ~ **synthesis** *n* PHOTO síntesis sustractiva *f*
subtractor *n* COMP&DP, ELECTRON substractor *m*
subtrahend *n* COMP&DP substraendo *m*
subtropical: ~ **anticyclone** *n* METEO anticiclón subtropical *m*; ~ **calms** *n pl* METEO, OCEAN calmas
subtropicales *f pl*
subtype *n* COMP&DP subtipo *m*
suburban: ~ **traffic** *n* TRANSP tráfico suburbano *m*
subway *n AmE* (*cf underground BrE*) RAIL ferrocarril
subterráneo *m*
succinate *n* CHEM succinato *m*
succinic *adj* CHEM succínico
succinimide *n* CHEM succinimida *f*
succinite *n* MINERAL succinita *f*, ámbar *m*
succinyl *n* CHEM succinilo *m*
succulage *n* AGRIC forraje suculento *m*
suck[1]: ~-**and-blow process** *n* C&G proceso de vacío y
soplo *m*
suck[2] *vt* TEXTIL aspirar
sucker *n* AGRIC chupón *m*, HYDRAUL émbolo *m*, INSTR
pistón *m*, ventosa *f*, MECH ENG chupador *m*, extractor
m, émbolo *m*, PRINT chupón *m*; ~ **rod** *n* FUELLESS
windmill pump árbol de bombeo *m*, MECH ENG *of
suction-pump* varilla del pistón *f*
sucrase *n* CHEM, FOOD invertasa *f*
sucrate *n* CHEM sucrato *m*
suction *n* MECH, MECH ENG aspiración *f*, succión *f*,
REFRIG, TEXTIL aspiración *f*; ~ **accumulator** *n*
REFRIG acumulador de aspiración *m*, acumulador
de succión *m*; ~-**and-filter installation** *n* SAFE
instalación de succión y filtros *f*; ~ **box** *n* MECH ENG
caja de succión *f*, PAPER caja aspirante *f*; ~ **box cover**
n PAPER recubrimiento de la caja aspirante *m*;
~ **carburetor** *AmE*, ~ **carburettor** *n BrE* AUTO, VEH
carburador de succión *m*; ~ **chamber** *n* TRANSP
cámara de succión *f*; ~ **circuit** *n* ELEC circuito de
succión *m*; ~ **couch press** *n* PAPER prensa a manchón
aspirante *f*; ~ **couch roll** *n* PAPER rodillo manchón
aspirante *m*; ~ **cover** *n* REFRIG recubrimiento de
aspiración *m*; ~ **dewatering** *n* TEXTIL desecación por
aspiración *f*; ~ **dredge** *n* OCEAN draga de succión *f*,
WATER draga aspirante *f*, draga de succión *f*;
~ **dredger** *n* WATER TRANSP draga de succión *f*;
~ **fan** *n* MECH ENG ventilador aspirante *m*;
~ **feeding** *n* C&G alimentación por succión *f*;
~ **filter** *n* PROD filtro por aspiración *m*, filtro por
succión *m*, WATER filtro de aspiración *m*, filtro de
succión *m*; ~ **filtration** *n* CHEM TECH filtración por
aspiración *f*; ~ **gage** *AmE see suction gauge BrE*;
~ **gas producer** *n* PROD gasógeno de succión *m*;
~ **gauge** *n BrE* REFRIG manómetro de aspiración *m*;
~ **head** *n* HYDRAUL, WATER altura manométrica de
aspiración *f*; ~ **hopper dredger** *n* WATER TRANSP
draga de succión con cántara *f*; ~ **hose** *n* WATER
manguera de succión *f*; ~ **hydroextraction** *n* TEXTIL
hidroextracción por aspiración *f*; ~ **lift** *n* WATER
altura de succión *f*; ~ **line** *n* PROD tubería de
aspiración *f*, tubería de succión *f*; ~-**line**

accumulator *n* REFRIG acumulador para el tubo de
aspiración *m*; ~ **machine** *n* C&G máquina de succión
f; ~ **mold** *AmE*, ~ **mould** *BrE n* C&G molde de
succión *m*; ~ **mount** *n* CINEMAT montura por succión
f; ~ **pickup transfer** *n* PAPER toma de la hoja por
aspiración *f*; ~ **pipe** *n* HYDROL, WATER, WATER
TRANSP *dredging* tubería de aspiración *f*; ~ **pit** *n*
PETR TECH barba de succión *f*, tanque de succión *m*;
~ **porosimeter** *n* PAPER porosímetro de aspiración *m*;
~ **porosity tester** *n* PAPER medidor de porosidad
mediante aspiración *m*; ~ **port** *n* PROD orificio de
aspiración *m*, orificio de succión *m*; ~ **pump** *n* FOOD
bomba aspirante *f*, bomba de succión *f*, HYDRAUL
bomba aspirante *f*, bomba de aspiración *f*, MECH ENG
bomba aspirante *f*, TEXTIL bomba de aspiración *f*,
WATER bomba aspirante *f*, bomba de aspiración *f*;
~ **ram** *n* PROD ariete aspirador *m*; ~ **roll** *n* PAPER
cilindro aspirante *m*; ~ **roll felt** *n* PAPER fieltro del
cilindro aspirante *m*; ~ **strainer** *n* PROD filtro rotativo
por succión *m*, REFRIG filtro de aspiración *m*;
~-**suspended vehicle** *n* TRANSP vehículo suspendido
por aspiración *m*; ~ **tank** *n* HYDRAUL depósito de
aspiración *m*; ~ **temperature** *n* REFRIG temperatura
de aspiración *f*; ~-**throttling valve** *n* AUTO válvula de
estrangulamiento de la aspiración *f*, válvula de
regulación de la aspiración *f*; ~ **tube** *n* HYDRAUL
tubería de descarga *f*, tubo de aspiración *m*, tubo de
exhaustación *m*; ~-**type governor** *n* AUTO regulador
tipo succión *m*; ~-**type valve** *n* AUTO, HYDRAUL, REFRIG
válvula de aspiración *f*
sud: ~-**channel** *n* MECH ENG *in machine-tool table*
canal de agua jabonosa *m*
sudan: ~ **grass** *n* AGRIC pasto sudán *m*
sudden: ~ **contraction of cross section** *n* HYDRAUL
contracción repentina de la sección transversal *f*;
~ **enlargement of cross section** *n* HYDRAUL estiramiento repentino de la sección transversal *m*; ~-**grip
rotary bench vice** *n BrE* MECH ENG tornillo rotatorio
de banco de sujeción instantánea *m*; ~-**grip rotary
bench vise** *AmE see sudden-grip rotary bench vice
BrE*; ~ **short-circuit test** *n* ELEC prueba de cortocircuito repentina *f*; ~ **storm commencement** *n*
(*SSC*) SPACE inicio repentino de tormenta *m*
suffix *n* COMP&DP sufijo *m*; ~ **notation** *n* COMP&DP
notación por sufijos *f*
sugar *n* AGRIC, C&G, CHEM, FOOD azúcar *m*; ~ **dye** *n*
COLOUR teñido al azúcar *m*; ~ **industry** *n* FOOD
industria azucarera *f*; ~ **nucleus** *n* FOOD núcleo del
azúcar *m*
suitcase: ~ **board** *n* PAPER cartón para maletas *m*
suite *n* COMP&DP serie *f*, TELECOM conjunto *m*, fila de
bastidores *f*, serie *f*; ~ **of switchboards** *n* TELECOM
fila de paneles conmutadores *f*
suiting *n* TEXTIL tela para trajes *f*
sulf- *AmE see sulph- BrE*
sullage *n* PROD *founding* nata de fundición *f*, suciedad
f; ~ **head** *n* PROD mazarota *f*; ~ **piece** *n* PROD
mazarota *f*
sulph- *pref BrE* CHEM sulf-
sulpha[1]: ~-**free** *adj BrE* CHEM sin sulfamida
sulpha[2]: ~ **drug** *n BrE* CHEM medicamento sulfamídico *m*, sulfamida *f*
sulphafurazole *n BrE* CHEM sulfafurazol *m*
sulphamate *n BrE* CHEM sulfamato *m*
sulphamic[1] *adj BrE* CHEM sulfámico

sulphamic^2: ~ **acid** n BrE CHEM, DETERG ácido sulfámico m
sulphamide n BrE CHEM sulfamida f
sulphanilamide n BrE CHEM sulfanilamida f
sulphanilate n BrE CHEM sulfanilato m
sulphanilic adj BrE CHEM sulfanílico
sulphapyridine n BrE CHEM sulfapiridina f
sulpharsenic adj BrE CHEM sulfarsénico
sulpharsenide n BrE CHEM sulfarsenido m, sulfarseniuro m
sulphate n BrE CHEM sulfato m, POLL sulfato m, tetraoxosulfato VI m; ~ **attack** n BrE CONST ataque de sulfato m; ~ **pulp** n BrE PAPER pulpa al sulfato f
sulphated: ~ **oil** n BrE DETERG aceite sulfatado m
sulphathiazole n BrE CHEM sulfatiazol m
sulphatide n BrE CHEM sulfatida f
sulphation n BrE CHEM, DETERG sulfatación f
sulphhydrate n BrE CHEM sulfhidrato m
sulphhydric adj BrE CHEM sulfhídrico
sulphide n BrE CHEM sulfuro m; ~ **ore** n BrE MINE mineral con sulfuros m; ~ **soil** n BrE COAL suelo sulfuroso m; ~ **toning** n BrE PHOTO viraje con sulfuros m
sulphinic adj BrE CHEM sulfínico
sulphinyl n BrE CHEM sulfinilo m
sulphite n BrE CHEM sulfito m; ~ **pulp** n BrE PAPER pulpa al sulfito f
sulphochlorination n BrE CHEM, DETERG sulfocloración f
sulpholane n BrE CHEM, PETR TECH sulfolano m
sulpholene n BrE CHEM, PETR TECH sulfoleno m
sulphonamide n BrE CHEM sulfonamida f
sulphonate n BrE CHEM sulfonato m
sulphonated adj BrE CHEM sulfonado
sulphonation n BrE CHEM, DETERG sulfonación f
sulphone n BrE CHEM, DETERG sulfona f
sulphonic adj BrE CHEM sulfónico
sulphonium n BrE CHEM sulfonio m
sulphonyl n BrE CHEM sulfonilo m
sulphosalicylic adj BrE CHEM sulfosalicílico
sulphur n BrE (S) CHEM, METALL, P&R, PETR TECH azufre m, sulfuro m (S); ~ **chloride** n BrE CHEM cloruro de azufre m; ~ **compound** n BrE GAS compuesto de azufre m; ~ **content** n BrE PETR TECH contenido de azufre m; ~ **cycle** n BrE POLL ciclo del azufre m; ~ **dioxide** n BrE CHEM anhídrido sulfuroso m, dióxido de azufre m, óxido de azufre IV m, CHEM TECH dióxido de azufre m, POLL dióxido de azufre m, dióxido sulfúrico m, óxido de azufre IV m; ~ **dioxide reduction** n BrE POLL reducción de contenido de dióxido de azufre f, reducción por dióxido de azufre f; ~**-ore** n BrE MINE mineral de azufre m; ~ **oxide** n BrE CHEM, POLL óxido de azufre m; ~ **trioxide** n BrE CHEM anhídrido sulfúrico m, trióxido de azufre m, óxido de azufre VI m, POLL anhídrido sulfúrico m, óxido de azufre VI m
sulphuration n BrE CHEM sulfuración f
sulphuric^1 adj BrE CHEM sulfúrico
sulphuric^2: ~ **acid** n BrE CHEM, DETERG ácido sulfúrico m, ácido vitriólico m, POLL tetraoxosulfato VI de hidrógeno m, ácido sulfúrico m, ácido vitriólico m; ~ **anhydride** n BrE CHEM anhídrido sulfúrico m, óxido de azufre VI m, POLL anhídrido sulfúrico m, trióxido de azufre m, óxido de azufre VI m
sulphuring n BrE C&G azufrado m
sulphurization n BrE CHEM sulfurización f

sulphurize vt BrE CHEM sulfurizar
sulphurous^1 adj BrE CHEM sulfuroso
sulphurous^2: ~ **acid** n BrE CHEM, POLL trioxosulfato IV de hidrógeno m, ácido sulfuroso m; ~ **combustible** n BrE POLL combustible con alto contenido de azufre m, combustible sulfuroso m; ~ **residue** n BrE GAS residuo sulfurado m
sulphuryl n BrE CHEM sulfurilo m
sultam n CHEM sultam m
sultone n CHEM sultona f
sumatrol n CHEM sumatrol m
summary: ~ **punch** n COMP&DP perforadora de resúmenes f, perforadora sumaria f; ~ **punching** n COMP&DP perforación de resúmenes f, perforación recapitulativa f; ~ **report** n PROD informe de conclusiones m, informe de resumen m
summation: ~ **hydrograph** n FUELLESS suma hidrográfica f
summer n CONST building jácena f, viga maestra f; ~ **beam** n CONST building jácena f, viga maestra f; ~ **calving** n AGRIC parición de vacas en verano f, paridera de verano f; ~ **fallow** n AGRIC barbecho de verano m; ~ **load waterline** n WATER TRANSP flotación de verano f, línea de carga de verano f; ~ **tree** n CONST traverso de viga maestra m
summit: ~ **canal** n WATER navigation nivel cumbre de un canal m
sump n LAB desagüe m, sumidero m, MINE pileta f (AmL), PETR TECH sumidero m, PROD colector m, colector de lubricante m, sumidero m, VEH colector de lubricante m, cárter inferior m, WATER sumidero m; ~ **guard** n VEH protector del cárter m; ~ **man** n CONST sumidero m; ~ **pump** n WATER bomba de sentina f, bomba de sumidero f; ~ **shaft** n MINE fondo del pozo m (Esp), pozo de franqueo m (AmL); ~**-type lubrication** n VEH lubricación por cárter de aceite f
sun: ~**-dried brick** n C&G ladrillo de milpa m, CONST ladrillo de milpa m, ladrillo secado al sol m; ~ **gear** n AUTO engranaje central m, engranaje planetario m; ~ **gear control plate** n AUTO plato de control de engranaje planetario m; ~ **gear lock-out tooth** n AUTO diente de bloqueo del engranaje planetario m; ~ **gear shift collar** n AUTO collar de desplazamiento del engranaje planetario m; ~ **interference** n SPACE interferencia solar f; ~ **sensor** n GEOPHYS sensor solar m; ~ **spectacles** n pl INSTR, OPT anteojos de sol m pl (AmL), gafas de sol f pl (Esp); ~**-synchronous orbit** n SPACE órbita solar síncrona f, órbita síncronosolar f; ~**-synchronous satellite** n SPACE satélite solar síncrona m, satélite síncronosolar m; ~ **tracker** n GEOPHYS rastreador solar m; ~ **visor** n BrE AUTO, VEH accessory parasol m (Esp), visera contra el sol f (AmL); ~ **vizor** AmE see sun visor BrE
sunfast adj COLOUR resistente al sol
S-universal: ~ **access** n TELECOM acceso universal S m; ~ **interface** n TELECOM interconexión universal S f; ~ **interface card** n TELECOM tarjeta de interconexión universal S f
sunk^1: ~ **into the wall** adj CONST embutido en la pared, empotrado en la pared; ~ **up** adj CINEMAT hundido
sunk^2: ~ **key** n MECH ENG chaveta encastrada f, chaveta hundida f; ~ **mount** n PHOTO montaje hundido m, of camera lens montaje encastrado m; ~ **setting** n PHOTO soporte encastrado m; ~ **well** n COAL pozo horadado m
sunken: ~ **rail** n RAIL carril al ras del pavimento m;

~ road n CONST carretera en desmonte f; **~ track** n RAIL vía al ras del pavimento f

sunlight n SPACE luz solar f; **~ resistance** n P&R resistencia a la luz solar f

sunspot n GEOPHYS mancha solar f; **~ cycle** n GEOPHYS ciclo de mancha solar m

sunstone n MINERAL oligoclasa f, piedra de sol f

super¹: **~-saturated** adj CHEM, PHYS, POLL sobresaturado

super² n AmE PRINT gasa para encuadernar f; **~ blanking pulse** n TV superimpulso de borrado m; **~ clean coal** n COAL carbón ultra limpio m; **~-high frequency** n (SHF) ELECTRON, SPACE, TELECOM frecuencia superalta f (FSA); **~-refraction** n SPACE superrefracción f, ultrarrefracción f

super³ vt CINEMAT superponer

supercalender n PACK machine to finish paper satinadora f, PAPER supercalandra f

supercalendered: **~ paper** n PAPER papel satinado m

supercalenderizing n PAPER supercalandrado m

supercarbonate n CHEM supercarbonato m

supercavitating: **~ propeller** n TRANSP hélice supercavitante f

supercharge n AIR TRANSP sobrealimentado m

supercharger n AUTO sobrealimentador m, MECH compresor para la sobrealimentación m, sobrealimentador m

supercharging n AUTO sobrealimentación f, RAIL sobrecarga f

superchilling n REFRIG refrigeración crítica f, refrigeración límite f

supercomputer n COMP&DP supercomputador m (AmL), supercomputadora f (AmL) superordenador m (Esp)

supercomputing n COMP&DP supercomputación f (AmL), superinformática f (Esp)

superconducting: **~ coil** n TRANSP bobina superconductora f; **~ device** n ELECTRON aparato superconductor m; **~ magnet** n PART PHYS imán superconductor m, TRANSP electroimán de arrollamientos superconductores m; **~ magnet levitation** n ELEC, PHYS, TRANSP levitación por electroimán superconductor f; **~ memory** n COMP&DP memoria superconducente f

superconductivity n COMP&DP superconductividad f, ELEC hiperconductividad f, superconductividad f, supraconductividad f, ELECTRON, PHYS superconductividad f

superconductor n ELEC hiperconductor m, superconductor m, supraconductor m, ELECTRON, PHYS, TELECOM superconductor m; **~ cable** n TELECOM cable superconductor m; **~ line** n TELECOM línea hiperconductora f, línea superconductora f

supercooled¹ adj PHYS superenfriado

supercooled²: **~ cloud** n METEO nube subfundida f; **~ water** n HYDROL agua subfundida f

supercooling n METALL sobrefusión f, PHYS superfrío m

supercritical¹ adj NUCL supercrítico

supercritical²: **~ reaction** n RAD PHYS reacción supercrítica f

superelevation n CONST sobreelevación f; **~ of the outer rail** n TRANSP peralte del rail exterior m; **~ of track** n RAIL peralte m

superfinishing: **~ honing stone** n MECH ENG piedra de pulir de super acabado f; **~ stone** n MECH ENG piedra de superacabado f

superfluid n PHYS superfluido m

superfluidity n PHYS superfluidez f

supergroup n TELECOM grupo secundario m, supergrupo m

superheat¹ n REFRIG recalentamiento m; **~ assembly** n NUCL conjunto de recalentado m

superheat² vt HEAT, HEAT ENG sobrecalentar

superheated: **~ steam** n HEAT, HEAT ENG vapor sobrecalentado m, PHYS vapor supercalentado m

superheater n HEAT, HEAT ENG sobrecalentador m, PROD recalentador m, sobrecalentador m; **~ damper** n PROD registro del sobrecalentador m; **~ element** n PROD elemento del recalentador m; **~ header** n PROD colector del recalentador m; **~ heating surface** n PROD superficie de caldeo del recalentador f; **~ manifold** n PROD colector del recalentador m; **~ pipe** n PROD tubo recalentador m; **~ unit** n PROD elemento sobrecalentador m

superheating n CHEM recalentamiento m, sobrecalefacción f, sobrecalentamiento m, METALL recalentamiento m, PHYS supercalentamiento m, PROD recalentamiento m, sobrecalentamiento m

superheavy: **~ nucleus** n PHYS núcleo superpesado m

superhigh: **~ cube** n (SHC) TRANSP hipercubo m; **~-speed traffic** n TRANSP tráfico de alta velocidad m

superimpose vt CINEMAT, PHOTO, TV sobreponer

superimposed: **~ interference** n TV interferencia superpuesta f

superinsulation n REFRIG aislamiento reforzado m

superlattice n CRYSTALL superred f

superluminescence n OPT, TELECOM superluminiscencia f

superluminescent: **~ diode** n OPT (SRD) diodo superluminiscente m, diodo superradiante m, TELECOM (SLD) diodo superluminiscente m; **~ LED** n TELECOM LED superluminiscente m

supermini n COMP&DP supermini m

supernatant adj CHEM sobrenadante

supernova n SPACE supernova f

superoxygenate vt CHEM superoxigenar

superphosphate n CHEM fosfato ácido m, superfosfato m; **~ of lime** n CHEM superfosfato de cal m

superplasticizer n CONST superplastificante m

superproton: **~ synchroton** n (SPF) PART PHYS super sincrotrón de protones m

superradiance n OPT, TELECOM superradiancia f

superradiant: **~ diode** n (SRD) OPT diodo superluminiscente m, diodo superradiante m, TELECOM diodo superradiante m

supersalt n CHEM supersal f

supersaturate vt CHEM, PHYS sobresaturar

supersaturated: **~ air** n METEO aire sobresaturado m; **~ solution** n CHEM solución sobresaturada f

supersaturation n CHEM sobresaturación f

superscript n COMP&DP exponente m, superíndice m, PRINT exponente m, letra volada f

supersonic¹ adj ACOUST supersónico

supersonic²: **~ frequency** n RAD PHYS frecuencia supersónica f; **~ speed** n PHYS velocidad supersónica f; **~ transport aircraft** n (SST) AIR TRANSP avión de transporte supersónico m

superstrings n pl PHYS supercadenas f pl

superstructure n CONST, CRYSTALL, WATER TRANSP superestructura f

supersymmetrical: **~ particle** n RAD PHYS partícula supersimétrica f

supersync: ~ **signal** *n* TV señal supersíncrona *f*
supertanker *n* TRANSP superpetrolero *m*
supertonic *n* ACOUST supertónica *f*
supertype *n* PRINT supertipo *m*
supervisor *n* COMP&DP, MAR POLL, SAFE supervisor *m*;
~ **call** *n* (*SVC*) COMP&DP llamada al supervisor *f*
supervisory: ~ **aid** *n* TELECOM ayuda supervisora *f*;
~ **announcement** *n* TELECOM anuncio supervisor *m*,
aviso supervisor *m*; ~ **message** *n* TELECOM mensaje
supervisor *m*; ~ **process** *n* PROD proceso supervisor
m; ~ **timer** *n* TELECOM temporizador supervisor *m*;
~ **tone** *n* TELECOM tono supervisor *m*
supplement: ~ **to refrigeration** *n* REFRIG complemento a la refrigeración *m*
supplementary: ~ **feeding** *n* AGRIC alimentación
suplementaria *f*; ~ **lens** *n* CINEMAT lente auxiliar *f*,
INSTR lente adicional *f*, PHOTO, TV lente auxiliar *f*;
~ **purification** *n* POLL depuración adicional *f*, purificación adicional *f*, purificación suplementaria *f*;
~ **service** *n* TELECOM servicio suplementario *m*
supplied: ~-**air breathing apparatus** *n* SAFE aparato
para respirar con inyección de aire *m*
supplier *n* COMP&DP distribuidor *m*, QUALITY proveedor *m*
supply[1] *n* ELEC *power*, FUELLESS abastecimiento *m*, GAS
suministro *m*, GEOL abastecimiento *m*, aporte *m*,
suministro *m*, SPACE abastecimiento *m*, WATER abastecimiento *m*, aprovisionamiento *m*, suministro *m*,
WATER TRANSP abastecimiento *m*; ~ **aircraft** *n* AIR
TRANSP, MILIT avión de aprovisionamiento *m*; ~ **base**
n PETR TECH base de aprovisionamiento *f*; ~ **boat** *n*
PETR TECH barco de abastecimiento *m*, barco de
suministro *m*, embarcación de abastecimiento *f*, WA-
TER TRANSP barco de abastecimiento *m*; ~ **cable** *n*
PROD cable de alimentación *m*; ~ **current** *n* ELEC ENG
corriente de alimentación *f*, corriente de suministro *f*;
~ **line** *n* WATER conducto de abastecimiento *m*; ~ **line
filter** *n* P&R filtro de línea de abastecimiento *m*;
~ **main** *n* ELEC ENG cable de distribución *m*;
~ **network** *n* ELEC red de distribución *f*; ~ **pipe** *n*
CONST tubería de abastecimiento *f*; ~ **pump** *n* MAR
POLL, WATER bomba de abastecimiento *f*; ~ **reel** *n*
CINEMAT carrete proveedor *m*, COMP&DP carrete de
entrega *m*, TV carrete alimentador *m*; ~ **roll** *n* TV
carrete de alimentación *m*; ~ **service** *n* ELEC *to
consumer* servicio de abastecimiento *m*, servicio de
suministro *m*; ~ **spool** *n* CINEMAT carrete proveedor
m; ~ **tank** *n* AIR TRANSP, AUTO depósito de suministro
m; ~ **vessel** *n* PETR TECH nave de abastecimiento *f*,
nave de suministro *f*, WATER TRANSP buque de
suministro *m*; ~ **voltage** *n* PROD tensión de alimentación *f*, voltaje de alimentación *m*
supply[2] *vt* ELEC *power*, FUELLESS, GEOL abastecer, PHYS
suministrar, SPACE, WATER, WATER TRANSP abastecer;
~ **with provisions** *vt* WATER TRANSP *ship* avituallar,
proveer de víveres, vituallar
supplying *n* PROD aprovisionamiento *m*, suministro *m*
support[1] *n* COMP&DP aceptación *f*, admisión *f*, apoyo
m, asistencia *f*, soporte *m*, CONST *of arch* pie *m*,
soporte *m*, *act* apoyo *m*, PHOTO soporte de película *m*;
~ **arm** *n* INSTR soportabrazos *m*; ~ **boat** *n* WATER
TRANSP embarcación de apoyo *f*; ~ **capacity** *n* PETR
TECH capacidad de apoyo *f*, capacidad de soporte *f*;
~ **pier** *n* MINE pilar de apoyo *m*, pilar de sustentación
m; ~ **pillar** *n* MECH ENG *diecasting die* columna de
soporte *f*, MINE pilar de apoyo *m*, pilar de susten-

tación *m*; ~ **pillar bush** *n* MECH ENG *injection mould*
casquillo de la columna de apoyo *m*; ~ **plate** *n* SPACE
chapa de montaje *f*; ~ **program** *n* COMP&DP programa de apoyo *m*, programa de soporte *m*; ~ **vessel**
n PETR TECH barco de apoyo *m*, nave de apoyo *f*,
WATER TRANSP buque de apoyo *m*, nave de apoyo *f*
support[2] *vt* COMP&DP aceptar, admitir, apoyar, asistir,
soportar, CONST soportar, MECH ENG apoyar, dar
sustento, demostrar, mantener, probar, sostener,
soportar
supported[1] *adj* PROD soportado
supported[2]: ~ **beam** *n* CONST viga apoyada *f*
supporting *n* CONST apoyo *m*, sostén *m*; ~ **fork** *n* MINE
llave de retenida *f*; ~ **pillar** *n* MINE pilar de apoyo *m*,
pilar de sustentación *m*; ~ **pylon** *n* ELEC *network* torre
de soporte *f*; ~ **rope** *n* CONST cuerda de sostén *f*;
~ **wall** *n* CONST pared de soporte *f*
suppress *vt* COMP&DP suprimir
suppressed: ~-**carrier system** *n* TV sistema de
portadora suprimida *m*; ~-**carrier transmission** *n*
ELECTRON transmisión por portadora suprimida *f*;
~-**carrier transmitter** *n* ELECTRON transmisor con
portadora suprimida *m*
suppression *n* COMP&DP, ELEC ENG supresión *f*;
~ **device** *n* PROD dispositivo de supresión *m*;
~ **factor** *n* SPACE factor de supresión *m*; ~ **grid** *n*
ELEC ENG rejilla supresora *f*
suppressor *n* ELEC ENG, ELECTRON supresor *m*, PROD
amortiguador *m*, eliminador *m*, supresor *m*, TELE-
COM supresor *m*; ~ **capacitor** *n* ELEC capacitor
supresor *m*, condensador supresor *m*; ~ **choke** *n*
ELEC amortiguador *m*; ~ **grid** *n* ELECTRON rejilla
supresora *f*
supratidal: ~ **deposits** *n* GEOL depósitos supramarea-
les *m pl*
surcharge *n* HYDROL sobrecarga *f*; ~ **load** *n* COAL
sobrecarga *f*
surcharged *adj* HYDROL sobrecargado
surd *n* MATH cantidad irracional *f*
surf[1] *n* OCEAN reventazón *f*
surf[2]: ~ **the net** *vi* COMP&DP correr tabla por la red,
surfear
surface[1] *adj* MINE del exterior, superficial; ~-**active** *adj*
CHEM tensioactivo, tensoactivo
surface[2] *n* COAL, GEOM, PHYS superficie *f*; ~ **acoustic
wave** *n* (*SAW*) ACOUST, ELECTRON, PHYS, TELECOM,
WAVE PHYS onda acústica de superficie *f* (*OAS*);
~ **acoustic wave device** *n* (*SAW device*) ELECTRON,
TELECOM dispositivo de onda acústica de superficie *m*
(*dispositivo de OAS, dispositivo OAS*); ~-**active agent**
n CHEM agente tensoactivo *m*, surfactante *m*, COAL
agente tensoactivo *m*, DETERG agente tensoactivo *m*,
surfactante *m*, FOOD agente tensoactivo *m*, MAR POLL
agente superficiactivo *m*, agente surfactante *m*,
agente tensoactivo *m*, P&R agente superficiactivo *m*,
agente tensoactivo *m*, agente surfactante *m*, POLL
agente tensoactivo *m*, surfactante *m*; ~ **air supply** *n*
OCEAN narguile *m*; ~ **application** *n* PAPER tratamiento superficial *m*; ~ **area** *n* POLL superficie *f*,
área superficial *f*; ~ **auger** *n* MINE cuchara de exterior
f; ~ **bonding strength** *n* PAPER resistencia al arrancado *f*, resistencia superficial *f*; ~ **boundary layer** *n*
METEO capa límite superficial *f*; ~ **boundary level** *n*
METEO nivel límite superficial *m*; ~ **burnishing facet**
n ACOUST faceta de superficie de bruñido *f*; ~ **burst** *n*
MILIT explosión superficial *f*; ~ **channel** *n* ELECTRON

canal de superficie *m*; ~ **charge** *n* ELEC, PHYS carga superficial *f*; ~ **charge density** *n* ELEC, PHYS, RAD PHYS densidad de carga superficial *f*, densidad superficial de carga *f*; ~ **color** *AmE see surface colour BrE*; ~ **coloring** *AmE see surface colouring BrE*; ~ **colour** *BrE n* COLOUR colorante de superficie *m*; ~ **colouring** *n BrE* PAPER coloreado en la superficie *m*; ~ **condenser** *n* PROD *steam* condensador de superficie *m*; ~ **conductance** *n* HEAT ENG conductancia de superficie *f*; ~ **connection** *n* TELECOM conexión de superficie *f*; ~ **of contact** *n* MECH ENG superficie de contacto *f*; ~ **conveyance** *n* MINE transporte a cielo abierto *m*; ~ **cooling** *n* REFRIG enfriamiento mediante superficie fría *m*; ~ **crack** *n* PROD *casting, founding* fisura *f*; ~ **current** *n* TELECOM, WATER TRANSP corriente superficial *f*; ~ **cut** *n* MINE rafadura a cielo abierto *f*, roza a cielo abierto *f*; ~ **defect** *n* QUALITY imperfección de superficie *f*; ~ **dehumidifier** *n* REFRIG deshumidificador de superficie *m*; ~ **demand lifeline** *n* OCEAN narguile *m*; ~ **demarcation** *n* CONST delimitación de un terreno *f*; ~ **density** *n* ELEC ENG densidad superficial *f*; ~ **development** *n* PHOTO revelado superficial *m*; ~ **discontinuities** *n pl* MECH ENG irregularidades de la superficie *f pl*; ~ **dressing** *n* CONST acabado de superficie *m*; ~ **drive** *n* MINE galería a cielo abierto *f*; ~-**drive reel** *n* PAPER bobina accionada en la superficie *f*; ~ **earthing connection** *n BrE* (*cf surface grounding connection AmE*) ELEC conexión de puesta a tierra superficial *f*; ~ **effect ship** *n* (*SES*) WATER TRANSP buque de sustentación hidrodinámica *m*; ~-**effect vehicle** *n* (*SEV*) TRANSP vehículo de efecto en superficie *m*; ~ **electron microscope** *n* (*SEM*) INSTR microscopio de exploración electrónica *m*, microscopio electrónico de exploración *m*; ~-**emitting electroluminescent diode** *n* ELECTRON, OPT, TELECOM diodo electroluminiscente de emisión superficial *m*; ~-**emitting light-emitting diode** *n* ELECTRON, OPT, TELECOM diodo electroluminiscente de emisión superficial *m*; ~ **energy** *n* PHYS energía superficial *f*; ~ **equipment** *n* MINE equipo de superficie *m*; ~ **erosion** *n* HYDROL erosión superficial *f*; ~ **finish** *n* PAPER acabado de la superficie *m*; ~-**finish microscope** *n* INSTR microscopio de asperezas superficiales *m*; ~ **float** *n* OCEAN flotador *m*, WATER TRANSP boya de superficie *f*; ~ **gage** *AmE*, ~ **gauge** *BrE n* MECH calibre de superficies *m*; ~ **geometry meter** *AmE*, ~ **geometry metre** *BrE n* METR metro de geometría de superficie *m*; ~ **grinder** *n* MECH amoladora de superficie *f*, MECH ENG amoladora de superficie *f*, esmeriladora *f*, rectificadora de superficies planas *f*; ~ **grinding** *n* MECH ENG esmerilado de superficies planas *m*, rectificación de superficies planas *m*; ~-**grinding machine** *n* MECH ENG rectificadora de superficies exteriores *f*; ~ **grounding connection** *n AmE* (*cf surface earthing connection AmE*) ELEC conexión de puesta a tierra superficial *f*; ~ **hardening** *n* METALL endurecimiento superficial *m*; ~ **hardness** *n* MECH ENG dureza de la superficie *f*; ~ **induction** *n* TV inducción del ruido de superficie *f*; ~ **integral** *n* PHYS integral de superficie *f*; ~ **layer** *n* MAR POLL capa de superficie *f*, capa superficial *f*, OCEAN capa superficial *f*; ~-**measuring instrument** *n* METR instrumento de medida de superficie *m*; ~ **milling** *n* MECH ENG fresado de superficies *m*; ~ **milling machine** *n* MECH ENG fresadora plana *f*;

~ **mirror** *n* INSTR espejo superficial *m*; ~-**mounted component** *n* (*SMC*) ELECTRON componente instalado en superficie *m*, TELECOM componente de montaje superficial *m*; ~-**mounted enclosure** *n* PROD cerramiento en superficie *m*; ~-**mounted socket** *n* ELEC enchufe hembra de montaje exterior *m*, enchufe hembra sobresaliente *m*; ~ **mounting** *n* COMP&DP montaje de superficie *m*, montura en superficie *f*, ELEC montaje de superficie *m*, montaje exterior *m*, ELECTRON instalación en superficie *f*; ~ **noise** *n* ACOUST, ELECTRON ruido de superficie *m*; ~-**piercing craft** *n* PETR TECH, PETROL buque perforador desde superficie *m*; ~ **planer** *n* MECH limadora *f*, MECH ENG desbastadora *f*, limadora *f*; ~ **planing** *n* MECH ENG cepillado *m*; ~ **planing machine** *n BrE* (*cf shaping planer AmE*) MECH ENG cepilladora *f*; ~ **plate** *n* MECH mármol *m*, MECH ENG, METR mármol de ajustador *m*, mármol de trazado *m*; ~ **power** *n* GAS potencia de superficie *f*; ~ **preparation** *n* CONST preparación de superficie *f*; ~ **pressure chart** *n* METEO mapa de presión de superficie *m*; ~ **protection** *n* COATINGS protección de la superficie *f*, protección superficial *f*; ~ **protection film** *n* PACK película protectora de la superficie *f*; ~ **protection tape** *n* PACK cinta protectora de la superficie *f*; ~ **resistance** *n* COAL, HEAT ENG resistencia de superficie *f*; ~ **resistivity** *n* ELEC ENG resistividad superficial *f*; ~ **of revolution** *n* GEOM superficie de revolución *f*; ~ **roughness** *n* CONST rugosidad de superficie *f*, MECH aspereza superficial *f*, irregularidad superficial *f*, rugosidad de superficie *f*, MECH ENG aspereza superficial *f*, PRINT rugosidad de superficie *f*; ~ **roughness standard** *n* METR estándar de aspereza superficial *m*; ~ **rust** *n* CONST óxido superficial *m*; ~ **sander** *n* MECH ENG arenadora *f*, lijadora *f*, pulidora *f*; ~ **search radar** *n* WATER TRANSP radar de exploración en superficie *m*; ~-**sized paper** *n* PAPER papel con encolado superficial *m*; ~ **sizing** *n* PAPER encolado superficial *m*; ~ **socket** *n* ELEC enchufe hembra superficial *m*; ~ **speed** *n* WATER TRANSP *submarines* velocidad en emersión *f*; ~-**speed indicator** *n* MECH ENG indicador de la velocidad superficial *m*; ~ **storage** *n* HYDROL depósitos en superficie *m pl*; ~ **strength** *n* PRINT resistencia de la superficie *f*; ~ **temperature limits** *n pl* SAFE límites de temperatura en superficie *m pl*; ~ **tension** *n* COAL, CONST, P&R, PHYS tensión superficial *f*; ~ **tension meter** *n* LAB tensiómetro *m*; ~-**tension modifier** *n* MAR POLL modificador de la tensión interfacial *m*; ~ **tension tank** *n* SPACE tanque de tensión superficial *m*; ~ **texture** *n* MECH ENG textura superficial *f*; ~ **texture measurement** *n* MECH ENG medición de la textura superficial *f*; ~-**to-air missile** *n* (*SAM*) MILIT misil de tierra a aire *m*, misil tierra-aire *m*; ~-**to-surface missile** *n* (*SSM*) SPACE misil superficie-superficie *m* (*SSM*); ~-**to-underwater missile** *n* MILIT misil desde la superficie a un blanco submarino *m*; ~ **treatment** *n* C&G tratamiento de la superficie *m*; ~ **ventilating fan** *n* MINE ventilador de superficie *m*; ~ **ventilation chimney** *n* MINE chimenea de ventilación de superficie *f*; ~ **ventilation duct** *n* MINE conducto de ventilación de superficie *m*; ~ **water** *n* COAL, CONST, HYDROL, WATER agua superficial *f*; ~ **water erosion** *n* COAL erosión por agua de superficie *f*; ~ **water load** *n* HYDROL volumen de agua superficial *m*; ~-**water management** *n* WATER administración de las aguas superficiales *f*; ~ **waters** *n pl* HYDROL, POLL aguas pluviales *f pl*; ~ **wave** *n* ACOUST onda superficial *f*, GEOPHYS onda de superficie *f*, OCEAN ola de superficie *f*, OPT onda superficial *f*; ~ **wind** *n* METEO viento de superficie *m*; ~ **worker** *n* MINE obrero que trabaja a cielo abierto *m*, obrero que trabaja en superficie *m*; **~-written videodisc** *BrE*, **~-written videodisk** *AmE n* OPT videodisco de escritura superficial *m*

surface³ *vt* MECH ENG desbastar, pulir, TEXTIL alisar, recubrir

surfacing *n* C&G aplanado *m*, CONST *civil engineering* tratamiento de la superficie *m*, MECH aplanado *m*, MECH ENG alisamiento *m*, nivelación *f*, pulimento *m*, revestimiento *m*, acabado *m*, *lathe work* cilindrado *m*, *wood working* aplanado *m*; **~-and-boring lathe** *n* MECH ENG torno de cilindrar y taladrar *m*; ~ **motion** *n* MECH ENG *lathe work* movimiento de avance transversal *m*, movimiento transversal *m*; ~ **of the road** *n BrE* RAIL nivelación de la vía *f*; ~ **sheet** *n* P&R hoja de material de revestimiento *f*; ~ **of the track** *n AmE* (*cf surfacing of the road BrE*) RAIL nivelación de la vía *f*

surfactant *n* CHEM agente tensoactivo *m*, surfactante *m*, surfactivo *m*, suspensión con superficie activa *f*, COAL, DETERG agente tensoactivo *m*, surfactante *m*, FOOD agente tensoactivo *m*, MAR POLL agente superficiactivo *m*, agente tensoactivo *m*, P&R agente superficiactivo *m*, agente surfactante *m*, agente tensoactivo *m*, PHYS sustancia con superficie activa *f*, POLL agente tensoactivo *m*, surfactante *m*; ~ **mud** *n* PETR TECH lodo surfactante *m*; ~ **sludge** *n* PETR TECH lodo surfactante *m*

surfing *n* WAVE PHYS surfing *m*

surge *n* AIR TRANSP *turbine engine* sobrecarga *f*, ELEC *voltage* sobretensión transitoria *f*, impulso *m*, ELEC ENG sobretensión transitoria *f*, corriente transitoria anormal *f*, PETR TECH surgencia *f*, PROD sobretensión *f*, sobrevoltaje *m*, WATER TRANSP resaca *f*; ~ **absorber** *n* ELEC *transmission* absorbedor de ondas *m*; ~ **arrester** *n* ELEC *transmission* disipador de sobretensiones *m*, ELEC ENG disipador de sobrevoltajes *m*; ~ **characteristic** *n* TV respuesta a transitorios *f*; ~ **current** *n* PROD sobrecorriente *f*, sobreintensidad *f*; ~ **diverter** *n* ELEC descargador de sobretensiones *m*, disipador de sobretensiones *m*; ~ **generator** *n* ELEC generador de impulsos *m*, generador de impulsos de alta tensión *m*, generador de impulsos de corriente *m*, generador de ondas *m*, generador de ondas de choque *m*, generador de picos de alta tensión *m*, generador de sobrecorrientes *m*, NUCL generador de impulsos *m*; ~ **impedance** *n* ELEC impedancia característica *f*, impedancia propia *f*; ~ **pressure** *n* PROD sobrepresión *f*; ~ **protection** *n* ELEC ENG protección contra sobrevoltaje momentáneo *f*; ~ **relay** *n* ELEC relé de máxima *m*, relé de sobreintensidad *m*, relé de sobretensión *m*; ~ **shaft** *n* FUELLESS chimenea de equilibrio *f*, HYDROL conducto de compensación *m*; ~ **suppressor** *n* PROD eliminador de sobrevoltaje *m*; ~ **tank** *n* FUELLESS tanque de equilibrio *m*, HYDROL cámara de compensación *f*

surgical: ~ **microscope** *n* INSTR microscopio quirúrgico *m*

surplus: ~ **water** *n* WATER excedente de agua *m*

surprint *n* PRINT sobreimpresión *f*

surround: ~ **sound** *n* CINEMAT sonido perimétrico *m*

surveillance *n* QUALITY supervisión *f*, SAFE inspección *f*, vigilancia *f*; ~ **approach radar rating** *n* AIR TRANSP clasificación de radar de búsqueda de aproximación *f*; ~ **balloon** *n* MILIT globo aerostático de vigilancia *m*; ~ **radar** *n* MILIT radar de vigilancia *m*; ~ **satellite** *n* SPACE satélite de vigilancia *m*

survey¹ *n* CONST levantamiento *m*, *public or other works* anteproyecto *m*, *with reference to value litigation* estudio *m*, peritación *f*, *on earth's surface* inspección *f*, GEOL prospección *f*, METR vigilancia *f*, WATER TRANSP inspección *f*; ~ **diving bell** *n* OCEAN torreta de observación *f*; ~ **traverse** *n* OCEAN itinerario *m*, itinerario de observación de mareas *m*

survey² *vt* CONST inspeccionar, MAR POLL efectuar un reconocimiento de, reconocer, METR inspeccionar, MINE efectuar un reconocimiento de, WATER TRANSP *ship, coast* hidrografiar, reconocer

surveying¹ *n* AGRIC agrimensura *f*, CONST *of character and position of rock, strata* levantamiento de planos *m*, *of public or other works* topografía *f*, *on earth's surface* agrimensura *f*, METR *quantity* vigilancia *f*, WATER TRANSP *ships, coast* hidrografía *f*, reconocimiento *m*

surveying² *vt* CONST nivelar

surveyor *n* AGRIC agrimensor *m*, CONST supervisor *m*, *of land* agrimensor *m*, inspector *m*, *of public works* topógrafo *m*, METR *quantity* vigilador *m*, WATER TRANSP perito *m*, inspector *m*; **~'s chain** *n* CONST cadena de agrimensor *f*; **~'s compass** *n* CONST brújula de agrimensor *f*; **~'s dial** *n* CONST cuadrante de agrimensor *m*; **~'s level** *n* CONST nivel de anteojo *m*; **~'s tape** *n* CONST cinta metálica *f*; **~'s transit** *n* CONST goniómetro de tránsito *m*, teodolito *m*

survival: ~ **kit** *n* AIR TRANSP, MILIT, SAFE equipo de supervivencia *m*, SPACE equipo de sobrevivencia *m*; ~ **wind speed** *n* FUELLESS velocidad de viento de supervivencia *f*

susceptance *n* ELEC *reactance*, ELEC ENG, PHYS susceptancia *f*

susceptibility *n* ELEC *reactance* propensión *f*, sensibilidad *f*, susceptibilidad *f*, PHYS susceptibilidad *f*

suspended: ~ **joint** *n* CONST junta suspendida *f*; ~ **lift** *n* MINE jaula elevadora colgada *f*, jaula elevadora suspendida *f*; ~ **liquid droplet** *n* POLL gotícula de líquido en suspensión *m*; ~ **load** *n* HYDROL arrastre en suspensión *m*; **~-load trolley set** *n* RAIL sistema de vagonetas suspendidas *m*; ~ **particle** *n* POLL partícula en suspensión *f*, partícula suspendida *f*; ~ **pump** *n* MINE bomba suspendida *f* (*Esp*), bomba volante *f* (*AmL*); ~ **scaffold** *n* CONST andamio colgante *m*; ~ **set** *n* MINE instalación de extracción volante *f* (*AmL*); ~ **system** *n* TRANSP sistema suspendido *m*; ~ **vehicle system** *n* (*SVS*) TRANSP sistema de vehículo suspendido *m*

suspension *n* CHEM, ELEC ENG suspensión *f*, MECH ENG colgador *m*, MINE suspendedor *m*, suspensión *f*, P&R, PHYS suspensión *f*; ~ **arm** *n* AUTO, VEH brazo de suspensión *m*; ~ **bridge** *n* CONST, MILIT puente colgante *m*; ~ **gear** *n* MINE dispositivo de suspensión *m*, mecanismo de suspensión *m*; ~ **hook** *n* MECH ENG gancho de suspensión *m*; ~ **insulator** *n* ELEC, ELEC ENG aislante de suspensión *m*; ~ **with linkages** *n* MECH ENG suspensión con juntas *f*; ~ **polymerization** *n* P&R polimerización en suspensión *f*; ~ **rod** *n* RAIL biela de suspensión *f*; ~ **of the rods** *n* MINE suspensión de la galería *f*; ~ **stud** *n* MECH ENG perno de suspensión *m*; ~ **system** *n* AUTO sistema de suspensión *m*

sustained: ~ **oscillation** *n* ELECTRON oscilación constante *f*; ~ **release pellet** *n* (*SRP*) AGRIC píldora de efecto retardado *f* (*PER*)

Sv *abbr* (*sievert*) NUCL, PHYS, RAD PHYS Sv (*sievert*)

SVC *abbr* COMP&DP (*supervisor call*) llamada al supervisor *f*, TELECOM (*signaling virtual channel AmE, signalling virtual channel BrE*) canal virtual de señalización *m*

SVS *abbr* (*suspended vehicle system*) TRANSP sistema de vehículo suspendido *m*

swab *n* PETR TECH limpiatubos *m*, PROD *moulder* mechón *m*; ~ **brush** *n* PROD *mould making* cepillo para frotar arena *m*

swabbing *n* C&G limpieza *f*, PETR TECH achique *m*, pistoneo *m*

swage[1] *n* MECH ENG triscador *m*, PROD abretubos *m*, enderezatubos *m*, *for shaping metal* estampa *f*, *saw set* triscador *m*, recalcador *m*; ~ **block** *n* PROD *forge* bloque de recalcar *m*, estampa *f*, estampa de forja *f*, tas de estampar *m*

swage[2] *vt* MECH estampar en caliente, forjar con estampa

swaging *n* PROD embutición *f*, estampado *m*, recalcado *m*; ~ **die** *n* MECH ENG *for forming* matriz para estampar en caliente *f*

swallow: ~ **hole** *n* GEOL sumidero *m*; ~~**tail joint** *n* CONST junta a media madera *f*

swanneck *n* CINEMAT, CONST cuello de cisne *m*; ~ **cock** *n* CONST grifo con cuello de cisne *m*; ~ **fly press** *n* MECH ENG balancín de cuello de cisne *m*, prensa de husillo de cuello de cisne *f*; ~ **screw press** *n* MECH ENG prensa de fricción de cuello de cisne *f*, prensa de husillo de cuello de cisne *f*

swap[1]: ~ **bodies** *n pl* RAIL cuerpos intercambiables *m pl*, unidades intercambiables *f pl*

swap[2] *vt* COMP&DP intercambiar, permutar

swapping *n* COMP&DP intercambio *m*, permutación *f*

sward *n* AGRIC pradera de pastos tiernos *f*

swarf *n* PROD *grindstone* barro de amolado *m*, *metal* virutas metálicas *f pl*

swash *n* OCEAN, WATER TRANSP *of wave* embate ascendente *m*; ~ **letter** *n* PRINT letra de adorno *f*

swatch *n* TEXTIL muestrario *m*; ~ **dyer** *n* COLOUR tinte de muestra *m*; ~ **type** *n* PRINT tipo de muestras *m*

swatching: ~~**out** *n* PRINT muestra *f*

swath *n* AGRIC andana de forraje *f*, hilera *f*, MAR POLL anchura de pasado *f*

sway: ~ **stabilization** *n* TRANSP estabilización por balanceo *f*

swaying *n* MECH ENG balanceo *m*, oscilación *f*, vaivén *m*

swealing *n* COLOUR migración *f*

sweat[1] *n* MINE condensación de la humedad sobre superficies metálicas *f*, sudación *f*; ~ **cooling** *n* REFRIG enfriamiento por condensación superficial *m*, SPACE enfriamiento por condensación superficial *m*, enfriamiento por porosidad del metal *m*, enfriamiento por transpiración *m*; ~ **roll** *n* PAPER cilindro enfriador *m*; ~~**type expansion valve** *n* REFRIG válvula de expansión con conexión soldada *f*

sweat[2] *vt* FOOD exhudar, sudar

sweating *n* PRINT, REFRIG condensación *f*; ~ **furnace** *n* PROD horno de licuación *m*

sweep[1] *n* ELECTRON barrido *m*, exploración *f*, HYDROL

of river revuelta *f*, curva *f*, PROD *strickle* terraja *f*, SPACE regresión *f*, misión ofensiva sobre territorio enemigo *f*, barrido *m*, vuelo de exploración *m*, TV barrido *m*, exploración *f*; ~ **aerial** *n* BrE (*cf sweep antenna AmE*) TELECOM antena de barrido electrónico *f*; ~ **angle** *n* AIR TRANSP ángulo de flecha *m*; ~ **antenna** *n* AmE (*cf sweep aerial BrE*) TELECOM antena de barrido electrónico *f*; ~ **board** *n* PROD terraja *f*; ~ **circuit** *n* TV circuito explorador *m*; ~ **frequency** *n* ELECTRON, TV frecuencia de barrido *f*; ~ **gas** *n* MILIT gas de ventilación *m*; ~ **microscope** *n* TELECOM microscopio de barrido *m*; ~ **mode** *n* ELECTRON función de barrido *f*; ~ **molding** AmE, ~ **moulding** BrE *n* PROD moldeo a la terraja *m*; ~ **plough** BrE, ~ **plow** AmE arado escardador *m*

sweep[2] *vt* CONST *chimney* barrer, deshollinar, PROD *founding* aterrajar; ~ **up** *vt* PROD *founding* aterrajar

sweeping *n* PETR TECH *of reservoir* barrido *m*, PROD *foundry* aterrajamiento *m*; ~ **up** *n* PROD aterrajamiento *m*

sweepings *n pl* PROD barreduras *f pl*

sweet: ~ **clover disease** *n* AGRIC enfermedad del trebol de olor *f*; ~ **crude** *n* PETR TECH crudo con poco azufre *m*; ~ **gas** *n* GAS, PETR TECH gas dulce *m*; ~ **natural gas** *n* GAS gas natural dulce *m*

sweetened *adj* FOOD edulcorado, endulzado

sweetener *n* FOOD edulcorante *m*, endulzante *m*

sweetening *n* PETR TECH extracción de gas sulfidrico de los hidrocarburos *f*, extracción de mercaptanes de gasolina *f*

swell[1] *n* METEO, OCEAN, WATER TRANSP mar de fondo *m*, mar de leva *m*; ~ **abatement** *n* OCEAN reducción de oleaje *f*; ~~**resistant finish** *n* COATINGS acabado a prueba de hinchazón *m*

swell[2] *vt* TEXTIL abombar

swell[3] *vi* PHYS inflar

swelled: ~ **coking coal** *n* COAL carbón de coque hinchado *m*

swelling *n* P&R dilatación *f*, hinchazón *f*, TEXTIL abullonado *m*; ~ **clay** *n* C&G arcilla dilatable *f*, PETR TECH arcilla dilatable *f*, arcilla expansible *f*; ~ **soil** *n* COAL terreno esponjoso *m*

swept: ~~**back wing** *n* AIR TRANSP, TRANSP ala de flecha positiva *f*; ~~**up casting** *n* PROD pieza aterrajada *f*; ~~**up core** *n* PROD macho aterrajado *m*; ~ **wing** *n* AIR TRANSP, TRANSP ala en flecha *f*

swift *n* TEXTIL tambor *m*

swimming: ~ **roll** *n* PAPER rodillo compensador del combado *m*

swing[1] *n* MECH ENG altura de puntos *f*, capacidad de torneado *f*, diámetro máximo admisible *m*, diámetro máximo torneable *m*, torneado máximo *m*, PAPER oscilación *f*; ~ **arm** *n* PROD brazo oscilante *m*; ~ **axle** *n* AUTO eje oscilante *m*; ~ **of the bed** *n* MECH ENG altura de puntos sobre la bancada *f*, diámetro admisible sobre la bancada *m*; ~~**bob lever** *n* MECH ENG palanca de volante *f*; ~~**bolt coupling** *n* MECH ENG acoplamiento de charnela *m*, acoplamiento de perno articulado *m*; ~ **bridge** *n* CONST puente basculante *m*, WATER TRANSP puente giratorio *m*; ~~**by** *n* SPACE vuelo de la cosmonave utilizando el campo de gravitación *m*; ~~**by effect** *n* SPACE efecto de catapulta del campo gravitatorio *m*, efecto del campo de gravitación sobre la nave *m*; ~ **crane** *n* CONST grúa giratoria *f*; ~ **door** *n* CONST puerta giratoria *f*; ~ **frame** *n* MECH ENG *of screw-cutting* *machine* lira *f*; ~ **gate** *n* CONST compuerta giratoria *f*; ~~**in filter** *n* PHOTO filtro giratorio *m*; ~ **in gap** *n* MECH ENG diámetro máximo admisible sobre la escotadura *m*; ~~**jib radial drill** *n* MECH ENG taladradora radial de brazo giratorio *f*; ~ **nose crossing** *n* TRANSP cruce de vías con corazón giratorio *m*; ~ **over bed** *n* MECH ENG diámetro admisible sobre la bancada *m*; ~ **over saddle** *n* MECH ENG diámetro admisible sobre la bancada *m*; ~ **radius** *n* PROD radio de oscilación *m*; ~ **of the rest** *n* MECH ENG diámetro admisible sobre la torreta *m*; ~ **sieve** *n* COAL criba oscilante *f*; ~ **ticket** *n* PACK billete de recorrido *m*; ~~**up mirror** *n* PHOTO espejo giratorio *m*; ~ **valve** *n* HYDRAUL válvula de bola *f*, válvula de charnela *f*

swing² *vt* MECH ENG dar vueltas, girar, virar

swing³ *vi* MECH ENG girar, virar; ~ **away** *vi* WATER TRANSP *ship* destacarse, zallarse

swinging¹ *adv* WATER TRANSP *mooring* borneando proa al viento

swinging² *n* MECH ENG balanceo *m*, oscilación *f*, pendulación *f*, vibración *f*; ~ **across the face** *n* WATER dragado circular *m*; ~ **back** *n* PHOTO tapa posterior giratoria *f*; ~ **choke** *n* ELEC bobina de reactancia de hierro saturado *f*, ELEC ENG bobina de reactancia de hierro saturado *f*, choque oscilante *m*, reactancia de acoplamiento *f*, reactor de autoinducción variable *m*; ~ **chute** *n* CONST conducto oscilante *m*; ~ **crusher** *n* MECH ENG rodillo perfilador giratorio *m*, triturador giratorio *m*, triturador oscilante *m*; ~ **door** *n* CONST puerta de vaivén *f*; ~ **movement** *n* MECH ENG movimiento de oscilación *m*, movimiento de péndulo *m*, movimiento oscilante *m*; ~ **post** *n* CONST poste de vaivén *m*; ~ **round** *n* CONST giro *m*; ~ **screen** *n* PROD criba oscilante *f*; ~ **valve** *n* PROD distribuidor oscilante *m*, válvula oscilante *f*

swipe: ~ **card** *n* TELECOM tarjeta de la palanca de arranque *f*

swirling: ~ **flow** *n* GAS flujo en remolino *m*; ~ **injection** *n* GAS inyección de remolino *f*

swish: ~ **pan** *n* CINEMAT panorámica muy rápida *f*

switch¹: ~~**selectable** *adj* PROD seleccionable por conmutador

switch² *n* CINEMAT conmutador *m*, COMP&DP conmutador *m*, interruptor *m*, CONST (*cf points, cf set of points*) cambios de vía *m pl*, aguja *f*, cambiavía *m*, juego de agujas *m*, ELEC *circuit breaker* interruptor automático *m*, disyuntor *m*, interruptor *m*, *circuit* conmutador *m*, ELEC ENG interruptor seccionador *m*, desviación *f*, llave *f*, conmutador *m*, interruptor *m*, PHYS interruptor *m*, RAIL (*cf points, cf set of points*) aguja *f*, juego de agujas *m*, cambiavía *m*, TELECOM conmutador *m*, TV interruptor *m*; ~ **assembly** *n* PROD montaje de aguja *m*; ~ **blade** *n* RAIL aguja de cambio *f*; ~ **body** *n* PROD cuerpo de aguja *m*; ~ **box** *n* CINEMAT caja de distribución *f*; ~ **clock** *n* ELEC, ELEC ENG interruptor horario *m*; ~ **cock** *n* CONST llave de paso *f*; ~ **cover plate** *n* PROD tapa de aguja *f*; ~ **engine** *n* AmE (*cf shunting engine BrE*) CONST, RAIL, TRANSP locomotora de maniobras *f*; ~ **fuse** *n* ELEC, ELEC ENG fusible del interruptor *m*; ~ **gears** *n pl* RAIL maniobra de agujas *f*; ~ **group assembly** *n* PROD montaje de grupos de agujas *m*; ~ **handle** *n* ELEC ENG pulsador del conmutador *m*; ~ **indicator** *n* PROD indicador de aguja *m*; ~ **lever** *n* ELEC ENG palanca del interruptor *f*, RAIL palanca de maniobra de agujas *f*; ~ **lock** *n* TV cerrojo de bloqueo *m* (*Esp*),

interruptor con traba *m* (*AmL*); ~~**mode power supply** *n* PROD suministro de potencia en modo de conmutación *m*; ~~**operating handle** *n* PROD palanca para accionar las agujas *f*; ~ **panel** *n* WATER TRANSP *electric circuit* cuadro de distribución *m*; ~ **relay** *n* ELEC relé de conmutación *m*; ~ **tongue** *n* RAIL aguja de cambio *f*; ~ **valve** *n* HYDRAUL válvula de desvío *f*, válvula de tres vías *f*

switch³ *vt* COMP&DP, TELECOM conmutar; ~ **in** *vt* ELEC ENG conmutar; ~ **off** *vt* COMP&DP interrumpir, ELEC ENG, MECH ENG cortar, desconectar, TV apagar, desconectar; ~ **on** *vt* ELEC conectar, conectar mediante interruptor, ELEC ENG conectar, dar corriente, encender, enchufar, poner en circuito, TELECOM enchufar, TV conectar, enchufar; ~ **to air** *vt* TV conectar al aire

switchable *adj* TV conmutable

switchboard *n* ELEC ENG cuadro de distribución *m*, TELECOM cuadro conmutador *m*, cuadro de conmutación *m*, cuadro de conmutación telefónica *m*, tablero de conmutación *m*, TV panel de conmutación *m*; ~ **operator** *n* TELECOM operador del cuadro conmutador *m*, operador del cuadro de conmutación *m*

switched¹ *adj* TELECOM conmutado

switched²: ~ **circuit** *n* TELECOM circuito conmutado *m*; ~ **current** *n* ELEC corriente conmutada *f*; ~~**loop console** *n* TELECOM consola de bucle conmutado *f*; ~ **multimegabit data service** *n* (*SMDS*) TELECOM servicio de conmutación de datos de multimegabits *m*, servicio de líneas conmutadas de datos de multimegabits *m*; ~ **network** *n* COMP&DP, ELEC ENG, TELECOM red conmutada *f*; ~ **network layer** *n* TELECOM capa de red conmutada *f*; ~ **service** *n* TELECOM servicio conmutado *m*; ~~**star network** *n* TELECOM red conmutada en estrella *f*; ~ **telephone network** *n* TELECOM red telefónica de líneas conmutadas *f*; ~ **virtual circuit** *n* TELECOM circuito virtual conmutado *m*

switcher *n* RAIL, TRANSP guardagujas *m*, locomotora para maniobras *f*, TV interruptor *m*

switchgear *n* ELEC aparato de conexión *m*, conmutador *m*, equipo de distribución *m*, equipos de conmutación y distribución *m pl*, interruptor *m*, mecanismo de control *m*, ELEC ENG aparamenta eléctrica *f*, aparatos de conexión *m pl*, equipo de maniobra *m*, órgano de conmutación *m*, NUCL equipos de conmutación *m pl*

switching *n* COMP&DP conmutación *f*, ELEC ENG conmutación *f*, disyunción *f*, RAIL desviación *f*, SPACE conexión *f*, conmutación *f*, derivación *f*, interrupción *f*, inversión *f*, TELECOM conmutación *f*; ~ **bar** *n* TV barra de conmutación *f*; ~ **call-in-progress** *n* TELECOM conmutación de llamada en curso *f*; ~ **center** AmE, ~ **centre** BrE *n* TELECOM, TV centro de conmutación *m*; ~ **circuit** *n* ELEC ENG circuito de conmutación *m*, circuito selector *m*, ELECTRON circuito de conmutación *m*, transistor de conmutación *m*; ~ **delay** *n* TELECOM retardo de conmutación *m*, retardo debido a la conmutación *m*; ~ **device** *n* ELEC ENG conmutador *m*, dispositivo de conmutación *m*, TELECOM aparato conmutador *m*, dispositivo de conmutación *m*; ~ **diode** *n* ELECTRON diodo de conmutación *m*, TELECOM diodo conmutador *m*, diodo de conmutación *m*, TV diodo de conmutación *m*; ~ **equipment** *n* COMP&DP equipo de conmutación *m*; ~ **frequency** *n* PROD frecuencia de conmutación *f*; ~-**in** *n* ELEC ENG entrada en circuito *f*; ~ **loss** *n* ELEC ENG pérdida por conmutación *f*; ~ **matrix** *n* SPACE, TELECOM, TV matriz de conmutación *f*; ~ **multiplexer** *n* TELECOM multiplexor de conmutación *m*; ~ **mux** *n* TELECOM multiplexión de conmutación *f*, multiplexor de conmutación *m*; ~ **network** *n* ELEC ENG, TELECOM red de conmutación *f*; ~ **network complex** *n* TELECOM complejo de red de conmutación *m*; ~ **point** *n* TELECOM nudo de conmutación *m*, punto de conmutación *m*; ~ **power supply** *n* ELEC ENG suministro de energía por conmutación *m*; ~ **process interworking telephony event** *n* (*SPITE*) TELECOM sistema de telefonía por interconexión de procesos *m*; ~ **processor** *n* TELECOM procesador de conmutación *m*; ~ **regulation** *n* ELEC ENG regulación de recorte *f*; ~ **regulator** *n* ELEC ENG regulador de recorte *m*; ~ **sequence** *n* ELEC secuencia de conmutación *f*; ~ **speed** *n* ELEC ENG rapidez de conmutación *f*, ELECTRON velocidad de conmutación *f*; ~ **stage** *n* TELECOM etapa de conmutación *f*; ~ **station** *n* ELEC estación de distribución *f*, estación de distribución de energía *f*, RAIL estación de maniobras *f*; ~ **statistical multiplexer** *n* TELECOM multiplexor estadístico de conmutación *m*; ~ **substation** *n* ELEC subestación de distribución de energía *f*, ELEC ENG subestación de distribución de energía *f*; ~ **system** *n* TELECOM, TV sistema de conmutación *m*; ~-**system processor** *n* TELECOM procesador del sistema de conmutación *m*; ~ **theory** *n* COMP&DP, ELECTRON teoría de conmutación *f*; ~ **time** *n* ELEC ENG tiempo de conmutación *f*; ~ **track** *n* RAIL vía de clasificación *f*, vías de maniobra *f pl*; ~ **tube** *n* ELECTRON tubo de conmutación *m*; ~ **unit** *n* TELECOM unidad conmutadora *f*, unidad de conmutación *f*; ~ **yard** *n* AmE (*cf marshalling yard BrE, shunting yard BrE*) RAIL estación de clasificación *f*, estación de maniobras *f*

switchpoint: ~ **light** *n* RAIL señal luminosa de punto de aguja *f*

swivel *n* MECH placa giratoria *f*, MECH ENG eslabón giratorio *m*, placa giratoria *f*, rótula giratoria *f*, MINE cabezal de sonda *m* (*AmL*), giratoria de perforación *f* (*Esp*), perforadora *f* (*AmL*), sonda *f*, giratoria *f*, PETR TECH cabeza de inyección *f*, cabezal giratorio *m*, rótula *f* (*Esp*), swivel *m* (*Esp*), unión giratoria *f*, PROD placa giratoria *f*, WATER TRANSP *fittings* grillete giratorio *m*; ~ **arm** *n* INSTR brazo basculante *m*; ~ **bearing** *n* MECH ENG cojinete de rótula *m*, cojinete esférico basculante *m*, soporte articulado *m*, soporte basculante *m*, soporte de rótula *m*; ~-**bearing motor** *n* ELEC ENG motor de apoyo giratorio *m*; ~ **block** *n* MECH ENG motón giratorio *m*; ~ **bridge** *n* CONST puente giratorio *m*; ~ **hanger** *n* MECH ENG soporte basculante *m*; ~ **hook** *n* MECH ENG alacrán *m*, gancho basculante *m*, gancho giratorio *m*, WATER TRANSP gancho giratorio *m*; ~ **joint** *n* MECH articulación giratoria *f*, MECH ENG articulación giratoria *f*, junta de rótula *f*, unión de nuez *f*, unión de rótula *f*, unión giratoria *f*; ~-**mounted reflector** *n* PHOTO reflector con montaje giratorio *m*; ~ **pipe connector** *n* MECH ENG conector basculante de tubo *m*; ~ **plummer block** *n* MECH ENG cojinete giratorio *m*; ~ **range clockwise** *n* MECH ENG alcance del balanceo hacia la derecha *m*; ~ **range counterclockwise** *n* MECH ENG alcance del balanceo hacia la izquierda *m*; ~ **rod** *n*

MINE cabezal de sonda *m* (*AmL*); ~ **slide rest** *n* MECH ENG portaherramientas basculante *m*, soporte de corredera oscilante *m*, soporte del carro basculante *m*; ~ **stirrup** *n* MECH ENG brida basculante *f*; ~ **vice** *n* BrE MECH ENG morsa giratoria *f*, tornillo de banco giratorio *m*, tornillo giratorio *m*; ~ **vise** *AmE see swivel vice BrE*

swiveling: ~ **roof** *AmE see swivelling roof BrE*

swivelling: ~ **roof** *n* BrE TRANSP techo giratorio *m*

SWR *abbr* (*standing-wave ratio*) PHYS, SPACE, TELECOM ROE (*relación de onda estacionaria*)

swung: ~ **baffle** *n* C&G obturador desviado *m*

syenite *n* CHEM, PETR TECH sienita *f*

syllabic: ~ **companding** *n* TELECOM compansión silábica *f*

syllable: ~ **articulation test** *n* TELECOM prueba de articulación silábica *f*

sylvanite *n* MINERAL silvanita *f*

sylvestrene *n* CHEM silvestreno *m*

sylvine *n* MINERAL silvita *f*

sylvinite *n* MINERAL silvinita *f*

sylvite *n* MINERAL silvita *f*

symbol *n* CHEM, COMP&DP símbolo *m*; ~ **set** *n* COMP&DP conjunto de símbolos *m*; ~ **string** *n* COMP&DP cadena de símbolos *f*, serie de símbolos *f*; ~ **table** *n* COMP&DP tabla de símbolos *f*

symbolic: ~ **addressing** *n* COMP&DP direccionamiento simbólico *m*; ~ **name** *n* COMP&DP nombre simbólico *m*; ~ **processing** *n* COMP&DP procesamiento simbólico *m*

symmetric[1] *adj* CHEM, COMP&DP, GEOM, MATH simétrico

symmetric[2]: ~ **matrix** *n* COMP&DP matriz simétrica *f*; ~ **pipe coupling** *n* MECH ENG acoplamiento simétrico de tubo *m*; ~ **saddle shape** *n* GEOM forma de silla de montar simétrica *f*, silla de montar de forma simétrica *f*; ~ **wave function** *n* PHYS, WAVE PHYS función de onda simétrica *f*

symmetrical[1] *adj* CHEM, COMP&DP, GEOM, MATH simétrico

symmetrical[2]: ~ **anastigmat lens** *n* CINEMAT, OPT, PHOTO objetivo anastigmático simétrico *m*; ~ **arrangement** *n* ELEC ENG disposición balanceada *f*; ~ **pair cable** *n* TELECOM cable de pares simétricos *m*; ~ **soundtrack** *n* ACOUST banda sonora simétrica *f*, pista de sonido simétrica *f*, CINEMAT banda sonora simétrica *f*; ~ **time matrix** *n* TELECOM matriz de tiempo simétrica *f*; ~ **transducer** *n* ELEC ENG transductor simétrico *m*; ~ **trapezoidal-screw thread** *n* MECH ENG hilo trapezoidal simétrico *m*

symmetry *n* CHEM, GEOM simetría *f*; ~ **elements** *n pl* CRYSTALL elementos de simetría *m*

sympathetic: ~ **detonation** *n* MINE detonación por simpatía *f*; ~ **ink** *n* COLOUR tinta invisible *f*, tinta simpática *f*

SYN *abbr* (*synchronous idle*) COMP&DP carácter de sincronismo *m*, carácter sincrónico *m*, inactivo síncrono *m*

synanthrose *n* CHEM sinantrosa *f*

sync[1]: **in** ~ *adj* CINEMAT sincronizado, TV en sincronizado

sync[2]: ~ **amplifier** *n* ELECTRON, TV amplificador síncrónico *m*; ~ **beep** *n* CINEMAT señal de sincronización *f*; ~ **blanking** *n* TV borrado síncrono *m*; ~ **cable** *n* CINEMAT cable de sincronización *m*; ~ **feedback** *n* TV realimentación síncrona *f*; ~ **generator** *n* CINEMAT generador de sincronización *m*, ELEC generador sincrónico *m*, TV generador de sincronización *m*, generador sincrónico *m*; ~ **input** *n* TV entrada de sincronización *f*; ~ **line-up** *n* TV alineación de sincronización *f*; ~ **mark** *n* CINEMAT marca de sincronización *f*; ~ **pulse** *n* CINEMAT impulso de sincronización *m*, pulso de reloj *m*; ~ **pulse cable** *n* CINEMAT cable de impulsos de sincronización *m*; ~ **pulse generator** *n* CINEMAT, TV generador de impulsos de sincronización *m*; ~ **separator** *n* TV sincronizador separador *m*; ~ **tip frequency** *n* TV frecuencia de pulsos de sincronización *f*

sync³ *vt* (*synchronize*) CINEMAT, TV sincronizar; ~ **dailies** *vt* CINEMAT sincronizar el rodaje diario

Synchro-Compur: ~ **shutter** *n* PHOTO obturador Synchro-Compur *m*

synchrocyclotron *n* PHYS sincrociclotrón *m*

synchrolock *n* CINEMAT, TV bloqueo de sincronización *m*

synchromesh *n* AUTO sincronizador *m*, sistema sincronizado del cambio de velocidades *m*; ~ **transmission** *n* AUTO transmisión sincronizada *f*

synchronism *n* ELECTRON sincronismo *m*, MECH ENG sincronismo *m*, sincronía *f*

synchronization¹: **in** ~ *adj* CINEMAT sincronizado

synchronization² *n* AUTO, MECH ENG, SPACE, TELECOM sincronización *f*; ~ **loss** *n* TV pérdida de sincronización *f*; ~ **network** *n* TELECOM red de sincronización *f*; ~ **pulse** *n* TV pulso de sincronización *m*; ~ **separator** *n* TV sincronizador separador *m*; ~ **transformer** *n* PROD transformador de sincronización *m*; ~ **window** *n* SPACE ventana de sincronización *f*

synchronize *vt* (*sync*) CINEMAT, TV sincronizar

synchronized: ~ **shooting** *n* CINEMAT rodaje sincronizado *m*; ~ **transmission** *n* AUTO transmisión sincronizada *f*

synchronizer *n* AUTO, CINEMAT, COMP&DP, ELEC, ELEC ENG sincronizador *m*

synchronizing¹ *adj* ELEC sincronización

synchronizing²: ~ **cone** *n* MECH ENG *tool* cono sincronizador *m*; ~ **relay** *n* ELEC relevador de sincronización *m*, relé sincronizador *m*

synchronous¹ *adj* COMP&DP síncrono, ELECTRON sincrono, GEOL contemporáneo

synchronous²: ~ **alternator** *n* ELEC, ELEC ENG alternador sincrónico *m*; ~ **belt** *n* MECH ENG polea síncrona *f*; ~ **belt drive** *n* MECH ENG polea conductora sincrónica *f*; ~ **capacitor** *n* ELEC ENG condensador síncrono *m*; ~ **character** *n* COMP&DP carácter sincrónico *m*; ~ **circuit** *n* TELECOM circuito sincrónico *m*; ~ **computer** *n* COMP&DP computador síncrono *m* (*AmL*), computadora síncrono *f* (*AmL*), ordenador síncrono *m* (*Esp*); ~ **converter** *n* ELEC *alternating current supply* convertidor sincrónico *m*, ELEC ENG conmutatriz, síncrona *f*, convertidor síncrono *m*; ~ **coupling** *n* ELEC acoplamiento sincrónico *m*; ~ **data-link control** *n* (*SDLC*) COMP&DP procedimiento de control de transmisión síncrona *m* (*SDLC*); ~ **detection** *n* ELECTRON detección síncrona *f*; ~ **digital hierarchy** *n* (*SDH*) TELECOM jerarquía digital sincrónica *f*, jerarquía digital síncrona *f*; ~ **digital hierarchy physical interface** *n* (*SDH physical interface*) TELECOM interfaz físico de jerarquía digital síncrona *m*; ~ **drive** *n* CINEMAT transmisión sincrónica *f*, TV accionamiento síncrono *m*; ~ **electric clock** *n* ELEC reloj eléctrico sincrónico

m; ~ **equipment management function** *n* (*SEMF*) TELECOM función de gestión del equipo sincrónico *f*; ~ **frequency encoding technique** *n* (*SFET*) TELECOM técnica de codificación de frecuencia síncrona *f*, técnica síncrona de codificación de frecuencia *f*; ~ **generator** *n* ELEC alternador *m*, generador sincrónico *m*, ELEC ENG, FUELLESS, PHYS, TRANSP alternador *m*, TV generador sincrónico *m*; ~ **idle** *n* (*SYN*) COMP&DP carácter de sincronismo *m*, carácter sincrónico *m*, inactivo síncrono *m*; ~ **induction motor** *n* ELEC motor asincrónico sincronizado *m*, motor sincrónico de inducción *m*, ELEC ENG motor sincrónico *m*; ~ **inverter** *n* ELEC ENG convertidor síncrono *m*; ~ **machine** *n* ELEC máquina sincrónica *f*, ELEC ENG mecanismo sincrónico *m*; ~ **modem** *n* ELECTRON módem sincrono *m*; ~ **motor** *n* CINEMAT, ELEC, ELEC ENG, PHYS, TRANSP motor síncrono *m*; ~ **multiplexer** *n* (*SM*) TELECOM multiplexor síncrono *m*; ~ **network** *n* COMP&DP red síncrónica *f*; ~ **port** *n* TELECOM puerto síncrono *m*; ~ **satellite** *n* SPACE satélite geoestacionario *m*, satélite síncrono *m*; ~ **speed** *n* ELEC, FUELLESS velocidad de sincronismo *f*, velocidad sincrónica *f*; ~ **transfer mode** *n* (*STM*) TELECOM modo de transferencia síncrona *m*; ~ **transmission** *n* COMP&DP, TELECOM transmisión síncrona *f*; ~ **transport module** *n* (*STM*) TELECOM módulo de transporte síncrono *m*; ~ **transport module-n** *n* (*STM-n*) TELECOM módulo-n de transporte síncrono *m*; ~ **videodisc** *BrE*, ~ **videodisk** *AmE n* OPT videodisco síncrono *m*

synchrotron *n* ELECTRON, NUCL, PART PHYS, PHYS acelerador de electrones *m*, acelerador de iones *m*, ciclotrón *m*, sincrotrón *m*; ~ **emission** *n* PHYS, RAD PHYS emisión sincrotrónica *f*; ~ **radiation** *n* RAD PHYS radiación sincrotrón *f*

synclinal: ~ **axis** *n* MECH ENG eje sinclinal *m*; ~ **flexure** *n* MECH ENG pliegue sinclinal *m*; ~ **fold** *n* MECH ENG pliegue sinclinal *m*

syncline *n* PETR TECH sinclinal *m*

synclinorium *n* GEOL sinclinorio *m*

syncword *n* TELECOM palabra de sincronización *f*

syneresis *n* CHEM, P&R sinéresis *f*

synergetic¹ *adj* CHEM sinergético

synergetic²: ~ **effect** *n* POLL efecto sinergético *m*; ~ **log** *n* PETR TECH perfil sinergético *m*

synergism *n* DETERG sinergismo *m*; ~ **effect** *n* P&R efecto de sinergia *m*, efecto de sinergismo *m*

synergist *n* DETERG producto sinergético *m*, FOOD sinergista *m*

synergistic: ~ **effect** *n* P&R efecto sinergético *m*, efecto sinérgico *m*

synergy *n* DETERG sinergia *f*

synform *n* GEOL siniforme *m*

syngenite *n* MINERAL singenita *f*

synoptical: ~ **switchboard** *n* ELEC tablero de distribución sinóptica *m*

synorogenic *adj* GEOL sinorogénico

synschistous *adj* GEOL sinesquistoso

synsedimentary: ~ **fault** *n* GEOL falla sinsedimentaria *f*

syntactic¹ *adj* CHEM, MINE sintáctico

syntactic²: ~ **analyser** *n* *BrE* TELECOM analizador sintáctico *m*; ~ **analysis** *n* TELECOM análisis sintáctico *m*; ~ **analyzer** *AmE see syntactic analyser BrE*

syntax: ~ **analyser** *n* *BrE* COMP&DP analizador sintáctico *m*; ~ **analysis** *n* COMP&DP análisis sintáctico *m*;

~ **analyzer** *AmE see syntax analyser BrE*; ~ **error** *n* COMP&DP error de sintaxis *m*, error sintáctico *m*; ~ **identifier** *n* TELECOM identificador sintáctico *m*; ~ **version** *n* TELECOM versión sintáctica *f*

syntectonic *adj* GEOL sintectónico

synthesis *n* CHEM, CHEM TECH, GAS síntesis *f*

synthesized: ~ **local oscillator** *n* ELECTRON oscilador local sintetizado *m*; ~ **music** *n* ELECTRON música sintetizada *f*; ~ **oscillator** *n* ELECTRON oscilador sintetizado *m*; ~-**signal generator** *n* ELECTRON generador de señal sintetizada *m*

synthesizer *n* ELECTRON, TELECOM sintetizador *m*; ~ **settling time** *n* TELECOM tiempo de establecimiento del sintetizador *m*

synthetic[1] *adj* CHEM sintético

synthetic[2]: ~ **crude** *n* PETR TECH crudo sintético *m*; ~ **detergent** *n* DETERG detergente sintético *m*; ~ **elastomer** *n* PETR TECH elastómero sintético *m*; ~ **enamel** *n* COLOUR esmalte sintético *m*; ~ **fault** *n* GEOL *mechanism* falla sintética *f*; ~ **fiber** *AmE*, ~ **fibre** *BrE* *n* HEAT ENG, TEXTIL fibra sintética *f*; ~ **gas** *n* GAS gas sintético *m*; ~ **gasoline** *n* *AmE* (*cf synthetic petrol BrE*) AUTO, PETROL, VEH gasolina sintética *f*; ~ **latex** *n* P&R látex sintético *m*; ~ **long oil varnish** *n* COATINGS, COLOUR barniz sintético de alto porcentaje en aceite *m*, barniz sintético largo en aceite *m*; ~ **membrane** *n* CONST membrana sintética *f*; ~ **natural gas** *n* (*SNG*) GAS, PETR TECH gas natural sintético *m* (*GNS*); ~ **petrol** *n* *BrE* (*cf synthetic gasoline AmE*) AUTO, PETROL, VEH gasolina sintética *f*; ~ **resin** *n* P&R, PETR TECH resina sintética *f*; ~ **rubber** *n* P&R, PETR TECH caucho sintético *m*; ~ **size** *n* TEXTIL apresto sintético *m*; ~ **varnish** *n* COATINGS, COLOUR barniz sintético *m*

synthol *n* CHEM sintol *m*

syntonin *n* CHEM sintonina *f*

syntonous: ~ **comma** *n* ACOUST coma sintónica *f*

syphon *n* *BrE* HYDROL, LAB, PHYS sifón *m*; ~ **conduit** *n* *BrE* HYDROL conducto sifónico *m*; ~ **spillway** *n* *BrE* FUELLESS sifón vertedero *m*, sifón vertedor *m*

syringe *n* LAB jeringa *f*

syringic *adj* CHEM siríngico

system *n* CONST, GEOL, TELECOM sistema *m*; ~ **with compulsory guidance by physical means** *n* TRANSP sistema de dirección obligatoria por medios físicos *m*; ~ **configuration** *n* ELEC configuración del sistema *f*; ~ **crash** *n* COMP&DP avería del sistema *f*, parada forzosa del sistema *f*; ~ **design review** *n* (*SDR*) SPACE revisión del diseño del sistema *f* (*SDR*); ~ **diagram** *n* ELEC diagrama del sistema *m*; ~ **disk** *n* COMP&DP disco del sistema *m*; ~ **earth** *n* *BrE* (*cf system ground AmE*) ELEC tierra de la red *f*, tierra de servicio *f*; ~ **with endless transportation units** *n* TRANSP sistema con unidades de transporte sin fin *m*; ~-**expander module** *n* PROD módulo de extensión

del sistema *m*; ~ **generation** *n* COMP&DP generación del sistema *f*; ~ **ground** *n* *AmE* (*cf system earth BrE*) ELEC tierra de la red *f*, tierra de servicio *f*; ~ **with guidance by adhesion** *n* TRANSP sistema de guiado por adherencia *m*; ~ **with intermediate stops** *n* TRANSP sistema con paradas intermedias *m*; ~ **load** *n* TELECOM carga del sistema *f*; ~ **management application entity** *n* (*SMAE*) TELECOM entidad de aplicación para la gestión del sistema *f*; ~ **management application entry** *n* TELECOM entrada de la aplicación para la gestión del sistema *f*; ~ **management application service element** *n* TELECOM elemento de servicio de la aplicación para la gestión del sistema *m*; ~ **operational diagram** *n* ELEC diagrama del proceso operativo del sistema *m*; ~ **pattern** *n* ELEC imágenes del sistema *f pl*; ~ **of pipes** *n* CONST red de tuberías *f*; ~ **pointer** *n* PROD indicador de sistema *m*; ~ **provider** *n* TELECOM proveedor del sistema *m*; ~ **providing a temporal resolution of 5 ns** *n* RAD PHYS sistema con una resolución temporal de 5 ns *m*; ~ **of satellite navigation** *n* WATER TRANSP sistema de radionavegación por satélite *m* (*satnav*); ~ **of seals** *n* CONST sistema de cierre *m*; ~ **security** *n* COMP&DP seguridad del sistema *f*; ~ **setup** *n* PROD montaje del sistema *m*; ~ **of shoring** *n* CONST *building* sistema de apuntalamiento *m*; ~ **startup** *n* PROD puesta en marcha del sistema *f*; ~ **status menu** *n* PROD menú del estado del sistema *m*; ~ **stock** *n* PROD existencias del sistema *f pl*; ~ **testing** *n* COMP&DP comprobación del sistema *f*, prueba del sistema *f*; ~ **with transportation units of intermediate length** *n* TRANSP sistema con unidades de transporte de longitud intermedia *m*; ~ **of units** *n* ELEC, METR, PHYS sistema de unidades *m*

systematic: ~ **absence** *n* CRYSTALL ausencia sistemática *f*; ~ **effect** *n* QUALITY efecto sistemático *m*; ~ **error** *n* METR, PHYS error sistemático *m*; ~ **sampling** *n* COMP&DP muestreo sistemático *m*; ~ **variation** *n* QUALITY desviación sistemática *f*

systems: ~ **analysis** *n* COMP&DP análisis de sistemas *m*; ~ **engineering** *n* COMP&DP ingeniería de sistemas *f*; ~ **library** *n* COMP&DP, PRINT biblioteca de sistemas *f*; ~ **management** *n* TELECOM gestión de sistemas *f*; ~ **network architecture** *n* (*SNA*) COMP&DP arquitectura de sistemas de redes *f*; ~ **network architecture** *n* TELECOM arquitectura de sistemas de redes *f*; ~ **programming** *n* COMP&DP programación de sistemas *f*; ~ **software** *n* COMP&DP software del sistema *m*, soporte lógico de sistemas *m*

systolic: ~ **architecture** *n* TELECOM arquitectura sistólica *f*; ~ **array** *n* COMP&DP arreglo sistólico *m*, matriz sistólica *f*

syzygy *n* FUELLESS *astronomy* tiempo de luna nueva o llena en el ciclo de fases *m*, GEOM sizigia *f*

T

T[1] *abbr* METR (*tera, tesla*) T (*tera, tesla*), PHYS (*tesla*) T (*tesla*)

T[2]: **~ operation** *n* PART PHYS operación de inversión del tiempo *f*

TA *abbr* (*terminal adaptor*) TELECOM adaptador terminal *m*

Ta *abbr* (*tantalum*) CHEM, ELEC ENG, METALL Ta (*tantalio*)

tab[1] *n* COMP&DP (*tabulator, tabulation*) tabulador *m*, tabulación *f*, MECH apéndice *m*, PACK lengüeta *f*, PROD apéndice *m*, lengüeta *f*, proyección *f*; **~ card** *n* PRINT tarjeta de pestaña *f*; **~ form** *n* PRINT forma de pestaña *f*; **~ stop** *n* PRINT fin de tabulación *m*; **~ washer** *n* MECH, MECH ENG arandela con lengüeta *f*

tab[2] *vt* (*tabulate*) COMP&DP tabular

TAB *abbr* COMP&DP (*tabulator key*) tecla de tabulación *f*, tecla tabuladora *f*, ELEC ENG (*tape-automated bonding*) empacado automático en cinta *m*

Tabakin: **~ potential** *n* NUCL potencial Tabakin *m*

tabbing *n* PRINT justificación *f*, troquelado de pestañas *m*

Taber: **~ abrasion** *n* P&R abrasión Taber *f*

tabergite *n* MINERAL tabergita *f*

table[1] *n* COAL cuadro *m*, faceta superior *f*, listado *m*, tabla *f*, COMP&DP tabla *f*, CONST *of prices, values, etc* cuadro *m*, MECH ENG *of machine tool, moulding machine* mesa *f*; **~ canting to any angle** *n* MECH ENG mesa de inclinación multidireccional *f*; **~ casting** *n* C&G vaciado en mesa *m*; **~ with compound slides** *n* MECH ENG mesa de deslizamiento múltiple *f*, mesa multidireccional *f*, mesa rotatoria *f*; **~ editing machine** *n* CINEMAT mesa de montaje *f*; **~ lookup** *n* COMP&DP consulta de tablas *f*, consulta en tabla *f*; **~ search** *n* COMP&DP búsqueda en tabla *f*; **~ with top and side faces** *n* MECH ENG mesa con caras superior y laterales *f*; **~-top tripod** *n* CINEMAT trípode de mesa *m*; **~ tripod** *n* PHOTO trípode de mesa *m*; **~ vice with clamp** *n* BrE MECH ENG tornillo de mesa con brida *m*; **~ vise with clamp** *AmE see table vice with clamp BrE*; **~ work surface** *n* MECH ENG superficie de trabajo de la mesa *f*

table[2] *vt* COAL catalogar, encajar, ensamblar, tabular

tablemount *n* OCEAN promontorio submarino *m*

tablet *n* COMP&DP tableta *f*; **~ bottle** *n* C&G botella para pastillas *f*; **~ sorting and inspection machine** *n* PACK máquina de clasificación e inspección de tabletas *f*

tableware: **~ and domestic glass industry** *n* C&G industria de la cristalería y vidrios domésticos *f*

tabular[1] *adj* COMP&DP tabular

tabular[2]: **~ work** *n* PRINT composición tabular *f*

tabulate *vt* (*tab*) COMP&DP tabular

tabulating: **~ card paper** *n* PAPER papel para fichas perforadas *m*

tabulation *n* (*tab*) COMP&DP tabulación *f*

tabulator *n* (*tab*) COMP&DP tabulador *m*; **~ key** *n* (*TAB*) COMP&DP tecla de tabulación *f*, tecla tabuladora *f*

TAC *abbr* (*total allowable catch*) OCEAN CMP (*captura máxima permitida*)

tach: **~ pulse** *n* TV pulso tacométrico *m*

tacheometer *n* CONST *surveying*, INSTR, PHYS taquímetro *m*

tacheometry *n* CONST *surveying*, PHYS taquimetría *f*

tachhydrite *n* MINERAL taquihidrita *f*

tachogenerator *n* MECH ENG generador tacométrico *m*, tacogenerador *m*

tachograph *n* TRANSP tacógrafo *m*

tachometer *n* AUTO, CINEMAT, INSTR, PHYS cuentarrevoluciones *m*, cuentavueltas *m*, tacómetro *m*, TV tacómetro *m*, cuentavueltas *m*, cuentarrevoluciones *m*, VEH cuentarrevoluciones *m*, cuentavueltas *m*, tacómetro *m*; **~ lock** *n* AUTO, CINEMAT, PHYS, TRANSP, TV, VEH bloqueo del tacómetro *m*

tachymeter *n* CONST *surveying*, INSTR, PHYS taquímetro *m*

tachyon *n* PHYS taquión *m*

tack[1] *n* MECH ENG *type of nail* clavito *m*, tachuela *f*, PACK, PRINT tiro *m*, WATER TRANSP *sailing* mura *f*, amura *f*, bordada *f*, *of sail* puño de amura *m*; **~ coat** *n* CONST capa adhesiva *f*, capa ligante *f*; **~ level** *n* PACK nivel de tiro *m*; **~ welding** *n* MECH soldadura por puntos *f*

tack[2] *vi* WATER TRANSP bordear, virar por avante

tackifying: **~ agent** *n* CHEM, P&R agente adherente *m*

tackiness *n* PAPER adhesividad *f*; **~ agent** *n* CHEM agente adhesivo *m*, agente de pegajosidad *m*

tacking *n* WATER TRANSP *sailing* virada *f*, voltejeo *m*

tackle *n* CONST *windlass or winch for raising ore* aparejo *m*, equipo *m*, MECH cuaderno *m*, aparejo *m*, MECH ENG extractor *m*, torno extractor *m*, maquinaria *f*, cuaderno *m*, PROD torno de extracción *m*, polipasto *m*, mufla *f*, aparejo *m*, aparejería *f*, jarcia *f*, WATER TRANSP *running rigging, lifting gear* aparejo *m*; **~ block** *n* PROD mufla *f*; **~ and fall** *n* PROD mufla *f*; **~ fall** *n* PROD cuaderno *m*; **~ hook** *n* PROD gancho de cuaderno *m*; **~ with hook block** *n* PROD aparejo con polea de gancho *m*, cuaderno de gancho *m*, polea de gancho *f*, polipasto con polea de gancho *m*

tackness: **~ agent** *n* P&R agente adhesivo *m*

tactical[1] *adj* MILIT *flight* táctico

tactical[2]: **~ radar** *n* (*TR*) TELECOM radar táctico *m*; **~ radius of action** *n* MILIT radio táctico de acción *m*

tactile: **~ feedback** *n* PROD retroalimentación táctil *f*

TACV *abbr* (*tracked air cushion vehicle*) TRANSP aerodeslizador sobre vía *m*

TADG *abbr* (*three-axis data generator*) SPACE TADG (*generador de datos triaxial*)

taffeta *n* TEXTIL tafetán *m*

taffrail *n* WATER TRANSP *boatbuilding* baranda *f* (*AmL*), barandilla *f* (*Esp*), coronamiento *m*

tag[1] *n* COMP&DP etiqueta *f*, marca *f*, PRINT marbete *m*, PROD distintivo *m*, herrete *m*, marbete *m*, TEXTIL etiqueta *f*

tag[2] *vt* COMP&DP etiquetar, marcar, PROD conificar el extremo de, reducir el diámetro de la punta, TEXTIL etiquetar

tagboard *n* TEXTIL tablón de etiquetas *m*

tagged: ~ **atom** *n* NUCL átomo marcado *m*

tagging *n* TEXTIL etiquetado *m*

tail[1] *n* C&G, CINEMAT cola *f*, COMP&DP cabo *m*, extremo *m*, CONST *of slate* cola *f*, extremo de cabio *m*, ELECTRON cola en T *f*, PRINT margen inferior *m*, pie *m*, VEH parte trasera *f*; ~ **assay** *n* NUCL *paper, board* concentración de colas *f*; ~ **bay** *n* WATER cola *f*; ~ **block** *n* PROD *pulley* motón de rabiza *m*; ~ **box** *n* WATER *of sluices* caja de cola *f*; ~ **disposal** *n* COAL colector *m*; ~ **edge** *n* PRINT borde inferior *m*; ~ **elevator** *n* WATER elevador en cola *m*; ~ **end** *n* PAPER punta para pasar la banda *f*; ~~**-end marker trackside detector** *n* RAIL dispositivo para evitar colisiones por detrás *m*; ~~**-end process** *n* NUCL reelaboración final *f*, tratamiento final *m*; ~ **fin** *n* AIR TRANSP *of aircraft* estabilizador vertical *m*, plano de deriva vertical *m*; ~ **heaviness** *n* AIR TRANSP pesadez de cola *f*; ~ **lamp** *n* VEH luz trasera *f*; ~ **leader** *n* CINEMAT guía de cola *f*; ~~**-lift lorry** *n* *BrE* (*cf tail-lift truck AmE*) TRANSP camión sustentado por la cola *m*; ~~**-lift truck** *n* *AmE* (*cf tail-lift lorry BrE*) TRANSP camión sustentado por la cola *m*; ~~**-loading gate** *n* TRANSP puerta de carga trasera *f*; ~ **lock** *n* WATER esclusa de salida *f*; ~ **miter sill** *AmE*, ~ **mitre sill** *BrE* *n* WATER *of canal lock* busco de aguas abajo *m*; ~ **piston rod** *n* MECH ENG contravástago del pistón *m*; ~ **propeller** *n* TRANSP hélice de cola *f*; ~ **pulley** *n* MECH ENG contrapolea *f*, polea de retorno *f*; ~ **rotor** *n* AIR TRANSP *of helicopter* rotor de cola *m*; ~ **sheave** *n* PROD polea de retorno *f*; ~ **shock wave** *n* AIR TRANSP onda de choque de cola *f*; ~ **slate** *n* CINEMAT claqueta de cola *f*; ~ **spindle** *n* MECH ENG *of lathe* husillo del contrapunto *m*; ~ **unit** *n* AIR TRANSP conjunto de cola *m*, empenaje *m*, plano de cola *m*; ~ **vice** *n* *BrE* MECH ENG tornillo de banco con cola *m*, tornillo de mano *m*; ~ **vise** *AmE see tail vice BrE*; ~ **wheel** *n* AIR TRANSP rueda de cola *f*

tail[2] *vt* CONST *architecture* agregar, añadir

tailback *n* TRANSP tope trasero *m*

tailband *n* PRINT margen de pie *m*

tailgate *n* CINEMAT compuerta trasera *f*, MECH compuerta inferior *f*, puerta de descarga *f*, TRANSP orificio de salida *m*, puerta trasera *f*, WATER *of canal lock* compuerta de cola *f*, compuerta de descarga *f*, contraalza *f*

tailing: ~ **pond** *n* COAL estanque colector *m*

tailings *n pl* AGRIC residuos de trilla *m pl*, COAL desechos *m pl*, ganga *f*, relave *m*, residuos *m pl*, CONST desechos *m pl*, residuos *m pl*, PAPER rechazos de depuración *m pl*; ~ **area** *n* MINE zona de desechos *f* (*AmL*), zona de estériles *f*, área de estériles *f* (*Esp*); ~ **dam** *n* CONST presa para almacenamiento de residuos *f*; ~ **elevator** *n* CONST elevador para residuos *m*

tailpiece *n* CONST pieza posterior *f*, WATER *pump* alcachofa de aspiración *f*

tailpin: ~ **thrust** *n* MECH ENG *of lathe* contrapunta del cabezal móvil *f*

tailpipe *n* AUTO tubo de escape *m*, CONST *of cock* tubo de cola *m*, VEH tubo de escape *m*, WATER *of pump* tubo de aspiración *m*; ~ **extension** *n* AUTO embellecedor del tubo de escape *m*

tailplane *n* AIR TRANSP estabilizador horizontal *m*, plano de cola *m*, plano horizontal de cola *m*

tailrace *n* HYDROL socaz *m*, canal de descarga *m*, canal de fuga *m*, *hydraulic engineering* caz de descarga *m*, *of water mill* canal de desagüe *m*, WATER canal de fuga *m*, canal de descarga *m*, caz de descarga *m*, canal de desagüe *m*, socaz *m*; ~ **tunnel** *n* HYDROL *recording*, WATER túnel de descarga *m*

tailrod *n* MECH ENG contra vástago *m*

tails *n pl* COAL finos *m pl*, relave *m*

tailskid *n* AIR TRANSP patín de cola *m*

tailsluice *n* WATER esclusa de descarga *f*

tailstock *n* MECH ENG cabezal móvil *m*

tailwater *n* FUELLESS agua de descarga *f*, HYDRAUL agua de descarga *f*, nivel de aguas abajo *m*, HYDROL, WATER agua de descarga *f*; ~ **level** *n* FUELLESS nivel del agua de descarga *m*

tailwind *n* METEO viento de cola *m*

taint *vt* FOOD contaminar, corromper

take[1] *n* CINEMAT toma *f*, PRINT porción de original que compone un tipógrafo *f*; ~~**-about chuck** *n* MECH ENG portabrocas intercambiable *m*; ~~**-away mechanism** *n* TEXTIL mecanismo extraíble *m*; ~~**-off reel** *n* CINEMAT carrete de demostración *m*; ~~**-up** *n* CINEMAT bobina de recogida *f*, MECH ENG compensación *f*, levantada *f*, TEXTIL acortado *m*, tirahilo de aguja *m*; ~~**-up cassette** *n* PHOTO chasis receptor *m*; ~~**-up drum** *n* PHOTO tambor receptor *m*; ~~**-up magazine** *n* CINEMAT chasis de recogida *m*; ~~**-up motion** *n* TEXTIL movimiento de arrollado *m*; ~~**-up reel** *n* CINEMAT carrete receptor *m*, COMP&DP carrete de enrollado *m*; ~~**-up spool** *n* TV carrete receptor *m*; ~~**-up sprocket** *n* CINEMAT engranaje receptor *m*; ~~**-up system** *n* TEXTIL sistema de arrollado *m*, sistema de tirahilos *m*; ~~**-up unit** *n* PROD unidad tensora *f*

take[2]: ~ **the burr off** *vt* MECH ENG *piece of metal* quitar la rebaba; ~ **down** *vt* CONST *scaffolding* retirar; ~ **the edge off** *vt* MECH ENG *chisel* quitar el filo; ~ **in** *vt* MECH ENG *cramp* aceptar, sujetar; ~ **on** *vt* WATER TRANSP *hands* enrolar; ~ **stock of** *vt* PROD evaluar, formarse un juicio de ~ **the wire-edge off** *vt* MECH ENG *chisel* quitar el filo

take[3]: ~ **a bearing** *vi* AIR TRANSP marcarse, WATER TRANSP *navigation* marcarse, tomar una marcación; ~ **effect** *vi* MECH ENG entrar en vigencia, hacer efecto; ~ **its rise** *vi* HYDROL, WATER *of river* nacer; ~ **on water** *vi* WATER TRANSP *of ship* hacer aguada

takeoff *n* AIR TRANSP despegue *m*; ~ **ability** *n* AIR TRANSP aptitud de despegue *f*; ~ **area** *n* AIR TRANSP zona de despegue *f*; ~ **distance available** *n* AIR TRANSP distancia disponible de despegue *f*; ~ **distance required** *n* AIR TRANSP distancia requerida de despegue *f*; ~ **flight path** *n* AIR TRANSP trayectoria de vuelo de despegue *f*; ~ **funnel** *n* AIR TRANSP embudo de despegue *m*; ~~**-monitoring system** *n* AIR TRANSP sistema monitor de despegue *m*; ~ **phase** *n* AIR TRANSP fase de despegue *f*; ~ **power rating** *n* AIR TRANSP potencia de despegue homologada *f*; ~ **reel** *n* CINEMAT carrete desenrollador *m*; ~ **run** *n* AIR TRANSP carrera de despegue *f*, recorrido de despegue *m*; ~ **speed** *n* AIR TRANSP velocidad de despegue *f*

takeout *n* C&G *action* sacado *m*, *device* sacador *m*; ~ **arm** *n* C&G brazo sacador *m*

taking[1]: ~ **lens** *n* PHOTO lente objetivo *f*; ~~**-off sheets materials** *n pl* PROD cubicación de obra hecha materiales *f*, introducción de datos en las casillas de un estado de obra según materiales *f*; **~-off sheets per hours** *n pl* PROD cubicación de obra hecha por horas *f*, introducción de datos en las casillas de un estado de obra por horas *f*

taking[2]: **~ out of wind** *phr* CONST *truing up to plane surface* extracción de aire *f*, extracción del viento *f*

talkback: **~ circuit** *n* TV circuito de intercomunicación *m*

talking: **~ road sign** *n* TRANSP señal hablante de carretera *f*, señal parlante de carretera *f*; **~ unit** *n* PROD entalcadora *f*

tall: **~ grass prairie** *n* AmE AGRIC *corn belt* pradera con pastos de alto porte *f*; **~-oil** *n* CHEM, P&R aceite de pulpa de madera *m*, aceite de resina *m*

tallow *n* CHEM, FOOD, TEXTIL sebo *m*; **~ oil** *n* CHEM, FOOD, TEXTIL aceite de sebo *m*

tallowy *adj* CHEM, FOOD, TEXTIL seboso

tally *n* COMP&DP *counter, sum* cuenta *f*, cómputo *m*, total *m*, OCEAN *network* recuento *m*, PROD cómputo *m*, inventario *m*, registro *m*; **~ light** *n* CINEMAT, TV luz indicadora *f*

talonic *adj* CHEM talónico

talose *n* CHEM talosa *f*

talus *n* GEOPHYS talud *m*

talweg *n* GEOL línea de fondo de un valle *f*, línea pendiente *f*, vaguada *f*, línea de valle *f*

tame: **~ pasture** *n* AGRIC pradera cultivada *f*

tamed: **~ frequency modulation** *n* TELECOM modulación de frecuencia regularizadora *f*

tamp *vt* CONST apisonar, MINE apisonar, atacar (*Esp*), atracar (*AmL*), consolidar, PROD apisonar, atracar, hincar, *areas* consolidar, RAIL batear

tamped: **~ carbon** *n* CHEM carbón aglomerado *m*

tamper *n* AGRIC *implement* apisonadora *f*, MINE *implement* apisonadora *f*, compactadora *f*, PROD *implement* apisonadora *f*, pisón *m*, *person* apisonador *m*; **~-evident closure** *n* PACK cierre que pone de manifiesto los intentos de violación *m*; **~-proof seal** *n* SAFE precinto a prueba de falsificaciones *m*

tamperproof[1] *adj* PACK garantizado contra falsificaciones

tamperproof[2]: **~ closure** *n* PACK cierre de garantía contra falsificaciones *m*

tamping *n* CONST apisonamiento *m*, MINE apisonamiento *m*, atacado *m* (*Esp*), atraque *m* (*AmL*), compactación *m* (*Esp*), PROD *act* apisonamiento *m*, *founding, of sand* apisonado *m*, compacción *f*, compactación *f*; **~ machine** *n* RAIL bateadora de traviesas *f*; **~ material** *n* MINE apisonadora *f*, equipo de apisonar *m*, PROD material de apisonar *m*; **~ rod** *n* CONST varilla compactadora *f*, MINE atacador *m*, pisón *m*; **~ stick** *n* MINE atacador *m*, pisón *m*

tan *abbr* (*tangent*) COMP&DP, CONST, GEOM, MATH tg (*tangente*)

TAN *abbr* (*total acid number*) CHEM VAT (*valor ácido total*)

tandem[1]: **~-mounted** *adj* PROD montado en tándem

tandem[2]: **~ arrangement** *n* ELEC ENG instalación en serie *f*; **~ axle** *n* VEH doble eje *m*; **~ connection** *n* ELEC ENG conexión en serie *f*, NUCL conexión en tándem *f*; **~ disc harrow** *BrE*, **~ disk harrow** *AmE n* AGRIC grada de discos de doble acción *f*; **~ exchange** *n* TELECOM central de tránsito *f*, central nodal de tránsito *f*, central telefónica intermedia *f*, central tándem *f*; **~ generator** *n* PHYS generador en tándem *m*; **~ mirror fusion reactor** *n* (*TMR*) NUCL reactor de fusión de espejos en tándem *m* (*TMR*); **~ rotor helicopter** *n* AIR TRANSP, TRANSP helicóptero de rotores en tándem *m*; **~-type press** *n* PRINT prensa de dos cuerpos *f*; **~ vibrating roller** *n* CONST apisonadora vibradora *f*

tang *n* MECH ENG *of file* espiga *f*, *of knife, chisel* rabera *f*, rabo *m*, cola *f*

tangency *n* GEOM, MECH, PHYS tangencia *f*

tangent *n* (*tan*) COMP&DP, CONST, GEOM, MATH *trigonometry* tangente *f* (*tg*); **~ circle** *n* GEOM círculo tangente *m*; **~ galvanometer** *n* ELEC *instrument*, ELEC ENG galvanómetro de tangentes *m*, PHYS galvanómetro tangente *m*; **~ key** *n* MECH ENG chaveta tangencial *f*; **~ plate** *n* MECH ENG *of screw-cutting lathe* lira *f*; **~ radius dresser** *n* MECH ENG rectificadora tangencial de curvas de unión *f*; **~ screw** *n* MECH ENG tornillo sin fin *m*; **~ to the circle** *n* GEOM tangente al círculo *f*

tangential[1] *adj* GEOM, MECH, PHYS tangencial

tangential[2]: **~ acceleration** *n* MECH, PHYS aceleración tangencial *f*; **~ component** *n* PHYS componente tangencial *f*; **~ control** *n* OPT control tangencial *m*; **~ diehead** *n* MECH ENG cojinete de roscar tangencial *m*, hilera tangencial *f*; **~ focal line** *n* PHYS línea focal tangencial *f*; **~ force** *n* COAL, MECH ENG fuerza tangencial *f*; **~ keys and keyways** *n pl* MECH ENG chavetas y chaveteros tangenciales *m pl*; **~ signal sensitivity** *n* PHYS sensibilidad de señal tangencial *f*; **~ strain** *n* MECH ENG tensión tangencial *f*; **~ stress** *n* MECH ENG esfuerzo tangencial *m*, fatiga tangencial *f*; **~ tectonics** *n* GEOL *communications* tectónica tangencial *f*; **~ threading die** *n* MECH ENG cojinete de roscar tangencial *m*; **~ velocity** *n* FUELLESS velocidad tangencial *f*

tangle: **~ net** *n* OCEAN red agallera *f*, red de enmalle *f*

tank *n* C&G horno *m*, tanque *m*, CONST, GAS tanque *m*, MECH depósito *m*, tanque *m*, MILIT carro de combate *m*, PAPER depósito *m*, tanque *m*, PETR TECH cisterna *f*, POLL almacén *m*, cuba *f*, depósito *m*, tanque *m*, tolva *f*, PROD algibe *m*, cisterna *f* (*AmL*), cubeta *f* (*Esp*), depósito *m*, estanque *m* (*AmL*), tanque *m* (*AmL*), *electric transformer* cuba *f* (*Esp*), REFRIG depósito *m*, tanque *m*, SPACE depósito *m*, tanque *m*, cisterna *f*, VEH depósito *m*, WATER TRANSP *boat building* tanque *m*; **~ barge** *n* TRANSP barcaza algibe *f*, gabarra algibe *f*; **~ block** *n* C&G piedra de la taza del horno *f*; **~ bulldozer** *n* MILIT explanadora de carros *f*; **~ cap** *n* VEH tapa del depósito *f*; **~ car** *n* AmE (*cf tank wagon BrE*) MINE, RAIL vagón cisterna *m*, vagón cuba *m*; **~ container** *n* TRANSP contenedor-tanque *m*; **~ developing** *n* CINEMAT revelado en tanque *m*; **~ development** *n* PHOTO revelado en tanque *m*; **~ dozer** *n* MILIT explanadora de carros *f*; **~ engine** *n* MINE locomotora cisterna *f* (*Esp*), locomotora ténder *f* (*AmL*); **~ filler cap** *n* AUTO tapón del depósito *m*; **~ furnace** *n* C&G taza del horno *f*; **~ hatch** *n* WATER TRANSP *of tanker* escotilla de acceso a un tanque *f*; **~ heater** *n* PHOTO calentador de tanque *m*; **~ locomotive** *n* MINE locomotora cisterna *f* (*Esp*), locomotora ténder *f* (*AmL*); **~ lorry** *n* BrE (*cf tank truck AmE*) TRANSP camión-cuba *m*; **~ neck** *n* C&G cuello del tanque *m*; **~ semitrailer** *n* TRANSP cisterna semi-remolque *f*, cisterna semi-trailer *f*; **~ storage** *n* PROD almacenaje en tanques *m*; **~ top** *n* WATER TRANSP *ship building* techo *m*; **~ top filter** *n* PROD filtro de la tapa del doble fondo *m*; **~ truck** *n*

AmE (*cf tank lorry BrE*) TRANSP camión-cuba *m*; ~ **valve** *n* HYDRAUL válvula del depósito *f*; ~ **wagon** *n BrE* (*cf tank car AmE*) MINE, RAIL vagón cisterna *m*, vagón cuba *m*

tankage *n* AGRIC residuo de frigoríficos *m*, residuo de mataderos *m*

tanker *n* AIR TRANSP avión cisterna de reaprovisionamiento en vuelo *m*, MAR POLL buque tanque *m*, PETR TECH buque petrolero *m*, buque cisterna *m*, PETROL buque petrolero *m*, TRANSP camión cisterna *m*, depósito-cisterna *m*, VEH camión cisterna *m*, WATER TRANSP *type of ship* buque tanque *m*; ~ **lorry** *n BrE* CONST camión cisterna *m*, camión tanque *m*; ~ **terminal** *n* TRANSP terminal de cisternas *f*; ~ **truck** *n AmE* CONST camión cisterna *m*, camión tanque *m*

tannage *n* CHEM curtido *m*

tannate *n* CHEM tanato *m*

tannic *adj* CHEM tánico

tannin *n* CHEM tanino *m*

tanning *n* CINEMAT endurecimiento *m*

tantalate *n* CHEM tantalato *m*

tantalic *adj* CHEM tantálico

tantalite *n* MINERAL tantalita *f*

tantalum *n* (*Ta*) CHEM, ELEC ENG, METALL tantalio *m* (*Ta*), tántalo *m* (*Ta*); ~ **anode** *n* ELEC ENG ánodo de tantalio *m*; ~ **capacitor** *n* ELEC ENG condensador de tantalio *m*; ~ **foil capacitor** *n* ELEC ENG condensador de láminas de tantalio *m*; ~ **oxide** *n* CHEM, ELEC ENG óxido de tantalio *m*; ~ **oxide capacitor** *n* ELEC ENG condensador de óxido de tantalio *m*; ~ **slug** *n* ELEC ENG ánodo sólido de tantalio *m*; ~ **slug capacitor** *n* ELEC ENG condensador con ánodo sólido de tantalio *m*; ~ **solid capacitor** *n* ELEC ENG condensador sólido de tantalio *m*; ~ **wet capacitor** *n* ELEC ENG condensador húmedo de tantalio *m*

tap[1] *n* CONST *BrE* (*cf faucet AmE*) *cock* grifo *m*, ELEC *winding* contacto *m*, conexión intermedia *f*, derivación *f*, toma *f*, ELEC ENG tomacorriente *m*, conexión intermedia *f*, LAB *BrE* (*cf faucet AmE*) llave de paso *f*, MECH grifo *m*, canilla *f*, macho de terraja *m*, MECH ENG *for cutting thread* macho de roscar *m*, macho *m*, macho de terraja *m*, PROD *furnace* sangría *f*, colada *f*; ~ **bolt** *n* MECH ENG perno completamente roscado *m*; ~ **change operation** *n* ELEC cambiador de relación de transformación *m*; ~ **changer** *n* ELEC *switch*, ELEC ENG conmutador de tomas *m*; ~ **with crutch key** *n* CONST grifo con llave de horquilla *m*; ~ **funnel** *n* LAB embudo con llave *m*; ~ **holder** *n* MECH ENG giramachos *m*, portamachos *m*; ~ **with metric thread** *n* MECH ENG arandela de asiento esférico *f*, cojinete radial sencillo de rótula *m*, cojinete sencillo de rótula *m*, cojinete sencillo esférico *m*, engranaje satélite *m*, macho de rosca métrica *m*, tornillo de sujeción del cojinete de roscar *m*; ~ **plate** *n* MECH ENG terraja de mano *f*; ~~**position indicator** *n* ELEC indicador de posición de tomas *m*; ~~**reseating tool** *n* MECH ENG macho de repasar roscas *m*; ~ **selector** *n* ELEC conmutador selector *m*, selector *m*; ~ **with square head** *n* MECH ENG macho de cabeza cuadrada *m*; ~ **switch** *n* ELEC conmutador de derivación *m*, conmutador de tomas *m*, conmutador selector *m*, llave de derivación *f*, selector *m*; ~ **washer** *n* MECH ENG arandela de canilla *f*, arandela de grifo *f*; ~ **with Whitworth thread** *n* MECH ENG macho con rosca Whitworth *m*; ~ **wrench** *n* MECH ENG bandeador

para roscar *m*, giramachos *m*, llave de machos de terraja *f*, llave giramachos *f*, volvedor *m*

tap[2] *vt* C&G *glass in melting furnace* vaciar, COAL sacar, derivar, horadar (*AmL*), puncionar, colar (*Esp*), taladrar, sangrar, FOOD sacar con espita, MINE horadar (*AmL*), extraer (*AmL*), taladrar, colar (*Esp*), PHYS dar golpecitos, PROD roscar, aterrajar, roscar con macho, golpear ligeramente, *to draw off by diverting* derivar, extraer

tape[1] *n* C&G, COMP&DP, MECH, P&R, TEXTIL cinta *f*, TV cinta magnetofónica *f*; ~ **advance** *n* TV avance de cinta *m*; ~ **alignment guide** *n* TV guiacinta de alineamiento *f*; ~~**automated bonding** *n* (*TAB*) ELEC ENG empacado automático en cinta *m*; ~ **backing** *n* TV cinta de emergencia *f*, cinta de respaldo *f*; ~ **base** *n* TV base de cinta *f*; ~ **cartridge** *n* COMP&DP cartucho de cinta *m*; ~~**coating material** *n* TV capa protectora de cintas *f*; ~ **condenser** *n* TEXTIL condensador de cintas *m*; ~~**controlled linecasting** *n* PRINT fundición de líneas de tipo controlado por cinta *f*; ~ **copy** *n* COMP&DP copia de cinta *f*; ~ **counter** *n* TV contador de cinta *m*, contador que indica la cantidad de cinta utilizada *m*; ~ **cupping** *n* TV escarificación de la cinta *f*; ~ **curvature** *n* TV curvatura de la cinta *f*; ~ **deck** *n* ACOUST platina magnetofónica *f*, COMP&DP mecanismo grabador de cinta *m*, unidad de cinta *f*; ~ **drive** *n* COMP&DP impulsor de cinta *m*, unidad de cinta *f*, TV mecanismo impulsador de cinta *m*; ~ **dump** *n* COMP&DP vuelco en cinta *m*, vuelco en cinta magnética *m*; ~ **file** *n* COMP&DP archivo de cinta *m*; ~ **guide** *n* TV guía de cinta *f*; ~~**hanging display reinforcement** *n* PACK refuerzo del expositor con cinta *m*; ~ **header** *n* COMP&DP cabecera de cinta *f*; ~ **input guide** *n* TV guía de entrada de la cinta *f*; ~ **label** *n* COMP&DP etiqueta de cinta *f*; ~ **leader** *n* COMP&DP enhebrador de cinta magnética *m*, TV conductor de cinta *m*; ~~**length indicator** *n* TV indicador de longitud de la cinta *m*; ~ **library** *n* COMP&DP biblioteca de cintas *f*, cintoteca *f*; ~ **lifter** *n* TV sustentadora de la cinta *f*; ~ **line** *n* METR metro agrimensor *m*; ~ **loop** *n* TV cinta continua *f*; ~ **loop cassette** *n* TV casete de cinta continua *f*; ~ **mark** *n* COMP&DP marca de cinta *f*; ~ **measure** *n* MECH, METR cinta de medir *f*, cinta métrica *f*; ~~**moistening device** *n* PACK dispositivo para humedecer la banda *m*; ~ **neutral plane** *n* TV plano neutro de la cinta *m*; ~ **output guide** *n* TV guía de salida de cintas *f*; ~ **oxide layer** *n* TV capa de óxido de la cinta *f*; ~ **punch** *n* COMP&DP perforadora de cinta *f*, troquel de cinta perforada *m*; ~ **reader** *n* COMP&DP lector de cintas *m*; ~ **recorder** *n* ACOUST, GEOPHYS magnetófono *m*; ~ **reproducer** *n* COMP&DP reproductor de cintas *m*; ~ **roller** *n* TV carrete de cinta *m*; ~ **run** *n* TV recorrido de la cinta *m*; ~ **sealer** *n* PACK aparato para cerrar o precintar con bandas *m*; ~ **skip** *n* COMP&DP omisión en la cinta magnética *f*, salto de cinta *m*; ~ **slippage** *n* TV deslizamiento de la cinta *m*; ~ **speed** *n* ACOUST, TV velocidad de cinta *f*; ~ **speed control** *n* TV control de la velocidad de la cinta *m*; ~ **splice** *n* CINEMAT empalme con cinta *m*; ~ **splicer** *n* CINEMAT empalmadora de cinta *f*; ~ **tension** *n* TV tensión de la cinta *f*; ~ **tension control** *n* TV control de la tensión de la cinta *m*; ~~**to-film transfer** *n* CINEMAT transferencia de cinta de vídeo a película *f*, TV transferencia de cinta a película *f*; ~ **transport** *n* COMP&DP transporte de cinta *m*; **~ unit** *n* COMP&DP unidad de cinta *f*; **~-wound core** *n* ELEC ENG núcleo enrollado de cinta *m*; **~ wrap** *n* OPT cinta enrollada *f*

tape² *vt* ELEC *insulation* medir

taped: **~ closure** *n* PACK cierre precintado *m*; **~ component** *n* ELEC ENG componente empacado en cinta *m*, componente encintado *m*, componente pegado con cinta *m*

taper *n* MECH ahusamiento *m*, conicidad *f*, cono *m*, unión cónica *f*, MECH ENG, PROD ahusamiento *m*; **~ bend** *n* MECH ENG *pipe fitting* codo cónico *m*; **~ bevel** *n* C&G bisel graduado *m*; **~ dowel** *n* MECH ENG pasador cónico *m*; **~ dowel with extracting thread** *n* MECH ENG pasador cónico con rosca extractora *m*; **~ key** *n* MECH ENG chaveta cónica *f*, cuña *f*; **~ key with gib head** *n* MECH ENG chaveta cónica con tacón *f*, cuña con tacón *f*; **~ key without gib head** *n* MECH ENG chaveta cónica sin tacón *f*, cuña sin tacón *f*; **~ keys and keyways** *n pl* MECH ENG chavetas y chaveteros cónicos *m pl*; **~ pin** *n* MECH pasador cónico *m*, MECH ENG aguja cónica *f*, clavija cónica *f*, pasador ahusado *m*, pasador cónico *m*; **~ pin with external thread** *n* MECH ENG pasador cónico con rosca exterior *m*; **~ pin with internal thread** *n* MECH ENG pasador cónico con rosca interior *m*; **~ pipe** *n* MECH ENG caño cónico *m*, tubo cónico *m*; **~ pipe thread** *n* MECH ENG rosca de tubo cónico *f*; **~ roller bearing** *n* MECH ENG cojinete de rodillos cónicos *m*; **~ sleeve** *n* MECH ENG manguito cónico *m*; **~ washer** *n* MECH ENG arandela cónica *f*

tapered: **~ axle end** *n* AUTO extremo cónico del árbol *m*; **~ compression ring** *n* AUTO anillo cónico de compresión *m*; **~ fiber** *AmE*, **~ fibre** *BrE* *n* OPT fibra de sección decreciente *f*, TELECOM fibra ahusada *f*, fibra cónica *f*, fibra de sección decreciente *f*; **~ hub** *n* VEH buje cónico *m*; **~ needle** *n* MECH ENG aguja cónica *f*; **~ roller bearing** *n* VEH rodamiento de rodillos cónicos *m*; **~ section** *n* ELEC ENG sección decreciente *f*; **~ transition** *n* OPT transición cónica *f*; **~ wing** *n* AIR TRANSP, TRANSP ala decreciente *f*, ala trapecial *f*

tapering *n* MECH ahusamiento *m*, MECH ENG afinamiento progresivo *m*, ahusamiento *m*, conicidad *f*, conificación *f*, PROD ahusamiento *m*

taphole *n* PROD *of furnace* agujero de colada *m*

taphrogenesis *n* GEOL tafrogénesis *f*

tapiolite *n* MINERAL tapiolita *f*

tapout: **~ block** *n* C&G bloque de vaciado *m*

tapped: **~ coil** *n* ELEC ENG bobina en derivación *f*; **~ control** *n* ELEC ENG control de toma intermedia *m*; **~ delay** *n* ELECTRON retardo por derivación *m*; **~ delay line** *n* ELECTRON línea de retardo por derivación *f*; **~ fitting** *n* MECH ENG *pipe* acoplamiento roscado *m*; **~ hole** *n* PROD agujero de colada *m*; **~ nut** *n* MECH ENG tuerca aterrajada *f*, tuerca roscada *f*; **~ primary winding** *n* ELEC ENG devanado primario derivado *m*; **~ resistor** *n* ELEC ENG resistencia derivada *f*; **~ secondary winding** *n* ELEC ENG devanado secundario derivado *m*; **~ substation** *n* ELEC *supply network*, MECH ENG subestación con tomas *f*; **~ transformer** *n* ELEC, ELEC ENG transformador con tomas *m*, transformador con tomas de regulación *m*; **~ winding** *n* ELEC ENG devanado con puntos intermedios *m*

tappet *n* AUTO balancín *m*, empujaválvulas *m*, excéntrica *f*, leva *f*, levantaválvulas *m*, taqué *m*, MECH botador *m*, MECH ENG botador *m*, pilón triturador *m*, VEH balancín *m*, levantaválvulas *m*; **~ adjuster** *n* MECH ENG ajustador del impulsor *m*; **~ stem** *n* AUTO vástago del levantaválvulas *m*; **~ valve drill** *n* CONST *rock drill* perforadora con válvula de platillo *f*

tapping *n* C&G vaciado *m* (*AmL*), ELEC *connection* toma intermedia *f*, bifurcación *f*, derivación *f*, derivación *f*, derivación de circuitos *f*, puesta en derivación *f*, ramificación *f*, acometida *f*, toma de corriente *f*, toma *f*, ELEC ENG acometida *f*, ramificación *f*, HYDRAUL grifo de dos vías *m*, MECH ENG roscado *m*, aterrajado *m*, PHYS golpeteo *m*, WATER *boat building* perforación *f*; **~ bar** *n* PROD *founding* pinzas para desatascar el agujero de colada *f pl*; **~ chuck** *n* MECH ENG boquilla para macho roscador *f*, plato portamachos *m*; **~ current** *n* ELEC *of winding* corriente de toma *f*; **~ drill** *n* MECH ENG broca de agujeros a roscar *f*; **~ duty** *n* ELEC rendimiento de toma *m*; **~ factor** *n* ELEC factor de toma *m*; **~ hole** *n* C&G orificio de vaciado *m*; **~ machine** *n* MECH ENG aterrajadora *f*, máquina de hacer tornillos *f*, máquina de taladrar y roscar tuberías *f*, máquina roscadora de interiores *f*; **~ the metal** *n* PROD *cast iron* colada de metal fundido *f*; **~ point** *n* ELEC ENG punto de toma *m*; **~ power** *n* ELEC *of winding* energía de toma *f*, potencia de toma *f*; **~ quantity** *n* ELEC cantidad de toma *f*; **~ range** *n* ELEC gama de tomas *f*; **~-screws thread** *n* MECH ENG hilo de los machos de roscar *m*; **~ step** *n* ELEC escalón de tomas *m*; **~ stream** *n* WATER toma en corrientes de agua *f*; **~ water** *n* MINE agua de extracción *f*

taproot *n* AGRIC raíz pivotante *f*

tar¹ *n* CHEM alquitrán *m*, brea *f*, CHEM TECH, COAL alquitrán *m*, CONST alquitrán *m*, brea *f*, ELEC, GEOL, MECH ENG alquitrán *m*, P&R alquitrán *m*, brea *f*, PETR TECH, PETROL, WATER TRANSP alquitrán *m*; **~ ball** *n* MAR POLL bola de alquitrán *f*; **~ boiler** *n* CONST caldera para calentar alquitrán *f*; **~ coating** *n* P&R pintura asfáltica *f*; **~ dye** *n* COLOUR colorante de alquitrán *m*; **~ paper** *n* PACK, PAPER papel bituminado *m*, papel embreado *m*; **~ sand** *n* PETR TECH arena impregnada de brea *f*; **~ sprayer** *n* CONST máquina para regar con alquitrán *f*; **~ sprinkler** *n* CONST regadera asfáltica *f*, rociador de alquitrán *m*

tar² *vt* GEN alquitranar

tare *n* PACK, TEXTIL tara *f*

target *n* CONST *surveying* mira *f*, tablilla *f*, ELEC, PART PHYS, PHYS anticátodo *m*, SPACE, TV blanco *m*, objetivo *m*; **~ burn-up** *n* NUCL valor objetivo de quemado *m*; **~ computer** *n* COMP&DP computador de destino *m* (*AmL*), computadora de destino *f* (*AmL*), ordenador de destino *m* (*Esp*); **~ designation laser** *n* ELECTRON láser de señalización del blanco *m*; **~ electrode** *n* ELEC ENG electrodo anticátodo *m*, TV electrodo del blanco *m*; **~-illuminating laser** *n* ELECTRON láser de iluminación del blanco *m*; **~ irradiation** *n* NUCL irradiación del blanco *f*, PART PHYS irradiación del anticátodo *f*, irradiación del ánodo *f*; **~ layer** *n* TV nivel del objetivo *m*; **~-leveling rod** *AmE* see *target-levelling rod BrE*; **~-leveling staff** *AmE* see *target-levelling staff BrE*; **~-levelling rod** *n* *BrE* CONST *surveying* mira de nivelación *f*; **~-levelling staff** *n* *BrE* CONST *surveying* mira de nivelación *m*; **~ mesh** *n* TV red del objetivo *f*; **~ tug** *n* MILIT remolcador de blancos *m*

tariff n ELEC, PACK, TELECOM tarifa f; ~ **structure** n TELECOM composición de tarifas f

tarmac n CONST tarmacadam f

tarmacadam n CONST tarmacadam f

tarpaulin n CONST tela alquitranada f, WATER TRANSP encerado m; ~-**covered container** n TRANSP contenedor cubierto con lona m

tarred: ~ **brown paper** n PACK, PAPER papel bituminado m, papel embreado m; ~ **cordage** n WATER TRANSP cabuyería alquitranada f; ~ **felt** n CONST fieltro alquitranado m, PAPER cartón piedra m

tarring n GEN alquitranado m

tartar n CHEM bitartrato de potasio m, tártaro m

tartaric[1] adj CHEM tartárico

tartaric[2]: ~ **acid** n CHEM, DETERG ácido tartárico m

tartrate n CHEM tartrato m

tartrated adj CHEM tartrado

tartronic adj CHEM tartrónico

tartronylurea n CHEM tartronilurea f

TAS abbr (true airspeed) AIR TRANSP velocidad anemométrica verdadera f, velocidad verdadera f

task n COMP&DP tarea f

tasmanite n MINERAL tasmanita f

tassel n AGRIC maize panoja f

taste: ~ **control** n WATER control de degustación m

tasting n FOOD cata f (Esp), cateo f (AmL)

tau: ~-**lepton** n NUCL, PART PHYS, PHYS leptón tau m; ~-**meson** n PART PHYS mesón tau m; ~ **neutrino** n PART PHYS, PHYS neutrino tau m; ~ **particle** n PART PHYS partícula tau f

tauon n PHYS tauón m; ~ **neutrino** n PART PHYS, PHYS neutrino tauón m

taurine n CHEM taurina f

tauriscite n MINERAL tauriscita f

taurocholate n CHEM taurocolato m

taurocholic adj CHEM taurocólico

taut: ~-**wire angle indicator** n OCEAN inclinómetro de cable en tensión m; ~-**wire indicator** n OCEAN medidor por hilo tenso m

tautomer n CHEM tautómero m

tautomeric adj CHEM tautómero

tautomerism n CHEM tautomerismo m

tautomerization n CHEM tautomerización f

taxi[1]: ~ **holding position** n AIR TRANSP punto de espera de rodaje m

taxi[2] vi AIR TRANSP rodar

taxiing n AIR TRANSP carreteo m, rodadura f, rodaje m

taximeter n VEH taxímetro m

taxiway n AIR TRANSP of airport pista de carreteo f, pista de rodaje f; ~ **centerline light** AmE see taxiway centreline light BrE; ~ **centerline marking** AmE see taxiway centreline marking BrE; ~ **centreline light** n BrE AIR TRANSP luz del eje de la pista de rodaje f; ~ **centreline marking** n BrE AIR TRANSP balizado del eje de la pista de rodaje m, marcación del centro de la pista f; ~-**edge marker** n AIR TRANSP balizado de los bordes de la pista de rodaje m, marcación lateral de la pista de rodaje f; ~ **intersection marking** n AIR TRANSP balizado de cruce de la pista de rodaje m, marcación de cruce de la pista de rodaje f; ~ **light** n AIR TRANSP luz de la pista de rodaje f

Taylor: ~ **cone** n RAD PHYS cono de Taylor m

taylorite n MINERAL taylorita f

Taylor-Orowan: ~ **dislocation** n CRYSTALL see edge dislocation dislocación de Taylor-Orowan f

Tb abbr (terbium) CHEM Tb (terbio)

TBC abbr (timebase corrector) TV corrector de base de tiempo m

T-beam n CONST viga en T f

TBF abbr (traveling belt filter AmE, travelling belt filter BrE) NUCL filtro de correa móvil m

T-bolt n (tee bolt) MECH ENG perno con cabeza de muletilla m, perno en T m

TBP abbr (tethered buoyant platform) PETR TECH plataforma flotante amarrada f

TC abbr (trunk code) TELECOM código interurbano m

Tc abbr (technetium) CHEM Tc (tecnecio)

TCE abbr (transit connection element) TELECOM elemento de comunicación en tránsito m, elemento de conexión en tránsito m

TCF: ~ **bleaching** n PAPER pulp blanqueo sin compuesto clorado m

T-connection n MECH ENG conexión en T f

T-core n CINEMAT núcleo T m

TCR abbr (telemetry command and ranging subsystem) SPACE communications TCR (control telemedida telemando y distancia)

T-cramp n CONST for stonework grapa en T f

TDC abbr AUTO, MECH (top dead center AmE, top dead centre BrE) PMS (punto muerto superior), PART PHYS (time-to-digital conversion) conversión temporal a digital f, VEH (top dead center AmE, top dead centre BrE) PMS (punto muerto superior)

TDF abbr (trunk distribution frame) TELECOM repartidor principal m

TDI abbr P&R (toluene diisocyanate) TDI (diisocianato de tolueno, toluendiisocianato), TELECOM (trade data interchange) intercambio de datos comerciales m

t-distribution n MATH distribución t f

TDM abbr (time-division modulation, time-division multiplexing) COMP&DP, ELECTRON, PHYS, SPACE, TELECOM TDM (modulación por división de tiempo, multiplexación por división de tiempo)

TDMA[1] abbr (time-division multiple access) COMP&DP, ELECTRON, SPACE, TELECOM acceso múltiple por división de tiempo m

TDMA[2]: ~ **terminal** n SPACE communications terminal TDMA f

TDN abbr (total digestible nutrients) AGRIC total de nutrientes digestibles m

Te abbr (tellurium) CHEM, ELEC ENG Te (telurio)

TE[1] abbr (transverse electric) ELEC ENG TE (transversal eléctrico)

TE[2]: ~ **mode** n (transverse electric mode) ELEC, ELEC ENG, OPT, PHYS, TELECOM modo TE m (modo eléctrico transversal); ~ **wave** n (transverse electric wave) ELEC, ELEC ENG, PHYS, TELECOM onda TE f (onda eléctrica transversal)

teak n CONST madera de teca f, WATER TRANSP madera de teca f, teca f

team n PROD equipo m, equipo de trabajo m, SPACE equipo m

tear[1] n C&G rasgadura f, PAPER desgarro m; ~ **fault** n GEOL falla de desgarramiento f; ~ **gas** n MILIT chemical warfare gas lacrimógeno m; ~ **grenade** n MILIT chemical warfare granada lacrimógena f; ~ **line** n PRINT línea de corte f; ~-**off** n PRINT arrancado m; ~-**off closure** n PACK cierre que se abre rasgando m; ~-**off pack** n PACK envase que se abre rasgando m; ~ **resistance** n P&R resistencia al desgarro f; ~ **strength** n P&R resistencia al desgarramiento f, resistencia al rasgado f, PAPER, PRINT, TEXTIL resistencia al desgarro *f*; ~ **strip** *n* PACK tira para rasgar *f*; ~ **tab lid** *n* PACK tapa lengüeta para rasgar *f*; ~ **tape** *n* PACK tira de rasgado *f*

tear² *vi* P&R romper

teardown *n* PROD desmontaje *m*

tearing *n* C&G rasgadura *f*, PAPER desgarro *m*, TV *cross-piece to which rail is attached* seccionamiento *m*; ~ **test** *n* P&R prueba de rasgado *f*; ~ **tester** *n* PAPER aparato para medir el desgarro *m*; ~ **wire** *n* PAPER hilo de desgarre *m*

teat: ~ **screw** *n* MECH ENG muñón roscado *m*, saliente roscada *f*

technetium *n* (*Tc*) CHEM tecnecio *m* (*Tc*)

technical: ~ **acknowledgement** *n* TELECOM reconocimiento técnico *m*; ~ **breakdown** *n* TELECOM fallo técnico *m*, interrupción en el servicio técnico *f*; ~ **breakthrough** *n* PROD avance técnico *m*; ~ **data management** *n* COMP&DP, PROD gestión de datos técnicos *f*; ~ **instructions** *n pl* MECH ENG, RAIL instrucciones técnicas *f pl*; ~ **product documentation** *n* SAFE documentación técnica del producto *f*; ~ **regulation** *n* CONST norma técnica *f*, normativa técnica *f*, TELECOM normativa técnica *f*; ~ **report** *n* TV informe técnico *m*; ~ **requirement** *n* METR requerimiento técnico *m*; ~ **safety requirement** *n* SAFE requisito técnico de seguridad *m*; ~ **school** *n* PROD escuela técnica *f*; ~ **service** *n* MECH ENG servicio técnico *m*; ~ **specification** *n* CONST especificación técnica *f*; ~ **stop** *n* AIR TRANSP *air transport* parada técnica *f*; ~ **viewpoint** *n* TELECOM punto de vista técnico *m*

Technical: ~ **and Operational Control Center** *n* AmE (*TOCC*) SPACE Centro de Control Técnico y de Operaciones *m* (*TOCC*)

technician *n* GEN técnico *m*

technological: ~ **restriction** *n* SPACE restricción tecnológica *f*

technology *n* GEN tecnología *f*

tectogene *n* GEOL orógeno *m*, tectógeno *m*

tectogenesis *n* PETR TECH tectogénesis *m*

tectonic¹ *adj* GEOL, PETR TECH tectónico

tectonic²: ~ **map** *n* GEOL mapa tectónico *m*; ~ **process** *n* PETR TECH proceso tectónico *m*; ~ **quake** *n* GEOPHYS movimiento tectónico *m*; ~ **setting** *n* GEOL contexto tectónico *m*

tectonics *n* GEOL, PETR TECH tectónica *f*

tectorial: ~ **membrane** *n* ACOUST membrana tectoria *f*

tedder *n* AGRIC oreador del heno *m*

tee¹: ~-**shaped** *adj* GEOM, MECH ENG en T

tee²: ~ **bolt** *n* (*T-bolt*) MECH ENG perno con cabeza de muletilla *m*, perno en T *m*; ~ **coupler** *n* OPT, TELECOM acoplador en T *m*; ~ **joint** *n* ELEC *cable* te de derivación *f*, unión en forma de T *f*; ~-**off substation** *n* ELEC *supply network*, ELEC ENG subestación de bifurcación *f*, subestación de derivación *f*; ~-**piece union** *n* CONST unión de una pieza en T *f*; ~ **slot** *n* (*T-slot*) MECH ENG ranura en T *f*; ~ **socket wrench** *n* MECH ENG llave de tubo en T *f*

teem *vt* C&G vaciar, PROD *founding* colar

teeming *n* PROD *moulds* colada de llenado *f*, llenado de lingoteras *m*, vaciado de metal fundido *m*; ~ **pouch** *n* MECH ENG bolsa de colada *f*

teetered: ~ **rotor** *n* FUELLESS rotor equilibrado *m*

teeth *n pl* MECH ENG *of gear wheel* dientes *m pl*

Teflon® *n* CHEM Teflón® *m*

TEI *abbr* (*terminal end-point identifier*) TELECOM identificador del punto final terminal *m*

teintochemistry *n* COLOUR química de la tintura *f*, química de tintes *f*

TEL *abbr* (*tetraethyl lead*) CHEM TEP (*tetraetilplomo*), plomo tetraetilo *m*

telecast *vt* TV televisar

telecine *n* TV telecine *m*; ~ **chain** *n* CINEMAT cadena de telecine *f*; ~ **machine** *n* TV máquina de telecine *f*; ~ **scan** *n* TV exploración de telecine *f*

telecommunications *n pl* COMP&DP, PHYS, WATER TRANSP telecomunicaciones *f pl*; ~ **cable** *n* TELECOM cable de telecomunicaciones *m*; ~ **management network** *n* (*TMN*) TELECOM red de gestión de telecomunicaciones *f*; ~ **network** *n* COMP&DP, TELECOM red de telecomunicaciones *f*; ~ **operator** *n* TELECOM operador de telecomunicaciones *m*

telecommuting *n* COMP&DP telecomnutación *f*

teleconference *n* COMP&DP, TELECOM teleconferencia *f*

teleconverter: ~ **lens** *n* CINEMAT lente teleconvertidora *f*

teledistribution *n* TV teledistribución *f*

teledynamic *adj* MECH ENG teledinámico

telegraph: ~ **cable** *n* ELEC ENG cable telegráfico *m*; ~ **exchange** *n* ELEC ENG central telegráfica *f*; ~ **installation** *n* TELECOM instalación telegráfica *f*; ~ **line** *n* ELEC ENG línea telegráfica *f*, sección de vía *f*; ~ **signal** *n* ELECTRON señal telegráfica *f*

teleinformatics *n* TELECOM telecomputación *f*, teleinformática *f*

telelens *n* PHOTO teleobjetivo *m*

telemarketing *n* TELECOM telecomercialización *f*, telemarketing *m*, telemercadeo *m* (*AmL*)

telematic¹ *adj* TELECOM telemático

telematic²: ~ **agent** *n* (*TLMA*) TELECOM agente telemático *m*

telematics *n* TELECOM telemática *f*

telemechanics *n* MECH ENG telemecánica *f*

telemechanism *n* MECH ENG telemecanismo *m*

telemeter *n* ELEC *measurement* aparato de telemedida *m*, distanciómetro *m*, teleindicador *m*, telemedidor *m*, telémetro *m*, MECH ENG distanciómetro *m*, medidor de distancia *m*, telemedidor *m*, telémetro *m*, MILIT telémetro *m*

telemetrograph *n* MECH ENG telemetrógrafo *m*

telemetry *n* COMP&DP telemetría *f*, ELEC *measurement* teleindicación *f*, telemedición *f*, telemedida *f*, telemetría *f*, MECH ENG telemetría *f*, telemedición *f*, telemedida *f*, MILIT, NUCL, PHYS, SPACE telemetría *f*, TELECOM telemetría *f*, telemedición *f*, telemedida *f*; ~ **command and ranging subsystem** *n* (*TCR*) SPACE *communications* control telemedida telemando y distancia *m*

telephone *n* TELECOM teléfono *m*; ~-**answering machine** *n* TELECOM aparato de contestación automática de llamadas telefónicas *m*, teléfono contestador *m*; ~ **bell** *n* TELECOM timbre de teléfono *m*; ~ **booth** *n* AmE (*cf telephone kiosk BrE*) TELECOM cabina telefónica *f*; ~ **cable** *n* ELEC ENG, TELECOM cable telefónico *m*; ~ **cable pair** *n* ELEC ENG, TELECOM par de cable telefónico *m*; ~ **call** *n* TELECOM llamada telefónica *f*; ~ **card** *n* TELECOM tarjeta telefónica *f*; ~ **conference** *n* TELECOM conferencia telefónica *f*; ~ **directory** *n* TELECOM directorio de teléfonos *m*, directorio telefónico *m*, guía telefónica *f*; ~ **dugout** *n* MILIT, TELECOM abrigo subterráneo telefónico *m*; ~ **earphone** *n* ACOUST, TELECOM auricular telefónico *m*; ~ **exchange** *n* TELECOM central telefónica *f*; ~ **extension** *n* TELECOM extensión telefónica *f*; ~ **extension cable** *n* TELECOM cable de extensión telefónica *m*; ~ **extension reel** *n* TELECOM carrete de extensión telefónica *m*; ~ **induction coil** *n* ELEC ENG, TELECOM bobina de inducción telefónica *f*; ~ **kiosk** *n* BrE (*cf telephone booth AmE*) TELECOM cabina telefónica *f*; ~ **line** *n* ELEC ENG, TELECOM línea telefónica *f*; ~ **network** *n* TELECOM red telefónica *f*; ~ **number list** *n* TELECOM lista de números de teléfonos *f*; ~ **operator** *n* TELECOM operador *m*, telefonista *m*; ~ **relay** *n* ELEC ENG, TELECOM relé telefónico *m*; ~ **switch** *n* ELEC ENG, TELECOM conmutador telefónico *m*; ~ **switchboard** *n* TELECOM conmutador *m*, conmutador telefónico *m*, cuadro conmutador *m*, cuadro de conmutación telefónica *m*, cuadro de operadora *m*, mesa de operadoras *f*, tablero de distribución telefónica *m*; ~ **switchgear** *n* ELEC ENG, TELECOM disyuntor telefónico *m*; ~ **terminal** *n* TELECOM terminal telefónico *m*; ~ **token** *n* TELECOM ficha telefónica *f*; ~ **transmitter** *n* ACOUST, TELECOM transmisor telefónico *m*; ~ **user** *n* TELECOM usuario del servicio telefónico *m*, usuario del teléfono *m*; ~ **wire** *n* ELEC ENG, TELECOM hilo telefónico *m*

telephonist *n* TELECOM operador *m*, telefonista *m*

telephony *n* COMP&DP, PHYS, TELECOM telefonía *f*; **~-rated device** *n* TELECOM dispositivo nominal telefónico *m*

telephoto: ~ **lens** *n* CINEMAT, PHOTO teleobjetivo *m*, PHYS lente telefoto *m*

telepoint *n* TELECOM telepoint *m*

teleprinter *n* BrE (*cf teletypewriter AmE*) COMP&DP, TELECOM teleescritor *m* (*Esp*), teleimpresor *m*, teleprinter *m* (*AmL*)

teleprocessing *n* COMP&DP teleproceso *m*

telerecorder *n* CINEMAT, TV telerregistrador *m*

telerecording *n* CINEMAT registro de programas de televisión *m*, telerregistro *m*, TV telerregistro *m*; ~ **equipment** *n* INSTR equipo de grabación a distancia *m*

telesales *n* TELECOM ventas por teléfono *f pl*

telescope *n* CONST, INSTR, OPT, PHYS, SPACE telescopio *m*, WATER TRANSP catalejo *m*; ~ **magnifier** *n* INSTR amplificador telescópico *m*; ~ **mount** *n* INSTR soporte telescópico *m*; ~ **mounting** *n* INSTR accesorio telescópico *m*; ~ **objective** *n* INSTR objetivo telescópico *m*

telescopic[1] *adj* INSTR, MECH, OPT, SPACE telescópico

telescopic[2]: ~ **alidade** *n* CONST, INSTR alidada telescópica *f*; ~ **arm** *n* CINEMAT brazo telescópico *m*; ~ **cylinder** *n* MECH ENG cilindro telescópico *m*; ~ **erector arm** *n* CONST brazo montador telescópico *m*; ~ **fork** *n* VEH horquilla telescópica *f*; ~ **guard** *n* SAFE *measuring* dispositivo protector telescópico *m*; ~ **jack** *n* MECH ENG gato telescópico *m*; ~ **joint** *n* MECH ENG junta telescópica *f*; ~ **leg** *n* PHOTO *process* pata telescópica *f*; ~ **shock absorber** *n* AUTO, VEH amortiguador telescópico *m*; ~ **sight** *n* INSTR visión telescópica *f*; ~ **spectacles** *n pl* INSTR, OPT lentes telescópicas *f pl*; ~ **support** *n* INSTR soporte telescópico *m*; ~ **tripod** *n* CINEMAT trípode telescópico *m*; ~ **tube** *n* PHOTO tubo telescópico *m*

telescoping *n* MECH ENG telescopiaje *m*

teleservice *n* TELECOM servicio por teléfono *m*

telesoftware *n* COMP&DP soporte lógico software remotamente disponible *m*, telesoftware *m*

teletext *n* COMP&DP teletexto *m*, texto a distancia *m*, TELECOM, TV teletexto *m*

teletype *n* (*TTY*) COMP&DP teletipo *m* (*TTY*), TELECOM impresor telegráfico *m*, teletipo *m* (*TTY*)

teletypesetting *n* PRINT teletipocomposición *f*

teletypewriter *n* AmE (*cf teleprinter BrE*) COMP&DP, TELECOM teleescritor *m* (*Esp*), teleimpresor *m*, teleprinter *m* (*AmL*)

televise *vt* TV televisar

television *n* (*TV*) TELECOM, TV televisión *f* (*TV*); ~ **broadcast satellite** *n* SPACE, TELECOM, TV *communications* satélite de radiodifusión televisiva *m*, satélite de televisión directa *m*; ~ **broadcasting** *n* TELECOM radiodifusión televisiva *f*; ~ **cabinet** *n* TELECOM, TV caja del televisor *f*, gabinete del televisor *m*; ~ **cable** *n* ELEC ENG, ELECTRON, PHYS, TELECOM, TV cable de televisión *m*; ~ **camera** *n* ELEC ENG, ELECTRON, PHYS, TELECOM, TV cámara de televisión *f*; ~ **camera tube** *n* ELEC ENG, ELECTRON, PHYS, TELECOM, TV tubo de cámara de televisión *m*; ~ **film** *n* TELECOM, TV película de televisión *f*; ~ **interference** *n* ELEC ENG, ELECTRON, PHYS, TELECOM, TV interferencia televisiva *f*; ~ **microscope** *n* INSTR, TELECOM, TV microscopio de televisión *m*; ~ **picture tube** *n* ELEC ENG, ELECTRON, PHYS, TELECOM, TV tubo de imagen televisiva *m*; ~ **receiver** *n* ELEC ENG, ELECTRON, PHYS, TELECOM, TV receptor de televisión *m*; ~ **relay** *n* ELEC ENG, ELECTRON, PHYS, TELECOM, TV retransmisión televisiva *f*; ~ **rights** *n pl* TELECOM, TV derechos de televisión *m pl*; ~ **set** *n* TELECOM, TV receptor de televisión *m*; ~ **signal** *n* ELEC ENG, ELECTRON, PHYS, TELECOM, TV señal televisiva *f*; ~ **standard** *n* TELECOM, TV norma de televisión *f*; ~ **transmitter** *n* ELEC ENG, ELECTRON, PHYS, TELECOM, TV emisor de televisión *m*, transmisor de televisión *m*; ~ **tube** *n* ELEC ENG, ELECTRON, PHYS, TELECOM, TV tubo de rayos catódicos para televisión *m*; ~ **viewer** *n* TELECOM, TV espectador de televisión *m*, teleespectador *m*

teleworking *n* TELECOM teletrabajo *m*

telewriter *n* TELECOM teleautógrafo *m*, teleinscriptor *m*

telewriting *n* TELECOM teleautógrafo *m*

telex *n* COMP&DP, TELECOM télex *m*; ~ **access unit** *n* TELECOM unidad de acceso télex *f*; ~ **exchange** *n* TELECOM central télex *f*; ~ **network identification code** *n* TELECOM código de identificación de la red télex *m*; **~-plus** *n* TELECOM télex-positivo *m*; ~ **position** *n* TELECOM posición télex *f*

telltale *n* MECH ENG *instrument* indicador *m*, avisador *m*, contador *m*, chivato *m*, PRINT indicador *m*; ~ **lamp** *n* RAIL faro testigo *m*, lámpara testigo *f*

tellurate *n* CHEM telurato *m*

tellurhydric *adj* CHEM telurhídrico

telluric[1] *adj* CHEM, FUELLESS *pertaining to Earth* telúrico

telluric[2]: ~ **ocher** *AmE*, ~ **ochre** *BrE n* MINERAL ocre de teluro *m*, telurita *f*; ~ **planet** *n* SPACE planeta telúrico *m*

telluride *n* CHEM telúrido *m*

tellurite *n* CHEM, MINERAL telurita *f*, telurito *m*

tellurium *n* (*Te*) CHEM, ELEC ENG telurio *m* (*Te*); ~ **nitride** *n* ELEC ENG nitruro de teluro *m*; ~ **nitride resistor** *n* ELEC ENG resistencia de nitruro de teluro *f*

tellurometer *n* CONST telurómetro *m*

tellurous *adj* CHEM teluroso

TEM[1] *abbr* ELEC ENG (*transverse electromagnetic*) TEM (*electromagnético transversal*), RAD PHYS (*transmission electron microscopy*) MET (*microscopía electrónica de transmisión*)

TEM[2]: **~ mode** *n* OPT, TELECOM modo TEM *m*; **~ wave** *n* (*transverse electromagnetic wave*) ELEC, ELEC ENG, PHYS onda TEM *f* (*onda electromagnética transversal*)

temper *n* C&G templado *m*; **~ brittleness** *n* METALL fragilidad por ductibilidad *f*, fragilidad por revenido *f*; **~ screw** *n* MECH ENG *adjusting screw* tornillo regulador *m*, tornillo de ajuste *m*, tornillo alimentador *m*, tornillo de graduar *m*, MINE cabeza de sonda *f*, tornillo regulador *m*

temperament *n* ACOUST temperamento *m*

temperate: ~ zone *n* METEO zona templada *f*

temperature[1]: **~-controlled** *adj* THERMO con temperatura controlada, con temperatura regulada; **~-dependent** *adj* THERMO termodependiente; **~-stable** *adj* THERMO termoestable

temperature[2] *n* GEN temperatura *f*; **~ alarm** *n* PROD alarma por temperatura *f*; **~ balance** *n* THERMO equilibrio térmico *m*; **~ coefficient** *n* ELEC ENG coeficiente de temperatura *m*, THERMO coeficiente de temperatura *m*, coeficiente térmico *m*, TV coeficiente de temperatura *m*; **~ coefficient of capacitance** *n* ELEC ENG coeficiente de temperatura de capacitancia *m*, coeficiente de variación de la capacidad con la temperatura *m*; **~ coefficient of resistance** *n* ELEC coeficiente de temperatura de resistencia *m*, ELEC ENG coeficiente de temperatura de resistencia *m*, coeficiente de variación de la resistencia con la temperatura *m*; **~-compensated crystal oscillator** *n* ELECTRON oscilador de cristal con temperatura compensada *m*; **~-compensated shadow mask mount** *n* TV tubo-máscara con compensación de temperatura *m*; **~-compensated Zener diode** *n* ELECTRON diodo Zener con temperatura compensada *m*; **~-compensating capacitor** *n* ELEC ENG condensador de compensación térmica *m*; **~-compensating network** *n* ELEC ENG red de compensación térmica *f*; **~ compensation** *n* ELEC ENG compensación térmica *f*, ELECTRON compensación de temperatura *f*, THERMO compensación térmica *f*; **~ control** *n* TEXTIL, THERMO control de temperatura *m*; **~ control regulation** *n* SPACE regulación del control de temperatura *f*; **~-controlled crystal** *n* ELECTRON cristal con temperatura controlada *m*; **~-controlled crystal oscillator** *n* ELECTRON oscilador de cristal con temperatura controlada *m*; **~-controlled inspection room** *n* MECH ENG habitación de inspección de temperatura regulada *f*; **~-controlled switch** *n* ELEC, ELEC ENG interruptor controlado por temperatura *m*; **~ controller** *n* REFRIG dispositivo de regulación de temperatura *m*, regulador de temperatura *m*; **~ curve** *n* THERMO curva de temperaturas *f*; **~ cycle** *n* THERMO ciclo de temperatura *m*; **~-dependent resistor** *n* ELEC ENG resistencia termodependiente *f*; **~ detector** *n* PROD, THERMO detector de temperatura *m*; **~ difference** *n* PHYS, THERMO diferencia de temperatura *f*; **~ drop** *n* GAS caída de temperatura *f*, descenso de temperatura *m*, THERMO caída de temperatura *f*; **~ equalization** *n* THERMO igualación de temperatura *f*; **~ equalizing** *n* THERMO igualación de temperatura *f*; **~ factor** *n*

CRYSTALL factor de temperatura *m*; **~ fluctuation** *n* REFRIG fluctuación de la temperatura *f*; **~ gradient** *n* HEAT gradiente de temperatura *m*, REFRIG velocidad de enfriamiento *f*, THERMO gradiente de temperatura *m*; **~-indicating lacquer** *n* COATINGS laca indicadora de temperatura *f*, laca termométrica *f*, THERMO laca termométrica *f*; **~ inversion** *n* METEO, POLL, THERMO inversión de temperatura *f*; **~ lag** *n* NUCL retardo térmico *m*, THERMO inercia térmica *f*; **~ log** *n* FUELLESS registro de temperatura *m*, PETROL perfil térmico *m*; **~ logging** *n* PETR TECH diagrafía de temperaturas *f*, perfilaje de temperaturas *m*, registro de temperatura *m*; **~-monitoring unit** *n* MINE unidad de control de temperatura *f*; **~ probe** *n* THERMO sonda de temperatura *f*; **~ profile** *n* THERMO perfil de temperaturas *m*; **~ range** *n* THERMO gama de temperaturas *f*, intervalo de temperatura *m*, rango de temperatura *m*; **~ ratio** *n* THERMO ratio de temperaturas *m*, razón de temperaturas *f*, relación de temperaturas *f*; **~ recorder** *n* TEXTIL registro de temperatura *m*; **~ regulator** *n* HEAT, PROD regulador de temperatura *m*; **~-related failure** *n* ELEC ENG, THERMO avería térmica *f*; **~ response** *n* ELEC ENG respuesta térmica *f*; **~ rise** *n* PHYS aumento de temperatura *m*, POLL aumento de temperatura *m*, calentamiento *m*, THERMO aumento de temperatura *m*; **~-salinity diagram** *n* OCEAN diagrama de temperatura-salinidad *m*; **~ saturation** *n* ELECTRON saturación térmica *f*; **~ scale** *n* THERMO escala de temperatura *f*; **~ sending device** *n* PROD dispositivo sensible a la temperatura *m*; **~ sensor** *n* AUTO, INSTR sensor de temperatura *m*, PROD sensor de temperatura *m*, termistor *m*, REFRIG sensor de temperatura *m*, THERMO sensor de temperatura *m*, termistor *m*; **~ switch** *n* PROD termostato *m*; **~ of touchable surfaces** *n* SAFE temperatura de superficies que se pueden tocar *f*; **~ variation** *n* REFRIG variación de temperatura *f*; **~ well logging** *n* PETR TECH diagrafía de la temperatura del pozo *f*, perfil de temperatura del pozo *m*, registro de temperatura del pozo *m*

tempered[1] *adj* CRYSTALL revenido, MECH templado

tempered[2]: **~ glass** *n* C&G, TRANSP vidrio templado *m*

tempering *n* CONST *concrete* templado *m*, METALL acritud *f*, revenido *m*, NUCL temple *m*

template *n* COMP&DP patrón *m*, plantilla *f*, ELEC *measurement in manufacture* escantillón *m*, patrón *m*, gálibo *m*, matriz *f*, plantilla *f*, modelo *m*, MECH patrón *m*, calibre *m*, modelo *m*, plantilla *f*, MECH ENG modelo *m*, patrón *m*, galga *f*, matriz *f*, plantilla *f*, calibrador *m*, PETR TECH placa-soporte *f*, losa-soporte *f*, PROD *loam moulding* plantilla *f*, modelo *m*, gálibo *m*, TEXTIL plantilla *f*, VEH plantilla *f*, WATER TRANSP *shipbuilding* calibrador *m*, gálibo *m*, plantilla *f*; **~ drilling** *n* PETROL perforación con plantilla *f*

temple: ~ spectacles *n pl* INSTR patilla de gafas *f*

templet *n* MECH ENG calibrador *m*, galga *f*, matriz *f*, modelo *m*, plantilla *f*, PROD *loam moulding* terraja *f*

tempo *n* ACOUST ritmo *m*

temporal: ~ coherence *n* (*cf time coherence*) OPT, PHYS, TELECOM coherencia temporal *f*; **~ fluctuation** *n* POLL evolución temporal *f*, fluctuación temporal *f*, tendencia en el tiempo *f*, variación temporal *f*; **~ resolution** *n* POLL análisis temporal *m*, resolución temporal *f*, separación temporal *f*, RAD PHYS resolución temporal *f*; **~ variation** *n* POLL evolución temporal *f*, fluctuación temporal *f*, tendencia en el tiempo *f*, variación temporal *f*

temporally: ~~**coherent beam** *n* ELECTRON haz de coherencia temporal *m*

temporary: ~ **bridge** *n* CONST puente provisional *m*; ~ **dam** *n* WATER presa provisional *f*; ~ **end instruction** *n* PROD instrucción final provisional para terminar temporalmente *f*; ~ **guide base** *n* PETROL base de guía transitoria *f*; ~ **load** *n* COAL carga temporal *f*; ~ **memory** *n* ELEC ENG memoria temporal *f*; ~ **road** *n* CONST carretera provisional *f*; ~ **set** *n* MECH ENG deformación elástica *f*; ~ **storage** *n* COMP&DP almacenamiento temporal *m*, memoria temporal *f*, NUCL almacenamiento provisional *m*; ~ **store** *n BrE* COMP&DP almacenamiento temporal *m*, memoria temporal *f*; ~ **stress** *n* C&G esfuerzo temporal *m*; ~ **threshold shift** *n* ACOUST desplazamiento temporal del umbral *m*; ~ **works** *n pl* CONST trabajos temporales *m pl*

ten: ~~**pole filter** *n* ELECTRON filtro de diez polos *m*, filtro decapolar *m*

tenacity *n* MECH ENG, TEXTIL tenacidad *f*

tendency: ~ **to reboil** *n* C&G tendencia a producir burbujas *f*

tender *n* MAR POLL buque auxiliar *m*, RAIL ténder *m*, WATER TRANSP buque nodriza *m*, embarcación auxiliar *f*

tenderizer *n* FOOD ablandador *m*

tenderometer *n* FOOD medidor de blandura *m*

tending: ~ **resistance** *n* P&R resistencia a la flexión *f*; ~ **side** *n* PAPER lado conductor *m*

tendon *n* NUCL varilla de pretensado *f*

tennantite *n* MINERAL tennantita *f*

tenon *n* CONST espiga *f*; ~ **drive** *n* MECH ENG *tools* herramienta de espigar *f*; ~ **joint** *n* CONST junta de espiga *f*; ~ **saw** *n* CONST sierra de dientes *f*

tenoned: ~ **and housed joint** *n* CONST junta encajada de espiga *f*

tenoning: ~ **machine** *n* MECH ENG espigadora *f*, máquina de espigar *f*

tenor *n* MECH ENG *grade* tenor *m*, MINE contenido *m*, curso *m* (*Esp*), ley *f* (*AmL*)

tenorite *n* MINERAL tenorita *f*

tensile[1] *adj* MECH ENG dúctil, extensible

tensile[2]: ~ **axis** *n* METALL tracción axial *f*; ~ **force** *n* MECH ENG fuerza de tensión *f*, fuerza de tracción *f*, PHYS fuerza de tensión *f*; ~ **impact test** *n* METALL prueba de impacto de tracción *f*; ~ **length** *n* PAPER longitud de rotura *f*; ~ **strain** *n* MECH ENG, METALL deformación por tracción *f*; ~ **strength** *n* MECH carga unitaria de rotura a la tracción *f*, resistencia a la tracción *f*, tenacidad *f*, MECH ENG fuerza de tracción *f*, resistencia a tensión *f*, P&R resistencia a la tensión *f*, PHYS resistencia tensional *f*, TELECOM resistencia a la tracción *f*, tenacidad *f*, TEXTIL resistencia a la tracción *f*; ~ **strength tester** *n* PAPER dinamómetro de tracción *m*; ~ **stress** *n* MECH carga unitaria a la tracción *f*, esfuerzo de tracción *m*, MECH ENG carga unitaria a la tracción *f*, resistencia a la tracción *f*, METALL carga unitaria de tracción *f*, esfuerzo de tracción *m*, NUCL esfuerzo de tracción *m*, PHYS fuerza de separación *f*; ~ **test** *n* MECH ENG ensayo de tracción *m*, prueba de tracción *f*, METALL prueba de tracción *f*, PHYS test tensional *m*; ~ **test piece** *n* MECH ENG pieza para ensayos de tracción *f*, pieza para pruebas de tracción *f*, probeta para ensayos de

tracción *f*; ~ **tester** *n* MECH ENG, P&R, PHYS instrumento para pruebas de tracción *m*

tensility *n* CRYSTALL, MECH ENG, METALL ductilidad *f*

tensiometer *n* OCEAN tensiómetro *m*

tension *n* ELEC ENG tensión *f*, voltaje *m*, MECH ENG *of spring* tensión *f*, tracción *f*, METALL, PHYS, TEXTIL tensión *f*; ~ **arm** *n* COMP&DP brazo de tensión *m*, brazo tensor *m*; ~ **bar** *n* TEXTIL barra de tensión *f*; ~ **block** *n* MECH ENG *counter motion* bloque de tensión *m*; ~ **device** *n* TEXTIL dispositivo de tensión *m*; ~ **efficiency** *n* ACOUST eficacia de tracción *f*; ~ **gash** *n* GEOL diaclasa de tensión *f*; ~ **member** *n* MAR POLL elemento tensor *m*, tirante *m*; ~ **piece** *n* MECH ENG pieza de tensión *f*; ~ **pulley** *n* MECH ENG polea tensora *f*; ~ **roller** *n* CINEMAT rodillo tensor *m*, MECH ENG cilindro tensor *m*, PAPER rodillo de tensión *m*; ~ **screw** *n* MECH ENG perno tensor *m*, tornillo tensor *m*; ~ **servo** *n* TV servo de tensión *m*

tensioner *n* PETROL, TEXTIL, VEH tensor *m*

tensioning: ~ **bar** *n* PRINT *of plate, blanket* barra de tensión *f*

tensor *n* MATH tensor *m*; ~ **calculus** *n* MATH cálculo tensorial *m*

tenterhook *n* CONST escarpia *f*

tentering *n* TEXTIL rameado *m*

tenthmo *n* PRINT décimo *m*

tephroite *n* MINERAL tefroíta *f*

tepid *adj* THERMO tibio

tera *pref* (*T*) METR tera (*T*)

terabyte *n* OPT terabyte *m*

terbium *n* (*Tb*) CHEM terbio *m* (*Tb*)

terchloride *n* CHEM tercloruro *m*

terebenthene *n* CHEM pineno *m*, terebenteno *m*

terebic *adj* CHEM térbico

terephthalate *n* CHEM tereftalato *m*

terephthalic *adj* CHEM tereftálico

tergal *n* CHEM, TEXTIL tergal *m*

term *n* COMP&DP, MATH término *m*

terminal *n* AIR TRANSP *airport* terminal *f*, AUTO *electricity* borne *m*, terminal *m*, CINEMAT, COMP&DP terminal *m*, ELEC *connection* terminal *f*, borne *m*, ELEC ENG *electricity* borne *m*, terminal *m*, PACK, PETR TECH, PHOTO, PHYS terminal *m*, PROD borne *m*, TELECOM *electricity* borne *m*, borna *f*, terminal *m*, TV borne *m*, terminal *m*, VEH terminal *m*, borne *m*, WATER TRANSP terminal *m*; ~ **adaptor** *n* (*TA*) TELECOM adaptador terminal *m*, adaptador del borne *m*; ~ **aigrette** *n* GEOPHYS corona terminal *f*; ~ **area** *n* AIR TRANSP *of airport* área de la terminal *f*; ~ **atom** *n* CHEM *of molecule* átomo terminal *m*; ~ **barrier strip** *n* ELEC bloque de terminales *m*, ELEC ENG, PROD bloque de terminales *m*, VEH regleta de conexiones *f*, bloque de terminales *m*; ~ **block** *n* ELEC *connection* bloque de conectores *m*, bloque de conexiones *m*, bloque de lengüetas de conexión *m*, bloque de terminales *m*, bloque terminal *m*, regleta de bornes *f*, regleta de terminales *f*, tablero de bornes *m*, tablero terminal *m*, ELEC ENG cuadro de terminales *m*, tablero de bornes *m*, bloque terminal *m*, bloque de terminales *m*, PROD bloque de bornas *m*, bloque de terminales *m*, bloque terminal *m*, VEH bloque terminal *m*, bloque de terminales *m*; ~ **box** *n* ELEC *cable accessory* caja de cables *f*, caja de empalme *f*, caja de terminales *f*, ELEC ENG caja de bornes *f*, caja de cables *f*; ~ **call forwarding** *n* TELECOM transmisión de una llamada terminal *f*; ~ **capacity** *n* PROD capacidad en los

terminales *f*; **~ cover** *n* PROD tapa de terminales *f*;
~ cover plate *n* PROD placa cubierta de terminales *f*;
~ crimper *n* MECH ENG engarzador terminal *m*,
plegador final *m*; **~ designation** *n* PROD designación
de terminales *f*; **~ device** *n* COMP&DP dispositivo
terminal *m*; **~ end-point identifier** *n* (*TEI*) TELECOM
identificador del punto final terminal *m*;
~ equipment *n* TELECOM equipo terminal *m*;
~ insulator *n* ELEC, ELEC ENG aislante del terminal
m; **~ lug kit** *n* PROD juego de lengüetas de conexión
para terminales *m*; **~ marking** *n* PROD indicación de
polaridad *f*; **~ platform** *n* PETR TECH plataforma
terminal *f*; **~ port** *n* COMP&DP portilla *f*, portilla para
terminal *f*, puerto de terminal *m*; **~ screw** *n* PROD
terminal de tornillo *m*; **~ server** *n* COMP&DP *networks*
procesador del terminal *m*, servidor terminal *m*;
~ station *n* TRANSP estación terminal *f*; **~ strip** *n*
PROD regleta de bornas *f*, regleta de conexiones *f*;
~-strip module *n* PROD módulo de regleta de
terminales *m*; **~ subaddressing** *n* TELECOM subdirección terminal *f*; **~ swing arm** *n* PROD brazo
oscilante terminal *m*; **~ symbol** *n* COMP&DP símbolo
terminal *m*; **~-tensioning screw** *n* PROD tornillo
tensor para terminales *m*; **~ tower** *n* ELEC *supply*
network torre de terminales *f*; **~ velocity** *n* PHYS
velocidad terminal *f*
terminate *vt* TELECOM conectar una impedancia
terminal
terminating *n* ELEC ENG terminal *f*; **~ element** *n* ELEC
ENG elemento terminal *m*; **~ equipment** *n* TELECOM
aparato terminal *m*; **~ exchange** *n* TELECOM central
de destino *f*; **~ impedance** *n* ELEC, ELEC ENG
impedancia de terminación *f*; **~ junctor** *n* TELECOM
conjuntor terminal *m*; **~ resistor** *n* ELEC ENG resistencia límite *f*; **~ stage** *n* TELECOM etapa terminal *f*;
~ traffic *n* TELECOM, TRANSP tráfico terminal *m*
termination *n* ACOUST, COMP&DP, ELEC, PRINT, PROD,
TELECOM terminación *f*
terminator *n* COMP&DP, PROD terminador *m*
terms: **~ of delivery** *n pl* PROD condiciones de entrega *f*
pl; **~ of the same degree** *n pl* MATH términos del
mismo grado *m pl*
ternary¹ *adj* CHEM, MATH ternario
ternary²: **~ alloy** *n* METALL aleación de tres componentes *f*, aleación ternaria *f*
ternitrate *n* CHEM ternitrato *m*
teroxide *n* CHEM trióxido *m*
terpadiene *n* CHEM terpadieno *m*
terpene *n* CHEM *compound* terpeno *m*
terpenic *adj* CHEM terpénico
terpin *n* CHEM terpina *f*
terpinene *n* CHEM terpineno *m*
terpineol *n* CHEM terpineol *m*
terpinol *n* CHEM terpinol *m*
terpinolene *n* CHEM terpinoleno *m*
terpolymer *n* CHEM, P&R terpolímero *m*
terrace *n* OCEAN, WATER TRANSP bancada de popa *f*,
banco *m*
terracer *n* AGRIC constructora de terrazas *f*
terracotta *n* C&G terracota *f*; **~ floor** *n* C&G piso de
loseta *m*, piso de terracota *m*; **~ statue** *n* C&G estatua
de terracota *f*
terrain *n* GEOL terreno *m*
terramycin *n* CHEM terramicina *f*
terrane *n* GEOL macizo autóctono *m*
terraplein *n* TRANSP terraplén *m*

terrestrial¹ *adj* SPACE terrestre
terrestrial²: **~ crust** *n* SPACE corteza terrestre *f*;
~ magnetism *n* GEOPHYS, PHYS magnetismo terrestre
m; **~ station** *n* SPACE *communications* estación
terrena *f*, estación terrestre *f*; **~ surface** *n* SPACE
superficie terrestre *f*; **~ telescope** *n* INSTR telescopio
terrestre *m*; **~ tide** *n* OCEAN marea terrenal *f*
terrigenous *adj* GEOL terrestre, terrígeno
territorial: **~ waters** *n pl* OCEAN aguas territoriales *f pl*
tert: **~-butylbenzene** *n* CHEM terc-butilbenceno *m*
tertiary: **~ creep** *n* METALL fluencia terciaria *f*;
~ crushing *n* COAL molienda terciaria *f*, triturado
terciario *m*; **~ fuel** *n* AUTO combustible terciario *m*;
~ recovery *n* PETR TECH recuperación terciaria *f*;
~ recrystallization *n* METALL recristalización terciaria *f*; **~ winding** *n* ELEC *of transformer* devanado
terciario *m*
Tertiary: **~ era** *n* GEOL, PETR TECH era Terciaria *f*
tervalence *n* CHEM trivalencia *f*
tervalent *adj* CHEM trivalente
Terylene *n* CHEM Terylene® *m*, terileno *m*, WATER
TRANSP *sailcloth* terileno *m*
tesla *n* (*T*) METR, PHYS tesla *f* (*T*)
Tesla: **~ coil** *n* ELEC ENG bobina Tesla *f*
tesselite *n* MINERAL tesselita *f*
tessera *n* C&G mosaico *m*, pieza de mosaico *f*
tesseral: **~ harmonic** *n* SPACE armónico teseral *m*
test¹ *n* CHEM ensayo *m*, prueba *f*, COAL comprobación
f, contraste *m*, dócima *f*, ensayo *m*, experimento *m*,
prueba *f*, COMP&DP prueba *f*, MECH ensayo *m*, examen
m, experimento *m*, prueba *f*, METALL ensayo *m*,
prueba *f*, PHYS prueba *f*, REFRIG ensayo *m*, prueba *f*,
SPACE ensayo *m*, prueba *f*, verificación *f*, TELECOM,
TEXTIL ensayo *m*; **~ assembly** *n* NUCL equipo de
prueba *m*; **~ bar** *n* MECH ENG barra de prueba *f*, barra
patrón *f*, barra testigo *f*; **~ basin** *n* WATER estanque de
prueba *m*; **~ bed** *n* COMP&DP banco de pruebas *m*,
lecho de prueba *m*, ELEC, MECH, MECH ENG, NUCL
banco de pruebas *m*, SPACE banco de ensayos *m*,
TELECOM banco de pruebas *m*; **~ bench** *n* COMP&DP,
ELEC, MECH banco de pruebas *m*, MECH ENG banco de
ensayos *m*, banco de pruebas *m*, NUCL, TELECOM
banco de pruebas *m*; **~ board** *n* ELEC panel de
pruebas y medidas *m*, tablero de pruebas *m*;
~ chart *n* CINEMAT carta de prueba *f*; **~ cock** *n*
WATER grifo de prueba *m*; **~ condition** *n* METR
condición de prueba *f*, PROD situación de prueba *f*;
~ continuous scan *n* PROD exploración continua de
prueba *f*; **~ cube** *n* CONST probeta cúbica *f*;
~ customer *n* TELECOM abonado de prueba *m*;
~ cylinder *n* CONST probeta cilíndrica *f*, cilindro
para pruebas *m*; **~ data** *n* COMP&DP datos de prueba
m pl; **~ data generator** *n* COMP&DP generador de
datos de prueba *m*; **~ equipment** *n* MECH ENG
instrumental de pruebas *m*; **~ facility** *n* MECH ENG
instalación de pruebas *f*; **~ firing** *n* SPACE disparo
experimental *m*; **~ flight** *n* AIR TRANSP vuelo de
pruebas *m*, SPACE vuelo experimental *m*; **~ flume** *n*
WATER canalón de prueba *m*; **~ for accuracy** *n* MECH
ENG prueba de fiabilidad *f*, prueba de precisión *f*;
~ for bending and for compression *n* MECH ENG
prueba de flexión y compresión *f*; **~ frequency** *n*
ELECTRON frecuencia de prueba *f*; **~ furnace** *n* PROD
horno de pruebas *m*; **~ ground** *n* VEH conexión a
masa de prueba *f*; **~ indicator** *n* TELECOM indicador
de ensayo *m*, indicador de prueba *m*; **~ jack** *n* ELEC

ENG conector de prueba *m*; ~ **laboratory** *n* QUALITY laboratorio de pruebas *m*; ~ **lead** *n* ELEC ENG conexión de prueba *f*; ~ **liner board** *n* PACK cartón tipo test liner *m*; ~ **load** *n* MECH ENG carga de prueba *f*; ~ **loading** *n* COAL carga de ensayo *f*, carga de prueba *f*; ~ **needle** *n* MECH ENG aguja de prueba *f*; ~ **oscillator** *n* ELECTRON oscilador de pruebas *m*; ~ **paper** *n* CHEM papel de prueba *m*, papel indicador *m*, papel tornasol *m*; ~ **pattern** *n* CINEMAT patrón de prueba *m*, ELECTRON imagen patrón de prueba *f*, TV carta de ajuste *f*; ~ **piece** *n* METALL muestra *f*, probeta *f*, PAPER probeta *f*, PHYS pieza de prueba *f*; ~ **piling** *n* COAL, MINE avance con agujas de sondeo *m*; ~ **pilot** *n* AIR TRANSP piloto de pruebas *m*; ~ **pit** *n* COAL pozo de sondeo *m*, GEOL calicata *f*; ~ **plate** *n* C&G placa de pruebas *f*, HYDRAUL timbre *m*; ~ **point** *n* TELECOM punto de prueba *m*; ~ **portion** *n* QUALITY muestra de prueba *f*; ~ **position** *n* TELECOM posición de pruebas *f*, posición de pruebas y medidas *f*; ~ **pressure** *n* HYDRAUL presión de ensayo *f*, presión de prueba *f*, REFRIG presión de prueba *f*; ~ **print** *n* PHOTO prueba de ensayo *f*, tira de prueba *f*; ~ **procedure for braking systems** *n* MECH ENG método de prueba para sistemas de frenado *m*, procedimiento de prueba para sistemas de frenado *m*; ~ **prod** *n* ELEC ENG pincho de pruebas *m*, sonda de prueba *f*; ~ **production** *n* PETROL producción de ensayo *f*; ~ **program** *AmE*, ~ **programme** *BrE* *n* METR programa de prueba *m*; ~ **pump** *n* WATER bomba de prueba *f*; ~ **record** *n* ACOUST grabación de prueba *f*; ~ **reel** *n* CINEMAT bobina de prueba *f*; ~ **report** *n* COMP&DP informe de prueba *m*; ~ **requirement** *n* PROD requisito de ensayo *m*, SAFE requisito de prueba *m*; ~ **rig** *n* MECH ENG dispositivo para pruebas *m*, instalación experimental *f*, NUCL instalación de pruebas *f*, instalación experimental *f*; ~ **rod** *n* PROD *blast furnace gauge* probeta cilíndrica *f*; ~ **room** *n* TELECOM sala de pruebas *f*; ~ **run** *n* COMP&DP ejecución de prueba *f*, pasada de prueba *f*, MECH ENG ensayo *m*, ensayo de programa *m*, período de marcha comprobatorio *m*, prueba *f*, prueba de duración *f*, prueba de funcionamiento *f*; ~ **section** *n* CONST tramo de pruebas *m*, PHYS *wire* sección de prueba *f*; ~ **shop** *n* MECH ENG taller de pruebas *m*; ~ **shot** *n* PHOTO toma de ensayo *f*; ~ **sieve** *n* MECH ENG tamiz de prueba *m*; ~ **sieving** *n* MECH ENG tamizado de prueba *m*; ~ **signal** *n* ELECTRON señal de prueba *f*; ~ **signal generator** *n* ELECTRON generador de señal de prueba *m*; ~ **single scan** *n* PROD exploración simple de prueba *f*; ~ **specification** *n* SPACE especificación experimental *f*; ~ **specimen** *n* METALL probeta de ensayo *f*, P&R espécimen de ensayo *m*, probeta de ensayo *f*; ~ **stand** *n* SPACE plataforma de pruebas *f*; ~ **strip** *n* CINEMAT, PHOTO tira de ensayo *f*; ~ **switch** *n* ELEC ENG interruptor de pruebas *m*; ~ **tape** *n* ACOUST, TV cinta de prueba *f*; ~ **terminal** *n* ELEC ENG terminal de pruebas *m*; ~ **tool** *n* LAB, QUALITY, SPACE útil de ensayo *m*; ~ **track** *n* TRANSP pista de pruebas *f*, vía de pruebas *f*; ~ **train** *n* RAIL tren de prueba *m*; ~ **transformer** *n* TELECOM transformador de prueba *m*; ~ **transmission** *n* TV transmisión de prueba *f*; ~ **tube** *n* C&G, CHEM, LAB tubo de ensayo *m*, PROD probeta *f*, tubo de ensayo *m*; ~ **tube holder** *n* LAB portatubos *m*; ~~**tube rack** *n* LAB *support* gradilla *f*;

~ **voltage** *n* ELEC prueba de tensión *f*, tensión de ensayo *f*, tensión de prueba *f*
test² *vt* GEN efectuar una prueba de, ensayar, probar
test³: ~ **a process** *vi* CHEM probar un proceso; ~ **the rope** *vi* MECH ENG probar la cuerda, probar la soga
tested¹: ~ **first** *adj* TELECOM de primera prueba
tested²: ~ **chain** *n* MECH ENG cadena probada *f*
testing *n* CHEM ensayo *m*, prueba *f*, COAL ensayo de producción *m*, prueba de producción *f*, verificación *f*, COMP&DP ensayo *m*, prueba *f*, comprobación *f*, MECH ENG comprobación *f*, constatación *f*, control *m*, ensayo *m*, prueba *f*, verificación *f*, QUALITY ensayo *m*; ~ **drill** *n* MINE perforación de comprobación *f* (*AmL*), perforación testiguera *f* (*Esp*); ~ **flame** *n* MINE gas de prueba *m*; ~ **machine** *n* MECH ENG máquina de verificación *f*; ~ **pressure** *n* HYDRAUL, REFRIG presión de prueba *f*; ~ **record sheet** *n* COLOUR protocolo de pruebas *m*; ~ **shop** *n* MECH ENG taller de verificación *m*; ~ **tank** *n* WATER TRANSP *hull, propeller* canal de experiencias hidrodinámicas *m*, canal de pruebas hidrodinámicas *m*
tethered¹ *adj* SPACE en cautividad
tethered²: ~ **buoyant platform** *n* (*TBP*) PETR TECH plataforma flotante amarrada *f*; ~ **satellite** *n* SPACE satélite en cautividad *m*
Tethyan: ~ **realm** *n* GEOL dominio Tetiense *m*
Tethys: ~ **Ocean** *n* GEOL mar Tethis *m*
TE/TM: ~ **mode** *n* PHYS modo TE/TM *m*
tetrabasic *adj* CHEM tetrabásico
tetrabromide *n* CHEM tetrabromuro *m*
tetrabromoethane *n* CHEM tetrabromoetano *m*
tetrabromoethylene *n* CHEM tetrabromoetileno *m*
tetracarbonyl *n* CHEM tetracarbonilo *m*
tetrachlorethane *n* CHEM tetracloroetano *m*
tetrachloroethylene *n* CHEM tetracloretileno *m*
tetrachloromethane *n* CHEM tetraclorometano *m*, tetracloruro de carbono *m*
tetrachord *n* ACOUST tetracordo *m*
tetradecanoic *adj* CHEM *acid* tetradecanoico
tetradymite *n* MINERAL tetradimita *f*
tetraethyl *n* CHEM tetraetilo *m*; ~ **lead** *n* (*TEL*) CHEM *antiknock additive* plomo tetraetilo *m*, teatrilplomo *m* (*TEP*)
tetragon *n* GEOM tetrágono *m*
tetragonal¹ *adj* CRYSTALL tetragonal
tetragonal²: ~ **system** *n* METALL sistema tetragonal *m*
tetrahedral *adj* CHEM *structure* tetrahédrico, CRYSTALL, GEOM tetraédrico
tetrahedrite *n* MINERAL tetrahedrita *f*
tetrahedron *n* CRYSTALL, GEOM tetraedro *m*
tetrahydride *n* CHEM tetrahidruro *m*
tetrahydrobenzene *n* CHEM tetrahidrobenceno *m*
tetrahydroglyoxaline *n* CHEM tetrahidroglioxalina *f*
tetrahydronaphthalene *n* CHEM tetrahidronaftaleno *m*
tetrahydroquinone *n* CHEM tetrahidroquinona *f*
tetrahydroxyquinone *n* CHEM tetrahidroxiquinona *f*
tetraiodofluorescein *n* CHEM tetrayodofluoresceína *f*
tetralin *n* CHEM tetralina *f*
tetrameric *adj* CHEM tetramérico
tetramethylene *n* CHEM tetrametileno *m*
tetramethylic *adj* CHEM tetrametílico
tetramine *n* CHEM tetramina *f*
tetranitrol *n* CHEM tetranitrol *m*
tetrapak *n* FOOD tetrapak *m*

tetraphonic: ~ **recording** *n* ACOUST grabación tetra-fónica *f*
tetrasulfide *AmE see tetrasulphide BrE*
tetrasulphide *n BrE* CHEM tetrasulfuro *m*
tetrathionic *adj* CHEM tetratiónico
tetratomicity *n* CHEM tetratomicidad *f*
tetravalence *n* CHEM tetravalencia *f*
tetravalency *n* CHEM tetravalencia *f*
tetravalent *adj* CHEM tetravalente
tetrazene *n* CHEM tetraceno *m*
tetrazine *n* CHEM tetrazina *f*
tetrazole *n* CHEM tetrazol *m*
tetrode *n* ELECTRON, PHYS tetrodo *m*; ~ **transistor** *n* ELECTRON transistor de tetrodo *m*; ~ **tube** *n AmE* (*cf tetrode valve BrE*) ELECTRON tubo de tetrodo *m*; ~ **valve** *BrE n* (*cf tetrode tube AmE*) ELECTRON tubo de tetrodo *m*
tetrolic *adj* CHEM tetrólico
tetrose *n* CHEM tetrosa *f*
tetroxide *n* CHEM tetróxido *m*
tetryl *n* CHEM tetrilo *m*
texasite *n* MINERAL texatita *f*
text: ~ **area** *n* PRINT área del texto *f*; ~ **editing** *n* TELECOM edición de textos *f*; ~ **editor** *n* COMP&DP, TELECOM editor de textos *m*; ~ **file** *n* COMP&DP archivo de texto *m*; ~ **formatter** *n* COMP&DP formatador de texto *m* (*AmL*), formateador de texto *m* (*Esp*); ~ **mailbox** *n* TELECOM buzón para textos *m*; ~ **matter** *n* PRINT composición tipográfica *f*; ~ **processing** *n* COMP&DP procesado de texto *m* (*AmL*) (*WP*), procesamiento de texto *m* (*WP*), tratamiento de texto *m* (*WP*); ~ **stream** *n* PRINT cadena de texto *f*
textile: ~ **glass fiber** *AmE,* ~ **glass fibre** *BrE n* C&G, TEXTIL fibra de vidrio textil *f*; ~ **labeling** *AmE,* ~ **labelling** *BrE n* TEXTIL etiquetado textil *m*; ~**-reinforced hose** *n* MECH ENG *hydraulic power* manguera con refuerzo textil *f*
texture *n* COAL textura *f*
textured: ~ **carpet** *n* TEXTIL alfombra texturada *f*; ~ **paint** *n* COLOUR, CONST pintura con textura *f*; ~ **vegetable protein** *n* (*TVP*) FOOD proteína vegetal texturizada *f* (*PVT*); ~ **yarn** *n* C&G fibra texturizada *f*
TFA *abbr* (*transfer allowed*) TELECOM transferencia permitida *f*
TFC *abbr* (*transfer controlled*) TELECOM transferencia controlada *f*
TFEL[1] *abbr* (*thin-film electroluminescence*) ELECTRON electroluminiscencia por capa delgada (*ELCD*)
TFEL[2]: ~ **display technology** *n* ELECTRON tecnología de visualización con ELCD *f*
T-flip-flop *n* ELECTRON basculador en T *m*, biestable tipo T *m*
TFP *abbr* (*transfer prohibited*) TELECOM transferencia prohibida *f*
TFR *abbr* (*transfer restricted*) TELECOM transferencia restringida *f*
TG *abbr* (*transcoding gain*) TELECOM ganancia de transcodificación *f*, ganancia debida a la codificación *f*
TGA *abbr* (*thermogravimetric analysis*) GEOPHYS, LAB, THERMO ATG (*análisis termogravimétrico*)
Th *abbr* (*thorium*) CHEM, RAD PHYS Th (*torio*)
thallic *adj* CHEM tálico
thallium *n* (*Tl*) CHEM talio *m* (*Tl*)
thallous *adj* CHEM talioso

thalweg *n* GEOL línea de fondo de un valle *f*, línea pendiente *f*, vaguada *f*, GEOL línea de valle *f*
thaw[1] *n* METEO deshielo *m*; ~ **rigor** *n* REFRIG contracción durante la descongelación *f*
thaw[2] *vt* FOOD, REFRIG derretir, derretirse, descongelar
thaw[3] *vi* METEO, THERMO derretir, derretirse, deshelarse
thawing *n* REFRIG descongelación *f*; ~ **point** *n* CHEM punto de descongelación *m*, punto de deshielo *m*
T-head: ~ **engine** *n* AUTO motor de culata en T *m*; ~ **valve train** *n* AUTO tren de válvulas en cabeza en T *m*
T-headed: ~ **bolt** *n* MECH ENG perno de cabeza en T *m*
thebaine *n* CHEM tebaína *f*
theft: ~**-alarm installation** *n* SAFE instalación de alarma contra robo *f*
theine *n* CHEM teína *f*
thenardite *n* MINERAL thenardita *f*
theobromine *n* CHEM teobromina *f*
theodolite *n* CONST, INSTR teodolito *m*
theophylline *n* CHEM teofilina *f*
theorem *n* ELEC, GEOM, PART PHYS, PHYS teorema *m*
theoretical: ~ **chemistry** *n* CHEM química teórica *f*; ~ **commercial dryness** *n* PAPER *of pulp* sequedad comercial teórica *f*; ~ **cutoff frequency** *n* ACOUST frecuencia de corte teórica *f*, ELEC frecuencia de corte teórica *f*, ELECTRON frecuencia de corte teórica *f*, PHYS, TELECOM frecuencia de corte teórica *f*; ~ **work** *n* PHYS trabajo teórico *m*
theory: ~ **of effective radius** *n* NUCL teoría del radio efectivo *f*; ~ **of numbers** *n* MATH teoría de números *f*; ~ **of transcendental numbers** *n* MATH teoría de números trascendentales *f*, teoría de números trascendentes *f*
thermal[1] *adj* PHYS, REFRIG, THERMO térmico
thermal[2]: ~ **accommodation coefficient** *n* SPACE coeficiente de acomodación térmica *m*; ~ **activation** *n* METALL, THERMO activación térmica *f*; ~ **agitation** *n* ELEC ENG agitación térmica *f*, termoagitación *f*, METALL, PHYS, THERMO agitación térmica *f*; ~ **ammeter** *n* ELEC *instrument* amperímetro de hilo caliente *m*, amperímetro térmico *m*, ELEC ENG, INSTR amperímetro térmico *m*, amperímetro de hilo caliente *m*; ~ **analysis** *n* CHEM, THERMO análisis térmico *m*; ~ **balance** *n* REFRIG, THERMO balance térmico *m*; ~ **barrier** *n* C&G, HEAT ENG, NUCL, SPACE, THERMO, TRANSP barrera térmica *f*; ~ **battery** *n* ELEC ENG, THERMO batería térmica *f*; ~ **beam time-of-flight experiment** *n* RAD PHYS experimento de tiempo de vuelo en un haz térmico *m*; ~**-bimetallic overlay relay** *n* PROD relé bimetálico térmico de capa *m*; ~**-bimetallic overload relay** *n* PROD relé bimetálico térmico de sobrecarga *m*; ~ **blooming** *n* ELECTRON floración térmica *f*; ~ **bonding** *n* P&R, PROD, THERMO unión térmica *f*; ~ **breakdown** *n* ELECTRON, THERMO disgregación térmica *f*; ~ **bulb** *n* AUTO bulbo térmico *m*; ~ **capacitance** *n* FUELLESS capacitación térmica *f*; ~ **capacity** *n* HEAT ENG, THERMO capacidad térmica *f*; ~ **center** *AmE,* ~ **centre** *BrE n* REFRIG centro térmico *m*; ~ **characteristic** *n* TELECOM característica térmica *f*; ~ **circuit breaker** *n* ELEC, ELEC ENG, THERMO disyuntor térmico *m*; ~ **column** *n* NUCL columna térmica *f*; ~ **component** *n* METALL componente térmico *m*; ~ **conductance** *n* HEAT ENG, PHYS conductancia térmica *f*; ~ **conductibility** *n* THERMO conductibilidad térmica *f*; ~ **conduction** *n* THERMO

conducción térmica *f*; ~ **conductivity** *n* CONST, GAS, HEAT ENG, P&R, PETR TECH, PHYS, THERMO conductividad térmica *f*; ~ **conductivity vacuum gage** *AmE*, ~ **conductivity vacuum gauge** *BrE n* REFRIG manómetro térmico *m*; ~ **conductor** *n* THERMO termoconductor *m*; ~ **content** *n* THERMO contenido térmico *m*; ~ **contraction** *n* MECH termocontracción *f*, THERMO contracción térmica *f*, termocontracción *f*; ~ **control** *n* SPACE control térmico *m*; ~ **control paint** *n* COLOUR pintura de control térmico *f*; ~ **converter** *n* ELEC ENG convertidor termal *m*; ~ **converter reactor** *n* NUCL reactor convertidor de calor *m*; ~ **cracking** *n* PETR TECH pirodesintegración *f*; ~ **current** *n* METEO corriente térmica *f*; ~ **cycle** *n* THERMO ciclo térmico *m*; ~ **cycling** *n* THERMO ciclado térmico *m*; ~ **decomposition** *n* P&R, THERMO descomposición térmica *f*; ~ **diffusion** *n* NUCL, PHYS, THERMO difusión térmica *f*; ~ **diffusion coefficient** *n* NUCL, PHYS, THERMO coeficiente de difusión térmica *m*; ~ **diffusion factor** *n* NUCL, PHYS, THERMO factor de difusión térmica *m*; ~ **diffusion process** *n* NUCL, PHYS, THERMO proceso de difusión térmica *m*; ~ **diffusion ratio** *n* NUCL, PHYS, THERMO cociente de difusión térmica *m*; ~ **diffusivity** *n* HEAT ENG, PHYS, THERMO difusividad térmica *f*; ~ **diode** *n* ELECTRON diodo térmico *m*; ~ **discharge** *n* RECYCL descarga de calor *f*, descarga térmica *f*, THERMO descarga térmica *f*; ~ **dissociation** *n* THERMO disociación térmica *f*; ~ **effect** *n* GAS efecto térmico *m*; ~ **efficiency** *n* AUTO eficacia térmica *f*, GAS eficiencia térmica *f*, rendimiento térmico *m*, HEAT ENG rendimiento térmico *m*, PHYS eficiencia térmica *f*, THERMO eficiencia térmica *f*, rendimiento térmico *m*; ~~**electric power plant** *n* ELEC ENG planta de energía termo-eléctrica *f*; ~~**electric power station** *n* ELEC ENG central de energía termo-eléctrica *f*; ~ **emission** *n* RAD PHYS emisión térmica *f*; ~ **emissivity** *n* THERMO emisividad térmica *f*; ~ **energy** *n* HEAT ENG, THERMO energía térmica *f*; ~ **energy storage system** *n* TRANSP sistema de almacenamiento de energía térmica *m*; ~ **engine** *n* THERMO motor térmico *m*; ~ **equilibrium** *n* HEAT ENG, THERMO equilibrio térmico *m*; ~ **equivalent** *n* THERMO equivalente térmico *m*; ~ **etching** *n* METALL ataque térmico *m*; ~ **evaporation** *n* METALL, THERMO evaporación térmica *f*; ~ **exchange** *n* GAS intercambio térmico *m*; ~ **exhaust manifold reactor** *n* TRANSP reactor-colector de escape térmico *m*; ~ **expansion** *n* P&R expansión térmica *f*, PETR TECH, TELECOM, THERMO *communications, antennae, aircraft* dilatación térmica *f*; ~ **expansion coefficient** *n* THERMO coeficiente de dilatación térmica *m*; ~ **expansion joint** *n* THERMO junta de dilatación térmica *f*; ~ **fatigue** *n* THERMO *communications, antennae, aircraft* fatiga térmica *f*; ~ **fission factor** *n* PHYS factor térmico de fisión *m*; ~ **flash** *n* NUCL fogonazo térmico *m*; ~ **gradient** *n* THERMO gradiente térmico *m*; ~ **gravimetric analysis** *n* CHEM TECH, COAL, GEOPHYS, PETR TECH, THERMO análisis gravimétrico térmico *m*; ~ **head** *n* THERMO carga térmica *f*; ~ **imager** *n* MILIT sistema de formación de imágenes térmicas *m*; ~ **imaging** *n* (*TI*) MILIT, RAD PHYS, THERMO formación de imágenes térmicas *f*, imagen térmica *f*, producción térmica de imágenes *f*; ~~**imaging sight** *n* THERMO *of liquids* mira de formación de imágenes térmicas *f*; ~~**imaging tube** *n* ELECTRON tubo de formación de

imagen térmica *m*; ~ **imbalance** *n* THERMO desequilibrio térmico *m*; ~ **inertia** *n* GAS, REFRIG, THERMO *of liquids* inercia térmica *f*; ~ **instability** *n* P&R, TELECOM, THERMO inestabilidad térmica *f*, termoinestabilidad *f*; ~ **instrument** *n* INSTR, THERMO instrumento térmico *m*; ~ **insulation** *n* CONST aislamiento térmico *m*, HEAT ENG aislación térmica *f*, aislamiento térmico *m*, MECH aislamiento térmico *m*, termoaislador *m*, PACK aislamiento térmico *m*, PETR TECH aislamiento térmico *m*, termoaislador *m*, RAIL aislamiento térmico *m*, THERMO aislamiento térmico *m*, termoaislador *m*, aislación térmica *f*, aislamiento isotermo *m*, WATER TRANSP aislamiento isotermo *m*; ~ **insulation coefficient** *n* PHYS, THERMO coeficiente de aislamiento térmico *m*; ~ **insulation index** *n* PHYS, THERMO coeficiente de termoaislamiento *m*, índice de aislamiento térmico *m*; ~ **jet engine** *n* AIR TRANSP motor termopropulsor *m*; ~ **lagging** *n* THERMO inercia térmica *f*, retardo térmico *m*; ~ **link** *n* THERMO *bead memory* enlace térmico *m*; ~ **load** *n* POLL descarga térmica *f*; ~ **mass** *n* THERMO masa térmica *f*; ~ **mixing** *n* NUCL mezcla térmica *f*; ~ **model** *n* SPACE modelo térmico *m*; ~ **neutron** *n* NUCL, PHYS, RAD PHYS neutrón térmico *m*; ~ **neutron fission** *n* NUCL, PART PHYS, PHYS fisión por neutrones térmicos *f*; ~ **neutron nonleakage probability** *n* NUCL probabilidad de permanencia de neutrones térmicos *f*; ~ **neutron yield** *n* NUCL rendimiento de neutrones térmicos *m*; ~ **noise** *n* ELECTRON, PHYS, SPACE *communications* ruido térmico *m*; ~ **noise generator** *n* ELECTRON generador de ruido térmico *m*; ~ **output** *n* MECH ENG producción térmica *f*, THERMO rendimiento térmico *m*; ~ **plasma** *n* GAS plasma térmico *m*; ~ **pollution** *n* POLL contaminación térmica *f*, THERMO polución calorífica *f*, polución térmica *f*; ~ **postcombustion** *n* TRANSP postcombustión térmica *f*; ~ **power** *n* THERMO energía térmica *f*; ~ **power plant** *n* NUCL central térmica *f*; ~ **power station** *n* THERMO central térmica *f*; ~ **printer** *n* COMP&DP, PRINT impresora térmica *f*; ~ **property** *n* CONST, THERMO propiedad térmica *f*; ~ **protection** *n* SPACE protección térmica *f*; ~ **protection tile** *n* SPACE teja de protección térmica *f*; ~ **radiation** *n* NUCL, PHYS, THERMO radiación térmica *f*; ~ **reactor** *n* RAD PHYS reactor térmico *m*; ~ **refiner mechanical pulp** *n* PAPER pasta mecánica de refino con tratamiento en caliente *f*; ~ **reforming** *n* PETR TECH reformado térmico *m*; ~ **relay** *n* ELEC, ELEC ENG relé térmico *m*; ~ **relief** *n* PROD alivio térmico *m*, descenso térmico *m*; ~ **resistance** *n* HEAT ENG, PHYS, THERMO resistencia térmica *f*; ~ **resistivity** *n* HEAT ENG, PHYS resistividad térmica *f*; ~ **runaway electron** *n* ELECTRON electrón fugitivo térmico *m*; ~ **screen** *n* SPACE pantalla térmica *f*; ~ **shield** *n* SAFE blindaje térmico *m*, SPACE pantalla térmica *f*, blindaje térmico *m*, THERMO blindaje térmico *m*; ~ **shock** *n* SPACE choque térmico *m*, THERMO cambio brusco de temperatura *m*, choque térmico *m*; ~ **shock chamber** *n* LAB cámara de choque térmico *f*; ~ **shutdown** *n* ELECTRON, THERMO interrupción térmica *f*; ~ **soaring** *n* THERMO vuelo en ascendencia térmica *m*; ~ **spectrum** *n* THERMO espectro térmico *m*; ~ **spike** *n* NUCL espiga térmica *f*; ~ **spraying** *n* COATINGS rociado térmico *m*; ~ **spring** *n* HYDROL fuente térmica *f*, manantial de aguas termales *m*, THERMO fuente térmica *f*, resorte térmico *m*;

~ stability n P&R, TELECOM, THERMO estabilidad térmica f; **~ steam generator output** n NUCL rendimiento térmico del generador de vapor m; **~ storage thermometer** n REFRIG termómetro de acumulación de calor m; **~ stress** n THERMO esfuerzo térmico m, termoesfuerzo m; **~ switch** n ELEC ENG conmutador térmico m; **~ transfer** n GAS transferencia térmica f; **~ transfer printer** n PACK termoimpresora f; **~ transmission** n HEAT ENG transmisión térmica f; **~ tuning** n ELECTRON sintonización térmica f; **~ utilization factor** n PHYS factor de utilización térmica m; **~ value** n THERMO valor térmico m; **~ wrap** n OPT, THERMO arrollamiento térmico m

thermalize vt CHEM termalizar

thermally: **~-induced buoyancy** n HYDRAUL, HYDROL, POLL flotabilidad inducida térmicamente f, flotación inducida térmicamente f; **~-pumped laser** n ELECTRON láser térmicamente bombeado m

thermic[1] adj THERMO térmico

thermic[2]: **~ effect** n GAS efecto térmico m; **~ exchange** n GAS intercambio térmico m; **~ inertia** n GAS inercia térmica f; **~ lance** n THERMO bisturí térmico m; **~ performance** n GAS eficiencia térmica f, rendimiento térmico m

thermion n THERMO termión m, termoelectrón m

thermionic[1] adj ELEC ENG, PHYS termoeléctrico, THERMO termiónico, termoeléctrico

thermionic[2]: **~ cathode** n ELEC ENG cátodo termiónico m; **~ conversion** n ELEC ENG, NUCL conversión termiónica f; **~ converter** n ELEC ENG convertidor termiónico m; **~ emission** n ELEC ENG, PHYS, RAD PHYS emisión termiónica f; **~ emission microscope** n INSTR microscopio de emisión termiónica m; **~ generator** n ELEC ENG generador termiónico m; **~ rectification** n ELEC ENG rectificación termiónica f; **~ rectifier** n ELEC ENG válvula termiónica f; **~ triode** n ELECTRON triodo termiónico m; **~ tube** n AmE (cf thermionic valve BrE) ELEC of radio válvula termoelectrónica f, tubo termiónico m, tubo de cátodo caliente m, válvula termiónica f, ELECTRON lámpara termiónica f, tubo termiónico m; **~ valve** BrE n (cf thermionic tube AmE) ELEC of radio válvula termoelectrónica f, tubo termiónico m, tubo de cátodo caliente m, válvula termiónica f, ELECTRON lámpara termiónica f, tubo termiónico m

thermistor n ELEC ENG resistencia variable con la temperatura f, termistor m, PHYS, REFRIG, TELECOM termistor m; **~ bridge** n ELEC ENG puente de termistores m; **~ circuit** n PROD circuito de termistor m; **~ control** n ELEC ENG control de termistores m; **~ mount** n ELEC ENG montaje de termistancia m

thermit, thermite: **~ welding** n CONST soldadura de termita f, soldadura aluminotérmica f, RAIL soldadura aluminotérmica f

thermoammeter n ELEC instrument amperímetro termoeléctrico m, amperímetro térmico m, termoamperímetro m, ELEC ENG, INSTR amperímetro termoeléctrico m, amperímetro térmico m

thermoanalysis n CHEM, THERMO termoanálisis m

thermobalance n CHEM termobalanza f

thermobank: **~ defrosting** n REFRIG termoacumulador para desescarche m

thermobonding: **~ fiber** AmE, **~ fibre** BrE n TEXTIL fibra de termoadhesión f

thermochemistry n CHEM termoquímica f

thermocline n OCEAN termoclina f

thermoconductor n THERMO termoconductor m

thermocouple n ELEC measurement termopar m, ELEC ENG pila termoeléctrica f, par termoeléctrico m, termocupla f, par térmico m, LAB communications, equipment, METALL, NUCL termopar m, PETR TECH termopar m, par térmico m, PHYS termocupla f, THERMO par termoeléctrico m, termopar m; **~ converter** n ELEC ENG convertidor de termopar m; **~ expander** n PROD expansor de termocupla m (AmL), expansor de termopar m (Esp), mecanismo de expansión de termopar m; **~ input** n PROD entrada de par termoeléctrico f, entrada de termopar f; **~ instrument** n INSTR instrumento termoeléctrico m; **~ thermometer** n ELEC ENG termómetro de termopar m

thermocurrent n NUCL corriente termoeléctrica f

thermodiffusion n THERMO termodifusión f

thermodynamic[1] adj CHEM, CONST, MECH ENG, PHYS, THERMO termodinámico

thermodynamic[2]: **~ cycle** n HEAT, THERMO ciclo termodinámico m; **~ equation of state** n THERMO ecuación de estado termodinámico f, ecuación termodinámica de estado f; **~ equilibrium** n SPACE equilibrio termodinámico m; **~ function** n THERMO función termodinámica f; **~ law** n THERMO ley de la termodinámica f, principio de la termodinámica m; **~ potential** n PHYS, THERMO potencial termodinámico m; **~ probability** n PHYS, THERMO probabilidad termodinámica f; **~ process** n THERMO proceso termodinámico m; **~ system** n THERMO sistema termodinámico m; **~ temperature** n PHYS temperatura termodinámica f; **~ transformation** n THERMO transformación termodinámica f

thermodynamics n CHEM, CONST, MECH ENG, PHYS, THERMO termodinámica f

thermoelastic: **~ distorsion** n SPACE distorsión termoelástica f; **~ martensite** n METALL martensita termoelástica f

thermoelectric[1] adj ELEC ENG, PHYS, THERMO termoeléctrico

thermoelectric[2]: **~ conversion** n ELEC ENG conversión termoeléctrica f; **~ cooling** n REFRIG enfriamiento termoeléctrico m; **~ effect** n ELEC of circuit, temperature efecto Seebeck m, efecto termoeléctrico m; **~ generator** n ELEC ENG generador termoeléctrico m; **~ power** n ELEC ENG energía termoeléctrica f, potencia termoeléctrica f, PHYS energía termoeléctrica f

thermoelectrical adj ELEC ENG, PHYS, THERMO termoeléctrico

thermoelectricity n ELEC ENG, PHYS, THERMO termoelectricidad f

thermoelectromotive: **~ force** n ELEC ENG fuerza termo-electromotriz f

thermofixing n TEXTIL dyeing termofijado m

thermoform: **~ machinery** n PACK termoformadora f

thermoforming[1] adj PACK, PAPER termoformado

thermoforming[2] n GAS, PACK termoformación f; **~ automatically from the reel** n PACK termoformación automática partiendo del material en bobina f; **~ packaging system** n PACK sistema de embalaje por termoformación m

thermogenerator n PHYS, THERMO termogenerador m

thermograph n LAB unit of measurement of absorbed

dose, NUCL, PHYS termógrafo *m*, THERMO termograma *m*, termógrafo *m*

thermographic: ~ **paper** *n* PAPER papel termográfico *m*

thermogravimetric: ~ **analysis** *n* (*TGA*) GEOPHYS, LAB, THERMO análisis termogravimétrico *m* (*ATG*)

thermogravimetry *n* P&R termogravimetría *f*

thermohaline: ~ **pumping** *n* OCEAN succión termohalina *f*

thermohygrograph *n* LAB *temperature recorder* termohigrógrafo *m*

thermolecular *adj* CHEM termolecular

thermoluminescence *n* PHYS, RAD PHYS, THERMO termoluminiscencia *f*

thermoluminescent[1] *adj* PHYS, RAD PHYS, THERMO termoluminiscente

thermoluminescent[2]: ~ **dosimeter** *n* RAD PHYS dosímetro termoluminiscente *m*

thermolysis *n* THERMO termólisis *f*

thermomagnetic *adj* THERMO termomagnético

thermomagnetism *n* THERMO termomagnetismo *m*

thermomechanical: ~ **effect** *n* THERMO efecto termomecánico *m*; ~ **pulp** *n* (*TMP*) PAPER pasta termomecánica *f* (*pasta TMP*)

thermometer *n* GEN termómetro *m*; ~ **glass** *n* C&G vidrio para termómetro *m*

thermometric[1] *adj* PHYS, THERMO termométrico

thermometric[2]: ~ **depth** *n* OCEAN profundidad termométrica *f*

thermometry *n* PHYS, THERMO termometría *f*

thermonatrite *n* MINERAL termonatrita *f*

thermoneutrality *n* CHEM termoneutralidad *f*

thermonuclear: ~ **combustion wave** *n* NUCL onda de combustión termonuclear *f*; ~ **power generation** *n* ELEC, NUCL generación eléctrica termonuclear *f*; ~ **reaction** *n* NUCL, PHYS reacción termonuclear *f*

thermophone *n* ACOUST termófono *m*

thermophosphorescence *n* THERMO termofosforescencia *f*

thermopile *n* ELEC ENG pila termoeléctrica *f*, termopila *f*, PHYS termopila *f*, SPACE pila termoeléctrica *f*, termopila *f*

thermoplastic[1] *adj* MECH, MECH ENG, P&R, TEXTIL, WATER TRANSP *polyester construction* termoplástico

thermoplastic[2] *n* MECH, MECH ENG, P&R, TEXTIL, WATER TRANSP *polyester construction* termoplástico *m*; ~ **component** *n* MECH ENG componente termoplástico *m*; ~ **mold** *AmE*, ~ **mould** *BrE n* MECH ENG molde termoplástico *m*; ~ **position switch** *n* PROD interruptor de posición termoplástico *m*; ~ **rubber** *n* P&R caucho termoplástico *m*, elastómero termoplástico *m*

thermoplasticity *n* P&R termoplasticidad *f*

thermoplastics *n* MECH ENG termoplástico *m*

thermosealing *n* PRINT termosellado *m*

thermoset[1] *adj* P&R termoestable

thermoset[2]: ~ **plastic** *n* (*cf thermosetting mould BrE*) MECH ENG plástico endurecido *m*, plástico termofraguado *m*

thermosetting[1] *adj* CHEM termoendurecible, termofraguable, termofraguante, MECH termoendurecido, P&R termoendurecible, termoendurente, THERMO termoendurecible, termoendurecido, termoestable

thermosetting[2] *n* MECH termofraguado *m*, THERMO termofraguado *m*; ~ **ink** *n* PRINT tinta que seca por calor *f*; ~ **mold** *AmE*, ~ **mould** *BrE n* (*cf thermoset plastic AmE*) MECH ENG molde de endurecimiento térmico *m*, molde de fraguado térmico *m*, molde termofraguante *m*

thermosiphon *AmE see thermosyphon BrE*

thermosphere *n* GEOPHYS termosfera *f*

thermostable *adj* CHEM, PETR TECH, THERMO termoestable

thermostat *n* GEN termostato *m*; ~ **control** *n* HEAT control termostático *m*; ~ **well** *n* PROD pozo termostático *m*

thermostatic[1] *adj* REFRIG, THERMO termostático

thermostatic[2]: ~ **element** *n* REFRIG elemento termostático *m*; ~ **expansion valve** *n* REFRIG válvula de expansión termostática *f*; ~ **valve** *n* MECH ENG válvula de acción termostática *f*, válvula de gobierno termostático *f*

thermostatically: ~-**controlled bath** *n* LAB baño con regulación termostática *m*; ~-**controlled developing dish** *n* PHOTO cubeta de revelado regulada termostáticamente *f*; ~-**controlled valve** *n* PROD válvula regulada termostáticamente *f*, REFRIG válvula termostática *f*

thermostatics *n* THERMO termostática *f*

thermosteric: ~ **anomaly** *n* OCEAN anomalía termostérica *f*

thermosyphon *n* BrE FUELLESS sifón térmico *m*

thermowell *n* PETR TECH pozo térmico *m*

thesaurus *n* COMP&DP *lexicon* diccionario de sinónimos *m*, tesoro *m*

Thévenin: ~'s **theorem** *n* PHYS teorema de Thevenin *m*

thevetin *n* CHEM tevetina *f*

thial *n* CHEM tial *m*

thialdine *n* CHEM tialdina *f*

thiation *n* CHEM tiación *f*

thiazine *n* CHEM tiacina *f*, tiazina *f*

thiazole *n* CHEM tiazol *m*

thiazoline *n* CHEM tiazolina *f*

thick[1] *adj* CHEM *solution* denso, espeso, viscoso; ~-**bedded** *adj* GEOL estratificación gruesa, estratificación potente

thick[2]: ~-**and-thin yarn** *n* TEXTIL hilo grueso y delgado *m*; ~ **film** *n* ELECTRON capa gruesa *f*, película gruesa *f*; ~-**film capacitor** *n* ELECTRON capacitor de capa gruesa *m*; ~-**film conductor** *n* ELECTRON conductor de capa gruesa *m*; ~-**film device** *n* ELECTRON dispositivo de capa gruesa *m*; ~-**film electroluminescent display** *n* ELECTRON visualizador electroluminescente de capa gruesa *m*; ~-**film hybrid circuit** *n* ELECTRON circuito híbrido de capa gruesa *m*; ~-**film hybrid circuit substrate** *n* ELECTRON substrato de circuito híbrido de capa gruesa *m*; ~-**film material** *n* ELECTRON material de capa gruesa *m*; ~-**film resistor** *n* ELECTRON resistencia de filamento grueso *f*, resistor de capa gruesa *m*; ~-**film technology** *n* ELECTRON tecnología de revestimiento grueso *f*, SPACE tecnología de capa gruesa *f*, tecnología de película gruesa *f*; ~-**layer integrated circuit** *n* TELECOM circuito integrado de capas gruesas *m*; ~ **oxide** *n* ELECTRON óxido espeso *m*; ~-**oxide metal gate MOS circuit** *n* ELECTRON circuito de SOM con puerta de metal de óxido espeso *m*; ~ **polished plate glass** *n* C&G vidrio plano, pulido y grueso *m*; ~ **roughcast plate glass** *n* C&G vidrio plano, grueso y vaciado en bruto *m*; ~-**seam winning** *n* COAL extracción de una capa espesa de carbón *f*; ~ **sheet glass** *n* BrE C&G vidrio plano grueso *m*; ~ **source** *n*

NUCL, RAD PHYS fuente radiactiva gruesa *f*; ~ **space** *n* PRINT espacio grueso *m*; ~ **stock** *n* PAPER pasta concentrada *f*; ~ **ware** *n* OCEAN loza industrial *f*; ~ **window glass** *n* AmE (*cf thick sheet glass BrE*) C&G vidrio plano grueso *m*

thicken[1] *vt* CHEM TECH espesar, PROD *core* aplicar una capa provisional de cera; ~ **by boiling** *vt* CHEM TECH espesar por ebullición

thicken[2] *vi* CHEM TECH espesarse, sedimentarse

thickened: ~ **slime** *n* COAL fangos espesos *m pl*; ~ **slurry** *n* COAL lodos espesos *m pl*

thickener *n* CHEM coagulante *m*, espesante *m*, CHEM TECH espesante *m*, COAL coagulante *m*, espesador *m*, espesante *m*, tanque de sedimentación *m*, FOOD espesante *m*, P&R, PAPER espesador *m*; ~ **drum** *n* CHEM TECH tambor del espesador *m*, tambor del separador sedimentario *m*; ~ **tank** *n* CHEM TECH tanque del espesador *m*, tanque del separador sedimentario *m*

thickening *n* C&G espesado *m*, COAL decantación *f*, espesamiento *m*, FOOD espesante *m*, espesado *m*; ~ **agent** *n* CHEM agente de espesamiento *m*, agente espesante *m*, DETERG agente de espesamiento *m*, agente espesante *m*, espesante *m*, FOOD agente de espesamiento *m*, agente espesante *m*; ~ **cone** *n* COAL tobera de decantación *f*

thickness *n* C&G espesor *m*, CHEM, MECH, P&R espesor *m*, grosor *m*, PAPER espesor *m*; ~ **calender** *n* PAPER calandra calibradora *f*; ~**cord ratio** *n* AIR TRANSP *of aerofoil section* proporción grosor-cuerda *f*; ~ **gage** AmE, ~ **gauge** BrE *n* C&G, LAB medidor de espesores *m*, MECH calibrador de espesores *m*, espesímetro *m*, galga de espesores *f*, MECH ENG calibrador de espesores *m*, espesímetro *m*, galga de espesores *f*, medidor de espesores *m*; ~ **of lines** *n* METR *brazing-lamp* espesor de líneas *m*; ~ **of lining** *n* MECH ENG espesor de la camisa *m*, espesor del revestimiento *m*, grosor del refuerzo *m*; ~ **loss** *n* TV pérdida de espesor *f*; ~ **margin** *n* MECH ENG tolerancia de espesor *f*

thicknessing *n* MECH ENG igualación de gruesos *f*, puesta a grueso *f*, regruesamiento *m*

thief[1]: ~**proof** *adj* SAFE a prueba de ladrones

thief[2]: ~ **formation** *n* PETROL formación absorbente *f*

Thiele: ~ **tube** *n* LAB *measuring* tubo de Thiele *m*

thimble *n* C&G dedal *m*, FOOD abrazadera *f*, NUCL *craft* tubo-guía *m*, PROD *boiler-tube ferrule* casquillo *m*, dedal *m*, distanciador tubular *m*, *rope eyelet* ojal *m*, WATER TRANSP *fittings* guardacabos *m*

thin[1] *adj* PROD tenue; ~**bedded** *adj* GEOL finamente estratificado; ~**walled** *adj* MECH ENG de pared delgada, de paredes de poco espesor

thin[2]: ~**edged weir** *n* HYDRAUL aliviadero en pared delgada *m*, vertedero de cresta aguda *m*, vertedero de cresta delgada *m*, vertedero en pared delgada *m*, WATER aliviadero en pared delgada *m*; ~ **film** *n* ELECTRON capa delgada *f*, capa fina *f*; ~**film capacitor** *n* ELEC capacitor de película delgada *m*, condensador de película delgada *m*, ELECTRON capacitor de capa delgada *m*; ~**film conductor** *n* ELECTRON conductor de filamento delgado *m*; ~**film device** *n* ELECTRON dispositivo de capa delgada *m*; ~**film electroluminescence** *n* (*TFEL*) ELECTRON electroluminiscencia por capa delgada *f* (*ELCD*); ~**film hybrid circuit** *n* ELECTRON circuito híbrido de capa delgada *m*; ~**film hybrid circuit substrate** *n* ELECTRON substrato de circuito híbrido de capa delgada

m; ~**film material** *n* ELECTRON material de capa delgada *m*; ~**film memory** *n* COMP&DP memoria de película delgada *f*, memoria de película magnética fina *f*; ~**film optical waveguide** *n* OPT guía de ondas óptica de película delgada *f*; ~**film resistor** *n* ELECTRON resistencia de capa delgada *f*, resistor de capa delgada *m*; ~**film technology** *n* ELECTRON tecnología de revestimiento delgado *f*; ~**film transistor** *n* ELECTRON transistor de capa delgada *m*; ~**film waveguide** *n* TELECOM guiaondas de película delgada *m*, guía de ondas de película delgada *f*; ~**layer capacitor** *n* TELECOM condensador de película delgada *m*; ~**layer chromatography** *n* (*TLC*) CHEM *analysis*, LAB cromatografía de capa delgada *f* (*CCD*), cromatografía de capa fina *f*; ~ **lens** *n* PHYS lente delgada *f*; ~ **negative** *n* CINEMAT negativo delgado *m*; ~ **print** *n* CINEMAT copia delgada *f*; ~ **ring bearing** *n* MECH ENG cojinete de anillo delgado *m*, cojinete de aro estrecho *m*; ~ **section** *n* CRYSTALL sección delgada *f*; ~ **sheet glass** *n* C&G vidrio plano sencillo *m*; ~ **source** *n* NUCL, RAD PHYS fuente radiactiva delgada *f*; ~ **space** *n* PRINT espacio fino *m*; ~ **spot detector** *n* C&G detector de puntos delgados *m*; ~ **stock** *n* PAPER pasta magra *f*; ~ **taper key** *n* MECH ENG chaveta cónica delgada *f*; ~**walled cylinder** *n* MECH ENG cilindro de pared delgada *m*; ~**walled half-bearing** *n* MECH ENG cojinete de dos mitades de pared delgada *m*; ~**walled spherical shell** *n* MECH ENG casco esférico de pared delgada *m*

thin[3] *vt* PROD adelgazar, disminuir, *paints* diluir; ~ **down** *vt* PROD *board* aligerar, *plate* reducir

thin[4]: ~ **out** *vi* PROD aligerarse, disminuir, disminuirse, enrarecerse, reducirse

thindown *n* NUCL degradación *f*

T-hinge *n* CONST bisagra en T *f*

thinly: ~**bedded** *adj* GEOL finamente estratificado

thinner *n* CHEM adelgazador *m*, diluyente *m*, disolvente *m*, COLOUR diluyente *m*, disolvente *m*, PETROL diluyente *m*

thinness *n* PROD raridad *f*, tenuidad *f*

thinning *n* AGRIC raleo *m*, CHEM, PROD dilución *f*; ~ **down** *n* PROD dilución *f*, disminución *f*, reducción *f*; ~ **out** *n* PROD disminución *f*, reducción *f*

thio- *pref* CHEM tio-

thioacetic *adj* CHEM tioacético

thioacid *n* CHEM tioácido *m*

thioalcohol *n* CHEM tioalcohol *m*

thioaldehyde *n* CHEM tioaldehído *m*

thioamide *n* CHEM tioamida *f*

thioarsenic *adj* CHEM tioarsénico

thiocarbamide *n* CHEM tiocarbamida *f*

thiocarbanilide *n* CHEM tiocarbanilida *f*

thiocarbonate *n* CHEM tiocarbonato *m*

thiocarbonic *adj* CHEM tiocarbónico

thiocyanate *n* CHEM tiocianato *m*

thiocyanic *adj* CHEM tiociánico

thiodiphenylamine *n* CHEM tiodifenilamina *f*

thioether *n* CHEM tioéter *m*

thioflavin *n* CHEM tioflavina *f*

thioglycolic *adj* CHEM tioglicólico

thioindamine *n* CHEM tiazina *f*, tioindamina *f*

thioindigo *n* CHEM tioíndigo *m*

thioketone *n* CHEM tiocetona *f*

thiol *n* CHEM alcohol de azufre *m*, mercaptán *m*, tiol *m*, FOOD alcohol de azufre *m*, POLL mercaptano *m*, tiol *m*

thiolate *n* CHEM tiolato *m*

thionaphthene *n* CHEM tionaftaleno *m*, tionafteno *m*
thionate *n* CHEM tionato *m*
thionation *n* CHEM tionación *f*
thione *n* CHEM tiona *f*
thioneine *n* CHEM tioneína *f*
thionic *adj* CHEM tiónico
thionine *n* CHEM tionina *f*
thionyl *n* CHEM tionilo *m*
thiopental *n* CHEM tiopental *m*
thiophene *n* CHEM tiofeno *m*
thiophenol *n* CHEM tiofenol *m*
thiophosgene *n* CHEM tiofosgeno *m*
thioplast *n* CHEM tiogoma *f*, tioplasto *m*
thiosulfate *AmE see thiosulphate BrE*
thiosulfuric *AmE see thiosulphuric BrE*
thiosulphate *n BrE* CHEM tiosulfato *m*
thiosulphuric *adj BrE* CHEM tiosulfúrico
thiourea *n* CHEM tiourea *f*
thioxanthone *n* CHEM tioxantona *f*
thioxene *n* CHEM tioxeno *m*
third: ~ **deck** *n* WATER TRANSP *ship design* tercera cubierta *f*; ~ **gear** *n* AUTO tercera marcha *f*; ~ **generation** *n* COMP&DP tercera generación *f*; **~-generation computer** *n* COMP&DP computador de tercera generación *m* (*AmL*), computadora de tercera generación *f* (*AmL*), ordenador de tercera generación *m* (*Esp*); ~ **harmonic** *n* ELECTRON tercer armónico *m*; ~ **harmonic distortion** *n* ELECTRON distorsión del tercer armónico *f*; ~ **law** *n* PHYS tercera ley *f*; **~-motion shaft** *n* AUTO, VEH árbol de tercer movimiento *m*; **~-order active filter** *n* ELECTRON filtro activo de tercer orden *m*; **~-order filter** *n* ELECTRON filtro de tercer orden *m*; ~ **party maintenance** *n* AIR TRANSP mantenimiento a terceros *m*; **~-party warning tone** *n* TELECOM tono de alerta para terceros *m*; ~ **rail** *n* RAIL tercer carril *m*, tercer riel *m*; ~ **stomach** *n* AGRIC omaso *m*, vientre *m*; ~ **tap** *n* MECH ENG tercer macho *m*; ~ **wire system** *n* ELEC sistema de conductor neutro *m*, sistema de hilo neutro *m*
thirty-sixmo *n* (*36mo, 36°*) PRINT pliego doblado para formar 36 hojas *m*
thirty-twomo *n* (*32mo, 32°*) PRINT pliego doblado para formar 32 hojas *m*
thistle: ~ **funnel** *n* LAB embudo con llave *m*
thixotropic[1] *adj* CHEM, COAL, P&R, PETR TECH, PHYS tixotrópico
thixotropic[2] *n* P&R tixotropía *f*
thixotropy *n* CHEM, COAL, PETROL, PHYS tixotropía *f*
tholoid: ~ **dome** *n* GEOL domo toloide *m*
thomsenolite *n* MINERAL thomselonita *f*
Thomson: ~ **bridge** *n* ELEC *instrument* puente Thomson *m*; ~ **coefficient** *n* PHYS coeficiente de Thomson *m*; ~ **cross-section** *n* PHYS sección eficaz de Thomson *f*; ~ **effect** *n* PHYS efecto de Thomson *m*; ~ **scattering** *n* PHYS difusión de Thomson *f*
thomsonite *n* MINERAL thomsonita *f*
thoria *n* CHEM óxido de torio *m*
thorianite *n* MINERAL torianita *f*
thoriated: ~ **tungsten filament** *n* ELEC ENG filamento de tungsteno toriado *m*
thoric *adj* CHEM tórico
thorite *n* MINERAL torita *f*
thorium *n* (*Th*) CHEM, RAD PHYS torio *m* (*Th*); **~-fueled reactor** *AmE*, **~-fuelled reactor** *BrE* *n* NUCL reactor con combustible de torio *m*, reactor de torio *m*; ~ **series** *n* RAD PHYS serie del torio *f*
thorn: ~ **apple** *n* AGRIC chamico *m*
thoroughfare *n* CONST paso *m*, vía pública *f*; ~ **hole** *n* CONST agujero pasante *m*
thousand *n* MATH mil *m*; **a ~ million** *n* MATH mil millones *m pl*
thrasher *n* PAPER batidor del fieltro *m*
thrashing *n* COMP&DP *memory* hiperpaginación *f*, pérdida de control *f*
thread[1] *n* C&G hebra *f*, hilo *m*, rosca *f*, MECH paso *m*, rosca *f*, MECH ENG *of nut* filete *m*, hilo *m*, paso *m*, MINE filamento *m*, PAPER, PRINT hilo *m*, PROD paso *m*, rosca *f*, hilo *m*, hebra *f*, filamento *m*, TEXTIL hilo *m*, enhebrar; ~ **chaser** *n* MECH ENG herramienta de roscar *f*, peine de roscar *m*; ~ **counter** *n* PAPER cuentahilos *m*; ~ **gage** *AmE*, ~ **gauge** *BrE n* MECH ENG calibrador de filetes de tornillos *m*, calibrador de roscas *m*, galga de roscas *f*, medidor de roscas *m*, METR galga de roscas *f*; ~ **grinding** *n* MECH ENG rectificado de roscas *m*; ~ **insert** *n* MECH ENG embutido de hilo *m*, insertado de hilo *m*, inserto de rosca *m*; ~ **lead angle** *n* MECH ENG ángulo de avance de la rosca *m*; ~ **microscope** *n* INSTR microscopio de rosca *m*; **~-milling cutter** *n* MECH ENG cortador rotatorio de roscas *m*, fresa de roscar *f*, fresadora de roscar *f*; ~ **pitch** *n* MECH ENG, VEH paso de rosca *m*; ~ **pitch gage** *AmE*, ~ **pitch gauge** *BrE n* MECH ENG galga de paso de rosca *f*; ~ **restorer** *n* MECH ENG repasadora de roscas *f*, restaurador de roscas *m*; ~ **run-out for fastener** *n* MECH ENG salida de rosca para fijador *f*; ~ **speed** *n* PROD velocidad de enhebrado *f*, velocidad lenta para recibir el tocho *f*; ~ **undercut** *n* MECH ENG rosca de poca altura *f*, rosca de poco diámetro *f*
thread[2] *vt* CINEMAT enhebrar
thread[3] *vi* PROD aterrajar, enfilar, enhebrar, pasar a través de, pasar por, roscar
threadbare *adj* TEXTIL raído
threaded[1] *adj* MECH roscado
threaded[2]: ~ **bolt** *n* VEH perno roscado *m*; ~ **bush** *n* MECH ENG casquillo roscado *m*; ~ **component** *n* MECH ENG componente roscado *m*; ~ **fastener** *n* MECH fiador roscado *m*, perno roscado *m*, MECH ENG abrazadera *f*, fijador roscado *m*, sujetador roscado *m*; ~ **fitting** *n* MECH ENG *of pipe* adaptador roscado *m*, conector roscado *m*, empalme roscado *m*; ~ **hole** *n* NUCL *circuit* orificio roscado *m*; ~ **joint** *n* NUCL unión roscada *f*; ~ **nut** *n* MECH ENG tuerca roscada *f*
threader *n* MECH ENG cortarroscas *m*, máquina de roscar *f*, roscadora *f*
threading *n* MECH ENG enrosque *m*, roscado *m*; **~-in** *n* PRINT *of tape into machine* posicionamiento *m*; ~ **of paper** *n* PAPER enganchado *m*; ~ **path** *n* CINEMAT trayectoria de enhebrado *f*; ~ **ring** *n* TELECOM anillo de roscar *m*; ~ **slot** *n* CINEMAT ranura de enhebrado *f*; ~ **tool** *n* MECH ENG *lathe* herramienta de roscar *f*
three[1]: **~-dimensional** *adj* PHYS tridimensional; **~-phase** *adj* ELEC *supply network* de tres fases, trifásico, ELEC ENG, PHYS trifásico; **~-way** *adj* MECH de tres vías, tridireccional
three[2]: **~-address instruction** *n* COMP&DP instrucción de tres direccionales *f*, instrucción de tres direcciones *f*; **~-axis data generator** *n* (*TADG*) SPACE generador de datos triaxial *m* (*TADG*); **~-axis gyro unit** *n* SPACE *spacecraft* unidad giroscópica triaxial *f*; **~-axis**

indicator *n* SPACE *spacecraft* indicador triaxial *m*; **~-axis stabilization** *n* SPACE *spacecraft* estabilización triaxial *f*; **~-beam color picture tube** *AmE*, **~-beam colour picture tube** *BrE n* ELECTRON tubo de imagen en color de tres haces *m*; **~-button mouse** *n* COMP&DP ratón de tres botones *m*; **~-cavity klystron** *n* ELECTRON klistron de tres cavidades *m*; **~-centered arch** *AmE*, **~-centred arch** *BrE n* CONST *curve described* arco apainelado *m*, *structure itself* arco de tres centros *m*; **~-circuit nuclear power plant** *n* NUCL central nuclear de tres lazos *f*; **~-color black** *AmE see* three-colour black *BrE*; **~-color map problem** *AmE see* three-colour map problem *BrE*; **~-color photography** *AmE see* three-colour photography *BrE*; **~-color plate** *AmE see* three-colour plate *BrE*; **~-color printing** *AmE see* three-colour printing *BrE*; **~-color process** *AmE see* three-colour process *BrE*; **~-colour black** *n BrE* PRINT grabado para tricromía *m*; **~-colour map problem** *n BrE* GEOM problema del mapa de tres colores *m*, problema del mapa tricolor *m*, problema del mapa tricromo *m* (*AmL*); **~-colour photography** *n BrE* PHOTO fotografía en triconomía *f*, fotografía tricroma *f*; **~-colour plate** *n BrE* PHOTO placa tricroma *f*; **~-colour printing** *n BrE* PRINT impresión tricromía *f*; **~-colour process** *n BrE* CINEMAT tricromía *f*; **~-component alloy** *n* METALL aleación de tres componentes *f*, aleación ternaria *f*; **~-conductor cable** *n* ELEC ENG cable de tres conductores *m*; **~-cone bit** *n* PETR TECH barrena tricónica *f* (*Esp*), mecha *f* (*AmL*), tricono *m* (*AmL*), trépano *m* (*AmL*); **~-cylinder engine** *n* MECH ENG motor de tres cilindros *m*, máquina tricilíndrica *f*; **~-dimensional form working** *n* MECH ENG trabajo tridimensional *m*; **~-dimensional graphic** *n* COMP&DP dibujo en tres dimensiones *m*, dibujo tridimensional *m*; **~-dimensional image** *n* TELECOM imagen tridimensional *f*; **~-dimensional integrated circuit** *n* ELECTRON circuito integrado tridimensional *m*; **~-dimensional integration** *n* ELECTRON integración tridimensional *f*; **~-dimensional machining** *n* MECH ENG maquinado tridimensional *m*, trabajo tridimensional a máquina *m*; **~-dimensional manifold** *n* GEOM variedad de tres dimensiones *f*, variedad tridimensional *f*; **~-electrode tube** *n* ELECTRON tubo de tres electrodos *m*; **~-emulsion film** *n* CINEMAT película de emulsión triple *f*; **~-fold rotation axis** *n* CRYSTALL eje de rotación ternario *m*; **~-grid tube** *n* ELECTRON tubo de tres rejillas *m*; **~-gun color picture tube** *AmE*, **~-gun colour picture tube** *BrE n* ELECTRON tubo de imagen en color de tres cañones *m*; **~-head battery** *n* MINE bocarte de cabezal triple *m*; **~-high mill** *n* MECH ENG laminador de tren trío *m*, laminador de tres cilindros superpuestos *m*, laminador de vaivén *m*, laminador trío *m*, tren trío *m*; **~-high rolls** *n pl* MECH ENG laminador de tren trío *m*, laminador de tres cilindros superpuestos *m*, laminador de tres rodillos *m*, laminador trío *m*; **~-high train** *n* MECH ENG laminador de tren trío *m*, laminador de tres cilindros superpuestos *m*, laminador de vaivén *m*; **~-hole torus** *n* GEOM toro de tres agujeros *m*; **~-input gate** *n* ELECTRON circuito de tres entradas *m*, puerta de tres entradas *f*; **~-input NAND gate** *n* ELECTRON puerta NO-Y de tres entradas *f*; **~-jaw chuck** *n* MECH ENG plato de tres garras *m*; **~-jaw concentric gripping chuck** *n* MECH ENG plato de

sujeción concéntrico de tres garras *m*; **~-jaw steady** *n* MECH ENG *of lathe* luneta fija de tres garras *f*; **~-jaw steady rest** *n* MECH ENG *of lathe* luneta fija de tres garras *f*; **~-lens turret** *n* CINEMAT torreta triple *f*; **~-level laser** *n* ELECTRON láser de tres niveles *m*; **~-level maser** *n* ELECTRON maser de tres niveles *m*; **~-level signal** *n* ELECTRON señal de tres niveles *f*; **~-lift cone pulley** *n* MECH ENG polea cónica de tres diámetros *f*, polea cónica de tres velocidades *f*; **~-month characteristic flow rate** *n* HYDROL porcentaje de caudal característico trimestral *m*; **~-necked flask** *n* LAB *15.432 grains or 0.03215 oz. troy* balón de tres bocas *m*, matraz de tres bocas *m*; **~-part flask** *n* PROD caja de tres partes *f*; **~-part two-stroke engine** *n* AUTO, VEH motor de dos tiempos de tres partes *m*; **~-parted box** *n* PROD *mould making* caja de tres partes *f*; **~-phase alternator** *n* ELEC, ELEC ENG *generator* alternador trifásico *m*; **~-phase alternomotor** *n* ELEC, TRANSP alternomotor trifásico *m*; **~-phase balanced condition** *n* PROD disposición trifásica equilibrada *f*; **~-phase circuit** *n* TELECOM circuito trifásico *m*; **~-phase current** *n* ELEC ENG corriente trifásica *f*; **~-phase current armature** *n* ELEC *generator* armadura de corriente trifásica *f*; **~-phase earthing transformer** *n* BrE (*cf three-phase grounding transformer AmE*) ELEC, ELEC ENG transformador de puesta a tierra trifásico *m*; **~-phase four-wire system** *n* MECH ENG sistema trifásico de cuatro hilos *m*, sistema trifásico tetrafilar *m*; **~-phase generator** *n* ELEC generador trifásico *m*; **~-phase grounding transformer** *n* AmE (*cf three-phase earthing transformer BrE*) ELEC, ELEC ENG transformador de puesta a tierra trifásico *m*; **~-phase induction motor** *n* ELEC ENG motor trifásico de inducción *m*, TRANSP motor de inducción trifásico *m*; **~-phase machine** *n* ELEC ENG mecanismo trifásico *m*, máquina trifásica *f*; **~-phase motor** *n* ELEC, ELEC ENG, PROD motor trifásico *m*; **~-phase neutral reactor** *n* ELEC reactor neutro trifásico *m*; **~-phase rotor** *n* ELEC ENG rotor trifásico *m*; **~-phase rotor winding** *n* ELEC ENG devanado del rotor trifásico *m*; **~-phase stator** *n* ELEC ENG estator trifásico *m*; **~-phase stator winding** *n* ELEC ENG devanado del estator trifásico *m*; **~-phase stepper motor** *n* ELEC ENG motor de velocidad gradual trifásico *m*; **~-phase supply** *n* ELEC alimentación trifásica *f*, ELEC ENG alimentación trifásica *f*, suministro trifásico *m*; **~-phase supply network** *n* ELEC red de distribución trifásica *f*; **~-phase synchronous motor** *n* ELEC ENG motor síncrono trifásico *m*; **~-phase system** *n* ELEC ENG sistema trifásico *m*; **~-phase transformer** *n* ELEC, ELEC ENG transformador trifásico *m*; **~-piece oil ring** *n* AUTO anillo de control de lubricación de tres piezas *m*, anillo de lubricación de tres piezas *m*, MECH ENG anillo de lubricación de tres piezas *m*, VEH anillo de control de lubricación de tres piezas *m*, anillo de lubricación de tres piezas *m*; **~-piece timber set** *n* MINE marco de entibación de triple sección *m*; **~-pin socket** *n* ELEC *connection* enchufe hembra de tres alfileres *m*, enchufe hembra de tres clavijas *m*; **~-ply belting** *n* MECH ENG correa de tres capas *f*, correa triple *f*; **~-ply wood** *n* CONST, PACK madera de tres capas *f*; **~-point bending** *n* METALL alabeo en tres puntos *m*; **~-point landing** *n* AIR TRANSP aterrizaje de tres puntos *m*; **~-point seat belt** *n* TRANSP cinturón de asiento de

tres puntos *m*, cinturón de seguridad de tres anclajes *m*; **~-point snap gage** *AmE*, **~-point snap gauge** *BrE n* MECH ENG calibrador de exteriores de tres puntos *m*, calibrador de herradura de tres puntos *m*, calibrador de horquilla de tres puntos *m*, calibre exterior *m*; **~-point switch** *n* ELEC conmutador de tres direcciones *m*, llave de tres puntos *f*; **~-pole switch** *n* ELEC ENG seccionador tripolar *m*; **~-position switch** *n* ELEC conmutador de tres posiciones *m*; **~-pronged chuck** *n* MECH ENG plato de tulipa *m*, portabrocas de tres mandíbulas *m*; **~-quarter tone** *n* PRINT tono a tres cuartos *m*; **~-sheave block** *n* MECH ENG bloque de tres poleas *m*; **~-sided cutting machine** *n* PRINT cortadora trilateral *f*; **~-slot winding** *n* ELEC devanado de tres ranuras *m*; **~-square file** *n* MECH ENG lima triangular *f*; **~-stage amplifier** *n* ELECTRON amplificador de tres etapas *m*; **~-stamp mill** *n* MINE molino de tres bocartes *m*, molino de tres pisones *m*; **~-state gate** *n* ELECTRON puerta de tres estados *f*; **~-state logic** *n* ELECTRON circuito lógico de tres estados *m*; **~-state output** *n* ELECTRON salida de tres estados *f*; **~-step cone pulley** *n* MECH ENG polea cónica de tres diámetros *f*; **~-step relay** *n* ELEC relé de avance de tres pasos *m*; **~-stranded line** *n* WATER TRANSP cabo colchado con tres cordones *m*; **~-strip camera** *n* CINEMAT cámara para película de tres capas de emulsión *f*; **~-strip negative** *n* CINEMAT negativo de tres capas de emulsión *m*; **~-threaded screw** *n* MECH ENG tornillo de tres entradas *m*; **~-throw crank shaft** *n* MECH ENG cigüeñal de tres codos *m*, cigüeñal de tres muñequillas *m*; **~-throw pump** *n* WATER bomba tricilíndrica *f*; **~-to-em space** *n* PRINT espacio de tres cuadratines *m*, espacio grueso *m*; **~-tube camera** *n* TV cámara de tres tubos *f*; **~-way call** *n* TELECOM llamada de tres direcciones *f*, llamada tridireccional *f*; **~-way cock** *n* CONST llave de tres vías *f*; **~-way conversation** *n* TELECOM conversación de tres direcciones *f*, conversación tridireccional *f*; **~-way switch** *n* ELEC conmutador de tres direcciones *m*, interruptor de tres direcciones *m*, llave de tres puntos *f*; **~-way valve** *n* HYDRAUL válvula de desvío *f*, válvula de tres vías *f*; **~-wheel tube cutter** *n* MECH ENG cortador de tubos de tres ruedas *m*; **~-winding transformer** *n* ELEC, ELEC ENG transformador de tres devanados *m*, transformador tri-devanado *m*; **~-wire current** *n* ELEC ENG corriente trifilar *f*; **~-wire generator** *n* ELEC generador de tres hilos *m*, generador trifilar *m*; **~-wire mains** *n pl BrE* (*cf three-wire supply network AmE*) ELEC ENG red trifilar *f*; **~-wire supply network** *n AmE* (*cf three-wire mains BrE*) ELEC ENG red trifilar *f*; **~-wire system** *n* ELEC ENG sistema trifilar *m*; **~-zeros anti-aliasing filter** *n* ELECTRON filtro anti-ajeno de tres ceros *m*; **~-zeros filter** *n* ELECTRON filtro de tres ceros *m*
3-D: **~ log** *n* PETROL perfil tridimensional *m*
threose *n* CHEM treosa *f*
threshing: **~ cylinder** *n* AGRIC cilindro desgranador *m*
threshold *n* ACOUST, COMP&DP, CONST, ELECTRON, GEOL, PHYS umbral *m*, SPACE comienzo *m*, entrada *f*, umbral *m*; **~ of audibility** *n* POLL umbral de audibilidad *m*; **~ audiometry** *n* ACOUST, SAFE audiometría de umbral *f*; **~ current** *n* ELEC, ELEC ENG, OPT, RAD PHYS, TELECOM corriente umbral *f*; **~ energy** *n* METALL energía crítica *f*; **~ extension demodulator** *n* SPACE *communications* desmodulador de umbral

extendido *m*, desmodulador de umbral mejorado *m*, TELECOM desmodulador de extensión umbral *m*; **~ frequency** *n* ELECTRON frecuencia crítica *f*, frecuencia umbral *f*, PHYS frecuencia umbral *f*, TELECOM frecuencia crítica *f*, WAVE PHYS frecuencia crítica *f*, frecuencia umbral *f*; **~ gate** *n* ELECTRON circuito umbral *m*; **~ of hearing** *n* POLL umbral de audibilidad *m*; **~ level** *n* PROD nivel de umbral *m*; **~ limit value** *n* (*TLV*) POLL valor límite umbral *m* (*TLV*); **~ limit value in the free environment** *n* POLL valor límite umbral en el medio ambiente *m*; **~ operation** *n* COMP&DP operación umbral *f*; **~ signal** *n* ELECTRON señal umbral *m*; **~ value** *n* ELECTRON valor umbral *m*; **~ voltage** *n* ELEC ENG tensión umbral *f*, TV umbral del voltaje *m*, voltaje de entrada *m*; **~ wavelength** *n* ELECTRON longitud de onda de entrada *f*
thresholding *n* ELECTRON formación de umbrales *f*, SPACE fijación del umbral *f*, formación de umbrales *f*
throat *n* ACOUST, C&G garganta *f*, CONST *of plane* cuello *m*, entrada *f*, garganta *f*, paso *m*, PROD *of blast furnace* tragante *m*, SPACE *nozzle of spacecraft* garganta *f*; **~ microphone** *n* ACOUST laringófono *m*
throttle[1] *n* AIR TRANSP *of aircraft* palanca de gases *f*, regulador de gases *m*, válvula de estrangulación *f*, HYDRAUL mariposa de válvula *f*, regulador *m*, toma de vapor *f*, VEH mariposa *f*; **~ control** *n* SPACE *spacecraft* control de gases *m*; **~ control lever** *n* AUTO palanca de control de la mariposa *f*; **~ control rod** *n* AUTO varilla de control de la palomilla *f*; **~ dashpot** *n* AUTO, VEH amortiguador de la válvula de mariposa *m*; **~ lever** *n* HYDRAUL palanca de admisión de gases *f*, palanca de la mariposa *f*; **~ linkage** *n* AUTO, VEH varillaje de mando de la mariposa *m*; **~ pintle nozzle** *n* AUTO boquilla de pivote del estrangulador *f*; **~ plate** *n* AUTO placa de la palomilla *f*; **~ pressure-boost valve** *n* AUTO válvula de sobrepresión de la mariposa *f*, válvula de sobrepresión del estrangulador *f*; **~-reach rod** *n* HYDRAUL varilla de accionamiento de la mariposa *f*; **~ rod** *n* HYDRAUL varilla de la mariposa *f*; **~ slide** *n* VEH regulador de la mariposa *m*; **~ stem** *n* HYDRAUL vástago de válvula de mariposa *m*; **~ stop screw** *n* VEH tornillo de regulación de la mariposa *m*; **~ valve** *n* AUTO válvula de estrangulación *f*, válvula de mariposa *f*, válvula de palomilla *f*, válvula reguladora *f* (*Esp*), COAL regulador de mariposa *m*, válvula de estrangulación *f*, válvula reguladora *f* (*Esp*), HYDRAUL válvula de admisión *f*, válvula reguladora de mariposa *f*, MECH ENG válvula de admisión *f*, válvula de estrangulación *f*, válvula de mariposa *f*, válvula de palomilla *f*, válvula de paso *f*, válvula reguladora *f* (*Esp*), MINE reguladora de mariposa *f* (*AmL*), válvula de estrangulación *f* (*AmL*), válvula de mariposa *f* (*Esp*), válvula reguladora *f* (*Esp*), PROD acelerador *m*, regulador *m*, regulador de mariposa *m*, válvula de estrangulación *f*, válvula reguladora *f* (*Esp*), VEH válvula de estrangulación *f*, válvula de mariposa *f*, válvula de palomilla *f*; **~ valve switch** *n* AUTO, VEH interruptor de válvula de estrangulación *m*
throttle[2]: **~ back** *vt* AIR TRANSP reducir gases
throttling *n* MECH ENG estrangulamiento *m*, obturación *f*, reducción de la sección de paso *f*, regulación *f*, RAIL estrangulamiento *m*; **~ device** *n* REFRIG dispositivo de estrangulación *m*
through[1]: **~-the-lens** *adj* CINEMAT a través del objetivo
through[2]: **~ band** *n* TRANSP banda transversal *f*;

~-**binder** n CONST *masonry* perpiaño m, piedra pasante f; ~ **bolt** n CONST tornillo pasante m, MECH ENG perno pasante m, tornillo pasante m; ~ **bridge** n CONST puente de tablero inferior m; ~-**connection** n TELECOM comunicación directa f, conexión de tránsito f; ~-**deck cable fitting** n WATER TRANSP paso de cables a través de cubierta m; ~-**drying machine** n PAPER secador con circulación de aire caliente a través del papel m; ~-**mortice** n CONST mortaja pasante f; ~ **parcel service** n RAIL servicio directo de paquetes m; ~-**rod cylinder** n MECH ENG cilindro de varilla pasante m; ~ **station** n TRANSP estación terminal f; ~-**stone** n CONST *masonry* perpiaño m; ~-**tenon** n CONST espiga pasante f; ~-**the-lens focusing** n CINEMAT enfoque a través del objetivo m; ~-**the-lens light meter** n (*TTL light meter*) CINEMAT fotómetro a través del objetivo m; ~-**the-lens reflex** n CINEMAT reflex a través del objetivo m; ~-**the-wall air-conditioning unit** n CONST, HEAT, REFRIG, THERMO acondicionador a través de la pared m; ~ **traffic** n TRANSP tráfico en tránsito m, tráfico interurbano m; ~-**wall crack** n NUCL grieta pasante f

throughfall n POLL precipitación no interceptada f

throughline n TELECOM línea directa f

throughput n COMP&DP capacidad de tratamiento útil f, rendimiento global m, PETR TECH caudal m, rendimiento total m, PROD capacidad de producción f, capacidad de tratamiento f, rendimiento total m, volumen global de consumo m

throw[1] n CINEMAT distancia de proyección f, tiro m, MECH ENG *eccentricity* alzada f, excentricidad f, TEXTIL cursa f, VEH *crankshaft* codo m; ~-**out bearing** n AUTO, VEH cojinete de desembrague m; ~-**out bearing sleeve** n AUTO, VEH manguito del cojinete de desembrague m; ~-**out fork pivot** n AUTO, VEH pivote de la horquilla de desembrague m; ~-**out fork strut** n AUTO, VEH puntal de la horquilla de desembrague m

throw[2] vt C&G modelar; ~ **back into alignment** vt CONST *wall* retranquear; ~ **back to waste** vt CONST desechar, rechazar; ~ **into action** vt MECH ENG poner en acción; ~ **into gear** vt MECH ENG engranar, poner en marcha; ~ **off** vt MECH ENG *belt* desprender, sacar; ~ **off center** AmE, ~ **off centre** BrE vt MECH ENG descentrar, desviar; ~ **on** vt MECH ENG *belt* poner; ~ **out of action** vt MECH ENG interrumpir la marcha, parar la marcha; ~ **out of gear** vt MECH ENG desengranar

throw[3]: ~ **a bridge over a river** vi CONST construir un puente sobre un río; ~ **out of feed** vi MECH ENG interrumpir el avance, parar el avance

throwaway: ~ **carbide drill** n MECH ENG broca de carburo al tungsteno descartable f, broca de carburo al tungsteno desechable f; ~ **tip** n MECH ENG *for tooling* cuchillas de herramientas descartables f pl, cuchillas de herramientas desechables f pl, pastilla desechable f, punta descartable f

thrower n C&G tornero m

throwing: ~ **wheel** n C&G rueda de alfarero f

thrust n AIR TRANSP empuje m, CONST *of ground* empuje m, presión f, falla f, corrimiento m, MAR POLL empuje m, MECH ENG empuje m, impulso m, tracción f, PHYS empuje m, PROD corrimiento m, empuje m, impulso m, SPACE empuje m, impulso m; ~ **augmenter** n AIR TRANSP *of aircraft* intensificador de empuje m; ~ **axis** n SPACE eje de empuje m, eje de tracción m; ~ **ball bearing** n MECH ENG cojinete de bolas de empuje m,

cojinete de empuje de bolas m; ~ **bearing** n FUELLESS, MECH cojinete de empuje m, MECH ENG cojinete de empuje m, pivote m; ~ **block** n MECH ENG pivote de empuje m, WATER TRANSP *of engine* chumacera de empuje f; ~ **chamber** n SPACE cámara de compresión f; ~ **coefficient** n SPACE coeficiente de empuje m; ~ **collar** n AUTO, VEH ollar de empuje m; ~ **cone** n SPACE tobera de inyección f; ~ **cutoff** n SPACE supresión del empuje f; ~ **decay** n SPACE disminución del empuje f; ~ **misalignment** n SPACE error de empuje m; ~ **modulation** n SPACE modulación de empuje f; ~ **plate** n MECH ENG plato de empuje m; ~ **program** AmE, ~ **programme** BrE n SPACE programa de empuje m; ~ **reverser** n AIR TRANSP *of aircraft*, TRANSP inversor de empuje m; ~ **subsystem** n SPACE subsistema de empuje m; ~-**to-mass ratio** n SPACE relación entre empuje y masa f; ~-**to-weight ratio** n SPACE relación entre empuje y peso f; ~ **vector** n SPACE vector de empuje m; ~ **vector control** n (*TVC*) SPACE control del vector de empuje m (*TVC*); ~-**vectoring nozzle** n AIR TRANSP *of aircraft*, SPACE tobera de empuje vectorial f, tobera orientable de empuje f; ~ **washer** n AUTO arandela de empuje f, arandela de presión f, MECH arandela de presión f, MECH ENG, PROD, VEH arandela de empuje f, arandela de presión f

thruster n SPACE propulsor m

thrusting n GEOL cabalgamiento m

thujane n CHEM tuyano m

thujene n CHEM tuyeno m

thujone n CHEM tuyona f

thujyl: ~ **alcohol** n CHEM alcohol tuyílico m

thulite n MINERAL thulita f

thulium n (*Tm*) CHEM tulio m (*Tm*)

thumb: ~ **bolt** n MECH ENG cerrojo de botón m; ~ **latch** n CONST picaporte m; ~ **wheel setting** n PROD ajuste accionado con el dedo pulgar m

thumbnut n MECH ENG mariposa f, tuerca de alas f, tuerca de mariposa f, tuerca de orejetas f, tuerca de palomilla f, tuerca manual f

thumbscrew n MECH ENG tornillo de apriete manual m, tornillo de cabeza moleteada m, tornillo de mariposa m, tornillo de orejetas m, tornillo de palomilla m, PROD tornillo de ajuste manual m, tornillo de mariposa m, tornillo de orejetas m

thumbwheel n CINEMAT ruedecilla f; ~ **switch** n ELEC conmutador de accionamiento con el pulgar m, PROD interruptor de rueda moleteada m

thumper n PETROL bobina de choque f

thunder[1] n METEO trueno m

thunder[2] vi METEO tronar

thunderbolt n METEO descarga a tierra f, rayo m

thunderclap n METEO tronido m

thundercloud n METEO nube de tormenta f

thunderstorm n METEO tormenta f

thuringite n MINERAL thuringita f

thymol n CHEM timol m

thymolphthalein n CHEM timolftaleína f

thyratron n CHEM, ELECTRON tiratrón m; ~ **inverter** n ELECTRON convertidor de tiratrón m

thyristor n ELEC, ELEC ENG, PHYS, TELECOM tiristor m; **off** ~ n ELECTRON tiristor en estado de desconexión m; ~-**controlled locomotive** n TRANSP locomotora controlada por tiristor f

thyronine n CHEM tironina f

thyroxine n CHEM tiroxina f

TI *abbr* (*thermal imaging*) MILIT, RAD PHYS, THERMO formación de imágenes térmicas *f*, imagen térmica *f*, producción térmica de imágenes *f*

Ti *abbr* (*titanium*) CHEM, METALL, SPACE Ti (*titanio*)

tick *n* AGRIC garrapata *f*

ticket: **~ machine** *n* TRANSP máquina expendedora de billetes *f*; **~ number** *n* PROD número de billete *m*, número de boleto *m*; **~ punch** *n* TRANSP picado del ticket *m*, taladradora de billetes *f*, taladradora de tickets *f*, taladro de billetes *m*; **~ slot machine** *n* TRANSP expendedora de billetes *f*

tidal: **~ basin** *n* FUELLESS, OCEAN dársena de marea *f*; **~ bore** *n* OCEAN macareo *m*; **~ capacity** *n* TRANSP capacidad en caso de afluencia masiva *f*; **~ channel** *n* OCEAN canal de resaca *m*; **~ component** *n* OCEAN componente de la marea *m*, onda fundamental *f*, onda principal *f*; **~ correction** *n* OCEAN corrección por la marea *f*; **~ creek** *n* OCEAN arroyuelo de marea *m*; **~ current** *n* FUELLESS, OCEAN, WATER TRANSP corriente de marea *f*; **~ delta** *n* OCEAN delta de marea *m*; **~ dock** *n* WATER TRANSP dársena de marea *f*; **~ energy** *n* OCEAN energía de la marea *f*, PHYS energía de mareas *f*; **~ epoch** *n* OCEAN atraso de la marea *m*, retardación de la marea *f*, retardo de la marea *m*; **~ fall** *n* OCEAN, WATER TRANSP bajada de la marea *f*; **~ flow** *n* HYDROL flujo de la marea *m*, TRANSP ritmo de afluencia de oleadas de tráfico *m*, ritmo de afluencia de tráfico *m*, WATER flujo mareal *m*; **~ harbor** *AmE*, **~ harbour** *BrE* *n* WATER TRANSP puerto de marea *m*; **~ height** *n* OCEAN, WATER TRANSP altura de la marea *f*; **~ inlet** *n* OCEAN angostura mareal *f*; **~ lock** *n* HYDROL compuerta de marea *f*; **~ movement** *n* FUELLESS, WATER TRANSP movimiento de la marea *m*; **~ port** *n* WATER TRANSP puerto de marea *m*; **~ power** *n* FUELLESS energía de la marea *f*, PHYS potencia de mareas *f*; **~ power plant** *n* ELEC ENG central maremotriz *f*; **~ power station** *n* FUELLESS central eléctrica maremotriz *f*, OCEAN central maremotriz *f*; **~ prism** *n* FUELLESS prisma de marea *m*; **~ range** *n* FUELLESS, GEOPHYS, HYDROL, WATER TRANSP alcance de marea *m*, amplitud de mareas *f*, carrera de la marea *f*, intervalo de mareas *m*; **~ scale** *n* OCEAN escala de mareas *f*; **~ stand** *n* OCEAN estoa *f*; **~ stream** *n* HYDROL, OCEAN, WATER TRANSP corriente de la marea *f*; **~ stream atlas** *n* WATER TRANSP atlas de corrientes *m*; **~ wave** *n* GEOPHYS ola de marea *f*, OCEAN onda de marea *f*, macareo *m*, ola de marea *f*, WATER TRANSP ola de marea *f*, onda de marea *f*

tide *n* FUELLESS, OCEAN, WATER TRANSP marea *f*; **~ chart** *n* WATER TRANSP *navigation* carta de corrientes de marea *f*; **~ curve** *n* OCEAN mareograma *m*; **~ duration** *n* OCEAN duración de la marea *f*; **~ flat** *n* OCEAN estero mareal *m*; **~ flow** *n* OCEAN reflujo *m*; **~ gage** *AmE see tide gauge BrE*; **~ gate** *n* WATER TRANSP canal de mareas *m*, esclusa de entrada mareal *f*; **~ gauge** *n* *BrE* FUELLESS mareógrafo *m*, GEOPHYS mareógrafo *m*, medidor de mareas *m*, OCEAN escala de mareas *f*, mareógrafo *m*; **~ level indicator** *n* GEOPHYS indicador de nivel de marea *m*; **~ lock** *n* WATER esclusa contra la marea *f*; **~ mill** *n* FUELLESS molino mareomotriz *m*, OCEAN, WATER TRANSP arte de estacas *m*; **~ phase** *n* OCEAN fase de la marea *f*; **~ pole** *n* GEOPHYS indicador de marea *m*; **~ race** *n* OCEAN, WATER TRANSP *of estuary* hilero de marea *m*; **~ record** *n* GEOPHYS record de marea *m*, registro de marea *m*; **~ recorder** *n* OCEAN mareógrafo *m*; **~ scale** *n* OCEAN escala de marea *f*; **~ station** *n* OCEAN estación mareográfica *f*; **~ table** *n* OCEAN, WATER TRANSP *navigation* anuario de mareas *m*, tabla de mareas *f*

tidemark *n* GEOPHYS marca de marea *f*, HYDROL línea de la marea alta *f*

tidewater *n* HYDROL, WATER agua de marea *f*

tideway *n* WATER TRANSP canal de mareas *m*

tie *n* (*cf sleeper BrE*) MECH ENG amarre *m*, atadura *f*, conexión *f*, enlace *m*, unión *f*, *tension member* barra *f*, tirante *m*, varilla *f*, RAIL *fixed equipment* traviesa *f*; **~ bar** *n* AIR TRANSP *helicopter* barra de unión *f*, CONST *of iron or steel roof-truss* traviesa de separación *f*, MECH ENG *tension member* barra de anclaje *f*, barra de conexión *f*, tirante *m*, varilla de unión *f*, RAIL *vehicles* traviesa *f*; **~ beam** *n* CONST *of wooden roof-truss* riostra *f*; **~ bolt** *n* MECH ENG *tension member* perno de fijación *m*, perno de sujeción *m*, perno sujetador *m*, tirante *m*; **~ circuit interface** *n* TELECOM interfaz del circuito de enlace *m*; **~ coat** *n* COATINGS capa de refuerzo *f*, capa de unión *f*; **~-down point** *n* ELECTRON punto de alineación *m*; **~-drilling machine** *n* RAIL *fixed equipment* máquina taladradora de traviesas *f*; **~-dyeing** *n* COLOUR teñido con nudos *m*; **~-in** *n* PETROL conexión *f*; **~ line** *n* METALL línea de conexión *f*, línea de contacto *f*, línea de unión *f*, TELECOM línea de enlace *f*; **~ plate** *n* NUCL *circuit* placa de sujeción *f*, WATER TRANSP *ship building* cuerda *f*; **~ rod** *n* AUTO barra de acoplamiento de las ruedas motrices *f*, varilla de conexión *f*, varilla de unión *f*, barra de acoplamiento *f*, C&G varilla de amarre *f*, CONST *of iron or steel roof-truss* tirante *m*, MECH ENG varilla de unión *f*, MECH ENG *tension member* varilla de conexión *f*, tensor *m*, barra tirante *f*, varilla de tensión *f*, PROD *founding* armadura *f*, VEH barra de acoplamiento de las ruedas motrices *f*, barra de acoplamiento *f*, WATER TRANSP *construction of engine* tirante *m*, barra tensora *f*, barra tensada *f*; **~ screw** *n* *AmE* (*cf sleeper screw BrE*) RAIL *fixed equipment* tirafondo *m*, tirafondo de traviesa *m*; **~ screwdriver** *n* *AmE* RAIL *fixed equipment* destornillador de traviesas *m*; **~ station** *n* *AmE* RAIL estación de enlace *f*; **~ wire** *n* ELEC ENG conexión alámbrica *f*; **~ wrap** *n* PROD arrollamiento de unión *m*

tieback *n* MECH ENG sujetado *m*, TEXTIL abrazadera *f*; **~ input** *n* PROD entrada de bucle *f*

tied: **~ letter** *n* PRINT letra atada *f*

tiemannite *n* MINERAL tiemannita *f*

ties: **~ per inch** *n pl* PRINT ataduras por pulgada *f pl*

tiffanyite *n* MINERAL tiffanyita *f*

TIG: **~ welding** *n* (*tungsten inert gas welding*) CONST soldadura de tungsteno a gas inerte *f*

tiger: **~'s eye** *n* C&G ojo de tigre *m*, MINERAL cuarzo amarillo con crocidolita *m*, ojo de tigre *m*

tight: **~ back** *n* PRINT lomo unido *m*; **~ buffer** *n* OPT protección apretada *f*; **~ buffering** *n* OPT protección apretada *f*; **~ closeup** *n* CINEMAT primerísimo primer plano *m*; **~ construction cable** *n* OPT cable de construcción apretado *m*; **~ corner** *n* CONST ángulo fijo *m*; **~ coupling** *n* ELEC, ELEC ENG acoplamiento fuerte *m*, PHYS acoplamiento ajustado *m*, TV acoplamiento cerrado *m*; **~ editing** *n* *BrE* (*cf flash cutting AmE*) CINEMAT, TV montaje rápido *m*; **~ end** *n* TEXTIL cabo tenso *m*; **~ formation** *n* PETROL formación compacta *f*; **~ framing** *n* CINEMAT encuadre ajustado *m*; **~ gravel** *n* CONST grava adherente *f*; **~ hole** *n* PETR

TECH hueco inestable *m*, pozo confidencial *m*; **~-jacketed cable** *n* OPT cable de construcción apretado *m*, TELECOM cable revestido compacto *m*; ~ **pick** *n* TEXTIL pasada apretada *f*; ~ **pulley** *n* PROD polea fija *f*; ~ **riveting** *n* CONST remache hermético *m*; ~ **selvage** *n* TEXTIL orillo tirante *m*; ~ **selvedge** *n* TEXTIL orillo tirante *m*; ~ **spooling** *n* PHOTO bobinado apretado *m* (*AmL*), rebobinado apretado *m* (*Esp*); **~-to-gage** *AmE*, **~-to-gauge** *BrE n* RAIL ajuste al gálibo *m*; ~ **winder** *n* CINEMAT bobinado apretado *m*

tighten *vt* C&G estrechar, MECH ENG *belt* apretar, estirar, estrechar, fijar, tensar; ~ **up hard** *vt* MECH ENG *screw* apretar al máximo

tightened: ~ **inspection** *n* QUALITY control reforzado *m*

tightener *n* MECH ENG apretador *m*, tensor *m*

tightening *n* MECH ENG apriete *m*, atesamiento *m*, tensión *f*; ~ **cord** *n* MECH ENG cordón tensor *m*; ~ **screw** *n* MECH ENG perno tensor *m*, tornillo tensor *m*; ~ **wedge** *n* MECH ENG cuña de apriete *f*, cuña de tensión *f*

tightness *n* MECH hermeticidad *f*, MECH ENG *of joint* apretura *f*, estanqueidad *f*, estrechez *f*, hermeticidad *f*, tirantez *f*, RAIL *vehicles* apretura *f*; ~ **test** *n* GAS prueba de apriete *f*

tiglic *adj* CHEM tíglico

tile[1] *n* C&G azulejo *m*, CONST *for roofing* teja *f*, azulejo *m*, *for flooring, paving* loseta *f*, mosaico *m* (*AmL*), baldosa *f*, P&R loseta *f*, SPACE *spacecraft* loseta *f*, teja *f*; ~ **burner** *n* C&G quemador de azulejos *m*; ~ **clay** *n* GEOL placa de arcilla *f*; ~ **cutter** *n* CONST cortadora de azulejos *f*, cortadora de baldosas *f*; ~ **factory** *n* C&G fábrica de mosaicos, azulejos y tejas *f*; ~ **floor** *n* CONST enlosado *m*, suelo de losas *m*; ~ **flooring** *n* CONST embaldosado *m*, suelo de baldosas *m*; ~ **kiln** *n* C&G horno de azulejos *m*; ~ **maker** *n* C&G *person* azulejero *m*, fabricante de azulejos *mf*, CONST azulejero *m*; ~ **press** *n* C&G prensa para azulejos *f*

tile[2] *vt* CONST *roof of building* tejar

tiled: ~ **window** *n* COMP&DP ventana en mosaico *f*

tiler *n* C&G *person* azulejero *m*, fabricante de azulejos *mf*, CONST azulejero *m*, *person* solador *m*, tejador *m*, alicatador *m*

tilery *n* C&G fábrica de mosaicos, azulejos y tejas *f*

tiling *n* C&G tejado *m*

till *n* COAL arcilla glaciárica *f*, residuos glaciales no estratificados *m pl*, GEOL arcilla glaciárica *f*

tiller *n* AGRIC cultivador *m*, hijo *m*, macollo *m*, MINE herramienta de giro *f*, llave de maniobra *f*, mango de maniobra *m* (*AmL*), palanca de maniobra *f*, WATER TRANSP *boat building* caña del timón *f*; ~ **axle** *n* WATER TRANSP *boat building* eje del timón *m*; ~ **plough** *n BrE* AGRIC arado rastra *m*; ~ **plow** *AmE* see *tiller plough BrE*; ~ **rope** *n* WATER TRANSP *boat building* guardín *m*

tilt[1] *n* CINEMAT panorámica vertical *f*, picado *m*, TV distorsión de la imagen *f*; ~ **bucket elevator** *n* TRANSP elevador de cubos basculantes *m*; ~ **container** *n* TRANSP contenedor de inclinación *m*; ~ **control** *n* CINEMAT control de panorámica vertical *m*, control de picado *m*; ~ **error** *n* GEOPHYS error de paralelismo *m*; ~ **hammer** *n* PROD martinete de báscula *m*, martinete de forja de palanca accionado por leva *m*; ~ **head** *n* PHOTO cabezal con movimiento panorámico vertical *m*; ~ **mixer** *n* TV corrector de

distorsión de imagen *m* (*Esp*), mezclador de la distorsión de la imagen *m* (*AmL*); ~ **shot** *n* CINEMAT toma con panorámica vertical *f*, toma picada *f*; ~ **table** *n* C&G mesa inclinable *f*; **~-top container** *n* TRANSP contenedor con inclinación superior *m*; **~-type semitrailer** *n* TRANSP semirremolque basculante *m*, semitrailer basculante *m*

tilt[2] *vt* CINEMAT picar, PRINT *essayer's mark* inclinar; ~ **down** *vt* CINEMAT picar hacia abajo

tiltable: ~ **tower** *n* FUELLESS *wind power* torre basculante *f*

tiltainer *n* TRANSP contenedor basculante *m*

tiltdozer *n* TRANSP explanadora de cuchilla basculante *f*, motoniveladora de cuchilla basculante *f*

tilted: ~ **block** *n* GEOL bloque inclinado *m*; ~ **shot** *n* CINEMAT toma inclinada *f*

tilter *n* PROD basculador *m*, horno basculador *m*, volcador *m*

tilth *n* AGRIC consistencia del suelo *f*

tilting *n* PROD basculamiento *m*, inclinación *f*, vuelco *m*; ~ **baseboard** *n* PHOTO tablero inclinable *m*; ~ **basket** *n* NUCL *steel rods* cesta basculante de manejo del combustible *f*; ~ **body** *n* TRANSP cuerpo basculante *m*; ~ **body coach** *n* TRANSP vagón pendular *m*; ~ **car** *n AmE* (*cf tilting wagon BrE*) TRANSP vagón pendular *m*; ~ **device** *n* NUCL dispositivo basculante *m*; ~ **dozer** *n* TRANSP explanadora pendular *f*; ~ **furnace** *n* HEAT horno oscilante *m*; ~ **gate** *n* FUELLESS *dams* compuerta basculante *f*; ~ **hammer** *n* PROD martinete de báscula *m*; ~ **head** *n* PHOTO cabezal inclinable *m*; ~ **mold** *AmE*, ~ **mould** *BrE n* C&G molde inclinable *m*; ~ **skip** *n* TRANSP cuba inclinable *f*; ~ **table** *n* MECH ENG mesa basculante *f*, mesa oscilante *f*; ~ **wagon** *n BrE* (*cf tilting car AmE*) TRANSP vagón pendular *m*

tiltmeter *n* GEOPHYS medidor de inclinación *m*

timber[1] *n* CONST, WATER TRANSP *shipbuilding* madera *f*, maderos *m pl*; ~ **bridge** *n* CONST puente de madera *m*; ~ **car** *n AmE* (*cf timber wagon BrE*) RAIL vagón para el transporte de troncos *m*; ~ **dog** *n* CONST *carpentry* perno para madera *m*; ~ **frame** *n* CONST *for wall* cerco de madera *m*, estructura de madera *f*, marco de madera *m*, MINE *mine-timbering* marco de madera *m*; ~ **framing** *n* CONST *for wall* entibación *f*; ~ **hitch** *n* WATER TRANSP *knot* vuelta de braza *f*; ~ **jack** *n* CONST soporte de madera *m*; ~ **raft** *n* CONST balsa de madera *f*; ~ **set** *n* MINE *mine-timbering* marco de ajuste *m pl* (*Esp*), marco de entibación *m* (*AmL*); **~-splitting wedge** *n* CONST cuña para partir madera *f*; ~ **suitable for conversion into market forms** *n* CONST madera convertible en elementos de dimensiones comerciales *f*; ~ **truss with iron bracing** *n* CONST viga de madera con arriostramiento de hierro *f*; ~ **wagon** *n BrE* (*cf timber car AmE*) RAIL vagón para el transporte de troncos *m*

timber[2] *vt* CONST entibar, revestir de madera

timbered: ~ **shaft** *n* CONST pozo entibado *m*

timbering *n* CONST entibación *f*, entibado *m*

timberline *n* AGRIC límite forestal *m*

timberyard *n* CONST, MINE almacén de maderas *m*

timbre *n* ACOUST timbre *m*, WAVE PHYS timbre *m*, tono *m*

time[1]: ~ **base** *n* ELECTRON, NUCL, PHYS, PROD, TELECOM, TV base de tiempo *f*; ~ **base error correction** *n* TV corrección del error de base de tiempo *f*; ~ **base frequency** *n* ELEC *cathode ray tube*

frecuencia de la base de tiempo *f*; ~ **base generator** *n*
TV, ELECTRON generador de base de tiempo *m*;
~ **bomb** *n* MILIT bomba de efecto retardado *f*;
~ **break** *n* GEOPHYS período de interrupción *m*;
~ **bucket** *n* PROD período *m*; ~ **card** *n* PROD tarjeta
de control del tiempo *f*; ~ **characteristic** *n* TELECOM
característica temporal *f*; ~ **charter** *n* PETR TECH flete
temporal *m*, WATER TRANSP *sea-transport* fletamento
a plazo *m*, fletamento a término *m*, fletamento por
tiempo *m*; ~ **code** *n* CINEMAT, TV código de tiempo
m; ~ **code editing** *n* CINEMAT, TV edición del código
de tiempo *f*, montaje con código de tiempo *m*;
~-**code generator** *n* CINEMAT, TV generador de
código de tiempo *m*; ~ **coherence** *n* OPT coherencia
temporal *f*, TELECOM coherencia de tiempo *f*;
~ **compression** *n* TELECOM compresión del tiempo
f, compresión en el tiempo *f*; ~-**consistent busy hour**
n TELECOM hora cargada acorde al tiempo *f*, hora
más cargada acorde al tiempo *f*; ~ **constant** *n* ELEC
AC circuit, PHYS constante de tiempo *f*; ~ **correlation**
n TELECOM correlación temporal *f*; ~-**correlation**
analysis *n* NUCL análisis por correlación de tiempo
m; ~ **delay** *n* ELECTRON tiempo de retardo *m*, TELE-
COM retardo *m*, tiempo de propagación *m*; ~-**delay**
circuit *n* ELECTRON circuito retardador *m*; ~-**delay**
distortion *n* ELECTRON distorsión del tiempo de
retardo *f*; ~-**delay generation** *n* ELECTRON generación de tiempo de retardo *f*; ~ **delay position switch**
n PROD interruptor de posición de tiempo retardado
m, temporizador *m*; ~-**delay relay** *n* ELEC relevador
con acción de retardo *m*, relevador de retardo *m*,
relevador retardado *m*, relé de acción diferida *m*, relé
de retardo *m*, relé de retardo de tiempo *m*, relé
retardado *m*, ELEC ENG relé temporizado *m*; ~-**delay**
starter *n* ELEC arrancador diferido *m*; ~-**dependent**
relay *n* ELEC relé dependiente del tiempo *m*, relé
variable en función del tiempo *m*; ~ **derivative** *n*
PHYS derivada temporal *f*; ~ **dilation** *n* PHYS dilatación temporal *f*; ~-**diversity reception** *n* TELECOM
recepción de diversidad temporal *f*; ~ **division** *n*
ELECTRON división de tiempo *f*; ~-**division**
demultiplexing *n* ELECTRON desmultiplexaje en el
reparto del tiempo *m*; ~-**division exchange** *n* TELE-
COM central temporizadora *f*, centro de
sincronización *m*; ~-**division modulation** *n* (*TDM*)
COMP&DP, ELECTRON, PHYS, SPACE, TELECOM, modulación por division de tiempo *f* (*TDM*); ~-**division**
multiple access *n* (*TDMA*) COMP&DP, ELECTRON,
SPACE, TELECOM acceso múltiple por división de
tiempo *m*; ~-**division multiplex** *n* TELECOM multiplex
de tiempo compartido *m*, multiplex por distribución
en el tiempo *m*, multiplex por división de tiempo *m*;
~-**division multiplexed signal** *n* ELECTRON señal
múltiple en la distribución del tiempo *f*; ~-**division**
multiplexer *n* ELECTRON multiplexor temporal *m*;
~-**division multiplexing** *n* (*TDM*) COMP&DP,
ELECTRON, PHYS, SPACE, TELECOM multiplexación
por división de tiempo *f* (*TDM*); ~-**division**
network *n* TELECOM red cronizadora *f*; ~-**division**
switching *n* COMP&DP conmutación por división de
tiempo *f*, TELECOM conmutación en el tiempo *f*,
conmutación temporal *f*; ~-**division switching**
system *n* TELECOM sistema de conmutación en el
tiempo *f*, sistema de conmutación temporal *m*;
~-**division system** *n* TELECOM sistema de distribución en el tiempo *m*, sistema de división de tiempo *m*;

~ **domain** *n* ELECTRON dominio temporal *m*;
~-**domain signal processing** *n* ELECTRON tratamiento de la señal en dominio temporal *m*; ~ **drift**
n ELECTRON tiempo de variación *m*; ~ **exposure** *n*
CINEMAT, PHOTO tiempo de exposición *m*; ~ **fence** *n*
PROD barrera de tiempo *f*; ~ **of flight** *n* (*TOF*) NUCL,
PART PHYS, RAD PHYS tiempo de vuelo *m*; ~-**footage**
calculator *n* CINEMAT calculadora de tiempo y
metraje *f*; ~ **frequency** *n* ELECTRON frecuencia
temporal *f*; ~ **grenade** *n* MILIT granada de efecto
retardado *f*; ~ **headway** *n* RAIL, TRANSP intervalos de
salida *m pl*; ~ **interval** *n* PROD intervalo de tiempo *m*;
~ **invariant signal** *n* ELECTRON señal invariable con el
tiempo *f*; ~ **jitter** *n* ELECTRON inestabilidad de la base
de tiempo *f*; ~ **key** *n* PROD pauta del tiempo *f*; ~ **lag** *n*
ELECTRON tiempo de retardo *m*; ~-**lag relay** *n* ELEC
relé retardado *m*; ~-**lapse photography** *n* CINEMAT,
PHOTO fotografía con cadencia temporizada de toma
de imágenes *f*; ~-**lapse survey** *n* TRANSP estudio
sobre frecuencias de tiempo *m*; ~-**lapse video tape**
recorder *n* PROD registrador de cintas de vídeo a
intervalos prefijados *m*; ~-**light output curve** *n*
PHOTO curva de rendimiento de tiempo-luz *f*;
~-**locking relay** *n* ELEC relé de acción diferida *m*,
relé temporizado *m*; ~ **marker** *n* ELECTRON cronometrador *m*; ~ **modulation** *n* ELECTRON modulación por
tiempos *f*; ~ **multiplex** *n* TV multiplex de tiempo *m*,
transmisión sucesiva de señales *f*; ~ **multiplexing** *n*
TELECOM multiplexión en el tiempo *f*; ~-**of-flight**
data analysis *n* (*TOF data analysis*) AIR TRANSP, RAD
PHYS análisis de datos de tiempo de vuelo *m*; ~-**of-**
flight detector *n* (*TOFD*) PART PHYS, RAD PHYS
detector de tiempo de vuelo *m*; ~-**of-flight velocity**
selector *n* NUCL, RAD PHYS selector de tiempo de
vuelo *m*; ~-**out** *n* COMP&DP interrupción *f*, tiempo de
espera *m*, TELECOM retraso *m*; ~-**out supervision** *n*
TELECOM supervisión del transcurso del intervalo de
retardo *f*; ~ **per piece** *n* PROD tiempo por pieza *m*;
~ **per unit** *n* PROD tiempo por unidad *m*; ~ **period** *n*
ELECTRON, PROD período de tiempo *m*; ~-**periodic**
field *n* ELEC ENG campo de periodicidad temporal *m*;
~ **phase** *n* PROD período de tiempo *m*; ~-**phased**
delivery *n* PROD entrega secuenciada *f*; ~ **phasing** *n*
PROD período de tiempo *m*; ~ **pulse modulation** *n*
(*TPM*) TELECOM modulación por tiempo de impulsos *f*; ~ **recorder** *n* INSTR registrador de tiempo *m*,
PROD *instrument* reloj para fichar *m*, reloj registrador
m, *person* controlador de rondas *m*; ~ **recording** *n*
INSTR, PROD cronografía *f*; ~-**related failure** *n* ELEC
ENG avería relativa a tiempo *f*; ~-**resolved**
radiography *n* NUCL radiografía de resolución
temporal *f*, radiografía resuelta en función del
tiempo *f*; ~-**resolved spectrum** *n* RAD PHYS espectro
de resolución temporal *m*, espectro resuelto en
función del tiempo *m*; ~ **reversal operation** *n* PART
PHYS operación de inversión del tiempo *f*; ~-**series**
analysis *n* ELECTRON análisis temporal *m*; ~ **sharing**
n TELECOM compartimiento del tiempo *m*, distribución de tiempo *f*, repartición de tiempo *f*, tiempo
compartido *m*; ~-**sharing** *n* COMP&DP tiempo compartido *m*; ~ **sheet** *n* PROD hoja de jornales *f*, tarjeta
para anotar la hora de entrada y salida *f*; ~ **shift** *n*
ELECTRON cronodesplazamiento *m*; ~ **signal** *n* ELEC-
TRON señal de tiempo *f*, WATER TRANSP señal horaria
f; ~ **slice** *n* COMP&DP fracción de tiempo *f*, unidad de
tiempo *f*, ELECTRON tramo de tiempo *m*; ~ **slicing** *n*

COMP&DP fraccionamiento del tiempo *m*, recorte de tiempo para uso múltiple *m*, ELECTRON división del tiempo *f*; ~ **slot** *n* ELECTRON ranura visualizadora de tiempo *f*, SPACE franja de tiempo *f*, TELECOM segmento de tiempo *m*, TV ranura de tiempo *f*; ~ **slot interchanger** *n* (*TSI*) TELECOM intercambiador de segmento de tiempo *m*; ~**-space diagram** *n* TRANSP diagrama espacio-tiempo *m*; ~ **stage** *n* (*T-stage*) TELECOM etapa de temporización *f*, etapa temporizadora *f*; ~ **stamp** *n* TELECOM reloj fechador *m*; ~ **switch** *n* CINEMAT interruptor temporizador *m*, ELEC conmutador de tiempo *m*, cronointerruptor *m*, interruptor de reloj *m*, interruptor de tiempo *m*, interruptor horario *m*, interruptor temporizado *m*, limitador horario *m*, ELEC ENG interruptor horario *m*, interruptor temporal *m*, TELECOM conmutador de tiempo *m*, cronointerruptor *m*, interruptor de reloj *m*, interruptor de tiempo *m*, interruptor horario *m*, interruptor temporizado *m*, limitador horario *m*; ~ **switching** *n* TELECOM conmutación en el tiempo *f*, conmutación temporal *f*; ~ **synthesis** *n* ELECTRON síntesis de tiempo *f*; ~ **synthesizer** *n* ELECTRON sintetizador de tiempo *m*; ~ **temperature curve** *n* CINEMAT curva de tiempo y temperatura *f*; ~**-temperature-tolerance** *n* (*t-t-t*) REFRIG *of frozen food* tiempo-temperatura-tolerancia *m* (*t-t-t*); ~ **to manoeuvre** *n* WATER TRANSP *radar* tiempo para maniobrar *m*; ~ **to rupture** *n* METALL duración hasta la rotura *f*; ~**-to-digital conversion** *n* (*TDC*) PART PHYS conversión temporal a digital *f*; ~ **trace** *n* GEOPHYS trazo del tiempo *m*; ~ **trend** *n* POLL evolución temporal *f*, fluctuación temporal *f*, tendencia en el tiempo *f*, variación temporal *f*; ~**-variable filtering** *n* GEOPHYS filtración cronovariable *f*, filtración variable en el tiempo *f*; ~ **variant** *n* PETROL variante temporal *f*; ~**-varying filter** *n* ELECTRON filtro variable con el tiempo *m*; ~**-varying signal** *n* ELECTRON señal variable con el tiempo *f*; ~ **zone** *n* WATER TRANSP huso horario *m*

time² *vt* CINEMAT cronometrar, PROD adaptar al tiempo, concertar, contar el tiempo, cronometrar, medir el tiempo, sincronizar, SPACE calcular, cronometrar, regular; ~**-tag** *vt* TELECOM marcar el sincronismo, marcar el tiempo

time³: ~ **out** *vi* PROD exceder el tiempo asignado

timebase: ~ **corrector** *n* (*TBC*) TV corrector de base de tiempo *m*; ~ **error** *n* TV error de base de tiempo *m*

timed¹: ~**-driven** *adj* PROD accionado y temporizado

timed²: ~ **defrosting** *n* REFRIG desescarche temporizado *m*; ~ **interval** *n* PROD intervalo cronometrado *m*; ~ **phased planning** *n* PROD planificación en períodos de tiempo *f*; ~ **print** *n* CINEMAT copia cronometrada *f*

timekeeper *n* PROD *person* controlador *m*, cronometrador *m*, cronometrista *m*

timekeeping *n* PROD cronometraje *m*, marcación en el reloj de entrada *f*

timeliness: ~ **rating** *n* PROD régimen de tempestividad *m*

timer *n* CINEMAT cronómetro *m*, COMP&DP marcador *m*, temporizador *m*, ELEC ENG temporizador *m*, LAB cronómetro *m* (*Esp*), medidor de intervalos de tiempo *m* (*AmL*), temporizador *m*, PHOTO reloj *m*, PHYS cronómetro *m*, PROD avance automático de encendido *m*, contador de tiempo *m*, cronógrafo *m*, cronómetro *m*, distribuidor de encendido *m*, regulador de tiempo *m*, relé temporizador *m*, temporizador

m, REFRIG reloj *m*, TELECOM cronómetro *m*, dispositivo de control de tiempo *m*, dispositivo eléctronico de control de tiempo *m*, medidor *m*, sincronizador *m*; ~ **address** *n* PROD dirección en función del temporizador *f*; ~ **bit** *n* PROD bit de temporizador *m*; ~ **clock bit** *n* PROD bit de temporizador *m*; ~ **instruction** *n* PROD instrucción del temporizador *f*; ~**-off delay** *n* PROD retardo en el cierre del temporizador *m*; ~**-off done bit** *n* PROD bit de cierre del temporizador *m*; ~**-on delay** *n* PROD temporizador en demora *m*; ~ **reset** *n* PROD reposición del temporizador *f*; ~ **rung** *n* PROD escalón del temporizador *m*; ~**-status bit** *n* COMP&DP, PROD bit de estado del temporizador *m*; ~**-timing bit** *n* PROD bit de cronometraje del temporizador *m*

timing *n* AUTO puesta a punto *f*, sincronización *f*, CINEMAT cronometraje *m*, COMP&DP, ELECTRON sincronización *f*, temporización *f*, TELECOM control de tiempo *m*, cronización *f*, cronomedición *f*, cronometración *f*, cronometraje *m*, medición de tiempo *f*, medida de tiempo *f*, registro de tiempo *m*, regulación en el tiempo *f*, sincronismo *m*, sincronización *f*, temporización *f*, VEH puesta a punto *f*, reglaje *m*; ~ **adjustment** *n* AUTO ajuste de sincronización *m*; ~ **analysis** *n* COMP&DP análisis de sincronismo *m*, análisis de temporización *m*, análisis de tiempo *m*, esquema de sincronismo *m*; ~ **angle** *n* AUTO, VEH ángulo de reglaje *m*; ~ **belt** *n* MECH correa de regulación *f*, VEH correa de distribución *f*; ~ **card** *n* CINEMAT tarjeta de cronometraje *f*; ~ **chain** *n* AUTO cadena de la distribución *f*, cadena de sincronización *f*, VEH cadena de la distribución *f*; ~ **cover** *n* AUTO cadena de distribución *f*, tapa del distribuidor *f*, VEH cadena de distribución *f*; ~ **diagram** *n* AUTO esquema de puesta a punto *m*, esquema de reglaje *m*, COMP&DP diagrama de temporización *m*, esquema de sincronismo *m*, PROD cronograma *m*; ~ **drum** *n* C&G tambor de tiempos *m*; ~ **gear** *n* AUTO engranaje de distribución *m*, engranaje de sincronización *m*, VEH engranaje de distribución *m*; ~**-gear housing** *n* AUTO, VEH alojamiento del engranaje de sincronización *m*; ~ **generator** *n* ELECTRON generador de medición de tiempo *m*; ~ **of the ignition** *n* AUTO puesta a punto del encendido *f*, sincronización del encendido *f*; ~ **line** *n* PETROL línea de sincronización *f*; ~ **mark** *n* AUTO marca de encendido *f*, marca de puesta a punto *f*, marca de sincronización *f*; ~ **pulse** *n* ELECTRON impulso de sincronización *m*, TV pulso de sincronización *m*; ~ **range** *n* PROD avance del encendido *m*; ~ **signal** *n* ELECTRON señal de tiempo *f*

tin *n* (*Sn*) CHEM estaño *m* (*Sn*), HYDRAUL bidón *m*, tambor *m*, METALL, MINE, PROD estaño *m* (*Sn*); ~**-closing machine** *n* BrE (*cf can-closing machine AmE*) PACK cerradora de botes *f*, máquina cerradora de latas *f*; ~ **delabelling** *n* BrE (*cf can delabeling AmE*) PACK desetiquetado de la lata *m*; ~**-filling line** *n* BrE (*cf can-filling line AmE*) PACK cadena de llenado de latas *f*; ~**-filling machine** *n* BrE (*cf can-filling machine AmE*) PACK llenadora de latas *f*, máquina llenadora de latas *f*; ~**-foiling machine** *n* PACK máquina para fabricar hojas de papel de estaño *f*; ~**-packing machine** *n* BrE (*cf can-packing machine AmE*) PACK empaquetadora de latas *f*, máquina enlatadora *f*; ~ **plate** *n* METALL hojalata *f*; ~**-plate pail** *n* PROD balde estañado *m*; ~**-plate varnish** *n* COATINGS, COLOUR barniz estañado *m*; ~ **plate**

worker *n* PROD estañador *m*; ~ **plate working** *n* PROD estañadura *f*; ~ **printing** *n* PRINT impresión metalgráfica *f*; ~ **pyrite** *n* MINERAL estannina *f*, pirita de estaño *f*; ~ **relabelling** *n* BrE (*cf can relabeling AmE*) PACK reetiquetado de latas *m*; ~**-sealing compound** *n* BrE (*cf can-sealing compound AmE*) PACK material usado para el sellado de la lata *m*; ~ **tack** *n* MECH ENG tachuela de estaño *f*; ~**-zinc finish** *n* COATINGS acabado de estañocincado *m*

tincalconite *n* MINERAL tinkalconita *f*

tinctorial *adj* COLOUR tintóreo

tincture[1] *n* COLOUR tintura *f*; ~ **of iodine** *n* COLOUR tintura de yodo *f*

tincture[2] *vt* COLOUR colorear, teñir

tine *n* AmE (*cf prong BrE*) CONST *of fork* diente *m*, púa *f*, MECH diente *m*, MECH ENG (*cf prong BrE, cf tooth BrE*) diente *m*, púa *f*

tinge[1] *n* COLOUR matiz *m*

tinge[2] *vt* COLOUR teñir, tinturar

tinkal *n* MINERAL atíncar *m*, tinkal *m*

tinman: ~**'s shears** *n pl* PROD cizallas de hojalatero *f pl*, tijeras de hojalatero *f pl*; ~**'s snips** *n pl* PROD cizallas de hojalatero *f pl*, tijeras de hojalatero *f pl*

tinned[1] *adj* C&G, CHEM, CONST, ELEC estañado, FOOD, PACK enlatado

tinned[2]: ~ **conductor** *n* ELEC *cable* conductor estañado *m*; ~ **food** *n* BrE (*cf canned food AmE*) FOOD, PACK alimento en conserva *m*, alimento enlatado *m*, comida enlatada *f*; ~ **wire** *n* ELEC ENG alambre estañado *m*

tinning *n* (*cf canning AmE*) C&G, CHEM, CONST estañado *m*, ELEC *of cable conductor* estañado *m*, estañadura *f*, FOOD, PACK enlatado *m*; ~ **industry** *n* BrE (*cf canning industry AmE*) AGRIC, FOOD, PACK industria conservera *f*

tinnitus *n* ACOUST acúfeno *m*

tinsel: ~ **conductor** *n* ELEC *cable with metal tapes* conductor de oropel *m*

tinsmith *n* PROD *person* hojalatero *m*

tinstone *n* MINERAL casiterita *f*, estaño vidrioso *m*

tint[1] *n* C&G tinte *m*, COLOUR matiz *m*, tintada *f*, tinte *m*, PHOTO tinte *m*, PRINT fondo de color *m*, matiz *m*; ~ **plate** *n* C&G placa de entintado *f*

tint[2] *vt* COLOUR colorear, matizar, teñir, PRINT, TEXTIL matizar

tinted[1] *adj* COLOUR teñido

tinted[2]: ~ **base** *n* CINEMAT soporte coloreado *m*; ~ **glass** *n* C&G vidrio de color *m*; ~ **laminated glass** *n* C&G vidrio de color laminado *m*

tinting *n* CINEMAT coloración *f*, P&R coloración *f*, tinción *f*, PRINT teñido *m*; ~ **strength** *n* PRINT intensidad de coloración *f*

tinware *n* PROD artículos de hojalata *m pl*

tip[1] *n* (*cf dump AmE*) COAL basculadora *f*, punta *f*, vagoneta *f*, ápice *m*, CONST *tipping-device* volquete *m*, POLL basurero *m*, PRINT encarte *m*, RAIL *of switch tongue* punta *f*, RECYCL basurero *m*, escombrera *f*, vertedero *m*, TELECOM hilo de punta *m*, hilo A *m*, WATER basurero *m*; ~ **area** *n* BrE MINE zona de cargamento *f*; ~ **box car** *n* COAL vagoneta basculadora *f*, volquete *m*; ~ **car** *n* AmE (*cf tip wagon BrE*) COAL vagoneta *f*, RAIL vagoneta basculante *f*; ~ **engagement** *n* TV fijación de inclinación *f*; ~ **heap** *n* BrE MINE montón exterior *m*; ~ **height** *n* TV altura de inclinación *f*; ~ **loss** *n* FUELLESS pérdida del flujo de aire a los extremos *f*; ~ **penetration** *n* TV

fijación de inclinación *f*; ~ **projection** *n* TV proyección de inclinación *f*; ~ **protrusion** *n* TV saliente de inclinación *m*; ~ **sampler** *n* COAL tomamuestras basculante *m*; ~**-speed ratio** *n* FUELLESS relación de la velocidad periférica *f*; ~**-up seat** *n* BrE (*cf folding seat AmE*) AUTO, VEH asiento abatible *m*, asiento plegable *m*; ~ **wagon** *n* BrE (*cf tip car AmE*) RAIL vagoneta basculante *f*

tip[2] *vt* CONST bascular, PROD calzar, herrar, poner placa postiza a herramientas; ~ **up** *vt* CONST bascular, volcar

tip[3] *vi* CONST inclinarse; ~ **up** *vi* CONST inclinarse

tipped: ~ **in** *adj* PRINT encartado

tipper *n* BrE (*cf dump truck AmE, cf dumper AmE, cf dumper truck AmE*) COAL basculador *m*, basculador de vagones *m*, camión volquete *m*, vagoneta basculante *f*, volcador de vagones *m*, volcador de vagonetas *m*, CONST basculante *m*, camión basculante *m*, TRANSP camión basculante *m*, dumper *m*, volquete *m*

tipping *n* BrE RECYCL vertido *m*; ~ **bucket** *n* BrE (*cf dump bucket AmE*) CONST balde basculante *m*, cubo basculante *m*; ~ **bucket conveyor** *n* TRANSP transportador de cuba basculante *m*; ~ **device** *n* CONST volcador *m*; ~ **mine car** *n* COAL vagoneta de minas basculante *f*; ~ **platform** *n* TRANSP plataforma basculante *f*

tire *AmE see tyre BrE*

tissue[1]: ~ **equivalent** *adj* NUCL equivalente a tejido

tissue[2] *n* PAPER papel tisú *m*; ~ **bank** *n* REFRIG banco de tejidos *m*; ~ **machine** *n* PAPER máquina de papel tisú *f*

tit *n* MECH ENG saliente *m*; ~ **screw** *n* MECH ENG tornillo de tetón *m*

titanate *n* CHEM titanato *m*

titanic[1] *adj* CHEM titánico

titanic[2]: ~ **acid** *n* CHEM ácido titánico *m*

titanite *n* MINERAL titanita *f*

titanium *n* (Ti) CHEM, METALL, SPACE titanio *m* (Ti); ~ **alloy** *n* METALL, SPACE aleación de titanio *f*; ~ **dioxide** *n* CHEM, P&R dióxido de titanio *m*; ~ **forging** *n* METALL aleación de titanio *f*, SPACE aleación de titanio *f*, forja de titanio *f*; ~ **iron oxide** *n* CHEM, MINERAL óxido de ferrotitanio *m*; ~ **nitride coating** *n* MECH ENG capa de nitruro de titanio *f*, revestimiento de nitruro de titanio *m*; ~ **nitride hardening** *n* MECH ENG endurecimiento por nitruro de titanio *m*; ~ **oxide** *n* CHEM óxido de titanio *m*; ~ **oxide pigment** *n* COLOUR pigmento de óxido de titanio *m*

titanous *adj* CHEM titanoso

titanyl *n* CHEM titanilo *m*

titer *AmE see titre BrE*

title *n* CINEMAT, PRINT título *m*; ~ **card** *n* CINEMAT tarjeta del título *f*; ~ **keyer** *n* TV manipulador de títulos *m*; ~ **page** *n* PRINT portada *f*; ~ **printer** *n* CINEMAT tituladora *f*

titrate *vt* CHEM titular, valorar, titrar, COAL dosificar, titrar, titular, DETERG, LAB titrar, titular

titration *n* CHEM análisis volumétrico *m*, titulación *f*, valoración *f*, COAL análisis volumétrico *m*, dosificación *f*, valoración *f*, DETERG valoración *f*, LAB análisis volumétrico *m*, titulación *f*, valoración *f*

titrator *n* CHEM, COAL, DETERG, LAB titulador *m*

titre *n* BrE CHEM *analysis* título *m*

titrimetry *n* CHEM *analysis* análisis por titulación *m*

T-joint *n* CONST *plumbing* unión en T *f*, ELEC *cable* empalme en T *m*, unión en forma de T *f*

T-junction *n* CONST, TRANSP cruce de carreteras en T *m*

TKO *abbr* (*trunk offer*) TELECOM enlace de oferta *m*

Tl *abbr* (*thallium*) CHEM Tl (*talio*)

TLC *abbr* (*thin-layer chromatography*) CHEM, LAB CCD (*cromatografía de capa delgada*), cromatografía de capa fina *f*

TLMA *abbr* (*telematic agent*) TELECOM agente telemático *m*

TLV[1] *abbr* (*threshold limit value*) POLL TLV (*valor límite umbral*)

TLV[2]: ~ **at place of work** *n* POLL TLV en el lugar de trabajo *m*, TLV en áreas de trabajo *m*; ~ **in the free environment** *n* POLL TLV en el medio ambiente *m*

Tm *abbr* (*thulium*) CHEM Tm (*tulio*)

TM[1] *abbr* (*transverse magnetic*) ELEC ENG TM (*magnético transversal*)

TM[2]: ~ **mode** *n* OPT, TELECOM modo TM *m*; ~ **wave** *n* (*transverse magnetic wave*) ELEC, ELEC ENG, PHYS onda TM *f* (*onda magnética transversal*)

TMN *abbr* (*telecommunications management network*) TELECOM red de gestión de telecomunicaciones *f*

TMP *abbr* (*thermomechanical pulp*) PAPER pasta TMP *f* (*pasta termomecánica*)

TMR *abbr* (*tandem mirror fusion reactor*) NUCL TMR (*reactor de fusión de espejos en tándem*)

TMUX *abbr* (*transmultiplexer*) TELECOM transmultiplexor *m*

T-network *n* ELEC ENG, PHYS, TELECOM red en T *f*

TNI *abbr* (*traffic noise index*) ACOUST TNI (*índice de ruido de tráfico*)

TNT *abbr* (*trinitrotoluene*) CHEM TNT (*trinitrotolueno*)

thrown: not to be ~ *phr* PACK no tirar

toboggan *n* SAFE *aircraft* rampa deslizante *f*, tobogán *m*

TOCC *abbr AmE* (*Technical and Operational Control Center AmE*) SPACE TOCC (*Centro de Control Técnico y de Operaciones*)

tocopherol *n* FOOD tocoferol *m*, vitamina E *f*

toe *n* CONST *of G cramp* base *f*; ~ **board** *n* CONST tablón de pie *m*; ~**-in** *n* VEH convergencia *f*; ~**-in angle** *n* AIR TRANSP *of runway lights* ángulo de convergencia *m*; ~**-out** *n* VEH divergencia *f*; ~ **region of characteristic curve** *n* PHOTO base de la curva característica *f*; ~**-to-top converter** *n* TEXTIL convertidor de cintas de filamentos continuos a discontinuos *m*; ~ **weighting** *n* CONST carga de base *f*

TOF[1] *abbr* (*time of flight*) NUCL, PART PHYS, RAD PHYS tiempo de vuelo *m*

TOF[2]: ~ **data analysis** *n* (*time-of-flight data analysis*) AIR TRANSP, PART PHYS, RAD PHYS análisis de datos de tiempo de vuelo *m*

TOFC *abbr* (*trailer on flatcar*) TRANSP remolque sobre vagón plataforma *m*

TOFD *abbr* (*time-of-flight detector*) PART PHYS, RAD PHYS detector de tiempo de vuelo *m*

toggle[1] *n* COAL basculador *m*, palanca acodada *f*, WATER TRANSP cazonete *m*; ~ **on-off switch** *n* PROD conectador/desconectador de palanca *m*; ~ **selection** *n* PROD selección por palanca basculante *f*; ~ **switch** *n* CINEMAT conmutador basculante *m*, ELEC conmutador de palanca acodillada *m*, interruptor de codillo *m*, interruptor de palanca *m*, interruptor de palanca acodada *m*, interruptor de palanca acodillada *m*, interruptor de palanquita *m*, interruptor de rótula *m*,

interruptor de volquete *m*, ELEC ENG conmutador eléctrico de palanca bidireccional *m*, ELECTRON interruptor de codillo *m*

toggle[2] *vt* COMP&DP, PROD bascular

tokamak *n* PHYS tokamak *m*

token *n* COMP&DP *ring network* señal *f*, testigo *m*; ~ **bus** *n* COMP&DP bus del testigo *m*, conductor común de la ficha *m*; ~**-passing network** *n* COMP&DP *ring network* red de paso de testigo *f*, red para alcanzar las fichas *f*; ~ **ring** *n* COMP&DP red en anillo *f*, red token ring *f*

tolerable: ~ gap *n* TRANSP distancia permitida *f*

tolerance *n* MECH tolerancia *f*, MECH ENG error máximo *m*, tolerancia *f*, variación permisible *f*, METR *for plastics*, TEXTIL tolerancia *f*; ~ **interval** *n* QUALITY intervalo de tolerancias *m*, zona de tolerancias *f*; ~ **limit** *n* MECH, METR, QUALITY límite de tolerancia *m*

tolerancing *n* MECH ENG, PROD indicación de las cotas con sus tolerancias *f*

toll: ~ bridge *n* CONST puente de peaje *m*; ~**-free call** *n* AmE (*cf freephone call BrE*) TELECOM comunicación interurbana no tasada *f* (*AmL*), llamada gratuita *f* (*Esp*); ~**-free number** *n* AmE (*cf freephone number BrE*) TELECOM número de llamada gratuita *m*, número de teléfono gratuito *m*; ~ **payment** *n* TRANSP pago de peaje *m*; ~ **road** *n* CONST carretera de peaje *f*; ~ **switch** *n* TELECOM conmutador interurbano *m*, cuadro conmutador para servicio interurbano *m*, cuadro interurbano *m*

toluate *n* CHEM toluato *m*

toluene *n* CHEM, DETERG, P&R, PETR TECH tolueno *m*; ~ **diisocyanate** *n* (*TDI*) P&R diisocianato de tolueno *m* (*TDI*), toluendiisocianato *m* (*TDI*)

toluic *adj* CHEM toluico

toluidine *n* CHEM toluidina *f*

toluldehyde *n* CHEM tolualdehído *m*

tolunitrile *n* CHEM tolunitrilo *m*

toluol *n* CHEM toluol *m*

toluquinoline *n* CHEM toluquinolina *f*

toluyl *n* CHEM toluilo *m*

toluylene *n* CHEM toluileno *m*

tolyl *n* CHEM tolilo *m*

tolylene *adj* CHEM tolilénico

tomography *n* MECH ENG radiotomografía *f*, tomografía *f*

ton *n* METR tonelada *f*; ~ **of displacement** *n* WATER TRANSP tonelada de desplazamiento *f*

TON *abbr* (*type of number*) TELECOM tipo de número *m*

tonal: ~ gradation *n* PHOTO graduación tonal *f*; ~ **inversion** *n* PRINT inversión de tonos *f*; ~ **note** *n* ACOUST nota tonal *f*; ~ **value** *n* PHOTO valor tonal *m*

tonalite *n* PETROL tonalita *f*

tonality *n* COLOUR tonalidad *f*

tone[1] *n* ACOUST acorde *m*, tono *m*, COLOUR, PHOTO tono *m*, PRINT tonalidad *f*, virado *m*, TELECOM tono *m*, WAVE PHYS timbre *m*; ~ **compression** *n* PRINT compresión de la gama tonal *f*; ~ **curve** *n* PRINT curva de virado *f*; ~ **disabler** *n* SPACE *communications* interruptor de tono *m*, neutralizador de tono *m*; ~ **generator** *n* ELECTRON generador de tonalidad *m*, TELECOM generador de audiofrecuencia *m*, generador de tono *m*; ~ **pager** *n* TELECOM paginador de tono *m*; ~ **pulse** *n* ACOUST, ELECTRON impulso acústico *m*; ~ **reproduction** *n* PRINT reproducción de tonos *f*; ~ **scale** *n* PRINT gradación de tonalidad *f*; ~ **signal** *n* ELECTRON señal acústica *f*; ~ **signaling** *AmE*,

~ signalling *BrE n* ELECTRON señalización de tonalidad *f*; **~ squelch system** *n* TELECOM sistema de sintonía silenciosa *m*, sistema de supresión *m*; **~ value** *n* PRINT valor de la tonalidad *m*

tone[2] *vt* PRINT virar; **~ down** *vt* PRINT esfumar; **~ up** *vt* PRINT tonificar

toned: ~ print *n* CINEMAT copia virada *f*

toner *n* PRINT tóner *m*

tong: ~ line *n* PETR TECH clave de las llaves *f*, línea de llaves *f*; **~ marks** *n pl* C&G marcas de las pinzas *f pl*; **~-test instrument** *n* ELEC, INSTR instrumento de prueba con tenazas *m*

tongs *n pl* CONST tenazas *f pl* (*AmL*), PETR TECH llaves *f pl*

tongue *n* C&G *of burner* lengua *f*, CONST *carpentry* lengüeta *f*, MECH ENG *of scale* fiel *m*, aguja *f*, *tang of knife, of chisel, of file* espiga *f*, TEXTIL lengüeta *f*; **~-and-groove joint** *n* CONST junta de ranura y lengüeta *f*; **~ weld** *n* PROD soldadura de lengüeta *f*; **~ welding** *n* PROD soldadura de lengüeta *f*

tongued: ~-and-grooved joint *n* CONST junta machihembrada *f*

tonguing: ~-and-grooving irons *n pl* CONST hierros machihembrados *m pl*; **~-and-grooving machine** *n* CONST máquina de machihembrar *f*; **~-and-grooving plane** *n pl* CONST cepillo para machihembrar *m*; **~ iron** *n* CONST hierro machihembrado *m*; **~ plane** *n* CONST cepillo para lengüeta *m*

toning *n* CINEMAT, PHOTO viraje *m*, PRINT virado *m*; **~ bath** *n* CINEMAT, PHOTO baño de viraje *m*; **~ solution** *n* PHOTO solución de viraje *f*

tonnage *n* METR tonelaje *m*, WATER TRANSP arqueo *m*

tonne *n* METR *metric* tonelada *f*

tonnes: ~ dead weight *n pl* PETR TECH toneladas de peso muerto *f pl*

tono *n* ACOUST acorde *m*

tool[1] *n* GEN instrumento *m*; **~ belt and pouches** *n* MECH ENG cinturón y bolsillo de herramientas *m*, cinturón y portacartuchera para herramientas *m*; **~ bit** *n* MECH, MECH ENG broca *f*; **~ box** *n* MECH ENG *chest of tools* caja de herramientas *f*, maletín de herramientas *m*, portaherramientas *m*, *of shaper, of planing-machine* carnero *m*, carro portaherramientas *m*; **~ with bright handle** *n* MECH ENG herramienta con mango brillante *f*; **~ carriage** *n* MECH ENG *of machine-tool* carro portaherramientas *m*; **~-changing system** *n* MECH ENG sistema de cambio de herramientas *m*; **~ crib** *n* PROD pañol para herramientas *m*; **~ grinder** *n* MECH afiladora de herramientas *f*, MECH ENG *machine* afiladora de cuchillas *f*, afiladora de herramientas *f*, máquina de amolar herramientas *f*, PROD afiladora de herramientas *f*; **~ grinding** *n* MECH afilado de herramientas *m*, MECH ENG, PROD afilado de herramientas *m*, amolado de herramientas *m*; **~ head** *n* MECH ENG *of shaping-machine* cabezal portaherramientas *m*; **~ holder** *n* MECH ENG mango de herramienta *m*, portaherramientas *m*; **~-holding fixture** *n* MECH ENG *for machine centres* dispositivo portaherramientas *m*; **~-holding slide** *n* MECH ENG carro portaherramientas *m*, corredera portaherramientas *f*; **~ life** *n* MECH ENG duración de la herramienta *f*, vida útil de la herramienta *f*; **~-life testing** *n* MECH ENG prueba de duración de herramientas *f*; **~ post** *n* MECH ENG *of lathe, of shaper, of planer, etc* portacuchillas *m*, portaherramientas *m*; **~ pusher** *n* PETR TECH capataz

de sondeo *m*, jefe de equipo *m*, jefe de taladro *m*, PETROL capataz de perforación *m*, jefe de perforación *m*; **~ ram** *n* MECH ENG *of slotting-machine* carnero portaherramientas *m*; **~ requisition** *n* PROD petición de herramientas *f*; **~ rest** *n* MECH ENG hembrilla del portaherramientas *f*, soporte de herramientas *m*; **~ sharpener** *n* MECH, MECH ENG, PROD afiladora de herramientas *f*; **~ sharpening** *n* MECH afilado de herramientas *m*, MECH ENG, PROD afilado de herramientas *m*, amolado de herramientas *m*; **~ shed** *n* CONST caseta de herramientas *f*; **~ slide** *n* MECH ENG *of slotting-machine* carnero portaherramientas *m*, carro portaherramientas *m*, corredera portaherramientas *f*; **~ trias** *n* MECH ENG tres herramientas *f pl*

tool[2] *vt* PROD *machine* mecanizar

tooling *n* PROD estampadura *f*, herramental *m*, maquinado *m*, *machining* mecanizado *m*; **~ allowance** *n* PROD *founding allowance* sobreespesor para el mecanizado *m*

toolkit *n* COMP&DP juego de herramientas *m*, conjunto de herramientas *m*

toolmaker *n* MECH, PROD fabricante de herramientas *m*, herramentista *m*; **~'s lathe** *n* MECH ENG torno de herramentista *m*; **~'s microscope** *n* METR microscopio *m*

toolroom *n* MECH taller de herramientas *m*

tooth *n* *BrE* (*cf tine AmE*) CONST, MECH diente *m*, MECH ENG diente *m*, púa *f*, PROD diente *m*; **~ lock washer** *n* MECH ENG arandela dentada de fijación *f*, arandela estriada de fijación *f*; **~ plane** *n* CONST cepillo dentado *m*; **~ profile** *n* MECH ENG *of gear* perfil del diente *m*

toothed: ~ drive belt *n* MECH ENG correa conductora dentada *f*; **~ rack** *n* NUCL eje dentado de accionamiento *m*; **~ ring armature** *n* ELEC *generator* armadura de anillo dentado *f*; **~ sector** *n* MECH ENG sector dentado *m*; **~ segment** *n* MECH ENG segmento dentado *m*; **~ wheel** *n* MECH ENG rueda dentada *f*, PROD rueda de engranaje *f*, rueda dentada *f*

toothing *n* CONST *masonry* dentellón *m*, MECH ENG *providing with teeth* dentado *m*, endentamiento *m*; **~ plane** *n* CONST cepillo dentado *m*; **~ stone** *n* CONST *masonry* piedra dentada *f*

top[1]: **~-dyed** *adj* TEXTIL teñido en peinado

top[2] *n* PRINT capa de protección al ácido *f*, TEXTIL cinta de fibras discontinuas *f*, peinado *m*; **~ assembly** *n* FUELLESS montaje superior *m*; **~ blanket** *n* PRINT mantilla superior *f*; **~ and bottom clearance** *n* MECH ENG *gearing* huelgo en el fondo de los dientes *m*, tolerancia máxima y mínima *f*; **~-bottom diffusion** *n* ELECTRON *of epitaxial impurities* difusión superior-inferior *f*; **~ and bottom stapling** *n* PACK grapado en la tapa del fondo *m*; **~ cap** *n* ELECTRON tapa superior *f*; **~ catch** *n* VEH enganche de capota del techo *m*; **~-cementing plug** *n* PETR TECH tapón de cementación superior *m*; **~ chrome** *n* COLOUR método de teñir con el mordiente después del colorante *m*; **~ coat** *n* COLOUR capa protectora *f*; **~ coat of paint** *n* P&R capa superior de pintura *f*, mano superior de pintura *f*; **~ compression ring** *n* AUTO, VEH anillo de compresión superior *m*; **~ of convertible** *n* AUTO capota de descapotable *f*, capota plegable *f*; **~ course of tank blocks** *n* C&G carrera superior *f*; **~ cross** *n* AGRIC *plant breeding* cruzamiento con probador *m*; **~ dead center** *AmE*, **~ dead centre** *BrE n* (*TDC*)

AUTO, MECH, VEH punto muerto superior *m* (*PMS*); ~ **of descent** *n* AIR TRANSP cumbre del descenso *f*; ~ **die** *n* PROD *of power hammer* calzo superior *m*, contraestampa *f*, estampa superior *f*; ~**-down construction** *n* CONST construcción de arriba hacia abajo *f*, construcción descendente *f*; ~**-down methodology** *n* COMP&DP metodología descendente *f*; ~ **dressing** *n* AGRIC abonadura sobre la superficie del suelo *f*; ~**-driving apparatus** *n* MECH ENG *of radial drilling-machine* aparato motor superior *m*; ~ **dyeing** *n* COLOUR teñido en cinta peinada *m*; ~ **fitting** *n* NUCL tobera superior *f*; ~ **flange** *n* CONST ala superior *f*; ~ **floor** *n* C&G piso superior *m*; ~ **gas** *n* GAS gas de alto horno *m*; ~ **hole** *n* MINE boca *f*, labor a cielo *f*, realce *m*; ~ **icing** *n* REFRIG recubrimiento de la carga con hielo triturado *m*; ~ **layer** *n* TEXTIL capa de tejido superior *f*; ~ **mark** *n* WATER TRANSP *buoys* marca de tope *f*; ~ **pallet** *n* PROD *of power hammer* contraestampa *f*, espiga de apoyo superior *f*, estampa superior *f*; ~ **plate** *n* MECH ENG chapa superior *f*, placa superior *f*, plato superior *m*, *of leafspring* hoja maestra *f*, PROD *founding* placa de recubrimiento *f*; ~ **plenum** *n* NUCL pleno superior *m*; ~ **ply** *n* TEXTIL capa superior *f*; ~ **pouring** *n* PROD *ingot mould* colada a chorro *f*, colada de pie *f*, colada en caída directa *f*, colada por arriba *f*; ~ **quark** *n* PART PHYS quark verdad *m*, t-quark *m*, truth quark *m*, PHYS quark top *m*; ~ **rail** *n* CONST *of door frame, sash frame* peinazo superior *m*; ~ **rake** *n* MECH ENG *of machine tool* complemento del ángulo de corte *m*, ángulo de despojo superior *m*, ángulo de rebaje superior *m*; ~ **road** *n* MINE galería de cabeza *f* (*Esp*), galería superior *f* (*AmL*); ~**-road bridge** *n* CONST puente de tablero superior *m*; ~ **roll** *n* MECH ENG *of rolling mill* cilindro de apoyo *m*, cilindro macho *m*, cilindro superior *m*, PAPER rodillo superior *m*; ~ **rounding tool** *n* MECH ENG estampa redonda superior *f*, estampa superior para hierros redondos *f*; ~ **side** *n* PAPER cara fieltro *f*; ~**-stabilized rapid transit system** *n* TRANSP sistema de tránsito rápido estabilizado al máximo *m*; ~ **station** *n* TRANSP estación superior *f*; ~ **of stroke** *n* MECH ENG *of piston* punto máximo de la carrera *m*; ~ **swage** *n* MECH ENG contraestampa *f*, estampa superior *f*, punzón de estampar *m*

top³: ~ **up** *vt* SPACE apretar, equilibrar, pesar, recargar a fondo

topaz *n* MINERAL topacio *m*

topazolite *n* MINERAL andradita *f*, melanita *f*, topazolita *f*

topgallant: ~ **bulwark** *n* WATER TRANSP *shipbuilding* baranda *f* (*AmL*), barandilla *f* (*Esp*), batayola *f*

topographer *n* CONST *person* topógrafo *m*

topographic: ~ **wave** *n* OCEAN ola topográfica *f*

topographical: ~ **survey** *n* CONST estudio topográfico *m*, investigación topográfica *f*, levantamiento topográfico *m*

topography *n* CONST topografía *f*

topological: ~ **property** *n* COMP&DP, GEOM propiedad topológica *f*

topologist *n* COMP&DP, GEOM topólogo *m*

topology *n* COMP&DP, GEOM topología *f*

topper *n* AGRIC desmochadora *f*

topping *n* AGRIC *tobacco* capado del tabaco *m*, FOOD aderezo *m*, cobertura *f*; ~ **charge** *n* ELEC ENG carga

superior *f*; ~ **cycle** *n* NUCL ciclo de contrapresión *m*; ~ **lift** *n* WATER TRANSP *rigging* amantillo *m*

topset: ~ **bed** *n* GEOL capa horizontal sobre la capa frontal del lecho *f*

topside *n* WATER TRANSP *shipbuilding* obra muerta *f*

topsoil *n* AGRIC capa arable *f*, COAL capa superficial del suelo *f*, CONST capa superior del suelo *f*, tierra vegetal *f*; ~ **stripping** *n* CONST eliminación de la capa superior del suelo *f*

torbernite *n* MINERAL torbernita *f*, NUCL chalcolita *f*, torbernita *f*

torch *n* CONST antorcha *f*, soplete *m*, ELEC, ELEC ENG lámpara de bolsillo *f*, GAS, MECH, PROD antorcha *f*, soplete *m*; ~ **brazing** *n* CONST soldadura a soplete *f*; ~ **for MIG-MAG welding** *n* CONST soplete para soldadura MIG-MAG *m*; ~ **for plasma welding** *n* CONST soplete para soldadura de plasma *m*; ~ **for TIG welding** *n* CONST soplete para soldadura TIG *m*

torching *n* CONST, GAS, MECH, PROD *founding, casting* flameado *m*

torn *adj* P&R rasgado

tornado *n* METEO tornado *m*

toroid *n* ELEC *coil* solenoide toroidal *m*, toroide *m*, NUCL toroide *m*

toroidal: ~ **aerial** *n* BrE (*cf toroidal antenna AmE*) TELECOM antena toroidal *f*; ~ **antenna** *n* AmE (*cf toroidal aerial BrE*) TELECOM antena toroidal *f*; ~ **coil** *n* ELEC, NUCL bobina toroidal *f*; ~ **core** *n* ELEC ENG, NUCL núcleo tórico *m*; ~ **electron gun** *n* TV cañón torroidal de electrones *m*; ~ **magnet** *n* PHYS imán toroidal *m*; ~ **pinch effect** *n* NUCL efecto de estricción toroidal *m*; ~ **sealing ring** *n* MECH ENG anillo de cierre hermético toroidal *m*, anillo de sello toroidal *m*, anillo obturador toroidal *m*; ~ **transformer** *n* ELEC, ELEC ENG transformador toroidal *m*

torpedo *n* (*cf detonator BrE*) MILIT, MINE, P&R torpedo *m*, RAIL petardo *m*, señal detonante *f*, WATER TRANSP *navy* torpedo *m*; ~ **boat** *n* MILIT buque torpedero *m*, WATER TRANSP *navy* torpedero *m*; ~ **furrow** *n* MILIT raya del torpedo *f*; ~ **gunboat** *n* MILIT, WATER TRANSP torpedero cañonero *m*; ~**-launching tube** *n* MILIT tubo lanzatorpedos *m*; ~ **net** *n* MILIT red antitorpedos *f*; ~ **track** *n* MILIT recorrido del torpedo *m*

torque *n* AUTO par motor *m*, ELEC ENG par de torsión *m*, MECH momento torsor *m*, par motor *m*, par torsor *m*, potencia *f*, MECH ENG momento de par *m*, momento de torsión *m*, momento torsor *m*, par de fuerzas *m*, torque *m*, PETR TECH momento torsor *m*, PHYS torque *m*, PROD momento de torsión *m*, momento de una fuerza *m*, par motor *m*, par torsor *m*, potencia *f*; ~ **arm** *n* AUTO barra de reacción del puente trasero *f*, barra de torsión *f*, brazo de torsión *m*, brazo del par *m*, barra de reacción *f*, VEH barra de reacción *f*, brazo de torsión *m*, brazo del par *m*, barra de reacción del puente trasero *f*, barra de torsión *f*; ~ **ball** *n* AUTO bola de torsión *f*; ~ **converter** *n* AUTO convertidor de par *m*, convertidor del par motor *m*, MECH ENG *of hydraulic transmission* convertidor de par *m*, convertidor de torque *m*, convertidor de torsión *m*, transformador de par *m*, VEH convertidor de par *m*, convertidor del par motor *m*; ~**-converter housing** *n* AUTO, VEH alojamiento del convertidor de torsión *m*, alojamiento del convertidor del par *m*; ~ **drive tube** *n* AUTO, VEH tubo del eje motor *m*; ~ **link** *n* AIR TRANSP enlace de par *m*; ~ **motor** *n* ELEC motor de par *m*, motor de par constante *m*, motor de par de torsión *m*, motor productor de par *m*; **~ multiplier** *n* MECH ENG multiplicador de par *m*; **~ nut** *n* PROD tuerca torsiométrica *f*; **~ screwdriver** *n* MECH ENG destornillador de par prefijado *m*, destornillador torsiométrico *m*; **~ spanner** *n* (*cf torque wrench*) MECH ENG llave de par *f* (*AmL*), llave inglesa torsiométrica *f* (*Esp*), llave con limitador de par *f*, llave de apriete prefijado *f*, llave de torsión *f*, llave dinamométrica *f*, llave torsiométrica *f*, VEH llave dinamométrica *f*; **~ stabilizer** *n* AUTO, VEH estabilizador del par *m*; **~ tube** *n* AUTO, VEH tubo de torsión *m*, tubo del eje propulsor del motor *m*; **~ wrench** *n* (*cf torque spanner*) MECH ENG llave con limitador de par *f*, llave de apriete prefijado *f*, llave de torsión *f*, llave dinamométrica *f*, llave torsiométrica *f*, llave de par *f* (*AmL*), llave inglesa torsiométrica *f* (*Esp*), VEH llave dinamométrica *f*

torr *n* PHYS torr *m*

torrefaction *n* PROD torrefacción *f*, tostadura *f*

torrefier *n* PROD torrefactor *m*

torrent *n* HYDROL crecida *f*, inundación *f*, torrente *m*

torrential *adj* METEO torrencial

torrid: **~ zone** *n* METEO zona ecuatorial *f*, zona tórrida *f*

torsion *n* MECH, MECH ENG torcedura *f*, torsión *f*, METALL, PHYS torsión *f*; **~ balance** *n* GEOPHYS, MECH ENG balanza de torsión *f*, PHYS equilibrio de torsión *m*, balanza de torsión *f*; **~ bar** *n* AUTO barra de torsión *f*, barra del par *f*, VEH barra de torsión *f*; **~ electrometer** *n* GEOPHYS electrómetro de torsión *m*; **~ meter** *n* INSTR torsiómetro *m*, LAB *rotating fluids* dinamómetro de torsión *m*, torsiómetro *m*; **~ spring** *n* MECH ENG muelle de torsión *m*, resorte de torsión *m*; **~ string** *n* ELEC ENG fibra de torsión *f*; **~-string galvanometer** *n* ELEC *instrument*, ELEC ENG galvanómetro de cuerda de torsión *m*, galvanómetro de fibras de torsión *m*; **~ test** *n* METALL prueba de torsión *f*

torsional[1] *adj* MECH de torsión, torsional

torsional[2]: **~ constant** *n* PHYS constante torsional *f*; **~ elasticity** *n* MECH ENG elasticidad de torsión *f*, elasticidad torsional *f*; **~ oscillation** *n* PHYS oscilación torsional *f*; **~ pendulum** *n* PHYS péndulo torsional *m*; **~ strain** *n* MECH ENG deformación torsional *f*; **~ strength** *n* MECH ENG resistencia a la torsión *f*; **~ stress** *n* MECH ENG esfuerzo torsional *m*; **~ tear tester** *n* PAPER aparato para medir la resistencia al desgarro por torsión *m*; **~ tenacity** *n* MECH ENG tenacidad torsional *f*; **~ test** *n* MECH ENG ensayo torsional *m*, prueba de torsión *f*, prueba torsional *f*

torulin *n* CHEM torulina *f*

torus *n* ELEC *coil* anillo *m*, toroide *m*, GEOM toro *m*, donut *m* (*infrml*), RAD PHYS cavidad toroidal *f*, toro *m*

tosyl *n* CHEM tosilo *m*

total: **~ absorption target** *n* PHYS objetivo de dosis absorvida total *m*, RAD PHYS objetivo de dosis absorbida total *m*; **~ acid number** *n* (*TAN*) CHEM valor ácido total *m* (*VAT*); **~ adherence train** *n* TRANSP tren de adherencia total *m*; **~ allowable catch** *n* (*TAC*) OCEAN captura máxima permitida *f* (*CMP*); **~ angular momentum** *n* PHYS momento angular total *m*; **~ angular momentum quantum number** *n* PHYS número cuántico del momento angular total *m*; **~ area** *n* CONST *of piece of ground* superficie total *f*; **~ atomic stopping power** *n* PHYS

poder total de frenado atómico *m*; **~ authorized catch** *n* OCEAN captura máxima autorizada *f*; **~ charge** *n* NUCL carga total *f*; **~ configuration** *n* TELECOM configuración total *f*; **~ cooling effect** *n* REFRIG potencia frigorífica total *f*; **~ denier** *n* TEXTIL denier total *m*; **~ deposition** *n* POLL deposición total *f*, electrodeposición total *f*, precipitación total *f*, sedimentación total *f*; **~ digestible nutrients** *n* (*TDN*) AGRIC total de nutrientes digestibles *m* (*TND*); **~ drag** *n* TRANSP resistencia total al avance *f*; **~ energy density** *n* ACOUST, PHYS densidad de energía total *f*; **~ evaporation** *n* HYDROL evaporación total *f*; **~ float** *n* PROD tiempo libre total *m*; **~ flow** *n* HYDROL *data* caudal total *m*; **~ height** *n* NUCL altura total de la vasija del reactor *f*; **~ internal reflection** *n* C&G, WAVE PHYS reflexión interna total *f*; **~ lift** *n* TRANSP sustentación total *f*; **~ line value** *n* PROD valor lineal total *m*; **~ linear stopping power** *n* PHYS poder total de frenado lineal *m*; **~ loss** *n* HYDROL pérdida total *f*; **~ loss refrigeration system** *n* REFRIG sistema de enfriamiento con refrigerante perdido *m*; **~ mass stopping power** *n* PHYS poder total masivo de frenado *m*; **~ mean free path** *n* NUCL recorrido libre medio total *m*; **~ oscillation amplitude** *n* ACOUST amplitud de oscilación total *f*; **~ permissible laden weight** *n* BrE (*cf total permissible loaded weight AmE*) VEH *regulations* carga máxima permitida *f*; **~ permissible loaded weight** *n* AmE (*cf total permissible laden weight BrE*) VEH *regulations* carga máxima permitida *f*; **~ permissible weight** *n* VEH *regulations* peso total autorizado *m*; **~ pitch** *n* MECH ENG *of screw* paso real *m*; **~ quality control** *n* (*TQC*) PROD, QUALITY control de calidad total *m* (*Esp*), maestría total de la calidad *f*; **~ quality management** *n* (*TQM*) QUALITY dirección total de la calidad *f*; **~ radiation pyrometer** *n* PHYS pirómetro de radiación total *m*; **~ radiator** *n* RAD PHYS radiador total *m*; **~ rate** *n* HYDROL *data* régimen total *m*; **~ reflection** *n* OPT, PHYS, TELECOM reflexión total *f*; **~ requirement** *n* PROD necesidad total *f*; **~ size** *n* METR tamaño total *m*; **~ storage volume** *n* GAS volumen total de almacenamiento *m*; **~ sulfur** *AmE*, **~ sulphur** *BrE* *n* P&R azufre total *m*; **~ width** *n* PAPER anchura total *f*

totally: **~-enclosed headstock** *n* MECH ENG cabezal blindado *m*, cabezal totalmente cerrado *m*, cabezal totalmente encastrado *m*; **~-enclosed motor** *n* ELEC motor acorazado *m*, motor blindado *m*, motor cerrado *m*, motor no ventilado *m*, motor totalmente encerrado *m*

tote: **~ box** *n* PACK bandeja para piezas *f*

totem: **~ pole arrangement** *n* ELECTRON *of amplifier with two bipolar transistors* disposición de simbología polar *f*

touch[1]: **~-and-go landing** *n* AIR TRANSP aterrizaje de toma de contacto y despegue *m*; **~-contact switch** *n* ELEC interruptor de contacto manual *m*; **~ needle** *n* MECH ENG aguja de contacto *f*, aguja de ensayar *f*, aguja de prueba *f*; **~ needle test** *n* MECH ENG ensayo de aguja de contacto *m*; **~-sensitive control** *n* COMP&DP control sensible al tacto *m*; **~-sensitive screen** *n* COMP&DP pantalla sensible a toque *f*, pantalla sensible al tacto *f*; **~ switch** *n* ELEC, ELEC ENG interruptor por contacto *m*; **~ trigger probe** *n* MECH ENG sonda de toque disparadora *f*, sonda interruptora de toque *f*, sonda interruptora de contacto *f*

touch[2]: **~ up** *vt* C&G, COLOUR, PHOTO, PRINT retocar

touch[3]: **~ bottom** *vi* WATER TRANSP *of ship* tocar fondo; **~ down** *vi* SPACE *spacecraft* aterrizar

touchdown *n* AIR TRANSP toma de contacto con tierra *f*, toque del tren de aterrizaje con la pista *m*, SPACE *spacecraft* aterrizaje *m*, toma de tierra *f*; **~ point** *n* SPACE *spacecraft* punto de contacto *m*; **~ speed** *n* AIR TRANSP velocidad de toma de contacto con tierra *f*; **~ zone** *n* AIR TRANSP zona de toma de contacto con tierra *f*

touching: **~ up** *n* C&G, COLOUR, PHOTO, PRINT retocado *m*, retoque *m*

touchpad *n* COMP&DP almohadilla de toque *f*, placa sensible al tacto *f*

tough: **~-brittle transition** *n* METALL transición de estado frágil a estado correoso *f*

toughened: **~ glass** *n* C&G, CONST vidrio endurecido *m*, SEG cristal reforzado, TRANSP cristal reforzado *m*, vidrio endurecido *m*, vidrio reforzado *m*

tour *n* AmE (*cf shift BrE*) PETR TECH turno de trabajo *m*

tourmaline *n* MINERAL, PHYS turmalina *f*

tow[1]: **~-dyed** *adj* TEXTIL teñido en cable

tow[2] *n* PROD *hemp or flax fibre* estopa *f*, TEXTIL cinta de filamentos continuos *f*, WATER TRANSP remolque *m*; **~ hook** *n* VEH gancho de tracción *m*; **~ net** *n* OCEAN red de arrastre *f*, red de tiro *f*; **~ strap** *n* TRANSP correa de remolcar *f*; **~ vehicle** *n* AUTO vehículo remolcado *m*

tow[3] *vt* MAR POLL, WATER TRANSP remolcar; **~ astern** *vt* WATER TRANSP remolcar en flecha

towage *n* WATER TRANSP derechos de remolque *m pl*

towbar *n* MECH barra de remolque *f*, VEH barra de tracción *f*

towed: **~ convoy** *n* TRANSP convoy remolcado *m*; **~ instrument** *n* OCEAN instrumento remolcado *m*; **~ submersible** *n* OCEAN sumergible remolcado *m*

towel: **~ rail** *n* HEAT toallero *m*

tower *n* CONST torre *f*, *trellis post* portacojinetes *m*, pedestal *m*, ELEC *supply network* torre *f*; **~ bolt** *n* CONST *locksmithing* pasador de cerrojo *m*; **~ crane** *n* CONST grúa torre *f*; **~ door** *n* C&G puerta de la torre *f*; **~ silo** *n* AGRIC silo torre *m*; **~ telescope** *n* INSTR telescopio de torre *m*

towing *n* AIR TRANSP remolque *m*, WATER TRANSP *vessels* atoaje *m*, remolque *m*; **~ bracket** *n* VEH horquilla de arrastre *f*, soporte de remolque *m*; **~ tank** *n* WATER TRANSP *hull, propeller* canal de experiencias hidrodinámicas *m*, canal de pruebas hidrodinámicas *m*; **~ vehicle** *n* VEH coche grúa *m*, vehículo remolcador *m*

towline *n* MAR POLL, WATER TRANSP estacha de remolque *f*

town: **~-and-country tire** *AmE*, **~-and-country tyre** *BrE n* VEH neumático para todo terreno *m*; **~ gas** *n* GAS gas ciudad *m*, gas para consumo urbano *m*, PETR TECH gas ciudad *m*; **~ planning map** *n* CONST plano de urbanismo *m*; **~ water** *n* HYDROL, WATER agua de ciudad *f*

Townsend: **~ discharge** *n* ELECTRON descarga Townsend *f*

towpath *n* CONST *on canal or river* zona de remolque *f*

towrope *n* MAR POLL, WATER TRANSP cable de remolque *m*, cabo de remolque *m*

toxic[1] *adj* COAL, PETR TECH, SAFE tóxico

toxic[2]: **~ effect** *n* POLL efecto tóxico *m*; **~ effluent** *n* RECYCL efluente tóxico *m*, emanación tóxica *f*; **~ gas** *n* GAS, SAFE gas tóxico *m*; **~ liquid** *n* SAFE líquido tóxico *m*; **~ material** *n* SAFE material tóxico *m*; **~ substance** *n* SAFE substancia tóxica *f*

toxicant *n* CHEM producto nocivo *m*, producto tóxico *m*

toxicity *n* CHEM, MAR POLL, P&R, PETR TECH, SAFE toxicidad *f*

toxicology *n* SAFE toxicología *f*

toxin *n* QUALITY toxina *f*

toxisterol *n* CHEM toxisterol *m*

TP *abbr* (*transaction processing*) COMP&DP procesado de transacciones *m*, procesamiento de transacciones *m*

TPDU *abbr* (*transport protocol data unit*) TELECOM unidad de transferencia de datos del protocolo *f*

TPE *abbr* (*transmission path endpoint*) TELECOM punto final de la vía de transmisión *m*

TPI *abbr* (*tracks per inch*) COMP&DP, PRINT PPP (*pistas por pulgada*)

T-piece *n* LAB *rotating fluids* pieza en T *f*; **~ union** *n* CONST unión de una pieza en T *f*

TPM *abbr* (*time pulse modulation*) TELECOM modulación por tiempo de impulsos *f*

TQC *abbr* (*total quality control*) PROD, QUALITY control de calidad total *m* (*Esp*), maestría total de la calidad *f* (*AmL*)

TQM *abbr* (*total quality management*) QUALITY dirección total de la calidad *f*

t-quark *n* PART PHYS t-quark *m*

TR[1] *abbr* ELECTRON (*transmit-receive*) ER (*emisión-recepción*), TELECOM (*tactical radar*) radar táctico *m*

TR[2]: **~ cell** *n* (*tactical radar cell*) WATER TRANSP conmutador TR *m*; **~ tube** *n* ELECTRON tubo de ER *m*

trace[1] *n* COMP&DP rastreo *m*, ELEC ENG trayectoria *f*, ELECTRON *on screen* línea *f*, GAS rastro *m*, traza *f* (*AmL*), huella *f* (*Esp*), GEOPHYS trazado *m*, señal *f*, registro *m*, MATH traza *f*, PETROL rastro *m*, traza *f*, vestigio *m*, huella *f*; **~ analysis** *n* WATER *fixed equipment* análisis de trazas *m*; **~ blanking** *n* ELECTRON supresión de línea *f*; **~ element** *n* CHEM oligoelemento *m*, GEOL elemento traza *m*, POLL elemento que se encuentra en una concentración pequeña *m*, oligoelemento *m*; **~ fossil** *n* GEOL fósil traza *m*; **~ integration** *n* ELECTRON integración de la señal *f*; **~ intensification** *n* ELECTRON intensificación de línea *f*; **~ interval** *n* TV duración de exploración de línea *f*, intervalo de trazo *m* (*AmL*); **~ mineral** *n* AGRIC microelemento *m*; **~ program** *n* COMP&DP programa de rastreo *m*, programa de trazado *m*

trace[2] *vt* COMP&DP rastrear, trazar, GEOM, MATH trazar, MECH ENG calcar, copiar

traceability *n* METR localización *f*

traced: **~ design** *n* PRINT diseño calcado *m*

tracer *n* AIR TRANSP, C&G, MAR POLL, MILIT, NUCL trazador *m*, PETROL indicador *m*, trazador *m*; **~ atom** *n* NUCL, PART PHYS átomo trazador *m*; **~ bullet** *n* MILIT bala trazadora *f*; **~ element** *n* CHEM elemento trazador *m*; **~ substance** *n* CHEM sustancia trazadora *f*

trachyandesite *n* PETROL traquiandesita *f*

trachybasalt *n* PETROL traquibasalto *m*

trachyte *n* PETROL traquita *f*

tracing *n* CINEMAT grabado *m*, MECH ENG *act* calcado

m, grabado *m*, PRINT calcado *m*; ~ **distortion** *n* ACOUST distorsión de contacto *f*; ~ **lathe** *n* MECH ENG torno copiador *m*; ~ **paper** *n* MECH ENG papel de calcar *m*, papel de calco *m*, papel tela *m*, papel vegetal *m*

track¹ *n* CINEMAT banda *f*, vía *f*, COMP&DP pista *f*, MECH banda de rodamiento *f*, carril *m*, MECH ENG *of lathe* guía *f*, NUCL *civil engineering* traza *f*, OCEAN *programming* derrota *f*, OPT traza *f*, pista *f*, surco *m*, canal *m*, PROD guía *f*, RAIL vía *f*, TV pista *f*, WATER TRANSP *of backstay, yachts* carril *m*, *of ship* eje *m*, eje de derrota *m*; ~ **adjustment** *n* TV ajuste de pista *m*; ~ **allocation** *n* RAIL asignación de vía *f*; ~ **and ballast renewal** *n* RAIL renovación de vías y balasto *f*; ~ **bed** *n* RAIL lecho para los rieles *m*; ~ **cable** *n* TRANSP cable-portante *m*, cable-vía *m*; ~ **channeler** *AmE*, ~ **channeller** *BrE* *n* MINE rafadora de deslizamiento *f*; ~ **chart** *n* WATER TRANSP *navigation* carta de derrotas *f*, trazado de la derrota *m*; ~ **circuit** *n* RAIL circuito de la vía *m*; ~ **configuration** *n* TV configuración de pista *f*; ~ **connection** *n* RAIL circuito de la vía *m*; ~ **density** *n* OPT densidad de traza *f*; ~ **diagram** *n* RAIL diagrama de vías *m*; ~ **gage** *AmE*, ~ **gauge** *BrE* *n* RAIL calibre para la separación entre ejes de carriles *m*; ~ **girder** *n* TRANSP traviesa *f*; ~**-guided transport system** *n* TRANSP sistema de transporte sobre raíles *m*; ~**-guided vehicle** *n* TRANSP vehículo guiado por raíles *m*; ~ **in service** *n* RAIL vía en servicio *f*; ~ **magnet** *n* RAIL imán de vías *m*; ~ **panel laying machine** *n* RAIL máquina para colocar vía prefabricada *f*; ~ **pitch** *n* COMP&DP separación entre pistas *f*, OPT, TV distancia entre pistas *f*; ~ **raising** *n* RAIL levante de la vía *m*, recalzo de la vía *m*; ~ **rod** *n* VEH tirante transversal *m*; ~ **roller** *n* MECH ENG *needle roller bearing* canal de deslizamiento *m*; ~ **section** *n* RAIL sección de vía *f*, tramo de vía *m*; ~ **selector** *n* TV selector de pistas *m*; ~ **strip** *n* CONST franja del camino *f*, oruga *f*, pista *f*; ~ **width** *n* AUTO ancho de vía *m*

track² *vi* CINEMAT seguir

trackball *n* COMP&DP bola de control del cursor *f*, boleador *m*, trackball *m*

tracked: ~ **air cushion vehicle** *n* (*TACV*) TRANSP aerodeslizador sobre vía *m*; ~ **armored fighting vehicle** *n* *AmE* MILIT vehículo blindado de combate sobre orugas *m*; ~ **armoured fighting vehicle** *BrE* *n* MILIT vehículo blindado de combate sobre orugas *m*; ~ **tractor** *n* CONST tractor de orugas *m*; ~ **vehicle** *n* TRANSP vehículo oruga *m*

tracker *n* SPACE observador *m*, rastreador *m*, seguidor *m*, señalador de recorrido *m*; ~ **register** *n* WATER TRANSP *radar* seguidor *m*

trackerball *n* COMP&DP bola de control del cursor *f*, boleador *m*, trackball *m*

tracking *n* AUTO ajuste *m*, ELEC *insulator fault* descarga superficial *f*, lectura *f*, MILIT *of aircraft missile*, OCEAN seguimiento *m*, SPACE alineación *f*, reglaje exacto *m*, seguimiento *m*, sondeo *m*, rastreo *m*, arrastre *m*, búsqueda *f*, determinación de la trayectoria *f*, TELECOM determinación de la trayectoria *f*, rastreo *m*, seguimiento *m*, trazado de la trayectoria *m*, TV seguimiento *m*; ~ **accuracy** *n* SPACE *communications* exactitud de pendiente *f*, exactitud de rastreo *f*; ~ **aerial** *n* *BrE* (*cf tracking antenna AmE*) SPACE antena de rastreo *f*, antena de seguimiento *f*; ~ **antenna** *n* *AmE* (*cf tracking aerial BrE*) SPACE

antena de rastreo *f*, antena de seguimiento *f*; ~ **camera** *n* SPACE cámara de observación *f*, cámara seguidora *f*; ~ **control** *n* TV control del seguimiento *m*; ~ **error** *n* METR, TELECOM error de seguimiento *m*; ~ **filter** *n* ELECTRON filtro de alineación *m*, filtro de reglaje *m*; ~ **filter demodulator** *n* SPACE *communications* desmodulador de filtro rastreador *m*; ~ **generator** *n* ELECTRON generador de exploración *m*, TV generador de seguimiento *m*; ~ **local oscillator** *n* ELECTRON oscilador local de exploración *m*; ~ **mechanism** *n* OPT mecanismo de seguimiento *m*; ~ **oscillator** *n* ELECTRON oscilador de búsqueda *m*; ~ **radar** *n* SPACE radar de exploración *m*, radar de rastreo *m*, radar de seguimiento *m*; ~ **shot** *n* CINEMAT toma de seguimiento *f*; ~ **station** *n* SPACE estación de rastreo *f*, estación de seguimiento *f*; ~ **system** *n* TELECOM sistema de rastreo *m*, sistema de seguimiento *m*; ~ **telemetry and command** *n* (*TTC*) SPACE *communications* telemetría y control de rastreo *f* (*TTC*)

tracklayer *n* AGRIC tractor de carriles *m*, RAIL instalador de carriles *m*

tracklaying *n* CINEMAT colocación de vías *f*, CONST, RAIL tendido de vía *m*; ~ **foreman** *n* RAIL capataz del tendido de la vía *m*

tracks: ~ **per inch** *n pl* (*TPI*) COMP&DP, PRINT pistas por pulgada *f pl* (*PPP*)

trackside: ~ **signaling** *AmE*, ~ **signalling** *BrE* *n* RAIL señalización lateral de la vía *f*

traction *n* CONST tracción *f*, MECH ENG adherencia *f*, arrastre *m*, tracción *f*, RAIL tracción *f*; ~ **cable** *n* TRANSP cable de tracción *m* (*Esp*); ~ **differential** *n* AUTO, VEH diferencial de tracción *m*; ~ **engine** *n* TRANSP motor de tracción *m*; ~ **locomotive** *n* RAIL locomotora de tracción *f*; ~ **network** *n* ELEC red de tracción *f*; ~ **rope** *n* MECH ENG cuerda de tracción *f*, soga de tracción *f*, TRANSP cable de tracción *m* (*Esp*)

tractive: ~ **force** *n* METR fuerza de tracción *f*; ~ **unit** *n* TRANSP unidad de tracción *f*, unidad tractora *f*

tractor *n* AGRIC, COMP&DP, CONST, MECH, MILIT tractor *m*, TRANSP conjunto de embarcaciones de desembarco *m*, tractor *m*, VEH tractor *m*; ~ **aircraft** *n* AIR TRANSP avión remolcador *m*; ~ **feed** *n* COMP&DP, PRINT arrastre de dientes *m*; ~ **propeller** *n* AIR TRANSP hélice tractora *f*; ~**-trailer lorry** *n* *BrE* VEH camión tractor de remolque *m*; ~**-trailer truck** *n* *AmE* VEH camión tractor de remolque *m*; ~ **unit** *n* TRANSP unidad de tracción *f*, unidad tractora *f*

trade: ~ **data interchange** *n* (*TDI*) TELECOM intercambio de datos comerciales *m*; ~**-in** *n* PROD cambio *m*, canje *m*, entrega a cuenta *f*, permuta *f*, trueque *m*; ~ **wind** *n* METEO viento alisio *m*

trademark *n* PROD marca de fábrica *f*

trading: ~ **port** *n* WATER TRANSP puerto comercial *m*

traditional: ~ **controls** *n pl* PROD controles tradicionales *m pl*; ~ **telephone network** *n* TELECOM red telefónica tradicional *f*

traffic *n* RAIL, TELECOM tráfico *m*, TRANSP circulación *f*, tráfico *m*, tránsito *m*, VEH tráfico *m*; ~**-actuated signal** *n* TRANSP *traffic control* señal activada por el tráfico *f*; ~**-adjusted controller** *n* TRANSP controlador ajustado al tráfico *m*; ~ **analyser** *n* *BrE* TRANSP analizador del tráfico *m*; ~ **analysis** *n* TELECOM análisis de tráfico *m*; ~ **analysis detector** *n* TRANSP detector de análisis del tráfico *m*; ~ **analyzer** *AmE* *see traffic analyser BrE;* ~ **assignment** *n* TRANSP asignación de tráfico *f;* ~ **assignment model** *n* TRANSP modelo de práctica de tráfico *m;* ~ **assignment program** *AmE,* ~ **assignment programme** *BrE n* TRANSP programa de asignación de tráfico *m;* ~ **burst** *n* SPACE *communication* aumento brusco del tráfico *m,* aumento repentino del tráfico *m;* ~ **carried** *n* TELECOM tráfico conducido *m;* ~**-carrying device** *n* TELECOM dispositivo de conducción de tráfico *m;* ~ **census** *n* TRANSP censo del tráfico *m;* ~ **center** *AmE,* ~ **centre** *BrE n* TRANSP centro de tráfico *m;* ~ **circle** *n AmE (cf roundabout BrE)* AUTO, CONST, TRANSP glorieta *f,* rotonda *f,* VEH glorieta *f;* ~ **circuit** *n* TELECOM circuito de tráfico *m;* ~ **computer** *n* TRANSP computador para tráfico *m (AmL),* computadora para tráfico *f (AmL),* ordenador para tráfico *m (Esp);* ~ **concentration** *n* TRANSP concentración de tráfico *f;* ~ **conditions** *n pl* TRANSP condiciones de tráfico *f pl;* ~ **cone** *n* CONST cono para señalización de tráfico *m;* ~ **control** *n* TRANSP control de tráfico *m,* control del tráfico aéreo *m,* demarcación de tráfico *m,* regulación de la circulación *f;* ~ **control installation** *n* TRANSP instalación de control del tráfico *f;* ~ **control program** *AmE,* ~ **control programme** *BrE n* TRANSP programa para controlar el tráfico *m;* ~ **count** *n* TRANSP recuento del tráfico *m;* ~ **counter** *n* TRANSP contador de tráfico *m;* ~ **cut** *n* TRANSP corte de tráfico *m;* ~ **demand** *n* TRANSP demanda por tráfico *f,* denuncia por infracción de tráfico *f,* reclamación de tráfico *f;* ~ **density** *n* TRANSP densidad de tráfico *f,* densidad de circulación *f;* ~ **detector** *n* TRANSP detector de tráfico *m;* ~ **distribution imbalance** *n* TELECOM desequilibrio de la distribución del tráfico *m;* ~ **division system** *n* TELECOM sistema de división de tráfico *m;* ~ **engineering** *n* TRANSP ingeniería de tráfico *f;* ~ **flow** *n* CONST volumen de tráfico *m,* TELECOM circulación de tráfico *f,* flujo de tráfico *m,* volumen de tráfico *m,* TRANSP afluencia de tráfico *f,* circulación del tráfico *f;* ~ **flow confidentiality** *n* TELECOM confidencialidad en la circulación de tráfico *f;* ~ **flow diagram** *n* TRANSP diagrama de la circulación del tráfico *m;* ~ **forecast** *n* RAIL previsión de tráfico *f;* ~ **forecasting** *n* TRANSP previsión de tráfico *f,* pronóstico de tráfico *m;* ~ **forecasting program** *AmE,* ~ **forecasting programme** *BrE n* TRANSP programa de previsión del tráfico *m,* programa de pronóstico del tráfico *m;* ~ **information** *n* TRANSP información del tráfico *f;* ~ **information identification signal** *n* TRANSP señal identificativa de información de tráfico *f;* ~ **island** *n* CONST isleta *f,* refugio *m;* ~ **jam** *n* TRANSP atasco de tráfico *m,* embotellamiento de tráfico *m;* ~ **lane** *n* OCEAN, WATER TRANSP *navigation* vía de circulación *f;* ~ **load** *n* TELECOM intensidad de tráfico *f,* TRANSP carga de explotación *f;* ~ **load imbalance** *n* TELECOM desequilibrio de la intensidad del tráfico *m;* ~ **management** *n* TRANSP dirección del tráfico *f;* ~ **network control** *n* TRANSP control de la red de tráfico *m;* ~ **noise index** *n (TNI)* ACOUST índice de ruido de tráfico *m (TNI);* ~ **offered** *n* TELECOM tráfico ofrecido *m;* ~ **operator position** *n* TELECOM puesto de operador de tráfico *m,* puesto de trabajo para operador de tráfico *m;* ~ **padding** *n* TELECOM relleno del tráfico *m;* ~ **parameter** *n* TRANSP parámetro de tráfico *m;* ~ **queue** *n BrE (cf line of cars*

AmE) TRANSP cola de coches *f;* ~ **radio transmitter** *n* TRANSP radio-transmisor de tráfico *m;* ~ **region** *n* TRANSP región de tráfico *f;* ~ **regulation system** *n* TRANSP sistema de regulación del tráfico *m;* ~**-routing program** *AmE,* ~**-routing programme** *BrE n* TRANSP programa de encaminamiento del tráfico *m,* programa de ordenación del tráfico *m,* programa para encaminar el tráfico *m;* ~**-routing strategy** *n* TELECOM estrategia para el enrutamiento del tráfico *f,* estrategia para el trazado de rutas de tráfico *f;* ~ **schedule** *n* RAIL horario de circulación *m;* ~ **semiactuated signal** *n* TRANSP señal de tráfico semi-activada *f;* ~ **separation scheme** *n* WATER TRANSP *navigation* dispositivo de separación del tráfico *m;* ~ **sign** *n* TRANSP señal de tráfico *f;* ~ **signal** *n* ELECTRON señal de circulación *f;* ~ **signal controller** *n* TRANSP controlador de señales de tráfico *m;* ~ **signals program** *AmE,* ~ **signals programme** *BrE n* TRANSP programa de señales de tráfico *m,* programa de señalización del tráfico *m;* ~ **simulation** *n* TRANSP simulación de tráfico *f;* ~ **simulator** *n* TRANSP simulador de tráfico *m;* ~ **situation** *n* TRANSP situación del tráfico *f;* ~ **stream** *n* TRANSP corriente de tráfico *f;* ~ **survey** *n* TRANSP estudio del tráfico *m;* ~ **unit** *n (TU)* TELECOM unidad de tráfico *f;* ~ **volume** *n* TRANSP volumen de tráfico *m;* ~**-volume meter** *n* TRANSP medidor del volumen del tráfico *m*

tragacanth *n* FOOD adragante *f,* goma *f*

trail: ~ **dredging** *n* WATER TRANSP dragado a remolque *m;* ~**-edge one-shot programming** *n* PROD programación paso a paso de trayectoria posterior *f*

trailer *n AmE (cf caravan BrE)* CONST remolque *m,* trailer *m,* MECH coche de remolque *m,* remolque *m,* MECH ENG remolque *m,* bogie *m (Esp),* boje *m (AmL),* RAIL remolque *m,* TRANSP caravana *f,* remolque *m,* trailer *m,* VEH trailer *m,* caravana *f,* remolque *m,* remolque articulado *m (AmL);* ~ **bogie** *n BrE (cf trailer car AmE)* RAIL carretón de remolque *m;* ~ **brake** *n* VEH freno del remolque *m;* ~ **car** *n AmE (cf trailer bogie BrE, trailer wagon BrE)* RAIL carretón de remolque *m;* ~ **label** *n* COMP&DP etiqueta de cola *f;* ~ **on flatcar** *n (TOFC)* TRANSP remolque sobre vagón plataforma *m;* ~ **record** *n* COMP&DP registro de cola *m;* ~**-towing machine** *n* TRANSP máquina de remolque *f;* ~ **wagon** *n BrE (cf trailer car AmE)* TRANSP vagoneta de remolque *f,* vagón de remolque *m*

trailing: ~ **arm** *n* VEH eje de salida *m;* ~ **axle** *n* VEH eje trasero portador *m;* ~**-blade coated paper** *n* PAPER papel estucado por cuchilla oscilante *m;* ~**-blade coating** *n* PAPER estucado por cuchilla oscilante *m;* ~ **cable** *n* ELEC ENG cable flexible de remolque *m,* cable móvil *m;* ~ **edge** *n* AIR TRANSP *of wing,* ELEC ENG flanco de bajada *m,* borde de caída *m,* ELECTRON borde de salida *m,* borde posterior *m,* PHYS borde trasero *m,* PROD borde de salida *m,* borde posterior *m,* TV flanco posterior de un pulso *m;* ~**-edge flap** *n* AIR TRANSP, TRANSP flap del borde de salida *m;* ~**-edge one-shot** *n* PROD único de borde posterior *m;* ~**-edge video track** *n* TV flanco posterior de la pista de video *m (AmL),* flanco posterior de la pista de vídeo *m (Esp);* ~ **load** *n* TRANSP carga relativa a rueda portante *f,* carga remolcada *f;* ~ **shoe** *n* VEH zapata posterior *f;* ~ **vector** *n* AIR TRANSP *sonic boom* vector de salida *m*

train: ~ **about to depart** *n* RAIL tren a punto de salir *m;* ~ **of action** *n* MECH ENG *gearing* normal de contacto *f*, tren de movimiento *m*; ~ **of bubbles** *n* C&G tren de burbujas *m*; ~ **connection** *n* RAIL conexión de trenes *f*; ~ **crew** *n* RAIL personal del tren *m*; ~ **ferry** *n* WATER TRANSP transbordador para trenes *m*; ~ **of gearing** *n* MECH ENG conjunto de engranajes *m*, sistema de engranajes *m*, tren de engranajes *m*; ~ **movement** *n* RAIL movimiento del tren *m*; ~ **printer** *n BrE* (*cf chain printer AmE*) COMP&DP, PRINT impresora de cadena *f*, impresora de tren *f*; ~~**protecting signal** *n* RAIL señal protectora de trenes *f*; ~ **of rolls** *n* MECH ENG tren de rodillos *m*; ~ **set** *n* RAIL composición del tren *f*; ~ **spacing** *n* RAIL espaciado del tren *m*; ~ **supervision** *n* RAIL inspección del tren *f*; ~ **supervision number** *n* RAIL número de identificación del tren *m*; ~~**through-the-lens mask** *n* PROD máscara abierta por la cámara *f*

trainer *n* AIR TRANSP *person* instructor *m*, *device, machine* aparato para enseñanza *m*, ELECTRON *device, machine* aparato para enseñanza *m*, *person* instructor *m*, SAFE *person* instructor *m*, *device, machine* aparato para enseñanza *m*, TRANSP, VEH *person* instructor *m*

training *n* MECH ENG *in speciality within company* especialización *f*, *of personnel* capacitación *f*, entrenamiento *m*, instrucción *f*, enseñanza *f*; ~ **flight** *n* AIR TRANSP vuelo de adiestramiento *m*; ~ **rack** *n* MILIT *artillery* cremallera circular de puntería azimutal *f*; ~ **reactor** *n* NUCL reactor de entrenamiento *m*; ~ **scheme** *n* MECH ENG programa de adiestramiento *m*, programa de capacitación *m*, programa de enseñanza *m*, programa de entrenamiento *m*; ~ **ship** *n* WATER TRANSP buque escuela *m*; ~ **simulator** *n* AIR TRANSP, NUCL, SPACE simulador de entrenamiento *m*; ~ **wheel** *n* MILIT *artillery* rueda de puntería azimutal *f*

trajectography *n* RAD PHYS, SPACE trayectografía *f*

trajectory *n* ELEC, MILIT, PHYS, SPACE trayectoria *f*

tram *n* MINE vagoneta de mina *f*, TRANSP tranvía *m*; ~ **stop** *n BrE* (*cf streetcar stop AmE*) TRANSP parada del tranvía *f*; ~ **system** *n* MINE sistema de arrastre *m*; ~ **track** *n BrE* (*cf streetcar track AmE*) TRANSP vía del tranvía *f*

tramlines *n pl* PHOTO *machines, workers* hojas en parejas paralelas *f pl*

trammel *n* MECH ENG *drawing* compás de elipses *m*, compás de varas *m*, elipsógrafo *m*; ~ **net** *n* OCEAN trasmallo *m*

tramway *n* TRANSP teleférico *m*, tranvía *m*; ~ **metro** *n* TRANSP tranvía metropolitano *m*, tranvía urbano *m*; ~ **motor unit** *n BrE* RAIL motor de tranvía *m*

trans: ~ **form** *n* CHEM *of molecule* forma trans *f*

transaction *n* COMP&DP operación *f*, transacción *f*; ~ **capabilities application part** *n* TELECOM solicitud de capacidades de transacción *f*; ~ **file** *n* COMP&DP archivo de movimientos *m*, archivo de transacciones *m*; ~ **management software** *n* COMP&DP software de administración de transacciones *m*, software de gestión de transacciones *m*; ~ **management subsystem** *n* TELECOM subsistema de gestión de la transacción *m*; ~ **processing** *n* (*TP*) COMP&DP procesado de transacciones *m*, procesamiento de transacciones *m*; ~ **record** *n* COMP&DP registro de operaciones *m*, registro de transacciones *m*

transactional: ~ **set-header** *n* TELECOM cabecera del aparato de transacción *f*, parte superior del equipo receptor de transacción *f*

transceiver *n* COMP&DP, TELECOM, WATER TRANSP *radio* transceptor *m*

transcendental *adj* MATH transcendental, transcendente

transcoder *n* TELECOM, TV transcodificador *m*

transcoding *n* TELECOM transcodificación *f*; ~ **gain** *n* (*TG*) TELECOM ganancia de transcodificación *f*, ganancia debida a la codificación *f*

transconductance *n* ELEC ENG, PHYS transconductancia *f*

transcontainer *n* TRANSP transcontenedor *m*, contenedor para transporte *m*

transcribe *vt* COMP&DP transcribir

transcurrent: ~ **fault** *n* GEOL falla transcurrente *f*; ~ **thrust** *n* GEOL cabalgamiento transcurrente *m*

transducer *n* GEN transductor *m*; ~ **efficiency** *n* ACOUST eficacia transductiva *f*; ~ **loss-factor** *n* ACOUST factor de pérdida transductiva *m*

transductor *n* ELEC ENG reactor de conmutación *m*, PHYS, PROD, SPACE transductor *m*

transfer[1] *n* (*cf decal AmE*) GEN transferencia *f*; ~ **acoustic impedance** *n* ACOUST, ELEC ENG, PHYS impedancia acústica de transferencia *f*; ~ **allowed** *n* (*TFA*) TELECOM transferencia permitida *f*; ~ **characteristic** *n* ELECTRON, PHYS característica de transferencia *f*; ~ **charge call** *n* TELECOM conversación tasable de transferencia *f*, conversación tasada de transferencia *f*, llamada cobrable de transferencia *f*, llamada con gastos de transferencia *f*, llamada tasable de transferencia *f*; ~ **controlled** *n* (*TFC*) TELECOM transferencia controlada *f*; ~ **die** *n* MECH ENG *press tools* molde de transferencia *m*; ~ **from tank** *n* SPACE transbordo desde el tanque *m*; ~ **function** *n* OPT, TELECOM función de transferencia *f*; ~ **gate** *n* ELEC ENG compuerta intermedia *f*; ~ **impedance** *n* ELEC *network*, TELECOM impedancia de transferencia *f*; ~ **inefficiency** *n* ELEC ENG ineficiencia de transferencia *f*; ~ **of licence** *n BrE* QUALITY transferencia de licencia *f*; ~ **of license** *AmE see transfer of licence BrE*; ~ **line** *n* MECH ENG línea de transferencia *f*; ~ **machine** *n* MECH máquina de transferencia *f*; ~ **matrix** *n* PHYS *measuring* matriz de transferencia *f*; ~ **mechanical impedance** *n* ACOUST, ELEC, ELEC ENG impedancia mecánica de transferencia *f*; ~ **mold** *AmE see transfer mould BrE*; ~ **molding** *AmE see transfer moulding BrE*; ~ **mould** *BrE n* MECH ENG *for rubber, for thermosetting* molde de dos fases *m*, molde de transferencia *m*; ~ **moulding** *n BrE* P&R moldeado en dos fases *m*, moldeado por transferencia *m*; ~ **orbit** *n* SPACE órbita de transferencia *f*; ~ **port** *n* NUCL abertura de transporte *f*, VEH lumbrera de transferencia *f*; ~ **prohibited** *n* (*TFP*) TELECOM transferencia prohibida *f*; ~ **pump** *n* MAR POLL bomba de trasiego *f*; ~ **rate** *n* COMP&DP velocidad de transferencia *f*, velocidad de traslado *f*, velocidad de transmisión *f*, OPT tasa de transferencia *f*, TELECOM velocidad de transferencia *f*; ~ **ratio** *n* TV factor de transferencia *m*; ~ **reaction** *n* NUCL reacción de transferencia *f*; ~ **restricted** *n* (*TFR*) TELECOM transferencia restringida *f*; ~ **stage** *n* SPACE etapa de transbordo *f*, fase de transbordo *f*; ~ **station** *n* MINE estación de transbordo *f*; ~ **syntax** *n* TELECOM sintaxis de transferencia *f*; ~ **tail** *n* TEXTIL cola de transferencia *f*; ~ **track** *n AmE* RAIL vía de transbordo *f*; ~ **tube** *n* PROD tubo de transferencia *m*

transfer[2] *vt* COMP&DP transferir, trasladar, PRINT transferir

transferred: ~-**electron diode** *n* ELECTRON diodo de transferencia de electrones *m*

transfinite *adj* MATH transfinito

transflective: ~-**back coating** *n* ELECTRON revestimiento con reverso transflexivo *m*; ~ **LCD** *n* ELECTRON DCL transflexivo *m*

transform[1] *n* ACOUST transformada *f*, COMP&DP transformación *f*, transformada *f*, CRYSTALL transformada *f*, ELECTRON, MATH transformación *f*, transformada *f*, PHYS transformada *f*; ~ **fault** *n* GEOL falla transformante *f*

transform[2] *vt* COMP&DP transformar

transformation *n* ELEC ENG conversión *f*; ~ **of electricity** *n* ELEC *supply network* transformación de electricidad *f*; ~ **point** *n* C&G punto de transformación *m*; ~ **process** *n* GAS proceso de transformación *m*; ~ **range** *n* C&G rango de transformación *m*; ~ **rate** *n* POLL grado de conversión *m*, grado de transformación *m*, razón de transformación *f*, ritmo de transformación *m*, velocidad de transformación *f*; ~ **temperature** *n* C&G temperatura de transformación *f*

transformer *n* GEN transformador *m*; ~ **core** *n* ELEC núcleo de transformador *m*, ELEC ENG núcleo del transformador *m*; ~ **coupling** *n* ELEC acoplamiento de transformador *m*, ELEC ENG acople por transformador *m*; ~ **efficiency** *n* ELEC eficiencia de transformador *f*; ~ **electromotive force** *n* ELEC, ELEC ENG, PHYS fuerza electromotriz estática *f*; ~ **EMF** *n* ELEC FEM del transformador *f*, PHYS transformador EMF *m*; ~ **isolation** *n* ELEC, ELEC ENG aislamiento de transformador *m*; ~ **loss** *n* ELEC ENG pérdida del transformador *f*; ~ **oil** *n* ELEC, ELEC ENG aceite del transformador *m*, aceite para transformadores *m*; ~ **primary switching** *n* PROD conmutación del primario del transformador *f*; ~ **substation** *n* ELEC *supply network* subestación de transformación *f*, subestación transformadora *f*, ELEC ENG subestación transformadora *f*, subestación de transformación *f*; ~ **tap** *n* ELEC ENG toma del transformador *f*; ~-**type dual input** *n* PROD entrada doble tipo transformador *f*

transformerless: ~ **power supply** *n* ELEC *supply network* suministro de energía sin transformador *m*

transfusion: ~ **bottle** *n* C&G botella para transfusión *f*

transgression *n* GEOL transgresión *f*

transient[1] *adj* ELEC ENG sobretensionado, transiente, NUCL transiente, transitorio, PHYS transiente, TELECOM transitorio; ~-**suppressed** *adj* PROD con supresión de corrientes momentáneas

transient[2] *n* ELEC ENG, NUCL, PHYS transiente *m*, transitorio *m*; ~ **analyser** *n BrE* ELECTRON analizador transitorio *m*; ~ **analysis** *n* ELECTRON análisis transitorio *m*; ~ **analyzer** *AmE see transient analyser BrE*; ~ **condition** *n* ELEC, ELEC ENG condición transitoria *f*; ~ **creep** *n* METALL fluencia transitoria *f*; ~ **current** *n* ELECTRON corriente transitoria *f*, PROD corriente de sobrevoltaje *f*, corriente momentánea *f*, onda errante *f*, perturbación momentánea *f*, TRANSP corriente momentánea *f*, corriente transitoria *f*; ~ **equilibrium** *n* PHYS equilibrio transiente *m*; ~ **error** *n* COMP&DP error transitorio *m*; ~ **fault** *n* ELECTRON avería transitoria *f*; ~ **fluctuation** *n* TELECOM componente en régimen transitorio *m*,

componente transitorio *m*, fluctuación transitoria *f*, onda errante *f*, perturbación transitoria *f*, variación transitoria *f*; ~ **globule of quark-gluon plasma** *n* PART PHYS glóbulo transitorio de plasma quark gluón *m*; ~ **oscillation** *n* PHYS oscilación transiente *f*; ~ **phase** *n* METALL fase transitoria *f*; ~ **phenomenon** *n* TELECOM fenómeno transitorio *m*; ~ **protection** *n* PROD protección temporal *f*, protección transitoria *f*; ~ **response** *n* ELEC ENG, ELECTRON respuesta transitoria *f*, TV respuesta en régimen transitorio *f*; ~ **short-circuit** *n* ELECTRON cortocircuito momentáneo *m*; ~ **state** *n* ELEC *general term* estado transitorio *m*, régimen transitorio *m*; ~ **suppression** *n* ELEC ENG supresión de transitorios *f*; ~ **suppressor** *n* ELEC ENG supresor de transitorios *m*; ~ **voltage** *n* ELEC sobretensión pasajera *f*, tensión momentánea *f*, tensión transitoria *f*, voltaje momentáneo *m*; ~ **voltage limitation** *n* PROD limitación de tensión transitoria *f*, limitación de voltaje momentáneo *f*

transistor *n* COMP&DP, ELECTRON, OPT, PHYS, SPACE transistor *m*; off ~ *n* ELECTRON transistor inactivo *m*; ~ **amplification** *n* ELECTRON amplificación con transistor *f*; ~ **amplifier** *n* ELECTRON amplificador con transistor *m*; ~ **base** *n* ELECTRON, TELECOM base de transistor *f*; ~ **bias** *n* ELECTRON polarización del transistor *f*; ~ **characteristic** *n* ELECTRON característica del transistor *f*; ~ **checker** *n* ELECTRON comprobador de transistores *m*; ~ **chip** *n* ELECTRON transistor *m*; ~ **collector** *n* ELECTRON, TELECOM colector de transistor *m*; ~ **control unit** *n* AUTO unidad de control transistorizado *f*; ~ **coupled logic** *n* ELECTRON lógica de transistores acoplados *f*; ~ **cutout frequency** *n* ACOUST, ELEC, ELECTRON, PHYS, TELECOM frecuencia de corte del transistor *f*; ~ **d-c load line** *n* ELECTRON recta de carga del transistor *f*; ~ **emitter** *n* ELECTRON emisor del transistor *m*, TELECOM emisor de transistor *m*; ~ **equivalent circuit** *n* ELECTRON circuito equivalente del transistor *m*; ~ **hybrid parameter** *n* ELECTRON parámetro híbrido del transistor *m*; ~ **ignition unit** *n* AUTO unidad de encendido transistorizado *f*; ~ **modulator** *n* ELECTRON modulador de transistor *m*; ~ **oscillator** *n* ELECTRON oscilador de transistor *m*; ~ **pair** *n* ELECTRON pareja de transistores *f*; ~ **power amplifier** *n* ELECTRON amplificador de potencia de transistor *m*; ~ **saturation** *n* ELECTRON saturación del transistor *f*; ~-**transistor logic** *n* (*TTL*) COMP&DP lógica transistor-transistor *f*, ELECTRON circuito lógico de transistor a transistor *m*; ~-**transistor logic family** *n* ELECTRON familia de circuito lógico de transistor a transistor *f*

transistorized: ~ **ignition system** *n* AUTO sistema de encendido transistorizado *m*; ~ **regulator** *n* AUTO regulador transistorizado *m*

transit *n* AIR TRANSP tráfico *m*, CONST tráfico *m*, tránsito *m*, NUCL tránsito *m*, WATER TRANSP *navigation* enfilación *f*; ~ **car** *n* MINE vagón de transporte *m*; ~ **connection element** *n* (*TCE*) TELECOM elemento de comunicación en tránsito *m*, elemento de conexión en tránsito *m*; ~ **exchange** *n* TELECOM central de tránsito *f*; ~ **fiber optic** *AmE*, ~ **fibre optic** *BrE n* OPT, TELECOM fibra óptica de tránsito *f*; ~ **passenger** *n* AIR TRANSP, TRANSP pasajero en tránsito *m*; ~ **switching center** *AmE*, ~ **switching centre** *BrE n* TELECOM centro de conmutación de tránsito *m*;

~ **telescope** *n* INSTR telescopio de anteojo central *m*; ~ **theodolite** *n* CONST teodolito *m*; ~ **time** *n* ELEC ENG tiempo de recorrido *m*, NUCL *heat unit*, PETROL tiempo de tránsito *m*, PHYS tiempo de transiente *m*, PROD tiempo de recorrido *m*, tiempo de tránsito *m*; **~-time device** *n* ELEC ENG dispositivo de tiempo de tránsito *m*; **~-time diode** *n* ELECTRON diodo de tiempo de tránsito *m*; **~-time reduction factor** *n* PROD factor de reducción del tiempo de tránsito *m*; ~ **traffic** *n* TELECOM tráfico de tránsito *m*

transition: ~ **contact** *n* ELEC *of transformer* contacto de transición *m*; ~ **curve** *n* CONST curva de transición *f*; ~ **element** *n* CHEM elemento de transición *m*; ~ **enthalpy** *n* NUCL entalpía de transición *f*; ~ **impedance** *n* ELEC *of resistor, reactance* impedancia de transición *f*; ~ **joint** *n* ELEC *cable connection* junta de transición *f*; ~ **lake** *n* POLL lago de enlace *m*, lago de transición *m*, lago de unión *m*; ~ **loss index** *n* ACOUST índice de pérdida de paso *m*; ~ **metal** *n* METALL metal de transición *m*; ~ **point** *n* NUCL punto de transición *m*; ~ **probability** *n* PHYS probabilidad de transición *f*; ~ **radiation detector** *n* RAD PHYS detector de radiaciones de transición *m*; ~ **segment** *n* AIR TRANSP *landing* segmento de transición *m*; ~ **temperature** *n* METALL, NUCL, PHYS, REFRIG temperatura de transición *f*; ~ **zone** *n* PETR TECH, PETROL zona de transición *f*

transitional: ~ **precipitate** *n* METALL precipitado de transición *m*

translate *vt* COMP&DP *image*, TELECOM traducir

translating: ~ **wheel** *n* MECH ENG *screw-cutting lathe* rueda de traslación *f*

translation *n* COMP&DP traducción *f*, GEOM traslación *f*, MECH ENG desplazamiento *m*, traslación *f*, traslado *m*, PHYS *of measuring instrument* traslación *f*; ~ **on a drawing** *n* PROD traducción a dibujo *f*; ~ **plane** *n* CRYSTALL, METALL plano de traslación *m*; ~ **speed** *n* TRANSP velocidad de traslación *f*; ~ **store** *n* TELECOM almacenamiento de compensación *m*, almacenamiento de corrección *m*, almacenamiento de traducción *m*, almacenamiento de traslación *m*

translator *n* COMP&DP traductor *m*, TELECOM traductor *m*, translador *m*; ~ **station** *n* TV estación de translación *f*

translatory: ~ **motion** *n* MECH ENG movimiento de traslación *m*, movimiento traslatorio *m*

transliterate *vt* COMP&DP transcribir, transliterar

translucence *n* CHEM, OPT translucidez *f*, RAD PHYS translucidez *f*, transparencia *f*

translucent[1] *adj* CHEM, OPT, RAD PHYS transluciente, translúcido

translucent[2]: ~ **drawing paper** *n* PAPER papel de calco *m*; ~ **glass** *n* C&G vidrio translúcido *m*; ~ **medium** *n* PHYS medio translúcido *m*; ~ **substance** *n* OPT superficie translúcida *f*, RAD PHYS sustancia translúcida *f*

transmissibility *n* ACOUST, TELECOM transmisibilidad *f*

transmission *n* (*TX*) GEN transmisión *f*; ~ **attenuation** *n* SPACE *communications* atenuación de la transmisión *f*; ~ **bearer** *n* TELECOM portador de emisión *m*, portador de transmisión *m*; ~ **block** *n* COMP&DP bloque de transmisión *m*; ~ **breakdown** *n* TELECOM corte de transmisión *m*, interrupción técnica del servicio *f*, TV corte de transmisión *m*; ~ **bridge** *n* TELECOM puente de transmisión *m*; ~ **bush chain** *n* MECH ENG cadena de buje de transmisión *f*;

~ **channel** *n* COMP&DP, TELECOM canal de transmisión *m*; ~ **characteristic** *n* TELECOM característica de transmisión *f*; ~ **coefficient** *n* ACOUST, PHYS coeficiente de transmisión *m*; ~ **control** *n* COMP&DP control de transmisión *m*; ~ **convergence** *n* TELECOM convergencia de transmisión *f*; ~ **convergence sublayer** *n* TELECOM subcapa de convergencia de transmisión *f*; ~ **copy** *n* CINEMAT copia de transmisión *f*, TV texto de transmisión *m*; ~ **electron microscope** *n* ELECTRON, INSTR microscopio electrónico de transmisión *m*, LAB microscopio electrónico de difracción por transmisión *m*, NUCL microscopio de electrones de transmisión *m*, PHYS, RAD PHYS microscopio electrónico de transmisión *m*; ~ **electron microscopy** *n* (*TEM*) RAD PHYS microscopía electrónica de transmisión *f* (*MET*); ~ **of energy** *n* ELEC ENG transmisión de energía *f*; ~ **error** *n* TELECOM error de transmisión *m*; ~ **function** *n* NUCL función de transmisión *f*; ~ **gain** *n* ACOUST, TELECOM ganancia de transmisión *f*; ~ **gear** *n* MECH ENG engranaje de transmisión *m*, *intermediate toothed gearing* engranaje intermedio de transmisión *m*; ~ **grating** *n* PHYS rejilla de transmisión *f*; ~ **highway** *n* TELECOM autopista de transmisión *f*, camino de transmisión *m*, vía de transmisión *f*; ~ **joint** *n* PROD junta de transmisión *f*; ~ **layer** *n* TELECOM capa de transmisión *f*; ~ **line** *n* CONST, ELEC línea de transmisión *f*, ELEC ENG línea de transporte de energía *f*, ELECTRON línea de transmisión *f*, PHYS, TELECOM línea de transmisión *f*; ~ **line network** *n* ELEC *supply* red de la línea de transmisión *f*; ~ **loss** *n* ACOUST, OPT pérdida por transmisión *f*, SPACE, TELECOM pérdida de transmisión *f*; ~ **main** *n* PETR TECH transmisión principal *f*; ~ **medium** *n* COMP&DP, OPT medio de transmisión *m*; ~ **mode** *n* ELECTRON *for LCDs* función de transmisión *f*, modo de transmisión *m*; ~ **network** *n* GAS, TELECOM red de transmisión *f*; ~ **node** *n* TELECOM nodo de transmisión *m*; ~ **overload** *n* TELECOM sobrecarga de transmisión *f*; ~ **path** *n* TELECOM vía de transmisión *f*; ~ **path endpoint** *n* (*TPE*) TELECOM punto final de la vía de transmisión *m*; ~ **pinion** *n* AUTO piñón de la transmisión *m*; ~ **priority code** *n* TELECOM código de prioridad de transmisión *m*, código de prioridad del circuito de transmisión *m*; ~ **quality** *n* TELECOM calidad de transmisión *f*; ~ **rate** *n* ELEC ENG velocidad de transmisión *f*; ~ **ratio** *n* AUTO proporción de transmisión *f*; ~ **recipient** *n* TELECOM receptor de transmisión *m* (*Esp*), recipiente de transmisión *m* (*AmL*); ~ **reduction** *n* AUTO reducción de transmisión *f*; ~ **requirement for ultraviolet filter** *n* SAFE norma de transmisión para filtros ultravioleta *f*; ~ **rod** *n* MECH ENG varilla de transmisión *f*; ~ **security** *n* COMP&DP seguridad de transmisión *f*; ~ **sender** *n* TELECOM emisor de transmisión *m*, transmisor *m*; ~ **sending** *n* TELECOM envío de transmisión *m*; ~ **shaft** *n* MECH ENG eje de transmisión *m*, eje motor *m*, eje transmisor *m*; ~ **spectrum** *n* NUCL espectro de transmisión *m*; ~ **speed** *n* COMP&DP, TELECOM velocidad de transmisión *f*; ~ **system** *n* ELEC ENG sistema de transmisión *m*; ~ **technique** *n* NUCL *heat unit* técnica de transmisión *f*; ~ **tower** *n* ELEC *supply network* castillete de transmisión *m*, mástil de transmisión *m*, torre de transmisión *f*; ~ **unit** *n* TELECOM unidad de transmisión *f*; ~ **window** *n* OPT ventana de transmisión *f*;

~ **wire** *n* WATER TRANSP *of rudder* cable de transmisión *m*, guardín *m*

transmissive: ~ **disc** *BrE*, ~ **disk** *AmE n* OPT disco transmisivo *m*; ~ **LCD** *n* ELEC ENG visor de cristal líquido transmisivo *m*, visor transmisivo de cristal líquido *m*

transmit[1]: ~ **aerial** *n BrE* (*cf transmit antenna AmE*) TELECOM, TV antena de transmisión *f*; ~ **antenna** *n AmE* (*cf transmit aerial BrE*) TELECOM, TV antena de transmisión *f*; ~ **channel** *n* TELECOM canal de transmisión *m*; ~ **fiber optic terminal device** *AmE*, ~ **fibre optic terminal device** *BrE n* TELECOM dispositivo terminal de fibra óptica de transmisión *m*; ~ **machine** *n* TELECOM máquina de transmisión *f*; ~**-receive** *n* (*TR*) ELECTRON emisión-recepción *f* (*ER*)

transmit[2] *vt* COMP&DP transmitir, WATER TRANSP *radio* emitir, transmitir

transmittance *n* CHEM TECH, OPT, PHYS transmitancia *f*, TELECOM transmisión *f*, transmitancia *f*, WAVE PHYS factor de transmisión *m*, transmitancia *f*; ~ **density** *n* OPT densidad de transmitancia *f*

transmitted: ~ **beam** *n* PHYS haz transmitido *m*; ~ **data** *n pl* TELECOM datos transmitidos *m pl*; ~ **light** *n* PHOTO, RAD PHYS luz transmitida *f*; ~ **light microscope** *n* INSTR microscopio de luz transmitida *m*; ~**-light microscope with polarizer** *n* INSTR microscopio de luz transmitida con polarizador *m*; ~ **wave** *n* PHYS onda transmitida *f*

transmitter *n* GEN transmisor *m*; ~ **failure** *n* TV fallo del transmisor *m*; ~ **identification signal** *n* TRANSP señal de identificación de transmisor *f*; ~ **of motive power** *n* MECH ENG transmisor de fuerza motriz *m*; ~ **power** *n* TV potencia de emisión *f*; ~**-receiver** *n* ELECTRON transmisor-receptor *m* (*TR*), TELECOM transmisor-receptor *m* (*TR*), emisor-receptor *m*, TV transceptor *m*, transmisor-receptor *m* (*TR*), WATER TRANSP *radio* transmisor-receptor *m* (*TR*); ~ **turn-on signal** *n* TELECOM señal de activación del transmisor *f*, señal de encendido del transmisor *f*; ~ **turn-on time** *n* TELECOM tiempo de activación del emisor *m*, tiempo de encendido del transmisor *m*

transmitting: ~ **aerial** *n BrE* (*cf transmitting antenna AmE*) TELECOM, TV antena transmisora *f*; ~ **aerial antenna** *n* PHYS antena aérea transmisora *f*; ~ **antenna** *n AmE* (*cf transmitting aerial BrE*) TELECOM, TV antena transmisora *f*; ~ **frequency** *n* ELECTRON, TELECOM, TV frecuencia de transmisión *f*

transmultiplexer *n* (*TMUX*) TELECOM transmultiplexor *m*

transmutation *n* NUCL, PHYS, RAD PHYS transmutación *f*

transom *n* CONST *architecture, carpentry* montante *m*, travesaño *m*, WATER TRANSP *boat building* bovedilla *f*, espejo *m*, peto de popa *m*; ~ **plate** *n* WATER TRANSP *shipbuilding* plancha del peto de popa *f*; ~ **stern** *n* WATER TRANSP *boat building* popa de espejo *f*

transonic[1] *adj* PHYS supersónico

transonic[2]: ~ **speed** *n* PHYS velocidad transónica *f*

transparency *n* P&R transparencia *f*, PHOTO diapositiva *f*, transparencia *f*, PRINT transparencia *f*, diapositiva *f*, TELECOM transparencia *f*

transparent[1] *adj* TELECOM transparente

transparent[2]: ~ **antitamper cover** *n* PROD tapa transparente contra toda falsificación *f*; ~ **bearer service** *n* TELECOM servicio transparente del portador *m*;

~ **coating** *n* COATINGS revestimiento transparente *m*; ~ **disc** *BrE*, ~ **disk** *AmE n* OPT disco transparente *m*; ~ **enamel** *n* C&G esmalte transparente *m*; ~ **film** *n* PACK película transparente *f*; ~ **glaze** *n* C&G vidriado transparente *m*; ~ **lacquer** *n* COATINGS, COLOUR laca transparente *f*; ~ **medium** *n* PHYS medio transparente *m*; ~ **overlay** *n* CINEMAT plantilla transparente *f*; ~ **positive** *n* PRINT diapositiva *f*; ~ **substance** *n* OPT superficie transparente *f*, RAD PHYS sustancia transparente *f*; ~ **transmission** *n* COMP&DP transmisión transparente *f*

transpiration: ~ **cooling** *n* GAS, REFRIG enfriamiento por transpiración *m*; ~ **of gases** *n* GAS transpiración de gases *f*

transplutonium: ~ **element** *n* NUCL elemento transplutónico *m*

transponder *n* PHYS transmisor-receptor *m*, PRINT repetidor *m*, SPACE *communications* baliza de radar *f*, contestador *m*, repetidor *m*, transpondedor *m*, TELECOM receptor-transmisor *m*, repetidor *m*, transpondedor *m*; ~ **beacon** *n* SPACE baliza transpondedora *f*

transport[1] *n* COMP&DP transporte *m*; ~ **by helicopter** *n* WATER TRANSP transporte por helicóptero *m*; ~ **capacity for solids** *n* HYDROL capacidad de transporte de sólidos *f*; ~ **and communications** *n pl* TRANSP transportes y comunicaciones *m pl*; ~ **glider** *n* MILIT planeador de transporte *m*; ~ **helicopter** *n* AIR TRANSP helicóptero de transporte *m*; ~ **in low-pressure tube** *n* TRANSP transporte por tubería a baja presión *m*; ~ **layer** *n* COMP&DP capa de transmisión *f*; ~ **mechanism** *n* TV mecanismo de transporte *m*; ~ **model** *n* POLL modelo de transporte *m*; ~ **protocol** *n* COMP&DP protocolo de transporte *m*; ~ **protocol data unit** *n* (*TPDU*) TELECOM unidad de transferencia de datos del protocolo *f*; ~ **and rescue helicopter** *n* AIR TRANSP, TRANSP helicóptero de transporte y rescate *m*; ~ **service access point** *n* (*TSAP*) TELECOM punto de acceso al servicio de transmisión *m*; ~ **under controlled temperature** *n* REFRIG transporte bajo temperatura controlada *m*

transport[2] *vt* HYDROL *floating body* transportar, TRANSP desplazar, transportar; ~ **by rail and road** *vt* TRANSP transportar por tren y carretera

transportable[1] *adj* COMP&DP transferible

transportable[2]: ~ **earth station** *n* SPACE *communications* estación terrestre transportable *f*; ~ **gas container** *n* SAFE contenedor para gases transportable *m*; ~ **reactor** *n* NUCL reactor transportable *m*

transportation *n* MINE transporte *m*; ~ **safety** *n* SAFE seguridad en el transporte *f*; ~ **source** *n* POLL fuente de transporte *f*; ~ **system** *n* CONST sistema de transporte *m*; ~ **time** *n* PROD tiempo de transporte *m*

transporter *n* MECH ENG transbordador *m*

transposing: ~ **frame** *n* PHOTO *device* bastidor de transposición *m*; ~ **instrument** *n* ACOUST instrumento de transposición *m*

transposition *n* ACOUST, ELEC *of insulated cables* transposición *f*; ~ **tower** *n* ELEC *supply network* torre de transposición *f*

transpressive: ~ **thrust** *n* GEOL cabalgamiento en zonas con comprensión oblicua *m*

transputer *n* COMP&DP transcomputador *m* (*AmL*), transcomputadora *f* (*AmL*), transordenador *m* (*Esp*)

transship *vti* PETR TECH, WATER TRANSP *passengers, cargo* transbordar

transshipment *n* PETR TECH, WATER TRANSP transbordo *m*; ~ **track** *n* BrE RAIL vía de transbordo *f*

transtainer *n* TRANSP puente rodante de carga *m*; ~ **crane** *n* TRANSP puente rodante de carga *m*

transuranic[1] *adj* CHEM, PHYS transuránico

transuranic[2]: ~ **waste** *n* NUCL residuos transuránicos *m pl*

transversal *n* GEOM transversal *f*; ~ **filter** *n* ELECTRON, TELECOM filtro transversal *m*; ~ **filtering** *n* ELECTRON filtrado transversal *m*; ~ **scratch** *n* CINEMAT raya transversal *f*

transverse[1] *adj* WATER TRANSP *ship design* transversal; ~ **electromagnetic** *adj* (*TEM*) ELEC ENG electromagnético transversal (*TEM*); ~ **magnetic** *adj* (*TM*) ELEC ENG magnético transversal (*TM*)

transverse[2]: ~ **beam** *n* WATER TRANSP *shipbuilding* bao transversal *m*; ~ **bulkhead** *n* WATER TRANSP *ship design* mamparo transversal *m*; ~ **chromatic aberration** *n* OPT, PHYS, RAD PHYS, TELECOM, TV aberración cromática transversal *f*; ~ **component** *n* PHYS componente transversal *f*; ~ **control arm** *n* VEH eje transversal *m*; ~ **current** *n* C&G corriente transversal *f*; ~ **electric** *n* (*TE*) ELEC ENG transversal eléctrico *m* (*TE*); ~ **electric mode** *n* (*TE mode*) ELEC modo eléctrico transversal *m* (*modo TE*), OPT modo eléctrico transversal *m* (*modo TE*), modo transversal eléctrico *m*, PHYS modo eléctrico transversal *m* (*modo TE*), TELECOM modo H *m*, modo eléctrico transversal *m* (*modo TE*), modo transversal eléctrico *m*; ~ **electric wave** *n* (*TE wave*) ELEC, ELEC ENG, PHYS, TELECOM onda eléctrica transversal *f* (*onda TE*); ~ **electromagnetic mode** *n* OPT, TELECOM modo electromagnético transversal *m*; ~ **electromagnetic wave** *n* (*TEM wave*) ELEC, ELEC ENG, PHYS onda electromagnética transversal *f* (*onda TEM*); ~ **energy distribution** *n* RAD PHYS distribución transversal de la energía *f*; ~ **engine** *n* (*see horizontal engine*) VEH motor horizontal *m*, motor transversal *m*; ~-**flux linear motor** *n* TRANSP motor lineal de flujo transversal *m*; ~-**flux machine** *n* TRANSP máquina de flujo transversal *f*; ~ **framing** *n* WATER TRANSP *shipbuilding* cuadernas transversales *f pl*; ~ **interferometry** *n* OPT, TELECOM interferometría transversal *f*; ~ **magnetic mode** *n* OPT, TELECOM modo magnético transversal *m*; ~ **magnetic recording** *n* ACOUST grabación magnética transversal *f*; ~ **magnetic wave** *n* (*TM wave*) ELEC, ELEC ENG, PHYS onda magnética transversal *f* (*onda TM*); ~ **magnification** *n* PHYS magnificación transversal *f*; ~ **member** *n* WATER TRANSP *shipbuilding* miembro transversal *m*; ~ **metacenter** *AmE*, ~ **metacentre** *BrE n* WATER TRANSP *ship design* metacentro transversal *m*; ~ **offset loss** *n* OPT, TELECOM pérdida por desplazamiento transversal *f*; ~ **recording** *n* TV grabación transversal *f*; ~-**scanning recorder** *n* TV grabador de exploración transversal *m*; ~ **section** *n* TELECOM corte transversal *m*, sección transversal *f*, WATER TRANSP *ship design* sección transversal *f*; ~ **slot** *n* TELECOM hendidura transversal *f*, ranura transversal *f*, rendija transversal *f*; ~ **spring** *n* RAIL muelle transversal *m*; ~ **stability** *n* WATER TRANSP *ship design* estabilidad transversal *f*; ~ **wave** *n* ACOUST, ELEC ENG, GEOL, PHYS, TELECOM onda transversal *f*, WAVE PHYS onda transversa *f*

tranverse: ~ **fracture** *n* C&G fractura transversal *f*

trap[1] *n* AGRIC piquete *m*, CHEM TECH, COMP&DP trampa *f*, CONST trampa *f*, colector *m*, válvula *f*, *plumbing* sifón *m*, CRYSTALL, GAS, GEOL, HEAT ENG, NUCL trampa *f*, PETR TECH separador *m*, trampa *f*, PETROL trampa *f*, PRINT aceptación del color siguiente en una impresión multicolor *f*, TRANSP *production*, TV trampa *f*; ~ **door** *n* CONST trampilla *f*; ~ **for vacuum pump** *n* LAB trampa para bomba de vacío *f*

trap[2]: ~ **air** *vi* PROD captar aire

TRAPATT: ~ **diode** *n* (*trapped plasma avalanche transit-time diode*) ELECTRON, PHYS diodo TRAPATT *m*

trapezium *n* GEOM trapecio *m*, trapezoide *m*

trapezoid *n* GEOM trapezoide *m*; ~ **arm-type suspension** *n* AUTO, VEH suspensión de tipo brazo trapezoidal *f*

trapezoidal[1] *adj* GEOM trapezoidal

trapezoidal[2]: ~ **blade** *n* MECH ENG hoja trapezoidal *f*; ~ **distortion** *n* ELECTRON distorsión trapezoidal *f*; ~ **thread** *n* MECH ENG *Acme thread* hilo trapezoidal *m*, *screws* rosca trapezoidal *f*

trapped: ~ **particle** *n* NUCL partícula retenida *f*; ~ **plasma avalanche transit-time diode** *n* (*TRAPATT diode*) ELECTRON, PHYS diodo TRAPATT *m*; ~ **rail system** *n* MINE red de ferrocarriles interceptada *f*

trapping *n* PRINT compatibilidad de sobreimpresión *f*, compatibilidad entre tintas *f*, SAFE atrapado *m*, entrampado *m*; ~ **site** *n* ELEC ENG emplazamiento de atrapado *m*

trash: ~ **fish** *n* OCEAN pescado desechado *m*; ~ **spring** *n* AGRIC cubrehierbas *m*; ~ **treader** *n* AGRIC azada compactadora *f*

travel[1] *n* MECH ENG *of carriage, valve* recorrido *m*, curso *m*, carrera *f*, desplazamiento *m*, NUCL desplazamiento *m*, recorrido *m*; ~ **follow-up** *n* AIR TRANSP control del viaje *m*; ~ **time** *n* GEOPHYS tiempo de recorrido *m*, SPACE tiempo de propagación *m*

travel[2] *vt* TRANSP viajar

traveler *AmE see* **traveller** *BrE*

traveling *AmE see* **travelling** *BrE*

traveller *n* BrE MECH ENG *runner, slider*, PROD *overhead crane* carro *m*

travelling *n* BrE PROD *of bridge of crane* traslación *f*; ~ **apron** *n* BrE PROD telera transportadora *f*, cinta transportadora *f*, correa transportadora *f*, *conveyor belt* transportador de banda articulada *m*; ~ **belt filter** *n* BrE (*TBF*) NUCL filtro de correa móvil *m*; ~ **belt screen** *n* BrE PROD criba corrediza *f*; ~ **block** *n* BrE PETR TECH bloque móvil *m*, bloque viajero *m*, PETROL aparejo móvil *m*, motón móvil *m*, polea móvil *f*; ~ **cradle** *n* BrE CONST *building* andamio móvil *m*, armazón móvil *m*; ~ **crane** *n* BrE MECH *lifting gear* grúa corrediza *f*, puente-grúa *m*, PROD grúa locomóvil *f*, puente-grúa *m*; ~ **dolly** *n* BrE CINEMAT, TV dolly para travelling *f*; ~-**field motor** *n* BrE TRANSP motor de campo desplazable *m*; ~ **gantry** *n* BrE WATER TRANSP grúa de pórtico móvil *f*; ~ **gantry crane** *n* BrE PROD grúa locomóvil *f*, pórtico acarreador *m*, WATER TRANSP grúa de pórtico móvil *f*; ~ **ladderway** *n* BrE CONST escalera corrediza *f*, escalera móvil *f*; ~ **matte** *n* BrE CINEMAT trama de traveling *f*; ~ **microscope** *n* BrE LAB *for length measurement* microscopio corredizo *m*; ~ **platform** *n* BrE CONST plataforma móvil *f*; ~ **pulley block** *n* BrE PROD polea móvil *f*, polipasto móvil *m*; ~ **runner** *n* BrE PROD *of* *overhead crane, ropeway* carro de rodadura *m*; ~ **staircase** *n BrE* CONST escalera corrediza *f*; ~ **table** *n BrE* MECH ENG *of rolling-mill* mesa de alimentación *f*, mesa movible *f*; ~ **trolley** *n BrE* PROD *of overhead crane, ropeway* carro de rodadura *m*; ~ **wave** *n BrE* ACOUST, ELECTRON onda progresiva *f*, PHYS onda viajera *f*, TELECOM, WAVE PHYS onda progresiva *f*; ~**-wave aerial** *n BrE* (*cf traveling-wave antenna AmE*) TELECOM, TV antena de onda progresiva *f*; ~**-wave amplifier** *n BrE* ELECTRON, TELECOM amplificador de ondas progresivas *m*; ~**-wave magnetron** *n BrE* ELECTRON magnetrón de onda progresiva *m*; ~**-wave maser** *n BrE* ELECTRON maser de onda progresiva *m*; ~**-wave motor** *n BrE* ELEC motor de ondas progresivas *m*; ~**-wave tube** *n BrE* (*TWT*) ELECTRON, PHYS, SPACE, TELECOM tubo de ondas progresivas *m* (*TOP*); ~**-wave tube amplifier** *n BrE* ELECTRON, SPACE, TELECOM amplificador de tubo de ondas progresivas *m*; ~ **waveguide** *n BrE* TELECOM guía de ondas progresivas *f*; ~ **waveguide amplifier** *n BrE* ELECTRON, TELECOM amplificador de las guías de ondas progresivas *m*; ~ **wheel** *n BrE* PROD *for crane* rueda de traslación *f*, rueda portadora *f*

traverse *n* CONST trazado de poligonal *m*, *crosspiece, crossbar, transom* travesaño *m*, cruce *m*, recorrido del carro *m*; ~ **feed** *n* MECH ENG *lathe-work* avance longitudinal *m*; ~ **motion bearing** *n* MECH ENG cojinete de movimiento longitudinal *m*; ~ **shaper** *n* MECH ENG limadora de carnero móvil *f*, limadora horizontal *f*

traversing *n* PROD *jenny of overhead travelling crane* traslación *f*; ~ **head shaping machine** *n* MECH ENG estampadora de cabeza horizontal *f*, limadora de cabeza horizontal *f*, limadora de carnero longitudinal *f*, limadora de carnero móvil *f*, prensa transversal *f*; ~ **jack** *n* MECH ENG gato de carrillo *m*, gato longitudinal *m*

travertine *n* FUELLESS travertino *m*

trawl[1] *n* MAR POLL, OCEAN arte de arrastre *m*, TEXTIL red barredera *f*, WATER TRANSP *fishing* arte de arrastre *m*; ~ **board** *n* MAR POLL, OCEAN compuerta *f*, puerta *f*, WATER TRANSP *fishing* compuerta *f*, puerta *f*; ~ **fishing** *n* MAR POLL, OCEAN, WATER TRANSP pesca por arrastre *f*; ~ **net** *n* MAR POLL, OCEAN, WATER TRANSP *fishing* red de arrastre *f*; ~ **warp** *n* MAR POLL, OCEAN, WATER TRANSP *fishing* cable de arrastre *m*; ~ **wing** *n* MAR POLL, OCEAN, WATER TRANSP *fishing* ala de la red de arrastre *f*, ala de red barredera *f*

trawl[2] *vi* OCEAN, WATER TRANSP *fishing* pescar con arte de arrastre

trawler *n* OCEAN arrastrero *m*, barco rastreador *m*, WATER TRANSP *fishing* arrastrero *m*

trawling *n* MAR POLL, OCEAN pesca por arrastre *f*; ~ **and dredging gear** *n* OCEAN, WATER TRANSP arte de arrastre y rastreo *m*

tray *n* C&G bandeja *f*, pálet *m* (*AmL*), CHEM bandeja *f*, caja *f*, placa *f*, plato *m*, LAB bandeja *f*, charola *f* (*AmL*), placa *f* (*Esp*), MECH ENG depósito debajo de la bancada *m*, bandeja *f*, PACK bandeja *f*, pálet *m* (*AmL*), PAPER, PHOTO bandeja *f*; out-~ *n* PROD bandeja de salida *f*; ~ **denesting-filling-and-lidding machine** *n* PACK máquina para extraer, llenar y tapar bandejas *f*; ~ **drying chamber** *n* REFRIG cámara de vacío con estanterías *f*; ~ **erector** *n* PACK armador de bandejas *m*; ~ **erector and loader** *n* PACK armador y

cargador de bandejas *m*; ~ **packaging** *n* PACK envasado en bandejas *m*; ~**-packing machine** *n* PACK envasadora en bandejas *f*; ~ **sealer** *n* PACK precintadora de bandejas *f*, sellador de bandejas *m*

trazer *n* INSTR trazador *m*

tread *n* AIR TRANSP *of landing gear* superficie de rodamiento del neumático *f*, vía *f*, banda de rodadura *f*, AUTO banda de rodadura *f*, CONST *of girder* superficie de rodadura *f* (*Esp*), oruga *f*, *of step* huella *f*, peldaño *m*, RAIL banda *f*, llanta *f*, VEH *of wheel* banda de rodadura *f*; ~ **depth gage** *AmE*, ~ **depth gauge** *BrE n* VEH galga para medir la profundidad del dibujo del neumático *f*; ~ **design** *n* VEH dibujo de la banda de rodadura *m*

treadle *n* MECH ENG pedal *m*; ~ **brake valve** *n* AUTO, MECH ENG válvula del pedal del freno *f*

treat *vt* COAL tratar

treatment *n* GEN tratamiento *m*

treble: ~**-pass boiler** *n* HEAT caldera de triple paso *f*

tree *n* COAL apea *f*, COMP&DP árbol *m*, MINE apea *f*, puntal *m*, tubo de la tubería de impulsión *m*; ~ **and branch network** *n* TELECOM red ramificada *f*; ~ **distribution** *n* TELECOM distribución ramificada *f*; ~ **network** *n* COMP&DP red en árbol *f*, TELECOM red en árbol *f*, red no mallada *f*, red ramificada *f*; ~ **search** *n* COMP&DP búsqueda en árbol *f*; ~ **structure** *n* COMP&DP, TELECOM estructura en árbol *f*; ~ **topology** *n* COMP&DP topología de árbol *f*

treed: ~ **system** *n* ELEC *supply network* sistema con múltiples derivaciones *m*, sistema ramificado *m*

treeing *n* PRINT descarga ramificada *f*

treenail *n* (*cf trunnel*) CONST espiga *f*

trefoil: ~ **formation** *n* ELEC *cable configuration* formación de trifolio *f*, formación de trébol *f*

trehalose *n* CHEM trehalosa *f*

trellis *n* CONST enrejado *m*, reja *f*; ~ **post** *n* CONST barrote de enrejado *m*

trelliswork *n* CONST enrejado *m*

trembler *n* ELEC ENG ruptor *m*; ~ **bell** *n* ELEC timbre intermitente *m*, timbre trepidante *m*

tremolite *n* MINERAL calamita *f*, tremolita *f*

tremolo *n* ACOUST trémolo *m*

tremorine *n* CHEM tremorina *f*

trench *n* COAL foso *m*, trinchera *f*, zanja *f* (*AmL*), CONST zanja *f* (*AmL*), GEOL, GEOPHYS fosa submarina *f*, MAR POLL zanja *f* (*AmL*), MILIT trinchera *f*, MINE foso *m*, trinchera *f* (*Esp*), zanja *f* (*AmL*), OCEAN fosa submarina *f*, zanja *f* (*AmL*), PETR TECH foso *m*, PETROL zanja *f* (*AmL*); ~ **cutter** *n* CONST zanjadora de cangilones *f*; ~ **silo** *n* AGRIC silo trinchera *m*; ~ **work** *n* CONST apertura de zanja *f*

trenching *n* CONST apertura de zanja *f*

trend *n* MINE dirección *f*, TEXTIL tendencia *f*

trepanner *n* MECH ENG trepanador *m*

T-rest *n* MECH ENG *lathe* portaherramientas en T *m*

trestle *n* CONST caballete *m*; ~ **bridge** *n* CONST puente de caballetes *m*; ~ **car** *n AmE* (*cf trestle wagon BrE*) RAIL *vehicles* vagón bastidor *m*; ~ **shore** *n* CONST *building* puntal de caballetes *m*; ~ **wagon** *n BrE* (*cf trestle car AmE*) RAIL *vehicles* vagón bastidor *m*

tri: ~**-blade cutting machine** *n* PRINT cortadora de tres cuchillas *f*; ~**-square file** *n* MECH ENG lima triangular *f*

triac *n* ELEC *thyristor* tiristor bidireccional *m*, triac *m*, ELEC ENG tiristor bidireccional *m*

triacetate *n* TEXTIL triacetato *m*; ~ **base** *n* CINEMAT soporte de triacetato *m*
triacetin *n* CHEM triacetina *f*
triacetonamine *n* CHEM triacetonamina *f*
triacid *n* CHEM triácido *m*
triad *n* CHEM tríada *f*
trial *n* AGRIC ensayo *m*, COAL comprobación *f*, ensayo *m*, experimento *m*, NUCL *of compound* prueba funcional *f*, TEXTIL prueba *f*; ~ **cock** *n* WATER grifo calibrador *m*; ~ **composite print** *n* CINEMAT copia de prueba combinada *f*; ~ **and error calculation** *n* GEOM cálculo por aproximaciones sucesivas *m*; ~ **and error method** *n* CRYSTALL método al tanteo *m*, método de tanteo *m*, método por aproximaciones sucesivas *m*; ~ **frame** *n* INSTR cuadro graduado *m*, marco de pruebas *m*; ~ **run** *n* NUCL *quality factor* prueba funcional *f*; ~ **speed** *n* WATER TRANSP velocidad en las pruebas *f*; ~ **strip** *n* CONST tramo de ensayos *m*; ~ **structure** *n* CRYSTALL estructura tentativa *f*
triamyl *n* CHEM triamilo *m*
triangle *n* CONST, GEOM, LAB, PHYS triángulo *m*; ~ **of forces** *n* CONST, PHYS triángulo de fuerzas *m*; ~ **test** *n* FOOD prueba triangular *f*; ~ **testing** *n* FOOD prueba triangular *f*
triangular[1] *adj* C&G, GEOM triangular
triangular[2]: ~ **arch** *n* CONST *structure, curve* arco triangular *m*; ~ **cam** *n* MECH ENG leva triangular *f*; ~ **matrix** *n* COMP&DP matriz triangular *f*
triangularity *n* C&G, GEOM triangularidad *f*
triangulate *vt* GEOM triangular
triangulation *n* CONST, GEOM, METR, SPACE triangulación *f*; ~ **point** *n* CONST punto de triangulación *m*
Triassic: ~ **period** *n* GEOL, PETR TECH período Triásico *m*
triaxial: ~ **pinch experiment** *n* NUCL experimento de estricción triaxial *m*; ~ **state of stress** *n* METALL estado triaxial de esfuerzo *m*; ~ **test** *n* CONST ensayo triaxial *m*
triazine: ~ **ring** *n* CHEM *structure* anillo de triazina *m*
triazoic *adj* CHEM triazoico
triazole *n* CHEM triazol *m*
tribasic *adj* CHEM *acid* tribásico
triboelectric *adj* ELEC, PHYS, TRANSP triboeléctrico
triboelectricity *n* PHYS, TRANSP triboelectricidad *f*
triboluminescence *n* PHYS triboluminiscencia *f*
tributary[1] *adj* HYDROL, TELECOM tributario
tributary[2] *n* HYDROL, TELECOM tributario *m*, WATER TRANSP *river* afluente *m*; ~ **channel** *n* HYDROL canal tributario *m*; ~ **unit** *n* (*TU*) TELECOM unidad tributaria *f*; --**unit group** *n* (*TUG*) TELECOM grupo de unidad tributaria *m*
tributyrin *n* CHEM tributirina *f*
tricarballylic *adj* CHEM tricarbalílico
trichite *n* PETROL triquita *f*
trichlorethylene *n* CHEM, DETERG tricloroetileno *m*
trichloride *n* CHEM tricloruro *m*
trichloroacetic *adj* CHEM tricloroacético
trichloroethylene *n* CHEM, DETERG tricloroetileno *m*
trichroic *adj* PHYS tricroico
trichroism *n* PHYS tricroismo *m*
trichromatic *adj* INSTR *of filter* tricromático
trick: ~ **printer** *n* CINEMAT impresora para trucado *f*
trickle[1]: ~ **charge** *n* CINEMAT carga lenta *f*, ELEC ENG carga de entretenimiento *f*, carga lenta *f*; ~ **charger** *n*

ELEC *accumulator* cargador de goteo *m*, cargador por goteo *m*, ELEC ENG cargador lento *m*
trickle[2] *vi* HYDROL gotear
trickling *n* HYDROL escurrimiento *m*, goteo *m*; ~ **filter** *n* POLL filtro de escurrimiento *m*, filtro de goteo *m*, filtro percolador *m* (*AmL*)
triclinic[1] *adj* CHEM, CRYSTALL triclínico
triclinic[2]: ~ **system** *n* METALL sistema triclínico *m*
tricone: ~ **bit** *n* PETR TECH barrena de arrastre *f*, barrena tricónica *f* (*Esp*), broca tricona *f*, mecha *f* (*AmL*), tricono *m* (*AmL*), trépano tricónico *m*
tricosane *n* CHEM tricosano *m*
tricresol *n* CHEM tricresol *m*
tricresyl *n* CHEM tricresilo *m*
tricycle: ~ **landing-gear** *n* AIR TRANSP tren de aterrizaje en triciclo *m*
tricyclic *adj* CHEM tricíclico
tridymite *n* MINERAL tridimita *f*
triester *n* CHEM triéster *m*
triethanolamine *n* CHEM, DETERG trietanolamina *f*
trifocal: ~ **glass** *n* C&G vidrio trifocal *m*
trifurcating: ~ **box** *n* ELEC *cable accessory* caja de derivación trifurcada *f*, caja de empalme para cable tripolar *f*; ~ **joint** *n* ELEC *cable connection* caja de derivación trifurcada *f*
trifurcator *n* ELEC *cable accessory* trifurcador *m*, trifurcante *m*
trig: ~ **point** *n* CONST punto de apoyo *m*
trigatron *n* ELECTRON trigatrón *m*
trigger[1] *n* CINEMAT, COMP&DP disparador *m*, ELEC *circuit breaker* circuito desconectador *m*, circuito de desenganche *m*, circuito de disparo *m*, MECH ENG mecanismo de disparo *m*, disparador *m*, gatillo *m*, MILIT *of firearm* disparador *m*, gatillo *m*, PHOTO disparador *m*; ~ **box** *n* AUTO, VEH caja disparadora *f*; ~ **circuit** *n* ELEC circuito activador *m*, circuito de activación *m*, circuito de disparo *m*, circuito de gatillado *m*, circuito de mando *m*, circuito disparador *m*, circuito excitador *m*, circuito gatillador *m*, circuito gatillo *m*, circuito tipo gatillo *m*, ELECTRON circuito activador *m*, circuito disparador *m*, PHYS circuito disparador *m*; ~ **contact** *n* AUTO contacto disparador *m*, MECH ENG contacto del disparador *m*; ~ **diode** *n* ELECTRON diodo activador *m*; ~ **grip** *n* CINEMAT mango disparador *m*, empuñadura con gatillo *f*; ~ **guard** *n* MILIT guardamonte *m*; ~ **level** *n* ELECTRON nivel de disparo *m*; ~ **pulse** *n* ELECTRON impulso activador *m*; ~ **relay** *n* PHOTO relevador de disparo *m*; ~ **wheel** *n* AUTO rueda disparadora *f*
trigger[2] *vt* COMP&DP, ELECTRON disparar, MECH ENG accionar, activar, disparar, gatillar, PHYS, SAFE, TELECOM *alarm* disparar
triggered: ~ **circuit** *n* ELECTRON circuito activado *m*
triggering *n* COMP&DP disparo *m*; ~ **circuit** *n* PHOTO circuito de disparo *m*; ~ **lead pulse** *n* TELECOM impulso activador de la línea *m*, impulso de disparo de la línea *m*, impulso de mando de la línea *m*, impulso disparador de la línea *m*, impulso iniciador de la línea *m*; ~ **pulse** *n* TV pulso activador *m*; ~ **system** *n* RAD PHYS sistema de disparo *m*; ~ **voltage** *n* TV voltaje de disparo *m* (*AmL*)
triglyceride *n* CHEM, DETERG triglicérido *m*
trigonal *adj* CRYSTALL romboédrico, trigonal
trigonometric *adj* GEOM trigonométrico
trigonometrical[1] *adj* GEOM trigonométrico
trigonometrical[2]: ~ **function** *n* GEOM función trigo-

nométrica *f*; ~ **ratio** *n* GEOM cociente trigonométrico *m*, razón trigonométrica *f*
trigonometry *n* GEOM trigonometría *f*
trihedral *adj* GEOM triedro, triédrico
trihedron *n* GEOM triedro *m*
trihydrate *n* CHEM trihidrato *m*
trihydric *adj* CHEM trihídrico
trihydrol *n* CHEM trihidrol *m*
triiodide *n* CHEM triyoduro *m*
trilateral *n* GEOM trilátero *m*
trill *n* ACOUST trino *m*
trim¹: **out of** ~ *adj* AIR TRANSP *aircraft* descompensado, desequilibrado
trim² *n* AIR TRANSP centrado *m*, compensado *m*, equilibrado *m*, estabilizado *m*, reglaje *m*, CINEMAT, PAPER, PRINT recorte *m* (*Esp*), SPACE *spacecraft* equilibrio en vuelo rectilíneo *m*, asiento *m*, WATER TRANSP *of boat, cargo* arrumaje *m*, arrumazón *m*, asiento *m*, romaneo *m*; ~ **bin** *n* CINEMAT recipiente para recortes *m*; ~ **capacitor** *n* ELEC capacitador variable *m*, condensador de ajuste de sintonía *m*, condensador variable *m*; ~ **control** *n* AIR TRANSP control de reglaje *m*; ~ **control switch** *n* AIR TRANSP interruptor de mando de reglaje *m*; ~ **mark** *n* PRINT línea de corte *f*; ~ **removal system** *n* PAPER sistema para eliminar los orillos *m*; ~ **shower** *n* PAPER rociador de refilar *m*; ~ **size** *n* PRINT tamaño final cortado *m*; ~ **stability** *n* AIR TRANSP estabilidad de compensación *f*; ~ **tab** *n* AIR TRANSP aleta compensadora *f*, ELEC ENG compensador *m*; ~ **washer** *n* PROD arandela de compensación *f*
trim³ *vt* AIR TRANSP estabilizar, CINEMAT recortar, CONST *joist* guarnecer, desbastar, cepillar, alisar, ribetear, MECH cepillar, rebabar, recortar, ajustar, PAPER desbarbar, PRINT recortar, PROD recortar, *wood* ajustar, cepillar, desrebabar, igualar, SPACE *spacecraft* asentar, equilibrar, estibar, WATER TRANSP *sailboat* arranchar, poner a son de mar; ~ **off the burr from** *vt* PROD desrebabar; ~ **off the rough edges from** *vt* PROD desrebabar
trimer *n* CHEM, P&R trímero *m*
trimerize *vt* CHEM trimerizar
trimesic *adj* CHEM trimésico
trimetallic: ~ **plate** *n* PRINT plancha trimetálica *f*
trimethylbenzene *n* CHEM trimetilbenceno *m*
trimethylcarbinol *n* CHEM trimetilcarbinol *m*
trimethylene *n* CHEM trimetileno *m*
trimethylpyridine *n* CHEM trimetilpiridina
trimmed¹: ~ **by the head** *adj* WATER TRANSP con asiento a proa; ~ **by the stern** *adj* WATER TRANSP con asiento a popa; ~ **off** *adj* PROD recortado
trimmed²: ~ **joist** *n* CONST brochal *m*, vigueta de unión *f*; ~ **size** *n* PACK tamaño final *m*, PAPER formato neto *m*, formato cortado *m*, PRINT formato cortado *m*, formato neto *m*
trimmer *n* COAL apilador de carbón *m* (*AmL*), extendedura de carbón *f* (*Esp*), CONST brochal *m*, ELEC capacitador variable *m*, condensador variable *m*, MECH ENG *for wood* desbastadora *f*, recortadora *f*, MINE apilador de carbón *m* (*AmL*), cargador de vagonetas *m*, extendedura de carbón *f* (*Esp*), PHOTO cortapruebas *m*; ~ **beam** *n* CONST viga rebajada *f*; ~ **capacitor** *n* ELEC ENG condensador de equilibrado *m*
trimming *n* AIR TRANSP compensación *f*, reglaje *m*, regulación *f*, PAPER orillo *m*, TEXTIL adorno *m*,

fornitura *f*; ~ **machine** *n* MECH ENG *grinder* agramiladora *f*, desbarbadora *f*, ribeteadora *f*; ~ **potentiometer** *n* ELEC *resistor* potenciómetro de ajuste *m*, potenciómetro de regulación *m*, ELEC ENG potenciómetro de regulación *m*; ~ **resolution** *n* ELEC ENG resolución de regulación *f*; ~ **tab** *n* AIR TRANSP aleta reguladora *f*; ~ **wheel** *n* MECH ENG muela desbarbadora *f*, muela rebarbadora *f*
trimolecular *adj* CHEM trimolecular
trimorphic *adj* CHEM trimórfico
trimorphism *n* CHEM trimorfismo *m*
trimorphous *adj* CHEM trimorfo
trimyristin *n* CHEM trimiristina *f*
trinitrate *n* CHEM trinitrato *m*
trinitrated *adj* CHEM trinitrado
trinitrin *n* CHEM trinitrina *f*
trinitro: ~-**compound** *n* CHEM trinitrocompuesto *m*
trinitrobenzene *n* CHEM trinitrobenceno *m*
trinitrocresol *n* CHEM trinitrocresol *m*
trinitrophenol *n* CHEM trinitrofenol *m*
trinitrotoluene *n* (*TNT*) CHEM trinitrotolueno *m* (*TNT*)
trinomial *n* MATH trinomio *m*
triode *n* ELECTRON, PHYS triodo *m*; ~ **action** *n* ELECTRON efecto de triodo *m*; ~-**hexode** *n* ELECTRON triodo-exodo *m*; ~ **oscillator** *n* ELECTRON oscilador de triodo *m*; ~ **tube** *n* AmE ELECTRON tubo de triodo *m*; ~ **valve** *BrE n* (*cf triode tube AmE*) ELECTRON tubo de triodo *m*
triol *n* CHEM triol *m*
triolein *n* CHEM oleína *f*, trioleína *f*
triose *n* CHEM triosa *f*
trioxane *n* CHEM metaformaldehído *m*, trioxano *m*
trioxide *n* CHEM trióxido *m*
trioxymethylene *n* CHEM trioximetileno *m*
trioxypurine *n* CHEM trioxipurina *f*
trip¹: ~-**free** *adj* PROD primario
trip² *n* MECH ENG desconexión *f*, desenganche *m*, disparo *m*, dispositivo de disparo *m*, dispositivo interruptor *m*, disyuntor *m*, fiador *m*, gatillo *m*, relé *m*, PETR TECH maniobra *f*, viaje *m*, PROD, SAFE dispositivo de disparo *m*, dispositivo interruptor *m*; ~ **catch** *n* CONST, MECH diente *m*, MECH ENG diente *m*, enganche *m*, fiador *m*, gatillo *m*, retén *m*; ~ **circuit** *n* ELEC circuito de disparo *m*, circuito desconectador *m*; ~ **coil** *n* ELEC bobina de disparo *f*, bobina de interrupción *f*; ~ **contact** *n* PROD contacto de disparo *m*; ~ **counter** *n* BrE (*cf trip odometer AmE*) AUTO, CONST, TRANSP odómetro *m*, VEH cuentakilómetros *m*, cuentakilómetros parcial *m*, odómetro *m*; ~ **curve** *n* PROD curva de disparo *f*; ~ **dog** *n* MECH ENG gancho disparador *m*, gatillo disparador *m*; ~ **free release** *n* ELEC *circuit breaker* escape libre *m*; ~ **gas** *n* GAS, PETR TECH gas de maniobra *m*, gas de viaje *m*; ~ **gear** *n* ELEC *circuit breaker* disparador *m*, órganos de desprendimiento *m pl*, mecanismo de báscula *m*, mecanismo de desenganche *m*, mecanismo basculador *m*, mecanismo desconectador *m*, mecanismo de disparo *m*, ELEC ENG órganos de desprendimiento *m pl*, MECH ENG disparador *m*, mecanismo de desenganche *m*, mecanismo disparador *m*; ~ **guard** *n* SAFE protección mediante disyuntor *f*; ~ **indicator** *n* CINEMAT indicador de desenganche *m*; ~ **logic signal converter** *n* NUCL convertidor de señales lógicas de disparo *m*; ~ **mileage indicator** *n* AUTO, VEH indicador de distancia *m*, indicador de kilometraje *m*;

~ odometer *n AmE* (*cf trip recorder BrE, cf trip counter BrE*) AUTO registrador de distancia *m*, odómetro *m*, CONST, TRANSP, VEH odómetro *m*; **~ pile driver** *n* CONST martinete de hinca pilotes *m*; **~ recorder** *n BrE* (*cf trip odometer AmE*) AUTO registrador de distancia *m*; **~ relay** *n* ELEC relé accionador *m*, relé de desenganche *m*, relé desconectador *m*, relé disparador *m*; **~ scale** *n* PROD escala de disparo *f*; **~ time** *n* PROD tiempo de disparo *m*, TRANSP tiempo de viaje *m*; **~ valve gear** *n* MECH ENG mecanismo de válvula disparadora *m*

trip³ *vt* MECH ENG interrumpir, PHYS viajar; **~ in** *vt* MECH ENG enganchar, engranar

trip⁴ *vi* MECH ENG desconectar, desenganchar, disparar; **~ anchor** *vi* WATER TRANSP zafar el ancla, zarpar

tripack: ~ film *n* PHOTO película tripack *f*

tripalmitin *n* CHEM tripalmitato de glicerilo *m*, tripalmitina *f*

triparanol *n* CHEM triparanol *m*

triphane *n* MINERAL trifana *f*

triphase *adj* ELEC ENG trifásico

triphasic *adj* CHEM trifásico

triphenol *n* CHEM trifenol *m*

triphenylmethyl *n* CHEM trifenilmetilo *m*

triphilic *adj* CHEM trifílico

triphyline *n* MINERAL trifilina *f*

triphylite *n* MINERAL trifilina *f*

triple: ~ alpha process *n* NUCL proceso alfa triple *m*; **~~beam coincidence spectrometer** *n* NUCL espectrómetro de coincidencia de haz triple *m*; **~ bond** *n* CHEM triple enlace *m*, triple ligadura *f*; **~~cavity mold** *AmE*, **~~cavity mould** *BrE n* C&G molde de triple cavidad *m*; **~~core cable** *n* ELEC cable de tres almas *m*; **~ expansion reciprocating engine** *n* WATER TRANSP máquina de triple expansión *f*; **~ junction** *n* CHEM TECH, CONST, GAS, MECH ENG, METALL, PETR TECH, WATER unión triple *f*; **~ ladder** *n* CONST escalera triple *f*; **~ pack** *n* PACK envase de tres paquetes *m*; **~~pass boiler** *n* HEAT caldera de triple paso *f*; **~ point** *n* METALL, PHYS, THERMO punto triple *m*; **~ valve** *n* HYDRAUL válvula de desvío *f*, válvula de tres vías *f*; **~~wound transformer** *n* ELEC, ELEC ENG transformador de triple arrollamiento *m*

triplet *n* NUCL *communications*, CHEM, PHYS triplete *m*; **~ lens** *n* CINEMAT, OPT, PHOTO objetivo triple *m*

triplex: ~ engine *n* MECH ENG máquina tricilíndrica *f*

triplite *n* MINERAL triplita *f*

tripod *n* GEN trípode *m*; **~ bush** *n* PHOTO casquillo del trípode *m*; **~ extension** *n* PHOTO extensión del trípode *f*; **~ head** *n* CINEMAT cabeza del trípode *f*, PHOTO cabezal del trípode *m*; **~ leg** *n* CINEMAT, INSTR, PHOTO pata del trípode *f*; **~ screw** *n* CINEMAT tornillo de trípode *m*; **~ stand** *n* PROD soporte de tres pies *m*

tripoli: ~ stone *n* GEOL roca de trípoli *f*

tripolite *n* MINERAL tierra de sílice *f*, trípoli *m*, PETROL trípoli *m*

tripper *n* MECH ENG basculador *m*, desenganchador *m*, disparador *m*, interruptor *m*, soltador *m*, trinquete *m*

tripping *n* AGRIC *legumes* desenlace *m*, MECH ENG desenganche *m*, desconexión *f*, disyunción *f*, interrupción *f*, desembrague *m*; **~ bracket** *n* WATER TRANSP *against curving* cartabón de arriostramiento *m*; **~ device** *n* MECH ENG basculador *m*, desconectador *m*, dispositivo de disparo *m*, dispositivo desconector *m*, dispositivo interruptor *m*, disyuntor *m*, PROD desconectador *m*, dispositivo de disparo *m*,

dispositivo interruptor *m*, disyuntor *m*, SAFE dispositivo de disparo *m*, dispositivo interruptor *m*; **~ line** *n* OCEAN cabo de disparo *m*, WATER TRANSP *to douse flags* cabo guía *m*, cargadura *f*, orinque *m*; **~ relay** *n* ELEC relé accionador *m*, relé de desenganche *m*, relé desconectador *m*, relé disparador *m*

tripropellant *n* SPACE tripropulsante *m*, tripropulsor *m*, THERMO tripropulsante *m*

triptane *n* CHEM triptano *m*

triptych: ~ screen *n* CINEMAT pantalla tríptica *f*

TRISEC: ~ ship *n* TRANSP barco TRISEC *m*

trisection *n* GEOM trisección *f*

trisilicate *n* CHEM trisilicato *m*

trisnitrate *n* CHEM trisnitrato *m*

trisodium¹ *adj* CHEM trisódico

trisodium²: **~ phosphate** *n* (*TSP*) DETERG fosfato trisódico *m* (*TSP*)

tristearin *n* CHEM triestearato de glicerina *m*, triestearina *f*

tristimulus: ~ paint *n* P&R pintura triestímulo *f*; **~ signal** *n* TV señal tricromática *f*

trisubstituted *adj* CHEM trisustituido

tritan *n* CHEM tritano *m*

trithionic *adj* CHEM tritiónico

tritiated¹ *adj* NUCL *coil* tritiado

tritiated²: **~ compound** *n* NUCL *labelled with tritium* compuesto irradiado con tritio *m*, compuesto tritiado *m*

triticin *n* CHEM triticina *f*

tritium *n* CHEM, PHYS tritio *m*; **~ extraction** *n* NUCL *ring winding* extracción de tritio *f*

tritoxide *n* CHEM tritóxido *m*

triturate *vt* CHEM triturar

trituration *n* CHEM trituración *f*

triturator *n* MECH ENG triturador *m*

trityl *n* CHEM tritilo *m*

trivalence *n* CHEM trivalencia *f*

trivalency *n* CHEM trivalencia *f*

trivalent *adj* CHEM trivalente

trivial: ~ name *n* CHEM *of element, compound* nombre vulgar *m*; **~ slip** *n* METALL error trivial *m*

trochoidal: ~ mass analyser *n BrE* NUCL analizador trocoidal de masas *m*; **~ mass analyzer** *AmE see trochoidal mass analyser BrE*; **~ mass spectrometer** *n* NUCL espectrómetro trocoidal de masas *m*

troctolite *n* PETROL troctolita *f*

troctolyte *n* PETROL troctolita *f*

troegerite *n* MINERAL trogerita *f*

troilite *n* MINERAL troilita *f*

Trojan: ~ horse *n* COMP&DP caballo de Troya *m*, caballo troyano *m*

troll *n* OCEAN curricán *m*

troller *n* OCEAN curricanero *m*

trolley *n* LAB *founding* carrillo *m*, NUCL *of a batch* carro *m*, PRINT caja con ruedas para transportar libros *f*, PROD *of overhead travelling crane, ropeway* carro de rodadura *m*, TRANSP trole *m*

trolleybus *n* TRANSP trolebús *m*

trolling: ~ fishing *n* OCEAN pesca a la cacea *f*, pesca al curricán *f*

trommel: ~ screen *n* COAL criba de tambor *f*, tromel *m*; **~ washer** *n* COAL lavador de tromel *m*

trona *n* MINERAL trona *f*

troop: ~~carrying vehicle *n* MILIT vehículo de transporte de tropas *m*

troopship *n* MILIT buque de transporte de tropas *m*

troostite *n* METALL, MINERAL troostita *f*

tropic *adj* CHEM *acid* trópico

tropical: ~ **air** *n* METEO aire tropical *m*; ~ **calm** *n* OCEAN calma tropical *f*; ~ **calms** *n pl* METEO calmas tropicales *f pl*; ~ **climate** *n* METEO clima tropical *m*; ~ **cyclone** *n* METEO ciclón tropical *m*; ~ **packaging** *n* PACK embalaje para climas tropicales *m*; ~ **revolving storm** *n* METEO tempestad tropical *f*

tropine *n* CHEM *compound* tropina *f*

tropopause *n* METEO tropopausa *f*

troposphere *n* METEO, SPACE troposfera *f*

tropospheric: ~ **scatter** *n* TELECOM dispersión troposférica *f*

trotyl *n* CHEM trotilo *m*

troubleshooter *n* MECH ENG buscador y reparador de averías *m*, especialista *m*, técnico en reparaciones *m*

trough *n* AGRIC bebedero *m*, C&G *used in manufacture of container glass* canal *m*, CONST artesa *f*, GEOL depresión *f*, LAB *founding* tina *f*, batea *f*, cuba *f*, METEO vaguada *f*, MINE gamella *f*, artesa *f*, OCEAN hondonada *f*, depresión angosta *f*, PROD bebedero *m*, cuba *f*, artesa *f*, WATER TRANSP *of wave* seno *m*; ~ **compass** *n* PROD brújula declinatoria *f*; ~ **conveyor** *n* PROD transportador de cinta cóncava *m*, transportador de cubetas *m*; ~ **cross-bedding** *n* GEOL estratificación cruzada en surco *f*; ~ **gutter** *n* CONST *building* canalón *m*; ~ **lip** *n* C&G labio del canal *m*; ~ **mixer** *n* C&G mezclador de canal *m*; ~ **washer** *n* MINE lavadora de cubetas *f*

trowel *n* CONST paleta *f* (*AmL*)

troy: ~ **ounce** *n* METR onza troy *f*; ~ **weight** *n* METR peso troy *m*

truck *n* AmE (*cf bogie BrE*, *cf lorry BrE*) AUTO camión *m*, bogie *m* (*Esp*), boje *m* (*AmL*), carretilla *f*, carretón *m*, remolque *m*, remolque articulado *m* (*AmL*), trailer *m* (*Esp*), vagón de mercancías *m*, GEN, MECH ENG, TRANSP vagón, WATER TRANSP *of mast* galleta *f*, perilla *f*; ~ **bolster** *n* AmE (*cf bogie bolster BrE*) RAIL *vehicles* traviesa del pivote del bogie *f*, traviesa del pivote del carretón *f*; ~ **car** *n* AmE (*cf truck wagon BrE*) TRANSP furgón *m*; ~ **car with swiveling roof** *n* AmE (*cf bogie wagon with swivelling roof BrE*) TRANSP carretón con techo giratorio *m*, furgón con techo corredizo *m*; ~ **crop** *n* AGRIC cultivo de hortalizas que se comercializan frescas *m*; ~ **factor** *n* AmE (*cf lorry factor BrE*) TRANSP factor de camión *m*; ~ **frame** AmE (*cf bogie frame BrE*) RAIL bastidor del bogie *m*, bastidor del carretón *m*; ~ **open self-discharge car** *n* AmE (*cf bogie open self-discharge wagon BrE*) TRANSP *railway* carretón de descarga auto-basculante *m*, vagón de auto-descarga con caja abierta *m*; ~ **pin** *n* AmE (*cf bogie pin BrE*) VEH pivote de remolque *m*, pivote del bogie *m*, pivote del enganche *m*; ~ **pivot** *n* AmE VEH pivote de arrastre *m*, pivote de remolque *m*, pivote del bogie *m*; ~ **shed** *n* AmE (*cf wagon shed BrE*) RAIL depósito de vagones *m*; **~-to-truck handling** *n* TRANSP manipulación de camión a camión *f*; **~-to-truck operation** *n* TRANSP operación de camión a camión *f*; **~-to-truck system** *n* TRANSP sistema de camión a camión *m*; ~ **wagon** *n* BrE (*cf truck car AmE*) TRANSP furgón *m*

trucked: ~ **troops** *n* AmE (*cf lorried troops BrE*) MILIT tropas transportadas por camión *f pl*

true[1]: ~ **airspeed** *n* (*TAS*) AIR TRANSP velocidad anemométrica verdadera *f*, velocidad verdadera *f*; ~ **anomaly** *n* SPACE anomalía real *f*, irregularidad

real *f*; ~ **course** *n* WATER TRANSP *navigation* rumbo verdadero *m*; ~ **density** *n* NUCL densidad verdadera *f*; ~ **digestibility** *n* AGRIC digestibilidad real *f*; **~-false check** *n* PROD verificación verdadero-falso *f*; ~ **fracture stress** *n* METALL esfuerzo de rotura uniforme *m*; ~ **half-width** *n* RAD PHYS verdadero espesor del valor mitad *m*; ~ **middlings** *n pl* COAL mixtos puros *m pl*, mixtos verdaderos *m pl*; ~ **motion** *n* WATER TRANSP *radar* movimiento verdadero *m*; ~ **north** *n* WATER TRANSP *navigation* norte verdadero *m*; ~ **pitch** *n* MECH ENG *of screw* paso real *m*; ~ **strain** *n* METALL tensión rectilínea *f*; ~ **stress** *n* METALL carga real *f*; **~-to-false transition** *n* PROD transición de verdadero a falso *f*; ~ **wind** *n* WATER TRANSP *navigation* viento verdadero *m*

true[2] *vt* MECH ENG alinear, centrar, corregir, enderezar, nivelar, rectificar; ~ **up** *vt* C&G alinear, MECH ENG afinar, alisar, centrar, igualar, nivelar, poner a escuadra, pulir, rebajar, retocar

truing *n* C&G alineación *f*; ~ **wheel** *n* MECH ENG muela rectificadora *f*, rueda rectificadora *f*

truncate *vt* COMP&DP, GEOM truncar

truncated: ~ **cone** *n* GEOM cono truncado *m*; **~-cone abrasive sheet** *n* MECH ENG chapa abrasiva de cono truncado *f*, hoja abrasiva de cono truncado *f*; ~ **pyramid** *n* GEOM pirámide truncada *f*; ~ **test** *n* SPACE prueba truncada *f*

truncating *n* GEOM truncamiento *m*

truncation *n* COMP&DP ruptura *f*, truncación *f*, GEOM truncamiento *m*; ~ **error** *n* COMP&DP error de ruptura *m*, error de truncamiento *m*

trunk *n* AUTO (*cf boot BrE*) funda *f*, maletero *m*, portaequipajes *m*, portamaletas *m*, COMP&DP (*cf link*) conductor común *m*, enlace de comunicaciones *m*, bus *m*, canal de comunicación *m* (*AmL*), conexión *f*, enlace *m*, eslabón de comunicación *m*, tronco *m*, MINE tina *f*, conducto *m*, cubeta *f*, TELECOM línea troncal *f*, línea troncal principal *f*, troncal *m*, tronco *m*, arteria *f*, enlace común *m*, línea *f*, línea auxiliar *f*, línea de enlace *f*, línea de unión *f*; ~ **cable** *n* ELEC ENG cable arterial *m*, cable de enlace *m*, TELECOM cable de unión *m*, cable para líneas auxiliares *m*, cable troncal *m*; ~ **channel** *n* TELECOM canal principal *m*, canal principal de una red *m*, vía principal *f*, vía principal de una red *f*; ~ **code** *n* (*TC*) TELECOM código interurbano *m*; ~ **distribution frame** *n* (*TDF*) TELECOM repartidor principal *m*; ~ **exchange** *n* TELECOM central interurbana *f*; ~ **feeder** *n* ELEC *supply* alimentador principal *m*, cable de unión de dos centrales generadoras *m*; ~ **handle** *n* AmE (*cf boot handle BrE*) VEH asa del portaequipajes *f*, manilla de apertura del maletero *f*; ~ **lid** *n* AmE (*cf boot lid BrE*) VEH tapa del maletero *f*; ~ **line** *n* ELEC *supply network* línea principal *f*, PETROL línea troncal *f*, RAIL línea principal *f*; ~ **main** *n* ELEC *supply* conductor principal *m*; ~ **network** *n* TELECOM red interurbana *f*; ~ **offer** *n* (*TKO*) TELECOM enlace de oferta *m*; ~ **piston engine** *n* WATER TRANSP máquina de pistón tubular *f*; ~ **switching** *n* TELECOM conexión *f*, conexión telefónica *f*; ~ **switching center** *n* AmE; ~ **switching centre** *n* BrE TELECOM centro de conexiones telefónicas *m*, centro de conexión *m*; **~-switching exchange area** *n* TELECOM red telefónica urbana de conexiones *f*, zona telefónica de conexiones *f*; ~ **system** *n* TELECOM sistema de conexiones *m*, sistema de enlaces *m*; ~ **transit exchange** *n* TELECOM central interurbana de tránsito *f*

trunked: ~ **dispatch system** *n* TELECOM sistema de expedición de enlaces *m*

trunking *n* ELEC ENG, TELECOM circuito de unión *m*, enlace *m*

trunkline: ~ **wiring** *n* PROD, TELECOM cableado del circuito principal *m*

trunnel *n* (*cf treenail*) CONST espiga *f*

trunnion *n* MECH muñón *m*, soporte giratorio *m*, MECH ENG amarre *m*, brida *f*, fijación *f*, gorrón *m*, muñón *m*, soporte giratorio *m*, NUCL *cockpit* muñón *m*, VEH soporte giratorio *m*

truss *n* CONST armadura de cubierta *f*; ~ **bridge** *n* CONST puente de celosía *m*; ~ **rod** *n* CONST *building* tirante de armadura *m*

trussed: ~ **beam** *n* CONST viga atirantada *f*, *underbraced type* viga armada *f*; ~ **girder** *n* CONST viga de celosía *f*; ~ **roof** *n* CONST techo reforzado *m*; ~ **wooden beam** *n* CONST *underbraced type* viga de celosía de madera reforzada *f*

trussing *n* CONST armadura *f*

trusted: ~ **functionality** *n* TELECOM funcionalidad fiable *f*

truth: ~ **quark** *n* PART PHYS quark verdad *m*; ~ **table** *n* COMP&DP tabla de decisión lógica *f*, tabla de verdad *f*

truxillic *adj* CHEM truxílico

truxilline *n* CHEM truxilina *f*

try[1]: ~ **cock** *n* WATER grifo de comprobación *m*; ~ **plane** *n* CONST cepillo de rafinar *m*; ~ **square** *n* MECH ENG escuadra *f*, escuadra de comprobación *f*, escuadra para verificar *f*

try[2] *vt* CONST *with trying plane* refinar; ~ **up** *vt* CONST *with trying plane* alisar, refinar

trying: ~-**up machine** *n* MECH ENG máquina de comprobación *f*, máquina de igualar tablillas *f*

tryout: ~ **facility** *n* MECH ENG dispositivo de comprobación *m*, equipo de ensayo *m*, instalación de prueba *f*; ~ **press** *n* MECH ENG prensa de comprobación *f*

tryptic *adj* CHEM tríptico

tryptomin *n* CHEM triptomin *m*

tryptomine *n* CHEM triptomina *f*

trysail *n* WATER TRANSP *sailing* vela de capa *f*

T-S: ~ **diagram** *n* OCEAN diagrama de temperatura-salinidad *m*

TS: ~ **network** *n* TELECOM red TS *f*

TSAP *abbr* (*transport service access point*) TELECOM punto de acceso al servicio de transmisión *m*

tscheffkinite *n* MINERAL tscheffkinita *f*

tschermakite *n* MINERAL tschernakita *f*

tschermigite *n* MINERAL tschermigita *f*

tschewkinite *n* MINERAL tscheffkinita *f*

T-section *n* ELECTRON sección en T *f*

T-shaped *adj* GEOM, MECH ENG en T, en forma de T

TSI *abbr* (*time slot interchanger*) TELECOM intercambiador de segmento de tiempo *m*

T-slot *n* (*tee slot*) MECH ENG ranura en T *f*; ~ **cutter** *n* MECH ENG fresa para acanaladuras en T *f*, herramienta de corte de ranuras en T *f*

TSP *abbr* (*trisodium phosphate*) DETERG TSP (*fosfato trisódico*)

T-square *n* MECH ENG cuadrado en T *m*, escuadra en T *f*, regla T *f*

T-stage *n* (*time stage*) TELECOM etapa de temporización *f*, etapa temporizadora *f*

T-stop *n* CINEMAT, PHOTO, TV abertura T *f*

tsunami *n* GEOPHYS, OCEAN tsunami *m*

TT: ~ **milk** *n* FOOD leche TT *f*

T-tail *n* AIR TRANSP *aircraft* cola en T *f*

TTC *abbr* (*tracking telemetry and command*) SPACE *communications* TTC (*telemetría y control de rastreo*)

TTL[1] *abbr* (*transistor-transistor logic*) COMP&DP lógica transistor-transistor *f*, ELECTRON CLTT (*circuito lógico de transistor a transistor*)

TTL[2]: ~ **light meter** *n* (*through-the-lens light meter*) CINEMAT fotómetro a través del objetivo *m*; ~ **logic family** *n* ELECTRON familia de CLTT *f*

t-t-t *abbr* (*time-temperature-tolerance*) REFRIG *of frozen food* t-t-t (*tiempo-temperatura-tolerancia*)

TTY *abbr* (*teletype*) COMP&DP, TELECOM TTY (*teletipo*), impresor telegráfico *m*

TU *abbr* TELECOM (*tributary unit*) unidad tributaria *f*, TELECOM (*traffic unit*) unidad de tráfico *f*

tub[1] *n* MINE caldero *m* (*AmL*), cangilón *m* (*Esp*), cubeta *f* (*AmL*), vagoneta *f*, PACK barril *m*, PROD cuba *f*, tina *f*, tonel *m*; ~ **controller** *n* MINE regulador de vagonetas *m*; ~ **wheel** *n* MECH ENG *emery cup-wheel* muela abrasiva de núcleo entrante *f*, rueda cilíndrica *f*

tub[2] *vt* MINE blindar, entubar, revestir (*AmL*)

tubbing *n* MINE entubación *f*, entubado *m*

tube *n* CONST *of lock* tubo *m*, *of key* cañón *m*, ELECTRON válvula electrónica *f*, tubo *m*, FUELLESS *flat plate collector*, GAS tubo *m*, HYDRAUL válvula *f*, LAB, OPT, PHYS tubo *m*, SPACE *communications* tubo *m*, estopín *m*, válvula *f*, TEXTIL tubo *m*; ~-**and-steel drill** *n* MECH ENG broca de tubos y acero *f*; ~ **bend** *n* MECH ENG codo *m*, codo de tubo *m*; ~ **brush** *n* LAB escobillón *m*; ~ **bundle** *n* NUCL *materials* haz tubular *m*; ~ **center** *AmE*, ~ **centre** *BrE n* INSTR hueco del tubo *m*; ~ **clip** *n* CONST abrazadera del tubo *f*; ~-**closing machine** *n* PACK cerradora de tubos *f*; ~ **column** *n* CONST columna tubular *f*; ~ **cutter** *n* LAB cortatubos *m*, MECH ENG cortador de tubo *m*, cortatubos *m*; ~-**drawing mandrel** *n* MECH ENG mandril extractor de tubos *m*; ~-**drawing press** *n* PROD prensa para estirar tubos *f*; ~ **expander** *n* CONST extensor de tubos *m*; ~-**filling and closing machine** *n* PACK máquina de llenado y cierre de tubos *f*; ~ **and fin radiator** *n* AUTO radiador de tubos y aletas *m*; ~ **gage** *AmE*, ~ **gauge** *BrE n* MECH ENG calibrador de tubos *m*, galga de tubo *f*; ~ **holder** *n* LAB portatubos *m*; ~ **mill** *n* COAL molino tubular *m*; ~ **neck** *n* TV cuello del tubo *m*; ~ **paint** *n* COLOUR pintura para tubos *f*; ~ **plate** *n* NUCL placa tubular *f*; ~-**scraper** *n* PROD limpiatubos *m*, rasqueta para tubos de caldera *f*; ~-**screwing machine** *n* MECH ENG máquina de aterrajar *f*, máquina de filetear tubos *f*, máquina roscadora de tubos *f*, roscadora de tubos *f*, terraja *f*; ~ **socket** *n* ELEC ENG soporte de tubo electrónico *m*, zócalo de tubo *m*; ~ **thickness gage** *AmE*, ~ **thickness gauge** *BrE n* NUCL galga de espesor de tubos *f*; ~-**type heat exchanger** *n* MECH ENG intercambiador de calor tubular *m*, termocanjeador de tubos *m*, termopermutador de tubos *m*; ~ **vehicle** *n* TRANSP vehículo subterráneo *m*; ~ **vehicle system** *n* (*TVS*) TRANSP sistema de vehículos subterráneos *m*, sistema de vehículos de tubos *m*; ~ **vise** *AmE see tube vice BrE*; ~ **vice** *n* BrE MECH ENG tornillo de tubos *m*; ~ **works** *n* PROD fábrica de tubos *f*; ~ **wrench** *n* MECH ENG llave de tubo *f*

tubeless: ~ **tire** *AmE*, ~ **tyre** *BrE n* VEH neumático sin cámara *m*

tuberin *n* CHEM tuberina *f*

tubing *n* CONST *system of tubes* sistema de tuberías *f*, FUELLESS *drilling*, PETROL tubería *f*; ~ **anchor** *n* PETR TECH anclaje de la tubería de producción *m*; ~ **glass** *n* C&G vidrio para tubos *m*; ~ **hanger** *n* PETROL sujeción para tubería de bombeo *f*

tubular[1] *adj* PROD tubular

tubular[2]: ~ **air heater** *n* HEAT calentador de aire tubular *m*; ~ **boiler** *n* FOOD caldera tubular *f*; ~ **ceramic capacitor** *n* ELEC ENG condensador cerámico tubular *m*; ~ **cooler** *n* FOOD refrigerador tubular *m*; ~ **dryer** *n* TEXTIL secadora tubular *f*; ~ **frame** *n* VEH bastidor tubular *m*, marco tubular *m*; ~ **furnace boiler** *n* HYDRAUL caldera de hogar tubular *f*; ~ **lamp** *n* ELEC lámpara tubular *f*; ~ **motor** *n* TRANSP motor tubular *m*; ~ **radiator** *n* AUTO radiador tubular *m*; ~ **scaffolding** *n* CONST andamiaje tubular *m*; ~ **sensor** *n* PROD sensor tubular *m*; ~ **transportation** *n* TRANSP transporte tubular *m*

Tuchel: ~ **connector** *n* CINEMAT conector Tuchel *m*

tuck: ~**-in closure** *n* PACK cierre remetiendo los bordes *m*; ~**-in flap** *n* PACK aleta para remeter *f*

tucking: ~ **blade** *n* PRINT cuchilla plegadora *f*; ~ **blades cylinder** *n* PRINT cilindro de cuchillas de solapa *m*

tuckstone *n* C&G cubretasa *f*

tue: ~ **iron** *n* AIR TRANSP, PHYS, PROD *blast furnace* tobera *f*

tufa *n* CONST, GEOL, PETR TECH, PETROL toba *f*

tuff *n* PETR TECH, PETROL toba *f*; ~ **deposit** *n* GEOL depósito de toba volcánica *m*

tuft *n* TEXTIL copo *m*

tufted: ~ **carpet** *n* TEXTIL alfombra empenachada *f*

tufting *n* AGRIC transplante de macollos *m*

tug *n* PETROL remolque *m*, WATER TRANSP remolcador *m*; ~ **aircraft** *n* AIR TRANSP avión remolcador *m*

TUG *abbr* (*tributary-unit group*) TELECOM grupo de unidad tributaria *m*

tugboat *n* MAR POLL remolcador *m*

tumble: ~ **dryer** *n* TEXTIL secadora por centrifugado *f*, secadora por volteo *f*; ~ **printing** *n* PRINT impresión a blanco y voltereta *f*

tumblehome *n* WATER TRANSP *ship building* cierre de boca *m*, entrada de obra muerta *f*

tumbler *n* AUTO, C&G tambor *m*, CONST *of lock* pestillo *m*, PROD tambor *m*, tumbador *m*, WATER *of dredge* prisma *m*, tambor *m*; ~ **lock** *n* CONST cerradura con pestillo *f*; ~ **switch** *n* ELEC ENG conmutador oscilante *m*, interruptor unipolar de bajo voltaje *m*

tumbleweed *n* AGRIC yuyo bola *m*

tumbling *n* PROD *founding* desarenado en el tambor giratorio *m*; ~ **barrel** *n* PROD tambor de limpieza *m*, tambor giratorio *m*; ~ **box** *n* PROD tambor giratorio *m*; ~ **drum** *n* PROD tambor giratorio *m*; ~ **mill** *n* PROD tambor giratorio *m*; ~ **shaft** *n* MECH ENG eje de levas *m*, *reverse-shaft* eje de inversión de marcha *m*, eje del cambio de marcha *m*

tuna: ~ **boat** *n* OCEAN atunero *m*

tunable: ~ **klystron** *n* SPACE klistron sintonizable *m*; ~ **magnetron** *n* ELECTRON magnetrón sintonizable *m*; ~ **oscillator** *n* ELECTRON oscilador sintonizable *m*

tune *vt* ACOUST acordar, sintonizar, afinar, AUTO, ELECTRON ajustar, sintonizar, TELECOM acordar, ajustar a resonancia, sintonizar, TV sintonizar, WAVE PHYS afinar, sintonizar

tuned[1] *adj* ACOUST, ELECTRON, TELECOM, TV, WAVE PHYS sintonizado

tuned[2]: ~ **amplifier** *n* ELECTRON amplificador sintonizado *m*; ~ **circuit** *n* ELECTRON circuito sintonizado *m*, PHYS circuito ajustado *m*; ~ **filter** *n* ELECTRON filtro ajustado *m*; ~ **impedance bond** *n* RAIL conexión inductiva reglada *f*; ~ **relay** *n* ELEC relé de resonancia *m*; ~ **transformer** *n* ELEC, ELEC ENG transformador sintonizado *m*

tuner *n* ACOUST sintonizador *m*, ELECTRON sintonizador *m*, unidad de sintonización *f*, RAD PHYS sintonizador *m*, TELECOM bloque de sintonía *m*, sintonizador *m*, unidad de sintonización *f*, TV sintonizador *m*, unidad de sintonización *f*

tungstate *n* CHEM tungstato *m*

tungsten *n* (*W*) CHEM, ELEC ENG, METALL tungsteno *m* (*W*), wolframio *m* (*W*); ~ **carbide** *n* MECH ENG carburo al tungsteno *m*, PETR TECH carburo de volframio *m*, carga de tungsteno *f*; ~**-carbide grit hole saw** *n* MECH ENG broca hueca cilíndrica con bordes de sierra de carburo al tungsteno *f*, sierra de perforación de filo de polvo de carburo al tungsteno *f*; ~**-carbide tooling** *n* MECH ENG equipo de herramientas de carburo al tungsteno *m*, maquinado con carburo al tungsteno *m*; ~**-carbide wire-drawing die** *n* MECH ENG trefilador de carburo al tungsteno *m*; ~**-carbide-tipped turning and planing tool** *n* MECH ENG herramienta de tornear y planear de placa de carburo al tungsteno *f*; ~ **filament** *n* ELEC *of lamp* filamento de tungsteno *m*; ~ **film** *n* CINEMAT película de tungsteno *f*; ~ **inert gas welding** *n* (*TIG welding*) CONST soldadura de tungsteno a gas inerte *f*; ~ **lighting** *n* CINEMAT iluminación de tungsteno *f*; ~ **spatter** *n* CONST salpicadura de tungsteno *f*; ~**-to-daylight** *n* CINEMAT lámpara de tungsteno a luz de día *f*

tungstic[1] *adj* CHEM túngstico

tungstic[2]: ~ **acid** *n* CHEM ácido túngstico *m*

tungstosilicate *n* CHEM tungstosilicato *m*

tuning *n* ACOUST afinación *f*, sintonización *f*, sintonía *f*, AUTO ajuste *m*, sintonización *f*, ELECTRON, RAD PHYS, TELECOM, TV, WATER TRANSP *of radar, radio* sintonización *f*, sintonía *f*; ~ **capacitor** *n* ELEC ENG condensador de sintonización *m*; ~ **characteristic** *n* RAD PHYS característica de sintonización *f*; ~ **circuit** *n* ELEC ENG circuito de sintonización *m*, ELECTRON circuito de sintonía *m*, TELECOM circuito de sintonía *m*, circuito sintonizable *m*, circuito sintonizador *m*; ~ **coil** *n* ELECTRON bobina de sintonización *f*, MILIT *army signals* bobina de sintonía *f*; ~ **indicator** *n* ELECTRON indicador de sintonización *m*; ~ **range** *n* RAD PHYS rango de sintonización *m*; ~ **screw** *n* ELEC ENG tornillo de sintonización *m*, PHYS tornillo de ajuste *m*; ~ **screwdriver** *n* MECH ENG destornillador de afinación *m*, destornillador de reglaje *m*, destornillador de sintonización *m*

tunnel *n* GEN túnel *m*; ~ **bar** *n* CONST *rock-drill mounting* perforadora de túneles *f*; ~**-boring machine** *n* CONST perforadora de túneles *f*; ~ **diode** *n* ELECTRON diodo Esaki *m*, diodo túnel *m*, PHYS diodo túnel *m*; ~**-diode amplifier** *n* SPACE *communications* amplificador por diodo de efecto túnel *m*; ~ **effect** *n* ELECTRON, PHYS, TRANSP efecto túnel *m*; ~ **kiln** *n* C&G, HEAT horno de túnel *m*; ~ **lehr** *n* C&G

templador de túnel *m*; ~ **vault** *n* CONST bóveda del túnel *f*

tunneling *AmE see tunnelling BrE*

tunnelling *n BrE* CONST perforación de túneles *f*, ELECTRON efecto túnel *m*, MINE perforación de túneles *f*, tunelización *f*; ~ **machine** *n BrE* CONST perforadora de túneles *f*, MINE máquina de tunelización *f*; ~ **mode** *n BrE* TELECOM modo de efecto túnel *m*; ~ **ray** *n BrE* TELECOM rayo de efecto túnel *m*; ~ **technique** *n BrE* CONST, MINE técnica de construcción de túneles *f*; ~ **work** *n BrE* CONST, MINE perforación de túneles *f*

tunny: ~ **boat** *n* OCEAN atunero *m*, cerquero atunero *m*, palangrero atunero *m*; ~ **fish net** *n* OCEAN almadraba *f*; ~ **fishery** *n* OCEAN almadraba *f*; ~ **net** *n* OCEAN almadraba *f*

tup *n* PROD *of pile-driver, drop-test machine* maza *f*, *of power hammer* calzo *m*; ~ **die** *n* PROD *power hammer* calzo de maza de martinete *m*; ~ **pallet** *n* PROD *of power hammer* espiga de apoyo de la maza *f*, estampa inferior *f*

turbid[1] *adj* WATER turbio

turbid[2]: ~ **water** *n* POLL, WATER agua turbia *f*

turbidimeter *n* CHEM, OCEAN turbidímetro *m*

turbidimetry *n* CHEM turbidimetría *f*

turbidite *n* GEOL turbidita *f*

turbidity *n* CHEM turbidez *f*, FUELLESS turbiedad *f*, HYDROL turbidez *f*; ~ **coefficient** *n* FUELLESS coeficiente de turbiedad *m*; ~ **current** *n* GEOL corriente de turbidez *f*, OCEAN corriente de fango *f*; ~ **layer** *n* OCEAN capa de turbidez *f*; ~ **meter** *n* CHEM nefelómetro *m*, LAB *ring winding* nefelómetro *m*, turbidímetro *m* (*Esp*), OCEAN turbidímetro *m*

turbine *n* GEN turbina *f*; ~ **blade** *n* MECH ENG pala de turbina *f*, paleta de turbina *f*, WATER TRANSP aleta de turbina *f*, álabe de turbina *m*; ~ **building** *n* NUCL edificio de turbinas *m*, sala de turbinas *f*; ~ **bypass system** *n* NUCL sistema de alivio de vapor al condensador *m*, sistema de baipás de la turbina *m*; ~ **casing** *n* WATER TRANSP carcasa de turbina *f*, envuelta de turbina *f*; ~ **chamber** *n* HYDRAUL cámara de turbina *f*; ~ **drilling** *n* PETR TECH perforación con turbina *f*; ~ **efficiency** *n* FUELLESS rendimiento de turbina *m*; ~ **engine** *n* AIR TRANSP, AUTO motor de turbina *m*, ELEC ENG turbomotor *m*, WATER TRANSP turbomotor *m*, turbomáquina *f*; ~ **fuel** *n* SPACE combustible de turbina *m*; ~ **house** *n* NUCL sala de turbinas *f*; ~ **meter** *n* GAS medidor de turbina *m*; ~ **milk cooler** *n* AGRIC, REFRIG enfriador de leche por turbina *m*; ~ **output** *n* FUELLESS rendimiento de turbina *m*; ~ **pit** *n* HYDRAUL cámara de turbinas *f*; ~ **propulsion** *n* WATER TRANSP turbopropulsión *f*; ~ **pump** *n* HYDRAUL bomba centrífuga con difusor *f*, bomba de turbina *f*, turbobomba *f*; ~ **seating** *n* WATER TRANSP polín de la turbina *m*; ~ **stop valve** *n* NUCL válvula de admisión de la turbina *f*; ~ **vessel** *n* WATER TRANSP buque de turbinas *m*, nave de turbinas *f*, turbonave *f*; ~ **wheel** *n* HYDRAUL rotor de turbina *m*, rueda de turbina *f*, WATER TRANSP rotor de turbina *m*; ~ **wheel with vanes** *n* HYDRAUL rueda de turbina con paletas *f*

turbine-engined: ~ **lorry** *n BrE* (*cf turbine-engined truck AmE*) AUTO camión con motor de turbina *m*; ~ **truck** *AmE n* (*cf turbine-engined lorry BrE*) AUTO camión con motor de turbina *m*

turbo: ~~**alternator** *n* ELEC *generator*, ELEC ENG turboalternador *m*: ~~**ramjet** *n* TRANSP turborreactor a postcombustión *m*; ~~**stapler** *n* TEXTIL cortadora con turbina *f*; ~~**top** *n* TEXTIL peinado mediante turbina *m*

turbocharged: ~ **engine** *n* WATER TRANSP *diesel* motor diesel sobrealimentado *m*, motor sobrealimentado *m*

turbocharger *n* MECH ENG turbosobrealimentador *m*, turbosoplante *m*, VEH turbocompresor *m*, WATER TRANSP *engines* turbosoplante *m*

turbocharging *n* WATER TRANSP *of engine* sobrealimentación *f*

turbocompressor *n* WATER TRANSP turbocompresor *m*

turbocruiser *n* WATER TRANSP turbocrucero *m*

turbodrilling *n* PETR TECH, PETROL turboperforación *f*

turboelectric *adj* ELEC ENG, TRANSP turboeléctrico

turboexpander *n* REFRIG turbina de expansión *f*

turbofan *n* AIR TRANSP *engine* turborreactor con soplante turbofan *m*, TRANSP turbohélice *f*; ~ **engine** *n* MECH ENG motor de turbo ventilador *m*, THERMO *vibration test* motor turboventilador *m*

turbogenerator *n* ELEC ENG turboalternador *m*, turbodínamo *m*, turbogenerador *m*

turbojet *n* AIR TRANSP *engine* turbina de reacción *f*, turborreactor *m*, THERMO turborreactor *m*; ~ **engine** *n* THERMO motor turborreactor *m*

turbomixer *n* PROD turbomezclador *m*

turbomolecular *adj* MECH ENG *pump* turbomolecular

turboprop *n* AIR TRANSP turbohélice *f*

turbopropeller *n* AIR TRANSP turbohélice *f*

turbopump *n* SPACE, WATER, WATER TRANSP turbobomba *f*

turboreactor *n* THERMO turborreactor *m*

turboseparation *n* FOOD turboseparación *f*

turbosupercharger *n* AUTO turbocompresor *m*, turbosobrealimentador *m*

turbotrain *n* RAIL, TRANSP turbotren *m*

turbulence *n* AIR TRANSP, AUTO, FUELLESS, METEO, SPACE turbulencia *f*; ~ **chamber** *n* AUTO cámara de turbulencia *f*; ~ **combustion chamber** *n* AUTO cámara de combustión de turbulencia *f*; ~~**generating grid** *n* FLUID rejilla generadora de turbulencia *f*

turbulent[1] *adj* FLUID, METEO turbulento

turbulent[2]: ~ **boundary layer** *n* FLUID capa límite turbulenta *f* (*Esp*); ~ **diffusion** *n* NUCL difusión turbulenta *f*; ~ **flow** *n* FLUID flujo turbulento *m*; ~ **layer** *n* METEO capa turbulenta *f*; ~ **plug** *n* FLUID islote de turbulencia *m*; ~ **reattachment** *n* FLUID readherencia de turbulencia *f*; ~ **separation** *n* FLUID separación turbulenta *f*; ~ **spot** *n* FLUID punto de turbulencia *m*; ~ **stream** *n* GAS corriente turbulenta *f*

turgite *n* MINERAL turgita *f*

turgor *n* FOOD turgor *m*

Turing: ~ **machine** *n* COMP&DP máquina Turing *f*

turmeric *n* CHEM cúrcuma *f*

turn[1] *n* ELEC *winding* espira *f*, ELEC ENG espira *f*, marcha *f*, MECH ENG *revolution* giro *m*, vuelta *f*, rotación *f*, revolución *f*, OCEAN *screen* repunte *m*, PHYS vuelta *f*, WATER TRANSP *of tide* repunte *m*; ~~**and-bank indicator** *n AmE* (*cf bank-and-pitch indicator BrE*) AIR TRANSP indicador de inclinación y cabeceo *m*, indicador de viraje e inclinación *m*; ~ **bar** *n* PRINT barra desviadora *f*; ~ **bridge** *n* CONST puente giratorio *m*, puente pivotante *m*; ~~**off** *n* ELEC ENG apagado *m*, corte *m*, desactivación *f*; ~~**off pulse** *n* ELECTRON impulso de interrupción *m*; ~~**off time** *n*

ELEC ENG tiempo de desconexión *m*; ~-on *n* CINEMAT encendido *m*, ELEC ENG conexión *f*, encendido *m*; ~-on pulse *n* ELECTRON impulso de conexión *m*; ~-on time *n* ELEC ENG tiempo de activación *m*, ELECTRON momento de conexión *m*; ~ plough *n* BrE AGRIC vertedera *f*; ~ plow *AmE see turn plough BrE*; ~ pulley *n* PROD polea de retorno *f*; ~ ratio *n* ELEC *transformer* razón de espiras *f*, razón de transformación *f*, relación de transformación *f*, relación de vueltas *f*; ~-to-turn winding *n* ELEC devanado entre espiras *m*

turn² *vt* MECH ENG tornear; ~ full on *vt* MECH ENG abrir completamente; ~ off *vt* CINEMAT apagar, ELEC ENG apagar, desactivar, desconectar, ELECTRON desconectar, interrumpir, poner a cero, PROD cerrar, desactivar, *electronics* cilindrar en el torno, WATER *tap* cerrar; ~ on *vt* ELEC ENG conectar, activar, encender, PROD abrir, encender, WATER *tap* abrir

turn³ *vi* SPACE dar vueltas, girar, virar, WATER TRANSP *navigation* evolucionar, realizar una evolución; ~ turtle *vi* WATER TRANSP enseñar la quilla al sol

turnaround *n* AIR TRANSP *airports* área de viraje *f*, *of aircraft* demora *f*; ~ card *n* PROD tarjeta de inversión *f*, tarjeta de recorrido *f*, tarjeta de viaje redondo *f*; ~ directive *n* PROD documento de respuesta *m*, orden de inspección general *f*, tiempo de respuesta *m*; ~ document *n* PROD documento de respuesta *m*, documento de carga y descarga *m*; ~ time *n* COMP&DP tiempo de cambio de sentido *m*, tiempo de giro total *m*, PROD tiempo de espera *m*, tiempo de respuesta *m*, tiempo de retorno *m*, RAIL, TELECOM tiempo de inversión *m*, tiempo de respuesta *m*; ~ time at terminus *n* RAIL tiempo de inversión en el terminal *m*

turnbuckle *n* CONST tensor *m*, MECH, MECH ENG tensor de tornillo *m*, OCEAN, WATER TRANSP *rigging* tensor *m*

turned¹: ~-off *adj* ELEC, ELEC ENG apagado

turned²: ~-and-bored pulley *n* PROD polea torneada y taladrada *f*; ~ letter *n* PRINT letra invertida *f*; ~-up flange *n* PROD *sheet metal work* brida rebatida *f*; ~ washer *n* MECH ENG arandela torneada *f*

turning *n* COAL recodo *m*, CONST *of crane* viraje *m*, MECH ENG *lathe-work* torneado *m*; ~ basin *n* WATER TRANSP *port* dársena de maniobra *f*; ~ between centers *AmE*, ~ between centres *BrE n* MECH ENG torneado entre puntos *m*; ~ bridge *n* CONST puente de maniobras *m*; ~ carrier *n* MECH ENG carretilla de torno para metales *f*, perro de arrastre *m*; ~ circle *n* VEH círculo de rotación *m*, WATER TRANSP *shiphandling* curva de evolución *f*; ~ diamond *n* MECH ENG diamante de tornear *m*; ~ gear *n* NUCL *element*, WATER TRANSP *engine* virador *m*; ~ gouge *n* MECH ENG escoplo para tornear *m*; ~ lathe *n* MECH ENG torno *m*; ~ mill *n* MECH ENG torno de barrenas horizontal *m*; ~ movement *n* TRANSP movimiento giratorio *m*; ~-off *n* WATER interrupción *f*; ~ on the face plate *n* MECH ENG torneado en el plato liso *m*; ~ point *n* CONST *surveying* punto de cambio *m*; ~ rest *n* MECH ENG *hand-rest of lathe* apoyamanos del torno *m*, *slide-rest of lathe* soporte del carro *m*; ~ saw *n* MECH ENG sierra giratoria *f*; ~ tool *n* MECH ENG herramienta de tornear *f*; ~ tool with carbide tip *n* MECH ENG herramienta de tornear con placa de acero al carbono *f*; ~ traffic *n* TRANSP tráfico de circunvalación *m*

turnings *n pl* PROD torneaduras *f pl*, virutas de torno *f pl*

turnkey *n* CONST llave en mano *f*; ~ installation *n* MECH ENG *complete installation* instalación completa *f*, instalación llave en mano *f*; ~ project *n* MECH ENG proyecto llave en mano *m*; ~ system *n* COMP&DP sistema de llave en mano *m*

turnout *n* CONST cambio de vía *m*, desvío *m*, RAIL cambio de vía completo *m*, ciclo de ocupación de vagones *m*, vía apartadero *f*, TEXTIL atuendo *m*; ~ on the curve *n* RAIL apartadero en curva *m*

turnover *n* C&G producción del día *f*, PROD rotación *f*, volumen de negocios *m*, volumen de ventas *m*, *lamination, rolling* volvedor de chapas *m*, WATER volumen *m*

turnpin *n* CONST *plumbing* mandril ensanchador *m*

turns: ~ per inch *n pl* TEXTIL vueltas por pulgadas *f pl*; ~ per meter *n pl* TEXTIL vueltas por metro *f pl*; ~ ratio *n* AUTO relación de espiras *f*, relación de transformación *f*, relación de vueltas *f*, ELEC razón de espiras *f*, razón de transformación *f*, relación de transformación *f*, relación de vueltas *f*, ELEC ENG relación de transformación *f*, relación entre el número de espiras del secundario y del primario *f*, PHYS cociente de vueltas *m*

turnscrew *n* MECH ENG *of screwdriver*, VEH llave inglesa *f*; ~ bit *n* MECH ENG punta del destornillador *f*

turnstile: ~ aerial *n* BrE (*cf turnstile antenna AmE*) TV antena cruzada *f*; ~ antenna *AmE* (*cf turnstile aerial BrE*) TV antena cruzada *f*

turntable *n* ACOUST tocadiscos *m*, AIR TRANSP plataforma giratoria *f*, MECH mesa giratoria *f*, soporte giratorio *m*, RAIL plataforma giratoria *f*, TRANSP elevadizo *m*, placa giratoria *f*; ~ feed *n* PACK dispositivo de alimentación mediante mesa giratoria *m*

turpentine *n* CHEM, COLOUR aguarrás *m*, trementina *f*, P&R aguarrás *m*; ~ substitute *n* COLOUR sucedáneo de aguarrás *m*; ~ varnish *n* COATINGS aguarrás *m*, barniz de trementina *m*, COLOUR barniz al aguarrás *m*, barniz de trementina *m*

turquoise *n* MINERAL turquesa *f*

turret *n* CINEMAT torreta *f*, MECH portaherramientas revólver *m*, torreta *f*, MECH ENG *of lathe*, MILIT *of tank* torreta *f*; ~ camera *n* CINEMAT cámara con portaobjetivos *f*; ~ cap *n* INSTR cubierta del cabezal del portaobjetivos *f*; ~ gun *n* MILIT cañón montado en torreta *m*; ~ head *n* MECH ENG *of lathe* torreta *f*; ~-head position switch *n* PROD interruptor de posición de la torreta *m*, interruptor de posición del portaherramienta revólver *m*; ~ lathe *n* MECH, MECH ENG torno revólver *m*; ~ slide *n* MECH ENG carro de la torreta *m*

turtle *n* CINEMAT tortuga *f*; ~ culture *n* OCEAN cría de tortugas *f*

tusk: ~ tenon joint *n* CONST junta de espiga dentada *f*

tuyere *n* AIR TRANSP, PHYS, PROD tobera *f*; ~ nozzle *n* PROD bocín de tobera *m*

TV¹ *abbr* (*television*) TELECOM, TV TV (*televisión*)

TV²: ~ academy leader *n* TV director de la academia de TV *m*; ~ bulb *n* C&G cinescopio *m*; ~ cutoff *n* TV corte en TV *m*

TVC *abbr* (*thrust vector control*) SPACE TVC (*control del vector de empuje*)

TVP *abbr* (*textured vegetable protein*) FOOD PVT (*proteína vegetal texturizada*)

TVS *abbr* (*tube vehicle system*) TRANSP sistema de vehículos subterráneos *m*

tweendeck *n* WATER TRANSP *shipbuilding* entrepuente *m*

tweezers *n pl* C&G tenazas *f pl*, LAB *coil* pinzas *f pl*, tenacillas *f pl*

twelve: **~-point recorder** *n* INSTR grabador de doce puntos *m*; **~-row punched card** *n* COMP&DP tarjeta perforada de doce columnas *f*; **~ ways back up** *n* PRINT impresión a blanco y vuelta *f*, retiro de pie con cabeza *m*

twice: **~ magic nuclide** *n* NUCL nucleido doblemente mágico *m*

twilight: **~ shot** *n* PHOTO toma crepuscular *f*

twill *n* TEXTIL sarga *f*

twin[1]: **~-engined** *adj* AIR TRANSP, MECH ENG bimotor, con dos máquinas, de dos motores

twin[2] *n* C&G gemelo *m*, CRYSTALL, METALL macla *f*; **~-axial cable** *n* PROD cable de conductores axiales retorcidos *m*; **~-bagging system** *n* PACK sistema de embolsado doble *m*; **~-barreled carburetor** *AmE*, **~-barrelled carburettor** *BrE n* AUTO, VEH carburador de cuba doble *m*; **~ boundary** *n* METALL contorno de la macla *m*; **~ cable** *n* ELEC, ELEC ENG cable de dos conductores aislados *m*; **~ carburetor** *AmE*, **~ carburettor** *BrE n* AUTO, MECH, VEH carburador doble *m*, carburador de doble cuerpo *m*; **~ cards** *n pl* TEXTIL cardas dobles *f pl*; **~-choke carburetor** *AmE*, **~-choke carburettor** *BrE n* AUTO, VEH carburador de estrangulador doble *m*, carburador de mariposa doble *m*; **~ cock** *n* WATER grifo de dos caras *m*; **~-cylinder engine** *n* MECH ENG motor bicilíndrico *m*, motor de cilindros gemelos *m*, motor de dos cilindros *m*; **~ ends** *n pl* TEXTIL cabos dobles *m pl*; **~ engine** *n* TRANSP motor bicilíndrico *m*, motor de dos cilindros *m*; **~-engine jet aircraft** *n* AIR TRANSP avión bimotor a reacción *m*; **~ engines** *n pl* MECH ENG motores gemelos *m pl*; **~ formation** *n* CRYSTALL formación de maclas *f*; **~ grinder** *n* C&G esmeril doble *m*; **~-ground plate** *n* C&G vidrio plano pulido por ambos lados *m*; **~-hull ship** *n* TRANSP barco catamarán *m*; **~ interlaced scanning** *n* TV doble exploración entrelazada *f*; **~-jet injection nozzle** *n* AUTO boquilla de inyección de chorro doble *f*; **~ lamella** *n* METALL laminilla de macla *f*; **~-lens reflex** *n* PHOTO cámara reflex de dos objetivos *f*; **~-lens reflex camera** *n* PHOTO cámara reflex de dos objetivos *f*; **~-line brake** *n* AUTO freno de línea doble *m*; **~ magazine** *n* PHOTO chasis doble *m*; **~ pack** *n* PACK paquete doble *m*; **~ paradox** *n* PHYS paradoja de los gemelos *f*; **~-piston engine** *n* AUTO motor de pistón doble *m*; **~ pole** *n* RAIL postes acoplados *m pl*; **~ polisher** *n* C&G pulidor doble *m*; **~ polishing** *n* C&G pulimiento doble *m*; **~ post** *n* RAIL postes acoplados *m pl*; **~ projectors** *n pl* CINEMAT proyectores dobles *m pl*; **~-reactor station** *n* NUCL central nuclear de dos grupos *f*, central nuclear de reactores gemelos *f*; **~-ribbon cable** *n* TRANSP cable de doble-conductor plano *m*, cable plano doble *m*; **~-rotor helicopter** *n* AIR TRANSP helicóptero de doble rotor *m*; **~-screw lathe** *n* MECH ENG torno de dos husillos de rosca *m*, torno de husillos gemelos de roscado *m*; **~-screw steamer** *n* WATER TRANSP buque de dos hélices *m*, vapor de hélices gemelas *m*; **~-spindle lathe** *n* MECH ENG torno de dos ejes *m*; **~-stream collator** *n* PRINT alzadora de doble flujo *f*; **~-tail unit** *n* AIR TRANSP

unidad de cola doble *f*; **~ wheels** *n pl* AIR TRANSP ruedas gemelas *f pl*; **~-wire board machine** *n* PAPER máquina de cartón de doble tela *f*; **~-wire paper machine** *n* PAPER máquina de papel de doble tela *f*, papel fabricado en máquina de doble tela *m*

twine *n* TEXTIL cordel *m*

twinned *adj* CRYSTALL *crystal* maclado

twinning *n* CRYSTALL maclado *m*, METALL formación de maclas *f*, germinación *f*, maclaje *m*; **~ plane** *n* METALL plano de maclado *m*, plano de maclaje *m*; **~ shear** *n* METALL cizallamiento de maclaje *m*; **~ system** *n* METALL sistema de maclaje *m*

twin-T: **~ network** *n* ELEC ENG red biconductora aislada en T *f*, red doble T en paralelo *f*

T-wire *n* TELECOM hilo A *m*, hilo de punta *m*

twist[1] *n* PAPER alabeo *m*, TEXTIL torsión *f*; **~ disclination** *n* METALL disclinación por alabeo *f*; **~ drill** *n* MECH broca helicoidal *f*, broca salomónica *f*, MECH ENG barrena espiral *f*, broca helicoidal *f*, broca para metal *f*, broca salomónica *f*; **~-drill grinder** *n* MECH ENG afiladora de brocas helicoidales *f*; **~ drill with parallel shank** *n* MECH ENG broca helicoidal con mango cilíndrico *f*; **~ drill with straight shank** *n* MECH ENG broca helicoidal con mango cilíndrico *f*; **~ drill with taper square shank** *n* MECH ENG broca helicoidal con mango cuadrado cónico *f*; **~ factor** *n* TEXTIL coeficiente de torsión *m*; **~ gimlet** *n* CONST barrena retorcida *f*; **~ grip** *n* VEH mangueta de torsión *f*; **~ hand reamer** *n* MECH ENG escariador helicoidal de mano *m*; **~ joint** *n* PROD *of wires* empalme por torcedura *m*; **~ lock plug** *n* CINEMAT enchufe de cierre por torsión *m*; **~ tap** *n* MECH ENG macho de roscar helicoidal *m*, macho roscador de ranuras helicoidales *m*; **~-to-release pull unit** *n* PROD unidad de tiro para torcer y soltar *f*; **~-to-release push unit** *n* PROD unidad de empuje para torcer y soltar *f*; **~-to-release unit** *n* PROD unidad para torcer hasta soltar *f*

twist[2]: **~-release** *vt* PROD torcer hasta soltar; **~ to release** *vt* PROD torcer hasta soltar

twisted[1]: **~ together** *adj* TELECOM trenzado

twisted[2]: **~ core** *n* TEXTIL alma torcida *f*; **~ pair** *n* COMP&DP par trenzado *m*, ELEC ENG conductor doble retorcido *m*, par trenzado *m*, PROD conductor doble torcido *m*, conductor doble trenzado *m*; **~-pair cable** *n* COMP&DP, TELECOM cable de par trenzado *m*; **~-pair flat cable** *n* ELEC ENG cable plano de par trenzado *m*; **~ waveguide** *n* ELEC ENG guiaondas revirado *m*

twister *n* TEXTIL continua de retorcer *f*, TRANSP ciclón *m*, tifón *m*, torbellino *m*

twisting *n* C&G *of tubes* torcido *m*, FLUID retorcimiento *m*, MECH ENG contorsión *f*, retorcedura *f*, retorcimiento *m*, torsionamiento *m*, torsión *f*; **~ closure** *n* PACK cierre por torsión *m*; **~ moment** *n* MECH ENG momento de torsión *m*, momento torsional *m*, momento torsor *m*

two[1]: **~-dimensional** *adj* PHYS bidimensional; **~-phase** *adj* ELEC *AC supply*, ELEC ENG bifásico

two[2]: **~-address instruction** *n* COMP&DP instrucción de dos direccionales *f*, instrucción de dos direcciones *f*; **~-bath method** *n* NUCL método de doble baño *m*; **~-bath processing** *n* PRINT procesado de dos baños *m*; **~-bath toning** *n* PHOTO viraje de doble tono *m*; **~-button mouse** *n* COMP&DP ratón de dos botones *m*; **~-cell capacitor** *n* ELEC capacitor de dos baterías *m*, condensador de dos baterías *m*; **~-circuit ignition**

system *n* AUTO sistema de encendido de dos circuitos *m*; **~-circuit nuclear power plant** *n* NUCL central nuclear de dos lazos *f*; **~-color press** *AmE see two-colour press BrE*; **~-color printing** *AmE see two-colour printing BrE*; **~-colour press** *n BrE* PRINT prensa de dos colores *f*; **~-colour printing** *n BrE* PRINT impresión bicolor *f*; **~'s complement** *n* COMP&DP complemento a dos *m*; **~-contact regulator** *n* AUTO regulador de dos contactos *m*; **~-contacts connector** *n* ELEC *capacitor* conector de dos contactos *m*; **~-cylinder press** *n* PRINT prensa de dos cilindros *f*; **~-disc clutch** *n BrE* AUTO embrague de doble disco *m*; **~-disk clutch** *AmE see two-disc clutch BrE*; **~-electron innermost shell** *n* NUCL capa interna de dos electrones *f*; **~-element relay** *n* ELEC relé de dos elementos *m*; **~-frequency channeling plan** *AmE*, **~-frequency channelling plan** *BrE n* TELECOM plan de canalización con dos frecuencias *m*; **~-frequency operation non-repeater mode** *n* TELECOM modo de no repetición de explotación en dos frecuencias *m*; **~-frequency relay system** *n* TELECOM sistema de relé hertziano en dos frecuencias *m*, sistema de retransmisión en dos frecuencias *m*; **~-frequency simplex** *n* TELECOM símplex con dos frecuencias *m*; **~-high mill** *n* PROD laminador dúo *m*, tren dúo *m*; **~-high roll** *n* PROD laminador dúo *m*, tren dúo *m*; **~-high train** *n* PROD laminador dúo *m*, tren dúo *m*; **~-hole torus** *n* GEOM toro de dos agujeros *m*; **~-layer board** *n* PAPER cartón de dos capas *m*; **~-layer paper** *n* PAPER papel de dos capas *m*; **~-leg puller** *n* MECH ENG extractor de dos brazos *m*; **~-nucleon system** *n* NUCL sistema de dos nucleones *m*; **~-part screw plate** *n* MECH ENG placa de roscar en dos partes *f*, placa de roscar en dos piezas *f*; **~-phase alternator** *n* ELEC, ELEC ENG *generator* alternador bifásico *m*; **~-phase carburetor** *AmE*, **~-phase carburettor** *BrE n* AUTO, VEH carburador bifásico *m*, carburador de dos fases *m*; **~-phase controller** *n* TRANSP controlador bifásico *m*; **~-phase cooling** *n* NUCL enfriamiento bifásico *m*; **~-phase current** *n* ELEC ENG corriente bifásica *f*; **~-phase flow** *n* GAS flujo bifásico *m*, REFRIG corriente bifásica *f*; **~-phase machine** *n* ELEC ENG mecanismo bifásico *m*; **~-phase motor** *n* ELEC, ELEC ENG motor bifásico *m*; **~-phase network** *n* ELEC *supply* red bifásica *f*; **~-phase rotor** *n* ELEC ENG rotor bifásico *m*; **~-phase rotor winding** *n* ELEC ENG devanado del rotor bifásico *m*; **~-phase stator** *n* ELEC ENG estator bifásico *m*; **~-phase stator winding** *n* ELEC ENG devanado del estator bifásico *m*; **~-phase system** *n* ELEC *network* sistema bifásico *m*, sistema de dos fases *m*, sistema difásico *m*, ELEC ENG sistema bifásico *m*; **~-piece connector** *n* ELEC ENG conector de dos piezas separadas *m*; **~-piece drive shaft** *n* AUTO, VEH eje de transmisión de dos piezas *m*; **~-piece propeller shaft** *n* AUTO eje propulsor de dos piezas *m*; **~-pin plug** *n* ELEC ENG clavija bipolar *f*; **~-plate clutch** *n* AUTO embrague de dos platos *m*; **~ plies of a two-ply yarn** *n pl* TEXTIL doblado de hilo a dos cabos *m*; **~-plus-one address instruction** *n* COMP&DP instrucción con direccional de dos más uno *f*, instrucción de dos más una direcciones *f*; **~-pole motor** *n* ELEC motor bipolar *m*; **~-pole switch** *n* ELEC ENG interruptor bipolar *m*; **~-pole system** *n* ELEC *of electrical machine* sistema bipolar *m*; **~-port network** *n* ELEC ENG red de dos accesos *f*; **~-revolution press**

n PRINT prensa de dos revoluciones *f*; **~-roll system** *n* PRINT sistema de dos rodillos *m*; **~-seat aircraft** *n* AIR TRANSP avión de dos plazas *m*; **~-side colored board** *AmE see two-side coloured board BrE*; **~-side colored paper** *AmE see two-side coloured paper BrE*; **~-side coloured board** *n BrE* PAPER cartón coloreado por ambas caras *m*; **~-side coloured paper** *n BrE* PAPER papel coloreado por ambas caras *m*; **~-sided disc** *BrE*, **~-sided disk** *AmE n* OPT disco de dos caras *m*; **~-slot module** *n* PROD módulo de dos ranuras *m*; **~-space compression** *n* MECH ENG *of air* compresión biescalonada *f*, compresión bietápica *f*; **~-speed counter motion** *n* MECH ENG contramovimiento de dos velocidades *m*, marcha atrás de dos velocidades *f*; **~-speed filling** *n* PACK llenado a dos velocidades *m*; **~-speed final drive** *n* AUTO transmisión de dos velocidades *f*; **~-stage fuel filter** *n* AUTO filtro de combustible de dos etapas *m*; **~-stage relay** *n* ELEC relé de dos etapas *m*; **~-state register** *n* TELECOM contador de dos etapas *m*, registrador de dos etapas *m*; **~-step cone** *n* PROD polea-cono de dos escalones *f*; **~-step cone pulley** *n* PROD polea-cono de dos escalones *f*; **~-stream instability** *n* NUCL inestabilidad de doble haz *f*; **~-stroke engine** *n* AUTO, MECH, MECH ENG, VEH, WATER TRANSP motor de dos tiempos *m*; **~-stroke oil** *n* AUTO aceite de dos tiempos *m*; **~-system contact breaker** *n* AUTO, VEH interruptor de contacto de dos sistemas *m*, interruptor de dos sistemas *m*, ruptor de dos sistemas *m*, ruptor doble *m*; **~-table machine** *n* C&G máquina de dos mesas *f*; **~-tanged file** *n* MECH ENG lima de dos mangos *f*; **~-terminal network** *n* PHYS red de dos terminales *f*; **~-throw crank shaft** *n* MECH ENG cigüeñal de dos muñequillas *m*; **~-tone dyeing** *n* COLOUR teñido de doble tono *m*; **~-way cock** *n* WATER grifo de dos vías *m*; **~-way damper valve** *n* AUTO, MECH ENG válvula de amortiguación bidireccional *f*, válvula de amortiguación de doble paso *f*, válvula de amortiguación de dos vías *f*; **~-way feed** *n* ELEC *supply* alimentador de doble vía *m*, alimentador de dos vías *m*; **~-way finned cooler** *n* REFRIG enfriador con aletas dobles *m*; **~-way mirror** *n BrE* C&G espejo falso *m*, falso espejo *m*; **~-way pallet** *n* TRANSP bandeja de dos accesos *f*, paleta de dos accesos *f*, pálet de dos accesos *m* (*AmL*); **~-way plough** *n BrE* AGRIC arado alternativo *m*, arado reversible de ida y vuelta *m*; **~-way plow** *AmE see two-way plough BrE*; **~-way restrictor** *n* PROD reductor bidireccional *m*; **~-way road** *n* CONST carretera de doble sentido *f*; **~-way switch** *n* ELEC conmutador de doble tiro *m*, conmutador de dos direcciones *m*; **~-way tap** *n* LAB *ring winding* llave de dos pasos *f*; **~-wheel grinding machine** *n* MECH ENG afiladora de dos muelas *f*; **~-wire circuit** *n* COMP&DP circuito de dos hilos *m*, ELEC circuito bifilar *m*, circuito de dos hilos *m*; **~-wire crosspoint** *n* TELECOM contacto bifilar *m*, contacto de dos conductores *m*, contacto de dos hilos *m*, punto de cruce bifilar *m*, punto de cruce de dos conductores *m*, punto de cruce de dos hilos *m*; **~-wire delta network** *n* ELEC *supply* red en delta bifilar *f*, red en triángulo bifilar *f*; **~-wire network** *n* ELEC *supply* red bifilar *f*; **~-wire switch** *n* TELECOM conmutador bifilar *m*, conmutador de dos conductores *m*, conmutador de dos hilos *m*; **~-wire switching system** *n* TELECOM sistema de conmutación bifilar *m*, sistema de conmutación de dos conductores *m*, sistema de conmutación de dos hilos *m*; **~-wire system** *n* ELEC *supply network* distribución bifilar *f*, sistema de dos hilos *m*, ELEC ENG sistema bifilar *m*, TELECOM sistema de dos hilos *m*

two-B-plus-D: **~ arrangement** *n* TELECOM circuito de dos B más D *m*, instalación de dos B más D *f*, montaje de dos B más D *m*

twofold: **~ rotation axis** *n* CRYSTALL eje binario de rotación *m*; **~ screw axis** *n* CRYSTALL eje binario de inversión *m*

TWT[1] *abbr* (*traveling-wave tube AmE, travelling-wave tube BrE*) ELECTRON, PHYS, SPACE, TELECOM TOP (*tubo de ondas progresivas*)

TWT[2]: **~ amplifier** *n* ELECTRON amplificador de TOP *m*; **~ transfer coefficient** *n* SPACE *communications* coeficiente de transferencia TOP *m*

TWTA *abbr* (*traveling-wave tube amplifier AmE, travelling-wave tube amplifier BrE*) ELECTRON, SPACE, TELECOM amplificador de tubo de ondas progresivas

TX *abbr* (*transmission*) TV transmisión *f*

tying: **~ closure** *n* PACK cierre por atado *m*

Tyler: **~ mount** *n* CINEMAT montura Tyler *f*

tymp *n* PROD *of blast furnace* timpa *f*

tympan *n* PRINT tímpano *m*; **~ paper** *n* PAPER papel para cubrir *m*

tympanic: **~ membrane** *n* ACOUST membrana timpánica *f*

tympanum *n* HYDRAUL tímpano *m*

Tyndall: **~ effect** *n* PHYS efecto Tyndall *m*

type[1]: **~ approval** *n* QUALITY aprobación de tipo *f*, SPACE prueba de homologación *f*; **~ color** *AmE*, **~ colour** *BrE* *n* PRINT color tipográfico *m*; **~ family** *n* PRINT familia de tipos *f*; **~ height** *n* PRINT altura del tipo *f*; **~ of number** *n* (*TON*) TELECOM tipo de número *m*; **~ plate** *n* PRINT plancha de tipos *f*; **~ section** *n* GEOL estratotipo *m*; **~ size** *n* PRINT medida del cuerpo *f*; **~ test** *n* AIR TRANSP *turbine engines* prueba de homologación de tipo *f*

type[2] *vt* COMP&DP escribir con el ordenador, escribir con el teclado

typeface *n* COMP&DP estilo de letra de imprenta *m*, PRINT ojo del tipo *m*, tipo de letra *m*, estilo de letra de imprenta *m*

typescript: **~ proof** *n* PRINT prueba mecanográfica *f*

typesetter *n* PRINT cajista *m*

typesetting *n* PRINT composición tipográfica *f*; **~ machine** *n* PRINT componedora tipográfica *f*

typewriter *n* COMP&DP máquina de escribir *f*; **~ face** *n* PRINT tipo de letra mecanográfica *m*

typhoon *n* METEO tifón *m*

typical: **~ deviation** *n* COMP&DP desviación típica *f*

typo *n* PRINT error tipográfico *m*

typographic: **~ point** *n* PRINT punto tipográfico *m*

typography *n* PRINT tipografía *f*

tyre *n* BrE RAIL bandaje *m*, VEH llanta *f*, neumático *m*; **~ groove** *n* BrE RAIL bandaje de rueda *m*; **~ profile** *n* BrE RAIL perfil del bandaje *m*; **~ reinforcement** *n* BrE TEXTIL refuerzo para neumáticos *m*; **~ tread** *n* BrE P&R superficie de rodadura de la cubierta *f* (*AmL*), superficie de rodadura del neumático *f*; **~ yarn** *n* BrE TEXTIL hilo para neumáticos *m*

tyrosamine *n* CHEM tiramina *f*, tirosamina *f*

tyrosine *n* CHEM tirosina *f*

U

U[1] *abbr* (*uranium*) CHEM, NUCL, RAD PHYS U (*uranio*)

U[2]: **~ bolt** *n* CONST perno en U *m*; **~ magnet** *n* MECH ENG imán en U *m*; **~ stage** *n* CRYSTALL *Fodorov stage, universal stage* platina universal *f*; **~ tube** *n* LAB *mass* tubo en U *m*

UA *abbr* (*user area, user agent*) COMP&DP, TELECOM agente usuario *m*, área de usuario *f*

UAS *abbr* (*unavailable second*) TELECOM segundo indisponible *m*, segundo inutilizable *m*, segundo no disponible *m*

UAT (*unavailable time*) TELECOM tiempo indisponible *m*, tiempo inutilizable *m*, tiempo no disponible *m*

UAX *abbr* (*unit automatic exchange*) TELECOM central automática unitaria *f*

ubitron *n* ELECTRON ubitrón *m*

U-bolt *n* VEH brida de ballesta *f*, WATER TRANSP *boatbuilding* perno en U *m*

UF *abbr* (*urea-formaldehyde resin*) ELEC, P&R resina de urea-formaldehido *f*

UFO *abbr* (*unidentified flying object*) AIR TRANSP, SPACE OVNI (*objeto volador no identificado*)

UHF[1] *abbr* (*ultrahigh frequency*) GEN UHF (*frecuencia ultra-alta, ultra-alta frecuencia*)

UHF[2]: **~ broadcasting** *n* TV radiodifusión por UHF *f*; **~ converter** *n* TV convertidor para UHF *m*; **~ signal** *n* ELECTRON señal de UHF *f*; **~ signal generator** *n* ELECTRON generador de señal de UHF *m*; **~ tuner** *n* TV sintonizador de UHF *m*

UHT *abbr* (*ultra heat treated*) FOOD UHT (*uperizado*)

UI *abbr* TELECOM (*unit interval*) intervalo unitario *m*, TELECOM (*unnumbered information*) información no numerada *f*

UIH: **~ control field** *n* TELECOM campo de control UIH *m*

UITS *abbr* (*unacknowledged information transfer service*) TELECOM servicio de transferencia de información no reconocido *m*

ULCC *abbr* (*ultralarge crude carrier*) PETR TECH super-transportador de crudo *m*

ulexine *n* CHEM ulexina *f*

ulexite *n* MINERAL ulexita *f*

ullage *n* CHEM *of container* hueco *m*, FOOD, MECH merma *f*, PETR TECH espacio vacío *m*, SPACE espacio vacío *m*, merma *f*

ulmic *adj* CHEM úlmico

ulmin *n* CHEM ulmina *f*

ulmous *adj* CHEM ulmoso

ultimate: **~ analysis** *n* GEOL análisis elemental *m*; **~ bending strength** *n* MECH ENG resistencia a la rotura por flexión *f*, resistencia máxima a la flexión *f*, resistencia máxima a la rotura por flexión *f*; **~ burn-up** *n* NUCL quemado final *m*; **~ elongation** *n* P&R alargamiento al fallar *m*, alargamiento de rotura *m*; **~ heat sink** *n* NUCL sumidero de calor final *m*; **~ load** *n* COAL carga límite *f*; **~ magnification** *n* METALL amplificación elemental *f*; **~ recovery** *n* PETR TECH producción final *f*; **~ shear strength** *n* MECH ENG fuerza límite de cizallamiento *f*, resistencia última al

corte *f*; **~ strength** *n* CONST resistencia a la rotura *f*, MECH ENG esfuerzo de rotura máximo *m*, fatiga de rotura *f*, límite de rotura *m*, resistencia a la rotura *f*, resistencia máxima *f*; **~ stress** *n* MECH ENG carga unitaria de rotura *f*, tensión de rotura *f*; **~ tensile strength** *n* MECH carga máxima unitaria a la tracción *f*, resistencia a la rotura traccional *f*, MECH ENG carga de rotura por tracción *f*, carga máxima unitaria a la tracción *f*, resistencia a la rotura traccional *f*, resistencia máxima a la tracción *f*, resistencia última a la tracción *f*, METALL carga de rotura por tracción *f*, carga máxima unitaria a la tracción *f*, P&R tensión de tracción a la rotura *f*; **~ tensile stress** *n* NUCL esfuerzo de tracción máximo *m*; **~ vacuum** *n* THERMO vacío absoluto *m*; **~ waste disposal** *n* NUCL almacenamiento definitivo de residuos *m*

ultra[1]: **~ heat treated** *adj* (*UHT*) FOOD uperizado (*UHT*)

ultra[2]: **~ large scale integration circuit** *n* TELECOM circuito integrado en escala ultra grande *m*

ultrabasic: **~ rock** *n* GEOL roca ultrabásica *f*

ultracentrifugation *n* CHEM ultracentrifugación *f*, NUCL ultracentrifugado *m*

ultracentrifuge *n* CHEM, LAB, NUCL, PHYS ultracentrífuga *f*; **~ enrichment plant** *n* NUCL planta de enriquecimiento por ultracentrifugado *f*

ultrachemical *adj* CHEM ultraquímico

ultrachromatography *n* CHEM, LAB ultracromatografía *f*

ultracold: **~ neutron** *n* NUCL neutrón ultrafrío *m*

ultrafilter *n* CHEM filtro para partículas coloidales *m*, ultrafiltro *m*

ultrafiltrate *n* CHEM ultrafiltrado *m*

ultrafiltration *n* CHEM ultrafiltrado *m*, CHEM TECH ultrafiltración *f*

ultrafine: **~ focus** *n* NUCL enfoque ultrafino *m*

ultrahigh: **~ accuracy weighing** *n* PACK pesada de muy alta precisión *f*; **~ frequency** *n* (*UHF*) ACOUST, CRYSTALL ultra-alta frecuencia *f* (*UHF*), ELEC, ELEC ENG hiperfrecuencia *f* (*HF, UHF*), ELECTRON frecuencia ultra-alta *f* (*FUA*), frecuencia ultraelevada *f*, hiperfrecuencia *f* (*HF, UHF*), ultra-alta frecuencia *f*, PHYS ultra-alta frecuencia *f*, SPACE hiperfrecuencia *f* (*HF, UHF*), TELECOM frecuencia ultra-alta *f* (*FUA*), frecuencia ultraelevada *f*, hiperfrecuencia *f* (*HF, UHF*), ultra-alta frecuencia *f* (*UHF*), TV frecuencia ultra-alta *f* (*FUA*), frecuencia ultraelevada *f*, hiperfrecuencia *f* (*HF, UHF*), WAVE PHYS frecuencia ultraelevada *f*, hiperfrecuencia *f* (*HF, UHF*), onda decimétrica *f*, ultra-alta frecuencia *f* (*UHF*); **~ ~speed photography** *n* CINEMAT, PHOTO fotografía ultrarrápida *f*; **~ ~speed traffic** *n* TRANSP tráfico ultra rápido *m*; **~ temperature reactor** *n* NUCL reactor de temperaturas muy elevadas *m*; **~ vacuum** *n* PHYS, REFRIG vacío ultra-alto *m*

ultralarge: **~ crude carrier** *n* (*ULCC*) PETR TECH super-transportador de crudo *m*

ultralight: **~ alloy** *n* SPACE aleación ultraligera *f*

ultramafic: **~ rock** *n* GEOL roca ultramáfica *f*

ultramafite *n* GEOL ultramafita *f*
ultramarine *n* CHEM lapislázuli *m*, ultramarino *m*; ~ **pigment** *n* COLOUR pigmento azul ultramar *m*
ultramicroanalysis *n* INSTR, LAB, NUCL ultramicroanálisis *m*
ultramicroscope *n* CHEM, LAB, METALL, OPT, PHYS ultramicroscopio *m*
ultramicroscopic *adj* CHEM, LAB, METALL, OPT, PHYS ultramicroscópico
ultramicroscopy *n* CHEM, LAB, METALL, OPT, PHYS ultramicroscopía *f*
ultramylonite *n* GEOL ultramilonita *f*
ultrapasteurization *n* FOOD ultrapasteurización *f*
ultrarapid: ~ **reaction** *n* CHEM reacción ultrarrápida *f*
ultrashort: ~ **wave** *n* WAVE PHYS onda ultracorta *f*; ~ **wave radar** *n* MILIT radar de ondas ultracortas *m*
ultrasmall *adj* PROD pequeñísimo, ultra pequeño
ultrasonic: ~ **bath** *n* LAB baño ultrasónico *m*; ~ **cleaning** *n* CINEMAT, TV limpieza ultrasónica *f*; ~ **detector** *n* TRANSP detector ultrasónico *m*; ~ **engineering** *n* MECH ENG ingeniería ultrasónica *f*; ~ **examination** *n* MECH examen ultrasónico *m*, NUCL inspección por ultrasonidos *f*, inspección ultrasónica *f*; ~ **frequency** *n* ACOUST, PHYS, RAD PHYS frecuencia ultrasónica *f*; ~ **fuel atomizer** *n* TRANSP atomizador ultrasónico de combustible *m*; ~ **generator** *n* RAD PHYS generador de ultrasonidos *m*, generador ultrasónico *m*; ~ **hazard** *n* SAFE peligro causado por ultrasonidos *m*, riesgo causado por ultrasonidos *m*; ~ **inspection** *n* WAVE PHYS examen ultrasónico *m*; ~ **machining** *n* NUCL maquinado por vibración ultrasónica *m*, RAD PHYS maquinado ultrasónico *m*; ~ **meter** *n* GAS medidor ultrasónico *m*; ~ **probe** *n* CONST sonda ultrasónica *f*, RAIL detector ultrasónico *m*; ~ **radar** *n* RAD PHYS radar ultrasónico *m*; ~ **sealing** *n* PACK cierre hermético ultrasónico *m*, estanqueidad ultrasónica *f*, herméticidad ultrasónica *f*, sellado ultrasónico *m*, soldadura por ultrasónico *f*, soldeo ultrasónico *m*, THERMO estanqueidad ultrasónica *f*; ~ **sounding** *n* ACOUST sondeo con ultrasonidos *m*, WAVE PHYS sondaje ultrasónico *m*, sondeo con ultrasonidos *m*; ~ **testing** *n* MECH ENG ensayo ultrasónico *m*, NUCL ensayo por ultrasonidos *m*, ensayo ultrasónico *m*; ~ **wave** *n* WAVE PHYS onda ultrasónica *f*; ~ **welding** *n* P&R soldadura por ultrasonido *f*, soldadura ultrasónica *f*, PACK estanqueidad ultrasónica *f*, THERMO cierre hermético ultrasónico *m*, estanqueidad ultrasónica *f*, hermeticidad ultrasónica *f*, sellado ultrasónico *m*, soldadura por ultraacústica *f*, soldeo ultrasónico *m*
ultrasonics *n* ACOUST, ELECTRON, PHYS ultraacústica *f*, WAVE PHYS supersónica *f*, ultraacústica *f*, ultrasónica *f*, ultrasónico *m*
ultrasound *n* ACOUST, ELECTRON, LAB, PHYS, WAVE PHYS ultrasonido *m*; ~ **generator** *n* LAB generador de ultrasonidos *m*, generador ultrasónico *m*; ~ **scan** *n* RAD PHYS barrido ultrasónico *m*
ultratrace *n* CHEM *analysis* ultratraza *f*
ultravacuum *n* THERMO ultravacío *m*
ultraviolet *n* (*UV*) OPT, PHYS, RAD PHYS, SPACE ultravioleta *m* (*UV*); ~ **catastrophe** *n* PHYS catástrofe ultravioleta *f*; ~ **erasing** *n* COMP&DP borrado por rayos ultravioleta *m*, borrado ultravioleta *m*; ~ **filter** *n* CINEMAT, PHOTO, SAFE filtro ultravioleta

m; ~ **lamp** *n* LAB lámpara de rayos ultravioleta *f*; ~ **light** *n* P&R, RAD PHYS luz ultravioleta *f*; ~ **microscope** *n* RAD PHYS microscopio de luz ultravioleta *m*; ~ **mirror** *n* RAD PHYS espejo ultravioleta *m*; ~ **photography** *n* RAD PHYS fotografía por luz ultravioleta *f*; ~ **photon** *n* PART PHYS fotón ultravioleta *m*; ~ **radiation** *n* FUELLESS, GEOPHYS, OPT, PHYS, POLL, RAD PHYS, SPACE radiación ultravioleta *f*; ~ **ray** *n* OPT rayo ultravioleta *m*; ~ **spectrophotometry** *n* CHEM *analysis* espectrofotometría de ultravioleta *f*, LAB espectometría de ultravioleta *f*; ~ **visible spectrophotometer** *n* CHEM LAB espectrofotómetro de ultravioleta visible *m*
umbellic *adj* CHEM umbélico
umbilical[1] *adj* GEOL umbilical
umbilical[2] *n* OCEAN tubo de supervivencia *m*; ~ **cable** *n* SPACE cable eléctrico para servicio de un equipo *m*, cable umbilical *m*; ~ **connector** *n* SPACE borne umbilical *m*, conector umbilical *m*; ~ **mast** *n* SPACE poste umbilical *m*
umbra *n* OPT, PHYS umbra *f*
umbrella *n* CINEMAT parasol *m*, sombrilla *f*; ~ **reflector aerial** *n* BrE (*cf* umbrella reflector antenna AmE) SPACE antena reflectora cónica *f*; ~ **reflector antenna** *n* AmE (*cf* umbrella reflector aerial BrE) SPACE *communications* antena reflectora cónica *f*; ~ **roof** *n* CONST marquesina *f*; ~**-type alternator** *n* ELEC, ELEC ENG *generator* alternador de eje vertical con rangua inferior *m*
Umklapp: ~ **process** *n* NUCL proceso Umklapp *m*
UNA: ~ **segment** *n* TELECOM segmento UNA *m*
unable: ~ **to comply** *adj* TELECOM incapaz de cumplir
unacceptable: ~ **quality** *n* TELECOM calidad inaceptable *f*
unacknowledged: ~ **information transfer service** *n* (*UITS*) TELECOM servicio de transferencia de información no reconocido *m*
unaltered *adj* GEOL inalterado
unamplified *adj* TELECOM no amplificado
unanswered: ~ **call** *n* TELECOM llamada no contestada *f*
unary[1] *adj* COMP&DP unario
unary[2]: ~ **operation** *n* COMP&DP operación unaria *f*
unattended[1] *adj* SPACE automático
unattended[2]: ~ **exchange** *n* TELECOM central no atendida *f*, central sin personal de guardia *f*, central sin personal permanente *f*; ~ **operation** *n* COMP&DP funcionamiento automático *m*, operación sin personal *f*
unauthorized: ~ **operation** *n* PROD operación inautorizada *f*
unavailability: ~ **time** *n* NUCL tiempo de indisponibilidad *m*
unavailable: ~ **second** *n* (*UAS*) TELECOM segundo indisponible *m*, segundo inutilizable *m*, segundo no disponible *m*; ~ **time** *n* (*UAT*) TELECOM tiempo indisponible *m*, tiempo inutilizable *m*, tiempo no disponible *m*
UNB: ~ **segment** *n* TELECOM segmento UNB *m*
unbaked *adj* THERMO *communications* crudo, no cocido
unbalance *n* ELEC asimetría *f*, MECH desequilibrio *m*, MECH ENG asimetría *f*, desequilibrio *m*, disimetría *f*, inestabilidad *f*
unbalanced[1] *adj* ELEC asimétrico, desequilibrado,

SPACE *communications* asimétrico, desequilibrado, inestable

unbalanced^2: ~ **input** *n* ELEC ENG cantidad de entrada de energía desequilibrada *f*; ~ **line** *n* ELEC, ELEC ENG línea desequilibrada *f*; ~ **output** *n* ELEC ENG salida de potencia desequilibrada *f*, SPACE *communications* salida asimétrica *f*, salida desbalanceada *f*; ~ **rudder** *n* WATER TRANSP timón ordinario *m*; ~ **system** *n* TELECOM sistema no balanceado *m*; ~ **three-phase system** *n* MECH ENG sistema trifásico desequilibrado *m*

unbiased^1 *adj* COMP&DP imparcial, impolarizado, insesgado *m*

unbiased^2: ~ **polarized relay** *n* ELEC relé impolarizado *m*, relé no polarizado *m*, relé sin polarizar *m*

unblanking: ~ **circuit** *n* TV circuito de permanencia *m*; ~ **pulses** *n pl* TV pulsos de borrado *m pl* (*AmL*), pulsos de permanencia *m pl* (*Esp*)

unbleached: ~ **mechanical pulp board** *n* PAPER cartón de pulpa mecánica sin blanquear *m*; ~ **pulp** *n* PAPER pulpa sin blanquear *f*

unbolt *vt* NUCL quitar los pernos

unbolting *n* MECH ENG destornillado *m*

unbonded: ~ **skin** *n* SPACE revestimiento suelto, abierto *m*

unbound: ~ **mode** *n* OPT, TELECOM modo no ligado *m*

unbroken: ~ **ore** *n* MINE mineral no fracturado *m*

unburnt: ~ **brick** *n* CONST ladrillo no cocido *m*, THERMO ladrillo crudo *m*, ladrillo no cocido *m*

UNC *abbr* (*unified coarse thread*) MECH ENG *systems of threads* UNC (*hilo de paso ancho unificado*)

uncanned: ~ **fuel element** *n* NUCL elemento de combustible desenvainado *m*, elemento de combustible sin vaina *m*

uncapping *n* MECH ENG desencasquetado *m*, desencasquillado *m*

uncased: ~ **hole** *n* PETR TECH pozo sin entubar *m*

uncemented: ~ **lens** *n* CINEMAT lente sin cementar *f*

uncertainty: ~ **of measurement** *n* METR ·error de la medida *m*; ~ **principle** *n* PHYS principio de incertidumbre *m*

uncharged *adj* ELEC neutro, sin carga, sin carga eléctrica, RAD PHYS no cargado

unclamp *vt* MECH ENG aflojar, desmontar, quitar la brida, soltar

unclocked: ~ **flip-flop** *n* ELECTRON biestable asíncrono *m*

unclutch^1 *n* AUTO, MECH ENG desembrague de transmisión *m*

unclutch^2 *vt* AUTO, MECH ENG desembragar

uncoated: ~ **fuel particle** *n* NUCL partícula de combustible no revestida *f*

uncoded *adj* TELECOM no codificado

uncollided: ~ **neutron** *n* NUCL neutrón que no ha entrado en colisión *m*

uncombined *adj* CHEM no combinado

uncommitted: ~ **transistor** *n* ELECTRON transistor libre *m*, transistor no afectado *m*

unconditional^1 *adj* COMP&DP, PROD incondicional

unconditional^2: ~ **end rung** *n* PROD último peldaño incondicional *m*; ~ **jump** *n* COMP&DP bifurcación incondicional *f*, salto incondicional *m*

unconditionally *adv* COMP&DP, PROD incondicionalmente

unconfined: ~ **ground water** *n* COAL agua subterránea

libre *f*; ~ **water** *n* HYDROL, WATER acuífero ilimitado *m*

unconformity *n* GEOL discontinuidad *f*, discordancia *f*, PETR TECH discordancia *f*; ~ **trap** *n* PETR TECH trampa de discordancia *f*

uncorking: ~ **machine** *n* PACK descorchadora *f*

uncorrected: ~ **lens** *n* CINEMAT, OPT, PHOTO lente sin corregir *f*; ~ **result** *n* METR resultado sin corregir *m*

uncouple *vt* RAIL desenganchar

uncoupling *n* NUCL desacoplamiento *m*, RAIL desenganche *m*, SPACE desacoplamiento *m*, desenganche *m*; ~ **rod** *n* MINE varilla desenganchada *f*

uncured^1 *adj* CHEM, ELEC, MECH no vulcanizado, P&R no curado, no endurecido, no vulcanizado, THERMO no vulcanizado

uncured^2: ~ **mat** *n* C&G colchoneta no curada *f*

uncut: ~ **length** *n* TELECOM longitud completa *f*; ~ **pile** *n* TEXTIL pelo sin cortar *m*

undecane *n* CHEM undecano *m*

undecanoic *adj* CHEM undecanoico

undecomposed *adj* CHEM no descompuesto

undecorated: ~ **dislocation** *n* METALL dislocación no decorada *f*

undecylenic *adj* CHEM undecilénico

undefined: ~ **error** *n* COMP&DP error indefinido *m*; ~ **key** *n* COMP&DP clave indefinida *f*, tecla indefinida *f*; ~ **statement** *n* COMP&DP declaración indefinida *f*, instrucción indefinida *f*, sentencia indefinida *f*

under^1: ~ **load** *adj* MECH ENG bajo carga, VEH cargado; ~ **repair** *adj* GEN bajo reparación, en reparaciones

under^2: ~ **canvas** *phr* WATER TRANSP con las velas desplegadas; ~ **control** *phr* MECH ENG bajo control; ~ **normal conditions of use** *phr* METR bajo condiciones normales de uso; ~ **steam** *phr* HYDRAUL bajo presión, MECH ENG a vapor, en presión; ~ **vacuum** *phr* THERMO bajo vacío

underbead: ~ **crack** *n* NUCL grieta debajo del cordón de soldadura *f*

underbody *n* VEH bajos de carrocería *m pl*, chasis inferior *m*; ~ **protection** *n* VEH protección de bajos *f*

underbunching *n* ELECTRON desagrupación *f*

undercarriage *n* AIR TRANSP tren de aterrizaje *m*, SPACE, TRANSP bastidor *m*, tren de aterrizaje *m*

undercoat *n* (*cf underseal BrE*) CHEM, COATINGS capa interior *f*, COLOUR mano interior *f*, CONST capa de imprimación *f*, primera mano *f*, VEH *body* aparejo *m*, imprimación *f*

undercoating *n* COATINGS revestimiento interior *m*

under-color: ~ **removal** *AmE see under-colour removal BrE*

under-colour: ~ **removal** *n BrE* PRINT reducción de color de fondo *f*

undercompacted^1 *adj* GEOL incompactado, PETR TECH incompactado, subcompactado

undercompacted^2: ~ **zone** *n* PETR TECH zona no compacta *f*

undercompaction *n* PETR TECH subcompactación *f*

undercrank *vt* CINEMAT, PHOTO, TV accionar a una velocidad menor que la normal

undercurrent *n* FUELLESS corriente de fondo *f*, OCEAN corriente submarina *f*, PROD corriente derivada *f*, corriente submarina *f*, WATER *sluices* corriente submarina *f*, WATER TRANSP *sea state* corriente subsuperficial *f*; ~ **relay** *n* ELEC relé de baja corriente *m*, relé de hipocorriente *m*

undercut *n* C&G muesca *f*, MECH ENG *incomplete thread*

corte sesgado *m*, hilo con poca altura *m*, PRINT
socabado *m*

undercutting *n* AGRIC socavación *f*; **~ saw** *n* MECH ENG
sierra de corte poco profundo *f*, sierra de rebaje *f*

underdevelop *vt* CINEMAT, PHOTO subrevelar

underdeveloped *adj* CINEMAT falto de revelado,
PHOTO, PRINT revelado insuficiente

underdriven *adj* MECH ENG accionado por debajo, con
excitación insuficiente, subexcitado

underexpose *vt* CINEMAT, PHOTO, PRINT subexponer

underexposed *adj* CINEMAT, PHOTO, PRINT, TV insufi-
cientemente expuesto

underexposure *n* CINEMAT, PHOTO, PRINT subexposi-
ción *f*

underfed *adj* AGRIC desnutrido

underfired: **~ furnace** *n* C&G horno *m*

underfishing *n* OCEAN subexplotación *f*

underfloor: **~ condenser** *n* NUCL condensador montado debajo de la turbina *m*; **~ engine** *n* AUTO motor
bajo el asiento *m*; **~ heating** *n* ELEC calefacción
debajo del piso *f*, HEAT ENG calefacción empotrada
en el suelo *f* (*Esp*), losa radiante *f* (*AmL*), THERMO
calefacción debajo del piso *f*; **~ ventilation** *n* REFRIG
ventilación por falso techo *f*

underflow *n* COAL corriente subterránea *f*, gruesos *m*
pl, OCEAN corriente de fondo *f*, WATER *sluices*
corriente de fondo *f*, corriente subfluvial *f*, corriente
subálvea *f*

underframe *n* MECH ENG armazón de sustentación *m*,
infraestructura *f*, NUCL *communications, equipment*
bastidor de soporte *m*, RAIL bastidor *m*

undergage: **~ hole** *AmE see undergauge hole BrE*

undergauge: **~ hole** *n BrE* PETR TECH, PETROL agujero
de diámetro demasiado pequeño *m*

underglaze: **~ painting** *n* COLOUR pintura previa al
barnizado *f*

undergrade: **~ bridge** *n* CONST puente inferior *m*

undergrazing *n* AGRIC subpastoreo *m*

underground[1] *adj* GEN subterráneo

underground[2] *n BrE* (*cf subway AmE*) RAIL, TRANSP
ferrocarril subterráneo *m*, subterráneo *m*; **~ bus** *n*
TRANSP autobús subterráneo *m*; **~ cable** *n* ELEC
supply network cable soterrado *m*, cable subterráneo
m, cable tendido bajo tierra *m*, ELEC ENG cable
subterráneo *m*; **~ cabling** *n* CONST cableado subterráneo *m*; **~ chamber** *n* TELECOM cámara
subterránea *f*; **~ drainage** *n* WATER drenaje subterráneo *m*; **~ exploration** *n* GAS exploración
subterránea *f*; **~ flow** *n* HYDROL corriente de agua
subterránea *f*, corriente subterránea *f*; **~ gasification**
n GAS, THERMO gasificación subterránea *f*; **~ line** *n*
ELEC ENG, TELECOM línea subterránea *f*; **~ mine** *n*
MINE mina subterránea *f*; **~ nappe** *n* HYDROL capa
freática *f*; **~ operation** *n* MINE trabajo subterráneo *m*;
~ railroad *n AmE* (*cf underground railway BrE*) RAIL
ferrocarril subterráneo *m*; **~ railway** *n BrE* (*cf
underground railroad AmE*) RAIL ferrocarril subterráneo *m*; **~ river** *n* HYDROL río subterráneo *m*;
~ storage *n* GAS, THERMO, WATER almacenamiento
subterráneo *m*; **~ storage system** *n* GAS sistema de
almacenamiento subterráneo *m*; **~ stream** *n* HYDROL
corriente de agua subterránea *f*; **~ tramway** *n*
TRANSP tranvía subterráneo *m*; **~ trolleybus** *n BrE*
(*cf underground trolleycar AmE*) TRANSP trolebús
subterráneo *m*; **~ trolleycar** *n AmE* (*cf underground
trolleybus BrE*) TRANSP trolebús subterráneo *m*;

~ waste disposal *n* WATER disposición subterránea
de basuras *f*; **~ water** *n* COAL, HYDROL, POLL agua
subterránea *f*; **~ working** *n* MINE trabajo subterráneo
m; **~ workings** *n* MINE laboreo subterráneo *m*,
trabajo subterráneo *m*

undergrounded: **~ system** *n* PROD sistema subterráneo *m*

underhung: **~ rudder** *n* WATER TRANSP timón colgado
m

underlap *n* TV no yuxtaposición de las líneas *f*

underlayer *n* TEXTIL basamento *m*, refuerzo de
alfombra *m*

underline *vt* PRINT subrayar

underliner *n* PAPER antecapa *f*

underload *n* NUCL subtensión *f*; **~ relay** *n* ELEC relé de
baja carga *m*, relé de carga mínima *m*, relé de mínima
m, relé de mínimo de carga *m*

underlying[1] *adj* GEOL subyacente

underlying[2]: **~ rock** *n* GEOL roca subyacente *f*

undermanned *adj* TRANSP con tripulación insuficiente

undermine *vt* CONST, MINE minar, socavar

undermining *n* CONST, MINE socavón *m*

undermodulation *n* ELECTRON submodulación *f*

underpass *n* CONST paso inferior *m*, RAIL paso inferior
m, paso subterráneo *m*

underpinning *n* CONST apuntalamiento *m*, recalce *m*

underpressure *n* MECH ENG presión insuficiente *f*,
subpresión *f*, subvoltaje *m*

underprinting *n* PRINT impresión de fondos *f*

underrange *n* PROD alcance inferior al normal *m*

underreaming *n* MINE ensanchamiento por trépano *m*

underrun: **~ bar** *n* AUTO, VEH barra flexible *f*;
~ bumper *n* VEH parachoques flexible *m*; **~ guard** *n*
VEH protección flexible *f*

undersaturated *adj* GEOL, METALL subsaturado

undersaturation *n* GEOL, METALL subsaturación *f*

undersea[1] *adj* OCEAN, WATER TRANSP submarino

undersea[2]: **~ habitat** *n* OCEAN habitáculo submarino
m

underseal *n BrE* (*cf undercoat*) VEH *body* aparejo *m*,
imprimación *f*

undersensitized *adj* PRINT poco sensibilizado

underset *n* OCEAN resaca *f*

undershoot[1] *n* AIR TRANSP aterrizaje corto *m*, entrada
corta *f*, ELECTRON impulso breve *m*, impulso corto *m*

undershoot[2] *vt* ELECTRON proyectar corto

undersize *n* COAL finos *m pl*, menudos de criba *m pl*

undersoil *n* MINE subsuelo *m*

understeer *n* VEH subvirador *m*

underswing *n* TV distorsión por sobremodulación *f*

underthrust *n* GEOL bajocorrimiento *m*

undertitration *n* CHEM subtitulación *f*

undertow *n* OCEAN resaca *f*, WATER TRANSP *sea*
contracorriente *f*, contracorriente submarina *f*,
resaca *f*

undervoltage *n* PROD hipovoltaje *m*, subvoltaje *m*

underwashing *n* OCEAN corriente submarina vaciante *f*

underwater: **~ acoustics** *n* ACOUST, OCEAN acústica
subacuática *f*; **~ camera** *n* PHOTO cámara fotográfica
submarina *f*; **~ cutting blowpipe** *n* CONST soplete de
corte bajo el agua *m*; **~ fishing** *n* OCEAN caza
subacuática *f*, pesca subacuática *f*; **~ habitat** *n*
OCEAN habitáculo subacuático *m*; **~ housing** *n*
CINEMAT, PHOTO carcasa submarina *f* (*Esp*), chasis
submarino *m* (*AmL*); **~ hull** *n* WATER TRANSP *ship
design* carena *f*, obra viva *f*; **~ photograph** *n* PHOTO

fotografía submarina *f*; ~ **photography** *n* PHOTO
fotografía submarina *f*; ~ **propagation** *n* TELECOM
propagación submarina *f*; ~ **reactor** *n* NUCL reactor
sumergido *m*; ~ **shot** *n* CINEMAT toma submarina *f*;
~ **vehicle** *n* PETR TECH vehículo submarino *m*, WATER
TRANSP vehículo subacuático *m*; ~ **welding** *n* PETR
TECH soldadura bajo agua *f*, THERMO soldeo submarino *m*

underway *adj* WATER TRANSP en movimiento, en navegación

underwriter *n* WATER TRANSP asegurador *m*, asegurador marítimo *m*

underwriting *n* WATER TRANSP *maritime insurance* comprobación y aceptación del seguro marítimo *f*

undiluted *adj* CHEM no diluido

undipped *adj* TEXTIL no bañado

undissociated *adj* METALL *transformer, electrical machine* no disociado

undistorted *adj* ELECTRON indistorsionado, sin distorsión

undisturbed: ~ **sample** *n* COAL muestra no alterada *f*

unducted: ~ **fan** *n* AIR TRANSP *engine* ventilador sin conductos *m*

undulant: ~ **fever** *n* AGRIC brucelosis *f*, fiebre de Malta *f*

undulating *adj* TELECOM ondulante, ondulatoria

undyed *adj* TEXTIL sin teñir

unenriched *adj* NUCL natural, no enriquecido

uneven: ~ **running** *n* RAIL circulación irregular *f*;
~ **temper** *n* C&G templado desigual *m*

unexpected: ~ **braking** *n* RAIL *vehicles* frenado inesperado *m*

unexploded: ~ **bomb** *n* (*UXB*) MILIT bomba sin detonar *f*, bomba sin explotar *f*

unexposed: ~ **film** *n* CINEMAT, PHOTO película sin exponer *f*, película virgen *f*

UNF *abbr* (*unified fine thread*) MECH ENG *system of threads* UNF (*hilo de paso fino unificado, rosca de paso fino unificado*)

unfasten *vt* CHEM desprender

unfavored: ~ **transition** *AmE see unfavoured transition BrE*

unfavoured: ~ **transition** *n* *BrE* NUCL transición desfavorecida *f*

unfenced *adj* CONST sin cercar, sin vallar

unfinished *adj* COATINGS *paper* semielaborado, PAPER sin acabar

unfired[1] *adj* C&G crudo, no cocido

unfired[2]: ~ **pot** *n* C&G vasija cruda *f*; ~ **tube** *n* ELECTRON tubo desactivado *m*

unfissioned *adj* NUCL, PART PHYS, PHYS no fisionado

unfit: ~ **for human consumption** *adj* FOOD no apto para consumo humano

unflavored *AmE see unflavoured BrE*

unflavoured *adj BrE* FOOD insípido

unfordable *adj* HYDROL invadeable

unforeseen: ~ **interruption** *n* TELECOM interrupción imprevista *f*

unfurlable *adj* SPACE *of antenna* desenrollable, desplegable, TELECOM desplegable

ungated: ~ **spillway** *n* HYDROL, WATER aliviadero sin compuertas *m*

unglazed *adj* C&G, CHEM no vidriado

ungraduated *adj* CHEM *of beaker*, LAB no graduado

UNH: ~ **segment** *n* TELECOM segmento UNH *m*

unhooking *n* MECH ENG desenganche *m*

UNI *abbr* (*user-network interface*) COMP&DP, TELECOM interfaz de la red del usuario *m*, interfaz usuario-red *f*

uniaxial *adj* CHEM, CRYSTALL, OPT, PHYS uniáxico

uniconductor: ~ **waveguide** *n* ELEC ENG guiaondas monoconductor *m*

unidentified: ~ **flying object** *n* (*UFO*) AIR TRANSP, SPACE objeto volador no identificado *m* (*OVNI*)

unidirectional[1] *adj* ACOUST *microphone* unidireccional, ELEC *current* de sentido único, unidireccional, unilateral, ELEC ENG unidireccional, TELECOM de sentido único, unidireccional

unidirectional[2]: ~ **transducer** *n* ELEC ENG transductor unidireccional *m*

unified[1] *adj* COMP&DP, SPACE *propulsion* unificado

unified[2]: ~ **bolt** *n* MECH ENG perno estándarizado *m*;
~ **coarse thread** *n* (*UNC*) MECH ENG *systems of threads* hilo de paso ancho unificado *m* (*UNC*);
~ **fine thread** *n* (*UNF*) MECH ENG *system of threads* hilo de paso fino unificado *m* (*UNF*), rosca de paso fino unificado *f* (*UNF*); ~ **screw thread** *n* MECH ENG tornillo de paso unificado *m*

unifilar: ~ **suspension** *n* ELEC suspensión unifilar *f*

unifining *n* CHEM unifinación *f*

uniflex: ~ **tray** *n* CHEM bandeja uniflex *f*

uniflow: ~ **compressor** *n* REFRIG compresor de flujo continuo *m*, compresor en equicorriente *m*

uniform[1] *adj* GEN uniforme

uniform[2]: ~ **corrosion** *n* METALL corrosión uniforme *f*;
~ **field** *n* PHYS campo uniforme *m*; ~ **flow** *n* HYDROL caudal uniforme *m*; ~**-index fiber** *AmE*, ~**-index fibre** *BrE* *n* OPT, TELECOM fibra de índice uniforme *f*;
~**-index profile fiber** *AmE*, ~**-index profile fibre** *BrE* *n* OPT, TELECOM fibra de perfil de índice uniforme *f*;
~ **layer winding** *n* ELEC arrollamiento uniforme en capas superpuestas *m*; ~ **line** *n* ELEC ENG línea uniforme *f*; ~ **motion** *n* PHYS movimiento uniforme *m*

uniformity: ~ **coefficient** *n* COAL coeficiente de uniformidad *m*

uniformly: ~**-excited column of gas** *n* RAD PHYS columna de gas uniformemente excitada *f*

unijunction: ~ **transistor** *n* ELECTRON transistor de una sola unión *m*

unilateral: ~ **track** *n* ACOUST banda unilateral *f*, pista unilateral *f*

uninflammable: ~ **coal** *n* COAL carbón no inflamable *m*

uninstrumented: ~ **fuel assembly** *n* NUCL elemento de combustible sin instrumentación *m*

unintended: ~ **actuation** *n* PROD actuación involuntaria *f*

uninterrupted: ~ **duty** *n* ELEC *equipment* servicio ininterrumpido *m*; ~ **flow** *n* TRANSP afluencia ininterrumpida *f*, circulación ininterrumpida *f*

union *n* COMP&DP unión *f*, CONST unión *f*, junta *f*, *pipecoupling* conexión *f*, empalme *m*; ~ **cloth** *n* TEXTIL tela con hilos mezclados *f*; ~ **cock** *n* CONST *with or without tail pipe* llave de conexión *f*; ~ **elbow** *n* CONST codo de empalme *m*, unión en L *f*; ~ **paper** *n* PAPER papel alquitranado de dos hojas *m*; ~ **screw** *n* MECH ENG perno de unión *m*; ~ **T** *n* CONST unión en T *f*

uniphase *adj* ELEC *conductor*, ELEC ENG monofásico

unipod *n* CINEMAT, PHOTO trípode de un pie *m*

unipolar[1] *adj* COMP&DP unipolar, ELEC *dynamo* unipolar, ELEC ENG monopolar, unipolar, ELECTRON *transistor* unipolar, NUCL unipolar ·

unipolar[2]: **~ integrated circuit** *n* ELECTRON circuito integrado unipolar *m*

unipole: **~ aerial** *n* BrE (*cf* unipole antenna AmE) TELECOM antena monopolo *f*; **~ antenna** *n* AmE (*cf unipole aerial BrE*) TELECOM antena monopolo *f*

unipotential[1] *adj* ELEC ENG equipotencial

unipotential[2]: **~ lens** *n* NUCL lente equipotencial *f*

unique: **~ I/O location addressing** *n* COMP&DP, PROD direccionamiento único de E/S *m*; **~ word** *n* (*UW*) SPACE *communications* grupo de señales único *m*, mandato único *m*, orden única *f*, sentencia única *f*; **~ word detection** *n* SPACE *communications* detección del grupo de señales único *f*

uniselector *n* ELEC ENG uniselector *m*

unison *n* ACOUST unísono *m*

unit *n* CHEM *of compound*, CINEMAT, COMP&DP, ELEC, GEOL unidad *f*, HYDRAUL elemento *m*, NUCL *measuring* grupo *m*, unidad *f*, PHYS unidad *f*, PRINT cuerpo impresor *m*, TELECOM unidad *f*, VEH conjunto de piezas *m*, equipo *m*; **~ of area** *n* METR unidad de área *f*; **~ automatic exchange** *n* (*UAX*) TELECOM central automática unitaria *f*; **~ auxilliary transformer** *n* NUCL transformador auxiliar de la unidad *m*; **~ capacity** *n* NUCL potencia del grupo *f*; **~ cell** *n* CRYSTALL celda unidad *f*, NUCL celda unitaria *f*; **~-cell parameter** *n* CRYSTALL parámetro de la celda unidad *m*; **~ conductance** *n* THERMO conductancia unitaria *f*; **~ construction body** *n* VEH carrocería desmontable *f*; **~-dose pack** *n* AmE PACK paquete de una dosis *m*; **~-dose packet** BrE *n* PACK paquete de una dosis *m*; **~-dose sachet** *n* PACK bolsita dosis unitarias *f*; **~ draft** *n* AGRIC coeficiente de labranza *m*; **~ of energy** *n* THERMO unidad de energía *f*; **~ of entropy** *n* THERMO unidad de entropía *f*; **~ of exposure** *n* RAD PHYS unidad de exposición *f*; **~ of fishing effort** *n* OCEAN unidad de esfuerzo pesquero *f*; **~ of force** *n* MECH ENG, PHYS unidad de fuerza *f*; **~ heater** *n* HEAT aerotermo *m*, THERMO *number* aerotermo *m*, calefactor unidad *m*; **~ housing** *n* REFRIG alojamiento de la unidad *m*; **~ interval** *n* (*UI*) TELECOM intervalo unitario *m*; **~ of length** *n* METR unidad de longitud *f*; **~ load vertical conveyor** *n* PROD transportador vertical de cargas unitarias *m*; **~ magnetic pole** *n* PETR TECH polo magnético unitario *m*; **~ of measurement** *n* METR, PETR TECH unidad de medida *f*; **~ output** *n* NUCL energía producida por la unidad *f*, producción de la unidad *f*; **~ pack** *n* PACK paquete unitario *m*; **~ string** *n* COMP&DP cadena unitaria *f*, serie unitaria *f*; **~ supervisor** *n* PROD supervisor de unidad *m*; **~ thrust** *n* SPACE *spacecraft* impulso unitario *m*; **~ time** *n* PROD tiempo unitario *m*; **~-type cable** *n* OPT cable de tipo unitario *m*; **~ vector** *n* PHYS vector unitario *m*; **~ weight** *n* COAL peso unitario *m*

unite *vt* CHEM unir

united: **~ injector** *n* AUTO inyector unido *m*

United: **~ States Nuclear Regulatory Commission** *n* (*US NRC*) NUCL Comisión Reguladora Nuclear de los Estados Unidos *f* (*US NRC*)

unitization *n* PETR TECH unificación *f*

unitized: **~ body** *n* VEH carrocería normalizada *f*

unity: **~ gain** *n* ELECTRON ganancia unidad *f*; **~-gain amplifier** *n* ELECTRON amplificador de ganancia unidad *m*

univalence *n* CHEM monovalencia *f*

univalent *adj* CHEM monovalente

universal: **~ bridge** *n* ELEC *measurement* puente de medida universal *m*, puente universal *m*; **~ centering apparatus** AmE, **~ centring apparatus** BrE *n* INSTR aparato de centraje universal *m*; **~ character set** *n* COMP&DP conjunto de caracteres universal *m*; **~ computer** *n* COMP&DP computador universal *m* (*AmL*) (*CU*), computadora universal *f* (*AmL*) (*CU*), ordenador universal *m* (*Esp*); **~ condenser** *n* INSTR condensador universal *m*; **~ developing tank** *n* PHOTO tanque de revelado universal *m*; **~ grinder** *n* C&G esmeril universal *m*; **~ grinding** *n* PROD esmerilado universal *m*; **~ jack** *n* AUTO gato universal *m*; **~ joint** *n* AUTO acoplamiento universal *m*, junta cardan *f*, junta cardánica *f*, junta de transmisión *f*, junta universal *f*, rótula cardan *f*, MECH junta cardan *f*, junta cardánica *f*, MECH ENG cruceta *f* (*AmL*), junta cardan *f*, junta cardánica *f*, junta universal *f*, VEH junta universal *f*, junta cardan *f*, junta cardánica *f*; **~ leader** *n* CINEMAT, TV guía universal *f*; **~ level protractor** *n* METR transportador de nivel universal *m*; **~ manipulator** *n* NUCL manipulador universal *m*; **~ milling machine** *n* MECH ENG fresadora universal *f*; **~ motion** *n* FLUID movimiento universal *m*; **~ motor** *n* ELEC, ELEC ENG motor universal *m*; **~ number** *n* TELECOM número universal *m*; **~ ripper-loader** *n* MINE arrancadora-cargadora para diversos usos *f*; **~ set** *n* COMP&DP conjunto universal *m*, juego universal *m*, MATH *basic term* conjunto universal *m*, universo *m*; **~ shears** *n* MECH ENG cizalla universal *f*; **~ shunt** *n* ELEC *resistance* derivación Ayrton *f*, derivador Ayrton *m*, derivador universal *m*, shunt Ayrton *m*, shunt universal *m*; **~ stage** *n* CRYSTALL platina de Fedorov *f*, platina universal *f*, INSTR plataforma universal *f*; **~ switch** *n* TELECOM conmutador universal *m*; **~ time coordinates** *n pl* (*UTC*) METEO, TELECOM coordenadas de hora universal *f pl*; **~ tool-and-cutter sharpener** *n* MECH, MECH ENG, PROD afiladora universal de herramientas de corte *f*; **~ viewfinder** *n* CINEMAT, PHOTO visor universal *m*; **~ wide-field microscope** *n* INSTR microscopio de campo ancho universal *m*

Universal: **~ Time** *n* SPACE *measures* hora universal *f*

unkeying *n* MECH ENG franqueo *m*

unknown: **~ message** *n* TELECOM mensaje desconocido *m*

unladen *adj* MAR POLL descargado

unlatch: **~ instruction** *n* PROD instrucción de apertura *f*; **~ rung** *n* PROD eslabón desbloqueado *m*

unlatching *n* NUCL desenganchado *m*

unlead *vt* PRINT sacar las interlíneas

unleaded: **~ gas** *n* AmE (*cf unleaded petrol BrE*) AUTO, PETR TECH, PETROL, POLL, VEH *fuel* gasolina sin plomo *f*; **~ gasoline** *n* AmE (*cf unleaded petrol BrE*) AUTO, PETR TECH, PETROL, POLL, VEH *fuel* gasolina sin plomo *f*; **~ petrol** BrE *n* (*cf unleaded gas AmE*, *cf unleaded gasoline AmE*) AUTO, PETR TECH, PETROL, POLL, VEH gasolina sin plomo *f*

unlike: **~ poles** *n pl* ELEC *magnetism* polos de nombre contrario *m pl*, polos de signo contrario *m pl*, polos opuestos *m pl*, PHYS polos opuestos *m pl*, polos de nombre contrario *m pl*, polos de signo contrario *m pl*

unlined *adj* CHEM liso, no rayado

unload[1]: **~ file** *n* PROD fichero memorizado *m*

unload[2] *vt* COMP&DP, MAR POLL, MILIT descargar, WATER TRANSP *cargo* descargar, desembarcar

unloaded[1] *adj* CINEMAT, PHOTO descargado

unloaded² : ~ **cable** *n* TELECOM cable no cargado *m*

unloader *n* MAR POLL buque descargador *m*, descargador *m*, REFRIG descargador *m*

unloading *n* CHEM, HYDRAUL, MECH ENG, METALL, MINE, PHYS descarga *f*; ~ **valve** *n* HYDRAUL, MECH ENG válvula de descarga *f*

unlock *vt* CINEMAT desbloquear, MILIT *artillery* abrir

unmake *vt* MECH ENG *joint* desmontar

unmaking *n* MINE desenganche *m*

unmanned¹ *adj* SPACE *spacecraft* automático, sin piloto, sin tripulación

unmanned² : ~ **exchange** *n* TELECOM central automática *f*, central no atendida *f*, central sin personal *f*; ~ **lander** *n* SPACE *spacecraft* módulo aterrizador automático *m*, módulo aterrizador no pilotado *m*, módulo de descenso automático *m*, módulo de descenso no pilotado *m*; ~ **landing stage** *n* SPACE fase de aterrizaje no pilotado *f*; ~ **passing point** *n* RAIL punto de paso sin personal *m*; ~ **submersible** *n* OCEAN sumergible telecomandado no tripulado *m*; ~ **turnout** *n* RAIL vía apartadero sin personal *f*

unmarried : ~ **sound** *n* CINEMAT sonido no sincronizado *m*

unmask *vt* MILIT *battery* despejar

unmoderated : ~ **fission neutron** *n* NUCL neutrón de fisión no moderado *m*

unmodulated *adj* SPACE *communications* inmodulado, no modulado

unmoor *vti* WATER TRANSP *ship* desamarrar, levar una de las dos anclas

unmooring *n* WATER TRANSP desamarre *m*

unmounted : ~ **tubing** *n* CONST tubo sin montar *m*

unnavigable *adj* HYDROL, WATER TRANSP no navegable

unnumbered : ~ **information** *n* (*UI*) TELECOM información no numerada *f*

unordered : ~ **tree** *n* COMP&DP árbol desordenado *m*

unoriented *adj* GEOL desorientado

unoxidizable *adj* CHEM inoxidable

unoxidized *adj* CHEM no oxidado

unpack *vt* COMP&DP desempaquetar, expandir

unpacked *adj* COMP&DP expandido

unpaired *adj* CHEM *electron*, ELEC ENG, ELECTRON no apareado, PART PHYS desapareado, PHYS desapareado, no apareado

unperforated *adj* TELECOM no perforado, sin perforar

unperturbed : ~ **orbit** *n* SPACE órbita no perturbada *f*

unplanned : ~ **maintenance** *n* QUALITY mantenimiento imprevisto *m*

unplasticized¹ *adj* P&R no plastificado

unplasticized² : ~ **PVC** *n* P&R *plastics* PVC no plastificado *m*

unplug *vt* ELEC *connection*, TELECOM desconectar, desenchufar, TV desenchufar

unpolled : ~ **mode** *n* PROD modo no inscrito *m*

unpressurized : ~ **line** *n* NUCL línea no presurizada *f*

unproved : ~ **area** *n* CONST zona sin ensayar *f*

unramming *n* MINE desatracamiento *m*

unravel *vt* OCEAN desenredar

unrectified : ~ **AC** *n* ELEC *supply network* CA sin rectificar *f*

unrefined *adj* FOOD no refinado

unregulated : ~ **bus system** *n* SPACE sistema de barras colectoras no regulado *m*; ~ **input** *n* PROD entrada no regulada *f*; ~ **voltage** *n* ELEC ENG voltaje no regulado *m*

unrestricted : ~ **bearer service** *n* TELECOM servicio del

portador sin restricciones *m*; ~ **digital data ratio** *n* TELECOM relación no restringida de datos digitales *f*; ~ **information transfer service** *n* TELECOM servicio de transferencia de información sin restricciones *m*; ~ **service** *n* TELECOM (*ISDN*) servicio sin restricciones *m*

unrevealed : ~ **failure** *n* QUALITY defecto no revelado *m*, falla no revelada *f*

unrig *vt* WATER TRANSP *mast, crane, etc* desaparejar, desguarnir, desnudar

unrigging *n* WATER TRANSP *mast, crane, etc* desaparejo *m*

unsafe¹ *adj* SAFE inseguro

unsafe² : ~ **act** *n* SAFE acción insegura *f*, acto inseguro *m*; ~ **conditions** *n pl* SAFE condiciones inseguras *f pl*; ~ **environmental conditions** *n pl* SAFE condiciones ambientales inseguras *f pl*

unsaturable *adj* CHEM insaturable

unsaturate *n* CHEM, FOOD, P&R, PETR TECH insaturado *n*

unsaturated¹ *adj* CHEM, FOOD, P&R, PETR TECH insaturado, no saturado

unsaturated² : ~ **carbon-to-carbon bond** *n* PETR TECH aglomerante carbón-carbón insaturado *m*; ~ **completely stable layer** *n* METEO capa estable totalmente sin saturar *f*; ~ **zone** *n* HYDROL zona no saturada *f*; ~ **zone water** *n* HYDROL zona no saturada de agua *f*

unscheduled : ~ **withdrawal** *n* NUCL *rotating fluids* extracción no programada *f*

unscramble *vt* TELECOM, TV descifrar

unscreened : ~ **coal** *n* COAL carbón sin tamizar *m*

unscrew *vt* NUCL destornillar

unscrewing *n* MECH ENG desatornillado *m*, desenganche *m*, desenroscado *m*; ~ **bush** *n* MECH ENG buje de desenroscar *m*; ~ **core** *n* MECH ENG *injection mould* molde de fijación por pernos *m*; ~ **parts mold** *AmE*, ~ **parts mould** *BrE n* MECH ENG molde de partes con pernos *m*, molde de piezas con pernos *m*

unseaworthy *adj* WATER TRANSP *ship* innavegable, inservible

unsettled *adj* WATER TRANSP *of weather* inseguro

unsewn¹ *adj* PRINT sin costura

unsewn² : ~ **binding** *n* PRINT encuadernación americana *f*, encuadernación sin costura *f*

unshielded : ~ **source** *n* NUCL fuente no blindada *f*

unship *vt* WATER TRANSP *cargo* desembarcar

unsized *adj* PAPER sin encolar

unslaked *adj* CHEM *lime* no apagado, no extinguido

unsoldering *n* MECH ENG desoldado *m*

unsplit : ~ **bush** *n* MECH ENG manguito de una pieza *m*

unspoilt : ~ **land** *n* POLL tierra vegetal *f*, tierra virgen *f*

unsprung : ~ **weight** *n* VEH peso no suspendido *m*

unsqueeze *vt* CINEMAT descomprimir

unsqueezed : ~ **image** *n* CINEMAT imagen descomprimida *f*

unstable¹ *adj* ELEC, METALL, METEO, PART PHYS, PHYS, TRANSP inestable

unstable² : ~ **air** *n* METEO aire inestable *m*; ~ **equilibrium** *n* PHYS equilibrio inestable *m*; ~ **flow** *n* FLUID, NUCL, TRANSP flujo inestable *m*; ~ **fracture** *n* METALL fractura inestable *f*; ~ **nucleus** *n* PART PHYS núcleo inestable *m*

unsteady : ~ **flow** *n* FLUID flujo no estacionario *m*, NUCL flujo inestable *m*

unstep *vt* WATER TRANSP *mast* desengastar

unstick: ~ **speed** *n* AIR TRANSP velocidad de despegue *f*

unstop *vt* CONST *pipe* abrir, dar paso

unstuff *vt* TRANSP desacolchar, desguarnecer

unstuffing *n* TRANSP vaciado *m*

unsulfonated: ~ **matter** *AmE see unsulphonated matter BrE*

unsulphonated: ~ **matter** *n* *BrE* DETERG material no sulfonado *m*

unsupercharged: ~ **engine** *n* AUTO motor sin sobrealimentación *m*

unsupported: ~ **beam** *n* CONST *strength of materials* viga sin apoyo *f*; ~ **shrink wrapping** *n* PACK empaquetadura al vacío sin apoyo *f*

unsymmetrical: ~ **arrangement** *n* ELEC ENG instalación asimétrica *f*

untapped *adj* ELEC *coil* sin derivaciones, sin tomas

unthread *vt* CINEMAT desenhebrar

unthreshed: ~ **head** *n* AGRIC espiga sin trillar *f*

untreated[1] *adj* HYDROL *of water* sin tratar

untreated[2]: ~ **sewage** *n* HYDROL, POLL, RECYCL, WATER aguas residuales no tratadas *f pl*; ~ **small** *n* COAL menudo no tratado *m*

untrimmed: ~ **machine width** *n* PAPER ancho útil de la máquina *m*; ~ **size** *n* PAPER formato bruto *m*, PRINT formato bruto *m*, tamaño bruto *m*, tamaño sin cortar *m*

untrussed: ~ **roof** *n* CONST tejado sin armadura *m*

untwisting *n* MECH ENG detorsión *f*

unvulcanized *adj* CHEM, ELEC, MECH, P&R, THERMO no vulcanizado

unwanted: ~ **emission** *n* TELECOM emisión no deseada *f*, emisión parásita *f*

unwashed[1] *adj* COAL no lavado

unwashed[2]: ~ **small** *n* COAL menudo no lavado *m*

unwind *vt* CINEMAT desbobinar

unwinder *n* TEXTIL desenrollador *m*

unwinding *n* MECH ENG desabobinado *m*, desenredado *m*, desenrollamiento *m*, RAIL devanado *m*; ~ **machine** *n* PACK desbobinadora *f*

UO₂[1] *abbr* (*uranium oxide*) CHEM UO_2 (*óxido de uranio*)

UO₂[2]: ~ **fuel** *n* NUCL combustible de UO_2 *m*; ~ **pellet** *n* NUCL pastilla de UO_2 *f*

UO₂-Gd₂-O₃: ~ **pellet** *n* (*urania-gadolinia pellet*) NUCL pastilla de UO_2-Gd_2-O_3 *f* (*pastilla de urania-gadolinia*)

up[1]: ~**-dip** *adv* GEOL contrariamente a la inclinación

up[2]: ~**-and-down motion** *n* MECH ENG movimiento alternativo *m*, movimiento alternativo vertical *m*, movimiento ascendente y descendente *m*, movimiento de vaivén vertical *m*, movimiento vertical *m*; ~ **count** *n* PROD conteo irreversible *m*; ~ **counter** *n* ELECTRON contador ascendente *m*, PROD contador irreversible *m*; ~ **counter rung** *n* PROD eslabón de contador irreversible *m*; ~**-down counter** *n* ELECTRON contador ascendente-descendente *m*, contador reversible *m*, PROD contador reversible *m*; ~ **and lower transistor switch** *n* PROD interruptor transisto de movimiento alternativo *m*; ~ **quark** *n* PART PHYS quark arriba *m*, up quark *m*, PHYS quark up *m*

upconverter *n* TELECOM convertidor ascendente *m*, convertidor elevador *m*, convertidor elevador de frecuencia *m*

update[1] *n* COMP&DP, PROD, TELECOM actualización *f*

update[2] *vt* COMP&DP actualizar, MECH ENG modernizar, poner al día, actualizar, PROD, TELECOM actualizar

updating *n* COMP&DP *of files*, PROD actualización *f*, TELECOM actualización *f*, puesta al día *f*

updip[1] *adj* GEOL de buzamiento ascendente, PETR TECH ascendente

updip[2] *n* GEOL buzamiento en sentido contrario a la inclinación *m*, PETR TECH buzamiento ascendente *m*, buzamiento hacia arriba *m*

updraft *AmE see updraught BrE*

updraught *n* *BrE* AUTO succión ascendente *f*

updraw: ~ **process** *n* C&G proceso de estirado vertical *m*

uperization *n* FOOD *food-processing machinery* uperización *f*

upfaulted: ~ **block** *n* GEOL bloque de dislocación ascendente *m*

upflow *n* NUCL flujo ascendente *m*

upgrade[1] *n* COMP&DP mejora *f*, CONST ascendente *m*, ascensión *f*, pendiente *f*

upgrade[2] *vt* CHEM refinar, COMP&DP mejorar, CONST ascender

upgrading *n* CHEM mejoramiento *m*, refinación *f*, COAL concentración *f*, enriquecimiento *m*

uphand: ~ **welding** *n* MECH soldadura *f*, soldadura a pulso *f*

uphill *adj* CONST cuesta arriba

upholstery *n* TEXTIL, VEH tapicería *f*

upkeep *n* PROD mantenimiento *m*, manutención *f*, sostenimiento *m*

upland: ~ **meadow** *n* AGRIC prado en altoplanicie *m*

uplift *n* FLUID sustentación *f*, GEOL, METEO levantamiento *m*, THERMO subpresión *f*

uplink *n* SPACE *communications*, TELECOM enlace ascendente *m*; ~ **block** *n* TELECOM bloque de enlace ascendente *m*; ~ **frequency** *n* SPACE *communications* frecuencia ascendente *f*; ~ **transmission phase** *n* TELECOM fase de transmisión del enlace ascendente *f*

upper: ~ **annealing temperature** *n* C&G temperatura superior de revenido *f*; ~ **bainite** *n* METALL bainita superior *f*; ~ **ball joint** *n* MECH junta de rótula superior *f*, MECH ENG junta de rótula superior *f*, rótula superior *f*; ~ **case** *n* PRINT caja alta *f*; ~ **containment pool** *n* NUCL piscina superior del recinto de contención *f*; ~ **control limit** *n* QUALITY límite superior de fiabilidad *m*; ~ **core** *n* NUCL interno superior del reactor *m*; ~ **deck** *n* WATER TRANSP cubierta superior *f*; ~ **end fitting** *n* NUCL tobera superior *f*; ~ **end plug** *n* NUCL tapón superior *m*; ~ **grid** *n* NUCL placa superior del núcleo *f*; ~ **internal** *n* NUCL interno superior del reactor *m*; ~ **ionosphere** *n* TELECOM ionosfera superior *f*; ~ **limit** *n* TELECOM límite superior *m*; ~ **limit of ozone layer** *n* METEO límite superior de la capa de ozono *m*; ~ **millstone** *n* FOOD muela superior *f*; ~ **part** *n* HYDROL *of river* curso superior *m*, tramo superior *m*; ~ **plenum** *n* NUCL pleno superior *m*; ~ **roll** *n* MECH ENG *rolling mill* cilindro macho *m*, cilindro superior *m*; ~ **sheet** *n* PRINT hoja superior *f*; ~ **shell assembly** *n* VEH tramo superior *m*; ~ **sideband** *n* COMP&DP, ELECTRON, PHYS, TELECOM, TV banda lateral superior *f*; ~ **stage** *n* SPACE última fase *f*; ~ **storage basin** *n* FUELLESS embalse de almacenamiento superior *m*; ~ **subfield** *n* TELECOM campo auxiliar superior *m*; ~ **surface** *n* AIR TRANSP *of wing*, PHYS superficie superior *f*; ~ **tie plate** *n* NUCL *vehicles* placa de sujeción superior *f*; ~ **wind** *n* METEO viento de la

atmósfera alta *m*, viento en altitud *m*; ~ **works** *n pl* WATER TRANSP *ship design* obra muerta *f*
upright *n* CONST *cross-piece to which rail is attached* subida *f*, montante *m*, soporte *m*, ascensión *f*, MECH ENG *post* apoyo *m*, paral *m*, poste de tabique *m*, soporte *m*, columna *f*, *of planing machine* montante *m*, MINE apoyo *m* (*AmL*), poste *m* (*Esp*), sustentación *f*, RAIL soporte *m*; ~ **burner** *n* PROD quemador recto *m*; ~ **fold** *n* GEOL pliegue simétrico *m*; ~ **freezer** *n* REFRIG congelador vertical *m*; ~ **radiator** *n* AUTO radiador derecho *m*, radiador vertical *m*; ~ **shaft** *n* MECH ENG eje vertical *m*; ~ **silo** *n* AGRIC silo vertical *m*
uprighter *n* C&G pie derecho *m*
uprush *n* OCEAN embate ascendente *m*
upset: ~ **welding** *n* THERMO soldeo por recalcadura *m*
upsetting: ~-**press** *n* MECH ENG prensa de recalcar *f*
upside-down: ~ **slate** *n* CINEMAT claqueta invertida *f*
upstream[1] *adj* FLUID, HYDROL ascendente, TV contracorriente, WATER aguas arriba
upstream[2] *adv* CONST, FLUID aguas arriba, río arriba, GAS aguas arriba, corriente arriba, río arriba, HYDROL aguas arriba, MECH, PHYS aguas arriba, río arriba, SPACE arriba, WATER TRANSP *river* a contra corriente, aguas arriba, contra la corriente, río arriba
upstream[3]: ~-**downstream symmetry** *n* FLUID simetría aguas arriba-aguas abajo *f*; ~ **fairing** *n* REFRIG carenado corriente arriba *m*; ~ **head** *n* FUELLESS salto de aguas arriba *m*; ~ **resistance** *n* PROD resistencia aguas arriba *f*; ~ **wake** *n* FLUID estela formada aguas arriba *f*
upstroke *n* AUTO, MECH ENG, VEH carrera ascendente *f*; ~ **press** *n* P&R prensa de carrera ascendente *f*
upsurge *n* HYDROL aumento del oleaje *m*
uptake *n* TEXTIL absorción *f*, WATER captación *f*, conducto ascendente *m*, toma *f*; ~ **crown** *n* AmE (*cf port crown BrE*) C&G corona del puerto *f*
upthrust *n* PHYS empuje hacia arriba *m*
upthrusted: ~ **wedge** *n* CONST *fixed equipment* cuña de falla inversa *f*
uptime *n* COMP&DP tiempo productivo *m*, tiempo útil *m*
U-Pu: ~ **cycle** *n* NUCL ciclo de U-Pu *m*
upward[1] *adj* GEOL ascendente; ~ **compatible** *adj* COMP&DP compatible hacia arriba
upward[2]: ~ **compatibility** *n* COMP&DP compatibilidad ascendente *f*, compatibilidad hacia arriba *f*; ~ **current classifier** *n* COAL clasificador de corriente vertical *m*; ~ **drilling** *n* C&G ataque a las piedras del horno por movimiento del vidrio *m*; ~ **flow** *n* NUCL flujo ascendente *m*; ~ **heave** *n* NUCL *founding* levantamiento *m*
upwash *n* AIR TRANSP *airworthiness* deflexión de flujo hacia arriba *f*
upwelling *n* OCEAN afloramiento *m*, surgencia *f*
upwind *adv* WATER TRANSP *sailing* al viento, contra el viento
uralite *n* MINERAL uralita *f*
uramido *adj* CHEM uramido
uranate *n* CHEM uranato *m*
urania: ~-**gadolinia pellet** *n* (*UO₂-Gd₂-O₃ pellet*) NUCL pastilla de urania-gadolinia *f* (*pastilla de UO₂-Gd₂-O₃*)
uranic[1] *adj* CHEM uránico
uranic[2]: ~ **fluoride** *n* NUCL fluoruro de uranio *m*
uranide *n* CHEM uranuro *m*
uraninite *n* MINERAL uraninita *f*

uranium[1]: ~-**bearing** *adj* CHEM, MINERAL, RAD PHYS uranífero
uranium[2] *n* (*U*) CHEM, NUCL, RAD PHYS uranio *m* (*U*); ~ **aluminide fuel** *n* NUCL combustible de aluminiuro de uranio *m*; ~-**bearing mineral** *n* NUCL mineral uranífero *m*; ~ **black** *n* NUCL negro de uranio *m*, uraninita *f*; ~ **compound** *n* NUCL compuesto de uranio *m*; ~ **concentrate** *n* NUCL concentrado de uranio *m*, torta amarilla *f*; ~-**conversion plant** *n* NUCL planta de conversión de uranio *f*; ~ **dicarbide** *n* CHEM, NUCL dicarburo de uranio *m*; ~ **dioxide fuel** *n* NUCL combustible de dióxido de uranio *m*; ~ **dioxide pellet** *n* NUCL pastilla de dióxido de uranio *f*; ~ **free from its daughters** *n* NUCL uranio sin sus hijas *m*; ~ **fuel element** *n* NUCL elemento de combustible de uranio *m*; ~ **galena** *n* NUCL galena de uranio *f*; ~ **heavy water reactor** *n* NUCL reactor de uranio moderado por agua pesada *m*; ~ **hexafluoride** *n* CHEM, NUCL hexafluoruro de uranio *m*; ~ **ingot** *n* NUCL lingote de uranio *m*; ~ **isotope separation plant** *n* NUCL planta de separación de isótopos de uranio *f*; ~ **milling** *n* NUCL tratamiento de minerales de uranio *m*; ~ **nucleus** *n* NUCL núcleo del uranio *m*; ~ **oxide** *n* (*UO₂*) CHEM óxido de uranio *m* (*UO₂*); ~-**plutonium cycle** *n* NUCL ciclo de uranio-plutonio *m*; ~ **preconcentrate** *n* NUCL preconcentrado de uranio *m*; ~ **reactor** *n* NUCL reactor de uranio *m*; ~ **refining** *n* NUCL refinado de uranio *m*; ~ **scrap** *n* NUCL restos de uranio *m pl*
uranous *adj* CHEM uranoso
uranyl *n* CHEM uranilo *m*
urazole *n* CHEM urazol *m*
urban: ~ **catchment** *n* WATER captación urbana *f*; ~ **cycle** *n* VEH recorrido en ciudad *m*, recorrido urbano *m*; ~ **electric vehicle** *n* TRANSP vehículo eléctrico urbano *m*; ~ **network** *n* TELECOM red urbana *f*; ~ **and regional metropolitan railroad** *n* AmE (*cf urban and regional metropolitan railway BrE*) TRANSP ferrocarril metropolitano urbano y de cercanías *m*; ~ **and regional metropolitan railway** BrE *n* (*cf urban and regional metropolitan railroad AmE*) TRANSP ferrocarril metropolitano urbano y de cercanías *m*; ~ **traffic** *n* TRANSP tráfico urbano *m*; ~-**water management** *n* WATER administración de aguas urbanas *f*
urea *n* CHEM, DETERG urea *f*; ~-**formaldehyde resin** *n* (*UF*) ELEC *insulation*, P&R resina de formaldehido de urea *f*, resina de urea-formaldehído *f*
ureal *adj* CHEM de la urea
ureic *adj* CHEM ureico
ureide *n* CHEM ureido *m*
ureotelic *adj* CHEM ureotélico
urethane *n* CHEM uretano *m*; ~ **buffer** *n* MECH ENG *die set* separador de uretano *m*
uric *adj* CHEM úrico
uridine *n* CHEM uridina *f*
urobilinogen *n* CHEM urobilinógeno *m*
uronic *adj* CHEM urónico
uropterin *n* CHEM uropterina *f*
urotropine *n* CHEM urotropina *f*
uroxanic *adj* CHEM uroxánico
US[1]: ~ **NRC** *abbr* (*United States Nuclear Regulatory Commission*) NUCL US NRC (*Comisión Reguladora Nuclear de los Estados Unidos*)
US[2]: ~ **standard thread** *n* MECH ENG hilo estándar de

los Estados Unidos *m*, rosca estándar de los Estados Unidos *f*

use: **~-by date** *n* PACK fecha de caducidad *f*; **~-surface** *n* COATINGS superficie de aplicación *f*

useful: **~ heat** *n* HEAT ENG calor útil *m*; **~ life** *n* PACK vida útil *f*; **~ rain** *n* METEO lluvia útil *f*; **~ refrigerating effect** *n* REFRIG potencia frigorífica útil *f*; **~ satellite load** *n* SPACE carga útil del satélite *f*; **~ surface** *n* MECH ENG superficie útil *f*; **~ working range** *n* TRANSP alcance útil de funcionamiento *m*

user[1]: **~-defined** *adj* COMP&DP definido por el usuario; **~-friendly** *adj* COMP&DP cómodo, fácil de manejar, fácil para el usuario

user[2] *n* GEN usuario *m*; **~ access** *n* COMP&DP, TELECOM acceso del usuario *m*; **~ agent** *n* (*UA*) COMP&DP, TELECOM agente usuario *m*; **~ area** *n* (*UA*) COMP&DP, TELECOM área de usuario *f*; **~-friendliness** *n* COMP&DP facilidad de manejo *f*; **~ group** *n* COMP&DP grupo de usuarios *m*; **~ guide** *n* TELECOM guía del usuario *f*; **~ interface** *n* COMP&DP interfase con el usuario *f*, interfaz del usuario *f*, TELECOM interfaz de usuario *f*; **~ manual** *n* COMP&DP manual del usuario *m*; **~ name** *n* COMP&DP nombre del usuario *m*; **~-network interface** *n* (*UNI*) COMP&DP, TELECOM interfaz de la red del usuario *m*, interfaz usuario-red *f*; **~ operating environment** *n* COMP&DP ambiente operacional del usuario *m*, entorno operativo del usuario *m*; **~ programmable device** *n* COMP&DP dispositivo programable por usuario *m*; **~ query** *n* COMP&DP consulta del usuario *f*, interrogación por el usuario *f*; **~-signaling bearer service** *AmE*, **~-signalling bearer service** *BrE n* TELECOM servicio portador de señalización al usuario *m*; **~-to-user indicator** *n* TELECOM indicador de usuario a usuario *m*; **~-to-user information** *n* (*UUI*) TELECOM información de usuario a usuario *f*; **~-to-user information message** *n* (*USR*) TELECOM mensaje de información de usuario a usuario *m*; **~-to-user signaling** *AmE*, **~-to-user signalling** *BrE n* TELECOM señalización de usuario a usuario *f*

U-shaped: **~ base plate** *n* MECH ENG *for drilling-machine* chapa de base en forma de U *f*, mesa de base en U *f*, plato de base en U *m*; **~ track girder** *n* TRANSP traviesa de vía en U *f*

USR *abbr* (*user-to-user information message*) TELECOM mensaje de información de usuario a usuario *m*

UTC *abbr* (*universal time coordinates*) METEO, TELECOM HUC (*coordenadas de hora universal*)

utensil *n* CONST elemento *m*, utensilio *m*

utility *n* PETR TECH servicio general *m*, PROD empresa de servicio público *f*, SPACE servicio *m*, utilidad *f*, TRANSP empresa de servicio público *f*; **~ knife** *n* MECH ENG cuchillo para uso general *m*; **~ program** *n* COMP&DP programa de utilidades *m*, programa de utilitarios *m*, programa utilitario *m*; **~ satellite** *n* SPACE *communications* satélite de utilidad *m*; **~ vehicle** *n* MILIT vehículo de uso general *m*, VEH vehículo utilitario *m*

utilization: **~ curve** *n* FUELLESS gráfico de utilización *m*

U-type: **~ engine** *n* AUTO motor tipo U *m*

UUI *abbr* (*user-to-user information*) TELECOM información de usuario a usuario *f*

UUS *abbr* (*user-to-user signaling AmE, user-to-user signalling BrE*), TELECOM señalización de usuario a usuario *f*

UV[1] *abbr* (*ultraviolet*) OPT, PHYS, RAD PHYS, SPACE UV (*ultravioleta*)

UV[2]: **~-absorbing** *adj* C&G absorbente de rayos Ultra Violeta; **~-transmitting** *adj* C&G transparente a los rayos Ultra Violeta *m*

UV[3]: **~ ray** *n* OPT rayo UV *m*

uvarovite *n* MINERAL uvarovita *f*

uvitic *adj* CHEM uvítico

UW *abbr* (*unique word*) SPACE *communications* grupo de señales único *m*, mandato único *m*, orden única *f*, sentencia única *f*

UXB *abbr* (*unexploded bomb*) MILIT bomba sin detonar *f*, bomba sin explotar *f*

V

V *abbr* CHEM (*vanadium*) V (*vanadio*), ELEC, ELEC ENG, METR, PHYS (*volt*) V (*voltio*)

vacancy *n* CRYSTALL *defect* vacante *m*, METALL laguna reticular *f*; **~-absorbing jog** *n* METALL desplazamiento por absorción de laguna reticular *m*; **~ diffusion** *n* METALL difusión de lagunas reticulares *f*; **~ disc** *BrE*, **~ disk** *AmE* *n* METALL disco de lagunas reticulares *m*; **~-emitting jog** *n* METALL desplazamiento por emisión de lagunas reticulares *m*

vacciniin *n* CHEM vaccinina *f*

vacuum[1]: **~-encapsulated** *adj* ELEC ENG encapsulado al vacío; **~-insulated** *adj* ELEC ENG aislado al vacío; **~-packed** *adj* FOOD envasado al vacío

vacuum[2] *n* GEN vacío *m*, SPACE subatmosférico *m*; **~ advance mechanism** *n* AUTO mecanismo de avance de vacío *m*, VEH mecanismo de avance *m*; **~ air pump** *n* FOOD bomba de vacío *f*; **~ arc** *n* ELEC, ELEC ENG arco de vacío *m*; **~ arc furnace** *n* HEAT horno de arco al vacío *m*; **~-assisted power brake** *n* AUTO freno mecánico de vacío *m*; **~ blowing** *n* C&G soplado con vacío *m*; **~ box** *n* PAPER caja aspirante *f*; **~ brake** *n* MECH ENG freno de vacío *m*, freno neumático *m*, vacuofreno *m*, RAIL freno de vacío *m*, vacuofreno *m*, VEH freno de vacío *m*; **~ brazing** *n* CONST soldadura al vacío *f*; **~ bubble** *n* C&G burbuja al vacío *f*; **~ capacitor** *n* ELEC ENG condensador de vacío *m*; **~ capstan** *n* TV cabrestante al vacío *m*; **~ casting** *n* NUCL fundición en vacío *f*; **~ chamber** *n* TV cámara de vacío *f*; **~ check valve** *n* AUTO válvula de control de vacío *f*; **~ cleaner for dusts hazardous to health** *n* SAFE aspirado al vacío de polvos peligrosos para la salud *m*; **~ cleaner for industrial purposes** *n* SAFE aspiradora para propósitos industriales *f*; **~-closing machine** *n* PACK máquina cerradora al vacío *f*; **~-coated film** *n* COATINGS revestimiento a vacío *m*; **~ contact element** *n* PROD elemento de contacto en vacío *m*; **~ contact plate process** *n* FOOD proceso de placa de contacto en vacío *m*; **~ contactor** *n* PROD contactor de vacío *m*; **~ cooling** *n* REFRIG enfriamiento de vacío *m*; **~-deposited film** *n* ELECTRON película depositada en vacío *f*; **~ deposition** *n* ELECTRON deposición en vacío *f*; **~ desiccator** *n* HEAT desecador por vacío *m*, LAB desecador al vacío *m*; **~ diode** *n* ELECTRON diodo de vacío *m*; **~ discharge** *n* ELEC, ELEC ENG descarga al vacío *f*; **~ distillation** *n* CHEM, CHEM TECH destilación al vacío *f*, FOOD, PHYS destilación en vacío *f*; **~ dryer** *n* COAL secador de vacío *m*, FOOD secador a vacío *m*, HEAT desecador por vacío *m*; **~ drying** *n* FOOD secador a vacío *m*; **~-drying cabinet** *n* MECH ENG armario de secado al vacío *m*, armario vacuosecador *m*, gabinete vacuosecador *m*; **~-drying oven** *n* FOOD horno de secado en vacío *m*; **~ engineering** *n* MECH ENG vacuoingeniería *f*, vacuotecnia *f*, vacuotécnica *f*; **~ equipment** *n* MECH ENG equipo de vacío *m*; **~ evaporator** *n* FOOD evaporador de vacío *m*; **~ filling** *n* FOOD llenado en vacío *m*; **~ filling machine** *n* PACK máquina de llenado al vacío *f*; **~ film holder** *n* PRINT portapelículas con disposi-

tivo de vacío *f*; **~ film transport system** *n* PACK sistema de transporte de película al vacío *m*; **~ filter** *n* CHEM TECH filtro al vacío *m*, COAL filtro de vacío *m*; **~ filtration** *n* CHEM TECH filtración al vacío *f*, filtrado en vacío *m*, COAL filtrado al vacío *m*, FOOD, LAB filtración al vacío *f*, filtrado en vacío *m*; **~ flask** *n* C&G termo *m*, LAB matraz de vacío *m*; **~-formed package** *n* PACK paquete conformado al vacío *m*; **~ forming** *n* P&R moldeado por vacío *m*, moldeo por vacío *m*; **~-forming mold** *AmE*, **~-forming mould** *BrE* *n* MECH ENG molde para formar por vacío *m*; **~ frame** *n* PRINT marco neumático *m*; **~ fuel pump** *n* AUTO, VEH bomba de combustible de vacío *f*; **~ furnace** *n* MECH ENG horno de vacío *m*, vacuohorno *m*; **~ gage** *AmE*, **~ gauge** *BrE* *n* FOOD manómetro de vacío *m*, INSTR vacuómetro *m*, MECH ENG indicador de vacío *m*, manómetro de vacío *m*, vacuómetro *m*, PETR TECH vacuómetro *m*, PHYS medidor de vacío *m*, PROD vacuómetro *m*, REFRIG manómetro de vacío *m*; **~-grating spectrograph** *n* WAVE PHYS espectrografía reticular en vacío *f*; **~ guide** *n* TV vacuómetro *m*; **~ guide system** *n* TV sistema de vacuometría *m*; **~ heat sealer** *n* PACK sellado hermético al vacío *m*, sellador hermético al vacío *m*; **~ heat treatment** *n* METALL tratamiento por calentamiento en el vacío *m*; **~ hose** *n* MECH ENG manguera de vacío *f*; **~ insulation** *n* ELEC, ELEC ENG aislamiento al vacío *m*, MECH ENG aislamiento por vacío *m*, vacuoaislamiento *m*; **~ lorry** *n* *BrE* (*cf vacuum truck AmE*) MAR POLL camión tanque con sistema de vacío *m*; **~ manifold** *n* INSTR tubería aspirante *f*; **~ melting** *n* METALL vacuofusión *f*; **~ metallization** *n* ELECTRON metalizado en vacío *m*; **~ metallizing** *n* C&G metalizado al vacío *m*; **~ mold** *AmE*, **~ mould** *BrE* *n* MECH ENG molde de vacío *m*; **~ oven** *n* LAB estufa al vacío *f*, horno al vacío *m*; **~ pack** *n* PACK paquete llenado al vacío *m*; **~-packaging machine** *n* PACK máquina empaquetadora al vacío *f*; **~-packaging tool** *n* MECH ENG, PACK máquina de empaquetado al vacío *f*; **~ pan** *n* LAB bandeja de vacío *f*; **~ phototube** *n* ELECTRON fototubo de vacío *m*, válvula de vacío *f*, INSTR fototubo de vacío *m*; **~ polarization** *n* NUCL *heat unit* polarización en vacío *f*; **~ pump** *n* FOOD, LAB, MAR POLL bomba de vacío *f*, MECH ENG bomba de vacío *f*, bomba neumática *f*, pulsómetro *m*, PHYS bomba de vacío *f*, bomba neumática *f*; **~ seal** *n* MECH ENG cierre hermético *m*, junta hermética *f*, obturador de vacío *m*, sello vacuoobturador *m*; **~-sealing machine** *n* PACK máquina selladora al vacío *f*; **~ shelf dryer** *n* FOOD secadero de estanterías a vacío *m* (*SCA*); **~ sintering** *n* METALL sinterización en el vacío *f*; **~ suspension** *n* TRANSP suspensión al vacío *f*; **~ switch** *n* ELEC *circuit breaker* conmutador al vacío *m*, conmutador de vacío *m*, interruptor de vacío *m*; **~ tanker** *n* MAR POLL buque tanque con sistema de vacío *m*; **~ technology** *n* MECH ENG tecnología del vacío *f*, vacuotecnología *f*; **~ test** *n* REFRIG prueba de vacío *f*; **~-thermoforming**

machine *n* PACK máquina termoformadora al vacío *f*; ~ **thrust** *n* SPACE empuje en vacío *m*; ~ **triode** *n* ELECTRON triodo de vacío *m*; ~ **truck** *n* AmE (*cf vacuum lorry BrE*) MAR POLL camión tanque con sistema de vacío *m*; ~ **tube** *n* COMP&DP tubo de vacío *m*, válvula de vacío *f*, ELECTRON, PHYS, TV tubo de vacío *m*; ~-**tube amplification** *n* ELECTRON amplificación de tubo de vacío *f*; ~-**tube amplifier** *n* ELECTRON amplificador de lámpara de vacío *m*, amplificador de tubo de vacío *m*; ~ **tube modulator** *n* ELECTRON modulador de lámpara de vacío *m*, modulador de tubo de vacío *m*; ~ **tube oscillator** *n* ELECTRON oscilador de lámpara de vacío *m*, oscilador de tubo de vacío *m*; ~ **ultraviolet** *n* SPACE ultravioleta en vacío *m*; ~ **unit** *n* MECH ENG unidad del sistema de vacío *f*; ~ **valve** *n* AUTO, VEH válvula de vacío *f*

VAD *abbr* (*vapor phase axial deposition AmE*, *vapour phase axial deposition BrE*) OPT, TELECOM deposición axial en fase vapor *f*, deposición axial por fase de vapor *f*

vadose: ~ **water** *n* WATER agua subterránea más arriba de la capa freática *f*

valence *n* CHEM, METALL, PHYS valencia *f*; ~ **band** *n* (*VB*) PHYS, RAD PHYS banda de valencia *f*; ~ **electron** *n* METALL, PHYS electrón de valencia *m*; ~ **electron concentration** *n* NUCL concentración de electrones de valencia *f*; ~ **state** *n* NUCL estado de valencia *m*

valency *n* CHEM valencia *f*

valentinite *n* MINERAL valentinita *f*

valeramide *n* CHEM valeramida *f*

valerate *n* CHEM valerato *m*

valeric *adj* CHEM valérico

valeryl *n* CHEM valerilo *m*

valerylene *n* CHEM valerileno *m*

validate *vt* COMP&DP, SPACE validar

validation *n* COMP&DP, QUALITY validación *f*

validity *n* TELECOM validez *f*; ~ **check** *n* COMP&DP control de validez *m*, verificación de validez *f*, TELECOM comprobación de validez *f*, prueba de validez *f*, verificación de validez *f*; ~ **period** *n* CONST período de validez *m*

valley *n* CONST *architecture* limahoya *f*; ~ **breeze** *n* METEO brisa de valle *f*; ~ **station** *n* TRANSP estación intermedia *f*

valuable: ~ **element** *n* NUCL *coil* elemento aprovechable *m*, elemento de valor *m*

value[1]: ~-**added** *adj* COMP&DP, TELECOM *services* de valor agregado (*AmL*), de valor añadido (*Esp*)

value[2] *n* REFRIG magnitud *f*, TELECOM valor *m*; ~-**added network** *n* (*VAN*) COMP&DP, TELECOM red de valor agregado *f* (*AmL*), red de valor añadido *f* (*Esp*); ~-**added service** *n* TELECOM servicio de valor agregado *m* (*AmL*), servicio de valor añadido *m* (*Esp*); ~ **analysis** *n* PROD análisis del valor *m*

valve *n* GEN válvula *f*; ~ **adaptor gasket** *n* REFRIG junta de estanqueidad del asiento de la válvula *f*; ~ **body** *n* AUTO cuerpo de la válvula *m*, MECH ENG cuerpo de válvula *m*; ~ **box** *n* HYDRAUL caja de válvulas *f*; ~ **cap** *n* VEH tapa de válvula *f*; ~ **chamber** *n* HYDROL cámara de compuertas *f*; ~ **chest** *n* HYDRAUL caja de válvulas *f*, cuerpo de la válvula *m*, cámara de distribución de vapor *f*, PETR TECH caja de distribución *f*, caja de válvulas *f*, cámara de distribución del vapor *f*; ~ **clearance** *n* AUTO holgura de la válvula *f*, holgura de taqués *f*, juego de la válvula *m*,

juego de taqué *m*, MECH ENG holgura de la válvula *f*, tolerancia de válvula *f*, VEH juego de la válvula *m*, juego de taqué *m*, holgura de la válvula *f*, holgura de taqués *f*; ~ **cock** *n* HYDRAUL distribuidor rotativo de válvula *m*; ~ **control** *n* AUTO mando de la válvula *m*; ~ **disc** *BrE*, ~ **disk** *AmE n* AUTO disco de válvula *m*; ~ **eccentric** *n* HYDRAUL excéntrica de válvula *f*; ~ **face** *n* VEH cara de empuje de la válvula *f*; ~ **flap** *n* NUCL charnela *f*; ~ **flutter** *n* REFRIG vibración de una válvula *f*; ~ **gear** *n* HYDRAUL mecanismo de distribución por válvulas *m*, mecanismo de mando del distribuidor *m*, VEH distribución por válvulas *f*; ~-**gear mechanism** *n* AUTO mecanismo de engranaje de las válvulas *m*; ~ **guide** *n* AUTO guía de válvula *f*, HYDRAUL alojamiento de válvula *m*, guía de válvula *f*, VEH guía de válvula *f*; ~ **head** *n* AUTO cabeza de válvula *f*; ~ **lap** *n* AUTO, HYDRAUL, VEH asiento de válvula *m*; ~ **lift** *n* HYDRAUL carrera de la válvula *f*, carrera del distribuidor *f*; ~ **lifter** *n* VEH empujador *m*, taqué *m*; ~ **liner** *n* HYDRAUL caja del distribuidor *f*; ~-**mating surface** *n* AUTO superficie de contacto de la válvula *f*; ~ **motion** *n* HYDRAUL desplazamiento de válvula *m*, distribución *f*; ~ **off** *n* NUCL válvula cerrada *f*; ~ **outlet** *n* MECH ENG salida de válvula *f*; ~ **push rod** *n* AUTO varilla empujadora de válvulas *f*, varilla empujaválvulas *f*; ~ **rocker** *n* HYDRAUL balancín de válvula *m*; ~ **rod** *n* HYDRAUL vástago de válvula *m*, vástago del distribuidor *m*, RAIL vástago del distribuidor *m*; ~ **rotator** *n* AUTO rotador de válvula *m*, VEH posicionador rotativo de la válvula *m*; ~ **seat** *n* AUTO asiento de válvula *m*, HYDRAUL alojamiento de válvula *m*, asiento de válvula *m*, espejo del distribuidor *m*, VEH asiento de válvula *m*; ~ **setting** *n* AUTO ajuste de válvula *m*, reglaje de taqué *m*, reglaje de válvula *m*; ~ **shaft** *n* AUTO eje de válvulas *m*; ~ **shaft seal** *n* AUTO sello del eje de válvulas *m*; ~ **spindle** *n* HYDRAUL vástago de válvula *m*; ~ **spool grinding** *n* PROD rectificado del carrete de la válvula *m*; ~ **spring** *n* AUTO, VEH muelle de válvula *m*; ~-**spring washer** *n* HYDRAUL, MECH ENG arandela de resorte de válvula *f*, arandela del muelle de válvula *f*; ~ **stem** *n* HYDRAUL, VEH vástago de válvula *m*; ~ **tappet** *n* AUTO empujaválvulas *m*, levantaválvulas *m*, HYDRAUL balancín de válvula *m*, empujador de válvula *m*, varilla de levantamiento de la válvula *f*, VEH levantaválvulas *m*; ~-**timing diagram** *n* AUTO diagrama de sincronización de válvulas *m*, esquema de sincronización de válvulas *m*; ~ **train** *n* VEH serie de válvulas *f*; ~ **travel** *n* HYDRAUL carrera de la válvula *f*, carrera del distribuidor *f*; ~ **yoke** *n* MECH ENG horquilla de válvula *f*, muletilla de válvula *f*

valveless: ~ **engine** *n* AUTO motor sin válvulas *m*

VAN *abbr* (*value-added network*) COMP&DP, TELECOM red de valor agregado *f* (*AmL*), red de valor añadido *f* (*Esp*)

Van Allen: ~ **belt** *n* RAD PHYS cinturón de Van Allen *m*; ~ **radiation belt** *n* GEOPHYS cinturón de radiación de Van Allen *m*, RAD PHYS cinturón de Van Allen *m*, cinturón de radiación de Van Allen *m*, SPACE cinturón de radiación de Van Allen *m*;

Van de Graaff: ~ **generator** *n* ELEC estatitrón *m*, generador Van de Graaff *m*, ELEC ENG generador Van de Graaff *m*, PHYS generador Van de Graaff *m*, estatitrón *m*

Van der Waals: ~ **bond** *n* CRYSTALL enlace de Van der

Waals *m*; ~ **equation** *n* PHYS ecuación de Van der Waals *f*; ~ **radius** *n* PHYS radio de Van der Waals *m*
vanadate *n* CHEM vanadato *m*
vanadic *adj* CHEM vanádico
vanadiferous *adj* CHEM vanadífero
vanadinite *n* MINERAL vanadinita *f*
vanadiolite *n* MINERAL vanadiolita *f*
vanadite *n* CHEM vanadito *m*
vanadium *n* (*V*) CHEM, METALL vanadio *m* (*V*)
vanadous *adj* CHEM vanadoso
vanadyl *n* CHEM vanadilo *m*
vane *n* AIR TRANSP *of turbine engine* álabe *m*, paleta *f*, CONST paleta *f*, tablilla *f*, álabe *m*, ELEC álabe *m*, FUELLESS paleta *f*, HYDRAUL *of turbine* álabe *m*, paleta *f*, pala *f*, INSTR aspa *f*, MECH álabe *m*, paleta *f*, MECH ENG *of turbine* pala *f*, paleta *f*, álabe *m*, NUCL álabe *m*, PROD álabe *m*, paleta *f*, aspa *f*, REFRIG, SPACE álabe *m*; ~ **axial fan** *n* REFRIG ventilador axial de paletas *m*; ~ **pump** *n* PROD bomba de paletas *f*, bomba rotativa de paletas *f*, WATER bomba de paletas *f*; ~**-type anode** *n* ELEC ENG ánodo tipo álabes *m*; ~**-type relay** *n* ELEC relé de aleta *m*; ~ **velocity** *n* FUELLESS velocidad de las paletas *f*; ~ **wattmeter** *n* ELEC, ELEC ENG, INSTR, PHYS vatímetro de paleta *m*
vanishing: ~ **line** *n* GEOM línea de fuga *f*; ~ **point** *n* GEOM punto de fuga *m*
vanity: ~ **mirror** *n* VEH espejo de cortesía *m*
vapor *AmE see vapour BrE*
vaporator *n* PROD vaporizador *m*
vaporization *n* GEN vaporización *f*
vaporize *vt* AUTO, CHEM, CHEM TECH, GAS, PHYS, THERMO vaporizar
vaporized *adj* AUTO, CHEM, CHEM TECH, GAS, PHYS, THERMO vaporizado
vaporizer *n* GEN vaporizador *m*
vaporizing: ~ **burner** *n* THERMO quemador nebulizante *m*
vaporous *adj* CHEM, GAS, PHYS vaporoso
Vapotron *n* ELECTRON Vapotrón *m*
vapour[1]: ~**-expanded** *adj* BrE CHEM TECH expandido por vapor; ~**-grown** *adj* BrE CHEM TECH crecido por vapor; ~**-proof** *adj* BrE SAFE a prueba de vapores
vapour[2] *n* BrE GEN vapor *m*; ~ **bath** *n* BrE CHEM TECH, LAB baño de vapor *m*; ~ **bubble** *n* BrE CHEM TECH burbuja de vapor *f*; ~**-catching cone cap** *n* BrE CHEM TECH tapa del cono atrapador de vapor *f*; ~ **compression** *n* BrE CHEM TECH compresión de vapor *f*; ~ **compression cycle** *n* BrE THERMO ciclo de compresión de vapor *m*; ~ **condensation** *n* BrE NUCL condensación de vapor *f*; ~ **density** *n* BrE CHEM, PHYS, THERMO densidad de vapor *f*; ~**-deposited layer** *n* BrE CHEM TECH capa obtenida por deposición de vapor *f*; ~ **deposition** *n* BrE ELECTRON deposición en vapor *f*, THERMO *for cable* deposición en fase vapor *f*, deposición en vapor *f*; ~ **deposition technique** *n* BrE CHEM TECH técnica de deposición en fase de vapor *f*; ~ **discharge lamp** *n* BrE THERMO lámpara de descarga de vapor *f*; ~ **dispersion** *n* BrE GAS dispersión de vapor *f*; ~ **generator** *n* BrE NUCL *ring winding* generador de vapor *m*; ~ **jet refrigerating cycle** *n* BrE REFRIG ciclo de refrigeración por chorro de vapor *m*, ciclo frigorífico de eyección de vapor *m*; ~ **line** *n* BrE HYDRAUL tubería de vapor *f*; ~ **lock** *n* BrE AUTO bolsa de vapor *f*, tapón de vapor *m*; ~ **permeability** *n* BrE HEAT ENG permeabilidad al vapor *f*, THERMO

permeabilidad de vapor *f*; ~ **permeance** *n* BrE HEAT ENG penetración del vapor *f*; ~ **phase** *n* BrE CHEM TECH, THERMO fase vapor *f*; ~ **phase axial deposition** *n* BrE (*VAD*) OPT deposición axial en fase vapor *f*, deposicíon axial por fase de vapor *f*, TELECOM deposición axial en fase vapor *f*, deposición axial por fase de vapor *f*; ~ **phase axial deposition technique** *n* BrE TELECOM técnica de depósito axial por fase de vapor *f*; ~ **phase chemical deposition** *n* BrE OPT, TELECOM deposición química en fase de vapor *f*; ~ **phase epitaxy** *n* BrE CHEM TECH epitaxia en fase vapor *f*; ~**-phase-grown epitaxial layer** *n* BrE ELECTRON estratificador epitaxial en fase de vapor crecida *m*; ~ **phase nitration** *n* BrE CHEM TECH nitración en fase vapor *f*; ~ **phase reaction** *n* BrE ELECTRON reacción en fase de vapor *f*; ~ **phase verneuil method** *n* BrE OPT método de Verneuil en fase vapor *m*; ~ **pressure** *n* BrE HEAT, PETR TECH, PHYS, REFRIG presión de vapor *f*; ~ **pressure thermometer** *n* BrE REFRIG termómetro de presión a vapor *m*; ~ **quenching** *n* BrE METALL temple instantáneo al vapor *m*; ~ **resistance** *n* BrE HEAT ENG resistencia del vapor *f*; ~ **resistivity** *n* BrE HEAT ENG resistividad del vapor *f*; ~ **return line** *n* BrE AUTO circuito de regreso del vapor *m*, línea de regreso del vapor *f*; ~ **trap** *n* BrE CHEM TECH trampa de vapor *f*
varactor *n* ELECTRON reactancia variable *f*, varactor *m*; ~ **chip** *n* ELECTRON chip varactor *m*; ~ **diode** *n* ELECTRON, PHYS, TV diodo varactor *m*; ~**-tuned oscillator** *n* ELECTRON oscilador de varactor ajustado *m*; ~ **tuning** *n* ELECTRON ajuste del varactor *m*
variable[1] *adj* MATH variable
variable[2] *n* COMP&DP, MATH variable *f*; ~**-amplitude recording** *n* ACOUST grabación de amplitud variable *f*; ~**-amplitude test** *n* METALL prueba de amplitud variable *f*; ~**-aperture shutter** *n* CINEMAT, PHOTO obturador de abertura variable *m*; ~**-area recording** *n* TV grabación de área variable *f*; ~ **attenuation** *n* ELECTRON atenuación variable *f*; ~ **attenuator** *n* ELECTRON atenuador variable *m*; ~**-bit rate** *n* (*VBR*) COMP&DP, TELECOM tasa de bits variable *f*; ~ **capacitor** *n* ELEC capacitador variable *m*, condensador variable *m*, ELEC ENG, PHYS condensador variable *m*; ~**-capacitor section** *n* ELEC ENG sección variable por condensador *f*; ~**-carrier modulation** *n* ELECTRON modulación de portadora variable *f*; ~ **coaxial attenuator** *n* ELECTRON atenuador coaxial variable *m*; ~ **delay** *n* TELECOM retardo variable *m*; ~**-delivery pump** *n* PROD bomba de caudal regulable *f*; ~**-density recording** *n* ACOUST grabación de densidad variable *f*; ~**-density track** *n* TV pista sonora de densidad variable *f*; ~**-discharge pump** *n* MECH ENG bomba de caudal regulable *f*, bomba de descarga variable *f*; ~**-displacement motor** *n* PROD motor de desplazamiento variable *m*; ~ **field** *n* COMP&DP, ELEC ENG campo variable *m*; ~ **flow** *n* HYDROL caudal variable *m*; ~ **focal length** *n* PHOTO distancia focal variable *f*; ~**-focus reflector** *n* PHOTO reflector de enfoque variable *m*; ~**-frequency oscillator** *n* ELECTRON oscilador de frecuencia variable *m*; ~**-gain amplifier** *n* ELECTRON amplificador de ganancia variable *m*; ~ **geometry inlet** *n* AIR TRANSP entrada de aire *f*, TRANSP admisión de aire con forma variable envuelo *f*, entrada de aire *f*, toma de aire de geometría variable en vuelo *f*; ~ **geometry intake** *n*

TRANSP toma de aire de geometría variable en vuelo *f*, toma de aire cuya sección puede cambiarse en vuelo *f*; ~ **geometry skirt** *n* TRANSP plinto de geometría variable *m*; ~ **inductance** *n* ELEC, ELEC ENG inductancia variable *f*; ~ **length** *n* COMP&DP longitud variable *f*; ~**-length code** *n* TELECOM código de longitud variable *m*; ~**-length record** *n* COMP&DP registro de longitud variable *m*; ~**-message sign** *n* TRANSP panel de mensaje cambiante *m*; ~**-microwave attenuator** *n* ELECTRON, TELECOM atenuador de microonda variable *m*; ~ **mixture** *n* AUTO mezcla variable *f*; ~ **moment of inertia model** *n* NUCL *coil* modelo de momento variable de inercia *m*; ~**-mu tube** *n* ELECTRON tubo de amplificación regulable *m*; ~ **name** *n* COMP&DP nombre de variable *m*; ~ **persistence** *n* ELECTRON persistencia variable *f*; ~**-persistence storage** *n* ELECTRON almacenamiento de persistencia variable *m*; ~**-persistence storage tube** *n* ELECTRON tubo de almacenamiento de persistencia variable *m*; ~ **pitch** *n* REFRIG paso variable *m*; ~**-pitch air propeller** *n* TRANSP hélice de aire de paso variable *f*; ~**-pitch inlet vane** *n* NUCL *ring winding* álabe de admisión de paso variable *m*; ~**-pitch propeller** *n* AIR TRANSP, MAR POLL, WATER TRANSP hélice de paso variable *f*; ~**-point representation** *n* COMP&DP representación de coma variable *f*; ~ **quantity** *n* ELEC ENG cantidad variable *f*; ~**-range marker** *n* WATER TRANSP *radar* anillo variable de distancia *m*, indicador variable de distancia *m*, selector de escala *m*; ~**-ratio transformer** *n* ELEC, ELEC ENG transformador de relación de voltaje regulable *m*; ~**-reluctance motor** *n* TRANSP motor de reluctancia variable *m*; ~**-reluctance stepper motor** *n* ELEC ENG motor paso a paso de reluctancia variable *m*; ~ **resistance** *n* ELEC ENG resistencia variable *f*, reóstato *m*; ~ **resistor** *n* ELEC resistencia variable *f*, resistor variable *m*, ELEC ENG resistor variable *m*, PHYS resistencia variable *f*; ~ **route sign** *n* TRANSP señal de cambios en la ruta *f*, señal indicadora variable *f*; ~ **shutter** *n* CINEMAT obturador variable *m*; ~**-slope delta modulation** *n* SPACE *communications* modulación delta de pendiente variable *f*; ~ **slow motion** *n* TV movimiento lento variable *m*; ~ **space** *n* PRINT espacio variable *m*; ~**-speed camera** *n* CINEMAT cámara de velocidad variable *f*; ~**-speed control** *n* TV control de velocidad variable *m*; ~**-speed conveyor belt** *n* TRANSP cinta transportadora de velocidad regulable *f*; ~**-speed message sign** *n* TRANSP panel de velocidad variable *m*; ~**-speed motor** *n* ELEC ENG motor de velocidad regulable *m*; ~**-speed scanning** *n* TV exploración a velocidad variable *f*, exploración de velocidad variable *f*; ~ **transformer** *n* ELEC, ELEC ENG transformador regulable *m*; ~**-valve timing** *n* TRANSP reglaje de válvulas variables *m*; ~ **velocity** *n* MECH ENG velocidad regulable *f*, velocidad variable *f*; ~ **venturi carburetor** *AmE*, ~ **venturi carburettor** *BrE* *n* AUTO, VEH carburador de venturi variable *m*; ~**-voltage generator** *n* ELEC generador de voltaje regulable *m*, generatriz de tensión variable *f*, ELEC ENG generador de voltaje regulable *m*; ~**-wordlength computer** *n* COMP&DP computador de longitud de palabra variable *m* (*AmL*), computadora de longitud de palabra variable *f* (*AmL*), ordenador de longitud de palabra variable *m* (*Esp*)

variamine *n* CHEM variamina *f*

variance *n* COMP&DP varianza *f*, MATH variancia *f*, varianza *f*, PHYS varianza *f*

variation *n* GEOPHYS, MECH ENG variación *f*, WATER TRANSP declinación *f*; ~ **compass** *n* GEOPHYS brújula de variación *f*; ~ **order** *n* CONST orden de desviación *m*, orden de variación *m*

variational: ~ **calculus** *n* MATH cálculo de variaciones *m*

varicolored *AmE see* varicoloured *BrE*

varicoloured *adj BrE* COLOUR multicolor, polícromo

varied: ~ **pitchblende** *n* NUCL pechblenda variada *f*

variegated[1] *adj* GEOL, MINERAL abigarrado

variegated[2]: ~ **copper** *n* MINERAL bornita *f*, cobre abigarrado *m*

varifocal: ~ **lens** *n* CINEMAT, INSTR, PHOTO objetivo de foco variable *m*

variocoupler *n* ELEC ENG acoplador variable *m*

variometer *n* ELEC ENG inductor regulable *m*

variscite *n* MINERAL variscita *f*

varistance *n* ELEC ENG resistencia de característica alineal *f*, varistor *m*

varistor *n* ELEC *resistor* resistencia de característica alineal *f*, resistencia no lineal *f*, varistancia *f*, varistor *m*, ELEC ENG resistencia de característica alineal *f*, varistor *m*, PROD varistor *m*

varnish[1] *n* CHEM, COLOUR, CONST, ELEC, P&R, PRINT barniz *m*; ~ **maker** *n* COATINGS fabricante de barniz *m*; ~ **maker's naphtha** *n* COATINGS disolvente para los fabricantes de barnices *m*; ~ **paint** *n* COATINGS, COLOUR pintura al barniz *f*; ~ **paint coat** *n* COLOUR capa de pintura al barniz *f*; ~ **run** *n* COATINGS barnizado *m*, pasada del barniz *f*; ~ **tear** *n* COATINGS descascarillado del barniz *m*

varnish[2] *vt* CINEMAT, COATINGS, COLOUR, CONST, PRINT, PROD barnizar

varnished *adj* COATINGS, COLOUR, CONST, PRINT barnizado

varnisher *n* COATINGS, COLOUR, CONST, PRINT barnizador *m*

varnishing *n* COATINGS, COLOUR, CONST, PRINT, PROD barnizado *m*; ~ **machine** *n* COATINGS, PROD máquina de barnizar *f*

varve *n* GEOL sedimentos cíclicos estacionales *m pl*, varva *f*

varying: ~ **loading** *n* METALL carga variable *f*

Vaseline ® *n* CHEM, PETR TECH, PETROL vaselina ® *f*, petrolato *m*

vasopressin *n* CHEM vasopresina *f*

vat *n* CHEM cuba *f*, tanque *m*, FOOD cuba *f*, tina *f*, tinaja *f*, PAPER cuba *f*, tina *f*, PROD artesa *f*, cuba *f*, tanque *m*, TEXTIL tina *f*; ~ **dye** *n* TEXTIL colorante tina *m*; ~ **dyeing** *n* COLOUR teñido con colorante de tina *m*; ~**-lined board** *n* PROD papel de tina revestido *m*; ~ **machine** *n* PAPER máquina de formas redondas *f*

vault *n* CINEMAT depósito *m*, CONST *architecture* bóveda *f*, *cellar* sótano *m*

vauquelinite *n* MINERAL vauquelinita *f*

Vauxhall: ~ **bevel** *n* C&G bisel Vauxhall *m*

VB *abbr* (*valence band*) PHYS, RAD PHYS banda de valencia *f*

V-belt *n* AUTO, MECH correa en V *f*, correa trapezoidal *f*, MECH ENG correa en V *f*, correa en cuña *f*, correa trapezoidal *f*, P&R correa en V *f*, correa trapezoidal *f*, VEH correa en V *f*; ~ **drive** *n* MECH ENG polea de correa trapezoidal *f*, transmisión de correa en V *f*, transmisión de correa trapezoidal *f*; ~ **speed**

transmission *n* MECH ENG transmisión de velocidad por correa trapezoidal *f*; ~ **tension** *n* MECH ENG tensión de correa en V *f*, tensión de correa trapezoidal *f*

V-belting *n* TEXTIL correa trapezoidal *f*

V-block *n* MECH ENG *draughtsman's* V de mecánico *f*, apoyo en V para trazar *m*, bloque metálico con ranura en V *m*, METR bloque metálico con ranura en V *m*

V-bob *n* MECH ENG balancín de escuadra *m*

VBR *abbr* (*variable-bit rate*) COMP&DP, TELECOM tasa de bits variable *f*

VC *abbr* (*virtual channel*) TELECOM canal virtual *m*

V-C: ~ **ratio** *n* TRANSP relación capacidad-volumen *f*

VCC *abbr* (*virtual channel connection*) TELECOM conexión de canal virtual *f*

VCCE *abbr* (*virtual channel connection endpoint*) TELECOM punto final de la conexión de canal virtual *m*

VCF *abbr* (*video command freeze-picture request*) TELECOM petición de imagen inmóvil de la videoseñal de mando *f* (*AmL*)

VCI *abbr* (*virtual channel identifier*) TELECOM identificador de canal virtual *m*

VC-n *abbr* (*virtual container-n*) TELECOM recipiente-n virtual *m*

VCO *abbr* (*voltage-controlled oscillator*) ELECTRON, SPACE, TELECOM OCT (*oscilador con voltaje controlado*)

V-connection *n* ELEC conexión en V *f*

VCR *abbr* (*videocassette recorder*) TV videograbador *m* (*AmL*), videograbadora *f* (*AmL*), vídeo grabador *m* (*Esp*)

VCS *abbr* (*virtual circuit switch*) TELECOM conmutador del circuito virtual *m*

V-cut *n* MINE cuele convergente *m*

V-cylinder: ~ **engine** *n* MECH ENG motor de cilindros en V *m*

VDA *abbr* (*video distribution amplifier*) TV amplificador de distribución de video *m* (*AmL*), amplificador de distribución de vídeo *m* (*Esp*)

VDU[1] *abbr* (*visual display unit*) COMP&DP , ELECTRON, INSTR, PRINT, TELECOM, TV VDU pantalla *f*, terminal de pantalla de visualización *f*, unidad de presentación visual *f*, unidad de visualización *f*, unidad de visualización virtual *f*

VDU[2]: ~ **operator** *n* COMP&DP, PROD operador de terminal de pantalla de visualización *m*

vector *n* GEN dirección *f*, rumbo *m*, vector *m*, translación de un punto a otro en un intervalo de tiempo *f*, portador *m*; ~ **coupling** *n* RAD PHYS acoplamiento vectorial *m*; ~ **field** *n* ELEC *electromagnetism*, ELEC ENG campo vectorial *m*; ~ **graphics** *n* COMP&DP gráficos vectoriales *m pl*; ~ **group** *n* ELEC *transformer* acoplamiento *m*; ~ **insect** *n* AGRIC insecto vector de la enfermedad *m*; ~ **model** *n* PHYS modelo vectorial *m*; ~-**network analyser** *n* BrE ELEC, ELEC ENG analizador de red vectorial *m*; ~-**network analysis** *n* ELEC, ELEC ENG análisis de red vectorial *m*; ~-**network analyzer** AmE *see vector-network analyser BrE*; ~ **potential** *n* ELEC ENG, PHYS potencial vector *m*; ~ **processing** *n* COMP&DP procesado vectorial *m*, procesamiento vectorial *m*; ~ **product** *n* PHYS producto vectorial *m*; ~-**scan cathode ray tube** *n* ELECTRON tubo de rayos catódicos de exploración vectorial *m*; ~-**scan electron-beam lithography** *n* ELECTRON litografía

por haz electrónico de exploración vectorial *f*; ~-**scanned beam** *n* ELECTRON haz de exploración vectorial *m*; ~ **scanning** *n* ELECTRON exploración vectorial *f*

vectored[1] *adj* SPACE orientable, vectorizado

vectored[2]: ~ **interrupt** *n* COMP&DP interrupción vectorial *f* (*Esp*), interrupción vectorizada *f* (*AmL*); ~ **thrust** *n* SPACE empuje orientable *m*; ~ **thrust engine** *n* SPACE motor de empuje orientable *m*

vectorial *adj* GEOM vectorial

vectorscope *n* TV vectorscopio *m*

VEE: ~ **foil craft** *n* TRANSP embarcación sobre aletas hidrodinámicas sustentadoras VEE *f*

veer *vi* WATER TRANSP *wind* girar en el sentido de los agujas del reloj, girar por redondo, rolar, *ships* virar por redondo; ~ **aft** *vi* WATER TRANSP *wind* alargarse; ~ **northward** *vi* WATER TRANSP *wind* llamarse al norte; ~ **off course** *vi* WATER TRANSP *ship* cambiar de rumbo virando por redondo

vegetable: ~ **cover** *n* AGRIC cubierta vegetal *f*; ~ **fat** *n* FOOD grasa vegetal *f*; ~ **glue** *n* PROD goma vegetal *f*, pegamento vegetal *m*; ~ **oil** *n* FOOD aceite vegetal *m*; ~ **parchment** *n* PAPER papel de pergamino vegetal *m*, papel sulfurizado *m*, PROD pergamino vegetal *m*; ~ **protein** *n* FOOD proteína vegetal *f*; ~ **seeder** *n* AGRIC sembradora de hortalizas *f*; ~ **size** *n* COLOUR cola vegetal *f*; ~-**sized paper** *n* PAPER papel apergaminado *m*

vehicle *n* CHEM medio *m*, vehículo *m*, MECH, PRINT vehículo *m*, SPACE excipiente líquido *m*, vehículo *m*, TRANSP vehículo *m*; ~-**actuated control** *n* AUTO control accionado por vehículos *m*; ~-**actuated signalization** AmE, ~-**actuated signallization** BrE *n* AUTO señalización accionada por vehículos *f*; ~ **characteristic detector** *n* TRANSP detector de características de vehículos *m*; ~ **extension period** *n* TRANSP período de aumento del número de vehículos *m*; ~ **intercept survey** *n* AUTO aviso para interceptar un vehículo *m*; ~ **location subsystem** *n* TELECOM subsistema de localización del vehículo *m*; ~-**mounted short primary linear motor** *n* AUTO motor primario en línea *m*; ~ **ramp** *n* AUTO rampa para vehículos *f*; ~ **tagging** *n* AUTO placa de identificación del vehículo *f*; ~ **tanker** *n* AUTO vehículo cisterna *m*

vehicular: ~ **flow at peak hour** *n* AUTO flujo rodado en hora punta *m*

V8: ~ **engine** *n* (*V-eight engine*) AUTO motor en V de ocho cilindros *m*

veil *n* CINEMAT velo *m*

Veil: ~ **Nebula** *n* SPACE nebula Veil *f*

vein *n* CONST *in wood, marble*, MINE veta *f*; ~ **wall** *n* GEOL pared de filón *f*

veined: ~ **board** *n* PAPER cartón jaspeado *m*; ~ **paper** *n* PAPER papel jaspeado *m*

Veitch: ~ **diagram** *n* COMP&DP diagrama de Veitch *m*

vellum: ~ **finish** *n* PROD acabado avitelado *m*; ~ **paper** *n* PAPER papel velín *m*, papel vitela *m*

velocimeter *n* PHYS tacómetro *m*

velocimetry *n* PHYS velocimetría *f*

velocity *n* GEN *of sound, waves* velocidad *f*; ~ **banding** *n* TV velocidad de bandas *f*; ~ **coefficient** *n* FUELLESS coeficiente de velocidad *m*; ~ **control servo** *n* TV servomecanismo para control de la velocidad *m*; ~-**depth curve** *n* PETR TECH curva velocidad-profundidad *f*; ~ **of detonation** *n* (*VOD*) MINE velocidad de detonación *f*; ~ **diagram** *n* FUELLESS diagrama de velocidad *m*, esquema de velocidad *m*, MECH ENG diagrama de velocidad *m*; ~ **error** *n* TV error de velocidad *m*; ~ **error compensator** *n* TV compensador del error de velocidad *m*; ~ **of flow** *n* REFRIG velocidad del flujo *f*; ~ **fluctuation** *n* FLUID fluctuación de velocidad *f*; ~ **head** *n* HYDRAUL altura cinética *f*, altura debida a la velocidad *f*, altura dinámica *f*, carga hidrostática *f*; ~ **increment** *n* SPACE incremento de velocidad *m*; ~ **inversion** *n* PETR TECH inversión de velocidad *f*; ~ **loss** *n* NUCL pérdida de velocidad *f*; ~ **microphone** *n* ACOUST micrófono de velocidad *m*; ~-**modulated amplifier** *n* ELECTRON amplificador de velocidad modulada *m*; ~-**modulated beam** *n* ELECTRON haz de velocidad modulada *m*; ~-**modulated oscillator** *n* ELECTRON oscilador de velocidad modulada *m*; ~-**modulated tube** *n* ELECTRON tubo de velocidad modulada *m*; ~ **modulation** *n* ELECTRON, PHYS, TV modulación de velocidad *f*; ~ **potential** *n* FUELLESS potencial de las alternancias en medio *m*; ~ **profile** *n* PHYS perfil de velocidad *m*; ~ **resonance** *n* PHYS resonancia de velocidad *f*; ~ **of sound** *n* WAVE PHYS velocidad del sonido *f*; ~ **stage turbine** *n* HYDRAUL turbina de expansión de impulsión *f*

velvet *n* TEXTIL terciopelo *m*; ~ **finish** *n* PAPER acabado mate antiguo *m*, aterciopelado artificial *m*; ~ **grass** *n* AGRIC sorgo lanudo *m*; ~ **leaf** *n* AGRIC malva india *f*; ~ **light trap** *n* PHOTO trampa de luz aterciopelada *f*; ~ **trap** *n* CINEMAT trampa de terciopelo *f*

venasquite *n* MINERAL venasquita *f*

vendor: ~ **scheduler** *n* PROD programador de proveedores *m*

veneer *n* CONST chapa *f*; ~ **board** *n* PROD chapa fina de madera revestida con cartón por ambas caras *f*; ~ **graft** *n* AGRIC injerto de hendidura *m*; ~-**splicing machine** *n* MECH ENG máquina de contrachapado *f*

veneering *n* CONST chapado *m*, revestimiento *m*; ~ **press** *n* MECH ENG prensa de contrachapado *f*, prensa de enchapar *f*

Venetian: ~ **blind effect** *n* TV efecto de persiana *m*

V-engine *n* AUTO motor en V *m*, WATER TRANSP motor con cilindros en V *m*

Venn: ~ **diagram** *n* COMP&DP, MATH diagrama de Venn *m*

vent[1] *n* C&G orificio de ventilación *m*, CONST *air hole* orificio de ventilación *m*, respiradero *m*, GEOL chimenea *f*, LAB tubo de ventilación *m*, MECH respiradero *m*, purga de aire *f*, tronera *f*, salida *f*, NUCL respiradero *m*, P&R abertura *f*, orificio de ventilación *m*, PROD *moulds* agujero de aire *m*, SPACE emisión *f*, manga de ventilación *f*, respiradero *m*; ~ **hole** *n* C&G, CONST orificio de ventilación *m*, HYDRAUL lumbrera de escape *f*, orificio de escape *m*, orificio de evacuación *m*, P&R orificio de ventilación *m*, PROD *moulds* agujero de aire *m*, SPACE orificio de despresurización *m*, orificio respiradero *m*; ~ **nozzle** *n* NUCL *heat unit* tobera de escape *f*; ~ **peg** *n* CONST clavija de ventilación *f*; ~ **pipe** *n* CONST tubería de ventilación *f*, NUCL *heat unit* tubo de venteo *m*; ~ **plug** *n* CONST tapón de cierre de la tubería de ventilación *m*; ~ **window** *n* AIR TRANSP ventana de ventilación *f*; ~ **wire** *n* PROD *moulds* aguja de ventear *f*, aguja para hacer agujeros *f*

vent[2] *vt* COAL purgar

vented: ~ **fuel assembly** *n* NUCL elemento de combustible venteado *m*; ~ **fuel rod** *n* NUCL varilla de combustible venteado *f*; ~ **nip press** *n* PAPER prensa ranurada *f*

ventiduct *n* CONST conducto de ventilación *m*

ventilate *vt* COAL airear, ventilar, CONST, PRINT, RECYCL airear, SAFE ventilar, airear, THERMO airear, ventilar, WATER TRANSP airear

ventilated[1] *adj* GEN ventilado

ventilated[2]: ~ **fan** *n* REFRIG ventilador ventilado *m*; ~ **froster** *n* REFRIG congelador ventilado *m*; ~ **motor** *n* ELEC motor ventilado *m*; ~ **nappe** *n* WATER napa ventilada *f*; ~ **propeller** *n* TRANSP hélice ventilada *f*; ~ **tank crew helmet** *n* MILIT casco ventilado para tripulación de carros *m*; ~ **vehicle** *n* REFRIG vehículo ventilado *m*

ventilating *n* CONST ventilación *f*; ~ **door** *n* CONST puerta de ventilación *f*; ~ **fan** *n* CONST, MINE ventilador *m*

ventilation *n* GEN ventilación *f*; ~ **breakdown** *n* COAL interrupción de la ventilación *f*; ~ **door** *n* MINE entrada de ventilación *f*, puerta de ventilación *f*; ~ **door opener** *n* SAFE abridor de puerta de ventilación *m*; ~ **drive** *n* COAL galería de ventilación *f*, MINE *tunnel* galería de ventilación *f*, túnel de ventilación *m*; ~ **duct** *n* CONST conducto de ventilación *m*; ~ **ducting** *n* MINE conducto de ventilación *m*; ~ **loss** *n* HEAT pérdida de ventilación *f*; ~ **pipe** *n* MINE tubería de ventilación *f*; ~ **shaft** *n* MINE pozo de ventilación *m*

ventilator *n* CONST, REFRIG, SAFE, WATER TRANSP *deck equipment* ventilador *m*; ~ **cowl** *n* WATER TRANSP *deck fitting* caperuza *f*, capuchón *m*; ~ **socket** *n* WATER TRANSP collarín *m*

ventimeter *n* FUELLESS, HYDROL, LAB, METEO, PHYS anemómetro *m*, WATER TRANSP anemómetro *m*, ventímetro *m*

venting *n* NUCL *mass* venteo *m*

venturi *n* AUTO venturi *m*, VEH difusor *m*, venturi *m*; ~ **effect** *n* METEO efecto Venturi *m*; ~ **meter** *n* PHYS medidor de Venturi *m*; ~ **nozzle** *n* MECH tobera de tipo Venturi *f*; ~ **scrubber** *n* COAL lavador Venturi *m*, POLL lavador Venturi *m*, venturi *m*; ~ **sludge** *n* COAL fango Venturi *m*; ~ **tube** *n* MECH ENG *for measuring flow rate* tubo de Venturi *m*, venturímetro *m*, PHYS tubo de Venturi *m*

Venturi-Parshall: ~ **flume** *n* HYDROL canal de esclusa Venturi-Parshall *m*

veratramine *n* CHEM veratramina *f*

veratric *adj* CHEM verátrico

veratrine *n* CHEM veratrina *f*

veratrol *n* CHEM veratrol *m*

verb *n* COMP&DP *COBOL* verbo *m*

verbena: ~ **oil** *n* CHEM esencia de verbena *f*

verdigris *n* CHEM acetato básico de cobre *m*, cardenillo *m*

verification *n* COMP&DP verificación *f*, MECH ENG comprobación *f*, constatación *f*, verificación *f*, *by means of limit gauge* calibración *f*; ~ **testing** *n* QUALITY ensayo de verificación *m*

verifier *n* COMP&DP verificador *m*

verify *vt* COMP&DP verificar

vermiculite *n* HEAT ENG *act*, MINERAL, REFRIG vermiculita *f*

vernal: ~ **equinox** *n* SPACE equinoccio de primavera *m*, equinoccio vernal *m*; ~ **point** *n* SPACE punto vernal *m*

vernier *n* MECH nonio *m*, MECH ENG nonio *m*, vernier

m, METR *blast furnace* nonio *m*; ~ **caliper** *AmE*, ~ **calliper** *BrE* *n* MECH calibre de nonio *m*, METEO calibre *m*, METR calibre de nonio *m*, pie de rey *m*, PHYS pie de rey *m*; ~ **depth gage** *AmE*, ~ **depth gauge** *BrE* *n* METR limnímetro de vernier *m*; ~ **height gage** *AmE*, ~ **height gauge** *BrE* *n* METR altímetro de vernier *m*; ~ **motor** *n* SPACE *on spacecraft* motor tipo nonio *m*, motor vernier *m*; ~ **potentiometer** *n* ELEC potenciómetro vernier *m*; ~ **scale** *n* MECH ENG escala de vernier *f*, escala del nonio *f*

veronal *n* CHEM veronal *m*
versals *n pl* PRINT iniciales decoradas *f pl*
versatility *n* SPACE pluriaplicación *f*, polivalencia *f*, versatilidad *f*
versene *n* CHEM versene *m*
version *n* COMP&DP versión *f*
verso *n* PAPER página izquierda *f*, página par *f*, PRINT página izquierda *f*, página par *f*, reverso *m*
vertex *n* CRYSTALL, GEOM, PHYS, TELECOM vértice *m*; ~ **angle** *n* PRINT, TELECOM ángulo del vértice *m*; ~ **feed** *n* TELECOM *of reflector antenna* alimentación en el vértice *f*; ~ **plate** *n* TELECOM *of aerial reflector* placa del vértice *f*; ~ **refractometer** *n* INSTR refractómetro del cénit *m*
vertical: ~ **alignment** *n* CONST alineación vertical *f*; ~ **amplifier** *n* ELECTRON amplificador vertical *m*; ~ **amplifier bandwidth** *n* ELECTRON ancho de banda de amplificador vertical *m*; ~ **amplifier dynamic range** *n* ELECTRON gama dinámica de amplificador vertical *f*; ~~**amplifier input** *n* ELECTRON entrada de amplificador vertical *f*; ~~**amplifier output** *n* ELECTRON salida de amplificador vertical *f*; ~ **amplitude** *n* TV amplitud vertical *f*; ~ **amplitude control** *n* TV control de la amplitud vertical *m*; ~ **angle** *n* GEOM ángulo vertical *m*; ~ **ascent** *n* SPACE ascenso vertical *m*; ~ **axis** *n* MATH eje de las y *m*, eje de ordenadas *m*, eje vertical *m*; ~~**axis wind turbine** *n* FUELLESS, MECH ENG turbina de viento con eje vertical *f*; ~ **bipolar transistor** *n* ELECTRON transistor bipolar vertical *m*; ~ **blanking** *n* COMP&DP borrado vertical *m*, ELECTRON supresión de línea *f*, TV borrado vertical *m*; ~~**blanking interval** *n* TV intervalo de borrado vertical *m*; ~~**blanking pulse** *n* TV impulso de borrado vertical *m*; ~ **cartoner** *n* PACK cartonaje vertical *m*; ~ **centering** *AmE see vertical centring BrE*; ~~**centering control** *AmE see vertical-centring control BrE*; ~ **centring** *n* *BrE* ELECTRON centrado vertical *m*; ~~**centring control** *n* *BrE* TV control de centrado vertical *m*; ~ **clamp** *n* INSTR barrilete vertical *m*; ~ **component** *n* PHYS componente vertical *f*; ~ **control** *n* CINEMAT, OPT control vertical *m*; ~ **convergence** *n* ELECTRON convergencia vertical *f*; ~ **curve radius** *n* CONST radio de la curva vertical *m*; ~ **cylinder-grinding machine** *n* MECH ENG rectificadora vertical *f*; ~ **deflecting plates** *n pl* PHYS placas deflectantes verticales *f pl*; ~ **deflection** *n* ELECTRON deflexión vertical *f*, desviación vertical *f*, TV deflexión vertical *f*; ~ **deflection coil** *n* ELEC ENG bobina de deflexión vertical *f*; ~ **deflection plate** *n* ELECTRON placa de deflexión vertical *f*; ~ **digester** *n* PAPER lejiadora vertical *f*, PROD digestor vertical *m*; ~ **dispersion** *n* POLL difusión vertical *f*, dispersión vertical *f*; ~ **drainage** *n* COAL desagüe vertical *m*, drenaje vertical *m*; ~ **engine** *n* AUTO, VEH motor vertical *m*; ~ **field-effect transistor** *n* ELECTRON

transistor de efecto de campo vertical *m*; ~ **format** *n* COMP&DP formato vertical *m*; ~ **gyro** *n* SPACE *on spacecraft* giroscopio vertical *m*, TRANSP giro en vertical *m*; ~ **handsaw** *n* MECH ENG sierra de mano vertical *f*; ~ **hold control** *n* TV control de sincronización vertical *m*; ~ **hole** *n* MINE pozo vertical *m*; ~ **and horizontal form-fill seal machine** *n* PACK máquina de conformado y sellado en vertical y horizontal *f*; ~ **illumination** *n* INSTR iluminación vertical *f*; ~ **interval** *n* TV intervalo vertical *m*; ~ **interval test signal** *n* TV señal de prueba de intervalo vertical *f*; ~ **lever** *n* PROD palanca vertical *f*; ~ **lime kiln** *n* HEAT, PROD horno de cal vertical *m*; ~~**linearity control** *n* TV regulación vertical de alineamiento *f*; ~ **lock** *n* TV enclavamiento vertical *m*; ~ **milling attachment** *n* MECH ENG acoplamiento de fresado vertical *m*; ~ **mode** *n* TV modo vertical *m*; ~ **MOS transistor** *n* ELECTRON transistor SOM vertical *m*; ~ **output stage** *n* ELECTRON fase de salida vertical *f*; ~ **parity** *n* COMP&DP paridad vertical *f*; ~ **plan** *n* GEOM plano vertical *m*; ~ **pneumatic pick longwall face** *n* MINE frente de tajo largo por elección neumática vertical *m*; ~ **polarization** *n* ELEC ENG, PHYS, TELECOM polarización vertical *f*; ~ **power MOS transistor** *n* ELECTRON transistor SOM de potencia vertical *m*; ~ **recording** *n* ACOUST grabación en profundidad *f*; ~ **redundancy check** *n* (*VRC*) COMP&DP comprobación vertical de la redundancia *f*, verificación de redundancia vertical *f*; ~ **reference unit** *n* SPACE unidad de referencia vertical *f*; ~ **scanning** *n* TV exploración vertical *f*; ~ **section** *n* CONST *of building* alzado *m*; ~ **seismic profile** *n* (*VSP*) PETR TECH perfil sísmico vertical *m*; ~ **seismograph** *n* GEOPHYS sismógrafo vertical *m*; ~ **separation** *n* PROD separación vertical *f*; ~ **shaft** *n* MINE pozo vertical *m*; ~ **shaft furnace** *n* HEAT horno vertical *m*; ~~**shaft Pelton wheel** *n* FUELLESS rueda tipo Pelton con árbol vertical *f*; ~ **shore** *n* CONST puntal vertical *m*; ~ **spacing** *n* PROD espaciado vertical *m*; ~ **speed** *n* SPACE velocidad vertical *f*; ~ **speed indicator** *n* (*VSI*) AIR TRANSP, SPACE indicador de la velocidad vertical *m* (*VSI*); ~ **stability** *n* TRANSP estabilidad vertical *f*; ~ **surface-type broaching machine** *n* MECH ENG fresadora de cremalleras tipo superficie vertical *f*; ~ **sweep** *n* ELECTRON barrido vertical *m*; ~ **sync pulse** *n* TV pulso sincronizador vertical *m*; ~ **tabulation** *n* (*VT*) COMP&DP tabulación vertical *f*; ~ **takeoff** *n* AIR TRANSP, MILIT despegue vertical *m*; ~ **takeoff and landing aircraft** *n* (*VTOL aircraft*) AIR TRANSP, MILIT avión de despegue y aterrizaje vertical *m*; ~~**tangent screw** *n* INSTR tornillo de precisión vertical *m*; ~ **temperature gradient** *n* METEO gradiente térmico vertical *m*, gradiente vertical de temperatura *m*, THERMO gradiente térmico vertical *m*; ~ **throw** *n* GEOL salto vertical *m*; ~~**tracking angle error** *n* ACOUST error de ángulo de seguimiento vertical *m*; ~ **traverse** *n* MECH ENG *of drilling spindle* avance vertical *m*, movimiento vertical *m*; ~~**type evaporator** *n* REFRIG evaporador de tipo vertical *m*; ~ **vacuum sealer** *n* PACK sellado en vertical al vacío *m*; ~ **water flow** *n* TEXTIL chorro de agua vertical *m*; ~ **wipe** *n* CINEMAT, TV transición donde una imagen quita a otra de la pantalla verticalmente *f*
vertically: ~~**adjustable table** *n* MECH ENG mesa de movimiento vertical *f*, mesa regulable vertical *f*

verticality: ~ **tolerance** *n* C&G tolerancia en la verticalidad *f*

vervein: ~ **oil** *n* CHEM esencia de verveína *f*

Very: ~ **light** *n* WATER TRANSP *signal* bengala de señales *f*; ~ **pistol** *n* MILIT, WATER TRANSP *distress signal* pistola de señales Very *f*

vesicular *adj* GEOL vesicular

vessel *n* LAB *container* recipiente *m*, MAR POLL *ship* embarcación *f*, barco *m*, buque *m*, OCEAN embarcación *f*, barco *m*, PHYS vasija *f*, TEXTIL recipiente *m*, TRANSP *ship* buque *m*, nave *f*, WATER TRANSP barco *m*, *container* recipiente *m*, *ship* nave *f*, buque *m*; ~ **equipment** *n* OCEAN avíos del buque *m pl*, equipo del barco *m*; ~ **location** *n* WATER TRANSP *by satellite navigation* localización de embarcaciones *f*; ~ **penetration** *n* NUCL penetración en la vasija del reactor *f*; ~ **support skirt** *n* NUCL *BWRs* faldilla de la vasija *f*; ~ **traffic services** *n pl* WATER TRANSP servicios de regulación del tráfico marítimo *m pl*

vestibule *n* HEAT, RAIL vestíbulo *m*

vestigial: ~ **sideband** *n* COMP&DP banda lateral residual *f*, ELECTRON, PHYS, TELECOM, TV banda lateral residual *f*, banda lateral vestigial *f*; ~ **sideband filter** *n* ELECTRON, TELECOM filtro de banda lateral residual *m*; ~ **sideband signal** *n* ELECTRON señal de banda lateral residual *f*

vesuvianite *n* MINERAL idocrasa *f*, vesubiana *f*

vesuvin *n* CHEM vesubina *f*

VF *abbr* (*voice frequency*) ELECTRON, RAD PHYS, TELECOM FV (*frecuencia acústica, frecuencia vocal, frecuencia de voz*)

VFA *abbr* (*volatile fatty acid*) AGRIC, CHEM AGV (*ácido graso volátil*)

V4: ~ **engine** *n* (*V-four engine*) AUTO motor en V de cuatro cilindros *m*

VGA *abbr* (*video graphics adaptor*) COMP&DP VGA (*adaptador de gráficos de video AmL, adaptador de gráficos de vídeo Esp*)

V-gage *AmE*, **V-gauge** *BrE n* C&G medidor en V *m*

V-gear *n* MECH ENG engranaje bihelicoidal *m*

V-groove *n* ELECTRON *transistors* acanalado en V *m*, ranura en V *f*, MECH ENG canal en V *m*, ranura en V *f*; ~ **clutch** *n* MECH ENG embrague cónico *m*, embrague de canal en V *m*, embrague de ranura en V *m*; ~ **etching** *n* ELECTRON *transistors* grabación de acanalado en V *f*

VHD *abbr* (*video high-density disc*) OPT videodisco de alta densidad *m*

VHF[1] *abbr* (*very high frequency*) GEN VHF (*frecuencia muy alta*)

VHF[2]: ~ **band** *n* TV banda VHF *f*, banda de muy alta frecuencia *f*; ~ **omnidirectional radio range** *n* (*VOR*) AIR TRANSP radiofaro omnidireccional de muy alta frecuencia *m*; ~ **radio telephone** *n* WATER TRANSP radioteléfono de ondas métricas *m*; ~ **signal** *n* ELECTRON señal de FMA *f*; ~ **signal generator** *n* ELECTRON generador de señal de FMA *m*; ~ **and UHF tuner** *n* TV sintonizador de UHF y VHF *m*

VHFO *abbr* (*very high-frequency omnirange*) AIR TRANSP, TRANSP RFMA (*radiofaro omnidireccional de alta frecuencia*)

VHS *abbr* (*video home system*) TV sistema doméstico de video *m* (*AmL*), sistema doméstico de vídeo *m* (*Esp*)

VHS-C: ~ **system** *n* (*video home system-compact*) TV sistema doméstico de video-compacto *m* (*AmL*)

VI: ~ **meter** *n* (*volume indicator meter*) TV contador

indicador de volumen *m*, medidor indicador de volumen *m*, registrador indicador de volumen *m*

VIA *abbr* (*video indicator active*) TELECOM videoindicador activo *m*

viable: ~ **bacterium** *n* HYDROL, RECYCL, WATER bacteria viable *f*

viaduct *n* CONST viaducto *m*

vial *n* AmE (*cf phial BrE*) C&G ampolleta *f*, botellita *f*, CHEM ampolleta *f*, frasco pequeño *m*, LAB *glassware* ampolleta *f* (*AmL*), frasco pequeño *m*

vibrate *vt* CONST vibrar

vibrated: ~ **concrete** *n* CONST concreto vibrado *m* (*AmL*), hormigón vibrado *m* (*Esp*)

vibrating: ~~**ball mill** *n* LAB *of compound* molino de bolas vibratorias *m*; ~ **feeder** *n* PROD alimentador vibrante *m*; ~ **feeders and conveyors** *n pl* MECH ENG alimentadores y transportadores vibratorios *m pl*; ~ **grizzly** *n* COAL cribón vibratorio *m*; ~~**reed frequency meter** *n* ELEC ENG medidor de frecuencia de lámina vibrante *m*; ~ **rod mill** *n* COAL laminador para redondos oscilantes *m*, tren de laminar redondos oscilantes *m*, PROD laminador para redondos oscilantes *m*; ~ **roller** *n* CONST rodillo vibratorio *m*, logotipo *m*; ~ **sample magnetometer** *n* NUCL magnetómetro vibratorio de muestreo *m*; ~ **screen** *n* CHEM criba vibratoria *f*, COAL criba vibradora *f*; ~ **sheepsfoot roller** *n* CONST apisonadora de rodillo vibratorio *f*; ~ **stirrer** *n* LAB agitador vibratorio *m*; ~ **string** *n* PHYS cuerda vibratoria *f*; ~ **system** *n* WAVE PHYS sistema vibratorio *m*; ~ **table** *n* C&G, COAL mesa vibratoria *f*

vibration *n* GEN vibración *f*; ~ **analysis** *n* MECH análisis de vibración *m*; ~ **calibrator** *n* ACOUST calibrador de vibraciones *m*; ~ **conveyor** *n* FOOD transportador vibratorio *m*; ~ **damper** *n* AIR TRANSP, AUTO, MECH, MECH ENG, REFRIG, VEH amortiguador de vibraciones *m*; ~ **damper and shock absorber** *n* SAFE amortiguador de vibraciones y absorbedor de choque *m*; ~ **galvanometer** *n* ELEC galvanómetro de resonancia *m*, galvanómetro de vibración *m*, ELEC ENG, PHYS galvanómetro de vibración *m*; ~ **generator** *n* SPACE generador de vibraciones *m*; ~ **hazard** *n* SAFE peligro originado por vibración *m*, riesgo originado por vibración *m*; ~ **isolator** *n* GEOPHYS aislador de vibración *m*; ~ **measurer** *n* INSTR medidor de vibraciones *m*; ~ **recorder** *n* INSTR grabador de vibraciones *m*; ~~**rotation spectrum** *n* PHYS espectro de vibración y rotación *m*; ~ **severity** *n* SAFE intensidad de la vibración *f*; ~ **and shock pick-up** *n* MECH ENG detector de vibraciones y choques *m*; ~ **test** *n* METR prueba de vibración *f*

vibrational: ~ **energy** *n* NUCL *heat unit* energía vibracional *f*; ~ **entropy** *n* METALL entropía vibracional *f*; ~ **quantum number** *n* PHYS número cuántico vibracional *m*; ~ **spectrum** *n* PHYS espectro vibracional *m*

vibrato *n* ACOUST vibrato *m*

vibrator *n* ACOUST, CONST, ELEC ENG vibrador *m*, PRINT rodillo oscilador *m*, SPACE oscilador *m*, vibrador *m*

vibratory: ~ **environment** *n* SPACE entorno vibratorio *m*; ~ **feeder** *n* MECH, PACK alimentador vibratorio *m*; ~ **hopper** *n* PACK tolva vibratoria *f*; ~ **sifter** *n* PACK cribador vibratorio *m*

vibrocompaction *n* NUCL vibrocompactación *f*

vice *n* BrE MECH prensa de tornillo *f*, tornillo de banco *m*, MECH ENG *flaw* imperfección *f*, defecto *m*, *tool* tornillo de banco *m*, prensa de banco *f*; ~ **bench** *n*

BrE PROD tornillo de banco *m*; ~ **cap** *n BrE* MECH ENG *of soft metal* mordaza *f*; ~ **clamp** *n BrE* MECH ENG *of wood, soft metal* tornillo de mano *m*; ~ **with clamp** *n BrE* MECH ENG tornillo con bridas *m*; ~ **with detachable jaws** *n BrE* MECH ENG tornillo con mandíbulas intercambiables *m*; ~ **grips** *n pl BrE* MECH ENG tornillos de mano *m pl*, alicates de sujeción *m pl*; ~ **with inserted jaws** *n BrE* MECH ENG tornillo con mandíbulas insertadas *m*; ~ **jaw** *n BrE* MECH ENG *of soft metal* mandíbula del tornillo *f*, mordaza del tornillo *f*; ~ **jaws** *n pl BrE* PRINT mordazas de prensa *f pl*; ~ **plate** *n BrE* MECH ENG *for drilling-machines* plato del tornillo *m*; ~ **press** *n BrE* MECH ENG prensa de tornillo *f*; ~ **with protected screw** *n BrE* MECH ENG tornillo con pernos protegidos *m*; ~ **sliding between parallel bars** *n BrE* MECH ENG *drilling-machine* tornillo deslizante con guías paralelas *m*, tornillo deslizante de barras paralelas *m*

vicinal *adj* CHEM vecinal, vecino

Vickers: ~ **hardness-testing machine** *n* MECH ENG durómetro Vickers *m*, máquina de prueba de dureza Vickers *f*

video *n* COMP&DP, TELECOM, TV video *m* (*AmL*), vídeo *m* (*Esp*); ~ **amplification** *n* ELECTRON videoamplificación *f* (*AmL*); ~ **amplifier** *n* ELECTRON videoamplificador *m* (*AmL*), PHYS, TV amplificador de video *m* (*AmL*), amplificador de vídeo *m* (*Esp*); ~ **assist** *n* CINEMAT asistencia de video *f* (*AmL*), asistencia de vídeo *f* (*Esp*); ~ **bandwidth** *n* COMP&DP, TV amplitud de banda de video *f* (*AmL*), amplitud de banda de vídeo *f* (*Esp*), ancho de banda de video *m* (*AmL*), ancho de banda de vídeo *m* (*Esp*); ~ **cable** *n* ELEC ENG cable de video *m* (*AmL*), cable vídeo *m* (*Esp*); ~ **carrier** *n* TV portadora de video *f* (*AmL*), portadora de vídeo *f* (*Esp*); ~ **channel** *n* TV canal de video *m* (*AmL*), canal de vídeo *m* (*Esp*); ~ **color analyzer** *AmE*, ~ **colour analyser** *BrE n* CINEMAT analizador de colores de video *m* (*AmL*), analizador de colores de vídeo *m* (*Esp*); ~ **command freeze-picture request** *n* (*VCF*) TELECOM petición de imagen inmóvil de la videoseñal de mando *f* (*AmL*); ~ **control room** *n* TV sala de control de video *f* (*AmL*), sala de control de vídeo *f* (*Esp*); ~ **display unit** *n* (*VDU*) PRINT terminal de pantalla de visualización *m* (*VDU*), TV unidad de display de video *f* (*AmL*), unidad de display de vídeo *f* (*Esp*), pantalla visual *f*; ~ **distribution amplifier** *n* (*VDA*) TV amplificador de distribución de video *m* (*AmL*), amplificador de distribución de vídeo *m* (*Esp*); ~ **feedback circuit** *n* TV circuito de realimentación de video *m* (*AmL*), circuito de realimentación de vídeo *m* (*Esp*); ~ **frequency** *n* ELECTRON, TELECOM, TV frecuencia de imagen *f*, frecuencia de video *f* (*AmL*), frecuencia de vídeo *f* (*Esp*); ~ **frequency converter** *n* TV convertidor de frecuencia de video *m* (*AmL*), convertidor de frecuencia de vídeo *m* (*Esp*); ~ **graphics adaptor** *n* (*VGA*) COMP&DP adaptador de gráficos de video *m* (*AmL*) (*VGA*), adaptador de gráficos de vídeo *m* (*Esp*) (*VGA*); ~ **head** *n* TV cabezal de video *m* (*AmL*), cabezal de vídeo *m* (*Esp*); ~ **head alignment** *n* TV alineación del cabezal de video *f* (*AmL*), alineación del cabezal de vídeo *f* (*Esp*); ~ **head assembly** *n* TV unidad del cabezal de video *f* (*AmL*), unidad del cabezal de vídeo *f* (*Esp*); ~ **head optimizer** *n* TV optimizador del cabezal de video *m* (*AmL*), optimizador del cabezal de vídeo *m* (*Esp*);

~ **high-density disc** *BrE*, ~ **high-density disk** *AmE n* (*VHD*) OPT videodisco de alta densidad *m*; ~ **home system** *n* (*VHS*) TV sistema doméstico de video *m* (*AmL*), sistema doméstico de vídeo *m* (*Esp*); ~ **home system-compact** *n* (*VHS-C system*) TV sistema doméstico de video-compacto *m* (*AmL*), sistema doméstico de vídeo-compacto *m* (*Esp*); ~ **indicator active** *n* (*VIA*) TELECOM videoindicador activo *m*; ~ **indicator ready-to-activate** *n* (*VIR*) TELECOM videoindicador listo para ser activado *m*; ~ **indicator suppressed** *n* (*VIS*) TELECOM videoindicador suprimido *m*; ~ **input** *n* TV potencia de entrada de video *f* (*AmL*), potencia de entrada de vídeo *f* (*Esp*); ~ **level** *n* TV nivel de video *m* (*AmL*), nivel de vídeo *m* (*Esp*); ~ **level indicator** *n* TV indicador de nivel de video *m* (*AmL*), indicador de nivel de vídeo *m* (*Esp*); ~ **loop** *n* TELECOM bucle de video *m* (*AmL*), bucle de vídeo *m* (*Esp*), circuito cerrado del video *m* (*AmL*), circuito cerrado del vídeo *m* (*Esp*), lazo de video *m* (*AmL*), lazo de vídeo *m* (*Esp*); ~ **output** *n* TV potencia de salida de video *f* (*AmL*), potencia de salida de vídeo *f* (*Esp*); ~ **phase reversal** *n* TV inversión de fase de video *f* (*AmL*), inversión de fase de vídeo *f* (*Esp*); ~ **pre-emphasis** *n* TV preacentuación de video *f* (*AmL*), preacentuación de vídeo *f* (*Esp*); ~ **projector** *n* TV proyector de video *m* (*AmL*), proyector de vídeo *m* (*Esp*); ~ **recorder** *n* TV grabador de cinta de video *m* (*AmL*), grabador de cinta de vídeo *m* (*Esp*), grabadora de cinta de video *f* (*AmL*), grabadora de cinta de vídeo *f* (*Esp*), magnetoscopio *m*, videograbador *m* (*AmL*), videograbadora *f* (*AmL*), vídeo grabador *m* (*Esp*); ~ **recording** *n* TELECOM grabación de video *f* (*AmL*), grabación de vídeo *f* (*Esp*), registro de video *m* (*AmL*), registro de vídeo *m* (*Esp*); ~ **signal** *n* ELECTRON videoseñal *f* (*AmL*), PHYS señal de video *f* (*AmL*), señal de vídeo *f* (*Esp*), SPACE *communications* señal de imagen *f*, señal de video *f* (*AmL*), señal de vídeo *f* (*Esp*), señal visual *f*, TELECOM señal de video *f* (*AmL*), señal de vídeo *f* (*Esp*), videoseñal *f* (*AmL*), TV señal de video *f* (*AmL*), señal de vídeo *f* (*Esp*); ~ **signal with blanking** *n* TV señal de video con borrado *f* (*AmL*), señal de vídeo con borrado *f* (*Esp*); ~ **signal pulse** *n* TV pulso de la señal de video *m* (*AmL*), pulso de la señal de vídeo *m* (*Esp*); ~ **switch** *n* TELECOM conmutador de video *m* (*AmL*), conmutador de vídeo *m* (*Esp*), conmutador mezclador de video *m* (*AmL*), conmutador mezclador de vídeo *m* (*Esp*); ~ **switching matrix** *n* TV matriz de conmutación de video *f* (*AmL*), matriz de conmutación de vídeo *f* (*Esp*); ~ **synthesizer** *n* TV sintetizador de video *m* (*AmL*), sintetizador de vídeo *m* (*Esp*); ~ **terminal** *n* COMP&DP terminal de video *m* (*AmL*), terminal de vídeo *m* (*Esp*); ~ **track** *n* TV pista de video *f* (*AmL*), pista de vídeo *f* (*Esp*); ~ **transmission** *n* TELECOM transmisión de video *f* (*AmL*), transmisión de vídeo *f* (*Esp*)

videocassette *n* TV videocasete *m*; ~ **recorder** *n* (*VCR*) TV grabador de videocasete *m*, videograbador *m* (*AmL*), videograbadora *f* (*AmL*), vídeo grabador *m* (*Esp*)

videoclip *n* TV videoclip *m*

videoconference *n* SPACE, TELECOM conferencia por video *f* (*AmL*), conferencia por vídeo *f* (*Esp*), videoconferencia *f* (*AmL*)

videodisc *BrE*, **videodisk** *AmE n* OPT, TV videodisco *m*; ~ **player** *n* OPT lector de videodisco *m*, reproductor de videodisco *m*; ~ **recording** *n* TV grabación en videodisco *f*; ~ **system** *n* COMP&DP, OPT sistema de videodisco *m*

videography *n* TELECOM videografía *f*

videophone *n* TELECOM videoteléfono *m*; ~ **switching system** *n* TELECOM sistema de conmutación del videófono *m*

videotape *n* PHYS cinta de video *f* (*AmL*), cinta de vídeo *f* (*Esp*), TELECOM cinta magnética de video *f* (*AmL*), cinta magnética de vídeo *f* (*Esp*), videocinta *f* (*AmL*), TV cinta de video *f* (*AmL*), cinta de vídeo *f* (*Esp*); ~ **dubbing** *n* TV doblaje de cinta de video *m* (*AmL*), doblaje de cinta de vídeo *m* (*Esp*); ~ **facility** *n* TV instalación para cintas de video *f* (*AmL*), instalación para cintas de vídeo *f* (*Esp*); ~ **library** *n* TV videoteca *f*; ~ **player** *n* TV reproductor de cintas de video *m* (*AmL*), reproductor de cintas de vídeo *m* (*Esp*); ~ **recorder** *n* (*VTR*) TV grabadora de cinta de video *f* (*AmL*), grabadora de cinta de vídeo *f* (*Esp*), videograbador *m* (*AmL*), videograbadora *f* (*AmL*), vídeo grabador *m* (*Esp*)

videotaping *n* TV grabación de cintas de video *f* (*AmL*), grabación de cintas de vídeo *f* (*Esp*)

videotex *n* COMP&DP videotex *m* (*Esp*), videotexto *m* (*Esp*), videtex *m* (*AmL*), TELECOM videotexto *m* (*Esp*), videtex *m* (*AmL*); ~ **gateway** *n* TELECOM medio de acceso al videotex *m* (*AmL*), medio de acceso al videotexto *m* (*Esp*); ~ **packet assembler-disassembler** *n* TELECOM armador-desarmador de paquetes de videotex *m* (*AmL*), armador-desarmador de paquetes de videotexto *m* (*Esp*); ~ **server** *n* TELECOM servidor de videotex *m* (*AmL*), servidor de videotexto *m* (*Esp*)

videoware *n* TV cintas de video *f pl* (*AmL*), cintas de vídeo *f pl* (*Esp*)

vidicon: ~ **camera** *n* TV cámara vidicón *f*; ~ **tube** *n* ELECTRON tubo vidicón *m*

view *vt* CINEMAT ver

viewdata: ~ **terminal** *n* TV terminal de videotexto *m*

viewer *n* TELECOM, TV espectador *m*

viewfinder *n* CINEMAT, PHOTO visor *m*, SPACE buscador *m*, visor *m*; ~ **eyepiece** *n* CINEMAT, PHOTO ocular del visor *m*; ~ **with hood** *n* PHOTO visor con caperuza *m* (*AmL*), visor con tapa *m* (*Esp*)

viewing *n* PRINT visualización *f*; ~ **angle** *n* CINEMAT ángulo de visión *m*; ~ **chamber** *n* INSTR recámara de observación *f*, recámara de visión *f*; ~ **lens** *n* CINEMAT, OPT, PHOTO, TV lente enfocadora *f*; ~ **magnifier** *n* PHOTO lente de aumento *f*; ~ **port** *n* SPACE puerto de observación *m*; ~ **theater** *AmE*, ~ **theatre** *BrE* *n* CINEMAT cine *m*, sala de proyección *f*; ~ **transformation** *n* COMP&DP transformación de visualización *f*; ~ **window** *n* COMP&DP ventana de visualización *f* (*Esp*), ventanilla de vista *f* (*AmL*), INSTR mirilla *f*, ventana de observación *f*

vigilance *n* RAIL vigilancia *f*; ~ **device** *n* RAIL dispositivo de vigilancia *m*

Vigneron-Dahl: ~ **trawl** *n* OCEAN, WATER TRANSP arte de arrastre de Vigneron-Dahl *m*

vignette *n* PHOTO, PRINT viñeta *f*

vignetting *n* PHOTO, PRINT viñeteado *m*

vineyard: ~ **plough** *BrE*, ~ **plow** *AmE* *n* AGRIC arado viñero *m*

vinic *adj* CHEM vínico

Vinten: ~ **crane** *n* CINEMAT grúa Vinten *f*

vinyl *n* CHEM vinilo *m*; ~**-coated fin** *n* REFRIG aleta

recubierta de vinilo *f*; ~ **lacquer** *n* CONST laca vinílica *f*

vinylacetylene *n* CHEM vinilacetileno *m*

vinylation *n* CHEM vinilación *f*

vinylbenzene *n* CHEM estireno *m*, vinilbenceno *m*

vinylidene *n* CHEM vinilideno *m*

vinylite *n* CHEM vinilita *f*

vinylog *n* CHEM vinílogo *m*

vinylogous *adj* CHEM vinílogo

vinylpyridine *n* CHEM vinilpiridina *f*

viocid *n* CHEM viocid *m*

violent: ~ **boiling** *n* NUCL ebullición violenta *f*

violuric *adj* CHEM violúrico

VIR *abbr* (*video indicator ready-to-activate*) TELECOM videoindicador listo para ser activado *m*

virgin[1] *adj* COMP&DP, PAPER virgen

virgin[2]: ~ **fiber** *AmE*, ~ **fibre** *BrE* *n* PAPER fibra virgen *f*; ~ **medium** *n* COMP&DP medio virgen *m*, soporte virgen *m*; ~ **neutron** *n* NUCL neutrón virgen *m*

virial: ~ **theorem** *n* PHYS teorema virial *m*

viridine *n* CHEM viridina *f*

virtual: ~ **call service** *n* COMP&DP servicio de llamada virtual *m*; ~ **channel** *n* (*VC*) TELECOM canal virtual *m*; ~ **channel connection** *n* (*VCC*) TELECOM conexión de canal virtual *f*; ~ **channel connection endpoint** *n* (*VCCE*) TELECOM punto final de la conexión de canal virtual *m*; ~ **channel connection-related function** *n* TELECOM función relacionada con la comunicación de canal virtual *f*; ~ **channel identifier** *n* (*VCI*) TELECOM identificador de canal virtual *m*; ~ **charged particle** *n* PART PHYS partícula de carga virtual *f*; ~ **circuit** *n* COMP&DP, TELECOM circuito virtual *m*; ~ **circuit bearer service** *n* TELECOM servicio portador del circuito virtual *m*; ~ **circuit switch** *n* (*VCS*) TELECOM conmutador del circuito virtual *m*; ~ **circuit switching node** *n* TELECOM nodo de conmutación del circuito virtual *m*; ~ **connection** *n* COMP&DP conexión virtual *f*; ~ **container** *n* TELECOM recipiente virtual *m*; ~ **container-n** *n* (*VC-n*) TELECOM recipiente-n virtual *m*; ~ **image** *n* CINEMAT, PHOTO, PHYS, TV, WAVE PHYS imagen virtual *f*; ~ **machine** *n* COMP&DP computador virtual *m* (*AmL*), computadora virtual *f* (*AmL*), ordenador virtual *m* (*Esp*); ~ **memory** *n* COMP&DP memoria virtual *f*; ~ **memory system** *n* (*VMS*) COMP&DP sistema de memoria virtual *m*; ~ **neutral particle** *n* PART PHYS partícula neutra virtual *f*; ~ **object** *n* PHYS objeto virtual *m*; ~ **particle** *n* PART PHYS partícula virtual *f*; ~ **path** *n* (*VP*) TELECOM vía de transmisión virtual *f*; ~ **path connection** *n* (*VPC*) TELECOM conexión de la vía de transmisión virtual *f*; ~ **path connection endpoint** *n* (*VPCE*) TELECOM punto final de la conexión de la vía de transmisión virtual *m*; ~ **path identifier** *n* (*VPI*) TELECOM identificador de la vía de transmisión virtual *m*; ~ **reality** *n* COMP&DP realidad virtual *f*; ~ **sound source** *n* ACOUST, POLL fuente sonora virtual *f*; ~ **terminal** *n* (*VT*) COMP&DP terminal virtual *m*

virus: ~ **disease** *n* AGRIC enfermedad viral *f*

VIS *abbr* (*video indicator suppressed*) TELECOM videoindicador suprimido *m*

visbreaker *n* PETR TECH desviscosificador *m*

viscid *adj* CHEM, FLUID viscoso

viscidity *n* FLUID viscosidad *f*

viscoelasticity *n* P&R viscoelasticidad *f*

viscometer n FLUID, LAB, P&R, PHYS viscosímetro m, viscómetro m

viscoplastic adj GAS viscoplástico

viscose n CHEM viscosa f; ~ **fiber** AmE, ~ **fibre** BrE n PROD fibra de viscosa f; ~ **pulp** n PROD pulpa de viscosa f

viscosimeter n FLUID, P&R viscosímetro m

viscosity n GEN viscosidad f; ~ **coefficient** n FLUID, THERMO coeficiente de viscosidad m; ~-**gravity constant** n THERMO constante de gravedad específica y viscosidad f; ~ **index** n FLUID, PETR TECH, THERMO índice de viscosidad m, VEH grado de viscosidad m; ~ **index improver** n PETR TECH mejorante del índice de viscosidad m; ~ **meter** n THERMO for cable viscosímetro m; ~-**temperature characteristics** n THERMO características de viscosidad y temperatura f pl; ~-**temperature coefficient** n THERMO coeficiente de viscosidad y temperatura m

viscostatic adj CHEM viscoestático

viscous[1] adj GEN viscoso

viscous[2]: ~ **action** n FLUID acción viscosa f; ~ **clutch** n VEH embrague hidráulico m, embrague por aceite m; ~ **damping** n MECH amortiguador de líquido viscoso m; ~ **flow** n ACOUST, AIR TRANSP, FLUID flujo laminar m, FOOD flujo viscoso m, MECH flujo laminar m, METALL flujo laminar m, flujo viscoso m, NUCL flujo laminar m, PHYS flujo laminar m, flujo viscoso m, REFRIG flujo laminar m; ~ **flow equation** n FLUID ecuación para el flujo viscoso f; ~ **force** n FLUID fuerza debida a la viscosidad f; ~ **incompressible flow** n FLUID flujo viscoso incompresible m; ~ **stress** n FLUID esfuerzo viscoso m

vise AmE see vice BrE

visibility n METEO, PHYS, TRANSP, WATER TRANSP visibilidad f; ~ **distance** n TRANSP distancia de visibilidad f; ~ **distance-measuring equipment** n TRANSP equipo para la medición de la distancia de visibilidad m

visible: ~ **grains** n pl GEOL for protection against particles granos visibles m pl; ~ **horizon** n WATER TRANSP celestial navigation horizonte visible m; ~ **light** n TELECOM, WAVE PHYS luz visible f; ~ **radiation** n OPT, SPACE, TELECOM radiación visible f; ~ **region** n FUELLESS campo visible m; ~ **spectrum** n PHYS espectro visible m

vision: ~ **carrier** n TV portadora de imagen f; ~ **clap** n CINEMAT claqueta visual f; ~ **control room** n TV sala de control de imagen f; ~ **mixer** n TV mezclador de imagen m

visor n SAFE ventana f, rotating fluids visor m

visual[1]: ~-**exempted** adj AIR TRANSP exento de visión

visual[2]: ~ **alarm** n TELECOM alarma visual f; ~ **approach** n SPACE aproximación visual f; ~-**audible signal** n COMP&DP señal visual-audible f; ~ **display unit** n (VDU) COMP&DP unidad de presentación visual f (VDU), unidad de representación visual f (VDU), unidad de visualización f (VDU), unidad de visualización virtual f (VDU), ELECTRON, INSTR unidad de presentación visual f (VDU), unidad de representación visual f (VDU), PRINT terminal de pantalla de visualización m (VDU), TELECOM unidad de visualización f (VDU), unidad de presentación visual f (VDU), TV pantalla f; ~ **inspection** n METR inspección visual f; ~ **leak test** n REFRIG prueba de fuga visual f; ~ **pack** n PACK paquete con contenido a la vista m; ~ **range meter** n INSTR medición del alcance visual f, medición del alcance óptico f; ~ **threshold of illumination** n AIR TRANSP umbral de iluminación visible m

visualization n COMP&DP visualización f

vital: ~ **stain** n COLOUR tintura de efecto retardado f

vitellin n CHEM vitelina f

Viterbi: ~ **decoding** n TELECOM decodificación Viterbi f

vitreous[1] adj C&G, CHEM, COATINGS, OPT, TELECOM vidrioso, vítreo

vitreous[2]: ~ **enamel** n C&G, COATINGS esmalte vítreo m; ~ **enamel label** n C&G etiqueta de vidrio f; ~ **silica** n C&G, OPT sílice vítrea f, TELECOM sílice vítrea f, óxido de silicio vítreo m; ~ **state** n C&G estado vítreo m

vitric: ~ **tuff** n GEOL tongue cut on one of boards toba vítrea f

vitrifiable: ~ **color** AmE, ~ **colour** BrE n C&G color vitrificable m

vitrification n CHEM vidriado m, vitrificación f, GEOL vitrificación f

vitrify vt COATINGS vitrificar

vitriol n CHEM vitriolo m

vitriolic: ~ **acid** n CHEM, DETERG, POLL ácido sulfúrico m, ácido vitriólico m

vitriolization n CHEM vitriolización f

vivianite n MINERAL vivianita f

VLCC abbr (very large crude carrier) PETR TECH supertransportador de crudo m, superpetrolero m

VLP abbr (long-playing video) OPT video de larga duración m (AmL), vídeo de larga duración m (Esp)

VLSI[1] abbr (very large-scale integration) COMP&DP, ELECTRON, PHYS, TELECOM integración en muy gran escala

VLSI[2]: ~ **chip** n COMP&DP chip VLSI m, plaqueta VLSI f; ~ **circuit** n PHYS, TELECOM circuito IMGE m

VMS abbr (virtual memory system) COMP&DP sistema de memoria virtual m

vocoder n COMP&DP codificador vocal m, vocoder m, vocodificador m, TELECOM aparato analizador codificador de las palabras m, codificador vocal m, vocoder m, vocodificador m

vocoding n TELECOM análisis y codificación de la palabra m, codificación vocal f

VODAS abbr (voice-operated device anti-singing) TELECOM telefonía simultánea de una única portadora f

vogesite AmE see vogesyte BrE

vogesyte n BrE PETR TECH vogesita f

voice[1]: ~-**activated** adj TELECOM activado por la voz; ~-**switched** adj TELECOM conmutado por la voz

voice[2] n COMP&DP, TELECOM voz f; ~ **activation** n TELECOM activación por la voz f, activación vocal f; ~ **amplifier** n TELECOM amplificador de voz m; ~ **annotation** n TELECOM anotación vocal f; ~-**band data detector** n TELECOM detector de datos de la banda de frecuencias telefónicas m, detector de datos de la banda de frecuencias vocales m; ~ **channel** n COMP&DP, TELECOM canal de voz m, canal vocal m; ~ **coder** n TELECOM codificador vocal m; ~ **control** n TELECOM control vocal m (AmL), modulación por la palabra f (Esp); ~-**controlled operation** n TELECOM operación controlada por la voz f; ~ **data entry** n COMP&DP entrada de datos de voz f; ~ **data packet switch** n TELECOM conmutador de paquetes de voz y datos m; ~ **detector** n SPACE communications detector vocal m; ~ **dialer** AmE see voice dialler BrE;

~ dialing *AmE see voice dialling BrE*; **~ dialler** *n BrE* TELECOM selector a distancia por frecuencia vocal *m*, selector por frecuencia vocal *m*, teleselector por frecuencia vocal *m*; **~ dialling** *n BrE* TELECOM selección a distancia por frecuencia vocal *f*, selección por frecuencia vocal *f*, teleselección por frecuencia vocal *f*; **~ digitization** *n* ELECTRON, TELECOM, TV digitalización de la voz *f*, digitización de la voz *f*; **~ frequency** *n* (*VF*) RAD PHYS frecuencia de voz *f*, frecuencia emitida por las cuerdas vocales *f*, frecuencia vocal *f* (*FV*), TELECOM frecuencia acústica *f*, frecuencia de voz *f*, frecuencia telefónica *f*, frecuencia vocal *f* (*FV*); **~ grade** *n* TELECOM *appliance, mechanism* calidad telefónica *f*; **~ mail** *n* TELECOM correo telefónico *m*, correspondencia radiotelefónica *f*, correspondencia telefónica *f*; **~ mailbox** *n* TELECOM buzón radiotelefónico *m*, buzón telefónico *m*; **~ message processor** *n* TELECOM procesador de comunicación hablada *m*, procesador de mensaje hablado *m*; **~ messaging** *n* TELECOM transmisión de mensajes hablados *f*; **~ network** *n* TELECOM red de conversación *f*, red telefónica *f*; **~-operated device anti-singing** *n* (*VODAS*) TELECOM telefonía simultánea de una única portadora *f*; **~-operated relay** *n* TELECOM relé accionado por la voz *m*, relé actuado por la voz *m*; **~-operated switch** *n* TELECOM conmutador activado por la voz *m*; **~-operated switching** *n* TELECOM conmutación activada por la voz *f*; **~-operated transmission** *n* TELECOM transmisión con portadora interrumpida *f*; **~ output** *n* COMP&DP salida vocal *f*; **~ privacy** *n* TELECOM privacidad de la voz *f*; **~ recognition** *n* TELECOM reconocimiento de voz *m*; **~ recognizer** *n* TELECOM reconocedor de voz *m*; **~ recorder** *n* SPACE grabador de voz *m*, grabadora de voz *f*; **~ response** *n* ELECTRON respuesta acústica *f*, TELECOM respuesta telefónica *f*; **~ response unit** *n* TELECOM unidad de respuestas telefónicas *f*; **~ sensor** *n* SPACE *communications* sensor acústico *m*; **~-switching equipment** *n* TELECOM equipo de conmutación por la voz *m*

voiceband *n* COMP&DP banda de voz *f*, banda vocal *f*, TELECOM banda de frecuencias telefónicas *f*, banda de frecuencias vocales *f*

void *n* GEN vacío *m*; **~ coalescence** *n* METALL combinación de huecos *f*, fusión de lagunas *f*; **~ detector** *n* PAPER detector de defectos *m*; **~ formation** *n* METALL formación de lagunas *f*; **~ growth** *n* METALL crecimiento de lagunas *m*; **~ ratio** *n* COAL porosidad *f*, PROD relación de vacío *f*; **~ volume** *n* TEXTIL volumen vacío *m*

voiding *n* NUCL formación de vapor en el primario *f*

voile *n* TEXTIL voile *m*

volatile[1] *adj* AGRIC, CHEM, COAL, COMP&DP, P&R, TEXTIL volátil

volatile[2]: **~ body** *n* COAL materia volátil *f*, volátiles *m*; **~ fatty acid** *n* (*VFA*) AGRIC, CHEM ácido graso volátil *m*; **~ memory** *n* COMP&DP, ELEC ENG memoria volátil *f*

volatility *n* CHEM, METALL, P&R, TEXTIL volatilidad *f*

volatilization *n* CHEM volatilización *f*

volatilize[1] *vt* CHEM volatilizar

volatilize[2] *vi* CHEM, TEXTIL volatilizarse

volborthite *n* MINERAL volborthita *f*

volcanic[1] *adj* GEOL, PETR TECH volcánico

volcanic[2]: **~ cinder** *n* GEOL escoria volcánica *f*; **~ ejecta** *n pl* GEOL eyecciones volcánicas *f pl*;

~ quake *n* GEOPHYS movimiento volcánico *m*; **~ rock** *n* PETR TECH roca volcánica *f*; **~ tuff** *n* PETR TECH toba volcánica *f*; **~ vent** *n* GEOL chimenea volcánica *f*, OCEAN conducto volcánico *m*

volcanism *n* GEOL volcanismo *m*

volley *n* MILIT *of firearm* descarga *f*, salva *f*

volt *n* (*V*) ELEC volt, voltio *m* (*V*), ELEC ENG, METR, PHYS voltio *m* (*V*)

voltage *n* ELEC, ELEC ENG tensión *f*, voltaje *m*, PHYS voltaje *m*, TELECOM, VEH tensión *f*, voltaje *m*; **~ amplification** *n* ELECTRON amplificación del voltaje *f*; **~ amplifier** *n* ELECTRON amplificador de voltaje *m*; **~ antinode** *n* ELEC ENG voltaje antinodal *m*; **~ balance** *n* ELEC equilibrio de tensiones *m*; **~ booster** *n* ELEC *transformer* sobrealimentador *m*, transformador elevador *m*, elevador de tensión *m*, amplificador *m*, rectificador excitador *m*, generador auxiliar *m*, elevador de voltaje *m*, ELEC ENG elevador de voltaje *m*, ELECTRON generador auxiliar *m*, elevador de voltaje *m*, sobrealimentador *m*, transformador elevador *m*, rectificador excitador *m*, amplificador *m*, elevador de tensión *m*, SPACE elevador de voltaje *m*, TV elevador de voltaje *m*, refuerzo de voltaje *m* (*AmL*); **~ comparator** *n* ELEC ENG comparador de voltaje *m*; **~ comparison** *n* ELEC ENG comparación del voltaje *f*; **~ control** *n* ELEC control de tensión *m*, regulación de tensión *f*; **~-controlled capacitor** *n* ELEC ENG condensador controlado por la tensión *m*; **~-controlled input** *n* ELEC ENG entrada de energía controlada por el voltaje *f*; **~-controlled oscillator** *n* (*VCO*) ELECTRON, SPACE, TELECOM oscilador controlado por voltaje *m* (*OCT*); **~-current characteristic** *n* ELEC ENG característica de corriente y voltaje *f*, curva característica voltaje-corriente *f*; **~-dependent resistor** *n* ELEC ENG resistencia dependiente de voltaje *f*; **~ difference** *n* ELEC, ELEC ENG, PHYS, TELECOM diferencia de tensión *f*; **~ divider** *n* ELEC divisor de potencial *m*, divisor de tensión *m*, divisor de voltaje *m*, reductor de voltaje *m*, ELEC ENG divisor de tensión *m*, partidor-reductor del voltaje *m*, PHYS divisor de voltaje *m*, TELECOM divisor de potencial *m*, divisor de tensión *m*, divisor de voltaje *m*, TV divisor de tensión *m*; **~ doubler** *n* ELEC *rectifier circuit* doblador de tensión *m*, doblador de voltaje *m*; **~ drop** *n* ELEC caída de potencial *f*, caída de tensión *f*, caída de voltaje *f*, ELEC ENG caída de tensión por resistencia *f*, caída de voltaje por resistencia *f*, PHYS caída de voltaje *f*, PROD caída de tensión *f*; **~-dropping resistor** *n* ELEC ENG resistencia de caída de voltaje *f*; **~ feedback** *n* ELEC ENG, ELECTRON realimentación de voltaje *f*; **~ fluctuation** *n* ELEC *supply* fluctuación de tensión *f*, fluctuación de voltaje *f*; **~ gain** *n* ELEC ENG amplificación del voltaje *f*, ganancia de tensión *f*; **~ generator** *n* PHYS generador de voltaje *m*; **~ gradient** *n* ELEC gradiente de potencial *m*, gradiente de tensión *m*; **~ indicator** *n* ELEC, ELEC ENG indicador de voltaje *m*; **~ jump** *n* ELEC salto de tensión *m*, salto de voltaje *m*; **~ level** *n* PROD nivel de tensión *m*; **~ limiter** *n* ELEC, ELEC ENG limitador de tensión *m*, limitador de voltaje *m*; **~ loss** *n* ELEC pérdida de tensión *f*; **~ multiplier** *n* ELEC *rectifier circuit* multiplicador de tensión *m*, multiplicador de voltaje *m*, ELEC ENG multiplicador de voltaje *m*; **~ polarity** *n* ELEC ENG polaridad del voltaje *f*; **~ pulse** *n* ELEC impulso de tensión *m*; **~ reference** *n*

ELEC ENG referencia de voltaje *f*; ~ **reference diode** *n* ELECTRON diodo de referencia de voltaje *m*; ~ **reference tube** *n* ELEC ENG tubo de referencia de voltaje *m*; ~-**regulated power supply** *n* ELEC, ELEC ENG alimentación de energía regulada por voltaje *f*; ~-**regulating transformer** *n* ELEC, ELEC ENG transformador regulador de la tensión *m*; ~ **regulation** *n* ELEC ENG regulación de voltaje *f*; ~ **regulator** *n* AUTO, COMP&DP regulador de tensión *m*, regulador de voltaje *m*, ELEC estabilizador de tensión *m*, regulador de tensión *m*, regulador de voltaje *m*, ELEC ENG, PROD, TV regulador de voltaje *m*, VEH regulador de tensión *m*, regulador de voltaje *m*; ~ **regulator diode** *n* ELECTRON diodo regulador de voltaje *m*; ~ **regulator tube** *n* ELEC ENG tubo regulador de voltaje *m*; ~ **relay** *n* ELEC ENG relé de tensión *m*; ~ **selector** *n* ELEC ENG selector de voltaje *m*; ~ **source** *n* ELEC ENG generador de voltaje *m*, PHYS fuente de voltaje *f*; ~ **spike** *n* ELEC *voltage*, ELEC ENG impulso parásito de voltaje *m*; ~-**stabilized power supply** *n* ELEC suministro de energía con estabilizador de tensión *m*, suministro de energía con estabilizador de voltaje *m*; ~ **stabilizer** *n* ELEC ENG estabilizador de voltaje *m*; ~ **stabilizer tube** *n* ELEC ENG tubo estabilizador de voltaje *m*; ~ **standing wave ratio** *n* (*VSWR*) SPACE *communications* relación de ondas estacionarias de tensión *f*; ~ **step** *n* PHYS escalón de voltaje *m*; ~ **surge** *n* ELEC ENG sobretensión *f*, sobrevoltaje *m*, TELECOM onda de sobretensión *f*, onda transitoria de tensión *f*, onda transitoria de voltaje *f*, sobretensión *f*, sobretensión inicial de encendido *f*, sobrevoltaje *m*; ~ **tester screwdriver** *n* MECH ENG destornillador de comprobación de corriente *m*, destornillador eléctrico de comprobación de fuerza *m*, destornillador para ensayos de tensión *m*, destornillador probador de tensión *m*; ~ **to earth** *n* BrE (*cf voltage to ground BrE*) ELEC ENG voltaje a tierra *m*; ~ **to ground** *n* AmE (*cf voltage to earth BrE*) ELEC ENG tensión a tierra *f*, voltaje a tierra *m*; ~ **to neutral** *n* ELEC tensión en estrella *f*, tensión entre fase y neutro *f*, voltaje entre fase y neutro *m*; ~-**to-frequency conversion** *n* ELEC ENG conversión de voltaje en frecuencia *f*; ~-**to-frequency converter** *n* ELEC ENG convertidor de voltaje en frecuencia *m*; ~ **transformer** *n* ELEC transformador de potencial *m*, transformador de tensión *m*, ELEC ENG transformador de potencial *m*, transformador de tensión *m*, transformador de voltaje *m*

voltaic: ~ **cell** *n* ELEC elemento voltaico *m*, pila voltaica *f*; ~ **pile** *n* ELEC ENG pila voltaica *f*

voltameter *n* BrE CHEM voltímetro-amperímetro *m*, ELEC ENG multímetro *m*, polímetro *m*, voltiamperímetro *m*, PHYS voltímetro-amperímetro *m*

voltammeter *AmE see voltameter BrE*

Volterra: ~ **dislocation** *n* METALL dislocación Volterra *f*

voltmeter *n* ELEC voltímetro *m*, ELEC ENG multímetro *m*, polímetro *m*, voltiamperímetro *m*, PHYS voltímetro *m*

volume *n* GEN *of tank* capacidad *f*, volumen *m*; ~-**capacity ratio** *n* TRANSP grado de capacidad-volumen *m*, relación capacidad-volumen *f*; ~ **change** *n* METALL cambio de volumen *m*; ~ **charge density** *n* ELEC, PHYS, RAD PHYS densidad de carga volumétrica *f*; ~ **compression** *n* ELECTRON *microphone signals* compresión de volumen *f*; ~-**density**

relationship *n* TRANSP relación densidad-volumen *f*; ~ **diffusion** *n* METALL difusión de volumen *f*; ~ **dosing** *n* PACK dosificado por volumen *m*; ~ **emission and absorption coefficient** *n* RAD PHYS coeficiente volumétrico de emisión y absorción *m*; ~ **expansion coefficient** *n* PHYS coeficiente de expansión volumétrica *m*; ~ **filling** *n* PACK llenado por volumen *m*, volumen de llenado *m*; ~ **flow rate** *n* REFRIG caudal volumétrico *m*; ~ **fraction** *n* METALL fracción de volumen *f*; ~ **indicator meter** *n* (*VI meter*) TV contador indicador de volumen *m*, medidor indicador de volumen *m*, registrador indicador de volumen *m*; ~ **integral** *n* PHYS integral de volumen *f*; ~ **label** *n* COMP&DP etiqueta de volumen *f*; ~-**limiting amplifier** *n* ELECTRON amplificador limitador de volumen *m*; ~ **rate** *n* PHYS tasa volumétrica *f*; ~ **resistivity** *n* ELEC ENG resistencia específica de volumen *f*; ~ **of rotation** *n* GEOM volumen de rotación *m*; ~ **size factor** *n* METALL factor específico de volumen *m*; ~ **unit** *n* ACOUST unidad de volumen *f*; ~ **velocity** *n* ACOUST *across surface element* velocidad de volumen *f*

volumeter *n* ACOUST volúmetro *m*

volumetric[1] *adj* MECH ENG, METALL *equation* volumétrico

volumetric[2]: ~ **analysis** *n* CHEM, COAL, DETERG análisis volumétrico *m*; ~ **efficiency** *n* AUTO eficacia volumétrica *f*, rendimiento volumétrico *m*, ELEC ENG, FUELLESS, SPACE, VEH *engine* rendimiento volumétrico *m*; ~-**filling unit** *n* PACK unidad de llenado volumétrica *f*; ~ **flask** *n* LAB *mass* matraz volumétrico *m*; ~ **strain** *n* MECH ENG deformación volumétrica *f*

volumic: ~ **power** *n* GAS potencia volúmica *f*

volunteer *n* AGRIC planta espontánea *f* planta guacha *f* (*AmL*), ricia *f*

volute: ~ **casing** *n* AUTO, VEH alojamiento en espiral *m*; ~ **chamber** *n* WATER canal colector *m*, *of centrifugal pump* caja espiral *f*, difusor *m*; ~ **spring** *n* MECH ENG muelle de hélice cónica *m*, resorte cónico en espiral *m*, resorte espiral cónico *m*

volutin *n* CHEM volutina *f*

vomicine *n* CHEM vomicina *f*

von: ~ **Neumann machine** *n* COMP&DP máquina von Neumann *f*

V1 *abbr* (*decision speed*) AIR TRANSP V1 (*velocidad de decisión*)

VOR *abbr* (*VHF omnidirectional radio range*) AIR TRANSP radiofaro omnidireccional de muy alta frecuencia *m*

vortex *n* COAL remolino *m*, torbellino *m*, vórtex *m*, vórtice *m*, FLUID torbellino *m*, HYDROL remolino *m*, MECH remolino *m*, vórtice *m*, PHYS vórtice *m*, SPACE torbellino *m*, vórtice *m*; ~ **effect** *n* GAS efecto de torbellino *m*; ~ **generator** *n* TRANSP generador de torbellinos *m*; ~ **meter** *n* GAS medidor de torbellino *m*; ~ **skimmer** *n* MAR POLL rasera vortical *f*; ~ **street** *n* FLUID calle de torbellinos *f*

vorticity *n* ACOUST, FLUID, PHYS vorticidad *f*; ~ **diffusion** *n* FLUID difusión de la vorticidad *f*; ~ **equation** *n* FLUID ecuación de vorticidad *f*

voussoir *n* CONST *archstone* dovela *f*

voyage: ~ **charter** *n* PETR TECH flete por viaje *m*, WATER TRANSP fletamento por viaje *m*, póliza de fletamento por viaje *f*

VP *abbr* (*virtual path*) TELECOM vía de transmisión virtual *f*

VPC *abbr* (*virtual path connection*) TELECOM conexión de la vía de transmisión virtual *f*

VPCE *abbr* (*virtual path connection endpoint*) TELECOM punto final de la conexión de la vía de transmisión virtual *m*

VPI *abbr* (*virtual path identifier*) TELECOM identificador de la vía de transmisión virtual *m*

V-pulley *n* MECH ENG polea en V *f*

VRC *abbr* (*vertical redundancy check*) COMP&DP comprobación vertical de la redundancia *f*, verificación de redundancia vertical *f*

V-shaped[1] *adj* GEOM, MECH ENG en V, en forma de V

V-shaped[2]: ~ **aerial** *n* BrE (*cf V-shaped antenna AmE*) TELECOM antena en V *f*; ~ **antenna** *n* AmE (*cf V-shaped aerial BrE*) TELECOM antena en V *f*; ~ **cylinder** *n* AUTO cilindro en V *m*; ~ **notch** *n* NUCL entalla en V *f*

VSI *abbr* (*vertical speed indicator*) AIR TRANSP, SPACE VSI (*indicador de la velocidad vertical*)

V6: ~ **engine** *n* (*V-six engine*) AUTO motor en V de seis cilindros *m*

VSP *abbr* (*vertical seismic profile*) PETR TECH perfil sísmico vertical *m*

VSWR *abbr* (*voltage standing wave ratio*) SPACE *communications* relación de ondas estacionarias de tensión *f*

VT *abbr* COMP&DP (*virtual terminal*) terminal virtual *m*, COMP&DP (*vertical tabulation*) tabulación vertical *f*

V-tail *n* AIR TRANSP *of aircraft* cola en V *f*

V-threaded: ~ **screw** *n* MECH ENG tornillo con hilo en V *m*, tornillo con rosca en V *m*

VTOL: ~ **aircraft** *n* (*vertical takeoff and landing aircraft*) AIR TRANSP, MILIT avión de despegue y aterrizaje vertical *m*

VTR *abbr* (*videotape recorder*) TV grabador de cinta de video *m* (*AmL*), grabador de cinta de vídeo *m* (*Esp*), grabadora de cinta de video *f* (*AmL*), grabadora de cinta de vídeo *f* (*Esp*), magnetoscopio *m*, videograbador *m* (*AmL*), videograbadora *f* (*AmL*), vídeo grabador *m* (*Esp*)

V-type: ~ **engine** *n* VEH motor de cilindros en V *m*

VU: ~**-meter** *n* ACOUST medidor VU *m*

vug *n* GEOL cavidad *f*

vuggy *adj* GEOL cavernoso, drusado, PETR TECH vacuolado, *ground* drusado

vughy *adj* (*see vuggy*) GEOL cavernoso

vugular *adj* GEOL cavernoso, PETR TECH vacuolar *m*

vulcanicity *n* GEOPHYS vulcanicidad *f*

vulcanite *n* CHEM, MECH vulcanita *f*, P&R ebonita *f*, caucho endurecido *m*, vulcanita *f*

vulcanization *n* CHEM, ELEC, MECH, P&R, THERMO vulcanización *f*

vulcanize *vt* CHEM, ELEC, MECH, P&R, THERMO vulcanizar

vulcanized[1] *adj* THERMO vulcanizado

vulcanized[2]: ~ **fiber disk** *AmE*, ~ **fibre disc** *BrE* *n* MECH ENG *abrasives* disco de fibra vulcanizada *m*

W

W[1] *abbr* CHEM (*tungsten, wolfram*) W (*tungsteno, wolframio*), ELEC, ELEC ENG, METR, PHYS (*watt*) W (*vatio*), WAVE PHYS (*angular frequency*) W (*frecuencia angular*)

W[2]: **~ particle** *n* PHYS partícula W *f*

wacke *n* GEOL *10% mud-supported grains in a micrite* vacka *f*

wackestone *n* GEOL roca carbonatada *f*

wad[1] *n* MINERAL ocre negro *m*, TEXTIL guata *f*, guateado *m*; **~ of cotton wool** *n* TEXTIL guata de algodón hidrófilo *f*, guateado de algodón hidrófilo *m*; **~ punch** *n* MECH ENG cortador de tacos *m*, punzón de guata *m*

wad[2] *vt* TEXTIL enguatar

wadding *n* CHEM empaque *m*, PACK guata *f*, PAPER guata *f*, revestimiento interior *m*, TEXTIL guateado *m*

wadi *n* HYDROL ued *m*, vado *m*, wadi *m*

wafer *n* AGRIC *hay* paca de heno muy compactada *f*, COMP&DP oblea *f*, ELEC ENG placa de contactos *f*, ELECTRON *semiconductors* pastilla *f*, oblea *f*, disco *m*; **~ distortion** *n* ELECTRON *semiconductors* distorsión de pastilla *f*; **~ fabrication** *n* ELECTRON *semiconductors* fabricación de pastillas *f*; **~ mask** *n* ELECTRON *semiconductors* máscara de pastilla *f*; **~ processing** *n* ELECTRON *semiconductors* tratamiento de la pastilla *m*; **~ scale integration** *n* COMP&DP integración a escala de oblea de silicio *f*, ELECTRON integración a escala de la pastilla *f*; **~ switch** *n* ELEC ENG conmutador de sectores *m*; **~ yield** *n* ELECTRON elasticidad de la pastilla *f*

wagnerite *n* MINERAL wagnerita *f*

wagon *n* BrE (*cf car AmE*) RAIL vagón de mercancías *m*, TRANSP carro *m* (*AmL*), coche *m* (*Esp*); **~ car** *n* BrE (*cf trailer wagon AmE*) TRANSP vagoneta de remolque *f*, vagón de remolque *m*; **~ distributor office** *n* BrE (*cf car distributor office AmE*) RAIL despacho del distribuidor de vagones *m*; **~ for internal yard use** *n* BrE (*cf car for internal yard use AmE*) RAIL, VEH vagón para uso interno en la estación *m*; **~ hoist** *n* RAIL montacargas para vagones *m*, montavagones *m*; **~ lift** *n* BrE (*cf car elevator AmE*) RAIL montacargas para vagones *m*, montavagones *m*; **~ shed** *n* BrE (*cf truck shed AmE*) RAIL depósito de vagones *m*; **~ sleeper train** *n* BrE (*cf car sleeper train AmE*) RAIL tren de coches-cama *m*; **~ vault** *n* CONST *architecture* bóveda de cañón *f*

wagonload *n* BrE (*cf carload AmE*) TRANSP carga de vagón *f*, vagón *m*

waist *n* TEXTIL cintura *f*, talle *m*; **~ dart** *n* TEXTIL pinza de talle *f*

wait: **~ loop** *n* COMP&DP bucle de espera *m*, lazo de espera *m*; **~ state** *n* COMP&DP estado de espera *m*

waiting: **~ call** *n* TELECOM llamada en cola de espera *f*; **~ on weather** *n* (*WOW*) PETR TECH espera por mal tiempo *f* (*WOW*)

wake *n* FLUID, MAR POLL, OCEAN, PHYS, WATER TRANSP *of ship* estela *f*; **~ of a cylinder** *n* FLUID estela de un cilindro *f*; **~ intensity** *n* FLUID intensidad de la estela *f*; **~ track** *n* WATER TRANSP *navigation* derrota

indicada por la estela *f*; **~ turbulence** *n* AIR TRANSP perturbación aerodinámica arrastrada *f*, turbulencia de la estela *f*

walchowite *n* MINERAL walchowita *f*

Walden: **~ inversion** *n* CHEM, OPT inversión de Walden *f*, inversión óptica *f*

wale *n* COAL carbón limpiado a mano *m*, TEXTIL columna *f*

waling *n* COAL extracción a mano *f*, extracción de piedras del carbón *f*, CONST cabecero *m*, larguero de entibación *m*

walk: **~ down** *n* COMP&DP pérdidas acumuladas *f pl*; **~-in freezer** *n* REFRIG congelador de acceso total *m*; **~-in refrigerator** *n* REFRIG cámara frigorífica pequeña *f*

walkaround: **~ inspection** *n* SPACE inspección de los alrededores *f*

walking: **~ accident** *n* SAFE accidente al caminar *m*; **~ beam** *n* MECH ENG balancín *m*, balancín de perforación *m*, viga balancín *f*, MINE balancín de perforación *m*; **~ dragline excavator** *n* CONST dragalina móvil *f*; **~ line** *n* CONST *stair-building* línea móvil *f*

walkway *n* CONST corredor *m*, pasillo *m*, MECH pasillo *m*, SPACE andén *m*, pasarela *f*, pasillo *m*

wall[1] *n* CONST *of rocks* muro *m*, *building* pared *f*, FLUID pared *f* (*Esp*), MINE *of break* respaldo *m* (*AmL*), *of vein* muro *m*, pared *f* (*Esp*), salbanda *f*, banco de roca natural *m*, PROD *of cylinder, boiler* pared *f*; **~ attachment** *n* FLUID adhesión a la pared *f*; **~ bearing** *n* MINE revestimiento de mampostería *m*; **~ box** *n* CONST caja en un muro *f*; **~ brace** *n* CINEMAT soporte de pared *m*; **~ bracket** *n* CONST palomilla *f*, MINE *shafting* apoyo empotrado *m*, brazo mural *m* (*AmL*), soporte de pared *m* (*Esp*), TELECOM apoyo empotrado *m*, brazo de pared *m*, consola mural *f*, ménsula de muro *f*, ménsula mural *f*; **~ coil** *n* REFRIG serpentín de pared *m*; **~ crane** *n* CONST grúa de pared *f*; **~ cupboard** *n* LAB *mass* gabinete de montaje mural *m*; **~ effect** *n* COAL acción de los muros *f*; **~-entrance insulator** *n* ELEC, ELEC ENG aislante de fijación mural *m*; **~ fitting** *n* CONST, ELEC, ELEC ENG aplique *m*; **~ holdfast** *n* CONST gato de pared *m*; **~ lamp** *n* ELEC *lighting*, ELEC ENG lámpara de pared *f*; **~ losses** *n* REFRIG pérdida por las paredes *f*; **~ mount enclosure assembly** *n* PROD conjunto de encerramiento montado en la pared *m*; **~ outlet** *n* ELEC *connection* conector mural *m*, enchufe mural *m*, tomacorriente de pared *m*, tomacorriente mural *m*; **~ paint** *n* COLOUR pintura para paredes *f*; **~ piece** *n* CONST *shoring* pieza de apoyo en pared *f*; **~ plate** *n* CONST larguero *m*, *roof-plate* pared por medio *f*, placa de asiento *f*; **~ socket** *n* ELEC *connection* enchufe de pared *m*, enchufe mural *m*; **~ string** *n* CONST *stair-building* zanca interior *f*; **~ thickness gaging** AmE, **~ thickness gauging** *n* BrE NUCL medición del grosor de paredes *f*

wall[2] *vt* MINE revestir de mampostería; **~ in** *vt* MINE fijar al muro; **~ up** *vt* CONST, MINE tapiar

walled: ~ **enclosure** n CONST cerramiento m

walling n CONST tabiquería f; ~ **scaffold** n MINE *blast furnace* desprendimiento del revestimiento m; ~ **stage** n MINE plataforma de entibado f

wallpaper n PAPER papel para tapizar paredes m; ~ **base** n PAPER papel soporte para papeles pintados m

walnut: ~ **oil** n FOOD aceite de nuez m

wand n COMP&DP lápiz lector m, varilla f, PRINT varilla f; ~ **scanner** n COMP&DP explorador a varilla m, lápiz lector m

wane n CONST *bevelled edge of board cut from log* bisel m, mengua f

Wankel: ~ **engine** n AUTO motor Wankel m, MECH ENG motor Wankel m, motor rotatorio m, THERMO, TRANSP motor Wankel m, VEH motor Wankel m, motor rotativo m

WANO abbr (*World Association of Nuclear Operators*) NUCL WANO (*Asociación Mundial de Operadores Nucleares*)

wanted: ~ **emission** n TELECOM emisión deseada f; ~ **signal** n ELECTRON señal requerida f; ~**-to-unwanted carrier-power ratio** n TELECOM razón de potencia de salida de portadora deseada a indeseada f

warble n ACOUST tono de frecuencia variable m, TELE-COM aullido m, ululación f; ~ **tone** n ACOUST tono modulado m

ward n CONST *of lock* guarda f

warded: ~ **lock** n CONST cerradura entallada f

warding: ~ **file** n MECH ENG lima de paletones f, lima para guardas f

Ward-Leonard: ~ **set** n ELEC ENG juego Ward-Leonard m

wardroom n WATER TRANSP *Royal Navy* cámara de oficiales f

ware: ~ **pusher** n C&G empujador de loza m

warehouse n PROD almacén m, bodega f, depósito m, WATER TRANSP almacén m; ~ **delivery** n PROD entrega en almacén f; ~ **management** n PROD administración de almacén f; ~ **order** n PROD orden de almacén f, pedido de almacén m; ~ **price** n PROD precio de almacén m

warehousing n PROD almacenaje m, almacenamiento m; ~ **charges** n pl PROD derechos de almacenaje m pl, derechos de depósito en aduana m pl

warfarin n CHEM warfarina f

warhead n MILIT, SPACE *missile* cabeza de combate f, cono de carga m

warm[1] adj THERMO caliente

warm[2]: ~ **air heating system** n HEAT sistema de calefacción por aire caliente m; ~ **air stream** n METEO corriente de aire caliente f; ~ **cloud** n METEO nube caliente f; ~ **front** n METEO frente caliente m; ~ **laboratory** n NUCL *of compound* laboratorio semi-caliente m, laboratorio tibio m; ~ **layer** n METEO capa caliente f; ~ **start** n COMP&DP arranque en caliente m, arranque secundario m (*Esp*), arranque tibio m (*AmL*), reanudación del sistema f; ~**-up time** n THERMO tiempo de calentamiento m; ~**-water sphere** n OCEAN esfera hidrotermal f

warm[3]: ~ **up** vt THERMO *spacecraft* calentar, encender

warming: ~**-in** n C&G calentamiento m; ~ **room** n REFRIG cámara de recalentamiento f

warmth n NUCL calor m, THERMO calor m, calor moderado m

warning n CONST, ELEC, LAB, MECH ENG, MINE alarma f, PROD advertencia f, alarma f, aviso m, SAFE, TELE-COM alarma f; ~ **bell** n SAFE campana de advertencia f; ~ **color** AmE, ~ **colour** BrE n COLOUR colorante de advertencia m; ~ **distance** n RAIL distancia de advertencia f; ~ **label** n SAFE etiqueta de advertencia f; ~ **light** n AIR TRANSP luz de aviso f, ELEC ENG luz de emergencia f, lámpara de advertencia f, SAFE luz de advertencia f; ~ **message** n TRANSP mensaje de advertencia m; ~ **sign** n CONST señal de peligro f, señal de precaución f, SAFE letrero de advertencia m; ~ **signal** n PROD señal de alarma f, WATER TRANSP señal de advertencia f, señal de aviso f; ~ **triangle** n SAFE señal triangular de peligro f

warp[1] n ACOUST alabeo m, C&G *of optical glass* torcedura f, PAPER alabeo m, TEXTIL urdimbre f, alabeo m, WATER TRANSP *towing* cable de remolque m, cabo de remolque m, remolque m; ~ **beam** n TEXTIL plegador de urdimbre m; ~ **break** n TEXTIL rotura de la urdimbre f; ~ **dyeing** n COLOUR teñido en urdimbre m; ~ **knitting** n TEXTIL género de punto por urdimbre m; ~**-knitting machine** n TEXTIL máquina de tricotar por urdimbre f; ~ **setting** n TEXTIL preparación de la urdimbre f; ~ **stop motion** n TEXTIL paraurdimbres m; ~ **yarn** n PAPER hilo de urdimbre m

warp[2] vt CONST *wood* alabear, deformar, WATER TRANSP *ship* espiar

warp[3] vi MECH, MECH ENG, WATER TRANSP alabearse, deformarse

warpage n C&G torcedura f

warped[1] adj MECH alabeado, deformado, oblicuo, torcido, MECH ENG alabeado, WATER TRANSP acalabrotado

warped[2]: ~ **sheet** n BrE (*cf bow and warp AmE*) C&G hoja pandeada f; ~ **timber** n CONST madera alabeada f

warper n TEXTIL urdidor m

warping n CONST *of wood* alabeo m, combadura f, PRINT *book binding* alabeo m, PROD *of castings*, RAIL deformación f, TEXTIL urdido m; ~ **creel** n TEXTIL fileta del urdidor f; ~ **drum** n WATER TRANSP *deck fittings* cilindro m, cilindro cabrestante m, tambor de chigre m, tambor de molinete m; ~ **head** n WATER TRANSP *winch* cabirón m; ~ **reed** n TEXTIL peine del urdidor m

warrant[1]: ~ **officers' wardroom** n WATER TRANSP camareta f

warrant[2] vt PROD *guarantee* garantizar

warranty n PROD certificado de garantía m, garantía f

Warren: ~ **engine** n TRANSP motor Warren m

warship n MILIT buque de guerra m, WATER TRANSP *navy* buque de guerra m, navío m

wash[1] n CHEM lavado m, CINEMAT baño de lavado m, CONST *of window* vierteaguas m, MECH ENG *water-colour drawing* dibujo al lavado m, PROD productos lavados m pl; ~ **boring** n COAL sondeo por inyección m, PETR TECH perforación por corriente de agua f, sondeo por corriente de agua m; ~ **bottle** n CHEM matraz de lavado m, piseta f, LAB piseta f; ~ **house** n PROD taller de lavado m; ~ **leather** n CONST cuero lavable m; ~ **primer** n COATINGS imprimación de revoque f, P&R pintura de imprimación anticorrosiva f, pintura de imprimación con propiedades adhesivas y protectoras f; ~ **tank** n PHOTO tanque de lavado m

wash[2] vt CHEM, COAL, MINE, TEXTIL lavar; ~ **away** vt

CHEM TECH eliminar, quitar, HYDROL eliminar por lavado; **~ with hot water** *vt* MAR POLL lavar con agua caliente; **~ with low pressure hoses** *vt* MAR POLL lavar usando mangas de agua a baja presión

washability *n* TEXTIL lavabilidad *f*

washboard *n* C&G lavadero *m*, CONST *skirting* rodapié *m*, WATER TRANSP *boat building* falca *f*

washed[1]: **~ out** *adj* CINEMAT descolorido; **~ overboard** *adj* WATER TRANSP barrido por la mar

washed[2]: **~ coal** *n* COAL carbón lavado *m*; **~ small** *n* COAL menudos lavados *m pl*; **~ and squashed consumer waste carton** *n* PACK caja de cartón usada, aplastada y limpia *f*

washer *n* CHEM TECH, COAL lavador *m*, CONST arandela *f*, MECH ENG *perforated disc* junta *f*, arandela *f*, PROD *washing machine* lavadora *f*, VEH dispositivo de lavado *m*, arandela *f*; **~ cutter** *n* MECH ENG cortaarandelas *m*, cortador de arandelas *m*; **~ for tapered guide pillar** *n* MECH ENG arandela para columnas de guías cónicas *f*

washery *n* MINE lavadero *m*

washing[1]: **--active** *adj* DETERG lavadoactivo

washing[2] *n* C&G, CHEM TECH, PROD, TEXTIL lavado *m*; **~ adjuvant** *n* DETERG adyuvante de lavado *m*, auxiliar de lavado *m*; **~ agent** *n* CHEM, DETERG agente de lavado *m*; **~ auxiliary** *n* DETERG auxiliar de lavado *m*; **~ bath** *n* DETERG baño de lavado *m*; **~ column** *n* CHEM TECH columna de lavado *f*; **~ drum** *n* PAPER tambor lavador *m*; **~ facilities** *n pl* TEXTIL instalaciones de lavado *f pl*; **~ instructions** *n pl* PACK, TEXTIL instrucciones de lavado *f pl*; **~ machine** *n* PROD lavadora *f*, TEXTIL máquina de lavar *f*; **~ out** *n* CHEM TECH ablución *f*, extracción de los depósitos solubles *f*, lavado interior con vapor *m*; **~ plant** *n* PROD instalación de lavado *f*, planta de lavado *f*; **~ powder** *n* DETERG polvo de lavado *m*; **~ powder slurry** *n* DETERG fangos del polvo de lavado *m pl*; **~ soda** *n* CHEM *hydrated sodium carbonate* sosa para lavar *f*; **~ tower** *n* CHEM TECH torre de lavado *f*; **~ tube** *n* LAB tubo de lavado *m*

washout *n* POLL eliminación de ciertas sustancias por la lluvia o viento *f*, escape *m*, fuga *f*, hundimiento por acción del agua *m*, RAIL hundimiento por la acción del agua *m*, socavón por la acción del agua *m*; **~ hole** *n* PROD *boiler* agujero de mano *m*, registro de limpieza *m*; **~ plug** *n* PROD macho para agujeros de limpieza *m*; **~ rate** *n* POLL velocidad de desagüe *f*, velocidad de vaciado *f*

washover *n* PETROL lavado *m*; **~ string** *n* PETR TECH sarta de lavar *f*

washup *n* PAPER, PRINT limpieza de los rodillos *f*

wasp: **--waisted tank** *n* C&G tanque cintura de avispa *m*

wastage *n* NUCL *mass* desgaste químico *m*, PROD *loss* despilfarro *m*, merma *f*, pérdida *f*, RECYCL desgaste *m*

waste[1] *n* FOOD residuo *m*, MINE escombrera *f*, estériles *m pl*, NUCL basura *f*, PAPER, POLL residuos *m pl*, PROD efluente *m*, desechos *m pl*, desperdicios *m pl*, despojos *m pl*, *loss* merma *f*, residuos *m pl*, basura *f*, pérdida *f*, RECYCL residuos *m pl*, desechos *m pl*, basura *f*, SAFE basura *f*, TEXTIL merma *f*, retales del corte *m pl*; **~ canister** *n* NUCL *mass* contenedor de residuos *m*; **~ cock** *n* CONST cañería de desagüe *f*, grifo de desagüe *m*; **~ collection** *n* RECYCL colecta de basuras *f*, colecta de desperdicios *f*, recogida de basuras *f*, recogida de desperdicios *f*, recolección de

basura *f* (*AmL*), recolección de desperdicios *f* (*AmL*); **~ condensate pump** *n* NUCL bomba del condensado de residuos líquidos *f*, bomba del residuo de la condensación *f*; **~ disposal** *n* NUCL almacenamiento definitivo de residuos *m*, RECYCL destrucción de la basura *f*, eliminación de desechos *f*, eliminación de la basura *f*, eliminación de residuos *f*, evacuación de residuos *f*, tratamiento de los efluentes *m*, WATER disposición de basuras *f*, eliminación de basuras *f*, eliminación de residuos *f*; **~ disposal by nuclear transmutation** *n* NUCL evacuación de residuos por transmutación nuclear *f*; **~ drift** *n* MINE galería de estériles *f* (*Esp*), galería de relleno *f* (*AmL*); **~ drum** *n* NUCL *mass* bidón de residuos *m*; **~ dump** *n* MINE escombrera *f*, escorial *m*, RECYCL vertedero *m*; **~ energy** *n* THERMO energía residual *f*; **~ of energy** *n* THERMO energía residual *f*; **~ evaporator** *n* NUCL *workmen* evaporador de residuos *m*; **~ extraction system** *n* PACK, POLL sistema de extracción de residuos *m*; **~ gas** *n* CHEM gas residual *m*, GAS gas de desecho *m*, gas de desperdicio *m*, gas sobrante *m*, NUCL residuos gaseosos *m pl*, POLL escape de gas *m*, fuga de gas *f*, gas residual *m*, gas sobrante *m*, PROD *of furnace* gas de exhaustación *m*, gas residual *m*; **~ gas heat** *n* THERMO calor de los gases de desecho *m*; **~ gas heat recovery** *n* THERMO *spacecraft* recuperación del calor de los gases de desechos *f*, recuperación del calor de los gases residuales *f*; **~ ground** *n* MINE terreno estéril *m*; **~ heap** *n* CONST, MINE escombrera *f*, RECYCL escombrera *f*, vertedero *m*; **~ heat** *n* HEAT ENG calor de desecho *m*, calor residual *m*, NUCL calor sobrante *m*, POLL calor residual *m*, calor sobrante *m*, THERMO calor residual *m*; **~ heat boiler** *n* HEAT caldera de calor de desecho *f*, THERMO caldera de recuperación *f*; **~ heat recovery** *n* THERMO recuperación del calor residual *f*; **~ land** *n* AGRIC erial *m*; **~ management** *n* RECYCL organización de la eliminación de desperdicios *f*; **~ outlet** *n* NUCL *workmen* salida de residuos *f*; **~ paper** *n* PAPER papel recuperado *m*, RECYCL papel de desecho *m*, papel usado *m*, papeles usados *m pl*; **~ paper contraries** *n* PAPER materias indeseables presentes en el papelote *f pl*; **~ pipe** *n* CONST tubería de desagüe *f*; **~ processing** *n* RECYCL tratamiento de la basura *m*; **~ product** *n* RECYCL desecho *m*, producto de desecho *m*; **~ recycling** *n* RECYCL reciclado de basura *m*, reciclado de residuos *m*; **~ rock** *n* MINE roca estéril *f*; **~ sheets** *n pl* PRINT pliegos sobrantes *m pl*; **~ sorting** *n* RECYCL clasificación de la basura *f*, separación de la basura *f*; **~ space** *n* HYDRAUL espacio perjudicial *m*; **~ steam** *n* HYDRAUL vapor de escape *m*, vapor de exhaustación *m*; **~ treatment** *n* RECYCL tratamiento de desechos *m*, tratamiento de la basura *m*, tratamiento de residuos *m*; **~ treatment plant** *n* RECYCL planta de tratamiento de basura *f*, planta de tratamiento de desechos *f*, planta de tratamiento de residuos *f*; **~ volume reduction factor** *n* NUCL factor de reducción del volumen de los residuos *m*; **~ water** *n* COAL, CONST aguas residuales *f pl*, HYDRAUL nivel de aguas abajo *m*, HYDROL agua sobrante *f*, aguas residuales *f pl*, aguas de desecho *f pl*, POLL aguas de albañal *f pl*, aguas de desecho *f pl*, aguas negras *f pl*, RECYCL aguas residuales *f pl*, WATER agua sobrante *f*, aguas de desecho *f pl*

waste[2] *vt* RECYCL agotar, gastar

wastewater: **~ disposal** *n* RECYCL eliminación de

aguas residuales *f*, evacuación de aguas residuales *f*; ~ **outfall** *n* WATER descarga de aguas residuales *f*; ~ **purification** *n* WATER depuración de aguas residuales *f*; ~ **recycling operation** *n* NUCL operación de reciclado de aguas residuales *f*; ~ **tank** *n* SPACE cisterna de agua de condensación *f*, cisterna de aguas residuales *f*; ~ **treatment** *n* HYDROL tratamiento de aguas residuales *m*, POLL tratamiento de aguas negras *m* (*AmL*), tratamiento de aguas residuales *m* (*Esp*), RECYCL tratamiento de aguas residuales *m*; **--treatment plant** *n* RECYCL planta de depuración de aguas residuales *f*, planta de tratamiento de aguas residuales *f*

wasteway *n* HYDRAUL canal de descarga *m*, canal de vertedero *m*, canal evacuador *m*, canal evacuador de crecidas *m*

watch[1]: **on** ~ *adj* WATER TRANSP *sailing* de guardia

watch[2]: ~ **casing** *n pl* MECH ENG caja de reloj *f*; ~ **casings** *n pl* MECH ENG relojeras *f pl*; ~ **glass** *n* LAB vidrio de reloj *m*; ~ **screw plate** *n* MECH ENG *very fine pitch* placa roscada de relojero *f*

watchdog: ~ **application** *n* COMP&DP aplicación de vigilancia *f* (*Esp*), aplicación tipo perro guardián *f* (*AmL*); ~ **timer** *n* COMP&DP marcador de perro guardián *m*, temporizador de vigilancia *m*, PROD temporizador controlador de secuencia *m*; **--timer set valve** *n* PROD válvula reguladora del temporizador controlador de secuencia *f*

watchman's: ~ **clock** *n* PROD controlador de rondas *m*

watchtower *n* MILIT garita *f*

water[1]: **--bearing** *adj* GAS, GEOL, HYDROL, MINE, PETR TECH, WATER acuífero; **--cooled** *adj* GAS enfriado por agua, PROD, TEXTIL refrigerado por agua, THERMO enfriado por agua, refrigerado por agua; **--eroded** *adj* HYDROL erosionado por el agua; **--hardened** *adj* THERMO *spacecraft* templado con agua; **--repellent** *adj* COATINGS, TEXTIL hidrófugo; **--resistant** *adj* PACK, TEXTIL resistente al agua; **--saving** *adj* HYDROL economizador de agua; **--soluble** *adj* CHEM, FOOD, TEXTIL soluble en agua

water[2]:

■ **a** ~ **absorption capacity** *n* WATER capacidad hidroscópica *f*; ~ **accumulator** *n* NUCL acumulador de agua *m*; **--activated battery** *n* ELEC ENG batería hidroactivada *f*; ~ **adit** *n* WATER galería de desagüe *f*; ~ **analysis kit** *n* LAB equipo de análisis de agua *m*; ~ **authority** *n* WATER autoridad de aguas *f*;

■ **b** ~ **balance** *n* HYDROL *software* equilibrador de agua *m*, WATER balance hídrico *m*; ~ **barrier** *n* MINE *to prevent propagation of coal dust* barrera de agua *f*; **--based backing adhesive** *n* PACK adhesivo de base acuosa *m*; **--based mud** *n* PETR TECH lodo a base de agua *m*; **--based paint** *n* CONST pintura al agua *f*; **--based sludge** *n* PETR TECH lodo a base de agua *m*; ~ **bath** *n* CHEM, LAB baño María *m*; ~ **bath evaporator** *n* NUCL evaporador de baño de agua *m*; **--bearing stratum** *n* GEOL manto freático *m*, HYDROL estrato acuífero *m*, WATER estrato acuífero *m*, horizonte acuífero *m*, manto freático *m*; ~ **box** *n* C&G, NUCL caja de agua *f*; ~ **budget** *n* WATER presupuesto de agua *m*; ~ **bus** *n* WATER TRANSP bus acuático *m*; ~ **butt** *n* CONST bota de agua *f*;

■ **c** ~ **can** *n* PROD *to wet an emery wheel or similar* surtidor de rociado *m*; ~ **carriage** *n* TRANSP *reservoirs* transporte de agua *m*; **--carrying capacity** *n* TEXTIL capacidad de transporte de agua *f*; ~ **catchment** *n*

WATER captación de agua *f*; **--cement ratio** *n* CONST relación agua-cemento *f*; ~ **channel** *n* COAL cebador *m*; ~ **chiller** *n* REFRIG enfriador de agua *m*; **--cleansing plant** *n* MINE estación depuradora de aguas *f*; ~ **clearance** *n* OCEAN profundidad de agua disponible *f*; ~ **cock** *n* CONST canilla del agua *f* (*AmL*), grifo del agua *m*; ~ **conditioning** *n* WATER tratamiento del agua *m*; ~ **conditioning process** *n* NUCL proceso de acondicionamiento del agua *m*; ~ **conduit** *n* WATER colector de agua *m*; ~ **conservation** *n* HYDROL conservación de agua *f*; ~ **container** *n* TEXTIL contenedor de agua *m*; ~ **content** *n* COAL, CONST contenido de agua *m*, GAS contenido acuoso *m*, contenido de agua *m*, METEO, OPT, PHYS contenido de agua *m*; **--cooled air-conditioning unit** *n* HEAT, REFRIG, THERMO acondicionador de aire con condensador de agua *m*; **--cooled condenser** *n* HEAT ENG condensador enfriado por agua *m*; **--cooled engine** *n* AUTO, VEH motor refrigerado por agua *m*; **--cooled furnace** *n* HEAT *text*, REFRIG, THERMO horno refrigerado por agua *m*; **--cooled heat trap** *n* CINEMAT trampa térmica enfriada por agua *f*; **--cooled reactor** *n* NUCL reactor refrigerado por agua *m*; **--cooled retort** *n* HEAT retorta refrigerada por agua *f*; **--cooled system** *n* MECH ENG sistema de enfriado por agua *m*, sistema de hidrorrefrigeración *m*, sistema de refrigeración por agua *m*; **--cooled transformer** *n* ELEC transformador de enfriamiento por agua *m*, transformador refrigerado por agua *m*, ELEC ENG transformador refrigerado por agua *m*; **--cooled tube** *n* ELECTRON tubo enfriado con agua *m*; ~ **cooling cascade** *n* MECH ENG *diecasting die* cascada de enfriamiento por agua *f*, cascada de refrigeración por agua *f*; ~ **curtain** *n* MINE *to prevent propagation of coal dust* barrera de agua *f*;

■ **d** ~ **decomposition under irradiation** *n* NUCL descomposición del agua por irradiación *f*; ~ **deficiency** *n* WATER deficiencia de agua *f*; ~ **defrosting** *n* REFRIG desescarche por aspersión *m*, desescarche por lluvia *m*; ~ **delivery** *n* WATER suministro de agua *m*; ~ **detector** *n* PROD hidoscopio *m*, hidróscopo *m*; ~ **distribution** *n* CONST, WATER distribución de agua *f*; ~ **drain cock** *n* WATER grifo de drenaje *m*; ~ **drive** *n* PETR TECH empuje de agua *m*, empuje por agua *m*, PETROL empuje hidrostático *m*;

■ **e** ~ **enamel** *n* COLOUR esmalte al agua *m*; ~ **equivalent** *n* PHYS equivalente de agua *m*; ~ **erosion** *n* HYDROL erosión debido al agua *f*; ~ **extraction structure** *n* CONST estructura para la extracción *f*;

■ **f** ~ **fall height** *n* HYDRAUL altura de la caída de agua *f*; ~ **feed** *n* PROD inyección de agua *f*; ~ **filter** *n* WATER, WATER TRANSP filtro de agua *m*; ~ **finish** *n* PAPER apresto de agua sobre calandria *m*, PROD acabado en agua *m*; **--finished board** *n* PAPER cartón alisado en húmedo *m*; **--finished paper** *n* PAPER papel alisado en húmedo *m*; ~ **finishing** *n* PAPER satinado en húmedo *m*, PROD acabado en agua *m*; ~ **fire-extinguisher** *n* SAFE extintor de fuego a base de agua *m*; ~ **fitting** *n* WATER acometida de agua *f*; ~ **flooding** *n* PETROL inyección de agua *f*; ~ **flow rate** *n* HEAT caudal de agua *m*;

■ **g** ~ **gage** *AmE see water gauge BrE*; ~ **gallery** *n* AUTO conducto de agua *m*; ~ **gap** *n* NUCL *measuring* huelgo entre elementos de combustible *m*; ~ **gas** *n*

GAS gas de agua *m*; ~ **gate** *n* WATER compuerta *f*, *gate-valve* válvula de compuerta *f*; ~ **gauge** *n* BrE COAL densímetro *m*, hidrómetro *m* (*Esp*), ELEC densímetro *m* (*AmL*), hidrómetro *m*, FOOD densímetro *m* (*AmL*), hidrómetro *m* (*Esp*), HYDROL densímetro *m* (*AmL*), hidrómetro *m* (*Esp*), indicador del nivel de agua *m*, MECH densímetro *m* (*AmL*), hidrómetro *m*, PETR TECH hidrómetro *m* (*Esp*), PHYS, VEH densímetro *m* (*AmL*), hidrómetro *m* (*Esp*), WATER hidrómetro *m* (*Esp*), indicador del nivel de agua *m*; ~ **glass** *n* C&G tubo de nivel *m*, DETERG cristal de agua *m*; ~ **gradient pressure** *n* TEXTIL gradiente de presión del agua *m*;

~ h ~ **hammer** *n* FLUID, PETR TECH golpe de ariete *m*; ~ **hardness** *n* WATER dureza del agua *f*; ~ **heater** *n* LAB, MECH ENG calentador de agua *m*; ~ **hose** *n* MINE manguera de agua *f*; ~ **hydrant** *n* WATER boca de riego *f*;

~ i ~ **indicator** *n* WATER indicador de agua *m*; ~ **inflow** *n* WATER golpe de agua *m*; ~ **ingress** *n* NUCL *communications* entrada de agua *f*; ~ **injection** *n* PETR TECH inyección de agua *f*; ~ **injection compressor** *n* HYDRAUL compresor de inyección de agua *m*; ~ **inlet** *n* REFRIG entrada de agua *f*, WATER orificio de entrada de agua *m*; ~ **intake** *n* CONST, FUELLESS, HYDROL toma de agua *f*;

~ j ~ **jacket** *n* AUTO camisa de agua *f*, PROD camisa exterior de agua *f*, THERMO camisa de agua *f*, camisa de refrigeración *f*, envuelta de agua *f*, VEH camisa exterior de agua *f*; ~ **jet** *n* WATER chorro de agua *m*; ~ **jet propulsion** *n* TRANSP propulsión por chorro de agua *f*;

~ k ~ **knockout** *n* PETR TECH eliminación de agua *f*;

~ l ~ **lacquer** *n* COATINGS, COLOUR laca al agua *f*; ~ **law** *n* WATER ordenanzas nacionales sobre el agua *f pl*; ~-**leakage alarm** *n* MINE alarma de escape de agua *f*, alarma de fugas de agua *f*; ~ **level** *n* CHEM nivel de agua *m*; ~-**level indicator** *n* HYDROL, WATER indicador del nivel de agua *m*; ~ **line** *n* CONST línea de flotación *f*, orilla del agua *f*, MAR POLL flotación *f*, línea de flotación *f*, TRANSP línea de flotación *f*, WATER TRANSP *of ship* flotación *f*, línea de flotación *f*; ~ **lines** *n pl* WATER TRANSP *naval architecture* líneas de agua *f pl*; ~-**logging** *n* NUCL encharcamiento *m*; ~ **lorry** *n* CONST camión cisterna para transporte de agua *m*;

~ m ~ **main** *n* WATER cañería principal del agua *f*, tubería principal del agua *f*; ~ **meter** *n* TEXTIL, WATER contador de agua *m*;

~ o ~-**oil ratio** *n* (*WOR*) PETROL relación agua-petróleo *f*; ~ **outlet** *n* REFRIG, WATER salida de agua *f*; ~ **outlet port** *n* WATER orificio de salida de agua *m*;

~ p ~ **parting** *n* HYDROL, WATER divisoria de aguas *f*; ~ **permeability** *n* P&R permeabilidad al agua *f*; ~ **pipe** *n* PROD conducto de agua *m*, WATER cañería de agua *f*, conducto de agua *m*, tubería de agua *f*; ~ **plug** *n* WATER boca de riego *f*; ~ **pollutant** *n* POLL contaminante del agua *m*; ~ **pollution** *n* HYDROL contaminación del agua *f*, POLL *unit of measurement of absorbed dose* contaminación acuática *f*, contaminación del agua *f*, WATER contaminación del agua *f*; ~ **port** *n* PROD agujero de agua *m*, paso de agua *m*; ~ **power** *n* FUELLESS, HYDRAUL, TEXTIL energía hidráulica *f*, THERMO energía hidroeléctrica *f*, energía hidráulica *f*, WATER energía hidráulica *f*; ~ **power station** *n* ELEC ENG central de energía hidroeléctrica

f; ~ **pressure** *n* CONST, HEAT presión del agua *f*, HYDROL presión hidráulica *f*, TEXTIL presión del agua *f*, WATER presión del agua *f*, presión hidráulica *f*; ~ **propeller** *n* BrE (*cf water screw AmE*) WATER TRANSP propulsor de hélice hidráulica *m*; ~ **pump** *n* AUTO, VEH bomba de agua *f*; ~ **pump housing** *n* VEH cuerpo de la bomba de agua *m*; ~ **purification** *n* CHEM TECH purificación del agua *f*, HYDROL depuración de las aguas *f*, WATER depuración de las aguas *f*, depuración del agua *f*; ~ **purification filter** *n* CHEM TECH, WATER filtro de purificación de agua *m*; ~ **purifier** *n* TEXTIL purificador del agua *m*;

~ q ~ **quality** *n* FUELLESS, HYDROL, POLL, QUALITY, WATER calidad del agua *f*; ~ **quality monitoring** *n* WATER supervisión de la calidad del agua *f*; ~ **quenching** *n* METALL enfriamiento por agua *m*;

~ r ~ **ram** *n* COAL, CONST, HYDRAUL, WATER ariete hidráulico *m*; ~ **ratio** *n* COAL contenido en agua *m*; ~-**regulating valve** *n* REFRIG válvula automática de agua *f*, válvula reguladora del agua *f*; ~ **repellency** *n* COATINGS impermeabilidad *f*; ~ **repellent coat** *n* COATINGS revestimiento hidrófugo *m*, revestimiento impermeable *m*; ~-**repellent finish** *n* COATINGS, TEXTIL acabado hidrófugo *m*; ~-**repellent impregnation means** *n* COATINGS medios de impregnación impermeables *m pl*; ~ **reservoir** *n* MINE acuífero *m*, depósito de agua *m* (*AmL*); ~ **resource development project** *n* HYDROL proyecto para el aprovechamiento de las aguas *m*; ~ **resources study** *n* HYDROL *programming* estudio sobre el aprovechamiento de las aguas *m*; ~ **retention** *n* HYDROL hidrorretención *f*, WATER retención de agua *f*; ~ **ring** *n* MINE poceta de recogida de aguas *f*;

~ s ~ **sampler** *n* LAB muestreador de agua *m*, tomamuestras *m*; ~ **saturation** *n* PETROL saturación de agua *f*; ~ **screw** *n* AmE (*cf water propeller BrE*) WATER TRANSP propulsor de hélice hidráulica *m*; ~ **slurry** *n* NUCL suspensión acuosa *f*; ~ **softener** *n* CHEM TECH, CONST, HYDROL, P&R, PRINT ablandador de agua *m*, TEXTIL suavizante del agua *m*, WATER ablandador de agua *m*; ~ **softening** *n* CHEM TECH, CONST, HYDROL, P&R, PRINT, WATER ablandamiento del agua *m*; ~-**soluble flux** *n* CONST fundente soluble en agua *m*; ~ **spray system** *n* NUCL sistema rociador de agua *m*; ~ **stain** *n* COLOUR pigmento semitransparente *m*, tintura de colorante vegetal *f*; ~ **storage coefficient** *n* HYDROL coeficiente de almacenamiento de agua *m*; ~ **strainer** *n* RAIL purgador *m*; ~ **supplier** *n* HYDROL abastecedor de agua *m*, POLL abastecedor de agua *m*, distribuidor de agua *m*, proveedor de agua *m*, WATER abastecedor de agua *m*; ~ **supply** *n* HYDROL abastecimiento de agua *m*, suministro de agua *m*, POLL abastecimiento de agua *m*, TEXTIL suministro de agua *m*, WATER *system* abastecimiento de agua *m*; ~ **supply line** *n* WATER acueducto *m*, cañería *f*, conducto *m*, tubería *f*; ~ **supply pipe** *n* WATER cañería de abastecimiento de agua *f*, tubería de abastecimiento de agua *f*; ~ **swivel** *n* MINE cabeza de inyección *f*, cabeza giratoria *f*, cabezal de inyección *m*; ~ **system** *n* HYDROL red hidráulica *f*, WATER TRANSP *circuits* servicio de agua *m*, sistema de agua *m*;

~ t ~ **table** *n* AGRIC napa de agua *f*, nivel freático *m*, FOOD *of transformer* tabla de actividad del agua *f*, HYDROL nivel de agua subterránea *m*, nivel freático *m*, PETR TECH capa freática *f*; ~ **table fluctuation** *n*

HYDROL fluctuación de la capa freática *f*, variación de la capa freática *f*; ~ **tank** *n* RAIL depósito de agua *m*, WATER depósito de agua *m*, tanque de agua *m*, WATER TRANSP tanque de agua *m*; ~ **tanker** *n* CONST depósito de agua *m*; ~ **tap** *n* LAB *mass* llave del agua *f*; ~ **temperature gage** *AmE*, ~ **temperature gauge** *n BrE* AUTO, VEH indicador de la temperatura del agua *m*; ~ **thermostat** *n* THERMO termostato de agua *m*; ~ **tide** *n* WATER TRANSP aguas de mareas *f pl*; ~ **tower** *n* CONST torre de elevación de agua *f*, HYDROL depósito elevado de agua *m*, MINE torre de enfriamiento *f*; ~ **transport** *n* WATER TRANSP transporte acuático *m*, transporte de agua *m*; ~ **treatment** *n* CHEM TECH tratamiento del agua *m*, COAL tratamiento de aguas *m*, NUCL tratamiento del agua *m*; ~ **treatment plant** *n* CONST planta de tratamiento de aguas *f*, HYDROL planta depuradora de aguas *f*, WATER instalación de tratamiento de agua *f*; ~ **truck** *n AmE* CONST camión cisterna para transporte de agua *m*; ~ **tube** *n* AUTO, HEAT ENG tubo de agua *m*; ~ **tube boiler** *n* HEAT, HEAT ENG caldera acuotubular *f*, caldera de tubos de agua *f*; ~ **turbine** *n* FUELLESS turbina hidráulica *f*, THERMO hidroturbina *f*, turbina hidráulica *f*;

▪ **u** ~ **under pressure** *n* WATER agua a presión *f*; ~**-use efficiency** *n* HYDROL eficiencia en la utilización del agua *f*;

▪ **v** ~ **valve** *n* CONST válvula de agua *f*; ~ **valve for firefighting** *n* MECH ENG válvula del sistema contraincendios *f*; ~ **vapor barrier** *AmE see water vapour barrier BrE*; ~ **vapor condensation test** *AmE see water vapour condensation test BrE*; ~ **vapour barrier** *n BrE* PACK barrera frente al vapor de agua *f*; ~ **vapour condensation test** *n BrE* MECH ENG *refrigerated cabinets* prueba de condensación de vapor de agua *f*;

▪ **w** ~ **wheel** *n* TEXTIL noria de agua *f*
water[3] ~**-free** *phr* CHEM, FOOD, HYDROL, PETR TECH anhidro, POLL anhidro, libre de humedad, sin humedad, TEXTIL sin agua, WATER anhidro
water[4] *vt* AGRIC abrevar, regar, CHEM diluir con agua, CONST *to sprinkle, irrigate* regar, HYDROL abrevar, WATER aguar, abrevar, regar; ~**-cool** *vt* CHEM enfriar con agua
water[5] *vi* WATER tomar agua
waterage *n* WATER TRANSP *water transport* barcaje *m*
waterborne *adj* CHEM transportado por agua, HYDROL arrastrado por las aguas, *illnesses* propagado por agua contaminada
watercourse *n* CONST *drain* vaguada *f*, corriente de agua *f*, HYDROL *stream,canal* corriente de agua *f*, POLL corriente de agua *f*, curso del agua *m*, línea de agua *f*, trayectoria del agua *f*
waterfall *n* HYDROL cascada *f*, salto de agua *m*
waterfront *n* WATER TRANSP barrio de los muelles *m*
watergel: ~ **explosive** *n* MINE explosivo del acuífero *m* (*AmL*), explosivo para aguas *m* (*Esp*)
waterglass *n* CHEM vidrio soluble *m*; ~ **color** *AmE*, ~ **colour** *n BrE* COATINGS vidrio coloreado *m*
waterleaf: ~ **paper** *n* PAPER papel sin encolar *m*
waterless *adj* DETERG deshidratado
waterlogged *adj* HYDROL anegado, anegado en agua, invadido por las aguas, WATER, WATER TRANSP *of ship* anegado
waterman *n* WATER TRANSP *boatman* barquero *m*, barquillero *m*, botero *m*

watermark *n* C&G marca de agua *f*, CINEMAT filigrana *f*, PAPER filigrana *f*, marca al agua *f*; ~ **roll** *n* PAPER rodillo afiligranador *m*, rodillo desgotador *m*
waterplane *n* WATER TRANSP *naval architecture* flotación *f*, plano de flotación *m*
waterproof[1] *adj* GEN impermeable
waterproof[2]: ~ **abrasive paper** *n* MECH ENG papel de lija impermeable *m*; ~ **adhesive** *n* P&R, PACK adhesivo resistente al agua *m*; ~ **coating** *n* COATINGS revestimiento impermeable *m*; ~ **paint** *n* COATINGS pintura impermeable *f*; ~ **painting** *n* COATINGS pintado impermeable *m*, recubrimiento de pintura impermeable *m*; ~ **sealed camera** *n* PHOTO cámara sellada impermeable *f*; ~ **sheet** *n* TEXTIL sábana impermeable *f*; ~ **tissue** *n* COATINGS tejido impermeable *m*
waterproof[3] *vt* GEN impermeabilizar
waterproofing *n* COATINGS, CONST, TEXTIL impermeabilización *f*; ~ **agent** *n* COATINGS agente impermeabilizador *m*; ~ **salts** *n pl* COATINGS sales impermeabilizadoras *f pl*
watershed *n* HYDROL cuenca hidrográfica *f*, divisoria de aguas *f*, vertiente *f*, WATER cuenca de captación *f*, cuenca hidrográfica *f*, hoya tributaria *f*, vertiente *f*
waterspout *n* METEO tromba *f*, tromba marina *f*, OCEAN, WATER TRANSP *sea state* tromba marina *f*
watertight[1] *adj* COATINGS impermeable, CONST estanco, impermeable, GAS, GEOL impermeable, HEAT ENG estanco al agua, HYDROL, MECH, P&R impermeable, PACK estanco al agua, impermeable al agua, impermeable, PAPER, PETR TECH, PETROL impermeable, PHYS hermético, TEXTIL estanco al agua, impermeable, WATER impermeable, WATER TRANSP *ship* estanco
watertight[2]: ~ **caprock** *n* GAS roca de cobertura impermeable *f*; ~ **socket outlet** *n* ELEC *connection* enchufe hermético *m*, enchufe hermético al agua *m*, enchufe impermeable *m*, enchufe impermeable al agua *m*
watertightness *n* CONST estanqueidad *f*, impermeabilidad al agua *f*
waterwall *n* OCEAN muro líquido *m*, pantalla de agua *f*
waterway *n* HYDROL conducto de agua *m*, río navegable *m*, WATER canal *m*, vía de agua *f*, vía fluvial *f*, WATER TRANSP canal de trancanil *m*, río navegable *m*, vía de navegación *f*
waterworks *n* WATER instalación de abastecimiento de agua *f*
watt *n* (*W*) ELEC, ELEC ENG, METR, PHYS vatio *m* (*W*); ~**-hour** *n* ELEC *unit of work* vatihora *m*, vatio-hora *m*, ELEC ENG, PHYS vatio-hora *m*; ~**-hour meter** *n* PHYS medidor de energía *m*
wattage *n* CHEM wataje *m*, ELEC ENG vataje *m*, vatiaje *m*
wattless[1] *adj* ELEC *alternating current* desvastado, desvatiado, deswatado, reactivo
wattless[2]: ~ **component** *n* ELEC *alternating current* componente desvastada *f*, componente desvatiada *f*, componente reactiva *f*, ELEC ENG componente reactivo *m*; ~ **current** *n* ELEC, ELEC ENG corriente reactiva *f*
wattmeter *n* ELEC vatímetro *m*, PHYS potenciómetro *m*
Watt's: ~ **fission spectrum** *n* NUCL espectro de fisión de Watt *m*
wave *n* ACOUST, ELEC onda *f*, ELEC ENG onda *f*, onda de baja frecuencia *f*, PHYS, TELECOM, WATER TRANSP,

WAVE PHYS onda *f*; ~ **amplificacion** *n* ELECTRON, WAVE PHYS amplificación de onda *f*; ~ **amplification** *n* TELECOM amplificación de onda *f*; ~ **amplitude** *n* FUELLESS, OCEAN, PHYS amplitud de onda *f*; ~ **analyser** *n* BrE ACOUST, ELECTRON analizador de onda *m*; ~ **analyzer** AmE *see wave analyser BrE*; ~ **base** *n* OCEAN nivel de base de las olas *m*; ~ **coherence** *n* TELECOM coherencia de onda *f*; ~ **coupling** *n* TELECOM, WAVE PHYS acoplamiento de onda *m*; ~ **crest** *n* FUELLESS cresta de una onda *f*; ~-**cut bench** *n* OCEAN plataforma de abrasión *f*, terraza de abrasión marina *f*; ~ **damper** *n* OCEAN amortiguador de olas *m*; ~ **damping** *n* OCEAN amortiguación de olas *f*; ~ **decay** *n* OCEAN disminución de amplitud de onda *f*; ~ **delta** *n* PETROL delta de onda *f*; ~ **diffraction** *n* TELECOM difracción de onda *f*; ~ **dispersion** *n* TELECOM dispersión de la onda *f*; ~ **drag** *n* TRANSP resistencia a la formación de olas *f*; ~ **duct** *n* ELEC ENG guiaondas cilíndrico *m*; ~ **energy** *n* OCEAN energía de las olas *f*, WAVE PHYS energía de onda *f*; ~ **equation** *n* ELEC, PHYS, RAD PHYS ecuación de onda *f*; ~ **filter** *n* WAVE PHYS filtro de ondas *m*; ~ **frequency** *n* RAD PHYS frecuencia de onda *f*; ~ **function** *n* PHYS, WAVE PHYS función de onda *f*; ~-**generating area** *n* OCEAN zona de generación de olas *f*; ~-**generating test tank** *n* WATER TRANSP *or boat design* canal de pruebas con generador de olas *m*; ~ **generating towing tank** *n* WATER TRANSP *ship or boat design* canal hidrodinámico con generador de olas *m*; ~ **generation** *n* TELECOM generación de ondas *f*; ~ **generator** *n* WAVE PHYS generador de ondas *m*; ~ **group** *n* PHYS, WAVE PHYS grupo de onda *m*; ~ **height** *n* FUELLESS altura de onda *f*, OCEAN altura de la ola *f*, PHYS altura de onda *f*, WATER TRANSP *sea state* altura de la ola *f*, WAVE PHYS altura de onda *f*; ~ **interference** *n* TELECOM interferencia *f*, interferencia de ondas *f*; ~ **maker** *n* WATER TRANSP *boat design* generador de olas *m*; ~ **mechanics** *n* ELEC ENG mecánica ondulatoria *f*, PHYS mecánica de ondas *f*, WAVE PHYS mecánica de ondas *f*, mecánica ondulatoria *f*; ~ **momentum per metre of crest** *n* FUELLESS energía cinética de onda por metro de cresta *f*; ~ **motion** *n* WAVE PHYS movimiento ondular *m*; ~ **number** *n* ACOUST, CHEM *of radiation*, WAVE PHYS número de onda *m*; ~ **optics** *n* OPT óptica de la onda *f*, óptica ondulatoria *f*, TELECOM óptica de la onda *f*; ~ **packet** *n* ELEC *waves propagation*, PHYS paquete de ondas *m*; ~-**particle duality** *n* PART PHYS dualidad onda-partícula *f*, dualidad onda-corpúsculo *f*, PHYS, WAVE PHYS dualidad onda-corpúsculo *f*, dualidad onda-partícula *f*; ~ **period** *n* WATER TRANSP *ship design* período de la ola *m*; ~ **polarization** *n* TELECOM polarización de la onda *f*; ~ **power** *n* FUELLESS energía de onda *f*, WAVE PHYS potencia de la onda *f*; ~-**propagating accelerator** *n* RAD PHYS acelerador por propagación de ondas *m*; ~ **propagation** *n* FUELLESS propagación de ondas *f*, PHYS propagación de onda *f*; ~ **propagation direction** *n* OCEAN dirección de propagación de las olas *f*; ~ **recorder** *n* OCEAN registrador de olas *m*; ~-**refraction diagram** *n* OCEAN diagrama de refracción de ondas *m*, WATER TRANSP *ship design* diagrama de refracción de las olas *m*, plano de refracción de las olas *m*; ~ **resistance** *n* WATER TRANSP *ship design* resistencia por formación de olas *f*; ~ **shadowing effects** *n pl* TELECOM efectos de pantalla de la onda

m pl; ~ **spectrum** *n* OCEAN espectro de ondas *m*, WAVE PHYS espectro de onda *m*; ~ **surface** *n* ACOUST, ELEC ENG superficie de onda *f*, PHYS onda superficial *f*; ~ **theory of light** *n* WAVE PHYS teoría ondulatoria de la luz *f*; ~ **train** *n* ACOUST, PHYS, WAVE PHYS tren de ondas *m*; ~ **transmission** *n* TELECOM transmisión de la onda *f*; ~ **trough level** *n* OCEAN nivel del seno de ola *m*; ~ **vector** *n* ELEC ENG, PHYS vector de onda *m*; ~ **velocity** *n* OCEAN velocidad de las olas *f*, WAVE PHYS velocidad de onda *f*; ~ **zone** *n* RAD PHYS zona de onda *f*

waveband *n* AIR TRANSP, COMP&DP, ELEC, ELECTRON banda de frecuencias *f*, RAD PHYS banda de frecuencias *f*, gama de longitud de ondas *f*, TELECOM, TV banda de frecuencias *f*, WATER TRANSP *radio* banda de frecuencias *f*, gama de longitud de olas *f*, WAVE PHYS banda de frecuencias *f*; ~ **switching** *n* TV cambio de bandas *m*

waveform *n* GEN forma de onda *f*; ~ **errors** *n pl* WAVE PHYS errores de forma de onda *m pl*; ~ **monitor** *n* TV monitor de forma de onda *m*; ~ **synthesis** *n* ELECTRON *signal generation* síntesis de la forma de onda *f*

wavefront *n* ACOUST, ELEC ENG, OPT, PETROL, PHYS, TELECOM frente de onda *m*, WAVE PHYS frente de onda *m*, guía de onda *f*; ~ **array** *n* COMP&DP arreglo de frente de onda *m*, matriz de frente de onda *f*

waveguide *n* ELEC ENG, PHYS, TELECOM, WATER TRANSP, WAVE PHYS guiaondas *m*, guía de ondas *f*; ~ **aerial** *n* BrE (*cf waveguide antenna AmE*) TELECOM antena de guía de ondas *f*, antena de guíaondas *f*, TV antena de guía de ondas *f*; ~ **antenna** *n* AmE (*cf waveguide aerial BrE*) TELECOM antena de guía de ondas *f*, antena de guíaondas *f*, TV antena de guía de ondas *f*; ~ **component** *n* ELEC ENG componente de guía de ondas *m*, componente de guíaondas *m*; ~ **coupling** *n* ELEC ENG acoplamiento de guía de ondas *m*, acoplamiento de guíaondas *m*; ~ **dispersion** *n* OPT, TELECOM dispersión de guía de ondas *f*, dispersión de guíaondas *f*; ~ **filter** *n* ELECTRON filtro de canal de ondas *m*; ~ **fixed load** *n* ELEC ENG carga fija guía de ondas *f*, carga fija guíaondas *f*; ~ **isolator** *n* ELEC, ELEC ENG aislante de guía de ondas *m*, aislante de guíaondas *m*; ~ **load** *n* ELEC ENG carga de guía de ondas *f*, carga de guíaondas *f*; ~ **mode** *n* TELECOM modo de guía de ondas *m*, modo de guíaondas *m*; ~ **phase shifter** *n* ELEC ENG desfasador de guía de ondas *m*, desfasador de guíaondas *m*, ELECTRON desfasador de guía de ondas *m*, NUCL desfasador de guía de ondas *m*, desfasador de guíaondas *m*, TELECOM, WAVE PHYS desfasador de guía de ondas *m*; ~ **plunger** *n* ELEC ENG émbolo de guía de ondas *m*, émbolo de guíaondas *m*; ~ **section** *n* ELEC ENG sección de guía de ondas *f*, sección de guíaondas *f*; ~ **sliding load** *n* ELEC ENG carga desplazable guía de ondas *f*, carga desplazable guíaondas *f*; ~ **slotted section** *n* ELEC ENG sección ranurada de guía de ondas *f*, sección ranurada de guíaondas *f*; ~ **transformer** *n* ELEC, ELEC ENG transformador de guía de ondas *m*, transformador de guíaondas *m*; ~ **transition** *n* ELEC ENG transición de guía de ondas *f*, transición de guíaondas *f*

wavelength *n* GEN longitud de onda *f*; ~ **division multiplexing** *n* (*WDM*) TELECOM multiplexión por división de longitud de onda *f*; ~ **division switch** *n* TELECOM conmutador de división de longitud de onda *m*; ~ **fluctuation** *n* OPT fluctuación de la longitud de onda *f*; ~ **multiplexing** *n* OPT multiple-xación de longitud de onda *f*, transmisión simultánea de varias longitudes de onda *f*; ~ **switching** *n* TELE-COM conmutación de longitud de onda *f*

wavelet *n* WAVE PHYS tren de ondas *m*

wavellite *n* MINERAL wavellita *f*

wavemeter *n* PHYS medidor de longitud de onda *m*, WATER TRANSP medidor de ondas *m*, WAVE PHYS cimómetro *m*, medidor de ondas *m*, ondámetro *m*

waves: ~ **travelling at the same speed** *n pl* RAD PHYS ondas que se desplazan a la misma velocidad *f pl*

waviness *n* PAPER ondulado *m*

wavy[1] *adj* C&G ondulado

wavy[2]: ~ **cord** *n* C&G cuerda ondulada *f*

wax[1] *n* GEN cera *f*, FOOD cera aislante *f*; ~ **content** *n* REFRIG contenido de parafina *m*; ~ **investment molds** *AmE*, ~ **investment moulds** *BrE n pl* MECH ENG moldes a la cera *m pl*

wax[2] *vt* GEN encerar

waxed: ~ **board** *n* PAPER cartón parafinado *m*

waxing *n* CINEMAT encerado *m*; ~ **machine** *n* CINEMAT enceradora *f*

way *n* CHEM camino *m*, procedimiento *m*, trayectoria *f*, CONST *method* método *m*, *path* camino *m*; ~ **freight train** *n AmE* (*cf way goods train AmE*) RAIL tren local de carga *m*, tren local de mercancías *m*; ~ **goods train** *n BrE* (*cf way freight train AmE*) RAIL *vehicles* tren local de carga *m*, tren local de mercancías *m*; ~ **out** *n* CONST salida *f*, OCEAN *programming* arrancada *f*, WATER TRANSP *of ship* salida *f*, arrancada *f*, viada *f*, andar *m*; ~ **point** *n* WATER TRANSP *navigation* punto de control de derrota *m*; ~ **and works department** *n BrE* RAIL departamento de vía y obras *m*

waybill *n* WATER TRANSP carta de porte *f*, hoja de ruta *f*, recibido para embarque *m*

Wb *abbr* (*weber*) ELEC, ELEC ENG, METR, PHYS Wb (*weber, weberio*)

weak: ~ **coupling** *n* NUCL acoplamiento débil *m*; ~ **force** *n* PART PHYS fuerza débil *f*, interacción débil *f*, partículas Z *f pl*; ~ **interaction** *n* NUCL interacción débil *f*, PART PHYS fuerza débil *f*, partícula W *f*, PHYS interacción débil *f*; ~ **inversion** *n* ELECTRON inversión ineficaz *f*; ~ **nuclear force** *n* NUCL fuerza nuclear débil *f*, PART PHYS fuerza nuclear débil *f*, interacción débil *f*; ~ **positron transition** *n* NUCL transición débil del positrón *f*

weakly: ~-**guiding fiber** *AmE*, ~-**guiding fibre** *BrE n* OPT, TELECOM fibra de guía débil *f*

weaning: ~ **weight** *n* AGRIC peso al destete *m*

weanling *n* AGRIC animal recién destetado *m*

weapons: ~ **system** *n* MILIT sistema de armas *m*

wear[1]: ~-**resistant** *adj* PACK resistente al desgaste

wear[2] *n* MAR POLL desgaste *m*, MECH, MECH ENG desgaste *m*, deterioro *m*, uso *m*, PAPER desgaste *m*, TEXTIL deterioro *m*, uso *m*; ~ **bushing** *n* PETROL cojinete de desgaste *m*; ~ **limit** *n* MECH ENG límite de desgaste *m*; ~-**out defect** *n* NUCL *communications* defecto por desgaste *m*; ~-**out failure** *n* ELEC ENG avería por desgaste *f*; ~-**out failure period** *n* QUALITY período de fallas por uso y desgaste *m*; ~ **pad** *n* MECH ENG zapata protectora *f*; ~ **part** *n* MECH ENG parte de desgaste *f*, parte protectora *f*, pieza desgastable *f*, pieza sujeta a desgaste *f*; ~ **plate** *n* MECH ENG plato de desgaste *m*, *press tools* placa de desgaste *f*, placa protectora *f*; ~ **rate** *n* CONST nivel de desgaste *m*;

~ **resistance** *n* TEXTIL resistencia al uso *f*; ~-**resistant coating** *n* COATINGS revestimiento resis-tente al desgaste *m*; ~ **strip** *n* MECH ENG cinta de desgaste *f*, cinta protectora *f*, listón de defensa *m*; ~ **and tear** *n* MECH ENG desgaste natural *m*, desgaste normal *m*, desgaste por el uso *m*, deterioro por uso *m*, uso y desgaste *m*, PROD uso y desgaste *m*, TEXTIL desgaste por el uso *m*

wear[3] *vt* MECH ENG consumir, gastar, usar, TEXTIL usar; ~ **down** *vt* MECH ENG desgastar, gastar; ~ **off** *vt* MECH ENG desgastar, usar; ~ **out** *vt* MECH ENG gastar, usar, TEXTIL desgastar

wear[4] *vi* WATER TRANSP *ship round* cambiar la proa y tomar la otra vuelta, virar por redondo

wearer: ~ **trial** *n* TEXTIL ensayo al uso *m*

wearing *n* MECH ENG desgaste *m*, deterioro *m*; ~ **course** *n* CONST capa de desgaste *f*; ~ **part** *n* COAL parte sujeta a desgaste *f*, GAS pieza de desgaste *f*; ~ **part of a machine** *n* MECH ENG parte desgastada de una máquina *f*, pieza desgastada de una máquina *f*; ~ **plate** *n* MECH ENG placa de desgaste *f*, plancha de desgaste *f*, plato de desgaste *m*; ~ **surface** *n* MECH ENG capa de desgaste *f*, superficie de desgaste *f*, superficie de rodamiento *f*, TEXTIL superficie desgas-tada *f*

weather[1]: ~-**beaten** *adj* WATER TRANSP *ship, person* castigado por el tiempo, estropeado por el tiempo; ~-**bound** *adj* WATER TRANSP *of ship* detenido por el mal tiempo

weather[2]: ~ **balloon** *n* METEO globo sonda *m*; ~ **bureau** *n* METEO instituto meteorológico *m*, oficina meteorológica *f*, servicio meteorológico *m*; ~ **chart** *n* METEO carta del tiempo *f*, carta sinóptica *f*, mapa del tiempo *m*, mapa sinóptico *m*; ~ **forecast** *n* HYDROL previsión del tiempo *f*, SPACE predicción meteorológica *f*, pronóstico del tiempo *m*, WATER, WATER TRANSP previsión del tiempo *f*; ~ **helm** *n* WATER TRANSP *boat* tendencia a orzar *f*; ~ **map** *n* WATER TRANSP carta meteorológica *f*; ~ **pattern** *n* SPACE diagrama meteorológico *m*, pauta meteoroló-gica *f*; ~ **report** *n* AIR TRANSP información meteorológica *f*, informe del tiempo *m*, informe meteorológico *m*, METEO boletín meteorológico *m*, información meteorológica *f*, informe del tiempo *m*, informe meteorológico *m*, POLL información meteoro-lógica *f*, SPACE información meteorológica *f*, informe del tiempo *m*, informe meteorológico *m*, WATER TRANSP parte meteorológico *m*, informe del tiempo *m*, informe meteorológico *m*; ~ **routing** *n* WATER TRANSP derrota meteorológica *f*, derrota óptima *f*; ~ **ship** *n* METEO buque meteorológico *m*, estación meteorológica oceánica *f*, WATER TRANSP buque meteorológico *m*; ~ **side** *n* WATER TRANSP *of ship* costado de barlovento *m*; ~ **station** *n* METEO, SPACE, WATER TRANSP estación meteorológica *f*; ~ **station cabinet** *n* WATER TRANSP estación meteo-rológica de buque *f*; ~ **system** *n* METEO sistema meteorológico *m*; ~ **warning** *n* AIR TRANSP adver-tencia meteorológica *f*, METEO, WATER TRANSP advertencia meteorológica *f*, aviso de mal tiempo *m*; ~ **watch** *n* SPACE observación del tiempo *f*, observación meteorológica *f*; ~ **window** *n* PETR TECH período de tiempo calmado entre períodos tormentosos *m*, ventana del tiempo *f*

weather[3] *vt* CONST desgastarse a la intemperie, secar al aire, GEOL alterar

weather[4] *vi* CONST secarse al aire; **~ a squall** *vi* WATER TRANSP *sailing* aguantar un chubasco; **~ a storm** *vi* WATER TRANSP *sailing* correr un temporal

weathered[1] *adj* AGRIC desgastado por las inclemencias

weathered[2]: **~ oil** *n* MAR POLL hidrocarburos alterados por exposición a la intemperie *m pl*, hidrocarburos intemperizados *m pl*

weathering *n* AGRIC meteorización *f*, COAL alteración atmosférica *f*, alteración meteórica *f*, meteorización *f*, oreo *m*, temperismo *m*, vierteaguas *m*, bocazo *m*, erosión eólica *f*, erupción *f*, estallido *m*, COATINGS alteración por acción de los agentes atmosféricos *f*, CONST deterioro por acción de la intemperie *m*, *of window* vierteaguas *m*, GEOL meteorización *f*, alteración de rocas *f*, MAR POLL intemperización *f*, exposición a la intemperie *f*, P&R alteración por acción de los agentes atmosféricos *f*, alteración a la intemperie *f*, PETROL meteorización *f*, erosión *f*, denudación *f*, TEXTIL intemperie *f*; **~ resistance** *n* CONST resistencia a la intemperie *f*

weatherproof[1] *adj* PAPER, SAFE a prueba de intemperie

weatherproof[2]: **~ clothing** *n* SAFE prendas impermeables *f pl*; **~ paint** *n* COLOUR pintura resistente a la intemperie *f*

weave[1] *n* TEXTIL ligamento *m*

weave[2] *vt* CONST *carpentry* entrelazar, TEXTIL tejer

weaver *n* OCEAN araña *f*

weaver's: **~ beam** *n* TEXTIL plegador de tejedor *m*

weaving *n* TEXTIL tejedura *f*, TRANSP rumbo en zigzag *m*, rumbo sinuoso *m*; **~ factor** *n* AIR TRANSP factor de rumbo sinuoso *m*, TRANSP factor de entrecruzamiento entre vehículos *m*, factor de rumbo sinuoso *m*; **~ maneuver** *AmE*, **~ manoeuvre** *BrE n* TRANSP maniobra en rumbo sinuoso *f*, maniobra en zig-zag *f*

web *n* AIR TRANSP *of spar* nervadura *f*, CONST *of girder, T iron* alma *f*, *of key* paletón *m*, MECH alma *f*, MECH ENG *of crank* brazo *m*, PAPER, PRINT banda *f*, VEH brazo *m*; **~ break** *n* PRINT rotura de la banda *f*; **~ break detector** *n* PRINT detector de rotura de la banda *m*; **~-fed offset rotary press** *n* PRINT rotativa offset de bobina *f*; **~ frame** *n* OCEAN, WATER TRANSP *shipbuilding* bulárcama *f*; **~ guide** *n* PRINT guía de la banda *f*; **~ lead** *n* PRINT extremo inicial de la banda *m*; **~ offset press** *n* PRINT máquina offset de bobina *f*; **~ page** *n* COMP&DP página web *f*; **~ path** *n* PRINT ruta de la banda *f*; **~ press** *n* PRINT rotativa de bobina *f*; **~ turning device** *n* PRINT dispositivo para girar la bobina *m*; **~ width** *n* PRINT anchura de la máquina *f*

Web: **the ~** *n* COMP&DP el Web *m*, la telaraña *f*

webbing *n* MAR POLL cincha *f*, OCEAN cincha *f*, mallas *f pl*, TEXTIL cincho *m*, cinta gruesa *f*

weber *n* (*Wb*) ELEC *unit of magnetic flux* weber *m* (*Wb*), weberio *m* (*Wb*), ELEC ENG, METR, PHYS weberio *m* (*Wb*), weber *m* (*Wb*)

Weber-Fechner: **~ law** *n* ACOUST ley de Weber-Fechner *f*

websterite *n* MINERAL aluminita *f*

wedge[1] *n* CINEMAT, CONST cuña *f*, MECH, MECH ENG calzo *m*, cuña *f*, MINE *quarrying*, PRINT cuña *f*; **~ brake** *n* MECH, MECH ENG *braking systems* freno de cuña *m*; **~ crack** *n* METALL fisuración en cuña *f*; **~ cut** *n* MINE excavación en cuña *f*; **~ densitometer** *n* PHOTO densímetro de cuña *m*; **~ disclination** *n* METALL disclinación en cuña *f*; **~ print** *n* CINEMAT copia de cuña *f*; **~-type combustion chamber** *n*

AUTO cámara de combustión tipo cuña *f*; **~-type fracture** *n* METALL fractura en forma de cuña *f*

wedge[2] *vt* MECH acuñar, calzar, MECH ENG acuñar

wedge[3]: **~ out** *vi* GEOL encajarse, encuñarse

wedged[1] *adj* MECH, MECH ENG acuñado

wedged[2]: **~ mortise-and-tenon joint** *n* CONST junta de mortaja de espiga con cuña *f*

wedging *n* MECH acuñado *m*, acuñadura *f*, MECH ENG acuñado *m*, acuñadura *f*, acuñamiento *m*, calce *m*, enchavetado *m*

weed: **~-killing train** *n* RAIL tren para rociar herbicidas sobre la vía *m*

weeder *n* AGRIC escardador *m*; **~-mulcher** *n* AGRIC desyerbador-acolchador *m*

weeding: **~ hoe** *n* AGRIC escardillo *m*

week: **~ utilization** *n* PROD utilización por semana *f*

weephole *n* CONST mechinal *m*

weft *n* PAPER trama *f*, SPACE banderín de señales *m*, fluctuación *f*, ráfaga de aire *f*, TEXTIL hilos para trama *m pl*, trama *f*; **~ break** *n* TEXTIL rotura de la trama *f*; **~ density** *n* TEXTIL densidad de la trama *f*; **~-knitted fabric** *n* TEXTIL tejido de punto por trama *m*; **~ stop motion** *n* TEXTIL paratramas *m*; **~ yarn** *n* PAPER hilo de trama *m*

Wehnelt: **~ cylinder** *n* INSTR, PHYS cilindro de Wehnelt *m*

weigh[1]: **~ bridge** *n* CONST puente báscula *m*

weigh[2] *vt* WATER TRANSP *anchor* levar; **~ down** *vt* CONST *a floor by overloading* sobrecargar

weighing: **~ boat** *n* LAB navecilla tarada *f* (*AmL*), pesasubstancias *m* (*Esp*); **~ bottle** *n* CHEM, LAB pesafiltro *m*; **~ dish** *n* LAB platillo tarado *m*; **~ machine** *n* PROD balanza *f*, báscula *f*, pesadora *f*; **~ and punnet filling** *n* *BrE* PACK llenado, apisonado y pesado *m*; **~ scale** *n* METR báscula de pesar *f*

weight *n* METR, PHYS peso *m*; **~ belt** *n* OCEAN cinturón de lastre *m*; **~ of face** *n* PRINT negrura del estilo *f*; **~ feeding** *n* PROD alimentación por peso *f*; **~ filling machine** *n* PACK máquina llenadora por peso *f*; **~ fraction** *n* NUCL fracción en peso *f*; **~ on bit** *n* (*WOB*) PETR TECH peso sobre el trépano *m* (*Esp*), peso sobre la barrena *m*, peso sobre la mecha *m* (*AmL*) (*PSM*), peso sobre la broca *m*; **~ optimization** *n* SPACE optimización del peso *f*, rendimiento máximo del peso *m*; **~ penetration test** *n* COAL prueba de penetración ponderal *f*; **~ strength** *n* (*WS*) MINE riqueza en peso *f*; **~ of type** *n* PRINT negrura del tipo *f*; **~ unit** *n* METR unidad de peso *f*

weighted: **~ average** *n* PROD media ponderada *f*, promedio ponderado *m*; **~ noise-level indicator** *n* ACOUST, POLL indicador del nivel de ruido medio *m*, indicador del nivel de ruido ponderado *m*

weighting *n* ACOUST, COMP&DP ponderación *f*; **~ curve** *n* ACOUST curva de ponderación *f*; **~ factor** *n* SPACE *communications* factor de pesada *m*, factor de ponderación *m*; **~ material** *n* PETROL material densificante *m*; **~ network** *n* ACOUST red de ponderación *f*

weightlessness *n* PHYS ingravidez *f*, SPACE estado sin pesadez *m*, ingravidez *f*

weights *n pl* METR pesas *f pl*; **~ and measures** *n pl* METR pesos y medidas *m pl*

weir *n* C&G vertedero *m* (*Esp*), vertedor *m* (*AmL*), CONST aliviadero *m*, FUELLESS presa sumergible *f*, HYDRAUL aliviadero *m*, rebosadero *m*, vertedero de aforo *m*, HYDROL aliviadero *m*, esclusa *f*, WATER *dam* presa *f*, vertedero *m*, *waste-weir* vertedero de crecidas *m*, aliviadero *m*, descargadero de crecidas *m*; ~ **bed** *n* OCEAN parque de cultivo *m*; ~ **boom** *n* MAR POLL barrera flotante con aliviadero *f*; ~ **skimmer** *n* MAR POLL rasera con aliviadero *f*, rasera de compuerta *f*, POLL desescoriador de vertedero *m*, desnatador de vertedero *m*, espumador de vertedero *m*; ~ **with vortex skimmer** *n* MAR POLL aliviadero con rasera vortical *m*

Weiss: ~ **domains** *n pl* PHYS dominios de Weiss *m pl*

Weissenberg: ~ **camera** *n* CRYSTALL cámara de Weissenberg *f*

weld^1 *n* METALL, NUCL, PROD, THERMO soldadura *f*; ~ **metal** *n* METALL metal de soldadura *m*; ~ **region** *n* NUCL zona de la soldadura *f*; ~ **strength check** *n* PROD verificación de la resistencia de la soldadura *f*

weld^2 *vt* MECH, PROD, THERMO soldar

weldability *n* MECH, MECH ENG, METALL soldabilidad *f*

welded^1 *adj* MECH, MECH ENG, METALL soldado

welded^2: ~ **body seam** *n* PACK junta de soldadura *f*; ~ **collar** *n* MECH ENG *pipe fitting* collar soldado *m*; ~ **fitting** *n* MECH ENG accesorio soldado *m*, pieza soldada *f*; ~ **tuff** *n* GEOL toba volcánica soldada *f*

welded^1: **as** ~ *adj* PROD tosco de soldadura *m*

welder *n* MECH soldador *m*, soldadora *f*, MECH ENG, METALL, SAFE soldador *m*; ~'**s goggles** *n pl* INSTR, SAFE anteojos de soldador *m pl* (*AmL*), gafas de soldador *f pl* (*Esp*); ~'**s hand shield** *n* SAFE careta de soldador de mano *f*; ~'**s hood** *n* SAFE careta de soldador *f*, casco de soldador *m*; ~'**s protective clothing** *n* SAFE prendas protectoras para soldador *f pl*; ~'**s protective curtain** *n* SAFE cortina protectora para soldador *f*; ~'**s safety helmet** *n* SAFE casco de seguridad para soldador *m*; ~'**s shield** *n* SAFE máscara protectora para soldador *f*

welding *n* C&G soldadura *f*, MECH ENG soldadura *f*, soldeo *m*, P&R, PROD, SAFE soldadura *f*, THERMO soldadura *f*, soldeo *m*; ~ **blowpipe** *n* CONST soplete de soldadura *m*; ~ **circuit** *n* CONST circuito de soldadura *m*; ~ **cycle** *n* CONST ciclo de soldadura *m*; ~ **goggles** *n pl* INSTR, SAFE anteojos para soldadores *m pl* (*AmL*), gafas para soldadores *f pl* (*Esp*); ~ **handshield** *n* CONST protector de manos para soldar *m*; ~ **hazard** *n* SAFE peligro originado por soldadura *m*, riesgo originado por soldadura *m*; ~ **helmet** *n* CONST casco protector para soldadura *m*, casquete de soldador *m*, SAFE careta de soldador *f*; ~ **machine** *n* PROD soldadora *f*; ~ **procedure** *n* CONST procedimiento de soldadura *m*; ~ **process** *n* CONST proceso de soldadura *m*; ~ **program** *AmE*, ~ **programme** *BrE n* CONST programa de soldadura *m*; ~ **protection** *n* SAFE protección de la soldadura *f*, protección en el trabajo de soldadura *f*; ~ **sequence** *n* CONST secuencia de soldadura *f*; ~ **smoke extraction system** *n* SAFE sistema de extracción de humos de soldadura *m*; ~ **station** *n* PETROL estación de soldado *f*; ~ **table with vacuum apparatus** *n* SAFE mesa de soldadura con aparatos de vacío *f*; ~ **torch** *n* THERMO soplete de soldeo *m*; ~ **transformer** *n* ELEC, ELEC ENG transformador de soldar *m*; ~ **visor** *n pl BrE* SAFE *protection* anteojos para soldar *m pl* (*AmL*), gafas para soldar *f pl*; ~ **vizor** *AmE see welding visor BrE*; ~ **wire** *n* CONST alambre para soldadura *m*

weldless *adj* PROD sin soldadura

weldment *n* MECH conjunto de piezas soldadas *m*, pieza formada por elementos soldados *f*

well *n* CONST *vertical opening contained within winding staircase*, HYDROL, PETR TECH, PETROL pozo *m*; ~ **bore** *n* PETR TECH agujero *m*, balsa *f*, hueco *m*; ~ **car** *n AmE* (*cf well wagon BrE*) RAIL vagón góndola *m*; ~ **casing** *n* COAL entubado del pozo *m*, recubrimiento del pozo *m*, FUELLESS *geothermal* tubería de revestimiento *f*; ~ **drill hole** *n* COAL, MINE agujero sondeador de pozos *m*; ~ **log** *n* GEOPHYS registro en pozo de perforación *m*, sondeo *m*; ~ **logging** *n* FUELLESS registro de perforación *m*, GEOL perfilado del sondeo *m*, GEOPHYS registro de sondeos *m*, PETR TECH diagrafía del pozo *f*, perfilaje del pozo *m*, registro del pozo *m*; ~**-moderated core** *n* NUCL *communications* núcleo bien moderado *m*; ~**-plugging block** *n* GAS bloque de taponamiento de pozo *m*; ~ **potential** *n* PETROL potencial del pozo *m*; ~ **sinking** *n* FUELLESS perforación de pozo *f*; ~**-sorted grains** *n pl* GEOL granos bien clasificados *m pl*, granos bien seleccionados *m pl*; ~ **wagon** *n BrE* (*cf well car AmE*) RAIL vagón góndola *m*; ~ **water** *n* AGRIC, COAL agua de pozo *f*, agua del subsuelo *f*, HYDROL agua de pozo *f*, agua freática *f*, agua del subsuelo *f*, WATER agua de pozo *f*, agua del subsuelo *f*, agua freática *f*, agua subterránea *f*, capa acuífera subterránea *f*

wellhead *n* FUELLESS boca de pozo *f*, GAS boca de pozo *f*, cabeza de pozo *f*, cabezal de pozo *m*, PETR TECH cabeza de pozo *f*, PETROL cabeza de pozo *f*, cabezal de pozo *m*; ~ **equipment** *n* PETROL equipo de cabezal de pozo *m*; ~ **pressure** *n* FUELLESS presión en boca de pozo *f*, PETROL presión en el cabezal del pozo *f*; ~ **temperature** *n* FUELLESS temperatura en boca de pozo *f*; ~ **valve** *n* FUELLESS válvula de boca de pozo *f*

welt *n* PROD cubrejunta *f*, refuerzo *m*

welted: ~ **joint** *n* PROD empalme con cubrejuntas *m*, junta engatillada *f*

wernerite *n* MINERAL wernerita *f*

west *adj* WATER TRANSP oeste, poniente

Westcott: ~ **model** *n* NUCL *communications* modelo de Westcott *m*

westerlies *n pl* METEO vientos del oeste *m pl*, zona de vientos del oeste *f*, OCEAN oestes *m pl*

Weston: ~ **standard cell** *n* ELEC pila patrón Weston *f*, ELEC ENG elemento estándar Weston *m*

westward *adj* WATER TRANSP que da al oeste, que mira al oeste

wet^1 *adj* THERMO mojado

wet^2: ~ **acidic fallout** *n* POLL polvo radiactivo ácido y húmedo *m*, precipitación acídica húmeda *f*, precipitación radiactiva ácida y húmeda *f*; ~**-air filter** *n* HEAT ENG filtro de aire húmedo *m*; ~**-aluminium capacitor** *n BrE* ELEC ENG condensador de aluminio húmedo *m*; ~**-aluminum capacitor** *AmE see wet-aluminium capacitor BrE*; ~ **ashing** *n* NUCL descomposición en ácido *f*; ~ **assay** *n* CHEM análisis por vía húmeda *m*, ensayo por vía húmeda *m*; ~ **board machine** *n* PAPER máquina de cartón húmedo *f*; ~ **break** *n* PAPER rotura en húmedo *f*; ~ **breaking length** *n* PAPER longitud de rotura en húmedo *f*; ~ **broke** *n* PAPER rotos húmedos *m pl*; ~**-bulb temperature** *n* HEAT ENG temperatura de bulbo húmedo *f*; ~**-bulb thermometer** *n* HEAT ENG, REFRIG, THERMO termómetro de bulbo húmedo *m*; ~ **cell** *n* ELEC ENG pila hidroeléctrica *f*; ~ **chamber** *n* OCEAN cámara húmeda *f*; ~**-collodion process** *n* PHOTO proceso con colodión húmedo *m*, PRINT procedimiento al colodión húmedo *m*; **~ compression** *n* REFRIG compresión húmeda *f*, funcionamiento en régimen húmedo *m*; **~ creping** *n* PAPER crespado en húmedo *m*; **~ cylinder liner** *n* AUTO camisa de cilindro húmedo *f*, camisa del cilindro húmeda *f*; **~ deposition** *n* POLL precipitación húmeda *f*, sedimentación húmeda *f*, deposición húmeda *f*; **~ desulfurization process** *AmE*, **~ desulphurization process** *n BrE* POLL proceso de desulfuración por vía húmeda *m*; **~ dock** *n* WATER TRANSP dique de marea *m*, dique flotante *m*; **~ and dry polishing** *n* C&G pulido mojado y seco *m*; **~-dry processing treatment** *n* TEXTIL tratamiento por el procedimiento húmedo-seco *m*; **~ dust removal installation** *n* SAFE instalación para remoción de polvos en húmedo *f*; **~ end** *n* CINEMAT extremo húmedo *m*, PAPER parte húmeda *f*; **~ felt** *n* PAPER fieltro húmedo *m*; **~ fog** *n* METEO niebla precipitante *f*, niebla que moja *f*; **~ gas** *n* GAS, PETROL, PHYS gas húmedo *m*; **~ gate** *n* CINEMAT ventanilla húmeda *f*; **~ gate printer** *n* CINEMAT positivadora de ventanilla húmeda *f*; **~ glue label** *n* PACK etiqueta que se pega húmeda *f*; **~ grinding** *n* COAL molienda en húmedo *f*; **~ hole** *n* MINE barreno húmedo *m*; **~ milling** *n* AGRIC molienda húmeda *f*; **~ natural gas** *n* PETR TECH gas natural húmedo *m*; **~ paint** *n* CONST pintura fresca *f*; **~ period** *n* POLL período húmedo *m*, época húmeda *f*; **~-plate process** *n* PRINT proceso de plancha humedecida *m*; **~ polishing** *n* C&G pulido húmedo *m*, PROD pulido en húmedo *m*; **~ precipitation** *n* POLL precipitación húmeda *f*, precipitación por vía húmeda *f*; **~ press** *n* PAPER prensa húmeda *f*; **~-press roll** *n* PAPER rodillo de prensa húmeda *m*; **~ pulp** *n* PAPER pulpa húmeda *f*; **~ radome** *n* TELECOM radomo húmedo *m*; **~ reaction** *n* CHEM reacción por vía húmeda *f*; **~ rot** *n* CONST *timber* caries húmeda *f*, pudrición *f*; **~ rub resistance** *n* PAPER resistencia al frotamiento en húmedo *f*; **~ screening** *n* COAL tamizado húmedo *m*; **~ scrubber** *n* POLL lavador de gases por vía húmeda *m*; **~-slug tantalum capacitor** *n* ELEC ENG condensador de tantalio por espira húmeda *m*; **~ standpipe** *n* CONST depósito regulador de humedad *m*; **~ steam** *n* FUELLESS vapor húmedo *m*; **~ stock** *n* PAPER pasta grasa *f*; **~ storage** *n* NUCL almacenamiento en húmedo *m*; **~ strength** *n* P&R resistencia en estado húmedo *f*, PAPER resistencia a la tracción en húmedo *f*; **~-strength paper** *n* PAPER papel resistente a la tracción en húmedo *m*; **~-strength resins** *n pl* PAPER resinas que imparten resistencia en húmedo *f pl*; **~-strength retention** *n* PAPER relación entre la resistencia en húmedo y en seco *f*; **~ track** *n* PRINT pista húmeda *f*; **~ treatment** *n* COAL, MECH ENG tratamiento húmedo *m*; **~ tree** *n* PETR TECH árbol húmedo *m*; **~-type cooler** *n* REFRIG enfriador húmedo de aire *m*

wet[3]: **~ on wet** *phr* P&R húmedo sobre húmedo

wet[4] *vt* CHEM humectar, FOOD humedecer, MAR POLL, MECH ENG humectar, PHYS humedecer, REFRIG humidificar, THERMO humectar, humedecer, humidificar, mojar

wether *n* AGRIC carnero castrado *m*

wetsuit *n* OCEAN traje abierto *m*, PETROL revestimiento húmedo *m*, WATER TRANSP ropa aceitada *f*, traje de buzo *m*, traje estanco *m*

wettability *n* P&R, PETROL humectabilidad *f*

wetted: **~-pad evaporative cooler** *n* REFRIG enfriador

de aire con relleno húmedo *m*; **~ surface** *n* WATER TRANSP *ship design* superficie mojada *f*

wetting[1] *adj* CHEM, MAR POLL, MECH ENG humectante

wetting[2] *n* MECH ENG *iron welding* desparramado de bronce fundido sobre las superficies *m*, humectación *f*, humectante *m*, humedecimiento *m*, humidificación *f*, mojadura *f*; **~ agent** *n* C&G, CHEM, CINEMAT, FOOD agente humectante *m*, MAR POLL agente humectante *m*, humectante *m*, P&R, PHOTO, PHYS, PRINT, TEXTIL agente humectante *m*; **~ of dry material** *n* TEXTIL mojado del material seco *m*

whale: **~ boat** *n* OCEAN ballenera *f*, ballenero *m*; **~ factory ship** *n* OCEAN ballenero factoría *m*

whaling: **~ ship** *n* OCEAN barco ballenero *m*

wharf *n* WATER TRANSP desembarcadero *m*, muelle con tinglados *m*, muelle de atraque con tinglados *m*

what: **~ you see is what you get** *phr* (*WYSIWYG*) COMP&DP lo que se ve es lo que se obtiene (*WYSIWYG*)

wheat: **~ bran** *n* AGRIC afrecho de trigo *m*; **~ brown shorts** *n* AGRIC subproducto de molienda de trigo *m*; **~ white shorts** *n* AGRIC subproducto de molienda del trigo *m*

wheatmeal *n* FOOD harina de trigo sin refinar *f*, harina entera *f*

Wheatstone: **~ bridge** *n* ELEC *instrument*, ELEC ENG, PHYS puente Wheatstone *m*

wheel *n* MECH ENG *hand-wheel* volante *m*, manivela *f*, muela abrasiva *f*, *pulley* polea *f*, muela de rectificar *f*, *small metal roller or runner* ruedecilla *f*, muela *f*, rueda *f*, PROD *of fan* rodete *m*, TRANSP, VEH rueda *f*, WATER TRANSP *boat building* rueda de gobierno *f*, rueda del timón *f*; **~ alignment** *n* AUTO, TRANSP, VEH alineación de ruedas *f*; **~-and-axle drive** *n* TRANSP tracción a ruedas y ejes *f*; **~ bearing** *n* VEH cojinete de rueda *m*, rodamiento de rueda *m*; **~ carriage** *n* MECH ENG *grinding-machine* carro portamuelas *m*; **~ clamp** *n* AUTO bloqueador de ruedas *m*, inmovilizador de ruedas *m*, VEH inmovilizador de ruedas *m*; **~ clearance** *n* RAIL holgura de rueda *f*; **~ cover** *n* VEH cubierta de rueda *f*; **~ crank** *n* MECH ENG manivela de plato *f*; **~ cylinder** *n* AUTO cilindro de la rueda *m*; **~ dresser** *n* MECH ENG *emery-wheel* reavivador de muelas abrasivas *m*, rectificador de muelas abrasivas *m*; **~-feed increment range** *n* MECH ENG proporción del incremento del avance de las ruedas *f*; **~ flange** *n* AUTO, RAIL, VEH pestaña de la rueda *f*; **~ flange lubricant** *n* RAIL lubricante de la pestaña de la rueda *m*; **~ flange roller** *n* MECH ENG rodillo de pestaña de la rueda *m*; **~ guard** *n* MECH ENG caja de ruedas *f*, cubremuelas *m*, cárter de engranajes *m*, SAFE *vehicles* cubremuelas *m*, protegemuelas *m*, PROD cabezal portamuelas *m*; **~ house** *n* WATER TRANSP *ships* caseta de gobierno *f*, puente de gobierno *m*; **~ load** *n* CONST carga por rueda *f*; **~ nut cross brace** *n* MECH ENG llave cruzada de tuercas de rueda *f*; **~ ore** *n* MINERAL bournonita *f*; **~ pit** *n* HYDRAUL cámara de turbina *f*; **~ rim** *n* VEH llanta de rueda *f*; **~ slide** *n* PROD carro portamuela *m*; **~ slide mark** *n* RAIL marca de patinaje de la rueda *f*; **~ slip** *n* AUTO patinaje estacionario de la rueda *m*; **~ slip mark on rails** *n* RAIL marca de patinaje de la rueda en el carril *f*; **~ spindle** *n* MECH ENG *grinding-machine* eje portamuelas *m*, muñón de la rueda *m*; **~ spindle speed** *n* MECH ENG velocidad del husillo *f*; **~-suspension lever** *n* AUTO palanca de suspensión de la rueda *f*; ~ **swarf** *n* PROD *grit from grindstone* fango de muela *m*, polvo de amolado *m*; ~ **tooth** *n* MECH ENG dientes de engranaje *m pl*; ~ **train** *n* MECH ENG tren de ruedas *m*; ~ **web** *n* RAIL centro de rueda *m*, plato de rueda *m*; ~ **well** *n* AIR TRANSP *landing gear* alojamiento de las ruedas *m*; ~ **which engages a worm** *n* MECH ENG rueda de conexión con tornillo sin fin *f*

wheelbarrow *n* CONST, TRANSP carretilla *f*

wheelbase *n* AIR TRANSP base de ruedas *f*, batalla *f*, VEH batalla *f*, distancia entre ejes *f*

wheeled: ~ **carriage** *n* MILIT *of gun* carro sobre ruedas *m*

wheelnut *n* BrE (*cf lug nut AmE*) AUTO tuerca de la rueda *f*, tuerca de orejetas *f*, tuerca de palomilla *f*, VEH tuerca de fijación de la rueda *f*

wheels: ~**-up landing** *n* AIR TRANSP aterrizaje con el tren replegado *m*

whetstone *n* PROD piedra de afilar *f*, piedra de amolar *f*

whetting *n* MECH ENG, PROD amolado *m*

whewellite *n* MINERAL whewelita *f*

whey *n* FOOD suero *m*; ~ **concentrate** *n* FOOD suero concentrado *m*; ~ **powder** *n* FOOD suero en polvo *m*

whip: ~ **aerial** *n* BrE (*cf whip antenna AmE*) SPACE antena de látigo *f*, TV antena de látigo *f*, antena vertical flexible *f*, WATER TRANSP antena de látigo *f*; ~ **antenna** *n* AmE (*cf whip aerial BrE*) SPACE antena de látigo *f*, TV antena de látigo *f*, antena vertical flexible *f*, WATER TRANSP *radio* antena de látigo *f*; ~ **pan** *n* CINEMAT panorámica rápida *f*

whiplash: ~ **effect** *n* TRANSP efecto sacudida *m*

whipping *n* WATER TRANSP *ropes* falaceado *m*

whipstock *n* PETR TECH bisel desviador *m*, cuña de desviación *f*, cuña desviadora *f*, whipstock *m*

whirling: ~ **of shafts** *n* MECH ENG vibración lateral *f*, vibración torsional *f*

whirlpool *n* HYDROL remolino *m*

whirlwind *n* METEO, WATER TRANSP remolino de viento *m*

whisker *n* CRYSTALL cristal filiforme *m*, ELECTRON *point-contact diodes* filamento fino *m*, METALL fibra cerámica refractaria formada por monocristales *f*, pelo de óxido metálico *m*, triquita *f*

whistle *n* ELECTRON silbato *m*; ~ **buoy** *n* WATER TRANSP *navigation marks, sound signal* boya de silbato *f*

whistler *n* SPACE *communications* atmosférico silbante *m*, perturbación silbante *f*

white[1]: ~**-hot** *adj* CHEM calentado al blanco, THERMO al rojo blanco, calentado al blanco, incandescente

white[2]: ~ **balance** *n* TV balance de blanco *m*; ~ **caps** *n* OCEAN cabrillas *f pl*; ~ **clip** *n* TV recorte de blanco *m*; ~ **compression** *n* TV compresión de blanco *f*; ~ **frost** *n* METEO escarcha *f*; ~ **heat** *n* THERMO calor blanco *m*; ~ **horses** *n* OCEAN cabrillas *f pl*; ~ **ice** *n* REFRIG hielo opaco *m*; ~ **iron pyrite** *n* MINERAL marcasita *f*, pirita blanca *f*; ~ **lead** *n* CHEM *basic lead acetate* azúcar de plomo *m*; ~ **leader** *n* CINEMAT guía blanca *f*; ~ **level** *n* TV nivel de blanco *m*; ~**-level frequency** *n* TV frecuencia de nivel de blanco *f*; ~ **light** *n* PHYS luz blanca *f*; ~**-light fringe** *n* PHYS franja de luz blanca *f*; ~ **limiter** *n* TV limitador de blanco *m*; ~ **lined board** *n* PACK cartón con la capa superior blanca *m*; ~ **metal packing** *n* RAIL revestimiento de metal antifricción *m*; ~ **mica** *n* P&R mica blanca *f*, mica moscovita *f*; ~ **noise** *n* ACOUST, COMP&DP ruido blanco *m*, ELECTRON ruido blanco *m*, ruido de secuencias de igual

amplitud *m*, PHYS ruido blanco *m*, SPACE ruido blanco *m*, ruido con espectro continuo y uniforme *m*, ruido de los motores a reacción *m*, ruido mezcla de múltiples frecuencias *m*, TELECOM ruido blanco *m*; ~ **noise generator** *n* ELECTRON generador de ruido blanco *m*; ~ **noise signal** *n* ELECTRON señal de ruido blanco *f*; ~ **noise source** *n* ELECTRON fuente de ruido blanco *f*; ~**-out** *n* METEO paisaje blanco *m*, resplandor blanco *m*; ~ **peak** *n* TV cresta de blancos *f*; ~ **photocopy** *n* PRINT fotocopia en negativo *f*; ~ **pigment** *n* COLOUR pigmento blanco *m*; ~ **pigmented powder** *n* COLOUR polvo pigmentado blanco *m*; ~ **product** *n* MAR POLL blancos *m pl*, hidrocarburos blancos *m pl*; ~ **radiation** *n* RAD PHYS, SPACE radiación blanca *f*; ~ **reference** *n* TV referencia de blanco *f*; ~ **room** *n* SPACE sala blanca *f*, sala esterilizada *f*; ~ **saturation** *n* TV saturación de blanco *f*; ~ **size** *n* COLOUR cola blanca *f*; ~ **squall** *n* OCEAN chubasco blanco *m*, chubasco seco *m*; ~ **vinegar** *n* FOOD vinagre blanco *m*; ~ **waters** *n pl* PAPER aguas blancas *f pl*

whiteness: ~ **degree** *n* PAPER índice de reflectancia en el azul *m*

whitewash[1] *n* CHEM blanqueado *m*, COATINGS lechada *f*, COLOUR encalado *m*, enjalbegado *m*, pintura a la cal *f*, CONST blanqueado *m*, pintura a la cal *f*; ~ **brush** *n* COLOUR brocha para encalar *f*, brocha para pintura a la cal *f*

whitewash[2] *vt* COLOUR blanquear

whitewashing *n* COATINGS, CONST blanqueado *m*

whiting *n* CHEM blanco de España *m*, blanco de yeso *m*

whitneyite *n* MINERAL whitneyita *f*

Whitworth: ~ **screw thread** *n* MECH ENG hilo Whitworth *m*, rosca Whitworth *f*; ~ **thread** *n* MECH ENG hilo Whitworth *m*, rosca Whitworth *f*

whole: ~ **food** *n* FOOD comida natural completa *f*; ~ **piece** *n* TEXTIL pieza entera *f*; ~**-rock analysis** *n* PETROL análisis de la roca intacta *m*; ~ **rock isochrone** *n* GEOL isocrona de roca total *f*; ~ **tone** *n* ACOUST tono completo *m*

wholesale: ~ **supplier** *n* PROD mayorista *m*, proveedor al mayoreo *m* (*AmL*), proveedor al por mayor *m* (*Esp*)

whorl *n* AGRIC espira *f*

wick *n* SPACE mecha trenzada *f*

wicket: ~ **gate** *n* HYDRAUL paleta directriz *f*

wide[1]: ~ **open** *adj* CINEMAT completamente abierto

wide[2]: ~**-angle converter** *n* PHOTO convertidor granangular *m*; ~**-angle instrument** *n* INSTR instrumento de ángulo amplio *m*; ~**-angle lens** *n* CINEMAT objetivo de foco variable *m*, objetivo gran angular *m*, INSTR, OPT objetivo gran angular *m*, PHOTO lente granangular *f*; ~**-angle scattering** *n* NUCL dispersión de gran ángulo *f*; ~ **aperture lens** *n* CINEMAT lente de gran abertura *f*; ~**-area network** *n* PRINT red de gran amplitud *f*; ~ **area system** *n* TELECOM sistema de amplio alcance *m*; ~**-band filter** *n* ELECTRON, TELECOM filtro de banda ancha *m*; ~**-band low-pass filter** *n* ELECTRON filtro de paso bajo de banda ancha *m*; ~**-bodied aircraft** *n* TRANSP avión reactor de fuselaje ancho *m*; ~**-body aircraft** *n* AIR TRANSP avión de fuselaje ancho *m*; ~**-bore tube** *n* LAB tubo de calibre ancho *m*; ~**-field metallurgical microscope** *n* INSTR microscopio metalúrgico de campo ancho *m*; ~**-field stereo microscope** *n* INSTR microscopio estereoscópico de campo ancho *m*;

~-**mouth bottle** *n* LAB botella de boca ancha *f*, frasco de boca ancha *m*; ~ **mouth container** *n* C&G brocal *m*; ~-**mouth neck** *n* PACK cuello de boca ancha *m*; ~-**necked flask** *n* LAB matraz de cuello ancho *m*; ~-**screen picture** *n* CINEMAT imagen de pantalla grande *f*; ~ **shot** *n* CINEMAT plano general *m*

wideband[1] *adj* COMP&DP, ELECTRON, TELECOM, TV de banda ancha

wideband[2] *n* COMP&DP, ELECTRON, TELECOM, TV banda ancha *f*; ~ **aerial** *n* BrE (*cf wideband antenna AmE*) SPACE antena multibanda *f*; ~ **amplification** *n* ELECTRON amplificación de banda ancha *f*; ~ **amplifier** *n* ELECTRON amplificador de banda ancha *m*; ~ **antenna** *n* AmE (*cf wideband aerial BrE*) SPACE antena multibanda *f*; ~ **axis** *n* TV eje de banda ancha *m*; ~ **beams** *n pl* RAD PHYS haces de banda ancha *m pl*; ~ **circuit** *n* TELECOM circuito de banda ancha *m*; ~ **filtering** *n* ELECTRON, TELECOM filtrado de banda ancha *m*; ~ **high-pass filter** *n* ELECTRON filtro de paso alto de banda ancha *m*; ~ **interference** *n* ELECTRON interferencia de banda ancha *f*; ~ **measurement** *n* ELECTRON medición de banda ancha *f*; ~ **modem** *n* ELECTRON módem de banda ancha *m*; ~ **modulation** *n* ELECTRON modulación de banda ancha *f*; ~ **noise** *n* ELECTRON, TELECOM ruido de banda ancha *m*; ~ **pipette** *n* CHEM pipeta de banda ancha *f*; ~ **power amplifier** *n* ELECTRON amplificador de potencia de banda ancha *m*; ~ **receiver** *n* TELECOM receptor de banda ancha *m*; ~ **signal** *n* ELECTRON, TELECOM señal de banda ancha *f*; ~ **switching network** *n* TELECOM red de conmutación de banda ancha *f*; ~ **transmission** *n* TELECOM, TV transmisión de banda ancha *f*; ~ **tube** *n* ELECTRON tubo de banda ancha *m*; ~ **tunable oscillator** *n* ELECTRON oscilador ajustable de banda ancha *m*

widmanstatten: ~ **plate** *n* METALL placa metálica widmanstatten *f*; ~ **structure** *n* METALL estructura widmanstatten *f*

widow *n* PRINT viuda *f*

width *n* CINEMAT ancho *m*, COMP&DP amplitud *f*, ancho *m*, anchura *f*, ELEC, ELECTRON, MECH ENG ancho *m*, PAPER ancho *m*, anchura *f*, PRINT anchura *f*, TEXTIL ancho *m*; ~ **of blade** *n* SAFE espesor de la hoja *m*; ~ **choke** *n* TV ancho de la bobina de reactancia *m*; ~ **coding** *n* ELECTRON *pulse-width modulation* codificación de la anchura *f*; ~ **in reed** *n* TEXTIL ancho en el peine *m*; ~ **jitter** *n* ELECTRON inestabilidad de la anchura *f*; ~ **of splitting** *n* METALL anchura del corte *f*

Wiedemann-Franz: ~ **law** *n* PHYS ley de Wiedemann-Franz *f*

Wien: ~ **bridge** *n* ELECTRON puente Wien *m*, PHYS puente de Wien *m*; ~-**bridge oscillator** *n* ELECTRON oscilador de puente Wien *m*; ~ **displacement law** *n* PHYS ley de desplazamiento de Wien *f*; ~ **law** *n* PHYS ley de Wien *f*

wig: ~-**wag signal** *n* RAIL señal oscilante *f*

Wigner: ~ **effect** *n* PHYS efecto Wigner *m*

wild: ~ **camera** *n* CINEMAT cámara no apta para sonido directo *f*; ~ **card character** *n* COMP&DP carácter comodín *m*; ~ **formation** *n* PAPER transparente irregular *m*; ~ **lookthrough** *n* PAPER transparente nuboso *m*; ~ **motor** *n* CINEMAT motor regulable *m*; ~ **oat** *n* AGRIC avena fatua *f*; ~ **shot** *n* CINEMAT toma sin sonido directo *f*; ~ **track** *n* CINE-

MAT banda libre *f*; ~ **well** *n* PETR TECH pozo en erupción *m*

wildcat *n* PETR TECH sondeo explorador *m*; ~ **drilling** *n* PETR TECH perforación exploratoria *f*; ~ **well** *n* PETROL pozo de cateo *m*, pozo de ensayo *m*, pozo de exploración *m*

willemite *n* MINERAL willemita *f*

williamsite *n* MINERAL williamsita *f*

Willison: ~ **coupling** *n* TRANSP acoplamiento Willison *m*

Wilson: ~ **cloud chamber** *n* PHYS cámara de niebla de Wilson *f*

wilt *n* AGRIC marchitamiento *m*

wilting: ~ **coefficient** *n* AGRIC coeficiente de marchitamiento *m*

wiluite *n* MINERAL wiluíta *f*

Wimshurst: ~ **machine** *n* ELEC ENG máquina Wimshurst *f*

winch[1] *n* CONST *cranked handle* cabrestante *m*, cigüeña *f*, chigre *m*, *windlass* torno *m*, MAR POLL chigre *m*, maquinilla *f*, TEXTIL barca de torniquete *f*, WATER TRANSP *deck fittings, hoarding* chigre *m*, maquinilla *f*, guinche *m*; ~ **drum** *n* OCEAN tambor de la maquinilla *m*, tambor del guinche *m*, WATER TRANSP *deck fittings* tambor *m*, tambor de la maquinilla *m*

winch[2]: ~ **into helicopter** *vt* WATER TRANSP *air-sea rescue* izar a bordo del helicóptero

Winchester: ~ **disk** *n* COMP&DP disco duro *m*

wind[1]: ~-**eroded** *adj* METEO erosionado por el viento

wind[2]: **off the** ~ *adv* WATER TRANSP *sailing* con el viento a popa del través

wind[3] *n* METEO, TEXTIL viento *m*; ~ **arrow** *n* METEO asta del viento *f*, flecha del viento *f*; ~ **bore** *n* WATER *of pump* alcachofa de aspiración *f*; ~ **brace** *n* CONST *building* contraviento *m*; ~ **bracing** *n* CONST arriostramiento contra vientos *m*; ~ **break** *n* METEO cortaviento *m*, protector contra el viento *m*; ~ **chart** *n* METEO mapa de los vientos *m*, WATER TRANSP *navigation* carta de los vientos *f*; ~ **conditions** *n pl* METEO condiciones del viento *f pl*; ~ **cone** *n* AIR TRANSP cono de viento *m*, manga *f*, manga indicadora del viento *f*, manga-veleta *f*; ~ **direction** *n* AIR TRANSP, METEO, WATER TRANSP dirección del viento *f*; ~ **dispersion** *n* GAS, POLL dispersión eólica *f*; ~-**driven generator** *n* ELEC ENG electrogenerador eólico *m*; ~-**driven sea** *n* OCEAN olas de viento *f pl*; ~-**electric power station** *n* ELEC ENG central de energía eólica *f*; ~ **energy** *n* FUELLESS, PHYS energía eólica *f*; ~ **erosion** *n* GEOL erosión eólica *f*; ~ **force** *n* METEO fuerza del viento *f*, potencia del viento *f*; ~ **gage** *n* AmE, ~ **gauge** *n* BrE FUELLESS, HYDROL, LAB, METEO, PHYS, WATER TRANSP anemómetro *m*; ~ **inclination meter** *n* METEO veleta *f*; ~ **machine** *n* CINEMAT máquina de viento *f*, ventilador *m*; ~ **power** *n* FUELLESS energía del viento *f*, METEO energía eólica *f*, PHYS potencia eólica *f*; ~-**powered generator** *n* ELEC aerogenerador *m*, generador eólico *m*, FUELLESS aerogenerador *m*; ~ **pressure** *n* METEO carga del viento *f*, presión del viento *f*; ~ **recorder** *n* METEO registrador del viento *m*; ~ **resistance** *n* FLUID resistencia debida al viento *f*; ~ **rose** *n* FUELLESS, METEO rosa de los vientos *f*; ~ **sail** *n* WATER TRANSP manguera de ventilación *f*; ~ **and sea state capability handling** *n* TRANSP manejo de capacidad del viento y del mar *m*; ~ **sensor** *n* METEO sensor de viento *m*, WATER TRANSP detector de viento *m*;

~ shaft n METEO asta del viento f, flecha del viento f; **~ shear** n METEO cizalladura de viento f, cortante del viento f; **~ sock** n AIR TRANSP cono de viento m, manga indicadora del viento f, manga-veleta f; **~ speed** n FUELLESS, METEO velocidad del viento f; **~-speed barb** n METEO barra indicatoria de la intensidad del viento f; **~ stress** n OCEAN carga ejercida por el viento f, presión del viento f; **~ stress sea** n OCEAN mar agitado m, mar de viento m; **~ stripping cropping** n AGRIC cultivo en franjas contraviento m; **~ telltale** n WATER TRANSP anemoscopio m, catavientos m, veleta f; **~ tunnel** n AIR TRANSP túnel aerodinámico m, túnel de viento m, CONST túnel aerodinámico m, PHYS túnel de viento m, SPACE túnel aerodinámico m; **~ tunnel balance** n AIR TRANSP balanza del túnel de viento f, equilibrio del túnel aerodinámico m; **~ tunnel testing** n SPACE spacecraft ensayo del túnel aerodinámico m; **~ turbine** n FUELLESS turbina de viento f, turbina eólica f, MECH ENG aeroturbina f, turbina de viento f, turbina eólica f; **~ turbine fan** n REFRIG ventilador con turbina eólica m; **~-turbine generator** n FUELLESS generador tipo turbina eólica m; **~-unwind equipment** n PACK equipo de enrollado-desenrollado m; **~-up** n TEXTIL bobinado m; **~-up apparatus** n TEXTIL aparato enrollador m; **~ velocity** n FUELLESS, METEO velocidad del viento f; **~ velocity cubed** n FUELLESS velocidad cubicada del viento f

wind⁴ vt CINEMAT bobinar, MECH ENG bobinar, encanillar, enrollar, PAPER, PHYS bobinar, TEXTIL enrollar; **~ up** vt MECH ENG coil spring dar cuerda a

wind⁵ vi CONST warp combarse, MECH ENG coil bobinar, enrollar

windage: ~ adjustment screw n INSTR tornillo de ajuste de la resistencia aerodinámica m; **~ loss** n ELEC electrical machine pérdida de energía por efecto del viento f, pérdida por rozamiento con el aire f

winder n C&G embobinador m, CONST escalón de escalera de curva m, peldaño de abanico m, PAPER enrollador m; **~ house** n MINE cámara de extracción f

winding n CONST warping alabeo m, bobinado m (AmL), combadura f, ELEC generator arrollamiento m, bobinado m (AmL), devanado m, ELEC ENG bobinado m, devanado m, MECH ENG enrollado m, bobinado m, enroscado m, PAPER enrollado m, PHYS bobinado m, VEH arrollamiento m, bobinado m, devanado m; **~ capacitance** n ELEC coil capacitancia de devanado f, ELEC ENG capacidad del bobinado f, capacitancia de devanado f; **~ drum** n PAPER tambor enrollador m; **~ engine** n MINE cabrestante m, máquina de extracción f (AmL); **~ and fanning** n PRINT aireado m; **~ inset** n MINE pozo de extracción m; **~ insulation** n ELEC coil aislación del devanado f, aislamiento del devanado m, ELEC ENG aislación del devanado f; **~ machine** n CINEMAT, PACK bobinadora f; **~ mechanism** n VEH mecanismo de bobinado m; **~ motion** n MECH ENG enrollamiento m, movimiento de bobinado m; **~ off** n PAPER desenrollado m; **~ pitch** n ELEC coil razón del arrollamiento m, paso del devanado m; **~ process** n TEXTIL proceso de bobinado m; **~ ratio** n ELEC transformer razón de transformación f, relación de transformación f; **~ RTD** n PROD PTC para enrollamiento m; **~ shaft** n MINE pozo de extracción m; **~ tackle** n WATER TRANSP sailing boats aparejo de estrellera m; **~ tension** n CINEMAT tensión de bobinado f;

~ tower n MINE caballete de extracción m, castillete m, torre de extracción f

windlass n CONST cabrestante m, guinche m, WATER TRANSP deck equipment, anchoring chigre m, molinete m

windmill: ~ pump n FUELLESS bomba de molino de viento f, bomba eólica f; **~ torque** n AIR TRANSP par en autorrotación m, par en régimen de molinete m

windmilling: ~ propeller n AIR TRANSP hélice en molinete f, hélice loca f; **~ restart** n AIR TRANSP rearranque en molinete m, reencendido en molinete m

window n COMP&DP, CONST ventana f, MECH ENG of vernier escala f, VEH ventanilla f; **~ air conditioning unit** n CONST, HEAT, REFRIG, THERMO acondicionador de ventana m; **~ bar** n CONST barrote m, reja f, removable bar to secure shutter separador de ventana m, traba f, wood division between panes of sash barra de la ventana f; **~ catch** n CONST cerrojo de ventana m; **~ clipping** n COMP&DP recorte de ventana m; **~ crank** n AmE (cf window regulator BrE) VEH manivela alzacristal f, manivela elevalunas f; **~ fastener** n CONST pasador de ventana m; **~ filter** n ELECTRON filtro de ventana m; **~ frame** n CONST, VEH marco de ventana m; **~ glass** n CONST vidrio común m; **~ opening** n CONST hueco de ventana m; **~ packaging** n PACK embalaje con ventana m; **~ rabbet** n CONST renvalso de ventana m; **~ regulator** n BrE (cf window crank AmE) VEH manivela alzacristal f, manivela elevalunas f; **~ seal** n VEH junta de estanqueidad de la ventanilla f; **~ transformation** n COMP&DP transformación en ventanas f; **~ winder** n AUTO manilla de la ventanilla f, manilla del elevalunas f

windowing n COMP&DP partición en ventanas f

windowsill n CONST antepecho de ventana m

windrow n AGRIC hilera de heno amontonada f

windrower n AGRIC hileradora f

windscreen n BrE (cf windshield) AIR TRANSP, AUTO, C&G parabrisas m, SPACE ojiva f, parabrisas m, TRANSP, VEH parabrisas m; **~ washer** n BrE (cf windshield washer AmE) AUTO, VEH lavaparabrisas m; **~ washer jet** n BrE (cf windshield washer jet AmE) AUTO chorro limpiaparabrisas m; **~ wiper** n BrE (cf windshield wiper AmE) AUTO, VEH limpiaparabrisas m

windshield n AmE (cf windscreen BrE) ACOUST antiviento m, AIR TRANSP, AUTO, C&G AmE (cf windscreen BrE) parabrisas m, CINEMAT antiviento m, SPACE AmE (cf windscreen BrE) ojiva f, parabrisas m, TRANSP parabrisas m, TV antiviento m, VEH parabrisas m; **~ washer** n AmE (cf windscreen washer BrE) AUTO, VEH lavaparabrisas m; **~ washer jet** n AmE (cf windscreen washer jet BrE) AUTO chorro limpiaparabrisas m; **~ wiper** n AmE (cf windscreen wiper BrE) AUTO, VEH limpiaparabrisas m

windward¹ adj METEO, WATER TRANSP navigation de barlovento

windward² adv METEO, WATER TRANSP navigation a barlovento

windward³: **~ side** n METEO, WATER TRANSP lado de barlovento m

windy adj METEO ventoso

wine: ~ carrier n WATER TRANSP buque tanque para el transporte de vino m

wing n AIR TRANSP, CONST ala f, MECH ENG of thumbscrew oreja f, aleta f, mariposa f, ala f, orejeta f, palomilla f, OCEAN, PHYS ala f, VEH aleta f, WATER

TRANSP ala *f*; ~ **bar light** *n* AIR TRANSP luz de barra del ala *f*; ~ **base** *n* MECH ENG *for slide units* base en T *f*; ~ **bolt** *n* MECH ENG perno de orejetas *m*, tornillo de orejas *m*; ~ **box** *n* AIR TRANSP caja alar *f*; ~ **compasses** *n pl* MECH ENG compás alado *m*; ~ **end** *n* OCEAN extremo de red de cerco *m*, extremo del ala *m*, punta de red de cerco *f* (*AmL*); ~ **flap** *n* AIR TRANSP flap alar *m*; ~ **lever knob** *n* PROD puño de palanca de aletas *m*; ~ **loading** *n* AIR TRANSP *aerodynamics* carga alar *f*; ~ **nut** *n* MECH ENG tuerca alada *f*, tuerca de alas *f*, tuerca de mariposa *f*, tuerca de orejeta *f*, tuerca de palomilla *f*, VEH tuerca de mariposa *f*, tuerca de palomilla *f*; ~ **rail** *n* RAIL contracarril *m*; ~ **root** *n* AIR TRANSP *aircraft* raíz alar *f*, raíz del ala *f*; ~ **screw** *n* MECH ENG tornillo alado *m*, tornillo de mariposa *m*, tornillo de orejetas *m*, tornillo de palomilla *m*; ~ **slot** *n* AIR TRANSP *aircraft* ranura del ala *f*; ~ **span** *n* AIR TRANSP envergadura alar *f*; ~ **tip** *n* AIR TRANSP *aircraft* extremo del ala *m*, punta del ala *f*; ~**-tip vortex** *n* AIR TRANSP torbellino de la punta del ala *m*, vórtice de la punta del ala *m*

winged: ~ **screw** *n* MECH ENG tornillo alado *m*

wingless: ~ **aphid** *n* AGRIC pulgón afidio *m*

wingwall *n* CONST muro lateral *m*

Winston: ~ **collector** *n* FUELLESS colector tipo Winston *m*

winter: ~ **annual** *n* AGRIC planta anual *f*; ~ **calving** *n* AGRIC parición invernal *f*; ~ **storage** *n* WATER TRANSP *vessel* invernada *f*

wintering: ~ **level** *n* AGRIC nivel de alimentación *m*

winterization *n* REFRIG *cooling of edible oils* enturbamiento de aceites por el frío *m*

winterize *vt* CHEM invernizar

winze *n* MINE calderilla *m*, coladero *m* (*Esp*), pozo de comunicación *m* (*AmL*)

wipe[1] *n* CINEMAT agrandamiento *m*, agrandamiento gradual de la imagen *m*, MECH ENG agrandamiento *m*, limpión *m*, soldadura *f*, TV agrandamiento gradual de la imagen *m*, agrandamiento *m*; ~ **joint** *n* CONST junta soldada *f*

wipe[2] *vt* CONST *joint* soldar

wiped: ~ **joint** *n* CONST junta soldada *f*

wiper *n* MECH ENG contacto deslizante *m*, contacto móvil *m*, excéntrica *f*, leva *f*, VEH escobilla *f*; ~ **arm** *n* AUTO, VEH brazo del limpiaparabrisas *m*; ~ **blade** *n* VEH escobilla del limpiaparabrisas *f*, rasqueta del limpiaparabrisas *f*; ~ **shaft** *n* MECH ENG eje de levas *m*

wiping *n* PRINT racleta *f*

wire[1] *adj* GEN alámbrico *m*

wire[2] *n* AGRIC, AUTO, CONST, ELEC alambre *m*, ELEC ENG alambre *m*, hilo metálico *m*, tendido de cables *m*, LAB, OPT, PACK alambre *m*, PAPER tela *f*, TELECOM cable *m*, hilo *m*, hilo metálico *m*, telegrama *m*, alambre *m*,, WATER TRANSP alambre *m*; ~ **aerial** *n* BrE (*cf wire antenna AmE*) TELECOM antena de hilo *f*, antena monofilar *f*, TV antena de hilo *f*; ~ **antenna** *n* AmE (*cf wire aerial BrE*) TELECOM antena de hilo *f*, antena monofilar *f*, TV antena de hilo *f*; ~ **bag tie** *n* PACK atado de la bolsa con alambre *m*; ~ **bonding** *n* ELEC ENG unión por hilo *f*; ~ **brush** *n* PROD *iron* cepillo de alambre *m*; ~ **bundle** *n* ELEC ENG carrete *m*; ~ **cloth** *n* PROD tela metálica *f*; ~ **cloth screen** *n* PROD criba de tela metálica *f*; ~**-coating machine** *n* PROD máquina revestidora de hilos *f*; ~ **core** *n* ELEC ENG núcleo alámbrico *m*; ~**-drag survey** *n* OCEAN explo-

ración con draga hidrográfica *f*; ~ **dragging** *n* OCEAN dragado hidrográfico *m*; ~ **drawing** *n* PROD estirado de hilos *m*, REFRIG laminado *m*; ~ **dredging** *n* OCEAN dragado hidrográfico *m*; ~ **drive roll** *n* PAPER rodillo de acondicionamiento de la tela *m*; ~ **edge** *n* MECH ENG *tool-sharpening* filo *m*; ~ **enamel** *n* COATINGS esmalte de alambre *m*; ~ **end** *n* ELEC ENG extremo alámbrico *m*, PAPER mesa de fabricación *f*; ~ **erosion** *n* MECH ENG *machining* desgaste del corte *m*, desgaste del filo de corte *m*; ~ **fence** *n* AGRIC, CONST alambrada *f*; ~ **frame** *n* PAPER bastidor de la tela *m*; ~ **fuse** *n* ELEC, MECH ENG fusible de alambre *m*; ~ **gage** *AmE*, ~ **gauge** *BrE* *n* METR calibrador de alambres *m*, galga de alambres *f*, manómetro de resistencia eléctrica *m*; ~ **gauze** *n* LAB malla de alambre *f*, PROD tela metálica fina *f*; ~ **guard** *n* PROD defensa de tela metálica *f*, rejilla de protección *f*; ~ **guide** *n* C&G guía de alambre *f*, PAPER guía de tela *f*; ~ **guide roll** *n* PAPER rodillo guía de la tela *m*; ~ **mark** *n* PRINT marca de la tela *f*; ~ **mesh** *n* C&G tela de alambre *f*, P&R rejilla de hilo metálico *f*, tela de alambre *f*, tela metálica *f*; ~ **mesh reinforcement** *n* C&G armadura de parilla *f*, refuerzo con malla de alambre *m*, refuerzo con tela de alambre *m*; ~**-mesh target** *n* RAD PHYS blanco reticular *m*, ánodo de rejilla *m*; ~ **mill** *n* MECH ENG *rolling* taller de producción de alambres *m*, trefilería *f*; ~ **netting** *n* CONST enrejado de alambre *m*; ~ **pair** *n* ELEC ENG par alámbrico *m*; ~ **pit** *n* PAPER fosa bajo la tela *f*; ~ **race ball bearing** *n* MECH ENG cojinete de bolas con pista de rodadura hecha de alambre de acero duro *m*; ~ **reel** *n* CONST tambor del cable *m*; ~**-reinforced hose** *n* MECH ENG, P&R manguera reforzada con alambre *f*, manguera reforzada con tela metálica *f*; ~**-return roll** *n* PAPER rodillo de retorno de tela *m*; ~ **roll** *n* PAPER rodillo-guía de tela *m*; ~ **rope** *n* MINE cable de perforación *m*, PROD cable metálico *m*; ~ **rope clamp** *n* PROD mordaza de cables metálicos *f*; ~ **rope sling** *n* SAFE eslinga de cable de acero *f*, estrobo de cable de acero *m*; ~ **screen** *n* PROD criba de tela metálica *f*; ~ **side** *n* PAPER cara tela *f*, lado tela *m*, PRINT lado tela *m*; ~ **sieve** *n* PROD criba de tela metálica *f*, tamiz de tela metálica *m*; ~ **spark machine** *n* ELEC ENG, MECH ENG máquina de electroerosión por cables *f*; ~ **stacking machine** *n* PACK apiladora y atadora con alambre *f*; ~ **staple** *n* CONST grada de alambre *f*; ~ **strainer** *n* CONST tamiz de alambre *m*; ~**-strapping equipment** *n* PACK equipo para el zunchado con alambre *m*; ~ **stretcher** *n* CONST enderezador de alambre *m*, PAPER tensor de la tela *m*; ~**-stripping pliers** *n pl* MECH ENG *tool* alicates de desenfundar cables *m pl*, alicates pelacables *m pl*; ~ **tray** *n* PAPER bandeja de tela *f*; ~ **wheel** *n* VEH rueda con radios de alambre *f*; ~ **wobble stick head** *n* PROD cabezal de retención oscilante del alambre *m*; ~ **works** *n* PROD trefilería *f*; ~**-wound armature** *n* ELEC *generator* armadura devanada *f*; ~**-wound coil** *n* ELEC bobina devanada *f*; ~**-wound core** *n* ELEC *transformer* núcleo bobinado *m*; ~**-wound potentiometer** *n* ELEC potenciómetro bobinado *m*, potenciómetro de alambre bobinado *m*, potenciómetro de alambre devanado *m*; ~**-woven screen** *n* PROD criba de tela tejida *f*; ~ **wrap** *n* MECH ENG alambre de envoltura *m*; ~ **wrapping** *n* ELEC ENG envoltura de alambre *f*

wire[3] *vt* ELEC, TV cablear

wired: ~ **broadcasting** n TV radiodifusión por hilo f, transmisión por cable f (AmL); ~ **cast glass** n C&G vidrio rolado acorazado m; ~**-logic system** n TELECOM sistema de lógica cableada m; ~**-programme control system** n (WPC system) TELECOM sistema de control de programas por conexionado m; ~ **safety glass** n C&G, SAFE vidrio de seguridad acorazado m

wiredrawer n PROD person trefilador m

wiredrawing: ~ **bench** n PROD banco de trefilación m

wireframe: ~ **representation** n COMP&DP representación en trama de alambre f

wireless: ~ **hearing-aid receiver** n TELECOM receptor inalámbrico de corrección auditiva m; ~ **microphone** n MILIT micrófono inalámbrico m; ~ **remote control** n CINEMAT control remoto inalámbrico m; ~ **telephony** n TELECOM telefonía inalámbrica f, telefonía sin hilos f

wireline: ~ **log** n PETR TECH perfil eléctrico m, registro eléctrico m

wirewound: ~ **resistor** n ELEC resistencia bobinada f, resistencia de alambre devanado f, resistencia de hilo bobinado f, resistencia devanada f, resistor de hilo arrollado m, ELEC ENG resistencia de hilo bobinado f, PHYS resistor de bobina m

wiring n ELEC connection tendido eléctrico m, alambrado m, canalización eléctrica f, conexionado m, conexiones eléctricas f pl, distribución eléctrica f, instalación de conductores f, instalación eléctrica f, cableado m, tendido de cables m, cableaje m, ELEC ENG cableado m, instalación f, SPACE bobinado de motores m, alambrado m, cableado m, conexionado m, distribución f; ~ **arm** n PROD brazo de cableado m; ~ **configuration** n PROD configuración del cableado f; ~ **diagram** n AUTO diagrama de conexiones m, diagrama eléctrico m, esquema de conexiones m, ELEC diagrama de cableado m, diagrama de conexiones m, diagrama eléctrico m, esquema de conexiones m, esquema eléctrico m, esquema eléctrico del circuito m, ELEC ENG, ELECTRON diagrama de cableado m, TELECOM diagrama de cableado m, diagrama de conexiones m, esquema de conexiones m, esquema eléctrico m, esquema eléctrico del circuito m; ~ **duct** n PROD conducto para cables m (Esp), ducto para cables m; ~ **error** n PROD error de cableado m; ~ **harness** n SPACE spacecraft cableado preformado m, mazo de cables m, modelo de cableado m; ~ **terminal** n PROD terminal de cableado m

witch: ~ **mirror** n C&G espejo de bruja m

withamite n MINERAL withamita f

withdrawal: ~ **current** n AmE (cf pull current BrE) C&G corriente de estiraje f

withdrawing: ~ **pin** n PRINT clavija de reposición f

withered adj AGRIC marchito, FOOD marchito, mustio, seco

witherite n MINERAL witherita f

withers n AGRIC cruz f

within[1]: ~**-plate** adj GEOL pipes de placa interna

within[2]: **to** ~ **an arbitrary constant** phr PHYS salvo una constante arbitraria

without[1]: ~ **finish** adj PAPER sin acabado

without[2]: ~ **interacting** adv RAD PHYS sin influirse mutuamente, sin interaccionar

withstand: ~ **current** n PROD corriente no disruptiva f; ~ **impulse** n PROD impulso no disruptivo m; ~ **impulse voltage** n ELEC, PROD voltaje impulsivo

no disruptivo m; ~ **voltage** n ELEC installation tensión no disruptiva f, voltaje no disruptivo m; ~ **voltage test** n ELEC installation prueba de tensión no disruptiva f, prueba de voltaje no disruptivo f

wittichenite n MINERAL wittichenita f

woad n COLOUR glasto m

WOB abbr (weight on bit) PETR TECH peso sobre la broca m, PSM (peso sobre la mecha), peso sobre el trépano m (Esp), peso sobre la barrena m

wobble[1] n SPACE giro excéntrico m, rotación fuera del plano normal al eje de rotación f; ~ **stick head** n PROD cabezal de retención oscilante m, interruptor de posición de palanca a resorte m; ~ **stick operating head** n PROD cabezal de funcionamiento oscilante m, cabezal de marcha oscilante m

wobble[2] vi SPACE balancearse, tambalearse

wobbulation n ELECTRON tambaleo m

wobbulator n ELECTRON modulador m

wohlerite n MINERAL wohlerita f

wolfram n CHEM (W, cf tungsten) tungsteno m (W), wolframio m (W)

wolframic adj CHEM wolfrámico

wolframite n CHEM, MINERAL wolframita f

wolfsbergite n MINERAL wolfsbergita f

wollastonite n MINERAL wolastonita f

wood: ~ **alcohol** n THERMO alcohol de madera m, metanol m; ~ **bit** n MECH ENG broca de madera f; ~ **brick** n CONST ladrillo de madera m; ~ **charcoal** n COAL carbón de madera m; ~ **coal** n COAL carbón de madera m; ~**-containing paper** n PAPER papel con pasta mecánica m; ~ **defect** n QUALITY defecto inherente a la madera m; ~ **flour** n P&R harina de madera f, polvo de madera m; ~ **lagging** n HYDRAUL revestimiento de madera m; ~ **paint** n COLOUR, CONST pintura para madera f; ~ **preservative** n CONST conservante para madera m; ~ **primer** n COATINGS imprimador de madera m; ~ **pulp** n PAPER pasta de madera f, pasta mecánica f; ~ **reinforcements** n pl WATER TRANSP for deck fittings refuerzos de madera m pl; ~ **resin** n P&R colofonía de madera f; ~ **saw** n CONST buck-saw sierra de madera f; ~ **screw** n CONST tornillo para madera m; ~ **shavings** n pl CONST virutas f pl; ~ **stain** n COLOUR tintura para madera f; ~ **suitable for building** n CONST madera para construcción f; ~ **tin** n MINERAL casiterita f, estaño leñoso m, estaño xiloide m; ~**-turner's lathe** n CONST torno para madera m; ~**-turning lathe** n CONST torno para madera m; ~ **wool** n PACK lana de madera f

woodchip: ~ **wall covering** n COATINGS revestimiento de madera para pared m; ~ **wallpaper** n COATINGS papel pintado de madera m

wooden: ~ **cradle** n PROD cuna de madera f; ~ **dunnage** n PROD durmientes de madera m pl, listones de madera m pl; ~ **mold** AmE, ~ **mould** BrE n WATER TRANSP molde de madera m; ~ **pile** n COAL pilote de madera m; ~ **plug** n WATER TRANSP boat building molde de madera m; ~ **sleeper** n BrE (cf wooden tie AmE) CONST durmiente de madera m (AmL), traviesa de madera f (Esp); ~ **tie** n AmE (cf wooden sleeper BrE) CONST railroad durmiente de madera m (AmL), traviesa de madera f (Esp); ~ **trough** n AGRIC comedero de madera m

woodruff: ~ **keys and keyways** n pl MECH ENG chavetas y chaveteros de media caña m pl

Woodruff: ~ **cutter** n MECH ENG cortador Woodruff m; ~ **key** n VEH chaveta Woodruff f, chaveta de disco f

woods n pl C&G maderos m pl

Wood's: ~ **glass** n C&G vidrio de Woods m

woodsawing: ~ **circular saw blade** n MECH ENG, PROD hoja de sierra circular para madera f

woodtype n PRINT tipo de madera m

woodwork n CONST maderaje m

woodworking: ~ **machinery hazard** n SAFE peligro originado por la carpintería m, riesgo originado por maquinaria de carpintería m

wool n C&G, TEXTIL lana f; ~ **count** n TEXTIL título de la lana m; ~ **merchant** n TEXTIL comerciante de lanas m

woollen: ~ **dyer** n COLOUR colorante para lanas m, tinte para lana m; ~ **spinning** n TEXTIL hilatura de lana cardada f

woolly adj TEXTIL lanoso

woolpack n TEXTIL fardo de lana m

word[1]: ~ **-oriented** adj COMP&DP orientado a la palabra, textual

word[2] n COMP&DP palabra f; ~ **address field** n PROD campo de direcciones de palabra m; ~ **delimiter** n COMP&DP delimitador de palabra m; ~ **generation** n ELECTRON generación de palabras f; ~ **generator** n ELECTRON generador de palabras m; ~ **length** n COMP&DP longitud de palabra f; ~ **processing** n (WP) COMP&DP procesado de texto m (WP), procesamiento de texto m (WP), tratamiento de texto m (WP), procesador de textos m; ~ **processor** n (WP) COMP&DP procesador de textos m; ~ **size** n COMP&DP tamaño de palabra m; ~ **time** n COMP&DP tiempo de palabra m; ~ **usage** n PROD uso de palabras m; ~ **wrap** n COMP&DP cambio automático de línea m, cambio de línea automático m, retorno automático de la última palabra m, PRINT alineado de palabras m

words: ~ **per second** n pl (wps) PRINT palabras por segundo f pl

work[1] n PHYS trabajo m; ~ **area** n COMP&DP área de trabajo f; ~ **assembly** n PROD ensamblajes m pl; ~ **and back** n PRINT impresión a blanco y retiración f; ~ **barge** n PETROL barcaza-taller f; ~ **boots** n pl SAFE founding botas de trabajo f pl; ~ **center** AmE see work centre BrE; ~ **center utilization** AmE, ~ **centre** BrE n PROD centro de trabajo m; ~ **centre utilization** n BrE PROD utilización del centro de trabajo f; ~ **file** n COMP&DP archivo de trabajo m; ~ **function** n ELEC ENG, PHYS función de trabajo f; ~ **handling** n PACK operaciones de manutención f pl; ~ **hardening** n CRYSTALL, MECH, METALL acritud f, endurecimiento por acritud m, endurecimiento por deformación m, endurecimiento por medios mecánicos m; ~ **-hardening coefficient** n CRYSTALL, MECH, METALL coeficiente de endurecimiento por medios mecánicos m; ~ **in hand** n PROD trabajo en curso de ejecución m; ~ **in process** n PROD trabajo en proceso m; ~ **-in-progress by employee** n PROD trabajo en curso de ejecución m; ~ **-in-progress control** n PROD control del trabajo en curso de ejecución m; ~ **load** n TEXTIL carga de trabajo f; ~ **order** n PROD orden de trabajo m; ~ **package** n SPACE paquete de trabajo m, plan de trabajo m, programa de trabajo m, propuesta de trabajo f; ~ **plate** n MECH ENG of machine mesa portapiezas f; ~ **print** n CINEMAT copia de trabajo f; ~ **rest blade** n MECH ENG for centreless grinding hoja del portapiezas f; ~ **safety** n SAFE seguridad en el

trabajo f; ~ **softening** n METALL reblandecimiento por acritud m; ~ **station** n COMP&DP estación de trabajo f, puesto de trabajo m, MECH ENG lugar de trabajo m, puesto de trabajo m, PACK lugar de trabajo m, PROD estación de trabajo f, punto de trabajo m; ~ **surface** n PROD superficie de trabajo f; ~ **traffic** n TRANSP tráfico para ir al trabajo m; ~ **underground** n CONST obras subterráneas f pl; ~ **and whirl** n PRINT imposición a blanco y voltereta f

work[2] vt C&G manufacturar, MECH ENG fashion elaborar, manufacturar, trabajar, METALL labrar, PROD manufacturar; ~ **out** vt COAL explotar

work[3]: ~ **against the grain** vi CONST wood trabajar contra veteado; ~ **to full capacity** vi MECH ENG trabajar a plena capacidad; ~ **loose** vi MECH ENG keying aflojarse, desenchavetarse, soltarse; ~ **with tripod** vi PHOTO trabajar con trípode; ~ **underground** vi CONST trabajar bajo tierra

workability n C&G maniobrabilidad f, CONST cualidad de trabajable f, docilidad f, MINE explotabilidad f

workable adj CONST dócil, trabajable, MINE explotable

workbench n INSTR banco de ajustador m, banco de taller m, PROD banco de taller m; ~ **unit** n INSTR, PROD banco de taller m

workday n CONST jornada laboral f

worked: ~ **-out lode** n MINE filón explotado m; ~ **-out vein** n MINE veta explotada f; ~ **thickness** n COAL coal seam anchura trabajada f, espesor trabajado m

workers': ~ **compensation** n SAFE indemnización a trabajadores f; ~ **protective clothing** n SAFE prendas protectoras de trabajo f pl; ~ **protective tents** n SAFE tienda protectora para trabajadores f

workholding: ~ **fixed table** n MECH ENG machine tools mesa fija portapiezas f; ~ **pallet** n MECH ENG machine tools fiador de la mesa portapiezas m

working[1] n MATH operación f, MECH ENG funcionamiento m, movimiento m, operación f, PROD of furnace marcha f; ~ **area** n COMP&DP área de trabajo f; ~ **beam** n MECH ENG balancín m; ~ **channel** n TELECOM canal activo m, canal de trabajo m; ~ **clothes** n pl CONST ropa de trabajo f, vestimenta de trabajo f, TEXTIL ropa de trabajo f; ~ **conditions** n pl PROD régimen de marcha m, SAFE vehicles condiciones de trabajo f pl; ~ **current relay** n ELEC relé de corriente activa m, relé de corriente de régimen m, relé de corriente de trabajo m; ~ **cycle** n AUTO ciclo de trabajo m; ~ **depth of tooth** n MECH ENG gearing altura de trabajo del diente de engranaje f; ~ **distance** n METALL distancia efectiva f, distancia útil f; ~ **end** n C&G lado caliente m; ~ **face** n COAL frente de arranque m (AmL), MINE frente de arranque m (AmL), frente de trabajo m (Esp); ~ **gloves** n pl SAFE guantes de trabajo m pl; ~ **gloves made of artificial rubber** n pl P&R, SAFE guantes de trabajo hechos de caucho artificial m pl, guantes de trabajo hechos de neopreno m pl; ~ **head** n HYDRAUL caída efectiva f, caída útil f; ~ **hours** n pl PROD horas de trabajo f pl; ~ **hours counter** n SAFE contador de horas trabajadas m; ~ **life** n C&G, PACK, PHOTO vida útil f; ~ **load** n MECH ENG carga de trabajo f; ~ **mechanism** n MECH ENG mecanismo de trabajo m, mecanismo en funcionamiento m; ~ **mine** n MINE minería f; ~ **part** n MECH ENG parte activa f, parte móvil f, parte útil f, pieza de trabajo f, NUCL parte móvil f, órgano activo m; ~ **platform** n C&G, CONST plataforma de trabajo f; ~ **pressure** n HYDRAUL chapa de caldera *f*, presión de régimen de trabajo *f*, presión efectiva *f*, *boiler* timbre *m*, timbre de la caldera *m*; ~ **range** *n* C&G rango de trabajo *m*; ~ **section** *n* PHYS sección eficaz *f*; ~ **speed** *n* MECH ENG velocidad de funcionamiento *f*, velocidad de trabajo *f*; ~ **standard** *n* PHYS sistema patrón de trabajo *m*; ~ **storage** *AmE*, ~ **store** *BrE n* COMP&DP almacenamiento de trabajo *m*, memoria de trabajo *f*; ~ **stress** *n* METALL esfuerzo efectivo *m*; ~ **temperature** *n* C&G temperatura de trabajo *f*; ~ **time percentage** *n* PROD porcentaje del tiempo de trabajo *m*; ~ **title** *n* CINEMAT título provisional *m*; ~ **voltage** *n* ELEC tensión de funcionamiento *f*, tensión de servicio *f*, tensión de trabajo *f*, voltaje de régimen *m*, voltaje de servicio *m*

working[2]: **in ~ order** *phr* MECH ENG en condiciones de servicio, en estado de servicio, en perfecto estado de funcionamiento, PROD en buen estado de funcionamiento

workmanship *n* PROD mano de obra *f*

workover *n* PETR TECH rehabilitación *f*, reparación *f*; ~ **barge** *n* PETR TECH barcaza de reparaciones *f*, gabarra de reparaciones *f*

workpiece *n* MECH pieza a máquina *f*, pieza de trabajo *f*

workplace *n* SAFE lugar de trabajo *m*; ~ **regulations** *n pl* SAFE normas sobre el lugar de trabajo *f pl*

works *n* PROD fábrica *f*, taller *m*; ~ **recording clock** *n* SAFE reloj de control *m*

workshop *n BrE* (*cf car repair shop AmE*) MECH taller *m*, PROD reunión de trabajo *f*, taller *m*, RAIL taller *m*, taller para la reparación de vagones *m*, SAFE taller *m*

World: ~ **Association of Nuclear Operators** *n* (*WANO*) NUCL Asociación Mundial de Operadores Nucleares *f* (*WANO*); ~ **Wide Web** *n* (*WWW*) COMP&DP World Wide Web *m* (*WWW*), telaraña mundial *f* (*WWW*)

worldwide[1] *adj* COMP&DP, SPACE, TELECOM mundial

worldwide[2]: ~ **communications** *n pl* TELECOM comunicaciones internacionales *f pl*; ~ **network** *n* SPACE *communications* red mundial *f*

worm *n* LAB serpentín *m*, MECH rosca *f*, tornillo sin fin *m*, MECH ENG *endless screw* tornillo sin fin *m*, *screw-thread* hilo *m*, rosca *f*, filete *m*; ~**-drive clamp** *n* MECH ENG *hose clip* abrazadera de tornillo sin fin para manguera *f*; ~ **gear** *n* MECH engranaje de tornillo sinfín *m*, engranaje helicoidal *m*, rueda de tornillo sinfín *f*, MECH ENG engranaje de tornillo sinfín *m*, engranaje helicoidal *m*, engranaje sinfín *m*, rueda dentada de tornillo sin fin *f*, WATER TRANSP mecanismo de tornillo sin fin *m*; ~ **gear final drive** *n* AUTO transmisión por tornillo sinfín *f*; ~ **gearing** *n* MECH ENG mando por tornillo sin fin *m*; ~ **rack** *n* MECH ENG cremallera sin fin *f*; ~ **roll** *n* PAPER rodillo con resaltes en espiral *m*; ~ **screw** *n* MECH ENG *wad-hook* tornillo sin fin *m*; ~ **wheel** *n* MECH ENG engranaje helicoidal *m*, rueda helicoidal *f*, rueda sin fin *f*

WORM *abbr* (*write-once read many times*) OPT escritura única lectura múltiple *f*

worn[1] *adj* MECH desgastado, usado, deteriorado, MECH ENG, TEXTIL deteriorado; ~**-out** *adj* TEXTIL desgastado, muy estropeado

worn[2]: ~ **bit** *n* PETR TECH barrena gastada *f*

worsted: ~ **spinning** *n* TEXTIL hilatura de estambre *f*

wort: ~ **cooler** *n* REFRIG enfriador de mosto *m*

wound[1]: ~ **onto the beam** *adj* TEXTIL enrollado sobre el plegador

wound[2] *n* SAFE herida *f*; ~ **rotor** *n* ELEC ENG rotor bobinado *m*; ~**-rotor induction motor** *n* ELEC ENG motor de inducción con rotor devanado *m*; ~ **rotor motor** *n* ELEC ENG motor con rotor bobinado *m*; ~ **stator** *n* ELEC ENG estator devanado *m*; ~ **stator motor** *n* ELEC ENG motor con estator devanado *m*

wove *n* PAPER vitela *f*; ~ **paper** *n* PAPER papel sin marca *m*

woven: ~ **carpet** *n* TEXTIL alfombra tejida *f*; ~ **fabric** *n* TEXTIL tejido de calada *m*

wow *n* ACOUST lloro *m*, TV fluctuación *f*; ~ **and flutter** *n* ACOUST, TV *acoustics* lloro y trémolo *m*

WOW *abbr* (*waiting on weather*) PETR TECH WOW (*espera por mal tiempo*)

WP *abbr* (*word processing, word processor*) COMP&DP WP (*procesado de texto, procesamiento de texto, tratamiento de texto, procesador de textos*)

WPC: ~ **system** *n* (*wired-programme control system*) TELECOM sistema de control de programas por conexionado *m*

wps *abbr* (*words per second*) PRINT palabras por segundo *f pl*

wrap[1]: ~ **around** *n* COMP&DP cambio automático de línea *m*, cambio de línea automático *m*, retorno automático de la última palabra *m*

wrap[2] *vt* MECH ENG *coil* enrollar, envolver, TEXTIL envolver

wraparound *n* PACK envoltura *f*, PRINT pliego inserto de cuatro páginas *m*; ~ **evaporator** *n* REFRIG evaporador envolvente *m*; ~ **label** *n* PACK etiqueta de la envoltura *f*; ~ **sleeving machine** *n* PACK envolvedora con manguitos *f*; ~ **tray** *n* PACK bandeja con embalaje envolvente *f*

wrapped: ~ **overlay** *n* PRINT superposición envuelta *f*; ~ **yarn** *n* TEXTIL hilo recubierto *m*

wrapper *n* TEXTIL bordadora *f*; ~ **fiber** *AmE*, ~ **fibre** *BrE n* TEXTIL fibra para recubrir *f*

wrapping *n* MECH ENG *coiling* envoltura *f*, PROD embalado *m*, empaquetado *m*, TEXTIL envoltura *f*; ~ **machine** *n* PACK máquina de envolver *f*; ~ **paper** *n* PACK, PAPER papel de embalaje *m*, papel de envolver *m*; ~ **tissue** *n* PAPER papel seda *m*

wrapround: ~ **plate** *n* PRINT plancha enrollable al cilindro *f*

Wratten: ~ **filter** *n* CINEMAT filtro Wratten *m*

wreck *n* WATER TRANSP *navigation* buque naufragado *m*, buque náufrago *m*, restos de naufragio *m pl* (*Esp*), restos de náufrago *m pl* (*Esp*), restos náufragos *m pl* (*AmL*)

wrecked: **be ~** *vi* WATER TRANSP perderse en un naufragio, sufrir un naufragio

wrecker *n* MILIT buque de salvamento *m*, TRANSP buque de salvamento *m*, grúa de auxilio *f*, tren de auxilio *m*

wrecking: ~ **crane** *n* RAIL grúa de auxilio *f*

wrench *n* (*cf spanner*) MECH llave de tuercas *f*, llave inglesa para tuercas *f*, MECH ENG llave de tuercas *f*, VEH llave de gancho *f*, llave de tetones *f*, llave de tuercas *f*; ~ **fault** *n* GEOL falla vertical de desgarre *f*

wring *vt* MAR POLL estrujar, TEXTIL escurrir

wringer *n* POLL exprimidor *m*, hidroextractor *m*, TEXTIL escurridora *f*; ~ **roll** *n* PAPER rodillo exprimidor *m*

wrinkle: ~ **paint** *n* COATINGS, COLOUR, P&R pintura rugosa *f*; ~**-resistant finish** *n* COATINGS acabado a prueba de arrugas *m*, acabado a prueba de rugosidades *m*, TEXTIL acabado a prueba de arrugas *m*

wrinkled: ~ **rim** *n* C&G borde arrugado *m*

wrinkling *n* CINEMAT reticulación *f*

wrist: ~ **pin** *n* *AmE* (*cf gudgeon pin BrE*) MECH muñequilla del pistón *f*, muñón del pistón *m*, perno de émbolo *m*, MECH ENG perno de la cruceta *m*, VEH *engine, piston* muñequilla del pistón *f*, pasador *m*; ~ **protector** *n* SAFE muñequera *f*

writable: ~ **disc** *BrE*, ~ **disk** *n* *AmE* OPT disco registrable *m*; ~ **optical disc** *BrE*, *n* **optical disk** *AmE n* OPT disco óptico registrable *m*; ~ **optical disc drive** *BrE*, ~ **optical disk drive** OPT unidad de disco óptico registrable *f AmE n*

write[1] *n* COMP&DP escritura *f*; ~ **error** *n* COMP&DP error de escritura *m*; ~ **head** *n* COMP&DP cabezal de escritura *m*; ~ **instruction** *n* COMP&DP instrucción de escritura *f*, instrucción de grabación *f*; ~**-once data disc** *BrE*, ~**-once data disk** *n* *AmE* OPT disco de datos para escribir una sola vez *m*; ~**-once disc** *BrE*, ~**-once disk** *n* *AmE* OPT disco de datos para escribir una sola vez *m*; ~**-once optical medium** *n* OPT medio óptico para escribir una sola vez *m*; ~**-once optical storage** *n* OPT almacenamiento óptico para escribir una sola vez *m*; ~**-once read many times** *n* (*WORM*) OPT escritura única lectura múltiple *f*; ~ **permit ring** *n* COMP&DP anillo de permiso de escritura *m*, anillo que permite escribir *m*; ~ **protect** *n* COMP&DP *floppy disk* protector contra escritura *m*; ~**-protect notch** *n* COMP&DP muesca de protección contra escritura *f*; ~ **protection** *n* COMP&DP *floppy disk* protección contra escritura *f*; ~ **pulse** *n* COMP&DP impulso de escritura *m*; ~ **ring** *n* COMP&DP anillo de escritura *m*; ~**-through capability** *n* ELECTRON capacidad de introducción de la información *f*; ~ **time** *n* COMP&DP tiempo de escritura *m*, ELEC ENG tiempo de grabación *m*

write[2] *vt* COMP&DP escribir

writing: ~ **gun** *n* ELECTRON *storage tubes* cañón de información *m*; ~ **speed** *n* ELECTRON *storage tubes* velocidad de grabación *f*; ~ **time** *n* ELECTRON tiempo de escritura *m*, tiempo de grabación *m*

written: ~ **state** *n* ELECTRON *storage tubes* fase escrita *f*, fase grabada *f*

wrong: ~ **color rendering** *AmE*, ~ **colour rendering** *n* *BrE* PRINT representación de color equivocada *f*; ~ **direction running** *n* RAIL circulación en sentido equivocado *f*; ~ **number** *n* TELECOM número equivocado *m*

wrought[1] *adj* CONST forjado, fraguado, MECH forjado, fraguado, labrado, MECH ENG forjado, fraguado, METALL forjado, fraguado, labrado, PROD forjado, fraguado

wrought[2]: ~**-copper alloy for plain bearings** *n* MECH ENG aleación de cobre forjado para cojinetes *f*; ~ **iron** *n* CONST, METALL hierro forjado *m*, hierro fraguado *m*; ~**-iron pipe** *n* CONST tubería de hierro forjado *f*

WRU *abbr* (*who-are-you*) TELECOM señal de identificación *f*

WS *abbr* (*weight strength*) MINE riqueza en peso *f*

W-type: ~ **engine** *n* AUTO motor tipo W *m*

wulfenite *n* COMP&DP wulfenita *f*, MINERAL plomo amarillo *m*, wulfenita *f*

wurtzite *n* MINERAL wurtzita *f*

WWW *abbr* (*World Wide Web*) COMP&DP WWW (*World Wide Web, telaraña mundial*)

wye: ~ **connection** *n* ELEC *transformer-reactor* conexión en Y *f*, conexión en estrella *f*

Wylie: ~ **relationship** *n* PETROL relación de Wylie *f*

WYSIWYG *abbr* (*what you see is what you get*) COMP&DP WYSIWYG (*lo que se ve es lo que se obtiene*)

X

X: **~ band** *n* ELECTRON banda X *f*; **~ plate** *n* TV placa de desviación horizontal (TRC) *f*

XALS *abbr* (*extended application layer structure*) TELECOM estructura en capas de aplicación extendida *f*

xanthate *n* CHEM xantato *m*

xanthein *n* CHEM xanteína *f*

xanthene *n* CHEM xanteno *m*

xanthic *adj* CHEM xántico

xanthine *n* CHEM dioxopurina *f*, xantina *f*

xanthocreatinine *n* CHEM xantocreatinina *f*

xanthogenic *adj* CHEM xantogénico

xanthone *n* CHEM xantona *f*

xanthophyl *n* AGRIC xantófila *f*

xanthophyllite *n* MINERAL xantofilita *f*

xanthoproteic *adj* CHEM xantoproteico

xanthosine *n* CHEM xantosina *f*

xanthous *adj* CHEM xantoso

xanthoxylin *n* CHEM xantoxilina *f*

xanthydrol *n* CHEM xantidrol *m*

xanthyl *n* CHEM xantilo *m*

x-arm: **~ machine** *n* C&G máquina de brazo X *f*

x-axis *n* CONST eje de abscisas *m*, eje de las x *m*, GEOM eje de abscisas *m*, eje de las x *m*, eje x *m*, MATH eje de abscisas *m*, eje de las x *m*, eje horizontal *m*, eje x *m*, PHYS eje x *m*, TV eje horizontal *m*

X-band: **~ magnetrons** *n* ELECTRON magnetrones de banda X *m pl*; **~ traveling wave tube** *AmE*, **~ travelling wave tube** *BrE n* ELECTRON tubo de ondas progresivas de banda X *m*; **~ TWT** *n* ELECTRON TOP de banda X *m*

x-coordinate *n* PHYS coordenada x *f*

x-deflection *n* TV desviación horizontal *f*

Xe *abbr* (*xenon*) CHEM Xe (*xenón*)

X-emitter *n* NUCL emisor de rayos x *m*

xenocryst *n* GEOL xenocristal *m*

xenolith *n* GEOL xenolito *m*

xenomorphic *adj* GEOL xenomórfico

xenon *n* (*Xe*) CHEM xenón *m* (*Xe*); **~ arc lamp** *n* CINEMAT lámpara de arco de xenón *f*; **~ arc projector** *n* CINEMAT proyector de arco de xenón *m*; **~ buildup** *n* NUCL *of sonic boom* acumulación de xenón *f*; **~ chloride** *n* ELECTRON cloruro xenónico *m*; **~ chloride laser** *n* ELECTRON láser de cloruro xenónico *m*; **~ effect** *n* NUCL efecto del xenón *m*; **~ poisoning effect** *n* NUCL efecto de envenenamiento por xenón *m*; **~ print** *n* CINEMAT copia de xenón *f*; **~ reactivity** *n* NUCL reactividad xenón *f*

xenotime *n* MINERAL espato de itrio *m*, xenotima *f*

xerography *n* COMP&DP, ELEC, ELECTRON, GAS xerografía *f*

xerophyte *n* AGRIC xerofita *f*

X-height *n* PRINT altura del núcleo de la letra *f*

xi: **~ hyperon** *n* PART PHYS, PHYS hiperón xi *m*; **~ particle** *n* PHYS partícula xi *f*

XLR: **~ connector** *n* CINEMAT, TV conector XLR *m*

XM: **~ synchronized shutter** *n* PHOTO obturador sincronizado XM *m*

XOR: **~ operation** *n* COMP&DP operación XOR *f*

X-radiograph *n* PHOTO *device* radiofotografía *f*

X-ray[1] *n* ELEC *radiation* rayo X *m*, rayo de Roentgen *m*, ELECTRON, METALL, PHYS, RAD PHYS rayo X *m*; **~ absorption** *n* RAD PHYS absorción de rayos X *f*; **~ absorption analysis** *n* RAD PHYS análisis de absorción de rayos X *m*; **~ absorption spectrum** *n* NUCL, PHYS espectro de absorción de rayos X *m*; **~ amplifier tube** *n* INSTR tubo amplificador de rayos X *m*; **~ analysis** *n* INSTR, RAD PHYS análisis por rayos X *m*; **~ apparatus** *n* INSTR aparato de rayos X *m*; **~ background radiation** *n* RAD PHYS radiación X de fondo *f*; **~ beam** *n* ELECTRON haz de rayos X *m*; **~ camera** *n* NUCL, RAD PHYS cámara de rayos X *f*; **~ cartridge** *n* INSTR rollo para rayos X *m*; **~ cassette** *n* INSTR casette de rayos X *f*; **~ cinematography** *n* CINEMAT cinematografía radiográfica *f*; **~ control room** *n* INSTR sala de control de rayos X *f*; **~ crystallography** *n* RAD PHYS cristalografía por rayos X *f*; **~ diagnostics** *n pl* INSTR diagnóstico por rayos X *m*; **~ diagram** *n* INSTR diagrama de rayos X *m*; **~ diffraction** *n* CRYSTALL, ELECTRON, METALL, SPACE, WAVE PHYS difracción de rayos X *f*; **~ diffraction analysis** *n* RAD PHYS análisis por difracción de rayos X *m*; **~ diffraction camera** *n* NUCL cámara de difracción de rayos X *f*; **~ diffraction pattern** *n* CRYSTALL diagrama de difracción de rayos X *m*, INSTR modelo de difracción de rayos X *m*; **~ diffractometer** *n* CRYSTALL, INSTR, RAD PHYS difractómetro de rayos X *m*; **~ dosimeter** *n* INSTR dosímetro de rayos X *m*; **~ escape peak** *n* RAD PHYS pico de fugas de rayos X *m*; **~ examination** *n* MECH inspección con rayos X *f*; **~ examination table** *n* INSTR mesa de examen para rayos X *f*; **~ film** *n* INSTR película de rayos X *f*; **~ flash** *n* INSTR disparo de rayos X *m*, flash de rayos X *m*; **~ fluorescence** *n* RAD PHYS fluorescencia X *f*, fluorescencia de rayos X *f*; **~ fluorescence analysis** *n* PHYS, RAD PHYS análisis por fluorescencia X *m*; **~ gate** *n* INSTR detector de rayos X *m*; **~ head** *n* INSTR cabezal de rayos X *m*; **~ image** *n* INSTR, LAB imagen de rayos X *f*; **~ image amplifier** *n* INSTR amplificador de imagen de rayos X *m*; **~ inspection** *n* NUCL, PHYS, RAD PHYS inspección por rayos X *f*, SPACE reconocimiento con rayos X *m*; **~ irradiation** *n* NUCL irradiación por rayos X *f*; **~ laser** *n* ELECTRON, NUCL, RAD PHYS láser de rayos X *m*; **~ lithography** *n* ELECTRON litografía por rayos X *f*; **~ luminescence** *n* NUCL luminiscencia por rayos X *f*; **~ mask** *n* ELECTRON máscara de rayos X *f*; **~ metallography** *n* NUCL metalografía por rayos X *f*, RAD PHYS radiometalografía *f*, renguenometalografía *f*; **~ microscope** *n* NUCL, RAD PHYS microscopio de rayos X *m*; **~ microstructure investigation** *n* NUCL investigación microestructural por rayos X *f*; **~ photoelectron spectroscopy** *n* PHYS espectroscopía de foto-electrones de rayos X *f*; **~ photoelectron spectroscopy XPS** *n* CHEM *analysis* espectroscopía fotoelectrónica de rayos X *f*; **~ photoelectron spectrum** *n* NUCL espectro fotoelectrónico de rayos X *m*; **~ photograph** *n* INSTR,

PHOTO fotografía por rayos X *f*, RAD PHYS fotografía por rayos X *f*, radiofotografía *f*, renguenografía *f*; ~ **photography** *n* INSTR, PHOTO, RAD PHYS fotografía por rayos X *f*; ~ **photon** *n* NUCL, PART PHYS fotón de rayos X *m*; ~ **protective glass** *n* C&G vidrio emplomado *m*, SAFE vidrio protector contra rayos X *m*; ~ **protective glasses** *n pl* INSTR, OPT, SAFE anteojos protectores de rayos X *m pl* (*AmL*), gafas protectoras de rayos X *f pl* (*Esp*); ~ **proximity printing** *n* ELECTRON radiografía por proximidad *f*; ~ **pulse** *n* ELECTRON impulso de rayos X *m*; ~ **quantum** *n* NUCL cuanto de radiaciones Roentgen *m*; ~ **radiation** *n* RAD PHYS radiación X *f*; ~ **reflection** *n* RAD PHYS reflexión de rayos X *f*; ~ **resist** *n* ELECTRON protección de rayos X *f*; ~ **scattering** *n* CRYSTALL dispersión de rayos X *f*; ~ **source** *n* NUCL *communications* fuente de rayos X *f*; ~ **spectrograph** *n* INSTR, RAD PHYS espectrógrafo de rayos X *m*; ~ **spectrography** *n* NUCL espectrografía por rayos X *f*; ~ **spectrometer** *n* RAD PHYS espectrómetro de rayos X *m*; ~ **spectrometry** *n* NUCL espectrometría de rayos X *f*; ~ **spectroscopy** *n* NUCL espectroscopía de rayos X *f*; ~ **spectrum** *n* RAD PHYS espectro de rayos X *m*; ~ **station** *n* PETROL estación de rayos X *f*; ~ **testing** *n* NUCL ensayo por rayos X *m*; ~ **topography** *n* CRYSTALL, METALL topografía de rayos X *f*; ~ **transformer** *n* INSTR transformador de rayos X *m*; ~ **tube** *n* CRYSTALL, ELECTRON, INSTR, RAD PHYS tubo de rayos X *m*; ~ **tube stand** *n* INSTR plataforma del tubo de rayos X *f*; ~ **unit** *n* INSTR unidad de rayos X *f*

X-ray[2] *vt* INSTR radiografiar

X-type: ~ **engine** *n* AUTO motor tipo X *m*

X-Y: ~ **alignment** *n* TV alineación X-Y *f*, alineación horizontal-vertical *f*; ~ **plotter** *n* SPACE trazador de curvas *m*, trazador gráfico X-Y *m*; ~ **recorder** *n* ELEC aparato de registro gráfico en coordenadas cartesianas *m*, registrador de XY *m*, registrador de coordenadas rectangulares *m*, registrador de curvas XY *m*, registrador gráfico en coordenadas cartesianas *m*, registrador para el trazado de curvas en coordenadas cartesianas *m*, SPACE registrador de dos coordenadas *m*

xylanthite *n* CHEM xilantita *f*

xylene *n* CHEM dimetilbenceno *m*, xileno *m*, DETERG, P&R, PETR TECH xileno *m*

xylenethiol *n* CHEM xilenetiol *m*

xylenol *n* CHEM dimetilfenol *m*, xilenol *m*

xylidine *n* CHEM dimetilanilina *f*, xilidina *f*

xylitol *n* CHEM xilitol *m*, FOOD xilita *f*

xylograph *n* PRINT xilografía *f*

xylol *n* CHEM xilol *m*

xylonite *n* P&R xilonita *f*

xylose *n* CHEM xilosa *f*

xylotile *n* MINERAL xilotila *f*

xylyl *n* CHEM xililo *m*

xylylene *n* CHEM xilileno *m*

Y

Y *abbr* (*yttrium*) CHEM, METALL Y (*itrio*)

yachting *n* WATER TRANSP salida programada *f*, travesía *f*

YAG[1] *abbr* (*yttrium aluminium garnet BrE, yttrium aluminum garnet AmE*) ELECTRON GAI (*granate alumínico de itrio*)

YAG[2]: ~ **laser** *n* ELECTRON láser GAI *m*

Yagi: ~ **aerial** *n* BrE (*cf Yagi antenna AmE*) SPACE, TELECOM antena Yagi *f*; ~ **antenna** *n* AmE (*cf Yagi aerial BrE*) SPACE *communications*, TELECOM antena Yagi *f*

yankee: ~ **cylinder** *n* PROD cilindro yanqui *m*; ~ **dryer** *n* PAPER secador Yankee *m*, cilindro satinador *m*

yapp: ~ **binding** *n* PRINT encuadernación con bordes cerrados *f*; ~ **edges** *n* PRINT bordes cerrados *m pl*

yard *n* CONST *storage-ground* patio *m*, zona de almacenaje *f*, METR yarda *f*; ~ **good knitter** *n* TEXTIL fabricante de género de punto por metros *m*; ~ **lumber** *n* PAPER madera secada al aire *f*

yardage *n* METR yardaje *m*, TEXTIL metraje *m*

yardarm *n* WATER TRANSP penol *m*

yardstick *n* TEXTIL metro de madera *m*

yarn[1] *n* C&G filamento *m*, P&R hilo *m*, TEXTIL hilado *m*, hilo *m*; ~ **applicator** *n* C&G aplicador de filamento *m*; ~ **carrier** *n* TEXTIL transportador de hilos *m*; ~ **carrier assembly** *n* TEXTIL montaje del transportador de hilos *m*; ~ **dyeing** *n* TEXTIL tintura en hilado *f*; ~ **end** *n* TEXTIL cabo del hilo *m*; ~ **feed control** *n* TEXTIL control de alimentación de hilo *m*; ~ **roll** *n* TEXTIL rodillo para el hilo *m*

yarn[2]: **--dye** *vt* TEXTIL teñir en hilado

yaw[1] *n* AIR TRANSP derrape *m*, guiñada *f*, FUELLESS guiñada *f*, PHYS desvío *m*, SPACE derrape *m*, guiñada *f*, oscilación *f*, ángulo de obliquidad *m*; ~ **adjustment** *n* FUELLESS ajuste de guiñadas *m*; ~ **angle** *n* SPACE, TRANSP ángulo de derrape *m*, ángulo de guiñada *m*; ~ **axis** *n* AIR TRANSP eje de derrape *m*, eje de guiñada *m*, SPACE eje de guiñada *m*, eje vertical *m*; ~ **control** *n* FUELLESS control de guiñadas *m*; ~ **rate** *n* SPACE velocidad de derrape *f*, velocidad de guiñada *f*

yaw[2] *vt* AIR TRANSP, SPACE guiñar

yaw[3] *vi* FUELLESS guiñar, dar guiñadas, SPACE dar bandazos, derrapar, guiñar, WATER TRANSP *navigation* guiñar

yawing *n* PHYS desvío *m*; ~ **moment** *n* AIR TRANSP, FUELLESS momento de guiñada *m*

yawl *n* WATER TRANSP yola *f*

y-axis *n* CONST eje de las y *m*, eje de ordenadas *m*, GEOM eje de las y *m*, eje de ordenadas *m*, eje y *m*, MATH eje de las y *m*, eje de ordenadas *m*, eje vertical *m*, eje y *m*, PHYS eje y *m*, TV eje vertical *m*

Yb *abbr* (*ytterbium*) CHEM, METALL Yb (*iterbio*)

y-branch *n* CONST bifurcación *f*, ramal *m*

y-cable *n* TV cable Y *m*

Y-connection *n* ELEC *transformer, reactor* conexión en estrella *f*, montaje en estrella *m*, ELEC ENG conexión en Y *f*, conexión en estrella *f*, PHYS conexión Y *f*

y-coordinate *n* PHYS coordenada y *f*

y-coupler *n* OPT, TELECOM acoplador en Y *m*

y-deflection *n* TV desviación vertical *f*

y-delta: ~ **starter** *n* ELEC arrancador y-delta *m*, interruptor de arranque y-delta *m*; ~ **starting switch** *n* ELEC interruptor de arranque y-delta *m*

year: **all ~ air conditioning** *n* CONST, HEAT, REFRIG acondicionamiento de aire para invierno y verano *m*

yearling *n* AGRIC animal de un año *m*

yeast: ~ **extract** *n* FOOD extracto de levadura *m*

yellow[1] *adj* COLOUR, PAPER, TEXTIL amarillo

yellow[2]: ~ **cake** *n* NUCL torta amarilla *f*; ~ **filter layer** *n* PRINT capa que actúa de filtro amarillo *f*; ~ **flag** *n* WATER TRANSP bandera amarilla *f*; ~ **straw pulp** *n* PAPER pulpa amarilla de paja *f*, pasta amarilla de paja *f*; ~ **strawboard** *n* PAPER papel de cartón *m*, papel de paja *m*; ~ **strawpaper** *n* PAPER papel de cartón *m*, papel de paja *m*

yellow[3] *vi* COLOUR, PAPER, TEXTIL amarillear

yellowing *n* COLOUR, PAPER, TEXTIL amarilleamiento *m*

yellowish *adj* COLOUR, PAPER, TEXTIL amarillento

yellowness *n* COLOUR, PAPER, TEXTIL amarilleamiento *m*

yeoman: ~ **of signals** *n* WATER TRANSP *crew* cabo de señales *m*, señalero primero *m*

yield[1] *n* AGRIC cosecha *f*, rendimiento *m* (*Esp*), rinde *m* (*AmL*), CHEM rendimiento *m*, COAL energía liberada *f*, producción *f*, rendimiento *m*, riqueza *f*, COMP&DP, ELECTRON, FUELLESS rendimiento *m*, GAS producción *f*, rendimiento *m*, MINE *pit* producción *f*, rendimiento *m*, riqueza *f*, NUCL, PETR TECH rendimiento *m*, PROD ganancia *f*, beneficio *m*, producción *f*, rendimiento *m*, TEXTIL rendimiento *m*; ~ **point** *n* METALL límite de elasticidad *m*, NUCL límite de elasticidad *m*, límite de fluencia *m*, límite de resistencia *m*, PHYS punto de producción *m*; ~ **strength** *n* NUCL *communications* límite de elasticidad *m*, P&R alargamiento en límite elástico *m*; ~ **stress** *n* METALL carga de deformación remanente *f*, límite de elasticidad *m*, PHYS fuerza de producción *f*

yield[2] *vt* TEXTIL rendir

yield[3] *vi* MECH ENG dar

yielding[1] *adj* TEXTIL productivo

yielding[2] *n* METALL, NUCL deformación permanente *f*

YIG[1] *abbr* (*yttrium iron garnet*) ELECTRON GFI (*granate férrico de itrio*)

YIG[2]: ~ **band-pass filter** *n* ELECTRON filtro de paso de banda de GFI *m*; ~ **filter** *n* ELECTRON filtro GFI *m*; ~ **tuned oscillator** *n* ELECTRON oscilador ajustado GFI *m*; ~ **tuned transistor oscillator** *n* ELECTRON oscilador de transistor ajustado GFI *m*; ~ **tuning** *n* ELECTRON ajuste GFI *m*

y-joint *n* ELEC *cable connection* unión en y *f*

Y-level *n* CONST *surveying* nivel de horquetas *m*

Y-network *n* PHYS red Y *f*

yoke *n* CHEM, ELEC yugo *m*, MECH ENG brida *f*, grapa *f*, horquilla *f*, yugo *m*, yunta *f*, *boreholes* garra de fijación *f*, *for lifting weights* balancín *m*, NUCL *spacecraft* yugo *m*, PHYS *magnets* culata *f*, VEH horquilla *f*; ~ **coil** *n* ELEC ENG *television* bobina de desviación *f*

you: who-are-~ *n* (*WRU*) TELECOM señal de identificación *f*

young: ~ **river** *n* HYDROL río joven *m*

Young: ~'s **law** *n* ACOUST ley de Young *f*; ~'s **modulus** *n* AIR TRANSP módulo de Young *m*, COAL coeficiente de Young *m*, módulo de Young *m*, CONST, MECH, MECH ENG módulo de Young *m*, METALL módulo de Young *m*, módulo de elasticidad longitudinal *m*, P&R módulo de Young *m*, PETR TECH coeficiente de elasticidad *m*, módulo de Young *m*, PETROL, PHYS módulo de Young *m*; ~'s **slits** *n pl* PHYS rendijas de Young *f pl*

Y-parameter *n* ELECTRON parámetro Y *m*

Y-piece *n* LAB acoplador en Y *m*

Y-signal *n* (*luminance signal*) TV señal Y *f*

ytterbia *n* C&G óxido de iterbio *m*, CHEM iterbia *f*, óxido de iterbio *m*

ytterbium *n* (*Yb*) CHEM, METALL iterbio *m* (*Yb*); ~ **oxide** *n* C&G, CHEM óxido de iterbio *m*

yttria *n* CHEM itria *f*, óxido de itrio *m*

yttrite *n* MINERAL itrita *f*

yttrium *n* (*Y*) CHEM, METALL itrio *m* (*Y*); ~ **aluminium garnet** *n* BrE (*YAG*) ELECTRON granate alumínico de itrio *m* (*GAI*); ~ **aluminum garnet** *AmE see yttrium aluminium garnet BrE*; ~ **iron garnet** *n* (*YIG*) ELECTRON granate férrico de itrio *m* (*GFI*); ~ **oxide** *n* C&G, CHEM óxido de iterbio *m*

yttrocerite *n* CHEM, MINERAL itrocerita *f*

yttrotantalite *n* MINERAL itrotantalita *f*

yttrotitanite *n* MINERAL itrotitanita *f*

Yukawa: ~ **potential** *n* PHYS potencial de Yukawa *m*; ~ **well** *n* NUCL pozo de Yukawa *m*

Z

Z¹ *abbr* (*atomic number*) CHEM, PART PHYS, PHYS Z (*número atómico*)

Z²: **~ boson** *n* PHYS bosón Z *m*; **~ coordinate** *n* PHYS coordenada z *f*; **~ particle** *n* PART PHYS, PHYS partícula Z *f*

zaratite *n* MINERAL zaratita *f*

z-axis *n* PHYS eje z *m*

z-direction: **~ tensile strength** *n* PROD resistencia a la tracción en la dirección z *f*

zeaxanthin *n* CHEM ceaxantina *f*

zebu *n* AGRIC cebú *m*

Zeeman: **~ component** *n* PHYS componente de Zeeman *f*; **~ effect** *n* NUCL, PHYS efecto Zeeman *m*

zein *n* CHEM, P&R ceína *f*, zeína *f*

Zeiss: **~ system transmitted-light microscope with polarizer** *n* INSTR microscopio de luz transmitida con polarizador Zeiss sistema *m*

Zener: **~ breakdown** *n* ELECTRON avería Zener *f*, perforación Zener *f*; **~ diode** *n* ELECTRON, PHYS, TELECOM diodo Zener *m*; **~ effect** *n* ELECTRON efecto Zener *m*; **~ voltage** *n* PHYS voltaje Zener *m*

Zener-Hollomon: **~ parameter** *n* METALL parámetro Zener-Hollomon *m*

zenith *n* FUELLESS, SPACE, WATER TRANSP *celestial navigation* cenit *m*, zenit *m*; **~ angle** *n* FUELLESS ángulo de cenit *m*; **~ carburetor** *n* *AmE*, **~ carburettor** *n* *BrE* AUTO, VEH carburador zenit *m*; **~ distance** *n* SPACE distancia cenital *f*; **~ point** *n* SPACE punto cenital *m*; **~ reduction** *n* SPACE reducción cenital *f*; **~ telescope** *n* INSTR, SPACE telescopio cenital *m*

zeolite *n* CHEM ceolita *f*, zeolita *f*, DETERG zeolita *f*, MINERAL ceolita *f*, zeolita *f*

zephyr *n* METEO céfiro *m*

zero¹ *n* GEN cero *m*; **~-address instruction** *n* COMP&DP instrucción de dirección cero *f*; **~ adjustment** *n* NUCL puesta a cero *f*; **~ anode** *n* ELEC ENG ánodo nulo *m*; **~ band** *n* NUCL *spacecraft* banda cero *f*; **~ beat** *n* TV oscilación cero *f*; **~ capacitance** *n* ELEC ENG capacitancia residual *f*; **~ carrier** *n* TV eliminación de la portadora *f*; **~ conductor** *n* ELEC ENG conductor nulo *m*; **~ creep** *n* METALL estiramiento nulo *m*; **~ crossing** *n* ELEC ENG cruce por cero *m*; **~-crossing switching** *n* ELEC ENG conmutación cruce cero *f*; **~ current** *n* ELEC ENG corriente residual *f*; **~ current turn off** *n* ELEC ENG desconexión de la corriente residual *f*; **~ degrees** *n* THERMO cero grados *m pl*; **~ displacement** *n* C&G desplazamiento cero *m*; **~ energy level** *n* NUCL nivel energético nulo *m*; **~-energy reactor** *n* NUCL reactor de potencia cero *m*; **~ frame** *n* CINEMAT cuadro cero *m*; **~ gravity** *n* (*zero-g*) GEOPHYS, PHYS, SPACE gravedad nula *f*; **~ impedance source** *n* ELEC ENG generador de impedancia nula *m*; **~ insertion force connector** *n* ELECTRON conector de fuerza de inserción nula *m*; **~ level** *n* CINEMAT nivel cero *m*; **~ lift angle** *n* AIR TRANSP, SPACE ángulo de elevación nula *m*; **~ loss circuit** *n* TELECOM circuito sin pérdidas *m*; **~ luminance** *n* TV luminancia cero *f*; **~-luminance**

plane *n* TV plano de luminancia cero *m*; **~ neutron-absorption cross-section** *n* NUCL sección eficaz de absorción neutrónica cero *f*; **~-pitch propeller** *n* MAR POLL hélice con paso nulo *f*; **~ point energy** *n* PHYS energía de punto cero *f*, RAD PHYS energía del punto cero *f*; **~ point fluctuation** *n* RAD PHYS fluctuación del punto cero *f*; **~ potential** *n* ELEC *voltage* potencial cero *m*, potencial nulo *m*; **~ power factor test** *n* ELEC prueba en factor de potencia cero *f*, prueba en factor de potencia nulo *f*; **~-power reactor** *n* NUCL reactor de potencia cero *m*; **~ power test** *n* NUCL prueba a cero potencia *f*; **~ pressure gradient** *n* FLUID gradiente nulo de presión *m*; **~ sequence impedance** *n* ELEC *polyphase winding* impedancia homopolar *f*; **~ setting** *n* NUCL *spacecraft* ajuste cero *m*, puesta a cero *f*; **~ span tensile strength** *n* PROD resistencia a la tracción de vano cero *f*; **~ suppression** *n* COMP&DP supresión de ceros *f*; **~ twist** *n* TEXTIL torsión cero *f*; **~ volt adjustment** *n* TV regulación a cero voltios *f*; **~ voltage** *n* ELEC ENG voltaje cero *m*; **~ voltage switching** *n* ELEC ENG conmutación de voltaje nulo *f*

zero² *vt* CHEM ajustar a cero, llevar a cero, poner a cero, CINEMAT, TV poner a cero; **~ fill** *vt* COMP&DP rellenar con ceros

zero-g *n* (*zero gravity*) GEOPHYS, PHYS, SPACE gravedad nula *f*

zeroize *vt* COMP&DP poner a cero

zeroth: **~ law** *n* PHYS, THERMO ley cero *f*, principio cero *m*

zerovalent *adj* CHEM cerovalente

zeunerite *n* MINERAL zeunerita *f*

z-fold *n* PRINT pliegue en z *m*

z-height *n* PRINT altura media *f*

zheta: **~-meson** *n* PART PHYS mesón zeta *m*

Ziegler: **~ alcohol** *n* DETERG alcohol de Ziegler *m*; **~ catalyst** *n* CHEM catalizador de Ziegler *m*

zietrisikite *n* CHEM zietrisikita *f*

zigzag: **~ connection** *n* ELEC *transformer, reactor* conexión en zigzag *f*; **~ dislocation** *n* METALL dislocación en zigzag *f*; **~ fold** *n* GEOL pliegue cabrío *m*, PRINT plegado en acordeón *m*, plegado en zigzag *m*; **~ rule** *n* *AmE* (*cf jointed rule BrE*) CONST metro plegable *m*, regla plegable *f*

zinc¹: **~-coated** *adj* COATINGS bañado de cinc, electrocinado, recubierto de cinc

zinc² *n* (*Zn*) GEN cinc *m* (*Zn*), zinc *m* (*Zn*); **~-air storage battery** *n* TRANSP batería de acumuladores de aire y zinc *f*; **~ battery** *n* ELEC ENG batería de zinc *f*; **~ blende** *n* CHEM, MINERAL blenda *f*, esfalerita *f*; **~-carbon cell** *n* ELEC ENG elemento de carbón-zinc *m*; **~ chloride** *n* ELEC ENG cloruro de zinc *m*; **~ chloride cell** *n* ELEC ENG elemento de cloruro de zinc *m*; **~ chromate pigment** *n* COLOUR pigmento de cromato de zinc *m*; **~ coating** *n* COATINGS baño de zinc *m*, cincado *m*, revestimiento de zinc *m*, P&R baño de zinc *m*, cincado *m*, galvanizado *m*, zincado *m*; **~ condensation** *n* COAL condensación de zinc *f*; **~ dust pigment** *n* COLOUR pigmento de polvo de zinc *m*; **~-manganese dioxide cell** *n* ELEC ENG célula de dióxido de manganeso-zinc *f*; **~ oxide** *n* CHEM, ELEC ENG óxido de zinc *m*; **~ oxide varistor** *n* ELEC ENG varistor de óxido de zinc *m*; **~ plate** *n* PRINT plancha de zinc *f*; **~-silver cell** *n* ELEC ENG célula de plata y zinc *f*; **~-silver oxide cell** *n* ELEC ENG célula de óxido de plata y zinc *f*; **~ vapor** *AmE*, **~ vapour** *BrE n* COAL vapor de zinc *m*; **~ wire** *n* ELEC ENG hilo de zinc *m*

zinc³ *vt* CHEM, COATINGS, CONST, ELEC, ELEC ENG, PROD galvanizar

zincate *n* CHEM cincato *m*

zincic *adj* CHEM cíncico, de cinc

zincite *n* MINERAL cincita *f*, zincita *f*

zinckenite *n* MINERAL zinkenita *f*

zincking *n* CHEM cincado *m*, galvanización *f*, COATINGS, ELEC, ELEC ENG, PROD galvanización *f*

zincky *adj* CHEM cincoso

zincoid *adj* CHEM cincoide

zincon *n* CHEM cincona *f*

zincosite *n* MINERAL cincosita *f*

zincous *adj* CHEM cincoso, zincoso

zincum *n* CHEM cincum *m*

zingiberene *n* CHEM zingibereno *m*

zinkosite *n* MINERAL cincosita *f*

zinnwaldite *n* MINERAL zinnwaldita *f*

zip¹ *n* *BrE* TEXTIL cremallera *f*; **~ fastener** *n* TEXTIL cierre de cremallera *m*; **~ lock bag** *n* PACK bolsa con cierre de cremallera *f*; **~ pan** *n* CINEMAT panorámica rápida *f*

zip² *vt* TEXTIL cerrar con cremallera; **~ in** *vt* TEXTIL unir con la cremallera

Zip: **~-a-tone** *n* PRINT trama impresa transparente adhesiva *f*

zipper *AmE see zip BrE*

zircaloy *n* NUCL zircaloy *m*; **~ cladding** *n* NUCL vaina de zircaloy *f*

zircon *n* C&G zircón *m*, MINERAL circón *m*; **~ refractory** *n* C&G refractario de zircón *m*

zirconate *n* CHEM circonato *m*, zirconato *m*

zirconia *n* C&G circona *f*, CHEM circonia *f*, óxido de circonio *m*; **~ refractory** *n* C&G refractario de circona *m*

zirconic *adj* CHEM circónico, zircónico

zirconifluoride *n* CHEM circonifluoruro *m*, zirconifluoruro *m*

zirconium *n* (*Zr*) CHEM, METALL circonio *m* (*Zr*); **~ base alloy** *n* METALL, NUCL aleación de circonio *f*

zirconyl *n* CHEM circonilo *m*, zirconilo *m*

Zn *abbr* (*zinc*) GEN Zn (*cinc, zinc*)

zoisite *n* MINERAL zoisita *f*

zonal: **~ harmonic** *n* SPACE armónico zonal *m*; **~ soil** *n* COAL terreno zonal *m*

zonation *n* GEOL *broadcasting* zonación *f*

zone *n* GEN zona *f*; **~ air conditioning unit** *n* REFRIG acondicionador de zona *m*; **~ axis** *n* CRYSTALL eje de zona *m*, eje zonal *m*; **~ formation** *n* METALL formación de zonas *f*; **~ melting** *n* METALL, NUCL fusión

por zonas *f*; **~ of petroleum accumulation** *n* PETR TECH zona de acumulación de petróleo *f*; **~ refining** *n* CRYSTALL refinamiento por zonas *m*, METALL purificación por fusión de zonas *f*, purificación por zonas *f*; **~ of saturation** *n* HYDROL zona de saturación *f*; **~ test** *n* PROD prueba de zona *f*; **~ time** *n* WATER TRANSP hora de huso *f*, hora de huso horario *f*; **~-toughened glass** *n* C&G vidrio endurecido por zonas *m*; **~ toughening** *n* C&G endurecido por zonas *m*

zoned: **~ fuel-loading** *n* NUCL carga de combustible por zonas *f*; **~ lens** *n* INSTR lente radioeléctrica escalonada *f*

zoning *n* GEOL *of ribbed bulkheads* zonificación *f*, PRINT división de impreso por zonas *f*; **~ plan** *n* CONST, WATER plano de restricción de nuevas construcciones *m*

zoogenic: **~ rock** *n* PETR TECH roca zoogénica *f*

zoom¹ *n* CINEMAT objetivo zoom *m*, COMP&DP ampliación *f*, aumento *m*, zoom *m*, INSTR objetivo de foco variable *m*, OPT objetivo zoom *m*, PHOTO objetivo de foco variable *m*, objetivo zoom *m*; **~-in** *n* COMP&DP acercamiento *m*, ampliación *f*, ampliación por acercamiento de la lente *f*, zoom *m*; **~ lens** *n* CINEMAT objetivo zoom *m*, INSTR objetivo de distancia focal regulable *m*, objetivo de foco variable *m*, zoom *m*, OPT objetivo zoom *m*, PHOTO objetivo de foco variable *m*, objetivo zoom *m*; **~ lever** *n* CINEMAT varilla de zoom *f*, TV manecilla del zoom *f*, palanca del zoom *f*, perilla del zoom *f*; **~-out** *n* COMP&DP alejamiento *m*, reducción *f*, reducción por alejamiento de la lente *f*; **~ range** *n* CINEMAT gama de zoom *f*, zoom *m*; **~ ring** *n* CINEMAT, PHOTO anillo de zoom *m*, aro de zoom *m*, TV anillo de zoom *m*; **~ stereomicroscope** *n* INSTR estereomicroscopio con zoom *m*, estereomicroscopio de distancia focal regulable *m*; **~ viewfinder** *n* CINEMAT visor de zoom *m*

zoom² *vi* CINEMAT, COMP&DP, INSTR, PHOTO, TV utilizar el zoom; **~ in** *vi* COMP&DP acercar, amplificar

zooming *n* COMP&DP acercamiento-alejamiento *m*, ampliación-reducción *f*, zoom *m*

zoosterol *n* CHEM zoosterol *m*

zootaxic *adj* CHEM zootáxico

zootaxy *n* CHEM zootaxia *f*

zooxanthine *n* CHEM zooxantina *f*

zorgite *n* MINERAL zorgita *f*

Z-parameter *n* ELECTRON parámetro Z *m*

Zr *abbr* (*zirconium*) CHEM, METALL Zr (*circonio*)

zunyite *n* MINERAL zuñita *f*

Zwicker: **~'s phon** *n* ACOUST, PHYS fonio Zwicker *m*

zygote *n* AGRIC cigoto *m*

zymase *n* CHEM cimasa *f*, zimasa *f*

zymic *adj* CHEM zímico

zymin *n* CHEM zimina *f*

zymohydrolysis *n* CHEM cimohidrólisis *f*

Tablas de conversión/
Conversion tables

1   Longitud / Length

		metro *metre*	pulgada *inch*	*pie *foot*	*yarda *yard*	*rod *rod*	*milla *mile*
1 metro *metre*	=	1	39,37	3,281	1,093	0,1988	$6,214 \times 10^{-4}$
1 pulgada *inch*	=	$2,54 \times 10^{-2}$	1	0,083	0,02778	$5,050 \times 10^{-3}$	$1,578 \times 10^{-5}$
1 pie *foot*	=	0,3048	12	1	0,3333	0,0606	$1,894 \times 10^{-4}$
1 yarda *yard*	=	0,9144	36	3	1	0,1818	$5,682 \times 10^{-4}$
1 rod *rod*	=	5,029	198	16,5	5,5	1	$3,125 \times 10^{-3}$
1 milla *mile*	=	1609	63360	5280	1760	320	1

1 yarda inglesa = 0,914 398 41 metros / 1 imperial standard yard = 0.914 398 41 metre
1 yarda científica internacional = 0,9144 metros (exactamente) / 1 yard (scientific) = 0.9144 metre (exact)
1 yarda americana = 0,914 401 83 metros / 1 US yard = 0.914 401 83 metre
1 milla marina inglesa = 6080 pies = 1853,18 metros / 1 English nautical mile = 6080 ft = 1853.18 metres
1 milla marina internacional = 1852 metros = 6076,12 pies / 1 international nautical mile = 1852 metres = 6076.12 ft

* unidad sin valor oficial en España / not recognized officially in Spain

2 Superficie / Area

		metro^2 *sq. metre*	pulgada^2 *sq. inch*	*pie^2 *sq. foot*	*yarda^2 *sq. yard*	*acre *acre*	*milla^2 *sq. mile*
1 metro^2 *sq. metre*	=	1	1550	10,76	1,196	$2,471 \times 10^{-4}$	$3,861 \times 10^{7}$
1 pulgada^2 *sq. inch*	=	$6,452 \times 10^{-4}$	1	$6,944 \times 10^{3}$	$7,716 \times 10^{-4}$	$1,594 \times 10^{-7}$	$2,491 \times 10^{-10}$
1 pie^2 *sq. foot*	=	0,0929	144	1	0,1111	$2,296 \times 10^{-5}$	$3,587 \times 10^{-8}$
1 yarda^2 *sq. yard*	=	0,8361	1296	9	1	$2,066 \times 10^{-4}$	$3,228 \times 10^{-7}$
1 acre *acre*	=	$4,047 \times 10^{3}$	$6,273 \times 10^{6}$	$4,355 \times 10^{4}$	4840	1	$1,563 \times 10^{-3}$
1 milla^2 *sq. mile*	=	$259,0 \times 10^{4}$	$4,015 \times 10^{9}$	$2,788 \times 10^{7}$	$3,098 \times 10^{6}$	640	1

1 rea = 100 metros cuadrados = 0,01 hectáreas / 1 are = 100 sq. metres = 0.01 hectare
1 milipulgada circular = $5,067 \times 10^{-10}$ metros cuadrados / 1 circular mil = 5.067×10^{-10} sq. metre
$\qquad$ = $7,854 \times 10^{-7}$ pulgadas cuadradas / $\qquad$ = 7.854×10^{-7} sq.inch
1 acre = 0,4047 hectáreas / 1 acre (statute) = 0.4047 hectare

* unidad sin valor oficial en España / not recognized officially in Spain

3 Volumen / Volume

		metro cúbico *cubic metre*	*pulgada cúbica *cubic inch*	*pie cúbico *cubic foot*	*galón imperial *UK gallon*	*galón americano *US gallon*
1 metro cúbico *cubic metre*	=	1	$6,102 \times 10^{4}$	35,31	220,0	264,2
1 pulgada cúbica *cubic inch*	=	$1,639 \times 10^{-5}$	1	$5,787 \times 10^{-4}$	$3,605 \times 10^{-3}$	$4,329 \times 10^{-3}$
1 pie cúbico *cubic foot*	=	$2,832 \times 10^{-2}$	1728	1	6,229	7,480
1 galón imperial† *UK gallon*	=	$4,546 \times 10^{-3}$	277,4	0,1605	1	1,201
1 galón americano‡ *US gallon*	=	$3,785 \times 10^{-3}$	231,0	0,1337	0,8327	1

† volumen de 10 libras de agua a 62°F / volume of 10lb of water at 62°F
‡ volumen de 8,328 28 libras de agua a 60°F / volume of 8.328 28 lb of water at 60°F
1 metro cúbico = 999,972 litros / 1 cubic metre = 999.972 litres
1 acre-pie = 271 328 galones imperiales = 1233 metros cúbicos / 1 acre foot = 271 328 UK gallons = 1233 cubic metres

* unidad sin valor oficial en España / not recognized officially in Spain

hasta 1976 el litro era igual a 1000,028cm^3 (volumen de 1kg de agua a máxima densidad) pero ha sido objeto de nueva definición y ahora vale 1.000cm^3 exactamente

until 1976 the litre was equal to 1000.028cm^3 (the volume of 1kg of water at maximum density) but then it was revalued to be 1000cm^3 exactly

4   Ángulo / Angle

		grado *degree*	minuto *minute*	segundo *second*	radián *radian*	revolución *revolution*
1 grado *degree*	=	1	60	3600	$1,745 \times 10^{-2}$	$2,778 \times 10^{-3}$
1 minuto *minute*	=	$1,677 \times 10^{-2}$	1	60	$2,909 \times 10^{-4}$	$4,630 \times 10^{-5}$
1 segundo *second*	=	$2,778 \times 10^{-4}$	$1,667 \times 10^{-2}$	1	$4,848 \times 10^{-6}$	$7,716 \times 10^{-7}$
1 radián *radian*	=	57,30	3438	$2,063 \times 10^{5}$	1	0,1592
1 revolución *revolution*	=	360	$2,16 \times 10^{4}$	$1,296 \times 10^{6}$	6,283	1

1 milésima angular (artillería) = 10^{-3} radianes / 1 mil = 10^{-3} radian

5   Tiempo / Time

		año *year*	día solar medio *solar day*	hora *hour*	minuto *minute*	segundo *second*
1 año *year*	=	1	365,24*	$8,766 \times 10^{3}$	$5,259 \times 10^{5}$	$3,156 \times 10^{7}$
1 día solar medio *solar day*	=	$2,738 \times 10^{-3}$	1	24	1440	$8,640 \times 10^{4}$
1 hora *hour*	=	$1,141 \times 10^{-4}$	$4,167 \times 10^{-2}$	1	60	3600
1 minuto *minute*	=	$1,901 \times 10^{-6}$	$6,944 \times 10^{-4}$	$1,667 \times 10^{-2}$	1	60
1 segundo *second*	=	$3,169 \times 10^{-8}$	$1,157 \times 10^{-5}$	$2,778 \times 10^{-4}$	$1,667 \times 10^{-2}$	1

1 año = 366,24 días sidéreos / 1 year = 366.24 sidereal days
1 día sidéreo = 86 164,090 6 segundos / 1 sidereal day = 86 164.090 6 seconds

* cifra exacta = 365,242 192 64 en el año 2000 de nuestra era / exact figure = 365.242 192 64 in A.D. 2000

6 Masa / Mass

		kilogramo *kilogram*	libra *pound*	*slug *slug*	*tonelada larga *UK ton*	*tonelada corta *US ton*	u
1 kilogramo *kilogram*	=	1	2,205	$6,852 \times 10^{-2}$	$9,842 \times 10^{-4}$	$11,02 \times 10^{-4}$	$6,024 \times 10^{26}$
1 libra *pound*	=	0,4536	1	$3,108 \times 10^{-2}$	$4,464 \times 10^{-4}$	$5,000 \times 10^{-4}$	$2,732 \times 10^{26}$
1 slug *slug*	=	14,59	32,17	1	$1,436 \times 10^{-2}$	$1,609 \times 10^{-2}$	$8,789 \times 10^{27}$
1 tonelada larga *UK ton*	=	1016	2240	69,62	1	1,12	$6,121 \times 10^{29}$
1 tonelada corta *US ton*	=	907,2	2000	62,16	0,8929	1	$5,465 \times 10^{29}$
1 u	=	$1,660 \times 10^{-27}$	$3,660 \times 10^{-27}$	$1,137 \times 10^{-28}$	$1,634 \times 10^{-30}$	$1,829 \times 10^{-30}$	1

1 libra imperial patrón = 0,453 592 338 kilogramos / 1 imperial standard pound = 0.453 592 338 kilogram
1 libra americana = 0,453 592 427 7 kilogramos / 1 US pound = 0.453 592 427 7 kilogram
1 libra internacional = 0,453 592 37 kilogramos / 1 international pound = 0.453 592 37 kilogram
1 tonelada = 10^3 kilogramos / 1 tonne = 10^3 kilograms
1 libra troy = 0,373 242 kilogramos / 1 troy pound = 0.373 242 kilogram

* unidad sin valor oficial en España / not recognized officially in Spain

7 Fuerza / Force

		dina *dyne*	neutonio *newton*	*libra fuerza *pound force*	*poundal *poundal*	gramo fuerza *gram force*
1 dina *dyne*	=	1	10^{-5}	$2,248 \times 10^{-6}$	$7,233 \times 10^{-5}$	$1,020 \times 10^{-3}$
1 neutonio *newton*	=	10^5	1	0,2248	7,233	102,0
1 libra fuerza *pound force*	=	$4,448 \times 10^5$	4,448	1	32,17	453,6
1 poundal *poundal*	=	$1,383 \times 10^4$	0,1383	$3,108 \times 10^{-2}$	1	14,10
1 gramo fuerza *gram force*	=	980,7	$980,7 \times 10^{-5}$	$2,205 \times 10^{-3}$	$7,093 \times 10^{-2}$	1

* unidad sin valor oficial en España / not recognized officially in Spain

8   Potencia / Power

		*Ucb por hora	*libra-pie por segundo	kilogramo-metro por segundo	caloría por segundo	caballo de vapor	vatio
		Btu per hr	ft lb s^{-1}	kg metre s^{-1}	cal s^{-1}	HP	watt
1 Ucb por hora Btu per hour	=	1	0,2161	$2,987 \times 10^{-2}$	$6,999 \times 10^{-2}$	$3,929 \times 10^{-4}$	0,2931
1 libra-pie por segundo ft lb per second	=	4,628	1	0,1383	0,3239	$1,818 \times 10^{-3}$	1,356
1 kilogramo-metro por segundo kg metre per second	=	33,47	7,233	1	2,343	$1,315 \times 10^{-2}$	9,807
1 caloría por segundo cal per second	=	14,29	3,087	$4,268 \times 10^{-1}$	1	$5,613 \times 10^{-3}$	4,187
1 caballo de vapor HP	=	2545	550	76,04	178,2	1	745,7
1 vatio watt	=	3,413	0,7376	0,1020	0,2388	$1,341 \times 10^{-3}$	1

1 vatio internacional = 1,000 19 vatios absolutos / 1 international watt = 1.000 19 absolute watt

* unidad sin valor oficial en España / not recognized officially in Spain

9 Energía, trabajo, calor / Energy, work, heat

		*Ucb Btu	julio $joule$	*libra-pie $ft\ lb$	cm^{-1} cm^{-1}	caloría cal	kilovatio-hora $kW\ h$	electrón-voltio $electron\ volt$	kilogramo kg	u†
1 Ucb Btu	=	1	$1{,}055 \times 10^{3}$	$778{,}2$	$5{,}312 \times 10^{25}$	252	$2{,}930 \times 10^{-4}$	$6{,}585 \times 10^{21}$	$1{,}174 \times 10^{-14}$	$7{,}074 \times 10^{12}$
1 julio $joule$	=	$9{,}481 \times 10^{-4}$	1	$7{,}376 \times 10^{-1}$	$5{,}035 \times 10^{22}$	$2{,}389 \times 10^{-1}$	$2{,}778 \times 10^{-7}$	$6{,}242 \times 10^{18}$	$1{,}113 \times 10^{-17}$	$6{,}705 \times 10^{9}$
1 libra-pie $ft\ lb$	=	$1{,}285 \times 10^{-3}$	$1{,}356$	1	$6{,}828 \times 10^{22}$	$3{,}239 \times 10^{-1}$	$3{,}766 \times 10^{-7}$	$8{,}464 \times 10^{18}$	$1{,}507 \times 10^{-17}$	$9{,}092 \times 10^{9}$
1 cm^{-1} cm^{-1}	=	$1{,}883 \times 10^{-26}$	$1{,}986 \times 10^{-23}$	$1{,}465 \times 10^{-23}$	1	$4{,}745 \times 10^{-24}$	$5{,}517 \times 10^{-30}$	$1{,}240 \times 10^{-4}$	$2{,}210 \times 10^{-40}$	$1{,}332 \times 10^{-13}$
1 caloría 15°C $cal\ 15°C$	=	$3{,}968 \times 10^{-3}$	$4{,}187$	$3{,}088$	$2{,}108 \times 10^{23}$	1	$1{,}163 \times 10^{-6}$	$2{,}613 \times 10^{19}$	$4{,}659 \times 10^{-17}$	$2{,}807 \times 10^{10}$
1 kilovatio-hora $kW\ h$	=	3412	$3{,}600 \times 10^{6}$	$2{,}655 \times 10^{6}$	$1{,}813 \times 10^{29}$	$8{,}598 \times 10^{5}$	1	$2{,}247 \times 10^{25}$	$4{,}007 \times 10^{-11}$	$2{,}414 \times 10^{16}$
1 electrón-voltio $electron\ volt$	=	$1{,}519 \times 10^{-22}$	$1{,}602 \times 10^{-19}$	$1{,}182 \times 10^{-19}$	$8{,}066 \times 10^{3}$	$3{,}827 \times 10^{-20}$	$4{,}450 \times 10^{-26}$	1	$1{,}783 \times 10^{-36}$	$1{,}074 \times 10^{-9}$
1 kilogramo kg	=	$8{,}521 \times 10^{13}$	$8{,}987 \times 10^{16}$	$6{,}629 \times 10^{16}$	$4{,}525 \times 10^{39}$	$2{,}147 \times 10^{16}$	$2{,}497 \times 10^{10}$	$5{,}610 \times 10^{35}$	1	$6{,}025 \times 10^{2}$
1 u	=	$1{,}415 \times 10^{-13}$	$1{,}492 \times 10^{-10}$	$1{,}100 \times 10^{-10}$	$7{,}513 \times 10^{12}$	$3{,}564 \times 10^{-11}$	$4{,}145 \times 10^{-17}$	$9{,}31 \times 10^{8}$	$1{,}660 \times 10^{-27}$	1

† partiendo de la relación energía-masa $E = mc^2$ / from the mass-energy relationship $E = mc^2$

* unidad sin valor oficial en España / not recognized officially in Spain

10 Presión / Pressure

	atmósfera patrón _standard atmosphere_	kg fuerza cm⁻² _kg force cm⁻²_	dina cm⁻² _dyne cm⁻²_	pascal _pascal_	*libra fuerza pulgada⁻² _pound force in⁻²_	*libra fuerza pie⁻² _pound force ft⁻²_	milibar _millibar_	torr _torr_	pulgada barométrica de mercurio _barometric in. Hg_
1 atmósfera patrón _standard atmosphere_	= 1	$1,033$	$1,013 \times 10^6$	$1,013 \times 10^5$	$14,70$	2116	1013	760	$29,92$
1 kg fuerza cm⁻² _kg force cm⁻²_	= $0,9678$	1	$9,804 \times 10^5$	$9,804 \times 10^4$	$14,22$	2048	$980,7$	$735,6$	$28,96$
1 dina cm⁻² _dyne cm⁻²_	= $9,869 \times 10^{-7}$	$10,20 \times 10^{-7}$	1	$0,1$	$14,50 \times 10^{-6}$	$2,089 \times 10^{-3}$	10^{-3}	$750,1 \times 10^{-6}$	$29,53 \times 10^{-6}$
1 pascal _pascal_	= $9,869 \times 10^{-6}$	$10,20 \times 10^{-6}$	10	1	$14,50 \times 10^{-5}$	$2,089 \times 10^{-2}$	10^{-2}	$750,1 \times 10^{-5}$	$29,53 \times 10^{-5}$
1 libra fuerza pulgada⁻² _pound force in.⁻²_	= $6,805 \times 10^{-2}$	$7,031 \times 10^{-2}$	$6,895 \times 10^4$	$6,895 \times 10^3$	1	144	$68,95$	$51,71$	$2,036$
1 libra fuerza pie⁻² _pound force ft⁻²_	= $4,725 \times 10^{-4}$	$4,882 \times 10^{-4}$	$478,8$	$47,88$	$6,944 \times 10^{-3}$	1	$47,88 \times 10^{-2}$	$0,3591$	$14,14 \times 10^{-3}$
1 milibar _millibar_	= $0,9869 \times 10^{-3}$	$1,020 \times 10^{-3}$	10^3	10^2	$14,50 \times 10^{-3}$	$2,089$	1	$0,7500$	$29,53 \times 10^{-3}$
1 torr _torr_	= $1,316 \times 10^{-3}$	$1,360 \times 10^{-3}$	$1,333 \times 10^2$	$1,333 \times 10^3$	$1,934 \times 10^{-2}$	$2,784$	$1,333$	1	$3,937 \times 10^{-2}$
1 pulgada barométrica de mercurio _barometric in Hg_	= $3,342 \times 10^{-2}$	$3,453 \times 10^{-2}$	$3,386 \times 10^4$	$3,386 \times 10^3$	$4,912 \times 10^{-1}$	$70,73$	$33,87$	$25,40$	1

1 torr = 1 milímetro de mercurio de una densidad de 13,5951g cm⁻³ a 0°C y para una aceleración de la gravedad de 980,665 cm/s⁻²
1 torr = 1 barometric mmHg density 13.5951 g cm⁻³ at 0°C and acceleration due to gravity 980.665 cm/s⁻²
1 dyne cm⁻² = 1 barad
* unidad sin valor oficial en España / not recognized officially in Spain

11 Flujo de inducción magnética / Magnetic flux

		maxvelio *maxwell*	kilolino *kiloline*	weberio *weber*
1 maxvelio (1 lino) *maxwell (1 line)*	=	1	10^{-3}	10^{-8}
1 kilolino *kiloline*	=	10^3	1	10^{-5}
1 weberio *weber*	=	10^8	10^5	1

12 Inducción magnética / Magnetic flux density

		gausio *gauss*	weberio m^{-2} (tesla) *weber m^{-2} (tesla)*	gamma *gamma*	maxvelio cm^{-2} *maxwell cm^{-2}*
1 gausio (lino cm^{-2}) *gauss (line cm^{-2})*	=	1	10^{-4}	10^5	1
1 weberio m^{-2} (tesla) *weber m^{-2} (tesla)*	=	10^4	1	10^9	10^4
1 gamma *gamma*	=	10^{-5}	10^{-9}	1	10^{-5}
1 maxvelio cm^{-2} *maxwell cm^{-2}*	=	1	10^{-4}	10^5	1

13 Fuerza magnetomotriz / Magnetomotive force

		*abamperio-vuelta *abamp turn*	amperio-vuelta *amp turn*	gilbertio *gilbert*
1 abamperio-vuelta *abampere turn*	=	1	10	12,57
1 amperio-vuelta *ampere turn*	=	10^{-1}	1	1,257
1 gilbertio *gilbert*	=	$7,958 \times 10^{-2}$	0,7958	1

* unidad sin valor oficial en España / not recognized officially in Spain

14   Intensidad de campo magnético / Magnetic field strength

		amperio-vuelta cm^{-1} *amp turn cm^{-1}*	amperio-vuelta m^{-1} *amp turn m^{-1}*	oerstedio *oersted*
1 amperio-vuelta cm^{-1} *amp turn cm^{-1}*	=	1	10^2	1,257
1 amperio-vuelta m^{-1} *amp turn m^{-1}*	=	10^{-2}	1	$1,257 \times 10^{-2}$
1 oerstedio *oersted*	=	0,7958	79,58	1

15   Iluminación / Illumination

		lux *lux*	fotio *phot*	*bujía-pie *foot-candle*
1 lux (1m m^{-2}) *lux (1m m^{-2})*	=	1	10^{-4}	$9,29 \times 10^{-2}$
1 fotio (1m cm^{-2}) *phot (1m cm^{-2})*	=	10^4	1	929
1 bujía-pie (1m pie^{-2}) *foot-candle (1m ft^{-2})*	=	10,76	$10,76 \times 10^{-4}$	1

* unidad sin valor oficial en España / not recognized officially in Spain

16 Luminancia / Luminance

		nit *nit*	estilbio *stilb*	*candela-pie^{-2} *cd ft^{-2}*	apostilbio *apostilb*	lambertio *lambert*	*lambertio-pie *foot-lambert*
1 nit (candela m^{-2}) *nit (cd m^{-2})*	=	1	10^{-4}	$9{,}29 \times 10^{-2}$	π	$\pi \times 10^{-4}$	0,292
1 estilbio (candela cm^{-2}) *stilb (cd cm^{-2})*	=	10^4	1	929	$\pi \times 10^4$	π	2920
candela-pie^{-2} *1 cd ft^{-2}*	=	10,76	$1{,}076 \times 10^{-3}$	1	33,8	$3{,}38 \times 10^{-3}$	π
1 apostilbio (1m m^{-2}) *apostilb (1m m^{-2})*	=	$1/\pi$	$1/(\pi \times 10^4)$	$2{,}96 \times 10^{-2}$	1	10^{-4}	$9{,}29 \times 10^{-2}$
1 lambertio (1m cm^{-2}) *lambert (1m cm^{-2})*	=	$1/(\pi \times 10^{-4})$	$1/\pi$	296	10^4	1	929
1 lambertio-pie *o* bujía-pie equivalente *foot lambert* or *equivalent foot candle*	=	3,43	$3{,}43 \times 10^{-4}$	$1/\pi$	10,76	$1{,}076 \times 10^{-3}$	1

intensidad luminosa de la candela = 98,1% de la bujía internacional
luminous intensity of candela = 98.1% that of international candle
1 lumen = flujo luminoso emitido por una fuente puntual uniforme, situada en el vértice de un ángulo
      sólido de 1 estereorradián y cuya intensidad es de 1 candela
1 lumen = flux emitted by 1 candela into unit solid angle

* unidad sin valor oficial en España / not recognized officially in Spain

Elementos químicos / Chemical elements

Símbolo/Symbol	Elemento	Element	Número atómico/ Atomic number
Ac	Actinio	Actinium	89
Ag	Plata	Silver	47
Al	Aluminio	Aluminium *(BrE)*	13
		Aluminum *(AmE)*	
Am	Americio	Americium	95
Ar	Argón	Argon	18
As	Arsénico	Arsenic	33
At	Astato	Astatine	85
Au	Oro	Gold	79
B	Boro	Boron	5
Ba	Bario	Barium	56
Be	Berilio	Beryllium	4
Bi	Bismuto	Bismuth	83
Bk	Berquelio	Berkelium	97
Br	Bromo	Bromine	35
C	Carbono	Carbon	6
Ca	Calcio	Calcium	20
Cd	Cadmio	Cadmium	48
Ce	Cerio	Cerium	58
Cf	Californio	Californium	98
Cl	Cloro	Chlorine	17
Cm	Curio	Curium	96
Co	Cobalto	Cobalt	27
Cr	Cromo	Chromium	24
Cs	Cesio	Caesium *(BrE)*	55
		Cesium *(AmE)*	
Cu	Cobre	Copper	29
Dy	Disprosio	Dysprosium	66
Er	Erbio	Erbium	68
Es	Einsteinio	Einsteinium	99
Eu	Europio	Europium	63
F	Flúor	Fluorine	9
Fe	Hierro	Iron	26
Fm	Fermio	Fermium	100
Fr	Francio	Francium	87
Ga	Galio	Gallium	31
Gd	Gadolinio	Gadolinium	64
Ge	Germanio	Germanium	32
H	Hidrógeno	Hydrogen	1
He	Helio	Helium	2
Hf	Hafnio	Hafnium	72
Hg	Mercurio	Mercury	80
Ho	Holmio	Holmium	67
I	Yodo	Iodine	53
	Iodo		
In	Indio	Indium	49
Ir	Iridio	Iridium	77
K	Potasio	Potassium	19
Kr	Cripton	Krypton	36
La	Lantano	Lanthanum	57
Li	Litio	Lithium	3

Lr	Laurencio	Lawrencium	103
Lu	Lutecio	Lutetium	71
Md	Mendelevio	Mendelevium	101
Mg	Magnesio	Magnesium	12
Mn	Manganeso	Manganese	25
Mo	Molibdeno	Molybdenum	42
N	Nitrógeno	Nitrogen	7
Na	Sodio	Sodium	11
Nb	Niobio	Niobium	41
Nd	Neodimio	Neodymium	60
Ne	Neón	Neon	10
Ni	Níquel	Nickel	28
No	Nobelio	Nobelium	102
Np	Neptunio	Neptunium	93
O	Oxígeno	Oxygen	8
Os	Osmio	Osmium	76
P	Fósforo	Phosphorus	15
Pa	Protactinio	Protactinium	91
Pb	Plomo	Lead	82
Pd	Paladio	Palladium	46
Pm	Promecio	Promethium	61
Po	Polonio	Polonium	84
Pr	Praseodimio	Praseodymium	59
Pt	Platino	Platinum	78
Ra	Radio	Radium	88
Rb	Rubidio	Rubidium	37
Re	Renio	Rhenium	75
Rh	Rodio	Rhodium	45
Rn	Radón	Radon	86
Ru	Rutenio	Ruthenium	44
S	Azufre	Sulphur *(BrE)*	16
		Sulfur *(AmE)*	
Sb	Antimonio	Antimony	51
Sc	Escandio	Scandium	21
Se	Selenio	Selenium	34
Si	Silicio	Silicon	14
Sm	Samario	Samarium	62
Sn	Estaño	Tin	50
Sr	Estroncio	Strontium	38
Ta	Tantalio	Tantalum	73
Tb	Terbio	Terbium	65
Tc	Tecnecio	Technetium	43
Te	Telurio	Tellurium	52
Th	Torio	Thorium	90
Ti	Titanio	Titanium	22
Tl	Talio	Thallium	81
Tm	Tulio	Thulium	69
U	Uranio	Uranium	92
V	Vanadio	Vanadium	23
W	Tungsteno	Tungsten	74
	Wolframio	Wolfram	
Xe	Xenón	Xenon	54
Y	Itrio	Yttrium	39
Yb	Iterbio	Ytterbium	70
Zn	Cinc	Zinc	30
	Zinc		
Zr	Circonio	Zirconium	40
	Zirconio